DOMI MINA
NVS TIO
ILLV MEA

THE OXFORD ENGLISH DICTIONARY

SECOND EDITION

THE OXFORD ENGLISH DICTIONARY

First Edited by

JAMES A. H. MURRAY, HENRY BRADLEY, W. A. CRAIGIE
and C. T. ONIONS

COMBINED WITH

A SUPPLEMENT TO THE OXFORD ENGLISH DICTIONARY

Edited by

R. W. BURCHFIELD

AND RESET WITH CORRECTIONS, REVISIONS
AND ADDITIONAL VOCABULARY

THE OXFORD ENGLISH DICTIONARY

SECOND EDITION

Prepared by

J. A. SIMPSON *and* E. S. C. WEINER

VOLUME XVII

Su–Thrivingly

CLARENDON PRESS · OXFORD

1989

Oxford University Press, Walton Street, Oxford OX2 6DP
Oxford New York Toronto
Delhi Bombay Calcutta Madras Karachi
Petaling Jaya Singapore Hong Kong Tokyo
Nairobi Dar es Salaam Cape Town
Melbourne Auckland
and associated companies in
Berlin Ibadan

Oxford is a trade mark of Oxford University Press

British Library Cataloguing in Publication Data
Oxford English dictionary.—2nd ed.
1. English language-Dictionaries
I. Simpson, J. A. (John Andrew), 1953-
II. Weiner, Edmund S. C., 1950-
423
ISBN 0-19-861229-X (vol. XVII)
ISBN 0-19-861186-2 (set)

Library of Congress Cataloging-in-Publication Data
The Oxford English dictionary.—2nd ed.
prepared by J. A. Simpson and E. S. C. Weiner
Bibliography: p.
ISBN 0-19-861229-X (vol. XVII)
ISBN 0-19-861186-2 (set)
1. English language—Dictionaries. I. Simpson, J. A.
II. Weiner, E. S. C. III. Oxford University Press.
PE1625.087 1989
423—dc19 88-5330

Data capture by ICC, Fort Washington, Pa.
Text-processing by Oxford University Press
Typesetting by Filmtype Services Ltd., Scarborough, N. Yorks.
Manufactured in the United States of America by
Rand McNally & Company, Taunton, Mass.

KEY TO THE PRONUNCIATION

THE pronunciations given are those in use in the educated speech of southern England (the so-called 'Received Standard'), and the keywords given are to be understood as pronounced in such speech.

I. *Consonants*

b, d, f, k, l, m, n, p, t, v, z *have their usual English values*

g as in *go* (gəʊ)
h ... *ho!* (həʊ)
r ... *run* (rʌn), *terrier* ('tɛrɪə(r))
(r) ... *her* (hɜː(r))
s ... *see* (siː), *success* (sək'sɛs)
w ... *wear* (wɛə(r))
hw ... *when* (hwɛn)
j ... *yes* (jɛs)

θ as in *thin* (θɪn), *bath* (bɑːθ)
ð ... *then* (ðɛn), *bathe* (beɪð)
ʃ ... *shop* (ʃɒp), *dish* (dɪʃ)
tʃ ... *chop* (tʃɒp), *ditch* (dɪtʃ)
ʒ ... *vision* ('vɪʒən), *déjeuner* (deʒøne)
dʒ ... *judge* (dʒʌdʒ)
ŋ ... *singing* ('sɪŋɪŋ), *think* (θiŋk)
ŋg ... *finger* ('fɪŋgə(r))

(FOREIGN AND NON-SOUTHERN)
ʎ as in It. *serraglio* (ser'raʎo)
ɲ ... Fr. *cognac* (kɔɲak)
x ... Ger. *ach* (ax), Sc. *loch* (lɒx), Sp. *frijoles* (fri'xoles)
ç ... Ger. *ich* (ɪç), Sc. *nicht* (nɪçt)
ɣ ... North Ger. *sagen* ('zaːɣən)
c ... Afrikaans *baardmannetjie* ('baːrtmanəci)
ɥ ... Fr. *cuisine* (kɥizin)

Symbols in parentheses are used to denote elements that may be omitted either by individual speakers or in particular phonetic contexts: e.g. *bottle* ('bɒt(ə)l), *Mercian* ('mɜːʃ(ɪ)ən), *suit* (s(j)uːt), *impromptu* (ɪm'prɒm(p)tjuː), *father* ('fɑːðə(r)).

II. *Vowels and Diphthongs*

SHORT
ɪ as in *pit* (pɪt), *-ness*, (-nɪs)
ɛ ... *pet* (pɛt), Fr. *sept* (sɛt)
æ ... *pat* (pæt)
ʌ ... *putt* (pʌt)
ɒ ... *pot* (pɒt)
ʊ ... *put* (pʊt)
ə ... *another* (ə'nʌðə(r))
(ə) ... *beaten* ('biːt(ə)n)
i ... Fr. *si* (si)
e ... Fr. *bébé* (bebe)
a ... Fr. *mari* (mari)
ɑ ... Fr. *bâtiment* (bɑtimɑ̃)
ɔ ... Fr. *homme* (ɔm)
o ... Fr. *eau* (o)
ø ... Fr. *peu* (pø)
œ ... Fr. *boeuf* (bœf) *coeur* (kœr)
u ... Fr. *douce* (dus)
ʏ ... Ger. *Müller* ('mʏlər)
y ... Fr. *du* (dy)

LONG
iː as in *bean* (biːn)
ɑː ... *barn* (bɑːn)
ɔː ... *born* (bɔːn)
uː ... *boon* (buːn)
ɜː ... *burn* (bɜːn)
eː ... Ger. *Schnee* (ʃneː)
ɛː ... Ger. *Fähre* ('fɛːrə)
aː ... Ger. *Tag* (taːk)
oː ... Ger. *Sohn* (zoːn)
øː ... Ger. *Goethe* ('gøːtə)
yː ... Ger. *grün* (gryːn)

NASAL
ɛ̃, æ̃ as in Fr. *fin* (fɛ̃, fæ̃)
ɑ̃ ... Fr. *franc* (frɑ̃)
ɔ̃ ... Fr. *bon* (bɔ̃)
œ̃ ... Fr. *un* (œ̃)

DIPHTHONGS, etc.
eɪ as in *bay* (beɪ)
aɪ ... *buy* (baɪ)
ɔɪ ... *boy* (bɔɪ)
əʊ ... *no* (nəʊ)
aʊ ... *now* (naʊ)
ɪə ... *peer* (pɪə(r))
ɛə ... *pair* (pɛə(r))
ʊə ... *tour* (tʊə(r))
ɔə ... *boar* (bɔə(r))

aɪə as in *fiery* ('faɪərɪ)
aʊə ... *sour* (saʊə(r))

The incidence of main stress is shown by a superior stress mark (') preceding the stressed syllable, and a secondary stress by an inferior stress mark (ˌ), e.g. *pronunciation* (prəˌnʌnsɪ'eɪʃ(ə)n).

For further explanation of the transcription used, see *General Explanations*, Volume I.

LIST OF ABBREVIATIONS, SIGNS, ETC.

Some abbreviations listed here in italics are also in certain cases printed in roman type, and vice versa.

a. (in Etym.)	adoption of, adopted from
a (as *a* 1850)	*ante*, 'before', 'not later than'
a.	adjective
abbrev.	abbreviation (of)
abl.	ablative
absol.	absolute, -ly
Abstr.	(in titles) *Abstract, -s*
acc.	accusative
Acct.	(in titles) *Account*
A.D.	*Anno Domini*
ad. (in Etym.)	adaptation of
Add.	Addenda
adj.	adjective
Adv.	(in titles) *Advance, -d, -s*
adv.	adverb
advb.	adverbial, -ly
Advt.	advertisement
Aeronaut.	(as label) in Aeronautics; (in titles) *Aeronautic, -al, -s*
AF., AFr.	Anglo-French
Afr.	Africa, -n
Agric.	(as label) in Agriculture; (in titles) *Agriculture, -al*
Alb.	Albanian
Amer.	American
Amer. Ind.	American Indian
Anat.	(as label) in Anatomy; (in titles) *Anatomy, -ical*
Anc.	(in titles) *Ancient*
Anglo-Ind.	Anglo-Indian
Anglo-Ir.	Anglo-Irish
Ann.	Annals
Anthrop., Anthropol.	(as label) in Anthropology; (in titles) *Anthropology, -ical*
Antiq.	(as label) in Antiquities; (in titles) *Antiquity*
aphet.	aphetic, aphetized
app.	apparently
Appl.	(in titles) *Applied*
Applic.	(in titles) *Application, -s*
appos.	appositive, -ly
Arab.	Arabic
Aram.	Aramaic
Arch.	in Architecture
arch.	archaic
Archæol.	in Archæology
Archit.	(as label) in Architecture; (in titles) *Architecture, -al*
Arm.	Armenian
assoc.	association
Astr.	in Astronomy
Astrol.	in Astrology
Astron.	(in titles) *Astronomy, -ical*
Astronaut.	(in titles) *Astronautic, -s*
attrib.	attributive, -ly
Austral.	Australian
Autobiogr.	(in titles) *Autobiography, -ical*
A.V.	Authorized Version
B.C.	Before Christ
B.C.	(in titles) British Columbia
bef.	before
Bibliogr.	(as label) in Bibliography; (in titles) *Bibliography, -ical*
Biochem.	(as label) in Biochemistry; (in titles) *Biochemistry, -ical*
Biol.	(as label) in Biology; (in titles) *Biology, -ical*
Bk.	*Book*
Bot.	(as label) in Botany; (in titles) *Botany, -ical*
Bp.	Bishop
Brit.	(in titles) *Britain, British*
Bulg.	Bulgarian
Bull.	(in titles) *Bulletin*
c (as *c* 1700)	*circa*, 'about'
c. (as 19th c.)	century
Cal.	(in titles) *Calendar*
Cambr.	(in titles) *Cambridge*
Canad.	Canadian
Cat.	Catalan
catachr.	catachrestically
Catal.	(in titles) *Catalogue*
Celt.	Celtic
Cent.	(in titles) *Century, Central*
Cent. Dict.	*Century Dictionary*
Cf., cf.	*confer*, 'compare'
Ch.	Church
Chem.	(as label) in Chemistry; (in titles) *Chemistry, -ical*
Chr.	(in titles) *Christian*
Chron.	(in titles) *Chronicle*
Chronol.	(in titles) *Chronology, -ical*
Cinemat., Cinematogr.	in Cinematography
Clin.	(in titles) *Clinical*
cl. L.	classical Latin
cogn. w.	cognate with
Col.	(in titles) *Colonel, Colony*
Coll.	(in titles) *Collection*
collect.	collective, -ly
colloq.	colloquial, -ly
comb.	combined, -ing
Comb.	Combinations
Comm.	in Commercial usage
Communic.	in Communications
comp.	compound, composition
Compan.	(in titles) *Companion*
compar.	comparative
compl.	complement
Compl.	(in titles) *Complete*
Conc.	(in titles) *Concise*
Conch.	in Conchology
concr.	concrete, -ly
Conf.	(in titles) *Conference*
Congr.	(in titles) *Congress*
conj.	conjunction
cons.	consonant
const.	construction, construed with
contr.	contrast (with)
Contrib.	(in titles) *Contribution*
Corr.	(in titles) *Correspondence*
corresp.	corresponding (to)
Cotgr.	R. Cotgrave, *Dictionarie of the French and English Tongues*
cpd.	compound
Crit.	(in titles) *Criticism, Critical*
Cryst.	in Crystallography
Cycl.	(in titles) *Cyclopædia, -ic*
Cytol.	(in titles) *Cytology, -ical*
Da.	Danish
D.A.	*Dictionary of Americanisms*
D.A.E.	*Dictionary of American English*
dat.	dative
D.C.	District of Columbia
Deb.	(in titles) *Debate, -s*
def.	definite, -ition
dem.	demonstrative
deriv.	derivative, -ation
derog.	derogatory
Descr.	(in titles) *Description, -tive*
Devel.	(in titles) *Development, -al*
Diagn.	(in titles) *Diagnosis, Diagnostic*
dial.	dialect, -al
Dict.	Dictionary; *spec.*, the *Oxford English Dictionary*
dim.	diminutive
Dis.	(in titles) *Disease*
Diss.	(in titles) *Dissertation*
D.O.S.T.	*Dictionary of the Older Scottish Tongue*
Du.	Dutch
E.	East
Eccl.	(as label) in Ecclesiastical usage; (in titles) *Ecclesiastical*
Ecol.	in Ecology
Econ.	(as label) in Economics; (in titles) *Economy, -ics*
ed.	edition
E.D.D.	*English Dialect Dictionary*
Edin.	(in titles) *Edinburgh*
Educ.	(as label) in Education; (in titles) *Education, -al*
EE.	Early English
e.g.	*exempli gratia*, 'for example'
Electr.	(as label) in Electricity; (in titles) *Electricity, -ical*
Electron.	(in titles) *Electronic, -s*
Elem.	(in titles) *Element, -ary*
ellipt.	elliptical, -ly
Embryol.	in Embryology
e.midl.	east midland (dialect)
Encycl.	(in titles) *Encyclopædia, -ic*
Eng.	England, English
Engin.	in Engineering
Ent.	in Entomology
Entomol.	(in titles) *Entomology, -logical*
erron.	erroneous, -ly
esp.	especially
Ess.	(in titles) *Essay, -s*
et al.	*et alii*, 'and others'
etc.	et cetera
Ethnol.	in Ethnology
etym.	etymology
euphem.	euphemistically
Exam.	(in titles) *Examination*
exc.	except
Exerc.	(in titles) *Exercise, -s*
Exper.	(in titles) *Experiment, -al*
Explor.	(in titles) *Exploration, -s*
f.	feminine
f. (in Etym.)	formed on
f. (in subordinate entries)	form of
F.	French
fem. (*rarely* f.)	feminine
fig.	figurative, -ly
Finn.	Finnish
fl.	*floruit*, 'flourished'
Found.	(in titles) *Foundation, -s*
Fr.	French
freq.	frequent, -ly
Fris.	Frisian
Fund.	(in titles) *Fundamental, -s*
Funk or *Funk's Stand. Dict.*	*Funk and Wagnalls Standard Dictionary*
G.	German
Gael.	Gaelic
Gaz.	(in titles) *Gazette*
gen.	genitive
gen.	general, -ly
Geogr.	(as label) in Geography; (in titles) *Geography, -ical*

Geol.	(as label) in Geology; (in titles) *Geology, -ical*
Geom.	in Geometry
Geomorphol.	in Geomorphology
Ger.	German
Gloss.	Glossary
Gmc.	Germanic
Godef.	F. Godefroy, *Dictionnaire de l'ancienne langue française*
Goth.	Gothic
Govt.	(in titles) *Government*
Gr.	Greek
Gram.	(as label) in Grammar; (in titles) *Grammar, -tical*
Gt.	Great
Heb.	Hebrew
Her.	in Heraldry
Herb.	among herbalists
Hind.	Hindustani
Hist.	(as label) in History; (in titles) *History, -ical*
hist.	historical
Histol.	(in titles) *Histology, -ical*
Hort.	in Horticulture
Househ.	(in titles) *Household*
Housek.	(in titles) *Housekeeping*
Ibid.	*Ibidem*, 'in the same book or passage'
Icel.	Icelandic
Ichthyol.	in Ichthyology
id.	*idem*, 'the same'
i.e.	*id est*, 'that is'
IE.	Indo-European
Illustr.	(in titles) *Illustration, -ted*
imit.	imitative
Immunol.	in Immunology
imp.	imperative
impers.	impersonal
impf.	imperfect
ind.	indicative
indef.	indefinite
Industr.	(in titles) *Industry, -ial*
inf.	infinitive
infl.	influenced
Inorg.	(in titles) *Inorganic*
Ins.	(in titles) *Insurance*
Inst.	(in titles) *Institute, -tion*
int.	interjection
intr.	intransitive
Introd.	(in titles) *Introduction*
Ir.	Irish
irreg.	irregular, -ly
It.	Italian
J., (J.)	(quoted from) Johnson's *Dictionary*
(Jam.)	Jamieson, *Scottish Dict.*
Jap.	Japanese
joc.	jocular, -ly
Jrnl.	(in titles) *Journal*
Jun.	(in titles) *Junior*
Knowl.	(in titles) *Knowledge*
l.	line
L.	Latin
lang.	language
Lect.	(in titles) *Lecture, -s*
Less.	(in titles) *Lesson, -s*
Let., Lett.	letter, letters
LG.	Low German
lit.	literal, -ly
Lit.	Literary
Lith.	Lithuanian
LXX	Septuagint
m.	masculine
Mag.	(in titles) *Magazine*
Magn.	(in titles) *Magnetic, -ism*
Mal.	Malay, Malayan
Man.	(in titles) *Manual*
Managem.	(in titles) *Management*
Manch.	(in titles) *Manchester*
Manuf.	in Manufacture, -ing
Mar.	(in titles) *Marine*
masc. (*rarely* m.)	masculine
Math.	(as label) in Mathematics; (in titles) *Mathematics, -al*
MDu.	Middle Dutch
ME.	Middle English
Mech.	(as label) in Mechanics; (in titles) *Mechanics, -al*
Med.	(as label) in Medicine; (in titles) *Medicine, -ical*
med.L.	medieval Latin
Mem.	(in titles) *Memoir, -s*
Metaph.	in Metaphysics
Meteorol.	(as label) in Meteorology; (in titles) *Meteorology, -ical*
MHG.	Middle High German
midl.	midland (dialect)
Mil.	in military usage
Min.	(as label) in Mineralogy; (in titles) *Ministry*
Mineral.	(in titles) *Mineralogy, -ical*
MLG.	Middle Low German
Misc.	(in titles) *Miscellany, -eous*
mod.	modern
mod.L	modern Latin
(Morris),	(quoted from) E. E. Morris's *Austral English*
Mus.	(as label) in Music; (in titles) *Music, -al; Museum*
Myst.	(in titles) *Mystery*
Mythol.	in Mythology
N.	North
n.	neuter
N. Amer.	North America, -n
N. & Q.	*Notes and Queries*
Narr.	(in titles) *Narrative*
Nat.	(in titles) *Natural*
Nat. Hist.	in Natural History
Naut.	in nautical language
N.E.	North East
N.E.D.	*New English Dictionary*, original title of the *Oxford English Dictionary* (first edition)
Neurol.	in Neurology
neut. (*rarely* n.)	neuter
NF., NFr.	Northern French
No.	Number
nom.	nominative
north.	northern (dialect)
Norw.	Norwegian
n.q.	no quotations
N.T.	New Testament
Nucl.	Nuclear
Numism.	in Numismatics
N.W.	North West
N.Z.	New Zealand
obj.	object
obl.	oblique
Obs., obs.	obsolete
Obstetr.	(in titles) *Obstetrics*
occas.	occasionally
OE.	Old English (= Anglo-Saxon)
OF., OFr.	Old French
OFris.	Old Frisian
OHG.	Old High German
OIr.	Old Irish
ON.	Old Norse
ONF.	Old Northern French
Ophthalm.	in Ophthalmology
opp.	opposed (to), the opposite (of)
Opt.	in Optics
Org.	(in titles) *Organic*
orig.	origin, -al, -ally
Ornith.	(as label) in Ornithology; (in titles) *Ornithology, -ical*
OS.	Old Saxon
OSl.	Old (Church) Slavonic
O.T.	Old Testament
Outl.	(in titles) *Outline*
Oxf.	(in titles) *Oxford*
p.	page
Palæogr.	in Palæography
Palæont.	(as label) in Palæontology; (in titles) *Palæontology, -ical*
pa. pple.	passive participle, past participle
(Partridge),	(quoted from) E. Partridge's *Dictionary of Slang and Unconventional English*
pass.	passive, -ly
pa.t.	past tense
Path.	(as label) in Pathology; (in titles) *Pathology, -ical*
perh.	perhaps
Pers.	Persian
pers.	person, -al
Petrogr.	in Petrography
Petrol.	(as label) in Petrology; (in titles) *Petrology, -ical*
(Pettman),	(quoted from) C. Pettman's *Africanderisms*
pf.	perfect
Pg.	Portuguese
Pharm.	in Pharmacology
Philol.	(as label) in Philology; (in titles) *Philology, -ical*
Philos.	(as label) in Philosophy; (in titles) *Philosophy, -ic*
phonet.	phonetic, -ally
Photogr.	(as label) in Photography; (in titles) *Photography, -ical*
phr.	phrase
Phys.	physical; (*rarely*) in Physiology
Physiol.	(as label) in Physiology; (in titles) *Physiology, -ical*
Pict.	(in titles) *Picture, Pictorial*
pl., plur.	plural
poet.	poetic, -al
Pol.	Polish
Pol.	(as label) in Politics; (in titles) *Politics, -al*
Pol. Econ.	in Political Economy
Polit.	(in titles) *Politics, -al*
pop.	popular, -ly
Porc.	(in titles) *Porcelain*
poss.	possessive
Pott.	(in titles) *Pottery*
ppl. a., pple. adj.	participial adjective
pple.	participle
Pr.	Provençal
pr.	present
Pract.	(in titles) *Practice, -al*
prec.	preceding (word or article)
pred.	predicative
pref.	prefix
pref., Pref.	preface
prep.	preposition
pres.	present
Princ.	(in titles) *Principle, -s*
priv.	privative
prob.	probably
Probl.	(in titles) *Problem*
Proc.	(in titles) *Proceedings*
pron.	pronoun
pronunc.	pronunciation
prop.	properly
Pros.	in Prosody
Prov.	Provençal
pr. pple.	present participle
Psych.	in Psychology
Psychol.	(as label) in Psychology; (in titles) *Psychology, -ical*
Publ.	(in titles) *Publications*
Q.	(in titles) *Quarterly*
quot(s).	quotation(s)
q.v.	*quod vide*, 'which see'
R.	(in titles) *Royal*
Radiol.	in Radiology
R.C.Ch.	Roman Catholic Church
Rec.	(in titles) *Record*
redupl.	reduplicating
Ref.	(in titles) *Reference*
refash.	refashioned, -ing
refl.	reflexive
Reg.	(in titles) *Register*

reg.	regular
rel.	related to
Reminisc.	(in titles) *Reminiscence, -s*
Rep.	(in titles) *Report, -s*
repr.	representative, representing
Res.	(in titles) *Research*
Rev.	(in titles) *Review*
rev.	revised
Rhet.	in Rhetoric
Rom.	Roman, -ce, -ic
Rum.	Rumanian
Russ.	Russian
S.	South
S.Afr.	South Africa, -n
sb.	substantive
sc.	*scilicet*, 'understand' or 'supply'
Sc., Scot.	Scottish
Scand.	(in titles) *Scandinavia, -n*
Sch.	(in titles) *School*
Sc. Nat. Dict.	*Scottish National Dictionary*
Scotl.	(in titles) *Scotland*
Sel.	(in titles) *Selection, -s*
Ser.	Series
sing.	singular
Sk.	(in titles) *Sketch*
Skr.	Sanskrit
Slav.	Slavonic
S.N.D.	*Scottish National Dictionary*
Soc.	(in titles) *Society*
Sociol.	(as label) in Sociology; (in titles) *Sociology, -ical*
Sp.	Spanish
Sp.	(in titles) *Speech, -es*
sp.	spelling
spec.	specifically
Spec.	(in titles) *Specimen*
St.	Saint
Stand.	(in titles) *Standard*
Stanf.	(quoted from) *Stanford Dictionary of Anglicised Words & Phrases*
str.	strong
Struct.	(in titles) *Structure, -al*
Stud.	(in titles) *Studies*
subj.	subject
subord. cl.	subordinate clause
subseq.	subsequent, -ly
subst.	substantively
suff.	suffix
superl.	superlative
Suppl.	Supplement
Surg.	(as label) in Surgery; (in titles) *Surgery, Surgical*
s.v.	*sub voce*, 'under the word'
Sw.	Swedish
s.w.	south-western (dialect)
Syd. Soc. Lex.	Sydenham Society, *Lexicon of Medicine & Allied Sciences*
syll.	syllable
Syr.	Syrian
Syst.	(in titles) *System, -atic*
Taxon.	(in titles) *Taxonomy, -ical*
techn.	technical, -ly
Technol.	(in titles) *Technology, -ical*
Telegr.	in Telegraphy
Teleph.	in Telephony
(Th.),	(quoted from) Thornton's *American Glossary*
Theatr.	in the Theatre, theatrical
Theol.	(as label) in Theology; (in titles) *Theology, -ical*
Theoret.	(in titles) *Theoretical*
Tokh.	Tokharian
tr., transl.	translated, translation
Trans.	(in titles) *Transactions*
trans.	transitive
transf.	transferred sense
Trav.	(in titles) *Travel(s)*
Treas.	(in titles) *Treasury*
Treat.	(in titles) *Treatise*
Treatm.	(in titles) *Treatment*
Trig.	in Trigonometry
Trop.	(in titles) *Tropical*
Turk.	Turkish
Typog., Typogr.	in Typography
ult.	ultimately
Univ.	(in titles) *University*
unkn.	unknown
U.S.	United States
U.S.S.R.	Union of Soviet Socialist Republics
usu.	usually
v., vb.	verb
var(r)., vars.	variant(s) of
vbl. sb.	verbal substantive
Vertebr.	(in titles) *Vertebrate, -s*
Vet.	(as label) in Veterinary Science; (in titles) *Veterinary*
Vet. Sci.	in Veterinary Science
viz.	*videlicet*, 'namely'
Voy.	(in titles) *Voyage, -s*
v.str.	strong verb
vulg.	vulgar
v.w.	weak verb
W.	Welsh; West
wd.	word
Webster	*Webster's (New International) Dictionary*
Westm.	(in titles) *Westminster*
WGmc.	West Germanic
Wks.	(in titles) *Works*
w.midl.	west midland (dialect)
WS.	West Saxon
(Y.),	(quoted from) Yule & Burnell's *Hobson-Jobson*
Yrs.	(in titles) *Years*
Zoogeogr.	in Zoogeography
Zool.	(as label) in Zoology; (in titles) *Zoology, -ical*

Signs and Other Conventions

Before a word or sense

† = obsolete
‖ = not naturalized, alien
¶ = catachrestic and erroneous uses

In the listing of Forms

1 = before 1100
2 = 12th c. (1100 to 1200)
3 = 13th c. (1200 to 1300), etc.
5–7 = 15th to 17th century
20 = 20th century

In the etymologies

* indicates a word or form not actually found, but of which the existence is inferred
:— = normal development of

The printing of a word in SMALL CAPITALS indicates that further information will be found under the word so referred to.

.. indicates an omitted part of a quotation.

- (in a quotation) indicates a hyphen doubtfully present in the original; (in other text) indicates a hyphen inserted only for the sake of a line-break.

PROPRIETARY NAMES

THIS Dictionary includes some words which are or are asserted to be proprietary names or trade marks. Their inclusion does not imply that they have acquired for legal purposes a non-proprietary or general significance nor any other judgement concerning their legal status. In cases where the editorial staff have established in the records of the Patent Offices of the United Kingdom and of the United States that a word is registered as a proprietary name or trade mark this is indicated, but no judgement concerning the legal status of such words is made or implied thereby.

su, dial. f. SHE; obs. f. SUE.

sua, obs. f. SO *adv.* and *conj.*

suabe (ˈswɑːbə, sweɪb). *Mus.* [It., ad. G. *Schwabe* SWABIAN.] ***suabe flute***: an organ flute-stop.
1855 E. J. HOPKINS *Organ* 119 *Suabe-flute*,..a tenor c Manual Stop of 4 feet, formed of wood pipes, with inverted mouths. It's tone is liquid and clear, and not so loud as the Wald-flute. **1907** *Musical Times* 1 Aug. 514/2 Swell Organ ..Voix celestes..Suabe flute 4 ft. **1954** *Grove's Dict. Mus.* (ed. 5) VI. 358/2 *Suabe flute*, a 4-ft open flute stop of medium scale, said to have been invented by William Hill. The tone is a soft variety of that of the Clarabella.

Suabian: see SWABIAN.

suability (sjuːəˈbɪlɪtɪ). *U.S.* [f. next: see -ITY.] Liability to be sued.
1798 in Dallas *Amer. Law* II. 470 Suability and suable are words not in common use, but they concisely and correctly convey the idea annexed to them. **1833** in Calhoun *Wks.* (1874) II. 302 The Senator cited the suability of the states as an evidence of their want of sovereignty.

suable (ˈsjuːəb(ə)l), *a.* Now chiefly *U.S.* Also **sueable.** [f. SUE *v.* + -ABLE.] Capable of being sued, liable to be sued; legally subject to civil process.
a **1623** SWINBURNE *Treat. Spousals* (1686) 120 The Parties contracting Spousals or Matrimony, under any such Conditions, are neither bound, nor suable, until the Condition be extant. **1693** *Mod. Rep.* XII. Case 93. 45 He cannot plead in bar *ne unques executor*,..because he allows him-self to be suable. **1810** J. MARSHALL *Const. Opin.* (1839) 137 A state which violated its own contract was suable in the courts of the United States. **1823** *Examiner* 78/2 If not a *femme sole*, she was not sueable at law. **1875** POSTE *Gaius* II. §282 A trustee is only suable for the simple amount of the subject of trust. **1903** *Times* 7 Jan. 6/2 Is a trade union to be regarded as a corporation sueable at law?
b. Capable of being sued for.
1726 AYLIFFE *Parergon* 343 Legacies out of Lands are properly suable in Chancery.

†**ˈSuada.** *Obs.* [L. *Suāda*, fem. of *suādus* persuasive, f. root *swād-* (see SUAVE). Cf. G. *suada, suade* (colloq.) gift of the gab.] The Roman goddess of persuasion; hence = persuasiveness, persuasive eloquence.
1592 HARVEY *Four Lett.* Wks. (Grosart) I. 242 How faine would I see..Suadas hoony-bees in you rehiu'd. **1593** —— *Pierce's Super.* Ibid II. 276 Euen the filed Suada of Isocrates, wanted the voyce of a Siren, or the sound of an Eccho. **1621** S. WARD *Happiness of Practice* 18 Irrisistable is the Suada of a good life, aboue a faire profession.

suade (sweɪd), *v.* Now *rare* or *dial.* Also 6 **swad(e**, 9 **'swade.** [Partly ad. L. *suādēre*, f. root *swād-* (see SUAVE); partly by aphæresis from PERSUADE. Cf. obs. F. *suader.*] = PERSUADE in various senses. Hence †**suading** *ppl. a.* (in *ill-suading*).
1531 CRANMER in Strype *Mem.* App. i. (1694) 3 He swadeth that with such goodly eloquence..that he were lyke to persuade many. **1548** BODRUGAN *Epit.* 248 There be diuerse whiche..swade the vnion of Scotlande vnto youre highnes. **1550** HOOPER *Serm. Jonas* iv. 69b, These comfortable promises, which the deuil auenturth to swad vs vnto. **1557** GRIMALDE in *Tottel's Misc.* (Arb.) 101 Flee then ylswading pleasures baits vntreew. **1589** *Mar-Martin* A 3 Thilke way & trood whilke thou dost swade, is steepe & also tickle. **1889** *N. W. Linc. Gloss.*, 'Swade. **1891** *Proving of Gennad* 121 So he..Agreed to work for her who suaded him.

†**ˈsuadible,** *a.* *Obs. rare*⁻¹. [ad. late L. *suādibilis*, f. *suādēre*: see prec. and -IBLE.] That may be easily persuaded; = SUASIBLE.
1382 WYCLIF *James* iii. 17 Wisdom that is fro aboue first ..it is chaast, aftirward pesible, mylde, suadible, and free.

‖**Suæda** (sjuːˈiːdə). [mod.L. (Forskål 1775).] A plant of the genus *Suæda* (N.O. *Chenopodiaceæ*), which comprises herbaceous or shrubby plants growing on the sea-shore or in saline districts.
1901 *Spectator* 26 Oct. 607/2 The three sea lavenders and *suæda*, which grows into bushes near Blakeney.

suagat, north. form of SO-GATE.

suage, obs. form of SEWAGE; variant of SWAGE.

suaif, obs. Sc. form of SUAVE *a.*

Suakin (ˈswɑːkɪn). Also **Suakim.** The name of a port on the Red Sea used as the distinctive epithet of a variety of gum arabic exported thence.
1874 FLÜCKIGER & HANBURY *Pharmacogr.* 210 Suakin Gum, Talca or Talha Gum..is remarkable for its brittleness. **1886** *Buck's Handbk. Med. Sci.* III. 409.

‖**suan-pan** (swæn pæn). Also **souan-, shwan-, swam-, swan-.** [Chinese, lit. reckoning board.] The Chinese abacus.
1736 tr. *Du Halde's Hist. China* III. 70 In casting up Accounts they [*sc.* the Chinese] make use of an Instrument called *Souan pan*. **1748** *Gentl. Mag.* July 295/2, I desire to give the public a Swan Pan that in my opinion is much preferable to that of the Chinese. **1833** *Penny Cycl.* I. 7/1 This instrument, called in Chinese Shwanpan. **1836** J. F. DAVIS *Chinese* II. xviii. 296 A little apparatus called a *Suân-pân*, or 'calculating dish'. **1875** *Encycl. Brit.* II. 526/1 The swan-pan, still in constant use among the Chinese. **1917** S. COULING *Encycl. Sinica* 1/1 *Suan p'an*, reckoning plate, the counting-board used by the Chinese. **1946** G. STIMPSON *Bk. about Thousand Things* 207 Virtually all calculations were performed on the abacus, an apparatus resembling the Chinese *suan pan* or the bead-and-frame affairs now used in kindergarten work. **1973** T. R. TREGEAR *Chinese* vi. 128 A further six hours a week is devoted to arithmetic, when calculating with the abacus or *suan p'an* is learnt.

suant, *sb.* ? *Obs.* Also 7, 9 **sewant** [? Var. of SEWIN¹.] App. a name for certain flat fish; see quots.
a **1609** DENNIS *Secrets of Angling* II. xxviii. (1613) C 7 b, To take the Sewant, yea, the Flounder sweet. *Ibid.* xlii. D 2 The Suant swift, that is not set by least. **1615** MARKHAM *Pleas. Princ.* vi. (1635) 32 The Flounder, and Sewant are greedy biters, yet very crafty. **1847** HALLIWELL *Dict. Sewant*, the plaice. *Northumb*

suant (ˈsjuːənt), *a.* Now *dial.* Forms: 5 **suante, suaunt,** 6–9 **sewant,** 8 **souant,** 9 **suent,** 8– **suant.** [a. AF. *sua(u)nt*, OF. *suiant, sivant*, pr. pple. of *sivre* (mod.F. *suivre*) to follow:—L. **sequere* for *sequī*.]
†**1.** Following, ensuing. *Obs.* (Cf. SUING.)
1422 YONGE tr. *Secr. Secr.* xxxvii. 195 Now will I retourn to that place..in this sam maner suante.
†**2.** ? Agreeing, suitable. *Obs.*
1418–20 J. PAGE *Siege of Rouen* in *Hist. Coll. Cit. Lond.* (Camden) 34 Kyngys, herowdys, and pursefauntys, In cotys of armys suauntys [*v.rr.* amyauntis, arryauntis].
3. Working or proceeding regularly, evenly, smoothly, or easily; even, smooth, regular. Also *advb.* = SUANTLY.
For other dial. meanings ('placid, equable', 'pleasing, agreeable', 'demure, grave') see *Eng. Dial. Dict.*
1547, etc. [implied in SUANTLY]. **1605** R. CAREW in *Lett. Lit. Men* (Camden) 100 By observing our wittie and sewant [*printed* servant] manner of deducing [words from Latin and French]. *a* **1722** LISLE *Husb.* (1757) 149 The middle-ripe barley..ripened altogether, and looked white and very suant [*marg.* kindly, flourishing]. **1787** GROSE *Prov. Gloss.*, *Zuant*, regularly sowed. The wheat must be zown zuant. **1796** W. H. MARSHALL *Rur. Econ. W. Eng.* I. 330 *Souant*: fair, even, regular (a hackneyed word). **1854** *N. & Q.* Ser. I. X. 420 A fisherman's line is said to run through his hand suant [*printed* suart] when he feels no inequality or roughness, but it is equally soft and flexible throughout. **1854** THOREAU *Walden* (1908) 28 Yet the Middlesex Cattle Show goes off here with *éclat* annually, as if all the joints of the agricultural machine were suent. **1899** BARING-GOULD *Bk. West* II. xvi. 252 Peter and his wife did not get on very 'suant' together.

ˈsuantly, *adv.* Now *dial.* [f. prec. + -LY².] Regularly, evenly, uniformly, smoothly.
The form *sewantly* of quot. 1592–3 was entered in Kersey's ed. of Phillips *World of Words* (1706) as *sevantly* with def. 'well, honestly'. Some mod. dicts. have copied this and have further invented a form *sevant* adj.
1547 RECORDE *Judic. Uryne* 18b, Not suantly and uniformly joyned together. **1592–3** *Act 35 Eliz.* c. 10 §1 That eche sorte of the saide Kersyes or Dozens shalbe sewantly woven throughout. **1865** JENNINGS *Obs. Dial. W. Eng.* 73 *Suently*, evenly, smoothly, plainly.

suarrow, variant of SAOUARI.

suasible (ˈsweɪsɪb(ə)l), *a.* *rare.* [ad. L. **suāsibilis*, f. *suās-*, ppl. stem of *suādēre* to SUADE: see -IBLE; cf. It. *suasibile.*] Capable of being persuaded; that is easily persuaded. (Cf. SUADIBLE.)
1582 *N.T.* (Rhem.) James iii. 17 Peaceable, modest, suasible [TINDALE easy to be entreated; *Wycl. 1st vers.* saudible, *2nd vers.* able to be counseilid]. **1656** BLOUNT *Glossogr.* **1832** *Fraser's Mag.* VI. 487 The want of mental strength rendering them so peculiarly suasible, that they possess no powers of resistance. **1851** I. TAYLOR *Wesley* 113 Throughout the Inspired Writings, men are dealt with by their Maker, [as] suasible, accountable, and free.

suasion (ˈsweɪʒən). Also 4 **suasioun,** 5 **-yon,** 6–7 **swasion.** [ad. L. *suāsio, -ōnem*, n. of action f. *suādēre* to SUADE. Cf. obs. F. *suasion* (14th c.).]
1. The act or fact of exhorting or urging; persuasion.
c **1374** CHAUCER *Boeth.* II. pr. i. (1868) 30 Com nowe furþe þerfore þe suasioun of swetnesse Rethoryen. **1432–50** tr. *Higden* (Rolls) VII. 93 Seynte Elphegus was made bischop of Wynchestre, thro the suasion off blissede Andrewe, apperynge to seynte Dunstan. **1528** MORE *Dyaloge* I. Wks. 157/1 Thei had ones at the subtill suasion of the deuill, broken the thirde comaundement. **1641** PRYNNE *Antipathie* 9 O perfidious, ungratefull counsell and swasion of this prelate. **1660** SOUTH *Serm.* (1727) IV. 34 It cannot be subdued by meer Suasion. **1720** WATTS in *Reliq. Juv.* (1789) 169 To address the ear With conquering suasion, or reproof severe. **1844** KINGLAKE *Eothen* xxviii, Men governed by reasons and suasion of speech. **1867** SMILES *Huguenots Eng.* v. (1880) 74 Conformity by force, if not by suasion.
b. *moral suasion*: persuasion exerted or acting through and upon the moral nature or sense.
1642 D. ROGERS *Naaman* 13 A cause of morall swasion to apprehend the truth. **1700** C. NESSE *Antid. Armin.* (1827) 112 Moral suasion will neuer prove effectual to open the heart of man. **1861** *Sat. Rev.* 14 Dec. 596 [They] might.. have found fitting occupation for their powers of moral suasion in the endeavour to avert a struggle far more ferocious. **1885** DILKE in *Leeds Merc.* 15 Dec. 5/3 Who thought that moral suasion needed to be aided by legislation.
c. *transf.*
1856 MASSON *Ess. Biog. & Crit.* 430 The occult suasion of the rhyme. *a* **1861** CLOUGH *Mari Magno* 383 The sinking stars their suasions urge for sleep. **1875** GLADSTONE *Glean.* VI. ii. 109 Introducing the Roman or Papal religion..under ..the silent but steady suasion of its ceremonial.
2. An instance of this.
c **1407** LYDG. *Reson & Sens.* 1994 With many mighty Argument, Tatteyne to ther entencion, By many strong suasion. *c* **1450** CAPGRAVE *Life St. Gilbert* 95 Ne pretyng of þe iuges, ne fayre suasiones of oþir. *c* **1555** HARPSFIELD *Divorce Hen. VIII* (Camden) 91 It is untrue that the state of the said 18 chapter standeth wholly upon dehortations but rather upon suasions and exhortations. **1642** D. ROGERS *Naaman* 149 Away with thy morality and morall swasions, bring them to the Spirit of Christ. **1663** HEATH *Flagellum* 7 Growing insolent and uncorrigible from those results and swasions within him. **1865** CARLYLE *Fredk. Gt.* XIX. v. (1872) V. 500 Suasions from Montalembert.

suasive (ˈsweɪsɪv), *a.* and *sb.* Also 7 **swasive.** [ad. L. **suāsivus*, f. *suās-*: see SUASIBLE; cf. obs. F. *suasif*, It., Sp. *suasivo.*]
A. *adj.* Having or exercizing the power of persuading or urging; consisting in or tending to suasion; occas. const. *of*, exhorting or urging to.
1601 WEEVER *Mirr. Mart.* A 3 b, Deliuer but in swasive eloquence Both of my life and death the veritie. **1660** WATERHOUSE *Arms & Arm.* 28 The puissant people of Rome, whose practice may be thought most swasive with this..military Age. **1662** SOUTH *Serm.* (1697) I. 62 Tho its command over them was but suasive, and political, yet it had the force of coaction. **1790** COWPER *Odyss.* x. 206 And in wing'd accents suasive thus began. **1871** EARLE *Philol. Engl. Tongue* 313 The genial and suasive satire of the *Biglow Papers*. **1888** T. E. HOLLAND in *Macm. Mag.* Sept. 359/1 These presents bore Latin inscriptions, suasive of eating and drinking. **1897** TROTTER *John Nicholson* 18 Thanks to the suasive influence of British gold.
B. *sb.* A suasive speech, motive, or influence.
1670 *Phil. Trans.* V. 1092, I shall not doubt but this Consideration will have the force of a great swasive. **1855** H. ROGERS *Ess.* (1874) II. vii. 335 By proper importunity, by flattering suasives. **1877** *Smith & Wace's Dict. Chr. Biog.* I. 476/2 Bribes, and tempting offers..were the suasives employed to induce the Armenians to renounce their faith.
b. *pl.* Used to render the title *Suasoriae* of one of the works of Seneca the rhetorician.
1856 MERIVALE *Rom. Emp.* xli. IV. 565 [Seneca] divides into the two classes of Suasives and Controversies the subjects of their scholastic exercises.

ˈsuasively, *adv.* [f. prec. + -LY².] In a suasive manner; so as to persuade.
1837 CARLYLE *Fr. Rev.* I. III. ii, Let a true tale, of his Majesty's..wretched pecuniary impossibilities, be suasively told them. **1871** HARDY *Desper. Remedies* xi, 'You must remember', she added, more suasively, 'that Miss Graye has a perfect right to do what she likes.'
So **ˈsuasiveness.**
1727 BAILEY vol. II. **1885** *Homilet. Rev.* June 481 The leading examples of the early style [of preaching].. characterized by much unction and suasiveness.

†**suaˈsorian,** *a.* *Obs. rare*⁻¹. [f. L. *suāsōri-us* (see next) + -AN.] = SUASORY *a.*
1646 J. TEMPLE *Irish Reb.* Pref. 7 The true Suasorian causes (if I may so tearm them) which enduced the Irish to lay the plot.

suasory (ˈsweɪsərɪ), *a.* and *sb.* Now *rare.* Also 7 **swas-.** [ad. L. *suāsōri-us*, f. *suās-*, ppl. stem: see SUASIBLE and -ORY. Cf. obs. F. *suasoire.*]
A. *adj.* Tending to persuade; persuasive.
1576 FLEMING *Panopl. Epist.* A j, Of Epistles, some be demonstratiue, some suasorie. **1645** PAGITT *Heresiogr.* (1647) 124 The most noble kinde of working, a mans conversion..is performed by swasory motives or advice. **1690** C. NESSE *Hist. & Myst. O. & N. Test.* I. 316 Using other suasory arguments. **1826** H. N. COLERIDGE *Six Months W. Ind.* (1832) 145 A singularly eloquent preacher in the pathetic and suasory style. **1853** WHEWELL *Grotius* II. 378 Some are justificatory or justifying, some suasory or impelling.
†**B.** *sb.* = SUASIVE *sb.*
1625 *Debates Ho. Commons* (Camden) 158 Drawing his swasorie from the answear in religion. **1654** GAYTON *Pleas. Notes* IV. i. 171 The Curate..had the happinesse to..have the advantage of her eare to convey his Consolatories, Suasories,..and the like fragments of his profession.
b. (See SUASIVE *sb.* b.)
a **1656** USSHER *Ann.* (1658) 694 The first Suasory of M. Seneca.
Hence **ˈsuasoriness** *rare*⁻⁰.
1727 BAILEY vol. II, *Suasoriness*, aptness to persuade.

suave (swɑːv, formerly also sweɪv), *a.* (†*adv.*) Also 6 **suafe, swave,** *Sc.* **suaif, swaif.** [a. F. *suave* (16th cent.), a 'learned' formation which took the place of the 'popular' OF. *soef, suef* (*suaif*):—L. *suāvis* sweet, agreeable:—**swādwis*, f. *swād-* (see SWEET *a.*).]
1. Pleasing or agreeable to the senses or the mind; sweet.
c **1560** A. SCOTT *Poems* (S.T.S.) vii. 29 Adew þe fragrant balme suaif, And lamp of ladeis lustiest! **1598** Q. ELIZ. *Plutarch* ix. 3 The suafes thing that Silence dothe Expres. **1694** MOTTEUX *Rabelais* v. Epist. 251 These Times.. alterate the suavest Pulchritude. **1849** C. BRONTE *Shirley* xxvi, To whom the husky oat-cake was from custom suave as manna. **1859** MISS MULOCK *Life for a Life* xvii, To break the suave harmony of things. **1878** H. S. WILSON *Alpine Ascents* iii. 99 The suaver white hoods of snow summits.
†**2.** Gracious, kindly. Also *advb. Sc. Obs.*
1501 DOUGLAS *Pal. Hon.* III. ii, Thir musis gudelie and suaue. *c* **1550** ROLLAND *Crt. Venus* II. 76 The nine Musis sweit and swaue. *c* **1560** A. SCOTT *Poems* (S.T.S.) i. 214 Resaif swaif, and haif ingraif it heir. *Ibid.* xxxvi. 73 Sweit Lord, to Syon be suave.

3. Of persons, their manner: Blandly polite or urbane; soothingly agreeable. (Cf. SUAVITY 4.)
1831 F. REYNOLDS *Playwright's Adventures* iv. 63 St Alm was anything but *suave*. **1847** C. BRONTË *Jane Eyre* xiv, He ..showed a solid enough mass of intellectual organs, but an abrupt deficiency where the suave sign of benevolence should have risen. **1853** —— *Villette* xxi, The rare passion of the constitutionally suave, and serene, is not a pleasant spectacle. **1853** LYTTON *My Novel* III. xxvi, A slight disturbance of his ordinary suave and well-bred equanimity. **1863** GEO. ELIOT *Romola* xxxi, Doubtless the suave secretary had his own ends to serve. **1898** J. A. OWEN *Hawaii* iii. 55 Oahumi was quite captivated by the plausible, suave manners of the ingratiating southern chief.
Comb. **1894** 'MAX O'RELL' *J. Bull & Co.* 30 These suave-looking people, far away in the Pacific Ocean.

suavely (ˈsweɪvlɪ), *adv.* [f. SUAVE *a.* + -LY².]
1. In a suave manner; with suavity.
1862 THORNBURY *Turner* I. 317 Mr. Judkins suavely waves his glass. **1873** BLACK *Pr. Thule* xxii, 'Oh, there is no use getting into an anger', said Mackenzie, suavely. **1902** HICHENS *Londoners* 38 'So glad to find you at home, dear Mrs. Verulam', the Duchess said suavely.
2. Agreeably, sweetly, gently.
1883 SYMONDS *Ital. Byways* vi. 103 Low hills to right and left; suavely modelled heights in the far distance. **1887** ANNE ELLIOT *Old Man's Favour* I. II. i. 204 Mrs. Hammond's voice..fell suavely on her ear.
So **ˈsuaveness**, suavity.
1905 W. E. B. DU BOIS *Souls Blk. Folk* iii. 58 We cannot settle this problem by diplomacy and suaveness.

suaveolent (sweɪˈviːələnt), *a. rare.* [ad. L. *suāveolens, -entem*, f. *suāve* advb. neut. of *suāvis* SUAVE + *olens, olent-*, pr. pple. of *olēre* to smell.] Sweet-smelling, sweet-scented.
1657 TOMLINSON *Renou's Disp.* 85 Medicaments are made more odoriferous and suaveolent. **1819** [H. BUSK] *Banquet* II. 544 Suaveolent, the viands valets bear. **1900** B. D. JACKSON *Gloss. Bot. Terms* 257.
So †**suaˈveolence**, fragrance.
1657 TOMLINSON *Renou's Disp.* 201 Accomodated to conciliate suaveolence to the skin or body.

†**suaviate**, *v. Obs. rare.* [f. L. *suāviāt-*, ppl. stem of *suāviārī*, f. *suāvium*, altered f. *sāvium* kiss, by assimilation to *suāvis* sweet.] *trans.* To kiss. So †**suaviˈation**, kissing.
1643 TRAPP *Comm. Gen.* xlvi. 29 What joy there will be, to see them and suaviate them, for whose sake, he shed his most pretious blood. **1656** BLOUNT *Glossogr.*, *Suavation* [sic], an amorous kissing. **1658** PHILLIPS, *Suaviation*.

suavify (ˈswævɪfaɪ), *v. rare*⁻¹. [ad. L. *suāvificāre*, f. *suāvis* SUAVE: see -FY.] *trans.* To make affable (Webster 1847).
1825 *Spirit of Public Jrnls. for 1823* (ed. 2) 444 Eating much tends to suavify the mood.

suaviloquence (sweɪˈvɪləkwəns). *rare.* [ad. L. *suāviloquentia*, f. *suāviloquens*, f. *suāvi-s* SUAVE + *loquens*, pres. pple. of *loquī* to speak.] Pleasing or agreeable speech or manner of speaking. So **suaˈviloquent, suaviˈloquious** (in Dicts.) *adjs.*, of sweet speech; **suaˈviloquy** [L. *suāviloquium*], suaviloquence.
a **1649** in *N. & Q.* Ser. I. X. 357 *Suaviloquence, sweetnes of language. **1805** T. HOLCROFT *Bryan Perdue* II. 18 Pray, Madam, are you acquainted with the word suaviloquence? **1860** HERVEY *Rhet. Convers.* 16 Even though you can deliver it with great suaviloquence. **1656** BLOUNT *Glossogr.*, **Suaviloquent*. **1659** (*title*), A collection of Authentique Arguments, swaviloquent Speeches, and prudent Reasons. **1658** PHILLIPS, **Suaviloquy*, a sweet, or pleasant manner of speaking.

†**ˈsuavious**, *a. Obs. rare*⁻¹. [f. L. *suāvi-s* (see SUAVE) + -OUS.] Pleasing, agreeable.
1669 WORLIDGE *Syst. Agric.* 211 Not a few, of our most suavious and delectable Rural Seats.

†**ˈsuavitude.** *Obs. rare.* Also 6 **savitude**. [ad. L. *suāvitūdo*, f. *suāvis*: see SUAVE and -TUDE.] Sweetness, gentleness.
1512 *Helyas* in Thoms *Prose Rom.* (1828) III. 35 He thanked God greatly of his divine savitude. *c* **1550** ROLLAND *Crt. Venus* III. 727 Plenist with sport, and sueit suauitude.

suavity (ˈswɑːvɪtɪ, older ˈswæv-). Also 5 **suavitee**, 6 **-ite, -yte**, 6–7 **-itie**. [ad. L. *suāvitās* (partly through F. *suavité*), f. *suāvis*: see SUAVE and -ITY.]
†**1.** Sweetness or agreeableness to the senses; *esp.* sweetness (of taste), fragrance (of odour). *Obs.*
c **1450** *Mirour Saluacioun* (1888) 144 There, is alle suavitee delitable to touching. **1513** BRADSHAW *St. Werburge* I. 3372 Suche a suauite and fragrant odoure Ascended from the corps. *Ibid.* II. 1907 O redolent rose repleit with suauite. **1646** SIR T. BROWNE *Pseud. Ep.* VII. vii. 351 Rachel.. desired them [*sc.* mandrakes] for rarity, pulchritude or suavity. **1658** R. WHITE tr. *Digby's Powd. Symp.* (1660) 51 The smell of beans..is a smell that hath a suavity with it. **1661** BOYLE *Style Script.* 253 Of both their Suavities [*viz.* of God's word and of honey], Experience gives much Adventageouser Notions than Descriptions can.
†**b.** Sweetness (of sound, harmony, expression).
1614 J. DAVIES *Commend. Poems* (1878) 10/1 Musickes haters haue no Forme, or Soule: For, had they Soules produc't in Harmony, They would be rauisht with her Suauity. *c* **1645** HOWELL *Lett.* (1655) II. lviii. 78 Touching her [*sc.* the Greek tongue's] degeneration from her primitive suavity and elegance. **1678** CUDWORTH *Intell. Syst.* I. iv. 296 Plato does..very much commend the Orphick Hymns, for their Suavity and Deliciousness. *a* **1821** V. KNOX *Ess.* cv. Wks. 1824 I. 517, I know not whether the *curiosa felicitas*.. may not be said to consist in delicacy of sentiment and suavity of expression.
2. Pleasurableness, agreeableness; *pl.* delights, amenities. Now only as coloured by sense 4.
1594 NASHE *Terrors Nt.* Wks. (Grosart) III. 268 One.. who in the midst of his paine falls delighted asleepe, and in that suauitie of slumber surrenders the ghost. **1619** HALES *Gold. Rem.* II. (1673) 65 The suavity of their Doctrine in the word Peace and Good things. **1656** EARL MONM. tr. *Boccalini's Advts. fr. Parnass.* II. lix. (1674) 211 To taste the sweet of Government, the suavity of Command. **1669** GALE *Crt. Gentiles* I. III. i. 18 The delights or suavities, which attend the teachings of Poesie. **1823** J. BADCOCK *Dom. Amusem.* 63 The common suavities of social life. **1860** O. W. HOLMES *Prof. Breakf.-t.* vi, The elegances and suavities of life.
†**b.** A state of sweet calm in the soul when specially favoured by God; *pl.* feelings of spiritual sweetness or delight. *Obs.*
[*c* **1610** *Women Saints* 55 Her bodie yielding a most fragrant odoure..a greate token of her ghostlie suauitie.] *a* **1617** BAYNE *Chr. Lett.* (1620) L 8, I thanke God in Christ, sustentation I haue,..but suauities spirituall I taste not any. **1648** BOYLE *Motives Love of God* (1659) 52 The unimaginable suavity, that the fixing of ones Love on God, is able to blesse the Soul with. **1671** WOODHEAD *St. Teresa* I. xv. 93 That, which the Soul is to do..is only to rest with suavity, and without noyse. *a* **1680** GLANVILL *Some Disc.* i. (1681) 55 The conceit of our special dearness to God..that goes no further than to some suavities, and pleasant fancies within our selves.
†**3.** Graciousness; sweetness of manner or treatment. *Obs.*
1508 FISHER *7 Penit. Ps.* Wks. (1876) 248 *Suauis dominus vniuersis*..In euery thynge that god dooth is suauyte. **1642** H. MORE *Song of Soul* IV. *Oracle* (1647) 297 Mild-smiling Cupid's there, With lively looks and amorous suavitie. *a* **1649** in *N. & Q.* Ser. I. X. 357 Suavitie, or sweetnes of carriage, is a wynning quality.
4. The quality or condition of being suave in manner or outward behaviour; bland agreeableness or urbanity.
1815 W. H. IRELAND *Scribbleomania* 252 Histories.. which uniformly tend to inculcate suavity of manners. **1818** SCOTT *Br. Lamm.* xxix, 'Lucy, my love,' she added, with that singular combination of suavity of tone and pointed energy which we have already noticed. **1848** DICKENS *Dombey* xxix, These words, delivered with a cutting suavity. **1878** BLACK *Green Past.* iii, Sometimes a flash of vehement enthusiasm..would break through the suavity of manner which some considered to be just a trifle too supercilious.
b. *pl.* Suave actions.
1852 MRS. STOWE *Uncle Tom's C.* viii, Cajoled by the attentions of an electioneering politician with more ease than Aunt Chloe was won over by Master Sam's suavities.

suay, obs. Sc. form of SO *adv.*

sub (sʌb), *sb.* [Short for various subst. compounds of SUB-.]
1. a. = SUBORDINATE.
Quot. 1696 may belong to 4; quot. 1708 is of uncertain meaning.
1696 PHILLIPS (ed. 5), *Ordinary*,..the Bishop of the Dioceses Sub [*ed.* 1706 Deputy] at Sessions and Assizes. **1708** *Brit. Apollo* No. 74. 2/2 Thou hast neither good humour, Policy, nor Common Civility to make a *Sub* dance attendance after you like any indifferent Querist.
1840 H. SPENCER in *Autobiogr.* (1904) I. xii. 173, I go..to complete sundry works which the Subs have left undone. **1846** MRS. GORE *Engl. Char.* (1852) 111 He is never.. tyrannical with his *subs*, like most great potentates. **1899** *Mary Kingsley's W. Afr. Studies* App. I. 546 Had the late Mr. Consul Hewett had the fiftieth part of the ability in dealing with the natives his sub and successor..showed.
b. For various titles of subordinate officials, as *sub-editor, sub-engineer, sub-lieutenant, sub-rector, sub-warden.*
1837 *Civil Engin. & Arch. Jrnl.* I. 43/1 The sub, or resident engineer. **1859** *Eclectic Rev.* Ser. VI. V. 253 The Newspaper—day and night. By a Quondam 'Sub'. **1863** P. BARRY *Dockyard Econ.* Pref. vi, The Editor lives in an atmosphere of care. His assistant, or sub, begins the day at nine o'clock at night. **1872** 'A. MERION' *Odd Echoes Oxf.* 38 Fear no more the snarl of the sub., Thou art past that tyrant's stroke. **1873** LELAND *Egypt. Sketch-bk.* 44 The two great men who filled our carriage were a couple of Levantine railroad subs. **1898** KIPLING *Fleet in Being* ii, The Sub wipes the cinders out of his left eye and says something.
2. = SUBALTERN *sb.* 2.
1756 WASHINGTON *Writ.* (1889) I. 293 Leaving Garrisons in them from 15 to 30 men under command of a sub or Trusty Sergeant. **1812** *Sporting Mag.* XXXIX. 245 A Sub' of Dragoons. **1865** LEVER *Luttrell* xxxvi. 262 Some hard-up Sub who can't pay his mess debts.
3. = SUBSALT. *rare.*
1807 T. THOMSON *Chem.* (ed. 3) II. 519 Besides the triple salts and the *subs* and the *supers*.
4. = SUBSTITUTE; *U.S.* esp. of substitute printers.
1830 GALT *Lawrie Todd* IV. iv, The agent..proposed that I should become sub for him there. **1864** *Field* 9 July 22/1 Lillywhite was caught by Yescombe, a 'sub'. **1875** KNIGHT *Dict. Mech.* 2433/2 *Sub* (Well-boring), a short name for *substitute*. A short section of rod for connecting tools or bars of different sizes. **1876** *Scribner's Monthly* Apr. 838/1 He consented finally to allow another printer to take his place in the 'Clarion' office—temporarily, and as his 'sub' only. **1887** *Irish Times* 24 May 7/7 D. Carbery c. sub. b. W. G. Downey 1. **1895** *Funk's Stand. Dict.*, *Sub-list*, a list of the subs or substitute printers who are allowed to supply the places of regular compositors. **1896** *Bootle Times* 18 Jan. 3/2 North End were short of two of their regular players,..but managed to find good subs in Davies and Reed. **1896** *Indianapolis Typogr. Jrnl.* 16 Nov. 407 Every one of these subs is working part of the time.
5. = SUBJECT. Common in *U.S.*
1838 BECKET *Parad. Lost* 8 (F. & H.) No longer was he heard to sing, Like loyal subs, 'God Save the King.' **1885** *N.Y. Merc.* May (in Ware *Passing English*), The Mercury will be pleased to hear from Mrs. Williams on this sub.
6. = SUBSCRIBER (*rare*), SUBSCRIPTION.
1805 M. L. WEEMS *Let.* 9 Jan. (1929) II. 310 In 18 hours subscriptioneering I obtaind from the Legislature 100 subs. to Sydney. **1833** J. ROMILLY *Diary* 12 Mar. (1967) 30 Fairly bullied Waud & Jones into subscribing to my Blencowe cause:—got 4 others subs today. **1838** HOOD *Clubs* 62 Indeed my daughters both declare Their Beaux shall not be subs. To White's, or Blacks. **1898** W. S. CHURCHILL *Let.* 5 Aug. in R. S. Churchill *Winston S. Churchill* (1967) I. Compan. II. 956, I have to pay £40 for one charger, £35 for the other & £20 subs to the mess. **1903** FARMER & HENLEY *Slang*, *Sub* ..(3) a subscription. **1912** *Daily News* 12 Nov. 6 He lets the party have an annual 'sub.'..of £10,000.
7. = SUBSIST (*money*): money in advance on account of wages due at the end of a certain period. Also *gen.*, an advance of money. *local.*
Cf. Cornish dial. *sist* (*money*).
1866 *Min. Evid. Totnes Bribery Comm.* 72/2, I do not think there was much money flying about before that, my bills were not paid; I was rather anxious about having my sub. *Ibid.*, Tell us the name of any voter who asked you about the sub. **1881** *Placard at Bury* (*Lancs.*), Wanted navvies, to work on the above Railway, good wages paid, and sub on the works daily. **1892** *Labour Comm.* Gloss. No. 9 *Sub*, money paid to workmen at the Scotch blast-furnaces on account, as there exists a monthly pay-day. **1897** BARRÈRE & LELAND *Dict. Slang* s.v., To do a sub is to borrow money..(Anglo-Indian). **1901** *Scotsman* 12 Apr. 9/5 Provided the men started to-morrow, each would receive a 'sub' of £1 on Saturday.
8. a. = SUBMARINE *sb.* 3. Also Comb., as ***subchaser*** = *submarine chaser* s.v. SUBMARINE *sb.* 3 b.
1917 J. M. GRIDER *Diary* 29 Sept. in *War Birds* (1927) 21 We were supposed to look out for gulls which they say usually follow in the wake of a sub. **1918** L. E. RUGGLES *Navy Explained* 124 *Sub-chaser*, a small, swift, light draft boat used to hunt submarines. **1931** 'TAFFRAIL' *Endless Story* xxi. 333 'Sub-chaser' 28, manned by the French, broke down in the Atlantic 700 miles from the Azores and was given up for lost. **1936** *Nat. Geogr. Mag.* LXIX. 799/1 Seamanship..includes instruction on how to..maneuver.. such craft as subchasers and motor launches. **1968** A. DIMENT *Bang Bang Birds* ii. 16 Boris snooping round Holy Loch and the nuclear subs. **1977** *New Yorker* 29 Aug. 20/1 A subchaser lurches forward on the calm water and comes to a stop as a black sub surfaces at its side.
b. = SUBMARINE *sb.* 4 b. *U.S. colloq.*
1955 *Sat. Even. Post* 1 Jan. 16 'I tell you,' a sandwich-shop operator said, 'Subs are taking over.' **1976** R. B. PARKER *Promised Land* ii. 5, I was ready to settle for Ugi's steak and onion subs.

sub (sʌb), *v.* Hence **subbing** *vbl. sb.* [Short for various verbal compounds of SUB-; or f. SUB *sb.*]
†**1.** = *sub-plough* vb. (see SUB- 3 c). *Obs.*
1778 [W. MARSHALL] *Minutes Agric.* 16 Aug. 1775, Nothing can equal sub-plowing, for clearing the surface from running weeds;..the second subbing was eight or nine inches deep. *Ibid.* 20 Oct., It was subbed by two oxen.
2. To work as a printer's substitute. In *gen.* use, to act as a substitute. Also *trans.*, to substitute (something). Chiefly *U.S.*
1853 'MARK TWAIN' *Let.* 26 Oct. (1917) I. i. 26, I am subbing at the Inquirer office. *Ibid.*, If I want it, I can get subbing *every night* of the week. **1879** *University Mag.* Nov. 589 At Cincinnati where he [Edison]..'subbed' for the night men whenever he could obtain the privilege. **1926** *Amer. Mercury* Dec. 465/2 When a new act was placed last on a programme, *Variety* put it: 'Fred and Daisy Rial subbed in the walk-out assignment.' **1943** *Sun* (Baltimore) 17 Sept. 8/2 (*heading*) Subbing camera for gun, corporal 'shoots' zeros. **1950** A. LOMAX *Mister Jelly Roll* (1952) 218 The lord of New Orleans piano was scratching hard for a living.., subbing for other piano players who showed up drunk on their jobs. **1974** *Globe & Mail* (Toronto) 24 July 10/2 Toronto Executive Alderman Arthur C. Eggleton subbing for Mayor David Crombie. **1981** B. GRANGER *Schism* (1982) x. 88 Father Malachy is subbing for the pastor at St. Mary's... The pastor broke his leg, jogging.
3. To pay or receive ('sub'); *occas.* to pay (a workman) 'sub'. Also *absol.* (see quots.), and *to* ***sub up***: to pay up or subscribe.
1874 C. HOLLOWAY *Jrnl. Visit to N.Z.* 22 Apr. (*typescript*) I. 57 In some instances the dissipated individual had to sub a few shillings of the Landlord to help him on the road. **1874** HOTTEN *Slang Dict.* 314 *Sub*, to draw money in advance. **1886** H. CUNLIFFE *Gloss. Rochdale-with-Rossendale*, *Sub*, to pay a portion of wages before all are due. **1891** *Pall Mall Gaz.* 19 Nov. 612 During the month there has been a more than usual amount of 'subbing'. **1892** *Labour Comm.* Gloss. No. 9 Some pieces of cloth cannot be finished in one week, therefore a weaver must either do without wages or *sub*. **1900** *N. & Q.* Ser. IX. VI. 354/1, 'I want you to go at once to London,'..'All right; but I shall want to be subbed.' **1901** *Ibid.* VII. 356/2 It was my daily duty to keep time and to 'sub' for some hundreds of men engaged on extensive railway..works in England. **1942** O. JESPERSEN *Mod. Eng. Gram.* VI. 546 *Sub* = subsidy or subsistence.., also subscription..and as a vb., esp. *sub up* 'subscribe'. **1958** G. MITCHELL *Spotted Hemlock* vii. 75 'Wasn't that rather expensive?'.. 'I believe Tony Biancini subbed up.'
4. = SUB-EDIT. Also, *to sub the purple*: see PURPLE *sb.* 7 b.
c **1890** *F. Wilson's Fate* 84 When Wilson, in 'subbing' his copy, cut out all the 'u's' from 'favour', 'honour', and so forth, there was a debating society of two. **1909** *Fabian News*

XX. 76/1 A certain amount of margin and space between the lines for any 'subbing' that may be required.

5. [SUBSTRATUM 4.] In the manufacture of photographic film: to coat with a substratum (see quot. 1965). Chiefly as *vbl. sb.*, the process of applying a substratum; the substratum itself.

1941 T. T. BAKER *Photographic Emulsion Technique* x. 179 The film base may be wiped or cleaned prior to subbing... The cleaned and substratumed film base is coated at a fairly rapid rate. **1958** H. BAINES *Sci. Photogr.* vi. 83 The rear side of roll film and sheet film is subbed (substratum coated). **1965** M. J. LANGFORD *Basic Photogr.* ix. 161 The manufacturer first 'keys' both sides of the film base or coats them with a foundation layer of gelatin and cellulose ester known as the 'subbing' layer. Next, the emulsion is coated over the subbing on the face of the film. **1977** J. HEDGECOE *Photographer's Handbk.* 263/1 Other non-porous surfaces should be pre-coated with the subbing which is normally supplied with the emulsion.

sub, obs. Sc. form of SIB.

‖**sub** (sʌb). *Lat. prep.* The Latin prep. *sub* (with the ablative) 'under', enters into a few legal and other phrases, now or formerly in common use, the chief of which are given below.

1. sub camino (?).

1734 SHORT *Nat. Hist. Min. Waters* 132 He posts off to one of the obscure Universities in Holland or France, gets dubbed Doctor with a *sub Camino* Degree in Physick.

2. sub dio, under the open sky, in the open air.

1611 CORYAT *Crudities* 28 He walked not *sub dio*, that is, vnder the open aire as the rest did. **1673** RAY *Journ. Low C.* 403 At Aleppo.. they set their beds upon the roofs of their houses, and sleep *sub Dio*, in the open air. **1704** SWIFT *T. Tub* ii, Attended the Levee *sub dio*. **1775** G. WHITE *Selborne, To Barrington* 2 Oct., The sturdy savages [*sc.* gipsies] seem to pride themselves.. in living *sub dio* the whole year round. **1880** SHORTHOUSE *John Inglesant* xviii, I would always.. be 'sub dio' if it were possible.

3. sub forma pauperis = *in forma pauperis* (see ‖IN 10).

1592 *Soliman & Pers.* I. iv. 89 Crie the chayne for me *Sub forma pauperis*, for money goes very low with me at this time. **1616** R. C. *Times' Whistle* 1492 Poor Codrus is Constraind to sue *sub forma pauperis*. **1654** WHITLOCK *Zootomia* 127 Should a Patient be bound to give all his Advisers a Fee, He must quickly be removed.. to the Hospital, there to bee sick *sub forma pauperis*.

4. sub hasta, lit. 'under a spear' [see SPEAR *sb.* 3 b], i.e. by auction (cf. SUBHASTATION).

1689 EVELYN *Let. to Pepys* 12 Aug., The humour of exposing books *sub hastâ* is become so epidemical.

5. sub Jove frigido, under the chilly sky, in the open air.

1818 SCOTT *Br. Lamm.* i, A peripatetic brother of the brush, who exercised his vocation *sub Jove frigido*. **1845** FORD *Handbk. Spain* I. 121 Not *sub Jove frigido*, but amid the bursting, life-pregnant vegetation of the South.

6. sub judice, lit. 'under a judge'; under the consideration of a judge or court; undecided, not yet settled, still under consideration.

1613 J. CHAMBERLAIN in *Crt. & Times Jas. I* (1848) I. 279 Lord Hay is like.. to be made an earl, but whether English or Scottish is yet *sub judice*. **1681** STAIR *Inst. Law Scot.* I. xvi. 334 The Relict did also claim a Terce out of that same one Tenement, which is yet *sub judice*. **1778** GEN. C. LEE in *Mem.* (1792) 426 Lingering in suspence, whilst his fame and fortune are *sub judice*. *a* **1817** T. DWIGHT *Trav. New Eng.*, etc. (1821) I. 104 They plainly consider the case as no longer *sub-judice*. **1828** DE QUINCEY *Rhetoric* Wks. 1890 X. 110 The relations of the People and the Crown.. continued *sub judice* from that time to 1688. **1897** *Daily News* 10 Dec. 8/3 He said the matter was being considered by the Committee, and therefore was sub judice.

7. sub lite, in dispute.

1892 *Nation* 8 Dec. 438/3 Mr. Petrie's dates are still, with good reason, *sub lite*.

8. sub modo, under certain conditions, with a qualification, within limits.

a **1623** SWINBURNE *Treat. Spousals* (1686) 139 If a Man and a Woman contract Matrimony *Sub modo*. **1726** AYLIFFE *Parergon* 336 That this *Paragium* or Legacy descends to her Executors like other Legacies bequeath'd purely and *sub modo*. **1765–8** ERSKINE *Inst. Law Scot.* III. i. §8 Obligations granted *sub modo*.. are not.. suspended until performance by the creditors in them. **1807** *Edin. Rev.* July 352 The opinion.. might be held *sub modo*, with perfect impunity. **1843–56** BOUVIER *Law Dict.* (ed. 6) s.v., A legacy may be given sub modo, that is, subject to a condition or qualification.

9. sub pede sigilli (see quot. 1843–56).

a **1676** HALE *Hist. Placit. Cor.* (1736) I. 171 Certificates, which are usually pleaded *sub pede sigilli*. **1843–56** BOUVIER *Law Dict.* (ed. 6) II. 554/2 *Sub pede sigilli*, under the foot of the seal; under seal.

10. sub plumbo, 'under lead', *i.e.* under the Pope's seal.

1522 J. CLERK in Ellis *Orig. Lett.* Ser. III. I. 314 The bull of the Kyngs title was made up *sub plumbo* bifore the Popis deth. **1535** *Lett. Suppr. Monast.* (Camden) 58 The pope.. gave hym licens to kepe an hore, and hath goode writyng *sub plumbo* to discharge his conscience.

11. sub pœna, under a penalty *of*.

1466 in *Archæologia* (1887) L. I. 52 Sub pena of a jd. to the Church to be payd.

12. sub rosa [see ROSE *sb.* 7], 'under the rose', in secret, secretly.

1654 GAYTON *Pleas. Notes* III. v. 93 What ever thou and the foule pusse did doe (*sub Rosa* as they say). **1772** J. ADAMS *Diary* 20 Dec. Wks. 1850 II. 305 This however, *sub rosâ*, because the Doctor passes for a master of composition. *a* **1834** COLERIDGE (in Dixon *Dict. Idiom. Phr.*), I wonder some of you lawyers (*sub rosa*, of course) have not quoted the pithy line of Mandeville. **1844** N. P. WILLIS *Lady Jane* II. lxxvii, Had he a 'friend' *sub rosa*? No, sir! Fie, sir!

13. sub sigillo [see SEAL *sb.*[2] 2 b], under the seal (of confession); in confidence, in secret.

1623 J. MEAD in *Crt. & Times Jas. I* (1848) II. 406 The forenamed Mr. Elliot told, *sub sigillo*, some suspicious passages. **1673** DRYDEN *Marr. à la Mode* II. 19, I may tell you, as my friend, *sub sigillo*, &c. this is that very numerical Lady, with whom I am in love. **1777** H. WALPOLE *Let. to H. S. Conway* 5 Oct., Remember, one tells one's creed only to one's confessor, that is *sub sigillo*.

14. sub silentio, in silence, without remark being made, without notice being taken.

1617–8 J. CHAMBERLAIN in *Crt. & Times Jas. I* (1848) II. 62 All things shut up *sub silentio* **1760** GILBERT *Cases in Law & Equity* 267 These are better than many precedents in the office, which have passed sub silentio without being litigated. **1843–56** BOUVIER *Law Dict.* (ed. 6) II. 555/2 Sometimes passing a thing sub silentio is evidence of consent. **1863** KEBLE *Life Bp. Wilson* xvi. 511 The Bishop would probably have passed over Mr. Quayle's second communication *sub silentio* as he had done the former.

15. sub specie æternitatis, 'under the aspect of eternity', i.e. viewed in relation to the eternal; in a universal perspective. [Cf. Spinoza *Ethices* (*a* 1677), in *Opera Posthuma*, 1677, v. xxix. 254.] Hence **sub specie temporis**, viewed in relation to time rather than eternity.

1896 W. CALDWELL *Schopenhauer's System* v. 268 Art enables us somehow to see things *sub specie aeternitatis*. **1911** *Encycl. Brit.* XXI. 441/2 The nature of any fact is not fully known unless we know it in all its relations to the system of the universe, or, in Spinoza's phrase, *sub specie aeternitatis*. **1925** A. HUXLEY *Let.* 21 Apr. (1969) 247 There, on the other side of the water, are one hundred and five million beings whose sole function—if you look at their lives sub specie aeternitatis—is to provide people like us with money. **1935** E. R. EDDISON *Mistress* 20 This man, as I have long observed him, looked on all things *sub specie æternitatis*; his actions all moved.. to slow perfection. **1952** V. A. DEMANT *Relig. & Decline of Capitalism* iii. 70 Hence what was true *sub specie aeternitatis* in the liberal aim is being lost. **1973** G. M. BROWN *Magnus* vii. 139 If.. we could look with the eye of an angel on the whole history of men, *sub specie aeternitatis*, it would have the brevity and beauty of this dance at the altar. **1928** L. HODGSON in A. E. J. Rawlinson *Essays on Trinity & Incarnation* viii. 378 Perhaps the best one can do is to speak of God as ἀπαθὴς *sub specie aeternitatis* but παθητικός *sub specie temporis*. **1944** W. TEMPLE *Let.* 12 Jan. (1963) 142, I have treated the Son and the Spirit as God *sub specie temporis* and the Father as God *sub specie eternitatis*. **1960** *Encounter* XV. 77 *Sub specie temporis* his Combination Rooms say more to us than Beckett's wet and windy plains.

16. sub specie mortis, in the face of death.

1955 *Times* 26 May 3/4 The ninth symphony, we are told, is poignant in that it was his last and written *sub specie mortis*. **1964** *Listener* 21 May 849/3 Written *sub specie mortis*, they are his [*sc.* Mahler's] most 'existentialist' works.

17. sub verbo = *sub voce*, sense 18; abbreviated *s.v.* (see S 4 a).

1902 J. M. BALDWIN *Dict. Philos. & Psychol.* II. 358/2 Many citations in Eisler, Wörterb. d. philos. Begriffe, sub verbo.

18. sub voce, under the word (so-and-so); abbreviated s.v. Cf. VOCE[2].

1859 *N. & Q.* 23 Apr. 341/1 Skinner, *Gloss.*, *sub voce*, evidently understands the word in this sense. **1871** *Ibid.* 9 Dec. 487/1 See Halliwell's *Dict.*, sub voce 'Braid'.

sub- (sʌb, səb), *prefix*, repr. L. *sub-* = the prep. *sub* under, close to, up to, towards, used in composition (cf. UNDER-) with the various meanings detailed below. (The related Skr. *upa-*, Gr. ὑπο- have a similar range of meaning.)

The *b* of L. *sub-* remained unchanged when it preceded a radical beginning with *s*, *t*, or *v*; before *m* and *r* it was frequently assimilated (see e.g. SUMMON, SURROGATE), and before *c*, *f*, *g*, and *p* it was almost invariably assimilated (see e.g. SUCCEED, SUFFER, SUGGEST, SUPPOSE). Variation is illustrated by L. *subfuscus* SUBFUSC beside L. *suffuscus*, *subrogātus* SUBROGATE beside *surrogātus* SURROGATE. A by-form *subs-* (cf. ABS-) was normally reduced to *sus-* in certain compounds with words having initial *c*, *p*, *t*, e.g. *suscipĕre*, *suspendĕre*, *sustinēre* (see SUSCEPTION, SUSPEND, SUSTAIN); and before *sp-* the prefix becomes *su-*, as in *suspicĕre*, *suspicio*, *suspirāre* (see SUSPECT, SUSPICION, SUSPIRE).

The original force of the prefix is either entirely lost sight of or to a great extent obscured in many words derived immediately or ultimately from old Latin compounds, such as *subject*, *suborn*, *subscription*, *subserve*, *subsist*, *substance*. (Where the prefix occurs in an assimilated form and is consequently disguised, as in *succeed*, *suffer*, *suppose*, an analysis of the compound does not readily suggest itself.) As a living prefix in English it bears a full meaning of its own and is freely employed in the majority of the senses defined below. Appropriate originally to composition with words of Latin origin it has become capable of being prefixed to words of native English or any other origin. This extension took place as early as the 15th c., but the beginnings of the wide use of which it is now capable date from the latter half of the 18th c., to which a large number of the earliest examples of scientific terms belong.

The more important and permanent compounds, whether general or technical, are entered in this Dictionary as main words; in the present article are treated such compounds of a general character as have not a permanent status in the language and scientific terms the meaning of which may (for the most part) be gathered from the meaning of the prefix and that of the radical element.

In Romanic, *sub-* was replaced by *subtus-* as a living prefix; e.g. *sublevāre* was ousted by **subtuslevāre*, whence OF. *souz-*, *souslever*, mod.F. *soulever*. (Cf. SOUTH-[2].) But *sub-* appears in OF. (1) from the 12th cent. in learned adoptions of old Latin compounds, e.g. *suborner* to SUBORN, *substance*, *subversion*, (2) from the 14th cent. (with variant *soub-*) in forms substituted for older compounds with *souz-*, *sous-*; e.g. *submayeur* (cf. *soubzmaire*) sub-mayor, *subprieur* (cf. *sousprieur*) SUBPRIOR, (AF.) *subtaxour* sub-taxer, *subvicaire* sub-vicar (see 6 below); *soubmetre* for *sousmetre* to SUBMIT.

Pronunciation. The prefix bears the main stress (1) in the following words derived from compounds of the old Latin stock, viz. *'subject* (sb.), *'subscript*, *'substance*, *'suburb*; *'subaltern*, *'subdolous*, *'subjugate*, *'sublimate*, *'subsequent*, *'subsidize*, *'subsidy*, *'substantive*, *'substitute*, *'subtrahend*; also in *'submarine*; (2) in words in which there is an implicit contrast with the simple word, e.g. *'subarch*, *'subclass*, *'subflavour*, *'subgenus*, *'sub-office*, *'subsection*, *'subsoil*. (As with other prefixes that express contrast, the principal stress is always on *sub-* when the contrast is explicit, as *deacon and 'subdeacon*, *to let or 'sublet*, *epithelial and 'subepithelial tissue*.) The prefix is stressless and the quality of its vowel is consequently reduced in *sub'duce*, *sub'due*, *sub'jective*, *sub'join*, *sub'junctive*, *sub'lime*, *sub'merge*, *sub'mit*, *sub'ordinate*, *sub'reption*, *sub'scribe*, *sub'serve*, *sub'side*, *sub'sidiary*, *sub'sist*, *sub'stantial*, *sub'stratum*, *sub'sume*, *sub'tend*, *sub'tract*, *su'burban*, *sub'vene*, *sub'vert*, and their derivatives. In other cases the prefix bears a stress varying from a light secondary to a stress even with that of the second element of the compound (the vowel being consequently unobscured), as in *ˌsub'acid*, *ˌsub'clavian*, *'sub'dean*, *ˌsubo'percular*, *ˌsubte'rranean*. In compounds belonging to branch II, even stress tends to prevail.

I. Under, underneath, below, at the bottom (of).

1. Forming adjs. in which *sub-* is in prepositional relation to the sb. implied in the second element, as in L. *subaquāneus* = that is *sub aquā* under water, SUBAQUANEOUS, *subdiālis* = that is *sub diō*, SUBDIAL, *subterrāneus* = that is *sub terrā*, SUBTERRANEAN, -EOUS.

a. Compounds of a general character (mainly nonce-wds.) and miscellaneous scientific terms.

subar'boreal, lying under a forest of trees. **sub'astral**, situated beneath the stars, mundane, terrestrial. **sub'cambrian** *Geol.*, lying beneath the Cambrian formation. **ˌsubcarbo'niferous** *Geol.*, designating the mountain-limestone formation of the carboniferous series or that lying beneath the millstone grit, lower carboniferous. †**sub'consulary**, being under the government of consuls. **sub'crustal**, lying under the crust of the earth. **sub'ferulary** [see FERULAR], under school discipline. **sub'fluvial**, extending under a river. **sub'glacial**, existing or taking place under the ice. **subla'custrine**, lying or deposited at the bottom of a lake. **sub'mundane**, existing beneath the world. **sub'niveal**, **-'nivean**, existing or carried on under the snow. **sub'nubilar**, situated beneath the clouds. **ˌsuboce'anic**, beneath the ocean. **ˌsubphoto'spheric**, produced under the photosphere. †**sub'renal**, occurring beneath the kidneys or in the region of the loins. **sub'ruinan**, underneath ruins. **subsca'larian** *a.* used as *sb.* (see quot.). **ˌsubsuper'ficial**, occurring below the surface. †**ˌsubtegu'laneous** [L. *subtegulāneus*, f. *tegula* tile], under the roof or eaves. **sub'tidal** *Ecol.*, situated or occurring below the low tide mark. **sub'undane** [L. *unda* wave], growing beneath the waves. **sub-'Wealden**, under the Wealden strata in Sussex (or similar strata elsewhere).

1886 GUILLEMARD *Cruise of Marchesa* II. 10 The explorer who penetrates the true primeval forest in a country such as Borneo finds himself at the bottom of a *subarboreal world. **1752** WARBURTON *Serm. Ps. cxliv.* 3 He compares this *sub-astral œconomy with the systems of the fixed stars. **1871** TYNDALL *Fragm. Sci.* (1879) II. ix. 172 The riddle of the rocks has been read from *sub-cambrian depths. **1849** DANA *Geol.* ix. (1850) 485 These *sub-carboniferous beds are well developed in Illawarra. **1654** H. L'ESTRANGE *Chas.*

I (1655) 55 In *subconsulary Rome, Athens or Sparta. **1898** *Geogr. Jrnl.* Nov. 545 Volcanic outflow of *subcrustal molten matter. **1852** Sir W. Hamilton *Discuss.* 118 Having in his tender years been *subferulary to some other kind of schooling. **1863** Hawthorne *Our Old Home, Up the Thames* II. 134 Making the *subfluvial avenue [*viz.* the Thames tunnel] only a little gloomier than a sheet of upper London. **1820** W. Scoresby *Acc. Arctic Reg.* I. 105 Pursuing their course through *subglacial channels to the front of the iceberg. **1860** Tyndall *Glac.* I. viii. 60 Strange subglacial noises were sometimes heard. **1859** Thirlwall *Rem.* (1878) III. 203 The prevailing notion of the *sublacustrine domains is, that they are full of countless treasures. **1832** *Examiner* 115/1 Yet have we our festivals Even in these *submundane halls. **1885** *Field* 12 Dec. 824/1 A favourite resort for these *sub-niveal operations is a steep bank where the heather is old and long. **1845** S. Judd *Margaret* I. xvii, Seizing a shovel he..commenced his *subnivean work. **1864-5** Wood *Homes without Hands* 38 In a subnivean abode. **1877** Dawson *Orig. World* ii. 63 That there is no *sub-nubilar solid sphere. **1858** *Rep. Brit. Assoc.* I. 22 *Suboceanic and subaerial volcanic ejecta. **1903** Agnes M. Clerke *Probl. Astrophysics* 66 *Sub-photospheric heat may be of almost any intensity. **1607** Topsell *Four-f. Beasts* 77 The humors which annoy the body of oxen are many, the first is a moist one called Malis;..the sixt a *Subrenall, when the hinder legs halte by reason of some paine in the loines. **1881** J. P. Briscoe *Old Nottinghamshire* 140 What is that sound! A subterranean, or *subruinan voice? **1790** Cowper *Let. to J. Johnson* 28 Feb., As to yourself, whom I know to be a **subscalarian*, or a man that sleeps under the stairs. **1899** *Smithsonian Rep.* 230 The superficial and *subsuperficial temperatures. **1656** Blount *Glossogr.*, **Subtegulaneous*, that is under the eaves or roofs of houses. **1878** *N. Amer. Rev.* CXXVII. 163 This subtegulaneous solitude. **1939** Clements & Shelford *Bio-Ecol.* x. 313 The *subtidal community reaches up into the tidal area. **1979** R. Brewer *Princ. Ecol.* v. 231 It is usual to recognize three zones on both sandy and rocky shores. These are the intertidal zone itself, a supratidal zone above it.., and the subtidal zone. **1851** D. Landsborough *Brit. Seaweeds* (ed. 2) 19 With bright festoons of gayer, gentler algues, *Subundane drapery. **1872** in *Rec. Sub-Wealden Explor.* (1878) 6 The thickness of the *Sub-Wealden strata in France and Belgium.

(*b*) In derived advbs., as **sub'glacially** *adv.*, under an ice sheet or glacier.

1909 Webster, *Subglacially. **1978** *Nature* 8 June 456/2 Lava flows which were erupted subglacially in southwestern Iceland.

b. *Anat.* (*Path.*, *Surg.*) and *Zool.* = Situated or occurring under or beneath (occas. behind) the part or organ denoted by the radical element, or lying on the ventral side of it or ventrally with respect to it; as in (late) L. *subālāris* that is *sub ālīs* under the wings, *suboculāris* SUBOCULAR, mod.L. *sublinguālis* SUBLINGUAL, etc.

Compounds of this class may coincide in form with compounds having a different analysis. Thus, *subabdominal* = under the abdomen, f. *sub abdōmine* + -AL[1], coincides with *subabdominal* = not quite abdominal, f. SUB- 21 d + ABDOMINAL; so SUBCARTILAGINOUS, SUBCENTRAL, SUBMUCOUS *subspinous*. Also, such a form as SUBUMBRELLAR may be analysed as (1) *sub umbrellā* + -AR[1] = situated beneath the umbrella, or (2) f. *subumbrella* (see f below) + -AR[1] = pertaining to the subumbrella; so SUBMENTAL. (In this second case the resultant signification is much the same whichever analysis is taken.)

In some of these compounds the implied regimen of the prep. is not a simple sb. but a group consisting of an adj. and a sb., the adj. being the element represented in the compound; e.g. *subdural*.

In the following list explanations of the radical element have been occasionally added in brackets; in most instances the meaning of the compound is readily inferred from that of the prefix and of the second element. Many more words of this class are to be found in the medical dicts. of Billings, Dorland, and others, *Sydenham Society's Lex.*, Allbutt's *Syst. Med.*, Buck's *Handbk. Med. Sci.*, etc.

subab'dominal (= situated or occurring under, below, or beneath the abdomen), ***suba'cromial***, ***sub'alar***, ***sub'anal***, ***subaponeu'rotic***, ***suba'stragaloid***, ***subau'ricular*** (an auricle), ***sub'cæcal***, ***sub'calcarine*** (the calcarine fissure), ***sub'capsular***, ***ˌsubcere'bellar***, ***subco'llateral*** (the collateral fissure of the brain), ***ˌsubconjunc'tival*** (the conjunctiva), ***sub'coracoid***, ***sub'cranial*** (the cranium, the cranial axis), ***subcu'ticular***, ***sub'deltoid***, ***sub'dermal***, ***-oid***, ***ˌsubdiaphrag'matic***, ***sub'discal*** (the discal shell), ***sub'dural*** (the dura mater), ***ˌsubecto'dermal***, ***-ic***, ***ˌsubendo'cardial***, ***ˌsubendo'stylar***, ***ˌsubendo'thelial***, ***ˌsubepi'dermal***, ***-ic***, ***ˌsubepi'thelial***, ***sub'falcial*** (the falx cerebri), ***sub'fascial***, ***sub'frontal*** (a frontal lobe), ***sub'genital***, ***sub-'genual*** (the knee), ***sub-'gingival*** (the gums, esp. between the gum-margins and the teeth), ***sub'glenoid*** (the glenoid fossa), ***sub'glottal***, ***sub'glottic*** (the glottis), ***sub'gular*** (the throat), ***sub'hæmal***, ***sub'hyoid***, ***ˌsubinte'stinal***, ***sub'labial***, ***subla'ryngeal***, ***sub'lobular*** (a lobule of the liver), ***sub'loral***, ***sub'mammary***, ***subman'dibular***, ***sub'mastoid***, ***subme'ningeal***, ***sub'muscular***, ***sub'nervian***, ***-'neural*** (a main neural axis or nervous cord), ***sub'nodal***, ***ˌsubœso'phageal***, ***-an***, ***sub'oral***, ***sub'ostracal*** (the shell, Gr. ὄστρακον), ***sub'pallial***, ***subpa'rietal*** (the parietal bone, lobe, etc.), ***subpe'duncular***, ***sub'pelvic***, ***ˌsubperi'cranial***, ***ˌsubperi'osteal***, ***ˌsubperito'neal***, ***ˌsubperito'neo-ab'dominal***, ***-'pelvic*** (the abdominal peritoneum, the peritoneum of the pelvis; applied to forms of extra-uterine pregnancy), ***subpe'trosal*** (the petrosal bone), ***sub'phrenic*** (the diaphragm), ***sub'pial*** (the pia mater), ***sub'pleural***, ***subpre'putial***, ***sub'pubic***, ***subpy'loric***, ***sub'radular***, ***sub'retinal***, ***sub'scrotal***, ***subsphe'noidal***, ***sub'spinal***, ***-'spinous***, ***sub'sternal***, ***sub'stigmatal***, ***sub'sylvian*** (the Sylvian fissure), ***subsy'novial*** (a synovial membrane), ***sub'tectal*** (the tectum of the skull), ***subtegu'mental***, ***sub'temporal*** (a temporal gyrus of the brain), ***subten'tacular*** (the tentacles or tentacular canal), ***subtra'pezial***, ***sub'ungual***, ***-'unguial***, ***subva'ginal***, ***sub'ventral***.

1840 *Cuvier's Animal Kingdom* 408 These branchiæ are situated..upon the *subabdominal appendages. **1839** *Dublin Jrnl. Med. Sci.* XV. 260 Symmetrical *Sub-acromial Luxations. **1834** G. Bennett *Wand. N.S.W.* II. 45 The beautiful *sub-alar plumage. **1889** *Q. Jrnl. Geol. Soc.* XLV. 644 The *subanal fasciole. **1868** Gay *Varicose Dis.* 150 The trunk veins, especially the *subaponeurotic. **1872** T. Bryant *Pract. Surg.* 1061 *Subastragaloid amputation. **1822** J. Parkinson *Outl. Oryctol.* 187 *Subauricular tooth in the larger valve. **1890** Billings *Nat. Med. Dict.*, **Subcæcal fossa*, pocket sometimes found in the peritoneum behind the cæcum. **1889** *Buck's Handbk. Med. Sci.* VIII. 154 The replacement of lingual lobule and fusiform lobule..by *subcalcarine gyre and *subcollateral gyre. **1889** *Lancet* 20 Apr. 787/2 The *subcapsular portion of the cortex. **1889** *Buck's Handbk. Med. Sci.* VIII. 240 The *subcerebellar veins. **1839-47** *Todd's Cycl. Anat.* III. 85/1 The cellular tissue..is sometimes the seat of..*subconjunctival ecchymosis. **1878** T. Bryant *Pract. Surg.* I. 308 Inflammation of the sclerotic or subconjunctival fascia. **1839** *Dublin Jrnl. Med. Sci.* XV. 251 Congenital *Subcoracoid Luxation. **1876** *Quain's Anat.* (ed. 8) II. 738 *Subcranial, Facial, or Pharyngeal Plates or Arches. **1855** Hyde Clarke *Dict.*, **Subcuticular*, under the cuticle. **1899** *Allbutt's Syst. Med.* VI. 575 The whitlow is often sub-cuticular. **1853** *Dublin Quart. Jrnl. Med. Sci.* XV. 6 The *subdeltoid bursa. **1887** Sollas in *Encycl. Brit.* XXII. 415/1 These cavities are known as *subdermal chambers. **1845** Todd & Bowman *Phys. Anat.* I. 425 They lie either in the cutis or *sub-dermoid tissue. **1844** Hoblyn *Dict. Terms Med.* (ed. 2) 293 **Sub-diaphragmatic*, the designation of a plexus, furnished by the solar plexus, and distributed to the diaphragm. **1902** *Proc. Zool. Soc.* II. 272 A *sub-discal series of internervular spots and dashes. **1875** W. Turner *Hum. Anat.* 219 A fine space containing a minute quantity of limpid serum..named the arachnoid cavity, or,..the *sub-dural space. **1888** *Q. Jrnl. Micros. Sci.* (N.S.) XXVIII. 381 The cutaneous muscles arise from the *subectodermal fibrous network. **1888** Rolleston & Jackson *Anim. Life* 784 A *sub-ectodermic plexus of ganglion cells in the subumbrella. **1897** *Allbutt's Syst. Med.* II. 827 *Sub-endocardial hæmorrhages. **1893** *Athenæum* 2 Dec. 774/1 The *subendostylar cœlom. **1875** W. Turner in *Encycl. Brit.* I. 848/2 The endothelial cells rest upon a *sub-endothelial tissue. **1853** *Pharmac. Jrnl.* XIII. 17 The *sub-epidermal cellular tissue. **1877** Huxley & Martin *Elem. Biol.* 65 The *subepidermic cells. **1873** T. H. Green *Introd. Pathol.* 264 The *sub-epithelial connective tissue. **1889** *Buck's Handbk. Med. Sci.* VIII. 121 The presence of a *subfalcial sinus. **1897** *Allbutt's Syst. Med.* IV. 601 Its source, a degenerate gland, is not only subcutaneous, but *subfascial also, that is, under the deep cervical fascia. **1877** Huxley *Anat. Inv. Anim.* vi. 260 The sternal surface presents, anteriorly, a flattened *sub-frontal area. **1888** Rolleston & Jackson *Anim. Life* 785 The membranes come to lie at the bottom of *subgenital cavities or lemnia. **1934** Webster, *Subgenual. **1935** R. E. Snodgrass *Princ. Insect Morphol.* xvii. 527 Proximally, below the 'knee', is a large fan-shaped subgenual organ. **1978** H. V. Daly *Introd. Insect Biol. & Diversity* vi. 109/1 Sub-genual organs are found in many insects but are lacking in Archeognatha, Coleoptera, and Diptera. **1898** H. H. Burchard *Text-bk. Dental Path. & Therapeutics* xxiv. 456 By *subgingival deposits are meant calculi which are first deposited in the annular depression between the gum-margin and a tooth. **1979** Williams & Elliott *Basic & Appl. Dental Biochem.* xii. 224 Dental plaque covers the tooth (supragingival plaque) and extends over the tooth surface of the gingival pocket (subgingival plaque). **1872** Humphry *Myology* 31 The palmar muscles take their origin from the coracoids, or *subglenoid part of the girdle. **1932** W. L. Graff *Language & Languages* i. 33 Even if we assume that the *subglottal force of expiration is the same.., on leaving the larynx its strength is..weakened. **1970** *Language* XLVI. 313 It would seem difficult to ascertain whether a change in fundamental frequency is due to a change in the tension of the laryngeal muscles or to a change in the subglottal air pressure. **1880** A. Flint *Princ. Med.* 304 Œdema in very rare instances occurs below the vocal cords. This is distinguished as *subglottic œdema. **1858** W. Clark tr. *Van der Hoeven's Zool.* II. 249 *Subgular vocal sac. **1872** Humphry *Myology* 8 The Cryptobranch is continued from the interior of the pelvis beneath the hæmal arches of the tail where it blends with the *subhæmal septum. **1876** *Quain's Anat.* (ed. 8) II. 740 The fourth arch, which has no special name, but might be called *sub-hyoid or cervical. **1870** Rolleston *Anim. Life* 125 Vessels..which pass round the intestine..to join a *sub-intestinal vessel. **1875** Blake *Zool.* 196 The nasal sacs are *sublabial. **1901** *Proc. Zool. Soc. London* I. 281 The *sub-laryngeal pouch is essentially a cæcal diverticulum of the ventral wall of the larynx, between the thyroid and cricoid cartilages. **1949** Koestler *Insight & Outlook* 391 A continuous flow of physiological processes, involving.. sublaryngeal movements (inner speech). **1839-47** *Todd's Cycl. Anat.* III. 173/1 The *sublobular veins are named from their position at the base of the lobules. **1896** *Brit. Birds, Their Nests & Eggs* I. 185 The superciliary and *sub-loral white streaks. **1857** Dunglison *Med. Lex.* s.v., '*Sub-mammary inflammation', inflammation of the areolar tissue beneath the mamma. **1875** Buckland *Log-Bk.* 118 The *submandibular..tissues. **1844** Hoblyn *Dict. Terms Med.* (ed. 2) 293 **Sub-mastoïd*, the name of a branch given off by the seventh pair of nerves, as it passes out from the stylo-mastoïd foramen. **1899** *Allbutt's Syst. Med.* VII. 569 Some injury during birth, such as usually results in *submeningeal hæmorrhage. **1855** Dunglison *Med. Lex.*, **Submuscular*, seated beneath muscles or a muscular layer. **1888** *Encycl. Brit.* XXIV. 679 In *Lumbricus* there are three longitudinal trunks which run from end to end of the body—(1) dorsal, (2) supranervian, (3) *subnervian. **1878** Bell tr. *Gegenbaur's Comp. Anatomy* 279 A *subneural cavity [in insects]. **1900** Lucas *Brit. Dragonflies* 53 The ultra-nodal sector is found between the principal and the *sub-nodal. **1835-6** *Todd's Cycl. Anat.* I. 547/2 A second [ganglion], which is *subœsophageal and anterior, supplies the buccal apparatus. **1858** W. Clark tr. *Van der Hoeven's Zool.* II. 59 Branchiæ open internally in a *subœsophagean tube. **1836-9** *Todd's Cycl. Anat.* II. 393/2 The *sub-oral ganglion is particularly subservient to mastication. **1883** *Encycl. Brit.* XVI. 675/2 A thin plate-like '*sub-ostracal' or (so-called) dorsal cartilage. **1854** Woodward *Mollusca* II. 195 A *sub-pallial expansion on the sides of the back. **1889** *Buck's Handbk. Med. Sci.* VIII. 152 *Subparietal [gyre]. **1815** J. Gordon *Syst. Hum. Anat.* I. 211 The *sub-peduncular Lobule of the Cerebellum. **1864** *Reader* No. 103. 771/1 The acute *subpelvic arch. **1872** T. Bryant *Pract. Surg.* 41 In the *subpericranial form [of contusions] the indurated base may organise. **1847-9** *Todd's Cycl. Anat.* IV. I. 713/2 In syphilis ..there is frequently *subperiosteal effusion of lymph. **1835-6** *Ibid.* I. 13/1 The *subperitoneal cellular tissue. **1896** *Nomencl. Dis.* 209 Affections connected with pregnancy... β. *Subperitoneo-abdominal. **1857** Bullock tr. *Cazeaux' Midwifery* 245 *Sub-peritoneo-pelvic Pregnancy..a species of extra-uterine pregnancy. **1889** *Buck's Handbk. Med. Sci.* VIII. 242 The oblique super- and *sub-petrosal sinuses. **1897** *Allbutt's Syst. Med.* III. 570 By *subphrenic abscess is understood a collection of pus in the hollow of the diaphragm. **1877** tr. *von Ziemssen's Cycl. Med.* XII. 465 Meshes or spaces in the tissue of the pia (*subpial space). **1862** H. W. Fuller *Dis. Lungs* 173 The *sub-pleural cellular tissue is injected and œdematous. **1872** T. Bryant *Pract. Surg.* 496 From retained *sub-preputial secretion or from adhesion between the glans and prepuce. **1831** R. Knox *Cloquet's Anat.* 198 *Sub-Pubic or Triangular Ligament. **1866** Huxley *Laing's Preh. Rem. Caithn.* 94 The sub-pubic arch. **1911** *Encycl. Brit.* (ed. 11) XVII. 166/2 The gastric glands, draining the stomach (these are divided into coronary, *sub-pyloric and retropyloric groups). **1877** Huxley *Anat. Inv. Anim.* viii. 488 The *subradular membrane is continued into a longer or shorter sac. **1847-9** *Todd's Cycl. Anat.* IV. I. 134/2 The submucous tissue of the gall-bladder; the subserous of the pleura..; the *subretinal. **1861** Bumstead *Ven. Dis.* 119 The *sub-scrotal cellular tissue. **1889** *Buck's Handbk. Med. Sci.* VIII. 241 The *subsphenoidal sinus. **1733** tr. *Winslow's Anat.* (1756) I. 259 The *Sub-Spinal..Fossa. **1878** Walsham *Handbk. Surg. Pathol.* 153 *Subspinous [dislocation]. The head of the bone is displaced on to the posterior margin of the glenoid cavity. **1831** R. Knox *Cloquet's Anat.* 772 The *substernal and pulmonary lymphatics. **1897** *Allbutt's Syst. Med.* III. 785 Dysphagia and substernal burning. **1896** *Proc. Acad. Nat. Sci. Philad.* 30 The marginal cell..may have the portion below the stigma (*substigmatal) longer than that beyond (poststigmatal). **1889** *Buck's Handbk. Med. Sci.* VIII. 152 Fissural connections..of the Sylvian with the basisylvian, presylvian, and *subsylvian. **1835-6** *Todd's Cycl. Anat.* I. 254/1 The *subsynovial cellular tissue. **1940** *Chambers's Techn. Dict.* 818/2 **Subtectal*, lying beneath the roof, as the roof of the skull. **1975** *Nature* 30 Oct. 738/1 In the vertebrates below mammals, the tectal and subtectal areas are the main centres of termination of sensory pathways. **1883** *Encycl. Brit.* XVI. 679/1 A pair of such spores [*sc.* tegumental] leading into *sub-tegumental spaces of considerable area. **1889** *Buck's Handbk. Med. Sci.* VIII. 153 The callosal,..precuneal, and *subtemporal fissures. **1877** Huxley *Anat. Inv. Anim.* ix. 586 The *subtentacular and cœliac canals. **1899** *Allbutt's Syst. Med.* VIII. 28 The *sub-trapezial plexus on the under surface of the trapezius muscle. **1855** Hyde Clarke *Dict.*, **Subungual*, under the nails. **1879** *St. George's Hosp. Rep.* IX. 755 The subungual wart. **1855** Dunglison *Med. Lex.*, **Subunguial*, belonging to parts under the nail; as subunguial exostosis. **1876** tr. *Wagner's Gen. Pathol.* 159 Coloring matter is..found..in the *sub-vaginal space. **1835** Kirby *Hab. & Inst. Anim.* I. ix. 267 No *subventral..foot.

(*b*) in derived advs.; e.g. ***subconjunc'tivally***, ***-'durally***, ***-'glottically***, ***-peri'osteally***, ***-'pially***; so SUBCORTICALLY.

1907 *Ophthalmoscope* V. 383 The conjunctival cicatrice had been divided *subconjunctivally. **1974** *Nature* 11 Oct. 553/2 Grafts..placed on Fischer hosts that had been inoculated subconjunctivally..were rejected abruptly. **1897** *Allbutt's Syst. Med.* II. 700 Injected *subdurally the results were not so constant. **1975** *Year Bk. Ear, Nose & Throat* 317 Direct laryngoscopy showed adducted cords with an absent lumen *subglottically. **1898** *Syd. Soc. Lex.*, **Subperiosteally*, in a subperiosteal manner. **1950** *Jrnl. Neurophysiol.* XIII. 192 A fine steel needle electrode thrust *subpially into the substance of the acoustic tubercle.

c. *Bot.* in the same sense as b; e.g. ***ˌsubarche'sporial***, ***subhy'menial***. Also SUBPETIOLAR.

1900 B. D. Jackson *Gloss. Bot. Terms*, **Subarchesporial Pad*, Bower's term for a cushion-like group of cells below the archesporium in *Lycopodium*. **1874** Cooke *Fungi* 57 The receptacle proper comprehends the *sub-hymenial tissue, the parenchyma, and the external membrane. **1882** Bennett *Text-bk. Bot.* (ed. 4) 288 The ascophorous hyphæ or subhymenial layer.

d. *Anat.* In adj. compounds in Latin form, of the type defined in b above, designating parts of the body, used absol. by ellipsis of sb. (e.g. *musculus* muscle, *membrāna* membrane): e.g. SUBANCONEUS, SUBCRUREUS, SUBMUCOSA.

(*b*) Adjs. of Eng. form are similarly used, esp. pl.; e.g. SUBCOSTAL, SUBORBITAL.

e. With sbs. forming attrib. compounds; e.g. ***'sub-ice***; ***sub-'cuticle*** = SUBCUTANEOUS; ***sub'solidus*** *Geol.*, existing or occurring in conditions corresponding to a point in a phase diagram below a solidus, i.e. when the system is wholly solid; ***sub-'turbary*** found under turf-ground.

1889 *Microcosm* Dec., His *subcuticle injections. 1959 *Times* 9 Jan. 11/6 Apart from the exposed mountains near the coast, *sub-ice hill and dale occur. 1973 *Nature* 20 Apr. 539/3 New chapters in the history of the continent will be based on the results of continued palaeomagnetic studies, much deep-sea drilling and to a lesser extent sub-ice drilling. 1900 *Pop. Sci. Monthly* Feb. 440 There would necessarily be a *submountain mass. 1895 *Westm. Gaz.* 7 Sept. 4/4 The whole of the *sub-river section of the line. 1952 B. MASON *Princ. Geochem.* x. 232 We must..consider the phase changes that may take place in solid solutions in the *subsolidus region. 1979 *Nature* 15 Mar. 220/1 This mineral assemblage could be produced by hot-pressing the above composition in subsolidus conditions. 1846 OWEN *Brit. Fossil Mammals* 512 The *sub-turbary shell-marl in various localities in Ireland. 1893 *Times* 24 June 7/6 The [latest] ships are practically the same with regard to the *sub-water structure.

f. With sbs. forming sbs. designating a part, organ, or substance lying under the part denoted by the radical element; e.g. SUBCOSTA, ***suben'cephalon***, ***subhy'menium***, SUBMENTUM, ***subpla'centa***, ***sub-'radius***, ***sub'testa*** (see quots.), SUBUMBRELLA.

1890 BILLINGS *Nat. Med. Dict.*, **Subencephalon*, Krause's name for combined medulla oblongata, pons Varolii, and corpora quadrigemina. 1900 JACKSON *Gloss. Bot. Terms*, *Sub-hymenial Layer* or **Subhymenium*, = Hypothecium. 1855 DUNGLISON *Med. Lex.*, **Subplacenta*, decidua membrana. 1897 PARKER & HASWELL *Zool.* I. 129 Half way between any ad-radius and the adjacent per- or inter-radius, a radius of the fourth order, of *sub-radius. 1816 P. KEITH *Syst. Physiol. Bot.* II. 374 The **Subtesta*, which is the inner coat of the seed and lies immediately under the *testa*.

g. Forming vbs., in L. *subhastāre* = 'hastæ subicĕre' (see SUBHASTATION), *subjugāre* to SUBJUGATE.

2. a. With adverbial force (= underneath, below, down, low, lower), prefixed to adjs., vbs., and pples. (and, less freq., sbs.), as in L. *subærātus* having copper underneath, *subjacens* underlying, SUBJACENT, *subscrībĕre* to write underneath, write down, SUBSCRIBE, *subsīdĕre* to sit down, SUBSIDE, *substernĕre* to strew or spread underneath, *subtendĕre* to stretch under, SUBTEND, late L. *subcavāre* to hollow out underneath; e.g. ***suba'djacent***, ***-'repent*** adjs.; ***subæ'rated***, ***-con'cealed***, ***-con'tained***, ***-'dented***, ***-'twined*** pples.; ***sub'cavate*** vb. **ˌsubline'ation**, underlining. **ˌsubpunctu'ation**, marking letters or words with dots underneath. † **sub'umbrage** *v.*, to overshadow. † **subun'dation**, the action of waves underneath. (Formations of this class are uncommon.)

1722 QUINCY *Lex. Physico-Med.* (ed. 2) 2 The superior Parts of the *subadjacent *Os Metacarpi*. 1922 JOYCE *Ulysses* 653 He..gained retarded access to the kitchen through the subadjacent scullery. 1771 *Phil. Trans.* LXII. 60 A *subærated..denarius of the Plætorian family. 1799 W. TOOKE *View Russ. Emp.* I. 115 A piece of mountain,..entirely bare of soil,..in conjunction with that mineral [*viz.* talc] *subcavating the trapp-stone. *a* 1734 NORTH *Exam.* III. vi. (1740) 430 To do it with Address, and *subconcealed Artifice. 1768 CHESELDEN *Anat. Hum. Body* 133 For the better understanding of the *sub-contained parts. 1836 SMART *Dict.*, **Subdented*, indented beneath. 1898 I. C. RUSSELL *River Developm.* 246 If a name were desired for this minor feature of the drainage of certain regions, it might be termed *subimposed. 1651 A. BOATE in *Ussher's Lett.* (1686) 564 He hath made use of..*Sublineation in lieu of Asterisks. 1908 *Times* 14 Mar. 14/1 The following whip..was marked with the sublineation of a thick black line. 1908 H. HALL *Stud. Eng. Off. Hist. Doc.* 384 Confession of a blunder by the process of *subpunctuation must have been particularly distasteful to a mediaeval scribe. 1650 BULWER *Anthropomet.* ii. 53 That they [hairs] should imbibe the afflux of *subrepent humours. 1908 *Daily Chron.* 25 July 1/4 A push-button *subtwined in a bower of red roses. 1581 *Satir. Poems Reform.* xliii. 82 Xerxes, quhose..schippis *subumbragit all the seyis on breid. 1552 HULOET s.v. *Banckes*, Banckes defensyue againste *subundation called Seabanckes.

b. Hence = in or into subjection, as in *subdĕre* to bring under, subdue, *subicĕre* to SUBJECT.

3. Prefixed to sbs. with adjectival force (partly on the analogy of L. *sublāmina* under-plate, *substrāmen* litter) = lying, existing, occurring below or underneath, under-, (hence, by implication) underground; e.g. ***sub-armour***, ***-trousers***, ***-vestment***; ***subcrust***, ***-current***, ***-deposit***, ***-flush***, ***-mind***; ***sub-note***; ***sub-crossing***, ***-railway***; in designations of architectural features, indicating a secondary member, feature, chamber, etc. placed under one of the same kind, e.g. ***sub-basement***, ***-cellar***, ***-hall***, ***-member***, ***-pier-arch***, ***-plinth***, ***-shaft***, ***-sill***, ***-store-room***, ***tower***; so ***sub-shelf***, ***subtrench*** (whence ***subtrenched*** adj.); **'sub-floor**, a floor serving as a base for another floor; **'sub-frame**, a secondary frame; *spec.* (*a*) in carpentry and building, the frame for the attachment or support of a window or door-frame, or of panelling; (*b*) in a vehicle, the frame on which the coachwork is built, as distinct from the chassis; **sub'stratosphere**, the upper part of the troposphere, immediately below the stratosphere. Also SUB-ARCH, etc. (Stress even, or on the prefix.)

1860 HEWITT *Anc. Armour* II. 132 The Hauberk of chain-mail is worn..not..as the principal defence..but as a *sub-armour. 1904 *Westm. Gaz.* 26 Apr. 5/1 Underneath, in the basement and *sub-basement, were many thousands of gallons of wines and spirits. 1894 *Outing* XXIV. 379/2 Gentlemen, I see I didn't examine your *sub-cellar. 1864 *Athenæum* 22 Oct. 530/3 If it be not found convenient to have *sub-crossings, surely light iron bridges would answer the purpose. 1886 *Ibid.* 4 Sept. 297/3 The intervening zone, or *sub-crust, which we should probably regard as being..in a state of hydro-thermal plasticity. 1902 *Westm. Gaz.* 14 Oct. 3/2 The *sub-current of American life. *a* 1828 SCHOOLCRAFT (Webster), **Subdeposit*. *a* 1846 LYELL (Worc.). 1893 J. P. ALLEN *Pract. Building Construction* viii. 122 Double floors may sometimes mean that the flooring or floor-boards are laid on the joists in two thicknesses..the bottom thickness being straight-jointed..; while the other..is laid in the ordinary way above the *sub-floor, as the bottom one is called. 1929 W. C. HUNTINGTON *Building Construction* vi. 264 This type of construction is greatly superior to that which rests the studs on a sole plate placed on top of the sub-floor. 1973 *Building Materials* (MTP Construction) 186 Any sub-floor can be levelled and smoothed. 1899 *Atlantic Monthly* LXXXIII. 759/1 A certain *subflush of overripe color beneath the dusky skin. 1929 *Motor* 1 Oct. 33 (Advt.), A *sub-frame, on which the body is built, isolates the coachwork from the chassis and prevents distortion; the sub-frame being mounted on the chassis by supports having a certain degree of flexibility. 1944 N. W. KAY *Pract. Carpenter & Joiner* vi. 138 Care must be taken to prevent any damage by shrinkage. One method..is to form a sub-frame within the main frame. D shows a sub-frame, to carry the glazing, tongued into the frame of the door. 1968 D. BRAITHWAITE *Fairground Archit.* v. 88 At least two further wagons were required for 'loose stuff'—sub-frames, gates and shutters, roundings and so on. 1979 *Daily Tel.* 1 Dec. 18 (Advt.), For Sale. Mini 850, 1969, 47,000 miles... New sub-frame, reconditioned gear-box. 1887 *Dict. Archit.*, **Sub-hall*, the place in the lower story under the hall or chief entrance, which last was usually on the first floor. 1875 BRASH *Eccl. Archit. Irel.* 133 These arches have each a chamfered *Sub-member. 1856 EMERSON *Eng. Traits, Lit.* Wks. (Bohn) II. 112 They exert every variety of talent on a lower ground, and may be said to live and act in a *sub-mind. 1824 DIBDIN *Libr. Comp.* 699 The *sub-note will shew that he possessed a few of his choicer works. 1835 R. WILLIS *Archit. Mid. Ages* vii. 94 Sometimes the *sub-pier-arch rests on a pilaster instead of a half shaft. 1836 PARKER *Gloss. Archit.* I. 61 A second or *sub-plinth under the Norman base. 1845 J. WILLIAMS (*title*), *Sub-Railways in London. 1835 R. WILLIS *Archit. Mid. Ages* iv. 34 *Sub-shafts sustain arches of which the upper side is united to the soffit of the next arch or wall. 1889 *Anthony's Photogr. Bull.* II. 415 Ten inches below the *sub-shelf is a sink. 1833 LOUDON *Encycl. Archit.* §867 The oak gate-posts are kept firm in their places, by the underground braces, to the *subsills. 1889 *Scribner's Mag.* Aug. 216/1 Distributions are made daily among the *substore-rooms. 1937 *Popular Sci. Monthly* Nov. 68/2 Aerial Battles miles above the earth..are foreshadowed by a *sub-stratosphere plane placed under test by the U.S. Army Air Corps. 1952 *Chambers's Jrnl.* Feb. 84/2 Another day Byrd flew over a never-ending succession of mountain-ranges, which looked as if they were suspended in the substratosphere. 1884 *Contemp. Rev.* July 104 A still better effect..was gained by placing an octagonal super-tower, or 'lantern', on a square *sub-tower. 1669 STAYNRED *Fortif.* 7 EFGH is the *Subtrench. *Ibid.*, Section of a Fort with a..Counterscarp; also *Subtrenched. 1890 *Columbus* (Ohio) *Disp.* 11 July, Four inches of white canvass *subtrousers was exposed between his pantaloons, spring-bottoms and shoe-tops. 1802 COLERIDGE *Lett.* (1895) 394 The diaper *subvestment of the young jacobin.

b. *Anat.* (*a*) Designating the lowest or basal part of the organ denoted by the second element (cf. med.L. *subjuga* lowest part of a yoke); e.g. ***subcutis***, ***subface***, ***subfacies***, ***subilium***.

1879 tr. *Haeckel's Evol. Man* (1905) 648 The corium is much thicker than the epidermis. In its deeper strata (the **subcutis*) there are clusters of fat-cells. 1826 KIRBY & SP. *Entomol.* III. 366 *Subfacies (the *Subface). The lower surface or underside of the head. 1898 *Syd. Soc. Lex.*, **Subilium*, the lowest portion of the ilium.

(*b*) Designating a part concealed or encroached upon; e.g. ***subfissure***, ***subgyre***.

1889 *Buck's Handbk. Med. Sci.* VIII. 160 Superfissures and *subfissures.—These terms are employed herein to designate the fissures which result from the formation of supergyres and *subgyres. 1903 *Amer. Anthropologist* (N.S.) V. 623 The occipital fissure..shows a number of well-marked subgyres in its depths. 1898 *Syd. Soc. Lex.*, **Sub-gyrus*, a gyrus that is encroached on or covered.

c. *Agric.* Short for *subsoil-*.

1778 [W. MARSHALL] *Minutes Agric.* 16 Aug. 1775, Put old Nimrod to the *sub-plow. 1778 *Ibid.*, Nothing can equal *sub-plowing for clearing the surface from running weeds. *Ibid.*, *Observ.* 97 After the Beans were drawn, the Soil was subplowed. 1866 C. W. HOSKYNS *Occas. Essays* 111 The well-known results of drainage and *subpulveration. 1856 MORTON *Encycl. Agric.* II. 647/2 Subsoil ploughs..are merely stirrers of the under soil, and might more properly be termed *sub-pulverizers.

4. *Mus.* With adj. force combining with sbs. to form terms designating: (*a*) an interval of so much below a given note; e.g. ***subdiapente***, ***subdiatessaron***; (*b*) a note or an organ-stop an octave below that denoted by the original sb.; e.g. SUBOCTAVE, ***subcontra octave***; ***sub-bass***, ***-bourdon***, ***-diapason***; cf. CONTRA- 4; (*c*) a note lying the same distance below the tonic as the note designated by the radical sb. is above it; e.g. SUBDOMINANT, SUBMEDIANT. (Cf. 13.)

1852 J. J. SEIDEL *Organ* 25 The organ at St. Elizabeth's at Breslau..contains a sub-diapason. 1869 *Engl. Mech.* 31 Dec. 385/3 Sub-bass is a 32 ft. tone stop. 1878 STAINER & BARRETT *Dict. Mus.*, *Subdiapente*, *Subdominant*, the fifth below or the fourth above any key note. 1879 *Organ Voicing* 18 All stops speaking at any interval other than the octave, *super* or *sub*. 1880 *Encycl. Brit.* XI. 483/2 The 'subbass'..an octave of 16 feet pitch. 1881 C. A. EDWARDS *Organs* 155 Sub-bourdon..is a rare manual stop of 32 ft. 1883 GROVE *Dict. Mus.* III. 747/2 A 'Canon in Subdiapente' was a canon in which the answer was a fifth below the lead. Similarly 'Subdiatessaron is a fourth below. 1901 TITCHENER *Exper. Psychol.* I. 32 Subcontra octave.

II. Subordinate, subsidiary, secondary; subordinately, subsidiarily, secondarily.

5. Having a subordinate or inferior position; of inferior or minor importance or size; subsidiary; secondary.

a. of persons; as in late L. *subadjuva* assistant, *subhēres* next or second heir; e.g. ***sub-advocate***, ***-deity***, ***-god***, ***-hero***, ***-substitute***, etc.

1645 MILTON *Colast.* Wks. 1851 IV. 351 The Laws of England, wherof you have intruded to bee an opiniastrous *Sub-advocate. 1641 —— *Ch. Gov.* I. vi, These two main reasons of the prelates..are the very wombe for a new *subantichrist to breed in. 1818 BENTHAM *Ch. Eng.*, *Catech. Exam.* 161 This newly commissioned Antichrist with his three Sub-Antichrists. *a* 1700 B. E. *Dict. Cant. Crew*, **Sub-beau*, or *Demibeau*, a wou'd-be-fine. *a* 1629 T. G[OFFE] *Careless Sheph.* I. i, It awes Not mortalls only; but makes other powers *Sub-Deities to thine. 1820 T. MITCHELL *Com. Aristoph.* I. 44 Some of the epithets applied to this sub-deity [Phales]. 1809 W. IRVING *Knickerb.* III. ii, Five schepens, who officiated as scrubs, *subdevils, or bottle-holders to the burger-meesters. 1680 SHADWELL *Woman-Capt.* I, Scarce any one is such a Fool, but he has a *sub-Fool that he can laugh at. 1679 DRYDEN *Limberham* v, Happily arriv'd, i'faith, my old *Sub-fornicator. 1726 DE FOE *Hist. Devil* II. i. 203 [Satan] had his *Sub-Gods, who under his several Dispositions receiv'd the Homage of Mankind. 1846 LADY EASTLAKE *Jrnls.* (1895) I. 189 Sir E. L. Bulwer..a man..reminding me of some of the *sub-heroes in his own books. 1649 WODENOTE *Hermes Theol.* 68 Saucy *Sub-Jacks possessed of the preferments of the Learned and Ancient. 1697 J. DENNIS *Plot & no Plot* v, They are my *Sub-pimps, and pick up a penny under me. 1899 SPENCER & GILLEN *Tribes Centr. Austral.* title-p., Special magistrate and *sub-protector of the aborigines, Alice Springs, South Australia. 1817 BENTHAM *Parl. Reform* Introd. 170 Dependance on an essentially insatiable shark with his *sub-sharks. 1788 HOLCROFT *Baron Trenck* (1886) II. vi. 99 The substitute of Kempf was Frauenberger, who..appointed one Krebs as a *sub-substitute. 1818 BENTHAM *Ch. Eng.* Introd. 17 Another body of divinity..to co-operate with the Catechism, and act under it, in the character of a sub-substitute to every thing that came from Jesus. *a* 1734 NORTH *Life Ld. Keeper North* (1742) 271 The Earl of Sunderland, Jeffries, and their *Sub-Sycophants. 1589 COOPER *Admon.* 93 Antichristian Prelates, Petie Antichrists, *Subvice-Antichrists, &c. as some..do terme them. *c* 1675 DRYDEN *Pref. to Notes Empr. Morocco* Wks. 1808 XV. 404 His king, his two empresses, his villain, and his *sub-villain, nay his hero, have all a certain natural cast of the father. 1840 MACAULAY *Ess.*, *Clive* (1854) 535/1 The villain or sub-villain of the story. 1692 SOUTH *Serm.* (1697) I. 204 The Repairer of a decayed Intellect, and a *Sub-worker to Grace, in freeing it from some of the inconveniences of Original Sin.

b. of material objects; e.g. ***sub-affluent***, ***-constellation***, ***-leader*** [LEADER[1] 12], ***-network***, ***-piston***, ***-totem***, etc.; **submu'nition** chiefly *U.S.*, (usu. *pl.*) small, short-range guided missiles; also *sing.*; **'substorm** *Meteorol.*, a disturbance of the earth's magnetic field restricted to certain, usu. polar, latitudes and typically manifested as an aurora and other upper atmospheric phenomena.

1873 tr. *Jules Verne's Meridiana* v, [The Kuruman] increased by the waters of a *sub-affluent, the Moschoria. 1744 *Phil. Trans.* XLIII. May 14 The cardinal and *subcardinal Points of the Compass. 1827 G. HIGGINS *Celtic Druids* 59 One of the very first *subcasts from the Asiatic hive. 1646 SIR T. BROWNE *Pseud. Ep.* v. xix. 262 If thereby be meant the Pleiades, or *subconstellation upon the back of Taurus. 1834–47 J. S. MACAULAY *Field Fortif.* (1851) 297 Keep their *sub-crests in the same plane as the sub-crests of the faces. 1859 MURCHISON *Siluria* vi. (ed. 3) 122 The whole of the calcareous courses of this *subformation. 1913 S. O'CASEY *Let.* 8 Mar. (1975) I. 23 The Editor recently, in a *sub-leader, advised all his readers to go and see pictures exhibited in the Central Branch of the Gaelic League. 1862 *Catal. Internat. Exhib.* II. XXXI. 20 The following *sub-master keys. 1975 *Aviation Week & Space Technol.* 6 Oct. 15/2 Improvement of the BLU-63 *submunition bomblet with two basic sizes of fragments. 1983 *Financial Times* 2 Dec. 2/3 Clusters of anti-armour submunitions which would be fired from stand-off positions. 1956 J. KLEIN *Study of Groups* iv. 50 This will be useful when we wish to analyse *sub-networks. 1978 *Sci. Amer.* June 95/1 Clos's design is based on the idea of building a large network out of smaller networks called subnetworks. 1895 *Outing* XXVI. 55/2 The serried ranks of *sub-pagodas in this strange, holy city. 1900 HISCOX *Horseless Vehicles* 66 When the ports in the *sub-piston close. 1879 G. PRESCOTT *Sp. Telephone* 434 M. Gaudoin also utilizes these different *subproducts in the manufacture of his carbons. 1961 AKASOFU & CHAPMAN in *Jrnl. Geophysical Res.* LXVI. 1339/2 Each such event, which Birkeland..called a polar elementary storm, is here called a *DP* *substorm. 1969 *New Scientist* 25 Sept. 669/3 These are the 'substorms' which manifest themselves as aurorae and associated magnetic disturbances. 1979 *Nature* 22 Feb. 649/1 Measurements were made during a magnetic substorm which appeared together with the polar light on 25–26 February, 1978. 1883 HOWITT in *Smithsonian Rep.* 818 A larger or smaller group of what I have called *subtotems, but which might be appropriately termed pseudo-totems.

c. of something immaterial, a quality, state, etc.; e.g. ***sub-cause***, ***-code*** [CODE *sb.*[1] 3 d], ***-cycle***, ***-entry***, ***-flavour***, ***-function***, ***-genre***, ***-hierarchy***, ***-idea***, ***-item***, ***-literature***, ***-part***, ***-plot*** [PLOT *sb.* 6], ***-problem***, ***-question***, ***-sense***, ***-society***, ***-substantiality***, ***-system***, ***-theme***, ***-theory***, ***-topic***, ***-war***, ***-world***, etc.; **sub-goal** *Psychol.*, something that must be achieved on the path to the main objective.

1898 *Engineering Mag.* XVI. 38 In all there are 149 *sub-accounts, under 24 general voucher titles. **1818** BENTHAM *Ch. Eng., Catech. Exam.* 331 In the principal article, they are stated as residing in the neighbourhood; whereas, in the *sub-articles, no statement to that effect is contained. **1825** COLERIDGE *Aids Refl.* (1848) I. 184 The cause of this, and of all its lamentable effects and *sub-causes. **1960** R. JAKOBSON in T. A. Sebeok *Style in Lang.* 352 For any speech community..there exists a unity of language, but this over-all code represents a system of interconnected *subcodes. **1967** *Language* XLIII. 752 Variants of one and the same code, realized by means of different information channels, are called 'subcodes'. **1973** S. HEATH in *Screen* Spring/Summer 215 The distinction between cinematic codes and sub-codes is initially made in *Langage et Cinéma* as that between general and particular cinematic codes. *a* **1631** DONNE *Serm.* xxxiv. (1640) 338 This part hath also two branches..in the first branch, there will bee two twiggs, two *sub-considerations. **1953** A. K. C. OTTAWAY *Educ. & Society* 45 A *sub-cycle was here set up within the whole economic setting. **1974** *Sci. Amer.* June 78/2, I have omitted the important subcycles of nitrogen and phosphorus, two elements that are strongly related to the origin of life and to biological processes in general. **1892** *Field* 18 June 942/1 [In whist] the *sub-echo is the showing of three trumps when a partner has led and called for them. This is accomplished by echoing in the usual manner. **1876** C. A. CUTTER *Rules for Dictionary Catalog* 13 Class entry with specific or class *subentry. **1979** G. N. KNIGHT *Indexing* vi. 106 If it is a sub-entry itself that errs with excessive references, then the remedy is to turn it into a cross-reference to a separate heading having its own sub-entries. **1895** *Daily News* 30 Nov. 6/3 Their manifest *sub-flavour of earnestness. **1949** KOESTLER *Insight & Outlook* x. 153 Like all means towards an end (or *subfunctions in non-teleological language) [etc.]. **1969** H. R. F. KEATING *Inspector Ghote plays Joker* iii. 35, I regard it as a sub-function of my post to make person-to-person contact with as many people in your department as possible. **1976** *N.Y. Times* 13 Jan. 40/5 This was because she belonged to, if in fact she hadn't pretty much created a *subgenre of the mystery novel. **1980** *Times Lit. Suppl.* 7 Nov. 1262/2 One of the major subgenres of science fiction (works dealing with robots and computers). **1932** E. C. TOLMAN *Purposive Behav.* 459/1 (*Index*) Sign-objects.. become *sub-goal-objects. **1967** M. ARGYLE *Psychol. Interpersonal Behaviour* v. 91 Driving a car from A to B involves the sub-goals of getting the engine started, getting the car moving in top gear, and getting to the intermediate points X, Y and Z. **1977** *Dædalus* Fall 121 The theory includes the representation of the task environment, the definition of goals and subgoals,..and the order in which alternative courses of action will be explored. **1962** H. C. CONKLIN in Householder & Saporta *Probl. Lexicogr.* 128 *Subhierarchies of varying 'depths' are often discernible within larger hierarchic structures. **1878** GROSART *G. Daniel's Poems* I. 217 'Antike' = ancient, with the *sub-idea of grotesqueness. **1855** BROWNING *Men & Women* II. 17 Sage provisos, *sub-intents, and saving-clauses. **1888** *Pall Mall Gaz.* 31 July 3/2 Whether the author is to be suspected of a satiric *sub-intention. **1928** in W. K. Hancock *Australia* (1930) v. 90 In the existing Customs tariff there are 259 items or *sub-items which provide *ad valorem* duties of 40 per cent. or over. **1781** *St. Trials* XI. 220/2 Upon this he makes many limitations; upon all of which he adds..this *sublimitation. **1840–1** DE QUINCEY *Style* Wks. 1862 X. 191 Where..the limitations and the sublimitations, descend, *seriatim*, by a vast scale of dependencies. **1961** WEBSTER, **Subliterature*,..inferior literature that does not survive the test of time. **1974** *Times Lit. Suppl.* 1 Feb. 105/1 Though it is important to acquaint oneself with best-sellers and sub-literature.., the chief stress should be on literature of enduring aesthetic worth. **1891** SCRIVENER *Fields & Cities* 150 Both these scourges [scrofula and dyspepsia], with the groups of families of *sub-maladies which grow in their wake. **1883** *Harper's Mag.* Jan. 179/2 Some subtle *sub-meaning [is] also conveyed. **1770** LUCKOMBE *Hist. Printing* 234 Prefaces, Introductions, Annotations..all which *sub-parts of a Work were formerly..put in Italic. **1949** KOESTLER *Insight & Outlook* x. 135 A sub-whole composed of sub-parts, which in themselves are sub-wholes, and so on. **1976** LIEBERMAN & RHODES *Compl. CB Handbk.* xi. 233 Each applicant..must follow the procedure prescribed by Subpart 1 of Part 1 of this chapter. **1916** C. HUGON tr. *Creizenach's Eng. Drama in Age of Shakespeare* v. 255 In those cases where a comic *sub-plot runs side by side with the main plot. **1962** G. K. HUNTER *John Lyly* iv. 237 The sub-plot episode of the pages and Grim the Collier of Croydon in Edwardes' Damon and Pithias. **1879** ROBY *Lat. Gram.* II. 8 Such a secondary predicate might..be called a *subpredicate. It is often called an apposition. **1907** W. JAMES *Mem. & Stud.* (1911) x. 236 So the great problem splits into two *sub-problems. **1980** *Sci. Amer.* Feb. 30/3, I shall treat such issues as special subproblems of allocation. **1899** F. J. MATHER *Chaucer's Prol.* p. xlii, The most serious passages of his poetry are seldom without a *sub-quality of humor. **1675** TULLY *Let. to Baxter* 27 There remaines yet one small *sub-question. **1619** R. JONES *Recant. Serm.* in *Phenix* (1708) II. 493 The reason of this Conjecture is [etc.]..The *sub-reason is [etc.]. **1856** EMERSON *Eng. Traits, Aristocracy* Wks. (Bohn) II. 83 Loyalty is in the English a *sub-religion. **1856** OLMSTED *Slave States* 292 The Second Auditor's General Report on Education..contains abstracts of *sub-reports. **1885** *Law Times Rep.* (N.S.) LIII. 566/2 If there was any doubt..it is entirely removed by the appropriate language used in *sub-rule 30. **1802–12** BENTHAM *Ration. Judic. Evid.* (1827) II. 150 These were mentioned as so many *sub-securities for correctness and completeness. **1890** *Academy* XXXVII. 218/1 A *subsensation of how, in Rossetti's weird phrase, his death was 'growing up from his birth'. **1947** E. PARTRIDGE *Usage & Abusage* 134/2 *Titanic*..is frequently employed with the *sub-sense of 'extraordinarily powerful'. **1981** *Dictionaries* II.–III. 168 Brockhaus lists it as an example illustrating a sub-sense of *Blut*. **1951** E. E. EVANS-PRITCHARD *Soc. Anthropol.* i. 13 Its boundaries include..peoples of near and further Asia, north Africa, and parts of Europe—an almost limitless number of..societies and *sub-societies. **1888** *Spectator* 30 June 910/2 There is a *sub-story dealing mainly with the amours of a disreputable young woman. **1922** JOYCE *Ulysses* 385 *Entweder* transsubstantiality *oder* consubstantiality but in no case *subsubstantiality. **1881** *Smithsonian Rep.* 203 Turning to the several *subsystems it appears that although it is possible that the orbits of the satellites of Mars, Jupiter [etc.]. **1957** V. W. TURNER *Schism & Continuity in African Society* i. 1 This book is..an attempt to analyse..the form and functioning of a sub-system, the village, within a wider system, the totality of Ndembu society. **1972** W. LABOV *Language in Inner City* ii. 64 BEV..is best seen as a distinct subsystem within the larger grammar of English. **1949** M. MEAD *Male & Female* xvii. 345 In this story there is a *sub-theme of the girl's mother's flirtation with a younger man. **1981** A. PATON *Towards Mountain* xxxiv. 307 The birth and rise of Afrikaner nationalism is one of the most powerful subthemes of my life story. **1951** PARSONS & SHILS *Toward Gen. Theory of Action* i. 28 Economic theory..only becomes a distinctive *subtheory of the general theory. **1897** O. J. NAVE *Topical Bible* 4 Under the *subtopic, *Instances of*, are grouped all the illustrative facts that occur in the Scriptures relating to each subject. **1923** *Notes from Ireland* Nov. 120/2 All this time a *sub-war rages. **1949** KOESTLER *Promise & Fulfilment* I. x. 114 The year..ended with the first encounters in the sub-war between the British Foreign Office and the future State of Israel. **1890** W. JAMES *Princ. Psychol.* II. xxi. 291 The popular mind conceives of all these *sub-worlds more or less disconnectedly. **1983** *Times* 10 Jan. 22/7 A sort of sub-world of smacked bottoms and scrawny mothers-in-law.

(*b*) With derived adjs., as ***sub-intentional***, ***-intentioned***, ***-systemic***.

1957 P. LAFITTE *Person in Psychol.* ix. 121 A projective test ..is designed to elicit what might be called sub-intentional behaviour, including the whole range of covert behaviour that the person cannot report directly. **1968** *Internat. Encycl. Soc. Sci.* XV. 387/2 Subintentioned deaths are those in which the deceased played an important indirect, covert, ..or unconscious role in his own demise. **1961** WEBSTER, Subsystemic. **1966** S. BEER *Decision & Control* xvi. 428 The prefrontal lobe of the cortex..has no specific sub-systemic control responsibilities. **1977** *Dædalus* Summer 81 The functionings of their subsystemic parts..and of the whole are to be understood with the aid of general systems theory.

d. of actions; e.g. ***sub-appearance***, ***-quarrel***, ***-smile***; **sub-optimi'zation** (see quot. 1967).

1820 LAMB *Elia* I. *Christ's Hosp.*, You never met the one by chance in the street without a wonder, which was quickly dissipated by the almost immediate *subappearance of the other. **1964** T. W. MCRAE *Impact Computers on Accounting* iii. 93 Cyberneticists are for ever emphasizing the dangers of *sub-optimization. **1967** E. DUCKWORTH in Wills & Yearsley *Handbk. Management Technol.* 119 *Sub-optimization*—the achievement of optimum working of, say, one department of a company without regard to the effect this may have on the rest of the organization. **1574** tr. *Josselin's Life 70 Abp.* Pref. to Rdr. D 2 b, A petye brawle and *subquarell betwen Yorke and duresme. **1799** S. TURNER *Hist. Anglo-Saxons* I. I. viii. 112 Amid this complexity of rebellion and *sub-rebellion. **1825** LAMB *Elia* II. *Stage Illusion*, The skilful actor, by a sort of *sub-reference, rather than direct appeal to us, disarms the character of a great deal of its odiousness. **1852** C. M. YONGE *Two Guardians* viii. 140 A certain *sub-smile about the corners of his mouth. **1882** 'F. ANSTEY' *Vice Versâ* iv, His cheeks were creased with a dimpling subsmile. **1879** HOWELLS *Lady of Aroostook* (1883) II. 158 With a knowing little look at Lydia, which included a *sub-wink for her husband.

6. a. With names of officials or persons occupying positions of authority, forming titles designating one immediately subordinate to the chief official, as in L. *subcenturio* (var. of *succenturio*) centurion's lieutenant, late L. *subdoctor* assistant teacher, *subscrībendārius* assistant secretary, eccl.L. *subdiāconus* SUB-DEACON, med.L. *subballīvus* SUB-BAILIFF, *subbedellus* under-beadle, *submagister* SUBMASTER, *subprior* SUBPRIOR, *subsecrētārius* under-secretary; e.g. ***sub-abbot***, ***-captain***, ***-conductor***, ***-king***, ***-vicar***, etc.

1767 BURN *Eccles. Law* (ed. 2) IV. 456 *marg.*, *Subabbat and subprior. **1818** BENTHAM *Ch. Eng.* 91 His Right Reverend Co-adjutors and Reverend *Sub-adjutors. **1729** FOXTON tr. *Burnet's App. St. Dead* 28 He commemorates their Deliverance out of Egypt,..Moses being the *Sub-administrator, with mighty Miracles and Prodigies. **1726** AYLIFFE *Parergon* 68 They ought not to execute these Precepts by simple Messengers or *Sub-Beadles. **1716** M. DAVIES *Athen. Brit.* II. 182 Schelstrat the Pope's *Subbibliothecarian. **1884** *Cyclist* 13 Feb. 242/1 The captain and *sub-captain..represent the club on the N.C.U. **1519** *Churchw. Acc. St. Giles', Reading* 3 Of the *Subchamberer of the Mon[astery] of Redyng. **1688** HOLME *Armoury* III. iii. 49/2 Officers..belonging to the Earl of Chester...Vice Chamberlain, or *Sub Chamberlain. **1858** GLADSTONE *Homer* III. 11 The subordination of the *sub-chief to his local sovereign. **1710** J. CHAMBERLAYNE *M. Brit. Notitia* II. 689 Mr. John Dundass, first Clerk of the Assembly...Nicol Spence, *Sub-Clerk. **1837** CARLYLE *Fr. Rev.* III. II. ii, Amid head-clerks and sub-clerks. **1688** *Lond. Gaz.* No. 2331/3 One of the King's Family shall succeed to the Bishoprick, as having been already designed by the Chapter for their *Sub-Coadjutor. **1947** H. G. FARMER *Royal Artillery Concerts* v. 15 For many years Zavertal would rehearse the orchestra for months without giving the slightest heed to the military band, which was left to the *sub-conductor (the Serjeant Major) and his subordinates. **1976** D. STEELE in H. Procter-Gregg *Beecham Remembered* I. 109 He came across the orchestra bridge to start untangling the confusion caused by Weingartner's being quite out of touch..with his sub-conductors. **1691** T. H[ALE] *Account New Invent.* p. cv, *Sub-Conservators for the River of Thames. **1670** COTTON *Espernon* I. II. 96 To importune the *Sub-Consul to conclude the Treaty. **1642–3** *Canterb. Marr. Licences*, Thomas Graunt, clerk, *subcurate of S. Mary's in Dover. **1580** in Picton *L'pool Munic. Rec.* (1883) I. 63 The same customer and *sub-customer shall yield and give their several accompts. **1672** *Ibid.* 284 William Galley Sub-customer. **1737** E. CHAMBERLAYNE *Angl. Notitia* II. 117 *Sub-director [of Ordnance]. **1896** HILPRECHT *Recent Res. Bible Lands* 87 Halil Bey, sub-director of the Museum in Constantinople. **1612** BRINSLEY *Lud. Lit.* 273 The particular help where either an Vsher is wanting, or else is not sufficient, is by a *Subdoctor. **1786** J. C. WALKER *Irish Bards* 83 This instrument was used..to assemble congregations [etc.]... Nor is it unlikely, that this office was performed by the *Sub-Druids. **1703** in J. Chamberlayne *M. Brit. Notitia* (1710) II. 561 The Office of Her Majesty's..Ordnance... Six Engineers..Four *Sub-Engineers. **1671** F. PHILLIPS *Reg. Necess.* 522 By fraud and collusion betwixt him and the said *Sub-Escheator. **1796** CHARLOTTE SMITH *Marchmont* IV. 433 Every fee, which the *sub-executors of our..laws are suffered to extort. **1809** W. TAYLOR in Robberd *Mem.* (1843) II. 277 Charon and his *subferrymen. **1883** *Harper's Mag.* Jan. 206/2 These Maine men are likely to become foremen, or *sub-foremen. **1774** MRS. DELANY *Life & Corr.* Ser. II. (1861) II. 70 Miss Goldsworthy is made *sub-governess to the young Royals at St. James's. **1876** E. JENKINS *Queen's Head* 4 The head waiter, and a lot of *sub-head-waiters. **1863** TREVELYAN *Compet. Wallah* (1866) 232 The *sub-inspector of police. **1684** BAXTER *Par. Congreg.* 38 [The Bishop] to be the *subintercessor, or the mouth of the Church in publick prayer. **1823** BENTHAM *Not Paul* 46 The *Sub-king of the Jews, Agrippa. **1848** LYTTON *Harold* III. iii, The lesser sub-kings of Wales. **1837** W. IRVING *Capt. Bonneville* I. 179 Mr. Walker, one of the *subleaders, who had gone with a band of twenty hunters. **1722** HEARNE *Collect.* (O.H.S.) VII. 385 The Fees being..1*s.* to the Head Librarian, 3*s.* 6*d.* to the *Sublibrarian, & 1*s.* 6*d.* to the Janitor. **1800** SOUTHEY *Lett.* (1856) I. 134 The sub-librarian is an intelligent man. **1733–4** MRS. DELANY *Let. to Mrs. A. Granville* 2 Mar., In what character is Miss Beal to go with the Orange family? A *sub-maid, I guess. **1883** *Manch. Exam.* 30 Oct. 5/2 Being *sub-manager for the last twenty-one years. *a* **1774** TUCKER *Lt. Nat.* (1834) II. 207 In order to gain favour with these inferior ministers or *sub-mediators. **1673** BAXTER *Let.* in *Answ. Dodwell* 82 Doth it follow that your Church Monarch can over-see them all himself without any *sub-overseers? **1685** —— *Paraphr. N.T.* John x. 3 To the Messiah God will open the door, and to *Sub-Pastors, they that by office are door-keepers to the Church, must open it. **1700** in *Cath. Rec. Soc. Publ.* (1909) VII. 69 The Pastor Tegers, and sub Pastor of St. Amand. **1617** MORYSON *Itin.* I. 210 The Patron ..made a solemne Oration to the *sub-Patron and the Marriners. **1671** E. CHAMBERLAYNE *Angl. Notitia* II. 228 Upon this Grand Office depends One hundred eighty two Deputy Post-Masters..and *Sub Post-Masters in their Branches. **1896** *Hansard's Parl. Debates* 18 Feb. 546/2 A number of messengers..employed by Sub-Postmasters. **1721** AMHERST *Terræ Fil.* No. 22. 112 Mr. Holt of Maudlin college, *sub-proctor at that time. **1688** HOLME *Armoury* III. iv. 181/2 The *Sub-Provincial, is to act the same things..as the Provincial. **1706** PHILLIPS (ed. Kersey), **Sub-Reader*, an Under Reader in one of the Inns of Court, who reads the Text of the Law the Reader is to Discourse upon. **1605** *Answ. Supposed Discov. Romish Doctr.* 20 They.. openly moued the greatest *Subregents in England to take armes against her. *a* **1711** KEN *Preparatives* Poet. Wks. III. 13 Neglect to thy Sub-regent's Throne Affronts thy own. **1673** BAXTER *Let.* in *Answ. Dodwell* 82 Doth it follow that your Church Monarch can..rule them without any *sub-rulers? **1860** W. L. COLLINS *Luck of Ladysmede* x, It was the *sub-sacrist approaching in the discharge of some of his duties. **1843** CARLYLE *Past & Pr.* II. vi, Our Lord Abbot..made him *Subsacristan. **1642** *Docq. Lett. Patent* (1837) 326 The Office of *Subsearcher w[th]: in the Porte of London. **1632** B. JONSON *Magn. Lady* Dram. Pers., Mr. Bias, A Vi-politique, or *Sub-secretary. **1678** *Trial of Coleman* 42 A Sub-Secretary, that did write very many things for him. **1826** SCOTT *Diary* 16 Nov. in *Lockhart*, Five Cabinet Ministers.. with sub-secretaries by the bushel. **1745** *Season. Adv. Prot.* 37 No Person shall be capable of acting as *Subsherriff.. who shall not have been a Protestant for five Years immediately before such his acting. **1737** J. CHAMBERLAYNE *M. Brit. Notitia* II. 80 The Chief Office..Head Sorter ..*Sub-Sorters. **1876** GLADSTONE *Homeric Synchr.* 124 Under the supremacy of Troy and of Priam, Anchises their king, seems to have been a *sub-sovereign. *a* **1715** BURNET *Own Time* (1766) I. 315 He had been his *subtutor and had followed him in all his exile. **1744** T. BIRCH *R. Boyle* 69 Mr. Tallents..had been..sub-tutor to several sons of the earl of Suffolk. **1706** PHILLIPS (ed. Kersey), **Sub-Vicar*, an Under-Vicar. **1600** W. WATSON *Decacordon* (1602) 105 Maister George Blackwell the new Archpriest of England: nay, the *Sub-uiceroy rather of all the Isles of Albion.

(*b*) in derived adjs.; e.g. ***subsecretarial*** pertaining to a sub-secretary.

1898 B. GREGORY *Side Lights* 499 From his sub-secretarial desk he spoke on a case.

b. In the designation of corresponding offices or functions; e.g. ***sub-administration***, ***-commissaryship***, ***-inspectorship***, etc.

1710 STEELE *Tatler* No. 193 ¶3 The *Sub-Administration of Stage Affairs. **1748** in Temple & Sheldon *Hist. Northfield* (1875) 273, I will..throw up my *sub-commissaryship. **1876** SMILES *Sc. Nat.* xiii. 268 The *subcuratorship could not be obtained. **1884** *Century Mag.* XXVIII. 134 One *sub-inspectorship of factories. **1839** J. ROGERS *Antipapopr.* x. §3. 253 We read nothing in Holy Scripture about the *submediation or the under-mediators. **1887** *Daily News* 1 Mar. 6/2 All the smaller *sub-postmasterships still continue to be in the gift of the Treasury. **1591** *Acts Privy Council* (1900) XXI. 105 The fee of the *Subproctorship for one whole yeare. **1881** *Athenæum* 15 Jan. 95/3 A *sub-professoriate of twenty readers. **1764** *Scott's Bailey*, **Sub-vicarship*, the office of an under vicar.

7. Compounded with sbs., to express division into parts, sections, or branches.

a. of material objects or of immaterial or abstract entities; e.g. ***substring*** (STRING *sb.* 15 c), ***-tree*** (TREE *sb.* 6 b (*e*)), ***-unit***, etc.; ***sub-areolet***, a division of an areolet; ***sub-cavity***, one of the smaller cavities into which a cavity is divided; ˈ***sub-channel*** *Radio*, a distinct division of a channel or frequency band; ***sub-folium***, a small or secondary folium; ˈ***subgrain***, a small grain contained within another grain in a metal; ***sub-hoˈrizon***, a layer within an existing archæological or soil horizon; ˈ***sublattice*** *Physics*, a coextensive part of a fuller lattice, obtained by considering all the members having some property not possessed by the other members; ˈ***sub-shell*** *Physics*, in an electron shell, the complete set of orbitals capable of being occupied by electrons of identical azimuthal quantum number *l*.

1852 DANA *Crust.* I. 192 From each lateral segment a small *subareolet is separated anteriorly. **1899** *Allbutt's Syst. Med.* VII. 647 The cavity of the cranium is divided into two *subcavities by the tentorium cerebelli. **1847–9** *Todd's Cycl. Anat.* IV. I. 99/1 The cells..containing no *sub-cells in their interiors. **1875** BRASH *Eccl. Archit. Irel.* 92 The chancel has a deep recess or *sub-chancel at the east end. **1959** *Wall St. Jrnl.* 30 June 1/4 Multiplexing...is a technique by which a radio station can divide its regular channels into *subchannels and transmit two or more sound signals at the same time. **1970** J. EARL *Tuners & Amplifiers* i. 24 Other features found in tuner-amplifiers..are automatic mono/stereo switching.., a low-pass filter for reducing the stereo sub-channel noise when the aerial signal is not quite strong enough for noise-free stereo reception, [etc.]. **1889** *Buck's Handbk. Med. Sci.* VIII. 127 The exact number and form of the cerebellar folia and *subfolia at birth. **1955** *Phil. Mag.* XLVI. 1343 Recent work..has shown that many of the dislocations left inside a metal after deformation are arranged along surfaces forming low angle boundaries between neighbouring regions of crystal, these latter being called *subgrains, cells, or particles. **1975** *Nature* 10 Apr. 489/1 Granular xenoliths..show various strain effects, including undulose extinction.., slip-planes, and subgrain development. **1928** *Bull. Amer. Soil Survey Assoc.* IX. 36 Other *sub-horizons are designated as A_1, A_2, etc. **1973** P. A. COLINVAUX *Introd. Ecol.* iii. 45 (*caption*) There may be several subhorizons in each of the main horizons and roots may penetrate them all. **1883** *Pall Mall Gaz.* 25 Sept. 10/1 What he might call *sub-houses, or a house within a house. **1641** MILTON *Animadv.* Wks. 1851 III. 226 An individuall cannot branch itselfe into *subindividuals. **1959** W. F. DE JONG *Gen. Crystallogr.* II. 101 Either the direct lattice..is congruent (similar) with the elementary Bravais lattice, or one is a *sub-lattice of the other. **1973** H. D. MEGAW *Crystal Structures* viii. 174 Physicists who are less used to describing any but very simple periodic structures,..use the very misleading term 'sublattice' for a Bravais array. **1976** *Physics Bull.* July 294/2 In a crystal the atomic lattice can divide into two interpenetrating sublattices so that most, if not all, of the neighbours of an atom on one sublattice belong to the other. **1885** WATSON & BURBURY *Math. The. Electr.* I. 237 The motions of the *submolecules. **1898** *Syd. Soc. Lex.*, **Subnucleus*, any one of the subdivisions into which a group of nerve-cells is divided by the passage through it of intersecting bundles. **1880** C. & F. DARWIN *Movem. Pl.* 223 The peduncle..bears three or four *sub-peduncles. **1836–9** *Todd's Cycl. Anat.* II. 910/1 The pro-thorax..is composed of four *sub-segments. **1930** RUARK & UREY *Atoms, Molecules & Quanta* ix. 272 The *n*, *l*, and *s* quantum numbers can still be assigned to individual electrons, and, therefore, the shells and *subshells can be designated in terms of these numbers. **1959** G. TROUP *Masers* 161 We take as an example Cr^{+++} which has 3 electrons in the unfilled outermost sub-shell. **1980** H. H. SISLER et al. *Chem.* viii. 209 For electrons in *s* subshells, we find that the probability distribution..is independent of direction in space and varies only with distance from the nucleus. **1955** N. CHOMSKY *Logical Struct. Linguistic Theory* (microfilm, Mass. Inst. Technol.) vi. 202b *Z'* differs from *Z* only in that it contains a *substring *Y* replacing the substring *X* of *Z*. **1966** D. G. HASS in *Automatic Transl. of Lang.* (NATO Summer School, Venice, 1962) 145 In natural languages, texts can be segmented into recurrent substrings. **1972** *Computer Jrnl.* XV. 232/2 Each co-ordinate of *T* specifies a set to which a substring of *A* belongs. **1947** *Proc. Cambr. Philos. Soc.* XLIII. 26 We call *S* a *subtree of *L* if $p_0(S)$ = 1 and $p_1(S)$ = 0. **1972** R. J. WILSON *Introd. to Graph Theory* iv. 51 Let T_1, ..., T_k be the subtrees obtained from *B* by removing the vertex *v* and every edge incident to *v*. **1976** J. S. GRUBER *Lexical Structures in Syntax & Semantics* II. i. 219 Instead of writing the lexical attachment rules as transformations, we will write them as terminal subtrees. **1936** *Economist* 7 Mar. 530/1 The promoters buy specified blocks of securities and deposit them with named trustees, who issue an agreed number of '*sub-unit certificates' against them. **1950** *Cold Spring Harbor Symp. Quantitative Biol.* XIV. 69/1 The phenomenon that the asymmetric unit in the crystal is a submultiple..of the molecular weights found in the ultracentrifuge, and..that excelsin..splits into 3n subunits. **1980** *Times* 15 Jan. 14 DNA is a long chain-like molecule composed of four different chemical subunits.

b. of a body or assembly of people, as in SUBCOMMITTEE, or of a division of animals or plants, as in SUBGENUS; e.g. ***sub-caste***, ***-clan***, ***-clone*** (also as vb. trans.), ***-flight*** [FLIGHT *sb.*[1] 1 h], ***-nation*** (also ***-nationalism***), ***-unit***; ***sub-band***, a division of a band; ***sub-breed***, a breed of animals constituting a marked division of a principal breed.

1808 PIKE *Sources Mississ.* (1810) I. App. 60 A young man, Wyaganage, has recently taken the lead in all the councils and affairs of state of this *sub-band. **1859** DARWIN *Orig. Spec.* iv. (1878) 87 The *sub breeds of the tumbler pigeon. **1896** *Daily News* 7 Apr. 3/3 The east *sub-brigade..supported by the west sub-brigade. **1892** H. H. RISLEY *Tribes & Castes Bengal* I. 78 The Bauris are divided into the following nine *sub-castes. **1974** tr. *Wertheim's Evolution & Revolution* iii. 240 Even if a sub-group within a caste..has constituted itself as a separate sub-caste, such a collective step will generally imply a disruption of recognized family ties. **1954** *Subclan [see PARAMOUNT *a.* 1 c]. **1961** *Virology* XIII. 160/2 *Subclones showing the morphology characteristic of the superinfecting virus were plated for virus release. *Ibid.*, Clones showing the morphology characteristic of the original virus were subcloned. **1977** *Jrnl. Protozool.* XXIV. 28/1 The plausible inference can be drawn that doublet and singlet subclones from a single source do not differ in the kinds of genes or of other molecules they contain. **1978** *Nature* 7 Dec. 579/2 We subcloned the mixed progeny of the cross. **1894** *Educ. Rev.* VII. 278 Every one of the *sub-conferences claims for its group of subjects an educational value equal to that of every other. **1908** *Westm. Gaz.* 8 Aug. 2/1 One Council, with *sub-councils corresponding roughly to the postal areas. **1877** LE CONTE *Elem. Geol.* (1879) 160 The fauna and flora of the United States are divided..into three *sub-faunæ and *sub-floræ. **1941** *Hutchinson's Pictorial Hist. War* 14 May–8 July 216/2 Dive-bombers usually approach at about eight thousand feet or so, and on arriving over the target break up into *sub-flights of three. **1833** CHALMERS in *Mem.* (1851) III. 381 The discussions of the separate or *sub-meetings. **1935** A. M. CARR-SAUNDERS in Huxley & Haddon *We Europeans* viii. 256 We might..contrast America with Europe, regarding the European nations as *sub-nations, that is as communities with a lower degree of distinction. **1967** M. AYUB KHAN *Friends not Masters* x. 183 We will remain 'sub-nations' if we do not join together to offer united resistance to power pressures. **1957** *Economist* 7 Sept. 739/2 This theoretically sensible policy ran up against the *sub-nationalism of the local peoples. **1974** G. W. CHOUDHURY *Last Days United Pakistan* i. 1 Emerging Bengali regionalism or sub-nationalism. **1860** MILL *Repr. Gov.* (1865) 115/2 Besides the controlling Council, or local *sub-Parliament, local business has its executive department. **1888** *Encycl. Brit.* XXIII. 473/1 Each of these phratries is subdivided into two *subphratries; and these subphratries are subdivided into an indefinite number of totem clans. **1888** *Ibid.* XXIV. 810/1 The main branchings [of a genealogical tree] were termed 'phyla', their branchings '*subphyla'. **1846** GROTE *Greece* II. ii. II. 324 Twelve *sub-races, out of the number which made up entire Hellas. **1894** W. WALKER *Hist. Congreg. Ch.* 299 With the two Edwardean divines..Emmons and Dwight,—the New Divinity may be said to have divided into two *subschools. **1824** SOUTHEY *Sir T. More* (1831) I. 362 Every Sect and every *Sub-sect has its magazine. **1868** GLADSTONE *Juv. Mundi* iv. 112 A *sub-sept of the Achaians. **1798** in Nicolas *Disp.* (1845) III. 49 He divided his force into three *Sub-squadrons. **1882** A. MACFARLANE *Consanguinity* 15 Each lineal ancestor forms a stock and his family breaks up into *sub-stocks. **1879** in Willis & Clark *Cambridge* (1886) III. 226 The *sub-Syndicate are of opinion that it would be undesirable. **1670** *Rec. Presbyt. Inverness* (1896) 2 To remitte the same [*sc.* names]..with the Moderator to the Bishope to yᵉ fors.ᵈ *Subsynode. **1885** *Athenæum* 28 Feb. 279/1 If the squadron is preferable to the troop as a *sub-unit. *a* **1944** K. DOUGLAS *Alamein to Zem Zem* (1946) 13 He allotted me two tanks, as a troop, there not being enough on the squadron strength to make *sub-units of more than two tanks.

(*b*) in derived adjs.; e.g. ***subphratric***, pertaining to a subphratry.

1977 *Jrnl. Commonwealth & Compar. Pol.* XV. 236 In 1968 the 81 successful UNIP candidates included 24 politicians at *subnational levels. **1887** J. G. FRAZER *Totemism* p. viii, *Subphratric and Phratric Totems. **1896** W. MACKAY *Rec. Presbyt. Inverness* 45 Among the *subsynodical refers read to-day.

c. of a region or an interval of time, as in SUB-DISTRICT; e.g. ***sub-age***, a division of an age.

1878 LOCKYER *Stargazing* 2 The Telescopic age..divides itself naturally into some three or four *sub-ages of extreme importance. **1926** *British Gaz.* 12 May 2/3 A service of corporation 'buses has been started in the *sub-area of Keighley. **1980** *Amer. Speech 1976* LI. 235 The second map ..shows the boundaries of twelve dialect areas and subareas of Scottish English. **1953** L. KUPER *Living in Towns* 304 Library books had been issued from *sub-centres in local schools. **1977** *Lancet* 5 Nov. 946/1 The health centre and subcentres provided additional support. **1826** KIRBY & SP. *Entom.* IV. 485 [Latreille] proposes further to divide his climates into *subclimates, by means of certain meridian lines. **1910** *Geol. Fören. i Stockholm Förhandl.* XXXII. 1146 (*heading*) Gothi- and Finiglacial *sub-epochs. **1940** A. H. SUTTON in *Bull. Geol. Soc. Amer.* LI. 1402 Subepoch —subseries. These terms as herein proposed are applicable to the first subdivisions of epochs and series respectively. **1867** G. F. CHAMBERS *Astron.* (1877) 23 The interval 11.11ʸ being divided into two unequal *sub-intervals of 4.77ʸ and 6.34ʸ. **1962** D. R. COX *Renewal Theory* ii. 30 To obtain (1) from first principles, divide the time interval (0, *t*) into a large number *k* of small subintervals of length Δt, where $k\Delta t = t$. **1980** A. J. JONES *Game Theory* ii. 109 Then divide the interval [0, 1] into three equal subintervals. **1936** *Discovery* Oct. 329/1 Measles and certain skin affections..are the result of these *sub-phase mutations. **1977** *Antiquaries Jrnl.* LVII. 392 It is simply a sub-phase of one phase..of a conservative..coinage. **1898** *Jrnl. Sch. Geog.* (U.S.) Oct. 286 The *sub-province known as the Great Plains. **1852** GROTE *Greece* II. lxxii. IX. 290 Each satrapy was divided into *sub-satrapies or districts. **1909** *Daily Chron.* 29 June 4/6 Cleveland,..stands with Holderness, Hallamshire, and Richmondshire as a *sub-shire of Yorkshire. **1903** *Subzone [see SECULE]. **1969** BENNISON & WRIGHT *Geol. Hist. Brit. Isles* ix. 213 The 6 goniatite stages called after goniatite genera..were formally called zones but they are stages further divided into 16 zones (and many subzones).

d. of a branch leading from or into the main body, or a subordinate section of a business or system of affairs; = branch-; e.g. ***sub-bureau***, a bureau depending on the principal bureau, ***sub-cash***, a deposit of cash at a branch, ***sub-office***, a branch office.

1896 *Pop. Sci. Monthly* Feb. 572 The bureau will be aided ..by *sub-bureaus. **1705** DE FOE *Consolidator* Wks. 1840 IX. 354 They brought all their running cash into one bank, and settled a *sub-cash, depending upon the grand bank, in every province of the kingdom. **1909** *Install. News* III. 29/1 Where wood casing is desired to be used for the *sub-circuits. **1892** *Daily News* 16 Sept. 5/4 A portion of the *sub-creek referred to, now being converted into a peaceful fishpond. **1804** *Edin. Rev.* V. 16 The other [college] is to consist of *sub-departments, one in each county. **1938** *Times* 13 Sept. 17/6 The opening of a further *sub-depôt for recruits at the air station at Dishforth, Yorks. **1976** *Daily Mail* (Hull) 30 Sept. 5/1 Councillors at Selby, concerned at the possibility of an Army Ordnance sub-depot being purchased by the Central Electricity Generating Board. **1958** W. STARK *Sociol. Knowl.* i. 31 The relation of the two *sub-disciplines to each other. **1982** *Sci. Amer.* Nov. 52/1 Answers to these questions call for close collaboration among earth scientists from many subdisciplines. **1897** MARY KINGSLEY *W. Africa* 139 Stopping at little villages to land passengers or at little *sub-factories to discharge cargo. **1902** W. JAMES *Var. Relig. Exper.* ix. 195 For them the soul is only a succession of fields of consciousness: yet there is found in each field a part, or *sub-field, which figures as focal and..from which..the aim seems to be taken. **1964** GOULD & KOLB *Dict. Soc. Sci.* 510/2 Political behaviour has come to be regarded as a sub-field, within the social sciences. **1968** N. CHOMSKY *Lang. & Mind* ii. 24 Linguistics..is simply the subfield of psychology that deals with these aspects of mind. **1977** *Dædalus* Fall 59 These subfields have been codified and systematized in an attempt to bring them into closer relation with theoretical frameworks. **1844** H. STEPHENS *Bk. Farm* I. 564 Where *sub-mains are employed in particular hollows, the ground comprehending the drainage belonging to each hollow should be distinctly marked off from the rest. *Ibid.*, A sub-main drain should be made along the lowest part of the hollow. **1907** *Nature* LXXVI. 554/2 The *submeter system is free from the objection of first cost to a great extent. **1876** PREECE & SIVEWRIGHT *Telegr.* 264 Every *sub-office on a circuit is called by the head office at the hour of commencing work. **1881** *Chicago Times* 17 June, Regarding the formation of a pool, the report..recommends three *sub-pools. **1901** *Daily Chron.* 27 Dec. 3/4 The Hammersmith *sub-post-office. **1862** H. SPENCER *First Princ.* II. xiv. §113 (1875) 324 The once independent *sub-sciences of Electricity, Magnetism, and Light. **1861** N. DAVIS *Carthage* 34 *Sub-sewers, and other..unsightly objects. **1971** *Optometry Today* 15 Vision care needs of the aging patient have virtually produced a *subspeciality within the opto-metric profession: vision care of the aging. **1980** *Jrnl. R. Soc. Med.* LXXIII. 758/1 Between four and seven reviews within six subspecialities of medicine. **1963** *Lancet* 5 Jan. 42/2 Some of the *subspecialties such as skins and eyes. **1961** *Communications Assoc. Computing Machinery* IV. 438/2 A request, by a task, to call in and execute a *subtask causes.. a new task (the subtask called) to be added to the task list, with the appropriate precedence and priority. **1971** *New Society* 26 Aug. 373/1 My first subtask is..to move the ramp... This sets up the subsubtask of computing the coordinates. **1982** *Sci. Amer.* Jan. 123/2 The several concurrent processes can be different subtasks of a single program. **1855** LEIFCHILD *Cornwall* 89 Divided lengthwise into other *sub-veins.

e. *Math.* Prefixed to sbs. to denote an entity which is contained in some similar entity, in that each of its elements is also an element of the latter and that it shares the characterizing properties of the latter, as ***subalgebra***, ***-field***, ***-formation***, ***-graph***, ***-manifold***, ***-matrix***, ***-module***, ***-object***, ***-ring***. Also SUBGROUP b, SUBSEQUENCE[2], SUBSET *sb.*[2]

1933 *Subalgebra [see LATTICE *sb.* 5]. **1979** *Proc. London Math. Soc.* XXXVIII. 315 Let A_N be the closed subalgebra of $L(H_N)$ generated by the operators $T_1, \ldots, T_N$ and set *H*. **1940** E. T. BELL *Devel. Math.* xi. 239 The final outcome may be roughly described as an analysis of the structure of fields with respect to their possible *subfields and superfields. **1971** G. HIGMAN in Powell & Higman *Finite Simple Groups* vi. 209 *Q*(α) is the real subfield of the field of the 5-th roots of unity. **1966** tr. *Gericke's Lattice Theory* iv. 71 We shall show that the set of *sub-formations of a formation.. relative to a given axiom system..that satisfies a condition yet to be formulated forms a complete lattice. **1931** *Proc. Nat. Acad. Sci.* XVII. 125 A *subgraph *H* of a graph *G* is a graph formed by dropping out arcs from *G*. **1979** PAGE & WILSON *Introd. Computational Combinatorics* iv. 76 Given a graph G = (P, L) then G' = (P', L') is a subgraph if P' is a subset of P and L' is a subset of L. **1963** H. FLANDERS *Differential Forms* v. 52 A manifold M is called a *sub-manifold of a manifold N provided there is a one-to-one smooth mapping *j*: M→N which has this..property. **1970** G. K. WOODGATE *Elem. Atomic Struct.* viii. 152 The matrix of *H'* which has to be diagonalized breaks up into *submatrices of given *M*. **1980** A. J. JONES *Game Theory* iii. 149 There are nine 2 × 2 submatrices obtained by deleting the ith row and j^{th} column from *A*. **1965** J. J. ROTMAN *Theory of Groups* iv. 68 A subset *W* of the *R*-module *V* is a *submodule of *V* in case it is a subgroup of *V* which is closed under scalar multiplication. **1981** *Amer. Math. Monthly* LXXXVIII. 53 Submodules of finitely generated free modules over a principal ideal domain are free and need no more generators. **1965** *Subobject [see PROPER *a.* 5 c (i)]. **1979** *Proc. London Math. Soc.* XXXVIII. 245 The subobjects of N^+ in *E* which contain the point ∞ are in 1–1 correspondence with closed ideals of subsets of N. **1937**, **1969** *Subring [see IDEAL *sb.* 3].

8. With advb. force, combined with adjs. and vbs. = in a subordinate or secondary manner or capacity, by subsidiary means, as ***sub-entitle*** vb., ***-functional*** adj.

1812 COLERIDGE in *Lit. Rem.* (1836) I. 366 The real value of melody in a language is considerable as *subadditive. **1716** M. DAVIES *Athen. Brit.* II. 368 His *Monarchia Dei* is directed against the Heathens for subjoyning and *sub-adoring several essentially subdistinguish'd Deities. **1901** *Daily News* 20 Feb. 6/5 The Assiut dam will be subsidiary to that at Assuan, inasmuch as it is..to be used *sub-conjunctively to that at Assuan. **1890** *Academy* 4 Jan. 7/3 Its anonymous author has *sub-entitled this book 'A New Story by an Old Hand'. **1845** POE in *Amer. Whig Rev.* II. 127/1 It is to be regretted that 'The Spanish Student' was not sub-entitled 'A Dramatic Poem', rather than 'A Play'. **1897–8** *Amer. Jrnl. Psych.* IX. 580 Pronunciation of an adjective..seems to *subexcite association tracts representing substantives. **1904** *Amer. Naturalist* Jan. 6 Hypohippus of the middle Miocene with *subfunctional lateral digits..is an instance of arrested evolution. **1871** Earle *Philol. Engl. Tongue* §464 The pronoun *I*..has..a sort of reflected or borrowed presentiveness;—what may be called a *sub-presentive power. **1828–9** Bentham *Offic. Apt. Maxim., On Militia* (1830) 4 The united wisdom and eloquence of the ruling one and the *sub-ruling few.

9. (*a*) On the analogy of SUBDIVIDE and SUBDIVISION, *sub-* is used to denote a further division or distinction; e.g. ***sub-classify***, ***sub-decimate***; ***sub-articulation***, ***-classification***, ***-component***, ***-kind***; (*b*) on the analogy of SUBCONTRACT *sb.* and *v.*, SUBINFEUDATION, SUBLET, to denote a second or further action or process of the same kind as that denoted by the radical; e.g. ***sub-colonize***, to colonize from a colony, ***sub-infer***, to draw as a further inference, ***sub-rent***, to rent from one who himself rents; ***sub-derivative***, a derivative of a derivative, ***sub-purchaser***, one who purchases from a previous purchaser, ***sub-reformist***, one who carries out a further reform, ***sub-vaccinee***, one who is vaccinated with lymph from a vaccinated person; ***sub-secession***, a secession from a body that has seceded. Also **'sub-carrier** *Telecommunication*, a carrier wave used to modulate another carrier; **'sublevel** *Physics*, each of a group of energy levels of an atom or nucleus which coincide under a coarse approximation or when some factor (as a magnetic field) is removed; **'subline** *Genetics*, a variant arising in an inbred line and distinguished by a trait usu. inherited from a genetically impure ancestor; **'subpassage** *sb. Biol.* and *Med.*, the passage of a strain of micro-organisms cultivated in one animal through another, esp. to increase the virulence; also as *v. trans.*; hence **'subpassaging** *vbl. sb.*; **sub'satellite** *Astronautics*, a satellite of a satellite; *spec.* a small artificial satellite released from another satellite or spacecraft; **sub-'underwriter** *Econ.*, one who underwrites part of a liability (esp. a share issue) underwritten by another; so **sub-'underwrite** *v. trans.*, **sub-'underwriting** *vbl. sb.*

1867 in Farrar *Ess. Lib. Educ.* 330 To imitate the copiousness and *subarticulation of Cicero's periods. **1953** Reed & Russell *Ultra High Frequency Propagation* xi. 411 *Subcarrier modulation, wherein a subcarrier spaced in the order of 10 kc from the highest modulating frequency is modulated with the desired intelligence, would provide all desired carrier amplitude variations at frequencies much in excess of any presently conceivable lobe modulation frequency. **1976** *Which?* Sept. 204/1 We measured how well the sets filtered from the audio output..the 38Hz sub-carrier frequencies—parts of the complex signal that tell the tuner that a stereo programme is being broadcast. **1873** M. Dewey in G. Dawe *Melvil Dewey* (1932) 320 Sub-classify each, or any, of these eighty-one (hundred) classes... A Dictionary of Science would receive no *sub-classification but remain simply with main class number. **1894** in *37th Rep. Columb. Inst. Deaf & Dumb* (1895) 9 We are required to have subclassifications by which we may know the.. specialized work to which it devotes itself. **1897** *Daily News* 16 Mar. 2/2 Abolition of sub-classification is recommended. **1873** *Sub-classify [see *sub-classification* above]. **1909** *Daily Chron.* 3 June 3/3 If you sub-classify 55,000 Germans into men, women and children. **1820** *Q. Rev.* XXIII. 73 A dependency upon that colony, from which it was *sub-colonized. **1965** N. Chomsky *Aspects Theory Syntax* i. 17 The syntactic component of a generative grammar contains a *transformational* *subcomponent. **1973** L. L. & J. M. Constantine *Group Marriage* xviii. 199 In the interpersonal dimension, we identified two subcomponents. **1704** J. Macmillan *True Narr.* in H. M. B. Reid *Camer. Apost.* (1896) 236 They draw a *sub-consequence, which is this, that it was contrar the protest and agreement. **1664** Power *Exp. Philos.* Pref. 12 All the fixed lights of Heaven are generally concluded to be pure Fire, and so consequently fluid also, and then *sub-consequentially in motion also. **1896** *Allbutt's Syst. Med.* I. 719 Large colonies [of bacteria] on *sub-cultivation will frequently appear as small ones. **1736** Bailey (folio) Pref., *To *Subdecimate*..to divide into tenths..as 10 Thousand into Hundredths. **1845** Jowett *Let. to B. C. Brodie* 28 Mar., [Rome] has defined, and *sub-defined, and deduced, and *subdeduced. **1856** R. A. Vaughan *Mystics* (1860) I. vi. vi. 209 Every definition and *subdefinition would be open to some doubt. **1884** *Law Rep. 13 Q.B. Div.* 466 Long leaseholds, which he had mortgaged by *sub-demise. **1880** *Westm. & Chelsea News* 2 Oct. Advt., A shop and Dwelling House..held for a term of 99 years, and *subdemised at £80 per annum. **1614** Raleigh *Hist. World* I. 142 For these *subderiuations [of the Turks] it were infinite to examine them. **1834** H. N. Coleridge *Grk. Poets* (ed. 2) 9 The modern derivative will, at some stage or other of its history, have been treated as an original substantive word..and associations connected only with its primary modern senses will have given birth to *sub-derivatives from it. *a***1661** Fuller *Worthies, Wiltshire* (1662) III. 150 Succeeding Princes, following this patern, have *sub-diminished their coin ever since. **1823** Bentham *Not Paul* 371 The name and person of his own *sub-disciple Apollos. **1643** J. M. *Sov. Salve* 26 To let in a deluge of forrein forces and so yet further *subdistract the remnant. **1662** Petty *Taxes* 13 How many retailers are needful to make the *subdistributions into every village of this nation. *a***1676** Hale *Prim. Orig. Man.* II. iv. (1677) 157 And possibly these variously *subdiversified according to the phantasy of the Artificer. **1863** Reade *Hard Cash* III. 74 What on earth was left for poor Dr. Wolf to do? Could he *sub-embezzle a Highlander's breeks? **1652** *Observ. touching Forms Govt.* 38 Constrained to epitomize, and *subepitomize themselves so long till at last they crumble away into the atomes of Monarchie. **1666** *Lond. Gaz.* No. 42/2 The Farmers of his Majesties Revenue of the Hearth-Duty, intending to *Sub-Farm several Counties. **1764** Gibbon *Misc. Wks.* (1814) III. 224 The lands were perhaps subfarmed by individuals. **1658** in *Dom. State Papers* 321 For seizure made by the *sub-farmers. **1857** Buckle *Civiliz.* I. ix. 568 The great lords having granted lands on condition of fealty and other services to certain persons, these last *subgranted them. **1885** *Law Rep. 28 Chanc. Div.* 121 An agreement of *sub-guarantee by which the signatories guaranteed the signatories of the original guarantee against loss. **1889** W. Rye *Cromer* 32 The *subholding created by Richard de Berningham. *a***1656** Bp. Hall *Rem. Wks.* (1660) 409 From the force then of this relation it is easily *subinfered that it is not lawful for Christian Churches..to forsake the communion of each other. **1905** *British Medical Journal* 27 May 1141 The injection in small amounts will not serve to infect the *subinoculated animal. **1843** Mill *Logic* II. III. xxii. 135 Examining every known *sub-kind included in the larger kind. **1968** *Listener* 4 July 6/1 The campus novel, a literary sub-kind that has languished these last years, is surely in for a revival now that dons have had the heady experience of being news. **1963** G. Troup *Masers & Lasers* (ed. 2) 183 Paramagnetic resonance is usually observed between *sub-levels of the term having lowest energy. **1971** *Sci. Amer.* Oct. 91/2 In a nonuniform [electrostatic] field such nuclei will exhibit energy levels that are split into a number of sublevels corresponding to the number of allowed orientations of the nucleus. **1948** *Jrnl. Genetics* XLIX. 92 A tumour arising in one *subline would be foreign, to some degree at least, to another subline. **1981** *Nature* 19 Feb. 626/1 Many of the major sublines of common inbred strains [of mice]..have arisen as a result of genetic contamination in the past. **1902** *Daily Chron.* 26 Nov. 6/6 The final *sub-lodger was squeezed out upon the landing for his sleeping-place. **1884** *Law Times* 29 Nov. 80/1 The mortgagees in fee of an hotel *sub-mortgaged to their bankers in 1879. **1883** *Law Times Rep.* (N.S.) XLIX. 556/1 The defendants last added are *sub-mortgagees of the trustee. **1872** E. W. Robertson *Hist. Ess.* 242 The client of that age was apparently a *sub-occupier of public land under his Patronus. **1934** Webster, *Subpassage, *sb.* **1947** *Ann. Rev. Microbiol.* I. 19 Pneumococci..maintained by rapid subpassage through mice. **1970** B. G. F. Weitz in H. W. Mulligan *African Trypanosomiases* vi. 114 Variants sometimes reverted to a 'parent' antigenic strain type when rodent subpassage was prolonged. **1969** *Parasitology* LIX. 352 Parasites isolated from the parasitaemia..were *subpassaged at 4-day intervals. **1978** *Nature* 14 Sept. 132/2 Tumours have been serially subpassaged 3× to date. **1970** *Ibid.* 12 Dec. 1061/1 Lincicome has shown that in calorically restricted mice the number of hosts that developed maximal infections and the intensity of the parasitaemia are increased by *subpassaging. **1866** *Law Rep. 1 Q.B. Cases* 589 On his seeking to get the pawn back from an insolvent *sub-pawnee. *Ibid.*, If the pawnee may repledge the pawn, the *sub-pledgee may do the same, and so on ad infinitum. **1755** *Gentl. Mag.* XXV. 354 They have successively come into the hands of many *sub-proprietors. **1855** Hyde Clarke *Dict.*, **Sub-purchaser*. **1643** Sir T. Browne *Relig. Med.* I. §54 The Church of Rome condemneth us, wee likewise them, the *Sub-reformists and Sectaries sentence the Doctrine of our Church as damnable [etc.]. **1826** Bell *Comm. Laws Scot.* I. 67 Possession of the *subrents. **1902** R. Bagot *Donna Diana* ii. 13 An apartment he had *sub-rented from a wealthy American widow. **1897** *Advance* (Chicago) 24 June 813/1, $500 of income from *sub-rental. **1849** Hooker *Himal. Jrnls.* (1854) I. xvii. 388 Through the medium of several *sub-renting classes. **1894** J. J. Astor *Journey in Other Worlds* II. i. 126 There will be no danger from meteors or *sub-satellites here..for anything revolving about the moon at this distance would be caught by the earth. **1956** *Time* (Canadian ed.) 24 Dec. 53/1 The inflated sub-satellite is a balloon of Mylar plastic ·0025 in. thick covered with an aluminium film ·0006 in. thick. **1978** *Nature* 5 Oct. 430/1 We have attempted..to interpret lunar palaeomagnetism as observed..in widespread crustal magnetic anomalies mapped by magnetometers on Explorer 35 and the Apollo 15 and 16 subsatellites. **1880** Burton *Reign Q. Anne* I. ii. 66 *Sub-secessions from the successive seceding bodies. **1680** Allen *Peace & Unity* Pref. 80 These seperations and *sub-seperations. **1894** *Daily Tribune* (N.Y.) 5 July, In not all of the cities is administration *sub-sold to confederated crime and to blackmailed business. **1895** *Pop. Sci. Monthly* Apr. 767 A *subspecialized descendant of an ancient generalized group. **1846** D. King *Lord's Supper* vii. 214 An endless splitting and *subsplitting of distinctions. **1897** Mary Kingsley *W. Africa* 393 These native *sub-traders have very risky lives of it. **1900** *Century Mag.* LIX. 493/2 The minister of the interior..whose touches thrill by devolution and *subtransmission throughout the mighty system. **1935** *Economist* 13 July 65/1 He did, however, *sub-underwrite the issue, which was discussed with him previous to the date of the prospectus. **1959** *Ibid.* 18 Apr. 256/1 The *sub-underwriters get 1 per cent of the amount they have underwritten. **1982** *Daily Tel.* 6 Mar. 1/7 A large proportion..is paid out to other financial institutions, called sub-underwriters. **1955** *Times* 11 July 14/1 Firm applications..have already been received..for 300,000 shares on *sub-underwriting terms. **1981** *Times* 8 Jan. 11/3 Brokers to the issue..completed the subunderwriting of the issue yesterday afternoon. **1897** *Allbutt's Syst. Med.* II. 592 All the *sub-vaccinees of the vaccinifer (who himself subsequently suffered from erysipelas) did not suffer from erysipelas. **1873** *Routledge's Young Gentl. Mag.* 85 *Sub-variation on White's thirteenth move.

10. *Math.* Compounded with adjs. expressing ratio, *sub-* denotes a ratio the opposite of that expressed by the radical element, as in L. *subduplus* SUBDUPLE, *subtriplus* SUBTRIPLE, late L. *submultiplus* SUBMULTIPLE; e.g. ***subdecuple*** = denoting the ratio 1 : 10, †***subdouble*** = SUBDUPLE, †***subnovitripartient*** = 1 : $9\frac{3}{8}$, i.e. 8 : 75, ***subsesquitertial*** = 3 : 4, ***subsuperparticular***, etc. Analogously, in SUBDUPLICATE, etc. the prefix is employed to express the ratio of the square (etc.) roots of quantities; but these compounds have been sometimes erron. used for *subduple*, etc. (cf. quot. 1657 below).

This use is modelled (in late L.) on that of Gr. ὑπο-, as in ὑποδιπλάσιος, late L. *subduplus*. Ratios of this kind were called ὑπόλογοι, the opposite πρόλογοι, ὑπο- app. expressing the notion of 'proportion of *lesser* inequality'. (Another arithmetical use of the Greek and Latin prefixes is unrepresented in Eng.; viz. that exemplified in ὑπότριτος, L. *subtertius*, lit. 'a third less', i.e. denoting a ratio $\frac{2}{3}$: 1, i.e. 2 : 3.)

1570 Billingsley *Euclid* 128 Comparing the lesse quantitie to the greater, it [*sc.* proportion] is called submultiplex, subsuperparticular, subsuperpartient, submultiplex superparticular, and submultiplex superpartient. **1648** Wilkins *Math. Magic* I. vii. 47 As one of these under Pulleys doth abate halfe of that heavinesse which the weight hath in it self, and cause the power to be in a sub-duple proportion unto it, so two of them doe abate halfe of that which remains, and cause a subquadruple proportion betwixt the weight and the power; three of them a subsextuple, four a sub-octuple. *Ibid.* 50 If unto this lower Pulley there were added another, then the power would be unto the weight in a subquintuple proportion. If a third, a subseptuple. **1652** Urquhart *Jewel* 288 It would bear the analogy..of a subnovitripartient eights; that is to say,..the whole being the Dividend, and my Nomenclature the Divisor, the quotient would be nine, with a fraction of three eights; or yet more clearly, as the Proportion of 72. to 675. **1653** H. More *Antid. Ath.* I. vi. §4 (1712) 19 The Notion of Sub-double, which accrued to that Lead which had half cut away. **1657** Hobbes *Absurd Geom.* Wks. 1845 VII. 375 It is but subquad[r]uplicate, as you call it, or the quarter of it, as I call it. **1674** Jeake *Arith.* (1696) 209 As the Series of the Numbers from the Units place are continued in a decuple proportion..so their value decreaseth in a subdecuple proportion. *a***1696** Scarburgh *Euclid* (1705) 181 The proportion is Subsuperparticular, and named Subsesquialteral, which is thus noted $\frac{2}{3}$. *Ibid.*, Subsuperpartient, as 5 to 8, or $\frac{5}{8}$ is subsupertriquintal: and 10 to 14, or $\frac{10}{14}$ is Subsuperbiquintal. **1709–29** V. Mandey *Syst. Math., Arith.* 37 Proportion Subduple, Subtriple, Sub-sesquialter, Subsuperbipartient. **1728** Chambers *Cycl.* s.v. *Ratio*, 3 to 2 is in a Sesquialterate Ratio; 2 to 3 in a Sub-sesquialterate. **1732** B. Robinson *Anim. Oecon.* 267 The simple and subquadruplicate Ratios of these Lengths. **1795** T. Maurice *Hindostan* (1820) I. I. ii. 75 The length of human life is diminished..in a subdecuple ratio.

III. Next below; near or close (to); subsequent (to). (As a living prefix *sub-* is restricted in this sense to prepositional uses: the advb. use is seen in SUBSEQUENT.)

11. Near to (a particular region or point), as in L. *suburbānus* SUBURBAN; e.g. SUB-BASAL, SUBDORSAL, SUB-LITTORAL, SUBMARGINAL.

Such words are often capable of another analysis (see 21 d).

12. *Geog.* and *Geol.* **a.** Lying about the base of or subjacent to mountains designated by the second element, hence, of less height than mountains of similar height to these, characteristic of regions of such altitude, as L. *subalpīnus* SUBALPINE; e.g. ***sub-Andean***, ***-Andine***, SUBAPENNINE, ***sub-Etnean***, ***sub-Himalayan***. Hence in the name of a district, e.g. ***sub-Himalaya(s***.

1875 *Encycl. Brit.* III. 744 The fourth and last Subregion of South America..may be most fitly named the *Subandean. **1885** *Linn. Soc. Jrnl., Bot.* XXII. 6 A *subandine as well as an andine zone. **1833** Lyell *Princ. Geol.* III. 76 The marine *sub-Etnean beds. **1847** *Sub-Himalayan [see SHERPA 1]. **1850** Ansted *Elem. Geol., Min.*, etc. 358 The formations composing the Sewalik hills, which have sometimes been called the Sub-Himalayans. **1851** *Jrnl. R. Geog. Soc.* XXI. 59 The Siwalik or sub-Himalayan range. **1851** Mantell *Petrifactions* v. §1. 413 Bones of mammalia from the *Sub-Himalayas. **1883** *Proc. R. Geog. Soc.* V. 617 The tertiaries of the Sub-Himalaya.

b. Denoting a region or zone adjacent to or on the borders of that designated by the second element; e.g. ***subantarctic***, ***-equatorial*** (also *fig.*), ***-frigid***, ***-torrid***.

1875 *Encycl. Brit.* III. 745 *Spheniscidæ*, a family limited to the Antarctic or *Subantarctic Ocean. **1909** (*title*) The Subantarctic islands of New Zealand. **1880** Dana *Man. Geol.* (ed. 3) 609 The corresponding zones in latitude..are 1. Equatorial, Lat. 0°–15°... 6. *Subarctic, 58°–66°. **1895** *Forum* June 468 There was once a widespread delusion in the *sub-arid belt..that rainfall follows the plough. **1909** Webster, *Subequatorial. **1935** H. H. Bashford *Lodgings for Twelve* 108 Apart from the excitements incident to the relief of Ladysmith and Mafeking, the Boer War—at any rate to the average undergraduate—was a sub-equatorial and not very important affair. **1977** *Sci. Amer.* Apr. 106/2 This is the earliest-known evidence of metallurgy in the entire subequatorial region. **1852** Dana *Crust.* II. 1472 Its southern portion..appears to pertain..to the *Subfrigid [Region]. **1896** *Yearbk. U.S. Dept. Agric.* 631 The *subhumid region. **1852** Henfrey *Veget. Eur.* 103 The regions which may be distinguished on the West side of the Scandinavian Alps are:—1. The Maritime region; 2. The *Subsylvatic region; 3. The Subalpine region; and 4. The Alpine region. **1852** Dana *Crust.* II. 1510 The genus *Porcellana* has but two-thirds as many species in the temperate as in the torrid zone. Yet the *sub-temperate region contains but one less than the *subtorrid.

13. *Mus.* Designating a note next to or next below some principal note, as in med.L.

subprincipālis SUBPRINCIPAL; e.g. SUBTONIC. (Cf. 4.)

14. a. Combined with adjs. (and in derived advbs.) with the sense 'of lower condition or degree (or size) than' or 'numerically less than' that denoted by the original adj.; e.g. Also (U.S.) in adjs. expressing an inferior educational status, as ***sub-angelical***, ***-divine***, ***-fresh*** (also ***-freshman***), ***-judicial***, ***-literary***, ***-maximal***, ***-miliary***, ***-molecular***, ***-morphemic***, ***-optimal*** (hence ***-optimally***), ***-optimum***, ***-phonemic*** (hence ***-phonemically***), ***-primary***, ***-regal***. **sub-bi'tuminous** *a. Geol.*, (of coal) of inferior quality to bituminous; intermediate in rank between bituminous coal and lignite; **sub'cellular** *a. Biol.*, smaller than a cell; occurring inside a cell; **subcom'pact** *a. U.S.*, designating a car which is smaller than a compact one (see COMPACT *ppl. a.*[1] II. 1 b); also *absol.* as *sb.*; **sub'freezing** *a.*, designating or characterized by a temperature lower than the freezing-point of water; **sub'luminal** *a.* [L. *lūmen*, *lūmin-* light], having or being a speed less than that of light.

This sense tends to blend with 19.

1652 BENLOWES *Theoph.* Pref., Man..is of all Creatures *sub-angelical the Almighties Masterpiece. **1908** *Econ. Geol.* III. 136 The term '*sub-bituminous' was recommended and formally adopted by the [U.S. Geological] survey for all official publications. **1949** F. J. PETTIJOHN *Sedimentary Rocks* xii. 366 Subbituminous, semibituminous, and semianthracite coals are transitional coal types. **1979** B. L. C. JOHNSON *Pakistan* xi. 161/1 The estimates of reserves of Lower Tertiary lignitic to sub-bituminous coal range between 449 and 478 million tonnes. **1608** HIERON *Defence* II. 83 These..maye be called conformable to the Canonicall or *subcannonical. **1953** *New Biol.* XV. 120 There are too many examples in which patterns arise..within single cells (and thus demand a theory dealing in *sub-cellular units). **1964** G. H. HAGGIS et al. *Introd. Molecular Biol.* ii. 20 Some enzymes are localized in certain sub-cellular structures. **1978** *Sci. Amer.* Dec. 68/2 Myoglobin combines with the oxygen released by red cells, stores it and transports it to the subcellular organelles called mitochondria. **1967** *Wall St. Jrnl.* 24 Feb. 1/1 AMC [*sc.* the American Motors Corporation] also is thinking of building a '*subcompact' car that would compete directly in size and price with Volkswagen. **1971** *Flying* Apr. 68/2 (Advt.), A different-looking subcompact with the spirit of a sporty car. **1980** *Times* 12 Dec. 24/3 Chrysler extended the close-down of its Belvidere, Illinois, assembly plant, which makes subcompact cars. **1610** DONNE *Pseudo-martyr* 185 Nor know we whether they will pleade Diuine Law, that is, places of Scripture, or *Sub diuine Law, which is interpretation of Fathers. **1652** BP. HALL *Invis. World* I. §2 O ye glorious Spirits..he that made you hath given us some little glimpse of your subdivine natures. **1958** *N.Y. Times* 15 Dec. 2/6 The Weather Bureau warned that *subfreezing temperatures would continue today. **1979** P. THEROUX *Old Patagonian Express* iii. 51 Two feet of snow in Boston. Chaos and death. Power cuts in sub-freezing weather. **1893** *Congregationalist* (Boston) 21 Sept., Enrollment as freshmen or '*sub-fresh' in the City College. **1896** *Living Topics Cycl.* (N.Y.) II. 264 Classical, scientific and mechanical *sub-freshman classes. **1808** BENTHAM *Sc. Reform* 67 All other persons who bear any part in the cause:—Judge, *sub-judicial officers, parties. **1872** SWINBURNE *Under Microscope* 79 'Ah, my lord..', says the jackal to the lion..'observe how all other living creatures belong but to some *sub-leonine class'. **1952** *New World Writing* Apr. 234 Even *aficionados* of murder fiction will concede..that except in the hands of a few writers it has been a *sub-literary product—characters unreal, dialogue artificial, plots highly improbable. **1980** *Jrnl. R. Soc. Arts* Apr. 302/1 He illuminates..this curious sub-literary genre in such a way that even serious students gain a profitable exposure to materials not often considered in length. **1969** *Physics Today* May 45/3 Particles traveling at *subluminal and those traveling at luminal velocities are two entirely distinct kinds of objects. **1980** *Sci. Amer.* Aug. 76/2 The expansion that appears from the earth to be superluminal would be relativistic but still subluminal when measured by the slower clocks of the source itself. **1890** W. JAMES *Princ. Psychol.* I. 235 *Submaximal nerve-irritations. **1880** A. FLINT *Princ. Med.* 194 The ultimate *submiliary granula coalesce to make..nodules. **1896** *Allbutt's Syst. Med.* I. 560 The body can resist the action of *subminimal doses of living bacteria. **1890** *Syd. Soc. Lex.*, *Subminimal stimulus*, a stimulus which is not strong enough to produce any obvious effect. **1935** *Discovery* Dec. 353/1 Raindrops may form on *sub-molecular electrically-charged units, or ions. **1964** G. H. HAGGIS et al. *Introd. Molecular Biol.* 338 Study of the mechanism of enzyme action is in a sense submolecular biology. **1947** C. F. HOCKETT in *Language* XXIII. 321 A scholar deciphering a dead language written in a non-phonetic or semi-phonetic orthography, may achieve good control of the tactics and semantics of the language, but remain in almost total ignorance of anything *sub-morphemic. **1964** E. A. NIDA *Toward Sci. Transl.* iii. 41 Certain submorphemic elements can also be recognized, e.g. the sound symbolism of *ush* in *gush*, *flush*, *blush*, *slush* and *mush*. **1901** *Amer. Jrnl. Physiol.* IV. 477 If the stimulation is *sub-optimal, the animal will seek the source of light. **1980** *Sci. Amer.* Sept. 134/1 On the whole, however, India remains a case of stunted, suboptimal growth, burdened as it is with the world's largest single national mass of poverty and unemployment. **1901** *Amer. Jrnl. Physiol.* IV. 478 The supra-optimally stimulated organism moves from the source, the *sub-optimally stimulated one moves towards the source, of light. **1958** *Times Rev. Industry* Sept. (London & Cambridge Economic Bull.) p. iii/1 A larger labour force..had to be..deployed sub-optimally. **1937** *Ann. Reg. 1936* 59 Attention was given to the social importance of nutrition due to the realisation that *sub-optimum nutrition is common and widespread. **1950** Suboptimum [see LINOLENATE]. **1935** *Language* XI. 102 A *sub-phonemic variation which the observer himself uses will generally escape his notice. **1969** *Archivum Linguisticum 1965* XVII. 109 By no means all subphonemic changes eventually become phonemic. **1981** *Amer. Speech 1977* LII. 171 Along the Atlantic seaboard, subphonemic vowel differences are common. **1955** C. F. HOCKETT *Man. Phonol.* 160 The worker who sets up fewer 'phonemes' must cover less '*subphonemically' but correspondingly more 'super-phonemically'. **1898** *Advance* (Chicago) 17 Feb. 206/2 The institution has never had a *sub-preparatory department, as several of the young colleges have. **1895** *Proc. 14th Conv. Instr. Deaf* 293 In *subprimary work there is surely an interesting field for the constructive talent. **1810** LAMB *Let. to T. Manning* 2 Jan., The ordinary titles of *sub-regal dignity. **1878** H. M. STANLEY *Dark Cont.* I. xv. 390 His sub-regal court. **1907** *Nature* LXXVI. 146/1 *Subthermal baths, given at temperatures below blood heat.

b. Similarly combined with sbs. (forming words used chiefly *attrib.*), as ***sub-cabinet*** (chiefly *U.S.*), ***-microgram***, ***-proletariat***, ***-threshold***, ***-zero***; **sub'millimetre** *a.*, less than a millimetre in size or length; pertaining to or employing electromagnetic waves of such a length; also **,submilli'metric** *a.*

1956 R. J. DONOVAN *Eisenhower* v. 66 Almost as soon as the Cabinet rises each week, Rabb meets with a group of *sub-Cabinet officers. **1974** P. GORE-BOOTH *With Great Truth & Respect* 389 The process of an important and difficult decision is remarkable... It passes through a hierarchy or a sort of sub-cabinet or both. **1981** *Economist* 24 Jan. 24/3 Lower appointments to sub-cabinet jobs are still being made and will be for some weeks. **1965** PHILLIPS & WILLIAMS *Inorg. Chem.* I. xvi. 576 Work on natural polonium has been limited to the *sub-microgram scale. **1976** *Nature* 10 June 454/1 Gibberellins are amongst the most potent of the naturally occurring plant growth regulators and exert maximal activity in most tissues when present in sub-microgram quantities. **1955** *Jrnl. Appl. Physics* XXVI. 1384/1 *Submillimeter radiation was produced when a pulsed, bunched high-energy electron beam was passed through a simple rectangular wave guide. **1973** *Physics Bull.* May 305/3 Submillimetre spectroscopy, or far infrared spectroscopy as it is more frequently termed, is a field in which there has been much activity during the last 15 years. **1976** *Sci. Amer.* June 127/1 All one had to do was to drop his view to the submillimeter level, where little creatures abound that are still new to science. **1975** *Nature* 6 Mar. 39/2 The mystery of the *submillimetric limb brightening [of the sun]. **1958** *Listener* 30 Jan. 186/1 Today the population of the delta belongs to the class which, I believe, sociologists call the rural *sub-proletariat. They are landless or almost landless peasants who seek casual employment in agriculture or anything that comes along. **1974** M. B. BROWN *Economics of Imperialism* iv. 87 Nor can we overlook..the role of migrant labour as a 'sub-proletariat' in Europe today. **1979** *Dædalus* Spring 105 The institutionalization of a subproletariat, and the creation of ethnic ghettos in the large urban areas are..examples of the changes taking place. **1937** BEST & TAYLOR *Physiol. Basis Med. Practice* lxiii. 1225 If a second stimulus also of *subthreshold strength..be sent into the nerve an impulse is set up. **1976** *Ann. Rev. Microbiol.* XXX. 234 Negative chemotaxis appears to be largely an all-or-none response to a threshold concentration, but weaker effects caused by prolonged exposure to subthreshold concentrations probably also occur. **1942** O. NASH *Face is Familiar* 137 And nobody is prompter In the face of hell, high water, and *sub-zero thermomter. **1980** R. MCCRUM *In Secret Place* xii. 113 He's having a sub-zero feud with Hayter.

c. Compounded with a further prefix, as **sub-'micro-** *Chem.*, involving amounts less than those typical of microanalysis; also used as an independent word.

1945 *Jrnl. Biol. Chem.* CLXI. 589 In order to estimate the P content of these solutions, a *submicroprocedure..having a range of 0·2 to 3 γ of P was employed. **1964** N. G. CLARK *Mod. Org. Chem.* xxiv. 495 The isolation of minute quantities of material from biological sources has necessitated even greater refinements, so that sub-micro techniques (requiring 30–50 μg) have been developed during recent years. **1974** [see MICRO- 8 b].

15. *Zool.* In names of divisions of animals regarded as having only imperfectly developed the characteristics denoted by the word to which *sub-* is prefixed, as *Subgrallatores*, *Submytilacea*, *Subungulata*. English derivatives have been occas. formed; e.g. ***subostracean***, a mollusc of the family *Subostracea*; ***subplantigrade***, of or resembling the group *Subplantigrada*, not quite plantigrade.

1836 *Penny Cycl.* V. 313/2 [De Blainville] allows that these last ought to form a distinct genus of the family of *Sub-ostraceans. **1883** *Encycl. Brit.* XV. 434 The greater number of the Carnivora..may be called '*subplantigrade', often when at rest applying the whole of the sole to the ground.

16. In craniometry, forming adjs. designating a type of skull having an index next below that of the type denoted by the second element; e.g. ***subbrachycephalic***, ***-ous*** (hence ***-cephaly***), ***subdolichocephalic***, ***-ous*** (hence ***-cephalism***).

These terms are based on Broca's classification, who used the L. forms (masc. pl.) *subbrachycephali*, *-dolichocephali*.

1863–4 THURNAM in *Mem. Anthropol. Soc.* I. 461 With M. Broca, it is desirable to admit a *sub-dolichocephalic and a *sub-brachycephalic class [of skulls]. *Ibid.* 510 Only about half [the skulls] are brachycephalous or *sub-brachycephalous. **1878** BARTLEY tr. *Topinard's Anthrop.* II. xii. 499 Low stature, woolly hair, black skin, and *sub-brachycephaly. **1895** *Smithsonian Rep.* I. 515 His cephalic index falls down to *subdolichocephalism. **1896** KEANE *Ethnol.* xii. 321 The shape of the head..is..here and there mesaticephalous and even *sub-dolichocephalous. **1890** BILLINGS *Nat. Med. Dict.*, **Sub-mesaticephalic*, having a cephalic index of 75 or 76. **1890** H. ELLIS *Criminal* iii. 52 Out of thirty criminals eight presented brains and skulls of a..capacity only found in *submicrocephalic subjects. **1863–4** THURNAM in *Mem. Anthropol. Soc.* I. 473 All these crania are very dolichocephalous. The first..is a remarkable specimen of synostosis... The form is *sub-scaphocephalic.

17. In the names of certain sectaries, = after, consequent upon, the opposite of SUPRA- (q.v.); e.g. SUBLAPSARIAN, SUBMORTUARIAN.

18. In designations of periods immediately 'below' or posterior to a particular period, as in ***sub-neolithic*** (also *fig.*), ***-Roman*** adjs.; SUBAPOSTOLIC.

1910 *Encycl. Brit.* (ed. 11) XII. 59 The following stages in the glaciation of North America:..The Aftonian (1st interglacial). The *sub-Aftonian or Jerseyan (1st glacial). **1902** *Encycl. Brit.* XXXI. 57 [Bugelkanne] is found everywhere in the area, made of various local clays, and it long survived into the 'Geometric' or *sub-Mycenaean period. **1905** A. J. EVANS in *Ann. Brit. School at Athens* X. 22 This stratum, to which the name 'Early Minoan I.' may be conveniently applied, shows naturally a greater survival of Neolithic elements... In its general complexion indeed it may be described as '*Sub-Neolithic'. **1956** E. E. CUMMINGS *Let.* 11 Mar. (1969) 248 Good Freudians were quick to suggest that my superego suffers from sub-neolithic trends. **1962** H. R. LOYN *Anglo-Saxon England* i. 39 Wheel-made pottery of *sub-Roman character. **1977** *History* LXII. 175 We cannot, however, expect that these works will ever provide information about the sub-Roman centuries.

IV. Incomplete(ly), imperfect(ly), partial(ly).

* *with adverbial meaning.*

19. a. Prefixed to adjs. or pples. of a general character, as in L. *subabsurdus* somewhat absurd, *subobscūrus* SUBOBSCURE; e.g. ***subanalogous***, somewhat similar; also ***sub-historical***, ***-literate***, ***-mature***, ***-moral***, ***-solid*** adjs. (The precise force of *sub-* may vary contextually from 'only slightly' to 'not quite, all but'.) **sub-eco'nomic** *a.*, not justifiable on purely economic grounds; **subin'hibitory** *a.*, (of a dose of a drug, chemical, etc.) enough to hinder but not prevent microbial growth; **sub'luminous** *a.*, dim; *spec.* in *Astr.*, of less luminosity than the normal; **sub'sexual** *a. Genetics*, characterized by or being a form of parthenogenetic reproduction in which the first division of meiosis occurs, with crossing-over, but not the second (reduction) division; **sub'social** *a. Biol.*, applied to species of spiders or insects that live gregariously but without a fixed social organization; **sub'vocal** *a.*, designating an unarticulated level of speech comparable to thought; hence **sub'vocally** *adv.*

1870 LOWELL *Study Wind.* 291 A thimbleful of ..*subacidulous Hock. **1767** *Phil. Trans.* LVII. 417 Little seeds *subanalogous, or somewhat resembling those we find in the fructification of the Fucus's. **1884** A. LANG *Custom & Myth* 236 A *sub-barbaric society—say that of Zululand. **1668** H. MORE *Div. Dial.* I. xxxvii. I. 160 This *subderisorious mirth. **1822–34** *Good's Study Med.* (ed. 4) I. 330 The mixture *sub-diluted for bathing. **1948** *Rep. Native Laws Commission 1946–48* (Dept. Native Affairs, S. Afr.) 4/2 Government assistance..in respect of *sub-economic schemes has all along been linked with the condition that the municipality should bear a share of the loss. **1971** *Leader* (Durban) 7 May 1/5 The Verulam Town Board has announced its intention to erect..100 sub-economic houses. **1980** *Sci. Amer.* Jan. 50/2 He created a two-way grid of categories based on the degree of geological knowledge (known deposits, inferred deposits and probable deposits) and on current economics (economic, subeconomic and uneconomic). *a* **1734** NORTH *Life Ld. Kpr. North* (1742) 228 The Spaniards have peculiar Councils, call'd Juntos,..which prevents such *sub-emergent Councils as these [*sc.* English cabinet councils]. **1842** LOUDON *Suburban Hort.* 17 *Sub-evergreen herbaceous plants are: Œnothera biennis and several other species, Pentstemon, Chelone, Asters. **1854** BADHAM *Halieut.* 180 Others, *subgregarious in their taste, swim about in small detached parties. **1940** K. MANNHEIM *Ideology & Utopia* 128 Besides this *sub-historical biological element a spiritual, transcendental element is also to be found in this sphere. **1973** R. J. W. EVANS *Rudolf II* ii. 45 Such a view.. has survived in sub-historical writing and belles-lettres. **1903** GEIKIE *Text-bk. Geol.* (ed. 4) I. 18 The coronal atmosphere..consists mainly of *subincandescent hydrogen. **1956** M. HYNES *Med. Bacteriol.* (ed. 6) ix. 123 Serial culture of susceptible organisms in the presence of *sub-inhibitory concentrations of an antibiotic results in the emergence of bacteria that can flourish in the presence of enormous concentrations of the antibiotic. **1976** *Ann. Rev. Microbiol.* XXX. 64 Some strains of *M. osloensis* produce such a preponderance of coccal cells that their true nature can only be ascertained in films from media with subinhibitory concentrations of penicillin. **1958** J. BERRY in J. A. Fishman *Readings Sociol. of Lang.* (1968) 743 In *subliterate societies (in most of Tropical Africa for example) where book-production is at the best financially hazardous, the need for exotic type can have a deterrent effect on book production. **1973** R. A. CRAMPSEY *Puerto Rico* 13 In 1940 the bulk of the people were subliterate or illiterate. **1864** *Spectator* 31 Dec. 1508 The sky is still *subluminous. **1959** *Encounter* July 53/2 The photography is that chocolate-marshmallow kind of subluminous chiaroscuro. **1969** O. J. EGGEN in S. S. Kumar *Low-Luminosity Stars* I. i. 22 Photometric parallaxes have been derived for the 27 stars in Table III which are very probably subluminous. **1976** *Progress in Sci. Culture* (E. Majorana Centre) Spring 52 Extragalactic sources can be classified in order of luminosity as follows (1) subluminous galaxies, such as M 31, (2) normal galaxies, [etc.]. **1899** *Submature [see PENEPLANATION]. **1922** C. A. COTTON *Geomorphol. N.Z.* I. xxviii. 415 The coast has passed through the stage of youth and has become sub-mature. **1951** *Jrnl. Sedimentary Petrol.* XXI. 128 Definition of the four stages of textural maturity. .. I. Immature stage... II. Submature stage. Sediment contains very little or no clay, but the non-clay portion..is still itself poorly sorted... III. Mature stage... IV. Supermature stage. **1965** G. J. Williams *Econ. Geol. N.Z.* xiii. 192/1 A submature valley formed on this surface, later to be dammed by a basalt flow. **1892** Zangwill *Bow Myst.* 87 A curious, *sub-mocking smile. **1946** *Mind* LV. 115 A will-less saint would be a *sub-moral being, a fine creature perhaps, but not a responsible moral agent. **1807** *Spirit Publ. Jrnls.* XI. 84, I swam with *subnatant tadpoles, I frisked with volatile newts. **1866** Odling *Anim. Chem.* 154, I now add to the free iodine some *suboxidised substance. **1650** Milton *Tenure of Kings* 59 Not prelatical, or of this late faction *subprelatical. **1817** Kirby & Sp. *Entomol.* (1818) II. 277 A *subputrescent stalk of Angelica. **1618** Hales in *Gold. Rem.* II. (1673) 23 That δυσωπία, that *subrustick shamefastness of many men. **1865** *Pall Mall Gaz.* 11 Nov. 9 It might be imagined that the advertisement conveyed a *subsarcastic touch. **1876** *Nature* XIV. 503/2 The *Sub-Semitic languages of Africa. **1937** C. D. Darlington in *Nature* 30 Oct. 761/2 Other mechanisms occur in the dog roses and with certain kinds of parthenogenesis whereby, as in *Œnothera*, a large part of the genes are prevented from recombining. With such systems stability has been achieved at the expense of variability, and we have arrived at what we may call a *sub-sexual method of reproduction. **1947** —— & Mather *Elements of Genetics* xii. 266 As compared with sexual species variation is much reduced but it still occurs. The new apomictic species is thus often subsexual. **1877** Swinburne *Note on C. Bronte* 11 Its superhuman or *subsimious absurdity. **1881** Westcott & Hort *Grk. N.T.* II. 230 What may be called '*subsingular readings' which have only secondary support. **1928** W. M. Wheeler *Social Insects* i. 13 The insects included in categories (1) to (5) may be designated as 'infrasocial'; those of (6), which are more interesting for our purposes may be called 'quasisocial' or '*subsocial'. **1958** *Science* 2 May 1046/1 Social organization in the main groups of social bees ..did not arise..through subsocial family groups. **1976** *Sci. Amer.* Mar. 101/3 Michener's second evolutionary route he calls subsocial. On this route only one level of behavior precedes eusociality; it is characterized by solitary rather than communal nest building. The solitary female [spider] remains at the nest, however, and cares for her young. **1922** Joyce *Ulysses* 674 The decocted beverages, allowing for *subsolid residual sediment of a mechanical mixture, water plus sugar plus cream plus cocoa, having been consumed. **1786** *Phil. Trans.* LXXVI. 319 Both of them immersed in *subtepid water. *a* **1734** North *Exam.* III. vii. (1740) 549 This put abundance of People of *subvirile Tempers, into a Twitter. **1934** M. Ten Hoor in *Jrnl. Philos.* XXXI. 534 The responsibility for descriptive analysis and psychological definition..has been accepted..by..the behaviorists... This theory..in its extreme form..contends that thought is nothing but *subvocal speech. **1980** A. Kenny *Aquinas* iii. 78 Aquinas has a clear grasp of the relationship between the intellect and the imagination when thought takes place in mental images or in subvocal speech. **1961** E. J. Furlong *Imagination* vii. 77 The words 'the Chapel' are *subvocally present to me along with the visual object. **1620** Venner *Via Recta* viii. 164 A *Subvulgar Diet is as it were a meane betweene the Accurate, and Vulgar.

(*b*) Such compounds are occas. used subst.

1635 Person *Varieties* II. 63 Whether that thing engendred bee a Star, or any other celestiall vertue, whereunto this *subdeficient striveth to attaine. **1633** Earl Manch. *Al Mondo* (1636) 86 There be certaine *subsapients so worldly wise, as they thinke all other men insipients.

b. In derived advbs., as ***submaturely***.

1900 *Proc. Boston Soc. Nat. Hist.* XXIX. 309 In central France..the initial form was an uplifted and submaturely dissected peneplain, in which valleys with incised meanders have been..developed. **1913** *Bull. Geol. Soc. Amer.* XXIV. 201 The submaturely dissected scarp.

20. a. With adjs. derived from the names of persons, used to designate something in the manner of but inferior to their work, characteristic style, etc. (Chiefly in nonce-formations.)

1934 E. Sitwell *Aspects Mod. Poetry* i. 18 Mr. Housman was followed by a school of poets, rather loosely held together by their sub-Wordsworthian ideals. **1959** *Listener* 5 Feb. 258/2 A laboured sub-Wodehousian straining after slapstick instead of farce. **1962** *John o' London's* 10 May 459/2 The opening has a sub-Chaplinesque quality. **1967** J. Philip et al. *Best of Granta* I. 16 Following the editorial come five sub-Miltonic stanzas. **1977** P. Johnson *Enemies of Society* xi. 154 One prominent sub-Marxist 'scientist' who constantly uses the crisis-mechanism, to justify, among other things, the use of positive censorship, when possible, is Herbert Marcuse.

b. Hence, prefixed simply to the names of persons.

1963 *Times Lit. Suppl.* 5 Apr. 235/2 Here is the eternal sex-life of the American college girl told in the eternal sub-Salinger..style. **1968** J. Bingham *I love, I Kill* xi. 132 It was called *Deeper in the South*..kind of sub-Tennessee Williams. **1977** *Listener* 28 July 122/3 A pregnant older lady who paints sub-Ernst surrealities.

21. In technical use, chiefly *Nat. Hist.*

A small proportion only of the more commonly used compounds are illustrated here.

a. With adjs. of colour, as in L. *subalbidus* somewhat white, whitish, *sublīvidus* somewhat livid, *subniger* blackish, *subviridis* greenish, late or mod.L. *subcitrinus* SUBCITRINE, *subpallidus* (for *suppallidus*) palish, *subrūfus* (for *surrūfus*) reddish; e.g. ***subalbid***, ***-luteous***, ***-pale***, ***-red***, ***-virid***.

c **1530** *Judic. Urines* II. viii. 33 b, Vryne pale or *subpale. *Ibid.* x. 37 Rudy vryne is moyst like fyne golde, and *subrufe goldysshe. *Ibid.* xi. 39 *marg.*, Rede or *subrede vryne. *Ibid.* xii. 41 Vryne Rubicunde or *Subrubicunde. *Ibid.* xiii. 42 Afore yt vryn were Rubie or *subrubie. **1590** Barrough *Meth. Physick* II. viii. (1596) 84 If his spittle..be yealow and *subpale. **1656** Blount *Glossogr.*, **Sub-albid*, somewhat white. **1657** Tomlinson *Renou's Disp.* 300 Seseli hath lignous..*subrubeous..surcles. *Ibid.* 610 A *subrufe ponderous Powder. **1661** Lovell *Hist. Anim. & Min.* 212 Tethyia. If red is edible, the pale and *subluteous are bitterish. **1694** Salmon *Bate's Disp.* (1713) 217/2 Of a *subvirid or greenish blue Colour. *Ibid.* 339/1 A *Subrubid or Livor coloured soft Calx. **1742** *Phil. Trans.* XLII. 125 A large tough *subrubicund Polypus. **1777** T. Percival *Ess.* I. 192 The portion with cantharides..neither assumed a *sublivid, nor an ash colour. **1800** Shaw *Gen. Zool.* I. 490 *Didelphis Obesula*,..*Subferruginous Opossum. **1802** *Ibid.* III. 397 *Coluber Nasicornis*,..*Subolivaceo-flavescent Snake. **1803** *Ibid.* IV. 556 *Holocentrus Bengalensis*,..*Subfulvous Holocentrus. **1804** *Ibid.* V. 282 *Raja Pastinaca*, ..*Subolivaceous Ray. **1809** *Ibid.* VII. 272 *Strix Caspia*, ..*Subluteous Owl. **1815** Stephens in Shaw's *Gen. Zool.* IX. 84 Of a *subrufous chesnut. **1817** *Ibid.* X. 626 *Subtestaceous Warbler, spotted with brown. **1846** Dana *Zooph.* (1848) 664 Colour *subminiaceous. **1847** *Proc. Berw. Nat. Club* II. v. 242 Elytra..of a dark *sub-æneous green. *Ibid.* 248 The margin often *sub-piceous. **1852** Dana *Crust.* I. 395 The legs are *subochreous. **1887** W. Phillips *Brit. Discomycetes* 13 Margin..*subcinnamomeous. **1898** *Syd. Soc. Lex.*, **Sub-flavous ligament*, short ligaments of yellow elastic tissue connecting the lamina of the vertebræ. **1900** *Westm. Gaz.* 29 June 2/1 Her complexion *sub-olive.

b. With adjs. denoting surface texture, contour, or marking, substance, consistency, composition, taste, odour, as in L. *subăcer* somewhat acrid, *subacidus* SUBACID, *subdūrus* somewhat hard, *subsalsus* saltish, mod.L. *sublānātus* somewhat woolly; e.g. ***subacerb***, ***-acrid***, ***-coriaceous***, †***-dure***, ***-granular***, ***-ate***, ***-ated***, ***-ose***, ***-hornblendic***, ***-membranous***, ***-stony***, ***-translucent***, ***-villose***, ***-villous***.

1638 Rawley tr. *Bacon's Life & Death* (1650) 40 It must be ordered..that the Juyce of the Body, bee somewhat hard, and that it be fatty, or *subroscide. **1657** Tomlinson *Renou's Disp.* 259 Its sapour is very sweet, *subamare, austere and somewhat aromatical. *Ibid.* 382 [Dates] are.. soft, but carnous, *subdure within. **1676** Grew *Anat. Plants* (1682) 246 Spirit of Nitre is a *subalkalizate Spirit. *Ibid.* 247 Spirit of Salt is a *subalkaline Acid. **1694** Salmon *Bate's Disp.* (1713) 248/2 These Tinctures are hot and dry, *substringent. **1694** *Phil. Trans.* XVIII. 15 A *subsaline and somewhat austere Serum. **1699** Evelyn *Acetaria* (1729) 129 Its pinguid, *subdulcid, and agreeable Nature. **1702** *Phil. Trans.* XXIII. 1165 *Alga Marina* is *Subacrid and Sweet. *Ibid.* 1171 The Roots are sweet and *subacerbe. **1756** P. Browne *Jamaica* 75 Its fibres are always rigid and *subdiaphane. **1760** J. Lee *Introd. Bot.* III. iv. (1765) 169 *Sarmentose*; when they are Repent and *subnude. **1777** Pennant *Brit. Zool.* IV. 3 A *sub-cordated body. **1777** S. Robson *Brit. Flora* 117 Leaves ovato-oblong, *subpilose. *Ibid.* 131 Branches *subvillose. **1781** *Phil. Trans.* LXXX. 375 A spissid *sub-pellucid liquid. **1785** Martyn *Rousseau's Bot.* xxvi. (1794) 387 The stem is *subherbaceous. **1787** tr. *Linnæus' Fam. Plants* 494 Legume rhombed, turgid, *subvillous. *Ibid.* 547 Pappus sessile, *subplumy. *Ibid.* 584 Seeds..*submembranous, inverse-hearted. *Ibid.* 683 Berry *substriated. **1792** Withering *Bot. Arrangem.* (ed. 2) III. 226 *Tremella Nostoc*...*Sub-gelatinous. **1817** Kirby & Sp. *Entomol.* (1818) II. 418 Both..have the material which diffuses their light included in a hollow *subtransparent projection of the head. *Ibid.* (1843) II. 44 Their abdomen swollen into an immense *sub-diaphanous sphere filled by a kind of honey. **1822** J. Parkinson *Outl. Oryctol.* 192 The operculum is small, elliptical, and *subosseous. *Ibid.* 201 *Voluta digitalina*: decussated, *subgranular. **1824** R. K. Greville *Scot. Cryptog. Flora* II. pl. 110 The surface covered with a minute *sub-pulverulent substance. **1826** Kirby & Sp. *Entomol.* III. 338 An internal *submembranaceous tooth or process. **1828** Stark *Elem. Nat. Hist.* II. 420 Axis slender, horny, or *sub-stony in the centre. **1829** Loudon *Encycl. Plants* (1836) 15 Leaves ..*sub-coriaceous. *Ibid.* 591 Leaves *subcordate sessile serrate *subvillous. *Ibid.* 1023 *Substriate or rugose. **1833** Hooker in Smith's *Eng. Flora* V. I. 46 Leaves *subopaque. **1833–4** J. Phillips *Geol.* in *Encycl. Metrop.* (1845) VI. 562/2 An irregular..bed..of serpentine..exhibits..a *sublaminated structure. **1839** De la Beche *Rep. Geol. Cornwall*, etc. iii. 64 The latter with a *sub-schistose structure. **1839** G. Roberts *Dict. Geol.*, **Sub-lamellar*.., extremely thin, like a sheet of paper. **1842** Percival *Rep. Geol. Connect.* 32 A dark grey *sub-porphyritic, *sub-hornblendic rock. **1846** Dana *Zooph.* (1848) 451 Branchlets ..*subterete and proliferous. *Ibid.* 590 Base *subgranulous. **1847** *Proc. Berw. Nat. Club* II. v. 236 Body slightly pubescent or *subglabrous. **1847** W. E. Steele *Field Bot.* 201 Bracts small, *sub-foliaceous. **1849** Dana *Geol.* xvii. (1850) 632 Hypersthene..having a pearly or *submetallic lustre. **1868** —— *Syst. Mineral.* (ed. 5) v. 194 Plasma... Rather bright-green to leek-green, also sometimes nearly emerald-green, and *subtranslucent or feebly translucent. **1870** Hooker *Stud. Flora* 196 Fruit compressed, obovate, *subhispid. **1871** W. A. Leighton *Lichen-flora* 27 Apothecia lecanorine or *sub-biatorine. **1880** Günther *Fishes* 66 Slender *subossified rings. **1895** J. W. Powell *Physiogr. Processes* in *Nat. Geog. Monogr.* I. 1 The interior of the earth is in a *subfluid condition. **1955** Brown & Dey *India's Mineral Wealth* (ed. 3) 623 The bloodstones are *subtranslucent, dark green chalcedony speckled with red; the moss agates..perfectly translucent stones.

c. With adjs. expressing shape, conformation, or physical habit, as in mod.L. *subæquālis* SUBEQUAL, *subamplexicaulis* slightly amplexicaul, *subobtūsus* somewhat obtuse, *subrepandus* somewhat repand, *subsessilis* SUBSESSILE; e.g. ***sub-acuminate***, ***-arborescent***, ***-cordate***, ***-ated***, ***-hooked***, ***-lunate***, ***-repand***, ***-simple***; ˌ**subacroˈcentric** *a. Cytology* = *subtelocentric* adj. below; **subˈhedral** *a.*, applied to crystals having partially developed faces, or incompletely bounded planes; ˌ**submetaˈcentric** *a. Cytology*, applied to a chromosome with the centromere almost in the middle, so that the two chromosome arms differ slightly in length; also *ellipt.* as *sb.*; ˌ**subteloˈcentric** *a. Cytology*, applied to a chromosome with a centromere near one end, but not as near as in an acrocentric chromosome; also *ellipt.* as *sb.*

1752 J. Hill *Hist. Anim.* 131 The *sublong and transversely radiated Buccinum. **1756** P. Browne *Jamaica* 101 The *subarborescent Polypodium with a large lobed foliage. **1775** J. Jenkinson *Linnæus' Brit. Plants* 148 The silicula is *subcordate. *Ibid.* 162 Crowfoot Cranesbill with two flowers on each peduncle, *subpeltated. **1777** S. Robson *Brit. Flora* 71 Leaves reniform, *subpeltate. *Ibid.* 124 Leaves *sub-hastate. *Ibid.* 138 Clusters *subimbricate. *Ibid.* 145 Petals *sublanceolate. *Ibid.* 159 Leaves lineari-lanceolate, *sub-serrate. *Ibid.* 170 Peduncles uniflorous, *subcorymbose. *Ibid.* 188 Leaves ovate, obtuse, *subcrenate. *Ibid.* 262 Females *subpedunculate. *Ibid.* 290 Leafits ovate, *subciliate. *Ibid.* 296 Leaves..lanceolate, *sublaciniate. *Ibid.* 304 Stem almost simple, *subventricose. **1785** Martyn *Rousseau's Bot.* xxiii. (1794) 321 The stem-leaves oblong and *Subsinuous. *Ibid.* 446 Balm of Gilead Fir has the leaves *subemarginate. **1787** tr. *Linnæus' Fam. Plants* 180 Cor[olla]. Universal not uniform, *subradiate. *Ibid.* 188 Petals five, endnick-inflected, *sub-unequal. *Ibid.* 282 Germ wedge-form, angular, *subpedicel'd. *Ibid.* 534 Cor[olla]. Compound *subimbricated. *Ibid.* 761 Seeds.. flat inwards, *subconvex outwardly. *Ibid.* 763 Villous-murex'd without, with *subrevolute margins. *c* **1789** *Encycl. Brit.* (1797) III. 447/2 The florets *subpedicellated, or standing on very short flower-stalks. **1800** Shaw *Gen. Zool.* I. 264 *Sub-auriculated dusky Seal. **1802** *Ibid.* III. 588 The tail abruptly *subacuminate. **1809** *Ibid.* VII. 313 *Sub-cristated ferruginous Shrike. **1815** Stephens in Shaw's *Gen. Zool.* IX. 92 Tail wedge-shaped with *sublunate ferruginous fasciæ. **1817** *Ibid.* X. 381 *Subcrested Flycatcher. **1819** *Ibid.* XI. 519 Beak..the apex *subtruncate. **1819** G. Samouelle *Entomol. Compend.* 93 Hands externally *subserrated. **1821** S. Gray *Brit. Plants* II. 3 Leaflets *sub-auricled at the base. **1822** W. P. C. Barton *Flora N. Amer.* II. 71 Corolla *sub-campanulate, five-lobed. **1822** J. Parkinson *Outl. Oryctol.* 38 *Subpediculated masses. *Ibid.* 56 With thick lamellæ windingly plaited, *subcristated. *Ibid.* 74 Granulated and *subdentated striæ. *Ibid.* 131 The mouth *subreniform, with five prominent lips. *Ibid.* 223 *Pecten discors*: *subinequivalved. *Ibid.* 224 *Plicatula tubifera*: *subirregular. **1823** R. K. Greville *Scot. Cryptog. Flora* I. pl. 46 Plants somewhat crustaceous or *substipitate. **1826** Kirby & Sp. *Entomol.* III. 170 The Libellulina MacLeay (whose metamorphosis that gentleman has denominated *subsemicomplete, a term warranted by their losing in their perfect state the mask before described). *Ibid.* 319 In *Scolia* ..&c.,..the antennæ are..in the females convolute or *subspiral. *Ibid.* 427 [The labial palpi] being most frequently filiform or *subclavate. **1826** Crouch *Lamarck's Conchol.* 15 Shell transverse, *subequivalve, inequilateral. *Ibid.* 18 Shell *subtransverse. *Ibid.* 19 Shell..*Sublobate at the base. *Ibid.* 20 Shell inequivalve,..the superior margin rounded, *subplicate. **1829** Loudon *Encycl. Plants* (1836) 7 Leaves ovate acute *sub-repand. *Ibid.* 17 Peduncle axillary *subracemose. *Ibid.* 701 Leaves *subamplexicaul. **1833** Hooker in Smith's *Eng. Flora* V. I. 107 The mouth truncated *subciliated. *Ibid.* 108 Stem..*subsimple. **1839–47** *Todd's Cycl. Anat.* III. 376/2 The coracoid..is a strong, *subcompressed, *subelongate bone. **1842** *Penny Cycl.* XXII. 53/1 Shell..painted with..transverse, *subfasciculated lines. **1846** Dana *Zooph.* (1848) 461 Branchlets *subdigitiform. *Ibid.* 527 Branches ..*subdilatate at apex. **1847** W. E. Steele *Field Bot.* 11 Heads *subumbellate. **1847** *Proc. Berw. Nat. Club* II. v. 240 Posterior tarsi with the first and last joints *subelongated. **1849** *Ibid.* vii. 371 With two curved *subpedicled claws. **1849** Dana *Geol.* App. I. (1850) 702 *Sub-alate above, sub-orbiculate behind. **1852** —— *Crust.* II. 703 The exterior plates of the abdomen have a triangular *subobtuse termination. **1853** Royle *Mat. Med.* 641 Leaves solitary, flat, *subpectinate. **1854** Hooker *Himal. Jrnls.* I. iii. 86 The larger, white flowered, *sub-arboraceous species prevailed. **1856** W. Clark tr. *Van der Hoeven's Zool.* I. 728 Shell.. furnished with small auriculæ, *subgaping at the side. **1858** *Ibid.* II. 390 Upper mandible with tip *subhooked. **1863** J. G. Baker *N. Yorksh.* 195 A native of Italy and Provence, which has been noted in a *subspontaneous state about the Yore. **1870** Hooker *Stud. Flora* 224 Campanulaceæ.. filaments free or *subconnate. *Ibid.* 301 Corolla ½ in., *subcampanulate. *Ibid.* 348 Shrubby, 1–5 ft., rarely *subarboreous (10–20 ft.). **1887** W. Phillips *Brit. Discomycetes* 145 Mouth *subconnivent. **1898** *Syd. Soc. Lex.*, **Subvermiform*, shaped somewhat like a worm. **1906** W. Cross et al. in *Jrnl. Geol.* XIV. 698 **Subhedral*, partly bounded by crystal faces, hypantomorphic, hypidiomorphic. **1961** M. J. D. White *Chromosomes* (ed. 5) ii. 23 Intermediate types exist..so that we may describe particular chromosomes '*subacrocentric' or 'metacentric'. **1963** *Austral. Jrnl. Zool.* XI. 8 Four pairs of *subacrocentrics, whose short arms are in most cases large enough to be distinctly visible in the preparations. **1963** *Jrnl. Nat. Cancer Inst.* XXXI. 642 The diploid complement of 22 pairs of chromosomes consists of 5 median metacentrics, 3 *subtelocentrics, [etc.]. **1964** *Ibid.* XXXII. 858 This system was arrived at by the arrangement of metacentric chromosomes in descending size order followed by *submetacentric and *subtelocentric chromosomes arranged in a similar manner. **1964** *Hereditas* LII. 211 Chromosomes..with arm ratios of 3·0 or higher are classed as ST ('*subtelocentric'). **1973** *Nature* 5 Oct. 262/1 The diploid karyotype of *U. limi* consisted of twenty-two chromosomes, eighteen metacentrics and four *submetacentrics. **1975** G. Anderson *Coring* ii. 35 (*caption*) Porous network of medium-grained euhedral to *subhedral dolomite rhombs. **1976** *Jrnl. Cellular Physiol.* LXXXVII. 104 The four groups (I, metacentric; II, *submetacentric; III, *subacrocentric; and IV, acrocentric) were defined for this purpose by the ratio, short/long arm length. **1980** *Canad. Jrnl. Genetics & Cytol.* XXII. 421 There are three SAT-chromosomes (arm ratio (r) = 1·74–1·92), four metacentric chromosomes (r = 1·07–1·14), seven *submetacentric chromosomes (r = 1·22–1·68) and seven subtelocentric chromosomes (r = 1·75–2·42).

d. With adjs. denoting position, as in SUBCENTRAL, SUBLATERAL; e.g. ***sub-ascending***, ***-erect***, ***-internal***, ***-opposite***, ***-terminal***.

1787 tr. *Linnæus' Fam. Plants* 501 Cor[olla] papilionaceous... Keel lanced, *subascending. *Ibid.* 761 Petals four..*subopposite to the calyx-divisions. **1822** J. Parkinson *Outl. Oryctol.* 208 Cancellated by transverse keels and *suboblique vertical striæ. **1826** Crouch *Lamarck's Conchol.* 18 Ligament marginal, *subinternal. **1826** Kirby & Sp. *Entomol.* III. 376 The *Subinterno-medial Nervure. *Ibid.*, The *Subexterno-medial Nervure. A nervure that..intervenes between the externo-medial and interno-medial. *Ibid.* 383 Postfurca... A process of the Endosternum, terminating in three *sub-horizontal acute branches, resembling..the letter **Y**. **1828** Stark *Elem. Nat. Hist.* II. 149 Peduncles of the eyes short and thick, and the eyes *sub-terminal. **1829** Loudon *Encycl. Plants* (1836) 269 Leaves about 12 *sub-erect. **1832** Lindley *Introd. Bot.* 94 If the angle formed by the divergence is between 10° and 20°, the vein may be said to be nearly parallel (*subparallela*). Index, *Subparallel. **1833** Hooker in Smith's *Eng. Flora* V. I. 24 Leaves..*subsecund rigid canaliculate. **1852** Dana *Crust.* II. 1184 Setæ..on the two *subultimate joints all shorter than the joints. **1856** Woodward *Mollusca* 207 Peristome thin,..nucleus *sub-external. **1870** Hooker *Stud. Flora* 474 Branches all *subradical or 0. **1880** Günther *Fishes* 473 Cleft of the mouth vertical or *sub-vertical. **1843** *Florist's Jrnl.* (1846) IV. 53 The plant has a rambling, *subscandent habit. **1901** *Jrnl. Sch. Geog.* Nov. 329/3 The channel walls are usually *sub-parallel and nearly straight.

e. With adjs. designating geometrical forms, as in mod.L. *subcylindricus* somewhat or approximately cylindrical, *subtriangulāris* SUBTRIANGULAR; e.g. ***subcircular, -conic(al, -cylindric(al, -pentagonal*** (= five-sided, but not forming a regular pentagon), ***-oblong, -rectangular, -spherical, -spheroidal.***

1752 J. Hill *Hist. Anim.* 91 The oblong Amphitrite..is of a *subcylindric figure. **1786** *Phil. Trans.* LXXVI. 166 A.. Helix of a *subconical form. **1787** tr. *Linnæus' Fam. Plants* 255 Anthers *suboblong. *Ibid.* 469 Berry subglobular, *subconic. **1792** Withering *Bot. Arrangem.* (ed. 2) III. 164 Thickly set with very small *sub-sphæroidal Tubercles. **1798** *Phil. Trans.* LXXXVIII. 440 He derives this variety, which he calls *subpyramidal, from a decrease of three rows of molecules, at the angles of the base of the two pyramids of the primitive rhomboid. **1804** Shaw *Gen. Zool.* V. 294 *Raja Giorna*,..*Subrhomboid brown Ray. *Ibid.* 425 *Subquadrangular-bodied Trunk-Fish. **1817** Stephens in Shaw's *Gen. Zool.* X. 501 Beak *subcylindrical, more or less thickened. **1819** Samouelle *Entomol. Compend.* 83 The fourth [abdomen joint] *subquadrate. *Ibid.*, Shell *subcircular. **1822** J. Parkinson *Outl. Oryctol.* 56 *A[lcyonium] trigonum.*—Carnous, cellular, *subtrigonal. *Ibid.* 80 The stars *subpentagonal. *Ibid.* 116 *Echinus rupestris.*—*Subelliptical. *Ibid.* 221 *Pinna subquadrivalvis* ..*subtetragonal. *Ibid.* 228 *Terebratula alata*: *subtrigonate, dilated. **1823** R. K. Greville *Scot. Cryptog. Bot.* I. pl. 31 Sporidia numerous, *subsphærical. *Ibid.* 52 Orbicular, *subhemispherical. **1826** Crouch *Lamarck's Conchol.* 26 Shell oblong, *subparallelipipedal. *Ibid.* 32 Spire very short, *sub-conoidal. **1838** *Penny Cycl.* XII. 269/1 Body..*Subprismatic. **1847** *Proc. Berw. Nat. Club* II. v. 250 Thorax..elongate, *sub-parallelo-grammic. **1852** Dana *Crust.* I. 193 Carapax broad *subrhombic. **1870** Hooker *Stud. Flora* 163 Umbels when in flower *subhemispheric. **1877** Huxley *Anat. Inv. Anim.* vi. 272 A *subquadrate labrum overhangs the mouth. **1880** Günther *Fishes* 38 The præoperculum, a *sub-semicircular bone. **1887** W. Phillips *Brit. Discomycetes* 301 A single layer of *subcubical cells. **1940** *Antiquity* XIV. 16 The hopelessly decayed traces of a large wooden object, apparently *subrectangular in plan. **1957** G. E. Hutchinson *Treat. Limnol.* I. ii. 171 *Subcircular, a less perfect approach to circular form. **1970** R. J. Small *Study of Landforms* iv. 121 King..has postulated that in many parts of Africa stream incision along joints has given rise to a *subrectangular drainage pattern. **1979** *Geogr. Mag.* July 668/3 *Subcircular pans on the Essex marshes.

f. With adjs. denoting a numerical arrangement or conformation, as in mod.L. *subbifidus, subtrifidus* imperfectly bifid, trifid, *subūniflōrus* having one or two flowers only or most commonly one; e.g. ***subbifid, -bipinnate, -trifid*** (**-3-*fid***), ***-triquetrous.***

1777 S. Robson *Brit. Flora* 238 Stem *subtriquetrous.. spike distich, involucrum monophyllous. *Ibid.* 284 Leaves *subbipinnate. *Ibid.* 287 Leaves *subtripinnate. **1816** *Edwards' Bot. Reg.* II. 130 b, Terminal lobe largest and *subtrilobate. **1821** W. P. C. Barton *Flora N. Amer.* I. 10 Calix *sub-bilabiate. *Ibid.* 55 Folioles ovate,..*sub-trilobed. **1822** J. Parkinson *Outl. Oryctol.* 126 The ambulacral lines *subbiporous. *Ibid.* 179 One short *subbifid cardinal tooth. *Ibid.* 215 The forepart beaked, *subbiangulated. **1829** Loudon *Encycl. Plants* (1836) 5 Nect[ary] wavy *sub-3-fid. *Ibid.* 25 [Leaves] rugose *sub 3-lobed. *Ibid.* 679 Leaves villous *sub-bipinnatifid at base. **1836** *Penny Cycl.* V. 312/2 Valves *sub-bilobated by the depression or emargination. **1852** Dana *Crust.* II. 769 The specimen..has all the three anterior pairs of legs *subdidactyle. **1857** T. Moore *Handbk. Brit. Ferns* (ed. 3) 48 Pinnæ..*sub-unilateral. **1870** Hooker *Stud. Flora* 114 Fragaria elatior..flowers *sub-1-sexual. *Ibid.* 208 Leaves broad, *sub-2-pinnatifid. *Ibid.* 364 Perianth irregular, *sub-2-labiate. *Ibid.* 379 Leaves alternate *subbifarious or secund. *Ibid.* 469 Capsules *sub-2-seriate on the segments. **1876** Harley *Royle's Mat. Med.* 376 Ovary *sub-trilocular.

g. *Med.*, as in SUBACUTE; e.g. ***subchronic***, not entirely chronic, more chronic than acute; ***sub-crepitant, -crepitating, -curative, -fertile, -resonant, -tympanitic; sub-febrile, -pyrexial***; **sub'clinical** *a.*, not giving rise to any observable symptoms; **sub'patent** *a.*, (of a parasite or parasitic infection) present but not detectable; of or pertaining to such an infection; **sub'tertian** *a. Med.*, applied to a severe form of malaria caused by the sporozoan *Plasmodium falciparum* and to the sporozoan itself; also *ellipt.* as *sb.*, subtertian malaria.

1834 J. Forbes *Laennec's Dis. Chest* (ed. 4) 77 There is only perceptible a very slight dull whistling... This variety of the phenomenon may be denominated *subsibilant respiration. **1849–52** *Todd's Cycl. Anat.* IV. 1402/1 Some slight *subinflammatory condition which varicose veins readily take on. **1853** Markham *Skoda's Auscult.* 284 The crepitating râle becomes *sub-crepitant, announcing the presence of œdema. *Ibid.* 122 No distinctive line can be drawn between crepitating, *sub-crepitating, and mucous râles. **1897** *Allbutt's Syst. Med.* II. 175 This *sub-pyæmic condition seems invariably to have supervened. *Ibid.* 427 In some cases a *subicteric tinge is observed. *Ibid.* 1137 A *subtympanitic or even a Skodaic note may be elicited. *Ibid.* III. 678 The whole tumour..is uniformly dull, unless on deep percussion, when a *subresonant note is elicited. *Ibid.* 894 A *sub-hepatic abscess due to disease of an appendix attached to an undescended cæcum. **1898** *Ibid.* V. 20 An habitually *subpyrexial temperature. *Ibid.* 527 A *sub-febrile temperature. **1899** *Ibid.* VII. 679 A form of subacute or *subchronic ophthalmoplegia. **1919** R. Ross *Suggestions for Care of Malaria Patients* 7 A severe type in which the paroxysms..are often found to recur every day and at irregular times..is caused by the malignant tertian parasite, sometimes called the '*subtertian' parasite (*Plasmodium falciparum*). **1926** *Q. Rev. Biol.* I. 399/2 In many infections the patent period is followed by a *Subpatent Period of indefinite length. **1930** M. F. Boyd *Introd. Malariol.* ii. 32 It would appear that resistance may be established earliest to *subtertian, and more slowly in tertian and quartan. **1946** *Nature* 17 Aug. 243/2 With the addition of *subcurative doses of 'Mapharsen', the amount of penicillin required to cure rabbit syphilis is reduced to a fraction of that required when penicillin is used alone. *Ibid.* 5 Oct. 487/2 L.V. is responsible for a certain number of cases of epididymal inflammations, many of them of a *subclinical type. **1947** *Ann. Rev. Microbiol.* I. 49 *Subpatent infections persisted in some individual ducks for as long as eight months after they had been inoculated with sporozoites. **1954** Martin & Hynes *Clin. Endocrinol.* (ed. 2) viii. 187 It is difficult to assess the efficiency of therapy in a *subfertile male. **1954** *Brit. Med. Jrnl.* 6 Feb. 293/2 It has been found that in indigenous East Africans the sickle-cell trait affords a considerable degree of protection against *subtertian malaria. **1971** *Observer* (Colour Suppl.) 31 Oct. 10/1 Like many men her husband seemed to be *subfertile but was by no means infertile. **1974** J. R. Baker in *Trypanosomiasis & Leishmaniasis* (Ciba Foundation Symposium No. 20) 32 Parasites may often be *subpatent, that is, too scanty to be detected by microscopic examination. **1978** *Jrnl. R. Soc. Med.* LXXI. 507 The spectrum of illness is wide, from severe and prostrating to mild and, probably, *subclinical. **1979** *Tropenmedizin u. Parasitologie* XXX. 239/1 Infected cows treated with *subcurative doses of trypanocidal drugs. **1979** E. Nnochiri *Textbk. Imported Diseases* iv. 59 *P[lasmodium] falciparum* infections, in contrast, are insidious in onset with irregular fever which subsequently becomes *subtertian (i.e. between 36 and 48 hours) in periodicity.

h. Forming advs. corresponding to adjs. of any of the above classes, as in ***subclinically, -terminally***; SUBACUTELY.

1833 Hooker in Smith's *Eng. Flora* V. I. 79 Leaves ..*subtrifariously imbricated. **1846** Dana *Zooph.* (1848) 683 Branchlets often *subreticulately coalescing. **1852** —— *Crust.* I. 167 Hand externally *sub-seriately small tuberculate. **1863** J. G. Baker *N. Yorksh.* 194 A species which..grows *sub-spontaneously in one or two places. **1870** Hooker *Stud. Flora* 115 Potentilla fruticosa..leaves *subdigitately-pinnate. *Ibid.* 222 Stem rigid leafy *subcorymbosely branched. **1871** W. A. Leighton *Lichen-flora* 12 *Subtransversely arranged in little heaps. **1888** *Q. Jrnl. Geol. Soc.* XLIV. 150 The fallen masses weathering *subspherically. **1954** *Amer. Jrnl. Public Health* XLIV. 575/2 It was ascertained that previous infection of a child with Type 2 or Type 3 virus failed to prevent his becoming infected *subclinically with Type 1 virus. **1963** R. P. Dales *Annelids* ix. 182 The rectum opening *subterminally at a dorsal anus.

22. With vbs., as in L. *subaccūsāre* to accuse somewhat, *subirascī* to be somewhat angry; e.g. ***sub-blush, -cachinnate, -deliquesce, -effloresce, -irasce, -understand***; † ***subinnuate*** to hint gently; † ***sub-murmurate***, to murmur gently or quietly.

1767 Sterne *Tr. Shandy* IX. xvii, Raising up her eyes, *sub-blushing, as she did it. **1822** *Blackw. Mag.* XII. 67 This *subcachinnating method of dissipating his spleen. **1806** *G. Adams' Nat. & Exp. Philos.* (Philad.) I. App. 549 Sulphat of Ammonia *Subdeliquesces. *Ibid.* 550 Borax *Subeffloresces. *c* **1645** Howell *Lett.* (1650) III. ix. 19 The most speculative..men *subinnuating that not only the sphear of the Moon is peepled. **1783** Parr *Let. to Rev. C. Burney* 8 Nov., You see I *subirasce. **1653** Urquhart *Rabelais* II. vi. 31 *Submurmurating my horarie precules. **1716** M. Davies *Athen. Brit.* III. 77 Their Master Blondel survening, and *subunderstanding it.

*** with adjectival meaning.*

23. With sbs. denoting action or condition, in the sense 'partial, incomplete, slight'; as in late L. *subdēfectio* slight failure; e.g. ***sub-animation, -saturation***; *Med.* often = 'less than the normal, mild, gentle'; e.g. ***sub-delirium, -fertility, -purgation***; also occas. with sbs. denoting material objects, e.g. ***sub-country, sub-relief***; **sub-song**, the part of a bird's song that is softer and less well defined than its characteristic series of notes and is believed to have no territorial significance.

1906 *Daily News* 23 Feb. 7 His speech had something of the *sub-animation which marks his later style. **1908** *Westm. Gaz.* 13 May 12/1 The London *sub-country. **1898** *Syd. Soc. Lex.*, **Subcrepitation*, the noise of subcrepitant râles. **1635** Person *Varieties* II. 63 Albeit the Heaven, Fire, and Ayre move in a circular motion, yet they move not all alike,..the Ayre as neerest to the Earth, is slower than the other two. By this *subdeficiency then, the Ayre..seemes but to goe about from Occident to Orient of its own proper motion. **1834** J. Forbes *Laennec's Dis. Chest* 235 With *sub-delirium and other signs of cerebral congestion. **1948** Martin & Hynes *Clin. Endocrinol.* viii. 157 Several examinations are advised before diagnosing *subfertility and they should be performed as soon as possible after ejaculation. **1962** H. Lourie *Question of Abortion* xxiii. 201 The sub-fertility clinics, the clinics dealing with sterile marriages. **1971** *Daily Colonist* (Victoria, B.C.) 21 Aug. 22/2 Male subfertility is the main factor in 45 per cent of childless marriages. **1818** *Art Pres. Feet* x, If such men cannot be dignified with a full diploma..it would be well if some species of *sub-graduation could be adopted. **1634** Bp. Hall *Contempl.*, *N.T.* IV. *Martha & Mary*, The just blame of this bold *sub-incusation; Lord, dost thou not care? **1855** Dunglison *Med. Lex.*, **Subinflammation*, a mild degree of inflammation, so slight as hardly to deserve the name inflammation... Lymphatic engorgements, scrofula, herpes, and cancer he [Broussais] considered subinflammations. **1664** H. More *Myst. Iniq.* 213 A modest *subinsinuation of the most perfect and full persecution. **1825** Lamb *Elia* II. *Stage Illusion*, The exquisite art of the actor in a perpetual sub-insinuation to us, the spectators,.. that he was not half such a coward as we took him for. **1872** T. G. Thomas *Dis. Women* (ed. 3) 47 The enfeebled woman is more liable to *subinvolution [of the uterus], passive congestion, and displacements, after delivery, than the strong. **1753** *Chambers' Cycl.* Suppl., **Subpurgation*, *subpurgatio*, a word used by some writers to express a gentle purgation. **1894** *Archæologia* LV. 28 *Sub-relief is the name I propose to give to that kind of sculpture which is by some called Egyptian relief. **1806** *G. Adams' Nat. & Exp. Philos.* (Philad.) I. App. 531 With the termination *ous*, when there is a *sub-saturation. **1897** *Allbutt's Syst. Med.* III. 177 The solvent relation of the bodily fluids to the material of gouty deposits is simply a question of saturation or subsaturation. **1898** *Syd. Soc. Lex.*, **Subsensation*, a moderate or lesser sensation. **1925** E. M. Nicholson in *Field* Dec. 31/3 Even the chaffinch..has a very low rambling, warbling *sub-song with no fire or decision about it. **1948** *Brit. Birds* XLI. 51 The sub-song was occasionally replaced by the typical loud burst of song characteristic of this species [*sc.* the redstart]. **1979** *New Scientist* 17 May 537/1 Subsong is a rather soft and rambling type of singing..in which the bird seems to try out various sounds for itself. **1855** *Fraser's Mag.* LI. 264 By acts of daily self-denial and much *sub-sustentation of body. **1817** Kirby & Sp. *Entomol.* (1818) II. 424 The ..*sub-transparency of the adjoining crust.

24. *Chem.* In names of compounds *sub-* indicates that the ingredient of the compound denoted by the term to which it is prefixed is in a relatively small proportion, or is less than in the normal compounds of that name; e.g. ***subacetate***, an acetate in which there are fewer equivalents of the acid radical than in the normal acetate, a basic acetate.

[**1839** Ure *Dict. Arts* 1085 The neutral state of salts is commonly indicated by their solutions not changing the colours of litmus, violets, or red cabbage; the sub-state of salts, by their turning the violet and cabbage green; and super-state of salts, by their changing the purple of litmus, violets, and cabbage, red.]

1797 *Phil. Trans.* LXXXVIII. 23 *Subcarbonate of potash being dropped into the solution. *Ibid.* 24 The fourth portion being boiled with 4 grains of *sub-phosphate of lime. **1801** *Ibid.* XCI. 197 *note*, A *subcarburet of potash. *Ibid.* 236 A real carbonate of *suboxide of copper. **1802** *Ibid.* XCII. 159 * *note*, It is..calomel, plus an insoluble *subnitrate of mercury. *Ibid.* 329 *Sub-borate of soda (borax). **1805** Saunders *Min. Waters* 374 A *sub-sulphat of iron. **1807** T. Thomson *Chem.* (ed. 3) II. 547 This [muriate of lead] being in the state of *submuriate. **1807** Aikin *Dict. Chem.* II. 23/2 A white *sub-nitrated oxyd. *Ibid.* 25/2 An acetite or *sub-acetite. **1819** Brande *Man. Chem.* 427 An insoluble *subacetate of copper. **1819** J. G. Children *Chem. Anal.* 311 A solution of a *suburate. **1826** Henry *Elem. Chem.* I. 646 This liquid Dr. Davy calls *sub-silicated, fluoric acid. *Ibid.* II. 289 The *sub-tannate contains $1\frac{1}{2}$ time as much base as the neutral tannate. **1833** *Phil. Trans.* CXXIII. 263 *Subsesquiphosphate of soda. **1838** T. Thomson *Chem. Org. Bodies* 152 *Subcrenate of lead is obtained by mixing subacetate of lead with crenic acid. **1854** *Jrnl. Chem. Soc.* VII. 26 *Subplatino-tersulphocyanide of mercury. **1857** Miller *Elem. Chem.*, *Org.* x. §1. 585 **Subcyanide of copper*, Cu_2 Cy. **1868** *Subsulphide [see PLUMBOUS *a.* 2]. **1859** Mayne *Expos. Lex.* 1221/1 **Subsulphurous acid*, i.e., containing less than sulphurous but more than hyposulphurous acid. **1871** *Jrnl. Chem. Soc.* XXIV. 999 *Subfluoride of silicon. **1892** *Photogr. Ann.* II. 229 A latent image of *sub-bromide of silver. **1899** *Allbutt's Syst. Med.* VIII. 516 Ammoniated mercury..is chiefly employed; but *subchloride (calomel) has a very similar action. **1976** *Nature* 15 Jan. 109/3 Vanadium *subsulphide β-V_3S is known to have a tetragonal unit cell.

V. 25. Secretly, covertly, as in L. *subaudīre* to SUBAUD, *subintrōdūcere* to SUBINTRODUCE, *subornāre* to SUBORN; e.g. SUBAID.

VI. 26. a. From below, up (hence) away, as in L. *subdūcere* to draw up or away, SUBDUCE, SUBDUCT, *subsistĕre* to stand up, SUBSIST, *subvertĕre* to turn up, overturn, SUBVERT.

This is the etymol. sense of the prefix in SUCCOUR, SUFFER, SUGGEST, SUSCEPTION, SUSPICION, SUSPIRE, SUSTAIN.

b. Hence *sub-* implies taking up so as to include, as in SUBSUME; so in the nonce-wd. ***subinclude*** vb., whence ***subinclusively*** adv.

1818 G. S. Faber *Horæ Mosaicæ* II. 137 The Law, which may well be viewed as subincluding its predecessor the Patriarchal dispensation. **1840** —— *Prim. Doctr. Regen.* 107 The females, as help-meets, were to be viewed as subincluded with the males. **1851** —— *Many Mansions* 14 Thus, again, subinclusively, the Official Dress of the High-Priest respected, in its arrangement, the System of the World.

VII. 27. In place of another, as in L. *subdĕre* to put in place of another (see SUBDITITIOUS), *substituĕre* to SUBSTITUTE; e.g. †***sub-elect*** to choose to fill another's place.

1600 HOLLAND *Livy* XXXIX. xxxix. 1049 The..assembly for subelecting of a Pretour in the place of the deceased.

VIII. 28. In addition, by way of or as an addition, on the analogy of L. *subjungĕre* to SUBJOIN, *subnectĕre* to SUBNECT; e.g. ***subinsert*** vb.

1621 BRATHWAIT *Nat. Embassie* 144 Therefore haue I subinserted this Satyre [viz. a 13th at the end of a set of 12].

¶**29.** Detached from the sb. to which it belongs it is used quasi-adj. in co-ordination with adjs. or attrib. sbs. qualifying the same sb.

1840 J. BUEL *Farmer's Comp.* 45 Trench ploughing mixes the sub with the surface soil. **1891** *Pall Mall Gaz.* 4 Dec. 6/3 The central, sub, and executive committees have been appointed.

¶**30.** Repeated (in senses of branch II) to denote further subordination or subdivision.

1651 C. CARTWRIGHT *Cert. Relig.* I. 41 The many Religions which are lately sprung up, and the sub, sub, subdivisions under them. **1811–31** BENTHAM *Logic* App. Wks. 1843 VIII. 289 Divisions, sub-divisions, and sub-subdivisions. **1868** SPENCER *Princ. Psychol.* (1870) I. 266 A particular feeling of redness associates itself irresistibly.. with the sub-class of visual feelings, with the sub-sub-class of reds. **1902** *Daily Chron.* 29 Apr. 3/5 Under sub-contracts or sub-sub-contracts. **1905** *Macm. Mag.* Dec. 126 This was divided, re-divided, sub-divided, and sub-sub-divided in every conceivable sort of way.

‖**suba** (ˈʃuba). [Hungarian.] A type of long sheepskin cloak worn by Hungarian shepherds.

1925 G. A. BIRMINGHAM *Wayfarer in Hungary* xiv. 130 The *suba* is a long cloak of sheepskin reaching to the ankles. It has no sleeves... Only when the weather is bad is the *suba* fastened in front. **1939** *Times Lit. Suppl.* 4 Nov. 636/4 The Hungarian shepherd's 'suba', a magnificently voluminous sheepskin cloak. **1971** *Nat. Geogr. Mag.* Apr. 481 (*caption*) Shepherds wear huge suba to escape autumn's chill. **1979** J. SNOWDEN *Folk Dress of Europe* 25 In the last century, the *suba*, a sheepskin cloak, was developed from primitve peasant wear to a garment of considerable elaboration and costliness... Circular, or nearly so,..the *suba* was cut with radial sections joined to a shoulder yoke. The long seams.. were decorated..on the skin side.

subacid (sʌbˈæsɪd), *a.* and *sb.* [ad. L. *subacidus*: see SUB- 21 b and ACID. Cf. It., Sp. *subacido*.]

A. *adj.* **1. a.** Somewhat or moderately acid.

1669 W. SIMPSON *Hydrol. Chym.* 328 It weeps forth a sub-acid liquor in great abundance. **1676** GREW *Anat. Plants* Lect. ii. (1682) 244 Mercury, with Oyl of Vitriol, will not stir, nor with Oyl of Sulphur. But with Spirit of Nitre presently boyls up. Hence Mercury is a subacid Metal. **1725** *Bradley's Fam. Dict.* s.v. *Sallet*, The sub-acid Orange, sharpens the Appetite. **1732** ARBUTHNOT *Rules of Diet* in *Aliments*, etc. (1736) 254 All Fruits which contain a sub-acid essential salt. **1836** LANDOR *Per. & Asp.* Wks. 1846 II. 385 He enjoys a little wine after dinner, preferring the lighter and subacid. **1891** SCRIVENER *Fields & Cities* 150 The food of the human being cannot be 'suitable' unless varied by sub-acid substances of some kind.

b. *Chem.* Containing less than the normal proportion of acid.

1855 J. SCOFFERN in *Orr's Circ. Sci., Elem. Chem.* 38 With regard to neutral and superacid, or subacid, salts.

2. Of character, temper, speech, etc.: Somewhat acid or tart; verging on acidity or tartness.

1765 STERNE *Tr. Shandy* VIII. xxvi, From a little sub-acid kind of drollish impatience in his nature, he would never submit to it. **1811** SYD. SMITH *Wks.* (1867) I. 205 A stern subacid Dissenter. **1829** SCOTT *Antiq.* Advert. ¶7 An excellent temper, with a slight degree of subacid humour. **1876** W. CLARK RUSSELL *Is he the Man?* II. 203 A hard, subacid expression..modified the character of her beauty. **1888** MRS. H. WARD *Robt. Elsmere* 428 Rose..was always ready to make him the target of a sub-acid raillery.

B. *sb.* **1.** Subacid quality or flavour, subacidity.

1785 A. SEWARD *Let.* 7 June (1811) I. 75 That tetchy unprovoked spleen..clouding and staining the lustre of fine talents, and many excellent qualities... Let us all take warning, and correct our acids and sub-acids of every sort. **1838** TICKNOR *Life, Lett. & Jrnls.* II. viii. 145 Rogers.. talked in his quiet way.., showing sometimes a little sub-acid. **1840** HOOD *Up Rhine* 198 You will perceive a little sub-acid in Markham's statement. **1884** *Harper's Mag.* July 241/1 The subacid of the strawberry.

2. A subacid substance.

1828–32 WEBSTER, *Subacid*, a substance moderately acid. **1891** SCRIVENER *Fields & Cities* 150 Sub-acids in their most convenient form cannot be put into a pill box.

Hence **subaˈcidity**, the quality or condition of being subacid; also, something slightly acid.

1833 CARLYLE *Misc. Ess., Diderot* (1888) V. 38 There is a certain sardonic subacidity in Père Hoop. **1886** *Law Jrnl.* 16 Jan. 37/2 The subacidity which gives special flavour to his style.

†**subact**, *pa. pple.* and *ppl. a. Obs.* [ad. L. *subact-us*, pa. pple. of *subigĕre*, f. *sub-* SUB- 2, 26 + *agĕre* to bring.] Subdued, reduced; brought under control or discipline; brought under cultivation.

1432–50 tr. *Higden* (Rolls) I. 287 At the laste Fraunce was subacte to Iulius Cesar, and occupyede by Romanes. *Ibid.* II. 103 The Danes other put to fliȝhte other subacte. *c* **1440** *Pallad. on Husb.* IV. 499 In Nouember & Marche her braunchis sette In donged lond, subact. *a* **1661** HOLYDAY *Juvenal* (1673) 11 The masculine and subact judgement of Juvenal. **1694** MOTTEUX *Rabelais* V. xxii. 103 A subact and sedate Intellection, associated with diligent and congruous Study. **1729** W. REEVE *Serm.* 353 The yoke of Christ is a reasonable service to a man of subact judgment.

†**suˈbact**, *v. Obs.* [f. L. *subact-*, pa. ppl. stem of *subigĕre* (see prec.).]

1. *trans.* To work up, as in cultivating the ground, kneading, the process of digestion, or the like.

1614 JACKSON *Creed* III. III. vii. §1 That faith could not take roote in them, vnlesse first wrought and subacted by extraordinary signes and wonders. **1615** CROOKE *Body of Man* 411 He thinketh, that the blood is carried..into the right ventricle of the Heart.., and is there boyled attenuated and subacted. **1626** BACON *Sylva* §27 Tangible Bodies haue no pleasure in the Consort of Aire, but endeauour to subact it into a more Dense Body. **1658** tr. *Porta's Nat. Magic* IV. xii. 137 He subacts the Barn-flores with Lees of Oyl, that Mice may not eat his Corn. **1697** EVELYN *Numismata* To Rdr., Some Corners, and little Wasts, not altogether subacted. **1822** GOOD *Study Med.* I. 10 Being softened or otherwise partially affected, instead of being entirely subacted, and reduced to chyme or chyle.

2. To bring into subjection; to subject, subdue.

1645 BP. HALL *Rem. Discontentm.* §19 The meek spirit is ..so throughly subacted, that he takes his load from God.. upon his knees. *a* **1680** T. GOODWIN *Life* Wks. 1703 V. I. p. xi, I lay bound as it were Hand and Foot, subacted under the Pressure of the Guilt of Wrath.

Hence †**suˈbacted** *ppl. a.*; †**suˈbacter**, one who works up substances.

1657 TOMLINSON *Renou's Disp.* 615 Anoint the hands of the subacter..with Oyl. **1679** EVELYN *Sylva* (ed. 3) To Rdr. a, Persons of right Noble and subacted Principles. *a* **1706** —— *Hist. Relig.* (1850) II. 375 A meek and subacted Christian. **1822** GOOD *Study Med.* IV. 272 The absorbents which drink up the subacted food from the alvine canal.

†**suˈbaction.** *Obs.* [ad. L. *subactiōnem*, n. of action f. *subact-*, *subigĕre* (see SUBACT *pa. pple.*).]

1. The action of working up, reducing, or kneading.

1626 BACON *Sylva* §838 There are of Concoction two Periods; The one Assimilation, or Absolute Conuersion and Subaction; The other Maturation. **1657** TOMLINSON *Renou's Disp.* 122 Now Unguents are made one while by the fire,..another while onely by long subaction. **1676** *Phil. Trans.* II. 771 In order to the subaction and detrusion of the aliments. **1706** PHILLIPS (ed. Kersey), *Subaction*,..Among Apothecaries, it is us'd for the working or soft'ning of Plaisters. **1822** GOOD *Study Med.* I. 324 The smaller ruminating animals, whose food, from the complexity of the organ, lies for a long time quiescent in a state of subaction.

2. Subjection, subdual. *rare*$^{-0}$.

1656 BLOUNT *Glossogr.* [citing Bacon; cf. quot. 1626 above].

subacute (sʌbəˈkjuːt), *a.* [SUB- 21.] Somewhat or moderately acute.

a. Of an angle.

1752 J. HILL *Hist. Anim.* 220 The pupil is..protended on the anterior part into a subacute angle.

b. *Zool.* and *Bot.*

1822 J. PARKINSON *Outl. Oryctol.* 222 *Plagiostoma.. sulcata*: ovate, lower part subacute. **1829** LOUDON *Encycl. Plants* (1836) 441 Sepals and petals subacute. **1872** OLIVER *Elem. Bot.* 307 Involucre..of..subacute, equal bracts.

c. *Med.* Between acute and chronic. ***subacute sclerosing panencephalitis***, a frequently fatal degenerative disease of the central nervous system, caused by reactivation of a measles virus some years after the original infection.

1833 *Cycl. Pract. Med.* II. 731/2 The fever..symptoms.. are..rather of a sub-acute than highly inflammatory character. **1878** HABERSHON *Dis. Abdomen* (ed. 3) 8 Mucous patches and gummata, which may be mistaken for abscesses or subacute glossitis. **1950** J. G. GREENFIELD in *Brain* LXXIII. 150 The name *subacute sclerosing encephalitis* therefore appears fully justified. Dr. van Bogaert's term 'leuco-encephalitis' emphasizes the characteristic damage to the white matter, but leaves out of account the cortical changes which are also important. Perhaps the term 'Panencephalitis' already adopted by Pette (1942) for forms which attack both grey and white matter could be usefully employed here, i.e. 'Subacute sclerosing panencephalitis'. **1967** *Brit. Med. Jrnl.* 5 Aug. 352/2 Measles complement-fixing and haemagglutination-inhibiting antibodies have been found in the serum of 22 patients with subacute sclerosing panencephalitis in significantly higher titre than in controls.

d. *gen.*

1861 *Sat. Rev.* 27 July 90 When a civil servant's mind has reached the stage of subacute discontent. **1896** MRS. CAFFYN *Quaker Grandmother* 139 The sub-acute passion of Harry Tryng blazed out in a few broken sentences.

So **subaˈcutely** *adv.*, with or in a subacute form.

1852 DANA *Crust.* II. 1194 Cephalothorax subacutely rostrate. **1872** H. A. NICHOLSON *Palæont.* 326 Fins sub-acutely lobate.

subadoˈlescent, *sb.* and *a.* [SUB- 19.] **A.** *sb.* = PREADOLESCENT *sb.* **B.** *adj.* = PREADOLESCENT *a.* a.

1957 R. A. HEINLEIN *Door into Summer* ii. 32 Did you ever try to discuss with a subadolescent something the child does not want to talk about? **1977** W. M. SPACKMAN *Armful of Warm Girl* 33 An enlarged snapshot of two baby boys and two sub-adolescent girls.

subadult (sʌbˈædʌlt, sʌbəˈdʌlt), *a.* and *sb.* [SUB- 19.] **A.** *adj.* Not fully adult. **B.** *sb.* A subadult individual.

Applied chiefly to animals (cf. *preadult* s.v. PRE- B. 1).

1903 *Nature* 3 Dec. 112/1 A subadult Australian barn-owl in which large bunches of the nestling down are retained on the legs. **1934** WEBSTER, Subadult *n.* **1946** *Nature* 28 Dec. 927/1 The author distinguishes between juvenile, young, sub-adult and adult, in that order of ascending age [of mammals]. **1962** B. HARRISSON *Orang-Utan* iii. 108 Sub-adults, who have left their mothers, cuddle in pairs to get additional warmth. **1975** *Sci. Amer.* May 56/3 Lions are termed cubs until they are two years old and subadults between the ages of two and four. **1976** *Ibid.* Apr. 118/3 Subadult crocodiles often form a semi-circle where a channel enters a pan, facing the inrushing water and snapping up the fish that emerge from the river.

subˈaerial, *a.* [SUB- 1 a. Cf. F. *subaérien*.] Chiefly *Geol.* and *Phys. Geog.* Taking place, existing, operating, or formed in the open air or on the earth's surface, as opposed to *subaqueous*, *submarine*, *subterranean*.

1833 LYELL *Princ. Geol.* III. 177 We think that we shall not strain analogy too far if we suppose the same laws to govern the subaqueous and subaërial phenomena. **1841** TRIMMER *Pract. Geol.* 172 Many subaërial volcanos have ejected trachyte and basaltic lava. **1852** DANA *Crust.* I. 5 Insects are essentially sub-aerial species. **1872** W. S. SYMONDS *Rec. Rocks* vi. 155 Vast masses of strata have been removed by subaerial denudation. **1880** DAWKINS *Early Man in Brit.* vii. 208 The rarity of sub-aerial refuse-heaps compared with those in caves and under rocks.

Hence **subˈaerially** *adv.*; **subˈaerialist**, one who holds the view that a certain formation is subaerial; also *attrib.*

1870 *Contemp. Rev.* XV. 625 It must have accumulated, subaërially, upon the surface of a soil covered by a forest of cryptogamous plants. **1887** *Athenæum* 24 Sept. 410/3 In 1865 the battle of the 'Uniformitarians' and 'Cataclysmists', 'Sub-aërialists' and 'Marinists', was still raging. *Ibid.*, The most extreme..sub-aërialist views.

sub-ˈagent. [SUB- 6.] A subordinate agent; the agent of an agent. (*spec.* in *U.S. Law.*)

1843–56 BOUVIER *Law Dict.* (ed. 6) II. 552/2 A sub-agent is generally invested with the same rights, and incurs the same liabilities in regard to his immediate employers, as if he were the sole and real principal. **1863** H. COX *Instit.* I. viii. 122 The candidate is responsible not only for his own acts, but for those of his agents, and for those of sub-agents appointed by them. **1881** *Instr. Census Clerks* (1885) 84 Persons working and dealing in various mineral substances. Sub-order 1.—Miners... Underground Agent, Sub-Agent.

Hence **sub-ˈagency**, the position, condition, or residence of a sub-agent.

1845 R. W. HAMILTON *Pop. Educ.* iv. (ed. 2) 64 The anti-christian usurpation..puts forth an unwonted vigour... An active..sub-agency is stalking through the land. **1900** *20th Rep. U.S. Geol. Surv.* IV. Pl. 44 Subagency of Southern Utes at Navajo Springs.

†**subˈagitate**, *v. Obs.* [f. L. *subagitāt-*, pa. ppl. stem of *subagitāre*, var. of *subigitāre*, f. *sub-* SUB-25 + *agitāre* to AGITATE.] *intr.* To have sexual intercourse. So †**subˈagitatory** *a.*, pertaining to sexual intercourse.

1637 HEYWOOD *Pleas. Dial.* ii. 113 Can they walke? Or do they sleepe? *Pam.* They do... Nay more than that, sometimes subagitate After their kinde. *a* **1693** *Urquhart's Rabelais* III. xii. 96 This grand subagitatory Atchievement.

†**subagiˈtation.** *Obs. rare.* [ad. L. *subagitātio*, *-ōnem*, n. of action f. *subagitāre* (see prec.).]

1. Carnal knowledge.

1658 PHILLIPS. **1675** J. SMITH *Chr. Relig. Appeal* I. vii. 56 That he might, by those Subagitations of their Wives, bolt out the secrets of their Husbands.

2. Used for SUBACTION (sense 1).

1653 R. G. tr. *Bacon's Hist. Winds*, etc. 366 With us by the subagitation [orig. *subactione*] and concoction of the Celestials, every tangible thing is not only not condensed to the height, but is also mixed with some spirit.

‖**subah** (ˈsuːbɑː). *Anglo-Indian.* Also **soubah**, **soobah**, **suba.** [Urdu = Arab. *çūbaʰ*.]

1. A province of the Mogul empire.

1753 HANWAY *Trav.* (1762) II. XIV. v. 362 Mahommed khan, was..dispatched..to demand..four provinces [*Note*, These the indians call soubahs.] **1796** MORSE *Amer. Geog.* II. 532 The names of the Soubahs, or Vice-royalties were Allahabad [etc.]. **1806** T. MAURICE *Ind. Antiq.* I. 134 So accurate an account of the geography of the Indian Subahs. **1858** BEVERIDGE *Hist. India* I. 141 [Akber's] administrative divisions of the empire into provinces or subahs.

2. = SUBAHDAR.

1753 ORME *Hist. Fragm.* (1805) 400 A Nabob, although appointed by a Subah, ought to have his commission confirmed by the King. **1788** BURKE *Sp. agst. W. Hastings* Wks. XIII. 96 There was not a captain of a band of ragged topasses that looked for any thing less than the deposition of soubahs. **1884** *Encycl. Brit.* XVII. 343/2 The revenue, when collected by the various sūbas, is transmitted under an escort to the Government treasury.

‖**subahdar** (suːbəˈdɑː(r)). *Anglo-Indian.* Also 7–9 **subidar**, 8 **sabahadaur**, 9 **sou-**, **soo-**, **subadar**, etc. [Urdu *çūbaʰdār*, f. SUBAH + Pers. *dār* possessor, master.]

1. A governor of a subah or province. Also, 'a local commandant or chief officer' (Y.).

1698 J. FRYER *Acc. E. Ind. & P.* 77 The Subidar of this Town being a Person of Quality. **1796** MORSE *Amer. Geog.* II. 532 Twelve grand divisions, and each was committed to the government of a Soobadar or Viceroy. **1858** J. B. NORTON *Topics* 18 The chief of Secundra Rao..has.. proclaimed himself Subadar, or governor, for the King of Delhi, of all the country between these towns and Allahabad. **1881** *Encycl. Brit.* XII. 796/1 The title of subahdar, or viceroy, gradually dropped into desuetude, as the paramount power was shaken off.

2. The chief native officer of a company of sepoys.

1747 (MS. in India Office) in Yule & Burnell *Hobson-Jobson* s.v., That..in a day or two they shall despatch another Subidar with 129 more Sepoys to our assistance. **1788** *Gentl. Mag.* LVIII. 68/1 A second flag, with a Sabahadaur and two Havildars, was sent in. **1841** *Penny Cycl.* XXI. 256/2 From 1748 to 1766 the sepoys were in separate companies of 100 each, commanded by subadars, or native captains, though under the superintendence of Europeans. **1890** KIPLING *Departm. Ditties* (ed. 4) 79 And there's Subadar Prag Tewarri Who tells how the work was done.

b. *attrib.*: **subahdar-major**, the native commandant of a regiment of sepoys.

1819 in *Engl. Hist. Rev.* (1913) Apr. 269 A brevet pay of 25 rupees per month is annexed to the Commission of Subadar-Major. **1849** EASTWICK *Dry Leaves* 80 The regiment shewed stronger excitement on this occasion of the arrest of their Subedár Major. **1857** —— *Autobiog. Lutfullah* vi. 185 A Súbahdár Major pensioner.

subahdary (su:bə'dɑ:ri:). *Anglo-Indian.* Also 8 su-, soubadary, -ee, -darr(e)y, 9 soobah-. [Urdu *çūbaʰdārī*, f. prec.] = next.

1764 *State Papers* in *Ann. Reg.* 190 We engage to reinstate the Nabob..in the subadarrey of..Bengal. **1800** *Asiatic Ann. Reg.* IV. 9/1 A firman, vesting Hyder with the subahdary of Sera. **1817** JAS. MILL *Brit. India* I. III. iv. 599 He was appointed to the regency or subahdarry of Deccan.

subahship ('su:bɑ:ʃɪp). [f. SUBAH + -SHIP.] The office or status of governor of a subah or province; also, the territory governed, = SUBAH I.

1753 ORME *Hist. Fragm.* (1805) 399 The Nabobs of Condanore, Cudapah,..the Kings of Tritchinopoly, Mysore, Tanjore, are subject to this Subahship. **1798** PENNANT *Hindoostan* II. 251 About Rhotas, and in the soubahships of Bengal and Orixa. **1897** G. SMITH *12 Ind. Statesmen* 296 Clive thought it necessary to obtain from Shah Aalum a blank firman for the Soobahship of the Deccan.

†**sub'aid**, *v. rare.* [f. SUB- 25 + AID *v.*] *trans.* To give secret aid to. Hence **sub'aiding** *ppl. a.*

1597 DANIEL *Civ. Wars* VI. i, That tumultuous rout, Whom close sub-ayding power, and good successe, Had made vn-wisely proud. **1609** *Ibid.* VIII. xlvii, To hold that Kingdome, from subayding such Who else could not subsist. **1630** R. N. tr. *Camden's Hist. Eliz.* Introd. 5 For that hee [the French King] had subayded the Scots [orig. *Scotis subsidia..submiserat*] against the English.

‖**subak** ('subak). Also soebak. [Balinese.] A Balinese rice-growers' co-operative, organized to ensure equitable distribution of water for irrigation.

1921 *Man. Netherlands India* (Admiralty) xi. 373 In the.. construction of aqueducts..the Balinese excels. Moreover, the natives have their own irrigation associations or *subaks*. **1926** H. NORDEN *Byways of Tropic Seas* ix. 159 Balinese economic life is governed by *Soebak*, a communistic organization which came into being for the joint irrigation of rice fields. **1937** M. COVARRUBIAS *Island of Bali* (1972) iii. 67 Disputes concerning ricefields or irrigation water are settled by the council of a special agricultural society, the *subak*. **1957** K. G. WITTFOGEL *Oriental Despotism* 25 In Bali the peasants are obliged to render labor service for the hydraulic regional unit, the *subak*, to which they belong. **1972** *Times* 11 Nov. 13/4 The brilliant green *sawahs*..are tended by village co-operatives, the *subaks*.

sub-'almoner. Also 7 -a(l)mner. [SUB- 6.] A subordinate almoner, one of the officials of the Royal Almonry.

1647 HAWARD *Crown Rev.* 31 Gentleman Amner: Fee, 11. 8. 1. *ob.* Sub-amner: Fee 6. 16 10. *ob.* **1710** J. CHAMBERLAYNE *M. Brit. Notitia* 106 One of the King's Chaplains, deputed by the Lord Almoner to be his Sub-Almoner. **1773** *Gentl. Mag.* XLIII. 200 The Rev. Mr. Kaye, Sub-almoner to his Majesty, preached at the Chapel Royal. **1886** *Encycl. Brit.* XXI. 37/1 The officers of the almonry, namely, the hereditary grand almoner, the lord high almoner, the sub-almoner, the groom of the almonry, and the secretary to the lord high almoner.

fig. **1654** CLEVELAND *Char. Diurn. Maker* 1 A Diurnal Maker is the Sub-Almner of History.

sub'alpine, *a.* (*sb.*) [ad. L. *subalpīnus*: see SUB- 12 and ALPINE. Cf. F. *subalpin*.]

1. Belonging to regions lying about the foot of the Alps.

1656 BLOUNT *Glossogr.*, *Subalpine*, under the Alps. **1829** MURCHISON in *Philos. Mag.* V. 402 The tertiary or subalpine deposits, which to the west of the Brenta are so much traversed by basaltic and trap rocks. **1833** LYELL *Princ. Geol.* III. 45 The fossil shells..of many of the Subalpine formations, on the northern limits of the plain of the Po. **1842** W. C. TAYLOR *Anc. Hist.* xiii. §1 (ed. 3) 365 Subalpine Italy received the name of Gaul from the Gallic hordes that settled in the northern and western districts. **1907** A. LANG *Hist. Scot.* IV. xvi. 412 A miserable little sub-Alpine inn.

b. *sb.* An inhabitant of such regions. *rare.*

1838 G. S. FABER *Inquiry* 479 Native Piedmontise Sub-alpines. *Ibid.* 503 The Subalpines or Vallenses.

2. Partly alpine in character or formation; pertaining to or characteristic of elevations next below that called *alpine*; belonging to the higher slopes of mountains (of an altitude of about 4,000 to 5,500 feet).

1833 HOOKER in Smith's *Eng. Flora* V. I. 71 Trees and rocks, in stony and subalpine countries. **1839** DE LA BECHE *Rep. Geol. Cornwall*, etc. i. 3 The hills and cliffs bordering the Bristol Channel..forming a coast remarkable for its general elevation and the sub-alpine character of some of its valleys. **1858** IRVINE *Brit. Plants* 78 The alpine and sub-alpine plants. **1870** HOOKER *Stud. Flora* 242 Wet sub-alpine limestone rocks of York and Durham. **1886** —— *Flora Brit. India* V. 57 Subalpine and Alpine Himalaya.

subaltern ('sʌbəltən, sə'bɔ:ltən), *a.* and *sb.* Also 6–7 -erne. [ad. late L. *subalternus* (Boethius, in sense 1 b): see SUB- III and ALTERN. Cf. F. *subalterne* (from 15th c.), It., Sp., Pg. *subalterno*.

Johnson 1755 has *'subaltern*, which is now the prevailing stressing in England, and, for the logical sense, in U.S. The stressing *su'baltern* first appears recorded in Bailey's (folio) Dict. of 1730.]

A. *adj.* †**1. a.** Succeeding in turn. *Obs. rare.*

1604 R. CAWDREY *Table Alph.*, *Subalterne*, succeeding, following by course and order. **1698** FRYER *Acc. E. India & P.* 363 Therefore God framed the first Intelligence, and that mediating the first Heaven, and so in their subaltern order to the Tenth. **1762** MILLS *Syst. Pract. Husb.* I. 469 The main stem, advancing higher and higher, left behind the subaltern blossom of a lower joint.

b. Logic. ***subaltern genus*** (or ***species***): a genus that is at the same time a species of a higher genus.

1654 Z. COKE *Logick* 21 Subaltern Genus is, that is successive and by turn, that is when it is genus of them contained under it, and species of that which is above it. **1692** RAY *Disc.* II. iv. (1732) 149 A distinct subaltern Genus. **1725** WATTS *Logic* I. iii. §3 This sort of universal Ideas, which may either be consider'd as a Genus, or a Species, is call'd Subaltern. **1826** WHATELY *Logic* I. ii. §5 (1827) 65 Iron-ore is a subaltern species or genus, being both the genus of magnet, and a species of mineral. **1864** BOWEN *Logic* iv. 72 The intermediate Concepts are the Subaltern Genera or Species.

2. Of inferior status, quality, or importance.

a. Of a person or body of persons: Subordinate, inferior. Now *rare.*

1581 LAMBARDE *Eiren.* I. v. 26 From the King..ought to flow all auctoritie to the inferiour and subalterne Iustices. **1597** SKENE *De Verb. Sign.* s.v. *Homagium*, Sum are maist chiefe and principall, sik as the King... Uther over-lordes are inferiour and subalterne. **1598** DALLINGTON *Meth. Trav.* Q 2 b, To this Parliament, they appeale from all other subalterne Courts throughout the Realme. **1622** MALYNES *Anc. Law-Merch.* 472 The Iudges for terme of life, and officers subalterne changing from yeare to yeare. **1695** BLACKMORE *Pr. Arth.* VI. 681 Inferiour, subaltern Divinities. **1728** CHAMBERS *Cycl.* s.v., The Subaltern Persons in an Epic Poem. **1734** tr. *Rollin's Anc. Hist.* (1827) I. 127 All such subaltern actors as played between the acts. **1809** MALKIN *Gil Blas* VIII. xiii. (Rtldg.) 309 Some subaltern attendants about the king's person. **1814** SCOTT *Wav.* li, He had been long employed as a subaltern agent and spy by those in the confidence of the Chevalier. **1875** GLADSTONE *Glean.* (1879) VI. 189 A case in which the statute prescribed a major amount of observance, but the subaltern or executive authority was content with a minor amount.

Const. *to.* **1597** *Extr. Aberd. Reg.* (1848) II. 154 Na maister..(except of the sang school), bot sic as sal be subalterne to the maister of the grammer school. **1609** OVERBURY *Observ. France* (1626) 17 Then hath euery Towne and Fortresse particular Gouernours, which are not subalterne to that of the Prouince. **1699** BURNET *39 Art.* i. 18 Others holding a vast number of Gods, either all equal or subaltern to one another. **1728** CHAMBERS *Cycl.* s.v., The Patriarchs..had several Wives..; but there were several subaltern to the principal Wife.

b. Hence, of rank, power, authority, action: Of or pertaining to a subordinate or inferior.

1581 MULCASTER *Positions* xxxv. (1888) 126 Where to much distraction is, and subalterne professions be made seuerall heads. **1601** J. WHEELER *Treat. Comm.* 25 A Deputie, and certaine discreet persons..who..haue subalterne power to exercise Merchants law. **1602** R. CAREW *Cornwall* 85 b, Neither can the parish Constables well brooke the same, because it submitteth them to a subalterne commaund. **1726** SWIFT *Gulliver* IV. vi. 295 They have a subaltern court paid to them by persons of the best rank. **1817** LADY MORGAN *France* I. (1818) I. 18 Gallantly fighting his way through every subaltern degree of his profession. **1822** SCOTT *Nigel* x, Protect the poor against subaltern oppression. **1868** GLADSTONE *Juv. Mundi* xi. 416 Sometimes the sovereignty was local, or subaltern.

c. Of immaterial things. (In recent use *U.S.*)

1644 DIGBY *Nat. Bodies* xxiii. 204 Which [motion] when it is once in act, hath..many other subalterne motions ouer which it presideth. **1654** H. L'ESTRANGE *Chas. I* (1655) 196 The vanity of that Faith, which is founded upon causes subaltern. **1750** JOHNSON *Rambler* No. 72 ⁋2 You have shown yourself not ignorant of the value of those subaltern endowments. **1776** BURNEY *Hist. Mus.* (1789) I. i. 61 These modes had other subaltern modes that were dependent on them. **1839** HALLAM *Lit. Eur.* III. iv. §55 All causes of wealth, except those he has enumerated, Serra holds to be subaltern or temporary. **1866** WHIPPLE *Char. & Char. Men* 22 The power and working intelligence of the subaltern natures it uses. **1893** in J. H. Barrows *World's Parl. Relig.* I. 256 Not a subaltern science to dogmatic theology.

†**d.** Of material things. *Obs.*

1733 tr. *Winslow's Anat.* (1756) I. 302 The Composition of the Fibres of this Muscle, and its division into several subaltern Muscles.

3. ***subaltern officer***: an officer in the army of junior rank, i.e. below that of captain. Hence ***subaltern rank***, etc.

1688 *Lond. Gaz.* No. 2396/3 Count Strozzi..was..Shot dead..and two or three Subalterne Officers wounded. **1702** *Milit. Dict.* (1704) s.v. *Officer*, *Subaltern-Officers*. The Lieutenant, Ensigns, and Cornets of Horse, Foot, and Dragoons, are so call'd. *a* **1721** PRIOR *Dial. Dead* (1907) 208 Had not I equally my Captains, and Subaltern Officers? **1807** *Med. Jrnl.* XVII. 222 The cries of the soldier were heard by the subaltern officer. **1811** *Regul. & Orders Army* 248 The Subaltern Officers, Non-Commissioned Officers, and Men, are to be divided into Watches. **1859** W. COLLINS *Q. of Hearts* iv, Have you any ears left for small items of private intelligence from insignificant subaltern officers?

4. Of a vassal: Holding of one who is himself a vassal. Hence of a feu or right.

1681 STAIR *Inst. Law Scot.* I. xiii. 252 The Vassals of the King, who only might grant subaltern Infeftments of their Ward Lands. *Ibid.* xxi. 420 If the major part be not alienate, Subaltern Infeudations..infer not recognition, when these rights are *disjunctim* of parts of the Fee. *Ibid.* 424 Seing all other Rights fall in *consequentiam*, as was found in Subaltern-rights, in the said case. *Ibid.* 429 Omitted not only by the immediat Vassal, but by all subaltern Vassals. **1723** *Bibl. Literaria* No. vi. 17 Reliefs, Fines, Duties upon the several subaltern Manors. **1765–8** ERSKINE *Inst. Law Scot.* II. vii. §8 Subaltern infeftments soon recovered force after the statute of Robert which abolished them. **1838** W. BELL *Dict. Law Scot.* 88 Suppose A to hold of the Crown blench, and that he subfeus his lands to B, to be held in feu. .. A's right is termed a public one; B's a base or subaltern right.

5. *Logic.* Of a proposition: Particular, in relation to a universal of the same quality.

subaltern opposition: opposition between a universal and a particular of the same quality. (Cf. SUBALTERNANT, SUBALTERNATE.)

1656 tr. *Hobbes' Elem. Philos.* I. iii. 30 Subaltern, are Universal and Particular Propositions of the same Quality; as, Every Man is a Living Creature, Some Man is a Living Creature. **1725** WATTS *Logic* II. ii. §3 Both particular and universal Propositions which agree in Quality but not in Quantity are call'd Subaltern. **1860** ABP. THOMSON *Laws Th.* §84. 151 Subaltern opposition is between any pair of affirmative or negative judgments, when the one has fewer terms distributed, that is, taken entire, than the other. **1864** BOWEN *Logic* vi. 162, I can immediately infer the truth of its Subaltern Opposite.

B. *sb.*

1. A person (†or thing) of inferior rank or status; a subordinate; *occas.* †a subaltern genus; †a subordinate character in a book.

1605 CAMDEN *Rem.* (1623) 4 When all Christianity in the Counsell of Constance was diuided into Nations, Anglicana Natio was one of the principall and no subalterne. *a* **1619** FOTHERBY *Atheom.* II. iii. §3 (1622) 219 The subalternes, are both, in their diuers relations; Genera, to their inferiors; and Species, to their superiors. *a* **1628** F. GREVIL *Life of Sidney* (1652) 14 They..both encourage, and shaddow the conspiracies of ambitious subalternes to their false endes. **1706** PHILLIPS (ed. Kersey), *Subalterns*, inferiour Judges, or Officers. **1765** H. WALPOLE *Otranto* (1886) 10 The art of the author is very observable in the conduct of the subalterns. **1787** CHARLOTTE SMITH *Rom. Real Life* II. 133 If the subalterns of the law once seize on the property. **1816** 'QUIZ' *Grand Master* I. 3 Passive obedience under wrongs, 'Tis thought, to subalterns belongs. **1860** EMERSON *Cond. Life, Power* Wks. (Bohn) II. 332 The geologist reports the surveys of his subalterns. **1885** 'MRS. ALEXANDER' *At Bay* v, The *chef de la sûreté* and his subaltern.

2. a. A subaltern officer in the army.

1690 *Lond. Gaz.* No. 2616/3 The Marquis de St. George, ..with his Lieutenant-Colonel, Major, 10 Captains, and 25 Subalternes are arrived here. **1760** *Caut. & Adv. Off. Army* 77 A Subaltern will find it extremely difficult to live upon his Pay, and support the Appearance of a Gentleman. **1796** MORSE *Amer. Geog.* I. 431 The respective companies choose their captain, and subalterns. **1811** *Gen. Regul. Army* 37 No Officer shall be promoted to the Rank of Captain, until he has been Three Years a Subaltern. **1846** BROWNING *Luria* III. 4 How could subalterns like myself expect Leisure or leave to occupy the field?

attrib. **1898** 'MERRIMAN' *Roden's Corner* x, Major White had, in his subaltern days, been despatched from Gibraltar on a business quest into the interior of Spain.

b. subaltern's butter, the fruit of *Persea gratissima* = AVOCADO, called also *midshipman's butter*; **subaltern's luncheon** (see quot. 1904).

1829 MARRYAT *Fr. Mildmay* xviii, Abbogada pears (better known by the name of subaltern's butter). **1904** A. GRIFFITHS *50 Yrs. Public Serv.* 50 The traditional 'subaltern's luncheon'—'a glass of water and a pull at the waistbelt'.

3. *Logic.* A subaltern proposition.

1685 tr. *Arnauld & Nicole's Logic* II. ii. 169 If they differ in Quantity only, and agree in Quality, as A.I. and E.O. they are call'd Subalterns. **1816** *Elements of Logic* II. iii. 47 Propositions which differ only in quantity are called subalterns. **1826** WHATELY *Logic* II. ii. §3, 1st. the two universals (A and E) are called contraries to each other; 2d. the two particular, (I and O) subcontraries; 3rd. A and I, or E and O, subalterns; 4th. A and O, or E and I, contradictories. *Ibid.*, Subalterns differ in quantity alone; Contraries, and also Subcontraries, in quality alone. **1870** JEVONS *Elem. Logic* ix. 78 Of subalterns, the particular is true if the universal be true.

Hence **'subalternhood, -ship**, the status or period of service of a subaltern.

1857 *Fraser's Mag.* LVI. 172 The Indian officer has to serve a long subalternhood. **1861** *Cornh. Mag.* Jan. 74 James Outram soon obtained the grand reward of efficiency in regimental subalternship, the adjutancy of a corps.

†**subaltern**, *v. Obs. rare.* [ad. med.L. *subalternāre*, f. *subalternus* (see prec.). Cf. OF. *subalterner*.] *trans.* To subordinate.

c **1400** *Pilgr. Sowle* (Caxton) I. xxx. (1859) 34 Al other worldly lawes ben..subalterned to gods lawe.

†**subal'ternal**, *a.* (*sb.*) *Obs.* [a. OF. *subalternal* (15th c.) or its source med.L. **subalternālis*, f. *subalternus* SUBALTERN: see -AL[1].]

1. Subordinate, inferior. Const. *to.*

c **1400** *Pilgr. Sowle* (Caxton) I. xxx. (1859) 33 Alle other lawes ordeyned of man be not subalternal for to serue the lawe of oure lord. **1588** FRAUNCE *Lawiers Logike* I. ii. 10 b, It were against..all arte to jumpe abruptly from the highest and most generall to the lowest and most speciall, without passing by the subalternal. **1607** TOPSELL *Four-f. Beasts* 714

Sundry Beastes haue not onely their diuisions, but subdeuisions, into subalternal kinds. **1625** DARCIE *Annales* a 4, Those subalternal Deities who, for putting themselues in Iupiters bedde, were .. metamorphosed into strange shapes. **1628** R. HEATH *Discov. Jesuit's Coll.* (Camden) 29 They acknowledg subjection to a foren power, and have setled a government amongst themselves subalternal therunto.

b. *sb.* A subordinate.

1673 MARVELL *Reh. Transp.* II. 227, I am not at all doubtful but that he [the Supreme Magistrate] may punish any such transgression in his Subalternals and Substitutes.

2. Succeeding in turn, alternating.

1588 J. HARVEY *Disc. Probl.* 23 There should euery 7000 yeere, insue a certaine subalternall time of peaceable calmenes, and transitory rest. **1657** *Penit. Conf.* v. 72 [74] Where the disease is sin, the remedy confession and prayer; the Physicians and Patients subalternal.

subalternant (sʌbɒlˈtɜːnənt). *Logic.* (More freq. in L. form.) [ad. mod.L. *subalternans, -ant-*, pr. pple. of *subalternāre* SUBALTERN *v.*] See quots.

1826 WHATELY *Logic* Index (1827) 347 Subaltern opposition, is between a Universal and a Particular of the same Quality. Of these, the Universal is the Subalternant, and the Particular the Subalternate. **1867** ATWATER *Logic* 109 In each pair of these the Universal is called the Subalternans, the Particular the Subalternate.

subalternate (sʌbɒlˈtɜːnət), *a.* (*sb.*) [ad. late L. *subalternātus* (*subalternātum genus* in Boethius), pa. pple. of *subalternāre*: see SUBALTERN *v.* and -ATE[2].] **A.** *adj.*

†**1.** Subordinate, inferior. Also const. *to*: Subordinate or subservient *to*. *Obs.*

1432-50 tr. *Higden* (Rolls) III. 123, iiij. principalle realmes, .. x. other realmes, subalternate to theyme. **1595** in *12th Rep. Hist. MSS. Comm.* App. IX. 173 What ministers of state and subalternat governors, as counsaile and magistrats. **1611** in *10th Rep. Hist. MSS. Comm.* App. I. 546 In putting so muche difference between an absolute king and a subalternate Queen. **1638** BAKER tr. *Balzac's Lett.* (vol. II) 79 As though the present time, were but subalternate to the future. **1670** CLARKE *Nat. Hist. Nitre* 51 Medicine being a subalternate Art to Philosophy. **1686** SPENCE tr. *Varillas' House of Medicis* 15 The Enditement was drawn up by the Subalternate Judges. **1701** NORRIS *Ideal World* I. ii. 104 So only the subalternate sciences suppose their objects, as taking them from the superior science wherein they are proved. **1704** *Phil. Trans.* XXV. 1702 An account of the several kinds of subalternate Species of Plants. **1874** in Manning *Ess. Relig. & Lit.* III. 317 Theology is a science subalternate to Revelation.

†**2.** Successive, succeeding by turns. *Obs.*

1706 PHILLIPS (ed. Kersey), *Subaltern* or *Subalternate*, that succeeds by turns.

†**b.** *Logic.* = SUBALTERN *a.* 1 b.

1658 E. PHILLIPS *Myst. Love* (1685) 285 The subalternate genus, as also the subalternate species, is that which is the species of this, but the genus of that.

3. [A new formation from SUB- 21 d and ALTERNATE *a.*] *Nat. Hist.* Alternate, but with a tendency to become opposite.

1829 LOUDON *Encycl. Plants* 571 Leaves pinnat[ifid]: segm[ents] stalked subalternate. **1846** DANA *Zooph.* (1848) 655 Polyps few and at distant intervals on the branches, subalternate. **1851** MANTELL *Petrifactions* iii. §5. 309 The subalternate arrangement and reversed position of the upper and lower series of teeth.

B. *sb. Logic.* A particular proposition.

1826, 1867 [see SUBALTERNANT].

Hence †**subal'ternately** *adv.*, subordinately, successively.

1606 B. BARNES *Foure Bks. Offices* 19 Subalternately respecting the purse. **1727** BAILEY (vol. II), *Subalternately*, .. successively.

sub'alternating, *ppl. a.* [f. **subalternate* vb. (cf. prec.) + -ING[2].] Succeeding by turns (1855 in Ogilvie Suppl.).

subalternation (ˌsʌbɒltəˈneɪʃən). [ad. med.L. *subalternātio, -ōnem*, n. of action f. *subalternāre*: see SUBALTERNATE.]

†**1.** Subordination. *Obs.*

1597 HOOKER *Eccl. Pol.* v. lxxiii. (1617) 397 Whereunto it was not possible they could concurre, vnlesse there were subalternation between them, which subalternation is naturally grounded vpon inequalitie.

†**2.** Succession by turn. *Obs.*

1616 BULLOKAR *Eng. Expos., Subalternation*, A succeeding by course. **1627** DONNE *Serm.* xliv. (1640) 441 That use of Subalternation in the service of God, of that, which we have called Antiphones, and Responsaries.

3. *Logic.* The relation between a universal and a particular of the same quality; the opposition which exists between propositions alike in quality but differing in quantity; also, 'an immediate inference from a universal to a particular under it' (*Cent. Dict.*).

1650 ELDERFIELD *Civ. Right Tythes* 35 It may be .. needful to consider her [the law's] several species, or indeed not so much their contradiction, as subalternation. **1677** GALE *Crt. Gentiles* Proem. 8 The Relate Affections of a Proposition are Conversion, Equipollence, Subalternation, and Opposition. **1697** tr. *Burgersdicius his Logic* I. xxxii. 127 By Subalternation we express our Meaning when we would signifie that one Enunciation is subordinated to another, and does necessarily follow from it. **1813-21** BENTHAM *Ontology* Wks. 1843 VIII. 203 Subalternation, viz. logical subalternation, opposition, and connexion, or the relation between cause and effect. **1864** BOWEN *Logic* vi. 155 But of these less perfect expressions some may more properly be regarded as inferences by Subalternation. **1867** ATWATER *Logic* 116 This is U, and by subalternation will give I also.

subalternity (sʌbɒlˈtɜːnɪtɪ). [f. SUBALTERN + -ITY. Cf. F. *subalternité*.] Subordinate position.

1620 T. GRANGER *Div. Logike* 178 Which respecteth not suppartitions, anatomical diuisions, or subalternities of members. **1773** H. WALPOLE *Let. to Mann* 4 Nov., I am sure I have none of the symptoms but the age and the subalternity. **1831** SOUTHEY in *Q. Rev.* XLV. 443 Christianity, they say, has raised the sex from servitude, but has condemned them to subalternity. **1850** tr. *Mazzini's Royalty & Republ.* Pref. 8 Redeeming by brilliant personal qualities the vice of subalternity, to which his position condemned him.

subalternize (ˈsʌbəltənaɪz), *v. rare.* [ad. F. *subalterniser*, f. *subalterne*: see SUBALTERN *a.* and -IZE.] *trans.* To subordinate.

1905 *19th Cent.* July 24 France was subalternised, domesticated everywhere; she suffered her greatest interests to be subordinated to those of an alien Power.

†**subalternly,** *a. Sc. Law. Obs.* [f. SUBALTERN *a.* + -LY[2].] By subinfeudation.

1681 STAIR *Inst. Law Scot.* I. xiii. 263 If the Lands .. be Disponed .. by the Vassal to others Subalternly Infeft.

suban'coneal, *a. Anat.* [See SUB- 1 b and next.] Situated beneath the anconeus.

1891 *Cent. Dict.* **1898** *Syd. Soc. Lex.*

‖**subanconeus** (ˌsʌbæŋkəʊˈniːəs). *Anat.* Also -æus. [mod.L. (sc. *musculus*), f. *sub-* SUB- 1 d + *ancōn* = Gr. ἀγκών elbow.] A small muscle arising from the triceps and humerus above the elbow-joint and inserted in the posterior ligament of the elbow. Hence ˌ**subanco'neous** *a.*

1848 *Quain's Anat.* (ed. 5) I. 330 On removing the triceps from the lower part of the humerus, some muscular fibres will be found connected with the capsule of the elbow-joint. Two slips extending from the bone above the fossa for the olecranon to the capsule have been described as distinct from the triceps, under the name sub-anconæus. **1887** *Buck's Handbk. Med. Sci.* V. 45 Subanconeous [muscle]. This consists of a few muscular fibres.

sub'angular, *a.* [ad. mod.L. *subangulāris*: see SUB- 21 c and ANGULAR.] Somewhat or slightly angular; having a blunt angle.

1777 PENNANT *Brit. Zool.* IV. 51 Ast[erias] with five rays depressed; broad at the base; sub-angular. **1849** DANA *Geol.* App. I. (1850) 685 Mesial fold large and subangular. **1873** GEIKIE *Gt. Ice Age* xvi. 202 Sprinkled with loose angular and subangular stones. **1894** *Geol. Mag.* Oct. 434 Each tubercle gives rise to three .. subangular ribs.

So **sub'angled, -'angulate(d** *adjs.*

1819 SAMOUELLE *Entomol. Compend.* 423 *Geometra .. strigilata.* The subangled Wave. **1822** J. PARKINSON *Outl. Oryctol.* 207 Turreted, with subangulated keels. *Ibid.* 210 Whirls round, but subangulate.

subapennine (sʌbˈæpənaɪn), *a.* (*sb.*) *Geol.* Also -appen(n)ine. [SUB- 12.] Applied to a series of strata of Pliocene age, such as are characteristic of the formation of the flanks of the Apennines in Italy; belonging to or characteristic of these strata.

1822 *Edin. Rev.* XXXVII. 50 Subappennine alluvial soils. **1833** LYELL *Princ. Geol.* III. 110 Throughout a great part of Italy, where the marls and sands of the Subapennine hills are elevated to considerable heights. **1851** RICHARDSON *Geol.* viii. 248 The subapennine beds of Piedmont. **1861** P. P. CARPENTER in *Rep. Smithsonian Instit.* 1860, 159 The Subappenine tertiaries of Piedmont.

b. *sb. pl.* The geological series bearing this name; a low range of hills skirting the slopes of the Apennines in Italy.

1830 LYELL *Princ. Geol.* I. 137 *note*, The newest tertiary strata of the age of the Subapennines. **1833** *Ibid.* III. 155 Brocchi, the first Italian geologist who described this newer group in detail, gave it the name of the Subapennines.

sub'apical, *a. Nat. Hist.* [SUB- 1 b, c, 11.] Beneath or near the apex; nearly apical.

1846 DANA *Zooph.* (1848) 445 The subapical calicles becoming very small. **1870** HOOKER *Stud. Flora* 78 Carpels hairy with an eglandular subapical pit. **1913** *Oxf. Univ. Gaz.* 4 June 955 The orange subapical bar to the fore wing.

ˌ**subapo'stolic,** *a.* [SUB- 18.] Belonging to or characteristic of the period in the history of the Church immediately following that of the apostles.

1880 *Encycl. Brit.* XI. 854/2 The history of the apostolic and subapostolic ages. **1881** WESTCOTT & HORT *Grk. N.T.* II. 296 Stray relics surviving from the apostolic or subapostolic age.

sub-aqua (ˌsʌbˈækwə), *a.* [Adj. use of L. phr. *sub aquā* under water: cf. SUB- I.] Of or pertaining to underwater swimming or diving performed (esp. as a sport) with the assistance of an aqualung. Also *ellipt.* as *sb.*, sub-aqua swimming.

1955 *Neptune* Aug. 31/1, I was .. surprised to learn that .. few members of the British Sub-Aqua Club were interested in .. spearfishing. **1959** *Listener* 8 Jan. 67/3 The 'sub-aqua-jet' which provides motive power for an under-water swimmer. **1962** *Underwater Swimming* ('Know the Game' Ser.) 3/1 The formation of sub-aqua clubs throughout the country. **1976** *Milton Keynes Express* 1 June 11/2 Saturday's attractions include demonstrations of .. swimming, life-saving, sub aqua and weight-lifting. **1978** *Times* 14 July 26/3 Sub-aqua diving is one of the country's leading growth sports.

†**suba'quaneous,** *a. Obs. rare*[−0]. [f. late L. *subaquāneus* (SUB- 1 a, *aqua* water) + -OUS.] = next, 1.

1656 BLOUNT *Glossogr.*

suba'quatic, *a.* [Cf. F. *subaquatique*.]

1. [SUB- 1 a.] = SUBAQUEOUS 1. Also, pertaining to plants growing under water.

1789 E. DARWIN *Bot. Gard.* II. 146 *note*, The subaquatic leaves of this plant .. are cut into fine divisions. **1800** —— *Phytol.* 76 The roots of .. water-plants, which might .. become articles of subaquatic agriculture. **1828** *Blackw. Mag.* XXIV. 316 Subaquatic paths for crossing the Nile. **1849** *Sk. Nat. Hist., Mammalia* III. 111 Tearing up the strong-fibred vegetables from their subaquatic bed by means of its tusks. **1874** COUES *Birds N.W.* 11 Ability to progress under water .. by a sort of subaquatic flying and scrambling.

2. [SUB- 20 c.] *Zool.* and *Bot.* Partly aquatic.

1844 H. STEPHENS *Bk. Farm* I. 483 Subaquatic plants, such as rushes. **1880** A. R. WALLACE *Isl. Life* II. xiii. 268 The large number of allied forms [*sc.* tortoises] which have aquatic or sub-aquatic habits. **1889** —— *Darwinism* 29 A large sub-aquatic dock.

subaqueous (sʌbˈeɪkwɪəs), *a.* [f. L. type **subaqueus*: see SUB- 1 a. Cf. It. *subaqueo*.]

1. a. Existing, formed, or constructed under water.

1677 PLOT *Oxfordsh.* 28 Terrestrial and subaqueous Plants. *a* **1711** KEN *Edmund* Poet. Wks. II. 26 As if subaqueous Fires .. Had boil'd the Waves. **1774** PENNANT *Tour Scot. in 1772*, 33 In some places are vast subaqueous precipices. **1776** —— *Brit. Zool.* I. 345 For the purpose of plunging into their subaqueous winter quarters. **1829** LANDOR *Imag. Conv.* Wks. 1853 I. 573/1 That dark colour which subaqueous weeds are often of. **1855** KINGSLEY *Westw. Ho!* xxxii, Tarn David, one of those strange subaqueous pebble-dykes. **1862** TOUNSEND *Man. Dates* s.v. *Submarine telegraph*, In 1848 successful subaqueous telegraphs were laid across the Rhine. **1903** MYERS *Hum. Pers.* I. 77 There is a rush upwards as of a subaqueous spring.

b. Performed or taking place under water; adapted for use under water.

1774 A. CAMPBELL *Lexiphanes* (ed. 4) 25, I risqued sub-aqueous voyage. **1839** *United Service Jrnl.* June 189 Subterraneous or subaqueous explosions. **1847** BARHAM *Ingol. Leg.* Ser. I. *Grey Dolphin*, As though the River god and Neptune were amusing themselves with a game of subaqueous battledore. **1875** KNIGHT *Dict. Mech., Sub-aqueous Helmet*, a diver's head-dress, supplied with air by pump from above.

c. *jocular.* That constructs works under water.

1844 THACKERAY *Contrib. to Punch* Wks. 1898 VI. 83 It weds the tunnel of the subaqueous Brunel with the mystic edifice of Cheops.

2. Below the sea-level. *nonce-use.*

1724 RAMSAY *Health* 397 Ye Dutch .. You scarce dare sleep in your subaqueous bowers.

3. Reflected as if in depths of water.

1798 W. MAVOR *British Tourists* V. 260 The shelving hills .. with their subaqueous images were of a faint grape-like hue. **1843** WORDSW. *Prose Wks.* (1876) III. 167 These specks of snow reflected in the lake, and so transferred, as it were, to the subaqueous sky.

4. In *fig.* use, lacking real substance or strength; wishy-washy.

1960 C. DAY LEWIS *Buried Day* i. 15 The whole picture, clear yet elusive, is bathed in a brooding, sub-aqueous light. **1970** H. BRAUN *Parish Churches* xix. 228 During the last fifty years an inevitable reaction has introduced pallid subaqueous treatments [of stained-glass windows], less obstructive to light but lacking all the ancient warmth and liveliness. **1977** *Listener* 28 July 122/3 A sort of subaqueous, loopy, transcendental speculation about female identity.

So **sub'aquean** *a. rare*[−1].

1782 W. STEVENSON *Hymn to Deity* 19 Subaquean monsters multiform in size.

suba'rachnoid, *a.* (*sb.*) *Anat.* and *Path.* [SUB- 1 b.] Situated or taking place beneath the arachnoid membrane. Also *sb.*, the subarachnoid space (between the arachnoid membrane and the pia mater).

1839-47 *Todd's Cycl. Anat.* III. 641/2 In apoplexy the blood escapes from the ventricle into the sub-arachnoid space. *Ibid.* 673/2 The subarachnoid fluid. **1843** R. J. GRAVES *Syst. Clin. Med.* ix. 97 Extensive thickening of the membranes of the brain, with subarachnoid effusion. **1893** W. R. GOWERS *Man. Dis. Nerv. Syst.* (ed. 2) II. 390 Subarachnoid hæmorrhage. **1896** *Allbutt's Syst. Med.* I. 189 The perivascular lymphatic sheaths and subarachnoid are filled with fatty products. **1902** HUGHES & KEITH *Man. Pract. Bot.* III. 305 To this subarachnoid tissue is given the name of Pia mater.

So ˌ**subarach'noidal, -'noidean** *adjs.*

1844 HOBLYN *Dict. Terms Med.* (ed. 2) 293 *Sub-arachnoïdean fluid*, an abundant serous secretion, situated between the arachnoïd and the pia mater. *Sub-arachnoïdean space*, the space between the arachnoïd and the spinal cord. **1871** W. A. HAMMOND *Dis. Nerv. Syst.* 51 Subarachnoidean effusion. **1876** tr. *Wagner's Gen. Pathol.* 229 The sub-arachnoidal connective-tissue bands and meshes.

subarbis, obs. pl. SUBURB.

'**sub-arch.** *Archit.* [SUB- 3, 5 b.] A subsidiary or secondary arch; one of two or more arches grouped in a larger arch; the lowest member in an arch of two or more 'orders'.

1835 R. WILLIS *Archit. Mid. Ages* vii. 91 The square body of the pier sustains the pier arches, while its lateral half shafts are appropriated to the sub-arches. **1849** PARKER *Introd. Gothic Archit.* iii. 133 Three or more lancet-lights under one arch, the points of the sub-arches touching the enclosing arch. **1879** *Cassell's Techn. Educ.* III. 40 The first of the three orders, or 'sub-arch'.

sub'arctic, *a.* (*sb.*)

1. [SUB- 12 b.] Nearly arctic; somewhat south of the arctic circle or regions; belonging to such a region. Also *sb. pl.*, subarctic regions.

1854 H. MILLER *Sch. & Schm.* (1858) 460 When subarctic molluscs lived in her [*sc.* Scotland's] sounds and bays. **1875** CROLL *Clim. & Time* xv. 236 As the ice began to accumulate during the cold periods in subarctic and temperate regions. **1892** STEVENSON *Across the Plains* vi. 204 It was still broad day in our subarctic latitude [in Caithness]. **1898** J. W. TYRRELL (*title*) Across the Sub-Arctics of Canada.

2. [SUB- 18.] Also **Subarctic**. Applied to a European climatic period that followed the Arctic and preceded the Preboreal.

1876 [see ARCTIC *a.* 3]. **1935** *Discovery* July 198/2 Relics from Arctic and Subarctic times during and soon after the last glaciation are still to be found in Scotland. **1973** P. A. COLINVAUX *Introd. Ecol.* vii. 93 There is peat between the Dryas-bearing bottom mud and the first line of stumps, a gradation probably, but one that could be used as a stratigraphic unit. It represented the sub-arctic period.

sub'arcuate, *a. Nat. Hist.* [SUB- 21 c.] Somewhat arcuate or bowed.

1819 SAMOUELLE *Entomol. Compend.* 87 Thumb subarcuate. **1846** DANA *Zooph.* (1848) 471 Branches.. subarcuate.

sub'arcuated, *a.*

1. [SUB- 21 c.] *Nat. Hist.* = prec.

1777 PENNANT *Brit. Zool.* IV. 71 Solen Pellucidus.. subarcuated and sub-oval.

2. [f. next.] *Archit.* Having two or more subordinate arches under a main arch.

1881 PARKER *ABC Gothic Archit.* 195 The mullions are carried up to the architrave, and the side lights only are subarcuated. **1886** WILLIS & CLARK *Cambridge* I. 582 Each of the three main divisions of the window is sub-arcuated.

ˌsubarcu'ation. *Archit.* [SUB- 2.] The construction of two or more subordinate arches under a main arch; the system of arches so constructed.

1845 J. INGRAM in *Builder* III. 465/2 The principle of subarcuation; that is the mode of constructing two inferior and subordinate arches under the third or main arch. *a* **1878** SIR G. SCOTT *Lect. Archit.* (1879) II. 112 The round pillar has lateral shafts to carry the sub-arcuation.

Subarian (sjʊəbə'riːən), *a.* and *sb.* Also **Subaraean**. [f. Akkadian *Subar(tu* 'Assyria' + -IAN.] **A.** *adj.* Of or pertaining to the Subarian people (see below) or their language. **B.** *sb.* **a.** (A member of) an ancient people of northern Mesopotamia in the 3rd and 2nd millennia B.C., sometimes identified with the Hurrians. **b.** The language (written in cuneiform) of this people. Cf. HURRIAN *sb.* and *a.*, MITANNI.

1923 C. J. GADD *Fall of Nineveh* 20 In his own building records Nabopolassar says, 'I slew the Subaraean, and turned the enemy's land into mounds and ruins.' *Ibid.*, Throughout these references, it is most probable that the enemy is the same, though described indifferently as Subaraean and Assyrian. **1926** —— in *Revue d'Assyriologie* XXIII. 63 The suffix *-ia* which is in constant use to form shortened names has long been established as a characteristic of Subaraean. **1939** [see PAPUAN *sb.* 2]. **1964** G. ROUX *Anc. Iraq* xi. 166 Babylon was attacked by a coalition of Elamites, Guti, 'Subarians' (Assyrians) and people from Eshnunna. **1974** *Encycl. Brit. Micropædia* V. 222/3 The Hurrian language, once improperly called Mitannian or Subarian, exists chiefly in four varieties of cuneiform.

‖**subarmale** (sʌbɑː'meɪliː). [L., neut. of *subarmālis*, f. *sub-* SUB- 1 a + *arma* ARMS: see -AL[1]. Cf. F. *subarmale.*] A coarse coat worn to protect the body from the pressure of the cuirass.

1825 FOSBROKE *Encycl. Antiq.* I. 784 The gambeson or wambais, or *subarmale.* **1849** [JAS. GRANT] *Mem. Kirkaldy* x. 97 The constable received a bullet through his steel cuisses and subarmale.

subarrhation (sʌbə'reɪʃən). Also **-arration**. [ad. med.L. *subarr(h)ātio, -ōnem*, n. of action f. *subarr(h)āre*, f. *sub-* SUB- 1 g + *arr(h)a* pledge.] An ancient form of betrothal in which pledges in the form of money, rings, etc. were bestowed by the man upon the woman.

a **1623** SWINBURNE *Treat. Spousals* (1686) 207 Forasmuch as Subarration, that is the giving and receiving of a Ring, is a Sign of all others, most usual in Spousals and Matrimonial Contracts. **1710** WHEATLY *Bk. Com. Prayer* x. §5. **1839** PALMER *Orig. Liturg.* II. 211 Subarrhation.

‖**subashi** (suː'bɑːʃɪ). Forms: 6 **subbassi**, 6–7 **subassi**, 7 **subashie, -sha, subbashaw, -bassawe, -bassa, sous-bashi, sous-basha**, 8 **sous-bachi**, 9 **soobashee, subasche, súbáshi**. [Turkish *sūbāshī* and *çūbāshī*, f. *çū* water + *bāsh* head, chief. (Some of the Eng. forms indicate an attempt to analyse the word as SUB- 6 + BASHAW.)] A Turkish official in command of a district or village; a 'police magistrate under the timariot system' (Redhouse).

1599 HAKLUYT *Voy.* II. I. 106 Yᵉ Subassi, & the Meniwe, with the Padre guardian. *Ibid.* 292 The Admirall.. appointeth the Subbassas. **1613** PURCHAS *Pilgrimage* (1614) 302 The Cadi and Subassi, if they finde any shops open, or any body eating in the day, set him on an Asse backwards. **1615** SANDYS *Trav.* 63 The Subashie is as the Constable of a Citie, both to search out and punish offences. **1632** LITHGOW *Trav.* IV. 136 In this Prison, are Bassawes, and Sub-bassawes imprisoned. **1687** Sous-basha [see SOUS-]. **1688** *Lond. Gaz.* No. 2336/5 The Sub-Bassa of this City. **1718** OZELL tr. *Tournefort's Voy.* II. 279, I promis'd them to pay the Tax for them, if the Sous-Bachi shou'd demand it. **1819** T. HOPE *Anast.* (1820) II. 377 A Tchawoosh.. summoned me before the Soo-bashee. **1823–4** *Encycl. Metrop.* (1845) XV. 509 A Jerí-báshi (Captain), Jerí-sureji (Corporal), and Súbáshi (Sergeant).. who have particular lands assigned to them on which they are obliged to reside. **1847** MRS. A. KERR tr. *Ranke's Hist. Servia* 115 In the villages, Subasches appeared as executors of the judicial and magisterial power.

sub-a'ssembly. [SUB- 7 a.] A unit assembled separately but designed to be incorporated, with other such units, into a larger manufactured product; also, the production of sub-assemblies. Cf. ASSEMBLY 1 c.

1919 *Brit. Manufacturer* Nov. 29/1 Parallel with the Finished Part Stores is the sub-assembly stores. **1924** W. J. HISCOX *Factory Lay-Out, Planning & Progess* ii. 29 The term 'sub-assembling' is used when two or more component parts are assembled together to form one part... Sometimes the 'sub-assembly' merely covers the fitting of a pin to a certain part. **1941** *Sun* (Baltimore) 21 Feb. 30/5 The Omaha plant will be used to assemble bombers from sub-assemblies and parts supplied by the automotive and other non-aeronautical enterprises. **1952** F. ALLEN *Big Change* II. vii. 111 The Ford assembly line, with its subassemblies, was unique. **1967** *Electronics* 6 Mar. 171/1 (*caption*) Three subassemblies constitute IBM's new mass production computer for varied aerospace applications. **1973** J. G. TWEEDDALE *Materials Technol.* II. iv. 73 Such mechanically-wrought products can form the primary material for further mechanical manipulation.. into fairly complex sub-assembly components.

Hence (as a back-formation) **sub-a'ssemble** *v. trans.*; **sub-a'ssembling** *vbl. sb.*

1924 Sub-assembling [see *sub-assembly* above]. **1940** *Sun* (Baltimore) 28 Nov. 1/2 Parts are manufactured and sometimes 'sub-assembled' at plants where idle machinery and man power are available.

suba'stringent, *a.* and *sb.* [SUB- 21 b.]

A. *adj.* Somewhat astringent.

1694 SALMON *Bate's Dispens.* (1713) 99/2 The Spirit of Mint,.. stomachick, cephalick, ..and subastringent. **1719** QUINCY *Lex. Physico-Med.* (1722) 40 A soft, healing, subastringent Balsamick. **1788** *Phil. Trans.* LXXX. 280 It had a slight saline, sub-astringent taste. **1887** MOLONEY *Forestry W. Afr.* 304 The plant yields a sub-astringent gum.

B. *sb.* A sub-astringent substance.

1756 P. BROWNE *Jamaica* 208 All the plants of this tribe are mild subastringents and vulneraries.

subat'lantic, *a.* Also **Subatlantic, sub-Atlantic.**

1. [SUB- 1 e.] Under the Atlantic Ocean.

1875 KNIGHT *Dict. Mech.* 2507/2 The subatlantic cable enterprise.

2. [SUB- 18.] Pertaining to or designating a European climatic period that followed the Sub-boreal and which is still current. Also *absol.*

1876 [see ARCTIC *a.* 3]. **1935** *Discovery* July 198/2 A fair number of these species has ever survived the last climatic phase, the humid Subatlantic time (after 500 B.C.). **1957** E. E. EVANS *Irish Folk Ways* xiv. 186 The onset of the sub-Atlantic climatic deterioration in the last millennium B.C. seems to have accelerated the peat-forming processes. **1975** J. G. EVANS *Environment Early Man Brit. Isles* vi. 149 The growing of cereals [in Yorkshire].. would have been difficult ..at any time since the onset of the Sub-atlantic.

'sub-atom. *Chem.* [SUB- 7.] A constituent part of an atom.

1880 CLEMINSHAW *Wurtz' Atomic Theory* 51 A primordial matter, the sub-atoms of which were grouped in different numbers to form the chemical atoms of hydrogen and the various simple bodies. **1904** A. J. BALFOUR *Refl. New Th. Matter* 9 There are those.. who think that the elementary atom of the chemist.. is but a connected system of monads or sub-atoms.

Hence **suba'tomic** *a.*

1903 *Edin. Rev.* Oct. 385 Sub-atomic physics. **1905** *Athenæum* 27 May 661 Experiments have been made with sub-atomic particles from one or other of these sources.

subaud (sə'bɔːd), *v. Gram. rare.* [ad. late L. *subaudīre* (tr. Gr. ὑπακούειν), f. *sub-* SUB- 25 + *audīre* to hear.] *trans.* To supply mentally or 'understand' (a word or words) to complete the sense or the construction.

1864 in WEBSTER.

sub'audible, *a.* [SUB- 14, 19.]

1. Not loud enough to be audible. Also *fig.*

1839 LEVER *Harry Lorrequer* vi, The faint sub-audible ejaculation of Father Luke, when he was recovered enough to speak. **1928** E. BLUNDEN *Undertones of War* vii. 109 A good joke: but with this sub-audible meaning.

2. Of a frequency: lower than the lowest audible frequency. Of a sound: too low-pitched to be audible.

1922 *Proc. IRE* X. 253 It may be at sub-audible, or super-audible frequencies. **1978** *Gramophone* June 128/2 Superimposed on this are subaudible tones successively at 4, 5, 6, 8, 10 and 12 Hertz.

subaudition (sʌbɔː'dɪʃən). [ad. L. *subaudītio, -ōnem*, n. of action f. *subaudīre* (see SUBAUD *v.*). Cf. F. *subaudition.*]

†**1.** Hearing a little. *Obs. rare*$^{-0}$.

1658 PHILLIPS.

2. Chiefly *Gram.* The act of mentally supplying something that is not expressed; something that is mentally supplied or understood; implied or understood meaning.

1798 TOOKE *Purley* II. (1805) 17 If it must have a name, it should rather be called *subaudition* than *abstraction. Ibid.* 121 Bond Band Bound—however spelled, and with whatever subaudition applied, is still one and the same word. **1839** *New Monthly Mag.* LVI. 455 There is a sub-audition of so many ifs. **1859** TRENCH *Study of Words* (ed. 9) iii. 87 'Policeman' has no evil subaudition. **1859** THACKERAY *Virgin.* lix, Taking the business-part for granted, and leaving it as it were for subaudition. **1905** *Sat. Rev.* 11 Mar. 311 A glorified subaudition of social compact lay also behind the Tudor despotism.

‖**subauditur** (sʌbɔː'daɪtə(r)). [L. = 'it is understood', 3rd pers. sing. pres. ind. pass. of *subaudīre* to SUBAUD.] = prec. 2. Phr. *in a subauditur*: by implication.

1803 BEDDOES *Hygëia* XI. 95 It will not pass like a *subauditur* in grammar. **1880** *Contemp. Rev.* Feb. 256 Our fiction.. is as much occupied, though in a subauditur, with the skeleton in the cupboard of daily life as [etc.]. **1885** J. MARTINEAU *Types Eth. Th.* I. I. ii. (1886) 313 You cannot tack on the word 'modes' immediately to 'substance' without a subauditur of attribute.

sub'axillary, *a.* (*sb.*) [SUB- 1 b, c.]

1. *Zool.* Situated beneath the axilla; *Ornith.* = AXILLARY. **b.** *sb. pl.* Axillary feathers or wing-coverts (*Cent. Dict.*).

1769 BANCROFT *Guiana* 304 Together with an inflammation and tumefaction of the lymphatic subaxillary glands. **1776** PENNANT *Brit. Zool.* II. 421 The subaxillary feathers [of the eared grebe].

2. *Bot.* Beneath the axil or the angle made by a branch with the stem or a leaf with the branch.

a **1802** E. DARWIN (Webster 1828–32). **1857** A. GRAY *First Less. Bot.* (1866) 232.

†**sub-'bailiff, -baily.** *Obs.* [a. AF. = OF. *sub(b)aillif, -balif* (cf. *southbaily* s.v. SOUTH-[2]) = med.L. *subballīvus*: see SUB- 6 and BAILIFF.] An under-bailiff.

14.. *Customs of Malton* in *Surtees Misc.* (1890) 59 The Balyffes or Subbalyffes of þe said Burgage. **1456** *Cov. Leet Bk.* (1908) 293 To take suerte of theire subbaillif and officers. *Ibid.* 322 The subbaylly and Constable. **1757** in Picton *L'pool Munic. Rev.* (1886) II. 149 The election of sub-bailiffs.

Hence †**sub'bailiwick**, the office or jurisdiction of an under-bailiff.

1452 *Cov. Leet Bk.* (1908) 274 Ye shall not set eny of your subbayliwikkes to eny certeyn ferm.

subbarbes, -ardes, obs. pl. SUBURB.

sub-'basal, *a.* [SUB- 1 b, 11.] Situated near or below the base of a part or organ. Also *sb.*, a sub-basal plate (*Funk's Standard Dict.* 1895).

1848 *Proc. Berw. Nat. Club* II. vi. 276 Nostrils sub-basal. **1870** HOOKER *Stud. Flora* 172 Cornus sanguinea.. lateral nerves subbasal. **1902** *Proc. Zool. Soc.* I. 48 The basal area of these wings irrorated with pearl-grey indicating two vague subbasal bands.

sub-base.

1. [SUB- 3.] **a.** *Archit.* The lowest part of a base which is divided horizontally.

1826 BRITTON *Exeter* 91 A charge of 5*l.* 6*s.* 8*d.* for four columns, with bases, sub-bases, and capitals. **1851** PUGIN *Chancel Screens* 29 [The screen] of S. Mark [Venice] is open above the subase [*sic*].

b. A base placed under the bottom of a machine or other apparatus to raise it higher from the ground.

1904 *Electr. Rev.* 24 Sept. 489 The whole turbine.. being mounted on a sub-base.

2. [SUB- 5 b.] A secondary base.

1903 *Science* 9 Oct. 478 Mr. Peary.. will.. after establishing a sub-base there, force his way northward to the northern shore of Grant Land.

†**subbasmont.** *Sc. Obs.* [a. OF. *soub-, subbassement* (mod.F. *soubassement*), app. f. *soubasse.*] The valance (of a bed).

1539 *Inv. Roy. Wardrobe* (1815) 45 Four grete beddis viz. ane of grene.. with ane subbasmont of grene velvett.

subber(be)s, obs. ff. pl. of SUBURB.

subbing: see SUB *v.*

†**sub-bois.** *Obs.* [AF. *subbois* = Law-Latin *subboscus*, f. *sub-* SUB- 3 + *boscus* wood. (Mod.F. has *sous-bois*; cf. *south-bois* s.v. SOUTH-[2].)] = UNDERWOOD.

1677 N. COX *Gentl. Recreat.* (ed. 2) 15 Of Sub-boys, some for Browse and Food of the Game, and for Shelter and Defence; as Maples, &c. Some for Browse and Defence; as Birch, Sallow, Willow. **1706** [see *south-bois* s.v. SOUTH-[2]]. **1708** *Les Termes de la Ley* 519 *Sylva cædua*.. is also called Subboys or Coppice Wood.

Sub-'boreal, *a.* Also sub-Boreal. [SUB- 18.] Pertaining to or designating a European climatic period that followed the Atlantic and preceded the Subatlantic. Also *absol.*

1876 [see ARCTIC *a.* 3]. **1935** *Discovery* July 198/2 The Atlantic period was followed by another drier, continental phase, the Subboreal, lasting from 2500 till 500 B.C. **1963** H. N. SAVORY in Foster & Alcock *Culture & Environment* iii. 27 Primitive man, at least under sub-Boreal climatic conditions, had a choice of two main routes which gave him relatively easy access to the Glamorgan uplands from the coastal area of settlement. **1975** J. G. EVANS *Environment Early Man Brit. Isles* iv. 84 The sequence is overlain by peat of Atlantic and Sub-boreal age.

subborn, obs. form of SUBORN.

† **subbosco.** *Obs.* Also subosco. [f. SUB- 3 + It. *bosco* wood.] A jocular word for: The hair that grows upon the lower part of the face.

1579 G. HARVEY *Letter-bk.* (Camden) 61 The clippings of your thrishonorable mustachyoes and subboscoes. **1654** GAYTON *Pleas. Notes* II. iii. 42 The boscos, and suboscos (I mean,) the dulapes and the jawy part of the face.

‖ **subbotnik** (suːˈbɒtnɪk). Pl. -niki, (anglicized) -niks. [a. Russ. *subbótnik*, f. *subbóta* Saturday: cf. SABBATH.] In the Soviet Union, the practice or an act of working voluntarily on a Saturday, for the benefit of the collective; = SATURDAYING *vbl. sb.*

The practice originated with workers on the Moscow-Kazan railway in Moscow on 10 May 1919. The meaning given in quot. 1920 is imprecise.

1920 *19th Cent.* Sept. 399 This mutilation was due to an accident which had happened to him while he was a *subbotnik*. *Subbotniki*.. are workmen who work on Saturday (*Subbota*) for the benefit of the Government: there is quite a large *subbotnik* movement in Russia. **1921** L. TROTSKY *Defence of Terrorism* viii. 136 The flourishing, unprecedented in the history of humanity, of labor voluntarism in the form of *subbotniks* (Communist Saturdays). **1959** C. LANDAUER *Europ. Socialism* I. xxvii. 772 The response to the call for *subbotnik* work left much to be desired. **1975** T. P. WHITNEY tr. *Solzhenitsyn's Gulag Archipelago* II. III. i. 14 Soon after that there began the Communist 'subbotniki'—'voluntary Saturdays'. **1979** *Nature* 16 Aug. 532/3 The Vietnamese economy is in such an urgent state that 75% of the proceeds of this year's *Subbotnik*, the Saturday in April when Soviet citizens contribute a day's work for the good of the economy, are to be devoted to Vietnam.

sub-'bottom, *a.* [SUB- 1 e.] Of or pertaining to what is underneath the sea-bed.

1949 *Trans. Amer. Geophysical Union* XXX. 7 The most clear-cut sub-bottom echoes are found in the region which shows least topographic relief. **1968** [see PROFILING *vbl. sb.* 3]. **1975** *Petroleum Rev.* XXIX. 103/1 Sub-bottom profiler.

sub'brachial, *a.* [ad. mod.L. *subbrachiālis*; see SUB- 1 b and BRACHIAL.]

1. *Ichth.* Situated under or near the pectoral fins; (of a fish) having the ventral fins so situated.

1836 *Partington's Brit. Cycl. Nat. Hist.* II. 556/2 *Gadoidæ*. .. A family of soft-finned fishes with sub-brachial fins. **1840** *Cuvier's Anim. Kingd.* 324 *Echeneis*. This genus, like Pleuronectes, might form a distinct family of Sub-brachial Malacopterygii.

2. Under the pectoral muscles.

1898 *Syd. Soc. Lex.*

3. Beneath the brachium (in cerebral anatomy).

1913 DORLAND *Med. Dict.* (ed. 7).

sub'brachian, *a.* and *sb.* *Ichth.* [As prec. + -AN.] **A.** *adj.* = prec. 1. **B.** *sb.* A subbrachiate fish; one of the *Subbrachiati* (formerly *-ata*).

1842 BRANDE *Dict. Sci.*, etc. 1183 *Subbrachians*, the name of the order of Malacopterygious fishes comprising those which have the ventral fins situated either immediately beneath and between, or a little in front or behind the pectoral fins. *a* **1843** in *Encycl. Metrop.* (1845) VII. 293/2 The Fish is designated Jugular or Subbrachian when the ventral fins are immediately beneath the pectoral and connected with their girdle, as the Cod.

So **sub'brachiate** [mod.L. *subbrachiātus*].

1859 MAYNE *Expos. Lex.*, *Subbrachiatus*,.. subbrachiate.

'sub-branch, *sb.* [SUB- 7.] A subdivision of a branch (in any sense).

1859 DARWIN *Orig. Spec.* iv. 124 In our diagram, this is indicated by the broken lines, beneath the capital letters, converging in sub-branches downwards towards a single point. **1875** JEVONS *Money* xx. 258 The National Bank of Ireland has about 114 branches and sub-branches.

So **'sub-branch** *v.*, **'sub-branched** *ppl. a.*

1676 GREW *Anat. Plants* Lect. iv. (1682) 266 Sprigs made up of four chief Branches standing crosswise, and those subbranched. **1857** DARWIN in *Life & Lett.* (1887) II. 125 Species.. always seem to branch and sub-branch like a tree from a common trunk.

ˌsub-briga'dier. [SUB- 6. Cf. F. *sous-brigadier.*] Formerly, an officer in the Horse Guards with the rank of a cornet.

1684 E. CHAMBERLAYNE *Angl. Notitia* (ed. 15) I. 200 Sub-Corporals, or Sub-Brigadiers. **1738** *Gentl. Mag.* VIII. 109/2 Mr Rastall,—Eldest Sub-brigadier of the first Troop of Horse-guards, in room of Capt. Prew decd. **1802** JAMES *Milit. Dict.* **1852** BURN *Naval & Milit. Dict.* (1863), *Sub-brigadier*, (second corporal of cavalry).

sub-'calibre, *a.* Also (*U.S.*) sub-caliber. [SUB- 5 c.] Of a projectile: smaller in calibre than the gun from which it is fired, and discharged from a secondary tube set inside the main barrel. Also, of, pertaining to, or employed in the firing of sub-calibre projectiles.

1876 E. H. KNIGHT *Amer. Mech. Dict.* III. 2434/2 *Subcaliber projectile*,.. a projectile for cannon or small-arms, of smaller diameter than the bore of the gun from which it is fired. **1909** *Teachers' Assembly Herald* 13 Apr. 19/1 Arms. Double-barreled shot-gun, pocket rifles, sub-calibre or auxiliary barrels. **1917** W. S. CHURCHILL in M. Gilbert *Winston S. Churchill* (1977) IV. Compan. I. 131 This after all is only applying the sub-calibre principle to actual service. **1946** T. C. OHART *Elements Ammunition* vii. 179 The subcaliber gun is mounted on a large gun tube for practical purposes. **1967** F. W. HACKLEY et al. *Hist. Mod. U.S. Mil. Small Arms Ammunition* I. II. vii. 93 *Subcaliber cartridges*. These.. were at first called 'ball cartridges for artillery drill cartridges'. They were designed to be fired from subcaliber barrels mounted within.. the main artillery gun tube. **1973** J. QUICK *Dict. Weapons & Mil. Terms* 426 Subcaliber ammunition is adapted for firing in weapons of larger caliber by subcaliber tubes.

ˌsubcarti'laginous, *a.*

1. [SUB- 21 b.] Somewhat, partly, or incompletely cartilaginous.

1541 COPLAND *Guydon's Quest. Cyrurg.* E iv, The sub-cartylagynous [substance of the nose; orig. L. *pars cartilaginosa*] is dowble one outwarde that maketh the typ of the nose and the other inwarde deuydeth the nosethyrlles. **1787** tr. *Linnæus' Fam. Plants* 487 The Fruit is a tongue pedicel'd, slender, subcartilaginous. **1835-6** *Todd's Cycl. Anat.* I. 37/1 Body.. gelatinous, supported by an internal, solid, subcartilaginous body. **1887** W. PHILLIPS *Brit. Discomycetes* 42 Pezizæ.. differs.. from Bulgariæ by not being.. subcartilaginous.

2. [SUB- 1 b.] Lying beneath the cartilage; hypochondrial.

1775 ASH, *Subcartilagenous*, lying under the gristles.

So **subcartila'gineous** *a.* *rare*$^{-0}$. [late L. *subcartilāgineus*] = sense 2 above.

1727 BAILEY (vol. II), *Subcartilagineous*, under the Gristles.

sub-'category. [SUB- 7 e, 9.] A subsidiary category; a subsection of a category; *spec.* in *Maths.* and *Linguistics.*

1909 WEBSTER, Sub-category *sb.* **1931** A. POPE *Introd. Lang. Drawing & Painting* II. iv. 63 It is well to stop in the joyous enthusiasm of thinking out new categories and subcategories. **1949** KOESTLER *Insight & Outlook* iv. 37 First, bisociation is not the same thing as ambiguity; ambiguity is merely a subcategory of it. **1956** R. REDFIELD *Peasant Soc. & Culture* 24 Typologies of Latin-American cultures or of the peasant subcategory of such cultures. **1972** A. G. HOWSON *Handbk. Terms Algebra & Anal.* xix. 98 Hence, *Ab* is a *functor* from G to the *subcategory* of Abelian groups and homomorphisms. **1982** *Sci. Amer.* Mar. 91/1 He divided the galaxies into two main classes, ellipticals and spirals, with several sub-categories.

Hence **sub-'categorize** *v. trans.*, to place in or divide into sub-categories; **ˌsub-categori'zation.**

1965 N. CHOMSKY *Aspects of Theory of Syntax* ii. 95 Rules .. which analyze a symbol in terms of its categorial context, I shall henceforth call *strict subcategorization rules*. **1965** Subcategorize [see *pre-adjectival* s.v. PRE- B. 1 d]. **1971** J. ANDERSON in A. J. Aitken et al. *Edin. Stud. Eng. & Scots* 69, I would like to consider some of the set of phenomena that we could reasonably require a subcategorisation of the modal verb in English to provide an explanation for. **1979** *Dictionaries* I. 14 The initial capitals are subcategorized and provided with lower-case letters and figures.

sub'caudal, *a.* (*sb.*) [SUB- 1 b, 11, 21 d.] Situated under or near the tail; not quite or almost caudal. **b.** *sb.* A subcaudal part; *esp.* a subcaudal plate in a serpent.

1777 PENNANT *Brit. Zool.* IV. 16 The sub-caudal fins. **1841** *Penny Cycl.* XIX. 404/2 All serpents which have abdominal scuta and subcaudal scales. **1877** COUES *Fur-Bearing Anim.* i. 16 In the Badgers.. a particular subcaudal pouch.. which produces a peculiar liquid. **1899** *Proc. Zool. Soc.* 671 The anterior subcaudals are purplish grey.

subce'lestial, *a.* and *sb.* [SUB- 1 a. Cf. OF. *sousceleste.*] **A.** *adj.* Situated or existing beneath or below the heavens; *rare* in literal sense; chiefly *transf.* Terrestrial, mundane, sublunary.

1561 EDEN *Arte Nauig.* I. v. 7 b, The Emperial heauen, conteyneth three.. *Hierarchias*,.. the fyrste.. called super-celestiall... The second is called Celestiall... The thyrde called Subcelestiall, conteyneth Virtutes, Archangels and Angels. **1627** HAKEWILL *Apol.* (1630) 45 All subcelestiall bodies.. consist of matter and forme. **1661** GLANVILL *Van. Dogm.* 4 The most refined glories of subcœlestial excellencies are but more faint resemblances of these. **1678** CUDWORTH *Intell. Syst.* I. iv. §32. 497 The *Dii Consentes*, were understood by Apuleius neither to be Celestial nor Sub-celestial Bodies, but a certain higher Nature perceptible only to our Minds. **1741-70** ELIZ. CARTER *Lett.* (1808) 35 Whether Mrs. Montagu may not be delighting herself with a tour through the coal mines, and have lost all remembrance of her subcelestial friends. **1911** WEBSTER, *Subcelestial*,.. *Astron.*, exactly beneath the zenith.

B. *sb.* A subcelestial being.

1652 BENLOWES *Theoph.* Pref., Sub-cœlestials, or Sublunaries have their Assignment in the lowest Portion of the Universe. **1708** H. DODWELL *Expl. Dial. Justin* 61 Speaking of the Difference between the Cœlestials and Subcœlestials, he makes their Life to be a Death to us, and our Life to be a Death to them.

† **sub'cellarer.** *Obs.* [f. SUB- 6 + CELLARER, after med.L. *subcell(er)ārius*, or obs.F. *soubscellerier*. Cf. ME. *sowcelerere* s.v. SOUS-, *sowthselerer* s.v. SOUTH-².] An under-cellarer in a convent.

c **1475** *Pict. Voc.* in Wr.-Wülcker 780/23 *Hic subselarius*, a subselerer. *c* **1702** in *Cath. Rec. Soc. Publ.* IX. 374 She was employed.. as subcellerere; Mrs of Novices, Conseler, and ward-robe.

sub'central, *a.*

1. [SUB- 11, 21 d.] Nearly or not quite central; near or close to the centre.

1822 J. PARKINSON *Outl. Oryctol.* 124 The mouth beneath, subcentral. **1836** *Penny Cycl.* V. 313/2 Fissure of adhesion in the lower valve subcentral. **1870** HOOKER *Stud. Flora* 461 Asplenium Trichomanes.. midrib subcentral.

2. [SUB- 1 a.] Being under the centre.

1828-32 in WEBSTER.

3. [SUB- 1 b.] *Anat.* Beneath the central sulcus of the brain; beneath the centrum of a vertebra.

1882 *Quain's Elem. Anat.* (ed. 9) I. 23 The precentral or subcentral parts or hypapophyses. **1890** BILLINGS *Nat. Med. Dict.*, *Subcentral arch*, hæmal arch. **1901** *Amer. Anthropologist* (N.S.) III. 461 The subcentral sulci of Eberstaller.

Hence **sub'centrally** *adv.*, under or near the centre or centrum. Also **sub'centrical** *a.* = 1 above.

1824 DU BOIS *Lamarck's Arrangem.* 302 The interior [of the Orthocera] is divided into many cells, transversely separated by septa, which are traversed by a subcentrical syphon. **1870** ROLLESTON *Anim. Life* 12 Several of the anterior.. vertebræ, have low hypapophysial ridges developed sub-centrally. **1872** H. A. NICHOLSON *Palæont.* 173 A pair of large compound eyes placed marginally or subcentrally.

sub'ception. *Psychol.* A blend of *subliminal perception* (see quot. 1949).

1949 MCLEARY & LAZARUS in *Jrnl. Personality* XVIII. 171 An experiment which confirms the notion that subjects give discriminatory galvanic skin responses to visual stimuli presented at tachistoscopic speeds too brief for correct verbal report. The implied perceptual process is termed by the authors *subception* (verb form—to *subceive*). *Ibid.* 179 It is suggested that the level of perceptual activity indicated by this finding be called *subception*. **1958** *New Biol.* XXVII. 29 The subject remains unaware not only of the stimulus but also of the fact that his 'guesses' are being biased. For this effect the word 'subception' has been coined. **1959** *Manch. Guardian* 2 July 4/6 The techniques of 'subception' would be of no value to advertising agents... Subception effects which could be obtained under laboratory conditions would be masked.. in real life. **1977** R. O. VIITAMÄKI in von Fieandt & Moustgaard *Perceptual World* xxi. 557 The subception effect has implications not only for perceptual theory but.. also.. in the fields of personality and clinical psychology.

† **sub'cernicle.** *Obs. rare.* [ad. late L. *subcerniculum*: see SUB- 5 b and CERNICLE.] ? A small sieve.

1657 TOMLINSON *Renou's Disp.* 484 Sieves made of Horses hairs.. called seraceous subcirnicles.

subcesive, obs. variant of SUBSECIVE.

'sub'chanter. [f. SUB- 6 + CHANTER. Cf. OF. *sou(b)chantre*, F. *sous-chantre.*] A precentor's deputy, succentor; now, a vicar choral or lay-clerk of a cathedral, who assists in chanting the litany.

The title is retained in York and Lichfield cathedrals.

1515 in W. Fraser *Sutherland Bk.* (1892) III. 60 Schir William Nory, subchantour of Murray. **1546** *Yks. Chantry Surv.* (Surtees) II. 438 Denis Heckylton, subchaunter there. *a* **1578** LINDESAY (Pitscottie) *Chron. Scot.* I. 200 The ..chanter and subchanter witht all kynd of wther officeis pertaining to ane colledge. **1637** GILLESPIE *Eng. Pop. Cerem.* III. viii. 161 Deanes, Vice-Deans,.. Sub-deacons,.. Chantours, Sub-chantours. **1703** M. MARTIN *Descr. W. Isl. Scot.* 362 A Sub-Chanter, who was bound to play on the Organs each Lords Day, and Festivals. **1825** (*title*) Expository Discourses, by the late Rev. Wm. Richardson, Subchanter of York Cathedral. **1876** J. GRANT *Burgh Sch. Scot.* I. 19 There are four principal persons in that cathedral [*sc.* Sarum], namely, the dean, chanter, chancellor, treasurer, besides a subdean and subchanter. **1898** *Daily News* 1 Apr. 7/6 Sub-chanter and priest vicar of Lichfield Cathedral.

transf. *a* **1618** J. DAVIES *Wittes Pilgr.* (1878) 52/2 That Holy, Holy, Holy, which They crie That are Sub-chaunters of Heau'ns Hermony.

Hence † **sub'chantership**, † **sub'chantress.**

14.. *Rule Syon Monast.* xiii. in *Collectanea Topogr.* III. (1836) 31 The chauntres and sub-chauntresses, the sexteyne and undersexteyne. **1546** *Yks. Chantry Surv.* (Surtees) II. 439 For his subchauntership, ijs.

'subcharge. [SUB- 5 b, c.]

† **1.** A second dish or course. Also *fig.* *Sc. Obs.*

c **1480** HENRYSON *Mor. Fab.* II. (*Town & C. Mouse*) xviii, Till eik thair cheir ane subcharge furth scho brocht, Ane plait of grottis [etc.]. *Ibid.* xxvii, The subcharge of thy seruice is bot sair. **1513** DOUGLAS *Æneid* XIII. ix. 118 All ar expert, eftir new mariage, On the first nycht quhat suld be the subcharge.

2. Subordinate charge.

1900 *Century Mag.* Feb. 503/2, I have seen M. Clémenceau as storm-fiend-in-chief, and M. Clovis Hugues in sub-charge of the Cave of the Winds.

sub-cheese (sʌbˈtʃiːz). *Mil. slang* (orig. *Anglo-Indian*). Also sub-cheeze, -chiz. [ad. Hind. *sab* all + *chiz* thing (see CHEESE sb.[2]).] The lot; everything; all that there is. Also in phr. *the whole sub-cheese*.

[**1864** HOTTEN *Slang Dict.* 98 The expression *cheese* may be found in the Gipsy vocabulary, and in the Hindostanee and Persian languages. In the last *chiz* means a thing. *Ibid.* 250 *Sub*, all. *Anglo-Indian.*] **1874** E. LEAR *Jrnl.* 4 May (1953) vii. 132 Then came the long and stumbling descent until the last village, where were all the coolies, and sub-cheese (everything). **1895** KIPLING *Day's Work* (1898) 181 She's as clever as a man... Settled the whole *subchiz* (outfit) in three hours. **1919** W. H. DOWNING *Digger Dialects* 60 Subcheese, the lot. **1962** M. MALGONKAR *Combat of Shadows* xxiv. 184 And the cricket pavilion, and the game cottage, the whole subcheeze. **1971** B. W. ALDISS *Soldier Erect* 251 Of course we were lugging our ammo, machine-guns, mortars, and the whole *subcheeze* with us.

sub'chela. [f. SUB- 23 + CHELA[1].] A form of chela characteristic of certain crustaceans, in which the terminal segment is bent back upon the next.

sub'chelate, *a.* **a.** [SUB- 21 c.] Imperfectly chelate. **b.** [f. prec.] Having a subchela.

1852 DANA *Crust.* II. 802 Four anterior legs subchelate. **1877** HUXLEY *Anat. Inv. Anim.* vi. 272 *Corycæus* has.. subchelate antennæ, and a rudimentary abdomen. **1893** STEBBING *Crust.* 45 The limb is.. said to be subchelate, the claw being in that case partial.

sub'cheliform, *a.* [SUB- 21 c.] = prec. a.

1835-6 *Todd's Cycl. Anat.* I. 762/1 In the first instance these instruments are denominated subcheliform claws, in the second chelæ simply, or cheliform claws. **1856** W. CLARKE *Van der Hoeven's Zool.* I. 649 First and second pairs of feet terminated by a large moveable hook, sub-cheliform.

subchet, ? error for SUBCHARGE.

1500-20 DUNBAR *Poems* lxvii. 19 Of quhais subchettis [*v.r.* surcharge] sour is the sals.

†**subcine'ritious,** *a. Obs.* [f. L. *subcinerīcius*, var. *succinerīcius*: see SUB- and CINERITIOUS.]

1. [SUB- 1 a.] Baked under ashes. *rare*⁻⁰.

1656 BLOUNT *Glossogr.*

2. [SUB- 21 a.] Somewhat ash-coloured, greyish. Hence **subcine'ritiously** *adv.*

1657 TOMLINSON *Renou's Disp.* 353 Subcineritiously virid. *Ibid.* 672 Balm flows from a.. Tree.. of a subcineritious colour. **1670** H. STUBBE *Plus Ultra* 130 A subcineritious or dirty-coloured putrilage.

‖**sub'cingulum.** [med.L.; see SUB- 3.] A broad belt or girdle worn beneath another.

1824 MEYRICK *Ant. Armour* Gloss., *Subcingulum*, when one belt was worn below another it was thus called. **1849** ROCK *Ch. Fathers* I. v. 492 Besides the girdle, our Anglo-Saxon bishops were girt with the sub-cingulum or broad belt.

subcisive, obs. variant of SUBSECIVE.

†**subcitrine,** *a. Obs.* [ad. mod.L. *subcitrīnus*: see SUB- 21 a and CITRINE *a.*] Of a somewhat yellow or greenish-yellow colour.

c **1530** *Judic. Urines* I. iii. 6 b, Theyr vryne is faynt of colour, as subcitrine or ȝelowysshe. **1572** J. JONES *Bathes Ayde* III. 26 b, Chaffie, or subcitrine coloure. **1637** BRIAN *Pisse-prophet* (1679) 85 Taking the Urinal out of the case, (perceiving it to be of a subcitrine or pale colour). **1702** *Phil. Trans.* XXIII. 1281 Of subcitrin colour.

subclass ('sʌbklɑːs, -æ-). [SUB- 7 b. Cf. F. *sous-classe.*] A subdivision of a class; *Nat. Hist.* a group of orders ranking next to a class.

1819 G. SAMOUELLE *Entomol. Compend.* 77 Dr. Leach considered the Malacostraca and Entomostraca as sub-classes. **1857** A. GRAY *First Less. Bot.* (1866) 177 Series, Class, Subclass, Order, or Family, Suborder, Tribe, Sub-tribe, Genus, Subgenus or Section, Species, Variety. **1880** GÜNTHER *Fishes* 65 The lowermost sub-class of fishes, which comprises one form only, the Lancelet. **1882** VINES tr. *Sachs' Bot.* 161 Dividing this class of structures into two sub-classes, hairs and emergences.

attrib. **1869** DK. ARGYLE *Primeval Man* II. 62 One of Cuvier's sub-class divisions.

So **'subclass** *v. trans.*, to place in a subclass.

1894-5 *16th Ann. Rep. Bur. Amer. Ethnol.* 72 The motive must be subclassed as sortilegic.

'sub-clause. [SUB- 5 c, 9.]

1. *Law.* A subsidiary section of a clause. Also *transf.*

1927 *Tax Cases* (1928) XI. x. 801 Notwithstanding anything in sub-clause (7) of Clause 20A contained the amounts credited to members under this clause shall not be deemed to be amounts withdrawn from Reserve Fund for the purposes of that sub-clause. **1946** *All England Law Reports* II. 577 In that sub-clause it is provided that the wife is to support, maintain and educate the child. **1959** I. & P. OPIE *Lore & Lang. Schoolch.* viii. 136 There are also some sub-clauses in the code [of oral legislation concerning possession]. **1974** *Williams' Law Wills* (ed. 4) v. 1067 My trustees shall hold such dwelling.. upon trust to sell the same with full power (subject to the provisions of sub-clause (e) of this clause) to postpone the sale.

2. *Gram.* A clause that is subordinate to a main clause.

1934 PRIEBSCH & COLLINSON *German Lang.* vi. 311 *So dass* (with *so* drawn out of the main clause into the sub-clause). **1957** R. W. ZANDVOORT *Handbk. Eng. Gram.* I. vi. 86 The subjunctive may be used in nominal sub-clauses depending on a main clause expressing will or wish. **1966** *English Studies* XLVII. 261 The independent use of subclauses in expressive speech is not restricted to *that*-clauses. **1983** *Times* 5 Oct. 32/7 He would launch into the last paragraph only to find that he had put in one sub clause too many.

‖**sub'clavia.** *Anat.* [mod.L. *subclāvia* (sc. *artēria* artery), fem. of *subclāvius* (see below).] The subclavian artery.

1733 tr. *Winslow's Anat.* (1756) II. 10 The Trachealis.. runs up from the Subclavia, in a winding Course. **1771** *Encycl. Brit.* I. 227/1 The Carotid arteries.. arise near each other,.. the left immediately, the right most commonly from the trunk of the subclavia on the same side.

†**sub'clavial,** *a.* and *sb. Anat. Obs.* [ad. mod.L. *subclāviālis*, f. SUBCLAVIUS.] = next.

1666 J. SMITH *Old Age* (1676) 236 The subclavial branch of the *Vena Cava*. **1670** *Phil. Trans.* V. 2078 Part of the Chyle is by the *Ductus Thoracicus* conveyed into the Sub-clavials, and so into the Cistern of the Breasts. **1674** *Ibid.* IX. 115 Whether through his *ductus* all the Chyle passeth to the subclavial vessel.

subclavian (sʌb'kleɪvɪən), *a.* and *sb. Anat.* [f. mod.L. *subclāvi-us* (see below) + -AN. F. has *sousclavier* (from 16th c.).] **A.** *adj.*

1. Lying or extending under the clavicle.

subclavian artery, the principal artery of the root of the neck, being the main trunk of the arterial system of the upper extremity. ***subclavian muscle*** = SUBCLAVIUS. ***subclavian vein***, the continuation of the axillary vein from the first rib till it joins the internal jugular vein.

1681 tr. *Willis' Rem. Med. Wks.* Vocab., Subclavian vessels; the vessels that belong to the little ribs of the breast. **1688** HOLME *Armoury* II. xvii. 423/1 The right Subclavian Arterie. **1702** *Phil. Trans.* XXIII. 1188 That part of the Axillary-Arteries, by some called the Subclavian Arteries. **1705** *Ibid.* XXV. 2010, I found the same Tumor comprehending the intercostals, Deltoides, Subclavian, and Subscapulary Muscles. **1770** FORDYCE in *Monthly Rev.* 310 The thoracic duct.. commonly terminates in the left sub-clavian vein. **1808** BARCLAY *Musc. Motions* 239 The difference of manner in which the carotid and subclavian arteries, on the two sides, arise from the aorta. **1834** J. FORBES *Laennec's Dis. Chest* (ed. 4) 19 Subclavian region. This includes merely the portion of the chest covered by the clavicle. **1887** CONAN DOYLE *Study in Scarlet* I. i, I was struck on the shoulder by a Jezail bullet, which shattered the bone and grazed the subclavian artery.

b. Pertaining to the subclavian artery, vein, or muscle, as ***subclavian groove***, etc. (see quots.).

1646 SIR T. BROWNE *Pseud. Ep.* IV. iv. 188 The Liver, which though it be seated on the right side, yet by the sub-clavian division doth equidistantly communicate its activity unto either arme. **1870** ROLLESTON *Anim. Life* 15 The right arteria innominata is seen to divide into its common carotid and subclavian trunks. **1890** BILLINGS *Nat. Med. Dict.*, *Subclavian glands*, lymphatic glands under the arch of the right subclavian artery. *Subclavian groove*, 1. That in which the subclavian artery lies on upper surface of first rib. 2. That into which the subclavius muscle is inserted on under surface of clavicle.

2. [As if f. L. *sub* under + *clāvis* key.] (See quot.) *rare*⁻⁰.

1656 BLOUNT *Glossogr.*, *Subclavian*, pertaining to that which is under lock and key.

B. *sb.* A subclavian vessel, nerve, or muscle.

1719 QUINCY *Lex. Physico-Med.* (1722) 241 The Vein [*Vena Pneumonica*] opens into the Subclavian. **1771** *Encycl. Brit.* I. 226/2 The subclavian on each side terminates at the upper edge of the first rib. **1888** ROLLESTON & JACKSON *Anim. Life* 365 The sub-clavians and carotids arise from the aortic arch in various ways.

subcla'vicular, *a. Anat.* and *Surg.* [ad. mod.L. *subclāviculāris*: see SUB- 1 b and CLAVICULAR.] Situated, occurring, or performed below or beneath the clavicle.

1656 BLOUNT *Glossogr.* s.v. *Vein*, *Subclavicular vein*, one of the two maine ascendant branches of the hollow veine, divided into six parts. **1853** MARKHAM *Skoda's Auscult.* 80 Weak bronchophony heard in the interscapular and sub-clavicular regions. **1872** BRYANT *Pract. Surg.* 218 The subclavicular operation. **1878** WALSHAM *Handbk. Surg. Pathol.* 151 Dislocation of the humerus... The head of the bone may be displaced.. Forwards and inwards beneath the clavicle (subclavicular).

subclavio- (sʌb'kleɪvɪəʊ), used as combining form of next, as in **sub,clavio-'axillary**, pertaining to the subclavian and axillary arteries.

1815 J. GORDON *Syst. Hum. Anat.* I. 69 The Subclavio-Jugular Veins. **1880** BARWELL *Aneurism* 38 A subclavio-axillary aneurism.

‖**subclavius** (sʌb'kleɪvɪəs). *Anat.* [mod.L. *subclāvius* (sc. *musculus*), f. *sub-* SUB- 1 b + *clāvis* key (cf. CLAVICLE[1] etym.).] In full ***subclavius muscle***: A small muscle extending from the first rib to the clavicle.

1704 J. HARRIS *Lex. Techn.* I. *Subclavius*, is a Muscle of the Thorax. **1733** tr. *Winslow's Anat.* (1756) I. 288 The Subclavius.. is a proper Depressor of the Clavicula. **1831** KNOX *Cloquet's Anat.* 31 Its anterior extremity [*sc.* of the first rib].. sometimes affords insertion above to the sub-clavius muscle. **1835-6** *Todd's Cycl. Anat.* I. 360/1 The thickened edge of the fascia which covers the subclavius.

sub'climax. *Ecol.* [f. SUB- 23 + CLIMAX 4 b.] A point in an ecological succession at which a plant community is prevented by climatic or other factors from reaching its natural climax.

1916 F. E. CLEMENTS *Plant Succession* vi. 107 Such apparent climaxes are always subordinate to the normal developmental or climatic climax, and may accordingly be distinguished as subclimaxes. **1926** TANSLEY & CHIPP *Aims & Methods in Study of Vegetation* ii. 9 Such an edaphic climax may be a climatic sub-climax. **1941** J. S. HUXLEY *Uniqueness of Man* iii. 104 If grassland is not the natural climax of plant life, but is only a 'sub-climax',.. then it will stand very heavy grazing. **1952** *Jrnl. Ecol.* XL. 105 It appears.. that this is in reality a grazing sub-climax vegetation. **1979** *Nature* 11 Oct. 425/2 Weedy herbs support fewer fungal parasites than do climax and subclimax herbs in the US.

subco'llector. [SUB- 6. OF. *soub(s)collecteur*, Sp. *subcolector.*] A deputy or assistant collector.

1558-9 *Act 1 Eliz.* c. 21 §22 No.. Commissioner, shalbe named or assigned to any Collector or Subcollector or presentor of the said Subsidie. **1687** *Lond. Gaz.* No. 2306/4 The Sub-Collector of the Tenths of the said Diocess due to His Majesty. **1758** J. BLAKE *Mar. Syst.* 29 The collector, or sub-collector, of the customs. **1837** *Lett. fr. Madras* (1843) 93 A Mr. Macdonald, the sub-collector. **1902** GAIRDNER *Engl. Ch. 16th c.* i. 12 Polydore Vergil was a native of Urbino, sent to England by Alexander VI. as sub-collector to Adrian.

subco'mmission. [Cf. F. *sous-commission.*]

1. [SUB- 5 c.] An under-commission.

1629 *Reg. Privy Council Scot.* Ser. II. III. 21 The commissioners.. have ordained sub-commissiouns to be granted to some selected persouns. **1648** HEYLIN *Relat. & Observ.* I. 119 Skippon.. authorized the said Commissioned Apprentices to grant Sub-commissions again to other Apprentices under them.

2. [SUB- 7 b.] A division of a commission.

1882 *Macm. Mag.* XLVI. 253 The President.. and the Minister.. name commissions, these name sub-commissions, and so we go on from day to day.

subco'mmissioner. [SUB- 6.] An assistant or subordinate commissioner.

1629 *Sc. Acts Chas. I* (1870) V. 199/2 The commissioners and subcommissioners alreadie appointed. **1696** *Lond. Gaz.* No. 3183/3 The Association of the Sub-Commissioners for Prizes, of the Port of Dover and its Districts. **1697** *View Penal Laws* 14 Offences against this Act.. to be determined by the Chief Commissioners.. then by the Subcommissioners. **1846** McCULLOCH *Acc. Brit. Empire* (1854) II. 289 The valuation was devolved on commissioners and sub-commissioners.

subco'mmit, *v. rare.* [SUB- 8.]

1. *trans.* To commit (something entrusted to one) to another.

1818 RANKEN *Hist. France* V. v. ii. 286 He subcommitted the publication of this dispensation.. to the friars of the Dominican order.

2. To refer to a sub-committee.

172. WODROW *Corr.* (1843) II. 582 At night the Instructions met, and we had a fast before us, which was sub-committed.

'subcommittee. Formerly **subco'mmittee.** [SUB- 7 b.] A committee formed from and acting under a main committee; a part of a committee appointed for special purposes.

1610 in *Crt. & Times Jas. I* (1848) I. 113 This day a sub-committee is appointed to consider [etc.]. **1621** ELSING *Debates Ho. Lords* (Camden) 98 Referred to the Sub-comittees of the priviledges. **1666** PEPYS *Diary* 5 Oct., The Sub-committee have made their report to the Grand Committee. **1790** BURKE *Fr. Rev.* 4 By acting as a sort of sub-committee in England for extending the principles of the National Assembly. **1823** JEFFERSON *Writ.* (1830) IV. 376 The committee of five met; no such thing as a sub-committee was proposed. **1898** 'MERRIMAN' *Roden's Corner* vii. 69 The meeting of the lady committees of the bazaar and ball sub-committees.

subconscious (sʌb'kɒnʃəs), *a.* and *sb.* [SUB- 19.]

A. *adj.* **1.** *Psychol.* **a.** Partially or imperfectly conscious; belonging to a class of phenomena resembling those of consciousness but not clearly perceived or recognized. **b.** Pertaining to the subconscious; belonging to that portion of the mental field the processes of which are outside the range of attention.

1832-4 DE QUINCEY *Cæsars* Wks. 1862 IX. 137 *note*, The Emperor Hadrian had taken one solitary step.. in the elevation of human nature; and not.. without some sub-conscious influence received directly or indirectly from Christianity. *a* **1841** —— *Pope* Wks. 1858 IX. 42 How much grander and more faithful to that great theme [Christianity] were the subconscious perceptions of his heart than the explicit commentaries of his understanding. **1886** MYERS *Phantasms of Living* II. 285 There exist sub-conscious and unconscious operations of many kinds; both organic, as secretion, circulation, &c.,.. and also mental, as the recall of names, the development of ideas, &c. **1886** *Encycl. Brit.* XX. 48/1 Subconscious presentations may tell on conscious life.. although lacking either the differences of intensity or the individual distinctness requisite to make them definite features. **1899** *Allbutt's Syst. Med.* VIII. 151 To cultivate the highest powers of the body and mind is to strengthen self-control and that subconscious inhibition which govern us in our habits of life.

c. *transf.*

1893 *Min. 8th Nat. Council Congr. Ch. U.S.* 54 This spirit that has always existed in the sub-conscious life of the Church is now rising into the light of consciousness. **1899** *Daily News* 7 Jan. 6/4 A sketch of himself.. has a subconscious humour one would not have suspected.

2. Partly or imperfectly aware.

1864 HAWTHORNE *Septimius* (1883) 352 He was subconscious that he was trying a bold experiment. **1879** LEWES *Probl. Life & Mind* Ser. III. I. vii. 104 While obeying the prevailing impulse we are conscious and sub-conscious of simultaneous solicitations in different directions.

B. *absol.* as *sb. Psychol.* The part of the mind that is not fully conscious but is able to influence actions, etc.

1886 *Encycl. Brit.* XX. 48/1 We cannot fix the limit at which the subconscious becomes the absolutely unconscious. **1890** J. M. BALDWIN *Handbk. Psychol.* (ed. 2) iv. 57 This whole field in its relation to consciousness has been well called the sub-conscious, from the fact that images formerly in consciousness have now fallen below the threshold, but may rise again..when the stimulation of the centres is sufficient. **1914** [see CO-CONSCIOUS *a.* and *sb.*]. **1928** H. G. & C. F. BAYNES tr. *Jung's Two Essays Anal. Psychol.* v. 67 The personal unconscious, of which I also speak as the 'subconscious', in contrast to the absolute or collective unconscious, contains forgotten memories, suppressed..painful ideas..apperceptions sometimes described as below the threshold (subliminal). **1934** J. M. CAIN *Postman always rings Twice* xvi. 187 There's a guy in No. 7 that murdered his brother, and says he didn't really do it, his subconscious did it. **1957** V. PACKARD *Hidden Persuaders* iii. 27 With all this interest in manipulating the customer's subconscious, the old slogan 'let the buyer beware' began taking on a new and more profound meaning. **1977** B. PYM *Quartet in Autumn* i. 6 Something of this may have been in Norman's subconscious as he turned the pages of his newspaper.

sub'consciously, *adv.* [f. prec. + -LY².] In a subconscious manner; with imperfect or feeble consciousness; in the region of subconsciousness.

1823 DE QUINCEY *Language* Wks. 1858 IX. 78 Whilst the finest models of style exist, and sub-consciously operate effectively as sources of delight, the conscious valuation of style is least perfectly developed. **1895** *Times* 17 Oct. 3/2 You do not feel as if you had had enough, but you are sub-consciously aware of having had too many. **1903** MYERS *Hum. Pers.* I. 378 Some of the associative consequents of the writing on the other [fragment of stone] were sub-consciously involved.

sub'consciousness. [f. as prec. + -NESS.]

1. Partial or imperfect consciousness; a state of consciousness in which perception is indistinct; that part of the mental field which is on the border of consciousness.

1874 G. H. LEWES *Probl. Life & Mind* (Ser. 1) I. 141 Neural processes which formerly were accompanied by Consciousness sink into Sub-Consciousness. **1879** *Ibid.* (Ser. III.) I. v. 88 There all the processes are blended, integrated, and in certain relative intensities become states of Consciousness; in lesser intensities, states of Subconsciousness. **1886** *Encycl. Brit.* XX. 47 The hypothesis of unconscious mental modifications, as it has been unfortunately termed,—the hypothesis of subconsciousness, as we may style it to avoid this contradiction in terms. **1904** *Brit. Med. Jrnl.* 17 Sept. 692 He probably projects into the mental life of others what is present in his own subconsciousness.

2. A condition of imperfectly realizing or being aware *of* something.

1881 *Nation* (N.Y.) XXXII. 290 Brady's consciousness or subconsciousness of the shortness and uncertainty of his own tenure. **1896** F. M. CRAWFORD *Corleone* xxxiii, He drove away the sub-consciousness that the thing was not yet done.

sub-'constable. Now *Hist.* [SUB- 6.] An under-constable, *esp.* in the Royal Irish Constabulary (see quots. 1814, 1883).

1512 *Act 4 Hen. VIII*, c. 19 §6 Preceptes to the Constables Hedbouroghes Thirdbouroghes Subconstables. **1558–9** *Act 1 Eliz.* c. 21 §16. **1814** *Act 54 Geo. III*, c. 131 §6 To appoint, for the Aid and Support of any such Chief Magistrates,..a Clerk, and also a Chief Constable, and any Number of Sub Constables, not exceeding Fifty in the whole. **1839** *Penny Cycl.* XIII. 25/2 The police..in 1836, consisted of..155 chief constables of the first and 59 of the second class; 1232 constables; 6233 subconstables. **1883** *Act 46 Vict.* c. 14 §12 After the first day of October one thousand eight hundred and eighty-three the sub-inspectors, constables, acting constables, and sub-constables of the Royal Irish Constabulary, shall respectively be styled district inspectors, sergeants, acting sergeants, and constables. **1886** BROPHY *Sk. R.I.C.* i. 7 Sub-Constable D—— was a scion of a family that were ruined chiefly by horse-racing. **1907** *Westm. Gaz.* 4 July 1/2 Sir Thomas Echlin..served..as sub-constable and constable in the ranks of the Royal Irish Constabulary.

'sub,continent. (Now also with main stress on second syllable.) [SUB- 5 b.] A land mass of great extent, but smaller than those generally called continents; a large section of a continent having a certain geographical or political independence; *spec.* applied formerly to South Africa, and more recently to India, Pakistan, Bangladesh, and Sri Lanka.

1863 HUXLEY *Man's Place Nat.* III. 154 From central Asia eastward to the Pacific islands and subcontinents on the one hand, and to America on the other. **1901** *Scotsman* 16 Oct. 11/1 In South Africa..the inhabitants of the sub-continent. **1911** *United Empire* June 389 Rhodesia might have seemed the Never-never-land of the sub-continent, a Cinderella among South African States. **1947** J. STEVENSON-HAMILTON *Wild Life S. Afr.* xiii. 94 The springbuck..is the only representative of the gazelle group, which is found in the sub-continent. **1954** B. & R. NORTH tr. *M. Duverger's Pol. Parties* II. i. 210 In Latin America, a general tendency towards the two-party system is perceptible, though it is generally..deformed by the revolutions, *coups d'état*, gerrymandering..characteristic of..that sub-continent. **1971** R. RUSSELL in *Aziz Ahmad's Shore & Wave* 7 The novel in Urdu, as in all the modern languages of the South Asian sub-continent, is of very recent growth. **1972** *Times of India* 28 Nov. 11/4 Mr. Azad outlined his Government's views on the political problems of the sub-continent. **1978** L. HEREN *Growing up on The Times* v. 175 Many Indians refused to accept the partition of the sub-continent.

,subconti'nental, *a.*

1. [SUB- 1 a.] Situated or occurring under a continent.

1900 SOLLAS in *Nature* LXII. 487/1 The sub-continental excess of temperature.

2. [SUB- 19.] Partly continental.

1897 *Pop. Sci. Monthly* L. 329 The occurrence of what are stated to be subcontinental or terrigenous deposits.

3. [SUB- 5 b.] Of or pertaining to a subcontinent, *spec.* the Indian subcontinent (see prec.).

1973 *Guardian* 5 Mar. 5/2 'I've been a Pakistani for 24 years,' she says, though her accent remains softly Irish and not at all subcontinental. **1975** R. JACKSON *S. Asian Crisis* iii. 66 The situation in East Pakistan had been represented..as yet another round in the perennial quarrel between the two sub-continental states.

†**subcon'tinuative,** *a. Gram. Obs.* [ad. late L. *subcontinuātīv-us* (in *conjunctiōnes subcontinuātīvæ*): see SUB- 8 and CONTINUATIVE. Cf. Gr. παρασυναπτικός applied to conjunctions used to introduce clauses implying a fact.] (See quots.)

1530 PALSGR. 148 Some [conjunctions] be subcontinuatyves whiche serve to contynue a mater whan..begon, or to begyn a mater at the first, as *povr autânt..si..combien..encore. Ibid.*, I have..called one of the vii modes..the subjunctyve mode or subcontinuatyve mode. **1798** TOOKE *Purley* (ed. 2) I. vii. 111 We shall get rid of that farrago of useless distinctions into *Conjunctive, Adjunctive, Disjunctive, Subdisjunctive,..Continuative, Subcontinuative.*

sub-con'tinued, *a. Med.* [SUB- 21 g.] Of a fever: Almost continuous, remittent.

1836 J. M. GULLY *Magendie's Formul.* (ed. 2) 60 Twenty-seven sub-continued, and eight remittent fevers, were cured. **1898** P. MANSON *Trop. Diseases* xxxvi. 543 Fever of an irregular, intermitting, or even of a sub-continued type.

So **sub-con'tinual** *a.*

1890 BILLINGS *Nat. Med. Dict.*, *Subcontinual fever*, malarial fever.

sub'contract, *sb.* [SUB- 9.] A contract, or one of several contracts, for carrying out a previous contract or a part of it.

1817 SELWYN *Law Nisi Prius* (ed. 4) IV. 1037 If the defendant was not liable, the plaintiff might be obliged to sue all the parties who had subcontracts before he could obtain redress. **1885** *Law Rep. 15 Q.B. Div.* 87 The contract with the plaintiff was to enable him to fulfil a sub-contract with his customer.

attrib. **1887** *Pall Mall Gaz.* 25 Nov. 11 Making it a condition of all Government clothing contracts that they must not be worked out under the sweating or sub-contract system.

subcon'tract, *v.* [SUB- 9.]

†**1.** *pass.* To be betrothed for the second time.

1605 SHAKS. *Lear* v. iii. 86 'Tis she is sub-contracted to this Lord.

2. *intr.* To make a subcontract.

1842 BURN *Naval & Milit. Dict.* (1863) s.v. *Sous, Sous-traiter*, to sub-contract. **1889** *Lancet* 9 Mar. 498 He..hands over what he cannot do himself to others with whom he subcontracts.

3. *trans.* To make a subcontract for. Formerly, of the sub-contractor; now often with contractor or work as subj. Also with *out*.

1898 *Westm. Gaz.* 26 Aug. 7/2 As to the food arrangements, they were not worked from London, but sub-contracted by people in the locality. **1939** *Daily Tel.* 18 Dec. 12/8 Outworkers required to sub-contract large and regular orders of light clothing. **1955** *Times* 19 Aug. 10/1 Hall Telephone will..be able to employ its factories to greater advantage by undertaking the manufacture of the James Gordon products, which hitherto have been sub-contracted by that company. **1972** *Daily Tel.* 20 Mar. 18/3 Most of the engineering parts are sub-contracted out. **1981** *Brit. Med. Jrnl.* 4 July 51/2 He worked on a commission of 15% on surgery sales, the middleman (the general practitioner) had nothing to do with it, and the surgical operation was subcontracted out.

Hence **subcon'tracted** *ppl. a.*, **subcon'tracting** *vbl. sb.*; **sub-con'tractor**, one who enters into a subcontract.

1842 *Civil Engin. & Arch. Jrnl.* V. 85/2 The sub-contractor..had to..lay down the temporary road. **1900** *Westm. Gaz.* 22 Oct. 8/1 Direct employment and no sub-contracting. **1902** *Daily Chron.* 29 Apr. 3/4 The conditions under which the sub-contracted work is carried out.

,subcontra'riety. *Logic.* [f. next: see CONTRARIETY.] The relation existing between subcontrary propositions.

1697 tr. *Burgersdicius his Logic* I. xxxiii, Subcontrariety is between two Particulars; Opposition Indefinite between two Infinites. **1864** BOWEN *Logic* vi. 162 It was convenient for Logicians to consider the relations of Subalternation and Sub-Contrariety.

sub'contrary, *a.* and *sb.* [ad. late L. *subcontrārius*, as a term of logic transl. late Gr. ὑπεναντίος: see SUB- 19 and CONTRARY *a.* Cf. OF. *subcontraire*, F. *sous-contraire*.]

A. *adj.* **1.** Somewhat or partially contrary.

1603 HOLLAND *Plutarch's Mor.* 1038 The other [number] which surmounteth, and is surmounted by the same part of their extremities, is named *Hypenantia*, that is to say, sub-contrary. **1697** J. SERGEANT *Solid Philos.* 314 Finding his Discourse in other Places Sub-contrary to what I took to be his Thoughts. **1897** BLACKMORE *Dariel* xxix, A conclusion not directly counter, but sub-contrary..to the view which her husband had ventured to form.

2. *Logic.* **a.** Applied to particular propositions (or the relation of opposition between them) agreeing in quantity but differing in quality.

1656 tr. *Hobbes' Elem. Philos.* I. iii. 31 Subcontrary, are Particular Propositions of different Quality; as Some Man is learned, Some Man is not learned. **1826** WHATELY *Logic* (1827) Index 347 Subcontrary opposition—is between two particulars, the affirmative and the negative. **1870** JEVONS *Elem. Logic* ix. 78 Of subcontrary propositions, one only can be false, and both may be true.

b. 'Applied to the relation between two attributes which co-exist in the same substance, yet in such a way that the more there is of one, the less there is of the other' (Webster 1864).

3. *Geom.* **a.** Applied to the relative position of two similar triangles having a common angle at the vertex and their bases not parallel, so that the basal angles are equal but on contrary sides. Also in a generalized sense (see quot. 1842).

1704 J. HARRIS *Lex. Techn.* I, *Subcontrary Position*, (in Geometry). **1842** *Penny Cycl.* XXIII. 185/1 When a figure or solid is symmetrical, so that equal lines or polygons can be drawn on two different sides, those equal lines or polygons may be called subcontrary.

b. Applied to any circular section of a quadric cone in relation to the base or to another circular section not parallel to it.

1706 W. JONES *Syn. Palmar. Matheseos* 254 If cut Parallel, or Subcontrary to the Base, the Section will be a Circle. **1842** *Penny Cycl.* XXIII. 185/1 The generating circle ABCD has a subcontrary circle EBFD, made by taking the line EF subcontrary to AC. **1877** *Encycl. Brit.* VI. 283/1 If a cone be cut by a plane which does not pass through the vertex, and which is neither parallel to the base nor to the plane of a subcontrary section.

B. *sb.* **1.** *Logic.* A subcontrary proposition.

1697 tr. *Burgersdicius his Logic* I. xxxiii, Subcontraries are, some man is just, some man is not just... Contraries, the negation added or taken away, contradict subcontraries. **1725** WATTS *Logic* II. ii. §3 If two particular propositions differ in quality, they are subcontraries. **1826** [see SUBALTERN *sb.* 3]. **1864** BOWEN *Logic* vi. 164 Sub-Contraries can be called 'opposites' only in a qualified and technical sense.

2. *Geom.* A subcontrary section of a cone.

1842 *Penny Cycl.* XXIII. 185/1 In a right cone every section has its subcontrary, except only the circle which generates the cone, and its parallels.

Hence **sub'contrarily** *adv.* (see quot.).

1728 CHAMBERS *Cycl.* s.v. *Subcontrary*, If the scalenous Cone BVD be so cut by the Plane CA, as that the Angle at C = D; the Cone is then said to be cut Subcontrarily to its Base BA.

sub'cortical, *a.* [SUB- 1 a.]

1. Lying, situated, or formed under the bark of a tree; (of insects) living or feeding under bark.

1815 KIRBY & SP. *Entomol.* (1818) I. 212 Wood-lice, ear-wigs, spiders, field-bugs, and similar subcortical insects. **1832** LINDLEY *Introd. Bot.* 213 To facilitate the descent of the subcortical fibres of the growing buds. **1851** MANTELL *Petrifactions* i. 43 These are not produced by the attachment of petioles, but are sub-cortical protuberances. **1866** RYE *Brit. Beetles* 89 *Omalium planum*..is, perhaps, as good a type of a subcortical insect as could be seen.

2. Situated under or pertaining to the region underlying (*a*) the cortex of a sponge, (*b*) the cortex of the brain.

1887 *Encycl. Brit.* XXII. 415 The roots of the incurrent sinuses form widely open spaces immediately beneath the cortex and are the rudiments of subcortical crypts. **1899** *Allbutt's Syst. Med.* VI. 810 Supra-nuclear paralysis (including the cortical and subcortical varieties). *Ibid.* VII. 422 The lesion was an essentially subcortical one.

Hence **sub'cortically** *adv.*, with reference to the region underlying the cortex.

1871 W. A. LEIGHTON *Lichen-flora* 150 The sub-cortically albo-maculate thallus.

‖**subcosta** (sʌb'kɒstə). *Entom.* [SUB- 1 f.] The subcostal vein of the wing of some insects; the vein just behind the costa.

1861 H. HAGEN *Synopsis Neuroptera N. Amer.* 343.

sub'costal, *a.* and *sb.* [ad. mod.L. *subcostālis*: see SUB- 1 b and COSTAL.]

A. *adj.* **1.** *Anat.* Situated below a rib or beneath the ribs; lying on the under side of a rib, as a groove for an artery.

1872 HUMPHRY *Myology* 19 The under or sub-costal parts of the broad pelvic shield. **1876** *Quain's Elem. Anat.* (ed. 8) I. 28 The inferior border [of a rib] presents on its inner aspect the subcostal groove. **1882** *Ibid.* (ed. 9) I. 30 The subcostal angle into the centre of which the ensiform process projects. **1890** BILLINGS *Nat. Med. Dict.*, *Sub-costal angle*, that formed by margins of costal cartilages at lower aperture of thorax. **1910** *Encycl. Brit.* (ed. 11) II. 667 Below the last rib a subcostal artery runs.

2. *Entom.* Situated behind or near the costal vein or nervure of an insect's wing.

1826 KIRBY & SP. *Entomol.* III. 376 Neuræ Subcostales (the Subcostal Nervures). Nervures springing from the under-side of the post-costal nervure, or from each other.

B. *sb.* A subcostal muscle (usually in L. form *subcostalis*); a subcostal artery, vein, or nervure.

[**1733** tr. *Winslow's Anat.* (1756) I. 319 The Sub-Costales having the superior Extremities of their Fibres much more distant from the Vertebral Articulation of the Ribs, than the lower Extremities.]

sub-cre'ation. [SUB- 5.] J. R. R. Tolkien's word for the process of inventing an imaginary or secondary world, different from the primary world but internally consistent.

1947 J. R. R. TOLKIEN in *Essays presented to Charles Williams* 51 This aspect of 'mythology'—sub-creation, rather than either representation or symbolic interpretation of the beauties and terrors of the world—is, I think, too little considered. **1974** R. HELMS *Tolkien's World* vi. 123 He needed to tell himself..that the cosmos is friendly to sub-creation, because it echoes its own chief and most joyous activity.

Also **sub-cre'ator**, one who engages in sub-creation.

1947 J. R. R. TOLKIEN in *Essays presented to Charles Williams* 51 In such 'fantasy', as it is called, new form is made; Faërie begins; Man becomes a sub-creator. **1972** P. H. KOCHER *Master of Middle-Earth* (1973) vii. 201 He..is lifted up to live above himself, as is the sub-creator of secondary worlds of fantasy at the height of his inspiration.

sub-cre'ative, *a.* [SUB- 5c(*b*), 8.] Of or pertaining to sub-creation or secondary creation. Hence **sub-cre'atively** *adv.*

Quot. 1860 shows a nonce-use of this word.

1860 O. W. HOLMES *Prof. Breakf-t.* ii, The 'subcreative centre', as my..friend has..called man. **1947** J. R. R. TOLKIEN in *Essays presented to Charles Williams* 71 To many, Fantasy, this sub-creative art which plays strange tricks with the world and all that is in it, combining nouns and redistributing adjectives, has seemed suspect, if not illegitimate. **1958** —— *Lett.* (1981) 286 In this Myth the rebellion of created free-will precedes creation of the World (Eä); and Eä has in it, subcreatively introduced, evil, rebellious, discordant elements of its own nature. **1974** R. HELMS *Tolkien's World* vi. 122 As artist, he is incomplete, impotent, without the presence of the other element in sub-creative activity—his community.

sub'critical, *a.* Also sub-critical. [SUB- 14.]

1. *Metallurgy.* Less than the critical temperature above which ferrite changes into austenite; ***subcritical annealing***, annealing in which the temperature is not raised above this.

1930 *Trans. Amer. Inst. Mining & Metall. Engineers, Techn. Publ.* No. 348. 5 The quenching to this subcritical temperature must be rapid enough to preserve the austenite essentially unchanged. **1935** M. A. GROSSMANN *Princ. Heat Treatment* viii. 113 Subcritical annealing will not induce as much softness as a full anneal. **1980** G. KRAUSS *Princ. Heat Treatment Steel* v. 115 Process and recrystallization annealing are similar subcritical annealing treatments usually applied to restore ductility to cold worked steel products.

2. Of a flow of fluid: slower than the speed at which waves travel in the fluid.

1941 *Civil Engin.* Mar. 171/1 The terms 'tranquil' and 'rapid' have been used..in connection with the Froude criterion... The frequently used terms 'low-velocity' and 'high-velocity' are..just as inept as the ambiguous 'subcritical' and 'supercritical'. **1943** R. C. BINDER *Fluid Mech.* xiv. 215 The hydraulic jump is an abrupt transition between what might be called supercritical and subcritical flow. **1981** *Sci. Amer.* Apr. 138/2 A ridge across a streambed provides an example of how a barrier can create supercritical flow, a standing wave and a hydraulic jump in an initially subcritical flow.

3. *Nucl. Physics.* Containing or being less than the critical mass (CRITICAL *a.* 7b).

1945 D. DIETZ *Atomic Energy in Coming Era* xii. 146 It was seen..that the mechanism of the bomb would have to bring sub-critical masses of the material together quickly. **1961** *Engineering* 7 Apr. 487/1 Two new light-water moderated and natural-uranium fuelled subcritical assemblies are appearing on the nuclear market in this country. **1978** *Nature* 9 Feb. 497/3 Chain reaction is unlikely, since the mass of uranium used in such satellites is normally subcritical.

subcru'real, *a.* *Anat.* Also -æal. [f. next.] Situated under the crureus; pertaining to the subcrureus. So **subcru'rean** *a.*

1839–47 *Todd's Cycl. Anat.* III. 49/1 We have known inflammation of the synovial membrane of the knee to have been the result of a wound of the subcruræal bursa. **1859** MAYNE *Expos. Lex.*, *Subcruræus*,..subcrurean.

‖**subcrureus** (sʌbkruə'riːəs). *Anat.* Also -æus. [mod.L. (sc. *musculus*), f. *sub-* SUB- 1d + *crūreus* (f. *crūs*, *crūr-* leg).] (See quot. 1848.)

1848 *Quain's Anat.* (ed. 5) I. 388 *Subcrureus.* Under this name is described a small band of muscular fibres, which extends from the anterior surface of the femur to the upper part of the synovial membrane of the knee-joint. **1887** *Buck's Handbk. Med. Sci.* V. 45 The subcrureus muscle found in the lower limb beneath the quadriceps extensor.

sub'cultural, *a.* Also sub-cultural. [SUB- 5, 7.] Of or pertaining to a subculture. Also, that is inferior to or below the general cultural level.

1933 *Brit. Jrnl. Psychol.* July 2 The residual group of patients..may be termed the subcultural type. This type is ..a collection of persons who are healthy, apparently sound neurologically.., but who lack intelligence. **1937** *Discovery* July 223/2 The sub-cultural social defective must be recognised as such..and the able child made an economic asset. **1958** B. BERNSTEIN in J. A. Fishman *Readings Sociol. of Lang.* (1968) 223 Within the last thirty years in both the fields of sociology and psychology there has been an increasing awareness of sub-cultural and social class influences upon behaviour and in particular learning. **1968** D. L. CLARKE *Anal. Archaeol.* vi. 234 Ethnologists..have drawn attention to the material equipment of the lower-level sub-cultural segments outlined by sociology. **1979** *Internat. Jrnl. Sociol. of Law* VII. 242 This order is not instilled by sanctions, at least not primarily so, but partly guaranteed by extra-legal normative structures (ethical norms, group norms, subcultural norms etc.).

'subculture, *sb.* Also sub-culture.

1. *Biol.* and *Med.* [SUB- 9.] A culture (of bacteria or the like) started from another culture; the process of starting a culture in this way.

1886 E. KLEIN *Micro-Organisms & Dis.* (ed. 3) v. 43 From the individual and separate colonies, it is then easy by re-inoculation of gelatine tubes..to start pure subcultures of the different species. **1899** *Allbutt's Syst. Med.* VII. 550 Growth..in subcultures may be recognisable within four hours. **1911** *Jrnl. Path. & Bacteriol.* XV. 94 In sub-culture it grew on plain agar. **1962** *Lancet* 5 May 933/1 Amongst the 240 staphylococcal strains tested..64 showed discrete colonies of this kind and they were tested by subculture on to the same concentration of drug. **1971** *Nature* 16 July 174/1 Subcultures of the bacterial cultures were carried out at 7 day intervals to maintain vigorous stocks.

2. [SUB- 7.] A group or class of lesser importance or size sharing specific beliefs, interests, or values which may be at variance with those of the general culture of which it forms part.

1936 R. LINTON *Study of Man* xvi. 275 While ethnologists have been accustomed to speak of tribes and nationalities as though they were the primary culture-bearing units, the total culture of a society of this type is really an aggregate of sub-cultures. **1937** *Brit. Jrnl. Psychol.* Apr. 358 We may regard the adjusted group..as a small culture pocket or subculture within the larger culture. **1948** T. S. ELIOT *Notes towards Definition of Culture* iv. 75 We may find ourselves led to the conclusion, that every sub-culture is dependent upon that from which it is an offshoot. **1955** T. H. PEAR *Eng. Soc. Differences* iii. 111 The extravert's and the introvert's idea of good manners and goodwill, even in the same sub-culture-pattern, are very different. **1963** T. PYNCHON *V.* xii. 361 Anyone who continues to live in a subculture so demonstrably sick has no right to call himself well. **1970** G. JACKSON *Let.* 4 Apr. in *Soledad Brother* (1971) 214 We are a subsidiary subculture, a depressed area. **1976** DEAKIN & WILLIS *Johnny go Home* v. 82 The [social] workers dress like their clients... Only their accents betray them as not being part of the sub-culture they are ministering to.

'subculture, *v.* *Biol.* and *Med.* [f. prec., sense 1.] *trans.* To produce a subculture of. Hence (with variable stressing) **subcultured** *ppl. a.*, **subculturing** *vbl. sb.*

1899 G. NEWMAN *Bacteria* 339 The contained bacteria will reveal themselves in characteristic colonies, which may be..sub-cultured. **1919** *Lancet* 2 Aug. 189/2 After eight subculturings in broth..all the strains had become agglutinable to para. B serum. **1930** *Forestry* IV. 66 Sub-culturing was done with small pieces of rhizomorph, and all cultures so made continued to produce rhizomorphs in great abundance. **1949** H. W. FLOREY in H. W. Florey et al. *Antibiotics* I. i. 18 This contaminating organism..was subcultured. **1967** M. E. HALE *Biol. Lichens* i. 8 Ideally the algae should be isolated and subcultured. **1970** *Nature* 25 July 383/1 Subcultured gonococci were exposed to antiserum alone. **1974** *Ibid.* 2 Aug. 383/2 Diploid fibroblast cultures can be propagated..only for a finite number of subculturings.

subcutaneous (sʌbkjuː'teɪnɪəs), *a.* [f. late L. *subcutāneus*, f. *sub-* SUB- 1b + *cutis* skin + *-āneus*: see -EOUS. Cf. It. *subcutaneo*; F. *souscutané*.]

1. Lying or situated under the skin.

1656 BLOUNT *Glossogr.*, *Subcutaneous*, between the skin and the flesh. **1698** A. DE LA PRYME *Diary* (Surtees) 180 A kind of a dropsy, or a gathering together of a subcutanious water. **1744** *Phil. Trans.* XLIII. 117 It is very probable, that none of the subcutaneous Juices are opaque. **1831** KNOX *Cloquet's Anat.* 141 The subcutaneous cellular tissue is traversed by large veins. **1835–6** *Todd's Cycl. Anat.* I. 466 *note*, In general the anomalous artery is the radial, and is subcutaneous in its course. **1872** BRYANT *Pract. Surg.* 12 The healing of subcutaneous wounds.

2. Living under the skin.

1664 POWER *Exp. Philos.* I. 22 This almost invisible sub-cutaneous Inhabitant. **1815** KIRBY & SP. *Entomol.* iv. (1818) I. 86 It does not appear..that the species..are..sub-cutaneous. **1849** *Proc. Berw. Nat. Club* II. vii. 361 The larva is subcutaneous in the leaves of the common Chickweed.

3. Of operations, etc.: Performed or taking place under the skin; characterized by application of a remedy beneath the skin; hence, of instruments by which such operations are performed or remedies administered; hypodermic.

1651 BIGGS *New Disp.* ¶241 A subcutaneous expurgation, should be sent out by the high way and sink of all sordid excrements. **1868** GARROD *Mat. Med.* (ed. 3) 381 The method of introducing medicine into the system by subcutaneous injection has gained much ground of late. **1875** KNIGHT *Dict. Mech.*, *Subcutaneous Syringe*, an instrument for injecting medicinal solutions beneath the skin. **1899** *Allbutt's Syst. Med.* VIII. 935 The subcutaneous administration of anti-toxic serum.

Hence **subcu'taneously**, *adv.*, under the skin, hypodermically; **subcu'taneousness.**

1727 BAILEY (vol. II), *Subcutaneousness*, the lying under the Skin. **1875** H. C. WOOD *Therap.* (1879) 231 When the drug is given subcutaneously. **1885** KLEIN *Micro-Org.* 46 Saliva of the healthy dog and of man inoculated subcutaneously into rabbits sometimes produces death.

subdane, -dayn, obs. forms of SUDDEN.

subdeacon (ˌsʌb'diːkən). *Eccl.* Forms: α. 4 sude(a)kne, 4–5 sodekene, 5 -en, -on, -un, -yn. β. 4–6 subdekin, -yn, -decon, (also 8) -diacon, etc. (see DEACON *sb.*[1]), 5– subdeacon. (See also *southdeacon* s.v. SOUTH-[2].) [a. AF., OF. *soudiakene*, *subdiacne*, f. *sou(s)-*, *sub-* (see SUB- 6) + *diacne* DEACON *sb.*[1], after eccl. L. *subdiāconus*, which was modelled on eccl. Gr. ὑποδιάκονος.]

1. The name of an order of ministers in the Christian church next below that of deacon.

The duty of subdeacons is to assist in the celebration of the Eucharist by preparing the sacred vessels and (in the Western Church) by reading the epistle. In the East the subdiaconate ranks as one of the minor, in the West as one of the major orders; it does not exist in the Church of England.

α. *c* **1315** SHOREHAM I. 1779 Sudeakne mey be ywedded nauȝt. *c* **1400** *Apol. Loll.* 39 þe clerkis of þi jurisdiccoun, þat are wiþ in þe ordre of sodeken, or a boue. *c* **1450** *Godstow Reg.* 471 Iames Vercellence, the popis sodekon. **1483** *Cath. Angl.* 371/1 A Sudekyn, *subdiaconus*.

β. **1303** R. BRUNNE *Handl. Synne* 1051 ȝyf þou..art a clerk, & hast þe los Of subdekene, or dekene by name. **1387** TREVISA *Higden* (Rolls) V. 359 Oon Arator, a subdecon of Rome. **1460** CAPGRAVE *Chron.* (Rolls) 74 He that schuld be mad a bischop schuld first be a benet,..and than a colet; and than subdiacone, diacone, and prest. **1555** WATREMAN *Fardle Facions* II. xii. 281 The Subdeacon mighte take the offring, and handle the Chalice, and the Patine. **1561** T. NORTON *Calvin's Inst.* IV. iv. 22b, As for Subdeacons, it is likely that at the beginnyng they were ioyned to the Deacons, that they should vse their seruice about the poore. **1615** WADSWORTH in Bedell *Lett.* 12 The Councels require the *ordines minores* of Subdeacon and the rest, to goe before Priesthood. **1635** PAGITT *Christianogr.* I. iii. (1636) 106 The Priests, Deacons, and Subdeacons of the Easterne Church. **1737** CHALLONER *Cath. Chr. Instr.* (1753) 154 From the minor Orders they are promoted to the Order of Sub-deacon, which is the first of those that are called Holy. **1859** NEWMAN *Serm. Var. Occas.* (1881) 254 At the age of twenty-four,..he was ordained sub-deacon. **1877** J. D. CHAMBERS *Div. Worship* 326 It was always the proper office of the Sub-deacon to read the Epistle.

†**b.** Applied to an order below the levites, the 'Nethinim' of Ezra ii. 70. *Obs.*

1382 WYCLIF *1 Esdras* ii. 70 The prestus and the Leuitus of the puple..and sodeknys [Vulg. *Nathinæi*]. **1546** LANGLEY tr. *Pol. Verg. de Invent.* IV. iii. 72 The ministers, whiche dyd make redye the sacrifice,..at the commaundement of the Leuites, these we may cal subdeacons.

2. The cleric (orig. one in subdeacon's orders) or lay clerk who acts as assistant next below the deacon at a solemn celebration of the Eucharist; the 'epistoler'.

1440 *Engl. Ch. Furnit.* (1866) 181 One whole vestment for Priest Deacon and Subdeacon. **1483** CAXTON *Gold. Leg.* 133/3 A preest a deken & a subdeken all reuested goyng to thaulter as for to saye masse. **1520** *Market Harborough Rec.* (1890) 215 To the parych clerke beynge subdeken iij[d]. *c* **1618** MORYSON *Itin.* IV. (1903) 439 When the Pope..sings Masse himselfe, with one Cardinall seruing him as Deacon, and another as subdeacon. **1701** in *Cath. Rec. Soc. Publ.* VII. 101 And his Dæcon, Subdiacon & Acolythe were his 3 sons, brothers to y[e] Nonne. **1851** PUGIN *Chancel Screens* 26 The Epistle and Gospel were sung by the deacon and sub-deacon, from marble desks enriched with carvings. **1865** *Directorium Anglicanum* (ed. 2) 2 *note*, The Epistoler or Subdeacon, if the ancient Sarum and modern Roman Rule be followed, should wear no stole at all.

†**b.** The vestment (viz. a tunicle) worn by the subdeacon at the Eucharist. *Obs.*

1521 in Strype *Stow's Surv.* (1754) I. 514/1, I wold that a Subdeacon of whyte Damask, be made. **1553** *Rec. St. Mary at Hill* (1904) 52 A preist & a subdeaken of blew bodkin. **1560** in *Trans. Essex Archæol. Soc.* (1863) II. 215, j vestement..of red velvet, wth a decon & subdecon.

Hence **sub'deaconate,** †**-'deaconhood,** †**-'deaconry, -'deaconship** = SUBDIACONATE.

1554 T. MARTIN *Marr. Priests* O ij (T.), Ye come to be promoted here to the holye order of subdeaconrie. **1587** *T. Norton's* tr. *Calvin's Inst.* IV. xix. 494b *marg.*, The order of Sub-deaconrie and the trifling vse thereof. **1615** WADSWORTH in Bedell *Lett.* 13 Subdeaconship [is giuen] by the deliuerie of the Patena alone, and of the Chalice emptie. **1728** CHAMBERS *Cycl.* s.v. *Sub*, 'Tis disputed among the Romanists, whether the Sub-deaconhood be a Sacrament or not. **1853** ROCK *Ch. Fathers* III. II. 50 The next step took the acolyte to the sub-deaconship. **1878** STUBBS *Const. Hist.* III. xix. 370 For the sub-deaconate and higher grades a knowledge of the New Testament..was requisite.

subdean (ˌsʌb'diːn). Forms: α. 4 soudene, 4–5 sodene, sud(d)ene, 6 sedeane. β. 5–7 subdeane, 6 -de(i)ne, 7 -dean. [a. AF. *sodean, *sudene, *subdene = OF. *sou(z)deien* (mod. *sousdoyen*), *soubdean*, f. *sou(s)-*, *sub-* (see SUB- 6) + *deien* DEAN[1], after med.L. *subdecānus*. Cf. *southdene* s.v. SOUTH-[2].] An official immediately below a dean in rank, and acting as his deputy.

α. **1362** LANGL. *P. Pl.* A. II. 150 Alle Denes and Sodenes [*v.rr.* southdenis, sudenes; B. II. 172 *MS. C.* subdeanes]. **1483** *Cath. Angl.* 371/1 A Svdene, *Subdecanus*. *a* **1529** SKELTON *P. Sparowe* 552 But for the egle doth flye Hyest in the skye, He shall be the sedeane, The quere to demeane.

β. **14..** [see α quot. 1362]. **1506** *Dunfermline Reg.* (Bannatyne Club) 375 Subdene of our souerane lordis chapell. *a* **1578** LINDESAY (Pitscottie) *Chron. Scot.* (S.T.S.) I. 200 The archedeine..and subdeine..witht all kynd of wther officeis pertaining to ane colledge. **1643** PRYNNE *Rome's Master-Peece* 29 Dr. Theodor Price, Subdean of Westminster. **1670** G. H. *Hist. Cardinals* I. III. 75 The Deans, and Sub-Deans of the Popes Chapel. **1715** HEARNE

MS. Diaries LVIII. lf. 68 b, Dr. Terry, the Subdean of Xt Church. **1876** [see SUBCHANTER].

Hence **sub'deanery**, the office, position, or residence of a subdean.

1579 *Reg. Privy Council Scot.* Ser. I. III. 139 Maister Andrew Polwart..hes obtenit a presentatioun to himself of the said subdenerie. **1786** J. BACON *Liber Regis* 1102 Subdeanry [of York], founded anno 1229. **1813** *Corresp. W. Fowler* (1907) 257 She came to the Subdeanery to see me. **1824** G. CHALMERS *Caledonia* III. 680 The subdeanry of Glasgow was taxed 26*l.* 13*s.* 4*d.*

sub-deb. *slang* (chiefly *U.S.*). Now *rare.* [SUB- 14 b.] A girl who will soon 'come out' as a social débutante. Hence, less specifically, a girl in her mid-teens. Also *fig.* and *attrib.*

1917 M. R. RINEHART (*title*) Bab: a sub-deb. *Ibid.* i. 14 Is it fair also, I ask, that in the best society a girl is a Sub-Deb the year before she comes out? **1930** *New Statesman* 1 Nov. 114/1 *The Little Review*, born in Chicago, a 'sub-deb' in California, debutante in New York, defunct in Paris. **1936** M. H. BRADLEY *Five-Minute Girl* 116 Margaret, two years older than Alva..and there was Joyce, the subdeb. **1939** [see DATING *vbl. sb.* c]. **1944** W. S. MAUGHAM *Razor's Edge* vii. 278 The living-room would do very well for the sub-deb dances which it would be her pleasant duty to give. **1947** *Time* 6 Jan. 20/3 The season's debutantes danced their way into society while eager sub-debs looked on.

Also **sub-'debutante** *U.S.*

1934 in WEBSTER. **1959** V. PACKARD *Status Seekers* xiii. 186 The girl..must be invited to the right sub-debutante parties.

subde'canal, *a. rare.* [f. med.L. *subdecānus* SUBDEAN + -AL[1].] Of or pertaining to a subdean or subdeanery.

1846 MCCULLOCH *Acc. Brit. Empire* (1854) II. 186 There are also Peculiars of various descriptions in most dioceses,.. royal, archiepiscopal, episcopal, decanal, sub-decanal, prebendal, rectorial, and vicarial.

‖**subdele'gado.** [Sp.: see SUB- 6 and DELEGATE *sb.*] An official in Spanish South America: see quot. 1845.

1845 *Encycl. Metrop.* XXIII. 78 These two classes of functionaries [viz. Commandants and Administrators] are under the immediate control of a *Subdelegado*, or Lieutenant of the Government, who has the chief command of all the country of the *Missions* [in Paraguay]. **1853** KINGSTON *Manco* i, In the house of a sub-delegado.

sub'delegate (-ət), *sb.* [f. SUB- 6 + DELEGATE, after AF., OF. *subdelegat*, med.L. *subdēlēgātus*; cf. OF. *sousdelegat*, F. *sous délégué*.] One who represents, or is deputy for, a delegate.

c **1550** ROLLAND *Crt. Venus* I. 215 Sa that thow mak me thy subdelegat. **1592** *Sc. Acts Jas. VI*, (1814) III. 557/2 The said mr of the mettallis..and his sub-delegattis..to be appointit be him. **1668** *Lond. Gaz.* No. 251/3 The Sub-deligate from the Marquiss Castel Rodrigo on the behalf of Spain. **1752** CARTE *Hist. Eng.* III. 320 Brooks, bishop of Gloucester, sitting as the pope's Subdelegate. **1794** GIFFORD *Reign Louis XVI*, 309 What then have they asked? —the suppression of aides and subdelegates. **1904** POLLARD *Cranmer* xii. 350 The subdelegate's court was opened in the Church of St. Mary.

sub'delegate (-eɪt), *v.* [f. SUB- 8, 9 + DELEGATE *v.* after F. *subdéléguer* or med.L. *subdēlēgāre*.] *trans.* †To appoint (a person) to act as a subdelegate; to transmit (power) to a sub-delegate.

1611 COTGR., *Subdeleguer*, to subdelegate, substitute, appoint another vnder him. *a* **1670** HACKET *Cent. Serm.* 354 All power and royalty is subdelegated from the Pope to other princes. **1891** *Spectator* 21 Feb., The ruler..delegates his power, which is again sub-delegated.

So †**sub'delegate** *pa. pple.* and *ppl. a.*, **sub'delegated** *ppl. a.*

1614 SELDEN *Titles Hon.* 252 Iudges of mean note sub-delegat by inferior Counts. **1706** PHILLIPS (ed. Kersey), *Sub-Delegate*, or *Judge Sub-Delegate*, a Judge appointed under another; a Deputy. **1709** *Lond. Gaz.* No. 4517/3 The Subdelegate Ministers of the Imperial Commission. **1726** AYLIFFE *Parergon* 310 A sub-delegated Judge, to whom only some part of the mesne Process in a Cause is committed in the second Place by a delegated Judge.

ˌ**subdele'gation.** [f. prec. Cf. F. *subdélégation.*] The action of subdelegating.

1611 COTGR., *Subdelegation*, a subdelegation, or substitution. **1684** *Lond. Gaz.* No. 1955/2 His Imperial Majesty's Subdelegation to his Commissioners here. **1752** CARTE *Hist. Eng.* III. 681 Upon producing the commissions on both sides, exceptions were made by the English to the form of subdelegation. **1824** SOUTHEY *Sir T. More* (1831) I. 105 Superintendence..is capable of being exercised..by delegation and subdelegation.

ˌ**subdenomi'nation.** [SUB- 7 b.] A subordinate denomination, category, class, or division.

1630 DELAMAIN *Grammelogia* a 2 b, What denomination you give unto any of the figures, the next great division is the next subdenomination. **1763** C. JOHNSTON *Reverie* II. 267 The mortgage affected only a very small part of his estate,.. a particular subdenomination only..being named in the deeds. **1802–12** BENTHAM *Ration. Judic. Evid.* (1827) II. 291 Applying to suits of the same denomination..plans of collection altogether different, according as this or that arbitrarily allotted sub-denomination happens to have given to them. **1896** *Daily News* 26 Feb., The table gives you their sub-denominations, from an analysis of the census returns.

subdi'aconal, *a.* [ad. med.L. *subdiācōnālis*, f. *subdiāconus* SUBDEACON.] Of a subdeacon.

1849 ROCK *Ch. Fathers* I. 390 The subdiaconal tunicle.

subdi'aconate. [ad. med.L. *subdiācōnātus*, f. *subdiāconus* SUBDEACON; cf. F. *sous-diaconat.*] The office or rank of subdeacon.

1725 tr. *Dupin's Eccl. Hist. 17th C.* I. v. 178 The Manner of conferring the Subdiaconate. **1847** MASKELL *Mon. Rit.* III. p. civ, These minor orders, and I now include the sub-diaconate, were not of divine institution. **1867** H. C. LEA *Sacerd. Celib.* iii. (1884) 54 The restriction on matrimony has never at any time extended below the subdiaconate.

†**subdial,** *a. Obs. rare.* [ad. L. *subdiālis*, f. *sub-* SUB- 1 a + *dī(v)um* sky; cf. *sub dio* s.v. ‖SUB.] Being in the open air, or under the open sky.

1647 N. BACON *Disc. Gov. Eng.* I. iv. (1739) 10 The Athenian Heliastick or Subdial Court. **1656** BLOUNT *Glossogr.*, *Subdial*, abroad in the Air, without the house, all open.

sub'dialect. [SUB- 7.] A subordinate dialect; a division of a dialect. Hence ˌ**subdia'lectal** *a.*, of or pertaining to a subdialect.

1642 HOWELL *For. Trav.* (Arb.) 48 The French have three dialects, the Wallon..the Provensall, (whereof the Gascon is a subdialect) and the speech of Languedoc. *c* **1645** —— *Lett.* (1650) I. 377 Yet hath she divers subdialects, as the Western and Northern English, but her chiefest is the Scotick. **1845** *Proc. Philol. Soc.* II. 171 With respect to the languages of Southern India not related to Sanscrit, the Tamul, of which the others are only sub-dialects, presents no direct analogy. **1862** LATHAM *Channel Isl.* III. xix. 439 A sub-dialect of the Jersey. **1875** WHITNEY *Life Lang.* xii. 245 The variety of sub-dialects, especially of the Lesghian, is very great. **1960** *Amer. Speech* XXXV. 218 Least likely to be widely accepted is Hoenigswald's general theory as to the origin of sound change... He revives the old substratum theory in a subdialectal setting. **1978** *Language* LIV. 10 The pattern of free variation (presumably representing subdialectal variation).

†**subdi'chotomize,** *v. Obs.* [SUB- 9.] *trans.* To subdivide.

1651 BIGGS *New Disp.* ¶235 Subdichotomise it by the severe incision knife of rationall argumentations.

So †**subdi'chotomy**, subdivision.

1644 MILTON *Areop.* Wks. 1851 IV. 445 Many subdichotomies of petty schisms.

subdi'chotomous, *a.* [SUB- 21 f.] Somewhat divided or branched. Hence **subdi'chotomously** *adv.*

1777 S. ROBSON *Brit. Flora* 305 Stem shrubby, subdichotomous. **1822** J. PARKINSON *Outl. Oryctol.* 91 A jointed arm dividing subdichotomously. **1880** SAVILLE KENT *Infusoria* I. 360 Contour of polythecium subdichotomous.

subdis'junctive, *a.* and *sb.* *Logic* and *Gram.* [ad. mod.L. *subdisjunctīvus*, = Gr. ὑποδιαζευκτικός: see SUB- 19 + DISJUNCTIVE.]

A. *adj.* Partly disjunctive (see quots.). **B.** *sb.* A subdisjunctive proposition or word.

1656 STANLEY *Hist. Philos.* VIII. (1687) 441 Contraries are either disjunctive or subdisjunctive... Subdisjunctive, are of two kinds, either in whole, betwixt Universals,..or in part, betwixt particulars... Of subdisjunctives in whole, both cannot be true, both may be false; both cannot be affirmative, both cannot be negative. Of subdisjunctives in part, both may be true, because they are taken in part. **1751** HARRIS *Hermes* 258 *note*, The Latins had a peculiar Particle for this occasion, which they called *Subdisjunctiva*, a Sub-disjunctive; and that was Sive. **1818** STODDART in *Encycl. Metrop.* (1845) I. 162/2 Priscian distinguishes the subdisjunctive from the disjunctive... In English we use the conjunction *or* indifferently as a disjunctive or subdisjunctive, that is, we say, 'Alexander *or* Paris', whether Alexander and Paris be two different persons, or only two different names for the same person. **1865** LIDDELL & SCOTT *Gr. Lex.* (ed. 5), ὑποδιαζευκτικός..as Gramm. word, subdisjunctive.

So **subdis'junction** *rare*⁻⁰.

1869 LIDDELL & SCOTT *Gr. Lex.* (ed. 6), ὑποδιάζευξις, sub-disjunction.

sub'distich, *a.* [SUB- 21 e.] Consisting of almost two rows. So **sub'distichous** *a.*

1777 S. ROBSON *Brit. Flora* 259 Spike compound, sub-distich. **1805–16** R. JAMESON *Char. Min.* 211 A Crystal is said to be..Subdistic (subdistique), when among the facets which are disposed in the same row around each base, there are two surmounted by a new facet, which is as it were..the rudiment of a second row. **1846** DANA *Zooph.* (1848) 650 Polyps subdistichous.

subdi'stinction. [In sense 1, ad. late L. *subdistinctio* (= Gr. ὑποστιγμή), f. *subdistinguĕre* (= Gr. ὑποστίζειν) to put a comma or one of the lesser stops: cf. SUB- 23. In senses 2 and 3, f. SUB- 5 c and 7 b + DISTINCTION.]

†**1.** A comma or semicolon. *Obs.*

1636 B. JONSON *Engl. Gram.* II. ix, A Sub-distinction is a meane breathing,..and is marked thus (;). **1825** FOSBROKE *Encycl. Antiq.* 460 A small pause or subdistinction.

2. A subordinate distinction.

1665 WALTON *Life of Hooker* (1670) F 5 By needless distinctions and sub-distinctions, to amuse his Hearers. **1727** *Narr. Proc. Synods Presbyt. Irel.* 111 Here, now, between Parties..there's a Party-Subdistinction made. **1847–8** DE QUINCEY *Protestantism* Wks. 1858 VIII. 154 Ten thousand evasions, distinctions, and subdistinctions. **1878** F. HARRISON in *Fortn. Rev.* Nov. 689 He disregarded the important subdistinction of the nature of the sanction and the kind of command.

†**3.** A subdivision, subspecies. *Obs.*

1725 *Bradley's Fam. Dict.* s.v. *Bohee-Tea*, As the Bohee and Green include all other Sub-distinctions, we shall have regard to no other. **1748** J. HILL *Hist. Fossils* 651 The *Spatagi* is a very comprehensive term, taking in most of the others as subdistinctions.

†**subdi'stinguish,** *v. Obs.* [SUB- 9. Cf. It. *suddistinguere*, Sp. *subdistinguir.*] *trans.* To distinguish into subordinate kinds, classes, species, etc.

1620 E. BLOUNT *Horæ Subs.* 218 But for more ease..all these particulars may be subdistinguished diuersly. **1633** T. ADAMS *Exp. 2 Peter* i. 16. 299 There are some sub-distinguished branches, which we referre to their owne places. **1766** *Complete Farmer* s.v. *Surveying* 7 E b/2 These three sorts of triangles may, according to the length and proportion of their sides, be sub-distinguished into seven. **1789** TWINING *Aristotle's Treat. Poetry* (1812) II. 186 The different parts of this long Episode were, again, subdistinguished by other titles.

'**sub-ˌdistrict.** [SUB- 7 c.] A division or subdivision of a district. Also *attrib.*

1816 BENTHAM *Offic. Apt. Maximized, Extr. Const. Code* (1830) 7 The Judicatory will be the immediate Judicatory of the sub-district in which the metropolis of the state is situated. **1871** *Parl. Papers, Acc. & Papers* XXXIX. 459 Statement of the Divisions of the Country into Military Districts and Sub-Districts, showing the Numbers of Regular and Auxiliary Forces in each. **1876** VOYLE & STEVENSON *Milit. Dict.*, *Brigade Depot*, the head-quarters of a sub-district of the army. Under the new localisation of the British army, the military districts of Great Britain and Ireland are divided into 12 districts, which are sub-divided into 70 infantry and 12 artillery sub-districts, and 2 cavalry districts. **1882** *Rep. Ho. Repr. Prec. Met. U.S.* 268 Pine Grove district..now generally regarded as a mining camp or subdistrict of the Tiger. **1909** *Westm. Gaz.* 1 Mar. 2/2 District boards and sub-district boards.

†**subdit,** *a.* and *sb.* Chiefly *Sc. Obs.* Also 5 -dyt(e, 5–6 -dite, -dict, 6 -det. [ad. L. *subditus* subject (in med.L. as sb. subject, vassal), pa. pple. of *subdĕre* to bring under, subdue, f. *sub-* SUB- 2 b + *-dĕre* to put. Cf. It. *suddito*, Sp., Pg. *subdito.*]

A. *adj.* Subject. Const. *to.*

c **1400** LOVE *Bonavent. Mirr.* (1908) 45 So that he myȝte knowe the noumbre of regiouns, of citees, and of the heuedes longynge to hem that weren subdyte to the Emperour of Rome. **1436** *Libel Engl. Policy* in *Pol. Poems* (Rolls) II. 197 For hym selfe and viij. kynges mo Subdite to hym. **1456** SIR G. HAYE *Law Arms* (S.T.S.) 180 [It] is nocht wele sittand that a grete lord suld be..subdyt till a symple knycht. *c* **1513** DOUGLAS *Let. Wolsey* in *Poet. Wks.* (1874) I. p. cvi, He is subdite to the King in France.

B. *sb.* A subject.

c **1375** *Sc. Leg. Saints* xvi. (*Magdalena*) 772 In þat land, til he lefit, [he] duelt, & with his subditis sa vele delt. **1450** in *Charters &c. Edin.* (1871) 70 Till all and sundry our lieges and subdictis. **1507** *Ibid.* 191 Oure officiaris, liegis, and subdictis. **1536** BELLENDEN *Cron. Scot.* (1821) I. 186 For administratioun of justice to his subdittis. **1555** WATREMAN *Fardle Facions* I. v. 59 The kinges vsing suche an equitie,.. towarde their subdites. **1596** DALRYMPLE tr. *Leslie's Hist. Scot.* I. 222 Eugenie the thrid..was meruellous clement toward his subdites.

†**subdi'titious,** *a. Obs. rare.* [f. L. *subditītius* (-*īcius*), f. *subdit-*, pa. ppl. stem of *subdĕre* (see prec.).]

1. Placed underneath; used as a suppository.

1657 TOMLINSON *Renou's Disp.* 182 These subdititious medicaments conduce much to the execution of small wormes. *Ibid.* 672 Laurel-berries..expressed..into a subdititious vessel.

2. Surreptitiously or fraudulently substituted, supposititious.

[**1625**: implied in *subdititiously* below.] **1656** BLOUNT *Glossogr.*, *Subdititious*, that is not properly ones whose it is feigned to be, that is put or laid in the place or room of another. **1668** WILKINS *Real Char.* II. i. 31 Stead, as substitute, subdititious, serve for, succedaneous, Deputy, Surrogate, Vicar, Delegate [etc.].

Hence †**subdi'titiously** *adv.*, by surreptitious substitution.

1625 PURCHAS *Pilgrims* II. 1375 That the Vizier determined to place subdit[it]iously in the roome of the Prince his owne Sonne.

subdi'vidable, *a. rare.* [f. SUBDIVIDE *v.* + -ABLE.] Capable of being subdivided.

1670 PETTUS *Fodinæ Reg.* 21 Those Shares subdividable into half and quarter parts.

subdi'vide, *sb.* [f. SUB- 5 b + DIVIDE *sb.* 2.] A subordinate division between rivers and their branches.

1902 W. M. DAVIS *Elem. Phys. Geogr.* 243 When a plain or plateau..is well dissected numerous..subdivides are developed between the smaller rivers and their branches.

subdivide (sʌbdɪ'vaɪd), *v.* [ad. late L. *subdīvidĕre*: see SUB- 9 and DIVIDE *v.* Cf. It. *suddividere*, Sp., Pg. *subdividir*; also F. *subdiviser.*]

1. *trans.* To divide (a part of a divided whole); to divide again after a first division. (Sometimes used loosely for *divide.*) *freq.* in passive.

a. in material sense.

1432–50 tr. *Higden* (Rolls) VI. 361 This kynge divided alle his proventes into ij. partes, oon parte whereof he subdivided ageyne into thre partes. **1483** CAXTON *Cato* 3 The second partye which is in uerse is subdyuyded in to foure partyes. **1626** BACON *Sylva* §104 If you diuide the Tones equally, the Eight is but Seuen whole and equall

Notes; And if you Subdiuide that into Halfe Notes, (as it is in the Stops of a Lute), it maketh the Number of thirteene. **1646** Sir T. Browne *Pseud. Ep.* 184 Below the cubit it divideth into two parts,..is at the fingers subdivided into three branches. **1758** J. Dalrymple *Ess. Feudal Property* (ed. 2) 11 The Folkland was divided and subdivided into Counties, Try-things,..and Hundreds. **1764** Harmer *Observ.* ii. §12. 68 Speaking of the tents of the Arabs, the Journal says, They are subdivided into three apartments. **1823** Lingard *Hist. Eng.* VI. 32 The army formed in two grand divisions, each of which was subdivided into a battle and two wings. **1870** *Sat. Rev.* 2 Apr., That all tenants should be allowed to subdivide their holdings amongst their relatives. **1870** F. R. Wilson *Ch. Lindisf.* 23 They subdivided their parish into five chapelries.

b. in immaterial sense.

a **1586** Sidney *Apol. Poetry* (Arb.) 28 These [*sc.* poets] be subdiuided into sundry more speciall denominations. The most notable bee the Heroick, Lirick [etc.]. **1641** *Termes de la Ley* 77 Some had that charge as incident to their offices..: some others had it simply as of it selfe... And both these sorts are againe subdivided by M. Lambert. *c* **1645** Howell *Lett.* (1650) I. 97 They were the first that subdivided the four cardinal winds to thirty two. *a* **1768** Sterne *Serm. Yorick* (1773) IV. 151 Mankind led to dispose of these attributes inherent in the Godhead, and divide and subdivide them again amongst deities. **1813** J. Thomson *Lect. Inflam.* 502 Attempts have..been made to subdivide the phenomena of mortification. **1868** Rogers *Pol. Econ.* ii. (1876) 16 The use of machinery tends still further to subdivide labour. **1887** Bentley *Man. Bot.* (ed. 5) 405 The Classes are also divided into Sub-classes, Series, Cohorts, or Alliances..in the same manner as the orders, genera, and species are subdivided.

c. *refl.*

1709 *Royal Proclam.* 27 Jan., The Commissioners..shall subdivide themselves,..so as three, at least, may be appointed for the Service of each Division. **1791** Paine *Rights of Man* (ed. 4) 21 The original hereditary despotism resident in the person of the King, divides and subdivides itself into a thousand shapes and forms.

d. *absol.*

1880 [see subdivider].

2. *intr.* To break up into subdivisions.

1597-8 Bacon *Ess., Faction* (Arb.) 78 When one of the Factions is extinguished, the remaining subdiuideth. **1682** Bunyan *Holy War* (1905) 293 They marched, they countermarched, they opened to the right and left, they divided, and subdivided. **1769** *Phil. Trans.* LIX. 200 From this part upwards those vessels divide and sub-divide. **1831** R. Knox *Cloquet's Anat.* 33 These laminæ subdivide into radiated fibrils. **1871** Tyndall *Fragm. Sci.* (1879) II. 243 Every string sub-divides, yielding not one note, but a dozen.

†**b.** Used loosely of two persons forming separate factions. *Obs. nonce-use.*

1625 Bacon *Ess., Faction* (Arb.) 80 When Brutus and Cassius were ouerthrowne, then soone after Antonius and Octauianus brake and Subdiuided.

Hence **subdi'vided** *ppl. a.*

a **1676** Hale *P. Atticus* iii. (1677) 98 One of the subdivided party, that finds it self weakest. **1777** S. Robson *Brit. Flora* 154 Stem subdivided. **1796** Withering *Brit. Plants* (ed. 3) II. 141 Panicles with subdivided branches. **1845** *Encycl. Metrop.* IV. 785 The first semi-oscillation will be performed as a whole, the next as a subdivided string. **1855** *Orr's Circ. Sci., Inorg. Nat.* 98 The middle oolite is almost as varied and subdivided as the lower.

†**sub'divident.** *Obs.* [f. subdivide, after *divident.*] That which subdivides.

1581 Mulcaster *Positions* xxxix. (1888) 197 All the people which be in our countrie be either gentlemen or of the commonalty. The common is deuided into marchauntes and manuaries generally, what partition soeuer is the subdiuident.

subdi'vider. [f. subdivide + -er[1].] One who subdivides; *spec.* one who carves out an estate; one who settles on a portion of an estate.

1880 *Daily News* 20 Dec. 5/6 To those who had already subdivided he offered new mountain farms, leaving the subdividers to decide who should remain and who should remove. **1885** Seebohm *Brit. Birds* III. 252 When Nature's natural divisions are interfered with, the subdivider is obliged to fall back upon specific characters to diagnose his genera. **1888** *Ohio State Jrnl.* (Columbus) 2 Mar., [City property] for sale at original subdivider's prices. **1889** *Blackw. Mag.* Oct. 527/1 It would thus seem to be absolutely necessary, in order that the crofter may enjoy a reasonable chance of retaining his holding, to free him from the incubus of the subdivider or squatter.

subdividing, *vbl. sb.* [-ing[1].] Subdivision.

1651 Baxter *Inf. Bapt.* 149 What dividing, and subdividing, and subdividing again!

subdividing, *ppl. a.* [-ing[2].] That subdivides.

1809 *Phil. Trans.* XCIX. 126 A little instrument which I denominate a subdividing sector. **1872** Symonds *Rec. Rocks* vi. 200 In the neighbourhood of Presteign the subdividing limestone is no longer seen.

Hence **subdi'vidingly** *adv.*, in subdivisions.

1842 De Quincey *Pagan Oracles* Wks. 1858 VIII. 193 What was the essential machinery by which the Oracles moved?—I shall inquire subdividingly.

†**subdi'vidual,** *a. Obs.* [f. subdivide *v.* after *dividual.*] Involving subdivision.

1716 M. Davies *Athen. Brit.* III. 55 To declare..new Articles of Faith in Popery and Arianism as subdividual Worship and individual Adoration.

subdi'visible, *a.* [f. subdivide *v.* after *divisible.* Cf. F. *subdivisible*, It. *suddivisibile.*] Capable of being subdivided.

1841 *Penny Cycl.* XIX. 312/2 Into how many parts soever a line may be divided, each part is a length, still subdivisible for ever. **1848** *Fraser's Mag.* XXXVIII. 51 The lands become divisible and sub-divisible.

subdivision (sʌbdɪ'vɪʒən, 'sʌb-). [ad. late L. *subdīvīsio, -ōnem*, n. of action f. *subdīvīs-*, *subdīvidĕre* to subdivide. Cf. F., Sp. *subdivision*, It. *suddivisione.*]

1. a. The act or process of subdividing, or fact of being subdivided.

1599 B. Jonson *Cynthia's Rev.* ii. iii, To come to your.. courtiers face, tis of three sorts, according to our subdiuision of a courtier, elementarie, practique, and theorique. **1622** Malynes *Anc. Law-Merch.* 360 The Denomination, Division and Subdivision of the moneys of all Countreys is most necessarie for Merchants. **1651** Hobbes *Leviath.* ii. xxiv. 128 There were twelve Tribes, making them thirteen by subdivision of the Tribe of Joseph. **1776** Adam Smith *W.N.* i. i. (1869) I. 12 This subdivision of employment in philosophy, as well as in every other business, improves dexterity, and saves time. **1845** *Encycl. Metrop.* IV. 802 The aliquot subdivision of a vibrating string. **1855** Bain *Senses & Int.* i. ii. §15 (1864) 43 The Cerebral Nerves are divided into nine pairs, some of these being considered as admitting of farther subdivision. **1855** Macaulay *Hist. Eng.* xx. IV. 490 The increase of wealth had produced its natural effect, the subdivision of labour. **1889** Welch *Naval Archit.* 113 Watertight Subdivision of Ships.

b. An instance of this.

a **1577** Sir T. Smith *Commw. Eng.* i. iii. (1584) 3 Of these maner of rulinges by one, by the fewer part [etc.]..they which haue more methodically..written vpon them, doe make a subdiuision. **1634** R. H. *Salerne's Regim.* Pref., The third Ranke..admits a Subdivision into Better and Worse, Wise and Foolish, Learned and Ignorant. **1776** Adam Smith *W.N.* i. xi. (1869) I. 175 The nature of their business admits of the utmost subdivisions of labour. **1861** Brougham *Brit. Const.* xix. 313 Too minute a subdivision of business tends to contract the minds of those who perform it.

2. a. One of the parts into which a whole is subdivided; part of a part; a section resulting from a further division; *Nat. Hist.* a subordinate division of a group.

1553 T. Wilson *Rhet.* (1580) 113 Of these three partes of Philosophie, I might make other three subdiuisions, and largely set them out. **1643** Sir T. Browne *Relig. Med.* i. §52 Methinks amongst those many subdivisions of hell, there might have bin one Limbo left for these. **1646** —— *Pseud. Ep.* 54 Chrystall..is..reduced by some unto that subdivision which comprehendeth gemmes. **1662** Stillingfl. *Orig. Sacræ* i. ii. §6 The Gnosticks and the severall subdivisions of them. **1777** S. Robson *Brit. Flora* 14 The petiole..subdivided, having two leafits on each subdivision. *Ibid.* 37 Orders are the subdivisions of Classes. **1825** Syd. Smith *Wks.* (1859) II. 197/2 A small subdivision of the clergy of the North Riding of Yorkshire. **1842** Gwilt *Archit.* §2848. 778 The subdivisions, apartments, or portions whereof a building consists. **1850** Ansted *Elem. Geol., Min.*, etc. 371 The deposits of the Secondary epoch.. may..be divided into four principal groups, each of which again presents well marked subdivisions. **1874** Stubbs *Const. Hist.* I. ii. 16 Their armies were arranged according to the contingents which represented the tribal subdivisions.

b. *Milit.* The half of a division (in first quot. the rear half). Also at various times, the half of a company; in the artillery, a gun with its waggons (now called subsection).

1625 Markham *Souldiers Accid.* 28 Whensoever this Bodie..(which containeth but ten persons in fyle) shall be devided in the midst betweene the Middlemen, then the last fiue Rankes to the Reareward are called by the name of Subdevision. **1702** *Milit. Dict.* (1704) s.v., *Subdivisions*, are the lesser parcels, into which a Regiment is divided in marching, being half the greater divisions. **1727** H. Bland *Milit. Discipl.* v. 60 When a Battalion is divided into three equal Parts or Divisions, each Division is then called a Grand-Division. Sub-Divisions are formed by dividing each Grand-Division into three, four or five equal Parts. **1796** *Instr. & Reg. Cavalry* (1813) 223 Subdivisions, Right Wheel! **1802** C. James *Milit. Dict.* s.v., A company divided forms two subdivisions. **1858** Beveridge *Hist. India* III. ix. iv. 635 The British force began to advance along the trunk road in a column of sub-divisions. **1876** Voyle & Stevenson *Milit. Dict.*, *Sub-division*, in artillery, a gun with its wagon. **1889** *Standing Orders Royal Regim. Artill.* 41 Four-gun Batteries will be divided into two Sections—Right and Left—of 2 Sub-Divisions each. **1913** *Times* 14 May 6/2 A bearer sub-division R.A.M.C.

c. *N. Amer.* An area of land subdivided into plots for the erection of houses; a housing estate.

1911 *Daily Colonist* (Victoria, B.C.) 29 Apr. 13/2 Willows Beach Subdivision... The subdivision adjoins the well known Uplands Subdivision. **1926** G. Frankau *My Unsentimental Journey* xv. 209 The straight road through your new 'sub-divisions' (Anglice—building lots). **1947** *Publ. Amer. Dial. Soc.* vii. 22 'Village' has always been the common term for a small settlement, but does not appear in the name itself unless this is a subdivision name: *Sunset Village, Pilgrim Village.* **1960** V. Packard *Waste Makers* (1961) xxiv. 299 The 'country' place in the suburbs loses its 'semirural' character as soon as a subdivision goes up beyond it..(even though a sub-division house..in the suburbs may be preferable to an old row house in the city). **1979** *Tucson* (Arizona) *Citizen* 20 Sept. 1A/1, 1,700 displaced residents..left flooded parts of 25 subdivisions in Harris and Galveston counties.

subdi'visional, *a.* [f. prec. + -al[1].] Of the nature of subdivision; pertaining to subdivision, or a subdivision; consisting of a subdivision.

1656 in Petty *Down Survey* (1851) 90 In making of provinciall lots, subdivisionall lotts must follow, soe far as they could be practized, to promote the settlement of the army. **1834** J. P. Smith *Script. & Geol. Sci.* (1839) 60 Particular formations, one, two, or more in a system or subdivisional group. **1847** Grote *Greece* ii. xxii. III. 463 The Italians or Itali.., the Morgetes, and the Chaones, all of them names of tribes either cognate or subdivisional. **1864** *Athenæum* No. 1920. 215/2 Subdivisional multiplications and production by budding. **1898** *Daily News* 24 Jan. 3/4 The station is a subdivisional one for the E Division.

†**subdi'visionate,** *v. Obs. nonce-wd.* [f. subdivision + -ate[3].] *trans.* To subdivide.

1578 Sidney *Wanstead Play* in *Arcadia*, etc. (1605) 574 *Secundum* their dignitie, which must also be subdiuisionated into three equall *species.*

subdi'visive, *a.* [f. L. *subdīvīs-*, pa. ppl. stem of *subdīvidĕre* to subdivide + -ive.] Resulting from subdivision.

1838 Sir W. Hamilton *Logic* xxv. (1860) II. 23 When a whole is divided into its parts, these parts may..be themselves still connected multiplicities; and if these are again divided, there results a subdivision (*subdivisio*), the several parts of which are called the subdivisive members (*membra subdividentia*).

subdolous ('sʌbdələs), *a.* Now *rare.* [ad. late L. *subdolōsus* or f. its source *subdolus*, f. *sub-* sub- 19 + *dolus* cunning.] Crafty, cunning, sly.

1588 A. King tr. *Canisius' Catech.* Riij, The subdolous crafte and deceate of Satan. **1637** Gillespie *Eng. Pop. Cerem.* Ep. A2b, The subdolous Machiavellian. *a* **1677** Barrow *Serm.* Wks. 1687 I. 65 Illusive simulations and subdolous artifices. **1828** D'Israeli *Chas. I*, I. 269 The King was troubled, lest this subdolous and eloquent man should shake his resolution. **1843** Syd. Smith *Lett. Amer. Debts* i, The subdolous press of America contends that the English..would act with their own debt in the same manner. **1880** W. Cory *Mod. Engl. Hist.* i. 102 Nor has any maxim so subdolous as this been devised to abridge the freedom of Britons.

Hence **'subdolously** *adv.*, **'subdolousness.**

1635 Person *Varieties* i. 28 Take heed of the subdolousnesse of their proposition, which is not universally true. **1643** Baker *Chron.* (1653) 554 See the subdolousnesse of this man. **1681** Evelyn *Let. to Pepys* 6 Dec. in *Diary & Corr.* (1852) III. 260, I neither would, nor honestly could, conceal..how subdolously they dealt. **1824** *Blackw. Mag.* XVI. 345 Whisky..mixed subdolously with burnt brown sugar. **1862** T. A. Trollope *Marietta* xxii, Nanni had subdolously stretched out his hand sideways..to administer a squeeze to a rosy little hand that timidly stole out half-way to meet his.

sub'dominant, *sb.*[1] *Mus.* [sub- 4. Cf. F. *sousdominante.*] The note next below the dominant of a scale; the fourth note in ascending and the fifth in descending a scale. Also *attrib.*

1793 *Encycl. Brit.* (1797) XII. 502/1 The chord of the sub-dominant. *Ibid.* 548/2 These three sounds, the tonic, the tonic dominant, and the sub-dominant, contain in their chords all the notes which enter into the scale of the mode. **1835** *Court Mag.* VI. 26/1 She might if she pleased break through that eternal descent by two semitones from the dominant to the sub-dominant. **1863** Atkinson *Ganot's Physics* §207 (1866) 162 The tonic, dominant, and sub-dominant chords. *Ibid.* 163 The dominant and sub-dominant bear major triads.

sub'dominant, *a.* (*sb.*[2]) [sub- 14.]

1. Less than dominant, not quite dominant. (See quots.)

1826 Kirby & Sp. *Entomol.* xlix. IV. 493 We may take *Scolia* for an example of a subdominant group beginning more southward. *a* **1909** *Buck's Med. Handbk.* III. 260 (Cent. Dict. Supp.) Those disturbances which are dominant become focal in consciousness, or the mind is fully conscious of such. Those that are sub-dominant bring about marginal or sub-conscious psychical states.

2. *Ecol.* Designating a species which is prevalent in a community, but below the dominant in precedence. Also as *sb.* Cf. dominant *a.* 8.

1909 Groom & Balfour tr. *Warming's Oecol. Plants* xxxv. 139 Every community consists of dominant and sub-dominant species, as well as of others that are more or less dependent upon these and occur only here and there. **1923** *Ecology* IV. 13 Species belonging to life-forms of subordinate rank (i.e. subdominant species) have also to be considered. **1933** [see co-dominant *sb.*]. **1969** *Gloss. for Landscape Work* (*B.S.I.*) v. 39 *Sub-dominant*..Of a species, that species in a mixed crop which is selected to come next in precedence to the dominant.

sub'dorsal, *a.* and *sb.* [Cf. F. *sous-dorsal.*]

A. *adj.* **1.** [sub- 1 a.] Pertaining to the part situated at the bottom of the back (*i.e.* the posteriors). *nonce-use.*

1800 in *Spirit Publ. Jrnls.* IV. 36 The vigorous posts which sustain the enormous subdorsal promontory of Lord G. *Ibid.* 371 He has ordered the dimensions of the subdorsal basis of each of the new scholars to be taken.

2. *Zool.* [sub- 11, 21 d.] Somewhat or almost dorsal; situated near the back.

1835-6 *Todd's Cycl. Anat.* I. 522/1 Fins advanced,.. distant and subdorsal. **1852** Dana *Crust.* i. 53 The feet of the two posterior pairs [of legs] are short and subdorsal.

B. *sb.* A subdorsal fin.

1856 Page *Adv. Text-bk. Geol.* xiii. 230 The dorsals differing from the sub-dorsals, and these again from the pectorals.

Hence **sub'dorsally** *adv.*, in a subdorsal position.

1902 *Proc. Zool. Soc.* II. 304 On 3rd. somite a pair of black 'eye-spots' surrounded by a white iris, subdorsally.

subduable (səb'djuːəb(ə)l), *a. rare.* [f. SUBDUE *v.* + -ABLE.] That may be subdued.

1611 COTGR., *Surmontable*,..subduable. **1662** H. MORE *Phil. Writ.* Pref. gen. (1712) p. x, A natural touch of Enthusiasm..such as, I thank God, was ever governable enough, and have found at length perfectly subduable. **1839** J. ROGERS *Antipapopr.* xii. §5. 277 If the love of sin be hardly subduable by the fear of hell. **1844** MRS. BROWNING *Drama of Exile* 1321 Who talks here..Of hate subduable to pity?

subdual (səb'djuːəl). [f. SUBDUE *v.* + -AL[1].]

1. The act of subduing or state of being subdued; subjection.

1675 BURTHOGGE *Causa Dei* 227 The Castigation and subdual of the affections. **1741–65** WARBURTON *Div. Legat.* v. iv. Wks. 1788 III. 139 Mahomet's work was not like Moses's, the subdual of a small tract of Country. **1864** PUSEY *Lect. Daniel* ii. (1866) 79 Permanent subdual distinguished the Roman Empire. Other Empires swept over like a tornado. **1882** H. S. HOLLAND *Logic & Life* (1885) 45 We are shut out from understanding this subdual which is belief. **1904** *Archæol. Æliana* XXV. II. 147 Their subdual lasted several years.

2. A becoming subdued or moderate. *rare.*

1884 J. TAIT *Mind in Matter* 72 In autumn, with the subdual of heat, there is annually, in Canada, a transformation of nature.

†**sub'duce**, *v. Obs.* [ad. L. *subdūcĕre*, f. *sub-* SUB- 26 + *dūcĕre* to lead, bring.]

1. *trans.* To take away, withdraw (*lit.* and *fig.*).

1626 BP. HALL *Contempl., O.T.* xx. iv, Else, had the chyld beene secretly subduced, and missed by his bloodie grandmother. **1632** —— *Hard Texts* Matt. xxviii. 20 Howsoever my bodily presence shall be subduced from you. **1664** OWEN *Vind. Animadv.* xvi. 422 No small part of the Territories of many Princes is subduced from under their power. *a* **1761** LAW *Comf. Weary Pilgrim* (1809) 55 They wanted not to have..their covetousness and sensuality to be subduced by a new nature from heaven derived into them.

b. To withdraw from allegiance; = SEDUCE *v.* 1.

a **1578** LINDESAY *Chron. Scot.* (S.T.S.) II. 297 [He] had subducit with his gould the men of weir that keipit the castell.

c. *refl.* (occas. *intr.*) To withdraw oneself or itself *from* a place or society, *from* allegiance, etc.; to escape *from*; to secede.

1542 BECON *Pathw. Prayer* ii. B vj b, It shalbe expedient for such as intende to exercyse prayer..to subduce & conuaye them selues from the company of the worldely people into some secrete..place. **1610** BP. HALL *Apol. Brownists* §7 You have separated from this Church..: If Christ haue taken away his word and Spirit [from it], you have justly subduced. **1636** T. GOODWIN *Child of Light* (1643) 112 A man can no way avoid his suggestions, nor subduce himself from them. *a* **1656** BP. HALL *Specialities Life* Rem. Wks. (1660) 21, I subduced myself speedily from their presence. *a* **1660** HAMMOND *19 Serm.* xiv. Wks. 1684 IV. 658 For never was the earth so peevish, as to..subduce it self from its [*sc.* the sun's] rayes.

2. To subtract, as a mathematical operation.

1571 DIGGES *Pantom.* I. xviii. F b, Subduce the first distance from the third. **1588** A. KING tr. *Canisius' Catech.* h vij, Thane subduce ye haill frome ye nombre of ye dayes of yat moneth. *a* **1676** HALE *Prim. Orig. Man.* 106 If out of that supposed infinite multitude of antecedent Generation, we should by the Operation of the Understanding subduce Ten.

3. To bring, lead *into. rare.*

1609 TOURNEUR *Funeral Poem Sir F. Vere* 278 Offences done against his owne estate..have oftentimes Subduc'd the malefactors for those crimes Into the hands of justice.

Hence †**sub'ducing** *vbl. sb.*, withdrawal.

1633 BP. HALL *Hard Texts* Neh. vi. 11 By weake subducing of my selfe, and hiding my head in the Temple. *a* **1660** HAMMOND *19 Serm.* xi. Wks. 1684 IV. 636 A cowardly, pusillanimous subducing of ones self.

†**subducend.** *Math. Obs. rare.* [ad. L. *subdūcendus*, gerundive of *subdūcĕre* (see prec.).] = SUBTRAHEND.

1706 W. JONES *Syn. Palmar. Matheseos* 16 If the Subducend be taken from the Minuend, there rests the Remainder.

†**subducion.** *Obs. rare*[−1]. [? f. SUBDUE + *-cion* = -TION.] ? Reduction to order. (Cf. SUBDUE 1 e.)

1455 *Rolls of Parlt.* V. 287/1 The conservation of the pease, and subducion of theym that entende to the breche therof.

subduct (səb'dʌkt), *v.* [f. L. *subduct-*, pa. ppl. stem of *subdūcĕre* to SUBDUCE.]

1. *trans.* To take away from its place or position, withdraw from use, consideration, influence, etc. Now *rare.*

a. with physical obj.

1652–62 HEYLIN *Cosmogr.* III. (1673) 61/1 The three Palestines..being subducted from the power of the see of Antioch. **1657** J. WATTS *Scribe, Pharisee*, etc. 205 One of the Elements is subducted from the people, and the other is adored by them. **1665–6** *Phil. Trans.* I. 382 For one determinate space of time it exhibits its lucid part to the Earth, for another, subducts it. **1715** M. DAVIES *Athen. Brit.* I. 141, I had but a bare sight of that Pamphlet, it being presently subducted from the Publick Perusal. *a* **1792** HORNE *Ess. & Th.* Wks. 1818 I. 363 The Chinese physicians never prescribe bleeding..; saying, that, if the pot boil too fast, it is better to subduct the fuel, than lade out the water. **1837** BARHAM *Ingol. Leg.* Ser. I. *Spectre of Tappington*, He replaced the single button [on his breeches] he had just subducted. **1844** H. ROGERS *Ess.* (1860) III. 119 All such as are inconsistent in their statements..are to be subducted from his catalogue.

b. with immaterial obj.

1614 JACKSON *Creed* III. III. vi. 151 Yet must all excesse in spirituall graces..be subducted from that prerogatiue which wee that are Christs messengers, haue in respect of Aarons successors. **1660** HEYLIN *Hist. Quinquart.* To Rdr., Nor have I purposely concealed or subducted any thing considerable which may seem to make for the advantage of the opposite party. **1754** EDWARDS *Freed. Will.* I. ii. (1762) 12 As having its Influence added to other Things, or subducted from them. **1840** G. DARLEY *Wks. Beaum. & Fl.* Introd., Subducting the devilish feature, it were well perhaps, if all Englishmen..resembled this portrait. **1843** MILL *Logic* III. viii. 465 Subduct from any phenomenon such part as is known by previous inductions to be the effect of certain antecedents. **1851** HERSCHEL *Study Nat. Phil.* II. vi. 156 When the effects of all known causes are estimated with exactness, and subducted.

c. *refl.*

1655 OWEN *Vind. Evang.* xxiii. 486 Sinne (which is the Creature's subducting its selfe from under the Dominion of God). **1668** —— *Expos. 130th Ps.* 76 From his providential presence he could never subduct himself.

2. a. To take away (a quantity) *from*, †*out of* another; to subtract, deduct. Now *rare.*

1571 DIGGES *Pantom.* IV. v. V iij, Your greater semidiameter, whiche subducted from youre former diuisor leaueth the semidimetient of the intrinsicall circle. **1649** ROBERTS *Clavis Bibl.* Introd. iii. 59 If out of the number of years..you subduct the years of the Oppressours of Israel under their Judges. **1674** MOXON *Tutor Astron.* II. (ed. 3) 70, 200 Years..which subducted out of 1000 leaves 800 Years. **1716** B. CHURCH *Hist. Philip's War* (1867) II. 85 William Fobes..was order'd to keep a just accompt of what each Indian had so that it might be subducted out of their wages at their return home. **1855** BREWSTER *Newton* I. iii. 42 Subducting the diameter of the hole from the length and breadth of the image, there remains 13 inches in the length and 2⅜ inches in the breadth. **1881** *Nature* XXIII. 558 When we..subduct the vapour pressure from the barometric height.

absol. **1646** *Recorde's Gr. Artes* 110 Therefore seeing 9 in the quotient, multiply, and subduct as before. **1662** HIBBERT *Body Div.* II. 86 They adde, they multiply; never subduct, never divide. **1706** W. JONES *Syn. Palmar. Matheseos* 14 According to their respective Value, take one of the next Denomination, out of which Subduct.

†**b.** *intr.* To take something away *from. Obs.*

1667 MILTON *P.L.* VIII. 536 Nature..from my side subducting, took perhaps More then enough. **1669** W. SIMPSON *Hydrol. Chym.* II. 124 The Spaw..helps the refining of the vessels..and so subducts from the Disease by hindring the affluent cause. **1798** W. MAVOR *Brit. Tourists* V. 193 Its neglected and languishing state still farther subducts from its picturesque effect.

3. To take away or remove surreptitiously or fraudulently. Also *absol.* Now *rare.*

1758 JOHNSON *Idler* No. 95 ¶11 Purchased with money subducted from the shop. **1760** C. JOHNSTON *Chrysal* (1822) I. 200 By subducting largely from the sums confided to him. **1824** LANDOR *Imag. Conv.* Wks. 1853 I. 53/1 If he had..brought down a brace out of a covey, instead of subducting them from the platter.

4. To draw up, lift. Now *rare.*

1837 BARHAM *Ingol. Leg.* Ser. I. *Spectre of Tappington*, Subducting his coat-tails one under each arm [etc.]. **1869** 'WAT BRADWOOD' *The O.V.H.* xxxi, Jemmy subducted his coat-tails, and sat him down.

5. *trans.* and *intr. Geol.* To move sideways and downwards underneath a neighbouring lithospheric plate.

1971 *Nature* 29 Jan. 309/2 A Mesozoic foldbelt..makes up the periphery of West Antarctica, suggesting that seafloor was once subducted along this margin. **1974** *Ibid.* 13 Sept. 102/3 Since the Lower Miocene eastern Sicily has been the border zone between colliding continental blocks and the oceanic lithosphere subducting beneath the Calabrian arc. **1975** *Sci. Amer.* Nov. 98/2 It is puzzling..that the Pacific plate can move laterally for 6,000 kilometers before it subducts. **1977** A. HALLAM *Planet Earth* 100 (*caption*) The dense oceanic plate..is being subducted beneath the lighter continental plate.

Hence **sub'ducted, sub'ducting** *ppl. adjs.*

1975 *Sci. Amer.* Nov. 93/1 If the subduction ceases altogether, the subducted segment of the lithosphere will lose its identity and become part of the surrounding mantle in roughly 60 million years. *Ibid.*, At a velocity of one centimetre per year the subducting plate will be assimilated at a depth of about 400 kilometres. **1980** J. G. NAVARRA *Earth, Space, & Time* i. 17/1 The subducted plate is believed to be more dense than the mantle into which it plunges because it is colder. **1980** *Economist* 16 Aug. 64 Where two plates collide, one plate plunges beneath the other... The world's deep ocean trenches mark the graves of such 'subducting' plate edges.

subduction (səb'dʌkʃən). [ad. L. *subductio, -ōnem*, n. of action f. *subdūcĕre* to SUBDUCE.] The action of subducting.

1. a. Withdrawal, removal. Now *rare.*

a **1620** J. DYKE *Sel. Serm.* (1640) 79 A quenching of fire by subduction of fuell. **1625** J. ROBINSON *Observ. Div. & Mor.* lv. 282 Unto whom..thought and care, in one night brought grey hayr, by subduction of nourishment. **1630** BP. HALL *Occas. Medit.* §66. (1634) 145 Oh that we were not more capable of distrust, then thine omnipotent hand is of wearinesse and subduction. **1730** *Hist. Lit.* I. 449 Fearing the Subduction of the King's Bounty, which he had hitherto supported it. **1839** *Blackw. Mag.* XLVI. 542 The withdrawal of a patriot from Parliament..is the subduction of parliamentary force. **1854** BUCKNILL *Unsoundn. Mind* 25 Terms signifying deprivation or subduction.

†**b.** Surreptitious or secret withdrawal. *Obs.*

a **1646** J. GREGORY *Posthuma* (1649) 88 The Corruption proceeded not by subduction from the Hebrew, but the accession to the Greek Scripture. **1721** BAILEY, *Subduction*, a taking privately from.

2. Subtraction, deduction. Now *rare.*

1579 DIGGES *Stratiot.* I. xv. 25 Subduction is the taking of the one Fraction from the other. **1608** BP. HALL *Epist.* I. vi. 284, I haue noted foure ranks of commonly-named Miracles: from which, if you make a iust subduction, how few of our wonders shall remaine either to beleefe or admiration! **1664** EVELYN *Pomona* Pref. 4 Brought thither without charge, or extraordinary subductions. **1706** W. JONES *Syn. Palmar. Matheseos* 16 Addition and Subduction, serve Reciprocally to prove each other. **1734** BERKELEY *Analyst* §5 Wks. 1871 III. 260 By the continual addition or subduction of infinitely small quantities. **1856** MASSON *Ess. Biog. & Crit.* 109 The property remaining..after the subduction of his own share as the eldest son.

†**3.** A drawing down or away (see quot. 1612); the evacuation (*of* excrement). (= Gr. ὑπαγωγή.)

1612 WOODALL *Surg. Mate* Wks. (1653) 274 Subduction is an abstraction of juyces, oyles, and other liquid matters downward by percolation, filteration, and the like. **1620** VENNER *Via Recta* vii. 111 They make the belly soluble, and helpe the subduction of excrements. **1688** HOLME *Armoury* III. xii. 446/2.

4. The action of subduing or fact of being subdued; subdual, subjection. (Const. *to.*) Now *rare.*

1670 G. H. *Hist. Cardinals* I. I. 11 Contriving, if not the destruction, at least the subduction of the Temporal Power to the Spiritual. **1717** L. HOWEL *Desiderius* (ed. 3) 157 Subduction of the Flesh. **1786** *Francis the Philanthropist* II. 33 The..celebrated fair, who boasts the subduction of whole regiments by the power of her charms. **1824** G. CHALMERS *Caledonia* III. 82 Edward assembled a large army ..for the subduction of Dumfries-shire. *Ibid.* 472 The ruling clergy..brought on the subduction of the kingdom.

†**5.** 'A reckoning or account' (1656 Blount).

6. *Geol.* [a. F. *subduction* (A. Amstutz 1951, in *Arch. des Sci.* IV. 326).] The sideways and downward movement of the edge of a lithospheric plate into the mantle beneath a neighbouring plate; **subduction zone**, a strip along which this is occurring.

1970 *Nature* 14 Nov. 659/1 The lateral displacement of continents involves at least partial destruction in subduction zones of either the plate on which they are borne or of another plate. **1972** *Sci. Amer.* Mar. 33/2 Along one edge of a crustal plate there is a subduction zone, usually marked by a trench. **1972, 1975** [see OBDUCTION 2]. **1975** *Sci. Amer.* Nov. 89/2 The deepest trenches of the world's oceans, including the Java and Tonga trenches and all others associated with island arcs, mark the seaward boundary of subduction zones. **1980** J. G. NAVARRA *Earth, Space, & Time* i. 17/2 Subduction along the Java Trench where the Indo-Australian Plate is moving under the Indonesian island chain..fueled the 1883 eruption of Krakatoa.

†**sub'ductive**, *a. Obs. rare*[−1]. [f. L. *subduct-* (see SUBDUCT) + -IVE.] That is to be subtracted.

1798 HUTTON *Course Math.* I. 170 That..changes its nature from a subductive quantity to an additive one.

†**subductory**, *a. Obs. rare*[−1]. [f. L. *subduct-* (see prec.) + -ORY.] Laxative. (Cf. SUBDUCTION 3.)

1620 VENNER *Via Recta* iv. 79 Why are Oysters vsually eaten a little before meale?.. By reason of their subductory qualitie, concerning the bellie.

†**subdue**, *sb. Obs.* Also 5 subdeue. [f. next.] Subdual, subjugation, conquest.

c **1465** *Pol. Rel. & L. Poems* (1903) 5 Wherefor, prince.., Remembere þe Subdeue of þi Regaly, Of Englonde, frawnce, & spayn trewely. **1482** *Rolls of Parlt.* VI. 223/1 In defens of this youre seid Reame, and subdue of youre Enemyes. *a* **1592** GREENE & LODGE *Looking Glasse* (1598) A 4 b, The worlds subdue.

subdue (səb'djuː), *v.* Forms: α. 4 so-, sudewe, so-, suduwe, sodeuwe. β. 5 subd(e)we, 5–6 -dew, 5–6 -dieu, 6 -deu, 5– subdue. [Of difficult etymology. ME. *sodewe, subdewe, -due*, represents formally AF. **soduer*, **su(b)duer* = OF. *so(u)duire, su(d)duire*, etc. (used with the meanings of L. *sēdūcĕre*) to deceive, seduce = OIt. *soddurre*:—L. *subdūcĕre* to draw up or away, withdraw, remove by stealth, purge, evacuate, calculate (see SUBDUCE, SUBDUCT). Neither L. *subdūcĕre* nor OF. *souduire* is recorded in the sense of 'subdue', so that it is to be presumed that the AF. form took over the sense from L. *subdĕre*, the pa. pple. of which is represented in Eng. by SUBDIT from *c* 1375.

There is no clear connexion in form or sense with the AF. *subduz* of Edw. III stat. ii. c. 17, ann. 1353; the meaning is app. 'attached' or 'arrested', not 'subdued'. The 15th c. AF. *subduer* (Littleton *Inst.*, ed. 1516, A vij b) was prob. modelled on the current Eng. form.]

1. a. *trans.* To conquer (an army, an enemy, a country or its inhabitants) in fight and bring them into subjection.

1387 TREVISA *Higden* (Rolls) III. 19 [He] wente and sodewed Siria. *Ibid.* 443 þanne he stood wiþ [*MS.* β suduweþ, *MS.* γ sodeuweþ] the peple þat woneþ at þe foot of þe hille mont Caucasus. *c* **1420** ? LYDG. *Assembly of Gods* 1651 Fooles..Wenyng to subdew, with her oon hande, That ys ouer mekyll for all an hoole lande. *c* **1460** FORTESCUE *Abs. & Lim. Mon.* xvi. (1885) 150 Is hyghnes shalbe myghty, and off poiar to subdue his ennemyes. **1486** in *Surtees Misc.* (1890) 54, I subdewid Fraunce. **1535** COVERDALE *Zech.* ix. 15 They shall consume and deuoure, and subdue them with slynge stones. **1553** EDEN *Treat. Newe Ind.* (Arb.) 21 How the Portugales subdued Malaccha, shalbe said hereafter. **1593** SHAKS. *3 Hen. VI*, III. iii. 82 Iohn of Gaunt, Which did subdue the greatest part of Spaine. **1653** HOLCROFT

Procopius, Goth. Wars 14 Since God hath given us Victory, and the glory of subduing a City. **1667** MILTON *P.L.* XI. 687 To overcome in Battel, and subdue Nations. **1788** GIBBON *Decl. & F.* xlvii. IV. 582 The Samaritans were finally subdued by the regular forces of the East: twenty thousand were slain. **1841** ELPHINSTONE *Hist. India* I. 397 They even assert that the same kings subdued Tibet on the east, and Cambója..on the west. **1879** FROUDE *Cæsar* xix. 330 He [*sc.* Cæsar] wished to hand over his conquests to his successor not only subdued but reconciled to subjection.

†**b.** Const. *to, unto, under* the conqueror or his rule. *Obs.*

1398 TREVISA *Barth. de P.R.* VI. xix. (Tollem. MS.), Whan y hadde sudewed all þe worlde to my lordschipe. *c* **1420** ? LYDG. *Assembly of Gods* 584 Owre gret rebell May we then soone euer to vs subdew. *c* **1460** FORTESCUE *Abs. & Lim. Mon.* ii. (1885) 111 Whan Nembroth..made and incorperate the first realme, and subdued it to hymself bi tyrannye. **1549** *Compl. Scot.* xi. 90 ȝour ald enemes hes intendit to..subdieu ȝou to there dominione. **1590** SPENSER *F.Q.* II. x. 13 Thus Brute this Realme vnto his rule subdewd. **1651** HOBBES *Leviath.* II. xvii. 88 When a man..by Warre subdueth his enemies to his will.

†**c.** To overcome or overpower (a person) by physical strength or violence. *Obs.*

1590 SPENSER *F.Q.* I. iv. 51 Rest a while Till morrow next, that I the Elfe subdew. *Ibid.* II. v. 26 Full many doughtie knights he..Had..subdewde in equall frayes. **1593** SHAKS. *2 Hen. VI,* III. ii. 173 As one that graspt And tugg'd for Life, and was by strength subdude. **1604** —— *Oth.* I. ii. 81 If he do resist Subdue him, at his perill.

d. *transf.* and *fig.*

1611 *Bible* Dan. ii. 40 Forasmuch as yron breaketh in pieces and subdueth all things. **1697** DRYDEN *Virg. Georg.* I. 228 Burrs and Brambles..th' unhappy Field subdue. *Ibid.* IV. 247 Subdu'd in Fire the stubborn Mettal lyes. **1799** COWPER *Castaway* 47 By toil subdued, he drank The stifling wave. **1883** R. BRIDGES *Prometheus* 761 The broad ways That bridge the rivers and subdue the mountains.

†**e.** To reduce to order or obedience. *Obs.*

1481 *Cov. Leet Bk.* 493 To subdue such personez as here late offended; diuerse of which personez be nowe late indyted of ryott & trasspas [etc.].

2. a. To bring (a person) into mental, moral, or spiritual subjection; to get the upper hand of by intimidation, persuasion, etc.; to obtain control of the conduct, life, or thoughts of; to render (a person or animal) submissive; to prevail over, get the better of. Const. *to* (that which exercises control, the control exercised).

1509 HAWES *Past. Pleas.* xxxiv. xii, He [*sc.* Cupid] is aduenturous To subdue mine enemies, to me contrarious. **1535** COVERDALE *Wisd.* xviii. 22 He ouercame not the multitude with bodely power..but with the worde he subdued him that vexed him. **1538** STARKEY *England* I. i. 12 Ther ys no best so strong..but to man by wysdom he ys subduyd. **1552** ABP. HAMILTON *Catech.* (1884) 48 Thai ar nocht subdewit to the rychteousness. **1560** DAUS tr. *Sleidane's Comm.* 405 The Prynces..by a certen feare and terrour subdued. **1588** SHAKS. *L.L.L.* I. ii. 187 His [Love's] disgrace is to be called Boy, but his glorie is to subdue men. **1610** —— *Temp.* I. ii. 489 This mans threats, To whom I am subdude, are but light to me. *a* **1721** PRIOR *Dial. Dead* (1907) 219 Swords Conquer some, but Words subdue all men. **1817** JAS. MILL *Brit. India* II. IV. vi. 156 Pigot, with a hardihood which subdued them,..declared that..he would furnish no money. **1833** HT. MARTINEAU *Brooke Farm* vi. 80 This recollection awakened others which subdued me completely. **1853** NEWMAN *Hist. Sk.* (1876) I. I. i. 31 He was subdued by the influence of religion. **1855** TENNYSON *Brook* 113 Claspt hands and that petitionary grace Of sweet seventeen subdued me ere she spoke.

absol. **1781** COWPER *Retirem.* 266 God has form'd thee with a wiser view, Not to be led in chains, but to subdue. **1837** CARLYLE *Fr. Rev.* I. I. ii, And so..did this [growth] of Royalty..spring up; and grow mysteriously, subduing and assimilating.

refl. **1513** DOUGLAS *Æneis* XIII. i. 37 The catall, quhilkis favorit langeyr The beist ourcummyn as thar cheif and heyr, Now thame subdewis vndir his ward in hy Quhilk has the ovirhand. **1833** TENNYSON *Dream Fair Women* lix, It comforts me in this one thought to dwell, That I subdued me to my father's will. **1870** DICKENS *Edwin Drood* ii, I must subdue myself to my vocation.

b. With a person's body, soul, mind, actions, etc. as obj.

c **1520** NISBET *N.T.*, Rom. ii. 15 marg., The fleische nother is nor cann be subdewit tharto. **1526** *Pilgr. Perf.* (W. de W. 1531) 148b, We must..subdue all our inordynate thoughtes. **1548** *Act 2 & 3 Edw. VI* c. 19 §1 Due and godlye abstynence ys a meane..to subdue mens Bodies to their Soule and Spirite. **1591** SHAKS. *1 Hen. VI,* I. ii. 109 My heart and hands thou hast at once subdu'd. **1603** —— *Meas. for M.* IV. ii. 84 He doth with holie abstinence subdue That in himselfe, which he spurres on his powre To qualifie in others. **1667** MILTON *P.L.* VIII. 584 If aught..were worthy to subdue The Soule of Man. **1769** *Junius Lett.* xxxv. 167 Before you subdue their hearts, you must gain a noble victory over your own. **1791** MRS. RADCLIFFE *Rom. Forest* ii, Having subdued his own feelings, he resolved not to yield to those of his wife. **1817** SHELLEY *Rev. Islam* Ded. xi, A prophecy Is whispered, to subdue my fondest fears. **1849** MACAULAY *Hist. Eng.* iv. I. 469 Those emotions were soon subdued by a stronger feeling. **1863** GEO. ELIOT *Romola* xx, She herself wished to subdue certain importunate memories.

c. *transf.*

c **1449** PECOCK *Repr.* I. xiv. 73 It miȝte seme that God wolde not subdewe or submitte..and sende him [*sc.* Holy Scripture] to resoun, for to be interpretid. **1535** COVERDALE *Phil.* iii. 21 Acordinge to ye workynge wherby he is able to subdue all thinges vnto himselfe. **1781** COWPER *Retirem.* 416 Wild without art, or artfully subdu'd, Nature in ev'ry form inspires delight.

†**d.** To achieve, attain (a purpose). *Obs. rare.*

1590 SPENSER *F.Q.* II. ix. 9 Perhaps my succour..Mote stead you much your purpose to subdew.

†**e.** To bring *to* a low state, reduce. *Obs.*

1605 SHAKS. *Lear* III. iv. 72 Nothing could haue subdu'd Nature To such a lownesse, but his vnkind Daughters. **1606** —— *Ant. & Cl.* IV. xiv. 74 His face subdu'de To penetrative shame.

f. In phr. ***to be subdued to what one works in***: to become reduced in capacity to the standard of one's material (in allusion to Shakes. *Sonnets* cxi.).

1907 W. RALEIGH *Shakespeare* iv. 107 Shakespeare accepted the facts, and subdued his hand to what it worked in. **1912** L. STRACHEY *Landmarks in French Lit.* iv. 92 Their [*sc.* the Elizabethans'] work has vanished from the stage, and is today familiar to but a few of the lovers of English literature. Shakespeare alone was not subdued to what he worked in. **1926** G. M. TREVELYAN *Hist. Eng.* v. iii. 559 When a man, in defending his country from foreign conquest, has to rely on certain forces, he ceases to be capable of criticizing them. He becomes subdued to the material in which he works.

3. To bring (land) under cultivation.

1535 COVERDALE *Gen.* i. 28 Growe, and multiplie, and fyll the earth, and subdue it. **1628** MAY *Virg. Georg.* I. 6 Nor is't unwholesome to subdue the Land By often exercise. **1677** W. HUBBARD *Narrative* 63 To engross more Land into their hands then they were able to subdue. **1794** S. WILLIAMS *Vermont* 307 Their lands, which they had..subdued by extreme labour. **1829** B. HALL *Trav. N. Amer.* I. 86 In proportion as the soil is brought into cultivation, or subdued, to use the local phrase. **1867** RUSKIN *Time & Tide* xxv. §176 Set..to subduing wild and unhealthy land.

4. In medical use: To reduce, allay. ? *Obs.*

1615 G. SANDYS *Trav.* 134 The iuyce of Cedars; which by the extreme..siccatiue faculty..subdued the cause of interior corruption. **1732** ARBUTHNOT *Rules of Diet* in *Aliments* etc. (1736) 262 Cresses, Radishes, Horse-Radishes, ..subdue Acidity. **1804** ABERNETHY *Surg. Obs.* 176 The inflammation of the brain was now subdued. **1809** *Med. Jrnl.* XXI. 52 Although the hysteric affections were still very troublesome, she could now completely subdue them by the use of pills. **1829** COOPER *Good's Study Med.* II. 515 The inflammation is to be subdued by blood-letting.

5. To reduce the intensity, force, or vividness of (sound, colour, light); to make less prominent or salient. (Cf. SUBDUED 2.)

1800 HT. LEE *Canterb. T.* (ed. 2) III. 139 A circular pavilion..Where both light and heat were subdued by shades. **1815** SHELLEY *Alastor* 165 With voice stifled in tremulous sobs Subdued by its own pathos. **1843** RUSKIN *Mod. Paint.* (1851) I. II. I. vii. §21 The warm colours of distance, even the most glowing, are subdued by the air. **1845** *Antiq. & Archit. Year Bk.* 319 Unable to subdue properly the red, blue, and gold of the niched hood mould. **1856** KANE *Arctic Expl.* I. ix. 102 Distance is very deceptive upon the ice, subduing its salient features.

subdued (səb'dju:d), *ppl. a.* [f. prec. + -ED[1].]

1. Reduced to subjection, subjugated, overcome. Also *absol.*

1604 SHAKS. *Oth.* v. ii. 348 One whose subdu'd Eyes,.. Drops teares as fast as the Arabian Trees Their Medicinable gumme. **1615** G. SANDYS *Trav.* 48 Strengthened both against forraine invasions and revolts of the subdued. **1660** MILTON *Dr. Griffith's Serm.* Wks. 1851 V. 397 [It] will in all probability subject the Subduers to the Subdu'd. **1812** CRABBE *Tales* xviii. 68 She had a mild, subdued, expiring look. **1837** CARLYLE *Fr. Rev.* III. IV. v, Lyons contains in it subdued Jacobins; dominant Girondins. **1890** 'R. BOLDREWOOD' *Col. Reformer* (1891) 202 A subdued, bronzed, resolved-looking man.

2. Reduced in intensity, strength, force, or vividness; moderated; toned down.

1822 [implied in SUBDUEDNESS]. **1835** LYTTON *Rienzi* IV. i, Censers of gold..steamed with the odours of Araby, yet so subdued as not to deaden the healthier scent of flowers. **1847** C. BRONTË *Jane Eyre* viii, My language was more subdued than it generally was when it developed that sad theme. *Ibid.* xiv, The subdued chat of Adèle. **1849** RUSKIN *Seven Lamps* iii. §17. 83 Many of the noblest forms are of subdued curvature. **1861** FLOR. NIGHTINGALE *Nursing* 59 There are acute cases (particularly a few eye cases..), where a subdued light is necessary. **1877** HUXLEY *Physiogr.* 203 The effects of subterranean heat in the locality may still manifest themselves in a subdued form. **1912** *Times* 19 Dec. 20/3 (Stock Exchange), There was a more subdued tone.

Hence **sub'duedly** *adv.*, with subdued sound, light, colour, etc.; **sub'duedness**, the condition of being subdued.

1822 COLERIDGE *Lett.* (1895) 718 In his freest..passages there is a subduedness, a self-checking timidity in his colouring. **1852** ROBERTSON *Serm.* Ser. IV. xxxix. (1863) 294 Meekness and subduedness before God. **1858** G. GILFILLAN *Life Sir T. Wyatt* W.'s Poet. Wks. p. xv, Homely natural feeling of the poetical and the subduedly sensuous. **1891** KIPLING *Light that Failed* xiii, Maisie was crying more subduedly.

sub'duement. *rare.* [f. SUBDUE *v.* + -MENT.] The action of subduing; subdual.

'A word not used, nor worthy to be used' (J.).

1606 SHAKS. *Tr. & Cr.* IV. v. 187, I haue seen thee.. scorning forfeits and subduments. *a* **1619** DANIEL *Coll. Hist. Eng.* (1626) 81 Hee sent a solemne Ambassage to Pope Adrian, to craue leaue for the subduement of that Country. **1807** G. CHALMERS *Caledonia* I. II. vii. 325 Anglo-Saxon.. on the subduement of the Romanized Ottadini, succeeded to the British tongue. **1860** FORSTER *Gr. Remonstr.* 89 That subduement of the Roman Catholic power on the continent.

subduer (səb'dju:ə(r)). [f. SUBDUE *v.* + -ER[1].] A person who or a thing which subdues, in the various senses of the verb.

c **1510** BARCLAY *Mirr. Gd. Manners* (1570) Div, Thus were they..by death subduers of their owne corps carnall. **1596** DALRYMPLE tr. *Leslie's Hist. Scot.* I. 73 The ald Romanis, subdueris of the Warlde. **1611** SPEED *Theat. Gt. Brit.* 39/2 Ostorius..Subduer of great Caractacus. **1732** ARBUTHNOT *Rules of Diet* in *Aliments* (1736) 253 Figs are great subduers of Acrimony. **1747** RICHARDSON *Clarissa* (1811) II. ii. 15 With some of the sex, insolent controul is a more efficacious subduer than kindness or concession. **1790** BURKE *Fr. Rev.* 322 By the laws of nature the occupant and subduer of the soil is the true proprietor. **1860** GEO. ELIOT *Mill on Fl.* I. v, It is a wonderful subduer, this need of love. **1860** PUSEY *Min. Proph.* 191 Such was He, the Subduer of all which exalted itself. **1900** DK. ARGYLL *Autobiogr.* (1906) II. 85 The subduer of a fierce enemy and the saviour of India.

sub'duing, *vbl. sb.* [f. SUBDUE *v.* + -ING[1].] The action of SUBDUE *v.*; subdual, subjugation.

c **1482** J. KAY tr. *Caoursin's Siege of Rhodes* (1870) ¶1 The subduynge and oppressynge of the..cytee of Constantynople. **1532** MORE *Confut. Tindale* Wks. 371 The subduyng of ye flesh and taming of bodily lustes. **1535** COVERDALE *1 Macc.* xiv. 34 What so euer was mete for the subduynge of the aduersaries. **1655** HUME in *Nicholas Papers* (Camden) III. 213 A combination made between France and Cromwell for the subduing of all the Spanish provinces of the Low Countries. **1690** CHILD *Disc. Trade* (1698) Pref. p. xv, The subduing [= abatement] of interest will bring in multitudes of traders. **1788** *Encycl. Brit.* (1797) I. 276/2 None of them [*sc.* harrows] are sufficient to prepare for the seed any ground that requires subduing. **1875** *Encycl. Brit.* I. 335/1 For the more speedy subduing of a rough uncultured surface.

sub'duing, *ppl. a.* [f. as prec. + -ING[2].] That subdues; tending to subdue.

1608 D. T[UVILL] *Ess. Pol. & Mor.* 66b, To polish and fashion out his then rough-hewen fortune, with the edge of his subduing sword. **1816** J. SCOTT *Vis. Paris* 118 A stimulating melange of what is most heating, intoxicating, and subduing. **1842** MANNING *Serm.* xvi. (1848) I. 228 Not because they are under any subduing dominion of indwelling sin. **1891** CONAN DOYLE *Adv. Sherlock Holmes* ii, There was something depressing and subduing in the sudden gloom.

Hence **sub'duingly** *adv.*, so as to subdue.

1833 *New Monthly Mag.* XXXVII. 301 What goes more subduingly to the heart than the author's poem to his sick child? **1880** MEREDITH *Tragic Com.* xviii, A hand that she had taken and twisted in her woman's hand subduingly!

subduple (sʌb'dju:p(ə)l, 'sʌbdju:p(ə)l), *a. Math.* [ad. late L. *subduplus*: see SUB- 10 and DUPLE *a.*] That is half of a quantity or number; denoting a proportion of one to two; (of a ratio) of which the antecedent is half the consequent.

1609 DOWLAND *Ornith. Microl.* 63 Euery Proportion is.. taken away by the comming of his contrary proportion... As by the comming of a subduple, a dupla is taken away, and so of others. **1648** [see SUB- 10]. **1706** W. JONES *Syn. Palmar. Matheseos* 55 The Ratio of 3 to 6 is 3/6 = ½ or sub-duple. **1715** tr. *Gregory's Astron.* (1726) II. 841 The number will be about subduple in a Jovial Year. **1728** CHAMBERS *Cycl.* s.v. *Subnormal*, The Subnormal PR is Subduple the Parameter. **1740** *Phil. Trans.* XLI. 426 Let us take..Two Points at Pleasure, the Point A in the Circumference of the Equator, and the Point C in the Circumference of a subduple parallel Circle.

sub'duplicate, *a. Math.* [SUB- 10.]

1. Of a ratio or proportion: Being that of the square roots of the quantities; thus, 2 : 3 is the subduplicate ratio of 4 : 9.

1656 tr. *Hobbes' Elem. Philos.* 121 A Proportion is said to be Divided, when between two quantities are interposed one or more Means in continual Proportion, and then the Proportion of the first to the second is said to be Subduplicate of that of the first to the third, and Subtriplicate of that of the first to the fourth. **1670** BOYLE *Usef. Exp. Nat. Philos.* II. iii. 15 The times are in Subduplicate Proportion to the lengths of the Pendulums. **1674** PETTY *Disc. Dupl. Prop.* 21 The First Instance, Wherein Duplicate, and Sub-duplicate Ratio or Proportion is considerable, Is In the Velocities of two equal and like Ships; which Velocities..are the square Roots of the Powers which either drive or draw them. **1706** W. JONES *Syn. Palmar. Matheseos* 288 The Times in which a Body runs thro' those Planes, shall be in a Subduplicate Ratio of their Altitudes. **1798** HUTTON *Course Math.* II. 358 The bodies descend by nearly uniform velocities, which are directly in the subduplicate ratio of the diameters.

¶**2.** = SUBDUPLE. (A misuse.)

1656 HOBBES *Six Lessons* Wks. 1845 VII. 277 It is the same fault when men call half a quantity subduplicate. **1755** JOHNSON, *Subduplicate*,..containing one part of two.

'subdwarf, *sb.* and *a. Astr.* [SUB- 23.] **A.** *sb.* A star which when plotted on the Hertzsprung–Russell diagram lies just below the main sequence, being less luminous than dwarf stars of the same temperature. Cf. SUBGIANT.

1939 G. P. KUIPER in *Astrophysical Jrnl.* LXXXIX. 548 Three classes of objects of special interest are expected to be found..: (1) white dwarfs; (2) intermediate white dwarfs or, more generally, stars not over 2 or 3 mag. below the main sequence... The second group extends almost along the whole main sequence. Since these stars merge into the main sequence and are much more similar to main-sequence stars than to white dwarfs.., the name 'subdwarfs' is suggested for this class of stars, in analogy with 'subgiants'. **1962** *New Scientist* 3 May 218/2 Some hot subdwarfs are found from their spectra to have helium but virtually no hydrogen. **1979** *Nature* 24 May 305/1 The observations of CH Cygni reported here were made to determine whether a symbiotic star is a binary system composed of an M6 giant and a hot subdwarf, or whether it is a cool star surrounded by a thick corona.

B. *adj.* Designating such a star.

1981 *Nature* 8 Oct. 432/2 The most likely explanation..is that the atmospheres are untypical of the subdwarf stars as a whole.

sub-'edit, *v.* [Back-formation f. next.] *trans.* To edit (a paper, periodical, etc.) under, to prepare (copy) for, the supervision of a chief editor. Also *absol.* Hence **sub-'editing** *vbl. sb.*

1855 D. G. ROSSETTI *Let.* 23 Jan. (1965) I. 241 He sub-edits the *Leader.* **1862** THACKERAY *Philip* xlii, I can tell you there is a great art in sub-editing a paper. **1880** *Trans. Philol. Soc.* 130 Several Americans have offered to undertake sub-editing [for the 'Oxford English Dictionary']. **1883** *Ibid.* Abstract p. iv, *S*,..partly arranged and sub-edited by Mr. C. Gray. **1915** WODEHOUSE *Psmith, Journalist* xx. 145, I am Psmith. I sub-edit.

sub-'editor. [SUB- 6.] A subordinate editor; one who sub-edits.

1834 [see *city-editor* s.v. CITY 9]. **1837** CARLYLE *Fr. Rev.* II. I. iii, Clerk Tallien, he also is become sub-editor; shall become able-editor. **1883** BLACK *Shandon Bells* xxx, I daresay I should..be the sub-editor of the *Cork Chronicle.*

Hence **sub-'editorship**, the position of sub-editor.

1855 HYDE CLARKE *Dict.* 383. **1862** THACKERAY *Philip* xxx, He had her vote for the sub-editorship.

,sub-edi'torial, *a.* [f. SUB-EDITOR + -IAL.] Pertaining to a sub-editor or sub-editorship.

1837 CARLYLE *Fr. Rev.* II. I. iv, While Tallien worked sedentary at the sub-editorial desk. **1850** THACKERAY *Pendennis* xxxiv, In a masterly manner he had pointed out what should be the sub-editorial arrangements of the paper. **1905** *Athenæum* 30 Sept. 437/2 The dry data were..set out skilfully enough in sub-editorial fashion.

'sub-,element. [SUB- 5.] A subordinate or secondary element.

1846 POE *N. P. Willis* Wks. 1864 III. 31 In addition to the element of novelty, there is introduced the sub-element of unexpectedness. **1882–3** *Schaff's Encycl. Relig. Knowl.* II. 1396 The good element..is God; and his personality comprises five spiritual and five material sub-elements.

,sub-ele'mentary, *a.* [SUB- 14.] Less than elementary, not quite elementary.

1626 DONNE *Serm.* lxxx. (1640) 823 In the Elements themselves, of which all sub-elementary things are composed. *a* **1835** MACCULLOCH *Attributes* (1837) II. 417 Disintegrated into those modes of elementary or subelementary matter whence it was first constructed.

sub'equal, *a.* [ad. mod.L. *subæquālis*: see SUB- 21 c and EQUAL.]

1. *Nat. Hist.* Nearly equal.

1787 tr. *Linnæus' Fam. Plants* 195 Florets all fertile. Proper one with petals five, heart-inflected, subequal. **1828** STARK *Elem. Nat. Hist.* II. 199 Eyes subequal. **1880** HUXLEY in *Times* 25 Dec. 4/1 The earliest known equine animal possesses four complete sub-equal digits on the fore foot. **1897** GÜNTHER in *Mary Kingsley's W. Africa* 704 Teeth small, subequal, with brown pointed tips.

2. Related as several numbers of which no one is as large as the sum of the rest.

In mod. Dicts.

Hence **sub'equally** *adv.*; **sube'quality**, the condition of being subequal.

1870 HOOKER *Stud. Flora* 200 Fruit glabrous, subequally ribbed all round. **1873** MIVART *Elem. Anat.* 172 In the number of these bones [metacarpals] and their sub-equality of development man agrees with many Vertebrates above Fishes.

‖**suber** ('sjuːbə(r)). *Bot.* (*Chem.*) [L. = cork, cork-oak.] The bark or periderm of the cork-tree; cork. Also, a vegetable principle found in this.

1800 HENRY *Epit. Chem.* (1808) 293 Suber,—this name is used to denote common cork wood. **1819** J. G. CHILDREN *Chem. Anal.* 298 Suber..is light, soft and elastic, burns with a bright flame and yields ammonia by distillation. **1826** HENRY *Elem. Chem.* II. 313 Of Suber and its Acid.

Hence **sube'ramic** *a.*, denominating the acid produced by the dry distillation of ammonium suberate. **sube'ramide**, the white crystalline compound formed by the action of aqueous ammonia on suberate of methyl or by heating suberic acid with phosphorus trichloride. **'suberane**, a liquid hydrocarbon (see quots.); hence **sube'ranic** *a.* **sube'ranilate**, a salt of **subera'nilic** *acid*, the acid remaining after suberanilide has been precipitated from a solution of fused suberic acid, aniline, and alcohol; so **sube'ranilide**.

1859 WATTS tr. *Gmelin's Handbk. Chem.* XIII. 221 *Suberamic Acid. $C^{16}NH^{15}O^{6}$. **1898** *Jrnl. Chem. Soc.* LXXIV. I. 125 *Suberamide melts at 216°. **1894** *Ibid.* LXVI. I. 265 The purified suberene (or heptamethylene, '*suberane') boils at 117–117·5° under 743 mm. pressure. **1911** *Encycl. Brit.* (ed. 11) XXII. 32/2 Cyclo-heptane (suberane), C_7H_{14}, obtained by the reduction of suberyl iodide. *Ibid.* 33/1 Cycloheptane carboxylic acid (*suberanic acid), $C_7H_{13}CO_2H$. **1859** WATTS tr. *Gmelin's Handbk. Chem.* XIII. 222 **Suberanilate of Ammonium.*—The acid dissolves easily in hot ammonia, and the salt is deposited in small granular crystals. *Ibid.*, *Suberanilic acid yields aniline when fused with potash. **1857** MILLER *Elem. Chem., Org.* iv. §2. 257 Dianilides... *Suberanilide 2 ($C_{12}H_5$), H_2N_2, $C_{16}H_{12}O_4$.

suberate ('sjuːbəreɪt). *Chem.* [ad. F. *subérate* (Lagrange 1797): see SUBER and -ATE[1].] A salt of suberic acid.

1800 tr. *Lagrange's Chem.* II. 297. **1806** *G. Adam's Nat. & Exp. Philos.* (Philad.) I. App. 547 Suberats. **1809** J. MURRAY *Syst. Chem.* (ed. 2) IV. 353 Suberate of potassa, formed by adding suberic acid to carbonate of potassa. **1862** MILLER *Elem. Chem., Org.* (ed. 2) xiv. §1. 888 Suberate of ethyl.

suberb, obs. form of SUBURB.

suberch. = SUBBOSCO.

1592 GREENE *Upst. Courtier* D 4 Whether hee will haue his crates cut low like a Juniper bush, or his suberches [? *read* suboschos] taken awaye with a Rasor.

subereous (sjuː'bɪərɪəs), *a.* [f. late L. *sūbereus*: see SUBER and -EOUS.] Suberous, suberose.

1826 KIRBY & SP. *Entomol.* xlvi. IV. 258 Substance.. Subereous... A soft elastic substance somewhat resembling cork. **1900** B. D. JACKSON *Gloss. Bot. Terms* 258/1.

suberic (sjuː'bɛrɪk), *a. Chem.* Also 8 -ique. [ad. F. *subérique* (Lagrange 1797): see SUBER and -IC.] Of or pertaining to cork. ***suberic acid***, a white crystalline dibasic acid prepared by the action of nitric acid on cork, paper, linen rags, fatty acids, and other bodies. Also ***suberic anhydride***, ***ether***, etc.

1799 *Monthly Rev.* XXX. 17 He was able to produce an acid nearly similar to the suberique, by digesting the nitrous acid on charcoal. **1806** *G. Adam's Nat. & Exp. Philos.* (Philad.) I. App. 562 Suberic [acid]. **1837** R. D. THOMSON in *Brit. Ann.* 355 Suberic ether. **1879** WATTS *Dict. Chem.* VI. 1040 Suberic aldehyde..is formed, together with suberic acid and palmitoxylic acid, by the action of fuming nitric acid on palmitolic acid. **1894** *Jrnl. Chem. Soc.* LXVI. I. 499 Suberic anhydride..is prepared by boiling suberic acid with acetic chloride.

sube'riferous, *a.* [f. SUBER + -(I)FEROUS.] Producing cork or suberin.

In mod. Dicts.

suberification (sjuː,bɛrɪfɪ'keɪʃən). *Bot.* [f. SUBER + -(I)FICATION.] = SUBERIZATION.

1885 GOODALE *Physiol. Bot.* 34 The principal modifications of the cell-wall are the following:..(3) Cutinization (or Suberification).

suberiform (sjuː'bɛrɪfɔːm), *a.* [f. SUBER + -(I)FORM.] Resembling cork, corky.

1841 *Penny Cycl.* XX. 423/2 The mass is composed of one (suberiform) substance. **1847–9** *Todd's Cycl. Anat.* IV. 19/1 Polypes distributed over the surface of a common mass, which is..composed of a suberiform substance supported by calcareous aciculi.

suberin ('sjuːbərɪn). *Chem.* Also -ine. [ad. F. *subérine* (Chevreul): see SUBER and -IN[1].] The cellular tissue which remains after cork has been exhausted by various solvents.

1830 LINDLEY *Nat. Syst. Bot.* 97 Cork..contains a peculiar principle called Suberin. **1885** GOODALE *Physiol. Bot.* 38 The substance which imparts the repellent character to the cell-wall is known as cutin; when restricted to cork it is called suberin.

Hence **'suberinate** *Chem.*, a salt of **sube'rinic** *acid*, an acid obtained indirectly from suberin.

1891 *Jrnl. Chem. Soc.* LX. 466 Suberinic acid, $C_{17}H_{30}O_3$, when gently warmed, forms a liquid miscible with alcohol, ether, and chloroform. *Ibid.*, Potassium suberinate is soluble in water and alcohol, but not in ether.

suberize ('sjuːbəraɪz), *v. Bot.* [f. SUBER + -IZE.] *pass.* To be converted into cork-tissue by the formation of suberin. Hence **suberi'zation**.

1882 VINES tr. *Sach's Bot.* 95 The suberisation of the newly-formed cells. **1884** BOWER & SCOTT *De Bary's Phaner.* 111 Often the wall is suberised all round and throughout its whole thickness. *Ibid.* 112 The totally suberised layers often separate in the section-cutting. **1885** GOODALE *Physiol. Bot.* 75 The walls of older cork-cells are cutinized or suberized throughout.

subero- ('sjuːbərəʊ), combining form of SUBER in names of chemical compounds containing or obtained from suberic acid.

1839 R. D. THOMSON in *Brit. Ann.* 354 Subero-pyroxylic ether. **1894** MUIR & MORLEY *Watts' Dict. Chem.* IV. 524/1 *Suberocarboxylic acid*, Hexane tricarboxylic acid. *Ibid.*, *Suberomalic acid*, Oxy-suberic acid.

suberone ('sjuːbərəʊn). *Chem.* [ad. F. *subérone* (Boussingault): see SUBER and -ONE.] An aromatic oil, formed by the distillation of suberic acid with lime.

1845 *Chem. Gaz.* III. 56. **1881** *Jrnl. Chem. Soc.* XXXIX. 540 Suberone readily combines with hydrocyanic acid.

Hence **sube'ronyl, -ylene** (see quots.).

1890 *Jrnl. Chem. Soc.* LVIII. II. 728 Suberone..is easily reduced to the corresponding alcohol, $C_7H_{13}.OH$, by the action of sodium in presence of alcohol. This suberonyl alcohol is a colourless, somewhat viscid liquid. *Ibid.*, Suberonyl iodide, when treated with alcoholic potash, yields suberonylene, C_7H_{12}.

suberose[1] ('sjuːbərəʊs), *a. Bot.* [ad. mod.L. *sūberōsus*: see SUBER + -OSE[1].] Having the appearance of cork; corky in form or texture.

1845–50 MRS. LINCOLN *Lect. Bot.* App. v. 204 *Suberose*, corky. **1846** DANA *Zooph.* (1848) 609 Suberose, of varying form. **1887** W. PHILLIPS *Brit. Discomycetes* 378 Disc.. encircled by a dehiscent,..distinct, suberose, friable ring.

suberose[2] (sʌbɪ'rəʊs), *a. Bot. rare*$^{-0}$. [ad. mod.L. *subērōsus*: see SUB- 21 c and EROSE.] Somewhat erose.

1828–32 in WEBSTER.

suberous ('sjuːbərəs), *a. Bot.* [f. SUBER or ad. mod.L. *sūberōsus* SUBEROSE[1]: see -OUS.] Corky; = SUBEROSE[1].

1679 EVELYN *Sylva* (ed. 3) 29 That..the sap should be so green on the indented leaves,..so Suberous in the Bark (for even the Cork-tree is but a courser Oak). **1776** J. LEE *Introd. Bot.* Explan. Terms 379 *Suberosus*, suberous, the outward Bark soft, but elastic like Cork. **1849** BALFOUR *Man. Bot.* §85 In some trees it [*sc.* the epiphlœum] consists of numerous layers, forming the substance called cork..; hence the name suberous, or corky layer, which is given to it. **1884** BOWER & SCOTT *De Bary's Phaner.* 550 Two forms of the superficial formation of cork may be distinguished..: namely, suberous crusts and suberous integuments.

sube'roxime. *Chem.* An oxime of suberyl.

1894 [see SUBERYLAMINE].

suberyl ('sjuːbərɪl). *Chem.* [ad. F. *subéryle* (Boussingault): see SUBER and -YL.] The diatomic radicle of suberic acid. Also *attrib.*

1852 W. GREGORY *Handbk. Org. Chem.* 245 It is probable that there exists a radical suberyle = C_8H_6O = Su. **1872** WATTS *Index to Gmelin's Handbk. Chem.*, Suberyl Hydride. **1874** *Jrnl. Chem. Soc.* XXVII. 935 On distilling suberic acid with lime he [*sc.* Boussingault] got a liquid boiling at 186°, which he called hydride of suberyl.

Hence **sube'rylamine, 'suberylene, sube'rylic** *a.* (see quots.).

1894 *Jrnl. Chem. Soc.* LXVI. I. 160 Suberylamine, $C_7H_{13}.NH_2$, may be obtained from suberoxime by reduction either with sodium in alcoholic solution or with sodium amalgam in alkaline aqueous solution. *Ibid.*, A monhydric alcohol, $C_7H_{13}.OH$, which the author calls suberylic alcohol or suberol. *Ibid.* 266 Suberylene, C_7H_{12}, is obtained when a mixture of equal volumes of suberylic iodide and alcohol is added to strong alcoholic potash.

†**subeth.** *Obs.* [a. med.L. *subet(h)*, ad. Arabic *subāt* 'somnus in capite apparens', lethargy, f. *sabata* to rest (cf. SABBATH). Cf. obs. F. *subet.*] Unhealthy or morbid sleep.

subeth Avicennæ was an old name for coma.

1398 TREVISA *Barth. De P.R.* v. iii. (1495) 107 Whan he slepith it happith him to haue Subeth, that is false reste. *c* **1550** LLOYD *Treas. Health* Y 7 Of the payne in the heade called subeth. **1626** MIDDLETON *Anything for Quiet Life* II. iv, Subject to Subeth, unkindly sleeps, which have bred opilations in your brain.

†**subethal**, *a. Obs. rare.* [ad. obs. F. *subethal*, f. *subeth*: see prec. For the etymol. sense cf. *carotid*, which is ult. f. Gr. καροῦν to plunge into heavy sleep.] The carotid (artery).

1541 COPLAND *Guydon's Quest. Cyrurg.* F iij, The greate veynes & arteres that are led by the furculles in stying vpwarde y[e] sydes of the necke to the superyour partyes, whiche be called Guy degi, and popleticis, depe & suberall [*read* subetall; orig. *subethalles*], Thyncysyon of the whiche be very peryllous.

'sub,factor. [SUB- 6.] A subordinate factor.

1705 tr. *Bosman's Guinea* vii. 94 When a Chief-Factor or Factor observes that his Sub-Factor or Ware-house Keeper are enclined to Extravagance. **1753** *Stewart's Trial* 159 He did,..for some time, employ the new pannel, as his sub-factor, in levying the rents of Ardshiel. **1818** SCOTT *Hrt. Midl.* xli, By going forward a little farther, they would meet one of his Grace's subfactors. **1872** YEATS *Growth Comm.* 348 Sub-factors ascended the rivers.

'sub,family. [SUB- 7 b.]

1. a. *Nat. Hist.* A primary subdivision of a family.

1833 *Penny Cycl.* I. 19/1 He denominates these subfamilies, cyprinoïdes, siluroïdes, salmonoïdes, clupeoïdes, and lucioïdes respectively. **1868** *Rep. U.S. Comm. Agric.* (1869) 87 The sub-family Melolonthidæ feed exclusively on vegetable matter. **1870** ROLLESTON *Anim. Life* 26 The congeneric subfamilies, under either great family of the Rasores and Columbidae respectively.

b. A subdivision of a human family, *spec.* one living within a primary family group (see quot. 1964).

1964 *Census of Population* 1960 (U.S. Dept. Commerce) I. I. p. lviii/2, A subfamily is a married couple with or without own children, or one parent with one or more own children under 18 years old, living in a housing unit and related to the head of the household or his wife. **1970** S. L. BARRACLOUGH in I. L. Horowitz *Masses in Lat. Amer.* iv. 129 Some such units have incomes close to those of sub-family producers.

2. *transf.*, esp. in *Linguistics.*

1856 W. D. WHITNEY in *Jrnl. Amer. Oriental Soc.* V. 195 The various sub-families and even closer kindred dialects had deviated too widely from their original and from one another. **1972** R. J. WILSON *Introd. Graph Theory* viii. 119 We call a transversal of a subfamily of *S* a partial transversal of *S*. **1978** *Language* LIV. 181 The Southern sub-family merged *ī* with *ĭ* and *u* with *ŭ*.

subferabylle, early var. of SUFFERABLE.

1483 *Cath. Angl.* 371/1 Subferabylle, *tollerabilis.*

subfeu ('sʌbfjuː), *sb. Sc. Law.* [f. SUB- 9 (*b*) + FEU *sb.*: cf. next.] A 'feu' or fief granted by a vassal to a subvassal.

1681 STAIR *Inst. Law Scot.* I. xxi. 420 All Sub-feues of Ward-lands, holden of Subjects without the Superiours consent, are declared null and void. **1758** J. DALRYMPLE *Ess. Feudal Property* (ed. 2) 84 As in subfeus at first, the original vassal remained still liable for the services. **1826** BELL

Comm. Laws Scot. (ed. 5) I. 29 If the condition be farther guarded with irritant and resolutive clauses, it seems that the subfeu may be challenged even before the necessity for a new entry with the superior arises. **1874** *Act 37 & 38 Vict.* c. 94 §4 Nothing herein contained shall be held to validate any subfeu in cases where subinfeudation has been effectually prohibited.

b. *attrib.*: **subfeu-duty** (cf. *feu-duty*, FEU *sb.* 3).
1826 BELL *Comm. Laws Scot.* (ed. 5) I. 25 Nothing more is demandable than the subfeu-duty.

subfeu (sʌbˈfjuː), *v. Sc. Law.* [f. SUB- 9 (*b*) + FEU *v.*; cf. med.L. *subfeodāre*.] Of a vassal: To grant (lands) in feu to a subvassal; to subinfeudate. Also *absol.*
1754 ERSKINE *Princ. Sc. Law* (1809) 137 The vassal who thus subfeus, is called the subvassal's immediate superior. **1758** J. DALRYMPLE *Ess. Feudal Property* (ed. 2) 88 In soccage fiefs the vassals subfeued their lands..to hold of themselves. **1826** BELL *Comm. Laws Scot.* (ed. 5) I. 24 Property subfeued as building ground in a city. *Ibid.* 29 When the prohibition to subfeu is effectually created as a real burden on the right of the vassal. **1876** *Encycl. Brit.* IV. 63/2 Every burgess held direct of the Crown. It was, therefore, impossible to subfeu the burgh lands.

Hence **subˈfeuing** *vbl. sb.*
1758 J. DALRYMPLE *Ess. Feudal Property* (ed. 2) 84 One thing which very much facilitated the progress of alienation, was the practice of subfeuing. **1826** BELL *Comm. Laws Scot.* (ed. 5) I. 29 In the New Town of Edinburgh, grants are generally made with a condition against subfeuing.

subfeudation (sʌbfjuːˈdeɪʃən). [f. SUB- 9 + FEUDATION, after SUBFEU *sb.*] The action or practice of granting subfeus; subinfeudation.
1681 STAIR *Inst. Law Scot.* I. xxi. 419 It is much debated ..whether by Sub-feudation, Recognition be incurred, or whether it be comprehended under alienation. **1835** *Tomlin's Law Dict.* s.v. *Tenure*, Very early they became hereditary, and that as soon as they did so, they led to the practice of sub-feudation. **1839** *Penny Cycl.* XIV. 105/1 Owing to the extensive system of subfeudation, or subtenure [in North Italy].

subfeudatory (sʌbˈfjuːdətərɪ). [f. SUB- 9 (*b*) + FEUDATORY, after prec. Cf. med.L. *subfeudātārius*.] One who holds a fief from a feudatory.
1839 *Penny Cycl.* XIV. 105/1 The political system of most towns of North Italy in the tenth and eleventh centuries consisted of the nobles, feudatories, and subfeudatories. *c* **1850** BROUGHAM (Ogilvie, 1882), The smaller proprietors or feudatories of the prince, had..proportionably few inferior vassals, or sub-feudatories.

subfief (ˈsʌbfiːf), *sb.* [f. SUB- 9 + FIEF *sb.* Cf. F. *sous-fief*.] A fief which is held of an intermediary instead of the original feoffor; *spec.* (now *Hist.*) in Germany, a minor state, holding of a more important state instead of directly of the German crown.
1845 S. AUSTIN *Ranke's Hist. Ref.* III. 515 He consented that Duke Ulrich should take possession of Würtenberg as a sub-fief of Austria. **1901** *Westm. Gaz.* 31 Jan. 3/1 In the German Empire the title of 'Lord' is connected mostly with subfiefs such as Rügen.

So **subˈfief** *v.* [cf. obs. F. *soubsfiefver*, Cotgr.] *trans.*, to grant as a subfief.
1903 E. MACCULLOCH *Guernsey Folk Lore* 61 In process of time they [*sc.* lands] came to be sub-fieffed by their possessors.

subˈfossil, *a.* [f. SUB- 21 + FOSSIL *a.*] Partly fossilized.
1832 DE LA BECHE *Geol. Man* (ed. 2) 161 A bed containing sub-fossil shells. **1851** WOODWARD *Mollusca* 130 Struthiolaria:..Australia and New Zealand, where alone it occurs sub-fossil. **1856** PAGE *Adv. Text-bk. Geol.* ix. 171 When petrifaction has not taken place, and the organism is merely embedded in superficial clays and gravels, the term sub-fossil is that more properly applied. **1880** A. R. WALLACE *Isl. Life* II. xix. 389 A small sub-fossil hippopotamus.

So **subˈfossil** *sb.*, a partly fossilized substance.
1873 GEIKIE *Gt. Ice Age* App. 516 Sub-fossils.

sub-ˈfraction. [SUB- 9.]
1. *Math.* A fraction of a fraction.
1612 W. COLSON *Gen. Tres., Art Arith.* A a a b/2 Subfraction, or fraction of fraction, as ½ of ⅓. **1817** COLEBROOKE *Algebra*, etc. 14 Assimilation of sub-fractions, or making uniform the fraction of a fraction.

2. *Biochem.* Any one of the portions into which a fraction may be further divided. Cf. FRACTION *sb.* 7.
1946 *Nature* 5 Oct. 474/1 The division of the combined cystine in wool into four sub-fractions of different chemical reactivity. **1962** V. N. OREKHOVICH et al. in A. Pirie *Lens Metabolism Rel. Cataract* 324 We succeeded in dividing β-crystallin of cattle lens into β_1- and β_2-crystallin..and γ-crystallin was divided into three sub-fractions. **1978** *Jrnl. Neurochem.* XXX. 563 A subfraction, derived from the microsomal fraction of rat cerebral cortex,..appears to be enriched in receptor sites for a number of potential neurotransmitters.

Hence ˌ**subfractioˈnation** *Biochem.*, the process of separating a fraction into further components.
1955 *Biochem. Jrnl.* LX. 615/1 This subfractionation has not brought to light any enzymic heterogeneity in the granules. **1978** *Jrnl. Neurochem.* XXX. 783 The possibility that these findings might reflect merely contamination of myelin with other membranes was tested by subfractionation.

†**subfumiˈgation.** *Obs.* = SUFFUMIGATION.
1390 GOWER *Conf.* III. 45 With Nigromance he wole assaie To make his incantacioun With hot subfumigacioun. **14..** *Chaucer's H. Fame* 1264 (Thynne), That vsen exorsisacions And eke subfumygacions. **1562** BULLEIN *Bulwarke, Bk. Simples* 26 The smoke of theim [marigold flowers] to bee made in a close subfumigacion. **1579** LANGHAM *Garden Health* 1 To stop fluxes, vse subfumigations thereof [acacia].

subfusc (ˈsʌb-, sʌbˈfʌsk), *a.* and *sb.* Also -fusk. [ad. L. *subfuscus*, var. of *suffuscus*: see SUB- 21 a + FUSK.] **a.** Of dusky, dull, or sombre hue; *spec.* of clothing: dark, as prescribed by the regulations of the Universities of Oxford and Cambridge for examinations and other formal occasions.
a **1763** SHENSTONE *Economy* III. 26 O'er whose quiescent walls Arachne's unmolested care has drawn Curtains subfusk. **1770** J. CLUBBE *Misc. Tracts* I. 4 Their subfusk complexions were probably acquired by greasy unguents and fuliginous mixtures dried in by the sun. **1853** 'C. BEDE' *Verdant Green* I. v, [University] statutes which required him ..to wear garments only of a black or 'subfusk' hue. **1887** W. BEATTY-KINGSTON *Mus. & Mann.* II. 321 The surface ..is become subfusk in hue with sheer feverish dryness. **1895** *Pall Mall Gaz.* 16 Dec. 11/1 The subfusc marbling of the convolvulus hawk [moth]. **1930** W. J. LOCKE *Town of Tombarel* v. 163 Cousin Hortense in some sort of unremarkable subfusc raiment. **1973** *New Society* 1 Nov. 259/3 His clothes very subfusc—grey suit polished black shoes, the only brightness a purple and red bowtie. **1978** G. GREENE *Human Factor* V. i. 232 Two women who might have been sisters in their similar subfusc clothing waited by what he guessed was a confessional box.
fig. **1893** E. GOSSE *Questions at Issue* 150 To overdash their canvases with the subfusc hues of sentiment. **1900** *Athenæum* 28 July 116/1 Such Philistines..provide a suitable and sub-fusk background for the real figures in the Italian family group. **1927** C. PARSONS in *Oxford Poetry* 24 Lost in what corner of this maze, With mind already dyed subfusc. **1949** C. P. SNOW *Time of Hope* v. xxxiii. 280 Allen ..made subfusc, malicious, aunt-like jokes at Getliffe's expense. **1958** L. DURRELL *Balthazar* x. 210 The frail subfusc moonlight glancing along the waves. **1970** N. MARSH *When in Rome* iv. 106 Mailer seemed to me to be, in a subfusc sort of way, cocksure.

b. (*a*) *absol.* with *the*; (*b*) as *sb.* Subfusc colour; subfusc dress.
1710 STEELE & ADDISON *Tatler* No. 260 ¶5 The Portuguese's Complexion was a little upon the Subfusk. **1882** *Blackw. Mag.* Aug. 234 The Apotheker had not deigned to alter or add to his ordinary suit of professional 'subfusk'. **1914** *Ibid.* Jan. 109/2 They give us drabs and subfuscs instead of the glowing colours of life. **1944** A. L. ROWSE *Eng. Spirit* xxxvii. 260 Black-gowned young men and women, all dutifully clad in *sub fusc*. **1961** E. WILLIAMS *George* xx. 320, I was able to keep up the illusion of study by twice donning sub-fusc and walking down to the Examination Schools in white tie and mortar-board.

subfuscous (sʌbˈfʌskəs), *a. rare.* [f. L. *subfuscus* (see prec.) + -OUS.] = prec.
1760 *Phil. Trans.* LII. 95 A paler yellow,..a few reddish and subfuscous spots. **1815** STEPHENS in Shaw's *Gen. Zool.* IX. I. 122 Cuckow with a..subfuscous body. **1904** *Sat. Rev.* 30 Jan. 140 Apart from the intellectual ravage, they should be restrained from blackening the sub-fuscous.

subgeneric (sʌbdʒɪˈnɛrɪk), *a.* [f. SUBGENUS after *generic*. Cf. F. *sous-générique*.] Of or pertaining to a subgenus; having the characteristics of, constituting, or typifying a subgenus.
1836 *Partington's Brit. Cycl., Nat. Hist.* II. 564/2 The trivial name of the common gade, *Mustela*, has been taken for the sub-generic name by many. **1852** DANA *Crust.* II. 1596 The form..is exceedingly various, and if adopted as subgeneric, the subdivisions will become very numerous.

Hence **subgeˈnerical** *a.* (in mod. Dicts.); **subgeˈnerically** *adv.*, so as to form a subgenus.
1851 MANTELL *Petrifactions* i. §2. 42 Plants belonging to the same family as the Lepidodendra, but supposed to be generically or sub-generically, distinct.

ˈ**subˌgenus.** Pl. ˈsubˌgenera. [f. SUB- 7 b + GENUS. Cf. F. *sous-genre* (Cuvier).] A subordinate genus; a subdivision of a genus of higher rank than a species.
1813 PRICHARD *Phys. Hist. Man* iii. §3. 110 The family of Mustelæ are distinguished by Cuvier into four departments or sub-genera. *Ibid.* 111 An American animal of the sub-genus Mephitis. **1849** BALFOUR *Man. Bot.* §708 Occasionally, a subgenus is formed by grouping certain species, which agree more nearly with each other in some important particulars than the other species of the genus. **1857** [see SUBCLASS]. **1885** *Encycl. Brit.* XVIII. 733/1 The well-known Gold and Silver Pheasants..each the type of a distinct section of sub-genus.

subget, obs. form of SUBJECT.

ˈ**subgiant.** *Astr.* [SUB- 23.] A star which when plotted on the Hertzsprung–Russell diagram lies between the main sequence and the giants; a star similar to a giant of the same spectral type but less luminous. Cf. SUBDWARF *sb* and *a.*
1937 *Astrophysical Jrnl.* LXXXV. 383 Three bright 'subgiants' having well-determined trigonometric parallaxes. **1943** W. W. MORGAN et al. *Atlas Stellar Structure* 6 For the stars of types F–K, class IV represents the sub-giants and class III the normal giants. **1978** H. L. SHIPMAN *Introd. Astron.* xi. 296 Star *A* becomes a rather unusual type of star, a subgiant—a low-mass, very dim, small red giant.

subˈglobose, *a.* [ad. mod.L. *subglobōsus*: see SUB- 21 c.] Somewhat or almost globose; almost spherical in shape.
1752 SIR J. HILL *Hist. Anim.* 200 The roundish or subglobose ones [*sc.* species of centronia], called by Klein and some others Cidares. **1775** J. JENKINSON *Linnæus' Brit. Plants* 67 The fruit is a subglobose capsule. **1826** KIRBY & SP. *Entomol.* III. 697 Supported..by triangular, conical, or subglobose props. **1872** OLIVER *Elem. Bot.* 308 Male flowers in pendulous, pedunculate, subglobose, silky catkins. **1879** E. P. WRIGHT *Anim. Life* 52 In..Micro-rhynchus, the head is short and sub-globose.

So **subgloˈboso-**, comb. form of SUBGLOBOSE.
1887 W. PHILLIPS *Brit. Discomycetes* 258 Cups scattered, sessile, subgloboso-hemispherical.

subˈglobular, *a.* [SUB- 21 c.] Somewhat or almost globular. So **subˈglobulose** *a.* (in Dicts.).
1787 tr. *Linnæus' Fam. Plants* 195 Stigma's subglobular. **1812** *New Bot. Gard.* I. 41 The pistillum is a subglobular germ. **1897** *Allbutt's Syst. Med.* III. 564 Circumscribed globular or subglobular tumours.

ˈ**subˌgovernor.** [SUB- 6.] An official next below a governor in rank.
Formerly the title of officials in royal and noble households, and in the South Sea and other companies.
1683 BAXTER *Dying Thoughts* 132 As now I am under the government of his Officers on Earth, I look for ever to be under subgovernours in Heaven. **1698** LUTTRELL *Brief Rel.* (1857) IV. 433 George Sayer, esq. a member of parliament, is made sub-governor to the duke of Gloucester. **1702** *Lond. Gaz.* No. 3772/4 The Royal African Company of England have appointed the Election of a Governour, Sub-Governor, and Deputy-Governor; on Tuesday the 13th Instant. **1721** *Act 7 Geo. I* c. 2. §1 The many Frauds..which were committed by the late Sub-Governor, Deputy-Governor, and Directors of the said [South-Sea] Company. **1725** DE FOE *Voy. round World* (1840) 282 The sub-governor and viceroy of New Spain. **1755** J. CHAMBERLAYNE *M. Brit. Notitia* II. 257 His Royal Highness the Prince of Wales's Officers and Servants. Governor..Preceptor.. Sub-Governor..Sub-Preceptor. **1822** *Edin. Rev.* XXXVII. 5 Stone, the subgovernor and confident of the Duke of Newcastle. **1849** GROTE *Greece* II. xxxviii. V. 2 [Darius] directed the various satraps and sub-governors throughout all Asia to provide troops.

b. Similarly ***subgovernor general.***
1784 J. KING *Cook's 3rd Voy.* V. vi, The Sub-governor General, who was at this time making a tour through all the provinces of the Governor General of Jakutsk.

ˈ**subgrade. 1.** *Road* and *Railway Engineering.* [SUB- 3 a.] The layer, either natural or constructed, lying immediately beneath the foundations of a road or railway line. Cf. SUBSTRATUM 4 b.
1893 G. A. PERKINS et al. in *Rep. Mass. State Highway Comm.* v. 78 The subgrade, or the ground on which the large stones rest, should be thoroughly compacted by rolling. **1906** *Engin. Rec.* 14 Apr. 478/3 The reduced quantity of broken stone required, when it is laid on a firm sub-grade. **1930** *Engineering* 1 Aug. 139/3 Maintenance of a mile of gravel road, including the sub-grade. **1962** *Ibid.* 30 Mar. 439 The stresses transmitted to the subgrade by a high quality structural are so small. **1979** *Railway Gaz. Internat.* Jan. 52/2 Protection of the sub-grade against frost.

2. [SUB- 9 (*a*).] A subsidiary grade; one within a grade.
1919 *Sociol. Rev.* XI. 90 We might perhaps recognise..an intermediate group, concerned chiefly with relations between sub-grades. **1931** J. S. HUXLEY *What dare I Think?* vi. 218 In this stage of thought there are, of course, many sub-grades.

ˈ**subgroup.** [SUB- 7 b.] **a.** A subordinate group; a subdivision of a group.
1845 DARWIN *Voy. Nat.* xvii. 379 One species of the sub-group Cactornis. **1859** —— *Orig. Spec.* iv. 126 Small and broken groups and sub-groups will finally tend to disappear. **1899** *Allbutt's Syst. Med.* viii. 772 The first three classes might be included in one group—Alopecia neurotica, with sub-groups universalis, localis, and circumscripta. **1935** *Planning* II. XLI. 6 Utility Services..has been working in three or four sub-groups, one of which dealing with transport has produced the survey contained in broadsheet No. 21. **1961** Y. OLSSON *Syntax Eng. Verb.* ii. 30 One sub-group is independent, for its extra-lingual correlation, of the speech-situation in which its terms are employed. **1978** K. HUDSON *Jargon of Professions* 10 Changes in the technology of communication have made it far easier for one cultural sub-group to hear the members of another group talking.

b. *Math.* A series of operations forming part of a larger group. More widely, any group all of whose elements are elements of a larger group.
1887 *Amer. Jrnl. Math.* IX. 51, I use 'self-conjugate sub-group' in translating Klein's 'ausgezeichnete Untergruppe' and Jordan's 'groupe permutable.' **1888** MORRICE tr. *Klein's Lect. Ikosahedron* 6 The simplest sub-group..is always that which arises from the repetitions of an individual operation. **1892** F. N. COLE tr. *Netto's Th. Substit.* 41 No two of these *a* subgroups have any element in common. **1937**, etc. [see PROPER *a.* 5 c]. **1975** I. STEWART *Concepts Mod. Math.* vii. 104 If I gave you a group of order 615 you would know, without any information about the multiplication table, that its subgroups cannot have any orders other than 1, 3, 5, 15, 41, 123, 205, and 615.

Hence ˈ**subgroup** *v. trans.*, to divide or classify into subgroups; **sub-grouping**, a subsidiary grouping or subgroup; the action of dividing or classifying into these.
1922 E. WALLACE *Flying Fifty-Five* xi. 67 They also were grouped and sub-grouped and indexed. **1956** J. KLEIN *Study of Groups* 168 It must be established that these sub-groupings are not thrown up by chance. **1960** *Amer. Speech* XXXV. 216 The two final chapters [of H. M. Hoenigswald,

Language Change & Linguistic Reconstruction] deal with.. the procedures for the sub-grouping of language families. **1977** *Lancet* 1 Jan. 9/1 The I.Q. data from this study have been subgrouped according to whether the immersion accident occurred in the hot or the cold months of the year. **1978** *Language* LIV. 468 Dyen concerns himself with three topics: the AN homeland, the subgrouping and external relationships of the AN language, and reconstruction.

subhar'monic, *sb.* and *a.* Also **sub-harmonic**. [SUB- 9.] **A.** *sb.* An oscillation with a frequency equal to an integral submultiple of another frequency. Freq. *attrib.*

1924 W. N. BOND in *Nature* 8 Mar. 355/2 The production of the half frequency easily, of the third frequency with care, and of the fourth frequency faintly.. leaves little doubt that the frequencies obtainable are all sub-multiples of the fundamental applied frequency... These forced vibrations might be described as sub-harmonics. **1940** H. F. OLSON *Elem. Acoustical Engin.* vii. 137 It has been analytically shown.. that subharmonics are possible in certain vibrating systems. **1952** [see *frequency divider* s.v. FREQUENCY 5]. **1961** M. L. GAYFORD *Acoustical Techniques & Transducers* III. 67 A curvature of the sides of the [loudspeaker] cone assists the suppression of sub-harmonics. **1976** *Gloss. Terms Mech. Vibration & Shock (B.S.I.)* 12 *Subharmonic response*, a response of a mechanical system exhibiting some of the characteristics of resonance at a frequency having a period that is an integral multiple of the period of the periodic excitation. **1978** A. B. PIPPARD *Physics of Vibration* I. ix. 253 Each sub-harmonic is stable over a limited range of excitation.

B. *adj.* Involving or being a subharmonic.

1940 H. F. OLSON *Elem. Acoustical Engin.* vii. 137 Another feature of subharmonic phenomena is the relatively long time required for 'build up'. **1962** A. NISBETT *Technique Sound Studio* 245 Paper cones are often corrugated to reduce any tendency to 'break up' radially and produce sub-harmonic oscillations. **1978** A. B. PIPPARD *Physics of Vibration* I. ix. 253 The pin is shown making contact with the cone every other cycle of the latter, and therefore responding in the octave subharmonic mode.

subhastation (sʌbhæ'steɪʃən). *Obs.* exc. *Hist.* [ad. L. *subhastātio, -ōnem*, n. of action f. *subhastāre*, f. *sub hastā* under the spear (see ‖SUB 4 and SUB- 1 g), from the Roman practice of setting up a spear where an auction was to be held. Cf. F. *subhastation*, It. *subastazione*, Sp. *subastacion*.] A public sale by auction.

1600 HOLLAND *Livy* XXXIX. xliv. 1052 The Censors by proclamation commaunded those to avoid farre from the subhastation, who had disanulled the former leases and bargains. **1625** DONNE *Serm.* (1626) 20 For that blasphemy then was David sold, under a dangerous sub-hastation. **1686** BURNET *Trav.* i. 10 The way of selling Estates, which is likewise practised in Switserland, and is called Subhastation.

'sub-'head. [SUB- 5, 6.]

1. An official next in rank to the head (of a college, etc.).

1588 in Ellis *Orig. Lett.* Ser. I. III. 27 The Hedds and Sub-Hedds of the said Colleges and Halls.

2. One of the subordinate divisions into which a main division of a subject is broken up.

1673 O. WALKER *Educ.* xi. 146, I have.. chosen to follow Matteo Pellegrini, who reduceth all Predicates that can be applied to a subject.. to twelve heads... I shall speak in order, shewing what sub-heads every place containeth. **1825** J. NICHOLSON *Oper. Mech.* 532 For further information on this head the reader is referred to the sub-head—Plastering. **1884** *Manch. Exam.* 6 Dec. 5/4 A question which occupies about thirty lines of print, and is divided into thirteen sub-heads. **1891** TUCKLEY *Under the Queen* 268 Making every head and every sub-head [of a sermon] stand out in bold relief.

3. A subordinate heading or title in a newspaper, book, chapter, article, etc.

1875 SOUTHWARD *Dict. Typogr.* 130 When an article or chapter is divided into several parts, the headings to those parts are set in smaller type than the full head, and are called Sub-heads. **1889** T. CAMPBELL-COPELAND *Ladder of Journalism* vi. 42 The first line.. should consist of from twelve to fifteen letters, presenting in the briefest form.. the subject of the article; beneath which, the sub-head of twelve words or thereabouts, making a line and a half, should be placed. **1903** MCNEILL *Egreg. Engl.* 98 It is essential.. that the episode should be reported with a separate sub-head and great circumstance in the Parliamentary report. **1914** *Temperance (Wales) Bill* (H.C. 72) Cl. 3 (*c*) Sub-heads (*h*), (*k*), and (*i*) of subsection (2). **1927** *Amer. Speech* II. 239/2 For a very long story, 'subheads' are usually provided, brief crosslines in bold face type the same size as the body type. **1961** C. WILLOCK *Death in Covert* xii. 203 One headline said: *Regency rakes ride again*, and the sub-head to the same story complained: *Last time a man was blown up.* **1979** D. ANTHONY *Long Hard Cure* vii. 64 The news story.. was on the front page, under the subhead: *Maniac claims fourth victim.*

So **'subheading** = SUBHEAD 2, 3. **'subhead** *v. trans.*, to furnish with a sub-heading; also *fig.*

1874 *Catal. Apprentices' Libr.* (N.Y.) p. v, Headings containing a large number of titles are subdivided into sub-headings to facilitate reference. **1877** *Harper's Mag.* Dec. 45/2 One of them was heading and sub-heading cable dispatches from the seat of war. **1889** WHEATLEY *How to Catal. Libr.* 197 In an index the headings will of course be in alphabet, and the sub-headings may be so also. **1902** *Daily Chron.* 10 Feb. 3/3 Each occurrence being ticketed in the margin with a funny little inset sub-heading. **1904** *Brit. Med. Jrnl.* 17 Dec. 1645 A chapter is devoted to this subject [of polysomatous terata] under the sub-headings of uniovular twins [etc.]. **1949** *Scrutiny* XVI. 52 He [*sc.* C. E. M. Joad] contrasts the present period, which he subheads as 'foreheads defiantly low', with the happy time of his youth. **1978** W. WHITE in W. Whitman *Daybks. & Notebks.* II. 415 The account, which totals more than 26 column inches in the *Times*, ends with a section subheaded 'The Poet Greets His Friends'.

sub-'human, *a.* (*sb.*) [SUB- 14, 19.]

1. a. Not quite human, less than human; *occas.* almost or all but human.

1793 J. WILLIAMS *Calm Exam.* 88 Perhaps the slumbers of Lord Thurlow are never broken by the.. interposition of thought; if they are not, the man is extra or sub-human. **1894** *Pop. Sci. Monthly* XLIV. 514 The mental operations of my subhuman dog. **1901** *Eng. Hist. Rev.* July 425 To imagine not only a king who is almost super-human in his self-will, but also a clergy and a nation which are sub-human in their self-abasement.

b. as *sb.* One who is less than human; a person of sub-human instincts.

1957 R. CAMPBELL *Portugal* iv. 62 This.. moray.. was fed chiefly on recalcitrant slaves.. devoured before the gloating eyes of the subhuman who was its owner. **1970** G. JACKSON *Let.* in *Soledad Brother* (1971) 247 Would you like to know a subhuman... I'm not a very nice person... more kin to the cat than anything else, the big black one.

2. Belonging to or characteristic of the part of creation that is below the human race.

1837 BEDDOES *Let.* in *Poems* (1851) p. ci, What my thoughts.. may be regarding things human, sub-human, and super-human. **1877** SWINBURNE *Note C. Brontë* 90 The typical specimen which then emitted in one spasm of sub-human spite at once the snarl and the stench proper to its place and kind. **1894** H. DRUMMOND *Ascent of Man* 28 He turns his back upon Nature—sub-human Nature, that is.

Hence **sub-hu'manity**, the quality of being sub-human, less than human existence; (*rarely*) a level of creation below the human race; **sub-'humanly** *adv.*, in a sub-human manner, bestially.

1909 G. B. SHAW in *Nation* 28 Aug. 787/2 Mr. Chesterton .. finally excogitates, as a proof of my superhumanity or sub-humanity, exactly the reason that would have been given by one of Wellington's private soldiers. **1929** A. HUXLEY *Do what You Will* 75 They live.. sub-humanly.. they sink.. towards a repulsive subhumanity. **1939** J. CARY *Mister Johnson* 157 They have become a new kind of creature, a sort of subhumanity which can smile and eat and live at a level of corruption and misery which would kill a real human being. **1966** 'H. MACDIARMID' *Company I've Kept* ii. 50 As soon as you make allowances.. then you are opening the floodgate for mediocrity and.. you are submerged under a tide of subhumanity. **1970** G. GREER *Female Eunuch* 262 Is it too much to ask that women be spared the daily struggle for superhuman beauty in order to offer it to the caresses of a subhumanly ugly mate?

†**sub'humerate**, *v. Obs. rare.* [f. SUB- 26 + L. (*h*)*umerus* shoulder + -ATE[3].] *trans.* To take up on the shoulders; to shoulder.

1628 FELTHAM *Resolves* II. lxxxii. 233 Nothing surer tyes a friend, then freely to subhumerate the burthen which was his. **1649** BULWER *Pathomyot.* II. i. 92 To bend their power to subhumerate.. the burden imposed upon them. **1656** BLOUNT *Glossogr.*

‖**subiculum** (sjuː'bɪkjʊləm). [mod.L. (Link), dim. f. *subic-*, stem of late L. *subices* (pl.) supports, f. *subicĕre* to throw or place under (see SUBJECT).]

1. *Bot.* In certain fungi, the modified tissue of the host bearing the perithecia.

1836 BERKELEY in Smith's *Engl. Flora* V. II. 370 Spots variegated with yellow and brown, subiculum rather thick. **1875** COOKE & BERKELEY *Fungi* 15 We have Pezizæ with a subiculum in the section Tapesia. **1887** W. PHILLIPS *Brit. Discomycetes* 226 Seated at first on a delicate white subiculum, which disappears as the plant advances to maturity.

2. *Anat.* The uncinate gyrus.

subidar, obs. var. SUBAHDAR.

†**subigate**, *v. Obs.* [irreg. f. L. *subigĕre* (f. *sub-* SUB- 26 + *agĕre* to bring) + -ATE[3].] *trans.* To knead or work up.

1657 TOMLINSON *Renou's Disp.* 172 Stir them together.. that the whole masse may be subigated.

subimago (sʌbɪ'meɪgəʊ). *Entom.* [SUB- 23.] In Ephemeridæ, the stage immediately preceding the imago, before the final pellicle has been cast; the insect at this stage. Also called *pseudimago* (see PSEUDO- 2).

1861 H. HAGEN *Synopsis Neuroptera N. Amer.* 343 *Subimago*, a state of Ephemera, &c., wherein the wings, &c., are covered with a membrane, which is cast off when it becomes an Imago. **1864** *Intell. Obs.* No. 33. 148 The immature sub-imago of the May-fly. **1889** CHOLMONDELEY-PENNELL *Fishing* 376 They avoid the subimago, and keep on feeding on the nymph. **1897** *Daily News* 27 July 8/1 The sober-tinted Iron Blue Dun again, is the imperfect form, or sub-imago, of the Jenny Spinner.

Hence **subi'maginal** *a.*, belonging to or characteristic of the subimago.

1878 *Encycl. Brit.* VIII. 458/1 The cast sub-imaginal skins of these insects.

subin'cision. [SUB- 2.] The cutting of an opening into the urethra on the under side of the penis: a practice prevalent in some primitive societies. So **subin'cise** *v. trans.*, to perform subincision upon.

1899 SPENCER & GILLEN *Native Tribes Central Australia* 263 The rite of sub-incision.. has frequently been alluded to by Curr and other writers under the name of the 'terrible rite'. **1904** —— *North. Tribes Central Australia* xi. 354 It was decided by the old men that, towards the close of these [ceremonies] three young men should be subincised.

,sub-incom'plete, *a. Entom.* [SUB- 21 c.] Designating a metamorphosis in which the active larva and pupa resemble the imago.

1838 *Penny Cycl.* XII. 494/1 Incomplete Pupæ are those without alary appendages... Sub-incomplete Pupæ are those which possess rudiments of wings.

sub'indicate, *v.* [f. pa. ppl. stem of late L. *subindicāre*: see SUB- 22 and INDICATE *v.*] *trans.* To indicate indirectly; to hint. So **subindi'cation**, a slight indication or token; **subin'dicative** *a.*, indirectly indicative or suggestive. (All *Obs.* or *arch.*)

1655–87 H. MORE *App. Antid.* (1712) 200 Rather obscure sub-indications of the necessary Existence of a God. **1659** —— *Immort. Soul* II. x. 222 This Spirit of the World has Faculties that work.. fatally or naturally, as several Gamaieu's we meet withall in Nature seem somewhat obscurely to sub-indicate. *a* **1677** BARROW *Serm.* (1686) III. 513 They served to the subindication and shadowing of heavenly things. **1681** H. MORE *Expos. Dan.* vi. 233 It is an hint and a sufficiently certain though something obscure subindication. **1822** LAMB *Elia* I. *Old Actors*, With that sort of subindicative token of respect which one is apt to demonstrate towards a venerable stranger.

subin'duce, *v. rare* or *Obs.* [Partly ad. late L. *subdūcĕre*, partly f. SUB- 25 + INDUCE.]

1. *trans.* To insinuate, suggest indirectly.

1640 SIR E. DERING *Sp. Relig.* 23 Nov. 14 Our Innovators by this artifice do alter our setled Doctrines; Nay they do subinduce points repugnant and contrariant.

2. To induce by indirect or underhand means.

a **1623** BUCK *Rich. III*, III. (1646) 60 His wife.. had made her subtill perswasions of stronger tye, and subinduced him to the Lancastrian side.

3. To bring about (a thing) as a result of or in succession to another.

1855 BROWNING *Epist.* 79 A case of mania—subinduced By epilepsy.

subin'feoff, *v.* [SUB- 9 (*b*).] = SUBINFEUD *v.*

1611 COTGR., *Subinfeudation*, a subinfeoffing. **1839** *Penny Cycl.* XIV. 387/2 Upon this subinfeudation being effected, A.. would have the seigniory of lands of which B and others had been subinfeoffed.

subin'feud, *v.* [SUB- 9 (*b*).]

1. *trans.* To grant (estates) by subinfeudation; in quot. *absol.*

1828 J. HUNTER *More's Life Sir T. More* Pref. p. xl, The two great houses of Newmarch and Fitzwilliam held Barnborough. Both subinfeuded.

2. To give (a person) possession *of* estates by subinfeudation.

1839 STONEHOUSE *Isle of Axholme* 291 The Abbot of Newburgh was subinfeuded of a small manor in this parish.

So **sub'infeudate** (occas. **-en-**) *v. trans.* = SUBINFEUD 1; also *fig.*

1839 KEIGHTLEY *Hist. Eng.* I. 130 A vassal of the crown.. might subenfeudate his lands, and have vassals bound to himself as he was to his superior lord. **1897** MAITLAND *Domesday Bk. & Beyond* 100 Justice, we may say, was already being subinfeudated.

,subinfeu'dation. *Feudal Law.* [ad. F. †*subinfeudation* (Cotgr.) or med.L. **subinfeudātio*: see SUB- 9 (*b*) and INFEUDATION. Cf. F. *sous-infeudation* (16th c.).]

1. The granting of lands by a feudatory to an inferior to be held of himself, on the same terms as he held them of his superior; the relation or tenure so established.

In England this practice was abolished in 1290 by the statute *Quia Emptores*, but in Scotland the principle of subinfeudation still survives.

1730 M. WRIGHT *Introd. Law Tenures* 156 *note*, Subinfeudation (by which a new inferior Feud was carved out of the old, the old one still subsisting). **1766** BLACKSTONE *Comm.* II. 91 The superior lords observed, that by this method of subinfeudation they lost all their feodal profits, of wardships, marriages, and escheats, which fell into the hands of these mesne or middle lords. *Ibid.* 136 The widow is immediate tenant to the heir, by a kind of subinfeudation or under-tenancy. *a* **1862** BUCKLE *Misc. Wks.* (1872) I. 353 Subinfeudation, so general in France, was checked by Magna Charta. **1876** BANCROFT *Hist. U.S.* I. vii. 182 To the proprietary was given the power of creating manors and courts baron, and of establishing a colonial aristocracy on the system of sub-infeudation. **1880** PHEAR *Aryan Village* vi. 154 This system of sub-infeudation.. prevails universally throughout Bengal.

2. An instance of this; also, an estate or fief created by this process.

1766 BLACKSTONE *Comm.* II. 257 In subinfeudations, or alienations of lands by a vasal to be holden as of himself. **1773** *Archæologia* II. 306 These land-holders of the first class, or barons, had a power of making subinfeudations of their land. **1832** AUSTIN *Jurispr.* (1879) II. 879 The statute 'Quia Emptores' 18 Edw. I prevented any new subinfeudations. **1870** LOWER *Hist. Sussex* I. 265 The manor is a sub-infeudation of Washington.

transf. **1840** *New Monthly Mag.* LIX. 161 What sub-infeudations of parentheses, what accumulations of paragraph upon paragraph.

So **subin'feudatory**, a sub-vassal holding by subinfeudation.

1886 *Encycl. Brit.* XX. 298/2 At the time of the Conquest the manor was granted to Walter d'Eincourt, and in the 12th century it was divided among the three daughters of his subinfeudatory Paganus.

†**sub'ingress.** *Obs. rare.* [SUB- 2.] The disappearance of a star or planet behind another in occultation.

1669 *Phil. Trans.* IV. 1109 If diligent heed be given to the times of the sub-ingress and emersion of the Star, and with what Spots on the Moons face it keeps in a right line.

†**subin'gression.** *Obs.* [SUB- 25.] Subtle or unobserved entrance.

1653 H. MORE *Antid. Ath.* II. ii. §9 (1712) 45 This forcible endeavour of the subingression of the air is not from the pressure of the ambient Air. **1660** BOYLE *New Exp. Phys. Mech.* iii. 44 The pressure of the ambient Air is strengthened upon the accession of the Air suck'd out; which, to make it self room, forces the neighboring Air to a violent-subingression of its parts. **1674** —— *Obs. Saltn. Sea* 8 That in the drawing up of the Vessel through the Salt water..the taste may have been alter'd by the subingression of Salt water.

sub'intellect, *v. rare.* [f. late L. *subintellect-*, pa. ppl. stem of *subintellegĕre* (see SUBINTELLIGITUR).] *trans.* To supply in thought, understand.

1811–31 BENTHAM *Logic* App. Wks. 1843 VIII. 283/2 The termination *cs*, as designative of an adjective, of which the substantive is subintellected, is preferred.

,subinte'llection. [ad. late L. *subintellectio, -ōnem*, n. of action f. *subintellegĕre* (see prec.).] The action of supplying in thought; subaudition.

1624 H. MASON *New Art of Lying* iv. 69 We may.. conceale the truth, or speake an vntruth, so as by subintellection, or a mentall reseruation, wee make vp the matter. **1808** T. F. MIDDLETON *Grk. Article* (1833) 25 The subintellection of the Participle of Existence as a Copula between the Article and its Predicate.

subin'telligence. *rare.* [f. SUB- 25 + INTELLIGENCE after prec. or next.] An implication.

1630 BP. HALL *Occas. Medit.* §100 (1634) 162 These, thy promises of outward favours are never but with a subintelligence of a condition, of our capablenesse.

So **subintelli'gential** *a.*, implying something beyond what is expressed.

1887 BROWNING *Parleyings* 115 So tells a touch Of subintelligential nod and wink—Turning foes friends.

‖**subintelligitur** (,sʌbɪntɛ'lɪdʒɪtə(r)). [L., 3rd pers. sing. pres. indic. pass. of *subintelligĕre* (var. of *-intellegĕre*), f. *sub-* SUB- 25 + *intellegĕre* (see INTELLECT).] An unexpressed or implied addition to a statement, etc. (Cf. SUBAUDITUR.)

1649 BLITHE *Engl. Improver Impr.* (1652) 174 Unless you please to take that for a Discovery which is by a Subintelligitur. **1681** T. FLATMAN *Heraclitus Ridens* No. 3 (1713) I. 13 You must, First, know that *We* and *Ours*, is to be construed with a *Subintelligitur*. *a***1734** NORTH *Exam.* I. ii. §8 (1740) 35 He took Sanctuary for Protection of Liberty and Life: Against what? The Tyranny of the then English Government. That's his *Subintelligitur*. **1817** COLERIDGE *Biog. Lit.* xii. (1907) I. 181 [The imagination] supplies, by a sort of *subintelligitur*, the one central power. **1886** JOWETT in *Life & Lett.* (1897) II. 313 We pray to God as a Person, a larger self; but there must always be a subintelligitur that He is not a Person.

subintrant (sʌb'ɪntrənt), *a.* (*sb.*) *Path.* [ad. L. *subintrant-em*, pr. pple. of *subintrāre* to steal into, f. *sub-* SUB- 25 + *intrāre* to ENTER. Cf. F. *subintrant*, It. *subentrante*.] Of fevers: Having paroxysms so rapidly that before one is over another begins; also said of the paroxysms. **b.** *sb.* A subintrant fever.

1684 tr. *Bonet's Merc. Compit.* VI. 231 In a subintrant (that is, when one fit comes before the other is off). **1747** tr. *Astruc's Fevers* 102 A subintrant tertian. **1886** *Lond. Med. Rec.* 15 Oct. 463/1 The hysterical attacks at this juncture were constant, sometimes subintrant. **1897** *Allbutt's Syst. Med.* II. 317 A remittent of the double tertian type, or double tertian with subintrant paroxysms. **1899** *Ibid.* VIII. 467 The fever..may be confined only to the eruptive period, and be ephemeral, remittent, subintrant [&c.].

,subintro'duce, *v.* [ad. L. *subintrōdūcĕre*: see SUB- 25 and INTRODUCE.] *trans.* To introduce in a secret or subtle manner. Chiefly in *ppl. a.*

In quot. 1886 with reference to the *mulieres subintroductæ* (Gr. συνείσακτοι), called also *extraneæ*, whom clerics were forbidden by the canons of various councils to have in their houses.

1664 JER. TAYLOR *Dissuas. Popery* I. §6 (1688) 44 To say that the first practise and institution is necessary to be followed, is called Heretical: to refuse the later subintroduc'd custom incurrs the sentence of Excommunication. **1844** GLADSTONE *Glean.* (1879) III. 16 The mode, in which the expression of it is subintroduced, seems to denote a repression of his own full meaning. **1886** CONDER *Syrian Stone-Lore* viii. (1896) 278 The practice of allowing 'sub-introduced sisters' to live in the houses of the celibates.

So †**,subintro'duct** *v.* in same sense; †**,subintro'duction,** surreptitious introduction.

1620 BP. HALL *Hon. Marr. Clergie* II. iv, The Canon alledged against the subintroduction of (*Mulieres extraneæ*) strange Women into the houses of Clergy-men. *a***1641** BP. MOUNTAGU *Acts & Mon.* (1642) 11 The only true God,.. no supposed,..subintroducted God or Gods.

subinvariant (sʌbɪn'vɛərɪənt). *Math.* [f. SUB- 23 + INVARIANT *sb.*] = SEMINVARIANT. Hence **subin'variantive** *a.*

1882 *Amer. Jrnl. Math.* V. 79 Any rational integer function of one or more subinvariants is itself one. *Ibid.* 81 *note*, Eventually I am inclined to substitute the word binariant for subinvariants, and to speak of simple, double, treble or multiple binariants. *Ibid.* 80 It must be capable of being satisfied by subinvariantive values of X_1 Y_1.

,sub-irri'gation. [SUB- 2 a.] The irrigation of land from beneath the surface, esp. by means of underground channels or pipes.

1880 *News & Press* (Cimarron, New Mexico) 19 Aug. 1/6 Sub irrigation for wheat would be too expensive. **1904** *Bull. Bur. Census, U.S. Dept. Comm. & Labor* No. 16. 25/1 In one of the systems of subirrigation the water is carried through pipes 14 inches below the surface. **1930** *Amer. Speech* VI. 11 Subirrigation is accomplished by allowing water to stand in deep ditches from which it soaks laterally. **1979** R. ADAMS et al. *Dry Lands* viii. 116/1 Sub-irrigation..is normally achieved either by creating an artificial water-table just below the ground surface or by burying a drip irrigation system or a network of perforated pipes.

Hence **sub'irrigate** *v. trans.* (also *absol.*), **sub'irrigated** *ppl. a.*

1903 *Sci. Amer. Suppl.* 17 Jan. 22616/3 Where the subsoil transmits water freely, irrigation ditches may subirrigate large tracts of country without rendering them marshy. **1933** *Nat. Geogr. Mag.* Feb. 189 (*caption*) The soil is remarkably fertile and is subirrigated by springs in the surrounding hills. **1950** H. B. ROE *Moisture Requirements in Agric.* viii. 229 On Elgin Bench..the subirrigated district includes an area of about 60,000 acres. **1976** D. GOLDBERG et al. *Drip Irrigation* i. 10 Drainage systems were utilized to function as a double action system, draining surplus water yet sub-irrigating through the same medium in a reverse operation.

†**subitane,** *a. Obs.* [ad. L. *subitāneus* (see next). Cf. OF. *subitain*.] Sudden; rash.

1633 PRYNNE *Histrio-m.* I. 701 The prejudicate erronious inconsiderate private and subitane Opinions of all ignorant novices. **1645** *Martin's Echo* in *Prynne's Fresh Discov.* 23 His midnight dreames, his distracted subitane apprehensions. **1648** PRYNNE *Plea for Lords* A ij b, These subitane indigested Collections.

b. *sb. pl.*

1645 MILTON *Colast.* Wks. 1851 IV. 344 It will bee..best for the reputation of him who in his *Subitanes* hath thus censur'd, to recall his sentence.

subitaneous (sʌbɪ'teɪnɪəs), *a.* [f. L. *subitān-eus* sudden (f. *subitus* SUBITE) + -OUS.] **a.** Sudden, hasty, unexpected; hastily produced or constructed. Now *rare.*

1651 BIGGS *New Disp.* ¶ 196 The argument of curing by the subitaneous precipitancy of cold. **1686** GOAD *Celest. Bodies* II. vii. 248 Some are Subitaneous, the Product of 24 Hours. **1751** *Chambers' Cycl.* s.v. *Bridge*, The Romans had also a sort of subitaneous bridges made by the soldiers, of boats [etc.]. **1760–72** tr. *Juan & Ulloa's Voy.* (ed. 3) I. 213 This almost subitaneous death of a person in the flower of his age. **1778** *Nat. Hist.* in *Ann. Reg.* 111/2 The rain waters, the subterraneous cavities, the absorptions, and sometimes more subitaneous agents, have made great ruins. **1822** T. TAYLOR *Apuleius* 304 He never either grieves or rejoices, nor wills, nor is averse to any thing subitaneous. **1892** 'DICK DONOVAN' *In Grip of Law* 246 The subitaneous clanging of a heavy bell.

b. *Biol.* Of the egg of a small aquatic invertebrate: hatching soon after it is laid. Cf. *resting egg* s.v. RESTING *ppl. a.* 1 b

1950 *Adv. Genetics* III. 240 From the fertilized eggs (the ephippial eggs) there emerge, after a shorter or longer resting period, exclusively females, the eggs of which (the subitaneous eggs) develop parthenogenetically in the brood chamber of the female. **1979** *Nature* 30 Aug. 722/1 Both quick-hatching (subitaneous) and resting eggs are produced but neither kind was believed to be fertilised, though in *Chaetonotus* two types of subitaneous egg have been reported.

Hence †**subi'taneousness.**

1727 BAILEY (vol. II), *Subitaneousness*,..Suddenness.

†**subitany,** *a. Obs.* [Formed as prec., after *momentany*.] = SUBITANEOUS.

1603 HOLLAND *Plutarch's Mor.* 8 To suffer yoong boies to make subitanie and inconsiderate orations. *a***1656** HALES *Gold. Rem.* I. (1673) 290 This which I now have commented is very subitany, and I confused.

†**subitary,** *a. Obs. rare.* [ad. L. *subitārius*, f. *subitus*: see next and -ARY.] Suddenly or hastily done, made, etc.

1600 HOLLAND *Livy* III. iv. 90 The Colonie Antium, were commaunded to send unto Quintius, subitarie souldiers. *Ibid.* XL. xxvi. 1077. **1661** BLOUNT *Glossogr.* (ed. 2).

†**subite,** *a. Obs.* Also 5 subytte. [a. OF. *subit*, fem. *subite*, or ad. L. *subitus*, pa. pple. of *subīre* to come or go stealthily, f. *sub-* SUB- 25 + *-īre* to go. Cf. It., Sp., Pg. *subito*.] Sudden, hasty.

1483 CAXTON *Cato* B vj, Thou oughtest to refrayne thyn yre. not onely the yre subdayn and subytte [etc.]. **1597** A. M. tr. *Guillemeau's Fr. Chirurg.* 51/3 All subite permutations are vnto our bodyes very preiudicialle. *a***1722** SIR J. LAUDER *Decis.* Suppl. 282 In phlebotomy or other manual operations,—the acts are subite or transient.

subitize ('sʌbɪtaɪz), *v. Psychol.* [f. L. *subitus* SUBITE *a.* + -IZE.] *intr.* and *trans.* To apprehend immediately (the number contained in a small sample). Hence **'subitizing** *vbl. sb.*

1949 E. L. KAUFMAN et al. in *Amer. Jrnl. Psychol.* LXII. 520 A new term is needed for the discrimination of stimulus-numbers of 6 and below... The term proposed is *subitize*... We are indebted to Dr. Cornelia C. Coulter, the Department of Classical Languages and Literatures, Mount Holyoke College, for suggesting this term. *Ibid.*, If no discontinuities had appeared in the results, no distinction between subitizing and estimating could have been drawn. **1971** *Jrnl. Gen. Psychol.* Jan. 121 The number of items in an array capable of being subitized. **1981** *Nature* 15 Oct. 569/2 Judgements of 'small' numerosities..are ordinarily attributed to subitizing.

‖**subito** ('subito), *adv. Mus.* [It.: cf. SUBITE *a.*] Quickly; usually in phr. ***volti subito***, turn quickly.

1724 *Short Explic. For. Wds. in Mus. Bks.* **1801** BUSBY *Dict. Mus.*

†**'subitous,** *a. Obs.* [f. L. *subitus* (see SUBITE) + -OUS.] Sudden.

1657 W. MORICE *Coena quasi Κοινὴ* 341 We find conversion..under the notion of such things as are not onely subitous but instantaneous. **1665** G. HARVEY *Advice agst. Plague* 3 An universal Lassitude, or Subitous soreness of all one's Limbs.

subjacency (səb'dʒeɪsənsɪ). [f. next: see -ENCY.] The state or condition of being subjacent.

In mod. Dicts.

subjacent (səb'dʒeɪsənt), *a.* [ad. L. *subjacentem*, pr. pple. of *subjacēre*, f. *sub-* SUB- 2 + *jacēre* to lie. Cf. F. *subjacent*.]

1. Situated underneath or below; underlying.

a. in general use.

1609 J. DAVIES *Holy Roode* (1878) 13/2 Such Sight a squemish stomacke ouerturnes, But comforts mine, with Matter subiacent. **1611** COTGR., *Subiacent*, subiacent; vnder-lying. **1660** BOYLE *New Exp. Phys. Mech.* i. 34 Not the incumbent Atmosphere, but onely the subjacent Air in the brass Cylinder. **1682** PIERS *Descr. W. Meath* (1770) 29 The subjacent liquor in the glass. **1754** *Phil. Trans.* XLIX. 144 Whatever part of this vapour begins to..subside first, will carry down with it part of the subjacent vapour. **1875** CROLL *Clim. & Time* x. 172 The whole of the surface-film, being chilled at the same time, sinks through the subjacent water.

b. *Anat.* and *Bot.* of nerves, bones, tissues, etc. (Const. *to.*)

1597 A. M. tr. *Guillemeau's Fr. Chirurg.* 10/3 The foresayed subiacent or subiectede membrane. **1758** *Phil. Trans.* LI. 176 The ramifications of the subjacent blood-vessels. **1787** tr. *Linnæus' Fam. Plants* 479 There are two concave impressions from the back, prominent underneath, which compress the subjacent wings. **1813** J. THOMSON *Lect. Inflam.* 2 The skin and subjacent cellular membrane. **1881** MIVART *Cat* 15 If the muscles be cut away, we come sooner or later to subjacent bones. **1896** *Allbutt's Syst. Med.* I. 238 Parts subjacent to cutaneous surfaces.

c. *Geol.* of strata, rocks, deposits, etc.

1695 WOODWARD *Nat. Hist. Earth* III. (1723) 137 The subjacent Strata. **1856** STANLEY *Sinai & Pal.* i. (1858) 6/2 This red colour I ascertained to be caused by the subjacent red sandstone. **1873** GEIKIE *Gt. Ice Age* ii. 5 Subjacent and intercalated beds. **1883** *Law Rep. 10 Q.B. Div.* 562 A piece of land was granted with a reservation of the whole of the subjacent minerals to the superior.

d. *transf.* and *fig.* Forming the basis or substratum. (Cf. SUBJECT *a.* 11, SUBJECTED 1 b.)

*a***1677** BARROW *Serm.* Wks. 1686 II. v. 74 The advantage of chusing one sutable to the subjacent matter and occasion. **1846** TRENCH *Mirac.* i. (1862) 118 The Lord..might have created, with no subjacent material, the wine with which He cheered these guests. **1880** *Academy* 14 Aug. 118/2 Anyone who will carefully compare the agreements and differences in Latin renderings, irrespective of the subjacent Greek text.

2. Lying or situated at a lower level, at or near the base (e.g. of a mountain).

1650 EARL MONM. tr. *Senault's Man bec. Guilty* 305 They built Citadels on the tops of mountains, to discover the subjacent Countreys. *a***1700** EVELYN *Diary* 4 Oct. 1641, Perceiving all the subjacent country, at so small a horizontal distance, to repercuss such a light as I could hardly look against. **1760** DERRICK *Lett.* (1767) I. 79 The rivers that water the subjacent plains. **1774** PENNANT *Tour Scotl. in 1772*, 327 Over the subjacent vales and lochs. **1837** LOCKHART *Scott* (1839) X. 84 Before the subjacent and surrounding lake and morass were drained. **1889** STEVENSON *Edinburgh* 22 The smoke of the Old Town blowing abroad over the subjacent country.

3. Taking place underneath or below. *rare.*

1862 WRAXALL tr. *Hugo's Les Miserables* IV. I. v. II. 293 The sign of a vast subjacent conflagration. **1898** P. MANSON *Trop. Diseases* xviii. 296 The superjacent mucous membrane sloughing or disintegrating in consequence of the subjacent destruction of its nutrient vessels.

Hence **sub'jacently** *adv.*, in a subjacent manner.

1882 G. MACDONALD *Castle Warlock* x, A new era in his life..., the thought of which had been subjacently present in his dreams.

subject ('sʌbdʒɪkt), *sb.* Forms: α. 4–5 sogett(e, sugett(e, 4–6 soget, sug(g)et, 4 *pl.* sugges, 5 sogete, sugete, seget (?), sewgyet, soiet, suiet, sogect, sugect. β. 4 subgit, soubgit, 4–5 subgett(e, 4–6 subiet, 5 subgyt, -gite, soubget, *pl.* subies, -jais, -gees, 5–6 subget, -giet. γ. 4–7 subiect, 5 -giect, 5–6 -iecte, 6 -gect, -yect, -iectt, subect, *Sc. pl.* subjeckis, 7– subject. [a. OF. *suget*, *soget* (12th c.), *sougiet*, *subjit*, *subg(i)et*, etc. (13th c.), *subject* (15–17th c.), also *soubject*, *suject*, mod.F. *sujet* (from 15th c.), repr. various stages of adoption of L. *subject-us* masc., *subject-um* neut., subst. uses of pa. pple. of *subicĕre* (see next). Cf. Prov. *subjet-z*, *suget-z*, It. *soggetto*, *suggetto*, and *sub(b)ietto*, Sp. *sugeto*, Pg. *sujeito*. The completely latinized spelling of the Eng. word became established in the 16th c.]

I. 1. a. One who is under the dominion of a monarch or reigning prince; one who owes allegiance to a government or ruling power, is subject to its laws, and enjoys its protection.

α. **1340** HAMPOLE *Pr. Consc.* 5578 Þa þat sugettes war til man, Sal accuse þair soveraynes þan. *c* **1394** *P. Pl. Crede* 650 Neþer souereyn ne soget þei ne suffreþ neuer. *c* **1449** PECOCK *Repr.* III. vi. 315 Thei were sugettis to the Emperour of Rome. *c* **1485** *Digby Myst.* (1882) III. 500, I wol a-wye sovereyns; and soiettes I dys-deyne. **1574** in *Maitl. Club Misc.* I. 111 Ane trew sugget to the Kingis Majestie.

β. **1399** GOWER *In Praise of Peace* 165 Crist is the heved and we ben membres alle, Als wel the subgit as the sovereign. *c* **1400** tr. *Secr. Secr.*, *Gov. Lordsh.* 51 Kynges.. large to subgitz. **1503** HAWES *Examp. Virt.* I. 14 Be to thy kynge euer true subgete.

γ. **1538** STARKEY *England* I. iii. 82 The commyns agayne the nobullys, and subyectys agayn they[r] rularys. *a* **1568** ASCHAM *Scholem.* I. (Arb.) 86 A quiet subiect to his Prince. **1593** SHAKS. *2 Hen. VI*, IV. ix. 6 Was neuer Subiect long'd to be a King, As I do long and wish to be a Subiect. *a* **1633** G. HERBERT *Jacula Prudentum* (1651) 62 For the same man to be an heretick and a good subject, is incompossible. **1649** [see LIBERTY *sb.*[1] 2]. *a* **1687** PETTY *Pol. Arith.* (1690) 75, I suppose that the King of England hath about Ten Millions of Subjects. **1765** BLACKSTONE *Comm.* I. 122 Every wanton and causeless restraint of the will of the subject.. is a degree of tyranny. **1849** MACAULAY *Hist. Eng.* iii. I. 308 These three Dukes were supposed to be three of the very richest subjects in England. **1858** FROUDE *Hist. Eng.* IV. xviii. 48 She had taught her son to suspect and dread the worthiest subject that he possessed.

(*b*) qualified by a possessive or equivalent phrase; also ***subject of the crown***.

α. *c* **1380** WYCLIF *Sel. Wks.* III. 28 Her regalte and her dignyte, by þe whiche þei schulen.. rulen hemsilf and her sogetis. *c* **1412** HOCCLEVE *De Reg. Princ.* 2212 Kynges of hir sogetz ben obeyed. **1483** *Cely Papers* (Camden) 137 To wryte unto the Kynges good grace that he wyll be faverabull unto hys sewgyettes. **1515** in *Douglas' Poet. Wks.* (1874) I. p. xxvii, The best belowyt prince and moost dred with lowff of his Lorddis and sugettis.

β. *c* **1374** CHAUCER *Boeth.* III. pr. viii. (1868) 80 Yif þou desiryst power þou shalt by awaites of þi subgitz anoyously be cast vndir many periles. ? *a* **1400** *Morte Arth.* 2314 Twa senatours we are, thi subgettez of Rome. **1415** in Ellis *Orig. Lett.* Ser. II. I. 48, I Richard York ȝowre humble subgyt and very lege man. **1456** SIR G. HAYE *Law Arms* (S.T.S.) 297 Alsmony princis with thair subjais. **1483** *Act 1 Rich. III*, c. 1 §1 The King's Subgiettis. **1524** in *Buccleuch MSS.* (Hist. MSS. Comm.) I. 220 Our officers, ministres, and subgiettes.

γ. *c* **1400** MAUNDEV. (Roxb.) xi. 41 He commaunded straitely til all his subiectes, þat þai schuld late me see all þe placez. *c* **1525** MORE *Hist. Rich. III*, Wks. 69/1 She said also y[t] it was not princely to mary hys owne subiect. **1560** DAUS tr. *Sleidane's Comm.* 283 b, The other William Gelluse was a subject of the Lantgraves. **1595** SHAKS. *John* II. i. 204 *Iohn.* You men of Angiers, and my louing subiects. *Fra.* You louing men of Angiers, Arthurs subiects. **1638** BAKER tr. *Balzac's Lett.* (vol. II) 14 Our Prince will put no yoke upon the consciences of his Subjects. **1733** SWIFT (*title*) A serious and useful Scheme to make an Hospital for Incurables; of universal Benefit to all his Majesty's Subjects. **1765** BLACKSTONE *Comm.* I. 263 The king has.. the prerogative of.. granting place or precedence to any of his subjects. **1827** HALLAM *Const. Hist.* (1842) II. 505 No subjects of the crown in Ireland enjoyed such influence, at this time, as the earls of Kildare. **1875** JOWETT *Plato* (ed. 2) IV. 504 The.. kings of our own day very much resemble their subjects in education and breeding.

(*c*) of a specified country or state; also, ***subject of the realm***.

α. **1436** in *Rep. Hist. MSS. Comm.* Var. Coll. IV. 199 To Us and to alle oure sugectis of the same [reame].

γ. *a* **1578** LINDESAY (Pitscottie) *Chron. Scot.* (S.T.S.) I. 16 To bring all the subjecttis of this realme to peace and rest. **1686** tr. *Chardin's Trav. Persia* 52 There was not any one Subject of the Republick who was a Knight of Malta. **1713** STEELE *Englishm.* No. 3. 15 When I say an Englishman, I mean every true Subject of Her Majesty's Realms. **1747** *State Trials* (1813) XVIII. 859 By naturalizing or employing a subject of Great Britain. **1912** *Times* 19 Oct. 5/1 Subjects of the Slav States throughout the Ottoman Empire.

(*d*) with adj. of nationality.

1810 BENTHAM *Packing* (1821) 253 Though a very obscure and insignificant person, I have the honour to be a British subject. **1886** FROUDE *Oceana* 98 Their Monro doctrine, prohibiting European nations from settling on their side of the Atlantic, except as American subjects.

† **b.** *collect. sing.* The subjects of a realm. ? Also *transf.* in quot. 1608. (Only Shaks.) *Obs.*

1602 SHAKS. *Ham.* I. ii. 33 In that the Leuies.. are all made Out of his subiect. **1603** —— *Meas. for M.* III. ii. 145 The greater file of the subiect held the Duke to be wise. **1608** —— *Per.* II. i. 53 How from the finny subject of the sea These fishers tell the infirmities of men.

† **2. a.** One who is bound to a superior by an obligation to pay allegiance, service, or tribute; *spec.* a feudal inferior or tenant; a vassal, retainer; a dependant, subordinate; an inferior. *Obs.*

α. *c* **1315** SHOREHAM *Poems* IV. 276 Ho hys þat neuer ne kedde woȝ In boste to hys sugges? *c* **1383** in *Engl. Hist. Rev.* (1911) Oct. 748 Seculer lordis owen.. to treete reesonabli & charitabli here tenauntis & sogetis. *a* **1400** *Minor Poems fr. Vernon MS.* 546/368 Haue mesure to þi soget. *a* **1400–50** *Wars Alex.* 2682 As soiet serued haue I þat sire many sere wyntir. *c* **1450** *Merlin* i. 6 Youre suster is elder than ye, and so she wolde alwey holde yow as her sogect.

β. *c* **1386** CHAUCER *Sompn. T.* 282 With-Inne thyn hous ne be thou no leoun, To thy subgitz do noon oppressioun. **1420** in Ellis *Orig. Lett.* Ser. III. I. 68 Hys heires, vassalles, and subgees. *a* **1475** ASHBY *Active Policy* 898 Saint petur saithe þat soubgettes shold be Buxom to thar lorde. *c* **1489** CAXTON *Sonnes of Aymon* i. 25 Thou knowest well that thou arte his man, vaysall, and subgette. *a* **1533** BERNERS *Huon* xlii. 142 Thou to be my subgett, and to pay me trybute.

γ. *c* **1430** LYDG. *Min. Poems* (MS. Harl. 2251 fol. 5 b), Ayenst thy felawe no quarele thow contryve: With thy subiect to stryve it were shame. *c* **1450** *Godstow Reg.* 1 Alle lordes þat.. forbedith her subiectes þat ben acursed to go out of þe church. **1530** PALSGR. 278/1 Subjecte or holder of house or lande, *uassal*. *c* **1530** *Pol. Rel. & L. Poems* (1903) 60 Selle no parte of thyne heritage vnto thy bettyr, but for lesse pryce selle yt to thy subiecte. **1593** SHAKS. *Rich. II*, v. ii. 39 To Bullingbrooke, are we sworne Subiects now. **1681** [see SUBFEU]. [**1728** CHAMBERS *Cycl.* s.v., Anciently, the Lords call'd, abusively, those who held Lands or Fees of them, or ow'd them any Homage, Subjects.]

† **b.** One who owes allegiance or obedience to a spiritual superior. *Obs.*

c **1380** WYCLIF *Sel. Wks.* III. 355 Þat ȝif he [*sc.* the pope] hadde siche power, he shulde assoile alle hise sugetis fro peyne and fro trespas. **1425** *Rolls of Parlt.* IV. 306/1 Ye said Lordes Spirituell hath promitted.. to calle yere subgettes to residence. *c* **1450** CAPGRAVE *Life St. Gilbert* vii, He chase on of his subiectis whom he knewe be þe Holy Goost þat he schuld succede in his office aftir his deth. **1513** BRADSHAW *St. Werburge* I. 3360 Her systers, and subiettes, a religious couent. **1552** ABP. HAMILTON *Catech.* (1884) 3 Al baith prelates & subjeckis.

† **c.** One who is under the spiritual oversight or charge of a parish priest; one of a 'curate's' parishioners. *Obs.*

c **1340** HAMPOLE *Prose Treat.* 24 Vnto thes men itt longith.. to vsene werkis of mercy.. in helpe and sustinaunce of hem silfe and of hir sugettis. *c* **1380** WYCLIF *Wks.* (1880) 73 Sugetis taken ensaumple at here curatis. *c* **1449** PECOCK *Repr.* II. xii. 219 A curat mai not.. alwey rynge at the eeris of hise suggettis. *c* **1450** *Lay Folks Mass Bk.* 68 God gyf þame grace so well for to teche þare sugettis ilke curet in his degre. [**1509** *Ibid.* 75.]

3. a. A person (rarely, a thing) that is in the control or under the dominion of another; one who owes obedience *to* another.

α. **13..** *Seuyn Sag.* (W.) 458 Kes me, leman, and loue me, And I thi soget wil i-be. *a* **1340** HAMPOLE *Psalter* ii. 10 Þai ere þe sugetis til þe deuel. *c* **1430** *Hymns Virgin* (1867) 63 Make him þi suget, to þee to swere þat he schal not discure þi name. *c* **1440** *York Myst.* iv. 16 All other creatours also there-tyll Your suggettes shall they bee. *c* **1450** *Mirk's Festial* 25 And soo schowe hym seruant and soget to hym, and knewlech þys schyld [= child] for hys God.

β. *c* **1374** CHAUCER *Troylus* II. 828 O loue to whom I haue and shal Ben humble subgit.

γ. *c* **1440** *Jacob's Well* xxxiii. 214 Resoun sufferyth his wyif, þat is, his subiecte coueytise, to spedyn in causes of falsnesse in ryche men. **1588** KYD *Househ. Phil.* Wks. (1901) 254 By Nature woman was made mans subiect. **1590** SHAKS. *Com. Err.* II. i. 19 The beasts, the fishes, and the winged fowles Are their males subiects. **1671** MILTON *Samson* 886 Nor was I their subject, Nor under their protection but my own. **1812** CRABBE *Tales* v. 201 Beauties are tyrants, and if they can reign, They have no feeling for their subject's pain. **1865** R. W. DALE *Jew. Temple* xxiv. 270 Every member of the human race is a subject of the Lord Jesus.

b. *transf.*

c **1520** NISBET *N.T.* Prol. (S.T.S.) I. 3 Thai were all in bondage and sugettis of syn. **1625** BACON *Ess.*, *Anger* (Arb.) 565 Anger is certainly a kinde of Basenesse: As it appeares well, in the Weaknesse of those Subiects, in whom it reignes. *a* **1721** PRIOR *Vicar of Bray & Sir T. Moor* Wks. 1907 II. 248 My knowledge in Divine and Human Law gave me to understand I was born a Subject to both. **1818** *Brathwait's Barnabee's Jrnl.* Introd. 67 It is of the essence of fashion to descend in the subjects of its dominion.

4. *Law.* **a.** A thing over which a right is exercised.

1765–8 ERSKINE *Inst. Laws Scot.* II. x. §32. 351 As orchards produce no fruits that are the subjects either of parsonage or vicarage tithes. **1875** DIGBY *Real Prop.* I. App. (1876) 266 By the subject of a right is meant the thing.. over which the right is exercised. My house, horse, or watch is the subject of my right of property. **1875** [see SUABLE].

b. *Sc.* A piece of property.

1754 ERSKINE *Princ. Sc. Law* II. i. §1 (1757) I. 105 The things or subjects to which persons have right, are the second object of law. The right of enjoying and disposing of a subject at one's pleasure is called property. *Ibid.* III. viii. §32 II. 376 Full inventory of all his predecessor's heritable subjects. **1819** J. MARSHALL *Const. Opin.* (1839) 154 The distinction between property and other subjects to which the power of taxation is applicable. **1864** *N. Brit. Advertiser* 21 May, Subjects in Nelson and Kent Streets to be exposed to sale by public roup. **1903** *Dundee Advertiser* 22 Dec. 5 Those holding 'subjects' of that kind.

c. Considered as the object of an agreement.

1838 W. BELL *Dict. Law Scot.* 581 Where the subject of the lease is rendered unfit for the purposes for which it was let, overblown with sand, inundated [etc.].

II. Senses derived ultimately (through L. *subjectum*) from Aristotle's use of τὸ ὑποκείμενον in the threefold sense of (1) material out of which things are made, (2) subject of attributes, (3) subject of predicates.

† **5.** The substance of which a thing consists or from which it is made. *Obs.*

c **1374** CHAUCER *Boeth.* v. pr. i. (1868) 150 Þei casten as a manere of foundement of subgit material [*de materiali subjecto*] þat is to seyn of the nature of alle resoun. **1398** TREVISA *Barth. De P.R.* III. xxi. (1495) 68 Yf the wytt of gropyng is all loste the subget of alle the beest [orig. *subjectum totius animalis*] is destroyed. **1590** MARLOWE *2nd Pt. Tamburl.* v. iii. [4557, 4561] *Amy*... Your soul giues essence to our wretched subiects, Whose matter is incorporoat [*sic*] in your flesh... *Tam.* But sons, this subiect not of force enough, To hold the fiery spirit it containes. **1651** FRENCH *Distill.* v. 109 Thus do these attractive vertues mutually act upon each others subject. **1669** WORLIDGE *Syst. Agric.* (1681) 9 That Universal Subject, or *Spiritus Mundi*, out of which they are formed. **1775** HARRIS *Philos. Arrangem.* Wks. (1841) 267 Every thing generated or made.. is generated or made out of something else; and this something else is called its subject or matter.

6. *Philos.* The substance in which accidents or attributes inhere. ***subject of inhesion*** or † ***inherence***: see these sbs.

c **1380** WYCLIF *Wks.* (1880) 19 Ȝif þei seyn, written and techen openly þat þe sacrament of þe auter þat men seen bitwen þe prestis hondis is accidentis wiþ-outen suget. **1398** TREVISA *Barth. De P.R.* XIX. cxvi. (1495) 920 As whan tweyne accidentes ben in one substaunce and subiecte: as colour and sauour. *c* **1400** in *Apol. Loll.* (Camden) p. vii, That the sacrid oost is.. accident withouten ony subiect. **1551** T. WILSON *Logic* C ij, Wee se heate in other thynges to be separated from the Subiecte. **1609** *Bible* (Douay) Gen. i. 16 *comm.*, Ancient Doctors judged it possible, that accidents may remaine without their subject. **1614** SELDEN *Titles Hon.* 126 It hath been questioned, which is the more both elegant and honorable.. whether to say *Serenissime Princeps à te peto*, or *A Serenitate Vestrâ peto*. And some haue thought the first forme the best, because in that the Accidents and Subiects are together exprest. **1616** BULLOKAR *Eng. Exp.* s.v., The body is the subiect in which is health, or sickenesse, and the minde the subiect that receiueth into it vertues or vices. **1678** GALE *Crt. Gentiles* IV. III. 5 Albeit sin be.. a mere privation, yet it requires some positive, real natural Being for its subject. **1728** CHAMBERS *Cycl.* s.v., Two Contraries can never subsist in the same Subject. **1762** KAMES *Elem. Crit.* (1833) 487 The same thing, in different respects, has different names; with respect to qualities of all sorts, it is termed a subject. **1836–7** SIR W. HAMILTON *Metaph.* viii. (1859) I. 137 That which manifests its qualities,—in other words, that in which the appearing causes inhere, that to which they belong, is called their *subject*, or *substance*, or *substratum*. *Ibid.* ix. 158 The general meaning of the word *subject* in its philosophical application,—viz. the unknown basis of phænomenal or manifested existence. **1858** WHEWELL *Hist. Sci. Ideas* I. 35 The mind is the subject in which ideas inhere.

† **b.** A thing having real independent existence.

1603 SHAKS. *Meas. for M.* v. i. 458 Thoughts are no subiects; Intents, but meerely thoughts.

7. *Logic.* **a.** That which has attributes; the thing about which a judgement is made.

1551 T. WILSON *Logic* M ij b, As touchyng wordes knitte, ye maie vnderstand, that they are ioyned outwardly to the Subiect, and geue a name vnto him, according as they are. **1697** tr. *Burgersdicius his Logic* I. xix. 72 A Subject is that to which something is adjoyn'd besides its Essence. And an Adjunct that which is adjoyn'd to something besides its Essence. **1838** [F. HAYWOOD] tr. *Kant's Crit. Pure Reason* Introd. iv. 10 Extending judgments.. add a predicate to the conception of the subject. **1843** MILL *Logic* I. ii. §5 By a subject is here meant any thing which possesses attributes. **1864** BOWEN *Logic* i. 5 The Concept.. brings together many objects into one Thought or many attributes into one subject. **1883** F. H. BRADLEY *Princ. Logic* 14 We shall see that the subject is in the end no idea but always reality.

b. The term or part of a proposition of which the predicate is affirmed or denied.

Earlier treatises on logic use the L. *subjectum*.

1620 T. GRANGER *Div. Logike* 178 The proposition hath two parts, the Subiect, and Predicate. **1697** tr. *Burgersdicius his Logic* I. xxvii. 109 Simple enunciation consisteth of a subject and a predicate. **1796** *Nitsch's View Kant's Princ.* 128 Collections of properties, which in a judgment are made the predicates of a subject. **1843** MILL *Logic* I. i. §2 The subject is the name denoting the person or thing which something is affirmed or denied of. **1870** JEVONS *Elem. Logic* vii. 62 It is.. usual to call the first term of a proposition the subject, since it denotes the underlying matter.

8. *Gram.* The member or part of a sentence denoting that concerning which something is predicated (i.e. of which a statement is made, a question asked, or a desire expressed); a word or group of words setting forth that which is spoken about and constituting the 'nominative' to a finite verb.

In the accus. and infin. construction the accus. is the subject of the infin.

a **1638** [see PREDICATE *sb.* 2]. **1733** J. CLARKE *Gram. Lat. Tongue* 68 *note*, The Nominative Case to a Verb.. is called by Grammarians the Subject of the Verb. **1751** J. H[ARRIS] *Hermes* II. i. 230 In English these are distinguished by their Position, the Subject standing first, the Predicate last. **1874** BAIN *Comp. Higher Eng. Gram.* (1877) p. xxiii, Infinitive (logical subject) anticipated by 'it', 'this', &c. (formal subject) comes after the predicate. *Ibid.* 299 Cases where the grammatical subject is a neuter pronoun—'it', 'this'—standing as a provisional anticipation of the real subject or fact predicated about. **1888** STRONG tr. *Paul's Princ. Hist. Lang.* 112 We have to distinguish between the psychological and the grammatical subject or predicate.

9. *Modern Philos.* More fully ***conscious*** or ***thinking subject***: The mind, as the 'subject' in which ideas inhere; that to which all mental representations or operations are attributed; the thinking or cognizing agent; the self or ego. (Correlative to OBJECT *sb.* 6.)

The tendency in modern philosophy after Descartes to make the mind's consciousness of itself the starting-point of enquiry led to the use of *subjectum* for the mind or ego considered as the subject of all knowledge, and since Kant this has become the general philosophical use of the word (with its derivatives *subjective*, etc.).

[The following quots. illustrate a transitional use:—

1682 RUST *Disc. Truth* xviii, Thus have we spoken concerning the truth of things, or Truth in the Object: It follows that we speak concerning Truth in the power, or faculty, which we call Truth in the Subject. **1697** NORRIS *Acc. Reason & Faith* i. (1724) 19, I consider..that the most general distribution of Reason is into that of the Object and that of the Subject; or, to word it more intelligibly, though perhaps not altogether so Scholastically, into that of the Thing, and that of the Understanding.] **1796** *Nitsch's View Kant's Princ.* 72 In every knowledge, perception, &c., there is something which refers to an object, and something which refers to the knowing or perceiving subject. **1817** COLERIDGE *Biog. Lit.* xii. (1907) I. 184 A spirit is..an absolute subject for which all, itself included, may become an object. **1829** *Edin. Rev.* L. 196 *note*, The thinking subject, the Ego. **1838** [F. HAYWOOD] tr. *Kant's Crit. Pure Reason* 293 The thinking subject is the object of Psychology. **1851** MANSEL *Proleg. Log.* i. 7 Every state of consciousness necessarily implies two elements at least; a conscious subject, and an object of which he is conscious. **1886** *Encycl. Brit.* XX. 39/1 The conception of a mind or conscious subject is to be found implicitly or explicitly in all psychological writers whatever.

III. 10. The subject-matter of an art or science.

1541 COPLAND *Guydon's Quest. Cyrurg.* Biij, Euery worke-man is bounde to knowe the subiect of his worke in whiche he worketh. **1563** FULKE *Meteors* 1 Whether we maye borowe ye name of meteoron to comprehende the whole subiect of oure woorke. **1656** tr. *Hobbes' Elem. Philos.* I. i. 7 The Subject of Philosophy, or the matter it treats of, is every Body of which we can conceive any generation. **1728** CHAMBERS *Cycl.* s.v., The Subject of Logic, is Thinking or Reasoning. *Ibid.*, *Subject* is also used for the Matter of an Art or Science..: Thus the human Body is the Subject of Medicine. **1875** JOWETT *Plato* (ed. 2) I. 4 All sciences have a subject, number is the subject of arithmetic. **1888** STRONG tr. *Paul's Princ. Hist. Lang.* 1 *marg.*, Subject of the Science of Language.

11. a. A thing affording matter for action of a specified kind; a ground, motive, or cause.

In some quots. a Gallicism.

1586 *Let. to Earle of Leycester* 6 The very ground and onely subject, whereupon such daungerous practises and complots had been founded. **1651** tr. *De-las-Coveras' Don Fenise* 115 Fenise asked him what subject he had to attempt against his life. **1652** LOVEDAY tr. *Calprenede's Cassandra* I. 15, I have my selfe as much or more subject to hate life than you. **1655** tr. *Sorel's Com. Hist. Francion* x. 10, I have subject enough to be angry with you. **1756** MRS. CALDERWOOD in *Coltness Collect.* (Maitland Club) 129 That had anybody been inclined to laugh, they might have had a good subject. **1831** SCOTT *Cast. Dang.* ix, Which had never given the English government the least subject of complaint. **1843** *Penny Cycl.* XXVII. 512/1 In such circumstances subjects of accusation are not long wanting. **1893** OMAN *Dark Ages* xx, We might perhaps have learnt that Charles also gave subjects for offence.

b. Const. *for*.

1598 SHAKS. *Merry W.* II. i. 3 What, haue scap'd Loue-letters in the holly-day-time of my beauty, and am I now a subiect for them? **1616** *Marlowe's Faustus* Wks. (1910) 222 Let them come in, They are good subiect for a merriment. **1780** *Mirror* No. 83 The great subject for wit and ludicrous representation arises from men's having a thorough knowledge of what is the fashionable standard of manners. **1816** J. WILSON *City of Plague* III. iv, I am no subject for your mirth.

c. That which can be drawn upon or utilized, means of doing something. *rare*.

1752 HUME *Ess. & Treat.* (1817) I. 265 Where they [*sc.* indulgences]..entrench upon no virtue, but leave ample subject whence to provide for friends, family, [etc.].

12. a. That which is or may be acted or operated upon; a person or thing towards which action or influence is directed, or that is the recipient of some treatment.

1592 SHAKS. *Rom. & Jul.* III. v. 212 Alacke, alacke, that heauen should practise stratagems Vpon so soft a subiect as my selfe. **1606** —— *Tr. & Cr.* II. ii. 160 There's..none so Noble, Whose life were ill bestow'd, or death vnfam'd, Where Helen is the subiect. **1611** TOURNEUR *Ath. Trag.* v. i, Nor could the first Man, being but the passiue Subiect not The Actiue Mouer, be the Maker of Himselfe. **1753** MISS COLLIER *Art Torment.* I. i. (1811) 37 All the pleasure of tormenting is lost, as soon as your subject is become insensible to your strokes. **1764** REID *Inquiry* i. §1 In the noblest arts, the mind is also the subject upon which we operate. **1777** PRIESTLEY *Matter & Sp.* (1782) I. Pref. 33 Power cannot mean anything without a subject. **1852** MRS. STOWE *Uncle Tom's C.* xx, She approached her new subject very much as a person might be supposed to approach a black spider. **1898** MORTIMER *Cath. Faith & Practice* I. 140 The subject of Baptism is any human being, whether an adult or an infant.

b. Const. *of* a specified action or activity.

1591 SHAKS. *1 Hen. VI*, IV. vi. 49 To be Shames scorne, and subiect of Mischance. **1605** —— *Macb.* III. iii. 8 And neere approches The subiect of our Watch. **1634** SIR T. HERBERT *Trav.* 117 [The Turks] haue made this Citie, a subiect of their bloudy cruelty. **1696** WHISTON *Th. Earth* 87 Not the vast Universe, but the Earth alone, with its dependencies, are the proper subject of the Six Days Creation. **1711** STEELE *Spect.* No. 53 ¶2 The Triumph of Daphne over her Sister Letitia has been the Subject of Conversation at Several Tea-Tables. **1796** ELIZA HAMILTON *Lett. Hindoo Rajah* (1811) I. 204 The many subjects of wonder with which a stranger is surrounded. **1823** SCOTT *Quentin D.* xix, The huge wains, which transported to and fro the subjects of export and import. **1831** —— *Cast. Dang.* vi, The most bold and fierce subjects of chase in the island of Britain. **1847** HELPS *Friends in C.* I. v. 73 Proficiency in any one subject of human endeavour. **1855** BAIN *Senses & Int.* II. ii. §45. 537, I may here refer to what is a common subject of remark. **1883** GILMOUR *Mongols* xvii. 207 Such..difficulties..are welcomed rather as subjects of debate than felt to be barriers to the acceptance of Christianity.

†**c.** One who or a thing which is subject *to* something injurious. *Obs.*

1592 MARLOWE *Mass. Paris* 222 [They will] rather seeke to scourge their enemies, Than be themselues base subiects to the whip. **1597** SHAKS. *2 Hen. IV*, I. iii. 61 Who..leaues his part-created Cost [viz. a half-built house] A naked subiect to the Weeping Clouds.

d. An object with which a person's occupation or business is concerned or on which he exercises his craft; †(one's) business; that which is operated upon manually or mechanically.

[**1541** COPLAND *Guydon's Quest. Cyrurg.* Biij, Yf it so be that the subiecte of the Cyrurgyen be the body of men-kynde.] **1766** W. GORDON *Gen. Counting-ho.* 102 Waste-book, containing an Inventory of my Subject. **1828** STEUART *Planter's Guide* (ed. 2) 267 The above Machine..is capable of removing subjects of from eighteen to about eight-and-twenty feet high. **1837** KEITH *Bot. Lex.* 22 The bark... In young subjects it is of a flexible and leathery texture. **1887** *Pall Mall Gaz.* 6 July 2/2 You must consider the capital we have to sink in our 'subjects' [*sc.* of a menagerie] when you calculate our expenses.

e. A body used for anatomical examination or demonstration; a dead body intended for or undergoing dissection.

1710 *Phil. Trans.* XXVII. 71 In our Subject the Hairs are every where pretty long. **1729** *Ibid.* XXXVI. 167 This Subject..had her Lungs full of small Tubercles. **1775** *True Patriot* IX. 330 The gentleman of the house [a surgeon] declared he had a very good subject above in the garret. **1829** SCOTT *Jrnl.* II. 219 The total and severe exclusion of foreign supplies raises the price of the 'subjects'. **1870** H. LONSDALE *Robt. Knox* 54 The supply of 'subjects' was so inadequate, that the surgeons' apprentices..determined upon the..step of procuring them from the graveyards.

f. A person who presents himself for or undergoes medical or surgical treatment; hence, one who is affected with some disease.

a good (bad) subject: a patient who has (has not) good prospects of improvement or recovery.

1822–34 *Good's Study Med.* (ed. 4) III. 285 The subject was forty-five years of age, and had evinced a slight rhachitic tendency from infancy. **1849** CUPPLES *Green Hand* xv, I asked if there wasn't any chance [of the captain's recovery]. 'Oh, the captain, you mean?' said he, 'don't think there is—he's a bad subject!' **1859** *Todd's Cycl. Anat.* V. 178/2 Two of the subjects died after severe instrumental labour. **1898** H. BROWN *Secret Gd. Health* 91 Smoking helps the subject to rest. **1898** *Allbutt's Syst. Med.* V. 276 A broad line of dilated venules is often seen in emphysematous subjects. **1905** ROLLESTON *Dis. Liver* 260 Patients with cirrhosis are..far from good subjects.

g. *Psychical Research*. A person upon whom an experiment is made.

1883 *Proc. Soc. Psych. Research* 18 July 251 A specific influence or effluence, passing from the operator to the 'subject'. **1886** GURNEY, etc. *Phantasms of Living* I. 16 The 'subject's' hand seemed to obey the other person's will with almost the same directness as that person's own hand would have done.

h. A person under the influence of religious enthusiasm. *rare*.

1820 SOUTHEY *Wesley* I. 417 Subjects began to cry out, and sink down in the meeting.

i. With epithet: A person in respect of his conduct or character. *rare*.

Cf. F. *mauvais sujet*.

1848 DICKENS *Dombey* xxxix, Unable..to satisfy his mind whether Mr. Toots was the mild subject he appeared to be.

13. a. In a specialized sense: That which forms or is chosen as the matter of thought, consideration, or inquiry; a topic, theme.

the human subject: man, regarded as a matter for study or observation.

1586 B. YOUNG *Guazzo's Civ. Conv.* IV. 208 Now that Lorde Hercules hathe geuen occasion to talke of this subiecte. **1667** *Decay Chr. Piety* 346 Here he would have us..fix our thoughts and studies: Nor need we fear that they are too dry a subject for our contemplation. *a* **1700** EVELYN *Diary* 13 June 1683, We shew'd him divers experiments on the magnet, on which subject the Society were upon. **1729** BUTLER *Serm.* Wks. 1874 II. 51 Justice must be done to every part of a subject when we are considering it. **1780** *Mirror* No. 89 As for politics, it was a subject far beyond the reach of any female capacity. **1794** MRS. RADCLIFFE *Myst. Udolpho* xxxviii, 'Alas! I know it too well,' replied Emily: 'spare me on this terrible subject.' **1828** MISS MITFORD in L'Estrange *Life* (1870) II. xi. 247 History never will sell so well as more familiar and smaller subjects. **1837** DISRAELI *Venetia* II. i, Her father had become a forbidden subject. **1872** MORLEY *Voltaire* (1886) 9/9 He always paid religion respect enough to treat it as the most important of all subjects. **1874** CARPENTER *Mental Phys.* I. ii. (1879) 70 The phenomena presented by the Human subject. **1902** VIOLET JACOB *Sheep-Stealers* viii, The Pig-driver seated himself beside him and plunged immediately into his subject.

b. With appositional phr. formed with *of* and expressing the nature of the subject.

1724 SWIFT *Drapier's Lett.* Wks. 1841 II. 34/1 In examining what I have already written..upon the subject of Mr. Wood. **1733** *Pres. St. Popery* 21 The late exceptions of a certain Lincolnshire minister on the subject of infallibility. **1765** *Museum Rust.* IV. 294 The subject of grasses is very nice. **1816** SCOTT *Old Mort.* xxxviii, After quoting Delrio, and Burthoog, and De L'Ancre, on the subject of apparitions. **1839** FR. A. KEMBLE *Resid. Georgia* (1863) 35 The indifference of our former manager upon the subject of the accommodation for the sick.

c. *on one's subject* (= F. *sur son sujet*): concerning one. (A Gallicism.)

1747 CHESTERF. *Lett.* cxviii, Two letters, which I have lately seen from Lausanne, upon your subject. **1775** W. MASON *Life of Gray* (ed. 2) 3 To make it necessary I should enlarge upon his subject.

d. An object of study in relation to its use for pedagogic or examining purposes; a particular department of art or science in which one is instructed or examined.

1843 *Penny Cycl.* XXVI. 29/1 An examination for honours in each subject is held subsequently. **1887** *Whitaker's Alm.* 540 If an officer only pass in the subjects necessary for a subaltern. **1913** *Rep. 7th Ann. Mtg. Hist. Assoc.* 8 Every man who teaches a subject well and with real enthusiasm.

14. a. The theme *of* a literary composition; what a book, poem, etc. is about.

a **1586** SIDNEY *Ps.* CIV. i, Make, O my soule, the subject of thy songe, Th'eternall Lord. **1596** WARNER *Alb. Eng.* x. lx. (1602) 266 Though stately be the subiect, and too slender be our Arte. **1638** BAKER tr. *Balzac's Lett.* (vol. II) 72, I did not think to have gone so far; it is the subject that hath carried me away. *c* **1645** MILTON *Sonn.* xi, A Book was writ of late call'd *Tetrachordon*;..The Subject new. **1667** —— *P.L.* IX. 25 Since first this Subject for Heroic Song Pleas'd me long choosing. **1780** *Mirror* No. 85 A poem may be possessed of very considerable merit,..though, from its subject, its length, or the manner in which it is written, it may not be suited to the Mirror. **1835** T. MITCHELL *Acharn. Aristoph.* 365 *note*, All of them subjects dramatized by Euripides. **1844** WHEWELL *Let. to J. G. Marshall* 29 Jan., The subject of my lectures is the difficulties of constructing a system of morals. **1903** A. B. DAVIDSON *Old Test. Prophecy* ix. 136 The developments of heathenism form the subject of Daniel.

b. The person of whom a biography is written.

1741 MIDDLETON *Cicero* I. Pref. p. xv, They [*sc.* writers of particular lives] are apt to be partial and prejudiced in favor of their subject. **1791** BOSWELL *Johnson* Adv. 1st ed., The delay of its publication must be imputed..to the extraordinary zeal which has been shewn..to supply me with additional information concerning its illustrious subject. **1885** *Pall Mall Gaz.* 18 Feb. 5/2 We think we like the book best because of the view it gives of the subject's character.

15. a. An object, a figure or group of figures, a scene, an incident, etc., chosen by an artist for representation.

1614 in *Archaeologia* XLII. 360 Another..picture of the same subject. **1695** DRYDEN tr. *Dufresnoy's Art Paint.* 11 The next thing is to make choice of a Subject beautifull and noble. *c* **1790** IMISON *Sch. Arts* II. 55 The subject to be painted should be situated in such a manner that the light may fall with every advantage on the face. **1859** REEVE *Brittany* 13, I was looking round the little knot of soldiers for a subject. **1872** RUSKIN *Eagle's Nest* §163 You must always draw for the sake of your subject—never for the sake of your picture. **1893** J. A. HODGES *Elem. Photogr.* 112 If the subject is so shaky as to render it impossible to take the portrait without its [*sc.* a headrest's] aid.

b. In decorative art, a representation of human figures or animals, an action or incident.

1828 DUPPA *Trav. Italy*, etc. 14 Ten compartments filled with subjects from the Old Testament. **1867** *Paris Exhib., Rep. Artisans Soc. Arts* 27 A pair of vases painted all round with subjects after Watteau.

16. *Mus.* The theme or principal phrase of a composition or movement; in a fugue, the exposition, dux, or proposition; ***first*** (***second***) ***subject***, the primary (or subsidiary) theme of a composition, esp. in sonata-form.

1752 C. AVISON *Ess. Mus. Expression* I. ii. 28 In the greater Kinds of musical Composition, there is a principal or leading *Subject* or Succession of Notes, which ought to prevail, and be heard throughout the whole Composition. **1753** *Chambers' Cycl.* Suppl. s.v. *Sogetto*, *Contrapunto sopra il sogetto*, a counterpoint above the subject, is that of which the subject is the bass. **1771** C. BURNEY *Present State Mus. in France & Italy* 49 The first subject is judiciously returned to while it still vibrates on the ear. **1801** BUSBY *Dict. Mus.*, *Subject*, the theme or text of any movement. **1876** STAINER & BARRETT *Dict. Mus. Terms* 411/1 In sonata form there should be two chief subjects, called first and second. **1883** ROCKSTRO in *Grove's Dict. Mus.* III. 747/2 The earliest known form of Subject is the Ecclesiastical *Cantus firmus*. **1883** GROVE *Dict. Mus.* III. 752/1 The Father of the Symphony [*sc.* Haydn] enriched his new Art-form with a Second Subject, so constructed as to enhance the beauty of the Primary Theme by the introduction of some form of expression distinctly opposed to it. **1898** G. B. SHAW *Perf. Wagnerite* 3 In classical music there are, as the analytical programs tell us, first subjects and second subjects, free fantasias, recapitulations, and codas. **1955** J. F. RUSSELL in H. Van Thal *Fanfare for Ernest Newman* 148 It is difficult to remember a Mozart first subject, for example, in which the common chord is not melodically employed. **1977** *Gramophone* June 90/2 Walton brilliantly exploits every conceivable kind of antiphony..the Worcester Cathedral choristers angelically distanced in the gentle second-subject at 'The glorious company of the Apostles'.

†**17.** That upon which something stands; a base. *Obs. rare*$^{-1}$.

1592 R. D. *Hypnerotomachia* 12 The Pægma base or subiect for this metaline machine to stand vpon, was of one solyde peece of marble.

IV. 18. *attrib.* and *Comb.*, as (sense 8) ***subject clause***, ***complement***, ***noun***, (also 7 b) ***part***, (also 13) ***-oriented*** adj.; (sense 13) ***subject-changer***; (sense 14, chiefly with reference to cataloguing books according to their subjects) ***subject card***, ***catalogue***, ***cataloguing***, ***entry***, ***heading***, ***index***, ***list***, ***reference***; **subject-monger**, one who exploits his subjects; **subject picture**, a genre painting; **subject-term** *Logic* = sense 7 b.

1869 C. A. CUTTER in F. L. Miksa *Charles Ammi Cutter* (1977) II. xxiv. 168 The *subject-cards would..be copied from these author-cards. **1982** D. L. FOSTER *Managing Catalog Department* (ed. 2) iii. 72 The best way to divide the catalog..is to divide the subject cards from the others within each drawer. **1873** M. DEWEY in G. Dawe *Melvil Dewey* (1932) 323 By this plan any books may be found without a catalogue since the library is in itself a full classed *subject catalogue. **1889** WHEATLEY *How to Catal. Libr.* 232 If he wants to find a manuscript upon a particular subject, he can look at the subject catalogue. **1900** E. W. HULME in *Libr. Assoc. Rec.* 5 Nov. 571 *(heading)* Principles of dictionary *subject-cataloguing in scientific and technical libraries. **1748** RICHARDSON *Clarissa* (1785) II. 160 But I asked him, If he had any news by his last letters from London: A question which he always understands to be a **subject-changer*; for otherwise I never put it. **1978** I. MURDOCH *Sea* 164 'Been to Ireland lately?' This always set Perry off and was a guaranteed subject-changer. **1957** R. W. ZANDVOORT *Handbk. Eng. Gram.* III. vi. 165 *What*..may introduce a *subject clause, an object clause,..a predicative clause, or a clause preceded by a preposition. **1939** H. E. PALMER *Gram. Spoken Eng.* (ed. 2) II. 80 A certain number of adverbs may be used as *subject-complements, i.e. as complements to..verbs of incomplete predication. **1869** C. A. CUTTER in *N. Amer. Rev.* CVIII. 115 In the New Catalogue, on the contrary, the *subject entry is the fullest. **1899** QUINN *Libr. Catal.* 71 The forms of subject entries in dictionary catalogues. **1874** *Catal. Libr. Mercantile Libr. Assoc. San Francisco* p. vi, *Subject-headings, when there are two or more titles, are denoted by a separate line in the same [fount]. **1973** M. AMIS *Rachel Papers* 60, I indent subject-headings, co-ordinate footnotes, mark cross-references in red and blue biros. **1861** *Catal. N.-Y. State Libr.: Gen. Libr., 1st Suppl.* p. xii, **Subject-Index.*—In the Index following the catalogue, the subjects of the books are arranged alphabetically. **1879** *Rep. Index Soc.* 3 Subject Indexes of Science, Literature, and Art. **1875** C. A. CUTTER in *Nation* 14 Oct. 252/1 'Analysis'—that is, reference under subjects to topics discussed in certain books incidentally but not at sufficient length to justify the insertion of the book in the *subject-list. **1902** *(title)* Subject List of Works on General Science [etc.]. **1630** LENNARD tr. *Charron's Wisd.* III. iii. §12 (1670) 363 A Prince must carefully preserve himself..from resembling, by over-great and excessive imposition, those tyrants, *subject-mongers, Cannibals. **1844** DISRAELI *Coningsby* III. iii, A cutting reply to Mr. Rigby's article with some searching mockery, that became the subject and the subject-monger. **1862** E. ADAMS *Elem. Eng. Lang.* (1870) 158 When the *subject noun is accompanied by qualifying or explanatory words, it is said to be enlarged. **1964** *Language* XL. 77 Middle voice embraces at least five subtypes: (1) *subject-oriented action, [etc.]. **1975** *Language for Life* (Dept. Educ. & Sci.) xii. 189 The primary school teacher is likely to conceive of his task in terms of integrated rather than subject-oriented work. **1628** T. SPENCER *Logick* 21 The first substance, or *subiect part of every sentence. *Ibid.* 255 The antecedent, or subiect part of the conclusion. **1862** THORNBURY *Turner* I. 257 His first *subject picture was 'Fishermen at Sea', 1796. **1876** *Public Libr. in U.S.A.* (U.S. Bureau Educ.) I. xxvii. 542 A dictionary catalogue (author- and anonymous-title entries with imprints,..*subject-references to the classed part). **1889** WHEATLEY *How to Catal. Libr.* 180 It is something appalling to conjecture what would be the size of the British Museum Catalogue if subject references were included in the general alphabet. **1880** W. H. S. MONCK *Introd. Logic* v. 39 A particular proposition is not limited to some *only* of the objects denoted by the *subject-term. **1980** A. KENNY *Aquinas* ii. 34 The word 'substance' can be used to refer to the thing that sentences such as the above are about: the object for which the subject-term of the sentences stands.

b. Used appositively in senses 7–9, as ***subject-object, -predicate, -verb*** adjs.

1933 *Jrnl. Philos.* XXX. 65 We have described those features of *subject-object situations whereby the narrowness of a point of view is escaped. **1936** J. R. KANTOR *Objective Psychol. Gram.* xvi. 222 The logical essense of these cases can be clearly discerned in the fact that the nominative and accusative are subject-object cases. **1977** DOUGLAS & JOHNSON *Existential Sociol.* p. xi, Experimental or other methodological protocol can produce the so-called subject-object dualism. **1900** B. RUSSELL *Leibnitz* ii. 12 The question whether all propositions are reducible to the *subject-predicate form is one of fundamental importance to all philosophy. **1980** A. KENNY *Aquinas* ii. 51 Sentences which are of subject-predicate form. **1935** G. K. ZIPF *Psycho-Biol. of Lang.* v. 234 One cannot determine *a priori* what actual proportion of spoken English consists of simple *subject-verb sentences. **1979** *Amer. Speech 1976* LI. 134 Of the nine problems covered, subject-verb agreement receives a thorough treatment.

subject ('sʌbdʒɪkt), *a.* Forms: α. 4 sug(g)ette, sougit, sujet, 4–5 suget(t, sogett(e, 4–6 soget, 5 sugget, soiet. β. 4 soubgit, subiet, 4–5 subgit, 5 subgyt, -gett, subiette, subyett, 5–6 subgette, 4–6 subget. γ. 4–6 subiect, 5 subyect, -iecht, 5–6 iecte, 6 -gecte, -jecte, 6– subject. [a. OF. *suget, subject* (12th c.), *sog(i)et, sougit, subg(i)et* (13th c.), mod.F. *sujet* (from 16th c.), repr. L. *subject-us*, pa. pple. of *subicĕre, subjicĕre*, f. *sub-* SUB- 3 + *jacĕre* to throw, cast.

Examples like the following are freq. in ME., where the word should prob. be construed as inflected adj., though formally indistinguishable from pl. sb.:—

c **1350** *Will. Palerne* 463 Min eiȝen sorly aren sogettes to serue min hert & buxum ben to his bidding. **1382** WYCLIF *1 Cor.* xv. 27 Whanne he seith, alle thingis ben sugetis to him. *c* **1386** CHAUCER *Pars. T.* ⁋634 Seint Paul seith O ye wommen, be ye subgetes to youre housbondes. **1456** SIR G. HAYE *Law Arms* (S.T.S.) 106 Thai realmes be nocht subjectes to the empire.]

I. 1. That is under the dominion or rule of a sovereign, or a conquering or ruling power; owing allegiance or obedience *to* a sovereign ruler or state, a temporal or spiritual lord, or other superior.

(*a*) in predicative position.

α. *c* **1330** R. BRUNNE *Chron. Wace* (Rolls) 14842 Þe Englys were nought of o wyl O kyng ouer þem to set, Ne for to be til on suget. *c* **1380** WYCLIF *Wks.* (1880) 44 And freris þat ben soget owen to þenke þat for god þei han forsaken here owen willes. **1387** TREVISA *Higden* (Rolls) II. 59 Al West Saxon was soget to hym. *Ibid.* 123 To þat see is sugett Barokschire, Wiltschire, and Dorsett. *c* **1450** *Mirk's Festial* 22 All þe world was suget to þe Emperour of Rome.

β. **1390** GOWER *Conf.* I. 26 Therwhiles that the Monarchie Of al the world in that partie To Babiloyne was soubgit. *c* **1425** *Engl. Conq. Irel.* 26 Þer was noght of þe lond-folke þat all nas subyett to hym. **1456** SIR G. HAYE *Law Arms* (S.T.S.) 218 Here speris the doctour, quhethir the king of Ingland be suget to the Emperour.., I ansuere..that thai ar nocht subget to the Empire. **1471** CAXTON *Recuyell* (Sommer) 509 Pannonye was subgette vnto kyng pryant. *c* **1511** *1st Engl. Bk. Amer.* (Arb.) Introd. p. xxxiv/2 All these be subgette to the great kynge of Israhel.

γ. *c* **1386** CHAUCER *Clerk's T.* 426 To been subiect, & been in seruage To the þat born art of a smal village. *c* **1400** *Destr. Troy* 5507 Dukes full doughty..þat subiect were sothely to þe same Perses. **1515** BARCLAY *Egloges* iv. (1570) C iv, What time a knight is subiect to a knaue. **1600** J. PORY tr. *Leo's Africa* VI. 265 All round about are subiect vnto the King of Tunis. **1662** J. DAVIES tr. *Olearius' Voy. Ambass.* 36 The Island was subject to the King of Denmark. **1842** W. C. TAYLOR *Anc. Hist.* xviii. (ed. 3) 573 The empire of India became subject to that of Persia. **1863** MARY HOWITT tr. *Bremer's Greece* I. vi. 161 The freest of all the states of the earth became subject to a despot.

(*b*) in attributive position. (Sometimes hyphened as if *subject* were regarded as the sb. used attrib.)

subject superior: see SUPERIOR *sb.*

1581 A. HALL *Iliad* I. 11 Many a subiect towne of his. *a* **1586** SIR P. SIDNEY *Arcadia* (1912) 246 He was not borne to live a subject-life, each action of his bearing in it Majestie. **1594** *Selimus* 890 (Malone Soc.), As if t'were lawfull for a subiect prince To rise in Armes gainst his soueraigne. **1595** SHAKS. *John* IV. ii. 171 O, let me haue no subiect enemies. **1690** LOCKE *Hum. Und.* IV. iii. §20 The Subject part of Mankind..might..with Egyptian Bondage expect Egyptian Darkness. **1781** GIBBON *Decl. & F.* II. 5 *note*, The names of his subject-nations. **1792** S. ROGERS *Pleas. Mem.* I. 180 As studious Prospero's mysterious spell Drew every subject-spirit to his cell. **1802** PINKERTON *Mod. Geog.* I. 309 Russia in Europe... Poland has been devoured; Denmark and Sweden may be considered as subject-allies. *a* **1859** MACAULAY *Hist. Eng.* xxv. V. 296 The Court which had dared to treat England as a subject province. **1871** MORLEY *Carlyle* in *Crit. Misc.* 197 The relations between.. governing race and subject race.

b. *to* a law, a jurisdiction.

1387 TREVISA *Higden* (Rolls) II. 391 Firste he sente messagers and heet his enemyes be soget to his lawe. *c* **1450** LOVELICH *Grail* xliv. 25 And þat to ȝoure lawe no more soiet þat ȝe be, but Only to the lawe Of Cristyente. **1490** CAXTON *Eneydos* viii. 34 Alle subgette and obeyssaunt vnto the lawes of her seygnorye. **1580** *Rot. Scacc. Reg. Scot.* XXI. 548 Alexander is nocht subject to the jurisdictioun of the saidis commissaris. **1690** LOCKE *Govt.* II. viii, To make him subject to the Laws of any Government.

2. *transf.* and *fig.* In a state of subjection or dependence; under the control, rule, or influence of something; subordinate.

(*a*) in predicative position.

α. *a* **1340** HAMPOLE *Psalter* xxxvi. 6 Be suget till lord, and pray hym. **1340** —— *Pr. Consc.* 1055 Þe mare world..suld be til man suggette, For to serve man. *c* **1350** *Will. Palerne* 473 My siȝt is soget to my hert. *c* **1380** WYCLIF *Serm.* Sel. Wks. I. 45 Þei wolden þat al þis world were suget unto þer sect. **1382** —— *Luke* ii. 51 He cam doun with hem..and was suget to hem. *c* **1430** *Hymns Virgin* (1867) 71 Deeþ is sugett to god to bende. *c* **1530** *Crt. Love* 1131 Us leffer were with Venus byden still,..and soget been Unto thise women.

β. *c* **1374** CHAUCER *Troylus* I. 231 He..wax sodeynly most subget vn to loue. *c* **1375** *Sc. Leg. Saints* xviii. (*Egipciane*) 34 His flesche sa dayntyt he had, þat to þe saule subiet he It mad. *c* **1407** LYDG. *Reson & Sens.* 6133 For crafte ys subget vn-to kynde. **1474** CAXTON *Chesse* II. iii. (1883) 37 A man is subgett vnto money may not be lord therof.

γ. *c* **1400** *Destr. Troy* 1846 As subiecte vnto syn. **1508** FISHER *7 Penit. Ps.* Wks. (1876) 48 The woman is subgecte to the man. **1538** STARKEY *England* I. i. 12 [Man] lord of al other bestys and creaturys, applying them al vnto hys vse, for al be vnto hym subiecte. *a* **1715** BURNET *Own Time* I. (1724) I. 46 The military power ought always to be subject to the civil. **1723** WATERLAND *2nd Vind. Christ's Div.* 38 Christ, since his Incarnation, has been subject to the Father. **1841** HELPS *Ess. Pract. Wisd.* (1875) 5 Imagination, if it be subject to reason, is its 'slave of the lamp'. **1847** YEOWELL *Anc. Brit. Ch.* iii. 24 Parts of Britain, inaccessible to the Romans, but subject to Christ. **1864** TENNYSON *Aylmer's Field* 71 Edith, whose pensive beauty, perfect else, But subject to the season or the mood.

(*b*) in attributive position.

1827 [TENNYSON] *Poems Two Bro.* (1893) 32 A subject world I lost for thee, For thou wert all my world to me. **1837** CARLYLE *Fr. Rev.* I. IV. iv, Upholstery, aided by the subject fine-arts, has done its best. **1875** JOWETT *Plato* (ed. 2) III. 56 The virtue of temperance is the friendship of the ruling and the subject-principle.

b. *to* the power, law, command, etc. of another.

c **1386** CHAUCER *Pars. T.* ⁋1045 Alwey a man shal putten his wyl to be subget to the wille of god. *c* **1400** tr. *Secr. Secr., Gov. Lordsh.* 55 Þat he ys subgyt to þe hegh myght of god. *c* **1450** tr. *De Imitatione* II. xii. 58 Þe worlde & þe flesshe shul be made suget to þi comaundement. **1590** SPENSER *F.Q.* III. vi. 40 All that liues, is subiect to that law. **1736** BUTLER *Anal.* I. v. Wks. 1874 I. 96 These affections are naturally..subject to the government of the moral principle. **1819** SCOTT *Ivanhoe* xxiv, Thou art the captive of my bow and spear—subject to my will by the laws of all nations. **1876** BLACK *Madcap Violet* xv, He would no longer be subject to the caprice of any woman.

c. Under obligation, bound *to*. *rare.*

1585 T. WASHINGTON tr. *Nicholay's Voy.* III. vij. 80 b, [They] are not subiect as the other are to watch or ward, nor goe vnto the Sarail. **1788** PRIESTLY *Lect. Hist.* lxiii. v. 504 He knows that if ever he be subject to pay, he will be proportionably able to do it.

†**d.** occas. uses: of a domestic animal; of a subordinate member of a series. *Obs.*

1633 T. ADAMS *Exp. 2 Peter* ii. 4 The first subject beast he [*sc.* a lion] met withall was an Asse. **1711** SHAFTESB. *Charac.* III. 284 Had the Author of our Subject-Treatises consider'd thorowly of these literate Affairs.

†**3.** ***to make, bring subject***: to bring into subjection or submission; to subdue, subjugate. *Obs.*

1382 WYCLIF *1 Cor.* xv. 26 He hath maad suget alle thingis vndir his feet. **1387** TREVISA *Higden* (Rolls) I. 277 Franci.. made alle þe lond sogett, ffrom Sicambria anon to þe Ryne. *c* **1440** *Gesta Rom.* lii. 232 Now he is takyn, & made soget to his Enmyes, & þou art free. **1500–20** DUNBAR *Poems* lxxxiv. 44 Suppois my sensualitie Subiect to syn hes maid my saull of syss. **1561** T. NORTON *Calvin's Inst.* I. 17 No man could then gesse that there should be any such Cyrus..that should bring subiect so mightie a monarchie vnder his dominion. **1587** HOLINSHED *Hist. Scot.* 258/1 Not ceassing till he had brought the Welshmen subiect at his pleasure. **1643** BURROUGHES *Exp. 1st 3 ch. Hosea* iv. 294 Conscience..is here made subject to low and vile things.

†**4.** Submissive; obedient. *Obs.*

1390 GOWER *Conf.* III. 52 His wif was such as sche be scholde, His poeple was to him sougit. *c* **1400** *Apol. Loll.* 42 To be mek and suget, and seruiciable, obedient and buxum to ilk man. **1474** CAXTON *Chesse* II. v. (1883) 61 The peple ..ryse agayn theyr lord and wole not be subget. **1508** DUNBAR *Tua Mariit Wemen* 327 Quhen I him saw subiect, and sett at myn bydding. **1601** R. JOHNSON *Kingd. & Commw.* (1603) 164 The Moscovite [hath] more subjectes and more subject; the Polonian better soldiers and more couragious.

†**b.** *transf.* Easily managed. *Obs. rare.*

1619 *Times' Storehouse* 690 [Rings] are..so subiect and light, that they may be worne on the least finger of the hand.

II. (Const. *to*.) **5.** Exposed or open *to*; prone *to* or liable to suffer from something damaging, deleterious, or disadvantageous.

c **1374** CHAUCER *Boeth.* III. pr. ii. (1868) 67 It nediþ nat to seie þat blisfulnesse be anguissous ne þorn ne subgit to greuances ne to sorwes [orig. *doloribus molestiisque subjectam*]. **1388** WYCLIF *Eccles.* iii. 20 Alle thingis ben suget to vanyte [orig. *cuncta subjacent vanitati*]. *c* **1450** *Myrr. our Ladye* 191 He that was vndedly was made subget to dethe. **1560** DAUS tr. *Sleidane's Comm.* 421 Therfore is he subjecte [orig. *objectum*] unto great perilles and daungers. **1671** MILTON *P.R.* II. 471 Subject himself to Anarchy within. **1682** DRYDEN *MacFl.* 1 All humane things are subject to decay. *a* **1700** EVELYN *Diary* 24 Mar. 1672, Lord! what miseries are mortal men subject to. **1748** HILL *Hist. Fossils* 346 It is of a very impure, irregular, and somewhat coarse texture, but not subject to spots or clouds. **1760** R. BROWN *Compl. Farmer* II. 28 These lands are very subject to worms. **1849** MACAULAY *Hist. Eng.* vii. II. 233 The disabilities to which the Roman Catholics were subject. **1912** SELBIE *Nonconf.* xii. 225 Here and there..Nonconformists will still often be subject to certain social disadvantages.

b. Exposed *to* violent treatment, damaging weather, or the like.

1490 CAXTON *Eneydos* i. 11 To that other she gyueth to be subgette to the face of the ryght blody swerde. **1585** T. WASHINGTON tr. *Nicholay's Voy.* IV. xxiii. 139 The citye..is very subiect vnto windes & Earthquakes. **1604** E. G[RIMSTONE] tr. *D'Acosta's Hist. Indies* II. x. 103 This Region is very moist and subiect to raine. **1615** G. SANDYS *Trav.* 48 The Sultans themselves have bene sometimes subject to their insolencies. **1631** GOUGE *God's Arrows* III. §6. 192 Gods true Church is subject to assaults in this world. **1726** LEONI *Alberti's Archit.* I. 7 The Isle of Lemnos..being very subject to Lightning. **1768** J. BYRON *Narr. Wager* (1778) 229 It is much too high built for a country so subject to earthquakes. **1833** HT. MARTINEAU *Tale of Tyne* vi, Naval seamen are..made subject to violence. **1853** NEWMAN *Hist. Sk.* (1876) I. I. ii. 64 The sands of the adjacent deserts..are subject to violent agitation from the action of the wind.

c. Liable *to* disease.

1577 GOOGE tr. *Heresbach's Husb.* 28 The stalke [of rye].. his eare hanging downewardes, and therefore more subiect to blasting. **1600** J. PORY tr. *Leo's Africa* VIII. 299 Some of the Egyptians are subiect vnto dangerous rheumes and feuers. **1663** GERBIER *Counsel* 23 The bording otherwayes is much subject to rott. **1756** C. LUCAS *Ess. Waters* I. 207 The more compound the water..the more subject will the patients be to fevers. **1863** *N. Brit. Rev.* May 375 The leaf and chaff of the cereals are subject to a disease called rust. **1879** FROUDE *Cæsar* xxviii. 483 He became subject to epileptic fits.

6. Liable *to* the incidence or recurrence of an action, process, or state.

1559 W. CUNNINGHAM *Cosmogr. Glasse* 97 That the supercelestiall bodies are subiect to alteration. **1577** *St. Aug. Manual* O vj b, Thou art not disseuered by places, nor altered by tymes, nor subiect vnto to & fro. **1598** SHAKS. *Merry W.* III. v. 117 A man of my Kidney..that am as subiect to heate as butter. **1625** B. JONSON *Staple of News* II. Interm. 33 Is there nothing to be call'd Infanta, but what is subiect to exception? **1710** ADDISON *Tatler* No. 192 ⁋5 A kind of good Nature, that is not subject to any Change of Health. **1772** PRIESTLEY *Inst. Relig.* (1782) I. Ded. 2 We are subject to successive impressions. **1817** JAS. MILL *Brit. India* II. v. ix. 715 The parties were rendered subject to personal examination upon oath. **1832** BREWSTER *Nat. Magic* v. 120 The nose..is more subject to change of perspective than any of the other features. **1855** FORBES *Gram. Hind. Lang.* 100 Accompanied by an adjective or pronoun subject to inflection. **1879** in *Cassell's Techn. Educ.* IV. 96/1 He discovered that plants were subject to a regular sleep at night like animals.

b. *Book-trade.* (*ellipt.*) Subject to discount.

1906 *Daily Tel.* 12 Oct. 10 What in the trade are known as subject-books..books that is to say which are subject to discount.

†**7.** Having a tendency, prone or disposed, *to* an action, or *to do* something. *Obs.*

c **1590** MONTGOMERIE *Sonn.* xxv. 5 Syn I am subject somtyme to be seik. **1595** SHAKS. *John* III. i. 14 A widdow, husbandles, subiect to feares. **1597** —— *2 Hen. IV*, III. ii. 325 How subiect wee old men are to this vice of Lying? *a* **1625** BOYS *Wks.* (1630) 751 Toll-gatherers, as being subject to many foule extortions and oppressions. **1643** in *Rep. Hist. MSS. Comm.* Var. Coll. IV. 286 Nere any howses or other materialls which are subiect to take fyer. **1666–7** Pepys *Diary* 20 Feb., How mean a thing a king is, how subject to fall. **1683** Moxon *Mech. Exerc., Printing* xxiv. ¶11 The Inck would be subject to run off. **1721** Bradley *Philos. Acc. Wks. Nat.* 95 The smaller Kinds of Animals, and such as are subject to be destroyed, encrease more plentifully. **1759** R. Brown *Comp. Farmer* 52 Some young sows..are subject to eat their pigs. **1793** Smeaton *Edystone L.* §170 Any thing being in the way..would be subject to hitch upon the stone.

†**8.** That may be brought under the operation of a faculty or sense. *Obs.*

1591 Harington *Orl. Fur.* Pref., The holy scriptures..are..not subiect to euerie weake capacitie. **1610** Shaks. *Temp.* I. ii. 301 Be subiect to no sight but thine, and mine. **1611** Tourneur *Ath. Trag.* III. i, I feele a substance warme, Subiect to the Capacitie of sense. **1620** T. Granger *Div. Logike* 41 The formes of artificiall things are subiect to our sence. **1667** Davenant & Dryden *Tempest* V. iii. (1674) 80 They are Spirits, with which the Air abounds..but that they are not subject To poor feeble mortal Eyes. **1668** Culpepper & Cole *Barthol. Anat.* I. xxii. 55 Scrotum or Scortum, hanging out like a purse or bag, and subject to the touch.

9. Dependent upon a certain correcting or modifying condition; conditional upon; resting upon the assumption of. Freq. *advb.*, conditionally upon, with the assumption of.

1832 Ht. Martineau *Ireland* v. 77 She wrote to her husband's dictation, subject to the suggestions of his companions. **1844** Disraeli *Coningsby* IX. vii, Subject to an ample annuity to Villebecque, she bequeathed the whole of her fortune to the husband of Edith. **1883** *Law Times* 10 Nov. 21/2 All other business should be transacted by single judges subject to appeal. **1890** *Law Times' Rep.* LXIII. 734/1 His power to institute criminal proceedings is subject to the conditions imposed by sect. 2 of that Act.

III. 10. Lying in the neighbourhood below a certain level, as that of a spectator; subjacent. *Obs.* or *arch.*

1432–50 tr. *Higden* (Rolls) I. 143 The region Hircany hathe on the este parte to hit the see of Caspy,..on the weste Hiberia, beenge subiecte to Caucasus. **1585** T. Washington tr. *Nicholay's Voy.* I. xvi. 17 This Bourg..is enuironed with great hilles, vnto which of all sides it is subiect. **1590** Spenser *F.Q.* I. xi. 19 Long he them bore aboue the subiect plaine. *Ibid.* III. vii. 4 A little valley, subiect to the same. **1695** Blackmore *Pr. Arth.* VI. 14 They ..all around the Subject Ocean view'd. **1795** Southey *Joan of Arc* v. (1853) 52 As o'er the subject landskip round I gazed. **1815** 'Agrestis' *Feudal Hall* xxii, The Baron's iron reign O'erawed, for leagues, the subject plain.

†**b.** Lying immediately below, underlying. *Obs.*

1578 Banister *Hist. Man* IV. 56 The viij Muscles of Abdomen..are propugnacles, and defences to the subiect partes. **1667** *Phil. Trans.* II. 497, I suppose, several subject Earths, Currents and Winds do vary it [phosphorescence of the sea].

†**c.** Laid open so as to be evident. *Obs. rare.*

1556 R. Robinson tr. *More's Utopia* S iv, So finely set furth..and so euidently subiect to the eye.

†**11.** Forming the substratum or substance. Chiefly in ***matter subject*** = subject-matter. *Obs.*

c **1374** [see matter *sb.*[1] 6]. **1586** T. B. *La Primaud. Fr. Acad.* I. 162 Aristotle saith, that nature in one respect is said to be the first and chiefe matter subiect of every thing that hath being. *Ibid.* 441 Looke out some matter subiect, apt, and fit to recreate our spirits withall. *Ibid.* 28 [see matter *sb.*[1] 9]. **1600** J. Pory tr. *Leo's Africa* II. 70 Hauing made sufficient digression, let us resume the matter subiect where we left. **1609** [see matter *sb.*[1] 6]. **1744** H. Brooke *Love & Vanity* 156 And let her form be what you will, I am the subject essence still.

subject (səbˈdʒɛkt), *v.* Forms: 4 suget(t)e, soget(t)e, sochete; 4–7 subiect(e, 6 *Sc.* subgek, *pa. t.* and *pple.* subie(c)kit, 6– subject. [ad. OF. *subjecter, -gecter, -getter*, or L. *subjectāre*, frequent. f. *sub(j)icĕre, subject-* (see prec.); cf. It. *soggettare, suggettare*, Sp. *sujetar, subjetar*, Pg. *sujeitar*. Some of the early Eng. forms are assimilated to the *a*-forms of the sb. and adj.]

1. *trans.* To make (persons, a nation or country) subject *to* a conquering or sovereign power; to bring into subjection *to* a superior; to subjugate. Also *refl.* *Obs.* or *arch.*

1382 Wyclif *2 Chron.* xxviii. 10 (MS. Douce 370) The sonis of Juda and of Jerusalem 3ee wiln subiecten to 3ou seruauntis and hond wymmen. **1387** Trevisa *Higden* (Rolls) VII. 169 þe forseide Harolde, kyng of Norway..subiectid unto hym Denmark. *c* **1460** in *Maitl. Club Misc.* III. (1855) 38 Efter that the Romanis subjectit the Britones. **1530** Palsgr. 742/1 They be nowe subjected to the emperour. **1565** *Reg. Privy Council Scot.* I. 362 Doand that in thame lyis to subject the haill stait of the commoun weill. **1601** R. Johnson *Kingd. & Commw.* (1603) 162 Some of them haue subiected themselues to this crowne. **1651** Hobbes *Leviathan* II. xix. 95 Men..consequently may subject themselves, if they think good, to a Monarch. **1667** Milton *P.L.* XII. 93 God in Judgement just Subjects him from without to violent Lords. **1734** tr. *Rollin's Anc. Hist.* (1827) I. Pref. 1 The Medes and Persians who were themselves subjected by the Macedonians.

b. *to* the rule, government, power, or service of a superior.

1552 Abp. Hamilton *Catech.* (1884) 3 All subjeckit to the service of ane lord. **1556** Lauder *Tractate of Kyngis* 362 How thay suld Instruct thare floke That ar subiectit to thare 3oke. *a* **1661** Fuller *Worthies, Derbyshire* (1662) I. 233 A meek..man, much beloved of such who were subjected to his jurisdiction. **1693** Dryden *Last Parting of Hector & Androm.* 125, I see thee, in that fatal Hour, Subjected to the Victor's cruel Pow'r. *a* **1700** Evelyn *Diary* Sept. 1646, Should the Swisse..be subjected to the rule of France or Spaine. **1835** Thirlwall *Greece* vii. I. 272 Phalces subjected Sicyon to the Dorian sway. **1839** Keightley *Hist. Eng.* II. 42 Subjecting them to an unheard of tyranny. **1853** Newman *Hist. Sk.* (1876) I. I. ii. 71 The service to which they were subjected was no matter of choice.

2. To render submissive or dependent; to bring into a state of subordination or submission.

1382 Wyclif *Ecclus.* iv. 31 (MS. Douce 369) Ne sochete thou thee to eche man for synne. *c* **1400** *Apol. Loll.* 75 Þe condicoun of Jewis..þat is sogetid not to mannis tradicoun, but to Goddis ordinaunce. *Ibid.* 109 Tul he soget him to þe biddingis of þe apostil. **1500–20** Dunbar *Poems* lxx. 20 Thy vengeance seiss on us to syn subjectit. **1568** Lauder *Godlie Tractate* 341 Least tha alwayis with Sin suld be subieckit. *a* **1590** in *Montgomery's Poems* Suppl. (S.T.S.) 199 Þai sleichtis sell neuir subgek me. **1605** *Play of Stucley* in Simpson *Sch. Shaks.* (1878) I. 227, I will not subject my desire herein And wait upon his leisure. **1614** Raleigh *Hist. World* II. 217 Altogether feminine, and subiected to ease and delicacie. **1643** Burroughes *Exp. 1st 3 ch. Hosea* ii. 39 If he subject that to his own base ends. **1654** Bramhall *Just Vind.* ii. 9 They have subjected Oecumenical Councels..to the Jurisdiction of the Papal Court. **1734** tr. *Rollin's Anc. Hist.* (1827) I. Pref. 51 In order the better to subject the minds of the people. **1744** Swift *Three Serm.* i. 10 This Doctrine of subjecting ourselves to one another. **1827** Scott *Surg. Dau.* i, He..was unwilling to subject himself to that which was exacted in polite society.

absol. **1667** Milton *P.L.* VIII. 607 Yet these subject not. **1692** Dryden *St. Euremont's Ess.* 342 [Religion] compells and doth not subject enough.

†**b.** To overawe, prevail upon. *Obs. rare.*

1605 *Play of Stucley* in Simpson *Sch. Shaks.* (1878) I. 214 To be threatened and subjected by him. **1670** Walton *Lives* I. 29 Sir Robert put on as suddain a resolution, to subject Mr. Donne to be his Companion in that Iourney.

†**c.** To master, overpower (one's desires). *Obs.*

1620 Venner *Via Recta* vii. 114 Such as respect their health, and can subiect their appetite. **1660** R. Coke *Justice Vind.* 15 Subjecting all their passions and affections.

†**3.** *intr.* To be or become subject, submit *to*. *Obs.*

c **1400** *Apol. Loll.* 76 New law techiþ þat no prest nor clerk ow to soget to no seculer lord. **1624** Bedell *Lett.* v. 90 Shee kils with the spirituall sword, those that subiect not to her. **1644** Hunton *Vind. Treat. Mon.* iv. 20 He is unresistible, and to be subjected to actively in lawfull things. **1720** Wodrow *Corr.* (1843) II. 477 His Majesty's government, which they most heartily pray for, and subject to in all things they possibly can.

†**4.** *trans.* To place *under* something or in a lower position; to make subjacent *to*. Chiefly *pass.* *Obs.*

1578 Banister *Hist. Man* v. 69 The rest of his way is subiected vnder Vena caua. **1594** R. Carew *Huarte's Exam. Wits* (1616) 116 Spaine is not so cold as the places subiected to the Pole. *a* **1676** Hale *Prim. Orig. Man.* II. vii. (1677) 190 The like Volcans..happen sometimes in the Land subjected to the Sea. **1807** J. Barlow *Columb.* I. 194 O'er the proud Pyrenees it looks sublime, Subjects the Alps, and levels Europe's clime.

†**b.** To place (the neck) under a yoke. Const. *to*. (Only in fig. context.) *Obs.*

c **1585** *Faire Em* I. 89 A number such as we subject Their gentle necks unto their stubborn yoke Of drudging labour. **1641** J. Jackson *True Evang. T.* II. 120 To subject their necks to the yoak of Christ.

†**c.** To lay before a person's eyes. Const. *to*. *Obs.*

1715–20 Pope *Ep. Addison* 33 In one short view subjected to our eye Gods, Emp'rors, Heroes, Sages, Beauties, lie. **1776** *Trial of Nundocomar* 106/2 It would be highly improper that their books should be..subjected to curious and impertinent eyes.

†**d.** To lay open, expose (physically). *Obs.*

1793 Smeaton *Edystone L.* §196 The work will always be dry, or subjected only to the rain.

5. To lay open or expose to the incidence, occurrence, or infliction of, render liable *to*, something. †Also *occas.* to render susceptible *to*, predispose *to*.

1549 *Compl. Scot.* xx. 171 Euerye thing is subieckit to the proces of the tyme. **1600** Shaks. *A.Y.L.* II. iii. 36, I rather will subiect me to the malice Of a diuerted blood, and bloudie brother. **1611** *Bible* Transl. Pref. ¶2 As oft as we do any thing of note or consequence, we subiect our selues to euery ones censure. *a* **1700** Evelyn *Diary* 12 Aug. 1641, It stands upon Contribution land, which subjects the environs to the Spanish incursions. **1701** Swift *Contests Nobles & Comm.* Wks. 1755 II. I. 42 One folly, infirmity, or vice, to which a single man is subjected. **1758** J. Dalrymple *Ess. Feudal Property* (ed. 2) 91 Clauses, subjecting the whole to forfeiture, in case the prohibition was infringed. **1770** Luckombe *Hist. Printing* 350 Having too much wooll in them..will subject them to soon hardening. **1792** Burke *Corr.* (1844) IV. 3 It would only subject the people to a renewal of the former outrages. **1830** D'Israeli *Chas. I*, III. 72 A mind thus deeply busied..was necessarily subjected to its peculiar infirmities. **1845** MacCulloch *Taxation* I. iv. (1852) 110 Is all that is upon the farm..subjected to taxation? **1861** M. Pattison *Ess.* (1889) I. 47 A blow or an abusive expression subjected the offender to a fine.

†**6.** *pass.* To be attributed *to*, inhere *in* a subject (subject *sb.* 6). *Obs.*

1606 B. Jonson *Masq., Hymenæi* Wks. (1616) 911 It is a noble and iust aduantage, that the things subiected to vnderstanding haue of those which are obiected to sense. **1649** Jer. Taylor *Gt. Exemp.* III. Disc. xiii. §13 When the relations are subjected in persons religious, and holy. **1659** Pearson *Creed* (1816) I. 293 That all the sufferings of our Mediator were subjected in his human nature. **1664** Jer. Taylor *Dissuas. Popery* II. Introd. B 2 b, I hope I. S. does not suppose it [*sc.* infallibility] subjected in every single Christian man or woman. **1690** Norris *Beatitudes* (1694) I. 92 For such and such Vertues as subjected in Man.

7. *Logic.* To make the subject of a proposition. (Cf. subjection 11.)

1628 T. Spencer *Logick* 129 How they be predicated, and how subiected. **1725** Watts *Logic* III. ii. §3 A fourth Figure wherein the middle Term is predicated in the major Proposition, and subjected in the minor.

8. To bring under the operation of an agent, agency, or process; to submit *to* certain treatment; to cause to undergo or experience something.

1794 R. J. Sulivan *View Nat.* I. 59 The polar parts being subjected to a colder medium, would be more compressed. **1801** *Encycl. Brit.* Suppl. II. 357/2 One knows not how to subject to the laws of our perceptions that which is absolutely independent of them. **1838** Thomson *Chem. Org. Bodies* 274 The alcohol is then to be separated by subjecting the matter to strong pressure in cloth. **1842** Loudon *Suburban Hort.* 94 This branch of garden management..has been subjected to scientific inquiry. **1855** Bain *Senses & Int.* III. ii. §8 (1864) 471 Subject the same persons to an extremely faint exhalation of the same substance. **1870** Max Müller *Sci. Relig.* (1873) 125 When people began to subject the principal historical religions to a critical analysis. **1907** J. H. Patterson *Man-Eaters of Tsavo* xix. 208 Just after this caravan had moved on we were subjected to some torrential rain-storms.

Hence **subˈjecting** *vbl. sb.* and *ppl. a.*

1760 Woolman *Jrnl.* vii. (1840) 83 The Spring of the Ministry was often low; and, through the subjecting Power of Truth, we were kept low with it. **1761** Hume *Hist. Eng.* I. ix. 185 The ambition of Henry had..been moved..to attempt the subjecting of Ireland. **1881** Fairbairn *Studies Life Christ* xvi. 302 The subject often suffers less than the subjecting people. **1912** *Engl. Rev.* Jan. 295 Science is a subjecting of the mind to things, Art is a subjecting of things to the mind.

†**subject**, *pa. pple.* *Obs.* [ad. L. *subject-us*, pa. pple. of *subicĕre* (see subject *a.*).] Subjected.

1526 *Pilgr. Perf.* (W. de W. 1531) 211 [He] hath subiect all thynges to hym, & put them vnder his fete. **1533** Gau *Richt Vay* 50 S. Paul vritis in the first chaiptur to the Ephesians, God hes subiect al thing onder his feit.

subjectable, -ible (səbˈdʒɛktəb(ə)l, -ɪb(ə)l), *a.* *rare.* [f. subject *v.* + -able, -ible. Cf. late L. *subjectibilis* (Vulgate).] That may be subjected *to*.

1802–12 Bentham *Ration. Judic. Evid.* (1827) III. 446 Under the assurance of his not being subjectable to eventual punishment. **1808** —— *Sc. Reform* 14 Not subjectible to counter-interrogation. **1831** *Jer. Taylor's Wks.* IV. 277 It was propounded to these fathers confessors as a thing not subjectable to their penitential judicature.

Hence **subjectaˈbility, -iˈbility.**

In recent Dicts.

†**subjectary.** *Obs. rare.* [f. subject + -ary[1].] One who is subject *to* another.

1485 *Digby Myst.* III. 752 He hathe made me clene and delectary, the wyche was to synne a subiectary.

†**subjectate**, *v.* *Obs. rare.* [f. subject *sb.* + -ate[3].] *pass.* To be inherent *in*.

1677 Gale *Crt. Gentiles* IV. 484 There is no moral evil, which is not founded and subjectated in some natural good.

subjectdom (ˈsʌbdʒɪktdəm). *rare.* [f. subject *sb.* + -dom.] The state or condition of being a subject.

1877 Rolleston in Greenwell *Brit. Barrows* 698 No clue to its nationality, except in the political sense of subjectdom, therefore is available.

subjected (səbˈdʒɛktɪd), *ppl. a.* [f. L. *subject-us* (see subject *a.*) or subject *v.* + -ed[1].]

1. Placed or set underneath; underlying, subjacent. *Obs.* or *arch.*

1597 A. M. tr. *Guillemeau's Fr. Chirurg.* 10/3 The foresayed subiacent or subiectede membrane. **1667** Milton *P.L.* XII. 640 The hastning Angel..Led them direct, and down the Cliff as fast To the subjected Plaine. **1673** Hale *Ess. Fluid Bodies* 5 The Gravitation or non-Gravitation of Fluids upon subjected Bodies. **1678** H. Vaughan *Thalia Rediv., Retirement* 225 Where he might view the boundless skie,..Subjected hills, trees, meads, and flowers. **1718** Prior *Solomon* I. 432 Where..Ascends my Soul? what sees She White and Great Amidst subjected Seas? **1820** Wiffen *Aonian Hours* (ed. 2) 8 The stockdove's plaintive wail Wins to the curious ear o'er the subjected vale.

†**b.** ***subjected matter*** = subject-matter. *Obs.*

1697 tr. *Burgersdicius' Logic* I. viii. 26 Creation is nothing else but the producing of something out of nothing; that is, out of no Subjected Matter.

2. Reduced to a state of subjection; under the dominion or authority of another. Hence, submissive, obedient.

a **1586** Sidney *Arcadia* I. xix. (1912) 123 With all subjected humblenes. **1595** Shaks. *John* I. i. 264 Needs must you lay your heart at his dispose, Subiected tribute to commanding loue. **1690** Locke *Hum. Und.* IV. xix. §6 He is certainly the most subjected, the most enslaved, who is so in his Understanding. **1719** De Foe *Crusoe* II. (Globe) 386 All the five were most willing,..subjected Creatures, rather like Slaves than Wives. **1763** J. Brown *Poetry & Mus.* 193 The Patrician Ladies, who lately had reveled amidst the Spoils of a subjected World. **1815** J. Cormack *Abol. Fem. Infanticide Guzerat* ii. 34 That a subsidiary and subjected tribe should have cherished such extravagant notions of their own superiority. **1876** Ruskin *Fors Clav.* VI. 88 To comply in all sweet and subjected ways with the wishes and habits of their parents. **1907** *Trans. Devon Assoc.* 48 The Welsh British had themselves absorbed a subjected race.

Hence **sub'jectedly** *adv.*, **sub'jectedness**.

1681 R. FLEMING *Fulfilling Script.* III. iii. (1726) 377 To dig in the town ditches, with a sweet subjectedness of spirit. **1839** *New Monthly Mag.* LV. 44 Licking his face, and subjectedly, as if in token of homage. **1885** MEREDITH *Diana* xxxviii, Notwithstanding her subjectedness to the nerves.

'subjectess. *nonce-word.* [f. SUBJECT *sb.* + -ESS[1].] A female subject.

1772 NUGENT *Hist. Fr. Gerund* I. 145 It being a plain case that men only ought to be called subjects, and women subjectesses.

'subjecthood. [-HOOD.]

1. [SUBJECT *sb.* I.] The state or condition of being a subject; = SUBJECTION 2.

1927 C. C. MARTINDALE *Christ is King* v. 93 The vast duty of our subjecthood almost narrows itself to this. **1968** *Economist* 17 Feb. 16/1 In the Kenya independence settlement devised by Mr Duncan Sandys in 1963,..they were offered the chance either to acquire Kenyan citizenship, or to have full rights of British subjecthood, including passports.

2. *Gram.* [SUBJECT *sb.* II.] The state of being a subject (of a sentence, etc.).

1976 *Classical Q.* XXVI. 38 The 'with' idiom expresses not the idea of means, but rather that of subjecthood or even agency. **1979** *Trans. Philol. Soc.* 223 The insertion of this reciprocal marker is shown to be sensitive to the transitive subjecthood, either actual or at some initial stage of derivation, of the affix it replaces.

subjectible: see SUBJECTABLE *a.*

subjectify (səb'dʒɛktɪfaɪ), *v.* [f. SUBJECT *sb.* + -IFY.] *trans.* To identify with or absorb in the subject; to make subjective.

1868 *Contemp. Rev.* VIII. 617 The oriental mind.. subjectifies the individuality, or, to frame a word for the occasion, *inwards* it. **1895** *Thinker* VII. 342 Destructive tendencies in human nature which subjectify themselves in the individual. **1900** SANTAYANA *Poetry & Relig.* 248 To subjectify the universe is not to improve it.

Hence **sub'jectifying** *ppl. a.*, viewing things subjectively; **subjectifi'cation**, the action of making or being made subjective.

1882 TRAILL *Sterne* xi. 170 The Uncle Toby of the subjectifying sentimentalist, surveying his character through the false medium of his own hypertrophied sensibilities. **1890** tr. *Pfleiderer's Devel. Theol.* II. iv. 186 The idealistic subjectification of the idea of God on the lines of Feuerbach. **1908** *Hibbert Jrnl.* Oct. 214 It would..be far more accurate to treat sensations as the subjectification of qualities than to treat qualities as the hypostases of sensations.

subjectile (səb'dʒɛktaɪl), *a.* and *sb. rare.* [f. SUBJECT *sb.* + -ILE.] Of material: Adapted to receive a 'subject' or picture. **b.** *sb.* A material on which a painting or engraving is made.

1859 GULLICK & TIMBS *Painting* 126 The metal..served as a subjectile to the opaque painting. *Ibid.*, The materials, or subjectiles, upon which paintings have been executed. **1881** *Oracles* 5 Nov. 294 The previous modes of printing in which the ink is contained in incisions..or upon reliefs.. and transferred thence to the paper or other subjectile material by pressure.

subjection (səb'dʒɛkʃən). Also 4–5 -iecciou*n*, -one, 4–6 -ieccion, 4–7 -iection, 5–6 -iectione, -geccion, -gection, -yon, 5–7 -iectioun, (4 subieccoun, 5 -ccyoun, -iounne, -iecctioun, -ione, -iectyon, supjection, 6 -ieccyon). [a. OF. *subjection* (12th c.), in mod.F. only in Rhet. sense, *sujétion* (17th c.) in other senses, ad. L. *subjectio, -ōnem*, n. of action f. *subicĕre* (see SUBJECT *a.*). Cf. Pr. *subjection*, It. *soggezione, suggezione*, and *subbiezione*, Sp. *sujecion*, in Rhet. sense *subjecion*, Pg. *sujeição, subjeição*.]

†**1.** The act, state, or fact of exercising lordship or control; dominion, domination, control. *Obs.*

c **1375** *Sc. Leg. Saints* vii. (*Jacobus*) 485 Dee þare þam leware wes ay, þane fore to thol subieccione of hyme þat segyt þan þar towne. *c* **1400** *Apol. Loll.* 59 þof þu desire to be prest, or be befor to hem þat þu coueitist..ouer proudly in coueiting subieccoun of hem. **1596** SPENSER *State Irel.* Wks. (Globe) 650/1 They should all rise generally into rebellion, and cast away the English subjection. **1667** MILTON *P.L.* x. 153 Lovely to attract Thy Love, not thy Subjection.

b. Phr. *in, into,* †*to,* †*unto,* †*under subjection*: in, into, under the dominion or control of a superior power.

Now felt as belonging to 2.

1340 HAMPOLE *Pr. Consc.* 4064 Swa þat it be put til destruccion Thurgh þam þat first was in subieccion. *c* **1386** CHAUCER *Monk's T.* 476 He..This wyde world hadde in subieccioun. **1390** GOWER *Conf.* I. 26 Of Babiloine al that Empire..[he] Put under in subjeccioun. *c* **1430** LYDG. *Min. Poems* (Percy Soc.) 90 Of Assurye to rekne the kynges alle, Whiche had that lond under subjeccioune. **1513** BRADSHAW *St. Werburge* I. 1544 Lowly submyttynge her vnder subieccyon. **1535** COVERDALE *Ps.* viii. 6 Thou hast put all things in subieccion vnder his fete. **1592** *Soliman & Pers.* III. i. 148 Till thou hast brought Rhodes in subiection. **1601** SHAKS. *All's Well* I. i. 6 To whom I am now in Ward, euermore in subiection. **1667** MILTON *P.L.* IX. 1128 Both in subjection now To sensual Appetite. *a* **1715** BURNET *Own Time* I. (1724) I. 46 They [*sc.* the military force] will ever keep the Parliament in subjection to them. **1758** J. DALRYMPLE *Ess. Feudal Property* (ed. 2) 3 The modern European colonies are kept in subjection..to their native country. **1853** NEWMAN *Hist. Sk.* (1876) I. I. ii. 91 The Caliph..was in subjection to a family of the old Persian race. **1862** SIR B. BRODIE *Psychol. Inq.* II. ii. 62 A well-regulated imagination, which is kept in subjection to the judgment.

c. with possessive pron. or phr. denoting the superior power or authority. *Obs.* or *arch.*

1340 HAMPOLE *Pr. Consc.* 4070 Fra þat tyme sal na land ne contre In subieccion of Rome langer be. **1390** GOWER *Conf.* III. 180 He..Which hath in his subjeccion Tho men whiche in possession Ben riche of gold. *c* **1400** MAUNDEV. (Roxb.) vi. 20 Oþer rewmes þat er vnder his subieccion. *c* **1407** LYDG. *Reson & Sens.* 5281 He kan make hem to lowte Vn-to his subieccion. *c* **1460** *Oseney Reg.* 110 This..graunt I made for A chaunterye..free and quietly fro the subieccion of the modur church. *c* **1489** CAXTON *Sonnes of Aymon* xix. 408 Whan he sawe that he was..in the subgectyon of Reynawde ..he was sore an angred. *c* **1500** *Melusine* 17 Al the Countre therabout he held vnder his subgection. **1530** PALSGR. 355 Whiche dyd submytte a great parte of Grece in their subjection. **1568** GRAFTON *Chron.* II. 885 To submit themselues to the subiection and grieuous yoke of the French king. **1584–5** *Act 27 Eliz.* c. 2. §4 Any Parson under her Majesties Subjection or Obedience. **1632** LITHGOW *Trav.* III. 78 [The Cretans] would rather..render to the Turke, then to liue vnder the subection of Venice. **1652** J. WRIGHT tr. *Camus' Nat. Paradox* I. 3 The Castellians are those who have Lands, Citties, Burroughs, Villages and Seignories under their subjection. **1800** *Asiatic Ann. Reg.* I *a.* 25/1 In reducing under his subjection the whole of the districts in which the best cinnamon is produced.

2. The act or fact of being subjected, as under a monarch or other sovereign or superior power; the state of being subject to, or under the dominion of, another; hence *gen.*, subordination.

1398 TREVISA *Barth. De P.R.* VI. xviii. (1495) 203 As the name seruaunt is a name of subieccion so the name lord is a name of soueraynte. *c* **1470** *Gol. & Gaw.* 441 Sauand my senyeoury fra subiectioun, And my lordscip vn-lamyt. **1563** WINȜET tr. *Vincent. Lirin.* Wks. (S.T.S.) II. 5 The subiectioun of the Israelitis amangis the Gentilis. **1596** SPENSER *State Irel.* Wks. (Globe) 612/2 That generall subjection of the land, wherof we formerly spake. **1611** SPEED *Theat. Gt. Brit.* I. xii. 23/2 [Bristol] because it is an entire County of it selfe, it denies subiection vnto either [Somersetshire and Glocestershire]. **1620** T. GRANGER *Div. Logike* 248 In regard of their conuenience, and subiection to the whole, they make no disiunction or opposition. **1641** 'SMECTYMNUUS' *Vind. Answ.* vii. 98 Now we read no where of the subjection of one Bishop and his charge to an other. **1651** HOBBES *Leviathan* I. viii. 39 Our obedience, and subjection to God Almighty. **1662** SOUTH *Serm.* Gen. i. 27 (1697) I. 67 The Will..was subordinate..to the Understanding..as a Queen to her King; who both acknowledges a Subjection, and yet retains a Majesty. **1814** WORDSW. *Excurs.* III. 268 By philosophic discipline prepared For calm subjection to acknowledged law. **1869** J. S. MILL (*title*) The subjection of women. **1872** YEATS *Growth Comm.* 58 The patriotic spirit..lost its force in a common subjection to Rome.

†**3.** Submission; obedience; homage. *Obs.*

1382 WYCLIF *1 Tim.* ii. 11 A womman lerne in silence, with al subiecciou*n*. **1387** TREVISA *Higden* (Rolls) II. 115 þe bisshop of Meneuia was i-sacred of þe bisshoppes of Wales ..and made non professioun noþer subiection to non oþer chirche. **1387–8** T. USK *Test. Love* I. ii. (Skeat) l. 10 A maner of ferdnesse crepeth in his herte, not for harme, but of goodly subjeccion. **1419** in Ellis *Orig. Lett.* Ser. II. I. 65 We ȝoure humble liges and servitours, with all subjection and humilitee. **1426** LYDG. *De Guil. Pilgr.* 1031 The body to the soule obeye In euery maner skylful weye, And bern to hym subieccion. **1460** CAPGRAVE *Chron.* (Rolls) Ded. 1 To my Sovereyn Lord Edward..a pore Frere..sendith prayer, obediens, subjeccion. **1526** *Pilgr. Perf.* (W. de W. 1531) 96 b, Good religyon and subieccyon sore reproueth contempte for his suggestyon. **1671** MILTON *Samson* 1405 Masters commands come with a power resistless To such as owe them absolute subjection. *a* **1674** CLARENDON *Surv. Leviathan* (1676) 91 To withdraw their subjection.

4. The action of making subject or bringing under a dominion or control; subjugation. *rare.*

1597 HOOKER *Eccl. Pol.* v. xlix. 104 The subiection of the body to the will is by naturall necessitie, the subiection of the will vnto God voluntarie. *a* **1676** HALE (J.), After the conquest of the kingdom and subjection of the rebels. **1849–50** ALISON *Hist. Eur.* VII. xlii. §43. 125 The conquest of Europe, or at least the subjection of all its governments to his control.

†**5.** The condition of a subject, and the obligations pertaining to it. *Obs.*

1599 SHAKS. *Hen. V*, IV. i. 153 The King..who to disobey, were against all proportion of subiection. **1611** —— *Cymb.* IV. iii. 19, I dare be bound hee's true, and shall performe All parts of his subiection loyally. *a* **1635** NAUNTON *Fragm. Reg.* in *Phœnix* (1707) I. 191 The Duke of Northumberland.. rose as high as subjection could permit, or sovereignty endure.

†**b.** *concr.* Subjects collectively. *Obs.*

1502 *Ord. Crysten Men* (W. de W.) v. iii. LL ij, The subgeccyon ayenst theyr prelates, the chyldren agayne the fader and moder. **1646** SIR T. BROWNE *Pseud. Ep.* 302 How populous the land from whence they came was, may be collected..from their ability in commanding so mighty subjections.

6. Legal or contractual obligation or liability.

c **1450** *Godstow Reg.* 342 With-out any subieccion as any of that same hold ought, sauf only the forsaide xij. d vnto the workes of the forsaid chirch yerely. **1456** SIR G. HAYE *Law Arms* (S.T.S.) 192 [If] a man suld..defend his frende in his presence injurit, sa is he nocht bounde to na subjectioun of law tharfore. **1760** T. HUTCHINSON *Hist. Mass.* ii. (1765) 251 They distinguished civil subjection, into necessary and voluntary. **1769** BLACKSTONE *Comm.* IV. ii. 28 The obligation of civil subjection, whereby the inferior is constrained by the superior to act contrary to what his own reason and inclination would suggest. **1843–56** BOUVIER *Law Dict.* (ed. 6) II. 553/2 *Subjection*, the obligation of.. persons to act at the discretion, or according to the judgment and will of others.

†**7.** The condition of being under some necessity or obligation; a duty or task; an 'infliction'. *Obs.*

1581 PETTIE *Guazzo's Civ. Conv.* I. (1586) 3, I feele it a great trauell..to obserue such circumstances, as the qualitie of the persons, and mine owne honor require: which is nothing else but paine and subjection. **1658** EVELYN *Fr. Gard.* (1675) 261 'Tis too great a subjection to gather their blossoms. **1659** —— *Let. to Boyle* 9 Aug., The many subjections, which I cannot support, of conversing with mechanical capricious persons. **1685** —— *Mrs. Godolphin* (1888) 183, I tell you she looked at it [*sc.* being obliged to play at cards] as a Calamity and subjection insupportable. **1719** LONDON & WISE *Complete Gard'ner* 313 The only Subjection we are obliged to in such Grounds, is, first, to weed much.

†**8.** The condition of being subject, exposed, or liable *to*; liability. *Obs.*

1593 MUNDY *Def. Contraries* 39 They are free from subiection to eie medicines, which they haue need to practise, that are subiect to the eyes inflamation. **1628** T. SPENCER *Logick* 128 His subiection to death; as a qualitie of his being. **1758** J. DALRYMPLE *Ess. Feudal Property* (ed. 2) 154 In respect of subjection to forfeiture.

†**9.** *Rhet.* An answer subjoined by a speaker to a question that he has just asked; the figure involving this; hence, a subjoined or additional statement, corollary. *Obs.*

1608 J. KING *Serm.* 5 Nov. 13 For what hath the righteous done? The subiection or answere implied must needs be, nihil, iust nothing. **1652** URQUHART *Jewel* 278 The refutative Schemes of Anticipation and Subjection. **1659** LEAK *Waterwks.* Pref. 3 If we should build upon this Rule of Archimedes, That the Superficies of the Water is Spherical ..there will follow a Subjection that we must hold in the Demonstrations; viz. That the Superficies of the Water is Circular. **1753** *Chambers' Cycl.* Suppl., *Subjection*..is used for a brief answer to a preceding interrogation.

†**10.** A putting under or placing before. *rare.*

1615 T. ADAMS *Leaven* 100 The most simple; who better vnderstand a spirituall doctrine, by the reall subiection of some thing familiar to their senses.

11. *Logic.* The act of supplying a subject to a predicate.

In mod. Dicts.

¶**12.** Misused for SUGGESTION. (Cf. SUBJESTION.)

c **1386** CHAUCER *Pars. T.* ⁋351 The firste thing is..thilke flesshly concupiscence, and after that comth the subieccion [*v. rr.* suggestion(e] of the deuel. *a* **1450** *Knt. de la Tour* (1868) 77 The kinge, thorughe her false subieccion, putte Ioseph into stronge prison.

subjectional (səb'dʒɛkʃənəl), *a. rare.* [f. prec. + -AL[1].] Involving or based upon subjection.

a **1617** BAYNE *Diocesan's Tryall* (1621) 18 By vertue of their subjectionall subordination. **1846** RUSKIN *Mod. Paint.* II. III. I. vi. §3 There is the Unity of different and separate things, subjected to one and the same influence, which may be called Subjectional Unity.

'subjectist. *rare.* 'One versed or skilled in the subjective philosophy', = SUBJECTIVIST.

a **1860** *Eclectic Rev.* (cited in Worcester).

subjective (səb'dʒɛktɪv), *a.* (*sb.*) [ad. late L. *subjectīvus*, f. *subjectus, -um* SUBJECT *sb.* So F. *subjectif*, It. *sobiettivo*, etc., G. *subjektiv*.]

†**1.** Pertaining or relating to one who is subject; belonging to or characteristic of a political subject; hence, submissive, obedient. *Obs.*

c **1450** tr. *De Imitatione* I. xiv. 16 If þou leene more to þin ovne reson þan to þe subiectiue vertu of Ihesu crist, it wol be late or þou be a man illuminate, for god wol haue us parfitly suget to him. **1595** in *Shaks. Cent. Praise* 16 For thousands vowes to them subjective dutie. **1606** J. DAVIES *Sel. Sec. Husb.* (1616) F 6 Who honor'd him..And no subiectiue dutie did forget. **1648** SYMMONS *Vind.* 336 Neither is the King,..of so subjective a nature as to submit his affairs wholly to his wife's guidance. *a* **1683** OWEN *Posth. Serm.* Wks. 1851 IX. 97 Subjective perfection, in respect of the person, obeying, in his sincerity and freedom from guile. **1706** DE FOE *Jure Divino* XI. 246 The great Subjective Article concurs, To make him all Mens King as well as ours.

2. Pertaining to the subject as to that in which attributes inhere; inherent; hence, pertaining to the essence or reality of a thing; real, essential.

1642 O. SEDGWICK *Eng. Preserv.* 34 Many prayings, and fastings,..and other doings have found no acceptation with God, nor wrought any subjective alterations in persons. **1647** JER. TAYLOR *Lib. Proph.* 133 That this confession [of St. Peter] was the objective foundation of Faith, and Christ and his Apostles the subjective, Christ principally, and S. Peter instrumentally. **1675** BURTHOGGE *Causa Dei* 395 All how Barbarous..soever, have..a Light within them, and a Light without them, Subjective and Objective Light. **1844** GLADSTONE *Glean.* (1879) V. 81 Nothing seems more plain than that her [the Church of England's] subjective materials are after all too solid..to permit..the serious apprehension of any such contingency. **1882** FARRAR *Early Chr.* I. 320 An illustration of the method whereby the subjective righteousness of God can become the objective righteousness (or justification) of man.

3. a. Relating to the thinking subject, proceeding from or taking place within the subject; having its source in the mind; (in the widest sense) belonging to the conscious life. (Correlative to OBJECTIVE *a.* 2 b.)

1707 OLDFIELD *Ess. Impr. Reason* II. xix, Objective certainty, or that of the thing, as really it is in itself..a Subjective certainty of it in the infinite Mind. **1725** WATTS

Logic II. ii. §8 Objective certainty, is when the proposition is certainly true in itself; and subjective, when we are certain of the truth of it. The one is in things, the other is in our minds. **1796** *Nitsch's View Kant's Princ.* 224 We are certain that every point in the circumference of a circle is at an equal distance from the centre; for we have sufficient objective and subjective reasons to this truth. **1798** W. TAYLOR in *Monthly Rev.* XXV. 585 Were we endeavouring to characterize this work, in the dialect peculiar to Professor Kant, we should observe, that its intensive like its extensive, magnitude is small:..its subjective is as slight as its objective worth. **1801** *Encycl. Brit.* Suppl. II. 356/1 The motives to consider a proposition as true, are either objective, i.e. taken from an external object,..or.. subjective, i.e. they exist only in the mind of him who judges. **1804–6** SYD. SMITH *Mor. Philos.* (1850) 54 His subjective elements, and his pure cognition. **1830** *Blackw. Mag.* XXVII. 10 Knowledge subjective is knowledge of objects in their relation to, and as they affect the mind knowing. **1832** AUSTIN *Jurispr.* (1879) II. 737 In the Kantian language subjective existences are either parcel of the understanding, or ideas which the understanding knows by itself alone. **1838** F. HAYWOOD tr. *Kant's Crit. Pure Reason* 651 Without a subjective property, nothing would be present to the being who perceives by intuition. **1864** BOWEN *Logic* xiii. 423 It appears to disprove..Kant's counter assertion that space is wholly subjective. **1877** E. CAIRD *Philos. Kant* II. iii. 241 Subjective ideas, ideas that have no root in actual experience, but only in the constitution of the faculties of perception. **1882** *Encycl. Brit.* XIV. 785/1 What is the ground of unity in things known, and in what way does thought unite the detached attributes of things into a subjective whole? **1883** *Ibid.* XVI. 91/2 The idea of truth or knowledge as that which is at once objective and subjective, as the unity of things with the mind that knows them.

b. Special collocations.

subjective idealism: see IDEALISM 1. ***subjective method***: the method of investigation which starts from conceptions and *a priori* assumptions, from which deductions are made. ***subjective selection***: the function of selection by or through consciousness.

1867 LEWES *Hist. Philos.* (ed. 3) I. Proleg. p. xxxiii, The Subjective Method which moulds realities on its conceptions, endeavouring to discern the order of Things, not by step by step adjustments of the order of ideas to it, but by the anticipatory rush of Thought, the direction of which is determined by Thoughts and not controlled by Objects. **1877, 1887** [see IDEALISM 1]. **1886** *Encycl. Brit.* XX. 73/2 Subjective selection, i.e...the association of particular movements with particular sensations through the mediation of feeling. **1911** *Encycl. Brit.* (ed. 11) XIV. 281/1 The doctrine which represents the subject itself and its state and judgments as the single immediate datum of consciousness, and all else..as having a merely problematic existence..is sometimes known as subjective or incomplete idealism.

4. a. Pertaining or peculiar to an individual subject or his mental operations; depending upon one's individuality or idiosyncrasy; personal, individual.

a **1767** T. BOSTON *Serm.* (1850) 77 There is an internal subjective discovery of Christ made in, and unto the soul, that finds him by the Holy Ghost. **1796** *Nitsch's View Kant's Princ.* 195 When any thing determines our will which is founded upon the subjective qualification of the individual, it is merely agreeable, though it may not be bad. **1818** HALLAM *Mid. Ages* (1872) I. 112 Sismondi never fully learned to judge men according to a subjective standard, that is, their own notions of right and wrong. **1858** O. W. HOLMES *Aut. Breakf.-t.* xi, The ingenuous reader will understand that this was an internal, personal, private, subjective diorama. *a* **1871** GROTE *Eth. Fragm.* ii. (1876) 42 This sentiment is..a subjective sentiment—that is, each individual experiences it in a degree and manner peculiar to himself.

b. *Art* and *Literature*. Expressing, bringing into prominence, or deriving its materials mainly from, the individuality of the artist or author.

1840 E. FITZGERALD *Lett.* (1889) I. 56 Enough of what is now generally called the subjective style of writing. **1846** *Ibid.* 161 The whole subjective scheme (damn the word!) of the poems I did not like. **1853** THOMSON *Laws Th.* (ed. 3) 25 *note*, A subjective tendency in a poet or thinker would be a preponderating inclination to represent the moods and states of his own mind. **1867** BRANDE & COX *Dict. Sci.* s.v., Rubens and Rembrandt were subjective painters. **1871** B. TAYLOR *Faust* (1875) I. 238 The subjective character of the early scenes in Faust is clearly indicated.

c. Tending to lay stress on one's own feelings or opinions; given to brooding over one's mental states; excessively introspective or reflective.

1842 KINGSLEY *Lett.* (1878) I. 88 Some minds are too subjective..they may devote themselves too much to the subject of self and mankind. **1856** R. A. VAUGHAN *Mystics* (1860) I. 207 A comparatively small measure of the subjective excess which we would call mysticism. **1871** MORLEY *Vauvenargues* in *Crit. Misc.* Ser. I. (1878) 25 A musing, subjective method of delineation.

d. Existing in the mind only, without anything real to correspond to it; illusory, fanciful.

1853 J. S. LE FANU in *Dublin Univ. Mag.* Dec. 723/1 Was this singular apparition..the invention of my poor stomach? Was it, in short, *subjective* (to borrow the technical slang of the day) and not the palpable aggression and intrusion of an external agent? **1869** HADDAN *Apost. Succ. Ch. Eng.* v. 107 A myth,..all in a moment received as a real history in the actual world, while in truth it had been a merely subjective fancy. **1870** MOZLEY *Univ. Serm.* iii. (1877) 69 This philosophy allows us..to take pleasure in a subjective immortality—which is practically posthumous reputation.

e. *Physiol.* and *Path.* Due to internal causes and discoverable by oneself alone: said of sensations, symptoms, etc.

subjective colours: the complementary colours of after-images arising from looking fixedly at coloured objects.

1855 DUNGLISON *Med. Lex.* s.v. *Sensation*, Subjective sensations, such as originate centrically, or in the encephalon,—as tinnitus aurium. **1860** TYNDALL *Glac.* 37 This green belonged to the class of subjective colours, or colours produced by contrast... The eye received the impression of green, but the colour was not external to the eye. **1876** *Trans. Clinical Soc.* IX. 97 The boomings in the ear and the subjective buzz. **1881** *Nature* No. 616. 359 All the combinational tones other than those of mistuned unisons must really arise in the ear itself and be subjective in character. **1899** *Allbutt's Syst. Med.* VI. 123 The subjective feelings of the patient must not be overlooked.

†**5.** ***subjective part*** (scholastic L. *pars subjectiva*): a part of which the corresponding whole is predicated. *Obs.*

1728 CHAMBERS *Cycl.* s.v. *Part*, A Subjective or Potential Part, is the same with a Logical one, viz. that contain'd in some universal Whole, not in Act, but only in Power; as Man and Horse are in Animal; Peter and Paul in Man.

6. *Gram.* **a.** Constituting, or having the function of, the subject of a sentence.

1862 E. ADAMS *Elem. Eng. Lang.* §456 When a subjective sentence is placed after the verb.

b. Having the character of the subject of a sentence as expressing the doer of an action; e.g. ***subjective genitive***.

1864 J. MANNING *Inq. Poss. Augment* 15 Subjective or active form (nominative). *Ibid.* 63 The confounding of subjective with objective genitives. **1873** [see PREPOSITIVELY]. **1880** E. A. ABBOTT *Via Latina* 221 Genitives may be divided into large classes, those in which the Gen. can be readily replaced (i.) by a Subject; (ii.) by an Object. The former are called Subjective; the latter, Objective.

7. Of the subjects treated, subject-. *rare.*

1881 *Times* 6 Jan. 11/1 The first addition to the evidence is a subjective index.

8. *absol.* with *the*: That which is subjective; rarely *sb.* a subjective fact or thing.

1817 COLERIDGE *Biog. Lit.* xii. (1907) I. 174 During the act of knowledge itself, the objective and subjective are so instantly united, that we cannot determine to which of the two the priority belongs. **1830** —— in *Lit. Rem.* (1838) III. 1 The Ipseity..; the relatively subjective, whose attribute is, the Holy One. **1853** SIR W. HAMILTON *Discuss.* 5 *note*, Psychology is nothing more than a determination of the Subjective and the Objective, in themselves. **1884** *Chr. Comm.* 20 Mar. 536/2 The real sweets of life..belong to the internals and subjectives of existence. **1894** CALDERWOOD *Vocab. Philos.* 321 In the wider sense, 'the subjective' includes the whole of the self-conscious life. **1897** tr. *Fichte's Sci. Ethics* 88 In cognition, an objective (the thing) is changed into a subjective, a representation.

subjectively (səb'dʒɛktɪvlɪ), *adv.* [f. prec. + -LY[2].]

†**1.** In subjection; as a subject or subjects; submissively. *Obs. rare.*

1579 W. WILKINSON *Confut. Fam. Love* 38 He willeth them to stand subiectiuely obedient to the Loue. **1678** R. BARCLAY *Apol. Quakers* ii. §11. 48 The Spirit doth now lead and influence the Saints, but..only subjectively, or in a blind manner.

†**2.** In a subject, as in that in which attributes inhere; with regard to the subject of inhesion; inherently. *Obs.*

1615 CROOKE *Body of Man* 695 Hence doth arise another especial difference betwixt a Sound and the obiects of other Senses, for these doe inhere in the sensible things actually and subiectiuely, both before, in, and after Sensation. **1626** YATES *Ibis ad Cæsarem* I. 26 Damnation is neither from God originally, nor in God subjectively. **1656** JEANES *Fuln. Christ* 195 The fulnesse in the text [Col. I. 19] regarded him subjectively, and intrinsecally, as *adjunctum receptum*, dwelling, and inhering in him. **1697** NORRIS *Acc. Reason & Faith* i. (1724) 21 Come we now to the Consideration of Reason as 'tis taken Subjectively. **1698** NORRIS *Pract. Disc.* (1722) IV. 167 By the Love of God we should..apprehend either that Love whereby a Man Loves God, taking the Term (God) Objectively, or that Love whereby he is beloved of him, taking the same Term Subjectively.

†**3.** In its (specific) nature; in itself. *Obs.*

1621 MOUNTAGU *Diatribæ* 302 First-fruits and Tithes were of the same extent subiectiuely; or if there were excesse vpon eyther side, it was in First-fruits. *a* **1641** —— *Acts & Mon.* (1642) 86 All the Propheticall blessings by Iacob.. concerning his sons, are not all of one nature..either subjectively for the matter, or objectively for the Persons and their Posterity. **1675** BURTHOGGE *Causa Dei* 42 Though Infernal Punishments be all of them Perpetual, and consequently Infinite protensively and in duration, yet that Intrinsically and Subjectively they are but Finite. **1697** BOLD *Reply to Mr. Edwards's Refl.* 45 That the Enquiry.. was not concerning Christian Faith considered subjectively, but objectively.

4. In relation to the thinking subject; by a subjective process; with reference to the mind or to mental representation; in the mind, in thought.

1796 *Nitsch's View Kant's Princ.* 222 To be of opinion, means, to take something for true, but from reasons that are neither subjectively nor objectively sufficient. **1803** *Edin. Rev.* I. 262 Man is known to himself by consciousness. All other beings he knows only subjectively. **1825** COLERIDGE *Aids Refl.* (1848) I. 138 An idea conceived as subsisting in an object becomes a law: and a law contemplated subjectively in a mind is an idea. **1855** [MISS COBBE] *Ess. Intuitive Mor.* 85 When our idea of the Divine Holiness is subjectively true—that is to say, when it is the very highest which our minds ..can apprehend. **1865** J. H. STIRLING *Secret of Hegel* I. 127 Kant conceived these relations [categories] subjectively, or from the point of view of our thought. **1880** E. WHITE *Cert. Relig.* Pref. 8, I have readily fallen into the popular usage [of Certainty and Certitude], which regards them as interchangeable expressions to denote subjectively the state of mind only.

5. With reference to the individual mind or the personal character, mental attitude, feelings, etc.; in *Art*, etc., in such a manner as to express the personality or idiosyncrasies of an artist or writer.

1841 TRENCH *Parables* ix. (1877) 186 The penny is very different to the different receivers; objectively the same, subjectively it is very different; it is in fact to every one exactly what he will make it. **1859** GULLICK & TIMBS *Painting* 41 A work of Art may be said to be subjectively treated when it is characterized more by the peculiar æsthetic or idiosyncratic development of the artist himself.

6. *Gram.* In the subjective relation; as a subjective genitive.

1864 J. MANNING *Inq. Poss. Augment* 20 The genitive of the Anglo-Saxon personal pronoun..may be used.. subjectively and objectively.

subjectiveness (səb'dʒɛktɪvnɪs). [Formed as prec. + -NESS.] The quality or condition of being subjective, subjectivity.

1855 HYDE CLARKE *Dict.*, *Subjectiveness.* **1880** LE CONTE *Light* 13 In smell, there is an equal commingling of subjectiveness and objectiveness.

subjectivism (səb'dʒɛktɪvɪz(ə)m). [f. SUBJECTIVE + -ISM. Cf. F. *subjectivisme.*]

1. The philosophical theory according to which all our knowledge is merely subjective and relative, and which denies the possibility of objective knowledge.

1857 W. FLEMING *Vocab. Philos.* 492 *Subjectivism* is the doctrine of Kant, that all human knowledge is merely relative; or rather that we cannot prove it to be absolute. **1872** tr. *Ueberweg's Hist. Philos.* I. 72 Protagoras the Individualist, Gorgias the Nihilist, Hippias the Polymathist, and Prodicus the Moralist..were followed by a younger generation of Sophists, who perverted the philosophical principle of subjectivism more and more, till it ended in mere frivolity. **1884** D. HUNTER *Reuss's Hist. Canon* xviii. 388 The eighteenth century..which gave birth to a subjectivism so boundless as to end in denying the reality of the world.

2. The subjective method (see SUBJECTIVE 3 b).

1882 T. DAVIDSON tr. *Rosmini's Phil. Syst.* p. xxvi, The subjectivism of Descartes and Malebranche.

3. A theory or method based exclusively on subjective facts.

1865 GROTE *Plato* II. 361 He cannot be content..to be a measure for himself and for those whom his arguments may satisfy. This would be to proclaim what some German critics denounce as Subjectivism. **1899** S. L. WILSON *Theol. Mod. Lit.* 420 In this strongly marked tendency to psychic analysis and searching subjectivism, Meredith is the true child of his time. **1900** *Pilot* 23 June 515/1 This would.. eliminate the danger of subjectivism, and secure that the points emphasized should not be merely personal or of local ..importance. **1905** J. ORR *Probl. Old Test.* v. (1906) 119 These methods seem to us eaten through with an arbitrary subjectivism which vitiates their application at every point.

b. An ethical theory which conceives the aim of morality to be based upon, or to consist in, the attainment of states of feeling.

1897 tr. *Külpe's Introd. Philos.* 111 The aim of morality is for subjectivism the production of a subjective state, that of pleasure or happiness (hedonism and eudæmonism). **1909** *Edin. Rev.* Oct. 350 So far from weakening religious beliefs of an enlightened kind, ethical subjectivism in no way affects the question of their veracity.

subjectivist (səb'dʒɛktɪvɪst). [f. prec.: see -IST.] One who believes in or advocates subjectivism. Also *attrib.* = SUBJECTIVISTIC.

1874 tr. *Ueberweg's Hist. Philos.* II. 65 This interpretation, which would make of Spinoza a Subjectivist. **1885** F. E. ABBOT *Sci. Theism* Introd. ii. 43 The subjectivist definition of knowledge. *Ibid.* 44 The utter indifference of subjectivists to their own innumerable self-contradictions. **1911** *Encycl. Brit.* VI. 850/2 The subjectivist principle that forms the starting-point of Berkley.

Hence **subjecti'vistic** *a.*

1884 W. JAMES in *Unitarian Rev.* Sept. 210, I will..speak rather of *subjectivism*, and the *subjectivistic* point of view. **1886** EDERSHEIM *Life Jesus* I. 208 *note*, True religion is ever objectivistic, sensuous subjectivistic. **1897** tr. *Kulpe's Introd. Philos.* 227 Subjectivistic ethics, following psychology, has taken two different forms, those of hedonism and eudæmonism.

subjectivity (sʌbdʒɪk'tɪvɪtɪ). [f. SUBJECTIVE + -ITY. So mod.L. *subjectivitas*, G. *subjectivität*, F. *subjectivité.*]

1. a. Consciousness of one's perceived states.

1821 COLERIDGE in *Blackw. Mag.* X. 249 In the object, we infer our own existence and subjectivity. **1874** SAYCE *Compar. Philol.* vii. 287 The idea of life, and therefore of subjectivity, is put out of sight. **1885** J. MARTINEAU *Types Eth. Th.* I. I. xi. §8. 211 They forbid us to appropriate to our own subjectivity the intelligent acts of which we are conscious.

b. A conscious being.

1830 COLERIDGE in *Lit. Rem.* (1838) III. 1 The Identity. The absolute subjectivity, whose only attribute is the Good. **1840** W. H. MILL *Applic. Panth. Princ.* I. 103 Individuals stand as 'the subjectivities that realize the substantial' of the Idea.

2. a. The quality or condition of viewing things exclusively through the medium of one's own mind or individuality; the condition of being dominated by or absorbed in one's personal feelings, thoughts, concerns, etc.; hence, individuality, personality.

[**1812** SOUTHEY *Omniana* I. 220 The nature of Bulls, which will be found always to contain in them a confusion of (what the Schoolmen would have called) Objectivety and Subjectivety, in plain English, the impression of a thing as it exists in itself and extrinsically, with the idea which the mind abstracts from the impression.] **1827** HARE *Guesses* (1859) 97 Often..the plural *we* is..a help to those who cannot get quit of their subjectivity, or write about objects objectively. **1844** W. G. WARD *Ideal Chr. Ch.* (ed. 2) 79 The vast increase of what is called subjectivity; the very much greater portion of man's life and interest which is occupied in observation of his own thoughts, feelings, and actions. **1871** R. H. HUTTON *Ess.* I. 248 'Subjectivity', as it is called, clouds the eyes; we want to know how far our own individual deficiencies, and sins, and impulses, colour our vision. **1880** *Scribner's Mag.* XX. 117 [Poe's] studies of character were not made from observation, but from acquaintance with himself; and this subjectivity, or egoism, crippled his invention. **1886** PATER *Ess. fr. Guardian* I. 11 This pioneer of an everybody's literature had his subjectivities.

b. That quality of literary or graphic art which depends on the expression of the personality or individuality of the artist; the individuality of an artist as expressed in his work.

1830 COLERIDGE *Table T.* 12 May, A subjectivity of the poet, as of Milton, who is himself before himself in everything he writes. **1882–3** *Schaff's Encycl. Relig. Knowl.* II. 953/2 Characteristics of Hebrew..poetry: 1. Subjectivity. The Hebrew poet deals only with what concerns him personally. **1889** SIR E. ARNOLD *Seas & Lands* iv. (1895) 49 'Fidelis' (Agnes Maude Machar), who is frequently called the first of Dominion poetesses, excels in a graceful subjectivity.

3. = SUBJECTIVISM 1.

1839 HALLAM *Lit. Eur.* IV. iii. §55 His [Malebranche's] philosophy..is subjectivity leading objectivity in chains. **1876** FAIRBAIRN in *Contemp. Rev.* June 133 Feuerbach.. developed the Hegelian subjectivity into the negation of objective reality.

4. The quality or condition of resting upon subjective facts or mental representation; the character of existing in the mind only.

1854 A. G. HENDERSON tr. *V. Cousin's Philos. Kant* viii. 177 The subjectivity of human reason; this it is that troubles Kant. **1877** E. CAIRD *Philos. Kant* II. iv. 262 The mere subjectivity of sensation. **1884** F. TEMPLE *Relat. Relig. & Sci.* v. (1885) 132 The pure subjectivity of Religion..is no more proved by this argument than the pure subjectivity of Science. **1888** *Mind* Oct. 596 Belief in the subjectivity of time, space and other forms of thought inevitably involves Agnosticism; belief in their objectivity in no way implies the rejection of Idealism.

subjectivize (səb'dʒɛktɪvaɪz), *v.* [f. SUBJECTIVE + -IZE.] *trans.* To make subjective. Hence **sub'jectivized** *ppl. a.*, **sub'jectivizing** *vbl. sb.*

1868 BAIN *Ment. & Mor. Sci.* II. 742 Kant even went so far as to make it [obligation] the principle of our morality; but this was subjectivizing good, as he had subjectivized truth. **1868** J. H. STIRLING tr. *Schwegler's Hist. Philos.* 336 Converting into objectivity, the subjectivized theoretical matter (truth). **1890–1** J. ORR *Chr. View God* v. (1893) 210 This weakening down and subjectivising of the idea of guilt.

subjec'tivo- (sʌbdʒɪk'taɪvɒ), comb. form of SUBJECTIVE = subjective and..., subjectively.

1846 SIR W. HAMILTON *Reid's Wks.* Note D. 845/2 The first of these [qualities of Body] I would denominate the class of Primary, or Objective, Qualities; the second, the class of Secundo-Primary, or Subjectivo-Objective Qualities. **1868** J. H. STIRLING tr. *Schwegler's Hist. Philos.* 276 A loosely connected intertexture of old subjectivo-idealistic views, and of new objectivo-idealistic ones. *Ibid.* 384 The cognized object..if itself mental, is subjectivo-objective.

'subjectless, *a.* [f. SUBJECT *sb.* + -LESS.]

1. Having no subject of interest.

1803 JANE PORTER *Thaddeus* (Warne) 101 Sick of his subjectless and dragging conversation. **1889** *Universal Rev.* 15 Feb. 249 The subjectless dulness of modern design.

2. With no subjects to rule.

1840 CARLYLE *Heroes* vi. 370 The subjects without King can do nothing; the subjectless King can do something.

3. Of a proposition, sentence, verb: Having no subject.

1874 *Supernat. Relig.* II. II. vi. 51 With nothing more definite than a subjectless φησί to indicate who is referred to. **1875** M. ARNOLD *God & Bible* v. 269 It is not true that the author..wields the *subjectless he says* in the random manner alleged. **1902** tr. *Brentano's Knowl. Right & Wrong* App. 115 Miklosich expressed the view that the finite verb of subjectless propositions always stands in the third person of the singular.

subject-like, *a.* or *adv. rare.* [-LIKE.] Like a subject; submissive(ly).

1553 in Kempe *Losely MSS.* (1836) 140 Being in his house..in perfecte quyettnes, good order, obedyence, and subjecte-lyke.

†**'subjectly,** *a. Obs. rare.* [f. SUBJECT *sb.* + -LY¹.] Obedient, submissive.

a **1603** T. CARTWRIGHT *Confut. Rhem. N.T.* (1618) 488 Our quiet and subiectly behauiour.

'subject-,matter. (Earlier *matter subject*: see SUBJECT *a.* 7; cf. F. *matière sujette*, from *c* 1500.) [= SUBJECT *a.* + MATTER *sb.*¹; tr. late L. *subjecta māteria* (Boethius), which represents Gr. ἡ ὑποκειμένη ὕλη (Aristotle).]

I. (Cf. ὑποκειμένη ὕλη in Arist. *Physics* B 1.)

1. The matter operated upon in an art, a process, etc.; the matter out of which a thing is formed.

[*c* **1374, 1586** *matter subject*: see MATTER *sb.*¹ 6.] *a* **1542** WYATT *7 Penit. Ps.* i. 58 Thy infynite mercye wante nedes it muste Subiect matter for hys operatyon. **1626** BACON *Sylva* §343 The Excluding of the Aire; And..the Exposing to the Aire..worke the same Effect, according to the Nature of the Subiect Matter. **1662** EVELYN *Sculptura* 6 Chalcography.. an Art which takes away all that is superfluous of the Subject matter, reducing it to that Forme or Body, which was disign'd in the Idea of the Artist. **1662** HIBBERT *Body Div.* II. 106 The infinite Creator..when he made him [*sc.* man] implyed by the subject-matter out of which she was made, mans soveraignty over her [*sc.* woman]. **1676** ALLEN *Addr. Nonconf.* 101 The whole body of a Nation who are baptized into the Universal Church..are in that respect subject matter of a Church. **1867** *Eng. Leader* 15 June 326 In every process whatever..the subject-matter, the hypostase, is not two instants in the same state.

†**2.** The ground, basis, or source *of* something. *Obs.*

1600 HOLLAND *Livy* I. 28 Let us therefore cherish..the subject matter of so great a publicke and private ornament [*materiem ingentis publice privatimque decoris.*] *a* **1683** OWEN *Disc. Holy Spirit* I. vi. (1693) 88 That God abideth in us and we in him is the subject matter of our Assurance.

II. (Cf. ὑποκειμένη ὕλη in Arist. *Eth. Nic.* I. iii, vii.)

3. Material for discourse or expression in language; facts or ideas as constituting material *for* speech or written composition, occas. for artistic representation; = MATTER *sb.*¹ 9.

[**1586** *matter subject*: see MATTER *sb.*¹ 9.] **1702** W. J. tr. *Bruyn's Voy. Levant* v. 12 The Rocks of Scylla and Charybdis, which afforded so much subject Matter to the ancient Poets. **1759** DILWORTH *Pope* 116 Subject-matter for his satyrical muse, he never wanted. **1854** tr. *Hettner's Athens & Pelop.* 89 The Persian wars, which..supplied subject-matter for the frieze of the Temple of Niké Apteros. **1875** M. ARNOLD *Ess. Crit.* i. (ed. 3) 43 The subject-matter which literary criticism should most seek. **1893** G. MOORE *Mod. Painting* 22 What..has this painter invented, what new subject matter has he introduced into art?

4. The subject or theme of a written or spoken composition; = MATTER *sb.*¹ 10.

1598 R. BERNARD tr. *Terence, Andria* Prol., [Menander's *Andria* and *Perinthia*] albeit they differ little in the subiect matter: yet notwithstanding they are vnlike in composition. **1649** ROBERTS *Clavis Bibl.* Introd. iii. 43 A summary Recapitulation..of the chief aime and subject-matter of every book. **1698** M. LISTER *Journ. Paris* (1699) 107 [A catalogue] is disposed according to the Subject Matter of the Books, as the Bibles and Expositors, Historians, Philosophers, &c. **1751** LABELYE *Westm. Br.* 105 The Number of Plates proper to illustrate the Subject-matter of each Volume. **1844** KINGLAKE *Eothen* iii. (1847) 36 The subject matters are slowly, and patiently enumerated, without disclosing the purpose of the speaker until he reaches the end of his sentence. **1877** J. D. CHAMBERS *Div. Worship* 377 The subject matter being proper for the Sermon.

5. The substance of a book, treatise, speech, or the like, as distinguished from the *form* or *style*; = MATTER *sb.*¹ 11.

1633 PRYNNE *1st Pt. Histrio-m.* III. i. 65 The Stile, and subiect Matter of most Comicall, and Theatricall Enterludes. **1752** EARL ORRERY *Rem. Swift* 181 The subject-matter of these pamphlets may perhaps be little worth your consideration; but their style will always command your attention. **1837** LOCKHART *Scott* IV. v. 153 Both as to subject-matter and style and method, remote *a Scævolæ studiis.* **1872** MINTO *Engl. Prose Lit.* Introd. 23 Had Campbell not been needlessly anxious to isolate the style from the subject matter. **1873** *Stud. Handbk. Univ. Oxford* 103 Candidates are expected to be able to translate the Greek text, and to answer questions on the subject-matter.

6. That with which thought, deliberation, or discussion, a contract, undertaking, project, or the like is concerned; that which is treated of or dealt with.

1657 CROMWELL *Sp.* 21 Apr., In considering and debating of those things that were the subject-matter of debate and consideration. **1669** CLARENDON *Ess.* Tracts (1727) 176 Let the law prescribe what it will, and the King command what he will, their obedience to either is not the subject-matter of this vow. **1692** LUTTRELL *Brief Rel.* (1857) II. 647 The lords intend to have another conference with the commons on the subject matter of the last. **1740** in Hanway *Trav.* (1762) I. I. viii. 33 We communicated to them captain elton's project, and have received their opinion..on the subject-matter thereof. **1826** BENTHAM *Humphrey's Prop. Code* in *Westm. Rev.* (1826) VI. 466 If the subject-matter be a fractional right, as a right of mine-working,..mention it accordingly. If subject-matters more than one are included in the deed, mention them accordingly. **1850** NEWMAN *Diffic. Anglicans* I. x. (1891) I. 304 A series of victories over human nature, which is the subject-matter of her [the Church's] operations. **1865** MOZLEY *Mirac.* v. 135 The individual uses the totally distinct principles of faith and reason according to the subject matter before him. **1875** MANNING *Mission Holy Ghost* xii. 330 There is a difference between the subject-matter of prudence and the subject-matter of counsel. **1875** DIGBY *Real Prop.* viii. (1876) 344 That a witness who had any interest in the subject-matter of his testimony was therefore not a credible witness at all. **1884** tr. *Lotze's Metaph.* 532 Those defects of memory that occur with regard to a certain definite subject-matter of our ideas; e.g. the forgetting of proper names.

b. That with which a science, law, etc. deals; the body of facts or ideas with which a study is concerned; = MATTER *sb.*¹ 12.

1660 JER. TAYLOR *Duct. Dubit.* III. vi. rule iii. §3 Some laws have in them a natural rectitude or usefulnesse in order to moral ends, by reason of the subject matter of the law. **1765** BLACKSTONE *Comm.* Introd. 60 As to the subject matter, words are always to be understood as having a regard thereto. **1818** HAZLITT *Engl. Poets* i. (1870) 1 In treating of poetry, I shall speak first of the subject-matter of it. **1864** BOWEN *Logic* xiii. 440 The subject-matter of calculations in the Theory of Probabilities is quantity of belief. **1874** SAYCE *Compar. Philol.* i. 52 Articulate speech itself, the subject matter of philology. **1895** *Educat. Rev.* Sept. 117 Those studies whose subject-matter is the direct product of intelligence.

c. *Law.* The matter in dispute.

1843–56 BOUVIER *Law Dict.* (ed. 6) II. 553/2 *Subject-matter*, the cause, the object, the thing in dispute. **1849** COBDEN *Speeches* 19 Each should be bound to submit the subject-matter of dispute to arbitration. **1888** *Weekly Notes* 22 Dec. 246/2 Because the parties had agreed to divide the subject matter of the litigation amongst themselves in a manner not in accordance with their actual title.

subject-object. *Philos.* A subjective object; the immediate object of cognition presented to the mind as distinguished from the real object; applied by Fichte to the ego.

1821 COLERIDGE in *Blackw. Mag.* X. 249/1 The subject witnesses to itself that it is a mind, *i.e.* a subject-object, or subject that becomes an object to itself. **1836–7** SIR W. HAMILTON *Metaph.* xxiii. (1859) II. 69 The immediate object, or object known in this act, should be called the *subjective object*, or *subject-object*, in contradistinction to the mediate or unknown object, which might be discriminated as the *object-object*. **1847** LEWES *Hist. Philos.* (1867) II. 485 The thought is necessarily and universally subject-object, matter is necessarily, and to us universally object-subject. **1897** tr. *Fichte's Sci. Ethics* 47 This whole Ego, in so far as it is neither subject nor object, but subject-object, has, in itself, a tendency to absolute self-activity.

Hence **,subject-objec'tivity,** a being that is subject and object, conscious being.

1848 W. SMITH *Fichte's Pop. Wks.* I. 440, I am subject and object:—and this *subject-object-ivity*, this return of knowledge upon itself, is what I mean by the term 'I'.

†**subjectory,** *a. Obs.* [f. SUBJECT *sb.* + -ORY.] ? Inherent.

1614 W. B. *Philos. Banquet* (ed. 2) Pref. 3 There are subiectory and pertinent peremptorie infirmities besides therevnto [*sc.* the eye] belonging ingendred, by Rheumes [etc.].

'subjectship. [f. SUBJECT *sb.* + -SHIP.] The condition or status of a subject.

1864 *Reader* 23 July 94 The rights and privileges of British subjectship. **1876** BATHGATE *Deep Things of God* vi. 131 The moral nature of man is the fact out of which both his sonship and his subjectship spring.

‖**subjee** (sʌb'dʒiː). Also sabji, sabzi, subzee, subdschi, (*erron.*) subjah. [ad. Urdu *sabzī* greenness, verdue, etc., bhang, f. *sabz*, a. Pers. *sebz* green.] The leaves and seed capsules of Indian hemp (*Cannabis indica*) used for making bhang; also, a drink made from an infusion of bhang.

1826 W. AINSLIE *Materia Indica* II. II. i. 39 Banghie..(Tam[ool])... Subjah..(Duk[hanie] and Hind[oostanie]). **1836** *Penny Cycl.* VI. 239/2 The drug obtained from hemp is called bang, or haschish, or cherris: gangika, or ganga, kinnab, subjah, majah, are other names for it. **1855** DUNGLISON *Med. Lex.*, *Bangue*,..*Subjee*. **1880** *Encycl. Brit.* XI. 648/2 *Bhang*, the Hindustani *siddhi* or *sabzi* ..is powdered and infused in cold water, yielding a turbid drink, *subdschi*. **1883** W. DYMOCK *Vegetable Materia Medica of Western India* 603 Cannabis sativa, Linn., Var. Indica... Leaves, Bháng, Siddhi, Sabzi (Hind. Beng. and Bomb.). **1887** BENTLEY *Man. Bot.* (ed. 5) 665 *Bhang*, *Subjee*, or *Sidhee*, the larger leaves and fruits without the stalks. **1893** —— et al. *Pharmacographia Indica* III. 320 *Sabzi* or *Sabji*, an infusion of Bhang with black pepper, anise and sugar. In Bengal milk, and cucumber and melon seeds are added. **1938** R. P. WALTON *Marihuana* xi. 190 Bhang. Also known as Subjee—is the larger leaves and capsules of the cannabis compressed in balls and sticky layers with here and there some flowers between. *Ibid.* 195 *Subzee*, an infusion of bang.

subjestion, refashioned form of SUGGESTION. Cf. SUBJECTION ¶ 12.

1556 J. HEYWOOD *Spider & Flie* xcii. 186 Serch their subiestions: how they maie agree: To be graunted, with honorable honeste. **1596** J. MELVILL *Diary* (Wodrow Soc.) 379 His prejudical dispositioun..conceavit against us be the maist subtill and importune subjestioun of craftie serpentes.

subjicible (səb'dʒɪsɪb(ə)l), *a. rare.* [f. L. *subjicĕre*, to SUBJECT + -IBLE.]

†**1.** Capable of being subjected *to* (dominion, control, etc.). (Only Jer. Taylor.) *Obs.*

1638 JER. TAYLOR *Serm. Gunpowder Treason* 50 A thing not subjicible to their penitentiall judicature. **1649** —— *Gt. Exemp.* Disc. ii. §6 Before the susception of it he was not a person subjicible to a command. **1660** —— *Duct. Dubit.* III. i. rule 5 §2 Actions..are subjicible to laws.

2. *Logic.* Capable of being made the subject of a predicate. Hence **subjici'bility**.

In mod. Dicts.

subjoin (səb'dʒɔɪn), *v.* Also 6 subion(n)e, 7 subjoyn(e. [In early use Sc.: ad. obs. F. *subjoindre* (15th–16th c.), ad. L. *subjungĕre*: see SUB- 28 and JOIN *v.*]

1. *trans.* To add at the end of a spoken or written statement, argument, or discourse; sometimes, to add (a note) at the bottom of a page.

a. with words denoting the form or contents of the addition as obj.

1573 TYRIE *Refut.* in *Cath. Tract.* 10/28, I will pass to the mater, first proponand my lettre, thairefter his ansuer..last of all I sall subione the refutatioun. **1588** A. KING tr. *Canisius' Catech.* h iiij, I haiff subionned thais twa tables following. **1656** JEANES *Mixt. Schol. Div.* 3 Having removed one feare..he subjoynes a command of an opposite fear. **1669** GALE *Crt. Gentiles* I. v. 27 To these we subjoyned the ancient Navigations of the Phenicians. **1683** MOXON *Mech. Exerc., Printing* i, In the same Book there are these written Notes subjoyned. **1727** *Col. Rec. Pennsylv.* III. 283 The several Persons whose names are subjoyned. **1785** COWPER *Let.* 5 Jan., According to your request I subjoin my Epitaph on Dr. Johnson. **1801** *Med. Jrnl.* V. 290 We shall subjoin, verbatim, an outline of the plan of such an institution. **1815** *Scribbleomania* 248, I will..subjoin the opinion of a very clever departed writer. **1835** THIRLWALL *Greece* vi. I. 187 He subjoins, as a reason, the comparatively late age of Homer and Hesiod. **1846** J. BAXTER *Libr. Pract. Agric.* (ed. 4) II. p. lix, We subjoin from a catalogue a list of prices. **1879** LUBBOCK *Addr. Pol. & Educ.* iii. 59, I subjoin the answers.

b. with quoted words or reported statement as obj.; †occas. almost = REJOIN *v.*

1646 SIR T. BROWNE *Pseud. Ep.* 217 Bodin explaining that of Seneca, *Septimus quisque annus ætati signum imprimit*, subjoynes, *hoc de maribus dictum oportuit* [etc.]. **1665** MANLEY *Grotius' Low C. Wars* 725 Subjoyning at last, that they were and would be safe against the punishments of that cruel Edict. **1670** G. H. *Hist. Cardinals* I. I. 20, I subjoyn'd, I do not wonder. **1784** tr. *Beckford's Vathek* 154 'We have here then,' subjoined Carathis, 'a girl both of courage and science.' **1853** C. BRONTE *Villette* xviii, 'She does several things very well.' (Flirtation amongst the number subjoined I, in thought.) **1862** GOULBURN *Pers. Relig.* II. i. 205 'Work out your own salvation', writes the Apostle, 'with fear and trembling';..but then he immediately subjoins, 'for it is God that worketh in you.'

2. To place in immediate sequence or juxtaposition; to add as a concomitant or related element.

1668 WILKINS *Real Char.* 371 They [vowels] may be both preposed and subjoyned to themselves and to one another. **1701** NORRIS *Ideal World* I. ii. 123, I have subjoined a minor to his major. **1716** [see *sub-adore*, SUB- 8]. **1751** HARRIS *Hermes* II. iv. 283 The Accusative is that Case, which to an efficient Nominative and a Verb of Action subjoins either the Effect or the Passive Subject. **1803** R. HALL *Sentiments Pres. Crisis* 9 The New Testament subjoins to the duty of fearing God, that of honouring the king. **1835** T. MITCHELL *Acharn. Aristoph.* 669 *note*, A single Bacchius appears to be subjoined to six anapæsts. **1856** M. C. CLARKE tr. *Berlioz' Instrumentation* 3 When Monteverde attempted to subjoin the chord of the seventh on the dominant without preparation.

†**3.** In occas. transf. uses: To attach in a subordinate position; to lie underneath and next to; to add as part of a treatment. *Obs.*

1632 LITHGOW *Trav.* VIII. 369 [Fez] may rather second Grand Caire, than subioyne it selfe to Constantinople. **1703** T. N. *City & C. Purch.* 26 The..last Fillet, which subjoyns the under side of the upper Thorus. **1706** E. WARD *Wooden World Diss.* (1708) 101 There's no bringing him to his true Temperament again, but by subjoining the Bilboes.

†**4.** To add to, strengthen, reinforce; to subscribe to, second (an opinion). *Obs.* ? *vulgar.*

1810 *Splendid Follies* I. 158 'Upon my word, sir' replied Seraphina, heartily subjoining his laugh. *Ibid.* III. 65 I'm sorry to subjoin your opinion,..by observing that gallantry is too often the only characteristic of a soldier. *Ibid.* 195 Report whispers that she means to subjoin her income with the widow's pittance.

Hence **sub'joined** *ppl. a.*

1812 G. CHALMERS *Dom. Econ. Gt. Brit.* 442 Let well intentioned men mark the subjoined detail of the real value of the imports, and exports of Ireland. **1857** MILLER *Elem. Chem., Org.* i. 18 The subjoined precautions are requisite. **1870** L'ESTRANGE *Life of Miss Mitford* I. v. 125 A mother's resentment at anything which could endanger her daughter's success is exhibited in the subjoined letter. **1879** *Encycl. Brit.* X. 224/1 The subjoined table gives the results of temperature observations at widely separated localities.

subjoinder (səb'dʒɔɪndə(r)). *rare*$^{-1}$. [f. SUBJOIN after *rejoinder*.] A remark subjoined to another.

1831 LAMB *Elia* II. *Ellistoniana*, 'I was hissed, Sir.' 'And you have the presumption to decide upon the taste of the town?' 'I don't know that, Sir, but I will never stand to be hissed,' was the subjoinder of young Confidence.

subjugable ('sʌbdʒəgəb(ə)l), *a. rare.* [f. L. *subjugāre* to SUBJUGATE + -ABLE.] That may be subdued or brought under cultivation.

1886 *Science* VII. 232 An abundance of good readily subjugable land, awaiting the settler.

subjugal (sʌb'dʒuːgəl), *a. rare.* [ad. late L. *subjugāl-is*, f. *sub-* SUB- 1 + *jugum* yoke: see -AL^{1}.]

†**1.** Under a 'yoke' or dominion. *Obs.*

c **1485** *Digby Myst.* (1882) III. 7, I am soveren of al soverens subjugal On-to myn empere.

†**2.** *Mus.* ? Plagal. *Obs.*

1609 DOWLAND *Ornith. Microl.* 89 The Songs of Authenticall Tones must be timed deepe, of the subiugall Tones high, of the neutrall, meanly.

3. Accustomed to the yoke: of a beast of burden.

1896 E. P. EVANS *Anim. Symb. Eccl. Archit.* 274 Lo, with what enormous ears This subjugal son appears, Most egregious ass.

4. *Anat.* [f. SUB- 1 b + JUGAL.] Under the jugal bone.

In mod. Dicts.

'**subjugate**, *pa. pple.* and *sb.* [ad. L. *subjugāt-us*, pa. pple. of *subjugāre* (see next).]

A. *pa. pple.* Subjugated. *Obs.* or *arch.*

1432–50 tr. *Higden* (Rolls) I. 347 For cause the peple off Englonde sayethe and cryethe Gurmunde to haue subiugate Irlonde. **1447** BOKENHAM *Seyntys* (Roxb.) 91 To his empere Many a cuntre he had subjugate. **1530** PALSGR. 742/1 For al their hye mynde they be now subjugate. **1535** STEWART *Cron. Scot.* I. 442 Vnto the Romanis subjungat [*sic*] to be. **1596** *Edw. III*, III. ii, Belike, you then despair of all success, And think your country will be subjugate. **1611** SPEED *Theat. Gt. Brit.* 75/1 Till it was first made subiugate to the Inuasion of the Danes. **1626** R. C. *Times' Whistle* 3495 Mans sence captivd'e, his reason subiugate. **1631** T. POWELL *Tom of All Trades* (1876) 147 The Lord Maior..to whose commandement they be immediately subjugate. **1901** *Westm. Gaz.* 18 Jan. 2/1 The spirit of revolt not subjugate but gone underground.

†**B.** *sb.* A subject. *Obs.*

1773 J. ROSS *Fratricide* I 791 (MS.) The dupe..The servile subjugate of Satan!

subjugate ('sʌbdʒəgeɪt), *v.* [f. L. *subjugāt-*, pa. ppl. stem of *subjugāre*, f. *sub-* SUB- 1 g + *jugum* yoke. (Cf. SUBJUGE.)]

1. *trans.* To bring under the yoke or into subjection; to reduce to the condition of a subject country or people.

1432–50 tr. *Higden* (Rolls) II. 37 That yle of Wiȝhte, whom Vespasian sende from Claudius did subiugate. **1530** PALSGR. 742/1, I subjugat, I bring under yoke or obeysaunce. **1654** COKAINE *Dianea* IV. 283 Arsinoe won, all is won, and the kingdome subjugated. **1718** PRIOR *Solomon* II. 184 O fav'rite Virgin, that hast warm'd the Breast, Whose sov'reign Dictates subjugate the East! **1845** *Encycl. Metrop.* II. 736/1 The special commissions given to the children of Israel to subjugate the land of Canaan. **1853** NEWMAN *Hist. Sk.* I. I. ii. 74 They neither subjugated the inhabitants of their new country..nor were subjugated by them. **1865** H. PHILLIPS *Amer. Paper Curr.* II. 96 The English..avowed their intention of making America a desert if they could not subjugate it.

absol. **1855** MILMAN *Lat. Christ.* IX. vii. (1864) V. 361 This inauspicious attempt to subjugate rather than win.

2. *transf.* and *fig.* To bring into bondage or under complete control; to make subservient or submissive.

1589 [? NASHE] *Almond for Parrat* 10 He wil needes haue subiects, before he can subiugate his affections. **1606** G. W[OODCOCKE] *Hist. Ivstine* XXXVI. 114 There was no soueraigne of Macedon able to subiugate their fealty by his dominion. **1611** BEAUM. & FL. *Four Plays, Tri. Hon.* i, His soul hath subjugated Martius soul. **1667** BOYLE *Orig. Formes & Qual.* (ed. 2) 298 To evince that the same Ingredient for instance, of Sulphur, is not as much subjugated by the Form of the intire Body, as that of the purgative portion of Rhubarb, by the Form of that Drugg. **1791** BOSWELL *Johnson* (1816) I. 394 Nor can history or poetry exhibit more than pleasure triumphing over virtue, or virtue subjugating pleasure. **1841** D'ISRAELI *Amen. Lit.* (1867) 650 Aristotle..had subjugated the minds of generation after generation. **1863** GEO. ELIOT *Romola* xxiii, His love and his hatred were of that passionate fervour which subjugates all the rest of the being. **1870** YEATS *Nat. Hist. Comm.* 99 The camel, an animal so early subjugated to the use of man. **1884** F. TEMPLE *Relat. Relig. & Sci.* iv. (1885) 118 Many species of animals perish as man fills and subjugates the globe.

†**3.** To place as if under a yoke. *Obs. rare.*

1660 F. BROOKE tr. *Le Blanc's Trav.* 190 This Prince hath a high veneration from his people, who subjugate their shoulders for his support [*qu'ils le portent sur leurs espaules*.]

Hence '**subjugated**, '**subjugating** *ppl. adjs.*

1656 EARL MONM. tr. *Boccalini's Advts. fr. Parnass.* I. xxi. (1674) 22 [They] took publick revenge for subjugated liberty. *Ibid.* II. lxxx. 232 The subjugated people may in time of Peace recover. **1782** MISS BURNEY *Cecilia* VIII. v, That noble and manly labour, which..disentangles them from such subjugating snares. **1872** YEATS *Growth Comm.* 34 The revenue was derived from tribute paid by subjugated races.

subjugation (sʌbdʒə'geɪʃən). [ad. late L. *subjugātio, -ōnem*, n. of action f. *subjugāre* to SUBJUGATE. Cf. F. *subjugation*.]

1. The action of subjugating or condition of being subjugated; the bringing of a country or nation under the yoke of a conquering power.

1658 PHILLIPS. *a* **1676** HALE *Prim. Orig. Man.* II. iv. 160 This was the condition of Greece the Learned Part of the World after their subjugation by the Turks. *a* **1806** HORSLEY *Serm.* viii. (1812) I. 143 The subjugation of nations, by the prosecution of this war. **1825** SCOTT *Talism.* vii, The English fighting for the subjugation of Scotland, and the Scottish..for the defence of their independence. **1883** H. WACE *Gospel & Witn.* iv. 74 The craving of the Jews for their temporal deliverance from subjugation to a heathen power. **1910** *Encycl. Brit.* (ed. 11) VI. 965/1 'There is subjugation', says Rivier.., 'when a war is terminated by the complete defeat of one of the belligerents so that all his territory is taken..and he ceases..to exist as a state.'

2. *transf.* and *fig.* Intellectual or moral subjection; reduction to a state of subserviency or submission; occas. the action of subduing (the soil).

1785 PALEY *Mor. Philos.* VI ii. 406 The almost universal subjugation of strength to weakness. **1849** RUSKIN *Seven Lamps* vii. §2. 184 Obedience is, indeed, founded on a kind of freedom, else it would become mere subjugation. **1856** KANE *Arctic Expl.* II. App. 305 The..exertions of Dr. J. J. Hayes..kept the scurvy in complete subjugation. **1858** B. TAYLOR *Northern Trav.* 307 The subjugation of virgin soil ..is a serious work. **1871** MORLEY *Carlyle* in *Crit. Misc.* 224 The essence of morality is the subjugation of nature in obedience to social needs.

subjugator ('sʌbdʒəgeɪtə(r)). [ad. late L. *subjugātor*, agent-n. f. *subjugāre* to SUBJUGATE.] One who subjugates; a subduer, conqueror.

a **1834** COLERIDGE (Worc.). **1858** GLADSTONE *Homer* I. 459 The subjugators of some race in prior occupancy of the soil. **1875** POSTE *Gaius* I. (ed. 2) 62 Paulus Aemilius, the subjugator of Epirus.

†**sub'juge**, *v. Obs.* Also 5 -iugue. [ad. F. *subjuguer* or L. *subjugāre* to SUBJUGATE.] *trans.* To subjugate. Also **sub'juging** *vbl. sb.*

1471 CAXTON *Recuyell* (Sommer) 367 They late yow wete that they haue good right to subiugue yow. **1474** —— *Chesse* III. v. (1883) 124 A knyght of rome..that had newly conquerid and subiuged the yle of Corsika. **1592** WYRLEY *Armorie* 26 Such people by plaine feate of Armes subjuged. **1660** A. SADLER *Subj. Joy* 29 Except thou..make Us bow, And yield our Necks, to thy Subjuging too.

subjunct ('sʌbdʒʌŋkt). *Gram.* [f. L. *subjunctus*, pa. pple. of *subjungĕre* SUBJOIN *v.*: cf. ADJUNCT *ppl. a.* and *sb.*] In Jespersen's terminology, a word or group of words of the third rank of importance in a phrase or sentence. Cf. PRIMARY *sb.* 9, ADJUNCT *sb.* 5 b.

1914 O. JESPERSEN *Mod. Eng. Gram.* II. xii. 283 The adjunct in *perfect simplicity* is a shifted subjunct of the adjective contained in the substantive *simplicity*, cf. *perfectly simple*. We may call these *shifted subjunct-adjuncts*. **1924** —— *Philos. Gram.* vii. 97 For tertiary we may use the term *subjunct*, and quaternary words..may be termed *sub-subjuncts*. **1935** [see ADJUNCT *sb.* 5 b].

subjunction (səb'dʒʌŋkʃən). Now *rare.* [ad. late L. *subjunctio, -ōnem*, n. of action f. *subjungĕre* to SUBJOIN.] The action of subjoining a statement, etc.; the condition of being subjoined, annexed, or closely attached.

1633 T. ADAMS *Exp. 2 Peter* iii. 18. 1591 Paul could not speake of this mercie without the subjunction of glorie. **1733** J. CLARKE *Gram. Lat. Tongue* 155 In Dependence upon, or in Subjunction to some other Verb. **1783** BLAIR *Lect.* xi. I. 218 The subjunction of Dolabella's character is foreign to the main object. **1869** WESSELY *Dict. Engl. & Germ.* II. *Beifügung*, addition, subjunction.

subjunctive (səb'dʒʌŋktɪv), *a.* and *sb.* [ad. L. *subjunctīv-us*, f. *subjunct-*, pa. ppl. stem of *subjungĕre* to SUBJOIN. Cf. F. *subjonctif*, It. *subiuntivo*, Sp. *subjuntivo*; also It. *soggiuntivo*.]

A. *adj.*

1. *Gram.* That is subjoined or dependent.

L. *subjunctivus* is a translation of Gr. ὑποτακτικός, which as a grammatical term was used variously with the meaning 'subjoined': see below.

†**a.** ***subjunctive article*** (Gr. ἄρθρον ὑποτακτικόν), the relative ὅς ἥ ὅ, as opposed to the 'prepositive article' ὁ ἡ τό; hence ***subjunctive pronoun, adverb*** = relative pronoun, adverb. ***subjunctive vowel*** (L. *vocalis subjunctiva*, Gr. φωνῆεν ὑποτακτικόν), the second vowel of a diphthong. ***subjunctive proposition***, a subordinate clause. *Obs.*

1583 subjunctive article [see PREPOSITIVE]. **1603** HOLLAND *Plutarch's Mor.* 1355 This particle or Conjunction Ει, that is to say, If, and..what Subjunctive proposition soever following after it. **1700** A. LANE *Key Art Lett.* (1705) 10 E Subjunctive is written at the end of a word, after a single Consonant to make the single Vowel before it long. **1751** HARRIS *Hermes* I. v. (1765) 79 We may with just reason..call this Pronoun the Subjunctive, because it cannot..introduce an original Sentence. **1818** STODDART in *Encycl. Metrop.* (1845) I. 43/1 The principal subjunctive pronouns in English are *who* and *which*, and sometimes *that*. **1824** L. MURRAY *Engl. Gram.* (ed. 5) I. 195 When we read the first chapter of Genesis, we perceive, that this subjunctive pronoun, as it may be called, occurs but seldom.

b. Designating a mood (L. *modus subjunctivus*, Gr. ὑποτακτικὴ ἔγκλισις) the forms of which are employed to denote an action or a state as conceived (and not as a fact) and therefore used to express a wish, command, exhortation, or a contingent, hypothetical, or prospective event. (The mood is used in both principal and subordinate clauses; cf., however, CONJUNCTIVE *a.* 3 c.) Also, belonging to this mood, e.g. ***subjunctive present*** or ***present subjunctive***.

So named because it was regarded as specially appropriate to 'subjoined' or subordinate clauses.

1530 PALSGR. 84 The subjunctive mode whiche they ever use folowyng an other verbe, and addyng this worde *que* before hym. **1612** BRINSLEY *Posing Pts.* (1669) 31 Why is it called the Subjunctive Mood? A. Because it dependeth upon some other Verb in the same sentence, either going before, or coming after it. **1669** MILTON *Acced. Gram.* 17 There be four Moods, which express the manner of doing; the Indicative, the Imperative, the Potential or Subjunctive, and the Infinitive. **1751** HARRIS *Hermes* I. viii. (1765) 143 This Mode, as often as it is in this manner subjoined, is called by Grammarians not the Potential, but the Subjunctive. **1839** T. MITCHELL *Frogs Aristoph.* 589 *note*, Examples of a subjunctive interrogative in the present tense ..are not wanting in the Greek writings. **1853** MAX MÜLLER *Chips* (1880) I. iii. 79 No subjunctive mood existed in the common Sanskrit. **1861** PALEY *Æschylus* (ed. 2) *Pers.* 120 To combine an aorist subjunctive with a future indicative.

c. Characteristic of what is expressed by the subjunctive mood; contingent, hypothetical.

1837 G. PHILLIPS *Syriac Gram.* 111 The tenses..in many cases express a potential, subjunctive, or hypothetical sense. **1866** R. CHAMBERS *Ess.* Ser. II. 214 One of the subjunctive heroes of literature and science. **1893** *Hansard's Parl. Debates* Ser. III. VIII. 1589 To make a subjunctive or contingent apology.

†**2.** In general sense: Additional *to*. *Obs. rare.*

a **1670** HACKET *Abp. Williams* I. 87 A few things more, subjunctive to the former, were thought meet to be Castigated in Preachers at that time.

†**3.** (See quot.) *Obs. rare*$^{-0}$.

1656 BLOUNT *Glossogr.*, *Subjunctive*, that under-sets, or joyns underneath.

B. *sb. Gram.*

1. The subjunctive mood; a form of a verb belonging to the subjunctive mood.

1622 J. W. tr. *Oudin's Sp. Gram.* 4 *Cogér*.. maketh in the Optatiue and Subiunctiue *Cója*. 1728 CHAMBERS *Cycl.* s.v. *Mood*, Men might have invented a particular Inflection... But they han't done it; and in lieu thereof, make use of the Subjunctive. 1835 T. MITCHELL *Acharn. Aristoph.* 253 *note*, The subjunctive thus used without ἂν has an interrogative and future signification. 1860 G. P. MARSH *Lect. Engl. Lang.* xiv. 317 The subjunctive is evidently passing out of use, and there is good reason to suppose that it will soon become obsolete altogether. 1875 POSTE *Gaius* I. (ed. 2) 36 The edicts and interdicts of the praetor are couched in the subjunctive (Exhibeas, Restituas, &c.), a milder form of imperative.

b. *Comb.*, as **subjunctive-equivalent**, an expression which conveys the subjunctive mood by a construction involving an auxiliary verb and an infinitive.

1927 E. A. SONNENSCHEIN *Soul of Grammar* ii. 87 Modern English makes a large use of 'subjunctive-equivalents,' e.g. expressions formed by combining a tense..of the verbs 'shall', 'will', 'may', 'let', with an infinitive. 1965 F. BEHRE in *English Studies* Apr. 89 But now is perhaps the right moment to question the fitness of using the term 'subjunctive-equivalent' in contemporary English.

†2. A relative. *Obs. rare.*

1818 STODDART in *Encycl. Metrop.* (1845) I. 83/2 *Where, whence*, and *whither*..serve indifferently for interrogatives and subjunctives.

Hence **sub'junctively** *adv.*, in the subjunctive mood, as a subjunctive.

1651 HOBBES *Leviathan* I. vi. 29 Deliberation is expressed Subjunctively; which is a speech proper to signifie suppositions. 1871 *Public School Lat. Gram.* §67. 167 Examples of the Conjunctive Mood used Subjunctively *accidit ut aegrotem.*

'sub,kingdom. [SUB- 7 b.] One of the primary groups into which the animal and vegetable kingdoms are divided.

1825 W. S. MACLEAY *Annulosa Javan.* 5 If we..descend from the consideration of the kingdom *Animalia* to the department or sub-kingdom *Annulosa*. 1851 CARPENTER *Man. Phys.* (ed. 2) 131 These Red Corpuscles can scarcely be said to exist in the blood of Invertebrated animals, and their proportion in the blood of Vertebrata varies considerably in the several groups of that sub-kingdom. 1870 H. A. NICHOLSON *Man. Zool.* (1875) 16 The six types or plans of structure, upon one or other of which all known animals have been constructed, are technically called 'sub-kingdoms', and are known by the names Protozoa, Cœlenterata, Annuloida, Annulosa, Mollusca, and Vertebrata. 1877 DAWSON *Orig. World* x. 213 The three Cuvierian sub-kingdoms of the Radiata, Articulata, and Mollusca. 1900 B. D. JACKSON *Gloss. Bot. Terms*, *Subkingdom*, the main division of a kingdom, a primary botanic division, as Phanerogams and Cryptogams.

†**sublabe.** *Obs. rare*⁻¹. [ad. L. *sublabium* (recorded only as a plant-name), f. *sub-* SUB- 3 + *labium* lip.] The underlip.

1577 GRANGE *Golden Aphrod.* E iv, Mundifiyng their beardes, cristalling their teeth, correcting their haires, cutting their sublabes.

'sublanguage. [SUB- 5 c.] A specialized language or system of notation that occurs only in certain contexts or is used only by certain people among those who speak the same ordinary language.

1934 WEBSTER, *Sublanguage*, a subordinate language; a dialect. 1951 J. HOLLOWAY *Lang. & Intell.* x. 182 These sub-languages include arithmetic and geometry..; chess notation; musical notation [etc.]. 1966 M. GROSS in *Automatic Transl. of Lang.* (NATO Summer School, Venice, 1962) 134 Of course a translation form L_1 to L_2 need not be an exact mapping L_1 and L_2, but there may be a large sublanguage of L_2. 1972 *Science* 23 June 1304/3 In a sub-language..such as the jargon of surgeons, the information is carried mainly by the kernels. 1973 G. W. TURNER *Stylistics* i. 26 Such sub-languages as the language of telegrams, newspaper headlines, advertisements or knitting patterns.

Sublapsarian (sʌblæp'sɛərɪən), *sb.* and *a. Theol.* [f. mod.L. *sublapsārius*, f. *sub-* SUB- 17 + *lapsus* fall, LAPSE: see -IAN. Cf. F. *sublapsaire*.]

A. *sb.* = INFRALAPSARIAN A, q.v.

1656 JER. TAYLOR *Deus Justificatus* 33 The Sublapsarians say, That God made it by his decree necessary, that all wee who were born of Adam should be born guilty of Originall Sin. *a* 1660 HAMMOND *Hell Torm.* (1665) 67 They which deny all irrespective decree of Reprobation or Præterition against Supralapsarians and Sublapsarians. 1765 MACLAINE tr. *Mosheim's Eccl. Hist.* Cent. XVII. II. ii. §12 The Reformed church was immediately divided into Universalists, Semi-universalists, Supralapsarians, and Sublapsarians. 1851 R. S. HAWKER in *Life & Lett.* (1905) 217 His little girl is a Sub-lapsarian. 1894 SIMKINSON *Laud* i. 13 The Puritan chiefs, divided into two hostile camps of sublapsarians and supralapsarians, argued interminably the question whether the Divine decrees of rigid election or reprobation dated from before or after the fall of Adam.

B. *adj.* = INFRALAPSARIAN B.

a 1660 HAMMOND *Pacif. Disc.* 14 The Decree of Reprobation according to the Sublapsarian Doctrine, being nothing else but a meer preterition or non-election of some persons whom God left, as he found. *a* 1751 DODDRIDGE *Lect.* (1763) 460 The Supralapsarian and Sublapsarian schemes agree in asserting the doctrine of predestination, but with this difference. 1765 MACLAINE tr. *Mosheim's Eccl. Hist.* Cent. XVII. II. II. ii. §10 The Sublapsarian doctors. 1885 *Encycl. Brit.* XIX. 671/1 The canons of Dort..are favourable to the sub-lapsarian view.

Hence **Sublap'sarianism**, the doctrine of the Sublapsarians. So †**Sub'lapsary** *a.* = SUBLAPSARIAN B.

1728 CHAMBERS *Cycl.*, *Sublapsary*, in Theology; or Infralapsary; a Term applied to such as hold, that God having foreseen the Fall of Adam, and in consequence thereof, the Loss of Mankind; resolved to give a Grace sufficient to Salvation to some, and to refuse it to others. 1865 *Pall Mall Gaz.* 20 Oct. 11 Predestinarianism, Supra-lapsarianism, Sublapsarianism, with all their various minor variations. 1875 SPURGEON *Lect. Stud.* Ser. I. 78 The great problems of sublapsarianism and supralapsarianism.

†**su'blate**, *pa. pple. Obs. rare*⁻¹. [ad. L. *sublāt-us* (see next).] Removed.

1694 MOTTEUX *Rabelais* v. 249 Then All arise, the Tables are sublate.

sublate (sə'bleɪt), *v.* [f. L. *sublāt-*, f. *sub-* SUB- 26 + *lāt-* (for **tlāt-*), pa. ppl. stem of *tollĕre* to take away.]

†1. *trans.* To remove, take away. *Obs.*

a 1548 HALL *Chron., Hen. VII*, 1 b, The aucthores of yᵉ mischiefe [were] sublated and plucked awaye. 1601 B. JONSON *Ev. Man in Hum.* (Qo. 1) II. iii, This brasse varnish being washt off, and three or foure other tricks sublated. 1657 HAWKE *Killing is M.* 46 Tiberius..was sublated by poison.

2. *Logic.* To deny, contradict, disaffirm: opposed to POSIT 2.

1838 SIR W. HAMILTON *Logic* xvii. (1866) I. 331 When of two opposite predicates the one is posited or affirmed, the other is sublated or denied. 1864 BOWEN *Logic* vi. 163 As both cannot be false, if I sublate one, the other is posited. 1867 ATWATER *Logic* 180 Whether, in the Subsumption, the Disjunct Members are properly sublated.

3. *Hegelian Philos.* (rendering G. *aufheben*, used by Hegel as having the opposite meanings of 'destroy' and 'preserve'): see quots. 1865.

1865 J. H. STIRLING *Secret of Hegel* I. 354 Nothing passes over into Being, but Being equally sublates itself, is a passing over into Nothing, Ceasing-to-be. They sublate not themselves mutually, not the one the other externally; but each sublates itself in itself, and is in its own self the contrary of itself. *Ibid.* 357 A thing is sublated, resolved, only so far as it has gone into unity with its opposite. 1868 —— tr. *Schwegler's Hist. Philos.* 401 The speculative of Hegel is also clear; it is what explanatorily sublates all things into the unity of God; or, in general, that is speculative, that sublates a many into one (or *vice versa*). A speculative philosophy, consequently, must be a chain of mutually sublating counterparts. 1877 E. CAIRD *Philos. Kant* II. x. 427 The material world exists only in so far as it goes into itself, or sublates its own self-externality. 1910 J. ORR in *Expositor* Apr. 367 High metaphysical theories, like Hegel's, which make sin..a moment of 'negation' to be afterwards sublated in a higher unity.

su'blated, *ppl. a.* [f. L. *sublātus* (see prec.) + -ED¹.]

†1. Exalted, excited. *Obs.*

1647 LILLY *Chr. Astrol.* xliv. 277 Their disease shall proceed from..high and sublated Pulses, keeping no order.

2. *Hegelian Philos.* (See SUBLATE *v.* 3.)

1868 J. H. STIRLING tr. *Schwegler's Hist. Philos.* 264 The non-ego has position only in the ego, in consciousness: the ego, consequently, is not sublated by the non-ego; after all the sublated ego is not sublated.

sublateral (sʌb'lætərəl), *a.* [f. SUB- 11 + L. *latus, later-* side + -AL¹.] Almost lateral; situated near the side.

1822 J. PARKINSON *Outl. Oryctol.* 188 The beaks sublateral, lying on the shorter side. 1870 HOOKER *Stud. Flora* 318 Radicle basal or sublateral. 1875 DARWIN *Insectiv. Pl.* x. 251 There are tentacles on the disc..near the extremities of the sublateral bundles.

sublation (sə'bleɪʃən). [ad. L. *sublātio, -ōnem*, n. of action f. *sublāt-* (see SUBLATE *v.*).]

†1. The middle part of a liquid that has thrown its sediment. *Obs.*

1533 ELYOT *Cast. Helth* (1541) 88 b, If lyke thynges be sene in the myddell of the urynall, they be called sublations. 1590 BARROUGH *Meth. Phisick* IV. vii. (1596) 233 Their vrine hath by and by a white cloude, or a laudable sublation in the middes.

2. The act of taking away, removal.

1626 J. YATES *Ibis ad Cæsarem* I. 18 The subversion of Sauls Kingdome, dispersion of the Iewes, rejection of the guests, sublation of the talents. *a* 1656 BP. HALL *Rem. Wks.* (1660) 188 He could not be forsaken by a sublation of union. 1913 DORLAND *Med. Dict.*, *Sublation*, the removal, detachment, or displacement of a part.

b. *Logic.* (See SUBLATE *v.* 2.)

1864 BOWEN *Logic* vii. 219 Only by the non-existence, or sublation, of all the others.

c. *Hegelian Philos.* (See SUBLATE *v.* 3.)

1865 J. H. STIRLING *Secret of Hegel* I. 356 Aufheben und das Aufgehobene (das Ideelle), sublation and what is sublated (and so only *idéellement*, not *réellement* is), this is.. a ground-form which repeats itself everywhere and always, the sense of which is to be exactly apprehended and particularly distinguished from Nothing.

†3. A lifting up, elevation. *Obs.*

1653 R. G. tr. *Bacon's Hist. Winds* 382 Let us enquire whether there be any such sublation or raising made by consent, or Magnetick power. 1656 BLOUNT *Glossogr.*, *Sublation*, a lifting up.

su'blative, *a.* [ad. L. **sublātīvus*, f. *sublāt-*: see SUBLATE *v.*] Annulling, negativing.

1751 HARRIS *Hermes* II. ii. 253 *note*, The conjunction ἢ being ἀναιρετικὸς, or sublative.

'sub-lease, *sb.* [f. SUB- 9 (e).] A lease granted by one who is a lessee or tenant, an underlease.

1826 BELL *Comm. Laws Scot.* (ed. 5) I. 67 In assigning a sublease, intimation to the principal tenant is not sufficient. 1838 W. BELL *Dict. Law Scot.* 582 Both the sublease and assignation are completed by possession. 1913 *Times* 7 Aug. 4/4 She had been the lessee, under a sub-lease, of the premises for something like eight years.

sub-'lease, *v.* [f. SUB- 9 (b).] *trans.* To sublet.

1828-43 TYTLER *Hist. Scot.* (1864) I. 174 In giving leases of houses..he prohibited his tenants and vassals from subleasing them to any except Englishmen. 1885 *Law Times* LXXIX. 233/1 A builder erects a row of cottages on the land subleased to him. 1898 TOBIAS *Freed, but not Free* 39 All the convicts whom he does not work himself are sub-leased by him to other employers, who may desire cheap labour.

So **sub-le'ssee**, one who holds or receives a sub-lease; **sub-'lessor**, one who grants a sub-lease.

1882 OGILVIE, *Sub-lessee.* 1884 *Law Times* 9 Feb. 259/1 To indemnify the sublessor against breaches of all covenants in the head-lease.

'sub-let, *sb.* [f. next.] A sub-lease.

1906 *Daily Chron.* 14 Sept. 4/5 The extensive shooting near Kingume,..which Lord Lilford has on a sub-let. 1906 A. B. TODD *Poet. Wks., Autobiogr.* iv. 36 My father had taken the place in sub-let from the late Mr. John Campbell.

sub-'let, *v.* [f. SUB- 9 (b) + LET *v.*¹] *trans.* To let (property, a tenement) to a subtenant; to lease out (work, etc.) under a subcontract; to underlet, sublease.

1766 SMOLLETT *Trav.* xxxix. II. 223 My landlord.. declared I should not be permitted to sub-let them to any other person. 1791 NEWTE *Tour Eng. & Scot.* 124 The Chieftain..lets the land..to renters; who sub-let it, again, in small parcels from year to year, to the lower class of the people. 1860 *All Year Round* No. 68. 427 This man employs the needlewomen, or perhaps sublets part of his contract to others who employ them. 1865 *Q. Rev.* July 31 Poulterers of Edinburgh and Glasgow rent ground, subletting the shooting, and furnishing the shops with the produce. 1871 AMY DUTTON *Streets & Lanes* i. 11 That house was occupied by a couple named Cripps, hard, griping people, who sublet most of the rooms. 1890 *Century Mag.* June 221/1 He's let and sublet, and every man has to make something out of him [the convict] each time.

absol. 1872-4 JEFFERIES *Toilers of Field* (1892) 242 He sub-lets, or takes lodgers, and sometimes these sub-let.

Hence **sub'lettable** *a.*, **sub'letter**, **sub'letting** *vbl. sb.*

1869 *Pall Mall Gaz.* 1 Sept. 3 It is, of course, to be saleable and devisable. Is it not also to be *sublettable? 1861 MAYHEW *Lond. Labour* II. 230 The *sub-lettors declaring.. that the rents were raised to them. 1812 SIR J. SINCLAIR *Syst. Husb. Scot.* II. 108 The *subletting of land. 1826 BELL *Comm. Laws Scot.* (ed. 5) I. 77 The right..of subletting. 1854 MᶜCULLOCH *Acc. Brit. Empire* I. 537 The legislature passed the Subletting Act, by which the underletting of farms was prohibited without the landlord's consent in writing. 1888 *Times* (weekly ed.) 11 May 15/2 He had known three or four sublettings before the work reached the workman.

sub-'lethal, *a.* [SUB- 19, 21.] **a.** *Med.* Of a drug, treatment, etc.: having an effect (only just) less than lethal.

1896 *Allbutt's Syst. Med.* I. 561 Beginning with minute sub-lethal doses of fully virulent poisons. 1910 HANSON & ZINSSER *Textbk. Bacteriol.* xii. 195 (*heading*) Active immunization with sublethal doses of fully virulent bacteria. 1937 *Ann. Reg.* 1936 59 Experimental epidemiologists showed the importance of latent and sub-lethal infection. 1947 *Radiology* XLIX. 303/1 At sublethal doses, the minimum granulocyte count occurs at about the same time as in non-survivors. 1977 J. L. HARPER *Population Biol. Plants* xvi. 493 These are the pathogens that kill young seedlings,..that convert sub-lethal damage done by other causes into lethal damage.

b. *Genetics.* Of an allele or a chromosomal abnormality: = SEMI-LETHAL *a.*

1935 *Jrnl. Heredity* XXVI. 357/2 Hadley reported the inheritance of a sub-lethal, hairless defect in Holsteins [*sc.* a breed of cattle]. 1946 *Nature* 16 Nov. 722/2 When a gene is sublethal, as are those for hæmophilia and achondroplasic dwarfism, its elimination by natural selection is in approximate equilibrium with its appearance by mutation. 1961 R. D. BAKER *Essent. Path.* xi. 274 'Sublethal genes' are those which produce malformations compatible with life in the uterus but responsible for death soon after birth.

Hence **sub'lethally** *adv.*

1958 *Science* 4 July 32 (*heading*) Delayed deaths in sublethally X-rayed F_1 hybrid mice injected with parental strain spleen cells. 1978 *Nature* 13 Apr. 625/2 Sub-lethally irradiated adult BALB/c mice.

†**suble'vaminous**, *a. Obs.* [f. L. **sublevāmin-*, *-āmen*, f. *sublevāre* (see SUBLEVE).] Supporting, sustaining.

1661 FELTHAM *Resolves* II. ii. 177 God..by his upholding and sub-levaminous Providence..governs all.

†**'sublevate**, *pa. pple. Obs.* [ad. L. *sublevātus*, pa. pple. of *sublevāre* (see SUBLEVE).] Raised, exalted.

1523 FITZHERB. *Husb.* (1525) 60 His hart..alway subleuate & lyfte vp to god in heuen.

† **'sublevate**, *v. Obs.* [f. L. *sublevāt-*, pa. ppl. stem of *sublevāre* (see next).]

1. *trans.* To raise, lift up, elevate.

1597 A. M. *Guillemeau's Fr. Chirurg.* 15 b/2 The groundedrawer, to subleuate out of the hoale, the Trepanede bone. **1613** JACKSON *Creed* II. 343 Whether God..cannot..by..subleuating their dull capacitie by facilitie and plentie of externall meanes, repaire whatsoeuer the iniuries of time. **1656** BLOUNT *Glossogr.*, *Sublevate*, to lift or hold up; Also to help, aid, ease, lighten or lessen. **1657** *Physical Dict.*, *Sublevated*, carried upward, as the vapors and spirits in distilation, or the dew when the sun riseth.

2. To sublimate.

1657 TOMLINSON *Renou's Disp.* 90 Which serves for distilling those things which are easily sublevated.

† **suble'vation.** *Obs.* [f. L. *sublevātio, -ōnem*, n. of action f. *sublevāre* (see next).]

1. The action of raising or lifting; elevation; also, a particular point of elevation or height.

1556 in Robinson *More's Utopia* S v b, The iust latitude therof, that is to say,..the subleuation or height of the pole in that region. **1658** PHILLIPS, *Sublevation*, a lifting up; also a helping, or easing. **1708** KEILL *Anim. Secret.* 179 The Remainder doubled gives 186 the Sublevation of the Weight Z.

2. A rising, revolt.

1613–18 DANIEL *Coll. Hist. Eng.* (1626) 32 Nothing could be done..but by a generall subleuation of the people. **1650** HOWELL *Giraffi's Rev. Naples* I. 9 Although the Nobility was then joyn'd with the people, that Sublevation was not very hurtfull. **1699** TEMPLE *Hist. Eng.* 211 The..Insurrections of the Nobles in England..were not followed by any general Commotion or Sublevation of the People.

† **subleve**, *v. Obs. rare*[−1]. [ad. L. *sublevāre*, f. *sub-* SUB- 26 + *levāre* to raise, lift, f. *levis* light.] *trans.* To succour.

1542 *St. Papers Hen. VIII*, IX. 188 *note*, He hath chef hope to be sublevid of somme smal reward by Your regal Mageste.

,sub-lieu'tenant. [SUB- 6. Cf. F. *sous-lieutenant*.]

1. An army officer ranking next to a lieutenant; formerly, an officer in certain regiments of the British Army, corresponding to the ensign in others.

1702–11 *Milit. & Sea Dict.* (ed. 4) I, *Sub-Brigadier*, *Sub-Lieutenant*, and the like, are Under-Officers appointed for the Ease of those over them of the same Denomination. Sub-Lieutenants of Foot take their Post at the Head of the Pikes. **1730** BAILEY (folio), *Sub-lieutenant*, an Officer in Regiments of Fusileers, where there are no Ensigns. **1736** *Milit. Hist. Pr. Eugene & Marlb.* I. 111 A Sub-Lieutenant of the Grenadiers of Geschwind. **1837** CARLYLE *Fr. Rev.* I. VII. vii, A patriotic Sub-lieutenant set a pistol to his ear.

2. An officer in the British Navy ranking next below a lieutenant. Formerly called *mate*.

1804 *Naval Chron.* XII. 510 A new Class of Officers, to be called Sub-Lieutenants, are to be appointed, selected from Midshipmen who have served their time. **1869** *Times* 15 Oct., That every midshipman or sub-lieutenant, on returning from his first long cruise, should pass not less than a year in a place of naval study. **1898** KIPLING *Fleet in Being* ii, By the time he has reached his majority a Sub-Lieutenant should have seen enough to sober Ulysses.

Hence **sub-lieu'tenancy**, the position or rank of a sub-lieutenant.

1837 CARLYLE *Fr. Rev.* II. II. ii, To such height of Sub-lieutenancy has he now got promoted, from Brienne School. **1893** F. F. MOORE *I Forbid Banns* liv, Charlie Barham passed a creditable examination for a sub-lieutenancy.

† **'subligate**, *v. Obs.* [f. L. *subligāt-*, pa. ppl. stem of *subligāre*, f. *sub-* SUB- 2 + *ligāre* to bind, tie.] Also **subli'gation.** (See quots.)

1656 BLOUNT *Glossogr.*, *Subligate*, to under-bind, to under-tye, to tye or hang at. **1658** PHILLIPS, *Subligation*, a binding, or tying underneath.

subligation, erron. form of SUPPLICATION.

1600 *Return fr. Parnass.* IV. i. 1249 The parish have put up a subligation against you.

sublimable (sə'blaɪməb(ə)l), *a.* Now *rare.* [f. SUBLIME *v.* + -ABLE.] Capable of sublimation or of being sublimated.

1666 BOYLE *Orig. Formes & Qual.* (1667) 128, I had subdivided the body of Gold into such minute particles that they were sublimable. *a* **1691** —— *Hist. Air* (1692) 47, I found the Salt it self to be sublimable. **1753** *Chambers' Cycl.* Suppl. s.v., They say that only those things are sublimable, which contain a dry exhalable matter in their original construction. **1869** PHILLIPS *Vesuv.* v. 152 [Ferric oxide] is not known to be sublimable per se.

Hence **su'blimableness**, the quality of being sublimable.

1661 BOYLE *Scept. Chym.* (1680) 391 He soon obtain'd such another Concrete, both as to tast and smell, and easie sublimableness as common Salt Armoniack.

† **su'blimary**, *a. Obs. rare*[−1]. [f. L. *sublīm-is* SUBLIME + -ARY[1].] Elevated, exalted.

a **1652** BROME *Painter's Ent.* ii, First to the Master of the feast, This health is consecrated; Thence to each sublimary guest. **1655** M. CARTER *Honor Rediv.* (1660) 2 Some men he hath..elevated..with the sublimary glories of Honor, Nobility, and Greatness.

sublimate ('sʌblɪmət), *sb.* [ad. L. *sublīmātum*, neut. pa. pple. (used subst. in med.L.) of *sublīmāre* to SUBLIME.]

1. A solid product of sublimation, *esp.* in the form of a compact crystalline cake.

a **1626** BACON *Art. Enq. Metals* (1669) 225 To enquire..what Metals endure Subliming; and what Body the Sublimate makes. **1694** SALMON *Bate's Dispens.* (1713) 359/2 In the other Part of the Neck you will have a kind of grey Sublimate. **1726** *Dict. Rust.* (ed. 3), *Sublimate of Arsenick*, is Arsenick corrected or freed from its more malignant Sulphurs, and rais'd to the top of the Matrass by the force of Fire. **1778** PRYCE *Min. Cornub.* 34 The sublimate of our white Mundick..may produce..some of the best white Arsenick. **1819** tr. *Berzelius* in *Ann. Philos.* XIII. 405 The sublimate was pure selenic acid. **1820** FARADAY *Exp. Res.* No. 13. 35 A sublimate of crystals filled the retort. **1869** ROSCOE *Elem. Chem.* 246 Chromic chloride ..is obtained as a sublimate, in beautiful violet crystals. **1894** *Times* 15 Aug. 12/2 The walls are nearly all covered by sublimates or dust that has adhered and crusted them over.

b. *fig.* A refined or concentrated product.

1683 NORRIS *Idea Happin* (1684) 27 Some have..grown mad with the Sublimate of Pleasure. **1872** LIDDON *Elem. Relig.* iii. 92 Man's soul is not a third nature, poised between his spirit and his body; nor yet is it a sublimate of his bodily organization.

2. 'Mercury sublimate'; mercuric chloride (bichloride or perchloride of mercury), a white crystalline powder, which acts as a violent poison.

In early times also used for arsenic (cf. RATSBANE 1).

1543 tr. *Vigo's Chirurg.* Interpr. (1550) AA aj b, Sublimate. Argentum sublimatum is made of Chalcantum, quycke-syluer, vyneger, and sal armoniake. **1594** PLATT *Jewell-h.* I. 10 Suger is a salt, Sublimate is a salt, Saltpeter is a salt. **1605** TIMME *Quersit.* I. vii. 26 White sublimate and arsnic..foster and hide a most burning and deadly fire. **1609** B. JONSON *Silent Wom.* II. ii, Take a little sublimate and goe out of the world, like a rat. *a* **1661** HOLYDAY *Juvenal* (1673) 122 Sublimate makes black the teeth; Cerusse makes gray the hair. **1789** W. BUCHAN *Dom. Med.* (1790) 513 To those whose stomach cannot bear the solution, the sublimate may be given in form of pill. **1842** BORROW *Bible in Spain* xvi, I have more than once escaped..having the wine I drank spiced with sublimate. **1899** *Allbutt's Syst. Med.* VIII. 605 A tar bath, with 15 gr. of sublimate added.

fig. **1633** G. HERBERT *Temple, Ch. Milit.* 132 Nay he became a poet, and would serve His pills of sublimate in that conserve. **1896** tr. *Huysmans' En Route* iii. 37 To cleanse it with the disinfectant of prayer and the sublimate of Sacraments.

b. Now usually ***corrosive sublimate***, formerly † ***sublimate corrosive***.

1685 BOYLE *Salubr. Air* 64 Though Corrosive Sublimate be so mischievous a Mineral Composition, that a few grains may kill a man. **1703** *Phil. Trans.* XXIII. 1325 Sublimate Corrosive. **1842** MACAULAY *Ess., Fredk. Gt.* (1851) II. 690 Pills of corrosive sublimate. **1874** GARROD & BAXTER *Mat. Med.* 103 Calomel is apt to contain a trace of corrosive sublimate.

c. ***sweet sublimate, blue sublimate*** (see quots.).

1725 *Bradley's Family Dict.* s.v., *Sweet Sublimate* is a Corrosive Sublimate, whose Points have been qualify'd by some Preparation. **1728** CHAMBERS *Cycl.* s.v., Sweet Sublimate, is the same with Corrosive, only temper'd and sweeten'd by the Addition of *Mercurius Dulcis*. **1753** *Ibid.* Suppl. s.v., *Blue Sublimate*, a preparation of mercury with some other ingredients, yielding a fine blue for painting.

d. *attrib.*: = containing or impregnated with corrosive sublimate, as ***sublimate bath, gauze, lotion, solution, water.***

1753 J. BARTLET *Gentl. Farriery* xxv. 226 Touch with a caustic, or wash with the sublimate water. **1843** R. J. GRAVES *Syst. Clin. Med.* xxvii. 339 During the year 1827 the venereal patients took..302 sublimate baths. *Ibid.* Corrosive sublimate baths. **1895** *Arnold & Sons' Catal. Surg. Instr.* 726 Sublimate Gauze. **1899** *Allbutt's Syst. Med.* VIII. 870 The parts were then disinfected with sublimate lotion.

3. *Mineral.* The deposit formed on charcoal or in a glass tube, when certain minerals are heated and subjected to the blowpipe.

1842 PARNELL *Chem. Anal.* (1845) 262 Metals. Produce a sublimate on charcoal—antimony; arsenic [etc.]... Give no sublimate on charcoal—mercury; osmium.

† **'sublimate**, *pa. pple.* and *ppl. a. Obs.* Also 5 -lymate, 6 -lemmat, 5, 7 -limat. [ad. L. *sublīmātus*, pa. pple. of *sublīmāre* to SUBLIME.]

A. *pa. pple.* **1.** Raised, elevated, exalted.

1460 CAPGRAVE *Chron.* (Rolls) 93 This man with sedicious knytis was sublimat in the empire. **1492** RYMAN *Poems* vi. 7 in *Arch. Stud. neu. Spr.* LXXXIX. 175 O spowse of Criste immaculate, Aboue alle aungellis sublimate. **1603** HARSNET *Pop. Impost.* 111 According as they are improued, sublimate, and aduaunced by the authority of holy church of Rome. **1612** DRAYTON *Poly-olb.* Notes 15 Some of them were sublimat farre above earthly conceit. **1646** SALTMARSH *Some Drops* ii. 95 This is Perfection and Prelacy sublimate.

2. Sublimated, distilled.

1471 RIPLEY *Comp. Alch.* III. xiv. in Ashm. (1652) 142 Thy Water must be seven tymes Sublymate.

B. *ppl. a.* **1.** ***mercury sublimate*** (occas. ***sublimate mercury***): = SUBLIMATE *sb.* 2.

1562 BULLEIN *Bulwarke, Bk. Simples* 74 With this Quickesiluer and Sal Armoniake, is made Marcurie sublemmat. **1610** B. JONSON *Alch.* II. i, Mercury sublimate, That keepes the whitenesse, hardnesse, and the biting. **1697** HEADRICH *Arcana Philos.* 118 Sublimate Mercury. **1770** *Phil. Trans.* LX. 187 A composition of sublimate mercury,..will prevent insects..from destroying the plumage. **1799** G. SMITH *Laboratory* I. 98 Ground and mixed with sublimate mercury.

2. Refined, purified; elevated, sublime.

1607 R. C[AREW] tr. *Estienne's World of Wonders* Ep. Ded., Others (of a more refined and sublimate temper) can sauour nothing but that which exceeds the vulgar capacitie. *Ibid.* 136 A most sublimate subtiltie. **1613** PURCHAS *Pilgrimage* (1614) 366 Offering her selfe more sublimate and pure, in the sacred name..of Religion. **1648** J. BEAUMONT *Psyche* X. lxv, So sublimate and so refining was That Fire, that all the Gold it turn'd to Dross. **1661** GLANVILL *Van. Dogm.* 124 The corporeal Machine, which even on the most sublimate Intellectuals is dangerously influential. **1676** HALE *Contempl.* II. *Medit. Lord's Pr.* 2 The most Exact Sublimate Wits inscribed their Altar, *To the Unknown God.* **1720** WELTON *Suffer. Son of God* I. x. 231 A Love Sublimate and Refined.

sublimate ('sʌblɪmeɪt), *v.* Also 7 -at. [f. L. *sublīmāt-*, pa. ppl. stem of *sublīmāre* to SUBLIME.]

† **1.** *trans.* To raise to high place, dignity, or honour. = SUBLIME *v.* 7. *Obs.*

c **1566** *Merie Tales of Skelton* in S.'s Wks. (1843) I. p. lxii, He that doth humble hymselfe..shalbe exalted, extoulled, ..or sublimated. **1631** WEEVER *Anc. Funeral Mon.* 868 Felix was..sublimated with an Episcopall Mitre. **1637** BASTWICK *Litany* I. 17 Sometime, forty at once or more, are mounted and sublimated into the high Commission Court. **1637** EARL MONM. tr. *Malvezzi's Rom. & Tarquin* 214 They..would sublimate themselves [orig. *accrescere volunt*] contrary to the will of fortune.

2. a. = SUBLIME *v.* 1. Now *rare.*

1591 PERCIVALL *Sp. Dict.*, *Sublimar*, to sublimate. **1631** BRATHWAIT *Whimzies, Metall-man* 62 Elevate that tripode; sublimate that pipkin; elixate your antimonie. **1651** WITTIE tr. *Primrose's Pop. Err.* IV. iii. 221 Honey thrice sublimated. **1706** PHILLIPS (ed. Kersey). **1858** SIMMONDS *Dict. Trade* 365 *Sublimate*,..to raise volatile substances by heat, and again condense them in a solid form.

b. *gen.* To act upon (a substance) so as to produce a refined product. Often in fig. context.

1601 DOLMAN *La Primaud. Fr. Acad.* III. xc. 401 A maruellous kinde of naturall chimistrie..so to sublimate that which of it selfe is poison. **1638** JACKSON *Creed* IX. xxiv. 169 None..would accuse an Alchimist..for wasting..copper, lead, or brasse, if hee could..sublimate them into pure gold. **1660** BRETT *Threnodia* 12 Tis chymick heat in's bloud doth swim, T'wil sublimate terrestr'al him And so make of a Duke a Cherubim. **1711** SHAFTESB. *Charac.* (1737) I. 134 The original plain principles of humanity..have, by a sort of spiritual chymists, been so sublimated, as to become the highest corrosives. **1747** HERVEY *Medit.* II. 30 December's cold collects the gross Materials, which are sublimated by the refining Warmth of May. **1750** G. HUGHES *Barbados* 32 The heat of the Sun..is so intense..that it sublimates their juices, salts, and spirits to a far greater degree of perfection. **1779** JOHNSON *L.P.*, *Milton* (1868) 71 The heat of Milton's mind may be said to sublimate his learning.

† **3. a.** To extract by or as by sublimation; = SUBLIME *v.* 2. Chiefly *fig. Obs.*

1614 T. ADAMS *Physic Heav.* Wks. (1629) 290 You that haue put so faire for the Philosophers stone, that you haue endeuoured to sublimate it out of poore mens bones, ground to powder by your oppressions. **1626** J. YATES *Ibis ad Cæsarem* II. 33 Words ænigmaticall, sublimated in the furnace of his owne braine. **1644** MILTON *Areop.* 9 It will be a harder alchymy then Lullius ever knew, to sublimat any good use out of such an invention.

b. *pass.* and *intr.* To be produced as the result of sublimation.

1682 J. COLLINS *Salt & Fish.* 127 This Salt was formerly found sublimated upon the superficies of the burnt Sands of that Country. **1799** G. SMITH *Laboratory* I. 327 The phosphorus, which in the receiver is sublimated of a yellowish colour. **1800** tr. *Lagrange's Chem.* I. 429 Towards the end of the operation, a little sulphur is sublimated. **1866** LAWRENCE tr. *Cotta's Rocks Classified* 74 Sulphur..sublimates in matrass. **1872** J. YEATS *Techn. Hist. Comm.* 321 Reducing the ore to powder, and afterwards by roasting it till the sulphur was sublimated. **1897** *Allbutt's Syst. Med.* II. 884 The chief part of this [morphia] literally burned and not sublimated at all.

4. a. To exalt or elevate *to* a high or higher state; = SUBLIME *v.* 4 c.

1599 B. JONSON *Cynthia's Rev.* (1616) I. iii, Knowing my selfe an essence so sublimated, and refin'd by trauell. **1600** W. WATSON *Decacordon* (1602) 97 A man in whose very countenance was pourtraid out a map of politicall gouernment.., sublimated with a reuerend maiestie in his lookes. **1614** JACKSON *Creed* III. IV. v. §8 This absolute submission of their consciences..sublimates them from refined Heathenisme or Gentilisme to diabolisme. **1673** *Lady's Calling* I. 32 This is it which sublimates and spiritualizes humanity. **1682** *Lond. Gaz.* No. 1711/4 Sedition and Rebellion, sublimated to the heighth, and as the very Extract of Disorder and Anarchy. **1781** HAYLEY *Tri. Temper* v. 288 Here grief and joy so suddenly unite, That anguish serves to sublimate delight. **1869** LECKY *Europ. Mor.* II. 295 Moral ideas in a thousand forms have been sublimated, enlarged and changed. **1884** AUG. J. E. WILSON *Vashti* x, Forced to lose faith in her..capacity to sublimate her erring nature.

b. *ironical.*

1822 in W. Cobbett *Rur. Rides* I. 89 The unnatural working of the paper-system has sublimated him out of his senses.

5. a. To transmute *into* something higher, nobler, more sublime or refined; = SUBLIME *v.* 5.

1624 [SCOTT] *Vox Regis* To Rdr. p. iv, It expresseth strength to haue words sublimated into works. **1672** STERRY *Serm.* (1710) II. 275 Holiness exalts and sublimates a Man into Spirit. **1676** HALE *Contempl.* II. 63 The Heart becomes ..the very sink..of all the Impure desires of the Flesh, where they are..sublimated into Impurities, more exquisite [etc.]. *a* **1708** BEVERIDGE *Priv. Th.* I. (1730) 159 By sublimating good Thoughts into good Affections. **1858** FROUDE *Hist. Eng.* IV. xviii. 59 Their understandings were too direct to sublimate absurdities into mysteries. **1884**

Contemp. Rev. Feb. 262 Sublimating into an ideal sentiment what..had been little more than an animal appetite.

b. *intr.* for *pass.* = SUBLIME *v.* 5 b.

1852 BRIMLEY *Ess.* (1858) 266 If Miss Rebecca Sharpe had really been..a matchless beauty,..she might have sublimated into a Beatrix Esmond.

c. *trans.* in *Psychoanal.* To refine or direct (instinctual energy), esp. that of the sexual impulse, so that it is manifested in more socially acceptable ways. Also *absol.* and *intr.*

1910 J. J. PUTNAM in A. A. Brill tr. *Freud's Three Contrib. Sexual Theory* p. vii, The instincts with which every child is born..may be refined ('sublimated')..into energies of other sorts. **1916** C. E. LONG tr. *Jung's Coll. Papers Anal. Psychol.* 141 Here we are confronted by an energetic effort to sublimate the fear into an eager desire for knowledge. **1921** R. MACAULAY *Dangerous Ages* vi. 112 You have some bad complexes, which must be sublimated. **1953** J. STRACHEY et al. tr. *Freud's Compl. Psychol. Wks.* VII. 50 The perversions ..—by being 'sublimated'—are destined to provide the energy for a great number of our cultural achievements. **1967** M. L. KING *Trumpet of Conscience* iv. 69 This rare opportunity for bloodletting was sublimated into arson. **1974** 'S. WOODS' *Done to Death* 195 If she had guilt feelings ..she might have sublimated them this way.

absol. and *intr.* **1933** J. JASTROW *House that Freud Built* vi. 136 We sublimate as we grow in psychic stature. **1955** H. HARTMANN in A. Freud *Psychoanal. Study of Child* X. 12 Melanie Klein..equates the capacity to cathect ego activities with libido with the capacity to sublimate. **1973** H. MCLEAVE *Question of Negligence* xxiii. 183 Some boy jilted her..thirty years ago. Now she sublimates like mad and expends all her pent-up emotion on her patients.

6. To refine away *into* something unreal or non-existent; to reduce to unreality.

1836-7 SIR W. HAMILTON *Metaph.* xxiii. (1859) II. 79 The materialist may now derive the subject from the object, the idealist derive the object from the subject, the absolutist sublimate both into indifference. **1867** *Morn. Star* 29 Jan., We are too much given to sublimate official responsibility until it becomes impalpable to ordinary senses. **1869** LECKY *Europ. Mor.* I. 342 While he..sublimated the popular worship into a harmless symbolism. **1910** W. S. PALMER *Diary Modernist* 264 A spiritual body is for him sublimated out of reality.

Hence **'sublimating** *vbl. sb.* and *ppl. a.*

1611 COTGR., *Sublimation*, a sublimating, raising, or lifting vp. **1612** W. PARKES *Curtaine-Dr.* 41 O this body of ours..what time doe wee bestow in the garnishment of the same (and especially our woemen)..in *Pomatums* for their skinnes, in *Fucusses* for their faces, by sublimatinge, and mercury. **1840** POE *Balloon Hoax* Wks. 1865 I. 97, I can conceive nothing more sublimating than the strange peril and novelty of an adventure such as this. **1913** E. JONES *Papers on Psycho-Anal.* xx. 416 (*heading*) The value of sublimating processes for education and re-education. **1923** J. S. HUXLEY *Ess. Biologist* vii. 276 Dominant ideas at work in the sublimating process.

sublimated ('sʌblɪmeɪtɪd), *ppl. a.* [f. prec. + -ED[1].]

1. a. Produced by sublimation.

1605 TIMME *Quersit.* II. v. 125 Then shal yee see the sublimated matter cleauing to the sides of the glasses. **1631** *Celestina* I. 16 Shee made sublimated Mercury. **1800** tr. *Lagrange's Chem.* I. 180 Half a part of sublimated sulphur. **1816** J. SMITH *Panorama Sci. & Art* II. 296 Sublimated metallic oxides.

†**b.** Mixed or compounded with corrosive sublimate (or arsenic). *Obs.*

1611 COTGR., *Sublimé*.. sublimated, or mixed with Arsenicke. **1631** MASSINGER *Believe as You List* II. i, A sublimated pill of mercurie.

2. *fig.* **a.** Of persons and immaterial things: Exalted, elevated; raised to a high degree of purity or excellence; lofty, sublime.

1599 SANDYS *St. Relig.* (1605) H 2 b, Of a more refined & sublimated temper, then that their country conceits can satisfie. **1612** DRAYTON *Poly-olb.* iv. 266 In words, whose weight best sute a sublimated straine. **1654** OWEN *Saints' Persev.* vii. 171 These latter, more refined, sublimated mercuriall wits. **1708** *Brit. Apollo* No. 105. 1/1 The Refin'd, the Sublimated precepts of the Gospel. *a* **1763** SHENSTONE *Economy* I. 122 Ye tow'ring minds! ye sublimated souls! **1812** JEFFERSON *Writ.* (1830) IV. 176 A sublimated impartiality, at which the world will laugh. **1823** LAMB *Guy Faux* in *Eliana* (1867) 19 Swallowing the dregs of Loyola for the very quintessence of sublimated reason. **1876** MISS BRADDON *Haggard's Dau.* xiii, Is this love, or only a sublimated friendship? **1901** R. GARNETT *Ess.* iii. 84 Poetry is neither exalted utility nor sublimated intellect.

†**b.** Puffed up, haughty. *Obs.*

1634 SIR T. HERBERT *Trav.* 130 The Kings of Pegu [etc.] are so sublimated, that when an Ambassadour comes before them, they must doe it creeping.

c. Condensed, concentrated. *rare.*

1884 *Harper's Mag.* Sept. 557/2 Paris is France, and Trouville a sublimated Paris.

3. Of physical things: Purified, refined, rarefied. *rare.*

a **1676** HALE *Prim. Orig. Man.* IV. ii. 297 The Æther, which is but a purer sublimated Air. **1860** MAURY *Phys. Geog.* i. 9 The sublimated air, diffusing itself by its mobility. **1862** MISS BRADDON *Lady Audley* xix, A sublimated meat that could scarcely have grown upon any mundane sheep.

4. *Psychoanal.* Of a (sexual) instinct, feeling, etc.: that has been refined and made more socially acceptable.

1911 *Amer. Jrnl. Psychol.* XXII. 436 If the transference is successful, be it a purely erotic feeling, or a sublimated one of respect.., there springs up the feeling of sympathy. **1923** J. S. HUXLEY *Ess. Biologist* vii. 271 A sublimated instinct has more and higher values attached to its satisfaction than one unsublimated. **1951** E. JONES *Ess. in Applied Psychol.* II. xiii. 320 A given sublimated interest..may represent one of the described stages. **1966** G. ONN tr. *Wyss's Depth Psychol.* I. ii. 194 Sublimated ideas may also temporarily sink back into the unconscious, regress and become symbols of complexes.

sublimation (sʌblɪ'meɪʃən). Also 4-5 **-acion**, 5 **-lym-**, **-acioun**, **-acyon**. [a. F. *sublimation* (from 14th c.), or ad. late L. *sublīmātio*, *-ōnem*, n. of action f. *sublīmāre* to SUBLIME. Cf. It. *sublimazione*, Sp. *sublimacion*, Pg. *sublimação.*]

1. a. The chemical action or process of subliming or converting a solid substance by means of heat into vapour, which resolidifies on cooling.

1390 GOWER *Conf.* II. 86 He mot..kepe in his entencion The point of sublimacion. *c* **1400** *Lanfranc's Cirurg.* 351 This is þe maner of sublimacioun, loke þou haue a strong vessel maad of glas þat it mowe dure in þe fier [etc.]. **1460-70** *Bk. Quinte Essence* 4 þe quint essencia þerof is naturaly incorruptible þe which ȝe schal drawe out by sublymacioun. **1594** PLAT *Jewell-ho.* III. 89 Distillations, calcinations, and sublimations. **1605** TIMME *Quersit.* I. vii. 28 The common armoniac..in the forme of most white and salt meale, may be carried up into the cloudes by sublimation. **1657** *Physical Dict.*, *Sublimation*, is a chymical operation, when the elevated matter in distillation, being carried to the highest part of the helm, and finding no passage forth, sticks to the sides thereof. **1719** QUINCY *Phys. Dict.* (1722) 414 The Sublimation of Camphire, Benzoin, and Arsenick. **1816** J. SMITH *Panorama Sci. & Art* II. 302 Sublimation is to dry matters, what distillation is to humid ones. **1867** BLOXAM *Chem.* 114 These crystals are moderately heated in an iron pan to deprive them of tar, and are finally purified by sublimation. **1880** STORY-MASKELYNE in *Nature* XXI. 204 It is possible..that the condition for its [viz. carbon's] sublimation in the form of crystals..is one involving a combination of high temperature and high pressure.

attrib. **1896** *Jrnl. Chem. Soc.* LXX. II. 635 Sublimation Temperatures in the Cathode-Light Vacuum. *Ibid.* 636 The sublimation tension of iodine at various temperatures.

b. *Geol.* Applied to a (supposed) analogous process by which minerals are thrown up in a state of vapour from the interior of the earth and deposited nearer its surface.

1829 *Phil. Mag.* Mar. 174 The conjecture, that galena in these veins has been in some instances supplied by sublimation from below. **1879** *Encycl. Brit.* X. 260/2.

attrib. **1881** RAYMOND *Mining Gloss.*, *Sublimation-theory*, the theory that a vein was filled first with metallic vapors. **1894** FOSTER *Ore & Stone Mining* 17 One great objection to the universal acceptance of the sublimation theory is that many of the minerals found in lodes would be decomposed at high temperatures. **1902** WEBSTER *Suppl.*, *Sublimation vein*,..a vein formed by condensation of material from the condition of vapor.

c. (The condition of) being in the form of vapour as the result of sublimation.

1808 *Med. Jrnl.* XIX. 12 Lead..taken in a state of sublimation into the lungs. **1856** PAGE *Adv. Text-bk. Geol.* xvi. 304 Products which issue in a state of sublimation from the craters of active volcanoes.

2. A solid substance deposited as the result of the cooling of vapour arising from sublimation or a similar process.

1646 SIR T. BROWNE *Pseud. Ep.* II. iv. 82 A fat and unctuous sublimation in the earth concreted and fixed by salt and nitrous spirits. **1652** BENLOWES *Theoph.* XIII. xxxvi, From pretious Limbeck sacred Loves distill Such Sublimations, as do fill Mindes with amazed Raptures of their Chimick Skill. **1867** J. HOGG *Microsc.* I. iii. 214 Dr. Guy brought under the notice of microscopists a plan for preserving metallic sublimations. **1869** PHILLIPS *Vesuv.* v. 152 Fenic chloride (muriate of iron) is found among the sublimations of Vesuvius. **1892** *Daily News* 3 Sept. 6/5 A magnificent lava-grotto all coated with beautiful sulphuric sublimations.

†**3.** = SUBLATION I. *Obs.*

1547 RECORDE *Urinal Phys.* (1651) 16 If it [*sc.* sediment] be so light, that it swim in the middle region of the urine, then it is called the sublimation or swim. **1625** HART *Anat. Urines* I. iii. 34 The urine in this disease was..variable and inconstant in the swimme and sublimation.

†**4.** Elevation to high rank. *Obs.*

c **1440** *Alphabet of Tales* 234 A hertelie ioy..þat he tuke when he hard tell of þe sublimacion of his fadur.

5. a. Elevation to a higher state or plane of existence; transmutation into something higher, purer, or more sublime.

1615 JACKSON *Creed* IV. III. viii. § 5 By the assistance of that grace whose infusion alone must worke the sublimation. *a* **1652** J. SMITH *Sel. Disc.* VII. iv. (1821) 334 That perfection of which they speak..was nothing else but a mere sublimation of their own natural powers and principles. **1764** REID *Inquiry* vii. 206 The new system by a kind of metaphysical sublimation converted all the qualities of matter into sensations. **1824** JEFFERSON *Writ.* (1830) IV. 387 Every individual of my associates will look..to the sublimation of its [the University's] character. **1866** F. HARPER *Peace through Truth* 299 This supernatural sublimation of man's nature.

b. An elated or ecstatic state of mind.

1816 T. L. PEACOCK *Headlong Hall* v, That enthusiastic sublimation which is the source of greatness and energy. **1884** *Harper's Mag.* LXIX. 469 The world has long sought an antidote to seasickness... It is sublimation. **1891** HARDY *Tess* xliii, Tess's unassisted power of dreaming..being enough for her sublimation at present, she declined except the merest sip.

c. *Psychoanal.* The refining of instinctual energy, esp. that of the sexual impulse, and its manifestation in ways that are socially more acceptable.

1910 A. A. BRILL tr. *Freud's Three Contrib. Sexual Theory* 58 It must be through these roads that the attraction of the sexual motive powers to other than sexual aims, the sublimation of sexuality, is accomplished. **1920** B. LOW *Outl. Psycho-Anal.* (ed. 2) iii. 81 If the sublimation-process can afford an adequate outlet for the psychic energy accompanying the primitive desires, we achieve a fairly satisfactory adjustment. **1925** I. A. RICHARDS *Princ. Lit. Crit.* xxxi. 232 If we do not extend the 'sublimation' theory too far..it may be granted that in some cases the explanation is in place. **1943** H. READ *Educ. through Art* vi. 177 Sublimation is thus the transformation of instinctive egoistic drives, wishes and desires onto socially useful or socially approved thoughts, ideals and activities. **1957** G. FABER *Jowett* v. 84 [His] extraordinary energy..may, perhaps, have been derived..from a perpetual 'sublimation' of the energy which most men release in acts of sex. **1977** R. L. WOLFF *Gains & Losses* vii. 404 *Zoe*..is the first novel to sound the notes which novelists were so often to repeat. Scepticism of Christian evidences, sublimation of doubt in sex, [etc.].

6. a. The result of such elevation or transmutation; the purest or most concentrated product (*of*); the highest stage or point (*of*); a height (*of*).

1691 *d'Emiliane's Frauds Rom. Monks* (ed. 3) 287 That they may authorize their neat Thoughts and high Sublimations of Wit. *a* **1693** SOUTH *Serm.* (1727) II. 199 It is (as it were) the very Quintessence and Sublimation of Vice, by which (as in the Spirit of Liquors) the Malignity of many Actions is contracted into a little Compass. **1828** DE QUINCEY *Rhet.* Wks. 1862 X. 39 The last sublimation of dialectical subtlety. **1831** D. E. WILLIAMS *Life Sir T. Lawrence* II. 37 The truth, the whole truth, and nothing but the truth, must be the sublimation aspired to. **1856** MISS MULOCK *John Halifax* xi, His demeanour..was the sublimation of all manly courtesy. **1863** MISS BRADDON *Eleanor's Vict.* xxiv, A woman's love is the sublimation of.. selfishness. **1874** HARDY *Far fr. Madding Crowd* xl, That acme and sublimation of all dismal sounds, the bark of a fox.

b. *Psychoanal.* The result of the refinement or transmutation of sexual or instinctual energy.

1926 *Internat. Jrnl. Psycho-Anal.* VII. 44 Thus Leonardo's genital activity..was wholly merged in his sublimations. **1955** H. HARTMANN in A. Freud *Psychoanal. Study of Child* X. 13 We know much more about the origin of specific contents of sublimations. **1973** *Jrnl. Genetic Psychol.* Mar. 153 It is out of the basic societal repression/inhibition of drives that sublimations are born.

Hence **subli'mational** *a.*

1934 in WEBSTER. **1935** *Mind* XLIV. 348 Sublimational, substitutional or Changeling psychology may be Freudian, but it surely is not the only 'scientific' psychology. **1943** A. HUXLEY *Let.* 4 Mar. (1969) 487 A revival of cerebrotonic philosophy in some..form, with a practical system of sublimational outlets, seems to be the only hope.

†**'sublimator.** *Obs. rare*[−1]. [f. SUBLIMATE *v.*: see -ATOR.] A thing which sublimates.

1752 *Phil. Trans.* XLVII. 549 The atmosphere of the earth is a more powerful sublimator than those of our chemists.

†**sublimatory**, *sb.* *Obs.* [ad. med.L. *sublīmātōrium*, neut. of *sublīmātōrius* (see next). Cf. F. *sublimatoire.*] A vessel used for sublimation, a subliming-pot.

c **1386** CHAUCER *Can. Yeom. T.* Preamb. 74 Oure.. descensories, Violes, crosletz, and sublymatories, Cucurbites, and Alambikes eek. **1584** R. SCOT *Discov. Witchcr.* XIV. i. 295. **1605** TIMME *Quersit.* II. v. 125 Smal long lymbeckes in forme of a sublimatorie. **1662** R. MATHEW *Unl. Alch.* 177 Grind them wel together, put them into a Sublimatory of good glass. **1694** SALMON *Bate's Dispens.* (1713) 484/2 The Volatile Sal-Armoniack is only the Volatile parts sublimed alone..the Acid..remaining behind at bottom of the Sublimatory.

sublimatory (stress variable), *a.* [ad. med.L. *sublīmātōrius*, f. *sublīmāt-*: see SUBLIMATE and -ORY[2].]

†**1.** Suitable for subliming. *Obs.*

1605 TIMME *Quersit.* II. v. 125 Thou shalt increase the fire ..until..the fire bee made sublimatorie.

†**2.** Used in sublimation. *Obs.*

1650 ASHMOLE *Chym. Coll.* 66 Take the pregnant Earth, and put it into a Sublimatory vessell luted and well shut up. **1666** BOYLE *Orig. Formes & Qual.* (1667) 240 Though these [sulphur, mercury, and vermilion] will rise together in Sublimatory Vessels.

3. *Psychoanal.* Pertaining to sublimation of instinctual energy or of the sexual drive.

1943 A. STRACHEY *New Ger.-Eng. Psycho-Anal. Vocab.* 66 Relating to sublimation; sublimatory. E.g...sublimatory processes. **1955** H. HARTMANN in A. Freud *Psychoanal. Study of Child* X. 16 We will tend to see in sublimation..a continuous process which..does not exclude temporary increases or decreases in sublimatory activities. **1968** *Psychoanal. Rev.* LV. 10 This concrete orientation occurred along with a reduced capacity for fantasy release or other sublimatory behavior. **1981** *Internat. Jrnl. Psychoanalytic Psychotherapy* VIII. 461 The newly liberated creative capacity permitted an important sublimatory release.

‖**subli'matum.** *Obs.* [neut. of L. *sublīmātus*: see SUBLIMATE *a.*] Corrosive sublimate.

1577 FRAMPTON *Joyfull News* 18 In the salt Fleume, he shall put with a Feather, a little of the water of Sublimatum. **1590** GREENE *Never too late* Wks. (Grosart) VIII. 16 Some sores cannot be cured but by Sublimatum. **1611** [see SUBLIMY].

sublime (sə'blaɪm), *a.* and *sb.* [ad. L. *sublīmis*, prob. f. *sub* up to + *līmen* lintel. Cf. F., It., Sp., Pg. *sublime.*] **A.** *adj.*

1. Set or raised aloft, high up. *arch.*

(*a*) in predicative use.

1604 R. CAWDREY *Table Alph.*, *Sublime*, set on high, lift vp. **1638** SIR T. HERBERT *Trav.* (ed. 2) 33 The element grew dreadfull,..the sea sublime and wrathfull. **1667** MILTON *P.L.* VI. 771 Hee on the wings of Cherub rode sublime On the Crystallin Skie. **1697** DRYDEN *Virg. Georg.* I. 331 Two Poles turn round the Globe... The first sublime in Heav'n, the last is whirl'd Below the Regions of the nether World. **1725** POPE *Odyss.* v. 212 Build the rising ship, Sublime to bear thee o'er the gloomy deep. **1784** COWPER *Task* I. 203 Cawing rooks, and kites that swim sublime In still repeated circles. **1842** TENNYSON *Vision of Sin* 103 To fly sublime Thro' the courts, the camps, the schools.

fig. **1646** SIR T. BROWNE *Pseud. Ep.* IV. i, Not..to gape, or look upward with the eye, but to have his thoughts sublime. **1786** BURNS *To J. S***** iv, My fancy yerket up sublime Wi' hasty summon.

(*b*) In attrib. use; †contextually = highest, top.

1612 WOODALL *Surg. Mate* (1639) 274 Sublimation is when that which is extracted is driven to the sublime part of the vessell. **1638** SIR T. HERBERT *Trav.* (ed. 2) 183 The sublime height did not disanimate us, as did the danger of descending. **1695** PRIOR *Ode to King* xi. Let Thy sublime Meridian Course For Mary's setting Rays attone. **1784** COWPER *Task* III. 157 Travel nature up To the sharp peak of her sublimest height. **1873** BROWNING *Red Cott. Nt.-cap* 239 A sublime spring from the balustrade About the tower.

b. Of the arms: Uplifted, upraised.

1754 GRAY *Progr. Poesy* 38 With arms sublime, that float upon the air.

c. Of flight; only in fig. context with implication of senses 4–7.

1684 BURNET tr. *More's Utopia* Pref. A4 We were beginning to fly into a sublime pitch, of a strong but false Rhetorick. **1838** EMERSON *Addr.* Wks. (Bohn) II. 193 In the sublimest flights of the soul, rectitude is never surmounted.

d. *Anat.* Of muscles: Lying near the surface, superficial. Also applied to the branch of anatomy treating of superficial muscles.

1855 DUNGLISON *Med. Lex.* **1891** *Century Dict.* s.v., The sublime flexor of the fingers (the flexor sublimis, a muscle).

2. Of buildings, etc.: Rising to a great height, lofty, towering. *arch.*

1635 HEYWOOD *Hierarchy* VIII. 532 Thunders at the sublimest buildings aime. **1657** BILLINGSLY *Brachy-Martyrol.* xxviii. 102 He'd rost her quick, and after throw her down From the sublimest tower in the town. **1799** in *Spirit Publ. Jrnls.* III. 322 Sublime their artless locks they wear. **1817** MOORE *Lalla Rookh* 209 Those towers sublime, That seem'd above the grasp of Time.

3. Of lofty bearing or aspect; in a bad sense, haughty, proud. Chiefly *poet.*

1596 SPENSER *F.Q.* v. viii. 30 The proud Souldan with presumpteous cheare, And countenance sublime and insolent. *a* **1639** WOTTON in *Reliq.* (1651) 171 His Limbs rather sturdy then dainty: Sublime and almost Tumorous in His Looks and Gestures. **1667** MILTON *P.L.* IV. 300 His fair large Front and Eye sublime declar'd Absolute rule. *Ibid.* XI. 236 Not terrible,..nor sociably mild,..But solemn and sublime. **1759** JOHNSON *Rasselas* xxxix, He was sublime without haughtiness, courteous without formality. **1844** MRS. BROWNING *Vis. Poets* c, There, Shakespeare, on whose forehead climb The crowns o' the world. Oh, eyes sublime, With tears and laughters for all time!

†**b.** Exalted in feeling, elated. *Obs.*

1667 MILTON *P.L.* X. 536 Sublime with expectation. **1671** —— *Samson* 1669 While thir hearts were jocund and sublime, Drunk with Idolatry, drunk with Wine.

4. Of ideas, truths, subjects, etc.: Belonging to the highest regions of thought, reality, or human activity. †Also *occas.* said of the thinker.

1634 MILTON *Comus* 785 Thou hast nor Eare, nor Soul to apprehend The sublime notion, and high mystery. **1647** H. MORE *Song of Soul* I. To Rdr. C2 The contemplation of these things is very sublime and subtile. **1674** PLAYFORD *Skill Mus.* (ed. 7) Pref. A4b, This [art] of Musick is the most sublime and excellent for its wonderfull Effects and Inventions. *a* **1721** KEILL *Maupertius' Diss.* (1734) 11 Let us leave it to sublimer Philosophers to search into the Cause of this Tendency. **1724** A. COLLINS *Gr. Chr. Relig.* 233 They despised the literal sense of the Old Testament, and employed their invention to find out sublime senses thereof. **1781** COWPER *Conversat.* 548 What are ages and the lapse of time, Match'd against truths, as lasting as sublime? **1819** KEATS *Fall Hyperion* I. 173 Whether his labours be sublime or low. **1848** MARIOTTI *Italy* II. iii. 82 The sublimest theories of divine doctrine. **1849** MACAULAY *Hist. Eng.* iii. I. 412 The most sublime departments of natural philosophy. *a* **1853** ROBERTSON *Lect.* (1858) 254 England's sublimer battle cry of 'Duty'.

†**b.** Of geometry: see quots. *Obs.*

1728 CHAMBERS *Cycl.* s.v. *Geometry*, The Higher, or Sublimer Geometry is that employ'd in the consideration of Curve Lines, Conic Sections, and Bodies form'd thereof. **1842** *Penny Cycl.* XXIII. 186/1 The term *sublime geometry* was technical, meaning the higher parts of geometry, in which the infinitesimal calculus or something equivalent was employed.

5. Of persons, their attributes, feelings, actions: Standing high above others by reason of nobility or grandeur of nature or character; of high intellectual, moral, or spiritual level. Passing into a term of high commendation: Supreme, perfect.

1643 BURROUGHES *Exp. 1st 3 ch. Hosea* vii. 385 Others are of more sublime spirits naturally, as if they were borne for great things. **1663** S. PATRICK *Parab. Pilgrim* (1687) 218 Nor is there any delight so noble and sublime, so pure and refined. *a* **1715** BURNET *Own Time* (1724) I. 215 He..was a very perfect friend, and a most sublime Christian. **1794** MRS. RADCLIFFE *Myst. Udolpho* xv, Emily's eyes filled with tears of admiration and sublime devotion. **1821** SHELLEY *Adonais* v, Others more sublime..Have sunk, extinct in their refulgent prime. **1838** LONGF. *Lt. Stars* ix, Thou shalt know..how sublime a thing it is To suffer and be strong. **1842** *Penny Cycl.* XXIII. 188/2 Lear, who appeals to the heavens, 'for they are old' like him, is sublime, from the very intensity of his sufferings and his passions. Lady Macbeth is sublime from the intensity of her will. **1852** TENNYSON *Ode Death Wellington* 34 And, as the greatest only are, In his simplicity sublime. **1872** GEO. ELIOT in Cross *Life* (1886) III. 159 Mr. Lewes makes a martyr of himself in writing all my notes and business letters. Is not that being a sublime husband?

b. *colloq.* with ironical force.

Mod. He has a sublime sense of his own importance. This is a sublime piece of impertinence.

6. Of language, style, or a writer: Expressing lofty ideas in a grand and elevated manner.

1586 A. DAY *Engl. Secretorie* I. (1595) 10 We do find three sorts [*sc.* of the style of epistles]..to haue bene generally commended. Sublime, the highest and stateliest maner, and loftiest deliuerance of any thing that may be, expressing the heroicall and mighty actions of Kings [etc.]. **1690** TEMPLE *Ess.* II. *Poetry* 19 It must be confessed, that Homer was..the vastest, the sublimest, and the most wonderful Genius. *a* **1718** PRIOR *Better Answer* vii, As He was a Poet sublimer than Me. **1728** CHAMBERS *Cycl.* s.v., The sublime Style necessarily requires big and magnificent Words; but the Sublime may be found in a single Thought, a single Figure, a single Turn of Words. **1756** WARTON *Ess. Pope* I. 18 Every excellence, more peculiarly appropriated to the sublimer ode. **1782** V. KNOX *Ess.* xv. (1819) I. 89 The Bible, the Iliad, and Shakspeare's works, are allowed to be the sublimest books that the world can exhibit. **1817** COLERIDGE *Biogr. Lit.* xvi. (1907) II. 22 The sublime Dante. **1839** DE QUINCEY *Milton* Wks. 1857 VII. 319 Whether he can cite any other book than the 'Paradise Lost', as continuously sublime, or sublime even by its prevailing character.

7. Of things in nature and art: Affecting the mind with a sense of overwhelming grandeur or irresistible power; calculated to inspire awe, deep reverence, or lofty emotion, by reason of its beauty, vastness, or grandeur.

a **1700** EVELYN *Diary* 12 Nov. 1644, Just before this portico stands a very sublime and stately Corinthian columne. **1762** KAMES *Elem. Crit.* iv. (1833) 110 Great and elevated objects considered with relation to the emotions produced by them, are termed grand and sublime. **1806** *Gazetteer Scot.* (ed. 2) 292 This fall of water..is indeed awful and sublime, but has too much of the terrible in its appearance. **1842** *Penny Cycl.* XXIII. 186/2 The stars are sublime, yet there is no terror in the emotion they excite. **1878** SMILES *Robt. Dick* vii. 78 After the cultivated fields, come the moors—quiet, solitary, and sublime.

8. Of rank, status: Very high, exalted. *arch.*

1702 EVELYN *Let. to Pepys* 20 Jan., Persons of the sublimest rank and office. *a* **1718** PRIOR *Ode to Queen* xix, Those Heights, where William's Virtue might have staid,.. the Props and Steps were made, Sublimer yet to raise his Queen's Renown. **1769** GRAY *Installat. Ode* 25 Meek Newton's self bends from his state sublime.

b. As an honorific title of the Sultan of Turkey or other potentates; also *transf.* of their actions. Cf. *Sublime Porte* (see PORTE), and SUBLIMITY 2d.

1820 BYRON *Juan* v. cxliv, Your slave brings tidings.. Which your sublime attention may be worth. **1821** SHELLEY *Hellas* 123 Your Sublime Highness Is strangely moved. **1855** MILMAN *Lat. Chr.* VII. iii. (1864) IV. 113 Gregory assumed the lofty tone of arbiter and commanded them to.. await his sublime award.

c. Refined: more recently used in trade names to designate the finest quality.

1694 SALMON *Bate's Dispens.* (1713) 299/2 It..will do that ..which others more esteemed sublime Medicines will not do. **1884** *Health Exhib. Catal.* 62/2 Jeyes' Sublime Disinfectant Toilet Soaps. **1897** *Daily News* 1 Oct. 7/7 A bottle upon which was a label 'Sublime Salad Oil'.

†**9.** *Med.* Of respiration: Of the highest degree.

1656 RIDGLEY *Pract. Physick* 224 Difficulty of breath is greater then in a Pluresy, which Hippocrates calleth sublime. **1668** CULPEPPER & COLE *Barthol. Anat.* II. iii. 92 The former Respiration Galen terms gentle or small,..the other strong,..a third sublime where the Diaphragma, intercostal..muscles, and muscles of the Chest do act all together

B. *sb.*

1. Now always with *the*: That which is sublime; the sublime part, character, property, or feature *of*. †Formerly with *a* and *pl.* and occas. without article, chiefly in contexts where SUBLIMITY would now be used.

a. in discourse or writing.

1679 SHADWELL *True Widow* I. 6 What is your opinion of the Play?.. There are a great many sublimes that are very Poetical. **1704** SWIFT *T. Tub* Pref. 22 Whatever Word or Sentence is printed in a different Character, shall be judged to contain something extraordinary either of Wit or Sublime. **1727** WARBURTON *Tracts* (1789) 115 With what a Sublime might that Flash of Lightning have been brought in. **1746** FRANCIS tr. *Hor., Art of Poetry* 561 Since I can write the true Sublime. **1749** FIELDING *Tom Jones* Contents IV. ii, A short hint of what we can do in the sublime, and a description of Miss Sophia Western. **1762** GIBBON *Misc. Wks.* (1814) V. 277 That sublime which results from the choice and general disposition of a subject. **1785** COWPER *Let. to J. Newton* 10 Dec., The sublime of Homer in the hands of Pope becomes bloated and tumid, and his description tawdry. **1847** TENNYSON *Princess* IV. 565 Feigning pique at what she call'd The raillery, or grotesque, or false sublime.

b. in nature and art.

1727 POPE, etc. *Art of Sinking* iv, The Sublime of Nature is the Sky, the Sun, Moon, Stars, &c. **1753** HOGARTH *Anal. Beauty* x. 51 What I think the sublime in form, so remarkably display'd in the human body. **1784** R. BAGE *Barham Downs* II. 320 The awful, the sublime of this reverend pile. **1820** W. IRVING *Sketch Bk.* I. 5 Never need an American look beyond his own country for the sublime and beautiful of natural scenery. **1842** *Penny Cycl.* XXIII. 188/1 The material sublime—or the sublime of nature.

c. in human conduct, life, feeling, etc.

1749 WARBURTON *Let. to Hurd* 13 June, His gravity and sublime of sentiment. **1756** BURKE *Subl. & Beaut.* I. vii. (1759) 58 Whatever is fitted in any sort to excite the ideas of pain, and danger, that is to say, whatever is in any sort terrible,..is a source of the sublime. **1789** BURNS *To Dr. Blacklock* ix, To make a happy fire-side clime To weans and wife, That's the true pathos and sublime Of human life. **1789** A. HAMILTON *Wks.* (1886) VII. 39 This was one of those strokes that denote superior genius, and constitute the sublime of war. **1804–6** SYD. SMITH *Mor. Philos.* (1850) 234 To harbour no mean thought in the midst of abject poverty, but..to found a spirit of modest independence upon the consciousness of having always acted well;—this is a sublime. **1847** PRESCOTT *Peru* (1850) II. 351 This was heroic, and wanted only a nobler motive for its object to constitute the true moral sublime. **1871** SMILES *Charac.* v. (1876) 134 The patriot who fights an always-losing battle —the martyr who goes to death amidst the triumphant shouts of his enemies..are examples of the moral sublime.

2. With *the*: The highest degree or point, summit, or acme *of*. Now *rare*.

1813 BYRON *Let. to Miss Milbanke* 26 Sept. Wks. 1899 III. 403 The moral of Christianity is perfectly beautiful—and the very sublime of virtue. **1817** —— *Beppo* lxxiii, The sublime Of mediocrity, the furious tame. **1818** —— *Juan* I. cli, With that sublime of rascals your attorney. **1838** DE QUINCEY *Shaks.* Wks. 1890 IV. 61 This is the very sublime of folly, beyond which human dotage cannot advance.

sublime (sə'blaɪm), *v.* [a. OF. *sublimer*, ad. L. *sublīmāre*, f. *sublīmis* SUBLIME *a.*]

1. *trans.* To subject (a substance) to the action of heat in a vessel so as to convert it into vapour, which is carried off and on cooling is deposited in a solid form.

c **1386** CHAUCER *Can. Yeom. T.* Preamb. 51 The care and wo That we hadden in oure matires sublymyng. **1460–70** *Bk. Quinte Essence* 4 By contynuel ascendynge and descendynge, by the which it is sublymed to so myche hiȝnes of glorificacioun. *Ibid.* 8 Take Mercurie þat is sublymed with vitriol, & comen salt, & sal armoniac .7. or .10. tymes sublymed. **1558** WARDE tr. *Alexis' Secr.* 102 b, To sublime Quicke Syluer, that is to saye, to make common sublyme. **1610** B. JONSON *Alch.* II. v, How doe you sublime him [mercury]? *Fac.* With the calce of egge-shels, White marble, talck. **1697** HEADRICH *Arcana Philos.* 27 Put the Mixture into a Sublimatory; from which sublime it ten or twelve times. **1730** CHAMBERLAYNE *Relig. Philos.* II. xviii. §9 Even a Metal..may be sublimed and mix'd with the Air by the Heat of Fire. **1774** J. HILL *Theophr.* (ed. 2) 235 Our factitious Cinnabar, made only by subliming Mercury and Sulphur together. **1827** FARADAY *Chem. Manip.* x. (1842) 262 It is easy to sublime and crystallize such bodies as camphor, iodine, naphthaline. **1869** ROSCOE *Elem. Chem.* 214 Ammonium Chloride..is obtained..by subliming a mixture of the commercial sulphate of ammonium with common salt.

absol. **1471** RIPLEY *Comp. Alch.* VIII. i. in Ashm. (1652) 171 We Sublyme not lyke as they do. **1596** FORMAN *Diary* (Halliw.) 28 The 27 of Aprill in subliming, my pot and glasse brok, and all my labour was lost pro lapide. **1610** B. JONSON *Alch.* II. v, Can you sublime, and dulcefie? **1678** R. RUSSELL tr. *Geber* II. I. IV. x. 108 This he well knows who hath sublimed in short Sublimatories.

2. *trans.* To cause to be given off by sublimation or an analogous process (e.g. volcanic heat); to carry over as vapour, which resolidifies on cooling; to extract by or as by sublimation.

1460–70 *Bk. Quinte Essence* 5 þe purete of þe quinte essencie schal be sublymed aboue. **1471** RIPLEY *Comp. Alch.* VIII. ii. in Ashm. (1652) 171 Som do Mercury from Vitriall and Salt sublyme. **1605** TIMME *Quersit.* I. xvi. 83 Glasse may be made of antimonie and of lead..by subliming flowers out of them. **1640** T. CAREW *Poems* (1651) 156 No more than Chimists can sublime True Gold. **1674** GREW *Anat. Pl.* (1682) 246 The saline Principle is altogether volatile, and sublimed away by the fire. **1791** E. DARWIN *Bot. Gard.* I. 94 *note*, This ponderous earth has been found ..in a granite in Switzerland, and may have thus been sublimed from immense depths by great heat. **1796** KIRWAN *Elem. Min.* (ed. 2) I. 419 Sulphur has been sublimed from it. **1827** FARADAY *Chem. Manip.* xxiv. (1842) 613 Put a portion of calomel into a Florence flask, and sublime it into the upper part by placing the bottom in sand. **1833** BREWSTER *Nat. Magic* xii. 299 We may yet study the lava which they have melted, and the products which they have sublimed. **1869** PHILLIPS *Vesuv.* iv. 107 Chloride of lead was among the substances sublimed.

3. *intr.* (†occas. *refl.*) **a.** To undergo this process; to pass from the solid to the gaseous state without liquefaction.

1622 MALYNES *Anc. Law-Merch.* 274 There remaineth a Paste..called the Almond Paste, which by a limbecke receiuing fire, causeth the Quicksiluer to subleme [*sic*]. **1651** FRENCH *Distill.* vi. 192 It will presently sublime in a silver fume, into the recipient. **1682** K. DIGBY *Chym. Secr.* 166 You shall see a little [Sal armoniac] sublime up to the discovered place of the Retort. **1683** PETTUS *Fleta Min.* I. 42 The Brimstone..doth roast away, and the Arsnick doth sublime it self with a strong heat. **1797** *Phil. Trans.* LXXXVII. 388 The acid will not sublime from it, but is decomposed by heat. **1823** FARADAY *Exp. Res.* No. 18. 82 It will.. sublime from one part of the bottle to the other in the manner of camphor. **1841** BRANDE *Man. Chem.* (ed. 5) 458 At higher temperatures it again liquifies, and at about 600° it boils, and sublimes in the form of an orange-coloured vapour. **1908** *Athenæum* 28 Mar. 390/1 All the 'non-valent' elements..should sublime, or pass from the solid into the gaseous state without liquefaction.

b. To be deposited in a solid form from vapour produced by sublimation.

1682 K. DIGBY *Chym. Secr.* 169 It will sublime with it in very red flowers. **1799** G. SMITH *Laboratory* I. 370 When the benjamin is heated the flowers will sublime. **1825** J. NICHOLSON *Oper. Mech.* 760 The arsenic sublimes..and adheres to the upper part of the vessel. **1856** MILLER *Elem.*

Chem., Inorg. xvii. §1. 1016 Calomel sublimes in quadrilateral prisms.

4. *trans.* To raise to an elevated sphere or exalted state; to exalt or elevate to a high degree of purity of excellence; to make (esp. morally or spiritually) sublime.

1609 G. BENSON *Serm. 7 May* 93 Let your thoughts be sublimed by the spirit of God. **1633** T. ADAMS *Exp. 2 Peter* ii. 4. 499 Persons so sublim'd, that what makes them everlastingly happy, shall never make them weary. **1649** JER. TAYLOR *Gt. Exemp.* II. 8 [Jesus] hallowed marriage..having new sublim'd it by making it a Sacramentall representment of the union of Christ and..the Church. *a* **1711** KEN *Psyche* Poet. Wks. IV. 253 As bless'd Elijah pray'd his Servants Eye Might be sublim'd the Angels to descry. **1729** SAVAGE *Wanderer* v. 521 No true benevolence his thought sublimes. **1765** GOLDSM. *Ess., Metaphor* Wks. (Globe) 331/1 A judicious use of metaphors wonderfully raises, sublimes, and adorns oratory or elocution. **1814** SOUTHEY *Roderick* III. 398 Call it not Revenge! thus sanctified and thus sublimed, 'Tis duty, 'tis devotion. **1819** BYRON *Juan* II. clxxx, The blest sherbet, sublimed with snow. **1858** MERIVALE *Rom. Emp.* liv. (1865) VI. 415 It sublimed every aspiration after the Good..by pronouncing it the instinct of divinity within us. **1861** M. ARNOLD *Pop. Educ. France* 146 Morality—but dignified, but sublimed by being taught in connection with religious sentiment. **1873** PATER *Renaissance* 176 The aspiring element, by force and spring of which Greek religion sublimes itself. **1880** HARDY *Trumpet-Major* xxxiii, Bob's countenance was sublimed by his recent interview, like that of a priest just come from the *penetralia* of the temple.

b. *above, beyond,* or *higher than* a certain state or standard.

a **1619** FOTHERBY *Atheom.* II. ix. §2 (1622) 296 The very end of Geometrie is nothing else, but onely to sublime mens mindes aboue their senses,..to the contemplation of Gods æternall Nature. **1651** JER. TAYLOR *Clerus Domini* v. §7. 31 Who can make it (ministerially I mean) and consecrate or sublime it from common..bread, but a consecrate..person? **1657** G. STARKEY *Helmont's Vind.* 15 [The Philosopher's] employment being sublimed a degree higher than Art, is ranked among the Liberal Sciences. **1820** HAZLITT *Lect. Dram. Lit.* 57 A personification of the pride of will and eagerness of curiosity, sublimed beyond the reach of fear and remorse. **1866** WHIPPLE *Char. & Charac. Men.* 1 A soul sublimed by an idea above the region of vanity and conceit. **1871** ALABASTER *Wheel of Law* 18 The existence of a God sublimed above all human qualities.

c. *into* a state or *to* a degree of purity, etc.

1643 J. M. *Sov. Salve* 35 That confirmation in grace by which free will is transfigured and sublimed into a state divine. **1651** JER. TAYLOR *Clerus Domini* iii. §11 An ordinary gift cannot sublime an ordinary person to a supernaturall imployment. **1774** PENNANT *Tour Scot. in 1772*, 5 Numbers of the discontented noblesse..resorted there,..sublimed the race into that degree of valour [etc.]. **1859** D. ANDERSON *Disc.* (1860) 55 The death of Matthew Henry's two children was designed to sublime his piety into that excellence which it attained.

†**d.** To purify (*from*). *Obs.*

1630 LORD *Banians* 52 The soule was impure..therefore it was needfull it should bee sublimed from this corruption. **1654** WHITLOCK *Zootomia* 406 Would we could light on some nobler principles that might sublime us from these Rellolacean Principles.

†**e.** With material obj. *Obs.*

1654 JER. TAYLOR *Real Pres.* 98 It is made Sacramental and Eucharistical, and so it is sublimed to become the body of Christ. **1667** MILTON *P.L.* v. 483 Flours and thir fruit Mans nourishment, by gradual scale sublim'd To vital Spirits aspire. **1740** CHEYNE *Regimen* 35 That spiritual Substance was analogous to Matter infinitely rarefied, refin'd or sublim'd. **1772–84** *Cook's 3rd Voy.* (1790) IV. 1254 The vines here being highly sublimed by the warmth of the sun and the dryness of the soil.

5. To transmute *into* something higher, nobler, or more excellent.

1695 DRYDEN tr. *Dufresnoy's Art Paint.* 7 Art being strengthned by the knowledge of things, may..be sublim'd into a pure Genius. **1706** PHILLIPS (ed. Kersey) s.v., To Sublime one's Flesh into a Soul. **1768** TUCKER *Lt. Nat.* (1834) II. 229 Our clay-built tabernacles sublimed into fit tabernacles of the Holy Ghost. **1790** BURKE *Fr. Rev.* Wks. V. 331 He, the œconomist,..subliming himself into an airy metaphysician. **1847** MILLER *First Impr. Eng.* xviii. (1857) 315 Those fictions of the classic mythology which the greater Greek and Roman writers have sublimed into poetry. **1855** MACAULAY *Hist. Eng.* xii. III. 193 His very selfishness therefore is sublimed into public spirit. **1864** LOWELL *Fireside Trav.* 36 F., whom whiskey sublimed into a poet.

b. *intr.* To become elevated, be transmuted *into* something higher.

1669 W. SIMPSON *Hydrol. Chym.* 76 The blood..begins to sublime or distil into more pure refined spirits. *a* **1711** KEN *Sion* Poet. Wks. IV. 381, I feel my Faith subliming into Sight. **1874** SEARS *Fourth Gospel* 172 This new faith subliming into knowledge.

6. *trans.* To raise up or aloft, cause to ascend.

1632 MASSINGER *City Madam* III. iii, I am sublim'd! grosse earth Supports me not. I walk on ayr! *c* **1650** DENHAM *Of Old Age* III. (1669) 34 Nor can thy head (not helpt) it self sublime. **1788** MME. D'ARBLAY *Diary* IV. VII. 344 With arms yet more sublimed, he..advanced, in silence and dumb heroics. **1845** BAILEY *Festus* (ed. 2) 241 Thoughts rise from our souls, as from the sea The clouds sublimed in Heaven.

b. To cause (vapour, etc.) to ascend, as by the action of the sun's heat.

1633 FOSBROKE *Chr. Race* 10 As clouds..being elevated and sublimed towards the upper region of the aire, are rarefied. **1655** VAUGHAN *Euphrates* 51 When the centrall Sun sublimes the Vapours. *a* **1691** BOYLE *Hist. Air* (1692) 186 There were great Store of Pieces of Brimstone, which are guessed to be sublimed up from the internal Parts of the Hill. **1705** J. PHILIPS *Blenheim* 8 As when two adverse Winds, Sublim'd from dewy Vapours, in mid Sky Engage with horrid Shock. **1871** C. KINGSLEY *At Last* vi, The malarious fog hung motionless.., waiting for the first blaze of sunrise to sublime it and its invisible poisons into the upper air.

†**c.** To cause (the juices of a plant, etc.) to rise, and thereby rarefy and purify them. *Obs.*

c **1645** HOWELL *Lett.* II. liv. (1892) 450 Wine itself is but Water sublim'd, being nothing else but that moisture and sap which is caus'd..by rain..drawn up to the branches and berries by the virtual attractive heat of the Sun. **1655** VAUGHAN *Euphrates* 46 There is a way made for the sperme to ascend more freely, which subliming upwards is attracted and intercepted by the vegetable Kingdom, whose imediat aliment it is. **1712** BLACKMORE *Creation* II. 234 Th' austere and ponderous Juices they sublime.

†**7.** To exalt (a person), raise to a high office or degree. *Obs.*

1557 NORTH *Gueuara's Diall Pr.* (1619) 706/1 Mardocheous [was] placed in his roome, and greatly sublimed and exalted. **1610** B. JONSON *Alch.* I. i, Haue I.. Sublim'd thee, and exalted thee, and fix'd thee I'the third region, call'd our state of grace? **1638** MAYNE *Lucian* (1664) 212/3 Gloriously crown'd..and sublimed, like one drest for a triumph.

sublimed (sə'blaɪmd), *ppl. a.* Also 4 sublymed, 5 sublimyd. [f. SUBLIME *v.* + -ED[1].]

1. That has undergone the chemical process of sublimation; produced by sublimation; = SUBLIMATE *a.* 1.

sublimed mercury: mercury sublimate. ***sublimed arsenic, sulphur***: flowers of arsenic, of sulphur.

c **1386** CHAUCER *Can. Yeom. T.* Preamb. 55 Oure Orpyment and sublymed Mercurie. *a* **1425** tr. *Arderne's Treat. Fistula*, etc. 83 Arsenic sublimed is of white colour. **1584** R. SCOT *Discov. Witchcr.* XIV. i. 295 Orpiment, sublimed Mercurie, iron squames, Mercurie crude. **1593** G. HARVEY *Pierce's Super.* Wks. (Grosart) II. 147 Mercurie sublimed, is somewhat a coy, and stout fellow. **1658** ROWLAND tr. *Moufet's Theat. Ins.* 926 Corrosives..(as Mercury sublimed, Vitriol, Orpiment, &c.). **1807** T. THOMSON *Chem.* (ed. 3) II. 26 It has no other smell than that of sublimed sulphur. **1811** A. T. THOMSON *Lond. Disp.* (1818) 535 Separate the sublimed matter from the scoriæ. **1842** PARNELL *Chem. Anal.* (1845) 26 Sublimed carbonate of ammonia, which is a sesquicarbonate. **1874** GARROD & BAXTER *Mat. Med.* 300 Collecting the sublimed acid by means of a cylinder of stiff paper inverted over the vessel.

b. *transf.* Refined. (Cf. SUBLIME *a.* 8 c.)

1905 *Brit. Med. Jrnl.* 25 Feb. 414 Using the very best sublimed olive oil.

†**2.** *fig.* **a.** Elevated, exalted, sublime; **b.** Purified, refined. *Obs.*

1600 W. WATSON *Decacordon* (1602) 334 Exhalated smokes of sparkling, hote, inflamed, dispersed, sublimed aspires. **1610** DONNE *Pseudo-martyr* 30 Shall the persons of any men..be thought to be of so sublimed, and spirituall a nature, that [etc.]. **1610** B. JONSON *Alch.* II. ii, Where I spie A wealthy citizen, or rich lawyer, Haue a sublim'd pure wife. *a* **1667** JER. TAYLOR *Serm. for Year* (1678) 355 The sobrieties of a graver or sublimed person. **1739** [BOYSE] *Deity* 151 Unmix'd his nature, and sublim'd his pow'rs. **1823** LAMB *Guy Faux* in *Eliana* (1867) 20 Erostratus must have invented a more sublimed malice than the burning of one temple.

†**c.** High and mighty. *Obs.*

1611 SPEED *Hist. Gt. Brit.* IX. viii. 39 In his sublimed Reply, hee snebs the King.

sublimely (sə'blaɪmlɪ), *adv.* [f. SUBLIME *a.* + -LY[2].]

†**1.** Aloft; highly; at or to a height. *Obs.*

a **1599** ROLLOCK *Passion* xli. (1616) 404 When thus way by checking, Hee hath beaten downe the imaginations..and cogitations that sublimely rose out of the minde. **1648** BOYLE *Motives Love of God* §14. 89 His soveraign Tranquillity is so sublimely plac'd, that 'tis above the reach of all Disquieting Impressions.

2. With sublimity of form, thought, expression, style; in a lofty or exalted manner. Also *ironical.*

1693 CONGREVE in *Dryden's Juvenal* (1697) 294 Verse so sublimely good, no Voice can wrong. **1700** *Luctus Brit., Death Dryden* 55 His Works are all sublimely Great. **1735** POPE *Prol. Sat.* 187 Whose fustian's so sublimely bad, It is not Poetry, but prose run mad. **1816** T. L. PEACOCK *Headlong Hall* vii, The sublimely romantic pass of Aberglaslynn. **1859** GEO. ELIOT *Adam Bede* xvii, There are ..few sublimely beautiful women. **1884** *Macm. Mag.* Oct. 443/1 Of this difficulty our Saxon-loving friends..are sublimely unconscious.

sublimeness (sə'blaɪmnɪs). [f. as prec. + -NESS.] The condition or quality of being sublime; sublimity.

1660 tr. *Amyraldus' Treat. conc. Relig.* I. v. 76 A matter of most divine sublimeness. **1683** CAVE *Ecclesiastici* 335 Neither does..the sublimeness of his Argument make his discourse obscure. **1734** *Burnet's Own Time* Life II. 675 Mr. Nairn was..remarkable for..Strength of Reasoning and Sublimeness of Thought. **1854** WISEMAN *Fabiola* II. xxxii. 343, I cannot see any way in which the sublimeness of the act could have been enhanced.

sublimer (sə'blaɪmə(r)). *rare.* [f. SUBLIME *v.* + -ER[1].] One who or a thing which sublimes.

a **1615** DONNE *Ess.* (1651) 68 That late Italian Distiller and Sublimer of old definitions.

sublimification (sə,blɪmɪfɪ'keɪʃən). [f. SUBLIME *v.* + -(I)FICATION.] The act or fact of making or being made sublime.

1791 W. GILPIN *Forest Scenery* I. 252 The poet has great advantages over the painter, in the process of sublim[if]ication, if the term may be allowed. **1868** *Pall Mall Gaz.* 22 Aug. 6 Mrs. Borradaile emerged from her baths in a state of sublimification which we should have thought would have made her marriage certain.

So **su'blimified** *ppl. a.*, rendered sublime.

1878 *Fraser's Mag.* XVII. 576 A sort of sublimified Berquin.

subliminal (sə'blɪmɪnəl), *a. Psych.* [f. SUB- 1 a + L. *līmin-, līmen* threshold + -AL[1]: coined to represent Herbart's *unter der Schwelle* sc. *des Bewusstseins* under the threshold of consciousness (*Psychol. als Wissenschaft* 1824, I. §47).] **a.** Below the threshold (see THRESHOLD *sb.* 2 c, LIMEN) of sensation or consciousness: said of states supposed to exist but not strong enough to be recognized. Also, pertaining to 'the subliminal self'.

1886 WARD in *Encycl. Brit.* XX. 48/1 Even if there were no facts to warrant this conception of a subliminal presentation of impressions and ideas. **1892** *Illustr. Lond. News* 8 Oct. 451/1 A pen, that strange conductor between the self he knows and the 'subliminal self' which is often flashing its surprises on him. **1892** MYERS in *Proc. Soc. Psychical Res.* Feb. 306 The subliminal memory includes an unknown category of impressions which the supraliminal consciousness..must cognise, if at all, in the shape of messages from the subliminal consciousness. **1902** PODMORE *Mod. Spiritualism* II. 31 The extraordinary outburst of subliminal or automatic activity.

b. *absol.* That which is subliminal; the subliminal self.

1901 W. JAMES in *Proc. Soc. Psychical Res.* May 18 Of the Subliminal, he [Myers] would say, we can give no ultra-simple account. **1903** MYERS *Hum. Pers.* I. ii. 347 Scenes.. which Sally as a subliminal noticed.

c. In collocations which denote exploitation of the idea that people can be unconsciously influenced by messages or other stimuli projected just below the threshold of awareness, as ***subliminal advertising, propaganda,*** etc.

1957 *Times* 18 Sept. 9/5 The report in your columns to-day from your New York Correspondent on subliminal advertising must be taken as a timely warning of an encroachment, if not upon the physical freedom, certainly upon the free will of the cinema and television audiences of the near future. **1957** *Technology* Nov. 328/4 The process —christened 'subliminal projection' because the message is transmitted at sub-threshold intensities—is ready for commercial exploitation. *Ibid.* 334/4 'Subliminal' propaganda—briefly flashing a suggestion on a cinema or television screen for subconscious observation. **1958** *Times* 5 July 7/2 A committee of the Institute of Practitioners in Advertising has reported on the subject of 'subliminal communication'. **1968** *Punch* 23 Oct. 563/1 Won't it [*sc.* the Government] use every trick in the book—including subliminal TV appeals and pressures—to make us buy more and more? **1975** *Perceptual & Motor Skills* XLI. 847 (*title*) Effect of subliminal stimuli on consumer behavior: negative evidence. **1981** J. E. ALCOCK *Parapsychol.* iv. 72 It is even unclear from the reports whether the increase in popcorn and cola sales occurred only after the exposure to subliminal advertising.

Hence **su'bliminally** *adv.*, in a manner which is subliminal or below the threshold of sensation or consciousness.

1892 F. W. H. MYERS in *Proc. Soc. Psychical Res.* VIII. 438 Similar subliminal activity is going on also along the *red to violet* spectrum of which we are supraliminally as well as subliminally cognisant. **1902** W. JAMES *Var. Relig. Exper.* x. 237 Subjects who are in possession of a large region in which mental work can go on subliminally. **1963** *Observer* 7 Apr. 22/2 The way it [*sc.* a book] is presented, with a cover more than subliminally reminiscent of the Leopard. **1977** J. GARDNER *Werewolf Trace* xxiv. 195 They also had a tape on the video link..which Harvester wanted to play through subliminally while Joseph watched the news.

subliming (sə'blaɪmɪŋ), *vbl. sb.* [f. SUBLIME *v.* + -ING[1].] The action of the verb SUBLIME.

1. = SUBLIMATION 1.

1471 RIPLEY *Comp. Alch.* VIII. ii. in Ashm. (1652) 171 Such Sublymyng accordyth never adele To our entent. **1584** R. SCOT *Discov. Witchcr.* XIV. i. 294 Their subliming, amalgaming, engluting. **1656** RIDGLEY *Pract. Physick* 248 Tartars use the thin part of Milk separated by subliming, to make themselves drunk. **1706** PHILLIPS (ed. Kersey), *Subliming-Pots*, the Vessels that serve for the Subliming of any Mixt Bodies. **1886** GUILLEMARD *Cruise of Marchesa* I. 23 The camphor, on subliming, is collected and packed in barrels.

†**2.** Exaltation. *Obs. rare.*

1641 SIR E. DERING *Sp. on Relig.* E ij b, This too elate subliming of one can not stand without a too mean demission of many other.

3. *attrib.*, as ***subliming dome*** (DOME *sb.* 5 a), ***-glass, -pot, vessel.***

1673 BOYLE *Ess. Effluviums* III. 13 The Subliming-glass. **1682** K. DIGBY *Chym. Secrets* II. 208 A Glass head upon your last Subliming-pot. **1719** QUINCY *Lex. Physico-Med.* (1722) 13 Aludels are subliming Pots used in Chymistry. *c* **1789** *Encycl. Brit.* (1797) IV. 446/1 The mouth of the subliming vessel. **1827** FARADAY *Chem. Manip.* xvi. (1842) 411 The bent tube being of such diameter as freely to pass over the subliming tube. **1881** GREENER *Gun* 309 The vapour..passes into the subliming dome, and is immediately precipitated into..flower of sulphur.

subliming (sə'blaɪmɪŋ), *ppl. a.* [f. as prec. + -ING[2].] That sublimes. **a.** That causes chemical sublimation. **b.** Undergoing sublimation. **c.** Rising, mounting. **d.** Elevating, exalting.

a. *a* **1631** DONNE *Valedict. of Bk.* 13 To all whom loves subliming fire invades. **1836** BRANDE *Man. Chem.* (ed. 4) 13 The mixture..is to be put into an aludel..and exposed to a subliming heat.

b. **1758** *Elaboratory laid open* 57 The sand should be removed from the retorts containing the subliming matter. **c.** **1666** [see SUBLINGUAL 1]. **d.** **1794** COLERIDGE *Relig. Musings* 107 His most holy name is Love. Truth of subliming import! **1823** MOORE *Rhymes on Road* vii. 72 Mingling earth's luxurious grace With Heaven's subliming thoughts.

sublimish (səˈblaɪmɪʃ), *a. rare.* [f. SUBLIME *a.* + -ISH[1].] Somewhat sublime.

1865 CARLYLE *Fredk. Gt.* XVI. vi. (1872) VI. 199 A man of some whims..but really honest, though rather sublimish in his interior.

sublimity (səˈblɪmɪtɪ). [ad. L. *sublīmitas, -tātem*, f. *sublīmis* SUBLIME: see -ITY. Cf. F. *sublimité*, etc.] The state or quality of being sublime.

†**1.** High or lofty position, height. *Obs.*

1563 *Homilies* II. *Agst. Peril Idol.* II. Hh iv, When Images are placed in Temples, and set in honorable sublimitie, and begin once to be worshipped. **1601** HOLLAND *Pliny* II. xvi. I. 11 The other cause of their [*sc.* the planets] sublimities is, for that [etc.]. **1665** SIR T. HERBERT *Trav.* (1677) 192 The subtility of the air and the sublimity of those Hills, which he says surpass the Alps. **1688** HOLME *Armoury* III. iii. 137/2 Geometrical Terms for their Plots, Figures, [etc.]. *Sublimities*, the heights or highness of things.

†**2.** High dignity *of* office, vocation, or the like.

1594 HOOKER *Eccl. Pol.* I. iv. 56 Being held with admiration of their own sublimitie and honor. *a* **1656** USSHER *Power of Princes* I. (1661) 43 The Regal sublimity is constituted by God. *a* **1700** EVELYN *Diary* 12 June 1650, He magnified the sublimity of the calling. *a* **1727** NEWTON *Chronol. Amended* ii. (1728) 226 Jupiter upon an Eagle to signify the sublimity of his dominion.

†**b.** A highly placed person. *Obs.*

1610 BOYS *Exp. Domin. Ep. & Gosp.* Wks. (1629) 163 Soueraigne Sublimities on earth are Gods among men.

†**c.** A high or dignified status. *Obs.*

1643 PRYNNE *Sov. Power Parl.* I. 41 If we be profitable servants, why doe we envy the eternall gaines of our Lord for our temporall sublimities or Prerogatives?

d. The status of one whose title is 'Sublime'; used with poss. pron. as a title of honour; in later use chiefly applied to the Sultan of Turkey or to the Sublime Porte.

So med.L. *sublimitas*.

1553 T. WILSON *Rhet.* (1580) 165, I beyng a Scholasticall panion, obtestate your sublimitie, to extoll myne infirmitie. **1589** [? NASHE] *Almond for Parrat* Ded. 1 Which if your sublimitie accept in good part,..I am yours. **1820** BYRON *Juan* IV. xci, In the Dardanelles, Waiting for his Sublimity's firman. **1892** *Sat. Rev.* 22 Oct. 466/1 Its Sublimity was unable to perceive any violation of the Treaty of Berlin.

3. Loftiness or grandeur of nature, character, conduct, or action; high excellence.

1526 *Pilgr. Perf.* (W. de W. 1531) 208 b, The length, the brede, the deepnes, and the sublimite or hye excellence of the crosse of Chryst. [See *Eph.* iii. 18, Vulg.]. **1597** HOOKER *Eccl. Pol.* V. lxvii. 181 Those things, which..for height and sublimitie of matter..weе are not able to reach vnto. **1614** RALEIGH *Hist. World* I. i. 11 In respect of Gods incomprehensible sublimitie, and puritie. **1655** M. CARTER *Honor Rediv.* (1660) 17 [Painting] hath been for its sublimity reckoned..among the liberall Sciences. **1756–7** tr. *Keysler's Trav.* (1760) I. 343 That, for truth and sublimity of doctrine, no book or system in the whole world came up to the holy scriptures. *a* **1812** BUCKMINSTER *Serm.* (1827) 36 Is there any thing to be learned..from the sublimity of the character, which is so much a subject of taste? **1851** MARIOTTI *Italy* 29 In 1846, France had not reached the acme of republican sublimity. **1870** MOZLEY *Univ. Serm.* iii. (1876) 67 In the Christian doctrine of a future state..the real belief in the doctrine goes together with..the moral sublimity of the state. **1874** L. STEPHEN *Hours in Libr.* (1892) I. v. 192 The genuine old Puritan spirit ceases to be picturesque only because of its sublimity.

b. An instance of this; a sublime thing or being.

1642 MILTON *Apol. Smect.* 17 Knowledge and vertue, with such abstracted sublimities as these. *a* **1715** BURNET *Own Time* (1766) I. 86 They..seemed to carry their devotions to a greater sublimity than others did. *Ibid.* 189 He loved to talk of great sublimities in religion. **1818** BYRON *Ch. Har.* IV. liv, The particle of those sublimities Which have relapsed to chaos. **1829** I. TAYLOR *Enthus.* ii. (1867) 27 Those false sublimities of an enthusiastic pietism. **1837** CARLYLE *Fr. Rev.* II. I. x, When such exhibition could appear a propriety, next door to a sublimity.

4. Loftiness *of* conception, sentiment, language, style, or treatment.

1624 GATAKER *Transubst.* 103 That subtilty and sublimitie of wit, that Jerome commandeth in Ephrems workes. **1676** HOBBES *Iliad* Pref. (1686) 5 The Sublimity of a Poet, which is that Poetical Fury which the Readers for the most part call for. **1685** BAXTER *Paraphr. N.T.* 1 Cor. ii. 6 Sublimity and accurateness of Speech. **1781** COWPER *Table-T.* 644 In him..Sublimity and Attic taste, combin'd. **1790** PALEY *Horæ Paul.* i. 7 Bursts of rapture and of unparalleled sublimity. **1841** W. SPALDING *Italy* I. 158 Polycletus,..a fellow-pupil of Phidias,..did not reach the sublimity of his rival in the representation of divinity. **1896** DK. ARGYLL *Philos. Belief* 280 It is impossible to deny the sublimity of this conception.

5. That quality in external objects which awakens feelings of awe, reverence, lofty emotion, a sense of power, or the like.

1779 JOHNSON *L.P.*, *Cowley* (1868) 9 Sublimity is produced by aggregation, and littleness by dispersion. **1787** POLWHELE *Engl. Orator* III. 512 His Voice Commanding..stern His Aspect and terrific..Sublimity his every Nod Attended. **1849** RUSKIN *Seven Lamps* iii. §9. 72 This expedient of continued series forms the sublimity of arcades and aisles. **1876** MISS BRADDON *Haggard's Dau.* x, Earth's loveliness or heaven's sublimity.

b. A sublime feature; a sublime expanse.

1819 in *Corr. Lady Lyttelton* (1912) 214 The sublimities of the Alps. *a* **1853** ROBERTSON *Lect.* i. (1858) 19 His character had been moulded by the sublimities of the forms of the outward nature. *a* **1869** LOWELL *Rhoecus* 157 The sky, With all its bright sublimity of stars.

6. The state of emotion produced by the perception or contemplation of the sublime.

1739 HUME *Hum. Nat.* II. 282 Any great elevation of place communicates a kind of pride or sublimity of imagination. *c* **1791** *Encycl. Brit.* (1797) VIII. 107/2 The emotions of grandeur and sublimity are nearly allied. **1887** A. BAIN *On Teaching Engl.* vi. 100 The Emotion termed Sublimity is connected with vastness of Power.

7. A high degree or standard, a height; with *the*, the highest degree, height, summit, acme.

1637 EARL MONM. tr. *Malvezzi's Romulus & Tarquin* 241 Bounding upon madnesse, it [*sc.* Melancholy] brings men to a sublimity, out of which one cannot passe. *a* **1667** JER. TAYLOR (Ogilvie 1882), The sublimity of wisdom is to do those things living, which are to be desired when dying. **1812** COLERIDGE *Friend* (1818) III. 34 There belong to it sublimities of virtues which all may attain, and which no man can transcend. **1823** LAMB *Guy Faux* in *Eliana* (1867) 20, I must make more haste; I shall not else climb the sublimity of this impiety. *Ibid.* 21 Such a sublimity of malice. **1883** tr. *Stepniak's Undergr. Russia* Introd. 42 He combines in himself the two sublimities of human grandeur: the martyr and the hero.

†**b.** A supreme or extreme phrase. *Obs.*

1651 N. BACON *Disc. Gov. Eng.* II. viii. (1739) 47 A qualified Legiance, without those sublimities of absolute, indefinite, immutable, &c.

Hence **suˈblimityship**, as a mock title.

1858 LYTTON *What will He do* I. xvii, Her Serene Sublimityship, Lady Selina Vipont.

sublimize (ˈsʌblɪmaɪz, səˈblaɪmaɪz), *v.* [f. SUBLIME *a.* + -IZE. Cf. F. *sublimiser.*] *trans.* To make sublime; to elevate, exalt, or refine.

1813 *Hervey's Medit.* Mem. Author p. xvi, She thought herself so completely sublimized as to stand in no need of religious instruction. **1841** HOR. SMITH *Moneyed Man* II. viii. 247 Solemn music and rich odours..sublimized devotion into ecstasy. **1880** 'OUIDA' *Moths* i, Baptiste sublimised and apotheosised by niello buttons, old lace, and genius.

Hence **sublimized** *ppl. a.*, elevated, exalted; refined in quality.

1849 *Benares Mag.* July II. 204 He declares..that the sublimized humanity of Feuerbach is almost as monstrous as Deity itself. **1896** *Daily News* 21 Apr. 6/4 It would seldom occur to anyone to recognise an affinity between the sack coverings to be seen on huge bales at warehouses and the sublimised fabric as applied to the bodices of ladies' dresses.

†**sublimy**, *a.* and *sb. Obs.* Also 6 **sublime, -yme.** [ad. F. *sublimé* sublimate, pa. pple. of *sublimer* to SUBLIME.] **A.** *adj.* ***mercury sublimy***: corrosive sublimate. **B.** *sb.* Mercury or arsenic sublimate.

1545 *Rates of Custome house* a ij b, Argente subline [*sic*] the c. li. xxxiii. s. iiii. d. *Ibid.* b viij, Mercury subline the pounde xii.d. **1558** W. WARDE tr. *Alexis' Secr.* 102 b, To sublime Quicke Syluer, that is to saye, to make common sublyme. **1580** HOLLYBAND *Treas. Fr. Tong.*, *Dux sublimé*, sublimie, a kinde of poison. **1611** COTGR., *Sublimé*, Sublimatum, or Sublimie, Arsenick, Ratsbane. **1706** PHILLIPS (ed. Kersey).

subˈlinear, *a.*

1. [SUB- 20 c.] Nearly linear (*Bot.* and *Zool.*: see LINEAR *a.* 4 b).

1777 S. ROBSON *Brit. Flora* 89 Leaves sublinear. **1852** DANA *Crust.* II. 887 The hand of the first pair of legs is sublinear. **1888** *Amer. Nat.* XXII. 1017 Suture sublinear above and slightly channeled below.

2. [SUB- 1 a.] Placed below a written or printed line.

Cf. *sublineation* s.v. SUB- 2.

1868 VISCT. STRANGFORD *Sel.* (1869) II. 254 The strange hooks or sub-linear commas by which the Poles denote certain nasal sounds in their language. **1909** *Bible in World* Aug. 239/2 There are two chief systems of punctuation known, sublinear and superlinear. *Ibid.*, All ordinary Hebrew manuscripts are vocalised or 'pointed' with the sublinear vowel signs.

‖**sublingua** (sʌbˈlɪŋgwə). *Zool.* [mod.L.: see SUB- 1 f and LINGUA.

(In medical L., *sublingua* was formerly used for 'uvula'.)]

In some animals, e.g. lemurs, a process consisting of a fold of mucous membrane under the tongue.

1878 BELL tr. *Gegenbaur's Comp. Anat.* 553 In many Prosimii and Chiroptera, as also in the platyrrhine Apes, there is a process below the tongue which is sometimes double; this is the so-called sublingua. **1896** tr. *Boas' Text Bk. Zool.* 487 *note*, On each side of the ventral surface of the tongue, there is a fold..; it is termed the 'sub-lingua', and attains its highest development in the Prosimii.

sublingual (sʌbˈlɪŋgwəl), *a.* (*sb.*) [ad. mod.L. *sublinguālis*: see SUB- 1 a, b and LINGUAL. Cf. F. *sublingual* (from 16th c.), etc.] **A.** *adj.*

1. *Med.* Of a pill, etc.: That is placed under the tongue to be sucked.

1661 LOVELL *Hist. Anim. & Min.* 515 Sublinguale troches. **1666** G. HARVEY *Morbus Angl.* (1672) 114 Those subliming humours ought..to be intercepted..by sublingual Pills. **1958** *Martindale's Extra Pharmacopœia* (ed. 24) I. 67 *Aleudrin*... Isoprenaline sulphate, available as Solution containing 1% for inhalation, and as Sublingual Tablets of 20 mg. **1980** *Amer. Speech* LV. 52 Nitroglycerine sublingual tablets given to heart patients for angina.

2. *Anat.* Situated under the tongue or on the under-side of the tongue. Also, belonging to the sublingua.

sublingual gland, the smallest salivary gland situated between the tongue on either side of the floor of the mouth. So *s. artery*, supplying the s. gland, side of the tongue, etc.; *s. cyst*, due to obstruction of the s. gland, etc., = RANULA; *s. fossa*, which lodges the s. gland. *s. nerve* = HYPOGLOSSAL nerve.

1694 *Phil. Trans.* XVIII. 229 [The use of] the *Musculus Mylohyoideus*..in Compressing its subjacent sublingual Glands. **1720** *Ibid.* XXXI. 7 The Buccal, Labial, internal Maxillar, and sublingual Glands, are of a yellow Colour. **1831** R. KNOX *Cloquet's Anat.* 653 The Sublingual Artery, which is sometimes a division of the submental. **1836–9** *Todd's Cycl. Anat.* II. 214/1 A depression (sublingual fossa) for the reception of the sublingual gland. **1872** BRYANT *Pract. Surg.* 256 *marg.*, Sebaceous sublingual cysts. **1875** *Encycl. Brit.* II. 165/1 In that genus [*Hylobates*] we first meet with a sub-lingual process (which becomes much larger in the lower apes). **1890** BILLINGS *Nat. Med. Dict.*, *Sublingual caruncle*, the papilla at which Wharton's duct opens, behind lower incisor teeth.

B. *sb.* A sublingual gland, artery, etc.

1720 *Phil. Trans.* XXXI. 7 They are as distinct from the Buccal, as the Sublinguals are from the internal Maxillars. **1840** G. V. ELLIS *Anat.* 182 One or two of them [*sc.* arteries] perforate the mylo-hyoid muscle, to anastomose with the sublingual.

Hence **subˈlingually** *adv.*, under the tongue.

1945 *Proc. Soc. Exper. Biol. & Med.* LVIII. 185/1, 4000 units of penicillin in 0·05 gm of zephiran was administered sublingually to a man. **1961** *Lancet* 9 Sept. 587/2 Testosterone was given sublingually. **1980** *Monthly Index Med. Specialities* Feb. 76/3 Lingraine... Ergotamine tartrate 2mg; green tab. Migraine [etc.]... 1 sublingually at onset of attack.

ˌsub-linˈguistic, *a.* **1.** [SUB- 19.] Not fully linguistic; expressed in a level below that of language.

1933 L. BLOOMFIELD *Language* ix. 148 These shortened forms occur in various languages; their relation to normal speech is obscure, but evidently they represent a kind of *sub-linguistic* communication, in which the ordinary meaning of the forms plays no part. **1956** J. WHATMOUGH *Language* I. 7 May 'thought' be not merely sub-linguistic, but also non-linguistic, or both? **1977** 'A. BURGESS' *Beard's Roman Women* v. 108 I'm American, so there won't be any language problem. Not that there'll be any need for language. Sublinguistic activity, let's call it.

2. [SUB- 5 c (*b*).] Of or pertaining to a sublanguage.

1976 *Amer. Speech 1974* XLIX. 266 The changes involved in these expressions are not sublinguistic.

†**suˈblition.** *Obs. rare*[−0]. [ad. L. **sublitio, -ōnem*, n. of action f. *sublinĕre, sublit-*, f. *sub-* SUB- 2 + *linĕre* to smear.] (See quot.)

1656 BLOUNT *Glossogr.*, *Sublition*, the ground colour, wherein the perfect colour is laid; it is called Grasing.

subˈlittoral, *a.* and *sb.* [SUB- 11.]

A. *adj.* Lying near the sea-shore or just below the shore-line or littoral zone. *spec.* in *Ecol.*, applied to the inshore biogeographic zone normally taken as extending from mean low tide to the edge of the continental shelf.

1846 SMART Suppl. **1849** *Sk. Nat. Hist.*, *Mammalia* IV. 180 The sublittoral formation in which they had been originally deposited. **1849** DARWIN in Herschel *Man. Sci. Enq.* 177 Our observations..on the alluvial and sub-littoral deposits of these latitudes. **1897** *Geogr. Jrnl.* Aug. 133, I should estimate that round the Pacific there are at least ten sub-littoral districts where earthquake-frequency may be about half that of Japan. **1909** E. WARMING *Œcol. Plants* IV. xli. 172 Sub-littoral 'region':—Ranges from below low-tide mark down to a depth of twenty fathoms (40 metres); here algae of all colours are represented. **1931** [see PROFUNDAL *a.* and *sb.*]. **1937** T. A. & A. STEPHENSON in *Trans. R. Soc. S. Afr.* XXIV. 360 It [*sc.* a particular zone of a beach] is occasionally exposed to a considerable extent, when maximal spring tides coincide with calm weather. This region we propose to call the Sublittoral Fringe. **1971** *Nature* 9 Apr. 402/2 In the Mediterranean, *Dardanus* inhabits sandy bottoms with some exposed rocks..from sublittoral to moderate depths down to 100 m.

B. *sb.* The sublittoral zone.

1961 in WEBSTER. **1964** V. J. CHAPMAN *Coastal Vegetation* i. 1 So far as algae are concerned, the sublittoral will extend downwards to the point where algae cease to grow. **1980** HISCOCK & MITCHELL in J. H. Price et al. *Shore Environment* II. i. 333 The real downward extent of the sublittoral..is often ignored by field workers.

Hence **subˈlittorally** *adv.*, in sublittoral regions.

1964 *Oceanogr. & Marine Biol.* II. 260 Sublittorally, the distribution of the radioactivity on the sea bottom is not uniform. **1971** *Nature* 9 Apr. 402/2 All are essentially warm temperate to tropical species occurring sublittorally in the Mediterranean, the Eastern and South Atlantic.

sublunar (sʌbˈl-, səˈbl(j)uːnə(r)), *a.* and *sb.* [ad. mod.L. *sublūnār-is* (cf. late Gr. ὑποσέληνος, ὑποσελήνιος): see SUB- 1 a and LUNAR. Cf. F. *sublunaire*, etc.]

A. *adj.* **1.** = SUBLUNARY A. Now *rare.*

1610 GUILLIM *Heraldry* III. iv. (1611) 94 Those cœlestiall creatures..being void of this corrupt mixture which is found in all creatures sublunar. **1667** MILTON *P.L.* IV. 777 Now had night measur'd with her shaddowie Cone Half way up Hill this vast Sublunar Vault. **1708** *Brit. Apollo* No. 85. 3/1 That all Sublunar Joys duration want. **1817** SHELLEY *Rev. Islam* V. i, The City's moonlit spires and myriad lamps, Like stars in a sublunar sky did glow. *a* **1857** D. JERROLD *John Applejohn* iv, To expire covered over with wounds was the only really desirable way of going out of this sublunar world.

2. *Navigation* and *Astr.* Applied to a point on the surface of the earth which lies on a line joining the centre of the moon and the centre of the earth, i.e. a point at which the moon is vertically overhead.

1938 P. V. H. WEEMS *Air Navigation* (ed. 2) xvi. 263 The geographical position of a heavenly body is the point on the earth's surface that has the body in its zenith; in other words the substellar, subsolar, or sublunar point. **1971** *Nature* 31 Dec. 537/2 Most large earthquakes occur after the epicentral region has passed the sublunar or subsolar point.

†**B.** *sb.* = SUBLUNARY B. *Obs.*

1613 CAMPION *Relat. Roy. Entert.* Descr., View these heau'n borne Starres, Who by stealth are become Sublunars. **1684** GADBURY (*title*) Cardines Cœli: or, an appeal to..observers of sublunars and their vicissitudes. **1686** GOAD *Celest. Bodies* II. iii. 180 The moon could claim no interest upon her Vicinity to us Sublunars.

sublu'narian, *a. rare.* [Formed as SUBLUNARY + -AN.] Existing or operating beneath the moon's surface.

1880 PROCTOR *Rough Ways* 108 The reinforcement of their action by the effects due to sublunarian energies. **1881** —— *Poetry Astron.* vi. 231 Sublunarian forces.

sub'lunariness. *rare*$^{-0}$. [f. next + -NESS.]

1727 BAILEY (vol. II), *Sublunariness*, the being under the Moon.

sublunary (sʌb'l(j)uːnərɪ, səb'l(j)uːnərɪ; older 'sʌbl(j)uːnərɪ), *a.* (*sb.*) [f. mod.L. *sublūnāris*: cf. LUNARY.] **A.** *adj.*

1. Existing or situated beneath the moon; lying between the orbit of the moon and the earth; hence, subject to the moon's influence.

1613 PURCHAS *Pilgrimage* (1614) 512 Patritius doth not onely auerre this, but that the Sea is as a sublunarie Planet. **1621** BURTON *Anat. Mel.* I. ii. I. ii. (1638) 46 Of these sublunary Devils..Psellus makes six kindes, fiery, aëriall, terrestriall, watery, and subterranean Devils. *a* **1649** CRASHAW *Carmen Deo Nostro* Poems (1904) 283 Starrs much too fair and pure to wait upon The false smiles of a sublunary sun. **1692** RAY *Disc.* (1732) 302 The sublunary Aereal Heavens. **1757** YOUNG *Last Day* I. 81 Ye sublunary worlds, awake, awake! **1848** MRS. JAMESON *Sacr. & Leg. Art* (1850) 168 The Four Doctors are in the centre of what may be called the sublunary part of the picture. **1850** S. DOBELL *Roman* i, Oh that bright realm of sublunary heaven.

†**b.** Inferior, subordinate (*to*). *Obs.*

1616 DONNE *Serm.* (Prov. xxii. 11) III. 337 Endymion loved the Moon. The sphear of our loves is sublunary, upon things naturally inferior to our selves. **1631** BRATHWAIT *Whimzies, Metall-man* 60 The arch-artist in this minerall is the alchymist; for the rest are all sublunarie unto him, hee only mercurie sublimate unto them.

2. Of or belonging to this world; earthly, terrestrial.

1592 GREENE *Groat's Wit* Ep. Ded., A witte that runnes in this sublunarie maze and takes but Nature for its original. **1615** W. LAWSON *Country Housew. Garden* (1626) 24 Euery thing sublunary is cursed for mans sake. **1632** B. JONSON *Magn. Lady* III. i, From all the points o' the Compasse, (That's all the parts of the sublunary Globe). **1650** J. HALL *Paradoxes* 38 The uncertainty of all sublunary things. *a* **1676** HALE *Prim. Orig. Man.* 83 Sublunary Bodies..are..subject to alteration and corruption. **1713** SWIFT *Apollo Outwitted* Wks. 1755 III. II. 109 Stroling Gods, whose usual trade is..To pick up sublunary ladies. **1782** COWPER *Let. to Jos. Hill* Nov., My eyes are, in general, better than I remember them to have been since I first opened them upon this sublunary stage. **1815** SCOTT *Guy M.* xlvi, The housekeeper..usually waylaid him on his return, to remind him of his sublunary wants. **1841** BREWSTER *Martyrs Sci.* v. (1856) 83 Like all sublunary blessings it was of short duration. **1873** BURTON *Hist. Scot.* VI. lxv. 3 For this too we may find a motive cause among sublunary human influences.

†**3.** Characteristic of this world and its affairs; mundane; material, gross; temporal, ephemeral.

1639 HABINGTON *Castara* II. (Arb.) 92 Tis no dull Sublunary flame Burnes in her heart and mine. **1643** MILTON *Divorce* I. ix. Wks. 1851 IV. 46 To remedy a sublunary and bestiall burning, which frugall diet without mariage would easily chast'n. **1648** BP. HALL *Breathings Devout Soul* 3 Can ye hope to finde rest in any of these sublunary contentments? **1742** YOUNG *Nt. Th.* VI. 206 And toil we still for sublunary pay? **1759** JOHNSON *Rasselas* xlvi, He began gradually to delight in sublunary pleasures. **1814** SCOTT *Wav.* xi, The Baron was exalted by wine, wrath, and scorn, above all sublunary considerations.

†**B.** *sb.* A sublunary thing or creature; chiefly *pl. Obs.*

1641 R. HARRIS *Abners Funerall* 8 We may say of all these Sublunaries, what Salomon saith of one particular; They are not. **1671** J. WEBSTER *Metallogr.* xii. 178 The mercurial part of it [*sc.* gold]..cannot be changed..by no sublunary except its compeer. **1720** *Humourist* Ded. p. xxiv, [To] publish to us Sublunaries..all the Secrets of your Honours Privy-Council. **1748** RICHARDSON *Clarissa* (1811) III. 310 Something extraordinary was to be done to keep her with us sublunaries.

subluxation (sʌblʌk'seɪʃən). *Path.* [ad. mod.L. *subluxātio, -ōnem*: see SUB- 23 and LUXATION. Cf. F. *subluxation*, etc.] A partial dislocation, a sprain.

1688 HOLME *Armoury* II. xvii. 448/2 *Sublaxation* [sic], a dislocation, or putting out of joynt. **1846** MILLER *Pract. Surg.* xxiii. 321 Subluxation forwards is by no means an uncommon result of falls on the palm. **1878** tr. *von Ziemssen's Cycl. Med.* XIV. 122 In the shoulder-joint an atonic subluxation often occurs, especially in children. **1893** W. R. GOWERS *Man. Dis. Nerv. Syst.* (ed. 2) II. 415 The persistent strong flexion may even lead to subluxation.

So **sub'luxate** *v.*, to dislocate slightly, sprain.

1893 W. R. GOWERS *Man. Dis. Nerv. Syst.* (ed. 2) II. 415 The fingers are..over-extended at the middle joint, which may be subluxated.

ˌsub-ma'chine-gun. [SUB- 5 b.] A light portable machine-gun firing ammunition of the same type and calibre as a pistol. Cf. THOMPSON.

1926 [see THOMPSON]. **1934** *Sun* (Baltimore) 4 Dec. 3/5 None of these companies manufacture the deadly submachine gun in popular use by criminals. **1942** J. STEINBECK *Moon is Down* 2 Grey-helmeted men who carried sub-machine-guns in their arms. **1951** 'J. WYNDHAM' *Day of Triffids* vi. 112, I dropped down, pulling Jocella with me as the clatter of a sub-machine gun began. **1965** J. A. MICHENER *Source* (1966) 816 Little Vered in her boxlike hat came darting in with her submachine gun spurting. **1973** G. GREENE *Honorary Consul* III. iii. 132 A stranger stood there waving a sub-machine gun at him.

'sub-man. [SUB- 14 b.] A man of markedly inferior development or capacities.

1921 R. A. FREEMAN *Social Decay & Regeneration* 248 As we are accustomed to speak of a man whose bodily and mental qualities are such as to lift him far above the common level, as a super-man, so we may conveniently refer to one who is to a like degree below the average as a sub-man. **1939** DYLAN THOMAS *Let.* 14 Sept. (1966) 237 Submen from the islands of crabs. **1951** N. M. GUNN *Well at World's End* xxix. 277 The Cromagnons, those sub-men who painted their bisons on the walls of far interior caves. **1964** *Punch* 28 Oct. 655/2 Peter Cook with his sub-man monologues. **1981** P. AUDEMARS *Gone to her Death* vii. 123 What do they do now? Send these apes—these sub-men—to a reform school.

sub'marginal, *a.* (*sb.*)

1. a. [SUB- 11.] Situated near the margin of a body or organ; (of cells in the wing of a hymenopterous insect) lying behind the marginal cell.

1829 LOUDON *Encycl. Plants* (1836) 877 Sori..marginal or submarginal. **1846** DANA *Zooph.* (1848) 142 Tentacles..submarginal. **1861** H. HAGEN *Syn. Neuroptera N. Amer.* 343 *Submarginal*, just behind the margin. **1872** H. A. NICHOLSON *Palæont.* 107 Most commonly the anus is marginal, or is sub-marginal.

b. *sb.* A submarginal cell.

1896 *Proc. Acad. Nat. Sci. Philad.* 30 There are but two submarginal cells;..The so-called second submarginal is morphologically the third, the true second of genera with three submarginals being absent.

2. [SUB- 19.] Of land: not capable of being farmed profitably.

1930 *Economist* 9 Aug. 272/1 It permits the survival of sub-marginal farms which plainly ought to be driven out of cultivation by the operation of economic forces. **1938** *Encycl. Brit. Bk. of Year* 24/2 In the autumn of 1937 a long-term programme for agriculture was announced [in the U.S.]. It included:..crop insurance, retirement of submarginal land, and price adjustment payments. **1970** E. FLORES in I. L. Horowitz *Masses in Lat. Amer.* ix. 336 Public lands could not be given to anybody simply because they were submarginal.

sub'marginate, *a. Nat. Hist.* [SUB- 21 b.] Imperfectly or nearly marginate; bordered with a mark slightly distant from the edge. So **sub'marginated, sub'margined**.

1856 W. CLARK *Van der Hoeven's Zool.* I. 155 Echinolampas... Disc *submarginate forwards. **1752** J. HILL *Hist. Anim.* 51 The brownish brassy Buprestis, with a *submarginated thorax. **1822** J. PARKINSON *Outl. Oryctol.* 202 Lip submarginated. **1787** tr. *Linnæus' Fam. Plants* 551 Tanacetum... Seeds solitary, oblong. Pappus *submargined. **1819** G. SAMOUELLE *Entomol. Compend.* 86 Shell submargined behind.

submarine ('sʌbməriːn, sʌbmə'riːn), *a.* and *sb.* [SUB- 1 a.] **A.** *adj.*

1. Existing or lying under the surface of the sea. Also *fig.*

1668 WILKINS *Real Char.* II. iii. 62 A sub-marine Plant. **1670** BOYLE *Tracts, Submarine Regions* i. 3 By the Appellation of Submarine Regions 'tis not to be supposed that the places so called are below the Bottom of the Sea, but only below the surface of it. **1796** WITHERING *Brit. Plants* (ed. 3) IV. 87 This Fucus is found on submarine rocks at very low water. **1833** LYELL *Princ. Geol.* III. 24 A vast submarine region, such as the bed of the western Atlantic. **1859** DARWIN *Orig. Spec.* xii. 395 The islands are situated on moderately deep submarine banks. **1877** HUXLEY *Physiogr.* 198 Submarine volcanoes occasionally give rise to new land. **1917** T. S. ELIOT *Prufrock & Other Observations* 35 His laughter was submarine and profound Like the old man of the sea's. **1925** A. HUXLEY *Those Barren Leaves* v. i. 348 He found himself adding, with a kind of submarine laughter below the surface of his voice: 'Do you think you *can* make an end?'

2. Operating or operated, constructed or laid, intended for use under the surface of the sea.

Later examples tend to merge with the recent *attrib.* use of the *sb.* (sense 3 b below).

submarine boat, a boat so designed that it can be submerged, and propelled when under water, used chiefly for carrying and discharging torpedoes. *submarine mine*, a charge of explosives, moored at or beneath the surface of the sea, intended by its explosion on impact to put a hostile vessel out of action immediately.

1648 WILKINS *Math. Magick* II. v. 178 Concerning the possibility of framing an Ark for submarine Navigations. *Ibid.* 182 These submarine Navigators will want the usuall advantages of winds and tides for motion. **1784** COWPER *Task* IV. 85 Submarine exploits. **1807** T. JEFFERSON *Let.* 16 Aug. in *Writings* (1853) V. 165, I have ever looked to the submarine boat as most to be depended on for attaching them [*sc.* torpedoes to the cable of a ship]. **1818** *Monthly Mag.* Feb. 46/2 His boat at this time he called the submarine boat, or the plunging boat. **1840** *Mech. Mag.* 19 Sept. 320 Spithead has been..a scene of diversified exertion in submarine work. **1855** *Lardner's Mus. Sci. & Art* III. 159 It is proposed to connect Orfordness..with the Hague, by seven separate submarine cables. **1860** PRESCOTT *Electr. Telegr.* 179 The wires of a submarine telegraph. **1860** MAURY *Phys. Geog.* ii. 30 Currents, for the most part, and for great distances, are submarine. **1861** *Jrnl. Chem. Soc.* XIV. 193 Applying the magneto-electric current to the ignition of submarine charges. **1867** SMYTH *Sailor's Wordbk.* 664 *Submarine Thermometer*, an instrument for trying the temperature of the sea at different depths. **1875** KNIGHT *Dict. Mech.*, *Submarine Boat*, a vessel constructed to navigate beneath the surface of the water. **1889** [see SUBMERSIBLE *a.*]. **1897** *Knowledge* 1 Jan. 20/1 All the great naval Powers are busily engaged in bringing submarine warfare to a perfect system of attack. **1900** *19th Cent.* May 722 Why it [*sc.* the naval programme] does not contain..any provision for submarine or submersible boats. **1919** *Daily Mail Year Bk.* 76/2 One and a half year's unrestricted submarine war. **1940** *Times* 11 June 7/4 Someone has blundered—Dr. Goebbels, or the German submarine command, or both. **1979** O. SELA *Petrograd Consignment* 17 The chiefs of the [German] civil, military and naval cabinets..had decided to end the blockade by declaring unrestricted submarine warfare.

B. *sb.*

1. A submarine creature; †a submarine plant, coral, etc.

1703 *Phil. Trans.* XXIII. 1419 A Description of some Coralls, and other curious Submarines. **1756** J. HILL *Brit. Herbal* 533 Grassy Alga..is the only submarine which has a regular root. **1839** HOOD *Sub-marine* 68 With open'd mouth and open'd eyes, Up rose the Sub-marine.

2. A submarine mine.

1886 *Pall Mall Gaz.* 28 July 6/2 Suppose you lay down submarines to help the defence; without a flotilla, how are you going to stop the enemy from taking them up or destroying them at night?

3. a. A submarine boat: see A 2 (now the dominant sense).

1899 *Westm. Gaz.* 2 Feb. 7/1 The submarine was no longer there. She was hidden from our fire and from our view. **1900** *Daily Mail* 4 May 4/3 The submarine has been adopted by the French navy as a means of gaining control of the Channel.

b. *attrib.* and *Comb.* in many obvious uses. Also **submarine chaser**, a small patrol boat equipped for military operations against submarines; **submarine pen**: see PEN *sb.*[1] 2 d; **submarine scout** = BLIMP 1.

1908 C. FIELD *Story of Submarine* 183 The rise of the Russian submarine flotilla. **1914** C. M. DOMVILLE-FIFE *Submarines* 9 The submarine fleets of England, France, Russia, [etc.]. **1915** W. E. DOMMETT *Aeroplanes & Airships* vi. 75 In place of an enemy camp or railway junction, we get the submarine base or dockyard. **1917** *Daily Mail* 5 Mar. 5/4 Expert officials of the [U.S.] Navy department devised a scheme for placing on board merchant ships..two or three small boats as submarine-chasers. **1917** *Jane's All the World's Aircraft* 78 c The 'Blimp' or Submarine Scout, evolved by the British Naval Air Service. **1931** W. G. CARR *By Guess & by God* 261 Lieutenant Johnson was 'submarine-minded'. He loved them. **1941** *Hutchinson's Pict. Hist. of War* 14 May–8 July 193 Fast revenue cutters of the U.S. coastguard service..are now in service with the Royal Navy as submarine chasers. **1942** *Sun* (Baltimore) 17 Mar. 1/5 That the submarine-killer is not instantly available is due to the same old cause—we did not start early enough. **1954** P. K. KEMP *Fleet Air Arm* 35 The first of the famous S.S., or Submarine Scout, airships. **1959** *Encounter* Jan. 13/1 The Polaris submarine-launched missile. **1975** B. MEYRICK *Behind Light* xiv. 190 They had to raise and lower the submarine nets. **1979** J. SHERWOOD *Hour of Hyenas* xiv. 163, I know Georgiades' boat..former Nazi navy submarine chaser.

4. *slang.* (Prob. transf. from sense 3.) †**a.** A doughnut. *U.S. Obs.*

1916 *Independent* 9 Oct. 77 'Two submarines and a mug of murk—no cow!' orders the waiter. **1942** BERREY & VAN DEN BARK *Amer. Thes. Slang* §91/25 *Doughnuts*,..sinkers, submarines.

b. A type of sandwich; = HOAGIE; *poor boy* (*sandwich*) s.v. POOR *a.* (*sb.*) 8. Freq. *attrib.* as ***submarine roll, sandwich***. Cf. SUB *sb.* 8 b. Chiefly *U.S.*

1955 *Sat. Even. Post* 1 Jan. 16/2 The submarine is a noble edifice built of meats, cheeses, fish—preserved and pickled—and fresh vegetables and greens, all stuffed into a whole long loaf of bread and laved generously with oil, herb-flecked vinegar and other delicious lubricants. **1961** WEBSTER, Submarine sandwich. **1967** *Amer. Speech* XLII. 279 (*title*) The submarine sandwich: lexical variations in a cultural context. **1973** Submarine roll [see HOAGIE]. **1973** *Kingston* (Ontario) *Whig-Standard* 11 July 7/2 Who are the biggest fans of the Jaycee beer garden where beer and submarine sandwiches are sold? **1979** *Tucson* (Ariz.) *Mag.* Sept. 68/2 Real bargains in pizzas, submarines and dinner platters.

Hence **submarine,** *v.* (*a*) *trans.*, to attack with a submarine; (*b*) *intr.*, to act or move like a submarine (*fig.*); **submariner** (-'mærɪnə(r)), a member of the crew of a submarine; **'submarining** (also -'riːnɪŋ) *vbl. sb.*, the use of or activity with submarines; also *attrib.* and as *ppl. a.*; **submarinism** *disused* = *submarining* vbl. sb. above; **subma'rinist**, an advocate of submarine boats.

1900 *19th Cent.* May 722 The confident statements of the French submarinists. **1911** *Chambers's Jrnl.* Feb. 170/1 'Ought to prove a tidy job for us, though,' he muttered with some anxiety, 's'long as she don't take to submarinin' first.' **1914** *Land & Water* 19 Sept. 17* Having been submarined and beached. **1915** *Times* 1 Feb. 9/3 All is fish which comes into the net of the submariner. **1915** *Glasgow Herald* 30 Mar. 8 The commander of the U16, which sank the British steamer Dulwich and the French vessels Ville de Lille and Dinorah, discussed 'submarinism' from the standpoint of one who had experience. **1915** *Spectator* 13 Nov. 645/2 America's last word as to submarining in the North Sea. **1917** R. LORD *Captain Boyd's Battery, A.E.F.* (1919) 24 *Submarine*,..let's submarine, etc.—to submerge, to make onself scarce in the presence of impending duty. **1918** G. FRANKAU *One of Them* xxii. 170 That Hand before whose Thumb the Cave-men bow, Whose oiled Palm guides the submarining mermans. **1927** *Westm. Gaz.* 23 May 6/2 The war advanced the study of submarinism and aviation. **1946** G. MILLAR *Horned Pigeon* viii. 96 A submariner named Mike Caplatt produced an original musical comedy. **1966** M. R. D. FOOT *SOE in France* iv. 62 The most active submarining spell. **1971** *Wall St. Jrnl.* 12 Mar. 1/4 Occupants [of a crashing car] could 'submarine' under an inflating bag and thus not be protected by it. **1972** J. BROOME *Convoy is to Scatter* I. 24 Submarining then was a human rather than a technological way of life, full of individuals who stamped one's memory with their character. **1976** J. LEE *Ninth Man* I. 5 If they stumbled into trouble on the beach, they could claim they were submariners. **1981** *Sunday Times* 26 Apr. 3/5 The 10-year-old dummy [in a test of safety belts] 'submarined'—that is, he slid forward under the belt, which tightened across his stomach and around his neck.

'subˌmarshal. *Obs.* exc. *Hist.* [SUB- 6.] A deputy or under-marshal; an official in the marshalsea acting as the knight-marshal's deputy.

1594 CROMPTON *Jurisd.* 104 Lopinion del Court fuit, que le Submarshal fuit deins le case del dit estat. **1607** COWELL *Interpr., Submarshall*,..is an officer in the Marshalsea. **1711** *Lond. Gaz.* No. 4797/1 The Count de Denhof, Sub-Marshal of Lithuania, hopes to succeed him.

'subˌmaster. [SUB- 6. Cf. med.L. *submagister*, F. *sous-maître*, formerly †*soubs-maistre*.] A subordinate, deputy, or assistant master.

14.. *Nom.* in Wr.-Wülcker 681/18 *Hic instructor*, a submastyr. **1517** in *Archæologia* LXI. 82 Sir Adam late submaister of the seid College. **1850** CHUBB *Locks & Keys* 15 With keys for the master, sub-master, and warders.

‖**submaxilla** (sʌbmæk'sɪlə). [mod.L.: see SUB- 3 and MAXILLA.] The lower jaw or jaw-bone.

sub'maxillary, *a.* (*sb.*) [f. mod.L. *submaxillāris*: see SUB- 1 b and MAXILLARY.]

1. Situated beneath the inferior maxilla.

submaxillary gland, a salivary gland situated on either side below the lower jaw; hence, pertaining to this gland, *esp.* of parts connected therewith, as *s. artery, duct, fossa, ganglion, vein*. Also as *sb.* (*ellipt.* for *s. artery*, etc.).

1787 *Med. Comm.* II. 369 The submaxillary glands were swollen. **1831** R. KNOX *Cloquet's Anat.* 73 An oblong superficial cavity, in which the submaxillary gland is placed. **1831** YOUATT *Horse* 120 The submaxillary artery, a branch of the jugular and the parotid duct. **1834** —— *Cattle* 335 The sub-maxillary vein returning the blood from the tongue, the mouth, and the face generally. **1836–9** *Todd's Cycl. Anat.* II. 214/1 A large depression (the submaxillary fossa) for the reception of the submaxillary gland. **1837** QUAIN *Elem. Anat.* (ed. 4) 812 The submaxillary ganglion, ..rests upon the gland just named [*sc.* the submaxillary]. **1871** DARWIN *Desc. Man* II. xii. 29 During the season of love, a musky odour is emitted by the submaxillary glands of the crocodile.

2. [f. prec.] Pertaining to the submaxilla.

1884 COUES *N. Amer. Birds* 98 On the under jaw, maxillary or submaxillary line.

sub'medial, *a.*

1. [SUB- 11, 20 d.] Near the middle or median line; almost medial.

1849 DANA *Geol.* App. I. (1850) 726 Beaks submedial.

2. *Geol.* [SUB- 1 a.] Lying below the middle group of rocks.

1855 OGILVIE Suppl., *Submedial*,..a term synonymous with transition, and applied to the lower secondary rocks, which bear a close resemblance to some of the primary rocks. **1855** J. PHILLIPS *Man. Geol.* 157 Scar limestone (submedial group).

So **sub'median** *a.*, near or behind a median part.

1851 MANTELL *Petrifactions* iii. §5. 293 The flattened angular spaces, and the sub-median trochanter. **1852** DANA *Crust.* II. 843 One tooth anterior, one submedian, and one posterior. **1861** H. HAGEN *Synopsis Neuroptera N. Amer.* 343 *Submedian nerve*, the longitudinal large nerve just behind the median.

sub'mediant. *Mus.* [SUB- 4 (*c*).] The sixth note of a scale, lying midway between the subdominant and the upper tonic. Also *attrib.*

1806 CALCOTT *Mus. Gram.* II. v. 135 The submediant.. varies also according to the Mode. **1889** PROUT *Harmony* i. 16 We..call this sixth note the Submediant, or lower mediant. *Ibid.* xii. 131 The submediant chord in the minor key. **1891** —— *Counterpoint* (ed. 2) 56 The submediant triad.

sub'mental, *a.* *Anat.* [SUB- 1 b, MENTAL *a.*[2]] Situated beneath the chin or under the edge of the lower jaw; chiefly in ***submental artery, vein***. Also, pertaining to the submentum.

1831 R. KNOX *Cloquet's Anat.* 653 The Sublingual Artery, which is sometimes a division of the submental. **1849–52** *Todd's Cycl. Anat.* IV. 1404/2 The submental vein, which arises in the sublingual gland. **1874** COUES *Birds N.W.* 617 Submental space partially feathered. **1883** *Encycl. Brit.* XV. 348/2 The submental gland of the Chevrotains.

‖**submentum** (sʌb'mɛntəm). *Entom.* [mod.L.; see SUB- 1 f.] The basal part of the labium.

1877 HUXLEY *Anat. Inv. Anim.* vii. 403 The submentum is not directly articulated with the cranial skeleton. **1888** ROLLESTON & JACKSON *Anim. Life* 141 The labium.. consists (1) of a large basal *sub-mentum*..(2) a *mentum*; (3) of two three-jointed *palpi*..(4) a *ligula*.

submerge (səb'mɜːdʒ), *v.* [ad. L. *submergĕre*, var. of *summergĕre*: see SUB- 2 and MERGE. Cf. F. *submerger*, It. *sommergere*, Sp., Pg. *sumergir*.]

1. *pass.* To be covered with water; to be sunk under water.

1606 SHAKS. *Ant. & Cl.* II. v. 94 So halfe my Egypt were submerg'd and made A Cesterne for scal'd Snakes. **1688** LUTTRELL *Brief Rel.* (1857) I. 453 That the island of Madera's..had been destroyed by an earthquake and submerg'd in the sea. **1794** R. J. SULIVAN *View Nat.* II. 430 Those lost people, whom we have supposed to have been submerged, when the present face of things was drawn into existence. **1833** LYELL *Princ. Geol.* III. 116 Tracts that may be submerged or variously altered in depth. **1853** KANE *Grinnell Exp.* xxxix. (1856) 359 The white whale..whistled, while submerged and swimming under our brig. **1877** HUXLEY *Physiogr.* 212 The remains of a vast forest..now submerged to a depth of perhaps twenty or thirty feet below high-water. **1880** DAWKINS *Early Man in Brit.* i. 1 He tells of continents submerged, and of ocean bottoms lifted up to become mountains.

fig. *a* **1625** BEAUM. & FL. *Love's Cure* v. iii, Many of his chief Gentry..spoyld, lost and submerged in the impious inundation and torrent of their still-growing malice. **1856** VAUGHAN *Mystics* (1860) I. 98 The miserable monks.. whose minds submerged in the 'mare tenebrosum' of the cloister, [etc.]. **1903** MYERS *Hum. Pers.* I. p. xxi, Faculty, which is kept thus submerged, not by its own weakness, but by the constitution of man's personality.

2. *trans.* To cause to sink or plunge into water; to place under water.

1611 COTGR., *Submerger*, to submerge; to plunge or sinke vnder, whirken or ouerwhelme by,..the water. **1726** BAILEY, To *Submerge*, to bend a Thing very low, to drown or dip. **1817** KIRBY & SP. *Entomol.* (1818) II. 212 Experimentalists may.., without danger, submerge a hive of bees, when they want to examine them particularly. **1870** YEATS *Nat. Hist. Comm.* 91 The shallow and tideless Baltic has scarcely a sounding that could submerge St. Paul's Cathedral.

fig. **1855** BAIN *Senses & Int.* II. ii. §19 (1864) 144 The magnitude of the sensation is attested by its power to submerge a great many irritations. **1907** FORSYTH *Posit. Preaching* iv. 124 Our demands must never be submerged by our sympathies.

3. *intr.* To sink or plunge under water; to undergo submersion.

1652 KIRKMAN *Clerio & Lozia* 123 A Cork sometimes elevateth it self, and then submergeth under the water. **1808** *Gentl. Mag.* LXXVIII. 670/2 Some say, they [*sc.* swallows] submerge in ponds. **1823** J. BADCOCK *Dom. Amusem.* 208 The ascending wires (where they submerge)..should be flattish at the sides. **1863** LD. LYTTON *Ring of Amasis* I. 48 He submerged, and we lost sight of him. **1903** A. H. BURGOYNE *Submarine Navigation* II. 162 Having reached the 'limit of visibility' it becomes necessary to submerge. **1915** *Glasgow Herald* 30 Mar. 8 In the vicinity of the enemy or when weather conditions make it necessary we submerge. **1930** W. FAULKNER *As I lay Dying* 146 We submerge in turn, holding to the rope, being clutched by one another. **1958** J. LEWIS in C. S. Lewis *Lett. to Amer. Lady* (1969) 72 He comes up for air now and then, blows a few pathetic bubbles, then submerges again. **1974** P. LOVESEY *Invitation to Dynamite Party* xiv. 172 Put the boat in diving trim... To submerge, push down the ballast-levers.

fig. **1837** CARLYLE *Fr. Rev.* II. III. iv, Plot after plot, emerging and submerging, like *ignes fatui* in foul weather. *Ibid.* III. II. v, This Question of the Trial..emerged and submerged among the infinite of questions and embroilments.

Hence **sub'merging** *vbl. sb.* and *ppl. a.*

1882 CROMMELIN *Brown-Eyes* viii, Alluvial deposit left there ages ago by the submerging waters. **1888** SCHAFF *Hist. Chr. Ch., Mod. Chr.* 219 Faith is the submerging of the old man, and the emerging of the new man. **1902** *Daily Chron.* 5 Apr. 7/6 The submerging was accomplished in 6 sec.

submerged (səb'mɜːdʒd), *ppl. a.* [f. prec. + -ED[1].] **a.** Sunk under water; covered or overflowed with water, inundated; *Bot.* growing entirely under water; *Naut.*, operating or being under water (esp. of or relating to a submarine).

1799 KIRWAN *Geol. Ess.* 81 The crash and ruin of the submerged continent. **1839** MURCHISON *Silur. Syst.* 503 One of these submerged forests is occasionally seen on the shore at Gupton Burrows. **1847** GROTE *Greece* II. xi. III. 197 The history of the vast submerged island of Atlantis. **1857** HENFREY *Bot.* 61 When they grow wholly under water (submerged leaves). **1884** BOWER & SCOTT *De Bary's Phaner.* 56 Hair-structures..under all states of adaptation, even in submerged species. **1902** H. C. FYFE et al. *Submarine Warfare* 258 When running submerged the submarine is lighter than her displacement. **1914** C. W. DOMVILLE-FIFE *Submarines* 10 Each of the 1,500 surface warships..carries the means for delivering submarine attacks in its torpedoes and surface and submerged discharging tubes. **1928** C. F. S. GAMBLE *N. Sea Air Station* 311 Their maximum submerged speed was, for a limited period, as much as 9 knots.

b. *fig.*; esp. in ***submerged tenth***, that part of the population which is permanently in poverty and misery. (Contrasted with *upper ten.*)

1837 CARLYLE *Fr. Rev.* I. v. iv, Happily, in place of the submerged Twenty-six, the Electoral Club is gathering. **1890** BOOTH *In Darkest Eng.* I. ii. 22 We have an army of nearly two millions belonging to the submerged classes. *Ibid.* 23 This Submerged Tenth—is it, then, beyond the reach of the nine-tenths in the midst of whom they live? *absol.* **1897** *Daily News* 31 Mar. 8/3 Those who seek to ameliorate the conditions of the submerged. **1903** *Westm. Gaz.* 18 Feb. 10/1 A..leader of hosts of submerged from the Egypt of slumdom.

c. Engin. ***submerged-arc welding***, a method of arc welding with a bare metal electrode in which both arc and electrode tip are entirely covered by a loose flux powder fed to the welding area.

1945 *Industry & Welding* Apr. 78 (*heading*) Submerged arc welding steps up production of invasion boat assemblies. **1952** [see BURDEN *sb.* 6]. **1975** BRAM & DOWNS *Manuf. Technol.* ii. 57 The submerged-arc welding process must be automatic.

sub'mergement. [f. SUBMERGE *v.* + -MENT.] Submersion.

1856 OLMSTED *Slave States* 524 When free from the social submergement and weight of disgrace which disabled them in England. **1884** *Daily News* 16 Sept. 5/7 With its incessant vibration and its state of almost continuous submergement, it is miserably uncomfortable for the crew.

submergence (səb'mɜːdʒəns). [f. SUBMERGE + -ENCE.] **a.** The condition of being submerged or covered with water (also *Geol.*, with glacier ice); the state of being flooded or inundated.

1832 LYELL *Princ. Geol.* II. 305 The proofs of submergence, during some part of the tertiary period,..are of a most unequivocal character. **1851** RICHARDSON *Geol.* ii. 21 The submergence of land by earthquakes. **1872** W. S. SYMONDS *Rec. Rocks* ix. 310 After the glacial submergence. **1875** DARWIN *Insectiv. Pl.* iii. 52 A submergence for forty seven hours had not killed the protoplasm.

b. *fig.*, e.g. a being plunged in thought; the 'swamping' of one thing by another; a sinking out of sight or into obscurity.

1871 GEO. ELIOT *Middlemarch* (1872) I. I. iii. 33 The secondary importance of ecclesiastical forms and articles of belief compared with that spiritual religion, that submergence of self in communion with Divine perfection. **1872** F. W. ROBINSON *Bridge of Glass* III. ix, The voice was so low, and the maiden's submergence so deep, that the grief-stricken figure did not move to the inquiry. **1898** *Chr. Herald* (N.Y.) 27 Apr. 368/4 An idea that death is the submergence of everything pleasant by everything doleful. **1903** MYERS *Hum. Pers.* I. p. xxviii, If the elements of emergence increase, and the elements of submergence diminish, the permeability of the psychical diaphragm may mean genius instead of hysteria.

sub'mergible, *a.* [f. SUBMERGE + -IBLE.] = SUBMERSIBLE.

1870 *Daily News* 18 Oct., To build a high-sided ship submergible in action. **1936** *World Petroleum* VII. 246 (*heading*) Submergible barges for Gulf Coast drilling. **1977** *Offshore Engineer* May 98/3 A submergible, electrically driven tide recorder is available from Benthos.

So **submergi'bility**.

1802–12 BENTHAM *Ration. Judic. Evid.* (1827) I. 130 Partaking in respect of submergibility of the nature of a ferry boat.

submerse (səb'mɜːs), *v. rare.* [f. L. *submers-*, pa. ppl. stem of *submergĕre* to SUBMERGE. Cf. next.] *trans.* To submerge, drown.

1837 *Fraser's Mag.* XVI. 344 [They] quietly submerse their memories in the waters of Lethe. **1905** *Daily Chron.* 15 June 6/7 The moving of the submersing lever from a perpendicular to a horizontal position.

submersed (səb'mɜːst), *pa. pple.* and *ppl. a.* [f. L. *submersus*, pa. pple. of *submergĕre* to SUBMERGE + -ED[1].] Submerged; covered with water, lying or growing under water. Now chiefly *Bot.*

a. *pa. pple.*

1727 BAILEY (vol. II), *Submersed*, plunged under Water, &c. **1776** J. LEE *Introd. Bot.* Explan. Terms 382 *Submersum*, submersed, sunk under the Surface of the Water. *c* **1789** *Encycl. Brit.* (1797) III. 444/2 A simple Leaf..may be Submersed, hid under the face of water. **1796** *Phil. Trans.* LXXXVI. 503 The fructification of the Chara being equally submersed. **1822** J. FLINT *Lett. Amer.* 214 A humane society for the resuscitation of persons submersed in water. **1836** MACGILLIVRAY *Trav. Humboldt* i. 23 A chain of mountains that has been broken up and submersed.

b. *ppl. a.*

1796 *Phil. Trans.* LXXXVI. 501, I do not hesitate to consider these grains of the submersed algæ to be..their effective seeds. **1807** SOUTHEY *Espriella's Lett.* II. 282 Submersed forests. **1836** MACGILLIVRAY *Trav. Humboldt* vi. 80 The islets of Coche and Cubagua are supposed to be remnants of the submersed land. **1847** W. E. STEELE *Field Bot.* 36 Submersed leaves multifid. **1866** *Treas. Bot.* 999/1 A submersed aquatic belonging to the order *Juncaginaceæ*. **1868** *Maidment's Scott. Ball.* I. 29 The submersed ecclesiastic was William de Perisbi.

submersible (səb'mɜːsɪb(ə)l), *a.* and *sb.* [f. L. *submers-*, pa. ppl. stem of *submergĕre* to SUBMERGE, prob. after F. *submersible*. Cf. mod.L. *submersibilis* and INSUBMERSIBLE (1865).]

A. *adj.* That may be submerged, covered with, plunged into, or made to remain under water; *esp.* of a boat (see quot. 1889).

1866 *Pall Mall Gaz.* 10 July 5 A German named Flack has invented a submersible vessel, to be used in laying torpedoes for the defence of harbours. **1889** SLEEMAN *Torpedoes* (ed. 2) 288 Torpedo boats which..are capable of being propelled at considerable depths below the surface of the water are usually termed 'submarine' torpedo boats; as however this is not the normal state of these vessels, they should rather be designated as 'submersible' torpedo boats. **1892** *Athenæum*

16 July 101/1 The place [Notre Dame de Londres] derives its name from Ondra, which in the local dialect signifies a humid or submersible country.

B. *sb.* A submersible boat; *spec.*, a small submersible vessel designed for use in underwater exploration or drilling or recovery operations, etc.

1900 *Daily Chron.* 8 Dec. 7 (Cass. Suppl.) The better type [of submarine boats] known as 'submersibles'. **1901** *Edin. Rev.* Apr. 343 Already in France the submarine is being displaced by the submersible. **1959** *Time* (Atlantic ed.) 23 Mar. 56/2 The *Skipjack* is the consummation of a long program to give the U.S. its first true submersible designed primarily for underwater work. **1967** *Listener* 18 May 657/2 Three of the bombs were soon recovered. The fourth—in the sea—nearly eluded an armada of warships, 'submersibles', and 'submarines'. **1973** D. KYLE *Raft of Swords* (1974) vi. 50 An oil company..had..been considering the purchase of a German submersible..small submarines for underwater industrial and defence use. **1980** *Daily Tel.* 14 Nov. 17 The film never gets round to it, being so preoccupied with salvage vessels, submersibles and diving bells, trying to locate, miles down, the dear old Titanic.

submersion (səbˈmɜːʃən). [ad. L. *submersio*, *-ōnem*, n. of action f. *submergĕre*, *-mers-* to SUBMERGE. Cf. F. *submersion*, It. *sommersione*, Sp. *sumersion*, etc.] The action of submerging or condition of being submerged; plunging into, sinking under, or flooding with water; *occas.* drowning.

1611 COTGR., *Submersion*, a submersion, plunging, sinking. **1653** RAMESEY *Astrol. Restored* 309 Many shipwracks and submersions of ships. **1692** RAY *Disc.* (1732) 242 The Submersion of the vast Island of Atlantis. **1781** COWPER *Retirem.* 584 All had long suppos'd him dead, By cold submersion, razor, rope, or lead. **1793** tr. *Buffon's Hist. Birds* VI. 471 The submersion of Swallows appears by no means ascertained. **1823** J. BADCOCK *Dom. Amusem.* 196 Half a pound of alum to every pint of water, which may be deemed necessary for the entire submersion of the article to be heated. **1856** STANLEY *Sinai & Pal.* ii. (1858) 144 Preserved by the salt with which a long submersion in those strange waters has impregnated them. **1910** *Encycl. Brit.* (ed. 11) III. 365 The earliest literary notices of baptism are far from conclusive in favour of submersion.

ˌsub-microˈscopic, *a.* [SUB- 14.] Too small to be seen even with the aid of a microscope; also *absol.*

1912 *Chem. Abstr.* VI. 1014 (*heading*) Methods for the recognition of submicroscopic structures. **1938** S. CHASE *Tyranny of Words* iii. 20 The submicroscopic, which we do not consciously see or feel. **1954** *Sat. Rev.* (U.S.) 19 June 48/1 'Reality' is apperceived on three levels: macroscopic, microscopic, sub-microscopic. **1978** H. MCLEAVE *Borderline Case* (1979) xiii. 133 A submicroscopic particle that struck and then went to earth.

Also **ˌsub-microˈscopical** *a.*; **ˌsub-microˈscopically** *adv.*

1934 *Amer. Jrnl. Sci.* CCXXVII. 284 A regularly repeated twinning of submicroscopically small units can give rise to an apparently homogeneous crystal. **1949** *Jrnl. Iron & Steel Inst.* CLXIII. 270/2 This heat might melt a sub-microscopically thin layer of metal. **1953** C. WAKELEY *Med. Dict.*, Sub-microscopical. **1954** *Ann. Reg.* *1953* 373 The determination of the structure of molecules in the sub-microscopical genes that regulate heredity. **1961** *Lancet* 2 Sept. 546/1 We have to continue the search for the basis of this specificity at the sub-microscopical level. **1976** *Dermatologica* CLIII. 209 No submicroscopical alterations of the cytoplasm were found in the interacting cells. **1981** *Acta Crystallogr.* A. XXXVII. 754/1 The diffraction of such submicroscopically intergrown twins is calculated for lamellae and blocks.

subˈminiature, *a.* [SUB- 14.] Even smaller than what is described as 'miniature'; very much reduced in size. Chiefly used in *Electronics* and *Photogr.*

1947 *Electronics* June 160/2 (caption) Oscillator circuits of the two units..are printed on the outer surface of a steatite cylinder housing the subminiature tube. **1956** *Spaceflight* I. 28/1 There are two alternative designs, one using subminiature valves and the other transistors. **1968** *Amateur Photographer* 1 May 13/2 Sizes [of camera] below 35mm are usually called sub-miniature. **1977** 'J. LE CARRÉ' *Hon. Schoolboy* vi. 123 Four lozenges of subminiature film..and a battered subminiature camera.

Hence **subˌminiaturiˈzation**, the development or use of subminiature devices, esp. in electronics.

1949 *Aviation Week* 11 Apr. 18/1 Not content with 'miniaturization' of electronic equipment for airborne installations, engineers are now utilizing 'subminiaturization' of this material to reduce its size and weight. **1957** *Circulation* XVI. 764/1 The transition from antisubmarine warfare to phonocardiography involved mainly subminiaturization of the transducer and adaptation of the amplifiers to the recording instruments used in routine clinical phonocardiography. **1960** *Analog Science Fact/Fiction* Nov. 108/2, I don't know what genius indulged his yen for subminiaturization,..but he carried it too far.

ˈsub-ˌminister, *sb.* Now *rare* or *Obs.* [f. SUB- 6 + MINISTER *sb.* Cf. med.L. *subminister*, F. *sous-ministre*, formerly †*subministre*.] A subordinate or deputy minister.

1565 HARDING *Answ. Jewel* 98 [Calvin's] disciple and subminister Theodore Beza. **1687** SETTLE *Refl. Dryden* 55 Why may not we suppose Subministers of the Fates to write their actions, some under Clarks to the Committee of Destinies? *c* **1800** R. CUMBERLAND *John de Lancaster* (1809) III. 200 The name of the sub-minister was now announced to Major Wilson. **1820** RANKEN *Hist. France* VIII. i. §2. 58 Tellier and Servien, subministers of Mazarin. **1823** BENTHAM *Not Paul* 371 As to Apollos, if so it was, that,..in the mind of our spiritual monarch, any such sentiment as jealousy, in regard to this sub-minister had place.

subminister (səbˈmɪnɪstə(r)), *v.* Now *rare.* [ad. L. *subministrāre* (var. *summ-*): see SUB- 8 and MINISTER *v.* Cf. F. *subministrer.*]

1. *trans.* To supply or furnish (sometimes in a secret manner).

1601 R. JOHNSON *Kingd. & Commw.* (1603) 262 Hauing subministred continuall supplies both of men and money, to their neighbors in flanders. **1669** GALE *Crt. Gentiles* I. III. iv. 56 A soil very fruitful, which subministered these fruits, of its own accord. *a* **1676** HALE *Prim. Orig. Man.* II. iv. 154 Even the inferior Animals have subministred unto Man the invention..of many things both Natural and Artificial and Medicinal. **1792** SIBLY *Occult Sci.* I. 56 As nothing can be produced, unless matter be subministered. **1857** *Truths Cath. Relig.* (ed. 4) II. 109 The blessed Virgin, subministering to him her flesh in the accomplishment..of the incarnation.

†**2.** *intr.* To minister *to* (lit. and fig.). *Obs.*

1611 COTGR., *Soubministrer*, to subminister vnto. *a* **1679** HOBBES *Rhet.* II. xviii. 76 They have wherewithal to subminister to their Lust. **1692** L'ESTRANGE *Fables* xxxviii. 38 Our Passions..are Good Servants, but Bad Masters, and Subminister to the Best, and Worst of Purposes, at once.

Hence **subˈministering** *ppl. a.*

a **1676** HALE *Prim. Orig. Man.* IV. iv. 327 The..accommodation of Faculties with subministring Faculties, and Organs subservient.

†**subˈministrant**, *a. Obs. rare.* [ad. med.L. *subministrans*, *-ant-*, pres. pple. of *subministrāre* (see prec.).] Subordinate.

a **1626** BACON *Cert. Consid. Ch. Eng.* Wks. 1778 III. 159 That which is most principal..to be left undone, for the attending of that which is subservient and subministrant [etc.].

†**subˈministrate**, *v.* [f. L. *subministrāt-*, pa. ppl. stem of *subministrāre* to SUBMINISTER.] *trans.* To supply, furnish.

1665 G. HARVEY *Advice agst. Plague* 15 Nothing subministrates apter matter to be converted into pestilent Seminaries than peoples steams and breaths. **1678** GALE *Crt. Gentiles* IV. III. 34 By permitting tentations, offering objects, subministrating occasions.

†**subminiˈstration.** *Obs.* [ad. late L. *subministrātio*, *-ōnem*, n. of action f. *subministrāre* to SUBMINISTER. Cf. OF. *soub-*, *subministration* (Cotgr.).] The action of subministering; ministering support; provision, supply.

1582 *N.T.* (Rhem.) Eph. iv. 16 The whole body being..knit together by al juncture of subministration. *Ibid.* Phil. i. 19 By your praier and the subministration of the Spirit of Jesus Christ. **1606** J. KING *Serm.* Sept. 39 Nourishment and raiment, and the subministration of necessary things. **1623** BP. HALL *Gt. Impostor* Wks. (1634) 462 The subministration of Vitall spirits, to the maintenance of the whole frame. **1678** GALE *Crt. Gentiles* IV. III. 57 Subministration of occasions.

So †**subˈministrator**, one who provides or supplies.

1611 COTGR., *Subministrateur*, a subministrator. **1625** tr. *Camden's Hist. Eliz.* I. 81 Some Marchants, which..became subministrators to the enemies of Christianity.

†**submise**, *v. Obs.* (Chiefly Caxton.) Also **-myse.** [app. f. OF. *soubmis*, var. of *sou(z)mis*, pa. pple. of *sou(z)metre* (:—L. **subtusmittĕre*) to submit.] *trans.* = SUBMIT 4, 5.

1471 CAXTON *Recuyell* (Sommer) 255 Loue in this nyght submysed and constrayned them to loue eche other with oute spekyng. **1483** —— *Gold. Leg.* 216/3 She submysed her body to delyte. **1491** —— *Vitas Patr.* (W. de W. 1495) II. 290 They haue submysed alle theyr wyll to the wyll of theyr soueraynes. **1502** *Ord. Crysten Men* (W. de W. 1506) IV. xxi. T viij b, The doubte, vnto the whiche the lenner [= lender] is submysed.

submiss (səbˈmɪs), *a.* Also 6–7 **-is, -isse.** [ad. L. *submissus*, pa. pple. of *submittĕre* to SUBMIT. Cf. SUMMISS.]

1. = SUBMISSIVE. (Const. *to.*) *Obs.* exc. *arch.*

a. Of persons.

1570 FOXE *A. & M.* I. 311/2 Neither was the kyng now and Archb. so submise: but [etc.]. **1580** LYLY *Euphues* (Arb.) 475 Be not too imperious ouer hir..nor too submisse. **1600** HEYWOOD *2nd Pt. Edw. IV*, II. ii. (1613) P 4 b, Was neuer Doue, or Turtle more submisse, Then I will be vnto your chastisement. **1612** BP. HALL *Contempl.*, *O.T.* III. iii. 207 To execute rigour vpon a submisse offender is more mercilesse then iust. **1625** MOUNTAGU *App. Cæsar* 110 It were to be wished, that such transported spirits were taught to be more submisse and sparing in their talk. **1667** MILTON *P.L.* VIII. 316 With aw In adoration at his feet I fell Submiss. **1708** J. PHILIPS *Cyder* I. 12 To foreign yoke submiss. **1735** SOMERVILLE *Chace* II. 112 Huntsman, lead on! behind the clust'ring Pack Submiss attend. **1813** SCOTT *Rokeby* III. xxi, Submiss he answer'd. **1862** CARLYLE *Fredk. Gt.* XII. iv. III. 213 To such of the Canons as he came upon, his Majesty was most polite; they most submiss. **1875** A. DE VERE *Mary Tudor* III. iii, Sir, you presume. Your station Is our confessional. There, as a daughter, I stand submiss.

absol. **1742** SHENSTONE *Schoolmistr.* xvii, To thwart the proud, and the submiss to raise.

b. Of actions, feelings, demeanour, etc.

a **1586** SIDNEY *Arcadia* (1622) 337 They would not equall them with those who were alreadie humbled, till they submitted in a more submisse manner. **1588** GREENE *Pandosto* (1607) A 3 b, Pandosto..entertained the Kings..& Noblemen with such submisse curtesie. **1622** BACON *Hen. VII*, 190 King Iames mollified by the Bishops submisse and eloquent Letters. **1659** HAMMOND *On Ps.* xcv. 6 Even the submissest and lowlyest gestures. **1702** C. MATHER *Magn. Chr.* Introd. C 3/2 A Simple, Submiss, Humble Style. **1817** COLERIDGE *Biog. Lit.* i. (1882) 5 The great works of past ages..in respect to which his faculties must remain passive and submiss. **1848** LYTTON *Harold* III. ii, Godwin prays with all submiss and earnest prayer. **1904** M. HEWLETT *Queen's Quair* I. xi, Every testimony of the submiss heart given him by my lady.

c. *fig.* Of material things.

1637 MARMION *Cupid & Psyche* I. i. 113 With her rosie feet insulting ore The submisse waves, a Dolphin she bestrides. **1868** GEO. ELIOT *Sp. Gipsy* II. 206 The loadstone draws, Acts like a will to make the iron submiss.

†**d.** Of buildings: ? Unpretentious. *Obs.*

1638 SIR T. HERBERT *Trav.* (ed. 2) 88 The buildings are generally submisse and low. **1664** J. WEBB *Stone-Heng* (1725) 40 Pylasters..ought not..to be of such stately Height as Pillars, but far more humble and submiss.

†**e.** With prefixed *too* forming subst. phr. *Obs.*

1606 WARNER *Alb. Eng.* XVI. ci. 399 And rather than in haughtiness did fault in too-submis.

†**2.** Of the voice, speech: Low, uttered in an undertone, subdued. *Obs.*

1604 E. G[RIMSTONE] *D'Acosta's Hist. Indies* V. xxx. 425 They said with a low and submisse voyce, Sir [etc.]. *a* **1638** MEDE *Wks.* (1672) 844 That submiss reading in Churches *sine cantu*, which we use now. **1666** J. SMITH *Old Age* 118 As Age enfeebleth a man the grindings are weaker, and the several voices of them more submiss. **1787** tr. *Klopstock's Messiah* IV. 182 Judas, then with submiss Voice said, Is it I?

subˈmissible, *a. rare.* [f. L. *submiss-*, pa. ppl. stem. of *submittĕre* to SUBMIT + -IBLE.] Capable of being submitted.

1837 LOCKHART *Scott* IV. i. 22, I..wish I could tell how [he]..translated [it] into any dialect submissible to Blackwood's apprehension.

submission (səbˈmɪʃən). Also 5 **-myssion, -mycion, -missioun,** 6 **-myssyon.** [ad. OF. †*submission* or its source L. *submissio*, *-ōnem* (var. *summ-*), n. of action f. *submittĕre* to SUBMIT. Cf. F. *soumission*, It. *sommessione*, etc. (see SUMMISSION).]

1. a. *Law.* Agreement to abide by a decision or to obey an authority; reference to the decision or judgement of a (third) party; in recent use *spec.*, the referring of a matter *to* arbitration; in *Sc. Law*, a contract by which parties agree to submit disputed matters to arbitration; also, the document embodying such a contract.

1411 *Rolls of Parlt.* III. 650/2 The forsaid Archebisshop, and Chamberleyn..by force of the submission that the said Robert in hem hath maad, haven ordeyned [etc.]. *c* **1450** *Godstow Reg.* 367 Next to this folowyth the Submyssion of the abbot and couent of Oseney to abide the ordeynyng. **1580** *Reg. Privy Council Scot.* Ser. I. III. 278 The submissioun maid and aggreit upoun..anent materis questionabill betuix thame. **1587** *Sc. Acts Jas. VI* (1814) III. 472/1 Submissioun of the contraversie betuix the erle of angus and lord flemyng. **1628** *Sc. Acts Chas. I* (1870) V. 189 The Submission made be the Lords of Erectiones Titulers Tacksmen and Gentrie Heretors of Lands To His Majestie anent their Superiorities and Teinds &c. **1697–8** *Act 9 Will. III* c. 15 §2 Where the Rule is made for Submission to such Arbitration or Umpirage. **1765–8** ERSKINE *Inst. Law Scot.* IV. iii. §29 Where the day within which the arbiters are to decide is left blank in the submission. **1854** *Act 17 & 18 Vict.* c. 125 §17 Every Agreement or Submission to Arbitration by Consent..may be made a Rule of any One of the Superior Courts of Law. **1875** *Encycl. Brit.* II. 312/2 A verbal submission..cannot be made a rule of court.

b. In wider use, the act of submitting a matter *to* a person for decision or consideration.

1911 *Concise Oxf. Dict.* s.v., The submission of the signature to an expert. **1914** *Times* 12 June 8/2 Amending Bill Drafted. Date of Submission to the Lords.

c. In legal use, a theory of a case put forward by an advocate. Cf. SUBMIT *v.* 7.

1922 *Westm. Gaz.* 20 Dec. 7/1 In my submission..this woman was called by the police as the only corroboration which they produced. **1923** *Ibid.* 4 Jan. 3/7 It was put to the Court that there should be no difference in the rates of wages for similar work in different localities,..but the Court could not uphold this submission. **1976** *Daily Tel.* 20 July 3/2 In my submission it is nonsense.

2. a. The condition of being submissive, yielding, or deferential; submissive or deferential conduct, attitude, or bearing; deference; †*occas.* humiliation, abasement. *arch.*

c **1449** PECOCK *Repr.* II. x. 207 More deuocioun, and louȝer submissioun thei myȝten not neither couthen araie forto bisette vpon Crist him silf. **1539** TONSTALL *Serm. Palm Sunday* (1823) 17 The bowynge down of euery knee, is ment the submyssyon of all creatures to theyr maker. **1560** DAUS tr. *Sleidane's Comm.* 10 Luther..writeth to the Bishop of Rome letters full of submission. *Ibid.* 273 Moste humbly and with great submission. **1591** SHAKS. *1 Hen. VI*, II. ii. 52 Tell her, I returne great thankes, And in submission will attend on her. **1643** BAKER *Chron.* (1653) 234 A Son of such submission. **1647** CLARENDON *Hist. Reb.* I. §110 He had not that..submission and reverence for the Queen as might have been expected. **1667** MILTON *P.L.* IV. 310 Subjection ..by her..Yeilded with coy submission, modest pride, And sweet reluctant amorous delay. **1720** SWIFT *Fates of Clergymen* Wks. 1755 II. II. 23 This sort of discretion is usually attended with..servile flattery and submission. **1855** MILMAN *Lat. Christ.* IX. II. xiii. IV. 357 They met, Frederick with dignified submission, the Pope with the calm majesty of age and position.

b. *pl.* Acts of deference or homage; demonstrations of submissiveness. *arch.*

1617 MORYSON *Itin.* II. 20 He failed not to mingle secretly the greatest Counsels of mischiefe with his humblest submissions. **1662** J. DAVIES tr. *Olearius' Voy. Amb.* 317 The Submissions, wherewith they express themselves in their Complements. *a* **1715** BURNET *Own Time* III. (1724) I. 522 He had really the submissions of a child to me. **1753** RICHARDSON *Grandison* V. xli. 254 To what submissions has your generous repentance subjected you. **1824–9** LANDOR *Imag. Conv.* Wks. 1846 I. 8 Those graceful submissions which afford us a legitimate pride when we render them to the worthy.

†**c.** Phr. ***with*** **(*great*)** ***submission***: subject to correction. Also *subst. Obs.*

1667 SIR T. HERBERT *Trav.* (1677) 31 Leaving every one to his own credulity, I shall only (but with submission) give my present apprehension of this Abassin Emperor. **1710** PALMER *Proverbs* 189 Two or three If you'll give me Leave's; as many Spare Me's, with Submission's and I humbly Conceive's. *a* **1721** PRIOR *Turtle & Sparrow* 126 With great Submission I pronounce, That People Die no more than Once. **1753** CIBBER *Lives Poets* I. 18 With great submission to his judgment, we think [etc.]. **1802–12** BENTHAM *Ration. Judic. Evid.* (1827) III. 644 With submission, suppositions of a contrary tendency might be raised in any number.

3. a. The action of submitting *to* an authority, a conquering or ruling power; the act of yielding to the claims of another, or surrendering to his will or government; the condition of having submitted; also, an instance of this.

1482 *Cov. Leet Bk.* 512 That þe seid Laurence shulde make his submission to such Meires as he had offended. **1575** GASCOIGNE *Glasse Govt.* Wks. 1910 II. 20 When the people of Israell provoked him at sundry times, he did yet at every submission stay his hand from punishment. **1584–5** *Act 27 Eliz.* c. 2. §13 All such..Submissions as shall be made by force of this Act..shall be certified into the Chancerie. **1617** MORYSON *Itin.* II. 19 A submission of the Rebels. *Ibid.* 279 Hee..made a most humble submission in writing. **1621** BACON in *Jrnl. Ho. Lords* III. 85/1 My humble Suit to your Lordships is, That my penitent Submission may be my Sentence, and the Loss of the Seal my Punishment. **1651** HOBBES *Leviath.* II. xx. 105 To save his own life..by submission to the enemy. **1729** BUTLER *Serm.* Wks. 1874 II. 203 Religion consists in submission and resignation to the divine will. **1831** SCOTT *Ct. Rob.* xxvi, By whose intervention you might have brought his empire to submission. **1833–5** NEWMAN *Hist. Sk.* (1876) II. I. viii. 150 The pursuit of gain may be an act of submission to the will of parents. **1874** GREEN *Short Hist.* vii. §2. 356 Mary was resolved to bring about a submission to Rome. **1878** *Encycl. Brit.* VIII. 334/2 The Act of Submission on the part of the clergy subordinated all ecclesiastical legislation within the kingdom to the royal will.

b. *transf.*

1781 COWPER *Charity* 158 All other sorrows virtue may endure, And find submission more than half a cure;..But slav'ry! **1790** —— *Mother's Pict.* 44, I learn'd at last submission to my lot. **1829** SCOTT *Anne of G.* xxiv, He recommends to us submission to our hapless fate.

†**4.** Used for: Admission, confession. (Shaks.)

1592 SHAKS. *Rom. & Jul.* III. i. 76 O calme, dishonourable, vile submission. **1598** —— *Merry W.* IV. iv. 11 Be not as extreme in submission, as in offence.

5. *attrib.*: **submission bond** (see sense 1), an arbitration bond.

1791 KYD *Law of Awards* 231 The party in whose favour the award was made, having no advantage from the submission being made a rule of court, brought a common action on the submission-bond.

†**sub'missioner.** *Obs. rare*$^{-1}$. [f. SUBMISSION + -ER[1].] One who makes his submission.

1593 NASHE *Christ's T.* (1613) 75 The Princes of the Iewes (which Titus as submissioners and succour-suers had received to mercy).

submissionist (səb'mɪʃənɪst). [f. SUBMISSION + -IST.] One who advocates submission; *spec.* in Spanish and U.S. history.

1828 *Lights & Shades* I. 209 Mr. Popjoy alluding to the submissionists at Cadiz. **1861** O. W. HOLMES in *Corr. Motley* (1889) I. 360 The Hunker or Submissionist, or whatever you choose to call the wretch who would sacrifice everything and beg the South's pardon for offending it. **1906** *Contemp. Rev.* July 118 Those organs which carried on a violent campaign against the submissionists.

submissive (səb'mɪsɪv), *a.* [ad. L. **submissīvus*, f. *submiss-*, pa. ppl. stem of *submittĕre* to SUBMIT. Cf. It. *sommessivo*.]

1. Of persons, their actions, words, attributes, etc.: Disposed or inclined to submit; yielding to power or authority; marked by submission or humble and ready obedience.

a **1586** SIDNEY *Arcadia* III. (1598) 335 With the most submissiue maner his behauiour could yeeld. **1588** SHAKS. *L.L.L.* IV. i. 92 Submissiue fall his princely feete before. **1596** —— *Tam. Shr.* Ind. i. 53 A lowe submissiue reuerence. **1640** BROME *Antipodes* III. ii, He bring him on submissive knees. **1670** PETTUS *Fodinæ Reg.* 34 It might be added with a submissive Confidence, that [etc.]. **1742** WESLEY *Hymn, 'O for a heart'*, An heart resign'd, submissive, meek. **1781** GIBBON *Decl. & F.* xxxvi. (1788) II. 326 His applications for peace became each hour more submissive. **1831** SCOTT *Ct. Rob.* xxv, With pious and submissive prayers, the Countess closed that eventful evening. **1841** D'ISRAELI *Amen. Lit.* (1867) 59 Feeble sovereigns and a submissive people could not advance into national greatness. **1868** FREEMAN *Norm. Conq.* (1877) II. App. 620 To represent Godwine as a model of submissive loyalty towards Eadward.

b. Const. *to*.

1686 tr. *Chardin's Trav. Persia* 238 This Prince is not..so submissive to his Orders, as the other Viceroys. **1757** WILKIE *Epigoniad* III. 56 His manly voice my horses will obey, And move submissive to his firmer sway. **1869** FREEMAN *Norm. Conq.* (1875) III. xii. 134 As little submissive to lawful authority as his forefather. **1907** *Verney Mem.* I. 458 Advising his quarrelsome sister..to be submissive to her husband.

c. *fig.* Of material things.

a **1721** PRIOR *2nd Hymn Callim.* 6 The sever'd Bars Submissive clink against their brazen Portals.

†**2. a.** = SUBMISS 2. *Obs. rare.*

a **1652** J. SMITH *Sel. Disc.* VI. vii. (1821) 253 Inquiring with a submissive voice, as if he had been at his private prayers, Shall I do so, or so?

†**b.** Restrained. *Obs. rare.*

1753 HANWAY *Trav.* (1762) II. I. xii. 62 If we consider what is due to health,..to moderate passions, submissive appetites.

sub'missively, *adv.* [f. prec. + -LY[2].] In a submissive manner, with submission.

c **1590** MARLOWE *Jew of Malta* [IV.] 1790 Write not so submissiuely, but threatning him. **1687** DRYDEN *Hind & P.* II. 509 The whole hierarchy, with heads hung down, Submissively declin'd the pondrous proffer'd crown. **1746** HERVEY *Refl. Flower Garden* (1818) 146 Under the heaviest tribulations most submissively patient. **1838** DICKENS *Nich. Nick.* xiv, 'Perhaps you are right, uncle,' replied Mrs. Kenwigs submissively. **1860** TYNDALL *Glac.* I. xxii. 153 He approached me submissively,..and declared his willingness to go on.

sub'missiveness. [f. as prec. + -NESS.] The quality or condition of being submissive.

1611 SPEED *Hist. Gt. Brit.* IX. xix. 714 We seeke rather by violence to extort, then by submissiuenes to beg his pardon. **1679** DRYDEN *Troil. & Cress.* Pref. b 2, With all the submissiveness he can practice, & all the calmness of a reasonable man. **1818** HALLAM *Mid. Ages* (1872) I. 125 The pope's knowledge of the personal submissiveness to ecclesiastical power. **1863** KINGLAKE *Crimea* (ed. 3) II. xii. 185 They approached him respectfully, but without submissiveness. **1890** F. W. ROBINSON *Very strange Fam.* 74 In all submissiveness [he] owned how deplorably wrong he had been.

submissly (səb'mɪslɪ), *adv. arch.* [f. SUBMISS + -LY[2].] With submission, submissively.

1595 in Birch *Mem. Q. Eliz.* (1754) I. 237, I beseech you most submissly, to use your excellent insight [etc.]. **1611** *Bible* Ecclus. xxix. 5 For his neighbours money he will speake submissely. **1650** JER. TAYLOR *Holy Living* ii. §4. 104 Humility consists not in..going softly and submissely. **1739** G. OGLE *Gualth. & Gris.* 104 Then chuse the Good! The Ill submissly bear. *a* **1851** MOIR *Castle of Time* xx, The heathen ..submissly owns His trust in Him who bled on Calvary!

sub'missness. *arch.* [f. as prec. + -NESS.] Submissiveness, submission.

1621 BURTON *Anat. Mel.* I. ii. III. xv, With all submissenes [I] prostrate my self to your censure and service. **1649** MILTON *Eikon.* xi. 104 Whether it were his envy, not to be over-bounteous, or that the submissness of our asking stirr'd up in him a certain pleasure of denying. **1664** BUTLER *Hud.* II. iii. 493 Whachum advanc'd with all submissness, T'accost 'em, but much more, their bus'ness.

submit (səb'mɪt), *v.* Also 4–6 **-mytte,** (4 *pa. t.* **-mytte,** 5 *pa. pple.* **-mytt**), 5 **-mett,** 5–6 **-myt,** 5–7 **-mitte,** 6–7 **-mitt.** [ad. L. *submittĕre*, var. of *summittĕre* (see SUMMIT *v.*[1]), f. *sub-* SUB- 2 + *mittĕre* to send, put; cf. OF. *soub-*, *submetre*, later var. of *sousmetre* (see note under SUB- *prefix*), mod F. *soumettre*, and Pr. *sob-*, *sotzmetre*, It. *sommettere* beside *sottomettere*, Sp. *someter*, Pg. *submetter*.]

I. 1. *refl.* and *intr.* To place oneself *under* the control of a person in authority or power; to become subject, surrender oneself, or yield *to* a person or his rule, etc.

†**a.** Const. *under*; *refl.* only. *Obs.*

c **1374** CHAUCER *Boeth.* II. pr. v. (Camb MS.), Syn ye demen þat tho fowlest thinges ben yowre goodys, thanne submitten [*v.r.* summytten] ye and putten yowre selven vndyr the fowleste thinges by yowre estimacion. **1471** CAXTON *Recuyell* (Sommer) 603/22 Sayng that they wold not submytte hem so many noble men vnder the strengthe of one man. **1535** COVERDALE *Gen.* xvi. 9 Returne to thy mastresse agayne, and submitte thyself vnder hir hande. **1574** tr. *Bale's Pag. Popes* Ep. Ded. *iv b, Although they were more in number,..yet woulde submitte them selues vnder their power, as though they were the inferiours. **1601** R. JOHNSON *Kingd. & Commw.* (1603) 109 They were enforced to submitte themselues vnder the protection of the Florentines.

b. Const. *to* (†*unto*) a person, his government, rule, will, etc.

(*a*) *refl.* *c* **1386** CHAUCER *Melib.* ¶854 We submytten vs to the excellence and benignitee of youre gracious lordshipe. **1411** *Rolls of Parlt.* III. 650/1 On whom, and to his ordenance, the forsaid Lord the Roos and Robert hadden submytted hem. **1490** CAXTON *Eneydos* xxi. 80 After that this dydo had vtterly submytted & dedicate her-self to eneas. **1526** TINDALE *Eph.* v. 22 Wemen submit youre selves vnto youre awne husbandes, as vnto the lorde. **1535** COVERDALE *1 Chron.* xxix [xxx]. 24 All kynge Dauids children submytted themselues vnto kynge Salomon. **1651** HOBBES *Leviathan* II. xvii. 88 When a man maketh his children, to submit themselves..to his government. **1686** tr. *Chardin's Trav. Persia* 149 He did not come and submit himself to him. **1859** GEO. ELIOT *Adam Bede* lii, We must submit ourselves entirely to the Divine Will. **1909** OXENHAM *Greatheart Gillian* xxvii, Submit yourself quietly to the law.

(*b*) *intr.* *c* **1460** SIR R. ROS *La Belle Dame* 234, I am hoole submytt to your seruise. **1608** SHAKS. *Per.* II. iv. 39 Your noble selfe..Were thus submit vnto. **1652** in *Cromwellian Union* (1902) 4 Several Troops of the Tories that are submitting to the Parliament. **1667** MILTON *P.L.* x. 196 To thy Husbands will Thine shall submit. **1745** BUTLER *Serm.* Wks. 1874 II. 284 Children..are..habituated..to submit to those who are placed over them. **1855** MACAULAY *Hist. Eng.* xii. III. 152 After the flight of James, those troops submitted to the Prince of Orange. **1877** FROUDE *Short Stud.* (1883) IV. I. iii. 34 He despatched a legate..to tell Becket that he must..submit to the king's pleasure.

c. Without const.: To yield, surrender, be submissive.

(*a*) *refl.* *c* **1440** *Partonope* 4621 (Univ. Coll. MS.), Myne heede ys naked, and I Submytte me. **1526** TINDALE *Matt.* xviii. 4 Whosoever..shall submit him silfe. **1568** GRAFTON *Chron.* II. 659 [They] came humbly and submitted themselues. **1595** SHAKS. *John* II. i. 159 Submit thee boy. **1638** BAKER tr. *Balzac's Lett.* (vol. II.) 13 The persecutors of those who submit themselves.

(*b*) *intr.* **1575** GASCOIGNE *Kenelworth* Wks. 1910 II. 93 Even gates and all..submitte and seeke your sheelde. **1593** SHAKS. *Rich. II*, III. iii. 143 What must the King doe now: must he submit? **1667** MILTON *P.L.* I. 108 Courage never to submit or yield. **1792** ALMON *Anecd. W. Pitt* III. xliv. 198 A Prince of the House of Savoy had his property seized by him: the injured Prince would not submit. **1852** MRS. STOWE *Uncle Tom's C.* xviii. 175 'Miss Marie', as Dinah always called her young mistress,..found it easier to submit than contend. **1871** FREEMAN *Norm. Conq.* (1876) IV. 164 That the greater part of the shire submitted easily after the fall of the Capital.

2. To surrender oneself *to* judgement, criticism, correction, a condition, treatment, etc.; to consent to undergo or abide by a condition, etc.

(*a*) *refl.* *c* **1430** LYDG. *Min. Poems* (E.E.T.S.) I. 62, I me submytte to alle that schall now heer This symple processe of my translacyoun. *c* **1430** *Stans Puer ad Mensam* 99 (Lamb. MS.), I submitte me to correccioun withoute ony debate. **1471** CAXTON *Recuyell* (Sommer) 367/2 That ye submette yow vnto theyr obeyssance. **1565** ALLEN *Def. Purg.* To Rdr. 6 b, I humbly submit my selfe to the iudgement of suche oure masters in faithe and religion, [etc.]. **1577–87** HOLINSHED *Chron.* III. 2/2 To submit themselues to bondage. **1594** KYD *Cornelia* IV. i. 160 Shall we then..Submit vs to vnurged slauerie? **1607** SHAKS. *Cor.* III. iii. 44 If you submit you to the peoples voices. **1617** MORYSON *Itin.* I. 122, I submitted my selfe to these conditions. **1621** BACON in *Jrnl. Ho. Lords* III. 84/2 [I] submit myself wholly to your Piety and Grace. **1629** *Sc. Acts Chas. I* (1870) V. 197 The saids persouns..did submitt thame selffes to ws and ar bound to stand and abyde at our determinatioun. **1667** MILTON *P.L.* IX. 919 Submitting to what seemd remediless. **17..** WHITE (T.), Christian people submit themselves to conformable observance of the.. constitutions of their spiritual rulers. **1819** SCOTT *Leg. Montrose* viii, 'May Heaven', he said,..'judge between our motives'... 'Amen', said Montrose; 'to that tribunal we all submit us'. **1913** *Times* 11 Aug. 3/1 The majority of cases would voluntarily submit themselves to treatment.

(*b*) *intr.* **1628** FELTHAM *Resolves* II. v. 11 A man that submits to reuerent Order. **1686** tr. *Chardin's Coronat. Solyman* 110 To which reasons of his sister the Prince submitted. *a* **1700** EVELYN *Diary* 2 Aug. 1665, That the meanes to obtaine remission of punishment was not to repine at it, but humbly submit to it. **1711** ADDISON *Spect.* No. 115 ¶1 Bodily Labour..which a Man submits to for his Livelihood. **1758** J. DALRYMPLE *Ess. Feudal Property* (ed. 2) 48 Perhaps the nobles more easily submitted to the uncertainty of relief. **1781** COWPER *Expost.* 633 Prove it —if better, I submit and bow. **1802** MAR. EDGEWORTH *Moral T.* (1816) I. 212, I must know my crime, before I submit to punishment. **1837** CARLYLE *Fr. Rev.* I. III. ii, Healing measures..such as..all men must, with more or less reluctance, submit to. **1874** MOZLEY *Univ. Serm.* ix. (1877) 200 To submit to trials for our own discipline.

transf. **1658** SIR T. BROWNE *Hydriot.* ii. (1736) 21 That Metal soon submitteth unto Rust and Dissolution.

†**b.** Const. *to* with inf. or gerund: To yield so far as *to do* so-and-so, consent *to*; *occas.* to condescend *to*. *Obs.*

(*a*) *refl.* *c* **1380** WYCLIF *Sel. Wks.* III. 457 þei submytten hem to be correctid. **1444** *Cov. Leet Bk.* 203 Submittyng themselffe with due submission to abyde the rule of the maiour. *a* **1533** BERNERS *Huon* lxxxi. 246, I submyt my selfe to receyue suche dethe that ye & youre barons can deuyse. **1549** COVERDALE, etc. *Erasm. Par. Gal.* vi. 4, 5 If he submitte him selfe to restore him againe.

(*b*) *intr.* *c* **1386** CHAUCER *Man Law's Prol.* Introd. 35 Ye been submytted thurgh youre free assent To stonden in this cas at my Iuggement. **1667** MILTON *P.L.* XII. 191 This River-dragon tam'd at length submits To let his sojourners depart. **1697** C. LESLIE *Snake in Grass* (ed. 2) 224 They, at last, submitted, to have these words left out. **1794** MRS. RADCLIFFE *Myst. Udolpho* xxviii, She submitted to humble herself to Montoni. **1818** CRUISE *Digest* (ed. 2) II. 158 Where the mortgagee submits to be redeemed. **1852** THACKERAY *Esmond* III. vii, I..affected gladness when he came, submitted to hear when he was by me.

†**3.** *refl.* To subject or expose oneself *to* danger, etc. *Obs.*

1471 CAXTON *Recuyell* (Sommer) 217/14 Your champion that for your loue submytteth hym self vnto the peryll of deth. *a* **1586** SIDNEY *Arcadia* III. xiv. (1912) 435 The dayly dangers Amphialus did submit himselfe into. **1601** SHAKS. *Jul. C.* I. iii. 47, I haue walk'd about the streets, Submitting me vnto the perillous Night.

II. 4. *trans.* To bring under a certain control, government, or rule; to make subject, cause to yield *to* a person; to cause (a thing) to be subordinated *to* another. Now *rare*.

In the first quot. a literalism of translation.

c **1374** CHAUCER *Boeth.* I. pr. iv. (1868) 19 What open confessioun of felonie hadde euer iugis so accordaunt in cruelte þat oþer errour of mans witte or ellys condicioun of fortune þat is vncerteyne to al mortal folk ne submyttede summe of hem? **1422** YONGE tr. *Secr. Secr.* xvii. 146 If þou wilt submyt or vndreset al thyngis to the. *c* **1449** PECOCK *Repr.* I. xiv. 73 It miȝte seme that God wolde not..submitte ..and sende him [*viz.* Holy Scripture] to resoun. **1530**

PALSGR. 355 Whiche dyd submytte a great parte of Grece in their subjection. **1558** T. WATSON *Seven Sacr.* 43 b, We submitte our reason to our fayth. **1590** C. S. *Right Relig.* 23 God..hath submitted all things vnder his feete. **1644** [H. PARKER] *Jus Populi* 28 Happy is that King which anticipates his subjects in submitting his own titles. **1850** TENNYSON *In Mem.* cxiv, Submitting all things to desire. **1863** GEO. ELIOT *Romola* xxxii, She was determined never to submit her mind to his judgment on this question.

5. To subject *to* a certain condition or treatment. Now *rare*.

c **1450** *Godstow Reg.* 507 The said Andrew bounde and submytted the same mese, with the pertynentis..to the distreynyng of the forsaid abbesse. **1490** CAXTON *Eneydos* Prol. 4, I submytte my sayd boke to theyr correctyon. **1528** MORE *Dyaloge* IV. Wks. 273/2 To submytte..the rebellion of theyr reason to the obedyence of faith. **1614** RALEIGH *Hist. World* V. iii. §15. 516 To submit learned Propositions, vnto the workemanship..of base handicrafts men. **1668** DRYDEN *Dram. Poesy* Ess. (ed. Ker) I. 56 Whether we ought not to submit our stage to the exactness of our next neighbours. **1758** J. DALRYMPLE *Ess. Feudal Property* (ed. 2) 214 That system..submitted its peculiar forms to the dispatch and ease required in the extended..dealings of mankind. **1861** M. PATTISON *Ess.* (1889) I. 47 The inmates of the Steelyard were submitted to an almost monastic discipline.

b. To subject *to* an operation or process.

1815 J. SMITH *Panorama Sci. & Art* II. 449 Till Sir H. Davy..submitted the earths to the same powerful means of analysis. **1837** GORING & PRITCHARD *Microgr.* 211 When submitted to the action of polarized light. **1857** MILLER *Elem. Chem., Org.* i. 42 When alcohol is submitted to distillation. **1885** *Sat. Rev.* 21 Feb. 235/2 Preparing their young horses for the wild rush of the hunting-field by submitting them to the milder yet stimulating excitement of coursing.

6. To bring under a person's view, notice, or consideration; to refer *to* the decision or judgement of a person; to bring up or present *for* criticism, consideration, or approval.

1560 DAUS tr. *Sleidane's Comm.* 31 b, To submitte his writynges to the knowledge of the Emperour. **1587** *Sc. Acts Jas. VI* (1814) III. 478/2 To quhome baith þe saidis pairties referrit and submittit þe foirsaid supplicatioun. **1644** *Sc. Acts Chas. I* (1870) VI. I. 179/2 Baith the saides pairties.. Submitted þe foirsaid Complant..before þe secreet Counsell. **1651** HOBBES *Leviathan* I. xv. 78 They that are at controversie, submit their Right to the judgement of an Arbitrator. *a* **1721** PRIOR *Prol. Delia's Play* 28 Dare to be true, submit the rest to Heaven. **1784** COWPER *Task* IV. 98 It [*sc.* the globe] turns submitted to my view, turns round With all its generations. **1856** FROUDE *Hist. Eng.* (1858) II. vi. 113 To prepare the measures which were to be submitted to Parliament by the government. **1860** TYNDALL *Glac.* II. xxvii. 384 It is indeed a grand experiment which Nature here submits to our inspection. **1891** *19th Cent.* Dec. 855 To submit a copy of his journal to the police before its publication could be sanctioned. **1905** *Act 5 Edw. VII*, c. 17 §5 In order that such proceedings may be submitted for the sanction of Parliament.

with clause.

1749 FIELDING *Tom Jones* Ded., How far I have succeeded ..I shall submit to the candid reader.

b. Without const.; in *Sc. Law*, to refer to arbitration.

1799 J. ROBERTSON *Agric. Perth* 374 An account of the quantity of corn shipped at this port..is submitted as deserving notice. **1838** W. BELL *Dict. Law Scot.* s.v. *Arbitration*, An order on the parties..mutually to discharge each other of the matter submitted. **1855** BAIN *Senses & Int.* III. i. §38 (1864) 378 On this question the following remarks are submitted. **1879** TOURGEE *Fool's Err.* xxv. 150 The conventions had..submitted constitutions which had been ratified by vote of the people. **1888** BRYCE *Amer. Commw.* xvi. I. 226 The officials of the government cannot submit bills.

c. *absol.* or *intr.*; in *Sc. Law*, to make a 'submission'.

1765–8 ERSKINE *Inst. Law Scot.* IV. iii. §35 Decrees-arbitral, as their force arises from the express compact of the parties submitting..could not be set aside. **1897** *Daily News* 4 Mar. 6/4 The latest Saturday outsiders may 'submit' will be the Saturday in next week.

7. To put forward as a contention or proposition; to urge or represent with deference (*that*...). Now freq. in legal parlance.

1818 CRUISE *Digest* (ed. 2) III. 226 He humbly presumed to submit to His Majesty, that, before any act was done [etc.]. **1863** MITCHELL *Sev. Stor. My Farm* 243 We submit that it looks a little yellow. **1875** E. WHITE *Life in Christ* IV. xxiv. (1878) 361 There is, I submit, no possibility of escape from the force of this argument. **1907** *Standard* 19 Jan. 4/4 Counsel, in concluding his speech, submitted that the plaintiff was entitled to recover damages.

III. 8. *trans.* To let or lay down, lower, sink, lay low; to place (one's neck) under the yoke or the axe. ***to submit the fasces*** (see FASCES 2). ? *Obs.*

c **1611** CHAPMAN *Iliad* XIII. 384 His shrunke knees, submitted him to death. *Ibid.* XX. 295 My lance, submitted [ἔγχος μὲν τόδε κεῖται ἐπὶ χθονός]. *a* **1634** RANDOLPH *Poems* (1638) 82 Rome did submit her Fasces. **1667** MILTON *P.L.* V. 784 Will ye submit your necks, and chuse to bend The supple knee? **1725** POPE *Odyss.* XI. 205 Since in the dust proud Troy submits her tow'rs. **1757** [see NECK *sb.*[1] 3 b]. **1807** ROBT. WILSON in *Life* (1862) II. 145, I will now submit my head to the block if [etc.]

†**b.** To put (the female) *to* the male. *Obs.*

1697 DRYDEN *Virg. Georg.* III. 104 Submit thy Females to the lusty Sire.

†**c.** *refl.* To become low or lower. *Obs.*

1662 DRYDEN *To Ld. Chanc.* 139 Sometimes the Hill submits itself a while In small Descents.

†**d.** To lower the standard of. *Obs.*

1556 R. ROBINSON tr. *More's Utopia* To Rdr. A ij b, To the meanesse of whose learninge I thoughte it my part to submit ..my stile.

submittal (səb'mɪtəl). *rare.* [f. SUBMIT + -AL[1].] The act of submitting.

1888 *Amer. Nat.* Mar. 262 The Report..having been.. called for at an unusually early date, as explained in the letter of submittal.

†**sub'mittance.** *Obs.* [f. as prec. + -ANCE.] Submission.

1605 *Answer Discov. Romish Doctr.* Ep. Ded. 5 That.. which your colleged Princes..doe offer to the so many yeares disobedient Netherlanders, vpon their temporall submittance. **1640** FULLER, etc. *Abel Rediv., Philpot* (1651) 223 Couragious Philpot..would not once allow The least Submittance to erronious powers. **1650** R. HOLLINGWORTH *Exerc. Usurped Powers* 18 There is a bar yet behind..to keep back such a submittance to the Usurper.

submitted (səb'mɪtɪd), *ppl. a.* [f. as prec. + -ED[1].]

1. Reduced to submission; that has surrendered to authority; subjugated.

In mod. use prob. after F. *soumis.*

1606 CHAPMAN *Gentl. Usher* IV. iii. 58, I..Easde with well gouerning my submitted payne. **1660** DRYDEN *Astræa Redux* 249 Proud her returning Prince to entertain With the submitted Fasces of the Main. **1837** CARLYLE *Fr. Rev.* II. III. iv, The wild submitted Titan. **1868** *Daily News* 7 Sept., The Turks..outraged some hapless families of 'submitted' peasants. **1900** *Westm. Gaz.* 17 Aug. 6/1 All foodstuffs, forage, and horses, whether in possession of submitted Boers or otherwise.

†**2.** Laid or put down. *Obs.*

c **1611** CHAPMAN *Iliad* XIX. 258 The bristled throat Of the submitted sacrifice with ruthless steel he cut.

†**3.** = SUBMISS *a.* 2. *Obs.*

1806 R. CUMBERLAND *Mem.* (1807) I. 396 He had spoken in a low and submitted voice.

4. Presented for judgement.

1897 *Westm. Gaz.* 26 Mar. 2/1 They must have judged the submitted works at the rate of more than two thousand a day.

sub'mitter. [f. SUBMIT + -ER[1].] One who submits.

1607 HIERON *Wks.* I. 384 Dorcas..a submitter of her selfe to the ordinance of God. **1635** D. DICKSON *Pract. Wks.* (1845) I. 25 Submitters turn in to Him acknowledging that they are dust and ashes. **1654** WHITLOCK *Zootomia* 118 The sick (but confident) submitters of themselves to this Empyricks cast of the Dye. **1782** J. BROWN *Nat. & Revealed Relig.* I. i. 25 The submitters, no doubt, insisted on the best terms, for their obedience, which they could obtain. **1840** *Tait's Mag.* VII. 68 The..trimmers, and submitters to expediency.

b. *Sc. Law.* One who makes a 'submission'.

1628 *Sc. Acts Chas. I* (1870) V. 191/2 This present Submission shall be no wayes prejudicial to whatsoever action of Warrandice competent to the saids Persones Submitters or any of them against their Authors. **1765–8** ERSKINE *Inst. Law Scot.* IV. iii. §32 If the submitters limit the power of the arbiters to any fixed day. **1804** *W. M. Morison's Decis. Crt. Session* XVII. 6900 According to the universal order taken by the submitters concerning kirklands.

†**submittie.** *Obs.* [f. SUBMIT + *-ie* = EE (cf. 16th–17th c. *committie*). The use of the suffix appears to be arbitrary.] One who has submitted.

1611 SPEED *Hist. Gt. Brit.* IX. viii. 9 To receiue peaceably all Submitties. **1617** MORYSON *Itin.* II. 154 Touching these submitties while they were in rebellion, he did spoile waste and kill many of them.

sub'mitting, *vbl. sb.* [-ING[1].] The action of the vb. SUBMIT; submission.

c **1460** *Oseney Reg.* 49 Of þ[e] which debates..þe parties.. haue i-putte þem-selfe in submittyng and ordinaunce of the bisshop of lincoln. *a* **1653** GOUGE *Comm. Heb.* xi. 18 This could not be without Isaac's voluntary submitting of himself. **1675** SHEFFIELD (Dk. Buckhm.) *Ess. Satire* 240 A life..Spent in base Injury, and low submitting. **1723** WATERLAND *2nd Vind. Christ's Div.* 62 The submitting to This Office is a great Instance of the Son's Condescension.

sub'mitting, *ppl. a.* [-ING[2].] That submits or makes a submission.

1791 KYD *Law of Awards* 238 Accounts..passed between both the submitting parties. **1805** ALEX. WILSON *Poems & Lit. Prose* (1876) II. 127 Butler's iron-hearted crew Doomed to the flames the weak submitting few. **1878** J. DAVIDSON *Inverurie* 51 Families the heads of which were able..to stand apart from the submitting majority.

Hence **sub'mittingly** *adv.*, submissively.

1825 R. P. WARD *Tremaine* I. xxxvii. 300 'True', said Georgina, submittingly.

†**sub'monish,** *v. Obs. rare*[−1]. [f. SUB- 22 + MONISH, after next.] To reprove gently.

1621 T. GRANGER *Eccles.* 56 Delights..which either by the wisedome of my minde, or by the submonishing inclinations of my senses I perceiued to affoord accesse of ioyfull contentment.

†**submo'nition.** *Obs.* [ad. L. **submonitio, -ōnem*, n. of action f. *submonēre* (var. *summ-*); see SUB- 22 and MONITION. Cf. OF. *submonicion.*] A gentle admonition, suggestion.

1562 WINȜET *Last Blast*, Ane Submonitioun to the Redar. **1621** T. GRANGER *Eccles.* 29 He should haue obeyed the submonitions of his owne conscience. **1650** ELDERFIELD *Civ. Right Tythes* 342 Under this very solemn protestation, submonition, and concluding asseveration.

sub'montane, *a.*

1. [SUB- 1 a.] Passing under, or existing below, mountains.

1819 *Blackw. Mag.* VI. 150 He sails along..till the shallop is driven into a cavern in the 'etherial cliffs of Caucasus'. It is scarcely to be expected that his submontane voyage should be very distinctly described. **1859** W. M. THOMSON *Land & Bk.* II. xvii. I. 377 The dark stairway..was a subterranean, or, rather, submontane path to the great fountain of Banias.

2. [SUB- 12 a.] Lying about the foot of mountains; belonging to the foot-hills of a range; also, belonging to the lower slopes of mountains.

1830 LINDLEY *Nat. Syst. Bot.* 287 Their principal station is on the sub-montane region between 1200 and 3600 feet of elevation. **1880** *Libr. Univ. Knowl.* VII. 161 The fertile submontane plains of Sialkot. **1888** *Encycl. Brit.* XXIV. 610/2 The submontane district around the town of Tokay. **1913** *Blackw. Mag.* Apr. 448/1 Hardy sub-montane savages armed with..deadly war-tools.

So †**submon'taneous** *a.* = 1 above.

1682 WHELER *Journ. Greece* VI. 465 These Subterraneous, or rather Submontaneous Passages of the Water, may..be reckoned amongst the greatest Wonders of the World.

,submortu'arian. *Theol. rare.* [f. SUB- 17 + L. *mortuus* dead (for *mors, mort-* death) + *-arian*; cf. SUBLAPSARIAN.] One who holds that a man's election to salvation or reprobation does not take place till after his death.

1700 C. NESSE *Antid. Armin.* (1827) 70 The Arminians.. may be called submortuarians for their holding no full election till men die.

†**submove,** *v. Obs. rare.* [ad. L. *submovēre* (var. *summ-*), f. *sub-* SUB- 26 + *movēre* to MOVE.] *trans.* To remove.

1542 BECON *Pathw. Prayer* xxix. M vij, Y[t] al Antechristes, Papistes [etc.]..submoued & put asyde, true Euangelystes..maye reygne among vs vniuersallye.

‖**submucosa** (sʌbmju:'kəʊsə). *Anat.* [mod.L., fem. (sc. *membrāna*) of *submūcōsus*: see SUBMUCOUS *a.*] The layer of areolar tissue lying beneath a mucous membrane; the submucous layer.

1885 KLEIN *Micro-Org.* 88 The submucosa of the inflamed Peyer's glands of the small intestine.

So **submu'cosal** *a.*, = SUBMUCOUS 2; **submu'cosally** *adv.*

1913 DORLAND *Illustr. Med. Dict.*, Submucosal. **1951** WHITBY & HYNES *Med. Bacteriol.* (ed. 5) v. 55 The sub-mucosal lymphatic plexus is much nearer to the surface than that of the skin. **1975** *New Yorker* 22 Dec. 75/1 There was no evidence of any intradermal, submucosal, or subcutaneous hemorrhaging. **1977** *Lancet* 8 Oct. 771/2, 0·5–1·0 ml was injected submucosally. **1978** *Jrnl. R. Soc. Med.* LXXI. 359 The ileal spout was excised and showed a significant submucosal haematoma.

sub'mucous, *a.* [ad. mod.L. *submūcōsus.*]

1. *Path.* [SUB- 21.] Somewhat mucous; partly consisting of or attended by mucus; of an indistinctly mucous character.

1684 tr. *Bonet's Merc. Compit.* I. 34 If both the Part be pained, and the Flesh be submucous [orig. (ten Rhyne) *si simul dolorosus sit locus et caro submucosa*]. **1904** *Appleton's Med. Dict.* s.v. *Râle, Subcrepitant r., Submucous r.*, a fine moist, bubbling sound, heard in inspiration or expiration or both.

2. [SUB- 1 b.] **a.** *Anat.* Situated beneath the mucous membrane; pertaining to the submucosa.

1835–6 *Todd's Cycl. Anat.* I. 180/2 The submucous tissue in the vicinity of the anus is very loose. **1847–9** *Ibid.* IV. I. 134/2 The submucous tissue of the gall-bladder. **1881** MIVART *Cat* 27 The mucous membrane is connected with the subjacent parts by submucous areolar tissue. **1902** HUGHES & KEITH *Man. Pract. Anat.* III. 137 The submucous tissue of the lip.

b. *Path.* and *Surg.* Occurring or introduced under the mucous membrane; affecting the submucosa.

1875 tr. *von Ziemssen's Cycl. Med.* X. 232 The submucous fibroid, growing inward into the cavity of the uterus. **1876** *Ibid.* IV. 96 Submucous injections. **1879** *St. George's Hosp. Rep.* IX. 31 Submucous abscesses the size of a bean in the wall of the stomach. **1897** *Allbutt's Syst. Med.* III. 962 Submucous hæmorrhages, leading to ulceration.

sub'multiple, *a.* and *sb.* [ad. late L. *submultiplus*: see SUB- 10 and MULTIPLE.]

A. *adj.* Of a ratio: In which the antecedent is an aliquot part of the consequent: the converse of *multiple*. Of a number, etc.: That is an aliquot part *of* another. Now *rare* or *Obs.*

a **1696** SCARBURGH *Euclid* (1705) 180, 12 compared to 4 is Multiple Proportion, and named triple: And 4 to 12 is Submultiple Proportion, and named Subtriple. **1704** J. HARRIS *Lex. Techn.* I, Submultiple Number, or Quantity, is that which is contained in another Number, a certain Number of Times exactly. **1728** CHAMBERS *Cycl.* s.v., The Ratio of 3 to 21 is Submultiple. **1739** in Rigaud *Corr. Sci. Men* (1841) I. 355 The sine of $1/n$ *A* (or submultiple part of the anomaly of the eccentric).

B. *sb.* A submultiple or aliquot part (*of*).

1758 *Phil. Trans.* L. 765 *note*, These arcs [are] the corresponding submultiples of those above. **1857** MILLER *Elem. Chem., Org.* xiv. §1. 773 Equivalent quantities of different salts when in solution occupy either the same volume, or volumes which are simple multiples or submultiples of each other. **1859** PARKINSON *Optics* (1866) 244 If the angle of a hollow cone.. be any sub-multiple of 180°. **1871** C. DAVIES *Metric Syst.* II. 40 [A] system of numbers where the multiples and submultiples are formed from a single unit. **1880** E. J. REED *Japan* I. 326 Its [the *yen's*] decimal submultiples being the *sen* (or cent) and the *rin*.

So †**submul'tiplicate** *a.* = A. above.

1656 tr. *Hobbes' Elem. Philos.* (1839) 364 The proportion of the altitudes decreasing to that of the ordinate lines decreasing, being multiplicate according to any number in the deficient figure, is submultiplicate according to the same number in its complement.

sub'nasal, *a.* **1.** [SUB- 1 b.] *Anat.* (See quots.)

1882 A. THOMSON et al. *Quain's Elem. Anat.* (ed. 9) I. 80 Subnasal or spinal point, the middle of the inferior border of the anterior nasal aperture at the base of the nasal spine. **1951** B. Z. SELIGMAN *N. & Q. Anthrop.* (R. Anthrop. Inst.) (ed. 6) I. 11 *Nasal height*,.. the distance between the nasion, which is the point of junction of the nasal and frontal bones in the midline, and the subnasal point, which is the point at which the lower end of the nasal septum meets the upper lip.

2. [SUB- 19.] Not quite or somewhat nasal in tone. *rare*$^{-1}$.

1936 R. LEHMANN *Weather in Streets* I. ii. 39 Cool voice, with an edge of sub-nasal gentility.

sub'nascent, *a.* [ad. L. *subnascens*, *-entem*, pr. pple. of *subnascī*: see SUB- 2 and NASCENT.] Growing underneath or up from beneath. Also *fig*.

1675 EVELYN *Terra* 93 The Vine.. imparts.. such a bitterness to the Mould, as kills Lettuce, and other subnascent Plants. *a* **1706** —— *Sylva* III. i. (1908) II. 5 Where their branches may freely spread.. without dripping and annoying the subnascent crop. **1707** *Phil. Trans.* XXV. 2422 The Royal Oak.. overspreading Subnascent Trees and young Suckers. **1853** WHEWELL *Grotius* III. 3 With reference to causes subnascent, that is, growing up during the progress of the war. **1900** B. D. JACKSON *Gloss. Bot. Terms*, *Subnascent*.., growing or arising from below some object.

†**sub'nect**, *v. Obs.* [ad. L. *subnectĕre*, f. *sub-* SUB- 2, 28 + *nectĕre* to bind.]

1. *trans.* To subjoin. Also *absol.*

c **1583** J. HOOKER *Descr. Exeter* in *Holinshed* III. 1027/1, I thought it good to subnect herevnto the description of the said church. **1586** —— *Hist. Irel.* ibid. II. 123/1 Of euerie of these houses.. we will breeflie subnect and declare particularlie in order as followeth. **1642** JACKSON *Bk. Consc.* 21 Let us here subnect two examples. **1677** GALE *Crt. Gentiles* IV. 354 Beatitude is the supreme end of al rational Appetition: therefore what men desire, they do, if they can, as Aristotle subnectes. **1704** HUSSEY (*title*) A Warning from the Winds... To which is Subnected a Laborious Exercitation upon Eph. 2. 2.

2. To fasten underneath. *rare*.

1710 POPE *Let. to Cromwell* 30 Dec., I was just going to say of his buttons; but I think Jupiter wore none (however I won't be positive.. but his robe might be subnected with a Fibula).

Hence **sub'nected** *ppl. a.*

1654 VILVAIN *Enchir. Epigr.* Pref. 1, I hav published.. two subnected Essais explicated in quarto.

†**sub'nex**, *v. Obs.* [f. L. *subnex-*, pa. ppl. stem of *subnectĕre* (see prec.).] = prec. 1.

1603 HOLLAND *Plutarch's Mor.* 1067 He subnexeth as touching evill things, these words. **1644** HUNTON *Vind. Treat. Mon.* v. 43, I had an intent to have subnexed other Arguments to make good those Assertions.

'subnormal, *sb.*

1. *Geom.* [ad. mod.L. *subnormalis* (sc. *linea* line): see SUB- 1 and NORMAL.] That part of the axis of abscissas which is intercepted between the ordinate and the normal at any point of the curve.

1710 J. HARRIS *Lex. Techn.* II. s.v., This Subnormal in the Common or Apollonian Parabola, is a Determinate Invariable Quantity; for 'tis always equal to half the Parameter of the Axis. **1715** in Rigaud *Corr. Sci. Men* (1841) II. 421 Because the curve AI is given, its subnormal GD will be given. **1842** FRANCIS *Dict. Arts* s.v., In all curves the subnormal is the third proportional to the subtangent and the ordinate. **1885** EAGLES *Constr. Geom. Plane Curves* 62 The focus *F* is found by drawing the normal at any point *D*, bisecting the sub-normal *NG* and setting off $AF = \frac{1}{2} NG$.

2. [SUB- 14: see sense b of the adj., below.] *Educ.* and *Psychol.* One who is below normal in academic or general ability.

1916 L. M. TERMAN *Measurement of Intelligence* vi. 78 Conversely, we may say regarding the subnormals that:—the child testing at (about) 90 is equaled or excelled by 80 out of 100. **1956** J. F. HORNER *Summary of Scientology* 15 The children who get extra attention are the subnormals. **1975** N. O'CONNOR in Kirman & Bicknell *Mental Handicap* iv. 102 The generally slowed reaction time to both visual and auditory, simple and complex stimulus-response situations which characterizes all subnormals.

sub'normal, *a.* [SUB- 14.] **a.** Less than normal, below the normal. Chiefly *Med.*

1890 BILLINGS *Nat. Med. Dict.*, *Subnormal*, less than usual. **1897** *Month* Sept. 329 All subnormal or supernormal phenomena of the soul. **1897** *Allbutt's Syst. Med.* III. 728 The temperature [in colic] is usually rather subnormal.

b. *Educ.* and *Psychol.* Of a level of intelligence and general ability which is below a predetermined standard of normality. See also *educationally subnormal* adj. phr. s.v. EDUCATIONALLY *adv.*

1919 H. WOODROW *Brightness & Dullness in Children* ii. 22 In 1904, the French Minister of Public Instruction made him [*sc.* Binet] a member of a commission appointed for the purpose of organizing classes for subnormal children... How were subnormal children to be positively distinguished? **1935** C. L. BURT (*title*) The subnormal mind. *Ibid.* ii. 77 In another 12 per cent. the parent, though not intellectually subnormal, was more or less unstable. **1940** A. O. HECK *Educ. Exceptional Children* xxiii. 342 Frequently, children are referred to as bright, average and subnormal. **1958** K. LOVELL *Educ. Psychol.* xii. 149 Those whose IQ's are within the range from about 80–55 will usually be classified as educationally subnormal. **1975** N. O'CONNOR in Kirman & Bicknell *Mental Handicap* iv. 102 Within the subnormal group, abnormal EEG was a poor indicator for prognosis.

subnor'mality. [f. prec. + -ITY.] **a.** The condition of being subnormal (*spec.* mentally subnormal); ***severe subnormality*** (see quot. 1959). Also *Comb.*, as **subnormality hospital**, a hospital for patients who are severely subnormal.

1890 *Lancet* 11 Jan. 105/1 Muscle soreness, and subnormality of temperature on the fourth day. **1935** C. L. BURT *Subnormal Mind* i. 8, I shall restrict myself to those forms of subnormality which seem to be chiefly mental in their origin. **1959** *Mental Health Act 7 & 8 Eliz. II* lxxii §4 (2) In this Act 'severe subnormality' means a state of arrested or incomplete development of mind which includes subnormality of intelligence and is of such a nature or degree that the patient is incapable of living an independent life. **1965** *Mod. Law Rev.* XXVIII. v. 580 Persons who.. receive local authority services for sub-normality. **1968** *Economist* 21 Dec. 37/2 Had she been of below average intelligence she could have been sent to a subnormality hospital. *a* **1974** R. CROSSMAN *Diaries* (1977) III. 644 No, out on tour studying the sub-normality hospitals, but I thought I would come down and put in an appearance.

subnotation (sʌbnəʊ'teɪʃən). [ad. L. *subnotātio*, *-ōnem*, n. of action, f. *subnotāre*: see SUB- 2 and NOTATION.] = RESCRIPT 2.

1843-56 BOUVIER *Law Dict.* (ed. 6) II. 554/1 *Subnotations*... The answers of the prince to questions which had been put to him respecting some obscure or doubtful point of law.

,subnoto'chordal, *a.*

1. [SUB- 21 b.] Somewhat of the nature of a notochord.

1872 H. A. NICHOLSON *Palæont.* 334 The vertebral column is sometimes composed of distinct vertebræ, sometimes cartilaginous or sub-notochordal. **1875** BLAKE *Zool.* 202 Endoskeleton cartilaginous, subnotochordal.

2. [SUB- 1 b.] Situated beneath the notochord.

1888 ROLLESTON & JACKSON *Anim. Life* 334 After the formation of the notochord a small sub-notochordal rod of cells is developed. **1909** J. W. JENKINSON *Exper. Embryol.* 134 Underneath the notochord is the subnotochordal rod.

sub'nuclear, *a. Physics.* [SUB- 14.] Smaller than or occurring in an atomic nucleus; relating to such particles or to phenomena involving them.

1964 *New Scientist* 20 Feb. 458/1 The frontier of physics has lain, since the war, in the field of sub-nuclear particles. **1964** M. GOWING *Britain & Atomic Energy 1939–45* 16 These two theories [of Schroedinger and Bohr].. form the basis of all modern atomic, nuclear, and sub-nuclear physics. **1969** *Times* 5 Feb. 13/7 The classification is part of the conceptual order which physicists are trying to impose on the sub-nuclear particles. **1981** C. H. L. SMITH in J. H. Mulvey *Nature of Matter* iii. 61 In the 1930s.. protons and neutrons were the only sub-nuclear particles known.

†**subob'scure**, *a. Obs.* [ad. L. *subobscūrus*: see SUB- 21 and OBSCURE.] Somewhat obscure.

1626 DONNE *Serm.* lxxvii. (1640) 786 In those sub-obscure times, S. Augustine might be excusable [etc.]. **1629** H. BURTON *Truth's Tri.* 219 Such vmbratilous and sub-obscure termes.

Hence †**subob'scurely** *adv.*, somewhat obscurely.

a **1625** DONNE *Ess.* (1651) 97 As these men were instruments of this work of God, so their names did sub-obscurely foresignifie it. **1624** —— *Devot.* (ed. 2) 207 The booke of Nature, where though subobscurely.. thou hast expressed thine own Image.

suboc'cipital, *a.* [ad. mod.L. *suboccipitālis*: see SUB- 1 b.]

1. Situated under the occiput or below the occipital bone.

suboccipital nerve, the first cervical nerve. ***s. triangle*** (see quot. 1911).

1733 tr. *Winslow's Anat.* (1756) II. 75 The Sub-Occipital Nerves. **1835-6** *Todd's Cycl. Anat.* I. 367/1 A.. depression, called the suboccipital fossa, or cervical fossa. **1877** HUXLEY & MARTIN *Elem. Biol.* 192 There is no suboccipital nerve in the Frog. **1890** BILLINGS *Nat. Med. Dict.*, *Suboccipital angle*, that between lines drawn from auricular point to inion and opisthion. **1911** *Encycl. Brit.* (ed. 11) XIX. 53/2 When the superficial muscles and complexus are removed from the back of the neck, the sub-occipital triangle is seen beneath the occipital bone.

2. Situated on the under surface of the occipital lobe of the brain.

1889 *Buck's Handbk. Med. Sci.* VIII. 152/2 Inconstant Fissures.. Adoccipital.. Suboccipital.

suboc'cipito-, [see SUB- 1 b and OCCIPITO-], as in **suboc,cipito-breg'matic** *a.*, pertaining to the region extending from the occiput to the bregma.

1857 BULLOCK tr. *Cazeaux' Midwifery* 220 The sub-occipito-bregmatic [diameter] extends from the middle of the space between the foramen magnum and the occipital protuberance.

sub'octave.

†**1.** [SUB- 10.] An eighth part. *Obs. rare.*

1705 ARBUTHNOT *Coins*, etc. (1727) 81 Our Gallon, which.. has the Pint for its Suboctave.

2. *Mus.* [SUB- 4 (*b*).] The octave below a given note. Also *attrib.* in ***suboctave coupler***.

1659 C. SIMPSON *Division-Violist* I. 7 With the Lowest String put down a Note, to make it a Sub-Octave thereunto. **1876** STAINER & BARRETT *Dict. Mus. Terms*, *Suboctave*, a coupler in the organ which pulls down keys one octave below those which are struck. **1884** *Encycl. Brit.* XVII. 834/2 The choir to great sub-octave coupler was used chiefly as a substitute for a double on the great organ.

subocular (sə'bɒkjʊlə(r)), *a.* (*sb.*) [ad. L. *suboculāris*: see SUB- 1 b and OCULAR. Cf. F. *suboculaire*.] Situated below or under the eyes.

1826 KIRBY & SP. *Entomol.* xlvi. IV. 315 [Stemmata] Sub-ocular... When placed in the space below the eyes. **1835-6** *Todd's Cycl. Anat.* I. 307/2 In the Woodpeckers it [*sc.* the nasal gland] is found in the sub-ocular air-cell. **1884** COUES *N. Amer. Birds* 152 The curved subocular or maxillo-palatine bar.

b. *sb.* A subocular scale.

1897 GÜNTHER in *Mary Kingsley's W. Africa* 697 Two rows of minute suboculars.

sub'odorate, *v. rare.* [f. L. *subodōrāt-*, pa. ppl. stem of *subodōrārī*, f. *sub-* SUB- 22 + *odōrārī* (f. *odor* ODOUR). Cf. It. *subodorare*, F. *subodorer*.] *trans.* To smell or scent out.

1606 WOTTON *Lett.* (1907) I. 354 This having been subodorated in Rome, they have there newly proposed [etc.]. **1837** *Fraser's Mag.* XVI. 660 Heyne, who, though no wizard, had subodorated the truth.

'sub-,officer. [f. SUB- 6 + OFFICER. Cf. F. *sous-officier*.] A subordinate officer.

a **1618** SYLVESTER *Maiden's Blush* 1353 Let him have pow'r.. underneath him to subordinate Sub-Officers. **1822** SYD. SMITH *Wks.* (1859) I. 358/2 The governor and sub-officers of the prison. **1837** CARLYLE *Fr. Rev.* II. I. ii, Sub-officers, soldiers, and sailors in mutiny. **1845** JAMES *Smuggler* xxx, A sub-officer of the Customs. **1913** *Daily Graphic* 24 Mar. 6/1 A sub-officer of the Fire Brigade.

subopercle (sʌbəʊ'pɜːk(ə)l). *rare.* [ad. mod.L. *suboperculum*. Cf. OPERCLE.] = SUBOPERCULUM.

1891 *Century Dict.* **1908** *Smithsonian Misc. Coll.* V. 16 Subopercle very broad.

subo'percular, *a.* (*sb.*) *Ichth.* [f. next + -AR¹.] Designating a bone in the lower part of the operculum of a fish; pertaining to the suboperculum.

1854 OWEN in *Orr's Circ. Sci.*, *Org. Nat.* I. 178 [The operculum] consists of four bones; the one articulated to the tympanic pedicle is called 'preopercular',.. the other three are, counting downwards, the 'opercular',.. the 'subopercular',.. the 'interopercular'. **1897** GÜNTHER in *Mary Kingsley's W. Africa* 699 Subopercular armature strong.

‖**suboperculum** (sʌbəʊ'pɜːkjʊləm). [mod.L., f. *sub-* SUB- 2 b (*a*) + OPERCULUM.]

1. *Ichth.* The bone situated below the operculum in the gill-cover of a fish.

1834 McMURTRIE *Cuvier's Anim. Kingd.* 191 A sort of lid, composed of three bony pieces, the operculum, the sub[o]perculum, and the interoperculum. **1878** BELL tr. *Gegenbaur's Comp. Anat.* 455 Behind the preoperculum is the suboperculum. **1888** ROLLESTON & JACKSON *Anim. Life* 93.

2. *Anat.* The part of an occipital orbital gyre which overlies the insula of Reil.

1889 *Buck's Handbk. Med. Sci.* VIII. 160/2 The insula.. becomes a subgyre, while the operculum, preoperculum, suboperculum, and postoperculum are supergyres.

Hence **,suboper'culiform** *a.*, of the form of a suboperculum.

1852 DANA *Crust.* I. 569 The outer maxillipeds are sub-operculiform.

subor'bicular, *a. Nat. Hist.* [SUB- 21 c.] Almost orbicular, nearly circular.

1753 *Chambers' Cycl.* Suppl. s.v. *Leaf*, Lunulated Leaf, one in form of a crescent: it is a suborbicular leaf hollowed at the base. **1822** J. PARKINSON *Outl. Oryctol.* 100 A sub-orbicular, depressed body. **1887** W. PHILLIPS *Brit. Discomycetes* 386 *Stictis punctiformis*... Gregarious, minute, immersed, urceolate, suborbicular.

Comb. **1870** HOOKER *Stud. Flora* 335 Populus tremula, leaves.. of branches suborbicular-ovate sinuate-serrate.

So **subor'biculate, -ated** *adjs.*

1775 J. JENKINSON *Linnæus' Brit. Pl.* 151 The silicula is erect, suborbiculated, compressed. **1825** MACLEAY *Annul. Javanica* 13 The thorax neither suborbiculate [n]or entire. **1847** *Proc. Berw. Nat. Club* II. v. 235 Head suborbiculate or subquadrate.

sub'orbital, *a.* and *sb.* [SUB- 1 b.]

A. *adj.* **1.** Situated below or under the orbit of the eye; infraorbital.

1822-7 GOOD *Study Med.* (1829) IV. 315 The sub-orbital branch of the fifth pair [of nerves]. **1854** LATHAM *Native Races Russ. Emp.* 28 The skin brown or brunette, and the suborbital portion of the face flattened. **1871** DARWIN *Desc. Man* II. xviii. 280 The so-called tear-sacks or suborbital pits. **1883** *Encycl. Brit.* XV. 348/2 The suborbital gland or 'crumen' of Antelopes and Deer.

2. [SUB- 19.] Being or having a trajectory that does not make a complete orbit of a planet.

1959 *N.Y. Times Mag.* 11 Oct. 18/1 The moment has come, after months of training, testing and short, sub-orbital flights, when one of seven carefully chosen men climbs into a space capsule perched high on the nose of an Atlas rocket. **1967** *New Scientist* 16 Nov. 424/1 The Soviet Union seems to have developed a sub-orbital missile, and the implications of the new weapon have been quickly realized. **1977** A. HALLAM *Planet Earth* 28/2 This hypothesis demands that the impact is sufficiently catastrophic to vaporize large amounts of surface and subsurface rock, the gases being ejected into suborbital trajectories.

B. *sb.* A suborbital structure; a suborbital bone, cartilage, nerve, etc.

1834 McMURTRIE *Cuvier's Anim. Kingd.* 192 The true Perches have the preoperculum dentated... Sometimes the sub-orbital and the humeral are slightly dentated. **1897** GÜNTHER in *Mary Kingsley's W. Africa* 709 The first sub-orbital is narrow, much narrower than the second and third, which nearly entirely cover the cheek.

So **sub'orbitar, -'orbitary** [mod.L. *suborbitārius*] *adjs.* and *sbs.*

1828 STARK *Elem. Nat. Hist.* I. 485 Preoperculi and *suborbitars dentated on their margin. *a* **1843** in *Encycl. Metrop.* (1845) VII. 300/2 The Suborbitar bones.. of Cuvier. **1890** BILLINGS *Nat. Med. Dict.*, *Suborbitar fissure*, infraorbital fissure. *Suborbitar fossa*, canine fossa. **1733** tr. *Winslow's Anat.* (1756) II. 64 The *Sub-Orbitary Ramus.. runs in the Canal of the inferior Portion of the Orbit. **1828** STARK *Elem. Nat. Hist.* I. 464 Suborbitaries dentated.

† **subor'dain**, *v. Obs.* [f. SUB- + ORDAIN, partly after med.L. *subordināre* to SUBORDINATE.]

1. [SUB- 27.] *trans.* To appoint in place of another.

1600 HOLLAND *Livy* XXXI. l. 804 In his place M. Acilius Glabrio was subordained [L. *suffectus*]. *Ibid.* XLI. xxi. 1109 Augures were subordained [L. *suffecti sunt*].

2. [SUB- 8.] To appoint to a subordinate position.

1602 J. DAVIES *Mirum in modum* (1878) 24/2 That Powre omnipotent, That Nature subordain'd, chiefe Gouernour, Of fading Creatures. **1602** DOLMAN *La Primaud. Fr. Acad.* (1618) III. 661 The first cause, through vertue whereof, the rest subordained vnder it do work.

3. To make subordinate or subject.

a **1617** BAYNE *On Eph.* (1643) 274 These may be subordeyned one to another. **1633** D. R[OGERS] *Treat. Sacr.* i. 16 The Covenant of obedience is subordeined to the covenant of grace.

4. To promulgate (an order) by a subordinate authority.

1654 EARL MONM. tr. *Bentivoglio's Wars Flanders* 154 No Order could issue forth from him, which was not to be subordained by the Councel of State.

'suborder.

1. [SUB- 7 b.] *Zool.* and *Bot.* A subdivision of an order; a group next below an order in a classification of animals or plants.

1826 KIRBY & SP. *Entomol.* IV. 391 If a subclass end in *ata*, a suborder might end in *ita*; a section in *ana*, a subsection in *ena*. **1840** *Cuvier's Anim. Kingd.* 411 The order contains two families, or rather sub-orders,.. Brachyura (short tailed) and Macroura or Macrura (long tailed). **1861** BENTLEY *Man. Bot.* 398 While all the above genera belong to the order Compositæ, they are at the same time placed in three different sub-orders. Thus the sub-order Cichoraceæ includes the Chicory, Dandelion, Sowthistle, and Lettuce [etc.]. **1898** *Guide Mammalia Brit. Mus.* 11 Man, Apes, and Monkeys constitute the suborder Anthropoidea.

b. *transf.*

1864 W. T. FOX *Skin Dis.* 42 Under the head of pustulæ, is a suborder, *furunculi*, to include anthrax, boils, and pustula maligna.

2. [SUB- 5 b.] *Arch.* A secondary or subordinate 'order' in a structure of arches.

1890 C. H. MOORE *Gothic Archit.* vi. 236 The hollow which is given to the soffit of the sub-order of the pier arcade in the nave of Malmesbury Abbey.

Hence **sub'ordered** *a.*, (of an arch) placed as a suborder.

1898 *Archæol. Jrnl.* Ser. II. V. 348 The subordered arch perhaps did not appear much.. before the eleventh century.

† **sub'ordering.** [SUB- 8.] Subordination.

1654 Z. COKE *Logick* 85 A perfect division also is either of The whole subordering [or] The Co-ordered.

subordinacy (sə'bɔːdɪnəsɪ). [f. SUBORDINATE *a.*: see -ACY.] The state of being subordinate; subordination.

1627 SPEED *England* xxviii. §5 In ackn[o]wledgement of subordinacie in that part of absolute power. **1673** TEMPLE *Ess. Irel.* in *Misc.* (1680) 102 This subordinacy [*ed.* 1709 subordinancy] in the Government, and emulation of parties. **1711** SHAFTESB. *Charac.* (1737) II. II. 98 To have.. Self-Affections too strong, or beyond their degree of subordinacy to the kindly and natural. **1820** T. L. PEACOCK *Misc.* Wks. 1875 III. 337 The subordinacy of the ornamental to the useful. **1891** *Temple Bar* Feb. 252 Her comparative subordinacy. **1893** *Advance* (Chicago) 9 Mar., Lifted out of subordinacy into supremacy.

su'bordinal, *a.* [f. mod.L. *subordo*, *-ordin-* (see SUB- 7 b, ORDER *sb.*) + -AL[1].] Of, pertaining to, or of the rank of, a suborder.

1870 ROLLESTON *Anim. Life* p. lxxxii, The two subordinal names above given. **1872** OLIVER *Elem. Bot.* II. 183 Upon these characters, derived from the face of the seed, subordinal divisions have been based. **1904** *Q. Rev.* Oct. 469 Africa has now no.. peculiar ordinal or subordinal groups of mammals of its own.

† **su'bordinance.** *Obs.* [f. SUBORDINATE *a.*, app. after *predominate* (for *predominant*) and *predominance*.] Subordination.

1642 H. MORE *Song of Soul* I. II. xii, We clearly see (As well as that pendent subordinance) The nearly couching of each realtie.

So † **su'bordinancy.**

1709 [see SUBORDINACY, quot. 1673]. **1768** in *Chauncy's Let.* 52 Government.. implies subordinancy and subjection.

† **su'bordinant,** *a. Obs.* [Alteration of SUBORDINATE by confusion with *predominant*.] Subordinate.

1697 J. SERGEANT *Solid Philos.* 458 Each of the Subordinant Sciences deduces Conclusions about its Proper Object.

su'bordinary, *sb. Her.* [f. SUB- 5 + ORDINARY *sb.*] A charge of frequent occurrence but considered as of less importance than an ordinary; a subordinate ordinary.

c **1791** *Encycl. Brit.* (1797) VIII. 445/2 All charges are distinguished by the names of honorable ordinaries, subordinaries, and common charges. **1842** BRANDE *Dict. Sci.* etc. 1183/2 According to some writers.. an ordinary, when it comprises less than one fifth of the whole shield, is termed a subordinary. **1880** *Encycl. Brit.* XI. 694/1 Very many both of these [ordinaries] and of the subordinaries.. are very frequent constituents in mouldings in the Norman style of architecture.

† **su'bordinary,** *a. Obs. rare.* [Alteration of SUBORDINATE by confusion with *ordinary*.] Subordinate.

1788 D. GILSON *Serm.* xii. 356 Let Women—know their sphere;.. Their rank is an.. honourable one—but it is a subordinary.

subordinate (sə'bɔːdɪnət), *a.* and *sb.* [ad. med.L. *subordinātus*, pa. pple. of *subordināre* to SUBORDINATE. Cf. It. *subordinato*, Sp. and Pg. *subordinado*; also F. *subordonné*.] **A.** *adj.*

1. a. Of a person or body of persons: Belonging to an inferior rank, grade, class, or order, and hence dependent upon the authority or power of another. Const. *to.*

1607 CHAPMAN *Bussy d'Ambois* III. i, Shew me a great man .. That rules so much more than his suffering King, That he makes kings of his subordinate slaues. **1624** FISHER in F. White *Repl. Fisher* 337 To make Saints Mediators subordinate vnto, and dependent of Christ, is to encrease his glorie. *a* **1626** BACON *Consid. Warre w. Spaine* Misc. (1629) 43 Two Generals.. assisted with Subordinate Commanders, of great Experience. **1669** GALE *Crt. Gentiles* I. I. i. 2 Neither is it possible to conceive, that a finite subordinate Being should be independent, or eternal. **1693** STAIR *Inst. Law Scot.* (ed. 2) IV. xxxix. §14 This defence extends to all Judges Supream and Subordinat. **1760–2** GOLDSM. *Cit. W.* c, The subordinate officer must receive the commands of his superior. **1827** SCOTT *Surg. Dau.* xiv, An act of deference.. paid by inferior and subordinate princes to the patrons whom they depend upon. **1863** H. COX *Instit.* I. x. 238 Elizabeth and her advisers attempted to render Parliament subordinate to the Privy Council. **1871** FREEMAN *Norm. Conq.* IV. 73 Besides these two great Viceroys, we also know the names of some of the subordinate captains who held commands under them.

b. Of power, position, command, employment.

1456 SIR G. HAYE *Bk. Knighthood* Wks. (S.T.S.) II. 1 Sa suld knychtis have dominacioun and seigneurye subordinate of the princis and lordis behalve. **1608** J. KING *Serm.* 24 Mar. 6 Nor by way of Lieutenantship, deputation, subordinate prefecture whatsoever, but as a King over subiects. **1622** CALLIS *Stat. Sewers* (1647) 231 An Ordinance is a subordinate direction, proceeding out of a more general power. **1681** STAIR *Inst. Law Scot.* I. xiii. 276 The Jurisdiction of all Barrons.. was.. subordinat to the Sheriffs. *a* **1700** EVELYN *Diary* 6 Feb. 1670, The lawfulnesse, decentnesse, and necessitie, of subordinate degrees and ranks of men and servants. **1765** MACLAINE tr. *Mosheim's Eccl. Hist.* Cent. IV. I. v. §10 [The Son] the instrument by whose subordinate operation the Almighty Father formed the universe. **1862** G. C. LEWIS *Let. to Earl Stanhope* 26 Apr., In his subordinate official position. **1874** STUBBS *Const. Hist.* I. iv. 68 His power is.. not subordinate.

c. Of things having an inferior rank in a series or gradation.

1456 SIR G. HAYE *Law Arms* (S.T.S.) 76 The hevynnis, be thair instrumentis subordinatis, sendis thair.. influencis in the materis that thir erdly thingis ar compound of. **1610** GUILLIM *Heraldrie* II. vi. (1611) 58 A couple-close is a subordinate charge deriued from a Cheuron. **1651** HOBBES *Leviathan* II. xxii. 115 Others [*sc.* systems] are.. Subordinate to some Soveraign Power. **1691** RAY *Creation* I. (1692) 8 Of both which kinds [of insects] there are many subordinate Genera. **1728** CHAMBERS *Cycl.* s.v. *Subordination*, In the Sciences, Trigonometry is subordinate to Geometry; and in the Virtues, Abstinence and Chastity are subordinate to Temperance. **1807** *Med. Jrnl.* XVII. 575 It was to that branch of it which bears the name of Therapeutics, that all the others were to have been subordinate. **1864** BOWEN *Logic* iv. 87 The other [Concept], having less Extension, or denoting fewer Individuals, is called Inferior, Lower, Narrower or Subordinate.

2. a. Of things, material and immaterial: Dependent upon or subservient *to* the chief or principal thing. Chiefly in technical use.

1588 FRAUNCE *Lawiers Logike* I. iv. 25 b, Subordinate is that which is not for it selfe desired, but referred to the chief end. **1597** HOOKER *Eccl. Pol.* v. lxii. (1611) 328 No circumstance but a subordinate efficient cause. **1621** BURTON *Anat. Mel.* I. ii. III. ii, Although this Phantasie of ours be a subordinate faculty to reason. **1625** N. CARPENTER *Geogr. Delin.* II. ix. (1635) 147 Subordinate causes can produce no other then subordinate effects. **1697** tr. *Burgersdicius' Logic* I. xviii. 69 A Subordinate End is that which is referred to some farther End. **1730** M. WRIGHT *Introd. Law Tenures* 159 *note*, The many subordinate Tenures and Manors subsisting at this Day. **1765** BLACKSTONE *Comm.* I. Introd. 98 As to Ireland, that is still a distinct kingdom; though a dependent, subordinate kingdom. **1818** STODDART in *Encycl. Metrop.* (1845) I. 18/2 Various aggregations of sentences in which the subordinate assertions are assumed by the mind in the manner already shown. **1844** *Proc. Philol. Soc.* I. 226 When a subordinate clause acts the part of object to a verb. **1857** J. W. GIBBS *Philol. Studies* 117 The more ancient languages had participials, where the more modern have subordinate clauses.

b. ***subordinate legislation*** Law (see quots.).

[**1841** G. C. LEWIS *On Govt. of Dependencies* 52 Legislation is subordinate when the sovereign person or body delegates the legislative power to an inferior authority, which issues or makes the law.] *Ibid.*, A power of subordinate legislation is sometimes *direct*;.. the laws made in virtue of it are issued avowedly.. by the subordinate legislature. **1901** C. ILBERT *Legislative Methods & Forms* p. v, Chapter III deals with what I have called subordinate legislation, that is to say, that part of the law which is enacted, not directly by the supreme legislature, but under delegated powers. **1917** *Erskine May's Treat. Laws Parl.* (ed. 12) xxiii. 567 Something must be said here of those administrative orders, rules and regulations which constitute what is sometimes called delegated or subordinate legislation. **1975** J. P. MORGAN *House of Lords & Labour Government* ii. 63 An equally important function is their work on subordinate legislation, a subject that requires a section to itself. **1980** *Oxf. Compan. Law* 758/1 Subordinate or delegated legislation takes many forms, rules, regulations, and orders made by Ministers of the Crown, frequently in the form of statutory instruments; [etc.].

3. Of inferior importance; not principal or predominant; secondary, minor.

a **1661** FULLER *Worthies, Northampton.* (1662) II. 288 Not to speak of his moral qualifications, and subordinate abilities. **1752** HUME *Ess. & Treat.* (1777) I. 236 Instances, where the subordinate movement is converted into the predominant. **1786** JEFFERSON *Writ.* (1859) II. 26 My expectations from it were of a subordinate nature only. **1808** SYD. SMITH *Wks.* (1859) I. 121/2 A very great proportion of all the curacies in England are filled with men to whom the emolument is a matter of subordinate importance. **1855** PRESCOTT *Philip II*, I. iv. I. 57 His haughty spirit could not be pleased by the subordinate part which he was compelled to play. **1887** *Dict. Archit.* s.v. *Sub Arch*, Subarcuation, that is, the mode of constructing two inferior and subordinate arches under the third or main arch. **1898** SWEET *New Engl. Gram.* II. 29 If a full word becomes subordinate in meaning, it can take weaker stress.

† **4.** In subjection; submissive. *Obs.*

1594 in *Cath. Rec. Soc. Publ.* V. 266 My direction was in all things to be subordinate to him y[t] should be Superior here of our Societye. **1784** COWPER *Task* II. 716 The mind was well inform'd, the passions held Subordinate.

† **5.** In physical senses: **a.** Placed underneath.

1648 WILKINS *Math. Magick* I. vii. 51 These Pulleys may be multiplyed according to sundry different situations, not onely when they are subordinate,.. but also when they are placed collaterally.

b. *Geol.* Underlying; subjacent.

1833 LYELL *Princ. Geol.* III. 170 Consisting.. partly of clay and sand, with subordinate beds of lignite. **1854** MURCHISON *Siluria* ii. 31 Containing the best roofing slates in the world, and subordinate courses of greywacke grit.

† **6.** advb. ***subordinate to***: in subordination or subjection to. *Obs.*

1642 *Lanc. Tracts Civil War* (Chetham Soc.) 73 We owe (subordinate to God) a great deal to Sir Iohn Seaton. **1737** *Gentl. Mag.* VII. 277 To inform and guide the People by it [*sc.* church authority], subordinate to holy Scripture. **1807** *Med. Jrnl.* XVII. 396 Subordinate to this will be given biographical notices of Authors.

B. *sb.*

1. A subordinate person; one in a position of subordination; one who is under the control or orders of a superior.

1640 G. SANDYS *Christ's Passion* 46 And so deny That Princes by Subordinates should die. **1667** MILTON *P.L.* v. 668 Satan.. his next subordinate Awak'ning. **1790** BURKE *Fr. Rev.* 218 What the jurisdiction of bishops over their subordinates is to be. **1856** *N. Brit. Rev.* XXVI. 185 All the heads of departments, civil and military, with a large proportion of their subordinates. **1898** 'H. S. MERRIMAN' *Roden's Corner* x. 100 Ready to prompt or assist, as behoved a merely mechanical subordinate.

2. A subordinate thing, matter, etc.

1839 *Penny Cycl.* XIII. 176/1 (*Kant*), The subordinates of modality are possibility, existence, and necessity. **1846** G. S. FABER *Lett. Tractar. Secess.* 248 Though there may be occasional disagreement in subordinates, there is a very singular and a very striking agreement in primaries.

subordinate (sə'bɔːdɪneɪt), *v.* [f. late L. *subordināt-*, pa. ppl. stem of *subordināre*, f. *sub-* SUB- 2 + *ordināre* to order, ORDAIN. Cf. It. *subordinare*, Sp., Pg. *subordinar*; F. *subordonner*.]

1. *trans.* To bring into a subordinate position; to render subordinate, dependent, or subservient; Const. *to.* Also †*occas.* (without *to*) to bring into subjection. Now *rare* with personal obj.

1597 HOOKER *Eccl. Pol.* v. lxxvi. (1617) 409 That what hee worketh, might.. be effected by.. instruments duely subordinated vnto the power of his owne Spirit. *a* **1600** —— *Disc. Justif.* §30 Things.. subordinated vnto Christ, by Christ himselfe. **1611** SPEED *Hist. Gt. Brit.* IX. xii. 154 Subordinating the Maior and Citizens to his gouernement. **1700** RYCAUT *Hist. Turks* III. 194 Under him six Agas were subordinated. *a* **1716** SOUTH *Serm.* Eph. iv. 10 (1744) VII. 23 The stars fight in their courses under his banner, and subordinate their powers to the dictates of his will. **1840** CARLYLE *Heroes* vi. (1841) 316 He to whose will our wills are to be subordinated. **1867** AUGUSTA WILSON *Vashti* xxviii, One whose every scheme shall be subordinated to your wishes, your happiness. **1889** *Spectator* 9 Nov. 632/2 They [the people of the U.S.] have subordinated their national aspirations to a detestable and narrow-minded race prejudice. **1898** SWEET *New Engl. Gram.* II. 33 The stress of the verb is often subordinated to that of its modifier.

2. To place in a lower order, rank, etc.; to make secondary or consider as of less importance or value. Const. *to*.

1624 WOTTON *Elem. Archit.* II. 107 As I haue before subordinated Picture, and Sculpture to Architecture, as their Mistresse. **1647** H. MORE *Poems* 308 That Kestrell kind Of bastard scholars that subordinate The precious choice induements of the mind To wealth. **1678** CUDWORTH *Intell. Syst.* I. iv. 596 Their Intention in thus Subordinating the Hypostases of their Trinity, was [etc.]. **1825** COLERIDGE *Aids Refl.* (1848) I. 22 The teacher, who subordinates prudence to virtue, cannot be supposed to dispense with virtue. **1872** LOWELL *Milton* Wks. 1890 IV. 84 There is an intolerable egotism which subordinates the sun to the watch in its own fob. **1876** GRANT *Burgh Sch. Scot.* II. xiii. 377 In the burgh Schools in which music . . was not subordinated to the other subjects of instruction.

3. *Archit.* To arrange (arches) in 'orders'.

a **1878** G. SCOTT *Lect. Archit.* (1879) I. 224 This suggested the system of sub-ordinating the rims, or recessing them.

Hence **su'bordinated** *ppl. a.*

1751 *Chambers' Cycl.* s.v. *Affection*, Affections: according to Aristotle, . . are either subordinating, or subordinated. **1899** *Westm. Gaz.* 29 Dec. 2/1 So vast was his system of subordinated labour, so numerous the army of pupils who worked under his controlling eye.

su'bordinately, *adv.* [f. SUBORDINATE *a.* + -LY².] In a subordinate, inferior, or dependent manner, degree, or position.

a **1633** AUSTIN *Medit.* (1635) 248 These [Angels] are held, to have . . the mooving (subordinately) of things beneath them. *a* **1667** COWLEY *Ess., Of Agric.* Wks. (1906) 400 Because he prayed for wisdom in the first place, he added all things else which were subordinately to be desir'd. *a* **1708** BEVERIDGE *Thes. Theol.* (1710) II. 378 Exerting the utmost of our power in doing good subordinately for our own safety, ultimately for God's glory. **1857** J. W. GIBBS *Philol. Studies* 116 The same thought . . may oftentimes be expressed either co-ordinately or subordinately. *a* **1890** LIDDON *Pusey* (1893) II. 19 Between the canonical books and those subordinately inspired works [etc.].

su'bordinateness. *rare.* [-NESS.] The quality or state of being subordinate; subordination.

1634 BP. HALL *Contempl., N.T.* IV. v. 126 The subordinatenesse of the creature doth not take away from the right . . of the first mover. *a* **1706** EVELYN *Hist. Relig.* (1850) I. 51 Who knows not that . . the subordinateness of the parts of Nature is not more astonishing than the subordinateness of thought and affections in the soul? **1871** MOZLEY *Univ. Serm.* v. (1877) 112 That freedom from all subordinateness to an authority above them.

su'bordinating, *vbl. sb.* [-ING¹.] Placing in a subordinate position.

a **1600** HOOKER *Eccl. Pol.* VII. xv. (1662) 43 The subordinating of inferiors to discharge some part of the same [office].

su'bordinating, *ppl. a.* [-ING².] That subordinates; involving subordination. ***subordinating conjunction*** (Gram.), one that serves to join a subordinate to a principal clause.

1751 [see SUBORDINATED *ppl. a.*]. **1850** GROTE *Greece* II. lxiv. VIII. 281 Constant subordinating control. **1857** J. W. GIBBS *Philol. Studies* 116 The subordinative or subordinating proposition. **1875** WHITNEY *Life Lang.* xii. 241 Relatives and subordinating conjunctions are wanting.

subordination (səbɔːdɪ'neɪʃən). [ad. late L. *subordinātio, -ōnem*, n. of action f. *subordināre* to SUBORDINATE. Cf. F. *subordination* (17th c.), It. *subordinazione*, etc.]

1. The arrangement *of* persons or things in a series of successively dependent ranks or degrees. †Also, an instance of this, a graded series of individuals or orders of beings. Now *rare* or *Obs.*

1616 BULLOKAR *Engl. Expos., Subordination*, an appointing or placing of one thing vnder another. **1646** H. LAWRENCE *Commun. Angels* 23 In this subordination, Angells come next to have an influence upon rationall creatures. **1672** GALE *Crt. Gentiles* I. I. i. (ed. 2) 2 Doth not Aristotle . . prove, that in Subordination of Causes there cannot be a progresse into infinit[ud]e? **1684** H. MORE *Answ.* 33 As if true Christianity took away all subordination of Ranks and Degrees in the world. **1750** JOHNSON *Rambler* No. 9 ⁋8 The endless subordination of animal life. **1758** J. DALRYMPLE *Ess. Feudal Prop.* (ed. 2) 200 The subordination of superior and vassal having soon ceased to be strict. *a* **1804** GILPIN *Serm.* III. xiv. 39 God hath bestowed . . different talents on different men: . . this subordination . . pervades all the works of God. **1837** WHEWELL *Hist. Induct. Sci.* III. 347 By arranging them [*sc.* animals] according to a subordination unknown to Aristotle himself. **1864** BOWEN *Logic* iv. 89 The Relations . . arising from the higher or lower position of a Concept in the series or hierarchy to which it belongs, are all denominated Relations of Subordination.

†**b.** The dependence of one part upon another in a piece of mechanism. *Obs. rare.*

1751 JOHNSON *Rambler* No. 126 ⁋7 One bar was secured by another with such intricacy of subordination—that he was himself not always able to disengage them in the proper method.

†**c.** A rank in a graded series. *Obs.*

a **1672** WILKINS *Nat. Relig.* II. iv. (1675) 333 Those several degrees and subordinations required to the order of the Universe. **1709** SWIFT *Adv. Relig.* Wks. 1755 II. I. 104 Persons, who in their several subordinations would be obliged to follow the examples of their superiors. **1712** STEELE *Spect.* No. 438 ⁋4 All the different Species and Subordinations of the Angry. **1751** JOHNSON *Rambler* No. 166 ⁋5 An insolent leveller, . . eager . . to confound the subordinations of society.

2. The condition of being subordinate, inferior, or dependent; subjection, subservience.

1651 HOBBES *Leviathan* III. xlii. 315 From the Subordination of a Government, cannot be inferred the Subjection of the Governor. **1710** STEELE *Tatler* No. 69 ⁋1 If we take too great an Idea of the Eminence of our Superiors, or Subordination of our Inferiors. **1715** M. DAVIES *Athen. Brit.* I. 127 By making use of that dangerous Term, Subordination, in explaining the eternal Filiation of the Divinity of our Saviour. **1788** GIBBON *Decl. & F.* liii. V. 507 Their independent spirit disdained the yoke of subordination. **1855** BREWSTER *Newton* II. xxii. 284 It might have been expected that a man of high principle would have kept in subordination his feelings as a rival. **1897** C. GORE in *Westm. Gaz.* 13 Apr. 6/2 That . . was no servile relationship, for subordination did not involve inferiority. **1910** *Encycl. Brit.* (ed. 11) XIII. 317/2 Without explaining the reason for the superior honour of the Saltire or for the subordination of the Quarter.

¶ ***under subordination***: under control.

1769 GOLDSM. *Hist. Rome* (1786) I. 373 The forces on the side of Marius were the most numerous, but those of Sylla better united and more under subordination. **1802** MARIAN MOORE *Lascelles* III. 190 Those whose actions are under the subordination of propriety.

b. Const. *to*. Phr. ***in (†with) subordination to.***

a **1600** HOOKER *Eccl. Pol.* VIII. iv. §6 (1648) 190 That Civill Authority is from God, but not immediately through Christ, nor with any subordination to God. **1687** DRYDEN *Hind & P.* II. 371 Nor can a council national decide, But with subordination to her Guide. **1766** BLACKSTONE *Comm.* II. 252 Escheat . . operates in subordination to this more antient and superior law of forfeiture. **1868** MILMAN *St. Paul's* xvii. 400 Porticos, large enough for effect, yet in humble subordination to the vast fabric which they enclose. **1884** tr. *Lotze's Logic* 91 The ground of all inferences is the subordination of the particular to the universal. **1884** *Law Rep. 14 Q.B. Div.* 266 The local board . . can only exercise their rights in subordination to the market rights.

†**c.** Subordinate agency. *Obs. rare.*

a **1676** HALE *Prim. Orig. Man.* 332 The like determination of the same Will was sufficient to form Man out of the Dust of the ground, without taking in a subordination or instrumentality of Angels.

d. *Gram.* The dependence of one clause upon another.

1857 J. W. GIBBS *Philol. Studies* 115 When two propositions . . are so united into a single thought or sentiment, that one proposition . . forms the complement of the other proposition, the former proposition is said to be subordinate to the latter, and this kind of union is called subordination. **1892** L. KELLNER *Engl. Syntax* 54 The first step towards the development of grammatical subordination was the use of a pronoun or a demonstrative adverb connecting the two sentences.

3. The condition of being subservient *to* some end, object, or need.

1673 STILLINGFL. *Serm.* I. iv. 67 All this it doth by way of subordination to the great end of it, which is the promoting mens eternal happiness. **1750** BEWICK *Hist. Quadr.* 21 A striking example of this subordination to the interests of mankind. **1839** *Penny Cycl.* XIII. 177/1 (*Kant*), The harmonious co-ordination of all things and their subordination to a general end. **1862** SPENCER *First Princ.* I. i. §2 (1875) 9 A certain subordination of individual actions to social requirements.

4. The condition of being duly submissive to authority or discipline; submission or subjection to the rule of a superior officer or the government of a higher power.

1736 BUTLER *Anal.* I. v. 122 The Subordination to which they [children] are accustomed in domestic life. **1760** *Caut. & Adv. Off. Army* 8 Subordination must be preserved in the Army. **1760–2** GOLDSM. *Cit. W.* xlii, Capable of behaving with just subordination to our superiors. **1838** PRESCOTT *Ferd. & Is.* II. viii. (1854) II. 120 They were without subordination, patience, industry, or any of the regular habits demanded for success in such an enterprise. **1857** RUSKIN *Pol. Econ. Art* 9 There has been wilfulness when there should have been subordination.

5. *Archit.* The act or fact of forming arches into 'orders'.

a **1878** G. SCOTT *Lect. Archit.* (1879) II. 75 The subordination of arches, by means of which, instead of going square through the thickness of a wall, they recede in orders or arched rims, each narrower than that above it. **1910** *Encycl. Brit.* (ed. 11) II. 402/1 The subordination of arches (arches built in rings, or orders, recessed one within the other).

¶ **6.** Misused for SUBORNATION.

1640 BP. HALL *Episc.* II. xi. 138 Charge him with corruption, and subordination. **1643** BAKER *Chron., Hen. VI* (1653) 273 Unlawful proceedings are used by subordination of witnesses, embracery of jurors. **1694** *S. Bethel's Provid. God* 76 The Subordination of Perjury.

subordinationism (səbɔːdɪ'neɪʃənɪz(ə)m). *Theol.* [f. prec. + -ISM.] The doctrine that the second and third persons of the Trinity are inferior, in order or in essence, to the first person. Hence **subordi'nationist**, one who maintains this doctrine; also *attrib.* or as *adj.*

1843 *Penny Cycl.* XXV. 243/1 The Father was regarded as the only supreme God, and as superior to the other persons of the Trinity, which is the doctrine called *Subordinationism.* **1880** *Encycl. Brit.* XI. 854/1 Hippolytus defended what is known as subordinationism against the patripassianism of the bishops. **1882** CAVE & BANKS tr. *Dorner's Chr. Doctr.* 204 The Subordinationist modification of the Ebionite tendency. *Ibid.* 208 Every form of Monarchianism, the Sabellian form as well as the Subordinationist.

⁋G. *Subordinatianismus* (an erron. formation after *Novatianismus*, etc.), used by Dorner, Döllinger, etc., is represented in Engl. translations by *subordinatianism*; similarly *Subordinatianer* by *subordinatianist*, and *subordinatianisch* by *subordinatian*.

1862 tr. *Dorner's Hist. Devel. Person of Christ* I. II. 58 The efforts made to exclude subordinatian elements from the conception of the Son. *Ibid.* 74 An Arian Subordinatianism was . . foreign to his mind. **1876** A. PLUMMER tr. *Döllinger's Hippol. & Callistus* iv. 191 *note*, The Subordinatianists of Alexandria.

su'bordinative, *a. rare.* [f. SUBORDINATE *v.* + -IVE.] Tending to subordinate, involving subordination.

1642 FULLER *Answ. Ferne* 3 England is not a simply subordinative, and absolute, but a Coordinative, and mixt Monarchy.

b. *Gram.* Containing a subordinate clause or clauses.

1857 J. W. GIBBS *Philol. Studies* 116 The subordinative proposition is not to be regarded as a composition of already existing parts to a whole, but as a development from the simple proposition.

su'bordinator. [f. SUBORDINATE *v.* + -OR.] Something which subordinates; *spec.* in *Gram.*, a subordinating conjunction.

1962 C. L. BARBER in F. Behre *Contrib. Eng. Syntax* 25 Clauses of time . . , most of them introduced by *when* . . ; the next commonest subordinators in these clauses are *until* . . and *while*. **1965** *Language* XLI. 242 Connectors are divided into subordinators (subordinating conjunctions) . . and coordinators. *Ibid.*, Subordinators link the sentence they introduce with either a preceding or a following superordinate structure. **1978** *Ibid.* LIV. 140 In only one case in our data did we observe Level I possibly in use as a status subordinator between adults.

suborn (sə'bɔːn), *v.* Also 6 subourne, *Sc.* suburn, 6–7 subborn, suborne. [ad. L. *subornāre*, f. *sub*- SUB- 25 + *ornāre* to equip, etc. Cf. F. *suborner* (13th c.), It. *subornare*, Sp. *sobornar*, Pg. *subornar*.]

1. *trans.* To bribe, induce, or procure (a person) by underhand or unlawful means *to* commit a misdeed. Usually const. *to do* a thing; also †*to* an act, †*against* a person or thing; when used *absol.* often = to draw away from allegiance, corrupt the loyalty of.

1534 *Act 26 Hen. VIII*, c. 4 §1 Kynsfolkes to suche offendours have resorted to the same Jurours, and have suborned them to aquyte dyvers murderers. **1555** EDEN *Decades* (Arb.) 71 This Katherine . . being suborned therto eyther by the kinge or his brothers promises. **1584** R. SCOT *Discov. Witchcr.* II. ii. 17 There must be suborned some craftie spie. **1590** SHAKS. *Com. Err.* IV. iv. 85 Thou hast subborn'd the Goldsmith to arrest mee. **1654** tr. *Scudery's Curia Pol.* 121 Seeing that Amurath hath invaded the Kingdom of his Allie, surprized his Townes, suborned his Subjects. **1663** S. PATRICK *Parab. Pilgrim* xxxvii. (1687) 491 He that hath thought there is a gain in friendship beside it self; may well be suborn'd against the same by the . . offers of a greater gain. **1783** W. THOMSON *Watson's Philip III*, v. 376 Different persons were suborned to cut off the duke by assassination. **1793** A. MURPHY *Tacitus* (1811) I. p. xxxv, Freedmen were suborned against their patrons. **1852** THACKERAY *Esmond* III. xiii, Had she not . . suborned servants, dismissed others, so that she might communicate with him? **1863** KINGLAKE *Crimea* I. 232 The President . . saw that the man could be suborned. He admitted him into the plot, [etc.]. **1911** *Act 1 & 2 Geo. V*, c. 6 §7 Every person who . . attempts to . . suborn another person to commit an offence against this Act.

fig. **1604** T. WRIGHT *Passions* II. i. 49 Vehement passions . . undermine the iudgement, and suborne it to give sentence in favour of them. **1645** MILTON *Tetrach.* Introd., Wks. 1851 IV. 140 It is not reason . . that . . suborns the common credence of men to yeeld so easily.

2. *spec.* To bribe or unlawfully procure (a person) *to* make accusations or give evidence; to induce *to* give false testimony or *to* commit perjury. Also, to procure (evidence) by such unlawful means. (Cf. SUBORNATION 2 b).

1557 *N.T.* (Geneva) Acts vi. 11 Then they subborned men, which sayd, We haue heard him speake blasphemous wordes. **1565** COOPER *Thesaurus* s.v. *Submitto*, To suborne or priuily to sende accusers to appeache one. *Ibid.*, *Subijcere testes*, to suborne false witnesses. **1603** SHAKS. *Meas. for M.* v. i. 106 Yᵘ knowst not what thou speak'st, Or else thou art suborn'd against his honor In hatefull practise. **1639** SALTMARSHE *Policy* 198 Wicked men suborne false witnesses when they are convicted. *a* **1680** BUTLER *Rem.* (1759) I. 303 Upon single Perjuries suborned by themselves they condemned Men unheard. **1711** ADDISON *Spect.* No. 171 ⁋9 A Witness, suborn'd by some of Mariamne's Enemies, who accused her to the King of a Design to poison him. **1736** FIELDING *Pasquin* I. i. 9, I would as soon suborn an Evidence at an Assize, as a Vote at an Election. **1777** SHERIDAN *Sch. Scandal* v. iii, I am so confounded, to find that Lady Sneerwell could be guilty of suborning Mr. Snake in this manner, to impose on us all. **1785** REID *Intell. Powers* I. ii. 46 If it can be shown that he is suborned, . . his testimony loses all its credit. **1864** KINGSLEY *Rom. & Teut.* v. (1875) 131 The Gothic courtiers . . suborned branded scoundrels to swear away his life. **1874** GREEN *Short Hist.* ix. §5. 645 The arrest of Shaftesbury on a charge of suborning false witnesses to the Plot. **1877** CONDER *Basis Faith* viii. 353 It is a kind of evidence which cannot be suborned.

b. To procure the performance or execution of (a thing) by bribery or other corrupt means.

1817 JAS. MILL *Brit. India* II. v. viii. 670 The letters which were written in the name of the Nabob,..were in fact suborned by the Governor-General. **1858** J. MARTINEAU *Stud. Christ.* 84 The public murder which they have privately suborned.

†**3.** To prepare, provide, or procure, *esp.* in a secret, stealthy, or underhand manner. *Obs.*

1540-1 ELYOT *Image Gov.* 93 [89] Where they be not therto sufficient, they wyll suborne some false quarrell to make a commotion. **1579-80** NORTH *Plutarch, Lucullus* (1595) 565 He beganne..to suborne the bands called Fimbrians, and to stirre them vp against Lucullus. **1615** CHAPMAN *Odyss.* x. 422 In a golden boule She then subornd a potion. **1667** MILTON *P.L.* IX. 361 Since Reason not impossibly may meet Some specious object by the Foe subornd. **1676** DRYDEN *State Innoc.* v. i, And those who, by Despair, suborn their Death. **1700** —— *Cymon & Iph.* 552 Then entring unexpected will we seize Our destin'd Prey,.. And hast'ning to the Seas suborn our Flight. *a* **1721** PRIOR *Truth & Falseh.* 33 Wks. 1907 II. 132 The Fraudful Dame, ..False sighs suborns, and artful tears.

†**4.** To furnish, equip, adorn. *Obs.*

1596 SPENSER *State Irel.* Wks. (Globe) 641/1 Evill thinges being decked and suborned with the gay attyre of goodly woordes. **1605** BACON *Adv. Learn.* II. xx. §3 Not to write at leasure that which men may read at leasure, but really to instruct and suborne action and active live.

†**5.** To give support to, aid, assist. *Obs.*

1568 GRAFTON *Chron.* II. 610 This Capteine [Jack Cade] not only suborned by teachers, but also enforced by priuie Scholemaisters, assembled together a great company of tall personages. *c* **1611** CHAPMAN *Iliad* VIII. 114 Let their brightnesse glase the skies, that night may not suborne The Greekes escape.

†**6.** To introduce or bring to one's aid with a sinister motive. *Obs.*

a **1619** FOTHERBY *Atheom.* I. ix. §1 (1622) 59 He [*sc.* Euripides] suborned, in his Tragœdie, the person of Sisyphus, to expresse all his vngodlinesse. **1649** MILTON *Eikon.* xxvi. 210 Nor is he onely content to suborne Divine Justice in his censure of what is past, but he assumes the person of Christ himself to prognosticate..what he wishes would come. **1677** *Let.* in J. Smith *Mem. Wool*, etc. (1757) I. lix. 215 Some Western Clothiers finding, so early, and upon other Reasons than are now suborned, that Trade decaying.

†**7.** [SUB- 27.] To commission (another) in one's place. *Obs. rare.*

1560 DAUS tr. *Sleidane's Comm.* 335 After they vnderstode, that it was not possible for them to go vnto al places, whiche had nede of remedy, of necessitie they suborned others [orig. *necessario summisisse alios*].

Hence **su'borning** *vbl. sb.* and *ppl. a.*

1578 WHETSTONE *2nd Pt. Promos & Cass.* II. iv, Against Vsurie, brybrie, and barrating, Suborning, extorcion, and boulstring. **1594** NASHE *Unfort. Trav.* L2b, Other superuising espialls to plie, follow, and spurre forward those suborning incensers. **1611** COTGR., *Subornation*, a subornation, or suborning. **1705** STANHOPE *Paraphr.* I. 72 The bribed Soldiers, and suborning Scribes, who by false Reports endeavoured to..destroy the Credit of that Resurrection.

†**subornate**, *pa. pple.* and *ppl. a. Obs.* [ad. L. *subornātus*, pa. pple. of *subornāre* to SUBORN.] Suborned.

1430-1 *Rolls of Parlt.* IV. 375/2 Certeyns subornatz proves and persones of hir assent and covyne. **1432-50** tr. *Higden* (Rolls) III. 63 Iulius Proculus, subornate by the Romanes, seide Romulus to haue apperede to hym. **1533** BELLENDEN *Livy* I. xvi. (S.T.S.) I. 91 Þe sonnys of Ancus (quhilkis has subornate þir lymmaris to sla þe king). **1560** *Maitl. Club Misc.* III. 225 Sche saw Jonet Watsone subornate and seducit be Williame and then repellet. **1590** BARROW & GREENWOOD in *Confer.* 33 Your subornate witnesses.

b. *adj.* ? Underhand, false.

a **1548** HALL *Chron., Hen. VI*, 169 The cloked gentlenes, and subornate fashion of the duke of Yorke.

†**subornate**, *v. Obs.* [f. L. *subornāt-*, pa. ppl. stem of *subornāre* to SUBORN.] = SUBORN.

1537 *Instit. Christen man* A7 Subornatynge fals wytnesse. *a* **1548** HALL *Chron., Edw. IV.* (1550) 40 The Frenche Kyng ..caused a varlet to be subornated, in a cote armure of Fraunce. **1553** BRENDE *Q. Curtius* x. 6 He did subornate certain lewde persons..to bring in false accusations against him.

subornation (sʌbɔː'neɪʃən). Also 6 **-acion**, **subborn-**, 7 **subernation**. [ad. L. *subornātio*, *-ōnem*, n. of action f. *subornāre* to SUBORN. Cf. F. *subornation*, It. *subornazione*, etc.]

1. The act of inducing or procuring a person to commit an evil action, by bribery, corruption, or the like; an instance of this. Also, †underhand action.

a **1548** HALL *Chron., Hen. VII*, 47b, He by his crafty subornacions had persuaded diuerse..to beleue..that he was the same verey person. **1579-80** NORTH *Plutarch, Solon* (1595) 99 Those that were compassed..by subornation at length to do a thing against their will. **1601** R. JOHNSON *Kingd. & Commw.* (1603) 225 By the subernation of the viceroy of Algier he was murdred in his tent by certain Turks. **1670** G. H. *Hist. Cardinals* III. III. 304 Without Bribery, or Subornation, he had attain'd to the dignity of the Purple. *a* **1715** BURNET *Own Time* (1724) I. 510 He protested ..that he knew of no subornation in all that matter. **1842** DE QUINCEY *Cicero* Wks. 1857 VII. 187 The sort of chicanery attending his subornation of managers in the Leibnitz controversy. **1853** GROTE *Greece* II. lxxxvi. XI. 291 By the hands of assassins and the treacherous subornation of his mother Eurydike.

2. The act of procuring a person to give false evidence. Also, an instance of this.

1528 MORE *Dyaloge* III. Wks. 211/2 For fere of subornacion & false instruction of witnesse. **1590** GREENE *Never too late* (1600) 82 Hee hath produced this younge man by a sinister subornation to periure himselfe. **1659** *Gentl. Calling* 420 If a witness prove a better pennyworth than the Judge, subornation shall do the business. **1748** SMOLLETT *Rod. Random* xxxi. (1760) I. 241 *chapter-heading*, I discover a subornation against me, by means of a quarrel between two of the evidences. **1792** BURKE *Corr.* (1844) IV. 74 A perjury as bloody as that of Oates and Bedlow;—a subornation as audacious. **1847** JAMES *Convict* xli, This is something like a subornation of witnesses.

b. ***subornation of perjury***: the act of procuring a witness on oath to commit perjury.

1588 FRAUNCE *Lawiers Logike* I. xix. 67 If any of them [*i.e.* jurors] bee discredited by Law as by attainder in conspiracy ..subornation of periury, or such like. **1678** MARVELL *Growth Popery* Wks. (Grosart) IV. 333 For subornation of perjury, tending to the defamation of his Majesty. **1765-8** ERSKINE *Inst. Laws Scot.* IV. iv. §75 Subornation of perjury consists in tampering with those who are to swear in judgement, by soliciting or directing them how they are to depose, without regard to truth. **1797** *Jacob's Law Dict.* (ed. 10) s.v. *Perjury*, If the person incited to take such oath do not actually take it, the person by whom he was so incited is not guilty of subornation. **1911** *Act 1 & 2 Geo. V*, c. 6 §8 Any offence punishable as perjury or as subornation of perjury.

transf. **1858** MERIVALE *Rom. Emp.* liv. (1865) VI. 405 A cheap subornation of flattery.

†**c.** A statement corruptly obtained. *Obs. rare.*

1737 WHISTON *Josephus, Antiq.* VII. viii. §4 The King perceived that this pretended story was a subornation derived from Joab, and was of his contrivance.

†**3.** The action of bringing a person to one's assistance or support. *Obs.*

1600 W. CORNWALLIS *Ess.* II. xlvi. Mm4b, Her [*sc.* Virtue's] counsels shall bee held so sincere, as they shall be accepted without the subornation of the nimph Egeria.

su'bornative, *a. rare.* [See SUBORN *v.* and -ATIVE.] Pertaining to subornation.

1802-12 BENTHAM *Ration. Judic. Evid.* (1827) I. 388 Any work..done..in the subornative line, for the purpose of giving existence to the lie.

suborned (sə'bɔːnd), *ppl. a.* [f. SUBORN *v.* + -ED[1].] In senses of the verb SUBORN; obtained by corrupt means; †supposititious, counterfeit.

1589 WARNER *Alb. Eng.* VI. xxx. (1602) 149 She baer'd so sweete a face, As from the sternest Godhood might extort suborned grace. **1594** NASHE *Unfort. Trav.* E3b, Because I was his suborned Lorde and master. **1598** DANIEL *Civ. Wars* v. lxxx, Suborned Iustice. **1610** CARLETON *Jurisd.* 72 The Fathers..reiecting this suborned and supposititious Canon. **1631** WEEVER *Anc. Funeral Mon.* 15 Suborned counterfeit hired mourners. **1676** MARVELL *Gen. Councils* Wks. (Grosart) IV. 94 By suborned witnesses, stirring up the rabble. **1860** ELLICOTT *Life Our Lord* vii. 335 To.. investigate the many suborned witnesses. **1860** FORSTER *Gr. Remonstr.* 105 Impositions by prerogative..were backed by suborned and scandalous decisions in the courts.

subornee (sʌbɔː'niː). [f. as prec. + -EE[1].] One who is suborned.

1894 *Law Times* XCVII. 384/1 Hireling subornees of perjury.

suborner (sə'bɔːnə(r)). [f. SUBORN *v.* + -ER[1].] One who suborns.

1593 NASHE *Christ's T.* Wks. (Grosart) IV. 163 Ambition & Auarice his suborner. **1602** FULBECKE *1st Pt. Parall.* 64 Suborners..which do minister occasion to the informer. **1629** T. ADAMS *Rage Oppress.* Wks. 607 Man is the maine suborner of mischiefe to his owne kind. **1632** BP. HALL *Hard Texts* Acts v. 3 Thou..hast drawne in the holy Ghost as a suborner, and abetter of thy wickednesse. **1769** BLACKSTONE *Comm.* IV. x. 137 The statute 5 Eliz. c. 9.. inflicts..a fine of 40*l.* on the suborner. **1817** COLERIDGE *Biog. Lit.* (1907) II. 214 His employer and suborner. **1823** BENTHAM *Not Paul* 251 Were they not..so many suborners of this same perjury? **1840** DICKENS *Old C. Shop* lxii, You perjurer, you suborner of evidence. **1874** MOTLEY *John of Barneveld* II. 440 The conspirator and suborner of murder.

subosco: see SUBBOSCO.

sub'oval, *a.* [SUB- 21c. Cf. F. *subovale.*] Somewhat or almost oval.

1752 J. HILL *Hist. Anim.* 9 The Macrocercus, with a suboval depressed body. **1777** S. ROBSON *Brit. Flora* 167 Corollulæ of the radius suboval. **1817** STEPHENS in Shaw's *Gen. Zool.* X. II. 564 Nostrils suboval and depressed. **1858** LEWES *Sea-side Studies* II. ii. 147 Minute suboval microscopic capsules.

sub'ovate, *a.* [ad. mod.L. *subōvātus*: see SUB- 21c.] Somewhat or almost ovate.

1752 J. HILL *Hist. Anim.* 98 [90] The Triton, with a subovate body. **1812** *New Bot. Gard.* I. 55 The pericarpium is a subovate, three-celled capsule. **1874** LUBBOCK *Orig. & Met. Ins.* i. 18 Hexapod antenniferous larvae, with a subovate body.

So †**sub'ovated** *a.*, = SUBOVATE *a.*; **sub'ovoid** *a.*, somewhat or almost ovoid.

1776 PENNANT *Brit. Zool.* II. 469 Nostrils..Small, subovated. **1828** STARK *Elem. Nat. Hist.* II. 289 Head subovoid. **1870** HOOKER *Stud. Flora* 121 Rosa spinosissima ..fruit subovoid.

†**subpand**. *Sc. Obs.* [f. SUB- 3 + PAND (OF. *pand*, var. of *pan* skirt).] A valance.

1578 *Inv. Roy. Wardrobe* (1815) 210 Ane auld bed of blak dames with the ruif and pandes and twa subpandis.

sub'pectoral, *a.* [SUB- 1a, b.]

1. *Zool.*, etc. Situated beneath the breast or *pectus*.

1834 McMURTRIE *Cuvier's Anim. Kingd.* 195 The subpectoral rays. **1872** T. BRYANT *Pract. Surg.* 154 The subpectoral glands.

2. Emanating from the depths of the chest.

1871 MEREDITH *Harry Richmond* xlvi, A muffled rattle of subpectoral thunder discharged at her in quick, heated snaps.

subpe'daneous *a.*, = SUPPEDANEOUS.

1656 BLOUNT *Glossogr.*, *Subpedaneous*, belonging to a foot-stool, or any thing under foot.

sub'pedital, = SUPPEDITAL, a shoe.

1526 *A C. mery talys* 3b, Set me .ii. tryangyls & .ii. semy cercles vppon my subpedytals.

sub'peditate *v.*, = SUPPEDITATE *v.*, to subdue.

1538 *St. Papers Hen. VIII* (1834) III. 78 The said Lord Deputie..hathe subpeditate..Murghe Obrene.

†**sub'penal**, *a. Obs. rare*[−1]. [f. L. *sub pœnā* + -AL[1]; cf. ‖SUB 11, SUBPŒNA, and PENAL.] Subject to penalties.

1659 GAUDEN *Tears Ch.* 483 These meetings of Ministers must be authoritative, not arbitrary, not precarious, but subpenall.

sub'petiolar, *a. Bot.* [SUB- 1c.] Situated under the petiole, as the buds of the plane-tree.

1891 *Century Dict.*

sub'petiolate, *a. Bot.* [mod.L. *subpetiolātus* (sense 1). Cf. F. *subpétiolé.*]

1. [SUB- 21c.] Somewhat petiolate; having a very short petiole.

1847 W. E. STEELE *Field Bot.* 25 Leaves..sub-petiolate.

2. = SUBPETIOLAR.

1900 B. D. JACKSON *Gloss. Bot. Terms.*

sub'petiole. *Bot.* [SUB- 5b.] A partial or secondary petiole, a petiolule.

1880 C. & F. DARWIN *Movem. Pl.* xii. 558 Each petiole, sub-petiole, and leaflet.

sub'petioled, *a. Bot.* [SUB- 21c.] = SUBPETIOLATE 1.

1800 *Asiatic Ann. Reg.* 269/1 Leaves..sub-petioled.

subplant *v.*, = SUPPLANT *v.*

1382 WYCLIF *Gen.* xxvii. 36 He forsothe hath subplauntid me. **1472** MARG. PASTON *Let. to J. Paston* 19 Nov., Mad to subplant you. **1603** OWEN *Pembrokeshire* iii. (1892) 35 The Normans haveinge subdued and subplanted the Saxon Kinges.

‖**subpœna** (səb'piːnə, sə'piːnə), *sb. Law.* Forms: 5-6 **suppena**, 5-7 **subpena**, 6 **supenea**, 6 **subpene**, 7 **sowpinee**, 8 **supœna**, 6- **subpœna**. [law-L., = L. *sub pœnā* under a penalty (cf. ‖SUB 11), being the first words of the writ.]

1. A writ issued by chancery commanding the presence of a defendant to answer the matter alleged against him. Also ***writ of subpœna***.

1422-61 in *Cal. Proc. Chanc. Q. Eliz.* (1827) I. Introd. 19 Graunte to the seid suppliant a writ sub pena direct to the seid Thomas. **1482** *Rolls of Parlt.* VI. 208/1 To graunte as many Writts of Sub pena out of the Court of Chauncerie. *a* **1517** in Scrope *Castle Combe* (1852) 294 A suppena brought agaynse me by hys false surmyse. **1543** tr. *Act 15 Hen. VI*, c. 4 For asmoche as dyuers persons haue before this tyme ben greatly greued by wryttes of sub pena. **1623** in *New Shaks. Soc. Trans.* (1885) 499 His Ma[ties] most gracious writt of Subpœna directed to the said James Baskervile.. and also to Susann Baskervile..comaunding them..to.. appeare..in his Ma[ties] high court of Chauncery. **1768** BLACKSTONE *Comm.* III. xxvii. 443 Upon common bills, as soon as they are filed, process of *subpoena* is taken out; which is a writ commanding the defendant to appear and answer to the bill, on pain of 100*l.* **1818** CRUISE *Digest* (ed. 2) I. 392. **1875** DIGBY *Real Prop.* vi. (1876) 286.

2. a. A writ issued from a court of justice commanding the presence of a witness under a penalty for failure.

1467 R. CALLE *Let. to Sir J. Paston* 3 Apr., He woll not come withoute he have a suppena. *c* **1550** *Wyll of Deuill* (? 1825) B4b, A Bouget too put their Sup penas in, to cracke the poore men with all in the countrey. *a* **1613** OVERBURY *Characters, Country Gentl.* Wks. (1856) 64 Nothing under a sub pœna can draw him to London. **1673** in *Canterbury Press* (1884) 26 Jan. 7/3 For a sowpinee For the witeneses 030. **1746** FRANCIS tr. *Hor., Sat.* I. ii. 13 By subpœnas dragg'd from home. **1818** SCOTT *Hrt. Midl.* xix, The worthy magistrate..had caused the ordinary citation, or *subpœna*, of the Scottish criminal court, to be served upon her. **1837** DICKENS *Pickw.* xxxi, It's only a subpœna in Bardell and Pickwick.

b. *attrib.* in ***subpœna office***.

1688 HOLME *Armoury* III. iii. 63/1 Officers belonging to the High Court of Chancery... The Clerk of the Subpena Office. **1797** *Jacob's Law Dict.* (ed. 10) s.v., The proper clerks of the Subpœna Office.

c. In Lat. phrases: ***subpœna ad testificandum*** [L., in order to testify], ***subpœna duces tecum*** [DUCES TECUM] (see quot. 1980).

1768 BLACKSTONE *Comm.* III. xxiii. 382 In the hands of third persons they [*sc.* books and papers belonging to the parties] can generally be obtained by rule of court, or by adding a clause of requisition to the writ of *subpoena*, which is then called a *subpoena duces tecum*. **1808** E. H. EAST *Rep.* IX. 476 The precedents of the common subpœna ad testificandum are scarcely more ancient than that of the subpœna duces tecum. **1891** *Weekly Notes* 12 Dec. 195/1

This was a motion..to set aside a writ of *subpœna duces tecum.* **1909** *Law Jrnl. Rep. King's Bench Div.* LXXVIII. 120/2 This case must not be taken as a precedent for any supposed rule that a person summoned on *subpœna ad testificandum* may get it set aside by swearing that he can give no relevant evidence. **1944** *All England Law Reports* (1945) I. 274 The party on whose behalf the motion is made has been required by a *subpœna ad testificandum* and *duces tecum* to appear before the district auditor. **1965** *Annual Practice* I. 881 Any party in any cause or matter may by *subpœna ad testificandum* or *duces tecum* require the attendance of any witness before an officer of the Court. **1980** *Oxf. Compan. Law* 1195/1 It [*sc.* a subpœna] takes two forms, *subpoena ad testificandum*, when the recipient is called to give evidence, and *subpoena duces tecum*, when he is required to bring documents or papers relevant to the controversy for examination by the court.

3. *fig.*

1593 *Tell-Trothe's N.Y. Gift* (1876) 36 What a cheape subpena is this to drawe an answere from the conscience. **1635** SHIRLEY *Lady Pleas.* I. (1637) B 2 b, To which appeare, As to the Court of Pleasure, all your gallants, And Ladies thither bound by a Subpena Of Venus. **1649** W. M. *Wand. Jew* (1857) 48 Shee serves me still with Subpœna upon Subpœna to answer to the Intergatories of her cruelty. **1906** *Hibbert Jrnl.* Jan. 265 That authority..is necessarily open to the challenge of criticism, liable to a subpœna before the higher bar of reason.

‖**sub'pœna,** *v. Law.* Also 7 **subpœne.** [f. prec.] *trans.* To serve with a writ of subpœna; to summon as a witness in a court of justice. (Chiefly in pa. pple.)

1640 in Rushw. *Hist. Coll.* (1692) III. I. 81 One Walker, and Cadwallader Powel,..subpœned to be made Defendants in a Third Information put into the High Court of Star-Chamber. **1693** *Humours Town* 6 My Cousin, here, and I, being subpœna'd up for Witnesses. **1710** P. BLAIR *Misc. Observ.* (1718) 66 The Physicians and Surgeons (being *subpena'd* as Evidences against him). **1755** *Gentl. Mag.* XXV. 329 The witnesses subpæna'd by the crown amounted to above 100. **1858** LYTTON *What will He do?* VII. vii, He would not even subpœna any of his old friends as to his general character. **1875** MISS BRADDON *Strange World* xi, Elgood and his daughter were both subpœnaed for the adjourned inquest. **1884** *Harper's Mag.* June 57/1 Other merchants may be subpœnaed to act as mercantile experts at the examination.

transf. **1755** CHESTERF. in *World* No. 151 ⁋1, I was lately subpœnaed, by a card, to a general assembly.

sub'polar, *a.* [Cf. Sp. *subpolar.*]

1. [SUB- 12 b.] Adjacent to the poles or polar sea.

1826 KIRBY & SP. *Entomol.* xlix. IV. 485 Beginning at 84° N. L. he [*sc.* Latreille] has seven Arctic ones, which he names polar, subpolar, superior, intermediate, supratropical, tropical, and equatorial.

2. [SUB- 1 a] Beneath the pole of the heavens.

1876 C. H. DAVIS *Polaris Exp.* iv. 96 The latitude of the southern entrance of Repulse Harbor, determined..by a meridian subpolar observation. **1883** PROCTOR *Gt. Pyramid* iii. 154 The subpolar meridional passage of [Alpha Draconis].

'subpopulation. 1. [SUB- 3.] A population living underground.

1890 *Daily News* 19 June 5/7 A sort of sub-population of elfin people, who live under the Treppe.

2. a. [SUB- 7 a] A population forming part of a larger population. **b.** [SUB- 9.] One derived or originating from some other population.

1959 *Heredity* XIII. 217 This gene flow..prevented the divergence of the two sub-populations. **1961** *Lancet* 9 Sept. 586/2 Serious outbreaks have occurred mainly because substantial poorly vaccinated subpopulation groups have remained—for example, lower socioeconomic groups in the U.S.A. **1964** S. LIEBERSON in J. A. Fishman *Readings Sociol. of Lang.* (1968) 553 Such subpopulations as social classes, juvenile delinquents, racial, ethnic, and tribal populations, age groups, regions, and occupational groups. **1971** J. Z. YOUNG *Introd. Study Man* xxvii. 385 Like all populations, ours is composed of many sub-populations, differing from each other not only outwardly but in their gene structure. **1974** J. W. DRAKE in Carlile & Skehel *Evolution in Microbial World* 53 Microbial subpopulations frequently become extinct. **1979** *Sci. Amer.* Mar. 53/1 Could it be that they represent a sub-population of tumor cells endowed with the particular characteristics making for successful metastasis?

subpouelle, variant of SUPPOWELL, to support.

14.. *MS. Cantab.* Ff. i. 6. fol. 123 Trustyng to Ihu..Tho send hys grace to subpouelle & Comffort Tho all that ys wyth wrong repourt.

'sub-pre,ceptor. *Obs.* exc. *Hist.* [SUB- 6.] An assistant preceptor or instructor. Hence **,subprecep'torial** *a.*

1698 LUTTRELL *Brief Rel.* (1857) IV. 406 The bishop of Salisbury, his preceptor, 1200£ per ann.; and Dr. Willis, his subpreceptor, 400£. **1755** [see SUBGOVERNOR]. **1827** *Gentl. Mag.* XCVII. II. 6 He had..been Sub-preceptor to his present Majesty, then Prince of Wales, and to the Duke of York. **1847** MEDWIN *Shelley* II. 221 Sub-preceptor to the Princess Charlotte. *Ibid.*, To relieve him from his sub-preceptorial duties.

'sub-,prefect. [SUB- 6. Cf. F. *sous-préfet.*] An assistant or deputy prefect; *spec.* an administrative official of a department of France immediately subordinate to the prefect; the administrator of a province of Peru.

1845 W. K. KELLY tr. *Blanc's Hist. Ten Yrs.* II. 175 The préfects, the sub-préfects, and the mayors. **1852** SHARPE *Hist. Egypt* xxi, Every deputy tax-gatherer, Every prefect, every sub-prefect. **1880** C. R. MARKHAM *Peruv. Bark* 125 The Sub-prefect, Don Pablo Pimentel. **1899** KIPLING *Stalky* 137 We aren't even sub-prefects.

Hence **,subprefec'torial** *a.* [cf. F. *sous-préfectoral*], pertaining to a subprefect or subprefecture; **subpre'fecture** [cf. F. *sous-préfecture*], the office or position of a subprefect, a division of a prefecture.

1837 *Penny Cycl.* IX. 105/2 (*Doubs*) The department is divided into four arrondissemens or sub-prefectures. **1870** *Illustr. Lond. News* 29 Oct. 438 Making of the five Roman provinces one only, with five sub-prefectures. **1879** STEVENSON *Trav. Donkey* 183 The subprefectorial map was fetched from the subprefecture itself.

subpress, obs. variant of SUPPRESS *v.*

1536 in Archbold *Somerset Relig. Houses* (1892) 56 To help me to the gifte of the priorie of ffynshed..yn case it be subpressed. **1542** BOORDE *Dyetary* ix. (1870) 250 That the lyuer, whiche is the fyre vnder the potte, is subpressed. **1637** PRYNNE *Docum.* (1877) 89 The clarke of the peace's deposition..which the judges had subprest as scandalous.

'sub,principal, *sb.*

†**1.** *Mus.* [med.L. *subprincipālis*, used to render Gr. παρυπάτη (sc. χορδή string): see SUB- 13.] = PARHYPATE. *Obs.*

1603 HOLLAND *Plutarch's Mor.* Explan. Wds., *Parhypate hypatôn*,..Subprincipall of principals... C, FA, UT. *Parhypate Mesôn*,..Subprincipall of meanes:..F, FA, UT.

2. [SUB- 6.] A vice-principal of a university, etc.

1597 *Sc. Acts Jas. VI* (1816) IV. 154/1 Þe principall subprinll regentis and remanent memberis of þe said college. **1615** *Reg. Mag. Sig. Scot.* 543/1 Mr Pat. Guthrie sub-principall of the said colledge. **1755** E. CHAMBERLAYNE *Angl. Notitia* II. 16 Eight Masters of Arts, of which, the first was Sub-Principal.

3. *Archit.* [SUB- 5 b.] (See quot.)

1842 GWILT *Archit.* Gloss., *Sub-principals*, the same as auxiliary rafters or principal braces.

4. [SUB- 13.] An open diapason sub-bass.

1876 STAINER & BARRETT *Dict. Mus. Terms*, *Subprincipal*, an organ stop consisting of open pipes, of 32 ft. pitch on the pedals, and of 16 ft. pitch on the manuals.

†**'subprincipal,** *a.* [SUB- II.] (See quot.)

1601 DOLMAN *La Primaud. Fr. Acad.* III. li. 236 Eight other windes, called sub-principall [orig. *souzprincipaux*], and which compound their names of their two next collaterall windes,..to wit, North-northeast, North-northwest.

'sub,prior. [a. OF. *subprieur* (14th c.), med.L. *subprior*, var. of *supprior* SUPPRIOR: see SUB- 6 and PRIOR *sb.* Cf. ME. *sousprior* s.v. SOUS-, and mod.F. *sousprieur* (from 13th c.).] A prior's assistant and deputy.

1340 *Ayenb.* 67 Þe abbottes and þe priours and hire officials ase subprior and þe opre. *c* **1440** *Promp. Parv.* 482/1 Subpriowre, *subprior.* **1540** *Act 32 Hen. VIII*, c. 24 §8 Subpriour of the said hospital of sainte John of Jerusalem. **1641** PRYNNE *Antipathie* 33 Hubert being dead the Monkes of Canterbury..elected Reginald their Sub-prior, for his Successour. **1767** BURN *Eccles. Law* (ed. 2) IV. 456 In every priory, next under the prior was the sub-prior, who assisted the prior whilst present, and acted in his stead when absent. **1868** MORRIS *Earthly Par.* (1890) 51/1 An old reverend man The sub-prior.

So **'sub,prioress.**

c **1660** in J. Morris *Troubles Cath. Forefathers* (1872) Ser. I. vi. 257 For Subprioress she appointed Sister Anne Tremaine. *c* **1789** in *Cath. Rec. Soc. Publ.* IX. 398 She fulfilled several important offices in the Community such as Subprioress, Mistress of Novices, and Cellerere.

'subprogram. *Computers.* [SUB- 5 c.] = SUBROUTINE.

1947 *Math. Tables & Other Aids to Computation* II. 358 Nor can it [*sc.* a computer] be directed to repeat automatically sub-programs within the same total program. **1965** *Math. in Biol. & Med.* (Med. Res. Council) IV. 205 All the sub-programs that enter into the FIDAC system are listed in a manual, which specifies for each what user-input parameters are required and what values they may take on. **1979** *Sci. Amer.* Dec. 87/1 The most important technique for limiting the complexity of computer programs is the use of subprograms: self-contained pieces of programming that are named, stored in a library and called on to perform their particular computation as part of the execution of other programs.

subpu'tation, variant of SUPPUTATION.

1905 J. B. BURY *St. Patrick* App. 382 It is to be noted that in the *Liber Armachanus* two divergent subputations of Patrick's age are found.

subra'mose, *a. Bot.* and *Zool.* [ad. mod.L. *subrāmōsus*: see SUB- 21 c.] Slightly ramose; having few branches; having a slight tendency to branch.

c **1789** *Encycl. Brit.* (1797) III. 444/2 Subramose, having only a few lateral branches. **1822** J. PARKINSON *Outl. Oryctol.* 42 Subramose tubes, everywhere muricated with acute tubercles. **1856** W. CLARK *Van der Hoeven's Zool.* I. 75 Polypary papyraceous, subramose.

transf. **1826** KIRBY & SP. *Entomol.* xxviii. III. 12 In the Supplement to the first volume, he has distributed the *Invertebrata* in a double subramose series.

So **sub'ramous** *a.*

1760 J. LEE *Introd. Bot.* (1794) 382 *Subramosus*, subramous, having few lateral Branches.

'sub-range. 1. [SUB- 5 b.] A subsidiary range (of mountains).

1859 R. F. BURTON in *Jrnl. Geogr. Soc.* XXIX. 125 §1 An extensive view of subrange and hill-spur.

2. [SUB- 7 c.] A range of values or conditions within a larger range.

1956 A. A. TOWNSEND *Struct. Turbulent Shear Flow* iii. 45 In this subrange [of Reynolds numbers], the motion is independent of the viscosity. **1968** FOX & MAYERS *Computing Methods for Scientists & Engineers* iii. 50 The computed value at r_c, and the given $y_o = a,$..provide boundary values for solution by linear equations in this first sub-range.

sub'rational, *a.*

1. [SUB- 14.] Below what is rational, less than rational.

1865 *Daily Tel.* 27 Nov. 2/3 The readiness..of a Tory, even of the sub-rational species, to entertain the question of Reform. **1896** *Expositor* Sept. 214 [Man is] incomparable with 'birds and four-footed beasts', and..with the entire subrational universe.

2. [SUB- 19 b.] *Math.* (See quot.)

1874-5 CAYLEY *Math. Papers* (1896) IX. 315 *note*, The expression 'subrational' includes irrational, but it is more extensive; if Y, X are rational functions, the same or different, of y, x respectively, and Y is determined as a function of x by an equation of the form $Y = X$, then y is a subrational function of x.

'sub,rector. [SUB- 6.] An official immediately below a rector in rank, and acting as his deputy.

1629 WADSWORTH *Pilgr.* vi. 55 The Sub-Rector and two of his schollers. **1678** WALTON *Life Sanderson* 28 b, In the year 1613, he was chosen Sub-rector of the Colledge. **1691** *Case of Exeter Coll.* 27 Differences arising betwixt the Rector and the Scholars, if not determined within twenty days by the Sub-Rector, the Dean, and three of the *Maximè Seniores* [etc.].

'sub,region. [SUB- 7 c.] A division or subdivision of a region.

1864 A. R. WALLACE in *Proc. Zool. Soc.* 273 Confining our attention now to the Australian region only, we may divide it into three subregions—Australia, the Pacific Islands, and the Austro-Malayan group—each of which has a distinctive character. **1869** SCLATER *Ibid.* 125 The true Australian sub-region (*Subregio australis*), comprising continental Australia, with, perhaps, the exception of the northern promontory of Cape York. **1882** MINCHIN *Unipl. Kinemat.* 194 That portion of the space bounded by the contour DEF which is not included in any of the sub-regions A, B, C. **1898** A. N. WHITEHEAD *Treat. Universal Algebra* I. i. 125 A region defined by any ρ independent letters lying in a region of $\nu-1$ dimensions, where ρ is less than ν, is called a subregion of the original region. **1959** G. & R. C. JAMES *Math. Dict.* 374/1 *Subregion*, a region within a region. **1974** *Nature* 11 Oct. 531/1 The periventricular areas of the hypothalamus were further dissected into four subregions and assayed for adrenaline. **1977** *Verbatim* Dec. 7/2 Cultural maps, such as those provided by Odum and Vance, would have been more useful than his reprinted essay from PMLA in identifying the subregions of the South.

Hence **sub'regional** *a.*, of or pertaining to a subregion.

1875 *Encycl. Brit.* III. 747 *marg.*, Their [*sc.* the Galapagos] Subregional assignation doubtful. **1946** *Richmond* (Va.) *News Leader* 7 Feb. 3/3 The Richmond sub-regional office of the Veterans Administration will be open ..until 5 P.M. **1966** [see LEISURE *sb.* 6 a and c]. **1977** *Lancet* 14 May 1054/1 We were surprised to read..that the treatment of leukæmia should no longer be regarded as regional or subregional.

sub'regular, *a.* [SUB- 19, 21.]

1. *Zool.* and *Bot.* Almost regular.

1822 J. PARKINSON *Outl. Oryctol.* 191 An unequal valved, subregular bivalve. **1870** HOOKER *Stud. Flora* 260 Corolla short subregular.

2. *Math.* (See quot.)

1886 CAYLEY *Math. Papers* (1897) XII. 444 An integral may be a regular integral, or it may be what Thomé calls a normal elementary integral: the theory of these integrals (which I would rather call subregular integrals) requires.. further examination.

subreption[1] (səb'rɛpʃən). [ad. L. *subreptio*, *-ōnem*, n. of action f. *subripĕre* (var. *surr-*), f. *sub-* SUB- 25 + *rapĕre* to snatch. Cf. F. *subreption*, Sp. *subrepcion*, Pg. *subrepção* and see SURREPTION.]

a. *Eccl. Law.* The suppression of the truth or concealment of facts with a view to obtaining a faculty, dispensation, etc. (Opposed to *obreption.*)

1600 W. WATSON *Decacordon* (1602) 343 [The bulls] were procured either merily by subreption, or..false information. **1644** BP. HALL *Modest Offer* (1660) 9 Lest there should be any subreption in this Sacred business, it is Ordered, that these Ordinations should be no other than solemn. **1706** tr. *Dupin's Eccl. Hist. 16th C.* II. III. xx. 361 Having a Power of enquiring into all Subreptions, Obreptions, or defects of Intention. **1728** CHAMBERS *Cycl.* s.v., Subreption differs from Obreption, in that Obreption is a false Expression of the Quality of a Thing or Fact, &c. And Subreption, a want of Expression. **1761** CHALLONER in E. Burton *Life* (1909) II. xxiv. 26 Purely in consideration of your request (tho' I apprehended he had obtained it by subreption) I consented to give him those faculties. **1876** tr. *Hergenröther's Cath. Ch. & Chr. State* II. 160 His rescript ..may have been obtained..by obreption..and by subreption. **1894** *Month* Mar. 391 If in a petition for a dispensation..it is the truth that is suppressed..there is said to be subreption.

b. *Sc. Law.* The act of obtaining gifts of escheat by suppression of the truth.

1752 MCDOUALL *Inst. Laws Scot.* II. III. III. i. 259 All rights of escheats..are granted by signatures or gifts from the crown, which may be stopt at their passing the seals, those being checks against subreption or obreption, *i.e.* their being obtained by concealing the truth, or expressing a falshood. **1838** W. BELL *Dict. Law Scot.*, *Subreption*, the obtaining gifts of escheat, &c. by concealing the truth.

c. A fallacious or deceptive representation; an inference derived from such a misrepresentation.

1865 J. H. STIRLING *Sir W. Hamilton* 47 Hamilton has long been aware of the inconveniences of sense. What are called its subreptions, its mistakes, blunders, errors [etc.]. **1877** WINCHELL *Reconcil. Sci. & Relig.* ix. 259 This form of expression is inexact, and opens the way to logical subreptions and other fallacious procedures. **1892** *Independent* (N.Y.) 21 July, This remark about 'climbing from a lower estate to a higher', is one of those neat little subreptions which sentimental recruits employ to deceive themselves. **1906** *Hibbert Jrnl.* July 793 There is a subreption also in the use of the term 'thought'; it truly refers to thought as a psychological process, but is taken as if it referred to thought as a metaphysical fact.

† **su'breption**[2]. = SURREPTION[2].

1632 SANDERSON *Serm.* (1674) II. 18 Miscarrying through his own negligence, incogitancy, or other subreption. **1634** —— *Two Serm.* ii. (1635) 64 Strength of temptation, sway of passion, or other distemper or subreption incident to humane frailty. **1640** —— *Serm.* (1674) II. 144 We.. break with him oftentimes through humane frailty and subreption. *a* **1658** FARINDON *Serm.* (1672) II. 603 To sin by ignorance or subreption, to feel those sudden motions and perturbations, those *ictus animi*, those sudden blows and surprisals of the mind.

subreptitious (sʌbrɛp'tɪʃəs), *a.* [f. L. *subrepticius, -itius* (f. *subrept-*, pa. ppl. stem of *subripĕre*): see prec. and -ITIOUS[1]. Cf. OF. *subreptice*, Sp., Pg. *subrepticio*.] **a.** *Law.* Obtained by subreption. **b.** Clandestine, SURREPTITIOUS.

1610 DONNE *Pseudo-martyr* 23 Whether that pretended Commandement from the Emperour were not subreptitious. *a* **1635** NAUNTON *Fragm. Reg.* (1641) 29 That he was a sub-reptitious Child of the Blood Royall. **1659** OSBORN *Misc.* To Rdr., The emendation of a subreptitious Copy. *a* **1660** *Contemp. Hist. Irel.* (Ir. Archæol. Soc.) I. 100 The lord Diggby alleadged against him that his comission was subreptitious. **1728** CHAMBERS *Cycl.* s.v., Papal Bulls and Signatures are Null and Subreptitious, when the true State of the Benefice.. and other necessary Matters, are not justly signified to the Pope. **1752** McDOUALL *Inst. Laws Scot.* II. 38 To prevent sub-reptitious grants. **1819** [H. BUSK] *Banquet* II. 533 The subreptitious theft.

Hence **subrep'titiously** *adv.*, by subreption.

1611 COTGR., *Subreptivement*, subrepticiously. **1890** T. E. BRIDGETT *Blunders & Forgeries* 18 That perhaps the rescript of which the Vicar of Mundeham boasted was obtained obreptitiously or subreptitiously.

subreptive (səb'rɛptɪv), *a.* [ad. late L. *subreptīvus*, f. *subrept-*, pa. ppl. stem of *subripĕre*. Cf. OF. *subreptif*.] Surreptitious; *spec.* in *Kantian Philos.* (see quot. 1877).

1611 COTGR., *Subreptif*, subreptiue. **1877** E. CAIRD *Philos. Kant* I. 151 'Many conceptions', he [Kant] says, 'arise in our minds from some obscure suggestion of experience, and are developed.. without any clear consciousness of the experience that suggests or the reason that developes them. These conceptions.. may be called *subreptive*'.

subresin ('sʌb,rɛzɪn). *Chem.* (Not in use.) [f. SUB- 3 + RESIN, after F. *sous-résine*.] That part of a resin which dissolves in boiling alcohol, and is deposited as the alcohol cools.

1838 T. THOMSON *Chem. Org. Bodies* 543.

† **su'bride**, *v. Obs. rare*[−0]. [ad. L. *subrīdēre* (var. *surr-*), f. *sub-* SUB- 22 + *rīdēre* to laugh.] To smile. So **su'brident** *a.*, smiling.

1623 COCKERAM I, *Subride*, to smile. **1897** *Athenæum* 6 Mar. 305/2 With some subrident joy.

† **subrige**, *v. Obs.* [ad. L. *subrigĕre* (*surr-*), by-form of *surgĕre* to SURGE.] *trans.* To raise up.

1623 COCKERAM II, To Lift up by little and little, *subrige*.

† **su'briguous**, *a. Obs.* [f. L. *subriguus*, f. *sub-* SUB- 2 + *riguus*, related to *rigāre* to water.] (See quot.)

1656 BLOUNT *Glossogr.*, *Subriguous*, moist, wet, and waterish underneath.

subrision (sə'brɪʒən). *rare.* [ad. L. **subrīsio, -ōnem*, n. of action f. *subrīdēre* to SUBRIDE.] The or an act of smiling.

1658 PHILLIPS, *Subrision*, a smiling. **1798** in *Spirit Publ. Jrnls.* (1799) II. 149 With an amiable subrision of countenance. **1860** J. H. STIRLING *Crit. Ess.*, *Macaulay* (1868) 133 In the act of enjoying a gentle subrision.

So **su'brisive**, **su'brisory** *adjs.*, smiling, playful.

1860 J. H. STIRLING *Crit. Ess.*, *Macaulay* (1868) 133 The following sentences.. if allowed to be subrisory. **1867** *Pall Mall Gaz.* 5 Jan. 1 This.. slight glimmer of subrisive irony. **1886** G. ALLEN *Darwin* i. 9 This half-hearted and somewhat subrisive denial.

† **'subrogate**, *pa. pple. Obs.* [ad. L. *subrogātus* (var. *surrogātus* SURROGATE), pa. pple. of *subrogāre* (see next).] Put in the place of another.

1432-50 tr. *Higden* (Rolls) III. 257 The x. men create were ammovede, and tribunes.. were subrogate. *Ibid.*, *Harl. Contin.* VIII. 440 Other laymen were subrogate in the places of theyme. **1526** in *Househ. Ord.* (1790) 146 Able, meete, honest, and sufficient persons, to be subrogate and put in their roomes and places.

subrogate ('sʌbrəgeɪt), *v.* [f. L. *subrogāt-*, pa. ppl. stem. of L. *subrogāre* (var. *surr-*), f. *sub-* SUB- 27 + *rogāre* to ask, offer for election.]

† **1.** *trans.* To elect or appoint in the place of another; to substitute in an office. *Obs.*

1538 ELYOT *Dict.*, *Subrogo*, to substitute or subrogate, to make a deputie in an office. **1538** STARKEY *England* (1878) 169 Our parlyament schold haue much to dow, yf, when so euer lakkyd any conseylar, hyt schold be callyd to subrogate other. *a* **1617** P. BAYNE *Diocesan's Tryall* (1621) 38 They were but subrogated to doe those supposed episcopall duties a while. *a* **1677** BARROW *Pope's Suprem.* (1680) 129 If he had ever been Bishop, he could not.. subrogate another, either to preside with him, or to succeed him. **1701** W. WOTTON *Hist. Rome* 391 The new secondary Consuls were.. subrogated in the place of him and of Adventus. **1728** CHAMBERS *Cycl.* s.v. *Subrogation*, The new Magistrates were also Subrogated in the Place of the old ones.

2. To substitute (a thing) for another; const. *in stead of*, *into the place of*, occas. *to*. Now *rare.*

a **1548** HALL *Chron.*, *Hen. VII* (1550) 2 b, Diuerse of the actes.. were adnulled.. & other more expedient for the vtilitie of the commen wealth were subrogated and concluded. **1624** DARCIE *Birth of Heresies* xii. 52 The Amict was subrogated in stead of the Iewish Ephod. **1651** JER. TAYLOR *Holy Dying* iv. §8 (1719) 168 The Christian Day is to be subrogated into the place of The Jews Day. **1657** TOMLINSON *Renou's Disp.* 627 In stead of Opobalsamum, which is most rare, subrogate Oyl of Cloves. *a* **1677** BARROW *Serm.* Wks. 1716 II. 288 The lives of beasts.. could [not] fitly be subrogated in stead of mens souls. **1892** A. E. LEE *Hist. Columbus* II. 435 Prompt to subrogate every party obligation to the higher one of maintaining.. the national compact.

3. *Law.* To put (a person) *in the place of*, or substitute (him) *for*, another in respect of a right or claim; to cause to succeed *to* the rights of another: see SUBROGATION 2.

1818 COLEBROOKE *Obligations* 176 When a bill of exchange is paid for the honour of any of the parties; the payer is thereby subrogated to the rights of the holder of the bill. **1866** MACLACHLAN *Arnould's Marine Insur.* III. vi. II. 869 The abandonment, although its effect is to subrogate the underwriters in the place of the assured, yet only does this to the extent of the insurance. **1882** *Act 45 & 46 Vict.* c. 61 §68 The payer for honour is subrogated for, and succeeds to both the rights and duties of, the holder as regards the party for whose honour he pays. **1883** *Law Rep. 11 Q.B. Div.* 383 The insurer is entitled to be subrogated into those rights of the assured which [etc.].

Hence **'subrogated** *ppl. a.*

1639 DU VERGER tr. *Camus' Admir. Events* 187 She conferres thereof with Isidorus her subrogated Gardian.

subrogation (sʌbrə'geɪʃən). [ad. L. *subrogātio, -ōnem*, n. of action f. *subrogāre* to SUBROGATE. Cf. F. *subrogation*, Sp. *subrogacion*, Pg. *subrogação* and see SURROGATION.]

† **1.** Substitution. *Obs.*

1418-20 LYDG. *Chron. Troy* IV. 334 [He] seide it was noon eleccioun, But a maner subrogacioun, Be-cause hym silfe in þe parlement At þe chesyng was nat þere present. **1611** COTGR., *Subrogation*, a subrogation, substitution, deputation. **1648** OWEN *Death of Death* III. x. 164 In the undergoing of death there was a subrogation of his person in the room and stead of ours. **1681** BAXTER *Answ. Dodwell* 119 To alter Gods Universal Laws by abrogation, subrogation, suspension, or dispensation.

2. *Law.* The substitution of one party for another as a creditor; the process by which a person who pays a debt for which another is liable succeeds to the rights of the creditor to whom he pays it; the right of such succession.

1710 J. HARRIS *Lex. Techn.* II, *Subrogation* in the Civil Law, is putting another Person into the Place and Right of him, that in any case, is the proper Creditor. **1818** COLEBROOKE *Obligations* 120 A surety, paying a debt without requiring subrogation or cession of the creditor's rights, has thereby extinguished the debt. **1866** MACLACHLAN *Arnould's Marine Insur.* III. vi. II. 875 The bottomry lender, who had become his creditor by the effect of this entire subrogation. **1910** *Encycl. Brit.* (ed. 11) XIV. 679/2 The payment of a partial loss gives the underwriter a similar subrogation but only in so far as the insured has been indemnified in accordance with law by such payment for the loss.

† **subroge**, *v. Obs. rare*[−1]. [ad. F. *subroger*, ad. L. *subrogāre* to SUBROGATE.] = SUBROGATE *v.* 1.

1600 HOLLAND *Livy* XLI. xviii. 1107 The other Consul.. subroged in the place of the deceassed.

sub rosa: see ‖SUB 12.

subro'tund, *a.* [ad. mod.L. *subrotundus*: see SUB- 21 c.] Somewhat or almost rotund, roundish.

1753 *Chambers' Cycl.* Suppl. s.v. *Leaf*, *Subrotund Leaf*, that approaching to the figure of the orbicular leaf, but departing from it, either in being too long, or too broad, or prominent. **1852** DANA *Crust.* I. 167 Two anterior teeth subrotund. **1861** BENTLEY *Man. Bot.* 167 When a leaf is perfectly round, it is orbicular.., a figure which is scarcely or ever found, but when it approaches to orbicular, as in *Pyrola rotundifolia*, it is subrotund or rounded.

So **subro'tundate**, **-ro'tundous** *adjs.*, in the same sense; **subro'tundo-**, combining form of SUBROTUND.

1775 J. JENKINSON *Linnæus' Brit. Pl.* 144 The dissepimentum is transverse, containing subrotundo-oblong seeds. **1775** ASH, *Subrotundous*, approaching to roundness. **1847** *Proc. Berw. Nat. Club* II. 240 Thorax quadrate, oblong, or sub-rotundate.

sub'round, *a.* [SUB- 21 d.] Subrotund.

c **1789** *Encycl. Brit.* (1797) III. 442/2 The figure of Similitudes is either.. Reniform, kidney-shaped, subround [etc.]. **1863** *Ann. Nat. Hist.* Ser. III. XII. 263 *Acanthocystis turfacea*... Globular, subround, of a green colour, loricated.

'subroutine. *Computers.* [SUB- 5 c.] A routine designed to be stored in a computer's memory so that longer, self-contained programs can make use of it any number of times without its being written into the program each time.

c **1946** GOLDSTINE & VON NEUMANN in J. von Neumann *Coll. Wks.* (1961) V. 25 Both.. machines are controlled by instructions punched into several tapes and they can be ordered to switch from one to the other as desired. They are usually referred to as 'master routine' and 'sub-routine' tapes. **1948**, **1951** [see ROUTINE *sb.* (*a.*) 1 d]. **1956** G. A. MONTGOMERIE *Digital Calculating Machines* xii. 248 We then transfer control to this subroutine whenever it is required, and arrange for its last action to be the transfer of control back to the main programme. **1959** M. H. WRUBEL *Primer of Programming for Digital Computers* iv. 100 Use the subroutine for sinh x and cosh x to construct a program for calculating $f = \sinh(x + y)/\cosh x \cosh y$. **1973** C. W. GEAR *Introd. Computer Sci.* iv. 156 Any built-in subroutines and functions required by the program are loaded with it. **1980** R. L. DUNCAN *Brimstone* xi. 272 'We.. can't handle the master program... So we'll attack the subroutines.'.. The computer responded.

sub-Sa'haran, *a.* [SUB- 1.] Situated or originating in regions of Africa south of the Sahara desert.

1955 *Ann. Amer. Acad. Political & Social Sci.* Mar. 13/1 The fact that sub-Saharan Africa has so large a number of distinguishable languages makes impressive documentation. **1969** *Times* 22 Oct. (Ghana Suppl.) p. i/2 Ghana was the pacesetter for modern Africa when it became the first sub-Saharan black country to move from colonial status to independence. **1978** J. UPDIKE *Coup* (1979) iii. 121 This French villa spun of sub-Saharan materials.

† **sub'salient**, *a. Obs. rare*[−1]. [ad. L. **subsaliens, -entem* (for *subsiliens*): see SUB- 26 and SALIENT.] Moving by leaps, spasmodic.

1716 M. DAVIES *Athen. Brit.* II. 145 Our rough and subsalient or subsulting Style of our uncouth Phraseological Latin.

subsalt ('sʌbsɒlt, -ɔː-), *sb. Chem.* (Not in use.) [f. SUB- 24 + SALT *sb.*[1] Cf. F. *sous-sel.*] A basic salt.

1806 *G. Adams' Nat. & Exp. Philos.* (Philad.) I. App. 547 Some [salts] are formed by an excess of their base.. and hence termed sub-salts. **1849** D. CAMPBELL *Inorg. Chem.* 5 Salts with less acid than base, are named basic salts, or subsalts, and are distinguished according to the proportion of base to acid; as bibasic subsalts, or tribasic subsalts. **1857** MILLER *Elem. Chem.*, *Org.* x. 595 Ferridcyanide of potassium.. gives.. with subsalts of mercury a brownish red.

† **subsalt**, *v. Obs. rare*[−0]. [ad. mod.L. *subsaltāre*, frequent. of *subsilīre* (see SUBSULT).] *intr.* To jump up.

1623 COCKERAM II, To Iumpe, *subsalt*.

subsaltatory (sʌb'sæltətərɪ), *a. rare*[−1]. [f. SUB- 22 + SALTATORY.] Characterized by a slight dancing motion.

1860 *Illustr. Lond. News* 11 Feb. 139/2 Undulatory, horizontal, vertical, and subsaltatory motions.

'subsample. [SUB- 9 (*b*).] A sample drawn from a sample.

1909 WEBSTER, Sub-sample, *n.* & *v.t.* **1913** *Econ. Geol.* VIII. 134 Each sample has thus been divided into 10 subsamples which may be used to estimate roughly the probable error. **1939** *Brit. Jrnl. Psychol.* XXX. 76 Burt chose his subsample of persons to be not only equal in average to one another, but equal to the average of all. **1959** H. BARNES *Oceanogr. & Marine Biol.* i. 32 (*caption*) Stempel (Suction) pipette. Used for taking an aliquot from a plankton sample. The sub-sample is contained between the curved part of the plunger and the barrel of the pipette. **1972** H. J. EYSENCK *Psychology is about People* ii. 92 The actual mean scores for P, E and N in the general population, and in various sub-samples graded by sex, age and class are known.

Hence **'subsample** *v. trans.*, **'subsampling** *vbl. sb.*

1909 Subsample *v.* [see the sb. above]. **1959** H. BARNES *Oceanogr. & Marine Biol.* i. 32 If larger nets are employed then it [*sc.* the catch] may have to be sub-sampled and only a fraction counted... There are various ways of such sub-sampling. **1969** R. LANGE *Chem. Oceanogr.* v. 79 It is.. useful to organize the numbers of the bottles for subsampling in such an order that [etc.]. **1971** *Nature* 4 June 290/2 They were subsampled for metal analysis and placed 0·8 m above ground in three locations down-wind of Swansea.

† **sub'sannate**, *v. Obs.* [f. late L. *subsannāt-*, pa. ppl. stem of *subsannāre*, f. *sub-* SUB- 22 + *sanna* mocking grimace.] *trans.* To deride, mock. Hence † **subsa'nnation**, mockery, derision; † **'subsannator**, a mocker; † **sub'sanne** *v.*, = SUBSANNATE.

1656 BLOUNT *Glossogr.*, **Subsannate*, to scorn or mock with bending the Brows, or snuffing up the nose. **1620** J. KING *Serm.* 24 Mar. 8 In scoffe and *subsannation of some Idoll-god. **1664** H. MORE *Myst. Iniq.* 231 Idolatry is as absolute a subsannation and vilification of God as malice could invent. **1517** H. WATSON *Ship of Fools* xli. Kiiij, Of *subsannatoures, calomnyatours and detractours. *a* **1619** FOTHERBY *Atheom.* Pref. (1622) Bj b, Who (like Sannioes) *subsanne all things, but onely their owne follies.

subscapular (sʌbˈskæpjʊlə(r)), *a.* [ad. mod.L. *subscapulāris*: see next. Cf. F. *sous-scapulaire.*]

a. *Anat.* Situated below, or on the under surface of, the scapula.

subscapular artery, the largest branch of the axillary artery; also, a branch of the suprascapular and the posterior scapular arteries. *subscapular fossa*, the concave ventral surface of the scapula. *subscapular muscle* = SUBSCAPULARIS.

1831 R. KNOX tr. *Cloquet's Anat.* 124 Behind the sub-scapular fossa. *Ibid.* 685 The Sub-Scapular Artery..is of considerable size. **1837** QUAIN *Elem. Anat.* (ed. 4) 350 In relation with the subscapular muscle and the axillary vessels. *Ibid.* 772 The sub-scapular nerves..are usually three in number. **1881** MIVART *Cat* 278 Another subscapular nerve is formed by the junction of very slender branches from the 6th and 7th cervical nerves. **1890** BILLINGS *Nat. Med. Dict.*, *Subscapular glands*, lymphatic glands along subscapular artery.

b. *Path.* Occurring under the scapula.

1897 *Allbutt's Syst. Med.* IV. 445 Subscapular hæmorrhage may result either from direct traumatism or indirect strain.

‖**subscapularis** (ˌsʌbskæpjʊˈlɛərɪs). *Anat.* [mod.L.: see SUB- 1 d and SCAPULAR.] In full *subscapularis muscle*: A muscle originating in the venter of the scapula and inserted in the lesser tuberosity of the humerus.

1704 J. HARRIS *Lex. Techn.* I, *Subscapularis*, or *Immersus*, is a Muscle of the Arm, so named from its Situation. **1733** tr. *Winslow's Anat.* (1756) I. 293 The Subscapularis hinders the Head of the Os Humeri from being luxated forward. **1831** R. KNOX tr. *Cloquet's Anat.* 124 Fasciculi of the sub-scapularis muscle. *Ibid.*, Anteriorly, where it is rounded, it furnishes points of insertion to the sub-scapularis. **1872** HUMPHRY *Myology* 36 The few fibres of the subscapularis constitute the only appearance of muscle upon the.. concave under surface of the coracoids and scapula. **1881** MIVART *Cat* 89 The subscapular fossa..affords attachment to the subscapularis muscle.

subscapulary (sʌbˈskæpjʊlərɪ), *a.* *Anat. rare.* [f. mod.L. *subscapulāris*: see SUB- 1 b and SCAPULARY.] = SUBSCAPULAR.

1705 *Phil. Trans.* XXV. 2010, I found the same Tumor comprehending the intercostals, Deltoides, Subclavian, and Subscapulary Muscles. **1855** DUNGLISON *Med. Lex.* 824 The subscapulary fossa. **1898** in *Syd. Soc. Lex.*

subscapulo- (sʌbˈskæpjʊləʊ), used as combining form of SUBSCAPULARIS, as in *subˌscapulo-capsuˈlaris*, *-hyˈoideus muscle* (see quots.).

1831 YOUATT *Horse* 119 The *subscapulo hyoideus*, from under the shoulder-blade, to the body of the *os hyoides*. **1873** *Quain's Elem. Anat.* (ed. 8) I. 203 A small additional muscle ..passing from the surface of the subscapularis over the capsular ligament,..the *subscapulo-capsularis* of Wenzel Gruber.

subscribable (səbˈskraɪbəb(ə)l), *a.* [f. SUBSCRIBE *v.* + -ABLE.] Capable of being subscribed.

1824 COLERIDGE *Aids Refl.* (1848) I. 310 A Church..is known to have worded certain passages for the purpose of rendering them subscribable by both A and Z.

subscribe (səbˈskraɪb), *v.* Also 6 -ybe. [ad. L. *subscrībĕre*, f. *sub-* SUB- 2 + *scrībĕre* to write. Cf. SUBSCRIVE.

From L. *subscrībĕre* are also It. *soscrivere*, Sp. *su(b)scribir*, Pg. *subscrever*; from L. type **subtusscrībĕre*, OF. *souzescrire*, *soubscrire*, mod.F. *souscrire*, Pr. *sotzescrivre*, It. *sottoscrivere*.]

1. *trans.* To write (one's name or mark) on, orig. at the bottom of, a document, esp. as a witness or consenting party; to sign (one's name) *to*. Now *rare.*

1425 *Rolls of Parlt.* IV. 297/2 In witnesse of whiche þing, ..my said Lord of Glouc' hath subscribed his name with his owne hand. H. Gloucestr'. *c* **1510** MORE *Picus* Wks. 3/2 Which questions..not a few famous doctours..had approued..and subscribed their names vndre them. **1511** in Ellis *Orig. Lett.* Ser. II. (1827) I. 182 That every gentilman answerer doo subscribe his name to the Articles. **1601** CHESTER *Love's Mart.* title-p., Seuerall moderne Writers, whose names are subscribed to their seuerall workes. **1643** *Decl. Commons Reb. Irel.* 49 The marke of Christopher Hassall is subscribed. **1676** *Office Clerk of Assize* B vij, Then must the Clerk of Assize direct the Cryer to call the Witnesses as they be subscribed to the Indictment. **1766** BLACKSTONE *Comm.* II. 377 They must all subscribe their names as witnesses. **1797** MRS. RADCLIFFE *Italian* xvii, Vivaldi was ordered to subscribe his name and quality to the depositions. **1816** SCOTT *Old Mort.* xxxvi, Subscribe your name in the record. [**1891** *Daily News* 9 Feb. 5/5 Could a signature be said to be sub-scribed when, strictly speaking, it was supra-scribed?]

b. To write, set down, or inscribe below or at the conclusion of something. Now *rare.*

1579 DIGGES *Stratiot.* I. iii. 3 Beginne your collection from the right hand to the lefte..& what Digit resulteth, subscribe. **1611** CORYAT *Crudities* 56 A goodly statue..with an honourable Elogium subscribed vnderneath the same. **1657** J. WATTS *Scribe, Pharisee*, etc. III. 101, I shall take my leave, and subscribe a friendly farewel to you. **1709–29** V. MANDEY *Syst. Math.*, *Arith.* 17 The Remainder being subscribed under the line drawn. **1777** *Ann. Reg.*, *Chron.* 239 His picture..with the words, 'The Atheist Parson', subscribed in capitals. **1860** ALB. SMITH *Med. Stud.* (1861) 72 In the space left for the degree of attention which the student has shown, it is better that he subscribes nothing at all than an indifferent report. **1866** MASSON tr. *Winer's Gram. N.T.* 59 In the earlier editions of the N.T. the Iota subscribed was too frequently introduced.

†**c.** To put (a person) down *for* so much. *Obs. rare.*

1593 SHAKS. *Rich. II*, I. iv. 50 Blanke-charters, Whereto when they shall know what men are rich, They shall subscribe them for large summes of Gold.

2. With compl.: **a.** *refl.* To put oneself down as so-and-so, at the foot of a letter or other document. Now *rare.*

1678 R. RUSSELL tr. *Geber* Transl. Pref. 4, I here conclude subscribing myself..your real Friend. **1711** STEELE *Spect.* No. 27 ⁋7, I am almost asham'd to Subscribe my self Yours, T. D. **1780** *Mirror* No. 81 A lady who subscribed herself S. M. *c* **1820** in *Corr. J. Sinclair* (1831) II. 400 Allow me to.. subscribe myself..your obedient, humble servant, J. R. Brancaleoni. **1827** SCOTT *Chron. Canongate* Introd., I beg leave to subscribe myself his obliged humble servant, Walter Scott. **1828** DARVILL *Race Horse* I. Ded., He who has the honour to subscribe himself,..Your most obliged And very humble Servant, R. Darvill.

†**b.** *trans.* To 'write (one) down' so-and-so. *Obs. rare.*

1599 SHAKS. *Much Ado* v. ii. 59 Claudio vndergoes my challenge, and either I must shortly heare from him, or I will subscribe him a coward.

3. To sign one's name to; to signify assent or adhesion to, by signing one's name; to attest by signing. (Cf. SUBSCRIPTION 5.)

Formerly often *to subscribe with one's (own) hand, to be subscribed with a name or names.*

1440 *Patent Roll 18 Hen. VI*, III, To thentente that these articles..should show of more record my true acquitail, I have subscribid them of my own hand. **1451** *Rolls of Parlt.* V. 218/1 That the seide Letters Patentes so subscribed with the names, be enrolled. *c* **1520** SKELTON *Magnyf.* 1685 With his hande I made hym to suscrybe A byll of recorde for an annuall rent. **1579** W. WILKINSON *Confut. Fam. Love* Brief Descr. iv, Their doctrine subscribed with his owne hand is this. **1651** N. BACON *Disc. Gov. Eng.* II. i. (1739) 6 He causeth the Judges to subscribe this Order, and so it becomes Law in repute. **1662** *Act 14 Chas. II*, c. 4 §6 Every ..person in Holy Orders..shall..subscribe the Declaration ..following scilicet. **1781** GIBBON *Decl. & F.* xix. (1787) II. 128 The emperor was persuaded to subscribe the condemnation of..Gallus. **1818** CRUISE *Digest* (ed. 2) VI. 69 He subscribed the will as a witness in the same room. **1843** GLADSTONE *Glean.* (1879) V. 38 On behalf of truth, we subscribe the protest against these preposterous impositions. **1849** MACAULAY *Hist. Eng.* ii. I. 171 Not content with requiring him to conform to their worship, and to subscribe their Covenant. **1888** *Q. Rev.* CLXVII. 209 At Oxford the matriculator subscribed the Thirty-nine Articles.

fig. **1847** DE QUINCEY *Sp. Mil. Nun* viii. Wks. 1853 III. 17 Chance is but the pseudonyme of God for those particular cases which he does not choose to subscribe openly with his own sign manual.

b. *pass.* (*a*) With a name or description: To be signed so-and-so. Now *rare.*

1640 in Rushw. *Hist. Coll.* (1692) III. I. 114 Fourteen Letters subscribed, W. Cant. **1725** *Lond. Gaz.* No. 6349/1 A Letter subscribed W. Baker. **1780** *Mirror* No. 84 A letter subscribed Censor.

†(*b*) *pass.* To be furnished with an inscription beneath. *Obs. rare.*

1688 HOLME *Armoury* III. ii. 33/2 An Escochion.. Subscribed, *Moneta Nova Ordin. Frisiæ.*

†**4.** To give one's assent or adhesion to; to countenance, support, favour, sanction, concur in.

1560 DAUS tr. *Sleidane's Comm.* 12 Manye do subscribe, and myghtye nations maynteine the cause. **1574** tr. *Marlorat's Apoc.* 15 They agree to the opinion of other men, and subscribe their sayings. **1603** SHAKS. *Meas. for M.* II. iv. 89 Admit no other way to saue his life (As I subscribe not that, nor any other, But in the losse of question). **1606** —— *Tr. & Cr.* II. iii. 156 *Aia.*.. Doe you not thinke, he thinkes himselfe a better man then I am? *Ag.* No question. *Aiax.* Will you subscribe his thought, and say he is? **1781** GIBBON *Decl. & F.* xxxvi. (1787) III. 494 Orestes..chose rather to encounter the rage of an armed multitude, than to subscribe the ruin of an innocent people.

†**5.** To sign away, yield up. *Obs. rare.*

1605 SHAKS. *Lear* I. ii. 24 (Qo.) The King gone to night, subscribd [*1st Fo.* Prescrib'd] his power, confined to exhibition, all this donne.

6. *intr.* To write one's signature; *esp.* to put one's signature *to* in token of assent, approval, or testimony; to sign one's name as a witness, etc. Also in *indirect pass.*

1535 COVERDALE *Isa.* xliv. 5 The thirde shal subscrybe with his honde vnto yͤ Lorde. **1560** DAUS tr. *Sleidane's Comm.* 140 This was the effect therof whereunto subscribed sixe and twenty Cardinalles. **1571** *Act 13 Eliz.* c. 12 §4 None ..shalbe admitted to thorder of Deacon or Ministerie, unles he shall fyrst subscribe to the saide Artycles. **159.** *Sir T. More* IV. ii. 74 [1235] His maiestie hath sent by me these articles..to be subscribed to. **1606** SHAKS. *Ant. & Cl.* IV. v. 14 Write to him, (I will subscribe) gentle adieu's, and greetings. **1611** *Bible* Transl. Pref. ⁋11 They could not with good conscience subscribe to the Communion booke. **1691** WOOD *Ath. Oxon.* I. 104 In 1546 he proceeded in Divinity, having about that time subscribed to the 34 Articles. *a* **1722** FOUNTAINHALL *Decis.* (1759) I. 12 Unless there be two Notaries, and..he gave them command to subscribe for him. **1724** SWIFT *Drapier's Lett.* Wks. 1755 V. II. 101 Many of those who subscribed against me. **1909** *Engl. Hist. Rev.* Apr. 242 Raignolds conformed, but in a vigorous..letter to Bancroft refused to subscribe.

†**b.** With compl. *Obs. rare.*

1641 MILTON *Ch. Govt.* II. Fj, Perceaving..that he who would take Orders must subscribe slave, and take an oath withall.

7. To give one's assent *to* a statement, opinion, proposal, scheme, or the like; to express one's agreement, concurrence, or acquiescence.

1549 CHALONER *Erasm. Praise Folly* Cj, If ye all doo subscribe to this opinion. **1588** SHAKS. *Tit. A.* IV. ii. 130 Aduise thee Aaron, what is to be done, And we will all subscribe to thy aduise. **1614** RALEIGH *Hist. World* II. 362 The Thracians againe subscribe to none of these reports. **1643** SIR T. BROWNE *Relig. Med.* II. §3. 143 The Foundations of Religion are already established, and the principles of Salvation subscribed unto by all. **1675** BAXTER *Cath. Theol.* II. I. 121 What Jesuite or Arminian will not subscribe to this? Who doubteth of it? **1699** BENTLEY *Phal.* 67 Clement's Computation is subscribed to..by Cyril. **1710** POPE *Let.* 20 July, I do not expect you shou'd subscribe to my private notions. **1765** *Museum Rust.* IV. 121 If they do not implicitly subscribe to his condemnation of other botanists. **1771** SMOLLETT *Humphry Cl.* (1815) 250 She enters into her scheme of economy..and..subscribes implicitly to her system of devotion. **1823** SCOTT *Quentin D.* Introd., I am contented to subscribe to the opinion of the best qualified judge of our time. **1877** GLADSTONE *Glean.* (1879) III. 207 That comparison..is not stated..in a manner to which I can subscribe. **1878** H. M. STANLEY *Dark Cont.* II. xi. 315 They readily subscribed to all the requirements of friendship.

b. To agree or be a party *to* a course of action or condition of things; to give approval, sanction, or countenance *to*; also *occas.* to consent or engage *to*; to agree *that*... Now *rare* or *Obs.*

1566 in Ellis *Orig. Lett.* Ser. I. II. 217 The Quene..wyll that all men that ar frends to anye of those that were previe to David deathe shall subscribe to pursue them... Some have subscribed, other have refused. *a* **1570** in Feuillerat *Revels Q. Eliz.* (1908) 407 He having ben required..to consent and subscribe to thaccomptes and reckoninges of the Revelles. **1596** LODGE *Wits Miserie* 68 The nobility amongst the Iewes..would subscribe to no election or superioritie. **1597** BEARD *Theatre God's Judgem.* (1612) 401 A certaine Cardinall committed daily Adulterie with a mans wife, that winked and as it were subscribed vnto it. *a* **1604** HANMER *Chron. Irel.* (1633) 32 They..yeelded to subscribe, that..they would not receive any Scot into their dominions. **1667** MILTON *P.L.* XI. 182 So spake, so wish'd much humbl'd Eve, but Fate Subscrib'd not. **1783** W. GORDON tr. *Livy's Rom. Hist.* II. xlv. (1809) 172 That the enemy should pass unpunished they could by no means subscribe to. **1825** HAZLITT *Spirit of Age* 173 The reverend divine might submit to the obligation, but he has no occasion to subscribe to the jest. **1844** LINGARD *Anglo-Saxon Ch.* I. iii. 141 Shall ..I..tamely subscribe to my own degradation?

8. To give one's adhesion or allegiance, make one's submission *to* another; *gen.* to submit, yield, give in. Now *rare* or *Obs.*

1590 GREENE *Never too late* (1600) 87 That he whom loue and errour did betray, Subscribes to thee [*i.e.* Reason]. **1591** *Troub. Raigne K. John* (1611) 58 Subscribe not Hubert, giue not Gods part away. *c* **1600** SHAKS. *Sonn.* cvii, Death to me subscribes; Since spight of him Ile liue in this poore rime. **1606** —— *Tr. & Cr.* IV. v. 105 Hector in his blaze of wrath subscribes To tender obiects. **1631** QUARLES *Samson* §7 Wks. (Grosart) II. 144/2 Passion replies, That feare and filiall duty Must serve affection, and subscribe to beauty. *a* **1652** BROME *City Wit* IV. i, As for Corantoes,..I speake it not swellingly, but I subscribe to no man. *c* **1665** MRS. HUTCHINSON *Mem. Col. Hutchinson* (1846) 69, I cannot subscribe to those who entitle that king to the honour of the reformation. **1851** HUSSEY *Papal Power* ii. 76 Anatolius required the Illyrian Bishops to subscribe to him, that is, profess canonical obedience.

†**b.** To submit or subject oneself *to* law or rule; to conform or defer *to* a person's will, etc. *Obs.*

1596 SHAKS. *Tam. Shr.* I. i. 81 Sir, to your pleasure humbly I subscribe. **1621** T. WILLIAMSON tr. *Goulart's Wise Vieillard* 119 To subscribe and submit himselfe to all his Statutes and Lawes. **1642** J. M[ARSH] *Argt. conc. Militia* 10 The will of the King ought to subscribe to the Law. **1760–72** H. BROOKE *Fool of Qual.* (1809) II. 134, I would make a.. narration to my child of all that had passed, but..would wholly subscribe to her pleasure.

†**c.** To admit one's inferiority or error, confess oneself in the wrong. *Obs. rare.*

1591 SHAKS. *1 Hen. VI*, II. iv. 44 If I haue fewest, I subscribe in silence. **1593** —— *2 Hen. VI*, III. i. 38 Which feare, if better Reasons can supplant, I will subscribe, and say I wrong'd the Duke.

9. Const. *to*: **a.** To admit or concede the force, validity, or truth of. Now *rare* or *Obs.*

1591 SHAKS. *Two Gent.* v. iv. 145, I..Plead a new state in thy vn-riual'd merit, To which I thus subscribe. **1753** RICHARDSON *Grandison* I. xx, One to whose superior merit, and to whose good fortune, I can subscribe. **1771** GOLDSM. *Hist. Eng.* I. Pref. p. vi, I must warmly subscribe to the learning..of Mr. Hume's history. **1838** LYTTON *Alice* I. xii, They have confided to me all the reasons of your departure and I cannot but subscribe to their justice.

†**b.** To make acknowledgement or admission of.

1601 SHAKS. *All's Well* v. iii. 96 When I had subscrib'd To mine owne fortune, and inform'd her fully.

†**10.** To make an undertaking *for*, vouch or answer *for* a person. *Obs.*

1599 SHAKS. *Much Ado* I. i. 41 He..challeng'd Cupid at the Flight: and my Vnckles foole reading the Challenge, subscrib'd for Cupid. **1601** —— *All's Well* III. vi. 89, I know th'art valiant, And to the possibility of thy souldiership, Will subscribe for thee.

11. *trans.* To promise over one's signature to pay (a sum of money) *for* shares in an undertaking, or *to* or *towards* a particular object; to undertake to contribute (money) in support of any object. Also, to take up (shares); = *subscribe for* (see 12).

1640 *Act 16 Chas. I*, c. 37 §1 Diverse great summes of money have beene subscribed some part whereof is already paid in. *a* **1700** EVELYN *Diary* 27 Nov. 1657, The stock resolv'd on was 800,000*l.* I tooke the oath at the E. India House, subscribing 500*l.* *Ibid.* 7 July 1664, I subscribed to Sir Arthur Slingsby's lottery a desperate debt owing me long since. **1762** T. MORTIMER *Ev. Man own Broker* (ed. 5) 171 The sum each subscriber has subscribed. **1792** ALMON *Anecd. W. Pitt* I. vii. 165 Pitt never subscribed one shilling into the funds. **1855** *Ann. Reg., Chron.* 117/2 Nearly 40,000,000*l.* was subscribed [for the new French loan]. **1863** FAWCETT *Pol. Econ.* I. iv. 42 Indian railways have been constructed by loans subscribed almost entirely in England. **1871** *Ann. Reg., Chron.* 113 The large sum of 10,000*l.* was subscribed at once. **1891** STUTFIELD *Rules Stock Exch.* 121 Vendors' or contractors' shares issued as paid up are not 'subscribed'. **1912** *World* 7 May 698/2 Over $300,000 was subscribed in Canada for ordinary shares.

b. *transf.* To contribute.

1902 *Daily Chron.* 28 June 9/2 The English team were engaged in an up-hill task against the Colonials, who.. subscribed the heavy score of 402.

12. *absol.* or *intr.* To undertake to contribute money *to* a fund, *to* a society, party, etc.

1642 in Rushw. *Hist. Coll.* (1692) III. I. 564 The Names of such Members of the Commons House of Parliament that Subscribed..for the speedy Reducing of the Rebels. **1701** EVELYN *Diary* 14 July, I subscrib'd towards rebuilding Oakwood Chapel. **1780** T. MORTIMER *Elem. Comm.* 386 To give them a fresh contributive faculty to subscribe to new loans. **1781** COWPER *Charity* 467 Extravagance and av'rice shall subscribe. **1792** in *Athenæum* (1887) 5 Nov. 604/3 Will you have the *Journal de Jacobins*? I'll subscribe on your answer. **1837** DICKENS *Pickw.* vii, I subscribe to the club here. **1848** THACKERAY *Van. Fair* xlv, He..subscribed handsomely to the county charities. **1856** HURLSTONE & GORDON *Exch. Rep.* XI. 715 Certain persons had subscribed to a steeple chase, to be run in the neighbourhood of Henley. **1876** 'L. CARROLL' *Hunting the Snark* v. xxii, In charity-meetings it stands at the door, And collects—though it does not subscribe.

b. *to subscribe for*: to put one's name down as a purchaser of shares, a periodical, newspaper, or book, etc.

1711 SWIFT *Jrnl. to Stella* 21 Sept., The maids of honour ..are teazing others to subscribe for the book. **1749** J. WOOD *Descr. Bath* (ed. 2) II. 445, I am well satisfied as many fifty Pound Tickets..would have been Subscribed for. **1829** LIPSCOMB *Buckingham* Prospectus, Subscribers are.. requested to transmit their names..through Messrs. Longman and Co..., by whom the respective Parts will be issued in the order subscribed for. **1890** SPRIGGE *Meth. Publ.* 19 When the libraries have subscribed for their copies. **1891** STUTFIELD *Rules Stock Exch.* 106 The loan may be subscribed for in amounts of £100.

13. *Book trade.* †**a.** *trans.* To issue (a book) to subscribers. *Obs.*

1701 *Advt.* in *De Royaumont's Hist. O. & N. Test.*, The Book will be Subscribed at one Pound in Quires. One Half down the other for Delivery, a 7th book gratis.

b. Of a bookseller: To agree beforehand to take (a certain number of copies of a book); also *subscribe for*. Also occas. *intr.* Of a book: To be taken by the trade.

1867 SPEDDING *Publ. & Authors* 37, I suppose that copies which are 'subscribed for' at the trade-sales are really sold to the subscribers at that rate of discount. **1873** CURWEN *Hist. Booksellers* 428 Of Mr. Disraeli's 'Lothair' 1500 copies were at first subscribed. **1887** *Athenæum* 25 June 833/1 The London trade have subscribed for 10,000 copies, which is said to be the largest number ever subscribed for a six-shilling novel. **1888** 'J. S. WINTER' *Conf. Publisher* xii. 87 Dayley's book 'Memory' came out. On the whole, it subscribed very well.

c. Of a publisher: To offer (a book) to the trade.

1910 *Encycl. Brit.* (ed. 11) IV. 234/2 At one of these establishments over 1,000,000 books are kept in stock. It is here that the publisher calls first on showing or 'subscribing' a new book, a critical process, for by the number thus subscribed the fate of a book is sometimes determined. **1913** *Early Life Mk. Rutherford* 83 My occupation now [185.] was to write Chapman's letters,..and, most disagreeable, to 'subscribe' his publications, that is to say, to call on booksellers and ask how many copies they would take.

¶A sense 'to publish by subscription' is given by some Dicts., but is not recognized by the trade.

subscribed (səb'skraɪbd), *ppl. a.* [f. prec. + -ED[1].] Contributed to a fund.

1841 THACKERAY *Gt. Hoggarty Diam.* vi, The subscribed and *bona fide* capital is five millions sterling.

subscriber (səb'skraɪbə(r)). [f. SUBSCRIBE *v.* + -ER[1].]

1. a. One who subscribes, or affixes his signature *to*, a letter or document, articles of religion, etc.

For spec. use in the history of Irish Presbyterianism, cf. NON-SUBSCRIBER 1 (*b*).

1599, **1650** [see NON-SUBSCRIBER 1]. **1651** J. DREW (*title*) The Northern Subscribers plea vindicated from the exceptions laid against it by the non-subscribing Ministers of Lancashire and Cheshire. *c* **1688** in Gutch *Coll. Cur.* I. 338 The Petition being finished, all the subscribers..went over to Whitehall to deliver it to the King. *a* **1700** EVELYN *Diary* 16 June 1687, It was reported the subscribers [to an Address] were above 1000. **1717** WODROW *Corr.* (1843) II. 335 The subscribers of that choice and invitation of a minister. **1789** MADISON in Sparks *Corr. Amer. Rev.* (1853) IV. 294 The letter was written by the first subscriber of it. **1886** *Law Rep. 31 Chanc. Div.* 223 A minority of the subscribers of the memorandum of association. **1912** SELBIE *Nonconf.* ix. 163 When..an attempt was made to obtain the assent of those present to a declaration of belief in the Doctrines of the Trinity and of the Divinity of our Lord, the company at once divided into subscribers and non-subscribers.

b. *transf.* One who assents.

1851 THACKERAY *Engl. Hum.* v. (1853) 222 It was as undoubting subscribers to this moral law, that Fielding wrote and Hogarth painted.

2. a. One who subscribes *to* a specified object or institution, the funds of a company, etc., *for* shares, a book, etc.

1697 DRYDEN *Æneid* Ded. e j b, Some of my Subscribers grew so clamorous, that I cou'd no longer deferr the Publication. **1721** SWIFT *South Sea* Wks. 1755 III. II. 134 Each poor subscriber to the sea sinks down at once. **1727** — *What passed in Lond.* Ibid. I. 179 Mr. Whiston held his lecture..to an audience of fourteen worthy citizens, his subscribers and constant hearers. **1776** ADAM SMITH *W.N.* v. i. III. art. i, Provided the subscribers were erected into a new East India company. **1780** T. MORTIMER *Elem. Comm.* 362 The original proprietors, or subscribers to the fund which formed the capital of the Bank of England. **1806** *Med. Jrnl.* XV. 359 By giving to a one guinea subscriber a privilege equal to that which is enjoyed by a three guinea subscriber. **1854** *Poultry Chron.* II. Pref., Our principal duty is to thank all our supporters, whether Subscribers, Advertisers, or Contributors. **1856** 'STONEHENGE' *Brit. Rural Sports* I. III. viii. 203 The Draw should be conducted on the following plan: first, the money for each stake should be paid to the secretary by the subscribers. **1873** CURWEN *Hist. Booksellers* 425 In 1842, Mr. Mudie commenced his system of lending out one exchangeable volume to subscribers at the rate of a guinea per annum. **1898** FRASER-MACKINTOSH *Minor Septs Clan Chattan* Pref. p. vi, My best acknowledgments are due..to Mr. John Mackay, the publisher, for the really handsome manner in which the book has been issued to subscribers.

b. *transf.* A contributor. *nonce-use.*

1773 GOLDSM. *Stoops to Conq.* IV, I was in for a list of blunders, and could not help making you a subscriber.

c. '*N.Y. Stock Exch.* Formerly, a speculator who, being a nonmember, was allowed on the floor of the Exchange outside of a certain rail' (Webster 1911).

d. One who pays a regular sum for the hire of a telephone line.

1878 (*title*) List of subscribers (Bell Telephone Co. of N.Y.). **1922** [see *dialling tone* s.v. DIALLING *vbl. sb.* 4]. **1934** HALDANE & HUXLEY *Animal Biol.* xii. 272 The telephone bells of all the subscribers would start ringing. **1978** *Broadcast* 6 Mar. 10/2 Viewdata is transmitted along normal telephone lines... Identifying the caller, the computer responds with a personalized greeting to the subscriber.

3. Special Comb.: **subscriber trunk dialling**, a telephone service by which subscribers can make trunk calls without the assistance of an operator, by dialling the exchange code and the number required; abbrev. *STD* (see S 4a).

[**1950** *Post Office Electr. Engineers' Jrnl.* XLIII. 170/2 If, at some future date, subscriber-to-subscriber trunk dialling is introduced, a national numbering scheme and a translator trunk dialling system may be introduced.] **1952** *Prof. Papers Inst. P.O. Electr. Engineers* No. 203. 1 Subscriber Trunk Dialling in the United Kingdom... The possibility of extending the range over which subscribers can dial their own calls has received increasing attention by many telephone administrations. **1979** M. UNDERWOOD *Victim of Circumstance* III. iii. 183 With subscriber trunk dialling and unitemised telephone accounts, it's very difficult to trace calls.

Hence **sub'scribership**.

1828 *Lancet* 26 July 539/2, I am now perfectly unconnected with its proprietorship, editorship, contributorship, subscribership, and readership!

subscribing (səb'skraɪbɪŋ), *vbl. sb.* [f. SUBSCRIBE *v.* + -ING[1].] The action of the verb SUBSCRIBE, subscription.

1602 *Archpriest Controv.* (Camden) II. 7 [Not] any subscribing of names to any thing we should make answere to. **1655** *Nicholas Papers* (Camden) II. 191 Since the subscribeing of this, I am informed y[t] it is very doubtfull whether Deuchry bee in Aberfoile or no. **1710** [BEDFORD] *Vind. Ch. Eng.* 121 Some Alterations were to be made to the Articles between their first Subscribing and their last Voting. **1751** WARBURTON *Note* Pope's Wks. IV. 166 The subscribing for a Book, which does honour to one's Age and Country. **1762** T. MORTIMER *Ev. Man own Broker* (ed. 5) 172 The first deposit..is made on or about the time of subscribing. **1845** STOCQUELER *Handbk. Brit. India* (1854) 285 The subscribing to a few regulations. **1855** *Poultry Chron.* 15 Aug. 555 The subscriptions shall be considered due at the time of subscribing. **1856** ELLIS & BLACKBURN *Cases Queen's Bench* IV. 454 But neither does the statute appoint where the will shall be subscribed by the attesting witnesses; and therefore a subscribing in any part may be sufficient.

attrib. **1712** ADDISON *Spect.* No. 271 ⁋2 The subscribing Part at the End of them [*sc.* Letters]. **1912** SHAYLOR *Fascin. Bks.* 220 It is to the subscribing department that publishers look for a tone and impetus to be given to a new book.

subscribing (səb'skraɪbɪŋ), *ppl. a.* [f. SUBSCRIBE *v.* + -ING[2].] That subscribes, attests or assents to a document, etc.

[**1651** implied in *non-subscribing*: see SUBSCRIBER 1.] **1808** W. WILSON *Hist. Diss. Ch.* I. 165 The unceremonious manner in which he treats Mr. Reynolds, and his subscribing brethren. **1855** in Ellis & Blackburn *Cases Queen's Bench* (1856) IV. 452 The execution of the will by the testator and by the other two subscribing witnesses. **1867** SPEDDING *Publ. & Authors* 40 For 5 copies sold to a subscribing bookseller, he receives 85*s.* **1872** YEATS *Growth Comm.* 211 Each of the subscribing cities [*viz.* to the Dutch East India Co.] was represented by a college or chamber.

1903 FAIRBAIRN in *Contemp. Rev.* Jan. 6 A subscribing..is not the only conservative church.

subscript ('sʌbskrɪpt), *sb.* and *a.* [ad. L. *subscript-us, -a, -um*, pa. pple. of *subscrībere* to write underneath, SUBSCRIBE.] **A.** *sb.*

1. That which is written underneath; a writing at the bottom or end of a document, etc.; a signature.

a **1704** T. BROWN *Ep. to C. Dives* Wks. 1711 IV. 179 By the Subscript, you'll quickly guess The Occasion of this odd Address. **1713** BENTLEY *Freethinking* §37 But be they Postscripts or Subscripts; your Translators neither made them, nor recommended them for Scripture. **1815** *Monthly Mag.* XXXIX. 307/2 The subscript, concerning which your correspondent..enquires. **1892** *Blackw. Mag.* Sept. 393 Monsieur Daudet hints that his captivating headline had not a little to do with the sale of its subscript.

2. a. A subscript letter or symbol.

1901 *Mod. Lang. Notes* June 323/1 Any of the accented letters, superscripts, subscripts and symbols found in the type-founder's catalogs.

b. *Computers.* A symbol (notionally written as a subscript but in practice usually not) used in a program, alone or with others, to specify one of the elements of an array.

1957 *Proc. Western Joint Computer Conf.* Feb. 190/1 The programmer may also employ subscripted variables having three independent subscripts. **1966** R. V. JAMISON *FORTRAN Programming* vi. 83 We cannot write these subscripts in the usual lowercase manner with an actual lowering of the subscript. Instead we write, for example, X(4), X(7) for x_4, x_7. **1973** C. W. GEAR *Introd. Computer Sci.* iii. 145 A three-dimensional array..is an array of two-dimensional arrays. It is accessed by specifying three subscripts. Thus, if the array is B, we can refer to B[I, J, K]. **1982** R. S. FORSYTH *Pascal at Work & Play* xii. 172 Execution errors occur when a program attempts something illogical or impossible... Typical examples are division by zero and trying to use a subscript outside the bounds set for the array. **1983** [see SUBSCRIPTED *a.*].

B. *adj.* Written underneath; chiefly in *iota subscript* (see IOTA 1), the small ι written underneath in ᾳ, ῃ, ῳ.

1871 WORDSWORTH *Gk. Primer* 6 The Dative Singular always ends in ι, which, however, is generally subscript. **1877** RAYMOND *Statist. Mines & Mining* 437 The subscript ω denoting that A is taken with reference to water. **1881** WESTCOTT & HORT *Grk. N.T.* Introd. §410 Analogy is distinctly in favour of allowing the Iota subscript. **1900** *N. & Q.* Ser. IX. VI. 485/2 The subscript cedilla is really a little *z*.

So **'subscripting** *vbl. sb.*, the action of providing with a subscript or subscripts; the use of subscripts.

1959 *Communications Assoc. Computing Machinery* Feb. 4/1 Unfortunately, many algebraic languages now in use.. do not allow subscripting of subscripts. **1972** BERGMANN & BRUCKNER *Introd. Computers & Computer Sci.* x. 342 In FORTRAN the subscripting is different; the subscripts run from 1 througn *n*. **1981** A. R. MILLER *BASIC Programs* iii. 39 A matrix is referenced by its name, which can be a single alphabetic character, or a string of characters. The indices are given as subscripts except in computer programs, where subscripting is not possible.

subscripted ('sʌb,skrɪptɪd), *a.* [f. SUBSCRIPT *sb.* + -ED[2].] Having a subscript, provided *with* a subscript; *spec.* in *Computing*, specified out of an array by means of a subscript or subscripts.

1957 [see SUBSCRIPT *sb.* 2b]. **1972** W. LABOV *Language in Inner City* iv. 153 The subscripted parentheses indicate optional elements that co-occur. **1983** *Daily Tel.* 19 Sept. 12/6 Subscripted variables take the form A(x), x being the value (or address) of the subscript... Subscripted string variables, needed to store strings of text, include a dollar sign, thus: 40 LET A$(6) = 'BUG'.

subscription (səb'skrɪpʃən). [ad. L. *subscriptio, -ōnem*, n. of action f. *subscript-*, *subscrībere* to SUBSCRIBE. Cf. OF. *sub-*, *soubscripcion*, mod.F. *souscription*, (Pr. *sotzescriptio*), It. *soscrizione*, Sp. *subscripcion*, Pg. *subscripção*.]

1. a. A piece of writing at the end of a document, *e.g.* the concluding clause or formula of a letter with the writer's signature, the colophon of a book, etc., the note appended to the epistles in the New Testament, etc.

c **1450** LYDG. *Secrees* 659 Off his pistil a breef Subcrypcyoun, Set lowly vndir. **1542–3** *Act 34 & 35 Hen. VIII*, c. 1 §6 Wherunto the same printers shalbe bounde to put the superscripcion and subscripcion in this forme, That is to saie: by the King and his Clergye, with addicion in the ende of the printers name..and yere of the printing of the same. **1586** A. DAY *Engl. Secretorie* I. (1625) 12 The manner of Salutation, the order of taking leave or farewell, the Subscription, and the outward direction. **1599** B. JONSON *Ev. Man out of Hum.* III. vii, How's this? Yours, if his owne? ..Belike this is some new kinde of subscription the gallants use. **1642** JER. TAYLOR *Episc.* (1647) 80 The subscription to the first Epistle to Timothy. **1727** W. MATHER *Yng. Man's Comp.* 104 Subscriptions for Letters. To the King; or To his most Excellent Majesty;..To the Queen, or, To the Queen's most Excellent Majesty. **1748** RICHARDSON *Clarissa* VII. 197 She dictated the farewel part, without hesitation; and when she came to the blessing and subscription, she took the pen, and..wrote the conclusion. **1790** PALEY *Horæ Paul.* xv. 378 The subscription of the first epistle to the Corinthians states that it was written from Philippi. **1816** SINGER *Hist. Cards* 170 Fust and Schoeffer, in the subscriptions to the books printed by them, lay no claim to the invention..of the art. **1882–3** *Schaff's Encycl. Relig. Knowl.* I. 102/1 The subscription [to the additions to *Esther*] ..refer to the whole book.

†**b.** Something written or inscribed underneath, *e.g.* a number written under another, an inscription or title underneath. *Obs.*

1631 WEEVER *Anc. Funeral Mon.* 772 These portraitures ..with the subscription following. *a* **1682** SIR T. BROWNE *Tracts* (1683) 206 A large Picture..with this Subscription. **1709–29** V. MANDEY *Syst. Math., Arith.* 68 Multiply the whole Subscription by the Quotient. **1814** *Gentl. Mag.* July 51 The..representation of a goat giving suck to the whelp of a wolf, with a subscription, which has been thus rendered.

2. A signature, signed name.

In Sc. *sign* (or *signet) and subscription manual* was formerly freq.

1483 *Sc. Acts* (1875) XII. 32/1 Lettrez of securite vndir þar Selis & subscripcions manualis. **1547** J. HARRISON *Exhort. Scottes* 226 The seales & subscriptions be so many, so auncient, and so faire, as cannot lightelie be counterfaicte. **1577** HANMER *Anc. Eccl. Hist.* VI. xlii. 118 Other epistles of Cyprian in the Romaine tongue with the subscription of diuerse other byshops. **1640** *Sc. Acts Chas. I* (1870) V. 268 Wch wordis he shall subscrybe with his signe and subscriptione manuell. **1690** in *Nairne Peerage Evid.* (1874) 27 Before thir witnesses to the subscriptions of the saids Marqueis and Marchiones of Atholl. *a* **1700** EVELYN *Diary* 29 Oct. 1662, The syngraphs and original subscriptions of divers Eastern Patriarchs. **1807** CRABBE *Par. Reg.* II. 284 All the blurr'd subscriptions in my book. **1831** SCOTT *Ct. Rob.* vii, Our sacred subscription is duly marked with the fitting tinge of green and purple. **1888** *Law Times Rep.* (N.S.) LIX. 3/2 A probative deed, which they attested by their subscriptions.

3. A signed declaration or statement; *Rom. Antiq.*, a rescript signed by the emperor. *Obs.* exc. *Hist.*

1599 Q. ELIZ. in Moryson *Itin.* (1617) II. 40 Though you think the allowance of that Counsell, whose subscriptions are your Ecchoes, should..satisfie us. **1609** HOLLAND *Amm. Marcell.* XV. vi. 42 This Athanasius..was by commandement from the Emperour warned by his subscription to depose from his sacerdotall See. **1647** CLARENDON *Hist. Reb.* II. §115 A Letter from the King, and a subscription from the Lords Commissioners. **1661** MARVELL *Corr.* Wks. (Grosart) II. 71 The way of maintenance layd out in your Act is directly opposed by a Subscription sent up to Colonell Gilby and my selfe. **1666** in *Extr. St. Papers rel. Friends* Ser. III. (1912) 259, I have sent you here inclosed a subscription which I have taken vnder his hand. **1773** BURKE *Sp. Relief Prot. Diss.* Wks. X. 33 There was no subscription, to which they were to set their hands. **1851** HUSSEY *Papal Power* ii. 80 It was argued, that they had no subscription from the Pope, nor ecclesiastical authority, to back them. **1864** POMEROY *Munic. Law* 41 An Annotation or Subscription was written to a private person, in answer to questions of a merely private application.

4. The action or an act of affixing a signature; the signing *of* one's name or *of* a document.

1492 EARL OF HUNTLY in *Thanes of Cawdor* (Spalding Club) 156 Writin at Lochcanmor under our signet, and with the subscriptioune of our hand. **1562** SANDYS in Strype *Ann. Ref.* (1735) I. 339 Every Bishop by the Subscription of his hand, promiseth, that he shall not..Alienate any of his Manors. **1592** *Sc. Acts Jas. VI* (1814) III. 586/1 Concerning subscriptioun of the signatures of the new infeftmentis of temporalities. **1689** *Col. Rec. Pennsylv.* I. 268 Vpon his subscription [he] was admitted to take his place in ye Councill. **1761** HUME *Hist. Eng.* (1806) IV. 127 The people ..flocked to the subscription of this covenant. **1765–8** ERSKINE *Inst. Law Scot.* III. ii. §8 A subscription by a cross or mark. **1825** SCOTT *Betrothed* xvii, The subscription of the contract of marriage had..been just concluded. **1885** *Law Rep. 14 Q.B. Div.* 715 The making and subscription of an oath in the House of Commons. **1912** *Signatures Jrnl. Bk. Roy. Soc.* Pref., The subscription of these signatures.

5. A declaration of one's assent *to* articles of religion, or some formal declaration of principles, etc. by signing one's name; *spec.* in the Church of England, assent to the Thirty-nine Articles.

1588 *Marprel. Epist.* (Arb.) 3 Any other of the holy league of subscription. *a* **1620** J. DYKE *Right Receiving* (1640) 8 Now that we have once said we are the Lords, and have subscribed to it, let us..have a care to say, we will be the Lords, and to stand to and make good our subscription. **1654** BRAMHALL *Just Vind.* vi. (1661) 155 We do indeed require subscription to our Articles. **1655** FULLER *Ch. Hist.* IX. 72 The persecuted Church of English in Frankford.. demanded subscription to their discipline of every man. **1721** [A. A. SYKES] (*title*) The case of subscription to the 39 Articles considered. **1782** PRIESTLEY *Corrupt. Chr.* I. I. 141 Application made to parliament..for relief in the business of subscription. **1868** M. PATTISON *Academ. Org.* i. 23 The Cambridge Act..abolished all subscription for degrees. *a* **1890** LIDDON *Pusey* (1893) I. 148 A check upon insurrectionary thought, such as is exerted by subscriptions to Confessions of Faith.

†**6. a.** Assent, approval. Also, an instance of this.

1580 G. HARVEY *Let. to Spenser* in S.'s Wks. (1912) 630/1 You shal neuer haue my subscription or consent..to make your *Carpĕnter* our *Carpēnter*. **1613** PURCHAS *Pilgrimage* (1614) 827 For the excellencie of the Tobacco there found, he should happily haue the smokie subscriptions of many Humorists. **1620** VENNER *Via Recta* (1650) 68 To their opinion..I see no reason why I should yeeld my subscription. *c* **1650** BRADFORD *Plymouth Plant.* (1856) 5 The more ye light of ye gospell grew, ye more yey urged their subscriptions to these corruptions.

†**b.** Submission, allegiance. *Obs. rare.*

1605 SHAKS. *Lear* III. ii. 18, I neuer gaue you Kingdome, call'd you Children; You owe me no subscription.

7. The action or an act of subscribing money to a fund or for stock; the raising of a sum of money for a certain object by collecting contributions from a number of people; †a scheme for raising money in this way. Also, an undertaking or agreement to subscribe so much.

1647 MAY *Hist. Parl.* II. vi. 122 The Treasurers appointed to receive the Moneys come in upon the Subscriptions for Ireland. *c* **1665** MRS. HUTCHINSON *Mem. Col. Hutchinson* (1885) II. 22 They hired him with a subscription of losses, for which they gave him public credit double to what he really had lost. *a* **1692** POLLEXFEN *Disc. Trade* (1697) 105 Without New Subscriptions there can be no way of coming into this Trade under this Charter, but by Buying Shares of the present Adventures *a* **1700** EVELYN *Diary* 9 Aug. 1682, The Academy which Monsieur Faubert did hope to procure to be built by subscription of worthy gentlemen and noblemen. **1740** CIBBER *Apol.* (1756) I. 142 Many people of quality came into a voluntary subscription of twenty.. guineas a-piece, for erecting a theatre. **1747** SHERLOCK in *10th Rep. Hist. MSS. Comm.* App. I. 299, I hear nothing from London of any moment, except the great Subscription for raising money next year. **1748** *Winter Even. Conv. Club of Jews*, etc. in *N. & Q.* Ser. v. V. 413/1 By stock-jobbers he means dose dat be not able to comply vit dare subscriptions. **1762** T. MORTIMER *Ev. Man own Broker* (ed. 5) 21 They will scarce better themselves by any new subscription. **1771** SMOLLETT *Humphry Cl.* (1815) 193 There is a public ball by subscription every night. **1818** SCOTT *Hrt. Midl.* xxvii, A certain hackney, which he..and another honest shopkeeper, combined to maintain by joint subscription. **1837** CARLYLE *Fr. Rev.* I. v. i, There has been erected, apparently by subscription, a kind of Wooden Tent. **1889** W. C. ANDERSON *Dict. Law* 986 (Cent. Dict.), Where an advance has been made..by others in consequence of a subscription, before notice given of a withdrawal, the subscription becomes obligatory. **1912** *World* 7 May 598/2, 100,000 cumulative 7 per cent. preference shares will be offered for subscription.

8. a. A contribution of money for a specified object; *spec.* the fixed sum promised or required as a periodical contribution by a member of a society, etc. to its funds, or for the purchase of a periodical publication, or in payment for a book published 'by subscription' (see 9).

Subscription and *donation* (to a charitable fund, a society, or the like) are usually contrasted, the former being a recurrent, the latter a single, contribution.

1679 in Willis & Clark *Cambridge* (1886) II. 567 Had not some of our benefactours been very slow in paying their subscriptions. **1710** J. CHAMBERLAYNE *M. Brit Notitia* II. 624 The Dean and Chapter have been no less bountiful, and the Clergy of the City are not backward in their Subscriptions. **1729** T. COOKE *Tales*, etc. 120 A Genius form'd like mine will soar at all, And boldly follow where Subscriptions call. *a* **1763** W. KING *Pol. & Lit. Anecd.* (1819) 183 Being applied to..for a charitable subscription. **1804** *Med. Jrnl.* XII. 11 That John Drew..and Tilden Sampson..be requested to receive subscriptions for the use of the institution. **1854** *Poultry Chron.* II. 126 Subscriptions and donations to be paid to the secretary. **1886** C. E. PASCOE *Lond. of To-day* xxxiii. (ed. 3) 300 The subscription to Almack's was ten guineas. **1912** *Nature* 26 Dec. 468/1 The temporary address of the society is the Natural History Museum, Cromwell Road, S.W. There is no subscription.

b. A sum of money subscribed by several parties; a fund: formerly *spec.* in Stock Exchange language. Now *U.S.* in phr. *to make* or *take up a subscription*, to make a collection.

1730 CHENY *List Horse-Matches* 125 On the 23d Day of June the 120 Guineas Subscription Money (and which Subscription is now expir'd) were run for at Richmond by five Year olds. **1756** J. COX *Narr. Thief-takers* 15 A gentleman in the Commission of the Peace in that Neighbourhood, and the Treasurer of that Subscription. *foot-note*, A Reward of 20l. for the taking of Thieves in Tottenham Division. **1762** T. MORTIMER *Ev. Man own Broker* (ed. 5) 46 *note*, A large quantity of any new fund, commonly called Subscription. **1785** GROSE *Dict. Vulgar T.* s.v. *Scrip*, Scrip is also a Change Alley phrase for the last loan or subscription. **1855** *Poultry Chron.* II. 530 A subscription is opened to present Mr. T. B. Wright, of Birmingham, with [etc.]. **1856** J. RICHARDSON *Recoll.* I. iii. 53 The parochial authorities..set on foot a subscription for the purchase of a piece of plate. **1865** H. PHILLIPS *Amer. Paper Curr.* II. 168 To relieve the army a subscription was taken up by the ladies of Philadelphia. **1897** *Daily News* 22 Apr. 6/3 [American sailor loq.] Let's make a subscription.

†**c.** *spec.* A share in a commercial undertaking or a loan. Also *collect. sing. Obs.*

1727 SWIFT *Circumcis. E. Curll* Wks. 1755 III. I. 166 Sir Gideon Lopez tempted him with forty pound subscription in Ram's bubble. **1728** CHAMBERS *Cycl.*, *Subscription*, in the English Commerce, is used for the Share or Interest, particular Persons take in a public Stock, or a Trading Company, by writing their Names, and the Shares they require, in the Register thereof. *a* **1744** POPE *Imit. Horace* I. vii. 65 South-sea Subscriptions take who please. **1762** T. MORTIMER *Ev. Man own Broker* (ed. 5) 108, I would farther recommend to you, by no means to lend your subscription, at the time of the coming out of the receipts:..for they [the Bears] borrow your Scrip to make good their illegal.. bargains.

9. *Book-trade.* **a.** A method of bringing out a book, by which the publisher or author undertakes to supply copies of the book at a certain rate to those who agree to take copies before publication. Freq. in phr. *by subscription.*

1706 PHILLIPS (ed. Kersey), *Subscription for a Book*, is when the Undertakers propose Advantages to those that take a certain Number of Copies at a set Price [*Bailey* 1730 *adds*: and lay down Part of the Money, before the Impression is finish'd]. **1715** (*Advt.*) Proposals for Printing by Subscription a new Edition of Marcus Tullius Cicero, by Thomas Hearne. **1728** CHAMBERS *Cycl.* s.v., Walton's Polyglot Bible, which is the first Book ever printed by Way of Subscription. **1771** SMOLLETT *Humphry Cl.* (1815) 151 The Scotchman gives lectures on the pronunciation of the English language, which he is now publishing by subscription. **1791** BOSWELL *Johnson* (1831) I. 222 In 1766 she published, by subscription, a quarto volume of miscellanies. **1807** DE LOLME *Const. Eng.* Advert. p. ii, In defect of encouragement from great men (and even from booksellers), I had recourse to a subscription. **1873** CURWEN *Hist. Booksellers* 25 He waited four years before he ventured to publish, and then only by the safe method of subscription. **1890** SPRIGGE *Meth. Publ.* 81 The system of publishing suggested by that firm..was that of 'subscription'.

b. (*a*) The taking up of a book by the trade; (*b*) The offering of a book to the trade.

1895 *Bookselling* June 163 Where the trade subscription may be..expected to cover the cost of the first edition. **1912** SHAYLOR *Fascin. Bks.* 145 Each new book when ready for publishing is brought to these establishments for 'subscription'—that is, to ascertain how many copies will be bought.

c. *U.S.* The house-to-house sale of books by canvassers. Freq. *attrib.*

1880 *Publisher's Weekly* (U.S.) 24 Apr. 425 There has been a great deal of grumbling in the retail trade..that so many good books have been taken out of its hands and put into those of subscription 'agents'. Many writers, such as Mark Twain, confine themselves, in fact, to subscription publishing. *Ibid.* 22 May 516 The important trade question of the ownership of subscription orders. **1897** G. H. P. & J. B. P[UTNAM] *Auth. & Publ.* (ed. 7) 51 Books sold by subscription (that is, through canvassers).

10. *attrib.* and *Comb.*, as (sense 8) ***subscription-money, -purse, -share; subscription-hunting*** ppl. adj.; **subscription book,** (*a*) a book containing the names of subscribers to any object (with the amounts of their subscriptions); (*b*) *U.S. Book-trade*, a book sold from house to house by canvassers; **subscription list,** a list of subscribers' names (with the amounts of their subscriptions); so †**subscription-paper,** †**-roll; subscription price,** (*a*) the price at which a book is offered before publication to those who promise to take copies, being usually lower than the price at which any unsubscribed copies will be sold on or after publication; (*b*) the price at which a periodical publication is supplied to those who promise to take so many numbers; †**subscription receipt** (cf. SCRIP *sb.*[4]), a receipt for a share or shares taken up in a loan or commercial undertaking; **subscription room,** a room (e.g. belonging to a club, an exchange) which is open to subscribers only; †**subscription-society,** a union of workmen to which each contributes a subscription; **subscription television** (also T.V.) *N. Amer.*, a television service which provides programmes for subscribers. (See also 9 c.)

1721 AMHERST *Terræ Fil.* No. 12 (1726) I. 65 *Subscription-books (by them call'd matriculation-books) were open'd, and most of the nobility and gentry subscribed their sons and their wards into them. **1771** SMOLLETT *Humphry Cl.* (1815) 64, I consulted the subscription-book; and, perceiving the names of several old friends, began to consider the group with more attention. **1784** *New Bath Guide* 65 Each Master has a ball in the winter and spring seasons, and subscription-books are also laid down at the Rooms, that all the company may have an opportunity of shewing those gentlemen marks of their respect. **1819** EGAN *Walks through Bath* 97 Ladies and gentlemen disposed to become members, are requested to have their names entered in the society's subscription-book. **1870** 'MARK TWAIN' *Lett. to Publishers* (1967) 31 You will make the finest success of it that has ever been made with a subscription book. **1880** *Publisher's Weekly* (U.S.) 24 Apr. 425 (*heading*) The trade and subscription books. **1897** *Boston* (Mass.) *Jrnl.* 16 Jan. 7/8 The Trustees of the Fenway Garden [Boston, Mass.].. have decided to keep the subscription-books open for the present. **1898** SHAW *Perf. Wagnerite* 134 Energetic *subscription-hunting ladies. **1843–56** BOUVIER *Law Dict.* (ed. 6) II. 555/1 **Subscription list*, the names of persons who have agreed to take a newspaper, magazine or other publication, placed upon paper, is a subscription list. **1880** *Publisher's Weekly* (U.S.) 22 May 516 That he be enjoined and restrained..from interfering with the subscription-lists of said publications, and from attempting to discharge any subscriber from his subscription thereto. **1887** *Spectator* 6 Aug. 1057/2 His name figured little in subscription-lists. *a* **1674** CLARENDON *Hist. Reb.* IX. §27 (an. 1645) The Letter Money and *Subscription Money being almost exhausted. **1715** *MS.* in Urry *Chaucer's Wks.* (B. Mus.), Books to be Delivered to the Subscribers Complt in Quires on paymt of their Subscription Money. **1730** [see sense 8 b]. **1774** FOOTE *Cozeners* I. Wks. 1799 II. 146 My expences in.. subscription-money to most of the clubs and coteries. **1780** *New Bath Guide* 26 The subscription to the dress-balls is one guinea to each person for the season, or as long as the subscription-money lasts. **1779** *Mirror* No. 2 ¶4 The *subscription-paper hung up fronting the door. **1886** *Perf. Bk. Kepinge Sparhawkes* Prospectus, *Subscription price, £1 1s; early application is needed to secure a copy. **1891** *Academy* 21 Feb. 185/2 The new publication..will be published monthly at a subscription price of eight rupees per annum, including postage. **1811** *Sporting Mag.* XXXVIII. 221 The *subscription-purse of a hunting club. **1762** T. MORTIMER *Ev. Man own Broker* (ed. 5) 172 The *subscription receipts thus paid in full, are called in the Alley, Heavy-Horse. **1780** —— *Elem. Comm.* 396 If the second or third purchasers in the course of circulation at market, are holders of the subscription receipts at the time of a payment. *a* **1676** HALE *Life P. Atticus* (1677) 142 They thought..that his Name should be the first in the *Subscription-Roll. **1812** COLERIDGE *Friend* (1818) III. 171 The innocent amusement..deserving of all praise as a preventive substitute for the stall, the kennel, and the *subscription-room. **1914** *Daily Tel.* 3 Aug. 5/1 The subscription-room of the Corn Exchange will..be open for the convenience of members. **1856** *Ann. Reg., Chron.* 52/2

The expenses of erecting the theatre are said to have amounted to 150,000*l.*; of which..50,000*l.* [was] raised by *subscription-shares of 500*l.* each. **1769** *Ibid.* 124 [Spitalfields] handkerchief-weavers..entered into a subscription of six-pence on every loom, to support their cause against the masters, one of whom..insisted..that his men should not belong to the *subscription-society. **1955** *How to unscramble Subscription T.V.* (Zenith Radio Corporation, U.S.), *Subscription T.V. can provide you and your family with the best of entertainment..major sports events..education..carefully prepared programs for your children..at a *nominal* price..when *you* want it..*if* you want it..and without ever having to leave the family room of your home. **1962** *Rep. Comm. Broadcasting 1960* 271 in *Parl. Papers 1961–2* (Cmnd. 1753) IX. 259 We now recommend that no service of subscription television be authorised. **1973** C. SAGAN *Cosmic Connection* viii. 62 An unmanned roving vehicle on Mars could probably be supported by subscription television.

b. in adj. use with the sense 'supported by subscription, maintained or provided by, open to, subscribers', as ***subscription ball***, ***charity-school***, ***club***, ***concert***, ***cricket-match***, ***dance***, ***house***, ***library***, ***masquerade***, ***music***, ***night***, ***school***.

1704 tr. *Moliere's* (*title*) Monsieur de Pourceaugnac... Acted at the Subscription Musick at the Theatre Royal. **1708** *New View Lond.* II. 762 A Subscription School for 50 Girls. **1749** H. WALPOLE *Lett.* (1846) II. 268 A subscription masquerade. **1753** *Scots Mag.* XV. 36/2 Sums laid out in.. subscription-concerts. **1779** C'TESS UPPER OSSORY in Jesse *Selwyn & Contemp.* (1844) IV. 176 A subscription ball is on foot, one hundred subscribers at twelve guineas each. **1808** SCOTT in *Lockhart* (1837) I. 37 A respectable subscription library. **1819** EGAN *Walks through Bath* 35 The Subscription-House..at York-Buildings. *Ibid.* 162 The Crescent-Fields,..with the addition of some charming subscription grounds. **1826** J. COOK *Fox-hunting* 149 A manager of a subscription pack. **1851** H. COLERIDGE *Ess.* I. 305 Suckling of infants will be exploded, as unproductive labour. Pap will be made by contract in subscription soup-kettles. **1859** MISS MULOCK *Life for a Life* xi, Charteris is opera-mad... Every subscription-night, there he is, wedged in the crowd. **1886** C. E. PASCOE *Lond. of To-day* vi, Subscription dances, under the patronage of a long list of names.

Hence (nonce-words) **sub'scriptionist**, one who begs for subscriptions; **sub'scriptionless** *a.*, without subscriptions.

1853 N. HAWTHORNE *Engl. Note-bks.* (1870) I. 59, I wish ..I had given the poor family ten shillings, and denied it to a begging subscriptionist, who has just fleeced me to that amount. **1897** *Westm. Gaz.* 9 Mar. 2/2 By depriving the school, already subscriptionless, of this aid grant.

subscriptive (səb'skrɪptɪv), *a. rare.* [f. L. *subscript-*, pa. ppl. stem of *subscrībĕre* to SUBSCRIBE + -IVE.]

1. Pertaining to the 'subscription' of a letter.

1748 RICHARDSON *Clarissa* VII. 197, I have endeavoured to imitate the subscriptive part [of the letter].

2. Pertaining to the subscribing of money.

1897 *Westm. Gaz.* 10 Mar. 2/2 Is it to be the population of a parish? or its subscriptive capacity?

†**sub'scrive**, *v. Sc. Obs.* [ad. OF. *soubscriv-*, pr. stem of *soubscrire*, mod.F. *souscrire* (see SUBSCRIBE). Cf. *descrive*, *inscrive*, *scrive*.] = SUBSCRIBE.

a. *trans.*

c **1470** HARDING *Chron.* CIII. vi, As Flores sayth and doeth it so subscrive. **1476** *Exch. Rolls Scot.* VIII. 344 *note*, Writtin and subscrivit at Edinburgh. **1535** STEWART *Cron. Scot.* II. 440 Peax tha maid, and band With letteris braid subscriuit with thair hand. *a* **1578** LINDESAY (Pitscottie) *Chron. Scot.* (S.T.S.) I. 286 He..tuike the pen in his hand and subscrywit the electioun. **1585** *Sc. Acts Jas. VI* (1814) III. 377 Euerie writtair subscriue his name on þe bak of signato[r] or lettre as allowit be him. *a* **1649** DRUMM. OF HAWTH. *Posth. Poems* (S.T.S.) II. 219 That our Confession is indeed Not the Apostolick Creed, Which of Negations we contrive, Which Turk and Jew may both subscrive. **1689** *Sc. Acts* (1875) XII. 48/2 To report what should be overtured be the Duke in wryting subscryved be the Duke. **1726** in *Nairne Peerage Evid.* (1874) 35, I have already granted and subscrived bonds of provisione to and in favours of my own children.

b. *intr.*

1490 *Munim. de Melros* (Bannatyne Club) 600 To thir my present lettres obl[i]gaitour I have affixit my seill & subscryffyt with my awin hand. **1567** *Satir. Poems Reform.* iii. 129 O ȝe that to our Kirk hes done subscriue. **1596** in T. Morris *Provosts of Methven* (1875) 88 With our handis on the pen led be the notaris vnderwrittin.., becaus we can nocht subscriue. **1640–1** *Kirkcudbr. War-Comm. Min. Bk.* (1855) 61 As for these that hes naither subscryvit nor will cum in, but stands owt, they are to be fyned. **1717** in *Nairne Peerage Evid.* (1874) 146 In the hands of me nottar publick subscriveing after the form..of the said heritable bond of provisione.

c. *pass.* To be engaged in a compact.

1583 *Leg. Bp. St. Androis* 536 Contempneris of our authoritie, Subscryvit aganist our Maiestie.

Hence **sub'scrived** *ppl. a.*, **sub'scriving** *vbl. sb.*, *ppl. a.*; **sub'scriver**, = SUBSCRIBER.

1562 *Maitl. Club Misc.* (1843) III. 291 Bye ye quhilk testimoniall ye said M[r] Thomas allegis hym injurit be ye subscriuaris yarof. **1564** in *Scott. Antiq.* (1901) Oct. 81 The gewing and subscryving of the said infeftment. [**1621**, **1638**: implied in *non-subscriver*, see NON-SUBSCRIBER 1]. **1651** *Caldwell Papers* (Maitland Club) I. 119 Item debursit be the tenents..conforme to the collectors subscryvit compt. **1681** *Sc. Acts Chas. II* (1820) VIII. 243 None but subscryving witnesses shall be probative in Executions of Messingers. **1696** *Ibid.*, *Will.* (1823) X. 63 The Subscriveing of Bonds.

sub'sea, *a.* and *adv.* Chiefly *Oil Industry.* Also **'subsea.** [SUB- 1 e.] **A.** *adj.* Situated or occurring beneath the surface of the sea.

1909 [see AIR-BORNE *a.*]. **1962** *Offshore* July 19 Equipment manufacturers have accelerated their research and development of sub-sea wellheads and auxiliary equipment. **1977** *Financial Times* 1 Apr. 11/1 Figures..suggest that over the life of North Sea oil development at least $20bn (at current prices) will be spent to make sure that platforms, pipelines, and sub-sea well systems are safe and in good working order. **1980** F. C. F. EARNEY *Petroleum & Hard Minerals from Sea* iv. 129 The oil companies' interest in subsea completion systems.

B. *adv.* Below the surface of the sea.

1971 *Bull. Amer. Assoc. Petroleum Geologists* LV. 1694/2 The gas-oil contact is at 6,636 ft subsea. **1977** *Offshore Engineer* May 49/1 The top of the reservoir formation is 1,800m subsea.

†**'subsecant.** *Math. Obs. rare.* [f. SUB- 1 + SECANT B 2 b.] That part of the axis of abscissas of a curve which is intercepted between a secant and the ordinate.

1816 tr. *Lacroix' Diff. & Int. Calc.* 655 Its subtangent P T must consequently be less than one of the subsecants.

subsecive ('sʌbsɪsɪv), *a.* Now *Obs.* or *rare.* Also 7 **subcisive**, **subcesive**, **subsicive**. [ad. L. *subsecīvus*, less correct f. *subsicīvus*, also (by transposition) *-cesīvus*, *-cisīvus* (cf. SUCCISIVE) cut off and left remaining, f. *sub-* SUB- 26 + *secāre* to cut (cf. SECTION).] Remaining over, spare: chiefly in ***subsecive hours***.

1613 JACKSON *Creed* I. To Rdr. C 3, The principal subiect of my subcisiue or vacant houres. *a* **1640** W. FENNER *Wilful Impen.* Ep. Ded., I had thought to have sent it to my Lord of Warwicke for his subcisive howers. **1652** NEDHAM *Dominium Maris* in Selden's *Mare Clausum* (1663) 128 The subcesive or remanent part onely is left out unassigned. **1832** SOUTHEY *Let. to J. W. Warter* 20 June, Next year it will become my chief object in those subsecive hours, for which I can find no English word.

†**sub'sect**, *v. Obs.* [f. SUB- 9 + L. *sect-*, pa. ppl. stem of *secāre* to cut.] *trans.* To subdivide.

1654 VILVAIN *Enchir. Epigr.* III. xcv. 79 The 7 Parts or Portions of the Earth, as som lat Authors now State or subsect them. **1654** GATAKER *Disc. Apol.* 93 You of the Calvinistical Sect, a Sect dissected, subsected, and resected.

'subsection. [f. SUB- 7 + SECTION.] A division of a section.

1621 BURTON (*title*) The Anatomy of Melancholy,..in Three Maine Partitions, with their seuerall Sections, Members, and Svbsections. *Ibid.* I. i. II. ix, In the precedent Subsections, I haue anatomised those inferiour Faculties of the Soule. **1841** DE QUINCEY *Style* Wks. 1859 XI. 228 Others who bring an occasional acuteness..to this or that sub-section of their duty. **1863** C. C. BLAKE in *Jrnl. Anthropol. Soc.* (1865) III. I. 5 A valuable..paper was read in subsection D [of the British Association], by Dr. Embleton. **1879** *Encycl. Brit.* X. 242/1 The behaviour of the lava as it issues and flows down the volcanic cones will be described in the next sub-section. **1885** *Act 48 & 49 Vict.* c. 70 §8 Sub-section one of section fifteen of the Sea Fisheries Act, 1883.

b. *Nat. Hist.* A subordinate division of a section or group.

1826 KIRBY & SP. *Entomol.* III. 414 In this subsection the *Diptera*, *Libellulina* and *Mantidæ* will find their place. **1826** [see SUBORDER 1]. **1840** *Cuvier's Anim. Kingd.* 415 Latreille divides this section [*sc.* Trigona] into sub-sections.

c. *Milit.* (See quot.)

1910 *Encycl. Brit.* (ed. 11) II. 690/1 Each section [of a battery]..consists of two sub-sections, each comprising one gun and its wagons, men and horses.

Hence **'subsectioned**, divided into subsections.

1820 KEATS *Cap & Bells* xi, With special strictures on the horrid crime, (Section'd and subsection'd with learning sage).

†**subsecute**, *v. Obs. rare.* [f. L. *subsecūt-*, pa. ppl. stem of *subsequī* (see SUBSEQUENT).] *trans.* To follow up, pursue.

a **1548** HALL *Chron.*, *Rich. III*, 46 b, Yf by any possibilitie he could be subsecuted and overtaken. **1569** STOCKER tr. *Diod. Sic.* II. xix. 70/2 Aristone..subsecuted and chased him through the countrey of Basalcie.

†**sub'secutive**, *a. Obs. rare*$^{-0}$. [f. as prec. + -IVE; cf. F. *subsécutif*.] Subsequent.

1611 COTGR., *Subsecutif*, subsecutiue.

‖**subsella** (səb'sɛlə). [mod.L., f. *sub-* SUB- 3 + *sella* a seat, after next.] = SUBSELLIUM 2.

1849 *Ecclesiol.* IX. 156 Seats placed stall-wise, with desks before them and subsellae beneath. **1861** NEALE *Notes Dalmatia* 117 On each side of the Choir are sixteen stalls,.. with subsellae.

‖**subsellium** (səb'sɛlɪəm). Pl. sub'sellia (-'sɛlɪə). [L., f. *sub-* SUB- 3 + *sella* seat.]

1. *Rom. Antiq.* A seat in an amphitheatre.

a **1701** MAUNDRELL *Journ. Jerus.* (1721) 16 Vaults which run under the Subsellia all round the Theatre.

2. *Church Archit.* = MISERICORD 2 c.

1806 J. DALLAWAY *Engl. Archit.* 118 The application of the ancient carved subsellia to the present reading-desks is a new idea. **1886** WILLIS & CLARK *Cambridge* I. 47 The stalls and subsellia..belong in style to the period of their construction.

'subsemitone. *Mus.* [ad. med.L. *subsemitonium*: see SUB- 13.] The leading note of a scale.

c **1800** BUSBY *Dict. Mus.*, *Sub-Semitone*, the name by which theorists distinguish the sharp seventh, or sensible, of any key. **1876** STAINER & BARRETT *Dict. Mus. Terms.*

sub'sensible, *a.* [SUB- 1 a.] Below or deeper than the range of the senses.

1863 TYNDALL *Heat* ii. 33 We can only reach the roots of natural phenomena by laying down, intellectually, a subsensible soil out of which such phenomena spring. **1871** —— *Fragm. Sci.* (1879) II. xv. 387 That subsensible world into which all natural phenomena strike their roots.

So **sub'sensual**, **-'sensuous** *adjs.*

1886 *Homilet. Rev.* July 73 The dark, *subsensual flow of a soul abandoned to vice. **1892** AGNES M. CLERKE *Fam. Stud. Homer* viii. 212 In some unexplained subsensual way. *a* **1834** COLERIDGE *Notes & Lect.* (1849) I. 164 Nationality in each individual, *quoad* his country, is equal to the sense of individuality *quoad* himself; but himself as *subsensuous, and central. **1898** HORTON *Commandm. Jesus* xvi. 290 In that subsensuous contact of spirit with spirit.

subsequence[1] ('sʌbsɪkwəns). [f. SUBSEQUENT: see -ENCE.]

1. That which is subsequent; a subsequent event; the sequel.

?*a* **1500** *Chester Pl.* I. 187 Yow shall well wyt the Subsequence, this Daunce will turne to teene and traye. **1592** WEST *1st Pt. Symbol.* §52 Let us enter into consideration of the subsequence or sequele thereof. **1610** HEALEY *St. Aug. Citie God* III. xxx. 150 Without any more stirre or other subsequence of war. *Ibid.* V. ix. 209 What auailes the subsequence? **1637** HEYWOOD *Descr. Sover aign of Seas* 34 As they comply in the premisses,..they differ not all in the subsequence. **1827** G. S. FABER *Sacr. Cal. Prophecy* (1844) III. 331 The predicted millennium with its concomitants and subsequences.

2. The condition or fact of being subsequent.

1668 WILKINS *Real Char.* I. iv. §1. 14 With such an order of precedence and subsequence as their natures will bear. **1701** GREW *Cosmol. Sacra* II. iii. 43 By which Faculty [*sc.* reminiscence], we are also able, to take notice of the Order of Precedence and Subsequence, in which they are past. **1846** TRENCH *Mirac.* No. 5 (1862) 159 The Scripture teaches the absolute subordination of evil to good, and its subsequence of order. **1854** THACKERAY *Newcomes* xxviii, An affair which appeared in due subsequence in the newspapers. **1884** BROWNING *Ferishtah*, *Bean-Stripe* 70 Joy, sorrow,—by precedence, subsequence—Either on each, make fusion.

sub-sequence[2] ('sʌbsiːkwəns). [SUB- 7 a, e.] A sequence contained in or forming part of another sequence; *spec.* in *Math.*

1908 [see OSCILLATORY *a.* 3]. **1958** R. C. MOORE *Introd. Hist. Geol.* (ed. 2) iv. 80 The second division of the Huronian Sequence, named the Cobalt Sub-sequence, has an aggregate thickness of more than 12,000 feet. **1972** A. G. HOWSON *Handbk. Terms Algebra & Anal.* xxii. 109 This definition formalises the notion of a subsequence as a sequence derived from the original sequence by the omission of a number (not necessarily finite) of terms. **1975** N. CHOMSKY *Logical Struct. Linguistic Theory* ix. 329 The term arrangement of t^* may not be the same as the term arrangement of the transformation T defined in the terms of t, although the latter term arrangement must be a subsequence of the former.

†**'subsequency.** *Obs. rare.* [f. SUBSEQUENT: see -ENCY.] The fact or condition of following.

1705 GREENHILL *Embalming* 336 The Heliotrope's subsequency to the Course of the Sun.

subsequent ('sʌbsɪkwənt), *a.* and *sb.* [a. F. *subséquent* (14th c. in Littré), or ad. L. *subsequens*, *-entem*, pr. pple. of *subsequī*, f. *sub-* SUB- III + *sequī* to follow.]

A. *adj.*

1. Following in order or succession; coming or placed after, *esp.* immediately after.

a **1460** J. METHAM *Wks.* (E.E.T.S.) 157/1, I rede in elde volummys this matere subsequent. **1599** A. M. tr. *Gabelhouer's Bk. Physicke* 346/1 Then applye theron the whytes of Egges..and then applye theron this subsequente playster. **1606** SHAKS. *Tr. & Cr.* I. iii. 344 Such Indexes, although small pricks To their subsequent Volumes. **1660** BARROW *Euclid* Pref. (1714) p. ij, The six precedent and the two subsequent [Books]. **1745** in *10th Rep. Hist. MSS. Comm.* App. I. 285 The Sentences precedent and subsequent. **1788** *Encycl. Brit.* (1797) I. 695/2 This, with the subsequent bones of the ear, are here delineated as large as the life. **1814** SCOTT *Wav.* ii, But more of this in a subsequent chapter. **1833** J. RENNIE *Alph. Angl.* 21 We shall see in a subsequent page the principle upon which this is founded.

absol. **1596** NASHE *Saffron-Walden* To Rdr. Wks. 1905 III. 22/31 The subsequent or hindermost of the paire.

2. a. Following or succeeding in time; existing or occurring after, *esp.* immediately after, something expressed or implied; coming or happening later.

† ***the subsequent*** (year, etc.), ***the*** (year, etc.) ***subsequent***, the year, etc. next following.

condition subsequent: see CONDITION *sb.* 2.

1503–4 *Act 19 Hen. VII*, c. 27 §6 To begyn and ende theyr accompt..in the yere subsequent for the yere precedent. **1651** G. W. tr. *Cowel's Inst.* 107 As if one gives any thing with such an intention that it shall be the Donees when a subsequent thing is performed. **1662** PETTY *Taxes* iv. 28 The envy which precedent missions of English [in Ireland] have against the subsequent. **1681** STAIR *Inst. Law Scot.* II. xxvii. 137 No Son of a subsequent Branch could be entered. **1762–71** H. WALPOLE *Vertue's Anecd. Paint.* (1786) V. 129 His other plates I will repeat briefly, as I shall those of subsequent engravers. **1800** COLQUHOUN *Comm. Thames* xi. 300 It was found needful to explain and amend this Charter by many others Subsequent. **1855** MACAULAY *Hist. Eng.* xvii. IV. 56 The day from which all his subsequent years took their colour. **1860** TYNDALL *Glac.* I. iii. 23 My subsequent destination was Vienna. **1905** R. BAGOT *Passport* xxxvi, Concetta delivered the letter, and another subsequent one.

b. Const. *to.* (Also advb. = *subsequently to.* Cf. *previous*, etc.)

1647 CLARENDON *Hist. Reb.* II. §12 The ill Consequences of it, or the Actions which were subsequent to it. *a* **1745** SWIFT *Some Remarks on Barrier Treaty* Wks. 1841 I. 430/1 This prodigious article is introduced as subsequent to the treaty of Munster. **1806** *Med. Jrnl.* XV. 141, I have not heard of any death but one shortly subsequent to cow-pox inoculation. **1822** HEBER *Wks. Jer. Taylor* (1828) I. p. xl, Subsequent to the suppression..he was..at large. **1871** SMILES *Charac.* ii. (1876) 39 It was long subsequent to the death of both his parents. **1911** *War Dept. Provis. Subsidy Scheme* 1 Lorries must have been built subsequent to 1st January, 1911.

c. Forming a sequel *to.* (*rare.*)

1779 JOHNSON *L.P.*, *Pope* (1868) 408 He had planned a work, which he considered as subsequent to his 'Essay on Man'.

d. *Phys. Geog.* Applied to a stream or valley that has developed its course so as to follow rock that is more easily eroded, and consequently in most cases following the strike of the rock.

[**1862** JUKES in *Q. Jrnl. Geol. Soc.* XVIII. 400 That the lateral valleys are the first formed..while the longitudinal valleys are of subsequent origin, gradually produced by atmospheric action on the softer and more easily eroded beds that strike along the chains.] **1895** W. M. DAVIS in *Geogr. Jrnl.* (R.G.S.) V. 131 The peculiarity of subsequent streams is..that they run along the strike of weak strata; while consequent streams run down the dip, crossing harder and softer strata alike. **1898** I. C. RUSSELL *River Developm.* vii. 185 Streams originate, the directions of which are regulated by the hardness and solubility of the rocks. Such streams appear subsequently to the main topographic features in their environment, and are termed subsequent streams. **1954** W. D. THORNBURY *Princ. Geomorphol.* v. 113 Because of the coincidence of subsequent valleys with belts of weak rock it is usually concluded that any valley which follows such a course is a subsequent valley. This may not be true, for the valley may have been on the weak rock from the beginning. **1970** R. J. SMALL *Study of Landforms* vii. 233 The most significant feature..will be the appearance and growth of 'subsequent' streams, which by the process of headward erosion will extend along lines of geological weakness.

e. *Geol.* = INTRUSIVE *a.* 2*b.*

1888 TEALL *Brit. Petrogr.* 449.

B. *sb.* †**1. a.** A person or thing that follows or comes after another. *Obs.*

1603 FLORIO *Montaigne* II. xii. 294 Deeming all other apprentiships as subsequents and of superarogation in regard of that [orig. *estimant tout autre apprentissage subsecutif à celuy-la & supernumeraire*]. **1623** BP. HALL *Serm. Reedified Chapell Earle of Exceter* Wks. (1634) 484 This conceit..is quite dissonant from the context, both in regard of the precedents, and subsequents. *a* **1676** HALE *Prim. Orig. Man.* II. vii. 179 It hath a most excellent congruity with the subsequents of the Holy History. **1685** *Coron. Jas. II* (Broadside), So Handsome that all other Ladies, Her Subsequents seem'd but her Shaddows. **1824** L. MURRAY *Engl. Gram.* (ed. 5) I. 241 As the relative pronoun, when used interrogatively, refers to the subsequent word or phrase containing the answer to the question, that word or phrase may properly be termed the subsequent to the interrogative.

†**b.** *these subsequents*: the persons or things mentioned immediately afterwards. *Obs.*

1612 STURTEVANT *Metallica* 57 These subsequents are most necessarie, as namely; Ioyners, Carpenters, Smithes, Brickelayers, Masons. **1637–50** ROW *Hist. Kirk* (Wodrow Soc.) 15 These subsequents..to be obserued in this Realme concerning Doctrine.

2. *Physical Geogr.* A subsequent stream (see sense A. 2d).

1895 W. M. DAVIS in *Geogr. Jrnl.* V. 144 The Welland, Gwash, Chater, and Eye being parts of consequent streams that have been captured by subsequents. **1956** D. L. LINTON *Sheffield* 42 Its headstream the Doe Lea has the aspect of a true subsequent, but from Staveley northwards though it maintains the direction of the Doe Lea this is no longer that of the strike of the rocks. **1970** R. J. SMALL *Study of Landforms* vii. 234 In an area where the structure comprises a series of anticlines and synclines, one is tempted ..to regard all synclinal streams as longitudinal consequents and all anticlinal streams as subsequents.

subsequential (sʌbsɪˈkwɛnʃəl), *a.* [f. SUBSEQUENT after *consequential.*] Subsequent.

1670 W. P[ENN] *Case Lib. Consc.* 29 No Temporary Subsequential Law whatever, to our Fundamental Rights, ..can invalid so essential a part of the Government. **1802–12** BENTHAM *Ration. Judic. Evid.* (1827) II. 582 Whether in their original character of advocates or in their subsequential..character of judges. **1829** —— *Justice & Cod. Petit.* 190 In another, say a subsequential judicatory, to which..the inquiry is..transferred. **1879** STEVENSON *Across the Plains* (1892) 9 It seems to fit some subsequential, evening epoch of the world.

Hence **subseˈquentially** *adv.*, subsequently.

1829 BENTHAM *Justice & Cod. Petit.* 127 Subsequentially applied instruments.

subsequently (ˈsʌbsɪkwəntlɪ), *adv.* [f. SUBSEQUENT *a.* + -LY².] At a subsequent or later time. Const. *to.*

1611 COTGR., *Subsecutivement*, subsequently. **1657** CROMWELL *Sp.* 21 Apr. (Carlyle), If any shall be subsequently named, after the Other House is sat. **1685** SOUTH *Serm.* Prov. xvi. 33 (1697) I. 337 They are forced to comply subsequently, and to strike in with things as they fall out. **1794** R. J. SULIVAN *View Nat.* II. 64 From the same cause, the natural character of nations may arise, however subsequently moulded. **1845** DARWIN *Voy. Nat.* viii. 174 In North America..the large quadrupeds lived subsequently to that period. **1863** LYELL *Antiq. Man* 2 The remains of living beings which have peopled the district at more than one era may have subsequently been mingled in such caverns. **1891** *Law Times* XCI. 142 Cases where a man becomes a soldier subsequently to the making of the order.

ˈ**subsere.** *Ecol.* [SUB- 5.] A secondary sere (see quot. 1926). Cf. PRISERE.

1916 [see PRISERE]. **1926** TANSLEY & CHIPP *Aims & Methods in Study of Vegetation* ii. 19 A new sere beginning after the succession has been stopped by the destruction of some later phase..we distinguish as a secondary sere or subsere. **1938** WEAVER & CLEMENTS *Plant Ecol.* (ed. 2) iii. 78 Seres..on secondary areas, such as lumbered, burned, flooded, or otherwise denuded ones, are termed subseres. **1964** V. J. CHAPMAN *Coastal Veg.* i. 3 Should an area of dune that has developed to forest become destroyed by burning a new succession would arise, but this would be known as a subsere.

‖**subserosa** (sʌbsɪəˈrəʊsə). *Anat.* [mod.L. (sc. *membrāna*): see SUB- 1 d and cf. next.] Subserous tissue.

1890 BILLINGS *Nat. Med. Dict.* **1901** *Jrnl. Exper. Med.* 29 Nov. 55.

subserous (sʌbˈsɪərəs), *a.* *Anat.* and *Path.* [f. SUB- + SEROUS.]

1. [SUB- 1 b.] **a.** *Anat.* Situated or occurring beneath a serous membrane, as ***subserous tissue.*** **b.** *Path.* Affecting the subserous tissue.

1833 *Cycl. Pract. Med.* II. 731/1 Its bloodvessels and those of the sub-serous cellular tissue are deeply injected. **1872** T. G. THOMAS *Dis. Women* (ed. 3) 276 Neoplasms, whether they be submucous, subserous or mural, keep up a constant nervous irritation. **1875** tr. *von Ziemssen's Cycl. Med.* X. 230 The subserous fibroid [of the uterus]. **1904** *Brit. Med. Jrnl.* 10 Sept. 597 The great numbers of cells which are found wandering far and wide in the submucosa, the musculature, and the subserous tissue.

2. [SUB- 21 b.] Somewhat serous.

In mod. Dicts.

†**subˈservant.** *Obs. rare*⁻¹. [SUB- 5 a.] An inferior servant, under-servant.

1661 K. W. *Conf. Charac.*, *Detracting Empirick* (1860) 64 A poor apothecaries subservant, whose work is to look to the stills, and sweep the shop.

subserve (səbˈsɜːv), *v.* [ad. L. *subservīre*, f. *sub-* SUB- 8 + *servīre* to SERVE *v.*¹]

1. *intr.* To be subservient *to.*

a **1619** FOTHERBY *Atheom.* II. i. §8 (1622) 186 Arts belonging to all these; and yet all of them subseruing vnto the Art of Riding. **1646** H. LAWRENCE *Commun. Angels* 10 All creatures shall subserve to that composition of which God is a part. **1677** GALE *Crt. Gentiles* III. 9 The manner of our disquisitions..is irregular... When we..make that subservient which should be ultimate, and that ultimate which should subserve. **1759** MARTIN *Nat. Hist.* II. 317 It subserves..to the Trade of this Place. **1822** L. HUNT *Indicator* No. 25 (1822) I. 193 Merely subserving to the worst taste of the times. **1860** WESTCOTT *Introd. Study Gosp.* v. 263 The historical framework of their writings subserved to a doctrinal development.

2. a. *trans.* To be instrumental in furthering or assisting (a purpose, object, action, function, or condition); to promote or assist by supplying an instrument or means.

1677 GALE *Crt. Gentiles* IV. 439 Is there not a world of men, which..subserve the Glorie of their Maker? **1685** BAXTER *Paraphr. N.T.* Matt. v. 9 That thou wilt..cause us to subserve thy Providence by our wise and diligent labours. **1687** *Lond. Gaz.* No. 2250/3 The free Exercise of Religion.. will..most truly subserve the Interest of Your Majesties Power. **1741** WATTS *Improv. Mind* I. xvii. (1801) 135 [The memory] uses all those parts..which subserve our sensations. **1786** tr. *Beckford's Vathek* 7 Even insensible matter shewed a forwardness to subserve his designs. **1815** KIRBY & SP. *Entomol.* x. (1816) I. 305 It might subserve the double purpose of ridding us of a nuisance, and relieving the public pressure. **1833–6** NEWMAN *Hist. Sk.* (1876) I. iv. v. 417 The cause of Protestantism..the Catholic Fathers certainly do not subserve. **1854** OWEN in *Orr's Circ. Sci.*, *Org. Nat.* I. 197 The ribs..subserve locomotion. **1896** *Allbutt's Syst. Med.* I. 109 The peripheral nervous system subserves sensation alone.

b. To be instrumental in furthering the purpose, interest, or function of (a person or thing). *rare.*

1661 BAXTER *Last Wk. Believer* (1682) 62 Christ will not take it ill..to have his Ministers subserve him in so excellent a work. **1669** GALE *Crt. Gentiles* I. I. 5 You see how the more imperfect subserve the perfect: the inanimate the animate; as the earth the plant. **1854** OWEN in *Orr's Circ. Sci.*, *Org. Nat.* I. 163 Portions of bone are also developed to protect and otherwise subserve the organs of the senses.

3. a. *intr.* To act in a subordinate position. *rare.*

1671 MILTON *Samson* 57 Not made to rule, But to subserve where wisdom bears command. **1840** BROWNING *Sordello* iii. 533 Old engagements out he blots For aye: Taurello shall no more subserve. **1968** T. KINSELLA *Nightwalkers* 60 We dwell together in urgency; Dominate, entering middle age; subserve, Aborting vague tendencies with buttery smiles.

†**b.** *trans.* To serve under, be subordinate to. *Obs. rare.*

1769 E. BANCROFT *Guiana* 319 The husband takes a second [wife]..who lives and subserves the former in all domestic employments.

4. *refl.* To avail oneself *of.* *rare.*

a **1834** COLERIDGE *Omniana* Lit. Rem. 1836 I. 373, I not merely subserve myself of them, but I employ them.

subserviate (səbˈsɜːvɪeɪt), *v.* [irreg. f. SUBSERVIENT + -ATE³.] *trans.* To make subservient or subordinate.

1893 CRONWRIGHT-SCHREINER in Farrelly *Settlem. S. Africa* (1900) 90 They would selfishly and foolishly subserviate the interests of the whole Colony to their own benighted wishes. **1906** CHURCHILL *Coniston* II. iii, The time would come when the railroads..would exterminate the boss, or at least subserviate him.

subservience (səbˈsɜːvɪəns). [f. SUBSERVIENT: see -ENCE.]

1. The condition or quality of being serviceable, as a means *to* an end.

a **1676** HALE *Prim. Orig. Man.* I All this accommodation ..and mutual subservience of the things in Nature. **1677** GALE *Crt. Gentiles* IV. 450 To order al means and affaires in subservience to his end and designe. **1793** BURKE *Obs. Conduct Minority* Wks. 1842 I. 614 It was in subservience to the general plan of disabling us from taking any steps against France. **1805** KNOX & JEBB *Corr.* I. 224 All events on this earth are regulated and directed, in subservience to the interests of that spiritual..kingdom of the Messiah. **1884** F. TEMPLE *Relat. Relig. & Sci.* iv. (1885) 119 We should trace the beneficent effects of pain and pleasure in their subservience to the purification of life.

†**b.** *pl.*

a **1693** *Urquhart's Rabelais* III. l. 402 The uses and subserviences they were fit for. **1802** PALEY *Nat. Theol.* xii, The plan is attended, through all its varieties and deflections, by subserviences to special occasions and utilities.

2. A condition of subordination or subjection *to* another. Now *rare* exc. as implied in 3.

1701 G. STANHOPE *Pious Breathings* v. xvii. (1720) 348 Grant that my sensual Affections may always continue in subservience to my reasonable mind. *a* **1704** T. BROWN *Praise of Wealth* Wks. 1730 I. 86 A change of power to subservience is a proof of folly. **1836** THIRLWALL *Greece* xxi. (1839) III. 173 They had secured the subservience of the whole island. **1902** W. BRIGHT *Age of Fathers* (1903) I. xv. 288 The sermon..asserted the absolute 'subservience' of the Son to the Father.

3. Subservient behaviour, attitude, or conduct; servile subordination, submissiveness, obsequiousness.

1819 SCOTT *Ivanhoe* xxiv, She could not indeed imitate his excess of subservience, because she was a stranger to the meanness of mind..by which it was dictated. **1849** GROTE *Greece* II. xxxviii. V. 23 A young Persian monarch, corrupted by universal subservience around him. **1873** HAMERTON *Intell. Life* IX. iii. 314 Johnson..is grander in his neglect of fashion than Goldsmith in his ruinous subservience. **1902** MATHIESON *Pol. & Relig.* I. x. 323 His subservience to the King..was due in part to the extreme weakness of his position.

subserviency (səbˈsɜːvɪənsɪ). [f. next: see -ENCY.]

1. = SUBSERVIENCE 1.

1651 BAXTER *Inf. Bapt.* 277 All things being..by him given out to the world, in subserviency to the ends of his design. **1662** STILLINGFL. *Orig. Sacræ* II. iv. §5 This Institution of them in the Schools of the Prophets was of great subserviency. **1732** BERKELEY *Alciphr.* III. §9 The Beauty of Dress depends on its subserviency to certain Ends and Uses. **1748** HARTLEY *Observ. Man* II. i. §3. 10 When we contemplate..the manifest Adaptations and Subserviencies of all these Things to each other. **1830** LYELL *Princ. Geol.* I. 479 The subserviency of our planet to the support of terrestrial as well as aquatic species. **1862** HOOK *Lives Abps.* II. 124 Persons, whom he intended to bring to a subserviency to his objects.

2. = SUBSERVIENCE 2. Now *rare* exc. as implied in 3.

1653 H. MORE *Conject. Cabbal.* (1713) 15 It is reasonable the worser should be in subserviency to the better. *a* **1665** J. GOODWIN *Being filled with the Sp.* (1867) 147 That subserviency which..seems to be attributed to the Holy Ghost. **1723** SWIFT *Argts. agst. Bps.* Wks. 1761 III. 263 Lords and squires—who..murmur at the payment of rent —as a subserviency they were not born to. **1896** DK. ARGYLL *Philos. Belief* 8 The subserviency of structure to function, and the priority in time of structural growth.

3. = SUBSERVIENCE 3.

a **1768** SECKER *Serm.* (1770) III. viii. 178 The obstructing of useful Measures by Opposition, forwarding bad ones by Subserviency. **1815** W. H. IRELAND *Scribbleomania* 57 *note*, Any stricture on the score of subserviency in style or composition. **1852** MRS. STOWE *Uncle Tom's C.* xxxix, That cringing subserviency which is one of the most baleful effects of slavery. **1878** LECKY *Eng. in 18th Cent.* I. i. 8 In no country have State trials been conducted with..a more scandalous subserviency to the Crown.

subservient (səbˈsɜːvɪənt), *a.* (*sb.*) [ad. L. *subserviens*, *-entem*, pr. pple. of *subservīre* to SUBSERVE.] **A.** *adj.*

1. Being of use or service as an instrument or means; serving as a means to further an end, object, or purpose; serviceable. Const. *to* a person or thing, a design, condition, process.

1632 TATHAM *Love crowns the end* I. Dram. Wks. (1878) 19 If these eyes be my own, I fondly trust They may be more subservient to me. **1651** BAXTER *Inf. Bapt.* 144 If they do preach any wholsom Doctrine, it is usually but subservient to their great Design. **1656** RIDGLEY *Pract. Physick* 55 The spirits..subservient to the imagination in the Brain. **1690** LOCKE *Hum. Und.* II. ix. §7 Ideas, which we may..suppose may be introduced into the Minds of Children in the Womb, subservient to the necessity of their Life..there. **1729** BUTLER *Serm.* Wks. 1874 II. 150 Every particular affection

..is subservient to self-love. **1781** GIBBON *Decl. & F.* xviii. (1787) II. 99 The arts of fraud were made subservient to the designs of cruelty. **1873** SYMONDS *Grk. Poets* vii. 189 The drama renders all arts subservient to the one end of action. **1879** HARLAN *Eyesight* ii. 18 All the other structures of the eye may be considered subservient to this one [the retina].

†**b.** Const. *to* with inf. or a prep. with gerund.

1668 DRYDEN *Dram. Poesy* Wks. 1725 I. 43 They dwell on him and his concernments, while the rest of the Persons are only subservient to set him off. **1714** R. FIDDES *Pract. Disc.* II. 145 Persons who are subservient in this respect towards promoting the honour of God. **1719** YOUNG *Revenge* III. i, This is a good subservient artifice, To aid the nobler workings of my brain. **1755** SMOLLETT *Quix.* (1803) II. 23 In making you subservient in facilitating our success.

†**c.** without construction. *Obs.*

1650 BULWER *Anthropomet.* 173 They are not in the number of them that perform an action, but of those that are subservient. **1661** J. FELL *Hammond* 112 Scarce ever reading any thing which he did not make subservient in one kinde or other. **1701** GREW *Cosmol. Sacra* II. i. 36 While we are awake, we feel none of those Motions, which are continually made, in the disposal of the Corporeal Principles Subservient herein.

2. Acting or serving in a subordinate capacity; subordinate, subject. Const. *to*.

a. of persons.

1647 CLARENDON *Hist. Reb.* I. §140 That the Queen might have solely that Power, and he only be Subservient to her. **1667** *Decay Chr. Piety* ii. ¶13 Can we think he will be patient thus to be made subservient to his enemy? **1711** G. HICKES *Two Treat. Chr. Priesth.* (1847) II. 79 The deacons as subservient inferior ministers. **1721** PRIOR *Predest.* 63 Wks. 1907 II. 347 Is God subservient to his own Decree? **1873** HAMERTON *Intell. Life* VII. vi. 258 Women are by nature far more subservient to custom than we are. **1880** 'VERNON LEE' *Italy* III. i. 73 They wanted the singer to remain subservient to the composer.

b. of things.

1641 MILTON *Ch. Govt.* iii. Wks. 1851 III. 109 Copies out from the borrow'd manuscript of a subservient scrowl. **1656** TUCKER *Rep.* in *Misc. Scott. Burgh Rec. Soc.* 19 The towne is a mercat towne, but subservient and belonging..to the towne of Lynlithquo. **1687** DRYDEN *Hind & P.* I. 88 Superiour faculties are set aside, Shall their subservient organs be my guide? **1709** POPE *Ess. Crit.* 263 Most Critics, fond of some subservient art, Still made the Whole depend upon a Part. **1864** PUSEY *Lect. Daniel* ii. 88 Antiochus Epiphanes..directed against God what was to be subservient to God. **1870** DISRAELI *Lothair* xii, Assuming that religion was true..then religion should be the principal occupation of man, to which all other pursuits should be subservient.

c. *Law.* (Cf. SERVIENT and SERVITUDE 7.)

1681 STAIR *Inst. Law Scot.* I. xvi. 327 Personal Servitudes are, whereby the property of one is subservient to the person of another. **1681** [see SERVITUDE 7]. **1884** *Law Rep. 25 Chanc. Div.* 580 The mortgagees of C, D, and E..acquiesced in those blocks being made subservient to the adjoining block B.

3. Of persons, their actions, etc.: Slavishly submissive; truckling, obsequious.

1794 MRS. RADCLIFFE *Myst. Udolpho* xlviii, Emily was.. disgusted by the subservient manners of many persons, who [etc.]. **1819** SCOTT *Ivanhoe* xxi, The foreigner came here poor, beggarly, cringing, and subservient. **1839** JAMES *Louis XIV*, IV. 251 He contrived to ally this subservient flattery to a degree of intemperate vehemence towards Louis. **1874** GREEN *Short Hist.* viii. §2 (1882) 472 The lawyers had been subservient beyond all other classes to the Crown.

B. *sb.* A subservient person or thing. *rare.*

1867 D. PAGE *Man* 143 The primitive notion that this earth was the centre of the universe, and the sun, moon, and stars, formed merely to be its subservients. **1898** MEREDITH *Odes Fr. Hist.* 35 The fair subservient of Imperial Fact.

subserviently (səb'sɜːvɪəntlɪ), *adv.* [f. prec. + -LY².] In a subservient manner.

1678 CUDWORTH *Intell. Syst.* 221 The worst of all Evils made..to contribute subserviently to the Good and Perfection of the Whole. **1795** *Ann. Reg., Hist.* 18 They acted subserviently to all its designs. **1823** W. SCORESBY *Jrnl.* p. xv, Discovery was an object, therefore, that could only be pursued subserviently to this. **1885** *Manch. Exam.* 26 Aug. 5/4 Unless it [*sc.* the Government] complies subserviently with the Nationalist demands.

So **sub'servientness** *rare*⁻⁰ (1727 Bailey Vol. II).

subserving (səb'sɜːvɪŋ), *ppl. a.* [f. SUBSERVE *v.* + -ING².] That subserves; subservient.

1621 BURTON *Anat. Mel.* I. i. II. ii, Ligaments, are they that tye the Bones together, and other parts to the Bones, with their subseruing tendons. **1893** *Advance* (Chicago) 2 Nov., Combine..against the ring and its boss and its subserving tool that now fills the Mayor's chair. [**1895** W. H. HUDSON *Spencer's Philos.* 124 In non-gregarious creatures, the only conflict is between self-subserving and race-subserving activities.]

subsesquialteral, etc.: see SUB- 10.

subsessile (sʌb'sɛsɪl), *a. Zool.* and *Bot.* [ad. mod.L. *subsessilis*: see SUB- 21 c.] Not truly sessile; almost sessile.

1760 J. LEE *Introd. Bot.* III. iv. (1765) 174 *Verticillus*, a Whorl, expresses a Number of Flowers that are subsessile. **1777** S. ROBSON *Brit. Flora* 104 Snow Saxifrage. Leaves obovate, crenate, subsessile. **1856** W. CLARK *Van der Hoeven's Zool.* I. 374 Abdomen subsessile, conico-acuminate.

'subset, *sb.*¹ [f. SUBSET *v.*] An act of subsetting or subletting.

a **1722**, **1765-8** [see SUBSETTING below].

'subset, *sb.*² [f. SUB- 5 c + SET *sb.*²] A subordinate set; a set all the elements of which are contained in another set.

1902 *Encycl. Brit.* XXIX. 121/1 It may be possible to divide the set into a number of subsets, no two of which contain a common object. **1911** *Trans. Amer. Math. Soc.* XII. 285 Among such [compact] assemblages one very important class are those which have the property that the first derived set (E') of every subset (E) of (D) is closed. **1928** *Amer. Jrnl. Math.* L. 521 In studying these difficulties we are led to the introduction of a new notion of a subset of a point set being connected through the complement of the point set. **1961** M. A. K. HALLIDAY in *Word* XVII. 276 Subsets progressively differentiated as the degree of collocational likeness set as defining criterion increases. **1968** E. T. COPSON *Metric Spaces* v. 67 Let a and b be two points of a subset A of a metric space M. **1977** J. L. HARPER *Population Biol. Plants* xiii. 416 There are 45 species of *Heliconius*, each specializing on its own sub-set of *Passiflora* species. **1980** *Amer. Speech 1976* LI. 165 We cannot always extrapolate from a corpus to the language in general or even to some subset of the language.

subset (sʌb'sɛt), *v. Sc.* [f. SUB- 9 (*b*) + SET *v.*¹] *trans.* To underlet, sublet.

1681 STAIR *Inst. Law Scot.* I. xiii. 253 As the half may be sub-sett, so any other right less then the value of the half, is sustained as an Infeftment of warrandice. **1752** *Scots Mag.* Nov. 551/2 A small farm.., which he had subset at about 6 l. Sterling *per annum*. **1801** *Farmer's Mag.* Nov. 381 A missive of tack,..which made no mention of assignees,.. was..found, neither capable of being assigned, nor subset. **1806** SCOTT *Fam. Lett.* (1894) I. 35, I have subset the whole of the sheep farm. **1838** W. BELL *Dict. Law Scot.* 582 To assign or subset a lease of the ordinary endurance of nineteen years.

b. *absol.* or *intr.*

1801 *Farmer's Mag.* Nov. 379 A tack of lands does not imply a power, either to assign, or even to subset. **1838** W. BELL *Dict. Law Scot.* 582 In such leases..an express authority to assign or subset must be given.

Hence **sub'setting** *vbl. sb.*; **sub'settable** *a.*, capable of being subset.

a **1722** FOUNTAINHALL *Decis.* I. 454 The axiom against sub-setting is only against an assignment... But a sub-set is lawful, and was so found 12 March 1686. **1765-8** ERSKINE *Inst. Law Scot.* II. vi. §33 (1773) 265 It remains a doubt, whether the power of subsetting is implied in the nature of a tack, without a special clause. *Ibid.*, By a subset the principal tacksman is not changed. **1801** *Farmer's Mag.* Nov. 379 All tacks, likewise, that are to subsist for a great length of time, are also assignable, as well as subsettable.

†**'subsettle.** *Obs.* [f. SUBSET *v.* + -LE, -EL; cf. *undersettle*.] An under-tenant; = UNDERSETTLE.

1583 in J. Guest *Rotherham* (1879) 361 Andrew Robinson sub setell for a horse on the comon contrary to our custome 6d.

subseyd, variant of SUBSIDE *sb.*

subshrub ('sʌbʃrʌb). *Hort.* [f. SUB- 3 + SHRUB *sb.*¹, to render mod.L. *suffrutex* (see SUFFRUTICOSE). Cf. the earlier *undershrub*.] An undershrub, or very small shrub.

1851 GLENNY *Handbk. Fl. Gard.* 11 The double-flowered varieties..may be..treated as perennial sub-shrubs. **1886** G. NICHOLSON *Illustr. Dict. Gardening* II. 168/1 Hypericum... An extensive genus..of greenhouse or hardy, evergreen or deciduous, herbs, shrubs, or sub-shrubs. **1957** R. E. WOODSON et al. *Rauwolfia* i. 11 The smallest species appears to be..a truly rhizomatous subshrub only six inches tall. **1980** *Country Life* 13 Mar. 790/1 Among sub-shrubs profitably treated as herbaceous and cut back to the ground now is mint-scented, sun-basking *Elsholtzia stauntonii*.

So **'subshrubby** *a.*, resembling a subshrub, suffruticose.

1843 *Florist's Jrnl.* (1846) IV. 140 It is a dwarf and compact-growing plant, apparently of an evergreen herbaceous or subshrubby habit. **1851** GLENNY *Handbk. Fl. Gard.* 67 Mathiola incana, the queen stock, is a sub-shrubby kind. **1856** DELAMER *Fl. Gard.* 107 The terms 'sub-shrubby plants' and 'suffruticose trees' have been invented, to designate those individuals which occupy intermediate positions in the long series of the vegetable kingdom.

†**subsidary**, *a. Obs.* Erron. f. SUBSIDIARY.

1628 H. BURTON *Israel's Fast* Ded. p. v, Who doe more hinder or preiudice the King in his necessarie and Royall Subsidarie Supplyes, then such Factours? **1688** HOLME *Armoury* III. iv. 195/2 Suffragan or Subsidary Bishops.

†**subsidate**, *v. Obs. rare*⁻¹. [irreg. f. L. *subsīdĕre* to SUBSIDE.] *intr.* To sink in.

1653 R. SANDERS *Physiogn.* 173 The eyes, being humble, subsidate.

So **subsi'dation**, a depression.

1838 *Fraser's Mag.* XVII. 24 The protuberances or subsidations of the cranium.

†**subside**, *sb. Obs.* Also -sede, -seyd, -syde. [a. F. *subside*, ad. L. *subsidium* SUBSIDY.] = SUBSIDY.

c **1450** *Brut* II. 329 He axed..a grete subsede to be graunted to hem, for defendyng of hem and of his reame. **1474** *Rental Bk. Cupar-Angus* (1879) I. 215 The byschoppis subseyd at his fyrst entre. **1502** ARNOLDE *Chron.* (1811) 193 The Rate of the Kyngis Custum and Subside of Marchaundises registred in the Escheker. **1542** *Yatton Churchw. Acc.* (Som. Rec. Soc.) 156 Payd for the Kyngs subsyde xiij s. iiij d. **1553** *Rec. St. Mary at Hill* (1904) 54 Aqvittaunce..for the Subsede of the Church for the Svmma of iij li vj s.

subside (səb'saɪd), *v.* [ad. L. *subsīdĕre*, f. *sub*- SUB- 2 + *sīdĕre* to sit down.]

1. *intr.* To sink down, fall to the bottom, precipitate. Also with *down*.

1681 tr. *Willis' Rem. Med. Wks.* Vocab., *Subside*, to sink down, or fall to the bottom. **1696** WHISTON *Th. Earth* III. (1722) 278 Their Shells were buried among the other Bodies or Masses which subsided down. **1721** BRADLEY *Philos. Acc. Wks. Nat.* 9 Bodies of no more weight than Shells, or Teeth of Fishes, would subside themselves down to the bottom. **1765** *Museum Rust.* IV. 98 Chalk laid on clay will, we know, subside. **1857** MILLER *Elem. Chem., Org.* (1862) ii. §1. 80 The precipitate is allowed to subside. **1877** HUXLEY *Physiogr.* 133 The gravel is the first to fall; then the sand subsides, and finally the mud settles down.

2. To sink to a low or lower level, *esp.* of liquids or soil sinking to the normal level; (of valleys) to form a depression; (of a swelling or something inflated) to be reduced so as to become flat.

1706 PHILLIPS (ed. Kersey) s.v., The Streams Subside from their Banks. **1729** T. COOKE *Tales*, etc. 46 Where shady Mountains rise, and Vales subside. **1731** ARBUTHNOT *Aliments* II. ii. (1735) 28 Small Air-Bladders..capable to be inflated by the Admission of Air, and to subside at the Expulsion of it. **1765** A. DICKSON *Treat. Agric.* (ed. 2) 151 When the earth hath fully subsided, and become firm and solid [etc.]. **1796** MORSE *Amer. Geog.* I. 609 The mountains converge into a single ridge, which..subsides into plain country. **1816** J. SMITH *Panorama Sci. & Art* II. 76 On pouring a quantity of water into one limb, the water will rise in the other, and when left undisturbed, will subside at an equal height in both. **1817** SHELLEY *Rev. Islam* VII. xxvii, The Eagle..The eager plumes subsided on his throat. **1844** H. STEPHENS *Bk. Farm* I. 513 A little [earth] is left elevated immediately over the drain, to subside to the usual level of the ground. **1863** LYELL *Antiq. Man* 34 The waters of the Nile had subsided. **1885** *Law Rep. 10 Prob. Div.* 87 A small blister, which subsided in a day or two.

b. Of a mass of earth, etc.: To fall or give way as the result of dynamic disturbance, etc.

1773 *Cook's Voy.* II. xiv. (1842) I. 329 A large tract of country, of which it was part, subsided by some convulsion of nature. **1840** LYELL *Princ. Geol.* III. xvi. (ed. 6) III. 345 Buildings which have at different times subsided beneath the level of the sea. **1879** *A. R. Wallace's Australasia* i. 11 The bottom of the ocean is itself even now subsiding more and more. **1884** *Pall Mall Gaz.* 29 July 5/1 We suspect that when the great basin of Taupo comes to be explored by the sounding lead, an extinct volcano, crater and all, will be found subsided in its midst.

c. Of persons: To sink down *into* or *on to* a chair, etc.

1879 F. W. ROBINSON *Coward Consc.* I. vi, She subsided into the easy-chair. **1888** 'J. S. WINTER' *Bootle's Childr.* ix, The subject of the joke subsided on to a chair where she sat giggling.

3. Of the sea, wind, storm: To sink to rest, abate.

a **1721** PRIOR *Tale from Boccace* 55 Wks. 1907 II. 343 Not Waves and winds Subside more sudden. **1740** PITT *Æneid* VII. 9 The Sea subsiding, and the Tempests o'er. **1839** THIRLWALL *Greece* xlix. VI. 168 The wind had already subsided. **1878** BROWNING *La Saisiaz* 54 Beneath where.. soft the tree-top swell subsides.

4. Of strong feeling, excitement, clamour, and the like: To cease from agitation, fall *into* a state of quiet or of less violence or activity.

a **1700** EVELYN *Diary* Sept. 1644, Our desire of revenge had by this time subsided. **1772** TOPLADY in R. Palmer *Bk. Praise* (1866) 436 Soon shall our doubts and fears Subside at His control. **1778** BURNEY *Evelina* xxxiii. (1791) I. 177 Her anger now subsiding into grief. **1783** CRABBE *Village* II. 183 Cease then that grief, and let those tears subside. **1824** SCOTT *St. Ronan's* iv, The clamour which attends the removal of dinner from a public room had subsided. **1855** *Poultry Chron.* III. 170 Buying and selling fowls has subsided from an excitement to a natural business transaction. **1863** GEO. ELIOT *Romola* xxix, They parted with softening, dropping voices, subsiding into silence. **1892** 'F. ANSTEY' *Voces Pop.* Ser. II. 156 The hubbub gradually subsides.

b. Of a condition: To die down, pass away, wear off. Of an action: To be discontinued.

1751 CHESTERF. *Lett.* cclviii, Your fencing likewise..may subside for the summer. **1762** T. MORTIMER *Ev. Man Own Broker* (ed. 5) 20 The probability of the premium (given on any Stock) totally subsiding. **1780** in *Lett. Earl Malmesbury* (1870) I. 460, I shall go when the novelty is a little subsided. **1813** SHELLEY *Q. Mab* III. 60 Too soon The slumber of intemperance subsides.

5. Of persons: To fall *into* an inactive or less active or efficient state.

1728 YOUNG *Love of Fame* VII. 196 His swelling soul subsides to native peace. **1847** MRS. GORE *Castles in Air* xix, I am not sure but I would rather live in the King's Bench.. than subside into a country Squire. **1865** DICKENS *Mut. Fr.* III. xv, 'That was well done!' panted Bella, slackening in the next street, and subsiding into a walk. **1885** *Manch. Exam.* 22 June 5/3 After a very promising career..he has subsided into a quiet and indifferent attitude.

b. To cease from activity; *esp.* to lapse into silence.

1871 *Cincinnati Comm.* Apr. (Schele de Vere *Americanisms* 638) Thereupon the doughty General subsided, but it would be a great mistake to suppose that he will remain silent. **1880** *Daily News* 1 July, Being told he must keep quiet or be arrested he subsided.

6. To be merged *in*; to pass *into*. *rare.*

1781 SIMES *Milit. Guide* (ed. 3) 4 Politeness should exceed authority, and the Officer subside in the gentleman. **1862** STANLEY *Jew. Ch.* I. xii. 267 The old life was..never entirely to subside into the new.

†**7.** *trans.* To cause to sink in. *Obs. rare.*

1650 BULWER *Anthropomet.* 75 The roots of that prominencie which subsides the apple of the eye.

subsided (səbˈsaɪdɪd), *ppl. a.* [f. prec. + -ED[1].] In senses of the verb: Sunk; precipitated; quieted.

1733 TULL *Horse-hoeing Husb.* xiii. 163 The Earth sinking away from the Roots, leaves the bottom of the Stalk higher than the subsided Ground. **1753** RICHARDSON *Grandison* VI. ix, When the contents are too much for me, I lay them down; and resume them, as my subsided joy will allow. **1758** *Elaboratory laid open* 63 Let the clear water be then poured back, into the first vessel, with great care not to disturb the subsided powder. **1839** URE *Dict. Arts* 1274 The muriate of copper is to be decanted from the subsided gypsum. **1844** H. STEPHENS *Bk. Farm* I. 504 All the sods just fill up the subsided drain. **1851** *Corr. Lady Lyttelton* (1912) 410, I.. woke with a pleasant subsided feeling.

subsidence (səbˈsaɪdəns, ˈsʌbsɪdəns). [ad. L. *subsīdentia* sediment, f. *subsīdĕre* to SUBSIDE: see -ENCE. Cf. It. *sussidenza* sediment.]

1. A sediment, precipitate. ? *Obs.*

1646 SIR T. BROWNE *Pseud. Ep.* 92 A Chalky earth, which ..steeped in water, affoordeth a cream..on the top, and a grosse subsidence at the bottome. **1650** VAUGHAN *Anthroposophia* 15 The Earth was an impure, Sulphureous subsidence, or *Caput mortuum* of the Creation. **1847** CLARKE in *Jrnl. R. Agric. Soc.* VIII. I. 109 The soil of the whole is the subsidence of a muddy water. **1890** GOULD *New Med. Dict.*, *Subsidence*,..in pharmacy, the sediment falling from a liquid.

2. The settling (of solid or heavy things) to the bottom, formation of sediment, precipitation.

1656 BLOUNT *Glossogr.*, *Subsidence*, a resting or setling in the bottom. **1696** WHISTON *Th. Earth* III. (1722) 278 The same Law..was also observ'd in the subsidence of the Shells of Fishes. **1765** *Museum Rust.* IV. 98 What I have written on the subsidence of chalk, and the simple method of recovering that almost-lost manure. **1799** *Monthly Rev.* XXX. 150 A force of subsidence, the natural consequence of gravity,..has produced similar effects. **1800** HENRY *Epit. Chem.* (1808) 125 Separate the liquid part by filtration or by subsidence. **1857** MILLER *Elem. Chem., Org.* (1862) iv. §1. 259 The clear oil is afterwards agitated.., again clarified by subsidence [etc.].

3. The sinking (of liquids) to a normal or lower level; also, a fall in the level of ground.

1669 BOYLE *Contin. New Exper.* xix. 62 The Quick-silver that before stood at 29 inches..would fall so low as to rest at 9 or 10 inches, (for once I measur'd the Subsidence beneath its former Elevation). **1837** SYD. SMITH *Wks.* (1850) 641 One of those Shem-Ham-and-Japhet buggies—made on Mount Ararat soon after the subsidence of the waters. **1839** G. BIRD *Nat. Philos.* 104 The subsidence of mercury in the barometer, as we ascend mountains..affords valuable data for calculating their vertical height. **1863** HAWTHORNE *Our Old Home* (1879) 104 The country..is a succession of the gentlest swells and subsidences. **1865** LIVINGSTONE *Zambesi* xxi. 429 Snags..left in the channel on the sudden subsidence of the water.

b. A fall in rhythm or accent.

1824 LANDOR *Imag. Conv.*, *Æschines & Phocion* Wks. 1853 I. 26/2 Concentrated are his arguments,..easy the swell and subsidence of his periods, his dialect purely attic. **1851** HAWTHORNE *Ho. Sev. Gables* x, He delighted in the swell and subsidence of the rhythm, and the happily-recurring rhyme.

4. A sinking *into* inactivity or quiescence.

a. of feelings, of a disturbance, of the attacks of a disease, etc.

1754 WARBURTON *Serm.* 27 Oct., Wks. 1788 V. 519 The mind..being, by the subdual or subsidence of the more violent passions, now become attentive to, and sensible of, the soft and gentle impressions of tranquillity. **1847** DICKENS *Haunted Man* ii. 70 A decided subsidence of her animosity. **1864** LOWELL *Fireside Trav.* 256 So these people burst out..into a noise and fury... And the subsidence is as sudden. **1890** GOULD *New Med. Dict.*, *Subsidence*,..in pathology, the gradual cessation and disappearance of an attack of disease.

b. Of physical phenomena or actions.

1731 ARBUTHNOT *Aliments* II. ii. (1735) 29 The alternate Motion of those Air-Bladders, whose Surfaces are by turns freed from mutual Contact, and by a sudden Subsidence meet again by the ingress and egress of the Air. **18..** *Edin. Rev.* (Seager), Subsidence of waves. **1860** TYNDALL *Glac.* I. 81 The subsidence of this action [throbbing] was always the signal for further advance. **1864** LOWELL *Fireside Trav.* 292 We awaited her subsidence as that of a shower. **1879** *Cassell's Techn. Educ.* I. 215 A second..fermentation takes place..; its subsidence diminishes the bulk of the wine.

c. Sinking into decline or decay.

1856 MERIVALE *Rom. Emp.* xxxiii. (1865) IV. 67 It was about the period of the Gracchi that this subsidence of the old aristocracy of birth began first to be remarked.

5. (orig. *Geol.*) A gradual lowering or settling down of a portion of the earth due to dynamic causes, mining operations, or the like.

1802 PLAYFAIR *Illustr. Hutton. Th.* 449 Though a local subsidence, or settling of the ground, could hardly account for this change,..yet a subsidence that has extended to a great tract..will agree very well with the appearances. **1854** MURCHISON *Siluria* vi. 131 The rock is..subject to slides or subsidences. **1856** PAGE *Adv. Text-bk. Geol.* ii. 39 Subsidences occasioned by earthquake and volcanic convulsions. **1912** *Standard* 20 Sept. 6/4 Streets and buildings..are being damaged by subsidences due to disused underground workings.

transf. **1861** *Morning Post* 27 Nov., They reached the door, but found it fixed by the subsidence of the walls.

6. *attrib.*, applied to vessels in which liquids are put in order to precipitate their suspended solid matter, as ***subsidence reservoir, vat.***

1858 SIMMONDS *Dict. Trade*, *Subsidence-vat*, a dyer's settling-vat. **1892** *Pall Mall Gaz.* 9 Sept. 2/1 All the companies supplying river water..have subsidence reservoirs, into which the water is first turned for the purpose of allowing such of the suspended solid matter as will to settle.

subsidency (sʌbˈsaɪdənsɪ, ˈsʌbsɪdənsɪ). Now *rare.* [ad. L. *subsīdentia*: see prec.] = prec.

1655-87 H. MORE *App. Antid.* (1712) 215 Bodies..in a confused agitation may very likely go together, as we see done..in the subsidency of this dreggish part of the World, the Earth. *a* **1661** FULLER *Worthies, Surrey* (1662) III. 79 Those who judiciously impute the sudden subsidency of the Earth in the interstice aforesaid to some underground hollowness. **1691** RAY *Creation* II. (1704) 261 So as to cause a Subsidency of the Lungs by lessening the cavity there. **1779** *Phil. Trans.* LXIX. 597 A strong and regular current in a river is the best of all means..for preventing the formation of banks in the bed by the subsidency of mud, &c. **1811** PINKERTON *Petral.* II. 216 Throughout all the space many fissures appeared and subsidencies of the ground. **1845** S. JUDD *Margaret* II. iii, In the subsidency and departure of love, the moral system is revolutionized.

subsident (sʌbˈsaɪdənt, ˈsʌbsɪdənt), *a. rare.* [ad. L. *subsīdens, -entem*, pr. pple. of *subsīdĕre* to SUBSIDE.] Precipitating.

1889 PENNELL *Fishing* 415 By subsequent treatment of the precipitated and subsident metals.

†**subsiˈdereal**, *a. Obs. rare*$^{-1}$. [SUB- 1 a.] Subcelestial, sublunary.

1636 in *Ann. Dubrensia* (1877) 57 This subsideriall rundle.

†**subˈsidial**, *a. Obs. rare*$^{-1}$. [f. SUBSIDY *sb.* + -AL[1].] = SUBSIDIARY *a.* 3 c.

1798 PENNANT *Hindoostan* II. 13 A subsidial ally of the English, who receive from its monarch the annual sum of £160,000.

subsidiarily (səbˈsɪdɪərɪlɪ), *adv.* [f. SUBSIDIARY *a.* and *sb.* + -LY[2].] In a subsidiary manner or position; subordinately, secondarily. (occas. const. *to.*)

1603 FLORIO *Montaigne* I. xxxii, At first sight he addresseth himselfe to this meane, which they never embrace but subsidiarily. **1625** *Docum. Impeach. Dk. Buckhm.* (Camden Soc.) 209 Three onely should speak, subsidiarily one to another. **1694** FALLE *Jersey* iv. 112 This Court was first brought in Subsidiarily, when Causes grew too numerous for Catel. **1818** H. T. COLEBROOKE *Obligations* 141 He is not bound subsidiarily for the remainder, in the event of insolvency of his coheirs. **1852** BROWNING *Shelley's Lett.* Introd. Ess. (1881) 7 Subsidiarily to the human interest of his work. **1897** MAITLAND *Domesday Bk. & Beyond* 148 The hundred being but subsidiarily liable.

subsidiarity (sʌbsɪdɪˈærɪtɪ). [tr. G. *subsidiarität* (1931, paraphrasing Pope Pius XI in *Rundschreiben über die gesellschaftliche Ordnung* (*Quadragesimo Anno* §80); cf. F. *subsidiarité* and SUBSIDIARY *a.*] The quality of being subsidiary; *spec.* the principle that a central authority should have a subsidiary function, performing only those tasks which cannot be performed effectively at a more immediate or local level.

1936 B. W. DEMPSEY tr. *O. von Nell-Breuning's Reorganization of Social Econ.* x. 206 The Pope repeats the same statement..: 'Of its very nature, the true aim of all social activity should be to help individual members of the social body, but never to destroy or absorb them.' This is the frequently mentioned and famous principle of *Subsidiarity of Social Activities*, also called the principle of *Subsidiarity of Associations*, a fundamental principle of Christian social doctrine. **1964** S. ATTANASIO tr H. Küng's *Structures of Church* vii. 215 Is there a *criterion* with respect to the exercise of the papal pastoral office in the individual dioceses?.. Post-Vatican theology developed a criterion: This is the *principle of subsidiarity* which, according to Pius XII, 'is valid for social life in all its organizations, and also for the life of the *Church* without prejudice to her hierarchical structure'. **1967** *New Catholic Encycl.* XIII. 762/1 The principle of subsidiarity is broadly concerned with the limits of the right and duty of the public authority to intervene in social and economic affairs. **1976** J. P. WOGAMAN *Christian Method of Moral Judgment* v. 142 According to the doctrine of subsidiarity, as developed in various papal encyclicals, social problems should be dealt with at the most immediate (or local) level consistent with their solution. **1980** J. H. WHYTE *Church & State in Mod. Ireland* (ed. 2) vi. 163 Concepts such as vocationalism, the principle of subsidiarity, and the danger of excessive State control **1982** *Times* 18 Sept. 7/5 The 'principle of subsidiarity'—a meaningless or even misleading phrase in English—is being discussed in the European Parliament in connection with eventual revision of the Treaty of Rome. It is defined to mean that the European Community's activities should be limited to those which are better performed in common than by member states individually.

subsidiary (səbˈsɪdɪərɪ), *a.* and *sb.* [ad. L. *subsidiārius*, f. *subsidium*: see SUBSIDIUM. Cf. F. *subsidiaire*, It. *sussidiario*, Sp., Pg. *subsidiario.*]

A. *adj.* **1. a.** Serving to help, assist, or supplement; furnishing assistance or supplementary supplies; auxiliary, tributary, supplementary. (Chiefly of things.)

1543 JOYE *G. J. confuteth Winch. Art.* fol. ij, Iustified by thonelye faith in him, and by nothing els as by any subsydiary attaynment..vnto this full iustificacion in christe. **1613** R. C. *Table Alph.*, *Subsidiarie*, that is giuen or set to aide another. **1615** CROOKE *Body of Man* 74 A bloud-like vapor which returneth into the veines, and so becommeth for want of better, a subsidiarie nourishment of the partes. **1627** DONNE *Serm.* xliv. (1640) 442 In these subsidiary gods, these occasional gods, there could be no Omnipotence, no Almightinesse. **1688** HOLME *Armoury* III. iii. 64/1 A Suffragan Bishop, or Subsidiary Bishop. **1731** ARBUTHNOT *Aliments* VI. viii. (1735) 235 Howsoever they [*sc.* bitter Substances] may be acceptable to some one Part, that is..that they are a sort of subsidiary Gall. **1776** ADAM SMITH *W.N.* v. iii. II. 545 [A sinking fund] is a subsidiary fund always at hand to be mortgaged in aid of any other doubtful fund. **1805-17** R. JAMESON *Char. Min.* 159 The decrements on these last faces are considered as subsidiary, to favour the action of the principal decrement. **1832** BREWSTER *Nat. Magic* v. (1833) 110 The inflammation..of the ignited gas will be sustained by these four subsidiary flames. **1864** BOWEN *Logic* vi. 150 Concerning the nature of the objects delivered by the Subsidiary Faculties. **1872** YEATS *Techn. Hist. Comm.* 211 We must mention the development of printing and the subsidiary art of paper-making. **1903** *Daily Chron.* 26 Oct. 3/5 Bishop Subsidiary of Caerleon.

b. Const. *to.*

1663 WATERHOUSE *Comm. Fortescue's De Laud. Legum Angliæ* 398 The Commoners of England being landed, are so subsidiary to their Princes and Laws in all kinds of aide and duty. **1679** EVELYN *Sylva* (ed. 3) To Rdr. A 3 An infinity of solitary, and loose Experiments subsidiary to it. *a* **1740** WATERLAND *Enq. conc. Inf. Commun.* v, As soon as Baptism became impaired, the Use of the Eucharist ought to come in as subsidiary, or supplemental to it. **1836** KEBLE *Serm.* viii. (1848) 200 A system of tradition, subsidiary to the Scriptures, might yet exist in the commonwealth or city of God. **1856** FROUDE *Hist. Eng.* (1858) I. v. 380 This was his first object, to which every other was subsidiary. **1868** M. PATTISON *Academ. Org.* v. 122 The College is subsidiary to the University. **1875** GLADSTONE *Glean.* VI. xxxix. 130 No ritual is too much, provided it is subsidiary to the inner work of worship.

c. Technical uses.

subsidiary cells (Bot.): certain epidermal cells which are less thickened or situated lower than the guard-cells which they surround. ***subsidiary coin***: coins of the lower denominations; *U.S.* silver coinage of lower denomination than the dollar. ***subsidiary company***, a company controlled by a holding company. Cf. B 2 c (*b*). ***subsidiary goal*** (Polo): see quot. 1899. ***subsidiary quantity*** or ***symbol*** (Math.): see quot. 1842.

1842 *Penny Cycl.* XXIII. 196 *Subsidiary*. A quantity or symbol is so called when it is not essentially a part of a problem, but is introduced to help in the solution. The term is particularly applied to angles, since the trigonometrical tables give a great power over their management, which causes their frequent introduction. **1863** FAWCETT *Pol. Econ.* III. xv. (1876) 480 Our copper and silver money are to be regarded as subsidiary coinage. **1884** BOWER & SCOTT *De Bary's Phaner.* 45 The superficial stomata first developed are surrounded by several partitioned zones of subsidiary cells. **1899** *J. M. Brown's Polo* 377 (Badm. Libr.), A subsidiary goal is obtained in the same way as a true goal, except that to score a subsidiary goal the ball must pass between the subsidiary goal mark and the goal-post which is nearest to it. Subsidiary goals are to be measured 11 feet from each goal-post on the outside. **1916** F. G. UNDERHAY *Income Tax* 272 (*Index*), Subsidiary company. **1928** *Daily Mail* 25 July 18/6 The net dividends received from the Subsidiary Companies amounted to £24,808 1s. 11d. **1970** M. GREENER *Penguin Dict. Commerce* 170 A subsidiary company must state in its accounts the name of its ultimate holding company and the country where this is incorporated.

d. Of a stream: Tributary. Similarly of a valley.

1834 PRINGLE *Afr. Sk.* vii. 246 We slept one night at the mouth of a subsidiary dell. **1837** CARLYLE *Fr. Rev.* III. II. i, All manner of subsidiary streams and brooks of bitterness flowing in. **1845** McCULLOCH *Acc. Brit. Empire* (1854) I. 39 The subsidiary streams that fall into the Trent. **1914** SIR J. FRENCH *Disp.* 8 Oct. in *Times* 19 Oct. 9/6 The general plateau on the south is divided by a subsidiary valley of much the same character, down which the small River Vesle flows to the main stream.

2. With the notion of helping or supplementing weakened or obscured: Subordinate, secondary.

1831 CARLYLE *Sart. Res.* (1858) 171 The others are only subsidiary species, or slight varieties. **1867** J. HOGG *Microsc.* I. ii. 68 When any system of waves meets with an obstacle, subsidiary systems of undulation will be formed. **1875** WHITNEY *Life Lang.* ix. 166 Its legion of subsidiary dialectic forms. **1883** R. H. SCOTT *Elem. Meteorol.* 380 Lesser eddies are found on the outskirts of the original depression... At times these latter 'secondary', 'subsidiary', or 'satellite' depressions, as they are called, develop greater energy than their primaries.

3. †**a.** Consisting of a subsidy or subsidies.

1608 WILLET *Hexapla Exod.* Ded. 1 That honourable assemblie hath..presented to your Maiestie a subsidiarie beneuolence. **1637** SALTONSTALL *Eusebius' Constantine* 7 The most royall Emperour after their departure, summoned those againe that had sent in their Subsidiary money. **1640** CULPEPPER in Rushw. *Hist. Coll.* (1692) I. 34 As soon as the House was setled, a Subsidiary Aid and Supply was propounded.

b. Depending on a subsidy or subsidies: in ***subsidiary treaty*** (cf. SUBSIDY 3 b, 4).

1755 H. WALPOLE *Lett.* (1840) III. 158 All the world revolted against subsidiary treaties. **1902** *Encycl. Brit.* (ed. 10) XXIX. 453/2 Lord Wellesley introduced that system of subsidiary treaties which has played so important a part in the expansion of British dominion.

c. Maintained or retained by subsidies.

1802 C. JAMES *Milit. Dict.*, *Subsidiary Troops*, troops of one nation assisting those of another for a given sum or subsidy. **1864** BURTON *Scot. Abr.* I. iii. 134 Both the British countries were in some measure subsidiary and protected states.

B. *sb.*

†**1.** The levy of a subsidy. *Obs. rare*$^{-1}$.

1592 GREENE *Upst. Courtier* (1871) 4 Their fathers were not above three pounds in the Kings books at a Subsidiary.

2. a. A subsidiary thing; something which furnishes assistance or additional supplies; an aid, auxiliary. Now *rare.*

1603 FLORIO *Montaigne* II. xii. 255 These considerations ought to be applied and employed to our beleefe, but as Subsidiaries. *a* 1660 HAMMOND *Serm.* (Phil. iv. 13) Wks. 1684 IV. 573 Which deceitful consideration drew on Pelagius himself, that was first only for nature, at last to take in one after another, five Subsidiaries more. 1697 EVELYN *Numismata* vii. 251 Images of the Gods and Goddesses, with other Subsidiaries. *a* 1706 —— *Mem.* (1819) II. 206, I.. shall not be able to do it with any satisfaction, unless yr Lop favour me with the com'unication of the subsidiaries in yr cabinet. 1796 BURNEY *Mem. Metastasio* I. 327 If, in despight of so many subsidiaries, you should be of a different opinion. 1808 HAN. MORE *Cœlebs* xxiii, As to the lectures.. they may be doubtless made very useful subsidiaries to instruction. 1824 L. MURRAY *Engl. Gram.* (ed. 5) I. 64 All other sorts of words must be regarded as subsidiaries.

b. An assistant.

1807 ROBINSON *Archæol. Græca* I. xiii. 58 The number of senators was again augmented... To these fifty a similar number of subsidiaries was added. 1881 *Blackw. Mag.* Apr. 507 The building is occupied by three priests and a few subsidiaries.

c. Technical uses: (*a*) *Mus.* A theme of inferior importance, subordinate to the first or second subject. (*b*) *Stock Exch.* A subsidiary company. (*c*) *Polo.* A subsidiary goal.

1883 *Grove's Dict. Mus.* s.v., In some cases a Subsidiary acquires so much importance in the working out as to rank as a third subject. 1898 *Westm. Gaz.* 22 Mar. 8/2 The whole question of the value of Randfontein lies.. in the way its numerous subsidiaries turn out. 1901 *Ibid.* 14 Jan. 9/1 The shares of the Corporation, which then stood at 1*s.* $1\frac{1}{2}$*d.*, now stand at 6*d.*, and it wants its shareholders to take the shares of these subsidiaries and provide more hard cash. 1903 *Daily Chron.* 27 Jan. 5/6 Three goals two subsidiaries to six goals two subsidiaries.

†**3.** A subsidized state. *Obs.*

1756 *Monitor* No. 30. I. 275 The immense treasure paid for those subsidiaries, which by their treaties are engaged to cover Hanover, at the sole expence of Great Britain.

subsiding (səb'saɪdɪŋ), *vbl. sb.* [f. SUBSIDE *v.* + -ING[1].] = SUBSIDENCE.

1672 BOYLE *New Exper. Flame & Air* 13 The subsiding of the Mercury. *a* 1676 HALE *Prim. Orig. Man.* II. vii. 190 Strabo.. attributes those great Floods and Inundations to the elevation and subsiding of the *Moles terrestris.* 1741 MONRO *Anat. Bones* (ed. 3) 17 A regular alternate Elevation and subsiding, or an apparent Pulsation. 1823 J. BADCOCK *Dom. Amusem.* 151 Mixing a small quantity of alum with the water accelerates the subsiding of the starch.

b. *attrib.* (cf. SUBSIDENCE 6.)

1892 *Pall Mall Gaz.* 9 Sept. 1/3 Subsiding beds were provided so that the fluid portion of the river was alone supplied to the consumers.

subsiding (səb'saɪdɪŋ), *ppl. a.* [f. SUBSIDE *v.* + -ING[2].] That subsides, in various senses of the verb.

1646 SIR T. BROWNE *Pseud. Ep.* 68 The subsiding powder dryed, retaines some magneticall vertue. 1694 SALMON *Bate's Dispens.* (1713) 353/1 Edulcorate the subsiding Pouder, by many affusions of fair Water. 1700 DRYDEN *Iliad* I. 711 With Terror trembled Heav'ns subsiding Hill. 1769 E. BANCROFT *Guiana* 279 The liquor is decanted from the subsiding bread, and drank. 1779 *Mirror* No. 66 Specifying .. the subsiding state of her affections towards them. 1839 DARWIN *Voy. Nat.* xxii. 561 That class of widely-encircling reefs, which indicate a subsiding land. 1889 LD. LYTTON *Let. to W. Ward* 25 Sept., The after effects of its subsiding eddies.

‖**subsidium** (səb'sɪdɪəm). Pl. sub'sidia. [L.: see SUBSIDY.] A help, aid, subsidy.

1640 in Rushw. *Hist. Coll.* (1692) I. 50 It was reasonable that in *Subsidium* they should contribute some help to their Neighbours. *a* 1676 HALE *Prim. Orig. Man.* 170 If left to it self without the continued *Subsidium* and Influence of the Divine Providence. 1729 SWIFT *Let. to Bolingbroke* 31 Oct., Because I cannot be a great Lord, I would acquire what is a kind of *subsidium.* 1817 T. L. PEACOCK *Melincourt* II. 182 They have at all times a little more than they actually need, a subsidium for age or sickness. 1878 M. PATTISON in *Encycl. Brit.* VIII. 517/2 Even if Erasmus had at his disposal the MSS. subsidia for forming a text.

subsidize ('sʌbsɪdaɪz), *v.* [f. SUBSIDY + -IZE.]

1. *trans.* **a.** To make a payment for the purpose of securing the services of (mercenary or alien troops).

1795 SEWARD *Anecd.* (1796) III. 382 Lord Chatham was obliged to call in to its aid the mercenary troops of other Nations: these.. he subsidised with a liberal.. hand. 1803 WELLINGTON in Gurw. *Desp.* (1835) II. 223 The latter has agreed to subsidize one company of artillery and two battalions of native infantry. 1838 PRESCOTT *Ferd. & Is.* II. xiv, He obtained a small supply of men from his Italian allies, and subsidized a corps of 8000 Swiss. 1878 LECKY *Eng. in 18th Cent.* I. iii. 350 An army of about 44000 Swedes, Danes, and Hessians was subsidised.

b. To furnish (a country, nation, princes) with a subsidy for the purpose of securing their assistance or their neutrality in war.

a 1797 H. WALPOLE *Mem. Reign Geo. III* (1845) I. vii. 105 Little Princes are subsidized, when not worthy of reciprocation. 1805 *Spirit Publ. Jrnls.* IX. 1, I have sought relief in hearing the censure of Administration for subsidizing the Continent. 1860 L. HARCOURT *Diaries G. Rose* I. 66 To subsidize one power against another.

2. *transf.* **a.** To secure the services of by payment or bribery.

1815 W. H. IRELAND *Scribbleomania* 26 *note*, Deigning to subsidize a venal pen in order to throw a gloss over the flagrant dereliction. 1871 *Daily News* 6 Nov., It was.. to abstain.. from subsidising the press. 1899 KIPLING *Stalky* 66 The three.. stood to attention.. in full view of all the visitors, to whom fags, subsidised for that end, pointed them out as victims of Prout's tyranny.

fig. 1862 F. HALL *Hindu Philos. Syst.* 122 In its operations, it [*sc.* the soul] subsidizes all the sense-organs.

b. To furnish funds for (a scheme or course of action). *rare.*

1858 FROUDE *Hist. Eng.* III. xvi. 431 Like so many of the northern abbots, he might have been hoarding a fund to subsidize insurrection.

c. To support by grants of money: now *esp.* of the government or some central authority contributing to the upkeep of an institution, etc.

1828 SOUTHEY in *Q. Rev.* XXXVIII. 592 For the British Government to pay the Roman Catholic clergy would be to subsidize the Court of Rome against itself. 1871 *Pall Mall Gaz.* 23 Aug. 10 M. Thiers' unhappy stroke of financial ingenuity actually subsidizes the detested Teuton. 1876 J. GRANT *Burgh Sch. Scot.* II. iii. 129 In several places, we find the councils actually subsidizing adventure schools. 1885 *Manch. Exam.* 17 Feb. 5/2 The schools.. have been subsidised by grants from the county magistrates. 1911 *War Dept. Provis. Subsidy Scheme* 1 The full terms under which the War Department will subsidize vehicles.

Hence **'subsidized, 'subsidizing** *vbl. sb.* and *ppl. a.*; **subsidi'zation, 'subsidizer.**

1817 COLERIDGE *Biog. Lit.* (1907) I. 142 The abandonment of the subsidizing policy, so far at least as neither to goad or bribe the continental courts into war. 1870 W. R. GREG *Pol. Probl.* 29 The encouragers and subsidisers of all other states through their crises of despondency and destitution. 1872 *Daily News* 25 Mar., Every country has its subsidized lines of steamers, which carry mails to all parts of the world. 1881 *Athenæum* 27 Aug. 274/1 The subsidizing of political benefit societies by well-to-do Conservatives. 1884 *Pall Mall Gaz.* 27 May 5/2 He.. put an extinguisher upon all hopes of a conference with the subsidizing nations, or the introduction of a countervailing tariff. 1907 *Daily Chron.* 1 Jan. 5/5 The statement as to Mr. Schiff's subsidisation of the alleged Galveston scheme is inaccurate. 1908 *Athenæum* 31 Oct. 545/3 It was about to cease as a subsidized publication of the French Government.

†**sub'siduous,** *a. Obs. rare*[−1]. [irreg. f. L. *subsidium* SUBSIDY *sb.* or F. *subside* SUBSIDE *sb.*: see -UOUS.] Assisting, subsidiary.

1490 CAXTON *Eneydos* xix. 71/29 Ye subsiduous [orig. F. *subcide*] modre that hath made the to be norysshed.. wyth the mylke of the tygres of Yrcanye.

subsidy ('sʌbsɪdɪ), *sb.* Also 4–7 **subsidie,** 5 **-sidee, -sydye,** 5–6 **-sidye,** 5–7 **-sedye,** 6 **subsedy, -sydy, -sidey, -sidwe** (?). [a. AF. *subsidie* = OF. (and AF.) *subside*, ad. L. *subsidium.* Cf. Pr. *subsidi*, It. *sussidio*, Sp., Pg. *subsidio.*]

1. Help, aid, assistance. Also with *a* and *pl. Obs.* or *arch.*

1387 TREVISA *Higden* (Rolls) III. 469 Everych [element of the body] schulde.. ȝeve us special helpe and subsidie by his owne dispensacioun. 1432–50 tr. *Higden* (Rolls) II. 189 A thowmbe in the ryȝhte foote of Pyrrhus kynge, the towchenge of whom ȝafe subsidy ageyne venom. 1492 RYMAN *Poems* lxxxi. 3 in *Archiv Stud. neu. Spr.* LXXXIX. 250 Petir and Paule and seintis alle.. For subsidie to you we calle. ? 1533 FRITH (*title*) An other boke against Rastel named the subsedye or bulwark to his fyrst boke. 1553 LATIMER *Serm. Lord's Prayer* vii. (1562) 53 [45] To cry vnto god.. for a subsidie against this.. enemy. 1557 PAYNELL *Barclay's Jugurth* 52 On the right winge.. he ordeyned as it were a forward enforced with a threfold subsidie or socour. 1639 FULLER *Holy War* IV. viii. 180 Before he began his voyage he craved a subsidie of prayers from the Monks of S. Albanes. 1675 ALSOP *Anti-Sozzo* iii. §2. 203 It's a very Ruful cause that needs such Subsidies to maintain it. 1830 SIR W. HAMILTON *Discuss.* (1853) 68 Dr. Brown.. rejects as unphilosophical, those hyperphysical subsidies.

2. *Eng. Hist.* A pecuniary aid granted by parliament to the sovereign to meet special needs.

In the 14th and 15th centuries the term (occurring, in the AF. form *subside*, in 1340 *Rolls Parlt.* II. 112/2, 117/1, 1353 27 *Edw. III* stat. i. c. 4, 1382 5 *Rich. II* stat. ii. c. 3) was applied mainly to the taxes on cloth, wool, leather, and skins, and the duties of tonnage and poundage. In Tudor times it was applied pre-eminently to a tax of 4*s.* in the pound on lands and 2*s.* 8*d.* in the pound on movables. Its application to tonnage and poundage was continued in acts of parliament until 1707 *Act 6 Anne* c. 48. In 1698 an increased percentage of duty charged upon certain articles was known as the New Subsidy.

The term has been extended by legal and historical writers to the aids derived from the tenth, the fifteenth, and other sources. The old lawyers, e.g. Coke, term the duties on wool, skins, and leather, 'perpetual' subsidies, the others being classed as 'temporary'.

† *book of subsidy*, = subsidy-book (see 4).

c 1380 WYCLIF *Wks.* (1880) 103 Whanne þe kyng & lordis axeden of grete prelatis subsidies & dymes for here temperaltes. 1422 [see TONNAGE *sb.* 1]. 1422 *Rolls of Parlt.* IV. 173/2 The forsaid pouere Commens.. graunton to oure said Lord the Kyng.. a subsidie of xxxiii s. iiii d... of every sak weight of Wolle, and of every ccxl. of Wolle felle. 1425 *Ibid.* 289/2 With oute any subsidee payng for the same [*sc.* Wool]. *c* 1460 FORTESCUE *Abs. & Lim. Mon.* vi. (1885) 122 The kynge hath therfore þe subsidie off pondage and tonnage. 1544 *Churchw. Acc. St. Giles, Reading* (ed. Nash) 70 To the kynges collectors for the subsidie ix[s] iiij[d]. *c* 1550 *Disc. Common Weal Eng.* (1893) 55 Which.. myght releue them [*sc.* breeders of wool] of theire subsidwes. 1571 *Acts Privy Council* VIII. 29 The assessing and taxing of the first payment of the Subsedye graunted by the Layetie at the last Parliament. 1581 LAMBARDE *Eiren.* II. ii. (1588) 109 Such as have their names registred in the Booke of Subsidie. 1593 SHAKS. *2 Hen. VI*, IV. vii. 25 He that made vs pay one and twenty Fifteenes, and one shilling to the pound, the last Subsidie. 1603–4 *Act 1 Jas. I*, c. 33 §2 Except and foreprised out of this Graunt of Subsidie & of Poundage, All maner of Woollen Cloth made or wrought. 1604 *Proclam.* in *Rates of Marchandizes* (*c* 1610) 5 Queene Mary.. did.. assesse vpon Clothes carried out of this Realme by way of Marchandize, a certaine rate for the Custome and Subsidie of them. 1647 CLARENDON *Hist. Reb.* I. §8 There was a mention.. of granting five Subsidies, a proportion.. scarce ever before heard of in Parliament. 1660 *Act 12 Chas. II*, c. 4 A Subsidy granted to the King of Tonnage and Poundage and other summes of Money payable upon Merchandize Exported and Imported. *a* 1700 EVELYN *Diary* 11 May 1671, The subsidie now given by Parliament to his Majesty. 1725 *Lond. Gaz.* No. 6366/2 All Goods.. which shall have remained in His Majesty's Warehouse for Security of the Duties Twelve Months, the Subsidies and Duties not paid. 1728 CHAMBERS *Cycl.* s.v., In the List of English Duties, or Impositions, are divers Kinds of Subsidies: Old Subsidy, Additional Imposition to the old Subsidy. New Subsidy, third Subsidy; Two-thirds Subsidy. 1845 McCULLOCH *Taxation* II. vi. (1852) 235 The new subsidy, granted in the reign of William III, was an addition of 5 per cent. to the duties on most imported commodities. 1874 GREEN *Short Hist.* vii. §5 (1882) 395 The perils of her reign drove her [Elizabeth] at rare intervals to the demand of a subsidy. 1876 FREEMAN *Norm. Conq.* V. xxiii. 181 In those days a subsidy took the form of a feudal grant.

b. *transf.* A pecuniary aid exacted by a prince, lord, etc.

a 1450 *Knt. de la Tour* (1868) 89 That quene.. dede mani aduersiteez to the pepille, by tailez and subsidiez. 1489 CAXTON *Faytes of A.* III. v. 176 Hys subgettes of ryht are holden to sette a subsydye upon them self. 1560 DAUS tr. *Sleidane's Comm.* 41 b, A subsidie is to be gathered in all countreis of the Empyre for the Turkishe warre. 1603 HOLLAND *Plutarch's Mor.* 403 Certaine paiments and subsidies which he would have to be levied of his subjects. 1609 SKENE *Reg. Maj.* II. lxxiii, Of helps and subsidies asked be the Lord fra his men... As quhen his sonne and heire is to be made knicht, or quhen he is to giue his eldest dochter in mariage. 1781 GIBBON *Decl. & F.* xxxi. (1787) III. 225 He stipulated an annual subsidy of corn and money. 1862 STANLEY *Jew. Ch.* I. xv. 347 From the treasury of the sanctuary.. they granted him a subsidy.

3. A grant or contribution of money. **a.** *gen.*

1421 *Cov. Leet Bk.* 36 The maiour to gyve a subsydye of money to the wardens of yche warde. *c* 1450 *Godstow Reg.* 394/7 And whan she wold entir religion, the forsaid hugh shold yeve to the same xx. marke into subsidie. 1560 DAUS tr. *Sleidane's Comm.* 286 He shall geve to his children as a subsidie an hondreth thousand crounes. 1711 STEELE *Spect.* No. 53 ¶10 Your Mention of a Subsidy for a Prince in Misfortune. 1862 THACKERAY *Philip* xvi, Out of small earnings [he] managed to transmit no small comforts and subsidies to old parents living somewhere in Munster.

b. A sum of money paid by one country to another for the promotion of war or the preservation of neutrality.

† *treaty of subsidy*, a subsidiary treaty.

1668 TEMPLE *Let. to Sir O. Bridgman* 27 Jan., Wks. 1720 II. 56 The hopes we must give him of obtaining Subsidies from Spain, which might countervail what they might lose from France. 1737 *Gentl. Mag.* VII. 705/2 This Court.. has push'd with so much Ardour the Treaties of Subsidy with Sweden and Denmark, as that they are both very far advanc'd. 1832 tr. *Sismondi's Ital. Rep.* xv. 324 Maximilian had never money enough to carry on the war without the subsidies of his allies. 1870 STANHOPE *Hist. Eng.* xii. 420 He proposed to contribute by monthly subsidies to the prosecution of the war against Philip if Philip persevered.

c. Financial aid furnished by a state or a public corporation in furtherance of an undertaking or the upkeep of a thing.

1867 SMYTH *Sailor's Word-bk.*, *Subsidy*.. a sum allowed for the conveyance of mails. 1881 H. FAWCETT *Free Trade & Prot.* (ed. 4) 38 The special object of assisting through postal subsidies the American shipping trade. 1882 D. A. WELLS *Merch. Mar.* 141 It seems clear.. that subsidies as a means of restoring American shipping cannot be made the policy of the United States. 1912 *War Dept. Subsidy Scheme* 1 Only those lorries which comply in every particular with the terms of this specification.. will be eligible for the grant of full subsidy.

d. *fig.*

a 1631 DONNE *Valed. Bk.* 42 Poems 1912 I. 31 Woman-kinde, Who though from heart, and eyes, They exact great subsidies, Forsake him who on them relies. ? *a* 1639 T. CAREW *Poems* (1651) 25 Universall losses may command A subsidie from every private eye.

4. *attrib.*, as ***subsidy act, fee***; † **subsidy book,** a book kept for recording the names of those liable to pay subsidy; † **subsidy citizen,** = *subsidy man*; † **subsidy man,** a person liable to pay subsidy; hence, a man of means or substance; † **subsidy money,** money derived from a subsidy; **subsidy roll,** = *subsidy book*; † **subsidy treaty,** a subsidiary treaty. **b.** (*temporary*) Applied to vehicles subsidized by the War Office in peace time while in their owners' hands and liable to be called upon at the outbreak of war; as ***subsidy lorry, machine.***

1910 *Encycl. Brit.* (ed. 11) XI. 86 Uniform rates of duty were fixed in England by the *Subsidy Act of 1660. 1575 LANEHAM *Let.* (1871) 35 Bear with me, though perchauns I place not thoz Gentlmen.. after theyr estatez: for I am neyther good heraud of armez, nor yet kno hoow they are set in the *Subsydy bookez. 1594 LYLY *Mother Bombie* II. v, He that had a cup of red wine to his oysters, was hoysted in the Queenes subsidie booke. *a* 1613 OVERBURY *Characters, Wise Man* Wks. (1856) 60 He chuseth not friends by the subsidy-book, and is not luxurious after acquaintance. 1663 MARVELL *Corr.* Wks. (Grosart) II. 93 The old way of rating in the subsidy-books. 1607 MIDDLETON *Michaelmas Term* III. iv, If we procure you two substantial *subsidy citizens to bail you. 1911 *War Dept. Provis. Subsidy Scheme* 2 A proportion of the initial *subsidy fee. 1913 *Leyland Motors Ltd.*, Standard War Office *Subsidy lurry.. War Office *Subsidy machines. 1591 PERCIVALL *Sp. Dict.*, *Canama*, *subsidie men, *Classis tributariorum.* **1597–8** *Act 39 Eliz.* c. 3 § 1 Fower substanciall Howsholders there beinge Subsidy men, or for wante of Subsidy men fower other substanciall Howseholders. **1618** *Archd. Essex & Colch. Depos. Rule* fol. 50 (MS.) He is worth (his debts beinge paid) a hundreth pounds, but is no subsidie man. **1626** DONNE *Serm.* lxvii. (1640) 680, I will be a Subsidy man so far, so far pay Gods debts, as to celebrate with condigne praise the goodnesse of that man. *a* **1676** HALE *Prim. Orig. Man.* II. x. 237 If we should..compare the numbers of Trained Souldiers then and now, the number of Subsidy-men then and now, they will easily give us an Account of a very great Increase and Multiplication of People. **1595** in *10th Rep. Hist. MSS. Comm.* App. v. 455 The *subsidey money groweing to the said towne. **1625–9** in Rushw. *Hist. Coll.* (1659) I. 188 Whether these Eight Ships lent to the French King..were not paid with the Subsidy-money? **1886** *Encycl. Brit.* XX. 313/1 The *subsidy rolls record the fifteenths and tenths, &c., granted by parliament to the crown. **1747** *Gentl. Mag.* XVII. 498 They continue to talk of the speedy march of a powerful body of troops to the assistance of the allies, in pursuance of a *subsidy-treaty. **1762** in *10th Rep. Hist. MSS. Comm.* App. I. 348 We did not renew last year the Subsidy Treaty with the King of Prussia.

Hence **'subsidy** *v.* (only in Carlyle), to subsidize.

1837 CARLYLE *Fr. Rev.* III. VII. iii, Austria hesitates; finally refuses, being subsidied by Pitt. **1858** —— *Fredk. Gt.* III. xx. I. 372 The English..fought and subsidied from side to side of Europe.

†**sub'sign**, *v. Obs.* [ad. L. *subsignāre*, f. *sub-* SUB- 2 + *signāre* to SIGN. Cf. OF. *soubsigner* (13th c.), mod.F. *soussigner* (16th c.).]

1. *trans.* To sign one's name under, subscribe, attest *with* one's signature or mark. Also, to subscribe (one's name).

1579 FENTON *Guicciard.* I. 19 He promised..by a writing subsigned with his owne hand, that [etc.]. **1589** HAKLUYT *Voy.* 418 A letter of the Sophie..subsigned with the hands both of the Sophie and his Secretarie. **1605** CAMDEN *Rem.* 93 Neyther have they seene..any deede..before the Conquest, but subsigned with crosses and single names. **1688** in Gutch *Coll. Cur.* II. 363 His Majesty intended..to require them to subsigne the Examinations. **1700** T. MADOX *Formulare Anglic.* (1702) p. xxvi, The Usage in This Kingdom was.., to Ratify their Charters by Subsigning their Names with Holy Crosses.

b. *pass.* To be signed so-and-so.

1583 STOCKER *Civ. Warres Lowe C.* II. 66 b, This sentence was pronounced the 4 of June 1568. And subsigned, Duke de Alua. **1687** N. JOHNSTON *Assur. Abby Lands* 189 Dated at Rome... Subsigned Beltradus. **1700** T. MADOX *Formulare Anglic.* (1702) p. xxvii, A Charter of K. Eadmund..is subsigned, Ego Eadmundus [etc.].

c. *pass.* To have a certain inscription underneath.

1572 BOSSEWELL *Armorie* III. 25 b, H. Hathe to hys Creste, a Verme hariante propre, subsigned about the tayle with a scrowe conteining thys Apothegme. *Est inclyta Virtus.*

2. *absol.* or *intr.* To append one's signature; (with cause) to testify *that*... In quots. *fig.*

1581 MULCASTER *Positions* iii. (1888) 10 Till iudgement haue subsigned, and circunstance sealed. *a* **1586** SIDNEY *Ps.* l. ii, The heav'ns subsigned with their handes, That God in justice eminentlie raignes.

3. *trans.* To sign away.

1605 SIR C. CORNWALLIS in Winwood *Mem.* (1725) II. 75 His owne Treasurie was exhausted, his Rents..susigned [*sic*] for the most parte for the Payment of Money borrowed.

†**subsig'nation.** *Obs.* [ad. late L. *subsignātio, -ōnem*, n. of action f. *subsignāre* to SUBSIGN.] Signature; affixing a seal. Also *fig.*

1590 SWINBURNE *Test.* 17 The presence of vij. witnesses, ..their subscription, their subsignation. **1612** SHELTON *Quix.* I. iv. iv. (1620) 328 This is as good as subsignation of your hands-writing. **1656** [? J. SERGEANT] tr. *T. White's Peripat. Inst.* App. 339 To fortify the Institutions, I would recommend to Thee, with a subsignation of Theology [orig. *Theologiæ chirographo*]. **1700** T. MADOX *Formulare Anglic.* (1702) p. xxvii, No great Stress can be laid upon the words of Subsignation to K. Edwy's Charter. **1726** AYLIFFE *Parergon* 482 The Subsignation or putting a Man's Mark or Signet.

†**sub'signed**, *ppl. a. Obs.* [Rendering F. *soussigné*, pa. pple. of *soussigner* to sign underneath.] Undersigned.

1565 in R. G. Marsden *Sel. Pleas Crt. Admir.* (1897) II. 56 We subsigned asseurers acknowledge and confesse to have asseured and doo assure to Pieter de Moucheron.

subsist (səb'sɪst), *sb.* [Shortening of SUBSISTENCE.] Payment of wages on account; = SUB *sb.* 7.

1855 LEIFCHILD *Cornwall* 146 There is a custom of advancing money to the miners called subsist, that they may live until the value of their two months' earnings is determined. **1886** J. BARROWMAN *Sc. Mining Terms* 65.

b. *attrib.*, in **subsist money**, = SUBSISTENCE MONEY I; **subsist week**, a week for which subsist money is paid.

1835 in *N. & Q.* Ser. IX. (1900) VI. 246/2 Agree to pay.. Subsist Money each and every fortnight in such sums as may be agreeable to the Parties. **1843** *Civil Engin. & Arch. Jrnl.* VI. 22/2 In the preceding account, no notice is taken of truck system, tommy shops..or subsist money. *Ibid.*, The cuttings are measured generally every fortnight, the intervening time being subsist weeks, when the pay is on account.

subsist (səb'sɪst), *v.* [ad. L. *subsistĕre* to stand still, stand firm, cease, be adequate to, support, f. *sub-* SUB- 26 + *sistĕre* to stand (see SIST *v.*). Cf. F. *subsister*, It. *sossistere, sussistere*, Sp., Pg. *subsistir*.]

I. 1. *intr.* To have an existence as a reality; to exist as a substance or entity. (Cf. SUBSISTENCE I.)

1549 *Bk. Com. Prayer, Quicunque vult*, Perfecte God, and perfecte man: of a resonable soule, and humayne fleshe subsisting. **1678** CUDWORTH *Intell. Syst.* I. iv. 499 Those Ideas, which Plato sometimes contends to be Substances, and to subsist alone by themselves. **1692** BENTLEY *Boyle Lect.* vi. 197 Matter abstractly consider'd cannot have subsisted eternally. **1701** NORRIS *Ideal World* I. iii. 145 That God is being itself subsisting by itself. **1847** EMERSON *Poems* 18 The young deities discussed..What subsisteth, and what seems. **1874** GEO. ELIOT *Coll. Breakf.-P.* 370 Define your Good..Next, how it may subsist without the Ill Which seems its only outline.

2. To have its being or existence *in* a certain manner, form, or state, or *by* a certain condition. *Obs.* or *arch.*

1594 HOOKER *Eccl. Pol.* I. ii. § 2 In which essentiall vnitie of God a Trinitie personall neuerthelesse subsisteth. **1614** RALEIGH *Hist. World* v. i. § 4. 331 The one [*sc.* cavalry] subsisting, by being at large; the other [*sc.* infantry], by close imbattailing. **1634** MILTON *Comus* 686 The unexempt condition By which all mortal frailty must subsist. **1649** J. ELLISTONE tr. *Behmen's Epist.* (1886) Pref. 7 All things proceed from God, subsist in God. **1684** *Contempl. St. Man* I. i. (1699) 2 The being of Time consists only of a succession of Instants..subsisting only by a flux of Moments. **1732** POPE *Ess. Man* I. 169 All subsists by elemental strife; And Passions are the elements of Life. **1784** COWPER *Task* I. 367 By ceaseless action all that is subsists.

3. †**a.** *Philos.* To exist *in* a substance or *in* accidents. *Obs.*

1599 SIR J. DAVIES *Nosce Teipsum* II. III. viii, If she were but the bodies accident, And her sole being did in it subsist, As white in snow. **1678** GALE *Crt. Gentiles* IV. III. 5 The wise Creator..has..so constituted al moral Beings, both Virtues and Vices, as that they cannot subsist but in something natural. **1690** LOCKE *Hum. Und.* II. xxiii. § 1 Not imagining how these simple Ideas can subsist by themselves, we accustom our selves, to suppose some Substratum, wherein they do subsist. **1686** SOUTH *Serm.* Isa. v. 20 (1727) II. 345 When they [*sc.* qualities] come to subsist in Particulars, and to be cloathed, and attended with several Accidents. **1821** COLERIDGE in *Blackw. Mag.* X. 219/2 The disciple of Malbranche, or of Berkeley, [affirms] that the objective subsists wholly and solely in the universal subject—God.

b. *gen.* To consist, lie, or reside *in* some specified thing, circumstance, fact, etc.

1633 G. HERBERT *Temple, Sacrifice* lvii, Your safetie in my sicknesse doth subsist. **1662** J. DAVIES tr. *Mandelslo's Trav.* 278 It subsists only in the opinion wherewith most sea-men are prepossessed, that, certainly there is an Island in those parts. **1707** FOUNTAINHALL *Decis.* (1759) II. 385 It [*sc.* a collegium] can subsist and continue in one. **1732** POPE *Ess. Man* IV. 38 The Universal Cause..makes what Happiness we justly call Subsist not in the good of one, but all. **1741** WARBURTON *Div. Legat.* II. II. 371 For the one God being the supreme Magistrate, it [*sc.* theocracy] subsisted in the Worship of that God alone. **1784** COWPER *Tiroc.* 390 His wealth, fame, honours, all that I intend, Subsist and centre in one point—a friend! **1882** COUES *Biogen* (1884) 60 If there be no chemical or physical difference [between a live amœba and a dead one], in what does the great difference subsist?

†**c.** To consist *of. Obs. rare.*

1631 BRATHWAIT *Whimzies, Pedler* 139 Would you have a true survey of his family and number them by the pole? you shall finde them subsist of three heads: himselfe, his truck, and her misset.

4. To preserve its existence or continue to exist; to remain in existence, use, or force.

c **1600** SHAKS. *Sonn.* cxxii. 5 So long as braine and heart Haue facultie by nature to subsist. **1662** STILLINGFL. *Orig. Sacræ* III. i. § 1 The souls of men are capable of subsisting after death. *a* **1715** BURNET *Own Time* III. (1724) I. 517 All ecclesiastical Courts subsisted now by this test only upon the King's permission. **1734** tr. *Rollin's Anc. Hist.* (1768) I. p. lvii, The equivocality..will not subsist in a translation. **1746** HERVEY *Medit.* (1818) 9 The exercises of gratitude subsisted in paradise. **1752** tr. *Rameau's Treat. Music* 115 As soon as a Discord can be prepared, the Syncope no longer subsists. **1762** T. MORTIMER *Ev. Man own Broker* (ed. 5) 59 The extensive scene of Jobbing, which has subsisted during the present war. **1794** S. WILLIAMS *Vermont* 161 The murders of the inquisition subsisted for centuries. **1811** JANE AUSTEN *Sense & Sensib.* xlv, His regard for her..has subsisted through all the knowledge of dear Marianne's unhappy prepossession for that worthless young man! **1813** PRICHARD *Phys. Hist. Man* vi. § 6. 311 The custom of eating their prisoners of war still subsists in the central parts of the island of Celebes. **1876** GLADSTONE *Homeric Synchr.* 189 He found that tradition subsisting among them. **1911** *Act 1 & 2 Geo. V*, c. 46 § 3 The term for which copyright shall subsist shall..be the life of the author and a period of fifty years after his death.

b. of physical things. Now *rare.*

1621 T. WILLIAMSON tr. *Goulart's Wise Vieillard* 2 Adam and all his posteritie had subsisted and continued long vpon earth. **1740** CHESTERF. *Let.* xxiii, Which charter subsists to this day, and is called Magna Charta. **1772** WESLEY *Jrnl.* 1 Feb. (1827) III. 439 Only the old chapel subsists. **1774** GOLDSM. *Nat. Hist.* (1862) I. vi. 30 Where men and animals have long subsisted. **1819** SHELLEY *Lett.* Pr. Wks. 1888 II. 285 The central arch..yet subsists. **1903** MYERS *Hum. Pers.* I. 244 The book, of course, subsists; it can be found in many libraries.

†**c.** To continue in a condition or position; to remain (so-and-so). *Obs.*

1607 SHAKS. *Cor.* v. vi. 73, I am return'd your Souldier:.. still subsisting Vnder your great Command. **1633** P. FLETCHER *Purple Isl.* II. xix, The wandring heat (which quiet ne're subsisteth). **1650** G. CAMPBELL in *Thanes of Cawdor* (Spalding Cl.) 293 Commending yow and your bed-fellow to the Lord, I subsist your loving freind Geo. Campbell.

†**5.** Of physical objects: To be or live in a certain place or state. *Obs.*

1655 STANLEY *Hist. Philos.* II. ii. (1687) 65/2 The Sea subsists upon the superficies of the Earth, which is flat. **1667** MILTON *P.L.* x. 922 Forlorn of thee, Whither shall I betake me, where subsist? *a* **1716** BLACKALL *Wks.* (1723) I. 97 A private Man may be consider'd..as a single Man subsisting by himself. **1813** W. TAYLOR *Engl. Syn.* (1856) 284 That is aquatile, which subsists in water.

6. Of a condition or quality: To exist.

1729 *Col. Rec. Pennsylv.* III. 362 That there should never any Uneasiness subsist between us. **1759** JOHNSON in *Boswell* (1831) I. 327 You have from me all the regard that can possibly subsist in the heart. **1777** WATSON *Philip II*, x. (1793) I. 422 Granted upon a condition which did not yet subsist. **1855** PRESCOTT *Philip II*, II. vi. I. 205 The best possible understanding seems to have subsisted between them.

II. †**7.** To make a stand, stand firm, hold out.

1643 CROMWELL in *Lett. & Sp.* (1850) I. xv. 219 Make them able to live and subsist. *a* **1662** HEYLIN *Laud* I. (1668) 162 If he cannot subsist, there is little or nothing left to hinder the House of Austria from being..Master of Germany. **1667** MILTON *P.L.* IX. 359 Firm we subsist, yet possible to swerve. **1671** —— *P.R.* III. 19 All the world Could not sustain thy Prowess, or subsist In battel. **1726** CAVALLIER *Mem.* IV. 290 There I gave Ravenal necessary Instructions either to avoid meeting the Enemy, or to subsist.

†**b.** To keep on, persevere. *Obs.*

1632 LITHGOW *Trav.* viii. 372 He succumb'd, and could not subsist, not beeing vsed to pedestriall trauayle.

†**8.** To stand, hold good. *Obs. rare.*

1747 J. HOWE *Let. to S. Thompson* 11 Sept., If this story subsists, I presume orders will be given.

†**9.** To cease, stop at a certain point. *Obs.*

a **1639** SPOTTISWOOD *Hist. Ch. Scot.* VI. (1677) 403 Nor did their folly, or madness rather, subsist here. *c* **1680** R. MACWARD *Contend.* (1723) 41 (Jam.), Here, at this time, I shall subsist, since I will have occasion to speak to this matter afterward. *Ibid.* 227, I might here subsist. But..I shall append..these few things.

III. 10. *trans.* To provide sustenance for; to support or maintain with provisions or funds; to maintain, support, keep: said of provisions, funds, etc., or of the persons dispensing them.

a **1683** SIDNEY *Disc. Gov.* II. xxvi. (1704) 187 Taking from them all ways of subsisting their Familys. **1698** FROGER *Voy.* 158 The Free-booters had contributed very much to subsist them for the first Years of the War. **1710** ADDISON *Tatler* No. 119 ¶ 2 We descry millions of species subsisted on a green leaf. **1725** BERKELEY *Let.* 16 July, When I accepted the Deanry it was not with any view of subsisting the College in Bermuda with its Income. **1725** *Bradley's Fam. Dict.* s.v. *Breeding of Milk*, A Cow, when she..has not Milk enough to subsist her Calf. **1749** FIELDING *Tom Jones* XV. xi, To be subsisted at her Expence from that little Fortune she had independent of her Father. **1854** *Blackw. Mag.* LXXVI. 1 Cultivating just as much land as would subsist them. **1879** H. GEORGE *Progr. & Pov.* I. v. (1881) 78 We have seen that capital does not advance wages or subsist labourers, but that its functions are to assist labour. **1901** P. FOUNTAIN *Deserts N. Amer.* x. 235 You can subsist them [*sc.* mules]..in a country where you could not find food for horses.

b. To maintain, provide for, provision (troops). Also formerly, to give pay or allowance (1802 C. James *Milit. Dict.*).

1687 T. BROWN *Saints in Uproar* Wks. 1730 I. 78 Explain to him after what manner you subsisted your cloven regiment. **1704** *Lond. Gaz.* No. 4045/3 The Charge of Subsisting these Officers and Men must be very great. **1799** HARRIS in Owen *Wellesley's Desp.* (1877) 120 We have a sufficient stock of provisions to subsist the troops. **1868** MENDELL & CRAIGHILL tr. *Jomini's Art of War* iii. 77 A French army upon the Elbe might be subsisted from Westphalia. **1898** MAHAN *Nelson* II. 241 If France..was.. subsisting an army corps upon Neopolitan territory.

refl. **1810** G. ROSE *Diaries* (1860) II. 456 Massena cannot long subsist himself in his position. **1841** CATLIN *N. Amer. Ind.* (1844) II. 39 The troops will be obliged to subsist themselves.

11. To maintain or support oneself; to live *upon* food or money, or *by* a particular occupation.

a. *intr.* (Also *fig.*)

1646 SIR T. BROWNE *Pseud. Ep.* I. vii. 26 Whose argument is but precarious and subsists upon the charity of our assentments. **1647** CLARENDON *Hist. Reb.* I. § 162 Ireland.. reduced to that good degree of Husbandry..that it not only Subsisted of itself..but really increased the Revenue of the Crown. **1672** in *Verney Mem.* (1907) II. 355, I have not wherewithall to subsist. **1777** SIR W. JONES *Ess.* i. Poems 189 Our European poetry has subsisted too long on the perpetual repetition of the same images. **1830** M. DONOVAN *Dom. Econ.* II. 291 Animals which subsist upon vegetables. **1865** DICKENS *Mut. Fr.* I. iv, Their forefathers had.. modestly subsisted on the Docks. **1885** *Encycl. Brit.* XIX. 255/2 From that time he subsisted by literature.

b. *refl.*

1719 DE FOE *Crusoe* II. (Globe) 556 He said no *Pecune* to carry him thither, or to subsist himself when he came there. **1756** BURKE *Vind. Nat. Soc.* 58 The people..began to subsist themselves from the publick Revenues. *a* **1806** HORSLEY *Serm.* (1811) 215 An idle peasantry subsist themselves by theft and violence. **1841** CATLIN *N. Amer. Ind.* xx. (1844) I. 142 The horses..subsist themselves, in winter and summer over the vast plains of prairie.

†**12.** *intr.* To support life, keep alive, live. *Obs.*

1727 SWIFT *Petit. Colliers* Wks. 1755 III. I. 130 Should it happen..that this city should be deprived of the sunbeams for several months; how will his majesty's subjects subsist? **1775** JOHNSON *Tax. no Tyr.* 29 The body may subsist, though less commodiously, without a limb. **1784** COWPER *Task* v. 79 How find the myriads..Due sustenance, or where subsist they now? **1794** S. WILLIAMS *Vermont* 388

Several colonies of white people have subsisted in the torrid zone of America.

b. Hyperbolically, with a negative expressed or implied.

1756 MRS. CALDERWOOD in *Coltness Collect.* (Maitland Club) 204 Hussy could not subsist without cards. **1758** JOHNSON *Idler* No. 7 ¶2 It is difficult to conceive how man can subsist without a News-paper.

†**13.** *trans.* **a.** To carry on, keep up. *Obs.*

1633 T. STAFFORD *Pac. Hib.* II. xxv. 254 The contents of the Letters, were to pray Aides to subsist the warre.

†**b.** To keep life in. *Obs.*

1716 *Phil. Trans.* XXIX. 493 It cannot be believed that a Supply, by this means obtained, can long subsist a Diver.

subsistence (səb'sɪstəns). Also 7– (now erron.) **subsistance.** [ad. late L. *subsistentia*, f. *subsistens* SUBSISTENT: see -ENCE. Cf. F. *subsistance* (from 16th c.), It. *sussistenza*, Sp., Pg. *subsistencia*. The L. word represents etymologically Gr. *ὑπόστασις* HYPOSTASIS.]

I. 1. Existence as a substance or entity; substantial, real, or independent existence.

1432–50 tr. *Higden* (Rolls) III. 221 Plato, whiche putte in God a cause of subsistence to be [*qui dixit in Deo causam esse subsistendi*]. **1603** HOLLAND *Plutarch's Mor.* 1032 It [*sc.* the soul] hath the subsistence and composition by harmony, but harmonie it is none. **1637** GILLESPIE *Engl. Pop. Cerem.* III. iv. 65 An abstract is no more an abstract, if it have a subsistence. *a* **1665** J. GOODWIN *Being filled with the Sp.* (1867) 209 The distinct manner of the subsistence of this one God—viz., that he subsists in three, which we call persons. **1680** BURNET *Rochester* (1692) 57 He believed the soul had a distinct subsistence. *a* **1711** KEN *Hymns Evang.* Poet. Wks. I. 28 A Drop, which has Subsistence when alone, Will loose it when into the Ocean thrown. **1736** CHANDLER *Hist. Persec.* 43 Beryllus also..taught that our Saviour had no proper personal subsistence before his becoming Man. **1738** WARBURTON *Div. Legat.* I. 47 This reason is a mere abstract Notion, which hath no real Subsistence. **1838** [F. HAYWOOD] tr. *Kant's Crit. Pure Reason* 654 Subsistence (*Subsistenz*) the existence of the substance, as inherence is that of the accident.

2. a. A thing that has substantial or real existence.

1605 TIMME *Quersit.* I. ii. 7 The soule and body of the world are knit together by the..æthereal spirits,..Joyning each part of the whole into one subsistence. **1650** EARL MONM. tr. *Senault's Man bec. Guilty* 50 When she [*sc.* the soul] withdraws within her self she knows subsistences, she treats with spirits. **1659** MOXON *Tutor Astron.* I. (1686) 1 They..concluded the parts to be Round: I mean, Every intire Subsistence, as the Stars, Planets, and the Earth. *a* **1774** TUCKER *Lt. Nat.* (1834) II. 191 Because substances cannot inexist in anything, much less coexist in the same subject; therefore he [*sc.* Plato] styled them hypostases or subsistences.

†**b.** The substance *of* a thing. *Obs.*

1605 BACON *Adv. Learn.* I. 27b, The one [*sc.* power] expressed in making the subsistence of the mater, & the other [*sc.* wisdom] in disposing the beauty of the fourme. **1653** H. MORE *Antid. Ath.* Pref. §8 (1712) 5 The framing of Matter into the bare subsistence of an Animal.

†**3.** The condition or quality of inhering or residing *in* something. *Obs.*

1628 T. SPENCER *Logick* 50 The forme is not the difference it selfe: for, a forme is a subsistence in an vnitie. **1650** HOBBES *De Corpore Politico* 133 The Subsistence and Migration of Accidents from place to place.

4. Continued existence; continuance. Now *rare*.

1616 BULLOKAR *Engl. Exp.*, *Subsistence*, the abiding or continuance of a thing in it owne estate. **1628** COKE *On Litt.* 122 A thing of perpetuall subsistance and continuance. **1642** in Rushw. *Hist. Coll.* (1692) III. I. 771 This time of urgent Necessity, which so much importeth the Safety, and even the very subsistence of Us and Our good People. **1649** MILTON *Eikon.* xxvii. 217 This Liberty of the Subject concerns himself and the subsistence of his own regal power. *a* **1687** H. MORE in *Glanvill's Sadducismus* (1689) 445 Believing no subsistence of the Soul of Christ after Death. **1729** BUTLER *Serm.* Wks. 1874 II. 100 It is necessary for the very subsistence of the world, that..injustice, and cruelty, should be punished. **1769** ROBERTSON *Chas. V*, VII. III. 3 This barbarous outrage committed during the subsistence of truce. *a* **1781** WATSON *Philip III*, III. (1793) I. 380 To rival the Dutch in those branches of commerce which they had engrossed during the subsistence of the war. **1875** GORMAN tr. *Swedenborg's Chr. Psychol.* ii. 19 Subsistence is the plain proof of existence. Hence the well-known maxim, Subsistence is perpetual existence.

†**5.** A state or mode of existence. *Obs.*

1597 HOOKER *Eccl. Pol.* V. li. §1 Euery person hath his owne subsistence which no other besides hath. **1627** in Rushw. *Hist. Coll.* (1659) I. 499 Let us all labor to get the King on our side, and this may be no hard matter, considering the neer subsistence between the King and people. *a* **1676** HALE *Prim. Orig. Man.* 299 The Watry Consistence, left in a circular subsistence by the subsiding of the Ball of Earth into the common Center of the Universe.

†**6.** *Theol.* Any of the three Persons of the Trinity; = HYPOSTASIS 5. *Obs.*

In late Gr. *ὑπόστασις* was used as the equivalent of L. *persona*; but in the treatise *Contra Eutychen et Nestorium* iii, ascribed to Boethius, it is stated that *subsistentia* in this sense renders Gr. *οὐσίωσις*.

1561 T. NORTON *Calvin's Inst.* I. xiii. 32, I call therefore a Persone, a subsistence in the essence of God. **1577** tr. *Bullinger's Decades* IV. iii. 624/1 We doe neither confound, nor yet denye or take away the three Subsistences or persons of the diuine essence. **1641** MILTON *Reform.* II. Wks. 1851 III. 68 The third subsistence of Divine Infinitude, illumining Spirit. *a* **1670** SOUTH *Serm.* Col. ii. 2 (1727) IV. 295 One single, undivided Nature's casting itself into three Subsistences, without receding from its own Unity. **1685** BAXTER *Paraphr. N.T.* Phil. ii. 5, 6 Christ,..the Brightness of his Father's Glory, and the express Image of his Subsistence, (or Person). *a* **1704** [see SUBSISTENT *sb.* 3].

II. †**7.** Basis, foundation; = HYPOSTASIS 2. *Obs.*

a **1631** DONNE *Selections* (1840) 78 Let us look first to.. reason; for if we lose that..there is no footing, no subsistence for grace. **1678** CUDWORTH *Intell. Syst.* 348 What is God, but the very Being of all things that yet are not, and the Subsistence of things that are?

†**8.** Sediment; = HYPOSTASIS 1 a. *Obs.*

1622 PEACHAM *Compl. Gent.* i. 16 The pure Oyle cannot mingle with the water, no more this extracted quintessence and Spirit of Vertue, with the dregges and subsistence of vnworthinesse.

III. 9. a. The provision of support for animal life; the furnishing of food or provender. Now *rare* exc. in ***means of subsistence***.

c **1645** HOWELL *Lett.* II. liv. (1892) 454 A Tree call'd *Manguais*, which affords..all things..that belong to the subsistence of man. **1655** CROMWELL *Let.* Nov. (1845) II. 390 What necessary supplies, as well for comfortable subsistence as for your security against the Spaniard, this place may afford. *a* **1704** T. BROWN *Praise Pov.* Wks. 1730 I. 104 Tilling their own few acres of ground for the subsistence of their families. **1767** A. YOUNG *Farmer's Lett. to People* 99 Furnishing turnips for the winter subsistance of the cattle. **1794** S. WILLIAMS *Vermont* 103 As the means of subsistence were destroyed, they removed further to the westward. **1833** HT. MARTINEAU *Brooke Farm* iii. 39, I should not wonder if you must pay for the subsistence of your cow this winter by extra labour. **1867** SMILES *Huguenots Eng.* xiv. (1880) 244 Finding the door to promotion or even to subsistence closed against him. **1884** *Law Times Rep.* L. 9/2 We submit that the court will not reduce the defendant to beggary by selling his only means of subsistence.

b. The upkeep *of* an army; the provision of supplies for troops.

1746 *Col. Rec. Pennsylv.* V. 41 The providing a sufficient quantity of Provisions for the subsistence of the Troops which shall be raised here. **1793** LINDSAY (*title*) Extracts from Colonel Tempelhoffe's History of the Seven Years' War; his Remarks..on the Subsistence of Armies, and On the March of Convoys. **1834** WELLINGTON in Stanhope *Convers.* (1888) 60, I have always taken most especial care of the subsistence of my troops.

10. a. Means of supporting life in persons or animals; means of support or livelihood. (In first quot. *transf.*)

1639 FULLER *Holy War* I. xxiv. 39 As for the brook Cedron, it was dried up, as having no subsistence of it self. **1687** DRYDEN *Hind. & P.* III. 245 If reduc'd subsistence to implore, In common prudence they wou'd pass your door. *a* **1700** EVELYN *Diary* 4 Feb. 1693, France in the utmost.. poverty for want of corn and subsistence. **1760** T. HUTCHINSON *Hist. Mass.* ii. (1765) 232 The country..but just affording subsistence. **1833** HT. MARTINEAU *Illustr. Pol. Econ.* IV. *Fr. Wines & Pol.* viii, I thought our poor helped out their subsistence by nettle broth and frog stew. **1834** L. RITCHIE *Wand. Seine* 183 The inhabitants..derive their subsistance chiefly from fishing. **1863** H. COX *Instit.* III. iii. 630 It is the interest of the monarch that his subjects should have subsistence and abundance.

b. With *a* and †*pl.* A living, livelihood.

1690 CHILD *Disc. Trade* (1698) 62 A trading country affording comfortable subsistances to more families than a country destitute of trade. **1693** DRYDEN *Disc. Satire* Ess. (ed. Ker) II. 38 My little salary ill paid, and no prospect of a future subsistence. *c* **1720** POPE *Let. to Buckingham* Wks. 1737 VI. 110 There is yet a small subsistance left them [*sc.* rats] in the few remaining books of the Library. **1832** HT. MARTINEAU *Hill & Valley* viii. 127 You offered your labour in return for a subsistence paid out of our capital. **1865** DICKENS *Mut. Fr.* I. vi, A knot of those amphibious human-creatures who appear to have some mysterious power of extracting a subsistence out of tidal water by looking at it.

†**c.** Food-supply, food, provender. *Obs.*

1697 DAMPIER *Voy.* I. 77 Their subsistence is much the same as in the other Islands..; they having some Goats [etc.]. **1774** PENNANT *Tour Scot. in 1772*, 278 All the subsistance the poor people have besides is curds milk and fish. **1776** ADAM SMITH *W.N.* I. xi. I. 286 They [*sc.* kinds of rude produce] have become worth..a greater quantity of labour and subsistence. **1788** *Encycl. Brit.* (1797) II. 756/1 The seal..being their principal subsistence.

d. = SUBSISTENCE MONEY 1.

1702 *Milit. Dict.* (1704), *Subsistance*, is Mony paid Weekly or Monthly, or otherwise to Soldiers, for them to subsist on till the general Pay days. **1798** R. JACKSON *Hist. & Cure Fever* 395 The pay of a soldier, while at home, the ration, on foreign service, with a small addition, or weekly stoppage from the subsistence, will be found equal to furnish every comfort..which a sick man can require. **1867** SMYTH *Sailor's Word-bk.*, *Subsistence*, the amount to be issued to troops as daily pay, after making the regulated deductions for rations, necessaries, etc.

11. *attrib.*, as ***subsistence dole***; with reference to farming, in which the produce is used for the producer's own subsistence and not for exchange; as ***subsistence agriculture, crop, economy, farming; subsistence farm, farmer***; **subsistence department** *U.S.*, the department that has charge of the provision of subsistence for troops; **subsistence diet**, the minimum amount of food requisite to keep a person in health; so ***subsistence quantity***; **subsistence level**, the economic level at which only the bare necessities of life can be provided; **subsistence stores** *U.S.*, stores required to keep an army in food, etc.; **subsistence wage**, the amount of money a person must earn in order to achieve a minimal standard of living. Also SUBSISTENCE MONEY.

1937 *Subsistence agriculture [see *cash-crop* s.v. CASH *sb.*[1] 3]. **1940** *Subsistence crop [see *subsistence farm* below]. **1863** *Congress. Globe* App. 184/2 That there be added to the *subsistence department of the Army one brigadier general, ..who shall be Commissary General of Subsistence. **1865** L. PLAYFAIR *Food of Man* 39 The urea secreted by a man living on a mere *subsistence diet. **1897** *Daily News* 30 Mar. 3/1, 330,000 gratuitously relieved by *subsistence doles. **1940** E. HUNTINGDON *Princ. Econ. Geogr.* 711 (Index), *Subsistence economy. **1962** R. S. THOMAN *Geogr.* III. viii. 150/1 The crudest of subsistence economies need not involve markets. **1971** *World Archaeol.* III. 171 Hunting.. is considerably less important in the overall subsistence economy than foraging. **1940** WHITBECK & WILLIAMS *Econ. Geogr. S. Amer.* (ed. 3) ii. 57 Subsistence crops are found both on tiny *subsistence farms and on the commercial plantations. **1951** A. L. ROWSE *England of Elizabeth* vi. 231 He was no mere *subsistence farmer. **1980** *Jrnl. R. Soc. Arts* Mar. 175/2 Let us take as an example..a subsistence farmer debating whether to produce a surplus for sale. **1949** W. SMITH *Econ. Geogr. Gt. Brit.* I. i. 44 As long as *subsistence farming was practised..price fluctuations had only a limited significance. **1962** *Listener* 22 Mar. 496/1 They are undergoing the transition from subsistence farming to being a landless proletariat. **1978** A. J. HUXLEY *Illustr. Hist. Gardening* i. 13 The final stage of collapse back into subsistence farming after conquest and pillage is..all too frequent. **1923** H. W. B. JOSEPH *Labour Theory of Value in Karl Marx* ii. 44 Marx believed in the so-called 'iron law of wages', in accordance with which there is a constant tendency under capitalism for wages to sink to the bare *subsistence-level. **1978** A. J. HUXLEY *Illustr. Hist. Gardening* i. 11 Communities have to raise themselves above the subsistence level before they can really afford to grow.. plants not strictly utilitarian. **1865** L. PLAYFAIR *Food of Man* 26 There is also included in this *subsistence quantity [of food] both a limited amount of mental work and a full proportional of assimilative work. **1895** *Funk's Stand. Dict.*, **Subsistence stores* (U.S.), the supplies of food required for the regular army. **1898** *Daily News* 30 June 5/4 Inability to bring the subsistence stores to the front rapidly enough. **1926** *British Worker* 10 May 3 Mr. Hebert Smith told to running bursts of sympathy the story of the miners' patient struggle to retain a *subsistence wage. **1982** *Washington Post* 17 July A4/4 Many..have also, it is alleged, worked long hours for subsistence wages.

subsistence money.

1. Money paid in advance to soldiers, workmen, etc. to supply their needs until the regular pay-day. (Cf. SUBSIST *sb.*, SUB *sb.* 7.)

1687 *Royal Order* 27 Nov. in *Lond. Gaz.* No. 2299/1 We do hereby..Require every..Officer..to pay..unto each Private Soldier..Three Shillings per Week,..as Subsistence-Money. **1743** BULKELEY & CUMMINS *Voy. S. Seas* 192 We should have a convenient House, with Firing, and eight Vintens a Man *per* Day Subsistence-Money. **1798** HUTTON *Course Math.* I. 33 *note*, Subsistence Money, is the money paid to the soldiers weekly... It is likewise the money advanced to officers till their accounts are made up. **1892** *Labour Comm.* Gloss. No. 9 s.v. *Money*, *Subsistence money*, a certain proportion of wages, equal to what one day's wages would be under the ordinary rate, *i.e.*, 6*d.* per hour, paid every day under the plus system.

2. An allowance for maintenance granted under special circumstances (see quots.).

1720 *Overseers' Acc. Holy Cross, Canterbury* (MS.), Paid Mrs. Yeats A Quarters subsistance Mony. **1847** C. G. ADDISON *Law of Contracts* I. i. (1883) 10 A parent..cannot be made liable,..unless..the child has become chargeable upon the parish, and the parish authorities sue for subsistence money in the mode provided by the poor laws. **1861** GEIKIE *Forbes* xiv. 518 The Professors..had to take their students to the country, live in expensive hotels, and received no subsistence money to defray their additional expenditure. **1876** VOYLE & STEVENSON *Milit. Dict.*, *Subsistence Money*, an allowance granted for the subsistence of soldiers who, whilst in imprisonment in cells, or confinement in the guard-room, forfeit their daily pay.

†**sub'sistency.** *Obs.* [ad. late L. *subsistentia* SUBSISTENCE.]

1. *Theol.* = SUBSISTENCE 6, HYPOSTASIS 5.

1592 tr. *Junius on Rev.* i. 4 This Spirit is one in person according to his subsistencie. **1652** BENLOWES *Theoph.* Pref., One Essence, Three Subsistencies. **1701** NORRIS *Ideal World* I. v. 240 The second of those three subsistencies which the Catholic Faith teaches us to believe and adore in the one undivided essence of God.

2. A thing that has a substantial existence; = SUBSISTENCE 2.

1652 BENLOWES *Theoph.* Author's prayer 17 Eternal Principle of all substances, essential Being of all Subsistencies. **1665** GLANVILL *Scepsis Sci.* iii. 11 We know as little how the union is dissolved, that is the chain of the so differing subsistencies that compound us, as how it first commenced. **1768** TUCKER *Lt. Nat.* (1834) I. 335 The ancients, holding the eternity of forms and ideas, supposed them subsistencies inexisting within the divine mind.

3. = SUBSISTENCE 4.

1628 T. SPENCER *Logick* 17 A first, or individuall substance, may be taken two wayes: one way, for every thing that hath a substance; another way, for a compleat subsistency, in the nature of any species.

4. Continued existence; = SUBSISTENCE 5.

1642 H. MORE *Song of Soul* II. III. iv. 21 Nor of well-being, nor subsistency Of our poor souls, when they do hence depart, Can any be assur'd. **1651** N. BACON *Disc. Gov. Eng.* II. xiii. (1739) 69 Maintaining thereby their subsistency by the consistence of the Members together. **1658** SIR T. BROWNE *Hydriot.* v. 28 A great part of Antiquity contented their hopes of subsistency with a transmigration of their souls. **1682** tr. *Erastus' Treat. Excomm.* 40 Whenever Christ made any new Institution, he omitted nothing that was requisite to its being and subsistency.

subsistent (səb'sɪstənt), *a.* and *sb.* Now *rare* or *Obs.* [ad. L. *subsistens, -ent-*, pr. pple. of *subsistĕre* to SUBSIST. Cf. F. *subsistant*.]

A. *adj.*

1. Existing substantially or really; existing of or by itself.

1617 COLLINS *Def. Bp. Ely* II. viii. 294 Things essentiall, or subsistent, not Chimeraes onely. **1646** SIR T. BROWNE *Pseud. Ep.* I. x. 42 Those which deny there are spirits subsistent without bodies. *a* **1688** CUDWORTH *Immut. Mor.* (1731) 17 The Modes of all Subsistent Beings..are immutably and necessarily what they are. **1701** NORRIS *Ideal World* I. iii. 145 Since God is very subsistent being nothing of the perfection of being can be wanting to him. **1911** WEBSTER, *Subsistent form, Schol.*, a form capable of existing apart from matter.

†**2.** Inherent or residing *in*. *Obs.*

1526 *Pilgr. Perf.* (W. de W. 1531) 197 b, How and after what maner those iii persones be subsistent in one deite. **1607** *Schol. Disc. agst. Antichr.* I. ii. 114 A gesture of prayer either explicit or implicit at the least, and that not by it selfe existent, but subsistent in prayer. **1692** BENTLEY *Serm.* ii. (1724) 62 No sensible Qualities, as Light, and Colour, and Heat, and Sound, can be subsistent in the Bodies themselves absolutely consider'd, without a relation to our Eyes, and Ears, and other Organs of Sense.

†**3.** Continuing in existence, lasting. *Obs.*

1603 FLORIO *Montaigne* II. xii. 350 Seeing all things are subject to passe from one change to another; reason..findes hir selfe deceived, as vnable to apprehend any thing subsistant and permanent.

4. Subsisting at a specified or implied time.

1832 CARLYLE *Misc. Ess., Death of Goethe* (1840) IV. 120 Men whose Impulse had not completed its development till after fifteen hundred years, and might perhaps be seen still individually subsistent after two thousand. **1849** *Blackw. Mag.* LXV. 206 Such words must be accepted as serious indications of subsistent evil.

5. Having means of subsistence. *nonce-use.*

1751 H. WALPOLE *Lett.* (1846) II. 383 The Prince's servants could no longer oppose, if they meant to be *consistent*. I told this to Mr. Chute, who replied instantly, 'Pho! he meant *subsistent*.'

B. *sb.*

†**1.** A subordinate, inferior. *Obs.*

1598 BARRET *Theor. Warres* V. ii. 151 Hee hath subsistants and ministers to performe their office.

2. A being or thing that subsists.

1656 STANLEY *Hist. Philos.* VIII. (1687) 433/2 The place of significats is divided into Phantasies, and subsistents on phantasie, dicibles, axioms, &c. **1694** BURTHOGGE *Reason* 244 It becomes a *Suppositum* or Subsistent by it self. **1906** *Athenæum* 17 July 204/1 These primary facts fall into three orders: the orders of physical and psychical *existents*, and objects of thought (such as relations, numbers, &c.), which may be called objective *subsistents*.

†**3.** *Theol.* = SUBSISTENCE 6. *Obs.*

1671 FLAVEL *Fount. Life* v. 11 The second person or subsistent in the glorious Godhead. *a* **1705** HOWE *Let. to Friend* Wks. 1724 II. 586 To say that all Perfection is in each subsistent; which I like better than Subsistence, as more expressive of the Concrete. *a* **1802** T. BELL *View Cov. Wks. & Grace* (1814) 434 The Father is a person, a subsistent in the Godhead.

subsistential (sʌbsɪ'stɛnʃəl), *a.* [f. late L. *subsistentia* SUBSISTENCE + -AL¹.] Pertaining to subsistence, *esp.* to the divine subsistence or hypostasis.

1620 T. GRANGER *Div. Logike* 310 His hypostaticall, or subsistentiall name. **1664** BAXTER *Div. Life* I. vii. 50 Having spoken of the effects of the Attributes of Gods Essence as such, we must next speak of the Effects of his three great Attributes which some call Subsistential, that is, his Omnipotency, Vnderstanding and Will. **1830** COLERIDGE in *Lit. Rem.* (1838) III. 2 The distinctities in the *pleroma* are the eternal ideas, the subsistential truths.

†**subsister,** †**subsistership.** *Obs.* ? Errors for, or jocular alterations of, SUBSIZAR, -SIZARSHIP.

1589 [? NASHE] *Almond for Parrat* Wks. 1905 III. 366, I am to tel you how laudibly he behaued himselfe in Peter-house, during the time of his subsistership. **1592** CHETTLE *Kind-harts Dr.* (1841) 45 You that was wont, like a subsister, in a gown of rugge, rent on the left shoulder, to sit singing the counter-tenor by the cage in Southwarke.

†**sub'sistible,** *a. Obs. rare*⁻¹. [f. SUBSIST *v.* + -IBLE.] Able to subsist.

1675 G. R. tr. *Le Grand's Man without Passion* To Rdr., [It] left Posterity in doubt, whether a man could be rendred sociable, that was not subsistible in Nature.

subsisting (səb'sɪstɪŋ), *vbl. sb.* [-ING¹.] The action of the vb. SUBSIST; SUBSISTENCE.

1597 HOOKER *Eccl. Pol.* v. lii. §3 By taking only the nature of man he still continueth one person, and changeth but the maner of his subsisting. **1603** in Moryson *Itin.* (1617) II. 276 The danger of his [*sc.* Tyrone's] subsisting as he doth, is.. to maintaine still a loose head of Rebellion. **1690** LOCKE *Hum. Und.* II. xxiii. §3 *note*, Your lordship has the idea of subsisting by itself. **1706** *Lond. Gaz.* No. 4195/1 His Majesty had received a..Supply of Money.., for the paying and subsisting..of his..troops. **1719** DE FOE *Crusoe* I. (Globe) 63, I had a tolerable View of subsisting, without any Want as long as I liv'd.

b. *attrib.* in **subsisting diet**, = *subsistence diet* (see SUBSISTENCE 11).

1865 L. PLAYFAIR *Food of Man* 8 In looking for a purely subsisting diet, we naturally turn to the experience of hospitals having convalescent patients unable still to take exercise.

sub'sisting, *ppl. a.* [-ING².]

†**1.** Existing substantially, substantial. *Obs.*

1674 OWEN *Disc. Holy Spirit* I. iii. 54 He [*sc.* the Holy Ghost] was represented by a subsisting Substance.

†**2.** Abiding, lasting. *Obs.*

1613 WITHER *Abuses Stript* I. Concl., Juvenilia (1633) 112 Shee hath no power to see The better things that more subsisting bee. **1678** J. BROWN *Life of Faith* (1824) I. vii. 138 Not only would the faith of this help to a subsisting life but ..to a life of joy.

3. Existing at a specified or implied time.

1765 BLACKSTONE *Comm.* I. viii. 276 Where there is a subsisting lease, of which there are twenty years still to come. **1794** PALEY *Evid.* III. i. (1800) II. 302 It appears in the Christian records..as being the subsisting opinion of the age and country in which his ministry was exercised. **1818** CRUISE *Digest* (ed. 2) II. 325 This not being a remainder created by that deed, but a conveyance of the then subsisting reversion or remainder expectant on the death of M. **1858** GLADSTONE *Homer* III. 9 Independently of sovereignties purely local.. we find a subsisting Pelopid empire. **1859** MILL *Liberty* i. (1865) 5 The still subsisting habit of looking on the government as representing an opposite interest to the public.

Hence †**sub'sistingly** *adv.*, enduringly.

a **1641** MOUNTAGU *Acts & Mon.* (1642) 72 But that Fabrick, whereon subsistingly doth it rely?

subsizar (sʌb'saɪzə(r)). Also 6 **subsiser, -cer,** 6–7 **-zer,** 7 **-cizer.** [SUB- 6.] In the University of Cambridge (latterly only at Trinity and Emmanuel colleges) an undergraduate (having special need of pecuniary assistance and formerly performing menial offices) ranking below a sizar.

c **1590** GREENE *Fr. Bacon* II. ii, Doth not all the towne crie out, and say, Frier Bacons subsiser is the greatest blockhead in all Oxford? *a* **1616** BEAUM. & FL. *Elder Brother* I. ii, [*Charles, a Scholar, loq.*] Bid my Subsiser carry my Hackney to buttry. **1618** D'EWES in *Autobiog.* (1845) I. 107 At the same time was admitted one Thomas Manning to be my sub-sizar. *a* **1635** CORBET *Poems* (1672) 102 The King being gone from Trinity, They make a Scramble for Degree; Masters of all sorts, and all Ages, Keepers, Subcizers, Lackeyes, Pages. **1691** WOOD *Ath. Oxon.* I. 227 John Penry ..became a Subsizer of Peter House in Cambridge, about 1578. **1853** *Camb. Univ. Comm.* Index 157 Trinity College: The number of sub-sizars is unlimited; the only advantage possessed by a sub-sizar is, that he pays 4*l.* instead of 10*l.* for tuition and that the admission fee is 2*l.* 15*s.* instead of 5*l.* **1866** *Stud. Guide Univ. Camb.* 371 The Subsizars succeed the Sizars in order of merit as vacancies occur. **1884** MULLINGER *Univ. Camb. fr. 1535 to Chas. I*, 339 The chapel clerk, the porter at the gate,..and the steward were.. generally recruited from the subsizars. **1902** *Stud. Handbk. Univ. Camb.* v. 97 Subsizarships are tenable for one year, but each Subsizar (if he has passed the Previous Examination..) will be elected into a Sizarship at the end of his first year.

†**b.** *fig.* A menial, lacquey. *Obs.*

1602 *2nd Pt. Return fr. Parnass.* IV. ii. 1565 Which that one ey'd subsicer of the skie, Don Phœbus empties by caliditie. **1644** CLEVELAND *Char. Lond. Diurn.* 5 O brave Oliver! Times voyder, Sub-sizer to the Wormes.

Hence **sub'sizarship** the position of a subsizar.

[**1589**: see SUBSISTERSHIP.]

1599 *Broughton's Lett.* i. 6 He pities your madnes (being acquainted therewith from your subsizership in Trinitie Colledge). **1853** *Camb. Univ. Comm.* Index 157. **1894** *Daily News* 14 June 7/7 The following scholarships will be offered: ..together with two subsizarships (limited to properly qualified candidates in need of assistance). **1902** [see above].

subsoil ('sʌbsɔɪl), *sb.* [f. SUB- 3 + SOIL *sb.*¹]

1. The stratum of soil lying immediately under the surface soil.

1799 J. ROBERTSON *Agric. Perth* 287 On light land, with a gravelly subsoil, thirty or thirty-five bolls are accounted a sufficient dose. **1850** ANSTED *Elem. Geol., Min.*, etc. §1018 In most cases the subsoil is immediately, and the soil intermediately, derived from the decomposition of the subjacent rock. **1879** JEFFERIES *Wild Life Southern Co.* 44 The chalky subsoil coming there nearer to the surface. **1890** *Hardwicke's Science Gossip* XXVI. 208 Barley with very short roots obtains its food from the surface-soil and does not affect the sub-soil, whence clover with very long roots draws its supply.

b. *transf.* and *fig.*

1839 CARLYLE *Chartism* iii. 123 This crude subsoil is the first subsoil of all true husbandry. **1852** M. PATTISON in *Westm. Gaz.* (1906) 15 Feb. 2/1 It would be the beginning of a system by which the University would strike its roots freely into the subsoil of society. **1871** BROWNING *Pr. Hohenstiel-Schwangau* 98 The subsoil of me, mould Whence spring my moods.

2. *attrib.* and *Comb.* (also SUBSOIL PLOUGH).

1831 JAS. SMITH *Thorough Draining* (1843) 23 For the purpose of breaking the subsoil furrow. **1840** BUEL *Farmer's Comp.* 103 Subsoil draining, or the drainage of waters that rise through the subsoil, or pass off at its outcroppings. **1851** H. STEPHENS *Bk. Farm* (ed. 2) II. 663/2 The subsoil-trenches of the Marquis of Tweeddale. **1860** O. W. HOLMES *Prof. Breakf.-t.* vi, Doctors assiduous,..undertakers solemn, but happy; then the great subsoil cultivator, who plants but never looks for fruit in his garden. **1879** *Cassell's Techn. Educ.* II. 171/2 Subsoil-trench plough. **1884** *Harper's Mag.* Apr. 761/2 This subsoil water..is scarcely less foul than sewage.

b. *fig.* with adj. force = penetrating deep down.

1882 W. CORY *Lett. & Jrnls.* (1897) 485 German is used by subsoil research men. **1894** *Advance* (Chicago) 12 Apr., Deep sub-soil repentance makes strong, healthy Christians who will stand wash and wear.

subsoil ('sʌbsɔɪl), *v.* [f. prec.] *trans.* To plough so as to cut into the subsoil, use a subsoil plough upon.

1840 *Trans. Yorkshire Agric. Soc.* 47 In September, 1838, I subsoiled two fields of ten acres each. **1875** ALEX. SMITH *New Hist. Aberd.* II. 1209 A considerable extent of the old tilly ground has been thorough drained, but not much of it subsoiled.

b. *fig.* or in fig. context.

1851 THACKERAY *Engl. Hum.* ii. (1900) 483 He had not worked crop after crop from his brain, manuring hastily, sub-soiling indifferently. **1878** CUYLER *Pointed Papers* 13 They subsoiled with the plough of Divine truth, which ripped to pieces self-righteousness and other secret sins.

Hence **'subsoiled** *ppl. a.*, **'subsoiling** *vbl. sb.* (also *fig.* = working below the surface, getting deep down); **'subsoiler**, an instrument for loosening the subsoil, a subsoil plough.

1840 *Trans. Yorkshire Agric. Soc.* 48 One of these *sub-soiled fields produced 35..bus. of wheat per acre. **1852** C. W. HOSKYNS *Talpa* 23 My first field was soon accomplished ..deep enough..to allow Exall and Andrews' *sub-soiler to follow the cross-ploughing. **1868** *Rep. U.S. Comm. Agric.* (1869) 414 Land broken in October with a two-horse Brinley plow, followed by a sub-soiler. **1879** *Cassell's Techn. Educ.* II. 171/2 The 'subsoil-trench plough'..consists in the first place of a subsoiler or coulter of iron. **1840** *Trans. Yorkshire Agric. Soc.* 48, I do not attribute this great falling off, per acre, altogether to the parallel *subsoiling. **1868** *Rep. U.S. Comm. Agric.* (1869) 215 The yield of fruit is largely increased by draining, trenching, and subsoiling. **1872** in *Sunday at Home* (1881) Dec. 841/2 We have participated.. in the subsoiling of English loyalty towards the Crown. **1888** BRYCE *Amer. Commw.* III. lxx. II. 555 Bosses begin the work of 'subsoiling', i.e. manipulating primaries and local conventions so as to secure the choice of such delegates..as they desire.

subsoil plough, *sb.*

A kind of plough with no mould-board, used in ploughed furrows to loosen the soil at some depth below the surface without turning it up.

1831 JAS. SMITH *Thorough Draining* (1843) 23 The Sub-soil Plough..was designed..for the purpose of opening up the close subsoil of the farm of Deanston. **1834** *Brit. Husb.* I. 465 In this operation, the subsoil plough..would no doubt be found a valuable acquisition. **1859** ALLEN *New Amer. Farm Bk.* (1884) 104 What is beyond it should be thoroughly broken up by the subsoil plow.

Hence **subsoil-plough** *v. trans.*, to use a subsoil plough upon; also **subsoil-ploughing** *vbl. sb.*, the use of a subsoil-plough.

1831 JAS. SMITH *Thorough Draining* (1843) 19 The charge of subsoil ploughing may be estimated at 24*s.* to 30*s.* per statute acre. **1840** BUEL *Farmer's Comp.* 45 In subsoil ploughing, no portion of the subsoil is brought to the surface, but merely loosened, and pulverized. **1844** H. STEPHENS *Bk. Farm* I. 659 It is cheaper to subsoil-plough land than to thorough-drain it. **1848** THACKERAY *Bk. Snobs* xxxi, I remember the conversations, O..how stupid they were! The subsoil ploughing;..the row about the representation of the county [etc.].

subsolar (səb'səʊlə(r)), *a.* [SUB- 1 a.]

†**1.** Exposed to the sun. *Obs. rare*⁻¹.

1657 TOMLINSON *Renou's Disp.* 44 From a subsolar place ..some are better or worse.

2. *Meteorol.* and *Astr.* Directly underneath the sun; having the sun in the zenith.

1860 FITZROY in *Merc. Marine Mag.* VII. 356 It is drawn towards, and after the 'sub-solar' rising part of the atmosphere. **1863** FITZROY *Weather Bk.* v. 71 The rising sub-solar or intertropical part of the atmosphere. **1910** G. L. HOSMER *Textbk. Pract. Astron.* xiv. 175 If an observer measures an altitude of the sun he locates himself on the circumference of a circle whose centre is the sub-solar point. **1938** [see SUBLUNAR *a.* 2]. **1970** N. ARMSTRONG et al. *First on Moon* ix. 195 As you get closer to the subsolar point you can definitely see browns and tans on the ground. **1978** PASACHOFF & KUTNER *University Astron.* xv. 409 Because of Mercury's slow rotation, the subsolar point is not always at the same place on the surface and so is not eternally heated.

3. Beneath the surface of the sun. *rare.*

1885 AGNES M. CLERKE *Pop. Hist. Astron.* II. ii. 211 In the penumbræ of spots, the glowing streams rushing up from the tremendous sub-solar furnace are bent sideways by the powerful indraught.

†**'subsolary,** *a. Obs. rare*⁻¹. [SUB- 1 a.] Subcelestial, sublunary.

1661 A. BROME *Par. 1st Chap. Eccles.* 70 Songs 198 Things done upon this subsolary ball.

sub'sonic, *a.* (and *sb.*) [SUB- 14.]

A. *adj.* **1. a.** Pertaining to, involving, capable of, or designating speeds less than the speed of sound. Cf. SUPERSONIC *a.* (and *sb.*) 2 a.

1937 *Jrnl. R. Aeronaut. Soc.* XLI. 1099 The drag coefficient rises..as the velocity of sound is reached, and.. remains very much higher than the sub-sonic figure. **1946** *Ibid.* L. 907/2 The National Physical Laboratory has examined the possibility of using flexible walls in high-speed subsonic tunnels. **1958** *Times* 9 Jan. 5/5 It is..to carry 95–100 passengers, cruising at high subsonic speeds of around 600 m.p.h. **1973** *Times* 5 Feb. 13/5 Capacity now exceeds demand for subsonic flight in the mass market. **1978** *Jrnl. R. Soc. Arts* CXXVI. 685/1 The break-down of the direct operating costs (DOC) per passenger mile for a typical subsonic aircraft is indicated in Table III.

b. *ellipt.* as *sb.* An aircraft not made to travel faster than sound. Cf. SUPERSONIC *a.* (and *sb.*) 2 b.

1970 *New Scientist* 10 Dec. 445/2 This aircraft will cruise at a higher altitude than the subsonics. **1975** *Nature* 31 Jan. 299/1 Ozone reduction could then be kept near the current reduction due to aircraft alone..for fleets up to 4,000 747-class subsonics at 11 km..or 1,000 at 13 km. **1977** *Jrnl. R. Soc. Arts* CXXV. 361/1, I originally planned to cover supersonics as well as subsonics.

2. = INFRASONIC *a.* 1. Cf. SUPERSONIC *a.* 1. *rare.*

1961 in WEBSTER. **1976** *Gramophone* Sept. 513/2 Arm mass problems are reduced on record warps, causing less intermodulation and unwanted sub-sonic cone movement of the loudspeakers.

Hence **sub'sonically** *adv.*

1962 *Economist* 8 Sept. 944/1 The aircraft have to fly mainly supersonically but in part subsonically. **1977** *Daily Tel.* 12 Dec. 2/7 The Indonesian decision to allow Concorde to fly subsonically through its air space.

†**subsor'tition.** *Obs. rare*$^{-0}$. [ad. L. *subsortītio, -ōnem*, n. of action f. *subsortīrī*: see SUB- 27 and SORTITION.] Selection by lot to fill the place of another. So **subsor'titiously** *adv.*

1654 H. L'ESTRANGE *Chas. I* (1655) 18 There being a hundred and fifty sick in the S. George, the councel ordered, ..that every ship should take to nurse a couple of the sick, and subsortitiously, by lot, to supply their places with as many sound. **1656** BLOUNT *Glossogr.*, *Subsortition*, a chusing by lots, after others have chosen, to fill up the number of those that before were refused.

'subspace. [SUB- 7 e.] **1.** *Math.* A space (SPACE *sb.*[1] 17) that is wholly contained in another space, or whose points or elements are all in another space.

1931 H. P. ROBERTSON tr. *Weyl's Theory of Groups & Quantum Mech.* i. 20 ℜ is decomposed into mutually perpendicular sub-spaces. **1946** *Nature* 12 Oct. 513/1 He has studied problems of deformation of sub-spaces, of 'imbedding', of automorphism, and of the variation of multiple integrals. **1968** P. A. P. MORAN *Introd. Probability Theory* v. 226 Particular subspaces of the space of all distributions. **1979** *Proc. London Math. Soc.* XXXVIII. 221 Let *X* and *Y* both be subspaces of the Hilbert space of all square summable sequences.

2. *Sci. Fiction.* A physical space in which motion and communication are supposed to occur free of their usual limitations, or subject to different laws.

1955 *Mag. Fantasy & Sci. Fiction* Aug. 106/1 The subspace radio had announced his coming, and preparations consonant with his exalted rank had been made. **1976** L. NIVEN in R. Bretnor *Craft Sci. Fiction* 180 *FTL, hyperdrive, hyperspace, subspace*, all refer to means of traveling faster than light in an otherwise relativistic universe.

'subspecies. [mod.L.; cf. F. *sous-espèce.*] A subdivision of a species; a more or less permanent variety of a species. Chiefly *Nat. Hist.*

1699 DAMPIER *Voy.* (1703) III. 75 There are..four sorts of these long-leg'd Fowls..as so many Sub-Species of the same Kind; viz. Crab catchers, Clocking-Hens [etc.]. **1807** AIKIN *Dict. Chem. & Min.* II. 13/2 Arseniat of Lead. Of this there are two subspecies. **1859** DARWIN *Orig. Spec.* ii. 51 No clear line of demarcation has as yet been drawn between species and sub-species..or, again, between sub-species and well-marked varieties, or between lesser varieties and individual differences. **1871** —— *Desc. Man* I. vii. I. 227 Some naturalists have lately employed the term 'sub-species' to designate forms which possess many of the characteristics of true species, but which hardly deserve so high a rank. **1880** WALLACE *Isl. Life* xvi. 339 A few flowering plants which, as varieties or sub-species, are apparently peculiar to our islands. **1881** J. C. MORRISON in *Encycl. Brit.* (ed. 9) XII. 19/1 Verse narrative..is..a sub-species by itself. **1898** *Atlantic Monthly* LXXXII. 492/1 Carolina snow-birds and mountain solitary vireos, two varieties ('subspecies' is the more modern word) originally described a few years ago.

Hence ˌ**subspeci'ation** [cf. SPECIATION], the evolutionary development of a subspecies or of subspecies.

1942 E. MAYR *Systematics & Origin of Species* vii. 169 Subspeciation, that is geographic variation, has acutally brought about the formation of unquestionably new species of birds. **1952** E. O. DODSON *Texbk. Evolution* xvi. 314 Subspeciation is the ordinary prerequisite to speciation in the neo-Darwinian scheme. **1956** PETERSON & FISHER *Wild America* iii. 43 Roger nearly always starts a difficult subject, like..subspeciation, when I'm threading my way through the stickiest London traffic. **1978** *Nature* 22 June 603/1 Four species [of *Plasmodium*]..are stipulated, three of which exhibit subspeciation.

subspe'cific, *a. Nat. Hist.* [f. prec. after *specific.*] Of, pertaining to, or of the nature of a subspecies.

1870 HOOKER *Stud. Flora* 246 Cuscuta Epithymum..does not seem entitled to sub-specific rank. **1883** W. S. KENT in A. J. Adderley *Fisheries Bahamas* 44 Three specific or sub-specific forms that correspond very closely with the three leading Mediterranean types above described. **1905** *Athenæum* 25 Feb. 246/3 Mr. Rothschild's opinion that *Gorilla castaneiceps* of Slack was an aberration, and not entitled to specific or subspecific rank.

Hence **subspe'cifically** *adv.*

1883 *Athenæum* 15 Dec. 781/2 A species of paradise bird of the genus *Drepanornis*..subspecifically different from *D. albertisi* of North-Eastern New Guinea. **1896** *Brit. Birds, Their Nests & Eggs* II. 60 The serin being only sub-specifically distinct from the canary.

sub'spinous, *a.*

1. [SUB- 21 b.] *Zool.* and *Bot.* Somewhat spinous.

1822 J. PARKINSON *Outl. Oryctol.* 45 Angulated branches, with subspinous and membranaceous expansions. **1870** HOOKER *Stud. Flora* 287 Marrubium, White Horehound.. subspinous, erect or spreading.

2. [SUB- 1 b.] *Anat.* and *Path.* **a.** Under the spinal column. **b.** Under the spine of the scapula.

In recent Dicts.

substage ('sʌbsteɪdʒ).

1. [SUB- 7.] *Geol.* A subdivision of a stage.

1859 DARWIN *Orig. Spec.* ix. 297 If the specimens come from different sub-stages of the same [geological] formation. **1906** CHAMBERLIN & SALISBURY *Geol.* III. 383 The following are the American stages of the glacial period now recognized in the interior of North America... The Champlain sub-stage (marine). The glacio-lacustrine sub-stage.

2. [SUB- 3.] An apparatus fixed beneath the ordinary stage of a compound microscope for the purpose of supporting mirrors and other accessories. Also *attrib.*

1888 RUTLEY *Rock-Forming Min.* 13 Generally speaking, a sub-stage is unnecessary. *Ibid.* 26 Examination by ordinary Transmitted Light (or Sub-stage Illumination). **1890** *Anthony's Photogr. Bull.* III. 96 A substage illuminator or condenser. **1896** *Allbutt's Syst. Med.* I. 506 Abbé's sub-stage-condenser. **1902** *Ross's Catal.*, Swing-out Substage.

substain, obs. form of SUSTAIN.

1401 *Pol. Poems* (Rolls) II. 108 The licnesse which that abidith therinne noon substeyned substans. **1556** ROBINSON tr. *More's Utopia* (Arb.) 59 Them whiche..substeyne losse and dammage.

substance ('sʌbstəns). Also 4–6 **substaunce,** (5 **sobstans,** 6 **supstance**). [a. OF. (mod.F.) *substance* (12th c.), ad. L. *substantia*, f. *substans, -ant-*, pr. pple. of *substāre* to stand or be under, be present, f. *sub-* SUB- 2 + *stāre* to stand. Cf. OF. *sustance*, Pr. *sustancia*, It. *sostanza, sustanza, -ia*, Sp., Pg. *su(b)stancia.*

L. *substantia* was adopted as the representative of Gr. οὐσία in its various senses.]

1. Essential nature, essence; *esp. Theol.*, with regard to the being of God, the divine nature or essence in respect of which the three Persons of the Trinity are one.

a **1300** *Cursor M.* 9762 An-fald godd vndelt es he, And a substance wit-in þir thre. *a* **1325** *Athan. Creed* 4 in *Prose Psalter* (1891) 194 Noiþer confoundand persons, ne departand þe substaunce. *Ibid.* 29. 195 He his God, of þe substaunce of þe fader biȝeten to-fore þe worldes; & man, of þe substaunce of þe moder born in þe world. *c* **1375** *Sc. Leg. Saints* i. (*Petrus*) 403 In þis symon dwellis ay twa substance, þat is to wyt, of devel and man, to-gyddir knete. **1450–1530** *Myrr. Our Ladye* 4 The glory of the blessyd endeles Trinite in onehed of substaunce and of Godhede. **1526** *Pilgr. Perf.* (W. de W. 1531) 197 The pure substaunce of god in his owne nature & deite. **1585** DYER *Prayse of Nothing* Writ. (Grosart) 77 That substance, which we communicate with Angels, being created of nothing. **1597** HOOKER *Eccl. Pol.* v. lii. §3 In Christ therefore God and man there is a two-folde substance, not a two-folde person, because one person extinguisheth an other, whereas one nature cannot in another become extinct. *c* **1610** *Women Saints* 173/11 [Arius] affirming the Sonne of god to be of inferiour substance to his Father. **1678** CUDWORTH *Intell. Syst.* 601 That Essence or Substance of the Godhead, which all the Three Persons or Hypostases agree in. **1833** NEWMAN *Arians* II. iv. (1876) 195 To protest..against the notion that the substance of God is something distinct from God Himself. **1860** PUSEY *Min. Proph.* 12 God giveth us of His Substance, His Nature,..making us partakers of the Divine Nature. **1876** NORRIS *Rudim. Theol.* I. iv. 73 It is God's nature to be one in substance, manifold (that is, threefold) in person.

2. *Philos.* A being that subsists by itself; a separate or distinct thing; hence *gen.*, a thing, being.

1340 *Ayenb.* 112 [Supersubstantial bread] þet is to zigge: þet paseþ and ouergeþ alle substances and alle sseppes be ver. **1382** WYCLIF *Gen.* vii. 4, I shal reyn vpon the erthe.. and I shal do awey al substaunce the which Y made, fro the ouermost of the erthe. **1551** T. WILSON *Logic* (1580) 33 b, A liuely bodie is a substaunce. *Ergo*, a man is a substaunce. **1599** SIR J. DAVIES *Nosce Teipsum* II. iii. 10 She [*sc.* the soul] is a substance, and a perfect being. **1616** R. C. *Times' Whistle* I. (1871) 8 God is an Essence intellectuall, A perfect Substance incorporeall. **1667** MILTON *P.L.* v. 408 Food alike those pure Intelligential substances require As doth your Rational. *Ibid.* VIII. 109 His Omnipotence, That to corporeal substances could adde Speed almost Spiritual. **1707** OLDFIELD *Ess. Impr. Reason* II. iii. 139 Minds, which are indiscerpible, are thinking Substances. **1725** WATTS *Logic* I. ii. §2 A Substance is a being which can subsist by itself, without dependence upon any other created being. **1818** STODDART *Gram.* in *Encycl. Metrop.* (1845) I. 8/1 We refer all our states of being to a substance called *self.* **1843** MILL *Logic* I. iii. §6 Substances are usually distinguished as Bodies or Minds. **1868** BAIN *Ment. & Mor. Sci.* App. 50 Mind being..expressed by the one attribute Thought (construed, however, as Thinking Substance), and..Body ..summed up in the one attribute Extension (Extended Substance). **1876** *Encycl. Brit.* V. 143/1 The question whether the material and the thinking substance are one does not meet us at the outset. **1910** T. CASE in *Encycl. Brit.* (ed. 11) II. 510/2 The doctrine that all things are substances which are separate individuals, stated in the Categories, is expanded in the Metaphysics.

b. *first* (*primary*) *substance, second* (*secondary, general*) *substance*: see quots.

In scholastic L. *substantia prima* and *substantia secunda*, translating πρώτη οὐσία and δευτέρα οὐσία (Aristotle *Categ.*).

1551 T. WILSON *Logic* C vj, The first substance is called euery singuler persone or propre name... The second substance comprehendeth both the general worde, and the kinde also of euery singuler persone. **1628** T. SPENCER *Logick* 129 The second substance: consisting in the Genus and Species. **1697** tr. *Burgersdicius' Logic* I. iv. 8 Substance is either First or Second. The First is a Singular Substance, or that which is not said of a Subject, as Alexander, Bucephalus. The Second..that which is said of a Subject, as Man, Horse. **1843** MILL *Logic* I. vi. §2 The well known dogmas of *substantiæ secundæ*, or general substances. **1876** *Encycl. Brit.* V. 223/1 The first category is subdivided into ..primary substance, which is defined to be..the singular thing in which properties inhere, and to which predicates are attached, and..genera or species which can be predicated of primary substances. **1903** W. TURNER *Hist. Philos.* 133 The first substance (οὐσία πρώτη) is the individual, which can neither exist in another nor be predicated of another. Second substance is the universal, which, as such, does not exist in another, but may be predicated of another.

3. a. *Philos.* That which underlies phenomena; the permanent substratum of things; that which receives modifications and is not itself a mode; that in which accidents or attributes inhere.

1398 TREVISA *Barth. de P.R.* XIX. cxvi. (1495) 920 Whan tweyne accidentes ben in one substaunce and subiecte: as colour and savour. **1402** in *Pol. Poems* (Rolls) II. 108 Thus leeveth not of the breed but oonli the licnesse which that abidith therinne noon substeyned substans. **1551** T. WILSON *Logic* C ij, The feare of God is an Accident, the soule is a Substaunce. **1606** BRYSKETT *Civ. Life* 116 The substance of euery thing is so called, by reason that it is subiect vnto accidents; neither can there be any accident (to which it is proper to be in some subiect) but it must fall into some substance. **1668** WILKINS *Real Char.* II. i. 26 Such things as..require a subject of inhesion..are indeed nothing but the modes of Substance. **1690** LOCKE *Hum. Und.* II. xxiii. §2 The Idea..to which we give the general name Substance, being nothing, but the supposed..support of those Qualities..which we imagine cannot subsist, *sine re substante*, without something to support them. **1762** KAMES *Elem. Crit.* (1774) II. App. 507 A being with respect to its properties or attributes is termed a subject, or substratum. Every substratum of visible qualities, is termed substance. **1781** COWPER *Anti-Thelyphth.* 42 Substances and modes of ev'ry kind. **1838** [F. HAYWOOD] tr. *Kant's Crit. Pure Reason* 174 The determinations of a substance, which are nothing else but its particular modes of existing, are termed accidents. **1872** MAHAFFY *Kant's Crit. Phil.* I. 268 Thus the pure Category of substance is that which can only be subject —and not predicate. **1876** *Encycl. Brit.* V. 155/1 The independent substantiality of mind and matter is withdrawn, and they are reduced into attributes of the one infinite substance.

b. in transf. and allusive uses.

c **1374** CHAUCER *Troylus* IV. 1505 Þenk þat folye is whan man may chese For accident [h]is substaunce ay to lese. *c* **1386** —— *Pard. T.* 77 Thise Cookes, how they stampe, and streyne and grynde And turnen substaunce in-to Accident. **1568** GRAFTON *Chron.* II. 570 The Capteynes there, myndyng not to lease the more for the lesse, nor the substance for the accident. **1579** G. HARVEY *Let. to Spenser* in S.'s Wks. (1912) 639/2 Vertue, the onely immortall and suruiuing Accident amongst so manye mortall and euer-perishing Substaunces. **1598** BARCKLEY *Felic. Man* VI. 568 Euill is no substance nor nature, but an accident that commeth to the substance. **1654** Z. COKE *Logick* 189 The causes are found out & put in substances, in respect of the Essence, Matter, and Form. **1790** BURKE *Rev. France* 28 Not changing the substance, but regulating the mode.

c. with reference to the doctrine of the Real Presence in the Eucharist.

1546 GARDINER *Detect. Deuils Sophistrie* 14 b, The substaunce of bred, beyng conuerted into the naturall bodely substaunce of our sauioure [*printed* souioure] Christe. **1565** HARDING *Answ. Jewel* 162 b, In this Sacrament after consecration there remayneth..onely the accidentes and shewes, without the substance of bread and wyne. **1597** HOOKER *Eccl. Pol.* v. lxvii. §10 How the wordes of Christ commaunding vs to eate must needes importe that as hee hath coupled the substance of his fleshe and the substance of bread together, so we together should receiue both. **1651** C. CARTWRIGHT *Cert. Relig.* I. 131 It doth argue an extra-ordinary power in Christ to give his Flesh to eat, though there be no turning of the substance of the Bread in the Sacrament into the substance of his Flesh.

†**4.** That which underlies or supports; a basis, foundation; a ground, cause. *Obs.*

1382 WYCLIF *Heb.* xi. 1 Feith is the substaunce of thingis to be hopid. *c* **1386** CHAUCER *Nun's Pr. T.* 37 And wel I woot the substance is in me If any thyng shal wel reported be. **1390** GOWER *Conf.* III. 68 Nectanabus, which causeth al Of this metrede the substance. *Ibid.* 222 Ther is nothing Which mai be betre aboute a king, Than conseil, which is the substance Of all a kinges governance. **1577** tr. *Bullinger's Decades* I. iv. 30 The substance or hypostasis is the foundation, or the vnmoueable proppe, which vpholdeth vs. **1595** *Locrine* I. i. 70 A greater care torments my verie bones, And makes me tremble at the thought of it, And in you, Lordings, doth the substance lie.

5. a. The matter, subject-matter, subject (of a study, discourse, written work, etc.).

1390 GOWER *Conf.* I. 10 Unto the god ferst thei besoughten As to the substaunce of her Scole, That thei ne scholden noght befole Her wit upon none erthly werkes, Which were ayein thestat of clerkes. *Ibid.* II. 84 Of bodies sevene in special With foure spiritz joynt withal Stant the substance of this matiere. *c* **1412** HOCCLEVE *De Reg. Princ.* 1030 Lo, fadir, tolde haue I yow þe substance Of al my greef. *c* **1420** ? LYDG. *Assembly of Gods* 1601 But forthe to shewe yow the substaunce Of thys matyr. *a* **1536** *Songs, Carols* etc. (E.E.T.S.) 106, I dare not, for þer dissplesans, Tell of þes maters half the substance. **1587** T. NORTON tr. *Calvin's Inst.* title-p., Notes conteyning in briefe the substance of the matter handled in each section. **1597** SHAKS. *2 Hen. IV*, IV. i. 32 Vnto your Grace doe I in chiefe addresse The substance of my Speech. **1600** J. PORY tr. *Leo's Africa* App. 400 Out of the relations..of these two woorthy authors..we will deriue the whole substance of our speech. **1665** BOYLE *Occas. Refl.* III. v. 44 This, if I forget not, was the substance of the Occasional Meditation, suggested to me by the Storm. **1875** *Encycl. Brit.* I. 498/2 There are two Alexandrian schools, distinct both chronologically and in substance. The one is the Alexandrian school of poetry and science, the other the Alexandrian school of philosophy.

b. Contrasted with form or expression.

1780 *Mirror* No. 80 Having thus done justice to the merit of those authors in point of substance, I proceed to shew their excellence in the composition and style of their productions. **1841** MYERS *Cath. Th.* III. §8. 29 This influence we may believe to have extended sometimes to the very words of the Revelation, but far more often only to the substance of it. **1877** R. W. DALE *Lect. Preach.* v. 118 The substance of our preaching has been given to us in a Divine revelation. **1888** *Encycl. Brit.* XXIII. 249 The doctrine of the Trinity is..one which..gives expression to the self-evidencing substance of revelation, and explains and supports religious experience.

†**c.** A subject-matter to be operated upon. *Obs.*

1390 GOWER *Conf.* III. 91 The hihe pourveance Tho hadde under his ordinance A gret substance, a gret matiere, Of which he wolde..These othre thinges make and forme.

6. a. That of which a physical thing consists; the material of which a body is formed and in virtue of which it possesses certain properties.

1398 TREVISA *Barth. De P.R.* VI. xx. (Bodl. MS.), Mete is a substaunce þat is able to be turned into þe substaunce of þe bodie þat is ifed. **1559** W. CUNNINGHAM *Cosmogr. Glasse* 43 The matter and substaunce of mans body. **1577** TUSSER *Husb.* (1878) 35 The soile and the seede..the lighter in substance, for profite the wurse. **1590** SIR J. SMYTHE *Disc. Weapons* 3b, Swords of conuenient length, forme and substance, haue been in all ages esteemed by all warlike Nations. *c* **1600** SHAKS. *Sonn.* xliv. 1 If the dull substance of my flesh were thought, Iniurious distance should not stop my way. **1613** SALKELD *Treat. Angels* 56 Angels haue somtimes beene knowne to eate..although they did not conuert the meate..into their owne substance. **1615** CROOKE *Body of Man* 628 The substance of it is soft, loose, rare and like a Sponge. **1667** MILTON *P.L.* II. 356 What creatures there inhabit, of what mould, Or substance? **1668** WILKINS *Real Char.* II. iv. 73 Stalk..of a woody substance. .. Head or spike.. having a soft downy substance. **1766** BLACKSTONE *Comm.* II. 4 It became necessary..to appropriate to individuals not the immediate use only, but the very substance of the thing to be used. **1829** LOUDON *Encycl. Plants* (1836) 1023 Epiphyllous scattered globular or subdepressed smooth pale at length black, Substance very corneous. **1846** LANDOR *Exam. Shaks.* Wks. 1846 II. 265 Give a countryman a plough of silver and he will plough with it all the season, and never know its substance. **1859** FITZGERALD *Omar* lxi, Surely not in vain My Substance from the common Earth was ta'en.

b. of incorporeal things.

c **1340** HAMPOLE *Prose Treat.* viii. 15 By abowndance of charite þat es in þe substance of þe saule. *c* **1384** CHAUCER *H. Fame* II. 260 Euery spech that ys yspoken..In his substaunce ys but aire. *a* **1475** G. ASHBY *Dicta Philos.* 234 A kynge sholde take of his olde acquaintance, His familier seruauntes vertuous,..of Substance, Wele disposed, trewe, not malicious. **1592** SHAKS. *Rom. & Jul.* I. iv. 99 Dreames.. Begot of nothing, but vaine phantasie, Which is as thin of substance as the ayre. **1667** MILTON *P.L.* IV. 585 Hard thou knowst it to exclude Spiritual substance with corporeal barr. **1668** WILKINS *Real Char.* I. i. 5 A great part of this Syriac tongue is for the substance of the words Chaldee, and Hebrew for the fashion. **1682** in *Verney Mem.* (1907) II. 311, I..am sorry that my Sonne should Be composed of such substance that nothing can shape Him for a Schollar. **1740** CHEYNE *Regimen* 35 That spiritual Substance was analogous to Matter infinitely rarefied, refin'd or sublim'd. **1862** SPENCER *First Princ.* I. iii. §20 (1875) 63 When, instead of the extent of consciousness, we consider its substance.

c. ***fifth substance*** = QUINTESSENCE.

1561 [see QUINTESSENCE 1].

7. a. The matter or tissue composing an animal body, part, or organ.

1398 TREVISA *Barth. De P.R.* v. v. (1495) giv/1 The humour cristallinus [of the eye]..is rounde in shape & sastaunce [*sic*]. *a* **1425** tr. *Arderne's Treat. Fistula* etc. 34 þe quitour, þerfore, bigynne to lessen somwhat, and the bolnyng somwhat to cese, and þe colour and þe substaunce of þe skynne for to turne to his owne naturel habitude. **1548** in *Vicary's Anat.* v. (1888) 41 [Cheeks] not fat in substaunce, but meanely fleshly. **1667** MILTON *P.L.* VI. 657 Thir armor help'd their harm, crush't in and brus'd Into thir substance pent. **1724** BLACKMORE *Treat. Consumptions* 9 An extraordinary Discharge of Flegmatick Matter,..while..the Substance of the Lungs remains sound. **1726** A. MONRO *Anat. Bones* 31 *Sinuses*, large Cavities within the Substance of the Bones, with small Apertures. **1804** ABERNETHY *Surg. Obs.* 178 Blood was discharged mixed with detached pieces of the substance of the brain. **1845** BUDD *Dis. Liver* 347 Irregular dilatation of the sac, so as to form additional pouches in the substance of the liver.

b. The muscular tissue or fleshy part of an animal body.

1695 *New Light Chirurg. put out* 23 Any Flesh-Wound where there is considerable loss of Substance. **1750** LADY LUXBOROUGH *Let. to Shenstone* 13 May, My plaisters are already reduced from eight or nine to two only: one over my eye,..and one just above my knee, where the loss of substance (as they call it) makes it longer in curing. **1831** YOUATT *Horse* 36 A three-fourth, or thoroughbred horse of sufficient substance and height. **1894** *Nature's Method in Evol. Life* iii. 45 The nervous system becomes highly strung, ..and the muscles deficient in size, with a general want of what is known as 'substance'.

†**c.** *Bot.* (See quots.) *Obs.*

1777 S. ROBSON *Brit. Flora* 15 *Bullate*, the substance of the leaf rising high above the veins, so as to appear like little blisters. **1793** MARTYN *Lang. Bot.* s.v. *Substantia*, The substance of a vegetable consists of the *Epidermis* or Cuticle, covering the *Cortex* or Outer Bark.

8. a. Any particular kind of corporeal matter.

1390 GOWER *Conf.* III. 89 Of man, of beste,..Of fissch, of foughl, of everychon That ben of bodely substance. **1541** COPLAND *Guydon's Quest. Cyrurg.* E iv, [The nose] is of thre substaunces, that is to wyt of substaunce flesshely, bony, and cartilagynous. **1644** DIGBY *Nat. Bodies* xiv. §11. 123 Our designe requireth more maniable substances. **1668** WILKINS *Real Char.* II. x. 259 Grain or some Vegetable, baked in a drier substance without any considerable mixture. **1774** PENNANT *Tour Scot. in 1772*, 169 The gills furnished with strainers of the substance of whalebone. **1774** GOLDSM. *Nat. Hist.* I. 75 This variety of substances, which compose the internal parts of our globe. **1802** PALEY *Nat. Theol.* v. §3. 65 That sort of substance which we call animal substance, as flesh, bone,..cartilage, etc. **1816** J. SMITH *Panorama Sci. & Art* II. 91 When a varnish of any kind is laid over a substance, to prevent it from absorbing water, some allowance should be made for such addition. **1827** FARADAY *Chem. Manip.* xix. (1842) 527 To perform the operation over a cloth or some other soft substance. **1839** LINDLEY *Introd. Bot.* (ed. 3) 472 Corky..; having the texture of the substance called cork. **1860** TYNDALL *Glac.* II. v. 250 Thus, from the mixture of two perfectly transparent substances, we obtain an opaque one.

b. A species of matter of a definite chemical composition.

1732 ARBUTHNOT *Rules of Diet* iv. in *Aliments* etc. 409 Substances abounding with volatile oily Salts. **1807** Simple substance [see PRIMARY *a.* 3d]. **1843** [see SIMPLE *a.* 13a]. **1856** *Orr's Circ. Sci., Mech. Philos.* 2 By simple substances, we mean those which cannot be resolved by the chemist into any simpler elements: thus gold, silver, and iron are simple substances... Copper, zinc, iron, and carbon are all considered elementary substances. **1864** *Intell. Obs.* No. 32. 93 A new substance..to which I gave the name Santoneine. **1876** *Jrnl. Chem. Soc.* I. 365 The saccharification of amylaceous substances.

(*b*) ***substance P*** (Biochem.): an undecapeptide thought to be involved in the synaptic transmission of nerve impulses, esp. pain impulses.

[**1931** EULER & GADDUM in *Jrnl. Physiol.* LXXII. 80 This standard preparation, which we call *P*, dissolved easily in water to form a practically clear solution.] **1934** GADDUM & SCHILD in *Ibid.* LXXXIII. 1 This unidentified substance has been known in the laboratory for some time as substance P, and will be referred to under this name. **1964** W. G. SMITH *Allergy & Tissue Metabolism* vi. 71 Substance P, which is a pharmacologically active polypeptide.., stimulates guinea pig ileum. **1979** *Sci. Amer.* July 69/3 Enkephalin and another peptide, substance P, have been implicated in pain perception, substance P with the transmission of pain-related impulses and enkephalin with their suppression.

c. *Anat.* and *Zool.* With qualifying word or phr. forming specific designations.

1815 J. GORDON *Syst. Hum. Anat.* I. 40 Adipose substance. **1855** DUNGLISON *Med. Lex.*, White Substance of Schwann. **1870** W. S. KENT in *Ann. Nat. Hist.* Mar. 217 The sarcodic substance lining all the interstitial cavities of the sponge.

9. A piece or mass of a particular kind of matter; a body of a specified composition or texture. Now *rare.*

c **1595** CAPT. WYATT *R. Dudley's Voy. W. Ind.* (Hakl. Soc.) 56 In the night a substance of fyre resemblinge the shape of a fierie Dragon should fall into our sailes and theare remaine some quarter of an ower. **1668** WILKINS *Real Char.* II. v. 133 That [fish] which hath..stiff substances on his head and back. *Ibid.*, A very rough skin, with finny substances, standing out from each side like wings. *Ibid.* vi. 172 Thin broad substances standing off from the body of the Fish. **1681** tr. *Belon's New Myst. Phys.* Introd. 32 Set the Water in a cold place, in a Glass Body, within eight Days, you will find a congealed Substance in the Bottom of the Vessel. **1725** *Bradley's Fam. Dict.* s.v. *White-Honey-Charge*, Continue boiling till the Roots and Herbs be reduced to a Mash..throwing away the gross Substance. **1726** SWIFT *Gulliver* III. i. 10, I..perceived a vast Opake Body between me and the Sun...it appeared to be a firm Substance. **1799** HT. LEE *Canterb. T., Wom. T.* (ed. 2) I. 351 Throwing from him, without examination, some hard substance that incommoded him.

10. a. A solid or real thing, as opposed to an appearance or shadow. Also, reality.

1576 FLEMING *Panopl. Epist.* 281 The ignoraunce of the world is grosse & palpable: for, touching Nature their skill is but superficiall, and like a shadowe destitute of substaunce. **1588** SHAKS. *Tit. A.* III. ii. 80 He takes false shadowes, for true substances. **1590** SPENSER *F.Q.* II. ix. 2 Full liuely is the semblaunt, though the substance dead. **1651** HOBBES *Leviathan* II. xxxi. 186 A Common-wealth, without Soveraign Power, is but a word, without substance. **1667** MILTON *P.L.* I. 529 With high words, that bore Semblance of worth not substance. *a* **1700** EVELYN *Diary* 27 Aug. 1667, One who kept up the forme and substance of things in the Nation. **1716** S. W. in *Nelson's Pract. True Devot.* (1784) p. xvi, Taught how to take the mystic Bread and Wine, T'adore the Substance, nor neglect the Sign. **1784** COWPER *Task* IV. 527 The poet's hand, Imparting substance to an empty shade, Impos'd a gay delirium for a truth. **1821** BYRON *Sardanap.* I. ii. 533 There needs too oft the show of war to keep The substance of sweet peace. **1836** MARRYAT *Japhet* lxiii, I would not lose the substance by running after shadows. **1856** MERIVALE *Rom. Emp.* l. V. 580 A mere honorary title, and only a presage of the substance that was to follow. **1914** *Daily Chron.* 28 July 6/3 The Austro-Hungarian communiqué..argues..that Servia conceded the shadows and withheld the substance.

b. *Westminster School.* An older pupil who is responsible for the proper conduct of a new boy, called his 'shadow'.

1845 *College & T.B. Life at Westm.* 25 Oct., After my first week at School, I started altogether on my own account, my Substance then having nothing more to do with me. **1899** W. K. R. BEDFORD *Outcomes of Old Oxford* 85 Every neophyte was consigned to the tutelage of some boy already in the school..the shortcomings of the shadow, or tyro, were credited to the preceptor, or substance, and visited with penalties upon the latter.

11. a. What is embodied in a statement; the meaning or purport of what is expressed in writing or speech; what a writing or speech amounts to.

1415 LD. SCROPE in *43rd Rep. Dep. Kpr. Publ. Rec.* 590 Ilche worde y kan nought remembr bot for the most sobstans as nye os y kan thinke. **1415** in Ellis *Orig. Lett.* Ser. II. I. 47 Yf heny of thes persones..woldyn contrary ye substaunce of yat i have wretyn at zys tyme. **1481** CAXTON *Myrr.* II. xxv. 117 Yf ye wyl here and wel reteyne the mater and substaunce of this present booke. **1502** *Ord. Crysten Men* (W. de W. 1506) I. ii. A vj b, I shall put the substaunce of the latyn afore sayd in englysshe. **1576** FLEMING *Panopl. Epist.* 17 So farre as I gather by the substance of your letters, a certaine kinde of suspicion is signified. **1597** SHAKS. *2 Hen. IV*, IV. i. 9, I haue receiu'd New-dated Letters from Northumberland: Their cold intent, tenure, and substance thus. **1612** BRINSLEY *Lud. Lit.* xxii. (1627) 256 Learning is not so much seen, in setting downe the words, as the substance. **1653** H. COGAN tr. *Pinto's Trav.* lxxix. 321 All of them together, seeming to be Merchants sons,..sung in verse with a very sweet and melodious voyce, words of this substance, 'High and mighty Lord' [&c.]. **1669** STURMY *Mariner's Mag.* I. ii. 3 But to come to the Substance of what is here intended. **1699** BENTLEY *Phal.* 233 The substance of the Epigram imports, that Thespis was the first contriver of Tragedy. *a* **1700** EVELYN *Diary* 5 Aug. 1670, This is the substance of what she told me. **1794** MRS. RADCLIFFE *Myst. Udolpho* xxxi, Who repeated the substance of what had passed between Montoni and herself. **1805** A. KNOX *Rem.* (1834) I. 1, I hope..that, if any thing..appeared exceptionable, it was in manner and expression only, and not in the substance of my sentiments. **1837** B'NESS BUNSEN in Hare *Life* (1879) I. x. 461 The whole substance of his communications proved a state of vicious disorganization. **1861** G. C. LEWIS *Let. to Reeve* 9 Apr., You may rely on the substance of this story being quite authentic. **1867** RUSKIN *Time & Tide* iii. §9 The substance of what I said to them was this.

†**b.** The main intent or purpose. *Obs. rare.*

1606 CHAPMAN *Gentl. Usher* IV. ii, To execute the substance of our mindes In honor'd nuptialls.

†**12.** The vital part. *Obs.*

c **1430** *Pol. Rel. & L. Poems* (1903) 233 'The kingis sone', sche seide, 'is deed, þe ioie, þe substaunce of my lijfe.' **1588** SHAKS. *Tit. A.* I. i. 374 Deare Father, soule and substance of vs all. **1605** *1st Pt. Jeronimo* I. iii, Come, my soules spaniell, my lifes ietty substance.

13. a. That which gives a thing its character; that which constitutes the essence of a thing; the essential part, essence.

c **1585** [R. BROWNE] *Answ. Cartwright* 55 To be able to teache is not of the substance of a minister, but onely of a lawful minister. *Ibid.* 56 If a man bee not a lawfull minister, hee hath no essence nor substance of a mynister. **1597** MORLEY *Introd. Mus.* 96 *Phi.* What doe you call keeping the substance of a note? *Ma.* When in breaking it, you sing either your first or last note in the same key wherin it standeth, or in his eight. **1620** T. GRANGER *Div. Logike* 94 The essences, or substances of things are not here meant. **1790** BURKE *Rev. France* 220 Miserable bigots..who hate sects and parties different from their own, more than they love the substance of religion. **1856** *N. Brit. Rev.* XXVI. 41 Modern thought, in its substance, is a congeries of all those refined theistic speculations, of all those baffled aspirations, of all those deep and distracting surmises. **1869** MOZLEY *Univ. Serm.* ii. (1876) 39 It is sufficiently clear that these are not the substance of the character.

b. in legal use. (Cf. SUBSTANTIAL A. 5b.)

1592 WEST *1st Pt. Symbol.* I. §22 The substance of this contract consisteth in the thing solde, and in the price thereof. **1596** BACON *Max. & Use Com. Law* I. (1630) 4 The intention is matter of substance. *Ibid.* xvi. 68 If a man bid one robbe I. S. as he goeth to Sturbridge-faire, and he robbe him in his house the variance seemes to be of substance. *a* **1623** SWINBURNE *Spousals* (1686) 141 Resisting the Substance of Matrimony, it overthroweth the Contract. **1843–56** BOUVIER *Law Dict.* (ed. 6) II. 555/2 *Substance*, evidence. That which is essential; it is used in opposition to form.

†**14.** The amount, quantity, or mass (*of* a thing).

c **1420** ? LYDG. *Assembly of Gods* 764 When Vertew sy the substaunce of hys oost, He prayed all the comons to the felde hem hy. *a* **1500** in *Rep. Hist. MSS. Comm.* Var. Coll. IV. 87 A vessaill called the Mighell of Brykelsey..in the whiche diuerse merchauntes of our Citie of London had goodes and merchandises to a grete value and substaunce. *c* **1500** *Lancelot* (S.T.S.) 1740 If..to the rich iftis of plesans, That thei be fair, set nocht of gret substans. **1520** *Cov. Leet Bk.* 675 What substance of malt was then brewede within the Cyte wokly by the comyn brewers. *a* **1548** HALL *Chron., Hen. V*, 57b, He found there innumerable substance of plate and money belongyng to the citizens. **1565** *Wills & Inv. N.C.* (Surtees 1835) 244 Raffe Vasye..oweth me for all my..muke..the substance by estimac[i]on come to or will come to..two hundrethe futhers. **1596** SHAKS. *Merch. V.* IV. i. 328 Be it so much As makes it light or heauy in the substance, Or the deuision of the twentieth part Of one poore scruple.

†**15. a.** The greater number or part, the majority, mass, or bulk *of*. *Obs.*

c **1374** CHAUCER *Troylus* IV. 217 It moste ben and sholde. For substaunce of þe parlement it wolde. **1435** *Cov. Leet Bk.* 185 That the maiour call the substaunce of the Crafte of Carpynters and sett hem to-geþer as one felawshipe. **1462** J. RUSSE *Let. to J. Paston* Sept., The substaunce of jentilmen and yemen of Lodyngland be assygned to be afore the seyd commesyoners. **1507** in Leadam *Sel. Cases Star Chamber* (Selden Soc.) 259 Robert..hath ered great substans of the ground of your seid besechers. **1512** *Act 4 Hen. VIII*, c. 1 §1 The said Countie [*sc.* Cornwall] is thre score and ten myle in lenght and the substance therof right litle more than six myle in brede. **1550–3** *Decaye Eng.* in S. Fish *Supplic.* (1871) 96 Many of them doeth kepe the most substaunce of theyr landes in theyr owne handes. **1552–3** *Act 7 Edw. VI*, c. 12 The Kynges Majesties Treasure..waasted, the greate Substaunce of the Moneyes molted and altered in bayse coyne.

b. ***sum*** (†***summary***) ***and substance***: see SUM *sb.*, SUMMARY *sb.*

16. a. Possessions, goods, estate; means, wealth. *arch.* (chiefly as a reminiscence of biblical language).

13.. *Cursor M.* 9538 (Gött.) Of his substance he gaf ilkan, And ilkan gaf he substance an. **1382** WYCLIF *Prov.* iii. 9 Honoure the Lord of thi substaunce. **1382** —— *Luke* xv. 13 He wastide his substaunce in lyuynge leccherously. *c* **1400** *Rom. Rose* 6595 Yit shulde he selle alle his substaunce And with his swynk haue sustenaunce. *c* **1430** LYDG. *Min. Poems* (Percy Soc.) 135 Abel..Gaff God his part, tethe of his substaunce. **1466** *Paston Lett.* Suppl. 108, I truste I am of that substans that, what soever caswelte fortunyd, yourre maistresship shuld not lese on pene of yourre dute. **1500–20** DUNBAR *Poems* lxxxviii. 7 London, thou art of townes A per se... Of merchauntis full of substaunce and myght. *c* **1520** SKELTON *Magnyf.* 1445 Take of his Substaunce a sure inuentory. **1535** COVERDALE *Job* i. 3 His substaunce was vij. M. shepe, iij. M. camels, v. C. yock of oxen, v. C. she asses, and a very greate housholde. **1535** —— *Ps.* xvii. 14 They haue children at their desyre, and leaue the rest of their substaunce for their babes. **1590** SHAKS. *Com. Err.* I. i. 24 Thy substance, valued at the highest rate, Cannot amount vnto a hundred Markes. **1634** SIR T. HERBERT *Trav.* 206 They will hazard all their worth..and other substance. *a* **1700** EVELYN *Diary* 3 Nov. 1685, Innumerable persons of the greatest birth and riches leaving all their earthly substance. **1794** WORDSW. *Guilt & Sorrow* xxvi, My father's substance fell into decay. **1849** MACAULAY *Hist. Eng.* ii. I. 156 A fortune raised out of the substance of the ruined defenders of the throne.

†**b.** With *a*: An amount of wealth, a fortune; *pl.* riches, possessions. *Obs.*

13.. [see sense 16]. **1382** WYCLIF *Ecclus.* xli. 1 Hauende pes in his substaunces [1388 richessis]. **1382** —— *Acts* ii. 45 Thei selden possesciouns and substaunces. **1382** —— *Heb.* x. 34 Knowynge ȝou for to haue a betere and dwelling substaunce. **1487** *Act 3 Hen. VII*, c. 2 Wymmen..havyng substaunces somme in goodes moveable, and somme in landes and tenements. **1560** DAUS tr. *Sleidane's Comm.* Pref. 5 b, Whose brother for the education of youth in true Religion & learning, imploied a wonderful substaunce. **1731–9** TULL *Horse-hoeing Husb.* (1822) 154 A small substance.

†**17. a.** A supply or provision *of*. *Obs.*

c **1385** CHAUCER *L.G.W.* 1560 Iason weddit was Vn-to this queen & tok of it substaunce What so hym leste onto his puruyaunce. *c* **1412** HOCCLEVE *De Reg. Princ.* 4909 If a man, in tyme of swich a nede, Of his goode ȝeue yow a goode substaunce. **1515** in Leadam *Sel. Cases Star Chamber* (Selden Soc.) II. 79 The said Towne [was] then in better substaunce of goodis good ordre and rule then it is nowe. **1535** COVERDALE *Eccl.* ii. 7 As for catell and shepe, I had more substaunce of them, then all they yᵗ were before me.

†**b.** Maintenance, subsistence. *Obs.*

c **1380** WYCLIF *Sel. Wks.* III. 67 Sees gendren manye fischis to substaunce of mankynde. **1502** *Ord. Crysten Men* (W. de W. 1506) I. iii. Cij, It is not gyuen to hym for substaunce or refeccyon corporell. *a* **1513** FABYAN *Chron.* VI. clxx. (1811) 164 All thynges..were than more wasted in glotony, and outrage of owners, than in substaunce and ayde of nedy men.

†**18.** Substantial existence, substantiality. *Obs.*

c **1366** CHAUCER *A.B.C.* 87 As j seide erst þou ground of oure substaunce Continue on us þi pitous eyen cleere. **1555** EDEN *Decades* (Arb.) 135 To gyue substance to priuation, (that is) beinge to noo beinge. **1628** [see SUBSISTENCY 3].

19. a. Substantial or solid qualities, character, etc.

c **1430** *Wyclif's Bible* Prol. I. 58 Symple men, that wolden for no good in erthe..putte awei..the leste..title, of holi writ, that berith substaunce, either charge. **1559** Q. ELIZ. in Strype *Ann. Ref.* (1709) I. II. 414 Dyvers reasons which appeare unto me to have in them small substance. **1581** RICH *Farew.* (1846) 159 Knowyng her housebande to be a man of no verie greate substaunce, and but slenderly stuffed in the hedpeece. **1858** HAWTHORNE *Fr. & It. Note-bks.* (1871) I. 221 Neither rulers nor people had any faith or moral substance. **1863** KINGLAKE *Crimea* (1876) I. 117 This fact gave great strength and substance to the pretensions of Russia.

b. That which makes a material firm, solid, and hard-wearing.

1833 HT. MARTINEAU *Loom & Lugger* I. ii. 21 You must learn from the French to give your fabrics more substance. *Mod.* There's hardly any substance in this material.

†**20.** The consistency *of* a fluid. *Obs.*

c **1450** *Mirk's Festial* 166/9 Take hede on watyr, and on yse, and on snow; how þay ben ych on dyverse in substance, and ȝet þay ben but watyr. **1541** COPLAND *Guydon's Quest. Cyrurg.* R j, When it [*sc.* blood] is drawen, consydre the substance and the colour yf it be so as is abouesayde. **1799** G. SMITH *Laboratory* I. 207 Give it the substance of thin paste.

21. in substance. **a.** In reality.

1390 GOWER *Conf.* II. 87 To receive Bothe in substance and in figure Of gold and selver the nature. **1667** MILTON *P.L.* XI. 771 Hee the future evil shall no less In apprehension then in substance feel Grievous to bear. **1785** BURKE *Sp. Nabob of Arcot's Debts* Wks. 1842 I. 339 The nabob of Arcot, and rajah of Tanjore, have, in truth and substance, no more than a merely civil authority. **1793** —— *On policy of Allies* Wks. 1842 I. 601 We know that the monarchy did not survive the hierarchy, no not even in appearance, for many months; in substance, not for a single hour.

†**b.** In general; generally speaking. (In ME. poetry used, esp. by Lydgate, as a metrical tag.)

c **1407** LYDG. *Reason & Sens.* 645 In especial ther be tweyne, And thou mayst chesen, in substaunce, Whiche ys most to thy plesaunce. *Ibid.* 894 And fynaly, as in substaunce, Do as the lyst, lo, this the ende. **1426** —— *De Guil. Pilgr.* 5881 Yt behoueth in sentence, That the fulfyllyng in substaunce To the fulle haue suffysaunce. *c* **1440** *Generydes* 1968 Now haue I here rehersid in substaunce xv kynges, As shortly as I myght, With ther powre and All ther hoole puysaunce. **1447** *Rolls of Parlt.* V. 129/2 In whos kepyng the Bokes, suretees and godes in substaunce holy remaigne.

†**c.** In the main, for the most part. *Obs.*

1475 *Rolls of Parlt.* VI. 151/1 The which forseid xᵗʰ part, and xvᵉ and xᵉ..been in substaunce levied and paied. *a* **1500** *Bale's Chron.* in *Six Town Chron.* (1911) 119 And the hertes of the comones in substaunce wer wᵗ þe Erle: And a geinst the seid priour.

d. In essentials, substantially.

1491 *Act 7 Hen. VII*, c. 22 *Preamble*, All whiche matiers afore rehercid is by the seid John Hayes in substaunce confessed and knowleged. **1581** in D. Digges *Complete Ambass.* (1655) 440 She used in substance the like speeches the King had done. **1687** A. LOVELL tr. *Thevenot's Trav.* II. 106 The Religion of the Persians is in substance the same with that of the Turks. **1737** *Gentl. Mag.* VII. 662 To this it was replied in Substance as follows. **1821** JEFFERSON *Writ.* (1830) IV. 344, I may misremember indifferent circumstances, but can be right in substance. **1857** KEBLE *Euch. Ador.* ii. 26 Whitgift..adds, in substance, the same account of it. **1908** *Progr. Modernism* 118 These are, in substance, our ideas upon the origin of religion.

e. In effect, virtually.

1834 H. TAYLOR *Artevelde* I. I. ii, Think well What you should say; for if it must be 'no' In substance, you shall hardly find that form Which shall convey it pleasantly.

†**f.** In a pure or unmixed state, in the natural state. (Cf. F. *en substance*.) *Obs.*

1621 BURTON *Anat. Mel.* I. ii. II. iii. 102 Theophrastus speakes of a Shepheard that could eat Hellebor in substance. *Ibid.* II. i. IV. ii. 303.

†**g.** ? Real, substantial. *Obs.*

1649 MILTON *Tenure of Kings* 4 When the Common wealth nigh perishes for want of deeds in substance, don with just and faithfull expedition.

22. of (..) substance: **a.** (often *of good* or *great substance*) Substantial, well-to-do, wealthy. (Cf. OF. *de substance*.)

1480 *Cov. Leet Bk.* 435 The Comien Counceill of þe Cite & other persones of substaunce. **1496** in *Rep. Hist. MSS. Comm.* Var. Coll. IV. 211 Suche inhabitantes of grete substans. *a* **1508** DUNBAR *Tua Mariit Wemen* 337 That syre of substance. **1528** MORE *Dyaloge* III. xv. Wks. 235/1 A very honest person, & of a good substaunce. **1660** SOUTH *Serm.* Matt. xiii. 52 (1727) IV. 11 A Man of Substance and Sufficiency. **1681** *Pennsylvania Arch.* I. 38 Men of substance and reputation. **1840** THACKERAY *Catherine* xxii, Hayes's father was reported to be a man of some substance. **1869** BLACKMORE *Lorna D.* i, My father being of good substance, at least as we reckon in Exmoor. **1889** JESSOPP *Coming of Friars* ii. 70 [He] was a man of substance and influence.

†**b.** Of immaterial things: Substantial, weighty.

c **1440** *Pilgr. Sowle* (Caxton 1483) IV. xxxiii. 82 The hygher that he is sette in estate the more shold his wordes be of substaunce and moost of reputacion. *a* **1456** LD. CROMWELL in *Paston Lett.* III. 425 There is a greet straungenesse betwix my right trusty frend John Radcliff and you, withoute any matier or cause of substaunce, as I am lerned. **1509** FISHER *Funeral Serm. C'tess Richmond* Wks. (1876) 291 Tryfelous thynges that were lytell to be regarded she wolde let passe by, but the other that were of weyght & substaunce [etc.].

†**c.** Of a meal: Sumptuous. *Obs.*

c **1485** *Digby Myst.* (1882) III. 574, I haue ordeynnyd a dyner of substawns, My chyff freyndes þerwith to chyr.

23. *Comb.*, as ***substance-yielding*** ppl. adj.

1611 COTGR., *Substantifique*, substantiell, or substance-yeelding.

substanced (ˈsʌbstənst), *pa. pple. rare.* [f. prec. + -ED².]

†**1.** Furnished with wealth. *Obs.*

1615 CHAPMAN *Odyss.* IV. 119 This Pallace here, (..furnished so well; And substanced with such a precious deale Of well-got treasure).

2. Made into a substance, made substantial, substantiated.

1873 WHITNEY *Other Girls* xxxiv. (1876) 443 If life were nothing but what gets phrased and substanced, the world might as well be rolled up and laid away again in darkness. **1890** J. PULSFORD *Loyalty to Christ* I. 129 Blessed are the appetites which feed on God's immortality; for His immortality shall be substanced in them.

3. Of a specified kind of substance. Chiefly in parasynthetic comb.

1624 QUARLES *Job Milit.* x. 71 Wks. (Grosart) II. 84/1 Your slender Maxims, and false Forgeryes, Are substanc't, like the dust, that flies besides me. **1753** *Chambers' Cycl.* Suppl. s.v. *Diamond*, The stone here described is said to be a full substanced Brilliant.

†**sub'stancefying**, *ppl. a. Obs. rare*⁻¹. ? = SUBSTANTIFIC.

1605 TIMME *Quersit.* III. 148 Those three substancefying beginnings are..found in al the things of nature.

substanceless (ˈsʌbstənslɪs), *a.* [f. SUBSTANCE *sb.* + -LESS.] Devoid of substance, unsubstantial.

1816 COLERIDGE *Hum. Life* Poems 316 If rootless thus, thus substanceless thy state. **1822** W. TENNANT *Thane of Fife* VI. 32 That conclave substanceless of gilded things. **1858** LYTTON *What will He do?* IX. i, You have made that life substanceless as a ghost—that future barren as the grave. **1895** MOIR in *Galt's Wks.* I. p. xci, The arguments..might be..too shadowy and substanceless to convey intellectual satisfaction.

sub-'standard, *a.* [SUB- 14.] **1.** Of a quality or size less than that which is normally or officially regarded as standard.

1909 in *Cent. Dict.* Suppl. **1930** *Daily Express* 6 Oct. 13/1 The famous 'Marshella'..sub-standard [stockings]... Special lot..slightly sub-standard. **1947** *Mind* LVI. 313 A race of philosophers from whom it is the fashion to expect somewhat sub-standard ratiocination. **1952** C. P. BLACKER *Eugenics: Galton & After* 312 The mother is frequently sub-standard mentally. **1964** D. MACARTHUR *Reminiscences* VI. 157 He took a substandard force and welded it into a weapon so deadly as to take command of the air whenever it engaged the enemy. **1975** M. SULLIVAN *Watch how you Go* i. 22 They lived all their long lives under sub-standard conditions, and accepted them.

2. Of speech: not conforming to standard usage; *spec.* employing forms which are widely used but are considered incorrect.

1933 L. BLOOMFIELD *Language* iii. 50 In such communities the non-standard language can be divided, roughly, to be sure, and without a sharp demarcation, into *sub-standard* speech, intelligible at least, though not uniform, throughout the country, and *local dialect*. **1951** TRAGER & SMITH *Outl. Eng. Struct.* 84, *I have knowed* can be called substandard or 'incorrect'. **1964** *English Studies* XLV. (Suppl.). 149 St. Mary's Lane, Lewes, is called 'Simmery Lane' in local sub-standard speech. **1977** *Word* 1972 XXVIII. 264 It is much more prevalent in the north, especially in substandard and rural speech.

3. *Cinemat.* Of film: less than 35 mm. wide; *spec.* 16 mm. wide.

1934 *Discovery* Feb. 47/2 [Films] shot on standard 35 mm film-stock before being reduced to the sub-standard non-flam 16 mm normally required for class-room use. **1940** *Chambers's Techn. Dict.* 818/1 Sub-standard sizes in use are 17·5, 16, 9·5 and 8 mm., as contrasted with the standard 35 mm. **1935**, **1959** [see NARROW GAUGE 2].

†**sub'stander.** *Obs.* [Rendering of L. *substans* (see SUBSTANCE *sb.*).] A thing that subsists. So **sub'standing** *ppl. a.*, subsisting.

1662 J. CHANDLER *Van Helmont's Oriat.* 144 A truly substanding or remaining Being [orig. *vere substantis entis*]. *Ibid.* 345 The Substance of that Substander or remainer [orig. *ejusque substantis substantia*].

substant (ˈsʌbstənt), *a.* and *sb. rare.* [ad. L. *substans*, *-ant-*, pr. pple. of *substāre* (see SUBSTANCE).]

A. *adj.* **1.** Substantial; subsistent.

1660 STANLEY *Hist. Philos.* IX. ii. (1687) 571/1 The Pythagoreans reduce all Beings, subsistent or substant, immediatly to Idæa's which truly are. **1838** J. E. READE *Italy* I. xxv, A substant and eternal memory.

2. Underlying.

1883 *Century Mag.* XXVII. 146 Its [*sc.* a glacier's] substant ice curls freely.

†**B.** *sb.* A subsisting thing. *Obs.*

1597 J. PAYNE *Royal Exch.* 24 The substants of bodie and soule have nothinge commune with this spirituall mariage.

substantia'bility. Error for SUBSTANTIALITY.

1836 MARRYAT *Japhet* lxii, The Quaker dress added very much to the substantiability of his appearance. **1839** *New Monthly Mag.* LVII. 143 The stalwart lover..does not relish having his identity, and still less his substantiability, called in question.

substantial (səbˈstænʃəl), *a.* (*adv.*) and *sb.* Forms: 4–8 **substancial**, (4 **-ciel**, 5 **-cyel**, 5–6 **-aunc-**, **-ciall(e**, **-cyall(e**, 5–7 **-tiall**), 6– **substantial**. [ad. late L. *substantiālis* (f. *substantia* SUBSTANCE), whence also F. *substantiel* (from 13th c.), Pr. *substancial*, Sp. *su(b)stancial*, It. *sostanziale*, *sustanziale*.] **A.** *adj.*

1. That is, or exists as, a substance; having a real existence; subsisting by itself.

1387–8 T. USK *Test. Love* II. xiii. (Skeat) l. 47 Naturel goodnesse of every substaunce is nothing els than his substancial being. **1488** CAXTON *Chast. Goddes Chyld.* 47 Eche thynge that is noo body if it be substancyall it is callid a spiryte. **1651** HOBBES *Leviathan* III. xxxiv. 211 Some such apparitions [*sc.* Dæmons] may be reall, and substantiall; that is to say, subtile Bodies, which God can form by the same power, by which he formed all things. *a* **1652** J. SMITH *Sel. Disc.* iv. (1821) 71 This hypothesis, that no substantial and indivisible thing ever perisheth. **1678** CUDWORTH *Intell. Syst.* Pref. 4 The general ranks of substantiall beings below the Deity. **1817** COLERIDGE *Biog. Lit.* xii. (1907) I. 169 The want of substantial reality in the objects of the senses, according to the sceptics.

absol. **1838** [F. HAYWOOD] tr. *Kant's Crit. Pure Reason* 327 That which..might yet seem to be an idea of transcendental reason, would be the conception of the substantial. **1856** FERRIER *Inst. Metaph.* XVI. (ed. 2) 328 There is a substantial in cognition; in other words, substance is knowable, and is known by us. *Ibid.* XVII. xvi. 348 The substantial in cognition (τὸ ὄν).

2. *Philos.* Of, pertaining or relating to, or inherent in substance (esp. as opposed to *accident*); that is substance. Also *transf.* and allusively.

1387–8 T. USK *Test. Love* II. vii. (Skt.) I. 147 Thilke thinges that we clepe power is but accident to the fleshly body; and so they may not have that suretee in might, whiche wanteth in the substancial body. **1526** *Pilgr. Perf.* (W. de W. 1531) 153 How to yᵉ actyue lyfe perteyneth accidentall ioye, but to the contemplatyue the substanciall crowne of glory. **1580** BLUNDEVIL *Horsemanship* IV. iv. 3 Sickness..is knowne..by inseparable or substantiall accidents, as by the shape, number, qualitie, & site of the part, or member diseased. **1581** FULKE in *Confer.* III. (1584) U iv, But bread is substance: Therefore he gaue them pieces of substance, or substantial pieces. **1642** DENHAM *Sophy* V. i If happiness be a substantial good, Not fram'd of accidents, nor subject to 'em. **1664** H. MORE *Apology* 498 Calvin seems to be affraid of the opinion of the Body being Spiritual, as implying a Substantial change.

3. ***substantial form*** [see FORM *sb.* 4 a: med.L. *substantialis forma* (Joannes Scotus Erigena), Gr. οὐσιῶδες εἶδος (Philoponus *Arist. Categ.*)]: the nature or distinctive character in virtue of possessing which a thing is what it (specifically or individually) is.

1413 [see FORM *sb.* 4 a]. **1477** NORTON *Ord. Alch.* v. in Ashm. (1652) 63 Coagulation is noe forme substantiall. **1666** BOYLE *Orig. Formes & Qual.* 45 Some Engines, which.. devoid of Substantial Forms, must do those strange things they are admir'd for, by vertue of those Accidents, the Shape, Size, Motion, and Contrivance of their parts. **1697** tr. *Burgersdicius' Logic* I. xvi. 56 Form is divided into Substantial and Accidental... The Substantial Form of a Musician, as he is a Man, is the Rational Soul; Accidental as he is a Musician, Musick. **1707** *Curios. Husb. & Gard.* 343 Salts.. he regarded as the Substantial Form of Bodies. **1728** CHAMBERS *Cycl.* s.v., Substantial Forms, *i.e.* Forms independant of all Matter; or Forms that are Substances themselves. **1741** WATTS *Improv. Mind* II. v. (1801) 214 A student who.. imagines certain immaterial beings, called substantial forms, to inhabit every herb, flower [&c.]. **1775** J. HARRIS *Philos. Arrangements* xvi. 387 *note.*

4. Relating to or proceeding from the essence of a thing; essential. Now *rare* or *Obs.*

c **1380** WYCLIF *Sel. Wks.* II. 285 Crist.. was of þe same kynde þat is ech man his broþer, and þis liknesse is in substancial kynde. **1509** HAWES *Past. Pleas.* XVIII. (Percy Soc.) 83 Your heart is your by substancyall lyne, It is not in my domynacyon. **1551** T. WILSON *Logic* (1580) 14 If he can learne firste to see the verie Nature, and, substanciall propertie of euery thyng. *a* **1653** H. BINNING *Princ. Chr. Relig.* Wks. (1735) 30/2 Christ may be called the Truth indeed, the substantial Word of God, for he is the very Substance of the written and preached Word. **1667** MILTON *P.L.* IV. 485 To give thee being I lent Out of my side to thee, neerest my heart Substantial Life. **1782** PRIESTLEY *Corrupt. Chr.* I. I. 127 Joachim.. denied that there was any essence, or any thing that belonged in common to the three persons, by which their substantial union was taken away, and nothing but a numerical or moral union was left.

5. a. That is, constitutes, or involves an essential part, point, or feature; essential, material.

Now said chiefly of immaterial things and often blending with 8, 9, or 14.

1432-50 tr. *Higden* (Rolls) VII. 399 A decrete was made that the substantialle partes of that rule scholde be kepede, and oþer thynges as superfluous to be refusede. **1467** in *Engl. Gilds* (1870) 385 It myght be ordeined a substancialle rule, that v. pagentes.. to be holden yerly, shuld not be to seche. **1528** MORE *Dyaloge* I. Wks. 174/1 That yͭ church can not erre in any such substauncyall article as God wyll haue vs bounden to beleue. **1541** COPLAND *Guydon's Quest. Cyrurg.* G j, Be the addicions abouesayd other bones than the bone of yͤ sholdre?.. No,.. but are substancyall party of it. **1567-9** JEWEL *Def. Apol.* (1611) 327 The Substantiallest points of all your Doctrine. **1588** KYD *Househ. Phil.* Wks. (1901) 269 Those compasses.. which, though they be diuers according to the variety of Countreys, is (notwithstanding) no occasion of substantiall difference. **1647** CLARENDON *Hist. Reb.* I. §20 The common misfortune of Princes, that in so substantial a part of their Happyness.. Themselves had never any part. **1686** GOAD *Celest. Bodies* II. viii. 273, I would not have it destitute of a Limme that is substantial, or one of its vital Parts. **1729** W. LAW *Serious C.* 52 Most of the employments of life are.. lawful; and all those that are so, may be made a substantial part of our duty to God. **1818** CRUISE *Digest* (ed. 2) II. 188 He could not find any substantial distinction between that case, and the principal one. **1867** RUSKIN *Time & Tide* viii. §35 Under.. Divine guidance, securing them from substantial error.

b. *Law.* Belonging to or involving essential right, or the merits of a matter.

[**1838** W. BELL *Dict. Law Scot., Substantialia*, those parts of a deed which are essential to its validity as a formal instrument.] **1843-56** BOUVIER *Law Dict.* s.v. *Form*, If the matter pleaded be in itself insufficient, without reference to the manner of pleading it, the defect is substantial. **1883** *Wharton's Law Lex.* (ed. 7) 739/1 The judge will consider what is the substantial fact to be made out, and on whom it lies to make it out. **1897** *Bouvier's Law Dict.* s.v. *Right to begin*,.. The party who asserts the affirmative of an issue has the right to begin and reply, as on him is the burden of proof. The substantial affirmative, not the verbal, gives the right.

6. Of food, a meal: Affording ample or abundant nourishment. (In later use the notion of solidity or quantity is predominant.)

1340 *Ayenb.* (1866) 113 þe more þet he [*sc.* food] is norissinde, me zayþ þet he is þe substancieler. *a* **1380** *S. Paula* 60 in Horstm. *Altengl. Leg.* (1878) 4 Cumforte þi brayn beter wiþ sum bred And wiþ sum substancial mete.

1578 *Chr. Prayers* in *Priv. Prayers* (1851) 451 We be able to brook substantialer meat, because we be grown to further years of discretion. **1626** SPEED *Adam out of Eden* v. (1659) 38 Clovergrass.. renders abundance of very exquisite hay, very great substantial and much desired. **1634** W. TIRWHYT tr. *Balzac's Lett.* (vol. I.) 115 Whilest others fill themselves with substantiall and most ponderous cates. *a* **1774** TUCKER *Lt. Nat.* (1834) II. 653 We say roast beef is good substantial food, but water-gruel not. **1822-7** GOOD *Study Med.* (1829) I. 210 One substantial meal of solid animal food daily. **1825** T. HOOK *Sayings* Ser. II. *Passion & Princ.* viii. III. 117 A good, substantial, hot luncheon. **1827** SCOTT *Chron. Canongate* iv, With something rather more substantial than bread and butter. **1902** VIOLET JACOB *Sheep-Stealers* xiv, Breakfast at nine, a substantial dinner at three, supper at eight.

7. Of structures, etc.: Of solid material or workmanship.

1390 GOWER *Conf.* III. 92 Erthe.. Which.. in his forme is schape round, Substancial, strong, sadd and sound. *c* **1412** HOCCLEVE *De Reg. Princ.* 5116 They made ware of a ribbe, ..Which more strong is, and substancial, þan slyme of eerthe. **1463** *Bury Wills* (Camden) 39 A substanciall and a sqwar dore of free stoon. **1512** *Act 4 Hen. VIII*, c. 1 §3 Goode and substanciall bulwarkes.. in every landyng place. **1551** ROBINSON tr. *More's Utopia* II. ii. (1895) 128 A brydge ..with gorgious and substanciall archeis. **1624** CAPT. J. SMITH *Virginia* v. 189 Then they built no more Cabbens, but substantiall houses. **1662** GERBIER *Principles* 19 Well-riveted Windowes, with substantiall Locks, Bolts, and Hinges. **1667** MILTON *P.L.* IV. 189 Some rich Burgher, whose substantial dores, Cross-barrd and bolted fast, fear no assault. **1707** MORTIMER *Husb.* (1721) I. 374 Country Houses ought to be substantial, and able to encounter all the shocks of the Wind. **1845** DISRAELI *Sybil* (1863) 129 Behind the substantial counter, which was an impregnable fortification. **1858** HAWTHORNE *Fr. & It. Note-bks.* II. 47 The clouds.. looking quite as substantial as the distant mountains. **1861** PARKER *Introd. Gothic Archit.* (ed. 2) iv. 103 Early Norman masonry is in general so massive and substantial that it is difficult to destroy all traces of it. **1879** STAINER *Mus. Bible* 5 Whose roof was never more substantial than a tent.

Comb. **1897** 'A. HOPE' *Phroso* iv. (1905) 73 He held a very substantial-looking whip in his hand.

†**8.** Of persons, their constitution, etc.: Sturdy, strong, burly. *Obs.*

c **1400** *Beryn* 2518 Natur was more substancial, when tho dayis were, Then nowe. **1533** ELYOT *Cast. Helthe* (1539) 52 b, [Vociferation] maketh the members of the body substancial and stronge. **1578** WHETSTONE *2nd Pt. Promos & Cass.* IV. i. (*heading*), Gresco, a good substantiall Offycer. **1602** in Moryson *Itin.* (1617) II. 250 Men broken, and not substantiall in war. **1657** BILLINGSLY *Brachy-Martyrol.* xiv. 48 Tormentors, pray procure Substantialler than these; these are too small.

9. Of ample or considerable amount, quantity, or dimensions. More recently also in a somewhat weakened sense, esp. 'fairly large'.

1454 *Rolls of Parlt.* V. 254/2 That substantiall provision be made in all hast. **1539** TONSTALL *Serm. Palm Sund.* (1823) 81 Yf a manne wolde offre a greatte substantiall suretie. *c* **1550** ROLLAND *Crt. Venus* II. 515 He thocht the price was ouir substanciall. **1616** in *Fortescue Papers* (Camden) 17 Although you are not capable (through your fulnes) of any substantiall addition from me. **1690** C. NESSE *Hist. & Myst. O. & N.T.* I. 138 The wealth of a man is.. reckoned.. by the substantial bills and bonds, &c. he is able to produce. **1728** MORGAN *Algiers* II. v. 319 Often.. one finds good substantial Leagues dwindling into even Liliputian Furlongs. **1780** JEFFERSON *Corresp.* Wks. 1859 I. 274 Were it possible to arm men, we would send on substantial reinforcements to you. **1897** MARY KINGSLEY *W. Africa* 335 One of us at least would.. have made something substantial by the venture. **1908** *Outlook* 8 Aug. 178/2 These two substantial volumes. **1957** W. S. CHURCHILL *Hist. Eng.-Speaking Peoples* III. 218 A substantial section of the population, which included the most prominent if not always the most powerful of French citizens, were largely exempt from taxation. **1976** *Sunday Times* 30 May 24/4 (Advt.), It is mandatory that candidates have experience of.. the control and motivation of a substantial work force.

10. Based upon a solid substratum; firmly or solidly established; not easily disturbed or damaged; of solid worth or value; weighty, sound. **a.** of statement, discourse, writing.

c **1430** LYDG. *Minor P.* (E.E.T.S.) I. 41 With Crystis worde substancial in sentence. **1468** *Engl. Misc.* (Surtees Soc.) 19 By substanciall wrytyng undre sealez. **1547** BOORDE *Brev. Health* in *Introd. Knowl.* (1870) 96 In great matters aske substancial counsell. **1576** FLEMING *Panopl. Epist.* 151 My letters cannot make you such substanciall assuraunce, of my desire touching your safetie, as it is in deede. *a* **1591** R. GREENHAM *Wks.* (1599) 56 The Lord.. vrgeth him with substantiall questions. **1602** in Moryson *Itin.* (1617) II. 238 We have not heard any such substantiall intelligence. **1691** WOOD *Ath. Oxon.* II. 607 His.. practical, spiritual, substantial preaching. **1710** ADDISON *Tatler* No. 158 ¶1 This he looks upon to be sound learning, and substantial criticism. **1742** in *10th Rep. Hist. MSS. Comm.* App. I. 277 Few words but substantial ones you will like best I suppose. **1863** GEO. ELIOT *Romola* xxxiv, His mind glanced round.. to see how far those words could have the force of a substantial threat. **1873** EARLE *Philol. Engl. Tongue* (ed. 2) §66 This division is substantial and useful.

b. of reasons, causes, evidence.

c **1513** MORE *Rich. III* Wks. 50/1 For that I se some men so gredye withowte any substauncial cause. **1528** in Pocock *Rec. Ref.* (1870) I. li. 121 Very good matter and substantial why the said matrimony should be dissolved. **1590** SHAKS. *Com. Err.* II. ii. 105 Your reason was not substantiall. *a* **1687** PETTY *Pol. Arith.* v. (1691) 88 Although there be not naturally substantial reasons.. why there should be such differences. **1845** M. PATTISON *Ess.* (1889) I. 19 No more substantial evidence being producible against the bishop, the synod broke up. **1846** GROTE *Greece* (1862) II. xvi. 394 In itself a substantial testimony. **1866** BARING-GOULD *Cur. Myths Mid. Ages* Ser. I. i. 23 How wanting they are in all substantial evidence which could make us regard the story in any other light than myth.

c. of actions, conditions, results, ideas.

1565 ALLEN *Defence Purg.* xvii. 282 Do yow not see here a trim faith and a substantiall? **1592** NASHE *P. Penilesse* Wks. 1904 I. 164 Now trust me, a substantiall trade. **1622** DRAYTON *Poly-olb.* XXIV. 240 The Christian Faith, for whose substantiall planting, Saint Augustine from Rome was to this Island sent. **1624** CAPT. J. SMITH *Virginia* III. xii. 94 Ten good workemen would haue done more substantiall worke in a day, then ten of them in a weeke. **1696** TATE & BRADY *Ps.* cxix. 165 Secure, substantial Peace have they. **1749** SMOLLETT *Regic.* v. i, Life with substantial ills enough is cursed. **1753** RICHARDSON *Grandison* V. xliii. 278 She has substantial notions still left, I find, of ideal Love. **1784** COWPER *Task* III. 300 Foolish man.. quits.. Substantial happiness for transient joy. **1812** COLERIDGE *Friend* (1818) III. 60 Where he deems his interference warranted by substantial experience. **1814** MISS MITFORD in L'Estrange *Life* (1870) I. viii. 256 The substantial comforts of a good coal fire. **1824** L. MURRAY *Engl. Gram.* (ed. 5) I. 543 The substantial enjoyments.. which result from piety and virtue. **1867** RUSKIN *Time & Tide* ii. §7 To.. complete his home gradually with more delicate and substantial comforts.

†**11.** Of acts, measures, etc.: Having weight, force, or effect; effective, thorough. *Obs.*

1461 *Cov. Leet Bk.* 314 The good & substanciall rule and guydyng that ye kepe theryn. **1485** *Ibid.* 523 Thobseruyng ..such sad direccions and substanciall ordinaunces. **1523** *Act 14 & 15 Hen. VIII*, c. 3 §1 The true and substanciall makyng of the said clothes. **1547** in Sir J. Williams *Accompte* (Abbotsf. Cl.) 4 That a substanciall Survey vue and true accompte.. shalbe taken. **1550** CROWLEY *Way to Wealth* 30 The most substanciall waye in curinge diseases is by puttinge awaye the causes. **1551** in Strype *Eccl. Mem.* (1721) II. II. iv. 272 That substantial Order be taken forth-with for the pulling down all Altars. **1683** MOXON *Mech. Exerc., Printing* xxiv. ¶19 There is no substantial remedying this fault, but by making a new Head.

12. a. Possessing 'substance', property, or wealth; well-to-do, wealthy; hence, of weight or influence.

c **1450** *Brut* 479 They.. ordeyned .iiij enquestes within the Cite, of substantiall peple. **1461** *Paston Lett.* II. 27 Any substancyall gentylman. *a* **1548** HALL *Chron., Hen. VI*, 169 b, The Maire.. assembled a great numbre of substanciall and grave citizens. **1593** NASHE *Christ's T.* 37 All which were of the Nobles, Gentlemen, and substantialest men of the Iewes. **1642** *Pr. Rupert his Declar.* 4 The Knights, Aldermen, and substantiall Citizens of London. **1714** FORTESCUE-ALAND *Pref. Fortescue's Abs. & Lim. Mon.* 10 A Jury of twelve upright and substantial Men, is by the Law, to be summon'd. **1771** SMOLLETT *Humphry Cl.* (1815) 104 The substantial tradesman, who was wont to pass his evenings at the alehouse for fourpence halfpenny, now spends three shillings at the tavern. **1823** SCOTT *Peveril* viii, Her father is a substantial yeoman. **1833** HT. MARTINEAU *Brooke Farm* viii. 94 In former times,.. the proprietor or occupier of thirty or forty acres was thought a substantial farmer. **1883** S. C. HALL *Retrospect* II. 276 Among our few fellow-passengers.. was a substantial Scottish grazier.

†**b.** *absol.* with *the*: Persons of influence. *Obs.*

1568 GRAFTON *Chron.* II. 331 The Maior of London, and the substanciall of the Citie toke counsaile together.

13. Of real worth, reliability, or repute; of good standing or status.

c **1449** PECOCK *Repr.* I. xvi. 85 Substancial clerkis weel leerned in logik. **1562** TURNER *Herbal* II. (1568) 72 Theophrast so ancient and substantiall autor. **1588** GREENE *Pandosto* (1843) 45 That he might go like an honest substantiall man to tell his tale. *a* **1687** PETTY *Pol. Arith.* (1690) 74 Another Book written by a substantial Author. **1814** W. WILSON *Hist. Diss. Ch.* IV. 310 Mr. Sheffield was a sound and substantial scholar. **1837** CARLYLE *Fr. Rev.* I. I. i, Dismissal of his last substantial man. **1863** FROUDE *Short Studies* (1867) I. 228 Till it be so agreed the substantial intellect of the country will not throw itself into the question.

14. Having a corporeal form; consisting of solid matter; corporeal, material. *Obs.* or *rare.*

1589 [? LYLY] *Pappe w. Hatchet* (1844) 36, I came so neere, that I could feele a substantiall knaue from a sprites shadowe. **1603** SHAKS. *Meas. for M.* III. ii. 290 To draw with ydle Spiders strings Most ponderous and substantiall things. **1653** H. MORE *Conject. Cabbal.* (1713) 184 He means no substantialler a Being by Matter than what may well be called Metaphysical. **1818** SCOTT *Br. Lamm.* xxiii, Neither was there pressure of the grass, nor any other circumstance, to induce him to believe that what he had seen was real and substantial.

15. Having substance; not imaginary, unreal, or apparent only; true, solid, real.

1592 SHAKS. *Rom. & Jul.* II. ii. 141 All this is but a dreame, Too flattering sweet to be substantiall. **1726-31** TINDAL *Rapin's Hist. Eng.* (1743) II. XVII. 115 Not only by words.. but by very substantial deeds. **1781** GIBBON *Decl. & F.* xvii. II. 23 The manly pride of the Romans, content with substantial power, had left to the vanity of the east the forms and ceremonies of ostentatious greatness. **1781** COWPER *Hope* 154 Hope sets the stamp of vanity on all That men have deem'd substantial since the fall. **1798** S. & HT. LEE *Canterb. T.* II. 15 His substantial wealth vanished, but the shadow still remained. **1862** SIR B. BRODIE *Psychol. Inq.* II. i. 27 We should.. not be led away from that which is real and substantial by the pursuit of the shadowy and fantastic.

16. a. Belonging to the component substance or matter of a thing.

1671 N. GREW *Anat. Pl.* I. iii. (1682) 13 In all such Roots, the Pith is.. of the same substantial nature. **1718** PRIOR *Solomon* I. 497 Now shine these Planets with substantial Rays?

b. Pertaining to the substance or tissue of the body or a part or organ.

1611 [see SUBSTANCE 23]. **1620** VENNER *Via Recta* viii. 189 The radicall or substantiall moysture of the body. *Ibid.* 192 By reason of much resolution of the nutrimentall and substantiall moisture through the pores. **1875** [see SUBSTANTIVE *a.* 8]. **1889** *Buck's Handbk. Med. Sci.* VIII. 120 Transition from substantial to membranous parietes.

†**17.** That is really such; thorough, real. *Obs.*

1663 S. PATRICK *Parab. Pilgr.* xx. (1687) 207, I mean.. that it must appear to the World, that you are a substantial Christian by all the acts of an Holy Life. *a* **1694** TILLOTSON *Serm.* liii. (1742) IV. 497 To become wise and peaceable and substantial Christians.

18. That is such in the main; real or true for the most part.

1771 *Junius Lett.* xliv. (1788) 256, I should be contented to renounce the forms of the constitution.., if there were no other way to obtain substantial justice for the people. **1790** PALEY *Horæ Paul.* i. 8 It establishes the substantial truth of the narration. **1841** MYERS *Cath. Th.* III. §24. I. 63 The question.. here is not concerning the substantial Divinity of the Jewish Scripture. **1852** H. ROGERS *Ecl. Faith* 322 They are certain of the substantial accuracy of their impressions. **1855** MACAULAY *Hist. Eng.* xviii. IV. 150 The Tories.. though they could not deny that there had been some hard cases, maintained that, on the whole, substantial justice had been done. **1875** JOWETT *Plato* (ed. 2) III. 115 He argues rightly for the substantial genuineness of the text.

†**B.** *adv.* = SUBSTANTIALLY. *Obs.*

1502 ARNOLDE *Chron.* 81 Consideryng that hys fee is competent for a substanciall lerned man. **1532** MORE *Confut. Tindale* Wks. 726/1 That substauncial wel learned man Lyre. *c* **1560** in *Anglia* XIII. 464 In the Latin tongue, and other substancial congrue languages.

C. *sb.*

1. a. *pl.* The things belonging to or constituting the substance; the essential parts or elements; the essentials.

1398 TREVISA *Barth. De P.R.* XVII. ci. (Bodl. MS.), Al þe substancials of þe tree haue sourenes & vertu of bindinge. **1567** *Reg. Privy Council Scot.* Ser. I. I. 547 Alwayis kepand all the uther substantiallis of the formar seill. **1652** GAULE *Magastrom.* 77 Neither doth nature prefer any creature for its adventitials or accidentals, but for its substantials or essentials. **1661** *Except. agst. Liturgy* 4 Those who in the substantials of the Protestant Religion are of the same perswasions with our selves. **1681** STAIR *Inst. Law Scot.* I. xiii. 262 The Clauses which are adjected in Infeftments, not being of the Substantials or Solemnities thereof. **1726** AYLIFFE *Parergon* 75 Altho' a Custom introduc'd against the Substantials of an Appeal be not valid..yet a Custom may be introduc'd against the Accidentals of an Appeal. **1816** J. SCOTT *Vis. Paris* (ed. 5) 181 In the substantials of knowledge and conduct they are below both these. **1845** M. PATTISON *Ess.* (1889) I. 8 One who is certainly not chargeable with neglect of the substantials of historical science. **1854** THOREAU *Walden* (1908) 41 A great proportion of architectural ornaments are literally hollow, and a September gale would strip them off, like borrowed plumes, without injury to the substantials. **1870** LOWELL *Among my Bks.* Ser. I. (1873) 26 Though his judgement in substantials, like that of Johnson, is always worth having.

†**b.** rarely *sing. Obs.*

1628 FELTHAM *Resolves* II. xlvii. 138 All this change, without the losse of any visible substantiall.

2. *pl.* Substantial or solid things.

a **1653** BINNING *Serm.* (1845) 570 All these substantials we let go, that we may get hold of some empty unedifying notions. **1796** MRS. M. ROBINSON *Angelina* I. 155 We look sharp after the substantials, and leave the shadows to your end of the town. **1824** MISS FERRIER *Inher.* xxviii, Too busy with the substantials of marriage, to have much time to bestow on the empty speculations of love.

3. *pl.* The substantial or solid parts of a meal.

1751 R. PALTOCK *P. Wilkins* (1884) I. 126 From day to day I found out something new to add to my repast, either in substantials or by way of dessert. **1765** H. WALPOLE *Let. to E. of Hertford* 7 Apr., Instead of substantials, there was nothing but a profusion of plates striped red, green, and yellow, gilt plate, blacks and uniforms! **1865** J. CAMERON *Malayan India* 301 Soup and fish generally both precede the substantials... The substantials are invariably followed by curry and rice. **1886** MISS BRADDON *One Thing Needful* v, The substantials were all on a side-table.

substantialism (səb'stænʃəlɪz(ə)m). *Philos.* [f. prec. + -ISM.] The doctrine that there are substantial realities underlying phenomena.

1881 W. JAMES in *Princeton Rev.* July 63 Agnostic substantialism like that of Mr. Spencer. **1888** *Microcosm* (N.Y.) Dec. 3 The fundamental tenet..of Substantialism maintains that besides the material substances in the general constitution of Nature there are also forms of immaterial substance.

substantialist (səb'stænʃəlɪst). [ad. G. *substantialist*, f. L. *substantiālis* SUBSTANTIAL: see -IST.]

1. One of a sect of Lutherans in the 16th century who held that original sin was not an accident in human nature but belonged to its substance; a Flacian.

1657 GAULE *Sapientia Just.* 10 That Original sin is not a vicious accident or adjunct, but is become our very Nature, Essence, and Substance;..so [maintain] the Flaccians, and Substantialists. **1847** [see FLACIAN].

2. One who holds a philosophical doctrine of substantialism.

1797 in *Monthly Mag.* (1819) XLVIII. 112 May not the substantialists retort, there can be no sensations or ideas; for, take away all substantial matter,..and what will then have become of ideas? **1836-7** SIR W. HAMILTON *Metaph.* xvi. (1859) I. 294 Philosophers..are divided into Realists or Substantialists, and into Nihilists or Non-Substantialists. **1888** *Microcosm* (N.Y.) Dec. 6 The conversational powers of the young substantialist [R. Rogers].

substantiality (səbstænʃɪ'ælɪtɪ). [ad. late L. *substantiālitas*, f. *substantiālis* SUBSTANTIAL; cf. F. *substantialité*, It. *sostanzialità*.]

1. The quality or state of being substantial; existence as a substance or substratum; substantial or real existence.

1545 BALE *Myst. Iniq.* 34 Substancialite, deificalite, carnalite, corporalite. **1651** [see MAGNESIA 1]. **1678** CUDWORTH *Intell. Syst.* I. v. 863 The Grand Objection against this Substantiality of Souls Sensitive, as well as Rational. **1683** PORDAGE *Mystic Div.* 79 This Love's Eternal Substantiality. **1760-72** H. BROOKE *Fool of Qual.* (1809) IV. 44 The clothing of our spirits with the heavenly substantiality of the spiritual body and blood of..Jesus himself. **1830** tr. *Tenneman's Man. Hist. Philos.* 344 Berkely ..maintaining that our senses..do not afford us any proof of the existence or substantiality of their objects. **1863** E. V. NEALE *Anal. Th. & Nat.* 45 The accidents of a substance while they are effects of its substantiality, determine the character of the substance which causes them. **1877** E. CAIRD *Philos. Kant* II. x. 419 The ascription of independent substantiality to each of the different phases of intellectual life. **1880** GREG *Across the Zodiac* I. vii. 167, I had afforded much stronger evidence, if not of my own substantiality, yet of the real existence of a repulsive energy.

attrib. **1897** tr. *Fichte's Sci. Ethics* 120 A mediating link between nature as mere mechanism (or the causality-relation); and freedom as the opposite of mechanism (or the substantiality-relation). **1902** *J. M. Baldwin's Dict. Philos. & Psychol.*, *Substantiality Theory* or *Substantialism*,..the theory that there are real substances, or distinct entities, underlying phenomenal facts or events.

†**b.** A substantial being or thing. *Obs.*

1651 BIGGS *New Disp.* Pref. 8 Real entities and substantialities. **1662** SPARROW tr. *Behmen's Rem. Wks.* 43 This very Substantiality or Corporeity..was Christs heavenly Flesh and Bloud.

2. Soundness, genuineness; solidity of position or status.

1660 R. BURNEY *Κέρδιστον Δῶρον* 19 He that is the Monarch is Ἄριστος, and Aristocraticall men do but creep under his feet, and have better cloathes then substantiality of Rule. **1865** M. ARNOLD *Ess. Crit.* x. (1875) 410 The substantiality, soundness, and precision of Mr. Long's rendering are.. conspicuous. **1876** GEO. ELIOT *Dan. Der.* xxiii, Whether she could not achieve substantiality for herself and know gratified ambition without bondage.

3. Solidity, firmness (of a structure).

1790 *Trans. Soc. Arts* VIII. 112 The substantiality of the new wall. **1879** W. L. LINDSAY *Mind in Lower Anim.* I. 113 Many of the lower animals build themselves dwellings that excel in substantiality..the huts or hovels of men. **1891** WINN *Boating Man's Vade-M.* 52 A boat of this kind..still survives, and vies in point of substantiality with many of more modern construction.

4. *concr.* (*pl.*) = SUBSTANTIAL C 3.

1813 LAMB *Recoll. Christ's Hosp.* Wks. 1818 I. 289 He.. partook in all the mirth, and in some of the substantialities of the feasting. **1842** *Blackw. Mag.* LI. 375 A ham and other substantialities composed our meal. **1842** J. WILSON *Recr. Chr. North* I. 213 If not all the delicacies, at least all the substantialities, of the season.

substantialize (səb'stænʃəlaɪz), *v.* [f. as prec. + -IZE.]

1. *trans.* To make substantial; to give reality to.

1821 H. REEDER *Dis. Heart* Pref., The diseases discriminated..and their nature substantialized by actual demonstration of morbid changes. **1866** HOWELLS *Venetian Life* iv. 50 That strange life, which even the stout..little Bohemian musicians..could not altogether substantialize. **1876** L. STEPHEN *Engl. Th. 18th C.* I. 65 The universe..is nothing but a series of abstract truths..substantialised by their reference to God.

2. *intr.* To become substantial in appearance.

1895 *Atlantic Monthly* Aug. 226 They then proceed to substantialize by darkening in tint.

substantially (səb'stænʃəlɪ), *adv.* [f. as prec. + -LY^2.]

1. In substance; in one's or its substantial nature or existence; as a substantial thing or being.

1398 TREVISA *Barth. De P.R.* XI. i. (1495) 381 Ayere is a symple element substancyaly moyste and hote. **14..** tr. *Honorius August. Elucid.* (1909) 3 þouȝ he [God] be ouer al wiþ his myght, he is substancialy in þe vndirstonding heuene. **1447** BOKENHAM *Seyntys* (Roxb.) 82 Ye al thre In personys distynct substancially Arn but oo god in trinite. **1564** T. DORMAN *Proufe cert. Art. Relig.* 83 b, Christes fleshe and bloud..is present..in humain substance, therefore substantially. **1577** tr. *Bullinger's Decades* (1592) 766 [The soul] doth not die with the bodie..bicause it liueth substantially. **1635** JACKSON *Creed* VIII. i. 6 Being first made substantially man, that hee might be for a time essentially and formally a servant. **1635** PAGITT *Christianogr.* I. iii. (1636) 137 The holy Ghost proceedeth from the Father by the Sonne, eternally, and substantially. **1667** MILTON *P.L.* III. 140 The Son of God was seen Most glorious, in him all his Father shon Substantially express'd. **1678** GALE *Crt. Gentiles* IV. III. 9 By actions modally evil, they generally understand such as are substantially good, yet have some modal accidental vitiositie. **1768** TUCKER *Lt. Nat.* I. I. i. 19 That which discerns is numerically and substantially distinct from that which is discerned. **1824** SCOTT *St. Ronan's* xxi, You have the said Willie corporally and substantially in presence before you. **1849** ROCK *Ch. Fathers* I. i. 15 That the Mass is a sacrifice in which the Body and Blood of Christ are truly and substantially present.

b. Essentially, intrinsically.

1649 JER. TAYLOR *Gt. Exemp.* Pref. §32 That which substantially distinguishes Man from Man, or an Angel from an Angel. *a* **1688** CUDWORTH *Immut. Mor.* (1731) 65 Tho' this Old Atomical Philosophy be most solidly and substantially true. **1842** H. ROGERS *Introd. Burke's Wks.* 48 An..exaggerated representation of what was substantially important truth.

c. Actually, really.

1802 WORDSW. *Misc. Sonn.* II. xi, There [in the glowing west] stood Indian citadel, Temple of Greece, and minster with its tower Substantially expressed. **1805** A. KNOX *Rem.* (1834) I. 16 In no human being, surely, was every possible part of this picture so substantially realised.

†**2.** In a sound or solid manner; on a firm or solid basis; effectively, thoroughly, properly, soundly.

a. qualifying verbs.

Freq. in the 16th and 17th c. in a large variety of contexts.

1505 *Facsimiles Nat. MSS.* I. 101 Whiche picture they shall substantially note and marke in every poincte soo that it agree in likenesse to the veray visage of the said Quene. *a* **1513** FABYAN *Chron.* VI. cxlv. (1811) 132 Charlis hauynge thus the rule & gouernaunce, rulyd it well & substancially. **1521** FISHER *Serm. agst. Luther* Wks. (1876) 327 Our souerayne lorde..hath with his pen so substauncyally foghten agaynst Martyn luther. **1523** in *Rep. Hist. MSS. Comm.* Var. Coll. IV. 213 To serve the Citie substantially unto Mighelmasse with candell after 1*d.* the li. ? *a* **1533** FRITH *Disput. Purgat.* (1829) 107, I pray you see how substantially he answereth the argument. **1573** *Art of Limming* 3 Laye on thy syse somewhat substancially. **1574** in *Vicary's Anat.* (1888) App. iii. 155 Yt was substancyally provyd..that he had verye..dysceytfully..behauyd him selfe. **1598** BARRET *Theor. Warres* II. i. 26 To see that the moneys collected..be substantially and throughly bestowed in pikes. *c* **1610** SIR J. MELVIL *Mem.* (1735) 335 They durst not yet take such a hazardous Course, till they might lay their Plots more substantially. **1668** R. STEELE *Husbandm. Call.* iii. (1672) 22 The poor prophet that had substantially warned others from the devil, could not escape himself. **1670** MILTON *Hist. Eng.* III. Wks. 1851 V. 99 To know.. what good laws are wanting, and how to frame them substantially. **1687** T. BROWN *Saints in Uproar* Wks. 1730 I. 74 I'll substantially thrash your jacket for you. **1696** R. BARCLAY (*title*) Baptism and the Lord's Supper; substantially asserted.

b. qualifying adjs. and advs.

c **1449** PECOCK *Repr.* I. xvi. 85 Substanciali leerned clerkis in logik. **1540-1** ELYOT *Image Gov.* 28 Lawiers substancially learned. **1583** GOLDING *Calvin on Deut.* 53 Surely hee were substantially well armed. *a* **1694** TILLOTSON *Serm.* Wks. (1714) 67 Substantially Religious towards God. **1711** *Vindic. Sacheverell* 82 It seems he got substantially drunk.

3. Of the construction of buildings, manufacture of fabrics, etc.: Solidly, strongly.

1463 *Bury Wills* (Camden) 19 To make..alle thing sewr that longith therto, and substancyally wrought to endure. **1517** TORKINGTON *Pilgr.* (1884) 6 It ys a good Cite, And.. substancially Edifyed. **1523** *Act 14 & 15 Hen. VIII*, c. 3 Worstedes..truely and substancially made and wrought. **1665** SIR B. G. D'OUVILLY *Brief Disc.* 18 These are substantially, strongly, and curiosly made Casements. **1702** *Lond. Gaz.* No. 3789/4 A Yacht..well, substantially, and lately built. **1845** STOCQUELER *Handbk. Brit. India* (1854) 393 The wall, substantially built of burnt brick. **1846** *Guide Archit. Antiq.* 76 The Register..being substantially bound in Russia. **1879** *Cassell's Techn. Educ.* IV. 1/1 A..lathe.. well and substantially made.

4. In all essential characters or features; in regard to everything material; in essentials; to all intents and purposes; in the main.

1781 COWPER *Hope* 398 For aught I see, Your faith and mine substantially agree. **1800** J. FOSTER in *Life & Corr.* (1846) I. 135 They substantially agree with me. **1855** MACAULAY *Hist. Eng.* xix. IV. 287 It is..reasonable to believe that his narrative is substantially true. **1856** FROUDE *Hist. Eng.* (1858) I. ii. 134 Demands..which, though taking many forms, resolved themselves substantially into one. **1865** MOZLEY *Miracles* i. 7 Extraordinary Divine agency partakes substantially of a miraculous character. **1875** WHITNEY *Life Lang.* xii. 240 It has maintained its own institutions..substantially unchanged from the very dawn of the historic period. **1881** WESTCOTT & HORT *Grk. N.T.* Introd. §17 Texts substantially free from the later corruptions.

†**5.** With substantial or ample comfort. *Obs.*

1663 PEPYS *Diary* 18 May, By seeing how much better and more substantially I live than others do. **1809** PINKNEY *Trav. France* 21 They seemed..to live very comfortably, not to say substantially.

substantialness (səb'stænʃəlnɪs). [f. as prec. + -NESS.] The condition or quality of being substantial; solidity, firmness, soundness.

1530 PALSGR. 278/1 Substancialnesse of any thyng, *solidité*. **1548** W. THOMAS *Ital. Gram.*, *Dict.*, *Efficacia*, substancialnesse, habilitie, or power. **1549** COVERDALE, etc. *Erasm. Par. 1 Peter* 8 Y^{t} excellent good womans maners & manly substauntialnes of mynde. **1555** HARPSFIELD in *Bonner's Homilies* 47 Peter, for the soundnes or substancialnes of hys deuotion, is called the rocke of the churches. **1587** GOLDING *De Mornay* x. (1617) 147 The substancialnesse of bones. **1624** WOTTON *Archit.* 36 In degree as in substantialnesse [the Ionic is] next aboue the Dorique. **1683** CAVE *Ecclesiastici* 335 The smartness of his Wit, the gravity and substantialness of his Sence. **1871** *Athenæum* 25 Nov. 685 Converts what is little more than nothing into something which has the semblance of rich, creamy substantialness. **1891** J. WINSOR *Columbus* 520 The substantialness of its structure gave rise to rumors that he was preparing a fortress for ulterior aims.

substantia nigra (sʌb'stænʃ(ɪ)ə 'naɪgrə). *Anat.* [mod.L., = black substance.] A curved layer of grey matter in the brain that extends from the pons to the subthalamic region on each side, separating the tegmentum of the midbrain from the crus cerebri, and forming part of the extrapyramidal system.

1882 *Quain's Elements Anat.* (ed. 9) II. 315 A section into the crus cerebri shows the two parts of which it is composed to be separated from one another by a tract of dark coloured grey substance known as the substantia nigra. **1923** [see PARKINSONISM]. **1961** *Lancet* 26 Aug. 446/1 A tiny old hæmorrhage in one substantia nigra, and a small periaqueductal glial scar, were the only focal lesions found. **1976** SMYTHIES & CORBETT *Psychiatry* iv. 41 The dopamine system is divided into several portions. The main one has its cell bodies in the substantia nigra.

substantiate (səb'stænʃɪeɪt), *v.* [f. mod.L. *substantiāt-*, pa. ppl. stem of *substantiāre*, f. *substantia* SUBSTANCE: see -ATE^3. Cf. It. *sostanziare*, Sp., Pg. *substanciar*.]

1. *trans.* To give substance or substantial existence to, make real or substantial.

1657 TRAPP *Comm. Ps.* xxviii. 7 Faith substantiateth things not yet seen. **1726** AYLIFFE *Parergon* 148 The Accidental of any Act, is said to be whatever advenes to the Act itself already substantiated. **1812** COLERIDGE *Friend* (1818) III. 187 Substantiating appearances into facts of science. **1863** COWDEN CLARKE *Shaks. Char.* iv. 107 The creative power of the fancy is a blessed gift in itself; but he substantiates that gift who converts it into the ordinary occurrences of daily life. **1877** E. CAIRD *Philos. Kant* iii. 44 Human thought substantiates accidents, and treats the finite as if it were infinite.

2. To give solidity to, make firm, strengthen.

1792 V. KNOX *Serm.* (Isa. xlvii. 8) Wks. 1824 VI. 99 He would sweeten and substantiate them [their enjoyments] by giving them a better foundation. **1827** HARE *Guesses* (1859) 242 Our lighter thoughts require the graver to substantiate them and keep them from evaporating. **1835** I. TAYLOR *Spir. Despot.* II. 55 In this endeavour of the clergy to substantiate their honours and revenues. **1858** FROUDE *Hist.*

Eng. III. 450 To pass through France..in a manner so.. confidential as..might contribute towards substantiating his relations with Francis.

3. To give substantial form to, embody, body forth.

1784 J. Barry *Lect. Painting* ii. (1848) 113 The difficulties of execution, which must embody and substantiate this conception. **1791** Boswell *Johnson* an. 1752, Particular qualities in the person he admires, the impressions of which are too..delicate to be substantiated in language. *c* **1811** Fuseli *Lect. Painting* iv. (1848) 448 That power which, in our days, substantiated humour in Sterne, comedy in Garrick. **1841** Emerson *Ess., Friendship* 196 As many thoughts in succession substantiate themselves.

4. To demonstrate or verify by proof or evidence; to make good.

1803 Malthus *Popul.* (ed. 2) 140 In a tribe on the frontiers of Junapore,..the practice of destroying female infants has been fully substantiated. **1808** Wellington in Gurw. *Desp.* (1835) IV. 165 If the Court should wish it, it can be substantiated by evidence. **1815** Kirby & Sp. *Entomol.* (1816) I. 55 That this substantiates the charge of cruelty against us I altogether deny. **1884** *Contemp. Rev.* Oct. 514 There is nothing to substantiate his integrity or competency.

Hence **sub'stantiating** *vbl. sb.* and *ppl. a.*; **sub'stantiative** *a.*, serving to substantiate; **substanti'ator**, one who substantiates.

1775 Ash, *Substantiating*, the act of making to exist. **1812** Coleridge *Friend* (1818) III. 264 The substantiating principle of all true wisdom. *c* **1814** —— in *Lit. Rem.* (1838) III. 71 The conscience is to the spirit or reason what the understanding is to the sense, a substantiative power. **1853** Ruskin *Stones Venice* III. iv. §23. 183 The difference between the substantiating and the imaginative methods of finish. **1884** *Pall Mall Gaz.* 27 Oct. 4/1 The untrimmed skirt..with only a few substantiating tucks round the bottom. **1906** *Cornh. Mag.* May 663 What value he has is that of the substantiator of other accounts.

substantiation (səbstænʃɪ'eɪʃən). [f. substantiate: see -ation.]

1. Embodiment. *rare.*

1760-72 H. Brooke *Fool of Qual.* (1809) IV. 87 Her whole form seemed a condensing or substantiation of harmony and light. *c* **1817** Fuseli *Lect. Painting* x. (1848) 528 These works are commonly considered as the produce of the school of Phidias, and the substantiation of his principles.

2. (See quot.)

1835 Coleridge in *Fraser's Mag.* XII. 623 All attempts at philosophical explication commenced in an effort of abstraction, aided by another function of the mind, for which I know no better name than substantiation; the identity of the thinker's own consciousness..was confounded with, and substituted for, the real substance of the thing.

3. The substitution of substance for shadow.

1863 A. B. Grosart *Small Sins* (ed. 2) 38 What was thus shadowed out and prefigured in the Old Testament received ..substantiation in the New Testament. **1870** Lowell *Study Wind.* (1871) 279 This substantiation of shadows.

4. The making good or proving a statement, etc.

1861 Garbett *Bible & Critics* i. 3 Such arguments, could they be substantiated, would destroy the Christian revelation at a blow. But this substantiation is found to be impossible. **1884** *American* VIII. 379 The fact as claimed will find lasting substantiation. **1886** *Pall Mall Gaz.* 7 Dec. 7/1 He failed to cite a single case in substantiation of his words.

†substan'tific, *a.* *Obs.* [ad. obs. F. *substantifique*, ad. med.L. *substantificus*, f. L. *substantia* substance: see -fic.] Producing substance.

1634 T. Johnson tr. *Parey's Chirurg.* iii. xviii. 109 Men.. have need of a great quantitie of bloud for the repairing of so many spirits, & the substantificke moisture. **1653** Urquhart *Rabelais* i. xix, The substantifick quality of the elementary complexion, which is intronificated in the terrestreity of their quidditative nature.

So **substan'tifical** *a.*, whence **†substan'tifically** *adv.*

1651 J. F[reake] *Agrippa's Occ. Philos.* 191 There are six substantificall qualities in the Elements, *viz.* Sharpness, Thinness, Motion, and the contrary to these. **1657** B. W. tr. *Bauderon's Expert Phisic.* xvii. 110 Moyst meat that is substantifically moyst, is good for all Feavers.

sub'stantify, *v.* *rare.* [ad. med.L. *substantificāre*, f. L. *substantia* substance: see -fy.] *trans.* To give substance to.

1605 Timme *Quersit.* iii. 143 Salt is firme, fixed, and substantifying beginning of all things.

†sub'stantious, *a.* Chiefly *Sc. Obs.* Also 5 substa(u)ncyous, 6 -cius, -tius (substentious), 6-8 -cious, (7 substanteious). [a. OF. *substantieux*, = It. *sostanzioso*, Sp., Pg. *substancioso*, ad. med.L. *substantiōsus*, f. *substantia* substance: see -ious.]

1. Weighty, important; solid, firm; effective.

1483 Caxton *Gold. Leg.* 431/2 Wyth shorte and substauncyous wordes. **1508** Dunbar *Tua Mariit Wemen* 248 God my spreit now inspir,..And send me sentence to say, substantious, et noble. **1535** Stewart *Cron. Scot.* (Rolls) I. 5 So that it be substantious of sentence. **1549** in R. Keith *Hist. Scot.* (1844) I. App. 435 The Lord Governour and Lordis of secret Counsall,..hes for substantious resistance thairof,..offerit thameselfis reddie to defend thair awin auld liberties. **1597** R. Bruce *Apol.* in Wodrow *Life* (1843) 175 To beseech him for some substantious remeed to all these evils. **1607** Gladstanes in *Orig. Lett. to Jas. I* (Bann. Cl.) I. 118 Thay find, in steid of superficiall.. inventiones, profitable and substantious theologie. **1640** R. Baillie *Canterb. Self-Convict.* 98 Of all the limbs of the masse the most substantious..are..the Offertorie, the Canon, the Communion. **1832** Southey *Lett.* (1856) IV. 284, I am glad that the political papers exist now in a substantious shape.

2. Of structures: Substantial, solid.

1529 *Aberdeen Reg.* (1844) I. 127 Ane nobill and substantius brig..completit and ended substantiuslie in all necessaries. **1541** Sir J. Sandilands *Deed* in *Proc. Antiq. Scot.* (1860) III. 162 To rais ane substantious wall of rouch werk.

3. Wealthy, well-to-do.

1517 *Acc. Ld. High Treas. Scot.* V. 153 The lordis, baronis, and uthiris substancius men. **1532** *Ibid.* VI. 117 All baronis, frehaldaris, and substantious gentilmen. **1545** *Reg. Privy Council Scot.* I. 11 It is necessar..to have with thame substantious freindis. **1560** *First & Sec. Bk. Discipl.* (1621) 46 Every fewar and substantious Gentlemans sonne. **1640** *Bk. War Committee of Covenanters* 54 Gif he be ane heritor or substantious soccarer [*read* cottarer] or yeoman.

b. Of provision: Ample.

1533 Bellenden *Livy* i. ix. (S.T.S.) I. 52 To mak provisioun in the maist riche and substancius maner þat þai mycht to Invaid vthir. **1561** in R. Keith *Hist. Scot.* (1734) I. 198 That thai with thair substancious Housaldis, weill bodin in feir of Weir, in thair maist substancious Maner, meit James Commendatour of Saintandrois. **1643** in Spalding *Troub. Scot.* (1792) II. 101 All the fencible persons..shall provide themselves..warlike provision..in the most substantious manner.

4. Considerable in number or amount.

1569 *St. Papers Eliz., For.* (1874) 154 [Some] substancious [force of footmen]. **1584** in *3rd Rep. Hist. MSS. Comm.* 414/1 Accumpaneit with a substantius number of your honest freindis.

†sub'stantiously, *adv.* *Sc. Obs.* [f. prec. + -ly².] With substantial means, support, effect.

1529 [see substantious 2]. **1533** *Acc. Ld. High Treas. Scot.* VI. 122 Sustantiuslie accumpanyit, weill bodin, etc., for defence of the realm. **1537** in Pitcairn *Crim. Trials* I. 251 Howbeit scho wes dotit substantiouslie. **1541** in *Exch. Rolls Scot.* XVII. 719 [Ane] honest mansion,..substantiously biggit. **1569** *Reg. Privy Council Scot.* Ser. i. II. 72 Gif thair attemptattis be nocht substantiouslie resistit. **1580** Jas. I *Let.* in W. Maitland *Hist. Edin.* (1753) i. iii. 39 Sa suirlie and substantiouslie gairdit. **1606** *Sc. Acts Jas. VI* (1816) IV. 288 To the effect the saidis vnlauchfull meitingis..may be substantiouslie suppressit.

†sub'stantiousness. *Sc. Obs. rare.* [f. as prec. + -ness.] Wealth.

1596 Dalrymple tr. *Leslie's Hist. Scot.* I 155 He is maid rich wt the money of Metellan..and wt his ample substantiousnes.

substantival (sʌbstən'taɪvəl), *a.* [f. substantive + -al¹.]

1. *Gram.* Of, belonging to, or consisting of, a substantive or substantives.

a **1832** Bentham *Language* Wks. 1843 VIII. 326/2 The substantival name of a quality presents the idea, in the character of a complete idea. **1843** *Proc. Philol. Soc.* I. 74 The substantival inflexions *ir*, *ar*. **1881** *Nation* (N.Y.) XXXII. 425 Nine-tenths of the New England Algonkin proper names..were composed of an adjectival and a substantival element.

2. Existing substantially.

1884 *Mind* IX. 128 The real is individual, self-existent, substantival.

Hence **substan'tivally** *adv.*, as a substantive.

1873 Earle *Philol. Engl. Tongue* (ed. 2) §479 The form *none* is only used substantivally. **1892** Earle & Plummer in *O.E. Chron.* Gloss. 373/2 Neuter used substantivally.

†substantivate, *pa. pple.* *Obs.* *rare*⁻¹. [f. med.L. *substantivāt-*, pa. ppl. stem of *substantivāre*, f. *substantivus* substantive.] Made into or used as a substantive.

a **1522** Lily *Gram.* in Colet *Æditio* (1537) Eiij b, An adiectiue standinge without a substantiue, shal be put in the neutre gendre substantiuate, as it is good. *Bonum est.*

substantive ('sʌbstəntɪv), *a.* and *sb.* Also 4 -if, -yf. [a. OF. *substantif* (from 14th cent.), ad. late L. *substantivus*, f. *substantia* substance: see -ive. Cf. OF. *sustentif*, Pr. *substantiu*, It. *so-, sustantivo*, Sp. *su(b)stantivo*, Pg. *substantivo*.]

A. *adj.*

1. a. Of persons, nations, etc.: That stands of or by itself; independent, self-existent, self-sufficient.

c **1470** Harding *Chron.* cxcii. v. 7 Thus were there dukes fiue Of newe create, and none was substantiue. *c* **1550** Rolland *Crt. Venus* i. 68 Umquhile agane serene and substantiue. **1626** Bacon *New Atl.* (1650) 15 How sufficient and substantive this Land was, to maintaine it selfe without any ayd (at all) of the Forrainer. **1792** Burke *Pres. St. Aff.* Wks. VII. 94 That Spain is not a substantive power: That she must lean on France, or on England. **1862** Rawlinson *Anc. Mon., Chald.* vii. I. 162 As a substantive deity, distinct from her husband. **1872** Geo. Eliot *Middlem.* lxxxvi, A pity that so substantive and rare a creature should have been absorbed into the life of another. **1882** T. H. Dyer *Imit. Art* 322 The chapel..could not have been in the church in Cimabue's boyhood, but it may have been a substantive building afterwards incorporated in it. **1888** R. L. Stevenson in *Scribner's Mag.* Jan. 126/2 He sees why I speak of the little people as of substantive inventors and performers.

b. Of immaterial subjects: Having an independent existence or status; not dependent upon, subsidiary to, or referable to something else.

1561 T. Norton *Calvin's Inst.* i. xiii. 33 b, This only name Jehouah whiche they call vnspeakable is a substantiue name to expresse hys essence. **1652** L. S. *People's Liberty* xxii. 57 An argument not so substantive but it will fall of it self. **1659** Fuller *Appeal Inj. Innoc.* (1840) 474 This dispute is substantive enough to stand by itself, and too large to be adjected to this book. **1805** *Ann. Rev.* III. 198 His Holland is still independent. His Poland has a substantive existence. **1835** Newman *Par. Serm.* (1837) I. xxi. 316 We haue no direct cognizance of what may be called the substantiue existence of the body. **1846** Grote *Greece* i. xxi. (1862) I. 555 Patroclus has no substantive position. **1850** Merivale *Rom. Emp.* xlv. (1865) V. 309 A mere title..rather than a substantive office and function. **1881** Westcott & Hort *Grk. N.T.* II. 36 Similar deductions are required in order to avoid being misled as to the substantive text of their exemplars. **1896** Purcell *Manning* I. 425 Archdeacon Manning, shortly before the close of the..meeting, proposed an Amendment, which finally took the form of a substantive Resolution. **1900** *Westm. Gaz.* 15 Jan. 3/1 It is a little remarkable..that the old judge has escaped for so long being made the subject of a substantive Life.

c. Of a dye: That attaches itself directly to the stuff, without the necessity of using a mordant. Also of pigments (see quot. 1902).

1794 Bancroft *Philos. Perm. Colours* 78 The colours of the first class I shall denominate *substantive*; using the term in the same sense in which it was employed by Bacon Lord Verulam, as denoting a thing solid by, or depending only upon itself. **1834-6** Barlow in *Encycl. Metrop.* (1845) VIII. 533/1 The cloth is then immersed in a bath composed of a substantive colour. **1902** *Encycl. Brit.* XXXI. 771/1 It is not unusual to arrange them [*sc.* pigments] into two groups, *substantive* and *adjective*. Amongst the members of the former group such a pigment as vermilion, where each particle is homogeneous, may be cited as an example.

d. *Med.* (See quot. 1844.)

1826 J. A. Paris *Treat. Diet* 90 The consideration..of the *Materia Alimentaria* necessarily embraces, not only the *substantive* agents above stated, but those which, from their *modus operandi*, are entitled to the distinctive appellation of alimentary *adjectives*. **1844** Hoblyn *Dict. Terms Med.* (ed. 2) 294 *Substantive*, a term applied by Dr. Paris to those medicinal agents which possess an inherent and independent activity.

e. *Milit.* Definitely appointed to the rank specified; also of an appointment or rank.

1854 T. Troubridge *Let.* 30 Dec. (MS.), I daresay they will make my Brevet rank *substantive* which is the new word they have coined for a *real* Lt. Colonelcy. **1883** H. B. Smith *Life Ld. Lawrence* I. vii. 177 It was not till towards the end of the following year that the 'substantive' post became vacant. **1883** *Pall Mall Gaz.* 14 Sept. 5/1 He..became 'officiating' Quartermaster-General..because, as Lieutenant-Colonel, he could not hold the substantive apppointment. **1898** *Geogr. Jrnl.* (R.G.S.) Nov. 530 When substantive major, he was also granted the local rank of lieut.-colonel.

2. *Gram.* a. Denoting a substance; in ***noun substantive*** (late L. *nomen substantivum*): = B. i.

nouns substantive is the correct pl.; *noun substantives* has also been used, and occas. †*nouns substantives*.

1509-1843 [see noun 2]. **1870** Jevons *Elem. Logic* iii. 17 No part of speech except a noun substantive. **1900** *Speaker* 23 June 374/1 Sir is a noun substantive, masculine.

fig. **1661** in *Verney Mem.* (1907) II. 100 To make the best agreement he can for the first yeare; after which he hopes your sonne will be a noune substantive. **1705**, **1741** [see noun 2].

b. Of the nature of, equivalent to or employed as a substantive; substantival.

1668 Wilkins *Real Char.* iv. vi. 446 All which difficulties will be most clearly stated by asserting it [*sc.* the infinitive] to be a Substantive Participle. For which this reason is to be given; because it hath all the signs both of a Noun Substantive and a Verb. **1824** L. Murray *Engl. Gram.* (ed. 5) I. 105 Some writers are of opinion, that the pronouns should be classed into substantive and adjective pronouns. *Ibid.* 287 A substantive phrase. **1857** J. W. Gibbs *Philol. Stud.* 167 Substantive clauses, expressing the subject, are placed at the commencement of the sentence. **1865** Tylor *Early Hist. Man.* iv. 62 The substantive-adjective is common enough in English.

3. *Gram.* Expressing existence; in ***substantive verb***, formerly ***verb substantive***: the verb 'to be'.

Late L. *verbum substantivum*, tr. Gr. ῥῆμα ὑπαρκτικόν.

1559 in Strype *Ann. Ref.* (1709) I. ii. App. ix. 434 The verbe substantyve *est* must be taken for *significat*. **1620** T. Granger *Div. Logike* 58 A verbe substantiue, or that which hath the force thereof gouerning two datiues. **1708** *Brit. Apollo* No. 97. 2/2 This Expletive is usually attendant on the Verb Substantive. **1764** in *Phil. Trans.* LIV. 422 The verb substantive, in conformity to the Hebrew and Phœnician custom, has been apparently suppressed here. **1824** L. Murray *Engl. Gram.* (ed. 5) I. 128 The substantive verb followed by a verb in the infinitive mood,..as, 'Ferdinand *is to command* the army'. **1826** Whately *Logic* ii. i. §2 (1850) 38 The substantive-verb is the only verb recognised by Logic. **1849** *Proc. Philol. Soc.* IV. 92 The original meaning of the so-called substantive verb. **1871** Earle *Philol. Engl. Tongue* §277.

4. a. Belonging to the real substance or essential nature of a thing; essential.

1858 Hawthorne *Fr. & It. Note-bks.* II. 81 Growing out of the back of the monster, without possessing any original or substantive share in its nature. **1858** J. Martineau *Stud. Christ.* 277 As a substantive part of their message. **1877** Owen *Wellesley's Desp.* p. xxi, The British Empire in India was already a great fact, and a substantive portion of the Empire at large.

b. Of law: Relating to or consisting of the rules of right administered by a court, as opposed to the forms of procedure (*adjective law*).

1786-9 Bentham *Princ. Intern. Law* Wks. 1843 II. 539 The laws of peace would..be the substantive laws of the international code: the laws of war would be the adjective laws of the same code. **1837** in W. Stokes *Anglo-Indian*

Codes (1887) I. Gen. Introd. p. xi, The Penal Code cannot be.. explicit while the substantive civil law and the law of procedure are.. confused. **1849** MACAULAY *Hist. Eng.* vi. II. 89 The substantive law remained; but it remained unaccompanied by any formidable sanction or by any efficient system of procedure. **1887** W. STOKES *Anglo-Indian Codes* I. Gen. Introd. p. ix, The first volume deals with Substantive Law, and contains the Penal Code, the Succession Act, the General Clauses Act, and the Acts relating respectively to Contract, Negotiable Instruments, Transfer of Property, Trusts, Easements and Specific Relief.

5. Existing as a substance or individual thing; having an actual or real existence; not imaginary or illusory; real.

1830 ARNOLD *Let.* in Stanley *Life* (1844) I. vi. 285 That our addresses should be those of substantive and tangible persons, not of anonymous shadows. **1850** GROVE *Corr. Phys. Forces* (ed. 2) 25 Let us now divest the mind of the impression that heat is in itself anything substantive. **1867** *Sat. Rev.* 8 June 735 The mythical Prester John, who really appears to have had a substantive original among the Mongols. **1869** J. MARTINEAU *Ess.* II. 351 The mind predicates nothing except about substantive objects of thought.

6. Having a firm or solid basis; not slight, weak, or transitory.

1809 SYD. SMITH *Serm.* I. 42 As much is felt for character as for the more gross, and substantive advantages of life. *Ibid.* II. 421 This load of solid substantive guilt. *c* **1820** HAZLITT (Ogilvie 1822), Strength and magnitude are qualities which impress the imagination in a powerful and substantive manner. **1847** GLADSTONE in Morley *Life* (1903) I. III. v. 375 It is a painful decision to come to,.. but the only substantive doubt it raises is about remaining in parliament. **1890** JAMES *Psychol.* I. 243 Let us call the resting-places the 'substantive parts', and the places of flight the 'transitive parts', of the stream of thought.

7. Having a value or effect because of numbers or quantity; of considerable amount or quantity.

1821 SOUTHEY *Lett.* (1856) III. 229 A poem of substantive length (above 600 lines) divided into several sections. **1844** H. H. WILSON *Brit. Ind.* III. viii. III. 389 As he grew up to manhood, Munir Mohammed claimed a substantive share in the administration. **1850** GROTE *Greece* II. lv. (1862) V. 13 By ensuring to every lesser state a substantive vote at the meetings of the confederacy. **1880** *Sat. Rev.* 3 Apr. 438 The work is far advanced at Newcastle, and a substantive beginning has been made at Wakefield.

8. Relating to or affecting the substance or tissue of an organ.

1875 tr. *von Ziemssen's Cycl. Med.* V. 346 Vesicular emphysema.. either occurs as an idiopathic disease, *i.e.* as substantive or substantial emphysema, or it is developed in connection with other affections of the pulmonary parenchyma. **1894** W. BATESON *Mat. Stud. Variation* Introd. 23 Variations in the actual constitution or substance of the parts themselves. To these Variations the name *Substantive* will be given.

B. *sb.*

1. a. (for *noun substantive.*) The part of speech which is used as the name of a person or thing; a noun.

1393 LANGL. *P. Pl.* C. IV. 338 As adiectif and substantyf vnite asken, Acordaunce in kynde, in cas and in numbre. **1520** WHITINTON *Vulg.* (1527) 5 b, Whan ij substantyues or moo come togyder. **1575** GASCOIGNE *Posies, Making of Verse* T iv b, The Latinists do commonly set the adiectiue after the Substantiue: As for example *Femina pulchra*. *a* **1633** AUSTIN *Medit.* (1635) 74 If you will but give leave to turne a Participle into a Substantive. **1669** *Croke's Rep.* II. (ed. 2) 345 Action for these words, Thou art a Bankrupt knave... It was held by the Court that the words were scandalous, and Actionable, being two Substantives. **1748** WESLEY in *Wks.* (1872) XIV. 1 Nouns are either Substantives or Adjectives. **1843** *Proc. Philol. Soc.* I. 142 Berber substantives have a distinction of gender into masculine and feminine. **1879** *Casssell's Techn. Educ.* IV. 95/2 Reducing the name of each plant to two words, the first substantive designating the genus.

fig. **1883** F. H. BRADLEY *Princ. Logic* I. i. §4. 4 A fact taken as a symbol ceases so far to be fact... It is no more a substantive, but becomes the adjective that holds of another. *a* **1892** MANNING in Purcell *Life* (1896) I. 583 Mr. Gladstone is a substantive, and likes to be attended by adjectives.

†**b.** ***substantives and adjectives***: the name of a game. *Obs.*

1658 E. PHILLIPS *Myst. Love* Gen. Lud. (1685) 4 A Description of the witty sport of Substantives and Adjectives. **1672** MARVELL *Reh. Transp.* I. 70 You would think he were playing at Substantives and Adjectives.

†**2.** A self-subsisting or independent person or thing. *Obs.*

1613 J. TAYLOR (Water P.) *Laugh & be Fat* Wks. (1630) II. 75/1 Now here's a Substantiue stands by himselfe. **1641** BAKER *Chron., John* 97 Now King John being a Substantive of himselfe. **1642** FULLER *Holy & Prof. St.* III. vii. 168 Countrey-houses must be Substantives, able to stand of themselves.

Hence †**'substantive** *v. Obs. trans.*, to make into a substantive.

1678 CUDWORTH *Intell. Syst.* 264 The word δαιμόνιον.. is.. an Adjective Substantiv'd; as well as το θεῖον is.

substantively ('sʌbstəntɪvlɪ), *adv.* [f. SUBSTANTIVE *a.* + -LY².]

1. *Gram.* As a substantive or noun.

1548 THOMAS *Ital. Gram., Dict., Somma*, substantiuely is the somme or full number in reckenyng. **1665** BRINSLEY *Posing Pts.* 131 These Genitives put Substantively, *Tanti, quanti*. *a* **1680** GLANVILL *Sadducismus* II. (1681) 34 To δαιμονιον, is to be understood Substantively for a Person, viz. an Evil Spirit. **1768** HOLDSWORTH *Rem. Virgil* 171 If Galbaneo cannot be used substantively. **1807** G. CHALMERS *Caledonia* I. III. ix. 447 Cainianog.. was formerly used substantively, for coin of different valuations.

2. As an independent or self-existing person or thing; substantially, inherently.

1598 BACON *Sacred Medit., Heresies* (Arb.) 129 Which actions, they will haue to depende substantiuely and originally, and without any.. subordination of causes vpon the will. **1844** S. R. MAITLAND *Dark Ages* 482 You are gods, and all of you the sons of the most High. But this adoptively, and not substantively. **1891** F. MARY WILSON *Browning Primer* 43 It may be said of Browning that, adjectively dramatic, he is not substantively a dramatist.

3. In substance or effect, substantially.

1828 *Examiner* 115/2 Substantively, we have alluded to all worth mentioning, it being unnecessary to dwell on some light attendant matter. **1858** PIRIE *Inq. Hum. Mind* ii. §2. 92 The French philosophers have.. substantively thrown off their allegiance to Reid.

substantiveness ('sʌbstəntɪvnɪs). [f. as prec. + -NESS.] The quality or condition of being substantive; independent or self-existent character.

1837 COLEBROOKE & WILSON *Sankhya Káriká* 44 Self-support, substantiveness, entireness. **1845** NEWMAN *Ess. Developm.* 33 Their contrariety, when explained, is an argument for its substantiveness and integrity. *Ibid.* 43 The Conference Connexion remains the representative of the Wesleyan ideas; in its gradual independence and growing substantiveness [etc.]. **1893** *Daily News* 14 Feb. 4/3 The masculine substantiveness of the character of the people.

substantivity (sʌbstən'tɪvɪtɪ). [f. SUBSTANTIVE *a.* + -ITY.] Substantiality.

1877 CONDER *Basis Faith* iv. 169 Unity and (if I may so call it) Substantivity—the capacity of possessing attributes. **1889** A. W. HALL in *Microcosm* (N.Y.) Dec., The mind naturally hesitates in conceding the substantivity of anything which eludes the senses as palpable material.

'substantivize, *v. Gram.* [f. SUBSTANTIVE *sb.* + -IZE.] *trans.* To convert into a substantive.

1866 MASSON tr. *Winer's Gram. N.T.* 340 The Inf[initive] directly substantivized by means of the Article. **1887** *Amer. Jrnl. Philol.* VIII. 104 The substantivized *être, pouvoir, vouloir, savoir*. **1901** M. CALLAWAY in *Publ. Mod. Lang. Assoc. Amer.* XVI. 141 The substantivized participle.

substantize, *v.* = prec.

1794 MRS. PIOZZI *Synonymy* I. 381 Nor would Dr. Johnson have endured with patience to hear this adjective substantized.

'substation. [SUB- 7 d.] **1.** A building or establishment subordinate to a principal station or office.

1881 *Rep. Indian Affairs* (U.S.) 45 The temporary establishing of two substations for the police.. resulted in the locking up of the offenders. **1891** *Advance* (Chicago) 12 Mar., Substations at convenient distances for the issuance of rations. **1933** *Jrnl. R. Hort. Soc.* LVIII. 162 Only two varieties have been recommended for extended trial at the sub-stations. **1982** 'M. HEBDEN' *Pel & Bombers* ii. 12 The sous-brigadier who ran the substation at St. Blaize.

2. A station at which electrical current is switched, transformed, or converted, intermediate in rank between a generating station and a low-tension distribution network.

1901 *Scotsman* 2 Mar. 12/5 Continuous current distribution from sub-stations. **1933** *Archit. Rev.* LXXIII. 2 The scheme of building included.. a university substation for electric power which supplies the laboratories. **1968** [see FEEDER 10 a]. **1976** P. R. WHITE *Planning for Public Transport* viii. 162 Substation costs were greatly reduced, and more powerful locomotives permitted.

3. *Telephony.* (See quots.)

1922 W. AITKEN *Automatic Telephone Systems* I. 3 We have, therefore, a *sub-station* at the subscriber's office, which may consist of one, or a plurality of direct lines, or a small switchboard. **1940** *Chambers's Tech. Dict.* 818/1 *Sub-station* or *subscriber's station* (*Teleph.*), a subscriber's telephone located on his premises.

sub'stellar, *a.* **1.** *Navigation* and *Astr.* [SUB- 1 a.] Applied to a point on the surface of the earth which lies on a line joining some particular star and the centre of the earth, i.e. a point at which the star is vertically overhead.

1910 C. L. POOR *Nautical Sci.* vii. 154 To find the substellar point.. it is necessary for the observer to know the sidereal time at which the observation is made. **1938** [see SUBLUNAR *a.* 2]. **1967** P. VAN DE KAMP *Princ. Astrometry* ii. 19 The terrestrial longitude and latitude of a substellar point equal the Greenwich Hour Angle (GHA) and declination of the star.

2. *Astr.* [SUB- 14.] Much smaller than a typical star.

1973 *Physics Bull.* Nov. 648/1 The shock wave preceding a black hole of substellar mass could explain both the scale of damage caused and the visual effects observed. **1978** *Nature* 24 Aug. 781/1 The resolution and sensitivity of the spinning infrared interferometer suggest other applications, for example, to cool features other than planets (such as dust rings or substellar companions).

substenance, substentation, obs. ff. SUSTENANCE, SUSTENTATION.

Cf. med.L. *substentare*, etc.

1483 *Rolls of Parlt.* VI. 256/2 Amonge other thyngs yeven.. for their substentacion. **1637** *Sc. Bk. Com. Prayer, Litany* B 6 All things necessary to their bodily substenance.

substile: see SUBSTYLE.

substituend (sʌb'stɪtjuːənd). [ad. L. *substituend-us*, gerundive of *substituĕre* SUBSTITUTE *v.*] A thing that can be put in the place of another, *spec.* in *Linguistics* or *Logic*.

1955 N. CHOMSKY *Logical Struct. Linguistic Theory* (microfilm, Mass. Inst. Technol.) viii. 432 We would naturally expect the substituend Y_1 to play the same role in the overall structure of the sentence as did the term Y_2 for which it is substituted. **1965** *Philos. Rev.* LXXIV. 473 We must have.. an appropriate nominal *substituend* of *x*. **1976** *Analysis* XXXVI. 81 The anaphoric substituend of a proform, if there is one, is (possibly a grammatical variant of) its antecedent.

substituent (səb'stɪtjuːənt). *Chem.* [ad. L. *substituens, -entem*, pr. pple. of *substituĕre* to SUBSTITUTE.] An atom or group of atoms taking the place of another atom or group in a compound.

1895-6 *Proc. Chem. Soc.* 51 The influence of ortho-substituents in preventing alkylation of the carboxyl group. **1905** *Brit. Med. Jrnl.* 27 May 1144 A substance having the structure of cinnamic acid, with a hydroxyl (OH) substituent.

'substitutable, *a.* [f. SUBSTITUTE *v.* + -ABLE.] Capable of being substituted.

1805 W. TAYLOR in *Ann. Rev.* III. 312 It will always bear a regular proportion to that of other substitutable food. *c* **1820** BENTHAM *Language* Wks. 1843 VIII. 314 Substitute the singular to the plural number when substitutable without impropriety! **1905** W. JAMES *Meaning of Truth* (1909) v. 132 Reality.. is always defined as a terminus within the general possibilities of experience; and what knows it is defined as an experience *that 'represents' it, in the sense of being substitutable* for it in our thinking. **1941** *Mind* L. 167 Both the original word and all signs substitutable for it stand independently for universals. **1961** R. BRAIN *Speech Disorders* v. 57 Even a phoneme is abstract, since it stands for and represents an indefinite variety of mutally substitutable phones. **1980** A. KENNY *Aquinas* ii. 58 It is tantamount to a predicate variable for which no predicate is substitutable.

Hence **substituta'bility**.

1907 W. JAMES *Meaning of Truth* (1909) vii. 175 The relations.. which we epistemologists study, relations of adaptation, of substitutability, of instrumentality, of reference and of truth. **1922** tr. *Wittgenstein's Tractatus Logico-Philosophicus* 171 Equations express the substitutability of two expressions. **1957** A. C. L. DAY *Outl. Monetary Econ.* xxxi. 395 There may also be a high or low degree of substitutability in consumption in each country. **1979** *Nat. Westminster Bank Q. Rev.* Nov. 33 Each occupation should be compared with a group of workers where there is some close, short-run substitutability i.e. where there is a fair degree of movement between the two labour markets.

substitute ('sʌbstɪtjuːt), *sb.* [ad. L. *substitūtus, -um*, masc. and neut. of *substitūtus* pa. pple. (see next). Cf. F. *substitut*, etc.]

I. A person acting in place of another.

1. a. One exercising deputed authority; a deputy, delegate.

c **1400** *Pilgr. Sowle* (Caxton 1483) IV. xxx. 78 Though a reame haue a noble kynge.. he ne suffiseth nought hym selue to gouerne.. his reame withouten other substitutes sett in diuerse places. **1456** SIR G. HAYE *Law Arms* (S.T.S.) 194 [He] has laiser.. to set his substitute with the tane and him self with the tothir. *a* **1513** FABYAN *Chron.* v. cxl. (1811) 125 He therefore puruayed vnder hym a substitute, named Nordobert, whyle he retornyd into Austracy or Lorayne. **1575** GASCOIGNE *Glasse Govt.* Wks. 1910 II. 29 These Magistrates must also bee.. honored because they are yᵉ substituts of yᵉ king. **1608** SHAKS. *Per.* v. iii. 51 When I did flie from Tyre, I left behind an ancient substitute. **1651** HOBBES *Leviathan* III. xlii. 274 The Power.. was given to the.. Apostles, and their Substitutes [etc.]. **1667** MILTON *P.L.* x. 403 My Substitutes I send ye, and Create Plenipotent on Earth. *a* **1721** SHEFFIELD (Dk. Buckhm.) *Wks.* (1753) I. 291 Here I stand the substitute of Rome. **1765** BLACKSTONE *Comm.* I. viii. 287 They belong to the king or his substitute without redemption. **1843-56** BOUVIER *Law Dict.* (ed. 6) II. 555/2 In letters of attorney, power is generally given to the attorney to nominate and appoint a substitute.

b. Of ecclesiastics.

1567 ALLEN *Def. Priesthood* 386 Excommunication.. may be exercised by the Bishops Legates or Substituts being no priestes. **1593** NASHE *Christ's T.* Wks. 1904 II. 129 Reuerend Ecclesiasticall Fathers, and other speciall-titled Church substitutes. **1837** CARLYLE *Fr. Rev.* I. v. v, Poor Bishop Pompignan withdraws; having got Lafayette for helper or substitute. **1873** HALE *In His Name* viii. 69 The archbishop's substitute.

†**c.** ***by substitute***: by proxy. *Obs. rare*⁻¹.

1594 SHAKS. *Rich. III*, III. vii. 181 First was he contract to Lady Lucie,.. And afterward by substitute betroth'd To Bona.

2. *Law.* A person nominated in remainder.

1758 J. DALRYMPLE *Ess. Feudal Property* (ed. 2) 135 That if any of the substitutes or their issue should alienate, then their right in the estate should cease. **1765-8** ERSKINE *Inst. Law Scot.* III. viii. §21 The person first called by the entail is the institute;.. the rest get the name of the heirs of entail, or substitutes. **1766** BLACKSTONE *Comm.* II. xxi. 355 The act of the ancestor shall bind the heir, and the act of the principal his substitute. **1838** W. BELL *Dict. Law Scot.* 950 *Substitutes in an entail*, are those heirs who are called failing the institute, whether disponee or grantee. **1869** *J. Austin's Jurispr.* (ed. 3) II. 864 *note*, In English law, in rights of.. limited duration, the party entitled cannot alienate so as to defeat the reversioners or substitutes.

3. *Mil.* One who for a remuneration agrees to serve in place of another balloted for the militia.

1777 *Jrnls. Continental Congress U.S.* (1907) IX. 1002 The laws which have been enacted in the State of Pennsylvania, permitting the furnishing of substitutes to perform militia duty. **1779** J. WOODFORDE *Diary* 30 Sept. (1924) I. 266, I let my man Ben have my little Mare to go to

Norwich this morning to try to get a Substitute to serve for him in the Militia. 1802 C. JAMES *Milit. Dict.*, *Substitute* in the Militia, a person who voluntarily offers to serve in the room of another that has been chosen by ballot... Substitutes may be provided for quakers. 1811 *Gen. Regul. Army* 201 No Soldier is to receive a Furlough on the plea of assisting to provide Substitutes for himself. 1840 HOOD *Up Rhine* 263 Every Prussian subject must be a soldier, consequently there can be no serving by substitute as in our militia. 1879 *Cassell's Techn. Educ.* III. 138 The proved inferiority in all respects of the substitutes provided.

4. a. *gen.* One who acts or is employed in place of another.

1836 J. GILBERT *Chr. Atonem.* iv. 166 We maintain..that some substitute to discharge the office of personal remorse must be demanded. 1873 SPENCER *Study Sociol.* i. 15 In China where a criminal can buy a substitute to be executed in his stead. 1886 *Encycl. Brit.* XXI. 136/1 The worshippers as a whole bear the guilt until they or the guilty man himself find a substitute. 1894 *Amer. Dict. Printing, Substitute*, one who works at case instead of another... In England a substitute is called a grass hand.

b. *spec.* in *Sport*, a player who replaces another after a match has begun. Abbrev. *sub* (see SUB *sb.* 4).

1849 in 'Bat' *Crick. Man.* (1850) 57 No substitute in the field shall be allowed to bowl. 1916 [see BENCH *sb.* 1 c]. 1951 *Sport* 30 Mar.–5 Apr. 6/1 Of course, the idea of substitutes in both Association and Rugby football is not new. 1976 *Southern Even. Echo* (Southampton) 17 Nov. 23/4 When Saints beat Wolves 6–2 in the Second Division last month, the appearance..of Martin Patching as substitute was lost into obscurity because of the emphatic margin of victory.

II. A thing put in the place of another.

5. a. That which is used or stands in place of something else. Usually const. *for*, occas. *of*, †*to*.

Quot. 1589 is an early isolated instance.

1589 PUTTENHAM *Engl. Poesie* (Arb.) 177 Then is it called by the Greekes *Hypozeuxis*, we call him the substitute after his originall, and is a supplie with iteration. *a* 1677 BARROW *Serm.* xliv. Wks. 1686 III. 513 Substitutes, and shadows of things more high in substance, and efficacy. 1756 C. LUCAS *Ess. Waters* III. 165 Such as can not afford wine may have recourse to it's substitute, beer. 1802 PALEY *Nat. Theol.* ix. 158 In every part of anatomy, description is a poor substitute for inspection. 1825 BENTHAM *Offic. Apt. Maximized, Observ. Peel's Sp.* (1830) 38 Salaries were substitutes to fees, and in that form the plague ended. 1828 SCOTT *F.M. Perth* xxxiv, Bearing branches of yew in their hands, as the readiest substitute for palm boughs, they marched..to hear High Mass. 1866 BRANDE & COX *Dict. Sci.* etc. II. 562/1 The French, whose franc or livre is the shrunken substitute of the ancient pound. 1870 F. R. WILSON *Ch. Lindisf.* 23 This is a miserable substitute for the old Norman chapel. 1871 L. STEPHEN *Playgr. Eur.* (1894) iv. 89 Till lately the natives used holes in their tables as a substitute for plates.

b. A person or thing that becomes the object of love (or another emotion) deprived of its natural outlet. Formerly only with qualifying noun, as ***father, mother substitute***: see the first elements. Cf. SURROGATE *sb.* (*a.*) 2.

1956 L. DURRELL *Justine* I. 78 For her we, her lovers, had become only mental substitutes for this first childish act—so that love, as a sort of masturbation, took on all the colours of neurasthenia. 1964 C. ISHERWOOD *Single Man* 23 Jim is the substitute I found for a real son. 1973 E. CALDWELL *Annette* (1974) II. iv. 50 I'd say that enormous teddy bear is a substitute till some boy comes along with the real thing she's after.

6. In technical use. †**a.** See quot. 1719. *Obs.*

1719–22 QUINCY *Lex. Physico-Med.*, *Substitute*, is said of one Medicine put in the room of another, nearest to it in Virtue, when that cannot be had. 1728 CHAMBERS *Cycl.* s.v., The Root of the great Centaureum, and sometimes Monk's Rhubarb, are used as Substitutes to Rhapontic.

b. An artificial food-stuff intended to supply the place of a natural food; also, a cheaper article or ingredient substituted for one that is recognized or patented.

1879 *Buck's Treat. Hygiene* I. 117 Animal Substitutes for Milk. *Ibid.* 119 Vegetable Substitutes for Breast-milk. 1888 *Times* 3 Jan. 9/5 Hereafter persons who eat butter substitutes will have to avow openly their meanness whether of spirit or of purse. 1903 *Lancet* 8 Aug. 417/1 The creed of the substitute-monger is always that the substitute is better than the real thing.

c. *Mech.* A short section used when a full-length section is not usable.

1875 [see SUB *sb.* 4].

d. *Chem.* A new compound formed by substitution.

1852 *Fownes' Chem.* (ed. 4) 599 Salicylamide..is converted by fuming nitric acid into the nitro-substitute, nitro-salicylamide.

e. *Philol.* A word that can stand in the place of another, e.g. a pronoun.

1807 WEBSTER *Philos. & Pract. Gram. Eng. Lang.* 15 *Substitutes*, words which are used in the place of other words or of sentences. 1933 L. BLOOMFIELD *Language* ix. 146 In every language we find certain forms, *substitutes*... In English, the pronouns are the largest group of substitutes. 1958 C. F. HOCKETT *Course in Mod. Linguistics* xxx. 253 The substitutes in this sentence are the morpheme *he* (in the word *his*) and the morpheme *do* (in the word *did*). *He* refers to *John*: it is John's hat which John puts on.

III. 7. *attrib.* and *Comb.*: **substitute-broker**, one who procures a substitute for a soldier balloted for the militia; so **substitute-brokerage**; **substitute-feeding**, a method of feeding with food-substitutes; **substitute-fibre** *Bot.* (see quot.).

1863 *Congress. Globe* 4 Feb. 714/3 As soon as it seemed to be understood that the Government was determined to force men into the army..these *substitute brokers made their appearance. 1865 LOWELL *Reconstruction* Pr. Wks. 1890 V. 212 We have had shoddy, we have had contracts, we have had *substitute-brokerage. 1897 *Trans. Amer. Pediatric Soc.* IX. 15 Dewees had a clearer idea of *substitute feeding than his predecessor. 1900 B. D. JACKSON *Gloss. Bot. Terms* 259 **Substitute Fibres*, like libriform fibres, but a much reduced form of prosenchyma, the 'Ersatzfasern' of Sanio.

b. *attrib.* passing into *adj.*

1899 *Westm. Gaz.* 4 Oct. 7/1 A substitute resolution was submitted. 1902 *Ibid.* 3 Mar. 7/3 The..possibility of using oil instead of coal as a substitute fuel. 1909 *Ibid.* 15 Feb. 8/1 A substitute vessel should be provided for every vessel so withdrawn.

substitute ('sʌbstɪtjuːt), *pa. pple.* and *ppl. a.* [ad. L. *substitūtus*, pa. pple. of *substituĕre* (see next).]

†**A.** *pa. pple.* Substituted. *Obs.*

1432–50 tr. *Higden* (Rolls) IV. 29 Elidurus..was substitute in to the kynge. 1533 MORE *Let. to T. Cromwell* Wks. 1427/2 It may well happen, that this pope may be deposed, & a nother substitute in his rome. 1555 EDEN *Decades* (Arb.) 109 A hundreth and fyftie fresshe men whiche were substitute in the place of suche as were deade. 1577–87 HOLINSHED *Hist. Scot.* II. 385/1 He was iudged..meet..to be chosen or substitute deputie and chancellor. 1680 tr. *Buchanan's De Jure Regni apud Scotos* (1689) 43 Robert the first was substitute in his stead. 1681 STAIR *Inst. Law Scot.* II. xxvi. 100 Different Lines Substitute in these Tailzies.

B. *ppl. a.* **1.** Substituted for or taking the place of another person or thing; (of officials) deputy. *Obs.* exc. *Sc.* in ***sheriff substitute*** (with incorrect pl. *sheriff substitutes*).

1615 tr. *De Montfart's Surv. E. Indies* Pref. B 2 My second and substitute Country. 1648 GAGE *West Ind.* xii. 42 Who send from thence their substitute Vicars to rule. 1685 BAXTER *Paraphr. N.T.* Acts xv. 5 Had not Apostolick Testimony..proved the abrogation, it would more hardly have been believed..than the substitute Canons of Bishops. 1754 in *Nairne Peerage Evid.* (1874) 50 John Richardson sheriff substitute of the shire of Perth. 1815, 1866, 1894 [see SHERIFF 2 b].

2. *Sc. Law.* Nominated in remainder.

1681 STAIR *Inst. Law Scot.* II. xxv. 101 The Children are but Heirs Substitute. 1816 SCOTT *Antiq.* xvi, No string of substitute heirs of entail.

substitute ('sʌbstɪtjuːt), *v.* Also occas. pa. t. 5 substitute. [f. L. *substitūt-*, pa. ppl. stem of *substituĕre*, f. *sub-* SUB- 27 + *statuĕre* to set up (see STATUTE).]

†**1. a.** *trans.* To appoint (a person) *to* an office as a deputy or delegate; occas. with compl. *Obs.*

1532 MORE *Confut. Tindale* Wks. 821/1 Yet can they not say nay, but that..he appointed saint Peter with other, and that they were all knowen heades. And they dyd also substytute other whyche were knowen heades also. 1564 HAWARD *Eutropius* x. Q viii b, They substituted vnder them .ii. Cesars. 1583 STUBBES *Anat. Abus.* II. (1882) 71 These graue fathers..do substitute vnder them in euerie particular church a minister. 1583 STOCKER *Civ. Warres Lowe C.* IV. 28 b, Those..whom his Maiestie had substituted, to the general. Gouernement of the Countreis. 1594 NASHE *Unfort. Trav.* Wks. 1904 II. 289 When death substitutes one frend his special baily to arrest another by infection. 1628 DIGBY *Voy. Mediterr.* (Camden) 4 Substituting him Commander in chiefe in case of my death. 1639 DU VERGER tr. *Camus' Admir. Events* 183 A man of..authority..was substituted to the Guardianship of her children. 1712 STEELE *Spect.* No. 509 ¶4 If a Man of a great Genius could..substitute slower Men of Fidelity to transact the methodical part of his Affairs.

†**b.** To set up or appoint as a ruler or official *in the place* (*stead, room*) *of* another. *Obs.*

1555 EDEN *Decades* (Arb.) 113 They contended whether it were beste to substitute Nicuesa in his place. 1582 T. WATSON *Centurie of Love* (Arb.) 128 Ioue..substituted Ganimedes into her [*sc.* Hebe's] office and place. 1596 DALRYMPLE tr. *Leslie's Hist. Scot.* I. 164 Emperour Domitian calling him vnto Italie substitute in his roume Julius Agricola. *a* 1619 FOTHERBY *Atheom.* I. xiii. §3 (1622) 138 The people should substitute him into his stead. 1639 FULLER *Holy War* III. xxv. 156 The Pope substituted John de Columna, a Cardinall, Legate in the place of Pelagius. 1722 DE FOE *Plague* (1884) 299 Neither did [these] go without substituting Curates..in their Places. 1831 SCOTT *Ct. Rob.* xx, Who shall assure me that vows which were made to the Saxon Bertha, will be binding if a French Agatha be substituted in her stead?

†**c.** To depute, delegate. *Obs.*

1597 SHAKS. *2 Hen. IV*, I. iii. 84 But who is substituted 'gainst the French, I haue no certaine notice. 1700 ASTRY tr. *Saavedra-Faxardo's Royal Polit.* II. 13 Necessity obliging a Prince to substitute his Power to several Ministers.

2. To put (one) in place of another.

a. const. *in* (occas. *into*) *the place, stead, room of.*

1588 SHAKS. *Tit. A.* IV. ii. 159 And how..their Childe shall be aduaunc'd,..And substituted in the place of mine. 1597 HOOKER *Eccl. Pol.* V. lxvii. §12 That Deitie which with the words of consecration abolisheth the substance of bread and substituteth in the place thereof my body. 1655 FULLER *Ch. Hist* I. v. 38 When the Golden Shields of King Solomon were taken away, Rehoboam substituted Shields of Brasse in their room. 1694 F. BRAGGE *Disc. Parables* iv. 138 By..substituting Him in our stead, to suffer, as the Representative of mankind, the punishment due to their iniquities. 1722 WOLLASTON *Relig. Nat.* vi. 140 Let a man substitute himself into the room of some poor creature dejected with invincible poverty. 1776 HAWKINS *Hist. Mus.* I. 342 Martianus Capella, who..was the first that substituted the term Tones in the room of Modes. 1802 PALEY *Nat. Theol.* i. 7 The expression, 'the law of metallic nature', may sound strange..to a philosophic ear, but it seems quite as justifiable as some others..such as the 'law of vegetable nature',..when it is substituted into the place of these. 1843 BETHUNE *Scott. Peas. Fire-side* 21 She could not at the time substitute any thing better in its stead.

b. Without const.

1620 T. GRANGER *Div. Logike* 300 Afterward hee substituteth the properties or powers thereof. 1697 DRYDEN *Virg. Georg.* III. 599 Reject him, lest he darken all the Flock, And substitute another from thy Stock. 1798 FERRIAR *Illustr. Sterne* ii. 51 Sterne has substituted a rich and beautiful chain of incidents. 1845 M. PATTISON *Ess.* (1889) I. 27 Chilperic had simply erased the word 'theft' from the parchment, and substituted that of 'murder'. 1870 JEVONS *Elem. Logic* xxii. 186 The reader by substituting various terms can easily make propositions.

†**c.** Const. *to.* *Obs.*

1681 BURNET *Hist. Ref.* II. I. 107 Christ substituting the Eucharist to the Paschal Lamb, used such an Expression, calling it his Body. 1769 GOLDSM. *Hist. Rome* II. 148 His own life was very opportunely substituted to that against which he aimed. 1804 *Med. Jrnl.* XII. 409 Substitute mild, cooling, subacid applications..to his tonics and stimulants. 1817 JAS. MILL *Brit. India* II. v. vii. 591 The Rajah would gladly have seen the authority of the English substituted..to that of the Vizir. 1830 W. TAYLOR *Hist. Surv. Germ. Poetry* I. 112 In a few generations, the court of France had substituted the French to the Frankish tongue.

d. Const. *for.*

1674 *Govt. Tongue* ii. 7 Tis sure he can substitute none for them that can equally conduce, either to his honor or interest. 1759 GOLDSM. *Bee* No. 1 ¶1 For real wit he is obliged to substitute vivacity. 1848 DICKENS *Dombey* lxi, Jackson..used to mention that in training for the ring they substituted rum for sherry. 1878 GLADSTONE *Primer of Homer* 104 Sacrifice could not be substituted for duty, nor could prayer. 1910 *Encycl. Brit.* IX. 51/2 The local priesthoods, who substituted their own favourite god for Re.

e. *Math.* and *Chem.* (See SUBSTITUTION 5, 7.)

1737 *Gentl. Mag.* VII. 675/1 Whose Value being substituted in the aforesaid Equation. 1845 DE MORGAN in *Encycl. Metrop.* II. 378/1 If in ψx we substitute ax for x. 1867 BLOXAM *Chem.* 23 The chemical equivalent of a metal expresses the weight which is required to be substituted for one part by weight of hydrogen in its compounds. 1885 WATSON & BURBURY *Math. Th. Electr.* I. 132 If before inversion we substitute for the charges at C_1 and O_2 their equivalent distributions on the plane *XEX'*.

3. *Law.* To nominate in remainder.

1560 DAUS tr. *Sleidane's Comm.* 277 b, He had by legacie made his son Edward of .ix. yeres his heire, & after him had substituted his daughter Mary. 1726 in *Nairne Peerage Evid.* (1874) 34 The next heir descending of my own body which faillieing my other heirs substituted. 1765–8 ERSKINE *Inst. Law Scot.* III. viii. §21 In the case of a land-estate which is settled in a long series of heirs, substituted one after another. 1788 J. POWELL *Devises* (1827) II. 317 If there are no such persons, it shall not suspend the right of others, but they shall take as if no such persons were substituted.

4. To take the place of, replace. **a.** (orig. in *pass.*)

Now regarded as incorrect.

(*a*) 1675 TEMPLE *Let. to Williamson* Wks. 1731 II. 350, I hear Don Emanuel de Lyra is like to be..one of the Plenipotentiaries, and come in as substituted by the Duke de Villa Hermosa. 1770 LUCKOMBE *Hist. Printing* 224 Double Pica..was..substituted by a new Letter. 1863 *Life in South* II. 198 Good brandy being substituted by vile whiskey. 1875 BENNETT & DYER tr. *Sachs' Bot.* II. v. 529 The diagram may..be substituted..by a formula composed of letters and numbers. 1900 *Archives Surg.* XI. 275 The medicine was continued a few days longer, and then substituted by the iodide of potassium.

(*b*) 1778 [W. MARSHALL] *Minutes Agric.* 13 Sept. 1775, Let straw substitute this, if possible. 1855 BAIN *Senses & Int.* II. ii. §16 (1864) 205 A means of judging how far touch can substitute sight. 1863 OLIVER *Less. Bot.* (1873) 162 Leafy stipules substituting true leaves. 1867 *Athenæum* No. 2084. 442/1 Miss Hughes substituted Miss Oliver. 1899 *Archives Surg.* X. 138 That 'varioloid' substituted in Bath the 'varicella' which was common in Bristol.

b. More recently, used incorrectly for REPLACE *v.* 3 a.

1974 *Daily Tel.* 25 July 6/7 The tribunal concludes that British Rail's proposal to compensate..at rates of four, five and six per cent. are inadequate and substitutes them with levels of five, 7½ and 10 per cent. 1978 *Maledicta* II. 176 Most commonly they are typically formed by substituting *diavolo* with other terms. 1980 *Coal: Energy for Future* (Shell Internat. Petroleum Co.) 3 OECD coal demand is likely to..grow much more rapidly as national actions to substitute oil by coal begin to take effect.

5. *intr.* To act as a substitute. Freq. with *for.*

1888 *Advance* (Chicago) 15 Nov., It was plain that the idea of substituting for Gertrude now thoroughly possessed her. 1913 *Cavalier* 23 Aug. 212/1 She is too busy now to look out for them, so I substitute. 1953 [see FURAN]. 1962 *Listener* 17 May 883/1 But how could it satisfactorily substitute for the complexity and psychological depth abandoned in hacking the novel down to size? 1965 *Language* XLI. 239 A construction..which may substitute for a word..is a phrase. 1975 *Sci. Amer.* Feb. 36/1 An ion of ferrous iron..can easily substitute for a magnesium ion.

substituted ('sʌbstɪtjuːtɪd), *ppl. a.* [f. SUBSTITUTE *v.* + -ED[1].] Put in place of another; created or produced by substitution.

1836 J. GILBERT *Chr. Atonem.* iv. 121 That the Divine Father either requires, or can accept of substituted suffering. 1840 W. H. MILL *Applic. Panth. Princ.* I. 83 The substituted step..is far less fitted to connect the ruptured parts together. 1876 DUNGLISON *Med. Lex.* 849/2 When a portion of the presenting mass of the fœtus becomes changed for another, in complicated presentations, the case has been termed one of substituted presentation. 1891 *Jrnl. Chem. Soc.* 62 By the action of primary amines on the hydrochlorides of glutarimido-ethers, substituted glutarimidines are formed. 1911 *Act 1 & 2 Geo. V*, c. 46 §24 He shall..be entitled to the substituted right set forth in the second column of that schedule.

substituteless, *a. rare.* [f. SUBSTITUTE *sb.* + -LESS.] Excluding the provision of substitutes.

1870 *Daily News* 6 Oct., Sufficient has..been said to show how satisfactory..as regards our Reserve Forces, would be the operation of a substituteless ballot.

substituter (ˈsʌbstɪtjuːtə(r)). Also 7 -tor. [f. SUBSTITUTE *v.* + -ER[1].] One who supplies the place of another; one who substitutes one thing for another.

1623 COCKERAM II, To Appoint one in anothers roome, *Substitute*, which is Appointed in that roome, *Substitude*, which Appointed him, *Substitutour*. **1635** J. HAYWARD tr. *Biondi's Banish'd Virg.* 81 The Prince answered, that he was sorry for his parting, but embraced the favour of his substitute, not to expect any service from him, but to doe him the service he owed his substitutor. **1830** *Fraser's Mag.* I. 617 The favour of Mr. Wilberforce..was at that time an object of importance to the right-minded substituter of the name. **1846** LANDOR *Imag. Conv., Albani & Pict.-Dealers* Wks. II. 6 This substituter of grass and moss for cabbage and onions. **1897** *Chr. Herald* (N.Y.) 15 Dec. 975/2 Substitutors drug their concoctions to give them a coffee flavor.

ˈ**substituting**, *ppl. a.* [-ING[2].] That substitutes; in quot., offering substitutes for drugs.

1902 *Pharmac. Jrnl.* 6 Sept. 268/2 All self-respecting chemists will agree that 'substituting' tradesmen are unfair dealers.

substitution (sʌbstɪˈtjuːʃən). [a. OF. (mod.F.) *substitution*, or ad. late L. *substitūtio, -ōnem*, n. of action f. *substituĕre* to SUBSTITUTE. Cf. OF. *sustitucion*, Pr. *sustitucio*, It. *so-, sustituzione*, Sp. *su(b)stitucion*, Pg. *substituição*.]

†**1. a.** The appointment of a deputy (or successor); deputation, delegation. ***by substitution***, by proxy.

1390 GOWER *Conf.* III. 178 Maximin..whanne he made a governour Be weie of substitucion Of Province or of region, He wolde ferst enquere his name. *c* **1450** CAPGRAVE *Life St. Gilbert* xii, Be-side þe myracle do in substitucion of his successour, þer fell many oþir grete..which wer cured. **1610** SHAKS. *Temp.* I. ii. 103 He did beleeue He was indeed the Duke, out o' th' Substitution. **1758** JOHNSON *Idler* No. 19 ¶ 11 Whoever is engaged in multiplicity of business, must transact some by substitution.

†**b.** A writ appointing a deputy official. *Obs.*

1754 ERSKINE *Princ. Sc. Law* (1809) 41 Sheriffs and stewarts-depute have a power to name a substitute or substitutes..within such a particular district as shall be mentioned in the substitution.

2. a. The putting of one person or thing in place of another. Const. *for*, †*to*.

1612 SELDEN *Illustr. Drayton's Poly-olb.* viii. 129 S. Peters own command, to make substitution of Arch-bishops or Patriarches to Arch-Flamins, and Bishops to Flamins. *a* **1626** MEVERELL in *Baconiana Physiol.* (1679) 117 Every part so separated, may easily be reduced into perfect Metal without Substitution of that, or those principles which Chymists imagin to be wanting. **1681-6** J. SCOTT *Chr. Life* (1747) III. 50, I shall explain his Subordination and Substitution to Christ in this Part of his Mediation. **1756** BURKE *Subl. & Beaut.* Wks. 1842 I. 73 Descriptive poetry operates chiefly by substitution; by the means of sounds, which by custom have the effect of realities. **1802** PALEY *Nat. Theol.* v. 76 A mere substitution of words for reasons. **1818** CRUISE *Digest* (ed. 2) IV. 265 A substitution of a new use, in the place of a former one. **1818** BENTHAM *Ch. Eng.* Pref. p. li, The substitution of the perfectly innoxious..ceremony, to the unfaithful imitation of a scene in private life. **1876** *Jrnl. R. Geogr. Soc.* XLVI. 42 The substitution of a yellow-stained belt for a plain uncoloured one.

b. With reference to the principle in religious sacrifices of replacing one kind of victim by another or a bloody by an unbloody offering; *esp.* in *Christian Theol.* used to designate a doctrine of the Atonement according to which Jesus Christ suffered punishment vicariously for man.

1836 J. GILBERT *Chr. Atonem.* ii. 71 What else but substitution can be understood by the innocent suffering for the guilty? **1856** VAUGHAN *Mystics* (1860) I. 235 Both Tauler and Luther believe in substitution. The substitution of Luther is external... The substitution of Tauler is internal. **1873** MOZLEY *Univ. Serm.* viii. (1876) 173 This..is the principle upon which the sacrifice of love acts, as distinguished from the sacrifice of mere substitution.

3. *Law.* **a.** The designation of a person or series of persons to succeed as heir or heirs on the failure of a person or persons previously named.

1590 SWINBURNE *Test.* 130 The fifte limitation is in vulgar or common substitutions. **1681** STAIR *Inst. Law Scot.* II. xxvi. 100 Where there are severall Substitutions of certain Persons, or Lines,..they are Specially called Heirs of Tailzie. **1765-8** ERSKINE *Inst. Law Scot.* III. viii. §21 Heirs pointed out in marriage-contracts, or in bonds containing clauses of substitution, are more commonly called heirs of provision. **1826** in *Nairne Peerage Evid.* (1874) 78 Notwithstanding the above substitution in favor of Margaret Harriet Stewart in the event of the decease of my wife it is my intention that if the fee of my property should devolve upon the said Caroline Oliphant..thro' the predecease of my son she shall have the absolute disposal thereof in the same manner as if the substitution to the said Margaret Harriet Stewart had never been insert. **1875** DIGBY *Real Prop.* v. (1876) 235 A thing may be given *inter vivos* or by will to A, subject to a condition that he should on the happening of a specified event..hand it over to B. In this case a substitution is created in favour of B.

b. (See quot.)

1843-56 BOUVIER *Law Dict.* (ed. 6) II. 556/1 *Substitution.* .. This takes place in a case where a creditor has a lien on two different parcels of land, and another creditor has a subsequent lien on one only of the parcels, and the prior creditor elects to have his whole demand out of the parcel of land on which the subsequent creditor takes his lien; the latter is entitled, by way of substitution, to have the prior lien assigned to him for his benefit.

†**4.** *Gram.* = SYLLEPSIS. *Obs.*

1728 CHAMBERS *Cycl.*, *Substitution*,..the using of one Word for another; or a Mode, State, Manner, Person or Number of a Word for that of another.

5. *Alg.* **a.** The method of replacing one algebraic quantity by another of equal value but differently expressed. **b.** The operation of passing from the primitive arrangement of *n* letters to any other arrangement of the same letters.

1710 in J. HARRIS *Lex. Techn.* II. **1842** *Penny Cycl.* XXIII. 198/2 A method of approximation, which is frequently used and of great importance, has obtained the name of successive substitution. **1845** DE MORGAN in *Encycl. Metrop.* II. 372/2 We may avoid this by allowing only what we will call lineal substitution. **1880** *Encycl. Brit.* XIII. 34/2 The method of integration by substitution corresponds to a change of the independent variable. **1892** F. N. COLE tr. *Netto's Th. Substitutions* 12 If an integral function of the elements $x_1, x_2, .. x_n$ is not symmetric, it will be changed in form, and consequently, if the x_λ's are entirely independent, also in value, by some of the possible interchanges of the x_λ's. The process of effecting such an interchange we shall call a *substitution.*

6. *Mus.* (See quot. *c* 1833.)

c **1833** GWILT in *Encycl. Metrop.* (1845) V. 777/1 *Substitution, Chords of*, names given to the two chords of the ninth major and minor. **1838** G. F. GRAHAM *Mus. Comp.* 29/1 Passing notes, notes of grace, anticipations, substitutions, altered or chromatic notes, and so on.

7. *Chem.* The replacement of one or more equivalents of an element or radical by a like number of equivalents of another. Also, the replacement of one atom or group of atoms in a molecule by another. Also *attrib.*

1848 FOWNES *Chem.* (ed. 2) 529 With ammonia the oil [of Gaultheria procumbens] yields salicylamide, and with fuming nitric acid a substitution-product, C_{16} H_7 NO_{10}. **1852** WATTS tr. *Gmelin's Handbk. Chem.* VII. 15 Dumas' Theory of Substitution and of Types. **1854** *Jrnl. Chem. Soc.* VII. 201 The Substitution-Compounds obtained by the Action of Nitric Acid on Cotton. **1857** MILLER *Elem. Chem., Org.* iii. §8. 213 A number of metallic substitution derivatives of alcohol. *Ibid.* iv. §2. 288 Strychnia, when pure, is turned yellow by concentrated nitric acid, and yields a nitrate of a new substitution base, nitrostrychnia. **1898** WADE *Introd. Org. Chem.* 91 The replacement of hydrogen by chlorine is termed direct substitution and that of chlorine by hydrogen inverse substitution. **1964** N. G. CLARK *Mod. Org. Chem.* xix. 381 The typical reactions of aromatic hydrocarbons are those of nuclear substitution, whereby one or more of the available hydrogen atoms attached to the nucleus are replaced by substituents derived from the reagent.

8. *Biol.* The replacement of one organ or function by another.

1870 *Henfrey's Bot.* §162 The modifications..dependent on the substitution of one organ for another, as in many double flowers where the stamens are replaced by petals. **1878** tr. *von Ziemssen's Cycl. Med.* XIV. 706 The law of substitution undergoes much limitation, and this alone can be granted, viz., that in the infracortical cerebral regions sensory elements can act for sensory, and motor for motor. **1902** *Rep. Brit. Assoc. Sci.* 631 The two post-Darwinian principles known as 'Substitution' and Isomorphism or 'Convergence'. The former may be exemplified by..the case of the Rays and Skates, in which..the tail, free to modify, becomes in one species a lengthy whiplash, in another, a vestigial stump.

9. *Philol.* A sound-change consisting in the replacement of one vowel or consonant by another.

1876 DOUSE *Grimm's Law* 25 Instead of the Differentiating Impulse, he here invokes Reciprocal Compensation as the operative cause of the later substitutions.

10. *Trade.* The dishonest replacement of one article of commerce by another; the passing off of one manufacturer's goods for another's.

1902 *Pharmac. Jrnl.* 6 Sept. 268/2 Several manufacturing firms which live on substitution. *Ibid.* 15 Nov. 508/1 Substitution, in essence and in fact, is palming off one article for another; thus in dispensing, by giving an imitation..for a proprietary or specific article.

11. *gen.* Replacement (*of* one thing) *by* another. See SUBSTITUTE *v.* 4.

1888 [see GRAVITATION 1]. **1938** R. D. CHARQUES *Footnotes to Theatre* II. 89 Some of the advocates of the..pictorial theatre went even so far as to recommend the substitution of the living actors by two-dimensional puppets. **1969** G. STEDMAN JONES in Cockburn & Blackburn *Student Power* 28 The political upheavals within the university in the last years are not the product of an imaginary substitution of workers by students. **1978** *Financial Results Oil Majors, 1977* (Shell Internat. Petroleum Co.) 7 In Europe, oil products demand declined by 1 per cent due to warmer weather, a generally weak economic performance and substitution by other energy sources, particularly hydro-electricity.

12. Special Comb. **substitution group** *Math.*, a group all the elements of which are substitutions (sense 5 b above); now usu. called *permutation group*.

1889 [see INTRANSITIVE *a.* 4]. **1916** G. A. MILLER et al. *Theory & Applications Finite Groups* i. 10 It will be proved ..that every finite group can be represented as a substitution group.

substitutional (sʌbstɪˈtjuːʃənəl), *a.* [f. prec. + -AL[1].]

1. *Theol.* Of or pertaining to, based upon the principle of, sacrificial substitution.

1786 A. M'LEAN *Commiss. Christ* III. Wks. 1847 I. 218 This points out the vicarious and substitutional nature of his death. *a* **1812** —— *Merit. Ground Justif.* ibid. III. 283 The merit and substitutional nature of Christ's obedience to the moral law throughout his life. **1893** *New Church Mess.* (N.Y.) 19 Apr. 244 This mercenary, substitutional theory of the atonement. **1897** *Advance* (Chicago) 4 Feb. 155/2 We need the divine sympathy, substitutional, because the Christ was tempted in all points as we are.

2. a. Involving a substitution; constituting or forming a substitute.

1820 J. FOSTER *Ess. Evils Pop. Ignor.* 166 While thus thrown loose from the former ties to the social order, their minds have not been seized upon to be put under the substitutional ones which sound instruction alone could impose. **1883** *Pall Mall Gaz.* 30 May 1/2 If he considered that he would not be fairly compensated under any substitutional private agreement. **1884** *Law Times Rep.* L. 619/2 Sect. 3 of the Act of 1878..is substitutional for sect. 62 of the Act of 1875. **1884** C. ROGERS *Soc. Life Scot.* x. II. 19 As a substitutional officer James I. appointed a Master of the Household. **1895** H. REYNOLDS *Anc. Dioc. Exeter* v. 127 This is the Pontifical of Edmund Lacy, a substitutional improvement on the order of Episcopal offices [etc.].

b. *Law.*

1883 *Law Rep. 23 Chanc. Div.* 738 W. Pearson, Q.C.,.. submitted that..the gift..was an original and not substitutional gift. **1894** *Daily News* 3 May 5/3 In other words, were the gifts substitutional or cumulative?

c. *Metallurgy.* Of an alloy: involving the substitution at certain lattice sites of atoms of the minor component for those of the major component; ***substitutional site***, a lattice site in an alloy at which atomic substitution occurs.

1940 [see INTERSTICE 1 b]. **1966** C. R. TOTTLE *Sci. Engin. Materials* viii. 186 Where complete or partial solid solubility exists and the solute atoms are too large to occupy interstitial positions, they replace solvent atoms at random in the lattice, and are accordingly referred to as substitutional. **1969** *Physics Bull.* May 167/2 To have the desired effects the implanted impurity atoms must eventually occupy isolated substitutional sites within the lattice. **1980** CHOMEL & COTTU in P. Haasen *Strength of Metals & Alloys* II. 1017 Substitutional alloy softening only results from a thermal component reduction of the flow stress.

Hence **substiˈtutionally** *adv.*

1874 WITHROW *Catac. Rome* (1877) 355 The Almighty Father, who is substitutionally represented by the Son in the adjoining scene. **1908** C. A. STRONG in *Ess. in honor of W. James* 172 The object..is not immediately (*i.e.*, without medium) but substitutionally known—known by the projection of a present experience, as truly possessed of definite qualities as the past experience it knows.

substitutionalism (sʌbstɪˈtjuːʃənəlɪz(ə)m). [f. prec. + -ISM.] (See quot.) Hence **substiˈtutionalist**.

1908 C. A. STRONG in *Ess. in honor of W. James* 171 The present experience does not intuite the past experience... It is a more or less perfect reproduction of it... It earns its title to be a memory by serving as a satisfactory substitute for the object in the regulation of conduct. We may call this the substitutional theory of knowledge, or, more briefly, substitutionalism. *Ibid.* 180 From this maze of misconceptions..the substitutionalist is saved by his insight that the proper thing to be called experience is not an experience projected into the place of another experience but an experience simply.

substitutionary (sʌbstɪˈtjuːʃənərɪ), *a.* [f. as prec. + -ARY.] = SUBSTITUTIONAL.

1842 J. P. SMITH *Four Disc.* (ed. 2) Notes 265 Other sacrifices also were symbols of a substitutionary death; for example, the sacrifice for ratifying a covenant;..and the sin-offering on account of a murder perpetrated by some unknown person. **1862** THRUPP *Anglo-Saxon Home* ii. 92 We find another lady with the substitutionary name of the Crow. **1872** SPURGEON *Treas. Dav.* Ps. lxxi. 15 The devil rages against the substitutionary sacrifice. **1874** W. P. ROBERTS *Law & God* (1878) 45 The first [of the three stages in the history of sacrifice] is the substitutionary human sacrifice. **1881** C. NEW *Serm. preached in Hastings* iii. 25 This substitutionary aspect of the Atonement. **1883** E. E. KAY in *Law Rep. 23 Chanc. Div.* 739 If the parent was dead at the date of the will..his issue are not able to take under the substitutionary gift. **1896** *Academy* 4 July 5/3 An editor ..errs gravely if he introduces thereinto one word of his own, be it substitutionary title or aught else. **1908** *Q. Rev.* July 98 He not only succeeded Geoffrey as substitutionary forester of North Petherton Park and Forest under the Mortimer régime, but was constable of Taunton Castle.

substitutive (ˈsʌbstɪtjuːtɪv), *a.* [ad. late L. *substitūtīvus*, f. *substitūt-* (see SUBSTITUTE *v.*): see -IVE. Cf. F. *substitutif*.]

†**1.** Belonging to, characteristic of, or involving the appointment of, a substitute or deputy. *Obs.*

1600 W. WATSON *Decacordon* (1602) 324 [Father Parsons has] authorized his subiect Master Blackwell with so ample immunities, priuiledges,..and substitutiue iurisdiction, as neither pope nor prince..may..haue to doe with him. **1616** CHAMPNEY *Voc. Bps.* 92 Christ..hath said it not only to his Apostles, but also to all Prelates, that shall suceede them by substitutive ordination. **1640** HOWELL *Dodona's Gr.* 130 His Highness might thinke fit to leave a substitutive power, with whom he pleased to bee contracted to the La: Amira.

2. Taking, or fitted to take, the place of something else: in various more or less technical applications (see quots.).

1668 WILKINS *Real Char.* III. ii. §5. 308 Those Substitutive Particles, which serve to supply the room of some sentence or complex part of it, are stiled Interjections. **1865** BRANDE & COX *Dict. Sci.*, etc. I. 601/2 *Currency*,..a generic term employed to designate the conventional measure of value, whether the measure be immediate, as gold and silver coin, or substitutive, as bank-notes and their analogies. **1876** DUNGLISON *Med. Lex.* 995/2 An agent is said to be 'substitutive', which—as in the case of nitrate of silver applied to inflammation of a mucous membrane—substitutes a temporary irritation for one tending to be more permanent. Such a mode of treatment is termed *substitutive medication.* **1903** MYERS *Hum. Pers.* II. 34 The question may be raised as to whether the second figure seen may not have been, so to say, substitutive. **1908** *Academy* 18 Jan. 356/1 He suggests instead that they should be allowed to record substitutive votes, by numbering the candidates '1,' '2,' '3,' etc. **1913** *Nation* 4 Jan. 605/1 'This tax is proposed to take the place of certain rates which politicians and economists of all sorts have long agreed should be national rather than local burdens'... I have insisted that this tax is substitutive, not cumulative.

b. *Logic.* Of a proposition or judgement: = CONDITIONAL *a.* 5.

1656 BLOUNT *Glossogr.*, *Substitutive*,.. It is also a term in Logick, as *Propositio substitutiva*, a conditional Proposition. **1822** T. TAYLOR *Apuleius* 376 The other [species of proposition is] substitutive or conditional. **1853** W. THOMSON *Laws Th.* (ed. 3) 155 The judgment in which definition is predicated, we call a substitutive judgment, because it furnishes a predicate identical with the subject as to sphere or extension, and therefore capable of being substituted for it. **1864** BOWEN *Logic* v. 109 In Substitutive Judgments the sign of equality may be used as the Copula.

3. *Theol.* Involving a theory of substitution.

1865 BUSHNELL *Vicar. Sacr.* I. iii. (1866) 43 The full vicarious typology and substitutive import of the original Greek version. **1882–3** *Schaff's Encycl. Relig. Knowl.* I. 205/1 A substitutive faith of the Church, by which the band of original sin is broken.

4. Dependent upon a legal substitution or designation of heirs in remainder.

1853 *Act 16 & 17 Vict.* c. 51 §2 Every..disposition of property, by reason whereof any person has..become beneficially entitled to any property..either originally or by way of substitutive limitation.

Hence '**substitutively** *adv.*, vicariously.

1890 *Lippincott's Mag.* Jan. 117 Thus did he execute his opponent..substitutively.

substitu'tivity. *Logic.* [f. SUBSTITUTIVE *a.* 2 b + -ITY.] The capacity of terms to function as logically equivalent substitutes for one another (see quot. 1965).

1940 W. V. QUINE *Math. Logic* 96 This restriction gives rise..to the following..substitutivity principle. **1943** [see IDENTICAL *sb.* 1]. **1945** *Mind* LIV. 358 Subject to certain important restrictions pointed out recently by Prof. W. V. Quine, we may accept what he calls the principle of substitutivity as applied to class-identity. **1959** K. R. POPPER *Logic of Sci. Discovery* 343 One of our axioms would become redundant, *i.e.* our axiom of substitutivity. **1965** *Jrnl. Philos.* LXII. 139 Quine, Frege, and Russell approach problems connected with *oratio obliqua* constructions determined to defend Leibniz's Law, the principle of substitutivity, sometimes referred to as 'the indiscernibility of identicals'. **1976** *Language* LII. 3 The sense of 'referential' represented by a pair of heavy parentheses is different from the standard one in terms of substitutivity of identicals.

substitutory ('sʌbstɪtjuːtərɪ), *a.* [f. L. *substitūt-* (see SUBSTITUTE *v.*) + -ORY.] Serving as a substitute.

1887 *Echo* 26 Feb. (Cassell), A few remarks on the proposed cultivation of tobacco as one of the substitutory crops for wheat, &c.

†'**substra**, *v. trans. Obs. rare.* [ad. med.L. *substrahe*, imper. of *substrahĕre* to SUBSTRACT. Cf. SUBTRAY.] *trans.* To subtract.

1557 H. BAKER *Rules Use Almanacs* D iij, You shall substra from the saide time the distaunce of the time proposed vntyll none.

substract (səb'strækt), *v.* Now *illiterate.* [f. med.L. *substract-*, pa. ppl. stem of *substrahĕre*, alteration of *subtrahĕre* to SUBTRACT after *abstrahĕre* to ABSTRACT. Cf. OF., Pr. *sostraire*, *substraire*, Sp. *su(b)straer.*] = SUBTRACT *v.*

†**1.** *trans.* To withdraw, withhold (a thing) *from* a person, etc. *Obs.*

1604 R. CAWDREY *Table Alph.* (1613), *Substract*, take from, withdrawe. **1607** TOPSELL *Four-f. Beasts* 80 Other put their Neckes into engins, and tame them by substracting their meate. **1647** N. BACON *Disc. Govt. Eng.* I. iii. (1739) 18 Where they shall know of the things belonging to the Crown,..to be concealed, intruded upon, or substracted. **1667** *Decay Chr. Piety* viii. §5. 266 This..substracts that spirit and vigour, which should carry us through the weary stages of duty. **1681** J. SCOTT *Chr. Life* I. iv. §5 (1683) 351 Whatso-ever Time and Attendance we bestow upon one thing, we must necessarily substract from another. **1710** PRIDEAUX *Orig. Tithes* i. 16 God charged the Jews with the Sin of Substracting these Tithes.

†**b.** *refl.* To withdraw oneself, retire *from. Obs.*

1550–60 BELLENDEN *Livy* I. (S.T.S.) I. 8, I will Desyre na thing erar..than to substract me fra þe sicht of sik miseriis.

2. *trans.* To take (one number or quantity) *from*, †*out of* another, as a mathematical process.

1588 A. KING tr. *Canisius' Catech.* hj, Swa yat ye anticipation being substractit, ye said æquinoxe micht be restoreit to ye 21 day of marche as it was before. **1647** LILLY *Chr. Astrol.* iv. 41 Added together, they make $43^h 03^m$, from which in regard they are more then 24 hours, I substract 24. **1656** H. PHILLIPS *Purch. Patt.* (1676) 83 You must substract the latter time out of the former time. **1660** BARROW *Euclid* v. xix. Coroll., If like proportionals be substracted from like proportionals. **1731** MILLER *Gard. Dict.* s.v. *Nature*, This Motion..if the Body were in Motion before, is either to be added to it, as if the Motions conspire, or substracted from it, as where contrary. **1800** *Phil. Trans.* XC. 624, 3″, 25, which, substracted from 110° 30′ 13″, 25, leaves 110° 30′ 10″. **1840** LARDNER *Geom.* 108 If from the square of the side opposite the right angle, the square of the given side be substracted, the remainder will be the square of the third side.

absol. **1626** J. YATES *Ibis ad Cæsarem* II. 156 Thereby declaring your selfe to be an exquisite Arithmetician, who can adde and substract at pleasure.

3. *transf.* and *gen.* To take away, deduct.

1613 HOBY *Counter-snarle* 25 My course hath euer beene ..to substract many ounces, from that ordinary opinion, which men of his profession doe..intertaine. **1641** EARL MONM. tr. *Biondi's Civil Wars* IV. 23 These must likewise bee substracted from the English, who were left to guard Jury. **1667** *Decay Chr. Piety* Pref. A 5 What vanity..have we substracted, upon the sense of Gods anger? **1744** HARRIS *Three Treat.* II. i. (1765) 57 There must be substracted from these [*sc.* media of visible objects] the Medium of Motion. **1755** LAVINGTON *Moravians Compared* 157 What are not found in their proper Places, these he substracted with equal Audaciousness. **1810** BENTHAM *Packing* (1821) 262 When all lawyers and all non-lawyers are substracted, how many have you left?

absol. **1656** HEYLIN *Extraneus Vapulans* 300 Our Authors false Arithmetique in Substracting from his own errours, and multiplying the supposed mistakes of the Observator. **1794** R. J. SULIVAN *View Nat.* I. 467 By evaporating, by cooling, or by substracting from the fluid. **1804** WELLINGTON in Gurw. *Desp.* (1835) III. 15 A..resistance to every thing like an abuse in the service which can tend to substract from the efficiency of the corps in the field. **1816** BENTHAM *Chrestom.* App., Wks. 1843 VIII. 188 So far from adding to, it will substract from, the quantity of labour necessary.

†**4.** To belittle, disparage. (? A blunder. Cf. SUBSTRACTOR.) *Obs.*

1728 NORTH *Mem. Music* (1846) 114 Every one.. spightfull to each other, and out of emulation substracting their skill in performing.

Hence **sub'stracting** *vbl. sb.*

1628 T. SPENCER *Logick* 18 The substracting of something inioyed, or the receiving of something that is added. **1667** *Decay Chr. Piety* 50 In artificial Movements, there is such a dependance of one part upon another, that the substracting of any one destroys the whole frame.

substraction (səb'strækʃən). Now *illiterate.* [ad. med.L. **substractio*, -*ōnem*, n. of action f. *substrahĕre* to SUBSTRACT. Cf. OF. *sustraction*, *substraction*, Sp. *substraccion.*] = SUBTRACTION.

1. The operation of taking one number or quantity *from* another; an instance of this. Also *transf.* and *gen.* Deduction, abstraction.

1596 NASHE *Saffron Walden* 141 Quarrelling by Diuision, getting wenches with childe by Multiplication, stealing by Substraction. **1601** W. BARLOW *Defence* 102 Euery addition or substraction is hie treason against his maiestie. **1613** W. BROWNE *Brit. Past.* I. iv. (1772) I. 136 Millions admit a small substraction. **1648** HEYLIN *Relat. & Observ.* I. 33 The same Ship..having been so often repaired, and thereby suffered so many substractions and additions, that hardly any part of the old Vessell remained. **1703** T. N. *City & C. Purchaser* 80 Substraction must have been made of all such Deductions. **1728** CHAMBERS *Cycl.* s.v., Substraction is the finding of a certain Number from two Homogeneous ones given, which, with one of the given Numbers, is equal to the other. **1818** BENTHAM *Ch. Eng.* Introd. 63 A course which, —after substraction made of all punishment and all reward ..would remain no less open to rulers than to subjects. **1827** CARLYLE *Germ. Rom.* II. 23 Rendering back to us with additions or substractions, the Beauty which existing things have of themselves presented to him.

2. The withdrawing or withholding of something necessary, due, essential, or customary.

1620 T. SCOTT *Highw. God* (1623) 74 Now there is cause to doubt rather substraction, then to hope for restitution. **1626** J. YATES *Ibis ad Cæsarem* I. 76 In the sorrowes of the soule there was..some substraction of divine consolation. **1643** PRYNNE *Opening Gt. Seal* 19 The great and privy Seales wilfully absence and substraction from the Parliament. **1660** R. COKE *Power & Subj.* 203 A Prior..may chuse either to sue for substraction of his Tithes in the Ecclesiastical court, or in the Exchequer. **1822** (*title*) Report of a trial in the Consistory Court at Durham in a Cause of Substraction of Easter Offerings.

Hence †**sub'stractionary** *a.*, of subtraction.

1674 JEAKE *Arith.* (1696) 54 If the Subtrahend and Remain be added, the Substractionary work will be proved.

†**sub'stractive**, *a. Obs. rare.* [f. L. *substract-* (see SUBSTRACT *v.*) + -IVE.] = SUBTRACTIVE.

1774 *Phil. Trans.* LXIV. 166, + $\frac{F - 40}{449}$ becoming negative or substractive.

†**sub'stractor.** *Obs. rare*$^{-1}$. [f. SUBSTRACT *v.* + -OR.] A detractor, calumniator.

1601 SHAKS. *Twel. N.* I. iii. 37 They are scoundrels and substractors that say so of him.

†'**substrahend.** *Obs.* [ad. med.L. *substrahendus* gerundive of *substrahĕre* to SUBSTRACT.] = SUBTRAHEND.

1713 WARD *Yng. Math. Guide* (1734) 148 Change all the Signs of the Substrahend.

‖**substramen** (səb'streɪmən). *rare*$^{-1}$. [L., f. *substernĕre* (see SUBSTRATE *a.*).] = SUBSTRATUM.

1807 HEADRICK *Arran* 56 Some contained various concretions, inserted in a sandy substramen.

substratal (səb'streɪtəl), *a.* [f. next or SUBSTRATUM + -AL[1].] Underlying; fundamental.

1851 *Jrnl. R. Agric. Soc.* XII. II. 495 This is the substratal view of the origin and relations of the surface soil. **1881** BLACKIE *Lay Serm.* iii. 115 The one proof or evidence that belongs to both is the reasonable substratal element which they imply.

substrate ('sʌbstreɪt), *sb.* [ad. mod.L. *substrātum.*] **1.** = SUBSTRATUM.

c **1810** COLERIDGE *Lit. Rem.* (1838) III. 379 The substrate or *causa invisibilis* may be the *noumenon* or actuality, *das Ding in sich*, of Christ's humanity, as well as the *Ding in sich* of which the sensation, bread, is the appearance. **1817** —— *Biog. Lit.* I. ix. 138 This again is no way conceivable, but by assuming as a postulate, that both are ab initio, identical and co-inherent; that intelligence and being are reciprocally each other's Substrate. **1822–7** GOOD *Study Med.* (1829) IV. 46 That common substrate which is diffused around us in every direction, and constitutes the whole of the visible world. **1839** *Penny Cycl.* XIII. 176/1 The notion of substance is..conceived..as a constant and persisting substrate of certain variable qualities or determinations. **1861** TRENCH *Comm. Ep. Churches Asia* 174 That the substrate of this language, and, so to say, the suggestion of this thought, is to be sought at Isaiah 22, there can be no reasonable doubt. **1886** *Encycl. Brit.* XXI. 428/2 Albert and Aquinas agree in declaring that the principle of individuation is to be found in matter, not, however, in matter as a formless substrate but in determinate matter (*materia signata*). **1897** tr. *Fichte's Sci. Ethics* 115 Let us assume an external cause directed upon the substrate of the impulse. **1899** J. W. POWELL *20th Ann. Rep. Bureau Amer. Ethnol.* (1903) p. clviii, The same deity can be invoked by many names,..and when another god is addressed, many of the same terms can be employed. The substrate of this custom is found in the concomitancy of qualities and properties. **1910** *Contemp. Rev.* July 28 There is reason to believe that the fur substrate [of the garment] was then withdrawn.

2. *Biochem.* The substance upon which an enzyme acts, i.e. whose reaction it brings about.

1907 *Bio-chem. Jrnl.* II. 143 When the relative amount of substrate is large, catalase is rapidly changed into an inactive form. **1938** [see ADENOSINE b]. **1962** VAN HEYNINGEN & WALEY in A. Pirie *Lens Metabolism Rel. Cataract* 336 Proteolytic enzymes are often characterized by their action on substrates which are not known to be the natural substrates of the enzyme *in vivo.* **1978** J. R. HOLUM *Org. & Biol. Chem.* xiii. 270 Many enzymes are named by attaching the suffix -ase to the name of the compound, called the substrate, whose reaction the enzyme catalyzes.

3. *Biol.* The surface or material on which any particular organism occurs or grows.

1908 W. M. BAYLISS *Nature of Enzyme Action* ii. 7 A name is frequently needed for the substances on which enzymes exert their activity... On the whole, 'substrate,' already used by many writers, seems to answer the purpose best. **1949** W. C. ALLEE et al. *Princ. Animal Ecol.* x. 158 The surface of water is an important substrate for life, though not nearly so important as the surface of land. **1967** M. E. HALE *Biol. Lichens* iv. 61 A large group of lichens..have high fidelity for limestone and other basic substrates. **1976** *Nature* 15 July p. xiii (Advt.), An order of Crustacea common on sandy or muddy substrates all round the European coasts. **1977** J. L. HARPER *Populations Biol. Plants* xxiv. 765 The variations in substrate that undoubtedly occurred..in the field were eliminated by using a standard potting compost throughout the experiment.

4. Any underlying bulk phase, layer, etc., on which something is deposited. Cf. SUBSTRATUM 4.

1937 *Nature* 24 July 158/1 In recent years, the practice has grown up among workers in surface chemistry of using the word 'substrate' to denote the bulk phase underlying a surface film, regardless of the fact that this word has been in general use for a much longer time to denote the substance upon which an enzyme acts. **1954** *Electronic Engin.* XXVI. 296 The applied metal film..adheres well to the substrate. **1960** [see EPITAXIALLY *adv.*]. **1967** *Times Rev. Industry* May 76/1 The use of polythene in coating paper and other substrates for packaging a variety of goods. **1974** *Physics Bull.* June 225/3 Spiller and Segmuller's x ray waveguide consists of a 30–50 nm thick layer of boron nitride between a substrate and cover layer of sapphire.

†'**substrate,** *a. Obs.* [ad. L. *substrātus*, pa. pple. of *substernĕre*, f. *sub-* SUB- 2 + *sternĕre* to throw or lay down.] Underlying; forming a substratum; constituting the subject-matter.

1678 GALE *Crt. Gentiles* IV. III. 2 Sin, as to its material constitution, has for its substrate mater or subject some natural good. **1684** tr. *Bonet's Merc. Compit.* XIV. 476 The Womb..has no proper Substrate Matter to breed a Callus. **1844** *Blackw. Mag.* LV. 668 The Thought..remains; the substrate, absolute, essential, generic notion.

†**substrate,** *v. Obs.* [f. L. *substrāt-* (see prec.).]

1. *trans.* To form a substratum to.

1578 BANISTER *Hist. Man* I. 10 It substrateth the brayne, no otherwise then a ground or foundation thereto.

2. *pass.* To be underlying or subjacent; to be or form a substratum (*to*).

1578 BANISTER *Hist. Man* I. 35 Talus..prostrated vnder Tibia, and Fibula, and subiect to their Appendances, although it seeme onely substrated to Tibia. **1654** VILVAIN *Enchir. Epigr.* I. ix. 4 Nature, Fate, Fortune, Chance in things created, Cleerly appear by Law divine substrated. **1701** BEVERLEY *Grand Apocal. Quest.* 17 From these two things Substrated, or lay'd in the Foundation, I proceed to raise the Convincing Proofs.

So †**substrated** *ppl. a.*, underlying.

1663 BOYLE *Usef. Exp. Nat. Philos.* II. App. 352 We have more then once had the bottom of the Retort melted, .. the melted glasse being supported by the substrated sand.

substration (səbˈstreɪʃən). [ad. late L. *substrātio*, *-ōnem*, n. of action f. *substrāt-*, *substernĕre* (see SUBSTRATE *a.*).]

†**1.** The prostration of the class of penitents known as *substrati*; also, the place where these penitents knelt. *Obs.*

1659 H. L'ESTRANGE *Alliance Div. Off.* 320 This place was called ὑποπτωσις Substration, because there they did .. throw themselves down to receive the Priests blessing. **1716** M. DAVIES *Athen. Brit.* II. 254 The different degrees of Penitential Fletion, Audition, Substration and Consistence, or Standing together with the Orthodox Flock.

2. A hypothesis.

1830 *Blackw. Mag.* XXVIII. 256 Theory is = Ordination. Hypothesis is = Substration.

substrative (səbˈstreɪtɪv), *a.* [f. L. *substrāt-* (see SUBSTRATE *a.*) + -IVE.] Underlying; forming a substratum.

1823 HONE *Anc. Myst.* 183 So large a substrative mass of superstition. *a* **1834** COLERIDGE in *Lit. Rem.* (1839) IV. 227 That *Idea Idearum*, the one substrative truth which is the form, manner, and involvent of all truths.

†**subˈstrator.** *Eccl. Obs. rare.* [f. L. *substrāt-* (see SUBSTRATE *a.*) + -OR.] One of a class of penitents in the early church called *substrati*; = KNEELER 2 a. (Cf. PROSTRATOR 2.)

1720 BINGHAM *Antiquities* XVIII. i. §1 The mourners or weepers, the hearers, the substrators, and the co-standers.

substratum (səbˈstrɑːtəm, -ˈstreɪtəm). Pl. substrata; also **substratums**. [mod.L., pa. pple. neut. sing. of L. *substernĕre* to spread underneath, f. *sub-* SUB- 2 + *sternĕre* to lay down, strew.]

1. *Metaph.* That which is regarded as supporting attributes or accidents; the substance in which qualities inhere.

1653 WHITFIELD *Treat. Sinf. Men* iv. 11 The *Substratum* or subject of sin, namely, the naturall motion or action whereto sin cleaves, is such a thing without which sin could not be. *a* **1676** HALE *Prim. Orig. Man.* I. i. 22 The Substance or the *Substratum* of those Accidents of things which are derived to us by our Sense. **1690** LOCKE *Hum. Und.* I. iv. §18 Something .. which we take to be the *substratum*, or support, of those Idea's we do know. **1740** CHEYNE *Regimen* 34 Material Substance is the *Substratum* of Extension, Impenetrability, Passivity and Figure. **1817** COLERIDGE *Biog. Lit.* (1907) I. 88 Different modes, or degrees in perfection, of a common substratum. **1838** [F. HAYWOOD] tr. *Kant's Crit. Pure Reason* 176 Substances (in the phenomenon) are the substrata of all determinations of time. **1874** SIDGWICK *Meth. Ethics* I. ix. 102 Permanent substrata or Noumena.

2. That which underlies, or serves as the basis or foundation of, an immaterial thing, condition, or activity; the basis on which an immaterial 'structure' is raised.

1631 J. BURGES *Answ. Rejoined* Manud. 32 It is their institution which imprints their signification, and not simply their owne similitude, which is but the *substratum*. *a* **1672** WILKINS *Nat. Relig.* I. xiv. (1675) 214 That *basis* or *substratum* upon which the Law is founded. **1798** J. BARRY *Let. Dilettanti Soc.* 65 As a totality which form the very *substratum* and essence of my Lectures to the Students of the Academy. **1816** COLERIDGE *Lay Serm.* (Bohn) 315 It is .. the realizing principle, the spiritual substratum of the whole complex body of truths. **1859** HELPS *Friends in C.* Ser. II. II. x. 244 All Aristotle's views were based upon a substratum of slavery. **1860** HOOK *Lives Abps.* I. 45 The simple patriarchal faith .. was never lost, and when the idolatrous superstitions were removed there still remained a substratum of truth. **1862** J. M. LUDLOW *Hist. U.S.* 4 There are in several places substrata of foreign blood, as the Dutch in New York and New Jersey, the Swedes in New Jersey and Delaware. **1870** NEWMAN *Gram. Assent* II. vii. 213 What in some minds seems like .. a faith founded on a perilous substratum of doubt. **1878** BOSW. SMITH *Carthage* 321 The stories themselves doubtless rest on a substratum of fact. **1900** W. L. COURTNEY *Idea Trag.* 58 In Henry Vth's character there was a substratum of common sense, of self-control.

3. That upon which a material thing is 'built up' or from which it is created; the subject-matter or matter operated upon.

a **1676** HALE *Prim. Orig. Man.* 345 He used the Matter which he had created to be the *substratum* of the Corporeal Natures, even of Man himself. **1708** *Brit. Apollo* No. 2. 2/1 That Hail and Snow are produc'd out of the same Substratum or matter. **1799** *Med. Jrnl.* I. 270 From a combination of the basis of vital air, with the substratum of carbon, sulphur, and phosphorus, arise the carbonic, sulphuric, and phosphoric acids. *c* **1825** T. CHALMERS in *Mem.* (1851) III. 65 *note*, With our Scottish peasantry, the substratum of the meal is either potatoes or bread. **1837** QUAIN *Elem. Anat.* (ed. 4) 9 The skeleton .. constitutes the substratum, to which the other parts are, as it were, applied. **1875** STEWART & TAIT *Unseen Univ.* vii. §213. 167 The atoms which form the material substratum of the present universe. **1878** BELL tr. *Gegenbaur's Comp. Anat.* 13 In the living body we observe a number of activities of its material substratum, by which the series of phænomena spoken of as life are conditioned.

4. a. An under-layer of any material substance.

1730 BAILEY (fol.), *Substratum*, .. any Layer of Earth or any other Thing that lies under another. **1764** BUSH *Hiber. Cur.* (1769) 79, I do not at all suppose that even the very first .. growth of this heath .. in any sense sprang from the fallen wood, its neighbouring substratum. **1846** R. RITCHIE *Railways* 10 Substrata of small stones, several feet in thickness. **1859** DICKENS *T. Two Cities* I. ii, A loaded blunderbuss lay at the top of six or eight loaded horse-pistols, deposited on a substratum of cutlass. **1878** ABNEY *Photogr.* xiv. 92 When it is required to cover the entire plate with either of these substrata, it is usual to wet the plate with distilled water. **1892** *Photogr. Ann.* 83 Coat the plates with an albumen substratum.

b. An under-layer of soil or earthy matter.

1730 [see above]. **1801** J. JONES tr. *Bugge's Trav. Fr. Rep.* i. 3 Where the substratum is gravel or sand. **1813** BAKEWELL *Introd. Geol.* 197 A proper knowledge of the quality of the sub-soil and the position of the sub-strata is necessary. **1824** G. CHALMERS *Caledonia* III. 596 Even the more level, and more genial soils are cold, from their substratums. **1872** A. C. RAMSAY *Phys. Geog.* (ed. 3) xvii. 268 The Vale of Clwyd, in Denbighshire—the substratum of which consists of New Red Sandstone.

c. *Bot.* The matter upon which a fungus or other plant grows.

1876 tr. *Wagner's Gen. Pathol.* 101 In the substratum the process of decomposition differs with the fungus present. **1882** VINES tr. *Sachs' Bot.* 307 Fungi grow exclusively upon organic substrata.

d. In immaterial sense.

1855 [J. D. BURN] *Autobiog. Beggar Boy* (1859) 2 Such as have passed through the various substrata of civilized society. **1873** CURWEN *Hist. Booksellers* 363 As the business is conducted by house to house visitation, a substratum of the public is reached which [etc.]. **1876** J. GRANT *Burgh Sch. Scot.* II. xi. 308 Children belonging to the substratum of society.

5. a. *Linguistics.* Elements or features of a language which are identified by linguists as being relics of, or due to the influence of, an earlier extinct language, usually of the same region. Cf. SUPERSTRATUM 2 a.

1922 O. JESPERSEN *Language* xi. 192 Many scholars have recently attached great importance to the .. influence exerted by one language on another in those cases in which a population abandons its original language and adopts that of another race... There is thus created what is now generally termed as *substratum* underlying the new language. **1933** L. BLOOMFIELD *Language* xxi. 386 There is no sense in the mystical version of the substratum theory, which attributes changes, say, in modern Germanic languages, to a 'Celtic substratum'. **1956** J. WHATMOUGH *Language* IV. 51 We have superimposed or adjacent languages (superstratum, substratum, and adstratum). **1972** H. KURATH *Studies in Area Linguistics* 120 The phonemic system of Gullah shows some clear influence of the African substratum.

b. *attrib.* and *Comb.*, as ***substratum influence***, ***language***, etc.; **substratum theory**, a theory that attributes linguistic change to the influence of a substratum language.

1933 L. BLOOMFIELD *Language* xxi. 386 The substratum theory attributes sound-change to transference of language: a community which adopts a new language will speak it .. with the phonetics of its mother-tongue. **1937** J. ORR tr. *Iordan's Introd. to Romance Linguistics* i. 12 An historical summary of the substratum problem. **1952** R. HALL in *Lingua* III. 144 The basic prerequisite for the possibility of substratum influence is a language transfer which takes place through a stage of bilingualism. **1954** *Word* X. 395 Diachronic dialectology deals .. with convergence, i.e. it studies partial similarities increasing at the expense of differences (traditionally, substratum and adstratum studies .. and the like). **1962** BURRILL & BONSACK in Householder & Saporta *Probl. Lexicogr.* 189 Words which had the force of generic terms in substratum languages may not be understood as generic terms by the present-day populace. **1973** *Archivum Linguisticum* IV. 110 In regard to the so-called Black English, William A. Stewart was the first to advocate a creole substratum theory. **1980** *English World-Wide* I. I. 150 It is not legitimate to compare a static description of creole with a static description of a substratum language.

†**subˈstrature.** *Obs. rare*[−1]. [f. L. *substrāt-* (see SUBSTRATE *a.*) + -URE.] A substratum.

1726 LEONI *Alberti's Archit.* I. 73/2 The substrature or layer under the pavement.

substruct (səbˈstrʌkt), *v. rare.* [f. L. *substruct-*, pa. ppl. stem of *substruĕre*, f. *sub-* SUB- 2 + *struĕre* to build, erect.] *trans.* To construct beneath; to lay as a foundation.

1847 EMERSON *Repr. Men, Plato* Wks. (Bohn) I. 295 The excellence of Europe and Asia are in his brain. Metaphysics and natural philosophy expressed the genius of Europe; he substructs the religion of Asia, as the base. *Ibid., Swedenborg* 328 A bird does not more readily weave its nest .. than this seer of the souls substructs a new hell and pit.

substruction (səbˈstrʌkʃən). [ad. F. *substruction* or L. *substructio*, *-ōnem*, n. of action f. *substruĕre* to SUBSTRUCT.]

1. *Arch.* The under-structure of a building or other work.

1624 WOTTON *Elem. Archit.* 23 We must first examine the Bed of Earth .. vpon which we will Build; and then the vnderfillings or Substruction, as the Auncients did call it. **1650** FULLER *Pisgah* II. xii. 259 It was contrived into rooms, and fortified with substructions therein, fit for the receipt of a Prince. **1717** BERKELEY *Jrnl. Tour Italy* Wks. 1871 IV. 532 A great quadrangular portico .., whereof the substructions only now remain. **1775** R. CHANDLER *Trav. Asia M.* (1825) I. 33 Higher up is the vaulted substruction or basement of a large temple. **1838** ARNOLD *Hist. Rome* v. I. 52 The massy substructions of the Capitoline temple. *a* **1842** *Ibid.* xliii. (1843) III. 91 The road therefore was restored, and supported with solid substructions below. **1866** FELTON *Greece, Anc. & Mod.* II. ii. 285 A part of this road is still to be seen .. with the ruined masses of the immense substructions which supported it. **1898** G. A. SMITH *Bk. Twelve Prophets* II. xxxvii. 530 Upon terraces and substructions of enormous breadth rose storied palaces, arsenals, barracks, libraries, and temples.

attrib. *c* **1676** WREN in Willis & Clark *Cambridge* (1886) II. 534 The Ground plot of the Substruction Cloister.

2. *fig.* A basis, foundation.

1765 BLACKSTONE *Comm.* I. xiii. 405 The laws of Oleron .. are received by all nations in Europe as the ground and substruction of all their marine constitutions. **1766** *Ibid.* II. iv. 51 A substruction and foundation of their new polity. **1822** T. ERSKINE *Ess. Faith* (1825) 33 A scaffolding or substruction for the doctrine. **1887** [E. JOHNSON] *Antiqua Mater* 232 The historic 'substruction' of a system supported by astrological calculation.

†**3.** (See quot.) *Obs. rare*[−0].

1656 BLOUNT *Glossogr.*, *Substruction*, an underpinning or grounselling of a house. **1728** CHAMBERS *Cycl.*

Hence **subˈstructional** *a.* (in recent Dicts.).

substructure (ˈsʌbstrʌktjʊə(r)). [f. SUB- 3 + STRUCTURE, after prec.] **a.** *Arch.* That part of a building which supports the superstructure; an under-structure, substruction.

1726 LEONI *Alberti's Archit.* I. 48/1 These .. Stones must be .. link'd with the under Courses, so as to make a kind of pavement at top to .. protect the Substructure. **1840** LONGF. *Skel. Arm.* Introd., The substructure of a windmill. **1861** BERESF. HOPE *Engl. Cathedral 19th C.* 89 The moderate scantlings .. obviate the risk of the roof crushing down the substructure. **1876** *Encycl. Brit.* IV. 284/1 The substructure of a bridge consists of foundations, abutments, and piers. **1884** *Manch. Exam.* 19 Dec. 5/3 The sub-structure of the pier.

b. *transf.* and *fig.*

1735 S. HARRIS *Comm. 53rd Ch. Isa.* Pref. 16 A substructure of their chronology, geography, and history. **1851** *Jrnl. Asiat. Soc. Bengal* 7 The kingdom of Menes .. rests upon a venerable substructure of several centuries of the Nile valley. **1856** KANE *Arctic Expl.* II. xxvii. 271 This glacier .. sloped gradually upward .. and then, following the irregularities of its rocky sub-structure, suddenly became a steep crevassed hill. **1875** E. WHITE *Life in Christ* I. viii. (1878) 73 No decisive anticipation of immortality for mankind as a substructure for religious faith can be deduced.

Hence **subˈstructural** *a.*, of the nature of a substructure; **ˈsubstructured** *a.* [-ED[2]], having a substructure.

1866 *Pall Mall Gaz.* 12 May 12 A narrative of long public services, mostly underground and substructural. **1884** *Homilet. Monthly* Sept. 684 These are the substructural truths of revelation. **1952** GERTH & MARTINDALE tr. *M. Weber's Anc. Judaism* III. x. 254 Babylonia and Egypt knew no unified, religiously substructured ethic. **1971** *Black Scholar* June 52/2 The substructured prison movements are gaining momentum.

substylar (ˈsʌbstaɪlə(r)), *a.* (*sb.*) Also **-ilar, -iler.** [ad. mod.L. *substylāris* (sc. *linea* line): see SUB- 1 and STYLAR.] ***substylar line*** = SUBSTYLE. Also *ellipt.* as *sb.*

1669 STURMY *Mariner's Mag.* VII. xi. 18 To find what Hour .. the Substiler is distant from the Meridian. *Ibid.* xxvii. 40 Chuse some convenient place in your Substiler Line .. and there draw the line FBA. **1764** J. FERGUSON *Lect.* 224 Draw the contingent line EQ, cutting the substilar line at right angles. **1795** HUTTON *Math. Dict.* II. 536 In easterly and westerly dials, the substilar line is the line of 6 o'clock.

substyle (ˈsʌbstaɪl). Also **-ile.** [See prec. and STYLE.] In dialling, the line on which the style or gnomon stands.

1593 FALE *Horologiogr.* 20 Extend your compasses, the one foote being placed in F. in the line of the Substile toward C. unto H. **1690** LEYBOURN *Curs. Math.* 704 To find the true Hour distances upon the Plain from the Substiles. **1715** tr. *Gregory's Astron.* (1726) I. 334 That they may be distinguished, and not confounded with the Substyle. **1764** J. FERGUSON *Lect.* 197 In all declining dials, the substile makes an angle with the hour-line of XII. **1795** HUTTON *Math. Dict.* II. 536.

b. *attrib.*

1636 in Rigaud *Corr. Sci. Men* (1841) I. 27 How it comes to pass that Mr. Gunter and yourself should differ in placing the substile line. **1669** STURMY *Mariner's Mag.* 57 There are two Lines called by the Names of Style and Substyle-Scale. **1764** J. FERGUSON *Lect.* 203 The line on which the stile or gnomon stands (commonly called the substile-line).

†**subˈsult,** *v. Obs. rare*[−0]. [ad. L. *subsultāre*, frequent. of *subsilīre*, f. *sub-* SUB- 26 + *salīre* to leap.] *intr.* To hop, jump about. Hence **subsulˈtation**, hopping, jumping up and down; **subˈsulting** *ppl. a.*

1656 BLOUNT *Glossogr.*, **Subsult*, to leap or hop under or about. **1650** H. MORE *Observ.* in *Enthus. Tri.*, etc. (1656) 71 The word Σκιρτηδον (which implies a *Subsultation, or Skipping this way and that way) .. seems to allude to .. Fire-crackers and Squibs rather than Cannons or Carbines. **1659** —— *Immort. Soul* III. xii. 452 If the meer motion of the material Aire caused the subsultation of the string tuned Unison. *a* **1688** CUDWORTH *Immut. Mor.* (1731) 114 Fortuitous Dancings or Subsultations of the Spirits. **1670** *Phil. Trans.* V. 1084 In those Earth-quakes .. a *subsulting perpendicular motion. **1679** LOCKE in H. R. F. Bourne *Life* (1876) I. 449, I found a subsulting something like the strokes of a pulse. **1716** M. DAVIES *Athen. Brit.* II. 145 Our rough and subsalient or subsulting Style of our uncouth Phraseological Latin.

subsultive (səbˈsʌltɪv), *a. rare.* [f. L. *subsult-*, pa. ppl. stem of *subsilīre* (see prec.) + -IVE.] Making or moving by sudden leaps, bounds, or starts.

1750 BERKELEY in *Gentl. Mag.* XX. 167/1 The earth .. moved up and down like the boiling of a pot... This sort of subsultive motion is ever accounted the most dangerous.

1770 LANGHORNE *Plutarch, Numa* I. 171 The Subsultive dance..which they [the Salii] lead up along the streets, when..they carry the sacred bucklers through the city. **1819** [H. BUSK] *Vestriad* v. 669 [His feet] slow, subsultive, graze the level floor. **1909** *Daily News* 2 July 5 A very severe shock of earthquake of a subsultive and undulating character was felt here.

subsultory (səb'sʌltərɪ), *a.* [Formed as prec. + -ORY.] = SUBSULTIVE.

1638 RAWLEY tr. *Bacon's Life & Death* 406 The Inordinate, and Subsultorie, Motion of the Spirits. **1715** *Phil. Trans.* XXIX. 326 Palpitation of the Heart, whose.. prodigious subsultory Motion..was easily felt. **1742** HORT *Instr. Clergy* 10, I am levelling this rule against that subsultory way of delivery that rises like a storm..and presently sinks into a dead calm. **1758** L. TEMPLE *Sketches* (ed. 2) 40 The Numbers ought to be accommodated to the Passion:..they ought..to run somewhat rambling and irregular, and often rapid and subsultory. **1822–7** GOOD *Study Med.* (1829) IV. 448 Clonus Palpitatio. Palpitation. Subsultory vibration of the heart or arteries. **1843** *Blackw. Mag.* LIV. 683 That subsultory movement from almost passive surveillance to the most intense development of power. **1887** *Science* (U.S.) 20 May 495/2 Within this tract, except near the edges of it, the motion was most conspicuously of subsultory character. **1905** *Edin. Rev.* Apr. 304 Shoals of deep-sea fish, killed by the impact of subsultory water. **1909** *Westm. Gaz.* 20 Jan. 9/3 A strong subsultory and undulatory shock, lasting six seconds.

absol. **1841** DE QUINCEY *Style* I. Wks. 1858 XI. 197 Flippancy opposed to solemnity, the subsultory to the continuous.

So **sub'sultorily** *adv.*, by sudden bounds or starts; **subsul'torious** *a.* = SUBSULTORY.

1626 BACON *Sylva* §326 The Spirits doe spread themselues Euen, and moue not *Subsultorily. **1898** in *Syd. Soc. Lex.* **1650** H. MORE *Observ.* in *Enthus. Tri.*, etc. (1656) 75 Meer vagrant imaginations seated in your own *subsultorious and skipjack phansie onely.

‖**subsultus** (səb'sʌltəs). *Path.* [mod. L., f. L. *subsult-*, *subsilīre* (see SUBSULT).] A convulsive or twitching movement. Often short for ***subsultus tendinum***, a convulsive twitching of the muscles and tendons present in certain fevers.

1806 ABERNETHY *Surg. Obs.* II. 7 *note*, The febrile actions are proportionately increased, attended by Subsultus of the Muscles and occasional convulsions. **1822–7** GOOD *Study Med.* (1829) IV. 686 A sense of tingling produced in the paralytic part, accompanied with some degree of subsultus, or a twitching or convulsive motion. **1825** WATERTON *Wand. S. Amer.* (1879) III. 141 There was no subsultus tendinum, or any visible alteration in its breathing. **1876** BARTHOLOW *Mat. Med.* (1879) 311 Belladonna is indicated when there is much low, muttering delirium, subsultus, and stupor.

sub'sumable, *a. rare.* [f. next + -ABLE.] Capable of being subsumed.

1882 STALLO *Concepts Mod. Phys.* xiv. 255 A concept may always be found under which things of whatever kind are subsumable.

subsume (səb'sjuːm), *v.* [ad. mod.L. *subsūmĕre*, f. *sub-* SUB- 2, 26 b + *sūmĕre* to take.]

†**1.** *trans.* To bring (a statement, instance, etc.) under another; to subjoin, add. *Obs.*

1535 STEWART *Cron.* III. 183 Neir be this tyme that ȝe heir me subsume. *Ibid.* 443 The ȝeir of God ane thousand and thre hunder And nyntie als syne for to subsume wnder. *a* **1660** HAMMOND *Serm.* viii. Wks. 1684 IV. 614 St. Paul.. cannot name that word, *sinners*, but must straight subsume in a parenthesis, *of whom I am the chief*.

2. *intr.* (*Logic.*) To state a minor premiss: freq. with the words of the proposition following.

1589 R. BRUCE *Serm.* 1 Cor. xi. 28 (1843) 110 There is not a law that ever was..devised, but of all the laws that ever was made, it is leisome to us to have a care of our health. Now, subsume; but the health of thy saull stands in the health of thy conscience..; therefore, be all laws, thou aught to attend to thy conscience. **1624** F. WHITE *Repl. Fisher* 323 Now then I subsume, no religious worship..is due to Saints... Inuocation of Saints is religious worship... *Ergo*, Inuocation is not due to Saints. **1644** DIGBY *Nat. Soul* ii. §6. 371 If any body..take this proposition rigorously and peremptorily, that what wise men affirme is true; and should there vpon subsume with evidence, that wise men say such a particular thing [etc.]. **1670** *Comenius' Janua Ling.* 156 The Major proposeth the basis or ground of the reasoning thus;..the Minor subsumeth,..the conclusion follows. **1733** W. CRAWFORD *Infidelity* (1744) 84 God..may unmake again what he has already made... But then I add, much more may he..annihilate an Offender... But I further subsume, if God can eternally annihilate even an innocent Being, he may do more eternally to the Guilty.

b. *spec.* in *Sc. Law* (see SUBSUMPTION 1 b).

1745 [H. HOME] *Ess. upon Several Subj.* iii. (1747) Suppl. Note, An Act of the 7th Parliament,..bearing That the Lands of Doun, &c. were feued by Queen Mary to Sir James Stewart..subsuming, that the said Sir James being descended of the Royal Blood [etc.]. **1747** in *Nairne Peerage Evid.* (1874) 148 Subsumeing that for the said James Fothringhame pursuer his greater security..they bound and obliged them..to warernd free relieve harmless and skaithless keep the said James Fothringhame.

3. *trans.* (*Logic.*) To state as a minor proposition or concept *under* another.

1697 J. SERGEANT *Solid Philos.* 427 It will not follow, from the Equal Application of it, by the respective Minors, to this or that Particular, Subsum'd under them, that the Assent to the two Conclusions,..will be Equal. **1828** DE QUINCEY *Rhet.* Wks. 1859 XI. 42 To judge, that is to subsume one proposition under another. **1838** [F. HAYWOOD] tr. *Kant's Crit. Pure Reason* 271 In every syllogism I first think a rule (major), by means of the understanding. Secondly, I subsume a cognition under the condition of the rule (minor), by means of the faculty of judgment. **1864** BOWEN *Logic* x. 319 Isolated cognitions..are not entitled to be called Sciences, until they are arranged in some Class, or subsumed under some comprehensive Law. **1876** W. FLEMING *Vocab. Philos.* (ed. 3) s.v. *Subsumption*, In the judgment, 'all horses are animals', the conception 'horses' is subsumed under that of 'animals'. **1887** ADAM *Platonis Apol. Socr.* Introd. (1889) p. xvi, No sooner has it [*sc.* induction] been attained than we ought (as in the practical syllogism) to subsume under it the special case.

4. To bring (one idea, principle, term, etc.) *under* another, (a case, instance) under a rule; to take up *into*, or include *in*, something larger or higher.

(*a*) **1825** COLERIDGE *Aids Refl.* (1848) I. 177 Under some one or other of these forms, the resemblances and differences must be subsumed in order to be conceivable. **1846** DE QUINCEY *Christ. Org. Pol. Movem.* Wks. 1859 XII. 279 In subsuming the given case proposed under the Scriptural principle. **1877** E. CAIRD *Philos. Kant* I. 138 To subsume the complexities of knowledge under its simplest principles. **1884** tr. *Lotze's Logic* 247 We must know beforehand that μ and ν can be subsumed under the species *m* and *n* of which the equation has been proved to be true. **1885** PATER *Marius* xv, A principle under which one might subsume men's most strenuous efforts after righteousness. **1887** W. T. MARTIN *Evol. Hypoth.* 42 A law may be subsumed under a higher law. **1899** MACKAIL *Morris* II. 197 Every form of decorative art could be subsumed under the single head of architecture. **1910** *Edin. Rev.* Apr. 461 Perhaps the wider term Aegean will come into general use; under it Minoan and Mycenean may be subsumed to describe successive stages in European developement.

(*b*) **1812** COLERIDGE *Friend* (1818) III. 255 Man in his idea, and as subsumed in the divine humanity, in whom alone God loved the world. **1871** MIVART *Gen. Spec.* 23 'Natural Selection' itself must be capable of being subsumed into some higher law. **1890** A. MOORE *Ess. Mental Evol.* 58 The child subsumes in its intellectual life the processes of the lower animals, but it rises above them. **1906** SAINTSBURY *Hist. Engl. Prosody* I. 288 The literature of the fifteenth century, with that first quarter of the sixteenth which is by pretty common consent to be subsumed in it for Southern England.

(*c*) **1869** *J. Austin's Jurispr.* (ed. 3) I. 506, I must correctly subsume the specific case as falling within the law. **1871** HUXLEY *Wks.* (1893) II. 182 These forces..operate according to definite laws..in accordance with some general law which subsumes them all. **1882** STEVENSON *Men & Bks.* 107 His cosmology must subsume all cosmologies. **1906** *Hibbert Jrnl.* Apr. 553 [Idealism] has shown how Spirit subsumes the world as its own.

b. *absol.*

1896 *Fortn. Rev.* July 146 Why continue to subsume when the only result will be to produce a formula which..may utterly fail?

†**5.** *gen.* To assume; to infer. *Obs.*

1643 HAMMOND *Serm.* vii. Wks. 1684 IV. 511 A Piece of the Philosopher there hath..had a great stroke in debauching the Divine, that the Understanding doth necessarily and irresistibly move the Will..from whence the Divine subsumes, that when Faith is once entered..these Works must..follow. **1678** *Hist. Indulgence* To Chr. Rdrs. 5 They must give me leave to assert and subsume..That.. I beleeve the Right that Christ hath bought, to be sole and supreme. **1694** S. JOHNSON *Notes Past. Lett. Bp. Burnet* I. 13 His Axiom or Postulatum is in the first Sentence, which I will allow..at present... But what he subsumes in the next Sentence is begging the Question.

†**6.** To resume, summarize. *Obs.*

a **1677** BARROW *Serm.* Wks. 1687 I. 123 The Apostle, after the proposing divers enforcements of this duty, subsumeth in the 8. verse, I will therefore, that men pray every-where [etc.]. **1678** R. BARCLAY *Apol. Quakers* ii. §4. 26 The Proposition..comprehendeth divers unquestionable Arguments, which I shall in brief subsume. *Ibid.* iii. §2. 72 The Sum whereof I shall subsume in one Argument.

Hence **sub'suming** *vbl. sb.*

1652 URQUHART *Jewel* 277 The pregnancy of the State, whose intuitive spirits can at the first hearing discerne the strength of manifold conclusions (without the labour of subsuming) in the very bowels and chaos of their principles. **1897** tr. *Fichte's Sci. Ethics* 116 In the first mode of proceeding, our judgment is what Kant calls *subsuming*, and in the latter work, what he calls *reflecting*.

subsumption (səb'sʌm(p)ʃən). [ad. mod.L. *subsumptio, -ōnem*, n. of action f. *subsūmĕre* to SUBSUME.]

1. *Logic.* A proposition subsumed under another; a minor premiss; *gen.*, an assumption.

1651 BIGGS *New Disp.* ¶182 Galen himself proveth the subsumption. **1662** J. CHANDLER *Van Helmont's Oriat.* 57 They shall sweat more than enough, before they will prove the subsumption or second Proposition. **1672** G. MACKENZIE *Pleadings* Pref. A iij b, It is the nature of a syllogisme to haue the subsumption in the second proposition. **1704** *Lond. Gaz.* No. 4037/5 This is not offered as an Elogie..on Her Majesty: She is far above what I can say, but it is an Antecedent to the following Subsumption. **1838** SIR W. HAMILTON *Logic* xvi (1866) I. 295 The proposition in which is expressed the relation of the middle term to the minor, is the Subsumption or Minor Premise. **1876** W. FLEMING *Vocab. Philos.* (ed. 3) s.v., Thus, if one were to say, 'No man is wise in all things', and another to respond, 'But you are a man', this proposition is a subsumption under the former.

b. *Sc. Law.* In full ***subsumption of the libel***: a narrative of the alleged crime, specifying the manner, time, and place of the crime, the person injured, etc. *Obs.* exc. *Hist.*

1639 *Declar. conc. Tumults Scot.* 256 The subsumptions of the particular faults committed by the Bishop of the Diocese. **1678** G. MACKENZIE *Crim. Laws Scot.* II. xxi. §i. (1699) 232 The Subsumption of the Libel, is the matter of Fact, which should condescend upon the Actors Names, and Designations. **1720** WODROW *Corr.* (1843) II. 491 Probably you will have heard the contents of it, and whether the subsumption relates to the stipend, or the five hundred pounds, or both. **1727** *Ibid.* III. 304 The whole of Mr. Dundas' arguments run upon this supposition, that heresy was to be the subsumption of the libel. **1838** in W. BELL *Dict. Law Scot.* 951.

2. Chiefly *Logic* and *Philos.* The bringing of a concept, cognition, etc. *under* a general term or a larger or higher concept, etc.; the instancing of a case *under* a rule, or the like.

1652 J. PAWSON *Vind. Free Grace* 7 The term (as many πᾶν ὁ quotquot) is too comprehensive and large to be restrained to so few as the Apostles; especially considering 'tis put as a sutable subsumption under that general term (all flesh) immediately foregoing. **1816** COLERIDGE *Lay Serm.* (Bohn) 339 The understanding..is the science of phenomena, and their subsumption under distinct kinds and sorts (genus and species). **1823** DE QUINCEY *Lett. to Yng. Man* Wks. 1860 XIV. 33 The minor is..distinguished from the major by an act of the judgment, namely, a subsumption of a special case under a rule. *Ibid.* 34 A casuistry, that is, a subsumption of the cases most frequently recurring in ordinary life. **1838** [F. HAYWOOD] tr. *Kant's Crit. Pure Reason* 290 The subsumption of the condition of another possible judgment under the condition of the rule, is the minor. **1855** SANDARS in *Oxford Ess.* 244 The administrative power, or the subsumption of different spheres and particular cases under the universal. **1864** BOWEN *Logic* vii. 188 The Judgment that a given 'Subject is contained under that intermediate Term or part', is the Subsumption of this Subject under the condition of that Rule. **1892** *Athenæum* 25 June 829/2 Is not the subsumption of fetishism under animism, as by Dr. Tylor, a self-contradictory confusing of two essentially different conceptions?

subsumptive (səb'sʌm(p)tɪv), *a. rare.* [ad. mod.L. *subsumptivus*, f. *subsumpt-*, pa. ppl. stem of *subsūmĕre* to SUBSUME: see -IVE.] Involving subsumption.

1807 R. KIRWAN *Logick* II. ix. 521 Those *subsumptive* and illative words, *but, now, therefore*. *a* **1834** COLERIDGE (Webster). **1884** tr. *Lotze's Logic* 97 Circle in the subsumptive syllogism.

subsuperparticular, etc.: see SUB- 10.

subsurface ('sʌbsɜːfɪs). [SUB- I.]

I. 1. That which lies immediately below the surface, e.g. the subsoil.

1778 [W. MARSHALL] *Min. Agric.* 12 Dec. 1776, Rough harrows, which tore up the plits, and shook still more of the seed down to the sub-surface. **1884** H. SPENCER in *Contemp. Rev.* July 31 The will of the majority is valid respecting the modes in which..parts of the surface or subsurface, may be utilized.

2. *Math.* In five-dimensional geometry, a three-dimensional continuum.

1873 CAYLEY *Math. Papers* (1896) IX. 79 *note*, In explanation of the nomenclature [*sc.* five-dimensional space], observe that in 5 dimensional geometry we have: space, surface, subsurface, supercurve, curve, and point-system, according as we have between the six coordinates 0, 1, 2, 3, 4, or 5 equations.

II. as *adj.* [see SUB- 1 e.] Existing, lying, or operating under the surface (as of the earth or water).

1875 CROLL *Clim. & Time* App. 553 Subsurface-water, or the stratum immediately below it. **1885** L. OLIPHANT *sympneumata* 101 The subsurface world. **1888** *Athenæum* 18 Aug. 215/1 Sympneumatic and subsurface consciousness. **1894** *Q. Rev.* Apr. 371 They are abundant in all surface and subsurface waters. **1894** *Geol. Mag.* Oct. 466 The downward creep of the surface and sub-surface soil. **1900** *Pop. Sci. Monthly* Mar. 533 Where sewers and subsurface pipes have not yet been laid. **1902** *Westm. Gaz.* 31 Dec. 6/3 The construction of sub-surface torpedo boats.

sub'tabulate, *v. Math.* [SUB- 9.] *trans.* To expand (a mathematical table) by systematic interpolation; to evaluate (a tabulated function) for a set of values of the argument in between the tabulated ones. Hence **sub'tabulated** *ppl. a.*; also **ˌsubtabu'lation**.

1924 WHITTAKER & ROBINSON *Calculus of Observations* iv. 57 We may obtain without difficulty formulae for subtabulation based on central-difference formulae. **1936** *Suppl. Jrnl. R. Statistical Soc.* III. 87 The differences of subtabulated values. *Ibid.* 93 Then..the original table is subtabulated over the range required to tenths, hundredths or thousandths. **1947** *Math. Tables & Other Aids Computation* II. 286 He had made independent subtabulations in each interval. **1952** D. R. HARTREE *Numerical Analysis* v. 78 A set of substabulated values. **1956** F. B. HILDEBRAND *Introd. Numerical Analysis* v. 146 This problem would occur..if a function were initially tabulated for increments of 0·1 in *x* and it were required to subtabulate the function for increments of 0·01. **1975** *Nature* 16 Oct. 541/1 The principle adopted in this project was to compute accurate values at rather widely spaced values of the argument, and to produce values at the required tabular interval by systematic interpolation or subtabulation.

'subtack. *Sc. Law.* [f. SUB- 9 (*b*) + TACK *sb.*[2]] A tack or lease granted by a superior to an inferior tenant.

1681 STAIR *Inst. Law Scot.* I. xix. §22. 384 A Sub-tack is that which is granted by the principal Tacks-man to his Subtennent. **1765–8** ERSKINE *Inst. Law Scot.* II. vi. §34 A subtack requires the same solemnities as a principal tack. **1792** SPALDING *Hist. Scot.* I. 338 He had already set in subtack these customs of Aberdeen and Banff to the town of Aberdeen. **1838** in W. BELL *Dict. Law Scot.* 951.

Hence **'subtacksman**, one who holds a subordinate tack at the hands of a tacksman.

1681 STAIR *Inst. Law Scot.* I. xix. §22. 385 The Heretor is not oblieged to know the Sub-tack, nor to call the Sub-tacksmen, in the Reduction of the principal Tack. **1733** P. LINDSAY *Interest Scot.* 213 The Sub-tacksman of this Duty can easily put the Law in Execution against them. **1765–8**

ERSKINE *Inst. Law Scot.* II. vi. §34 The subtacksman is tenant, not to the proprietor, but to the principal tacksman.

'subtangent. *Math.* [ad. mod.L. *subtangens, -entem*: see SUB- 1 and TANGENT.] That part of the axis of a curve which is contained between the tangent and the ordinate.

1715 *Phil. Trans.* XXIX. 196 He determines the Proportion of the Subtangent to the Ordinate. **1798** HUTTON *Course Math.* II. 306 The Method of Tangents, is a method of determining the quantity of the tangent and subtangent of any algebraic curve; the equation of the curve being given. **1816** tr. *Lacroix' Diff. & Int. Calc.* 75 The line PS will constantly tend to become equal to the subtangent PT. **1827-8** HAMILTON in *Encycl. Metrop* (1845) I. 740/1 The subtangent is bisected by the curve, whether the coordinates are rectangular or oblique.

'subtarget. [SUB- 5 b.] (See quots.)

1904 *Westm. Gaz.* 6 July 10/2 The 'Sub-Target Gun Machine' is the latest invention whose object is to afford indoor practice in rifle shooting... The technical description of the invention defines it as 'a firearm holder with no aiming-point-of-rest, having the capacity to move with the firearm carried by it, and electrically controlled recording mechanism including a miniature target offset from the trajectory of the firearm, to record the direction of trajectory. **1906** *Ibid.* 9 May 5/2 A miniature rifle range provided with the sub-target rifle.

subtar'tarean, -ian, *a.* [tr. Gr. ὑποταρτάριος: see SUB- 1 a and TARTAREAN *a.*[1], TARTARIAN *a.*[2]] Being or living under Tartarus.

1676 HOBBES *Iliad* XIV. (1686) 211 Then Juno, as she was required sware By all the Subtartarian Gods. **1718** POPE *Iliad* XIV. 314 The queen..from the infernal bowers Invokes the sable subtartarean powers. **1794** T. TAYLOR *Pausanias' Descr. Greece* III. 280 Some [of the mundane gods] are.. subtartarean. **1820** *Blackw. Mag.* VII. 358 Invoking from the realms below The subtartarean gods, the Titan train.

So **subtartarus'd** *a.*

1856 S. R. MAITLAND *False Worship* 36 It was the place of the Titans; of those whom Hesiod calls 'Subtartarus'd Titans', τιτῆνες θ' ὑποταρτάριοι.

†sub'tectacle. *Obs. rare.* [f. L. *sub* under + *tectum* roof, probably after *tabernacle.*] Covering, protection.

1609 J. DAVIES *Holy Roode* (1878) 20/1 This is true Faiths intire Subtectacle; Propitiatorie Sacrifice for Sinne: This is God crucifi'd. **1612** —— *Muse's Sacr.* (1878) 10/1 Th abuse of Men, and Shames Subtectacle.

sub'teen, *sb.* (and *a.*) orig. *U.S.* [SUB- 14 b.]

a. A child belonging to the age-group next below teenage. Freq. *pl.*

1952 *Amer. Speech* XXVII. 73 Bonds department store, 16 Feb.: Adv. announcing opening of 'Infants to *Subteens* Shop'. **1960** *Twentieth Cent.* Nov. 389 The sub-teens, the pocket-money market,..have never been considered anything but children. **1964** *Discovery* Oct. 31/2 Even the sub-teens of the 1960's interpret all too readily the Freudian symbolism of Peter Pan. **1976** *Publishers Weekly* 7 June 75/1 Subteens and teens with an ambition to get into journalism.

b. *attrib.* passing into *adj.*, esp. with reference to clothing designed for the older pre-teenage girl.

1953 *Sun* (Baltimore) 22 July 5/5 (Advt.), Very special purchase! Regular 5.98 and 7.98 sub-teen cottons. **1962** *Sunday Express* 4 Feb. 14/6 Dating is now an accepted thing in the age group known as 'subteen'. **1968** P. WELLES *Babyhip* xxii. 151 Armed with enormous shopping bags, they descended on the subteen department. **1978** M. FARREN *Feelies* 146 The sub-teen girls in the crowd went even wilder.

Also **sub'teenage** *a.*; **sub'teenager.**

1959 *New Statesman* 7 Nov. 631/3 He is a pervert.. interested emotionally only in pubescent girls, subteenagers as they are known in American advertising. **1960** P. GOODMAN *Growing up Absurd* v. 117 This is the meaning, surely, of the publicity that has been trumped up for the Little League, the baseball teams of subteenagers sponsored and underwritten by various business firms. **1963** *Times Lit. Suppl.* 8 Feb. 91/4 (Advt.), He lives in Switzerland and is married with two sub-teenage daughters. **1968** *Punch* 3 July 3/2 A friend is worried at Wimbledon's chauvinistic effect on his sub-teenage kids. **1977** *Washington Post* 20 Feb. D4/2 He keeps horses and a pony for two subteenage daughters. **1980** *Ibid.* 5 Oct. A 22/3 There are a 'tremendous' number of subteenagers who abuse a variety of drugs and alcohol.

subtegulaneous: see SUB- 1 a.

subtelitie, obs. form of SUBTILITY.

'sub,tenancy. [f. next.] The status, right, or holding of a subtenant.

a **1861** PALGRAVE *Norm. & Eng.* (1864) III. 405 The others who received their rewards by Vavassories or Subtenancies. **1882** *Encycl. Brit.* XIV. 276/1 The determination of a lease by forfeiture has the same effect as its determination in any other way, in destroying subtenancies or other rights created under it.

subtenant (ˌsʌb'tɛnənt). Chiefly *Sc.* Also 5 **-ten(n)and,** 6 **-tenent, sibtennend,** 6-7 **-tennent,** 7 **-tennat.** [SUB- 9 (*b*). In med.L. *subtenens.*] One who holds of a tenant; an undertenant.

1445 in *14th Rep. Hist. MSS. Comm.* App. III. 12 Twenty schillingis..to be pait to me be the Saide Androu Kere or his facturis or subtenandis. **1474** in *Acc. Fam. of Innes* (Spalding Cl.) 81 To be haldin and had all and hale the saidis landis..to the foresaid James his airis assigneis and subtennandis for al the termis of threttein yeris. **1541** *Rec. Elgin* (New Spalding Cl. 1903) I. 66 Tha that ar sibtennendis to the burgh for the landis of Duuellegrene. **1586** in *Exch. Rolls Scot.* XXI. 418 Sett in assedatioun for the space of fyve yeiris..to Uthrid Makdowell of Garthland, his airis, assignais, and subtennentis. **1681** STAIR *Inst. Law Scot.* I. xix. §23. 385 Where the Sub-tennent was warned, tacite Ralocation alledged by the Sub-tennent, was not sustained without producing a standing Tack to the principal Tacksman. **1703** in M. A. Mills *Stat. Laws I. of Man* (1821) 175 The said Tennants and Inhabittants dwelling in and possessing those Cottages and Intacks shall henceforward become Sub-tennants to the said Farmers, Tennants, and other Persons. **1846** MCCULLOCH *Acc. Brit. Empire* (1854) II. 215 Sub-tenants or assignees to the leases specified in the article immediately preceding..can also vote. **1861** BROUGHAM *Brit. Const.* x. 136 There were smaller owners or sub-tenants, holding of the eleven thanes, as these held of the Crown.

b. *fig.*

1804 BEWICK *Brit. Birds* II. Introd. p. vi, They [*sc.* land birds] are the subtenants of the cultivated world.

subtend (səb'tɛnd), *v.* [ad. L. *subtendĕre*, f. *sub-* SUB- 2 + *tendĕre* to stretch, TEND. Cf. Sp., Pg. *subtender.*]

1. *trans.* (*Geom.*) To stretch or extend under, or be opposite to: said *esp.* of a line or side of a figure opposite an angle; also, of a chord or angle opposite an arc.

1570 BILLINGSLEY *Euclid* I. iv. 14 That angle is said to subtend a side of a triangle, which is placed directly opposite, and against that side. **1571** DIGGES *Pantom.* I. xviii. Fj, This done conioyne their endes togither and the angle subtended of the longest staffe is a right. **1646** SIR T. BROWNE *Pseud. Ep.* I. vii. 25 In rectangle triangles the square which is made of the side that subtendeth the right angle, is equall to the squares which are made of the sides containing the right angle. **1681** COLVIL *Whigs Suppl.* (1710) 13 The truth is, they [*sc.* a man's legs] in every thing Resemble do a Bow and String. The one strait to the other bending, Is like a Chord an Arch subtending. *c* **1791** *Encycl. Brit.* (1797) VII. 666/2 An angle at the circumference is measured by half the arc it subtends. **1798** HUTTON *Course Math.* I. 292 In any Triangle, the square of the Side subtending an Acute Angle, is Less than the Squares of the Base and the other Side, by Twice the Rectangle of the Base and the Distance of the Perpendicular from the Acute Angle. **1862** TODHUNTER *Euclid* 19 The greater angle of every triangle is subtended by the greater side or has the greater side opposite to it. **1885** LEUDESDORF *Cremona's Proj. Geom.* 227 The angle subtended at any point on the curve by a fixed diameter would be a right angle. **1885** WATSON & BURBURY *Math. Th. Electr.* I. 137, 2β is the angle of the cone subtended by the disc at *M*.

b. in *Astron.* and *Optics.*

1722 WOLLASTON *Relig. Nat.* iii. 54 He must be a brute.. who does not know, that the same line (*v.g.* the diameter of the Sun) at different distances subtends different angles at the eye. *c* **1790** IMISON *Sch. Arts* I. 196 The best eye can hardly distinguish a particle of matter that subtends at the eye an angle less than half a minute. **1821** CRAIG *Lect. Drawing*, etc. vi. 362 The same angle which the picture subtends with the eye. **1833** M. ARNOTT *Physics* (ed. 5) II. 241 The fly then would subtend a larger visual angle than he, that is to say, would be forming on the retina a larger image than the man. **1835** POE *Adv. Hans Pfaall* Wks. 1864 I. 36 Whose apparent diameter subtended at the balloon an angle of about sixty-five seconds. **1907** HODGES *Elem. Photogr.* (ed. 6) 24 The visual angle subtended on the plate.

c. *transf.* and *gen.*

1859 MURCHISON *Siluria* (ed. 3) iii. 53 The Llandeilo formation is subtended on the north, south, and west by younger Silurian deposits. **1860** MOTLEY *Netherl.* (1868) I. 140 The river..subtends the arc into which the place [*sc.* Antwerp] arranges itself. **1867** MURCHISON *Siluria* (ed. 4) xx. 493 The chalk-cliffs which subtend the Wealden area. **1868** KINGLAKE *Crimea* III. vii. 117 Standing upon a semi-circular tract of ground, subtended by the great bay or roadstead. **1873** SYMONDS *Grk. Poets* ix. 282 This large arc was subtended by a long straight line—the σκηνή, or background of the stage. **1880** *Nature* XXI. 212/2 Tracts such as the great deserts or prairies might subtend a sufficient angle to preserve their natural hue.

d. *fig.*

1866 FELTON *Greece, Anc. & Mod.* I. 33 It takes but a few moments to tell in outline this traveller's story; but how many ages does it subtend. **1869** SPENCER *Princ. Psychol.* (1872) I. II. iv. 217 The angle it subtends in consciousness when we are reminded of it a year after, is very small. **1898** P. MANSON *Trop. Dis.* Introd. p. xiv, When this third animal happens to be a tropical species, the disease it subtends, so to speak, is in natural conditions, necessarily tropical also.

†2. *pass.* Of an angle, a side of a figure: To be extended *under*, to be opposite *to*. *Obs.*

1570 BILLINGSLEY *Euclid* I. iv. 14 Euery angle of a triangle is contayned of two sydes of the triangle, and is subtended to the third side. **1660** BARROW *Euclid* I. iv, The remaining angles B, C, shall be equal to the remaining angles E, F, each to each, under which the equal sides are subtended.

3. *trans.* (*Bot.*) To extend under, so as to embrace or enfold.

1871 W. A. LEIGHTON *Lichen-flora* 94 Apothecia.. subtended by the very short deformed divaricate extremities of the laciniæ. **1872** OLIVER *Elem. Bot.* II. 237 A 3-lobed bract, subtending a single nut.

Hence **sub'tended** *ppl. a.*, (*a*) stretched underneath; (*b*) of an angle opposite a side.

1679 EVELYN *Sylva* (ed. 3) 56 To clip, and let the leaves fall upon a subtended sheet. **1824** SMYTH in Duppa *Trav. Italy*, etc. (1828) 185 *note*, The subtended angles carefully corrected. **1884** tr. *Lotze's Logic* 248 The formula we are seeking must mention the subtended angle.

†sub'tendent, *a.* and *sb.* *Obs.* Also 7 **-ant.** [ad. L. *subtendens, -entem*, pr. pple. of *subtendĕre* to SUBTEND.]

A. *adj.* That subtends.

1571 DIGGES *Pantom.* I. vi. C iij b, In equiangle triangles, al their sides are proportional aswel such as conteyne the equall angles, as also their subtendente sides. *Ibid.* xx. F ij b, The subtendent staffe or side of the triangle. **1688** HOLME *Armoury* III. iii. 139/2 A *Cord, Chord*, or *Subtendant Line*; is a streight Line which joyns to an Arch or Bow by its ends.

B. *sb.* A subtending line or side.

1570 DEE *Math. Pref.* 30 Square then, halfe the Subtendent of that watry Superficies. **1673** in Rigaud *Corr. Sci. Men* (1841) II. 569 *A, E*, are the subtendants of two arches which together make up ⅓ the circumference.

sub'tending, *ppl. a.* [-ING[2].] That subtends.

1571 DIGGES *Pantom.* I. xx. F ij b, Make a fyne notche, or marke vpon that subtending staffe. **1660** R. COKE *Justice Vind.* 20 What proportion..the subtending side of an isosceles right-angle triangle hath to one of the comprehending sides. **1859** R. F. BURTON *Central Afr.* in *Jrnl. Geogr. Soc.* XXIX. 237 The Tanganyika cannot be drained eastward by rents in a subtending mountain ridge. **1882** VINES tr. *Sachs' Bot.* 599 If..the subtending leaf (bract) is developed later than the axillary branch (inflorescence). **1900** B. D. JACKSON *Gloss. Bot. Terms* 250/2 *Subtending Leaf*, that leaf whose axil gives rise to a bud or peduncle.

‖sub'tenia. *Arch. rare.* [f. SUB- 1 + *tenia*, TÆNIA.] The narrow listel under the lower tænia of the Doric entablature; the guttæ band.

1563 SHUTE *Archit.* C iij b, Geue Tenia..the seuenth parte, and geue Subtenia, and Gutta pendante..the sixte part of a modulus to their height.

subtense (səb'tɛns), *sb.* *Geom.* [ad. mod.L. *subtensa* (sc. *linea* line), fem. pa. pple. of *subtendĕre* to SUBTEND. Cf. Sp., Pg. *subtensa.*]

a. A subtending line; *esp.* the chord of an arc. Also, the angle subtended by a line at a point.

1614 HANDSON tr. *Pitiscus' Trigonom.* 31 A subtense is a right line, inscribed in a Circle, dividing the whole Circle into 2. Segments. **1656** tr. *Hobbes' Elem. Philos.* (1839) 193 The subtenses of equal angles in different circles..are to one another as the arches which they subtend. **1678** CUDWORTH *Intell. Syst.* I. iv. 653 Nor doth every one, who hath an Idea of a Rectangular Triangle, presently understand, that the Square of the Subtense, is Equal to the Squares of both the Sides. **1713** DERHAM *Phys. Theol.* I. iv. (1727) 30 *note*, The whole Diameter of the Orb, viz. 20000, made the Subtense but of one Minute to one of the fix'd Stars. **1733** TULL *Horse-hoeing Husb.* xxi. 305 Plow-Wrights always take this Subtense at the Fore-End of a Beam, whether it be a long Beam or a short one. **1803** *Phil. Trans.* XCIII. 396 The total extent of the arch is about 15°, having half of its subtense on each side zero. **1958** *Engineering* 21 Feb. 231/3 Fig. 4 shows the composite picture for the Horseshoe Falls, the angles signifying the angular subtense of any part of the Falls at the floodlights. **1974** *Nature* 3 May 86/2 The test strips..had a subtense of between 1° and 2°. *Ibid.* 13 Dec. 535/2 Stereo blending does not work well when the angular subtense of the line joining the speakers exceeds about 60°.

b. *attrib.*: **subtense method**, a method of tacheometry in which the angle at the instrument is variable and the distance base is either constant or specially measured.

1897 *Geogr. Jrnl.* (R.G.S.) X. 469 We..then made a traverse of the valley on the bar-subtense method. **1902** *Encycl. Brit.* XXXIII. 143/2 Subtense method. **1905** C. F. CLOSE *Topogr. & Geogr. Surv.* 51 The general principle of subtense work and tacheometry is the measurement of the angle subtended at the observer by a short measured length at a distance.

†sub'tention. *Obs.* [f. L. *subtent-*, pa. ppl. stem of *subtendĕre* to SUBTEND: see -TION.] = SUBTENSE *sb.*

1610 HOPTON *Baculum Geodæt.* VII. ii. 297 Any right lines being applied to a circle is called a subtention, which may be Sines, Tangents, or Secants.

subtenure ('sʌbˌtɛnjʊə(r)). [f. SUB- 9 (*b*) + TENURE.] The subfeudation of land; the holding of land, or land held, by a lease from a superior tenant.

1839 *Penny Cycl.* XIV. 105/1 Owing to the extensive system of subfeudation, or subtenure. **1862** H. BEVERIDGE *Hist. India* III. VII. iv. 125 The sale of a zemindary abolished all sub-tenures. **1911** E. BEVERIDGE *N. Uist* 24 It became necessary for King Alexander III. to deal with the subtenure of the Hebrides.

subter- ('sʌbtə(r)), *prefix*, repr. L. *subter-* = the adv. and prep. *subter* below, underneath, used in composition = (1) below, beneath; (*a*) advb. as in *subterfluĕre* to flow beneath (see SUBTERFLUOUS), (*b*) prep. as in *subtercutāneus* lying under the skin (*cutis*); (2) secretly, as in *subterfugĕre* to flee secretly (see SUBTERFUGE); and, in some rare Eng. compounds, = (3) lower or less than (cf. SUB- 14). The following are instances either of little-used adoptions of L. compounds or mere nonce-words (in some cases suggested by antithesis to compounds of *super-*).

subte'rrannuating *vbl. sb.*, the placing of an event later than its actual date. **subter-'brutish** *a.*, lower than (that of) the brutes. **ˌsubter-ce'lestial** *a.*, below the heavens. **subter-'conscious** *a.*, = SUBCONSCIOUS. **†subter'cubant** [L. *cubāre* to lie down] (meaning unknown). **ˌsubtercu'taneous** [L. *-eus*], = SUBCUTANEOUS. **subter'duction** [cf. L. *subterdūcĕre*], a carrying away secretly. **ˌsubterero'gation**, the performance of less than is required. **ˌsubtere'therial** *a.*, subaerial. **†subter'fluent, †sub'terfluous** *adjs.*, flowing underneath. **subter'human** *a.*, below what is human. **subter'jacent** *a.* [L. *subterjacēre*], underlying, subjacent. **ˌsubterlap'sarian** [properly **subtersublapsarian*] *a.*, pertaining to a view of redemption which conceived a sufficiency of grace for all, but a positive decree to save restricted to some. **'subtermarine**, one who works under the sea. **subter'sensual, -'sensuous** *adjs.*, = SUBSENSUAL, -SENSUOUS. **ˌsubtersu'perlative**, a degree lower than that expressed by an ordinary superlative of inferiority. **'subterˌsurface** *a.*, lying below the surface, subsurface.

1656 HEYLIN *Extraneus Vapulans* 102 The superannuating in the business of the Councel of Dort, (a *subteranannuating call'd in the true sense of the thing). **1831** CARLYLE *Sart. Res* I. viii, O *subter-brutish! vile! most vile! **1665** SIR T. HERBERT *Trav.* (1677) 253 By the Fiat of the Almighty the *subter-celestial waters were separated from the super-celestial. **1856** BAGEHOT *Biogr. Studies* (1880) 15 There is a kind of eruption of ideas from a *subter-conscious world. **1597** HARVEY *Trimming of Nashe* Wks. (Grosart) III. 69 The..grand Commander of all the superrants & *subtercubants of Englands great Metropolis. **1748** tr. *Vegetius Renatus' Distemper of Horses* 9 There are seven Species of this Maul: The moist, the dry, the *subtercutaneous, the articular [etc.]. **1656** BLOUNT *Glossogr.*, **Subterduction*, a private stealing or leading away. **1617** COLLINS *Def. Bp. Ely* II. ix. 346 It is certaine that Supererogation there can be none, though praeterogation we should graunt you, howbeit *subtererogation were the fitter word. **1686** GOAD *Celest. Bodies* III. iii. 456 The *Subter-Ætherial Globe. **1755** JOHNSON, **Subterfluent*, running under. **1656** BLOUNT *Glossogr.*, **Subterfluous*, which runs or flows under. **1833** CARLYLE *Misc. Ess.*, *Cagliostro* (1888) 88 He were no man but some other kind of creature, superhuman or *subter-human. **1839** J. STERLING *Ess.*, etc. (1848) I. 264 The universe presents itself to them as a conflux of forces, subter-human, human, and superhuman. **1597** A. M. tr. *Guillemeau's Fr. Chirurg.* 25/2 As then not parte of the corrosive fall on any of the *subteriacent partes. **1762** tr. *Busching's Syst. Geog.* III. 29 A delightful prospect over the subter-jacent plain. **1893** FAIRBAIRN *Christ Mod. Theol.* I. viii. 173 The *Subterlapsarian School, which had hypothetical universalism as its note. **1891** MEREDITH *One of our Conq.* xxvi, A diver's wreck, where an armoured livid *subter-marine, a monstrous puff-ball of man, wandered seriously light in heaviness. **1885** —— *Diana* III. xii. 219 To pursue the thing would be to enter the *subtersensual perfumed caverns of a Romance of Fashionable Life. **1878** P. W. WYATT *Hardrada* 43 Sailing on one vast *subtersensuous greed Their smuggling life-craft ply. **1655** FULLER *Ch. Hist.* VI. 271 The Apostles words of himself, who am lesse than the least of all saints... As I may say, a *subter-subterlative [*sic*] in his humility. **1659** —— *App. Inj. Innoc.* III. 18 Because he was Ἐλαχισ[τ]ότερος, (and if there be a more subter-superlative) the least of the least of his brethren. **1831** *Fraser's Mag.* IV. 322 He never fails to sink to the *subter-surface level of Joseph Hume.

subteraquean (sʌbtə'reɪkwɪən), *a.* *rare.* [Formed as next + -AN.] = next.

1865 *Morning Star* 21 July, The people ascended from the subteraquean chamber.

subteraqueous (sʌbtə'reɪkwɪəs), *a.* *rare.* Also *erron.* subterr-. [f. L. **subteraqueus*: see SUBTER- (1) and AQUEOUS.] Living, situated, performed, etc. under water.

1682 H. MORE *Annot. Glanvill's Lux O.* 139 By those inevitable Laws of the subteraqueous Sandalphon. **1733** TULL *Horse-hoeing Husb.* iii. 26 The Effect the vicissitudes of Winter and Summer have upon Subterraqueous Vegetables. **1823** BYRON *Juan* XIV. lxxxi. 'An oyster may be cross'd in Love,'—and why? Because he mopeth idly in his shell, And heaves a lonely subterraqueous sigh.

subterfuge ('sʌbtəfjuːdʒ), *sb.* [ad. L. *subterfugium*, f. *subterfugĕre*, f. *subter-* SUBTER- (2) + *fugĕre* to flee. Cf. F. *subterfuge*, It. *sutterfugio*, Sp., Pg. *subterfugio*.]

1. An artifice or device to which a person resorts in order to escape the force of an argument, to avoid condemnation or censure, or to justify his conduct; an evasion or shift. Chiefly of discourse, argument, debate, but also of action in general.

1573 J. TYRIE *Refut.* in *Cath. Tractates* (S.T.S.) 29, I dout na thing, gif thay ansver directlie without all subterfuge,.. that it salbe easie to everie man to espy quha defendis the richt caus. **1611** COTGR., *Subterfuge*, a subterfuge; a shift; a priuie slip, craftie euasion, cunning escape. **1637–50** Row *Hist. Kirk* (Wodrow Soc.) 268 That no such subterfuge be left unto impious and wicked men. **1651** CHAS. II. *Let.* 24 May in *10th Rep. Hist. MSS. Comm.* App. I. 42 That without delays or subterfuges the goods be restored. **1659** H. MORE *Immort. Soul* III. xiv. 475 The Fifth and last is rather a Subterfuge then an Objection. **1665** GLANVILL *Scepsis Sci.* vii. 39 All their shifts, subtilties, newly invented Words and Modes, sly subterfuges and studyed evasions. **1741** WATTS *Impr. Mind* I. x. (1801) 87 Do not affect little shifts and subterfuges to avoid the force of an argument. **1781** COWPER *Friendship* 189 No subterfuge or pleading Shall win my confidence again. **1784** —— *Task* II. 670 By forgery, by subterfuge of law. **1829** LYTTON *Disowned* vi By what subterfuge, or cavil, does the present claimant of these estates hope to dislodge their rightful possessor. **1843** R. J. GRAVES *Syst. Clin. Med.* x. 106, I speak here without any subterfuge. **1849** MACAULAY *Hist. Eng.* v. I. 564 It was answered that the earl was asleep. The privy councillor thought that this was a subterfuge, and insisted on entering. **1895** RIDER HAGGARD *Heart of World* xvi, I will answer you, and, scorning subterfuge or falsehood, set out the whole matter in the hearing of the people.

b. contextually: A means of escape (*from* censure, etc.); an excuse.

1755 SMOLLETT *Quix.* (1803) 122 You have no subterfuge nor the least room to say you was deceived. **1761** HUME *Hist. Eng.* II. xxxix. 377 The queen of Scots had no other subterfuge from these pressing remonstrances. **1828** SCOTT *F.M. Perth* xxxiv, You seek but a subterfuge, that you may say when you are defeated..that it was for want of the number of your band fully counted out.

†**2.** A place to which a person escapes; a retreat, refuge. *Obs.*

1616 BULLOKAR *Engl. Expos.*, *Subterfuge*,.. a place to hide or saue one in. **1660** in *Sel. Harl. Misc.* (1793) 379 My lord of Derby had taken this place for a subterfuge, after the defeat given him by Colonel Lilburn. **1665** MANLEY *Grotius' Low C. Wars* 363 There were in the Castle Subterfuges and Scluces, to prevent the inraging [orig. *iram*] of the Enemy. **1737** WHISTON *Josephus* II. VI. vii. 941 They depended on these under ground subterfuges.

fig. **1720** WELTON *Suffer. Son of God* I. iv. 68 We have now a Subterfuge to flee to; under which, we are sure to be shelter'd from the Justice and Wrath of God. **1844** THIRLWALL *Greece* lxvi. VIII. 426 This proposal drove the senate out of its last subterfuge.

†**3.** That which conceals; a 'cloak'. *Obs.*

1635 BRATHWAIT *Arcadian Princ.* 55 Connivence gives impunity to impiety, and greatnesse becomes a Subterfuge to guiltinesse. *a* **1718** PRIOR *Knowledge* 710 They..sculk behind the Subterfuge of Art. **1733** CHEYNE *Engl. Malady* II. viii. §3. 194 The Spleen or Vapours..is a common Subterfuge for meer Ignorance of the Nature of Distempers.

†**'subterfuge**, *v.* *Obs. rare.* [ad. L. *subterfugĕre* (see prec.).]

1. *intr.* To employ subterfuges.

1637 in *Prynne's Disc. Prel. Tyrr.* (1641) II. 95 Upon paine of suspention of the parties offending, or subterfuging.

2. *trans.* To escape, evade, get out of.

1641 J. SHUTE *Sarah & Hagar* (1649) 59 Jonah had a plot to subterfuge his employment to Nineveh. *a* **1643** —— *Judgem. & Mercy* (1645) 80 Whatsoever plea he hath before thought of to subterfuge the judgement.

So †**'subterfuging** *ppl. a.*, employing subterfuges; evasive.

1802 in *Ann. Rev.* (1803) I. 391/2 No little, narrow policy, will do; no partial meanness, no monopoly, no jobbing business, nor subterfuging tricks of avarice!

†**'subterfugy.** *Obs. rare.* [ad. L. *subterfugium*: see SUBTERFUGE *sb.*] A subterfuge.

1637 GILLESPIE *Engl. Pop. Cerem.* Ord. C 3 The lurking places of their elaborate subterfugies. **1655** FULLER *Ch. Hist.* XI. xvii. 230 Many more are their subterfugies.

subter'natural, *a.* [SUBTER- (3).] Below what is natural, less than natural.

1870 LOWELL *Among my Bks.* Ser. I. (1873) 87 We must be content to call hypochondria subternatural, because the tone of the instrument is lowered. **1880** GLADSTONE in W. O'Brien *Recoll.* (1905) 262 The expression of subter-natural glee which sits upon the visage of the hon. member for Cavan. **1890** *Q. Rev.* Apr. 296 Shakspere's preternatural or subternatural creations.

subterpose (sʌbtə'pəʊz), *v.* *rare.* [f. SUBTER- (1) + *-pose*, as in *superpose*, *impose*.] *trans.* To place underneath.

1894 BARING-GOULD *Deserts S. France* I. 149 Their remains may be discovered at a lower level, though not subterposed.

So **ˌsubterpo'sition**, a placing below, position underneath.

1833 LYELL *Princ. Geol.* III. 388 Subterposition in the plutonic, like superposition in the sedimentary rocks, being ..characteristic of a newer age. **1851** GLADSTONE *Let. to Manning* 26 Jan., It will bring about a great shifting of parts, much super- and much subter-position.

sub-terra, *a.* *rare*⁻¹. [L. *sub* under + *terra* ground.] Subterranean.

1841 CATLIN *N. Amer. Ind.* x. (1844) I. 76, I have subjoined a sketch of one of these sub-terra communities.

subterrane ('sʌbtəreɪn), *a.* and *sb.* Now *rare.* Also 9 -ain. [ad. L. *subterrāneus*, f. *sub-* SUB- 1 a + *terra* earth. Cf. OF. *soub-*, *subterrain* (F. *souterrain*), It. *sotterrano*, *-aneo*.]

A. *adj.* = SUBTERRANEAN *a.*

1614 RALEIGH *Hist. World* II. 650 By this secret subterrane vault, Zedechias making his stealth, recouered.. the plaines or deserts of Iericho. **1633** T. ADAMS *Exp. 2 Peter* ii. 4. 513 Hell is a subterrane treasure of hidden fire. **1712** *Phil. Trans.* XXVII. 481 As to the Age in which those Trees were interred, it is hard to determine. Many think they have lain in that Subterrane State ever since Noah's Flood. **1824** BYRON *Def. Transf.* I. i. 79 The waters stir, Not as with air, but by some subterrane And rocking power of the internal world. **1830** W. PHILLIPS *Mt. Sinai* I. 550 From all its vasty antres subterrane. **1831** KEIGHTLEY *Mythol. Greece & Italy* 68 Hades, the brother of Zeus and Poseidon, was lord of the subterrane region, the abode of the dead. **1842** J. F. WATSON *Ann. Philad. & Penn.* (1877) I. 412 A subterrane tunnel. **1861** D. GREENWELL *Poems* 95 Some echo subterrain.

B. *sb.* = SUBTERRANEAN *sb.* 3.

1774 J. BRYANT *Mythol.* I. 116 It was a cave in the rock, abounding with variety of subterranes, cut out into various apartments. **1816** G. S. FABER *Orig. Pagan Idol.* III. 260 Like the subterrain of mount Olivet, it resembled the mouth of an oven or a well. **1830** W. PHILLIPS *Mt. Sinai* II. 34 Mystic subterrane From surface down to centre is commoved. **1843** tr. *Custine's Empire of Czar* II. 18 The submarine dungeons of Kronstadt,..and..many other subterranes.

†**subte'rraneal**, *a.* (*sb.*) *Obs.* [f. L. *subterrāneus* (see prec.) + -AL¹.]

A. *adj.*

1. Underground; = SUBTERRANEAN *a.* 1.

1592 R. D. *Hypnerotomachia* 30 Feareful vaultes, and subterraneal buttresses. **1639** G. PLATTES (*title*) A Discovery of Subterraneall Treasure: viz. of all manner of Mines and Minerals. **1651** J. F[REAKE] *Agrippa's Occ. Philos.* 404 Subterraneall and dark Demons. **1671** BOHUN *Disc. Wind* Contents, The 2ᵈ Locall Origine of Winds in Generall from the Earth or Seas, as from Submarine or Subterraneall Eruptions. **1673** BOYLE *Ess. Effluviums* III. 51 The more agile Corpuscles of Subterraneal Salts. **1681** GREW *Musæum* I. §ii. i. 14 He catcheth Ant's by scratching open their subterraneal Hives. **1690** C. NESSE *Hist. & Myst. O. & N. Test.* I. 7 Mountains not cast up by the flood, nor by the subterraneal spirits. **1741** *Phil. Trans.* LV. 239 The subterraneal damps and mineral spirit of fountains seem.. exactly to resemble each other.

2. Belonging to the lower regions; infernal; = SUBTERRANEAN *a.* 2.

1651 T. STANLEY *Plat. Disc. Love* 222 The World her self being one, can have but one soul; which as it animates the subterraneal parts, is called Pluto; the sublunary Neptune; the celestial, Jupiter. **1803** SHAW tr. *Bacon's Fables Anc.* xi, [Pluto] hurrying her to his chariot, carried her with him to the subterraneal regions.

B. *sb. pl.* Underground strata.

1652 FRENCH *Yorksh. Spaw* iii. 32 How variously subterraneall communicate their vertues to this Element [*viz.* water].

subterranean (sʌbtə'reɪnɪən), *a.* and *sb.* [f. L. *subterrāneus* (see SUBTERRANE) + -AN.]

A. *adj.*

1. a. Of inanimate objects: Existing, lying, or situated below the surface of the earth; formed or constructed underground, either by nature or by the hand of man; underground.

1610 HOLLAND *Camden's Brit.* 747 Their further inquiery, whether there are not Subterranean trees growing under earth. *a* **1625** CHALONER *Six Serm.* (1629) 24 Even the Labyrinthes of Dedalus haue left their subterranean habitations. **1634** SIR T. HERBERT *Trav.* 95 [The Caspian Sea] has no..entercourse with any Sea, except (as is credible) it be subterranean, into the Euxine. **1712** BLACKMORE *Creation* I. 34 Tell, by..what subterranean Ways, Back to the Fountain's Head the Sea conveys The refluent Rivers. **1718** LADY M. W. MONTAGU *Lett.* II. xlix. 64, I was..led into one of the subterranean apartments, which they call 'The Stables of the Elephants'. **1835** LYELL *Princ. Geol.* (ed. 4) IV. 6 The relative date of rocks formed in the subterranean regions during the Newer Pliocene ages. *Ibid.* Index 450 Subterranean lava causes elevation of land. **1849** MACAULAY *Hist. Eng.* iii. I. 316 In 1685 the tin of Cornwall..was still one of the most valuable subterranean productions of the island. **1856** MACAULAY *Johnson* in *Encycl. Brit.* (ed. 8) XII. 795 His taste in cookery, formed in subterranean ordinaries and *Alamode* beefshops, was far from delicate. **1856** STANLEY *Sinai & Pal.* xiv. (1858) 439 The subterranean vault, over which..the whole structure was erected. **1860** PRESCOTT *Electr. Telegr.* 169 The idea of building subterranean lines in this country! **1863** DANA *Man. Geol.* 647 Subterranean streams, which have their rise in hills and mountains, and are fed, like the surface-rivers, by the rains and snows. **1877** NORTHCOTE *Rom. Catac.* I. v. 71 The ceilings of their subterranean chapels. **1878** *Encycl. Brit.* VIII. 685/1 Along the French coast several subterranean affluents of the Mediterranean have been discovered.

b. Of animate beings: Living or working under ground.

1621 BURTON *Anat. Mel.* I. ii. I. ii, Of these sublunary Diuels, *Psellus* makes six kindes, fiery, aeriall, terrestriall, watery, and subterranean Diuels. **1642** HOWELL *Twelve Treat.* (1661) 50 Ther were subterranean invisible troups (at Ragland Castle) mustered under-ground in Wales. **1753** RICHARDSON *Grandison* (1754) VI. ix, Subterranean colliers, tinners, [&c.] **1835** KIRBY *Creat. Anim.* II. 420 Baron Humboldt has given an account of a wonderful eruption of subterranean fishes.

c. Of physical phenomena, forces or movements, actions, etc.: Operating or performed under ground.

1603 HOLLAND *Plutarch's Mor.* 1190 The casting up aloft into the aire of stones & cinders by subterranean windes under the earth. **1667** MILTON *P.L.* I. 231 When the force Of subterranean wind transports a Hill Torn from Pelorus. **1813** BAKEWELL *Introd. Geol.* Pref. 6 All rocks or strata have been either formed or consolidated by central subterranean fire. **1825** SCOTT *Betrothed* xxiv, Immured as she seemed to be, to perish by a strange and subterranean death. **1829** —— *Anne of G.* ii, A noise like subterranean thunder. **1855** J. PHILLIPS *Man. Geol.* 585 The same localities..were during later periods influenced by more gradual and continual subterranean expansion. **1877** HUXLEY *Physiogr.* 186 This region is peculiarly subject to subterranean disturbances.

d. *Bot.* Of parts of a plant: Growing under ground.

1839 LINDLEY *Introd. Bot.* (ed. 3) 491 *Subterranean*.., growing under the earth. **1849** BALFOUR *Man. Bot.* §70 Stems have been divided into *aerial*, or stems which appear wholly or partially above ground; and *subterranean*, or those which are entirely under ground. **1884** BOWER & SCOTT *De Bary's Phaner.* 349 The subterranean shoots of the rhizome.

e. Of trees or a forest: Buried in the earth.

1813 BAKEWELL *Introd. Geol.* 11 On the coast of Lincolnshire and part of Yorkshire there is a subterranean forest about seventeen feet under the present high-water mark.

2. Existing under the earth; belonging to the lower regions or underworld; infernal.

1619 GORGES tr. *Bacon's Wisd. Anc.* 156 He [Pluto] caught vp Proserpina..and caried her away with him in his Coach to the Subterranean dominions. *a* **1700** EVELYN *Diary* 20 Feb. 1645, The celestial, terrestrial, and subterranean deities. *a* **1806** HORSLEY *Serm.* xx. (1816) II. 176 The consolation which the preaching of our Lord in the subterranean regions afforded to these prisoners of hope. **1837** CARLYLE *Fr. Rev.* I. I. i, And ye, as subterranean Apparitions are wont, vanish utterly,—leaving only a smell of sulphur!

3. *fig.* Existing or working out of sight, in the dark, or secretly.

1651 JANE *Εικων Ακλαστος* 230 They never pretended priviledge of Parliament further then the subterranean junto. **1855** MOTLEY *Dutch Rep.* VI. i. (1866) 782 His subtle, unscrupulous, and subterranean combinations of policy. **1879** FARRAR *St. Paul* I. 570 They saw through the subterranean injustice and virulent animosity of the Jews in bringing false charges against innocent men. **1882** LECKY *Eng. in 18th Cent.* III. 68 The subterranean and more ignoble works of faction. **1891** HALL CAINE *Scapegoat* xxvi, The entire town..was honeycombed with subterranean revolt.

B. *sb.*

1. One who lives under ground; a cave-dweller.

1625 B. JONSON *Staple of News* I. vi. 44 Her Graces Grandfather, Was Duke, and Cousin to the King of Ophyr, The Subterranean. **1691** R. KIRK *Secret Commw.* i. (1815) 5 These Subterraneans eat but little in their Dwellings. **1833** L. RITCHIE *Wand. Loire* 61 An anecdote..will convey a better idea..of the habitations and manners of the subterraneans.

2. An inhabitant of the lower regions.

1836 I. TAYLOR *Phys. Theory* xvi. 219 That very ancient, and may we not say biblical classification of all intelligent orders, under the three heads of celestials, terrestrials, and subterraneans.

3. An underground cave, chamber, or dwelling.

1797 in C. K. Paul *W. Godwin* (1876) I. 259 We proceeded to about the middle of the subterranean. *c* **1800** R. CUMBERLAND *John de Lancaster* (1809) III. 251, I have..a subterranean of strong beer to set the antient Britons a-dancing on their heads. **1836** WISEMAN *12 Lect. Sci. & Rev. Relig.* II. 146 The hypogeæ, or subterraneans of Eilithyia. **1855** NEWMAN *Callista* (1890) 333 The passage..was only one of several natural subterraneans..opening into each other. **1906** R. WHITEING *Ring in the New* 66 Prue found an ample subterranean, neatly furnished.

b. *fig. pl.* Depths.

1912 *Engl. Rev.* Dec. 27 Down into subterraneans within myself that were positively frightening.

subterraneanly (sʌbtəˈreɪnɪənlɪ), *adv.* [-LY².] Under the ground.

1888 ROLLESTON & JACKSON *Anim. Life* 534 Eyes are absent in some Crustaceans which live subterraneanly. **1892** AGNES M. CLERKE *Fam. Stud. Homer* x. 259 They are commonly disguised under some form of ore, subterraneanly bestowed.

†**subterraˈneity.** *Obs. rare.* [f. next + -ITY.] The condition of being subterraneous; *concr.*, a place or thing found under ground.

1686 *Sir T. Browne's Pseud. Ep.* II. i. 42, I fear we commonly consider subterraneities [*earlier edd.* subterranities], not in Contemplations sufficiently respective unto the Creation. **1721** BAILEY, *Subterraneity*, a being subterraneous. **1807** tr. *Three Germans* I. 69 The flight of steps by which they had been conducted to the subterraneity.

subterraneous (sʌbtəˈreɪnɪəs), *a.* Now *rare.* [f. L. *subterrāneus* (see SUBTERRANE) + -OUS.]

1. a. = SUBTERRANEAN *a.* 1 a.

1607 J. KING *Serm.* 5 Nov. 29 They saie to the ground couer vs, and to a subterraneous vault, keep vs close. **1646** SIR T. BROWNE *Pseud. Ep.* II. i. 55 Yet are they not to be closed up in the generall name of concretions, or lightly passed over as onely Elementary, and Subterraneous mixtions. **1662** STILLINGFL. *Orig. Sacræ* III. iv. §6 Those subterraneous waters which pass up and down through the bowels of the earth. **1667** *Decay Chr. Piety* xii. ¶1 There are many subterraneous springs which feed this ocean. **1712** E. COOKE *Voy. S. Sea* 84 The River..having run subterraneous for two Leagues, rises again. **1725** POPE *Lett.* (1737) VI. 69 In my garden..I have happily finished the subterraneous way and grotto. **1775** JOHNSON *West. Isl.* 164 Being subterraneous, they must be always damp. **1776** GIBBON *Decl. & F.* ii. I. 45 The subterraneous prisons were abolished. **1813** SOUTHEY *Nelson* II. 28 Lady Hamilton..explored..a subterraneous passage, leading from the palace to the sea side. **1842** LOUDON *Suburban Hort.* 227 The sources of cold..are, rain at a lower temperature than the soil,..and where draining has been neglected, subterraneous water. **1875** JOWETT *Plato* (ed. 2) V. 332 Let them bring together the streams in subterraneous channels. **1900** *Q. Rev.* July 93 The area of those subterraneous riches is limited.

b. = SUBTERRANEAN *a.* 1 b.

1727 SWIFT *Wonder Wond.* Wks. 1755 II. II. 52 Certain subterraneous nymphs. **1832** G. DOWNES *Lett. Cont. Countries* I. 193 The *Proteus anguineus*—a creature, which is in a manner both subaqueous and subterraneous. **1832** J. RENNIE *Butterfl. & M.* 51 The Subterraneous Rustic (*Agrotis annexa*). **1860** SMILES *Self Help* ii. 29 Occupying an underground cellar, over which he put up the sign, 'Come to the subterraneous barber'.

c. = SUBTERRANEAN *a.* 1 c.

1658 SIR T. BROWNE *Hydriot.* 34 The Stoicks who thought the souls of wise men had their habitation about the Moon, might make slight account of subterraneous deposition. **1664** POWER *Exp. Philos.* I. 63 Subterraneous Damps do some-times..grow to that over-height of fermentation, that they fire of themselves. *a* **1682** SIR T. BROWNE *Tracts* (1683) 154 There can be no assured decision without an ocular exploration and subterraneous enquiry. **1703** *Phil. Trans.* XXIII. 1327 Venomous Steems and Damps..are frequent in Countries that abound with Minerals or Subterraneous Fires. *a* **1774** TUCKER *Lt. Nat.* (1834) II. 121 The subterraneous thumps of the miner's spade and pickaxe. **1803–5** WORDSW. *Matron of Jedborough & her Husb.* 27 He breathes a subterraneous damp. **1832** BREWSTER *Nat. Magic* ix. 240 Camels are..rendered furious when they hear these subterraneous sounds. **1855** *Orr's Circ. Sci., Inorg. Nat.* 49 This matter, in a melted state, has been from time to time agitated, disturbed, and forced out by subterraneous forces.

d. = SUBTERRANEAN *a.* 1 d.

1777 S. ROBSON *Brit. Flora* 136 *Trifolium subterraneum*,.. Subterraneous Trefoil. **1829** T. CASTLE *Introd. Bot.* 45 Subterraneous—when they are in the ground, as with the snow-drop and most plants. **1833** HOOKER in Smith's *Engl. Flora* V. I. 117 Perianth subterraneous oblong fleshy.

e. = SUBTERRANEAN *a.* 1 e.

1704 J. HARRIS *Lex. Techn.* s.v., Those Trees, which being left there at the Universal Deluge, are so plentifully found buried in the Earth, in many Countries, are called Subterraneous Trees, and by some Fossile-wood. **1712** *Phil. Trans.* XXVII. 478 The Subterraneous Trees, uncovered by an Inundation of the River of Thames in Dagenham and Havering Marshes. **1728** CHAMBERS *Cycl.* s.v., Mr. Boyle gives us an Instance..of a huge Subterraneous Oak dug out of a Salt Mine in Transylvania. **1830** HERSCHEL *Study Nat. Phil.* 346 The subterraneous 'Flora' of a geological formation. **1887** CASSELL s.v., Subterraneous forest.

f. (See quot.)

1781 *Ann. Reg.* III. 248/2 The application of the principles of ordinary geometry to the working of mines is what the author of this work calls subterraneous geometry.

2. = SUBTERRANEAN *a.* 2.

1633 PRYNNE *Histrio-m.* I. 260 She obtained the subterraneous places of Hell in stead of an inheritance. **1678** CUDWORTH *Intell. Syst.* I. i. §19. 19 [Pluto's] Subterraneous Cave. *Ibid.* iv. §17. 308 Calling him in the Starry Heaven and Æther, Jupiter; in the Air, Juno; in the Winds, Æolus; in the Sea, Neptune; in the Earth and Subterraneous Parts Pluto.

3. = SUBTERRANEAN *a.* 3.

1660 R. BURNEY *Κέρδιστον Δῶρον* 130 All other leagues and combinations are subterraneous, when they either trust to or fear the Arm of flesh. **1682** *2nd Plea Nonconf.* 44 It was as cunning a subterraneous Conveyance for Popery, as could be thought of. **1735** H. WALPOLE *Let.* 9 Sept. in *10th Rep. Hist. MSS. Comm.* App. I. 259 These dark & subterraneous negociations wth ye promise of secrecy in all events. **1759** —— *Mem. Geo. II* (1847) III. vii. 176 He might have discovered some of Legge's subterraneous intrigues. **1856** DE QUINCEY *Confess.* Pref. Notice, So obstinately has this malady pursued its noiseless, and what I may call subterraneous, siege.

subteˈrraneously, *adv.* [-LY².]

1. Below the surface of the ground.

1859 R. F. BURTON *Central Afr.* in *Jrnl. Geogr. Soc.* XXIX. 218 An edible white fungus growing subterraneously. **1890** *Hardwicke's Science Gossip* XXVI. 73 At no great depth beneath London and the south-eastern counties there lay the continuation subterraneously of the chain of hills represented by the Mendips in the West of England, and the Ardennes of Belgium.

2. Secretly; in the dark.

1791–1823 D'ISRAELI *Cur. Lit., Buckhm.'s Pol. Coquetry* III. 349 He winded the duke circuitously,—he worked at him subterraneously. **1833** T. HOOK *Parson's Dau.* II. xi, From the elder Miss Lovell to her brother this news was thus as it were subterraneously conveyed. **1856** DE QUINCEY in H. A. Page *Thomas De Quincey* (1877) II. 123 What more, then, was it, my dear girls, that you were subterraneously seeking? **1912** A. HARRISON in *Engl. Rev.* Mar. 676 It is a force growing subterraneously.

subteˈrraneousness. *rare.* [-NESS.] The quality of being subterranean.

1727 BAILEY (vol. II), *Subteraneousness*, the being under the Earth, or inclosed within the Surface, Bowels, or hollow Parts of the Earth. **1851** G. S. FABER *Many Mansions* 345 We find the same character of Centrical Subterraneousness given to the Locality of Hades in two Cognate passages of the Apocalypse.

subteˈrranity. *Obs.* or *rare.* Irreg. var. of SUBTERRANEITY.

1646 SIR T. BROWNE *Pseud. Ep.* II. i. 55, I feare we commonly consider subterranities not in contemplations sufficiently respective unto the creation. **1656** BLOUNT *Glossogr.*, *Subterranity*, the being under ground. **1877–8** HENLEY in *Ballades & Rondeaus* (Canterb. Poets) 83 We search the stars for Fame, Or sink her subterranities; The legend's still the same:—'O Vanity of Vanities!'

†**ˈsubterrany,** *a.* (*sb.*) *Obs. rare.* [ad. L. *subterrāneus* (see SUBTERRANE): cf. *momentany*.] = SUBTERRANEAN.

1626 BACON *Sylva* §326 The Making of Gold did require a very temperate Heat, as being in Nature a Subterrany worke, where little Heat commeth. *Ibid.* 354 We see that in Subterranies there are, as the Fathers of their Tribes, Brimstone and Mercury: In Vegetables, and Liuing Creatures there is Water and Oyle. **1651** R. CHILD in *Hartlib's Legacy* (1655) 73 It is necessary for him to know all subterrany things. **1651** J. F[REAKE] *Agrippa's Occ. Philos.* 393 Innumerable unclean spirits..; under these they place a kind of spirits, subterrany or obscure, which the Platonists call Angels that failed. **1656** BLOUNT *Glossogr.*

subterrene (sʌbtəˈriːn), *a.* and *sb.* Also 7 -en. [ad. L. *subterrēnus*: see SUB- 1 a and TERRENE.]

A. *adj.*

1. Underground; = SUBTERRANEAN 1.

1610 HEALEY *St. Aug. Citie God* x. ix. 372 Sixe kindes of Dæmones. First the fiery,..5. the subterrene, that liue in caues. **1615** G. SANDYS *Trav.* 302 The earth is full of subterrene fires. *a* **1711** KEN *Hymnarium* Poet. Wks. II. 127 Shew me the Gulph, that's fix'd between The upper Hades, and the sub-terrene. **1829** I. TAYLOR *Enthus.* ix. 228 Those dungeons of dimness,..those labyrinths of subterrene communication. **1862** *Macm. Mag.* May 64 The inconvenience of the subterrene trains. **1878** PROCTOR *Pleas. Ways Sci.* ix. (1879) 181 The activity thus exhibited..had its origin in the same subterrene or submarine region as the Peruvian earthquake.

2. Infernal; = SUBTERRANEAN 2.

1836 I. TAYLOR *Phys. Theory* xvi. 219 *note*, The three great orders of the intelligent economy—the heavenly, the earthly, and the subterrene. **1858** CASWALL *Poems* 80 Dread Angels subterrene Mighty in works of ill.

B. *sb.* An underground dwelling, etc.; (with *the*) the underworld.

1854 S. DOBELL *Balder* xviii. 75 Have we shut thee forth, poor child, And wist not of thy journey, nor the end And exit of that gloomy subterrene Which thou didst enter? **1856** *Tasso & Leonora* 95 Being as transparent as Montesino's glass Castle, while he fancied himself as impenetrable as the said Montesino's Subterrene. **1867** J. B. ROSE tr. *Virg. Æneid* Notes 404 The urns and sarcophagi in these subterrenes bear purely native mythological subjects. *c* **1873** J. ADDIS *Eliz. Echoes* (1879) 94 Th' uncertain hum Of hosts upsweeping from the subterrene.

†**subteˈrrenean,** *a.* *Obs. rare*⁻¹. [Formed as prec. + -AN.] Subterranean.

1670 PETTUS *Fodinæ Reg.* Introd., Many do write of Subterrenean Trees, Serpents, Fishes, &c.

subterrestrial (sʌbtəˈrɛstrɪəl), *a.* and *sb.* Now *rare.* [See SUB- 1 a and TERRESTRIAL.] **A.** *adj.*

1. = SUBTERRANEAN 1. Now *rare.*

1613 M. RIDLEY *Magn. Bodies* Pref. 2 For searchers of minerals, mettals, sea-coles, and other subterrestrial bodies. **1658** ROWLAND tr. *Moufet's Theat. Ins.* 891 Bees subterrestrial have another form and nature. **1686** PLOT *Staffordsh.* 87 Hot Springs or subterrestrial Exhalations. **1730** FIELDING *Tom Thumb* Pref., Wks. 1882 VIII. 351 Those two extremities of style Mr. Dryden illustrates by the familiar image of two inns, which I shall term the aërial and the subterrestrial. **1885** W. K. PARKER *Mammal. Desc.* vi. 148 The mole did not become subterrestial just lately.

†**2.** = SUBTERRANEAN 2. *Obs.*

1615 W. HULL *Mirr. Maj.* 68 The Popes pretended Supremacie ouer coelestiall, terrestriall, and subterrestriall creatures. **1643** R. O. *Man's Mort.* v. 27 Angels that are highest in dignitie, and so coelesteiall;..Divels and Death the lowest, and so subterrestriall. *a* **1653** GOUGE *Comm. Heb.* ii. 8 Every creature, invisible or visible,..celestiall or supercelestiall, terrestriall or subterrestriall. **1702** T. BROWN *Lett. fr. Dead to Living* Wks. 1760 II. 209 The most reputable way of entring into this subterrestrial country [*viz.* Hell] is to come in at the fore-door.

B. *sb.* A creature living under ground.

1800 COLERIDGE *Piccolom.* I. xi. 91 Mole-eyed, thou mayest but burrow in the earth, Blind as that subterrestrial.

ˈsubtest. [SUB- 5 c, 7 a.] A test which is subsidiary to or forms part of a main test, esp. (*Psychol.*) in aptitude assessment.

1939 *Brit. Jrnl. Psychol.* July 21 In normal mental test theory there is a test variable (consisting, if need be, of several sub-tests which are used additively). **1961** *Lancet* 26 Aug. 487/1, I also heartily endorse his call for a refinement in the constituent subtests of psychological batteries, so that intellectual functions may be more precisely identified. **1968** W. E. LAMBERT in J. A. Fishman *Readings Sociol. of Lang.* (1968) 480 It is clear from these analyses that the subtests of the Modern Language Aptitude Test..are generally highly correlated with intelligence. **1976** *Word 1971* XXVII. 320 It includes subtests of vocabulary, oral comprehension, sentence completion, spelling, and grammar.

ˈsubtext. †**1.** [SUB- 3 a] Text appearing below other text on a page. *Obs.*

1726 J. LOWE *Lat. Gram.* ix, The Fundamental rules in Text; the Less-necessary sub-joined in Subtext.

2. [SUB- 5 c.] An underlying theme in a piece of writing (esp. in a novel or play). Also *transf.*

1950 E. R. HAPGOOD tr. *C. Stanislavski's Building Character* viii. 113 What do we mean by subtext? What is it that lies behind and beneath the actual words of a part?.. It is the manifest, the inwardly felt expression of a human being in a part, which flows uninterruptedly beneath the words of the text, giving them life and a basis for existing. **1960** S. MOORE *Actor's Training: Stanislavski Method* iii. 27 An artistic, rich imagination will also contribute a great deal when an actor interprets the lines and fills them with the meaning that lies behind, the 'subtext'. **1964** *Evergreen Rev.* Dec. 78/1 The modern style of interpretation..digs 'behind' the text, to find a sub-text which is the true one. **1973** *Times* 2 Jan. 7/8 Also admirable was the manner in which Prince underlined the subtext of naturalism that lies beneath the very obvious symbolic superstructure. **1978** G. VIDAL *Kalki* i. 16 Whenever I got the chance I gave my pitch, which, basically, is the subtext of *Beyond Motherhood*.

subˈthalamic, *a.* *Anat.* [SUB- 1 b.] Situated below the thalamus.

1882 *Quain's Elements Anat.* (ed. 9) II. 326 The fibres [of the crura]..are seen diverging at the side of the subthalamic tegmental region into the inner capsule. **1962** *Gray's Anat.* (ed. 33) 1025 The floor of the diencephalon..forms the subthalamic tegmental region. This, together with the anterior part of the floor and the immediately adjacent parts of the side wall, comprise the hypothalamus. From the functional point of view, however, the subthalamic tegmental region is usually excluded from the hypothalamus. **1973** *Brit. Med. Jrnl.* 15 Dec. 666/1 A vascular lesion of the subthalamic nucleus results in sudden onset of violent choreic movements in the contralateral half of the body.

subˈthalamus. *Anat.* [SUB- 1 f.] A region of grey and white matter in the brain at the base of the diencephalon, below the thalamus and adjacent to the substantia nigra and the red nucleus.

1920 S. W. RANSON *Anat. Nervous Syst.* xiv. 222 The hypothalamus consists of three parts: (1) the pars optica hypothalami, . . (2) the pars mamillaris hypothalami, and (3) the subthalamus. **1946** F. W. JONES *Buchanan's Man. Anat.* (ed. 7) 1378 The inferior surface of the thalamus is related to . . the subthalamus, which intervenes between the thalamus and the tegmental part of the mid-brain. **1974** D. & M. WEBSTER *Compar. Vertebr. Morphol.* xi. 261 Just ventral to the dorsal thalamus is the ventral thalamus (sometimes called the subthalamus), which is primarily concerned with somatic motor functions.

Subtiaba (suːbtɪ'ɑːbə). [The name of a village, (San Juan Bautista de) *Subtiaba*, earlier *Sutiaba*, (see quot. 1891): perh. of Nahuatl origin.] **a.** (A member of) an Indian people of western Nicaragua. **b.** The Tlapanec language of this people (no longer spoken), formerly considered to have Hokan affinities but now regarded as Otomanguean. Formerly also **Subti'aban**. Also *Comb.*, as **Subtiaba-Tlapanec**, a group of related central American Indian languages, including Subtiaba.

[**1878** S. HABEL in *Smithsonian Contrib. Knowl.* No. 269. 24, I proceeded to Leon. Here I collected as many words and sentences as I could of the *Raburochi* language, spoken in the neighboring village of Sutiaba.] **1891** D. G. BRINTON *Amer. Race* 159 The Subtiabas are inhabitants of the valley of that name near the modern city of Leon in Nicaragua. **1911** THOMAS & SWANTON *Indian Languages of Mexico & Central Amer.* 77 Mangue . . was the most northwesterly tribe of the series, the area occupied extending . . northwards from the territory of the Subtiaba (Squier's Nagrandans) 'along the Gulf of Fonseca'. . . *Subtiaban* (*Synonyms*: Nagrandan, Maribi). This language . . forms a distinct family. **1925** E. SAPIR in *Amer. Anthropol.* XXVII. 402 Subtiaba, a language now spoken by only a small number of Indians in a village near Léon, on the Pacific slope of Nicaragua. . . For a long time the language was believed to be an isolated one . . But it appeared later that it is very closely related to Tlappanec or Yopi, a language spoken in the state of Guerrero in Southern Mexico. **1935** P. RADIN in *Internat. Jrnl. Amer. Linguistics* VIII. 45/1 Lehmann succeeded in demonstrating quite clearly that Tlappanec was closely related to the Subtiaba language of Nicaragua. **1965** *Canad. Jrnl. Linguistics* Spring 100 The third constituent of Hokan-Coahuiltecan, Subtiaba-Tlappanec. **1978** *Language* LIV. 507 Both papers are crucially concerned with a particular language known in two dialectal forms, Subtiaba (extinct, of Nicaragua) and Tlapanec (still spoken in Guerrero, Mexico).

subtile ('sʌtɪl, 'sʌbtɪl), *a.* (*sb.*) Forms: 4–6 **subtyl, -yll, 4–7 -ill,** (4 **soubtil, -tiel,** 5 **subtille,** 5–6 **-tyle,** 6 **-tylle,** *Sc.* **-tel(l, sobtyll, suptel),** 4– **subtil, subtile.** [a. F. *subtil* (from 14th c.), latinized refashioning of OF. *s(o)util* SUBTLE *a.*]

1. Chiefly of fluids: Not dense, thin, rarefied; penetrating, etc. by reason of tenuity; = SUBTLE *a.* 1.

1390 GOWER *Conf.* III. 92 This soubtil water myhtely . . The strengthe of therthe perceth ofte. **1398** TREVISA *Barth. De P.R.* III. xvii. (1495) 63 Subtyl humour temprith and purith that that is in the lymmes of the syȝte. *Ibid.* V. xix. 124 The ayre and brethe drawen in by the mouth is amended and puryd, and made subtyll therin. *a* **1425** tr. *Arderne's Treat. Fistula* etc. 59 If it be for humour, þat is . . for it is scharp, or subtile, or watrye. **1509** FISHER *Funeral Serm. C'tess Richmond* Wks. (1876) 304 It [*sc.* the risen body] shall be subtyle that it shall perce thorowe the stone walles. *c* **1530** *Judic. Urines* II. xii. 41 b, It maketh the vryne subtyle and thynne. **1533** ELYOT *Cast. Helthe* 33 The rayne water . . is most subtyl & penetratiue. **1590** SPENSER *F.Q.* III. vii. 39 An Egle, that with plumy wings doth sheare The subtile ayre. **1616** SURFL. & MARKH. *Country Farm* 630 The . . red-like wines which are of a thin and subtile substance. *c* **1645** HOWELL *Lett.* (1655) IV. l. 120 As if they had som subtile invisible Atomes wherby they [*sc.* thoughts] operat. **1661** LOVELL *Hist. Anim. & Min.* 150 The fat, is hot, subtile and better than the rest. **1742** *Lond. & Country Brewer* III. (ed. 2) 233 By the subtile Salts of the Lime, it will make its Way into the Pores . . of the Wood. *a* **1774** GOLDSM. *Surv. Exp. Philos.* (1776) II. 4 Some have thought that air is nothing more than earth or water expanded and assuming a more subtil form. **1784** COWPER *Task* VI. 135 The vital energy that mov'd . . the pure and subtile lymph Through th'imperceptible meand'ring veins Of leaf and flow'r. **1839** HALLAM *Lit. Eur.* III. iii. §149 The belief in ghosts, or spirits of subtile bodies. **1858** SEARS *Athan.* xviii. 160 The luminiferous ether is still more subtile, and eludes the analysis of the chemist. **1872** J. G. MURPHY *Comm. Lev.* vii. 37 The fat and the flesh turned by the fire of the altar into a subtile fume.

transf. **1642** H. MORE *Song of Soul* II. ii. III. 18 Corporeall wight such subtile virtue never has. **1844** EMERSON *Nature, Discipline* Wks. (Bohn) II. 158 The air resembles the light which traverses it with more subtile currents.

fig. **1681–6** J. SCOTT *Chr. Life* (1747) III. 628 The Arguments of it would be too thin and subtil for vulgar Capacities. **1829** I. TAYLOR *Enthus.* ii. (1867) 22 The region of abstract conceptions . . has an atmosphere too subtile to support the health of true piety.

b. ***subtile matter***: see MATTER *sb.*[1] 5 b.

†**c.** Of a voice: Thin. *Obs.*

1398 TREVISA *Barth. De P.R.* XIX. cxxxi. (1495) 942 In subtyll voys the spyryte is not stronge.

2. Of fine or delicate texture; also, delicately formed or moulded; = SUBTLE *a.* 2.

c **1381** CHAUCER *Parl. Foules* 272 A subtyl couercheif of valence. **1398** TREVISA *Barth. De P.R.* III. ix. (1495) 54 The soule that yeueth felynge hathe place in the moost subtill chambres of the brayne. **1474** CAXTON *Chesse* III. i. (1883) 79 More subtile & more deyntous metes. **1481** CAXTON *Myrr.* II. x. f viij, Trees the whiche in stede of leues bere wulle of whiche is made cloth right fair & subtyle. **1579** LANGHAM *Gard. Health* 535 Rose water . . maketh the skinne subtill and thinne. **1599** SIR J. DAVIES *Nosce Teipsum* II. 12, I do distinguish plaine Each subtill line of her immortall face. *Ibid.* 11 Her subtile forme thou onely canst define. **1608** B. JONSON *Masques, Beauty* Wks. (1616) 906 A thinne subtile vaile ouer her haire. *a* **1648** DIGBY *Closet Opened* (1677) 90 Strain the[m] clean through a subtil strainer. **1668** CULPEPPER & COLE *Barthol. Anat.* I. xiv. 35 A certain little lobe . . compassed with a thin and subtile Membrane.

3. Of small thickness, thin, fine; = SUBTLE *a.* 3.

a **1425** tr. *Arderne's Treat. Fistula* etc 68 Wolle y-tesed or subtile stupez of line. **1555** EDEN *Decades* (Arb.) 222 He putteth his toonge to one of the ryftes . . being as subtyle as the edge of a swoorde. **1612** SHELTON *Quix.* (1620) I. iii. 18 Some slight and subtill wallets, which could scarce be perceiued. **1616** B. JONSON *Devil an Ass* Prol. 5 Though you presume Satan a subtill thing, And may haue heard hee's worne in a thumbe-ring. **1665** BOYLE *Occas. Refl.* IV. iv. 69 The subtil threds of Silk-worms. **1742** POPE *Dunc.* IV. 590 Arachne's subtile line.

fig. **1870** LOWELL *Among my Bks.* Ser. I. (1873) 158 Every subtilest fibre of feeling.

†**b.** Of ships: Narrow, slender. Cf. OF. *galere subtile*. *Obs.*

c **1489** CAXTON *Blanchardyn* 151, xxx grete shyppes and four score galeys subtyl. **1599** HAKLUYT *Voy.* II. i. 78 Gallies, aswell bastards as subtill mahonnets.

4. Of powder, etc.: Fine, minute; = SUBTLE *a.* 4.

a **1425** tr. *Arderne's Treat. Fistula* etc. 41 þe moste subtile mele of barly. **1513** *Life Hen. V* (1911) 110 Many heapes of sand, wch was so subtill and smale, that it mooued wth everie wynde. **1545** RAYNALDE *Byrth Mankynde* (1552) 136 b, Beynge fyrst beaten to subtyle powdre. *c* **1600** CHAPMAN *Iliad* IX. 629 The subtile fruit of flax. **1683** K. DIGBY *Chym. Secrets* 77 Take Antimony Mineral . . in subtil Powder. **1697** HEADRICH *Arcana Philos.* 30 Of this Marchasite . . make a subtile Powder. **1797** *Encycl. Brit.* (ed. 3) XI. 447/1 Beat your ore into a most subtile powder.

5. Involving careful discrimination or fine points; †difficult, abstruse; = SUBTLE *a.* 5.

c **1386** CHAUCER *Man of Law's T.* 80 Many a subtil resoun forth they leyden. **1390** GOWER *Conf.* III. 331 In proverbe and in probleme Sche spak, and bad he scholde deme In many soubtil question. **1456** SIR G. HAYE *Law Arms* (S.T.S.) 14 It be sum part subtile to under-stand. **1560** DAUS tr. *Sleidane's Comm.* 13 b, Let vs not throughe a subtill interpretation accompt king Charles a Germaine. **1565** COOPER *Thesaurus* s.v. *Abstrusior*, *Disputatio abstrusior*, a more subtill, hard, or obscure disputacion. **1598** STOW *Surv.* 44 Halfe pence and Farthinges, the account of which is more subtiller then the pence. **1610** HOLLAND *Camden's Brit.* 352 [Odo] was committed to prison by a subtile distinction, as Earle of Kent, and not Bishop of Baieux. **1651** HOBBES *Leviathan* I. xv. 79 This may seem too subtile a deduction of the Lawes of Nature, to be taken notice of by all men. **1664** *Comenius' Janua Ling.* 755 The study of the Mathematicks is as profitable, as subtil (deep). **1788** REID *Active Powers* III. iv. 162 There has been much subtile disputation in ancient and modern times.

6. Fine, delicate; = SUBTLE *a.* 6.

1599 SIR J. DAVIES *Nosce Teipsum* II. Introd. xxiv, But of that clocke within our breasts we beare, The subtill motions we forget the while. **1625** B. JONSON *Staple of N.* II. iv. 164 Like a knitting needle, To serve by subtill turnes. **1634** W. TIRWHYT tr. *Balzac's Lett.* (vol. I.) 305 These other more fine, and subtile vertues I cannot learne at Court. **1752** HUME *Pol. Disc.* i. 3 Some principles . . which may seem too refin'd and subtile for such vulgar subjects. **1858** LONGF. *M. Standish* VI. 4 As if thought had the power to draw to itself . . Whatsoever it touches, by subtile laws of its nature. **1871** *Edin. Rev.* Apr. 428 The subtilest differences of perception and emotion. **1885** F. B. VAN VOORST *Without a Compass* 20 Those intricate questions that possess so subtile a charm. **1888** E. CLODD *Story Creation* xi. 216 Their subtile shades of meaning.

†**7.** Of persons: Clever, dexterous, skilful; = SUBTLE *a.* 7. *Obs.*

c **1374** CHAUCER *Anel. & Arc.* 88 He was . . subtill in þat Crafte. *c* **1385** —— *L.G.W.* 572 Sche . . made hire subtyl werkemen make a schryne. **1390** GOWER *Conf.* III. 114 It causeth yit A man to be soubtil of wit To worche in gold. *c* **1450** *Merlin* i. 21 This Blase was a nobill clerk and subtile. **1456** SIR G. HAYE *Law Arms* (S.T.S.) 38 [He] was rycht subtile in spech of Latyn. *c* **1489** CAXTON *Sonnes of Aymon* xi. 277 He was the subtillest nygramancer that ever was in the worlde.

†**8.** Cleverly devised; ingeniously contrived; ingenious; = SUBTLE *a.* 8. *Obs.*

c **1384** CHAUCER *H. Fame* 1188 Many subtile compassinges Babewynnes and pynacles Ymageries and tabernacles I say. **1390** GOWER *Conf.* III. 40 A wonder soubtil thing he wroghte. *c* **1391** CHAUCER *Astrol.* II. §40, I tok a subtil compas. **1484** CAXTON (*title*) Here begynneth the book of the subtyl historyes and Fables of Esope. **1577–87** HOLINSHED *Chron.* III. 833/2 Blew veluet and cloath of siluer, all to cut in subtill knots. **1585** T. WASHINGTON tr. *Nicholay's Voy.* I. viii, By great artifice and subtill architecture builded. **1659** LEAK *Waterwks.* 23 A very Subtile Engin, to raise a standing Water, by means of the Sun.

9. Of persons, animals, their actions, etc.: Crafty, artful, sly, cunning; = SUBTLE *a.* 10.

c **1385** CHAUCER *L.G.W.* 2519 Be war ȝe wemen of ȝoure subtyl fo. **1386** *Rolls of Parlt.* III. 225/1 Many wronges subtiles, and also open oppressions. **1390** GOWER *Conf.* I. 231 To voide with a soubtil hond The beste goodes of the lond And bringe chaf and take corn. **1513** DOUGLAS *Æneis* VI. ii. 43 In subtell wordis of obscurite Involupand the trewth and verite. **1549** LATIMER *Ploughers* (Arb.) 32 He goeth aboute bi his sleyghtes and subtyle meanes, to frustrate the same. **1575** GASCOIGNE *Kenelworth* Wks. 1910 II. 108 In sweetest flowres the subtyll Snakes may lurke. **1591** SHAKS. *Two Gent.* IV. ii 95 Thou subtile, periur'd, false, disloyall man. **1611** *Bible* Gen. iii. 1 The serpent was more subtill [COVERDALE sotyller] then any beast of the field. **1628** FELTHAM *Resolves* II. ix. 23 Taken with the subtile cozenages of Vice. **1634** SIR T. HERBERT *Trav.* 199 Their [crocodiles'] condition is subtile (such their bloudie teares when they haue deuoured a man proue them for). **1646** SIR T. BROWNE *Pseud. Ep.* I. iii. (1686) 8 They are mocked into Error by subtiler devisors. **1719** DE FOE *Crusoe* I. 71 The Goats were so shy, so subtile, and so swift of Foot. **1814** SOUTHEY *Roderick* x. 346 And with such subtile toils enveloped him. **1850** HARE *Mission Comf.* 137 To overcome sin's fiercest and subtilest temptations.

†**b.** Of looks: Sly. *Obs.*

c **1386** CHAUCER *Squires T.* 277 Swich subtil lookyng and dissymelynges. **1500–20** DUNBAR *Poems* lxxxiv. 35 Be subtill winkis, and thair desaitfull talis. **1513** DOUGLAS *Æneis* VII. Prol. 100 Hir subtell blenkis sched and wattry lycht.

10. Characterized by sagacity or penetration; discriminating, discerning; = SUBTLE *a.* 9.

1474 CAXTON *Chesse* II. v. (1883) 65 Ther was a kynge of so subtyll engyne That [etc.]. *a* **1533** BERNERS *Huon* lvii. 194 Frenchemen are ryght subtyl in gyuyng of good counsell. *Ibid.*, Gerames, who was subtyl, wel perceyued the mynde of the lady. **1600** SHAKS. *A.Y.L.* I. iii. 79 She is too subtile for thee. **1611** *Bible* 2 Sam. xiii. 3 Ionadab was a very subtill man. **1612** BACON *Ess.*, *Studies* (Arb.) 11 Histories make men wise, Poets wittie, the Mathematickes subtill [1598 subtle]. **1691** RAY *Creation* I. (1692) 71 How or why that should have such influence upon the Spirits . . I am not subtil enough to discern. **1718** PRIOR *Solomon* II. 224 With subtil Wit and fair Discourse. **1741** BETTERTON *Hist. Engl. Stage* iii. 34 This was a Nicety in Acting that none but the most subtile Player could so much as conceive. **1826** DISRAELI *Viv. Grey* V. vi. 200 The most subtile diplomatist. **1875** STEDMAN *Vict. Poets* (1887) xi. 411 A subtile observer would perceive how truly he [*sc.* Shelley] represents his own time.

11. Of feeling, sense: Acute, keen.

1610 GUILLIM *Heraldry* III. v. (1660) 123 By reason that our sight is far more subtill and apprehensive than is our hearing. **1662** J. DAVIES tr. *Olearius' Voy. Ambass.* 2 The stinch also offends it, and makes those heart-sick whose smelling is subtile. **1718** PRIOR *Solomon* III. 136 Pass we the slow Disease, and subtil Pain. **1721** BRADLEY *Philos. Acc. Wks. Nat.* 54 In which I suppose there is contained their most Subtile sense of feeling. **1847** LONGF. *Evang.* II. iv, A secret Subtile sense crept in of pain. **1913** DORLAND *Med. Dict.* (ed. 7) 917/2 *Subtile*, keen and acute, as, a subtile pain.

12. †**a.** Of weight, after tare has been deducted. Cf. SUBTLE *a.* 12. *Obs.*

1502 ARNOLDE *Chron.* (1811) p. xvi, The rekenynge of grocery, and weight sobtyll and grosse. **1660** T. WILLSFORD *Scales Comm.* 107 What those gross or subtile summes do make in pence.

†**b.** Of a quantity: Belonging to a lower denomination. *Obs.*

15.. *MS. Harl.* 660 lf. 81 b, Euery subtylle grayne [doth] contayne 20 mytes. **1542** RECORDE *Gr. Artes* (1640) 120 Whatsoever thing is compared to other, if it be greater, and containeth many of them, it is a grosse denomination: but if it be lesser . . then are they called the subtile denominations. **1579** DIGGES *Stratiot.* I. vi. 10 Grosse to subtile by Multiplication, Subtile, to grosse by partition is performed.

13. *Comb.*, as ***subtile-pated***, ***-witted*** adjs.

1591 SHAKS. *1 Hen. VI*, I. i. 25 The subtile-witted French. *c* **1595** DONNE *Sat.* i. 62 Our subtile-witted antique youths. **1655** GURNALL *Chr. in Arm.* I. 103 The subtilest-pated men.

†**B.** *sb. pl.* Fluids. *Obs. rare.*

a **1585** MONTGOMERY *Sonn.* lvi. 9 Suppose the solids subtilis ay restrantis.

†**subtile**, *v.* *Obs.* Also 6 suptyle. [ad. med.L. *subtiliāre* (whence OF. *soutillier*, *subtilier*, It. *sottigliare*): see SUBTILIATE *v.*]

1. *trans.* To make subtile or thin; to rarefy.

1471 RIPLEY *Comp. Alch.* I. vii. in Ashm. (1652) 130 Lat the Body be sotelly fylyd With Mercury, as much then so subtylyd. **1495** *Trevisa's Barth. De P.R.* XIX. xi. 871 Whyte colour is gendrid for thynnynge and subtyllynge of partyes of the matere. **1528** PAYNELL *Salerne's Regim.* Yj b, Heatynge, subtilynge & dissoluynge hit [*sc.* phlegm]. *c* **1530** *Judic. Urines* II. viii. 33 b, Whan kynd hete hath more suptyld & maystred y[e] mater than appereth. *c* **1550** LLOYD *Treas. Health* I viij, By subtyllynge the humore. **1605** TIMME *Quersit.* III. 189 All the humours of our body are made thinne and subtiled.

2. To imagine craftily.

1537 *Instit. Chr. Man* A 3 Charmes, wytche-craftes, or any other false artes subtiled and inuented by the dyuell.

subtilely: see SUBTILLY.

†'**subtileness**. *Obs.* [f. SUBTILE *a.* + -NESS.]

1. Thinness, tenuity.

1398 TREVISA *Barth. De P.R.* IV. i. (1495) e iij b/2 The symplynes of a boystous thynge is subtylnes in that comyth in by wythdrawynge of fastnes & thycnes of partyes. **1528** PAYNELL *Salerne's Regim.* b iv, The subtilnes [ed. 1541, subtile parte] of the bloud burneth hit selfe and tourneth in to coler and grossely into melancoly. **1597** A. M. tr. *Guillemeau's Fr. Chirurg.* 41/1 Because of the subtilenes thereof [*sc.* of the cautery], and the virtues of his substance. **1617** MORYSON *Itin.* III. 45 The subtilenesse of the Ayre. **1676** WISEMAN *Chirurg. Treat.* I. vi. 34 The *Erysipelas à Sanguine bilioso*, from cholerick Bloud, . . affects onely the outward Parts, none of which escape its tenuity and subtilnes.

2. Cunning, craftiness.

1474 CAXTON *Chesse* II. v. (1883) 60 Thou hast vaynquyshid them . . by thy newe deceyuable falsenes and by subtilnes. **1509** HAWES *Past. Pleas.* XX. iv. (1555) M iij b, Ye shall be ryght well vyctoryous Of all your enemyes so full of subtylnes. *c* **1511** *1st Engl. Bk. Amer.* (Arb.) Introd. 33/2 The Lyon sleeth the vnicorne with subtylnes. **1641** EARL MONM. tr. *Biondi's Civil Wars* III. 123 Had the Dolphin lived he had runne no danger; for in time he might easily have won him by his subtilnesse.

3. Subtlety (of argument).

1591 GREENE *Farew. to Folly* Wks. (Grosart) IX. 251 As well to imitate Aristotle in the sumptuousnes of his apparell as the subtilnesse of his arguments.

†**'subtilesse.** *Obs. rare*$^{-1}$. In 5 subtyllesse. [a. OF. *subtilesse*, var. *soutilesse*, f. *soutil* SUBTLE *a.* + *-esse* -ESS[1]. Cf. It. *sottigliezza*.] Subtlety.

1471 CAXTON *Recuyell* (Sommer) 384 He chaungyd hym self in guyse of a serpent this is to vnderstande in subtyllesse and in malyce.

†**sub'tiliate,** *pa. pple.* and *ppl. a. Obs. rare.* [ad. med.L. *subtīliātus*, pa. pple. of *subtīliāre* (see next).] Made thin or fine; rarefied.

1471 RIPLEY *Comp. Alch.* II. i. in Ashm. (1652) 135 Of ther hard and dry Compactyon subtylyat. **1555** EDEN *Decades* (Arb.) 294 All whiche are moued, digested, subtiliate, attenuate, ryped, and made sweete. **1610** HEALEY *St. Aug. Citie God* 563 Augustine giues the Angels most subtiliate bodies, invisible, actiue, and not passiue.

†**sub'tiliate,** *v. Obs.* Also 5 sutilyate. [f. med.L. *subtīliāt-*, pa. ppl. stem of *subtīliāre*, f. *subtīlis* SUBTLE *a.*: see -ATE[3].] *trans.* To make thin or tenuous; *esp.* to rarefy (a fluid); to sublime; to refine, purify.

14.. *MS. Ashm.* 1408 XI. 31 Whosoever knowethe to sutilyate [quicksilver]. **1579** FULKE *Heskins' Parl.* 169 He supposeth the body of Christe might be subtiliated, by his Diuine power, to passe through the doores. **1582** HESTER *Secr. Phiorav.* I. xxxviii. 45 Our Quintaessentia solutiua.. subtiliateth the humors, and evacuateth them dounewards. **1594** PLAT *Jewell-ho.* 88 Sol so subtiliated by often reiteration of Aqua Regis vpon it, as that it becam almost an impalpable powder. **1601** HOLLAND *Pliny* XXXII. ix. II. 443 The same being washed after the manner of lead, be singular for to subtiliat the thicke eye-lids. **1603** —— *Plutarch's Mor.* 1318 Being of this opinion, that the flame doth subtiliate and rarefie the aire. **1630** LORD *Banians* 54 Those spirits that are subtiliated by Stils and Lymbecks, the fire is effectuall to their subliming. **1651** BIGGS *New Disp.* ⁋157 Subtiliated into a jubilee of spiritual *Aporhæa's* or evaporations. **1655** T. VAUGHAN *Euphrates* 67 The earth thickens the water, and on the contrary the water subtiliates the earth. **1678** R. RUSSELL *Geber* I. i. 4 Much more attenuated and subtiliated than it was before.

Hence †**sub'tiliated**, †**sub'tiliating** *ppl. adjs.*

1603 HARSNET *Pop. Impost.* 159 To our subtiliated, sublimated new spirits of the Sorbon. **1650** CHARLETON *Paradoxes* Prol. 14 A streame of subtiliated Atomes. **1665** G. HARVEY *Adv. agst. Plague* 6 A very dry and warm or subtiliating air.

†**subtili'ation.** *Obs.* [ad. med.L. *subtīliātio, -ōnem* (Albertus Magnus), n. of action f. *subtīliāre* (see prec.) Cf. OF. *subtiliation*, It. *sottigliazione*.] The action of making a thing 'subtile', thin, or fine; rarefaction; purification by separating the fine parts from the coarse; reduction (of a solid) to a liquid, reduction to powder; also the condition resulting from this; a 'subtile' particle, etc.

1398 TREVISA *Barth. De P.R.* IV. v. (1495) 87 There is none euaporacyon, neyther delyueraunce of the superfluytees, neyther subtilyacyon of the spyrytes. *Ibid.* IX. i. (Tollem. MS.) Meuynge is cause of generacion and of all chaungynge of neþer þinges,.. and of subtiliacion of water and of þee ayer. **1471** RIPLEY *Comp. Alch.* Pref. in Ashm. (1652) 126 Tyll thy Base by ofter subtylyatyon Wyll lyghtly flow as Wex uppon Mettall. **1594** *Mirr. Policy* (1599) Lj, We must first.. purifie it from the earthlinesse, and.. bring it to the subtiliation and simplicitie of fire. **1612** WOODALL *Surg. Mate* Wks. (1653) 274 Subtiliation is dissolution, separating the subtil parts from the grosse. **1650** CHARLETON *Paradoxes* Prol. 19 Minute Subtiliations.. interposed betwixt the.. Object and the body exhalant. **1662** H. STUBBE *Indian Nectar* iii. 34 The due comminution, and subtiliation of food. **1678** R. RUSSELL tr. *Geber* I. iii. 9 Vinegars, of what kind soever, acute and harsh are cleansed by Subtiliation. **1685** BOYLE *Enq. Notion Nat.* 358 Rational Souls,.. not capable to be produc'd by any Subtiliation or other Change of Matter whatsoever.

†**sub'tiliative,** *a. Obs. rare.* [f. med.L. *subtīliāt-*, pa. ppl. stem of *subtīliāre* to SUBTILIATE + -IVE. Cf. It. *sottigliativo*.] Having the property of thinning, rarefying, dissolving.

c **1425** tr. *Arderne's Treat. Fistula*, etc. 89 þis alkenet.. is subtiliatyue and resolutyue without mordicacion. **1528** PAYNELL *Salerne's Regim.* 4 Whey is subtiliative washyng & lewsynge. **1543** TRAHERON tr. *Vigo's Surg.* III. xv. 106 b/2 The medicines.. must be subtiliatiue and liquide.

subtilin ('sʌbtɪlɪn). *Pharm.* [f. L. *subtil-is* slender + -IN[1].] Any of a group of polypeptides of differing antibiotic activity (***subtilin A, B, C***) derived by culture from *Bacillus amyloliquefaciens* (orig. identified as *B. subtilis*), the most potent of which are used against Gram-positive bacteria and certain pathogenic fungi.

1944 JANSEN & HIRSCHMANN in *Arch. Biochem.* IV. 298 The substance thus differing from tyrothricin has been named *subtilin* by the authors. **1948** *Sun* (Baltimore) 9 Jan. 5/1 Recently publicized 'wonder drugs' include.. subtilin. **1948** C. H. HASSAL in *Nature* 28 Feb. 318/1 By use of the latter procedure, followed by dilution of the alcoholic extract with adjustment of the *p*H to 2·3, an active concentrate, which we will term subtilin *C*, was obtained. **1966** *McGraw-Hill Encycl. Sci. & Technol.* XIII. 230/2 Subtilin A, the major component of the subtilin family, is separated by partition chromatography. **1976** J. S. GLASBY *Encycl. Antibiotics* 334/1 A further antibiotic isolated from cultures of *Bacillus subtilis*, subtilin may be produced by both surface and submerged growth on various media. The associated antibiotic subtilin C.. appears to be identical.. in all respects except that it gives no colour reaction with $FeCl_3$ solution.

subtilisin (sʌb'tɪlɪsɪn). *Biochem.* [f. L. *subtīlis* slender + -IN[1].] Any of a group of extracellular proteinases derived from strains of *Bacillus amyloliquefaciens* (orig. identified as *B. subtilis*).

1953 GÜNTELBERG & OTTESEN in *Compt. Rend. des Travaux du Laboratoire Carlsberg: Ser. Chim.* XXIX. 47 Since.. the *B. subtilis* proteinase appears to be a rather well defined enzyme.. we feel that it will be appropriate to give it a name, and we propose to call it 'subtilisin'. **1968** A. WHITE et al. *Princ. Biochem.* (ed. 4) xii. 255 This is indicated by the finding that the subtilisins, proteolytic enzymes of *Bacillus subtilis* of different genetic origin, possess entirely different amino acid sequences. **1980** *Developmental Biol.* LXXVIII. 383/2 Protease activity of subtilisin and trypsin was confirmed with Azocoll.. as substrate at pH 7·0.

subtilism ('sʌ(b)tɪlɪz(ə)m). *rare*$^{-1}$. [f. SUBTILIZE: see -ISM.] Subtle doctrine.

1855 MILMAN *Lat. Christ.* XIV. iii. VI. 470 The high orthodox subtilism of Duns Scotus.

subtilist ('sʌ(b)tɪlɪst). *rare.* [f. SUBTILIZE: see -IST.] = SUBTLIST.

1667 WATERHOUSE *Narr. Fire in London* 49 The many forraign minded and addicted subtilists amongst us. **1829** CARLYLE in *For. Review & Cont. Misc.* IV. 126 The true Scholastic is a mystical Subtilist [1840 *Misc.* II. 237 Subtlist].

subtility (səb'tɪlɪtɪ). Forms: α. 4 soutilete, sutilite, suttellite, 5 sotyllyte, sutillyte. β. 4 soubtilite, subtilitee, 4–6 -tylyte, -tilite, 5 -tylytee, 6 -tel(l)itie, -tillite, -ie, -tellyte, 6–7 -tilitie, 6– subtility. [a. OF. (1) *soutilite*, *sutelite*, (2) *subtilite*, = Pr. *subtilitat*, It. *sottilità*, Sp. *sutilidad*, Pg. *subtilidade*, ad. L. *subtīlitas, -ātem*, f. *subtīlis* SUBTLE *a.* Cf. SUBTILTY, SUBTLETY.

Now used as the noun of quality of SUBTILE chiefly in the physical senses.]

1. Acuteness, perspicacity; = SUBTLETY 1.

1388 WYCLIF *Ecclus.* i. 6 To whom was the roote of wisdom schewid? and who knewe the sutilites therof? *a* **1578** LINDESAY (Pitscottie) *Chron. Scot.* (S.T.S.) I. 18, I knew the subtillitie that he hes ane merwellous foirsicht of all kynd of suspitioun. **1632** LITHGOW *Trav.* II. 62 Vlysses.. excelled all other Greekes in.. subtility of wit. **1866** ALGER *Solit. Nat.* IV. 187 Masters whose comprehensiveness and subtility of thinking have scarcely been surpassed.

†**2.** Skill, cleverness, ingenuity; = SUBTLETY 2.

α. *c* **1375** *Sc. Leg. Saints* ii. (*Paulus*) 751 þai.. throw thar suttellite In his wame gert it fosterit be. **1426** LYDG. *De Guil. Pilgr.* 5473 For hyr gret sotyllyte, Thys lady.. Prayede hyr ..For to helpe make thys bred.

β. **1375** BARBOUR *Bruce* XX. 305 The gud lord of Dowglass syne Gert mak ane cass of siluir fyne, Anamalyt throu subtilite. *c* **1386** CHAUCER *Can. Yeom. T.* 818 (Lansd. MS.) And men knewe al my subtilite Be god men wolde haue so grete envie To me.. I sholde be dede. **1470–85** MALORY *Arthur* II. xix. 99 Merlyn lete make by his subtylyte that Balyns swerd was put in a marbel stone. **1483** CAXTON *Gold. Leg.* 333/2 He had subtylytee for teschewe the lyggynge in a wayte of his enemyes. **1484** —— *Fables of Auian* v, I.. canne gyue remedy to al manere of sekenes by myn arte and subtylyte. **1662** J. DAVIES tr. *Mandelslo's Trav.* 34 It hath the subtility to swallow down Muscles, and keep them in the stomack, till the heat thereof hath opened the shell. **1669** GALE *Crt. Gentiles* I. Introd. 4 It is the part of a Student, to require subtilitie or exactnesse in every kind.

†**3.** Cunning, craftiness; = SUBTLETY 3. *Obs.*

1375 BARBOUR *Bruce* X. 38 The king, that in all assays Wes fundyn wiss and awerte, Persauit thair subtilite. **1390** GOWER *Conf.* I. 239 With sleihte and with soubtilite. **1567** *Gude & Godlie B.* (S.T.S.) 99 Defend me from the fals subtellitie Of wickit men. **1567** *Satir. Poems Reform.* iv. 116 And mylde meiknes sylit with subtilitie. **1607** TOPSELL *Four-f. Beasts* 228 To signifie how irreligious pastors in holy habittes beguile the simple with subtility. **1611** *Bible* 2 Kings x. 19 Iehu did it in subtiltie.. that hee might destroy the worshippers of Baal. *a* **1761** LAW *Comf. Weary Pilgr.* (1809) 59 An earthly animal that only excelled.. the beasts, in an upright form and serpentine subtility.

†**4.** An instance of this; a cunning or crafty scheme, an artifice, dodge; = SUBTLETY 4. *Obs.*

α. **1390** GOWER *Conf.* II. 199 Nou herkne the soutilete.

β. *c* **1386** CHAUCER *Merch. T.* 3 (Harl. MS.) Lo swiche sleighthes and subtilites In wommen. **1484** CAXTON *Fables of Æsop, Life* 2 b, I shalle fynde a subtylyte that we shall haue no blame ne harme therfore. **1673** *Lady's Call.* I. 28 It needs none of those subtilities and simulations, those pretences and artifices.

5. (Excessive) nicety or refinement in argument, etc.

c **1384** CHAUCER *H. Fame* 855 Haue y not preved thus symply With-outen any subtilite Of speche or grete prolixite? *c* **1400** *Pilgr. Sowle* (Caxton 1483) IV. xxviii. 75 Amonges the Romayns at that tyme was had greete subtylite in philosophye. **1534** WHITINTON *Tullyes Offices* II. M, The substylyte [*sic*] and quiddyte is a nother maner of thynge, whan truthe it selfe is fyled or subtylly handled in disputacyon. **1605** BACON *Adv. Learning* I. 20 This same vnprofitable subtilitie or curiositie is of two sorts.

6. An instance of this; esp. *pl.* = SUBTLETY 7.

1589 PUTTENHAM *Engl. Poesie* II. xi. [xii.] (Arb.) 104, I being very inquisitiue to know of the subtillities of those countreyes, and especially in matter of learning. *c* **1643** LD. HERBERT *Autobiog.* (1824) 42 Their tutors commonly spend much time in teaching them the subtilities of Logic. **1764** *Mem. Geo. Psalmanazar* 41 Controversies clogged.. with sophistry and endless subtilities. **1845** LINGARD *Anglo-Saxon Ch.* II. 178 *note*, The subtilities of philosophers.

7. Tenuity, fineness; = SUBTLETY 8.

c **1400** *Lanfranc's Cirurg.* 43 þe medicyn þanne muste be hoot & drie with subtiliate [*read* subtilite] as terebentine to moiste bodies. **1526** *Pilgr. Perf.* (W. de W. 1531) 229 The fourth dowry [*sc.* of the body] is subtilite. **1552** LYNDESAY *Monarche* 6169 Subtellyte thay [*sc.* the blessed] sall haue maruellouslye. **1652** BENLOWES *Theoph.* VI. lxxv, They.. far surpasse the sun-beams in subtilitie. **1707** *Curios. Husb. & Gard.* 69 There is no part.. in which the Subtility and Suppleness of the Sap more claim our Admiration, than in Trees that are grafted. **1801** *Phil. Trans.* XCII. 46 The utmost imaginable subtility of the corpuscles of light.

8. Delicacy, intricacy; = SUBTLETY 9.

1601 HOLLAND *Pliny* XXII. xxiv. II. 136 There is a reason rendred, full of infinit subtilitie,.. Why the same things seem not alwaies bitter or sweet alike in every mans tast. **1855** BAIN *Senses & Int.* III. i. §15 (1864) 352 An operation of great subtility.

subtilization (ˌsʌ(b)tɪlaɪ'zeɪʃən). [ad. med.L. *subtīlizātio, -ōnem*, n. of action f. *subtīlizāre* to SUBTILIZE. Cf. F. *subtilisation* (from 16th c.), Sp. *su(b)tilizacion*.]

1. The action of the vb. SUBTILIZE; the sublimation or rarefaction of a substance.

1603 HOLLAND *Plutarch's Mor.* 1318 They burne incense by kindling Rosin, for to clense and purifie the aire by this rarefaction and subtilization. **1705** PURSHALL *Mech. Macrocosm* 85 By divers Percolations, and Subtilizations, to get their specifying Parts for the Meliorating of Mettals. **1715** CHEYNE *Philos. Princ.* I. i. 14 It having been always found that their [*sc.* fluids'] Resistances were proportional to their Densities. So that no Subtilization, Division of parts, or Refining can alter their Resistances. **1726** *Gentl. Mag.* LVI. 169 It is.. inconceivable.. that any.. subtilisation, or modification of matter should render it capable of perceiving. **1837** HARRIS *Gt. Teacher* 213 If the soul resulted from any subtilization, juxtaposition, or combinations of brute atoms.

fig. **1856** R. A. VAUGHAN *Mystics* (1860) I. IV. ii. 96 The excessive subtilisation of the One contributes toward the worship of the Manifold. **1882** STALLO in *Nature* XXVI. 542 To convert facts into ideas by a process of dwindling or subtilisation.

2. The drawing of subtle distinctions; over-refinement of argument, etc.

1755 JOHNSON, *Subtilization*,.. Refinement; superfluous acuteness. **1812** W. TAYLOR in *Monthly Rev.* LXVIII. 503 Saint John of Damascus.. introduced to Europe the oriental subtilizations about points of faith. **1833** *New Monthly Mag.* XXXVII. 339 Is his plan practicable? It is not destroyed by its very subtilization?

subtilize ('sʌ(b)tɪlaɪz), *v.* Also 6 subtelise, 7 subtillize, 7– subtilise. [ad. med.L. *subtīlizāre*, f. *subtīlis* SUBTLE *a.*: see -IZE. Cf. F. *subtiliser*, It. *sottilezzare*, Sp. *sutilizar*, Pg. *subtilisar*.]

1. *trans.* To render thin or rare, less gross or coarse, more fluid or volatile; to rarefy, refine. (occas. const. *into*.) Now *rare* or *Obs.*

1597 LOWE *Chirurg.* IX. Cc 3 If the bloud be grosse, vse frictions to subtilize it and make it runne. **1603** HOLLAND *Plutarch's Mor.* 1339 For aire is engendred by the extinction of fire: and the same againe being subtilized and rarefied, produceth fire. **1662** MERRETT tr. *Neri's Art of Glass* xliii, That the water may penetrate and subtilise the ingredients. **1680** BOYLE *Exper. Chem. Princ.* I. 26 Fermentation rarefy's the oyly parts of the Juice of Grapes, and subtilizes them into vinous spirits. **1731** MILLER *Gard. Dict.* s.v. *Leaves*, To subtilize.. the Abundance of nourishing Sap, and to convey it to the little Buds. **1758** REID tr. *Macquer's Chym.* I. 43 Fire only subtilizes and attenuates the earthy matter. **1863** KIRK *Chas. the Bold* I. 61 There [*sc.* Flanders] the products of the earth are mingled, subtilized, shaped into new forms, exchanged, and redistributed.

absol. **1612** *Benvenuto's Passenger* I. ii. 103 Those preserued in pickle doe astringe, subtilize, cut, obsterpe and open. **1725** *Bradley's Fam. Dict.* s.v. *Saxifrage*, The properties of it are to.. Cleanse, Open, Subtilize and Dissolve.

†**b.** To sublimate. *Obs.*

1611 COTGR. s.v. *Sublimé, Argent sublimé*, Mercurie subtilized by the Limbecke. **1799** G. SMITH *Laboratory* I. 120 Repeat this till you can subtilize no more of calx.

†**c.** To comminute. *Obs.*

a **1722** LISLE *Husb.* (1757) 7 Stirring the earth, subtilizing it's parts, and turning it up to the air. **1739** tr. *Algarotti on Newton's Philos.* (1742) II. 102 When they are ground (that is, when their Parts are subtilised) their Colours change.

2. *fig.* To exalt, elevate, sublime, refine.

1638 T. WHITAKER *Blood of Grape* 34 What panick feares doth wine prevent in the Souldier subtilizing their drooping spirits. **1652** J. WRIGHT tr. *Camus' Nat. Paradox* I. 20 What cannot this Passion do when it refineth and subtilizeth thus such young Souls! **1750** JOHNSON *Rambler* No. 114 ⁋5 The art of thievery is.. subtilized to higher degrees of dexterity. **1774** J. BRYANT *Mythol.* II. 276 He tries to subtilize, and refine all the base jargon about Saturn. **1836** *Blackw. Mag.* XL. 329 We subtilize this conception till we fit it to make part of our notion of matter in its utmost abstraction. **1856** R. A. VAUGHAN *Mystics* (1860) I. III. ii. 61 By reducing the soul to its most abstract simplicity, we subtilise it so that it expands into the infinite. **1870** R. C. JEBB *Sophocles' Electra* (ed. 2) p. ix, The mythus.. has been.. gradually subtilized by touches palliating the crime. **1910** *Even. Post* (N.Y.) 15 Jan. 6 The attempt to subtilize and mysticize the plain old freebooting narrative.

b. const. *into, to*; also with *away*.

1644 DIGBY *Nat. Bodies* 3 b, Sence with distinctions they so nicely pare, They subtilize it quite away to aire. **1661** GLANVILL *Van. Dogm.* xvii. 167 The most obvious Verity is subtiliz'd into niceties, and spun into a thread indiscernible by common Opticks. **1742** YOUNG *Nt. Th.* v. 9 To raise the low, to magnify the mean, And subtilize the gross into refin'd. **1852** HAWTHORNE *Blithedale Rom.* xii. (1879) 124 By long brooding over our recollections, we subtilize them into something akin to imaginary stuff.

3. To render (the mind, the senses, etc.) acute or penetrating.

1642 H. MORE *Song of Soul* III. i. xxxii, Rayes down sent From higher sourse the mind do maken pure, Do clear, do subtilise. **1652** J. WRIGHT tr. *Camus' Nat. Paradox* x. 239 See.. how the extremity of danger doth subtilize men's

Wits. **1725** *Bradley's Fam. Dict.* s.v. *Air*, Good Air.. exhilarates the Heart, subtilizes the Senses, sharpens the Understanding. **1865** *Daily Tel.* 9 Nov. 6/6 Subtilising and strengthening his intellect by familiarity with the psychological and ontological problems of the schools.

4. To render subtle, introduce subtleties or nice distinctions into; also, to argue subtly upon.

1599 Sandys *Europæ Spec.* (1629) 155 They which do subtilize the points of goodnes more curiously, will say that Pivs Quintvs was a good Prælat, but no good Prince. **1635** J. Hayward tr. *Biondi's Banish'd Virg.* 33 Speculation too much subtilized makes a man unfit.. for the contemplative life. **1690** Locke *Hum. Und.* iii. x. §7 'Tis no wonder if the wit of man so employ'd, should perplex, involve, and subtilize the signification of sounds. **1732** Waterland *Chr. Vind. agst. Infid.* 48 The Mysticks followed, and deviated in like manner with the former, by over-refining and subtilizing plain Things. **1745** Warburton *Serm.* (2 Pet. i. 6) Wks. 1788 V. 134 They spent their whole lives in agitating and subtilizing questions of faith. **1814** D'Israeli *Quarrels Auth.* (1867) 260 Plain words were subtilised to remove conceits. **1826** Disraeli *Viv. Grey* ii. i, He commented upon expressions, he split and subtilized words.

5. *intr.* To make subtle distinctions; to argue or reason in a subtle manner; to split hairs.

1592 Daniel *Compl. Rosamond* xxxii, Th' one autentique made her fit to teach, The other learnt her how to subtelise. **1606** Sylvester *Du Bartas* ii. iv. *Magnificence* 476 In doubtfull Cases he can subtilize. *a* **1754** Maclaurin *Serm. & Ess.* (1755) 330 It should make us very cautious how we subtilize against it. *a* **1797** H. Walpole *Geo. II* (1847) II. iv. 115 We were not.., by being taught to subtilize, to lose respect for the essential. **1873** Symonds *Grk. Poets* vii. 203 Wrangling, perorating, subtilizing, seeking victory in strife of words.

b. Const. *on, upon, about.* Also in *indirect pass.*

1644 Digby *Nat. Bodies* vi. §1. 40 Of such nature, are the qualities and moodes, that some moderne Philosophers haue so subtilized vpon. **1653** R. G. tr. *Bacon's Hist. Winds* 174 They would not subtilize about that subject in infinitum. **1662** Evelyn *Sculptura* 107 However afterwards subtilized upon and cultivated. **1758** Goldsm. *Mem. Prot.* (1895) II. 103 But what will not Men do.. who subtilize upon the commonest Duties until they no longer appear binding? **1843** Mrs. Browning *Lett. R. H. Horne* (1877) I. 70 It [*sc.* shyness] is a species of consciousness which is.. resolvable into self-love, subtilise about it as we may. **1858–9** G. P. Marsh *Engl. Lang.* xiii. (1862) 193 Rask.. has subtilized so far upon them [*sc.* intonations], that few of his own countrymen, even, have sufficient acuteness of ear to follow him.

Hence **'subtilized** *ppl. a.*

1674 A. G. *Quest. conc. Oath Alleg.* 21 Heat first extenuates, and then draws away the subtiliz'd parts. **1719** Quincy *Compl. Disp.* 9 What passes for Spirit as a Principle, is no other than an highly subtilized Salt. **1741** Middleton *Cicero* II. 549 The Stoics fancied, that the soul was a subtilized, fiery substance. **1858** Sears *Athan.* vii. 64 Not that the spiritual world is a subtilized natural one on the plane of materialism. **1878** Hardy *Ret. Native* iii. viii, Brimming with the subtilised misery that he was capable of feeling.

†**'subtilizer.** *Obs. rare.* [f. prec. + -er¹.] One who makes subtle distinctions or reasons subtly.

1611 Cotgr., *Subtiliseur*, a subtilizor. *a* **1734** North *Life Ld. Kpr. North* (1742) 64 A Slave to Prejudice, a Subtiliser, and Inventor of unheard of Distinctions.

'subtilizing, *vbl. sb.* Also 6–7 -tell-. [-ing¹.]

1. = subtilization 1.

1662 Merrett tr. *Neri's Art of Glass* xvi, *Crocus Martis* is nothing else but a subtilising and Calcination of Iron. **1693** tr. *Blancard's Phys. Dict.* (ed. 2) 89/2 *Sublimatio*..is a Subtilizing of things by gradually Dissolving them, and Exalting them into a purer.. degree of their own Qualities.

2. = subtilization 2.

1596 Warner *Alb. Eng.* x. lix. (1602) 262 For Salomon, diuinely wise, could Subtellizings sound. **1676** Marvell *Mr. Smirke* 20 By which sort of subtilizing the Church hath in former Ages much suffered. **1701** Norris *Ideal World* i. i. 11 A subtilising upon a fine nothing. *a* **1754** Maclaurin *Serm. & Ess.* (1755) 331 These things shew the tendency of incautious subtilizing on the differences between the will and the affections. **1837** Whewell *Hist. Induct. Sci.* (1857) I. 49 The love of subtilizing and commenting.

'subtilizing, *ppl. a.* [-ing².]

†**1.** Rarefying, attenuating. *Obs.*

1611 Cotgr., *Subtiliant*, extenuating, subtilizing. **1673–4** Grew *Anat. Pl.* iii. ii. iv. 132 That so the attenuating and subtilizing Aer, may have a more easie.. admission at the Trunk. **1725** *Bradley's Fam. Dict.* s.v. *Broom*, It's of a provoking and subtilizing nature, and injurious to the Heart and Stomach. *Ibid.*, *Goose-Grass*, It's somewhat abstersive and desiccative, and its Parts are a little subtilizing.

2. That draws subtle distinctions; given to or characterized by subtle reasoning or disputation.

1839 De Quincey *Recoll. Lakes* Wks. 1862 II. 146 Raising a cross-fire of artillery from the subtilizing intellect. **1872** Minto *Engl. Prose Lit.* i. i. 71 His subtilising turn of mind. **1881** A. P. Stanley in *Macm. Mag.* XLIII. 208/1 The liberty sought for was not to be attained by open and legal methods, but by crooked and subtilizing explanations.

subtilly, subtilely ('sʌtɪlɪ, 'sʌbtɪlɪ), *adv.* Now *rare* or *Obs.* Forms: α. 4, 6 subtyly, 5 -tylliche, -telly, 5–6 -tylly, 5–7 -tily, 6 -til(l)ie, 7 -tilley, 4– subtilly. β. 6– subtilely. [f. *subtil*, subtile *a.* + -ly². (Cf. subtly.)]

1. Thinly; finely; in a rarefied manner or form.

α. *a* **1425** tr. *Arderne's Treat. Fistula*, etc. 86 Ich on of þise bi þamself be ful subtily gronden on a stone. **1613** Purchas *Pilgrimage* (1614) 369 The aire was full of formes.. which subtilly and as it were by euaporation, infuse themselues into the eies. **1646** Sir T. Browne *Pseud. Ep.* ii. v. 84 A dram thereof [*sc.* glass], subtilly powdered in butter. **1711** J. Greenwood *Engl. Gram.* 297 If the Breath go more subtilly or thinly out of the Mouth. **1799** G. Smith *Laboratory* I. 107 Subtilly pulverized Venice glass. **1811** Pinkerton *Petral.* II. 423 This iron being unoxygenated, subtilly divided, and dispersed through the whole mass.

β. **1597** A. M. tr. *Guillemeau's Fr. Chirurg.* 28/3 If.. the blood issue out of the same to subtilely. **1757** *Phil. Trans.* I. 164 Whilst the gold continues subtilely divided. **1794** R. J. Sulivan *View Nat.* I. 428 Provided its particles be so subtilely divided and suspended [etc.]. **1823** J. Badcock *Dom. Amusem.* 152 The vapour from the ley.. will penetrate the goods, and operate so subtilely as to disengage the carbonic resin.

2. Craftily, cunningly, insidiously; = subtly 3.

α. *c* **1385** Chaucer *L.G.W.* 797 *Thisbe*, At nygh[t] sche stal a wey ful pryuyly With hire face I-wymplid subtyly. *c* **1386** —— *Pard. T.* 237 This wyn of Spaigne crepeth subtilly In othere wynes growynge faste by. *c* **1386** —— *Merch T.* 759 And subtilly this lettre doun she threste Vnder his pilwe. **1509** Hawes *Past. Pleas.* xi. vi. (1555) Fj, Pryuely The morall sense they cloke full subtyly, In prayse or dysprayse. **1592** Shaks. *Rom. & Jul.* iv. iii. 25 A poyson which the Frier Subtilly hath ministred to haue me dead. **1611** *Bible* Ps. cv. 25 To deale subtilly with his seruants. **1625** Bacon *Ess.*, *Envy* (Arb.) 517 Enuy worketh subtilly, and in the darke. **1660** R. Coke *Power & Subj.* 207 Divers persons having provisions of the Pope.. have.. subtilly excluded divers persons of their benefices. **1667** *Decay Chr. Piety* ii. 214 When he sees his light serve only to aid us the more subtilly to contrive our deeds of darkness. **1668** Rolle *Abridgm.* 91/11 Le Defendant Craftily and subtilly intending to deceive and cozen the Plaintiff.. affirmed.. that the said Gelding was then his own. **1794** G. Adams *Nat. & Exp. Philos.* I. i. 9 This mischief diffuses itself still more subtilly in philosophy.

β. **1658–9** *Burton's Diary* (1828) IV. 261 It was said it was so subtilely and dangerously laid, that it was impossible to prevent it, if divers of them had not been committed. **1727** De Foe *Syst. Magic* i. iv. (1840) 101 You will find the Devil subtilely insinuating dreams into the heads of.. great Men. **1831** Napier *Penins. War* xii. i. (1840) III. 418 The majority of that assembly were so subtilely dealt with by Pedro Souza, that they privately admitted Carlotta's claims. **1837** Carlyle *Fr. Rev.* ii. iii. ii, Our glorious Revolution is subtilely, by black traitors.. perverted to do it.

3. Cleverly, dexterously; = subtly 1. Also, with acuteness or perspicacity.

c **1400** *Pilgr. Sowle* (Caxton) v. v. (1859) 76 Among [the precious stones].. ben sette, wonder subtylly, sterres of huge light. **1484** Caxton *Fables of Æsop* iii. i, The shepherde.. with a nydle subtylly drewe oute of his foote the thorne. **1500–20** Dunbar *Poems* xviii. 48 Gude James the Ferd.. said full subtillie, 'Do weill, and sett not by demying'. **1513** Douglas *Æneis* viii. x. 70 The speyr, and eyk the scheild so subtylly Forgit. **1541** Copland *Guydon's Quest. Cyrurg.* L iij b, Whan they be drye sewe them subtylly, and the lyppes wyl reioyne togydre. **1590** Spenser *F.Q.* ii. ix. 46 They of liuing fire most subtilly Were made, and set in siluer sockets bright. **1750** tr. *Leonardus' Mirr. Stones* 44 They fill the hole with a tincture, or bind it with a ring, or more subtilly, when they work up the leaves of the balasius into the form of diamonds.

†**4.** Of physical perceptions: Keenly, acutely. *Obs.*

c **1430** *Pilgr. Lyf Manhode* i. lxxii. (1869) 42 This heeringe knoweth more subtylliche, and apperceyueth more cleerliche.

5. With subtle distinctions; by subtle argument; = subtly 2.

1678 Cudworth *Intell. Syst.* 586 Sometimes again, this Philosopher subtilly distinguisheth, betwixt νόησις αὐτή.. and τὸ νοοῦν or τὸ ἔχον τὴν νόησιν. *a* **1694** Tillotson *Serm.* (Phil. iii. 8) Wks. (1714) 65 Others have sought to ease themselves of all the evil of affliction by disputing subtilly against it. **1853** Whewell *Grotius* II. 295 These matters might be divided more subtilly. **1860** S. Wilberforce *Addr. Cand. Ordin.* 69 That vast and subtilly contrived system of external formalism.

subtilty ('sʌ(b)tɪltɪ). Forms: 4 subtilete, 4–6 subtilte(e, 5–6 -tylte(e, 5–7 -tialtie, -tiltye, 8 -tilety, 5– subtilty. [Alteration of ME. *sutiite*, subtlety after subtile. Cf. subtility.

Now used as an occas. variant of subtlety in moral and intellectual senses.]

†**1.** Acuteness, penetration, perspicacity; = subtlety 1. *Obs.*

c **1386** Chaucer *Sompn. T.* 582 They seyde subtiltee And heigh wit made hym speke as he spak. **1560** Daus tr. *Sleidane's Comm.* 3 Commonly called thangelical doctor, for the subtiltie of his witte [orig. *ob acumen ingenii*]. **1611** *Bible* Prov. i. 4 To giue subtiltie to the simple, to the yong man knowledge and discretion. **1651** Hobbes *Leviathan* i. xi. 49 A better stratagem, than any that can proceed from subtilty of Wit. **1748** Hartley *Observ. Man* i. i. §1. 298 The Subtilty and Extent of his intellectual Faculties.

†**2.** Skill, cleverness, dexterity; = subtlety 2.

c **1386** Chaucer *Nun's Pr. T.* 499 Ther nys no comparison Bitwixe the wisedom and discrecion Of youre fader and of his subtiltee. **1474** Caxton *Chesse* iii. viii. (1883) 148 Hit is gretter subtilte to kepe well his owne goodes. **1565** Cooper *Thesaurus*, *Solertia*,.. craftinesse, or subtiltie in practisinge good or ill. **1660** H. Bloome *Archit.* C j b, Wit and subtilty in the Art of working in stone.

3. Cunning, craftiness, guile; = subtlety 3.

c **1374** Chaucer *Troylus* v. 1254 What subtilte, what newe lust.. haue ye to me? *c* **1386** —— *Sqr.'s T.* 132 She shal his treson see, His newe loue, and al his subtiltee. **1515** Barclay *Egloges* iii. (1570) C j/1 Blinded with fraude and subtiltie. **1568** Grafton *Chron.* II. 525 The Englishemen entered by subtiltie into the gate, and so gat the Dongeon. **1594** Nashe *Unfort. Trav.* 3 That olde adage, Much curtesie, much subtiltie. **1617** Moryson *Itin.* ii. 16 Having experienced his false subtiltie, and knowing that he sought delaies onely till he could have aide from Spaine. **1671** Milton *P.R.* i. 144 Let him [*sc.* Satan] tempt and now assay His utmost subtilty. **1751** Johnson *Rambler* No. 144 §1 Subtilty furnishes Arms to Impudence, and Invention leads on Credulity. **1834** Newman *Par. Serm.* I. xix. 294 Beware then of the subtilty of your Enemy.

†**4.** A cunning or clever device, artifice, stratagem; = subtlety 4. *Obs.*

c **1386** Chaucer *Can. Yeom. T.* 291 To lerne a lewed man this subtiltee. *c* **1386** —— *Wife's Prol.* 576 (Selden MS.) I bar him on honde he had enchaunted me, My dame taughte me that subtilte. *c* **1440** *Pallad. on Husb.* xi. 290 Grekis haue an other subtiltee. **1471** Caxton *Recuyell* (Sommer) 229 He began to.. auyse hym of a grete subtylte for to come to hys entente. **1558** G. Cavendish *Poems* (1825) II. 142 At the last this subtiltie I fand. **1576** Turbervile *Venerie* xvi, Of the Nature and Subtilties of Hartes. **1655** E. Terry *Voy. E. India* ii. 103 Nature hath taught them this subtilty.. to build their Nests in the twigs, and the utmost boughs of those Trees. **1722** De Foe *Plague* (1754) 38 A Subtilty of one of those Quack-operators with which he gull'd the poor People. **1734** tr. *Rollin's Rom. Hist.* (1827) III. 97 A treasure of subtilties and stratagems of infinite value.

†**5.** *Cookery.* = subtlety 5. *Obs.*

c **1504** in Leland *Collectanea* (1715) VI. 25 A Subtiltie, a Kyng syttyng in a Chayre with many Lordes about hym. **1513** *Bk. Keruynge* in *Babees Bk.* (1868) 272 Fruyter vaunte, with a subtylte. *a* **1548** Hall *Chron.*, *Hen. VIII*, 216 b, The first course.. was xxviii dishes besides subtilties and shippes made of waxe mervailous gorgious to beholde. [**1861** *Our Engl. Home* 70 Notices of the 'subtilties', as the ornamental dishes were called, are curious.]

†**6.** Thinness, tenuity, rarity; = subtlety 8.

a **1395** Hylton *Scala Perf.* (W. de W. 1494) ii. xlvi, By the self lyght maye the soule see the fairhede of angels.. the subtylte of hem in substaunce. **1579** Fulke *Heskins' Parl.* 167 He.. doeth transfourme the bodye of Christe into the subtiltie and thinnesse of a spirite. **1599** Sir J. Davies *Nosce Teipsum* ii. clxxx, Nought tyes the Soule, her subtiltie is such. **1626** Bacon *Sylva* §216 The Sutbilties of Articulate Sounds.. may passe thorow Small Crannies, not confused. *a* **1676** Hale *Prim. Orig. Man.* i. i. 8 Some things though they are.. near unto us, yet are of that subtilty that they escape our Senses. **1815** J. Smith *Panorama Sci. & Art* ii. 179 He supposes the subtilty of this fluid to be so great, that it penetrates the pores of all bodies.

fig. **1750** Johnson *Rambler* No. 13 §14 The Threads of Reasoning.. are frequently drawn to such Subtilty, that common Eyes cannot perceive.. them.

†**b.** Acuity, pungency, penetratingness. *Obs.*

1661 Lovell *Hist. Anim. & Min.* 101 The fat of a Leopard is grosse and sharp, it's subtiltie appeares in those that have a pulse in their temples, and the vertigo, the smell thereof being taken whilest it is rosting. **1794** G. Adams *Nat. & Exp. Philos.* I. i. 28 From the subtilty of the effluvia of bodies retaining their particular properties.

7. Excessive nicety or refinement in argument, etc.

c **1550** Rolland *Crt. Venus* ii. 111 In argumentis full of subtialtie. **1790** Burke *Rev. France* 86, I have nothing to say to the clumsy subtilty of their political metaphysics. **1818** Cruise *Digest.* (ed. 2) V. 452 These reasons savour of a wonderful subtilty. **1869** Lecky *Europ. Mor.* I. 236 Subtilty of motives, refinements of feeling.

b. An instance of this, esp. *pl.*; = subtlety 7.

1474 Caxton *Chesse* iii. v. (1883) 120 He is reputed most sage and wise that argueth and bryngeth in moste subtyltes. **1651** G. W. tr. *Cowel's Inst.* 125 All those Roman subtilties are dissolved into the ancient Law of Nations. **1668** Hale *Rolle's Abridgm.* Pref., Conversant in subtilties of Logick, Philosophy and the Schoolmen. **1681** Stair *Inst. Law Scot.* ii. xxvi. 89 A new Subtilty was invented, to frustrat the Falcidian Law. **1713** Derham *Phys. Theol.* 3 Such as are unacquainted with the Subtilties of Reasoning and Argumentation. **1758** Johnson *Idler* No. 11 ¶2 The numerous lovers of subtilties and paradoxes. **1830** Mackintosh *Eth. Philos.* Wks. 1846 I. 55 Some part of the method and precision of the Schools was lost with their endless subtilties and their barbarous language. **1866** Felton *Greece, Anc. & Mod.* II. 194 In the courts.. the subtilties of argument.. had.. long been.. reduced to system.

†**8.** Delicacy, fineness (of physical objects, movements). *Obs.*

1616 B. Jonson *Devil an Ass* ii. i. 86 The subtilty o' my yest. **1626** Bacon *Sylva* §98 Whatsoeuer is Inuisible, either in respect of the Finenesse of the Body it selfe;.. Or of the Subtilty of the Motion. **1660** Bloome *Archit.* B j b, The one after mans shape,.. the other with womans subtilty. **1691** Ray *Creation* i. (1704) 197 How would he have admired the immense Subtilty of their Parts. **1794** G. Adams *Nat. & Exp. Philos.* III. xxix. 186 An active medium.. which.. can so far deceive us by the subtilety of its vibrations.

'sub-,title, *sb.* [sub- 5 b.]

1. A subordinate or additional title of a literary work.

1825 T. H. Horne *Outlines for Classification of Library* 86 To each Volume should be prefixed.. an Alphabetical Table of th several Titles and sub-titles. **1865** Geo. Eliot *Let.* 16 Sept. (1956) IV. 203 Mr. Lewes.. thinks my suggestion as to the sub-title acceptable. **1878** *N. Amer. Rev.* CXXVII. 346 It is the sub-title rather than the title that indicates the chief importance of his work. **1884** Jennings *Croker Papers* III. p. xxiii, 'Sybil, or the New Nation', as the book was at first called, the sub-title being afterwards changed to 'The Two Nations'. **1895** *Bookman* Oct. 20/1 She should either have called it 'Rome in the Dark Ages', or have added 'The Dark Ages' as a subtitle.

2. A repetition of the chief words of the full title of a book at the top of the first page of text; also, a half-title.

1890 *N. & Q.* Ser. vii. IX. 143/2 Title and contents, xii, followed by sub-title to whist. **1896** *Moxon's Mech. Exerc.*, *Printing* p. xviii, The running title and the sub-titles.

3. *Cinemat.* and *Television.* A caption which appears on a cinema or television screen, esp. to translate the dialogue or to explain the action. Freq. in *pl.*

1909 *Moving Picture World* 27 Feb. 235/1 If the audience is not given time to read the sub-titles or if they are indistinct..the spectators lose the thread. **1924** WODEHOUSE *Leave it to Psmith* i. 30 What he did not know about erring wives and licentious clubmen could have been written in a sub-title. **1931** B. BROWN *Talking Pictures* xi. 287 Another [camera].. photographs a sub-title tablet about a foot across and illuminated by a couple of arc lamps. **1944** [see DUB *v.*[5]]. **1957** M. SUMMERTON *Sunset Hour* x. 140 The French film was mediocre. I ignored the sub-titles, testing my ear on the dialogue. **1975** G. HOWELL *In Vogue* 5/1 The subtitles to films brought American slang to Britain... 'Beatrix Esmond goes nix on the love-stuff.'

So **'subtitle** *v. trans.*, (*a*) to furnish with a specified sub-title; (*b*) *Cinemat.* and *Television*, to furnish (a film or programme) with subtitles. Also **'subtitled** *ppl. a.*; **'subtitler**; **'subtitling** *vbl. sb.*

1891 J. W. EBSWORTH *Roxb. Ball.* VII. 358 Another ballad, sub-titled, 'The Willow Green turned into Carnation'. **1895** *Advance* (Chicago) 15 Aug. 236/3 The *Countess Bettina* is subtitled the History of an Innocent Scandal. **1930** E. V. KNOX in *Living Age* 1 Apr. 188 It is a *lingua franca*, or a *lingua californica*... The subtitlers have created a wilderness and called it prose. **1948** *Brit. Film Rev.* Apr. 10 The Cinemas of Great Britain are now showing the sub-titled films so well known to readers in other parts of the world. *Ibid.*, It cannot be said that subtitling in England is uniformly good. **1950** *Jrnl. Soc. Motion Picture & Television Engin.* Nov. 536 Several operations are necessary in order to subtitle pictures. **1968** *Punch* 31 Jan. 154/3 The sub-titler.. can sum up a passage of flashy philosophy in one profound-seeming sentence. **1979** K. CONLON *Move in Game* vi. 71 'Tell me some more about academic life.'.. 'Well... There were subtitled foreign films.' **1982** *English World-Wide* III. I. 53 Films are virtually all subtitled.

subtle ('sʌt(ə)l), *a.* Forms: *α.* 3–7 sotill, 4–5 -el, il(le, -yl(e, 4–6 -ell, 5–6 -yll, (4 -ele, -ile, -ylle, soutil, -yle, 5 sotule, 6 sot(t)le); 4–5 sutell, -il, 4–6 -el, 5–6 suttell, -ill, 5–7 suttle, 6–7 sutle (4 sutile, -ill, 5 -elle, -ille, suttyle, *Sc.* sutaille, suttale, sittell, 6 sut(t)yll). *β.* 6– subtle. [a. OF. *soutil*, *sotil*, *sutil* (12th c.), mod.F. *subtil* (see SUBTILE) = Pr. *sotil*, It. *sottile*, Sp. *sutil*, Pg. *subtil*:—L. *subtīlem*, nom. *-īlis*, for **subtēlis*:—**subtexlis* app. finely woven, f. *sub* under + **texlā*, *tēla* woven stuff, web (cf. TEXTURE).

In the 1st Folio of Shakspere the instances are about equally divided between the spellings *subtle* and *subtil(e, -ill*. In the first editions of Milton's poems the spelling *suttle* (with *suttlety*, *suttly*) is the only one, except in *Paradise Regained*, which has *subtle* (with *subtilty*).]

1. Of thin consistency, tenuous; not dense, rarefied; hence, penetrating, pervasive or elusive by reason of tenuity (now chiefly of odours).

13.. *E.E. Allit. P.* A. 1050 Þurȝ woȝe & won my lokyng ȝede, For sotyle cler moȝt lette no lyȝt. *c* **1400** MAUNDEV. (Roxb.) iii. 9 Abouen on þir hilles es þe aer so clere and so sutill þat men may fele na wynd þare. **1422** YONGE tr. *Secr. Secr.* lxiv. 240 Sutil and thyn spetil that descendyth..fro the Palete of the mouth to the tonge. *a* **1566** R. EDWARDS *Damon & Pithias* (1571) Cij b, But mee thinkes, this is a pleasant Citie, The Seate is good,.. The Ayre subtile and fine. **1660** BOYLE *New Exp. Phys.-Mech.* ix. 74 The most subtle Chymical Spirits. **1665** DRYDEN *Ind. Emp.* II. i, Arise ye subtle Spirits, that can spy. **1799** *Med. Jrnl.* I. 250 There was only one part of the air, namely, the most subtle and elastic, that could be called vital. **1842** BROWNING *In a Gondola* 33 The Arab sage In practising with gems can loose Their subtle spirit in his cruce And leave but ashes. **1863** TYNDALL *Heat* ii. 23 The material theory supposes heat to be..a subtle fluid stored up in the inter-atomic spaces of bodies. **1891** FARRAR *Darkness & Dawn* xix, A sweet and subtle odour seemed to wrap her round in its seductive atmosphere.

2. Of fine or delicate texture or composition. *Obs.* exc. *arch.*

1382 WYCLIF *Isa.* xix. 9 Plattende and weuende sotile thingus. *a* **1662** HEYLIN *Laud* II. (1668) 331 Many a fine and subtle Carpet. **1705** ATTERBURY *Serm.* Luke xvi. 31 (1726) II. ii. 65 Their fine and subtle Texture [*sc.* of the works of nature]. **1790** COWPER *Odyss.* XIX. 173 A robe Of amplest measure and of subtlest woof. **1827** KEBLE *Chr. Y.*, *Sun. bef. Adv.* x, Thinner than the subtlest lawn.

†**b.** Of food: Delicate, light. *Obs.*

a **1400–50** *Wars Alex.* 2923 Þare sesonde was a soper þe sotelest vndire heuen. **1422** YONGE tr. *Secr. Secr.* lxii. 239 Sotyll diet is beste. *c* **1450** CAPGRAVE *Life St. Aug.* 47 Grete wast was not in his hous of sotil metes.

†**3.** Of small thickness or breadth; thin, slender, fine. *Obs.*

1382 WYCLIF *Lev.* xiii. 30 The heer ȝalow, and sotiler than it is wont. *c* **1386** CHAUCER *Knt.'s T.* 1172 The sharpe swerd ouer his heed Hangynge by a soutil twynes threed. *c* **1407** LYDG. *Reason & Sens.* 1150 Hir clothing..Wroght and wove..With sotil thredes softe and smale. **1460–70** *Bk. Quinte Essence* 9 If ȝe wole not make lymayl of gold, þanne make þerof a sotil þinne plate. **1606** SHAKS. *Tr. & Cr.* v. ii. 151 No Orifex for a point as subtle, As Ariachnes broken woofe to enter. *a* **1680** BUTLER *Rem.* (1759) I. 129 Tools of sharp and subtle Edges.

†**b.** Of a ship: = SUBTILE 3 b. *Obs.*

1511 *Guylforde's Pilgr.* (Camden) 7 An C Galyes, grete bastardes and sotell.

†**4.** Finely powdered; (of particles) fine, minute.

1394 in Heath *Grocers' Comp.* (1869) 60 [The unjust mode of garbling spices and other] sotill wares. **1426** LYDG. *De Guil. Pilgr.* 16818 The Sotyl smale Sandys and gravell off the See. *c* **1460** J. RUSSELL *Bk. Nurture* 57 Loke þy salte be sutille, whyte, fayre and drye. **1460–70** *Bk. Quinte Essence* 4 Selid with þe seel of lute of wijsdom, maad of þe sotillest flour. **1753** *Chambers' Cycl.* Suppl. s.v. *Sublimable*, Giving wings, as it were, to its subtle particles, so that they may ascend with its easily sublimable matter.

5. Of immaterial things: Not easily grasped, understood, or perceived; †intricate, abstruse. (Now merged in sense 6.)

1340 HAMPOLE *Pr. Consc.* 1794 Þe dede es swa sutil and pryve, þat na man may it properly se. *c* **1350** *Will. Palerne* 2603 Sechande towarde cisile þe sotilest weyes. **1357** *Lay Folks' Catech.* (L.) 244 We schul wele wyte þat þese thre thyngys ben wel sotel and diuers. **1377** LANGL. *P. Pl.* B. xv. 48 Alle þe sciences vnder sonne and alle þe sotyle craftes I wolde I knewe. **1387** TREVISA *Higden* (Rolls) VII. 69 Curious and sotil artes and sciens. **1616** B. JONSON *Devil an Ass* II. i. 114 There's not place, To gi' you demonstration of these things. They are a little to subtle. **1667** MILTON *P.L.* VIII. 192 Things remote From use, obscure and suttle. *a* **1680** BUTLER *Rem.* (1759) II. 167 The subtler Words and Notions are, the nearer they are to Nonsense.

6. Fine or delicate, esp. to such an extent as to elude observation or analysis.

1639 W. CARTWRIGHT *Royal Slave* II. i, Kings' pleasures are more subtle than to be Seen by the vulgar. *a* **1648** LD. HERBERT *Hen. VIII* (1683) 449, I told her it should be no pain, it was so sotell (for so is his word). **1805** WORDSW. *Prelude* I. 549 How other pleasures have been mine, and joys of subtler origin. **1849** RUSKIN *Seven Lamps* v. §9. 144 The seven are in a most subtle alternating proportion. **1855** BAIN *Senses & Int.* II. iii. §20. 569 Many inconsistencies are too subtle for the detection of an ordinary mind. **1856** FROUDE *Hist. Eng.* (1858) II. vi. 7 The influence of the popes in England was of that subtle kind which was not so readily defeated. **1879** *Good Words* Dec. 831/1 What subtle associations will recall the phantoms of the past.

7. Of craftsmen, etc.: Skilful, clever, expert, dexterous. (Const. *of*.) *arch.*

a **1300** *Cursor M.* 325 First in his witte he all purueid His werc, als dos þe sotill wright. ? *a* **1366** CHAUCER *Rom. Rose* 688 Of song sotil and wys. **13..** *Minor Poems fr. Vernon MS.* xlix. 339 Þe more sotil he is of þat art. *c* **1450** *Merlin* 362 [He] made..a Chekier of golde and Ivory half parted, ffor he was right sotill of soche crafte. **1821** BYRON *Two Foscari* IV. i, I..bribed no subtle master Of the destructive art. **1859** FITZGERALD *Omar* xliii, The subtle Alchemist that [can] in a Trice Life's leaden Metal into Gold transmute.

b. *transf.*

c **1386** CHAUCER *Knt's. T.* 1191 With soutil pencel was depeynted this storie. **1422** YONGE tr. *Secr. Secr.* lviii. 220 He is of sotille ymagynacion as of hand-werkys. **1703** PRIOR *Advice to Painter* 22 Wks. 1907 II. 290 All Nature's Gifts refin'd by subtlest Art. **1867** RUSKIN *Time & Tide* ii. §7 To attain..more subtle and exemplary skill in his own craft. **1880** SMILES *Duty* iii. 50 The Indians are clever workmen, with ingenious, subtle fingers.

c. Of animals. *rare.*

† *subtle jack*: ? the weaver-bird.

1605 SHAKS. *Macb.* III. i. 96 The valued file Distinguishes the swift, the slow, the subtle. **1699** DAMPIER *Voy.* II. II. 68 Subtle Jacks are Birds as big as Pigeons... They are called by the English *Subtle Jacks*, because of this uncommon way of building. **1854** *Poultry Chron.* I. 419 The..most subtle, cunning, sharpest-flying Pigeon for Homeing.

†**8.** Of things: Characterized by cleverness or ingenuity in conception or execution; cleverly designed or executed, artfully contrived. *Obs.*

a **1300** *Cursor M.* 4750 In sum bok find i þar a wile þat ioseph fand þat was sutile. **1375** BARBOUR *Bruce* XIX. 32 Sa sutell purchass can he ma, That he gert tak thame euirilkane. **1393** LANGL. *P. Pl.* C. XI. 207 For god seith hit hymself 'shal neuere good appel þorw no sotel science on sour stock growe'. **1473** WARKW. *Chron.* (Camden) 26 He..with a sotule poynte of werre, gate and enteryd Seynt Michaels Mount. **1667** MILTON *P.L.* I. 727 From the arched roof Pendant by suttle Magic many a row Of Starry Lamps.

9. Of persons, their faculties, actions: Characterized by penetration, acumen, or discrimination. Now with implication of (excessive) refinement or nicety of thought, speculation, or argument.

α. **13..** *Cursor M.* 13443 (Gött.) Of godspellers he was þe ferth. Marc, luca, mathe, his felaus, Bot iohn was sotilest in saus. **1340** *Ayenb.* 24 Sotil wyt wel uor to vynde. *c* **1386** CHAUCER *Merch. T.* 183 Sondry scoles maken sotile clerkis. ? *a* **1400** *Morte Arth.* 808 Two phylozophirs..In the seuyne scyence the suteleste fondene. *c* **1440** *Gesta Rom.* xvi. 55 (Add. MS.), The second best counseilour, and the thirde the sotelest enserchour. **1502** ATKYNSON tr. *De Imitatione* I. v. (1893) 157 The fame of sotell phylosophers. **1579** G. HARVEY *Letter-bk.* (Camden) 71 Y[e] suttle and intricate acumen of Aristotle. *c* **1597** in *Harington's Nugæ Ant.* (1804) I. 188 The narrowest examiners and suttellest distinguyshers of wordes. **1644** MILTON *Areop.* (Arb.) 68 A Nation not slow and dull, but..acute to invent, suttle and sinewy to discours.

β. **1597** HOOKER *Eccl. Pol.* v. lxvii. 176 Not for the exercising of our curious & subtle wits. **1769** ROBERTSON *Chas. V*, VII. III. 62 The subtle dexterity of a scholastic metaphysician. **1807** CRABBE *Par. Reg.* III. 115 The young how brave, how subtle were the old. **1814** BYRON *Ode Napoleon* viii, A subtle disputant on creeds. **1840** MACAULAY *Ess.*, *Ranke's Hist.* (1897) 549 Subtle speculations touching the Divine attributes. **1842** H. ROGERS *Introd. Burke's Wks.* I. 40 A close and subtle analysis of the mental phenomena. **1844** DICKENS *Mart. Chuz.* xxvi, The laws of sympathy between beards and birds ..are questions for the subtle reasoning of scientific bodies. **1872** FREEMAN *Gen. Sk. Eur. Hist.* v. 97 As the Greeks had in old times produced so many subtle philosophers, so they now produced equally subtle divines.

†**10.** Of persons or animals: Crafty, cunning; treacherously or wickedly cunning, insidiously sly, wily. *Obs.*

α. **1357** *Lay Folks' Catech.* (L.) 1220 Þey be mysdoers, sotel, and slyhtful dysseyuers. **1446** LYDG. *Night. Poems* I. 136 Whom that the sotell serpent can deceyue. *c* **1470** HENRY *Wallace* I. 273 Suthroun ar full sutaille euirilk man. **1535** COVERDALE *Gen.* iii. 1 The serpent was sotyller then all the beastes of the felde. **1559** *Mirr. Mag.* (1563) Dj, The Wolfe doth spoyle, the suttle Fox doth pyke. **1583** GOLDING *Calvin on Deut.* iii. xvi. 94/1 He that is suttlelest and fullest of shiftes. **1631** MILTON *Sonn.* vii. 1 How soon hath Time the suttle theef of youth, Stoln on his wing my three and twentith yeer! **1667** —— *P.L.* VII. 495 The Serpent suttl'st Beast of all the field.

β. **1593** SHAKS. *2 Hen. VI*, v. i. 191 A subtle Traitor needs no Sophister. **1598** —— *Merry W.* III. i. 103 Am I subtle? Am I a Machiuell? **1671** MILTON *P.R.* I. 465 The subtle Fiend..Dissembl'd, and this answer smooth return'd. **1709** E. W. *Donna Rosina* 67 I'll tell you what I would do, said this Subtle Baggage. **1781** COWPER *Conversat.* 809 The subtle and injurious may be just, And he grown chaste that was the slave of lust.

†**b.** Of actions, thoughts, etc. *Obs.*

α. *c* **1380** WYCLIF *Wks.* (1880) 278 Þe sotil amortasynge of seculer lordischipis þat is don bi menene hondis in fraude of þe kyngis statute. **1382** —— *2 Cor.* xi. 3 The serpent disceyuede Eue with his sutil wordis. **1429** *Rolls of Parlt.* IV. 349/1 Grete damagis and sotil deceitis. *c* **1470** HENRY *Wallace* I. 84 Be suttale band thai cordyt of this thing. *c* **1510** MORE *Picus* Wks. 23 Against euery sottle suggestion of vice. *a* **1568** ASCHAM *Scholem.* I. (Arb.) 55 The sotle inticement of som lewd seruant. **1667** MILTON *P.L.* IX. 184 His head.., well stor'd with suttle wiles.

β. **1607** SHAKS. *Timon* IV. iii. 515 Is not thy kindnesse subtle, couetous? **1671** MILTON *P.R.* IV. 308 All his tedious talk is but vain boast, Or subtle shifts conviction to evade.

†**c.** Of ground: Tricky. *Obs.*

1607 SHAKS. *Cor.* v. ii. 20 Like to a Bowle vpon a subtle ground I haue tumbled past the throw. **1630** B. JONSON *Chloridia* B, Vpon Tityus his brest, that (for sixe of the nine acres) is counted the subtlest bowling-ground in all Tartary.

11. Working imperceptibly or secretly, insidious.

1601 SHAKS. *Twel. N.* I. v. 316, I feele this youths perfections With an inuisible, and subtle stealth To creepe in at mine eyes. **1788** GIBBON *Decl. & F.* xliii. IV. 331 The winds might diffuse that subtle venom. **1818** BYRON *Ch. Har.* IV. cxxxvi, From the loud roar of foaming calumny To the small whisper of the as paltry few, And subtler venom of the reptile crew. **1878** *Masque Poets* 25 What subtle drug shall give release with slightest pain before it slay.

†**12.** Of weight: = SUBTILE 12 a; now SUTTLE. *Obs.*

1622 MALYNES *Anc. Law-Merch.* 22 The Custome of Antuerp is to weigh by the hundreth pounds euen weight called Subtle, for the which commonly there is allowed at the weigh-house 101 lb. **1636** in Foster *Crt. Min. E. Ind. Comp.* (1907) 203, 500. wt. subtle of pepper.

13. *Comb.* chiefly parasynthetic adjs., as ***subtle-brained***, ***-cadenced***, ***-headed***, ***-meshed***, ***-nosed***, ***-paced***, ***-scented***, ***-shadowed***, ***-souled***, ***-thoughted***, ***-tongued***, ***-witted***. Also objective, as ***subtle-subtilising*** vbl. sb.

1603 FLORIO *Montaigne* II. xvii. (1632) 366 The more ..*subtle-brained a man is, the more is he hated. **1818** KEATS *Endym.* I. 493 'Twas a lay More *subtle cadenced.. Than Dryope's lone lulling of her child. **1571** GOLDING *Calvin on Ps.* xvii. 4 There bee some *suttleheaded persones, which mark other mennes dooinges narowly. **1596** SPENSER *View St. Ireland* Wks. (Globe) 618/2 Yet will some one or other suttle-headed fellowe..pike some quirke. **1907** *Academy* 10 Aug. 766/1 On that side he laid a *subtle-meshed web from end to end. **1561** T. NORTON *Calvin's Inst.* I. 32 The *suttlenosed [F. *gaudisseurs*] and babbling men do easily mock out this. **1830** TENNYSON *Isabel* 21 A most silver flow Of *subtle-paced counsel in distress. **1871** ROSSETTI *Poems*, *Love's Nocturn* xv, So do mounting vapours wreathe *Subtle-scented transports. **1609** DANIEL *Civ. Wars* VII. xiv, Here Scottish border broyles, and feares of Fraunce,..Brought forth a *suttle-shadowed countenance. **1819** SHELLEY *Peter Bell 3rd* v. ii, He was a mighty poet—and A *subtle-souled psychologist. **1860** SYMONDS in *Life* (1895) I. 362 Refinements and *subtle-subtilisings of all sorts. **1830** TENNYSON *Ode to Memory* 118 Those whom passion hath not blinded, *Subtle-thoughted, myriad-minded. **1639** G. DANIEL *Ecclus.* xxi. 22 The proud Orator And *Subtle-Tongu'd Man. **1553** GRIMALDE *Cicero's Offices* III. (1558) 137 It is a part not..of a good man: but rather of a *suttlewitted. **1664** BUTLER *Hud.* II. iii. 470 But Sidrophel more subtle-witted, Cry'd out. **1820** SHELLEY *Hymn Merc.* lxvi, Jupiter..Laughed heartily to hear the subtle-witted Infant give such a plausible account.

†**'subtle**, *v.* *Obs.* Also 4–5 so-, sou-, sutille, -ele, -ile. [a. OF. *soutill(i)er* = It. *sottigliare* :—med.L. *subtīliāre*, f. *subtilis* SUBTLE *a.*]

1. *refl.* and *intr.* To devise subtleties or subtle distinctions, to argue subtly.

a **1340** HAMPOLE *Psalter* ii. 2 Whan þa þat sould gif þaim hally til godis luf..sutils þaim in swilk thynge þat draghs þaim fra thoght of heuen in till werldis besynes. **1362** LANGL. *P. Pl.* A. XI. 139 Hit [*sc.* Theology] is no science forsoþe to sotilen þer-Inne.

2. *intr.* To scheme, plan craftily. Also with clause.

c **1380** WYCLIF *Sel. Wks.* II. 379 Þe fend sutilliþ evere aȝens holy chirche. **1393** LANGL. *P. Pl.* C. XXI. 336 Ich sotilede how ich myghte Lette hem þat louede hym nat lest þei wolde hym martrye.

3. *trans.* To devise cleverly.

1377 LANGL. *P. Pl.* B. x. 214 Alle þise science I my-self sotiled and ordeyned. *Ibid.* XIX. 454 Eche man sotileth a sleight synne forto hyde.

4. To attenuate, reduce.

c **1400** *Lanfranc's Cirurg.* 229 Þou must sotile his dietyng, & he schal not ete to miche.

5. ? To pulverize, reduce to ashes. *nonce-use.*

1624 FLETCHER *Rule a Wife* IV. i, A fire subtle ye, are ye so crafty?

Hence †**'subtling** *vbl. sb.* (in 5 **sotelinge, sutiling**), = SUBTILIZATION.

1398 TREVISA *Barth. De P.R.* XIX. xi. (Bodl. MS.), White coloure is igendred for þynnynge & sotelinge of parties of þe mater. *c* **1449** PECOCK *Repr.* II. ix. 195 Of al such craft and sutiling ouȝten alle Cristen men be waar, that thei therbi be not bigilid.

†**'subtlehead.** *Obs. rare.* In 4 sotylhede. [f. SUBTLE *a.* + -HEAD. Cf. MHG. *subtîlheit.*] Subtlety.

1340 *Ayenb.* 117 He ne may him-zelue yknawe, ne him uestni ine þe strengþe of his uyendes, ne hare sotylhede.

subtleness ('sʌt(ə)lnɪs). [-NESS.] Subtlety.

1398 TREVISA *Barth. De P.R.* V. xxxviii. (Bodl. MS.) He [*sc.* the stomach] is senewy to resceyue and haue þe sotilnes of feling and vertu and strengþe of appetitee. *c* **1430** *Syr Gener.* (Roxb.) 8297 Yf she had wist of this sotelnes She wold not haue goote the ring I-wis. *c* **1560** A. SCOTT *Poems* (S.T.S.) xxix. 17 Thair hairtis ar sett wᵗ sittelness. **1836** SMART, *Subtleness, Subtlety*, artfulness, cunning. **1870** *Daily News* 7 Oct., Its occasional subtlenesses of thought. **1909** H. M. GWATKIN *Early Ch. Hist.* xix. II. 178 The subtleness of sin.

†**'subtleship.** *Obs. rare*⁻¹. [-SHIP.] Subtlety.

1614 SYLVESTER *Bethulia's Rescue* IV. 28 Wks. (1641) 495/1 Let the smooth cunning of my soothing lips Surprise the fell Fox in his Suttleships.

subtlety ('sʌt(ə)ltɪ). Forms: α. 4 sotilti, sutil(l)te, suttilte, 4–5 sotelte(e, -ilte(e, -ylte(e, sutelte(e, 4–6 soteltie, 5 -ty, -ellte, sutiltee, sutteltee, 5–6 sotyltie, suttelte, 5–7 suttleti e, -ty, 6 sotiltie, -tye, sottelte, souttiltey, sutteltie, suttelte, suttylt(e)y, -ie. β. 5–6 subtelte, 6 -tie, 6–7 subtletie, 6– subtlety. [a. OF. *su-*, *soutilte:*—L. *subtīlitās*, *-ātem*, n. of quality f. *subtīlis* SUBTLE. The spelling was latinized in the 16th c. like that of *subtle*. Cf. SUBTILITY, SUBTILTY.]

1. Of persons, the mind, its faculties or operations: Acuteness, sagacity, penetration: in modern use chiefly with implication of delicate or keen perception of fine distinctions or nice points.

α. **1340** HAMPOLE *Pr. Consc.* 5903 Gudes of grace may þir be, Mynde, and witte, and sutilte. **1422** YONGE tr. *Secr. Secr.* vi. 134 What aualyth Sotilte of vndyrstondynge and connynge? **1538** STARKEY *England* I. iv. 116 Ther ys nothyng so true and manyfest, but the suttylty of mannys reson may deuyse somethyng to say contrary.

β. *c* **1400** *Rom. Rose* 7471 Who so that hath hadde the subtelte The double sentence for to se. **1553** EDEN *Treat. Newe Ind.* (Arb.) 24 They greatly excel all other men in subteltie of wit and knowledge. **1597** HOOKER *Eccl. Pol.* v. lxvii. (1611) 363 They labour..by subtletie of wit to make some shew of agreement. **1638–56** COWLEY *Davideis* III. *note* 32 Some with much subtlety, and some probability, understand a Pillar of Salt, to signifie only an Everlasting Pillar, of what matter soever. **1780** HARRIS *Philol. Enq.* Wks. (1841) 508 Though that subtlety might sometimes have led them into refinements rather frivolous, yet have they given eminent samples of penetrating ingenuity. **1855** MACAULAY *Hist. Eng.* xiv. III. 409 Wit, taste, amplitude of comprehension, subtlety in drawing distinctions. **1872** MINTO *Engl. Prose Lit.* I. i. 47 His subtlety in distinguishing wherein things agree and wherein they differ.

†**2.** Skill, cleverness, dexterity. *Obs.*

c **1375** *Sc. Leg. Saints* xi. (*Symon & Iudas*) 271 A kyste þat wrocht is all with costlyke wark & sutelte. *c* **1400** *Destr. Troy* 8395 Miche soteltie, for-sothe, settyng of notes, Crafte þat was coynt, knawyng of tymes.

3. Craftiness, cunning, esp. of a treacherous kind; guile, treachery.

α. **1375** BARBOUR *Bruce* I. 172 Throuch gret sutelte and ghyle,..He was arestyt syne and tane. *c* **1394** *P. Pl. Crede* 56 Ʒet seyn they in here sutilte to sottes in townes, þei comen out of Carmeli Crist for to followen. *c* **1410** HOCCLEVE *Mother of God* 46 Lest our fo, the feend, thurgh his sotiltee, ..Me ouercome with his treecherie. **1456** SIR G. HAYE *Law Arms* (S.T.S.) 18 To wirk with sutelte of ypocrisy. **1526** TINDALE *Matt.* xxvi. 4 The chefe prestes..heelde a counsell, howe they mygt take Jesus by suttelte, and kyll him. **1577** GRANGE *Golden Aphrod.* G iv, She turned him for his suttlety in stealyng the same into a wylie Foxe. **1667** MILTON *P.L.* IX. 93 In the wilie Snake, What-ever sleights none would suspicious mark, As from his wit and native suttletie Proceeding.

β. **1532** *Rom. Rose* 6172 in *Chaucer's Wks.* 160b/1, I dwell with hem that proude be And ful of wyles and subtelte. **1548–9** (Mar.) *Bk. Com. Prayer, Litany*, Those euyls, whiche the crafte and subteltie of the deuyll or man worketh against us. **1656** BRAMHALL *Reply S.W.* 3 To observe with what subtlety this case is proposed, that the Church of England agreed with the Church of Rome. **1781** GIBBON *Decl. & F.* xvii. II. (1787) 73 The laws were violated by power, or perverted by subtlety. **1821** BYRON *Cain* III. i, Surely a father's blessing may avert A reptile's subtlety.

†**4.** An ingenious contrivance; a crafty or cunning device; an artifice; *freq.* in unfavourable sense, a wily stratagem or trick, something craftily invented. *Obs.*

α. **1375** BARBOUR *Bruce* III. 611 Bot giff we fynd sum sutelte, Ourtane all sone sall we be. *c* **1380** WYCLIF *Wks.* (1880) 20 Bi false procurynge of matrymonye bi soteltees and queyntese. *c* **1420** *Liber Cocorum* (1862) 5 Anoþer sotelte I wylle telle. Take harpe strynges made of bowel [etc.]. *c* **1450** *Bk. Curtasye* 758 in *Babees Bk.*, Yf þo syluer dysshe wylle algate brenne, A sotelte I wylle þe kenne. ? **1545** BRINKLOW *Compl.* vii. (1874) 20 How many gyles and suttylteys be there, to auoyde and escape the seruyng of the kyngs wrytt. **1671** MILTON *Samson* 56 Liable to fall By weakest suttleties.

β. **1576** TURBERV. *Venerie* xxix, Let him marke the place where he hath fed, and whereon also to marke his subtelties and craftes. **1654** BRAMHALL *Just Vind.* vii. (1661) 224 It hath been an old Subtlety of the Popes..to make the world believe that nothing could be done without them.

5. *Cookery.* A highly ornamental device, wholly or chiefly made of sugar, sometimes eaten, sometimes used as a table decoration. *Obs.* exc. *Hist.*

? *c* **1390** *Form of Cury* in Warner *Antiq. Culin.* (1791) 4 It techith for to make curious potages and meetes, and sotiltees. *c* **1440** in *Househ. Ord.* (1790) 450 A soteltee Seint-jorge on horsebak, and sleynge the dragun. **1467–8** *Durham Acc. Rolls* (Surtees) 92 Pro le Tynfole empt. pro ornacione et pictura del soteltez erga festum Natal. Domini. **1517** TORKINGTON *Pilgr.* (1884) 7 They mad vs goodly Chere wᵗ Diverse Sotylties as Comfytes and Marche Panys. **1552** LATIMER *Serm. Par. King* (Parker Soc.) II. 139 At the end of the dinner they have certain subtleties, custards, sweet and delicate things. [**1768** H. WALPOLE *Let. to Cole* 6 June, I am no culinary antiquary: the Bishop of Carlisle, who is, I have often heard talk of a *sotelte* [printed *sotelle*], as an ancient dish. **1852** MISS YONGE *Cameos* II. xxxi. (1877) 327 The feast was entirely of fish: but they were of many kinds, and were adorned in the quaintest fashions, with sotilties, or subtleties. **1875** JEAFFRESON *Bk. Table* I. 133 A subtelty, representing a pelican on a nest with her birds.]

†**6.** Abstruseness, complexity, intricacy; also *pl.*, abstruse or intricate matters. *Obs.*

13.. *Seuyn Sag.* (W.) 48, I wil that ye teche him euyn The sutelte of sience seuyn. **1387** TREVISA tr. *Higden* (Rolls) I. 15 Nouȝt sotilte of sentence, noþer faire floriscynge of wordes, but swetnesse of deuocion of þe matire schal regne in þis book. *c* **1407** LYDG. *Reason & Sens.* 1700 [Mercury] doth habounde In sotyltes ful profounde. **1535** COVERDALE *Wisd.* viii. 8 She knoweth yᵉ sotilties of wordes, & can expounde darke sentences. **1591** SPARRY tr. *Cattan's Geomancie* A 4, The..suttletie of this Science.

7. A refinement or nicety of thought, speculation, or argument; a fine distinction; a nice point.

1654 BRAMHALL *Just Vind.* ii. (1661) 28 That prefers not a subtlety or an imaginary truth before the bond of peace. *a* **1680** BUTLER *Rem.* (1759) II. 486 They that are curious in Subtleties, and ignorant in things of solid Knowledge. **1760** STERNE *Tr. Shandy* IV. xxix, My father delighted in subtleties of this kind. **1837** WHEWELL *Hist. Induct. Sci.* (1857) I. 191 The..unprofitable subtleties of the schools. **1868** MILMAN *St. Paul's* vi. 115 The lecturer had no logical subtleties. **1876** FREEMAN *Norm. Conq.* V. xxiv. 369 [He] held that land as a plain matter of fact, and without any legal subtleties, as a personal gift from King William. **1903** LD. HALSBURY in *Law Rep.* 1 *K.B. Div.* 413 By ingenious subtleties to bring within the grasp of the tax something which was not intended.

8. Thinness, tenuity, exility; penetrativeness arising from lack of density.

1691 RAY *Creation* I. (1704) 109 The subtlety, activity, and penetrancy of its effluvia. **1748** HARTLEY *Observ. Man* I. i. §1. 24 Admitting the Existence and Subtlety of the Aether. **1779** JOHNSON *L.P., Cowley* (1781) I. 31 Subtlety..in its original import means exility of particles. **1855** BREWSTER *Newton* I. vi. 146, I will suppose ether to consist of parts differing from one another in subtlety by indefinite degrees. **1893** SIR R. BALL *Story of Sun* 120 Such is the wondrous subtlety of the ethereal fluid.

9. Fineness or delicacy of nature, character, manner, operation, or the like; an instance of this.

1820 HAZLITT *Lect. Dram. Lit.* 17 Religious controversy sharpens the understanding by the subtlety and remoteness of the topics it discusses. **1840** CARLYLE *Heroes* (1858) 204 Who knows to what unnameable subtleties of spiritual law all these Pagan Fables owe their shape! **1879** SWINBURNE *Stud. Shaks.* (1880) 7 The delicate and infinite subtleties of change and growth discernible in the spirit and the speech of the greatest among poets. **1888** BRYCE *Amer. Commw.* cvii. III. 549, I doubt whether democracy tends to discourage originality, subtlety, refinement, in thought and in expression.

subtlist ('sʌt(ə)lɪst). [f. SUBTLE *a.* + -IST. Cf. SUBTILIST.] One who is addicted to subtleties.

1840 [see SUBTILIST, quot. 1829]. **1887** HARDY *Woodlanders* III. xii. 239 A subtlist in emotions, he cultivated as under glasses strange and mournful pleasures.

'subtlize, *v. rare.* [f. SUBTLE *a.* + -IZE. Cf. SUBTILIZE.] *intr.* To indulge in subtleties.

1821 *Blackw. Mag.* IX. 301 The human mind is displayed ..in its acuteness, subtleizing to infinity.

subtly ('sʌtlɪ), *adv.* Forms: α. 4–5 sotel(l)y, -illy, -ylly, sutely, 4–6 suttelly, 5–6 suttely, (4 sotelliche, -elych, -il(l)iche, -ylleche, suteli, -elly, -il(l)i, -illy, 5 sotelyche, -yly, *Sc.* sutailly, -ellye, suttilly, 6 sottelye, sut(t)ellie, suttully), 6–7 suttly. β. 6 subtel(l)y, 6–7 (9) subtlely, 6– subtly. [f. SUBTLE *a.* + -LY². Cf. SUBTILLY.]

1. Cleverly, dexterously, skilfully; ingeniously, artfully, cunningly. *arch.*

α. *c* **1350** *Will. Palerne* 3117 We be so sotiliche be-sewed in þise hides. **1387** TREVISA *Higden* (Rolls) VI. 425 It was i-made sotilliche by gravynge craft. *c* **1400** *Destr. Troy* 3038 Hir ene..Full sutelly set, Serklyt with heris On the browes so bryght. *c* **1440** *Gesta Rom.* xliii. 170 (Harl. MS.) To have a sherte sotelyche I-made for his body. *c* **1550** ROLLAND *Crt. Venus* I. 140 Tabletis of gold,..With Saphiris set so suttellie and sound. **1667** MILTON *P.L.* VIII. 207 Thou seest How suttly to detaine thee I devise.

β. **1687** SETTLE *Refl. Dryden* 65 Subtly contrived too. **1859** FITZGERALD *Omar* lxi, That He who subtly wrought me into Shape Should stamp me back to common Earth again.

2. With subtle thought or argument; with nice or fine-drawn distinctions.

c **1315** SHOREHAM VII. 203 Hare oȝe wyt, hyt hym bykecheþ, Þat god so sotylleche secheþ, Þat syt so heȝe. *a* **1513** FABYAN *Chron.* VII. ccxlv. (1811) 288 It is ouer subtely excused, or soo darkely..wryten, that the reder therof shall hardely come to yᵉ knowlege of the trouthe. **1561** T. NORTON *Calvin's Inst.* I. xiii. (1634) 54 In too subtlely pearcing into the high misterie. **1591** SYLVESTER *Du Bartas* I. ii. (1641) 18/1, I know how subtly greatest Clerks Presume to argue in their learned Works. **1749** HARTLEY *Observ. Man* I. iv. Concl. 512 Matter and Motion, however subtly divided, or reasoned upon, yield nothing more than Matter and Motion still. **1829** LYTTON *Devereux* II. viii, Let us not talk of these Matters so subtly. **1884** *Punch* 23 Feb. 87 The subtly-woven length Of his audacious argument.

†**3.** With craft or guile; craftily, treacherously, deceitfully, insidiously. *Obs.*

α. *c* **1325** *Poem Times Edw. II*, lxiv. (Percy Soc.) 29 Sotelych for-sothe Thei don the kyngs hest; Whan ech man hath his parte The kyngs hath the lest. **1340** *Ayenb.* 26 Þo byeþ ypocrites sotyls, þet sotilliche wylleþ heȝe cliue. **1414** *26 Pol. Poems* xiii. 63 Mede wiþ poyson sotyly is maynt. *a* **1508** DUNBAR *Tua Mariit Wemen* 254, I wes dissymblit suttelly in a sanctis liknes. **1535** COVERDALE *Acts* vii. 19 The same dealte suttely with oure kynred. **1600** HOLLAND *Livy* XXXV. xiv. 896 How suttelly and cauteloulsy he had like a cunning Carthaginian, couched his words in a certeine kind of flatterie. **1641** MILTON *Ch. Gov.* I. v. 15 Suttly to cast a jealousie upon the Crowne.

β. *a* **1548** HALL *Chron., Hen. VIII*, 220b, Utteryng wonderous woordes, as she was before subtelly and craftely induced and taught. *c* **1585** [R. BROWNE] *Answ. Cartwright* 24 Why did M. C. so subtlely set contrary to dumbe ministers, sufficient ministers? **1658** T. WALL *Charact. Enemies Ch.* 62 Let them subtlely insinuate necessary defence, sure enough the preparations they make shew a delight in war. **1727** DE FOE *Syst. Magic* I. iv. (1840) 95 The Devil takes this for a handle, and subtly makes Canaan dream.

4. Delicately, finely.

1732 POPE *Ess. Man.* I. 219 In the nice bee, what sense so subtly true, From pois'nous herbs extracts the healing dew? **1849** RUSKIN *Seven Lamps* v. §12. 147 The Pisan front is far more subtly proportioned. **1876** G. ELIOT *Dan. Der.* lxvi, This subtly-poised physical susceptibility.

5. In a manner that defies observation, analysis, or explanation.

1854 MILMAN *Lat. Chr.* IV. i. II. 9 [Mohammedanism] dealt prodigally in angelic appearances, and believed in another incorporeal, or, rather, subtly-corporeal race, between angels and men. **1874** GREEN *Short Hist.* iv. §1. 157 The song passes swiftly and subtly into a world of romantic sentiment. **1879** FARRAR *St. Paul* I. 157 Apology and demonstration are subtly blended throughout his appeal. **1890** *Scribner's Mag.* Jan. 191 A very strong impression of French superiority was very subtly instilled. **1912** *Times* 19 Oct. 5/2 A religious intolerance as subtly vicious as was ever the fanatical impetus of the Crescent.

subtone ('sʌbtəʊn). [f. SUB- 5c + TONE *sb.*]

1. A subordinate tone; an undertone.

1894 *Yellow Bk.* I. 190 The river was wrapped in a delicate grey haze with a golden sub-tone. **1906** *Daily Chron.* 4 May 5/3 Those delicate tones and sub-tones of feminine feeling which 'mere man' is..too dense to appreciate.

2. *Mus.* A subordinate sound.

1894 *Daily News* 10 Sept. 2/4 He [*sc.* Wheatstone] was the first..to give a physical explanation of the sombre effect of the minor chord, which sounds prosaic to the æsthetic critic, for it is dependent on the theory of sub-tones just mentioned. [Wheatstone used 'subordinate sounds'.]

subtonic (sʌb'tɒnɪk), *a.* and *sb.* [In A and B 1 f. SUB- 19, in B 2 f. SUB- 13.]

A. *adj. Phonetics.* (See quot.)

1833 J. RUSH *Philos. Human Voice* (ed. 2) 54 A number of sounds, possessing..properties analogous to those of the tonics; but differing in degree... From their inferiority to the tonics,..whilst they admit of being intonated or carried concretely through the intervals of pitch, I have called them Subtonic sounds. *Ibid.*, Some of the subtonic vocalities are purely nasal, as: *m, n, ng, b, d, g.*

B. *sb.*

1. *Phonetics.* A 'subtonic' sound.

1833 J. RUSH *Philos. Human Voice* (ed. 2) 55 This vocality of the subtonics..is variously modified by the nose, tongue, teeth and lips.

2. *Mus.* The note a semitone immediately below the upper tonic of a scale; the leading note.

1854 MOORE *Compl. Cycl. Music.* **1889** E. PROUT *Harmony* i. §13 The seventh note of the scale..is sometimes..called the 'Subtonic'.

subtopia (sʌb'təʊpɪə). Also Subtopia. [Blend of SUBURB and UTOPIA: cf. SUBURBIA.] A disparaging term for: Suburbia regarded as an ideal place. Applied more generally to areas of undifferentiated, ill-planned, and ugly sub-urban development; unsightly suburbs which encroach on the countryside.

1955 I. NAIRN in *Archit. Rev.* CXVII. 365 There will be no real distinction between town and country. Both will consist of a limbo of shacks, bogus rusticities, wire and aerodromes, set in some fir-poled fields... Upon this new Britain the *Review* bestows a name in the hope that it will stick—*Subtopia.* **1960** KOESTLER *Lotus & Robot* II. 277, I loathe crooners and swooners,..neon and subtopia. **1963** A. ROSS *Australia 63* iv. 102 The descent from Utopia to Subtopia is steep and short. **1971** *Country Life* 2 Sept. 566/1 Will there still be English villages as we know them, or will they have merged into an unending subtopia in which town and country have become indistinguishable? **1976** W. J. BURLEY *Wycliffe & Schoolgirls* vii. 123 The killer was a man of the suburbs..at home in a neatly patterned subtopia.

sub'topian, *a.* and *sb.* Also Subtopian. [f. prec. + -AN.] **A.** *adj.* Of, pertaining to, or characteristic of subtopia.

1955 I. NAIRN in *Archit. Rev.* CXVII. 372 The other is the panic reflex to the spread of Subtopia, which attempts improvements using standards which are themselves Subtopian. **1963** *Times Lit. Suppl.* 3 May 321/2 For a man with such a harrowing tale to tell Mr. Camp ought not to be so reassuringly readable.. He will be avidly read by the subtopian commuters and their desperate wives. **1973** J. LEASOR *Host of Extras* i. 24 This subtopian hinterland of back-to-back houses and outside privies.

B. *sb.* A resident of subtopia.

1958 N. MACKENZIE *Conviction* 11 Those parts of it [*sc.* Britain] that remain unspoiled are falling into the hands of the subtopians. **1972** I. BROAT (*title*) The Subtopians.

Hence **sub'topianism**, the characteristics or ideals of subtopia; **sub'topianize** *v. trans.*, to render subtopian.

1959 *Cambr. Rev.* 25 Apr. 447/2 One can imagine some of them.. trying to show that this eclipse was a bad thing, for which broadcasting, subtopianism, Trade Unions and the Welfare State were jointly to blame. *a* **1963** C. S. LEWIS *Poems* (1964) 62 One huge celestial charabanc, will stink and roll Through patient heaven, subtopianized from pole to pole. **1970** *New Scientist* 13 Aug. 342/2 It needed the motor-car to.. subtopianize suburbia.

subtotal, *sb.*, *a.* (and *v.*) [f. SUB- + TOTAL *a.* and *sb.*, *v.*] **A.** *sb.* (stressed '*subtotal*) [SUB- 9.] An intermediate total; a total of part of a group of numbers to be added.

1906 *U.S. Patent 823,474*, Fig. 4, showing means for printing marks or characters indicating both totals and subtotals. **1921** J. A. V. TURCK *Origin Mod. Calculating Machines* 168 A feature common to recording of added columns of numerical items is the distinguishing characters for clear, sub-totals and totals by the use of letters, stars and other marks. **1952** D. R. HARTREE *Numerical Analysis* ii. 20 After each contribution is added, a subtotal is taken, then the next contribution is set and added. **1977** *New Yorker* 29 Aug. 54/2, I kept the new totals in conformity with their figures but changed the supporting details and some subtotals.

B. *adj.* (stressed *sub'total*) *Surg.* [SUB- 21 g.] Involving the removal of only part of an organ or tissue.

1908 *Practitioner* Dec. 788 Surgeons adopted what has been called hysterectomy with intraperitoneal treatment of the stump, or subtotal hysterectomy. **1977** *Lancet* 29 Oct. 899/2 The natural history of the disease may be interrupted by ablative therapy (subtotal thyroidectomy or the use of radioiodine).

Hence '**subtotal** *v. trans.*, (*a*) to add (numbers) so as to obtain a subtotal; (*b*) to obtain a subtotal from the contents of (a register, etc.).

1936 *Suppl. Jrnl. R. Statistical Soc.* III. 95 The contents of any register may be totalled,.. or sub-totalled, i.e. printed without clearing the register. *Ibid.* 99 Several prints of the function may be obtained by inserting more non-add steps after position 8, and sub-totalling register 5 on each of these. **1956** G. A. MONTGOMERIE *Digital Calculating Machines* xii. 250 This causes the accumulator to be sub-totalled into register 117.

†**subtract**, *sb. rare. Obs.* [ad. L. *subtractus*, pa. pple. of *subtrahĕre* to SUBTRACT.]

1. ? A remainder.

a **1635** NAUNTON *Fragm. Regalia* (1641) 27 Sir Iohn Perrot was a goodly Gentleman.. and he was of a very ancient discent, as an heire to many Subtracts [*other ed. of* 1641 abstracts] of Gentry.

2. A subtrahend.

1690 LEYBOURN *Curs. Math.* 341 If he be carefull to make his Canon right, the Letters themselves will direct him how to frame his Divisors and Subtracts.

subtract (səb'trækt), *v.* Also 6 -track. [f. L. *subtract-*, pa. ppl. stem of *subtrahĕre* (whence OF. *subtraire*, It. *sottrarre*, Pg. *subtrahir*) f. *sub-* SUB- 26 + *trahĕre* to draw, carry. See also SUBSTRACT.]

1. *trans.* To withdraw or withhold (a thing that is or may be used or enjoyed). *Obs.* exc. *arch.*

1548 *Act 2 & 3 Edw. VI*, c. 13 §13 Yf anye person doe subtracte or withdrawe any manner of tithes. **1559–60** *MS. Cott. Calig.* B. IX, Let not men.. move zow to subtract zour helping hand. **1581** MARBECK *Bk. Notes* 588 They did not subtract from them their ciuill obedience or counted them from that day forward, no longer to be their kings. **1607** *Statutes* in *Hist. Wakefield Gram. Sch.* (1892) 69 To subtract so much of the Ushers wages. **1846** GROTE *Greece* I. iii. I. 105 His ill will is thus raised, and he tries to subtract from man the use of fire.

†**2.** To remove *from* a place or position. *Obs.*

1574 *Reg. Privy Council Scot.* Ser. I. II. 374 The merchandis.. traffiquand betuix Berwick and Edinburgh salbe subtractit and withdrawin. **1640** BP. HALL *Episc.* II. vii. 187 And yet none of the ancient burdens subtracted. **1659** BP. PEARSON *Creed* (1839) 303 Should we imagine Christ to anticipate the time of death, and to subtract his soul from future torments necessary to cause an expiration. **1676** GLANVILL *Ess. Philos. & Relig.* III. 27 Let him then subtract his Finger, and he will perceive the Quicksilver to descend from the Tube into the subjacent Vessel.

b. *refl.*

c **1540** *Bellenden's Livy* (S.T.S.) I. 8 (MS. A) To subtract [*MS. B* substract] me fra sicht of sic miserijs as oft occurris in to oure dayis. **1657** J. SERGEANT *Schism Dispach't* 74 If they.. would subtract themselves from her obedience. *Ibid.* 511 Whoever subtracts himself from a former actuall governour. **1889** *Daily News* 28 Feb. 4/2 Whether steps will be taken.. to prevent Houston from subtracting himself from the jurisdiction of one of her Majesty's Courts.

3. *Math.* To take away or deduct (one quantity *from*, †*out of* another): see SUBTRACTION 3. Also *absol.* or *intr.*

1557 RECORDE *Whetst.* K ij, Wherfore I subtract 16. out of 18. **1574** W. BOURNE *Regim. Sea* xx. (1577) 53 Subtract or take away the stars declination from the heigth. **1652** *News fr. Low Countr.* 8 Podex can.. Adde, Multiply, Subtract, Divide. **1774** M. MACKENZIE *Marit. Surv.* 62 Subtract the Complement of the Declination from the half Sum, and take the Remainder. **1838** DE MORGAN *Ess. Probab.* 72 Remembering to subtract at the last step instead of adding. **1882** MINCHIN *Unipl. Kinemat.* 53 We should get a better approximation still by subtracting the temperature at 12 from the temperature at 1 second past 12, and multiplying the difference by 3600.

b. *transf.* and *fig.*

a **1676** HALE *Prim. Orig. Man.* (1677) 123 What is so subtracted or subducted out of the extent of the Divine Perfection, leaves still a Quotient, if I may so call it, Infinite. **1838** [F. HAYWOOD] tr. *Kant's Crit. Pure Reason* 415 A law of the understanding, from which it is permitted to deviate under no pretence, or therefrom to subtract any phenomenon. **1863** GEO. ELIOT *Romola* ix, The transient pink flush.. subtracted nothing from her majesty. **1875** JOWETT *Plato* (ed. 2) I. 474 That is what I suppose you to say,.. you may, if you wish, add or subtract anything.

Hence **sub'tracting** *vbl. sb.* and *ppl. a.*

1691 RAY *Creation* I. (1692) 109 The same Swallow by the subtracting daily of her Eggs proceeded to lay nineteen successively. *c* **1850** *Rudim. Navig.* (Weale) 46 There is to be no adding or subtracting. **1956** J. L. STEWART *Circuit Theory & Design* ix. 289 (*caption*) A two-tube subtracting circuit.

sub'tracter. *rare.* [f. prec. + -ER[1].]

1. One who subtracts.

1828–32 WEBSTER.

†**2.** = SUBTRAHEND. *Obs.*

1818 TODD.

3. *Electronics.* = SUBTRACTOR 2.

1950 W. W. STIFLER *High-Speed Computing Devices* xiii. 284 The subtracter which is subtracting a large number from a smaller generates an extra carry pulse at the end of the arithmetic operation. **1970** *IEEE Trans. Computers* XIX. 720/1 A cascade of these subtracters, controlled by a multiplier recorder, provides multiplication.

subtraction (səb'trækʃən). Also 5 subtraccio(u)n, 5–6 -tractioun(e, 6 sotraccion. [ad. late L. *subtractio*, *-ōnem* (in Vulgate tr. Gr. ὑποστολή), n. of action f. *subtrahĕre* to SUBTRACT. Cf. It. *sottrazione*, Pg. *subtracção*. See also SUBSTRACTION.]

†**1.** Withdrawal or removal from a place. *Obs.*

c **1400** *Sc. Trojan War* (Horstm.) II. 369 He.. wylfully in-to þat stede Hath graunted þe subtractioune Of þat relyk of gret renowne To Anthenor. **1432–50** tr. *Higden* (Rolls) II. 155 As in the subtraccion of Danes as vn to the maner and chaunce þer of croniclers make noo mencion [etc.].

2. The withdrawal or withholding *of* something due, necessary, or useful. Also, an instance of this. *Obs.* exc. *arch.*

c **1450** tr. *De Imitatione* II. x. 53 He þat is tauȝt wiþ þe ȝifte of grace, and lerned wiþ þe betyng of subtraccion [orig. *subtractionis verbere*]. **1552** ABP. HAMILTON *Catech.* (1884) 33 This plaige of subtractioun of grace. **1598** in *Archpriest Controv.* (Camden) I. 96 By ye addicions & sotraccions affirmacions & negacions, etc., of the particul[rs] of his autority. *a* **1656** BP. HALL *Rem. Wks.* (1660) 163 A subtraction or diminution of the maintenance of studied Divines. **1818** HALLAM *Mid. Ages* (1872) II. 242 A second subtraction of obedience, or at least declaration of neutrality. **1833** WADDINGTON *Hist. Ch.* xxiii. 524 The party in France, which for some time had been opposed to the subtraction of obedience.. declared its adhesion.

b. *Law.* The withdrawal or withholding from a person of any right or privilege to which he is lawfully entitled.

1660 R. COKE *Power & Subj.* 21 Ecclesiastical laws relate to.. subtraction and right of tythes, oblations, &c. **1768** BLACKSTONE *Comm.* III. 94 The suit for restitution of conjugal rights.. is brought whenever either the husband or wife is guilty of the injury of subtraction, or lives separate from the other without any sufficient reason. *Ibid.* 231 The subtraction or non-observance of any of these conditions, by neglecting to swear fealty, to do suit of court, [etc.] is an injury to the freehold of the lord. **1835** *Tomlins' Law-Dict.*, *Subtraction of Rents and Services.*

c. *Logic.* The exception of one class from another in which the excepted class is naturally included.

In recent Dicts.

3. *Math.* The taking of one quantity *from* (†*out of*) another; the operation of finding the difference between two quantities, the result being termed the *remainder*. Also, an instance of this.

compound subtraction: see COMPOUND *a.* 2 b.

c **1425** *Crafte Nombrynge* (E.E.T.S.) 10 þou most know þat subtraccion is drawynge of one nowmber oute of anoþer nomber. **1542** RECORDE *Gr. Artes* (1575) 95 Subtraction or Rebating is nothing els, but an arte to withdrawe and abate one summe from another, that the Remainer may appeare. **1571** DIGGES *Pantom.* I. xviii. Fj, Nowe by subtraction subduce 100 from 120, there remayneth your diuisor 20. **1612** DRAYTON *Poly-olb.* iv. 390 *note*, Subtraction of this number, and, in some, addition.. will rectifie many gross absurdities in our Chronologies. **1706** PHILLIPS (ed. Kersey) s.v., *Compound Subtraction*, is the Method of taking a Summ compounded of several different Species, from another Summ Compounded likewise of the same sorts of Species. **1854** *Orr's Circ. Sci., Math.* 22 Proceed in like manner with each denomination till the subtraction is finished. **1910** *Encycl. Brit.* (ed. 11) II. 538/2 We.. perform the subtractions independently, and then regroup the results as the remainder.

b. *transf.* and *fig.* Abstraction, deduction, removal.

1534 WHITINTON *Tullyes Offices* I. (1540) 27 That we maye be as good accompters of our offyces and dutyes, and se bothe in addycion and subtraction what somme may surmounte of the remaynes. **1738** T. BIRCH *App. Life Milton* I. 72 By comparing it with his other Account, we shall perceive.. that there is not an entire Agreement in any one of the Paragraphs,but there are either Alterations, or Additions, or Subtractions, or Contradictions. **1820** R. JACKSON *Sk. Febrile Dis.* (ed. 2) I. 227 Dr. Rush, and other American physicians carried subtraction of blood to great extent in the American epidemic. **1828** P. CUNNINGHAM *N.S. Wales* (ed. 3) II. 325 The gift of a single million out of this vast amount is about as insignificant as the subtraction of a grain of wheat from a peck measure. **1857** MILLER *Elem. Chem., Org.* xiii. §1. 723 From it all the varieties of organized products might be obtained, by the addition or subtraction of water, oxygen, and ammonia. **1864** LOWELL *Fireside Trav.* (1909) 25 The world can endure the subtraction of even a justice of the peace with provoking equanimity.

4. Detraction, depreciation. (Cf. SUBTRACTOR.) *rare.*

1890 *Century Mag.* XXXIX. 624/2 Of Shakspere he [*sc.* Emerson] talked much, and always without a word of subtraction.

subtractive (səb'træktɪv), *a.* and *sb.* [ad. med.L. *subtractīvus*, f. *subtract-*: see SUBTRACT *v.* and -IVE. Cf. Pg. *subtractivo*.]

A. *adj.* **a.** Involving or denoting subtraction, deduction, or diminution; also in *Linguistics*, of a morph or morpheme (cf. REPLACIVE *a.*); (of a mathematical quantity) that is to be subtracted, negative, having the minus sign.

1690 LEYBOURN *Curs. Math.* 808 We have therefore now three *Prosthaphæreses* of the Moon... Which since they are all of the same sort, to wit, each of them subtractive [etc.]. **1699** *Phil. Trans.* XXI. 352 *Subtractive Ratio* is that whose Terms are dispos'd to Subtraction, that is, to Division. **1812** WOODHOUSE *Astron.* xiv. (1821) 381 The resulting numerical values.. if additive of the north polar distance, are subtractive of the zenith distance. **1813** *Monthly Mag.* XXXVI. 307 *However—Yet—Notwithstanding—Nevertheless.* These may be called subtractive conjunctions: they all concede something, and deduct something else. **1824** R. JACKSON *View Formation* etc. *Armies* 505 Besides measured diet,.. there are other means.. diminishing the volume of the fluids... These are subtractive, viz. blood letting and purging. **1829** BENTHAM *Justice & Cod. Petit.* Prelim. Explan. p. vi, To employ either draft, with.. amendments, whether additive, subtractive, or substitutive. **1890** H. B. FINE *Number-Syst. Algebra* 102 In reducing equations.. subtractive terms in either member are rendered additive by transposition to the other member. **1948**, etc. [see REPLACIVE *a.*]. **1953** [see PORTMANTEAU *sb.* 4 d]. **1968** *Amer. Speech* XLIII. 203 Primary graphemic shortenings.. may be divided into the subtractive and the replacive.

b. *Cryst.* (See quot. 1805–17.)

1805–17 R. JAMESON *Char. Min.* (ed. 3) 147 Tetrahedral and prismatic molecules are always arranged in such a manner in the interior of primitive and secondary crystals, that, taking them in groups of 2, 4, 6, 8 they compose parallelopipeds... These parallelopipeds are by Hauy named subtractive molecules. **1823** BROOKE *Crystallogr.* 66 A more simple theory of decrement.. may be substituted for that which has been established upon the assumption of the irregular tetrahedron as the integrant molecule, and the obtuse rhomboid as the subtractive molecule.

c. *Photogr.* Of or pertaining to the production of a coloured photographic image by passing white light through a series of filters which absorb or subtract different parts of the spectrum. Cf. ADDITIVE *a.* c.

1906 E. J. WALL tr. *Konig's Natural-Color Photogr.* I. 23 (*heading*) Three-color printing, or the subtractive method of three-color photography. **1916** G. L. JOHNSON *Photogr. in Colours* ix. 141 Processes.. which depend on the 'three-colour' principle are daily growing in favour... There are two forms of this process, the 'subtractive' one.. and the 'additive' method. **1935** [see ADDITIVE *a.* c]. **1957** V. J. KEHOE *Technique Film & Television Make-Up* 219 The dye images form the composite color pictures by subtractive synthesis. **1978** *SLR Camera* Dec. 61/1 This subtractive method is the most commonly used in modern colour printing.

B. *sb.* Something that is subtracted or deducted from another quantity; *spec.* in *Linguistics*, a subtractive morph or morpheme.

1949 E. A. NIDA *Morphology* (ed. 2) iv. 103 Such bound forms are either (1) nonclitics—additives, replacives, subtractives. **1954** *Word* X. 224 The same comment applies to 'subtractives'. **1979** *Daily Tel.* 21 Nov. 18 Apart from the purchase of a stamp.. the ½p is no more than an additive to or subtractive from some other price.

sub'tractor (sʌb'træktə(r)). [f. SUBTRACT *v.* + -OR.]

1. (Substituted by Warburton, 1747, for SUBSTRACTOR of the folios in Shaks. *Twel. N.* I. iii. 37.)

2. *Electronics.* A circuit or device that produces an output dependent on the difference of two inputs or of multiples of them. Cf. SUBTRACTER 3.

1950 W. W. STIFLER *High-Speed Computing Devices* 450/1 (Index), Subtractor [*in text as* subtracter]. **1953** A. D. & K. H. V. BOOTH *Automatic Digital Calculators* vi. 36 An adder or subtractor requires the provision of some form of register in which the sum is to be stored. **1970** J. EARL *Tuners & Amplifiers* v. 118 The signals from these [microphones] are fed into an 'adder/subtractor' network, giving two outputs, one L + R and the other L − R. **1977** J. G. GRAEME *Designing with Operational Amplifiers* vii. 177 To combine addition and subtraction with integration, the summing and differencing techniques of adders and subtractors are applied to integrators.

subtrahend ('sʌbtrəhɛnd). *Math.* [ad. L. *subtrahendus* (sc. *numerus* number), gerundive of *subtrahĕre* to SUBTRACT.] The quantity or number to be subtracted.

1674 JEAKE *Arith.* (1696) 18 The number to be substracted ..called the Subtrahend. **1714** CUNN *Treat. Fractions* 39 Then substract the Numerator of the Subtrahend from the common Denominator. **1826** in *Encycl. Metrop.* (1845) I. 428/1 The next digit in the subtrahend is greater than the one corresponding to it in the minuend.

b. *transf.* A sum of money to be deducted.

1845 CARLYLE *Cromwell* (1871) I. 98 Subtracting the due subtrahend. **1858** —— *Fredk. Gt.* IX. x, Here is the Princess's account; with the subtrahend, twenty-five or seventy-five per cent, *not* deducted. **1911** *Edinb. Rev.* Jan. 138 Her wages..are liable to a serious subtrahend for the loss..caused by leaving her house..in the hands of another.

† **subtray**, *v. Obs.* Also 5-6 subtrahe, 6 -trah. [f. imper. sing. *subtrahe* or stem *subtrah-* of L. *subtrahĕre* to SUBTRACT. Cf. SUBSTRA.] To subtract (*trans.* and *intr.*).

c **1425** *Crafte Nombrynge* (E.E.T.S.) 13 Here he teches þe Craft how þou schalt know, whan þou hast subtrayd, wheþer þou hast wel ydo or no. *c* **1430** *Art Nombryng* (E.E.T.S.) 16 And so forthe subtrahe fro the totalle nombre in respect of þe digit. **1477** NORTON *Ord. Alch.* v. in Ashm. (1652) 81 Your Liquors be ordained to add and subtray, To make equalitie by wisdome of assay. **1549** CHALONER *Erasm. on Folly* G ij, From howe many..euilles I haue subtraied these my selie paches. **1579** DIGGES *Stratiot.* I. xv. 26 The last Fraction being lesse then ⅜ enforceth you to Subtrahe one out of 4. **1588** J. MELLIS *Briefe Instr.* D viij, To make the summes equall, gather the total hereof..and subtray it from the totall summe of your Creditor opposite.

'sub,treasurer. [SUB- 6.] An assistant or deputy treasurer.

The specific designation of an official of Hereford and Truro Cathedrals, and of the Inner Temple; formerly in *U.S.* of the official in charge of a subtreasury.

1546, **1786** [implied in SUBTREASURERSHIP]. **1821** LAMB *Elia, Old Benchers Inner T.*, But the worthy sub-treasurer—who respects his old and his new masters—would but have been puzzled. **1849** EASTWICK *Dry Leaves* 172, I suddenly reflected that the treasurer—with all the race of sub-treasurers—had departed. **1882** AINGER *Lamb* vi. 103 His father's old and loyal friend Randal Norris, the sub-treasurer of the Inner Temple.

Hence **sub'treasurership**, the office of a subtreasurer.

1546 *Yks. Chantry-Surv.* (Surtees) II. 363 The Subtresorer-shyppe in the saide Churche. **1786** J. BACON *Liber Regis* 1102 Diocese of York. The Cathedral Church... Sub Treasurership.

'sub,treasury. [SUB- 7 d.] A subordinate or branch treasury; *U.S.* the organization by which the separate safe-keeping of the public funds is entrusted to specially appointed officers; any of the branches of the Treasury established in certain cities of the States for the receipt and safe-keeping of public monies.

1837 CALHOUN *Wks.* III. 81 This proposed reorganization has been called a sub-treasury. **1837–42** HAWTHORNE *Twice-told T.* (1851) II. viii. 118 With their interminable brawls about Banks and the Sub-Treasury, Abolition [etc.]. **1858** HOMANS *Cycl. Comm.* 1765/2 The failures of many of these [banking institutions] during the years 1837–1842 led to the establishment, on the 6th August, 1846, of the Independent Treasury, or Sub-treasury... The sub-treasuries for the reception of the public funds are at Boston, New York, Philadelphia, and other cities. **1896** *Daily News* 24 July 8/5 A telegram from Washington says that the Treasury Department has been advised that over 23 million dollars in gold will be turned into the sub-treasuries by the banks. **1901** ALLDRIDGE *Sherbro* xxvii. 313 There was a sub-treasury at the port of Sulima; the sub-accountant forwarded down..revenue to the amount of £1,000.

attrib. **1888** *Encycl. Brit.* XXIII. 766/2 Van Buren..after a four years' struggle,..succeeded in making the 'sub-treasury scheme' law (1840).

'subtri,angular, *a.* Chiefly *Zool.* and *Bot.* [ad. mod.L. *subtriangulāris*: see SUB- 21 e.] Approaching the form of a triangle; somewhat triangular.

1787 tr. *Linnæus' Fam. Plants* 763 Calodendron... Seeds two in each cell, subtriangular. **1824** DU BOIS *Lamarck's Arrangem.* 45 The Mactræ..are marine shells..almost always subtriangular. **1854** OWEN in *Orr's Circ. Sci., Org. Nat.* I. 192 The exoccipitals..are very irregular subtriangular bones. **1881** *Nature* XXIII. 605 A sub-triangular wedge-shaped implement.

So **'subtri,angulate** *a.*, with combining form **,subtriangu'lato-**.

1849 HARDY in *Proc. Berw. Nat. Club* II. vii. 361 Head sub-triangulate. **1852** DANA *Crust.* I. 118 Carapax sub-triangulato-ovate.

'subtribe. [SUB- 7 b.] A subdivision of a tribe.

1836–9 *Todd's Cycl. Anat.* II. 860/1 The second sub-tribe, *Hydradephaga*, includes the predaceous water-beetles. **1857** [see SUBCLASS]. **1857**, etc. [see HAPU]. **1859** R. F. BURTON *Centr. Afr.* in *Jrnl. Geog. Soc.* XXIX. 84 The Wazaramo number many sub-tribes, the principal of which are the Wákámbá. **1870** HOOKER *Stud. Flora* 150 Tribe iv. Seselineæ... Sub-tribe 2. Coriandreæ. **1958** G. LIENHARDT in Middleton & Tait *Tribes without Rulers* 103 A tribe is divided into subtribes, its largest political segments. **1977** *Time* 19 Dec. 21/3 Its population of 2·5 million citizens includes members of 76 ethnic groups, mostly subtribes of the Tswana.

Hence **'subtribual** *a.*, pertaining to a subtribe.

1881 BENTHAM in *Jrnl. Lin. Soc.* XVIII. 287 The most important tribual and subtribual characters.

'subtriple, *a.* [ad. late L. *subtriplus*: see SUB- 10 and TRIPLE *a.*]

1. *Math.* That is one third of a quantity or number; denoting a proportion of 1 to 3; (of a ratio) of which the antecedent is one third of the consequent.

1644 DIGBY *Nat. Bodies* viii. §6. 60 Which must be in sub-triple proportion of the diameter of the sunne to the diameter of the great orbe. *a* **1696** SCARBURGH *Euclid* (1705) 180 As 13 to 4 inverted, is 4 to 13 viz. Subtriple sesquiquartal. **1719** QUINCY *Compl. Disp.* 14 The Proportion of White Lead to Lead itself comes out still less, i.e. sub-triple. **1728** CHAMBERS *Cycl.*

2. *sub-triple spot*, a moth (see quot.).

1832 J. RENNIE *Butterfl. & M.* 179 The Sub-triple Spot (*Paramesia subtripunctulana*).

'sub triplicate, *a. Math.* [SUB- 10.]

1. Of a ratio or proportion: Being that of the cube roots of the quantities; thus, 2 : 3 is the subtriplicate ratio of 8 : 27.

1656 [see SUBDUPLICATE]. **1710** J. HARRIS *Lex. Techn.* II, *Paraboloids*, are Paraboliform Curves in Geometry; whose Ordinates are supposed to be in a Subtriplicate, Subquadruplicate, &c. Ratio of their respective Abscissæ. **1781** *Phil. Trans.* LXXI. 316 Let us see how near they come to the reciprocal sub-triplicate ratio of their weights.

¶ **2.** = SUBTRIPLE. (A misuse.)

1656 HOBBES *Six Lessons* Wks. 1845 VII. 277 It is the same fault when men call..a third part subtriplicate of the whole.

sub'triplicated, *a.* [SUB- 21 f.] Imperfectly divided into three sections.

1822 J. PARKINSON *Outl. Oryctol.* 212 Lip bordered internally; columella subtriplicated.

subtrist (sʌb'trɪst), *a. rare.* [ad. L. *subtristis*, f. *sub-* SUB- 19 + *tristis* sad.] Somewhat sad.

1820 SCOTT *Abbot* xxix, You look subtrist and melancholic.

'sub tropic, *a.* and *sb.* [SUB- 12 b, 19.]

A. *adj.* = SUBTROPICAL.

1891 in *Cent. Dict.* **1900** B. D. JACKSON *Gloss. Bot. Terms*, *Subtropic*, applied to half-hardy plants which in temperate climates can thrive in summer only.

B. *sb. pl.* **subtropics**: the regions adjacent to or bordering on the tropics.

1886 *Times* (Philad.) 3 May (Cent.), There are but two counties [of Florida] in the sub-tropics—Dade and Monroe. **1898** P. MANSON *Trop. Diseases* I. i. 1 The principal cause of morbidity in the tropics and sub-tropics.

sub'tropical, *a.* Also ,sub'tropical. [SUB- 12 b, 19.]

1. Bordering on the tropics.

1865 *Englishman's Mag.* Nov. 393 Some currents convey ice into subtropical countries. **1807** LYELL *Princ. Geol.* (ed. 10) I. I. x. 200 A climate approaching that now only experienced in sub-tropical regions. **1883** *Chamb. Jrnl.* 142 The sponges of commerce are almost wholly obtained from tropical or sub-tropical seas.

2. Characteristic of subtropical regions; of a climate, character, habit, etc. between temperate and tropical; almost tropical.

1842 LOUDON *Suburban Hort.* 527 Climates sub-tropical, or tropical. **1863** DANA *Man. Geology* 534 The Miocene flora of the vicinity of Vienna the same author pronounces to be subtropical. **1868** *Rep. U.S. Commissioner Agric.* (1869) 6 The..culture of tropical and sub-tropical fruits in the southern States. **1880** DAWKINS *Early Man in Brit.* ii. 21 The sub-tropical members decreased, and the temperate forms..preponderated.

subtrude (səb'tru:d), *v.* [f. L. *sub-* SUB- 2, 26 + *trūdĕre* to thrust.]

1. *trans.* To thrust under.

a **1846** *Dublin Rev.* (Worc.).

2. *intr.* To thrust itself in stealthily.

1898 HARDY *Wessex Poems* 129, I see the nightfall shades subtrude.

'subtype. [SUB- 5 c.] A subordinate type; a type included in a more general type; *spec.* a subdivision of a type of micro-organism.

1862 MILLER *Elem. Chem., Org.* (ed. 2) i. §2. 50 The hydrochloric acid type..forms a subtype which comprehends the chlorides, fluorides, bromides, iodides, and cyanides. **1872** OLIVER *Elem. Bot.* II. 122 In some Natural Orders the amount of variation..is so considerable that we shall find it needful to employ subtypes. **1951** WHITBY & HYNES *Med. Bacteriol.* (ed. 5) xii. 203 By preparing specific Vi phages more than 20 types and sub-types of the typhoid bacillus have been recognized. **1963** *Lancet* 12 Jan. 92/2 Three serotypes are known, but subtypes of type 2 have recently been demonstrated in some animal species. **1979** *Sci. Amer.* Jan. 66/1 That particular subtype of the influenza virus had been the agent of the pandemic of 1918, which killed 20 million people worldwide.

Hence as *v. trans.*, to assign to a subtype; to classify in terms of subtypes; **'subtyping** *vbl. sb.*

1973 *Lancet* 20 Oct. 867/1 Relatives of 9 blood-donors were also subtyped; all had the same subtype as the index case to which they were related. *Ibid.* 869/1 The value of subtyping as an epidemiological tool. **1977** *Ibid.* 15 Oct. 803/2 A multiply resistant strain of type-19 (not yet subtyped) *Streptococcus pneumoniæ* was isolated. **1980** *Brit. Jrnl. Psychiatry* CXXXVII. 502/1 Subtyping of schizophrenia into paranoid and non-paranoid subtypes.

'sub,typical, *a.* [SUB- 19.] **a.** Of the character of a subtype. **b.** Not quite typical; lying between the typical and aberrant forms.

1837 SWAINSON *Nat. Hist. Birds* II. 4 The first three of these sub-families constitute the aberrant circle... The fourth is the sub-typical. *Ibid.* 76 The *Piprinæ* constitute the subtypical group of this family [*sc.* the *Ampelinæ*]. **1854** WOODWARD *Mollusca* II. 241 The Bivalve Shell-fish.. constitute the second or sub-typical group in the quinary system.

‖ **subucula** (sə'bju:kjʊlə). Also anglicized (*rare*) subucule. [L. dim. f. *sub* under + **uĕre* to put, as in *exuĕre*, *induĕre*.] **a.** A kind of shirt or under-tunic worn by the ancient Romans. **b.** In the Anglo-Saxon Church, a tunic worn beneath the alb, serving as a kind of cassock.

[Cf. *c* **1450** CAPGRAVE *Life St. Gilbert* 125 My auctor her setteth a word 'subucula' whech is both an awbe and a schert.]

1660 R. COKE *Power & Subj.* 162 That every Priest celebrating Mass, hath his Corporal, and Subucule [*mispr.* Subumle] under his Alban. **1849** ROCK *Ch. Fathers* I. v. 460 Besides the alb..the Anglo-Saxons wore another garment.. the subucula. **1877** *Encycl. Brit.* VI. 456/2 It was a custom of the Romans to wear two tunics... The one next the skin was known as the *subucula*.

Subud (sʊ'bʊd). [Contraction of Skr. *suśīla* good disposition, *budh* to awake, learn, *dharma* custom (see quot. 1968).] A system of exercises by which the individual seeks to approach a state of perfection through the agency of the divine power; hence, a movement (founded in 1947 and led by the Javanese mystic Pak Muhammad Subuh, b. 1901) based on this system.

1958 J. G. BENNETT *Concerning Subud* vi. 111 *Subud*..the perfect harmony of the inner life (Budhi) and outer life (Suśila) that is attained when our entire being is submitted to the Will of God. **1959** A. HUXLEY *Let.* 12 Aug. (1969) 874 Subud is simply a technique for reproducing the quaking of the early Quakers—a release via the muscles. **1962** *Lancet* 26 May 1125/2 As Subud has taken some hard knocks in your columns, I feel that someone ought to speak up for the 5000–6000 members of the Subud movement in this country. **1968** E. VAN HIEN *What is Subud?* ii. 25 Subud is a contraction of three Sanskrit words: Susila Budhi Dharmi. In Subud terminology, these have been interpreted as follows: Susila means 'right living'. Budhi refers to 'the higher powers and capacities latent in man himself'. Dharma means 'submission to the Will of God'. Taken together, they mean 'Right living according to the highest that is possible for man in submission to God's Will'. **1969** M. SUBUH *Basis & Aim of Subud* 5 It is also necessary to explain that Subud is neither a kind of religion nor a teaching, but it is a spiritual experience awakened by the Power of God. **1972** N. SAUNDERS *Alternative London* xviii. 176 Subud forms a link between psychotherapy and mysticism as roads to self-realisation.

subulate ('sju:bjʊlət), *a. Bot.* and *Zool.* [ad. mod.L. *sūbulātus*, f. *sūbula* awl: see -ATE[2]. Cf. F. *subulé*.] Awl-shaped; slender and tapering to a point.

1760 J. LEE *Introd. Bot.* I. xiii. (1765) 31 *Subulate*, Awl-shaped. **1785** *Phil. Trans.* LXXV. 9 Our bird..has a weak, slender, subulate bill. **1785** MARTYN *Lett. Bot.* xiii. (1794) 132 Flowers in a spike, with a subulate receptacle. **1817** KIRBY & SP. *Entomol.* xvii. II. 33 Their long and large head, armed with very long subulate mandibles. **1887** W. PHILLIPS *Brit. Discomycetes* 303 Margin unevenly fringed with somewhat roughened subulate hairs.

Comb. **1845** LINDLEY *Sch. Bot.* viii. (1858) 136 Radical leaves subulate-striated. **1870** HOOKER *Stud. Flora* 206 Involucral bracts..subulate-lanceolate.

So **'subulated** *a.*, with comb. form **'subulato-**.

1752 HILL *Hist. Anim.* 495 The beak of the Sturnus is of a subulated figure. **1760** J. LEE *Introd. Bot.* II. xx. (1765) 118 The upper Filament is subulato-setose. **1773** G. WHITE *Selborne, To Barrington* 8 July, The *hippoboscæ hirundinis*, with narrow subulated wings. **1833** HOOKER in Smith's *Eng. Flora* V. I. 21 Leaves subulato-setaceous.

subuliform (sju:'bju:lɪfɔ:m), *a.* [ad. mod.L. *sūbuliformis*, f. *sūbula* awl: see -FORM.] Subulate.

1859 MAYNE *Expos. Lex.* **1866** *Treas. Bot.*

† **subulon.** *Obs.* [ad. L. *sūbulo*, f. *sūbula* awl.] A young hart (with straight unbranched horns).

1607 TOPSELL *Four-f. Beasts* 122 *marg.*, Of Spittards & Subulons. *Ibid.* 133 The dung of Harts cureth the dropsie, especially of a Subulon or young Hart. **1688** HOLME *Armoury* II. viii. 160/2 He beareth Argent, a Subulons (or a Brocards) head, proper... This head of a Subulon, is born by the name of Subell.

† **sub'umber**, *v. Obs. rare*[−1]. [f. L. *sub* SUB- 2 + *umbra* shadow. Cf. *subumbrage* s.v. SUB- 2.] *trans.* To shelter.

c **1470** HARDING *Chron.* LXIII. vi, Under shryne buryed and subumbred Emong al Christen kynges worthy to be remembred.

‖ **subum'brella.** *Zool.* [mod.L.; see SUB- 1 f.] The internal ventral or oral disk of a hydrozoan; the concave muscular layer beneath the umbrella of a jelly-fish.

1878 BELL tr. *Gegenbaur's Comp. Anat.* 108 In the Medusæ it [*sc.* a muscular layer] is limited to the surface which carries the gastric apparatus, where it forms the 'sub-umbrella'. **1888** ROLLESTON & JACKSON *Anim. Life* 248

Scattered ganglion cells in connection with this [inner nerve] ring lie in the ectoderm of the sub-umbrella.

Hence **subum'brellar** *a.* [SUB- 1 b.], beneath the umbrella; pertaining to the subumbrella.

1877 HUXLEY *Anat. Inv. Anim.* iii. 137 A sub-umbrellar cavity with a roof formed by the umbrella.

†**sub'union.** *Obs. rare.* [ad. mod.L. *subūnio*, rendering late Gr. ὑφέν (= ὑφ', ὑπό under + ἕν one) HYPHEN: see UNION.] Incomplete union (of words or syllables).

[The L. word is used = hyphen; cf.:—**1665** R. JOHNSON *Scholars Guide* 2 A Subunio (-) used 1. when two whole words are united, as pale-faced. 2. when one part of the word is writ at the end of one line, and the other at the beginning of the next. **1685** MATLOCK *Fax Nova Artis Scrib.* 20.]

1648 HEXHAM *Du. Dict.* II. *Gram.* B bb, Hyphen is a Note of Sub-union, either of two words..or of the Connexion of two or more Syllables together. **1688** HOLME *Armoury* III. v. 251/1 *Hyphen*, is a mark of subunion either of two words, as Self-love; or of the connection of two Syllables at the end of a Line, and the beginning of the succeeding Line thus =.

suburb ('sʌbɜːb). Forms: *pl.* 4–5 sub(b)arbes, -is, (-ys), -urbis, 5–7 suburbes, 6–7 subburbs, suberbs, (4 subaarbis, 5 -orbz, sowbarbys, subbardes, -ars, -ers, 6 -arbs, -ardes, subberbes, -is, -urbes, -ys, -orbes, sub-vrbs), 5– suburbs; also 5 sowthbarbys, -ez, 6 southebarbis (see SOUTH-²); *sing.* 4–7 suburbe, 5 sub(b)arbe, subbarde, 7– suburb. [a. OF. *sub(b)urbe*, pl. *-es*, ad. L. *suburbium*, pl. *-ia* (med.L. also *suburbii*), f. *sub* SUB- 11 + *urbs* city. Cf. Sp., Pg. *suburbio*.]

1. The country lying immediately outside a town or city; more particularly, those residential parts belonging to a town or city that lie immediately outside and adjacent to its walls or boundaries.

a. *collect. pl.*

c **1380** WYCLIF *Wks.* (1880) 364 þai hadden subarbis to fede þer þe beestis þat schuld be offred sacrifice to god in þe temple. *c* **1386** CHAUCER *Can. Yeom. Prol.* 104 In the suburbes of a toun..Lurkynge in hernes and in lanes blynde. **1387** TREVISA *Higden* (Rolls) IV. 211 An oxe spak to a plowȝ man in þe subarbes of Rome. **1398** —— *Barth. de P.R.* XIV. xii. (Tollem. MS.) Sichem, þat was a cite of socoure with subbarbes [*ed.* **1535** subardes, **1582** suburbes] þerof in mounte Effraym. *c* **1430** LYDG. *Min. Poems* (Percy Soc.) 4 Florentynes, and Venycyens, And Esterlinges,.. aftyr the maier riding, Passid the subbarbis to mete withe the Kyng. **1439** *Rolls of Parlt.* V. 23/1 Fletestrete in the subbardes of London. *c* **1460** *Oseney Reg.* 6 þᵉ church of seynte marye Mawdeleyn the which is i-sett in the subbarbis of oxonforde. **1493** in Young *Ann. Barber-Surg. Lond.* (1890) 67 Withyn this cyte or subbers of the same. **1523** *Act 14 & 15 Hen. VIII*, c. 3 §5 Withyn either of the said Townes of Lyn and Great Yarmouth or Suburbes of the same. **1592** GREENE *Vision* Wks. (Grosart) XII. 259 He trudgeth towards Antwerpe, where in the suberbes, hee heard of his wife. **1593** NASHE *Christ's T.* Wks. 1904 II. 148 London, what are thy Suburbes but licensed Stewes? **1613** SHAKS. *Hen. VIII*, v. iv. 76 Theres a trim rabble let in: are all these Your faithfull friends o' th' Suburbs? **1665** *Baker's Chron.*, *Contin. Chas. I*, 501 That part of the Suburbs of London commonly called Covent Garden. *a* **1720** SEWEL *Hist. Quakers* (1795) II. VII. 2 At London, and in the suburbs. **1845** S. AUSTIN *Ranke's Hist. Ref.* III. 223 They..had resolved to burn the suburbs, in order to preserve the city within the walls. **1875** HELPS *Soc. Press.* iv. 59 How this ugly lot of suburbs would join with that ugly lot, and that there would soon be one continuous street.

†**b.** *collect. sing.*

1395 *E.E. Wills* (1882) 9 In the parosch of seynt sepulcre in the suburbe of london. *c* **1440** *Promp. Parv.* 482/1 Suburbe, of a cyte or wallyd towne (*K.* suburb or sowthbarbys of cyte), *suburbium, suburbanum.* **1691** WOOD *Ath. Oxon.* I. 9 He was sent to Gloucester College, in the Suburb of Oxon. **1706** PHILLIPS (ed. Kersey). [**1853** NEWMAN *Hist. Sk.* (1873) I. I. ii. 70 Its cities..were surrounded beyond their fortifications by a suburb of fields and gardens.]

2. Any of such residential parts, having a definite designation, boundary, or organization.

a. *sing. form.*

1433 LYDG. *St. Edmund* App. 395 Not ferre out of the toun In a subarbe callyd Rysbygate. **1665** MANLEY *Grotius' Low C. Wars* 955 Suddenly a suburb beyond the River, that might have been defended, was quitted. *a* **1700** EVELYN *Diary* 15 Jan. 1645, I went to the Ghetto, where the Jewes dwell as in a suburbe by themselues. **1727** DE FOE *Tour Gt. Brit.* III. II. 34 This Street is call'd the Cannon-Gate,.. which Part, tho' a Suburb, is a Kind of Corporation by itself, as Westminster to London. **1836** MACGILLIVRAY *Trav. Humboldt* v. 68 Crossing the Indian suburb, the streets of which were very neat. **1869** FREEMAN *Norm. Conq.* (1877) III. xii. 109 The monks of Saint Stephen already dwelt in their suburb beyond the walls of Caen. **1913** *Standard* 20 June 7/7 The people of Clapham, or Cricklewood, or Clapton, or any other suburb.

†**b.** *pl. form with sing. concord.*

1610 HOLLAND *Camden's Brit.* 810 The suburbs of Gates-head, which is conioined to New-castle. *a* **1668** LASSELS *Voy. Italy* (1698) I. 58 A continual Suburbs of stately villas and villages. **1753** *De Foe's Tour Gt. Brit.* (ed. 5) III. 214 The Market-place and St. Nicolas's Church, from whence, for a good Way, shoots out a Suburbs to the North-east,.. and each Suburbs has its particular Church.

3. *transf.* and *fig.* (*pl.*, rarely *sing.*) Outlying parts, ouskirts, confines, purlieus. **a.** of localities.

1382 WYCLIF *Ezek.* xlv. 2 On eche part it shal be halewid in fyue hundrid by fyue hundrid, four maner by cumpas, and in fifti cubitis in to the suburbis therof bi cumpas. **1601** DENT *Pathw. Heaven* 313 Ill company is the suburbs of Hell. **1604** E. G[RIMSTONE] *D'Acosta's Hist. Indies* III. iv. 128 They come to the Ilands of Guadelupe Dominique,..and the rest, which..be as it were, the suburbs of the Indies. **1613** PURCHAS *Pilgrimage* (1614) 91 Constantine raised these suburbes of Hell, and destroyed both the customes, statues, and temple it selfe. **1635** QUARLES *Embl.* v. vi. (1718) 270 To heav'n's high city I direct my journey, Whose spangled suburbs entertain mine eye. **1655** FULLER *Ch. Hist.* VI. §2 II. 285 The Kitchin..with the Larder and Pantrey the necessary suburbs thereof. **1667** MILTON *P.L.* I. 773 [Bees] Flie to and fro, or on the smoothed Plank, The suburb of thir Straw-built Cittadel,..confer Thir State affairs. *a* **1703** BURKITT *On N.T.* Luke xxiii. 42 Even then, when he is in the suburbs of hell, he will blaspheme.

b. of immaterial things.

1599 NASHE *Lenten Stuffe* Wks. 1905 III. 174 The vaward or subburbes of my narration. **1642** D. ROGERS *Naaman* 363 They would never come within the condition or suburbes of mercy. **1650** TAYLOR *Holy Living* ii. §6. 142 When our fortunes are violently chang'd, our spirits are unchang'd, if they alwayes stood in the Suburbs and expectation of sorrowes. **1655** FULLER *Best Act Obliv.* 2 Lent is a season for sorrow, this Week is the suburbs of Lent. **1822–56** DE QUINCEY *Confess.* Wks. 1890 III. 293 In summer, in the immediate suburbs of midsummer. **1848** LONGF. *Fireside, Resign.* v, This life of mortal breath Is but a suburb of the life elysian. **1863** COWDEN CLARKE *Shaks. Char.* xvii. 445 Silence is an embryo of a man,..a man dwelling in the suburbs of sense.

c. *jocular.*

a **1658** CLEVELAND *Poems* (1687) 326 The Suburbs of my Jacket are so gone, I have not left a Skirt to sit upon.

4. *attrib.* and *Comb.* **a.** Simple attrib. (rarely in pl. form) passing into adj. = Belonging to a suburb or the suburbs, SUBURBAN. Now *rare*.

1592 *Nobody & Someb.* I, Heares queanes maintaind in euery suburb streete. **1593** MARLOWE *Lucan's 1st Bk.* 569 Those that inhabited the suburbe fieldes Fled. **1662** GERBIER *Brief Disc.* 19 The Windows on the London and Suburbs Houses. **1680** OTWAY *Orphan* Prol. 20 The harmless Life Of Suburb Virgin or of City Wife. *a* **1721** PRIOR *Turtle & Sparrow* 424 Hear thy dirty Off-spring Squall From Bottles on a Suburb-Wall. **1811** SCOTT *Don Roderick* II. xxxix, The spark that, from a suburb-hovel's hearth Ascending, wraps some capital in flame. **1820** KEATS *Lamia* II. 26 From the slope side of a suburb hill. **1883** *Century Mag.* Oct. 821/1 The houses..grow up stories higher—villas—suburb houses.

†**b.** = Belonging to or characteristic of the suburbs (of London) as a place of inferior, debased, and *esp.* licentious habits of life (cf. quots. 1593, 1613, in sense 1). (*freq.* in 17th cent.) *Obs.*

suburb sinner: a loose woman, prostitute.

1598 B. JONSON *Ev. Man in Hum.* I. iii, If I can but hold him vp to his height,..it will do well for a suburbe-humor. **1599** —— *Cynthia's Rev.* II. iv, We cannot haue a new peculiar court-tire, but these retainers will haue it; these Suburbe-sunday-waiters. **1608** DEKKER *Lanth. & Candle Lt.* Wks. (Grosart) III. 266 Belzebub..knowes, that these Suburb sinners haue no landes to liue vpon but their legges. **1633** MARMION *Fine Companion* G 2 There's a wench that has her Suburb trickes about her, I warrant. **1638** NABBES *Bride* I. iv, You malkin of suburb authority set up only to fright crows. **1649** MILTON *Eikon.* Pref., Dissolute swordmen and Suburb roysters. **1664** COTTON *Scarron.* IV. (1667) 136 Some durty Suburb drab. *a* **1668** DAVENANT *News fr. Plimouth* III. i, You look in this light habit Like one of the Suburb-Sinners.

c. = SUBURBICARIAN. *rare*.

1813 *Examiner* 1 Mar. 131/2 The six suburb Bishopricks shall be re-established.

d. †**suburb dross**, bee-glue, PROPOLIS (see quot. and cf. quot. 1667 in sense 3 a).

1657 S. PURCHAS *Pol. Flying-Ins.* 158 Propolis is as much as suburbe dross, with which the Bees fasten the skirts of the Hive to the board.

suburban (sə'bɜːbən), *a.* and *sb.* [ad. L. *suburbānus*, f. *sub* SUB- 11 + *urbs* city: see -AN. Cf. F. *suburbain*, It., Sp., Pg. *suburbano*.] **A.** *adj.*

1. Of or belonging to a suburb or the suburbs of a town; living, situated, operating, or carried on in the suburbs.

a **1625** FLETCHER *Faithf. Friends* II. ii, To yield At first encounter may befit the state Of some suburbane strumpet, but not her. **1631** BRATHWAIT *Whimzies, Apparator* 131 A pestilent headpeece hee ha 's to blow up suburbane traders: with whom hee trucks. *a* **1661** HOLYDAY *Juvenal* (1673) 18/2 The Rich had stately Monuments on the sides of the publick ways in their own suburbane fields. **1671** MILTON *P.R.* IV. 243 Athens..native to famous wits Or hospitable, in her sweet recess, City or Suburban, studious walks and shades. **1751** T. EDWARDS in *Richardson's Corr.* (1804) III. 19, I will hope that..the air of your agreeable suburbane North-End, will restore you. **1781** COWPER *Retirem.* 481 Suburban villas, highway-side retreats, That dread th' encroachment of our growing streets. **1824** LOUDON *Encycl. Gard.* (ed. 2) §7285 The suburban villa..is of limited extent, but contains a small kitchen-garden and stables... Such villas are occupied more by professional men and artists. **1837** LOCKHART *Scott* I. iv. 120 His chosen intimate..continued to be..Mr. John Irving—his suburban walks with whom have been recollected so tenderly. **1849** MACAULAY *Hist. Eng.* iii. I. 351 They reside..at suburban country seats surrounded by shrubberies and flower gardens. **1855** *Ibid.* xviii. IV. 243 Among the suburban residences of our kings, that which stood at Greenwich had long held a distinguished place. **1883** *Law Times* LXXV. 130/2 The speculative builder..has become the pest of suburban London.

2. *transf.* Having characteristics that are regarded as belonging especially to life in the suburbs of a city; having the inferior manners, the narrowness of view, etc., attributed to residents in suburbs.

1817 BYRON *Beppo* lxvi, A fifth's look's vulgar, dowdyish, and suburban. **1860** EMERSON *Cond. Life, Worship* Wks. (Bohn) II. 403 If you follow the suburban fashion in building a sumptuous-looking house for a little money, it will appear to all eyes as a cheap dear house.

3. = SUBURBICARIAN. *rare*.

1858 J. MARTINEAU *Stud. Chr.* 204 Two names are given in.., those of Hyppolytus, a suburban clergyman, and of Caius, whose charge lay within the city itself.

4. Special collocations: ***suburban line***, a railway line which runs between the centre of a city and its suburbs; ***suburban neurosis***, a form of neurosis said to occur esp. among suburban housewives which is associated with feelings of boredom, loneliness, and lack of personal fulfilment; ***suburban sprawl***, the straggling and often ill-planned expansion of the suburbs of a city over a large area of adjacent countryside; an instance of this.

1869 *Bradshaw's Railway Man.* XXI. 379 The *Suburban line, from the Salt River station to Wynberg, is now open. **1926** *Times* 6 May 3/1 Skeleton services were run on main and suburban lines, and more trains are promised to-day. **1972** C. FREMLIN *Appointment with Yesterday* i. 10 South Coast, this [ticket] office... Suburban line, opposite Platform Six. **1938** S. J. L. TAYLOR in *Lancet* 26 Mar. 759/1, I hope to show that environment plays no less a part in the production of what I venture to call 'the *suburban neurosis' than it does in the production of physical disease. **1962** *Listener* 6 Dec. 948/2 The so-called 'suburban neurosis' is due to society's having failed to provide a constructive role for these mothers. **1983** *Jrnl. Amer. Acad. Child Psychiatry* XXII. 172 (*heading*) The nuclear family, suburban neurosis, and iatrogenesis in Auckland mothers of young children. **1949** H. BLUMENFELD in *Social Forces* Oct. 59/1 The Association poses the alternative of 'self-contained towns' versus '*suburban sprawl'. **1958** *Listener* 19 June 1022/3 The transformation of most of the country into a gigantic suburban sprawl. **1972** *Country Life* 6 Jan. 18/1 The suburban sprawl that characterises much of the eastern seaboard of the northern United States.

B. *sb.*

†**1.** *sb. pl.* Suburbs. *Obs.*

a **1340** HAMPOLE *Psalter* Cant. 520 þe suburbanys of gomor.

2. a. A suburban residence. **b.** A resident in the suburbs.

1841 S. BAMFORD *Passages in Life of Radical* (ed. 2) I. xxxiv. 203 He passed on, leaving those warm-hearted suburbans capering and whooping like mad. **1856** NEWMAN *Callista* xxii. 195 Can truth give me a handsome suburban with some five hundred slaves. **1906** *Westm. Gaz.* 1 Sept. 3/1 All good suburbans congratulate themselves on the choice of their abode. **1926** R. MACAULAY *Crewe Train* II. vi. 129 Don't waste time arguing about the accepted premises of life, of which one is that suburbans are dull. **1977** *Transatlantic Rev.* LX. 197 She laughed..being confused by Mr and Mrs Superb the Semi-Detached Suburbans strolling their Sealyhams, for woodpeckers.

Hence **su'burbandom, -hood,** suburban conditions of life, the residents of the suburbs collectively; **su'burbanism,** the characteristics of suburban life; a suburban peculiarity; **su'burbanite,** a resident in the suburbs; **subur'banity,** the condition of being suburban; an instance of this, a suburban characteristic, feature, locality; **suburbani'zation,** the act of suburbanizing or the condition of being suburbanized; an instance of this; **su'burbanize** *v. trans.*, to render suburban; **su'burbanized** *ppl. a.*, rendered suburban; **su'burbanly** *adv.*

1902 *Speaker* 13 Dec. 284/1 The respectabilities and genteelness of mere *suburbandom. **1879** *Macm. Mag.* XLI. 188/1 There is..another side to this story, which the *suburbanhood of Manchester would like greatly to tell. **1888** MRS. H. WARD *Robt. Elsmere* II. xi, A county [*sc.* Surrey], which is throughout a strange mixture of *suburbanism and the desert. **1907** *Sat. Rev.* 6 Apr. 423 She..is a symbol of middle-aged suburbanism rejuvenated and illuminated by fresh experience. **1911** TYRRELL in *19th Cent.* Apr. 693 There seem to have been suburbanisms and provincialisms, like the Praenestine vulgarism..of dropping the first syllable of a word. **1890** *Advance* (Chicago) 20 Feb., Much dissatisfaction among *suburbanites over the proposed change. **1896** *Westm. Gaz.* 9 Nov. 7/2 The Lord Mayor's Show brings out the suburbanite in full force. **1623** COCKERAM, Neighbourhood in the Subburbs, **Suburbannitie.* **1833** *New Monthly Mag.* XXXVII. 50 The pipe he smoked of an evening, under certain circumstances of suburbanity. **1848** *Illustr. Lond. News* 17 June 387/1 Erith is the prettiest of pretty suburbanities. **1884** *Spectator* 4 Oct. 1320/2 Suburbanity, with its combined characteristics of money, scandal, and church going. **1926** *Daily Tel.* 3 Aug., In the urbanisation or *suburbanisation of the country motor transport is destined to be even more effective than railways. **1938** *Archit. Rev.* LXXXIII. 216/3 It is gratifying to find *Country Life* adding its own opposition to a tendency which, if not soon halted, will result in literally nation-wide suburbanization. **1951** N. PEVSNER *Middlesex* 55 Finchley Parish had only 1,500 inhabitants in 1801 and still only 7,000 in 1871. Thereafter suburbanization set in. **1978** H. CARPENTER *Inklings* iv. 64 They still went on walking tours, until the increasing suburbanisation of the countryside and the outbreak of war brought that annual event finally to a halt. **1893** C. E. NORTON in *Lowell's Lett.* (1894) I. 2 The whole district, though so near the city, was not yet *suburbanized. **1901** *Daily Chron.* 13 May 5/2 The district is..becoming suburbanised and unfit for sport. **1921** *Edin. Rev.* Jan. 111 The local feeling of the less *suburbanised Home Counties continues to object. **1977** *Time* 25 Apr. 35/2 We are going to go on with suburbanized homes. **1963** S. S. IKRAMULLAH *Purdah to Parliament* ii. 17 The mentality and attitude of those who lived in these parts were also *suburbanly correct.

†**suburbars**, *sb. pl.* ? Error for *suburbans* (cf. prec. B. 1). But cf. SUBURBLES.

1530 *Test. Ebor.* (Surtees) V. 290 To every hospitall wᵗin the citie of York, and also unto the subarbars of the same.

†**suburbed**, *a. Obs. rare*$^{-1}$. [f. SUBURB + -ED^2.] Having a suburb or suburbs.

1602 R. CAREW *Cornwall* 120 Bottreaux Castle, seated on a bad harbour of the North Sea, and suburbed with a poore market towne.

Suburbia (sə'bɜːbɪə). Now often **suburbia**. [f. SUBURB + -IA^1.] A quasi-proper name for: The suburbs (*esp.* of London). Freq. rather disparagingly. Also in N. Amer. and general contexts, and (*poet. nonce-use*) as quasi-*adj.*

1895 E. PUGH (*title*) A street in Suburbia. **1896** *Westm. Gaz.* 20 Apr. 8/1 Suburbia also was very great in primroses and maiden-hair fern posies. **1907** H. WYNDHAM *Flare Footlights* xix, Adrian took a leisurely survey of the room and its occupants. Both reflected Suburbia very strongly. **1922** L. MUMFORD in H. E. Stearns *Civilization in U.S.* 13 'Suburbia' is used here in both the accepted and in a more literal sense. On one hand I refer to the fact that the growth of the metropolis throws vast numbers of people into distant dormitories where..life is carried on without the discipline of rural occupations and without the cultural resources that the Central District of the city still retains. **1925** WODEHOUSE *Sam the Sudden* xiv. 99 The early morning patois of Suburbia, which is the English language filtered through toast and marmalade. **1936** T. SHARP *Eng. Panorama* vi. 94 H. G. Wells..anticipated with extraordinary accuracy (and, as it seems to-day, with a maddening optimism) the universal suburbia which is already upon us. **1947** AUDEN *Age of Anxiety* III. 76 A married tribe commutes, mild from suburbia. **1967** MCLUHAN & FIORE *Medium is Massage* 72 It gave us darkest suburbia and its lasting symbol: the lawnmower. **1970** G. F. NEWMAN *Sir, You Bastard* iii. 92 The deposit on their admission to suburbia was managed jointly.

†**su'burbial**, *a. Obs. rare.* [f. L. *suburbium* SUBURB + -AL^1.] = SUBURBAN.

1602 R. CAREW *Cornwall* 101 Yet do they prescribe in a suburbiall market (as I may terme it) to Plymmouth for their reliefe. **1778** T. WARTON in Johnson & Steevens *Shaks.* V. 266 Moor-ditch..opened to an unwholesome and impassable morass, and consequently not frequented by the citizens, like other suburbial fields which were remarkably pleasant. **1861** STEPHENS & BURN *Bk. Farm-Build.* Index 560/2 Suburbial dairy farming.

†**su'burbian**, *a.* and *sb. Obs.* [f. L. *suburbium* SUBURB + -AN.] **A.** *adj.* Suburban; in 17th cent. often with reference to the licentious life of the (London) suburbs (cf. SUBURB 4 b).

1606 HOLLAND *Sueton.* 39 There is yet to be seene the place of his nourcery, within a suburbian house belonging to his Auncesters. **1609** ROWLEY *Search for Money* (Percy Soc.) 37 We should returne back to the suburbian bordello (before mentioned). **1632** MASSINGER *City Madam* III. i, I know them—swaggering, suburbian roarers. **1653** *Consid. Dissolv. Crt. Chancery* 47 Some of the Middlesex or Suburbian Justices. **1675** T. DUFFETT *Mock Tempest* III. i, Not pledge me, thou salt Suburbian Hackney, not pledge me. **1732** *Lond. Mag.* I. 334 Give some share of credit to the out-lying night-walkers, and Suburbian ghosts. **1810** CRABBE *Borough* xviii. 244 Suburbian prospects, where the traveller stops To see the sloping tenement on props.

B. *sb.* A resident in the suburbs.

1607 DEKKER *Knt's Conjur.* (1842) 55 All the brokers in Long Lane Houns-ditch, or else wher, with all the rest of their colleagued suburbians that deale vppon ouerworne commodities. **1679** DRYDEN *Limberham* IV. i, Down with the Suburbians, down with them. *a* **1704** T. BROWN *Lett. fr. Dead* Wks. 1720 II. 248 A true profligate Suburbian. **1760** FOOTE *Minor* I. Wks. 1799 I. 232 You cockneys now beat us suburbians at our own weapons. **1825** C. M. WESTMACOTT *Engl. Spy* I. 287 Scum of the suburbians.

suburbican (sə'bɜːbɪkən), *a.* [ad. L. type **suburbicānus*, f. *suburbium* SUBURB, after *suburbicārius*.] = SUBURBICARIAN.

1659 GAUDEN *Tears Ch.* I. i. 27 One Ecclesiasticall polity [which]..extended, not onely to the walls of that city, but to the suburbican distributions. **1681** R. L'ESTRANGE *Apol. for Protest.* III. i. 51 The Suburbican Places of about an hundred Italian Miles from Rome. **1687** W. JOHNSTON *Assur. Abby Lands* 16 The Suburbican Diocess of Rome. **1782** PRIESTLEY *Corrupt. Chr.* II. xi. 289 The popes..had no ..authority beyond the suburbican provinces. **1884** *Times* 1 Feb. 6 Two of the six Suburbican Sees being vacant at the same time. **1894** *Tablet* 4 Aug. 174 St. Bonaventure..was compelled to accept the Suburbican See of Albano.

†**suburbi'carial**, *a. Obs. rare*$^{-1}$. [Formed as next + -AL^1.] = next.

1688 *Proc. Parl. of Paris upon Pope's Bull* 15 Is he persuaded that His Power reaches no farther than the Diocess of Rome, and his Patriarchship than the Neighbouring Provinces, stiled Suburbicarial?

suburbicarian (ˌsʌbɜːbɪ'kɛərɪən), *a.* [f. late L. *suburbicārius*, f. *suburbium* SUBURB, after *urbicārius* URBICARY. Cf. F. *suburbicaire*, Pg. *suburbicario*.] Applied to the dioceses (now six in number) around Rome, and to their churches, etc., which are subject to the jurisdiction of the Pope as metropolitan and the bishops of which form the body of cardinal bishops. (The term has been more widely used by some.)

1654 OWEN *Doctr. Saints' Persev.* Pref. E 2, I have spent some time in the consideration of mens conjectures of those suburbicarian Churches. **1657** HEYLIN *Ecclesia Vind.* 305 His first Epistle, inscribed to the Bishops of Lucania, another of the Suburbicarian Provinces, which made up that Patriarchate. **1715** BENTLEY *Serm.* x. 354 When the empire was first Christian the Bishops of Rome had no more under their Inspection than the Suburbicarian Regions. **1840** MILMAN *Hist. Chr.* III. 371 Within the city, he [*sc.* the Pope] presided over above forty churches, besides the suburbicarian districts. **1853** E. H. BROWNE *Expos. 39 Art.* xxxvii. §2 II. 635 It has been proved, that the suburbicarian Churches meant those within the district, which belonged to the *Vicarius Urbis.* **1893** F. W. PULLER *Prim. Saints & See of Rome* 14 The relations of the Bishop of Rome to his suburbicarian suffragans.

suburbicary (sə'bɜːbɪkərɪ), *a.* (*sb.*) [ad. late L. *suburbicārius* (see prec.).]

1. = SUBURBICARIAN.

1654 BRAMHALL *Just Vind.* v. (1661) 93 One who understood the ancient proper bounds of the Roman Patriarchate as well as any man, doth limit it to the Suburbicary Churches, that is a part of Italy, and three Islands, Sicilia, Sardinia and Corsica. **1692** SIR T. P. BLOUNT *Ess.* 11 The Suburbicary Region of Italy. **1725** tr. *Dupin's Eccl. Hist. 17th C.* I. II. v. 152/1 Some Provinces of Italy were distinguish'd by the Names of Suburbicary and Annonary. **1853** E. H. BROWNE *Expos. 39 Art.* xxxvii. §2 II. 635 As to the limits of the Roman Patriarchate, much depends on what is meant by the term *Suburbicary Churches.* **1908** *Ch. Times* 5 June 761/1 Rome, with the suburbicary region, had long enjoyed a certain political independence.

†**b.** *sb. pl.* The suburbicarian provinces of Italy.

1665 STILLINGFL. *Grounds Protest. Relig.* II. vi. Wks. 1709 IV. 426 All the Provinces in the Diocese of Italy..which Provinces the Lawyers and others term Suburbicaries.

†**2.** Suburban. *Obs.*

1654 H. L'ESTRANGE *Chas. I* (1655) 124 Such numerous rows of stately and ambitious buildings, as made old London envy the magnificence of her Sub-urbicary sister.

†**suburbles**, *sb. pl.* In 5 subarblis, 6 suberbillis. Obscure pl. form of SUBURB.

14.. *Chaucer's Can. Yeom. Prol.* 104 (MS. Camb.), In the subarblis of a toun. **1536** BELLENDEN *Cron. Scot.* XVI. v. (1821) II. 461 He brint the suberbillis of Carlele.

†**'suburbless**, *a. Obs.* [f. SUBURB + -LESS.] Without suburbs.

1650 FULLER *Pisgah* v. 190 Ierusalem..being on the East and South suburbless.

†**Subu'traquian**. *Obs. rare.* [f. L. *sub utrāque*, scil. *specie* under both kinds.] One who advocates the administration of the Sacrament in both kinds; = UTRAQUIST. (Cf. CALIXTIN 1.)

1649 OWEN *Shak. & Transl. Heaven & Earth* 22 Hath not Germany..Hierome and Subutraquians to answer for? **1662** —— *Animadv. on 'Fiat Lux'* ii. 74 Poor men.. whom they called Waldenses, Albigenses, Lollards,.. Subutraquians, Picards.

'subvaˌriety. [SUB- 7 b.] A subordinate or minor variety, *esp.* of a domestic animal or cultivated plant.

1802-12 BENTHAM *Ration. Judic. Evid.* (1827) IV. 536 Men of the class of professional lawyers..being, under all their varieties and sub-varieties, men. **1811** PINKERTON *Petral.* Introd. p. ii, Some [writers] have Varieties; and Werner, with a truly German want of taste, has added Sub-species and Sub-varieties. **1822-7** GOOD *Study Med.* (1829) II. 405 Some pathologists have set down *Arachnitis* as a sub-variety of the meningic form. **1868** DARWIN *Anim. & Pl.* I. i. 18 There is not sufficient evidence that any of these ancient dogs belonged to the same identical sub-varieties with our present dogs. **1875** E. WHITE *Life in Christ* III. xxiii. (1878) 336 The original distinct kinds of living things, out of which all subvarieties have sprung.

'subˌvassal. Chiefly *Sc. Obs.* exc. *Hist.* [SUB- 9 (*b*).] An under-vassal; a vassal of a vassal.

1480 *Acta Dom. Conc.* (1839) 52/1 His landes of Wyndale quhilk he haldes of þe lard of ȝestre in preiudice and skath of þe said Richart his subvassale & tennand. **1565** *Reg. Privy Council Scot.* I. 358 Gif he be Erle, Lord, Barroun, frehaldar, wassale, subwassall, fewar, or heritour. **1606** *Acts Parl. Scot., Jas. VI* (1816) IV. 287/1 Act anent setting of fewis be subvassellis of waird landis. **1681** STAIR *Inst. Law Scot.* I. xiii. 236 Charters granted by his [*sc.* the king's] Vassals to their Sub-vassals. **1750** CARTE *Hist. Eng.* II. 290 The subvassals were..subject, in cases of rebellion, to the same forfeitures and penalties, as the immediate vassal. **1838** W. BELL *Dict. Law Scot.* 88 B, the subvassal, has thus two superiors; A, from whom he derives his right..and the Crown, which is his mediate superior. **1858** CARLYLE *Fredk. Gt.* III. vi. (1872) I. 251 They shall be Subvassals under us as Hereditary Duke. **1878** LECKY *Eng. in 18th Cent.* I. ii. 171 The great charter compelled the barons to grant their subvassals mitigations of feudal burdens.

Hence **'subˌvassalage**, the condition of being a subvassal; a property held by a subvassal.

1775 L. SHAW *Hist. Moray* II. 123 On the West side of the river..is Coulclachie, a subvassalage of Angus MacIntosh. **1838** W. BELL *Dict. Law Scot.* 88 This would be to deprive A of his subvassalage, which no act of the Crown or of B can accomplish.

†**subvassour**. *Sc. Obs. rare*$^{-1}$. Also **subvavassour**. [ad. med.L. *subvassor*, for **subvavassor*: see SUB- 9 (*b*) and VAVASOUR.] = prec.

14.. *Act Malcolm II*, c. 9 þai þat haldis of knychtis þe quhilkis are callit subuauasouris [Skene *Reg. Maj.* 3 subvassours; orig. *subvassores*].

†**sub'vect**, *v. Obs. rare*$^{-1}$. [f. L. *subvect-*, pa. ppl. stem of *subvehĕre*, f. *sub-* SUB- 26 + *vehĕre* to carry.] *trans.* To bring forward.

1641 J. JACKSON *True Evang. T.* II. 158 To this purpose then, let us here subvect such safe and necessary rules.

†**sub'vene**, *v. Obs. rare*$^{-1}$. [ad. L. *subvenīre*, f. *sub-* SUB- 26 + *venīre* to come.] *intr.* To come as a relief or remedy.

1756 WARBURTON *View Bolingbroke's Philos.* iv. 213 A future state must needs subvene, to prevent the whole Edifice from falling into ruin.

sub'vent, *v.* [f. L. *subvent-*, pa. ppl. stem of *subvenīre* (see prec.).] †**1.** *trans.* To come to the help of. *Obs. rare*$^{-1}$.

a **1630** S. PAGE *Expos. Ld.'s Prayer* (1631) 26 That none but the preseruer of man, can either preuent the euill that we feare, or subuent vs in the euill wee feele.

2. = SUBVENTION *v.*

1921 *Discovery* Nov. 293/1 The excavations authorised and subvented by the French Government began in 1880 and have been continued to the present time. **1965** *New Statesman* 23 Apr. 646/1 The only question is, should the taxpayer continue to subvent [the Catholic education system]? **1976** *Times Lit. Suppl.* 25 June 793/2 A..fear of subventing the profits of commercial firms.

†**subven'taneous**, *a. Obs.* [f. mod.L. *subventāneus*, f. L. *sub* SUB- 1 a + *ventum* wind: see -EOUS. Cf. obs. F. *subventané*.] Windy; *esp.* of unfertile eggs.

1646 SIR T. BROWNE *Pseud. Ep.* III. xxi. 162 The relation of the Mares in Spaine, and their subventaneous conceptions, from the westerne winde. **1666** S. PARKER *Free & Impart. Censure* (1667) 79 Theories in Philosophie.. impregnate the mind with nothing but Ayerie and Subventaneous Phantasmes. **1686** PLOT *Staffordsh.* 272 Whether the Egg it self at first was imperfect or subventaneous. **1688** HOLME *Armoury* II. xiii. 313/2 *Subventaneous Eggs*, such as the Hen brings forth without the Treading of the Cock.

subvention (səb'vɛnʃən). [a. OF. *subvencion*, *-tion*, = Pr. *subventio*, It. *sovvenzione*, Sp. *subvencion*, Pg. *subvenção*, ad. late L. *subventio*, *-ōnem*, n. of action f. *subvenīre* to SUBVENE.]

1. A subsidy levied by the state. *Obs.* exc. *Hist.*

14.. *Secr. Secr.* MS. Ashm. 396 fo. 2 Of kynges aides and subvencioun. **1426** LYDG. *De Guil. Pilgr.* 1818 Grace Dieu ffor to exile By dyuers extorsyons Of dymes or Subvencions, or taylladges iffounde newe. **1868** MILMAN *St. Paul's* iv. 89 Convocation proceeded to the less important affair of a subvention to the King.

†**2.** The provision of help, support, or relief. Also, an instance of this. *Obs.*

1535 W. MARSHALL (*title*) The Forme and Maner of Subvention, or Helpying for pore People, devysed and practysed in the Cytie of Hypres in Flanders. **1570** FOXE *A. & M.* (ed. 2) I. 6/2 Suche goods were geuen to the church .. to serue the publique subuention of the nedy. **1625** USSHER *Answ. Jesuit* 374 By way of subuention, in helping those out whom at the time of his death he found there. **1657** TWYSDEN *Vindic. Ch. Eng.* iv. 80 They sometimes exhorted Christians to the subvention of the Holy Land. **1737** STACKHOUSE *Hist. Bible* VI. ii. (1749) 845 The Manner, in which he is said to have been carry'd up, was, by the Subvention of a Cloud.

3. A grant of money for the support of an object or institution; *occas.* a grant in aid of necessitous persons; now *esp.* a grant from government or some other authority in support of an enterprise of public importance.

1851 GALLENGA *Italy* 85 By screening from losses the *appaltatori*, or shop-keepers, who farmed the public revenues, by private subventions. **1854** MILMAN *Lat. Chr.* I. Introd. 3 They [*sc.* the Greek churches] were often bound together by mutual charitable subventions. **1858** CARLYLE *Fredk. Gt.* I. iii. (1872) I. 22 The Crown-Prince..begged some dole or subvention for these poor people. **1860** MRS. W. P. BYRNE *Undercurr. Overl.* II. 96 Subventions to madhouses, foundling hospitals, &c. **1881** *Nature* XXIV. 426 The French Government have resolved to grant a subvention for erecting a statue. **1891** *Spectator* 27 June, The resources of English wealth for the purpose of providing subventions for the Colonial Episcopate.

4. The granting of pecuniary aid for the support of an undertaking.

1868 ROGERS *Pol. Econ.* ix. (1876) 97 By inducing the possessor to export his capital in foreign loans, or for the subvention of foreign industry. **1876** BANCROFT *Hist. U.S.* V. xxxii. 119 The ministry confessed its inability to reduce the colonies except by the subvention of foreign troops. **1894** *Daily News* 8 June 3/4 They had not to pay anything towards the subvention of rural roads.

Hence **sub'vention** *v.* [cf. F. *subventionner*] *trans.*, to support or assist by the payment of a subvention. (Only in pa. pple.)

1868 *Daily News* 10 Nov., That national and subventioned establishment [the Théâtre Français]. **1880** *Sat. Rev.* No. 1289. 52, 12 per cent. were French vessels subventioned by the Government. **1885** *American* IX. 362 The society has from time to time subventioned learned works. **1904** *Daily Tel.* 18 July 8/6 The German subventioned steamer Prinz Heinrich. **1909** *Expositor* July 85 The German Oriental Society, subventioned by the German Emperor.

sub'ventionary, *a.* [f. prec. + -ARY.] Of the nature of a subvention.

1866 CARLYLE *Remin.* (1881) II. 42 Which annual sum.. I could not..have dreamt of accepting as gift or subventionary help from any fellow-mortal.

sub'ventionize, *v.* [f. SUBVENTION *sb.* + -IZE.] = SUBVENTION *v.*

1879 *Daily Tel.* 22 July, The Empress Eugenie has told M. Rouher that she will not continue to subventionise the Imperialist newspapers. **1886** *Ibid.* 2 Mar. (Cassell), The managers of subventionized theatres.

†**subven'titious**, *a. Obs. rare*⁻¹. [f. L. *subvent-*, pa. ppl. stem of *subvenīre* to SUBVENE + -ITIOUS.] Of the nature of a subvention.

a **1693** *Urquhart's Rabelais* III. xxxiii, He should never help, aid, supply, succour nor grant them [*sc.* delinquents] any subventitious Furtherance.

sub'ventive, *a. rare*⁻¹. [Formed as prec. + -IVE.] Giving help or support.

1871 CARLYLE in *Mrs. Carlyle's Lett.* (1883) I. 16 [He] had a great admiration..for Leigh Hunt, to whom John was often actually subventive.

subversal (səbˈvɜːsəl). *rare.* [f. L. *subvers-* (see next), after *reversal*.] Subversion.

1893 *Nat. Observer* 11 Nov. 654/1 Endless subversals of 'public form'. **1898** H. B. M. WATSON *Advent.* vii. 98 My ideas were destined to a rude subversal.

subverse (səbˈvɜːs), *v. rare.* [f. L. *subvers-*, pa. ppl. stem of *subvertĕre* to SUBVERT.] *trans.* To subvert, upset.

1590 SPENSER *F.Q.* III. xii. 42 Those goodly roomes.. Now vanisht vtterly, and cleane subuerst She found. **1730–46** THOMSON *Autumn* 1128 Empires subvers'd, when ruling Fate has struck Th' unalterable hour. **1870** MISS BROUGHTON *Red as Rose* I. 24 The fear of subversing the table.

subversion (səbˈvɜːʃən). Also 4–5 -cioun, -sioun, 4–6 -cion, -cyon, 6–7 -tion. [a. OF. *subversion* (from 12th c.), = It. *sovversione*, Sp. *su(b)version*, Pg. *subversão*, ad. late L. *subversio*, *-ōnem*, n. of action f. *subvertĕre* to SUBVERT.] The action of subverting or state of being subverted.

1. Overthrow, demolition (of a city, stronghold, etc.). ? *Obs.*

1382 WYCLIF *Gen.* xix. 29 He..dylyueride Loth fro the subuersioun of citees in whiche he had dwellid. *c* **1400** MAUNDEV. (Roxb.) xvii. 77 Þis Loth was he þat was saued at the subuersioun of Sodom. **1412–20** LYDG. *Chron. Troy* II. 2946 For þis þe fyn þat þer folwe schal: Subuersioun, bothe of tour and wal. **1547** J. HARRISON *Exhort. Scottes* 208 Sackyng of tounes, subuersion of holdes, murder of men. **1589** PUTTENHAM *Engl. Poesie* I. xxiv. (Arb.) 62 Nowe are the causes of mans sorrowes many:..the ouerthrowes and discomforts in battell, the subuersions of townes and cities, the desolations of countreis. **1605** B. JONSON *Volpone* II. i, A whale..that had waited there..for the subuersion Of the Stode-Fleet. **1615** G. SANDYS *Trav.* 205 Beseiged by an hundred and fifty thousand Mahometans, Acre received an utter subversion. **1618** BOLTON *Florus* II. xvii. (1636) 144 That Gracchus who was father of the Gracchi punished them with the subversion of one hundred and fifty of their cities. **1856** STANLEY *Sinai & Pal.* vii. (1858) 289 Bela, the old name of Zoar, was understood..to allude to the fact of its frequent subversion by earthquakes.

2. The turning (of a thing) upside down or uprooting it from its position; overturning, upsetting (of an object). Now *rare.*

1670 COTTON *Espernon.* I. IV. 181 The violence of the powder was so great, that it blew up the floor where the Duke sate at dinner,..the Duke only by a miracle of Fortune remaining still sitting, and upright in the midst of this subversion. **1684** T. BURNET *Theor. Earth* I. vii. 91 The opening and shutting the Abysse, with the dissolution or subversion of the Earth. **1703** EVELYN *Diary* 26 Nov., The subversion of woods and timber..through my whole estate ..is almost tragical. *c* **1791** *Encycl. Brit.* (1797) VII. 374/1 Others think, that the waters of the sea..turned the whole surface of the earth upside down;..and that in this general subversion, the shells came to be interred here, fishes there, trees there, &c. **1816** T. L. PEACOCK *Headlong Hall* x, The subversion of a cup of chocolate..into the nape of the neck of Sir Patrick O'Prism.

†**3.** *Med.* **subversion of the stomach**: nausea. *Obs.*

Cf. med.L. *subversio animæ* (Sinon. Barth.).

1615 CROOKE *Body of Man* 145 The great consent betweene the stomacke and the kidneyes, and the subuersion of the stomacke, and frequent vomits. **1628** VENNER *Baths of Bathe* (1650) 355 Weaknesse and subversion of the stomack.

4. In immaterial senses: Overthrow, ruin.

a. of a law, rule, system, condition, faculty, character, etc.

1399 *Rolls of Parlt.* III. 451/2 Subversion of lawe of the lond. **1488–9** *Act 4 Hen. VII*, c. 19 To the subvercion of the polecy and gode rule of this lond. **1502** *Ord. Crysten Men* (W. de W.) v. iv, Manyfested subuercyon of the trouth of god. **1558** T. WATSON *Seven Sacr.* 34 b, Wherupon foloweth the decaye of healthe, and subuersion of reason. **1669** GALE *Crt. Gentiles* I. Introd. 9 A Discourse..which directly tendes to the subversion of my main Hypothesis. **1681** FLAVEL *Meth. Grace* xxvii. 461 The crucifixion of sin necessarily implies the subversion of its dominion over the soul. **1757** W. PITT *Desp.* 23 Aug. in *10th Rep. Hist. MSS. Comm.* App. I. 213 The Danger to Great Britain and her Allies, resulting from a total Subversion of the System of Europe. **1757** GRAY *Let.* in *Poems* (1775) 252 It is the brokenness, the ungrammatical position, the total subversion of the period that charms me. **1849** MACAULAY *Hist. Eng.* ix. II. 412 The violent subversion of one free constitution would have been a strange prelude to the violent restoration of another. **1863** H. COX *Instit.* I. vii. 64 The Norman Conquest was a subversion of the titles to land. **1880** E. WHITE *Certainty in Relig.* 103 Under conditions which expose your faith to ever-imminent subversion.

b. of persons, countries, peoples, or their lives or fortunes.

1470–1 *Rolls of Parlt.* VI. 233/2 The seid Duke and Erle intended..the subversion of this his Reaume. **1531** ELYOT *Gov.* III. xv, Many a valyaunt capitayne and noble prince haue..brought all their contrayes in daungeour, and often tymes to subuercion and ruyne. *a* **1578** LINDESAY (Pitscottie) *Chron. Scot.* I. 31 He drew..to his assistance.. the erle of Douglas and mentenit him onlie for the chancellaris subuerssioun and ruwyne. **1593** SHAKS. *2 Hen. VI*, III. i. 208 These great Lords..Doe seeke subuersion of thy harmelesse Life. **1608** WILLET *Hexapla Exod.* 827 The ouerthrow and subuersion of the Cananites. **1643** FULLER *Serm. Reform.* 17 We have so long waited for their conversion, we have almost seene our subversion. **1737** WATERLAND *Eucharist* 599 The common methods of Subversion begin with lessening the Work of Preparation. **1755** W. DUNCAN *Cicero's Sel. Orat.* viii. §27 (1841) 143 His pursuit of new praise threatens the entire subversion of his former fortune. **1798** LD. AUCKLAND in *Corr.* (1862) III. 386 The subversion of several powers and states upon the continent.

sub'versionary, *a. rare.* [f. prec. + -ARY.] = SUBVERSIVE.

a **1846** *Ch. Ob.* (Worc.). **1894** *Speaker* 30 June 712/2 Firmness and courage in dealing with subversionary forces during his Premiership.

subversive (səbˈvɜːsɪv), *a.* [ad. L. **subversīvus*, f. *subvers-*, pa. ppl. stem of *subvertĕre* to SUBVERT: see -IVE. Cf. F. *subversif*, Sp. *su(b)versivo*, Pg. *subversivo*.] Having a tendency to subvert or overthrow; tending to subversion.

1644 HUNTON *Vindic. Treat. Mon.* iv. 22 Who have.. actually used forceable Resistance against subversive Instruments of their Soveraignes Will. **1730** WATERLAND *Rem. Clarke's Expos. Ch.-Catech.* 92 If we once yield to go farther than is reasonable..in the subversive Way, there is no knowing where..to stop. **1858** STANLEY *Life Arnold* II. ix. 156 One fatal error, subversive indeed, in its consequences. **1885** R. L. & F. STEVENSON *Dynamiter* 88 Whether it was the salt or the mustard, or the mere combination of so many subversive agents,..the young sufferer obtained relief. **1887** LOWELL *Democracy*, etc. 12 Nor was it among the people that subversive or mistaken doctrines had their rise.

b. Const. *of.*

1724 A. COLLINS *Gr. Chr. Relig.* 245 They put a sense upon the words subversive of the true literal sense. **1762** KAMES *Elem. Crit.* (1763) II. xviii. 433, I know no other fault more subversive of the melody. **1769** BLACKSTONE *Comm.* IV. 52 The principles of the papists being deservedly looked upon to be subversive of the civil government. **1812** D'ISRAELI *Calam. Auth.* (1879) 177 There is a poignant delight in study, often subversive of human happiness. **1849** MACAULAY *Hist. Eng.* I. i. 121 Liberties which, if allowed to any other troops, would have proved subversive of all discipline.

c. Const. *to.* (*rare.*)

1786 *Francis the Philanthropist* III. 163 To obviate inconveniences so subversive to their interests. **1879** *Cassell's Techn. Educ.* II. 55/1 That same system..was.. doomed to the most violent opposition as subversive to the Christian faith. **1912** *Ulster Covenant* in *Standard* 20 Sept. 8/4 Being convinced in our conscience that Home Rule would be..subversive to our civil and religious freedom.

sub'versive, *sb.* [f. the adj.] A subversive person; one who wishes to overthrow a political regime. Also *transf.* and *fig.*

1887 G. MEREDITH *Let.* Feb. (1970) II. 853 Londoners,.. ladies, dandies, mild revolutionists, total subversives, would mob together. **1927** *Weekly Dispatch* 23 Oct. 1/2 The fight against subversive anti-Fascism ceased. The subversives were crushed. **1951** *Manch. Guardian* 30 June 5/5 They [*sc.* the Chinese] have had quite a lesson in Korea and would hesitate before moving into Burma, except as subversives. **1954** I. DEUTSCHER *Age of Permanent Revolution* 14 He [*sc.* Trotsky] stakes everything on the change and upheaval that Time, the great subversive, must bring about. **1977** F. ORMSBY *Store of Candles* 49 At high tide the sea is under the city, A natural subversive. **1978** 'J. HIGGINS' *Day of Judgment* v. 75 You specialized in handling subversives, revolutionary movements generally and so on.

†**sub'versor**. *Obs. rare*⁻¹. [ad. L. *subversor*, agent-n. f. *subvertĕre* to SUBVERT.] = SUBVERTER.

a **1548** HALL *Chron., Hen. VIII*, 138 b, All people curssed the Cardinall..as subversor of the Lawes..of Englande.

subvert (səbˈvɜːt), *v.* [ad. OF. *subvertir* (from 13th c.), or L. *subvertĕre*, f. *sub-* SUB- 26 + *vertĕre* to turn. Cf. It. *sovvertere*, Sp. *subvertir*, Pg. *subverter*.]

†**1.** *trans.* To overthrow, raze to the ground (a town or city, a structure, edifice). *Obs.*

1382 WYCLIF *Gen.* xix. 29 Whan forsothe God had subuertid the citees of that regioun. **1422** YONGE *Secr. Secr.* 163 The excellent Cite of troy for aye Subuertid and destrued was. **1513** *Life Henry V* (1911) 117 Some others labored to subuert and ouerthrowe the walls. **1591** SHAKS. *1 Hen. VI*, II. iii. 65 These are his substance, sinewes, armes, and strength, With which he..Razeth your Cities, and subuerts your Townes. **1610** HOLLAND *Camden's Brit.* 361 When those more ancient Churches were subverted, Aldred ..erected another. **1632** LITHGOW *Trav.* II. 64 Earthquakes ..often-times subuert their houses. **1665** MANLEY *Grotius' Low C. Wars* 255 He easily recovered what ever had been conquered by..Mansfeldt,..and utterly subverted all that was unnecessary. **1775** R. CHANDLER *Trav. Asia M.* (1825) I. 331 Many villages were absorbed, the city Sipylus was subverted, and marshes were changed into lakes.

†**b.** in fig. context. *Obs.*

1661 BOYLE *Scept. Chem.* II. (1680) 162 Something that Subverts another Foundation of the Chymical Doctrine. *a* **1677** BARROW *Serm.* xxix. (1687) I. 401 To dissolve those sacred bands, by which its union is conteined, and to subvert the onely foundations of publick tranquillity. **1775** DE LOLME *Constit. Eng.* I. i. 9 William of Normandy.. subverted the ancient fabric of the Saxon Legislation. **1792** BURKE *Corr.* (1844) III. 392 They began its destruction by subverting..the foundations of civil society itself.

†**2.** To upset, overturn (an object); *occas.* to break up (ground). *Obs.*

1543–4 *Act 35 Hen. VIII*, c. 10 §2 The Partie.. whose Lande or Soile shalbe so herafter subverted and broken. **1563** *Homilies* II. I. II. Dd ij, He..ouertourneth the tables of thexchaungers, subuerteth the seates of them that sold doues. **1697** DRYDEN *Virg. Georg.* IV. 312 They themselves contrive To rob the Honey, and subvert the Hive. *a* **1700** EVELYN *Diary* 17 Feb. 1662, The tempest of wind..which subverted besides huge trees, many houses, innumerable chimnies.

†**3.** To evert (the eyelid). *Obs.*

1547 BOORDE *Brev. Health* ccv. (1557) 70 b, Blere eyes whiche is when the vnder lid of the eye is subuerted.

†**4.** To upset (the stomach, appetite). *Obs.*

1620 VENNER *Via Recta* Introd. 13 The Bathes..doe weaken and subuert the stomacke. *Ibid.* 98 The sweet Orenges are not fit for sauce, because they subuert the appetite, and cause loathsomnesse in the stomacke. **1661** LOVELL *Hist. Anim. & Min.* 186 Their eggs or spawn are poysonsome,..subverting the stomack, especially in May.

5. To undermine the character, loyalty, or faith of, corrupt, pervert (a person). Now *rare.*

c **1375** *Sc. Leg. Saints* i. (*Peter*) 82 He askit petir, quharfor he Subuertit men of þat cuntre. **1382** WYCLIF *Tit.* iii. 11 Schonye thou a man heretyk,..witinge for he that is such maner man is subuertid, and trespassith. **1552** ABP. HAMILTON *Catech.* (1884) 47 He that is siclike is subvertit and synnis. **1615** J. WRIGHT *Acc. Lady Jane Grey* in *Phenix* (1708) II. 29 Whom..desire of Life hath subverted, and made of a Christian an Infidel. **1633** STAFFORD *Pac. Hib.* II. iii. (1821) 255 Hee was at that time reclaimed, and subverted to bee a good Catholike. **1715** [A. A. SYKES] *Innoc. Error* 38 If he be subverted, yet 'twill be hard to prove Sin or Self-Condemnation upon a Man. **1914** *Times* 21 Oct. 7/5 These ringleaders..dispose of large means with which they are able to subvert workmen of their country engaged in the dockyard.

6. To disturb (the mind, soul); to overturn, overthrow (a condition or order of things, a principle, law, etc.).

c **1386** CHAUCER *Pars. T.* ¶ 561 It reueth hym the quiete of his herte and subuerteth his soule. **1426** LYDG. *De Guil. Pilgr.* 16471 Yff he contynue in hys malys..to subuerten myn hope. **1474** CAXTON *Chesse* 46 The mynystres by theyr pryde and orgueyl subuerte justyce. **1530** PALSGR. 742/2 This cursed opynion, if it may contynewe a whyle, it wyll subvert all good lawes. **1596** SPENSER *F.Q.* v. ix. 2 After that he..with dreadfull fate Had vtterly subuerted his vnrighteous state. **1639** DANIEL *Ecles.* xiii. 26 Hee.. Promises mountaines, brings thee to his feast, And doth subvert thy Reason, in thy Tast. **1654** H. L'ESTRANGE *Chas. I* (1655) 30 To the end he might..have perverted the Prince, and subverted the true Religion established in England. **1741** BUTLER *Serm.* Wks. 1874 II. 267 Nor can this obligation be denied..upon any principles, but such as subvert all other obligations. **1786** BURKE *Art. agst. W. Hastings* Wks. 1842 II. 205 In order to subvert the plain and natural interpretation given by the council to the orders of the court of directors. **1803–6** WORDSW. *Excurs.* IX. 132 Our active powers..become Strong to subvert our noxious qualities. **1830** HERSCHEL *Study Nat. Phil.* III. v. (1851) 338 The strongest chemical affinities were thus readily subverted by the decomposing action of the pile. **1844** H. H. WILSON *Brit. India* I. 507 If the constitution of the British Indian empire were subverted, the civil and military services would be broken down. **1861** BUCKLE *Civilisation* II. iii. 259 James..attempted..to subvert the liberties of Scotland.

absol. **1790** BURKE *Rev. France* 102 They have a power given to them, like that of the evil principle, to subvert and destroy.

7. To bring about the overthrow or ruin of (a †person, people, or country, a dynasty, etc.).

1529 MORE *Suppl. Soulys* Wks. 302/2 To make an open insurreccion & subuerte all the realme. **1535** COVERDALE *Isa.* xxxvii. 9 Thou knowest well, how the kinges of Assiria haue handled all the londes, that they haue subuerted. **1549–62** STERNHOLD & H. *Ps.* cxlv. (1566) 367 But he them al that wicked are, wil vtterly subuert. **1610** HEALEY *St. Aug. Citie God* 389 Hee [*sc.* Scipio] subdued Africa, and subverted Haniball. **1667** MILTON *P.L.* XII. 568 By things deemd weak Subverting worldly strong. **1827** HALLAM *Const. Hist.* iii. (1876) I. 135 Nothing so much strengthens any government as an unsuccessful endeavour to subvert it. **1841** ELPHINSTONE *Hist. India* I. 403 The inscriptions lead us to think that the dynasty subverted by the Mussulmans was of more recent origin. **1869** GLADSTONE *Juv. Mundi* vi. 156 That the Pelopids did not simply subvert, or succeed to, a prior dynasty, but that they held a new dominion.

sub'vertant, *a. Her.* [f. SUBVERT *v.* + -ANT.] = REVERTANT.

1688 [see SUBVERTED 2].

sub'vertebral, *a. Anat.* [SUB- 1 b.] Situated under or below a vertebra or the vertebral column.

1851 MANTELL *Petrifactions* iv. §2. 372 The first and second vertebræ..have additional sub-vertebral, wedge-shaped bones. **1872** HUMPHRY *Myology* 11 In the deepest stratum of all the muscular fibres with their intermuscular septa extend, under the surface of the bodies of the vertebræ, as far as the middle line... They..constitute what may be designated a 'subvertebral rectus'. **1879** HUXLEY & MARTIN *Pract. Biol.* 165 The sub-vertebral lymph sinus.

sub'verted, *a.* [f. SUBVERT *v.* + -ED¹.]

1. Overturned, overthrown.

1749 JOHNSON *Van. Hum. Wishes* 216 Did no subverted Empire mark his End? **1776** PENNANT *Tour Scot. in 1772* II. I. 241 Beneath one foot, a subverted vase, expressive of her character as a nymph of the fountains. **1822** MRS. PLUNKET in C. Butler *Hist. Mem. Eng. Cath.* (ed. 3) IV. 336 He prefers a protestant establishment and an unimpaired state to a roman catholic establishment and a subverted one.

2. *Her.* Reversed, turned in a direction contrary to the usual one.

1688 HOLME *Armoury* II. xiv. 340/2 *Reversed, Everted, Subverted, Subvertant,* or *Debased*: is when a thing from its proper nature and use, is turned over, or downwards. *Ibid.* II. xviii. 454/2 Party per pale, A. and G. three Cressants subverted in pale O.

sub'verter. [f. SUBVERT *v.* + -ER[1].] One who subverts or overthrows.

1515 in Leadam *Sel. Cases Star Chamber* (Selden Soc.) II. 80 The said mayre and Aldremen..be the brekers and subuerters of the good ordre and rule of the said Towne. **1526** *Pilgr. Perf.* (W. de W. 1531) 298 b, The subuerter & deceyuer of the people. **1612** TAYLOR *Comm. Titus* iii. 1. (1619) 547 How haue Christians..beene alwaies charged, that they were the onely subuerters of the place where they liued? **1697** DRYDEN *Life Virgil* (1721) I. 44 Virgil..might deserve the Title of Subverter of Superstitions, as well as Varro. **1764** GIBBON *Tri. Romans* Misc. Wks. 1814 IV. 380 The subverters of liberty. **1838** THIRLWALL *Greece* xxviii. IV. 60 Cries which threatened the subverters of the constitution with death. **1863** DE MORGAN in *Athenæum* 10 Oct. 467/3, I will not, from henceforward, talk to any..constructor of perpetual motion, subverter of gravitation, ..&c.

sub'vertible, *a.* *rare*$^{-1}$. [f. SUBVERT *v.* + -IBLE.] Capable of being subverted.

1817 COLERIDGE *Biog. Lit.* (1907) II. 29 Some [principles] which are unsteady and subvertible from the narrowness or imperfection of their basis.

sub'verting, *vbl. sb.* [-ING[1].] The action of overturning or overthrowing.

1382 WYCLIF *2 Tim.* ii. 14 To no thing it is profitable, no but to the subuertyng of men heeringe [**1611** the subuerting of the hearers]. **1580** HOLLYBAND *Treas. Fr. Tong, Subornement,*..a subuerting, a corrupting. **1611** COTGR., *Bouleversement*, an ouerturning, subuerting.

†**subvertise,** *v.* *Obs.* *rare*$^{-1}$. [ad. OF. *subvertiss-*, pres. stem of *subvertir* to SUBVERT.] *trans.* To subvert.

1484 CAXTON *Fables of Æsop* III. vi, They that setten alle theyr malyce ageynste fortune ben subuertysed and ouerthrawen by her.

subvirate ('sʌbvɪreɪt). *nonce-wd.* [f. SUB- 19 + L. *vir* man + -ATE[4].] One whose manhood is imperfect. (Used jocularly as if the name of a chemical salt.)

1861 O. W. HOLMES *Old Vol. Life* Wks. 1891 VIII. 9 Even these poor New England Brahmins of ours, *subvirates* of an organizable base as they often are, count as full men.

sub'vital, *a.* (*sb.*) [SUB- 19 a.] **a.** *Genetics.* Of a gene: causing the death of a significant proportion of the individuals carrying it, but not as many as a semi-lethal gene. Also as *sb.* Cf. LETHAL *a.* 1 d, SEMI-LETHAL *a.* and *sb.*

1948 E. HADORN in *Symp. Soc. Exper. Biol.* II. 181 We may even come across mutants, or organ systems of lethals, that behave during a first sensitive period as subvital factors, during a second period as semi-lethals, and during a third period as true lethals. **1951** T. DOBZHANSKY *Genetics & Origin of Species* (ed. 3) iii. 67 About 57 percent of the second and 49 percent of the third chromosomes which were free of lethals or semilethals were 'subvital' in homozygotes. A subvital is a deleterious gene or gene complex which causes..the death of less than half of the homozygotes. **1962** [see LETHAL *a.* 1 d]. **1978** *Acta Embryol. Exper.* I. 101, 80·9% of them survive the ill effects of the mutation; it is, therefore, considered a subvital mutation.

b. *Biol.* Not fully alive; having only some of the characteristics of living systems.

1954 *New Biol.* XVI. 10 Amongst the energy-providing materials are needed also 'sub-vital' systems which, using the energy provided, can grow and split and thus reproduce themselves.

,subvocali'zation. [SUB- 23; cf. *subvocal* s.v. SUB- 19.] The act or process of articulation with the lips or other speech organs silently or with barely audible sound, esp. while reading.

1947 G. T. BUSWELL in *Scientific Monthly* June 542/2 Completely silent reading, or 'nonoral' reading..is carried on without subvocalization. **1960** A. W. EDFELD *Silent Speech* II. vi. 88 The quotient between the rate of oral reading and the rate of silent reading was used as the measure of subvocalization. **1966** *New Scientist* 29 Dec. 738/1 'Subvocalization' in its most familiar form..consists of audible whispering while reading to oneself. **1974** *Nature* 8 Nov. 121/1 They were instructed to hold their tongues firmly between their teeth and lips while listening and were told to minimise subvocalisation.

Hence [as a back-formation] **sub'vocalize** *v. trans.* and *intr.*, to utter or form (words) by subvocalization; **sub'vocalizer**; **sub'vocalizing** *ppl. a.*

1947 G. T. BUSWELL in *Scientific Monthly* June 542/2 Few persons listening to a lecture follow the speaker by subvocalizing after him the words he speaks. **1947** —— in *Elem. School Jrnl.* Dec. 193/2 Persons who subvocalize in silent reading have a much slower rate than those who suppress all tendencies to deal with words separately. *Ibid.* 194/2 They were subvocalizers, the victims of a method of teaching reading that fixed oral-reading habits first. **1964** *Jrnl. Educ. Psychol.* LV. 339 Subvocalizers exhibited a higher mean lip movement and a slower mean breathing rate than did nonsubvocalizers. **1966** *Science* 16 Dec. 1467/2 An individual who subvocalizes to any great extent is limited to a top reading speed of approximately 150 words per minute —a maximum attainable while reading aloud. **1966** *New Scientist* 29 Dec. 738/3 Of 17 subvocalizing college students out of 50..nearly all managed to reduce their involuntary vocal activity to nil within five minutes. **1978** K. AMIS *Jake's Thing* xv. 153 Jake had subvocalized an oath.

'sub,warden. [SUB- 6.] An under or deputy warden.

1661 WOOD *Life* (O.H.S.) I. 390 Sir Thomas asked where Mr. Fisher the subwarden was? Mr. Brent, the senior fellow, answer'd: 'Sir, Mr. subwarden keeps his chamber'. **1688** HOLME *Armoury* III. iv. 199/2 *Vice-Principle*, the second person in the Colledg, which in some particular Halls or Colledges are termed *Vice-Masters, Sub-Wardens*, [etc.]. **1908** *Westm. Gaz.* 24 Feb. 4/1 He was for a brief period Sub-Warden of Bishop's College. **1911** F. HARRISON *Autobiogr. Mem.* ii. I. 83 The Sub-Warden whom I afterwards came to know..as a very worthy..gentleman.

'subway, *sb.* [SUB- 3.]

1. a. An underground passage for conveying water-pipes, gas-pipes, telegraph wires, etc.; an underground tunnel by which pedestrians or vehicles may pass from one point to another below a road or roads, or a river, railway, etc.

1825 HOOD & REYNOLDS *Odes & Addresses* 7 Speak up —or hath he hid his name To crawl thro' 'subways' unto fame Like Williams of Cornhill? **1828** J. WILLIAMS (*title*) An historical account of subways in the British Metropolis, for the flow of pure Water and Gas into the houses of the Inhabitants, without disturbing the pavements. **1834** *Penny Cycl.* II. 263/1 By means of it [*sc.* an arched structure].. subways, or sewers, are made to pass under heavy structures and along streets, with..safety. **1869** *Bradshaw's Railway Man.* XXI. 454 Thames Subway. Incorporated..for making and maintaining a subway, under the river Thames, from Deptford to the Isle of Dogs. Length, 582 yards, with various roads and approaches. **1884** *Law Times Rep.* N.S. LI. 540/1 There was no bridge or subway for passengers to cross the line by. **1954** *Gloss. Highway Engin Terms* (*B.S.I*) 25 *Subway*, an underground passageway or tunnel to permit traffic movement or to accommodate pipes and cables underneath a structure, road or railway.

attrib. **1887** *Dict. Archit.* s.v., The city of London and Southwark subway company. **1888** *Advance* (Chicago) 26 Apr. 260 A subway commission that for two years have drawn good salaries for not putting their wires under ground.

b. chiefly *N. Amer.* (orig. *U.S.*). An underground railway. Freq. *attrib.*

1893 *Massachusetts Acts & Resolves* 1420 The mayor of the city of Boston shall appoint..three commissioners..to be known as the board of subway commissioners. **1904** *Daily Chron.* 29 Oct. 3/7 The subway is being extended to Brooklyn by tunnel under the East River. **1905** *Ibid.* 8 Mar. 5/4 The collision on the subway line occurred on the north-bound track at Twenty-third Street. **1906** *Daily Colonist* (Victoria, B.C.) 27 Jan. 2/5 An aged woman was killed by a subway train today while trying to get into a car in which the door had been closed. **1911** *N. & Q.* 2nd Ser. IV. 487/1 The New York Subway, with an extent of some 25 miles, including the tracks for local and express trains, has been so designated since it was opened in 1905. **1919**, etc. [see METRO[2]]. **1941** B. SCHULBERG *What makes Sammy Run?* i. 22 They were walking down the steps to the subway arm in arm. **1951** E. PAUL *Springtime in Paris* v. 106 They stood there staring at the subway map. **1968** *Globe & Mail* (Toronto) 17 Feb. 48/3 (Advt.), An apartment..minutes from the Davisville subway station. **1971** *New Society* 18 Aug. 322/2 The [Glasgow] underground (never called the tube)... Glaswegians persist in calling it the subway. **1979** R. JAFFE *Class Reunion* (1980) I. viii. 117 The subway kiosk in Harvard Square.

2. Special Comb.: **subway alumni** *sb. pl.* (U.S. slang), city-dwelling supporters of a college football team who, though not graduates of the college, attend games or follow the results through the news media (also *transf.*).

1947 *Sun* (Baltimore) 3 Nov. 15/8 Many letters have come in attacking Army for dropping Notre Dame... These letters came from Notre Dame's subway alumni, not from Notre Dame. **1960** *Washington Post* 7 Apr. D7 Silky Sullivan, the hero of the 'subway alumni', went into the 1958 Derby as the sentimental favorite. **1982** *Chicago Sun-Times* 26 Oct. 91 Faust would be having a devil of a time staying in the good graces of Notre Dame alumni (real and subway).

Hence as *v. intr.* (N. Amer. colloq.), to travel by subway or underground railway.

1929 M. LIEF *Hangover* 307 He subwayed up to Times Square. **1945** *PM* (N.Y.) 13 Apr. M4/2 We subwayed to Brooklyn. **1968** *Globe & Mail* (Toronto) 17 Feb. 46 (Advt.), You drive a Mercedes, but want to subway to the office.

subzee, var. SUBJEE.

sub'zonal, *a.* *Embryol.* [SUB- 1 b.] Designating a layer of cells beneath the zona pellucida of an ovum, constituting the basis of the chorion.

1877 W. TURNER *Hum. Anat.* 864 The sub-zonal membrane consists essentially of a layer of cells, which was originally continuous with the cellular layer lining the inner surface of the proper amnion. *Ibid.*, The formation of the amnion and sub-zonal outer layer of the persistent chorion.

'subzone. *Geol.* [SUB- 7 c.] A subdivision of a zone.

1888 A. GEIKIE in *Q. Jrnl Geol. Soc.* XLIV. 403 At the top of the fourth subzone..an interesting discovery was made of a thin band containing Serpulites. **1894** *Geol. Mag.* Oct. 442 Showing five sub-zones..with names of all the genera and species found in each.

†**suc.** *Obs.* Also succe. [a. F. *suc*, or ad. L. *sūcus* SUCCUS. Cf. SUCK *sb.*[3]] Juice, sap.

1551 TURNER *Herbal* I. F v b, The frenche men seth out of it [*sc.* the birch tree] a certain iuce or suc[*ed.* 1568 suck] other-wise called bitumen. **1630** LENNARD tr. *Charron's Wisd.* (1658) 13 *Chyle*, that is to say, a kinde of white *Suc*, fit for the nourishment of the body. **1657** *Physical Dict.*, *Succe*, juyce, vital moisture either of a plant, or of an humane body.

suc, obs. form of SICK.

succade (sʌ'keɪd). Also 5 socade, 6 sukcade, 7 succad. [a. AF. *sukade* (15th c.) = OF. (north-eastern) *succade*, also *chuc(c)ade*, of uncertain origin (see -ADE 1 c): cf Du. *sukade*, G. *succade*. See also SUCCATE and SUCKET.] Fruit preserved in sugar, either candied or in syrup; *pl.* sweetmeats of candied fruit or vegetable products.

1463 *Mann. & Househ. Exp.* (Roxb.) 217 Item, in a pott off socade, ij. d. **1502** *Priv. Purse Exp. Eliz. York* (1830) 43 A present of oranges and sukcades. **1542** BOORDE *Dyetary* xix. (1870) 278 The rootes of Alysaunder soden tender and made in succade. **1597** GERARDE *Herbal* II. cclxvi. 650 [The root of elecampane] is especially preserued by those that make succade and such like. **1690** CHILD *Disc. Trade* (1698) 112 Italian, Spanish, Portugal, and French commodities viz. oil, wine, fruit, sugar, succads, shoomack. **1719** DE FOE *Crusoe* I. (Globe) 195, I found two Pots of very good Succades, or Sweet-meats. **1821** J. SMYTH *Pract. Customs* 244 The peel of Citron preserved in sugar, and all other moist sweetmeats not particularly enumerated in the table of duties, are denominated Succades. **1836** in R. Ellis *Customs* (1840) IV. 292 Peaches..even, although they may be dry, if sugar has been the material of preservation, they must be treated as succades. **1863** *Act 26 Vict.* c. 22 Succades, including all Fruits and Vegetables preserved in Sugar, not otherwise enumerated.

b. succade gourd, the vegetable marrow.

1866 *Treas. Bot.* 358/2 The Egg-shaped or Succade Gourd, or Vegetable Marrow, *Cucurbita ovifera succada*.

†**su'ccado.** *Obs.* [See prec. and -ADO 2.] ? Fruit syrup.

c **1530** in Gutch *Coll. Cur.* II. 297 Oone depe Goblit fer suckado. **1537** in *Lett. & P. Hen. VIII* (1890) XII. I. 451 Two little barrels of suckat, weighing 18 lbs., the one of flowers of oranges, the other of fine succado, at 9*d.* the lb.

‖**succah** ('sʊkə, ‖su'ka). Also sukkah, [Heb. *sukkāh*, lit. 'hut'.] One of the booths in which a practising Jew spends part of the Feast of the Tabernacles. Cf. SUCCOTH.

[**1819** *Christian Spectator* I. 126/2 They made booths, in Hebrew *succoth*, that is, sheds or hovels of thorn bushes.] **1875** J. PICCIOTTO *Sk. Anglo-Jewish Hist.* xvi. 140 The Succoths [*sic*] or tabernacles were then, as at present, decorated with fruits and flowers. **1905** *Jewish Encycl.* XI. 660/2 The sukkah or booth was to be a structure especially built for the festival. **1925** *Public Opinion* 4 Sept. 220/3 A sukkah for use during the Feast of Tabernacles. **1970** *New Yorker* 20 June 32/2 The Rabbi's disciples escorted her personally into the *sukkah*. **1979** *Jewish Chron.* 7 Dec. 39/1 Tradition has it that the minute Yom Kippur ends, you dash out and erect the first plank of the Succah. Tradition in our house has it that as soon as Succot is over, you dash out looking for the first Chanucah presents. **1981** C. POTOK *Bk. of Lights* (1982) vi. 191 'What do you want built, chaplain?' 'It's called a succah. It's a kind of booth or hut with wooden sides and an open roof covered with leaves and branches.'

succar, obs. Sc. form of SUGAR *sb.*

†**succarath.** *Obs.* Also sucaratha. [Cf. SUE *sb.*] (See quots.)

1594 BLUNDEVIL *Exerc.* v. (1636) 566 This dangerous beast is called *Sucaratha*, which being chased of Hunters, doth take her young ones upon her backe. **1635** NIEREMBERG *Hist. Nat.* IX. lxxiv. 189 Belluam rapacem apud Patagones *su*, id est aquam vocant nonnulli, quòd plerumque iuxta fluuios degat. Alij dicunt *succarath*. **1688** HOLME *Armoury* II. x. 212/2 A Monster like Beast, inhabiting in the Newfound World; and is of some termed a *Succarath*.

succatash, -osh, -ush, variants of SUCCOTASH.

†**'succate.** *Obs.* Also 6 socate, -atte, suckat, succot, 6, 8 succat. Obscure variant of SUCCADE. Also *fig.* (Cf. med.L. *succātum* (15th c.) 'safftgetranck', 16th cent. Du. *sucate* = *sukade*.)

1481–90 *Howard Househ. Bks.* (Roxb.) 506 Item..for caryeng of spyces oranges and succate vj.s. viij.d. **1536** *Acc. Ld. High Treas. Scot.* VI. 287 Tua barrellis and ane halff of succatis. **1562** TURNER *Herbal* II. 24 b, Som vse to make succat wyth hony or sugar of the yonge nuttes [of the Walnut tree]. **1562** BULLEIN *Bulwarke, Bk. Simples* (1579) 44 b, The rootes must be tenderly sodden, and preserued in Succate. **1593** G. HARVEY *Pierce's Super.* 136, I haue giuen you a tast of his Suger-loafe, that weeneth..Cheekes succats,..and Mores iunkets nothing comparable to his pap. **1715** D'ANOIS *Wks.* 503 b, Succats [*printed* Succals] and Sugar-Plumbs were devour'd by Cart-loads.

Comb. **1562** TURNER *Herbal* II. 22 The succot makers.

†**succa'toon.** *Obs.* [Of unascertained origin. Cf. SUCCOTA.] A kind of cloth.

1703 *Lond. Gaz.* No. 3933/4 The Cargo of the Star of the East, consisting of Long Cloth,..Succatoons, Silks, Red-Sanders, Rice, &c. **1825** DALBY *Hume & Smollett's Hist. Eng.* V. 241 *note*, The trade..at Pondicherry..consists of long cloths.., ginghams, and succatoons.

†**suc'cease,** *v.* *Obs.* Also 6 suckeses. Altered form of SURCEASE.

1551 *Gray's New Year's Gift* 31 in Furnivall *Ballads fr. MSS.* I. 420 The Iusteses, that sholde se this suckeses [*Camb. MS.* surcesse], stand by and her yt, and kepe the kynges pese. 1630 J. TAYLOR (Water P.) *Wks.* III. 92/1 This riff raff rubbish..Came to vs as our fire began to smother.. Commanding that our bonfire should succease.

†**succedane.** *Obs. rare.* Anglicized form of SUCCEDANEUM.

1601 HOLLAND *Pliny* II. 5 The ashes also made thereof, be counted a good Succedane of Spodium. *Ibid.* 158.

†**succe'daneal,** *a. Obs. rare.* [f. L. *succēdāneus* (see next) + -AL[1].] = next.

1633 AMES *Fresh Suit agst. Cerem.* II. 173 As succedaneall instances to the former,..the Rejoynder bringeth in diverse, out of the..Ceremoniall law. 1669 W. SIMPSON *Hydrol. Chym.* 121, I haue by a succedaneal preparation so opened the body.

†**succe'daneous,** *a. Obs.* [f. L. *succēdāneus* (*succīdāneus*), f. *succēdĕre* to SUCCEED. Cf. F. *succédané*, It. *succedaneo*.]

1. Taking, or serving in, the place of something else; acting as a succedaneum or substitute. Const. *to* (*unto*).

In the 17th c. said esp. of medicinal applications or ingredients.

1646 SIR T. BROWNE *Pseud. Ep.* 114 He prescribeth the stones of the Otter, or River-dog, as succedaneous unto *Castoreum.* 1657 G. STARKEY *Helmont's Vindic.* 295 By succedaneous secrets the same diseases may be restored, although not with the same speed or universality. 1686 HORNECK *Crucif. Jesus* iii. 40 It being taken for granted that the Lord's Supper was succedaneous to the Passover. *a* 1722 LISLE *Husb.* (1757) 245 Being bit off, it has similar succedaneous parts. 1775 JOHNSON *West. Isl.* 302 The Islanders are obliged to content themselves with succedaneous means for many common purposes. 1802–12 BENTHAM *Ration. Judic. Evid.* (1827) IV. 122 In what cases ..a succedaneous security shall be accepted at the hands of the plaintiff. 1816 *Monthly Rev.* LXXIX. 506 Some intelligent editor should undertake to re-engrave the old, and to insert in its proper place the succedaneous matter.

2. Supplementary. *rare.*

1665 *R. Scot's Discov. Witchcr.* (*title-p.*), In two Books: The First by the aforesaid author: The Second now added in this Third Edition, as Succedaneous to the former. 1800 BENTHAM *Corr.* Wks. 1843 X. 345/2 If your succedaneous volumes should be as yet unbound. 1808 —— *Sc. Reform* 38 In the succedaneous or supplemental plan.

‖**succedaneum** (sʌksɪ'deɪnɪəm). (Also 8–9 *erron.* succeedaneum.) Pl. **-ea, -eums.** [mod.L., neut. sing. of L. *succēdāneus* SUCCEDANEOUS.]

1. A thing which (*rarely*, a person who) replaces or serves in the place of another; a substitute.

1662 PETTY *Taxes* 82 Almost all commodities haue their substitutes or *succedanea.* 1679 J. GOODMAN *Penit. Pard.* II. ii. (1713) 182 Others..will part with a sin without a *succedaneum*, or entertaining any other in its room. *a* 1734 NORTH *Examen* III. viii. §63 (1740) 632 Where Reason and Justice is wanted, a Face of Assurance is the *Succedaneum.* 1774 GOLDSM. *Nat. Hist.* (1824) I. xv. 103 A kind of succedaneum which has been lately conceived to answer the purpose of fresh water. 1774 H. WALPOLE *Lett.* (1857) VI. 124 In lieu of me, you will have a charming succedaneum, Lady Harriet Stanhope. 1844 STEPHENS *Bk. Farm* II. 193 But independent of all succedanea, which may be given to horses at times as a treat,..there should be a regular feed prepared for farm-horses. 1860 KINGSLEY *Limits Exact Sci.* 17 They are..apt..to patch them where they are weakest, by that most dangerous succedaneum of vague and grand epithets. 1911 F. A. MACCULLOCH *Relig. Anc. Celts* ix. 162 As kings were represented by a substitute, so the sacred tree ..may also have had its *succedaneum.*

b. Const. *for.*

1662 H. STUBBE *Indian Nectar* iii. 56 It is impossible to provide any succedanea, or substitutes for these kind of Commodities. 1699 *Phil. Trans.* XXI. 311 How the Arabians fell first into the use of Coffee is hard to tell, perhaps 'twas their Succedaneum for Wine. 1772–84 *Cook's Voy.* (1790) V. 1620 Green plantains are an excellent succedaneum for bread. 1806 A. HUNTER *Culina* (ed. 3) 227 A Succedaneum for green Pease in Winter. 1834 PRINGLE *Afr. Sk.* iii. 165 A pan of live charcoal or embers from our wooden fires was the usual succedaneum for a blazing hearth. 1848 DICKENS *Dombey* xxiii, A pair of dreadnought pilot-trousers, whereof the waistband was so very broad and high, that it became a succedaneum for a waistcoat. 1891 'ROY TELLET' *Draught of Lethe* II. 225 If you cannot afford a conscience, the best succedaneum for it is a keen sense of professional propriety.

†**c.** Const. *to.*

1667 *Phil. Trans.* II. 516 The continual motion of their Gills, a *Succedaneum* to Lungs. 1733 TULL *Horse-hoeing Husb.* vii. 56 This is but an Imitation of the Hand-Hoe, or a *Succedaneum* to it. 1755 H. WALPOLE *Lett.* (1857) II. 477 He has contracted for a *succedaneum* to the Mingotti. 1802–12 BENTHAM *Ration. Judic. Evid.* (1827) III. 143 Self-inculpative discourse..can never be an adequate succedaneum to judicial confession.

d. Const. *of.* (*rare.*)

1651 FRENCH *Distill.* vi. 183 This Oil may be the *Succedaneum* of true gold. 1791 W. GILPIN *Forest Scenery* I. 81 The most beautiful succedaneum of the stone-pine, which these climates afford is the pinaster. 1837 CARLYLE *Fr. Rev.* I. II. i, Paper; which in many ways is the succedaneum of Gold.

2. *Med.* A drug, frequently of inferior efficacy, substituted for another.

c 1643 LD. HERBERT *Autobiog.* (1824) 45 It being the manner of Apothecaries so frequently to put in the Succedanea that no man is sure to find with them Medicines made with the true drugs. *a* 1661 FULLER *Worthies, Brecknockshire* (1662) IV. 21 Physicians have their Succedanea, or Seconds, which well supply the place of such Simples, which the Patient cannot procure. 1748 SMOLLETT *Rod. Random* xix, The most expert man at a succedaneum, of any apothecary in London. 1822–7 GOOD *Study Med.* (1829) IV. 461 In such cases, we must find out, by trial, what is its best succedaneum. 1866 A. FLINT *Princ. Med.* II. I. xi. 258 For this end the succedanea of opium, viz., conium, belladonna, and hydrocyanic acid may be prescribed.

†**3.** Misused for: A remedy, cure. *Obs.*

1737 LD. CHESTERF. in *Gentl. Mag.* VII. 498 Their Case is certainly above Comfort, and, I own, I am at a Loss what to recommend to 'em. Succedaneums there are none, I shall only endeavour to suggest Lenitives. 1785 H. WALPOLE *Let. to Mann* 24 June, Italian summers are a good succedaneum, and, I hope, will be more efficacious than our north-easterly winds. 1789 J. WILLIAMS *Min. Kingd.* I. 179, I am politician enough to be able to suggest the proper remedy or succedaneum for all these difficulties.

†**succedany.** *Obs. rare*[−1]. Anglicized f. prec.

1657 TOMLINSON *Renou's Disp.* 625 There are many simples most convenient..as the fruit of Balm and its fit succedany, Dittany.

succedent (sək'siːdənt), *a.* and *sb.* Now *Obs.* or *rare.* Also 6–9 **succedant,** 9 **succeedant, -ent.** [ad. L. *succēdens, -ent-*, pr. pple. of *succēdĕre* to SUCCEED.] **A.** *adj.*

1. Following, succeeding, subsequent. Const. *to.*

c 1450 *Mirour Saluacioun* (Roxb.) 35 First lef and then flowres and grapes succedent. 1577 HARRISON *England* I. vii. 7 b in *Holinshed*, That after death it [*sc.* the soul] went in to another bodye, the seconde or succedent, being alwayes, eyther more noble, or more vile than the former. 1587 —— *Ibid.* II. v. 157 in *Holinshed*, Few of them doo agree vpon forme of discipline and gouernement of the church succedent. 1607 WALKINGTON *Optic Glass* 63 Which causeth a great heate to be ingendered ther by the coughing motion, which heat draws a succedent phleum. 1614 W. BEDWELL *Nat. Geom. Numbers* iv. 63 The quotient 2 I place in the quotient for the side of the succedent cube. 1677 CARY *Palæol. Chron.* II. I. §1. xx. 144 The making of those XIV Dynasties succedent one to another, which for severals of them were coeval. 1797 *Monthly Mag.* XXXVI. 214 There must have been a precedent, and there also must be a succedent state. 1887 A. M. BROWN *Anim. Alkaloids* 158 Each having an existence of its own, but presenting in its terms antecedent and succedant, analogies which [etc.].

b. *Her.*

1688 HOLME *Armoury* II. 485/2 *Succedant*, succeeding, following one another. 1828–40 BERRY *Encycl. Her.* I.

2. Astrol. ***succedent houses***: the 2nd, 5th, 8th, and 11th houses (see quots.).

1591 SPARRY tr. *Cattan's Geomancie* 64 The 2. 5. 8. and 11. be called the houses Succedants. 1601 DOLMAN *La Primaud. Fr. Acad.* (1618) III. 690 Those fowre [houses of heaven] which begin at the foure foresaid angles, are named Angularie houses: the next fowre following are called Succedent, and the rest Cadent. 1671 BLAGRAVE *Astrol. Pract. Phys.* 164 For common signs, and succedant houses we usually allow somewhat above half so much as we do for first signs. 1679 MOXON *Math. Dict.*, *Succedent-Houses*, Are so called, because they succeed or follow Angles in a Celestial Figure; as the 11*th.* the 2*d.* the 5*th.* and the 8*th.* which succeeding, is yet not so much in Order, as in Condition and Dignity. 1819 JAS. WILSON *Dict. Astrol.* 165 In a succeedent house, moveable signs give months.

B. *sb.*

†**1.** A thing that follows another. *Obs.*

c 1440 *Pallad. Husb.* III. 1124 This Greek auctorite So macth to craft nature a succedent. 1608 J. KING *Serm.* 5 Nov. 17 A succedent I graunt, nearest vnto it of al others.

2. *Astrol.* A 'succedent house' (see A 2).

c 1391 CHAUCER *Astrol.* II. §4 The lord of the assendent.. is fortunat, whan he is..in a succedent, where-as he is in his dignite & conforted with frendly aspectys of planetes. 1591 SPARRY tr. *Cattan's Geomancie* 176 There be foure called angles, and foure succedants, and foure cadants. 1653 R. SANDERS *Physiogn.* 32 In the succedent was Aquarius.

†**3.** A result, issue. *Obs. rare.*

1627 E. F. *Hist. Edw. II* (1680) 143 Such is the mutability of the inconstant Vulgar..; despising the time being, extolling that of their Forefathers, and ready to act any mischief to try by alteration the succedent.

succeed (sək'siːd), *v.* Forms: 4 *Sc.* **succed,** 4–6 **succede,** 6–7 **succeede** (4, 6 *Sc.* **succeid,** 6 **-eyd,** 8 **suckseed**), 6– **succeed.** [a. OF. *succeder* (from 14th c.) or ad. L. *succēdĕre*, to go under, go up, come close after, go near, f. *suc-* = SUB- III + *cēdĕre* to go. Cf. Pr. *succedir*, It. *succedere*, Sp. *suceder*, Pg. *succeder*.]

1. a. *intr.* To come next after and take the place of another, either by descent, election, or appointment, in a position of rule or ownership; to be the immediate successor in an office or in an estate.

1375 BARBOUR *Bruce* I. 64 Than the neyst cummyn off the seid, Man or woman, suld succeid. *c* 1386 CHAUCER *Clerk's T.* 576 Whan Walter is agon, Thanne shal the blood of Ianicle succede And been oure lord. *c* 1400 *Apol. Loll.* 5 Bi þe slownes of þe pope, and of prelats succedand in his place, and bi her peruerse werkis, moost iuil comiþ to vs. 1538 STARKEY *England* I. iv. 108 You know by the ordur of our law, the eldyst brother succedyth. 1590 SPENSER *F.Q.* II. x. 68 After him Vther, which Pendragon hight, Succeding There abruptly it did end. 1608 HEYWOOD *Lucrece* II. ii, Barren Princes Breed danger in their singularitie; Having none to succeed, their claime dies in them. 1891 E. PEACOCK *N. Brendon* I. 59 When Sir Ralf died, Sir John succeeded.

b. Const. *to* (a person): = 2.

c 1375 *Sc. Leg. Saints* xii. (*Mathias*) 71 Gyf þu myn awne ware, & mycht as ayr succed to me. 1387 TREVISA *Higden* (Rolls) VII. 119 Þis ȝere deide þe secounde Richard, þe fourþe duke of Normandie, to whom succedid his sone Richard þe þridde. 1456–70 in *Acts Parlt. Scot.* (1875) XII. 27/1 Eftyr the deceiss of this lard of Meldrum succedit tyll hyme ane othir lard. 1529 *Reg. Privy Seal Scot.* I. 585 The aire or airis maile or femaile..succedand to the said umquhile erle. 1613 PURCHAS *Pilgrimage* (1614) 280 Saracon ..was appointed Sultan,..to whom Saladine his Nephew succeeded. 1831 SCOTT *Nigel* Introd., A young heir, who has totally altered the establishment of the father to whom he has succeeded. 1874 MARKBY *Elem. Law* (ed. 2) §564 Neither the heir nor the legatee has a right to claim any portion of the moveable estate;..they do not in any way *succeed* to the deceased. 1908 R. BAGOT *A. Cuthbert* vi. 52 It was his duty to marry again, and to have children to succeed to him.

fig. 1500–20 DUNBAR *Poems* xii. 22 Evirmair vnto this warldis joy As nerrest air succeidis noy.

c. To follow in office in order of seniority. *rare.*

1764 FOOTE *Mayor of G.* I. Wks. 1799 I. 166 We always succeeded of course; no jumping over heads.

d. Const. †(*a*) *in, into*, (*b*) *to* (an estate, a position of rule or ownership).

(*a*) *c* 1386 CHAUCER *Clerk's T.* 1079 His sone succedeth in his heritage..after his fader day. 1482 in *Eng. Hist. Rev.* XXV. 123 Alle oyere yat shalle succede in that office. 1520 CAXTON *Chron. Eng.* I. 6 b/1 His sone Heleazarus succeded in yᵉ bysshopryche. 1585 T. WASHINGTON tr. *Nicholay's Voy.* II. xix. 53 If shee be brought to bed of a manchild, the same may by order and course succeed in the Empyre. 1590 SPENSER *F.Q.* II. x. 41 Next them did Gurgunt, great Bellinus sonne In rule succeede. 1597 *Reg. Mag. Sig. Scot.* 303/2 Rob. Scot..and Barbara Scott his spous..ar and hes bene maist kyndlie to succeid in the tak. 1643 BAKER *Chron.* (1653) 60 Rodolph succeeded in the See of Canterbury. 1690 LOCKE *Govt.* I. ix. Wks. 1714 II. 135 David by the same title that Saul Reigned..succeeded in his Throne, to the exclusion of Jonathan.

(*b*) 1563 in Strype *Ann. Ref.* (1709) xxxviii. 400 The advancement of the Scotch Title to succede to the English Crown. *a* 1578 LINDESAY (Pitscottie) *Chron. Scot.* (S.T.S.) I. 194 Nor zit succeidand to na grett heretaige. 1596 DALRYMPLE tr. *Leslie's Hist. Scot.* I. 88 Quhen the peychtis doubted quha suld succeid to the kingdome law-fullie. 1765 BLACKSTONE *Comm.* I. iii. 199 Henry the eighth..succeeded to the crown by clear indisputable hereditary right. 1891 *Speaker* 2 May 564/1 When he succeeded..to the family estates, he found them heavily encumbered. 1912 *Eng. Hist. Rev.* Jan. 44 There seems to be some ground for surmising that Henry wished him to succeed to Neville's office.

e. *transf.* Const. *to* (†*into*): To follow another in the enjoyment or exercise of; to be the next to share or take part in.

1612 BREREWOOD *Lang. & Relig.* 178 Mozal, as I said afore, is either Seleucia, or succeeded into the dignity of it. 1670 DRYDEN *Conq. Granada* II. III. i, Take breath; my guards shall to the fight succeed. 1693 —— *Disc. Satire* Ess. 1900 II. 22 Some witty men may perhaps succeed to their designs. 1782 PRIESTLEY *Corrupt. Chr.* I. IV. 363 The christian saints succeeded..to the honours. 1866 R. W. DALE *Disc. Spec. Occ.* v. 156 We have succeeded to the honours and responsibilities of our predecessors.

2. a. *trans.* To take the place of, as successor in an office or heir to an estate; to follow (another) in ownership or the occupation of a position or office; to be successor or heir to.

1503–4 *Act 19 Hen. VII*, c. 25 §2 They that soo shall succede them..in the seid Sees & Bisshopprikkes. 1513 MORE *Life Rich. III*, Wks. 70/2 So was I to king Edward faithfull chapleyn, & glad wold haue bene yᵗ his childe had succeded him. 1583 STUBBES *Anat. Abus.* II. (1882) 90 Matthias succeeding Iudas the traitour in the administration of the apostleship. 1611 *Bible* Deut. ii. 12 The children of Esau succeeded them when they had destroyed them from before them, & dwelt in their stead. 1675 WOOD *Life* (O.H.S.) II. 310 His brother Ralph succeeds him in the estate. 1702 N. BLUNDELL *Diary* (1895) 6 Eliz. Sumner Dary-Maid left my Service and was sucksееded by Mary Formby. 1841 ELPHINSTONE *Hist. India* II. 63 When they retired, they were succeeded by the Gakkars. 1860 R. ROSS *Engl. Hist.* 149 Richard Cromwell succeeded his father. 1892 GARDINER *Student's Hist. Eng.* 13 In 47 Aulus Plautius was succeeded by Ostorius Scapula. 1897 J. W. CLARK *Barnwell* Introd. 13 Prior Geoffrey..was succeeded by Prior Gerard.

†**b.** *fig.* To follow by imitating. *Obs.*

1577 HANMER *Anc. Eccl. Hist.* (1619) 507 Succeed your fathers and ancestors in obedience. 1601 SHAKS. *All's Well* I. i. 70 Succeed thy father In manners as in shape.

†**3.** To fall heir to, inherit, come into possession of; = *succeed to*, 1 d, e. *Obs.*

1490 *Cov. Leet Bk.* 537 Ye must hastely procede vnto theleccion off an-other personne to succede the said office. 1561 NORTON & SACKV. *Gorboduc* III. i. 73 Egall in degree With him that claimeth to succede the whole. 1603 SHAKS. *Meas. for M.* II. iv. 123 Else let my brother die, If not a fedarie but onely he Owe, and succeed thy weaknesse. 1606 G. W[OODCOCKE] *Lives Emperors* in *Hist. Ivstine* Kk4 Mychaell, the son of Constantinus Ducas, sur-named.. Parapinaceus succeedeth the Empire. 1725 RAMSAY *Gentle Sheph.* To C'tess Eglintoun 131 Thrice happy! who succeed their mother's praise, The lovely Eglintouns of other days.

4. a. *intr.* To come next or immediately afterwards in an order of individual persons or things; to follow on; also, †to occupy the space vacated by something. (Sometimes const. *to.*)

c 1391 CHAUCER *Astrol.* II. §12, & next him [*sc.* Mercury] succedith the Mone; & so forth by ordre, planete aftur planete. *c* 1485 *Digby Myst.* II. 344 Go forth yowur way; I wyll succede In-to what place ye wyll me lede. *a* 1548 HALL *Chron., Edw. IV*, 28 b, Thys battayl on both sides was sore fought & many slayn, in whose romes succeded euer fresh, and freshmen. 1596 DALRYMPLE tr. *Leslie's Hist. Scot.* I. 52 To the Mernes neist succeidis Angus. 1690 LOCKE *Hum. Und.* II. xxiii. §24 The ambient Fluid, having a full Liberty to succeed in each Point of Space. 1692 RAY *Disc.* 131 The Waters rising up out of the subterraneous Abyss the Sea must needs succeed. *a* 1700 EVELYN *Diary* 11 Mar. 1651, There was another Malefactor to succeede. 1715 DESAGULIERS *Fires Impr.* 25 The cold Air all the while coming down and succeeding at D till the whole Air in the Room has pass'd thro'. 1798 R. BLOOMFIELD *Farmer's Boy*,

Spring 179 Sub-ordinate they one by one succeed; And one among them always takes the lead. **1908** A. Dobson *De Libris* Prol. p. v, I can't pretend to read You the pages that to this succeed.

†**b.** *trans.* To follow, walk after. *Obs.*

c **1485** *Digby Myst.* II. 589, I wyll yow succede, for better or wors, To the prynces of pristes. **1781** Cowper *Hope* 14 As in a dance the pair that take the lead Turn downward, and the lowest pair succeed.

†**5.** *intr.* To be continued, go on. *Obs.*

1486 *Bk. St. Albans, Her.* a j, How bondeage began first in aungell and after succeded in man kynde. **1605** Verstegan *Dec. Intell.* vi. 156 The old grownded opinion, that hath by ancient tradition succeeded from age to age. **1609** Rowlands *Whole Crew Kind Gossips* 17 My discontent succeedeth day by day.

6. a. To follow or come *after* in the course of events, the sequence of things, the order of development, etc.; to take place or come into being subsequently. †*to succeed*: to come; future.

c **1450** *Godstow Reg.* 352 In the which..mese..the Chapelayn.. shold haue a dwellyng to serue by the tymys succedyng. *a* **1533** Ld. Berners *Gold. Bk. M. Aurel.* (1546) B iij, As the ages hath succeded, so are discouered the sciences. **1570** *Satir. Poems Reform.* xvii. 117 We se and spyis not our sorrowis to succeid. **1583** Foxe *A. & M.* (ed. 4) 1397/2 The Masse Priests succeede after Christ, doing the same sacrifice (as they say) which he did before. **1593** Shaks. *2 Hen. VI*, II. iv. 2 After Summer, euermore succeedes Barren Winter. **1613** —— *Hen. VIII*, v. v. 24 A Patterne to all Princes liuing with her, And all that shall succeed. **1622** Peacham *Compl. Gentl.* x. (1906) 95 After him [*sc.* Gower] succeeded Lydgate, a Monke of Bury, who wrote that bitter Satyre of Peirs Plow-men. **1667** Milton *P.L.* iv. 535 Enjoy, till I return, Short pleasures, for long woes are to succeed. *Ibid.* x. 733 Who of all Ages to succeed, but feeling The evil on him brought by me, will curse My Head. **1678** Marvell *Corr.* Wks. (Grosart) II. 619 Those ill consequences which have since succeeded both at home and abroade. **1781** Cowper *Hope* 749 And when.. This earth shall blaze, and a new world succeed. **1847** C. Brontë *Jane Eyre* v, Half an hour's recreation succeeded, then study. **1875** Jowett *Plato* (ed. 2) V. 56 The age of reverence is gone, and the age of irreverence and licentiousness has succeeded.

†**b.** To follow as a consequence *of* or *upon*; to proceed *from* a source; to ensue, result. *Obs.*

1537 Starkey in Strype *Eccl. Mem.* (1721) I. App. lxxxi. 194 Al worldly respects set aside, and al dangerous success, which might succede of the same. **1632** Lithgow *Trav.* iii. 117 Curing a festered soare with a poysoned playster; whence succeeded a dismall discord. **1652** Nedham tr. *Selden's Mare Cl.* 7 Any innovation of wrongs succeeding thereupon. **1697** Dryden *Virg. Georg.* iv 771 The Cause is known, from whence Thy Woe succeeded. **1710** Prideaux *Orig. Tithes* v. 225 The Normans having conquered this Realm, a thorough abolition of the whole [uniformity of laws, etc.] had like to have succeeded.

c. Const. *to*: = 9.

1687 A. Lovell tr. *Thevenot's Trav.* i. Pref., Those Exercises, which in the breeding of Youth, commonly succede to their School Education. **1700** Dryden *Pal. & Arc.* iii. 346 While Day to Night, and Night to Day succeeds. **1703** Rowe *Ulysses* Dedic., That this Glorious End may very suddenly succeed to your Lordship's Candor and Generous Endeavours after it. **1833** Tennyson *Two Voices* 205, I know that age to age succeeds, Blowing a noise of tongues and deeds.

†**7. a.** To follow *in*, or come *into*, *the place of* someone or something. *Obs.*

1551 Robinson *More's Utopia* ii. (1895) 283 They succede into the places of the other at theyre dyinge. **1638** Junius *Paint. Ancients* 100 Masters..should take the scholars in hand with a fatherly minde, esteeming themselves to succeed in their place that committed the children unto them. **1667** Milton *P.L.* xii. 508 But in thir room..Wolves shall succeed for teachers. **1690** Locke *Hum. Und.* ii. iv. §3 The Idea of the Motion of one single Body alone, without any other succeeding immediately into its place. **1701** Stanhope *Pious Breathings* iv. xii. (1704) 277 When these Spirits are dispossessed, the Spirit of God will succeed into their place.

b. Const. *to*: To take the place of.

a **1700** Dryden (J.), Revenge succeeds to love, and rage to grief. **1807** G. Chalmers *Caledonia* I. ii. vii. 325 Anglo-Saxon..on the subduement of the Romanized Ottadini, succeeded to the British tongue. **1819** Shelley *Cenci* ii. i. 52 What can now Have given you that cold melancholy look, Succeeding to your unaccustomed fear? **1883** *Manch. Exam.* 30 Nov. 5/3 Something like consternation succeeded to the benevolent interest with which the earlier movements of the Mahdi had been regarded.

†**c.** *trans.* (*causative*) To cause to take the place of another. *Obs. rare.*

1666 Dryden *Ann. Mirab.* clxxv, Young Hollis.. Impatient to revenge his fatal Shot, His right hand doubly to his left succeeds.

†**8.** Of an estate, etc.: To descend in succession; to devolve *upon*, to come down *from*. Chiefly *Sc.*

1536 *Abst. Protocols Town Clerks Glasgow* (1897) IV. 92 That the landis and tenement suld succeyd to hym in heretage. **1549** *Compl. Scot.* xvii. 155 Considerand that the crop ande rute of our gentreis and genologie hes succedit fra adam. **1596** Dalrymple tr. *Leslie's Hist. Scot.* I. 82 Quhais Impire..athir succeiding to thair awne eftircumers, or be violence..occupied be strangeris. **1601** Shaks. *All's Well* iii. vii. 23 A ring the Countie weares, That downward hath succeeded in his house From sonne to sonne. **1604** —— *Oth.* v. ii. 367 (1st Qo.) Ceaze vpon the fortunes of the Moore: For they succeed to [*1st Fol.* on] you.

9. *trans.* To come after or follow in the course of time or the sequence of events. (In first quot., to live after, be posterior to.)

c **1525** Fisher *Serm. conc. Heretickes* B ij, Tyll vs (that succede the commynge of our sauiour) the same thynges be disclosed. **1608** Shaks. *Per.* i. iv. 104 The Curse of heauen and men succeed their euils. **1646** Sir T. Browne *Pseud. Ep.* v. iv. 238 If..those destructive effects they now discover succeeded the curse, and came in with..thornes and briars. **1647** Cowley *Mistr., Dial.* i, Shame succeeds the short-liv'd pleasure. *a* **1774** Goldsm. *Surv. Exp. Philos.* (1776) II. 1 The natural philosophers that just succeeded the ages of obscurity. **1784** Cowper *Task* vi. 259 This smiling sky, So soon succeeding such an angry night. **1816** Scott *Antiq.* xxxi, These alternate feelings of embarrassment, wonder, and grief, seemed to succeed each other more than once upon her torpid features. **1864** Bryce *Holy Rom. Emp.* vi. (1875) 85 The rule of Alberic had been succeeded by the wildest confusion. **1913** *Times* 14 May 6/1 An ideal day for manœuvres, clear and cool, succeeded yesterday's rain.

†**10. a.** *intr.* To happen, fall out, come to pass, take place. *Obs.*

1537 Cromwell in Merriman *Life & Lett.* (1902) II. 63 Nothing is succeded sythens my last writing. *a* **1548** Hall *Chron., Hen. VI*, 79 From thensefurth daily succeded, murder, slaughter, & discencion. **1606** G. W[oodcocke] *Hist. Ivstine* xvi. 68 By force whereof, it succeded that.. they died and their Countrey not deliuered. **1653** tr. *Carmeni's Nissena* 78 She desired to be inform'd of..what had suceeded since the Prince Doralbo's expedition.

†**b.** To happen *to*, fall as a portion *to* a person.

a **1533** Ld. Berners *Gold. Bk. M. Aurel.* (1546) N v, If yl succede to him..it is by reason of the ignoraunce of him selfe. **1622** Mabbe tr. *Aleman's Guzman d'Alf.* ii. 259 Lest that succeed vnto them, which happened vnto Don Quixote de la Mancha. **1669** W. Penn in *Extr. St. Papers rel. Friends* Ser. iii. (1912) 280 The honner which will redownd to thee, exceeds farr the advantage that Can succeed to me.

†**11. a.** Of an enterprise, etc.: To have a certain issue; to turn out (one way or another, well or ill).

1540–1 Elyot *Image Gov.* (1549) 33 But it succeeded all other wise. **1560** *Bible* (Geneva) Tob. iv. 6 If yu deale truely, thy doings shal prosperously succede to thee. *a* **1586** Sidney *Ps.* xxxvii. i, Though ill deedes well succeeding be. **1595** Daniel *Civil Wars* i. xliv, But euery day things now succeeded worse. **1600** Fairfax *Tasso* iv. lxxxii, Yours be the thanks, for yours the danger is, If ought succeed (as much I feare) amis. **1605** Shaks. *Lear* i. ii. 157, I promise you, the effects he writes of, succeede vnhappily. **1684** R. Waller *Nat. Exper.* 40 Whether the manner of their operation would succeed contrary, or any way different to what they appear.

†**b.** To turn out *to* one's advantage or disadvantage. *Sc. Obs.*

1533 Bellenden *Livy* ii. xvi. (S.T.S.) I. 191 Bot his tary and Inobedience succedit to his hevy dammage. **1549** *Compl. Scot.* viii. 72 The proditione of ane realme succedis to the hurt of the public veil.

12. a. To have the desired or a fortunate issue or conclusion; to turn out successfully.

c **1450** [see succeeding *vbl. sb.* 1]. **1595–9** [see succeeding *ppl. a.* 5 b]. **1617** Moryson *Itin.* i. 161 Since..this our meeting hath not succeeded,..there is no other remedie but to make our peace at leasure by exchange of letters. **1667** Milton *P.L.* i. 166 Our labour must be..out of good still to find means of evil; Which oft times may succeed. **1685** Dryden *Sylvæ* Pref., This was impossible for Virgil to imitate; because the severity of the Roman language denied him that advantage. Spencer endeavour'd it in his Sheperd's Calendar; but neither will it succeed in English. **1738** Wesley *Ps.* i. iv, His happy Toil shall all succeed Whom God himself delights to bless. **1808** *Med. Jrnl.* XIX. 331, I only used it in two instances, in both of which it succeeded. **1856** Froude *Hist. Eng.* (1858) I. v. 464 There was no reason why an attempt which had succeeded once might not succeed again. **1861** Buckle *Civiliz.* (1873) II. viii. 577 When the spirit of the age is against those remedies, they can at least only succeed for a moment.

b. Of growing plants: To meet with success, do well, thrive.

1812 *New Bot. Gard.* I. 4 Layers and cuttings likewise sometimes succeed. **1816** Tuckey *Narr. Exped. R. Zaire* i. (1818) 28 We..were told that wheat succeeds perfectly when sown in the dry plains in the rainy season. **1880** C. R. Markham *Peruv. Bark* 468 There the North American cottons succeed.

13. a. Of persons: To attain a desired end or object; to be successful in an endeavour; to bring one's labours to a happy issue. Also formerly, with adv., to have 'good' or 'ill success'. Also in proverbial phr.

1509 Hawes *Past. Pleas.* xiv. (Percy Soc.) 55 Above al other he did so excell, None sith his time in arte wolde succede, After their death to have fame for their mede. **1678** Dryden *All for Love* Pref., Ess. 1900 I. 197 Thus the case is hard with writers: if they succeed not, they must starve. **1731–8** Swift *Pol. Conversat.* Introd. 24 Nor did the late D. of R—— and E. of E—— succeed much better. **1735** Pope *Prol. Sat.* 362 Alike my scorn, if he succeed or fail. **1765** *Museum Rust.* IV. 368 In this I was told it was impossible to succeed, because a very sensible farmer..had tried the experiment, and failed. **1866** G. Macdonald *Ann. Q. Neighb.* vii. (1878) 124, I have succeeded very badly. **1884** *Manch. Exam.* 16 May 4/7 If he had studiously endeavoured to be unjust he could not have succeeded more completely. *Prov.* **1840** T. H. Palmer *Teacher's Man.* 223 'T is a lesson you should heed, Try, try again; If at first you do n't succeed, Try, try again. **1857** W. E. Hickson *Try Again* in *Moral Songs* 8 'Tis a lesson you should heed, Try, try, try again. If at first you don't succeed, Try, try, try again. **1915** E. B. Holt *Freudian Wish & its Place in Ethics* iii. 103 The child is frustrated, but not instructed; and it is in the situation where, later on in life, we say to ourselves, 'If at first you don't succeed, try, try again!' **1960** I. Jefferies *Dignity & Purity* v. 91 Not to worry... If at first you don't succeed, try, try, try again. *a* **1976** A. Christie *Miss Marple's Final Cases* (1979) 39 You mustn't give up, Mr. Rossiter. 'If at first you don't succeed, try, try, try again.'

b. Const. *in* with gerund. (Also *transf.* of things.)

1839 Keightley *Hist. Eng.* II. 67 Cranmer succeeded in obtaining a mitigation of the provisions. **1869** Tozer *Highl. Turkey* II. 232 Bold touches..succeed in leaving a distinct impression on the mind. **1898** Flor. Montgomery *Tony* 11 She succeeded in finding an empty carriage.

†**14.** *trans.* (*causative*) To give success to; to prosper, further. *Obs.*

1613 Tourneur *P. Henry* 135 Whose influence makes that His own virtues are succeeded justly. **1626** Shirley *Maid's Rev.* v. iii, Good Ansilva, give't her, And heavens succeed the operation! **1651** Baxter *Inf. Bapt.* 193, I leave that which I have written to God to succeed as he please. **1654** Owen *Saints' Persever.* ii. §20. 44 This way of Disputing will scarce succeed you, in this great undertaking. **1717** Pope *Iliad* x. 352 Pallas..succeeds their enterprise. **1760–72** H. Brooke *Fool of Qual.* (1809) IV. 72 May Heaven succeed your..wish. **1825** E. Irving *Word God* ii. Wks. 1864 I. 18 God, being ever willing and ever ready to second and succeed His word. **1843** J. Perkins *8 Yrs.' Resid. Persia* 219 (Bartlett *Amer.*), Sincerely praying and desiring..the Smiles of Heaven to succeed your..embassy.

†**15.** *intr.* To come up or near *to*, approach. *Obs. rare.*

1596 Spenser *F.Q.* vi. iv. 8 Who euer, as he saw him nigh succeed, Gan cry aloud with horrible affright. **1697** Dryden *Virg. Past.* v. 7 Will you to the cooler Cave succeed? *Ibid.*, *Georg.* iii. 632 Snakes, familiar, to the Hearth succeed. *Ibid.* 758 To his rough Palat, his dry Tongue succeeds.

suc'ceedable, *a. nonce-wd.* [f. prec. + -able.] Likely to succeed.

1817 Byron *Let. to Murray* 9 Mar., I should have thought the Assyrian tale very succeedable.

succeedant, -ent, var. succedent.

suc'ceeded, *ppl. a.* [f. succeed *v.* + -ed[1].] That has succeeded to a dignity, position, etc.

1891 *Daily News* 27 June 3/1 The newly succeeded Lord Tollemache.

succeeder (sək'siːdə(r)). Also 5 succidur, 6 -ceder, 7 -cedor. [f. succeed *v.* + -er[1].]

1. One who (*occas.* a thing which) succeeds another; a successor. Now *rare.*

c **1440** *Alph. Tales* 60 His succidur þe homycide, at garte sla hym, ioyes of his dignytie at he hase after hym. **1570** Foxe *A. & M.* (ed. 2) I. 77/1 Alexander,..whose succeeder next was Xistus or Sixtus. **1579** W. Wilkinson *Confut. Fam. Love* 1 b, They rayled on them calling them.. succeders of the Pharisees. **1594** Shaks. *Rich. III*, iv. iv. 128 Ayery succeeders of intestine ioyes. **1595** Daniel *Civ. Wars* i. xxiv, But now this great succeeder all repaires, And rebrings-backe that discontinued good. **1615** Crooke *Body of Man* 970 The Dog-teeth also do fall out and the place of the succeeder is a little of the one side the roote of the former. **1620** E. Blount *Horæ Subs.* 286 That if his owne issue failed, hee might leaue a succeeder, such as his owne affection should make choyce of. **1688** J. Renwick *Dying Test.* in *Biogr. Presbyt.* (1827) II. 291, I am the more willing to pay this Cost, for their Instruction, and my Succeeder's ease. **1864** Tennyson *Aylmer's F.* 294 The sole succeeder to their wealth,..The last remaining pillar of their house.

2. One who is successful.

1836 L. Hunt in *New Monthly Mag.* XLVIII. 56 The first undoubted succeeders in raising a man into the air.. were the brothers Stephen and Louis de Montgolfier. **1884** Browning *Ferishtah* Epil. 19 Each as on his sole head, failer or succeeder, Lay the blame or lit the praise.

succeeding (sək'siːdɪŋ), *vbl. sb.* [-ing[1].]

1. Successful issue, success.

c **1450** tr. *De Imitatione* iii. xxxv. 104 Lest þou be lifte up in succedyng of þi desire [orig. *in bono successu*]. **1671** Milton *P.R.* ii. 143 Lest confidence Of my success with Eve in Paradise Deceive ye to perswasion over-sure Of like succeeding here. **1730** A. Gordon *Maffei's Amphith.* 80 For the better succeeding in the important Undertaking he has in hand. **1768–74** Tucker *Lt. Nat.* (1834) II. 137 Their succeeding throws no obstacle against his success. **1847** G. Harris *Life Hardwicke* II. vii. 129 Failure in such a case, where all the qualifications for succeeding were possessed.

†**2.** Succession. *Obs.*

c **1460** *Oseney Reg.* 204 Last that the trowth of this thyng by succedyng of tyme myȝght be callyd in-to dowte. **1482** *Monk of Evesham* (Arb.) 70 They..begunne to goo fro ful bittyr peynys to wars and so by succeding of her peynys dayly her tormentys besyly encresyn. **1596** Dalrymple tr. *Leslie's Hist. Scot.* I. 58 Heir now, be a commoune vse of succeiding, thay entir at thair awne hand without ony mair. **1679** [see succedent A. 2].

†**3.** Consequence, result. *Obs.*

1601 Shaks. *All's Well* ii. iii. 199 Is it not a Language I speake? *Par.* A most harsh one, and not to bee vnderstoode without bloudie succeeding.

†**4.** The act of following *in the place of* something. *Obs.*

1644 Digby *Bodies* viii. 55 A violent succeeding of ayre in the roome of the fire.

suc'ceeding, *ppl. a.* [-ing[2].] That succeeds.

1. Following in a line of rulers or heirs, in the course of time or events, in the process of development, etc.; coming after or later; subsequent.

1561 T. Norton *Calvin's Inst.* i. 13 The orderly succeding course of daies and nightes. **1593** Shaks. *Rich. II*, i. iii. 20 My King, and his succeeding issue. **1594** —— *Rich. III*, iii. i. 71 He did..begin that place, Which since, succeeding Ages haue re-edify'd. **1600** W. Watson *Decacordon* 264 The succeeding occasions of erronious conceipts, hath been our owne faultes. **1624** Quarles *Job Milit.* Med. iii. 24 Hath Heauen..Nipt thy succeeding Blossoms? *a* **1700** Evelyn *Diary* 17 Jan. 1653, This was the beginning of all the succeeding gardens, walks,..and plantations there. **1767** Young *Farmer's Lett. to People* 212 So much succeeding bad weather came, that the crops were

..damaged. **1769** E. BANCROFT *Guiana* 27 The pistil.. contains the embryo of the succeeding berry. **1781** COWPER *Expost.* 308 Successive loads succeeding broils impose. **1807** T. THOMSON *Chem.* (ed. 3) II. 468 These compounds shall be the subject of the five succeeding Chapters. **1854** *Poultry Chron.* I. 524 At each succeeding show, there is manifest improvement in these birds. **1884** *Athenæum* 19 Jan. 88/2 This index has served as a model to many succeeding librarians. **1906** *Lit. World* 15 Nov. 518/2 Each succeeding page is the prelude to new adventures.

†**b.** Coming, to come, future. *Obs.*

1676 MARVELL *Mr. Smirke* Wks. (Grosart) IV. 5 They are the succeeding hope of our church, the youth of our clergy. **1676** HALE *Contempl.* II. (1677) 177 These I shall carry with me into the succeeding World. **1763** CHURCHILL *Confer.* Poems 281 May to succeeding times..my crimes Stand blazing forth.

†**2.** *Astrol.* = SUCCEDENT A. 2. *Obs.*

1594 BLUNDEVIL *Exerc.* IV. xxxvi. (1636) 493 Those that do follow next any of these principall Angles, are called succeeding houses. **1653** R. SANDERS *Physiogn.* 220 Of these houses, some are Cardinal, some are succeeding, some cadent.

3. Following in immediate succession; immediately following; next following.

[*c* **1586** C'TESS PEMBROKE *Ps.* XLIX. v, Loe, the first succeeding light perceaves The just installed in the great mans steed. **1685** H. MORE *Paralip. Prophet.* ix. 62 To place the Epocha of Herod's Reign in his immediate succeeding Hyrcanus. **1905** *Act 5 Edw. VII*, c. 6 §2 At any period not later than the next succeeding quarter to that in which the money was borrowed.]

1639 in *Shropsh. Par. Doc.* (1903) 30 The said parishioners may yearely and without molestac'on of him or the succeedinge incumbent freely enjoy the liberty thereof. **1748** *Anson's Voy.* II. viii. 220 The succeeding four months in which we continued at sea. *a* **1771** GRAY *Dante* 58 All that whole Day, or the succeeding Night. **1911** *Act 1 & 2 Geo. V.* c. 16 §2 The income which that person may reasonably expect to receive during the succeeding year in cash.

b. Coming next in order.

1838 BELL *Dict. Law Scot.* 953 First, descendants; failing them, collaterals; and, last of all, ascendants succeeding.

†**4.** Following one after another; successive; consecutive. *Obs.*

1602 CHURCHYARD & ROBINSON (*title*) A True Discovrse Historicall of the svcceeding Governovrs in the Netherlands. **1670** PETTUS *Fodinæ Reg.* 12 Most of which Laws are agreeable to the Grants and Powers of our succeeding Kings. **1697** DRYDEN *Virg. Georg.* I. 99 That while the Turf lies open..Succeeding Suns may bake the Mellow Ground. *a* **1718** PRIOR *Knowledge* 271 Poems (1905) 271 See daily Show'rs..bless the flow'ry Buds succeeding Birth. **1763** CHURCHILL *Apol.* Poems (1767) I. 72 Waller, whose praise succeeding bards rehearse.

†**5. a.** With prefixed adv.: Having a (happy or unhappy) issue. *Obs.*

1561 NORTON & SACKV. *Gorboduc* I. ii. 31 As the blame of yll succedyng thinges Shall light on you. *a* **1586** SIDNEY *Ps.* I. ii, All the things whereto that man doth bend Shall prosper still with well succeeding end.

†**b.** Successful. *Obs.*

1595–9 DANIEL *Civ. Wars* V. lxxvii, Frends, opinion, & succeeding chaunce, Which wrought the weak to yeld. **1654** FULLER *Two Serm.* 25 God..sometimes is delighted to offer to himselfe the fattest Malefactors, fed in the state of succeeding wickednesse.

Hence †**suc'ceedingly** *adv.*, successively, consecutively.

1600 W. WATSON *Decacordon* (1602) 291 Iustinus Martyr, Athenagoras, and Tertullian, succeedingly did write diuers discourses. **1624** CAPT. J. SMITH *Virginia* VI. 205 To continue the History succeedingly as neere with the day and yeere as may bee.

†**'succeless**, *a. Obs. rare*$^{-1}$. [f. *succe*, SUC + -LESS.] Juiceless.

1657 TOMLINSON *Renou's Disp.* 447 All cocks are fleshless and succeless.

†**suc'cend**, *v. Obs.* [ad. L. *succendĕre*, f. *suc-* = SUB- 2 + **candĕre*, related to *candēre* to glow with heat.] *trans.* To set on fire, kindle, burn.

1432–50 tr. *Higden* (Rolls) III. 85 A potte succendede. *Ibid.* 249 Esdras the scribe repairede the lawe brente and also succendede by men of Calde. **1477** NORTON *Ord. Alch.* v. in Ashm. (1652) 64 Ruby colour is of a thinn fume succended In a cleere Body.

succent (sək'sɛnt), *v.* [f. L. *succent-*, pa. ppl. stem of *succinĕre* (see next).] To sing the second part of a verse, etc. (*trans.* and *intr.*).

1880 SMITH & CHEETHAM *Dict. Chr. Antiq.* II. 1745/1 One voice sang the first part of a verse..and the rest of the congregation all together succented it, that is, sang the close of it. *Ibid.* 1942/1 The passages already quoted point to this officer's duty of 'succenting' in the service of the church. **1904** J. CAMPBELL *Ch. & Par. Kirkcaldy* i. 18 Every psalm was sung in a different manner; one would be sung as a solo ..another by a leader 'incepting' the verse, while the congregation 'succented' the second halves of the verses.

succentor (sək'sɛntə(r)). Also 7 -our. [a. late L. *succentor*, agent-n. f. *succinĕre* to sing to, accompany, 'chime in', agree, f. *suc-* = SUB- 8 + *canĕre* to sing. In sense 3, as correlative to *præcentor* PRECENTOR, associated with SUB- 6 (cf. SUBCHANTER).]

†**1. a.** A chanter who takes up the chant after the precentor, or who presides over the left choir. (Also *allusively*.) *Obs.*

1647 TRAPP *Comm. Rev.* v. 14 The Saints were the Precentors in this blessed Quire, and now they are the Succentors also. They began the Song, and so conclude it. **1697** O. HEYWOOD *Heavenly Converse* Wks. 1826 IV. 525 We find precentors and succentors in this blessed quire, saints above and saints below. **1817** FOSBROOKE *Brit. Monachism* 182 The Succentor or Subchantor presided over the left Choir; the Chantor began, and the Subchantor answered.

†**b.** One who sings the bass in a choir. *Obs. rare*$^{-0}$.

1656 BLOUNT *Glossogr.*

†**2.** *fig.* An abettor. *Obs. rare*$^{-1}$.

1609 HOLLAND *Amm. Marcell.* XIX. xii. 141 Paulus.. was the prompter and succentor of these cruell enterludes.

3. A precentor's deputy.

1642 in *Chas. I. Wks.* (1662) II. 230 The Bill for the utter abolishing and taking away of all Archbishops, Bishops,.. Succentors, [etc.]. **1691** WOOD *Ath. Oxon.* II. 19 Cartwright ..had the Succentors place in the Church of Salisbury confer'd on him. **1771** *Antiq. Sarisb.* 140 Walter de la Wyle was Succentor or Subdean of Sarum. **1865** *Churchman* 9 Nov. 1283 Mr. Precentor is to have a Vicar Choral to act as succentor or precentor's deputy. **1904** *Times* 17 Mar. 5/5 The posts of succentor and librarian at St. Paul's are not held by the same person.

Hence **suc'centorship**, the office of succentor.

1691 WOOD *Ath. Oxon.* II. 19 In his Proctorship succeeded Joh. Maplet..and in his Succentorship Rob. Joyner. **1829** CASSAN *Bps. Bath & Wells* 104 The Succentorship and the Provostship..were..suppressed.

succenturiate (sʌksɛn'tjʊərɪət), *pa. pple.* and *a.* [ad. L. *succenturiātus*, pa. pple. of *succenturiāre* (see next).]

†**1.** *pa. pple.* Substituted. *Obs. rare.*

1641 H. L'ESTRANGE *God's Sabbath* 70 His dominion was not onely over the old Sabbath, to abrogate that; but over the new also, to surrogate that as succenturiate to the other.

2. *adj.* ***succenturiate gland, kidney*** (Anat.): one of the suprarenal capsules, small bodies in front of the upper part of the kidneys.

1836–9 *Todd's Cycl. Anat.* II. 417/1 The female organs of the Scorpion..open by two canals,..each having a small cæcum or succenturiate gland appended near its termination. **1843** WILKINSON tr. *Swedenborg's Anim. Kingd.* I. viii. 224 The succenturiate kidneys, which appear to be made up of glandular forms and corpuscles.

†**succenturiate** (sʌksɛn'tjʊərɪeɪt), *v. Obs.* [f. L. *succenturiāt-* pa. ppl. stem of *succenturiāre* to receive as a recruit, f. *suc-* = SUB- 27 + *centuria* CENTURY.]

1. *trans.* (See quots.) *rare*$^{-0}$.

1623 COCKERAM, *Succenturate* [sic]. **1656** BLOUNT *Glossogr.*, *Succenturiate*, to fill up the number of the Band, for them that are dead or absent; to recruit.

2. To supply what is lacking in; to supply (a want); to supplement. Also *absol.*, to provide a supplement *to*.

1622 MISSELDEN *Free Trade* (ed. 2) To Rdr., For supply of other mens learning, to succenturiat my wants, I needed it, I confesse, but took it not. *a* **1680** T. GOODWIN *Blessed St. Saints* xi. Wks. 1703 V. III. 75 Faith thus ceasing, if this Salvation of the Soul did not succenturiate and recruit it anew [etc.]. *a* **1680** —— *Unregen. Man* XIII. ix. Wks. 1692 III. 610 Christ..doth..make this same Exhortation; I say to you..and I will forewarn you,..Fear him that is able to destroy Body and Soul. The Apostle succenturiates, We know him that hath said, Vengeance is mine [*Heb.* x. 30].

3. To put *instead of* another; to substitute (const. *to*).

1647 TRAPP *Comm. Matt.* xxi. 32 *Ye repented not afterwards.* No, not after his death, though ye saw me succenturiated to him. **1659** H. L'ESTRANGE *Alliance Div. Off.* 25 Had the edification of the people been better provided for by certain Lessons of the Canon succenturiated ..in their stead.

4. *intr.* To come in the place of something, fill a place, fill up a gap.

1630 *Cal. St. P., Domestic* (1860) 357 [The late King named the Earl of Northampton in their charter as the first steward; the Earl of Pembroke succeeded. If he pleases to] succenturiate, *sic ab Jove tertius Ajax*. **1660** W. WINSTANLEY *Eng. Worthies* Pref. p. v, To remedy that, procure in them what you can to succenturiate in the History diligently. **1684** HOWE in H. Rogers *Life* (1863) viii. 216 The order (to which the subjoined directions of your lordship do succenturiate).

5. *trans.* To take the place of.

1650 MASSEY *Microcosm.* 23 Most honoured Sir,..give me leave to speak one word to you, you succenturiate him.

†**succenturi'ation.** *Obs.* [f. prec.: see -ATION.] The supply of recruits to fill up a 'century' or company; *gen.* the supply (of persons or things).

1643 M. NEWCOMEN *Craft Ch. Advers.* 32 Such a succenturiation there hath been of plots, that we may say of them, as she of Gad, A Troope commeth. **1654** H. L'ESTRANGE *Chas. I* (1655) 161 Then they entered into consideration of constituting the Third Estate, and what succenturiation, what supplement should be resolved upon in the lieu of Bishops. **1658** PHILLIPS, *Succenturiation*,..a filling up the number of Souldiers wanting in any Company. **1676** W. HUBBARD *Happiness People* 51 The.. succenturiation of the persons called to supply the room of them that having served their generation, are now fallen asleep.

†**succernate**, *v. Obs. rare*$^{-0}$. [irreg. f. L. *succernĕre*, f. *suc-* = SUB- 2 + *cernĕre* to sift: see -ATE[3].] *trans.* To sift. Also **succer'nation**.

1623 COCKERAM, *Succernate*, to bolt or range meale. **1658** PHILLIPS, *Succernation*, a bolting, or sifting of Meal.

‖**succès** (syksɛ). [Fr., = SUCCESS *sb.*] Used in phrases with reference to types of artistic success or acclaim, as ***succès de scandale*** (də skɑ̃dal), success due to notoriety or scandalous character; ***succès d'estime*** (dɛstim), a critical rather than a popular or commercial success; ***succès fou*** (fu), a success marked by wild enthusiasm. Also *transf.* and *fig.*

[**1826** *New Monthly Mag.* Dec. 578 Merely that lukewarm approbation, which in Paris is termed *un succès d'estime*.] **1859** *Once a Week* 13 Aug. 136/1 My second attempt..will be something more substantial than a mere *succès d'estime*. **1878** J. A. C. MORISON *Gibbon* vi. 86 The book was..a *succès fou*. **1887** R. CHURCHILL *Let.* 2 Mar. in W. S. Churchill *Lord Randolph Churchill* (1906) II. xvii. 291, I think the Government are earning a rather second-rate kind of *succès d'estime*. **1896** G. B. SHAW *Our Theatres in Nineties* (1932) II. 35 Mr Cartwright..enjoyed..a sort of *succès de scandale*. **1908** MRS. H. WARD *Diana Mallory* III. xvi. 331 She would find herself a *succès fou*—people tumbling over each other to invite her, and make a show of her. **1919** 'C. DANE' *Legend* 56 The first two books were a *succès d'estime*. **1928** *Observer* 1 Jan. 8 The success which Victor Margueritte's novel 'La Garçonne' made all over Europe..was chiefly a succès de scandale. **1948** W. FORTESCUE *Beauty for Ashes* xix. 142 It was hard work creating something from nothing, but very great fun, and had the usual *succès fou* of all dramatic performances coached by the founder. **1965** A. J. AYER in *Listener* 4 Nov. 700/2 The result was *Language, Truth and Logic*... Though it had an almost immediate *succès de scandale*, its tenets..had a respectable philosophical ancestry. **1977** *Daily Tel.* 17 Mar. 14/3 It has already won a *succès d'estime* in the United States, and seems likely also to become a cult work here. **1978** *Christian* V. 86 What caught on with a succès fou and drew in the spiritual élite of the generation in tens of thousands was a Benedictine reform movement. **1979** M. HILEY *Victorian Working Women* I. iv. 48 *The Pictorial World*..was obviously hoping for some *succès de scandale* by splashing women in trousers across its front page.

success (sək'sɛs), *sb.* Also 6 **sukces**, 6–7 **succes(se, suckses**, (7 **sucksess**, 8 **-cess**). [ad. L. *successus*, f. *succēdĕre* (*success-*) to SUCCEED. Cf. F. *succès*, It., Pg. *successo*, Sp. *suceso*.]

†**1. a.** That which happens in the sequel; the termination (favourable or otherwise) of affairs; the issue, upshot, result. *Obs.*

1537 STARKEY *Let. to Pole* in Strype *Eccl. Mem.* (1721) I. App. lxxxi. 194 That you should al worldly respects set aside & al dangerous success which might succede of the same. **1548** W. THOMAS *Let. to Hen. VIII* ibid. II. App. X. 77 Neither do I trust mine authors so much as not to mistrust contrary successes, both to their rules & their examples. **1555** EDEN *Decades* III. x. (Arb.) 182 Whose prosperous begynnynges ended with vnfortunate successe. **1561** NORTON & SACKV. *Gorboduc.* 1543 One sort that saw the dangerous successe Of stubborne standing in rebellious warre. **1563** *Homilies, Agst. Idolatry* III. Mmiij, Ye haue harde..out of hystories Ecclesiasticall, the begynnyng, proceadyng, and successe of Idolatry by Images. **1601** SHAKS. *All's well* III. vi. 86, I know not what the successe wil be my Lord, but the attempt I vow. **1642** J. M[ARSH] *Arg. conc. Militia* 12 Who shall live to see an end of that rebellion and what the successe of it will be? **1667** MILTON *P.L.* II. 9 Insatiate to pursue Vain Warr with Heav'n, and by success untaught. **1668** MARVELL *Corr.* Wks. (Grosart) II. 249 The successe of Wednesday's debate..was a question to desire his Majesty to call before him some persons. **1733** NEAL *Hist. Purit.* II. 329 The success of this war will fall within the compass of the next year.

†**b.** An event. *Obs.*

1588 PARKE tr. *Mendoza's Hist. China* 324 The company which went with him were very fewe to make resistance against such successes as might happen. **1658** EARL MONM. tr. *Paruta's Wars Cyprus* 78 Troubled at the loss of Nicossia and at the other successes, which fell out..quite contrary to ..hopes. **1753** L. M. *Accompl. Wom.* I. 12 To read..so many different successes, wherein we feel our Passions moved according to the Adventures treated of.

†**c.** The result (of an experiment), the effect (of a medicine). *Obs.*

1606 BRYSKETT *Civ. Life* 6 M. Smith the Apothecary was come..to vnderstand what successe the physick he had prepared for me did take. **1684** R. WALLER *Nat. Exper.* 55 This Experiment was often repeated, always with the same success. **1756** in *Med. Observ.* (1776) I. 390 So intent on trying..the success of the sublimate in the cure of the *Lues Venerea*.

†**d.** ***in the success***: eventually. *Obs.*

a **1676** HALE *Prim. Orig. Man.* (1677) 144 Their Predictions..flattered both Cæsar and Pompey with long Lives..both which fell out in the success, to both extremely contrary. **1738** *Gentl. Mag.* VIII. 152/1 An Attempt which would never answer in the Success.

2. a. The fortune (good or bad) befalling anyone in a particular situation or affair. Usually with qualifying adj. *good success* = sense 3; *ill success*: failure, misadventure, misfortune. *arch.*

a **1548** HALL *Chron., Hen. VII*, 39 Although thei had knowlege what good successe Perkyn had enjoyed in al his former attemptes. **1577** HANMER *Anc. Eccles. Hist.* (1619) 495 After that the assault of Adaarmanes tooke no prosperous successe at Antioch. **1579** LYLY *Euphues* (Arb.) 104 Philautus hauing intellygence of Euphues his successe, and the falsehoode of Lucilla. **1596** RALEIGH *Discov. Guiana* 17 The hard successe which all these & other Spaniards found in attempting the same. *Ibid.* 28 Berreo..looked for no other successe than his predecessors in this enterprize. **1619** in Foster *Eng. Factories India* (1906) 74, I am sorrye to heare of John Younges disaster etc., yett am in good hope of better sucksess. **1671** MILTON *P.R.* IV. 1 Perplex'd and troubl'd at his bad success. *a* **1700** EVELYN *Diary* 26 Nov. 1657, After a sermon and prayers for good successe. **1704** N. BLUNDELL *Diary* (1895) 25, I went to wish good Suckcess to Mr. Molineux of Croxtath ere he went a Courting. **1764** GOLDSM. *Hist. Eng. in Lett.* (1772) II. 208 The bad success of his admirals at sea. **1823** SOUTHEY *Hist. Penins. War* I. 470 With so little accuracy do the French relate the circumstances of their ill success. **1839** KEMBLE *Resid.*

Georgia (1863) 126, I was recalled to a most ludicrous perception of my ill success.

†**b.** In particularized use. *Obs.*

1590 SPENSER *F.Q.* I. v. 25 The..good successes, which their foes ensew. 1607 SHAKS. *Cor.* I. vi. 7 The Roman Gods, Leade their successes, as we wish our owne. 1612 DRAYTON *Poly-olb.* x. 14 *note*, After diuers unfortunat successes in warre. 1661 PEPYS *Diary* 25 Sept., Sir W. Pen told me that I need not fear any reflection upon my Lord for their ill successe at Argier... My Lord Crewe,..I see,..is afraid my Lord's reputacon will a little suffer in common talk by this late successe. 1764 GOLDSM. *Hist. Eng. in Lett.* II. 225 The reduction of this..fortress served to interrupt the prosperous successes of the English company.

3. a. (= the older *good success.*) The prosperous achievement of something attempted; the attainment of an object according to one's desire: now often with particular reference to the attainment of wealth or position.

a 1586 SIDNEY *Ps.* XXX. vii, While I my race did runne, Full of successe, fond I did say, That I should never be undone. 1592 KYD *Sp. Trag.* III. iii. 3 Giue but successe to mine attempting spirit. 1617 MORYSON *Itin.* II. 49 The Rebels being swolne to the height of pride..by continual Successe in their actions. 1697 DRYDEN *Virg. Georg.* III. 760 A Drench of Wine has with Success been us'd. 1713 ADDISON *Cato* I. ii, 'Tis not in mortals to Command success, But we'll do more, Sempronius; we'll Deserve it. 1765 BLACKSTONE *Comm.* I. iii. 198 A title the most remote and unaccountable that was ever set up, and which nothing could have given success to. 1827 SCOTT *Highl. Widow* ii, His success in fishing and the chase was able to add something to her subsistence. 1848 THACKERAY *Van. Fair* xiv, It was George who had interrupted the success of her first love-passage. 1863 GEO. ELIOT *Romola* xix, That argument of success which is always powerful with men of the world. 1885 O. W. HOLMES *Emerson* xi. 260 'Success' in its vulgar sense,—the gaining of money and position,—is not to be reached by following the rules of an instructor. 1895 *Law Times* XCIX. 476/2 It requires the talents of a Boileau, Molière, or La Fontaine to play the part of a *flâneur* with any success.

proverb. 1868 HELPS *Realmah* v, Nothing succeeds like success. [Cf. F. *Rien ne réussit comme le succès.*]

b. An instance of this; a successful undertaking or achievement. ***success of esteem, success of scandal***, tr. *succès d'estime, succès de scandale* s.v. SUCCÈS.

1666 DRYDEN *Ann. Mirab.* ccx, Swell'd with our late Successes on the Foe. 1740 CIBBER *Apol.* (1756) I. 50 Before her time our ancestors had many successful contests with their sovereigns..: yet what did those successes amount to? 1857 DUFFERIN *Lett. High Lat.* vii. 133 To convert a questionable success into an undoubted triumph. 1880 *Daily News* 19 Oct. 4/7 The dustbin absorbs scores of..poems that win a 'success of esteem'. 1891 *Spectator* 2 May 615/1 The mass comprehends nothing except a visible success. 1916 G. SAINTSBURY *Peace of Augustans* iii. 144 The extraordinary power of the close of *Vathek* has secured it..a success of esteem. 1926 C. E. MONTAGUE *Rough Justice* III. vii. 99 Notorious novels, successes of scandal, that lived as hard and about as long as super-impudent ball-dresses. 1939 D. CECIL *Young Melbourne* vii. 191 *Glenarvon* had a success of scandal; three editions were called for within a few weeks. But it dealt the death blow to..Caroline's social position. 1958 W. PLOMER *At Home* xii. 175 They [*sc.* publishers' readers] are liable to advise the rejection of typescripts that might have popular success and be moneymakers, or success of esteem followed perhaps by durability and influence.

c. *transf.* One who or a thing which succeeds or is successful.

1882 L. C. LILLIE *Prudence* 63 To be a success in this circle, is to contribute to the beauty..or the effect of the hour. 1884 *Daily News* 27 Feb., Should Mr. Peel prove as great a success in the Speaker's chair, as he proved in oratory before he entered it [etc.]. 1885 'MRS. ALEXANDER' *Valerie's Fate* v, Mrs. Hartwell's dance was a great success.

†**4. a.** Succession or sequence in time or occurrence. ***in success of time***: in course or process of time. *Obs.*

1546 GARDINER *Declar. Joye* 85 The sonne sheweth her selfe in the mornynge, in whome there is encrease by successe tyll the sonne come to the highest at noone. 1547 BALDWIN *Mor. Philos.* (1564) 18 The successe of thinges to come. 1549–62 STERNHOLD & H. *Ps.* xix. 2 The wondrous workes of God appeare, By euery dayes successe. 1553 EDEN *Treat. Newe Ind.* (Arb.) 41 In successe of time, foure of the greatest Ilandes embrased the Christian faith. 1611 MUNDAY (*title*) A briefe Chronicle of the Successe of Times from the Creation of the World to this Instant. 1611 SPEED *Hist. Gt. Brit.* IX. xv (1623) 780 This King, of whose life by order and successe of Storie wee are now to write. 1626 C. POTTER tr. *Sarpi's Hist. Quarrels* 338 This difficultie found Padauin in the successe of his iourney [*così andaua difficoltando il suo camino*]. 1656 HEYLIN *Surv. France* 282, I shall draw down the successe of their affairs from the beginning of the Reformation. 1690 C. NESSE *Hist. & Myst. O. & N.T.* I. 103 An house..will contract new..filth in success of time.

†**b.** An instance of this; a succession. *Obs.*

1610 GUILLIM *Heraldry* II. vii. (1660) 81 Causing a success of surging billowes. *a* 1676 HALE *Prim. Orig. Man.* (1677) 37 Otherwise we must of necessity make all successes in the World purely natural and necessary.

†**c.** Subsequent history. *Obs.*

1555 EDEN *Decades* III. VII. (Arb.) 166 As generally to lerne thoriginall & successe of thynges: And particularlye to reherse the noble factes of their ..auncestours. 1681 H. MORE *Expos. Dan.* App. i. 250 Can a man believe that the Original or success of that people was ἀχειροποίητόν τι?

†**5.** Succession as of heirs, rulers, etc. *Obs.*

1587 GOLDING *De Mornay* Ep. Ded. to K. Hen., After a long successe of these Herauldes, came the Sauiour. 1590 SPENSER *F.Q.* II. x. 45 Then all the sonnes of these fiue brethren raynd By dew successe. 1597 SHAKS. *2 Hen. IV*, IV. ii. 47 And so, successe of Mischiefe shall be borne, And Heire from Heire shall hold this Quarrell vp. 1611 —— *Wint. T.* I. ii. 394 Our Parents Noble Names, In whose successe we are gentle.

6. a. *attrib.*, as ***success ethic, hunter, rate, value***, etc.

1923 W. STEVENS *Let.* 11 Feb. (1967) 236 Aside from this absurd hero-worship, or success-worship, the town is purely a business place. 1946 *Nature* 17 Aug. 242/2 A success-rate of syphilis prevention of more than 97 per cent was claimed to be unequalled by any other mode of treatment. 1949 *Success-goal* [see *open-class* s.v. OPEN *a.* 22 a]. 1951 M. MCLUHAN *Mech. Bride* (1957) 35/2 They remain avid customers for the success manuals and beauty treatments which by themselves constitute a large line of merchandise. 1955 KOESTLER *Trail of Dinosaur* 93 The same is true of obsessional success-hunters in every field. 1957 R. K. MERTON *Social Theory* (rev. ed.) v. 170 The distribution of success-values among economic and social strata. 1965 H. HENDIN in A. Giddens *Stud. in Social & Polit. Theory* ix. 311 His legal ambitions were excessive and he found it impossible to compromise with his grandiose success fantasies. 1977 *Time* 13 June 44/2 They are an uncommonly interesting lot, whose lives and habits illuminate what achievement means today in the society that invented the success ethic.

b. *Comb.*, as **success story** *colloq.* (orig. *U.S.*), (*a*) an account of a success; (*b*) an instance of a successful venture, an achievement, etc.

1925 *Ladies' Home Jrnl.* Feb. 28/2 (*heading*) A great success story. 1938 *Time* 14 Nov. 84/2 Last year, when the U.S. Circuit Court of Appeals ruled that physicians might send contraceptives by mail her career became a 'success story'. 1954 W. K. HANCOCK *Country & Calling* vii. 203 Departments would naturally prefer to get 'a good press', whereas we were bound by our instructions to write critical history, not 'a success story'. 1973 *Nature* 9 Nov. 58/1 The study of X-ray sources is one of the great success stories of present-day astrophysics. 1978 *Jrnl. R. Soc. Arts* CXXVI. 755/2 A comparative success story is the inundation of the ancient city of Nagarjunakonda to make way for a great hydro-electric project.

†**suc'cess**, *v. Obs. rare.* [f. prec.] *intr.* **a.** To be a successor. **b.** To happen.

1545 *St. Papers Hen. VIII* (1849) X. 576 By my last of the 13 of thinstant I signified to the same of the case successid to the Signor Ludovico de Larme. ?1560 BALE *Chron. Sir J. Oldcastle* Pref. A viij b, His sonne Henry the sixt successed [*ed.* 1544 succeded] in hys rome. 1567 TURBERV. *Ovid's Ep.* 131 b, A blissefull signe that all Shall not successe aright.

†**succe'ssanean**, *a. Obs. rare*$^{-1}$. [f. L. *success-*, pa. ppl. stem of *succēdĕre* to SUCCEED, ? after *succēdāneus* SUCCEDANEOUS.] Marked by succession or transition.

1635 PERSON *Varieties* I. viii. 28 Things of a fluid and successanean nature, such as time is.

†**suc'cessantly**, *adv. Obs. rare*$^{-1}$. [Arbitrarily f. L. *success-, succēdĕre* to SUCCEED + -ANT + -LY^{2}.] ? In succession.

1588 SHAKS. *Tit. A.* IV. iv. 113 Then goe successantly and plead for him.

†**successary.** *Obs. rare.* [f. L. *success-, succēdĕre* to SUCCEED + -ARY.]

1. A successor.

1486 *Bk. St. Albans, Her.* cj b, That he and his successaries all way with bataill and swereddys shulde be punyshid. 1520 *Caxton's Chron. Eng.* 58 b/1 This man ordeyned y^{t} no bysshop sholde ordeyne his successary.

2. Succession.

a 1616 BEAUM., etc. *Laws Candy* I. ii, My peculiar honours, not deriv'd From successary, but purchas'd with my blood.

successful (sək'sɛsfʊl), *a.* [f. as prec. + -FUL.]

1. Of persons: That succeeds or achieves success, *esp.* (in recent use), that attains to wealth or position, that 'gets on'.

1588 SHAKS. *Tit. A.* I. i. 66 The good Andronicus,..Successefull in the Battailes that he fights. 1617 MORYSON *Itin.* II. 24 The Iris Kerne..became so disasterous to the English, and successefull in action.., as they shaked the English governement. 1661 BOYLE *Style Script.* Ep. Ded., It hath been observ'd, that Secular Persons of Quality..are generally much Successfuller in Writing of Religion..than ..Men in Orders. 1725 DE FOE *Voy. round World* (1840) 351 They had been..pretty successful in their navigation. 1805 SCOTT *Let.* in *Lockhart* (1837) II. ii. 54 If I have been at all successful in the paths of literary pursuit. 1860 TYNDALL *Glac.* I. xi. 83 It failed; we tried again, and were successful. 1870 E. PEACOCK *Ralf Skirl* II. 271 Mackenzie was a successful man. 1878 JEVONS *Primer Polit. Econ.* 60 Educated men who have not been successful become secretaries, house-agents,. and the like.

b. *transf.* of things.

1848 J. FORSTER *O. Goldsm.* 377 There was nothing to make the town half so fond of a man..as a successful play. 1855 *Orr's Circ. Sci., Inorg. Nat.* 132 Great and successful works of art are among the most noble..of all human triumphs. 1879 *Cassell's Techn. Educ.* I. 166/2 The clock was a highly successful work of the art of the period. 1890 W. J. GORDON *Foundry* 200 The *Times*, and..the *Daily News*, and many others of the successful papers in the provinces and on the Continent.

2. Of actions, conditions, etc.: Attended with, characterized by, or resulting in success.

1588 SHAKS. *Tit. A.* I. i. 172 And welcome Nephews from succesfull wars. 1596 —— *Tam. Shr.* I. ii. 158 And perhaps with more successful words Then you. 1638 JUNIUS *Paint. Ancients* 79 In..rare workes of Art, we are not so much taken with the beautie it selfe, as with the successfull boldnesse of Art. 1651 HOBBES *Leviath.* Rev. 392 They justifie all the successefull Rebellions. 1766 GOLDSM. *Vicar W.* vii, At this he laughed, and so did we: the jests of the rich are ever successful. 1865 CARLYLE *Fredk. Gt.* XIX. v. V. 502 The successfullest campaign that ever was. 1891 *Speaker* 2 May 532/2 The jugglery of words was never more successful than in this distinction without a difference.

†**3. a.** Bringing success, propitious. *Obs. rare.*

c 1592 MARLOWE *Jew of Malta* I. i, Making..the winds To driue their substance with successefull blasts.

†**b.** Conducive or necessary to success. *Obs.*

1657 AUSTEN *Fruit Trees* I. 135 It is very succesfull that we proportion Grafts and stocks in Grafting.

suc'cessfully, *adv.* [f. prec. + -LY^{2}.]

1. In a successful manner; with success.

1588 SHAKS. *Tit. A.* I. i. 194, I haue bene thy Souldier forty yeares, And led my Countries strength successefully. 1647 CLARENDON *Hist. Reb.* I. §36 In order to move him the more successfully thereto, they procured the Pope to write a Letter himself to his Highness. 1709 ADDISON *Tatler* No. 24 ¶2 He is very successfully loud among the Wits. 1826 LAMB *Pop. Fallacies* v, A domestic..cut his throat, but not successfully. 1898 'H. S. MERRIMAN' *Roden's Corner* i. 8 His ..phlegmatic calm successfully concealed the fact.

†**b.** ***to look successfully***: to seem likely to succeed. *Obs. rare.*

1600 SHAKS. *A.Y.L.* I. ii. 165 He is too yong: yet he looks successfully.

†**2.** Successively. *Obs.*

1651 DAVENANT *Gondibert* Pref., Brief hints such as, if all the arguments were successfully read, would make him easily remember the mutual dependencies of the general design.

suc'cessfulness. [f. as prec. + -NESS.] The condition or quality of being successful.

1649 ROBERTS *Clavis Bibl.* 180 Their victorious successfulnesse in military exploits against their enemies. 1754 EDWARDS *Freed. Will* IV. v. 220 The Successfulness, or Unsuccessfulness of Means in order to an Effect,..consists in those Means being connected or not connected with the Effect. 1879 MEREDITH *Egoist* xliii, Its prevailing successfulness in the country where he was placed.

succession (sək'sɛʃən). Also 4–5 -oun(e, -yon, etc. [ad. OF. *succession* (from 13th c.) or its source L. *successio, -ōnem*, n. of action f. *succēdĕre* to SUCCEED. Cf. Pr. *successio*, It. *successione*, Sp. *sucesion*, Pg. *successão.*]

I. 1. a. The action of a person or thing following, or succeeding to the place of, another; the coming of one person or thing after another; also, the passing from one act or state to another; an instance of this.

c 1386 CHAUCER *Knt.'s T.* 2156 He hath so wel biset his ordinaunce, That speces of thynges and progressions Shullen enduren by successions. 1577 tr. *Bullinger's Decades* (1592) 6 Least peraduenture their children shuld be ignorant of the beginning and succession of worldly things. 1605 BACON *Adv. Learn.* II. 113 b, The future succession of all ages. 1624 GATAKER *Transubst.* 148 Such a succession is to be found in euery substantiall conuersion, whereby one substance is destroyed, and other succeedeth in the roome of it. 1690 LOCKE *Hum. Und.* II. xiv. §6 By reflecting on the appearing of various Ideas, one after another in our Understandings, we get the Notion of Succession. 1738 WESLEY *Hymn 'God is a Name my Soul adores'* iii, Thy Being no Succession knows And all thy vast Designs are one. 1764 GOLDSM. *Trav.* 116 Whatever blooms in torrid tracts appear, Whose bright succession decks the varied year. 1847 TENNYSON *Princess* III. 312 We..live, perforce, from thought to thought, and make One act a phantom of succession. 1866 OWEN *Anat. Vertebrates* I. §70. 381 The reproduction of the component denticles in horizontal succession. 1874 GREEN *Short Hist.* vi. §6 (1882) 330 The series of measures which in their rapid succession changed the whole character of the English Church. 1875 JOWETT *Plato* (ed. 2) IV. 416 The ideas of men have a succession in time as well as an order of thought.

†**b.** The act of passing by continuous movement *into* a place. *Obs.*

1691 RAY *Creation* I. (1692) 69 The Air accompanies and follows it by a constant Succession. 1729 T. DALE tr. *Freind's Emmenol.* (1752) xii. 154 Nutrition being nothing else than the apposition of any Juice, or a perpetual succession of aliment into the Pores of the Fibres.

†**c.** The act of following another in a course of conduct. *Obs. rare.*

1601 SHAKS. *All's Well* III. v. 24 The miserie is example, that so terrible shewes in the wracke of maiden-hood, cannot for all that disswade succession.

2. *Phr.* **a.** ***in succession***, one after another in regular sequence, successively.

c 1449 PECOCK *Repr.* III. v. 306 Forto abide in thilk sufficience thoruȝ manye ȝeeris in successioun. 1668 MOXON *Mech. Dyalling* 46 Mark them in succession from the beginning with 10, 20, 30, to 90. 1690 LOCKE *Hum. Und.* II. xiv. §10 'Tis as clear as any Demonstration can be, that it must..touch one part of the Flesh first, and another after; and so in Succession. 1801 *Farmer's Mag.* Apr. 149 In the period I have taken, we have had three unfavourable seasons, and two in succession, worse than any other in the memory of any man living. 1827 FARADAY *Chem. Manip.* xix. (1842) 505 On one end of the tube the parts will be bent and curved in succession as they become heated. 1868 LOCKYER *Elem. Astron.* iii. §12 (1879) 69 The rotation of the Earth bringing each part in succession from sunshine to shade. 1914 *Infantry Training* 73 When a column is on the march, platoons may, if desired, advance in fours in succession.

†**b.** ***by succession(s***: successively. *Obs.*

1432–50 tr. *Higden* (Rolls) II. 271 After that other realmes were made in Grece by succession. 1591 SYLVESTER *Du Bartas* I. ii. Wks. (1641) 11/1 Because the Matter, wounded deep in Heart With various Love..by successions, Form after Form receives.

†**c.** ***in a succession***: continuously. *Obs.*

a **1715** BURNET *Own Time* (1724) I. 173 If the money.. had been raised all in a succession, as fast as the work could be carried on.

†**3.** The course, lapse, or process *of time*. *Obs.*

1456 SIR G. HAYE *Law Arms* (S.T.S.) 229 A thing that is nocht of valew be the law as ground of rycht in the begynnyng, the successioun of tyme may never mak it rycht. **1620** E. BLOUNT *Horæ Subs.* 328 This was the true Originall, by which in succession of time the Empire was translated. **1655** M. CARTER *Honor Rediv.* (1660) 90 Succession of time hath converted it into another custom.

4. The transmission (or mode of transmission) *of* an estate, royal or official dignity, or the like.

a **1325** *MS. Rawl. B. 520* fol. 59 þoru maner of ȝifte þe womman passez bifore þe man, in succession. **1375** BARBOUR *Bruce* I. 57 Thai said, successioun of kyngrik Was nocht to lawer feys lik; For thar mycht succed na female. **1387** TREVISA *Higden* (Rolls) II. 147 The moder blood schulde be putt to fore in successioun of heritage. **1432-50** tr. *Higden* (Rolls) III. 403 Philippus the kynge of Macedony, sollicitate and besy for the succession of þat realme [orig. *de regni successore*]. **1538** STARKEY *England* II. ii. 195 As touchyng the successyon and intaylyng of landys, ther must nedys be prouysyon. **1641** EARL MONM. tr. *Biondi's Civil Wars* IX. 223 So long as the Earl of Warwick lived, he was not certaine of the Kingdoms succession. **1682** DRYDEN *Mac Fl.* 10 To settle the Succession of the State. **1690** in *Nairne Peerage Evidence* (1874) 26 To provyde and secure the successione of the lands. **1826** BELL *Comm. Laws Scotl.* (ed. 5) I. 100 The equal partition of the succession which prevailed in the Roman law, has place also in the law of Scotland in the succession of moveables.

5. a. The process by which one person succeeds another in the occupation or possession of an estate, a throne, or the like; the act or fact of succeeding according to custom or law *to* the rights and liabilities of a predecessor; the conditions or principles in accordance with which this is done.

the succession: the conditions under which successors to a particular estate, throne, etc. are appointed. ***war of succession***: a war to settle a dispute as to the succession to a particular throne.

a **1513** FABYAN *Chron.* VII. ccxxvi. (1811) 254 That he shulde haue MMM. markes yerelye, as before was promysed vnto hym.. with other condycions of successyon. **1533-4** *Act 25 Hen. VIII* c. 22 An Acte for the establishement of the Kynges succession. **1593** SHAKS. *3 Hen. VI*, II. i. 172 He swore consent to your Succession. **1607** CHAPMAN *Bussy d'Ambois* III. ii. 385 Why wrongful to suppose the doubtless right To the succession worth the thinking on? **1643** BAKER *Chron.* (1653) 99 King Richard being dead, the right of Succession remained in Arthur, Son of Geoffry Plantagenet. **1697** DRYDEN *Virg. Georg.* IV. 303 Th' immortal Line in sure Succession reigns. *a* **1700** EVELYN *Diary* 16 May 1681, Lord Sunderland.. having fallen into displeasure of the King for siding with the Commons about the Succession. **1701** FARQUHAR *Sir H. Wildair* IV. i, What, sir? the Succession!—Not mind the Succession! **1708** CHAMBERLAYNE *M. Brit. Notitia* II. II. ii. (1710) 385 The succession to the Crown of Scotland. **1714** SWIFT *Pres. St. Aff.* Wks. 1755 II. I. 214 The security of the protestant succession in the house of Hanover. **1766** BLACKSTONE *13 Comm.* II. The power of the laws in regulating the succession to property. **1790** BURKE *Fr. Rev.* Wks. 1808 V. 64 The course of succession is the healthy habit of the British constitution. **1832** LD. MAHON (*title*) History of the War of the Succession in Spain. **1839** KEIGHTLEY *Hist. Eng.* II. 44 The dangers of a disputed succession being now terminated. **1853** *Act 16 & 17 Vict.* c. 51 (*title*) An Act for granting to Her Majesty Duties on Succession to Property. **1879** DIXON *Windsor* II. xvi. 169 She stood in order of succession to the duchy.

b. Phr. (*a*) ***by succession***: according to the customary or legal principle by which one succeeds another in an inheritance, an office, etc. by inherited right.

1412-20 LYDG. *Chron. Troy* I. 2889 Sche þat.. schulde haue ben by successioun Eyre by dissent of þat regioun. *c* **1430** —— *Min. Poems* (Percy Soc.) 17 The degré be just successioune,.. Unto the kyng is now descended doune, From ether parte righte as eny lyne. **1474** CAXTON *Chesse* II. ii. (1883) 27 For better is to haue a kynge by succession than by eleccion. **1593** SHAKS. *Rich. II*, II. i. 199 How art thou a King But by faire sequence and succession? *c* **1600** —— *Sonn.* ii, Prouuing his beautie by succession thine. **1668** DRYDEN *Def. Dram. Poesy* Ess. 1900 I. 111, I am only a champion by succession. **1865** F. M. NICHOLS tr. *Britton* I. 219 *marg.*, Title by succession.

(*b*) (To have, hold, take) ***in succession***.

1472-3 *Rolls of Parlt.* VI. 4/2 Londes.. which eny persone temporell.. hath.. in fee symple, eny maner fee tayle, or in succession. **1835** TOMLINS *Law Dict.* s.v. *Successor*, Such a corporation cannot regularly take in succession goods and chattels. **1890** GROSS *Gild Merch.* I. 95 The borough.. was an aggregate body acting as an individual,.. having a common seal, holding property in succession.

c. *pregnantly* for: The line or order of succession.

[**1533-4**: see sense 5.] **1708** SWIFT *Sentim. Ch. Eng. Man* ii. Wks. 1841 II. 214/1 Thus hereditary right should be kept so sacred as never to break the succession. **1849** MACAULAY *Hist. Eng.* xx. II. 460 He was in the succession to an earldom. **1874** GREEN *Short Hist.* vii. §2 (1882) 353 Mary.. had been placed next in the succession to Edward by her father's will.

6. (A person's) right or privilege of succeeding to an estate or dignity.

1461 *Rolls of Parlt.* V. 490/2 Any persone or persones corporat, or havyng succession perpetuell. **1477** *Ibid.* VI. 172/2 Any persone or persones havyng succession. **1571** GOLDING *Calvin on Ps.* LXI. vii, He dyed full of dayes.. having delivered the succession of his kingdome to his Sonne. **1583** *Reg. Privy Council Scot.* Ser. I. III. 568 To denude him of his heretage and rychteous successioun dew to him as eldest sone. **1651** tr. *De-las-Coveras' Don Fenise* 314 He without regarding the ordinance of his mother would possesse himselfe of the succession. *a* **1700** DRYDEN (J.) What people is so void of common sense, To vote succession from a native prince? **1828** SCOTT *F.M. Perth* xiv, He could achieve such a purpose without endangering both his succession and his life. **1875** MAINE *Hist. Instit.* i. 16 Each tract was the property.. of some body of persons who, in modern legal phrase, had perpetual succession. **1894** SIR W. HARCOURT in *Daily News* 17 April 2/7 The right to make wills or settlements or successions is the creation of positive law.

7. The act of succeeding to the episcopate by the reception of lawfully transmitted authority by ordination. ***apostolic(al) succession*** (or ***the succession***), the continued transmission of the ministerial commission, through an unbroken line of bishops from the Apostles onwards.

1565 HARDING *Confut. Apol. Ch. Eng.* 57b, To go from your succession, which ye can not proue, and to come to your vocation, how saye you, Syr? **1567** JEWEL *Def. Apol.* II. 129 Haue these menne their owne succession in so safe Record? Who was then the Bishop of Rome nexte by succession vnto Peter? **1577** HANMER *Anc. Eccl. Hist.* 55 Obtayning the first stepp of Apostolical Succession, and being deuine Disciples of the.. principall men. **1653** CROMWELL *Sp.* 4 July (Carlyle), I speak not.. for a Ministry deriving itself from the Papacy, and pretending to that which is so much insisted on, 'Succession'. **1845** BP. WILBERFORCE in Ashwell *Life* (1880) I. viii. 314 Instead of taking as your prominent subject the 'Succession'.. you would take the more spiritual view of the Ministry. **1847** YEOWELL *Anc. Brit. Ch.* ix. 99 We have an account of their [*sc.* the bishops'] successions for some ages. **1879** HADDON *Apost. Success. Ch. Eng.* ii. 35 Foreign or other Protestants, who either disclaim or do not possess the Succession. *Ibid.* 30 The historical and canonical objections advanced.. against the validity of the English Succession.

II. †**8.** Successors, heirs, or descendants collectively; progeny, issue. *Obs.*

a **1340** HAMPOLE *Psalter* Cant. 496 My generacioun, þat is, succession of childire. *c* **1400** *Rom. Rose* 4857 Bycause alle is corrumpable And faile shulde successioun. **1432-50** tr. *Higden* (Rolls) II. 441 The sonnes of Hector recurede and toke þe cite of Troye, expellenge the succession of Antenor. **1459** *Rolls of Parlt.* V. 351/2 Eny other succession of youre body lawefully commyng. **1533-4** *Act 25 Hen. VIII* c. 22 To.. provyde for the perfite suertie of both you and of your moste lawfull succession and heires. **1555** EDEN *Decades* (Arb.) 296 When they [*sc.* beasts] shulde bringe furth theyr broode or succession. **1605** in *Abst. Protocols Town Clerks Glasgow* (1896) II. 121 Prayeris.. for.. the Kingis Majestie, his hienes Quein, and thair successioune. **1611** SHAKS. *Cymb.* III. i. 8 Cassibulan.. for him, And his Succession, granted Rome a Tribute. **1697** DRYDEN *Virg. Georg.* IV. 78 Their young Succession all their Cares employ: They breed, they brood, instruct and educate.

†**9. a.** A generation (of men); chiefly *pl.* (future or successive) generations. *Obs.*

c **1430** LYDG. *Minor Poems* (Percy Soc.) 85 The chieldren of Seth in story ye may se, Flowryng in vertu by longe successiouns. **1593** NASHE *Christ's T.* 26b, So exceeding are mine aduersities, that after successions which shall heare of them; will euen be desolate.. with the hearing. **1611** BEAUM. & FL. *Maid's Trag.* IV. i, Found out with every finger, made the shame Of all successions. **1659** HAMMOND *On Ps.* lxxix. 13 Our posterity to all successions joyning with us. **1685** BURNET tr. *More's Utopia* 98 Ancestors, who have been held for some Successions rich. **1720** SWIFT *Mod. Educ.* Wks. 1755 II. II. 39 The sloth, luxury, and abandoned lusts, which enervated their breed through every succession.

†**b.** Posterity. *Obs.*

1628 HALL *Contempl.*, *O.T.* XIII. 1098 If we sow good workes succession shall reape them. **1655** STANLEY *Hist. Philos.* I. (1701) 13/1 To propagate his Doctrine to Succession. **1704** INETT *Orig. Anglic.* I. xi. §14. 183 Succession so far justified this Proceeding, that this Council of Sardice was never receiv'd by the Eastern Churches. **1704** NELSON *Fest. & Fasts* (1705) xvi. 185 He.. provided for Succession by constituting Bishops, and other Officers and Pastors.

10. a. A series of persons or things in orderly sequence; a continued line (*of* sovereigns, heirs to an estate, etc.); an unbroken line or stretch (*of* objects coming one after another). Also, †a continued spell (*of* weather).

1579 W. WILKINSON *Confut. Fam. Love* Aiij, The succession of Popes, and that body and kingdome is the very Antichrist. **1594** HOOKER *Eccl. Pol.* II. vi. §4 St. Augustine.. saith.. In all this order of succession of Bishops [of Rome] there is not one Bishop found that was a Donatist. **1603** KNOLLES *Hist. Turks* (1638) 231 The Greeke Historiographers (best like to know the Turkish succession). **1662** STILLINGFL. *Orig. Sacræ* II. iv. §1 In that same place God doth promise a succession of Prophets. **1667** MILTON *P.L.* XII. 331 A long succession must ensue, And his next Son.. The clouded Ark of God.. shall in a glorious Temple Enshrine. **1734** tr. *Rollin's Anc. Hist.* I. Pref. p. vi, The entire succession of ages is present to him. **1796** MORSE *Amer. Geog.* I. 168 An agreeable succession of small points of land. **1797** JANE AUSTEN *Pride & Prej.* I. xvii. (1813) 203 Such a succession of rain. **1831** BREWSTER *Optics* iv. 34 When we consider the inconceivable minuteness of the particles of light, and that a single ray consists of a succession of those particles. **1849** MACAULAY *Hist. Eng.* vii. II. 189 The House of Austria had, by a succession of victories, been secured from danger on the side of Turkey. **1874** GREEN *Short Hist.* vii. §7 (1882) 418 Every progress of Elizabeth from shire to shire was a succession of shows and interludes.

†**b.** The followers collectively, or a sect of followers, of a school of thought. (Rendering Gr. διαδοχή.) *Obs.*

1653 MORE *Antid. Ath.* Gen. Pref. p. xvii, I omitted to set down the succession of the Pythagorick school. **1656** STANLEY *Hist. Philos.* IV. (1701) 133/1 The Succession of the Ionick Philosophy, which before Socrates was single: after him was divided into many Schools. **1699** BENTLEY *Phal.* 80 The Successions of the Pythagorean School.

11. A set of persons or things succeeding in the place of others.

1647 CLARENDON *Hist. Reb.* I. §165 That That which looked like Pride in some, and like Petulance in others, would.. be in time wrought off, or in a new Succession reformed. **1821** SHELLEY *Adonais* xliii, While the one Spirit's plastic stress Sweeps through the dull dense world, compelling there All new successions to the forms they wear. **1865** W. B. CARPENTER in Youmans *Corr. & Conserv. Forces* 418 (Cent. Dict.) The leaves of 'evergreens'.. are not cast off until the appearance of a new succession.

†**12.** That to which a person succeeds as heir; an inheritance. *Obs. rare.*

1382 WYCLIF *Deut.* xviii. 8 Out take that, that in his cytee of the fadre successyoun is owed to hym. **1587** GOLDING *De Mornay* xxvii. 479 Now let vs see what we our selues haue brought to this decayed succession. **1706** PHILLIPS (ed. Kersey), *Succession*,.. an Inheritance or Estate come to one by Succession. **1751** *Female Foundling* II. 80, I can, indeed, leave him a good Succession.

III. †**13.** The result, issue. *Obs.* (Cf. late L. *successio*.)

1514 in Ellis *Orig. Lett.* Ser. II. I. 228 Any prousperous succession of your Graces causes. **1549** LATIMER *1st Serm. bef. Edw. VI* (Arb.) 36 According to the aduyse of his friend the one of them wroght where the succession was not good. **1557** CARD. POLE in Strype *Eccl. Mem.* (1822) III. II. 494 As the successyon shewede he dyd.

IV. 14. In technical use: **a.** *Astron.* (See quots.)

1679 MOXON *Math. Dict.*, *Succession of the Signs*, Is that order in which they are usually reckoned; as first Aries, next Taurus, then Gemini, &c. **1728** CHAMBERS *Cycl.* s.v., When a Planet is direct, it is said to go according to the Order and Succession of the Signs,.. when Retrograde, it is said to go contrary to the Succession of the Signs.

b. *Mus.* 'The order in which the notes of a melody proceed'. Also = SEQUENCE *sb.* 3b.

1752 tr. *Rameau's Treat. Mus.* 85 A Sequence, or Succession of Harmony, is nothing else but a Link or Chain of Keys and Governing-notes. **1801** BUSBY *Dict. Mus.* (1811) s.v., Of succession there are two kinds, conjunct and disjunct. Conjunct Succession is when the sounds proceed regularly, upward or downward, through the several intervening degrees. Disjunct Succession is when they immediately pass from one degree to another without touching the intermediate degrees. **1875** STAINER & BARRETT *Dict. Mus. Terms* s.v., A sequence is sometimes spoken of as a succession, and passages of similar chords or progressions are described as a succession of thirds [etc.].

c. *Milit.* (See quots.)

1745 J. MILLAN (*title*) The Succession of Colonels to All His Majesties Land Forces, from their Rise, to 1744. **1802** JAMES *Milit. Dict.*, *Succession of Rank*, relative gradation according to the dates of commissions. *Ibid.*, *A Commission in succession*, a commission in which an individual has an inherent property from having purchased it, or raised men. **1805** —— *Milit. Dict.* (ed. 2), *Succession of colonels*, a particular part of the official army list is so called. The dates of the several appointments are therein specified, together with the numbers and facings of the different regiments.

d. *Agric.* and *Hort.* (*a*) The rotation (of crops); (*b*) the maturing of crops of the same kind by a system of successive sowings so that as one is declining another is coming on.

1778 [MARSHALL] *Observ. Agric.* 168 The Succession of Crops (or rather of the Occupants of the Soil, whether Crops, or Fallow) may be regular or irregular. **1796** —— *Rural Econ. W. Eng.* II. 144 The succession is similar to that of West Devonshire: ley ground, partially fallowed for wheat, with one or two crops of oats; grass seeds being sown with the last crop. **1842** LOUDON *Suburban Hort.* 505 In order to have a succession of fruit, it is requisite to sow the seed at three different times. **1900** *Daily News* 5 May 4/3 Almost every kind of vegetable may now be sown for succession.

e. *Geol.*, etc. The continued sequence in a definite order of species, types, etc.; *spec.* the descent in uninterrupted series of forms modified by evolution or development.

1834 DARWIN *Jrnl.* in *Voy. Beagle* (1839) III. 210 The law of the succession of types. **1836** BUCKLAND *Geol. & Min.* I. vi. 54 To refer the origin of existing organizations.. to an eternal succession of the same species. **1842** SEDGWICK in *Hudson's Guide Lakes* (1843) 188 Phenomena which not only indicate succession, but were elaborated during vast intervals of time.

f. *Ecol.* The sequence of ecological changes in which one group of plant or animal species is replaced by another.

1860 H. D. THOREAU in *N.Y. Weekly Tribune* 6 Oct. 6/6 (*heading*) The succession of forest trees. **1899** *Bot. Gaz.* XXVII. 95 The ecologist.. must study the order of succession of the plant societies in the development of a region. **1904** *Univ. Nebraska Stud.* IV. 332 Such succession herbaria are the natural outgrowth of formational ones. **1926** TANSLEY & CHIPP *Aims & Methods in Study of Vegetation* ii. 7 Vegetation, when left to itself, tends to change in a definite direction.. and this change we call succession. **1957** G. E. HUTCHINSON *Treat. Limnol.* I. xv. 834 It is not impossible that the element plays some part in regulating phytoplankton succession. **1975** *Sci. Amer.* May 90/1 Forest succession proceeds too slowly for it to be observed directly.

g. *Geol.* A group of strata whose order represents a single chronological sequence.

1940 *Bull. Amer. Assoc. Petroleum Geologists* XXIV. 309 Near Las Vegas an apparently conformable succession of marine beds, mostly limestone, is designated as the Bird Spring formation. **1976** *Jrnl. Geol. Soc.* CXXXII. 121 The study area covers.. the eastern half of the flysch succession. **1979** D. ATTENBOROUGH *Life on Earth* ii. 36 The limestones at the top of the Moroccan succession are about 560 million years old.

V. 15. *attrib.*: **succession bath**, a bath in which hot and cold water are used in succession (*Cent.*

Dict.); **succession-crop**, a crop of some plant coming in succession to another; **succession duty**, a duty assessed upon succession to estate; **succession flowers**, a crop of flowers following an earlier crop; **succession house**, one of a series of forcing-houses having regularly graded temperatures into which plants are moved in succession; so ***succession-pine***; **succession powder** (F. *poudre de succession*), a poison supposed to have been made of lead acetate; **succession state**, a state which comes into existence after the overthrow or division of a previous state (used orig. of those states which succeeded the dismembered Austro-Hungarian Empire in 1919); **succession tax**, a tax similar to succession duty; **succession war** = 'war of succession' (see 5).

1864 MRS. A. GATTY *Parab.fr. Nat.* 21 A narrow slip..for *succession-crops of mustard and cress. **1853** *Act 16 & 17 Vict.* c. 51 §45 The Commissioners..may assess the *Succession Duty on the Footing of such Account and Estimate. *Ibid.* 55 This Act may be cited for all Purposes as 'The Succession Duty Act, 1853'. **1894** *Act 57 & 58 Vict.* c. 30 §18 (2) The principal value of real property for the purpose of succession duty shall be ascertained in the same manner. **1841** *Florist's Jrnl.* (1846) II. 25 Some amends is, however, made for this, in the readiness with which the *succession-flowers come on. **1792** CHARLOTTE SMITH *Desmond* II. 93 An immense range of forcing and *succession houses. **1798** JANE AUSTEN *Northang. Abb.* (1833) II. vii. 147 How were Mr. Allen's succession-houses worked? **1857** MRS. MARSH *Rose Ashurst* I. iii. 77 He went on, opening succession house after succession house. We ended by the garden door at which we had entered. **1786** ABERCROMBIE *Gard. Assist.* 59 Young *succession pines—or last years crowns and suckers retained in nursery bark pits or beds. *a* **1821** MRS. PIOZZI in A. Hayward *Autobiogr., Lett. & Lit. Remains Mrs. Piozzi* (1861) I. 356 In Italy it was supposed to have been the *succession powder mingled with chocolate whilst in the cake, not in the liquid we drink. Acqua Toffana, and succession powder (polvere per successione) were administered, as I have heard, with certain although ill-understood effects. **1824** LD. J. RUSSELL *Mem. Aff. Europe* I. 192 The Countess of Soissons..Being accused of having bought some of the poison, called by the dealers *succession powder*. **1846** A. AMOS *Great Oyer Poisoning* 347 In more modern times the like powers have been attributed to the *Aqua Tophana*, and the *Succession Powder*. **1924** *Succession state [see NATIONALISTICALLY *adv.*]. **1943** C. HOLLINGWORTH *German just behind Me* ii. 14 Like Romania it [*sc.* Yugoslavia] is a 'Succession State'. **1973** *Times Lit. Suppl.* 23 Mar. 318/2 Now that the breakaway of Bangladesh has effected a second partition of the Indo-Pakistani subcontinent, there has been renewed interest in all three succession states in the long-standing controversy over whether the first partition was either inevitable or necessary. **1858** BRIGHT *Sp., Reform* 27 Oct. (1869) 281 A law to impose a *Succession-tax. *a* **1823** PENNEY *Linlithgowshire* (1832) 151 This barony was probably forfeited during the *succession war. **1867** *Chambers' Encycl.* IX. 177/2 Succession wars were of frequent occurrence in Europe, between the middle of the 17th and the middle of the 18th centuries, on the occasion of the failure of a sovereign house.

successional (sək'sɛʃənəl), *a.* [f. prec. + -AL[1].]

1. Pertaining to, characterized by, or involving the succession of persons as heirs, rulers, or the like; passing or proceeding by succession or descent; often with special reference to the apostolic succession.

1600 W. WATSON *Decacordon* (1602) 306 To bring this whole monarchiall Isle from the name, honor and title of successionall regality, to be vnder a Viceroyes gouernment. **1637** HEYLIN *Antid. Lincoln.* xi. 87 Many things come unto our hands by a successionall tradition. **1652** —— *Cosmogr.* II. 61 [Alsatia] Governed for the Emperours by Provinciall Earls,..accomptable to the Emperours under whom they served; in the end made hereditarie and successionall unto their posterities. **1653** GAUDEN *Hierasp.* 53 Christ, the Institutor of an authoritative and successional Ministry. **1835** *Fraser's Mag.* XI. 283 He might have had the civility to predict a successional husband. **1845** D. KING in *Ess. Chr. Union* v. 245 He..had them regularly consecrated by English bishops, and so qualified to keep up and transmit the successional virtue! *a* **1854** W. JAY *Autobiogr.* (1855) xiv. 127 The system of providing for places by a merely successional supply.

2. a. Of things: Following one upon another; occurring in succession; involved in a succession.

1685 H. MORE *Paralip. Prophet* xxxix. 340 Both the Cause and the Effect is successional through many Ages. **1711** SHAFTESB. *Charac.* III. Misc. iv. i. 194 The Question is, 'What constitutes the We or I?' And, 'Whether the I of this instant, be the same with that of any instant proceding, or to come.'.. So that the same successional *We* or *I* must remain still, on this account, undecided. **1827** DE QUINCEY *Lessing* Wks. 1859 XIII. 289 Successional signs can express none but successional objects, or those of which the parts are in succession. **1872** HUMPHRY *Myology* 8 The peculiar vibratory or successional manner of action of the several parts of a fibre. **1875** CROLL *Clim. & Time* x. 181 In a successional descent of surface-films from above downwards.

b. In technical use (chiefly *Hort.*; cf. SUCCESSION 15).

1786 ABERCROMBIE *Gard. Assist.* 100 The pine apple plants—now in fruit, must not be shifted, only the young successional pines. **1829** LOUDON *Encycl. Plants* (1836) 623 The winter variety [of pea] is sown in September and October, and the summer at different periods, from February to June, for successional cuttings. **1842** —— *Suburban Hort.* 435 Successional cropping is that in which the ground is wholly occupied with one crop at one time, to be succeeded by another crop, also wholly of one kind. **1866** R. OWEN *Anat. Vertebrates* I. §70. 375 The floor of the alveolus..forms..the roof of a lower vault, in which the germ of a successional tooth..is in course of developement. **1881** *Encycl. Brit.* XII. 249/2 If sown in spring it [*sc.* the Intermediate Stock] blooms in autumn, and furnishes a useful successional crop of flowers. **1892** *Gardener's Chron.* 27 Aug. 239/3 The flowers are successional for many months.

c. *Ecol.* Of or pertaining to ecological succession. Cf. SUCCESSION 14 f.

1922 R. H. YAPP in *Jrnl. Ecol.* X. 13 The Successional Habitat practically agrees with Clements' developmental concept of habitat. **1967** M. E. HALE *Biol. Lichens* vii. 99 Successional stages leading to forested stands. **1979** *Sci. Amer.* Feb. 73/2 The Swiss have come increasingly to rely on natural tree types and natural successional trends as a basis for their silviculture.

Hence **suc'cessionally** *adv.*, by succession.

1846 in Worcester (citing *Ecl. Rev.*).

successionist (sək'sɛʃənɪst). [f. SUCCESSION + -IST.] One who maintains the validity or necessity of a succession; *esp.* one who upholds the doctrine of the apostolic succession. (Also ***apostolic successionist***.)

1846 in Worcester (citing *Ecl. Rev.*). **1895** J. ALISON in *Romanism & Ritualism* 18 To the Ritualist, the Sacerdotalist, and the Apostolic Successionist, we say the body is more than raiment [etc.].

successionless (sək'sɛʃənlɪs), *a.* [-LESS.] Without succession; having no successors.

1623 DRUMM. OF HAWTH. *Flowers of Sion* Wks. (S.T.S.) II. 38 And as ends and beginnings Thee not clame, Successionlesse that Thou bee still the same. **1854** E. G. HOLLAND *Mem. J. Badger* 15 Like the priesthood of Melchizedek, successionless and without descent.

successive (sək'sɛsɪv), *a.* [ad. med.L. *successivus*, f. *success-*, *succēdĕre* to SUCCEED. Cf. F. *successif*, It., Pg. *successivo*, Sp. *sucesivo*.]

1. a. With pl. or compound sb.: Coming one after another in an uninterrupted sequence; following one another in order.

1432-50 tr. *Higden* (Rolls) II. 117 Yorke hathe but ij. suffraganes subiecte to it onely,..of the successiue institucions of whom somme thynges ar to be seide here by ordre. **1606** G. W[OODCOCKE] *Lives Emp.* in *Hist. Ivstine* L12 Three successiue Bishops, Iohn, Benedict, and Clement..excommunicated him. **1628** FELTHAM *Resolves* II. lxii. 177 Furies..alwaies deliuers the author into successiue mischiefes. **1690** LOCKE *Hum. Und.* II. xiv. §6 A constant train of successive ideas. **1719** I. WATTS *Bk. Praise* 92 Jesus shall reign where'er the sun Does his successive journeys run. **1788** PRIESTLEY *Lect. Hist.* III. xvi. 137 A view of the successive changes of the English coin to the present time. **1827** FARADAY *Chem. Manip.* xiii. (1842) 291 These crucibles gradually deteriorate and become injured by successive operations. **1838** DE MORGAN *Ess. Probab.* 15 The multiplication of all the successive numbers from 1 up to some high number. **1860** TYNDALL *Glac.* I. ii. 16 By repeated reflection, successive echos are sent to the ear. **1880** GEIKIE *Phys. Geog.* iv. 305 In countries where the winters are severe, ordinary building-stones and mortar are found to peel off in successive crusts.

predicative passing into *adv.* **1667** MILTON *P.L.* IV. 614 Since God hath set Labour and rest, as day and night to men Successive. **1716** POPE *Iliad* VI. 184 They fall successive and successive rise. **1791** COWPER *Iliad* IV. 510 So moved the Greeks successive, rank by rank.

b. With sing. sb.: Following another of the same kind in a regular sequence or series. Somewhat *rare.* Also quasi-*adv.*

1597 MORLEY *Introd. Mus.* 9 *Phi.* What is a stroke? *Ma.* It is a successiue motion of the hand, directing the quantitie of euery note and rest in the song, with equall measure. **1609** DANIEL *Civ. Wars* IV. l, And three..he assailes;..each successiue after other quailes. **1633** P. FLETCHER *Purple Isl.* IX. xxiv, When he fell, and left the barren heath, His parent straight inspir'd successive breath. **1686** GOAD *Celest. Bodies* I. xvi. 101 The Celerity of a Boat is continued by a successive dip of the Oar. **1746** FRANCIS tr. *Hor., Epist.* I. vi. 53 Then raise a second Plumb; A third successive be your earnest Care. **1822** SCOTT *Nigel* vii, He..took his leave, promising to be equipped and in readiness to embark with him on the second successive morning at ten o'clock. **1842** MRS. BROWNING *Grk. Chr. Poets* (1863) 114 What is this accent but a stroke, an emphasis, with a successive pause to make complete the time?

†**c.** Of a condition, influence, etc.: Continuous, uninterrupted. *Obs.*

1586 WARNER *Alb. Eng.* II. ix, He divers yeares good fortune had, successive in each thing. **1631** WEEVER *Anc. Funeral Mon.* 350 Her successive prosperitie. **1652** FELTHAM *Low Countries* (1677) 45 A strong Earth Quake would shake them to a Chaos, from which the successive force of the Sun..hath a little amended them.

2. Characterized by or involving succession; brought about or produced in succeeding stages.

1685 H. MORE *Let.* in J. Norris *Theory Love* (1688) 152 Successive Quantity seems more capable of being infinite then permanent Quantity. **1728** CHAMBERS *Cycl.* s.v. *Action*, Actions are..divided into Instantaneous, where the whole Effect is produced in the same Moment;..And Successive, where the Effect is produced by degrees. **1786** GILPIN *Mount. & Lakes Cumb.* (1792) I. viii. 119 The successive fall; in which the water, instead of making one continued shoot, falls through a succession of different stories. **1799** G. SMITH *Laboratory* II. 11 We might, indeed, make a successive collection of the coins of the western emperors. **1835** LYELL *Princ. Geol.* (ed. 4) I. 242 Doctrine of successive development not confirmed by the admission that man is of modern origin. **1842** [see SUBSTITUTION 5]. **1900** B. D. JACKSON *Gloss. Bot. Terms*, *Successive Whorl*, one whose members did not originate simultaneously, but in succession.

†**3.** = HEREDITARY. **a.** Of things: Descending or transmitted by succession or inheritance. *Obs.*

1432-50 tr. *Higden* (Rolls) VI. 283 This Kenulphus.. havynge successyve hate of Offa his predecessor ageyne men of Kente. **1588** SHAKS. *Tit. A.* I. i. 4 Pleade my Successiue Title with your Swords. I was the first borne Sonne. **1594** T. BEDINGFIELD tr. *Machiavelli's Florentine Hist.* (1595) To Rdr., To liue in the obedience of a successiue royall Monarchie. **1609** HEYWOOD *Brit. Troy* XVII. lxxvi, Leauing the Crowne successiue to his son. **1613** PURCHAS *Pilgrimage* (1614) 752 This function is successiue, and by tradition they teach their eldest sonnes the mysterie of this iniquitie. **1640** FULLER *Joseph's Party Col. Coat* 175 First for the Hereditarinesse of it, it [*sc.* leprosy] is a successive disease. **1698** G. THOMAS *Pensilvania* 50 Their Government is Monarchical, and Successive.

†**b.** Of persons: Succeeding by inheritance. *Obs.*

1592 KYD *Sp. Trag.* III. i. 14 Your King, By hate depriued of his dearest sonne, The onely hope of our successiue line. **1622** DRAYTON *Poly-olb.* xxvii. 276 Her Pedigrees to show, her right successiue Kings. **1649** MILTON *Tenure of Kings* 21 Jehu had special command to slay Jehoram a successive and hereditarie Tyrant. **1683** CREECH *Lucret.* (ed. 2) Notes 52 Every King whether Elective or Successive, Rules by the same Authority.

†**c.** Next in order of succession. Also *transf.*

1595 T. P. GOODWINE *Blanchardyn* liv. 212 The princely mariage which now was fully concluded betweene his successiue heire..with the renouned Lady and Queene of Tormaday. *c* **1600** SHAKS. *Sonn.* cxxvii, Blacke..now is blacke beauties successiue heire. **1632** H. SEILE *Augustus* 212 Hee should resemble old Ianus with the two faces; with th'one looking on the King Regnant; with th'other, on the Prince successive. **1726** POPE *Odyss.* XIX. 208 His son Deucalion bore successive sway.

†**4.** Attended or fraught with success; successful.

1582 [implied in SUCCESSIVELY 6]. **1593** *G. Harvey's Pierce's Super.* To Harvey, If..the doubtlesse successiue benefit thereof..may worke any plausible..motions with you. **1597** BEARD *Theatre God's Judgem.* (1612) 347 In this successive battell it is to be noted..how religiously the Emperour both began and finished it. **1620** BRATHWAIT *Five Senses* in *Archaica* (1815) II. 45 Weak is he in his resolves, unbounded in his desires, and seldom successive in his dispatch. **1659** *Lady Alimony* III. i, His prosperous exploits abroad, then which none more successive.

‖**successive** (sʌksɪ'saɪviː), *adv.* [med.L., adv. of *successīvus* SUCCESSIVE.] In succession.

1593 in T. Morris *Provosts of Methven* (1875) 82 To the saidis Johnne Grahame, and Mariorie Rollok, his spous, and the langar levar of thame tua successiue. **1681** in *Nairne Peerage Evidence* (1874) 15 Failing of heirs male the eldest daughter or heir female to be procreate betwixt them successive without division. **1687** WINSTANLEY *Lives Engl. Poets* 71 He was successive a Musician, Schoolmaster, Servingman, Husbandman, Grasier, Poet.

successively (sək'sɛsɪvlɪ), *adv.* Also 5 sussessiffly, successevely, 5-6 -yvely. [-LY[2].]

1. By successive stages (of increase or decrease); †by degrees. Now *rare.*

a **1425** tr. *Arderne's Treat. Fistula*, etc. 58 When þe pacientes felen þamself more heuy..þan is þe flwyng ouer mych; wherfor it is alsone successyuely to be restreyned and turned away. *a* **1548** HALL *Chron., Hen. VI*, 105 b, A pestilent humor, which successively a litle and litle corrupteth all the membres. **1620** E. BLOUNT *Horæ Subs*, 262 To doe that at once, which must bee done successiuely, is an argument of a rash, and intemperate man. **1715** DESAGULIERS *Fires Impr.* 23 The Air goes into the Hollows, is warm'd, and then successively warms the whole Air of the Room. **1743** EMERSON *Fluxions* Pref. p. vii, What a continual and successively variable Velocity can produce. **1827** FARADAY *Chem. Manip.* xx. (1842) 545 Now and then the stoppers of bottles become fixed.., in which case means of loosening them, successively increasing in power..must be resorted to. **1862** MILLER *Elem. Chem., Org.* (ed. 2) iii. §1. 152 The higher terms of the series becoming successively more viscid and oily.

2. In succession.

1439 *E.E. Wills* (1882) 114 The wardeyns of Seynt Austyns church..sussessiffly beyng. **1462** *Rolls of Parlt.* V. 489/1 Henry the Vth..and Henry the VIth..successevely Kynges of Englond. **1503** *Ibid.* VI. 522/2 They..and their successours, and the successours of every of them, shall have successyvelye for ever, lyke auctorite. **1521** in Ellis *Orig. Lett.* Ser. III. I. 258 [He] opennyd the boke..and begynning the prohem, redde therof successyvely v. lefes. **1590** SPENSER *F.Q.* II. x. 44 Fiue sonnes he left begotten of one wife, All which successiuely by turnes did raine. **1617** MORYSON *Itin.* I. 170 It was subject to the Emperour Otho the first, by right of his wife, and successively to the Emperours. **1651** HOBBES *Leviath.* III. xxxviii. 245 Everlasting Fire,..(into which men may be cast successively one after another for ever). *a* **1700** EVELYN *Diary* 9 Feb. 1671, The famous play call'd 'The Siege of Granada', (Dryden) two days acted successively. **1712** STEELE *Spect.* No. 400 ¶9 The Disappointment of four or five Passions which she has successively had for different Men. **1776** GIBBON *Decl. & F.* xiii. I. 356 Diocletian was successively promoted to the government of Mæsia, the honours of the consulship, and the important command of the guards of the palace. **1818** SCOTT *Hrt. Midl.* l, The lad ..fetched an earthen jar and a horn cup,..and offered them successively to the lady and to the boy. **1854** BREWSTER *More Worlds* x. 163 If we suppose ourselves placed successively on Mars, Jupiter, Saturn, Uranus, and Neptune, the Sun will appear smaller and smaller. **1874** GREEN *Short Hist.* ix. §1 (1882) 593 He became successively Solicitor and Attorney-General.

†**3.** Continuously or without interruption (for a certain period). *Obs.*

1531 ELYOT *Gov.* I. ii, And so successiuely one kynge gouerned all the people of Israell unto the time of Roboaz. **1550** *Hall's Chron.* (*title-p.*) Beginnyng at the tyme of kyng Henry the fowerth, the first aucthor of this deuision, and so successively proceading to yᵉ reigne of..kyng Henry the eyght. **1627** W. BEDELL in *Lett. Lit. Men* (Camden) 136 It begins much about the Conquest..and continues successively to Calixtus the 3rd. **1683** MOXON *Mech. Exerc., Printing* i. 5 And there [*sc.* Oxford] the excercise of Printing hath continued successively to this day. **1709** STEELE *Tatler* No. 107 ¶14 Repeat this every Day for a Month successively. **1748** WASHINGTON *Jrnl.* 7 Apr., Writ. 1889 I. 5 Raind successively all last night. *c* **1790** *Encycl. Brit.* (1797) VI. 739/2 For 18 years successively.

†**4.** In the course of events, subsequently, eventually. *Obs.*

1600 FAIRFAX *Tasso* I. xxiv, What to this howre successiuely is donne Was full of perill. **1612** DRAYTON *Poly-olb.* ii. 156 And all that there-vpon successiuely befell. **1654** EARL MONM. tr. *Bentivoglio's Wars Flanders* 277 Which they..were not long adoing, as we shall successively relate.

†**5.** By succession or inheritance. *Obs.*

1594 SHAKS. *Rich. III*, III. vii. 135 Not as Protector..But as successiuely, from Blood to Blood. **1597** —— *2 Hen. IV*, IV. v. 202 So thou, the Garland wear'st successiuely.

†**6.** Successfully, propitiously. *Obs.*

1582 MUNDAY *Disc. E. Campion* F iij, Howe all thinges went successivelie foreward. **1597** A. M. tr. *Guillemeau's Fr. Chirurg.* 54/2 Beinge verye successivelye cured of Mr. Martel, Chyrurgiane to the Kinge. **1630** BRATHWAIT *Engl. Gentlem.* 62 Any exploit, how successively or prosperously soever managed. **1683** KENNET tr. *Fragm. on Folly* (1709) 33 A battle shall be more successively fought by serving men.. than by the most accomplished philosophers.

suc'cessiveness. [-NESS.] The state or quality of being successive.

a **1676** HALE *Prim. Orig. Man.* I. vi. (1677) 119 The Image whereby it [*sc.* the Understanding] conceives it, is partly by the successiveness of its own operations. **1829** MILL *Hum. Mind* xiv. §2 II. 68 The process of having two ideas in succession, in which process the being sensible of the successiveness is part. **1851** RUSKIN *Stones Venice* I. xxvii. §18 They are all conventionalised into a monotonous successiveness of nothing. **1878** BARTLEY tr. *Topinard's Anthrop.* Introd. 19 Nature does not make sudden jumps. There is a successiveness observable throughout.

So **succe'ssivity.**

1866 *Examiner* 3 Feb. 70/1 An absolute Being, whose nature..precludes..all successivity and change.

successless (sək'sɛslɪs), *a.* Now *rare*; freq. in 17th and 18th c. [f. SUCCESS *sb.* + -LESS.] Without, or having no, success; unsuccessful.

1584 PEELE *Arraignm. Paris* I. v, How mighty men made foul successless war Against the gods. **1589** WARNER *Alb. Eng.* VI. xxx. (1612) 149 Successlesse..and inraged. **1615** G. SANDYS *Trav.* 9 Divers great Princes,..with Successlesse labor, have attempted to make that rockie streight a navigable passage. **1641** *Remonstr. Commons* in Rushw. *Hist. Coll.* (1692) III. I. 440 An expenceful and successless attempt upon Calez. **1665** DRYDEN *Ind. Emp.* II. i, The hopes of thy successless love resign. **1682** SIR T. BROWNE *Chr. Mor.* I. §18 That may succeed with one which may prove successless with another. **1713** ADDISON *Cato* I. i, Passion unpity'd, and successless love Plant daggers in my heart. **1782** MISS BURNEY *Cecilia* II. v, Belfield fired first, and missed; the Baronet was not so successless. **1820** J. CLARE *Poems Rural Life* (ed. 3) 138 By successless sallies wearied quite. **1875** BROWNING *Aristoph. Apol.* 134 He sympathizes, he concerns himself, He pens epistle, each successless play. **1891** J. R. LOUNSBURY *Stud. Chaucer* I. i. 56 To make out the best showing possible for the English of a successless campaign.

Hence **suc'cesslessly** *adv.*, **suc'cesslessness.**

1642 O. SEDGWICK *Eng. Preserv.* 40 Like him in the Gospel who began to build, but did not make an end: Whereupon results a vanity and successelesnesse to our workes. **1652** HEYLIN *Cosmogr.* IV. 110 Successlessly again attempted. **1744** BIRCH *Life of Boyle* 27 After the queen's and others doctors remedies had been successlessly tried. **1827** *Blackw. Mag.* XXI. 790 We tried..on three days, successively and successlessly. **1906** B. CAPES *Loaves & Fishes* 204 He permitted his employers so to presume upon his reputation for successlessness.

successor (sək'sɛsə(r)). Forms: 3–8 **successour**, 4–6 **successoure**, (7 **-er**), 4– **successor**. [a. OF. (AF.) *successour*, *-or* (mod.F. *successeur*), = Pr., Pg. *successor*, It. *successore*, Sp. *sucesor*, ad. L. *successor*, *-ōrem*, agent-n. f. *success-*, *succēdĕre* to SUCCEED.] **a.** One who succeeds another in an office, dignity, function, or position. Const. *of*, *to* (the predecessor), *in*, *to*, †*of* (the thing succeeded to). (Correlative to *predecessor*.)

singular successor (Sc. Law): see SINGULAR *a.* 4 b.

1297 R. GLOUC. (Rolls) 10440 Of him & of his successours of rome To holde euere engelond. **1338** R. BRUNNE *Chron.* (1810) 72 To Frankis & Normanz..To Flemmynges & Pikardes..He gaf londes bityme, of whilk þer successoure Hold ȝit þe seysyne. **1382** WYCLIF *Dan.* v. 31 Darius of Mede was successour in the rewme. *c* **1400** MAUNDEV. (1839) v. 43 He was Successour to Machomete, and of his Generatioun. *c* **1450** *Mirk's Festial* 189 He toke Clement by þe hond..and made hym pope and successor aftyr hym. **1546** *Reg. Privy Council Scot.* Ser. I. I. 37 Air and successour of tailze of umquhile Duncane Lawmond. **1571** GOLDING *Calvin on Ps.* lxxi. 1 David..did carefully comend untoo God his sonne whom he should leave successor of his kingdom. **1611** *Bible* Ecclus. xlvi. 1 The successor of Moses in prophesies. **1671** MILTON *Samson* 1021 Thy Paranymph, ..Successour in thy bed. **1679** DRYDEN *Troil. & Cress.* Prol. 17 Where are the Successours to my name? **1766** BLACKSTONE *Comm.* II. 430 A gift to such a corporation, either of lands or of chattels, without naming their successors, vests an absolute property in them so long as the corporation subsists. *Ibid.* 431 The word *successors*, when applied to a person in his politic capacity, is equivalent to the word *heirs* in his natural. **1841** ELPHINSTONE *Hist. India* II. 359 Ahdád, the grandson and spiritual successor of Báyazid. **1864** BRYCE *Holy Rom. Emp.* xii. (1875) 188 Henry VI, the son and successor of Barbarossa.

b. *transf.* of a thing.

c **1386** CHAUCER *Man of Law's T.* 323 O sodeyn wo that euere art successour To worldly blisse. **1863** H. COX *Instit.* III. viii. 703 Intervals between the expiration of one Mutiny Act and the enactment of its successor.

c. *attrib.*, as ***successor-designate***; **successor state** = *succession state* s.v. SUCCESSION 15.

1958 D. TAIT in Middleton & Tait *Tribes without Rulers* 197 His companion is generally his successor-designate in the office. **1974** P. GORE-BOOTH *With Great Truth & Respect* 388, I set up a committee of three, consisting of Colin Crowe, Dennis Greenhill, my successor-designate, representing the Foreign Office and Jack Johnston representing the Commonwealth Office, to meet daily. **1930** *Economist* 9 Aug. 274/1 A century ago the present 'successor States' of the Hapsburg and Ottoman Empires might have been economically self-sufficient. **1971** H. MACMILLAN *Riding Storm* xvi. 537 The complicated intrigues and rivalries among the successor states of the old Turkish Empire.

Hence **suc'cessorship** [-SHIP], the condition or position of successor, succession.

1627 H. BURTON *Baiting Pope's Bull* 84 What is this to the purpose, to proue the Popes Vicarship or his Successorsship? **1720** GORDON & TRENCHARD *Independ. Whig* (1728) 436 Nor is there a Word in Scripture, whereby we can guess that they were intended to be Successors to the Apostles, much less that the Successorship was to continue to the End of the World. **1886** ROGERS *Soc. Life Scotl.* III. xx. 265 A class of persons might have existed..without any successorship. **1895** *Cath. News* 27 July 6 Three Irish Priests have been selected..in connection with the successorship to the late Most Rev. Dr. Moran, in the Bishopric of Dunedin N.Z.

†**suc'cessory**, *a. Obs.* [ad. late L. *successōrius*, f. *successor* SUCCESSOR: see -ORY. Cf. It., Pg. *successorio*.] Succeeding by inheritance, hereditary.

1610 DONNE *Pseudo-martyr* 288 Which may often fall out in states, which elect their Princes, because there are many limitations, but in Successorie princes, it cannot hold. **1619** *Time's Store House* v. xxiii. 518/2 It is manifest, dignities which were but the bare names of personal Offices, to haue at length become hereditary and successory. **1641** *Mann. Holding Parl. in Eng.* 27 Our King's..granted an hereditary and successory perpetuity unto honourable titles.

†**suc'cide**, *v. Obs. rare*$^{-1}$. [ad. L. *succīdĕre*, f. *suc-* = SUB- 26 + *cædĕre* to cut.] *trans.* To cut off, shorten.

1432–50 tr. *Higden* (Rolls) II. 185 The breste is constreynede with mony sighes, the brethe is succidede.

suc'ciduous, *a. Obs. rare*$^{-0}$. [f. L. *succiduus*, f. *succidĕre*, f. *suc-* = SUB- 2 + *cadĕre* to fall.] Ready to fall; tottering.

1656 BLOUNT *Glossogr.*

succiferous (sʌk'sɪfərəs), *a. Bot. rare.* [f. mod.L. *succiferus*, f. *succus*: see SUCCUS and -FEROUS.] Producing or bearing sap.

1655–87 H. MORE *App. Antid.* (1712) 232 The modern Philosophers..who have not only observ'd the succiferous but also airiferous vessels of Plants. **1672–3** GREW *Anat. Pl., Roots* (1682) 70 The Lignous Part, if not always, yet usually, is also Compounded of Two Kinds of Bodies, *scil.* Succiferous or Lignous and Aer-Vessels.

†**,succifi'cation.** *Obs. rare.* [f. SUCCUS + -FICATION.] The production of sap.

1733 TULL *Horse-hoeing Husb.* ii. 19 If Leaves did not perform this necessary work of Succification, the Lives of Plants would not..so entirely depend on the use of Leaves, as they appear to do.

succin ('sʌksɪn). *rare.* Also 6 **succine**. [ad. L. *succinum*, *sūcinum*. Cf. F. *succin*, It., Sp., Pg. *succino*.] Amber.

1596 DALRYMPLE tr. *Leslie's Hist. Scot.* I. 47 Succine, or ambre, quhilke the Greikis calles Electre. [In some mod. Dicts.]

succin- (sʌksɪn), comb. form (before a vowel) of L. *succinum* amber, in the names of various amide and anilide derivatives of SUCCINIC acid, e.g. ***succinamic acid***, ***succinanil***; also ***succinasphalt***: see quots. Cf. SUCCINO-.

1838 T. THOMSON *Chem. Org. Bodies* 594 When succinamide is treated with potash, ammonia is disengaged, and the temperature rises. **1857** MILLER *Elem. Chem., Org.* iv. §1. 242 Succinimide is metameric with succinamic acid. *Ibid.* §2. 257 Succinanile $C_{12}H_5N$, $C_8H_4O_4$. *Ibid.*, Succinanilic acid HO, $C_{12}H_5$, HN, $C_8H_4O_5$. *Ibid.*, Succinanilide 2 $(C_{12}H_5)$, H_2N_2, $C_8H_4O_4$. **1868** WATTS *Dict. Chem.* V. 453 *Succinasphalt*, a resinous substance resembling amber, and apparently related to retinite, obtained from the granular clay iron-ore of Bergen in Bavaria. *Ibid.* 460 Succinamate. *Ibid.* 461 Succinanilate of Ammonium is very soluble in water.

succinate ('sʌksɪneɪt). *Chem.* Also **-at**. [ad. F. *succinate* (Lavoisier): see SUCCINIC + -ATE⁴.] A salt of succinic acid.

1790 KERR tr. *Lavoisier's Elem. Chem.* 273 All the succinats were unknown to the ancient chemists. **1805** DAVEY *Alkali* in *Phil. Trans.* XCV. 232, I have separated.. the oxide of iron by succinate of ammonia. **1876** tr. *Schützenberger's Ferment.* 28 The calcium succinate is easily purified by treating it with alcohol.

succinated ('sʌksɪneɪtɪd), *a. Chem.* [f. mod.L. *succinātus*, f. *succinum* amber.] Containing or combined with amber.

1698 *Phil. Trans.* XX. 257, I then gave her Spirit of Sal. Armon. Succinated. **1800** tr. *Lagrange's Chem.* II. 79 The scoriæ which float at the top have been called *Succinated Scoriæ*.

succinct (sək'sɪŋkt), *pa. pple.*, *ppl. a.*, and *a.* [ad. L. *succinctus*, pa. pple. of *succingĕre*, f. *suc-* = SUB- 2, 26 + *cingĕre* to gird. Cf. F. *succinct*, It., Pg. *succinto*, Sp. *sucinto*.]

A. *pa. pple.* and *ppl. a.*

1. Girt, engirdled.

1432–50 tr. *Higden* (Rolls) II. 369 Thei feyne Scylla to be a woman succincte with the hedes of dogges. **1634** SIR T. HERBERT *Trav.* 115 The towne is most beautified by a vast garden of the Kings, succinct with a great towred mud-wall. **1656** BLOUNT *Glossogr.*, *Succinct*, enuironed, fenced about; girt, compassed. **1830** W. PHILLIPS *Mt. Sinai* I. 279 The Everlasting Form—If form there were—of lineament, was void, Succinct with shadows.

fig. **1706** J. PHILIPS *Cerealia* 97 Wks. (1781) 140 Soon she shakes Her drowsy wings, and follows to the war With speed succinct. [Cf. quot. 1667 in B. 3.]

2. a. Of garments, etc.: Girded up; confined by or as by a girdle. Also of persons.

1604 R. CAWDREY *Table Alph.*, *Succincte*..close girt up. **1616–61** HOLYDAY *Persius* (1673) 324 And when my golden boss I newly had Hung up to my succinct house gods. **1726** POPE *Odyss.* XVII. 200 Aside they lay Their garments, and succinct, the victims slay. **1841** TRENCH *Parables* xxvii. 437 The waiting at table with the dress succinct, was a mark of servitude. **1843** R. H. HORNE *Orion* I. 86 The form Succinct ..Of Artemis. **1866** J. B. ROSE tr. *Ovid's Fasti* I. 344 The Priest..succinct for sacrificial feast. **1876** LOWELL *Ode Fourth July* I. i. 18 Over her broad brow in many a round,.. Succinct, as toil prescribes, the hair was wound In lustrous coils.

b. *Ent.* Of certain pupæ: Supported by a silken filament round the middle.

In mod. Dicts.

B. *adj.*

1. a. Of a narrative, etc.: Compressed into small compass; expressed in few words; brief and concise.

1585 T. WASHINGTON tr. *Nicholay's Voy.* I. xv. 16 b, A succinct description of the yland. **1596** T. BELL *Surv. Popery* (*title-p.*) A succinct and profitable enarration of the state of Gods Church. **1634** R. H. *Salernes Regiment* 207 A Succinct and plaine Discourse of the Nature and nourishment of divers kinds of Fish. **1711** HEARNE *Collect.* (O.H.S.) III. 107 A full, though succinct and sober Narrative. **1760–72** J. ADAMS tr. *Juan & Ulloa's Voy.* (ed. 3) I. p. ix, They give us a succinct account of the Creoles. **1781** COWPER *Convers.* 235 A tale should be judicious, clear, succinct; The language plain, and incidents well link'd. **1839** HALLAM *Lit. Eur.* III. 278 This account of the original of language appears in general as probable as it is succinct and clear. **1864** BOWEN *Logic* vii. 184 We need some more succinct mode than that of severally applying to each Syllogism all these Rules.

b. *transf.* Compact.

1635 HEYWOOD *Hierarchy* II. 83 Hee [*sc.* man] is stiled a little and succinct world within himselfe. **1800** HURDIS *Fav. Village* 84 Beyond yon humble and succinct abode.

†**c.** *advb.* Concisely, briefly. *Obs.*

1593 NASHE *Christ's T.* 77 Very largely haue I inueighed against this vice elswhere, wherefore heere I will trusse it vp more succinct [*printed* surcinct].

2. Of persons, their speech, style, etc.: Characterized by verbal brevity and conciseness; terse.

1603 HOLLAND *Plutarch's Mor.* 203 Apollo himselfe loveth brevitie, and is in his oracles verie succinct and pithy. **1606** —— *Sueton.* To Rdr., His succinct style and termes. *a* **1637** B. JONSON *Discov.* (1641) 119 A strict and succinct style is that, where you can take away nothing without losse, and that losse to be manifest. **1670** MILTON *Hist. Eng.* v. Wks. 1851 V. 223 The Saxon Annalist wont to be sober and succinct..runs..into such extravagant fansies [etc.]. **1712** STEELE *Spect.* No. 468 ¶8, I must grow more succinct. **1759** ROBERTSON *Hist. Scot.* (1817) 211 A succinct and dry writer. **1958** S. J. PERELMAN *Most of S. J. Perelman* 491 Now, Messieurs, exposition is wearisome, so I will be succinct.

3. Of garments: Not ample or full, close-fitting, scant. *arch.* or *poet.*

[**1667** MILTON *P.L.* III. 643 His habit fit for speed succinct.] **1712–14** POPE *Rape Lock* III. 41 Four Knaves in garbs succinct, a trusty band. **1725** —— *Odyss.* XIV. 83 His vest succinct then girding round his waste. **1746** BERKELEY in Fraser *Life* viii. 306 If any other [dress] can be contrived yet more succinct and tight. **1755** *Monitor* No. 21. I. 182 Some novelties of dress, viz. very low stays, and very succinct petticoats. **1831** SCOTT *Cast. Dang.* xi, [She] exchanged her stole, or loose upper garment, for the more succinct cloak and hood of a horseman. **1858** CARLYLE *Fredk. Gt.* VI. iii. (1872) II. 161 Mere soldier uniform, succinct blue coat, white linen gaiters. **1893** SYMONDS *Life M. Angelo* I. ii. 66 Tuscan lads half draped in succinct tunics.

4. Of short duration, brief, curt.

1796 MME. D'ARBLAY *Camilla* IV. 331 With a succinct bow..he took a hasty leave. **1837** CARLYLE *Fr. Rev.* II. I. ii, With the rope round their neck, their destiny may be succinct! **1892** STEVENSON & L. OSBOURNE *Wrecker* xi. 175 Captain Nares acknowledged our previous acquaintance with a succinct nod.

succinctly (sək'sɪŋktlɪ), *adv.* [-LY².]

1. In a succinct manner; with brevity and conciseness.

c **1537** PAYNEL in De Benese *Measur. Lande* Pref. + iiij, Thys..boke..Where in is succinctly and breflye conteyned the perfect fourm and rule of measurynge. **1599** B. JONSON

Cynthia's Rev. IV. iii, *Hed.* In the behalfe of the males, I gratifie you, Amorphus. *Pha.* And I, of the females. *Amo.* Succinctly return'd. **1605** BACON *Adv. Learn.* II. xxiii. §8 The Examples alledged for the discourses sake, are cited succinctly, and without particularity. **1653** H. COGAN tr. *Pinto's Trav.* xxi. 73, I have labored to speak succinctly in divers places, where possibly better wits then mine would amplifie matters. **1714** PRIOR *Viceroy* xxxi, Succinctly thus to you I've told, How this Viceroy did reign. **1850** JAMIESON *Sacred & Leg. Art* 195, I will give you the story as succinctly and as properly as I can. **1876** DUHRING *Dis. Skin* 70 Atrophy, succinctly stated, is want of balance between the nutritive supply and the part to be nourished.

b. *transf.* In a brief space of time; with summary treatment.

1837 CARLYLE *Fr. Rev.* II. I. ii, So shall the Parlements perish, succinctly; and innumerable eyes be dry. **1856** KANE *Arctic Expl.* II. xii. 127 He was dealt with more succinctly by his neighbor..who..pushed him into the sea, after harpooning him.

†**2.** Without fullness or ampleness. *Obs.*

1743 *Davidson's Virg., Æneid* VII. II. 187 Picus..in his scanty Robe succinctly dressed [Virg. *succinctus trabea*].

succinctness (sək'sɪŋktnɪs). [-NESS.]

1. The quality or condition of being succinct; conciseness.

1609 HEYWOOD *Brit. Troy* To Rdrs., I haue taskt my selfe to such succinctnesse and breuity, that [etc.] **1644** DIGBY *Nat. Soul* Pref. 352 To serue for conueniency and succinctenesse of discourse. *a* **1716** SOUTH *Serm.* Eccl. v. 2 (1727) II. 128 Brevity and Succinctness of Speech, is that, which in Philosophy or Speculation we call *Maxim*, and First Principle. **1864** BURTON *Scot. Abr.* I. v. 279 John Hamilton.. states with much succinctness..a favorite charge of that day against Knox. **1884** *Athenæum* 11 Oct. 459/3 A critic is always loth to quarrel with succinctness.

2. The condition of being close-fitting or without fullness.

1818 *Blackw. Mag.* III. 277 Grave academics..started forth in the unwonted and unnatural succinctness of the sagum. **1891** FARRAR *Darkness & Dawn* II. 261 He wore the dress of a jockey of the green faction, and its succinctness revealed his thin legs and protuberant person.

‖**succinctorium** (sʌksɪŋk'tɔərɪəm). [late L., f. *suc-* = SUB- + *cinctorium* girdle, f. *cingĕre* to gird.] A band or scarf (resembling a maniple) embroidered with an Agnus Dei, worn pendant from the girdle by the Pope on certain occasions.

1688 HOLME *Armoury* III. iv. 175/2 A Bishops Vestments, or Pontifical Symbols of Ecclesiastical Regencie... *Succinctorium*, a kind of Girdle.

Hence **succinctory** (sək'sɪŋktərɪ), in same sense.

1572 R. T. *Discourse* 28 To glorifie, our holie father the Pope, dothe note Buechingerus and Innocentius..affirme that there are 9 special ornamentes: his hose, his shoes, or sandalles, his succynctory or girdell [etc.]. **1583** STUBBES *Anat. Abus.* I. (1879) 48 Girded with a thong of the skin of the same, in sted of a girdle or succinctorie about his loines. **1868** WALCOTT *Sacred Archæol.* 273 In lieu of a maniple, he has a succinctory.

succincture (sək'sɪŋktjʊə(r)). *rare.* [ad. mod.L. *succinctūra*, f. *succinct-*, *succingĕre*: see SUCCINCT and CINCTURE.]

†**1.** ? A ligature. *Obs.*

1597 A. M. tr. *Guillemeau's Fr. Chirurg.* 16 b/1 We must cutt it [*sc.* black or leadish gut] of vnder the foresayed succincture.

2. The action of girding the loins.

1894 BLACKMORE *Perlycross* 349 But why are we told to gird our loins,—of which succincture the Spencer is expressive.

‖**succinea** (sək'sɪnɪə). *Zool.* Pl. -eæ, eas. [mod.L. (Draparnaud), fem. of *succineus*, f. *succinum* amber, SUCCIN.] Any gasteropod of the genus of this name: so called from the transparent texture and amber colour of the shell.

1840 *Cuvier's Anim. Kingd.* 349 The *Succinea*..has an ovate shell, with an aperture longer than its width. **1863** LYELL *Antiq. Man* xvi. 332, I found the fluviatile loam or brick-earth, enclosing the usual helices and succineæ. **1902** CORNISH *Natur. Thames* 16 Tiny physas and succineas, no larger than shot.

suc'cineous, *a.* *rare*⁻⁰. [f. L. *succineus* (see prec.).] Resembling amber.

1656 BLOUNT *Glossogr.*

†**suc'cinge**, *v.* *Obs.* *rare*⁻¹. [ad. L. *succingĕre* (see SUCCINCT).] *trans.* To engirdle.

1578 BANISTER *Hist. Man* I. 24 The ribbes, in their inner region or side, are succinged and clothed with a most sensible Membran called Pleura.

†**suc'cingent**, *a.* *Obs.* [ad. L. *succingens*, *-entem*, pr. pple. of *succingĕre* (see prec.).] Engirdling, embracing.

1578 BANISTER *Hist. Man* VII. 90 Beside this succingent coate [*sc.* the pleura], the ribbes haue to them, one peculiar [*sc.* the periosteum]. **1684** tr. *Bonet's Merc. Compit.* v. 142 Pus..enclosed in a bag, made by the connexion of the Lungs with the succingent membrane. *Ibid.* XII. 388 Unless..its Coat be so round and soft, that the Pulp, as well as the succingent Coat, is consumed.

succinic (sək'sɪnɪk). [ad. F. *succinique* (Lavoisier), f. L. *succinum* amber, SUCCIN: see -IC 1 b.]

1. *Chem.* *succinic acid*: a dibasic acid obtained by the dry distillation of amber. (Formerly called *salt* or *spirit of amber*.)

1790 KERR tr. *Lavoisier's Elem. Chem.* 190 Succinic acid, [old name] Volatile salt of amber. **1836–41** BRANDE *Chem.* (ed. 5) 1160 When succinic acid is obtained in the form of crystals from its aqueous solutions, it is in a hydrated state. **1876** HARLEY *Mat. Med.* (ed. 6) 360 Succinic acid is supposed to be expectorant.

b. Similarly ***succinic amide, anhydride, chloride, ether, oxychloride***. Also attrib. ***succinic test***.

1805 SAUNDERS *Min. Waters* 386 Various experiments respecting alumine and its relations with the succinic test. **1857** MILLER *Elem. Chem., Org.* iii. §4. 153 The formula of the oxalic, carbonic, and succinic ethers, must be taken as containing one equivalent of the dibasic acid and two equivalents of oxide of ethyl. *Ibid.* vi. §3. 426 Succinic oxychloride ($C_8H_4O_4Cl_2$). **1862** *Ibid.* (ed. 2) v. §1. 294 Benzoic and succinic anhydrides. **1868** WATTS *Dict. Chem.* V. 460 Succinic Amides.

2. Found in amber, as an insect.

1836 F. W. HOPE in *Trans. Entomol. Soc. Lond.* I. 133 Observations on Succinic Insects.

succiniferous (sʌksɪ'nɪfərəs), *a.* *Bot.* [f. SUCCINUM + -FEROUS.] Resin-producing.

1896 *Nat. Sci.* Sept. 161 Only such specimens as are enclosed by the fossil resin belong with certainty to the succiniferous trees.

succinimide (sʌk'sɪnɪmaɪd). *Chem.* [f. SUCCINIC + IMIDE.] A crystalline substance obtained by the action of dry ammonia gas on succinic anhydride. So **succi'nimidate**.

1857 MILLER *Elem. Chem., Org.* iv. §1. 242 Succinimide is metameric with succinamic acid. It yields a crystallizable compound with silver, termed succinimidate of silver. **1868** WATTS *Dict. Chem.* V. 460 Argentic succinimide. **1890** *Lancet* 11 Oct. 778/2 The succinimide appears to be about as efficacious as the yellow oxide.

succinite ('sʌksɪnaɪt). [f. SUCCINUM + -ITE.]

1. *Min.* **a.** A granular garnet of the colour of amber.

After F. *succinite* (Bonvoisin, 1807).

1816 P. CLEAVELAND *Min.* (1822) I. 363. **1854** DANA *Syst. Min.* (ed. 4) II. 191.

b. Amber.

After G. *succinit* (Breithaupt, 1820).

1854 DANA *Syst. Min.* (ed. 4) II. 466 Amber. Yellow Mineral Resin,..Succinite. **1896** *Nat. Sci.* Aug. 100 Succinite is the most common and the best known of the Baltic ambers.

2. *Chem.* The insoluble resinous element in amber.

1868 DANA *Syst. Min.* (ed. 5) 740 Amber is not a simple resin. According to Berzelius..it consists mainly..of a resin which resists all solvents (properly the species succinite), along with two other resins soluble in alcohol and ether.

succino- ('sʌksɪnəʊ), used as comb. form (before a cons.) of L. *succinum* amber: see quots. (Cf. SUCCIN-.)

1868 WATTS *Dict. Chem.* V. 460 *Succinonitrile (Cyanide of Ethylene) $C^4H^4N^2$. **1901** DORLAND *Illust. Med. Dict.* (ed. 2), **Succinoresinol*, a resinol from amber. **1862** MILLER *Elem. Chem., Org.* (ed. 2) v. §3. 369 Succinic acid combines ..with sulphuric anhydride, and forms a deliquescent crystallizable compound acid, termed *succino-sulphuric acid.

succinol ('sʌksɪnɒl). [f. L. *succinum* amber + -OL.] Purified amber tar-oil, used in the treatment of skin diseases.

1913 DORLAND *Med. Dict.*

succinous ('sʌksɪnəs), *a.* *rare.* [f. SUCCINUM + -OUS.] Of or pertaining to amber.

1658 PHILLIPS. **1794** R. J. SULIVAN *View Nat.* I. 233 The succinous [acid] is found only in amber. **1796** KIRWAN *Elem. Min.* (ed. 2) II. 4 The Succinous Acid, has been found in mineral Coal.

‖**succinum** ('sʌksɪnəm). [L.] Amber.

1608 MIDDLETON *Mad World* III. ii, No poorer ingrediences then the liquor of Currall, cleere Amber, or Succinum. **1666** *Phil. Trans.* I. 345 What is to be observed about *Succinum* or Amber. **1783** *Ibid.* LXXIII. 226 Nor has it, like succinum, a polished appearance or transparency. **1821** J. SMYTH *Pract. Customs* 169 Oil..of Amber or Succinum the lb. 5*s.* 6*d.* **1876** HARLEY *Mat. Med.* (ed. 6) 360.

succinyl ('sʌksɪnɪl). *Chem.* [f. SUCCINIC + -YL.] The radical of succinic acid. Hence **succi'nylic** *a.* = SUCCINIC.

1868 WATTS *Dict. Chem.* V. 464.

succinylcholine (ˌsʌksɪnaɪl'kəʊliːn). *Pharm.* Also succinyl choline. [f. SUCCINYL + CHOLINE.] The ion $[-CH_2COO{\cdot}(CH_2)_2\overset{+}{N}(CH_3)_3]_2$ formed by esterification of succinic acid with choline; also, a halogen salt of this, given intravenously as a short-acting muscle relaxant and local anæsthetic; = SUXAMETHONIUM.

1950 *Chem. Abstr.* XLIV. 2124 It is shown that succinyl choline produces strong curarizing effects. **1952** [see SCOLINE]. **1965** J. POLLITT *Depression & its Treatment* vi. 80 Occasionally recovery from succinyl choline is delayed and artificial respiration required for an extended period. **1974** M. C. GERALD *Pharmacol.* iii. 52 Alcohol..and the skeletal muscle relaxant succinylcholine are broken down by the enzymes alcohol dehydrogenase and pseudocholinesterase, respectively.

succinylsulphathiazole (ˌsʌksɪnaɪlsʌlfə'θaɪəzəʊl). *Pharm.* Also -sulf-. [f. SUCCINYL + SULPHATHIAZOLE.] A poorly absorbed sulphonamide derivative which is used in the treatment of gastrointestinal infections and is inactive until hydrolysed to sulphathiazole in the body; 4'-(thiazol-2-ylsulphamoyl)-succinanilic acid, $C_3H_2NS{\cdot}NH{\cdot}SO_2{\cdot}C_6H_4{\cdot}NH{\cdot}CO{\cdot}(CH_2)_2COOH$.

1941 *Proc. Soc. Exper. Biol. & Med.* XLVIII. 129 (*heading*) Succinyl sulfathiazole, a new bacteriostatic agent locally active in the gastrointestinal tract. **1981** H. J. ROGERS et al. *Textbk. Clinical Pharmacol.* xix. 647 Only 5–10% of these drugs are absorbed... Examples are phthalylsulphathiazole and succinylsulphathiazole, both of which hydrolyse to sulphathiazole.

succise (sək'saɪs), *a.* *Bot.* [ad. L. *succīsus*, pa. pple. of *succīdĕre* to SUCCIDE.] Shaped as if abruptly cut or broken off at the lower end.

1880 A. GRAY *Struct. Bot.* 436.

†**suc'cision.** *Obs.* *rare*⁻¹. [ad. late L. *succīsio*, *-ōnem*, n. of action f. *succīdĕre* to SUCCIDE.] A felling or lopping down.

a **1626** BACON *Case Impeachm. Waste* Wks. 1730 IV. 107 Upon waste brought and assigned in the succision of trees.

†**suc'cisive**, *a.* *Obs.* [ad. L. *succīsīvus*, partly metathetic var. of *subsicīvus* SUBSECIVE, partly f. *succīs-*, pa. ppl. stem of *succīdĕre* to SUCCIDE.] Spare (hours).

1619 W. SCLATER *Expos. 1 Thess.* (1629) To Rdr., My succisiue houres..I promise to be wholly imployed that way. **1629** H. BURTON *Truth's Tri.* Pref., It was borrowed from the interrupted succisiue houres of my court-attendance. **1656** BLOUNT *Glossogr.*

†**suc'city.** *Obs.* *rare*⁻¹. [f. L. *succus* juice, sap + -ITY. But ? an error for *succosity*.] Moisture.

1646 SIR T. BROWNE *Pseud. Ep.* II. i. 42 A lapidifical succity, and principle which determins prepared materials unto specificall concretions.

†**succla'mation.** *Obs.* [ad. L. *succlāmātio*, *-ōnem*, n. of action f. *succlāmāre*, f. *suc-* = SUB-28 + *clāmāre* to call.] Outcry, applause.

1566 PAINTER *Pal. Pleas.* (1575) I. 15 b, This succlamation and pitifull complaint, so stirred the multitude. **1600** HOLLAND *Livy* XLII. liii. 1146 All the while that he delivered this speech, there might be heard secret succlamations often-times. **1623** COCKERAM.

succle, obs. form of SUCKLE.

succollate, *v.* *rare*⁻⁰. [ad. L. *succollāre*, f. *suc-* = SUB- 26 + *collum* neck.] So **succo'llation**.

1623 COCKERAM, *Succollate*, to beare on ones shoulders. *Ibid.*, *Succollation*, a bearing on the shoulders.

†**succontrary**, ? *a.* *Obs.* *rare*⁻⁰. [f. L. **succontrārius* = *subcontrārius* SUBCONTRARY.] ? Subcontrary.

a **1500** *Medulla Gram.* (Bodl. MS. Top. gen. c. 20 lf. 463), *Succontrarior*, to stonde to succontrarye.

succor: see SUCCOUR, SUGAR.

succorance ('sʌkəræns). *Psychol.* Also **succourance**. [f. SUCCOUR *v.* + -ANCE.] A term used in some forms of personality assessment to describe the need for help, sympathy, and affection as a psychogenic force. Hence **'succorant** *a.*

1938 H. A. MURRAY *Explorations in Personality* ii. 83 *Succorance* (Succorant attitude), to seek aid, protection or sympathy. *Ibid.* iii. 181 The Succorance drive seeks a nurturant O. *Ibid.* 182 The Succorant need is always a sub-need. **1944** L. MUMFORD *Condition of Man* ii. 75 He builds his life around the themes of rejection and succorance. **1953** *Brit. Jrnl. Psychol.* Nov. 333 *Succourance*: some heroes show their great need of support, encouragement, care and protection. **1973** *Jrnl. Genetic Psychol.* June 185 Femininity involved being more..succorant. **1977** H. G. BURGER in B. Bernardi *Concept & Dynamics of Culture* 421 The nine behavioral systems of man were stated on unclear empirical grounds by Beatrice Whiting (1963:7): succorance, or asking help from others, [etc.].

†**succo'rrosive**, *a.* *Obs.* *rare*⁻¹. In 6 -yfe. [ad. L. **succorrōsīvus*: see SUB- 19 and CORROSIVE.] Tending to corrode.

1541 COPLAND *Galyen's Terap.* 2 Bj, It is an humour gnawynge aboute succorosyfe.

succory ('sʌkərɪ). Forms: 6 suckorie, -ery(e, -erie, succoury, -arie, -orye, succhory, 6–7 succorie, 7 suckary, succoreye, 8 succury, 6– succory. [Alteration of *cicoree*, *sichorie*, *sycory*, old forms of CHICORY, q.v., after MLG. *suckerîe*, MDu. *sûkerîe* (Du. *suikerei*, older Flem. *suykerey*, *succory*).]

1. The plant *Cichorium Intybus* (N.O. *Compositæ*), with bright blue flowers, found wild in England, esp. by roadsides. Also, its leaves and roots used medicinally and as food (cf. CHICORY, ENDIVE).

Also called for distinction *wild succory*.

1533 ELYOT *Cast. Helth* (1541) 28 b, Cykorie or suckorie is lyke in operation to lettise. 1548 TURNER *Names Herbes* (E.D.S.) 44 Intybus syluestris is of two sortes, the one is called in latin Cichorium, and in englishe Succory or hardewes. *c* 1550 LLOYD *Treas. Health* G j b, The ioyce of Succorye put into the eare or nostrel that is on the contrary syde to the grefe taketh away vtterly the tooth ache. 1655 CULPEPPER, etc. *Riverius* I. i, In Summer we can allow a moderate use of Herbs, . . as Endive, Succory, Sorrel. 1697 DRYDEN *Virg. Georg.* I. 182 And spreading Succ'ry choaks the rising Field. 1736 BAILEY *Househ. Dict.* s.v., Succory pounded and put under the left nipple eases the heart-ache. 1750 *Phil. Trans.* XLVI. 377 He had taken, for some Days, a Decoction of wild Succory. 1833 MACAULAY *Ess.*, *War Success. Spain* (1897) 239 The conquerors were trying to manufacture coffee out of succory, and sugar out of beet-root. 1880 JEFFERIES *Gt. Estate* 131 The blue succory and the scarlet poppies stand side by side in the yellow wheat.

2. Applied with qualifying words to other composites, chiefly of the tribe *Cichoriaceæ*:

garden succory: = ENDIVE 1 b. **gum succory**: see GUM *sb.*[2] 9 b. **hog succory**; = *swine's succory* (*b*). **lamb succory**, the genus *Arnoseris* (Treas. Bot.). **poison succory**, *Aposeris fœtida* (ibid.). †**rush (rushy) succory**: see RUSH *sb.*[1] 7. **swine's succory**, (*a*) dwarf nipplewort, *Arnoseris* (*Lapsana*) *pusilla*; (*b*) the genus *Hyoseris*. **wart succory**: = *swine's succory* (*a*). † **yellow succory**, *Picris hieracioides*.

1538 TURNER *Libellus*, *Intubum*, Suckery, Ryght gardyn wylde. 1548 [see GUM *sb.*[2] 9 b, RUSH *sb.*[1] 7]. 1548 TURNER *Names Herbes* (E.D.S.) 42 Hieracium . . may be called in englishe greate Haukweede or yealowe Succory. *Ibid.* 44 Intybus hortensis is of two sortes, the one is called Endyue, or whyte Endyue, & the other is called gardine Succory. 1597 GERARDE *Herbal* II. xxix. 224 Blewe gum Succorie. *Ibid.* 225 Yellowe gum Succorie. *Ibid.*, Rushie gum Succorie hath a tough and harde roote. *Ibid.* 226 The male Swines Succorie hath a long and slender roote. 1601 CHESTER *Love's Mart.*, etc. (1878) 82 Mosse of the Sea, and yellow Succorie, Sweete Trefoile, [etc.]. 1728 BRADLEY *Dict. Bot.*, Swine's Succory or Hawksweed. 1760 J. LEE *Introd. Bot.* App. 328 Succory, Wart, *Lapsana*. 1776 WITHERING *Arrangem. Veget.* 493 *Hyoseris Minima* . . Small Swine's Succory. 1829 LINDLEY *Synops. Brit. Flora* 157 *L*[*apsana*] *pusilla*. . . Swine's succory.

3. *attrib.*, as ***succory leaf***, ***plant***, ***powder***, ***root***, ***seed***; **succory broth, water**, a decoction made from succory, used as a cooling draught; **succory dock-cress**, nipplewort, *Lapsana communis*; **succory hawkweed**, the genus *Crepis*.

1809 *Med. Jrnl.* XXI. 393 It may be taken . . mixed with syrup of *succory broth. 1857 PRATT *Flower. Pl.* III. 218 Common Nipple-wort . . is sometimes called Swine's-cress, and *Succory Dock-cress. 1776 WITHERING *Arrangem. Veget.* 486 *Crepis Tectorum* . . Smooth *Succory Hawk-weed. 1688 HOLME *Armoury* II. iv. 60/1 He beareth Argent, a *Succory Leaf, Vert. 1831 J. DAVIES *Manual Mat. Med.* 122 Succory leaves. 1876 *Encycl. Brit.* V. 614/2 The Chicory or *Succory plant. 1867 BRANDE & COX *Dict. Sci.*, etc. III. 637/2 If *succory powder be present [in coffee]. 1570 in Gutch *Coll. Cur.* (1781) II. 7 *Suckerye rotes and parsnip rotes. 1832 *Veg. Subst. Food of Man* 304 The succory root . . is . . cut in pieces, and . . dried to admit of its being . . ground. 1665 HOOKE *Microgr.* 156 *Succory Seeds are like a Quiver full of Arrows. 1670 TEMPLE *Lett.* Wks. 1731 II. 222 A Glass of *Succory-Water. 1822 SCOTT *Nigel* xvi, Drink succory-water to cool your blood. 1839 JAMES *Louis XIV*, III. 296 And drinking a glass of succory water, she was suddenly seized with violent pain.

succose ('sʌkəʊs), *a.* *Bot.* *rare*$^{-0}$. [ad. L. *succōsus*, f. *succus* juice. Cf. SUCCOUS.] Full of juice or sap.

1859 MAYNE *Expos. Lex.* s.v. *Succosus*.

† **su'ccosity.** *Obs.* In 6 **sucosyte, succozitie, -site.** [ad. mod.L. *succōsitās*, f. *succōsus* (see prec.).] Juice, moisture.

c 1530 *Judic. Urines* II. vii. 28 To drawe to hym sucosyte, that is to say, humidyte. 1548–77 VICARY *Anat.* viii. (1888) 70 These *Miseraices* . . bring to *Vena porta* the succozitie of Chiley gooing from the stomacke. 1579 G. BAKER *Guydo's Quest.* 29 To . . beare awaye the saide succosite from the liuer.

succot, obs. form of SUCCATE.

† **su'ccota.** *Obs.* [Cf. SUCCATOON.] A kind of cloth.

1780 *Phil. Trans.* LXX. App. p. vii, As the Dutch Company do not pay duty in Japan, either on their exports or imports, they send an annual present to the court, consisting of cloth, chintzs, succotas, cottons, stuffs, and trinkets. 1796 MORSE *Amer. Geog.* II. 589.

succotash ('sʌkətæʃ). Also 8–9 **suckatash, succatosh,** 9 **sagatash, succatras, suckertash, succatash, suc-ca-tush.** [a. Narragansett *msiquatash* (inanimate pl.), of which divergent explanations are given.] A dish of North America Indian origin, usually consisting of green maize and beans boiled together.

1751 J. MACSPARRAN *Diary* 4 Aug. (1899) 47 Mo^{r} dined with us upon Suckatash and Ham. 1778 J. CARVER *Trav. N. Amer.* vi. 263 This [dish] is composed of their unripe corn . . and beans in the same state, boiled together with bears flesh . . They call this food Succatosh. 1792 BELKNAP *Hist. New Hampsh.* III. 93 Their *samp* and *homony*, . . their *nokehike*, . . their *suckatash*, which is a mixture of corn and beans boiled, are much used. 1826 J. F. COOPER *Mohicans* xxviii, The wise Huron is welcome, . . he is come to eat his 'suc-ca-tush' with his brothers of the lakes! 1876 E. W. CLARK *Life Japan* 61 There were roast ducks and chickens, . . tomatoes, succotash, and potatoes.

succoteague, variant of SQUETEAGUE.

1888 GOODE *Amer. Fishes* 111.

‖**Succoth** (su'kot). Also †**Souccoth; Succot, Sukkot(h.** [a. Heb. *sukkôṯ*, pl. of *sukkah*: cf. SUCCAH.] = *Feast of Tabernacles* s.v. TABERNACLE *sb.* 1 b.

1882 tr. *L. Kompert's Scenes from Ghetto* 102, I hope you will be back in time for the *Souccoth*. 1888 H. POLANO *Talmud* III. 244 Making a tabernacle for thyself during Succoth. 1905 *Jewish Encycl.* IX. 583/1 Number of days on which the several ceremonies of Sukkot are observed. 1907 I. ZANGWILL *Model of Sorrows* ii, in *Ghetto Comedies* 20 When *Succoth* (Tabernacles) came, again no money, no bread. 1921 *Daily Colonist* (Victoria, B.C.) 16 Oct. 15/7 The Jewish folk of Victoria will observe Succoth, the original Thanksgiving Day of ancient Israel, better known as the Feast of the Tabernacle—on October 16. 1944 M. SAMUEL in M. W. Weisgal *Chaim Weizmann* I. 88 The Jews were more transfigured by *their* celebration of Shavuoth and Sukkoth than the Russian peasants by *their* thanksgiving celebrations. 1973 *Synagogue Light* Sept., Passover and Succoth are of seven days duration. 1974 *Times* 8 Oct. 10/1 The Soviet authorities allowed . . about 90 Jews to hold a picnic . . to mark the *Sukkot*, a religious festival. 1979 [see SUCCAH].

succotrine, variant of SOCOTRINE.

succour ('sʌkə(r)), *sb.* Forms: α. 3 **sucurs, sukurs,** 4 **socurs, -ourse,** *Sc.* **succouris,** 4–5 **socoures,** 4–6 **socours,** *Sc.* **succourss,** 5 **socors, socouris,** 5, 7 **secours,** 6 **souc(c)oures,** *Sc.* **succurss, -urris,** 6–7 **succors, succours,** 7 **succourse.** β. 3–5 **socur,** 3–6 **socour,** 4 **succure, sukour, soker,** 4–5 **sokour, socure,** 4, 6 **succur,** 4–6 **socoure,** 5 **soucour, socor, socowre, sokoure,** 5–6 **sucour,** 6 **suc(c)oure, socowr,** *Sc.* **suckyr,** 6–7 **sucker,** 8 **souccour,** 6– (now *U.S.*) **succor,** 4– **succour.** [ME. *sucurs*, *socurs*, *socours*, etc., a. OF. (AF.) *sucurs*, *soc*(*c*)*ours*, etc. (mod.F. *secours*) = It. *soccorso*:—med.L. *succursu-s*, n. of action f. *succurrĕre* to SUCCOUR. The final *-s* was at an early date apprehended as the plural suffix and a new singular (*succour*) came into existence, the plural of which is identical with the old singular.

G. *succurs* (from OF.) is used in the military sense, and MDu. *secors*, *socoers*, in the general sense.]

1. Aid, help, assistance.

α. *a* 1225 *Ancr. R.* 244 Inward, . . bonen biwinneð sone sucurs & help . . aȝean flesches fondunges. *c* 1325 *Metr. Hom.* 136 Thai waken Crist and askes socoures Wit orisoun. 1375 BARBOUR *Bruce* I. 328 Till god sum succouris till him send. *c* 1385 CHAUCER *L.G.W.* 1341 Withouten hys socourse, Twenty tyme y-swowned hath she thanne. *c* 1460 SIR R. ROS *La Belle Dame* 847, I can no mor, but aske of hem socours. 1533 BELLENDEN *Livy* (B. M. MS.) III. v. (S.T.S.) II. App. 306 Þe romans knew vele þai war freyndis cumin to þair succurss. *a* 1542 WYATT '*So feble is the threde*' 3 But it have elleswhere some aide or some socours The runnyng spyndell of my fate anon shall end his cours. 1548 UDALL, etc. *Erasmus Par. Matt.* iii. 11 b, Who so euer distrusting god doe leane vnto the souccoures of this world. 1605 BACON *Adv. Learn.* I. iv. §2 Luther . . being no waies ayded by the opinions of his owne time, was enforced . . to call former times to his succors.

β. *c* 1290 *Beket* 60 in *S. Eng. Leg.* 108 Þoruȝ grace þat heo hadde Of Iesu crist, and socur of men þat hire ouer ladden. *a* 1300 *Cursor M.* 24479 Her-wit come me son succur And sum lightnes o mi langur. *c* 1315 SHOREHAM II. 5 Gode atende to my socour. *c* 1320 *Sir Tristr.* 3284 Þe folk fleiȝe vnfain And socour criden schille. 1390 GOWER *Conf.* II. 293 Clepende and criende al the day For socour and deliverance. *c* 1450 *Merlin* iii. 50 We haue heere no vitaile to abide after socour of oure frendes. 1500–20 DUNBAR *Poems* lxxxvi. 29 At hellis ȝettis he gaf hyme na succour. 1523 *Act 14 & 15 Hen. VIII*, c. 13 The said Haven [was] greatly amended to the sucour and comfort of all the marchauntes ther resortyng. 1551 CROWLEY *Pleas. & Payne* 221 No man shall him heare Nor at his nede shewe him succoure. 1600 SHAKS. *A.Y.L.* II. iv. 75 Here's a yong maid with travaile much oppressed, And faints for succour. 1613 —— *Hen. VIII*, v. iv. 55, I might see from farre, some forty Truncheoners draw to her succour. 1681 BELON *New Myst. Physick* Introd. 23 To this purpose, we must fly again to Chymistry for Succor. 1748 *Anson's Voy.* II. iii. 151 Indians . . bartered their fish . . with our people. This was indeed some little succour. 1758 JOHNSON *Idler* No. 4 ¶6 The devotion of life or fortune to the succour of the poor. 1849 MACAULAY *Hist. Eng.* vi. II. 80 Many exiles, who had come . . to apply for succour, heard their sentence, and went brokenhearted away. 1891 FARRAR *Darkn. & Dawn* lvi, Paul's first impulse was to fly to the succour of his Roman brethren.

† **b.** *to do succour*, to give assistance to. *Obs.*

a 1300 *Cursor M.* 4903 He þat has yow don socur Stoln haue yee of his tresur. *c* 1374 CHAUCER *Compl. Mars* 292 Her that, with vnfeyned humble chere, Was euere redy to do yow socoure. *a* 1533 LD. BERNERS *Huon* lxv. 224 Oberon . . dyd me such socoure and ayde, that I came to my purpose.

2. One who or that which helps; a means of assistance; an aid.

a 1300 *Cursor M.* 21846 To be vr socur at vr end. ? *a* 1366 CHAUCER *Rom. Rose* 1606 Ther may no thyng ben his socour. 1382 WYCLIF *2 Sam.* xxi. 17 Abisay, the sone of Saruye, was to hym a socour. *c* 1440 *Pallad. on Husb.* I. 1019 Eek the blossom greet socour is Of euery tre ther swetnesse in the flour is. *c* 1450 *Merlin* 11 God be my socoure in my moste nede as I haue seide trouth. 1535 COVERDALE *Ps.* xxi. 19 Thou art my sucoure, haist the to helpe me. 1560 *Bible* (Geneva) Wisd. xvii. 11 Feare is nothing els, but a betraying of the succours, which reason offreth. 1620 FLETCHER, etc. *Double Marr.* v. ii, You have lost two noble succors. 1696 STANHOPE *Chr. Pattern* (1711) 79 Since then so little confidence is due to his succours, the concern ought not to be great, if he withdraw . . them. 1750 JOHNSON *Rambler* No. 167 ¶6 The succours of sickness ought not to be wasted in health. 1829 I. TAYLOR *Enthus.* x. 264 Christianity . . even when unaided by those secular succours.

3. Military assistance in men or supplies; *esp.* auxiliary forces; reinforcements.

sing. α. *a* 1225 *Ancr. R.* 232 Hwoso is siker of sukurs þet him schal sone kumen, & ȝelt tauh up his kastel to his wiðer-wines. 1375 BARBOUR *Bruce* XIX. 641 In thar cuntre heir ar we, Quhar that may cum vs na succourss. 1489 CAXTON *Faytes of A.* II. viii. 106 He had but a fewe folke but he wayted after a grete secours. 1523 *Acc. Ld. High Treas. Scot.* V. 212 That my lord of Arrane and succurris suld haist thaim to him. 1533 BELLENDEN *Livy* v. ii. (S.T.S.) II. 147 Mvniciouns . . to resist euery succurss or supple þat mycht cum þarefra. 1608 CHAPMAN *Byron's Conspir.* I. i. 26 Spaines colde friendship, and his lingring succours. *a* 1648 LD. HERBERT *Hen. VIII* (1683) 621 To send several Ambassadors into England and France to demand succours.

β. 1297 R. GLOUC. 11980 Þat hom ne com no socour hii seie al so wel, So þat . . hii ȝolde vp þen castel. 1340–70 *Alisaunder* 148 Þei see no succour in no syde aboute, That was come to hur koste þe king for to lett. *c* 1400 *Destr. Troy* 9700 Prayond hom . . For to buske hym to batell, & þo buernes helpe In offence of hor fos, and hor fuerse socour. 1470–85 MALORY *Arthur* III. xi. 113 Kyng Pellinore . . gaf hym an old courser, and kyng Arthur gaf hym armour and a swerd, and els had he none other socour. *a* 1548 HALL *Chron.*, *Edw. IV*, 18 b, He was required to make hast, . . although he brought no succor with him. 1666 DRYDEN *Ann. Mirab.* lxxiii, Our watchful General had discern'd from far This mighty succour, which made glad the Foe. 1802 JAMES *Milit. Dict.*, *Succour*, in war, assistance in men, stores, or ammunition. 1867 SMYTH *Sailor's Word-bk.* 665 *Succour*, an enterprise undertaken to relieve a place besieged or blockaded, by either forcing the enemy from before it, or throwing in supplies. 1876 VOYLE & STEVENSON *Milit. Dict.* (ed. 3) 414/1 *To throw succour* or help into a place means to introduce armed men, ammunition, provisions, &c. into a besieged place.

pl. *a* 1548 HALL *Chron.*, *Hen. V*, 79 Perceivyng that their succours were taken, [they] playnely judged that the toune could not long continue. 1625–8 tr. *Camden's Hist. Eliz.* II. (1688) 226 To provoke them to Battel, before all their Succours were come together out of France and Germany. 1663 WHARTON in *11th Rep. Hist. MSS. Comm.* App. v. 13 A great defeat given the Dutch by the Bishop . . upon which the French succours are returned, *re infecta*. 1741 MIDDLETON *Cicero* II. x. 417 Antony had invested it so closely . . that no succours could be thrown into it. 1768 BOSWELL *Corsica* ii. (ed. 2) 114 The succours which he left were not of much avail. 1805 JAMES *Milit. Dict.* (ed. 2), *To throw in succours*, to introduce armed men, ammunition, provisions, &c. into a besieged place. 1842 MACAULAY *Lake Reg.* xiii, There rode the Volscian succours. 1854 J. S. C. ABBOTT *Napoleon* (1855) I. xiii. 223 The French hoped that they were French ships conveying to them succors from Alexandria or from France.

4. Shelter, protection; a place of shelter, sheltered place, refuge. *Obs.* exc. *dial.*

a 1300 *Cursor M.* 5600 Þe kinges kin . . O quam sprang of þe sauueur þat broght vs all in-to socur. *c* 1380 WYCLIF *Sel. Wks.* III. 323 Alle þat drawen men out of þe chirche or seintuarie, whanne þei fleen þeder for sukour after here manslauȝter or þefte, ben cursed. 1387 TREVISA *Higden* (Rolls) IV. 137 Of þe oþer deel he made places of socour for pore men. *c* 1450 in Kingsford *Chron. London* (1905) 132 A ffalse Breton morderyd a wedew . . and aftyrward he toke socor of Holy Chirche at Seynt Georgis in Suthwerk. 1458 in Turner *Dom. Archit.* (1851) III. 43 It was a greet socour of erthe & of sonde. 1573 TUSSER *Husb.* (1878) 62 In tempest . . warme barth vnder hedge is a sucker to beast. 1622 R. HAWKINS *Voy. S. Sea* (1847) 100 It is full of good succors for shipping. 1628 in Foster *Eng. Factories India* (1909) III. 217 This is noe good place to winter in, it being . . noe sucker for them from the wether. 1636 in *Wilts Arch. Mag.* XXIII. 259 A place that in winter time was a special and usual succour for preserving the breed of young deer belonging to the Chace. 1641 BEST *Farm. Bks.* (Surtees) 72 Riggons neaver goe well of but att one time of the yeare, . . unlesse it bee with such as have good succour for them. 1850 *Jrnl. R. Agric. Soc.* XI. II. 687 The young beech plants must have 'succour', that is shelter, themselves, or they will not grow. 1893 *Wilts. Gloss.* s.v., On bleak parts of the Downs the cottages are mostly to be found in the succours.

† **5.** A tributary (of a river). *Obs.*

1570–6 LAMBARDE *Peramb. Kent* (1826) 199 One of the succours to Medway. 1613 PURCHAS *Pilgrimage* (1614) 644 Hauing gotten fresh helpe of some other streames, that send in their succours.

† **6.** A pecuniary aid, subsidy. *Obs.*

1605 VERSTEGAN *Dec. Intell.* x. (1628) 322 A certaine payment was wont to be made among the souldiers like vnto that which is now called succors. 1619 CARLETON in *Eng. & Germ.* (Camden) 51 The succours of this State wilbe . . 50^{m} florins a monthe for the space of a yeare.

7. *Comb.*, as ***succour-giver***, ***-suer***.

1593 Succour-suer [see SUBMISSIONER]. *c* 1600 J. BRYAN in Farr *S.P. Eliz.* (1845) II. 333 God help to me doth send, And to my succour-giuers Is an assisting friend.

succour ('sʌkə(r)), *v.* Forms: 3–5 **socur(e,** 3–6 **socoure,** 4–5 **-owre, sokoure, -ere, soccoure,** 4–6 **socour, succur,** 5–6 **succoure,** 6– 7 **sucker,** (3 **sucuri, soco(u)ri, -y,** 4 **socurry, soucouri, sokore, socre, succure, sukere,** *pa. pple.* **ysucrod, y-, i-socoured,** 4–6 **soker,** 5 **socowryn, sokery, socore, sucor,** 5–6 **succurre,** 6 **suckar, socker,** 7 **sucurre),** 6– (now *U.S.*) **succor,** 5– **succour.** [a. OF. (i) *socorre*, *suc*(*c*)*urre*, *secourre*:—L. *succurrĕre*, f. *suc-* = SUB- 26 + *currĕre* to run; (ii) *suc*(*c*)*urir* (with change of conjugation), mod.F. *secourir*. Cf. Pr. *socorre*, *secorrer*, It. *soccorrere*, Sp., Pg. *socorrer*.]

1. *trans.* To help, assist, aid (a person, etc.).

c **1250** *Kent. Serm.* in *O.E. Misc.* 32 Hit is us nyede þet se þet sucurede hem ine þa peril þet us sucuri ine ure niedes. *a* **1300** *Cursor M.* 4608, I red þat þou, onan, Do gett þe a god purueur þat in þis nede þe mai socur. **1340** *Ayenb.* 186 Wel ssolle we..helpe and soucouri þe on þe oþer. *c* **1380** *Sir Ferumb.* 172 He þat scholde me socoury to ȝen myn enymys. **1387** TREVISA *Higden* (Rolls) VIII. 41 He..socrede Thomas of Caunturbury whan he was exiled. **1390** GOWER *Conf.* I. 256 So schal his Soule be socoured Of thilke worschipe ate laste. *c* **1400** *Anturs of Arth.* xvii, Were thritte trentes of masse done,..My saule were socurt ful sone, And broȝte un-to blys. *c* **1430** LYDG. *Min. Poems* (Percy Soc.) 131 Ther is no gayne may us socoure. **1526** TINDALE *Heb.* ii. 18 He is able to sucker them that are tempted. *a* **1548** HALL *Chron., Edw. IV*, 4 Duke Charles..succored them with a small pencion. **1548–9** (Mar.) *Bk. Com. Prayer, Catechism*, To loue, honour, and succoure my father and mother. **1651** HOBBES *Leviath.* II. xix. 97 There is no Favourite of a Monarch, which cannot as well succour his friends, as hurt his enemies. **1718** PRIOR *Solomon* II. 571 We raise the sad, and succour the distress'd. **1865** KINGSLEY *Herew.* xix, It would behove me..to succour this distressed lady. **1867** SMILES *Huguenots Eng.* xi. (1880) 184 The fugitives were everywhere made welcome, and succoured and helped.

absol. **1535** BOORDE *Let.* in *Introd. Knowl.* (1870) 56 God succuryng, who euer kepp yow in helth & honer.

b. *transf.*

1390 GOWER *Conf.* III. 213 Whan he the comun riht socoureth. ?*a* **1400** *Morte Arth.* 2276 Thare myghte no siluer thaym saue, ne socoure theire lyues. **1549** *Compl. Scot.* Ep. 4 That his..entreprise vas conuoyit & succurrit be ane diuyne miracle, rather nor be the ingyne of men. **1578** LYTE *Dodoens* 473 Garden Smilax hath long and small branches growing very high..when they be succoured with rises or long poles. *Ibid.* 653 The white Rose, whose stalkes ..are..x. xii. or xx. foote high, and sometimes longer, if they be staied vp or suckered. **1599** SHAKS., etc. *Pass. Pilgr.* xiv. 28 Yet not for me, shine sun to succour flowers.

absol. *a* **1850** ROSSETTI *Dante & Circle* II. (1874) 279 Of all that thou or I can say, But one word succoureth.

2. To furnish with military assistance; to bring reinforcements to; *spec.* to relieve (a besieged place).

1297 R. GLOUC. (Rolls) 8233 Folc of ierusalem & of damache come...& to socouri antioche uaste þuderward drou. *c* **1330** R. BRUNNE *Chron. Wace* (Rolls) 12778 Sex þousand sent he..To socoure þeym. *c* **1380** *Sir Ferumb.* 2610 Or we mowen bet y-socoured be wiþ Charlis & ys ferede. *c* **1400** *Destr. Troy* 8466 All the kynges..þat comyn were to Troy, The citie to socour, with þere sute hoole. **1470–85** MALORY *Arthur* x. i. 413, I will socoure hym with all my puyssaunce. *a* **1548** HALL *Chron., Hen. IV*, 18 Yf the castel were not suckered within iii monthes. **1585** T. WASHINGTON tr. *Nicholay's Voy.* I. xv. 16b, The place.. coulde not haue bin fortified nor succoured. **1613–18** DANIEL *Coll. Hist. Eng.* (1626) 24 [He] brings a mighty Army to succour Arques, assieged by..the Dukes Generall. **1706** PHILLIPS (ed. Kersey), *To Succour a Place*, is to raise the Siege of such a Place, driving the Enemy from before it. **1876** VOYLE & STEVENSON *Milit. Dict.* (ed. 3) 414/2 *To succour*,..to relieve a force requiring assistance.

†**3.** To relieve or remedy (a state of want, weakness, etc.); to relieve (a diseased condition). *Obs.*

1526 TINDALE *Mark* ix. 24 Sucker myne vnbelefe. **1526** —— *2 Cor.* viii. 14 Let youre aboundaunce socker their lacke. **1590** SPENSER *F.Q.* II. iii. 31 To succour the weake state of sad afflicted Troy. **1613** PURCHAS *Pilgrimage* (1614) 602 The outward members are forced to yeeld their bloud, to succour any sudden oppression of the heart. *c* **1645** MILTON *Sonn., Forcers of Consc.* 18 That so the Parliament May..succour our just Fears.

absol. **1657** TOMLINSON *Renou's Disp.* 301 It efficaciously sucurres in pestilentious diseases.

4. To shelter, protect. Now *dial.*

1398 TREVISA *Barth. De P.R.* XVII. lxxxi. (1495) 653 Greynes ben warded and socoured wyth ryndes..for to saue the inner pyth and kynde hete. **1563** SHUTE *Archit.* Bj, Some succoured them selues vnder the shadowe of trees. **1617** MORYSON *Itin.* II. 67 The Haven was commodious to succour weather-beaten ships. **1684** BUNYAN *Pilgr.* II. 157 That by these Waters they [*sc.* sheep] might be housed, harbored, suckered, and nourished. **1893** *Wilts. Gloss.* s.v., An old-fashioned bonnet is said to 'succour' the ears. A cold wind cuts up cabbages, except where they are 'succoured' by bushes or walls.

5. *Naut.* To strengthen, make firm or taut.

1688 HOLME *Armoury* III. xv. (Roxb.) 44/1 To succour and ease the sheat, least it break in great winds. **1706** PHILLIPS (ed. Kersey) s.v., Among Sea-men, to *Succour* is to strengthen or make more firm; as To Succour a Cable, Mast, &c. *c* **1850** *Rudim. Navig.* (Weale) 152 Its use is to succour the scarphs of the apron.

succour, obs. form of SUGAR *sb.*

succourable ('sʌkərəb(ə)l), *a.* [a. OF. *so-*, *sucurable*, etc., chiefly active, rarely passive (mod.F. *secourable*), f. *secourir* to SUCCOUR: see -ABLE. Cf. It. *soccorrevole*.]

1. Affording succour, helpful. *Obs.* exc. *arch.*

c **1400** *Ragman Roll* 175 in Hazl. *E.P.P.* I. 76 Releuer to the pore, and socourabill Ben ye. *c* **1450** *Mirour Saluacioun* (Roxb.) 128 Oure lady marie..softned hire dere sons ire with hire sucurable prayere. *c* **1477** CAXTON *Jason* 50b, I think well that fortune hath ben socourable to the noble lady. **1591** SPARRY tr. *Cattan's Geomancie* 153 Good friendes and succorable. **1615** CLEAVER *Explan. Prov.* 434 The goodnes of God which is very succourable. **1619** *Times Store-House* 780/2 Perceiuing him [*sc.* a physician] not so succourable, as hee desireth or would haue. **1620** THOMAS *Lat. Dict.*, *Auxiliaris*..succourable. *c* **1765** FLLOYD *Tartarian T.* (1785) 61/2 Succourable Fairy,..furnish me.. with means. **1880** BROWNING *Dram. Idyls, Pan & Luna* 34 What help? When, lo, A succourable cloud with sleep lay dense.

2. Capable of being helped or relieved. *rare.*

1654 EARL MONM. tr. *Bentivoglio's Wars Flanders* 77 But the Town being munited, and at all times succorable, and he having but a few men with him, he could not doe it.

†**'succourer.** *Obs.* [a. OF. *secourere*, etc. (mod.F. *secoureur*), f. *secourir* to SUCCOUR.] One who, or that which aids or assists.

1442 *Rolls of Parlt.* V. 61/1 Socorours and Helpers to the Enemyes of the Cristien feith. *c* **1450** LOVELICH *Merlin* 9577 Behe'd sire Gyrflez, his socourer. **1495** *Act 11 Hen. VII* c. 64 Preamble, The same persones..were..favourers gydantis helpers socourers and comforteris. **1611** *Bible* Rom. xvi. 2 She hath beene a succourer of many, and of my selfe also. **1623** SANDERSON *Serm., Ad Magist.* I. (1632) 137 To each of these the Magistrate must be a succourer to his power. **1686** BUNYAN *Bk. Boys & Girls* 41, I will be thy Succourer.

Hence †**'succouress** *rare*^{−1}, a female helper.

1582 STANYHURST *Æneis* I. (Arb.) 37 Of trauayl of Troians, O Queene, thee succeres only.

succourful ('sʌkəfʊl), *a. rare.* [f. SUCCOUR *sb.* + -FUL.] Helpful.

1898 MEREDITH *Odes Fr. Hist.* 70 Succourful daughters of men.

succouring ('sʌkərɪŋ), *vbl. sb.* [-ING[1].] The action of the vb. SUCCOUR; assistance.

c **1330** *Arth. & Merl.* 8301 Þer was ioie..þer miȝt be no more þan was þer of þat socouringe. *c* **1400** *Laud Troy Bk.* 5777 Ne hadde Tentan come to his socouryng, He hadde be brouȝt to his endyng. *c* **1450** LOVELICH *Merlin* 859, J schal comen to ȝow jn Socowrenge. **1530** PALSGR. 272/1 Socouryng, *secovrs, ayde.* **1538** *Test. Ebor.* (Surtees) VI. 84 To the sokeringe of his childer. **1626** E. MOUNTAGU in *Buccleuch MSS.* (Hist. MSS. Comm.) I. 265 The defence of the realm, the succouring of the allies of the same.

'succouring, *ppl. a.* [-ING[2].] That succours; bringing or affording help or assistance.

a **1616** JONSON *Epigr., Voyage* 30 Alcides, be thou succouring to my song. **1704** TRAPP *Abra-Mulé* I. i, Leading on His succ'ring Troops to raise the Siege of Buda. **1782** MISS BURNEY *Cecilia* v. xi, The soothing recompense of succouring benevolence. **1836** NEWMAN in *Lyra Apost.* (1849) 111 Each trial has its weight; which whoso bears, Knows his own woe, and need of succouring grace. *a* **1901** W. BRIGHT *Age Fathers* (1903) I. xix. 381 He wrote..to express his regret that as yet no succouring hand had been held out to the suffering Eastern Church.

succourless ('sʌkəlɪs), *a.* Now *rare.* [f. SUCCOUR *sb.* + -LESS.]

1. Of persons or conditions: Without help, helpless; *freq.* without resources or means of subsistence, desititute.

1412–20 LYDG. *Chron. Troy* III. 1357 Pollidamas..stood, Socourles from al remedie. **1535** COVERDALE *Prov.* xxxi. 8 Be thou an aduocate..to speake for all soch as be domme & sucourles. **1568** GRAFTON *Chron.* II. 412 Beyng succourlesse, and wandering vp & downe, at the last he was taken in a towne called Plashey in Essex. **1621** BURTON *Anat. Mel.* II. ii. VI. i, Whose speech may ease our succourlesse estate. **1632** LITHGOW *Trav.* x. 506 These once happy Iles..are Metamorphosed in the Anatomy of succourlesse oppression. **1641** *Stockton on Tees Par. Reg.*, A poor succourless boy was buried 28 March. **1661** MORGAN *Sph. Gentry* III. ix. 112 Fighting alone succourlesse with five of the King of Portugal's ships. **1736** THOMSON *Liberty* V. 120 What Conflagrations Earthquakes, Ravage,.. succourless, and bare, the poor Remains Of Wretches forth to Nature's Common cast? **1828** LYTTON *Pelham* III. xi, The hopeless and succourless bed of death. **1876** *Daily News* 18 Dec. 5/2 On the Hattia island, where the people were three days succourless.

absol. **1443** *Pol. Poems* (Rolls) II. 210 Visite the poore, and of compassioun, Nakyd and needy, and hungry socourlees. **1536** WYATT *Penit. Ps., 2nd Prol.* 20 Wks. (1913) 216 A.. refuge for to save The Socourles. *a* **1586** SIDNEY *Ps.* x. viii, The succour of the succourles. *a* **1658** CLEVELAND *Poems*, etc. (1677) 152 You are tyed by your Order to give Protection to the Weak and Succourless.

b. *transf.* of a thing.

1613–16 W. BROWNE *Brit. Past.* I. iv, Cold Winter's rage ..makes the sap leave succourlesse the shoot.

†**2.** Affording no refuge. *Obs.*

1601 DEACON & WALKER *Spirits & Divels* 233 You are now fledde..to the succourlesse shelter of that your weather beaten action.

succous ('sʌkəs), *a. rare.* [ad. L. *succōsus*, f. *succus* juice.] Containing juice or sap; juicy.

1694 WESTMACOT *Script. Herb.* 8 The Fruit or Apples of this green succous Shrub, are round. **1859** CHRISTINA ROSSETTI *Goblin Market* 258 Must she no more that succous pasture find? **1859** MAYNE *Expos. Lex.* 1224/1 *Succosus*,.. succous or succose.

†**su'ccrescent,** *a.* *Obs. rare*^{−1}. [ad. L. *succrescent-*, *-ens*, pres. pple. of *succrescĕre* to grow up, f. *suc-* = SUB- 26 + *crescĕre* to grow.] Arising afterwards, succeeding.

1653 ASHWELL *Fides Apost.* 276 The Workes of Athanasius..were alleaged by after Ages against succrescent Heresies.

‖**succuba** ('sʌkjʊbə). *Pl.* -bæ (8 -a's). Also 8 sucuba. [late L. = strumpet, f. *succubāre*, f. *suc-* = SUB- 2 + *cub-* to lie.] = SUCCUBUS.

1587 *Mirr. Mag., Humfrey Dk. Glouc.* xi, That his auncient Grandame..Was a Feend of the kind that (Succubæ) some call. **1610** B. JONSON *Alch.* II. ii, I walke Naked betweene my *succubæ.* **1619** FLETCHER, etc. *Knt. Malta* v. ii, We'll call him Cacodemon, with his black gib there, his *Succuba.* **1620** T. SCOTT *God & King* (1623) 80 Looke in the streete, if you can distinguish men and women asunder..if euery *Succuba* seemes not an *Incubus.* **1662** M. W. *Marriage Broaker* 54 What's she must be my Masters Succuba. **1708** *Brit. Apollo* No. 45. 2/1 As to the Succubusses, or Succuba's, the Case is..different. **1788** PASQUIN *Childr. Thespis* (1792) 187 By the Sucubae spawned. **1873** LELAND *Egypt. Sketch-Bk.* 175 The fair Hermelina, a charming Succuba, who had..been the true love for forty years of Benedict Berna. **1900** ELWORTHY *Horns of Honour* ii. 88 Female demons, or succubæ, were the constant tempters of both St. Jerome and St. Anthony. **1906** B. CAPES *Loaves & Fishes* 143 That dead rogue is already forgathering with his succuba.

succube ('sʌkju:b). *rare.* Also succub. [ad. L. *succuba*, *-us*: see prec. Cf. F. *succube* m.] = prec.

1721 D'URFEY *Athenian Jilt* Operas, etc. 164 Our Succub Satanick now found She touch'd his Soul in place unsound. **1889** E. SALTUS *Tristrem Varick* 152 There would be no insomnia now. In the magic of a cablegram that succube had been exorcised forever.

succubine ('sʌkjʊbaɪn), *a. rare.* [f. SUCCUBA or SUCCUBUS + -INE[1].] Of or pertaining to a succubus.

[**1533–4** *Image Ipocr.* IV. 278 And ffryer Incubyne And ffryer Succubine.] **1838** BARHAM *Ingol. Leg.* Ser. I. *St. Nicholas* liv, Oh! happy the slip from his Succubine grip, That saved the Lord Abbot.

succubous ('sʌkjʊbəs), *a. Bot.* [f. L. *suc-* = SUB- 2 + *cub-* (*cumbĕre*) to lie + -OUS.] Having the upper margin of each leaf covered by the lower margin of the one succeeding it: applied to some of the *Jungermanniaceæ*.

1857 [see INCUBOUS]. **1861** H. MACMILLAN *Footn. Page Nat.* 49 [The leaves of the liverworts] are disposed either in a spiral which turns from left to right, in which case they are called succubous, or in a spiral which turns from right to left, when they receive the name of incubous leaves.

succubus ('sʌkjʊbəs). *Pl.* -bi (7–8 -busses). [med.L., masc. form (with fem. meaning) corresp. to SUCCUBA, after INCUBUS.]

1. A demon in female form supposed to have carnal intercourse with men in their sleep. (Cf. INCUBUS.)

1387 TREVISA *Higden* (Rolls) I. 419 That fend þat gooþ a nyȝt, Wommen wel ofte to begile, Incubus hatte be ryȝt; And gileþ men oþer while, Succubus is þat wight. **1547** BOORDE *Brev. Health* cxix. (1870) 78 *Incubus* doth infeste and trouble women, and *Succubus* doth infest men. **1584** R. SCOT *Discov. Witchcr.* III. xix. (1886) 56 The divell plaieth *Succubus* to the man and carrieth from him the seed of generation, which he delivereth as *Incubus* to the woman. **1644** *Merc. Brit.* No. 23. 178, I think Incubusses and Sucubusses are Angells of light to these. **1647** COWLEY *Mistr., Not Fair* 14 So men (they say) by Hells delusions led, Have ta'ne a *Succu'bus* to their bed. **1691** R. KIRK *Secret Commw.* i. (1815) 13 For the Inconvenience of their Succubi, who tryst with Men, it is abhominable. **1797** *Encycl. Brit.* (ed. 3) XVIII. 52/2 The truth is, the succubus is only a species of the nightmare. **1818** C. K. SHARPE *Law's Memorialls* Pref. p. xx, For forty years, he [*sc.* Benedict of Berne] had kept up an amatory commerce with a Succubus, called Hermeline. **1950** A. CLARKE *Coll. Plays* (1963) 315 Branduv is sleeping with a succubus. **1958** L. DURRELL *Balthazar* vii. 167 Thirst *can* be quenched like this, by inviting a succubus to one's bed. **1969** J. UPTON tr. *R. Diaz Sánchez's Cumboto* 261 The dream reoccurred many times, it was the work of a clever succubus who came to my cot regularly to conduct her oneiric concert. **1977** A. CARTER *Passion of New Eve* ii. 27, I would..remember the myth of the succubus, the devils in female form who come by night to seduce the saints.

attrib. **1619** PURCHAS *Microcosmus* l. 479 If the Deuill cannot turne himselfe into a *Succubus* Spirit, to be, or seeme to be a transubstantiate Woman.

2. *transf.* **a.** A demon, evil spirit; *occas.* a familiar spirit.

1601 WEEVER *Mirr. Mart.* A vij, A swaggering humour, Of some shape-altring Succubus begot. **1634** SIR T. HERBERT *Trav.* 169 An old Tartarian Hecate..inuocated her *Succubi* to succour mee. **1727** WARBURTON *Enq. Prod.* I. 63 A Church-yard Carcass raised and set a strutting by the Inflation of some hellish Succubus within. **1840** BARHAM *Ingol. Leg.* Ser. I. *Lady Rohesia*, The most impudent *Succubus*..dare as well dip his claws in holy water as come within the verge of its [*sc.* the passing bell's] sound. **1868** BROWNING *Ring & Bk., Ct. Guido Franc.* 1137 The witches' circle intact, charms undisturbed That raised the spirit and succubus.

b. A strumpet, whore; a term of abuse for a low woman, *occas.* applied to a man.

1622 J. TAYLOR (Water P.) *Whore* Wks. (1630) II. 106/1 A Succubus, a damned sinke of sinne. **1684** OTWAY *Atheist* I, Nor got no meat, but such as the old Succubus his wife bought at a stinking price. **1699** FARQUHAR *Const. Couple* IV. iii, Here is an old succubus, madam, that has stole two silver spoons, and says she's your nurse. **1706** T. BAKER *Turnbridge Walks* IV. i, A flinching son of a succubus, to pretend to call for a looking glass and sneak away. **1748** SMOLLETT *Rod. Random* xlvi, 'Yes, thou barbarian,' said she, turning to Wagtail, 'thou tiger, thou succubus!' **1803** C. K. SHARPE *New Oxf. Guide* i. Corr. 1888 I. 13 [A bedmaker] Like any fell Succubus, wrinkled and old, With the lip of a shrew, and the nose of a scold.

†**succudrous,** *a. Sc. Obs.* In 4–5 succud(e)rus, 6 succuidrus. [Variant of SURQUIDROUS.] Presumptuous, arrogant.

c **1475** *Rauf Coilȝear* 909 Ȝe Sarazeins are succuderus and self willit ay. **1513** DOUGLAS *Æneis* XIII. vi. 111 Syk succuidrus ondertakyng.

So †**su'ccudrously** *adv.*, presumptuously, arrogantly.

c **1375** *Sc. Leg. Saints* x. (*Mathou*) 369 Bot gyf a seruand now vald ta His kingis wyfe succudrusly. *c* **1475** *Rauf*

Coilȝear 856 Then said the Sarazine to Schir Rauf succudrously.

†**succudry.** *Obs. Sc.* Also 4–5 succuddry, -quidry, -cowdry, sukudry, 6 sucquedry, 5 succeudry. [Variant of SURQUIDRY.]

Presumption, arrogance.

1375 BARBOUR *Bruce* XI. 11 It wes gret succuddry [*var.* E. sukudry, H. sucquidry] That set thame apon sic folye. *Ibid.* XVI. 327 His outrageouss succudry And will, that mar wes than hardy, Of purposs letit hym. *c* **1425** WYNTOUN *Cron.* IV. vi. 51 As Daryus tynt in til Sythi Throw his hawtane succudry. *c* **1470** *Gol. & Gaw.* 278 Spekis na succeudry, for Cristis sone deir! **1553** DOUGLAS *Æneis* XIII. vi. 111 (1710) 467 For sic sucquedry vndertakin now, His awne mischeif.. He fundin has. [Cf. 1513 in SUCCUDROUS.]

succulence (ˈsʌkjʊləns). [Formed as next: see -ENCE.] The quality or condition of being succulent; juiciness. Also, succulent part.

1787 MARSHALL *Rur. Econ. Norfolk* I. 257 It is allowed to stand the winter better, and to preserve its firmness and succulence. **1824–9** LANDOR *Imag. Conv.* Wks. 1846 II. 59 The latter math has less substance, succulence, and fragrance than the Summer crop. **1842** LOUDON *Suburban Hort.* 337 Though the fruit would be more numerous it would be deficient in succulence and flavour. **1883** G. ALLEN in *Nature* 29 Mar. 512 The succulence here acts as a reservoir for water.

succulency (ˈsʌkjʊlənsɪ). [ad. med.L. *succulentia*, f. *succulentus*: see next and -ENCY.] = prec.

1616 DONNE *Serm.* Prov. xxii. 11 (1661) III. 330 Pith and marrow to give a succulencie, and nourishment, even to the bones, to the strength and obduration of sin. *a* **1620** J. DYKE *Sel. Serm.* (1640) 271 The.. chewing of the meate.. expresses.. the juyce and succulency of it. **1664** BEALE in *Evelyn's Pomona* 25 [Quinces] will bear with some degrees of hungry land, if they be supplied with a due measure of succulency, and neighbouring moisture. **1738** KINNEIR *Ess. Nerves* 55 The succulency of the Nerves in a healthy man, depends upon the goodness and due quantity of the blood, that enters the vessels of the brain. **1815** KIRBY & SP. *Entomol.* (1816) I. 321 These branches.. are.. exposed to the open air under a shed, where from their succulency they [*sc.* cochineal insects] continue to live for several months. **1842** LOUDON *Suburban Hort.* 437 The nature of the changes intended to be made on them by cultivation, such as blanching, succulency, magnitude, &c. **1890** H. M. STANLEY *Darkest Africa* II. xxx. 297 The grass was void of succulency and nutriment.

succulent (ˈsʌkjʊlənt), *a.* and *sb.* [ad. L. *succulentus* (*sūculentus*), f. *succus* (*sūcus*) juice: see -LENT, -ULENT. Cf. F. *succulent.*] **A.** *adj.*

1. Full of juice; juicy. **a.** Applied to plants and their parts having a fleshy and juicy substance.

1601 HOLLAND *Pliny* I. 444 Their [*sc.* figs'] succulent substance.. when they begin to ripen, is white like milke. **1626** BACON *Sylva* §507 Such Plants, as are very Succulent. **1668** WILKINS *Real Char.* II. iv. §3. 70 Texture of the Leaf; .. Succulent; having thick juicie leaves, covered with a close membrane, through which the moisture cannot easily transpire, which makes them continue in dry places. **1756** C. LUCAS *Ess. Waters* I. 43 The succulent tribe of aloes and ficoides. **1785** MARTYN *Lett. Bot.* vii. (1794) 75 The fruit, which.. is succulent in the peach. **1813** SIR H. DAVY *Agric. Chem.* (1814) 280 All green succulent plants contain saccharine or mucilaginous matter. **1837** M. DONOVAN *Dom. Econ.* II. 323 The carrot is valuable on account of the facility with which it is kept in a recent and succulent state for a length of time. **1882** VINES tr. *Sach's Bot.* 417 These peculiar stipules remain fresh and succulent not only during the life of the leaves but also after they have fallen. **1908** [MISS E. FOWLER] *Betw. Trent & Ancholme* 49 The succulent house-leek, green and red.

b. Of various other things.

1615 CROOKE *Body of Man* 30 From the substance some [parts] are dense, others rare and succulent or iuicy, others spongie & soft. **1666** BOYLE *Orig. Formes & Qual.* II. 245 That it [*sc.* coral] is oftentimes found very succulent. **1877** BLACK *Green Past.* xliv. 357 Rich, deep black, succulent mud. **1878** T. BRYANT *Pract. Surg.* I. 116 Each tumour.. becomes solid, more succulent, and more rapid in its growth.

c. Of food or articles of food.

1669 W. SIMPSON *Hydrol. Chym.* 66 The succulent parts of the aliment. **1725** *Fam. Dict.* s.v. *Gravy*, Such Messes, into which some of it is to be put to render them more Succulent. **1831** SCOTT *Ct. Rob.* xii, The succulent and highly-spiced messes indulged in by the nations of the East. **1907** S. ELLIOT *Rom. Plant Life* 181 Sussex downs so famous for succulent mutton.

†**d.** Of persons: Well nourished. (Cf. SAPPY 4.)

1673 R. HEAD *Canting Acad.* 147 Her name was.. Wheedle, a plump succulent Girl.

2. *transf.* and *fig.* 'Juicy', 'sappy', rich.

1626 BACON *Sylva* §512 Yellow is a lesse Succulent Colour than Green. **1660** WATERHOUSE *Arms & Arm.* 147 In short, from these the learned Nobility and Gentry.. grow to be succulent Philosophers. **1692** BENTLEY *Boyle Lect.* iv. 127 In the flower of her Youth, while she [*sc.* the Earth] was succulent and fertil. **1827** HALLAM *Const. Hist.* iv. (1876) I. 224 The queen and her courtiers.. continued to prey upon their succulent victim [*sc.* the Church]. **1859** MEREDITH *R. Feverel* xii, Pluming a smile upon his succulent mouth. *Ibid.* xxxv, His air of rather succulent patronage. **1866** GEO. ELIOT *F. Holt* xl, It occurred to her that when she had known about them a good while they would cease to be succulent themes of converse or meditation. **1898** G. B. SHAW *Plays* II. *You never can tell* II. Stage-direct., He.. is at present reduced to the advertisements, which are not sufficiently succulent to induce him to persevere with them.

3. *Comb.*, as ***succulent-fruited, -leaved*** adjs.

1830 LINDLEY *Nat. Syst. Bot.* 183 The berries of the succulent-fruited kinds. **1842** LOUDON *Suburban Hort.* 267 Sedums, and other succulent-leaved plants.

B. *sb. Bot.* A succulent plant.

1825 *Greenhouse Comp.* I. 105 Green-house succulents are of the easiest possible culture and propagation. **1842** LOUDON *Suburban Hort.* 267 The leaves of such succulents as cacalia,.. cactus, and similar plants. **1914** *Daily News & Leader* 25 June 4 The succulents growing in the desert.

Hence **ˈsucculently** *adv.*, in a succulent manner.

1892 E. REEVES *Homeward Bound* 174 Transparent, grey, pure, succulently inviting snails. **1899** KIPLING *Stalky* 69 Mr. King was pleased to smile succulently in form.

succulous (ˈsʌkjʊləs), *a.* [irreg. f. L. *succulentus* SUCCULENT + -OUS.] Succulent.

1846 in WORCESTER citing *For. Q. Rev.*

succumb (səˈkʌm), *v.* Also 5 subcombe, succombe, 5–7 succumbe, 7–8 succomb. [a. OF. *succomber*, also *subcomber*, ad. L. *succumbĕre* (*subc-*), f. *suc-* = SUB- 2 + *-cumbĕre* to lie. Cf. It. *soccombere*, Sp. *sucumbir*, Pg. *succumbir*.

Noted by Johnson 1755 and Sinclair *Obs. Sc. Dial.* (1782) 94 as a peculiarly Scottish word.]

†**1.** *trans.* To bring down, bring low, overwhelm. *Obs.*

c **1489** CAXTON *Blanchardyn* xxviii. 104 In their folysshe pryde I shal succombe & brynge a lowe their corage. **1490** —— *Eneydos* xxii. 81 For to distroye her, & vtterly subcombe her in-to persecucyon extreme. **1549** *Compl. Scot.* Ep. 1 Thre vehement plagis quhilk hes al maist succumbit oure cuntre in final euertione. *Ibid.* vii. 71 My triumphant stait is succumbit in decadens.

†**2.** *intr.* To fail in a cause. *Sc. Obs.*

1561 *Reg. Privy Council Scot.* Ser. I. I. 174 To have succumbit in his said caus. **1586–7** *Ibid.* IV. 141 Succumband and failyeand nochtwithstanding heirin.

3. To sink under pressure or give way to superior force, authority, etc.: said properly of persons or communities, and *transf.* of conditions, designs, occas. of material things.

1604 EARL STIRLING *Aurora* El. iii. 34 Surcharg'd with sorowes I succomb. **1632** LITHGOW *Trav.* VIII. 372 The eight day.. he succumb'd, and could not subsist, not beeing vsed to pedestriall trauayle. **1637–50** ROW *Hist. Kirk* (Wodrow Soc.) 500 As in all nationall tryells some succumbs, sundrie did adhere to their subscription of the King's Covenant. **1751** *Philos. Lett. on Physiogn.* 259 (T.) Our fortitude.. may bend under the weight of malignancy and opposition, yet not succumb. **1754** FOOTE *Knights* II, That I who have rejected so many matches should instantaneously succumb. **1846** TRENCH *Mirac.* 76 This scheme of interpretation, thus assailed from so many sides, .. quickly succumbed. **1847** CALHOUN *Speeches* Wks. 1861 IV. 354 So completely did the National party succumb, that .. the word 'National' was not named. **1851** GALLENGA *Italy* vii. 499 Italy.. had stood up for a wrestle with Austria, and succumbed. **1886** C. E. PASCOE *Lond. of To-day* xxx. (ed. 3) 273 After suffering from conflagrations on many occasions, the crypt finally succumbed in the year 1834.

b. Const. *to.* (In first quot., to yield the palm *to.*)

1632 LITHGOW *Trav.* v. 181 The now decayed Towne of Tharsus, who for antiquity will not succumbe to any City of Natolia. **1663** BUTLER *Hud.* I. iii. 459 And to their wills we must succumb, *Quocunque trahunt*, 'tis our doom. **1716** M. DAVIES *Athen. Brit.* II. 255 The pretended Infallibility of Pope Liberius, succumb'd at the same time to the same Arian Coercive Politicks. **1738** A. HILL *Let. Ld. Bolingbroke* 25 June Wks. 1753 I. 274 One is involved by events, and succumbs to, and subsists by expedients. **1825** LYTTON *Zicci* 27 Pardon me if I do not succumb to curiosity. **1828** CUNNINGHAM *N.S. Wales* (ed. 3) II. 84 The small trader and settler must they knew succumb to the price they chose to fix. **1848** W. K. KELLY tr. *L. Blanc's Hist. Ten Y.* II. 578 The honourable conviction, that Belgium ought not to give way to threats, however it might be doomed to succumb to force. **1878** PROCTOR *Pleas. Ways Sci.* x. (1879) 201 Even the most powerful and ferocious beasts must succumb in the long run to man. **1889** G. FINDLAY *Engl. Railway* 8 Those rails were of so light a description that they soon succumbed to heavy wear and tear.

c. Const. *under*, *beneath*, occas. *before*.

a **1734** NORTH *Exam.* III. vi. §47 (1740) 457 Men seem to succumb under it, as a Process, now become of Course. **1808** BP. WATSON *Charge in 1805*, 40 Thinking that Popery is every where succumbing under the general diffusion of knowledge. **1833** I. TAYLOR *Fanat.* v. 97 The noble may be readily made to succumb beneath the base. *a* **1862** BUCKLE *Misc. Wks.* (1872) I. 12 The men of facts at length succumbed before the man of ideas.

4. *spec.* To yield to the attacks of a disease, the effect of wounds, an operation, etc.; hence, to die.

1849 EASTWICK *Dry Leaves* 205 Half the sipáhis succumbed;—the doctor was so terrified at the number of deaths that he became deranged. **1865** LIVINGSTONE *Zambesi* xx. 404 He succumbed in a few months to fever. **1886** BARING-GOULD *Court Royal* xlviii, I think he caught a chill, and being below par he succumbed. **1891** *Pall Mall Gaz.* 10 Jan. 6/2 Mr. Picken has since succumbed to his injuries.

†**5.** *trans.* To abandon, give up. *Obs.*

1632 LITHGOW *Trav.* x. 435 Arguments of Religion.. they succumbe, their conference onely pleading mutuall forbearance.

Hence **suˈccumber**, **suˈccumbing** *vbl. sb.*

1844 GLADSTONE *Let.* in Purcell *Life Manning* (1895) I. xiv. 297, I am not sure.. of your whole assertion that subscribers were mere succumbers. **1885** *Athenæum* 3 Jan. 7/1 Was it a sudden succumbing of Becket's keen intelligence to those superstitions of a dark age?

succumbence (səˈkʌmbəns). *rare.* [f. SUCCUMB *v.* + -ENCE.] A giving way or yielding.

1837 C. LOFFT *Self-formation* II. 78 One unlucky succumbence to idleness turns the tide at once.

succumbency (səˈkʌmbənsɪ). Now *rare.* [f. next: see -ENCY. Cf. med.L. *succumbentia* failure in a cause.] A giving way or yielding; submission.

1653 R. G. tr. *Bacon's Hist. Winds* 371 The means and wayes of the succumbency and yieldings of Motions are carefully to be looked into. **1668** HOWE *Bless Righteous* (1825) 258 Thy vile succumbency gives him the day and his will upon thee. **1698** —— *Serm. Duty Magistr.* Wks. 1863 V. 396 A timorous fainting and succumbency. **1820** FOSTER *Ess. Evils Pop. Ignor.* 163 This.. unquestioning, unmurmuring, succumbency under the actual allotment.

†**suˈccumbent**, *a.* (*sb.*) *Obs. rare.* [ad. L. *succumbens, -entem*, pr. pple. of *succumbĕre* to SUCCUMB. In sense 1 after It. *soccombente.*]

A. *adj.* **1.** Subject, submissive *to.*

c **1645** HOWELL *Lett.* II. ix. (1890) 387 Christianity.. makes not Sense so much subject to Reason, as Reason succumbent to Faith. **1660** —— *Parly of Beasts* 2 Queen Morphandra.. useth to make Nature her self not only succumbent and passive to her desires, but [etc.].

2. Underlying.

1664 POWER *Exp. Philos.* II. 114 Water, by its weight onely, and no innate Elatery, did depel the Succumbent Quicksilver in the Tube.

3. Succumbing.

1812 J. J. HENRY *Camp. agst. Quebec* 81 The humanity of Morgan and Humphreys, towards a succumbent foe.

B. *sb.* (See quot. 1661 and KNEELER 2 a.)

1661 BLOUNT *Glossogr.* (ed. 2), *Succumbents*,.. antiently it signified those penitents or excommunicate persons that fell down on their knees and prayed in a certain place behind the Quire or Pulpit. [**1850** NEALE *Hist. East. Ch.* Introd. I. I. 210 The Succumbentes were passing the silver gates on their way out.]

succur, obs. form of SUCCOUR, SUGAR.

†**suˈccurrance.** *Obs.* In 5 socurraunce. [a. OF. *socorrance*, f. *socorre* to SUCCOUR.] Succour.

c **1450** *Cov. Myst.* (Shaks. Soc.) 220 Gracyous prophete of socurraunce.

succursal (səˈkɜːsəl), *a.* and *sb.* [ad. F. **succursal*, only in fem. *succursale* (sc. *église* church), ad. L. **succursālis*, f. *succursus* SUCCOUR. Cf. It. *soccorsale.*]

A. *adj.* Subsidiary; applied *esp.* to a religious establishment dependent upon a principal one.

1844 [C. MACFARLANE] *Camp of Refuge* I. 9 From the grand abbey of Crowland to the dependent house or succursal cell of Spalding. **1855** MILMAN *Lat. Christ.* XIV. viii. VI. 564 Its Cathedral, surrounded by its succursal churches. *Ibid.* 574 The building, with its succursal aisles. **1889** *Tablet* 16 Feb. 243/1 The more recent institution of the latter and its succursal office.

B. *sb.* A subsidiary establishment; a branch institution, society, business, etc. (Const. *to*, *of*.)

1859 SALA *Tw. round Clock* (1861) 221 The 'Virtuous Club,' established as a succursal to the Royal Society. **1862** —— *Accepted Addr.* 86 The undertaking business.. was a succursal to his trade. **1884** *Athenæum* 22 Mar. 376/1 Freston, or Frieston, was a succursal of the Benedictine Abbey of Croyland.

‖**b.** In F. form **succursale** (sb. fem. sing.).

1882 *Times* 11 Sept. 7/4 The new docks on the London, Tilbury, and Southend Railway, a sort of succursale of the East and West India Dock system. **1885** *Ibid.* 18 Sept. 13/4 Six of the monks emigrated last year to America, and 32 have been detached to a *succursale* in Tipperary. **1901** A. C. WELCH *Anselm & His Work* v. 87 So many monks passed between the two, that St. Saviour's became practically a succursale of Le Bec. **1910** *Nation* 16 July 568/2 Mexico.. has become a mere 'succursale' of the United States.

‖**succus** (ˈsʌkəs). Pl. succi (ˈsʌksaɪ). [L.] A juice; in scientific terminology applied to (*a*) fluid secretions in an animal or vegetable body, (*b*) juices extracted from plants.

[**1719** QUINCY *Lex. Physico-Med.* (1722), *Succus*, is any Juice.] **1771** BP. WATSON *Ess. Subj. Chem.* Chem. Ess. 1787 V. 137 Wherever there is a vascular system, containing a moving nutritive succus, there is life. **1874** GARROD & BAXTER *Mat. Med.* (ed. 4) 263 He regards the succus [of hemlock] as the only reliable preparation of the drug for internal use.

succuss (səˈkʌs), *v.* [f. L. *success-*, pa. ppl. stem of *succutĕre*, f. *suc-* = SUB- 26 + *quatĕre* to shake.] **a.** *trans.* To shake up; *spec.* to shake (a patient) to elicit the splashing sound in pneumothorax.

1865 *Athenæum* No. 1975. 307/3 The violent shock which closes the rapid descent is expected to *succuss* the patient into proper shape.

b. *Homœopathy.* To shake (a preparation of a drug) vigorously.

1910 *Encycl. Brit.* XIII. 646/1 To make the 2 × potency, 10 drops or 10 grains of this first dilution or trituration are mixed with 90 drops of pure alcohol.. and are succussed or triturated. **1938** D. SHEPHERD *Magic of Minimum Dose* 264 The 12th potency.. is prepared.. by diluting one drop in a hundred and shaking or succussing violently. **1974** *Homoeopathy* June/July 86 Between each dilution he [*sc.* Hahnemann] succussed (shook vigorously) the medicine.

†**succuˈssation.** *Obs.* [ad. L. **succussātio, -ōnem* (altered in med.L. to *succursātio* in the sense 'trotting'), n. of action f. *succussāre*, f.

success- (see SUCCUSS). Cf. F. *succussation* (Cotgr.).] Shaking up, violent shaking, jolting.

1649 BULWER *Pathomyot.* II. ii. 126 That succussation of the Lungs and agitation of the Midriff. **1682** *Weekly Memorials* 231 That motion which does not affect our bodies with Succussation.. is esteemed rest. **1706** RENEU *Let.* in C. Wordsworth *Scholæ Acad.* (1877) 297 The succussation of your Horse is so great, only to come to london upon him. **1760** STERNE *Tr. Shandy* IV. xxii, The succussations of the intercostal and abdominal muscles in laughter. **1774** A. CAMPBELL *Lexiph.* (ed. 4) 17, I suffered from some artificial excoriations which I had contracted..by the severe successations of a conductitious steed.

b. Trotting (of a horse). Cf. 1706, 1774 above.

1646 SIR T. BROWNE *Pseud. Ep.* IV. vi. 193 Lifting one foot before, and the crosse foot behinde, which is succussation or trotting. **1663** BUTLER *Hud.* I. ii. 48 Whether Pace or Trot, (That is to say, whether Tolutation, As they do term't, or Succussation). **1681** COLVIL *Whigs Supplic.* (1751) 120 His horses grievous succussation Had so excoriat his foundation.

succussion (sə'kʌʃən). [ad. L. *succussio, -ōnem*, n. of action f. *succuss-, succutĕre* to SUCCUSS. So F.] **a.** The action of shaking or condition of being shaken, esp. with violence; an instance of this.

1622 WOTTON *Lett.* (1907) II. 259 He was taken with a trembling and sudden succussion. **1660** STANLEY *Hist. Philos.* XIII. IV. ii. (1687) 880/1 We see whole Houses shake, by reason of the jumbling, and succussion of Carts and Chariots. **1713** DERHAM *Phys.-Theol.* III. iii. 69 Dreadful Succussions and Convulsions of the Earth. **1733** CHEYNE *Engl. Malady* II. ix. §2 (1734) 206 Vomits..by their Successions and Action..open the Obstructions. **1824** MCCULLOCH *Highlands Scot.* II. 319 The very act of riding, serves, by its fundamental succussions, to nail and fix the observations in the sensorium. **1867** BLOXAM *Chem.* 205 The acid boils with succussion or violent bumping. **1885** W. ROBERTS *Urin. & Renal Dis.* III. xiv. (ed. 4) 678 Violent running, dancing, riding, or severe muscular effort or succussion of the body. **1898** P. MANSON *Trop. Diseases* xxiii. 359 This blood comes from the wall of an abscess jarred and torn by the succussion of the harassing cough.

b. *spec.* (*Med.*) An act or method of diagnosis in pneumothorax, etc. which consists in shaking the thorax to detect the presence of fluid.

1747 *Gentl. Mag.* XVII. 77/2 If the infirm cannot stir out of their bed or chair,..they may make a succussion by heaving up and letting down their shoulders. **1833** *Cycl. Pract. Med.* I. 222/1 The operator stopping the succussion suddenly, and listening for the sound of fluctuation. **1858** COPLAND *Dict. Pract. Med.* III. II. 933/2 Laennec first clearly demonstrated the conditions upon which the evidence furnished by succussion depends. **1865** *Athenæum* No. 1975. 307/3 The operation of succussion, as Hippocrates used to perform it, at Larissa. **1866** A. FLINT *Princ. Med.* 148 Succussion in most cases develops a splashing sound frequently having the same kind of musical intonation as the respiration, voice, and tinkling sounds.

attrib. **1883** F. T. ROBERTS *Th. & Pract. Med.* (ed. 5) 358 *Succussion-signs*... The signs produced by shaking a patient are:—1. A splashing-sensation felt by the hand. 2. A splashing-sound. **1886** FAGGE *Princ. Med.* I. 940 Another sign of pneumothorax..is that which is termed 'succussion-splash'. **1897** *Allbutt's Syst. Med.* IV. 661 This succussion sound..is specially interesting as having been observed by Hippocrates.

c. *Homœopathy.* The vigorous shaking of a preparation of a drug.

1848 HEMPEL & QUIN tr. *Jahr's New Manual* II. 1059 *Succussion*, shaking. **1910** *Encycl. Brit.* XIII. 646/1 The continuation of the dynamization of trituration or succussion develops a spiritual acurative agency. **1938** D. SHEPHERD *Magic of Minimum Dose* 21 This trituration or succussion is a most important part of the preparation of the drug. **1974** *Homoeopathy* June/July 86 This process of dilution and succussion seemed to give the remedy more energy and a greater healing effect.

successive (sə'kʌsɪv), *a. rare.* [f. L. *succuss-*: see SUCCUSS.] Characterized by a shaking motion.

1742 *Phil. Trans.* XLII. 84 It began by a successive Motion, and followed by a sort of Blow with the horrible Violence. **1864** in WEBSTER citing DANA.

sucgen, obs. form of SAY *v.*[1]

such (sʌtʃ), *dem. adj.* and *pron.* Forms: see below. [OE. *swelc, swilc, swylc*, corresp. to OFris. *sellich, -ik, selk, sek, sullik, sulch, sulk* (mod.Fris. *suk, sok*), OS. *sulîk*, (*solîk*), MLG. *sol(l)ik, sollek, solk* (LG. *sü(l)k, sö(l)k*), MDu. *sulc, selc, solc, swilc, swelc*, also *sulic, -ec* (Du. *zulk*, WFlem. also *zuk*), OHG. *sulîh, -ich, -ech, solîh, -ech, solch-, sol-* (MHG. *solich, solch, solh*, also *sölch, sölh, sülich, sülc, sölk, selch, silch*, mod.Ger. *solch*), ON. *slíkr* (MSw. *sliker*, Sw. *slik*, Da. *slig*) whence SLIKE *a.*, Goth. *swaleiks*:—OTeut. **swalîko-*, **swilîko-*, lit. so formed, f. *swa* SO *adv.* + **līko-* body, form (cf. LIKE *a.*).

The OE. *swelc* and *swilc* represent primitive **swalîko-* and **swilîko-* respectively, the latter being an analogical formation on **hwilîko-* WHICH; cf. OE. *hwilc* beside *hwelc* (:—**hwalîko-*), and Goth. *hwileiks*. Evidence for the rounding of *swilc* to *swylc* appears late in the 9th c., and a sporadic spelling *swulc* is found from *c* 1000. *Swylc* and *swulc* became in ME. *swülch, swulch*, which, by the absorption of *w* and loss of *l*, gave *such* (in ME. written also *soch*), the modern standard form. The dropping of *w* was carried through into the other types *swe(l)ch* and *swi(l)ch*, whence the widespread dial. forms *sech* and *sich*. Thus, and by similar cross-influences, a large variety of forms arose, which can be grouped according to (1) the quality of the vowel, (2) the retention or loss of *w*, (3) the retention or loss of *l*, as well as (4) the palatalization or non-palatalization of *c*. The unpalatalized forms SWILK and SIC (*swelk, swik, silk*, etc.) are treated separately in their alphabetical places.

The vocalism of the continental forms is in many points obscure. Some of them indicate the possibility of there having been new formations distinct from the original types, and there has no doubt been interaction of the forms of WHICH, the development of which, presumably on account of the difference of the initial sound, has not been entirely parallel.]

A. Illustration of Forms.

1. α. 1 **swelc, suelc, suælc, swælc, suoelc.** Also 5 **swelk, suelk,** (see SWILK).

[*c* **725** *Corpus Gloss.* (Hessels) A 204 *At queue*, end suelce.] *c* **831** *Charter* in *O.E. Texts* 446 Suelc man se ðisses landes bruce. *c* **888** ÆLFRED *Boeth.* xix, Ne se deað þeah swelces ne recþ. *c* **950** *Lindisf. Gosp.* Matt. ix. 8 *Potestatem talem*, mæht suælc.

β. 1 **swilc,** 1–2 **suilc,** 2–3 **swilch, suilch.** (See also SWILK.)

[*c* **725** *Corpus Gloss.* (Hessels) A 881 *Atqueve*, onsuilce.] *c* **831** *Charter* in *O.E. Texts* 446 Suilc man sue hit aweʒe. *c* **995** *Anc. Charters B. Mus* Cott. VIII. 38 On bocum & an swilcum lytlum. **1154** *O.E. Chron.* (Laud MS.) an. 1137 þe land was al fordon mid suilce dædes. *c* **1160** *Hatton Gosp.* Matt. ix. 8 Swilcne anweald. *a* **1200** *Moral Ode* 220 Swilche freonde. *c* **1200** *Trin. Coll. Hom.* 11 Alle þo þe leueð þat swilch þing hem muge furðrie oðer letten. *Ibid.* 165 Of swilch mai grisen men þe ani god cunnen.

γ. 1–2 **swylc,** (**swylic**), 1, 3 **swulc,** 3 **swulc(c)h,** *masc. acc. sing.* **swulne**

c **897** ÆLFRED *Gregory's Past. C.* xxxvii. 264 (Cott. MS.) Ða swylcan. *a* **950** *Ælfred's Boeth.* xxxix. §2 (Cott. MS.) He ne con onʒitan..forhwy swylc God ʒeþafað. *c* **1000** *Judith* 65 Hæfde ða his ende ʒebidenne..swylcne he ær æfter worhte. *c* **1000** *Beowulf* 880 Swulces hwæt. **1032** in *Anglia* XI. 9 Na hyrde we..ænig wurde hus aræred swylic þæt mære wæs. *c* **1175** *12th Cent. Hom.* 2 Swylce tacnæ wurcen swylce ðu wyrcst. *c* **1200** *Trin. Coll. Hom.* 135 Swulc se he hit here makeð. *c* **1205** LAY. 5333 Sone swa heo ihurden swulch worde. *Ibid.* 5345 þane we nimen swulne ræd. *a* **1225** *Ancr. R.* 382 Ich wot swulne þet bereð..heui brunie and here.

2. α. 3 **suweche,** 3–5 **sweche,** (4 **swheche,** *Kent.* **zuech,** 5 **schwe(s)che).**

a **1250** *Owl & Night.* (Jesus MS.) 1711 Heo wolde..yeue answere..myd sweche worde. *a* **1300** *Deb. Body & Soul* in *Map's Poems* (Camden) 338 Suweche fyve els is in werld of alle thinges. **1340** *Ayenb.* 156 Be zueche fables wes y-woned þe wyse man teche his mayre. *c* **1340** *Leg. Rood* 223 Swech deþ he under feng. *c* **1450** CAPGRAVE *Life St. Aug.* 1 Swech tresour as I haue in possession. **1466–7** *Mann. & Househ. Exp.* (Roxb.) 171 At schwesche a pryse as ʒe kane akorde.

β. 2–5, 9 *Glouc. dial.* **swich,** 3–5 **suich, suych,** 4–5 **swiche, swych(e,** (3, **swic, swyhc, svich, siwiche, suwiche, schuuych,** 4 *Kent.* **zuich, zuych,** 5 **swyhche, sqwyche).** Also 4–5 **swyk,** etc. (see SWILK).

c **1175** *Lamb. Hom.* 157 Swiche teres schedde ure drihten. *a* **1200** *Moral Ode* 80 Nis na lauerd swich se is crist, ne king swuch ure drihten. *c* **1290** *S. Eng. Leg.* 459 Men þat schuuych torment iseiʒen. **13..** *Cursor M.* 10 (Gött.) King arthour, þat was so riche, Was non in his time funden suiche. **1340** *Ayenb.* 37 Of zuichen þer byeþ uele maneres. *c* **1391** CHAUCER *Astrol.* Prol. (1872) 2 Swich a child. **1426** LYDG. *De Guil. Pilgr.* 17162 In Thapocalyps off Johan Swych a beste fond I noon. *c* **1440** *Promp. Parv.* 483/2 Swyche (*H.* swyhche, *P.* suche), *talis*. *c* **1450** J. METHAM *Wks.* (E.E.T.S.) 45 In sqwyche a case, or sqwyche a chauns. **1461** *Paston Lett.* II. 18 Suyche as arn right credible. **1462** *Ibid.* 82 Swyche talkynge.

γ. 2–4 **swuch,** 3 **swucch, swuc, shwuch,** 4 **swoch.**

a **1200** [see 2β]. *c* **1205** LAY. 18351 Ofte heo eoden to ræde of swucchere neode. *a* **1225** *Ancr. R.* 112 Swuc grure he hefde. *Ibid.* 312 Wreððen swuch feder, & sweamen swuchne warden. *c* **1290** *S. Eng. Leg.* 384 I nam no kyng swuch þing to habbe. *a* **1399** *Pol. Poems* (Rolls) I. 271 Swoch claterers.

3. α. 3 **sulch, swlc(h, solch.**

An early northern example of absorption of the *w* is given by *soelce* adv. in *Rituale Eccl. Dunelm.* 19, 69.

c **1205** LAY. 671 Brutus hine bi-þohte of swlchere [*c* **1275** solchere] neode. *Ibid.* 282 Swlc werc him þuhte swiðe muri.

β. 3 **selk(e,** 3–4 **sulk(e,** 4–5 **silk(e** (see SWILK).

4. α. 4–5 **seche,** 9 *dial.* and *vulgar* **sech, setch.**

13.. *Gaw. & Gr. Knt.* 1543 A hundreth of seche As I am. *c* **1400** *Anturs of Arth.* xxxi. (MS. Ireland), Seche game, and siche glee, Seʒhe he neuyr are. *c* **1450** *Mirk's Festial* 51 Seche he avaunset. **1848** THACKERAY *Van. Fair* xvi, Sech a business. **1885** LELAND *Brand-new Ballads* (ed. 2) 126 Setch a set of scallawags as these I never saw.

β. 3– (now *dial.*) **sich;** also 4–5 **sych(e,** 4–6 **siche,** 8– **sitch,** *s.w.* and *Irel.* **zitch, zich;** 4 **schych,** 6 **schiche, shyche, scheich, shytt.**

c **1250** *Kent. Serm.* in *O.E. Misc.* 32 Swiche lorde þet siche miracle mai do. *c* **1380** WYCLIF *Serm.* Sel. Wks. II. 317 Worldly men ben siche men þat þe world hab overcomen. *c* **1400** [see 4α]. *c* **1400** *Destr. Troy* 11340 Syche counsell.. kepe I none of. *a* **1425** tr. *Arderne's Treat. Fistula*, etc. 92 With þis puluis haue I cured sich fikez. **1487** *Cely Papers* (Camden) 168 The ceson ys syche at Bruges now that [etc.]. *c* **1550** CHEKE *Matt.* iii. 15 Let sich thinges go now. **1746** *Exmoor Scolding* (E.D.S.) 24 Ees dedent thenk tha had'st a be' zich a Labb o' tha Tongue. **1782** ELIZ. BLOWER *Geo. Bateman* I. 86 I had *sitch* an affection for him **1846** DICKENS *O. Twist* (rev. ed.) xv. 81 Oh, you naughty boy, to make me suffer sich distress. *a* **1847** *George Ridler's Oven* vii. in Halliwell *Dict.* p. xviii, My dog has gotten zitch a trick. **1848** DICKENS *Dombey* xxxix, Sitch is his conscience! **1863** *Southern Confederacy* (Atlanta) 13 May 2/1 The buryal squad organized *fust* and foremost, and begun to inter ther money and spoons and 4 pronged forks and sich like. **1867** ROCK *Jim an' Nell* lxxxvii. (E.D.S.) Ha isn't worth zich trouble. **1890** KIPLING in *Scots Observer* 28 June 149 Don't call your Martini a cross-eyed old bitch; She's human as you are—you treat her as sich. **1938** M. K. RAWLINGS *Yearling* xvi. 185 'Is that true, Buck?' Buck whittled busily. 'Now if you was to tell me a tale,' he said, 'I'd not ask you no sich of a question.' **1953** E. SIMON *Past Masters* III. 191 'But I did it in my own time,' said Monro... 'There ain't no sich thing, old son.' **1981** P. MACDONALD *One Way Street* i. 9 These bloody English..have put their imprint on this place in sich a way as to make yew want to heave.

? *a* **1400** *Kyng & Hermyt* 281 in *E.P.P.* (1864) I. 24 Aboute schych mastery. **1512–13** *Trevelyan Papers* III. (Camden) 9 Schiche mo[r]tuaries as ys due. *Ibid.*, He sayth that Jamys Clarke..wyll no paye yᵉ scheichys dwttes. **1556** MACHYN *Diary* (Camden) 119 Ane shytt person. *Ibid.* 133 Shyche a man.

γ. 3– **such;** also 3–5 **succh,** 3–6 **soch,** 4–6 **soche,** 4–7 **suche,** (3 **socch,** 4 **sooche, suuche, swche,** 5 **sucche,** 5–7 **souche,** 6 **souch, sutche, soyche,** *s.w. dial.* **zutche,** 6–7 **sutch);** 3 **shuc, scuch,** 4 **shoch,** 5 **schwsche,** 6 **scwch,** 6–7 **shuch(e,** 9 *dial.* **shut.**

c **1205** LAY. 491 To wroþer heore hele habbeð heo such [*c* **1275** such] werc idon. *a* **1250** *Owl & Night.* (Jesus MS.) 1511 þe vle wes glad of suche tale. **1377** LANGL. *P. Pl.* B. XVI. 112 Ofte he heled suche. *c* **1380** WYCLIF *Sel. Wks.* III. 455 Alle men tristynge in socche indulgencis. *c* **1400** *Brut.* I. lxxxv. 87 The Emperour loste soche foure of his folc as dede Kyng Arthur. **1487** *Paston Lett.* III. 463 Specially souche as have knowen me. **1530** *Proper Dyaloge* in Roy *Rede me*, etc. (Arb.) 134, I and suche other. **1535** COVERDALE *Bible* Ep., To make soch meanes for vs vnto his heauenly father. **1551** T. WILSON *Logic* (1580) 15 b, To keepe sutche Ceremonis. **1555** *Cal. Anc. Rec. Dublin* (1889) 442 Whoosomever doo not observe souche ordre. *a* **1568** ASCHAM *Scholem.* II. (Arb.) 123 Any soch thing. **1574** in W. H. TURNER *Select. Rec. Oxford* 354 Soyche as should plye ther bockes. **1577–82** BRETON *Flourish upon Fancie* Wks. (Grosart) I. 6/2 Sutch his Schollers are. **1585** in *Eng. Hist. Rev.* (1914) Jan. 113 Souche of the comen howse as they made choice of. **1586** FERNE *Blaz. Gentrie* 188 Giffe she put zutche a vermine beast, in trust to keepe it. **1661** PR. RUPERT in *11th Rep. Hist. MSS. Comm.* App. v. 8 Souche that comands those that stay on these frontirs.

c **1250** *Long Life* 27 in *O.E. Misc.* 156 Weilawei shuc weneð to lede. *c* **1250** *Moral Ode* 222 in *E.E.P.* (1862) 29 God sculde alle godes frend a wihd scuche freonde. **1303** R. BRUNNE *Handl. Synne* 3044 No shoch kote to þe shulde be. **1466–7** *Mann. & Househ. Exp.* (Roxb.) 172, I have ʒeffen ʒowe no schwsche kawse. **1501** *Cal. Anc. Rec. Dublin* (1889) 388 A resonable day scwch as pleaser to the maysteres to gywe. *c* **1538** in Archbold *Somerset Relig. Houses* (1892) 85 Schuche as were as warthy as some other. **1549** LATIMER *Ploughers* (Arb.) 31 There was neuer shuch a preacher..as he is. **1556** *Chron. Grey Friars* (Camden) 55 Then was made a proclamacyon agayne shoche sayers. **1638** *Hamilton Papers* (Camden) 34 All shuch horses that should pase through that toune. *Mod.* (*Birmingham*). Shut a lot.

B. Signification.

Such is a demonstrative word used to indicate the quality or quantity of a thing by reference to that of another or with respect to the effect that it produces or is capable of producing. Thus, syntactically, *such* may have backward or forward reference; in the uses of branch I it has the former, in those of branch II mainly the latter.

The use of *such* and *such a* in the attributive position is illustrated in detail only in sense 1, but the same rules apply to the adj. generally; for special uses see branch IV.

I. 1. Of the character, degree, or extent described, referred to, or implied in what has been said.

a. with sing. sb.

(*a*) With a concrete sb., or an abstract sb. used in a particularized sense; now superseded by *such a* (see (*c*) below) except *poet.*

971 *Blickl. Hom.* 189 Hwa lyfde þe þæt þu swylce scylde ʒefremedest? *a* **1122** *O.E. Chron.* (Laud MS.) an. 1087 [1086] Hwam ne mæʒ earmian swylcere tide? *c* **1205** LAY. 5421 To swulche forward we beoð hidere isende. *a* **1250** *Owl & Night.* (Jesus MS.) 1496 Hw may þer eny luue beo, Hwar such mon gropeþ hire þeo? *c* **1385** CHAUCER *L.G.W.* 474 Prol., To be war from falsenesse & from vice By swich ensaumple. *a* **1425** *Cursor M.* 4379 (Trin.) Whoso bigynne wol siche þing him owe to þinke on þe endyng. **1589** PUTTENHAM *Engl. Poesie* II. ix. (Arb.) 94 If one should rime to this word *Restore* he may not match him with *Doore*.. such rime is strained. **1646** CRASHAW *Sospetto d' Herode* li, She thinks not fit such he her face should see. **1749** JOHNSON *Van. Hum. Wishes* 298 Such Age there is, and who could wish its End? **1805** WORDSW. *Elegiac Stanzas* 30 Such Picture would I at that time have made. **1842** MACAULAY *Horatius* l, Was none who would be foremost To lead such dire attack. *a* **1849** BEDDOES *Dream-Pedlary* ii, Such pearl from Life's fresh crown Fain would I shake me down.

(*b*) With an abstract sb. used in a general sense.

971 *Blickl. Hom.* 85 Ne us næfre swylce eʒe ne wearþ ..ʒeendebyrded. *c* **1100** *O.E. Chron.* (MS. F) an. 995 Hi wurðan ða swyðe bliþe þurh swilce wissunge. *c* **1275** *Sinners Beware* 171 in *O.E. Misc.* 77 From succhе lecherye Heo schule to helle cume. ? *a* **1366** CHAUCER *Rom. Rose* 697 Than wist I.. That ydelnesse me serued well That me putte in sich Iolite. *c* **1460** *Emare* 626 Be stylle, syr,.. Lette syche mornynge bene. **1535** COVERDALE *2 Sam.* xiii. 12 Do not thou soch foly. **1590** SPENSER *F.Q.* III. i. 50 Such loue is hate, and such desire is shame. **1700** DRYDEN *Flower & Leaf*

95 Such Joy my Soul, such Pleasures fill'd my Sight. **1777** BURKE *Corr.* (1844) II. 158 Such partiality to his endeavours. **1802** MAR. EDGEWORTH *Moral T.* (1816) I. 220, I little thought, that I should so soon be in such need. **1844** MRS. BROWNING *Lost Bower* xxxix, She never sings such music.

(*c*) ***such a***: see (*a*). (Cf. G. *solch ein.*)

c **1205** LAY. 18881 For ȝet næt hit neoðer..þat of Vðere Pendragune scal arisen swilc a sune. *c* **1290** *Beket* 1255 in *S. Eng. Leg.* 142 He þonkede god þat swuch a prelat under him moste beo. **13..** *Bonaventura's Medit.* 813 þere was neuer womman bare swyche a chylde. **1390** GOWER *Conf.* I. 42 Ther may noman finde The rihte salve of such a Sor. *c* **1400** MAUNDEV. (1839) Prol. 3 Righte wel oughte us for..to drede and serven suche a Lord. *c* **1500** *Melusine* 360 Sayeng þat neuer tofore they herd of suche a thing. **1606** CHAPMAN *Gentl. Usher* II. i, Now such a huddle and kettle neuer was. **1664** BUTLER *Hud.* II. ii. 862 Else when we put it to the push, They had not giv'n us such a brush. **1711** ADDISON *Spect.* No. 23 ¶2 He does not believe any the most Comick Genius can censure him for talking upon such a Subject at such a Time. **1821** SCOTT *Kenilw.* xxii, Thou didst ill to speak to such a man of such matters. **1849** MACAULAY *Hist. Eng.* ix. II. 436 The Prince declared that to avert the horrors of such a persecution was one of his chief objects.

†(*d*) ***a such.*** (Cf. F. *un tel*, G. *ein solcher.*)

a **1240** *Sawles Warde* in *O.E. Hom.* I. 251 To a swuch bale. **1297** R. GLOUC. (Rolls) 379 Lute wonder it was þat strange men in is owe lond dude a such trespas. **1307** *Elegy on Edw. I*, ix, Wel longe we mowe clepe & crie, Er we a such kyng han y-founde!

b. with pl. sb.

a **950** *Boeth. Metr.* x. 55 Se [hlisa] is eac to lytel swelcra lariowa. *c* **1175** *Lamb. Hom.* 157 Swiche teres scedde M. Magdalene þa heo wosch ure drihtenes fet. **1297** R. GLOUC. (Rolls) 154 þat water of baþe is þat on þat euere is iliche hot. .. Swiche baþes þer beþ fale. **1362** LANGL. *P. Pl.* A. Prol. 32 Summe chosen Chaffare to cheeuen þe bettre, As hit semeþ to vre siht þat suche men scholden. **1393** *Ibid.* C. I. 64 Bote holy churche & charite choppe a-doun swich shryuers. *a* **1425** [see A. 4*β*]. **1526** TINDALE *Rom.* ii. 2 That the iudgement of God is accordynge to trueth, agaynst them which commit soche thynges. **1579** GOSSON *Sch. Abuse* (Arb.) 30 The abuse of such places was so great that [etc.]. **1667** MILTON *P.L.* v. 401 Such high advantages thir innocence Gave them above thir foes. **1725** WATTS *Logic* 332 Such indirect and remote arguments may also be sometimes used to confirm a proposition which has been before proved by arguments more direct and immediate. **1808** SCOTT *Marm.* I. xxv, I love such holy ramblers. **1881** MIVART *Cat* 128 Some muscles attached to a long bone which is relatively fixed at one end, tend to make it describe..a movement of circumduction. Such muscles are termed Rotators. **1892** MRS. OLIPHANT *Hist. Sk. Q. Anne* vi. (1894) 304 [He] was ..indignant with the highflyers for expressing such opinions.

2. Standing predicatively at the head of a sentence or clause, and referring summarily to a statement or description just made.

In ME. *such is* (+ inf.) often = This is what it is (to be, etc.). *such is life!*: an exclamatory phrase now often used trivially as an expression of resignation or acquiescence in things as they are.

1297 R. GLOUC. (Rolls) 8675 Such it is to be ssrewe. *Ibid.* 11736 Suich was þe morþre of einesham, uor bataile non it nas. *c* **1320** *Cast. Love* 1161 Such beo þe duntes of batayle þat he polede for vs. *a* **1330** *Roland & V.* 75 þai toke him þe letter & kist his hand, Swiche was þe lawe of þe land. *c* **1381** CHAUCER *Parl. Foules* 570 Lo sich it is to haue a tunge loos. *c* **1386** —— *Prol.* 485 And swich he was y-preued ofte sithes. *c* **1450** *Merlin* 632 Soche was the a-vision that I saugh in my slepe. **1567** PAINTER *Pal. Pleas.* II. 508 Sutch was the desyres of these two lovers. **1697** DRYDEN *Virg. Georg.* IV. 701 He first, and close behind him follow'd she, For such was Proserpine's severe Decree. **1716** POPE *Iliad* VIII. 595 For such is Fate, nor can'st thou turn its course. **1774** GOLDSM. *Nat. Hist.* (1776) IV. 197 Such these animals appeared when brought into Europe. **1818** SCOTT *Hrt. Midl.* xxviii, The Lady..did not..ring a bell, because such was not the fashion of the time, but she whistled on a silver-call. **1837** LOCKHART *Scott* I. vi. 178 Such was the germ of the magnificent library and museum of Abbotsford. **1855** MACAULAY *Hist. Eng.* xi. III. 71 His Majesty,—such was now the language of too many Anglican divines,—would have been [etc.]. **1865** DICKENS *Mut. Fr.* I. ii, With a mournful air—as who should say, 'Here is another wretched creature come to dinner; such is life!' **1890** DOYLE *White Company* v, At the end of a year he would be free to return to the cloisters, for such had been his father's bequest. **1896** *Law Q. Rev.* July 201 If such be the law, we are pretty sure it is not the law Parliament intended to make.

3. Of the same kind or class as something mentioned or referred to; of that kind; similar, the like. *Obs.* or *arch.*, exc. in collocation with a numeral, indef. adj., etc. (see V).

c **1200** *Trin. Coll. Hom.* 45 Mid þese þre lokes..and mid swiche weldede. *c* **1205** LAY. 6564 Æuere he þohte embe uuel and swulche weoren his dede. **1390** GOWER *Conf.* III. 312 Anon was mad a cofre sich. *c* **1400** MAUNDEV. (1839) xix. 205 A Pipe or a Penne or suche a thing. *c* **1450** *Two Cookery Bks.* 83 Take faire peces of paynmain, or elles of such tendur brede. **1596** SHAKS. *Merch. V.* IV. i. 97 Let their beds Be made as soft as yours: and let their pallats Be season'd with such Viands. *c* **1600** —— *Sonn.* liv, The Canker bloomes haue full as deepe a die, As the perfumed tincture of the Roses, Hang on such thornes, and play as wantonly. **1613–16** W. BROWNE *Brit. Past.* II. i. (1772) II. 19 Of rotchets, whitings or such common fish. **1697** DAMPIER *Voy.* (1729) I. 97 Penguins..are a Sea-Fowl, about as big as a Duck, and such Feet. **1771** *Encycl. Brit.* II. 698/1 The protractor is a small semicircle of brass, or such solid matter. **1796** MRS. INCHBALD *Nature & Art* xi. (1820) 27 You *are* my father—you have just such eyes, and such a forehead. **1829** SCOTT *Anne of G.* vii, Fustian, hides, peltry, and such ordinary articles.

4. Equivalent to a descriptive adj. or adv. on which it follows closely and the repetition of which is thus avoided. (Cf. 22.)

So is now preferred.

c **897** ÆLFRED *Gregory's Past. C.* xvi. 101 Hu he wolde ðæt mon him miltsode ȝif he suelc wære. *a* **1225** *Ancr. R.* 208 Iseliliche muwun heo siggen þet þene teil swuch ivindeð. **1340** *Ayenb.* 51 'Ich habbe a to kuead heaued.' And he zayþ zoþ, uor he heþ hit zuych ymad. *c* **1386** CHAUCER *Prol.* 313 Discreet he was, and of greet reuerence. He semed swich. *c* **1400** LOVE *Bonavent. Mirr.* (1908) 58 They wolde not be seyn suche in other mennes siȝt. **1590** SPENSER *F.Q.* III. vii. 29 [He] rather ioyd to be, then seemen sich. **1667** MILTON *P.L.* III. 100 Such I created all th' Ethereal Powers And Spirits. *Ibid.* v. 521 That thou art happie, owe to God; That thou continu'st such, owe to thy self. **1697** DRYDEN *Æneid* Ded., Ess. 1900 II. 154 A heroic poem, truly such. **1825** SCOTT *Talism.* xxviii, The pointless lances of the preceding day were certainly no longer such. **1865** KINGSLEY *Herew.* ix, Robert, who thought himself as good as his brother (though he was not such, save in valour).

5. The previously described or specified; the (person or thing) before mentioned.

In this sense *such* (not *such a*) is usual with a sing. sb.

c **1375** *Cursor M.* (Fairf.) 10869 Thow shalt conceyve a child..And his name shalle þou Ihesu calle... Suche wordis were seid to mary. **1452** in *Rep. Hist. MSS. Comm.* Var. Coll. IV. 201 Unto the tyme they have founde suerte of ther gode beringe; and yf they fynde not suche suerte [etc.]. **1491** *Newminster Cartul.* (Surtees) 252 If eny..recouere happyn agenste eny of yᵉ said partiez..yᵗ partie..ayenst whome sich recouere is had [etc.]. **1551** SIR J. WILLIAMS *Accompte* (Abbotsf. Club) 1 All and singuler souche Redye money. **1667** MILTON *P.L.* v. 26 Such whispering wak'd her. **1680** *New Hampsh. Prov. Papers* (1867) I. 388 If any Christian.. shall speak contempteously of the Holy Scriptures..such person or persons shall be punished. **1771** *Encycl. Brit.* II. 698/2 Any number of inches,..with any part of an inch, can be taken.., providing such part be greater than the one hundredth part of an inch. **1818** CRUISE *Digest* (ed. 2) VI. 332 For default of *such* issue, viz. that issue which is before mentioned. **1828** MOORE *Pract. Navig.* 120 As ships never run such dist[ance] in 24 hours. **1835** CARLYLE in Froude *Life Lond.* (1884) I. ii. 43 My true wish is that such creed may long hold compactly together in you. **1878** *Act 41 & 42 Vict.* c. 53 §2 A gratuity awarded..to any clerk shall be estimated according to the period during which such clerk has served.

II. Where the meaning is determined by reference to a correlative or dependent clause.

6. a. With *such* in both clauses: in OE. ***swelc.. swelc***; later ***such as..such*** = L. *qualis..talis*, except in proverbial sentences of the type 'Such master, such man'.

Beowulf 1328 (Gr.) Swylc scolde eorl wesan, æþeling ærgod, swylc Æschere wæs! *a* **901** *Laws Ælfred* I. xi, Mid swelce hræȝle he ineode, mid swelce gange he ut. **971** *Blickl. Hom.* 59 Eal swylce seo lange mettrumnes biþ þæs seocan mannes, þonne [etc.]..swylc is þæt lif þysses middanȝeardes. **1340** *Ayenb.* 235 To zuiche lhorde zuich maine. **1390** GOWER *Conf.* I. 360 Such Capitein such retenue. *c* **1400** *Pilgr. Sowle* (Caxton) IV. xxix. (1859) 61 Suche as is the kynge,..suche is the peple. **1474** CAXTON *Chesse* II. ii. (1883) 33 Suche moder, suche doughter, comunely. *a* **1540** [see LETTUCE 2]. **1548–9** (Mar.) *Bk. Com. Prayer, Athan. Creed,* Such as the father is, suche is the sonne. **1549** LATIMER *Ploughers* (Arb.) 28 Such as the noble men be, suche wyll the people be. **1560** *Bible* (Geneva) 2 Cor. x. 11 Suche as we are in worde by letters when we are absent; suche wil we be also in dede, when we are present. **1586** A. DAY *Engl. Secretorie* I. (1625) 134 Consider that such as is the tree such is the fruit. **1618** BOLTON *Florus* (1636) 151 Such as the Captaine is, such is the Souldier. **1725** BERKELEY *Proposal* Wks. 1871 III. 223 Such as their trade is, such is their wealth. **1821** SCOTT *Pirate* xxx, He is dame Norna's servant it's like,—such man, such mistress! **1898** BESANT *Orange Girl* II. xxvi, Such as they are, such they have been made.

†**b.** With one of the correlatives omitted: = Such as. *Obs.*

Beowulf 72 (Gr.) And þær on innan eall ȝedælan ȝeongum and ealdum, swylc him god sealde. *a* **1000** *Cædmon's Dan.* 66 ðehlodon him to huðe hordwearda ȝestreon, fea & freos, swilc þær funden wæs. *a* **1200** *Moral Ode* 80 Nis na lauerd swich se is crist ne king swuch ure drihten. *Ibid.* 120 Al his lif scal bon suilch boð his endinge. *c* **1205** LAY. 4153 He somenede færd swulc nes næuere eær on erde. *c* **1275** —— 3892 Her com a selcouþ tockne soch neuere ne com.

c. With *what* as the correlative in the dependent clause. *rare.*

1834 *Tracts for Times* No. 24. 5 What the Apostles are in St. Paul's Epistles, such the Bishops are in those of Ignatius. **1850** NEWMAN *Diffic. Anglicans* I. xii. (1891) I. 379 What Arius, Nestorius, or Eutyches were then, such are Luther and Calvin now.

†**d.** With advb. *as* as the correlative in the dependent clause. *Obs.*

1535 COVERDALE *Judg.* viii. 21 As the man is, soch [**1611** so] is also his strength. *a* **1611** CHAPMAN *Iliad* XXIII. 517 As corn-ears do shine with dew..When fields set all their bristles up, in such a ruff wert thou, O Menelaus. **1658** DRYDEN *Cromwell* xiii, He..made to Battels such Heroick Haste As if on Wings of Victory he flew. **1790** BURNS *Ballad Dumfries Elect.* xiv, As flames amang a hundred woods, As headlong foam a hundred floods—Such is the rage of battle.

7. a. With correlative *as* pron. (see AS 23), ME. also *as that*, taking the place of OE. *swelce, swá.* ***such as*** = Of the kind or degree that; the kind of (person or thing) that.

According to the syntax of the subordinate clause, *as* may be equivalent to a relative in an oblique case = of, in, with (etc.) which.

c **888** ÆLFRED *Boeth.* xxxiv. §10 Be swelcum ȝesceaftum swelce nane sawle nabbað. **971** *Blickl. Hom.* 95 Ealle hie sceolan þonne arisan..on swylcum heowe swa hie ær hie sylfe ȝefrætwodan. *c* **1100** *O.E. Chron.* (MS. D) an. 1058 Mid swilcan weorðscipe swa nan oðer ne dyde ætforan him. *a* **1122** *Ibid.* (Laud MS.) an. 1009 þa com him swilc wind onȝean swilce nan mann ær ne ȝemunde. *c* **1175** *Lamb. Hom.* 83 þe sunne schineð þer þurh, and ho nimeð al swuch hou alse ho þer on uint. *a* **1225** *Leg. Kath.* 1852 Wið swuch dream..as drihtin deah to cumene. *c* **1230** *Hali Meid.* 5 Of ..swuch wurðschipe, as hit is to beo godes spuse. *c* **1290** *Beket* 1204 in *S. Eng. Leg.* 141 Of swuch a frere ase ich am. **1340–70** *Alex. & Dind.* 855 Swiche werkus to swinke as oþur swainus vsen. **1377** LANGL. *P. Pl.* B. XIII. 433 What dauid seith of suche men as þe sauter telleth. **1480** *Cov. Leet Bk.* 473 Before such persones and at such places as this case shall require. **1546** GARDINER *Detect. Devils Sophistrie* 228 Christ ..is..mocked..wᵗ such toyes and termes, as the Jewes deuised not more spitefull. *a* **1586** SIDNEY *Arcadia* II. (Sommer) 126b, When..Musidorus tooke on such shepherdish apparell..as I now weare. **1638** FORD *Fancies* I. iii, Thy growth to such perfection, as no flattery Of art can perish now. **1774** GOLDSM. *Nat. Hist.* (1776) VI. 82 If it be true that such meat as is the most dangerously earned is the sweetest. **1815** SCOTT *Let.* in *Lockhart* (1837) III. x. 318 To finish an odd little tale within such time as will mistify the public, I trust. **1857** HUGHES *Tom Brown* II. ii, We'll each of us give you such a thrashing as you'll remember. **1877** RUSKIN *St. Mark's Rest.* v. 65 Such a cloak for their commercial appetite as modern church-going is for modern swindling.

ellipt. **1586** W. BAILEY *Preserv. Eye-sight* (1633) 35 We must use topicall meanes, and such as are discussive. **1695** DRYDEN tr. *Dufresnoy's Art. Paint.* Pref. p. xii, In these pompous Expressions, or such as these. **1737** POPE *Hor. Epist.* II. ii. 2 You love a Verse, take such as I can send. **1780** *Mirror* No. 94 To guard such of my readers as should be disposed to indulge in it, against its..consequences. **1821** SCOTT *Kenilw.* xviii, He is to have no access to the lady but such as I shall point out. **1891** FARRAR *Darkn. & Dawn* xl, All the ordinary conventions of a Roman marriage were carried out, except such as were purely pagan.

†**b.** With *as* omitted. *Obs. rare.*

1613 SHAKS. *Hen. VIII*, II. ii. 101 They haue sent me such a Man, I would haue wish'd for.

†**8.** With *as* followed by a relative usually in an oblique form. *Obs.*

1579 FENTON *Guicciard.* Ep. Ded., The man..was such a one, as whose virtues were farre from all suspition of partialitie. **1618** BOLTON *Florus* I. xvi. (1636) 48 Our army being..shut up within such a fastnesse as out of which it could not escape. **1678** CUDWORTH *Intell. Syst.* 17 Such a System of it, as from whence it would follow, that there could not be any God. *Ibid.* 198 By such a nature as which ..is..nescient of what it doth.

9. In uses marked by special word-order.

a. In predicative use.

1154 *O.E. Chron.* (Laud MS.) an. 1135 þa..uuard þe sunne suilc als it uuare thre-niht ald mone. *c* **1205** LAY. 7048 His hæð wes swulc swa beoð gold. **1377** LANGL. *P. Pl.* B. x. 253 Suche as þow semest in syȝte be in assay y-founde. **1421** *26 Pol. Poems* 83 Be suche wiþ-ynne, as ȝe outward seme. *c* **1450** CAPGRAVE *Life St. Aug.* 38 Loke if ȝe be swech as þei be. Wold God ȝe were swech as I fynde hem. **1597** HOOKER *Eccl. Pol.* v. liv. §5 His [right] beeing such as we cannot reach. **1630** HALL *Occas. Medit.* §9 (1633) 23 O God, wee are such as thou wilt bee pleased to make us. **1794** MRS. RADCLIFFE *Myst. Udolpho* lv, Her conduct was such as might have been expected from the weakness of her principles. **1817** JAS. MILL *Brit. India* II. v. vii. 598 Be the other virtues belonging to it such as they may. **1859** RUSKIN *Two Paths* iii. §96 Your stuffs need not be such as would catch the eye of a duchess.

b. ***such as one*** or ***it is***: having the character that he (it) has, no more and no less; used chiefly with a depreciatory or contemptuous reference, or apologetically.

a **1240** *Ureisun* in *O.E. Hom.* I. 201 þet wule bi-cluppen þe þer swuch ase þu ert þer louerd of leoue. *a* **1240** *Wohunge, Ibid.* 285 A wrecche bodi..bere ich ouer eorðe, and tat swuch as hit is haue ȝiuen..to þi seruise. *c* **1386** CHAUCER *Reeve's T.* 201 If ther be eny Swich as it is, yet shal ye haue youre part. **1538** STARKEY *England* (1878) 134 They haue theyr seruyce, such as hyt ys, al in theyr vulgare tong openly rehersyd. **1546** J. HEYWOOD *Prov.* (1867) 42 Many men wishte..Some well fauourd vysor, on hir yll fauourd face. But with visorlyke visage, suche as it was, She smirkt, and she smylde. *a* **1700** DRYDEN *Pref. to Fables* Ess. 1900 II. 249 Thoughts, such as they are, come crowding in so fast upon me, that [etc.]. **1719** DE FOE *Crusoe* II. (Globe) 363 To get up upon their Feet, and perhaps put on a Coat, such as it was, and their Pumps. **1855** MACAULAY *Hist. Eng.* xx. IV. 463 Such as his mind was, it had been assiduously cultivated. **1878** HARDY *Ret. Native* VI. i, But, such as the rooms were, there were plenty of them.

c. In attributive use after its sb.

c **1000** ÆLFRIC *Saints' Lives* xxix. 263 þa com þær heofonlic leoht..swilc swa hi ær ne ȝesawon. **1340** *Ayenb.* 56 þer huer he makeþ his miracles zuiche ase behoueþ to þe dyeule. **1460** CAPGRAVE *Chron.* (Rolls) 84 With words.. swech as Seint Augustin wold nevir write. *a* **1533** LD. BERNERS *Huon* cxi. 385 A fyne shyrte and dobelet..such as he wold chose. **1590** SHAKS. *Com. Err.* I. i. 81 A small spare Mast, Such as sea-faring men prouide for stormes. **1667** MILTON *P.L.* I. 620 Tears such as Angels weep. **1757** W. WILKIE *Epigoniad* IV. 95 Its music such, as when a stormy gale Roars thro' a hollow cliff. **1820** KEATS *Lamia* I. 36 A mournful voice, Such as once heard,..destroys All pain but pity. **1859** TENNYSON *Guinev.* 545 Beauty such as never woman wore.

d. Hence *such as* is used to introduce examples of a class: = for example, *e.g.*

1695 DRYDEN tr. *Dufresnoy's Art Paint.* Pref. p. xvi, If.. their Characters were wholly perfect, (such as for Example, the Character of a Saint or Martyr in a Play). **1774** GOLDSM. *Nat. Hist.* (1776) III. 198 All of the cat kind, such as the lion, the tiger, the leopard, and the ounce. **1779** *Mirror* No. 31 Writers, such as Theophrastus and La Bruyere. **1842** LOUDON *Suburban Hort.* 282 The grafting of plants of one family on those of another totally opposite, such as the jessamine on the orange. **1875** JEVONS *Money* xiii. 159 Many large gold coins, such as the..doubloon.

10. a. The principle clause may be reduced to *such* and the words qualified by it for the purpose of producing a terse (exclamatory) form.

c **1420** *Sir Amadace* (Camden) xlix, Seche a storme as thou was inne, That thou myȝte any socur wynne, A fulle fayre happe hit wase! **1779** WARNER in Jesse *Selwyn & Contemp.* (1844) IV. 271 Such a dinner as we had to-day! *Mod.* Oh dear! Such a fuss as never was!

b. The clause introduced by *as* may be reduced to the subj. only; when this is a pron., it may be either nom. or acc., *e.g.* 'such as *me*' or 'such as *I*' (*sc.* am).

c **1000** ÆLFRIC *Hom.* II. 162 Se wolde habban swilcne hlisan swa Benedictus. *c* **1412** HOCCLEVE *De Reg. Princ.* 1144 Erthen vessel, to swich a man as me Ful sittyng is. **1588** SHAKS. *L.L.L.* IV. iii. 131 As his, your case is such. **1611** —— *Wint. T.* II. i. 191 Others such as he. **1617** DONNE *Serm.* Luke xxiii. 40 (1660) III. 2 The Revelations of Brigid, and of Katherine, and such She-fathers as those. **1712** ADDISON *Spect.* No. 317 ¶3 Such a Road of Action as that I have been speaking of. **1716** HEARNE *Collect.* (O.H.S.) V. 292, 4 Pillars, ..of such Marble as the Pillars of Sarum Cathedral. **1717** ADDISON *Notes Ovid* Wks. 1721 I. 234 This way of joining two such different Ideas as Chariot and Counsel to the same verb. **1740** RICHARDSON *Pamela* (1741) I. xxiv. 67 He.. look'd at me, and, as I thought afterwards, as sillily as such a poor girl as I. **1831** SCOTT *Ct. Rob.* xviii, Instead of such language as this. **1841** ELPHINSTONE *Hist. India* I. 595 He replied..that barbarity such as his was unexampled among princes. **1885** 'MRS. ALEXANDER' *At Bay* ii, Deering could not endure the companionship of such a man as Vincent.

c. ***there is such a thing as***: a phrase used to hint or suggest that the thing referred to exists and therefore must be taken into account; often used *colloq.* to convey a veiled threat.

1729 BUTLER *Serm.* Wks. 1874 II. 132 It is manifest, that there is such a thing as this self-partiality and self-deceit. **1767** *Woman of Fashion* II. 114 There is such a Thing as a Letter miscarrying. **1818** T. L. PEACOCK *Nightmare Abbey* xiii, There is a girl concealed in this tower, and find her I will. There are such things as sliding panels and secret closets. **1889** *Sat. Rev.* 23 Mar. 335/1 It may be said that there are such things as horsewhips, and it is thought that men have backs.

11. ***such..as*** (OE. *swá*): the..that, *pl.* those.. that; any or all..that; as many (or as much)..as.

a **1000** *Soul's Addr.* 103 (Gr.) Sculon wit..brucan swylcra yrmþa swa þu unc ær scrife. *c* **1375** *Cursor M.* 259 (Fairf.) Suche worde and werkis as we in lyue redy acountes mone we gyue. *c* **1386** CHAUCER *Can. Yeom. Prol.* 166 Swich thyng as that I knowe, I wol declare. **1390** GOWER *Conf.* I. 70 Glad was hire innocence tho Of suche wordes as sche herde. **1470** in *Camden Misc.* (1847) I. 6 A remembrance of suche actez and dedez as oure souveraigne lorde hadde done. **1534** CROMWELL in Merriman *Life & Lett.* (1902) I. 387 Certayne besynes..to be done..with soche spede and diligence as they conveniently may. **1539** TAVERNER *Erasm. Prov.* (1552) 49 Such ale as he hath brued, let him drynke him self. **1601** DOLMAN *La Primand. Fr. Acad.* (1618) III. 848 All these things proceede from the diuersitie of the nature..of such humours as haue engendred them. *a* **1715** BURNET *Own Time* VII. (1823) V. 147 The electress..was forced to submit to such terms as were imposed on her. **1835** J. DUNCAN *Beetles* (Nat. Lib.) 182 This genus..comprehends such insects as have the antennæ slightly compressed. **1867** RUSKIN *Time & Tide* ii. §5 There is a root of the very deepest ..truth in the saying, which gives to it such power as it still retains.

predic. **1737** *Gentl. Mag.* VII. 261/2 These, being such as occur to my Memory at present.

12. With relative *who*, *which* (*whence*, *where*, etc.) or *that* (OE. *þe*, *se þe*): = 'such..as' (in senses 6 and 11). Now *rare* and regarded as incorrect.

c **831** *Charter* in *O.E. Texts* 446 Suelc mon se ðet lond hebbe. *c* **1000** ÆLFRIC *Hom.* II. 162 þæt he ðone cwelmbæren hlaf..on swilcere stowe awurpe, ðær hine nan man findan ne mihte. *c* **1000** —— *Saints' Lives* Pref. 62 Buton he hæbbe..swylce þening men þe þeawfæstnysse him ȝebeodon. *c* **1205** LAY. 4242 Swulc for-wonde man þe mid sorwe at-wand. *Ibid.* 18934 Ich con swulche leche-craft þe leof þe scal iwurðen. **1340** *Ayenb.* 139 Alle zuiche þinges þet þe kueade poure deþ and þoleþ. *c* **1386** CHAUCER *Prol.* 3 Whan that Aprille with hise shoures soote..hath..bathed euery veyne in swich licour Of which vertu engendred is the flour. *c* **1386** —— *Monk's T.* 741 Swich a reyn doun fro the welkne shadde That slow the fyr. **1390** GOWER *Conf.* I. 57 Such thing wherof a man may lere That to vertu is acordant. *c* **1400** tr. *Secr. Secr., Gov. Lordsh.* 106 þat þou chese of wyse men..sweche þat hauyn perfeccion of enournede eloquence. **1419** *26 Pol. Poems* 70 He þat..wole..suche games bygynne Where þat he wot he may not wynne. *c* **1489** CAXTON *Sonnes of Aymon* ix. 233 Lordes, lete vs doo suche a thyng, wherof we shall gete worshyp. **1515** in Leadam *Sel. Cases Star Chamber* (Selden Soc.) II. 95 To occupie eny misterye or craft without thagrement of suche Craft that he desireth to be of. **1552–3** *Act 7 Edw. VI*, c. 12 §11 At suche place, where he and his Familie..shall kepe his house. **1601** SHAKS. *Jul. C.* II. i. 130 Such suffering Soules That welcome wrongs. **1662** STILLINGFL. *Orig. Sacræ* II. i. §2 Such a person..who gave..evidence..that he acted no private design. **1709** SWIFT *Adv. Relig.* Wks. 1755 II. I. 109 Such men are often put into the commission of the peace, whose interest it is, that virtue should be utterly banished. **1709** STRYPE *Ann. Ref.* lii, 524 These..seemed to him..such which he never thought..would be seriously opposed. *a* **1774** GOLDSM. *Hist. Greece* I. 227 Such of his friends that had not forsaken him. **1818** CRUISE *Digest* (ed. 2) V. 211 The husband and wife had not such an estate in the land whereof a fine could be levied. **1829** SCOTT *Anne of G.* xiv, Such prisoners from whom he was desirous of extorting.. information. **1873** NEWMAN *Idea Univ.* (ed. 3) 431 In spite of such [*ed.* 1859 whatever] deductions from it that have to be made in detail. **1888** 'SARAH GRAND' *Ideala* (1893) 229 Only such intellectual pursuits which are pleasant.

13. a. Followed by a dependent clause introduced by *that*, †*so* (*that*), †*as*, *as that* (now rare), or by *as to* (formerly only †*to*) with infin., expressing a consequence. The meaning of *such* tends to be intensive = so great, etc.

(*a*) *c* **1100** *O.E. Chron.* (MS. F) an. 995 þes ȝeares..wearð swylc mancwealm þæt na belaf binnan Cristes cyrcan butan fif munecan. *a* **1200** *Moral Ode* 395 Crist ȝyue us leden her swilc lif and habben her swilc ende þat we moten þuder come. **1297** R. GLOUC. (Rolls) 252 To such prowesse he drou þat al þe kun þat him iseiȝ adde of him ioye inou. **13..** *Guy Warw.* (A.) 266 Swiche iuel is comen him on þat he weneþ his liif forgon. *c* **1386** CHAUCER *Knt.'s T.* 4 He was.. in his tyme swich a Conquerour, That gretter was ther noon vnder the Sonne. *c* **1450** *Merlin* 694, I am soche a fole that I love a-nother better than my-self. *a* **1533** LD. BERNERS *Huon* xciv. 304 He sounded the trompettes with suche brute that merauyle it was to here. **1600** J. PORY tr. *Leo's Africa* III. 109 There was such hauock made..that a sillie remnant of them was left alive. **1712** ADDISON *Spect.* No. 499 ¶3 This filled my Mind with such a huddle of Ideas, that..I fell into the following Dream. *a* **1715** BURNET *Own Time* II. (1724) I. 189 He was a very prudent man; and had such a management with it, that I never knew any Clergy-man so universally esteemed. **1800** WORDSW. *Pet Lamb* 11 'Drink, pretty creature, drink,' she said in such a tone That I almost received her heart into my own. **1891** *Law Times* XC. 411/2 Allowing a foundry and other property to fall into such a state of disrepair that it was impossible to let them.

without conj. *c* **1205** LAY. 31585 Oswy is a swulc mon þine scome he wulle don. *c* **1386** CHAUCER *Can. Yeom. Prol. & T.* 849 Lo swich a lucre is in this lusty game A mannes myrthe it wol turne vn-to grame. *a* **1400** *Minor Poems fr. Vernon MS.* xlii. 9 þou art wrouht of such a kynde: Wiþ-outen loue maiȝt þou not be. **1470–85** MALORY *Arthur* VIII. xxxi. 320 He was in suche a study he herd not what Gouernayle said. **1573** TUSSER *Husb.* (1878) 123 Such season may chance, it shall stand thee vpon, till it againe, er an Sommer be gon. **1700** DRYDEN *Pal. & Arc.* II. 325 Such Pity wrought in ev'ry Ladies Mind, They left their Steeds, and prostrate on the Place..implor'd th' Offenders Grace.

(*b*) *c* **1369** CHAUCER *Dethe Blaunche* 28 Suche fantasies ben in myn hede So I not what is best too doo.

(*c*) **1417** [see 37 c]. **1560**, *c* **1600** [see 34 b]. **1610** B. JONSON *Alch.* IV. i. 6, I ha' told her such braue things, o' you,..As shee is almost in her fit to see you. **1625** BACON *Ess., Vicissit Things* (Arb.) 570 They haue such Powring Riuers, as the Riuers of Asia..are but Brookes to them. **1769** GOLDSM. *Hist. Rome* (1786) I. 372 Having disposed his army in such a manner as that none of the defendents could escape. **1883** *Trans. Amer. Philol. Assoc.* 54 (Art. 'Southernisms'), The Faculty are favorable to *such* a reduction of studies *as that* a man can do his work well.

(*d*) *a* **1450** [see 37 b]. **1581** PETTIE tr. *Guazzo's Civ. Conv.* III. (1586) 151 Thinking that his sonne was such a foole to accept his offer. **1599** *George a Greene* D ij b, This is wondrous, being blinde of sight, His deepe perseuerance should be such to know vs. **1779** *Mirror* No. 31 They may be expressed in such vague..terms, as to lay before the reader no marked distinguishing feature. **1825** J. NICHOLSON *Oper. Mech.* 41 The upper part M M X Y of the cup should be of such a form as to have the sides covered only with a thin film of the fluid. **1892** BIERCE *In Midst of Life* 109 He..had borne himself with such gallantry as to attract the attention of his superior officers.

b. predicative.

c **1200** *Trin. Coll. Hom.* 95 Two þeroffe ben swiche þat no man ne mai underfo [etc.]. **1340** *Ayenb.* 8 Zuych may by þe onboȝsamnesse þet hit is dyadlich zenne. **1474** CAXTON *Chesse* IV. v. (1883) 175 The moeuynge of hem is suche That the whyte may goo in to the space of the alphyn. **1591** SHAKS. *1 Hen VI*, V. iii. 70 Beauties Princely Maiesty is such, Confounds the tongue, and makes the senses rough. **1611** CORYAT *Crudities* 170 The variety of the curious obiects which it exhibiteth..is such, that a man shall much wrong it to speake a little of it. *a* **1700** in *Cath. Rec. Soc. Publ.* IX. 343 Infirmitys, wch were such y^t^ she was not able to take rest in a bed. **1829** SCOTT *Anne of G.* xxx, Such and so gentle is René's temper, that even my unfilial conduct will not diminish my influence over him. **1895** *Law Times* C. 3/1 The system by which solicitors are paid is such that only by circumlocution and red tape can they make a living. **1911** *Act 1 & 2 Geo. V*, c. 50 §15 A certificate..to the effect that his eyesight is such as to enable him to make accurate tests for inflammable gas.

c. In attributive use after its sb.

1771 *Encycl. Brit.* II. 695/2 At the point..K, such that the points K, H, and B may be in the same right line, let there be fixed a fourth staff. **1840** LARDNER *Geom.* 288 Let a distance CB be taken on the conjugate axis, such that the square of CB shall bear to the square of CA, the same ratio [etc.]. **1876** TREVELYAN *Macaulay* II. ix. 137 Statesmen, who had assumed an attitude such that they could not.. avoid being..insincere. **1895** THOMPSON & THOMAS *Electr. Tab. & Mem.* 60 The number of them is chosen such that in a cross section of the field [etc.].

d. With the clauses in reverse order, that containing *such* being explanatory of what precedes.

1362 LANGL. *P. Pl.* A. VII. 121 We mowe nouþur swynke ne swete, such seknes vs eileþ. **1567** ALLEN *Def. Priesth.* To Rdr., They remember well (such is theyr exercise in ye woord) how [etc.]. **1579** A. M[UNDAY] *Captiv. John Fox* in Hakluyt *Voy.* (1589) 154 There was no man that would take charge of a gally, the weather was so rough, and there was such an amasednes amongst them. *c* **1600** SHAKS. *Sonn.* lxxxi, You still shall liue (such vertue hath my Pen). **1673** G. FOX in *Jrnl. Friends' Hist. Soc.* (1914) July 98 The poore people ar redy to mutany in the market her is such a cry for corne to make them bread.

14. a. By suppression of the clause expressing comparison or relativity, *such* acquires an emphatic force = so great, so eminent, and the like.

c **893** ÆLFRED *Oros.* VI. i. 252 Mid þæm bryne hio wæs swa swiþe forhiened þæt hio næfre siþþan swelc næs. **1297** R. GLOUC. (Rolls) 796 Leuere he adde wende & bidde is mete ..in a strange londe þan þere as he him sulf king was & such þing adde an honde. *c* **1400** *Destr. Troy* 1725 My suster Exiona in seruage is holdyn, þat is comen of soche kyn, coldes my hert. *Ibid.* 11680 Seche trust haue the troiens truly þerin. **1598** SHAKS. *Merry W.* II. i 45 If it were not for one trifling respect, I could come to such honour. **1697** DRYDEN *Virg. Georg.* III. 717 When, after such a length of rowling Years, We see the naked Alps. **1849** MACAULAY *Hist. Eng.* x. II. 600 Never had there been such crowds in the churches.

b. *colloq.* Used as an absolute intensive, the implied clause of comparison being indeterminate and quite lost sight of.

ever such: see EVER *adv.* 9 b.

a **1553** UDALL *Royster D.* III. iii. (Arb.) 44 Ye shall not.. marry... Ye are such a calfe, such an asse, such a blocke. *a* **1616** BEAUM., etc. *Laws Candy* I. ii, How have I lost a Father? Such a Father! Such a one Decius! **1780** *Mirror* No. 93 He does little things, and talks of little things, with an air of such importance! *Ibid.*, A sad affair happened last night: my brother and sister had such a tiff! **1803** MARY CHARLTON *Wife & Mistress* IV. 87 'Lord bless me, no, Ma'am!' replied she: 'it's ever such a way off.' **1818** SCOTT *Br. Lamm.* x, To express himself churlishly..towards an old man, whose daughter (and *such* a daughter) lay before them. **1849** R. CURZON *Visits Monast.* 417 They were marvellously cool and delicious, and there were such quantities of them. **1891** 'J. S. WINTER' *Lumley* xiv, Oh! yes—such a happiness that it has all come right. **1900** W. GLYN *Visits of Elizabeth* (1906) 27 You would be amused at Vernon, where we stayed the night in *such* an inn!

15. a. Preceding an adj. used attrib., *such*, *such a* becomes advb. = so, so...a.

1522 SKELTON *Why not to Court* 652 Suche a madde bedleme For to rewle this reame, It is a wonders case. **1553** T. WILSON *Rhet.* 107 b, Mithridates..hadde suche an excellent memorie that [etc.]. **1591** SHAKS. *1 Hen. VI*, V. v. 84, I feele such sharpe dissention in my breast, Such fierce alarums both of Hope and Feare, As I am sicke with working of my thoughts. **1621** MOUNTAGU *Diatribæ* 507 Not to play such vnwise a part as those Thoes did. **1711** ADDISON *Spect.* No. 68 ¶3 If I were to give my Opinion upon such an exhausted Subject. **1742–3** LD. HERVEY in *Johnson's Debates* (1787) II. 320 This mighty army..collected from such distant parts. **1823** SCOTT *Quentin D.* xxxi, All comes of his gaining an archer's place at such early years. **1848** DICKENS *Dombey* xliv, His visage was in a state of such great dilapidation, as to be hardly presentable. **1863** MRS. OLIPHANT *Salem Chapel* ix. 143 In such a dark night as this, with such wet gleams about the streets. **1902** *Westm. Gaz.* 17 Dec. 12/1 Yes, I always liked Shakespeare; you know, he has *such* a nice face!

b. ***not such*** (***a***): = 'no such' (27 b).

1896 SAINTSBURY *Donne's Poems* I. p. xix, Chalmers, a very industrious student, and not such a bad critic.

III. (See also *such a one* 28 d.)

16. a. Used to indicate or suggest a name, designation, number, or quantity, where the speaker or writer prefers or is obliged to substitute a general phrase for the specific term that would be required in a particular instance.

c **1460** METHAM *Wks.* (E.E.T.S.) 155 Yff a man or a woman be born on sqwyche a day off the mone, ye schal conceyue that he ys, or sche ys, dysposyd so as to haue wurchyp, or ellys troubyl. **1526** TINDALE *James* iv. 13 Let vs go into soche a citie. **1544** tr. *Littleton's Tenures* 79 b, That the feoffour pay to the feoffee..such a sume at such a day. **1564** *Brief Exam.* C iiij b, It is..the part of..charitie..to leaue such vse of suche signes in such a Churche, free. **1664** in *Extr. St. Papers rel. Friends* Ser. III. (1912) 226, I inform'd my Lord..that..a greate number would meete att 2 of ye Clocke att such a house. **1755** SMOLLETT *Quix.* Pref. (1803) I. 6 The giant Golias,..whom the shepherd David slew..as it is written in such a chapter of the book of Kings. **1868** FREEMAN *Norm. Conq.* (1877) II. App. 588 The form always is that the King grants the bishopric or abbacy to such a person. **1913** *Oxf. Univ. Gaz.* 19 Feb. 495/2 This Diploma is to certify that A. B...attended a prescribed course of lectures..and (on such a date) satisfied..the examiners.

b. ***such and such.*** (rarely predicative.)

Hence ***such-and-suchness***, the quality or condition of being so-and-so.

1551 *Bible* 2 Kings vi. 8 In suche a place and in suche a place [**1560** *Geneva* In suche and suche a place] wyl I pitch. **1560** *Ibid.* (Geneva) 2 Sam. xii. 8, I..wolde moreouer.. haue giuen thee suche and suche things. **1565** J. HALLE *Hist. Expost.* 6 Suche men and suche enformed me that he can tell of thynges loste. **1611** SHAKS. *Cymb.* I. iii. 28 How I would thinke on him at certaine houres, Such thoughts, and such. **1625** HART *Anat. Ur.* II. v. 82 Vpon the feeding on such and such food it was no vncouth thing for him to voyd such an vrine. **1710** BERKELEY *Princ. Hum. Knowl.* §31 Wks. 1871 I. 171 Such and such ideas are attended with such and such other ideas. **1818** COBBETT *Pol. Reg.* XXXIII. 114, I shall.. proceed upon the supposition that the contents are such and such. **1855** THACKERAY *Newcomes* xlv, Lord and Lady Blank, of Suchandsuch Castle. **1861** T. A. TROLLOPE *La Beata* I. i. 2 Number so-and-so in such-and-such a street. **1885** SETH *Scot. Philos.* ii. 57 Every event has a character; is such-and-such an event. *Ibid.*, It is at its such-and-suchness, at its character—in other words, at the universal in it—that we have to look. **1899** E. CALLOW *Old Lond. Tav.* I. 247 It became the custom to ask what coffee-house such-and-such a man frequented.

†**c.** ***such or such***: this or that. *Obs.*

c **1530** *Judic. Urines* II. ii. 13 As ofte as I say suche vryne, or suche went beforn suche, or suche. **1676** GLANVILL *Ess. Philos. & Relig.* v. 23 Though I deny such, or such a sense [of a text]. **1695** DRYDEN tr. *Dufresnoy's Art. Paint.* Pref. p. xxxvii, The Posture of a Poetique Figure is as I conceive, the Description of his Heroes in the performance of such or such an Action. **1796** H. HUNTER tr. *St. Pierre's Study Nat.* (1799) I. 292 There is a greater distance between the understanding of Newton, and that of such or such a man, than between the understanding of that man and the instinct of an animal.

17. *Comb.* (parasynthetic.)

1591 SHAKS. *Two Gent.* IV. iv. 196 Such a colour'd Perrywig. **1597** BEARD *Theatre God's Judgem.* (1612) 425 Oh that we had..such minded captaines, that would sharply represse the wrongs..which are so common. **1711** STEELE *Spect.* No. 96 ¶4 A Lady that saw such a Gentleman at such a Place in such a coloured Coat.

IV. Absolute and pronominal uses.

†**18.** The persons or things before mentioned; those, they; also with sing. reference, that person or thing. *Obs.*

c **1000** ÆLFRIC *Hom.* I. 84 Eadiȝe sind þa innoðas þe hi ȝebæron, and ða breost þe swylce ȝesihton. *a* **1250** *Owl & Night.* (Jesus MS.) 1324 Hwat constu..of storre?.. Al so doþ mony deor and man, þeo of suyche no wiht ne can. *c* **1330** *Arth. & Merl.* 673 Swiche schuld acomber also fele, So þat oþer had brouȝt to wele. **1535** COVERDALE *Rom.* ii. 2 For we are sure that the iudgement of God is..ouer them that do soch. **1655** FULLER *Ch. Hist.* VIII. ii. §33 Such set to order Kingston Bridge did their work by halves.

19. a. Persons or things such as those mentioned, described, or referred to.

c **897** ÆLFRED *Gregory's Past. C.* xxxvii. 265 Oft eac ða swelcan monn sceal forsion mid eallum forsewennessum. **1382** WYCLIF *Gen.* xli. 19 Thes folweden other seuen oxen, in as myche defourme and leene, that neuer siche..Y sawȝ. **1390** GOWER *Conf.* I. 13 In the worldes reverence Ther ben of suche manie glade. *Ibid.* II. 43 Sone, thou art non of swiche, For Love schal the wel excuse. *c* **1450** tr. *De Imitatione* III. xxxv. 104 He takiþ non hede wheþer he illude ..by true or by false... Lete not þin herte þerfore be troubled ner drede suche. **1573** in Bridgett & Knox *Q. Eliz. & Cath. Hier.* (1889) vii. 112 Her Maiestie had choise ynough of souch at that tyme, and yet hath. **1634** MILTON *Comus* 15 To such my errand is. **1867** ROCK *Jim an' Nell* (E.D.S.) lxxxix, Let un beckon Hagegy Bess; wi' zich, I reckon, Ha now delight'th vor mang.

b. ***and such***: and suchlike, and the like.

[*a* **1400–50** *Wars Alex.* 1889 Þe somme of siluer & of siche & of sere stanes.] **1652** *News fr. Lowe-Countr.* 6 Cures Collicks, Belly-Ach, and such. **1849** J. G. SAXE *Poems, Proud Miss MacBride* xix, Little by little he grew to be rich, By saving of candle-ends and sich. **1894** MRS. DYAN *Man's Keeping* (1899) 203 A smaller table held ices, squashes, and such. **1904** *Windsor Mag.* Jan. 296/2 A little place hung about with Eastern draperies and altar-cloths and such.

20. a. With dependent rel. pron.: Such people *as*, those (people) *who*, *whose*, etc.; all or any *that*.

In OE. and ME. also sing. = such a man.

835 *Charter* in *O.E. Texts* 448 Swælcum se hit ȝeðian wile. *a* **1225** *Ancr. R.* 84 He misseið bi swuche þet is cwic in God. *Ibid.* 382 Ich wot swulne þet bereð boðe togedere heui brunie and here. **1377** LANGL. *P. Pl.* B. x. 26 Þe sauter seyth þe same bi suche þat don ille. *c* **1386** CHAUCER *Melib.* ¶45 By ..assent of swiche as weren wise. *c* **1400** *Pilgr. Sowle* (Caxton 1483) IV. xxxiv. 82 The gouernement of a reame shold be..executed by suche as were of grettest bounte. *c* **1489** CAXTON *Sonnes of Aymon* ix. 208 Ye aske counseyll of suche that canne not counseyl theymselfe. **1523** LD. BERNERS *Froiss.* I. ccvii. 245 We may fortune to mete with suche that shall pay for our scotte. **1563** HYLL *Art Garden.* (1593) 143 This being also drunk, helpeth such which be stopped in the brest. **1613** SHAKS. *Hen. VIII*, I. i. 76 Such To whom as great a Charge, as little Honor He meant to lay vpon. **1625** MASSINGER *New Way* II. i, Such whose fathers were right worshipful. **1748** G. WHITE *Serm.* (MS.) To such from whom we look for advantages. **1777** W. CAMERON in *Transl. & Paraphr. Ch. Scot.* xiv. 1 Let such as would with Wisdom dwell, frequent the house of woe. **1800** SYD. SMITH *Six Serm.* 65 Such of their fellow-creatures who have fixed their faith in an amiable and benevolent religion. **1829** in *Nairne Peerage Evidence* (1874) 76 Such of you to whom it may appertain to issue and pay..the said annuity. **1876** SWINBURNE *Note Engl. Repub.* 21 The mere love-offering of preserved souls and such whose minds are dedicated to nothing temporal.

b. People of the same kind *as*.

1823 SCOTT *Quentin D.* xvi, Such as I are free in spirit when our limbs are chained. **1850** TENNYSON *In Mem.* xxxiv, What then were God to such as I? **1869** SIR F. H. DOYLE *Lect.* iii. 96 To consider whether it be not to such as him, rather than to such as them, that we ought to look.

21. a. Such a thing; the thing mentioned or referred to.

Beowulf 996 Wundorsiona fela secga ȝehwylcum, þara þe on swylc starað. *a* **900** CYNEWULF *Elene* 571 (Gr.) Cwædon þæt hio on aldre owiht swylces ne ær ne sið æfre hyrdon. **1154** *O.E. Chron.* (Laud MS.) an. 1137 Suilc & mare þanne we cunnen sæin we þolenden. *c* **1175** *12th Cent. Hom.* 30 Heo dweloden swyðe þa ða heo swylces axoden. *c* **1380** WYCLIF *Sel. Wks.* III. 436 Ȝif a best bad a man do siche. **1845** BAILEY *Festus* (ed. 2) 77 Do Thou grant, Lord! That when wrongs are to be redressed, such may Be done with mildness. **1885** LELAND *Brand-New Ball.* 127 Ye are goin' for the summer to the islands by the sea,..setch is not for setch as me.

†**b.** With correl. or rel. Such a thing..(as). *Obs.*

c **893** ÆLFRED *Oros.* I. x. 48 Hit is scondlic..ymb swelc to sprecanne hwelc hit þa wæs. *a* **1250** *Prov. Ælfred* 83 in *O.E. Misc.* 106 Hwych so þe mon soweþ al swuch he schal mowe. **1390** GOWER *Conf.* I. 178 Ofte swich as men beginne Towardes othre, swich thei finde, That set hem ofte fer behinde, Whan that thei wene be before.

†**c.** ***such as***: that which, what, whatever.

c **1340** *Medit. Passion* in *Hampole's Wks.* (1895) I. 92 Graunte me grace..euere to knouleche me for sich as I am, a sinful wrecche. *c* **1440** *Alphabet of Tales* 184 He sett befor þaim suche as he had in his cell. *c* **1460** *Towneley Myst.* xxvii. 278 Ye ar welcom..To sich as we haue. **1474** CAXTON *Chesse* II. iv. (1883) 51 After that he had eten suche as plesid hym he voyded the mete. **1484** —— *Fables of Æsop* I. xi, He that is wyse must not..take hede to his wordes but lete hym go for suche as he is. **1568** tr. *Thevet's New found worlde* xxv. 41 The Indians..brought vs thither suche as the land.. bringeth forth.

22. Referring to a descriptive sb. or phrase (cf. 4).

c **1430** *Pilgr. Lyf Manhode* IV. xxxi. (1869) 193 Alle knyhtes that hauen swerdes resceyuen not swiche colees. Gret joye it were..if thei hadden swiche. **1477** EARL RIVERS (Caxton) *Dictes* 11 b, Ware the of the wordes of lyers, and suche punysshe. **1565** HARDING *Answ. Jewel* 211 If he had offered bread and wine onely,..it had ben no newe oblation, for such had been made by Melchisedech. **1581** MARBECK *Bk. Notes* 494 With him that is holie, virtuous, and good, a man (keeping companie with such) shall have a smacke of his holinesse. *a* **1637** B. JONSON *Discov., De vita humana* (1640) 105 Like Children, that imitate the vices of Stammerers so long, till at last they become such. **1662** J. DAVIES tr. *Olearius' Voy. Ambass.* 402 They were forc'd to..travel so arm'd to secure themselves against the Robbers thereabouts: but they looked more like such themselves. *a* **1700** EVELYN *Diary* 2 Dec. 1666, To examine whether the soile..would be proper to make clinker-bricks, and to treate with me about some accomodation in order to making such. **1771** *Encycl. Brit.* II. 698/1 It were easy to transfer to the diameter of a circle the chords of all arches to the extent of a semicircle; but such are rarely found marked upon rules. **1828** SCOTT *Aunt Marg. Mirror* ii, Two or three low broad steps led to a platform in front of the altar, or what resembled such. **1848** THACKERAY *Bk. Snobs* xiii, He will not have his young friends to be snobs in the future, or to be bullied by snobs, or given over to such to be educated. **1889** GEIKIE in *Nature* 19 Sept. 486 To call for more facts and experiments, if such are possible. **1912** *Eng. Hist. Rev.* Jan. 27 A forest became such by a stroke of the pen, not by any physical change.

23. ***such and such***: such and such persons or things; also *sing.*, this and this.

a **1450** *Knt. de la Tour* xv, He saide..that suche and suche had saine her do hit. **1574** HELLOWES *Gueuara's Fam. Ep.* (1577) 310 Not contented to take the wheat, [etc.]..to giue vnto such and such out of yᵉ doores. **1576** FLEMING tr. *Caius' Dogs* (1880) 34 Giuing warnyng to them of the house, that such & such be newly come. **1602** SHAKS. *Ham.* II. i. 57, I saw him yesterday, or tother day; Or then or then, with such and such. **1893** F. ADAMS *New Egypt* 147 We have done such, and such, and such.

V. Uses with special classes of words and in idiomatic phrases.

* *In collocation with indef. adjs., numerals, etc.*

When used absol. the phrases in 24–27 become a kind of composite pronouns.

24. With *many* (*more*), *any*, *some*, *all*, *every*: many (etc.)...of the (same) kind, many...like this. Also in phr. ***or some such*** (also ***somesuch***): or some such thing.

With a sing. sb. the construction *many a such*, *any such a*, etc. was formerly common.

c **888** ÆLFRED *Boeth.* xxxiv. §6 Ðeþyld & rihtwisnes & wisdom, & maneȝe swelce cræftas. *a* **1225** *Ancr. R.* 382 Ȝif eni mon ei swuch þing ortroweð bi him. *c* **1380** WYCLIF *Sel. Wks.* III. 443 When ony suche men asken þe sacrid ooste. **1382** —— *Eph.* v. 27 Not hauynge wem, or spot,..or ony such thing. *c* **1400** *Rom. Rose* 7123 Many a such comparisoun. *a* **1425** *Cursor M.* (Trin.) 13712 Moises wol we alle suche stone. **1526** TINDALE *Mark.* ix. 37 Whosoever receave eny soche a chylde in my name, he receaveth me. **1548** UDALL, etc. *Erasm. Par. Luke* xvii. 134 Beefore ye haue any perceiueraunce that any suche thyng is to come. **1548–9** (Mar.) *Bk. Com. Prayer, Litany*, All suche as haue erred and are deceyued. **1549** T. SOME *Latimer's 2nd Serm. bef. Edw. VI* To Rdr. (Arb.) 53 A fewe moo suche Preachers. **1550** CRANMER *Let. to Voysey* in *Misc. Writ.* (Parker Soc.) 428 All such benefices..as..have been..impropried. **1570** GOOGE *Pop. Kingd.* III. 33 Masse blesseth euery such as seekes in welthie state to bee. **1599** SHAKS. *Much Ado* V. iv. 49 Some such strange bull leapt your fathers Cow. **1607** HIERON *Wks.* I. 241 Euery such shall bee cut off by the hand of God. **1653** H. MORE *Antid. Ath.* (1662) 97 A many such miracles. **1663** BUTLER *Hud.* I. i. 356 He ne'er gave quarter t' any such. **1778** MISS BURNEY *Evelina* xvi, I never kept company with any such gentry. **1832** BREWSTER *Nat. Magic* xiii. 331 Several such strata. **1836** THIRLWALL *Greece* xviii. (1839) 77 If we may properly attribute any such objects to him. **1837** LOCKHART *Scott* IV. vii. 222 Some such excursion had been ..recommended to him by his own physicians. **1895** BARING-GOULD *Noémi* xxiv, Some such a colourless, cadaverous light as that which [etc.]. **1967** D. FRANCIS *Blood Sport* iii. 35 He was in France on business wasn't he, or somesuch. **1972** *Daily Tel.* 11 Apr. 22/5 Plan will be to approach them with proposals for short and sharp bursts of selling with stamps—stamp weeks or somesuch. **1973** R. PARKES *Guardians* vii. 122 The doctor believed it might aid expiation or abreaction or some such.

25. ***such other*** (arch.), †***other such***; as pron. ***such others***, arch. ***other such***. Phr. †***and such other***, and the like, and such-like.

c **888** ÆLFRED *Boeth.* xxiv. §3 On swilcum & on oðrum swelcum lænum & hreosendum weorðscipum. *c* **1000** ÆLFRIC *Exod.* vii. 11 Hiȝ worhton oðer swilc þing þurh hira dry-cræft. *a* **1225** *Ancr. R.* 242 Þeos & oðer swuche dredfule þouhtes. *a* **1425** LANGL. *P. Pl.* A. I. 104 (MS. U) [Cherubin and Seraphin] and siche mo oþere. *c* **1450** *Brut.* II. ccxxvii. 299 Ploghmen, & such oþer laborers. *c* **1482** J. KAY tr. *Caoursin's Siege of Rhodes* ¶5 Gorones, culuerynes, serpentines and such other. **1530** PALSGR. 463/2, I brede a chylde, or brede yonge, as a woman or any other suche beest dothe. **1532** *Dial. on Laws Eng.* II. xlii. 106 A Captayne.. shall be bounde for the offence of hys squyres And an hoste for his ghest and such other. **1588** KYD *Househ. Philos.* Wks. (1901) 268 By fires, tempests, inundations, and other such. **1600** J. PORY tr. *Leo's Africa* II. 94 Either cheese, butter, milk, or any other such commoditie. **1707** FREIND *Peterborow's Cond. Sp.* 131 Such other place as shall be judged proper. **1725** DE FOE *Voy. round World* (1840) 86 Roots, yams, mangoes, and such other articles. **1762** KAMES *Elem. Crit.* xviii. §iv. (1774) II. 122 *Observance, opponent*,.. and such others of three syllables. **1867** SWINBURNE *Blake* (1868) 150 Behmen, Swedenborg, or such others. **1871** RUSKIN *Fors Clav.* x. 15 There are, indeed, other such in the world.

26. a. ***such another***, ***another such***: another... of the kind, another similar. (Rarely ***another such a***, †***such a...such another***: one... another, with a sing. sb.)

Such another is used idiomatically in Shakespeare, where we should now say simply either (*a*) 'such (a)', as in *Two Gent.* III. i. 133, *Tr. & Cr.* I. ii. 282 (Fo. 1), or (*b*) 'another', 'a second', as in *Merry W.* I. iv. 160.

a **1300** *Sat. People Kildare* iv. in *E.E.P.* (1862) 153 Soch an oþir an erþe i note. *c* **1375** *Cursor M.* 1942 (Fairf.) For nankyn chaunce sal I take suche a-noþer veniaunce. *a* **1553** UDALL *Roister D.* III. v. (Arb.) 56 *R. Royster.* Did not you make me a letter brother? *Scriuener.* Pay the like hire, I will make you suche an other. **1594** SHAKS. *Rich. III*, I. iv. 5, I would not spend another such a night. **1597** —— *2 Hen IV*, II. iv. 275 Such other Gamboll Faculties hee hath..for the which the Prince admits him; for the Prince himselfe is such another. **1620** E. BLOUNT *Horæ Subs.* 352 Heere are besides the ancient Statues of the Horatij and Curiatij, and such another of Neroes Mother as I haue mentioned to be in the Capitoll. **1623** MIDDLETON *More Dissemblers* V. ii, How? such another word, down goes your hose, boy. **1684** ROSCOMMON *Ess. Transl. Verse* 258 Another Such had left the Nation thin, In spight of all the Children he brought in. **1720** *Humourist* 65 Such a Person can do nothing ill, and such another..nothing well. **1756** AMORY *Buncle* (1770) I. 173 She was such another genius as Chubb. **1852** MRS. STOWE *Uncle Tom's C.* xxix. 273 We'll never get another such a master. **1861** T. L. PEACOCK *Gryll Grange* xxxii, That chance has passed from her; and she will not easily find such another. **1867** SWINBURNE *Blake* (1868) 180 The 'frowning babe' of the last stanzas is..the same or such another as the one whose birth is first spoken of. **1871** RUSKIN *Fors Clav.* v, No foolish being..will ever be capable of saying such another foolish thing.

b. Similarly ***such a second***.

1828 SCOTT *Tapestr. Chamb.* (*ad med.*), I would not run the risk of such a second night.

27. ***no*** (†***none***) ***such*** adj., rarely †***no such a***; absol. or as pron. now only ***none such*** (cf. NONESUCH, NONSUCH), formerly ***no such*** (and †***such none***). **a.** No (person or thing) of the kind; none of the kind.

a **900** CYNEWULF *Crist* 290 Nan swylc ne cwom æniȝ oþer ofer ealle men. *a* **1122** *O.E. Chron.* (Laud MS.) an 1032 Her ..atywde þæt wildefyr ðe nan mann æror nan swylc ne ȝemunde. *a* **1225** *Ancr. R.* 96 Ne chastie ȝe neuer nenne swuchne mon bute o þisse wise. **1297** R. GLOUC. (Rolls) 3063 In þe world such non is. **13..** *Guy Warw.* (C.) 122 On this half the see noon suche was. *a* **1400** *Minor Poems fr. Vernon MS.* xxix. ii. 69 Þe Iew..seide þer nas non such child þrinne. *c* **1430** *Pilgr. Lyf Manhode* IV. lix. (1869) 205 Ther sook neuere noon non swich milk ne droouh noon swich brest. **1535** COVERDALE *Ecclus.* xlv. 13 Before him were there sene no soch fayre ornamentes. **1535** —— *Acts* xxi. 25 We haue wrytten, and concluded, that they shulde obserue no soch, but onely [etc.]. **1582** STANYHURST *Æneis*, etc. (Arb.) 145 Syth mye nose owtpeaking, good syr, your liplabor hindreth, Hardlye ye may kisse mee, where no such gnomon apeereth. **1601** R. HOLTBY in *Archpr. Controv.* (Camden) I. 185 They had no such ignorance that could excuse them admittinge that he was a superior. **1607** HIERON *Wks.* I. 237 No such shall inherite the kingdome of Christ and of God. **1647** TRAPP *Marrow Gd. Authors* in *Comm. Ep.* 697 The Emperour Commodus would needs be stiled ὑπεραίρων, or the Surpasser, as if there were none such. **1663** BUTLER *Hud.* I. i. 44 'Tis plain enough he was no such. **1749** BERKELEY *Word to Wise* Wks. 1871 III. 440 There can be no such thing as happy life without labour. **1774** tr. *Helvetius' Child of Nature* II. 86, I would..have no such a tête à tête with such a man. **1831** SCOTT *Cast. Dang.* ix, 'Who was it passed through your post even now, with the traitorous cry of Douglas?' 'We know of no such.' **1849** MACAULAY *Hist. Eng.* vi. II. 119 Objection was taken by some zealous Protestants to the mention made of the Roman Catholic religion. There was no such religion. **1867** SWINBURNE in *Fortn. Rev.* Oct. 428 There is no such thing as a dumb poet or a handless painter.

b. No great; advb. qualifying as adj. (cf. 15 b) = not (a) very, not a. †***nothing such***: nothing of any account.

1579 SPENSER *Sheph. Cal.* Sept. 79, I thought the soyle would haue made me rich: But nowe I wote, it is nothing sich. **1606** SHAKS. *Ant. & Cl.* III. iii. 44 Why me think's by him, This Creature's no such thing. **1612** BACON *Ess., Death* (Arb.) 384 Death is no such enemy, when a man hath so many followers about him. **1663** DRYDEN *Wild Gallant* I, If that be all, there's no such hast. **1695** CONGREVE *Love for L.* V. i, Fifty in a hale constitution, is no such contemptible age. **1773** GOLDSM. *Stoops to Conq.* V. ii, Five-and-twenty miles in two hours and a half is no such bad driving. **1782** MISS BURNEY *Cecilia* v. xii, As you happen to be quite alone, a little agreeable company would be no such bad thing. **1867** M. ARNOLD *Celtic Lit.* 87 So long as Celt and Teuton are.. at least, no such great while out of their cradle. **1870** W. MORRIS *Earthly Par.* III. 279 Clad in attire of no such wretched price.

c. Phr. ***no such*** †***matter*** or ***thing***: nothing of the kind; also exclamatorily, = not at all, not a bit of it, quite the contrary.

1538 POLE *Let.* in Strype *Eccl. Mem.* (1721) I. App. lxxxiii. 213 Neither you nor no man else..can bring no such thing against mine opinion. **1560** *Bible* (Geneva) 2 Sam. xiii. 12 No suche thing oght to be done in Israel: commit not this folie. **1584** PEELE *Arraignm. Paris* I. i, *Pan.* We meet not now to brawl. *Faun.* There's no such matter, Pan. **1588** GREENE *Pandosto* Wks. (Grosart) IV. 267 The goodman..desired her to be quiet, for there was non such matter. *c* **1600** SHAKS. *Sonn.* lxxxvii, In sleepe a King, but waking no such matter. **1755** GRAY *Let. to Chute* 14 Aug., They thought me rheumatic and feverish, no such thing! **1814** L. HUNT *Feast Poets*, etc. (1815) 60 The vices..are only 'imputed' to him; —to use a pithy and favourite mode of quotation, 'There's no such thing!' **1867** AUGUSTA WILSON *Vashti* xv, I shall do no such thing.

28. such a(n) one, formerly also †**such one**, freq. as one word †**suchon**.

a. Such a person or thing as that specified or referred to; one of that kind.

c **1375** *Cursor M.* 85 (Fairf.) Of suche an [*Cott.* suilk an] sulde men mater take. *c* **1380** WYCLIF *Wks.* (1880) 47 Þei schullen presenten hym to þe nexte custode of þat place where euere þei fynden sychon. **1390** GOWER *Conf.* I. 47 Ther is manye of yow Faitours, and so may be that thow Art riht such on. *c* **1400** *Pilgr. Sowle* (Caxton 1483) IV. xxxiii. 82 Good ryght is that vpon suche one be take vengeaunce. **1535** COVERDALE *Job* xiv. 3 Thinkest thou it now well done, to open thine eyes vpon soch one? **1559** AYLMER *Harborowe*

F ij, It is a great enterprise..to pulle a quenes crowne of hir head: and specially such a ones. **1594** O. B. *Quest. Profit. Concern.* L ij b, Such ones are said to harrow hell, to make their sonnes Gentlemen. **1654** O. SEDGWICK *Fun. Serm.* 15 The death of such a one is an exceeding loss. **1732** MANDEVILLE *Enq. Origin Honour* 166 To such a one, a Clergyman should preach the Strictness of Morality. **1816** HAZLITT *Pol. Ess.* (1819) 82 A Jacobin is one who would haue his single opinion govern the world... Such a one is Mr. Southey. **1885** SWINBURNE *Misc.* (1886) 298 Such an one..is by common consent a blackguard.

b. Followed by rel. pron. *as*, formerly †*that*, etc.: One of the kind that; one who, a thing which.

1390 GOWER *Conf.* I. 96 He mot him binde To such on which of alle kinde Of wommen is thunsemlieste. *c* **1400** MAUNDEV. (1839) 287 Suche an on as is of gode maneres. **1530** CROMWELL in Merriman *Life & Lett.* (1902) I. 330 Dilligent and honest And suchon that..wilbe gladde to serue your grace in any thing. **1539** *Great Bible* Ps. lxviii. 21 The hearie scalpe of soch one [**1611** such a one] as goeth on still in his wyckednes. **1583** STOCKER *Civ. Warres Lowe C.* IV. 23 He was a verie noble young Prince, and such a one as in whom, was great hope of good. **1599** SHAKS. *Much Ado* V. i. 7 Such a one whose wrongs doth sute with mine. **1673** O. WALKER *Educ.* 235 Such a one..as is a discreet and virtuous person. **1884** SWINBURNE *Misc.* (1886) 28 He was merely a royalist, and such an one as may be bred and reared out of the middle class.

c. Followed by rel. adv. *as*: One of the same kind as; one like (so-and-so).

c **1400** *26 Pol. Poems* 111 Wiþ suchon as I to make debat. **1535** COVERDALE *Ps.* xlix. 21 Thou..thinkest me to be euen soch one as thy self. **1596** HARINGTON *Apol. Ajax* (1814) 21 A passing proud fellow. Such a one as Naaman the Syrian. **1611** *Bible* Philem. 9 Being such a one as Paul the aged. **1726** WELSTED *Dissemb. Wanton* Wks. (1787) 5 By marrying some commodious person; such a one as Mr. Toby. **1868** THIRLWALL *Lett.* (1881) II. 195 It was just such a one as that which was the occasion of Wordsworth's sonnet. **1885** SWINBURNE *Misc.* (1886) 225 Such an one as these.

d. A certain one not specifically named (see 16); So-and-so. *Obs.* or *arch.*

1560 *Bible* (Geneva) Ruth iv. 1 Ho, suche one [**1611** such a one], come, sit downe here. **1566** *Pasquine in Traunce* 24 Then did the coniurer aske, whether he was such a one or such a one, naming many and sundry persons that dyed long ago. **1603** SHAKS. *Meas. for M.* II. i. 114 That such a one, and such a one, were past cure of the thing you wot of. **1678** OTWAY *Friendship in F.* I. i, He hath been with my Lord such-a-one. **1712** ARBUTHNOT *John Bull* II. iii, Instead of plain Sir and Madam..he calls us Goody and Gaffer such a one. **1798** W. HUTTON *Life* (1816) 52 [She] mentioned several such-a-ones who solicited her hand. **1812** BYRON *Waltz* xiii, Sir—Such-a-one. **1832** HT. MARTINEAU *Hill & Valley* (1843) 162 They said that 'neighbour such-a-one was a prisoner'.

†**e.** As adj. following the sb.: Such *as*. *Obs.*

1535 COVERDALE *1 Macc.* iv. 47 They..buylded a new aulter soch one as was before. **1546** J. HEYWOOD *Prov.* (1867) 64 A larom suche one As folke ring bees with basons. *a* **1716** SOUTH in Chambers *Cycl. Eng. Lit.* I. 465/1 Sensuality is..one kind of pleasure, such a one as it is.

29. Miscellaneous.

a. ***such much***: so much, thus much.

1832 CARLYLE *Let. to J. Carlyle* 2 July, Such much for Annandale, where you see there are..many mercies still allotted to us.

†**b.** ***what such***: of what kind. *Obs.*

1671 H. M. tr. *Erasm. Colloq.* 152 What such soever an one thy husband be. *Ibid.* 555 Consider here with me what such they be.

†**c.** ***who such***: such as, whoever. *Obs.*

1667 MARVELL *Corr.* Wks. (Grosart) II. 226 That you may returne who such take it [*sc.* an oath].

†**d.** ***such a like, such...like***: = SUCH-LIKE.

1474 *Cov. Leet Bk.* 389 Intrelles of bestes or such filthy thyng like. **1541** SIR T. WYATT *Let. to Privy Counc.* in *Poet. Wks.* (1858) p. xxxiv, Alleging that he had once swerved from him in such a like matter. **1577** VAUTROUILLIER *Luther on Ep. Gal.* 95 Such a like thing of late happened to that miserable man Doctor Kraus of Hal. **1608** [see LIKE *a.* 1 d].

e. ***such a few, such a many*** (colloq.): so few, so many.

1841 THACKERAY *Gt. Hogg Diam.* xiii, No one could have thought it could have done such a many things in that time.

30. Preceding a poss. pron., as ***such his*** = that or this (those or these) of his. Rarely with correlative *as*. *Obs.* or *arch.*

1565 ALLEN *Def. Purg.* (1886) 6, I..submit myself to the judgment of such our masters..as..are made the lawful pastors of our souls. **1581** —— *Apologie* 121 God giueth not the tast of such his comfortes to any, but [etc.]. **1600** W. WATSON *Decacordon* (1602) 265 Such their friends as they themselues made choice of. **1647** CLARENDON *Hist. Reb.* IV. §13 The Minister..Resisted such their Licence. **1709** STEELE *Tatler* No. 1 ⁋1, I shall..publish such my Advices and Reflections. **1787** *Minor* IV. xix. 307 A few words of such my personages as have not previously been..disposed of. **1837** SIR F. PALGRAVE *Merch. & Friar* Dedic. p. xxi, When you pay such your visit to the civic muniment room.

31. With a cardinal numeral, which now always precedes *such*: (So many) of that kind, or of the kind *that*.

1297 R. GLOUC. (Rolls) 439 Hii hadde suche þritti men as were in hor side. **1377** LANGL. *P. Pl.* B. I. 106 Cherubyn and seraphin suche seuene and an-othre. *c* **1530** LD. BERNERS *Arth. Lyt. Bryt.* (1814) 334 He had to do all at ones wyth suche vi. as syr Rowland is. *a* **1568** ASCHAM *Scholem.* II. (Arb.) 107 This golden sentence, diuerslie wrought upon, by soch foure excellent Masters. **1575** GASCOIGNE *Posies, Notes Instruct.* Wks. 1907 I. 471 Rythme royall is a verse of tenne sillables, and seven such verses make a staffe. **1582** N. LICHEFIELD tr. *Castanheda's Conq. E. Ind.* 16 Since it was so expedient to have a Pilot, the Generall then requested to have two such. **1600** SHAKS. *A.Y.L.* IV. i. 119 *Orl.* And wilt thou haue me? *Ros.* I, and twentie such. **1634** MILTON *Comus* 575 The..innocent Lady..gently ask't if he had seen such two. **1709** J. WARD *Introd. Math.* IV. ii. (1734) 367 By the Rectangle of any two Abscissa's is meant the Rectangle of such two parts as, being added together, will be equal to the Transverse Diameter. **1766** FORDYCE *Serm. Yng. Women* (1767) I. i. 70 What is the shallow admiration of an hundred such? **1820** BYRON *Juan* III. lxxxvi. x, Of two such lessons, why forget The nobler and the manlier one?

†**32.** With a cardinal numeral *such* is used to denote multiplication by the number in question; e.g. ***such five*** (*as* or *so*) = five times as many or as much (as). *Obs.*

OE. *oþer swilc* = as much or as many more; *swilc healf* = half as much.

Beowulf 1583 Slæpende fræt folces Denigea fyftyne men and oðer swylc ut offerede. *c* **1000** *Sax. Leechd.* II. 180 ðenim þæs selestan wines & grenes eles swilc healf. *Ibid.* 214 þry lytle bollan fullan gemengde wiþ swilc tu wæteres. *c* **1290** *S. Eng. Leg.* 102 þat is suych a pouſent more wurth þanne al þat þing þat is. *a* **1300** *Floriz & Bl.* 360 Grante him þat þu wilt so, And tak mid amoreȝe suche two. *c* **1369** CHAUCER *Dethe Blaunche* 408 To have moo floures swiche seven As in the walkene sterris bee. **1387** TREVISA *Higden* (Rolls) VI. 83 He hadde suche þre so hardy men in his oost as þe oþer hadde in his. *c* **1412** HOCCLEVE *De Reg. Princ.* 1195, I se þou woldest sorowe swyche two As I. **1470–85** MALORY *Arthur* X. viii. 426 He is able to bete suche fyue as ye and I be.

** *In phrases with sbs.*

33. ***such kind***, † ***sort***, † ***such*** (***a***) ***manner*** (***of***), † ***of such manner***: of such a kind.

1303 R. BRUNNE *Handl. Synne* 243 þy god ys of swych manere, þogh þou forsake hym ryght now here, To-morwe mayst þou com aȝeyn. *Ibid.* 1737 Aȝens swyche maner wyuys þat wyl nat amende here lyuys. *a* **1325** *MS. Rawl. B. 520* lf. 52 Of suuche manere felonies. **1340** *Ayenb.* 10 Kueade wordes of zuyche manere. *c* **1380** WYCLIF *Wks.* (1880) 390 To occupie siche maner londe or lordeschip. **1382** —— *Gen.* xliii. 32 A fowle thing thei wenen sich a manere feeste. *a* **1450** MYRC 39 Wrastelynge, & schotynge, & suche maner game. **1470–85** [see MANNER *sb.*[1] 9]. **1513** MORE in Grafton *Chron.* (1568) II. 788 If suche kind of wordes had not bene. *a* **1542** WYATT in *Tottel's Misc.* (Arb.) 37, I am not of such maner condicion. *c* **1645** HOWELL *Lett.* II. liv. (1892) 453 A holy kind of liquor made of such sort of flowers. **1670** ROBERTS *Advent. T.S.* 200 When such kind of Reports are imprinted into the Fancy of the People. **1709** J. WARD *Introd. Math.* III. i. §5. (1734) 290 Of such kind of Polygons there are infinite Varieties. **1804–6** [see SORT *sb.*[2] 7 b]. **1841** F. E. PAGET *Tales of Village* (1852) 488 Such kind of things are not uncommon..among gay young men.

34. a. † ***in such manner***: in this or that way. ***in such manner*** or † ***sort as***: in the way that, as.

1297 R. GLOUC. (Rolls) 7779 So þat þe king in such manere suluer wan ynou. **1484** CAXTON *Fables of Auian* vii, He prayd in suche maner as foloweth. **1552** WEST *1st Pt. Symbol.* §100 g, The one doth..couenant with the other to doe..some..thing or things in such sort as they haue concluded therof amongst themselues. **1628** HOBBES *Thucydides* (1822) 47 In such sort as it should seem best. **1709** BERKELEY *Th. Vision* §72 The Faintness, which enlarges the Appearance, must be applied in such Sort, and with such Circumstances, as have been observed to attend the Vision of great Magnitudes. **1818** CRUISE *Digest* (ed. 2) IV. 395 In such sort, manner, and form..as the husband should thereafter..appoint.

b. ***in such*** (***a***) ***manner*** or ***sort*** (arch.) ***as, as that, that***: in such a way that, so that.

1449 J. METHAM Wks. (E.E.T.S.) 301 Help me to adorune ther chauns in sqwyche manere, So that [etc.]. **1560** DAUS tr. *Sleidane's Comm.* 169 b, Themperour answereth yᵉ protestantes Ambassadours..in suche sorte as it coulde not be wel perceived, whether [etc.]. **1576** FLEMING *Panopl. Epist.* 59, I will write of my selfe..in such sort, that I varie not from the president..of many noble..personages. *c* **1600** SHAKS. *Sonn.* xcvi. 13, I loue thee in such sort As thou being mine, mine is thy good report. **1625** BACON *Ess., Cunning* (Arb.) 437 Let him..moue it himselfe, in such sort, as may foile it. **1665** BUNYAN *Holy Citie* To Rdr. A ij b, That one so low..as I, should busie my self in such sort, as to meddle [etc.]. **1668** MOXON *Mech. Dyalling* 10 Apply one of the sides of your Clinatory..to the Plane, in such sort that the Plumb-line..may fall upon the Circumference of the Quadrant. **1712** ADDISON *Spect.* No. 321 ⁋30 In such a manner as they shall not be missed. **1771** *Encycl. Brit.* II. 693/2 An index..which..is joined to the centre A, in such manner as that it can move round. **1821** SHELLEY *Let. to Ollier* 8 June in *Mem.* (1859) 135 In such a manner as it shall be difficult for the reviser to leave such errors. **1825** SCOTT *Betrothed* Concl., Damian shrunk together in such sort that his fetters clashed. **1885** FINLAYSON *Biol. Relig.* 31 But the man who is spiritually dead is, at the same time, in such sort living, that [etc.].

†**35.** ***such-a-thing*** = Thingumbob, What's-his-name. (Cf. F. *Monsieur Chose.*) *Obs.*

1756 MRS. CALDERWOOD in *Coltness Collect.* (Maitland Club) 185 Who knows who Mr. Such-a-thing is?

36. ***such time as*** (or ***that***): the time when, the moment at which. (rarely with *as* omitted.) Occas. used (quot. 1634) as conjunctional phr. = When, while; also pleonastically with *when* (quot. 1607). *Obs.* or *arch.*

1411 *Rolls of Parlt.* III. 650/2 Atte such resonable tyme as it likyth the forsaid Lord the Roos to assigne. **1518** in Leadam *Sel. Cases Crt. Requests* (Selden Soc.) 15 Vnto suche tyme as he..payde vnto the seid John for his fees ix.s. **1550** in *Rep. Hist. MSS. Comm.* (1907) Var. Coll. IV. 220 Untyll suche tyme that Mr. Meyor..shall take any order for the same. **1607** SHAKS. *Cor.* III. iii. 19 And when such time they haue begun to cry, Let them not cease. **1611** *Bible* Transl. Pref. ⁋2 At such time as the professours and teachers of Christianitie..were liberally endowed. **1634** SIR T. HERBERT *Trav.* 82 He attained the Georgian Confines, in a darke night, such time as the Persians slept. **1660** WOOD *Life* (O.H.S.) I. 349 Till such time the sickness is ceased in their house. *a* **1761** LAW *Comf. Weary Pilgr.* (1809) 16 Till such time as something has disturbed his state.

37. (See also SUCHWISE.) **a.** ***in*** (†***on***) ***such*** (***a***) ***wise***: in such a manner, so, thus. *arch.*

c **1375** *Cursor M.* 3292 (Fairf.) He..saide til hir on suche a wise, mayden saide he [etc.]. **1390** GOWER *Conf.* I. 1 So that it myhte in such a wyse..Beleve to the worldes eere. *c* **1440** *Generydes* 34 Gret pite that she in suche a wyse Shuld sette hyr wurchippe atte so litill prise. *a* **1555** LATIMER *Serm. & Rem.* (Parker Soc.) 149 Whoso in such wise fighteth with the devil, shall have the victory. **1838** MRS. BROWNING *Isobel's Child* vii, All smiles come in such a wise, Where tears shall fall or have of old. **1887** MORRIS *Odyss.* XII. 294 Eurylochus spake in suchwise. **1913** D. BRAY *Life-Hist. Brahui* i. 5 She believes that in such wise will it be given life.

b. ***in*** (†***by***, †***on***, †***upon***) ***such wise***: in such a manner, so *that*, *as to*.

a **1225** *Leg. Kath.* 1956 þis pinfule gin wes o swuch wise iginet, þet [etc.]. *a* **1450** *Knt. de la Tour* xvii, To be ielous..in suche wise as to shame hym selff and his wiff. *c* **1477** CAXTON *Jason* 24 The raynes of his horse fayled..in suche wise as he tumblid the hede vnder. *c* **1489** —— *Sonnes of Aymon* i. 28 He smote a knyghte..by suche a wyse that he ouerthrewe hym doun deed. **1568** GRAFTON *Chron.* II. 10 He destroyed the land..in such wise, that .ix. yeres after it lay vnlaboured. **1858** SEARS *Athan.* x. 80 The pneumatology of the sacred writers brings home to us the doctrine of the resurrection in such wise as to give it [etc.]. **1903** *Westm. Gaz.* 12 Jan. 10/1 He..gave proof of a cruel..disposition, in suchwise that [etc.].

†**c.** ***in such wise as***: in the way that, as. *Obs.*

1390 GOWER *Conf.* I. 106 In such wise as he compasseth, His wit al one alle othre passeth. **1417** HEN. V in Ellis *Orig. Lett.* Ser. III. I. 61 [They] have..doon theire Ambassiat in suche wyse as we halde us wel apaide. **1534** MORE *Comf. agst. Trib.* II. xvi. Wks. 1192/1 He that is illuded by the dyuell, is in suche wise deceiued and worsse to, then be they by their dreame. **1630** PRYNNE *Anti-Armin.* 9 We must receiue Gods promises in such wise as they are generally set forth vnto vs.

*** **38.** As such. **a.** As being what the name or description implies; in that capacity.

1711 STEELE *Spect.* No. 41 ⁋5 When she observed Will. irrevocably her Slave, she began to use him as such. **1712** *Ibid.* No. 386 ⁋2 Witty Men are apt to imagine they are agreeable as such. **1797** *Encycl. Brit.* XVI. 566/2 Her son was proclaimed *her* heir, and *as such* great duke of all the Russias. **1831** SCOTT *Cast. Dang.* xx, A Welsh knight, known as such by the diminutive size of his steed. **1851** CARPENTER *Man. Phys.* (ed. 2) 434 Biliary matter does not pre-exist *as such* in the blood. **1851** PUGIN *Chancel Screens* 10 No parochial churches, built as such, ever had close screens. **1891** EDGE in *Law Times* XC. 395/1 The defendant is the rector of the parish, and, as such, occupies the glebe land. **1911** *Act 1 & 2 Geo. V*, c. 48 §4 The trade or business carried on in the house or place by the licence holder as such.

b. The sense 'in that capacity' passes contextually into: Accordingly, consequently, thereupon. *colloq.* or *vulgar.*

1721 in Swayne *Churchw. Acc. Sarum* (1896) 351 [He] did ..publickly Declare..That he had chosen the said William Clemens to be his parish Clerk..And bid the Congregation to..accept him—as such Witness Henry Biggs, F. Barber, [etc.]. **1800** J. KING in *Corr. W. Fowler* (1907) 33, I very much longed to hear from you..and as such I did not the least esteem it for its having been delayed for the reasons assigned. **1814** W. FOWLER *Ibid.* 297 H. R. H. Princess Augusta..motioned for me to come to her Highness. As such she addressed me in the most pleasant manner possible.

c. (Earlier †*as it is such*, etc.) Intrinsically considered; in itself; *quâ* (so-and-so).

1654 Z. COKE *Logick* 2 Philosophy, which comprehends Metaphysicks, which considereth things as they are such. **1670** MILTON *Hist. Eng.* VI. 291 True fortitude glories not in the feats of War, as they are such, but as they serve to end War soonest by a victorious Peace. **1678** CUDWORTH *Intell. Syst.* 839 If Matter as such, had Life, Perception, and Vnderstanding belonging to it. **1732** BERKELEY *Alciphr.* II. §4 Is there anything in the nature of vice, as such, that renders it a public blessing? **1777** COWPER *Let. J. Hill* 25 May, His later Epistles, I think, are worth little, *as such*, but might be turned to excellent account by a young student of taste and judgement. **1849** RUSKIN *Seven Lamps* vi. §7. 169 History, as such, was indeed entrusted to the painters of its interior. **1884** tr. *Lotze's Metaph.* 68 The abstract conception of a *Thing as such.*

†**such**, *adv.* and *conj.* *Obs.* Also 1 **swelce, swilce, swylce,** (etc.) 2 **swice, swilc,** 2–3 **swulche,** 3 **swulc, swich, suich, suych, swlc(h, sulc(h,** 6 **suche.** [OE. *swelce*, etc., f. *swelc* SUCH *a.*]

A. *adv.* In correlation: So. *rare.*

In OE. the advb. meanings are 'in like manner, likewise, also, as well, too', 'as, like', 'in such a manner, so'.

a **831** *Charter* in *O.E. Texts* 444 Mid suilce godcunde gode suilce iow cynlic ðynce. *c* **1386** CHAUCER *Prol.* 243 Vn to swich a worthy man as he. *Ibid.* 684 Swiche glarynge eyen hadde he as an hare. **1390** GOWER *Conf.* I. 28 As Stiel is hardest in his kynde Above alle othre that men finde Of Metals, such was Rome tho The myhtieste. *c* **1430** *Pilgr. Lyf Manhode* IV. xii. (1869) 182 It is a meevinge sercleliche suich in the ende as at the firste. **1509** BARCLAY *Shyp of Folys* (1874) I. 208 None lyueth..Suche meke so holy, so wyse or pacyent, Whiche can hym selfe at euery tyme so gyde To please eche fole.

b. To such an extent, so much (that).

1776 HERD *Scottish Songs* I. 103 The Hogan Dutch they feared such, They bred a horrid stink then.

B. *conj.* As if.

c **888** ÆLFRED *Boeth.* xxxv. §7 Wildu dior ðær woldon to irnan & stondan swilce hi tamu wæren. *a* **1175** *Cott. Hom.* 227 Swice hi godes were. *c* **1175** *Lamb. Hom.* 91 þa iweorden alle þos ilefede men swulche hi alle hefden ane heorte. **1205** LAY. 3070 þe king Leir iwerðe swa blac swilch hit a blac cloð weoren. *Ibid.* 28009 He aras up and adun sat, swulc he weore swiðe seoc. *a* **1250** *Owl & Night.* (Jesus MS.) 1533 He chid & gred such he beo wod.

suche, obs. form of SEEK *v.*

†**suchkin**, *a. Obs.* In 3 **swulches cunnes**, 4 **suchekin**, 5 **sichekyns**. [f. SUCH *a.* + KIN *sb.*[1] 6 b. Survives in dial. (chiefly n.midl.) *suchen a*, *sichen a.* Parallel forms are SWILKIN, SICCAN.] Of such a kind, this kind of.

c **1205** LAY. 20337 Mid swulches cunnes ginnes Baldulf com wið innen. *c* **1375** *Cursor M.* 15253 (Fairf.) I salle noȝt of na suchekin [*Cott.* suilkin] drink na mare drink wiþ ȝou. *c* **1425** *St. Elizabeth of Spalbeck* in *Anglia* VIII. 111 After sichekyns merueilous.. disciplyne.

'such-like, 'suchlike, *a.* and *pron.* [f. SUCH *a.* + LIKE *a.* Cf. SIC-LIKE, SWILK-LIKE.]

A. *adj.* Of such a kind; of the like or a similar kind; of the before-mentioned sort or character.

1422 YONGE tr. *Secr. Secr.* 239 Suche-like dyuersite may a man fynde in dyuerses stomakis. **1526** TINDALE *Mark* vii. 8 Many other suche lyke thinges ye do. *a* **1557** MRS. M. BASSET tr. *More's Treat. Pass.* Wks. 1357/1 Hunger, thyrste, slepe, werines, & such like disposicions. *c* **1610** *Women Saints* 160 As for paynted face, or colouring of eyes, and such like brickle brauerie. **1660** FULLER *Mixt Contemp.* (1841) 177 An old ship, some few rotten nets, and such-like inconsiderable accommodations. **1732** BERKELEY *Alciphr.* vi. §19 Glaucus, or such-like great men in the minute philosophy. *a* **1774** GOLDSM. *Surv. Exp. Philos.* (1776) I. 314 A piece of butter, or some such like substance. **1822** LAMB *Elia* I. *Dream Childr.*, Peaches, nectarines, oranges, and such-like common baits of children. **1844** KINGLAKE *Eothen* viii, She said.. that the practice of such-like arts was unholy as well as vulgar. **1910** *Encycl. Brit.* (ed. 11) XIV. 167/2 When a dog, then, is observed to gnaw and eat suchlike matters,.. it should be suspected.

†**b.** With quantitative adjs. and ellipt. *Obs.*

1489 *Rolls of Parlt.* VI. 434/2 Shetis, Dyapers, Pottes,.. and other siche like. **1535** JOYE *Apol. Tindale* (Arb. 38) He calleth the same the lyfe of condempnacion or dampnable lyfe.. with many siche lyke. **1614** SELDEN *Titles Hon.* 6 Such like more occurre in ancient.. Storie very frequent.

c. predicatively. (*rare.*)

1535 COVERDALE *Ecclus.* xlv. 6 He chose Aaron his brother .., exalted him, & made him soch like. **1767** MICKLE *Concub.* II. lix, Such was his Life;.. And suchlich [*sic*] was his Cave. **1874** SAYCE *Compar. Philol.* ii. 69 Suchlike were the answers readily given to the inquirer.

d. Having forward reference, usually with correlative *as.* (*rare.*)

1591 SHAKS. *Two Gent.* IV. i. 52 Such like petty crimes as these. **1598** BARNFIELD '*As it fell upon a day*' 39 Poems (Arb.) 121 If that one be prodigall, Bountifull, they will him call. And with such-like flattering, Pitty but hee were a King. **1623** in Rushw. *Hist. Coll.* (1659) I. 288 Such-like course shall be taken as was in a like occasion at his Majesties coming into England. **1870** MORRIS *Earthly Par.* III. IV. 276 Suchlike hearts As ye have.

B. *pron.* Usually *pl.* Such-like persons or things; also *sing.*, something of that kind; the like. Chiefly in ***and such-like, or such-like.***

a **1425** tr. *Arderne's Treat. Fistula*, etc. 74 Bark-duste, psidie, balaustie, mumme and sich like. **1535** COVERDALE *Ps.* xv. 3 All my delyte is vpon the sanctes that are in the earth, and vpon soch like. **1535** —— *Ezek.* xviii. 14 A sonne.. that seith all this fathers synnes,.. feareth, nether doth soch like. **1535** —— *Gal.* v. 21 The dedes of y[e] flesh are manifest, which are these:.. dronkennes, glotony, and soch like. **1571** DIGGES *Pantom.* I. xxviii. I j, Marked uppon a slate or such like. **1579** *Mem. St. Giles's, Durham* (Surtees) 1 Payde to Richard Gylson.. for laying up earthe to y[e] whicke ij.s. vj.d. Item payde to Rycharde Robinson for suche lyke ii.s. iij.d. **1592** in J. Morris *Troubles Cath. Forefathers* (1877) 32 Those letters are carried to Topcliffe or such like. **1669** WORLIDGE *Syst. Agric.* (1681) 214 These Bushes, Brakes, and suchlike. *a* **1774** GOLDSM. *Surv. Exp. Philos.* (1776) I. 191 A smooth marble hearth-stone, or such like. **1865** KINGSLEY *Herew.* xl, He has a ring or two left, or an owch, or such like. **1869** *Routledge's Ev. Boy's Ann.* 6 There's thorns and such-like as high as my head. **1878** BROWNING *Poets Croisic*, etc. 193 A bard, sir, famed of yore, Went where suchlike used to go.

†**b.** In A. d. *Obs. rare.*

1676 HALE *Contempl.* I. 7 These, and such like as these.

suchness ('sʌtʃnɪs). [f. SUCH *a.* + -NESS.] The condition or quality of being such; quality.

In occasional use only, exc. in the language of modern philosophy.

c **960** ÆTHELWOLD *Rule St. Benet* (Schröer 1885) 89 Sy ȝebroðrum reaf ȝeseald be swilcnesse and staþele þære stowe þe hy on wuniað. *c* **1000** *Sax. Leechd.* I. 260 Mid sumum oðrum mete ȝemengcedne be þære swylcnysse þe seo untrumnys þonne byð. **1674** N. FAIRFAX *Bulk & Selv.* To Rdr., Either as they have Beings from God, or a Suchness of being from our handy-work. *Ibid.* 94, 182. **1842** SIR W. HAMILTON *Diss.* in *Reid's Wks.* (1846) 856/2 The Primary [Qualities of Body] are less properly denominated Qualities (Suchnesses). **1878** W. BARNES *Engl. Speech-craft* 12 Mark-words.. of suchness, as *good, bad.* **1899** DZIEWICKI *Wyclif's De Logica* III. Introd. p. xxvii, Becoming is a change, not of the subject, but of its 'suchness'.

suchon: see SUCH *a.* 28.

suchwise ('sʌtʃwaɪz), *adv. rare.* [Short for *in such wise*: see SUCH *a.* 37. Cf. G. *solcherweise.*] In such a manner.

c **1375** *Cursor M.* 11971 (Fairf.) Wirk noȝt suche wise [*Cott.* þis wise]. **1556** *Aurelio & Isab.* A vij, Suche wise that the great loue that the father bore her, greued her meruelouslie sore. **1875** MORRIS *Æn.* v. 303 And now amidmost of all these suchwise Æneas spake. **1890** —— *Earthly Par.* 293/2 Such-wise [*ed.* 1870 so far] things went With Ingibiorg, that [etc.].

suck (sʌk), *sb.*[1] Also 4–5 **souke**, 6 *Sc.* **sowk, sulk**, 6–7 **sucke**, 8–9 *dial.* **souk, sook.** [f. SUCK *v.* Cf. SOCK *sb.*[3]]

1. a. The action or an act of sucking milk from the breast; the milk or other fluid sucked at one time. ***at suck***, engaged in sucking.

13.. *S. Gregory* (Vernon MS.) 191 Whon heo hedde iȝiue þe child a souke. **1500–20** DUNBAR *Poems* lxxv. 24 My new spanit howffing fra the sowk. **1535** COVERDALE *Isa.* xxviii. 9 The children, which are weened from suck or taken from the brestes. *a* **1586** SIDNEY *Arcadia* (1622) 412 O mother of mine, what a deathfull sucke haue you giuen me? **1851** MRS. BROWNING *Casa Guidi Wind.* I. 1193 Who loved Rome's wolf, with demi-gods at suck, Or ere we loved truth's own divinity. **1912** D. CRAWFORD *Thinking Black* I. vii. 117 He wants everything, even a literal suck of your blood.

b. The application of suction by the mouth either to an external object (e.g. a wound, a pipe) or internally.

1760 STERNE in Traill *Sterne* v. (1882) 53, I saw the cut, gave it [*sc.* my finger] a suck, wrapt it up, and thought no more about it. **1849** CUPPLES *Green Hand* iii, A rough voice .. was chanting the sea-song.. in a curious sleepy kind of drone, interrupted every now and then by the suck of his pipe. **1864** LATTO *Tam. Bodkin* ii. 12 Toastin' his taes at a roarin' peat-fire, an' takin' a quiet sook o' his rusty cutty. **1896** HARDY *Jude* I. vi, She gave.. an adroit little suck to the interior of each of her cheeks.

c. An act of fellatio. *coarse slang.*

1941 G. W. HENRY *Sex Variants* II. 1177 A real suck seems to be one in which orgasm and ejaculation are induced. **1972** *Screw* 12 June 21/2 They start their separate ways through a variety of fucks and sucks and lesbian encounters.

2. A small draught of liquid; a drink, a sup.

1625 MASSINGER *New Way* I. i, *Wellborn.* No bouse, nor no tobacco? *Tapwell.* Not a suck, sir, Nor the remainder of a single can. **1792** BURNS *Weary Pund o' Tow*, There sat a bottle in a bole... And ay she took the tither souk, To drouk the stourie tow. **1861** READE *Cloister & H.* I. 27 'Tis a soupe-au-vin... Have a suck.

†**3. a.** Milk sucked (or to be sucked) from the breast; mother's milk. *Obs.*

1584 COGAN *Haven Health* ccxvii. (1636) 244 To old men, wine is as sucke to young children. **1591** *Child-Marriages* 144 If the said John Richardson.. doe cause the said Bastard Childe to be sufficiently nursed.. and kept, with apparell, Suck, attendinge, and all other necessaries nedfull or belonging to such a childe. **1596** SPENSER *State Irel.* Wks. (Globe) 638/2 Yong children.. drawe unto themselves, togither with theyr sucke, even the nature and disposition of theyr nurses. **1607** TOPSELL *Four-f. Beasts* 111 Their dam hath no suck for them, til she hath bene six or seauen houres with the male. **1655** CULPEPPER, etc. *Riverius* VI. v. 136 Therefore when Children have it from their Suck, let the Nurse be changed.

†**b.** *fig.* Sustenance. *Obs.*

1584 COGAN *Haven Health* (1636) 214, I had rather be without sucke, than that any man, through his intemperate feeding, should have cause to fee mee or feed me.

†**4.** Strong drink; tipple. *slang. Obs.*

a **1700** B. E. *Dict. Cant. Crew*, *Suck*, Wine or strong Drink. *This is rum Suck*, it is excellent Tipple.

5. The drawing of air by suction; *occas.* a draught or current of air; *spec.* in *Coal-mining*, the backward suction of air following an explosion of fire-damp.

1667 BOYLE in *Phil. Trans.* II. 582 About the seventh suck, it [*sc.* phosphorescent rotten wood] seemed to grow a little more dim. **1848** KINGSLEY *Yeast* i, A cold suck of wind just proved its existence by tooth-aches on the north side of all faces. **1880** *Leeds Mercury* 13 Sept. 8 The pit took a 'suck' again and the air current, such as it was, came right.

6. The sucking action of eddying or swirling water; the sound caused by this; *locally*, the place at which a body of water moves in such a way as to suck objects into its vortex.

suck of the ground: see quot. 1893.

c **1220** *Bestiary* 578 Ðe sipes sinken mitte suk, ne cumen he nummor up.

1778 T. HUTCHINS *Descr. Virginia* 32 About 200 miles above these shoals, is, what is called, the Whirl, or Suck, occasioned, I imagine, by the high mountain, which there confines the River. **1849** CUPPLES *Green Hand* xviii, By this time we were already in the suck of the channel. **1863** W. LANCASTER *Praeterita* 41 Its hissing suck of waves. **1878** CUYLER *Pointed Papers* 112 When the pilot.. finds that she will not obey the helm, he knows that he is within the suck of the whirlpool of Charybdis. **1891** C. ROBERTS *Adrift Amer.* 227 The suck of the water was very strong, and I could feel it pull me back like a strong current. **1893** *Leisure Hour* 679 A ship is always faster in deep water than in shallow, owing to what seamen call the suck of the ground, which is only a way of saying that the bulk a ship displaces must be in small proportion to the depth beneath her keel if it is to spread itself readily around her. **1904** W. CHURCHILL *Crossing* II. x. 364 The mighty current.. lashed itself into a hundred sucks and whirls.

7. *slang.* A deception; a disappointing event or result. Also *suck-in.*

1856 DOW *Serm.* II. 316 (Bartlett) A monstrous humbug —a grand suck in. **1872** S. DE VERE *Americanisms* 639 *Suck in*, as a noun and as a verb, is a graphic Western phrase to express deception. **1877** *N.W. Linc. Gloss.*, *Suck, Suck-in*, an imposition, a disappointment.

8. *pl.* Sweetmeats. Also *collect. sing. colloq.*

1858 HUGHES *Scour. White Horse* vi. 110 Nuts and apples, and ginger-bread, and all sorts of sucks and fun. **1865** *Good Words* 125 They sometimes get a 'knob o' suck' (a piece of sweetstuff) on Saturday.

†**9.** A breast-pocket. *Criminals' slang. Obs.*

1821 D. HAGGART *Life* 26 He returned the screaves to his lil, and placed it in his suck. **1923** *Chambers's Jrnl.* 6 Oct. 716/1, I.. pulled the dub of the outer jigger from his suck.

10. *slang.* A sycophant; esp. a schoolboy who curries favour with teachers. Cf. SUCK *v.* 26 e; *sucker-up* s.v. SUCKER *sb.* 14.

1900 FARMER *Public School Word-Bk.* 197 *Suck, subs.* (University), a parasite, a toady. **1907** B. M. CROKER *Company's Servant* xx. 213 He was just a suck—that's all. **1916** JOYCE *Portrait of Artist* (1969) i. 11 We all know why you speak. You are McGlade's suck. **1955** W. GADDIS *Recognitions* II. ii. 373 The shade of the boy whom he had not seen since they were boys together (Martin was Father Joseph's 'suck') lived on the air as though they had parted only minutes before.

11. *pl.* as *int.* Used as an expression of contempt, chiefly by children. Also in phr. ***sucks to you*** and varr. *slang.*

1913 C. MACKENZIE *Sinister Street* I. I. vii. 98 This kid's in our army, so sucks! **1922** F. HAMILTON *P.J.: Secret Service Boy* iv. 178 'S', he announced, '*u,c,k,s,t,o,y,o,u*.' **1935** N. MITCHISON *We have been Warned* I. 28 Brian is a baby. Oh sucks, oh sucks on Brian. **1945** E. WAUGH *Brideshead Revisited* II. v. 287 It's great sucks to Bridey. **1952** 'C. BRAND' *London Particular* xv. 191 A most regretable air of sucks to you. **1968** *Melody Maker* 30 Nov. 24/5 This is a rotten record—yah boo and sucks. **1974** *Times* 4 Mar. 9/5 Sucks boo, then, with acting like this, to that new National Theatre down the road. **1978** 'J. LYMINGTON' *Waking of Stone* ii. 45 'Sucks to you!' she said.. tossing her head so her pigtails swung. **1983** *Listener* 19 May 11/1 The council treated the urbane Mr Cook to the politician's equivalent of 'Yah, boo, sucks'.

12. *Canad. slang.* A worthless or contemptible person. Cf. SUCK *v.* 15 f; *suck-hole* s.v. SUCK-.

1974 *Globe & Mail* (Toronto) 8 Mar. 1/6 The teachers are copping out. They're now saying, if we can't have our way, then we're going to be sucks and refuse to work. **1975** *Citizen* (Ottawa) 28 Oct. 1/1 A neighbor described Rob as 'a quiet guy who was always getting put down a lot. Lots of people used to call him a suck... He didn't do much socially or in the way of sports.'

¶ ***to give suck***: see SUCK *v.* 16.

suck (sʌk), *sb.*[2] Chiefly *n.w.* and *w.midl.* Also 6 **sucke.** [app. var. of SOCK *sb.*[2] Cf. SOUGH *sb.*[3]] A ploughshare.

1499 [see SUCKING *sb.*]. **1570** LEVINS *Manip.* 185/1 Ye Sucke of a plow. **1588** *Lanc. & Cheshire Wills* (Chetham Soc.) II. 149 One sucke and one cultur. **1688** HOLME *Armoury* III. viii. 333/2 The Sough, or Suck, is that as Plows into the ground. **1725** *Fam. Dict.* s.v. *Earth* Bbb/1 The Plowman.. will not.. be able to point the Suck where he would. **1798** *Trans. Soc. Arts* XVI. 166 For hoeing, I have shares or sucks, in the shape of a trowel, which I can fix on the points of the drills. **1800** *Rob. Nixon's Chesh. Prophecies* Verse (1873) 41 Between the sickle and the suck, All England shall have a pluck. **1879** MISS JACKSON *Shropsh. Word-bk.* **1886** *Cheshire Gloss.*

†**suck**, *sb.*[3] *Obs.* Also **sucke.** Variant spelling of SUC, prob. influenced by SUCK *v.*

1560 WARDE tr. *Alexis' Secr.* II. 14 b, The suck or iuice of a radish roote. **1567** PAINTER *Pal. Pleas.* II. 146 The sucke & marrow of his bones. **1621** LODGE *Summary of Du Bartas* I. 270 A liquid and fluent matter, composed of that sucke which furnisheth the Stomacke. **1631** A. B. tr. *Lessius' De Prov. Num.* 110 The fruit serues for the continuance of the seed,.. and therefore they are more full of suck. **1635** SWAN *Spec. Mundi* vi. (1643) 297 Succinum is a Bituminous suck or juice of the earth.

suck (sʌk), *v.* Forms: *Pres. stem.* 1 **sucan**, 2–3 **suke(n**, 3–4 **souken**, 4–6 **souke, sowke**, 4–7 **soke**, 5–7 **sucke**, (4 **soke, soukke, socon, sugke, suk**, *Sc.* **swk**, *Kent.* **zouke**, 4, 9 *Sc.* **sook**, 6 **soucke, sowk, suke, soulk**, *Sc.* **soik, sulk**, 6, 9 **souk**, 6–7 **souck**, 7 *Anglo-Irish* **shoke**, 8 *dial.* **seawke**), 6– **suck.** *Pa. t.* α. *strong.* 1 ***seac**, (*pl.* **sucon, -un**), 2–3 **suke**, 3 **sæc, soc**, 3–4 **sec, sok, sek(e**, 3–5 **soke**, 4–5 **secke, sak, souk(e, sowk(e, swoke**, 5 **sook**; β. *weak.* 4 **soukid, sowkid**, *Sc.* **swkyt**, 4–5 **souked**, 5–6 **sowked**, 6 **sokid**, 6–8 **suck'd, suckt**, 6– **sucked.** *Pa. pple.* α. *strong.* 1 **-socen**, 4 **sokun, suken, soke, i-soke**, 5 **soken, -yn**, 7 **sucken**; β. *weak.* 4 **soukid**, *Sc.* **sukit**, 5–6 **sowked**, 6 **souked, -it, sowkit**, 6–8 **suck'd, suckt**, 7 **suckd**, 6– **sucked.** [OE. *súcan*, corresp. to L. *sūgĕre*, OIr. *sūgim*, f. root *sūg-*. A parallel root *sūk-* (cf. L. *sūcus* juice) is represented by OE. *súgan*, MLG., MDu. *sûgen* (Du. *zuigen*), OHG. *sûgan* (MHG. *sûgen*, G. *saugen*), ON. *súga.*

This verb is related by ablaut to *soak*, with which there is some contact of meaning, see sense 21 below, SUCKING *ppl. a.* 5, and SOAK *v.* 8 b, c, 10.]

I. 1. a. *trans.* To draw (liquid, *esp.* milk from the breast) into the mouth by contracting the muscles of the lips, cheeks, and tongue so as to produce a partial vacuum.

c **825** *Vesp. Hymns* vii, Sucun huniȝ of stane & ele of trumum stane. *c* **1000** *Ags. Ps.* (Thorpe) viii. 2 Of ðæra cild muðe, þe meolc sucað, þu byst hered. *c* **1000** ÆLFRIC *Hom.* II. 488 Ða ongunnon ealle ða næddran to ceowenne heora flæsc and heora blod sucan. *a* **1225** *Ancr. R.* 330 He sec þe milc þet hine uedde. *a* **1300** *X Commandm.* 39 in *E.E.P.* (1862) 16 Besech we him.. þat sok þe milk of maid-is brest. **13..** *K. Alis.* 6119 They.. Soken heore blod, heore flesch to-gnowe. *c* **1440** *Gesta Rom.* ii. 5 (Harl. MS.) So sat þe tode alle þat ȝere, and secke his blod. **1523** FITZHERB. *Husb.* §69 The calfe wyll soucke as moche mylke, er it be able to kyll, as it is worthe. **1588** SHAKS. *Tit. A.* II. iii. 144 The milke thou suck'st from her did turne to Marble. **1710** W. KING *Heathen Gods & Heroes* xi. (1722) 45 He is said to have gain'd his Immortality by the Milk he suckt from her. **1774** GOLDSM. *Nat. Hist.* (1776) IV. 70 The weasel, where it once fastens, holds, and continuing also to suck the blood at the same time, weakens its antagonist. **180.** in Dickson *Pract. Agric.* (1805) II. 1058 If an ewe gives more milk than its lamb will suck. **1825** SCOTT *Talism.* xxi, Suck the poison from his wound, one of you. **1848** STEINMETZ *Hist. Jesuits* I. 212 Ignatius..even applied his mouth to their ulcers, and sucked the purulent discharge. **1848** THACKERAY *Van. Fair* lxii, The knowing way in which he sipped, or rather sucked, the Johannisberger.

b. Of flies, etc. drawing blood, bees extracting honey from flowers; also of flowers 'drinking' the dew, etc.

1340 *Ayenb.* 136 þe smale uleȝe þet..of þe floures zoucþ þane deau huerof hi makeþ þet hony. **1422** YONGE tr. *Secr. Secr.* 180 The flyes thyke lay on hym that his blode soke. **1474** CAXTON *Chesse* II. v. (1883) 66 Many flyes satte vpon the soores and souked his blood. **1593** SHAKS. *2 Hen. VI*, IV. i. 109 Drones sucke not Eagles blood, but rob Bee-hiues. **1637** MILTON *Lycidas* 140 Throw hither all your quaint enameld eyes, That on the green terf suck the honied showres. *c* **1645** HOWELL *Lett.* III. iv. (1892) 517 The Bee and the Spider suck honey and poison out of one Flower. **1820** SHELLEY *Prometh. Unb.* III. iii. 102 Night-folded flowers Shall suck unwithering hues in their repose. **1833** WORDSW. *Warning* 33 Like the bee That sucks from mountain-heath her honey fee.

c. *to suck the blood of* (fig.): to exhaust the resources of, drain the life out of. (Cf. BLOOD-SUCK *v.*)

1583 STUBBES *Anat. Abus.* II. (1882) 7 He meaneth to sucke thy bloud. **1584** GREENE *Mirr. Modestie* Wks. (Grosart) III. 17 These two cursed caitifes..concluded when they might finde hir alone, to sucke the bloude of this innocent lambe. **1610** HOLLAND *Camden's Brit.* (1637) 49 The Lieutenant, cruelly to suck their bloud, and the Procuratour as greedy to preie upon that substance. **1819** SCOTT *Ivanhoe* vii, The wealth he had acquired by sucking the blood of his miserable victims, had but swelled him like a bloated spider.

d. *to suck one's fill*: see FILL *sb.*[1] 1.

c **1475** *Songs & Carols* xlvi. (Percy Soc.) 50 He toke hyr lovely by the pape,..And sok hys fyll of the lycowr. **1798** WORDSW. '*Her Eyes are Wild*' 84 My little babe! thy lips are still, And thou hast almost sucked thy fill. **1805** DICKSON *Pract. Agric.* II. 981 Young calves when permitted to suck their fill are often seized with a looseness. **1818** SCOTT *Hrt. Midl.* xxxix, I wad wuss ye, if Gowans, the brockit cow, has a quey, that she suld suck her fill of milk.

e. *transf.* and *fig.* or in fig. context.

13.. *Bonaventura's Medit.* 277 Þys sermoun at crystys brest slepyng he soke. **1393** LANGL. *P. Pl.* C. XIII. 55 Crist ..bad hem souken of hus brest sauete for synne. **1580** J. STEWART *Poems* (S.T.S.) II. 103/5 Thocht source I souck not on the sacred hill. *a* **1586** SIDNEY *Astr. & Stella* Sonn. lxxiii, Because a sugared kiss In sport I suckt. **1592** SHAKS. *Rom. & Jul.* V. iii. 92 Death that hath suckt the honey of thy breath. **1592** —— *Ven. & Ad.* 572 Had she then gaue ouer, Such nectar from his lips she had not suckt. **1600** *Cath. Tract.* 245 Ye may sie what venemous poyson thay souk out of the Ministers breists. **1601** SHAKS. *Jul. C.* II. ii. 87 From you great Rome shall sucke Reuiuing blood. **1602** MARSTON *Antonio's Rev.* IV. i, Studious contemplation sucks the juyce From wisards cheekes. **1604** EARL STIRLING *Crœsus* I. i, Faire Citie, where mine eyes first suck't the light. **1842** TENNYSON *Will Waterproof* 213 Thou shalt from all things suck Marrow of mirth and laughter.

f. (See quot. 1960.) With person or part as obj. Cf. sense 24 below. *coarse slang.*

1928 in A. W. Read *Lexical Evidence from Folk Epigraphy Western N. Amer.* (1935) 78, I suck cocks for fun. **1960** WENTWORTH & FLEXNER *Dict. Amer. Slang* 527/2 *Suck v.i., v.t.* 1 [taboo] to perform cunnilingus or, esp., fellatio. **1972** *Screw* 12 June 21/2 Characters fuck and suck each other like *real* people do. **1973** E. BULLINS *Theme is Blackness* 79 You heard what I said, bitch..take me to dinner and suck mah dick and et cetera fa dessert.

2. To imbibe (qualities, etc.) *with* the mother's milk. (Cf. 5.)

1586 T. B. *La Primaud. Fr. Acad.* I. 166 As if we had sucked iniquitie togither with our nurses milke. **1588** KYD *Househ. Philos.* Wks. (1901) 259 That first and tender age of infancie..oftentimes with the milke sucketh the conditions of the Nursse. **1607** SHAKS. *Cor.* III. ii. 129 Thy Valiantnesse was mine, thou suck'st it from me. **1639** MASSINGER *Unnat. Comb.* I. i, I think they suck this knowledge in their milk.

3. To extract or draw (moisture, goodness, etc.) *from* or *out of* a thing; to absorb into itself.

1398 TREVISA *Barth. De P.R.* XVII. cxxvi. (1495) 686 The pyth of the russhe is good to drawe water of out of the erthe for it soukyth it kyndly. **1585** JAS. I *Ess. Poesie* (Arb.) 14 Fra tyme that onis thy sell [Phœbus] The vapouris softlie sowkis with smyling cheare. **1593** SHAKS. *Rich. II*, III. iv. 38 The noysome Weedes, that..sucke The Soyles fertilitie from wholesome flowers. **1657** AUSTEN *Fruit Trees* 71 Great and large Trees do suck and draw the fertility of the ground exceedingly. **1697** DRYDEN *Virg., Georg.* I. 438 Oft whole sheets descend of slucy Rain, Suck'd by the spongy Clouds from off the Main. *Ibid.* III. 222 Let 'em [*sc.* Mares] suck the Seed with greedy Force; And close involve the Vigour of the Horse. **1847** TENNYSON *Princ.* VII. 24 She..sees a great black cloud..suck the blinding splendour from the sand. **1880** *Scribner's Mag.* Mar. 756 Treat all suckers as weeds, cutting them down..before they have sucked half the life out of the bearing hill.

†**4.** To draw or extract (money, wealth) from a source. Also in early use *intr.* with partitive *of. Obs.*

c **1380** WYCLIF *Serm.* Sel. Wks. II. 187 Þes prelatis.. cunnen summone þe Chirche..from oo place to anoþer, to sooke of her moneye. *c* **1386** CHAUCER *Cook's T.* 52 To sowke Of that he brybe kan or borwe may. **1399** LANGL. *Rich. Redeles* IV. 9 Sellynge, þat sowkid siluer rith ffaste. **1610** HOLLAND *Camden's Brit.* (1637) 756 Having first cunningly suckt a great masse of money from the credulous king.

5. To derive or extract (information, comfort, profit, etc.) *from*, †*of*, or *out of*. (Cf. 2.)

1535 COVERDALE *Ps.* lxxii. 10 There out sucke they no small auauntage. **1539** CROMWELL in Merriman *Life & Lett.* (1902) II. 176 Communications at large sucked of hym. **1565** T. STAPLETON *Fortr. Faith* 10 He made those notes sucked out of John Bale. *c* **1600** CHALKHILL *Thealma & Cl.* (1683) 95 Ægypt Schools..From whence he suckt this knowledg. **1605** *1st Pt. Jeronimo* II. iii. 8 Hast thou worne gownes in the Uniuersity, Tost logick, suckt Philosophy? **1625** BACON *Ess., Travel* (Arb.) 523 In Trauailing in one Country he shall sucke the Experience of many. **1715** HEARNE *Collect.* (O.H.S.) V. 109 Spinosa..suck'd the first Seeds of Atheism from the famous Francis Vanden Ende. **1784** COWPER *Task* IV. 111 He sucks intelligence in ev'ry clime. **1822** LAMB *Elia* I. *Compl. Decay of Beggars*, Much good might be sucked from these Beggars. **1908** M. S. RAWSON *Easy go Luckies* xxi, Had he been a scholar he might have sucked a sort of delicately pungent comfort from an epigram of Tacitus. **1914** MARETT in *Folk-Lore* XXV. 20 The active conditions that enable us to suck strength and increase out of the passive conditions comprised under the term environment.

†**6.** To draw (air, breath) into the mouth; to inhale (air, smoke, etc.). *Obs.*

1590 SHAKS. *Com. Err.* II. ii. 194 They'll sucke our breath, or pinch vs blacke and blew. ? **1614** D. MURRAY in Drumm. of Hawth. *Poems* (S.T.S.) I. 95 To them who on their Hills suck'd sacred Breath. **1634** SIR T. HERBERT *Trav.* 150 Tobacco suckt through water by long canes or pipes. **1712–14** POPE *Rape Lock* I. 83 Some [spirits]..suck the mists in grosser air below. **1717** —— *Eloisa* 324 See my lips tremble, and my eye-balls roll, Suck my last breath, and catch my flying soul!

7. To draw (water, air, etc.) in some direction, esp. by producing a vacuum. Also *intr.* for *pass.* of the wind.

1661 BOYLE *Certain Physiol. Ess.* (1669) 216 Having by a certain Artifice out of a large glass..caus'd a certain quantity of air to be suck'd, we [etc.]. **1730–46** THOMSON *Autumn* 768 Old Ocean too, suck'd thro' the porous globe, Had long ere now forsook his horrid bed. **1847** TENNYSON *Princ.* v. 339 Right and left Suck'd from the dark heart of the long hills roll The torrents. **1849** CUPPLES *Green Hand* ii, The [gulf] stream *sucks* the wind with heat. *Ibid.* xiii, The air aloft appeared in the mean time to be steadying and *sucking*. **1857** MILLER *Elem. Chem., Org.* i. 17 Instead of sucking air through the apparatus, heat is to be very cautiously applied to the chlorate.

8. a. To draw in so as to swallow up or engulf.

1523 FITZHERB. *Husb.* §2 The lande is verye toughe, and wolde soke the ploughe into the erthe. *c* **1590** *Sir T. More* (Malone Soc.) 1306 As when a whirle-poole sucks the circkled waters. **1697** DRYDEN *Æneid* III. 538 Charibdis..in her greedy Whirl-pool sucks the Tides. **1817** SHELLEY *Rev. Islam* XII. ix, Like the refluence of a mighty wave Sucked into the loud sea.

b. *fig.* To draw *into* a course of action, etc.

1771 SMOLLETT *Humphry Cl.* (1815) 266, I am insensibly sucked into the channel of their manners and customs. **1779** J. MOORE *View Soc. Fr.* (1789) I. i. 9 Small chance will remain of his being sucked into the old system. **1840** DE QUINCEY *Essenes* Wks. 1862 IX. 287 He is now rapidly approaching to a torrent that will suck him into a new faith. **1899** LD. ROSEBERY in *Daily News* 6 May 4/1 We were sucked into a house dinner.

II. 9. a. To apply the lips to (a teat, breast, the mother, nurse, or dam) for the purpose of extracting milk; to draw milk from with the mouth.

c **1000** ÆLFRIC *Saints Lives* viii. 125 Ne sceamode þe to ceorfanne þæt þæt ðu sylf suce? *c* **1000** *Ags. Gosp.* Luke xi. 27 Eadig is se innoð þe þe bær & þa breost þe ðu suce. *c* **1205** LAY. 5026 Þa tittes þet þu suke [*c* **1275** soke] mid þine lippes. *Ibid.* 12981, & Vther his broðer þa ȝæt sæc [*c* **1275** soc] his moder. *c* **1275** *XI Pains of Hell* 135 in *O.E. Misc.* 151 Neddren heore [*sc.* the women's] breosten sukeþ. **1303** R. BRUNNE *Handl. Synne* 546 Hyt shulde a go, and sokun ky. *c* **1350** *Will. Palerne* 2702 For þe blissful barnes loue þat hire brestes souked. **1387** TREVISA *Higden* (Rolls) III. 267 Hir moder..schewed hir brestes þat eiþer of hem hadde i-soke. *a* **1400** *Octouian* 566 We segh..a wonder happe; A manchyld swoke a lyones pappe. *c* **1450** *Merlin* 88 To put youre owne childe to sowken a-nother woman. **1538** *Test. Ebor.* (Surtees) VI. 85 The foll that soukes olde maire. **1588** SHAKS. *Tit. A.* IV. ii. 178 Ile make you..feed on curds and whay, and suck the Goate. **1697** J. LEWIS *Mem. Dk. Gloucester* (1789) 6 He ordered her to go to bed to the young prince, who soon sucked her. **1781** COWPER *Expost.* 473 Thou wast born amid the din of arms, And suck'd a breast that panted with alarms. **1805** DICKSON *Pract. Agric.* II. 986 When the calf is suffered to suck the mother, it should have the first of the milk.

b. of bees, etc., as in 1 b.

1426 LYDG. *De Guil. Pilgr.* 17560 As an yreyne sowketh the flye, And hyr entroylles draweth oute. **1665** BOYLE *Occas. Refl.* 67 How busie the Bees are in sucking these [blossoms]. **1812** KIRBY in K. & Spence *Introd. Entom.* (1816) I. 164 *note*, A small Melitta, upon which some of these creatures were busy sucking the poor animal. **1889** *Science-Gossip* XXV. 270/2 Union of many flowers on one inflorescence, which is therefore more conspicuous, and more easily sucked by insects, than single flowers.

c. *to suck the hind tit* or *teat*: to be inferior or have no priority. Also *intr.* with *on. slang* (orig. *U.S.*).

1940 W. V. T. CLARK *Ox-Bow Incident* iv. 244 'Well,' he said, 'if you like to suck the hind tit.' **1951** N. MONSARRAT *Cruel Sea* III. vi. 179 You haven't a hope... As far as radar is concerned, corvettes are sucking on the hind tit. **1963** *Time* 8 Nov. 47, I don't want these kids around here to suck on a hind tit when it comes to getting a good education. **1975** *Weekend Mag.* (Montreal) 31 May 20/2 Radio, no matter what you've read about the Radio Revolution, still sucks the hind teat at the CBC.

10. a. To apply the lips and tongue (or analogous organs) to (an object) for the purpose of obtaining nourishment; to extract the fluid contents of by such action of the mouth; to absorb (a sweetmeat) in the mouth by the action of the tongue and the muscles of the cheeks.

to suck** a person's **brains: see BRAIN *sb.* 4 b. ***to teach one's grandmother to suck eggs***: see EGG *sb.* 4 b. † ***to suck the eggs of***: to extract the 'goodness' of, cause to be unproductive. ***to suck the monkey***: see MONKEY *sb.* 12. ***suck it and see*** (see quot. 1951); now used *attrib.* and *absol.* (also with hyphens) to denote experimental methods.

1340 HAMPOLE *Pr. Consc.* 6764 Þai sal for threst þe hevedes souke Of þe nedders þat on þam sal rouke. *c* **1450** *Cov. Myst.* (Shaks. Soc.) 28 That sory appyl that we han sokyn To dethe hathe brouth my spouse and me. **1576** GASCOIGNE *Philomene* Wks. 1910 II. 179 Such unkinde, as let the cukowe flye, To sucke mine eggs. **1599** SHAKS. *Hen. V*, I. ii. 171 The Weazell (Scot) Comes sneaking, and so sucks her Princely Egges. **1602** *2nd Pt. Return fr. Parnass.* IV. ii, This sucks the eggs of my inuention. **1658** ROWLAND tr. *Moufet's Theat. Ins.* 1067 When he hath his belly full, he laies up the rest of his provant, and hangs them up by a thred to suck them another time. **1706** E. WARD *Wooden World Diss.* (1708) 81 They may suck their Paws at Home in a whole Skin. **1750** GRAY *Long Story* 48 A wicked Imp..Who prowl'd the country far and near,..And suck'd the eggs, and kill'd the pheasants. **1774** GOLDSM. *Nat. Hist.* (1776) IV. 322 It is a common report, that during this time, they [*sc.* bears] live by sucking their paws. **1780** COWPER *Progr. Err.* 530 If some mere driv'ler suck the sugar'd fib, One that still needs his leading-string and bib. **1851** MAYHEW *Lond. Labour* I. 204/2 The old ones wants something to suck, and not to chew. **1852** THACKERAY *Esmond* I. iii, A grand, languid nobleman in a great cap and flowered morning-gown, sucking oranges. **1908** M. S. RAWSON *Easy go Luckies* xviii, The policeman's five children (all sucking sweets). **1951** PARTRIDGE *Dict. Slang* (ed. 4) Add. 1189/2 *Suck it and see!* A derisive c[atch-]p[hrase] retort current in the 1890's. **1968** *New Scientist* 3 Oct. 10/1 Biologists..prefer to employ the 'suck it and see' approach adopted by Harold Wilson to politics rather than the impractical (?) idealism of Michael Foot. **1973** *Nature* 2 Mar. 16/2 In the best tradition of 'suck it and see' Fowlis has attempted to use such a velocimeter to measure the flow of both mercury and the liquid alloy NaK. **1976** *New Scientist* 16 Dec. 636/1 Types of experiment that could be usefully or uniquely performed in space:..'suck-it-and-see' experiments to explore a new environment (such as the plant growth and spider-web-spinning variety). **1979** *SLR Camera* June 42/3 It's difficult to lay down any hard and fast recommendations for using fill-in lighting; it's really a suck-it-and-see situation.

b. To apply the tongue and inner sides of the lips to (one's teeth) so as to extract particles of food.

1595 SHAKS. *John* I. i. 192 When my knightly stomacke is suffis'd Why then I sucke my teeth. **1901** W. R. H. TROWBRIDGE *Lett. her Mother to Eliz.* xxii. 106 The people at Croixmare couldn't have eaten worse than Mr. Sweetson; ..he sucked his teeth when he had finished.

11. *transf.* **a.** To draw the moisture, goodness, etc. from.

1693 EVELYN *De la Quint. Compl. Gard.* I. 51 Without doubt the Earth would not grow Lank, Meagre, and Hungry, as it does, if the Plants did not Suck it just as Animals do their Dams. **1733** TULL *Horse-hoeing Husb.* xvi. 246 'Tis certain that Turneps, when they stand for Seed, suck and impoverish the Ground exceedingly. **1879** E. ARNOLD *Lt. Asia* v. 134 In forest glades A fierce sun sucked the pools.

b. To work (a pump) dry. (Cf. 19.)

1753 *Scots Mag.* Mar. 156/2 About four in the afternoon the pump was sucked. **1857** in *Merc. Marine Mag.* (1858) V. 8 After sucking the pumps, I had to keep one pump..at work.

c. To cling closely to.

1859 TENNYSON *Marr. Geraint* 324 Monstrous ivy-stems ..suck'd the joining of the stones.

12. To draw money, information, or the like from (a person); to rob (a person or thing) of its resouces or support; to drain, 'bleed'.

1558 in Feuillerat *Revels Q. Eliz.* (1908) 17 He will..make waiste, sucke the Quene, or pynche the poore or all thre. **1617** SIR T. ROE in *Embassy* (1899) 419 In hope to gett, no man can escape him [the King]; when hee hath suckd them, hee will not knowe them. **1752** CHESTERF. *Lett.* cclxxii, When you are with *des gens de robe*, suck them with regard to the constitution and civil government. *a* **1774** FERGUSSON *Plainstanes & Cawsey* Poems (1845) 48 And o' three shillin's Scottish suck him. **1847** EMERSON *Repr. Men, Napoleon* Wks. (Bohn) I. 374 The land sucked of its nourishment, by a small class of legitimates. **1856** KINGSLEY in *N. Brit. Rev.* XXV. 22 Fathers became gradually personages who are to be disobeyed, sucked of their money, [etc.]. **1874** GEO. ELIOT *Coll. Breakf.-P.* 617 Who..suck the commonwealth to feed their ease.

13. a. With predicative adj.: To render so-and-so by sucking.

1530 PALSGR. 742/2 You shall se hym sucke him selfe asleepe. **1606** SHAKS. *Ant. & Cl.* v. ii. 313 Dost thou not see my Baby at my breast, That suckes the Nurse asleepe. **1607** TOPSELL *Four-f. Beasts* 302 In the next morning let them [*sc.* foals] be admitted to sucke their belly full. **1715** F. SLARE *Vindic. Sugars* 54 This Liquor invited all Sorts of Flies to it, ..many of them did suck themselves drunk. **180.** in Dickson *Pract. Agric.* (1805) II. 1058 [The ewes] are..held by the head till the lambs by turns suck them clean. **1879** BURROUGHS *Locusts & Wild Honey* 11 Bees will suck themselves tipsy upon varieties like the sops-of-wine.

b. *to suck dry*, to extract all the moisture or liquid out of by suction; *fig.* to exhaust.

1592 *Arden of Feversham* II. ii. 119 When she is dry suckt of her eager young. **1593** SHAKS. *3 Hen. VI*, IV. viii. 55 My Sea shall suck them dry. **1598** STOW *Surv.* 470 London felt it most tragicall; for then he both seysed their liberties, and sucked themselues dry. **1647** H. MORE *Poems* 266 Abhorred cugs by devils sucken dry. *a* **1719** ADDISON tr. *Virg. Fourth Georg.* 195 Wks. 1721 I. 24 Some [bees]..Taste ev'ry bud, and suck each blossom dry. **1771** *Ann. Reg.* 207/1 After one had sucked the bones quite dry,..I have seen another take them up,..and do the same. **1865** DICKENS *Mut. Fr.* III. v, A crew of plunderers, who would suck me dry by driblets.

14. To produce as by suction. *rare.*

1849 T. Woolner *My Beautiful Lady, My Lady in Death* xvi, The heavy sinking at her heart Sucked hollows in her cheek.

III. 15. a. *intr.* Of the young of a mammal: To perform the action described in sense 1; to draw milk from the teat; to feed from the breast or udder.

c **1000** [see sucking *ppl. a.* 1]. *c* **1175** *Lamb. Hom.* 5 He mihte ridan..uppon þa lutthle fole þat ȝet hit wes sukinde. *c* **1205** Lay. 13194 Vther wes to lutel þa ȝet he moste suken. *c* **1290** *Beket* 1460 in *S. Eng. Leg.* 148 Ne womman þat was with childe, Ne þe children þat soukinde weren. **1303** R. Brunne *Handl. Synne* 6022 Com a pore womman..And bare a chylde..þe pappe yn þe mouþe as hyt had soke. *c* **1375** *Sc. Leg. Saints* xvi. (*Magdalena*) 679 þai..fand þe child at þe pape, lyand rycht as he sukit had. *c* **1440** *Sir Gowther* 113 He sak so sore thei [*sc.* the nurses] lost here lyfes. **1513** Douglas *Æneis* iii. vi. 74 A grete sow fereit of grysis thretty heid, Liggin on the ground..About hir pappis sowkin. **1523** Fitzherb. *Husb.* §39 Let them sucke as longe as the dammes wyll suffre theym. **1542** Boorde *Dyetary* xvi. (1870) 275 All thynges the whiche dothe sucke, is nutrytyue. **1600** Shaks. *A.Y.L.* iii. ii. 81 To see my Ewes graze, & my Lambes sucke. **1606** —— *Tr. & Cr.* i. iii. 292 Tell him of Nestor, one that was a man When Hectors Grandsire suckt. **1687** A. Lovell tr. *Thevenot's Trav.* i. 167 There we saw a great many Women, and little Children, most of them Sucking. **1799** *Med. Jrnl.* II. 44 The wet-nurse having presented it the breast, it took it with avidity, but it could suck but little, in consequence of its weak state. **1820** Shelley *Œd. Tyr.* i. 51, I suck, but no milk will come from the dug. **1858** Churchill *Dis. Childr.* 30 It is desirable that a child should not be weaned before nine months, nor suck after twelve.

b. *at*, †*of*, †*on* the breast or the mother.

c **1330** *Arth. & Merl.* 8466 þou souke of hir tat. **1377** Langl. *P. Pl.* B. xi. 116 He..badde hem souke for synne saufly at his breste [**1393** C. xiii. 55 Souken of hus brest]. *c* **1386** Chaucer *Prioress' Prol.* 6 Children..on the brest soukynge. *a* **1400** *Octouian* 555 A man chyld..Sok of her as of a woman That wher hys dame. *c* **1460** *Towneley Myst.* xxi. 57 Of my dame sen I sowked had I neuer sich a nyght. **1486** *Bk. St. Albans, Hunting* e iv, A fawne sowkyng on his dam. **1549** *N. Country Wills* (Surtees 1908) 204 Two mares..and two feles sucking upon theym. *a* **1578** Lindesay (Pitscottie) *Chron. Scot.* (S.T.S.) II. 53 The zoung babe of hir breist sucand. **1590** Spenser *F.Q.* i. i. 15 A thousand yong ones.. Sucking vpon her poisonous dugs. **1645** *Relation late Witches* 19 The said Anne offered to give unto her daughter Sarah Cooper an Impe in the likenes of a gray Kite, to suck on the said Sarah. **1691** Ray *Creation* i. (1692) 117 Such as are nourished with Milk, presently find their way to the Paps, and suck at them.

c. of flies drawing blood, etc., as in 1 b.

1610 Shaks. *Temp.* v. i. 88 Where the Bee sucks, there suck I. **1728** Pope *Dunc.* i. 130 How there he plunder'd snug, And suck'd all o'er, like an industrious Bug. **1780** Cowper *Progr. Err.* 326 These flesh-flies of the land; Who fasten without mercy on the fair, And suck, and leave a craving maggot there. **1870** Wilson *Austral. Songs* 99 Honey-birds loitered to suck at the wattle.

†**d.** *transf.* and *fig.* *Obs.*

a **1548** Hall *Chron., Edw. IV*, 229 b, Suche other as daily flatered hym for their peculier profites (as he had many in deede that daily sucked at his elbowe). **1571** Digges *Pantom.* A iv, Such two footed Moules and Todes whom..nature hath ordayned to craule within the earth, and suck upon the muck. *a* **1626** Bacon *Hen. VIII* in *Misc., Wks.* (1629) 165 The Crowne, which had sucked too hard, and now being full,..was like to Draw lesse.

e. To practise fellatio (or cunnilingus). *coarse slang.*

1928 in A. W. Read *Lexical Evidence from Folk Epigraphy Western N. Amer.* (1935) 78 My cock is only 10 ins long so if any one would like to suck meet me here 9 pm. **1960** [see sense 1 f above]. **1975** E. Hannon *Doors* 123 White chicks dig suckin, that's a fact. That's cause suckin's sophisticated. **1977** M. T. Bloom *13th Man* (1978) viii. 148 The pimp said: 'She wouldn't suck so she couldn't make a living. I had to send her back.'

f. To be contemptible or disgusting. *slang.* Cf. suck *sb.*[1] 12.

1971 *It* 2–16 June 3/2 Polaroid sucks! For some time the Polaroid Corporation has been supplying the South African government with large photo systems..to use for photographing blacks for the passbooks..every black must carry. **1976** G. V. Higgins *Judgment of Deke Hunter* vi. 59, I had a lousy summer... I thought it sucked, and I bet next summer'll suck too. **1978** M. Gordon *Final Payments* xi. 193 All the hotels have the same pictures. The last one, the food sucked.

16. a. to give suck (occas. † *to give to suck*): to give milk from the breast or udder, to suckle. Const. simple dat. or *to*. Now *arch.*

Suck, properly infin. (cf. G. *zu saugen geben*, Du. *te zuigen geven*), is now felt as a sb.; cf. suck *sb.*[1] 1 a.

c **1330** *Arth & Merl.* 2694 Late..þi wiif it loke Of hir milk & ȝiue it souke. **1340** *Ayenb.* 60 þe blonderes byeþ þe dyeules noriches þet his children yeueþ zouke. *c* **1386** Chaucer *Reeve's T.* 237 To rokken and to yeue the child to sowke. *c* **1400** *Pilgr. Sowle* (Caxton 1483) iv. xx. 65 Eke the to sowken of my brestes yafe I. **1471** Caxton *Recuyell* (Sommer) 12 Am y not he that ye bare and gaf me souke of your brestes? **1588** Kyd *Househ. Phil.* Wks. (1901) 237 Mothers ought to giue their owne Children sucke. **1653** H. Cogan tr. *Pinto's Trav.* lxiv. 257 If a mother hath a child which she cannot give suck unto for some valuable consideration. **1786** J. Hunter *Treat. Ven. Dis.* vii. i. 388 She gave suck to this second child. **1801** *Med. Jrnl.* V. 504 A poor woman, who gave suck to a child about a year old. **1858** Churchill *Dis. Childr.* 30 The mother may give the child suck during the night or day only.

b. without personal obj. Now *arch.*

1382 Wyclif *Luke* xxiii. 29 Wombis that han not gendrid, and the teetis whiche han not ȝouun souke. **1526** Tindale *Matt.* xxiv. 19 To them that are with chylde, and to them that geve sucke [Wyclif noryschinge]. **1605** Shaks. *Macb.* i. vii. 54, I haue giuen Sucke, and know How tender 'tis to loue the Babe that milkes me. **1674** tr. *Scheffer's Lapland* 131 Those [does] that have young ones never are housed, but give suck without. **1691** Ray *Creation* i. (1692) 107 Seeing it would be for many reasons inconvenient for Birds to give Suck.

17. *to suck at*: (*a*) to take a draught of; to inhale: (*b*) to take a pull at (a pipe, drinking vessel).

1584 Cogan *Haven Health* ccxxi. (1636) 256 Mervaile it is to see how the Welchmen will lye sucking at this drinke [*sc.* Metheglin]. **1607** Dekker *Knt.'s Conjur.* (1842) 49 Snakes euer sucking at thy breath. **1815** J. Smith *Panorama Sci. & Art* II. 124 Drawing out the air with the mouth by sucking at the orifice *c.* **1855** Browning *Grammar. Funeral* 96 Back to his studies..He..Sucked at the flagon. **1872** E. Yates *Castaway* i. ix, He sat quietly sucking away at his long pipe.

18. Of inanimate objects: To draw by suction.

c **1220** *Bestiary* 568 Ðer ðe water sukeð [*MS.* sinkeð], sipes ge sinkeð. [*Cf.* suk *in l.* 578.] **1573** Tusser *Husb.* (1878) 47 Weede and the water so soketh and sucks, that goodnes from either it vtterly plucks. **1871** *Trans. Amer. Inst. Mining Eng.* I. 53 If the stamps are left..standing in the pulp, between blows, the material settles around them and they 'suck' when the lift commences.

19. Of a pump: To draw air instead of water, as a result of the exhaustion of the water or a defective valve.

1627 Capt. J. Smith *Sea. Gram.* ii. 9 The Pumpe sucks, is when the water being out, it drawes vp nothing but froth and winde. **1769** Falconer *Dict. Marine* (1780) s.v. *Pompe*, The pump sucks, or is dry. **1831** Jane Porter *Sir. E. Seaward's Narr.* I. 61 It [*sc.* the pump] sucked, that is no more water remained within reach. **1899** F. T. Bullen *Log Sea-waif* 170 Of course she leaked..but still in fine weather the pumps would 'suck' in ten minutes at four-hour intervals.

fig. **1854** Lowell *Jrnl. in Italy* iii. Prose Wks. 1890 I. 129 Even Byron's pump *sucks* sometimes, and gives an unpleasant dry wheeze. **1854** Emerson *Lett. & Soc. Aims, Resources* Wks. (Bohn) III. 197 This pump [*sc.* our globe] never sucks; these screws are never loose.

transf. **1710** C. Shadwell *Fair Quaker Deal* ii. 27 The Bowl sucks; Empty is the Word.

†**IV. 20.** *trans.* To give suck to, suckle. *Obs.*

1607 Topsell *Four-f. Beasts* 671 So is this beast enabled by nature to beare twice in the yeare, and yet to sucke her young ones two monthes together. **1612** [see opossum 1]. **1680** R. L'Estrange *Erasm. Colloq.* ii. 29 He had the Happiness to taste the Milk of the same Breast that suck'd our Saviour.

†**V. 21.** In trans. senses of soak *v.*: **a.** To cause to sink in, instil. **b.** *to suck one's face*, to drink. *Obs.*

a. 1549 Coverdale, etc. *Erasm. Par. 1 Tim.* 16 Not bryngynge the sentence with the, that fauoure or malyce or dyspleasure or any other affeccion hath secretlye sowked into thee, but of the thing selfe in dede knowen.

b. *a* **1700** B. E. *Dict. Cant. Crew* s.v., *We'll go and Suck our Faces*,..let's go to Drink... *He loves to Suck his Face*, he delights in Drinking.

VI. Specialized uses with advs.

22. a. *trans.* With various advs.: To draw by suction in some direction.

1570 *Satir. Poems Reform.* xxiv. 80 That bludy Bouchour ever deit of thrist, Soukand the soules furth of the Sanctis of God. **1599** Shaks. *Hen. V*, iv. ii. 17 Your faire shew shall suck away their Soules, Leauing them but the shales and huskes of men. **1687** A. Lovell tr. *Thevenot's Trav.* i. 3 Two contrary Eddies.., which making Vessels turn round for some time, suck them down to the bottom without remedy. **1784** Cowper *Task* ii. 103 The fixt and rooted earth, Tormented into billows,..with..hideous whirl Sucks down its prey. **1806** J. Beresford *Miseries Hum. Life* (ed. 3) ii. x, One shoe suddenly sucked off by the boggy clay. **1873** G. C. Davies *Mount. & Mere* ii. 7 A head would pop up to suck some insect down. **1879** Browning *Ivan Ivanovitch* 26 The monstrous wild a-hungered to resume Its ancient sway, suck back the world into its womb.

b. suck (a)round. *intr.* To go about behaving sycophantically. Occas. *ellipt.* Cf. sense 26 e. *slang* (orig. and chiefly *U.S.*).

1931 *Princeton Alumni Weekly* 22 May 798/1 If 'drag' or 'hot dope' is necessary one usually 'sucks around' for it. **1934** G. Ade *Let.* 27 June (1973) 186 As for the Landis party on July 10th I have had no invitation but maybe I could suck around and get one. **1940** M. Marples *Public School Slang* 169 Thus a boy is said to *suck round*, if he tries to ingratiate himself. **1941** B. Schulberg *What makes Sammy Run?* xi. 209 The tycoon who spends the first part of his life sucking and crushing, and the last part giving away dimes. **1979** 'A. Hailey' *Overload* iii. xiv. 273 Logically, she should go to the city editor. She might have done it, too, if the son-of-a-bitch hadn't handed her that coach-and-team crap earlier today. Now it would look as if she was sucking around him because of it.

23. suck in.

a. *trans.* To draw into the mouth by suction; to inhale (air, etc.); *occas.* to draw in (one's breath), etc.

c **1220** *Bestiary* 514 Ðis cete ðanne hise chaueles lukeð, ðise fisses alle in sukeð. *c* **1400** Maundev. (1839) 205 Whan thei schulle eten or drynken, thei taken thorghe a Pipe..and sowken it in. *c* **1460** *Promp. Parv.* (Winch.) 461 Sokyn in diuers þyngis, or drynkyn yn, *imbibo*. **1686** tr. *Chardin's Trav. Persia* 341 There they suck in the fresh Air. **1706** E. Ward *Wooden World Diss.* 85 He sucks in Smoak like a Virginia-Planter. **1845** Disraeli *Sybil* (1863) 282, I have breathed this air for a matter of half a century. I sucked it in when it tasted of primroses. **1885** E. Greey *Bakin's Captive of Love* iv. (1904) 28 Sucking in his breath as he bowed respectfully.

b. To imbibe (qualities, etc.) *with* one's mother's milk, *with* a draught.

1622 Fletcher *Beggar's Bush* ii. iii, I suck'd not in this patience with my milk. **1732** Berkeley *Alciphr.* i. v, The notions you first sucked in with your milk. **1781** Cowper *Hope* 518 The wretch, who once..suck'd in dizzy madness with his draught. **1848** W. K. Kelly tr. *L. Blanc's Hist. Ten Y.* II. 201 That fatal diversity which these different races had sucked in with their mother's milk.

c. *gen.* To draw or take in (*lit.* and *fig.*); to absorb.

1597 Donne *Lett. Sev. Pers., Storme* 62 Pumping hath tir'd our men, and what's the gaine? Seas into seas throwne, we suck in againe. **1603** B. Jonson *Sejanus* i. ii, Those deeds breath honor, that do suck in gaine. **1606** Shaks. *Tr. & Cr.* ii. ii. 12 There is no Lady..More spungie, to sucke in the sense of Feare. **1678** Bunyan *Pilgr.* i. (1900) 56 These infirmities possessed me in thy Country, for there I suckt them in. **1728** Pope *Dunc.* iii. 58 As..whirligigs twirl'd round by skilful swain, Suck the thread in, then yield it out again. *a* **1774** Goldsm. *Surv. Exp. Philos.* (1776) I. 64 Sometimes electric bodies suck in the electric fire, and sometimes they throw it out.

d. To take in by means of the perceptive faculties.

c **1600** Chalkhill *Thealma & Cl.* (1683) 10 With desire Her ears suck'd in her speech. **1667** Pepys *Diary* 17 Aug., I have sucked in so much of the sad story of Queen Elizabeth,..that I was ready to weep for her. **1669** Gale *Crt. Gentiles* i. ii. viii. 116 This Persian Idolatrie, which the Israelites had suckt in. **1745** P. Thomas *Jrnl. Anson's Voy.* 240 They could not shake off the Prejudices they had sucked in. **1780** Mme. D'Arblay *Lett.* 27 April, The portion you allowed me of your..Journal, I sucked in with much pleasure and avidity. **1793** D'Israeli *Cur. Lit.* II. 112 He [*sc.* Jonson] would sit silent in learned company, and suck in (besides wine) their several humours into his observation.

e. To draw in, as into a whirlpool or vortex.

1616 J. Lane *Contn. Sqr.'s T.* ix. 273 Which..bothe sokes and bringes men in, Wheare none, at last, shall either save or winn. **1663** S. Patrick *Parab. Pilgr.* xxxvii. (1687) 486 The waters began to suck him in. **1728** Pope *Dunc.* ii. 332 Sinking to the chin, Smit with his mien the Mud-nymphs suck'd him in. **1807** Wordsw. *Blind Highland Boy* 155 The tide retreated from the shore, And sucked, and sucked him in. **1849** Lyell *2nd Visit U.S.* (1850) II. 168 He had seen the water rush through the opening at the rate of ten miles an hour, sucking in several flat boats. **1856** Emerson *Eng. Traits, Wealth* Wks. (Bohn) II. 75 The poor-rate was sucking in the solvent classes.

f. *dial.* and *slang.* To take in, cheat, deceive.

1842 'Mrs. Clavers' *Forest Life* I. xiii. 135, I a'n't bound to drive nobody in the middle of the night,..so don't you try to suck me in there. *c* **1850** 'Dow jr.' in Jerdan *Yankee Hum.* (1853) 113 The British got pretty nicely sucked in, when our Dutch grandaddies went to smoking on the Battery, and concealed it beneath a cloud of tobacco fume. **1909** *Westm. Gaz.* 15 May 2/3 You've tried to run a ship on the cheap and been sucked in.

g. *intr.* To curry favour *with*. *Sc.*

1899 Crockett *Kit Kennedy* 239 He tells tales on the rest of the scholars, to sook-in wi' the maister.

24. suck off. *trans.* To cause (someone) to experience an orgasm by fellatio or cunnilingus. *coarse slang.* Cf. sense 1 f above.

1928 in A. W. Read *Lexical Evidence from Folk Epigraphy Western N. Amer.* (1935) 79 When will you meet me to suck me off? **1941** G. W. Henry *Sex Variants* II. 1176 The object of *suck* can be either the organ or the person; but the object of *suck off* is usually the person, who is mentioned within the idiom, e.g. 'to suck him off'. **1959** W. Burroughs *Naked Lunch* 76 Equilibrists suck each other off deftly. **1969** Fabian & Byrne *Groupie* (1970) vii. 50 He listened superciliously..and, spreading his legs, asked me to 'suck him off' to make him less uptight. **1971** *Guardian* 27 Sept. 14/5 One American GI is forcing a Vietnamese woman to suck him off. **1976** J. Crosby *Snake* (1977) xxxv. 222 Elf has had a busy night... Sucking me off till all hours.

25. suck out.

a. *trans.* To draw out or extract by or as by suction. Also in fig. context.

c **1375** *Sc. Leg. Saints* xi. (*Symon & Judas*) 321 þa..bad þe edris suk owt faste al þe venyme. **1398** Trevisa *Barth. De P.R.* iv. vii. (1495) 90 Flyes and wormes that sytt on flesshe and sucke out the blode. *c* **1440** *Pallad. on Husb.* xi. 16 Sowe hit not, hit sowkith out the swete Of euery lond. **1535** Coverdale *Ps.* lxxiv. 8 As for the dregges therof, all ye vngodly of the earth shal drynke them, & sucke them out. **1563** T. Gale *Antidot.* i. ii. 2 It [a medicine] sucketh oute superfluous moysture in dropsyes. **1611** *Bible* Ezek. xxiii. 34 Thou shalt euen drinke it and sucke it out. **1618–19** Fletcher, etc. *Q. Corinth* ii. iv, They look like potch'd Eggs with the souls suckt out Empty and full of wind. *a* **1700** Evelyn *Diary* 24 Aug. 1678, The flannell sucking out the moisture. **1753** *Chambers' Cycl.* Suppl. s.v. *Sucking*, The tip [of the tongue] is again employed to the sucking out more milk. **1843** Carlyle *Past & Pr.* ii. iv. 78 Every fresh Jew sticking on him like a fresh horseleech, sucking his and our life out. **1865** Tylor *Early Hist. Man.* xiii. 363 They pretend to cure the sick by sucking out stones through their skin.

†**b.** To extract (information or profit). *Obs.*

1546 *St. Papers Hen. VIII*, XI. 14 His Majestes pleasure is, that sucking out as moche as ye may to what other condicions they will descende, you shall [etc.]. **1604** E. G[rimstone] *D'Acosta's Hist. Indies* To Rdr., Every one may sucke out some profit for himselfe.

†**c.** To drain. *Obs.*

1687 Miège *Gt. Fr. Dict.* ii. s.v., He suckt out (or suckt up) the Bottle.

26. suck up.

a. *trans.* To draw up into the mouth by suction. Also, †to drain the contents of.

a **1450** Myrc (1902) 1811 ȝef a drope of blod..Falle vp-on þe corporas, Sowke hyt vp a-non-ryȝt. **1560** *Bible* (Geneva) Job xxxix. 33 His yong ones also sucke vp blood. **1577** B. Googe *Heresbach's Husb.* iv. (1586) 188 The Toade bloweth them, and sucketh them [*sc.* bees] vp at their owne doores. **1601** Shaks. *Jul. C.* ii. i. 262 Is it Physicall to walke vnbraced, and sucke vp the humours Of the danke Morning? **1668** Wilkins *Real Char.* ii. ix. §2. 236 Sucking up the breath. **1687** [see 25 c.]. **1774** GOLDSM. *Nat. Hist.* (1776) IV. 264 The elephant dips the end of its trunk into the water, and sucks up just as much as fills that great fleshy tube. **1840** *Cuvier's Anim. Kingd.* 207 The Sun-birds.. subsist on the nectar of flowers, which they suck up.

b. To draw up as by suction or the creation of a vacuum; to absorb (liquid); to draw up (moisture) by heat; also, to draw up moisture from.

1530 PALSGR. 742/2 As the yerthe, or a sponge sucketh up water. **1590** SHAKS. *Mids. N.* II. i. 89 The Windes..haue suck'd vp from the sea Contagious fogges. **1604** JAS. I. *Counterbl. to Tobacco* (Arb.) 104 The smoakie vapours sucked vp by the Sunne. **1630** DRAYTON *Muses Eliz., Noah's Flood* 106 By this the Sunne had suckt vp the vaste deepe. **1683** MOXON *Mech. Exerc., Printing* xxiv. ¶ 19 He rubs it [*sc.* the sponge] over..the Tympan, to Suck up the Water. **1825** J. NICHOLSON *Oper. Mech.* 102 To prevent the formation of a vacuum in the rising bucket, or what is called by the miller 'sucking up the tail-water'. **1863** KINGSLEY *Water-Bab.* (1874) 55 The burning sun on the fells had sucked him up; but the damp heat of the woody crag sucked him up still more. **1877** HUXLEY *Physiogr.* 71 The thread constantly sucks up the liquid.

†**c.** To absorb by a mental process; to drink in.

1602 MARSTON *Antonio's Rev.* V. vi, May his stile..have gentle presence, and the sceans suckt up By calme attention of choyce audience. *c* **1610** *Women Saints* 89 The holie virgin..sucked vp and exhaled her maisters..praises of her celestiall Loues excellencie.

d. To swallow up.

1611 SHAKS. *Cymb.* III. i. 22 Roaring Waters, With Sands that will not beare your Enemies Boates, But sucke them vp to' th' Top-mast. **1650** *Contemp Hist. Irel.* (Ir. Archæol. Soc.) II. 101 This good service they haue don to his Majestie after shokinge up the sweete and substance of his Catholicke subjects of Monster. **1795** GOUV. MORRIS in Sparks *Life & Writ.* (1832) III. 52 Britain will suck up that commerce which formerly flowed to Amsterdam. **1869** LOWELL *Dara* v, Wise Dara's province, year by year, Like a great sponge, sucked wealth and plenty up.

e. *intr.* **to suck up to**, to curry favour with; to toady to. (Also without *to.*) *slang* (orig. *Schoolboys*'). Cf. *sucker-up* s.v. SUCKER *sb.* 14.

1860 *Hotten's Slang Dict.* (ed. 2) 231 *Suck up*, 'to suck up to a person', to insinuate oneself into his good graces. **1876** ANNIE THOMAS *Blotted out* xvi, I can't suck up to snobs because they happen to be in power and to have patronage. **1899** E. PHILLPOTTS *Human Boy* 203 Fowle sucked up to him..and buttered him at all times. **1905** H. A. VACHELL *Hill* vi, 'Afterwards', John continued, 'I tried to suck-up. I asked you to come and have some food.' **1936** M. MITCHELL *Gone with Wind* xl. 719 We hear how you suck up to the Yankees..to get money out of them. **1945** E. WAUGH *Brideshead Revisited* II. iv. 261, I imagine she's been used to bossing things rather in naval circles, with flag-lieutenants trotting round and young officers on-the-make sucking up to her. **1957** R. K. MERTON *Social Theory* (rev. ed.) viii. 270 Data in *The American Soldier* on what was variously called brown-nosing, bucking for promotion, and sucking up. **1963** D. OGILVY *Confess. Advert. Man* (1964) i. 15, I despise toadies who suck up to their bosses; they are generally the same people who bully their subordinates. **1966** [see CRAWL *v.*[1] 3 c]. **1979** J. COOPER *Class* (1980) vi. 131 Harry Stow-Crat also has to suck up to neighbouring farmers in case he should want to hunt over their land.

suck-, the verb-stem used in combination: **suck-fish** = SUCKER *sb.* 11; †**suck-fist** [FIST *sb.*[2]], a toady; †**suck-giver** [f. phr. *give suck*: see SUCK *v.* 16], a wet-nurse; **suck-hole**, †(*a*) ? (see quot. 1626); (*b*) *U.S.*, a whirlpool, a pond; (*c*) *Canad.* and *Austral. slang*, a term of abuse (cf. SUCK *sb.*[1] 12); hence as *v. intr. slang* (orig. and chiefly *Canad.*), to curry favour; **suck-jack** [partial transl. of Pg. *papa-jaca*, f. *papar* to swallow + *jaca* (locally) little crab], a fish (see quot.); **suck-lamb** [tr. G. *sauglamm*; cf. SOCK-LAMB], a sucking lamb; †**suck-nurse**, a wet-nurse; †**suck-pint** = SUCK-BOTTLE 2; †**suck-purse**, an extortioner; †**suck-spigot** = SUCK-BOTTLE 2; also *attrib.*; †**suck-stone**, a remora or sucking-fish; **suck-(a)-thumb**, a child that sucks its thumb; also *attrib.*

1753 *Chambers' Cycl.* Suppl., **Suck-fish*,..an English name for the *remora*, or *echeneis* of Artedi. **1758** W. BORLASE *Nat. Hist. Cornw.* 269, I found on Careg-killas, in Mount's Bay, a particular kind of suck-fish [*Lepadogaster cornubiensis*]. **1876** GOODE *Fishes of Bermudas* 61 *Leptecheneis naucrates*..and *Ptheirichthys lineatus*..are probably the most common species of 'Suck-fish' found here. **1611** COTGR., *Humevesne* [read *vesse*], a *sucke-fist. **1551** T. WILSON *Logic* (1580) 80 b, Wee Englishemen knowe (not onely by hearesaie, but also by good experince) that custome is the mother, and the *sucke giuer vnto all erroure. **1626** MIDDLETON *Mayor of Queenb.* III. iii, I will learn the villany of all trades;..if in the brewer, I will taste him throughly, and piss out his iniquity at his own *suckhole. **1909** *Dialect Notes* III. 377 *Suck-hole, n.*, a whirlpool. Common [in East Alabama]. **1961** PARTRIDGE *Dict. Slang* Suppl. 1302/2 *Suck-hole, v.*, to toady, as in 'He won't suck-hole to anyone'; hence, to cringe; low Canadian; C. 20. **1964** F. O'ROURKE *Mule for Marquesa* 200 They rode on toward the small water hole... Dolworth led them off a plateau down the rocky trail to the suckhole under the rock ledge. **1966** P. MATHERS *Trap* 12 Our progressive mayor..and his pack of scabby suckhole mates. **1968** J. WAINWRIGHT *Edge of Extinction* 48 He can roast to hell—then go suckholing to Old Nick. **1970** *Globe Mag.* (Toronto) 31 Oct. 4/2 No matter how strong I could become there was still someone in this city of 470,000 who thought I was a suckhole. **1972** J. METCALF *Going down Slow* vii. 128 Can't even fix yourself a sandwich without suckholing round that man. **1843** LOWE *Fishes Madeira* 177 *Sebastes Maderensis*..Little Rock-fish, or *Suck-jack. *Ibid.* 178 Its second Portuguese name of 'Papa-Jaca', or Suck-jack, it has earned by its troublesome addiction to hooks baited with the little crab 'Jaca'. **1887** *Daily News* 20 June 2/6 German *suck lamb, 5s 4d. *c* **1640** H. BELL *Luther's Colloq. Mens.* (1652) 315 They compelled women with childe and *suck-nurses to fast. **1611** COTGR., *Humeux*, a *sucke-pinte, or swill-pot; a notable drunkard. **1586** SIR E. HOBY tr. *Coignet's Polit. Disc. Truth* 41 [They] winde themselues out of the handes of these *suckpurses [orig. *succebourses*]. **1585** HIGINS *Junius' Nomencl.* 425 *Ebriosus*,.. a dronkard: a *suckspigget. **1639** HORN & ROB. *Gate Lang. Unl.* lxxxiv. §823 A common crunkard (a suck-spiggot, swill-bowl) that is alwaies bibbing. **1661** K. W. *Conf. Charac., Cambr. Minion* (1860) 82 She's a fine finacle Cambridge production, got by and aiming no higher then some suckspicket sophister. **1602** *Withals' Dict.* 37 A little Fishe called a *Suckstone, yt staieth a ship vnder saile. **1661** LOVELL *Hist. Anim. & Min.* 235 Suckstone. *Remora.* They are said by their magnetick vertue to stop ships. **18..** *Shock-headed Peter*, I said the Scissors Man would come, To disobedient *Suck-a-Thumb. **1890** E. WARREN *Laughing Eyes* 50 A helpless suck-thumb infant.

suckable ('sʌkəb(ə)l), *a.* and *sb. rare.* [f. SUCK *v.* + -ABLE.] **A.** *adj.* That can be sucked. **B.** *sb.* A suckable kind of food.

1846 M. WILLIAMS *Sanscr. Gram.* p. 9 This division of food into four kinds, lickables, drinkables, chewables, and suckables, is not unusual in Indian writings. **1865** *Morn. Star* Sept. 25 They sucked the sweets of all that was suckable.

suckabob ('sʌkəbɒb). *rare.* [f. SUCK *v.*] A sweetmeat that is sucked in the mouth.

1888 J. PAYN *Myst. Mirbridge* v, The British lollipop or suckabob.

'suck-,bottle. [f. SUCK- + BOTTLE *sb.*]

1. An infant's feeding-bottle. (Cf. SUCKING-BOTTLE.)

1641 BROME *Joviall Crew* v. Wks. 1873 450 Nephew Martin, still the Childe with a Suck-bottle of Sack. **1674** tr. *Scheffer's Lapland* xxvi. 123 Rain-deers milk..is grosser and thicker then they can well draw out of a suck-bottle. **1709** [W. KING] *Usef. Trans. Philos.* Mar. & Apr. 56 The Child must have Presents of Silver Caudle-Cups, Porringers, Spoons, and Suck-Bottles. **1853** *Househ. Words* VIII. 146/1 They will furnish you with every assistance you can want; a valet-de-chambre,..a nurse-maid, and, thanks to the suck-bottle, even a nurse.

2. A tippler. Also as a quasi-proper name.

a **1652** BROME *Love-sick Crt.* v. ii, What sayes old Suck-bottle? **1707** WARD *Terræ-filius* No. 2. 9 Such a Swill-Belly'd Suck-Bottle.

sucked (sʌkt), *ppl. a.* [f. SUCK *v.* + -ED[1].] In various senses of the verb; extracted, absorbed, or depleted by suction.

sucked orange: see ORANGE *sb.*[1] 1 b.

1600 SHAKS. *A.Y.L.* IV. iii. 127 Did he leaue him there Food to the suck'd and hungry Lyonnesse? **1667** MILTON *P.L.* x. 633 Nigh burst With suckt and glutted offal. **1824** MISS FERRIER *Inher.* lxxii, Pretty!—what makes her pretty? —wi' a face like a sooket carvy! **1857** W. E. GLADSTONE in Morley *Life* (1903) I. IV. viii. 561 But for Disraeli, who could not be thrown away like a sucked orange. **1881** ENSOR *Journ. Nubia* viii. 73 The sucked and marrowless bones. **1904** *Brit. Med. Jrnl.* 17 Sept. 665 Some half dozen [maggots] which were filled with recently sucked blood. **1906** C. MANSFIELD *Girl & Gods* xxiii, The streets seemed filled with drunkards, sucked oranges, hot chestnuts, sore noses and chilblains. **1909** OXENHAM *Great-Heart Gillian* xliii. 310 Baby Gillian ..waved a sucked pink thumb at him and his men.

b. *sucked stone*, a honeycombed stone occurring in the tin lodes of Cornwall.

1778 PRYCE *Min. Cornub.* 90 The Lode itself..is cavernous, and full of holes, thence called a Sucked Stone by the Tinners. **1814** W. PHILLIPS in *Trans. Geol. Soc.* II. 118.

'suck-egg. [f. SUCK- + EGG *sb.*[1]] **a.** An animal that is reputed to suck eggs, e.g. a weasel, cuckoo; *fig.* an avaricious person. **b.** A young fellow; *slang.* 'a silly person' (Barrère & Leland).

1609 ARMIN *Maids of More-Cl.* C iij b, Where's this suck-egge, wheres Jack a boy? **16..** MIDDLETON, etc. *Old Law* III. ii, This beard cannot get children, you lank suck-eggs, Unless such weasels come from court to help us. *c* **1640** [SHIRLEY] *Capt. Underwit.* v. i. in Bullen *Old Pl.* (1883) II. 395 *Con.* Is there not a weesill crept into your Chamber, lady?..A Mounsier sucklegge [*sic*]. *Sis.* Do you take my Chamber for a henns neast? **1685** CROWNE *Sir C. Nice* II, A Scholler Madam? a Schollers Egg—emptyed by old suck-Eggs, of all that Nature gave me. **1836** HALIBURTON *Clockm.* Ser. I v. (1839) 12, I guess, said he, if General Campbell knew what sort of a man that are magistrate was, he'd disband him pretty quick, he's a regular suck-egg. **1851** STERNBERG *Dial. Northants.* 109 *Suck, Suck-egg*, the cuckoo; also applied to a stupid fellow.

c. *attrib.* That sucks eggs. Also *U.S. dial* (chiefly *South* and *Midland*), used to designate a dog regarded as the type of viciousness or worthlessness (also *transf.*).

1631 QUARLES *Hist. Samson* Wks. (Grosart) II. 141 The suck-egge Weasell. **1658** ROWLAND tr. *Moufet's Theat. Ins.* 934 Of the first kinde is the Flesh-fly, Horse-fly, Oxe-fly, the Suck-egge-fly. **1892** *Dialect Notes* I. 232 He is as mean as a suck-egg dog. **1927** P. GREEN *Unto Such Glory* in *One-Act Plays for Stage & Study* 3rd Ser. 104 He's a dirty low-down suck-egg dog. **1931** *Virginia Q. Rev.* Jan. 102 Hayes got up and slunk off like a suck-egg dog caught in the hen-house. **1958** 'W. HENRY' *Seven Men at Mimbres Springs* ix. 107 But I will be a suck-egg son of a bitch if I can't tie my good arm behind me, stand on my bad leg only, and still whup me the living daylights out of any skinny little Alabama bast—.

sucken ('sʌkən), *sb.*[1] *Sc.* Forms: 5 sukkin, swken, 5–7 suckin, 6 su(c)kyn, 9 shucken, 7– sucken. [Variant of SOKEN. The orig. meaning is 'resort' (*sc.* to a particular mill).]

1. The duty and liability of tenants within a district astricted to a mill. (See THIRLAGE 2 and cf. SOKEN 2 b.) †Also *occas.* the meal ground at such a mill.

1423 *Charters*, etc. *of Edinb.* (1871) 55 With the suckins, thryl multris, and al freedomes langand thairto. **1488** *Acta Dom. Audit.* (1839) 124/2 Þe wrangwis withhalding of þe þrell multure and sukkin awing to þe said alexandris mylne. **15..** *Aberd. Reg.* V. 16 (Jam.), He com nocht to grynd his quhyt in thair mill as he that aucht suckyn thareto. **1641** *Acts Parl. Scot., Chas. I* (1814) V. 657/1 Sex bollis of moulter or sucking quhilkis perteinet to the Carmelite freires of the said burcht. **1711** in *Nairne Peerage Evidence* (1874) 138 All and haill the lands of Hardhaugh and Chimieshill with ye multures suckens sequells and knaveship therof. **1806** R. JAMIESON *Pop. Ballads* I. 294 Her daddie, a cannie ald carl, Had shucken and mouter a fouth.

2. The lands astricted to a mill; = THIRL *sb.*[2] 1 c; also, the population of such lands.

Cf. INSUCKEN, OUTSUCKEN.

1754 ERSKINE *Princ. Law Scot.* II. ix. (1757) 210 The lands astricted, (which are called also the thirle or sucken). **1799** J. ROBERTSON *Agric. Perth* 397 The greatest difficulty arises, where the mill belongs to one proprietor and the sucken to another. **1820** SCOTT *Monast.* xiii, Those of the Sucken, or enthralled ground, were liable in penalties, if, deviating from this thirlage,..they carried their grain to another mill. **1872** INNES *Lect. Scot. Legal Antiq.* ii. 47 The sucken, as we call the population thirled to a mill.

b. *transf.* The area of a bailiff's jurisdiction; the district within which one practises or carries on business.

a **1688** J. WALLACE *Descr. Orkney* (1693) 93 Sucken, A Bailiffrie, so much ground as is vnder the Bailiffs Jurisdiction. **1871** W. ALEXANDER *J. Milne's Songs & Poems* Introd. p. ix, He afterwards commenced business as a shoemaker..in the parish of Durris, where he had a sufficient 'sucken' to employ two men besides himself. **1871** —— *Johnny Gibb* (1873) 117 The younger Dr. Drogemweal, who had settled 'doon throu'', so as to be beyond the limits of his father's 'sucken'.

Hence **'suckener**, a tenant of a sucken; **'suckening**, the astriction of tenants to a mill.

1636 *Reg. Mag. Sig. Scot.* 215/2 In *lie suckning, thirling*, et astringendo burgenses. **1754** ERSKINE *Princ. Law Scot.* II. ix. (1757) 214 Where there is neither an explicite constitution of thirlage, nor proof of services of any sort, performed by the suckeners, the dominant tenement can claim none. **1797** *Statist. Acc. Scot.* XIX. 67 The millers.. oppress the suckeners. **1820** SCOTT *Monast.* xiii. *note*, Perquisites demanded by the miller, and submitted to or resisted by the Suckener as circumstances permitted.

'sucken, *sb.*[2] *dial.* Also **-an.** [Obscure formation on the root of SUCK *v.*] Wet, moisture; liquid manure; = SOCK *sb.*[3] 2, 2 b. Hence **'suckeny** *a.*

1615 W. LAWSON *Country Housew. Garden* (1626) 7 The sucken of your Dwelling-house, descending into your Orchard (if it be cleanly conueighed) is good. *Ibid.* 41 The earth that feeds them decaying..must either haue supply of sucken, or else leaue thriuing and growing. **1878** *Cumberld. Gloss., Suckan* [mispr. *Suckam*]..*Suckeny land*, moist land of good quality.

'sucken, *a. rare.* [Short for *bond-sucken* (cf. *love-soken* s.v. LOVE *sb.*[1] 16), properly a sb. = compulsory resort of a tenant to a mill for the grinding of his corn.] Astricted *to* a mill; = THIRL *a.*

[**1523** FITZHERB. *Surv.* 9 b, The lordes tenauntes be called bonde socon. **1859** DICKINSON *Gloss. Words & Phr. Cumberld.* 11 Some farms are bound by tenure to carry their corn to the manorial mill to be multured and ground, and are 'bond-sucken' to that mill.]

1878 J. DAVIDSON *Inverurie* Introd. 7 The corns sucken to the mill. *Ibid.* v. 178 Conglass and Drimmies were sucken to the very ancient Mill of Inveramsay. **1882** in *Jamieson's Sc. Dict.*

†**sucken**, obs. Sc. pa. pple. of SINK *v.* (Cf. *drucken.*)

1535 STEWART *Cron. Scot.* (Rolls) I. 20 His cristell eyne wes suckin in his heid.

'suckeny. *Hist.* Also 4 sukkenye, 7 surkney, 9 suckeney. [a. OF. *soucanie*, also *sor-*, *surquanie* (earlier *soschanie*, *sousquenie*, cf. med.L. *soscania*) of Slavonic origin (cf. Polish *suknia* coat), whence also MHG. *sukkenîe.*] A smock.

? *a* **1366** CHAUCER *Rom. Rose* 1232 She hadde on a sukkenye [*16th c. edd.* suckeny; orig. F. *sorquanie*] That not of hempe ne heerdis was. **1658** PHILLIPS, *Surkney*, a kind of white garment like a rotchet. [**1834** PLANCHÉ *Brit. Costume* 113 The sosquenie, surquayne, or suckeney was an exterior garment at this period [viz. temp. Edw. I]. **1885** DILLON *Fairholt's Costume Eng.* II. 387 *Sukkenye*, a loose frock.]

sucker ('sʌkə(r)), *sb.* Forms: 4 souker(e, 5 sokare, -ere, sowker, sucour, 6 socar, *Sc.* soukar, 6–7 succor, suckar, 7 soker, succur, shucker, 9 (in sense 4) succour, *dial.* sooker, 6– sucker. [f. SUCK *v.* + -ER[1].]

I. 1. a. A young mammal before it is weaned; †a child at the breast (*even-sucker*, see EVEN- 2); now *spec.* a sucking-pig; a young whale-calf.

See also RABBIT-SUCKER (†*rabbit's sucker*).

1382 WYCLIF *2 Macc.* ix. 29 Philip, his euen souker [Vulg. *collactaneus ejus*]. *c* **1440** *Promp. Parv.* 463/1 Sokere, or he þat sokythe, *sugens.* *c* **1460** [see RABBIT-SUCKER 1]. *a* **1549** in *Gentl. Mag.* (1813) May 427 Rabbetts socars the dozen, xviij *d.* **1591** PERCIVALL *Sp. Dict.*, *Mamanton o mamon*, a sucker. **1607** TOPSELL *Four-f. Beasts* 673 Although the fœcundity of Swine bee great, yet it is better to kil off two or three,..for this multitude of suckers do quickly draw away all nourishment from the dam. *c* **1614** FLETCHER *Wit at Sev. Weapons* III. i, *Sir Gr.* I promise you, not a house-Rabbit, Sir. *Old K.* No sucker on 'em all. **1701** C. WOOLEY *Jrnl. New York* (1860) 38 Their [*sc.* whales'] young Suckers come along with them their several courses. **1836** *Uncle Philip's Convers. Whale Fishery* 253, I saw the whale with its sucker. **1878** *Ure's Dict. Arts* IV. Suppl. 380 Racks, or young rabbits about two months old..and suckers, or very young rabbits. **1883** *Standard* 11 June 6/3 The inquiry [for pigs] was restricted, at less money for suckers. **1902** T. F. DALE *Riding & Polo Ponies* iii. 45 Fillies should be taken off the moors as suckers.

b. *fig.* A greenhorn, simpleton. orig. *N. Amer.*

1838 *Patriot* (Toronto) 29 May 1/2 It's true that pigs has their troubles like humans..constables catches 'em, dogs bites 'em, and pigs is sometimes as done-over suckers as men. **1857** *San Francisco Call* 5 Dec. (Thorton *Amer. Gloss.*), You may think I'm a sucker. **1904** E. ROBINS *Magnetic North* viii. 153 Goin' out to stir up a boom, and sell his claim to some sucker. **1927** A. CONAN DOYLE *Case-Bk. Sherlock Holmes* 92 I'll see this sucker and fill him up with a bogus confession. **1941** [see PLAY *v.* 24 a]. **1957** *Essays in Crit.* VII. 47, I confess to being a sucker myself, if not for Malory, for Welsh legend. **1960** P. GOODMAN *Growing up Absurd* iii. 65 Our present poor are absolute sheep and suckers for the popular culture which they cannot afford, the movies, sharp clothes, and up to Cadillacs. **1973** L. MEYNELL *Thirteen Trumpeters* iv. 57 He got..a tiny percentage out of the total takings of the Casino. The more suckers who turned up the the more each sucker spent the better pleased he was. **1979** *Financial Rev. Survey* (Sydney) 22 Oct. 11/2 Look at the advertising man himself. He's the biggest sucker in town. From rotary engines to studded blue jeans—you'll find 'em at the agency. **1981** M. GEE *Dying, in Other Words* 58 Elsie laughed when she told about Pelham and called her a sucker, and said that she ought to ask him for money, men often liked giving you money, it was part of the game.

2. One who or that which sucks with the mouth.

Cf. the animal-names BLOOD-SUCKER, GOATSUCKER, HONEYSUCKER.

c **1440** *Promp. Parv.* 463/1 Sokare of mylke, or sokerel that longe sokythe, *mammotrepus*. **1598** *Extr. Aberd. Reg.* (1848) II. 168 Devoraris and suckeris of the blude and substance of the pure. **1611** COTGR. s.v. *Tetard*, A great sucker, a child that sucketh much. **1861** *Jrnl. R. Agric. Soc.* XXII. I. 147 The fastest sucker will have an undue share of the milk.

3. One who lives at the expense of another; one who draws profit or extorts subsistence from some source; *U.S. slang*, a sponger, parasite.

1500–20 DUNBAR *Poems* lxiii. 41 Soukaris [*pr.* sonkaris], groukaris, gledaris, gunnaris. *a* **1548** HALL *Chron., Hen. VI*, 159 Flatterers to the kyng.., suckers of his purse and robbers of his subiectes. **1589** [? LYLY] *Pappe w. Hatchet* To Rdr., I knowe there is none of honour so carelesse..that wil succor those that be suckers of the Church. **1728** RAMSAY *Gen. Mistake* 140 This sucker thinks nane wise, But him that can to immense riches rise. **1856** DOW *Serm.* III. (Bartlett) Those suckers belonging to the body loaferish, whose sole study appears to be to see how much they can get without the least physical exertion.

4. a. A shoot thrown out from the base of a tree or plant, which in most cases may serve for propagation; now *esp.* such a shoot rising from the root under ground, near to, or at some distance from, the trunk; also (now *rare*), a runner (as of the strawberry); also, a lateral shoot; in the tobacco plant, an axillary shoot (cf. SUCKER *v.* 2).

1577–82 BRETON *Toyes of Idle Head* Wks. (Grosart) I. 54/1 If suckers draw the sappe from bowes on hie, Perhaps in tyme the top of tree may die. **1591** PERCIVALL *Sp. Dict.*, *Pimpollo*, a succor that groweth out of the bodies of trees, *Stolo*. **1615** W. LAWSON *Country Housew. Garden* (1626) 4 The roots of Apples and Peares..will put foorth suckers, which are a great hinderance. **1669** WORLIDGE *Syst. Agric.* (1681) 129 Filberds are generally drawn as Suckers from the old Trees. **1682** G. ROSE *Sch. Instruct. Officers Month* 154 Take the Succors or Stalks of these Roman Lettice, and peel of the leaves and skins. **1688** *Phil. Trans.* XVII. 982 When the top-bud [of the tobacco plant] is gone, it puts forth no more Leaves, but Side-branches, which they call Suckers. *a* **1700** EVELYN *Diary* 12 Sept. 1641, Out of whose stem, neere the roote, issue 5 upright and exceeding tall suckers or boles. **1707** MORTIMER *Husb.* (1721) II. 188 Spanish Broom is not much unlike the yellow Jessamine... It..is increased by Seeds or Suckers. **1766** *Complete Farmer* s.v. *Quince-tree*, Suckers are the worst to raise them from; and cuttings are generally preferred to layers. **1772–84** *Cook's Voy.* (1790) I. 279 Pine-apples..grow so luxuriantly that seven or eight suckers have been seen adhering to one stem. **1807** *Med. Jrnl.* XVII. 374 Stem upright,..bare at base, at top leafy, branched, never throwing out succours. **1815** J. SMITH *Panorama Sci. & Art* II. 688 Clear the strawberries from suckers. **1842** LOUDON *Suburban Hort.* 239 Plants are propagated either by seed, or by division: the latter mode including cuttings, joints, leaves, layers, suckers, slips, budding, grafting, and inarching. **1870** HOOKER *Stud. Flora* 107 The Dwarf Cherry forms a bush with copious suckers. **1877** AUG. MORRIS *Tobacco* 45 The tobacco plant shoots up its stalk at top, sending out some four or five main suckers branchwise.

b. *fig.* (freq. with reference to the withdrawal of nourishment from the parent stem).

1591 GREENE *2nd Pt. Conny Catch.* Ep. Ded., Wks. (Grosart) X. 73 If the honorable and worshipfull of this land looke into their liues, and cut off such vpstarting suckars that consume the sap from the roote of the Tree. **1642** FULLER *Holy & Prof. St.* III. v. 163 If thou payest nothing, they will count thee a sucker, no branch. **1688** NORRIS *Theory & Regul. Love* II. iii. 113 This [*sc.* self-love] is the great Sucker of Society, and that which robbs the Body Politick of its due nourishment. **1777** SHERIDAN *Sch. Scandal* II. iii, For my part I hate to see prudence clinging to the green suckers of youth. **1792** in *Ld. Auckland's Corr.* (1861) II. 428, I have no olive-branches round my table, and I stand like a blasted pollard without a sucker to survive me. **1818** HALLAM *Mid. Ages* VIII. ii. (1819) III. 382 A manufacturing district.. sends out, as it were, suckers into all its neighbour-hood. **1827** J. F. COOPER *Prairie* III. v. 160, I am a sycamore, that once covered many with my shadow... But a single succour is springing from my roots. **1858** STANLEY *Life of Arnold* I. v. 215 A living sucker from the mother country. **1876** GEO. ELIOT *Dan. Der.* xxx, This woman whose life he had allowed to send such deep suckers into his had a terrible power of annoyance in her.

5. An organ adapted for sucking or absorbing nourishment by suction, *e.g.* the proboscis of an insect, the mouth of a cyclostomous fish, a siphonostomous crustacean, etc.

1685 *Phil. Trans.* XV. 1158 The Sucker or Proboscis.. wherewith the Bee sucks the Honey from the flowers. **1771** *Ann. Reg.* II. 169/1 Corals and sea-pens protrude or draw back their suckers. **1817** KIRBY & SP. *Entomol.* xvii. II. 88 Their sucker being inserted in the tender bark, is without intermission employed in absorbing the sap. **1828** STARK *Elem. Nat. Hist.* II. 247 The mouth consisting of a rostrum, from which a syphon or sucker is protruded at will. *Ibid.*, Pediculus..; mouth consisting of a rostrum, inclosing an exsertile sucker. **1899** *Allbutt's Syst. Med.* VIII. 866 When the sucker [of the louse] is taken out a tiny blood mark appears on the surface [of the human skin].

6. a. Any fish having a conformation of the lips which suggests that it feeds by suction; *esp.* North American cyprinoid fishes of the family *Catostomidæ*.

1772 *Phil. Trans.* LXIII. 155 The fourth and last fish brought from Hudson's Bay is there called a Sucker, because it lives by suction. **1806** PIKE *Sources Mississ.* (1810) 60 They..raise plenty of Irish potatoes, catch pike, suckers, pickerel, and white fish in abundance. **1848** BARTLETT *Dict. Amer.*, *Sucker*, a very common fish of the genus *labeo*, and of which there are many varieties, including the Chub, Mullet, Barbel, Horned Dace, etc. **1888** GOODE *Amer. Fishes* 16 The destructive inroads of sturgeon, cat-fish and suckers upon the spawning beds in Lake Pepin.

b. *U.S.* An inhabitant of the state of Illinois.

For the alleged origin of the term see quot. 1833.

1833 C. F. HOFFMAN *Winter in Far West* (1835) I. 207 There was a long-haired 'hooshier' from Indiana, a couple of smart-looking 'suckers' from the southern part of Illinois, a keen-eyed leather-belted 'badger' from the mines of Ouisconsin. [*note*, So called after the fish of that name, from his going up the river to the mines, and returning at the season when the sucker makes its migrations]. **1838** HALIBURTON *Clockm.* Ser. II. xix. (1839) 258 There's the hoosiers of Indiana, the suckers of Illinoy, the pukes of Missuri [etc.]. **1856** EMERSON *Eng. Traits, Race*, I found abundant points of resemblance between the Germans of the Hercynian Forest and our 'Hoosiers', 'Suckers', and 'Badgers', of the American woods.

7. Used as a book-rendering of *Suctoria*, the name of various groups of animals having a sucking apparatus.

1835–6 *Todd's Cycl. Anat.* I. 771/1 The suckers..live almost invariably attached to their prey. *a* **1843** SOUTH *Zool.* in *Encycl. Metrop.* (1845) VII. 275/1 Edwards..arranges the Crustaceans in the three sub-classes: 1. Suckers..; 2. Xyphosures..; 3. Masticators.

8. The embolus, piston, or rising-valve of a pump; the piston of a syringe or an air-pump.

1611 COTGR., *Soupape*,..the Supper, or Sucker of a Pumpe. **1634** J. B[ATE] *Myst. Nat.* 7 No engine for water workes..can be made without the help of Succurs, Forcers, or Clackes. **1653** H. MORE *Antid. Ath.* II. ii. §9 The Sucker of the Air-pump, the Cylinder being well emptied of the Air, should draw up above an hundred pound weight. **1712** J. JAMES tr. *Le Blond's Gardening* 192 Almost all Water-Engines are reducible to the Bucket and Sucker. **1837** W. B. ADAMS *Carriages* 113 If the sucker of a pump be allowed to get dry it fails to draw up the water. **1862** SMILES *Engineers* III. 10 When the pump descends, there is heard a plunge..: then, as it rises, and the sucker begins to act [etc.].

9. †**a.** *Anat.* = EMULGENT *sb. Obs.*

1615 CROOKE *Body of Man* 145 The other veine, of his office is called the emulgent or sucker.

†**b.** An absorbent substance. In *fig.* context.

1605 BACON *Adv. Learn.* II. 34 The entrie of doubts are as so many suckers or sponges, to drawe vse of knowledge.

†**c.** One of a number of 'buckets' attached to a moving chain. *Obs.*

1686 PLOT *Staffordsh.* 148 The chain is made with leather suckers upon it at little distances, which bring up water, and discharge themselves into a trough.

d. A pipe or tube through which anything is drawn by suction; *locally*, a hood over a fire-place.

1755 *Churchw. Acc. Wolsingham* (MS.) Sucker in yᵉ Vestery Chimnay, 3s. od. **1838** T. THOMSON *Chem. Org. Bodies* 602 All the oil passed over with the water... It was separated from the water by means of a sucker. **1848** BARTLETT *Dict. Amer.*, *Sucker*, a tube used for sucking sherry-cobblers. They are made of silver, glass, straw, or sticks of maccaroni. **1876** *Whitby Gloss.*, *Sooker*, in old dwellings, a brick hood or canopy..projecting over the fire for focalizing the air current.

e. An air-hole fitted with a valve; a valve for the regulation of the flow of air.

1797 *Monthly Mag.* III. 303 When the bellows is opened, one of its sides becomes filled with ordinary air, by means of a sucker placed next to the moving leaf. **1833** LOUDON *Encycl. Archit.* §1975 In long conduit pipes, air-holes.. terminating in inverted valves or suckers, should be made at convenient distances. **1881** C. A. EDWARDS *Organs* 42 In the middle-board are placed suckers, *i.e.*, holes provided with leather valves on the top.

f. *Bot.* = HAUSTORIUM.

1849 BALFOUR *Man. Bot.* §122 In parasites..such as Dodder.., roots are sometimes produced in the form of suckers, which enter into the cellular tissue of the plant preyed upon. **1856** HENSLOW *Dict. Bot. Terms*, *Sucker*,..a tubercular process..on the stems of certain flowering parasites.

g. *Golf.* (See quot. 1931.) orig. *U.S.*

1931 *Daily Express* 2 Sept. 1/5 The United States Golf Association passed a special rule permitting 'suckers'—that is, balls embedded in the mud—to be lifted and cleaned without penalty. **1963** *Times* 9 Jan. 4/3 There do not seem to have been any 'suckers', although some of Ray's towering drives were repeatedly expected to produce them.

II. 10. A part or organ adapted for adhering to an object; the adhesive pad of an insect's foot, etc.; a suctorial disk, foot, etc.

1681 GREW *Musæum* I. 105 This Fish [*i.e.* Remora] is able to fasten himself to any great Fish, Boat, or Ship, with the help of the Coronet or Sucker on his Head. **1817** KIRBY & SP. *Entomol.* xxiii. II. 320 Those [insects] that climb by the aid of suckers, which adhere..by the pressure of the atmosphere. **1851** CARPENTER *Man. Phys.* (ed. 2) 521 The arms of the Cuttle-fish, which are furnished with great numbers of contractile suckers. **1897** *Allbutt's Syst. Med.* II. 1007 These, the suckers and hooklets, serve to attach the parasite to the mucous membrane of the alimentary canal of the host.

11. Any fish characterized by a suctorial disk by which it adheres to foreign objects; *e.g.* fishes of the genus *Cyclopterus* (cf. *lump-sucker* s.v. LUMP *sb.*²), the genus *Liparis* (sea-snails or snail-fishes), the remora (*Echeneis*).

1753 *Chambers' Cycl.* Suppl. App., *Sucker*, or *Suck-fish* [i.e. *Remora*]. **1776** PENNANT *Brit. Zool.* III. pl. xxi, Unctuous Sucker. *Ibid.* pl. xxii, Bimaculated Sucker. Jura Sucker. **1828** FLEMING *Hist. Brit. Anim.* 189 *L[epadogaster] cornubiensis*. Cornish Sucker. **1863** COUCH *Brit. Fishes* II. 195 Network Sucker..*Liparis reticulatus*. **1898** MORRIS *Austral Eng.* 443 *Sucker*, name given in New Zealand to the fish *Diplocrepis puniceus*.

12. A toy, consisting of a round piece of leather with a string attached at the centre, which, laid wet upon a solid surface and drawn up by the string, adheres by reason of the vacuum created.

1681 GREW *Musæum* I. 105 Those round Leathers, where-with Boys are us'd to play, called Suckers, one of which, not above an inch and ½ diametre, being well soaked in water, will stick so fast to a Stone [etc.]. **1832** BREWSTER *Nat. Magic* x. 260 The leathern suckers used by children for lifting stones. **1906** O. ONIONS *Drakestone* xxix, The lad was.. cutting a round sucker of leather.

III. 13. *colloq.* (orig. *local*). A sweet, a 'suck'. Also *spec.* (chiefly *N. Amer.*), a lollipop; ***all-day sucker***: see ALL *a.* IV. b.

1823 E. MOOR *Suff. Words* 408 *Suckers*, a longish sort of a sweety. **1893** KIPLING *Many Invent.* 168 We've played 'em for suckers so often. **1898** *Tit-Bits* 30 Apr. 85/2 'Young bloods' of the town who buy their 'Suckers' and weeds at the shop. **1907** *Dialect Notes* III. 250 *Sucker, n.*, a kind of hard candy held by a small wooden stick and sucked. 'Let's buy suckers.' **1938** *Times* 13 Jan. 14/5 One of them said: 'I'll buy some suckers.' **1956** J. SYMONS *Paper Chase* xii. 91 A window in which gobstoppers, liquorice bootlaces and sherbet suckers nestle. **1962** J. LUDWIG in R. Weaver *Canad. Short Stories* (1968) 2nd Ser. 242 'I got no money for suckers,' the woman said nastily. **1971** *Islander* (Victoria, B.C.) 19 Sept. 4/3 The small children eagerly hunted suckers that had been hidden in a large hay wagon. **1977** E. JONG *Loveroot* 45 Little sugar suckers with sour centers.

IV. 14. *attrib.* and *Comb.*, as (sense 1 b) ***sucker bait, bet, list, punch, trap***; (sense 10) ***sucker-bearing, -like, -shaped*** ppl. adjs.; **sucker-bashing** *Austral. slang* (see quots. 1945, 1953); **sucker-cup, -foot** = *sucking-cup, -foot* (see SUCKING *vbl. sb.* 3 b); **sucker-disk** = sense 10; **sucker-fish** = senses 6 and 11, SUCKING-FISH; **sucker-rod** (see quots.); **sucker-up** = SUCK *sb.*¹ 10 (cf. SUCK *v.*¹ 26 e).

1939 *Amer. Speech* XIV. 80/2 *Mootch* is a derisive term applied to a careful customer... Retailers lose money on the 'mootch', because he buys only those things offered as '*sucker bait' or 'specials'. **1976** 'TREVANIAN' *Main* (1977) xiii. 249 'Have you any reason to think you might be in trouble?' he asks. But she is not taking sucker bait like that. She smiles. **1945** J. A. ALLAN *Men & Manners in Austral.* 89 Before that the settlers had cut the scrub a foot above ground, piled the refuse round the stumps, and fired it as the new shoots appeared. Even after that, '*sucker bashing'—which had raised the cost of clearing to 15/- an acre—had still been needed. **1953** BAKER *Australia Speaks* iii. 80 *Sucker bashing*, work at cutting down saplings. **1962** *Australasian Post* 25 Oct. 40 Whilst sucker-bashing at Mirambigo Station. **1857** GOSSE *Omphalos* vii. 171 In the adult the *sucker-bearing shoots frequently run to a considerable distance. **1883** *Encycl. Brit.* XVI. 674/2 The sucker-bearing arms of male Dibranchiate Siphonopods. **1920** *Collier's* 26 Mar. 22/3 You actually intend *makin'* a *sucker bet like that? **1979** *Tucson* (Arizona) *Citizen* (Weekender Mag.) 28 Apr. 9/3 Don't buy much insurance. Cover your potential catastrophic losses with insurance, but not your minor setbacks. Remember that the way insurance companies make money is by taking as many sucker bets as possible. **1845** GOSSE *Ocean* vi. (1849) 306 There is placed in each *sucker-cup of the long feet [of squids, etc.], a sharp projecting hook. **1964** *Oceanogr. & Marine Biol.* II. 412 The functional histology of the *sucker-disk of two British regular echinoids..has been described. **1977** *Playgirl* May 76/2 The sucker-disc mouth [of a lamprey] was stuck solidly to the smooth skin on J. T.'s right side. **1867** SMYTH *Sailor's Word-bk.* 568 The *sucker-fish. It has a long oval plate on the top of the head, by which..it clings to a ship's bottom. **1889** *Nature* 17 Jan. 285/2 The Employment of the Sucker-fish (Echeneis) in Turtle-fishing. **1898** *Proc. Zool. Soc.* Nov. 589 A small sucker-fish of the genus *Lepadogaster*. **1870** ROLLESTON *Anim. Life* 141 The water-vascular canal supplying the ambulacral *sucker-feet. **1846** DANA *Zooph.* iv. (1848) 31 Tentacles, which affix themselves by a *sucker-like action. **1910** *Collier's* 17 Dec. 25/1 '*Sucker lists', as the promoters call the roster of victims..are traded and passed on. **1966** T. PYNCHON *Crying of Lot 49* v. 114 After a week of anxiously watching the mailbox..getting nothing but sucker-list stuff through the regular deliveries. **1981** E. AMBLER *Care of Time* v. 65 If they're pulling names on the sucker list, they can forget mine. I'm not available. **1947** *Amer. Speech* XXII. 122/2 **Sucker punch*, a hit or punch delivered without warning. **1950** J. DEMPSEY *Championship Fighting* 50 The right lead is called a sucker punch. **1979** N. HYND *False Flags* xxii. 201 It was a sucker punch... The fist landed, breaking his nose. **1865** *Harper's Mag.* Apr. 571/1 Small engines are used in most cases, with hardly sufficient power ro raise the *sucker-rod out of a deep well. **1875** KNIGHT *Dict. Mech.* 2442/2 *Sucker-rod*, a rod connecting the brake of a pump with the bucket. **1881** RAYMOND *Mining Gloss.*, *Sucker-rod*, the pump-rod of an oil-well. **1840** *Cuvier's Anim. Kingd.* 471 *Limnochares*, Latr., has the mouth *sucker-shaped. **1953** POHL & KORNBLUTH *Space Merchants* xvi. 156 Warren Astron had never returned to his *sucker-trap on Shopping One. **1973** *Sunday Advocate-News* (Barbados) 16 Dec. 3/5 So this Christmas, shop wisely, avoid the sucker traps. **1911** F. SWINNERTON *Casement* ii. 66 '*Suckers-up' (those who sought by illegitimate means to ingratiate themselves with the manager). **1976** P. LIVELY *Stitch in Time* i. 10 Toady, said Maria to it [*sc.* a cat] silently, sucker-up.

sucker ('sʌkə(r)), *v.* Also 8 succour. [f. prec.]

†**1.** *trans.* To fit or provide with a sucker or valve. *Obs. rare*$^{-1}$.

1660 R. D'ACRES *Elem. Water-drawing* iv. 33 The water will not follow after, though you suck never so strongly, and sucker it never so closely.

2. To remove superfluous young shoots from (tobacco or maize plants); †also, to remove (the shoots).

a **1661** FULLER *Worthies, Glouc.* (1662) 349 Many got great estates thereby, notwithstanding the great care and cost in.. suckering, topping,..making and rowling it [*sc.* tobacco]. **1705** R. BEVERLEY *Virginia* II. §20 (1722) 128, I am inform'd they [*sc.* Indians] used to let it all run to Seed, only succouring the Leaves, to keep the Sprouts from growing upon, and starving them. **1779** *Ann. Reg.* 107/1 Care must be taken to nip off the sprouts that will be continually springing up at the junction of the leaves with the stalks. This is termed 'suckering the tobacco'. **1817–18** COBBETT *Resid. U.S.* (1822) 94 Fifteen acres of good Indian corn, well planted, well suckered, and well tilled in all respects. **1908** MARY JOHNSTON *Lewis Rand* xiv. 162 I've wanted power ever since I went barefoot and suckered tobacco.

3. *intr.* To throw up suckers. Also occas. *pass.*, to be thrown up as a sucker.

1802 *Trans. Soc. Arts* XX. 369 When those [plants] I have now planted begin to sucker. **1894** *Times* 21 Feb. 4/3 Plants of Sisal hemp suckered in fourteen months. **1894** BLACKMORE *Perlycross* 256 As straight as a hazel wand sucker'd from the root.

4. *trans.* To cheat, to trick. *slang* (orig. and chiefly *U.S.*).

1939 *Sat. Even. Post* 14 Oct. 78/1 It was a little deal I got suckered on. **1948** *Chicago Tribune* 27 Mar. 1. 1/4 Apparently we are again going to be suckered into approval of a glorified world WPA. **1958** J. & W. HAWKINS *Death Watch* (1959) 87 We're going to sucker the killer out in the open. **1971** L. GRIBBLE *Alias the Victim* xii. 184 He had been suckered badly. What had to be done was to get away. **1978** J. GORES *Gone, no Forwarding* (1979) xv. 90 Delaney suckered us into making a payment which he now claims is an admission of guilt because we made it.

Hence **suckering** *vbl. sb.* in sense 2 (also *attrib.*).

1817–18 COBBETT *Resid. U.S.* (1822) 138 Where would the hands come from to do the marking; the dropping and covering of the Corn;..the suckering when that work is done, as it always ought to be? **1877** AUG. MORRIS *Tobacco* 44 In suckering, the work is done with both hands, commencing at the top of the plant. **1881** *Encycl. Brit.* XII. 235/1 The soil should be carefully opened and the shoots removed with a suckering iron.

sucker: see SUCCOUR, SUGAR.

suckered ('sʌkəd), *ppl. a.* [f. SUCKER *sb.* + -ED².] Of an organ: Provided with suckers.

1855 KINGSLEY *Glaucus* (1878) 163 Small cuttle-fish.. with a ring of suckered arms round their tiny parrots' beaks. **1879** SPENCER *Data of Ethics* ii. §4. 12 The cephalopod.. using its suckered arms at one time for anchoring itself and at another for holding fast its prey.

suckered, Sc. form of SUGARED.

suckerel ('sʌkərəl). Also 5 sokerel. [f. SUCK *v.*: see -REL.]

1. A suckling; *esp.* a sucking foal.

c **1440** *Promp. Parv.* 463/1 Sokare of mylke, or sokerel that longe sokythe, *mammotrepus.* **1813** *Sporting Mag.* XLI. 37 Six suckerels averaged the sum of 37^{l} 16^{s} 8^{d} each.

2. A catostomous fish, *Sclerognathus* (*Cycleptus*) *elongatus*, of the Mississippi and Ohio Rivers.

1888 GOODE *Amer. Fishes* 436 The Black Horse,..also called 'Missouri Sucker',..'Suckerel' and 'Shoenaher'.

'**sucket.** Now rare exc. *arch.* and *Hist.* Forms: 5 soket, 6 suckitte, -ette, succet, suk(k)ett, sok(k)ett, 6–7 socket, suckett, 6–8 sucket. [Altered form of SUCCATE after SUCK *v.* and -ET¹.] **a.** = SUCCADE.

1481–90 *Howard Househ. Bks.* (Roxb.) 42 Item, soket viij. li. vj. onces viij.s. vj.d. **1509** *Test. Ebor.* (Surtees) V. 5 Comfettes, sugir plattes, and suckittes. **1542** *Ibid.* VI. 167 A longe silver spone for sokett, a longe forke of silver for sokett. **1544** PHAER *Regim. Lyfe* (1553) E.ij, Sucket of citrons. **1611** COTGR., *Carbassat*, wet sucket, made of the vpper part of the long white Pompion, cut in slices. **1615** MARKHAM *Eng. Housew.* ii. 78 Your preserued fruites shall be disht vp first, your Pastes next, your wet Suckets after them, then your dried Suckets. **1662** HIBBERT *Body Div.* I. 77 Pope Alexander poysoned the Turks brother in candid suckets. **1688** HOLME *Armoury* III. iii. 8c/1 Dried Sweet-meats & Suckets of Oranges. **1751** *Affect. Narr. H.M.S. Wager* 7 Here is plenty of Citrons, of which they make a fine Sweet-meat, or Sucket. **1929** E. LINKLATER *Poet's Pub* xii. 144 The table already gleamed with..jumbals and marchpane and suckets of one kind and another. **1959** P. VANSITTART *Tournament* xiv. 115 Suckets shaped as unicorns, swans, frogs.

b. *transf.* and *fig.*

1607 WALKINGTON *Optic Glass* 27 This made the Castalianist..to bee esteemed..the Marmalade and Sucket of the Muses. **1635** BRATHWAIT *Arcadian Princ.* III. 214 Celsus a theevish Poet..was arraign'd..For stealing Suckets from an others hive. **1654** CLEVELAND *Poems* 4 Natures confectioner, the Bee, Whose suckets are moist Alchimie. **1917** A. WAUGH *Loom of Youth* 10 'Those who can, do, while those who can't, teach.' This choice sucket.. comes consolingly to the ears of one whom the chances and caprices of life may have thrown casually on the preceptorial beach.

c. As a term of endearment.

1605 *Tryall Chev.* II. i, Peace, good Thomasin, silence, sweet socket.

d. *attrib.* and *Comb.*

1575 LANEHAM *Let.* (1871) 23 The brideeup, foormed of a sweet sucket barrell. **1636** DAVENANT *Wits* II. i, Now does my blood wamble! you! Sucket eater! **1938** CURRIER & BUHLER *Marks Early Amer. Silversmiths* 165 Forks were apparently unknown except for serving—to which use were doubtless put the small sucket-forks..for sweetmeats. **1956** G. TAYLOR *Silver* v. 112 The three prongs were curved, unlike the two prongs of the sucket fork. **1977** FLEMING & HONOUR *Penguin Dict. Decorative Arts* 768/2 *Sucket fork*, an implement with a spoon at one end and a two-pronged fork at the other, intended for eating fruit, especially *succade*.

¶Reliable evidence for the survival of *sucket* in mod. dialects is wanting. Halliwell's entry *sucket*, a young rabbit, is clearly an error for *sucker*.

†'**suckey**, *a. slang. Obs. rare*$^{-0}$. [f. SUCK *sb.*¹ or *v.* + -EY, -Y.] (See quot.)

a **1700** B. E. *Dict. Cant. Crew*, *Suckey*, drunkish, maudlin, half Seas o'er.

suck-eye, variant of SOCKEYE.

†**sucking**, *sb. Obs.* [f. SUCK *sb.*²] (See quot.)

1499 *Placitum* in Blount *Law Dict.* (1691) s.v., Per *Sucking*, hoc est fore quiet. de illis amerciamentis, quando *le Burlimen*, id est, supervisores del Ringyord,..præmonit. fuerint ad imparcand. & faciend. clausuras illas simul cum vicinis suis, ille qui non venit ad talem præmonitionem amerciatus erit ad pretium unius vomeris, Anglice a *Suck*, prætii quatuor denar.

sucking ('sʌkɪŋ), *vbl. sb.* [f. SUCK *v.* + -ING¹.]

1. a. The action of the verb SUCK; suction. Also, an instance of this.

c **1375** *Sc. Leg. Saints* xi. (*Symon & Iudas*) 324 þai wechis, þat had mare care of þat swkyne þan þai had yare. **1382** WYCLIF *Gen.* xxi. 8 Thanne the child growide and was don awey fro sowkyng. **14..** *Tundale's Vis.* 123 Thou blestful quene of kyngis emperes That gaf thi son sowkyng in a stall. *c* **1440** *Jacob's Well* 231 Whan þe modyr wanyth here child, sche wetyth here tetys wyth sum byttere thyng, & so þe chyld felyng ofte þat bytternes leuyth his soukyng. **1573** TUSSER *Husb.* (1878) 84 Otes with hir sucking a peeler is found. **1581** *Satir. Poems Reform.* xliii. 44 Freseruit from slauchter be souking of a beir. **1596** DALRYMPLE tr. *Leslie's Hist. Scot.* I. 91 Meil quhilke throuch souking thay fed vpon. **1599** A. M. tr. *Gabelhouer's Bk. Physicke* 267/2 Nether must we afther his meates and suckinges, dandle it much. **1688** HOLME *Armoury* III. xx. (Roxb.) 234 An Instrument or pipe..made of this forme, will cause the water by sucking to rise vp and run forth. **1727** *Philip Quarll* (1816) 61 Reserving only one for sucking of the old ones, to keep them in milk. **1885** *Daily News* 13 Feb. 5/1 There are very powerful engines which do the blowing and the sucking through these tubes. **1892** CARMICHAEL *Dis. Children* 287 The child should be fed at regular intervals from both breasts at each sucking.

†**b.** *transf.* = SUCTION 1 c. *Obs.*

1656 RIDGLEY *Pract. Physick* 10 Appetite wanting. If there be no sucking, the forces cannot fail, and there are signs of repletion.

2. *pl.* What is obtained by suction. *rare.*

1387–8 T. USK *Test. Love* I. iv. (Skeat) I. 27 The olde soukinges whiche thou haddest of me arn amaystred and lorn fro al maner of knowing. **1809** MALKIN *Gil Blas* x. x. (Rtldg.) 371 To dip in my four fingers and thumb, and then to sup like a bear upon suckings.

3. *attrib.* and *Comb.*, as *sucking operation*, *power*; †**sucking-bone**, ? a marrowbone; **sucking-cushion, -pad**, a lobulated mass of fat occupying the space between the masseter and the external surface of the buccinator; †**sucking-pipe**, a pipe used for drawing air or water in some direction; **sucking-pot** = SUCKING-BOTTLE 1; **sucking reflex** *Biol.*, the instinct to suck as possessed by the young of all mammals; **sucking response** *Biol.*, the action of sucking as a response to some stimulus or influence; †**sucking-tooth** = MILK-TOOTH; **sucking-tube**, a tube through which liquid is sucked into the mouth; **sucking-up** *slang*, sycophancy; †**sucking-young** *adj.*, young enough to be still sucking the dam.

1648 HEXHAM II, *Een Zuygh-been*, a *Sucking-bone. *a* **1907** SUTTON in *Piersol's Human Anat.* 493 The *sucking cushions sometimes enlarge in adults. **1896** HARDY *Jude* I. vi, She had managed to get back one dimple by..repeating the odd little *sucking operation before mentioned. **1889** MACALISTER *Human Anat.* 566 The buccal fat in the child forms a lobulated..*sucking-pad. **1699** *Phil. Trans.* XXI. 228 [In a Draught of Savery's Engine] *G* The Force Pipe. *H* The *sucking Pipe. **1731** *Ibid.* XXXVII. 7 A Sucking Pipe and Grate..going into the Water, which supplies all the four Cylinders alternately. **1735** *Ibid.* XXXIX. 42 The Sucking-Pipe receives its Air only from the Room where the Machine stands. **1552** HULOET, *Suckyng pot for chyldren, *aliphanus.* **1843** C. A. F. PARKE *Let.* 19 Aug. in U. Ridley *Cecilia* (1958) xi. 125 She uses a sucking pot, but the Old Crab thinks that she sucks in wind. **1774** GOLDSM. *Nat. Hist.* (1776) VI. 272 On this occasion their *sucking power is particularly serviceable. **1923** T. P. NUNN *Education* 167 An infant is born in vigorous possession of the *sucking reflex. **1974** *Biol. Abstr.* LIX. 2593/2 An otherwise normally developed female rabbit without ears may have lost them when still in the nest due to a 'sucking-reflex' among its siblings, such as that which occurs among young mice. **1938** *Jrnl. Genetic Psychol.* LIII. 369, 49 per cent of sleeping infants gave *sucking responses to stimulation of the lips. **1975** *Jrnl. Compar. Physiol. & Psychol.* LXXXVIII. 796 Monitoring sucking responses to a rubber teat revealed that ..the vigorous oral activity continued largely unabated. **1601** HOLLAND *Pliny* I. 338 A guelding never casts his teeth, no not his *sucking teeth, in case he were guelded before. **1875** KNIGHT *Dict. Mech.* 2442/2 The *sucking-tube was used by the ancients as a domestic utensil, and also in the temples. **1946** B. MARSHALL *George Brown's Schooldays* ii. 7 'Thank heaven my people sent me here with a decent grub box.' 'But what has a grub box to do with being caned..?' Brown asked. 'The gentle art of *sucking-up, of course... Not to the beaks.' **1978** 'M. INNES' *Ampersand Papers* I. v. 44 He wasn't doing any sucking-up act on Archie. **1657** W. RAND tr. *Gassendi's Life Peiresc* II. 110 It was a most swift Beast, and such as could not be taken, save when it was *sucking-young.

b. Applied to various organs in fishes, crustaceans, etc. adapted for use as suckers, e.g. ***sucking-bowl***, ***-cup***, ***-disk***, ***-foot***, ***-mouth***, ***-spear***, ***-tube***.

1841 T. R. JONES *Anim. Kingd.* §171 In the male *Actheres*, the *sucking-bowl possessed by the female does not exist. **1840** *Cuvier's Anim. Kingd.* 446 The two anterior [legs].. exhibiting, on the inside, a kind of rosette, formed by the muscles, and seeming to act as a *sucking-cup. **1830** J. E. GRAY in *Encycl. Metrop.* (1845) XXI. 592/1 A dorsal tail, ending in a *sucking disk. **1883** *Science* I. 195/2 Ambulatory tentacles..terminating..in expanded sucking-disks. **1855** KINGSLEY *Glaucus* (1878) 167 The bird's foot star..which you may see crawling by its thousand *sucking-feet. *a* **1843** SOUTH *Zool.* in *Encycl. Metrop.* (1845) VII. 279/2 The *Sucking Mouth exhibits..three different forms, the proboscis, the promuscis, and the antlia. **1895** D. SHARP *Insects* in *Cambr. Nat. Hist.* V. 467 The *sucking-spears of this Insect are so long and slender as to look like hairs. **1868** *Rep. U.S. Commissioner Agric.* (1869) 310 The *sucking tube, or tongue [of hymenoptera].

sucking ('sʌkɪŋ), *ppl. a.* [f. SUCK *v.* + -ING².]

1. a. That sucks milk from the breast; that is still being suckled, unweaned.

†*sucking fere* [FERE *sb.*¹, companion], a foster brother. (Cf. *even-sucker* s.v. SUCKER *sb.* 1.)

c **1000** ÆLFRIC *Hom.* I. 246 Æȝðer ȝe men ȝe ða sucendan cild. *c* **1205** LAY. 20973 þa sukende children þeo adrenten inne wateren. *c* **1375** *Sc. Leg. Saints* vii. (*Jacobus*) 689 Hyre sowkand sowne þane cane scho ta. **1382** WYCLIF *Acts* xiii. 1 Manaen, that was the sowkynge feere of Eroud tetrarke. *c* **1491** *Chast. Goddes Chyld.* 14 A louynge moder listeth to play with her souking childe. **1560** DAUS tr. *Sleidane's Comm.* 466 A sucking babe in the cradell, not fully halfe a yeare olde. **1611** *Bible* Isa. xlix. 15 Can a woman forget her sucking child? **1743** *Pol. Ballads* (1860) II. 302 And ev'ry parish sucking-babe Again be nurs'd with Gin. **1845** G. JOHNSON *Mat. Med.* in *Encycl. Metrop.* VII. 508/1 If infusion of senna be given to the nurse, the sucking infant becomes purged.

†**b.** *absol.* transl. L. *lactens*, etc.: Suckling. *Obs.*

c **975** *Rushw. Gosp.* Matt. xxi. 16 Of muðe cildra & sukendra. *c* **1000** ÆLFRIC *Deut.* xxxii. 25 Cniht and mædenu, sucende mid ealdum men. *a* **1325** *Prose Psalter* cxxx. 4 As þe souking is vp his moder. **1382** WYCLIF *1 Sam.* xv. 3 Sle fro man vnto womman, and litil child, and soukynge.

2. a. Of an animal: That is still sucking its dam. See also SUCKING-PIG.

1382 WYCLIF *1 Sam.* vii. 9 O sowkynge loomb. **1398** TREVISA *Barth. De P.R.* XVIII. lxiii. (Bodl. MS.), Flesche of souking calues. *c* **1440** *Promp. Parv.* 463/2 Sokynge gryce, *nefrendus.* **1513** DOUGLAS *Æneis* VIII. x. 81 The sowkin wolff furth streking brest and vdyr. **1535** COVERDALE *Ecclus.* xlvi. 16 What tyme as he offred the suckynge lambes. **1557** *Richmond Wills* (Surtees) 94 Soulkynge calves. **1596** SHAKS. *Merch. V.* II. i. 29 Plucke the yong sucking Cubs from the she Beare. **1833** W. H. MAXWELL *Field Bk.* Introd., A sucking-mastiff.

b. Of a bird: That is still with its mother. Now chiefly in ***sucking dove***, echoed from Shaks. (see quot. 1590); also *attrib.*

Cf. dial. *sucking duck*, *gander*, *turkey*, used fig. = simpleton.

1590 SHAKS. *Mids. N.* I. ii. 85, I will aggrauate my voyce so, that I will roare you as gently as any sucking Doue. **1634** *Althorp MS.* in Simpkinson *Washingtons* (1860) App. p. xxii, For 5 dozen and 1 sucking chickinges at 2d. ob the chick, 00 12 03^{ob}. **1821** SCOTT *Kenilw.* xxiv, He never had so much [brains] as would make pap to a sucking gosling. **1837** CARLYLE *Fr. Rev.* II. I. iv, Some loud as the lion; some small as the sucking dove. **1846** MRS. GORE *Eng. Char.* (1852) 157 From the sucking-dove eloquence of Private Secretaryship, he suddenly thundered into a Boanerges! **1858** TROLLOPE *Dr. Thorne* xxvi, No young sucking dove could have been more mild than that terrible enemy [etc.].

3. *fig.* **a.** Not come to maturity; not fully developed; budding.

1648 J. BEAUMONT *Psyche* XIII. lviii, Some petty sucking Knaves their best did try. *Ibid.* XIX. cxvii, From sucking sneaking Schisms, they boldly broke Into the monstrous amplitude of those Black Heresies [etc.]. **1678** DRYDEN *All* *for Love* Pref., Ess. 1900 I. 193 My enemies are but sucking critics, who would fain be nibbling ere their teeth are come. **1681** —— *Span. Friar* III. i, This is no Father Dominic..; this is but a diminutive sucking Fryar. **1708** *Brit. Apollo* No. 50. 3/2 You are as yet, but a sucking Young Lover. **1834** MARRYAT *P. Simple* iv, He looks like a sucking Nelson. **1853** 'C. BEDE' *Verdant Green* II. ii, Told you he was a sucking Freshman, Giglamps! **1876** *Nature* 13 Jan. 202/2 The book before us, however, is not the book we should recommend to a sucking geometer.

transf. **1854** MRS. GASKELL *North & S.* viii, Most of the manufacturers placed their sons in sucking situations at fourteen or fifteen years of age.

b. Infantile, childishly innocent.

1842 LOVER *Handy Andy* x. 96 To see their simplicity—sucking simplicity, I call it.

4. That sucks down, under water, into a whirlpool, etc. †*sucking sand* = QUICKSAND.

1513 DOUGLAS *Æneis* I. iii. 42 The sowcand sweltht. *Ibid.* VII. vi. 45 Quhat proffitit me Sirtis, that soukand sand? **1670–1** NARBOROUGH *Jrnl.* in *Acc. Sev. Late Voy.* I. (1694) 118 Sucking Rocks lie on the North-side of the Streights. **1818** KEATS *Endym.* III. 249 Where through some sucking pool I will be hurl'd With rapture to the other side of the world! **1853** R. S. HAWKER *Prose Wks.* (1893) 28 There's a nine-knot breeze above, And a sucking tide below. **1910** B. CAPES *J. Abercraw* II. xviii. 259 It was like a nightmare race over sucking quicksands.

†**5.** Tending to drain or exhaust; = SOAKING *ppl. a.* I. *Obs.*

c **1440** *Pol. Rel. & L. Poems* 246 'Accidia' ys a souking sore, he traveylyth me from day to day.

6. Special collocations: **sucking carp**, the carp-sucker, *Ictiobus carpio*; **sucking louse**, a blood-sucking ectoparasite of mammals belonging to the order Siphunculata (or Anoplura); †**sucking-paper**, blotting-paper; **sucking stomach** *Zool.*, a stomach in certain invertebrates that expands so as to provide a food reservoir (formerly interpreted as the means by which the animal imbibed fluid); †**sucking stone**, pumice.

1804 SHAW *Gen. Zool.* V. I. 237 *Sucking Carp. *Cyprinus Catastomus*..: said to live chiefly by suction. **1910** R. DOANE *Insects & Disease* iv. 54 The *sucking lice..are suspected of carrying some of these same diseases. **1950** *N.Z. Jrnl. Agric.* Jan. 68/1 Sucking louse: This parasite [of pigs] is very common in New Zealand. **1962** GORDON & LAVOIPIERRE *Entomol. for Students of Med.* xxxvi. 223 Members of the order Anoplura, all of which are known as 'sucking lice' possess 'sucking' mouthparts borne on an elongated head. *a* **1648** DIGBY *Closet Opened* (1677) 227 Filter it through *sucking-paper. **1886** F. R. CHESHIRE *Bees & Bee-Keeping* I. vii. 94 Cook calls the honey-sac the '*sucking stomach', using an old, but extremely misleading, title. **1925** A. D. IMMS *Gen. Textbk. Entomol.* 98 The organ is then known as the food-reservoir or 'sucking stomach', but the latter expression is misleading and incorrect. **1664** *Comenius' Janua Ling.* 582 *marg.*, A *sucking stone ful of little holes.

'sucking-,bottle.

1. An infant's feeding-bottle. Now *local.* (Cf. SUCK-BOTTLE I.)

1632 SHERWOOD, A sucking bottle, *succeron.* **1660** *Act 12 Chas. II*, c. 4. Sched. s.v. *Bottles*, Bottles of Wood vocat. sucking bottles the Groce..x.s. **1690** LOCKE *Hum. Und.* IV. vii. §9 A Child..knows..that its Sucking-bottle is not the Rod. **1825** in *Trans. Amer. Pediatric Soc.* (1897) IX. 13 The child should be fed by means of a sucking-bottle.

b. *transf.* and *fig.*

1636 MASSINGER *Bashf. Lover* III. i, *Octavio pours a cordial into the mouth of Ascanio. Gothrio (to Hortensio).* You may believe him. It is his sucking-bottle, and confirms 'An old man's twice a child'. **1668** H. MORE *Div. Dial.* II. xxiv. (1713) 168, I am of that childish humour, that I do not relish any drink so well as that out of mine own usual Sucking-bottle.

†**2.** A breast-pump. *Obs.*

1688 HOLME *Armoury* III. xii. 435/2 A Nipple pipe, or Sucking bottle,..haveing an hole..at one end, which is as large as to receive the nipple of a Womans brest.

†**3.** A West-Indian plant (see quot.). *Obs.*

1750 G. HUGHES *Nat. Hist. Barbados* v. 139 Bread and Cheese; or, Sucking-Bottle. This is a ligneous Wyth, with dark Iron-coloured Leaves... The Flowers are succeeded by yellow conic capsular Pods, somewhat in Shape like a Bottle.

'sucking-fish. A fish furnished with a sucker or adhesive organ. **a.** The REMORA, *Echeneis remora.*

1697 DAMPIER *Voy.* I. iii. 64 The Sucking-fish is about the bigness of a large Whiting. **1756** P. BROWNE *Jamaica* 493 The Sucking Fish. This fish is remarkable on account of its *scuta*,..by whose *setulæ*..it fastens itself to the sides of ships, planks, fishes, or other bodies. **1880** GÜNTHER *Introd. Study Fishes* 461 A somewhat ingenuous way of catching sleeping turtles by means of a Sucking-fish held by a ring fastened round its tail. **1884** *Longman's Mag.* Mar. 524 Few sharks are caught in tropical seas that have not one or more sucking fish attached to them.

b. Applied to various other fishes, *e.g.* the Cornish sucker, the lump-sucker.

1776 PENNANT *Brit. Zool.* III. 120 Lesser Sucking Fish... Lepadogaster. **1867** *Chambers' Encycl.* IX. 181/1 *Sucking Fish*, a name sometimes given..to fishes of the family Discoboli.

'sucking-pig. A new-born or very young pig; a young milk-fed pig suitable for roasting whole. (Formerly often called *roasting pig.*)

1566 WITHALS *Dict.* 17 Yonge suckyng pigges, *porci delici.* **1606** *Shuttleworths' Acc.* (Chetham Soc.) 166 For one souckinge pigge, ij^s viij^d. **1632** MASSINGER *City Madam* II. i, There were three sucking pigs served up in a dish. *c* **1746** J. COLLIER (Tim Bobbin) *View Lanc. Dial.* Wks. (1862) p. xxxvii, I know no moor on um neaw, than a seawking-pig. **1834** MARRYAT *P. Simple* (1863) 198 A roast sucking pig came on as a second course. **1846** YOUATT *Pig* (1847) 130 Those intended to be killed for 'sucking-pigs' should not be above four weeks old. **1886** W. J. TUCKER *E. Europe* 73 'You like sucking-pig?' he asked. 'Not particularly.' 'Ah! you never ate them as they ought to be eaten!'

'sucking-pump.

†**1.** An air-pump. *Obs.*

1660 BOYLE *New Exp. Phys. Mech.* Proem 12 A Sucking Pump, or as we formerly call'd it, an Air Pump.

2. A suction pump. Now *rare.*

1660 D'ACRES *Art Water-drawing* 5 As it is every day to be seen in sucking Pumps, whose water will not follow the Bucket much above the said hight. **1707** MORTIMER *Husbandry* (1721) I. 92 Those continual Repairs and Mendings, that the least Defects in Sucking-pumps are constantly requiring. **1815** J. SMITH *Panorama Sci. & Art* II. 116 A contrivance for converting the common sucking-pump into a lifting-pump. **1830** HERSCHEL *Study Nat. Phil.* III. i. 228 On the occasion of a sucking-pump refusing to draw water above a certain height.

suckle ('sʌk(ə)l), *sb.*[1] Also 5 succle, sokel, -yl, 6 suckell. [app. short for HONEYSUCKLE. Cf. SUCKLING *sb.*[2]]

a. Clover. Also called †*lamb-suckle.* **b.** *attrib.* in †*suckle-bloom* glossing L. *locusta.* = HONEYSUCKLE 1, 1 b. *Obs.*

14.. *Medical MS.* in *Anglia* XIX. 78 Succle, a good medycyne for þe web in þe eye. *c* **1475** *Pict. Voc.* in Wr.-Wülcker 787 *Hec locusta*, a sokylblome. **1597** GERARDE *Herbal* II. ccccclxxvii. 1018 Medow Trefoile is called..of some Suckles, and Honisuckes. **1709** T. ROBINSON *Vindic. Mosaick System* 91 Honey..which they suck out of the Honey-Flowers, as the Honey-Suckle, Lamb-Suckle, the Clover Flowers. **1728** R. BRADLEY *Dict. Bot.*, *Suckles* is Honeysuckle.

c. = HONEYSUCKLE 2. Also *suckle bush.*

1816 L. HUNT *Rimini* II. 192 And ivy, and the suckle's streaky light. **1886** BRITTEN & HOLLAND *Plant-n.*, Suckle-bush, *Lonicera Periclymenum.*

d. *fig.*

c **1425** *Cast. Persev.* 976 in *Macro Plays* 106 *Luxuria.* With my sokelys of swettnesse, I sytte & I slepe.

suckle ('sʌk(ə)l), *sb.*[2] [f. next.]

†**1.** A suckling organ. *Obs. rare.*

1638 SIR T. HERBERT *Trav.* (ed. 2) 26 The body of this fish [*sc.* the manatee]..wanting fins, in their place ayded with 2 paps which are not only suckles but stilts to creep a shoare upon.

2. A suckling-house for lambs. *local.*

1805 R. W. DICKSON *Pract. Agric.* II. 1056 In order to conduct this sort of fattening with..success, a lamb-house or suckle of proper dimensions must be provided.

suckle ('sʌk(ə)l), *v.* Also 5 sukle, 6 soc(k)le. [Of obscure formation.

Usually taken to be f. SUCK *v.* + -LE, but the ordinary frequentative meaning of this suffix is not appropriate. Possibly a back-formation from SUCKLING *sb.*, first recorded *c* 1440.]

1. a. *trans.* To give suck to; to nurse (a child) at the breast.

1408 *Wyclif's Bible* Job iii. 12 (MS. Fairf. 2) Whi was j suklid wiþ tetis? **1604** SHAKS. *Oth.* II. i. 161 *Iago.* She was a wight... *Des.* To do what? *Iago.* To suckle Fooles, and chronicle small Beere. **1607** —— *Cor.* I. iii. 44 The brests of Hecuba When she did suckle Hector, look'd not louelier Then Hectors forhead. **1697** DRYDEN *Virg. Past.* III. 41 My Brinded Heifer..Two Thriving Calves she suckles twice a-day. *a* **1704** T. BROWN *Satire Quack* Wks. 1730 I. 63 Some she-bear..Suckled thee young. **1789** BUCHAN *Dom. Med.* (1790) 233 If she continue to suckle the child, it is at the peril of her own life. **1828** SCOTT *F.M. Perth* xxvi, The misery of the mother's condition rendered her little able to suckle the infant. **1844** STEPHENS *Bk. Farm* II. 470 A calf is suckled for 10 weeks. **1879** DIXON *Windsor* I. iv. 35 An English prince, ..suckled by an English nurse.

absol. **1839–47** *Todd's Cycl. Anat.* III. 361/2 The specific gravity of the milk appears to increase as the woman continues suckling.

b. *fig.* To nourish *with*, bring up *on.*

1654 JER. TAYLOR *Real Pres.* A 3, It began in the ninth age, and in the tenth was suckled with little arguments and imperfect pleadings. **1721** BRADLEY *Philos. Acc. Wks. Nat.* 35 The Roots..are till that time in a manner suckled by the Mother Plant. **1732** POPE *Ess. Man* I. 134 For me kind Nature..Suckles each herb, and spreads out ev'ry flow'r. **1781** COWPER *Expost.* 364 Though suckled at fair freedom's breast. **1807** WORDSW. '*The world is too much with us*' 10 A Pagan suckled in a creed outworn. **1883** G. MOORE *Mod. Lover* xvii, The great artist..is born in the barren womb of failure and suckled on the tears of impotence.

2. To cause to take milk from the breast or udder; to put to suck. Also with *up.* Now *rare.*

1523 FITZHERB. *Husb.* §38 Put the lambe to her, and socle it. **1566** PAINTER *Pal. Pleas.* I. 78 If kiddes be sockled vp wyth ewes milke. **1778** [W. MARSHALL] *Minutes Agric.* 28 Feb. an. 1776 Suckling calves after they are ten weeks old, is bad management. *a* **1796** VANCOUVER in A. Young *Agric. Essex* (1813) II. 284 A third [purpose] may be added, that of suckling, or feeding calves for the London market. **1834** L. RITCHIE *Wand. Seine* 131 [The Jews] were forbidden to suckle their children by means of Christian nurses.

3. *intr.* To suck at the breast.

1688, etc. [? implied in SUCKLING *ppl. a.* 2.] **1823** MME. P. PANAM *Mem. Yng. Gr. Lady* 102 The child who was suckling at my bosom. **1966** P. SCOTT *Jewel in Crown* I. 28 Their children, three girls and two boys to date (apart from the one still suckling..) sat on the front benches. **1977** *Sci. Amer.* Aug. 80/3 Since the evicted joey may continue to suckle for another four months, the female red kangaroo may have three offspring in the 'pipeline' at any one time: a dormant blastocyst, a small joey nursing and developing in the pouch and a larger young-at-foot still suckling.

suckler ('sʌklə(r)). Also *Sc.* 5 suclar, 6 sowklar. [f. SUCKLE *v.* + -ER[1].]

1. An unweaned mammal (rarely an infant); *esp.* a sucking calf. Also *attrib.*

1473 *Rental Bk. Cupar-Angus* (1879) I. 166 Twa cupyl of suclar kyddis. **1791** J. LEARMONT *Poems* 269 This day we hae our suckler lambs to spane. *c* **1800** ABDY in A. Young *Agric. Essex* (1813) II. 277 Sucklers of a week old, sold at Ongar market for 40s. each. **1832** L. HUNT tr. *Theocritus' Hercules & Serp.* 61 When they saw the little suckler, how He grasped the monsters. **1892** *Wilts Co. Mirror* 5 Aug. 4/2, 30 Fat and Suckler Calves.

†**b.** as a term of endearment. *Obs.*

1500–20 DUNBAR *Poems* lxxv. 53 My sowklar [*Bann. MS.* sucker] sweit as ony vnȝoun.

2. An animal that suckles its young; a mammal. Also, with epithet, an animal that suckles its young in a specified manner. *rare.*

1850 *Jrnl. R. Agric. Soc.* XI. II. 577 They are moderately prolific and excellent sucklers. **1861** *Zoologist* Ser. I. XIX. 7303 The sucklers and birds of the island have already been enumerated. *a* **1866** WHEWELL (Ogilvie).

3. One who rears young calves or lambs. *local.*

1750 W. ELLIS *Mod. Husbandm.* IV. I. 116 (E.D.S.). **1778** [W. MARSHALL] *Minutes Agric.* 29 Oct. 1775 Last night, the Suckler, in a great hurry, drove one of the cows out of the suckling-house into the yard. **1784** ROBINSON *Let.* in *N. & Q.* 3rd Ser. IV. 342, I sold the butcher a fat calf and the suckler a lean one.

4. *pl.* The flowering heads of clover. Also *attrib.* in *sing.* Cf. SUCKLING *sb.*[2] 1.

1725 RAMSAY *Gentle Sheph.* IV. ii, On the Suckler brae. **1853** G. JOHNSTON *Nat. Hist. E. Bord.* I. 54 The flowered heads are called by the common people *sookies* or *sucklers.* **1893–4** *Northumbld. Gloss.* II. 706 *Sucklers*, white clover.

5. = SUCKER *sb.* 4. *dial.* Cf. SUCKLING *sb.* 2.

1796 H. HUNTER tr. *St. Pierre's Study Nat.* (1799) II. 178 A very lofty tuft of oats..consisting of thirty-seven stalks,..without reckoning a multitude of other small sucklers. **1851** STERNBERG *Dial. Northants.* 109 *Sucklers*, slips of willow, &c., used for planting.

suckling ('sʌklɪŋ), *sb.*[1] Forms: 5 suklinge, sukkelyng, 5–6 sokelyng(e, 6 suc(k)lynge, -elynge, 7 sucklin, 6– suckling. [f. SUCK *v.* + -LING[1]. Cf. MDu. *sôgeling* (Du. *zuigeling*, WFlem. *zoogeling*), MHG. *sôgelinc*, *sûgelinc* (G. *säugling*).]

1. a. An infant that is at the breast or is unweaned.

c **1440** *Promp. Parv.* 463/1 Sokelynge, or he þat sokythe, *sububer.* **1535** COVERDALE *Ps.* viii. 2 Out of the mouth of the very babes & sucklinges thou hast ordened prayse. **1578** BANISTER *Hist. Man* I. 8 The place, that in infantes, and late borne sucklynges, is so soft, and tender. **1601** DENT *Pathw. Heaven* 389 A louing mother, though her yoong suckling crie all night,..when she ariseth, she loueth it neuerthelesse. **1845** WORDSW. '*Young England*' 14 Let Babes and Sucklings be thy oracles. **1897** *Allbutt's Syst. Med.* III. 129 In this country at any rate, rickets is practically unknown amongst sucklings.

b. A young animal that is suckled; *esp.* a sucking calf; cf. SUCKLER 1.

1530 PALSGR. 272/1 Sokelyng a yong calfe. **1577** B. GOOGE *Heresbach's Husb.* 43 b, Here next to my house, are my Sucklings, that are brought to their dammes to sucke thrise a day. **1655** MOUFET & BENNET *Health's Improv.* (1746) 136 Calves are either Sucklings or Wainlings. **1693** CONGREVE in *Dryden's Juvenal* XI. (1697) 285 The tend'rest Kid And Fattest of my Flock, a Suckling yet. **1731** ARBUTHNOT *Aliments* iv. (1735) 92 When an Animal that gives Suck turns feverish,..the Milk turns..to Yellow; to which the Suckling has an Aversion. **1821** BYRON *Cain* II. ii, I lately saw A lamb stung by a reptile: the poor suckling Lay foaming on the earth. **1822–7** GOOD *Study Med.* (1829) II. 590 Half the dogs pupped there are supposed to die of it while sucklings.

c. *fig.*

1806 H. K. WHITE *Let. to R. W. A.* 18 Aug., This island, and its little suckling the Isle of Wight.

2. = SUCKER *sb.* 4. *dial.* Cf. SUCKLER 5.

1798 *Trans. Soc. Arts* XVI. 345 The sucklings of my old trees transplanted.

suckling ('sʌklɪŋ), *sb.*[2] Also 5 suklynge, 5–6 sokelyng(e. [app. f. SUCKLE *sb.*[1]]

1. Clover. (Also *lamb-sucklings.*) *dial.* †Also glossing L. *locusta.* = HONEYSUCKLE 1, 1 b; SUCKLE *sb.* 1 a.

c **1440** *Promp. Parv.* 463/1 Sokelynge, herbe (or suklynge), *locusta.* *c* **1450** *Cov. Myst.* (Shaks. Soc.) 270 As we with swete bredys have it [*sc.* the passover lamb] ete And also with the byttyr Sokelyng. [Cf. *Exodus* xii. 8.] **1530** PALSGR. 272/1 Sokelyng an herbe. *a* **1682** SIR T. BROWNE *Extr. Common-Pl. Bks.* Wks. 1835 IV. 379 The flowers of sorrel are reddish,..of sweet trefoil or suckling three-leaved grass, red or white. **1765** *Museum Rust.* IV. 123 The white or Dutch clover... Probably from the apparent advantage which sheep receive from this admirable grass, is it called lamb's sucklings. **1798** *Hull Advertiser* 24 Mar. 2/1 Clover seed, trefoil, sainfoin, red suckling. **1895** *Gloss E. Anglia*, *Suckling*..(2) The common purple clover. In Suffolk, however, the red clover is never called *suckling*, but that term is generally used for the white or Dutch clover. **1898** RIDER HAGGARD *Farmer's Year* (1899) 61 The suckling is already thick in the grass, making patches of green carpeting.

2. = HONEYSUCKLE 2 (*Lonicera Periclymenum*). *Obs.* exc. *dial.*

1653 LAWES *Ayres & Dial.* II. 16 The wanton Suckling and the Vine. **1664** in *Verney Mem.* (1907) II. 208 To smell the sucklins and the stocks and to see the new trees grow. **1678** R. Ferrier *Jrnl.* in *Camden Misc.* (1895) IX. 32 Fine walks covered overhead with roses and sucklings. **1823** E. Moor *Suffolk Words* 408 *Sucklin*,..the honey-suckle.

suckling (ˈsʌklɪŋ), *vbl. sb.* [f. suckle *v.* + -ing[1].]

1. a. The feeding of infants at the breast. **b.** The rearing of young calves, etc. in suckling-houses.

1799 *Syn. Husb.* in R. W. Dickson *Pract. Agric.* (1805) II. 978 In suckling..the charges are much heavier than when the milk is sold out of the pail. **1842** Prichard *Nat. Hist. Man* 64 The processes connected with reproduction and suckling. **1892** J. Carmichael *Dis. Childr.* 288 Irregular Suckling is a fruitful cause of illness in the infant.

c. *transf.* (see quot.)

1855 Delamer *Kitch. Gard.* (1861) 153 The Lancashire exhibitors..leave but very few [gooseberries] on each bush, and increase the size of those..by a process called 'suckling', *i.e.*, placing a pan of water under each berry, that it may swell from the vapour given out.

2. *attrib.*, as ***suckling time***; **suckling assistant**, a device for relieving nursing mothers when suffering from sore nipples; †**suckling box**, ? a feeding-bottle of wood; **suckling-house**, a house or hut in which young calves or lambs are brought up; †**suckling meats**, food suitable for infants.

1803 *Med. Jrnl.* X. 353 Relfe's *suckling assistant. **1679** C. Nesse *Antichrist* 97 Milk in a warm breast is more effectual nourishment, than milk in a cold *suckling box. **1778** [W. Marshall] *Minutes Agric.* 29 Oct. 1775 The Suckler..drove one of the cows out of the *suckling-house into the yard. *c* **1610** *Women Saints* 111 Then had she nyne poore infants..whome she fedd on her knees, with tender and *suckling meates agreeable for their infancie. **1818** Keats *Endym.* iii. 456 She took me like a child of *suckling time, And cradled me in roses.

suckling (ˈsʌklɪŋ), *ppl. a.* [f. suckle *v.* + -ing[2].]

1. a. Giving suck. **b.** Rearing young calves, etc. in suckling-houses.

1799 Underwood *Dis. Childhood* (ed. 4) I. 293 Infants at the breast necessarily lying so much on the arm of the suckling mother. *c* **1800** Abdy in A. Young *Agric. Essex* (1813) II. 278 In the dairy farms the calves are generally sold at a week old, to the suckling farmer. **1805** R. W. Dickson *Pract. Agric.* II. 979 The calf-suckling farmer.

2. = sucking *ppl. a.* 1, 2.

In earlier quots. possibly attrib. use of suckling *sb.*[1]

1688 *Lond. Gaz.* No. 2357/4 Lost..a black and white suckling Spaniel Bitch. **1732** Arbuthnot *Rules of Diet* in *Aliments* etc. 404 Most of the Diseases of suckling Infants proceed from Milk growing sour and curdling in the Stomach. **1819** Scott *Ivanhoe* xxxii, Though thou art not so tender as a suckling pig. **1835** Wordsw. *Sonn.* '*While poring Antiquarians*', The Wolf, whose suckling Twins [etc.]. **1896** *Allbutt's Syst. Med.* I. 163 Milk, the natural food of the suckling animal.

b. *transf.* and *fig.*

1866 Swinburne *Laus Veneris* lxxix, O breast whereat some suckling sorrow clings. **1882** Coues *Biogen* (1884) 43 Some German metaphysicians and their suckling converts.

suckyr, obs. form of succour.

sucrase (ˈs(j)uːkreɪz). *Biochem.* [f. F. *sucre* sugar *sb.* + -ase.] An enzyme that catalyses the hydrolysis of disaccharides to monosaccharides; *spec.* that which catalyses the hydrolysis of sucrose to glucose and fructose; = invertin, invertase, saccharase.

1900 in B. D. Jackson *Gloss. Bot. Terms.* **1901** *Jrnl. Chem. Soc.* LXXX. i. 180 The isolation of 'sucrase' the actual enzyme of cane sugar inversion from yeast in a pure form appears..to be hopeless. **1954** A. White et al. *Princ. Biochem.* xvii. 397 Specific disaccharases for sucrose and lactose, named sucrase and lactase, respectively, are supposed to occur also in the intestinal juice. **1974** *Encycl. Brit. Micropædia* IX. 640/1 Sucrase is produced by the mucous membrane cells lining the walls of the small intestine. **1981** M. Toporek *Basic Chem. Life* xix. 271 Evidence at present indicates that..maltase, sucrase, and lactase are not actually secreted into the intestinal lumen.

sucrate (ˈs(j)uːkreɪt). *Chem.* [a. F. *sucrate*, f. *sucre* sugar + -ate[4].] A compound of a substance with sucrose.

1868 Fownes *Chem.* (ed. 10) 686 Cane-sugar does not turn brown when triturated with alkalis..: it combines with them, however, forming compounds called sucrates.

‖**sucre** (sukre). [f. the name of Antonio José de *Sucre*, a South American patriot.] A basic monetary unit of Ecuador, consisting of 100 centavos; a coin of this value.

In 1915 the *sucre* was worth about 2 shillings.

1886 *Rep. Sec. Treasury* 230, 412, 413 (Cent. Dict.). **1897** *Westm. Gaz.* 12 May 1/3 The Government of Guayaquil recently made a special issue of postage-stamps of the value of 1 c., 2 c., 5 c., 10 c., 20 c., 50 c., and 1 sucre. **1902** *Encycl. Brit.* (ed. 10) XXVII. 649/2.

‖**sucrier** (sykrie). [Fr.] A sugar-bowl, usu. made of porcelain and with a cover.

1869 C. Schreiber *Jrnl.* 9 Oct. (1911) I. 50 A Bow (sprigged) sucrier with cover and acorn top. **1904** E. Dillon *Porcelain* p. xxi, *Sèvres* porcelain. Two small *sucriers*..*Gros bleu* and green ground, with birds on branches painted in white reserves. **1960** *Times* 18 June 11/2 But odd pieces—*sucriers*, cup and saucers, teapots—can be obtained at moderate cost. **1975** *Country Life* 4 Dec. (Suppl.) 43/1 Chelsea-Derby sucrier, c. 1770.

sucro- (s(j)uːkrəʊ), used as combining form of F. *sucre* sugar, as ***sucro-acid***, an acid obtained by the action of an acid on a sugar.

1862 Miller *Elem. Chem.*, *Org.* (ed. 2) iv. §3. 288 The following equations will serve to elucidate the composition of some of these sucro-acids:—1. Sucro-tartaric acid, dibasic:—Tartaric acid + Sucrose = Sucro-tartaric acid. **1913** Dorland *Illust. Med. Dict.* 918/1 *Sucroclastic*, splitting up sugar; as, a sucroclastic enzyme.

sucrose (ˈs(j)uːkrəʊs). *Chem.* [f. F. *sucre* sugar + -ose[2].]

1. †**a.** Any one of the sugars having the composition ($C_{12}H_{22}O_{11}$) and properties of cane-sugar; = saccharose. *Obs.*

1862 [see prec.]. **1866** Roscoe *Elem. Chem.* 322 Saccharine ..Bodies..may be divided into three classes: (1) Sucroses ..(2) Glucoses..(3) Amyloses. **1897** *Allbutt's Syst. Med.* III. 200 The sucroses..cane-sugar, maltose, and lactose.

b. *spec.* a white crystalline sugar, $C_{12}H_{22}O_{11}$, which can be derived from sugar-cane, sugar beet, and in lesser quantities from most other plants, and is used as a sweetener; = saccharose.

In chemical terms, sucrose is an optically active disaccharide composed of D-fructose and D-glucose and having a structure described by the systematic name α-D-glucopyranosyl-(1,2)-β-D-fructofuranoside.

1857 W. A. Miller *Elem. Chem.* III. ii. 54 Cane sugar or Sucrose ($C_{12}H_{11}O_{11}$).—This variety of sugar is chiefly obtained from the sugar cane. **1888** Bloxam *Chemistry* (ed. 6) 644 Sucrose fuses at 160°C. (320°F.), and does not crystallize on cooling. **1903** A. J. Walker tr. *Holleman's Textbk. Org. Chem.* i. 274 On hydrolysis sucrose yields *d*-glucose and *d*-fructose in equal proportions. **1964** N. G. Clark *Mod. Org. Chem.* viii 138 Molasses is the dark syrup remaining after the removal of crystallized sugar from evaporated sugar-cane juice or the aqueous extract of sugar beet; it contains between 40 and 50 per cent of sucrose (table sugar). **1980** C. W. Spangler *Org. Chem.* i. xii. 248 Lactose and sucrose are two of the more common disaccharides.

2. *attrib.* and *Comb.*, as **sucrose (density) gradient** *Biochem.*, a gradient of sucrose concentration used in the centrifugation of biological media to prevent convection currents; freq. *attrib.*; **sucrose phosphate**, any of the esters that can be formed between sucrose and phosphoric acid; **sucrose phosphorylase**, a bacterial enzyme which catalyses the breakdown of sucrose, ultimately producing glucose-1-phosphate and fructose.

1944 *Jrnl. Exper. Med.* LXXIX. 304 Concurrent experiments..performed without the protective action of a *sucrose gradient showed no indication of a sedimentation boundary. **1947** *Ann. Rev. Microbiol.* I. 362 Friedewald & Pickels.., by centrifugation in a sucrose density gradient so as to reduce convection, noted differences between PR8 and Lee strains. **1968** H. Harris *Nucleus & Cytoplasm* iii. 43 (*caption*) Sucrose-density-gradient sedimentation pattern of a crude extract of *Escherichia coli* cells exposed to [^{14}C] uracil for 20 seconds. **1979** *Biochim. & Biophysica Acta* DLXIV. 191 Sucrose density gradient analysis of the postribosomal fraction of muscle and liver revealed that the sedimentation profiles of the synthetases of the two tissues were similar. **1938** *Chem. Abstr.* XXXII. 5920 The rabbit paw was injected with 10 cc. of 2% aq. solns. of..Ca *sucrosephosphate. **1960** *Plant Physiol.* XXXV. 269/2 Any sucrose-phosphate which is formed is ultimately dephosphorylated by enzymes in sugar beet tissue at some stage prior to storage in the root. **1979** *Infection & Immunity* XXIV. 868/1 Hydrolysis of sucrose phosphate would be expected to yield glucose 6-phosphate and fructose. **1943** *Jrnl. Biol. Chem.* CLI. 360 It is possible to obtain active preparations of *sucrose phosphorylase relatively free of invertase and phosphatase. **1977** *Jrnl. Molecular Catalysis* II. 453 The interest in sucrose phosphorylase lies in the fact that a stable and re-usable insoluble preparation can be useful for both preparative and analytical purposes.

sucst, sucþ: see see *v.*

suction (ˈsʌkʃən). [ad. L. *suctio*, *-ōnem*, n. of action f. *suct-*, *sūgĕre* to suck. Cf. F. *succion* (OF. *suction*).]

1. a. The action of sucking with the tongue and lips (or analogous organs). Also, an instance of this.

Applied to a method of extracting soft cataract (and the instruments used) by sucking the liquid from the lens through a tube (cf. *suction tube* in 4 b).

1626 Bacon *Sylva* §191 Sounds..may be made, as well by Suction, as by Emission of the Breath: as in Whistling, or Breathing. **1749** Hartley *Observ. Man* i. ii. §2. 169 The Motions dependent on the Sensations of the Tongue..: Suction, Mastication [etc.]. **1800** *Med. Jrnl.* III. 376 The author asserts, that..all the parts [in insects] derive their aliment from simple suction. **1840** L. Hunt *Seer* i. x. 25/1 His [*sc.* a fly's] suctions of sugar. **1841** T. R. Jones *Anim. Kingd.* 194 The internal digestive apparatus [of the leech] is evidently adapted..to form a capacious reservoir for the reception of fluids taken in by suction. **1862** Calverley *Verses & Transl.* (ed. 2) 2 When I..sent those streaky lollipops home for your fairy suction. **1868** E. Edwards *Ralegh* I. xxv. 615 He was unable to take sustenance, except by suction. **1869** Lawson *Dis. Eye* (1874) 130 Extraction of Soft Cataract by Suction... Two, three, or four days having elapsed, the second stage or suction part of the operation may be performed.

b. Imbibing strong drink, drinking. *slang.*

1817 Scott *Let. to Morritt* 11 Aug. in Lockhart, A man.. cannot easily spend much money in liquor, since he must walk three or four miles to the place of suction and back again. **1837** Dickens *Pickw.* xxiii, Wery good power o' suction, Sammy. **1913** *Daily Mail* 25 Apr. 5/1 'What was this debt for?' asked Judge Snagge. 'Suction, my lord,' was the reply.

†**c.** *transf.* The craving of appetite. *Obs.*

1615 Crooke *Body of Man* 169 Least the parts shoulde pine away when they are..hunger-starued, nature hath framed one part of exquisite and perfect sense, which alone fore-apprehending the suction and so the want of the rest [etc.]. **1661** Lovell *Hist. Anim. & Min.* 365 A continual and unsatiable desire of eating caused, by a vehement sense of suction in the mouth of the ventricle.

d. *fig.*

1851 Hawthorne *Ho. Sev. Gables* xvii, They had been drawn into the great current of human life, and were swept away with it, as by the suction of fate itself. **1903** *Westm. Gaz.* 24 Oct. 8/1 If we had joined the movement we should have been drawn into it through suction.

2. The production of a more or less complete vacuum with the result that external atmospheric pressure forces fluid into the vacant space or causes the adhesion of surfaces.

1658 R. White tr. *Digby's Powd. Symp.* (1660) 53 One may remark within the..œconomy of nature, sundry sorts of attractions: as that of suction. **1669** W. Simpson *Hydrol. Chym.* 129 The pressure would not be so much..unless at the time of the suction of the air. **1674** Boyle *Excell. Theol.* ii. v. 212 Suction and the ascension of water in pumps. **1702** Savery *Miner's Friend* 20 The external Pressure of the Atmosphere or what is vulgarly called Suction. **1793** W. & S. Jones *Catal. Optical* etc. *Instr.* 6 A model of a water pump, exemplifying the nature of pumps, and proving the absurdity of what is called suction. **1878** Meredith *Teeth* 222 That adaptation of the plate to the mucous membrane which is necessary to keep out particles of food, or to make perfect suction. **1899** Baring-Gould *Bk. West* II. vi. 86 The suction had been so great as to tear the leather gaiters I wore off my legs.

3. Short for *suction-pipe*.

1886 J. Barrowman *Sc. Mining Terms* 65 *Suction*, or *Suction pipe*, the tail pipe of a pump; that part of a pump where the water enters. **1889** Welch *Text Bk. Naval Archit.* xi. 124 Its length is sufficient to enable it to be screwed at its other end to any of the suctions.

4. *attrib.* and *Comb.* **a.** Simple attrib.

1847–9 *Todd's Cycl. Anat.* IV. i. 145/1 Air entering veins lying within the suction-influence of the chest. **1855** Dunglison *Med. Lex.*, *Suction power*, the force presumed to be exerted on the blood in the veins by the active dilatation of the heart. **1899** *Allbutt's Syst. Med.* VII. 250 The alternate compressive action of the abdominal wall and suction action of the thorax.

b. Special comb.: **suction box, chamber**, a chamber in a pump into which the liquid is conveyed by the suction-pipe; **suction dredge** *Engin.*, a type of dredge employing a suction pump, used in the dredging of soft material from sea-beds and river bottoms; hence **suction dredger**, a vessel which carries a suction dredge; **suction dredging** *vbl. sb.*; **suction fan**, (*a*) a fan used to increase or diminish the draught in a furnace; (*b*) a fan for withdrawing chaff and dirt from grain, or steam and hot air from meal, as it comes from the burrs (Knight, 1884); **suction gas**, the town gas produced by a suction plant; **suction lift** *Mech.*, the height to which a liquid can be drawn up a pipe by suction; **suction pipe**, (*a*) the pipe leading from the bottom of a pump barrel to the reservoir from which fluid is to be drawn; (*b*) a pipe for the extraction of dust from tow; **suction plant**, a form of gas producer (see producer 3) in which the blast is induced by suction; **suction-plate**, (*a*) a dental plate kept in position by atmospheric pressure; (*b*) (see quot. 1889); **suction pressure** *Bot.* [tr. G. *saugkraft* suction force (Ursprung & Blum 1916, in *Ber. d. Deutsch. bot. Ges.* XXXIV. 539)], the force with which a cell can imbibe water, being the difference between the pressure exerted by the cell walls on the cell contents and the osmotic pressure of the contents; **suction primer** (see quots.); **suction pump**, a pump of the type in which the barrel is placed above the level of the reservoir, and is connected therewith by a suction pipe; **suction stop**, any of the 'clicks' peculiar to certain South African languages; **suction stroke**, in an internal-combustion engine, a piston stroke in which fresh mixture is drawn into the cylinder; **suction tube**, (*a*) = *suction-pipe* (*a*); (*b*) a tube used in an operation for cataract; **suction valve**, (*a*) the valve at the bottom of the cylinder of a suction pump, below the piston; (*b*) the valve in a steam engine through which the water is drawn from the hot-well into the feed-pump (Knight, 1875). Also in various names of machines which perform their operations by suction or the creation of a vacuum; e.g. ***suction cleaner***, ***gas engine***, ***hose***, ***sweeper***.

1889 Welch *Text Bk. Naval Archit.* xi. 124 A *suction-box or valve chest..is fitted beneath the pump. **1864** Webster, **Suction-chamber*, the chamber of a pump into which the suction pipe delivers. **1904** *Westm. Gaz.* 14 Sept. 9/3 Their fight with *suction cleaners alone had cost them £3,750. **1901** *Daily Colonist* (Victoria, B.C.) 27 Oct. 3/2 Next Monday..the first *suction dredge ever operated in the western part of the Dominion will be given a trial. **1940** *Sun* (Baltimore) 4 Dec. 6/3 Excavations by huge dipper and suction dredges already are under way at both ends of the canal. **1977** *New Yorker* 20 June 68/2 Suction dredges are portable, cheap, irresistible to a certain class of lone, adventuring miner. **1911** *Daily Colonist* (Victoria, B.C.) 6 Apr. 14/5 Plans are being prepared for a new *suction dredger of the type of the King Edward for use in British Columbia coast waters. **1930** *Engineering* 13 June 760/1 The sand backing was filled in over the bank by suction dredgers. **1974** H. R. Cooper *Pract. Dredging* (ed. 2) i. 10 (*caption*) A powerful pump, a floating platform, a pipe and disposal system...that is the simple anatomy of the Suction Dredger. **1965** G. V. Williams *Econ. Geol. N.Z.* vii. 69/2 These sands were washed beyond the narrow confines of the Ohinemuri River..where they were worked by *suction-dredging some years ago. **1974** H. R. Cooper *Pract. Dredging* (ed. 2) p. x, During the 12 years since the first edition of *Practical Dredging* was published, trailing suction dredging methods have become increasingly important. **1874** Raymond *Statist. Mines & Mining* 400 A *suction-fan wherewith to increase or diminish the draught, and to cause the effectual passage of the gases and fumes through even a compact mass of ore. **1907** *Daily Mail Year Bk.* 75/2 *Suction-gas has been adapted to marine purposes. **1936** Bone & Himus *Coal* xxiv. 417 By the year 1901 'Suction-Gas Plants' were established on the market. *Ibid.* 418 A typical 'suction gas', generated from gas-coke, with air saturated with steam at 51·7°C, contains CO_2 = 5·15, CO = 25·45, H_2 = 13·10, CH_4 = 0·30, and N_2 = 56·00 per cent. **1906** *Westm. Gaz.* 2 Oct. 5/2 The householder must supply himself with a small *suction gas-engine. **1888** *Daily News* 2 July 5/5 The Grinder and Manly tugs got to work with their *suction hose. **1909** N. Hawkins *Mech. Dict.* 559/2 *Suction lift. **1940** Kristal & Annett *Pumps* ii. 103 It is a generally accepted rule that 15-ft. suction lift is a safe operating condition. **1976** C. P. Kittredge in I. J. Karassik et al. *Pump Handbk.* II. 148 A positive value of h_s is called a suction head while a negative value of h_s is called a suction lift. **1793** *Trans. Soc. Arts* V. 209 A proper length of *suction pipe. **1835** Ure *Philos. Manuf.* 215 Arrangements ..for cleaning the tow by a blowing-machine, with dust suction-pipes. **1909** *Rep. Brit. Assoc. Adv. Sci. 1908* 826 A *suction plant costs less and occupies less ground space, but the gas made in it is not so strong as in the older form of pressure plant. **1920** H. C. Greenwood *Industr. Gases* III. 344 Suction plants have an advantage in the reduction of risk of carbon monoxide poisoning owing to the prevailing negative pressure. **1875** Knight *Dict. Mech.* 2442/2 **Suction-plate* (*Dental*). **1889** Welch *Text Bk. Naval Archit.* xi. 124 A deck- or suction-plate.., to the under side of which, at its centre, the tail pipe from the pump is attached. **1922** W. Styles in *Biochem. Jrnl.* XVI. 728, I propose for this quantity, already described as a force and a power, but which is in reality a pressure, the term '*suction pressure'. **1958** *New Biol.* XXV. 38 Water moves from the soil to the leaves along a gradient which most European workers call a gradient of suction pressure or suction force and most Americans, a gradient of diffusion pressure deficit. **1978** *Physiol. Plant Path.* XIII. 275 Infection of tomato plants by *Meloidogyne javanica* resulted in increased suction pressure in the root system. **1875** Knight *Dict. Mech.* 2442/2 **Suction-primer*, a small force-pump worked by hand and used in charging a main-pump. **1884** *Ibid.* Suppl. 871/1 *Suction Primer*, a device to charge a steam pump ready for starting. **1825** J. Nicholson *Oper. Mech.* 635 Two or three kinds, used for domestic purposes, of which the *suction and lifting pumps are the chief. **1883** *Science* I. 524/1 It has long been discussed whether the ventricle of the heart is not only a force-pump in systole, but also a suction-pump in diastole. **1887** H. Sweet in *Academy* 10 Dec. 394 The *suction-stops or 'clicks' of the South-African languages. **1904** R. T. Mecredy *Dict. Motoring* 169 The *Suction Stroke... The descent of the piston naturally causes a vacuum in the combustion chamber, which at first was air and gas tight. **1933** V. L. Maleev *Internal-Combustion Engines* v. 59 Temperature t_d of the gases in the cylinder at the end of the suction stroke is higher than the outside temperature t_o. **1941** Newton & Seeds *Motor Vehicle* (ed. 3) xi. 172 The displacement of the piston on the suction stroke represents potential ability for forming a vacuum in the cylinder. **1920** *Chambers's Jrnl.* Nov. 830/1 A *suction-sweeper that we have examined recently runs the electric type very close indeed. **1926–7** *Army & Navy Stores Catal.* 114/1 Whirlwind Suction Sweeper. Its revolving Brush sweeps the carpet... Its powerful suction sucks the dust into the dustproof container. **1863** Atkinson tr. *Ganot's Physics* (1866) 131 A *suction tube,..which dips into the reservoir from which water is to be raised. **1879** *St. George's Hosp. Rep.* IX. 502 One, resulting from the prick of a thorn, in a man, aged 28, was extracted with the suction-tube. **1831** Lardner *Pneumatics* v. 294 Probably the most simple and the best contrivance [for an air pump] is one in which the *suction valve is altogether dispensed with.

c. *spec.* in *Aeronaut.*, used *attrib.* to designate various devices concerned with controlling flow conditions in the boundary layer, as ***suction aerofoil, control, slot***, etc.

1933 *Gloss. Aeronaut. Terms* (*B.S.I.*) VII. 58 *Suction face*, the side of an airscrew blade formed by the upper surfaces of its aerofoil elements. **1946** *Jrnl. R. Aeronaut. Soc.* L. 431/1 The suction aerofoil exhibits a large discontinuous fall of velocity followed by a gentle rising velocity from the position of the suction slot to the trailing edge. **1950** *Ibid.* LIV. 159/2 The suction wing principle must be associated with the flying wing layout for it to be truly advantageous. **1960** *Aeroplane* XCIX. 268/2 In spite of official reluctance to admit the potentialities of suction control of the boundary layer, the enthusiasts persist in their efforts. **1977** *Jrnl. R. Soc. Arts* CXXV. 350/1 The US..flew a modified twin-jet reconnaissance aircraft..in 1966 with suction slots which also achieved a high degree of wing laminar flow.

Hence **'suctional** *a. rare*$^{-1}$, having a power of suction (*fig.*); **'suctionist** *nonce-wd.*, one who favours a theory of suction.

1707 *Phil. Trans.* XXV. 2415 Several Phænomena of which, being liable to be accounted for by the Suctionists, and Funicularians, to proceed from some (unintelligible) Internal Cause. **1872** Ruskin *Munera P.* 32 The holder of wealth..may be regarded..as a money-chest with a slit in it, not only receptant but suctional.

suctorial (sʌk'tɔərɪəl), *a. Zool.* [f. mod.L. *suctōrius* (n. pl. *Suctōria*, sc. *animālia*, the name of various zoological Groups), f. *suct-*, *sūgĕre* to suck *v.*] Of an organ: Adapted for sucking. Of an animal: Having organs adapted for sucking or having the power of suction; belonging to any of the groups named Suctoria in which the mouth is adapted for sucking, or which possess sucking disks, or the like. Of a habit, etc.: Involving or characterized by suction.

1833 Owen *Descr. Catal. Comp. Anat.* II. 80 When the Lamprey is firmly attached..to foreign bodies by means of its suctorial mouth. **1835–6** *Todd's Cycl. Anat.* I. 267/2 The *Tenuirostres*..or suctorial birds. **1846** Patterson *Zool.* 61 Suctorial discs, such as those of the leeches. **1851** Richardson *Geol.* viii. 267 The Hemiptera..are suctorial insects. **1880** Bastian *Brain* vi. 99 Owing to the suctorial habits of these fierce and predatory creatures, the œsophagus is very narrow. **1900–13** Dorland *Med. Dict.* 672/1 Suctorial pad.

So **suc'torian**, a member of the Suctoria; *esp.* a cyclostomous fish; in mod. use *spec.* a protozoan of the class or subclass Suctoria, the adult form of which is usually sessile, lacking cilia and feeding by the use of suctorial tentacles; also as *adj.* = suctorial *a.*

1842 Brande *Dict. Sci.*, etc. **1931** R. R. Kudo *Handbk. Protozool.* xxxiii. 399 The body of a suctorian may be spherical, elliptical, dendritic, etc. **1939** *Jrnl. Cellular & Compar. Physiol.* XIV. 410 The tentacles of the suctorian protozoan Ephelota coronata..are very long and thin. **1975** *Nature* 7 Aug. 467/2 Microtubules have also independently evolved into many other organelles of motility, such as.. suctorian tentacles and haptonemata. **1980** J. N. Farmer *Protozoa* xvii. 678/1 The tentacles of suctorians included in this family are of one type, the feeding tentacles.

suctorious (sʌk'tɔərɪəs), *a. Zool.* Now *rare.* [Formed as suctorial *a.* + -ous.] = suctorial.

1815 Kirby & Sp. *Entomol.* (1816) I. 167 The larvæ of Dytisci fixing themselves by their suctorious mandibles to the body of fish. **1835–6** *Todd's Cycl. Anat.* I. 519/2 Both kinds of prehensile organs are provided with acetabula, or suctorious discs for adhesion.

So **'suctory** *a. rare*$^{-1}$.

1826 Kirby & Sp. *Entom.* III. xxxiv. 464 *Rostellum*, which I employ to denote the suctory organs of the louse tribe.

sucupira (ˌsʊkə'piːərə). [a. Pg., f. Tupi *sucupira.*] A dark brown hardwood obtained from trees of the genus *Bowdichia* or *Diplotropis*, both native to South America, esp. Brazil, and belonging to the family Leguminosæ; also, a tree of either of these genera.

1924 Record & Mell *Timbers Trop. Amer.* II. 270 The woods commonly known as 'sucupira' are of a deep chocolate-brown color. **1950** *Archit. Rev.* CVII. 124 The photograph..shows..an office partition in 'sucupira', a rich purple hardwood. **1977** *Transatlantic Rev.* LX. 86 The colossal Ceibas, para nuts and sucupiras with their blue flowers high in the sun.

sucuri, -urris, -urs(s: see succour *sb.* and *v.*

sud *sb.*, sing. of suds, q.v.

†**sud**, *v. Obs.* [f. prec.]

1. *trans.* To befoul, soil.

1593 Nashe *Christ's T.* (1613) 164 Recouer your soules though you haue sudded your bodies.

2. *intr.* To foam. (See sudding *ppl. a.*)

1603 G. Fletcher *Canto Death of Eliza* i, The streame, That sudding on the rocke, would closely seeme To imitate her whitenesse with his frothy creame.

3. *pass.* To be covered with drift sand left by a flood.

1787 Grose *Provinc. Gloss.* s.v. *Sudded*, The meadows are sudded; i.e. covered with drift sand left by the floods. W.

sud, dial. var. *should*: see shall A 7 *β*.

sudaine, -te, obs. forms of sudden, -ty.

‖**sudak** (su'dak). [Russian *sudák.*] A species of pike-perch.

1799 W. Tooke *View Russian Emp.* III. 151 Still in greater plenty in the subordinate streams are the sudak, pearch, and innumerable kinds of scale-fish. **1973** *Nat. Geogr. Mag.* May 612/1 All the strange but delicious bounty of the Volga, handsome, fat fish with names like sazan, sudak.

‖**sudamina** (s(j)uː'dæmɪnə), *sb. pl. Path.* [mod.L., pl. of *sūdāmen*, f. *sūdāre* to sweat.] Minute whitish vesicles or pustules caused by the accumulation of sweat in the upper layers of the skin after copious perspiration, esp. in certain fevers.

1671 Salmon *Syn. Med.* I. xlviii. 113 'Ἱδρῶα *Sudamina* the Measles are pustules like Millet-seed which ulcerate the Skin. **1844** Hoblyn *Dict. Terms Med.* (ed. 2). **1862** H. W. Fuller *Dis. Lungs* 245 A vesicular eruption of sudamina. **1906** *Daily Chron.* 6 Apr. 5/5 Suffering from an outbreak of 'sudamina', consequent on eating putrid meat.

Hence **su'daminal** *a.*, pertaining to or consisting of sudamina.

1899 *Allbutt's Syst. Med.* VII. 709 There is a great tendency to profuse sweating after fits, and this may lead to sudaminal rashes.

Sudan (suː'dɑːn, -æn). Also **Soudan.** [Name for the part of Africa lying between the Sahara and the Equator, orig. embracing the whole region as far west as the Atlantic Ocean, but now restricted to the country lying to the south of Egypt, a. Arab. *sūdān*, pl. of *sūdā* black.]

1. = Sudanese *sb.* Also *attrib.*

1867 'Ouida' *Under Two Flags* I. xiii. 297 Chasseurs, Zouaves..mingled with jet-black Soudans. **1889** W. F. Butler *Charles George Gordon* iii. 58 Some of his old Soudan soldiers.

2. *Chem.* Used *attrib.* to designate various azo and diazo dyes mostly derived from 2-hydroxynaphthalene and anthraquinone, used as industrial dyes and biological stains: as ***Sudan I*** (also *1*), the orange-yellow azo dye, C_6H_5ROH (where R = $-N{:}N{\cdot}C_{10}H_6-$); ***Sudan II*** (also *2*), the brown azo dye, $(CH_3)_2{\cdot}C_6H_3{\cdot}N{:}N{\cdot}C_{10}H_6OH$; ***Sudan III*** (also *3*), the red diazo dye, $C_6H_5{\cdot}N{:}N{\cdot}C_6H_4{\cdot}ROH$; ***Sudan IV*** (also *4*), the scarlet diazo dye, $CH_3{\cdot}C_6H_4{\cdot}N{:}N{\cdot}C_6H_4(CH_3){\cdot}ROH$; ***Sudan black*** (*B*), the black diazo dye,

$$C_6H_5{\cdot}R{\cdot}R \overset{NH}{\underset{NH}{\diamond}} C(CH_3)_2.$$

1894 A. G. Green tr. *Schultz' & Julius' Syst. Survey Org. Colouring Matters* 66 (*table*) Sudan I..Benzene-azo-*β*-naphthol. $C_{16}H_{12}N_2O$. *Ibid.* 70 (*table*) Sudan II.. Xylene-azo-*β*-napthol. $C_{18}H_{16}N_2O$. *Ibid.* 86 (*table*) Sudan III..Benzene-azo-benzene-azo-*β*-naphthol. $C_{22}H_{16}N_4O$. **1907** *Practitioner* Nov. 635 Fresh sections stained with Sudan III. **1956** [see polybase]. **1961** R. D. Baker *Essent. Path.* iv. 40 The lipid is bound in the organ and does not have the physicochemical form necessary to absorb Sudan dye. **1966** T. S. & C. R. Leeson *Histology* i. 16/1 Fat can be detected in sections which have not been exposed to fat solvents by stains such as Sudan III, Sudan IV, and Sudan black B. **1974** Passmore & Robson *Compan. Med. Stud.* III. I. xxi. 14/2 Sudan black B stains the cytoplasm of the myeloid series, the intensity of the staining increasing with maturation.

3. ***Sudan grass*** (*U.S.*), a tall annual grass, *Sorghum sudanense*, which is cultivated for hay in dry regions of the United States. Also *ellipt.*

1912 *Yearbk. U.S. Dept. Agric. 1911* 72 Sudan grass..is another example of a new forage crop that has become popular almost in one season. **1929** C. C. Deam *Grasses of Indiana* 325 Sudan grass has only recently been introduced into Indiana and its use as a hay crop is on the increase. **1949** *Hoard's Dairyman* 25 Oct. 756/3 Frost-nipped cane, sudan, pig weeds, Johnson grass, and flax are poisonous to cattle. **1964** Mrs. L. B. Johnson *White House Diary* 6 July (1970) 176 You can look down on the church spire in the valley below and the fields in between, with Sudan grass waving in the wind. **1978** J. Updike *Coup* (1979) i. 28 In the wide belt of transition between withered sudan and stark desert, there were islands of what had been, before the drought, pasture land.

Hence **ˌsudano'philia** *Med.* [-philia], the condition in which cells containing particular fatty or lipid structures can be stained with a Sudan dye; hence **ˌsudano'philic** *a.*, capable of taking up Sudan stains.

1911 Stedman *Med. Dict.* 840/2 *Sudanophilia*,..a condition in which the leucocytes contain minute fat droplets which take a brilliant red stain when treated with 0·2 per cent Sudan III. **1954** E. W. Dempsey in R. O. Greep *Histology* xxvii. 745 (*caption*) The two sections are from two phases of secretion and illustrate the increased sudanophilia of the rodlike mitochondria during the phase of extrusion of fat from the cells. **1956** *Nature* 7 Jan. 48/1, I observed certain sudanophilic corpuscles which do not appear to have been previously described. **1961** R. D. Baker *Essent. Path.* iv. 40 Fat occurring normally in adipose tissue, adrenal cortex and corpus luteum absorbs Sudan dyes and is called sudanophilic. **1979** *Atherosclerosis* XXXIII. 486 Sudanophilia is evident in the upper thoracic portion and in the area of the renal arteries. **1980** *Ibid.* XXXV. 103 Polar coordinate mapping was used to determine the rate of progression of spontaneous sudanophilic coeliac lesions on the aortic wall in White Carneau pigeons.

sudand, -anetee, obs. forms of sudden, -ty.

Sudanese (suːdə'niːz), *a.* and *sb.* Also **Soudanese.**

A. *adj.* Of or pertaining to the Sudan. **B.** *sb.* An inhabitant or the inhabitants of the Sudan. Also in *Comb.*, as **Sudanese-Guinean** (see quots.).

1875 Gordon in *G. in Central Africa* (1881) 77 Cowardly, lying, effeminate brutes these Arabs and Soudanese! **1884** Keane *Ethnol. Egyptian Sudan* 17 Subjoined are tabulated schemes of all the Eastern Sudanese and contiguous ethnical groups. **1884** E. W. Hamilton *Diary* 13 May (1972) II. 615 In the House of Commons yesterday there was an abnormal display of excitement..on the occasion of the Soudanese or Gordonese vote of censure moved by Sir M. H. Beach. **1887** *Encycl. Brit.* XXII. 277/2 The well-watered and arable Soudanese lands. *Ibid.* 279/1 The Sudanese Negro peoples. **1905** Sayce in *Contemp. Rev.* Aug. 267 The Egyptian has never been fond of military service, whereas, we all now know, the Sudanese is essentially a fighting animal. **1954** Pei & Gaynor *Dict. Linguistics* 207 *Sudanese-Guinean*, a family of African Negro languages, spoken by an estimated total of 50,000,000 persons... Some linguists consider Sudanese and Guinean as two independent families. **1967** M. Schlauch *Language* ii. 39 In a wide belt stretching across Northern Africa, bounded on the South by a line extending Eastwards from the shores of the Gulf of Guinea and then dipping still farther to the South, we find a chain of languages grouped together and known as Sudanese-Guinean.

Also **Suda'ni** (also **Sudany**) *a.* and *sb.* in the same sense; **Sudanian** (suːˈdeɪnɪən) *a.* [f. mod.L. *Sudania*, the Sudan], Sudanese.

1842 PRICHARD *Nat. Hist. Man* 305 The black Súdanian nations. **1896** *Daily News* 20 May 5/1 He is a Sudani, and was one of Gordon's soldiers. **1906** PETRIE *Relig. Anc. Egypt* ix. 63 The Sudany dancer. **1908** SIR H. JOHNSTON *Grenfell & the Congo* II. xxiii. 587 Sudanian Africa.

Sudanic (suːˈdænɪk), *a.* and *sb.* [f. SUDAN + -IC.] **A.** *adj.* = SUDANESE *a.*; *spec.* of or pertaining to the Sudan or an extensive group of African languages spoken there and elsewhere in central, northern, and eastern Africa. **B.** *sb.* (One of) the Sudanic group of languages.

1912 D. WESTERMANN *Shilluk People* 1. 32 Hamitic languages..differ from the Sudanic languages chiefly in the grammatical gender. *Ibid.*, Numerous Shilluk-words, which most probably are Sudanic, are found in languages generally counted as Hamitic. **1913** N. W. THOMAS *Anthrop. Rep. Ibo-Speaking Peoples of Nigeria* 1. 141 The languages of West Africa, commonly called Sudanic, and spoken by the true negro, have been classified into four main groups—Eastern Sudanic, Central Sudanic, Middle and Western Sudanic. **1931** C. K. MEEK *Sudanese Kingdom* iv. 184 Mlle. Homburger has recently written a paper attempting to prove a close connection between Ancient Egyptian, Fulani, Sudanic, and Bantu. **1936** *Discovery* June 171/1 The Nilotes of the Nile Valley, speaking Negro (Sudanic) languages and extending from the Anglo-Egyptian Sudan some 200 miles south of Khartum into Uganda. **1956** E. E. EVANS-PRITCHARD *Nuer Relig.* iii. 104 They think easily in terms of Spirit but not in terms of medicines, the idea of which as it obtains among their Sudanic neighbours they seem scarcely able to grasp. **1956** A. W. SOUTHALL *Alur Society* ii. 24 The Bendi are also Sudanic speakers. **1957** LD. HAILEY *African Survey 1956* iii. 84 Negro (including Sudanic, Bantu, and Nilotic), and Hamito-Semitic. **1972** J. BIGGS-DAVISON *Africa—Hope Deferred* iii. 24 The Sudanic economy was mainly rural and pastoral. **1977** *Sci. Amer.* Apr. 110/3 Ehret suggests that the names applied to cattle and sheep by many modern Bantu-speakers were probably derived from the non-Bantu languages known collectively as Central Sudanic. **1980** *Cambr. Encycl. Archaeol.* 342/1 The formative processes of the Early Iron Age complex took place in the country to the north-west, in the 'sudanic' belt of open grassland savanna on the northern fringes of the equatorial forest.

Sudanization (ˌsuːdənaɪˈzeɪʃən). [f. as prec. + -IZATION.] The action or process of making Sudanese in character, *spec.* with reference to the independence of the Sudan from Great Britain in 1956.

1951 *Britannica Bk. of Year* 44/1 The year was one of progress towards the government's declared object—the Sudanization and independence of the Sudan. **1955** *Times* 2 Aug. 5/2 The first stage in the 'Sudanization' of important posts held by foreigners, had been completed. **1970** H. TREVELYAN *Middle East in Revolution* 19 Commissions were to be established to guide the Governor-General, to supervise Sudanisation of the Civil Service,..and to supervise the formation and work of the Constituent Assembly. **1978** S. LLOYD *Suez 1956* i. 12 A Sudanisation Committee to deal with the administration and defence forces.

So **'Sudanize** *v. trans.*

1884 *Pall Mall G.* 5 May 11/2 Let it be supposed that the Soudan..is tranquillized, its administration 'Soudanized', native Mudirs appointed [etc.].

Sudano- (suːˈdɑːnəʊ), used as comb. form of SUDAN and its derivatives, as in **Sudano-Sahelian** adj.; **Sudano-Guinean** = *Sudanese-Guinean* s.v. SUDANESE *sb.* Cf. SUDANOPHILIA (s.v. SUDAN).

1939 [see NILO-]. **1954** PEI & GAYNOR *Dict. Linguistics* 207 Some linguists consider Sudanese and Guinean as two independent families; others, notably Delafosse, consider Sudano-Guinean and Bantu to be members of a larger linguistic group. **1979** *Nature* 18 Jan. 167/3 UNCOD therefore proposed giant transnational projects like..a joint livestock management programme in the Sudano-Sahelian countries.

‖**sudarium** (s(j)uːˈdɛərɪəm). [L.: see next.] **1.** A napkin or cloth for wiping the face; a handkerchief (in quot. 1801 *jocular*); *spec.* the cloth with which, according to legend, St. Veronica wiped the face of Christ on the way to Calvary, and on which his features were impressed; hence, any similar cloth venerated as a relic; a portrait of Christ on a cloth. (Cf. VERNICLE, VERONICA.)

1601 W. BIDDULPH in T. Lavender *Trav. Four Englishmen* (1612) 115 A woman called Veronica..brought forth a *Sudarium*..to wipe his face. *a* **1700** EVELYN *Diary* 17 Nov. 1644, The miraculous Sudarium indued with the picture of our Saviour's face. **1801** SYD. SMITH in Lady Holland *Mem.* (1855) I. iii. 46 The most intrepid veteran of us all dares no more than wipe his face with his cambric sudarium. **1816** J. DALLAWAY *Stat. & Sculpt.* 312 He..holds a sudarium in his right hand and in his left a roll. **1859** GULLICK & TIMBS *Painting* 61 A representation of this kind—the head of the Saviour on a cloth, and called a 'sudarium' is common in the works of early painters.

†**b.** = MANIPLE 3. *Obs.*

1688 HOLME *Armoury* III. iv. 187/1 The *Manipulus* or *Sudarium*, called also *Mappula* or *Phanon*.

2. = SUDATORIUM. Also *fig.*

1852 G. W. CURTIS *Wand. in Syria, Damascus* vii. 329 You rise and enter the Sudarium beyond. **1863** TREVELYAN *Compet. Wallah* 171 [In India] the mind, like the body, becomes languid and flabby and nerveless... While this sudarium continues to be the seat of government [etc.].

sudary (ˈs(j)uːdərɪ). *Obs.* or *arch.* Also 4–5 sudare, 4–6 sudarie, 5 seou-, sewdarie, (shouldarye), sodary, sudurye, 5–6 sudarye, 6 sudari, sudere; also (disyll.) 5 sudayr, *Sc.* swdour. [ad. L. *sūdārium*, f. *sūdor* sweat: see -ARY[1] 2. Cf. It., Sp., Pg. *sudario*, Pr. *suzari*, F. *suaire*. Gr. σουδάριον, from L., is used in Luke xix. 20, John xi. 44, xx. 7, Acts xix. 12.]

1. A napkin or handkerchief used to wipe sweat or tears from the face; a sweat-cloth; *esp.* such a napkin venerated as a relic of a saint.

a **1350** *St. James* 137 in Horstm. *Altengl. Leg.* (1881) 98 Þe childe þan toke þe appostels sudary. *c* **1375** *Sc. Leg. Saints* i. (*Petrus*) 53 In his bosum ay he bare a sudare, to wepe his Ene. **1382** WYCLIF *Acts* xix. 12 On syke men the sudaries [*later vers.* napkins]..or nyȝt clothis..weren borun fro his body. *c* **1430** LYDG. *Min. Poems* (Percy Soc.) 30 For eyen and nose the nedethe a mokadour, Or sudary. **1483** CAXTON *Gold. Leg.* 426/2 He came to the sudayr of the saynt & with grete deuocion kyssed it. **1623** COCKERAM, *Sudorne* [? *Sudorye*], a handkerchefe. **1835** BROWNING *Paracelsus* III. 438 A monk fumbled at the sick man's mouth With some undoubted relic—a sudary Of the Virgin.

2. The napkin which was about Christ's head in the tomb; hence, a shroud or winding-sheet. Also attrib. *sudary cloth*.

a **1300–1400** *Cursor M.* 17288 + 193 (Cott.) Peter..saȝe þe schetez spred, and þe sudary þore leued þat was in þe sepulcre laide on our lordez heued. *c* **1380** WYCLIF *Serm.* Sel. Wks. II. 99 His face was bounden wiþ a sudarie. *c* **1440** *York Myst.* xxxvi. 387 A sudarye Loo here haue I, Wynde hym for-thy. *c* **1450** in *Maitland Club Misc.* III. 204 Ane gret sepultur with ane ymage of our Saluiour..and ane swdour of quhit silk abon the sam. **1483** CAXTON *G. de la Tour* a iij b, Moo than a thousand men in sudaryes lyke dede men. **1485** *Digby Myst.* III. 1049 Here is nothyng left butt a sudare cloth. ? *a* **1500** *Chester Pl.* xix. (Shaks. Soc.) II. 98 My Lorde Jesu is awaye! But his shouldarye south to saye, Lyinge here I fynde. **1517** TORKINGTON *Pilgr.* (1884) 3 Ther in a Castyll ys a ffayer Churche where ys the sudary of ower Savyor Crist Jhu. **1538** *Prymer Salisb. Use* in Maskell *Mon. Rit.* (1846) II. p. xiii, The body of Jesu Was wraped and bounde in a sudary. **1756–7** *Keysler's Trav.* (1760) I. 342 The holy Sudary at Turin.

3. *Eccl.* A ceremonial cloth of linen or silk, often fringed; *esp.* a humeral veil. *arch.*

1431 *Rec. St. Mary at Hill* (1904) 27 Also vj seoudaries corporas & a case. *c* **1450** in Aungier *Syon* (1840) 367 Sudaryes longyng to the awtres. **1488** in *Archæologia* XLV. 116 A Sewdarie of grene tarterne ffringed with silke on bothe endis. *c* **1500** *Order Consecr. Nuns* in Maskell *Mon. Rit.* (1846) II. 327 Every virgyn shall have a long sudary or towell uppon both hir handys. **1523** [COVERDALE] *Old God* (1534) M iij b, Yᵉ chapleins armed euery one of theym with an ob. do cast theyr ob. in to the basen kyssyng yᵉ sudary. **1549** EDW. VI. *Injunct.* in Burnet *Hist. Ref.* (1681) II. II. I. No. 33. 165 Blessing his Eyes with the Paten or Sudary. **1891** LEGG *Missale Westm.* p. xv, The fifth is the initial of St. Stephen's office, and represents the saint as a deacon holding up stones in a sudary.

†**'sudate**, *v. Obs.* [f. L. *sūdāt-*, pa. ppl. stem of *sūdāre* to sweat.] *intr.* To sweat, perspire.

1599 A. M. tr. *Gabelhouer's Bk. Physicke* 125/1 Drincke then the wine as warm as you may,..cause yourselfe to be well deckede, because you might sudate. **1623** COCKERAM. **1644** *Vind. Anglicus* 6.

†**su'dation.** *Obs.* [ad. L. *sūdātio, -ōnem*, n. of action f. *sūdāre* (see prec.). Cf. F. *sudation*.] Sweating, perspiration. Also *fig.*

1599 A. M. tr. *Gabelhouer's Bk. Physicke* 157/1 If the Patient can attayne to sudatione before he goe to bedde. **1623** COCKERAM. **1656** BLOUNT *Glossogr.*, *Sudation*, a sweating: a taking of pains. **1844** HECKER *Epid. Mid. Ages* 266 An advocate of the twenty-four hours' sudation.

‖**sudatorium** (s(j)uːdəˈtɔːrɪəm). [L., neut. sing. of *sūdātōrius*: see next and -ORIUM.] A room in which hot-air or steam baths are taken to produce sweating; a sweating-room (esp. *Rom. Antiq.*).

1756–7 tr. *Keysler's Trav.* (1760) III. 421 A Sudatorium has also been built here, the effect of which is caused by the steam of the water. **1820** T. S. HUGHES *Trav. Sicily* I. iii. 74 A sudatorium, or sweating-room. **1835** *Penny Cycl.* IV. 37/1 A convenient apparatus for applying it [*sc.* heated air] was invented by the late Dr. Gower, called a *Sudatorium*. **1851** D. WILSON *Preh. Ann.* (1863) II. III. ii. 25 The Roman mansion with its hypocaust and sudatorium. **1899** F. T. BULLEN *Idylls Sea* iv. 20, I awoke streaming as if in the sudatorium of a Hammam.

sudatory (ˈs(j)uːdətərɪ), *a.* and *sb.* Also 6 -orye. [ad. L. *sūdātōrius*, f. *sūdāt-*, *sūdāre* to sweat: see -ORY. Cf. F. *sudatoire*, It., Sp. *sudatorio*.]

A. *adj.* Producing, accompanied by, or connected with sweating. *rare.*

1597 A. M. tr. *Guillemeau's Fr. Chirurg.* 51/1 Those which have passede throughe the Sudatorye regione. **1599** —— tr. *Gabelhouer's Bk. Physicke* 157/2 Make therof a sudatorye bath. **1656** BLOUNT *Glossogr.* **1847** *Blackw. Mag.* LXI. 737 All shrivelled up as we were by the heat—for we were almost past the sudatory stage. **1861** *Illustr. Lond. News* 5 Jan. 10/1 Turkish baths. These sudatory institutions..get a man's extra flesh down. **1911** J. WARD *Roman Era in Brit.* v. 94 It is usual to have..two or more sudatory rooms at different temperatures.

B. *sb.* **1.** = SUDATORIUM

1615 G. SANDYS *Trav.* 289 This Sudatory is entred by a long narrow passage hewne into the rock. *a* **1700** EVELYN *Diary* 8 Feb. 1645, Neere to this cave are the natural stoves of St. Germain, of the nature of sudatories. *Ibid.*, These sudatories are much in request for many infirmityes. **1753** *Scots Mag.* Aug. 418/2 This antique piece appears to be a floor of a Roman sudatory. **1840** HODGSON *Hist. Northumb.* III. II. 319/2 This seems to have been the principal laconicum, caldarium, vapour room, or sudatory. **1841** CATLIN *N. Amer. Ind.* xiii. I. 97 Their vapour baths, or sudatories, of which each village has several. **1884** *Contemp. Rev.* Aug. 321 His house..having baths and sudatories.

fig. **1824–9** LANDOR *Imag. Conv.* Wks. 1853 I. 340/2 We rush out of the sudatory of Byron to roll in the snow of Wordsworth.

¶**2.** Misused for SUDARY 1.

1828 DE QUINCEY *Toilette of Heb. Lady* Wks. 1859 XII. 140 The girdle..continued to be the appropriate depository for the napkin..or sudatory.

‖**sudd** (sʌd). Also sadd. [Arab. *sudd*, n. of action to *sudd* to obstruct.] An impenetrable mass of floating vegetable matter which obstructs navigation on the White Nile.

1874 BAKER *Ismailïa* II. xiii. 488 To remove the sudd or obstruction to the navigation of the great White Nile. **1881** *Proc. R. Geog. Soc.* (N.S.) III. 301 A survey of the Nile, from the Sobat upwards, to the obstructive *sudd* in the Bahr el Gebel. **1898** *Nat. Rev.* Aug. 796 The gunboat's business after Fashoda will be to cut through the *sudd* and reach Beden as soon as possible.

b. *transf.* A temporary dam constructed across a river.

c **1900** SIR B. BAKER in *Daily Chron.* 10 Dec. 9/2 The method of working was to erect temporary dams or 'sudds', formed of various materials. **1903** *Sci. Amer.* 28 Feb. 152/2 To inclose the area, upon which it was intended to work during the season, by temporary dams or 'sadds' in November.

c. *attrib.* and *Comb.*

1900 *Westm. Gaz.* 10 July 2/1 The 'sudd' regions of the White Nile. **1900** *Daily News* 14 July 4/5 Major Peake's sudd-cutting party. **1911** *Chamb. Jrnl.* 28 Jan. 142/1 A factory is to be established in the sudd-country for the production of briquetted water-weed on an extensive scale.

Hence **'sudded** *ppl. a.*, obstructed by sudd.

1900 *Westm. Gaz.* 10 July 2/2 In 1898 Lord Kitchener found the Gebel River sudded.

suddain, -ain(s)ly, -ant(i)e, obs. forms of SUDDEN, -LY, -TY.

†**'suddart.** *Sc. Obs.* Also 6 suddard, suddert, su(l)dart, soudart, so(w)ldart, 6–7 souldart. [a. OF. *so(u)ldard, -art*, mod.F. *soudard, -art*, f. *soude, so(u)lde* pay: see SOLD *sb.*[1] and -ARD.] A mercenary soldier. Also Comb. *suddart-like* adj. or adv.

1542 *Records of Elgin* (New Spald. Cl.) I. 69 The sudaart [*sic*] decernit and deliuerit that [etc.]. **1549** *Compl. Scot.* xi. 90 Mortal veyr amang the soudartis. **1567** *Reg. Privy Council Scot.* Ser. I. I. 560 The pretendit licence unlauchfullie grantit to Johnne Mortoun suddart for the transporting of sex lastis of talloun. **1575–6** *Ibid.* II. 482 Cumpaneis of suddartis and utheris brokin men. **1587** W. FOWLER *Wks.* (S.T.S.) I. 101 Skairslie I can tell, Now whidder he as chiften did, or suldartlyke, excell. *a* **1599** A. HUME *Poems* vii. 199 Conquerers, and soldarts of the Lord. *a* **1614** J. MELVILL *Diary* (Wodrow Soc.) 429 At unawars behind his bak, They interprys'd thair limmers crewaltie, Quhilk souldart-like they durst nocht undertak.

fig. **1573** J. DAVIDSON *Poet. Rem.* (1829) 3 All the rabill of Sathanis suddartis, in Scotland, Ingland, and France.

sudden (ˈsʌd(ə)n), *a.*, *adv.* and *sb.* Forms: 3–6 soden, sodan(e, -ayn(e, 4–6 sudayn(e, *Sc.* sud(d)an(e, 4–7 sodain(e, -ein(e, -eyn(e, 6–7 sodyne, 6–8 suddain(e, (4 soudein, sudein(e, -en, -eyn(e, *Sc.* sowdane, soudan, swdan, 5 sothen, -eyn, 6 soddaine, -ayn, soudain(e, -eine, -en, soodain, suddayne, -eyn(e, -ein(e, *Sc.* soddan(e, suiden, 6–7 sodden, 7 sudain(e), 6– sudden. Also *β.* 5 soubdayne, subdayn, 6 subdain, *Sc.* subdane; *γ. Sc.* 4 so-, sudende, soudande, 4–6 sud(d)and, 5 sodand, sothent, 6 -end, suddant(e; *dial.* 8 sudent, 9 suddent, -int. [a. AF. *sodein, sudein* = OF. (mod.F.) *soudain*, also †*soubdain*, †*subdain* = Pr. *sub-*, *sob(i)tan, sobtan, soptan*, It. *subitano* :—pop.L **subitānu-s*, for L. *subitāneus* (whence Sp., Pg. *subitaneo*), f. *subitus*: see SUBITE.

The present spelling was not finally established till after 1700; by far the commonest spelling in the 1st folio of Shaks. is *sodaine*, and *suddain* lasted on into the first quarter of the 18th c.]

A. *adj.* **1. a.** Of actions, events, conditions: Happening or coming without warning or premonition; taking place or appearing all at once.

In some contexts the implication is rather 'Unexpected, unforeseen, unlooked-for', or 'Not prepared or provided for'.

1340 HAMPOLE *Pr. Consc.* 1951 What es til man mare certayn þan þe dede es þat es swa sodayn? *Ibid.* 5129 Right swa þe commyng of man son sal be, Sodayne and bright and dreful to se. *c* **1386** CHAUCER *Clerk's T.* 260 This sodeyn cas this man astonyed so That reed he wax. **1390** GOWER *Conf.* I. 78 The Schip with sodein blast, Whan men lest wene, is overcast. *c* **1440** *York Myst.* xvii. 42 A sodayne sight was till vs sente. *c* **1460** *Merita Missæ* 125 in *Lay Folks Mass Bk.* 151 What sothen a wenture the be-falle. **1514** BARCLAY *Cyt. & Uplondyshm.* (Percy Soc.) 8 Tempest & sodayne storme of rayne. **1548–9** (Mar.) *Bk. Com. Prayer, Litany*, From battaile and murther, and from sodain death: Good lorde deliuer us. **1549** LATIMER *Ploughers* (Arb.) 36 The people wyll not beare sodayne alterations. **1595** SHAKS. *John* v. vi.

26 That you might The better arme you to the sodaine time, Then if you had at leisure knowne of this. **1615** Sandys *Trav.* 6 Here a garrison is kept; supplyed by the townes-men vpon each sodaine summons. **1658** *Whole Duty Man* v. §30 His death may be sudden to him, though it comes by never so slow degrees. **1683** Pettus *Fleta Min.* i. (1686) 33 When the Oar is set alone upon the Test, that it may not be put into a violent suddain heat. *a***1700** Evelyn *Diary* 12 Nov. 1643, Hayle, rain, and suddaine darknesse. **1781** Cowper *Conversat.* 281, I interrupt him with a sudden bow. **1794** Mrs. Radcliffe *Myst. Udolpho* xxx, She heard a sudden step behind her. **1855** Tennyson *Brook* 24, I come from haunts of coot and hern, I make a sudden sally. **1874** Green *Short Hist.* vii. §7 (1882) 419 Few events in our literary history are so startling as this sudden rise of the Elizabethan drama. **1887** Ruskin *Præterita* II. 189, I..am simply helpless on any sudden need for decision like this.

β. **1489** Caxton *Faytes of A.* i. xxii. 69 The soubdayne necessitees that may fall. *c***1489** —— *Blanchardyn* xxiv. 92 A soubdayne sparkle of Ialousye cam to hym. **1563** Winȝet *Bk. 83 Quest.* Pref., Wks. (S.T.S.) I. 49 The subdane change of sum cunning clerkis.

γ. [*c***1375**: see suddenly 2.] *c***1470** Henry *Wallace* iii. 418 It was wicht Wallace, Had thaim our set in to that sodand cas. **1535** Stewart *Cron. Scot.* II. 124 At set purpois and nocht of suddante cace. **1556** *Peebles Burgh Rec.* (1872) 234 Gif ony..sudand fyre occurris. *a***1578** Lindesay (Pitscottie) *Chron. Scot.* (S.T.S.) I. 63 Ewerie man iudgit that suddand and prosperous succes sould haue ane schort end.

b. Of emotions, impulses, etc.

1382 Wyclif *Prov.* iii. 25 Ne drede thou with sodeyn gastnesse. **1390** Gower *Conf.* I. 290 Thurgh his sodein Malencolie To do so gret a felonie. **1575** Gascoigne *Kenelworth* Wks. 1910 II. 121 Into deepe admiration and suddayne perplexitie. **1581** Pettie tr. *Guazzo's Civ. Conv.* i. (1586) 12 b, Moued by some sodaine toie which taketh them in the head. **1667** Milton *P.L.* v. 452 Sudden mind arose In Adam, not to let th' occasion pass. **1784** Cowper *Task* vi. 550 His horse,..Snorting, and starting into sudden rage. **1831** Scott *Ct. Rob.* xix, After a sudden start of surprise, he recognised his acquaintance Sylvan. **1898** 'H. S. Merriman' *Roden's Corner* ii. 21 Checked in a moment of earnest endeavour by a sudden perception of the humorous.

c. Of a turning, etc.: Abrupt, sharp. In *Zool.* and *Bot.* applied to parts that are sharply marked off from the neighbouring parts (cf. suddenly 1 b).

1390 Gower *Conf.* II. 293 It hapneth at a soudein wente, ..He fell unwar into a pet. **1680** Moxon *Mech. Exerc.* xi. 194 The swift coming about of the Work would..draw or job the suddain edge into the Stuff. **1784** Cowper *Task* i. 267 Descending now..A sudden steep. **1837** Carlyle *Rev. France* i. i. iv, At some sudden turning in the Wood of Senart. **1891** *Cent. Dict.* s.v., A sudden antennal club; a sudden truncation.

d. Of physical objects: Appearing or discovered unexpectedly. Now *arch.* or *poet.*

*c***1460** Fortescue *Abs. & Lim. Mon.* vii. (1885) 125 Ther come a sodayne armye vpon this londe by see or by lande. **1596** Dalrymple tr. *Leslie's Hist. Scot.* I. 192 The King of the Pechtes..wastes, with a suddane power, the nerrest cuntreyes perteyneng to the Scottis. **1648** J. Beaumont *Psyche* iv. lxxxviii, Up sprung a suddain Grove. **1712** Pope *Messiah* 68 See lilies spring, and sudden verdure rise. **1712–14** —— *Rape Lock* v. 127 A sudden Star, it shot thro' liquid air. **1819** Keats *Otho* i. i. 47 The Hungarians.. Appear'd, a sudden host, in the open day. **1841** Browning *Pippa Passes* ii. Poems (1905) 176 When o'er the sudden specks my chisel trips. **1855** —— *Childe Roland* xix, A sudden little river crossed my path As unexpected as a serpent comes. **1879** E. Arnold *Lt. Asia* 4 And Earth put forth a thousand sudden flowers.

†**e.** Of diseases. ***sudden stroke***: apoplexy. ***sudden taking*** (see quot. 1688). *Obs.*

*a***1548** Hall *Chron., Hen. IV* (1550) 32 b, He was taken with a sore sodayn disease [*Grafton adds* called an Apoplexie]. *a***1568** Coverdale *Treat. Death* i. ix. Wks. (Parker Soc.) II. 57 The gout, frenzy, the sudden stroke, and such like. **1651** T. de Grey *Compl. Horsem.* i. (1656) 66 And it also preventeth suddain sicknesse, if you haue anie suspect thereof. **1688** Holme *Armoury* ii. 151/1 The Sudden taking [is] when he [*sc.* a horse] is deprived of his feeling and motion, not being able to stir any way.

2. a. Of actions, feelings: Unpremeditated, done without forethought. *Obs.* or *arch.*

*a***1300** *Cursor M.* 28653 Als wreth þat scort, and soden es [*MS.* sodenes]. **1390** Gower *Conf.* III. 192 How he..Of sodein wraththe and nought of riht Forjugged hath. **1483** [see subite]. **1594** T. B. *La Primaud. Fr. Acad.* ii. 230 It is a sodain & tumultuous iudgement, of which a man may truly say, a short sentence of a sottish iudge. **1596** Bacon *Max. & Use Com. Law* ii. (1635) 2 If one kill another upon a suddaine quarrell, this is manslaughter. **1658** *Whole Duty Man* iv. §7 He that swears commonly, is not only prepared to forswear when a solemn Oath is tendered him, but in all probability does actually forswear himself often in these suddener Oaths. **1729** Butler *Serm.* Wks. 1874 II. 93 Sudden anger, upon certain occasions, is mere instinct. **1781** Cowper *Hope* 390 If sentence of eternal pain belong To ev'ry sudden slip and transient wrong.

b. Of persons: Acting without forethought or deliberation; hasty, impetuous, rash. *Obs.* or *arch.*

*c***1374** Chaucer *Troylus* v. 1024 Retornyng in here soule ay vp and doun The wordes of þis sodeyn Diomede. **1530** Palsgr. 325/1 Sodayne, hasty of condycions, *soudayn*. *a***1585** Montgomerie *Cherrie & Slae* 513 Be not soddane, sir, The mater is of wecht. **1607** Tourneur *Rev. Trag.* iv. i, His Grace is old, and sudden. *a***1631** Donne *Poems* (1650) 2 Cruell and sodaine, hast thou since Purpled thy Nayle, in bloud of innocence? **1667** Milton *P.L.* ii. 738 My sudden hand Prevented spares to tell thee yet by deeds What it intends. **1825** Scott *Talism.* xx, Neither provoke me to be sudden by any unfit reply. **1850** Newman *Diffic. Anglicans* 252 Some men, or races of men, are more sudden in their tempers than others.

3. a. Performed or taking place without delay; speedy; prompt, immediate. *Obs.* exc. of death.

*a***1375** *Joseph Arim.* 390 Vppon sodeyne deþ þou schalt sone dye. **1450–80** tr. *Secr. Secr.* 18 Takyng on him hasty and sodeyne vengeaunce. **1557** *Tottel's Misc.* (Arb.) 243 If I do false my faith in any point or case, A sodein vengeance fall on me. **1591** Shaks. *1 Hen. VI*, i. iv. 48 None durst come neere, for feare of suddaine death. **1650** Cromwell *Let. Gov. Edinb. Castle* 13 Dec. (Carlyle), Expecting your sudden answer, I rest, Your servant, Oliver Cromwell. *a***1658** Cleveland *Rustick Rampant* Wks. (1687) 449 He acquaints the Citizens with the Kings Peril and his own, and requests their sudden Assistance. **1671** Milton *P.R.* i. 96 Our danger..which admits no long debate, But must with something sudden be oppos'd. **1678–9** Dryden & Lee *Œdipus* iv. i, I charge him on his life To speak; concealment shall be sudden death. **1831** Scott *Jrnl.* 21 Dec., If I were worthy I would pray God for a sudden death, and no interregnum between I cease to exercise reason and I cease to exist.

b. ***sudden death*** (slang): (*a*) a single toss used to decide an issue; hence in *Lawn Tennis*, a game played to break a tie; also in general sporting use (usu. *attrib.*), designating an additional competition or period of extra time in which the first to concede a game or score is immediately eliminated; (*b*) *U.S.*, a potent alcoholic drink; (*c*) (see quot. 1886).

1834 *Blackw. Mag.* May 752/1 'Which', said he, 'is it to be—two out of three, as at Newmarket, or the first toss to decide?' 'Sudden death', said I, 'and there will soon be an end of it.' **1863** C. Reade *Hard Cash* I. vii. 205 America is fertile in mixtures: what do we not owe to her? Sherry-cobbler, gin-sling..sudden death. **1865** *Slang Dict.* 250 *Sudden death*, the first toss in a bet, to be decided by *skying* a copper. **1865** 'Mark Twain' in *Californian* 18 Mar. 8/3 Our reserve (whom we had..kept out of sight and full of chain-lightning, sudden death and scorpion-bile all day..) came filing down the street as drunk as loons. **1886** Yule & Burnell *Hobson-Jobson, Sudden death*, Anglo-Indian slang for a fowl served as a spatchcock. **1927** W. E. Collinson *Contemp. Eng.* 36 *Sudden death* [is used] for a game played to bring a set to a sudden, decisive conclusion without playing out the full number. **1939** *Sun* (Baltimore) 21 July 15/8 Skipper Bill Barrow, of the Rochester Yacht Club, sailed his Thisbe II to victory today in a sudden-death race against defending champion Aphrodite. **1945** *Ibid.* 3 Mar. 7/2 Tech meets the winner tonight, and got this break by having its name picked out of a hat when the 'sudden death' playoff plan was decided on. **1946** L. P. Hartley *Sixth Heaven* viii. 162 'Game-ball all,' was called... 'Shall we play it out?' said Dick, 'or shall we have sudden death?' **1961** *Times* 29 Aug. 3/4 Player and..J. Herbert tied for the lead ..and then had a sudden-death play-off. **1972** 'E. Lathen' *Murder without Icing* xxvi. 224 'I hear that it wasn't a bad game.'.. 'Not bad! When it went into sudden death overtime?' **1974** *Times* 22 Jan. 10/7 The WCT circuit as a whole contains a controversial innovation: a 13-point tie-break with a 'sudden death' finish. This means that the first player to score seven points wins the tie-break whether he leads by two points or not. **1977** *Evening Gaz.* (Middlesbrough) 11 Jan. 14/6 These matches are 'sudden death' affairs, a single match in each round either home or away depending on the luck of each draw.

†**4. a.** Of persons: Swift in action, quick to perform, prompt, expeditious. Also, peremptory, sharp. *Obs.*

1591 *Troub. Raigne K. John* (1611) 18 Speake man, be sodaine, who thy Father was. **1601** Shaks. *Jul. C.* iii. i. 19 Caska be sodaine, for we feare preuention. **1622** Fletcher *Span. Cur.* iv. vii, A suddain witty thief. **1630** *R. Johnson's Kingd. & Commw.* 193 The French is of so sudden and busie disposition, that he quickly yeelds to that a man demands. **1716** Pope *Iliad* vii. 282 No more—be sudden, and begin the fight. **1753** Richardson *Grandison* III. xvii. 135 You are a little sudden upon me.

†**b.** Of mental faculties: Quick, sharp. *Obs.*

1608 *Pennyless Parl.* xlvi. in *Harl. Misc.* (1744) I. 181 There shall so many sudden, or rather sodden Wits, step abroad, that a Flea shall not frisk forth, unless they comment upon her. **1630** *R. Johnson's Kingd. & Commw.* 190 Men of light and unsteady braines, have commonly sudden and sharpe conceits. **1742** Pope *To Mr. T. Southern* 11 The feast, his tow'ring genius marks In yonder wild goose and the larks! The mushrooms shew his wit was sudden!

†**c.** Of the eye: Glancing quickly. *Obs.*

1590 Spenser *F.Q.* i. v. 10 The Paynim chaunst to cast his eye, His suddein eye,..Vpon his brothers shield. **1649** Milton *Eikon.* xxiv. 492 Like the Apples of Asphaltis, appearing goodly to the sudden eye, but look well upon them, or at least but touch them, and they turne into Cinders. **1651** Davenant *Gondibert* i. vi. 59 [He] Bids both their Breasts be eithers open book, Where nought is writ too hard for sodain Eies.

5. Made, provided, or formed in a short time. *Obs.* or *arch.*

1599 Shaks. *Hen. V*, i. i. 32 Neuer was such a sodaine Scholler made. **1617** Moryson *Itin.* ii. 187 How dangerous it is, that the Army should depend on sudden provisions. **1697** Dryden *Virg. Georg.* iii. 554 Swift Rivers are with sudden Ice constrain'd. **1812** *Sporting Mag.* XXXIX. 101 A sudden dinner was provided. **1870** Lowell *Study Wind.*, *Chaucer* (1871) 173 Nothing is more certain than that great poets are not sudden prodigies, but slow results.

6. Prompt in action or effect; producing an immediate result. *poet.*

*c***1586** C'tess Pembroke *Ps.* lxiv. iv, Thou, O God, from sodain bow Death striking them a shaft shall send. **1592** Shaks. *Rom. & Jul.* iii. iii. 45 Had'st thou no poyson mixt, no sharpe ground knife, No sudden meane of death? **1819** Shelley *Cenci* ii. i. 142 How just it were to hire assassins, or Put sudden poison in my evening drink? **1826** Milman *A. Boleyn* 165 There's no disease will let the spirit loose With less keen anguish than the sudden axe! **1865** Swinburne *Atalanta* 44 Hast not thou One shaft of all thy sudden seven that pierced Seven through the bosom?

†**7.** Done, performed, or prepared on the spur of the moment; extempore, impromptu. *Obs.*

1591 Shaks. *Two Gent.* iv. ii. 12 Notwithstanding all her sodaine quips, The least whereof would quell a louers hope. **1591** —— *1 Hen. VI*, iii. i. 6 Doe it without inuention, suddenly, As I with sudden, and extemporall speech, Purpose to answer what thou canst obiect. *a***1656** Bp. Hall *Let. to Person Qual.*, Your love will put the best construction upon these sudden lines. **1741** Watts *Improv. Mind* Pref., Imperfect sketches, which were designed by a sudden pencil, and in a thousand leisure moments.

†**8.** Brief, momentary, lasting only a short time.

1561 T. Norton *Calvin's Inst.* i. ix. (1634) 30 God brought not his word among men for a sodaine shew [*vne monstre et parade de petite duree*]. **1567** Maplet *Gr. Forest* 29 The race of this life was so sodaine and short so often perilled and every eche moment at death his nod and beck. *c***1595** Carew *Excell. Eng. Tongue* in G. G. Smith *Eliz. Crit. Ess.* II. 287 A fuller obseruation of what my soddaine memorye cannott represent vnto mee.

†**9.** Happening at an early date; shortly to come or to be. *Obs.* (Cf. suddenly 4.)

1594 Shaks. *Rich. III*, iii. iv. 45 We haue not yet set downe this day of Triumph: To morrow, in my iudgement, is too sudden. **1607** Tourneur *Rev. Trag.* ii. i, The Dukes sonne..One that is like to be our suddaine Duke. **1621** Elsing *Debates Ho. Lords* (Camden) 122 To represent the daungers and the present and sodeyne occasions which may be loste. **1712** R. Gale in *Mem. W. Stukeley* (Surtees) I. 149, I will make up the first summe by a sudden opportunity. **1749** Fielding *Tom Jones* xv. ix, I must pray for a sudden opportunity of returning those pecuniary obligations.

B. *adv.* (So F. *soudain*.)

1. = suddenly. Chiefly *poet.*

?**1404–8** *26 Pol. Poems* 24 Deþ claymeþ eche man for hesse, And sodeyn, deþ no dayes selle. **1588** Shaks. *L.L.L.* ii. i. 107 Pardon me, I am too sodaine bold. **1590** Spenser *F.Q.* i. i. 6 The day with cloudes was suddeine overcast. **1652** in Gilbert *Contemp. Hist. Irel.* (Ir. Archæol. Soc.) III. 76 If I cannot be sudaine in the heade of a considerable armie, I am likly to be founde in the counties of Sligoe or Letrim. **1667** Milton *P.L.* v. 650 Pavilions numberless, and sudden reard. **1742** Blair *Grave* 63 Sudden! he starts. **1810** Scott *Lady of L.* v. xix, As up the flinty path they strain'd Sudden his steed the leader rein'd. **1833** Tennyson *Dream Fair Wom.* xxxi, Sudden I heard a voice that cried, 'Come here'. **1884** Browning *Ferishtah, Eagle* 13 Sudden there swooped An eagle downward.

2. When qualifying an adj. in the attrib. position *sudden* is often hyphened to it.

1730 Thomson *Autumn* (ed. 2) 951 The sudden-starting tear. **1836** Newman in *Lyra Apost.* (1849) 10 Sudden-whelming storm. **1859** Tennyson *Elaine* 327 There brake a sudden-beaming tenderness Of manners and of nature.

C. quasi-*sb.* and *sb.*

1. In advb. phr. formed with preps. = suddenly (chiefly in sense 1).

a. ***of a sudden*** (earlier †***of the sudden***): now usually with preceding *all*.

1570 Dee *Math. Pref.* d iij b, I thinke, that none can iustly account them selues Architectes, of the suddeyne. **1590** H. Barrow in Greenwood *Coll. Art* D ij b, I was..compelled.. to answere of the sodaine vnto such articles. **1596** Shaks. *Tam. Shr.* i. i. 152 Is it possible That loue should of a sodaine take such hold? *a***1648** Digby *Closet Opened* (1669) 188 When all is heated through, it [*sc.* gravy] will quicken of a sudden. **1681–6** J. Scott *Chr. Life* (1747) III. 66 All of a sudden, and without any..previous Instructions, they were heard to speak..in the fifteen several Tongues of fifteen several Nations. **1864** Mrs. Lloyd *Ladies of Polcarrow* 103 And then Prudy, all of a suddent, began to keep company with that little Preventative fellow. **1890** Doyle *White Company* xxx, As he gazed, he saw of a sudden a man steal forth from the wood. **1891** Farrar *Darkn. & Dawn* xvii, Then all of a sudden appears Caligula, and demands that Claudius should be recognised as his slave.

b. ***on*** or ***upon a*** (or ***the***) ***sudden*** (also †***on sudden, o' the sudden***). Very common *c* 1560–1700.

1558 in Feuillerat *Revels Q. Eliz.* (1908) 17 To be..done ..for more reasonable hier in hope of present payment then can be had or done upon the soden. **1565** Cooper *Thesaurus* s.v. *Subitarius, Subitarij milites*, souldiours mustred..vpon a sodayne. **1581** T. Howell *Deuises* G iij, Who running well, at first, on sodaine slakes. **1611** *Bible* Ecclus. xi. 21 It is an easie thing in the sight of the Lord, on the sudden to make a poore man rich. **1630** Ussher *Lett.* (1686) 449 For the Bargain which you mention of Ancient Coins,.. I cannot upon the sudden say any thing; for my own Purse is too shallow. **1647** Clarendon *Hist. Reb.* i. §23 He did not upon the Suddain comprehend the consequences. *a***1700** Evelyn *Diary* 15 Oct. 1644, It pleas'd God on the suddaine to appease the wind. **1719** De Foe *Crusoe* i. 136 My Crop promis'd very well, when on a sudden I found I was in Danger of losing it all again. **1825** Scott *Talism.* xii, At length, and upon a sudden, the gallant stag-hound bayed furiously. **1843** F. E. Paget *Warden of Berkingholt* 118 He became on the sudden, moody, sullen and reckless. **1849** Macaulay *Hist. Eng.* ii. I. 152 On a sudden a gleam of hope appeared. **1868** Browning *Ring & Bk.* ix. *Bottinius* 1303 O' the sudden, as good gifts are wont befall.

†(*b*) as *adj.* Prompt, speedily made. *Obs.*

1683 Temple *Mem.* Wks. 1720 I. 439, I was surpriz'd to hear a Proposition so on the sudden, so short, and so decisive.

†**c.** ***at a*** (or ***the***) ***sudden***. *Obs.*

1560 Whitehorne *Ord. Souldiours* (1588) 3 To know how many men may march in a rancke, & at a sudden to bring them into a fouresquare battaill. **1574** Hellowes *Gueuara's Fam. Ep.* (1577) 70 When they shoulde haue done a thing at the soudaine, they haue sit downe with great leysure to take counsell. **1589** Puttenham *Engl. Poesie* iii. xxiv. (Arb.) 287 When Parmenio..perswaded king Alexander..to set vpon Darius at the sodaine. **1632** Sir T. Hawkins tr. *Mathieu's*

Unhappy Prosp. 170 Caligula seeing many Senators at his table, laughed at a sudden.

†**d.** ***in a sudden.*** *Obs.*

1560 WHITEHORNE *Arte Warre* 60 Parte of thy men maie be well hidden, to be able in a sodain, and contrary to thenemies opinion to assaut him. *Ibid.* 69 The other twoo shal remain behinde, distaunte other thirtie yardes: the which facion maie bee ordained in a sodaine.

†**e.** ***on (upon, with) such a sudden,*** so suddenly; ***of (upon) this sudden,*** on the spur of the moment; ***upon a very great sudden, in great sudden,*** very suddenly. (Cf. 2.) *Obs.*

1572 in Ellis *Orig. Lett.* Ser. I. II. 267 If I could make them [*sc.* lodgings] better upon suche a sodeyn, then wold I. **1575** GASCOIGNE *Kenelworth* Wks. 1910 II. 102 These verses were devised..upon a very great sudden. **1582** N. LICHEFIELD tr. *Castanheda's Conq. E. Ind.* I. xlvii. 103 b, And indeed with such a sodaine came upon him, that [etc.]. **1600** SHAKS. *A. Y. L.* I. iii. 27 Is it possible on such a sodaine, you should fall into so strong a liking with old Sir Roulonds yongest sonne? **1600** *1st Pt. Sir J. Oldcastle* I. iii. 116 You are welcome, Sir, what ere you be; But of this sodaine, Sir, I do not know you. **1617** USSHER *Lett.* (1686) 60, I have nothing that upon this sudden I can well write of. *a* **1674** MILTON *Hist. Moscovia* v. Wks. 1851 VIII. 513 Wherat the Emperor in great sudden bid him get home.

†**2.** A sudden need, danger, or the like; an emergency. *Obs.*

Chiefly governed by preps. *at, on* (cf. 1 b, c).

1559 BERCHER *Nobylytye Wymen* (Roxb. Club) 102 Howe redye they be in matters of dowbte, howe constant in the Sodeyne of dayngers. *Ibid.* 119 Wymen be best at the sodeyne. **1585–6** EARL LEYCESTER *Corr.* (Camden) 228 When parliaments be called vppon suddens. **1589** BIGGES *Summarie Drake's W. Ind. Voy.* 44 The helpe of marriners for that sudden to make trenches could not be had. **1608** CHAPMAN *Byron's Conspir.* II. ii. 221 On any sudden, upon any ground, And in the form of all occasions. *a* **1639** WOTTON in *Reliq.* (1651) 331, I would wish Parents to mark ..the witty excuses of their Children, especially at Suddains and Surprizals. **1704** S. SEWALL *Diary* 22 May, He had.. called me back again; At such a Sudden I knew not what to doe.

†**3.** Suddenness. *Obs. rare.*

1575 GASCOIGNE *Glasse Govt.* Wks. 1910 II. 63 The sodaine of our departure seemeth somewhat straunge unto me.

†**4.** ***for a sudden***: for an instant. *Obs.*

1688 BUNYAN *Heavenly Footman* (1724) 84 Agrippa gave a fair Step for a sudden.

sudden, obs. pa. pple. of SEETHE *v.*

suddene, obs. form of SUBDEAN.

suddenly (ˈsʌd(ə)nlɪ), *adv.* (*a.*) Forms: see SUDDEN; also 4–5 **sodonly,** 7 **suddainsly, sudingly.** [f. SUDDEN + -LY².]

1. Without warning or preparation; all at once, all of a sudden.

In some contexts the implication is rather 'At an unexpected moment, unexpectedly'.

c **1290** *S. Engl. Leg.* 19 In ȝwuche manere it were þat it queinte so sodeinliche al þat liȝt þat huy bere. *a* **1300** *Cursor M.* 11609 Vte o þis coue þan sagh þai glide Mani dragons wel sodanli. *c* **1330** *Spec. Guy Warw.* 882 Worch while þu mait, For sodeyneliche þu miht be caiht. **1375** BARBOUR *Bruce* VII. 505 He thoucht than with his cheuelry To cum apon hym sodanly. **1390** GOWER *Conf.* II. 21 As a man that sodeinli A gost behelde, so fare I. *c* **1400** *Destr. Troy* 12494 Sodonly the softe winde vnsoberly blew. **1470–85** MALORY *Arthur* III. xii. 114 Ye cam in sodenly ther as we were at the hyghe feest and tooke awey this lady. **1508** FISHER *7 Penit. Ps.* cxxx. Wks. (1876) 202 The cogytacyons whiche come sodeynly vnto the mynde. **1530** RASTELL *Bk. Purgat.* III. xv. L iv b, Yf such a synner dye sodenly, and before he haue had any tyme to take any repentaunce. **1577–82** BRETON *Flourish upon Fancie* Wks. (Grosart) I. 9/2 Ouer this lies a Bridge, but trust mee, verie weake: For when you are in midst therof, then sodenly twyll breake. **1615** SANDYS *Trav.* 7 Cowardize is joyned with their crueltie, who dare do nothing but sodainly, vpon advantages. **1671** MILTON *P. R.* II. 298 He view'd it round, When suddenly a man before him stood. **1736** BUTLER *Anal.* I. ii. Wks. 1874 I. 41 These natural punishments or miseries often come, not by degrees, but suddenly. **1774** PENNANT *Tour Scot. in 1772,* 331 Here the water suddenly narrows. **1860** TYNDALL *Glac.* I. xi. 73 One star..suddenly made its appearance above one of the Aiguilles. **1879** FARRAR *St. Paul* (1883) 166 No one likes to be suddenly awakened.

b. *Zool.* and *Bot.* Sharply, abruptly.

1843 [see 5]. **1847** W. E. STEELE *Field Bot.* 189 Leaves suddenly acuminate.

†**2.** Without delay, forthwith, promptly, immediately, directly, at once. *Obs.*

c **1330** *Arth. & Merl.* 607 Þat þai schuld sodeinliche Smite of his heued hastiliche & no word no speke him to. *c* **1375** *Sc. Leg. Saints* xxxii. (*Justin*) 424 He hyr herd sodendely, & gert cese þat mortalyte. *c* **1386** CHAUCER *Merch. T.* 165, I prey yow shapeth for my mariage Al sodeynly, for I wol nat abyde. **1423** JAS. I *Kingis Q.* cxxvi, Straught vnto the presence sodeynly Off dame Minerue,..Gude hope..led me. *c* **1475** *Harl. Contin. Higden* (Rolls) VIII. 556 As soone as he was crowned, enoynted, and sacred, anone sodaynly he was chaunged into a new man. **1513** BRADSHAW *St. Werburge* II. 1409 Wherwith saynt Werburge departed sodeinly To the blys of heuyn. **1593** SHAKS. *3 Hen. VI,* IV. ii. 4 Speake suddenly, my Lords, are wee all friends? **1650** BULWER *Anthropomet.* 116 When the water enters the Weazon, men are suddenly drowned. **1669** STURMY *Mariner's Mag.* v. xiii. 85 Be sure when you have Fired the Fuse, suddenly to cast it [*sc.* the grenade] out of your hand. **1682** NORRIS *Hierocles* 82 If we fall into sin, suddenly to betake ourselves to Justice as to a soveraign Medicine.

†**3.** Without premeditation; on the spur of the moment; extempore. *Obs.*

1340 *Ayenb.* 64 Huanne me zuereþ be tyene, and sodaynlyche, huer-of him uorþinkþ efterward. *a* **1450** MYRC 1485 He þat doth hyt sodenlyche, And afterwarde hym reweth myche. *c* **1450** HOLLAND *Howlat* 120, I can nocht say sudanelye..Bot I sall call my cardinallis and my counsall. **1591** [see SUDDEN A. 7]. **1593** SHAKS. *2 Hen. VI,* II. i. 130 Sight may distinguish of Colours: But suddenly to nominate them all, It is impossible. **1656** N. BERNARD *Life J. Usher* 22 Their readinesse in the Scripture was marvellous, being able suddainly to have repeated any part of the Bible.

†**4.** After a comparatively short time; at an early date, early; soon, speedily; shortly (*after*).

This sense tends to coalesce with 1.

c **1500** *Lancelot* 1874 Qwho that sal exced His rent, he fallith sodandly in nede. **1588** KYD *Househ. Philos.* Wks. (1901) 271 Salt and Vineger doo not onely keep flesh long time sweete and seazoned, but fish and fowle, which will bee suddainly corrupt. **1634** SIR T. HERBERT *Trav.* 210 Cut a small hole in euery tree, into which immediatly effudes the liquour, so that suddenly all the holes..are full. **1645** G. DIGBY in *Nicholas Papers* (Camden) 65 You shall as suddainly as may be receive a particular accompt of them both. **1671** MILTON *Samson* 1565, I refrain, too suddenly To utter what will come at last too soon. **1681** KNOX *Ceylon* III. iv. 78 Either just before or very suddenly after this Voice, the King always cuts off People. **1766** GOLDSM. *Vic. W.* xx, How he had been taught the art of a cognoscento so very suddenly.

†**b.** Not long after the time of speaking or writing; shortly; very soon. *Obs.*

1544 in Froude *Hist. Eng.* (1858) IV. 305, I will not bid you good night. Suddenly we shall meet again in the kingdom of heaven. **1596** SHAKS. *1 Hen. IV,* I. iii. 294 When time is ripe, which will be sodainly. **1661** PR. RUPERT in *11th Rep. Hist. MSS. Comm.* App. v. 9, I hope the Duke of Yorke will have given order for a Fregatte for me, soe that I hope suddainsly to see you. **1676** ETHEREDGE *Man of Mode* I. i, Now practising a famous Ballat, which will Be suddenly danc'd at the Bear-Garden. **1680** *Bunyan's Mr. Badman* Bookseller's Advt. (1905) 15 There is now in the Press, and will be suddenly published, An Exposition on the 6, 7, 8, 9, and 10th, Chapters on the Hebrews. **1703** PETIVER *Musei Petiv.* 95 Plants and Insects..some of which I shall suddenly figure. **1711** ADDISON *Spect.* No. 239 ¶12, I shall very suddenly give my Reader an Account of the whole Art of Cavilling.

5. When qualifying an adj. in the attrib. position *suddenly* is often joined to it by a hyphen.

1772 NUGENT *Hist. Fr. Gerund* II. 147 One of those lazy, suddenly-learned gentry. **1843** *Penny Cycl.* XXV. 269/2 It tends to *Trochus acutus* in its suddenly-pointed spire. **1900** *Westm. Gaz.* 16 Aug. 1/2 One of those suddenly-arising emergencies.

†**6.** Used as *adj.* Quick, rapid. *Obs. rare*⁻¹.

1556 *Aurelio & Isab.* (1608) I vij, Youre thoughte is soudainlier than ower tonge. [**1600** *Gowries Conspiracie* B ij, The suddainly comming of his Maiestie vnlooked for there.]

suddenness (ˈsʌd(ə)nnɪs). Forms: see SUDDEN *a.*; also 4 **sodeynesse,** 7 **suddeness.** [f. SUDDEN *a.* + -NESS.]

1. The quality of taking place without warning or preparation; unexpectedness.

1382 WYCLIF *Wisd.* v. 2 Seende thei..shul merueilen in the sodeynesse [Vulg. *subitatione*] of the vnhopid helthe. *a* **1586** SIDNEY *Arcadia* III. xxiv. Wks. 1912 I. 492 Who when he saw her fal, had his owne rage stayed a little with the soddennes of her destruction. **1624** MASSINGER *Renegado* II. v, The suddennesse Of their departure.. Deterr'd us. **1685** BAXTER *Paraphr. N. T.,* 1 Tim. iii. 6 The suddenness of the Light which they have received so transporteth them, that [etc.]. **1797** S. & HT. LEE *Canterb. T.* (1799) I. 6 The suddenness of his excursion had caused Montford to be but ill provided with letters of recommendation. **1838** THIRLWALL *Greece* xxx. IV. 161 The suddenness of the calamity which had deprived Athens of her navy had prevented the laying in a stock of provisions to meet a long siege.

2. Hastiness, precipitancy. Now *rare.*

1580 HOLLYBAND *Treas. Fr. Tong., Hastiveté,* hastinesse, sodennesse. **1651** HOBBES *Leviath.* II. xxvii. 158 There is no suddennesse of Passion sufficient for a totall Excuse. **1876** HARDY *Ethelberta* (1890) 188, I will not urge you to be precipitate... My suddenness perhaps offended you.

3. The quality of being quick to act; immediateness or promptitude in action or movement.

This sense tends to coalesce with 1.

1596 SPENSER *State Irel.* Wks. (Globe) 615/2 [He] speedely rann forward, accounting his suddaynesse his most advauntage. **1599** SANDYS *Europæ Spec.* (1632) 188 They have..ruined those powerfull..Empires in the sodainnesse of an instant. **1615** CROOKE *Body of Man* 543 The swiftnesse and suddennesse of the motion of the eye-liddes. *a* **1661** FULLER *Worthies, Staffordsh.* (1662) 39, I know not whether more to admire at the suddeness of payment, or vastness of the Sum. **1750** CARTE *Hist. Eng.* II. 2 The suddenness of whose coronation did not prevent protests being made against it. **1837** CARLYLE *Fr. Rev.* II. I. xi, Sharp Bretons, with their Gaelic suddenness. **1841** SPALDING *Italy* III. 286 The suddenness of the chill which accompanies the evening twilight. **1885** *Manch. Exam.* 5 Nov. 5/3 With surprising suddenness and heartiness they broke out in loud cheers.

†**4.** Steepness, abruptness. *Obs. rare.*

1594–7 DONNE *Sat.* iii. 82 On a huge hill,..Truth stands, and hee that will Reach her, about must, and about must goe; And what the hills suddennes resists, winne so.

suddenty (ˈsʌd(ə)ntɪ). Chiefly *Sc. Obs.* exc. *dial.* Forms: see SUDDEN. [a. OF. *sodeinete* (mod.F *soudaineté*), f. *sodein* SUDDEN: see -TY.]

1. = SUDDENNESS 1; *occas.* an instance of this, an unexpected attack.

1388 WYCLIF *Wisd.* v. 2 Thei schulen wondre in the sudeynte of heelthe vnhopid. **1536** BELLENDEN *Cron. Scot.* (1821) I. 23 That he micht, be untraist suddante, the more cruelte exerce. *a* **1586** MONTGOMERY *Misc. Poems* xlv. 9 Come, gentill Death, and that with suddentie. **1596** DALRYMPLE tr. *Leslie's Hist. Scot.* I. 166 Feiring the suddantie and craftines of the cuntrey men. *Ibid.* II. 135 The Bartains in respect of that suddentie, resist and defend al tha mycht. **1611** SPEED *Hist. Gt. Brit.* IX. xx. §12 These short dangers and troubles, by reason of their suddainty did worthily make the King wakefull. **1633** SIR A. JOHNSTON *Diary* (S.H.S.) 15 The sudainte of it confounds me yet.

b. Phr. ***of (a) suddenty, on*** or ***upon (a) suddenty, in*** or ***on a great, in sic a suddenty,*** etc.: all of a sudden, (so, very) suddenly.

c **1440** *Alphabet of Tales* 19 As he was drawand, þer happend of Sodentie a fyssh to com in-to þe bukett. *c* **1557** ABP. PARKER *Ps.* xc. 254 As early grasse in sodentye doth change hys hue and plight. **1582–8** *Hist. Jas. VI* (1804) 77 The regent thus endit his..dayes in sic suddainty..as ye haue heard. **1587** *Reg. Privy Council Scot.* Ser. I. IV. 167 The said Maister, upoun suddentie, devisit the secund [device]. **1596** DALRYMPLE tr. *Leslie's Hist. Scot.* I. 165 Thairfor vpon Angus he brekis in vpon a suddentie. **1633** SIR A. JOHNSTON *Diary* (S.H.S.) 13 That it pleased God upon a sudainty..to separat thos saules quhilk he had joined out of his love. **1650** R. BAILLIE *Lett. & Jrnls.* (Bannatyne Club) III. 120 He left the west in a great suddentie and demi-disorder. **1818** SCOTT *Hrt. Midl.* xviii, It is not likely that he should have joined them on a suddenty. **1824** —— *Redgauntlet* let. xi, My father's tongue was loosed of a suddenty. **1876** ROBINSON *Gloss. Whitby* 189/1 It cam doon amang us all on a suddenty.

2. (In Sc. legal language.) An unpremeditated outburst of passion. ***on, upon,*** rarely ***of, in (a) suddenty***: without premeditation.

1469 *Acts Parl. Scot., Jas. III* (1814) II. 95/2 Gret slachteris quhilkes has bene Richt commone..of late baith of fore thocht felony and of suddante. **1496** *Reg. Privy Seal Scot.* I. 10/1 The slauchter of John Thomsoun committit apon suddante alanerly. *c* **1575** *Balfour's Practicks* (1754) 519 Gif..it..out of ane *chaud-melle,* or suddentie, that ilk ane of thame slay uther. **15..** *Aberd. Reg.* (Jam.), Spokin in suddanty, in the first motioune of yre. **1609** SKENE *Reg. Maj.* 46 b (tr. Stat. Dav. II.), Crymes (committed be ane suddentie, or ane chaud-mellee). **1637–50** ROW *Hist. Kirk* (Wodrow Soc.) 36 He who slayes any upon suddentie and inadvertence. **1678** G. MACKENZIE *Crim. Laws Scot.* I. xi. §xi. (1699) 64 *Chaudmella,* or Slaughter committed upon suddenty. **1776** SIR D. DALRYMPLE *Annals Scot.* I. 4 If he.. committed slaughter of suddenty. **1785** ARNOT *Crim. Trials* (1812) 195 That there is no distinction between..deliberate assassination and killing of a suddenty.

‖**Sudder** (ˈsʌdə(r)), *a.* (*sb.*) *Anglo-Indian.* [a. Urdu = Arab. *çadr* foremost or highest part of a thing, chief place or seat, etc., used in comb. with adj. sense.] Chief, supreme: applied esp. to high government departments or officials.

1787 *Gentl. Mag.* 1181/2 The Court of Sudder Dewannee Adaulet. **1835** [see MOONSIF]. **1845** STOCQUELER *Handbk. Brit. India* (1854) 342 Hydrabad is a collectorate, or Sudder station. **1850** *Directions Rev. Off. N.W. Prov.* 99 The Sudder Board of Revenue. **1897** G. SMITH *Twelve Indian Statesm.* x. 253 The Supreme and Sudder Courts were amalgamated at the Presidency Towns.

b. *ellipt.* as *sb.* = Sudder Court.

1834 *Baboo* I. iii. 50 (Stanf. Dict.), I was trying to save myself from appearing a fool before my masters in the Sudder to morrow. **1858** J. B. NORTON *Topics* 150 In Madras, the Sudder consists of only three judges.

sudding (ˈsʌdɪŋ), *vbl. sb.* [f. SUD(S + -ING¹.] The action of putting through a sud.

1909 *Stores' List,* No labour being necessary beyond sudding and rinsing.

†**ˈsudding,** *ppl. a. Obs.* [f. SUD *v.* + -ING².] Foaming.

1633 P. FLETCHER *Purple Isl.* II. xi, All froths his yellow streams with many a sudding fall. *Ibid.* IV. vii, The big-grown main with fomie billows swelling, Stops there the sudding stream.

suddite (ˈsʌdaɪt). [f. SUDD + -ITE¹.] A kind of fuel manufactured from sudd.

1911 *Daily News* 20 April 6 The new fuel is to be known as Suddite.

suddle (ˈsʌd(ə)l), *sb. Sc.* [f. the vb.] A stain, spot.

1861 R. QUINN *Heather Lintie* (1863) 239 Nature's touch sae pure an' bricht, But blemish, flaw, or suddle.

†**suddle,** *a. Sc. Obs.* In 5 **suddill.** [See next and cf. SUDDLY.] Filthy.

a **1500** *Colkelbie Sow* I. 171 The suddill sow of the sord.

suddle (ˈsʌd(ə)l), *v. Sc.* and *north. dial.* Also 6 **suddill,** 8 **sudle.** [Immediate source uncertain. Cf. MHG. *sudeln, sudlen* to wallow in mire, G. *sudeln* to soil, defile.] *trans.* To soil, sully, defile. Hence **suddled** *ppl. a.*

1513 DOUGLAS *Æneis* XII. ii. 124 That..I may..in the dusty puldyr.. Suddill and fyle hys crysp and ȝallow hayr. **1696** A. TELFAIR *True Relat. Appar.* 10 Seven small bones, with Blood, and some Flesh, all closed in a peice of Old suddled Paper. **1722** HAMILTON *Wallace* 12 She..A sudled Curch o'er Head and Neck let fall. [Cf. SUDDLY, quot. *c* 1470.] *c* **1820** HOGG *Poems* (1865) 279/2 His gravat was suddled. *a* **1825** *Ld. Thomas & Fair Annet* vi. in Child *Ballads* (1885) II. 186/1 She must put on her suddled silks, That she wears every day.

†'**suddly**, *a. Obs. Sc.* In 5 soudly, 6 sudly. [f. SUDDLE *v.* + -Y.] Soiled, dirty.

c **1470** HENRY *Wallace* I. 241 A soudly courche our hed and nek [scho] leit fall. *c* **1560** in *A. Scott's Poems* (E.E.T.S.) 90 Rycht as the sone schynis on the sudly schaw.

suddrone, suddroun, obs. ff. SOUTHRON.

†'**suddy**, *a. Obs.* [f. SUD(S + -Y.] Turbid, thick; also *fig.* 'muddy'.

1587 HARRISON *Descr. Brit.* xiv. 87/1 in *Holinshed*, The water of this riuer is for the most part sore troubled, as comming thorough a suddie or soddie more. **1614** LATHAM *Falconry* (1633) 27 Between a blacke & a tawnie, as it were of a suddie colour. **1657** G. STARKEY *Helmont's Vindic.* 314 Not as Sope which makes a troubled suddy water.

sude(n, obs. pa. t. pl. of SEETHE *v.*

sude(a)kne, -decon, obs. ff. SUBDEACON.

sudene, obs. f. SUBDEAN.

Sudeten (su:'deɪtən), *a.* and *sb.* [Ger., the name of the *Sudeten* mountains in northeastern Czechoslovakia.] **A.** *adj.* Of, pertaining to or designating the predominantly German-speaking area of Czechoslovakia in the vicinity of the Sudeten mountains (the Sudetenland) which was annexed by Germany from 1938 to 1945. Freq. as ***Sudeten German***.

1937 *Times* 20 Oct. 13/2 (*heading*) Czechoslovakia and the Sudeten Germans. *Ibid.* 6 Dec. 11/5 (*heading*) Sudeten German quarrels. *Ibid.*, Dissensions within the Sudetendeutsch Party. **1939** *Encycl. Brit. Bk. of Year* 526 At the time of the annexation by Germany of the Sudeten areas of Czechoslovakia there were in the country some 5,000 refugees from the old Reich and from Austria. **1946** W. S. CHURCHILL *Victory* 131 Henlein, Sudeten-German leader, committed suicide. **1959** W. F. LEOPOLD in J. A. Fishman *Readings Sociol. of Lang.* (1968) 355 Sudeten Germans with Bavarian dialect adapt themselves slowly to Swabian. **1966** S. MANN *Collecting Playing Cards* iv. 84 (*heading*) The Franconian or Sudeten pattern (Sudetendeutsch). **1968** [see the *sb.* below]. **1974** *Listener* 25 Apr. 530/2 The Sudeten 'problem' was being manipulated both by appeasers here and..by Hitler. **1982** S. G. DUFF *Parting of Ways* xv. 135 Gradually, up to 1933, the Sudeten Germans had become reconciled to the [Czechoslovak] Republic.

B. *sb.* An inhabitant of the Sudetenland; a Sudeten German.

1938 H. NICOLSON *Diary* 13 May (1966) 341 The Sudetens could not approve of a pro-Russian and anti-German policy. **1943** *Amer. Speech* XVIII. 200 The term *Sudetens*, extremely frequent in the news columns of 1938, did not exist before that year. **1968** K. MARTIN *Editor* xii. 252 The Sudetens had some real grievances, even though they were the best-treated minority in Europe... The Czech government knew that their real problem had nothing to do with Sudeten grievances.

Sudetic (su:'deɪtɪk), *a.* Now *rare.* [f. SUDET(EN *sb.* + -IC: cf. G. *sudetisch.*] Of or pertaining to the Sudeten region of Czechoslovakia.

1907 *Muret-Sanders Encyclopaedic Eng.-German & German-Eng. Dict.* II. 710/3 *Sudetan..Gebirge*,..Sudetic Mountains. **1928** C. DAWSON *Age of Gods* xii. 270 A movement of population was certainly taking place at this period, for the skulls of the Lengyel people belong not to the old 'Sudetic' type of the Danube region, but are distinctively Nordic. **1928** P. SELVER tr. *Benes' My War Memoirs* xix. 481 The Austrian Minister..sent..the..Allied Governments a protest against the attempt to retain the Sudetic Germans within Czechoslovakia. **1934** PRIEBSCH & COLLINSON *German Lang.* I. ii. 37 Of less moment..are..the fair broad-heads of East Baltic type on the eastern periphery and a very primitive strain, called by Günther Inner Asiatic or Sudetic (from the Sudetes). **1938** *Manch. Guardian* 12 May 6/3 It is not clear what is meant by the 'extreme limit' to which the Czecho-Slovak Government is asked to go in its 'concessions' to the Sudetic German minority.

sudewe, obs. f. SUBDUE *v.*

sudge(o)rne, obs. ff. SOJOURN.

sudiform ('s(j)u:dɪfɔ:m), *a. rare.* [f. L. *sudis* stake, pile + -FORM.] Shaped like a stake.

1822 J. PARKINSON *Outl. Oryctol.* 120 Their [*sc.* the sea-urchins'] spines are various, never uniformly setous, but either large and sudiform and as if truncated, or long and crenulated.

sudiorne, -journe, obs. forms of SOJOURN.

sudoite ('su:dəʊaɪt). *Min.* [ad. G. *sudoit* (G. Müller 1962, in *Naturwissenschaften* XLIX. 205/2), f. the name of Toshio *Sudo* (b. 1911), Japanese mineralogist and crystallographer: see -ITE[1].] (See quot. 1963.)

1963 *Amer. Mineralogist* XLVIII. 214 G. Müller (1962) proposes 'sudoite' as a name for this dioctahedral series of phyllosilicates, as chlorite is the name of the analogous trioctahedral series. **1977** *Mineral. Abstr.* XXVIII. 16/1 An essentially regular interstratification of mica (sericite) and chlorite (sudoite) was found in an alteration area of the Matsumine Kuroko deposit of the Hanaoka mine.

sudoral ('s(j)u:dərəl), *a.* and *sb. Path. rare.* [f. L. *sūdor* sweat + -AL[1]. Cf. OF. *sudoral.*] Characterized by a disturbance of the function of sweating.

1876 DUNGLISON *Med. Lex.* 313/2 *Diarrhœa, Sudoral*, diarrhœa associated with a disturbance of the functions of the skin, preventing the secretion of sweat. **1892** OSLER *Princ. & Pract. Med.* I. i. 16 Jaccoud and others in France have especially described this sudoral form of typhoid fever.

‖**sudoresis** (s(j)u:də'ri:sɪs). [mod.L., irreg. f. L. *sūdor* sweat + *-esis* as in DIAPHORESIS.] Sweating, exudation.

1834 MCMURTRIE *Cuvier's Anim. Kingd.* 405 The Gall-insects appear to injure trees by a superabundant sudoresis through the punctures they make in them. **1901** DORLAND *Illust. Med. Dict.*, *Sudoresis*, profuse sweating.

sudoric (s(j)u:'dɒrɪk), *a. Chem.* [f. L. *sūdor* sweat + -IC. Cf. F. *sudorique.*] ***sudoric acid***, an acid said to be present in human sweat. (Cf. HIDROTIC.)

1856 *Orr's Circ. Sci.*, *Pract Chem.* 318, I call them caseic, sudoric, and capric acids (capronic, caprylic, and caprinic acids of other authors).

sudoriferous (s(j)u:də'rɪfərəs), *a.* [f. late L. *sūdōrifer* or mod.L. *sūdōriferus*: see -FEROUS. Cf. F. *sudorifère*, It., Sp., Pg. *sudorifero.*]

1. = SUDORIFIC I.

1597 A. M. tr. *Guillemeau's Fr. Chirurg.* 49/1 Sudoriferouse medicaments. **1694** WESTMACOTT *Script. Herb.* 26 The extract of the wood of Box is sudoriferous. **1833** M. SCOTT *Tom Cringle* vii, The temper of the people.. is hotter than the climate, and that, God knows! is sudoriferous enough.

2. = SUDORIPAROUS.

1713 DERHAM *Phys.-Theol.* v. vii. 338 The sudoriferous Glands and Vessels. **1849–52** *Todd's Cycl. Anat.* IV. II. 841/1 The cutaneous secretion is formed by the spiral sudoriferous canals. **1856** TODD & BOWMAN *Phys. Anat.* II. 387 These glands..are..related rather to the sudoriferous than to the salivary system. **1877** BURNETT *Ear* 23 The sudoriferous glands are most abundant on the posterior surface of the auricle.

Hence **sudo'riferousness**.

1727 BAILEY (vol. II.), *Sudoriferousness*, aptness to cause Sweat.

sudorific (s(j)u:də'rɪfɪk), *a.* and *sb.* Also 7 -iphicke, 7–8 -ifick. [ad. mod.L. *sūdōrificus*: see -FIC. Cf. F. *sudorifique*, It., Sp., Pg. *sudorifico.*]

A. *adj.*

1. Promoting or causing perspiration; diaphoretic.

1626 BACON *Sylva* §706 A Decoction of Sudorifick Herbs. **1634** *Lowe's Chirurg.* (ed. 3) v. xii. 153 Decoct on sudoriphicke. **1732** ARBUTHNOT *Rules of Diet* in *Aliments*, etc. 271 Many things which are diuretick are likewise sudorifick. **1811** A. T. THOMSON *Lond. Disp.* (1818) 584 This oil is stimulant, anti-spasmodic, anodyne, and sudorific. **1850** S. DOBELL *Rom.* v. Poet. Wks. (1875) 59 Sudorific toil. **1869** CLARIDGE *Cold Water Cure* 203 Sudorific Process.

2. Connected with the secretion and the exudation of sweat; sudoriparous, perspiratory.

c **1720** W. GIBSON *Farrier's Dispens.* vii. (1734) 184 The Sudorifick Pores. **1799** UNDERWOOD *Dis. Childhood* (ed. 4) II. 169 *Hydroa*, or *Sudamina* is a trifling eruption from the sudorific glands. **1878** HAMILTON *Nervous Dis.* 74 During the warmer season, when the sudorific apparatus requires a free capillary circulation.

3. Consisting of sweat. *rare.*

1807 SYD. SMITH *Wks.* (1850) 85 A miraculous image of our Lady of Serdenay, which always sweats—not ordinary sudorific matter—but an oil of great ecclesiastical efficacy. **1837** BARHAM *Ingol. Leg.* Ser. I. *Leech Folkstone*, Did you ever..burst out into sudorific exudation like a cold thaw, with the thermometer at zero?

4. Of limestone caves, etc.: That exudes.

1828 DUPPA *Trav. Italy*, etc. 142 The steam-baths of Dædalus..consist of several sudorific grottos.

B. *sb.* A medicine or remedy which promotes perspiration; a diaphoretic.

1667 *Phil. Trans.* II. 547 She never swet in her life, nor could it be procur'd by ordinary Sudorificks. **1728** CHAMBERS *Cycl.* s.v., Sudorificks only differ from Diaphoreticks in the Degree of their Action; the one promoting sensible Perspiration, the other insensible. **1756** C. LUCAS *Ess. Waters* III. 171 This bath becomes the most powerful and certain sudorific known. **1841** BREWSTER *Martyrs Sci.* II. iv. (1856) 159 Antimony..a well known sudorific in the present practice of physic. **1883** J. MACKENZIE *Day-dawn Dark places* 42 They actually rolled the miserable man in the burning sand as a sudorific! **1908** SIR H. JOHNSTON *G. Grenfell & Congo* II. xxii. 557 A treatment of disease by massage or sudorifics.

b. *transf.*

1777 H. WALPOLE *Let. to C'tess Upper Ossory* 29 June, We will keep ourselves warm with hot cockles and blind-man's-buff, and other old English sudorifics.

†**sudo'rifical**, *a. Obs. rare.* [f. as prec. + -AL[1].]

1. = SUDORIFIC I.

1651 FRENCH *Distill.* i. 34 There will come forth an insipid water, sudorificall and laxative.

2. Sweaty, perspiring.

1828 *Blackw. Mag.* XXIV. 350 He deterges his brow sudorifical.

†**sudorifi'cation**. *Obs. rare*[−1]. [f. L. *sūdor* sweat + -(I)FICATION.] Sweat, perspiration.

1708 *Brit. Apollo, Q. Paper* No. 1. 3/1 It makes my.. Carcase..in a humid Sudorification.

sudoriparous (s(j)u:də'rɪpərəs), *a. Phys.* [f. mod.L. *sūdōriparus*, f. *sūdor* sweat: see -PAROUS. Cf. F. *sudoripare.*] Secreting sweat.

1851 CARPENTER *Man. Phys.* (ed. 2) 446 The Sudoriparous or sweat-glands. **1876** DUHRING *Dis. Skin* 18 Certain gases, as carbonic acid, and other substances, are eliminated from the body through the sudoriparous glands.

b. Used loosely for: Connected with the production of sweat or with the sweat-glands.

1899 *Allbutt's Syst. Med.* VIII. 676 Both the sudoriparous and sebaceous functions may be abolished. *Ibid.* 825 They originate in the sweat-glands, and are usually found about the forehead or skin of the scalp (sudoriparous adenoma).

sudorous ('s(j)u:dərəs), *a. rare.* [f. late L. *sūdōrus*, f. L. *sūdor* sweat: see -OUS.] Sweaty.

1646 SIR T. BROWNE *Pseud. Ep.* II. v. 85 The strigments and sudorous adhesions from mens hands. *Ibid.* v. xxi. 270 The sudorous or thin serosity perspirable through the skin. **1893** DOUGHTY *Wherry in Wendish Lands* 274 Four backs, weary and sudorous.

‖**Sudra** ('su:drə). *Anglo-Indian.* Forms: 7 *pl.* **Shudderies, -yes,** 7, 9 **Soudra,** 8 **Tschud(d)irer, Sudder,** 8–9 **Soodera, Sooder,** 9 **S(h)uder, Shudra, Soodra, Çudra,** 8– **Sudra.** [a. Skr. *śūdra* (Hindi *shūdr*, Urdu *sūdr*), of doubtful etym. Cf. F. *Soudra*, Pg. *Chudrer.*] A member of the lowest of the four great Hindu castes.

1630 LORD *Banians* xii, The third Tribe or Cast, called the Shudderies. **1678** J. PHILLIPS tr. *Tavernier's Trav.* II. III. iii. 162 The fourth Caste is that of the *Charados* or *Soudras*. **1717** J. T. PHILLIPS *People of Malabar* 20 As for the *Tschudirers*, they have Licence only to read the six Systems. **1794** SIR W. JONES *Instit. Hindu Law* Wks. 1799 III. 357 For a *Súdra* is ordained a wife of his own class. **1796** ELIZA HAMILTON *Lett. Hindoo Rajah* (1811) I. 115 Any base born sooder. **1796** MORSE *Amer. Geog.* II. 544 The fourth tribe is that of *Sudder*. **1800** *Asiat. Ann. Reg.* 55/2 A Vaisya, unable to subsist by his own duties, may descend to the servile acts of a Súdra. **1858** BEVERIDGE *Hist. India* II. IV. i. 13 The modern Sudra is no longer a slave. **1910** *Encycl. Brit.* XIII. 503/1 Whilst the Arya was thus a *dvi-ja*, or twice-born, the Sudra remained unregenerate during his lifetime.

attrib. **1794** SIR W. JONES *Instit. Hindu Law* Wks. 1799 III. 333 A *Bráhmen* may seize without hesitation..the goods of his *Súdra* slave. **1828** *Asiatic Costumes* 60 Hindoos of the soodra caste. **1829** *Encycl. Metrop.* (1845) XX. 677/2 Nanda, the son of a Súdra mother. **1876** *Encycl. Brit.* V. 190/2 After Buddha, Sudra dynasties ruled in many parts of India.

sudroun, obs. form of SOUTHRON.

suds (sʌdz), *sb. pl.* Forms: 6 sudes, 6–7 suddes, 7–8 sudds, 6– suds. Also *sing.* sud (7 sudd). [Of uncertain etymology.

With the existing evidence it is difficult to establish the chronology of the senses. Sense 2 is perhaps the original: in which case the immediate source may be MLG., MDu. *sudde* (WFris. *sodde*), or MDu. *sudse*, in Kilian *zudse* (WFris. *sodze*) marsh, bog.]

†**1.** Dregs, leavings; hence, filth, muck. Also *fig.* or in fig. context. *Obs.*

1548 UDALL *Erasm. Par.* Pref. 2 b, He had so infected the clere fountaine of Goddes woorde with the suddes of humain tradicions. **1563** *Mirr. Mag.*, *Rivers* iv, Oft causyng good to be reported yll, Or dround in suddes of Lethes muddy swyll. **1576** TURBERV. *Venerie* xxxv. 93 Perchance the fight..Amasde your mynde, and for a whyle did draw Your noble eyes, to settle on such suddes. **1581** *Lanc. & Cheshire Wills* (Chetham Soc.) II. 3, I geue and bequeath vnto James hamer my sone all the dust and sudes towardes the keepinge of a swine. **1594** *Manch. Crt. Leet Rec.* (1885) II. 90 That Roberte Marshall shall not cast any suddes or bludye water one..his backside. **1596** NORDEN *Progr. Pietie* (1847) 178 The dangerous estate of thy church, which is much pestered and infected with the suds of error. **1609** J. DAVIES *Hum. Heaven on Earth* clix. Wks. (Grosart) I. 21/1 Swimming in Suddes of all sorditie. **1622** DONNE *Serm.* John i. 8 (1649) II. 344 Those that lye in the suddes of nature. *c* **1645** HOWELL *Lett.* II. iii, The base Suds which Vice useth to leave behind it.

†**2.** Flood-water; the water of the fens; water mixed with drift-sand and mud; drift-sand left by a flood. Also *transf.* (quot. 1599). *Obs.*

The authors here quoted belong to E. Anglia.

1599 NASHE *Lenten Stuffe* Wks. 1905 III. 196 Leander.. when hee sprawled through the brackish suddes to scale her [*sc.* Hero's] tower. **1621** QUARLES *Esther* Wks. (Grosart) II. 63/2 [God's] lesser breath..can drowne The spacious Vniuerse in suds of Clay. **1629** H. C. *Disc. conc. Drayning Fennes* B, To be surrounded, or to lye in the suds, as we say, three quarters or halfe a yeere..doth mischiefe..the ground. **1635** QUARLES *Embl.* IV. i. Wks. (Grosart) III. 79/1 Thus am I driven upon these slipp'ry suds,..My life's a troubled sea, compos'd of Ebs and Flouds. **1851** T. STERNBERG *Dial. Northants.* 109 *Suds*, floods. Water mixed with sand and mud; formerly applied to the water of the fens.

3. a. Water impregnated with soap for washing, esp. when hot. **b.** The frothy mass which collects on the top of soapy water in which things are washed; in early use *esp.* a barber's lather. (More fully SOAP-SUDS.) Also in fig. and allusive use (cf. sense 5).

1581 PETTIE tr. *Guazzo's Civ. Conv.* (1586) I. 41 b, Hee which washeth his mouth with his owne praise, soyleth himselfe with the suddes that come of it. **1593** G. HARVEY *New Letter* Wks. (Grosart) I. 281, I haue some suddes of my mother witt, to sowse such a Dish clowte in. **1594** PLAT *Jewell-ho.* I. 34 Maister Barnabe Googe will haue all the suddes of his landery conueied thereon. **1596** NASHE *Saffron Walden* 16 Thou that hast made so manie men winke whyles thou cast suds in their eyes. **1606** DEKKER *Seuen Deadly Sinnes* Wks. (Grosart) II. 62 Barbers..throwing all their Suddes out of their learned Latin Basons into my face. **1606** MARSTON *Fawne* IV. i, Alas my miserable maister, what suds art thou washt into? **1611–** [see SOAP-SUDS]. **1612** WEBSTER *White Devil* v. iii, She simpers like the suds A collier hath been wash'd in. **1688** HOLME *Armoury* III. 98/2 Beating the

Soap and Water together, to make it rise to a Froth, which they [*sc.* Laundresses] call Suds. **1749** FIELDING *Tom Jones* VIII. iv, The shaver was very tedious in preparing his suds. *a* **1756** ELIZA HAYWOOD *New Present* (1771) 268 Let them be washed in strong clear suds. **1844** DICKENS *Mart. Chuz.* xxix, He lathered him bountifully. Mr. Bailey smiled through the suds. **1873** BROWNING *Red Cott. Nt.-cap* 1576 The brilliant bubble burst in suds! **1887** MEREDITH *Young Reynard* i. Poet. Wks. (1912) 286 Light as a bubble that flies from the tub, Whisked by the laundry-wife out of her suds. *a* **1893** W. BURNS THOMSON *Remin.* (1895) 33 She stroked the suds off her hands and arms.

c. *sing.* A soap solution.

1835 URE *Philos. Manuf.* 129 It [*sc.* the grease of the fleece] serves to facilitate the scouring of wool by means of water alone, with which it forms a kind of sud or emulsion. **1884** W. S. B. MCLAREN *Spinning* (ed. 2) 32 A moderately good washing in a warm sud, with a neutral soap.

4. a. Foam, froth. Also *sing.*

1592 GREENE *Upst. Courtier* D iv b, They lookte like foure blowne bladders..washt ouer with the suds of an old stale die. **1607** MIDDLETON *Fam. Love* III. ii, Like the suds of an ale-fat or a washing-bowl. **1906** F. S. OLIVER *Alex. Hamilton* IV. ii. 279 Opinions which never at any point touched a firm bottom, but merely swam like a kind of 'sud' upon the stream of expediency. **1913** J. G. FRAZER *Golden Bough, Balder* II. 231 While one medicine-man whirls a bull-roarer, another whips up a mixture of water and meal into frothy suds symbolic of clouds.

b. *Whaling.* The foam churned up by a wounded whale.

1850 SCORESBY *Cheever's Whalem. Adv.* xii. (1858) 164 Let us be up among the suds.

c. *slang* (orig. and chiefly *U.S.*) Beer.

1904 G. V. HOBART *I'm from Missouri* iii. 52 Who..hoists a few dippers of suds?.. Dad! **1907** *Daily Chron.* 16 May 6/7 A 'tub of suds,' the name for a glass of low quality beer. **1924** *Truth* (Sydney) 27 Apr. 6 *Suds*, beer. **1925** FRASER & GIBBONS *Soldier & Sailor Words* 273 *Suds*, ale. **1926** *Flynn's* 16 Jan. 638/2 The boozeclerk give us th' high sign he had doped th' suds or skat. **1931** 'D. STIFF' *Milk & Honey Route* 177 Fill up on 'suds' for a dime. **1943** C. L. SONNICHSEN *Roy Bean* 171 The bear..was still consuming his free bottle of suds. **1962** *Radio Times* 17 May 43 Let's split to your pad for some suds. **1975** *Globe & Mail* (Toronto) 8 Feb. 1/2 Before then, Labatt had only a marginal share of the suds market in Quebec. **1977** *Mod. Boating* (Austral.) Jan. 30/1 The figure propped half-standing on a bar stool, with his face in a glass of suds. **1979** *Tucson* (Arizona) *Mag.* Sept. 60/3 Sip suds out of glass jars while you wait.

5. in the suds († *in suds, in the sud*): chiefly in *to lie* or *be in the suds*; *to lay, leave in the suds.*

a. In difficulties, in embarrassment or perplexity. *Obs.* or *slang.*

c **1572** GASCOIGNE *Posies, Fruites Warre* Wks. 1907 I. 161 He..sought with victuall to supplie, Poore Myddleburgh which then in suddes did lie. **1603** KNOLLES *Hist. Turks* (1621) 426 Whilest Scodra thus lay in the suds. **1617** in *Crt. & Times Jas. I* (1848) I. 468 The Lord Coke is left in the suds. **1653** H. MORE *Conject. Cabbal.* (1713) 230 After the hurry of his inordinate pleasures and passion, when he was for a time left in the suds, as they call it. **1730** SWIFT *Death & Daphne* Misc. 1735 V. 109 Away the frighted Spectre scuds And leaves my Lady in the Suds. **1775** S. J. PRATT *Liberal Opin.* cxxxiv. (1783) IV. 216 This proves, *logicè*, that you are in the suds; which is, *Anglicè*, being interpreted, that you will be hanged. *a* **1800** *Jolly Beggar* xii. in Child *Ballads* V. 114/2 When that some have got their wills They'l leave you in the suds. **1816** U. BROWN *Jrnl.* 28 Sept. in *Maryland Hist. Mag.* (1916) XI. 234 We both in the sudds pretty much. *Ibid.* 29 Sept. 235 Thinking that I was not out of the sudds yet. **1887** R. T. COOKE *Happy Dodd* xxvii. 295, I shan't leave Mis' Payson in the suds.

†**b.** Undone; done for; in disgrace. Similarly, *into the suds.* *Obs.*

1611 SPEED *Hist. Gt. Brit.* IX. xxiv. 222 The glory of the Spaniards laid in the suds. **1613** FLETCHER, etc. *Captain* III. vi, I'le fuddle him Or lye 'ith sudd [*2nd Fol.* suds]. **1631** [MABBE] *Celestina* xxi. 197 Our solace is in the suds! our joy is turn'd into annoy! **1632** MASSINGER *Maid of Hon.* I. ii, Look not with too much contemplation on me; If you do, you are in the suds. **1633** ROWLEY *Match at Midnight* v. i, There's one Iaruis, a rope on him has juggled me into the sudds too.

c. In the sulks; in the blues. *dial.*

1611 COTGR. s.v. *Vilain*, Being in the suds, or sullens. **1631** R. H. *Arraignm. Whole Creature* xvi. 280 So long he is sicke in the suds, and diseas'd in the sullens. **1807** R. ANDERSON *Cumbld. Ball.* 139 Some lasses thought lang to the weddin—Unax'd, others sat i' the suds. **1840** LADY C. BURY *Hist. of Flirt* xxv, Mary does not look very well, and you are in the suds.

†**d.** In an unfinished state or condition. *Obs.*

a **1592** GREENE *Orpharion* Wks. (Grosart) XII. 7 It hath line this twelve months in the suds. Now at last it is crept forth in the Spring. **1615–20** C. MORE *Sir T. More* (*c* 1627) 242 Some [actions-at-law] lye in the suddes by the space of diuerse yeares. **1642** FULLER *Holy & Prof. St.* IV. xvi. 319 Who so trimly dispatch'd his businesse, that he left it in the suddes.

e. †(*a*) Being lathered. *Obs.* (*b*) Being washed, 'in the wash'.

c **1626** *Dick of Devon* II. i. in Bullen *O. Pl.* (1883) II. 29 We may hap to be in the suddes ourselves. *c* **1640** [SHIRLEY] *Capt. Underwit* I. *Ibid.* 327, I thought you by the wide lynnen about your neck have been under correction in the suds, sir. **1766** SMOLLETT *Trav.* v. Wks. (1841) 699/1 Captain B——, ..with the napkin under his chin, was no bad representation of Sancho Panza in the suds. **1788** *Times* 1 Jan., Though his Lordship has been so long in the suds, it is not thought that shaving will take place till the day of Judgment. **1863** MRS. GASKELL *Sylvia's Lovers* xvii, Thy best shirt is in t' suds, and no time for t' starch and iron it.

†**f.** Slightly intoxicated, fuddled. *Obs.*

1770 *Gentl. Mag.* XL. 559 He is said to be..a little in the suds.

6. *attrib.* and *Comb.*: **sud-dish**, a barber's soap-dish; †**suds-monger** *contemptuous*, a barber; **suds-tub**, a washing-tub.

1892 *Pall Mall Gaz.* 16 Feb. 3/1 His shop..is still to be seen with..its emblematic *sud-dish hanging in front. **1638** FORD *Fancies* I. ii, A dry shaver, a copper-bason'd *suds-monger. **1805** *Spirit Publ. Jrnls.* IX. 113 Poor Mungo came out of the *suds tub no whiter than when soused in!

suds (sʌdz), *v.* [f. the sb.]

1. *trans.* To lather; to cover with soap-suds, or wash in soapy water.

1834 'C. PACKARD' *Recoll. Housekeeper* 12 Ma'am Bridge was *sudsing* the clothes in a tub before her. **1939** N. S. COLBY *Remembering* ii. 62 She dipped my hair in a basin of hot water, sudsed it, rinsed it, and dried it with a towel. **1976** *S. Wales Echo* 27 Nov. 6/3 (Advt.), Rub-a-Dub Doll. Soap her and suds her. See how much fun a bath can be. **1981** P. THEROUX *Mosquito Coast* xv. 185 The..splash of our foot-operated wheel sounded like a washing machine sudsing clothes.

2. *intr.* To form suds. *U.S.*

1893 M. A. OWEN *Voodoo Tales* 5 An impertinent housewife had dared to affirm that her soap wouldn't 'suds'. **1972** *Fortune* Jan. 73/1 Detergent foam first became a matter of national concern in the early 1960's, when Representative Henry S. Reuss of Wisconsin, among others, pointed out that detergents were persisting, and sometimes sudsing, in the environment.

So **'sudsing** *vbl. sb.* and *ppl. a.*

1844 'J. SLICK' *High Life N.Y.* II. 20 I'd gin myself a good sudsing in the wash hand basin. **1879** *Scribner's Monthly* Oct. 940/2 As soon as they begin to boil, remove them to the 'sudsing'-water. **1881** S. P. MCLEAN *Cape Cod Folks* 167 A good poundin', and boilin', and sudzin', you need. **1957** T. STURGEON in D. Knight *100 Yrs. Sci. Fiction* (1969) 334 Slim heard more water running and sudsing noises, and, by ear, followed the operation through a soaping and two rinses. **1971** *New Yorker* 6 Nov. 5 (Advt.), This rich, sudsing, mentholated cleanser was developed by dermatologists. **1978** *Nature* 6 Apr. p. xxvii/2 The concentrated detergent powder dissolves quickly to provide fast action, minimal sudsing, and free rinsing.

sudsable ('sʌdzəb(ə)l), *a.* [f. SUDS *v.* + -ABLE.] Capable of forming soap-suds; also of garments: washable in soapy water. Hence **sudsa'bility**.

1951 *Sun* (Baltimore) 15 Dec. 10 (Advt.), She never has too many blouses..so lovable..so wearable..so sudsable. **1959** *Wall St. Jrnl.* 16 Dec. 9/2 More folks are becoming more conscious of the sudsability of their tap water. **1970** *Globe & Mail* (Toronto) 25 Sept. 16/2 (Advt.), Tam-and-scarf set in thick suds-able hand-crocheted acrylic.

sudser ('sʌdzə(r)). *U.S. slang.* [f. SUDS *sb. pl.* + -ER[1].] A soap opera.

1968 *New Yorker* 30 Mar. 114/2 It has the suggestions of sadness and 'depth' that make it a kind of high-class sudser for women. **1975** *Ibid.* 5 May 31/1 This NBC half-hour TV sudser expired after fifteen months. **1982** *Washington Post* 8 Dec. C10 Clooney's autobiography..has been turned into another drably shabby TV sudser.

sudsy ('sʌdzɪ), *a.* *U.S.* [f. SUDS + -Y.] Consisting of, full of, or characterized by soap-suds. Also *transf.* and *fig.*

1866 *Harper's Mag.* Sept. 544/2 He's gone! across the sudzy sea. **1884** *Ibid.* Sept. 528/2 Washers..laving their linen in the sudsy stream. **1891** *Advance* (Chicago) 5 Nov., The steaming, sudsy tub. **1901** *Munsey's Mag.* XXV. 441/2 A pleasant, sudsy cleanliness about the two little rooms. **1980** *Times Lit. Suppl.* 17 Oct. 1160/1 Thanks to Arianna Stassinopoulos's votive ministrations, Maria Callas has graduated from opera to the sudsier, sublimer realm of soap opera.

suduwe, obs. form of SUBDUE.

sudyakne, obs. form of SUBDEACON.

†**sue**, *sb.* *Obs.* Also su. [Cf. SUCCARATH.] (See quots.)

1607 TOPSELL *Four-f. Beasts* 660 There is a region in the new-found world, called Gigantes, and the inhabitants thereof are called Pantagones;..they cloath themselues with the skins of a beast called in theyr owne toong *Su*, for by reason that this beast liueth for the most part neere the waters, therefore they cal it by the name of *Su*, which signifieth water. **1623** COCKERAM III, *Sue*, a most cruell fierce beast, carrying her young vpon her backe to shadow them from the heat with her huge taile. **1688** HOLME *Armoury* II. x. 212/2 He beareth Argent; a *Sue* Sable.

sue (sjuː), *v.* Forms: 3–5 **suwe, siwe, sywe**, 3–7 **sewe**, 4–5 **seue, suy(e**, 4–6 **swe**, (*pa. t.* and *pple* **sude**), 5–6 **sew, seu**, 5–7 **siew, shue**, (3 **suu, siu suhe, siwi, sywi, siwy**, 4 **siue, s(e)wy, seuwe, suie**, 5 **su, suew, seewe, sieu, syew, svyn**, 6 **suw, seyv**), 4– **sue.** [a. AF. *suer, siwer, sure, suir(e* = OF. *sivre*, also *sevre, sievre*, etc. (pres. stem *siu-, sieu-, seu-*), mod.F. *suivre*:—pop. L. **sequĕre* (cf. Pr. *segre, seguir*, It. *seguire*, Sp., Pg. *seguir*), for L. *sequī* to follow.]

I. Transitive senses.

†**1.** To follow (a person or thing in motion); *occas.* to tend (cattle). Also with *forth.* *Obs.*

c **1290** *St. Brandan* 460 in *S. Eng. Leg.* 232 So þicke huy [*sc.* fish] werena-boute þis schip And euere syweden it so. **1377** LANGL. *P. Pl.* B. v. 550, I haue ben his folwar al þis fifty wyntre; Bothe ysowen his sede and sued his bestes. **1421–2** HOCCLEVE *Complaint* 321 My wyckednesses evar followe me, as men may se the shadow a body swe. **1426** LYDG. *De Guil. Pilgr.* 8763, I ha founde a chaumberere, Me suyng at my bak behynde. *c* **1450** *Mirk's Festial* 49 Þes kynges sudyn þys sterre forth, tyll þay come ynto Bedeleem. *c* **1485** *Digby Myst.* III. 532 Go ȝe be-fore; I sue yow ner. **1590** SPENSER *F.Q.* III. iv. 50 It was a knight, which now her sewd.

†**b.** To follow (a person's steps, a track, path). Also in fig. context. *Obs.*

c **1380** WYCLIF *Wks.* (1880) 481 Þis was lymytid to petre & hise þat suyden þe steppis þat petre wente. *c* **1410** *Master of Game* (MS. Digby 182) xxv, Come ageynn þer as he gan to sewe and sewe forth þe right. *c* **1450** *Godstow Reg.* 23 Wold god I cowth þy steppes wel to sewe! **1548** FORREST *Pleas. Poesye* 55 In suynge the Steppes of suche men approbate. **1596** SPENSER *F.Q.* IV. ix. 26 As when two Barkes, this caried with the tide, That with the wind, contrary courses sew.

†**c.** To follow with the eyes. *Obs.*

a **1425** *Cursor M.* 12200 (Trin.) Þe lettres fro alpha to tayu Wiþ dyuerse siȝte may men sew. *c* **1435** *Torr. Portugal* 89 Thow darryst full evyll with thy Ey hym sewe.

†**2. a.** To come after, follow, succeed (in time).

1377 LANGL. *P. Pl.* B. XVIII. 190 Þat Adam & Eue and alle þat hem suwed Shulde deye doune riȝte and dwelle in pyne after. *c* **1450** *Mirk's Festial* 28 Þes þre festys þat seuþe þe byrth of Crist. **1450** *Rolls of Parlt.* V. 212/1 The oure of mydnyght next suyng the seid Tuesday. **1491** *Ibid.* VI. 443/2 That no Collectour be charged of any Colleccion of II XVmes and X^mes togeders, oon ymmediatly suyng another.

†**b.** To follow as a consequence or result. *Obs.*

c **1400** tr. *Secr. Secr., Gov. Lordsh.* 43 Of euels þat seuen flesshly apetit. **1493** *Festivall* (W. de W. 1515) 5 b, Lechery that sueth alwaye glotony. **1559** *Mirr. Mag., Rich. II*, i, Shame sueth sinne, as rayne drops do the thunder.

†**3.** To go in pursuit of; to chase, pursue. *Obs.*

c **1275** LAY. 16437 Aurelie him siwede forþ. **1297** R. GLOUC. (Rolls) 2941 Þo hengist ysey þe cristinemen sywi him so vaste. **13..** *K. Alis.* 1198 (W.) No scholde foul, gret no smal, Have y-siwed Bulsifall! **1388** WYCLIF *Prov.* x. 4 The same man sueth briddis fleynge. *c* **1460** *Towneley Myst.* viii. 403 We shall not seasse to thay be slayn, For to the see we shall thaym sew. **1596** SPENSER *F.Q.* VI. ix. 2 Great trauell hath the gentle Calidore..sith I left him last Sewing the Blatant beast.

†**b.** Said of misfortune, etc. *Obs.*

a **1310** in Wright *Lyric P.* iv. 24 In sunne ant sorewe y am seint, that siweth me so fully sore. *c* **1400** tr. *Secr. Secr., Gov. Lordsh.* 50 Myshappe shal sone sewe him. **1510** *Treat. Galaunt* in Furnivall *Ballads fr. MSS.* I. 448 Dyuers aduersytees seweth vs yere be yere.

†**4.** To follow (a person) as an attendant, companion, or adherent; to accompany, attend upon; *occas.* to follow (a banner or the like); to frequent (a person's company). *Obs.*

a **1250** *Owl & Night.* 1526 (Jesus MS.) Þat..syweþ þare þat noht naueþ, & haueþ atom his riche spuse. *c* **1275** LAY. 1387 And ich þe wolle siwi mid mine gode folke. *c* **1320** *Cast. Love* 1274 And elles-wher þer he eode, Muche folk him suwede of feole þeode. **1377** LANGL. *P. Pl.* B. XI. 414 That clergye þi compaignye ne kepeth nouȝt to sue. **1382** WYCLIF *Matt.* viii. 19 Maistre, I shal sue thee, whidir euer thou shalt go. ? *a* **1400** *Morte Arth.* 81 Wyth sextene knyghtes in a soyte, sewande hym one. *c* **1400** MAUNDEV. (1839) 226 He..commanded hem anon to make hem redy, and to sewen his Banere. *c* **1450** *Merlin* 210 Than cried Merlin, 'Gentill knyghtes, what tarye ye heere so longe? suweth me!' **1483** CAXTON *Gold. Leg.* 134 b/1 Ther were vii wymen that siewed hym whyche gadred up the dropes of hys blood. **1522** *Mundus & Infans* 170 For seuen kynges sewen me, Bothe by daye and nyght.

†**b.** Phr. *to serve and sue*: to give 'suit and service' to (see SUIT *sb.* 2). *Obs.*

c **1380** ? CHAUCER *Balade Compl.* 12 My worldes Ioye, whom I wol serve and sewe. **1590** SPENSER *F.Q.* II. vii. 9 Wherefore if me thou deigne to serue and sew, At thy commaund lo all these mountaines bee.

†**5.** To take as guide, leader, or pattern; to follow as a disciple or imitator. *Obs.*

a **1300** *Fall & Passion* 105 in *E.E.P.* (1862) 15 Hou hi lord ssold siu þe. **1382** WYCLIF *Prol. Bible* i. 1 Jerom, in suynge Ebreyes, comprehendith alle these bookis in xxij. *a* **1400** *Minor Poems fr. Vernon MS.* 591 Suwe no wikked mon In wille nouþer in þouht. **1426** LYDG. *De Guil. Pilgr.* 12040 That thow mayst swen cryst ihesu. **1430–40** —— *Bochas* VIII. Prol. (1494) C ij, I shall procede as it is to me due In these two bokis Bochas for to sue. **1493** [H. PARKER] *Dives & Pauper* (W. de W.) I. xvi. 49/1 To lette the people to sue the Jewes in manner of worshyppyng. **1509** BARCLAY *Shyp of Folys* (1874) I. 183 Beware his wayes, fle hym on euery syde, Who that hym sueth both hurte and shame shall fynde.

†**6.** To conform to, comply with the conditions of. *Obs.*

a **1300** *Fall & Passion* 97 in *E.E.P.* (1862) 15 Þroȝ is deþ he ouer cam as he is manhed siwed. **1390** GOWER *Conf.* I. 277 And for this cause I thenke suie The forme bothe and the matiere. **1422** YONGE tr. *Secr. Secr.* 218 The Sowle..sueth the kynde and the complexcion and the propyrteys of the body. **1463–4** *Rolls of Parlt.* V. 501/2 That every of the seid Clothes..folowe and sue..oon ordre of makyng.

†**7.** To comply with (a person's will), follow (another's advice or one's own inclinations or devices). *Obs.*

1362 LANGL. *P. Pl.* A. II. 56 To be Boxum and Boun his Biddyng to folfulle,..And, as sir Simonye wol sigge, to suwen [*v.rr.* suyen, sewen] his wille. *a* **1400–50** *Wars Alex.* 3534 Ne neuire ȝour rialte renay bot rede to sewe. **1422** YONGE tr. *Secr. Secr.* 209 Yf a man yeuyth good consaill, thou mayste hit Su. **1509** BARCLAY *Shyp of Folys* (1874) I. 2 Suche Unthriftes as sue theyr carnal lust. *Ibid.* 60 He sholde sue the counsayle of men wyse and prudent. **1642** H. MORE *Song of Soul* I. i. 3 When skilfull limmer 'suing his intent Shall fairly well pourtray..The true proportion of each lineament. **1767** MICKLE *Concub.* I. xxxiv, She conns, and freely sues her native Bent.

†**8.** To follow, adopt, put into practice (a form of belief, a manner of life, a virtue or vice, an occupation or profession); to engage in, occupy oneself with (a pursuit). *Obs.*

c **1290** *Beket* 249 in *S. Eng. Leg.* 113 Pley he siwede of hauekus and of houndes. **1362** LANGL. *P. Pl.* A. XI. 242 To suche þat sewen oure beleue. *c* **1374** CHAUCER *Troilus* I. 379

Thus toke he purpos loues craft to suwe. *c* **1380** WYCLIF *Wks.* (1880) 17 Hou suen þei charite? **1382** —— *1 Pet.* iii. 11 Seke he pees, and parfijtly sue it. **1390** GOWER *Conf.* I. 118 With low herte humblesce suie. *a* **1400–50** *Wars Alex.* 795* (Dubl.) As he þe sadyll hed sewyd seuenten wynter. *c* **1407** LYDG. *Reason & Sens.* 503 Me to excite Alle vertues for to sywe And vices pleynly to eschiwe. *c* **1430** —— *Min. Poems* (Percy Soc.) 28 He sued bad doctryne. *c* **1430** *Hymns Virgin* (1867) 67 Goo, Conscience, þou lewide asse, I kepe not þi maneris to sue. *c* **1450** *St. Cuthbert* (Surtees) 1047 He suld noght childres gammys su. **1470–85** MALORY *Arthur* XIII. xx. 641 The good man Ioyned syr launcelot..to sewe knyghthode. **1509** BARCLAY *Shyp of Folys* (1874) I. 19 Thus am I a foole and all that sewe that guyse. **1575** GASCOIGNE *Glasse of Government* Wks. 1910 II. 43 That they may shun the bad, & sew the best. **1590** SPENSER *F.Q.* II. ii. 17 Since errant armes to sew he first began. **1591** —— *M. Hubberd* 743 At other times he casts to sew the chace Of swift wilde beasts. **1799** WORDSW. *Two April Mornings* 29 With rod and line I sued the sport Which that sweet season gave.

†**9.** To prosecute, carry out (an action); to pursue (a subject); also, to follow up (an achievement). *Obs.*

1297 R. GLOUC. (Rolls) 10320, & to sywi þis mansinge, & þe asoylinge al so, We asigneþ þe bissop of winchestre þer to. **1393** LANGL. *P. Pl.* C. XXI. 361 Suynge my teme! *c* **1460** SIR R. ROS *La Belle Dame* 227 Though y sue so grete an entirprise. **1559** BALDWIN *Mirr. Mag., Salisbury* xxxvii, I, suing this so good successe, Layd siege to Orlyaunce. *c* **1565** in R. G. Marsden *Sel. Pleas Crt. Admir.* (1897) II. 56 They maye not macken and seyv there voyage. **1596** SPENSER *F.Q.* VI. x. 2 He meanes no more to sew His former quest.

†**10.** To take (legal action); to institute (a legal process); to plead (a cause). Phr. *to sue the law* (LAW *sb.*[1] 8). *Obs.*

c **1400** tr. *Secr. Secr., Gov. Lordsh.* 93 He..leuys faith, and suys þe lawe aȝeyn perfeccioun of lordshipe. **1449** *Rolls of Parlt.* V. 146/2 If the seid Tresorer and Vitaler..be remysse or negligent, and..will not effectuely sue such actions. **1460** *Cal. Anc. Rec. Dublin* (1889) 304 Ani maner of materys that may othyr oght be syewyt befor Mayr and Baylyffes. **1523** FITZHERB. *Husb.* §170 Though thou sue the lawe with charytie. **1538** STARKEY *England* (1878) 199 That ther be no cause sewyd out of the reame, except causys of scysme. **1572** HULOET (ed. Higins), Sue action of debte vpon a byll.

11. To institute a suit for, make a legal claim to; hence *gen.* to petition or appeal for; to seek to obtain. Now *rare* (superseded by *sue for*, 21 b).

1297 R. GLOUC. (Rolls) 1232 In is owe court he ssolde Ansuerie þat echman to him siwi wolde. **1390** GOWER *Conf.* I. 168 The more he lest of that he suieth, The mor me thenketh that I winne. **1426** LYDG. *De Guil. Pilgr.* 9285 Myn hertys ese for to swe, I wolde abyde (& nat remewe). **1446** in *3rd Rep. Hist. MSS. Comm.* 360/1 Your Aumener hath sieued [of the Pope] Provision of the Deanery of youre Church of Wellys. **1475** *Bk. Noblesse* (Roxb.) 41 A man shulde not be discouraged alway to sew his right. **1500** DAUS tr. *Sleidane's Comm.* 215 b, They both are wont to swe and crave hys frendship right busyly. **1695** PRIOR *Prol.* 21 Not that from this confession we would sue Praise undeserv'd. **1799** S. TURNER *Hist. Anglo-Sax.* II. vi. 287 He went with twelve soldiers to sue peace of the Welchman. **1824** SCOTT *St. Roman's* xvi, They had prevented him from suing an augmentation of stipend.

with clause. **1452** *Cal. Anc. Rec. Dublin* (1889) 277 No maner of men that dwellyth wythin the seid cite shuld not sywe that himselffe shoulde be in no queste of enditemet.

b. Const. inf. (occas. gerund): To petition to be allowed, (hence) to seek *to do* or *to be* something. *arch.*

c **1407** LYDG. *Reason & Sens.* 586 Yf he by vertu siwe kan To be lyke in condicion. **1509** FISHER *Funeral Serm. C'tess Richmond* Wks. (1878) 292 Many sued to haue had her to maryage. **1593** SHAKS. *3 Hen. VI*, III. ii. 61 What Loue, think'st thou, I sue so much to get? **1606** —— *Ant. & Cl.* I. iii. 33 When you sued steying, Then was the time for words. **1624** QUARLES *Job Milit.* Wks. (Grosart) II. 91/1 I'm turn'd a laughing-stock To boyes, and those that su'd to tend my Flock. **1630** *R. Johnson's Kingd. & Commw.* 328 The liberty to weare which [*sc.* arms] causes divers to sue to be souldiers. **1799** SHERIDAN *Pizarro* I. i, With weariless remonstrance he sued to win me from my purpose. **1821** JOANNA BAILLIE *Metr. Leg., Columbus* xlii, The ship's brave captain..kindly sued to set him free.

12. *spec.* To make application before a court for the grant of (a writ or other legal process): often with implication of further proceedings being taken upon the writ, etc.; hence, to put in suit, to enforce (a legal process).

a **1325** *MS. Rawl. B.* 520 fol. 52 b, Therfore ne be ileued þat te atachemens ne ben uersliche isiwede [orig. *qe les attachementz ne soient fetz freschement sur les felonies faites*]. *c* **1412** HOCCLEVE *De Reg. Princ.* 4097 Golde wolde, for false emprisonyng, a writ Sue agayn þe, if he at large were. **1503–4** *Act 19 Hen. VII*, c. 36 The same sir William suyde appele of mayme ayenst the seid sir Edward. **1507** *Cal. Anc. Rec. Dublin* (1889) 394 No maner persones..schall swe or cawse to be swyt anny writes of subpena. **1534** *Star Chamber Cases* (Selden Soc.) II. 309 Your said oratour sued assise in the comon lawe against the said mulso. **1613** SHAKS. *Hen. VIII*, III. ii. 341 Because all those things you haue done of late..Fall into th' compasse of a Premunire; That therefore such a Writ be sued against you. **1632** MASSINGER *City Madam* I. iii, *Sir John.* How much owes Penurie? *Goldwire.* Two hundred pounds: His Bond three times since forfeited. *Sir John.* Is it su'd? *Goldwire.* Yes Sir, and execution out against him. **1680** FILMER *Patriarcha* iii. §18. 140 If a Writ of Errour be sued in Parliament upon a Judgment given in the Kings Bench. **1817** SELWYN *Law Nisi Prius* (ed. 4) II. 858 A particular chattel, which the owner might be for ever deprived of, if he could not sue replevin. **1818** CRUISE *Digest* (ed. 2) I. 494 If a trustee has conveyed away the lands, by the direction of the *cestui que trust*, before execution sued, they cannot be taken in execution.

b. more freq. *to sue out*, †*forth.*

c **1412** HOCCLEVE *De Reg. Princ.* 1501 If a wyght haue any cause to sue To vs, som lordes man schal vndertake To sue it out. **1440** *Let.* in J. Stevenson *Lett. & P.* (Rolls) II. 306 The place in Corylonde..ys sesyde in to the cheffe lordes handes of the fee for defaute of claym of yow; the whiche youre frendes wolde have sewede ouȝt, yf theye hadde wyst ..that ye hadde been alyve. **1534** *Star Chamber Cases* (Selden Soc.) II. 214 Your saide subiect..hathe sewyd owte of your courte of Chanceryе your wrytez of Replegiare alios [= alias] and plures [= pluries]. **1572** GRINDAL *Injunct. Dean & Chapter York* in *Remains* (1843) 150 When extracts ..of testaments and obligations should be sued forth, oftentimes the same could not be found. **1573** in Feuillerat *Revels Q. Eliz.* (1908) 204 Bryan Dodmer for Botehier and charges in suyng owte the privie seale. **1596** BACON *Max. & Use Com. Law* I. (1630) 33 It putteth him to sue out his pardon of course. **1656** PRYNNE *2nd Pt. Short Demurrer Jews* 11 He sued forth Letters by way of Proces against him, both for the Debt and interest. **1691** *Act 3 Will. & Mary* c. 14 §5 Before any Action brought, or Process sued out against him [etc.]. **1714** *Lond. Gaz.* No. 5254/4 A Commission of Bankrupt Su'd forth by the said Anthony Soleirol. **1768** BLACKSTONE *Comm.* III. xviii. 273 To this end he is to sue out, or purchase by paying the stated fees an original or original writ, from the court of chancery. **1779** WARNER in Jesse *Selwyn & Contemp.* (1844) IV. 35 Mrs. Newgate is suing out her habeas. **1827** HALLAM *Const. Hist.* xiii. (1876) III. 14 A party detained without any warrant must sue out his habeas corpus at common law. **1875** POSTE *Gaius* III. 343 After a man's body was taken in execution, no other process could be sued out against his lands or his goods.

transf. and *fig.* **1577** HANMER *Anc. Eccl. Hist.* (1619) 376 He got him in all the haste to Constantinople, and sued out a commandement from the Lieutenant of that province for [etc.]. **1583** BABINGTON *Commandm.* (1590) 139 Let all flesh fall downe before His footstoole and sewe out pardon. **1852** SIR W. HAMILTON *Discuss.* (1853) 6 *note*, If these [words] did not already enjoy a prescriptive right, as denizens of the language.., they would be well entitled to sue out their naturalization.

c. *to sue, sue out, sue forth* (*one's*) *livery*: see LIVERY *sb.* 5 a.

13. To institute legal proceedings against (a person); to prosecute in a court of law; to bring a civil action against. In full, *to sue at* (†*at the*, †*in the*, †*to the*) *law.*

Prov. *sue a beggar and catch a louse*: see BEGGAR 1 c.

14.. *Customs of Malton* in *Surtees Misc.* (1890) 59 No Burgese, nor noo odyr man..schall sew one a nodyr bot alonely in yᵉ cowrtte of yᵉ Burgage. **1438** in Gross *Gild Merch.* (1890) II. 65 Non of them shall sew oþir at lawe. **1526** TINDALE *Matt.* v. 40 Yff eny man will sue the at the lawe. **1530** CROMWELL in Merriman *Life & Lett.* (1902) I. 329 He ys Swed in a primineri by burges. **1530** PALSGR. 716/2 Gyve me my monaye, or I wyll sewe the in the law. **1570** LEVINS *Manip.* 94/32 To Sew one to the lawe, *in ius vocare.* **1588** *Marprel. Epist.* (Arb.) 33 Sir (sayd they) shew vs your discharge, and wee are satisfied. No (quoth-he) I will shew you none, go sue me, go sue me. **1589** [? LYLY] *Pappe w. Hatchet* in *L.'s Wks.* (1902) III. 413 If thou sue me for a double maime, I care not though the Iurie allow thee treble damages. **1670** in *Verney Mem.* (1907) II. 296 My opinion is that he will not pay a peny till he is sued. **1711** ADDISON *Spect.* No. 122 ¶4 There is not one in the Town where he lives that he has not sued at a Quarter-Sessions. **1845** POLSON *Eng. Law* in *Encycl. Metrop.* II. 825/1 A partner cannot sue his co-partner at law in respect of anything connected with or involving the consideration of the partnership accounts. **1858** J. B. NORTON *Topics* 266 A timber merchant in Malabar sued the proprietress of a forest for non-delivery of certain logs of wood. **1882** G. SETON *Mem. A. Seton* ii. 35 Having been deprived of his stipend by the king, Bruce sued the Crown in the Court of Session, and obtained a decision in his favour.

†**b.** In collocation with other verbs expressing annoyance or persecution. *Obs.*

a **1500** in *Archaeologia* LIX. 9 Thomas Dyconson..hath of his grete malice trobolid, swed and arrested your said supplyant. **1538** in Leadam *Sel. Cases Star Chamber* (Selden Soc.) II. 64 Henry did wrongfully seu vex and trouble your saide subiecte. **1648** *Bury Wills* (Camden) 214 Such of my said two brothers as..shall..sewe, molest, and trouble mine executoʳˢ.

14. To petition, appeal to. *rare.*

c **1521** R. PACE in Ellis *Orig. Lett.* Ser. III. I. 277, I sywdde hys Grace to signe the Popis lettre. **1560** DAUS tr. *Sleidane's Comm.* 352 b, His sonnes obey him herein, and sending Ambassadours most earnestly and oft admonish and sue them [*monent atque citant*]. *a* **1674** CLARENDON *Surv. Leviath.* (1676) 88 To sue the Soveraign, and to demand the hearing of his Cause. **1813** BYRON *Giaour* 1194 Then will I sue thee to forgive.

15. To woo, court. Also *fig. arch.*

1596 SPENSER *F.Q.* VI. viii. 20, I was..sude and sought with all the seruice dew. *c* **1648–50** BRATHWAIT *Barnabees Jrnl.* IV. (1818) 153 Farewell Tank-hill, which I viewed, Lemnian Lydia, whom I sewed. **1764** GOLDSM. *Trav.* 173 No zephyr fondly sues the mountain's breast. **1830** TENNYSON *Mermaid* 43 They would sue me, and woo me, and flatter me. **1856** MISS MULOCK *John Halifax* xviii, For a penniless youth to sue a lady with a fortune.

II. Intransitive senses.

†**16.** To continue, proceed, go on. *Obs.*

c **1200** *Trin. Coll. Hom.* 85 Sume men leden erest iuel liflode, and turnen eft to god, and þeron seweð alse seinte poul. **1390** GOWER *Conf.* I. 131 Of Pride, which I schal eschuie, Now axeth forth, and I wol suie. *c* **1400** *Destr. Troy* 1475 Of his sonnes to say or I sew ferre, Ector was oldist & heire to hym seluyn.

†**17.** To follow after a person or thing in motion; to follow as an attendant or adherent; to go in chase or pursuit: freq. with *after*, *on*, *upon* preps. and advs. *Obs.*

c **1290** *Beket* 419 in *S. Eng. Leg.* 118 Þe Mannes frend þat was a-slawe siweden ope him so faste. **1297** R. GLOUC. (Rolls) 460 Hii þat miȝte ofscapie bigonne to fle vaste Hii of troye siwede wiþ oute eni feintise. **13..** *Coer de L.* 5040 He smot Favel with spores off golde, Sewe hym that sewe wolde. *c* **1330** *Arth. & Merl.* 9367 Arthour wald after sue. **13..** *E.E. Allit. P.* B. 87 Swyerez þat swyftly swyed on blonkez. *a* **1375** *Joseph Arim.* 668 Now þe kyng comes to sarras and mony on him suwen. *c* **1440** *Pallad. on Husb.* v. 173 Thiderward ek wol she fle; But sewe vppon. **1441** *Plumpton Corr.* (Camden) p. lx, [He] sewed with his said fellowship upon them & followed them unto the said towne of Helperby. *c* **1475** *Partenay* 137 The best for noyse A-forn the hundys ran, The houndes sewing after ful strongly. **1555** PHAER *Æneid* II. Ej, Euen among the middes he lept, with will to die, and wee Him after sued.

†**b.** To go along with or accompany something mentioned or implied. *Obs.*

c **1400** *Laud Troy-bk.* 8060 Erbe-de-bothe, & Cassidone, And euere among the dyamaund, Sewed wel with gode orfoyle-suand. **1418–20** J. PAGE *Siege Rouen* in *Archaeologia* XXI. 51 Hyt [*sc.* the ditch] was depe..Wyth a trenche suwynge on every syde. *c* **1420** *Liber Cocorum* (1862) 35 Rostyd..With neck and hede suande in fere.

†**18.** To proceed, move, go, esp. with speed; to sally *out*, *forth*. *Obs.*

c **1395** *Plowman's Tale* III. 928 The damoseles that to the daunce sewe. *c* **1400** *Destr. Troy* 687 Þen suet þai with solas into a sure chamber. *Ibid.* 820 He sues furth on þe soile to Chethes the kyng. *Ibid.* 11109 Yet sadly ho sete, sewit hym agayne. *c* **1471** *Pol. Poems* (Rolls) II. 279 Thay seuyd owte freshly, thay kepud none araye. *c* **1500** *Lancelot* 3145 The blak knycht, horsit, to the feld can sew.

†**19.** To do service or homage: chiefly in phr. *serve and sue* (cf. 4 b). *Obs.*

a **1300** *Leg. Rood* (1871) 52 [He] let hem cristny echon and siwy after his wille. *c* **1350** *Will. Palerne* 581 Þanne hadde þis menskful melior maydenes fele a-segned hire to serue & to seuwe hire a-boute. **1583** BABINGTON *Commandm.* (1590) 11 O how doo men..seeke it, sew and serve for it, their care both day and night is how to attaine the fastest to it. **1590** SPENSER *F.Q.* III. v. 47 What bootes thy seruice bace To her, to whom the heauens do serue and sew? *Ibid.* x. 9 He did her seruice dewtifull, and sewed At hand with humble pride.

†**20. a.** To follow in time or in a succession of persons. Nearly always in pr. pple. *Obs.*

13.. *Gaw. & Gr. Knt.* 501 Vche sesoun serlepes sued after oþer. **1382** WYCLIF *Luke* xx. 30 The firste took a wyf, and is deed, with outen sones; and the brother suwinge took hir. **1387** TREVISA *Higden* (Rolls) VII. 91 In the Satirday sewynge. **1390** GOWER *Conf.* III. 123 Octobre, which bringth the kalende Of wynter, that comth next suiende. *c* **1400** *Destr. Troy* 13658 When Idumius was ded..Two sones of hym-selfe suet hym after. *c* **1450** LOVELICH *Grail* lii. 971 Þat with-Inne two dayes Aftyr Sewynge he browhte hem Alle to Cristenynge. **1502** ARNOLDE *Chron.* (1811) 114 From the day of makyng herof vnto the feste of M. next suyng. *a* **1513** FABYAN *Chron.* VII. (1811) 488 Of Englysshe kynges here lyeth the beauteuous flour Of all before passyd, and mirrour to them shall sue. *a* **1642** GATAKER *Whitgift* in Fuller *Abel Rediv.* (1867) II. 197 Being an understanding man, he might shrewdly guess at those things that shortly after sued.

†**b.** To follow in the sequence of events, as a consequence or result; to ensue. *Obs.*

a **1225** *Ancr. R.* 208 Auh ȝif hit ne suweð [*v.r.* suheð] her, þe teil & þe attri ende is þe eche pine of helle. **13..** *Bonaventura's Medit.* 402 Þy pyne shal sone be ouerpaste, And ioye shal sewe euer for to last. *c* **1386** CHAUCER *Melib.* ¶463 The perils and yueles þat myghte sewe of vengeance takynge. *c* **1422** LYDG. *Serpent of Divison* (1911) 57 Þe habowndawnt schedynge of blod þat is likely to sewe. *c* **1450** *Pol. Poems* (Rolls) II. 226 Shame sewith sone, whenne syn gooth by-fore. *a* **1550** *Hye Way to Spittel Ho.* in Hazl. *E.P.P.* IV. 22 Wherby dooth sue suche inconuenyence, That they must ende in meschaunt indygence. **1563** *Mirr. Mag., Collingbourne* xxxix, Sith the gylty alwayes are suspicious, And dread the ruyne that must sewe by reason. **1567** GOLDING *Ovid's Met.* v. 58 There came a Dart a skew And lighted in his Coddes the place where present death doth sew. **1597** HALL *Sat.* I. Prol. 16 Infamy dispossest of native due Ordained of old on looser life to sue.

†**c.** To follow in an arrangement, in the sequence of a discourse, etc. *Obs.*

a **1325** *MS. Rawl. B.* 520 lf. 55 After þat hit sewe plenerliche in oþer stude biþinne [orig. *secundum quod inferius dicetur plenius*]. **1390** GOWER *Conf.* II. 340 Nou herkne a tale next suiende. *c* **1400** *26 Pol. Poems* 72 Skynes is oon, and sorw doþ sewe, Þe thridde hat 'deþ', and þe fierþe 'drede'. *c* **1400** *Pilgr. Sowle* (Caxton 1483) IV. xxxiii. 81 After this it seweth to speke of the brest. **1414** *Rolls of Parlt.* IV. 57/1 After the forme that sueth. **1482** *Ibid.* VI. 198/2 All severall summes of money hereafter suyng in writyng assigned. **1513** BRADSHAW *St. Werburge* I. ccxxxiv, Nexte in ordre suynge sette in goodly purtrayture, Was our blessed lady.

†**d.** To follow by logical reasoning. *Obs.*

1390 GOWER *Conf.* III. 236 Be weie of skile it suieth, The man is cause, hou so befalle. *c* **1400** *Pilgr. Sowle* (Caxton 1483) V. xiv. 108 Yf he were myghty, than myght he gette connyng, but he maye not gete it, why hit seweth that in hym is feblesse and grete vnmyght.

21. To make legal claim; to institute legal proceedings; to bring a suit.

a **1400** *Olde Vsages Winchestre* in *Eng. Gilds* (1870) 361 Ȝif he in þe fourty dayes comeþ in-to towne, and he wele sewy, be a-ȝen somened vp-on þe somaunce a-fore y-seyd. **1579** *Expos. Termes Lawes* 156 b, Playntife is hee that sueth or complayneth in an assyse or in an actyon personall. **1588** SHAKS. *L.L.L.* v. ii. 427 How can this be true, That you stand forfeit, being those that sue? **1613** PURCHAS *Pilgrimage* 211 Dayes, in which schoole masters may not beat their schollers, nor any man will sue at the law. **1783** BURKE *Rep. Aff. India* Wks. 1842 II. 71 The moment he attempts to sue, the money may be paid into the company's treasury. **1817** SELWYN *Law Nisi Prius* (ed. 4) II. 752 Infant executors may sue by attorney. **1898** J. MEWS *Digest Cases* 51 The person seeking to enforce it must prosecute for the criminal offence before he can sue in a civil action. **1911** WILSHERE *Elem. Crim. Law.* (ed. 2) 4 When a person sues in an action for libel or assault he does not sue on behalf of the public.

b. Const. *for* (†*upon*) that in respect of which a claim is made.

1393 LANGL. *P. Pl.* C. IV. 370 Þat is noȝt reisonable ne rect to refusy my syres sorname, Sitth y, his sone and seruaunt, suwe for his ryghte. *c* **1400** *Beryn* 2075 Þe blynd man wist..

he shuld have lost his while, To make his pleynt on Beryn, & suyd oppon his good. **1598** R. BERNARD tr. *Terence, Andria* IV. v, He is now at law for his inheritance. Hee sues for his patrimonie. **1651** HOBBES *Leviath.* II. xxi. 113 He hath the same Liberty to sue for his right. **1673** R. HEAD *Canting Acad.* 146 She sued for Alimony. *a* **1768** ERSKINE *Inst. Law Scot.* I. vi. §44 That first [husband] hath it in his power.. to sue for a divorce against her. **1856** FROUDE *Hist. Eng.* (1858) I. ii. 115 The Prince of Wales.. was under the age at which he could legally sue for such an object. **1858** LD. ST. LEONARDS *Handy-Bk. Prop. Law* xxii. 175 To sue for a debt. **1901** W. R. H. TROWBRIDGE *Lett. her Mother to Eliz.* xxii. 105 Connie Metcalfe is suing for breach of promise,—ten thousand pounds damages.

c. phr. ***to sue and be sued.***

1540 *Act 32 Hen. VIII*, c. 42 §1 Whiche company of Barbours be incorporated to sue and be sued by the name of Maistres.. of the.. commynaltie of the Barbours of London. **1712** PRIDEAUX *Direct. Ch.-wardens* (ed. 4) 78 They are a Corporation.. and can sue or be sued. **1844** *Act 7 & 8 Vict.* c. 113 §47 Every Company [of Bankers] of more than Six Persons.. shall have the same Powers and Privileges of suing and being sued in the Name of any one of the public Officers of such Copartnership. **1857** TOULMIN SMITH *Parish* 99 [The churchwardens] can sue and be sued, as a corporation, in respect to it.

d. In marine insurance policies (see quots.).

1622 MALYNES *Lex Merc.* xxv. 154 That in case of any misfortune, it is lawfull for him [*sc.* the assured].. to sue, labour and trauell for in and about the defence, safegard, or recouerie of the goods. **1787** DURNFORD & EAST *Rep. Cases* I. 612 There is.. in every policy a clause which enables the assured, in case of any loss or misfortune, to sue, labour, and travail, for the recovery of the goods, without prejudice to the insurance. **1899** R. G. MARSDEN *Digest Cases Shipping*, etc. 1268 Sue and Labour Clause.

22. To make one's petition or supplication *to* a person *for* a person or a thing; to plead, appeal, supplicate. (Also in indirect passive.)

c **1400** *Destr. Troy* 1854 All he grauntes to forgyue.. Iff ye send hom þat semly þat I sew fore. *c* **1412** HOCCLEVE *De Reg. Princ.* 1499 If a wyght haue any cause to sue To vs. *c* **1440** *York Myst.* xxix. 212 Gose nowe and suye to hym selfe for þe same thyng. *a* **1500** *Assemb. Ladies* 332 Be nat aferd; unto her lowly sew. **1526** *Pilgr. Perf.* (W. de W. 1531) 277 They be than constrayned to sue to god for succour & helpe. **1560** DAUS tr. *Sleidane's Comm.* 95 They have sued for peace in vayne. **1576** GASCOIGNE *Kenelworth Castle* Wks. 1910 II. 124 Bacchus shalbe sued unto for the first fruits of his Vineyards. **1593** SHAKS. *Rich. II*, I. i. 196 *King.* We were not borne to sue, but to command. **1598** —— *Merry W.* II. ii. 170 *Fal.* Good Master Broome, I desire more acquaintance of you. *Ford.* Good Sir Iohn, I sue for yours. *a* **1661** FULLER *Worthies, Norfolk* (1662) 250 Crouds of Clients sued to him for his counsel. **1667** MILTON *P.L.* I. 111 To bow and sue for grace With suppliant knee. **1762–71** H. WALPOLE *Vertue's Anecd. Paint.* (1786) III. 105 He sued in vain to the king for delivery. **1770** LANGHORNE *Plutarch* (1879) I. 118/2 He permitted all to sue for the consulship. **1808** WELLINGTON in Gurw. *Desp.* (1837) IV. 127 We ought not to be kept for ten days on our field of battle before the enemy (who sued on the day after the action) is brought to terms. **1862** GOULBURN *Pers. Relig.* I. xi. 175 A Liturgy.. necessarily secures exact agreement among the worshippers as to the things sued for. **1865** DICKENS *Mut. Fr.* III. iv, A blessing for which many of his superiors had sued and contended in vain. **1879** LUBBOCK *Addr. Pol. & Educ.* vii. 143 But what country would be compelled to sue for peace by the loss of its shipping?

†**b.** Const. inf. or clause denoting what is sought for. *Obs.*

c **1420** ? LYDG. *Assembly of Gods* 238 Yet shall he su to me to haue hys pese. **1513** *Life Hen. V.* (1911) 138 They labored and sewde vnto him to haue there olde priuiledges confirmed. *a* **1529** SKELTON *Bouge of Courte* 121 Of martchauntes a grete route Suwed to Fortune that she wold be theyre frynde. **1587** TURBERV. *Trag. Tales* 43 Haue you forgotten how you sude to him, to take a wife? **1604** SHAKS. *Oth.* III. iii. 79 'Tis as I should.. sue to you, to do a peculiar profit To your owne person. **1732** *Col. Rec. Penn.* III. 440 Divers other Nations have.. sued to them.. to come into Alliance with them.

c. *transf.* and *fig.*

c **1430** *Hymns Virgin* (1867) 20 In þi doom lete merci sue! **1592** SHAKS. *Ven. & Ad.* 356 Her eyes petitioners to his eyes suing. **1657** J. SMITH *Myst. Rhet.* 147, I perswade you not to let slip occasion, whilst it.. offers, nay sues to be taken. **1759** GOLDSM. *Bee* No. 2 ¶7 Her bosom.. rose suing, but in vain, to be pressed. **1859** MEREDITH *R. Feverel* xv, 'Pray let me', she pleaded, her sweet brows suing in wrinkles.

†**d.** To seek *after*. *Obs.*

1548 UDALL, etc. *Erasm. Par., Matt.* vi. 45 Which sueth after earthly thynges. **1553** GRIMALDE *Cicero's Offices* (1558) Pref., In case a man loue any one parte of himselfe to much: or sew after the end therof by a wrong way.

23. To be a suitor *to* a woman. *arch.*

1588 SHAKS. *L.L.L.* III. i. 191 What? I loue, I sue, I seeke a wife. **1591** —— *Two Gent.* II. i. 143 My Master sues to her: and she hath taught her Sutor, He being her Pupill, to become her Tutor. **1596** SPENSER *F.Q.* VI. xi. 5 Yet ceast he not to sew and all waies proue, By which he mote accomplish his request. *a* **1687** COTTON *Ode Love* iii, With judgment now I love and sue, And never yet perfection knew, Until I cast mine eyes on her. **1805** MRS. H. TIGHE *Psyche* I. vi, Low at her feet full many a prince had sued. **1826** WORDSW. '*Ere with cold beads of midnight dew*' 3, I grieved, fond Youth! that thou shouldst sue To haughty Geraldine.

sue: see SEE, SEW, SHOE *v.*, SOW.

sueable, variant of SUABLE.

Suebic ('swi:bɪk), *a.* [f. L. *Suēbus* + -IC. Cf. SUEVIC.] = SUEVIC *a.*

1907 H. M. CHADWICK *Orig. Engl. Nat.* vi. 137 There is no satisfactory evidence for the existence of Suebic tribes in north-west Germany.

suech, variant of SWESH *Sc.*, drum.

Sueco-Gothic, *a.* [Alteration of *Sueo-*, SUIOGOTHIC after mod.L. *Suecus* Swedish, *Suecia* Sweden.] Swedish.

1824 WATT *Bibl. Brit., Authors* II. 532 *x*, He [*sc.* Ihre] was the Author.. of an explanation of the old Catalogue of the Sueco-Gothic Kings.

sued (s(j)u:d), *ppl. a.* [f. SUE *v.* + -ED[1].] See SUE *v.* 13. ***sued-for***: see SUE *v.* 22.

1607 SHAKS. *Cor.* II. iii. 215 And now againe, of him that did not aske, but mock, Bestow your su'd-for Tongues? **1621** G. SANDYS *Ovid's Met.* VI. (1626) 115 The su'd-for Delia. **1647** STAPYLTON *Juvenal* VIII. 118 When.. thy su'd-for Province hath at length receiv'd thee. **1775** DE LOLME *Constit. Eng.* I. x, Concerning the arrests of sued persons.

suede (sweɪd, Fr. sɥɛd). Also **suède**. [a. F. (*gants de*) *Suède* (gloves of) Sweden.] **1.** Orig. in ***suede gloves***, gloves made of undressed kid-skin; hence *suede* is used for the material and the colour of it. Now also applied to other kinds of leather finished to resemble undressed kid-skin; also an article, usu. a shoe, made of suede.

1859 *Habits of Gd. Society* iv. 178 Soft gloves of the kind termed *gants de suède* [misprinted *gants de siècle*]. **1884** *Health Exhib. Catal.* 57 Kid and Suède gloves made in their manufactories at Paris, Grenoble and Brussels. **1888** *Daily News* 23 April 6/4 A girl in a well-made gown of pale suède silk, striped with openwork. **1894** *Ibid.* 22 Nov. 8/1 Now, suèdes and silk gloves are permitted, and in a couple of months are succeeded by French kid. **1923** [see SAND *sb.*[2] 1 i]. **1957** M. B. PICKEN *Fashion Dict.* 211/1 *Suede*.., leather, usually calf, finished by special process, with flesh side buffed on emery wheel to produce napped, velvety surface. **1968** V. CANNING *Melting Man* viii. 237 The only spare shoes were a pair of ginger suèdes. **1970** *Daily Tel.* 2 Mar. 14 Ankle-length, shiny, wet-look coats, suèdes and leathers were often trimmed with fur. **1975** C. CALASIBETTA *Fairchild's Dict. Fashion* 324/2 *Suede*, leather, usually lambskin, doeskin, or splits of cowhide.. that has been buffed on the flesh side to raise a slight nap. **1982** T. HEALD *Masterstroke* v. 103 A heavy dew underfoot.. soaked through Bognor's suedes, moistening his socks.

2. *attrib.* and *Comb.*, as ***suede-coloured***, ***-gloved***, ***-like***, adjs.; **suede brush**, a brush with which to brush suede; **suede cloth** = SUEDETTE; **suede-footed** *a.* = *suede-shoed* adj. below; **suedehead** *slang* (see quot. 1970); **suede shoe**, a shoe made with a suede upper; chiefly used *attrib.* to denote: (*a*) resemblance to the rough texture of suede; (*b*) *fig.*, something which displays a spurious smartness (*U.S. colloq.*); **suede-shoed** *a.*, wearing suede shoes.

1951 *Catal. of Exhibits, South Bank Exhib., Festival of Britain* 30/1 *Suede brush; Federation of British Rubber Manufacturers Association. **1967** 'K. O'HARA' *Unknown Man* ix. 81 A rubber suede-brush she used to buff the key-case. **1930** *Daily Express* 30 July 5/4 *Suede cloth, which made its real appearance in furnishing last year. **1979** *Arizona Daily Star* 5 Aug. J 5/2 (Advt.). Soft supple suedecloth is in several styles. **1897** *Daily News* 17 April 6/6 A visiting costume in *suède-coloured cashmere. **1938** J. W. DAY *Dog in Sport* iv. 64 It will take many generations of stupid women in Bayswater and *suède-footed young men in Kensington to ruin the character of this eminently sensible working dog. **1979** —— in *East Anglian Mag.* Aug. 531/2 None of your suede-footed, whey-faced, sniffling little intellectuals. **1981** J. JOHNSTON *Christmas Tree* 121 Her *suede-gloved hands clasped on her knee. **1970** *Time* 8 June 37 The skinheads are lineal descendants of the rockers—with an added touch of mindless savagery. When their hair grows a trifle longer, they refer to themselves as *suedeheads. Skins or suedes, they specialize in terrorising such menacing types as hippies and homosexuals, Pakistani immigrants and little old ladies. **1974** P. CAVE *Mama* (new ed.) iv. 25 The suedehead kids weren't expecting any 'bovver'. **1971** *Country Life* 28 Oct. 1107/1 When some browsing animal blunders against them bursting their [*sc.* the puffballs'] *suede-like skin. **1952** *News* (San Francisco) 27 Feb. 10/1 (*heading*) '*Suede-shoe boys' renew racket here. Homeowners warned on repair work. **1973** M. AMIS *Rachel Papers* 29 Chronic bronco was reserved for nicotined oldsters with suede-shoe lungs. **1979** *Tucson* (Arizona) *Citizen* 20 Sept. 1B/6 There are also a lot more 'pseudo-high rollers' in Phoenix, too, which is Mano's police description of a phony. 'Suede shoe types,' he calls them. **1980** D. MARLOWE *Rich Boy from Chicago* iv. 52 He edited the college magazine (pre-Beat poetry, suede-shoe satire). **1938** *New Statesman* 21 May 863/2 The abusive semi-illiterate or the sleek, shinily tailored, down-at-heel, *suède-shoed playboy, who hawks inferior goods on their doorstep.

sueded ('sweɪdɪd), *a.* [f. SUEDE + -ED[2].] Of leather: buffed on the flesh side to raise a slight nap. Also of fabrics, etc.: provided with a nap.

1956 *Gloss. Leather Terms* (*B.S.I.*) 5 A fine soft leather.. sueded on the flesh side. **1962** *L. L. Bean Catal.* Spring 12 Ladies' bush coat and pant.. styled from sueded cotton poplin. **1971** *Leader* (Durban) 7 May 5/5 (Advt.), Men's bri-nylon sueded warm winter shirts. **1976** *National Observer* (U.S.) 30 Oct. 9/3 (Advt.), Made of strong and supple full grain steerhide with the rough side out. Rich, sueded finish. **1978** *Textiles* (Manchester) VII. 46/2 Patterned and sueded fabrics.

suedette (sweɪ'dɛt). Also **suèdette**. [f. SUEDE – -ETTE.] A material designed to imitate the texture of suede, esp. a type of cotton or rayon fabric with a suede-like nap.

1915 *Chambers's Jrnl.* May 413/1 A cover of waterproofed suedette. **1930** *Daily Express* 30 July 4/5 To make a smart.. tea cosy, cut out four pieces of material.. in suede, velvet, or suedette. **1960** *Pract. Wireless* XXXVI. 350/2 The cabinet is finished in cream rexine with a royal blue suedette surround and a blue and gold scale. **1962** *Punch* 23 May 785/3 Massive Mums in tartan trews and suèdette jackets. **1963** *Punch* 10 July 54/2 Apple-green suedette wallpaper. **1971** *Sunday Times* 6 June 33 Swimming in suede is the new thing; swimming in cotton suedette the next best. **1977** *Cosmopolitan* Feb. 19/1 Wore brown suedette shoes with thin black suits and thick regional accents.

suein, obs. form of SWAIN.

sueing, obs. form of SEWIN[1], bull-trout.

1603 OWEN *Pembrokeshire* (1892) 117 Sueinges, Mullettes and botchers.

sueird, sueit, suelhu, suelle, suelt, suely, suemme: see SWORD, SWEAT, SWEET, SWALLOW, SWELL, SWELT, SWALLOW, SWIM.

suen, obs. form of SEWIN[1], bull-trout.

c **1640** J. SMYTH *Hund. Berkeley* (1885) 319 The salmon, wheat trout or suen.

suen, obs. f. SEE *v.*

suench, var. SWENCH.

suent, variant of SUANT *a.*

Sueogothic: see SUIOGOTHIC.

†'**suer**. *Obs.* [f. SUE *v.* + -ER[1].]

1. A pursuer.

1388 WYCLIF *Lam.* i. 6 The princes therof.. ȝeden forth withouten strengthe bifore the face of the suere.

2. A follower, disciple.

c **1380** WYCLIF *Sel. Wks.* III. 511 Jesus Crist and his apostilis and here beste seweres. *c* **1394** *P. Pl. Crede* 148 Crist.. saide to his sueres forsoþe on þis wise. **1395** PURVEY *Remonstr.* (1851) 47 Be ye my sueris as and I am the suere of Crist [cf. *1 Cor.* xi. 1].

3. One who follows (a course of action).

1382 WYCLIF *Titus* ii. 14 A peple acceptable to him silf, suere of good werkis. *a* **1420** *Wyclif's Bible, Ecclus.* xli. 8 *gloss*, The sones of synneris; that is, sueris of the fadris synnes. *c* **1510** BARCLAY *Mirr. Gd. Manners* (1570) A iij, That is the foure Vertues surnamed Cardinall,.. For them and their suers God doth alway commende.

4. One who sues or petitions; *esp.* a plaintiff.

1423 *Rolls of Parlt.* IV. 256/2 That the partie so founden in defaute, paie to the suer.. half as muche as the forfaiture amounteth too. **1461** *Cal. Anc. Rec. Dublin* (1889) 311 Halfe to the courte and half to the suere. **1495–6** *Plumpton Corr.* (Camden) 114 That no privie seal shold goe against no man, but if the suer therof wold find suerty to yeld the parties defendants ther damages. *a* **1565** RASTELL *Bew. M. Iewel* Pref. A ix b, If the Suer for it be *notus Pontifici*. **1593** [see SUBMISSIONER].

suer, obs. form of SURE *a.*, SWEAR.

suerd, suere, suerliche, etc., **suersby, suertie**, etc., **sueryar**: see SWORD, SWEAR, SWEER, SWIRE, SURELY, SURESBY, SURETY, SWEARER.

‖**suerte** ('swerte, su:'ɛəteɪ). [Sp., lit. 'chance, fate, luck': cf. SORT *sb.*[1]] An action or pass performed in bull-fighting; one of the three stages of a bull-fight; = TERCIO, TERTIO 2 a.

1838 *Q. Rev.* LXI. 418 'Suertes' or manners of killing the bull. **1893** CHAPMAN & BUCK *Wild Spain* v. 58 It is in this phase of the fight that we trace the origin of several of the *suertes* which are practised in the modern Corrida de Toros. **1910** *Encycl. Brit.* IV. 790 The fight is divided into three divisions (*suertes*). *Ibid.*, Then begins the *suerte de picar*, or division of lancing. **1932** R. CAMPBELL *Taurine Provence* 61 The estocada is the climax, to hasten.. which, all the other suertes (actions, passes, and feats) must be devoted. **1957** A. MACNAB *Bulls of Iberia* v. 53 The *banderilla* act is a 'decorative' *suerte* rather than one of 'punishment'. **1967** MCCORMICK & MASCAREÑAS *Compl. Aficionado* i. 24 'The suerte of the varas' means the picador's work.

Suess (su:s). The name of Hans E. *Suess* (b. 1909), Austrian-born U.S. chemist, used *attrib.* to designate certain phenomena in radio-carbon dating, as **Suess effect**, the reduction in the proportion of carbon 14 in the atmosphere and plant life during the twentieth century as a result of the increased burning of fossil fuels, which lack that isotope; **Suess wiggle**, each of a series of relatively short-term irregularities, of disputed existence and origin, in the calibration curve obtained by dendrochronology for radio-carbon dating.

1957 *Proc. R. Soc.* A. CCXLIII. 562 An accurate assessment of the Suess effect can yield valuable data on the carbon cycle. **1976** *Nature* 8 July 128/1 There have probably also been periods of irregular fluctuation spanning a few hundred years (the so-called Suess 'wiggles'). **1977** *Sci. Amer.* May 86/3 There is uncertainty in interpreting the present era of solar activity from carbon-14 evidence because of the Suess effect. **1979** *Nature* 5 July 48/1 (*heading*) Confirmation of the Suess wiggles: 3200–3700 BC.

suet ('s(j)u:ɪt). Forms: 4–5 **suette**, 4–8 **sewet** (4 **swhet(t**, 5 **sweth**, **swette**, **swet(e**, **svette**, 6 **suete**, **sewett(e**, **suyt**, **showitt**, 6–7 **shewet**, 7 **sueete**, **shuet**, **sewed**, **suit**, 8 **suett**), 4– **suet**. [App. a. AF. **suet*, **sewet*, f. *su(e*, *seu* = OF. *seu*, *sieu* (mod.F.

suif) = Pr. *ceu*, *seu*, *sef*, It. *sevo*, *sego*, Sp., Pg. *sebo*:—L. *sēbum* tallow, suet, grease.]

1. a. The solid fat round the loins and kidneys of certain animals, *esp.* that of the ox and sheep, which, chopped up, is used in cooking, and, when rendered down, forms tallow. (Occas. applied to the corresponding fat in the human body.)

1377 *Durham Acc. Rolls* (Surtees) 46 In iiij *li.* Swhet emp. in villa, viij *d.* **1398** TREVISA *Barth. De P.R.* XVI. xliv. (Bodl. MS.), Yren schal not ruste if it is ismered wiþ suette..of an herte. *a* **1400** in *Rel. Ant.* I. 53 Tak..fresch swyne grees or of a bare, and fresch sewet of a herte, and fresch talgh of a schepe. *c* **1430** *Two Cookery bks.* 41 Take Percely, & Swynys grece, or Sewet of a schepe. *c* **1440** *Promp. Parv.* 483/1 Swete, of flesche or fysche or oþer lyke (*P.* suet, *due sillabe*), *liquamen, sumen.* **1486** *Bk. St. Albans, Hunting* e viij, She beerith booth sewet and pure greece Yit wolde I mayster.. fayne witt more Where lyth the suet of the haare be hynde or befoore. **1562** TURNER *Herbal* II. 125 Bulles tallowe or gote buckes swet. **1563** in W. M. Williams *Ann. Founders' Co.* (1867) 63 Payde for viij pounds of Showitt & longe Marybones iij s. iiij d. **1615** R. COCKS *Diary* (Hakl. Soc.) I. 93 Cows shewet for shipps use for chirurgion. **1634** PEACHAM *Compl. Gent.* (ed. 2) xxi. 253 For your Maggots or Ientles they are fed with Sheepes shuet. **1675** HOBBES *Odyssey* (1677) 218 There are o' th' fire good puddings full of suit. **1712** ADDISON *Spect.* No. 317 ¶8 Too many Plumbs, and no Sewet. **1844** H. STEPHENS *Bk. Farm* II. 97 The kidney is extracted from the suet. **1855** *Ibid.* (ed. 2) II. 703/2 Mutton suet is used in the manufacture of common candles. **1889** J. M. DUNCAN *Clin. Lect. Dis. Wom.* xxx. (ed. 4) 244 Remote parametritis may affect the region of the psoas muscle or may affect the suet.

†**b.** *Hunting.* The fat of deer. *Obs.*

a **1400** *Parlt. 3 Ages* 83, I soughte owte my sewet and semblete it to gedre. **1576** TURBERV. *Venerie* lxxvii, I haue termed their [*sc.* bears'] fatte greace, and so is it to be called of all beastes which praye: and of all Deare and other fallow beasts, it is to be called Sewet. **1610** GUILLIM *Heraldry* III. xiv. (1660) 166. *a* **1700** B. E. *Dict. Cant. Crew, Sewet*, Deer's Grease.

2. *attrib.*, as ***suet-chopper***, ***dumpling***; **suet affection**, a diseased condition of the fat surrounding the kidneys; **suet-brained** *a.*, stupid; **suet crust**, a form of heavy pastry made with suet, esp. used for meat or fruit puddings; **suet face**, a face of a pale complexionless appearance; hence **suet-faced**; **suet-headed** *a.*, stupid; **suet pudding**, a pudding made of flour and suet and usually boiled in a cloth.

1889 J. M. DUNCAN *Clin. Lect. Dis. Wom.* xxx. (ed. 4) 244 Whether the *suet affection explains the frequent occurrence of albuminuria in parametritic cases, it is to be remembered as an important concomitant of the disease. **1921** *Public Opinion* 26 Aug. 199/2 Even among the most *suet-brained readers of the Morning Post there are some [etc.]. **1858** SIMMONDS *Dict. Trade*, **Suet-chopper*, a mincing knife for cutting up suet. **1845** E. ACTON *Mod. Cookery* xvi. 406 (*heading*) Common *suet-crust for pies. **1906** *Mrs. Beeton's Bk. Househ. Managem.* xxxi. 889 Suet crust..flour..suet..baking-powder..salt..water. **1951** *Good Housek. Home Encycl.* 671/1 Make 6–8 oz. suet-crust pastry. **1977** 'E. CRISPIN' *Glimpses of Moon* xii. 231 Mrs Clotworthy is making a steak-and-kidney pudding with a thick suet crust. *a* **1756** ELIZA HAYWOOD *New Present* (1771) 205 *Suet Dumplings. **1874** RUSKIN *Fors Clav.* xlviii. IV. 273 We will..have suet dumpling instead of pudding. **1897** RHOSCOMYL *White Rose Arno* 52 The chair of Gwgan Maddox was shadowed by the *suet face of the servant. **1922** JOYCE *Ulysses* 166 A pallid *suetfaced young man polished his tumbler knife fork and spoon with his napkin. **1937** E. POUND *Let.* 10 Mar. (1971) 291 Make it clear..that 200 words per subject is all that wildcat editing can get over on the *suet-headed Brits. *a* **1756** ELIZA HAYWOOD *New Present* (1771) 196 A *Suet Pudding, Take half a pound of fine beef suet, [etc.]. **1906** BEATRICE HARRADEN *Scholar's Dau.* xi. 213 Big suet pudding with treacle.

suet(e, obs. ff. SUIT, SWEET.

sueter, obs. f. SUITOR.

suetnes, obs. Sc. f. SWEETNESS.

suety ('s(j)uːɪtɪ), *a.* Also **-etty**. [f. SUET + -Y[1].]

1. Of the nature of suet.

1730 BAILEY (fol.), *Steatocele*, a preternatural Tumour in the Scrotum of a suety or Suet-like Consistence. **1739** SHARPE *Surg.* xxv. 125 If the Matter forming them resembles Milk-Curds, the tumour is call'd *Atheroma*;..if compos'd of Fat, or a suety Substance, *Steatoma.* **1802** *Med. Jrnl.* VIII. 564 That rare change of structure in the ovarium in which it is found to contain masses of suetty matter. **1871** SCOFFERN in *Belgravia* III. 442 The fat is hard or suety.

b. *fig.* Pale-faced.

1801 SOUTHEY *Lett.* (1856) I. 152 Do you remember the suetty, small-pox man at Gray's Inn?

2. Full of suet; made with suet.

1807 LAMB *Let. to J. Hume* 29 Dec., I always spell plumb-pudding with a *b*, p-l-u-m-*b*—I think it reads fatter and more suetty. **1897** *Daily News* 3 May 4/1 Great, round, soft, suetty puddings, pitted black with plums. **1903** FARMER & HENLEY *Slang, Suetty-Isaac*,..suet pudding.

Sueve (swiːv). [ad. L. *Suēvus*.] = SUEVIAN *sb.*

a **1901** W. BRIGHT *Age Fathers* (1903) II. xxxiii. 179 Vandals, Alans, and Sueves..had lately invaded the peninsula. **1911** T. S. HOLMES *Chr. Ch. Gaul* xi. 302 An enormous army of Vandals, Alans, and Sueves..crossed the Rhine.

sueven, variant of SWEVEN, dream.

Suevian ('swiːvɪən), *a.* and *sb.* [f. L. *Suēvus*, var. *Suēbus* (see SUEBIC) + -IAN. Cf. SWABIAN.]

A. *adj.* Of or belonging to a confederation of Germanic tribes called by the Romans *Suēvī* (*Suēbī*), which inhabited large territories in Central Europe to the east of the Rhine. **B.** *sb.* Any individual of these tribes.

1617 [see SLOVENLINESS]. *a* **1727** NEWTON *Observ. Dan.* I. v. (1733) 39 The Quades and Marcomans were Suevian nations; and they and the Suevians came originally from Bohemia. **1845** *Encycl. Metrop.* XI. 246/1 The mixed host of Vandals, Burgundians, Alans, and Suevians. **1889** J. B. BURY *Hist. Later Rom. Emp.* II. vi. I. 155 The Vandals abandoned their blockade of the Suevians.

So **'Suevic**, †**'Suevical** *adjs.*

1560 DAUS tr. *Sleidane's Comm.* 53 b, George Truckese, chiefe capitaine of the Suevical league. **1776** GIBBON *Decl. & Fall* x. I. (1782) 315 A king of the Marcomanni, a Suevic tribe. **1861** J. G. SHEPPARD *Fall Rome* iii. 129 The second great Suevic tribe, or federation of tribes, were the Alemanni. **1909** *Contemp. Rev.* Sept. 331 Visigothic Spain ..had absorbed the Suevic kingdom of Galicia.

suevite ('sweɪvaɪt). *Petrogr.* [ad. G. *suevit*, f. L. *Suēvia*, *Suēbia*, name of a region in W. Germany (see prec. and SWABIAN *a.* 1 a): see -ITE[1].] A type of welded braccia found associated with impact craters, similar to a tuff but showing signs of impact metamorphism; orig. such a rock from the Ries crater near Nördlingen in W. Germany.

1938 *Mineral. Abstr.* VII. 74 The tuffs (suevite) of the Nördlinger Ries are supposed to be rocks fused by the impact of the meteorite. **1970** *New Scientist* 23 July 174/3 The so-called 'suevite' rocks of the Ries are almost indentical to some of the surface samples from the fragmented lunar 'regolith'.

suey, sueyn, obs. ff. SWAY, SWAIN.

suey pow ('suːɪ paʊ). *U.S. slang.* Also **sueypow**, **sui pow**. [Orig. unknown.] (See quot. 1914.)

1914 JACKSON & HELLYER *Vocab. Criminal Slang* 82 *Suey pow, noun*, current amongst opium smokers. A sponge or rag used to cool and cleanse the face of an opium bowl. **1926** *Variety* 29 Dec. 7/4 The dopes and hop heads, with their 'stem',..'sui pow', [etc.]. **1939** [see *joy-pop* s.v. JOY *sb.* 10].

Suez ('suːɪz, 'suːəz). The name of an Egyptian port [Arab. *al-Suways*] at the head of the Red Sea, used *attrib.* and *absol.* to denote the military and political crisis which resulted from the nationalization of the Suez Canal in 1956; ***Suez group*** (now *Hist.*), a group of Conservative MPs who opposed the withdrawal of British troops from the Suez Canal Zone in 1954; hence applied to other groups advocating the presence of British troops in the Middle or Far East.

1955 *Ann. Reg. 1954* 34 Anglo-Egyptian talks have been recently renewed in Cairo..and the so-called 'Suez group' in the Conservative Party, about 40 in number and led by Captain Waterhouse, had consequently become restive. **1958** H. NICOLSON *Diary* 18 June (1968) 350, I am very worried about the Lebanon situation, fearing it may prove a repetition of Suez. **1961** *Guardian* 6 Dec. 18/1 Captain Charles Waterhouse, one of the original 'Suez rebels' in the winter of 1956–7. **1962** *Hansard Commons* 13 Nov. 281/1 The hon. Member for Leeds, East spoke of my hon. Friend the Member for Inverness as being a member of the Suez Group. **1966** *New Statesman* 3 June 804/1 The cabinet's Suez Group (Wilson, Healey, Stewart and Bottomley) are prepared to bring back a good many servicemen following the end of Confrontation but want to maintain the bases till the late 1970s. **1968** M. JONES *Survivor* iii. 55 She could not remember events like Suez and Hungary. **1972** R. R. JAMES *Ambitions & Realities* ii. 104 What became known as 'the Suez Group' constituted the first orgainzed element in the Conservative Party that viewed Heath with hostility. **1981** A. PRICE *Soldier no More* ix. 122 Ever since Suez the Americans had been bad friends with the Israelis.

†**suff.** *Obs.* Also 6–7 **suffe**, 7 **zuft** (?). [Of unascertained origin; the relation to *surf* is obscure.] The inrush (of the sea) towards the shore.

An early instance is perhaps to be found in *c* 1475 *Pict. Voc.* in Wr.-Wülcker 800/25 *Hec ledonis*, a sulse [? *read* suffe].

1599 HAKLUYT *Voy.* II. I. 227 The Suffe of the Sea setteth her lading dry on land. **1600** *Ibid.* III. 848 So neere the shore, that the counter-suffe of the sea would rebound against the shippes side. **1621** in Foster *Eng. Factories Ind.* (1906) 262 The suffe of the seaes caried us violently on the shoule. **1625** J. GLANVILLE *Voy. Cadiz* (Camden) 99 The workeing high goeing (or Zuft as they call it) of the Sea against the same shore. **1687** *Phil. Trans.* XVI. 496 After what manner they were to make their Descent, particularly in relation to the Suff of the Sea.

†**su'ffarcinate**, *v. Obs. rare*[−0]. [f. ppl. stem of late L. *suffarcīnāre*: see SUB- and FARCINATE.]

1656 BLOUNT *Glossogr.*, *Suffarcinate*, to truss or stuff up, to load or burthen.

†**suffa'rraneous**, *a. Obs. rare*[−0]. [f. L. **suffarrāneus*, a spurious word etymologized as f. *suf-* = SUB- + *far* grain, meal.] (See quots.)

1656 BLOUNT *Glossogr.*, *Suffarraneous*, that carrys meal or flower to any place to sell. **1658** PHILLIPS, *Suffarraneous* or *Subfarraneous*, being under another servant; it being an ancient custome among the Romans, that the chief servant took his portion of corn from the master, the under servant from him.

suffaryng, obs. form of SOVEREIGN.

Suffean, variant of SUFIAN.

suffeat, obs. form of SOFFIT.

1714 STEELE *Lover* No. 33 ¶2 The Oval is fastened to a great Suffeat adorned with Roses in Imitation of Copper.

suffeceant, obs. form of SUFFICIENT.

suffect (sə'fɛkt), *a.* (*sb.*) *Rom. Antiq.* [ad. L. *suffectus*, pa. pple. of *sufficĕre* to substitute (see SUFFICE).] Applied to the office of those additional consuls (or to the consuls themselves) who were elected, as under the Empire, during the official year. Also *sb.*, a consul suffect.

1862 MERIVALE *Rom. Emp.* lxvi. VII. 410 *note*, The innovation of the suffect consulship. **1883** *Athenæum* 3 Mar. 286/2 T. Sextius Africanus, a colleague of Ostorius Scapula in the suffect consulate A.D. 59. *a* **1908** C. BIGG *Orig. Christ.* (1909) xi. 122 Granianus and Fundanus had been consuls suffect. **1913** G. EDMUNDSON *Church in Rome* 252 The three suffects for 93 A.D.

†**su'ffect**, *v. Obs. rare*[−1]. [f. L. *suffect-*, pa. ppl. stem of *sufficĕre* (see prec.).] *trans.* To substitute.

1620 BP. HALL *Hon. Marr. Clergie* I. §24 When the question was of suffecting Amadeus Duke of Sauoy, a maried man, in the roome of Eugenius.

So †**su'ffection** [late L. *suffectio*], substitution.

1612 COTTA *Disc. Dang. Pract. Phys.* I. vi. 48 Where.. with a sufficient supply by others, the suffection or deputation may ease of a burden. **1671** [? R. MACWARD] *Case Accomod. Exam.* 78 The *Episcopus Praeses*, who when present is to preside, and when absent, doth, at best, only permit a precarious suffection.

Suffee, obs. form of SOPHY[1], SUFI.

1698 FRYER *Acc. E. India & P.* 108 *Mogul*, which is as much as *Suffet* in Arabic, from whence the Persian Emperor is called *Suffee*.

suffeit, obs. form of SOFFIT.

1774 *Oxford Jrnl.* 15 Jan. 3/2 The Diameter of the Arch is forty one feet nine inches and the suffeit twenty five feet six inches.

suffer ('sʌfə(r)), *v.* Forms: 3–4 **so-**, **suffri**, 3–5 **soffre**, 3–6 **sofre**, 3–7 **suffre**, 4–5 **suffere**, **-yr**, **soeffre**, 4–6 **soffur**, **-ir**, 4–7 **sufer**, 5–6 **sofer**, (3 **soffry**, 4 **soffer**, **-or**, **soffrie**, **suffire**, **sufre**, 5 **sufferne**, **sofyr**, **suffyre**, **-ur**, **souer**, 6 **syffyr**), 4– **suffer**. [a. AF. *suffrir*, *soeffrir*, *-er* = OF. *sof(f)rir*, mod.F. *souffrir*, corresp. to Pr. *suffrir*, *so-*, It. *sofferire*, Sp. *sufrir*, Pg. *sof(f)rer*:—pop. L. **sufferīre*, for *sufferre*, f. *suf-* = SUB- 26 + *ferre* to bear.]

I. To undergo, endure.

1. *trans.* To have (something painful, distressing, or injurious) inflicted or imposed upon one; to submit to with pain, distress, or grief.

a. pain, death, punishment, †judgement; hardship, disaster; grief, †sorrow, care.

a **1225** *Ancr. R.* 274 Þenc oðe attrie pinen Þet God suffrede oðe rode. *c* **1250** *Kent. Serm.* in *O.E. Misc.* 27 He..Þet diath solde suffri for man-ken. *a* **1300** *Cursor M.* 4050 Ioseph ..Þat was Þe chast and Þat gentil Þat siÞen sufferd sa fele peril. **13..** *E.E. Allit. P.* B. 718 Such domez, Þat Þe wykked & Þe worÞy schal on wrake suffer. *c* **1374** CHAUCER *Anel. & Arc.* 167 Þe helle Which sufferith faire Anelyda Þe Quene. **1390** GOWER *Conf.* I. 195 Of me no maner charge it is What sorwe I soffre. *Ibid.* III. 7, I..suffre such a Passion, That men have gret compassion. **1482** *Monk of Evesham* (Arb.) 67 The greuys peyne of that same stenche ys more intollerable ..than any other peynys that synners sofryn. **1526** TINDALE *2 Cor.* xi. 25, I suffered thryse shipwracke. **1560** DAUS tr. *Sleidane's Comm.* 74 b, He suffered the lyke punyshment. **1651** HOBBES *Leviath.* II. xxviii. 163 If a subject shall..deny the authority of the Representative of the Common-wealth, .. he may lawfully be made to suffer whatsoever the Representative will. **1676** *Charge in Offce of Clerk of Assize* 102 The offender shall suffer Imprisonment for a year. **1736** BUTLER *Anal.* I. ii. Wks. 1874 I. 35 All which we enjoy, and a great part of what we suffer, is put in our own power. **1875** JOWETT *Plato* (ed. 2) V. 166 Every one who does wrong is to suffer punishment by way of admonition. **1903** J. H. MATTHEWS *Mass & its Folklore* 113 The names of those Romans who had suffered martyrdom prior to the..final settlement of the Canon.

b. wrong, injury, loss, shame, disgrace.

c **1275** LAY. 24854 Ne solle hii in londe soffri none sconde. *a* **1300** *Cursor M.* 10394 Iesu crist..for vs sufferd gret despite. **1390** GOWER *Conf.* II. 381 Strong thing it is to soffre wrong, And suffre schame is more strong. *c* **1400** MAUNDEV. (Roxb.) Pref. 1 He sufferd many reprufes and scornes. *c* **1450** *Godstow Reg.* 176 For her expenses & harmys Þat they sofred by the occasyon of Þe seyde rent not I payde in Þe tyme I-sette. **1502** ARNOLDE *Chron.* (1811) 129 The most greuos sorous losses..that he hath suffred. **1640–1** *Kirkcudbr. War-Comm. Min. Bk.* (1855) 76 Besyde the disgrace that our nation sufferis throw thair goeing naked in a strange countrie. **1849** MACAULAY *Hist. Eng.* ii. I. 175 Men..whose minds had been exasperated by many injuries and insults suffered at the hands of the Roundheads. **1891** *Law Rep.*, *Weekly Notes* 79/2 The defendant contended that the plaintiff had suffered no loss. **1912** *Times* 19 Oct. 7/3 Montenegro..has suffered some eclipse of her first flush of enthusiasm.

c. bodily injury or discomfort, a blow, wound, disease. *arch.*

a **1300** *Cursor M.* 25490 Iesus, þat wald . . suffer . . Boffetes on þi soft chin. *c* **1330** *King of Tars* 57 Crist ur saveour, That soffrede woundes fyve. **13 . .** *E.E. Allit. P.* A. 554 We . . þat suffred han þe dayez hete. *a* **1425** tr. *Arderne's Treat. Fistula* etc. 1 The forsaid sir Adam . . suffrand fistulam in ano. *c* **1450** CAPGRAVE *Life St. Aug.* xxiv, þoo woundis whech þi son souered in his body. **1539** *Great Bible* Ps. xxxiv. 10 The lyons do lacke, and suffre hunger. **1576** FLEMING *Panopl. Epist.* 28 The woundes which I suffered long agoe. **1617** MORYSON *Itin.* III. 90 For feare that hee should suffer thirst. **1687** A. LOVELL tr. *Thevenot's Trav.* II. 26, I suffered much cold that Night, though I had on my Capot. **1819** SCOTT *Ivanhoe* xliv, Complaints in the bowels and stomach, suffered by himself and his monks.

2. To go or pass through, be subjected to, undergo, experience (now usually something evil or painful).

a **1300** *Cursor M.* 15563 Bot sal we elles suffre samen, bath soft and sare. **1362** LANGL. *P. Pl.* A. XI. 113 From hennes to soffre-Boþe-weole-and-wo. **1399** —— *Rich. Redeles* Prol. 36 Mekely to suffre what so him sente were. *c* **1420** ? LYDG. *Assembly of Gods* 1638 What may worse be suffryd than ouer mykyll weele? *a* **1500** *St. Margaret* 62 in *Brome Bk.* 109 How they syffyryd wyll and woo And how thye dede ther merty[r]dam take. **1530** RASTELL *Bk. Purgat.* I. v, Ease & pleasure doth comforte the nature of that thyng whych suffereth that ease and pleasure. **1598** SYLVESTER *Du Bartas* II. ii. II. Wks. (1641) 123/1 And, for each body acts, or suffers ought, Having made Nouns, his Verbs he also wrought. *a* **1656** STANLEY *Hist. Philos.* V. xi. (1701) 185/2 Whensoever they seem to effect any thing, we shall find that they suffer it long before. **1662** TUKE *Adv. 5 Hours* IV. i, W' had better suffer than deserve our fate. **1766** GOLDSM. *Vic. W.* xxiii, Here they suffered a siege. **1839** KEIGHTLEY *Hist. Eng.* II. 28 Three more . . suffered the same fate.

3. a. *intr.* To undergo or submit to pain, punishment, or death.

a **1300** *Cursor M.* 20280 He wel i suffer o na care. **13 . .** *E.E. Allit. P.* A. 940 þat is þe cyte þat þe lombe con fonde To soffer inne sor for manez sake. *c* **1380** WYCLIF *Serm.* Sel. Wks. I. 65 We shulden maken us redy to suffre in oure body for þe name of Crist. *a* **1400** *Minor Poems fr. Vernon MS.* 156 He feled neuere lisse ne lith, þerfore hym þouȝte beter legles þen so to suffre þer-wyþ. *c* **1450** tr. *De Imitatione* III. lxii. 144 Suffre paciently, if þou can not suffre ioingly. **1546** GARDINER *Declar. Joye* 38 S. Paule sayth, he suffreth for the electes that they myght be salued. **1548–9** (Mar.) *Bk. Com. Prayer, Catech,* Jesus Christ . . Whiche . . Suffered under Ponce Pilate, was crucified, dead, and buried. **1686** tr. *Chardin's Trav. Persia* 118 We suffer'd for no want of any thing. *a* **1721** PRIOR *Dial. Dead* (1907) 258 Every Man is obliged to suffer for what is right, as to oppose what is Unjust. **1772** W. WILLIAMS in *Bk. Praise* (1863) 244 In Thy Presence we can conquer, We can suffer, we can die. **1841** THACKERAY *Gt. Hoggarty Diam.* ix, Gracious Heavens! . . a lady of your rank to suffer in this way! **1848** —— *Van. Fair* xxviii, He suffered hugely on the voyage, during which the ladies were likewise prostrate. **1856** FROUDE *Hist. Eng.* (1858) II. vii. 227 It was a hard thing to suffer for an opinion; but there are times when opinions are as dangerous as acts. **1889** *Sat. Rev.* 9 Feb. 145/2 A brave man suffers in silence. **1905** C. G. HARTLEY *Weaver's Shuttle* 268 The child who moves restlessly when suffering.

b. *from* or (now rare) *under* a disease or ailment.

1800 *Med. Jrnl.* III. 422 She had suffered much from disease. **1836** DICKENS *Let.* 15 Nov. (1965) I. 195, I . . am still suffering under . . a head-ache. **1848** THACKERAY *Van. Fair* lv, It was only one of Mrs. Wenham's headaches which prevented us—she suffers under them a good deal. **1884** M. MACKENZIE *Dis. Throat & Nose* II. 176 He had suffered from delirium tremens. **1898** FL. MONTGOMERY *Tony* 10 She was suffering from what she was pleased to call a fit of depression.

4. To be the object of an action, be acted upon, be passive. Now *rare*.

c **1374** CHAUCER *Boeth.* V. met. iv. (1868) 167 Yif þe þriuyng soule . . ne doþ no þing by hys propre moeuynges, but suffriþ. **1548** VICARY *Anat.* ix. 79 So that eche of them [*sc.* man's and woman's seed in generation] worketh in other, and suffereth in other. **1587** GOLDING *De Mornay* x. (1592) 145 The Elements haue power and force to do, whereas matter hath abilitie but onely to suffer or to be wrought vpon. **1656** STANLEY *Hist. Philos.* V. vi. (1701) 161/2 These principles are called Elements, of which Air and Fire have a faculty to move and effect; the other parts, Water and Earth to suffer. **1667** MILTON *P.L.* I. 158 Fall'n Cherube, to be weak is miserable Doing or Suffering. **1818** STODDART *Gram.* in *Encycl. Metrop.* (1845) I. 5/1 In language, a verb is a word which signifies to do, or to suffer, as well as to be.

†**5.** *trans.* To submit patiently to. *Obs.*

1297 R. GLOUC. (Rolls) 7281 Some . . sofrede as hii noȝt ne miȝte al þe oþeres wille. **1382** WYCLIF *1 Pet.* ii. 19 If . . ony man suffrith [Vulgate *sustinet*] sorewes, or heuynesses, suffringe [*patiens*] vniustly. **1390** GOWER *Conf.* III. 71 Wher as sche soffreth al his wille, As sche which wende noght misdo. *c* **1400** *Cursor M.* 29103 (Cott. Galba) To luke if þai in gude life lend, And suffers what he will þam send.

†**6.** *intr.* To endure, hold out, wait patiently. (Often with *abide, bide.*) ***to suffer long***: to be long-suffering. *Obs.*

1362 LANGL. *P. Pl.* A. IV. 18 Sette my Sadel vppon Soffre-til-I-seo-my-tyme. *c* **1375** *Sc. Leg. Saints* xvi. (*Magdalena*) 19 þou bidis & sufferis, til þat we thru repentance wil turne to þe. *c* **1380** *Sir Ferumb.* 808 Firumbras was hard, & suffrede wel, þoȝ hit him greuede sare. *a* **1400** *Minor Poems fr. Vernon MS.* 731 Of alle þe vertues þat þer beone, To suffre, hit is a þing of prys. *c* **1450** *Merlin* 165 Marganors . . badde hem suffre and a-bide, while thei myght, for to socour theire peple. **1523** LD. BERNERS *Froiss.* I. clxxii. 209 He was sore displeased therwith, and suffred tyll he herde howe they were put to their raunsome. **1526** TINDALE *1 Cor.* xiii. 4 Love suffreth longe, and is corteous. **1535** COVERDALE *Ecclus.* ii. 4 Suffre in heuynesse, and be pacient in thy trouble. **1563** B. GOOGE *Eglogs* viii. (Arb.) 65 God . . suffers long, reuengyng slow.

†**7.** *trans.* To resist the weight, stress, or painfulness of; to endure, bear, stand. *Obs.* exc. *dial.*

1387 TREVISA *Higden* (Rolls) I. 217 Whan þei myȝte nouȝt in þe holy day suffre on hire piliouns and here cappes for hete. **1388** WYCLIF *Exod.* xviii. 18 The werk is aboue thi strengthis, thou aloone maist not suffre it. **1481** CAXTON *Godfrey* viii. 29 That they shold charge them with suche tributes that they myght not suffre. **1551** T. WILSON *Logic* (1580) 51 Children can suffer muche colde. **1592** WEST *1st Pt. Symbol.* § 102 b, Any such corrasiue . . medicine . . as the said H. shal think his nature is vnable to suffer or abide. **1634** SIR T. HERBERT *Trav.* 146 Some [Persians] . . can suffer short wide stockings of English cloth or Kersies. **1640** T. BRUGIS *Marrow of Physicke* II. 140 Let the pan be no hotter than you can suffer your hand on it. **1673** RAY *Journ. Low C.* 70 These Waters [*sc.* Baths of Aken] . . are very easie to suffer. **1684** *Contempl. State of Man* II. vii. (1699) 202 If one cannot tell how to suffer the Tooth-ach, Head-ach, or the Pain of the Chollick.

absol. **1615** MARKHAM *Eng. Housew.* II. i. (1668) 15 Drink thereof morning and evening as hot as you can suffer.

8. To be affected by, subjected to, undergo (an operation or process, *esp.* of change). Now only as *transf.* of 1.

a **1425** tr. *Arderne's Treat. Fistula*, etc. 31 If it be nede for to chaufe it more for þe terebentyne, loke þat it suffre noȝt mych hete. *Ibid.* 80 þe membrez . . may noȝt withstande to þe strength of þe vitriol; and so þai suffre liquefaccion of it. **1610** SHAKS. *Temp.* I. ii. 400 Nothing of him that doth fade, But doth suffer a Sea-change Into something rich, & strange. **1659** PEARSON *Creed* (1839) 361 He suffered a true and proper dissolution at his death. **1678** G. MACKENZIE *Crim. Laws Scot.* I. vi. § 19. 51 Their goods should be put under sicker Burrows, . . under which they must remain ay and while they suffer an Assize. **1756** C. LUCAS *Ess. Waters* I. 80 Bodies void of aqueous humidity can neither suffer fermentation nor putrefaction. **1787** JEFFERSON *Writ.* (1859) II. 89 The conveyance of the treaty itself is suffering a delay here at present. **1793** BURKE *Corr.* (1844) IV. 158 The very language of France has suffered considerable alterations since you were conversant in French books. **1816** SINGER *Hist. Cards* 33 Bullet allows this explanation to be very plausible, but says it suffers some very material difficulties. **1831** BREWSTER *Optics* i. 12 Let rays AM, AD, AN, . . fall upon the mirror at the points M, D, and N, and suffer reflexion at these points. **1860** TYNDALL *Glac.* II. xvii. 319 Along these lines the marginal ice suffers the greatest strain. **1877** HUXLEY *Physiogr.* xix. 318 The figure of the ship suffers a change.

9. a. *intr.* To undergo the extreme penalty; to be put to death, be executed. Now *rare* in literary use exc. of martyrdom.

1570 FOXE *A. & M.* (ed. 2) III. 1972/2 *marg.*, The chief dispatcher of al Gods Sainctes that suffered in Q. Maries time. **1581** ALLEN *Apologie* 87 b, England can not lacke Albans, whose Protomartyr being of that name . . suffered . . to saue his Christian guest. [**1638** NABBES *Covent Garden* IV. iii. in Bullen *O.P.* N.S. I. 73 The Gentlewomen will not see us hang'd. But they may suffer us, and that's a word for hanging.] **1652** LAMONT *Diary* (Maitland Club) 46 He was . . sent to Stirling . . wher he was appointed to suffer, and was executed there. *a* **1700** EVELYN *Diary* 13 June 1649 Sir John Owen, newly freed from sentence of death among the Lords that suffer'd. **1752** *Miss Blandy's Own Acc.* 65 Miss Blandy suffered in a black Bombazine short Sack and Petticoat, with a clean white Handerchief drawn over her Face. **1818** SCOTT *Br. Lamm.* xix, She is a witch, that should have been burned with them that suffered at Haddington. **1828** P. CUNNINGHAM *N.S. Wales* (ed. 3) II. 279, 'I have received a letter since, acquainting me that he has suffered.' 'Suffered! . . dear me, what has he suffered?' 'He has been hanged, sir.' **1861** BROUGHAM *Brit. Const.* xv. 238 Several of his adversaries were condemned to death, and suffered accordingly. **1877** J. MORRIS *Troubles Cath. Forefathers* Ser. III. 38 *note*, Edward Transham or Stransham, . . suffered at Tyburn.

†**b.** To be killed or destroyed. *Obs.*

1605 SHAKS. *Macb.* III. ii. 16 But let the frame of things dis-ioynt, Both the Worlds suffer. **1610** —— *Temp.* II. ii. 39 This is no fish, but an Islander, that hath lately suffered by a Thunderbolt.

10. To sustain injury, damage, or loss; to be injured or impaired. Const. *from, under*.

c **1600** SHAKS. *Sonn.* cxxiv, It suffers not in smilinge pomp, nor falls Vnder the blow of thralled discontent. **1601** —— *Twel. N.* II. v. 144 *Mal. M.* But then there is no consonancy in the sequell that suffers vnder probation: *A.* should follow, but *O.* does. **1697** H. WANLEY in *Bodl. Q. Rec.* (1915) Jan. 107 In the Library, many such [*sc.* books of Prints] haue suffered extreamly. **1756** C. LUCAS *Ess. Waters* I. 156 The teeth suffer in mastication or chewing the aliments. **1796** CHARLOTTE SMITH *Marchmont* IV. 222 Suffering from the fatal law entanglements of his father. **1815** SCOTT *Guy M.* xl, How must he in the meantime be suffering in her opinion? **1841** THACKERAY *Shrove Tuesday in Paris* Wks. 1900 XIII. 569 Debt is a staple joke to our young men, 'Who suffers for your coat?' is, or used to be, a cant phrase. **1870** F. R. WILSON *Ch. Lindisf.* 68 The edifice suffered in the civil wars under Cromwell. **1894** P. FITZGERALD in *Daily News* 26 Sept. 6/4 It [*sc.* the Cathedral] has not suffered—the correct phrase—from the restorers. **1915** *Times* 26 April 10/3 Other Army Corps suffered even more severely.

11. *causative.* To inflict pain upon. *Obs.* exc. *dial.*

c **1500** *Lancelot* 1368 Yow sufferith them, oppressith & anoyith. **1593** SHAKS. *2 Hen. VI*, V. i. 153 A hot ore-weening Curre, . . Who being suffer'd with the Beares fell paw, Hath clapt his taile, betweene his legges. **1893** *Wiltshire Gloss.*, *Suffer*, to punish, to make suffer. 'I'll suffer you, you young rascal!'

II. To tolerate, allow.

12. *trans.* To endure the existence, presence, or activity of (a person); to bear with, put up with, tolerate. Now *rare* and *arch.*

a **1300** *Cursor M.* 14749 Ferli thinc vs Quarfor þat we þe suffer þus, Quatkin thing can þou sai to Do, quar-for we suld þe bu? **1340** *Ayenb.* 38 þe kueade domesmen þet hise soffreþ. *c* **1380** WYCLIF *Sel. Wks.* III. 178 A man schulde suffur anoþur, and muche more a prelate schulde wisely suffur hys sugettis. *a* **1400** *Minor Poems fr. Vernon MS.* 494 Hou þat he suffreþ þe and me Wiþ miht al þat he may. **1470–85** MALORY *Arthur* VII. xi. 229 Euer curtoisly ye haue suffred me. **1487** *Cely Papers* (Camden) 166 The Comyns wyll nott suffur hym. **1535** COVERDALE *Judg.* ii. 23 Thus the Lorde suffred all these nacions. *c* **1585** [R. Browne] *Answ. Cartwright* 73 They are to bee suffered as brethren in the churche. **1712** STEELE *Spect.* No. 438 ¶4 How pityful is the Condition of being only suffered? **1848** THACKERAY *Van. Fair* xxxviii, He suffered his grandmother with a good-humoured indifference. **1872** HOWELLS *Wedd. Journ.* 99 They are suffering and perpetuating him.

13. a. To allow (a thing) to be done, exist, or take place; to allow to go on without interference or objection, put up with, tolerate. *arch.* or *dial.*

c **1290** *Beket* 1601 in *S. Eng. Leg.* 152 I-nelle none costomes soffri . . þat aȝein sothnesse beoth. *c* **1350** *Will. Palerne* 3337 Men, for youre manchipe na more þat suffreþ. **1377** LANGL. *P. Pl.* B. II. 174 Erchdekenes and officiales . . Lat sadel hem with siluer owre synne to suffre. *c* **1385** CHAUCER *L.G.W.* 1846 *Lucrece*, That nolde she suffre by no wey. *c* **1400** *Destr. Troy* 5081 It falles to a fole his foly to shew, And a wise man witterly his wordes to suffer. *c* **1430** LYDG. *Min. Poems* (Percy Soc.) 67 Suffre at thy table no distractioun. **1523** FITZHERB. *Husb.* § 20 The sede [*sc.* of Cockole] is rounde and blacke, and maye well be suffred in a breade-corne. **1584** LODGE *Alarm agst. Usurers* 15 Our lawes . . although they suffer a commoditie, yet confirme not they taking. **1592** SHAKS. *3 Hen. VI*, VI. viii. 8 A little fire is quickly trodden out, Which being suffer'd, Riuers cannot quench. **1604** E. G[RIMSTONE] TR. *D'Acosta's Hist. Indies* III. iv. 128 The Easterly winds raine continually, not suffering their contraries. **1660** JER. TAYLOR *Worthy Commun.* ii. § 2. 124 We suffer religion, and endure the laws of God but we love them not. **1716** LADY M. W. MONTAGU *Lett.* I. vi. 19, I have . . here . . had the permission of touching the relics, which was never suffered in places where I was not known. **1806** GOUV. MORRIS in Sparks *Life & Writ.* (1832) III. 229 France will no longer suffer the existing government. **1894** HALL CAINE *Manxman* VI. xiii. 405 They wouldn't have me tell thee before because of thy body's weakness, but now they suffer it.

†**b.** To allow to remain; to leave. *Obs. rare.*

c **1450** *Merlin* 104 Syr, we pray yow that the swerde be suffred yet in the ston to Passh. **1584** COGAN *Haven Health* (1636) 101 A rosted apple, suffered untill it were cold, and then eaten last at night . . hath loosed the belly.

†**c.** To admit of. *Obs. rare.*

a **1300** *Cursor M.* 13037 Sco wist þat rightwis was his sau, Moght noght suffer na gain-sau. **1793** BURKE *Corr.* (1844) IV. 199 It is not permitted to Sir Gilbert Elliot to be an ordinary man; neither his nature nor the times will suffer it.

14. Const. *acc.* and *inf.* (†*pple., compl. phr.*) or *clause*: To allow or permit a person, animal, or inanimate thing to be or to do so-and-so.

a. a person or animal.

with acc. and inf. c **1290** *Beket* 1283 in *S. Eng. Leg.* 143 þat o Man ne beoi-soffred to gon forth mid is wille. *c* **1386** CHAUCER *Knt.'s T.* 87 He . . wol nat suffren hem . . Neither to been yburyed nor ybrent. **1453** *Cal. Anc. Rec. Dublin* (1889) 279 The suynerd of the towne shulde not suffre the swyne to cum into the strone. *a* **1466** GREGORY *Chron.* in *Hist. Coll. Cit. Lond.* (Camden) 146 They of the sayde markett shalle nought ressayvyn nor sufferne to entre, any preson . . in to the sayde markett. **1486** *Bk. St. Albans* f v b, Who that . . suffrith hys wyfe to seche mony halowys. **1540–1** ELYOT *Image Gov.* (1549) 50 In offices he seldome suffred to be any deputies. **1583** STOCKER *Civ. Warres Lowe C.* III. 99 [They] woulde not suffer the persons aforesayde come in. **1658** EARL MONM. tr. *Paruta's Wars Cyprus* 121 He conjured them, not to suffer the victorious army incur any shame. *c* **1665** MRS. HUTCHINSON *Mem. Col. Hutchinson* (1846) 28 Greatness of courage would not suffer him to put on a vizor. **1760–2** GOLDSM. *Cit. W.* cxix, I was not suffered to stir far from the house, for fear I should run away. **1813** MISS MITFORD in L'Estrange *Life* (1870) I. vii. 245 Maria fell into a sort of hysteric of fright . . and anger because she was not suffered to wear a diamond necklace. **1833** HT. MARTINEAU *Vanderput & S.* vi. 91 He has suffered the storks to build on the summer house. **1898** BESANT *Orange Girl* II. ix, Her sins lie upon the head of those who suffer her . . to grow up without religion.

with acc. and pple. a **1400** *Minor Poems fr. Vernon MS.* 494 What mon wolde now suffre so His sone I-slayen. **1560** DAUS tr. *Sleidane's Comm.* 5 Neyther would Duke Frederick . . unlesse he judged him to be an honest man, suffer him so long unpunyshed. **1562** WINȜET *Cert. Tractates* Wks. (S.T.S.) I. 110 To suffir an harlot in his wyfes tyme lyand with an wthir harlot? **1606** CHAPMAN *M. D'Olive* II, What meanes your Grace to suffer me abus'd thus?

with acc. and compl. phr. **1593** SHAKS. *2 Hen. VI*, III. ii. 262 It were but necessarie you were wak't, Least being suffer'd in that harmefull slumber, The mortall Worme might make the sleepe eternall. **1624** CAPT. J. SMITH *Virginia* V. 179 Master More . . by no meanes would admit of any diuision, nor suffer his men from finishing their fortifications. **1705** tr. *Bosman's Guinea* 336 He is obliged to suffer the King of Popo in quiet Possession of his Island.

with clause. **13 . .** R. GLOUC. 1794 (MS. B), þe kyng hym wolde ȝeue lyf, ac ys men nolde noȝt, Ne suffre, þat þer were o liue eny of here fon. **1340–70** *Alex. & Dind.* 1056 Suffre ȝe nolle þat we by-wepe in þis word ȝour wikkede dedus. *c* **1386** CHAUCER *Sompn. Prol.* 7, I yow biseke, that of youre curteisye, . . As suffereth me I may my tale telle. *c* **1400** MAUNDEV. (1839) xxiii. 252 And therfore thei suffren, that folk of alle Lawes may peysibely duellen amonges hem. **1457** HARDING *Chron.* Proem xiv. in *Eng. Hist. Rev.* (1912) Oct. 743 But so was sette your noble chaunceller, He wolde nought suffre I had such waryson. **1611** *Bible* Judges xvi. 26 Suffer mee, that I may feele the pillars whereupon the house standeth. **1720** OZELL *Vertot's Rom. Rep.* II. xiv. 320 He ought not to suffer that one of his Fathers Assassins should enjoy the Fruit of his crime.

b. an inanimate or immaterial thing.

with acc. and inf. *a* **1300** *Cursor M.* 19809 To suffer þar na wrang be don. *c* **1400** MAUNDEV. (Roxb.) Pref. 2 His precious blude, þe whilk he sufferd be schedd for vs. **1481** *Cov. Leet Bk.* 475 Nor..suffryng eny thyng to be commytted..wherby the seid trewes..myght fall in vyolacion. *a* **1548** HALL *Chron., Edw. IV*, 57 b, To suffer the sayde mencioned mariage, to take effect. **1622** S. WARD *Christ All in All* (1627) 31 He would neuer suffer any part of the repute or honour of any his acts or labours, rest vpon his owne head. *a* **1700** EVELYN *Diary* 2 Nov. 1644 A sea of thick cloudes..every now and then suffering the top of some other mountaine to peepe through. **1774** BURKE *Corr.* (1844) I. 502 If..we should suffer any thing to be lost..by our remissness. **1827** SCOTT *Highl. Widow* v, She suffered his complaints..to die away without returning any answer. **1849** MACAULAY *Hist. Eng.* vi. II. 120 The answer was so unpleasing to James that he did not suffer it to be printed in the Gazette. **1871** B. STEWART *Heat* (ed. 2) §115 The acid will retain the water and will not suffer it to evaporate.

with acc. and pple. *a* **1325** *MS. Rawl. B. 520* lf. 31 b, Hoe ..wollez bluþeloker suffren felonies idone to straunge passen biþoute peine þane aditi þe felons. **1563** *Homilies* II. *Agst. Peril Idol.* I, Joas, and other Princes whiche eyther sette vp, or suffred suche aultars of Images vndestroyed. **1589** COOPER *Admon.* 217 They..striue against God.., who wil not suffer it unpunished. **1592** KYD *Sp. Trag.* III. xiii. 3, I, heauen will be reuenged of euery ill; Nor will they suffer murder vnrepaide. **1615** CHAPMAN *Odyss.* XIV. 133 These men..will never suffer left Their vniust wooing of his wife.

with acc. and compl. phr. *c* **1375** *Cursor M.* 22620 (Fairf.) Quy þi wrecched hande-werk in wa in þis fire þou suffris squa. *c* **1380** WYCLIF *Sel. Wks.* III. 344 þis lif is ful of sorowe..þat suffriþ not blis wiþ it. **1390** GOWER *Conf.* I. 361 The faucon which..soeffreth nothing in the weie, Wherof that he mai take his preie. **1477** EARL RIVERS (Caxton) *Dictes* 21 b, He that wol not suffre the stenche of my careyn aboue the erthe. **1525** LD. BERNERS *Froiss.* II. lxxx. 242 Nowe we wyll suffre in rest a season the armye of Castell.

15. To allow oneself, submit *to be* treated in a certain way; to endure, consent *to be* or *to do* something.

a. *refl. arch.*

a **1300** *Cursor M.* 17239, I sufferd me for þe be slain. *c* **1450** *Mirour Saluacioun* (Roxb.) 72 Sampson soeffred hym self be bonden. **1526** TINDALE *1 Cor.* vi. 7 Why rather suffre ye not youre selves to be robbed? **1671** WOODHEAD *St. Teresa* II. xi. 92 Love beginning to afford them sensible consolations, they too much suffer themselves to be carried away therewith. **1743** BULKELEY & CUMMINS *Voy. S. Seas* 197 This is a Place that a Man is oblig'd sometimes to suffer himself to be used ill. **1837** LOCKHART *Scott* iv. (1871) 174 Brown Adam [*sc.* Scott's horse] never suffered himself to be backed but by his master. **1877** in Bryce *Amer. Commw.* (1888) li. II. 285 Considerable proportions of them in their devotion to politics suffer themselves to be driven from the walks of regular industry.

†**b.** *intr. Obs.*

c **1315** SHOREHAM I. 780 He soffreþ noȝt to be to-trede, And of bestes deuoured. *a* **1325** *MS. Rawl. B. 520* lf. 32 b, Ȝif a nellez noȝt suffri to ben resteid. **1474** CAXTON *Chesse* I. i. (1883) 9 He might not suffre to be repreuid and taught of hym. **1500–20** DUNBAR *Poems* lxxii. 94 Thus Jesus with his woundis wyde, As martir suffrit for to de. **1538** STARKEY *England* (1878) 178 Our cuntrey, wych wyl not suffur to be so ornat and so beutyful, in euery degre, as other cuntreys be. **1632** SIR T. HAWKINS tr. *Mathieu's Unhappy Prosp.* 80 He..endured contradiction, and sometime suffered to be cut off in his opinions. *a* **1665** SIR K. DIGBY *Priv. Mem.* (1827) 278 As long as I can march at ease by myself, I will never suffer to be carried away from myself by the throng. **1764** GOLDSM. *Hist. Eng. in Lett.* (1771) II. 308, I must not suffer to have the laws broken before my face.

16. *trans.* (by ellipsis of *inf.*) To permit or allow (a person) to do a certain thing; †to let alone. Also occas. *absol. arch.*

1387 TREVISA *Higden* (Rolls) VII. 187 So hadde Alfrede my broþer helped me, if Godwyn had i-suffred [**1432–50** hade suffrede hym]. **1477** EARL RIVERS (Caxton) *Dictes* I As fer as myn fraylnes wold suffre me. **1523** FITZHERB. *Husb.* §39 Let them [*sc.* lambs] sucke as longe as the dammes wyll suffre theym. **1530** PALSGR. 742/2 Let us suffer hym and se what he wolde do. **1590** GREENE *Orl. Fur.* Wks. (Grosart) XIII. 135, I wish thee well, Orlando; get thee gone, Say that a centynell did suffer thee. **1604** DEKKER *King's Entert.* 277 Even children (might they have been suffred) would gladly have spent their little strength. **1663** WOOD *Life* (O.H.S.) I. 483 Then all went in, soe many that were suffered. **1700** T. BROWN tr. *Fresny's Amusem.* 97 One of them would have been poking a Cranes Bill down his Throat,..but the Doctors would not suffer him. **1818** COBBETT *Pol. Reg.* XXXIII. 492 Let us hear him now, if indignation will suffer us. **1878** J. P. HOPPS *Jesus* x. 37 How would I have blest you if you would have suffered me!

†**17.** With two objects (or the equivalent): To allow a person to have a certain thing. *Obs.*

c **1290** *Beket* 1615 in *S. Eng. Leg.* 152 Bote þov suffri him is riȝte lawes Ichulle bi-come þi fo. *c* **1385** CHAUCER *L.G.W.* 1575 *Hypsipyle*, Alle tho that sufferede hym his wille. **1481** CAXTON *Godfrey* lxx. 115 The turke..wold not suffre them of nothyng, sauf to occupye and laboure therthe.

†**18.** *intr.* **a.** Of a person (*transf.* of a thing): To allow a certain thing to be done. *Obs.*

1297 R. GLOUC. (Rolls) 4198, & þe wule he wolde þis tendre þing weneþ foule ynou, & heo ne miȝte sofry noȝt, Mid lecherye he hire slou. **1382** WYCLIF *Luke* xxii. 51 Suffre ȝe til hidur [TINDALE, Soffre ye thus farre forthe]. *c* **1400** *Destr. Troy* 8094 A gloue of þat gay gate he belyue,..None seond but hir-selfe, þat suffert full well. **1605** B. JONSON *Sejanus* iv, Still, do'st thou suffer Heau'n? will no flame, No heate of sinne make thy iust wrath to boile? **1613** PURCHAS *Pilgrimage* IV. xviii. (1614) 437 The name..remayning as diuers languages and dialects will suffer, almost the same.

†**b.** Of a condition of things: To allow or admit of a certain thing being done. *Obs.*

1548–9 (Mar.) *Bk. Com. Prayer, Priv. Baptism*, And saye the Lordes prayer, yf the tyme will suffre. **1573** TUSSER *Husb.* (1878) 47 If weather will suffer, this counsell I giue, Leaue sowing of wheat before Hallomas eue. **1612** BRINSLEY *Lud. Lit.* xxii. (1627) 256 If his leisure will suffer.

suffer, variant of SOVER *a.* and *v. Sc.*

sufferable ('sʌfərəb(ə)l), *a. Obs.* exc. *arch.* Forms: 4 **suffrabil, suffreable,** 4–6 **suffrable,** 5 **souffrable, suffyrabyl, sufferabylle, suffurable,** 6 **sufferabil,** *Sc.* **suffrabile,** 4– **sufferable.** Also SUBFERABYLLE. [a. OF. *suffrable* = It. *sofferevole*, ad. med.L. *sufferābilis*, f. *sufferre* to SUFFER. Subsequently modified in form by assimilation to SUFFER *v.*

A L. type *sufferibilis is represented by It. *soffribile*, Sp. *sufrible*, Pg. *sof(f)rivel*.]

†**1.** Patient, long-suffering. Also const. *of*: Willing to submit to. *Obs.*

1303 R. BRUNNE *Handl. Synne* 8641 þey ogh to be suffrable and meke, And no foly on ouþer men seke. *c* **1386** CHAUCER *Wife's Prol.* 442 Oon of vs two moste bowen doutelees, And sith a man is moore resonable Than womman is, ye moste been suffrable. *c* **1412** HOCCLEVE *De Reg. Princ.* 2934 Of swich writyng be of right suffrable. *Ibid.* 4423 Thogh he to venge hym tarie, & be suffrable. **1568** E. TILNEY *Flower Friendsh.* C ij b, Sufferable in the importunities of his wyfe. **1577** STANYHURST *Descr. Irel.* viii. in *Holinshed* 28/1 The [Irish] people are thus enclined, religious, franke, amorous, irefull, sufferable of infinite paynes, very glorious. **1611** SPEED *Theat. Gt. Brit.* (1614) 132/2 They rather live rudely..and with a sufferable ease, ignorant of ambition, enjoy those contentments.

†**b.** Capable of endurance. *Obs.*

1482 CAXTON *Godfrey* cxlix. 221 He toke with hym a lytil companye of them that were moost suffrable.

2. That can be 'suffered' or put up with; bearable, tolerable, endurable. Also, tolerably good.

a **1340** HAMPOLE *Psalter* cvi. 29 þe persecuciouns he tempird and made þaim suffrabil. **1382** WYCLIF *Matt.* x. 15 It shall be more suffreable to the lond of men of Sodom and Gomor in the day of iugement, than to that citee. **1440** *Alphabet of Tales* 345 It was mor suffrable vnto hur, þe sorow of dead, þan was þe mirthe of life. **1493** [H. PARKER] *Dives & Pauper* (W. de W.) VII. v. 281/1 The lordshyp of this worlde is sufferable & worshypfull. **1574** NEWTON *Health Mag.* 35 Let us touche suche sortes of fyshes as are best and most sufferable. **1578** TIMME *Calvin on Gen.* 94 The more sufferable..that the Commandment of God was the less tolerable was their Crookedness in refusing to obey. **1654** GATAKER *Disc. Apol.* 84 Manie Anabaptists..are more justifiable before God, and more sufferable with man, then Presbyterians and strict Calvinists. **1725** DEFOE *Voy. round World* (1840) 92 Insolent to a degree beyond what was sufferable. **1814** EARL DUDLEY *Lett.* 9 Aug. (1840) 58 There must be some great defect in his mind, or he would try to make himself a little more sufferable. *a* **1843** SOUTHEY *Common-pl. Bk.* (1849) Ser. II. 248 His funereal elegies are ..not quite worthless; that to Antonio Ferreira on his wife's death is sufferable. **1852** THACKERAY *Esmond* II. i, During the time, the suffering is at least sufferable. **1872** HOWELLS *Wedd. Journ.* (1892) 69 It was something..that made the air so much more sufferable than it had been.

†**3.** That may be allowed, permissible. *Obs.*

a **1395** HYLTON *Scala Pref.* (W. de W. 1494) II. xxxii, This maner syghte is sufferable to symple soules that can noo better. **1480** *Cov. Leet Bk.* 472 That comen-wele is nott sufferable by the kynges lawes. *a* **1571** JEWEL *On 1 Thess.* (1611) 84 And how is that sufferable by any Law, that by so many Lawes is condemned? **1598** MANWOOD *Lawes Forest* i. (1615) 20 It is not..sufferable for any other person, to hunt or hauke after any of those wilde beastes. **1653** A. WILSON *Jas. I*, 20 For the Clericks..they are no way sufferable to remain in this Kingdom.

†**4. a.** Capable of suffering, passible. *Obs.*

c **1400** LOVE *Bonavent. Mirr.* vii. 52 For withouten dowte he hadde verray flesche and kyndely sufferable as haue othere children. *c* **1430** *Life St. Kath.* (Roxb. Club) 36 Of þe experience of his suffrable nature he scheude to vs þat he was bothe verray god & man.

†**b.** Attended with suffering. *Obs.*

1548 GESTE *Agst. Priv. Masse* D j b, Christes sufferable and bloudy sacrifice.

†**c.** That may suffer injury or loss. *Obs.*

1651 BAXTER *Inf. Bapt.* 312 In the conferring of this (he saith) baptismall Regeneration is defined. But yet this is sufferable and loseable.

†**5.** *Logic.* Producing an effect on the senses.

Cf. *Burgersdicius' Logic* I. vi. (1697) 17 Patible Quality, in Greek ποιότης παθητική.

1654 Z. COKE *Logick* 32 Quality hath four kinds or specials. 1. Habit. 2. Natural power. 3. Sufferable quality. 4. Figure.

'**sufferably**, *adv. rare.* [f. prec. + -LY[2].]

†**1.** With patient endurance. *Obs.*

1483 CAXTON *Gold. Leg.* 300 b/2 They..knelynge on their knees receyued Suffrably wyth a Joyous herte the Swerdes of them that martryd them.

†**2.** To the accompaniment of suffering. *Obs.*

1548 GESTE *Agst. Priv. Masse* F v b, Els he shuld not haue bene eaten whole & vnbroken vnsufferably but by pecemele and sufferably as the lambe was.

3. So as to be tolerable, tolerably. *arch.*

1702 ADDISON *Dial. Medals* ii. 92 An infant Titan held she in her arms Yet sufferably bright, the eye might bear The ungrown glories of his beamy hair. **1875** *Contemp. Rev.* XXVII. 68 He can write sanely and sufferably when he pleases.

†'**sufferage.** *Obs. rare.* [f. SUFFER *v.* + -AGE.] Permission, approval.

1622 F. MARKHAM *Bk. War* v. ix. 195 In this mans power (under the sufferage of the Generall) is the election of many Captaines. **1650** B. *Discolliminium* 28, I will grant him as he saith, if he will hold to his spelling, that all is now united in the Sufferage of the People, though not in their Suffrage.

sufferaine, obs. form of SOVEREIGN.

sufferance ('sʌfərəns). Forms: 4 **sufrance, soffra(u)nce,** 4–6 **suff(e)raunce,** 4–7 **suffrance,** 5 **souerans(e, soferons, -aunce, sofferaunce,** 5–6 **sufferans, souerance,** 6 **souffrance, suffrans,** 7–8 **sufference,** 4– **sufferance.** [a. AF., OF. *suf(f)rance*, *soffrance* (mod.F. *souffrance*) = Pr. *sofransa, -ensa*, It. *sofferenza*, Sp. *sufrencia*, ad. late L. *sufferentia*, f. *sufferre* to SUFFER: see -ANCE. Subsequently modified in form by assimilation to SUFFER *v.*]

I. 1. Patient endurance, forbearance, long-suffering. *arch.* (See also LONG-SUFFERANCE.)

a **1300** *Cursor M.* 29106 þe preist..Agh to sceu þe, sinful man, þat he ta sli thing in sufferance, To stand him in stede o penance. *c* **1330** *Spec. Guy Warw.* 571 Houre swete lord ..bad hem ben of god suffraunce In alle manere destourbaunce. **13..** *E.E. Allit. P.* C. 417 Wel knew I þi cortaysye, þi quoynt soffraunce. *c* **1386** CHAUCER *Clerk's T.* 1106 For oure beste is al his [*sc.* God's] gouernance; Lat vs thanne lyue in vertuous suffrance. *c* **1450** *Mirk's Festial* 214 God, forto preue hym and his meke suffrance, made hym blynd. **1531** ELYOT *Gov.* 12 Wher vertue is in a gentleman, it is commonly mixt with more suffraunce..than..it is in a person rural. *a* **1596** *Sir T. More* III. i. 173 That awefull Iustice, Which looketh through a vaile of sufferaunce Uppon the frailtie of the multitude. **1642** MILTON *Apol. Smect.* Wks. 1851 III. 252, I will not deny but that the best apology against false accusers is silence and sufferance. **1680** OTWAY *Orphan* I. ii, Bear it With all the suffrance of a tender Friend.

2. The suffering or undergoing *of* pain, trouble, wrong, etc. *arch.*

1426 LYDG. *De Guil Pilgr.* 7486 Lyk a myghty champyoun, Thow shalt with laurer crownyd be, By suffraunce off adversyte. **1502** ATKYNSON tr. *De Imitatione* III. xx. (1893) 212 From the houre of my byrthe vnto my deth vpon the crosse, I neuer cessed of suffraunce of peynes. **1528** MORE *Dyaloge* III. Wks. 219/2 Yf a man..after repenting his sin would..willyngly offer hym selfe to the sufferaunce of open shame. **1539** TONSTALL *Serm. Palm Sund.* (1823) 16 His..sufferaunce of deathe for mankynde. **1614** JACKSON *Creed* III. 156 Vnder pain of eternall damnation, or sufferance of greater thirst in hell. **1794** MRS. RADCLIFFE *Myst. Udolpho* xxx, To glory in the quiet sufferance of ills. **1842** G. S. FABER *Prov. Lett.* (1844) II. 295 The Holy Catholic Church..has been exempt from the sufferance of persecution for these fifteen hundred years. **1856** H. BONAR *Hymn*, '*Calm me, my God*' v, Calm in the sufferance of wrong.

†**b.** The suffering of a penalty. *Obs.*

1599 SHAKS. *Hen. V*, II. ii. 159 God be thanked for preuention, Which [I] in sufferance heartily will reioyce. **1599** NASHE *Lenten Stuffe* 57 The Cardinalles..held this suffocation a meete sufferance for so contemning the king of fishes. **1640** SIR E. DERING *Sp. on Relig.* 18 Dec. 22, I proceed to his second sufferance, which was by the Vice-chancellour of Oxford.

†**c.** Damage, injury. *Obs. rare.*

1604 SHAKS. *Oth.* II. i. 23 A Noble ship of Venice, Hath seene a greeuous wracke and sufferance On most part of their Fleet. **1823** JEFFERSON *Writ.* (1830) IV. 369 The trappings of such a machinery..by the inequalities they produced, exposed liberty to sufferance.

†**3.** (tr. L. *passio.*) Passivity, receptivity. *Obs.*

c **1374** CHAUCER *Boeth.* v. met. iv. (1868) 167 þe passioun þat is to seyn þe suffraunce or þe wit in þe quike body.

4. = SUFFERING *vbl. sb.* 3. *arch.*

1422 YONGE tr. *Secr. Secr.* 169 In full grete Sufferaunce haue I be so many Ieris. *c* **1485** *Digby Myst.* III. 864 Alle þis xall be þe soferons of my deite. **1563** *Homilies* II. *For Good Friday* I, Not that the sufferaunce of thys transitory lyfe, shoulde be worthy of that glory to come. **1603** SHAKS. *Meas. for M.* II. iv. 168 Thy vnkindnesse shall his death draw out To lingring sufferance. *Ibid.* III. i. 80 The poore Beetle that we treade vpon In corporall sufferance, finds a pang as great, As when a Giant dies. **1628** DIGBY *Voy. Mediterr.* (Camden) 13 *note*, A most resupine patience in their sufferance. **1711** SHAFTESB. *Charac.* (1737) II. II. 164 To see the Sufferance of an Enemy with cruel Delight may proceed from the height of Anger, Revenge, Fear, and other extended Self-Passions. **1795** BENTHAM *Escheat vice Tax.* 38 It can save me..from ideal hardship, but not from corporal sufferance. **1819** SCOTT *Ivanhoe* xxix, Nature exhausted by sufferance. **1861** J. A. ALEXANDER *Gospel Christ* vii. 100 She looked back, and became a pillar of salt, perhaps without a pang of corporal sufferance.

†**b.** *pl.* = SUFFERING 3 b. *Obs.*

1597 HOOKER *Eccl. Pol.* v. xlviii. §8 To say he knew not what waight of sufferances his heauenly Father had measured vnto him, is somewhat hard. **1628** FELTHAM *Resolves* II. lxxxii, There is a Sympathie of soules..which makes them sensible of one anothers sufferances. **1656** S. HOLLAND *Zara* 211 How joyous our Champion and Soto were to behold this Mansion.., let those that have been sensible of their sufferances relate.

†**5.** Capacity to endure, endurance. *of bare sufferance*, barely endurable. *Obs.*

1544 BETHAM *Precepts War* II. lxx. L viij, Nothynge is so vnweldable, that by manlye prowes, and sufferaunce, may not be conquered and vndertroden. **1584** R. SCOT *Discov. Witchcr.* III. xi. 45 This melancholike humor..maketh sufferance of torments. **1604** EDMONDS *Observ. Cæsar's Comm.* 62 The two chiefest parts of a soldier, Valour and Sufferance. **1621** FLETCHER *Isl. Princ.* II. i. 3, I nere saw before A Man of such a sufferance; he lies now Where I would not lay my dog, for sure 'twould kill him. **1690** LOCKE *Hum. Und.* II. xxviii. §12 This is a Burden too heavy for human Sufferance. **1702** ROWE *Tamerl.* IV. i, Griefs beyond a mortal Sufferance. **1823** J. BADCOCK *Dom. Amusem.* 139 Give it a heat to the temperature of bare sufferance to the hand.

II. 6. Sanction, consent, or acquiescence, implied by non-intervention; permission, leave; toleration, indulgence. Now *rare* exc. as in d.

a **1300** *Cursor M.* 747 Wit his suffrance he it lete. **1303** R. BRUNNE *Handl. Synne* 12365 Hyt was but suffraunce, Nat hys wyl, nat hys ordynaunce. *c* **1386** CHAUCER *Frankl. T.* 60 And therfore hath this wise worthy knyght To lyue in ese suffrance hire bihight. **1464** *Cov. Leet Bk.* 323 Maruayllyng gretely not only the presumpcion of the said persones, but also of your suffrance in that partie. **1488** *MSS. Acc. Maldon* (Essex) *Liber B.* fol. 39 The barreris, gate, and fence there stondith at the sufferance of the tovne. *c* **1550** L. WAGER *Life Marie Magd.* (1904) 175 Of parentes the tender and carnall sufferance Is to yong maidens a very pestilence. **1554** *Act 1 & 2 Phil. & Mary* c. 11 §1 Coines..of other Realmes..by the suffrance and consent of the King and Quene..be currant in paiment within this Realme. **1579** SPENSER *Sheph. Cal.* Feb. 187 Nought aske I, but onely to holde my right: Submitting me to your good sufferaunce. **1625** K. LONG tr. *Barclay's Argenis* III. iv. 158 That easinesse and too much sufferance toward your Nobility.. hath betrayed the chiefe strength of your Kingdome. **1768** BLACKSTONE *Comm.* III. 87 They subsist and are admitted in England, not by any right of their own, but upon bare sufferance and toleration from the municipal laws [etc.]. **1817** JAS. MILL *Brit. India* II. v. iv. 421 The Company.. possessing their privileges through his sufferance, and owing obedience to his throne. **1854** J. S. C. ABBOTT *Napoleon* (1855) II. xiii. 221 The supplies of his troops, the advance of his reenforcements, etc., all depended upon their sufferance. **1875** MAINE *Hist. Instit.* iii. 95 The temporary occupation of the common tribe-land tends to become permanent, either through the tacit sufferance or the active consent of the tribesmen.

b. Const. *of* (that which is allowed or tolerated), *to* with inf.

† *sufferance of peace*, a grant of peace, truce.

1338 R. BRUNNE *Chron.* (1810) 267 In þe sufferance of pes [orig. *En suffraunce de pees*]. **1463–4** *Rolls of Parlt.* V. 506/1 The sufferaunce wherof hath caused grete ydelnes. **1534** MORE *Comf. agst. Trib.* III. Wks. 1212/1 Disparsing them for slaues among many sundry countreys of hys, verye farre fro their owne, without ani sufferaunce of regresse. **1547–64** BAULDWIN *Mor. Philos.* 70 b, Justice exalteth the people: but sufferance to sinne maketh the people most wretched & miserable. **1611** SPEED *Hist. Gt. Brit.* IX. ix. (1632) 618 The too-patient sufferance of some forraine grieuances. *Ibid.* xxiv. 1192 Their offer and sufferance to carry with them many voluntary English souldiers. [**1706** PHILLIPS (ed. Kersey), *Sufferentia Pacis*,..a Sufferance or Grant, of Peace or Truce.] **1840** THACKERAY *Shabby-genteel Story* v, Young ladies had been brought, from dislike to sufferance of a man, from sufferance to partiality.

†**c.** of God: freq. in the formula ***by the sufferance of God*** = by divine permission. *Obs.*

Cf. AF. *par divine soeffrance.*

c **1386** CHAUCER *Parson's T.* 551 Peyne is sent by the rightwys sonde of god, and by his suffrance. *c* **1400** MAUNDEV. (Roxb.) xvii. 76 It befell thurgh þe sufferaunce of Godd þat sudaynely he fell to grete mischeffe. **1439** *Charters &c. of Edinb.* (1871) 64 Patrike be the souerance of God Abbot of Halyrudhouse. **1470–85** MALORY *Arthur* XVIII. xix. 760 Sythen hit is the sufferaunce of god that I shalle dye for the loue of soo noble a knyghte. **1477** *MS. Rawl. B. 332* lf. 42, I purpose with Goddis sufferaunce for to be here with you in my proper persone. **1528** *St. Papers Hen. VIII*, IV. 497, I shall provide, by the soverance of God, that [etc.]. **1540** *Act 32 Hen. VIII* c. 25 §1 Thomas and Edwarde by the sufferaunce of God Archebishops of..Caunterbury and Yorke. **1559** *Bk. Presidentes* 8 Thomas by diuine suffraunce archbyshop of Canterbury. **1655** FULLER *Ch. Hist.* I. 11 Take ye a Law, and by that Law (through Gods sufferance) rule your Kingdome of Britain. **1879** R. K. DOUGLAS *Confucianism* iii. 77 Kings rule by its [*sc.* Heaven's] sufferance, and are deposed by its decree.

d. ***on*** or ***upon*** (formerly †*by*) ***sufferance***: by virtue of a tacit assent but without express permission; under conditions of passive acquiescence or bare tolerance.

1562 COOPER *Answ. Priv. Masse* (1850) 135 Neither those things which some did..upon Simplicity by sufferance should be brought as testimonies what the Church..ought ..to do. **1758** JOHNSON *Idler* No. 21 ⁋ 11 The ignominy of living by sufferance. **1846** LYTTON *Lucretia* 36 It is humiliating to me to know that I woo clandestinely and upon sufferance. **1864** MISS BRADDON *H. Dunbar* xii. 91, I will not accept my liberty on sufferance. **1879** MCCARTHY *Own Times* xxiii. II. 186 They were a Ministry on sufferance when they appealed to the country.

†**e.** An instance of this, a licence. *Obs.*

1547–55 RIDLEY *Wks.* 269 My lord, such things as St. Paul enjoined to the Gentiles for a sufferance..were only commandments of time. **1601** W. CORNWALLIS *Ess.* II. I, Let them take my papers, and doe with them what they will. Sufferances of some kinde are holesomer then reuenge. **1645** MILTON *Tetrach.* Wks. 1851 IV. 178 Our Saviour himself allows divorce to be a command. Neither doe they weak'n this assertion, who say it was only a sufferance.

f. *Customs.* In full, ***bill of sufferance***: a licence to ship or discharge cargoes at specified ports.

1670 BLOUNT *Law Dict.*, *Bill of Sufferance*, is a Licence granted at the Custom-house to a Merchant, to suffer him to trade from one English Port to another, without paying Custom. **1676** in *Rep. Comm. H. Comm.* (1803) XIV. 541 A sufferance granted to Mr. Jackson, to land salmon at St. Saviour's Dock. **1750** BEAWES *Lex. Merc.* (1752) 393 Coast Sufferances, are to be given without Fees. **1789** in *Rep. Comm. H. Comm.* (1803) XIV. 540 Resolved that no sufferance be granted for landing foreign goods on any public wharf beyond the wharf commonly called Brown's. **1832** *Gen. Order* in R. Ellis *Customs* (1841) II. 52 Application must be made..for a baggage-sufferance..to authorize the landing..of such part..as may be unaccompanied by the proprietor. **1867** SMYTH *Sailor's Word-bk.* 693 *Transire*, a custom-house document specifying the goods shipped by a coasting vessel, docketted with a sufferance for their discharge on arriving at the place of destination.

7. *Law.* The condition of the holder of an estate who, having come in by lawful right, continues to hold it after the title has ceased without the express leave of the owner. *Phr.* ***tenant, estate at sufferance*** (*† in sufferance*).

Cf. AF. *par lounge suffraunce sauntz autre title* (Britton II. xxiv).

1579 SPENSER *Sheph. Cal.* May 106 The time was once,.. When shepeheards had none inheritaunce, Ne of land, nor fee in sufferaunce. **1592** WEST *1st Pt. Symbol.* §42 d, A particuler estate in certaine, is an estate at will, or at sufferance. **1628** COKE *On Litt.* §460 A Release to a Tenant at sufferance is voyd because he hath a possession without privity. **1766** BLACKSTONE *Comm.* II. 150 An estate at sufferance, is where one comes into possession of land by lawful title, but keeps it afterwards without any title at all. **1818** CRUISE *Digest* (ed. 2) I. 288 There is no privity of estate between a tenant at sufferance, and the owner of the land; for this tenant only holds by the laches of the owner. **1829** SCOTT *Rob Roy* Introd., The family..occupied a good deal of property there,—whether by sufferance, by the right of the sword,..or by legal titles of various kinds [etc.]. **1867** BRANDE & COX *Dict. Sci.*, etc. III. 638/2 Tenancy at or by Sufferance.

b. *transf.*

1570 T. NORTON tr. *Nowel's Catech.* (1853) 157 Foreign kings that held the kingdom of sufferance under the Roman empire. *a* **1633** AUSTIN *Medit.* (1635) 266 This is no highway, but a way of Sufferance, by favour **1680** MORDEN *Geog. Rect., E. & W. Indies* (1685) 257 The French..upon Sufferance or Incroachment..pretend to that which we call Nova Scotia. **1722** DE FOE *Plague* 136 This is not the king's highway, it is a way upon sufferance. **1784** COWPER *Task* v. 363 Whose freedom is by suff'rance, and at will Of a superior, he is never free. **1801** S. & HT. LEE *Canterb. T.* IV. 16 The very house lately lent on sufferance to the Kruitzners. **1836** THIRLWALL *Greece* xxv. (1839) III. 365 If they were called upon to resign what they had occupied by abuse and held by sufferance.

†**8.** Suspension, delay; respite. (Chiefly after OF. or med.L.) *Obs.*

1523 LD. BERNERS *Froiss.* I. xxiii. 32 There was no delacyon of sufferaunce, nor mercy, but incontynent he was drawen..and quartered. *Ibid.* xxv. 36 To treat for a peace, and sufferaunce of warr. **1652** NEDHAM tr. *Selden's Mare Cl.* 404 This special kind of Truce was called Sufferance of War. **1738** CHAMBERS *Cycl.* (ed. 2), *Sufferance*, in ancient customs, a delay, or respite of time, which the lord granted his vassal, for the performance of fealty and homage.

9. *attrib.* **sufferance goods**, goods shipped or landed under a sufferance; **sufferance quay, wharf**, a quay or wharf at which cargo could be shipped or landed under a sufferance (see 5 f).

1774 *Hull Dock Act* 6 To ship off..all goods called *Sufferance Goods. *Ibid.* 33 The first *sufferance quay or wharf shall be erected. **1882** *Encycl. Brit.* XIV. 831/1 The frontage of the legal quays in 1795 was only 1419 feet, and of the sufferance quays about 3500 feet. **1784** in *Rep. Comm. H. Comm.* (1803) XIV. 541 The petition of Mr. David Griffin, wharfinger, praying that a wharf purchased by him ..may be used as a *sufferance wharf. **1796** W. VAUGHAN *Exam.* 7 Coasters generally load and discharge at Sufferance-Wharfs; some few of them at the Legal Quays. **1838** in R. Ellis *Customs* (1840) IV. 271 Landing-surveyor at legal quays to attend at sufferance wharfs for approval of values on application being made.

sufferande, obs. form of SOVEREIGN.

†**'sufferant**, *a.* *Obs.* Also 4 **suffra(u)nt**, 6 **sufferaunt, -ent.** [a. AF. *suffrant*, Of. *soffrant*, pr. pple. of *suffrir*, *soffrir* to SUFFER.] Long-suffering, patient.

c **1330** *Spec. Guy Warw.* 587 Or pine of bodi or shame in londe, Off al þis þou most suffraunt be. *c* **1369** CHAUCER *Dethe Blaunche* 1010 So pure suffraunt was hir wytte..Hyt folowed wel she koude goode. **1594** R. CAREW *Huarte's Exam. Wits* (1596) To Rdr., If thou be discreet, well compounded and sufferent.

b. *absol.* One who is patient or long-suffering.

c **1374** CHAUCER *Troylus* IV. 1584 Sle with reson al þis hete; Men seyn þe suffraunt ouercometh.

Hence †**'sufferantly** *adv.*, ? submissively.

a **1536** *Songs, Carols*, etc. (E.E.T.S.) 58 'Hayle, holy moder!'.. So said owr Savyowr sufferently Vnto the lady.

sufferante, -tie, etc., obs. ff. SOVEREIGN, -TY.

suffered ('sʌfəd), *ppl. a.* [-ED¹.] Endured.

1610 SHAKS. *Temp.* I. ii. 231 The Marriners..Who, with a Charme ioynd to their suffred labour I haue left asleep.

sufferent(e, obs. ff. SOVEREIGN.

sufferer ('sʌfərə(r)). Also 5–6 **suffrer**, 6 *Sc.* **sufferar.** [f. SUFFER *v.* + -ER¹.]

1. One who suffers pain, tribulation, injury, wrong, loss, etc.; one who suffers *from* disease or ill health.

c **1450** tr. *De Imitatione* III. li. 123, I knowe hov all þinge is doon, I knowe þe wronge doer & suffrer. **1579** RICE *Invect. agst. Vices* D ij b, The sufferers of persecution for his names sake. **1671** MILTON *Samson* 1525 The sufferers then will scarce molest us here. **1684** WOOD *Life* (O.H.S.) III. 94 Basill Wood, sometimes a captaine in the king's army and a great sufferer for the king's cause. **1781** COWPER *Retirem.* 343 Sad suff'rer under nameless ill. **1825** SCOTT *Betrothed* iv, A severe discharge of missiles with the Welsh, by which both parties were considerable sufferers. **1888** MISS BRADDON *Fatal Three* I. v, He had made up his mind that Dr. Hutchinson must come to see these humble sufferers, and to investigate the cause of evil.

b. One who suffers death; one who is killed (now only in reference to martyrdom).

1721 WODROW *Hist. Suff. Ch. Scot.* III. iv. §5. II. 147, I know well, by subdolous Proposals, and captious Questions, great Endeavours were used to shake the Sufferers. **1815** SCOTT *Guy M.* x, On one side of this patch of open ground, was found the sufferer's naked hanger. **1828** —— *F.M. Perth* xxiv, When thrown off from the ladder, the sufferer will find himself suspended, not by his neck,..but by the steel circle. **1836** GEN. P. THOMPSON *Exerc.* (1842) IV. 103 The 'poor sufferers', as we say at York in assize time. **1849** MACAULAY *Hist. Eng.* vii. II. 176 A few years later a more illustrious sufferer, Lord Russell, had been accompanied by Burnet from the Tower to the scaffold in Lincoln's Inn Fields.

c. A patient. Now *rare.*

1809 *Med. Jrnl.* XXI. 180 To such as have been in the habit of watching the various changes in this disease at the bedside of the unfortunate sufferer. **1848** THACKERAY *Van. Fair* xiv, A generous rivalry..as to which should be most attentive to the dear sufferer in the state bedroom.

†**2.** That which undergoes some operation; a passive thing. *Obs. rare*⁻¹.

1587 GOLDING *De Mornay* x. (1592) 146 Whereof then.. so great ods betwixt them, sith we holde opinion that God is Good, and the verie worker or Doer, and contrariwise that Matter is Euill, and but onely a Sufferer?

†**3.** One who permits something to be done. *Obs.*

a **1533** LD. BERNERS *Gold Bk. M. Aurel.* xi. (1537) 19 b, No bablers, but small spekers: no quarellers, but suffrers. **1560–1** *First Bk. Discipl. Ch. Scot.* in Knox's *Wks.* (1848) II. 188 Thair sall Goddis wraith reigne, not onlie upone the blind and obstinat idolater, but also upone the negligent sufferaris. **1627** SANDERSON *Serm.* (1674) I. 273 As for the very formality it self of the sin, God is (to make the most of it) but a sufferer.

suffering ('sʌfərɪŋ), *vbl. sb.* [f. SUFFER *v.* + -ING¹.]

†**1.** Patient endurance; long-suffering. *Obs.*

a **1340** HAMPOLE *Psalter* xxvi. 20 Suffire þat þou suffirs for god and of god, for wa is þaim þat losis suffrynge. **1382** WYCLIF *James* v. 11 ȝe herden the suffring [*gloss*, or pacience] of Job.

2. The bearing or undergoing of pain, distress, or tribulation. In early use const. *of* the thing suffered.

c **1340** HAMPOLE *Prose Treat.* 5, I ȝode by sufferynge of werynes and I fand Ihesu wery in þe way. *c* **1380** WYCLIF *Sel. Wks.* III. 304 Wilful sofforyng of deþ. **14..** *Pol. Rel. & L. Poems* (1903) 277 In suffryng Of trokys [? crokys] & naylis clynkyng. **1534** TINDALE *Heb.* ii. 9 Jesus which is crouned with glory and honour for the sofferinge of death. **1597** HOOKER *Eccl. Pol.* v. liii. §1 Both working of wonders and suffering of paines. **1607** SHAKS. *Cor.* v. ii. 71 I'th state of hanging, or of some death more long in Spectatorship, and crueller in suffering. **1667** MILTON *P.L.* XI. 375, I..to the evil turne My obvious breast, arming to overcom By suffering. *a* **1716** SOUTH *Serm.* (1823) IV. 401 The Christian religion..[is] a religion teaching suffering, enjoining suffering, and rewarding suffering. *a* **1845** S. SMITH *Wks.* (1859) I. 142 Suffering is not a merit, but only useful suffering. **1873** MOZLEY *Univ. Serm.* viii. (1876) 192 The generous suffering of one person for another.

attrib. **1662** GURNALL *Chr. in Arm.* III. v. ii. §1 Even he comes forth to meet thee,..willing to impart some of his Suffering-skill unto thee.

†**b.** The action of suffering death; execution; martyrdom. *Obs.*

1651 G. FOX in *Jrnl.* (1911) I. 14 Two men sufferd for small thinges: & I was moved..to Incourage yᵐ concerneinge there suffringe. *a* **1700** EVELYN *Diary* 12 Nov. 1644, The suffering of St. Laurence painted *a fresca* on the wall.

c. The incurring of loss. *rare.*

1805 COLLINGWOOD *Let.* in *Daily Chron.* (1905) 10 July 3/4 This Great day has not been without a considerable suffering on our part in loss of Officers and Men.

3. A painful condition; pain suffered.

c **1392** CHAUCER *Compl. Venus* 45 Thus be we euyr in drede and suffrynge. *a* **1771** GRAY *Dante* 66 Far less shall be Our Suffering, Sir. **1818** BYRON *Ch. Har.* IV. xxii, All suffering doth destroy, or is destroy'd, Even by the sufferer. **1829** LYTTON *Devereux* IV. i, I rose from the bed of suffering and of madness,..altered, but tranquil. **1890** *Science Gossip* XXVI. 53/2 It is just those energetic, matter-of-fact people, who..are the most likely to interfere and to aggravate suffering.

b. In particularized use, chiefly *pl.*

1609 DANIEL *Civ. Wars* IV. lxxv, Future ill On present suffrings, bruted to aryse. **1611** *Bible* Rom. viii. 18 The sufferings of this present time. **1667** MILTON *P.L.* IV. 26 Of worse deeds worse sufferings must ensue. **1736** BUTLER *Anal.* I. ii. Wks. 1874 I. 35 We cannot find by experience, that all our sufferings are owing to our own follies. **1764** BURN *Poor Laws* 197 The sufferings indeed of the poor are less known, than their misdeeds. **1780** BENTHAM *Princ. Legisl.* xiv. §1 This is a suffering common to all. **1862** M. NAPIER *Mem. Claverhouse* II. 84 All were expected, under the Orange Revolution, to contribute a suffering, however small, to this grand Commination of the governments of the Restoration. **1877** MRS. FORRESTER *Mignon* I. 221 She is callous to his sufferings.

c. In the Society of Friends, the hardships of those who were distrained upon for tithes, etc. ***Meeting for Sufferings***: an organization for investigating and relieving these: see also quot. 1906.

1657 G. FOX *Epistles* No. 141 All Friends everywhere, that are in any sufferings, let your sufferings be gathered up together in every County. **1661** F. HOWGILL in *Extr. St. Papers rel. Friends* Ser. II. (1911) 129 Wee haue made it our work to collect vp all the sufferings from all partes & to make what vse wee cann of them. **1683** SARAH MEADE in *Jrnl. Friends' Hist. Soc.* (1914) Oct. 165 An exact Accᵗ of all youʳ sufferings..sent up hitheʳ to the meettinge of sufferrings, in ordeʳ to bee putt to the rest of ffriends sufferrings, yᵗ are presented to yᵉ Kinge. **1708** CHAMBERLAYNE *M. Brit. Notitia* I. III. i. 200 Their Meetings..are..Monthly, Quarterly, Yearly, Second-Days Meetings, and Meeting of

Sufferings. **1837** W. ALLEN *Jrnl.* in *Life* (1847) III. 265 Fifty Friends of the Meeting for Sufferings met. **1906** *Christ. Discipl. Soc. Friends* II. xi. 59 The Meeting for Sufferings (so called from the nature of its original object) is a standing representative committee of the Yearly Meeting, and is entrusted with a general care of whatever may arise during the intervals of the Yearly Meeting affecting the Society.

†**4. a.** Permission. **b.** Tolerance. *Obs.*

c **1460** *Oseney Reg.* 135 Frere William Sutton By þe suffryng of god Abbot of Oseneye. **1523** LD. BERNERS *Froiss.* I. cccxciii. 677 Ye haue had a fayre sufferyng. *a* **1578** LINDESAY (Pitscottie) *Chron. Scot.* (S.T.S.) II. 315 About the sufferring of ane day of law anens the clairk of Sanctandros. **1637** *Decr. Star Chamber* in *Milton's Areop.* (Arb.) 15 He..shall first giue notice..of such demise, or suffering to worke or print there.

†**5.** Passive reception of action. *Obs.*

1548 VICARY *Anat.* ix. 79 Lyke as the Renet of the Cheese hath by him selfe the way or vertue of working, so hath the mylke by way of suffering. **1587** GOLDING *De Mornay* xiv. 241 What els is corrupting, but suffering? And what els is suffering, but receyuing?

ˈsuffering, *ppl. a.* [f. SUFFER *v.* + -ING².]

†**1.** That endures patiently, LONG-SUFFERING; inured to suffering; submissive. *Obs.*

a **1340** HAMPOLE *Psalter* vii. 12 God rightwis iuge, stalworth and soffrand. *c* **1400** tr. *Secr. Secr., Gov. Lordsh.* 108 þat þou ert..lastyng, wys, and sufferand. **1470–85** MALORY *Arthur* VII. xx. 244 He is curteis and mylde and the moost sufferynge man that euer I mette with al. **1601** SHAKS. *Jul. C.* II. i. 130 Such suffering Soules That welcome wrongs. **1605** B. JONSON *Sejanus* IV, Whome hee (vpon our low, and suffering neckes) Hath rays'd, from excrement, to side the Gods. **1679** W. PENN in *Wks. I. Penington* (1784) I. p. x, By nature he was suffering to a degree of letting his mercy to others almost wound his own soul. **1694** J. KETTLEWELL *Comp. for Persecuted* Wks. 1718 II. 295 O Almighty..God!..in these Suffering Times, give me a Suffering Spirit.

†**2.** Passive. *Obs.*

1398 TREVISA *Barth. De P.R.* VI. xii. (Bodl. MS.) In þe male beþ vertues formale and schaping..and in þe female materialle suffring and passiue. **1792** COWPER *Let. to Mrs. King* 26 Jan., The infallible Judge of human conduct may possibly behold with more complacency a suffering than an active courage.

3. a. Of persons, their character, condition, etc.: That suffers, or is characterized by the suffering of, pain, affliction, or distress.

1597 SHAKS. *Lover's Compl.* 178 Gentle maid Haue of my suffering youth some feeling pitty. *a* **1643** LD. FALKLAND, etc. *Infallibility* (1646) 102 It is well knowne that..where both religions are professed..none be on the suffering hand but we, none persecutes but they. **1659** *Gentl. Calling* Pref. §3 The Martyrologie even of these suffering times. **1687** DRYDEN *Hind & P.* III. 138 You have your day, or you are much bely'd, But I am always on the suff'ring side. **1705** STANHOPE *Paraphr.* I. 11 We can feed and cloath hungry and naked Christ in his suffering Members. *a* **1716** SOUTH *Serm.* (1823) IV. 401 The Christian religion..is a suffering religion. **1790** BURKE *Rev. France* 123 Deserters from principle,..they never see any good in suffering virtue. **1814** JANE AUSTEN *Mansf. Park* I. xviii. 357 Such nature and feeling in it as must..make it a very suffering exhibition to herself. **1820** SHELLEY *Prometh. Unb.* I. 630 Many..live among their suffering fellow-men As if none felt. **1828** LYTTON *Pelham* II. xiii, Mr. Chitterling Crabtree.. subscribed to the aid of the suffering friends of freedom. **1885** *Athenæum* 18 July 79/3 Her verse is characterized by.. keen sympathy with suffering man and woman.

b. In Puritan use, with reference to hardships endured for the sake of religion, esp. in ***suffering saint.***

1661 J. PERROT (*title*) To the Suffering Seed of Royalty, Wheresoever Tribulated upon the Face of the whole Earth. **1664** BUTLER *Hud.* II. II. 406 That Sinners may supply the place Of suff'ring Saints is a plain Case. **1667** *Epil. Dryden's Secret Love,* A whipt Fanatick who does not recant Is by his Brethren call'd a suffring Saint. [**1682** CLAVERHOUSE *Let. to Queensberry* 1 Mar., I would desire leave to draw out of the two regiments a hundred of the best musketeers had served abroad; and I should take horses here, amongst the *suffering sinners*.] **1896** MRS. CAFFYN *Quaker Grandmother* 317 Harry was as yet scarcely in fit condition for any suffering-saint phase to be foisted upon him.

c. [After F. *souffrant.*] Ill, indisposed. *rare.*

1885 'MRS. ALEXANDER' *Valerie's Fate* iii, My poor friend is very suffering and anxious to press on to Mentone.

d. ***suffering cat(s)!*** an exclamation expressing surprise or annoyance. Also ***the suffering Moses*** (cf. MOSES 1 c), etc.

1869 'MARK TWAIN' *Innocents Abroad* v. 52 The suffering Moses!—there ain't money enough in the ship to pay that bill! **1897** KIPLING *Captains Courageous* vi. 134 'Sufferin' Christianity!' sez Counahan (he always said that whin..he was not feelin' good). **1907** S. E. WHITE *Arizona Nights* xv. 217 Suffering cats, think how that fellow sized us up for a lot of pattern-made fools. **1931** S. LEWIS *Sel. Short Stories* (1935) 162 Suffering cats! You might have been one of your uncles still puttering around with dirty pitchforks back on the farm! **1948** G. H. JOHNSTON *Death takes Small Bites* v. 122 She doesn't think I've got any guts.' 'Well, sufferin' cat! What does she want? Alexander the Great?' **1977** J. PORTER *Who the Heck is Sylvia?* vi. 54 Oh, suffering cats, with that bunch of lecherous thugs it could have been *anybody*!

†**4.** *transf.* Becoming impaired by use. *Obs.*

1601 B. JONSON *Poetaster* I. i. 77 The suffering ploughshare, or the flint may weare.

5. *Comb.*, as ***suffering-minded*** adj.

1598 CHAPMAN *Iliad* v. 276 Most suffering-minded Tydeus sonne.

suffering, obs. or illiterate f. SOVEREIGN *sb.*

ˈsufferingly, *adv. rare.* [-LY².]

†**1.** With patient endurance. *Obs.*

a **1340** HAMPOLE *Psalter* xciii. 13 þat he bere suffrandly what sa be done. *c* **1440** *York Myst.* xxii. 204 [Who] thre temptacions takes expres, þus suffirrantly. *c* **1450** *Pol. Rel. & L. Poems* (1903) 136 þou sett my saule, myn hert, in ese, ..soferandely þe for to plese.

†**2.** Passively. *Obs.*

1682 *Cabbalist. Dial.* 8 An ὑλοπάθεια, or an affect or moving sufferingly to become Matter.

3. With suffering.

1860 *Chamb. Jrnl.* XIV. 96 Sadly and sufferingly passed the day.

suffes, obs. form of SUFFICE.

ˈsuffet, *v. dial.* [? Imitative.] = BUFFET *v.*

c **1440** *Promp. Parv.* 41/2 Buffetyn or suffetyn. **1891** *Sheffield Gloss.* Suppl., *Suffit*, to beat... This word is used about Eccleshall, near Sheffield.

suffete (ˈsʌfiːt). *Antiq.* [ad. L. *suffes, sūfes, -et-*, of Phœnician origin (cf. Heb. *shōphēt* judge). Cf. F. *suffète.*] One of the supreme executive magistrates of the ancient republic of Carthage.

1600 HOLLAND *Livy* xxx. vii. 743 All men thought verily that Scipio would..lay siege unto Carthage: whereupon their Suffetes (who are the Consuls as it were, of the citie) called the Senate. **1701** SWIFT *Contests Nobles & Comm.* Wks. 1755 II. I. 25 The suffetes at Carthage. **1839** *Penny Cycl.* XV. 441/2 The judges [in Israel] seem to have been somewhat analogous to the Carthaginian suffetes. **1884** SAYCE *Anc. Emp. East* 210 In time the monarchy disappeared altogether, its place being supplied by suffetes or 'judges'.

suffiand: see SUFFIE.

‖**suffibulum** (səˈfɪbjʊləm). *Rom. Antiq.* [L. *suffibulum*, f. *suf-* = SUB- 1 + *fībula* brooch.] A rectangular veil, white with a purple border, worn by vestals at the time of sacrifice.

1753 *Chambers' Cycl.* Suppl. **1886** *Encycl. Brit.* XX. 819/2 *note*, The only statue known on which the *suffibulum* is represented. **1891** FARRAR *Darkn. & Dawn* xxxiii, 'Thanks, kindest of Vestals,' said Titus, gratefully kissing the purple hem of her *suffibulum*.

suffice (səˈfaɪs), *v.* Forms: 4 **suffische,** 4–5 **suffich;** 4 **sofise,** 4–5 **-ice,** 4–6 **suffyse, -yce,** 4–7 **suffise,** 5 **suffis, -icy, -ys(s, -es, sofyse,** 5–6 **suffyze,** 5–7 **-ize,** 4– **suffice.** [f. OF. *suffis-*, pres. stem of *suffire*:—L. *sufficĕre*, f. *suf-* = SUB- + *facĕre* to make, do.]

1. *intr.* To be enough, sufficient, or adequate for a purpose or the end in view.

c **1340** HAMPOLE *Prose Treat.* (1866) 19, I haue tolde þe in þis mater a lyttill as me thynke; noghte affermande þat þis suffisches, ne þat þis es þe sothefastnes in þis mater. **1390** GOWER *Conf.* II. 138 He..the richesse of gold despiseth, And seith that mete and cloth sufficeth. *a* **1425** tr. *Arderne's Treat. Fistula* etc. 28 And þis sufficeþ of þe kuttyng of þe fistule. **1528** MORE *Dyalogue* IV. Wks. 264/2 Yet yf he lacked charite, all hys fayth suffised not. **1596** SHAKS. *Tam. Shr.* I. ii. 66 'Twixt such friends as wee, Few words suffice. **1646** *Hamilton Papers* (Camden) 133 This shall suffice from.. Your Grace's humblest seruant, R. Moray. **1667** MILTON *P.L.* II. 411 What art can then Suffice, or what evasion bear him safe Through the strict Senteries? **1718** HICKES & NELSON *J. Kettlewell* I. xviii. 41 To omit other Instances.. let this which followeth suffice. **1818** CRUISE *Digest* (ed. 2) II. 340 So a seisin at one time would suffice; for the statute said 'seised at any time'. **1847** EMERSON *Poems, Day's Ration* Wks. (Bohn) I. 482 Why need I volumes, if one word suffice?

†**b.** Const. *to* (a person): To be enough for, satisfy the requirements of; = sense 5. *Obs.*

1340–70 *Alex. & Dind.* 61 To us silf sofisen þis cauus. **1382** WYCLIF *John* xiv. 8 Schewe to vs the fadir, and it suffisith to vs. *c* **1400** MAUNDEV. (Roxb.) xxxii. 145 Qwhat thing myght suffice to þat man, to wham all þe werld will noȝt suffice? **1426** LYDG. *De Guil. Pilgr.* 5206 Swych ten.. Wolde nat suffysen vn-to me At O dyner..To fulfylle myn appetyt. **1484** CAXTON *Curiall* I b, Late hyt suffyse to the and to me that one of us tweyne be infortunat. *a* **1533** LD. BERNERS *Huon* lxvi. 229 All this suffyseth not to me for I wolde haue parte of yᵉ seygnory.

c. Const. *for* in the same sense.

c **1386** CHAUCER *Knt.'s T.* 375 Oonly the sighte of hire whom þat I serue..Wolde han suffised right ynough for me. *a* **1513** FABYAN *Chron.* VI. cciv. (1811) 215 Why is nat this kyngdom suffycyent for twayne yᵗ somtyme suffysed for .vii.? **1791** COWPER *Iliad* IV. 426 Short reprimand and exhortation short Suffice for thee. **1807** CRABBE *Par. Reg.* I. 80 Such all the rules, and they suffice for all.

d. Const. *for* (a thing): To be of sufficient quantity, capacity, or scope for; to provide enough material or accommodation for.

1393 LANGL. *P. Pl.* C. xx. 203 Yf hit sufficith nat for a-seth ..Mercy..wil make good þe remenant. **1422** YONGE *Secr. Secr.* xxiii. 151 Suffysid a lytill garde of yᵉ foote for his Pallis, for his halle, and for his roob. **1611** *Bible* 1 Kings xx. 10 If the dust of Samaria shall suffice for handfuls for all the people that follow me. **1703** POPE *Thebais* 216 For crimes like these, not all those realms suffice, Were all those realms the guilty victor's prize! **1847** MRS. A. KERR t. *Ranke's Hist. Servia* 115 The Janissaries by whom they were surrounded sufficed not for their purposes. **1866** GEO. ELIOT *F. Holt* (1868) 46 The book-shelves did not suffice for his store of old books. **1875** SPENCER *First Princ.* II. v. §59 (ed. 3) 189 *note*, This mode of conceiving the phenomena suffices for physical inquiries.

†**e.** Const. *to*: To be adequate or equal to; to avail for. *Obs.*

c **1325** *Song of Yesterday* 136 in *E.E.P.* (1862) 136 Al þi wit schal be þorw souȝt To more good þen þou may suffise. **13..** *E.E. Allit. P.* A. 135 Vrþely herte myȝt not suffyse To þe tenþe dole of þo gladnez glade. **1375** BARBOUR *Bruce* I. 12, I wald fayne set my will, Giff my wyt mycht suffice thartill, To put in wryt a suthfast story. *c* **1400** *Destr. Troy* 6747 All-þof Ector was on, þat odmony slogh,..Hymselfe might not suffise to þat soume hoge. **1496–7** *Act 12 Hen. VII*, c. 13 § 1 The graunt of the seid too xvᵐᵉˢ and xᵐᵉˢ doth not suffise nor extende to the behoufull chargis and expencis. **1526** *Pilgr. Perf.* (W. de W. 1531) 13 He wolde not that his worde onely sholde suffyse to our example of lyuynge.

f. Const. *for* with a noun of action or gerund.

1475 *Rolls of Parlt.* VI. 150/2 The somme..wold not suffise for the contentation of the wages. **1577** B. GOOGE tr. *Heresbach's Husb.* 19 b, Such store of Poultrie..as the doung of them suffised for the manuring of theyr ground. **1653** W. RAMESEY *Astrol. Restored* 20 This may suffice for the silencing of such simpletons. **1815** J. SMITH *Panorama Sci. & Art* II. 627 A lighter harrow..will suffice for covering seed. **1856** FROUDE *Hist. Eng.* (1858) II. vi. 37 The evidence of the most abandoned villains sufficed for their conviction.

g. Const. *to* with inf.

1390 GOWER *Conf.* I. 153 Al the world ne may suffise To stanche of Pride the reprise. **1480** CAXTON *Cron. Eng.* cii. 82 The lyuyng peple ne suffysed not to burye the dede bodyes. **1500–20** DUNBAR *Poems* xxiii. *heading*, Be mirry and glaid, honest and vertewous, Ffor that suffisis to anger the invyous. **1614** RALEIGH *Hist. World* II. xxvii. 617 The same occasions sufficed also, to procure the deliuerie of Manasses. **1667** MILTON *P.L.* VII. 113 To recount Almightie works What words or tongue of Seraph can suffice? **1741–2** GRAY *Agrip.* 59 The world, you gave him, Suffices not to pay the obligation. **1839** KEMBLE *Resid. Georgia* (1863) 259 A very short time would suffice to teach him to read. **1860** TYNDALL *Glac.* I. xiv. 97 The fog..every trace of which a few minutes sufficed to sweep away. **1883** *Manch. Guard.* 12 Oct. 5/3 A little thing has sufficed to destroy the balance of a structure that was already tottering.

†**h.** ***to suffice to oneself***: to be self-sufficient. *Obs.*

c **1400** *Apol. Loll.* 109 þei þat sufficy to hemsilf. **1587** GOLDING *De Mornay* iii. 32 The onely one God,..Suffizing to himselfe.

†**2.** *impers.* It is enough. *Obs.*

1382 WYCLIF *Mark* xiv. 41 He cam the thridde tyme, and seith to hem, Slepe ȝe nowe, and reste ȝe; sothli it sufficith. *c* **1386** CHAUCER *Shipman's T.* 52 Na moore of this as now, for it suffiseth. **1390** GOWER *Conf.* III. 245 Whan kinde is dueliche served, It oghte of reson to suffise. *c* **1400** *Rule St. Benet* (verse) 1824 Sese! it suffes now. **1530** PALSGR. 743/1 Syth he hath made his confessyon with his awne hande, it suffyseth, I aske no more.

b. Const. inf. or clause with, or (formerly) without, anticipatory subject *it*. Now chiefly in the subjunctive, ***suffice it***, sometimes short for ***suffice it to say.***

1390 GOWER *Conf.* I. 14 To studie upon the worldes lore Sufficeth now withoute more. **1426** LYDG. *De Guil. Pilgr.* 6864 Than suffysede, stedefastly To loue god, our creatour. **1548–9** (Mar.) *Bk. Com. Prayer, Publ. Baptism*, If the childe be weake, it shall suffice to powre water upon it. **1557** NORTH *Gueuara's Diall Pr.* II. xxxiv. (1568) 153 For to be a good captayne, sufficeth only to be hardy, and fortunate. **1692** DRYDEN *St. Euremont's Ess.* 25 It suffices to say that Xantippus becoming the manager of affairs, altered extreamly the Carthaginians Army. **1779** *Mirror* No. 8 Suffice it to say, that my parting with the Dervise was very tender. **1898** 'H. S. MERRIMAN' *Roden's Corner* x. 100 Suffice it to say that there are many such reasons.

1422 YONGE tr. *Secr. Secr.* 178 Hit suffichyth that..we fyndyth y-writte, that oone forcible kynge of grete Pouer, assiget the Cite of Rome. **1552** *Bk. Com. Prayer, Communion*, It shall suffyse that the bread be suche, as is vsuall to bee eaten. **1582** STANYHURST *Æneis* II. (Arb.) 64 Sufficeth yt also That Troians misery dyd I liue too testifye mournefull. **1590** SPENSER *F.Q.* II. viii. 56 Suffise, that I haue done my dew in place. *a* **1593** MARLOWE *Hero & Leander* I. 71 Let it suffise, That my slacke muse sings of Leanders eies. **1596** SHAKS. *Tam. Shr.* I. i. 252 If thou ask me why, Sufficeth my reasons are both good and waighty. **1646** CRASHAW *Steps to Temple* 71 Angels cannot tell; suffice, Thyself shalt feel thine own full joys. **1671** MILTON *Samson* 63 Suffices that to me strength is my bane. *a* **1764** LLOYD *New-River Head* Poet. Wks. 1774 II. 68 Suffice it, that my goody's care Brought forth her best, tho' simple fare. **1812** BYRON *Ch. Har.* I. iii, Suffice it, that perchance they were of fame. **1841** THACKERAY *Gt. Hoggarty Diam.* vii, I have passed over a great deal of the religious part of Mr. Brough's behaviour: suffice it, that religion was always on his lips.

c. With dative pron. added. *arch.*

c **1385** CHAUCER *L.G.W.* 573 Suffiseth me thou make in þis manere [etc.]. *c* **1392** —— *Compl. Venus* 65 To the hit ought ynogh suffise, that love so highe a grace to yow sent. **1484** CAXTON *Fables of Æsop* v. xii, Wel hit maye suffyse the to haue had tweyne of them. *c* **1520** NISBET *N.T.* Matt. x. 25 It sufficis to the discipile that he be as his maistir. **1592** KYD *Sp. Trag.* III. xv. 20 Sufficeth thee that poore Hieronimo Cannot forget his sonne Horatio. **1598** SHAKS. *Merry W.* II. i. 10 Let it suffice thee (Mistris Page)..that I loue thee. **1667** MILTON *P.L.* XI. 88 Had it suffic'd him to have known Good by it self. **1690** LOCKE *Hum. Und.* II. ix. §15 It suffices me only to have remark'd here, that [etc.]. **1833** TENNYSON *Two Voices* 386 Suffice it thee Thy pain is a reality. **1875** HAYWARD *Love agst. World* 80 Let it suffice you that I will see you on the subject.

d. Const. *for* with acc. and inf.

1848 THACKERAY *Van. Fair* lxiii, It sufficed for our Minister to stand up for Madame Strumpff.

†**3.** To have the necessary ability, capacity, or resources for doing something; to be competent or able *to do* something. Chiefly const. inf. *Obs.* (in later use coloured by 1 g.)

a **1325** *MS. Rawl. B. 520* lf. 32 b, Ȝif þe lord ne mai noȝt suffisen to uellen þe vnder wode þe contreie him sal helpe. *c* **1383** *Concl. Loll.* in *Eng. Hist. Rev.* (1911) Oct. 748 In vsinge medeful werkis..as moche as þei suffisen. **1390** GOWER *Conf.* III. 21, I schal do, fader, as ye sein, Als ferforth as I mai suffise. *c* **1400** MAUNDEV. (1839) xx. 221 The Lordes here han folk of certeyn nombre, als thei may suffise. **1406** HOCCLEVE *La Male Regle* 400 To recorde it vnnethe I may souffyse. *c* **1450** HOLLAND *Howlat* 96, I may nocht suffyss to se ȝour sanctitud sad. **1523** SKELTON *Garl.*

Laurel 875 Of all your bewte I suffyce not to wryght. **1743** WARBURTON *Ric. Arist.* in *Pope's Dunc.* p. xxxiv, If so many and various graces go to the making up a Hero, what mortal shall suffice to bear this character? **1823** SCOTT *Quentin D.* Introd., A Frenchman..can..address himself to a variety of services, and suffice in his own person to discharge them all.

†**b.** *trans.* To be capable of. *Obs.*

1390 GOWER *Conf.* I. 89 That thou to loves heste obeie Als ferr as thou it myht suffise. **14..** *Chaucer's H. Fame* 1180 (Caxton) My wytt [ne] may it [*v.r.* me] not suffyse.

†**4.** *intr.* Contextually, of a quality or condition: To provide adequate means or opportunity; to allow or admit of a certain thing being done. Also *trans. Obs.*

c **1369** CHAUCER *Dethe Blaunche* 1094 As my wytte koude best suffyse..I besette hytte To loue hir yn my beste wyse. **1423** JAS. I *Kingis Q.* cxl, Quhill my yf may suffise. **1425** *Rolls of Parlt.* IV. 296/2 My said Lordes..shall as ferforth as her cunnyng and discretions suffisen, trewely..avise ye Kyng. *c* **1440** *Generydes* 1150 When they came ther they sawe a faire cite, As full a pepill as it cowde suffice. *c* **1450** in Aungier *Syon* (1840) 311 Yf the tyme wylle suffise it, the abbes..may exorte them in thys wyse. **1477** EARL RIVERS (Caxton) *Dictes* 1 As fer as my wrecchednes wold suffyse.

5. *trans.* To be enough for; to meet the desires, needs, or requirements of (a person); to satisfy. *arch.* †Also *impers.*

The object is of datival origin: cf. 1 b. † (*it*) *sufficeth me*: I am satisfied, content.

1390 GOWER *Conf.* I. 290 Al that mihte him noght suffise, That he ne bad to do juise Upon the child. *c* **1400** *Rom. Rose* 6005 Therfore it suffisith me Her good herte and her beaute. *c* **1400** *Beryn* 1219 The halff of our lyvlode Wold scarsly suffise hym selff aloon. *c* **1440** *York Myst.* xxiii. 18 þat suffice vs with-outen more. **1481** CAXTON *Godfrey* viii. 30 They were so grete plente of peple that no londe myght suffyse them. **1550** CROWLEY *Last Trumpet* 417 Let this example suffice the. **1583** STOCKER *Civ. Warres Lowe C.* III. 112 A pound of bread, which oftentimes would scarcly suffice some trauellers to breakfast. **1592** KYD *Sp. Trag.* III. xv. 35 Sufficeth me; thy meanings vnderstood. **1794** MRS. RADCLIFFE *Myst. Udolpho* xxviii, It is my will that you remain here, let that suffice you. **1803–5** WORDSW. *Rob Roy's Grave* 38 The good old rule Sufficeth them. **1854** NEWMAN *Hist. Sk.* (1876) I. I. iv. 173 Barbarian minds remain in the circle of ideas which sufficed their forefathers.

transf. **1643** J. M. *Sov. Salve* 13 A weak reason may suffice so strong a cause.

†**b.** Const. *of* (the thing). *Obs.*

c **1440** *Gesta Rom.* I. xxxii. 125 (Harl. MS.), He that pleithe with me, shall neuer be suffisid of my pley. **1483** CAXTON *G. de la Tour* c viij, For it suffyseth them ynowe of one masse. **1611** BIBLE *Ezek.* xliv. 6 O yee house of Israel, let it suffice you, of all your abominations.

c. *pass.* To be satisfied or content. *arch.*

c **1430** LYDG. *Min. Poems* (Percy Soc.) 200 Whoos boody may not suffysed been. **1483** CAXTON *G. de la Tour* e ij, Therwith she myght haue be pleased and suffised. **1531** ELYOT *Gov.* I. xiii. (1880) I. 115 The parentes..being suffised that their children can onely speke latine proprely. **1598** SYLVESTER *Du Bartas* II. ii. III. (1641) 132/1 Whose searching soule can hardly be suffiz'd With Vulgar Knowledge. *c* **1600** SHAKS. *Sonn.* xxxvii, I in thy abundance am suffic'd. **1700** DRYDEN *Theod. & Honoria* 194 Not half suffic'd, and greedy yet to kill. **1850** T. T. LYNCH *Theoph. Trinal* v. 71 One half hour, solemnity may fill his heart; the next, pleasantry; by each shall his heart be for the time sufficed.

†**d.** *refl.* To satisfy oneself. *Obs.*

† *suffice thee, you*: be content.

1484 CAXTON *Fables of Æsop* IV. ix, Suffyse the, For ther to I shalle put al my dylygence. *a* **1533** LD. BERNERS *Huon* lxxxv. 268 Suffyce you with the gyft that I haue gyuen you. **1597** A. M. tr. *Guillemeau's Fr. Chirurg.* t v, I suffise my selfe with my accustomed manner. **1601** SHAKS. *All's Well* III. v. 10 Come lets returne againe, And suffice our selues with the report of it.

†**6.** To provide enough food for, satisfy the appetite of; also, to satisfy (the appetite). Chiefly *pass. Obs.*

c **1450** LOVELICH *Grail* xlviii. 428 The tenthe part Of theke Meyne with that fisch suffised not scholde be. **1526** TINDALE *Mark* viii. 4 From whence myght a man suffyse them with breed? *Ibid.* 8 They ate and were suffysed. **1595** SHAKS. *John* I. i. 191 And when my knightly stomacke is suffis'd, Why then I sucke my teeth. **1596** SPENSER *F.Q.* V. iii. 4 When all men had..Of meates and drinkes their appetites suffiz'd. **1609** *Man in Moone* (1849) 30 He is none of your ordinarie fellowes, which will suffice nature for threepence;..a rabbit is but a bitte with him. **1687** DRYDEN *Hind & P.* I. 554 When the herd suffis'd, did late repair To ferney heaths. **1791** COWPER *Iliad* I. 577 They feasted, and were all sufficed.

†**7.** To satisfy, meet the 'calls' of (a desire, need, sense, emotion, etc.) *Obs.*

1533 in Leadam *Sel. Cases Star Chamber* (Selden Soc.) II. 301 What [meat] shulde suffice their necessitie. **1547–64** BAULDWIN *Mor. Philos.* (Palfr.) 60 Sleepe no more then shall suffice the sustentation of your bodies. *c* **1585** *Faire Em* I. i. 67 Let my vttermost wealth suffice thy worth. **1598** CHAPMAN *Iliad* XVIII. 316 Then Ioue askt Iuno, if at length, she had suffisde her splene. **1651** DAVENANT *Gondibert* III. iv, The King has now his curious sight suffis'd With all lost Arts. **1667** MILTON *P.L.* I. 148 Strongly to suffer and support our pains, That we may so suffice his vengeful ire. **1725** POPE *Odyss.* II. 63 Scarce all my herds their luxury suffice. **1737** WHISTON *Josephus, Antiq.* XVI. vii. §1 There was..indeed enough to suffice all his wants.

†**8.** *intr.* with *unto*: To be satisfied with. *rare.*

c **1390** CHAUCER *Truth* 2 Suffise vnto þyn þyng þow it be smal.

†**9.** *trans.* To make or be sufficient provision for; to supply *with* something. Also, to replenish (a supply). *Obs.*

c **1440** *Pallad. on Husb.* IV. 56, V sester shal suffice an aker lond. *Ibid.* IX. 191, Xij hundrid pounde of metal shal suffise A thousand feet in lengthe of pipis sure. **1600** HAKLUYT *Voy.* III. 381 Oxen,..whereof..they killed fourescore, which sufficed the armie with flesh. **1697** DRYDEN *Æneid* IX. 1085 Nor Juno, who sustain'd his arms before, Dares with new strength suffice th' exhausted store. **1700** —— *Iliad* I. 653 The Pow'r appeas'd, with Winds suffic'd the Sail.

†**10.** To supply, furnish (a product, etc.). *Obs.*

1626 BACON *Sylva* §510 The Iuyce, as it seemeth, not being able to suffice a Succulent Colour, and a Double Leafe. **1725** POPE *Odyss.* XIII. 292 The rugged soil..Suffices fulness to the swelling grain.

su'fficeable, *a. nonce-wd.* [f. prec. + -ABLE.] Capable of being satisfied.

1864 CARLYLE *Fredk. Gt.* XVI. vi. IV. 329 A sum-total of actual desire to live with King Friedrich, which might..have almost sufficed even for Voltaire..; nor was Voltaire easily sufficeable!

†**su'fficed**, *ppl. a. Obs.* [f. as prec. + -ED[1].] Satisfied.

1590 SPENSER *F.Q.* I. ii. 43 Time and suffised fates to former kynd Shall vs restore. **1624** QUARLES *Sion's Sonn.* iv, O Thou, the joyes of my sufficed heart.

su'fficer. *rare.* [f. as prec. + -ER[1].] A satisfier.

1900 P. C. SIMPSON *Fact Christ* ii. 33 He regarded Himself as the sufficer of all others' need.

sufficience (sə'fɪʃəns). *arch.* Forms: 4–6 **sufficiens**, 5 **suffisiance, suffycyence, -ens**, 5–6 **sufficians**, 5–7 **-aunce**, 6 **suficiens, suffiecence**, 4– **sufficience**. [a. OF. *sufficience* or ad. late L. *sufficientia*, f. *sufficient-, -ens*, SUFFICIENT: see -ENCE; cf. next and SUFFISANCE.]

1. The quality or condition of being sufficient or enough; sufficient supply, means, or resources.

c **1380** WYCLIF *Serm.* Sel. Wks. II. 44 Siþ alle þingis is bifore Crist, þis sufficience lastiþ longe. **1460** CAPGRAVE *Chron.* (Rolls) 92 If we be bisi for to gete us tresoure in Hevene, God schal send us sufficiens in erde. **1500–20** DUNBAR *Poems* lxvii. 1 Quho thinkis that he hes sufficence Of gudis hes no indigence. **1546** LANGLEY tr. *Pol. Verg. de Invent.* I. cxv. 27 b, If it [*sc.* the Nile] increse unto the depth of twelue or thurtene Cubites it portendeth lacke of Sufficience. *a* **1578** LINDESAY (Pitscottie) *Chron. Scot.* (S.T.S.) I. 57 Thinkand gif they saiffit thame selffis they had suffiecence quhill ane better fortoun. **1695** LD. PRESTON *Boeth.* III. pr. ii. (1712) 109 That they may have Sufficiences and Abundance within themselves. **1873** MORLEY *Rousseau* II. 113 This full and perfect sufficience of life was abruptly disturbed.

†**b.** *phr.* (Sc.) *at* or *to sufficience* (= F. *à suffisance*): in sufficient quantity, sufficiently. *in sufficience*: in comfort. *Obs.*

c **1430** *Pilgr. Lyf Manhode* I. lxxxiii. (1869) 48 Now needeth it thanne quod sapience that fulfillinge to sufficience thow fynde it. *c* **1470** HENRY *Wallace* IX. 1174 Ȝon folk has fud, trast weill, at sufficians. *Ibid.* X. 551 Off nolt and scheip thai tuk at sufficiens. **1535** W. STEWART *Cron. Scot.* (Rolls) II. 705 He wes richt weill sustenit,..At sufficience that neidfull wes to haif, With sic prouisioun that that armet [= hermit] had. **1549** *Compl. Scot.* iii. 26 Ȝe sal eyt ȝour breyde in suficiens.

†**2.** Capacity; ability; competence. Also, a capable or competent person. *Obs.*

1382 WYCLIF *2 Cor.* iii. 5 Not that we ben sufficient for to thenke ony thing of vs, as of vs, but oure sufficience is of God. **1432–50** tr. *Higden* (Rolls) I. 201 The chiefe cite of whom is callede Capua, namede so of the capacite of sufficiaunce. **1607** ROWLANDS *Hist. Guy War* Ep. Ded., These Artless Lines, which in the silence of greater sufficiences, serve only to keep Valour from Oblivious destruction. **1669–70** MARVELL *Corr.* Wks. (Grosart) II. 303 They are the judges of the sufficience of the securityes. **1676** *Ibid.* 498 [He] is very well known for his sufficience and integrity.

†**3.** That which suffices for one's needs; satisfaction of one's needs; sustenance. *Obs.*

c **1450** *Mankind* 731 in *Macro Plays* 27 Wepynge, sythynge, & sobbynge, were my suffycyens. **1500–20** DUNBAR *Poems* lxxxi. 100 With gredines I se this world ourgane, And sufficence dwellis nocht bot in heavin. **1578** *Chr. Prayers in Priv. Prayers* (1851) 513 Draw the soul, that thirsteth after thee, to the rivers of everlasting sufficience, which are above. **1613** PURCHAS *Pilgrimage* (1614) 15 This whereof wee treat they neede not, as finding all sufficience in their All-sufficient Creator. **1620** T. GRANGER *Div. Logike* 168 God is all sufficient, *Gen.* 17. 1. and giues sufficience to all his creatures.

†**4.** = SELF-SUFFICIENCE. *Obs.*

1382 WYCLIF *2 Cor.* ix. 8 To make al grace abounde in ȝou, that ȝe in alle thingis euermore hauynge al sufficience. **1669** GALE *Crt. Gentiles* I. I. i. 4 God contemplating himself beholds in his Divine Essence or Sufficience.

sufficiency (sə'fɪʃənsɪ). Also 5–7 **-encie**, 8 **-entcy**. [ad. L. *sufficientia* (see prec. and -ENCY). Cf. It. *soffic(i)enza, -ia*, Sp. *suficiencia*.]

†**1.** Sufficient means or wealth; ability or competence to meet pecuniary obligations. *Obs.*

1495 *Act 11 Hen. VII*, c. 24 §3 Iffe ther be not persones of suche sufficiencie within the Shyre. **1601** F. TATE *Househ. Ord. Edw. II* §1 (1876) 5 This stewarde shall be a man of good sufficiency. **1611** *Bible* Lev. v. 7 *marg* His hand cannot reach to the sufficiencie of a lambe. *Ibid.* Job xx. 22 In the fulnesse of his sufficiencie, he shalbe in straites. **1682** SCARLETT *Exchanges* 48 The one as well as the other [*viz.* the drawer and the remitter], must be careful, and enquire into each others Sufficiency. **1747** *Act 20 Geo. II*, c. 43 §36 The Clerk of Court shall be answerable for the Sufficiency of such Cautioner.

b. A sufficient supply; a competence.

1608 D. T[UVILL] *Ess. Pol. & Mor.* 50 b, The powerfull hand of irreprooueable wisdom, hath divided our sufficiencie into little portions. **1645** CROMWELL *Let. to Lenthall* 14 Sept. (Carlyle), The same spirit of faith by which we ask all our sufficiency, and have received it. **1682** W. PENN in *Life* Wks. 1782 I. p. lxxx, Let your industry..go no farther than for a sufficiency for life. **1728–46** THOMSON *Spring* 1157 An elegant sufficiency, content, Retirement, rural quiet. **1898** 'H. S. MERRIMAN' *Roden's Corner* viii. 78 Holland suggests..an elderly gentleman..who, having laid by a small sufficiency, sits peaceably by the fire.

c. Adequate provision of food or bodily comfort.

1796 CHARLOTTE SMITH *Marchmont* I. 169 [He] could not afford to repair or to live in it [*sc.* the house] with any degree of comfortable sufficiency for years before his death. **1837** HT. MARTINEAU *Soc. Amer.* III. 139 She and her daughter..kept the house, which might vie with any nobleman's for true luxury; perfect sufficiency and neatness. **1848** MILL *Pol. Econ.* IV. ii. §4. 256 There is..sufficiency everywhere when anciently there would have been scarcity in some places and superfluity in others.

2. The condition or quality of being sufficient for its purpose or for the end in view; adequacy.

1565 STAPLETON tr. *Staphylus' Apol.* 161 b, The sufficiency of only faith to saluation. **1589** *Hay any Work* 27 We know the sufficiencie of it [*sc.* a book] to be such, as the Puritans are not able to answere it. *c* **1650** BRADFORD *Plymouth Plant.* (1856) 75 Perceiveing y[e] mariners to feare y[e] suffisiencie of y[e] shipe. **1661** PEPYS *Diary* 15 July, I read over the will, and had their advice therein, who as to the sufficiency thereof confirmed me. **1726** AYLIFFE *Parergon* 116 The Competency or Sufficiency of an Ecclesiastical Benefice, ought to be considered..in respect of the..Charges incumbent on such a Benefice. **1755** YOUNG *Centaur* (1757) IV. i. 112 The sufficiency of human reason. **1839** HALLAM *Lit. Eur.* II. viii. §8 Montuela calls him the model of commentators for the pertinence and sufficiency of his notes. **1863** H. COX *Instit.* III. v. 658 Surveyors, who report on the sufficiency of river steam-vessels before they are entitled to ply for passengers. **1884** *Law Rep.* 27 *Chanc. Div.* 630 There is a doubt about the sufficiency of the assets. **1912** *Oxf. Univ. Gaz.* 6 Nov. 149/1 The Board shall in writing report to the Regius Professor of Divinity as to the sufficiency of the Candidate's work.

3. (A) sufficient number or quantity *of*; enough.

1531 TINDALE *Expos. 1 John* (1537) 88 We ought to aske of God only sufficyency of all worldly thynges. **1598** BARCKLEY *Felic. Man* (1631) 491 That which bringeth forth contentation, is a sufficiency of things. **1623** BINGHAM *Xenophon* 93 If we shall finde such sufficiencie of shipping, that not one of vs shall need to be left behinde. *a* **1640** T. JACKSON *Treat. Signs Times* Wks. 1673 II. 380 The daily sacrifice of beasts did cease for want of provision, they having plenty, or sufficiency of nothing but of famine. **1747** WESLEY *Prim. Physick* (1755) Pref. p. xiii, There is Sufficiency of other Medicines. **1774** GOLDSMITH *Nat. Hist.* (1862) I. II. v. 321 When he has eaten a sufficiency, he then retires. **1832** LYELL *Princ. Geol.* II. xv. 244 So as to afford sufficiency of wood for fuel. **1859** CORNWALLIS *New World* I. 353 For practical mining purposes it contained no sufficiency of gold. **1901** ALLDRIDGE *Sherbro* xv. 145 None of the women wear any clothes, there is simply a sufficiency of strung beads around their waists.

4. Sufficient capacity *to* perform or undertake something; adequate qualification; ability, competency. *Obs.* or *arch.*

1567 *Reg. Privy Council Scot.* Ser. I. I. 539 The honestie, habilitie,..and sufficiency of oure said dearest brother to have the cure..of oure said..sone. **1583** STUBBES *Anat. Abus.* II. (1882) 54 Their knowledge, discretion, and sufficiencie in their art. **1590** SIR J. SMYTHE *Disc. Weapons* (title-p.), The great sufficiencie, excellencie and wonderful effects of Archers. **1604** SHAKS. *Oth.* I. iii. 224 We haue there a Substitute of most allowed sufficiencie. **1627** HAKEWILL *Apol.* (1630) 220 Well knowne in London for his Sufficiencie in his profession. **1690** LOCKE *Hum. Und.* II. xxvii. §8 So able a Man as he, who had Sufficiency enough to warrant all the Testimonies he gives of himself. **1786** BURKE *Art. agst. W. Hastings* Wks. 1842 II. 200 The nabob's sufficiency for the management of his own affairs. **1800** MORNINGTON in Owen *Wellesley's Desp.* (1877) 653 The state..has already supported them at a considerable expense, under the presumption of their sufficiency to discharge the duties. **1866** GEO. ELIOT *F. Holt* xli, Their sufficiency to judge the men who make love to them.

†**b.** An instance of this; a qualification; also, an accomplishment. *Obs.*

1590 SIR J. SMYTHE *Disc. Weapons* Dedic., To set foorthe and beautifie their owne sufficiencies. **1599** B. JONSON *Cynthia's Rev.* I. iv, I feare I may doe wrong to your sufficiencies in the reporting them. **1601** —— *Poetaster* I. ii. 132 It shall neuer put thee to thy Mathematiques, Metaphysiques, Philosophie, and I know not what suppos'd sufficiencies. **1635** R. N. tr. *Camden's Hist. Eliz.* III. 254 The..Privy Councell taking notice of his sufficiencies, made use of his counsaile. **1691** WOOD *Ath. Oxon.* I. 85 By recommendations made to the King of his great sufficiencies in..Oratory. **1713** STEELE *Guard.* No. 13 ¶4 One may have an air, which proceeds from a just sufficiency and knowledge of the matter before him.

†**5.** = SELF-SUFFICIENCY 1. *Obs.*

1635 SWAN *Spec. Mundi* iii. §1 (1643) 42 God..whose sufficiencie and efficiencie is altogether absolute.

6. = SELF-SUFFICIENCY 2. *arch.*

1638 ROUSE *Heav. Acad.* ix. 135 They thought their own eyes sufficient to see, and their own eares to heare; and resting in this insufficient sufficiencie [etc.]. **1690** TEMPLE *Ess., Anc. & Mod. Learn.* 3, I could not read either of this Strain, without some indignation, which no quality among men is so apt to raise in me as sufficiency, the worst composition out of the pride and ignorance of mankind. **1711** SHAFTESB. *Charact.* (1737) II. I. ii. 207, I cou'd never have the Sufficiency to shock my Spiritual and Learned Superiours. **1734** tr. *Rollin's Belles Lettres* (1783) I. 280 By this air of sufficiency they think they gain the esteem of others, though they only procure their contempt. **1893** STEVENSON *Catriona* viii, Who effer heard of such suffeeciency as tell a shentlemans that is the king's officer he cannae speak Cot's English?

sufficient (sə'fɪʃənt), *a.* (*adv.*, *sb.*) Forms: 4 *Sc.* **sufficyand, -yciand,** 4–5 **-icia(u)nt(e,** 4–6 **-icyent,** *Sc.* **-iciand,** 5 **-isia(u)nt, -yceant, -ycient, -ycyaunt, -ysyent, -eceant,** 5–6 **-ycyent, -iente,** 6 **-iecient,** 6–7 **-itient,** (7 **sophytient),** 4– **sufficient.** [a. OF. *sufficient*, *-ant*, or ad. its source L. *sufficiens*, *-ent-*, pr. pple. of *sufficĕre* to SUFFICE. Cf. It. *soffic(i)ente*, Sp. *suficiente*, Pg. *sufficiente*. In ME. the word was partially assimilated in spelling to SUFFISANT.

Formerly †*sufficient enough* was used in various senses.]

A. *adj.*

1. a. Of a quantity, extent, or scope adequate to a certain purpose or object.

c **1380** WYCLIF *Wks.* (1880) 260 ȝif þei tellen a good sufficient cause, telle we þe same cause whi we bileuen þat þis is cristis gospel. *a* **1400–50** *Wars Alex.* 4396 Þat seising burde sufficiant, þofe soȝt ȝe na ferre. *a* **1533** LD. BERNERS *Huon* lxxxi. 242 Ye hadde mete and also good wynes suffycyent at home. **1583** STUBBES *Anat. Abus.* II. (1882) 32 In former times a mans bare word was sufficient, now no instrument, band, nor obligation can be sure inough. **1614** DAY *Festivals* xi. (1615) 318 Should we..praise our God whole Daies, and whole Nights.., it were not sufficient enough. **1667** MILTON *P.L.* VIII. 5 What thanks sufficient.. have I to render thee? **1721** BRADLEY *Philos. Acc. Wks. Nat.* 186 Some Variety of such exotick Rarities from the hotter Climates, as afford the curious sufficient matter of Admiration. **1817** JAS. MILL *Brit. India* II. IV. v. 177 Intelligence was in sufficient time received..to enable him to collect an army. **1865** S. WILBERFORCE *Sp. Missions* (1874) 166 It will be quite sufficient if, in the fewest words, I venture to suggest one or two considerations which [etc.]. **1884** GILMOUR *Mongols* xxxi. 361 Many a lama who has nominally a sufficient income never receives more than half of his due.

b. Const. *for*: (*a*) = to furnish means or material for, to supply, to provide for the performance of (a thing).

c **1380** WYCLIF *Sel. Wks.* III. 346 For noumbre of preestis brouȝt in bi Crist was sufficient for Cristis hous... Who mai denye þat ne þis noumbre of þes officeris is now to myche? *c* **1460** FORTESCUE *Abs. & Lim. Mon.* viii. (1885) 126 How necessarie it is þat livelod sufficient be asseigned ffor the kynges ordinarie charges. *a* **1548** HALL *Chron., Hen. IV*, 32 b, Treasure sufficient..for such a iourney roiall. **1561** T. HOBY tr. *Castiglione's Courtyer* I. (1577) G ij, My talke hath not beene..sufficient ynough for the weightinesse of the matter. **1715** ATTERBURY *Serm.* (Matt. xxvii. 25) (1734) I. 132 These Prophecies..were sufficient for the Conviction of any Men, who did not lie..under a Judicial Infatuation. **1774** CHESTERF. *Lett.* xv, Romulus..not having sufficient inhabitants for his new city. **1892** *Photogr. Ann.* II. 557 That is sufficient range for any purpose.

(*b*) = to provide for the needs or accommodation of, to satisfy (a person or animal). Also with acc. and inf.

1535 FISHER *Wayes perf. Relig.* Wks. (1876) 382 Yet hath he still in him self loue suffitient for infinite moe. **1577** HOLINSHED *Hist. Scot.* 432/1 It appeareth to be sufficient ynough for vs. **1585** *Knaresb. Wills* (Surtees) I. 150 Sufficient hay for his horse. **1611** *Bible* Transl. Pref. ⁋4 A doctrine..so tempered, that euery one may draw from thence that which is sufficient for him. *a* **1700** EVELYN *Diary* 17 Oct. 1644, The publiq armoury..sufficient for 30,000 men. *a* **1720** SEWEL *Hist. Quakers* (1795) II. VII. 1 There was not sufficient room for all to sit down at once. **1832** BREWSTER *Nat. Magic* x. 252 A few general observations will perhaps be sufficient for ordinary readers. **1876** E. MELLOR *Priesth.* iv. 164 If the sacrament in one kind is sufficient for the people it is sufficient for the priest.

c. Const. *to* in the same senses. *rare* exc. in allusion to or imitation of Matt. vi. 34.

1539 *Great Bible* Matt. vi. 34 Sufficient vnto the daye, is the trauayle therof. **1647** SALTMARSH *Spark Glory* (1847) 20 It ought to be sufficient to us, that the Scriptures [etc.]. **1718** ATTERBURY *Serm.* (Acts i. 3) (1734) I. 174 It was sufficient to that Purpose. **1751** EARL ORRERY *Rem. Swift* (1752) 78 His wit was sufficient to every labour. **1766** A. ADAMS *Let.* 13 Oct. in L. H. Butterfield et al. *Adams Family Corr.* (1963) I. 56 Sufficient to the Day is the Evil thereof. **1886** SAINTSBURY *Ess. Eng. Lit.* (1891) 439 He..is very sufficient also to the tastes of all those who love good English. **1917** H. B. TWYFORD *Purchasing & Storing* 323 A 'sufficient unto the day' policy has brought some rude jolts to many manufacturing establishments. **1921** GALSWORTHY *To Let* I. xii. 114 He never looks happy—not really happy. I don't want to make him worse, but of course I shall have to, when Jon comes back. Oh! well, sufficient unto the night! **1928** D. H. LAWRENCE *Lady Chatterley's Lover* ii. 18 Sufficient unto the day is the evil thereof. Sufficient unto the moment is the *appearance* of reality. **1960** C. DAY LEWIS *Buried Day* ii. 34 They watch the spring rise inexhaustibly—a breathing thread out of the eddied sand, sufficient to their day. **1967** S. BECKETT *Stories & Texts for Nothing* v. 93, I haven't been damned for what seems an eternity, yes, but sufficient unto the day, this evening I'm the scribe. **1983** E. ROSSITER *Lemon Garden* v. 72 'What about this hospital business?' Sufficient, I thought, unto another day.

¶ Construed as pr. pple. with dative regimen.

1423 *Acts Privy Counc.* III. 95 Wee consideringe yᵉ saide some..nought suffeceant yow to yᵉ..redy paiement of youre saide wages.

d. Const. *to* with inf.

c **1380** WYCLIF *Sel. Wks.* III. 413 Siþ þo gospel is.. sufficyent in treuthe to governe Cristis Churche. **1527** in Leadam *Sel. Cases Star Chamber* (Selden Soc.) II. 166 They can not fynde..that ther is corne sufficient in the same shyre to susteyne the people. **1579–80** NORTH *Plutarch* (1595) 80 The ouer excessiue speeches..were not sufficient enough to expresse the peaceable raign. *a* **1586** SIDNEY *Arcadia* I. xv. (1912) 97 He..having a fortune sufficient to content, & he content with a sufficient fortune. **1597** MORLEY *Introd. Mus.* 115, I cannot cease to praie you diligentlie to practise, for that onelie is sufficient to make a perfect Musician. **1667** MILTON *P.L.* II. 102 And by proof we feel Our power sufficient to disturb his Heav'n. **1688** *Col. Rec. Pennsylv.* I. 228 A sufficient number to make a Quorum. **1736** BUTLER *Anal.* I. i. Wks. 1874 I. 31 The same kind of force which is sufficient to suspend our faculties..will be sufficient to destroy them. **1820** W. IRVING *Sketch Bk.* II. 99 The beauty of the day was of itself sufficient to inspire philanthropy. **1890** *Law Times Rep.* LXIII. 765/1 Even a threatened interference with a plaintiff's rights..is sufficient to justify him in taking proceedings.

e. *impers.* with dependent clause or inf.

1538 STARKEY *England* (1878) 44 Suffycyent hyt ys that no man by nature ys excludyd from felycyte. **1553** EDEN *Treat. Newe Ind.* (Arb.) 5 They thought it not sufficiente in their life time to deserue prayse. **1667** MILTON *P.L.* XI. 252 Sufficient that thy Prayers are heard. **1797** S. & HT. LEE *Canterb. T.* (1799) I. 390 It is sufficient that I know thy guilt.

†**f.** Satisfactory. *Obs. rare.*

1375 BARBOUR *Bruce* I. 368 With a wertu of leavte A man may ȝeit sufficyand be.

g. Achieving its object; effective. *rare.*

1831 SCOTT *Ct. Rob.* xi, She..dealt him so sufficient a blow, that Toxartis lay lifeless on the plain. **1897** 'A. HOPE' *Phroso* vii. (1905) 130 Phroso paused in her recital of the savage, simple, sufficient old trick.

2. In technical language. **a.** Of legal documents, securities, etc.

1461 *Paston Lett.* II. 34 [They] shall have a signement sufficient to hem aggreabill for the seid payment. **1472–3** *Rolls of Parlt.* VI. 40/2 That the seid writyng endented..be lawfull and sufficient warant and discharge ayenst your Highnes. **1495, 1523** [see DISCHARGE *sb.* 4 e]. **1551** in Feuillerat *Revels Edw. VI* (1914) 56 This our Lettre shalbe your sufficient discharge for the same. **1592** WEST *1st Pt. Symbol.* § 103 d, That then the suruiuor..shall with ij. other sufficient suerties..by their sufficient & lawfull writing obligatory become.. bound [etc.]. **1628** COKE *On Litt.* 270 If the lessee enter into the land, and hath possession of it by force of the said lease, then such release made to him by the feoffor, or by his heire is sufficient to him. *a* **1768** ERSKINE *Inst. Law Scot.* IV. iv. § 90 (1773) 737 Libels might be so laid as to deprive the pannel of every article of exculpation, let it be ever so sufficient. **1820** GIFFORD *Compl. Eng. Lawyer* 82 The sheriff..is obliged to take (if it be tendered) a sufficient bail-bond. *Ibid.* 662 The said H. B. doth hereby agree, by good and sufficient conveyance in the law..to assign..unto the said C. D...all those three houses [etc.].

b. Theol. ***sufficient grace***: see GRACE *sb.* 11 b.

1728 *Chambers Cycl.* s.v. *Grace*, Grace..is Efficacious, or Efficient, when it has the Effect; and Sufficient when it has it not, tho' it might have had it. **1898** MORTIMER *Cath. Faith & Pract.* I. 120 Exciting grace regarded in its result is called (1) Sufficient and (2) Efficient grace.

c. Modern Philos. (***principle*** or ***law of***) ***sufficient reason***: see quot. 1717. ***sufficient condition*** (see quot. 1930); cf. *necessary condition* s.v. NECESSARY *a.* 1 d.

Sufficient reason is a translation of Leibnitz's 'raison suffisante' (*Monadologie*, 1714, §§31, 32), for which he had previously suggested 'raison déterminante' (*Réfl. sur le livre de Hobbes*, 1710); he may have been influenced in his final selection of the adj. by the use of *sufficient cause* in:

1656 HOBBES *Quest. conc. Liberty, Necessity & Chance* 294, I hold that to be a sufficient cause to which nothing is wanting that is needful to the producing of the effect. The same is also a necessary cause.

1717 S. CLARKE tr. *Leibnitz's 2nd Paper* in *Coll. Papers* 21 In order to proceed from Mathematicks to Natural Philosophy, another Principle is requisite, as I have observed in my *Theodicæa*: I mean, the Principle of a sufficient Reason, *viz.* that nothing happens without a Reason why it should be so rather than otherwise. *Ibid.* (tr. *5th Paper*) 207 The Principle of the Want of a sufficient Reason does alone drive away all these Spectres of Imagination. **1838** DE MORGAN *Ess. Probab.* 10 Many of our conclusions are derived from this principle, which is called in mathematics *the want of sufficient reason.* **1839** *Penny Cycl.* XIII. 398/2 The fundamental principles of all reasoning, namely, the principle of contradiction and the law of sufficient reason. *Ibid.* 399/1 This adjustment of the monads was in accordance with certain sufficient reasons in each monad..; this sufficient reason was their comparative perfection. **1857** MAURICE *Mor. & Met. Philos.* IV. viii. § 72. 516 The sufficient reason must be found seeing it is implied in all demonstrations. **1914** B. RUSSELL *Our Knowledge of External Wrld.* iv. 109 In the hypothetical sense, continuity may be allowed to be a *necessary* condition if two appearances are to be classed as appearances of the same thing. But it is not a *sufficient* condition, as appears from the instance of the drops in the sea. **1923** C. D. BROAD *Sci. Thought* xiii. 499 Certain brain-events are the necessary and sufficient conditions of the occurrrence of all our different sensations. **1930** L. S. STEBBING *Mod. Introd. Logic* xv. 271 A condition X is a *sufficient condition* of an occurrence A provided that whenever X is present A occurs. But if A may occur when X is absent, then X, though a sufficient is not a *necessary* condition of A. **1948** AMBROSE & LAZEROWITZ *Fund. Symbolic Logic* v. 83 The sufficient condition for *q*'s truth is given by '$p \supset q$'. **1949** [see NECESSARY *a.* 1 d]. **1965** E. J. LEMMON *Beginning Logic* i. 28 Hence we shall say that, whenever it is the case that if *P* then *Q*, *P* is sufficient condition for *Q*, and, whenever it is the case that only if *P* then *Q*, *P* is a *necessary condition* for *Q*.

d. ***sufficient statistic***, a statistic that contains all the information in the observations it is based on that is relevant to the estimate being made.

[**1922** R. A. FISHER in *Phil. Trans. R. Soc.* A. CCXXII. 316 The statistic chosen should summarise the whole of the relevant information supplied by the sample. This may be called the Criterion of Sufficiency.] *Ibid.* 359 In the case of the normal curve of distribution it is evident that the second moment is a sufficient statistic for estimating the standard deviation. **1972** A. W. F. EDWARDS *Likelihood* ii. 18 If we were certain that no other model would ever be contemplated, then the sufficient statistic could replace the original data as raw material for inductive inference.

†**3. a.** Qualified by talent or ability; competent, capable, able. *Obs.*

c **1385** CHAUCER *L.G.W.* 1067 *Dido*, That he was lyk a knyght, And sufficiaunt [*v.rr.* suffisa(u)nt] of persone & of mygh[t]. **1424** *Cov. Leet Bk.* 85 One or ij sufficiante men to ouerse the Collectours. **1576** ABP. GRINDAL *Let. Ld. Burleigh* in *Rem.* (1843) 360, I pray your lordship's help that Mr Redmayn..may be archdeacon of Canterbury. He is a very sufficient man. **1603** KNOLLES *Hist. Turks* (1621) 332 Where they were by sufficient teachers, first instructed in the principles of the Mahometan religion. **1659** RUSHW. *Hist. Coll.* I. 605 A sufficient preaching Minister shall be provided..to serve the Cure. **1667** MILTON *P.L.* II. 404 Whom shall we send In search of this new world, whom shall we find Sufficient? **1719** LONDON & WISE *Compl. Gard.* p. xiii, Those that..have a sufficient Gardener. **1817** JAS. MILL *Brit. India* II. V. v. 497 Sir Eyre Coote should be requested to take upon himself, as alone sufficient, the task [etc.].

†**b.** Const. *to*, *for* (a function, work), *to do* something. *Obs.*

1382 WYCLIF *2 Cor.* iii. 5 Not that we ben sufficient [L. *sufficientes*, Gr. ἱκανοί] for to thenke ony thing of vs. *c* **1440** *Jacob's Well* 295 To holdyn offyse þat a man is noȝt suffycyent to. **1456** SIR G. HAYE *Law Arms* (S.T.S.) 23 He was nat sufficiand to governe the office. ? **1598** in *Lismore Papers* Ser. II. (1887) I. 14 A Master of Artes, and euery waie uery sufficient to be the Warden. **1611** *Bible* Transl. Pref. ⁋6 Who had bene so sufficient for this worke as the Apostles or Apostolike men? **1639** S. DU VERGER tr. *Camus' Admir. Events* 69 Sufficient to performe their huswifery. **1667** MILTON *P.L.* III. 99, I made him just and right, Sufficient to have stood, though free to fall.

†**4.** Of persons: Of adequate means or wealth; having a competence, substantial, well-to-do; hence, qualified by means or status for an office or duty. (Const. *of* = in respect of; *to* with inf.) *Obs.*

1436 *Rolls of Parlt.* IV. 501/2 The more sufficient that men be of liflode..ye more [etc.]. *c* **1482** in *Cal. Proc. Chanc. Q. Eliz.* (1830) II. Pref. 63 The same Robert is not sufficient to pay and content the said arrerages. **1590** PAYNE *Brief Descr. Ireland* (1841) 11 [He] hath gotten more sufficient tennauntes into his said countrie then any other two. **1596** SHAKS. *Tam. Shr.* IV. iv. 95 Some sufficient honest witnesses. **1655** R. YOUNGE *Charge agst. Drunkards* 2 More is thrown out of one swines nose, and mouth, and guts, then would maintein five sufficient familes. *c* **1672** WOOD *Life* (O.H.S.) I. 178 An honest and sufficient farmer. **1678** PENN in *Life* Wks. 1782 I. p. lxiv, How many sufficient and trading families are reduced to great poverty by it. **1679** —— *Addr. Prot.* II. 226 Many, once sufficient, are expos'd to Charity. **1782** ELIZ. BLOWER *Geo. Bateman* II. 157 A great many very sufficient people.

†**5.** Of things: Of adequate quality; of a good standard; substantial; in good condition. *Obs.*

1473 *Rental Bk. Cupar-Angus* (1879) I. 165, ij bollis of hors corn sufficiand. **1490** *Munim. de Melros* (Bann. Club) 600 Of þe quhilk viij chalder five salbe of gud sufficient qwheit. **1507** *Reg. Privy Seal Scot.* I. 209/2 Sufficiand merchand gudis. **1682** in *Thanes of Cawdor* (Spald. Club) 360 Guild and sufficient work built according to airt. **1699** *Ibid.* 393 Ane sufficient stair caise. *c* **1800** TENNANT in *Southey's Comm.-pl. Bk.* Ser. II. (1849) 422 Their enlargement gradually loosens and shatters the most sufficient buildings. [**1837** CARLYLE *Fr. Rev.* I. IV. iv, Making shoes,—one may hope, in a sufficient manner.]

6. In full, ***sufficient for*** (†***to***) ***oneself***: = SELF-SUFFICIENT 1.

1388 WYCLIF *Prov.* xii. 9 A pore man, and sufficient to him silf. **1850** NEWMAN *Diffic. Anglic.* I. (1891) 21 The English people is sufficient for itself. **1872** RUSKIN *Eagle's N.* § 77 The first order of Charity is to be sufficient for thyself.

1382 WYCLIF *Phil.* iv. 11, I haue lerud, in whiche thingis I am, sufficient [L. *sufficiens*, Gr. αὐτάρκης] for to be. **1502** ATKYNSON tr. *De Imitatione* III. xxiii. (1893) 216 Thou, good lorde, amonge all thinges art best, hyest, moost mighty & moost sufficient.

†**7.** = SELF-SUFFICIENT 2. *Obs.*

1620 FLETCHER *Chances* v. ii, Thou art the most sufficient, (I'le say for thee) Not to believe a thing. **1671** TEMPLE *Let. to J. Temple* Wks. 1731 II. 246 Sufficient and confident that no Endeavours can break the Measures between us and Holland. **1709** STEELE *Tatler* No. 51 ⁋5 A sufficient self-conceited Coxcomb. **1709** CIBBER *Rival Fools* III, The dull Stupidity of a sufficient Fool!

†**B.** *adv.* = SUFFICIENTLY. *Obs.*

1509 HAWES *Conv. Swearers* xliv, Am not I wounded for the suffycyent? **1560** WHITEHORNE *Ord. Souldiours* (1588) 15 b, A triangle battaile, may be always sufficient able to breake al maner of foure square battailes. **1592** *Arden of Feversham* I. i, I haue talkt sufficient. **1625** FLETCHER & SHIRLEY *N. Walker* III. i, Was I not late in my unhappy marriage, Sufficient miserable? **1762** FALCONER *Shipwr.* II. 146 When down sufficient, they securely brace [the yard]. **1826** W. A. MILES *Deverel Barrow* 17 When it takes a sufficient southerly course to admit of avoiding the mound.

C. *sb.* (This is prob. in origin partly a reduced form of *sufficiante*, SUFFICIENCY.)

†**1.** The quality or condition of being sufficient; sufficiency. *Obs.*

a **1450** *Lett. Marg. Anjou & Bp. Beckington* (Camden) 140 His suffisiant of cunnyng and habilite thereto. **1600** W. CORNWALLIS *Ess.* I. xix, I know not much of want, neither desire I Riches: I am borne to sufficient.

2. A sufficient quantity or supply; sufficient means; enough.

1470–85 MALORY *Arthur* XX. xvii. 828 For haue I suffycyaunt that may longe to my person I wylle aske none other ryche araye. **1523** LD. BERNERS *Froiss.* I. 60 b, They founde reasonably sufficyent therof. **1526** TINDALE *1 Tim.* v. 16 Let not the congregacion be charged: that hytt maye have sufficient for them that are widdowes in dede. **1587** *Mirr. Mag., Porrex* xii, Sufficient here is sayd to warne the wise. **1807–8** W. IRVING *Salmag.* (1824) 155, I have not, nor perhaps ever shall acquire, sufficient of the philosophic policy of this government. **1818** CRUISE *Digest* (ed. 2) III. 498 Whether sufficient appeared by the special verdict in this case, to prevent the lessor of the plaintiff..from recovering in the ejectment? **1860** TYNDALL *Glac.* I. ii. 14 We saw sufficient to account for the noise.

†**su'fficientize**, *v. Obs. rare*$^{-1}$. [f. prec. + -IZE.] *trans.* ? To make 'sufficient' or competent.

1693 BEVERLEY *Gospel Truth* 35 This sufficiency, saith he [St. Paul], is of God, who hath therein Sufficientized [? us; *2 Cor.* iii. 6 ἱκάνωσεν ἡμᾶς] to Minister the New Testament.

sufficiently (sə'fɪʃəntlɪ), *adv.* (*sb.*) [f. SUFFICIENT *a.* + -LY^{2}.] In a sufficient manner.

1. In a manner or to an extent calculated to satisfy the circumstances of the case or adequate to a certain purpose or object; enough for the purpose (expressed or implied).

Formerly also in phr. † *sufficiently enough.*

1375 BARBOUR *Bruce* I. 322 Thar wes nane that euir him kend Wald do sa mekill for him, that he Mycht sufficiantly fundyn be. *c* **1380** WYCLIF *Wks.* (1880) 386 þat þe clergy was sufficyently purveyed for lyfelode. *c* **1430** *Pilgr. Lyf Manhode* I. lxx. (1869) 41 Thouh swiche ten j hadde had to a dyner, j hadde not be fed sufficientliche. **1503–4** *Act 19 Hen. VII*, c. 19 Many Tanners put their hydes and ledder to sale before they be sufficiantly dryed. **1556** OLDE *Antichrist* 108 b, I suppose it be sufficiently ynough declared, that the B. of Rome deserueth this thrid title. **1592** *Arden of Feversham* v. iii. 15 His pursse and girdle found at thy beds head Witnes sufficiently thou didst the deede. **1638** JUNIUS *Paint. Ancients* 33 Never..to swallow doune our meale, before it be sufficiently chewed. **1658** W. BURTON *Itin. Anton.* 123 Upon a hill sufficiently enough steep, to which there was no accesse. **1667** MILTON *P.L.* VIII. 404 Seem I to thee sufficiently possest Of happiness, or not? *a* **1700** EVELYN *Diary* 4 Nov. 1644, The..never to be sufficiently admir'd Torso of Amphion and Dirces. **1769** *Junius Lett.* ix. (1788) 66 The subject too has been already discussed, and is sufficiently understood. **1878** LECKY *Eng. in 18th Cent.* II. vii. 283 The strength of their principles was sufficiently shown by their almost unanimous refusal of the abjuration oath. **1885** 'MRS. ALEXANDER' *Valerie's Fate* i, You are not sufficiently clad. I must insist on your taking my shawl again.

b. Const. †*to*, *for* (a purpose, etc.).

1560 DAUS tr. *Sleidane's Comm.* 30 Thou aunswerest Luther..not sufficientlye to the matter [*non satis ad rem*]. **1764** *Museum Rust.* IV. 27 A soil..made sufficiently moist for vegetation. **1809** MALKIN *Gil Blas* I. viii. ¶2 A volley, for which I was not sufficiently case-hardened. **1884** F. TEMPLE *Relat. Relig. & Sci.* i. (1885) 20 The rule is sufficiently general for all practical purposes.

c. Const. *to* with inf.

1759 ROBERTSON *Hist. Scot.* I. III. 162 Nor were they sufficiently skilful in the art of war to reduce the place by force. **1857** MILLER *Elem. Chem., Org.* iii. §8. 222 Air is.. admitted to the distillate, sufficiently slowly to prevent it from taking fire. **1860** TYNDALL *Glaciers* I. xxii. 153 The slope..was just sufficiently steep to keep the attention aroused. **1895** *Law Times Rep.* LXXIII. 702/2 The thing saved was held to be sufficiently like a ship to be not unfairly treated as a ship.

2. Adequately, satisfactorily; hence, fully, completely, quite; now chiefly with adjs., as... as well could be.

c **1375** *Sc. Leg. Saints* vi. (*Thomas*) 402 þe tothir ensampil tane ma be sufficiandly be þe wyne-tre. *c* **1440** *Alphabet of Tales* 336 A clerk þat was wele and sufficientlie letterd. **1447** BOKENHAM *Seyntys* (Roxb.) 10 My wyt and my penne so to enlumyne..that suffycyently Thy legende begunne, I may termyne. *c* **1510** MORE *Picus* Wks. 2/1 If no man should dooe it, but he that might sufficientlye dooe it, no man should dooe it. **1577** HANMER *Anc. Eccl. Hist.* (1619) 436 There was such a maruellous great earthquake,..that it cannot sufficiently be described. **1611** SHAKS. *Wint. T.* IV. ii. 16 Businesses, (which none (without thee) can sufficiently manage). **1621** in Foster *Eng. Factories Ind.* (1906) 239 Itt is suffitiently probable a greater prejudice will enforce them to petition for his licence. **1662** J. DAVIES tr. *Olearius' Voy. Ambass.* 165 We entertained them with certain Gobelets of Aquavitae and sent them sufficiently drunk to the Ship. **1674** in *Verney Mem.* (1907) II. 317 All this has sophytiently vexed me. **1759** JOHNSON *Rasselas* iv, The old man went away sufficiently discontented. **1845** PATTISON *Ess.* (1889) I. 13 The style of Bede, if not elegant Latin, is yet correct, sufficiently classical. **1884** F. M. CRAWFORD *Rom. Singer* I. 3 He is still sufficiently ugly. **1905** R. BAGOT *Passport* xxxiv. 396 The last hour or so has been sufficiently trying to the nerves.

†**3.** Of workmanship: Substantially. *Obs.*

1387–8 T. USK *Test. Love* III. ix. (Skeat) l. 58 No man wene this werke be sufficiently maked; for goddes werke passeth mannes. **1393** *Reg. de Aberbrothoc* (Bann. Club) II. 42 William Plumer sal theke the mekil quer..wyth lede and guttir yt al abowt sufficiandly with lede. **1460** in *Rec. City of Norwich* (1910) II. 94 So þ^{t} þe cloth which shall be sufficiantely made shall be tokened. **1477** *Rolls of Parlt.* VI. 180/2 If any of the seid persone or persones..make not the seid pavement sufficienly. **1537** *Registr. Aberdon.* (Maitl. Club) I. 414 Sir Wilȝame..sall ouphald..þe foirsaid tenment..in all necessar thingis sufficientlie. **1639** in *Thanes of Cawdor* (Spalding Club) 284 Withe armes names and siferis..weill and sufficientlie wrocht. **1699** *Ibid.* 394 To finish the said work weel suffeciently neetly and compleetly.

4. Contemptuously. *pseudo-dial.* (Cf. SUFFICIENCY 6.)

1893 STEVENSON *Catriona* viii, I think I was used extremely suffeeciently myself to be set up to fecht with an auld wife.

†**5.** As *sb.* (after uses of late L. *sufficienter*). Sufficient means; sufficient; enough. *Obs.*

1456 SIR G. HAYE *Law Arms* (S.T.S.) 123 Gif he had nede, and had nocht sufficiandly to mak were with. *c* **1520** BARCLAY *Jugurth* (ed. 2) 58 From the heven descended.. plenty of rayne-water, that it was more than sufficiently to all the army. **1585** T. WASHINGTON tr. *Nicholay's Voy.* III. xix. 106 b, There is not brought sufficiently vnto them for the maintenance of their ydle life. **1586** BRIGHT *Melanch.* 128 Sufficiently hath bene saide. **1609** *Bible* (Douay) Nahum ii. 12 The lion hath caught sufficiently [Vulg. *cepit sufficienter*] for his welpes.

†**su'fficienty.** *Obs.* Also 5 -ia(u)nte. [a. AF. **sufficiaunte*, f. *sufficiant*, *-ent* SUFFICIENT: see -Y. Cf. SUFFISANTEE.] = SUFFICIENCY.

1450 in *Antiq. Rep.* (1809) IV. 639 Ordeyne and appoynte suche sufficiante of men and stuffe, as it may be sufficiante for the defence of the Castell and Ile. **1450–80** tr. *Secr. Secr.* 53 Surtee and sufficiante to þy gouernaille. **1461** *Rolls of Parlt.* V. 495/2 Yf there be not so many dwellyng within the same Shire of that sufficiaunte. **1592–3** A. HALL in Ellis *Orig. Lett.* Ser. II. III. 170, I..am hereupon, knowing his sufficienty,..humbly to beseeche your Honnor to stand my good Lord in my sonnes suite.

sufficing (sə'faɪsɪŋ), *ppl. a.* [f. SUFFICE *v.* + -ING^{2}.] That suffices *for* a purpose or object; sufficient, adequate, satisfying. (Cf. *all-sufficing*, quot. 1623 s.v. ALL- 7, SELF-SUFFICING *ppl. a.*)

1606 SHAKS. *Ant. & Cl.* IV. xiv. 117 Draw thy sword, and giue mee, Suffising strokes for death. *a* **1640** WOTTON in Farr *S.P. Jas. I* (1848) 248 Nor shrubs alone feel thy sufficing hand. **1642** MILTON *Apol. Smect.* Wks. 1851 III. 255, I had no fear but that the authors of *Smectymnuus*.. were prepar'd..to returne a suffizing answer. **1827** SCOTT *Highl. Widow* ii, The death of MacTavish Mhor was, in her apprehension, a sufficing reason. **1860** GEN. P. THOMPSON *Audi Alt.* cii. III. 4 And if the representation was such as to send sufficing men to parliament, it would be known which. **1905** E. CLODD *Animism* §7. 41 The sufficing materials for belief in an entity *in* the body, but not *of* it.

Hence **su'fficingly** *adv.*, so as to suffice; **su'fficingness**, sufficiency (cf. SELF-SUFFICINGNESS)

1821 *Examiner* 316/2 [She] is consequently more sufficingly suited to the various demands of the character. **1841** L. HUNT *Seer* (1864) II. 3 Beautiful present sufficingness of a cat's imagination!

suffiction (sʌ'fɪkʃən). [f. *suf-* = SUB- + FICTION *sb.*, after *supposition*.] A fiction taken as a hypothesis.

1817 COLERIDGE *Biog. Lit.* v, In the majority of instances these hypotheses or suppositions better deserve the name of ὑποποιήσεις, or *suffictions*. *Ibid.* xii, Arbitrary suppositions, or rather suffictions. **1833** —— *Table-t.* (1835) II. 197 It seems to me a great delusion to call or suppose the imagination of a subtle fluid, or molecules penetrable with the same, a legitimate hypothesis. It is a mere *suffiction*.

†**suffie**, *v. Obs. rare.* [ad. F. *suffire* (see SUFFICE).] *intr.* To suffice. Also †**suffiand** *a.* [after *suffisand*, SUFFISANT], sufficient.

c **1380** WYCLIF *Serm.* Sel. Wks. I. 120 Philip seide to Crist þat looves of two hundrid pens suffiden not to hem, þat ech man take a litil what. **1456** *Extr. Burgh Rec. Peebles* (1872) 116 To geyf hym a sufiand lewyn.

†'**suffiment.** *Obs. rare.* [ad. L. *suffīmentum* smoke of burnt sacrifice, f. *suffīre* (see SUFFITE).] A perfume burned or smoked as a medicinal remedy.

1650 H. BROOKE *Conserv. Health* To Rdr. A ix, Errhina for the Nose: Sneezing-powders, Suffiments. **1670** H. STUBBE *Plus Ultra* 62 The giving of Sandaracha, or Orpiment inwardly for old coughs; and the suffiment made out of it, are recorded by Dioscorides. **1862** MAYNE *Med. Vocab.* (ed. 2) s.v. *Suffimentum*.

'**suffisance.** Also 4–5 **souffisaunce**, (4 **sufficance**), 5 **suffishance**, **souffisance**, 5–6 **suffysaunce**, 6 **suffisans**, **-zaunce**, *illit.* **-gance**, 6–7 **suffizance**. [a. OF. *suff-*, *soffisance* (in Gower *sufficance*), ad. late L. *sufficientia* SUFFICIENCE.]

†**1.** (A) sufficient provision or supply; enough to supply one's needs. *Obs.*

c **1381** CHAUCER *Parl. Foules* 637 Which I have wroght so wel to my plesaunce; That to yow oghte been a suffisaunce. *c* **1386** —— *Sompn. T.* 135 Haue I nat of a capon but the lyuere And of youre softe breed nat but a shyuere And after that a rosted pigges heed..Thanne hadde I with yow hoomly suffisaunce [*v.r.* sufficeance]. *c* **1400** *Pol. Rel. & L. Poems* (1866) 27 Be payed with litelle, content with suffisance. **1484** CAXTON *Fables of Auian* xii, Euerychone ought to haue suffysaunce and to be content of that that he hath. *c* **1510** BARCLAY *Mirr. Gd. Maners* (1570) Cj, Wherfore on suffisaunce set thy pleasour and ioy, And couet not to climbe. **1568** *Jacob & Esau* IV. ix, A litle thing God wotte to me is suffisance. **1632** HOLLAND *Cyrupædia* 186 And when I have gotten it: locke what surplusage I see over and above suffisance.

†**2.** Sufficient quantity *of*; = SUFFICIENCY 3. *Obs.*

1387–8 T. USK *Test. Love* III. viii. (Skeat) l. 116 Suffisaunce of covenable comoditees without any maner nede. **1390** GOWER *Conf.* III. 28 Him thenkth..that he hath ful sufficance Of liflode. **1449** *Respect. Truce w. Scot.* in Rymer *Fœdera* (1710) XI. 244 Souffisaunce, of Gresse, Hay. *c* **1500** *Lancelot* 2004, I shal fulfill and do yowr ordynans Als far of wit as I have suffisans. *c* **1510** *Kal. Sheph.* F iiij, Suffysaunce of all thyngs necessary for salute & helpe of our soules & of our bodyes. **1544** BETHAM *Precepts War* II. lxxxiii. M ij b, To prouyde that thyne armye maye haue suffysaunce of vytayle.

†**3.** Abundance, ample means, wealth. *Obs.*

1390 GOWER *Conf.* III. 161 He liveth to the sufficance Of his havinge. *c* **1400** *Sc. Trojan War* (Horstm.) II. 3058 Thelamocus regned..In Achaia ȝeris sevynty, That in tyme of his governance It eked in-to gret suffisance. **1454** *Rolls of Parlt.* V. 273/1 Merchauntz..beyng many in nombre, and of greet suffisaunce. *c* **1470** HARDING *Chron.* XXX. x. (MS. Seld.), Leving his lond..In suffisaunce, and alle prosperite. **1574** A. L. tr. *Calvin's Foure Serm.* Ep., We see some flowing in earthly wealth and suffisance.

†**4.** Ability; = SUFFICIENCY 4. *Obs.*

c **1392** CHAUCER *Compl. Venus* 17 Not withstondyng al his suffisaunce, His gentil hert ys of so grete humblesse [etc.]. **1426** LYDG. *De Guil. Pilgr.* 8286 He that hath no suffysaunce Wyth-Inne hym-sylff tendure peyne. **1426** *Pol. Poems* (Rolls) II. 140 God of nature hath yoven him suffisaunce, Likly to atteyne to grete honure and pris. **1483** CAXTON *G. de la Tour* d iij b, Other ther ben that haue grace, wytte and suffisaunce ageynste couetyse. **1627** J. CARTER *Plain Expos.* 84 So in like manner are we, for competencie and suffizance in outward things, to vse the best industrie and prouision that wee can.

†**5. a.** Satisfaction, contentment. *Obs.*

c **1374** CHAUCER *Boeth.* III. pr. iii. (1868) 70 þou..in alle þe plente of þi rycchesse haddest þilke lak of suffisaunce. *c* **1386** —— *Pars. T.* ¶833 Suffisance, that seketh no riche metes ne drinkes. *c* **1407** LYDG. *Reason & Sens.* 190 Euery hert..him reioysseth with plesaunce, For the grete suffysaunce That they ha founde by disport. *c* **1430** —— *Min. Poems* (Percy Soc.) 123 Covetise oppressithe souffisaunce. **1484** CAXTON *Curiall* 3 Yf thou be in mene estate of whyche thou hast not suffysaunce thou shalt stryue for to mounte and ryse hyer. **1586** A. DAY *Engl. Secretorie* II. (1625) 97 In couetousnesse there is neuer any suffizance. **1590** SPENSER *Muiop.* 207 In the warme Sunne he doth himselfe embay, And there him rests in riotous suffisaunce Of all his gladfulnes.

b. A source of satisfaction. *Obs.*

c **1369** CHAUCER *Dethe Blaunche* 1038 She was, that swete wife, My suffisaunce, my luste, my lyfe. *c* **1430** LYDG. *Min. Poems* (Percy Soc.) 2 The vj^{te}. Herry, roote of her gladnes, Ther hertes joy, ther worldis suffisaunce. *Ibid.* 10 Sovereigne lord, welcome to youre citee!.. Welcome oure gladness, welcome oure suffisaunce! **1502** *Ord. Crysten Men* (W. de W.) I. vii, I graunte that Ihesu cryste is very redemptor & suffysaunce of all the worlde.

c. The satisfying (*of* a desire). *Obs.*

1548 UDALL, etc. *Erasm. Par. Luke* iv. 54 More then for the suffisaunce of nature is necessarie. **1574** tr. *Marlorat's Apoc.* 113 Not to hunger nor to thirst is taken for the full suffizance of all desires.

†**6.** Self-sufficiency, independence. *Obs.*

a **1450** *Knt. de la Tour* 202 And by cause I shold haue suffysaunce, he commaunded and charged me that neuer I shold put my self in subiection of none offyce vnder my souerayne lord.

7. (With Fr. pronunc. sufizɑ̃s). [After mod.F. *suffisance*.] Excess of self-confidence, conceit. (Cf. SUFFICIENCY 6.)

1781 BENTHAM in *Tait's Mag.* (1840) VII. 703 Pratt has more distance and more suffisance than either of the others. **1781** —— *Mem. & Corr.* Wks. 1843 X. 100 In his conversation there is..nothing of that hauteur and suffisance one would expect. **1917** D. H. LAWRENCE *Phoenix II* (1968) 82 The police-officer turned, saluted politely, and said, with the polite, intolerable *suffisance* of officialdom: 'Good evening! Trouble here!' **1925** —— *St. Mawr* 25 At the same time he was free of the Englishman's water-tight *suffisance*. **1957** S. SMITH *Coll. Poems* (1975) 344 Ah me the *suffisance* I drew therefrom What strength, what glory from that fattening fluid.

†'**suffisant**, *a. Obs.* Forms: 4 **suffis(c)haunt**, **-yssaunt**, **-icant**, *Sc.* **-icent**, 4–5 **-isant**, 4–6 **-isaunt**, 5 **-ysa(u)nt**, **-ischande**, **-issant**, **souffis(s)ant**, **suffissand**. [a. OF. *suffisant*, *soufisant*, in Gower *-cant* (whence also MDu. *soff-*, *suffisant*), pr. pple. of *suffire* to SUFFICE. Cf. SUFFICIENT.]

1. = SUFFICIENT 1 (with various const.)

a **1340** HAMPOLE *Psalter* cxxvi. 2 Bot if oure lord be kepere of oure saulis, all oure besynes is noght suffyssaunt. *c* **1380** WYCLIF *Serm.* Sel. Wks. I. 85 Cristis reule were fulli suffisant to alle men. *c* **1386** CHAUCER *Miller's T.* 365 Loke þat they..han ther-Inne vitaille suffisant But for a day. **1390** GOWER *Conf.* I. 153 Me thenketh that this evidence As to this point is sufficant. *c* **1391** CHAUCER *Astrol.* Prol. 63 Ther folwith a canon, suffisant to teche..the maner of the wyrkyng of þat same conclusioun. *c* **1400** *Rom. Rose* 5608 Mete and drynke and esy foode..And also suffisaunt clothyng. **1450** HEN. VI in *Rep. Hist. MSS. Comm.* Var. Coll. IV. 85 There vitailes ben not suffisant to serue them for iij wekes. *c* **1450** *St. Cuthbert* (Surtees) 1300 Halfe a hate lafe and soule he fande, þat to a male was suffischande. **1471** CAXTON *Recuyell* (Sommer) 135 Whan they fonde hem in nombre suffisant for to entre in to bataylle. *a* **1500** *Craft of Deyng* in *Ratis Raving*, etc. 3 þocht..he had neuer ben schrewyne befor..sa at thare-of he mycht haf suffissand contriscione, he war sauf. *c* **1570** *Pride & Lowl.* (1841) 82 These for our life we holden suffisaunt.

2. Of things (chiefly immaterial): Satisfactory in quality or efficacy; effective.

1340 HAMPOLE *Pr. Consc.* 3874 If it [*sc.* a bishop's pardon] be noght swa suffishaunt Als þe papes es. *c* **1386** CHAUCER *Wife's T.* 54 To seche and leere An answere suffisant [*v.rr.* sufficia(u)nt, sufficant] in this mateere. **1389** in *Eng. Gilds* (1870) 8 þat þey leye a suffisaunt wed, or elles fynde suffisaunt borwes of þe broþerhede. **1390** GOWER *Conf.* I. 81 Thei..token what thei myhten wynne Of such good as was sufficant. *Ibid.* 250 The tokne was so sufficant That it ne mihte be forsake. **1455** *Paston Lett.* I. 365 As it apperith by writing suffisaunt.

3. Of persons: = SUFFICIENT 3.

c **1385** CHAUCER *L.G.W.* 2524 *Phyllis*, Ye be nat suffisaunt to bere the peyne. *c* **1386** —— *Pard. T.* 470 That ye mowe haue a suffisant Pardoneer Tassoille yow. *c* **1400** *Pilgr. Sowle* (Caxton) IV. xxix. (1859) 61 An vnwyse kyng..lesith his people; but by the wytte of a suffysaunt souerayne, the peple is saued. *c* **1412** HOCCLEVE *De Reg. Princ.* 362 þe worþi prelacie, And vnder hem þe suffissant clergye. **1489** CAXTON *Faytes of A.* III. viii. 184 In his place he wyl leue for hym a suffysaunt man. **1491** —— *Vitas Patr.* (W. de W. 1495) I. Prol. 1 We ben not couenable ne suffisaunt to telle & recompte soo grete thynges.

4. Of persons: = SUFFICIENT 4.

1483 Caxton *G. de la Tour* b j, He sente certayne knyghtes and ladyes of the most suffisaunt of his royamme. **1491** *Cal. Anc. Rec. Dublin* (1889) 374 So that he fyn[d]e suffisaunt suertes therto.

5. = sufficient 6.

Chiefly after L. *sufficiens (sibi)*.

a **1340** Hampole *Psalter* xxii. 1 Na thynge sall me want, þat is, in him i sall be sikere and suffisaunt. *c* **1374** Chaucer *Boeth.* iii. pr. iii. (1868) 70 þanne may nat rycchesse maken þat a man nis nedy ne þat he be suffisaunt to hym self. **1382** Wyclif *Prov.* xii. 9 Betere is a pore man, and suffisaunt to hymself, than a glorious, and nedi bred.

†**suffisantee.** *Obs. rare.* [a. AF. *suffisante*, f. *suffisant* (see prec.). Cf. sufficienty.] Property.

1436 *Rolls of Parlt.* IV. 501/2 No persone of lesse suffisantee of Freehold then of the yerly value of xx li.

†**suffisantly,** *adv. Obs.* [f. suffisant + -ly[2]. Cf. MDu. *soffisantelike.*] Sufficiently, adequately, competently.

a **1340** Hampole *Psalter* Cant. 498 Whaim sa þou has punysst suffysaauntly here þou will noght punyss eft. *c* **1374** Chaucer *Boeth.* iv. pr. vi. (1868) 133 Vnneþes is þer suffisauntly any þing to answere perfitly to þi questioun. **1426** Lydg. *De Guil. Pilgr.* 21904 Now thow hast ynowh plente Off water..Suffysauntly a bath to make. **1483** Caxton *Gold. Leg.* 224/2 He cam agayn to his owen place and ete suffysauntly twyes a day of the same loof. **1489** —— *Faytes of A.* iii. viii. 184 With peyne he shulde fynde one that shulde suffysauntly kepe his rowme. **1502** *Ord. Crysten Men* (W. de W.) iv. vi, That the synner sayth not suffysauntly his synnes.

suffise, obs. form of suffice.

suffisticate, obs. erron. f. sophisticate.

1638 H. Shirley *Mart. Soldier* iii. F 2 b, We finde the spirits often suffisticated By many accidents, but yet not mortified.

suffit: see soffit, suffet.

†**suffite,** *sb. Obs. rare.* [ad. L. *suffītus*, f. *suffīt-*, *suffīre* to fumigate, f. *suf-* = sub- 2 + **fīre* (prob. related to *fūmus* smoke).] = suffiment.

1621 Burton *Anat. Mel.* i. iii. iii. 267 Suffites, perfumes, and suffumigations.

So †**suffite** *v.*, to fumigate; †**su'ffition** [L. *suffītio*], fumigation, perfume.

1656 Blount *Glossogr.*, *Suffition*, a purfume, a fumigation. **1657** Tomlinson *Renou's Disp.* 215, I saw a waiting man..so suffited by a woman. **1753** *Chambers' Cycl.* Suppl., *Suffition*, among the Romans, a kind of lustration, practised by persons who had attended a funeral; it was performed by walking over fire, and being sprinkled with water.

suffito, obs. var. of soffit.

suffix ('sʌfɪks), *sb.* [ad. mod.L. *suffixum*, subst. use of neut. of *suffixus*, pa. pple. of *suffigĕre*, f. *suf-* = sub- 2 + *figĕre* to fix. Cf. F. *suffixe.*]

1. *Gram.* A verbal element attached to the end of a word to form an entirely new word (e.g. *short*, *short-age*, *short-en*, *short-er*, *short-est*, *short-ish*, *short-ly*, *short-ness*) or as an inflexional formative (e.g. *ox*, *ox-en*).

1778 Bp. Lowth *Transl. Isaiah* Notes 243 These being all the places, where this word occurs without a suffix. **1864** I. Taylor *Wds. & Places* 124 The suffixes which occur most frequently in Anglo-Saxon names denote an enclosure of some kind. **1900** Sweet *New Engl. Gram.* 459 This suffix is frequent in names of animals, generally expressing youth or smallness, as in *youngling*. **1904** H. Bradley *Making of English* 133 The freedom with which we can still form new derivatives by means of suffixes inherited from Old English.

2. *Math.* An inferior index written to the right of a symbol.

1842 *Penny Cycl.* XXIII. 211/1 *Suffix*, a term lately employed in mathematical language to denote the indices which are written under letters, as in a_0, a_1, a_2, a_3. **1882** Minchin *Unipl. Kinemat.* 14 The suffixes signifying that *n* is to receive all integer values from 1 to ∞.

3. *attrib.*: **suffix ablaut**, variation in the vowel of a suffix; **suffix language**, a language inflected by means of suffixes; **suffix-pronominal** *a.*, having suffixal pronouns.

1869 Bleek *Comp. Gram. S. Afr. Lang.* ii. 136 One of these families of languages (either the Prefix-Pronominal or the Suffix-Pronominal). **1874** H. Bendall tr. *Schleicher's Compar. Gram.* 3 The Indo-European is therefore a suffix-language, together with the neighbouring languages of the Finnish stem. **1879** A. R. Wallace *Australasia* i. 7 The Australian idioms are characterised exclusively by suffix formations. **1881** Whitney *Mixt. in Lang.* 21 A prefix-language..might live in contact with a suffix-language forever without finding out the latter's character..until, perchance, it should have borrowed suffix-words enough to create in its own usage an analogy [etc.]. **1900** E. Björkman *Scand. Loan-Words in M.E.* i. 112 Here *aȝ* might depend on suffix-ablaut as in O.E. *faȝen*, *faȝ(e)nian.* **1977** *Archivum Linguisticum* VIII. 80 We must now examine cases where SF apparently fails, despite a following [l] rather than [ł]. Several cases, such as *falaed*, *alaer* may be explicable on grounds of 'suffix ablaut'.

Hence '**suffixal** *a.*, of the form or nature of a suffix; **suffix'ation**, formation by means of a suffix; **su'ffixion** [after prefixion], the act of suffixing or state of being suffixed; '**suffixment**, use as a suffix; '**suffixual** *a.* = suffixal *a.*

1874 A. B. Davidson *Introd. Hebr. Gram.* 101 The cons. and *suffixal forms of sing. and plur. coincide in spelling. **1899** Fay in *Amer. Jrnl. Philol.* XX. 449 After composition had sunk to *suffixation. *a* **1860** Worcester (citing *N. Brit. Rev.*), *Suffixion. **1879** Earle *Philol. Engl. Tongue* (ed. 3) §356. 331 An old French form *-ie*, now become *y*, of whose various *suffixment mention has been made above. **1901** J. Huguenin *Secondary Stress in Anglo-Saxon* 13 The inflected cases in which the *suffixual syllable is lengthened by position are, the genitive and dative singular feminine, the accusative singular masculine, and the genitive plural. **1964** [see mora[1] 3 b].

suffix (sə'fɪks, 'sʌfɪks), *v.* Chiefly in *pa. pple.* [Partly f. L. *suffixus* (see prec.), partly f. suffix *sb.*]

1. *trans.* To fix or place under; to subjoin.

1604 R. Cawdrey *Table Alph.*, *Suffixed*, fastned vnto. **1891** *Downside Rev.* X. 179 These are the words or letters which are suffixed to the larger part of the unacknowledged verse. **1900** *19th Cent.* Aug. 240 That splendid outburst of indignant eloquence which he suffixed as a dedicatory epilogue to the *Idylls of the King*.

2. To add as a suffix.

1778 Bp. Lowth *Transl. Isaiah* Notes 243 It occurs in other instances with a Pronoun suffixed. **1837** Richardson *Dict.* I. 64 From which by suffixing *ed*, we form a new participle. **1869** Peile *Gk. & Lat. Etym.* (1875) 55 If pronominal, they must have been suffixed at first to modify the root in a general way.

So **suffixed** *ppl. a.*, used as a suffix.

1869 Bleek *Comp. Gram. S. Afr. Lang.* ii. 136 *note*, The use of such a suffixed article. *a* **1902** A. B. Davidson *O. T. Proph.* (1903) xx. 348 All the suffixed pronouns.

suffizance, -ant, var. suffisance, -ant *Obs.*

†**sufflame,** *v. Obs. rare.* In 6 **-flawme.** [ad. late L. *sufflammāre*, f. *suf-* = sub- 26 + *flammāre* to flame.] *intr.* To rise like flame.

c **1530** *Judic. Urines* ii. xi. 39 b, Corrupt vapures sufflawmyng vp about the herte.

sufflaminate (sə'flæmɪneɪt), *v.* Now *rare.* [f. L. *sufflāmināt-*, *-āre*, f. *sufflāmen*, *-min-*, f. *suf-* = sub- 2 + **flāmen:—*flagmen* (cogn. with balk *sb.*[1]) beam, balk.] *trans.* To put an obstacle in the way of, obstruct.

1656 Blount *Glossogr.*, *Sufflaminate*, to skatch, scotch, or trig a wheel. **1660** H. More *Myst. Godl.* To Rdr. 24 All their superstitious Ceremonies put together adde nothing to them, but rather stifle and sufflaminate them. *a* **1672** Wren in Gutch *Coll. Cur.* I. 252 By long speeches..to sufflaminate the progress of business. **1683** *Phil. Trans.* XIV. 467 These ponds or Cisterns that sufflaminate the Current of the Aqueducts. **1836** *Tait's Mag.* III. 8 The movement and play of public business is sufflaminated. **1907** *Athenæum* 27 July 98/2 An advertisement of..'the..gas microscope,'..which gave Sam Weller an occasion to sufflaminate Mr. Buzfuz.

Hence †**sufflami'nation** (see quot.) *rare*[—0].

1658 Phillips, *Sufflamination*, a stopping the wheels of a Coach, or Cart, with an Instrument called a Sufflamen, or Trigger.

†**su'fflate,** *v. Obs.* [f. L. *sufflāt-*, pa. ppl. stem of *sufflāre*, f. *suf-* = sub- 26 + *flāre* to blow.] *trans.* To blow up, inflate; also *fig.*

1616 J. Lane *Contn. Sqr.'s T.* v. 110 As sensual vsurpers them sufflate. **1623** Cockeram, *Sufflated*, blowne up. *a* **1708** T. Ward *Eng. Ref.* etc. iii. (1710) 24 An inflam'd-zeal-burning Mind Sufflated by the Holy-Wind. **1778** [W. H. Marshall] *Min. Agric.* 21 Feb. 1777, The same cow again sufflated by cabbages. **1791** —— *Rural Econ. W. Eng.* (1796) II. 299.

†**su'fflation.** *Obs.* [ad. L. *sufflātio*, *-ōnem*, n. of action f. *sufflāre* (see prec.).] The action of blowing (up); inflation (*lit.* and *fig.*); distension with wind; inspiration (by the 'breath' of the Holy Ghost); expiration.

1599 A. M. tr. *Gabelhouer's Bk. Physicke* 121/2 When anye mans Bellye with sufflationes is straygned. **1631** R. H. *Arraignm. Whole Creature* xi. §2. 102 As the wandring Starres in their motions, yea as the Windes in their sufflations. **1660** R. Burney *Κέρδιστον Δῶρον* (1661) 65 There is no other Canker to Nobility and Gentry but sufflation. **1663** Waterhouse *Fortescue's De Laud. Legum Angliæ* 396 If any of them act above the sphear of vulgarity, 'tis by the sufflation of a miracle. **1778** [W. H. Marshall] *Min. Agric.* 27 Feb. 1776 It seems fully proved, that salt and water will cure a sufflation. **1797** Geddes *Transl. Bible* II. Pref. p. v, The admission..of a perpetual and unerring sufflation.. destroys their [*viz.* the Scriptures] credibility throughout. **1800** T. Green *Diary Lover of Lit.* (1810) 233 Discanting largely on the consequences of such a sufflation [*viz.* the explosion of gunpowder by the contending armies on the continent]. **1817** Coleridge *Lay Serm.* ii. (1852) 145 With strange sufflations he exorcised me.

†**su'fflature.** *Obs. rare*[—1]. [f. L. *sufflāt-* sufflate + -ure.] Distension with wind, flatulence.

1660 tr. *Paracelsus' Archidoxis* ii. 111 Camphyr..is..a most present help in Sufflatures, (or Windy-swellings).

†**suffle,** *sb. Obs. rare*[—1]. ? Commotion, disturbance. (Perhaps a misprint for *ruffle.*)

1650 A. A[scham] *Reply to Sanderson* 13 Hee might put all the World into an endlesse suffle, before he should finde such Persons.

†**suffle,** *v. Obs. rare.* [app. ad. F. *souffler*:—L. *sufflāre* (see sufflate).]

1. *intr.* To blow. (Cf. ruffle *v.*[2] 3.)

1622 R. Hawkins *Voy. S. Sea* (1847) 22 The wind began to suffle with fogge and misling rayne.

2. *trans.* To blow *up.*

1632 Lithgow *Trav.* ix. 382 Its Kind Is nurs'd by Raine, and suffled vp with wind.

suffling ('sʌf(ə)lɪŋ), *vbl. sb.* [f. suffl(e *v.* + -ing[1].] A sound as of blowing or heavy breathing.

1904 H. F. Day *Kin O'Ktaadn* i. 11 The..whummle of horses and..sufflings of..cattle hint that 'fodder-time' is at hand. **1933** W. de la Mare *Lord Fish* 37 It was so full of the suffling and sighing, the music and murmuration of water.

sufflue (sʌ'fluː). *Her.* Also 7 *erron.* **surflewe.** [Of unknown origin; perhaps f. *suf-* = sub- 1 + flue *sb.*[3]] = clarion *sb.* 2, rest *sb.*[3] 2 b.

1562 Legh *Armory* 88 b, Geules, three Sufflues Or, [borne] by the name of Verst. **1572** Bossewell *Armorie* ii. 124 b, I haue harde some boldely affirme it to be called a Rest,..where in deede it serueth to an other purpose, as to convey the winde from the Bellowes to all the pipes of the Organes: and by propre name is called a Sufflue. *a* **1661** Fuller *Worthies, Cornw.* (1662) 210 What usually are termed therein *Rests*..are called by some Criticks, *Surflewes.* **1682** J. Gibbon *Introd. ad Lat. Blazon.* 56. **1849** Planché in *Jrnl. Brit. Archæol. Assoc.* IV. 349.

†'**suffocate,** *pa. pple.* and *ppl. a. Obs.* Also 5–6 **-at.** [ad. L. *suffōcātus*, pa. pple. of *suffōcāre* (see next).]

1. Suffocated by deprivation of air.

1460 Capgrave *Chron.* (Rolls) 267 In which first day the duke of Gloucetir was suffocat at Caleys. **1555** Eden *Decades* (Arb.) 152 The moonkey..helde hym so fast aboute the throte, that he was suffocate. **1593** Shaks. *2 Hen. VI*, i. i. 124 For Suffolkes Duke, may he be suffocate. **1632** Lithgow *Trav.* iv. 148 Pilgrimes were often suffocate to death.

2. Smothered, overwhelmed.

1471 Ripley *Comp. Alch.* i. xii. in Ashm. (1652) 132 In mynd..bare thys, That never thyne Erth wyth Water be suffocate. **1526** *Pilgr. Perf.* (W. de W. 1531) 48 The wedes had suffocat and destroyed his corne. **1584** Cogan *Haven Health* ccxiv. (1636) 229 In a cold stomack the little heat is suffocate with grosse meate. **1606** Shaks. *Tr. & Cr.* i. iii. 125 This Chaos, when Degree is suffocate, Followes the choaking.

suffocate ('sʌfəkeɪt), *v.* [f. L. *suffōcāt-*, pa. ppl. stem of *suffōcāre*, f. *suf-* = sub- 1 + *faucēs* throat.]

1. *trans.* To kill (a person or animal) by stopping the supply of air through the lungs, gills, or other respiratory organs.

1599 A. M. tr. *Gabelhouer's Bk. Physicke* 231/2 Ether in his mothers bodye, or els in the birth it might be suffocatede. **1641** J. Jackson *True Evang. T.* i. 44 Others inverted..and a fire being underneath, were so smoaked and suffocated to death. **1681** Chetham *Angler's Vade-m.* xxxviii. §11 (1689) 248 Fishes are suffocated in Waters if they be..frozen. **1791** Mrs. Inchbald *Simple Story* III. ii. 16 Half suffocated with the loss of breath. **1803** *Med. Jrnl.* IX. 488 The violent irritation and spasm..which so often suffocate children. **1817** Byron *Beppo* xvii, A Husband whom mere suspicion could inflame To suffocate a wife. **1873** Mivart *Elem. Anat.* xii. 465 To suffocate a frog it is sufficient to keep its mouth open.

2. To interrupt or impede respiration in (a person); to stifle, choke. †Also, to throttle (the windpipe), stifle (the breath).

1599 Shaks. *Hen. V*, iii. vi. 45 Let not Hempe his Windpipe suffocate. **1660** R. Coke *Power & Subj.* 72 The night-mare; which..makes men think they are invaded, oppressed and suffocated with great weight. **1784** Cowper *Task* ii. 819 Ev'ry plague that can infest Society..meets the eye, the ear, And suffocates the breath at ev'ry turn. **1800** Mrs. Hervey *Mourtray Fam.* II. 27, I am suffocated in this crowd. **1848** Dickens *Dombey* l, He had like to have suffocated himself with this pleasantry. **1854** J. S. C. Abbott *Napoleon* (1855) II. xxii. 418 The soldiers were suffocated with sorrow.

3. To destroy as if by the exclusion of air; to smother, overwhelm, extinguish.

a. something material or physical.

1584 R. Scot *Discov. Witchcr.* xii. vi. 223 Manie lewd persons..with incantations..doo..extinguish, suffocate, and spoile all vineyards, ortchards, medowes [etc.]. **1614** T. Adams *Diuells Banket* iii. 109 The thicke spumy mists, which vapour vp from the..earth, doe often suffocate the brighter aire. **1652** French *Yorksh. Spaw* iv. 46 The use of cold baths is not..for old men, because that little heat which they have is thereby suffocated. **1758** Reid tr. *Macquer's Chym.* I. 122 By distillation..it [*sc.* acid of Vinegar] may be freed..from the great quantity of water which in a manner suffocates it. **1793** *Trans. Soc. Arts* V. 54 The plants..will suffocate every kind of weed near them. **1797** *Phil. Trans.* LXXXVII. 421 A mass sufficiently thick to suffocate the whole of the light which enters it. **1807** J. Barlow *Columb.* ii. 330 His fleet high flaming suffocates the skies. **1842** Loudon *Suburban Hort.* 386 The roots are suffocated and rotted from their delicacy.

b. something immaterial, esp. a mental attribute.

1526 *Pilgr. Perf.* (W. de W. 1531) 76 b, Labour..to expell the same venym..or..to suffocate or smere it within y[e]. *c* **1550** Rolland *Crt. Venus* ii. 720 Thay wald him mak sum aid,..Or his sorrow in sum part suffocat. **1644** Prynne & Walker *Fiennes' Trial* 39 It being a meere artifice..to suffocate the truth. **1664** H. More *Myst. Iniq.* 257 The being inveigled in idolatrous Worship does not quite suffocate and dead that Divine sense. **1749** Hartley *Observ. Man* i. §1. 44 Blood and Serum..lying in the Ventricles, suffocate Sensations. **1868** Milman *St. Paul's* vi. 112 That ..superstition which..had suffocated the higher truths of religion.

4. *intr.* To become stifled or choked. *rare.*

1702 De Foe *Mock Mourners* (ed. 3) 77 Convulsions follow, and such Vapours rise, The Constitution Suffocates and Dies. **1730** *Phil. Trans.* XXXVI. 449 The Disease continued so obstinate, and the Patient so like to suffocate, that [etc.]. **1883** *Harper's Mag.* Jan. 237/2, I suffocate in a stuffy room. **1888** *Daily News* 9 July 5/7 Whilst he was suffocating he remained calm and still.

Hence 'suffocated *ppl. a.*, 'suffocating *vbl. sb.*

1621 T. Williamson tr. *Goulart's Wise Vieillard* 23 Death is a suffocating and quenching of the naturall heate of the body. **1737** Whiston *Josephus, Hist.* v. xi. §4 As the suffocated materials were now gradually consumed. **1793** Beddoes *Scurvy*, etc. 50 In suffocated animals the left cavities of the heart are full of venous blood. **1898** G. B. Shaw *Plays* II. *Candida* 148 In a suffocated voice.

'suffocating, *ppl. a.* [-ING^{2}.]

1. That causes suffocation; stifling.

1604 Shaks. *Oth.* iii. iii. 389 If there be Cords, or Kniues, Poyson, or Fire, or suffocating streames, Ile not indure it. **1667** *Phil. Trans.* II. 416 The hot winds blowing..with such a suffocating heat. **1764** Harmer *Observ.* i. §16. 39 These hot winds are not deadly at Aleppo... They are very incommoding and suffocating in Barbary and Egypt too. **1807** T. Thomson *Chem.* (ed. 3) II. 172 The dense and suffocating odour of muriatic acid. **1817** Shelley *Rev. Islam* i. xiii. 3 Would the Snake Relax his suffocating grasp. **1829** Lytton *Disowned* lxxxiv, Throwing, as it were, in that exclamation, a whole weight of suffocating emotion from his chest. **1860** Tyndall *Glac.* i. xviii. 133 The dead suffocating warmth of the interior of an oven. **1879** Froude *Cæsar* xxii. 391 The hills were waterless, the weather suffocating.

fig. **1875** Helps *Soc. Press.* viii. 101, I hope he told you of the suffocating interest I take in your present subject.

†**b.** *suffocating damp*, = choke-damp. So *suffocating shaft. Obs.*

1695 Woodward *Nat. Hist. Earth* iv. (1723) 227 One is called the *Suffocating*, the other the *Fulminating Damp.* **1778** Pryce *Min. Cornub.* 201 If faggots on fire..be thrown into a suffocating Shaft, it will rarify the bad air.

2. Accompanied by suffocation.

1748 *Anson's Voy.* ii. v. 184 That uneasy and suffocating sensation. **1818–20** E. Thompson *Nosologia* (ed. 3) 222 Convulsive suffocating cough. **1838** Thackeray *Yellowpl. Corr.* iv. (1887) 26 She gev a suffycating shreek. **1900** *Westm. Gaz.* 10 Sept. 6/2 A hoarse, suffocating sound.

3. That undergoes suffocation. *rare.*

1869 *Daily News* 2 July, The mute agonies of the suffocating lobster before he is boiled alive in a pot.

4. as *adv.* = suffocatingly. *rare.*

1737 Whiston *Josephus, Hist.* iii. ix. §1 It was suffocating hot.

Hence '**suffocatingly** *adv.*, so as to cause suffocation.

1822 *Blackw. Mag.* XII. 434, I never felt more suffocatingly hot. **1854** Dickens *Hard T.* ii. iv, The.. suffocatingly close Hall. **1885** 'Mrs. Alexander' *Valerie's Fate* vi, Her heart suddenly waking from its torpor to beat wildly, suffocatingly.

suffocation (sʌfəˈkeɪʃən). Also 6 -cion. [ad. L. *suffōcātio-, -ōnem*, n. of action f. *suffōcāre* to suffocate. Cf. F. *suffocation*] The act of suffocating or condition of being suffocated.

a **1577** Sir T. Smith *Commw. Eng.* ii. xxiii. (1589) 95 He ..that violently commeth to his death, whether it bee by knife, poison, cord, drowning, burning, suffocation, or otherwise. **1598** Shaks. *Merry W.* iii. v. 119 It was a miracle to scape suffocation. **1620** Venner *Via Recta* viii. 190 They ..that..surcharge their bodies with ouer-much meat.. incurre suddaine and perilous suffocations. **1737** Whiston *Josephus, Antiq.* vi. viii. §2 Some..demoniacal disorders.. brought upon him such suffocations as were ready to choke him. **1819** Scott *Leg. Montrose* xiii, Departing quietly by suffocation, like your ancestors before you. **1846** J. Baxter *Libr. Pract. Agric.* (ed. 4) I. p. xxiv, The large ball room.. was crammed to suffocation. **1875** A. S. Taylor *Poisons* (ed. 3) 107 A lady who had been rendered unconscious by chloroform died from suffocation, as a result of the food finding its way into the air passages.

b. *transf.* and *fig.*

1567 Fenton *Trag. Disc.* i. (1898) I. 76 To dye afore my tyme by suffocacion of pynnynge dollour. **1651** Wittie tr. *Primrose's Pop. Err.* iii. 150 The suffocation of heat. **1744** *Phil. Trans.* XLIII. 130 Blackness is brought on, by an Extinction or Suffocation of those same mixed Rays. **1824** Loudon *Encycl. Gard.* (ed. 2) §893 *Suffocation* [in plants]. Sometimes it happens that the pores of the epidermis are closed up, and transpiration consequently obstructed. **1837** Carlyle *French Rev.* iv. iv, Is it not..the very murkiness, and atmospheric suffocation, that brings the lightning?

†**c.** [medical L. *suffocatio hysterica* or *uterina.*] In full *suffocation of the womb, matrix, mother* (see mother *sb.*^{1} 12 b), *bairn's bed* (see bairn *Comb.*): hysteria. *Obs.*

1549 *Compl. Scot.* vi. 67 Muguart, that is gude for the suffocatione of ane vomans bayrnis bed [*read* bed]. **1578** Lyte *Dodoens* 19 The same is good against the Suffocation of the Matrix (that is the stopping and hardnesse of the Mother). **1603** E. Jorden (*title*), A Briefe Discovrse of a Disease called the Suffocation of the Mother. **1607** Topsell *Four-f. Beasts* 652 The fat of a sheep..cureth the suffocation of the womb. **1719** Quincey *Lex. Physico-Med.* (1722), *Suffocation*, Choaking. This is used in Hysterick Cases, wherein the Uterus is imagined to be..as it were suffocated with ill Humours.

suffocative (ˈsʌfəkeɪtɪv), *a.* [ad. mod.L. *suffōcātīvus*, f. *suffōcāt-*: see suffocate *v.* and -ive.] Tending to suffocate; causing or inducing suffocation; attended by suffocation.

Chiefly *Med.*, esp in *suffocative catarrh* = capillary bronchitis.

1605 Timme *Quersit.* iii. 157 Violent catarres which are called suffocatiue. **1753** *Chambers' Cycl.* Suppl., *Suffocative catarrh*,..the name of a disease, which consists in a copious eruption of a serous and mucous humor into the vesicles of the lungs. **1758** *Monthly Rev.* 507 Nervous suffocative asthmas. **1791** E. Darwin *Bot. Gard.* i. iv. 64 The fell Syroc's suffocative breath. *Ibid.* ii. iii. 61 With quick sighs, and suffocative breath, Her interrupted heart-pulse swims in death. **1869** E. A. Parkes *Pract. Hygiene* (ed. 3) 114 Sextons..are subject to..suffocative catarrhs. **1876** *Trans. Clinical Soc.* IX. 129 She has suffocative attacks, in which she can hardly breathe. **1908** G. W. E. Russell *Threepenny Bits* vii. 47 Forging their way through suffocative crowds.

†**suffoke,** *v. Obs. rare*$^{-1}$. [a. F. *suffoquer*, = Pr. *sofogar*, ad. L. *suffōcāre* to suffocate.] *trans.* To suffocate, drown.

1490 Caxton *Eneydos* xxi. 77 Wythout to suffoke me now ..in-to the depe see of amaritude.

Suffolk (ˈsʌfək). **a.** The name of one of the counties of East Anglia; used attrib. in designations of things produced in or peculiar to the county, as *Suffolk butter, cheese, cow, dumpling, dun, ham, pig*; **Suffolk bang** (see quot.); **Suffolk coprolite**, a phosphatic nodule occurring in the Red Crag of Suffolk; **Suffolk crag**, a Pliocene formation occurring in Suffolk (see quot. 1852); **Suffolk grass**, the annual meadow grass, *Poa annua*; **Suffolk latch** (see quot. 1972); **Suffolk punch**, a small but strong and hardy horse bred largely in Suffolk; **Suffolk sheep**, a black-faced hornless sheep of a breed first developed in East Anglia, distinguished by a short fleece, large size, and the production of lean meat; **Suffolk thump** = *Suffolk bang.*

1867 Smyth *Sailor's Word-bk.*, *Suffolk Bang, a very poor and hard kind of cheese. **1735** J. Kirby *Suffolk Trav.* 2 In this Part is made the *Suffolk Butter, so managed by the Neat Dairy-Wife, that it is justly esteemed the pleasantest and best in England. **1636** Davenant *Wits* iii. i, Some *Suffolk Cheese. **1661** Pepys *Diary* 4 Oct., I found my wife vexed at her people for grumbling to eat Suffolk cheese. **1797** Young *Agric. Suffolk* 203 Cheese 5d., but Suffolk 3½d. and 4d. **1867** Sibson *Agric. Chem.* 249 *Suffolk Coprolites are amongst the first known phosphatic minerals. **1797** T. M. in Young *Agric. Suffolk* 180 *note*, The true *Suffolk polled cow. **1834** [Youatt] *Cattle* (Lib. Usef. Knowl.) 175 The milking properties of the Suffolk cow. **1852** Lyell *Man. Elem. Geol.* (ed. 4) 162 The *Suffolk crag is divisible into two masses, the upper of which has been termed the Red, and the lower the Coralline Crag. **1824** *New Syst. Cookery* (new ed.) 234 Yeast or *Suffolk Dumplings. **1834** [Youatt] *Cattle* (Lib. Usef. Knowl.) 174 The *Suffolk Dun used to be celebrated..on account of the extraordinary quantity of milk that she yielded. **1875** *Encycl. Brit.* I. 389/1 A polled breed of cattle, the prevailing colour of which is dun or pale red, from which they are known as the *Suffolk Duns.* **1759** B. Stillingfleet *Observ. Grasses* in *Misc. Tracts* (1762) 367 What is known in some few counties by the name of the *Suffolk grass. **1846** J. Baxter *Libr. Pract. Agric.* (ed. 4) I. 368 The *Pōa ánnua*, or Suffolk grass, is so short of growth..as to render it an encumberer of the soil. **1855** E. Acton *Mod. Cookery* (rev. ed.) xiii. 256 The receipt for the *Suffolk ham. **1966** *Times* 28 Dec. 9/6 A genuine Suffolk ham man is Mr. R. Stiff of Kersey. He uses his own pigs and douses the hams in black treacle, spices and stout. They are then floated in tubs of sweet pickle. **1940** *Chambers's Techn. Dict.* 819/2 **Suffolk Latch (Join.)*, a variant of the *Norfolk Latch.* **1972** *Country Life* 13 Jan. 98/1 The great variety of country door-latches would reward a study in depth: the well-known type, the 'Suffolk latch', is usually operated by a pivoted blade, which passing through the door and depressed by thumb pressure, lifts the latch. **1981** 'G. Gaunt' *Incomer* xviii. 117 Les Taunton thumbed down the Suffolk latch of the Queen's Head taproom and entered. **1842** *Penny Cycl.* XXIII. 214/1 *Suffolk pigs are perhaps..the most profitable breed in England. **1784** Cullum *Hist. Hawsted* 222 This breed is well known by the name of *Suffolk Punches. **1816** J. Smith *Panorama Sci. & Art* II. 644 The Suffolk-punches, which are common in the district called High Suffolk. **1850** Dickens *Dav. Copp.* xix, A Suffolk Punch, when he's a good 'un, is worth his weight in gold. [**1794** A. Young *Gen. View Agric. Suffolk* xiii. 33 The Norfolk breed of sheep spread over almost every part of the county; and as the most famous flocks are about Bury.. it has been observed, that they ought rather to be called the Suffolk breed.] **1893** J. Wrightson *Sheep* viii. 75 The original *Suffolk sheep existed in famous flocks during Arthur Young's time. *a* **1825** Forby *Voc. E. Anglia* s.v. *Bang*, *Suffolk Thump.

†**b.** **Suffolk powder**: see quot. *Obs.*

1753 *Chambers' Cycl.* Suppl., *Suffolk powder* the name of a medicinal powder, good for the bite of a mad dog. It had its name from a Countess of Suffolk, who used to give it with great success.

c. *absol.* = Suffolk cow, pig, punch, or sheep.

[**1797** in Young *Agric. Suffolk* 185 The Suffolk milk gave two and one-third ounces more cream than the horned one.] **1831** W. Youatt *Horse* 39 The immense power of the Suffolk is accounted for by the low position of the shoulder. **1834** [——] *Cattle* (Lib. Usef. Knowl.) 175 In no part of the kingdom were the farmers more careless as to the breed, providing only that the cows were true Suffolks. **1846** —— *Pig* 66 A cross between the Suffolk and Lincoln. **1902** *Encycl. Brit.* XXV. 193/2 The Suffolk..probably took its origin in the crossing of improved Southdown rams with the old horned Norfolk ewes. **1928** [see actioned *ppl. a.*]. **1960** G. E. Evans *Horse in Furrow* xiii. 181 He knew the Suffolks so well..that he could pick out a horse's breed by studying him. **1979** C. MacLeod *Luck runs Out* (1981) ii. 21 Those gorgeous Clydesdales and Percherons and Belgians and Suffolks..with their brasses polished like gold. **1980** 'D. Shannon' *Felony File* vii. 173 He's found the sheep... They're sixty dollars each. They're Suffolks.

Hence **Suffolkian** (in 7 -cean), *a.*, of or belonging to the county of Suffolk; '**Suffolkism** (-cism), a Suffolk idiom or peculiarity.

1622 Drayton *Poly-olb.* xix. 399 From the Suffolcean side yet those which Stour prefer Their princely Orwell praise. **1823** E. Moor *Suffolk Words* 23 Where words occur, not readily understood by the Unsuffolked reader, he is to take them as Suffolcisms.

Suffolker (ˈsʌfəkə(r)). [f. Suffolk + -er^{1}.] A native or inhabitant of Suffolk.

1849 Dickens *Dav. Copp.* (1850) xi. 117 The men generally spoke of me as..'the young Suffolker'. **1910** H. M. Doughty *Chron. Theberton* iii. 40 We Suffolkers never misplace H's. **1952** M. Allingham *Tiger in Smoke* vi. 100 We come from the same part of the country, sir. We're all Suffolkers. **1978** *East Anglian Daily Times* 7 Dec. 8/6 First was depicted the hitherto unseen paintings of a dead Suffolker, the late Cecil Howard Lay.

†**su'ffossion.** *Obs. rare.* [ad. L. *suffossio, -ōnem*, f. *suffodĕre*, f. *suf-* = sub- 3, 26 + *fodĕre* to dig.] Digging under or up; undermining.

1623 Cockeram, *Suffossion*, an undermining. *c* **1625** Bp. Hall *St. Paul's Combat* i. Wks. 1634 II. 440 Those suffossions of walls [etc.]. **1648** —— *Select Th.* i. §32 What is it to tell of the suffossion of her vineyards? vastation of her tents?

†**suffounge,** *v. Obs. rare*$^{-1}$. [a. OF. **suffongier* (cf. AF. *fungier* to smoke):—L. *suffūmigāre*, f. *suf-* = sub- 26 + *fumigāre* to fumigate.] *trans.* To fumigate.

1490 Caxton *Eneydos* xxiv. 87 [She] toke herself for to encence it, and to suffounge the place.

suffragan (ˈsʌfrəgən), *sb.* and *a.* Forms: 4 **suffrigane, soffragan,** 4–7 **suffragane,** 5 **suffragann, -igan(n, -ygane, -ann, sofregann,** 5–6 **suffrygan,** 6 **suffregan(e, -ragene, (suffryngham),** 4– **suffragan;** β. 5 **suffrecan, -ykayn, soffrycan,** 5–6 **soffrecan,** 6 **suffrecane, -ykane, soufrecan.** [a. AF., OF. *suffragan* (13th c.), occas. *-ain* (mod.F. *suffragant*), corresp. to It. *soffraganeo, -ano*, Sp. *sufraganeo, -ano*, Pg. *suffraganeo*, repr. med.L. *suffrāgāneus*, f. stem of *suffrāgium* suffrage.

The earliest OF. examples, being in the pl. *suffragans*, are ambiguous for the form of the sing., but it is probable that **suffragan* was the older form (cf. MDu. *suffragaen*), and that *suffragant* (1451 in Du Cange) is due to etymologizing alteration (see -ant); cf. however Pr. *suffraguant*, It. *suffragante*.]

A. *sb.*

1. A bishop considered in regard to his relation to the archbishop or metropolitan, by whom he may be summoned to attend synods and give his suffrage.

c **1383** *Concl. Loll.* xxvii. in *Eng. Hist. Rev.* (1911) Oct. 746 Decrees..þat ȝeuen þe chesigne of þe erchebisshop to alle his suffragans. **1387** Trevisa *Higden* (Rolls) II. 115 þe primat of ȝork haþ but tweie suffragans in Engelond, þat beeþ þe bisshoppis of Caerlile and of Duram. *c* **1440** *Jacob's Well* 17 Which sentence was ȝouyn..be Boniface, erchebysschop of cauntyrbury, and be v. oþere bysschoppys, his suffraganys. **1534** *Lyndewode's Const. Provinc.* 3 We.. commaunde all and euerye our Cobysschoppes and suffragans. **1611** Coryat *Crudities* 532 He had no lesse then sixteene Bishops vnder him that were subiect to his iurisdiction as his Suffragrans [*sic*]. **1716** M. Davies *Athen. Brit.* III. 28 The two High-flying Suffragans to AB. Laud. **1768** Boswell *Corsica* iii. (ed. 2) 164 The Corsican bishops, who are..suffragans of the archbishop of Pisa. **1862** Hook *Lives Abps.* II. ii. 121 The suffragans of the province were summoned as usual to assist at the consecration of their metropolitan. **1876** Freeman *Norm. Conq.* V. xxiii. 214 The Bishop of Orkney, more strictly a suffragan of Trondhjem, is seen acting as a suffragan of York.

transf. **1877** C. Geikie *Christ* lii. (1879) 619 The Jewish primate and his suffragans kept steadily in view his arrest.

2. An assistant or subsidiary bishop, performing episcopal functions in a certain diocese but having no jurisdiction; in the Church of England, since the passing of Act 26 Hen. VIII, c. 14, a bishop appointed to assist a diocesan bishop in a particular part of his diocese.

Suffragan bishops take their title from certain towns named in the above act or (according to the Suffragans Nomination Act of 1888) from 'such other towns as Her Majesty may..by Order in Council direct shall be taken'.

c **1380** Wyclif *Wks.* (1880) 225 þat þei ben not maad bischopis of heþene men..& þanne meyntened to be suffragans & sellen sacramentis. **14..** *S.E. Leg.* (MS. Bodl. 779) fol. 102 Suþþe he made him bysschop..& makid him his suffragan & in his stede prechour. **1483** *Cath. Angl.* 371 Suffragane, *Coepiscopus.* **1511–12** *Rec. St. Mary at Hill* 277 Paid the Suffregan for haloyng of a Chales [etc.]. **1534** *Act 26 Hen. VIII*, c. 14 §1 Everie Archebyshope and Byshop of this Realme,..beynge dysposed to have any Suffragane. **1536** Boorde *Let.* in *Introd. Knowl.* (1870) 58, I was.. dyspensyd with þe relygyon by the byshopp of Romes bulles, to be suffrygan off chychester. **1587** Harrison *England* ii. ii. 49 in *Holinshed*, Which function peraduenture he [*sc.* the Bishop] committed to his suffragane. **1615** Wadsworth in Bedell *Lett.* (1624) 13 One Hodgeskin Suffragan of Bedford. **1654** Gataker *Disc. Apol.* 101 Dr. Stern..was at that time Suffragane of Colchester. **1885** *Life & Lett. A. Monod* 58 M. Charles Barde of Geneva who had been called to act as suffragan at Lyons. **1912** *Cath. Encycl.* XIV. 324/2 It is presumed that the cardinal-bishop has given his suffragan all the faculties necessary for the government of his diocese.

β. **1470–85** Malory *Arthur* xii. xiv. 611 Thenne the suffrecan lete fylle a grete vessel with water. **1493–4** *Rec. St. Mary at Hill* 198 Payd to þe soffrycan of london for halowyng of sentt stevyn ys autyr, xs. iiij d. **1530** Palsgr. 273/1 Soufrecan, *suffragan, penitencier.* **1556** *Chron. Grey Friars* (Camden) 78 There the suffrecane gave them their dyssipline.

†3. A coadjutor, assistant; a deputy, representative. *Obs.*

1481 in Legg *Clerk's Bk.* 1549, 66 Howe the Clerke And the Suffrigann of Seynt Nicholas Churche Aught to do...

The suff[r]ygann Augh to fastenn the Church Dorys [etc.]. **1500–20** DUNBAR *Poems* xlviii. 173 The nychtingaill song [to the rose], 'Haill, naturis suffragene'. *Ibid.* lxxxv. 68 Oratrice, mediatrice, salvatrice, To God gret suffragane! **1577** B. GOOGE tr. *Heresbach's Husb.* 3, I haue..my maide, so skilfull in huswyferie, that she may well be my wyues suffragan. **1647** C. WALKER *Myst. Two Junto's* 6 The remaining part of the House are but..Suffragans to ratify what is forejudged. **1687** *Lond. Gaz.* No. 2242/3 The Elector of Trier has named the Bishop his Suffragan to go and compliment the King. **1748** RICHARDSON *Clarissa* (1768) VIII. xix. 53 Her [*sc.* a strumpet's] bed-side, surrounded..by her suffragans and daughters. **1760** H. WALPOLE *Let. to Mann* 7 May, She made her suffragan, Whitfield, pray for and preach about him.

†**b.** Of things: A help, aid. *Obs.*

1644 BULWER *Chiron.* 16 So these suffragans of speech [*sc.* hands] by a lively sense afford that shadow which is the excellencie of the vocall pourtraicture. **1693** *D'Emilianne's Hist. Monast. Orders* 35 The Canons of those times.. frequently..were Helps and Suffragans to the Bishops.

B. *adj.*

1. *bishop suffragan*, *suffragan bishop*: = A. 1, 2.

1475 *Voc.* in Wr.-Wülcker 629 Prelatte or byschop suffrygane. **1534** *Act 26 Hen. VIII*, c. 14 §1 Everie suche personne..shalbe callyd Byshop Suffragane of the same See wherunto he shalbe namyd. **1538** AUDLEY in *Lett. Suppr. Monast.* (Camden) 240 William More, clerk, byshopp suffragan of Colchester. **1671** F. PHILLIPS *Reg. Necess.* 442 The Arch-bishop of York, and his Suffragan Bishops. *c* **1676** T. BARLOW *Rem.* (1693) 162 A Co-adjutor or Suffragan Bishop is, *quoad Ordinem*, really and properly a Bishop. **1726** AYLIFFE *Parergon* 69 No Suffragan Bishop shall have more than one riding Apparitor in his Diocess. **1846** MCCULLOCH *Acc. Brit. Empire* (1854) II. 301 The total income of the two archbishops, and of their ten suffragan bishops, will then be 70,938*l.* **1888** *Act 51 & 52 Vict.* c. 56 It was enacted that the towns therein named should be taken ..for sees of bishops suffragans. **1907** *Cath. Encycl.* I. 691/2 In regard to his suffragan bishops the metropolitan may compel them to assemble in provincial council every three years.

2. Of a see or diocese: Subordinate *to* a metropolitical or archiepiscopal see.

1712 E. COOKE *Voy. S. Sea* 399 Valladolid, a Bishoprick, suffragan to Mexico. **1907** *Cath. Encycl.* I. 692/1 To-day archbishops cannot visit a suffragan diocese, unless [etc.]. **1913** T. F. TOUT in *Reg. J. de Halton* Introd. 24 The see of Sodor, which, until the fifteenth century, was supposed to be suffragan to..Trondhjem.

fig. **1784** H. WALPOLE *Let. to H. S. Conway* 14 Aug., That the King of Spain, now he has demolished Algiers, the metropolitan see of thieves, will come and bombard Richmond, Twickenham, and all the suffragan cities that swarm with pirates and banditti.

Hence **'suffraganal** *a.*, pertaining to a suffragan bishop; **'suffraganate**, the seat of a suffragan bishop; **'suffragancy**, the office or tenure of a suffragan; **'suffraganship**, the office or status of a suffragan.

1892 *Times* 14 Oct. 11/2 The *suffraganal or nominal sees are as absolute shams as Wiseman's original Bishopric of Melipotamos *in partibus infidelium*. **1879** *Echo* 11 July 2/5 Bedford is the town nearest to London that is mentioned in the Act of Henry VIII. as a suitable place for a *suffraganate. **1888** *Guardian* 8 Feb. 186/2 The appointment of Sir Lovelace Stamer to the Suffraganate of Shrewsbury. **1864** *Spectator* 25 June 742 The refusal of the Presbyteral Council of Paris to renew the '*suffragancy' of the younger Athanase Coquerel. **1549** LATIMER *5th Serm. bef. Edw. VI* (Arb.) 135, I meane not hallowers of belles, nor Christiners of belles, that is a popysh *suffraganship. **1583** STOCKER *Civ. Warres Lowe C.* I. 5 b, There were certaine Suffraganeships of cathedral churches conuerted into Bishopricks. *a* **1661** FULLER *Worthies*, *Cumbld.* (1662) 220 He was.. made *Episcopus Pissinensis*..and therewith held the Suffraganeship under Henry Beaufort Bishop of Lincoln.

suffra'ganean, *a. rare.* [f. med.L. *suffrāgāneus* (see prec.) + -AN.] Suffragan. So **suffra'ganeous** *a.*, pertaining to a suffragan.

1704 *Collect. Voy.* (Churchill) III. 641/1 The Patriarch.. has eight..Suffraganean Bishops. **1904** *Times, Lit. Suppl.* 4 Nov. 338/2 The dreary round of suffraganeous functions.

†**'suffragant**, *sb.* and *a. Obs.* [a. F. *suffragant*, ad. L. *suffrāgans, -ant-*, pr. pple. of *suffrāgārī* (see next).] **A.** *sb.* **1.** = SUFFRAGAN *sb.* 2.

1611 COTGR., *Suffragant*, a Suffragant, or Suffragan, a Bishops deputie.

2. One who gives his suffrage or vote; a voter; hence, a supporter, witness.

1627 JACKSON *Holy Cath. Faith* I. xxi. 181 Wee haue euery member of the Romish Church a suffragant or witnesse for vs. **1656** *Artif. Handsom.* 118 Hoping to find them more friends and suffragants to the virtues..of sober women than enemies to their beauty. **1678** R. L'ESTRANGE *Seneca's Mor.* II. xx. 261 When they are no longer Candidates, they are Suffragants. **1697** POTTER *Antiq. Greece* I. ix. (1715) 44 The Prytanes, who were also oblig'd to provide a sufficient number of Stones for the Suffragants.

B. *adj.* **1.** Auxiliary, subordinate.

1603 FLORIO *Montaigne* I. lvi. (1632) 175 She [*sc.* Divinity] ought to be chiefe ruler..and not suffragant and subsidiary.

2. Giving support or witness.

a **1656** BP. HALL *Rem. Wks.* (1660) 302 If..I should let my pen loose to the suffragant testimonies..I should trye your patience.

†**'suffragate**, *v. Obs.* [f. L. *suffrāgāt-*, pa. ppl. stem of *suffrāgārī*, f. stem of *suffrāgium* SUFFRAGE.]

1. *trans.* To delegate, appoint.

1600 W. WATSON *Decacordon* (1602) 273 Suffragating Arrian Bishops and others in their places.

2. *intr.* To testify, to bear witness *to.*

1620 T. GRANGER *Div. Logike* 233 Verbes, to witnes, testifie,..Suffragate. **1629** PRYNNE *Old Antith.* 73 All these doe fully suffragate to this our third Ante-Arminian Conclusion. **1633** —— *Histrio-m.* 77 All Times, All Ages.. Subscribe, and Suffragate with these our Authors to our Minor. **1665** GLANVILL *Scepsis Sci.* viii. 45 Now this seems bigg of repugnancies, though Sense it self suffragate to its truth. *a* **1676** HALE *Prim. Orig. Man.* I. ii. (1677) 62 Unless there were some common consonancy and congruity of somewhat inherent in Nature which suits, corresponds and suffragates to that Tradition.

3. To vote (*for*).

1630 PRYNNE *Anti-Armin.* 2 If all these suffragate or passe their Verdict for the Arminians. **1691** WOOD *Fasti Oxon.* (1820) II. 345 Michael Ward..was incorporated in the said degree, with liberty given him to suffragate in congreg. and convoc.

Hence †**'suffragating** *ppl. a.*, voting; assenting.

1684 DRYDEN *Prol. to Univ. Oxford* 31 Nations su'd to be made free of Rome: Not in the suffragating Tribes to stand, But in your utmost, last, Provincial Band. **1850** BLACKIE *Æschylus* II. 119 These words the Argive people Answered with suffragating hands.

†**suffra'gation.** *Obs. rare.* [ad. L. *suffrāgātio, -ōnem*, n. of action f. *suffrāgārī* to SUFFRAGATE.] The giving of a vote.

1576 FLEMING *Panopl. Epist.* 12 Our suffragation, or consenting voices. **1652** GAULE *Magastrom.* 176 A diabolicall..contract, sacrament, suggestion, suffragation, operation, and delusion. **1656** in BLOUNT *Glossogr.*

So †**'suffragator** [L. *suffrāgātor*], a voter, supporter; witness; †**'suffragatory** *a.* [L. *suffrāgātōrius*], exercising a right to vote.

1617 COLLINS *Def. Bp. Ely* II. vii. 262 Did euer any man make them his suffragators or spokes-men to god? **1618** T. MORTON in *Ussher's Lett.* (1686) 67 The Synod..is held at Dort, the most of their Suffragators are already Assembled. **1813** *Monthly Mag.* XXXV. 427/1 Suffragatory institutions were to be solicited.

suffrage ('sʌfrɪdʒ), *sb.* Also 5 **souffrage, sofrage,** 6 *Sc.* **sufferagh,** 6–7 **sufferage,** 7 **suff'rage.** [ad. L. *suffrāgium*, partly through F. *suffrage* (from 13th c.). Cf. It., Pg. *suffragio*, Sp. *sufragio*. An earlier anglicization of the L. pl. is SUFFRAGIES.]

1. *collect. pl.* and *sing.* Prayers, *esp.* intercessory prayers, intercessions. *arch.*

c **1380** WYCLIF *Wks.* (1880) 303 In alle þise wordis ben feyned of gostliche suffrage wiþ-oute grounde. **1432–50** tr. *Higden* (Rolls) I. 431 Vn til thei aske the suffrage and helpe of Seynte Wenefride. *c* **1450** *Godstow Reg.* 182 In massys, in matyns, in oþer owrys, suffrages, almys, fastynges. **1513** BRADSHAW *St. Werburge* I. 3259 Also by her merite, suffrage and peticion Euery humble creature had helpe and succour. **1553** BECON *Reliques of Rome* (1563) 197* The Suffrages and sacrifices of the Masse. **1602** WARNER *Alb. Eng.* XIII. lxxvii, Not tedious suffrages they ask't, nor Sacrifices strate. **1660** WOOD *Life* (O.H.S.) I. 345 The chappell being onlie for privat or secret suffrages. **1681** BURNET *Hist. Ref.* II. I. 64 That the Sacrifice might bring to them a greater Indulgence, being offered up by the Suffrages of the Saint. **1865** KINGSLEY *Herew.* i, Of what use to you then the suffrages of the saints? **1904** M. HEWLETT *Queen's Quair* I. viii. 110 The Queen was at prayers—which is more than can be said for the priest who should have lifted up her suffrages.

b. *spec.* Prayers for the souls of the departed: *esp.* in phr. *to do suffrage*. *arch.*

c **1440** *Alphabet of Tales* 58 He..garte do message & oders prayers & suffrage of halie kurk for hym. *c* **1450** *Godstow Reg.* 206 So þat þey scholde haue in mynde the sowlys Afore in alle here prayeris suffrages & benefettes for euer. **1483** CAXTON *Gold. Leg.* 348/2 That generalle Suffrages temporal myght be done for them. **1521** *Extr. Burgh Recs. Stirling* 14 Oct. (1887) 13 Twa markis of obit silver..for sufferagh to be doun for the saullis of wmquhill Allexander lord Elphinstoun and Sir Johen Elphinstoun, his fader. *c* **1554** in *10th Rep. Hist. MSS. Comm.* App. I. 87 To do suffrage for the sawll of the deid. **1584** R. SCOT *Discov. Witchcr.* XV. xxii. 434 Whose soule art thou?.. Wantest thou any suffrages, masses, or almes? **1596** R. H. tr. *Lavaterus' Ghostes & Spir.* 107 Whether he require any aide by prayers and suffrages? **1848** K. H. DIGBY *Broad Stone Hon.* III. *Morus* 280 Their prayers and suffrages for the dead.

†**c.** phr. ***suffrages of prayers***; cf. med.L. *orationis suffragium*, OF. *suffrages d'oroisons*. *Obs.*

The original sense was prob. 'help given by (intercessory) prayer': cf. sense 2.

1447 in Anstey *Epist. Acad. Oxon.* (O.H.S.) I. 261 We commend us unto ȝowr goode lordschipe wᵗ the gostly suffrages of oure prayers. *c* **1613** in *Cath. Rec. Soc. Publ.* (1914) XIV. 34 We humbly request the Suffrages of your Devout Prayers of Charity.

d. *pl.* Liturgical intercessory petitions; *esp.* in the Book of Common Prayer, (*a*) the intercessory petitions pronounced by the priest in the Litany (also *sing.*, any one of these); (*b*) a series of petitions pronounced by the priest with the answers of the people, a set of versicles and responses.

Also by some writers (see quots. 1657, 1732, 1796) used for a responsive petition (or response to a versicle, etc.).

1532 ELYOT *Let.* in *Gov.* (1880) I. p. lxxix, [In Germany] the Preest [at mass] in vestmentes after oure manner singith everi thing in Latine as we use, omitting suffrages. **1548–9** (Mar.) *Bk. Com. Prayer, Evensong*, Then the suffrages before assigned at Matins. *Ibid., Litany*, The Letany and Suffrages. **1587** HARRISON *England* II. i. 138/1 in *Holinshed*, After morning praier also we haue the letanie and suffrages. **1657** SPARROW *Bk. Com. Prayer* 95 These Forms of prayers, (where the peoples devotion is so often excited..by continual Suffrages, such as *Good Lord deliver us*; *We beseech thee to hear us good Lord,*) were called ἐκτενεῖς δεήσεις, earnest or intense Petitions. **1662** *Bk. Com. Prayer, Form of Prayer 5 Nov.*, In the Suffrages after the Creed, these shall be inserted and used for the King. **1697** J. LEWIS *Mem. Dk. Glocester* (1789) 78 He..would answer very properly at prayers, in the Suffrages and different parts of the Liturgy. **1714** *Order in Council* 1 Aug. in *Lond. Gaz.* No. 5247/3 In the Suffrages next after the Creed, instead of *Queen* read *King.* **1732** NEAL *Hist. Purit.* I. 54 They compiled a Litany consisting of many short petitions interrupted by Suffrages. **1796** PEGGE *Anonym.* (1809) 145 *Tu autem*..is the beginning of the suffrage, which was supposed to follow the reading of the Scripture, which the reading scholar was to continue, by saying, *Miserere mei, Domine.* **1855** PROCTER *Bk. Com. Prayer* 255 After the suffrage for the Church, those for the ecclesiastical orders usually come first. **1882–3** *Schaff's Encycl. Relig. Knowl.* II. 1327 A brief litany, in which the people continually respond to the various suffrages, 'Lord, have mercy upon us'. **1885** *Pall Mall Gaz.* 23 May 7/2 Installation of the Dean of Gloucester... The Bishop then said some suffrages. **1885** DIXON *Hist. Ch. Eng.* III. 496 The Suffrages which the clerks were wont to sing in the time of the communion [*viz.* the Agnus Dei, etc.].

transf. **1701** NORRIS *Ideal World* I. ii. 35 This great and solemn suffrage of the adorable Trinity, Let us make man.

†**2.** Help, support, assistance. Also, one who helps, a support. *Obs.*

c **1460** *Promp. Parv.* 483/2 *K., P.* Suffrage, or helpe, *suffragium.* *c* **1480** HENRYSON *Orpheus & Eurydice* 174 And had noucht bene throu suffrage of his harp, Wyth scharp pikis he had bene schorne & schent. **1513** BRADSHAW *St. Werburge* I. 420 Moost blessed Werburge..Our synguler suffrage, and sterre of our clerenes. *Ibid.* 3055 Than she requyred with humylyte The spyrytuall sufferage of holy vnccyon. **1528** ROY *Rede me* (Arb.) 86 Thorowe his passion, For vs he made satisfaccion, Withoute eny mans suffrage. **1613** R. C. *Table Alph., Suffrage*, consent, or voyce, or helpe.

3. a. *orig.* A vote given by a member of a body, state, or society, in assent to a proposition or in favour of the election of a person; in extended sense, a vote for or against any controverted question or nomination.

1534 MORE *Comf. agst. Trib.* III. xxvi. Wks. 1259/2 Euery mans assent was called his suffrages:..one kinde of those suffrages, was by certayn thynges that are in latine called *calculi.* **1588** SHAKS. *Tit. A.* I. i. 218 People of Rome, and Noble Tribunes heere, I aske your voyces and your Suffrages. *c* **1600** DRAYTON *Miseries Q. Margaret* cliv, The Spirituall Lords, and Temporall,..who farre more ready are To giue, then he their suffrages to craue. **1651** HOBBES *Leviath.* III. xlii. 290 The manner of choosing Magistrates.. was by plurality of suffrages. *a* **1707** S. PATRICK *Autobiog.* (1839) 43 The fellows came up one by one, and in a paper wrote their suffrages. **1765** BLACKSTONE *Comm.* I. 170 In all democracies..it is of the utmost importance to regulate by whom, and in what manner, the suffrages are to be given. **1781** J. MOORE *View Soc. It.* (1790) I. viii. 79 When the election took place, all the suffrages fell upon Paul Lue. **1809–10** COLERIDGE *Friend* (1865) 127 Each of these [*sc.* inhabitants] has a right to a suffrage. **1848** MILL *Pol. Econ.* II. i. §2 (1876) 125 A magistrate or magistrates, whom we may suppose elected by the suffrages of the community. **1873** C. ROBINSON *N.S. Wales* 91 Those whose suffrages are to determine its [*i.e.* the State's] future should be able to give an intelligent vote.

b. An object, as a pebble, a marked paper, or the like, used to indicate a vote given. *rare.*

1534 MORE *Conf. agst. Trib.* III. Wks. 1259/2 Vnto him which ouercometh, he will geue a white suffrage. **1665** J. BUCK in Peacock *Stat. Cambr.* (1841) App. B. p. lxxviii, The Scrutators..put their suffrages into one of the Hats. **1819** SCOTT *Ivanhoe* xxxvii, The Grand Master had collected the suffrages. **1835** T. MITCHELL *Acharn. of Aristoph.* 543 *note*, Ψηφίζεσθαι, to vote by suffrages thrown into jars.

4. *gen.* A vote in support of or an opinion in favour of some person or thing; hence (now *Obs.* or *arch.*), in neutral sense, an opinion.

1594 *Selimus* E, The loue I beare to my deare Acomat, Commands me giue my suffrage vnto him. **1610** B. JONSON *Alch.* To Rdr., If it were put to the question..the worse would finde more suffrages. **1640** HALL *Episc.* II. xiii. 166 Tertullian was..not at all below him [*sc.* Irenæus] in the clearnesse of his suffrage, *Edant origines &c.* **1653** *Nicholas Papers* (Camden) II. 24, I have herein sent you an Extract of the Substance of that Elector's Suffrage there concerning his Majesty. **1660** H. MORE *Myst. Godl.* To Rdr. 25 He that is a perfect Papist being of one mind and suffrage with his Church. **1726** POPE *Odyss.* XIX. 181 My anxious parents urge a speedy choice, And to their suffrage gain the filial voice. **1750** JOHNSON *Rambler* No. 11 ¶9 He that finds his knowledge narrow,..and by consequence his suffrage not much regarded. *c* **1804** JANE AUSTEN *Watsons* in Austen-Leigh *Mem.* (1871) 322 'Oh uncle! do look at my partner; she is so pretty!'.. Charles was hurried off without being able to receive his uncle's suffrage. **1822–7** GOOD *Study Med.* (1829) I. 423 It has not fallen to my lot..to add my suffrage in its favour. **1850** WHIPPLE *Ess. & Rev.* (ed. 3) I. 13 He has the hesitating suffrages of men of taste, and the plaudits of the million. **1883** 'OUIDA' *Wanda* I. 216 The world would not be as much so if I really wanted its suffrages.

5. a. Approval, sanction, consent. Const. *to. arch.*

1598 CHAPMAN *Iliad* VIII. 7 That God nor Goddesse may attempt, t' infringe my soueraigne mind: But all giue suffrage. **1609** B. JONSON *Sil. Wom.* I. ii, I'll giue no suffrage to't. *a* **1652** BROME *Novella* V. i, Let me beg Your suffrage Lady, I may bid them welcome. **1668** *Rolle's Abridgm.* Publ. Pref. a 2, The Common-Law of England..hath had the suffrage of the whole Kingdome in all Ages. **1704** EVELYN *Diary* Dec., My Lord of Canterbury wrote to me for suffrage for Mr. Clarke's continuance..in the Boyle Lecture. **1787** J. BARLOW *Oration 4th July* 12 The system to be established by his suffrage is calculated for the.. purposes of extending peace. **1825** SCOTT *Jrnl.* 20 Nov., To gain your suffrage to his views, he endeavours [etc.]. **1873**

H. ROGERS *Orig. Bible* ii. (1875) 80 Those religious systems which happen to have the suffrage of the government.

†**b.** An instance of this; an expression or token of approval. *Obs.*

1603 KNOLLES *Hist. Turks* (1621) 304 Such was the glorie and valour of Huniades..as..procured vnto him the generall fauour and suffrages of all. **1607** TOPSELL *Four-f. Beasts* 470 The man was pardoned, and the lion was giuen vnto him for a reward or suffrage. **1610** HEYWOOD *Gold. Age* I. i, The Queene, the Peeres, And all the people with lowd suffrages, Haue shrild their Auees. **1788** T. TAYLOR *Proclus* I. 9 They openly presaged, that this gift..was a future suffrage of his succession confirmed by divine events. **1829** I. TAYLOR *Enthus.* viii. 195 A system..which had won for itself a suffrage so general if not universal.

†**6.** The support or assurance of evidence or testimony in favour of something. *Obs.*

1606 S. GARDINER *Bk. Angling* 50 We list first to conclude our iudgement by suffrages of scriptures. **1650** BULWER *Anthropomet.* 4 In the opinion of Claramontius, the reason of the thing gives a suffrage unto it. *a* **1677** BARROW *Serm.* (1686) III. ii. 17 Precepts are delivered in an universal and abstracted manner,..without any intervention, assistence, or suffrage of sense. *a* **1718** W. PENN *Tracts* Wks. 1726 I. 570 We herein are not without the Suffrage of the Scriptures to our Defence.

7. The collective vote of a body of persons.

1610 HEYWOOD *Gold. Age* I. i, I choose it as my right by gift of heauen, The peoples suffrage, the dead Kings bequest. *a* **1700** EVELYN *Diary* 6 Jan. 1661, I was now chosen (and nominated by his Majestie for one of the Council) by suffrage of the rest of the Members, a Fellow of the Philosophic Society. **1776** GIBBON *Decl. & F.* (1782) I. xii. 384 The election of a new emperor was referred to the suffrage of the military order. **1823** BENTHAM *Not Paul but Jesus* 221 Philip,..one of the seven trustees, who..had been chosen by universal suffrage.

8. a. The collective opinion of a body of persons; hence, contextually, consensus of opinion; (common or general) consent.

1576 FLEMING *Panopl. Epist.* 111 In this suffrage or voyce of consent. **1611** CORYAT *Crudities* 627 Mercator..who by the vniuersall suffrage of all the learned is esteemed the most excellent cosmographer. **1662** GUNNING *Lent Fast* 79 The Apostles by their common suffrage sanctified..these 7 weeks of fastings. **1697** EVELYN *Numismata* vii. 240 Head..cut in Onyx, comparable by universal Suffrage to any of the Old Masters. **1794** R. J. SULIVAN *View Nat.* II. 232 To prefer their own judgment to the general suffrage of mankind. **1861** MILL *Utilitar.* ii. 16 What means are there of determining which is the acutest of two pains..except the general suffrage of those who are familiar with both? **1882** HINSDALE *Garfield & Educ.* II. 361 He draughted a paper,..and submitted it to the suffrage of the republic of scientific scholars.

†**b.** Repute; = OPINION 6. *Obs.*

1667 WATERHOUSE *Narr. Fire in London* 90 She hath the suffrage abroad to be one of the most August..Governments in the world.

9. The casting of a vote, voting; the exercise of a right to vote; election by voting.

1665 MANLEY *Grotius' Low C. Wars* 907 They..should have right of suffrage in their Dyets and Assemblies. **1667** MILTON *P.L.* II. 415 Here he had need All circumspection, and wee now no less Choice in our suffrage. **1709** STRYPE *Ann. Ref.* I. xxix. 299 They went to the Suffrage in the Afternoon, and such of the House as were against the Six Articles..carried it. **1760–72** J. ADAMS tr. *Juan & Ulloa's Voy.* (ed. 3) II. 45 In the former [university] are chairs for all the sciences, and filled by suffrage. **1850** MARSDEN *Early Purit.* (1853) 300 A successor was chosen by general suffrage. **1887** LOWELL *Democracy* etc. 32 The right of suffrage is not valued when indiscriminately bestowed.

†**10.** A voice or voting power in a matter. *Obs.*

a **1662** HEYLIN *Laud* (1668) 375 The Covenanters had so laid the Plot, that none but those of their own Party should have Suffrage in it. **1673** *Lady's Call.* Pref., The Gyneceum has still had a rival suffrage with the Senate.

11. a. The right or privilege of voting as a member of a body, state, etc. (orig. *U.S.*)

1789 *Constit. U.S.* v, No state shall be deprived of its equal suffrage in the Senate. **1817–8** COBBETT *Resid. U.S.* (1822) 220 The suffrage, or qualification of electors, is very various. **1840** ARNOLD *Hist. Rome* II. 313 The survivors..were obliged to become Roman citizens without suffrage. **1867** LATHAM *Black & White* 114 No territories shall be admitted as States in which there is not an equal suffrage of all races and colours.

b. With prefixed word denoting the extent, as ***adult, female, household, manhood, universal, woman('s, women's suffrage***.

1798 W. NARES *Jacobin* vi. in *Anti-Jacobin* No. 22, I pant and sigh for univers——al suffrage. **1866** [see HOUSEHOLD 8]. **1873** [see MANHOOD 7]. **1877** GLADSTONE *Glean.* (1879) I. 147 Is not Mr. Lowe a little hard on the universal suffrage of France, when he charges on it a protective tariff, seeing that the no-suffrage of Russia has one tenfold more protective? **1884** [see FEMALE *a.* 4 b]. **1906** W. R. CREMER in *Hansard Commons* 25 Apr. 1572 If they once opened the door and enfranchised ever so small a number of females..it ultimately meant adult suffrage... Hon. Members had not really thought out what adult suffrage must lead to. **1910** *Hansard Commons* 11 July 55 The Member for Clitheroe explained with great explicitness what his object is. The hon. Gentleman's object is adult suffrage. That adult suffrage, of course, includes the vote for all adult women... The result of this adult suffrage, when it does come, will be a total electorate of 23,000,000 instead of 7,000,000. In that total electorate there will be a considerable majority of women. **1939** G. B. SHAW *Geneva* I. 16 The president and parliament are elected by adult suffrage every two years.

†ˈ**suffrage**, *v.* *Obs.* [f. prec. or ad. L. *suffrāgārī* (see SUFFRAGATE).]

1. *intr.* To vote *for* or *against*; hence, to agree or side *with*, to give support *to*.

1613 T. GODWIN *Rom. Antiq.* (1614) 97 Neither children ..nor old men..were allowed to suffrage in these assemblies. **1652** L. S. *People's Liberty* ix. 60 They are not to be permitted to suffrage in state affairs. **1657** TOMLINSON *Renou's Disp.* 237 Yet Matthiolus will not suffrage herewith, but contends [etc.]. **1657** W. MORICE *Coena quasi Κοινη* ix. 93, I never voted for exorbitant Episcopacy, nor should I have ever suffraged against a regulated. *Ibid.* Diat. vi. 309 Some, that suffrage for the Presbyterial Government. **1661** GLANVILL *Van. Dogm.* 179 What he hath of this, was never learnt from his Hypotheses; but forcibly fetch'd in to suffrage to them.

2. *trans.* To elect by vote; hence, to give support to; to side with.

1641 MILTON *Reform.* II. Wks. 1851 III. 57 As well as their worldly wisedomes are priviledg'd as members of the State in suffraging their..Burgesses. **1641** *Anc. Customs Eng.* in *Harl. Misc.* (Malh.) IV. 368 Every particular subject, who is either present personally, or consenting by his assignee, suffraged by himself. **1838** S. BELLAMY *Betrayal* 17 When the false god call'd Upon her tempest breath to suffrage him.

Hence †ˈ**suffrager** *Obs. rare*, a voter.

1613 T. GODWIN *Rom. Antiq.* (1614) 98 Little coffers, into which the suffragers which did approue the law did cast in the first table; those that disliked it, did cast in the second. **1701** *Enq. Inconv. Public & Adv. Priv. Elect.* 22 An Election ..is a Majority of Votes including the Sense of a Majority of Suffragers.

suffragette (sʌfrəˈdʒɛt). [f. SUFFRAGE *sb.* + -ETTE.] A female supporter of the cause of women's political enfranchisement, *esp.* one of a violent or 'militant' type. Also as *v. intr.* (in quot. *fig.*); **suffraˈgetism**; **suffraˈgettish, suffragetty** *adjs.*

1906 *Daily Mail* 10 Jan., Mr. Balfour and the 'Suffragettes'... It was not surprising that Mr. Balfour should receive a deputation of the Suffragettes. **1907** *Athenæum* 28 Sept. 358/2 [Aristophanes] who represented Cleon as noisy, Euripides as sentimental, Socrates as pedantic, and women as 'suffragettes'. **1909** H. G. WELLS *Ann Veronica* vii. 134 And her straight hair was out demonstrating and suffragetting upon some independent notions of its own. **1912** C. S. CHURCHILL *Let.* 7 Feb. in M. Soames *Clementine Churchill* (1979) vi. 76 Amy is kind, but more Suffragetty, Christian Sciency and Yankee Doodle than ever. **1913** G. B. SHAW *Let.* 4 Feb. in *B. Shaw & Mrs. Campbell* (1952) 79 That is the sort of thing that you vaguely lump into a cloud of abomination as Suffragettism. **1957** E. HYAMS *Speaking Garden* 75 What, in their time, were more ludicrous than suffragettism or antisepsis or anti-slavery? **1970** G. GREER *Female Eunuch* 295 The history of suffragettism..is beyond the scope of this book. **1974** V. NABOKOV *Look at Harlequins* (1975) IV. iv. 173 Mrs. Noteboke, a stout dark lady in suffragettish tweeds.

suffragi (sʊˈfrɑːgiː). Also **suffraggi**. [a. *sufragī*, repr. Egyptian Arab. pronunc. Turk. *sofraji*, f. Arab. *sufra* food, dining-table + Turk. agent-suffix *-ji*.] A waiter, butler or steward.

1924 *Blackw. Mag.* Feb. 245/2 Our suffragi and cook led a sort of troglodyte life for days. **1959** W. THESIGER *Arabian Sands* xiii. 247 In the new 'hotel'..there was electric light, fans, and tinned food served by a Sudanese suffragi. **1972** R. MAUGHAM *Escape from Shadows* iii. 136 Suffragis sprang up from nowhere with drinks, and I was offered one. **1979** *Stand* XX. IV. 34/2 The suffraggi puts a whisky before me.

suffragial (səˈfreɪdʒɪəl), *a.* *nonce-wd.* [f. L. *suffrāgium* SUFFRAGE + -AL[1].] Pertaining to voting.

1844 MOZLEY *Ess.* (1878) II. 40 The two rights, commercial and suffragial.

†**suffragies**, *sb. pl.* *Obs.* Also 3 -iis, 4–5 ijs, 5 -iez, -yes, -is, 6 -ees. [ad. L. *suffrāgia*, pl. of *suffrāgium* SUFFRAGE *sb.*]

1. Prayers, *esp.* on behalf of the departed.

a **1225** *Ancr. R.* 22 A morwen, oþer a niht efter þe suffragiis of Uhtsong, sigge3 Commendacium. *c* **1380** WYCLIF *Sel. Wks.* III. 259 No prelat may assoylle, ne graunte hevenely suffragies. **1432–50** tr. *Higden* (Rolls) VI. 195 Suffragyes doen for dedde men. **1450** *Rolls of Parlt.* V. 188/1 A solempne Obite..to be..founden with other certayn observauncez and suffragiez. *a* **1533** FRITH *Disput. Purgat.* I. Wks. (1573) 17 He shal lye in the paynes of purgatory, vntill he be deliuered thence by Masse pence, the Popes pardon or certaine other Suffragies. **1555** EDEN *Decades* (Arb.) 293 They..thinke that the soules of deade menne are not helped with the suffragies of preestes.

2. Votes, opinions, testimonies.

1587 D. FENNER *Def. Ministers* 26 Lett him neither be a Commaunder or Lorde, nor a slaue vnto the suffragies, but a fellowe & a discerner. **1593** R. HARVEY *Philad.* 9 If nothing be true in one country which hath not suffragees from another Countrey, I cannot tell what historie may stand.

†ˈ**suffraging**, *vbl. sb.* *Obs.* [f. SUFFRAGE *v.* + -ING[1].] The exercise of the suffrage, voting.

1613 T. GODWIN *Rom. Antiq.* (1614) 101 They also having freedome of suffraging. **1691–2** WOOD *Fasti Oxon.* II. 107 An equal power of suffraging did not now pertain to all masters.

†**suˈffraginous**, *a.* *Obs.* *rare*[−1]. [ad. L. *suffrāginōsus*, f. *suffrāgin-*, SUFFRAGO.] Of, belonging to, or affecting the hocks of animals.

1646 SIR T. BROWNE *Pseud. Ep.* III. i. 106 The bought of the fore-legs [in the elephant] not directly backward,..the hough or suffraginous flexure behinde rather outward. **1656** BLOUNT *Glossogr.*, *Suffraginous*, that is diseased in the houghes or pasterns.

suffragism (ˈsʌfrədʒɪz(ə)m). [f. next + -ISM.] The advocacy of an extension of the suffrage, e.g. to women (***women's suffragism***).

1888 BRYCE *Amer. Commw.* xciii. III. 301 Women's suffragism is thought 'bad form'. **1908** *Lit. Guide* 1 Aug. 123/2 He does, indeed, make a remark on feminine achievement in those spheres, but we dare not repeat it in this year of suffragism.

suffragist (ˈsʌfrədʒɪst). [f. SUFFRAGE + -IST.] An advocate of the extension of the political franchise, *esp.* (after about 1885) to women. Often with prefixed word (cf. SUFFRAGE *sb.* 11 b), as ***complete suffragist, universal suffragist, woman suffragist***.

1822 *Blackw. Mag.* XII. 156 If they come back Universal Suffragists, we offer to turn Radicals. **1845** *Tait's Mag.* XII. 67 The Complete-suffragists, will say, that..the League are practically admitting the truth of what they have always urged... Which..furnishes one reason the more why the Suffragists should help the League. **1865** *Pall Mall Gaz.* 17 Oct. 5 The anti-negro-suffragists in Connecticut. **1883** *American* VI. 7 The most persistent suffragist claims no more than this. **1900** *N. Eng. Hist. & Gen. Reg.* Suppl. cxxi, The cause of the woman suffragists. **1914** *Daily Mail* 8 June 6/6, I am a woman and a suffragist.

Hence **suffraˈgistic** *a.*, **suffraˈgistically** *adv.*

1907 M. BEERBOHM in *Sat. Rev.* 13 Apr. 457/2 The shrill suffragistic cheers which punctuated the first performance. **1909** *Daily Chron.* 13 Nov. 6/4 The pageant had been preceded by an excellent entertainment, including several 'suffragistic' and other playlets. **1923** K. D. WIGGIN *My Garden of Memory* (1924) xiii. 121 Ella intrusively and suffragistically fluttered into the nest,..sadly complicating the family arrangements.

‖**suffrago** (səˈfreɪgəʊ). *Anat.* [L.] The 'heel' at the junction of the tibia and the tarsus in quadrupeds and birds.

1842 BRANDE *Dict. Sci.* etc., *Suffrago*, in Mammalogy and Ornithology, the joint of the tibia with the tarsus. **1872** COUES *N. Amer. Birds* 240 The feathers rarely reach the suffrago.

suffraine, -ayn(d, obs. forms of SOVEREIGN.

†**suˈffrete.** *Obs.* Also 5 **-aite**. [a. OF. *s(o)uffrete, -aite* = Pr. *sofracha*, It. †*soffratta*:—L. *suffracta-m*, pa. pple. fem. (used as sb.) of *suffringĕre* to break up, f. *suf-* = SUB- 26 + *frangĕre* to break.] Want, need.

c **1450** *Merlin* iii. 59 Many provertees [*sic*] and grete suffraites suffred oure lorde her in erthe for oure sake. **1481** CAXTON *Godfrey* xciii. 144 Vytayll began to faylle, And was grete suffrete and scarsenes in thoost.

†**suffretous**, *a.* *Obs.* Also 5 **suffretouse, -ateuse, -atous.** [a. OF. *suffretous, -aitous* (mod.F. *souffreteux*), = Pr. *sofrachos*; f. *suffraite* (see prec.).] Needy, in want, miserable.

c **1450** *Merlin* xiii. 201 He knoweth beste the pore and the suffretouse. **1481** CAXTON *Godfrey* ccix. 306 The hoost.. were but fewe and suffretous by cause they had no shippes. **1490** —— *Eneydos* i. 13 Now was that pyetous cyte..putte in desolacyon suffretous. **1491** —— *Vitas Patr.* (W. de W. 1495) I. xli. 64 b/2 Tyll that thou haste dystrybuted alle thyse goodes..to the suffretous, poore and nedy.

suffreyn, obs. form of SOVEREIGN.

14.. in *Tundale's Vis.* (1843) 149 Fyrst hyle to hym honowre That suffreyn is and socowre.

†ˈ**suffriate**, *v.* *Obs.* *rare*[−0]. [f. pa. ppl. stem of L. **suffriāre*, f. *suf-* = SUB- 26 + *friāre* (see FRIABLE).]

1623 COCKERAM, *Suffriate*, to crumble bread.

†**suffricate**, *v.* *Obs.* *rare*[−0]. [f. pa. ppl. stem of L. *suffricāre*, f. *suf-* = SUB- 26 + *fricāre* to rub.]

1623 COCKERAM, *Suffricate*, to rub off.

†**suffront.** *Obs.* [app. f. *suf-* = SUB- 3 + FRONT *sb.* (9 b).] ? An altar-frontal.

1516 in G. Oliver *Lives Bps. Exeter* etc. (1861) 364 Suffront, stayned de blodio bokeram cum ymagine Crucifixi. **1668** BP. HACKET *Let.* in T. T. Carter *Life J. Kettlewell* (1895) 49 In velvet, purple and azure, fifty pounds worth..to serve as paraphront or suffront, and carpet for the Altar. *a* **1670** —— *Abp. Williams* II. (1693) 107 Paraphront, Suffront, for the Hangings above and beneath the Table.

suffrutescent (sʌfruːˈtɛsənt), *a.* *Bot.* [ad. mod.L. *suffrutescens, -ent-*, f. *suf-* = SUB- 21 c + *frutescens* FRUTESCENT. So F.] Somewhat woody or shrubby at the base.

1816 *Edwards' Bot. Reg.* II. 130 *Arctotis maculata*. White tawny-stained suffrutescent Arctotis. **1829** LOUDON *Encycl. Plants* (1836) 729 Stem suffrutescent. **1880** A. GRAY *Struct. Bot.* iii. §3. 50 Undershrubs or Suffruticose plants, are woody plants of humble stature... If less decidedly woody, they are termed Suffrutescent.

‖**suffrutex** (ˈsʌfruːtɛks). *Bot.* Pl. **suffrutices** (sʌˈfruːtɪsiːz); also 7 *erron.* **-ages** (but cf. FRUITAGE 3). [mod.L., f. *suf-* = SUB- 23 + FRUTEX.] A plant having a woody base, but a herbaceous annual growth above.

1567 MAPLET *Gr. Forest* 27 A fourth kind [of plant] which they cal Suffutrex [*sic*] a mean betwene the Herbe and the shrub. **1691** RAY *Creation* I. (1692) 154 Odoriferous and ever-green Shrubs and Suffrutices. *a* **1706** EVELYN *Silva* (1776) 509 Herbaceous Suffrutages. **1726** *Dict. Rust.* (ed. 3), *Suffrutex*, is a low Woody perennial Plant, that sends out no leaves from its Roots; and beginning to be branch'd from the very bottom of the Stalk, as Lavender, Sage, Rue, and the like. **1866** in *Treas. Bot.*

†**suffru'ticeous, -ious,** *a. Bot. Obs.* [f. mod.L. *suffrutic-* (see prec.) + -EOUS, -IOUS.] = next.

1657 TOMLINSON *Renou's Disp.* 283 Kermes.. is the name of a Suffruticeous Plant. **1657** *Physical Dict., Suffruticious*, between a shrub and an herb.

suffruticose (sʌ'fruːtɪkəʊs), *a. Bot.* [ad. mod.L. *suffruticōsus*, f. *suffrutic-*, SUFFRUTEX + -OSE.] Of the character of a suffrutex; woody at the base but herbaceous above.

1793 MARTYN *Lang. Bot., Suffruticosus*, Suffruticose, Undershrubby. **1842** LOUDON *Suburban Hort.* 430 Raspberries being suffruticose plants. **1842** BRANDE *Dict. Sci.* etc. s.v., Lavender is an instance of a suffruticose plant. **1876** HARLEY *Mat. Med.* (ed. 6) 362 Litmus Lichens are rigid suffruticose lichens.

So †**su'ffruticous** *a. Obs. rare.*

1776 J. LEE *Introd. Bot.* Explan. Terms 378 *Suffruticosus*, suffruticous, half-shrubby.

†**su'ffulce,** *v. Obs. rare.* [ad. L. *suffulcīre*, f. *suf-* = SUB- 26 + *fulcīre* to prop, but ? confused with *suffarcināre* to stuff.] *trans.* To stuff.

1599 A. M. tr. *Gabelhouer's Bk. Physicke* 106/2 For Asthmasye.. Take 14 or 15 figges, suffulce, or fille the same with Mustard seed. *Ibid.* 111/2 Gird the bodye.. with the suffulced little pillowes.

†**su'ffult,** *v. Obs. rare*⁻¹. [f. L. *suffult-*, pa. ppl. stem of *suffulcīre* (see prec.).] *trans.* To support.

c **1540** tr. *Pol. Verg. Eng. Hist.* (Camden 36) 181 Hee minded to have suffultid and releeved relligion with his goods.

suffulted (sʌ'fʌltɪd), *a. Ent.* [f. L. *suffultus*, pa. pple. of *suffulcīre* (see above) + -ED.] See quot.

1826 KIRBY & SP. *Entomol.* IV. xlvi. 287 Suffulted Pupil (*Pupilla suffulta*). When the pupil shades into another colour.

†**su'ffume,** *v. Obs. rare*⁻¹. [ad. L. **suffūmāre*, f. *suf-* = SUB- 2, 26 + *fūmāre* to FUME.] *trans.* To suffumigate. Hence †**su'ffume** *sb.*, a suffumigation.

1540 R. JONAS *Byrth Mankynde* 19 b, It shalbe also verye profytable for her to suffume the nether places with muske. **1656** RIDGLEY *Pract. Physick* 20 Resolving suffumes are profitable.

suffumigate (sʌ'fjuːmɪgeɪt), *v. rare.* Also 6 *pa. pple.* (*Sc.*) **suffumigat.** [f. pa. pple. of L. *suffūmigāre*, f. *suf-* = SUB- 2, 26 + *fūmigāre* to FUMIGATE.]

1. *trans.* To fumigate from below.

1588 ALEX. HUME *Hymns* vii. 35 Suffumigat with nard and cinnamon. **1612** WOODALL *Surg. Mate* Wks. (1653) 202 The patients hinder parts well suffumigated with the same decoction. **1623** COCKERAM, *Suffumigate*, to smoake underneath. **1910** KIPLING *Rewards & Fairies* 270, I sprinkled sulphur on the faggots whereby the on-lookers were as handsomely suffumigated.

†**2.** *intr.* To rise in smoke or vapour. *Obs.*

1599 A. M. tr. *Gabelhouer's Bk. Physicke* 219/2 Take greene Corne or seede, lay it on coales, and it will suffumigate.

suffumigation (sʌfjuːmɪ'geɪʃən). Now *arch.* or *Hist.* [ad. L. *suffūmigātio, -ōnem*, n. of action f. *suffūmigāre* to SUFFUMIGATE. Cf. OF. *subfumigation*, F. *suffumigation.*] The action of suffumigating or fumigating from below; an instance of this; chiefly *concr.* (usually *pl.*): fumes or vapours generated by burning herbs, incense, etc.; also *occas.*, a substance used for this purpose.

a. *Med.* used to produce a therapeutic effect by penetration of the body.

1422 YONGE *Secr. Secr.* lxiii. 239 Aftyr that man sholde vse suffumygacionys of herbis. *a* **1425** tr. *Arderne's Treat. Fistula* etc. 74 Afterward be þer done suffumigacion or fomentacion. **1540** R. JONAS *Byrth Mankynde* 26 Yf this profet nothynge, then vse this suffumigation. Take myrrhe, galbanum, castorium [etc.]. **1599** A. M. tr. *Gabelhouer's Bk. Physicke* 65/1 Let the suffumigatione therof ascende to thy Eares. **1601** HOLLAND *Pliny* II. Expl. Wds. Art, *Suffumigation*, is the smoke that is received into the body from under a stoole, for the diseases of the guts, fundament, or matrice. **1604** JAS. I *Counterbl. to Tobacco* (Arb.) 100 The stinking Suffumigation whereof [*sc.* of tobacco] they yet vse against that disease. **1635** BRATHWAIT *Arcadian Princ.* 235, I meane by sweatings and suffumigations to extract all those viscid and oily humours. **1684** tr. *Bonet's Merc. Compit.* xiv. 494 A Phthisical Person [cured].. by a Suffumigation of Amber. **1769** E. BANCROFT *Guiana* 87 The Indians.. often use it by way of suffumigation, for rheums, head-achs etc. **1835** BROWNING *Paracelsus* III. 442 Such a suffumigation as, once fired, Had stunk the patient dead ere he could groan.

b. used in incantations, in the offering of sacrifices, and in witchcraft to excite evil spirits.

[**1390, 14..**: see SUBFUMIGATION.]

1565 JEWEL *Repl. Harding* (1611) 427 The Sacrifices, that in Old times were made vnto Fides, and Terminus,.. consisted only in Suffumigations, and Odors. **1567** FENTON *Trag. Disc.* iii. (1898) 153 Diverse suffumigacions incident to witchecrafte. **1614** SELDEN *Titles Hon.* 9 To these were.. giuen diuine worship and ceremonies with suffumigations, crownes of flowers, and other rites. **1646** J. GREGORY *Notes & Obs.* (1650) 97 They observed such a place of the Moone, made such a suffumigation, uttered such and such words at the graffing of one Tree upon another. **1652** GAULE *Magastrom.* 222 A suffumigation made with the congealed blood of an Asse, and the fat of a wolfe, and Storax. **1696** AUBREY *Misc.* (1721) 172 Evil Spirits are pleased and allured and called up by Suffumigations of Henbane &c. stinking Smells, &c. **1830** SCOTT *Demonol.* i. 46 The nostrils are made to inhale such suffumigation, as well as the mouth. **1856** R. A. VAUGHAN *Mystics* (1860) II. VIII. iii. 179 *note*, The sympathetic influence.. of stones and metals, ointments and suffumigations.

†**c.** *gen.* A fume, vapour. *Obs.*

1567 MAPLET *Gr. Forest* 72 Suffumigation of Brimstone. *a* **1612** HARINGTON *De Valet. Conserv.* (1624) 43 Your parlors or Chambers being first purged and ayred with suffumigations. **1614** T. ADAMS *Diuells Banket* III. 109 As the suffumigations of the oppressed stomach, surge vp and cause the head-ach. **1651** H. MORE *Enthus. Tri.* (1712) 5 A little reek or suffumigation.

Hence †**suffumi'gatious** *a.*, used for suffumigation.

1688 HOLME *Armoury* II. vi. 119/3 Suffumigatious Gums, or such as are for Perfumes.

†**suffumige.** *Obs. rare.* [ad. med.L. *suffūmigium* (whence It., Pg. *suffumigio*), f. *suffūmigāre* to SUFFUMIGATE.] = SUFFUMIGATION.

1666 G. HARVEY *Morb. Angl.* xx. 245 Drying suffumiges or smoaks are oft prescribed with good success. [**1855** DUNGLISON *Med. Lex.*, *Suffimentum*, a perfume; suffumige; fumigation.]

†**su'ffund,** *v. Obs. rare*⁻¹. [ad. L. *suffundĕre* (see SUFFUSE).] *trans.* To suffuse.

1657 TOMLINSON *Renou's Disp.* 68 Many stones may be ignified.. and still suffunded with a certain humour.

†**suffurate,** *v. Obs. rare.* [f. pa. ppl. stem of L. *suffurārī*, f. *suf-* = SUB- 26 + *furārī*, f. *fur* thief.] *trans.* To steal away.

1549 E. BECKE *Bible* Pref. A A vi, If all magistrates.. wolde.. vouchsafe to suffurate & spare an houre or ii in a day, from theyr worldly busines. *a* **1564** BECON *Nosegay* Pref., Wks. (1843) 195 At such hours as I could conveniently suffurate and steal away from the.. teaching of my scholars.

Hence †**suffu'ration**, a drawing away.

1651 BIGGS *New Disp.* ¶297 The Spagyrick art.. doth debilitate many things by a privie and insensible suffuration.

suffuse (sə'fjuːz), *v.* [f. L. *suffūs-*, pa. ppl. stem of *suffundĕre*, f. *suf-* = SUB- 2, 26 + *fundĕre* to pour.]

1. *trans.* To overspread as with a fluid, a colour, a gleam of light.

a. of tears, moisture. Chiefly *pass.*

1590 [see SUFFUSED 1]. **1600** FAIRFAX *Tasso* XII. lxxiv, His eies vnclos'd, with teares suffused. **1754** HUME *Hist. Eng., Chas. I*, x. I. 461 Hamilton long followed him with his eyes, all suffused in tears. **1773–83** HOOLE *Orl. Fur.* XVIII. 1162 While tears his cheeks suffuse. **1797** S. & HT. LEE *Canterb. T.* (1799) I. 352 His whole frame [was] suffused with a cold dew. **1838** PRESCOTT *Ferd. & Is.* xiii. II. 115 Every eye was suffused with tears.

b. of light, air, fire, colour. Often in fig. context.

1728–46 THOMSON *Spring* 1086 Dark looks succeed; Suffus'd, and glaring with untender fire. **1786** tr. *Beckford's Vathek* (1883) 33 To hide the blush of mortification that suffused their foreheads. **1813** SHELLEY *Q. Mab* VI. 25 A kindling gleam of hope Suffused the Spirit's lineaments. **1818** WORDSW. *Even. Volunt.* ix. 45 Yon hazy ridges.. Climbing suffused with sunny air. **1860** TYNDALL *Glac.* I. xxv. 184 The glorious light.. suffused with gold and crimson the atmosphere itself. **1877** BLACK *Green Past.* xxxv. 283 The beautiful colour that for a second suffused her blushing face. **1882** *Garden* 5 Aug. 119/1 Sepals and flowers white, suffused at base with rosy lilac.

c. *transf.* and *fig.*

1813 COLERIDGE *Night-scene* 43 Eyes suffused with rapture. **1848** W. H. BARTLETT *Egypt to Pal.* v. (1879) 101 The life and literature of the nation were suffused with these reminiscences. **1867** J. B. ROSE tr. *Virg. Æneid* 160 The crowded ranks Of disembodied Shades suffused the banks. **1868** HELPS *Realmah* ii. (1876) 10 The most commonplace objects being suffused with beauty. **1876** HOLLAND *Sev. Oaks* xv. 234 The amused expression suffused the lawyer's face.

2. To pour (a liquid) over a surface. (Also *refl.*) Chiefly in fig. context.

1734 tr. *Rollin's Roman Hist.* (1827) III. VII. 328 Suffusing over the study of philosophy the dye of rhetoric. **1815** *Ann. Reg., Chron.* 92/2 Water, sugar, &c. from the boiler and pans.. suffused thickly upon the trees. **1829** I. TAYLOR *Enthus.* x. 282 The healing flood of Christian truth shall suffuse itself in all directions. **1854** *Jrnl. R. Agric. Soc.* XV. II. 427 Springs, suffused from higher grounds.

suffused (sə'fjuːzd), *ppl. a.* [f. prec. + -ED¹.]

1. Overspread as with fluid, light, colour, etc.

1590 SPENSER *F.Q.* III. vii. 10 Wiping the teares from her suffused eyes. **1629** QUARLES *Argalus & Parthen.* II. Wks. (Grosart) III. 264/2 Which strongly did importune A world of teares from these suffused eyes. **1805** *Med. Jrnl.* XIV. 201 The eyes became more suffused and dull. **1878** BROWNING *La Saisiaz* 71 How suffused a cheek You had turned me had I sudden brought the blush into the smile.

2. Spread over a surface like water. Also *fig.*

1851 MRS. BROWNING *Casa Guidi Wind.* I. 817 The deep look which shall drain Suffused thought into channelled enterprise. **1873** BLACK *Pr. Thule* xxvi. 432 There was a faint suffused sense of joy in her heart.

Hence **su'ffusedly** *adv.*, in a suffused manner.

1895 MEYRICK *Brit. Lepidopt.* 461 Forewings whitish.. dorsum suffusedly fuscous.

suffusion (sə'fjuːʒən). Also 7 **-tion.** [ad. L. *suffūsio, -ōnem*, n. of action f. *suffūs-* (see SUFFUSE). Cf. F. *suffusion*, It. *suffusione*, etc.]

1. The defluxion or extravasation of a fluid or 'humour' over a part of the body; †*concr.* the fluid itself; *spec.* in *Old Med.*, cataract.

1398 TREVISA *Barth. De P.R.* XVII. xli. (Bodl. MS.) An oynemente þat.. helpeþ aȝens suffusion of yȝen. **1575** TURBERV. *Faulconrie* 235 Ther is a cataract which doth light upon the eyes of a hawke whome we may tearme a suffusion. **1608** TOPSELL *Serpents* 209 The braine [*sc.* of lizards] is profitable for suffusions. **1667** MILTON *P.L.* III. 26 So thick a drop serene hath quencht thir Orbs, Or dim suffusion veild. **1674** W. BATES *Harmony Div. Attrib.* vii. 140 As the Eye that is clouded with a Suffusion, so that all things appear yellow to it. **1688** BOYLE *Vit. Sight* 251, I have observed them [*sc.* flyes in the eye] to continue many years without being more than a bastard suffusion, as Physicians speake. **1726** *Dict. Rust.* (ed. 3), Suffusion of the Eye, in a Horse, is a Sort of Pin and Web. **1728** *Chambers' Cycl.* s.v., The Jaundice is a Suffusion of Bile over the whole Body. **1748** V. RENATUS *Dis. Horses* 70 A Suffusion or Defluxion in their Feet. **1859** MAYNE *Expos. Lex.* s.v., A suffusion, or extravasation of some humour, as of blood in the eye.

2. The action of suffusing a surface with fluid, moisture, or colour; the condition of being suffused or overspread. Also, an instance of this.

1611 COTGR., *Suffusion*, a suffusion, or powring vpon; a spreading abroad. **1642** H. MORE *Song of Soul* III. iii. 49 Miry clods of this accursed earth; Whose dull suffusions make her often sown. **1789** E. DARWIN *Bot. Gard.* II. (1791) 65 In dim suffusion lies The glance divine, that lighten'd in their eyes. **1813** SCOTT *Trierm.* III. xxx, The golden glow.. O'er which in slight suffusion flows A frequent tinge of paly rose. **1843** R. J. GRAVES *Syst. Clin. Med.* xi. 127 He had.. a furious aspect, suffusion of the eyes.. and perfect sleeplessness. **1872** DARWIN *Emotions* viii. 218 The suffusion of the eyes with tears.

fig. **1676** CUDWORTH *Intell. Syst.* I. iv. 224 Because he.. being deeply tinctured, as it were, with the Suffusions of it [*sc.* a doctrine], every thing which he look'd upon, seem'd to him coloured with it. **1792** A. YOUNG *Trav. France* I. 251 There is in this painting such a suffusion of grace, and such a blaze of beauty [etc.]. **1852** LD. COCKBURN *Life Jeffrey* I. 91 A clear sweet voice, and a general suffusion of elegance.

3. A colouring or tint spread over a surface, *esp.* over the skin by the action of the blood, etc.; *freq.* a flush of colour in the face, a blush.

1700 DRYDEN *Ovid's Met.* xv. 287 The Disk of Phœbus when he climbs on high, Appears at first but as a bloodshot Eye; And when his Chariot downward drives to Bed, His Ball is with the same Suffusion red. **1712** STEELE *Spect.* No. 390 ¶1 Would she not be much more modest without that ambiguous Suffusion? **1745** AKENSIDE *Odes, Agst. Suspicion* ii, Already in your eyes I see a pale suffusion rise. **1763** *Phil. Trans.* LIII. 232 He.. had a yellow suffusion over his skin. **1777** G. FORSTER *Voy. round World* I. 102 A beautiful suffusion of purple. **1818** SCOTT *Br. Lamm.* ix, The deadly paleness.. gave place to a deep and rosy suffusion. **1843** R. J. GRAVES *Syst. Clin. Med.* viii. 93 The tunica adnata was of a pearl-white colour, without the slightest suffusion.

suffusive (sə'fjuːsɪv), *a.* [f. L. *suffūs-* (see SUFFUSE) + -IVE.] Tending to suffuse or spread.

1872 GEO. ELIOT *Middlem.* I. II. xvi. 295 That agreeable after-glow of excitement when thought lapses from examination of a specific object into a suffusive sense of its connections with all the rest of our existence. **1889** J. M. ROBERTSON *Ess. Crit. Meth.* 152 Interest in the love-stories and satisfaction in the minor character-drawing have passed into retrospection and suffusive musing. **1891** *Harper's Mag.* June 65/1 Purple and saffron and a suffusive blood-red flush.

‖**Sufi**¹ ('suːfɪ). Forms: 7 **Suffi**, 7, 9 **Sofee**, 8 **Souffee**, 8–9 **Sofi**, 9 **Soof(f)ee, Soofi, Soophee**, 9 **Sufi.** [a. Ar. *çūfī* lit. 'man of wool', f. *çūf* wool (see Margoliouth *Early Devel. Mohamm.*, 1914, 141). Cf. F. *sofi*, *soufi*. It has often been erron. associated with SOPHY¹, q.v.] One of a sect of Muslim ascetic mystics who in later times embraced pantheistic views.

1653 GREAVES *Seraglio* 178 Those Turks which.. would be accounted Sofees [*marg.* Puritans] do commonly read, as they walk along the streets. **1796** MORSE *Amer. Geog.* II. 571 Some of them called Souffees, who are a kind of quietists. **1815** ELPHINSTONE *Acc. Caubul* (1842) I. Introd. 83 The mystical doctrines of the Sofees. **1872** LOWELL *Dante* Prose Wks. 1890 IV. 149 A Soofi who has passed the fourth step of initiation. **1875** *Encycl. Brit.* II. 677/2 The Persian Sufis specially distinguished themselves by their practice of abstinence and solitary meditation.

attrib. **1815** ELPHINSTONE *Acc. Caubul* (1842) I. 273 The beauty of the Soofee system. **1886** CONDER *Syrian Stone-Lore* ix. (1896) 342 *note*, The 'path', the final 'unity' with God, the disbelief in all creeds, [etc.].. which form the great Sufi doctrines, are purely Buddhist.

Sufi², erron. form of SOPHY¹.

1876 *Encycl. Brit.* IV. 707/1 The Sophi or Sufi of Persia. *Ibid.* V. 175/1 The palace of the Sufi princes.

†'**Sufian,** *a.* and *sb. Obs.* Also 6 **Sophian,** 7 **Suffean.** [f. SUFI¹ + -AN.] **A.** *adj.* Belonging to the Sufis. **B.** *sb.* A Sufi.

1585 T. WASHINGTON tr. *Nicholay's Voy.* III. xx. 108 For that in the Arabian tongue wool is called Sophy, those which are of this sect are called Sophians... The Sophians whiche are the Persians, weare redde ones [*sc.* turbans]. **1698** FRYER *Acc. E. India & P.* 268 One of the Suffean Creed is Constituted Governor.

Sufic ('suːfɪk), *a.* [f. SUFI¹ + -IC.] Pertaining to the Sufis or their mystical system.

1884 *Encycl. Brit.* XVII. 522/2 There are frequent Súfic allegories [in the *Iskandarnáma*], just as in the *Makhzan*.

1914 MARGOLIOUTH *Early Devel. Mohamm.* 153 To a certain extent the Sûfic fasting and simplicity of diet was based on medical theory.

Sufiism ('su:fɪɪz(ə)m). Also **Sooffeeism, Sufyism, Suffeeism, Sufeism.** [f. SUFI[1] + -ISM.] = next.

1817 C. MILLS *Hist. Muhammedanism* 407 The.. visionary doctrines of Sooffeeism. **1844** H. H. WILSON *Brit. India* I. 101 The blended abstractions of Sufyism and the Vedanta. **1864** *Lond. Rev.* 28 May, Hafiz, with his mystic Suffeeism. **1880** *Encycl. Brit.* XI. 368/1 The system of philosophy professed by Persian poets and dervishes..is called Sufiism.

So **Sufi'istic** *a.*, pertaining to Sufiism.

1880 *Encycl. Brit.* XI. 368/1 The Sufiistic system of philosophy.

Sufism ('su:fɪz(ə)m). Also **Sofism.** [f. SUF(I[1] + -ISM.] The mystical system of the Sufis.

1836 *Partington's Brit. Cycl. Lit.*, etc. III. 854 Sufism, the pantheistic mysticism of the East. **1847** in WEBSTER. **1898** E. P. EVANS *Evol. Ethics* iv. 126 In Persia a highly mystical and poetical sofism has grown up.

Also **'Sufist** = SUFI[1] (in quot. *attrib.*); **Su'fistic** *a.*, pertaining to Sufism.

1854 LOWELL *Journ. Italy* Prose Wks. 1890 I. 199 He should take his motto from Bishop Golias's '*Mihi est propositum in tabernâ mori*', though not in the sufistic sense of that misunderstood Churchman. **1913** *Everyman* 13 June 269/1 The Sûfist mystic, Jelalu' d' Din Rumi.

sufon, obs. form of SEVEN.

† **sug**, *sb.*[1] *Obs.* Variant of SOG *sb.*

1578 LYTE *Dodoens* 511 The Rushes grow in low moyst sugges [*edd.* **1595**, **1610** sugs], or waterie places.

† **sug**, *sb.*[2] *Obs.* Also 7 **sugg.** [Origin unknown.] A species of fish-louse parasitic on the trout.

1653 WALTON *Angler* iii. 90 Many of them [*sc.* trout] have sticking on them Sugs or Trout lice, which is a kind of a worm, in shape like a Clove or a Pin with a big head. **1668** WILKINS *Real Char.* II. v. §2. 125. **1688** HOLME *Armoury* II. ix. 190. **1758** BINNELL *Descr. Thames* 176.

sug (sʌg), *v. dial.* (chiefly west-country). Also **sugg.** [Variant of SOG *v.*] To soak (*trans.* and *intr.*).

1633 T. ADAMS *Exp. 2 Peter* ii. 5 As land by long sugging under the waters hath the heart of it eaten out. **1706** PHILLIPS (ed. Kersey), To *Sug*, to soak in Water. **1733** W. ELLIS *Chiltern & Vale Farm.* 276 Its spungy, deep Roots will sugg, rot, and die here in a few Years.

sugan, variant form of SUGGAN *sb.*

sugar ('ʃʊgə(r)), *sb.* Forms: see below. [a. OF. *çucre* (12–14th c.), *çuquere, zuchre, sukere*, north-east. *chucre*, mod.F. *sucre* (from 13th c.), = Pr. *sucre*, It. *zucchero*, ad. (prob. through OHG.) med.L. *zuccarum, succarum*, ad. Arab. *sukkar* (with prefixed article *assukkar*, whence Sp. *azucar*, Pg. *assucar*). The phonological history of the Eng. forms is in several points obscure. (1) The *g* of the modern form (see γ-forms below) cannot be accounted for by any known OF. or AF. forms (but med.L. *zugurum* occurs); cf., however, AF. *segerstaine*, Norman F. *segrestein* = OF. *secrestain* (see SEXTON), and Eng. *flagon* representing F. *flacon*. (2) The quantity of the vowel of the first syllable appears to have been variable from early times (cf. the spellings *suigur, sewger, seukere*, and *suggur*), but the development of initial (sj) into (ʃ) makes it probable that the long *ū* (u:) prevailed (cf. *sure*), and that shortening took place afterwards; ('sju:gə(r)) survives in some north midl. districts. (3) The Sc. forms (δ) pronounced ('sʌkər) show a survival of the short vowel type from F. (sykr), but LG. influence is also possible.

The relation of Arab. *sukkar* to Gr. σάκχαρον, σάκχαρ (whence L. *saccharon*, SACCHARUM), Pers. *shakar*, Skr. *śarkarā* (Prakrit *sakkara*) ground or candied sugar, orig. pebble, grit (cf. JAGGERY), is not clear. Forms representing one or other of the types are found in most European languages: e.g. MLG. *sucker*, MDu. *sucker, sûker, suycker* (mod.Du. *suiker*), OHG. *zucura* (MHG. *zu(c)ker*, G. *zucker*), Icel. *sykr*, MSw. *so(c)ker, sucker* (Sw. *socker*, Da. *sukker*), Lit. Russ. *cukor*, Serb. *cukar*, Boh. *cukr*, Pol. *cukier*, Turk. *sukker*; Rum. *zahăr*, Russ. *sakharŭ*, Serb. *šećer*, †*cahara*, †*cakara*, Bulg. *sheker, zahar'*, Turk. *sheker*.]

1. a. A sweet crystalline substance, white when pure, obtained from a great variety of plant juices, but chiefly from those of the sugar-cane and sugar-beet, and forming an important article of human food.

α. 3–4 **zuker**, 4 **-ur, zucur, -er, zuccor, zukre, couker,** 5 **zucre, zuccary;** 5 **zugere, -ure.**

In med.L. documents it is often impossible to determine whether a form is intended for Latin or for latinized English.

c **1299** *Durham Acc. Rolls* (Surtees) 494 Zuker Roch. *Ibid.* 495 Zuker Marrokes. *c* **1310** *Ibid.* 510 In 3 *li.* et di. de Couker de Rupe. In 31 *li.* de Couker de Marrok. **1340** *Ibid.* 37 In di. li. zukur emp., 3*d.* **1364** in *Exch. Rolls Scotl.* II. 182 Per empcionem 434 librarum, cum quartario, zucure, xlij *li.* xviij *d.* **1419** *Lib. Alb. Rolls* Ser. I. 224 Kark de zucre, xij d. *a* **1425** tr. *Arderne's Treat. Fistula* etc. 68 Recipe cynamom [etc.]..to which be done zuccary euenly. **14..** *Nom.* in Wr.-Wülcker 714 *Hec zucurca* [sic], zugure.

β. 4 **sucere, -ore, suker, (seukere),** 4–5 **sucre,** 5 **sucure, sukyr.**

[**1289–90** *Househ. Exp. R. de Swinfield* (Camden) 1 :6 In .xix. lī sucar, .viij.s. .viij. d. ob... Item in .xxix. libr sucur in duobus panibus .xvj. s. xj. d.] **1308** *Durham Acc. Rolls* (Surtees) 4 In 1 libra de sucore, 9*d.* **1309–10** *Ibid.* 6, 3 *li.* de sucere. *a* **1310** in Wright *Lyric P.* v. 26 Such sucre mon secheth that saveth men sore. **1340** *Ayenb.* 83 þet is þe zuete sucre and of guod ssmak. **1390** GOWER *Conf.* II. 222 Whan venym melleth with the Sucre And mariage is mad for lucre. **14..** *Langl. P. Pl.* B. v. 122 (MSS. B R) Sucre. *c* **1440** *Promp. Parv.* 484/1 Sukyr, *zucura.*

γ. 4–5 **sugure,** 4–6 **sugur, sugre,** 4–7 **suger,** 5–6 **sugour,** (4 **suigur,** 4, 6 **surger** (?), 5 **sewger, sugyr, -or, sogyr, suggir,** 6 **sugare, -ir, suggur, suuger,** 6–8 **suggar,** 7 **shugar),** 6– **sugar.**

1334–5 *Abingdon Rolls* (Camden) 4 Item pro surger viij s. x d. **1377** LANGL. *P. Pl.* B. XIV. 312 The nyneth is swete to þe soule, no sugre is swettere. *c* **1386** CHAUCER *Squire's T.* 606 Yeue hem sugre [*v. rr.* sugere, sucre, suger], hony, breed and Milk. *c* **1400** MAUNDEV. (Roxb.) xvii. 76 Swetter þan sugur or hony. **1440–1** *Durham Acc. Rolls* (Surtees) 78 Item 1 layf de sugre. *Ibid.*, Di. 1 aff de Sogyr. **1491** in *Rep. Hist. MSS. Comm.* Var. Coll. IV. 211, 6 loves of sewger, 10. *s.* **1530** PALSGR. 176 *Sucre*, sugar. **1562** TURNER *Herbal* II. 36 b, The pouder of it [*sc.* liverwurt] taken wyth suggar. **1607** DEKKER & WEBSTER *Northw. Hoe* II. i, The warres in Barbary make Suger at such an excessiue rate. **1682** WILDING in *Collect.* (O.H.S.) I. 255 For shugar..00 00 02. **1756** C. LUCAS *Ess. Waters* I. 73 The like effect is produced by dropping oils on sugar. **1788** COWPER *Pity for Africans* 6 How could we do without sugar and rum? Especially sugar, so needful we see? **1898** G. B. SHAW *Plays* I. *Widowers' Houses* 8 Do you take sugar, Mr Cokane?

δ. *Sc.* 5–7 **succour,** 8– **succar, sucker,** (5 **sucur,** 6 **sukkoure, suckar, succur(e,** 7 **sucre,** 8 **soukar).**

1495 *Ledger A. Halyburton* (1867) 41, 12 li. sucur valens, ..½ sucur lacrissye. **1496** *Acc. Ld. High Treas. Scot.* I. 284, viij pund and x vnce of succour. **1549** *Compl. Scotl.* xvii. 145 Spicis, eirbis, drogis, gummis, & succur for to mak exquisit electuars. **1629** Z. BOYD *Last Battell* 958 (Jam.) Poyson, confected with sucre, is moste piercing and deadlie. **1644** Row *Extr.* in *Hist. Kirk* (Wodrow Soc.) p. xxvi, Two of them..misbehavit themselfes..in drinking wine, sek, and succour. **1786** BURNS *Scotch Drink* ix, Just a wee drap sp'ritual burn in, An' gusty sucker! **1852** J. FRASER *Poet. Chimes, Jas. V*, III. ii, Neeps, like sucker, wha'll buy neeps?

b. With qualifying adj., sb., or phr. indicating: (*a*) the place of origin or manufacture, as † ***sugar of Alisaunder*** (= Alexandria), ***Babylon, Barbary, Candy*** (cf. SUGAR-CANDIAN), ***Cipre*** (= Cyprus), ***Marrokes*** (= Morocco); see also LISBON; (*b*) colour, as ***black,*** † ***blanch, brown*** (see BROWN *a.* 7), ***green, white, yellow sugar;*** see also ROSET; (*c*) the stage of boiling, purification, or crystallization at which, or the form in which, the particular kind is produced, as ***blown, boiled, burnt, caramel, centrifugal, clarified, coarse, cracked, crashed, crude, crushed, crystal, crystalline, crystallizable, -ized, double-refined, form, granular, -ated, hard, high, liquid, low, pounded, raw, refined, refining, refuse, sifted, stamped, strained, uncrystallizable, unrefined sugar;*** † **ambered, female, fluid, male, pulled, store, true sugar,** † **sugar royal** (see quots.); see also BARLEY B. 2, BASTARD A. 10, CANDIED 2, CANDY *sb.*[1] 2, CLAYED 1, FEATHERED 9, LOAF-SUGAR, LUMP *sb.*[1] 9, MOIST *a.* 7, MUSCOVADO, PEARL *sb.*[1] 13, PEARLED 4, POWDER *sb.*[1] 5 b, POWDERED 6, ROCK *sb.*[1] 4 a, 9, SOFT *a.* 29; (*d*) its use, as ***coffee, kitchen, preserving sugar;*** (*e*) the plant from which it is made; see BEET *sb.* 2, BEETROOT, CANE *sb.*[1] 9 a, DATE *sb.*[1] 4, MAPLE 3, PALM *sb.*[1] 7 c.

c **1430** *Two Cookery-bks.* 50 Caste a-bouyn Sugre of *Alysaundre. *a* **1648** DIGBY *Closet Opened* (1669) 131 *Ambered-sugar is made by grinding very well, four grains of Amber-greece, and one of Musk, with a little fine Sugar. *c* **1330** *Durham Acc. Rolls* (Surtees) 518, 20 li. zukur *Babilon. **1592** *Wills & Inv. N.C.* (Surtees 1860) 212, x lbs. of *Barbarye sugar 10s. **1607** MARSTON *What You Will* I. i, Ha sweete, hunny barbary suger sweete Maister. *c* **1430** *Two Cookery-bks.* 7 Take *blake sugre, an cold water. **1408–9** *Durham Acc. Rolls* (Surtees) 608 It. 1 lb. suger *blanch, 2s. **1725** *Fam. Dict.* s.v., To have *Blown Sugar; when it has boiled a few more Walms, hold the Skimmer in your hand, and having, as before, shaken it a little, beating the Sides of the Pan, blow through the Holes. **1843** PEREIRA *Food & Diet* 119 When sufficiently heated, sugar becomes brown,..in this state it is called Caramel or *Burnt Sugar. **1553** EDEN *Treat. New Ind.* (Arb.) 41 Suger which excelleth the sugre of *Candye or Sicilia. **1725** *Fam. Dict.* s.v., These boilings are perform'd by Degrees... Sugar may be boil'd till it becomes Smooth, Pearled, Blown, Feather'd, *Crack'd and *Caramel. **1884** KNIGHT *Dict. Mech.* Suppl. 872 Soft *centrifugal sugar. **1725** *Fam. Dict.* s.v., Two Ladles full of *clarify'd Sugar are put to one of Water. **1753** *Chambers Cycl.* Suppl. s.v., *Coarse sugar, in which there is more oil than in refined sugar, is recommended as a good medicine. **1875** KNIGHT *Dict. Mech.* 2443/1 The crystals are separated in the centrifugal machine, and sold as a very light-colored *coffee-sugar. *a* **1834** in MCulloch *Dict. Comm.* (ed. 2) 1095 Different Sorts of *crashed Sugar to be kept separate. **1728** CHAMBERS *Cycl.* s.v., *Crude Sugar, or Moscouade, is that first drawn from the Juice of the Cane. **1857** MILLER *Elem. Chem., Org.* ii. §1. 66 The syrup..is boiled down again in the vacuum pan, and is obtained in the form of what is termed *crushed sugar. **1867** *Chambers' Encycl.* IX. 192/1 *Crystal Sugar. **1839** URE *Dict. Arts* 1209 The liquor..can dissolve none of the *crystalline sugar. *Ibid.* 1203 Not only is the *crystallizable sugar blackened, but its faculty of crystallizing impaired. *Ibid.* 1207 Nearly 35 cwt. of *crystallized sugar. **1316** *Durham Acc. Rolls* (Surtees) 11, 18 *li.* de sucore de *cipre. *c* **1450** *Two Cookery-bks.* 95 Take resons of corance,..Maces, sugur of Cipris. **1755** *Dict. Arts & Sci.* IV. s.v., The *double refined sugar of the shops. **1845** *Encycl. Metrop.* VIII. 498/1 That which is obtained from Muscovado, the crystals of which are sweeter, and less hard and fine, is named *female sugar. **1884** KNIGHT *Dict. Mech.* Suppl. 872 *Form sugar (nearly white). **1839** URE *Dict. Arts* 1203 Concentrated cane-juice, containing nearly half its weight of *granular sugar. **1842** *Penny Cycl.* XXIII. 225/1 The difficulty of extracting *granulated sugar from a fruit containing so much mucilage. **1875** KNIGHT *Dict. Mech.* 2447/2 Cones of sugar, containing 100 pounds each of *green sugar. **1755** *Dict. Arts & Sci.* IV. s.v., They put it up in hogsheads,..under the name of *grey or brown sugar. **1624** *Althorp MS.* in Simpkinson *Washingtons* (1860) App. p. lv, *Hard sugar for conserve of redd roses. **1848** *Chambers' Inform. for People* I. 727/2 According to the quantity of water which any sugar contains, so it is denominated *high or *low; that from the cane being a higher or stronger variety than that from the grape, and sugar-candy a higher form than that of raw sugar. **1607** TOPSELL *Four-f. Beasts* 238 They are serued vpon the table, and strewed ouer with *kitchen suger. **1681** GREW *Musæum* II. ii. ii. 224 By placing a great many slender sticks across a Vessel of *liquid Sugar. **1835** *Partington's Brit. Cycl. Arts & Sci.* II. 795/2 [The key] on being..turned round, unlocks the socket and plug at the bottom of the tube, and allows the liquid sugar to flow through the apertures. **1845** *Encycl. Metrop.* VIII. 498/1 That which is obtained from cakes of sugar is very white and hard, resembling crystal; it is called *male sugar. **1299** *Durham Acc. Rolls* (Surtees) 495 In 25 *li.* de Zuker *Marrokes. *c* **1340** *Ibid.* 36 In 12 *li.* succuris Marrok'. **1728** CHAMBERS *Cycl.* s.v., They strew the Surface over with the same *pounded Sugar. **1851** MAYHEW *Lond. Labour* I. 204 *Pulled sugar, or penides. **1797** *Encycl. Brit.* (ed. 3) XVIII. 59/2 After the melasses are drained off, the sugar becomes pretty dry and fair, and is then called muscovado or *raw sugar. **1712** tr. *Pomet's Hist. Drugs* I. 57 As much as the *Refined-Sugar wants of its first Weight. **1845** *Act 8 & 9 Vict.* c. 5 §10 Bastard or Refined Sugar. **1834** McCULLOCH *Dict. Comm.* (ed. 2) 1089 The *refuse sugar.. remaining after the process of refining. *c* **1299** *Durham Acc. Rolls* (Surtees) 494 In 10 *li.* de Zuker *Roch. **1326–7** *Ibid.* 15, 5 li. Zukur de Roche. **1712** tr. *Pomet's Hist. Drugs* I. 55 This *Sugar-Royal is extreamly white throughout the whole. **1714** *Fr. Bk. of Rates* 102 Double refined Sugar, called, Sugar Royal. **1845** ELIZA ACTON *Mod. Cookery* xvi. (ed. 2) 335 The pastry must be..well covered with *sifted sugar. **1867** *Tomlinson's Cycl. Arts* II. 687/1 A description of sugar, called *stamped sugar, is prepared from the inferior qualities..in such a manner as to have the shape and appearance of first quality refined. **1728** CHAMBERS *Cycl.* s.v., *Strain'd or Brown Sugar..does not differ much from the crude Sugar. **1812** HOWARD in *Partington's Brit. Cycl. Arts & Sci.* II. 793/2 Water dissolves the most *uncrystallizable sugar in preference to that which is most crystallizable. **1834** McCULLOCH *Dict. Comm.* (ed. 2) 1092 The Quantity of *Unrefined Sugar imported into the United Kingdom. *c* **1430** *Two Cookery-bks.* 7 Take *whyte sugre an caste þer-to. **1546** J. HEYWOOD *Prov.* (1867) 5 When time hath tournd white sugar to white salte. **1774** GOLDSM. *Nat. Hist.* (1824) I. 135 White sugar will sometimes be full of maggots. **1867** *Tomlinson's Cycl. Arts* II. 677/2 The juice being decanted off and boiled down.. furnished a pure white sugar. **1834** McCULLOCH *Dict. Comm.* (ed. 2) 1097 Sugar..Bengal, *yellow.

c. *pl.* Kinds of sugar; also, †cargoes or stocks of sugar.

1570 *Act 13 Eliz.* c. 25 §8 The said Acte..is not meant to extend..to any Wynes Oyles Sugers. **1607** [HARINGTON] *Englishm. Docter* Ad Libr., Nor of Barbary, Those luscious Canes, where our rich Sugars lie. **1695** *Disc. Duties on Sugars* 4 Every one that hath been acquainted with the Importing Sugars. **1714** MANDEVILLE *Fab. Bees* (1733) I. 52 Decio got five hundred pounds by his sugars. **1800** *Asiat. Ann. Reg.* II. 58/2 Sugars manufactured in India. **1847** *Simmonds's Colon. Mag.* Dec. 413 Sugars had evidently risen.

† **d.** = SUGAR-CANE. *Obs.*

1593 MUNDAY *Def. Contraries* 93 In Madera, Cyprus, and other Islandes, where the Sugars doe grow. **1660** F. BROOKE tr. *Le Blanc's Trav.* 111 The country abounds in Sugars, which they make great and many uses of. **1785** MARTYN *Lett. Bot.* xiii. (1794) 153, I have not told you..that Sugar is a grass of the first division.

e. *colloq.* A lump or teaspoonful of sugar.

1962 L. DEIGHTON *Ipcress File* xxiii. 150 He poured coffee into a black wedgwood cup and put four sugars in. 'Raise the sugar count,' he said. **1978** C. MACLEOD *Rest you Merry* (1979) ii. 18 'Why don't I make us a cup of coffee?' 'Great idea. Three sugars in mine.' **1982** *Sunday Tel.* 18 Apr. 8/6 How many sugars they were allowed in their tea.

2. *transf.* and *fig.* uses, phrases, etc.

a. *fig.* or in fig. context: Sweetness; also, sweet or honeyed words.

c **1374** CHAUCER *Troylus* III. 1194 To whom this tale sucre [*v.rr.* seukere, sugre] be or soot. **1412–20** LYDG. *Chron. Troy* I. 218 Galle in his breste and sugre in his face. *Ibid.* IV. 2794 þin hony mouþe þat doth with sugre flete. *c* **1430** —— *Min. Poems* (Percy Soc.) II. 160 Galle under sugre hath doubyl bitternesse. *c* **1530** *Crt. Love* 542 That they be bound by nature to disceive, and sugre strewe on gall. **1713** S. SEWALL *Diary* 22 Oct., Mr. Noyes..said Love was the Sugar to sweeten every Condition in the married Relation. **1890** BARRÈRE & LELAND *Slang Dict.* (1897), *Sugar*,..(Amer.) flattery, praise, gammon. **1895** *Cornh. Mag.* Oct. 398 She was all sugar and honey.

b. Proverbial and allusive phr. ***to be neither sugar nor salt, not to be made of sugar or salt:*** not likely to be injured by a wetting; not afraid of wet weather.

1600 SHAKS. *A.Y.L.* III. iii. 31 Honestie coupled to beautie, is to haue Honie a sawce to Sugar. **1655** MOUFET & BENNET *Health's Improv.* 251 Sugar never marred sawce. **1842** LOVER *Handy Andy* i, Sure he's neither sugar nor salt, that he'd melt. **1855**, **1870** [see SALT *sb.*[1] 2 f].

c. *slang.* Money.

1862 *Cornh. Mag.* Nov. 648 We have just touched for a rattling stake of sugar at Brum. **1884** *Punch* 11 Oct. 180/1 Political Picnics mean sugar to them as is fly to wot's wot. **1890** 'R. BOLDREWOOD' *Col. Reformer* (1891) 308 He's always got the sugar, consequence he always gets the worth of his money.

d. *slang* (orig. *U.S.*). A narcotic drug: spec. (*a*) heroin; ***brown sugar*** (see quot. 1974); (*b*) LSD (taken on a lump of sugar).

1935 A. J. POLLOCK *Underworld Speaks* 116/2 *Sugar and salt*, poisonous habit forming drugs; any of the white narcotics. **1951** *Evening Sun* (Baltimore) 27 Mar. 4/1 Dope in general was 'cement'..'sugar', etc. **1956** H. GOLD *Man* who was not with It (1965) iii. 27 You'll dream about the sugar yet. You'll wake up hot for it. No joy-popping, hear? Stay off, kid. **1967** M. M. GLATT et al. *Drug Scene* Gloss. 116 *Sugar*, dose of LSD on sugar lump. **1973** K. ROYCE *Spider Underground* viii. 118 We sat in a corner of this dark, smoke-infested hole that smelled of..third-rate pot... 'What a place to pick,' I complained. 'It's the sort of dump the fuzz raid three times a week.'.. 'Relax, man. They hit us last night... That makes it safe, man. I'm not carrying sugar or anything. I don't touch the stuff.' **1974** *Indonesian Observer* 26 July 3/2 French police said this year they have seized 50·6 pounds (23 kilograms) of 'brown sugar' in the suitcases of 13 Chinese arriving at Orly airport enroute to Amsterdam. The brown sugar is 33 per cent heroin diluted with 60 per cent caffein and strychnine. **1978** D. MACKENZIE *Raven settles Score* (1979) 32 No more Hong Kong brown sugar. We'll be out of business. **1979** *Observer* 25 Nov. 4/1 Detectives call them the 'sugar people' and they are young, rich and blue-blooded. They are also heroin addicts. It is in an ironic double reference to the 'sugar daddy' parents and to the expensive white powder they inject or sniff.

e. *colloq.* A term of endearment. Also in Comb., as ***sugar-babe, -baby, -pie***, etc.

1930 *Dialect Notes* VI. 85 *Sugar-pie*,..common term of endearment. **1930** J. H. COMBS in B. A. Botkin *Folk-Say* v. 245 A-settin' on the ice till my feet got cold, sugar-babe. **1936** M. MITCHELL *Gone with Wind* xxvi. 455 Scarlett said gratefully: 'Thank you, Sugarbaby.' **1936** J. CURTIS *Gilt Kid* vi. 68 When am I going to see you again, sugar? **1944** L. A. G. STRONG *Director* xvii. 135 See here, sugar. I'll take care of you. **1951** S. SPENDER *World within World* i. 26 No, you don't, sugar, you don't go out with your cold. **1962** J. D. MACDONALD *Girl, Gold Watch & Everything* vii. 87 What you do for a living, sugar? **1976** P. FLOWER *Crisscross* i. 10 'What's funny, sugar?' Sibyl said... Would he ever get Sibyl to stop calling him sugar? **1980** D. BRIERLEY *Blood Group O* 76 Okay, sugar, what are you looking for?

3. *Chem.* **a.** In old terminology, applied (with qualification) to certain compounds resembling sugar in form or taste (cf. SALT *sb.*[1] 5). † ***sugar of iron, steel***: ? an oxide or chloride of iron; ***sugar of lead*** or † ***Saturn*** (also ***English sugar***): lead acetate. ***acid*** (or ***essence***) ***of sugar***: oxalic acid. † ***sugar of milk*** = ***milk sugar*** (MILK *sb.* 10).

1652 FRENCH *Yorksh. Spaw* x. 92 To mix some Sugar of steel, or steel wine with the first glass. *Ibid.* xii. 99 Unless it be corrected..with Sugar of Iron, made out of the very Mine of Iron. **1661** BOYLE *Scept. Chym.* VI. 383 Sugar of Lead, which though made of that insipid Metal and sour salt of Vinager, has in it a sweetnesse surpassing that of common Sugar. **1662** R. MATHEW *Unl. Alch.* §108. 176 It wil shoot into most transparent Christals, which is called the Sugar of Saturn. **1753** *Chambers' Cycl.* Suppl., Sugar of milk. **1756** BURKE *Subl. & Beaut.* IV. xxii. (1759) 297 The component parts of this [*sc.* milk] are water, oil, and a sort of a very sweet salt called the sugar of milk. **1776** *Edinb. Med. Comm.* IV. 260 Six parts of a fine volatile alkali, can be saturated with one of the acid of sugar. **1800** B. MOSELEY *Treat. Sugar* (ed. 2) 112 The acid thus obtained I call acid of sugar..because sugar affords it more pure..than any other matter hitherto tried. **1843** R. J. GRAVES *Syst. Clin. Med.* xxv. 314 In Egypt acetate of lead, under the name of *English sugar*, is in great request for making eye-water. **1847** C. J. HEMPEL tr. *Rau's Organon of Specific Healing Art* lxii. 128 If triturated with sugar of milk, it [*sc.* phosphorus] changes to phosphoric acid in a very few hours. **1859** MAYNE *Expos. Lex.* 1225/2 *Acid of Sugar, Essence of Sugar*, common terms for..oxalic acid. **1864** P. SQUIRE *Compan. Brit. Pharmacopœia* 161 *Sugar of Milk*... Crystallized Sugar obtained from the Whey of Cow's Milk by evaporation. **1895** *Montgomery Ward Catal.* Spring & Summer 252/3 Artists Tube Oil Colors..Silver White, Sugar of Lead, Terre Verte. **1975** *Nature* 23 Oct. 632/2 Something needed to be done to stop the watering of milk..and even so flagrant a malpractice as the use of 'sugar of lead', as lead acetate was called, to sweeten beer.

b. In modern terminology, a chemical compound having the composition of ordinary sugar and forming a constituent of many substances; also, in wider sense (with distinctive qualifying word), any member of the SACCHAROSE and GLUCOSE groups of carbohydrates, all of which are soluble in water, more or less sweet to the taste, and either directly or indirectly fermentable.

sugar of acorns = QUERCITE. ***animal sugar, sugar of flesh*** or ***muscle*** = INOSITE. ***hepatic sugar*** = LIVER *sugar*. ***liquid sugar***, uncrystallizable glucose. See also APHIS 2, DIABETES, DIABETIC 1, FRUIT *sb.* 9, GELATIN 3, GRAPE *sb.*[1] 9, INVERT *a.*, INVERTED 6, LIVER *sb.*[1] 7, MALT *sb.*[1] 5, MANNA[1] 9, MUSHROOM *sb.* 6c, NEST *sb.* 8, POTATO *sb.* 6a, SORGHUM 4, STARCH *sb.* 5b, URINE, VEGETABLE.

sugar of milk, milk-sugar (= LACTOSE) is a sugar in the modern chemical sense, but the term belongs in origin to the old nomenclature (see a).

1826 HENRY *Elem. Chem.* II. 403 Sugar enters pretty largely into the composition of milk; and into the urine, when altered by disease. **1838** T. THOMSON *Chem. Org. Bodies* 1034 Sugar is the essential constituent in liquors to be converted into vinegar. **1866** ROSCOE *Elem. Chem.* 322 (1) Sucroses, or the sugars proper, (2) Glucoses, or the grape sugars. **1891** F. TAYLOR *Man. Pract. Med.* (ed. 2) 777 This quantity of urine contains half a grain of sugar.

1868 WATTS *Dict. Chem.* V. 6 *Sugar of* *Acorns... A saccharine substance contained in acorns. **1826** HENRY *Elem. Chem.* II. 403 *Animal Sugar. **1867** BLOXAM *Chem.* 615 A sweet substance called inosite or sugar of *flesh. **1857** DUNGLISON *Med. Lex.* s.v. *Saccharum, Liver* or **Hepatic Sugar.* **1838** T. THOMSON *Chem. Org. Bodies* 636 *Liquid sugar was first pointed out by Proust... It is distinguished from every other species of sugar, by being incapable of crystallizing. **1852** W. GREGORY *Handbk. Org. Chem.* 370 Inosite or sugar of *muscle. **1857** DUNGLISON *Med. Lex.*, Sugar, muscle.

4. *attrib.* and *Comb.* **a.** *attrib.* Of, pertaining to, derived or made from, connected with sugar or the sugar-cane, belonging to or involved in the cultivation or manufacture of sugar, as ***sugar-adulteration, -barrel, -basin, basket, -beer, bin, -boilery, -bounty, cube, -culture, dish, factory, icing, industry, kettle, knife, lump, mill, mule, ration, refinery, scoop, thermometer, trade, worker***, etc.; also, producing sugar, as ***sugar-climate, -colony*** (hence ***-colonist***), ***estate, field, grove, -island (-islander), land, plantation***.

1856 *Orr's Circ. Sci., Pract. Chem.* 409 Any processes..of *sugar adulteration. **1837** CARLYLE *Fr. Rev.* III. III. i, *Sugar-barrels rolled forth into the street. **1785** *Daily Universal Reg.* 1 Jan. 3/2 (Advt.), Oval pierced *sugar and cream basons, 10 oz. to 15 oz. a pair. *a* **1828** D. WORDSWORTH *Jrnl.* (1941) II. 81 A sugar-basin made of cocoa-nut. **1851** *Catal. Great Exhib.* III. 755/1 Two satin-wood sugar-basins. **1917** F. H. BIGELOW *Historic Silver of Colonies* 472/1 (Index), *Sugar baskets. **1981** *Sunday Tel.* 18 Jan. 13/2 Garrads have augmented the exhibition with antique castors.., as well as sugar baskets, boxes, tongs and nippers. **1880** C. R. MARKHAM *Peruv. Bark* xvi. 160 This *sugar-beer is called *huarapu*. **1792** (*title*) Remarks on the New *Sugar Bill. **1848** LD. G. BENTINCK in Disraeli *Life* (1905) 375 Six days' discussion on the sugar bill. **1922** JOYCE *Ulysses* 58 There he is,..leaning against the *sugar-bin in his shirtsleeves. *a* **1774** R. FERGUSSON *Rising of Session* xi. Poems (1789) 47 In wine the *sucker biskets soom As light's a flee. **1837** CARLYLE *Fr. Rev.* II. v. iv, Of *sugar-boileries, plantations, furniture. **1840** R. ELLIS *Customs* IV. 243 *marg.* *Sugar Bounty. **1888** *Pall Mall Gaz.* 14 Apr. 10/2 The International Conference upon Sugar Bounties. **1822** AINSLIE *Land of Burns* 232 Cadging about the track-pats, pouries an' *succar bowls. **1834** MARIA EDGEWORTH *Helen* xxxvi, She set sugar-bowl and cream before him. **1688** HOLME *Armoury* III. xxii. (Roxb.) 281 Sugar Boylers Instruments..a *sugar brush. **1861** THACKERAY *Four Georges* i. 26 In the *sugar-chamber there were four pastrycooks. **1830** T. BURGES *Debates in Congress* 10 May 929 Men have..emigrated from South Carolina to the *sugar climate..of Louisiana. **1839** URE *Dict. Arts* 1203 Our *sugar colonists. **1702** LUTTRELL *Brief Rel.* (1857) V. 196 Our *sugar collonies in the West Indies. **1733** *Act 6 Geo. II*, c. 13 (*title*) An Act for the better..encouraging the Trade of his Majesty's Sugar Colonies in America. **1833** *Act 3 & 4 Will. IV*, c. 56 §9 The Island of Mauritius shall be deemed to be one of His Majesty's Sugar Colonies. **1591** *Exch. Rolls Scotl.* XXII. 156 For certane *succour confectis and sweit meit furneist to bancatis. **1897** *Sugar cube [see CUBE *sb.*[1] 1 b]. **1978** T. ALLBEURY *Lantern Network* xi. 169 She was screwing up the paper from the sugar cubes. **1742** W. ELLIS *Timber-Tree Improved* II. 151, I was told..that this Wood makes fine *Sugar-dishes, and other Turners-ware. **1765** J. WEDGWOOD *Let.* 17 June (1965) 34 The articles are..a slop basin, sugar dish with cover, [etc.]. **1771** *Ann. Reg.* 131/1 For stealing a silver tea-pot and sugar-dish. **1908** *Daily Chron.* 23 May 1/7 This *sugar dust is heavily charged with ether. **1834** MCCULLOCH *Dict. Comm.* (ed. 2) 1094 Mr. Grant's motion for a reduction of the *sugar duties, 25th of May, 1829. **1796** STEDMAN *Surinam* I. 314 The *sugar estates in this colony contain five or six hundred acres. **1870** KINGSLEY *At Last* x, Managers of sugar-estates. **1908** KIPLING *Actions & Reactions* (1909) 96 They [*sc.* bees] took to cadging round *sugar-factories and breweries. **1958** O. CAROE *Pathans* xxvi. 429 Peshawar, always famous for its sugar-cane, has been enriched with finer varieties which have turned the old village industry of *gur* into the great sugar-factories which now sustain the life of Pakistan. **1613** DEKKER *Strange Horse-Race*, etc. Wks. (Grosart) III. 316 Before either this Masque, or *Suger-feast come marching in their true and most sweet state. **1930** W. K. HANCOCK *Australia* iv. 81 Polynesians in their wild state never clamoured for admission to the Queensland *sugar-fields. *a* **1700** EVELYN *Diary* 27 June 1654 A collation of eggs fried in the *suggar furnace. **1875** KNIGHT *Dict. Mech.* 2446/1 *Sugar-furnace*, one in which pans are set for boiling sugar-cane juice. **1792** G. IMLAY *Topogr. Descr. Western Terr. N. Amer.* 136 Luxuriant *sugar groves. **1847** *Ex. Doc. 31st U.S. Congress 1 Sess. House* (1849) No. 5. III. 629 A ridge covered with sugar maples, formerly an Indian sugar grove. **1948** E. N. DICK *Dixie Frontier* 247 A clump numbering from one hundred to three hundred trees was chosen for the operation. Such a clump came to be called a sugar grove. **1769** MRS. RAFFALD *Eng. Housekpr.* (1778) 265 To make *Sugar Iceing for the Bride Cake. **1930** E. WAUGH *Labels* vii. 180 Gaudi has again introduced his 'sugar-icing' motive, translating it from tile and mosaic into carved stone. **1979** 'M. HEBDEN' *Pel & Faceless Corpse* xii. 123 The pink shirt had suddenly become sugar icing-coloured and hideously wrong. **1887** *Encycl. Brit.* XXII. 628/1 There are numerous modified and subsidiary processes connected with refining, as well as with all branches of the *sugar industry. **1714** *Observ. Trade Sugar Colonies* 5 How near the Desolation of the *Sugar Islands is at hand. **1779** Sugar island [see SCUTTLE *v.*[2] 1 a]. **1980** *Jrnl. R. Soc. Arts* Apr. 271/1 The UK has traditionally bought 50 per cent of the sugar consumed here on the world market, principally from the Sugar Islands of the Caribbean. **1764** J. OTIS *Rights Brit. Colonies* 29 That..brutal barbarity that has long marked the general character of the *sugar-islanders. **1728** CHAMBERS *Cycl.* s.v., The *Sugar Juice is purified. **1834** J. KEMPER in *Wisconsin Hist. Coll.* (1898) XIV. 444 If ardor leads some of the [Sioux] hunters beyond the boundary stake, they can be punished by the soldiers by having their *sugar kettles broken or their lodges torn down. **1847** *Webster's Dict.* (ed. 2), *Sugar-kettle*, a kettle used in boiling down the sap or juice from which sugar is made. **1728** CHAMBERS *Cycl.* s.v., When it has been a Quarter of an Hour in the Forms, 'tis cut with a *Sugar-Knife. **1949** *Caribbean Q.* I. 8 It was..the stalwart, armed with hoes and..sugar knives.., whose work would 'make or break' the proprietor. **1692** *Calendar Virginia State Papers* (1875) I. 44 We marcht to the *Suggar Land. **1883** SWEET & KNOX *On Mexican Mustang through Texas* vii. 82 A great deal of the finest sugar-lands in the world. **1974** *Guardian* 23 Jan. 12/6 As far as sugar lands are concerned,..the Government is now the largest landowner. Tate and Lyle sold their lands to the last government. **1901** KIPLING *Kim* xii. 307 She chuckled like a contented parrot above the *sugar lump. **1964** D. FRANCIS *Nerve* ix. 122 The dope has been given to the horses on sugar lumps. **1858** SIMMONDS *Dict. Trade* 366/1 **Sugar-machinery*, the rolling mills necessary for squeezing out the sap of the sugar-cane. **1600** HAKLUYT *Voy.* III. 718 His owne Ingenios or *sugar-milles. **1800** B. MOSELEY *Treat. Sugar* (ed. 2) 33 Water or Horse sugar Mills. **1882** W. D. HAY *Brighter Britain!* I. viii. 221 If all the farmers in the district were to combine to grow beet-root on every acre they could plough,..even then it would hardly pay the sugar-mills, or possibly the farmers either. **1971** *Advocate-News* (Barbados) 24 Apr. 10/1 (Advt), ½ acre house plots and/or cottage with sugarmill and swimming pool. **1681** GREW *Musæum* IV. §i. 353 Sal Ammoniac sublim'd in a *Sugar-Mould. **1861** BENTLEY *Man. Bot.* 699 Treacle [is] the thick juice which has drained from refined sugar in the sugar-moulds. **1908** *U.S. Dept. Agric. Farmers' Bull.* No. 334. 24 *Sugar mules are those shipped south to use on the sugar farms of Georgia, Louisiana, and other Southern States. **1960** V. WILLIAMS *Walk Egypt* 71 A sugar mule, now, was a big fellow. He ate big, but he pulled big, and he would look big before the wagon. **1844** G. DODD *Textile Manuf.* ii. 55 Copper vessels heated by steams, like *sugar-pans,..&c. **1809** NEUMANN *Sp.-Engl. Dict.*, *Alfeñique*, a *sugar-paste made with oil of sweet almonds. **1728** CHAMBERS *Cycl.* s.v., Some have imagined, that the ancient and modern *Sugar-Plant were different. **1714** *Observ. Trade Sugar Colonies* 4 The English *Sugar Plantations are upon small Islands. **1834** MCCULLOCH *Dict. Comm.* (ed. 2) 1087 The Spanish sugar plantations. **1883** 'MARK TWAIN' *Life on Miss.* xl. 419 The great sugar plantations border both sides of the [Mississippi] river. **1978** 'A. YORK' *Tallant for Disaster* ii. 28 The burnt earth roadway which led to the sugar plantation. **1681** GREW *Musæum* II. §ii. ii. 224 Permitting the Molosses to drain away through a hole at the bottom of the *Sugar-Pots. **1731** *Gentl. Mag.* I. 137 *Sugar Powder best 59s per C. **1553** EDEN *Treat. Newe Ind.* (Arb.) 40 In the Ilande of Hispana..were erected 28. *suger presses. **1870** KINGSLEY *At Last* x, A small sugar-press..under a roof of palm-leaf. **1890** D. DAVIDSON *Mem. Long Life* x. 261 The cog-wheels of the Indian sugar-presses were invariably cut at an angle of 45°. **1917** *Sugar ration [see RATION 3 c]. **1978** L. DEIGHTON *SS-GB* xxv. 237 Drink up your tea, that's a good boy. It's the last of the sugar ration. **1794** A. YOUNG *Trav. France* (ed. 2) II. xix. 539 The *sugar refinery is a considerable business, there are 10 large and 17 smaller houses engaged in it. **1833** M. SCOTT *Tom Cringle* xvi, Bullock's blood is..used in the sugar refineries in England. **1896** G. MEREDITH *Let.* 17 June (1970) III. 1236, I..can own her sweet to the ear, wondering what it is in her that extracts her deadly bitter from a sugar-refinery. **1855** STEPHENS *Bk. Farm* (ed. 2) II. 440/2 The following analysis of *sugar refuse was made by Professor Johnston. **1780** J. HOWARD *Prisons in Eng. & Wales* 71 *Sugar-saucers of brass wire. **1916** *Daily Colonist* (Victoria, B.C.) 1 July 8/2 Mothers had been remembered by most of the workers, for there were bread boards, and sleeve holders, *sugar scoops and wooden spoons. **1960** R. A. PARKER *Family of Friends* 89 The old days of the Quaker garb and the sugar-scoop bonnet were gone forever. **1977** *Time* 14 Nov. 21/1 The Concordski whistled down the runway for 33 seconds, sucking in air through four 'sugar scoop' intakes slung beneath its body. **1805** DICKSON *Pract. Agric.* I. 209 **Sugar scum*, which consists of lime and bullocks' blood. **1840** MARRYAT *Poor Jack* xliv, He had.. worked his passage home in a *sugar ship. **1688** HOLME *Armoury* III. xxii. 281 A *Sugar Sive. **1868** WATTS *Dict. Chem.* V. 472 Suppose..a *sugar-solution before inversion turns the plane of polarisation..to the right. **1598** SYLVESTER *Du Bartas* I. iii. (1641) 26/1 The precious Reed Whence *Sugar sirrops in abundance bleed. **1842** *Penny Cycl.* XXIII. 231/2 Animal charcoal is variously applied in the bleaching of sugar-syrup. **1913** M. H. NEIL *Candies & Bonbons & how to make Them* 24 A *sugar thermometer is generally used for testing the boiling syrup. **1695** *Disc. Duties on Sugars* 14 This Gentleman seems very unwilling to allow any thing of the Merchant to be concern'd in the *Sugar-Trade. **1714** *Observ. Trade Sugar Colonies* 4 Jamaica could never be kept and improved so as to support the Sugar Trade to this Kingdom. **1887** *Encycl. Brit.* XXII. 625/1 Within the first twenty years of the 16th century the sugar trade of San Domingo expanded with great rapidity. **1677** *Phil. Trans.* XII. 819 Vinous shrubs are now coming into fashion; of these do some make *Sugar-wines by art. **1973** *Sunday Express* (Trinidad) 1 Apr. 12/5 A delegation of *sugar workers is to..protest what they call the 'abandonment of the cane-growing industry'. **1826** *Art of Brewing* (ed. 2) 31 The brewing of *sugar worts.

b. Objective, with agent-nouns, vbl. sbs., and ppl. adjs., as ***sugar-boiler, -boiling, -broker, -growing, -maker, -making, -planter, -producer, -producing, rationing, -refiner***, etc.; also in the names of implements used in manufacturing or preparing sugar, as ***sugar-chopper***, etc.

1688 HOLME *Armoury* III. xxii. (Roxb.) 279 Instruments ..usefull to the *sugar Boyler or Baker. **1856** *Orr's Circ. Sci., Pract. Chem.* 388 Iron-melters, sugar-boilers and cooks. **1688** HOLME *Armoury* III. xxii. (Roxb.) 279 That hot and Laborious imploy of *Sugar Boyling, and refineing. **1851** MAYHEW *Lond. Labour* I. 357, I purchased a small tin saucepan, a piece of marble slab, and commenced sugar-boiling. **1866** W. REED *Hist. Sugar* 54 Whilst the sugar boiling season lasted. **1841** *Picayune* (New Orleans) 10 June 2/3 Several dealers in sugar and *sugar brokers were yesterday summoned before Recorder Bertus. **1858** SIMMONDS *Dict. Trade* 366/1 **Sugar-chopper*, a small hatchet for breaking up loaf-sugar. **1881** *Instr. Census Clerks* (1885) 63 Sugar Merchant, Chopper, Cutter. **1898** *Allbutt's Syst. Med.* V. 406 A *sugar-destroying body or ferment. **1875** KNIGHT *Dict. Mech.* 2446/1 Hersey's *sugar-dryer is for granulating damp sugar. **1844** BREEN *St. Lucia* 296 In 1840 the *sugar-grower took the alarm. **1816** *Niles' Reg.* 6 Apr. 81/1 The representatives of the *sugar-growing states insist on a certain duty upon that article. **1856** *Orr's Circ. Sci., Mech. Philos.* 326 In sugar-growing countries. **1870** KINGSLEY *At Last* xvi, The profits of sugar-growing..have been of late very great. **1598** *Sugar-maker [see CANDIER]. **1750** T. SHORT *Disc. Tea, Sugar*, etc. 80 With the Skimmings of the Juice of the Cane..the Sugar-makers feed their Swine and Poultry. **1835** J. J. AUDUBON *Ornith. Biogr.* III. 439 With large ladles the sugar-makers stirred the thickening juice of the maple. **1899** W. A. MACKAY *Pioneer Life in Zorra* 171 Not infrequently would the sugar-makers remain in the woods most of the night boiling down the sap.

1753 *Chambers' Cycl.* Suppl. s.v., The whole art of *sugar-making, or the reducing vegetable juices to what we call sugar. **1796** Stedman *Surinam* I. 316 The..dangers to which the sugar-making negroes are exposed. **1828** M. O'Brien *Jrnls.* (1968) I. iii. 27 During sugar-making time it will contain a furnace and other vessels. **1953** R. F. V. Heuston *Salmond's Law of Torts* (ed. 11) xiv. 566 In *Indermaur* v. *Dames* itself the hole in the floor was a defect but a necessary incident of sugar-making. **1839** Ure *Dict. Arts* 1200 Each *sugar manufacturer has a warehouse. **1747** *State of Sugar-Trade* 3 British *Sugar Planters. **1842** *Niles' Reg.* 14 May 176/3 (*caption*) Sugar planters of Louisiana. **1926** J. Masefield *Odtaa* i. 4 In the seventies others, from all parts of England, settled as sugar-planters along the northern sea coast in the Pituba country. **1983** A. Brookner *Look at Me* iv. 56 The wealthy sugar planter's daughter. **1807** *Edin. Rev.* Oct. 151 The profits of *sugar planting. **1881** *Harper's Mag.* Apr. 646 We met one of the largest *sugar producers. **1974** *Guardian* 23 Jan. 12/4 Jamaica is the biggest sugar producer in the Commonwealth Caribbean. **1866** 'Mark Twain' *Lett. from Hawaii* (1967) 135 Maui.. that deservedly famous *sugar-producing region. **1868** Watts *Dict. Chem.* V. 354 *Sorgho*,..a sugar-producing grass. **1918** *Times* 20 Jan. 3/1 When *sugar rationing actually came into operation, the workers..had to face considerable pressure. **1976** J. Lee *Ninth Man* 77 Talking about sugar rationing. **1688** *Sugar refiner [see sugar-baker 2]. **1755** *Dict. Arts & Sci.* IV. s.v., Our sugar refiners first dissolve it [*sc.* coarse sugar] in water. **1879** G. W. Bagby *Canal Reminiscences* 10 What was their petty thieving compared to the enormous pillage of the modern sugar refiner and the crooked-whiskey distiller? **1979** *Dædalus* Summer 113 Sugar refiners, soap boilers, glass blowers, and brewers..depended on continuously fired furnaces. **1835** *Partington's Brit. Cycl. Arts & Sci.* II. 793/2 The process of *sugar-refining is now carried to so high a degree of perfection. **1839** Ure *Dict. Arts* 1201 It is curious to find in the antient arts of Hindostan exact prototypes of the *sugar-rollers. **1688** Holme *Armoury* iii. xxii. (Roxb.) 281 A *Sugar Skimmer..is a round plate of Brass a little hollow in the midle and made full of round holes. **1866** W. Reed (*title*) The History of Sugar and *Sugar Yielding Plants.

c. Instrumental and parasynthetic, as ***sugar-cured***, ***-free***, ***-iced***, etc.; similative, as ***sugar-coloured***, ***-pink***, †***-sweet***; also ***sugar-like***.

1887 W. Phillips *Brit. Discomycetes* 231 Externally *sugar-coloured. **1848** A. Prentice *Let.* 20 June in *Tour in U.S.* vi. 56, I tasted some excellent *sugar-cured ham. **1889** *Judge* (U.S.) 12 Jan. 222/2 Beautiful red, sugar-cured ham. **1897** *Daily News* 16 Dec. 7/2 A sugar-cured ham. **1924** *Amer. Jrnl. Physiol.* LXVII. 635 Three other totally depancreatized dogs had been used for studying the administration of insulin..for several weeks, during which time their urine was never *sugar-free for a period of more than 6 or 7 hours at a time. **1978** *N.Y. Times Mag.* 23 July 22/3 The absence of what had formerly been desirable is now proudly advertised: not only lead-free gas, but salt-free diets and sugar-free soft drinks. **1805** Nelson *To Dk. Clarence* 12 June in Nicolas *Disp.* (1846) VI. 455, 200 and upwards of *sugar-laden Ships. **1879** *Jrnl. Chem. Soc.* Abstr. 360 Its granular, *sugar-like appearance. **1805** Nelson *To A. Davidson* 12 June in Nicolas *Disp.* (1846) VI. 454 More than two hundred Sail of *sugar-loaded Ships. **1961** *House & Garden* Feb. 48 A..sofa covered in *sugar-pink tafetta. **1978** 'M. M. Kaye' *Far Pavilions* xxi. 299 Rajastham..where..men..painted their houses blinding white or sugar-pink. **1600** Breton *Pasquils Fooles-cappe* Wks. (Grosart) I. 18/2 *Sugar sweete, or bitter as the gall, Tis Pasquils humour. **1612** J. Davies *Muse's Sacrifice* Wks. (Grosart) II. 44/2 And Gall itselfe, to them made Sugar-sweet! **1906** Kipling in *Tribune* 15 Jan. 4/4 *Sugar-topped biscuits.

5. a. Special combs.: **sugar-almond**, a sweetmeat consisting of an almond coated with sugar; †*transf.* a stone resembling this; **sugar aquatint**, a method of etching in which the artist draws his dark areas on a copper plate with a solution of black water-colour and sugar; **sugar-bag**, (*a*) a bag or sack for containing sugar, *esp.* a bag made of coarse thick paper specially coloured or (*Austral.* and *N.Z.*) of fine sacking; also used as a measure of quantity; (*b*) (in Austral. Aborigines' speech) a wild bees' honeycomb; **sugar-box**, †(*a*) a sugar-basin or sugar-caster; (*b*) a box in which sugar is packed; †**sugar-bread**, a species of confectionery; **sugar-butter sauce**, a sauce made with sugar and butter; **sugar-cake**, a rich cake made with sugar, butter, and cream; also *fig.*; **sugar-camp** *U.S.*, a place in a maple forest or plantation where the sap is collected and boiled for sugar; **sugar card**, a ration card entitling the holder to a ration of sugar; **sugar-caster, -castor** (see castor[2]); **sugar-coat** *v.*, to coat with sugar; *fig.*, to make palatable; *esp.* in **sugar-coated** *ppl. a.* (of pills); so **sugar-coating** *vbl. sb.*; **sugar-cone**, a conical mould used in making loaf-sugar; **sugar-crusher**, (*a*) a machine for crushing sugar-cane; (*b*) an implement for crushing sugar for use at table; **sugar daddy** [cf. daddy 3] *slang* (orig. *U.S.*), an elderly man who lavishes gifts on a young woman; also *transf.*; **sugar-disease**, diabetes; †**sugar-garden**, **sugar-house**, a sugar-factory, sugar-works; **sugar-house molasses**, a low-grade molasses produced at sugar-factories, now chiefly used in the preparation of certain medicines and chemicals; **sugar-lime**, lime formed in the process of preparing sugar from beet-root; †**sugar-man**, a sugar-maker or confectioner; †**sugar-meat**, a sweetmeat, comfit, confection; **sugar mouse**, a sweet made of sugar in the shape of a mouse; **sugar nippers**, (*a*) an implement for cutting loaf sugar into lumps; (*b*) a pair of sugar tongs; **sugar-on-snow** *U.S.*, a delicacy made by pouring hot maple syrup on snow (snow *sb.*[1] 5 a); **sugar-orchard** *U.S.* = sugar-bush 1; **sugar-paper**, coarse paper such as that used for making sugar-bags; **sugar-pellet**, a pellet of sugar; †a piece of sugar-paste; †**sugar-penide** [cf. MLG. *suckerpenit* (see penide)], corruptly *-pennye*, barley-sugar; **sugar puff**, (*a*) a puff (see puff *sb.* 5) made with sugar; (*b*) *pl.*, the proprietary name of a breakfast cereal; **sugar rag** *U.S.* = *sugar-teat*; †**sugar-roll**, (*a*) ? a sweetened bread roll; (*b*) a sugar-mill roller; **sugar sack**, a bag made of fine sacking for containing sugar; the sacking itself; **sugar sand** *U.S.*, a fine sand raised by the sap of the maple tree which results in a gritty sediment in maple syrup unless removed; **sugar shell** *N. Amer.*, a spoon with a shell-shaped bowl for serving sugar; **sugar sifter**, (*a*) see quot. 1875; (*b*) = *sugar caster*; **sugar snow**, (*a*) snow (snow *sb.*[1] 5 a) made with sugar; (*b*) *N. Amer.*, a snow-fall in the maple sugar season (see quot. 1932); †**sugar-snuff**, a snuff compounded of powdered sugar-candy and oil of nutmegs; **sugar soap**, an alkaline abrasive used to remove paint, and in solution for cleaning paintwork; †**sugar-spar**, †**sugar-spirit** (see quots.); **sugar stick**, a stick of sweetstuff; also *fig.*; **sugar-teat** (see quot. 1847); in quot. 1856, *transf.*; also **sugar-tit**; **sugar-tongs**, a metal implement for taking hold of pieces of lump sugar (to put them into a beverage), consisting of two limbs connected by a flexible back (or a hinge) and furnished at each end with claws or a spoon-shaped plate; **sugar trough** *U.S.*, a wooden trough used for collecting maple sap; **sugar vase**, a tall sugar-container for use at table; **sugar-vinegar**, vinegar made from the waste juice and washings in sugar-manufacture; **sugar-wash** (see quot.); **sugar-water**, †(*a*) water in which sugar has been dissolved; (*b*) see quot. 1753; (*c*) *U.S.* the sap of the sugar-maple; **sugar-weather** *Canad.*, spring weather, characterized by cold nights and warm days, that starts the sap running in maple trees.

1594 Marlowe & Nashe *Dido* ii. i. Wks. 1904 II. 359 Ile giue thee *Sugar-almonds. **1681** Grew *Musæum* iii. §i. v. 296 The Sugar-Almond..so like to the rougher sort which Confectioners sometimes make, that, excepting the Tast, nothing can be liker. **1935** *Amer. Speech* X. 193/2 The 'bonton [fashion] shades' included *icing blue* and *sugar almond pink*. **1973** G. Greene *Honorary Consul* iii. ii. 124 It [*sc.* a missal] might have been a first Communion present, for it closely resembled the sugar almonds..distributed on such occasions. **1962** D. Bland *Illustration of Bks.* (ed. 3) viii. 155 Picasso used *sugar aquatints in his Buffon, making two plates, one to print grey and the other black. **1764** *New Hampsh. Hist. Soc. Coll.* (1889) IX. 156, [I sent] also lb 14½ *Sugar bag with it. **1830** R. Dawson *Present State of Australia* 136 The strange native pointed with his tomahawk to the tree and..repeated the words 'Choogar-bag, choogar-bag, choogar-bag!' (sugar-bag) their English expression for honey, or anything sweet. **1864** R. Henning *Let.* 27 Nov. (1966) 185 The other [aboriginal] has been.. climbing gum-trees after 'sugar-bags', or wild honeycombs. **1882** *Cassell's Family Mag.* Nov. 756/2 The crowns..have two square corners like the bottom of a sugar-bag. **1913** D. H. Lawrence *Sons & Lovers* vii 164 There's something very blue; is it a bit of sugar-bag? **1927** M. Terry *Through Land of Promise* 104 We found the others clustered round a bauhinia tree... 'We've got a sugar bag.' **1928** V. Palmer *Passage* i. v. 44 It was Uncle Tony standing with a sugar-bag over his shoulders. **1948** F. A. Iremonger *William Temple* v. 81 A nine-year-old boy in a Bethnal Green school, who handed to his teacher one morning an untidy piece of blue paper torn from a sugar-bag. **1963** *N.Z. Listener* 6 Sept. 9/2 Reference to the price of a 'sugar' bag full of oysters. It drew my attention to the frequency with which we in New Zealand refer to a 'sugar bag' as a basic unit of quality. **1967** A. & D. Reid *Paddle Wheels on Waganui* 71 On another trip the same cabin boy acquired a sugar-bag of apples. **1620** *Unton Inv.* (1841) 27 A *sugar boxe,..one sugar boxe spoone. **1639** *12th Rep. Hist. MSS. Comm.* App. ix. 8, 1 Scollup Suger boxe. **1669** R. Montagu in *Buccleuch MSS.* (Hist. MSS. Comm.) I. 448 A vinegar pot, oil pot, and sugar box. **1747** in *Nairne Peerage Evidence* (1874) 81 Silver milk pott..suggar box..silver salvar. **1796** Stedman *Surinam* I. 361 Placing my sugar-boxes in the middle of a tub, and on stone. **1858** Simmonds *Dict. Trade* 366/1 *Sugar-box*, a kind of long case in which Havana and some other sugars are imported. **1587** Harrison *England* ii. v. in *Holinshed*, Marchpaine, *sugerbread [*ed.* 1577 sugred bread], gingerbread. **1901** *Daily Chron.* 16 Nov. 8/5 A Plum Pudding, with beaten *sugar-butter sauce, after the receipt of Merton College, Oxford. **1600** Breton *Pasquils Fooles-cappe* Wks. (Grosart) I. 26/1 Such vile coniunctions such constructions make, That some are pois'ned with a *Sugar Cake. **1716** W. Moffett *Hesperi-neso-gr.* ii. 9 This grunting Sow would sooner take, And eat a T——d than Sugar-Cake. **1801** S. & Ht. Lee *Canterb. T.* IV. 14 Pots of conserves, sugar cakes, and such other housewifely presents as..gratify the appetites common to children. **1819** Keats *Otho* i. ii, Who..dares to give An old lion sugar-cakes of mild reprieve? **1923** Sugar cake [see sauerbraten]. **1977** A. Wilson *Strange Ride of Rudyard Kipling* ii. 110 The Durbar Room at the Queen's beloved Osborne House—not a very happy sugar-cake Moghul decoration. **1779** M. Patten *Diary* (1903) 400, I went to our *shugar Camp and covered some fire steads with brush where we had Cabbage and french Turnip seed sowed to preserve them from Cattle. **1805** Pike *Sources Mississ.* (1810) 49 He informed me that.. the sugar camp near the stockade was where he made sugar. **1805** R. Sutcliff *Trav. N. Amer.* (1811) 184, I saw several sugar camps..where the sap is collected in small wooden troughs. **1959** R. Campbell *I would do it Again* ii. 7 The neighbours gathered at the sugar camps. **1966** *Publ. Amer. Dial. Soc.* xxxviii. 66 *Sugar camp.* This characteristically Midland [Illinois] term appears only once in the field interviews but with much more frequency in the checklists. **1917** H. H. Henson *Jrnl.* 11 Dec. in *Retrospect* (1942) I. vi. 217, I started the day by filling up the new *sugar cards for the household. **1676** *Sugar-castor [see castor[2] 1]. **1763** Colman *Prose Sev. Occas.* (1787) I. 251 A queer sort of building Ma'am, said young Bonus,—a mere pepper-box, and there,—(pointing to the turrets of All Souls) there are the sugar-casters. **1878** Pollen *Anc. & Mod. Gold & Silver Wk.* 160 Sugar caster: silver-gilt, chased with figures of virtues. **1870** *Eng. Mech.* 18 March 660/3 He can have his pills..*sugar-coated by any druggist. **1910** J. J. Reeve in *The Fundamentals* III. 99 The little truth in it served to sugar-coat and give plausibility to some deadly errors that lurked within. **1875** 'Mark Twain' in *Atlantic Monthly* Aug. 195/1 Stephen sweetened him up and put him off a week. He called then..and came away *sugar-coated again. **1876** Dunglison *Med. Lex.* 998/1 Sugarcoated pills are prepared like the sugarplums of the confectioners. **1935** *Motion Picture* Nov. 81/1 That keen humor, barbed sometimes, pointed always, but never other than good-natured and sugar-coated, has passed beyond our ken. **1977** R. L. Wolff *Gains & Losses* ii. 197 The earliest [High Church] novelists..whose fiction amounted to little more than sugar-coated tracts. **1908** *Westm. Gaz.* 21 Jan. 12/1 Who used his great gift of humour as a *sugar-coating for the great things he has had to say. **1856** *Orr's Circ. Sci., Pract. Chem.* 410 *Sugar-cones painted with white-lead are avoided. **1870** A. S. Stephens *Married in Haste* 366 He held a *sugar-crusher in one hand. **1901** Kipling *Kim* xv. 403 He felt..that his soul was out of gear with its surroundings—a cog-wheel unconnected with any machinery, just like the idle cog-wheel of a cheap Beheea sugar-crusher laid by in a corner. **1962** J. B. Priestley *Margin Released* i. i. 11 In winter, toddy, for which we had those silver sugar-crushers. **1926** G. Frankau *My Unsentimental Journey* ii. 32 There came another woman to the sofa; and spoke to me of '*sugar-daddies'. **1935** Wodehouse *Luck of Bodkins* xxi. 266 The morning papers had come aboard, reassuring citizens..that sugar daddies were still being surprised in love-nests. **1959** [see door-mat b]. **1973** *Times* 13 July (Motor Racing Suppl.) p. iii/2 The oil and petrol companies, for a long time the sugar-daddies of top class motor racing. *Ibid.* 20 Sept. 3/7 Norma Levy, a prostitute, had a 'sugar daddy' called Bunny who paid her rent and gave her a Mercedes car. **1847–9** *Todd's Cycl. Anat.* IV. i. 100/2 The chemical mechanism of *sugar-disease. **1613** Purchas *Pilgrimage* (1614) 630 His provisions for his Ingenewes or *Sugar-gardens. **1600** J. Pory tr. *Leo's Africa* v. 52 To every of the Ingenios or *sugar-houses..do belong Negro-slaves, for the planting of their canes. **1769** *Ann. Reg.* 111 Mr. Derman's sugar-house, in Black-friers, was burnt to the ground. **1812** Brackenridge *Views Louisiana* (1814) 175 The sugar houses..were easily distinguished by the vast columns of smoke they sent up into the air. **1848** W. E. Burton *Waggeries* 35 Encomiums on the sweets of married life were drowned in sugar-house molasses. **186.** Walt Whitman *To Working Men* vi. Poems (1868) 110 White-lead-works, the sugar-house, steam-saws. **1886** B. P. Poore *Perley's Reminisc.* I. 39 Many of the passengers visited the bar to imbibe Holland gin and sugar-house molasses—a popular morning beverage. **1890** Billings *Nat. Med. Dict.*, *Treacle*, sugar-house molasses, the uncrystallizable residue of the refining of sugar. **1868** Watts *Dict. Chem.* V. 469 The calcareous thin syrup..is..filtered through bone-black, which removes a small quantity of *sugar-lime. *a* **1626** Breton *Figure of Foure* ii. No. 78 Wks. (Grosart) II. 7/1 Foure sweet Trades in a Citie: *Sugar-men, Comfit-makers, Perfumers and Nose-gay-makers. **1688** Holme *Armoury* iii. xxii. (Roxb.) 280/2 A Sugar mans Lip Bason. **1587** *Holinshed's Chron.* III. 1490/1 A most sumptuous banket prepared of *sugar meats for the men of armes, and the ladies. **1613** Wither *Sat. Ess.*, *Vanity* M 6 Sweet sugar meats, and spice. **1931** A. Uttley *Country Child* xii. 115 She pinched the stocking from the toe to the top... There was a tin ball..filled with comfits, and an orange, and a *sugar mouse. **1965** 'M. A. Gibbs' *Sugar Mouse* xv. 155 A sugar mouse, its chocolate eyes run to smudges, its paper ears flattened,..and its sugar hardened into rock. **1790** *Pennsylvania Packet* 1 Mar. 1/1 This Day..will commence the Sale of a Large and General Assortment of..screw drivers, iron holders, *sugar nippers. **1840** Barham *Ingol. Leg.* 1st Ser. 240 With those great sugar nippers they nipp'd off his 'flippers'. **1858** P. L. Simmonds *Dict. Trade Products*, *Sugar-nippers*, tools for cutting loaf-sugar into lumps. **1921** *Glasgow Herald* 14 July 5 A pair of George II. silver sugar nippers. **1981** Sugar nippers [see *sugar basket*, sense 4 a above]. **1947** *Publ. Amer. Dial. Soc.* viii. 9 **Sugar on snow*, ..'waxed' maple sugar served on snow. **1948** *Richmond* (Va.) *Times-Dispatch* 9 Jan. 16/1 As serious a breach of etiquette as eating 'sugar-on-snow' with a knife or beating one's grandmother in public. **1973** M. Crowell *Greener Pastures* 173 It never fails to remind me..of our introduction to sugar-on-snow. **1848** Bartlett *Dict. Amer.* 344 **Sugar orchard*, a collection of maple trees selected and preserved in the forest for the purpose of making sugar therefrom. **1926** *Paper Terminol.* (Spalding & Hodge, Ltd.) 24 **Sugar paper*, a common quality of wrapping paper made principally from paper waste. Used..for sugar bags. **1972** *Guardian* 5 Dec. 16/7 Drawing paper..Grey or off-white, good quality sugar paper. **1591** Percivall *Sp. Dict.*, *Alfenique*, *suger pellets, *Saccari gluten.* **1613** Dekker *Strange Horse-Race*, etc. Wks. (Grosart) III. 372 [Dishes] heaped full to the brim with Sugar-pellets. **1830** *Edin. Rev.* L. 517 For administering all kinds of homoopathic medicine the little sugar pellets are the favourite medium. **1599** A. M. tr. *Gabelhouer's Bk. Physicke* 108/2 Then take *Sugerpennye as much as is needfulle with Lettis, and fragrant Rosewater. *c* **1623**, **1683** [see penide]. **1712** tr. *Pomet's Hist. Drugs* I. 55 The first Sort,..call'd Sugar-

Penids, is boil'd till the Sugar becomes brittle. **1711** *Sugar puff [see RATAFIA 1]. **1736** BAILEY *Household Dict.* Mm 3 b, To make all Sorts of Sugar Puffs. **1957** *Trade Marks Jrnl.* 1 May 460 Sugar Puffs... Cereal preparations coated with sugar and flavoured with honey... Quaker Oats Limited. **1959** *Elizabethan* Apr. 10/1 You've taken all the Sugar Puffs which are sweet already and left me with one mouldy old bit of Shredded Wheat. **1962** J. BRAINE *Life at Top* xiii. 173, I want Sugar Puffs, Daddy, I do. And yoggy. And cheese. **1855** J. E. COOKE *Ellie* 203 Are you going.. to make a *sugar-rag for that baby up there? **1895** 'MARK TWAIN' in *Harper's Mag.* Dec. 136/1 Somebody fetch this sick doll a sugar-rag. **1938** *Daily Progress* (Charlottesville, Va.) 15 Feb. 1/6 Mayor J. Fulmer Bright.. dubbed the concessions offered by the State a 'sugar-rag dipped in paregoric'. **1727** *Coll. Epigrams* ccxii, All their cheer was *sugar-rolls and sack. **1758** in *6th Rep. Dep. Kpr. Rec.* App. II. 129 A new method of Casting Guns or Cannon, Fire Engines, Cylinders, Pipes, and Sugar Rolls,.. in dried sand. **1767** in *N. & Q.* 9th S. VII. (1901) 148/1 It is customary with us [at Caius Coll., Camb.].. to have sugar-roll and sack standing in the hall. **1891** KIPLING *Light that Failed* ii. 18 Has any man here a needle? I've got a piece of *sugar-sack. **1929** B. L. BURMAN *Mississippi* 78 Two beds, one made of automobile cushions nailed together and covered with a few folded sugar-sacks. **1965** S. T. OLLIVIER *Petticoat Farm* x. 140 The thin tired figure with the.. sugar-sack apron and dishevelled hair. **1882** *Vermont Agric. Rep.* VII. 64 In the process of sugar making there was a point where it would combine with the lime, making '*sugar sand' or the malate of lime. **1949** [see NITRE *sb.* 1 d]. **1975** *Islander* (Victoria, B.C.) 25 May 5/3 The strained [maple] syrup should sit to allow sugar sand to settle to the bottom of the mixture. **1895** *Sugar shell [see *flat-ware* s.v. FLAT A. *adj.* 15]. **1916** *Daily Colonist* (Victoria, B.C.) 12 July 7/1 Sale Goes Merrily On!.. Sugar Shells, fine silver plate, plain, for 50c. **1875** KNIGHT *Dict. Mech.* 2452/1 **Sugar-sifter*, a machine for sorting grades of crushed or ground sugar according to fineness of grain. **1906** GALSWORTHY *Man of Property* I. vi. 88 Now, what did you give for that sugar-sifter? **1976** *Deeside Advertiser* 9 Dec. 9/6 She presented a cut glass sugar sifter to Mrs. Brockley, past president. **1611** J. DAVIES *Sco. Folly, To Worthy Persons* Wks. (Grosart) II. 64/1 If a storme should rise.. Of *suger-snowes and haile of care-a-wayes. **1826** A. ANDERSON *Diary* 20 Mar. in G. Sellar *Narrative* (1916) viii. 124 Gordon awakened us by shouting 'A sugar snow.' There had been a light shower of it during the night, and the air was soft. Holes were rebored, and there was a fine run of sap. **1932** L. I. WILDER *Little House in Big Woods* 92 It's called sugar snow, because a snow this time of year means that men can make more sugar... The snow will hold back the leafing of the trees, and that makes a longer run of sap. **1973** M. CROWELL *Greener Pastures* 149 Sugar snow is falling in those distinctive great feathery flakes that foretell the beginning of a maple sap run. **1715** F. SLARE *Vindic. Sugars* 6, I have.. recommended the Use of *Sugar-Snuff to several Friends. **1930** C. H. EATON *Painting & Decorating* IV. XIII. 843 *Sugar soap has a softening action on the water, and is not so liable [as soda].. to cause undue softening of the paint film. **1958** *Woman* 22 Feb. 14/3 Walls must be washed, brushed... Paintwork washed with sugar-soap, rinsed and allowed to dry. **1963** W. TEE *Painting & Decorating* viii. 67 When you have removed all traces of the sugar soap, mop up surplus moisture. **1729** *Phil. Trans.* XXXVI. 31 Those which they call *Sugar-spars, are those whose Crystallisations are very small, and so on crumbling to Pieces have the Appearance of powdered Sugar. **1731** P. SHAW *Ess. Artif. Philos.* 126 By *Sugar-Spirit is here understood, the Spirit prepared from the Washings, Scummings, Dross and Waste of a Sugar-Baker's Refining House. **1811** *Ann. Reg., Hist.* 33/1 He.. proposed an increase of one halfpenny per gallon on the wash of sugar-spirits. **1825** HONE *Every-day Bk.* I. 51 Their upright cylinder-shaped show-glasses, containing peppermint-drops,.. *sugar-sticks, hard-bake [etc.]. **1892** *Irish Daily Independent* 4 July 5/5 We are not sugarsticks. *Ibid*, Sugarsticks.. men whose steadfastness would melt away before a passing cloud. **1914** CHESTERTON *Flying Inn* xxi. 255 When the three boys last met in the village market-place, they were all sucking sugar-sticks. **1936** W. B. YEATS *Let.* 21 Dec. (1940) 124 He [*sc.* Wilfred Owen] is all blood, dirt & sucked sugar stick. **1847** HALLIWELL, **Sugar-teat*, a small portion of moist sugar tied up in a rag of linen of the shape and size of a woman's nipple, given to quiet an infant when the mother is unable to attend. **1856** KANE *Arctic Expl.* II. v. 63 Sugar-teats of raw meat are passed around. **1938** M. K. RAWLINGS *Yearling* v. 51 The 'coon nibbled at his flesh and cried again. 'He wants his sugar-teat,' Fodder-wing said maternally. **1892** *Dialect Notes* I. 232 *Sugar-tit. **1936** M. MITCHELL *Gone with Wind* viii. 145 Prissy produced the sugar-tit.. and the baby's wails subsided. **1958** S. A. GRAU *Hard Blue Sky* 118 So she went into the bedroom and picked up the sugar tit and tucked it into his mouth. **1708** W. KING *Cookery* 70 For want of *Sugar-tongs or Spoons for Salt. **1874** RUSKIN *Fors Clav.* IV. 272 Because people are now always in a hurry to catch the train, they haven't time to use the sugar-tongs. **1779** in *Proc. Mass. Hist. Soc.* (1886) 2nd Ser. II. 453 Made *Sugar Troughs and Katch.[d] some Sap. **1837** R. BIRD *Nick of Woods* II. iv. 90 What should I do but see the old sugar-trough floating in the bushes. **1946** C. RICHTER *Fields* 17 She lifted the long bundle from out of the sugar trough. **1848** H. R. FORSTER *Stowe Catal.* 144 A pierced *sugar-vase—with goats' heads. **1956** G. TAYLOR *Silver* ix. 202 *Sugar Vases.* Among the many varieties of vases is one based on the Greek volute-krater. **1981** *Sunday Tel.* 18 Jan. 13/1 Tate and Lyle's own collection.. includes silver gilt sugar vases with tops, and the pierced ladles used with them. **1839** URE *Dict. Arts* 1 Vinegar may be distinguished into four varieties,.. 1. Wine vinegar. 2. Malt vinegar. 3. *Sugar vinegar. 4. Wood vinegar. **1812** *Ann. Reg., Gen. Hist.* 9 '*Sugar wash' i.e. the liquid prepared in order to distil spirits from it. *c* **1430** *Two Cookery-bks.* 7 Take almaundys,.. an stampe hem, an draw hem, with þe *sugre water thikke y-now, in-to a fayre vessel. *c* **1450** *Ibid.* 85 Grynde hem with sugour water into faire mylke. **1753** *Chambers' Cycl.* Suppl. s.v. *Sugar spirit*, Sugar-water, which is no other than the water in which the aprons, moulds, and other utensils, employed in the refining of sugar, are washed. **1843** PEREIRA *Food & Diet* 118 Sugar water is frequently used at the table on the continent. **1875** KNIGHT *Dict. Mech.* 2267/2 A spout for sugar-water (the sap of the sugar-maple tree). **1826** A. ANDERSON *Diary* 18 Mar. in G. Sellar *Narrative* (1916) viii. 124 Have had no *sugar-weather this week; frosty with strong winds, and some snow. **1942** G. CAMPBELL *Thorn-Apple Tree* 97 When the March sun began to honeycomb the snow, and the sun was warm on the south side of the house, then came sugar weather.

b. In names of birds, insects, and other animals that feed upon or infest sugar or sweet things, as ***sugar-acarus, -ant, -worm***; **sugar-creeper** (see CREEPER 3); **sugar-eater**, = SUGAR-BIRD 2, 3; **sugar glider**, a flying phalanger, *Petaurus breviceps*, found in Australia and New Guinea; **sugar-louse, -mite**, (*a*) a springtail or silverfish, *Lepisma sacchari*; (*b*) a mite of the genus *Tyroglyphus* or *Glyciphagus*; **sugar squirrel**, a species of flying-squirrel found in Australia, which lives partly on honey; = *sugar glider* above.

1856 *Orr's Circ. Sci., Pract. Chem.* 409 The theory which refers grocers' psora to the *sugar acarus is exceedingly probable. **1790** *Phil. Trans.* LXXX. 346 The *Sugar Ants, so called from their ruinous effects on the sugar-cane. **1898** MORRIS *Austral English* 443/2 *Sugar-Ant*, a small ant, known in many parts of Australia by this name because of its fondness for sweet things. **1811** SHAW *Gen. Zool.* VIII. I. 258 *Sugar Creeper, *Certhia saccharina.* **1796** NEMNICH *Polyglot.-Lex.* VI. 910 *Sugar eater, *Certhia flaveola.* **1845** RICHARDSON in *Encycl. Metrop.* XXII. 464/2 *Nectarinia*,.. Sugar-eater. **1937** *Discovery* Dec. 365/1 Only fifteen inches in total length, with a lovely ash-grey coat.., the *Sugar Glider is usually a gregarious creature. **1941** E. TROUGHTON *Furred Animals of Australia* 95 'Sugar Glider' is now adopted as being brief and suitable for popular use. **1972** *Sci. Amer.* Sept. 56/1 Males of the sugar glider.. go even further. **1817** KIRBY & SP. *Entomol.* xxiii. II. 320 The common *sugar-louse. **1796** NEMNICH *Polyglot.-Lex.* VI. 910 *Sugar mite, *Lepisma saccharina.* **1828–32** WEBSTER *Dict.*, *Sugar-mite*,.. lepisma. **1884** OGILVIE *Dict.* (ed. 2), *Sugar-mite*, a species of Acarina or mite, *Acarus sacchari.* **1846** WATERHOUSE *Mammalia* I. 331 *Petaurus* (*Belideus*) *Sciureus.* Squirrel Flying-Phalanger... *Sugar Squirrel of the colonists of New South Wales. **1932** *Victorian Naturalist* XLIX. 97 When one has kept the 'Sugar Squirrel' in captivity and suffered keen bites from its long piercing teeth, one is able to appreciate the spitfire temper concealed in these beautiful little creatures. **1658** ROWLAND tr. *Moufet's Theat. Ins.* 1087, I assert that a little worm is bred in Sugar, long, black as a flea,.. like to a Weevil; and therefore we may justly call it a *Sugar-worm.

c. In the names of plants or fruits, so called on account of their sweetness or their yielding sugar: **sugar-apple**, either of two West Indian trees of the N.O. *Anonaceæ* or their fruits, *Anona squamosa* and *Rollinia Sieberi*; **sugar-bean**, *Phaseolus saccharatus* and *Phaseolus lunatus* (1858 Simmonds *Dict. Trade*); **sugar beet**, any variety of the beetroot plant from which sugar is manufactured; **sugar-berry**, the North American nettle-tree, *Celtis occidentalis*, = HACKBERRY 2; also, one of several other North American species of *Celtis*; **sugar-birch**, a N. American species of birch, as *Betula lenta* or *Betula nigra*, from the sap of which sugar is obtained; **sugar-fungus**, the fungus of yeast, *Saccharomyces cerevisiæ*; **sugar-grass**, (*a*) = SORGHUM 1 b; (*b*) the Australian grass *Pollinia fulva* or *Erianthus fulvus*; **sugar-gum**, the Australian *Eucalyptus corynocalyx* and *E. Gunnii*; **sugar-melon**, a sweet melon (cf. F. *melon sucrin*); **sugar-millet** = SORGHUM 1 b; **sugar (snap) pea** (†**-pease**): see quots. 1707, 1866; = MANGE-TOUT; †**sugar-pear**, a very sweet variety of pear; **sugar-pine** (see quots.); **sugar-pumpkin** (see quot.); †**sugar-reed** [cf. Du. *suikerriet*] = SUGAR-CANE; **sugar-tree**, (*a*) = SUGAR-MAPLE; (*b*) = SUGAR-BUSH 2; (*c*) an Australian shrub, *Myoporum platycarpum*; **sugar-wood** = SUGAR-MAPLE; **sugar-wrack**, *Laminaria saccharina.*

1738 *Phil. Trans.* XL. 347 The Fruit of this and most other Anonas are Food for Lizards... Some of these Fruits have, from their Taste, been called Custard-apple, *Sugar-apple, and Sour-sops. **1750** G. HUGHES *Barbados* 179 It bears about April a great many flowers very much resembling those of a sugar apple. **1874** STEWART & BRANDIS *Flora N. West India* 6 Custard-apple (Sweet-sop or Sugar-apple in America). **1831** SIR J. SINCLAIR *Corr.* II. 422 Information regarding.. the *sugar beet, will be found in .. 'Crud's Economie de l'Agriculture', p. 285. **1887** *Encycl. Brit.* XXII. 626/1 The sugar beet is a cultivated variety of *Beta maritima.* **1818** W. P. C. BARTON *Compendium Floræ Philadelphicæ* I. 151 Celtis occidentalis... *Sugar-berry Tree. American Nettle Tree. **1846** LINDLEY *Veget. Kingd.* 580 The drupes of Celtis occidentalis, the Nettle-tree or Sugar-berry, are administered in the United States in dysentery. **1896** *Chicago Rec.* 17 Feb. 4/6 He laid the groundwork.. by cutting a sugarberry sprout. **1948** *Florida Anthropologist* May 19 This vegetation includes sugarberry, banyan, mulberry, papaya, saw palmetto and small plants. **1969** T. H. EVERETT *Living Trees of World* xiv. 129/1 The closely related sugarberry (*C. laevigata*), native from Indiana and Illinois southward,.. has a maximum height of 90 feet. **1751** J. BARTRAM *Observ. Trav. Pennsylv.* etc. 27 The timber was *sugar birch, sugar maples, oak and poplar. **1857** *G. Bird's Urin. Deposits* (ed. 5) 398 The *penicillium glaucum*, though distinct from the *sugar-fungus, yet is not unfrequently found associated with it. **1862** ANSTED *Channel Isl.* IV. xx. 476 The *sugar grass, or sorgho. **1889** MAIDEN *Usef. Pl.* 106 The 'Sugar Grass' of colonists, so called on account of its sweetness. *Ibid.* 27 *Eucalyptus Gunnii*,.. In Tasmania this is known as 'Cider Gum', and in South-Eastern Australia occasionally as the '*Sugar Gum'. *Ibid.* 442 *Eucalyptus corynocalyx*,.. Sometimes called 'Sugar Gum', on account of its sweetish foliage, which attracts cattle and sheep. **1616** SURFL. & MARKH. *Country Farm* 195 To make Cucumbers or Pompions sugred [*marg.* *Sugar-Melons]. **1629** PARKINSON *Parad.* 525 Some are called Sugar Melons, others Peare Melons, and others Muske Melons. **1707** MORTIMER *Husb.* (1721) II. 156 The *Sugar Pease, which being planted in April is ripe about Midsummer, its Cods.. boiled with the unripe Pease in them, is extraordinary sweet. **1710** *Tusser Redivivus* in *Tusser's Husb.* (1878) 89 *note*, Runcival pease find now very little Entertainment in Gentlemen's Gardens... In their room are got the Egg pea, the Sugar pea,.. etc. **1866** *Treas. Bot.* 897/2 There is a section [of peas] denominated Sugar-peas, which is remarkable in that the pods are destitute of the inner film peculiar to the pods of the other kinds of Peas. **1907** A. FRENCH *Bk. Veg.* 198 Pea, edible-podded or sugar, is a type of pea with tender pods, which are eaten. **1951**, **1972** Sugar pea [see MANGE-TOUT]. **1980** *Ecology Center* (Berkeley, Calif.) *Newslet.* Oct. 6/2 A great crop of Sugar Snap Peas. **1664** EVELYN *Kal. Hort.* Aug. 72 Pears.. Summer Poppering, *Sugar Pear, Lording Pear. **1766** *Complete Farmers* s.v. *Pear*, The green sugar-pear. **1855** DUNGLISON *Med. Lex.* s.v. *Arrow Root*, Florida arrow-root is derived from *Zamia integrifolia* or *Z. pumila*, *Sugar pine. **1857** J. D. BORTHWICK *Three Yrs. California* xi. 188 In this part of the country the pine-trees are of an immense size... The most graceful is what is called the 'sugar pine'. **1876** *Encycl. Brit.* IV. 704/1 The sugar pine (*Pinus Lambertiana*). **1905** *Trade Catalogue* (Cent. Dict. Suppl.), Negro or Nantucket *Sugar Pumpkin. The true old-fashioned black-warted, shelled pumpkin. **1719** QUINCY *Compl. Disp.* 227 The *Sugar-Reed or Cane. **1705** R. BEVERLEY *Hist. & Present State Virginia* II. 21 The Honey and *Sugar-Trees are likewise spontaneous, near the Heads of Rivers. **1717** *Petiveriana* III. 246 Sugar-tree, grows at the Heads of Rivers, and near Mountains. **1801** J. BARROW *Trav.* I. 62 One.. called here the sugar-tree, from the great quantity of saccharine juice contained in the bottom of its vase-shaped flowers. **1866** *Treas. Bot.* 1110/1 Sugar-tree, *Myoporum platycarpum.* **1872** S. DE VERE *Americanisms* 418 The Sugar-Tree or Sugar-Maple (Acer saccharinum). **1949** *Chicago Tribune* 13 Mar. I. 6/4 The Crane Naval depot encroached upon some fine old sugar trees in Martin county. **1809** A. HENRY *Trav.* 68 Covered with the rock or sugar maple, or *sugar-wood. **1882** *Encycl. Brit.* XIV. 29/2 Kelp .. is prepared from the deep-sea tangle (*Laminaria digitata*), *sugar wrack (*L. saccharina*).

†**6. a.** in *fig.* use, passing into adj. (with superlative ***sugarest, sug(e)rest***): Sugary, sweet. *Obs.*

c **1530** *Crt. Love* 22 Thy suger-dropes swete of Elicon Distill in me.. I pray. **1578** T. PROCTOR *Gorg. Gallery* L iv, Our sugarest sweetes reapes sorowing sobs in fine. **1596** SHAKS. *Merch. V.* III. ii. 119 Here are seuer'd lips Parted with suger breath. **1599** —— *Hen. V*, v. ii. 303 You haue Witch-craft in your Lippes, Kate: there is more eloquence in a Sugar touch of them, then in the Tongues of the French Councell. **1604** DEKKER *Honest Wh.* Wks. 1873 II. 97 Our Country Bona Robaes, oh! are the sugrest delicious Rogues. **1687** in *Magd. Coll. & Jas. II* (O.H.S.) 167 They were wheedled.. by.. sugar words.

†**b.** In parasynthetic compounds, as ***sugar-chopped, -lipped, mouthed*** adjs. *Obs.*

1553 *Respublica* III. iii. 680 A slypper, suger-mowthed howrecop as can bee. *a* **1652** BROME *New Acad.* I. i, Do you tell me Of your sweet sugar-chop't nestle coxscombe? **1827** SCOTT *Surg. Dau.* Concl., All that sugar-lipped raillery which is fitted for the situation of a man about to do a foolish thing.

sugar ('ʃʊgə(r)), *v.* Forms: 5–6 **sugre**, 6–7 **suger**, 7– **sugar**. [f. SUGAR *sb.*]

1. a. *trans.* To mix, cover, sprinkle, or sweeten with sugar.

1530 PALSGR. 743/1, I suger, I make swete with suger, *je sucre.* **1626** BACON *Sylva* §16 With Water thick Sugred. **1736** BAILEY *Househ. Dict.* Mm 3 b, To Sugar all Sorts of small Fruit. **1806** SOUTHEY *Let. to Mary Barker*, Rum and water.. sugared to the utmost. **1824** LD. GRENVILLE *Nugæ Metricæ* 87 We now sugar our cups as freely as our ancestors spiced and drugged them. **1872** GEO. ELIOT *Middlem.* li, When I sugar my liquor.

absol. **1834**, **1850** [see CREAM *v.* 6].

b. in fig. context (cf. 2).

1610 T. ABBOTT *Old Way* 9 To Suger the brims of their intoxicated Cups, that men the more greedily.. may drinke those venimous potions. **1642** D. ROGERS *Naaman* 320 Instead of (Master) call him (Father) sugering the bitter potion they were to minister. **1654** FULLER *Comm. Ruth* (1868) 137 One dram whereof is able to sugar the most worm-wood affliction. **1740** [see SUGARING *vbl. sb.* 1].

c. *intr.* To spread sugar mixed with beer, gum, etc. upon trees or the like in order to catch moths. Also *trans.* with the tree as obj.

1857, **1882** [see SUGARING *vbl. sb.* 3]. **1889** *Pall Mall Gaz.* 20 Aug. 3/1 They were out late 'sugaring for moths'. **1892** F. E. BEDDARD *Anim. Coloration* iii. 84 Any lepidopterist who has 'sugared' in the New Forest. **1902** S. S. SPRIGGE *Industr. Chevalier* vii. 165 There are crowds of them,.. who go out beating bushes, tapping palings, and sugaring trees.

2. *fig.* To make sweet, agreeable, or palatable. ***to sugar the pill*** = *to gild the pill* s.v. GILD *v.*[1] 1 b.

1412–20 LYDG. *Chron. Troy* Prol. 57 That wyth thyn hony swete Sugrest tongis of rethoricyens. **1429** *Pol. Poems* (Rolls) II. 145 Thy right ay sugre with remyssioun. *a* **1586** SIDNEY *Arcadia* III. xxvii, The messenger,.. having ever used to sugre any thing which his Maister was to receave. **1613–18** DANIEL *Coll. Hist. Eng.* (1626) 51 To baite the people, and sugar their subiection. **1639** S. DU VERGER tr. *Camus' Admir. Events* 194 Bad love is sugered full of quaint wantonesses. **1681** T. FLATMAN *Heraclitus Ridens* No. 23 (1713) I. 152 *Jest.* Oh, Mr. Sham's.. turn'd true Protestant! *Earn.* Nay, I thought so by their sugaring the Oaths. **1794** LD. ST. HELENS *Let.* 14 Oct. in A. Paget *Paget Papers* (1896) I. 66 They [*sc.* the Prussian Cabinet] have no right to complain, as I observe that you continued to gild and sugar over the pill which you were directed to administer. [**1878**

C. GIBBON *For the King* iii, Madam, I can sugar my pills, but I cannot sugar my words.] **1936** V. W. BROOKS *Flowering of New England* xv. 287 He liked to administer doses of moral quinine, and he never thought of sugaring his pills. **1954** N. MITFORD *Madame de Pompadour* xviii. 237 To sugar the pill of what was, in fact, his dismissal, a Cardinal's hat was procured for Bernis by Stainville. **1955** E. POUND *Section: Rock-Drill* lxxxix. 55 Louis Philippe suggested that Jackson stand firm And not sugar his language. **1978** J. CARROLL *Mortal Friends* v. ii. 521 The bishop sugared the request with his smile. **1978** [see PILL *sb.*[2] 1 b].

absol. **1604** SHAKS. *Oth.* I. iii. 216 These Sentences, to Sugar, or to Gall, Being strong on both sides, are Equiuocall.

b. with *over*.

1603 SHAKS. *Ham.* (Qo. 1) 1768 Then I perceiue there's treason in his lookes That seem'd to sugar o're his villanie. **1649** MILTON *Eikon.* Pref. Wks. 1851 III. 330 The common grounds of Tyranny and Popery, sugard a little over. **1686** H. MORE *Let.* in Norris *Th. Love*, etc. (1688) 217 A sin.. sugar'd over with the circumstance of *Jucundum* or *Vtile* or both. **1830** CUNNINGHAM *Brit. Paint.* II. 77 Burke.. endeavoured to soothe down his rugged spirit and sugar over the bitterness of his nature. **1849** ROBERTSON *Serm.* Ser. I. ix. (1866) 152 Names.. with which this world sugars over its dark guilt.

c. To flatter. Also const. *up*.

1923 J. MANCHON *Le Slang* 300 *To sugar a person up*, flatter quelqu'un. **1939** R. CHANDLER *Big Sleep* ii. 25 It won't get you anything. Sugaring them never does. **1958** R. STOUT *And four to Go* iii. 172 There was no point in trying to sugar him. The damage.. had been done the second he saw me. **1962** W. FAULKNER *Reivers* x. 219 When I sugars up a woman, it aint just empty talk.

3. *intr.* usually ***sugar off***: in U.S. and Canada, in the manufacture of maple-sugar, to complete the boiling down of the syrup in preparation for granulation.

1836 in [Mrs. Traill] *Backw. Canada* App. 316 Those that sugar-off outside the house have a wooden crane fixed against a stump. **1845** [see SUGARING *vbl. sb.* 2]. **1884** BLAKELEE *Indust. Cycl.* 432 If it is noticed while sugaring off that the syrup is scorched. **1892** HOWELLS *Mercy* 17 Families that you find up in the hills, where the whole brood study Greek while they are sugaring off in the spring.

4. *Cambridge Univ. Rowing slang.* To shirk while pretending to row hard. Also *transf.*

1882 'F. ANSTEY' *Vice Versa* viii. 166 Although (to use a boating expression) he 'sugared' with some adroitness, he was promptly found out, for his son had been a dashing and plucky player. **1890** BARRÈRE & LELAND *Slang Dict.* (1897) 307/2. **1894** *Daily News* 6 Feb. 3/5 Now do look alive, number ninety and five, You're 'sugaring'. **1898** *Blackw. Mag.* Jan. 48 Don't sugar—four. **1906** G. B. SHAW *Let.* 4 Apr. in *Florence Farr, Shaw, Yeats* (1946) 26 Your standard of work [*sc.* in acting].. is far too low... You sugar disgracefully except where you see your way to an effect.

5. Used in imprecations, esp. as pa. pple.: = BLOW *v.*[1] 29. *euphem.*

1886 MRS. H. WOOD in *Argosy* XLI. 270 'Stephenson says he had blue eyes. Now Dick's are brown.' 'Eyes be sugared,' retorted the lawyer. **1903** [see AMATEUR 3 b]. **1903** KIPLING *Traffics & Discov.* (1904) 107 War's declared at midnight. *Pedantics* be sugared! **1942** *Tee Emm* (Air Ministry) II. 78 Real pilot be sugared. Real little show-off, more like! **1962** B. GLANVILLE *Diamond* xxi. 339 'They wouldn't talk to me.' .. 'Sugar them; you're too good for them.'

6. *trans.* To 'cook' or 'doctor'; *spec.* to give a specious impression of the amount of trade done by (a place of business, etc.). *colloq.*

1892 STEVENSON & OSBOURNE *Wrecker* xv. 239 Out of six thousand mats [*sc.* bags of rice], only twenty were found to have been sugared; in each we found.. about twelve pounds of drug. **1894** *Daily News* 26 Dec. 5/3 'Sugaring a house'.. in Birmingham.. denoting a system of creating a fictitious appearance of business by privately giving away money to be spent at its bars.

sugarallie (ʃugəˈralɪ). *Sc. colloq.* Also **sugarellie** (-ˈɛlɪ), **-olly** (-ˈɑlɪ), etc. [A shortened form of *sugar alicreesh*, 16th-cent. Sc. *sukker lagrace*, *succour alacreische*, f. SUGAR *sb.* + Du. *lakk(e)ris* LIQUORICE, LICORICE.] **a.** Liquorice.

1812 P. FORBES *Poems* 21 Sulphur, salt fish, sugar allie. **1842** *Children in Mines Rep.* App. 465 in *Parl. Papers 1842* XVI. 1 Mother gives me 3d., which I spend in sugar-alleys and sweeties. **1876** S. R. WHITEHEAD *Daft Davie* iii. 53 The stock of candy and liquorice (known in that countryside by the name of 'sugar-ally'). **1915** A. S. NEILL *Dominie's Log* xviii. 206 To-night I have a great craving for a stick of twisted sugarelly—the polite call it liquorice. **1921** — *Carroty Broon* xvii. 229 Long tubes of sugarella. **1947** L. DERWENT *Clashmaclavers* 87 Whiles a lucky-bag I'd try, Or sticky sugar-alla buy.

b. *Comb.* **sugarallie button** a round sweet made of liquorice; **sugarallie hat**, a tall cylindrical hat, esp. as formerly worn by policemen; **sugarallie water**, a drink made by vigorously shaking a container in which water and a stick of liquorice have been placed.

1887 A. D. WILLOCK *Rosetty Ends* xx. 148 Havin' discovered that Flossie had a weakness for sugarellie buttons, Simpson has made it a habit to hae ane or twa o' thae sweetmeats in his pouch on courtin' nichts. **1887** J. McBAIN *Arbroath* 104 Their bonnets were replaced by 'sugarellie hats'. **1904** 'H. FOULIS' *Erchie* 65 The sugaraully hats the polis used to hae. **1953** J. J. LAVIN *Compass of Youth* I. vi. 54 Yelling derisively: 'Sugarawlly Hat,' to the might and majesty of the law. **1889** J. M. BARRIE *Window in Thrums* xxii. 207 Bairns.. shook their bottles of sugarelly water into a froth. **1923** W. D. LYELL *Justice-Clerk* I. iv. 26 What say ye to a sma' bottle o' sugaralie water? **1947** J. F. HENDRY *Fernie Brae* 10 Shall we make some sugarolly water?

ˈsugar-ˌbaker. [Cf. Du. *suikerbakker*, G. *zuckerbäcker*.]

† **1.** A confectioner. *Obs.*

1650 *Comenius' Janua Ling.* §408 The Sugar baker make's readie sweet-meats.

2. A sugar-refiner. *Obs.* exc. *Hist.*

1688 HOLME *Armoury* III. xxii. (Roxb.) 281 The coat of Armes of the Sugar bakers or Refiners. **1727** DE FOE *Eng. Tradesm.* iv. (1841) I. 26, I have seen a confectioner turn a sugar-baker. **1777** SHERIDAN *Sch. Scand.* II. ii, Her mother was a Welsh milliner and her father a sugarbaker at Bristol. **1834** *Brit. Husb.* I. 426 Sugar-bakers' scum is the skimmings of the sugar during the operation of refining. **1836–7** DICKENS *Sk. Boz, Tales* x, Mr. Gabriel Parsons.. was a rich sugar-baker, and mistook rudeness for honesty. **1858** SIMMONDS *Dict. Trade.*

So **ˈsugar-ˌbakehouse**, a sugar-refinery; **ˈsugar-ˌbakery**, (*a*) a sugar-refinery; (*b*) the occupation of a sugar-refiner; **ˈsugar-ˌbaking** *vbl. sb.*

1815 *Ann. Reg., Chron.* 91 A *sugar bakehouse. **1794** *Debates U.S. Congress* 5 May (1849) 635 There were only seventeen *sugar-bakeries in the United States. **1860** THACKERAY *Lovel* i. (1861) 43 He had embarked in many businesses besides the paternal sugar-bakery. **1714** *Fr. Bk. of Rates* 103 The said Manufacture of *Sugar-Baking and Refining in France. **1805** FORSYTH *Beauties Scot.* III. 36 There are few manufactures here [*sc.* Greenock] carried on.. excepting of cordage.. sugar-baking, and some few others. **1902** *Encycl. Brit.* XXXIII. 48/1 In former days, when refining sugar or 'sugar baking' was supposed to be a mystery.

ˈsugar-bird. [G. *zuckervogel* is used in senses 1 and 2. Sense 3 is after Du. *suikervogel*.] A name applied to various small birds which feed (or were supposed to feed) on the nectar of flowers.

† **1.** = CANARY-BIRD. *Obs.*

1688 HOLME *Armoury* II. xi. 242/2 The Canary Bird, or Sugar Bird.. is as big as a common Titmouse.

2. A bird of the genus *Certhiola*, belonging to the family *Cærebidæ*, in the W. Indies and S. America; also applied to the genera *Certhia* and *Dacnis*.

1787 LATHAM *Gen. Synop. Birds* Supp. 128 Famous Creeper... A Specimen of this, in the collection of the late Mr. Boddam, was called by the name of Sugar-Bird. **1879** E. P. WRIGHT *Anim. Life* 255 The Sugar-birds, or *Cerebidæ*, are confined to the tropical parts of America. **1894** NEWTON *Dict. Birds* III. 761 The Banana Quit is the Sugar-bird. **1902** *Nature* 25 Sept. 541/2 A Blue Sugar-bird (*Dacnis cayana*) from Brazil.

3. Applied to various members of the family *Nectariniidæ* or Sun-birds of Africa. Also, an African honey-eater of the genus *Promerops*.

1798 LADY A. BARNARD *Jrnl.* Apr. in *Lives of Lindsays* (1849) III. 408 The sugar-bird's tail.. is long and elegantly formed. **1822** W. J. BURCHELL *Trav. S. Afr.* I. ii. 18 The delicate Humming-birds (*Trochili*) of South America are, in Southern Africa, represented by the Nectarinæ, here called by the Dutch colonists *Suiker-vogels* (sugar-birds), from having been observed.. to feed principally on the honey of the flowers of the *Suiker-boscä* (sugar-bush). **1834** PRINGLE *Afr. Sk.* 22 Brilliant as the glancing plumes Of sugar-birds among its blooms. **1908** *Chr. Express* 1 Apr. 55/1 A male Long-tailed sugar-bird (Promerops cafer). **1913** D. FAIRBRIDGE *That which hath Been* 30 The emerald-throated sugar-birds.. darted from one pink protea to another. **1973** S. CLOETE *Company with Heart of Gold* 155 A sugar bird returned to its infinitesimal nest in the grey bush.

ˈsugar-bush.

1. A grove or plantation of sugar-maples.

1823 COOPER *Pioneers* xx, We will stop and see the 'sugar-bush' of Billy Kirby. **1836** [MRS. TRAILL] *Backw. Canada* 315 The sap having been boiled down in the sugar-bush. **1842** [see EIGHTY 2 c]. **1896** *Vermont Agric. Rep.* XV. 38 Does the location of a sugar bush determine the quality of the sugar? **1950** *N.Y. Times Mag.* 23 Apr. 46/2 'Sugar bush' is rarely heard in New Jersey, but in Pennsylvania it is the normal term. **1973** L. RUSSELL *Everyday Life Colonial Canada* xi. 144 The settler who would exploit his grove of maple trees or 'sugar-bush' cleared narrow roads through the woods.

2. [Cape Du. *suikerbos*.] The South African shrub *Protea mellifera*; also, any of several other species of *Protea* rich in nectar. Cf. PROTEA.

1822 [see SUGAR-BIRD 3]. *a* **1823** J. EWART *Jrnl.* (1970) ii. 14 The Protea of Linn[æus] called by the colonists the sugar bush, from the quantity of sweet juices the large and beautiful flowers contain. **1880** *Silver's S. Africa* (ed. 3) 127 It covers extensive grounds.. associating with the Kreupelboom, the Sugar-bush and other shrubs. **1931** V. SAMPSON *Kom Binne* 28 The wild arums, the sugar-bush goblets of pink or cream. **1970** M. MULLER *Cloud across Moon* 239 The masses of white and pink sugar bushes were covered with nearly opened sticky, stiff flowers.

3. *U.S.* An evergreen shrub, *Rhus ovata*, native to southwestern North America and bearing yellow flowers followed by dark red berries.

1900 *West Amer. Sci.* X. 61 The Sugar-bush is a handsome evergreen shrub. **1931** G. H. VANSELL *Nectar & Pollen Plants California* 49 Sugar bush.. of coastal southern California blossoms in winter. **1949** *Nature Mag.* Nov. 424/1 There is the gray of some manzanitas, the silver of white sage, the dark green of sugar bush. **1982** M. MILLAR *Mermaid* vi. 57 Drought-resistant native plants like ceanothus and sugar-bush.

† **sugar-candian.** *Obs.* Etymologizing alteration of SUGAR-CANDY as if f. *Candia*, Crete. (Cf. med.L. *sucura de candia*, MLG. *sucker van kandea*.)

In J. Taylor (Water-P.) *Pennyless Pilgr.* (1618) F 3 'Sugar-carrion' has been altered by editors to 'Sugar-candian'.

1597 BP. HALL *Sat.* II. iv, If not a dramme of Triacle soueraigne, Or Aqua vitæ, or Sugar Candian,.. can it remedie.

† **sugar-candied**, *sb. Obs. rare.* Perverted form of SUGAR-CANDY.

1599 B. JONSON *Cynthia's Rev.* Induct., I would thou hadst some sugar-candied, to sweeten thy mouth.

sugar-candied, *a.* Also 7 -candid. [f. SUGAR-CANDY + -ED[2].]

1. Coated with (fine white) sugar; hence, white as if candied over with sugar.

1592 NASHE *P. Penilesse* Wks. 1904 I. 180 Their cheeks suger-candied and cherry blusht so sweetly. **1673** W. H[ICKES] *Lond. Drollery* 44 Thy lips are white as Tallow, never man did Buss sweeter things, sure they'r Sugar-candid.

2. *fig.* Sweet, sugared, honeyed. (Cf. CANDIED 3.)

In recent use only with pun on *candid*.

1650 A. B. *Mutatus Polemo* 23 We.. accosted them with the most prestigious sugar-candid words we could invent. **1893** R. WALLACE in *Daily News* 14 July 2/7 Governments had generally two classes of friends, the candid and the sugar-candied. (Loud laughter.)

sugar-candy (ʃugəˈkændɪ). [ad. F. *sucre candi* (in which *candi* was at an early date apprehended as a pa. pple.; cf. 15th c. *chucre candit*, and It. *zucchero candito*), corresp. to Pr. *sucre cande*, Sp. *azucar candi*, Pg. *assucar candi*, MLG. *suckercandi* (also *-it*), early mod.Du. *suycker candye* (Du. *kandij-suiker*), G. *zuckerkand* (16th c.), med.L. *succar-candi*; repr. Arab. *sukkar* SUGAR + *qandī* of sugar, f. *qand* sugar, a. Pers. *kand* = Skr. *khaṇḍa* sugar in pieces (cf. *khaṇḍa śarkarā* candied sugar), orig. piece, fragment, f. root *khaṇḍ* to break.]

1. Sugar clarified and crystallized by slow evaporation.

brown (or †***red***) ***sugar-candy***: that obtained at the first crystallization. ***white sugar-candy***: that obtained by reboiling the former and allowing it to crystallize.

[**1390** *Earl Derby's Exped.* (Camden) 19 Pro vj lb. sucri candy.] **1392** *Ibid.* 219 Pro diversis speciebus.. emptis.. viz. croco,.. gariofilis, sugre candy, sugre caffetin. *c* **1420** *Liber Cocorum* (1862) 7 With sugur candy, thou may hit dowce. *c* **1460** J. RUSSELL *Bk. Nurture* 757 Whot appuls & peres with sugre Candy. [**1510** tr. *Rentale Dunkeld.* (S.H.S.) 213 Zucro candey.] **1584** COGAN *Haven Health* cxxix. (1636) 128 White sugar is not so good for flegme, as that which is called Sugar Candie. **1596** SHAKS. *1 Hen. IV*, III. iii. 180 One poore peny-worth of Sugar-candie to make thee long-winded. **1610** *Shuttleworths' Acc.* (Chetham Soc.) 191 Halfe a pound of brown suger candie, xij[d]. **1611** *Ibid.* 196 White suger candie. **1620** VENNER *Via Recta* vi. 102 Red Sugar-Candy, which is only good in glysters. **1664** POWER *Exp. Philos.* I. 27 Diaphanous like Sugar-Candy. **1755** SMOLLETT *Quix.* (1803) IV. 8, I thought.. his voice as sweet as sugar-candy. **1836–41** BRANDE *Chem.* (ed. 5) 115 Thus we see sugar-candy crystallized upon strings, and verdigris upon sticks. **1864** GARROD *Mat. Med.* (ed. 2) 316 Cane sugar.. crystallized from a strong solution with the addition of spirit.. forms oblique four-sided prisms, sugar candy.

2. *fig.* Something sweet, pleasant, or delicious.

1591 GREENE *Farew. Follie* Wks. (Grosart) IX. 294 Sugar candie she is, as I gesse, fro the waist to the kneestead. **1591** HARINGTON *Orl. Fur.* Pref. ¶8 In verse is both goodnesse and sweetnesse, Rubarb and Sugercandie, the pleasaunt and the profitable. **1593** G. HARVEY *Pierce's Super.* Wks. (Grosart) II. 254 O the sugarcandy of the delicate bag pipe there. **1817** BYRON *Beppo* lxxx, Oh, for old Saturn's reign of sugar-candy! **1889** GRETTON *Memory's Harkback* 94 Lord John Russell, to whom a rap at the University was always sugar-candy.

b. *attrib.* or as *adj.* Sugared, honeyed, deliciously sweet.

1575 G. HARVEY *Letter-bk.* (Camden) 91 The goodliest suugercandye style That ever cam neere me a mile. **1602** *2nd Pt. Return fr. Parnass.* III. iv. 1377 Give him some sugar candy tearms. **1602** MIDDLETON *Blurt, Master-Constable* v. ii, No, no, my sugar-candy mistress, your goodman is not here. **1903** LD. R. GOWER *Rec. & Rem.* 149 The party in that sugar-candy, cake-like house of wits was a small one. **1909** *Daily Chron.* 20 Sept. 4/6 Sugar-candy hymns.

3. *attrib.*, as ***sugar-candy powder, stick***; also applied locally to crystallized geological formations (see quots. 1778, 1876).

1683 TRYON *Way to Health* xv. (1697) 368 Take.. White-Sugar candy-powder one Dram and half. **1706** E. WARD *Wooden World Diss.* (1708) 77 A mere Sugar-candy Stick, in Comparison to his Cat of Nine-Tails. **1778** W. PRYCE *Min. Cornub.* 92 A white candied, or pellucid Crystal, commonly termed a White Sugar Candy (Spar) Crystal. **1876** WOODWARD *Geol. Eng. & Wales* 204 The beds at Portland and Tisbury contain beautiful yellow crystals of sulphate of barytes (sugar candy stone).

Hence **sugar-ˈcandyish** *a.*, resembling sugar-candy.

1874 DISRAELI *Let.* Aug. in *Lett. to Lady Bradford* (1929) I. vii. 135 Her manners not only sugary but sugar-candyish. **1927** J. MASEFIELD *Midnight Folk* 172 A bowl of raspberries and cream with blobs of sugar-candyish brown sugar.

ˈsugar-cane. [f. SUGAR *sb.* + CANE *sb.*[1] Cf. F. *canne à sucre*, †*de sucre*, Sp. *caña de azucar*, Pg. *canna d'assucar*.] A tall stout perennial grass, *Saccharum officinarum*, cultivated in tropical and sub-tropical countries, and forming the chief source of manufactured sugar.

African or *Chinese sugar-cane*: see IMPHEE, SORGHO b, SORGHUM 1 b.

1568 tr. *Thevet's New found Worlde* lxxvii. 126 The stalke groweth like to Suger Canes. 1582 N. LICHEFIELD tr. *Castanheda's Conq. E. Ind.* I. xi. 28 By these messengers were presented..three Sheepe, many Orenges, and Sugar Canes. *c* 1592 MARLOWE *Jew of Malta* IV. 1814 The Meads, ..Instead of Sedge and Reed, beare Sugar Canes. 1624 CAPT. J. SMITH *Virginia* IV. 149 Their mighty wealth of Sugar canes, being first transported from the Canaries. 1662 J. DAVIES tr. *Mandelslo's Trav.* 135 Sugar Canes, eighteen foot long, and seven inches about. 1779 HERVEY *Nav. Hist.* II. 203 The first introduction of the sugar-cane into the English West-India settlements, is said to be in the year 1641. 1832 *Veg. Subst. Food of Man* 382 The Sugar-Cane.. must be considered..a native of China. 1857 H. S. OLCOTT (*title*) Sorgho and Imphee, the Chinese and African Sugar Canes. 1861 BENTLEY *Man. Bot.* 697 *Holcus saccharatus* or *Sorghum saccharatum*, is called the North China Sugar-cane or Sweet Sorgho. 1878 MORLEY *Diderot* II. 243 A gang of negro-slaves work among the sugar-canes.

attrib. 1838 T. THOMSON *Chem. Org. Bodies* 625 The substances which he found in sugar-cane juice. 1839 URE *Dict. Arts* 1195 Sugar-cane mill. 1876 *Nature* 14 Dec. 150 The Sugar-Cane Disease in the May River District, Queensland.

† '**sugar-chest.** *Obs.* Also *Sc.* **suckar kist.**

1. A chest for sugar.

1549 *Acc. Ld. High Treas. Scot.* IX. 345 For..careing of ane suckar kist furtht of Leytht to Edinburght..vj s.

2. Applied to the hard wood of various trees and to the trees themselves: see quots.

1545 ASCHAM *Toxoph.* (Arb.) 123 Steles be made of dyuerse woodes, as..Sugercheste. 1567 GOLDING *Ovid's Met.* IX. (1593) 230 From underneath a sugarchest [tr. *sub ilice*]. 1585 HIGINS *Junius' Nomencl.* 149/1 *Alnus nigra*,..the blacke alder tree: some take it to be that which is commonly called sugerchest. 1591 PERCIVALL *Sp. Dict.*, *Evano*, *Ebenus*, sugarchest. 1609 J. DAVIES *Holy Roode* Ep. Ded. 14 To Flesh and Blood this Tree but Wormewood seemes, How ere the same may be of Suger-chest. 1683 MOXON *Mech. Exerc.*, *Printing* vii, I us'd to make them of Sugar-Chest; That Stuff being commonly well-season'd, by the long lying of the Sugar in it, and is besides a fine hard Wood.

sugared ('ʃʊgəd), *ppl. a.* Forms: 4–5 **sucred**; 4–7 **sugred** (5 **-id, -yd, -et, sugird, -urd, sugurt, sugeryd**, 6 **-ed**, *Sc.* **sug(g)urit, sugorit**, 7 **suger'd, sugg'red, sugr'd, sug'red**), 6– **sugared** (7–8 **sugar'd**); *Sc.* 7 **succred**, 8–9 **suckered**. [f. SUGAR *sb.* or *v.* + -ED. Cf. med.L. *zucarata*, *sugurata* (*aqua*), F. *sucré*.]

1. Containing or impregnated with sugar; sweetened with sugar.

c 1420 *Liber Cocorum* (1862) 53 Ȝet sugurt soppes I nyl forȝete. 1567 MAPLET *Gr. Forest* Ep. Ded., Ambrosia, a sugred and confect kinde of Wine. 1576 GOSSON *Spec. Hum.* in *Sch. Abuse* (Arb.) 77 The tender floure..Whose sugred sap sweet smelling sauours yeeldes. 1577 HARRISON *England* III. i. in *Holinshed*, Marchepaine, sugred bread [*ed.* 1587 sugerbread], gingerbreade. 1626 BACON *Sylva* §726 Wine Sugred inebriateth lesse, than Wine Pure. 1633 P. FLETCHER *Pisc. Eclogues* VII. xxxvii, No sugred made confection. 1685 HEDGES *Diary* (Hakl. Soc.) I. 209 Sugared Biskett. 1763 MILLS *Pract. Husb.* IV. 368 Phials half filled with sugared water. 1886 D. C. MURRAY *First Pers. Sing.* ii, He asked for a glass of sugared water and a match. 1889 J. M. DUNCAN *Clin. Lect. Dis. Wom.* xxii. (ed. 4) 190 By the sugared urine irritating the skin.

b. ***sugared pumpkin***: = *sugar-pumpkin* (SUGAR *sb.* 5 c).

[1600 SURFLET *Countrie Farme* 252 To make cucumbers or pompions sugred, you must steepe the seed in water that is well sweetned with sugar or honie,..and so sowe them.] 1884 *De Candolle's Orig. Cultivated Pl.* 254 The sugared pumpkin, called Brazilian.

c. Resembling (that of) sugar; sugary. *rare.*

1725 *Fam. Dict.* s.v. *Pears*, A very muskish sugared Taste.

d. Sugar-coated; candied, 'crystallized'.

1855 DICKENS *Househ. Words* XII. 133/2 Bonbons made of sugared nuts and almonds. 1874 BLACK *Pr. Thule* xiv. 228 Her pockets stuffed with packages of sugared fruits. 1878 C. GIBBON *For the King* iii, Pills and words come to the same effect in the end, whether sugared or no. 1892 GARRETT *Encycl. Pract. Cookery* I. 15/1 Sugared Almonds.

e. Smeared with a mixture of sugar, beer, etc. for the purpose of catching moths.

1887 *Cassell's Dict.* s.v. *Sugaring*, The collector visits the sugared trees after dark with a bull's-eye lantern.

2. *fig.* Full of sweetness; honeyed, luscious, delicious. **a.** With lit. language retained.

1426 LYDG. *De Guil. Pilgr.* 14287 Flaterye, The wych, with hys sugryd galle, Euery vertu doth appalle. 1523 SKELTON *Garl. Laurel* 73 Sith he hath tastid of the sugred pocioun Of Elyconis well. 1576 GASCOIGNE *Kenelworth* Wks. 1910 II. 108 The Sugred baite oft hides the harmefull hookes. 1629 Z. BOYD *Last Battel* 950 (Jam.) All fleshlie pleasures are both vain and vile... Beware of such succred poison. 1663 S. PATRICK *Parab. Pilgr.* xv. (1687) 132 These sugared drops do love most to stay in the solitary places.

b. Of actions, states, etc.: *freq.* having an attractive outward appearance, alluring.

c 1374 CHAUCER *Troylus* II. 384 So lat youre daunger sucred [*v.r.* sugred] ben a lyte. 1569 in Burnet *Hist. Ref.*, *Rec.* (1681) II. II. III. xii. 369 Her cunning and sugred entertainment of all Men that come to her. *a* 1586 SIDNEY *Apol. Poetry* (Arb.) 28 His sugred inuention of that picture of loue. *c* 1590 GREENE *Fr. Bacon* vii. 68 Whose face, shining with many a sugar'd smile. 1607 SHAKS. *Timon* IV. iii. 259 Thou would'st haue..followed The Sugred game before thee. 1633 G. HERBERT *Temple*, *Glance* i, I felt a sugred strange delight. 1651 JER. TAYLOR *Serm. for Year* II. xix. 248 If we retain..any one beloved lust, any painted devil, any sugar'd temptation. 1890 *Spectator* 18 Oct., Davies was afterwards more successful in his offers of sugared law.

†**c.** Of sound, melody, harmony: Dulcet, mellifluous. *Obs.*

c 1430 LYDG. *Min. Poems* (Percy Soc.) 11 To practyse withe sugrid melody. 1500–20 DUNBAR *Poems* xlvi. 13 A nychtingall, with suggurit notis new. 1580 GIFFORD *Posie Gillofl.* Wks. (Grosart) 93 Her sugred descant. 1648 J. BEAUMONT *Psyche* XI. ccxvii, What Ear could now Disrelish such a sugar'd Noise as this!

†**d.** Of the tongue, mouth, lips (*occas.* of persons), with reference to eloquence or tone. *Obs.*

c 1440 LYDG. *Amor vincit omnia* v. (MS. Ashm. 59) þe greke Omerus w^t his sugred mouþe. 1508 DUNBAR *Gold. Targe* 263 Your sugurit lippis and tongis aureate. 1560 ROLLAND *Seven Sages* 63 O Pantillas with thy sweit suggurit toung. 1573 L. LLOYD *Pilgr. Princes* (1586) 24 b, Demosthenes that sugred Orator. 1635 SWAN *Spec. Mundi* vii. §3 (1643) 348 The harmlesse Choristers..do then begin to tune again their sugred throats.

e. Of words, speech, eloquence. (The commonest use.)

1387–8 T. USK *Test. Love* I. iv. (Skeat) l. 34 She..gan deliciously me comforte with sugred wordes. *c* 1440 LYDG. *St. Albon* (1534) A ij, Sugred deties of Tullius Cicero. *c* 1450 —— *Secrees* 220 Thorugh his sugryd Enspyred Elloquence. 1539 TAVERNER *Gard. Wysed.* I. 30 His wordes were more sugred than salted, more dilectable then profytable. 1591 SHAKS. *1 Hen. VI*, III. iii. 18 Faire perswasions, mixt with sugred words. 1633 G. HERBERT *Temple*, *Rose* i, This world of sugred lies. 1664 H. MORE *Antid. Idolatry* x. 140 The fair words and sugar'd speeches of that cunning Woman. 1789 WOLCOT (P. Pindar) *Expost. Ode* x. Wks. 1812 II. 236 Like Children, charm'd with Praise's sugar'd song. 1863 KINGLAKE *Crimea* (1877) II. 165 The cheap sugared words are quickly forgotten. 1891 FARRAR *Darkn. & Dawn* xxxv, She understood that sugared letter which had summoned her from Antium!

†**f.** Of kisses. *Obs.*

a 1586 SIDNEY *Astr. & Stella* Sonn. lxxiii, A sugared kiss In sport I suckt. 1599 B. JONSON *Cynthia's Rev.* IV. iii, So sugred, so melting, so soft, so delicious. 1658 E. PHILLIPS *Myst. Love* Gen. Lud. (1685) 17 Kisses. Tempting,.. sugred, lingring.

†**g.** Of persons: Sweet, precious. *Obs.*

c 1475 *Partenay* 3848 Adieu, my sugret suete souerain lorde! 1583 WASTNES in *Melbancke's Philotimus* To Author, God prosper thee (my sugred darling boy).

sugarellie, var. SUGARALLIE.

sugarer ('ʃʊgərə(r)). *slang.* [f. SUGAR *v.* + -ER[1].] One who shirks, *spec.* at rowing. Cf. SUGAR *v.* 4.

1904 W. G. EAST *Rowing & Sculling* 20 A sugarer, a man who, whilst rowing correctly, avoids putting in a full share of work. 1925 W. DEEPING *Sorrel & Son* xviii. 171 It was necessary to be neither a funk nor a sugarer.

sugariness ('ʃʊgərɪnɪs). [f. SUGARY *a.* + -NESS.] The quality or condition of being sugary; luscious sweetness.

1848 LOWELL *Biglow P.* Introd., Poet. Wks. (1879) 174 The sugariness of tamed and cultivated fruit. 1899 *Pall Mall Gaz.* 26 Dec. 3/3 That 'sugariness' of diction which has endeared the author to a wide circle of readers.

sugaring ('ʃʊgərɪŋ), *vbl. sb.* [f. SUGAR *v.* + -ING[1].]

1. Sugary or sweet matter; sweetening. Also, the adding of sugar.

1740 CHEYNE *Regimen* 339 Noviciats in the spiritual Life are often gratified with such Sugarings for their Encouragement; but Bread is for grown Persons. 1887 *Cassell's Dict.*, *Sugaring*,..Sugar used for sweetening, &c. 1892 *Daily News* 16 Sept. 5/5 The California prune..will keep better and longer without sugaring than the latter. 1907 *Westm. Gaz.* 1 June 2/1 The less alcoholic wines of the North, artificially strengthened by sugaring.

2. *U.S.* The manufacture of sugar from the maple. Also ***sugaring off*** (see SUGAR *v.* 3).

1836 in [Mrs. Traill] *Backw. Canada* App. 316 The best rule I can give as to the sugaring-off, as it is termed, is to let the liquid continue at a fast boil. 1845 S. JUDD *Margaret* II. i. (1871) 151 The neighbors, boys and girls, come in at the 'sugaring off'. 1872 S. DE VERE *Americanisms* 206 The verb to sugar off is derived from the custom of winding up the sugaring at a certain period. 1904 W. CHURCHILL *Crossing* xi. 136 Then came the sugaring, the warm days and the freezing nights.

attrib. 1836 [MRS. TRAILL] *Backw. Canada* 156 Till it has arrived at the sugaring point. 1897 *Advance* (Chicago) 8 Apr. 455/2 The sugaring parts of Ohio. 1899 *Atlantic Monthly* Apr. 561 In sugaring time, Deacon Abram deliberately lets five barrels of maple soak.

3. (See SUGAR *v.* 1 c.) Also *attrib.*

1857 *Zoologist* Ser. I. XV. 5649 Sugaring by night is certainly very profitable for Lepidoptera, ants and cockroaches. 1882 *Cassell's Nat. Hist.* VI. 32 This mode of collecting is called 'sugaring', and is somewhat uncertain, as on some nights the sugar will be covered with Moths, and on others you will scarcely find one. 1902 S. SQUIRE SPRIGGE *Industr. Chevalier* vii. 170 A midnight sugaring expedition.

4. Bribery.

1891 J. P. QUINN *Fools of Fortune* 285 This payment is what the 'fakirs' call 'sugaring', and I have never known one of these officials for whom the dose could be made too sweet. 1902 S. E. WHITE *Blazed Trail* xvi. 117 The old-time logger found these two individuals susceptible to the gentle art of 'sugaring'.

sugarish ('ʃʊgərɪʃ), *a. rare.* Also 5 **zucrish, -ys.** [f. SUGAR *sb.* + -ISH[1].] Sugary, sweet.

c 1450 *Mirour Saluacioun* (Roxb.) 27 Hire speche was lawe and soft..Neure fell to sharp nor bittere bot hevenly zucrish swete. *Ibid.* 126 His hevenly zucrys halsinges ineffable and gloriouse. 1857 *Tait's Mag.* XXIV. 6 The latter being of a sacchrarineish and sugarish taste.

sugarless ('ʃʊgəlɪs), *a.* [f. SUGAR *sb.* + -LESS.] Without sugar, unsugared.

1785 COWPER *Let. to Newton* 27 Aug., Wks. 1836 V. 153 His dishes of sugarless tea. 1896 *Allbutt's Syst. Med.* I. 408 Green vegetables and sugarless wines and spirits. 1898 *Pall Mall Mag.* Sept. 97 A cup of lukewarm coffee, sugarless and milkless.

'**sugar-loaf.** [f. SUGAR *sb.* + LOAF *sb.*[1] 3.]

1. A moulded conical mass of hard refined sugar (now rarely made).

1422 *Durham Acc. Rolls* (Surtees) 59 In 1 Sugyrlaffe, 8*s.* 4*d.* 1452 *Paston Lett.* I. 236, I pray yow that ye woll vouchesaff to send me an other sugor loff, for my old is do. 1555 EDEN *Decades* (Arb.) 380 Teneriffa is..a greate hyghe picke lyke a suger lofe. 1585 T. WASHINGTON tr. *Nicholay's Voy.* III. i. 69 b, Wearing on their heads a hygh yealow hatte made after the fashion of a suger loofe. 1604 [? CHETTLE] *Wit of Woman* G 4, Giue the gentlewoman a leashe of angells, to buy a sugar loafe. 1660 BOYLE *New Exp. Phys. Mech.* xxxiii. 247 A Gardiner's watering Pot shap'd conically, or like a Sugar-Loaf. 1707 LADY GRISELL BAILLIE *Househ. Bk.* (S.H.S.) 69 For a suger lofe £3. 7s. 6d. 1800 B. MOSELEY *Treat. Sugar* (ed. 2) 113 The blue paper for covering sugar-loaves. 1835 *App. Munic. Corpor. Rep.* IV. 2896 (Kingston-upon-Thames), The High Steward..is entitled to 18 sugar loaves every year. These are worth about 9*l.*, and are usually distributed in charity. 1876 W. H. G. KINGSTON *Banks Amazon* 112 The snow-capped, truncated peak of Cotopaxi, looking like a vast sugar-loaf.

2. *transf.* A thing having the shape of a sugar-loaf. **a.** Usually ***sugar-loaf-hat*** (see 3): A conical hat, pointed, rounded or flat at the top, worn during the Tudor and Stuart periods and after the French Revolution.

1607 DEKKER & WEBSTER *Westw. Hoe* v. iii, Do not I know you, grannam? and that sugar-loaf?

b. A high conical hill.

a 1691 BOYLE *Hist. Air* (1692) 184 Till they arrived at the top of the sugar-loaf, or highest pile of the mountain. 1715 *Phil. Trans.* XXIX. 318 The white Cloud still hiding the greatest part of the Sugar-loaf [*sc.* Teneriffe]. 1862 *Chambers' Encycl.* IV. 745/2 The rock [of Gibraltar], at its highest point, the Sugar Loaf, attains an elevation of 1439 feet above the sea. 1879 STEVENSON *Trav. Donkey* (1886) 30 The outline of a wooded sugar-loaf in black.

c. A kind of cabbage.

1766 *Complete Farmer* 7 P 4/1, I have not one cabbage this year of the sort I intended to have; what I have being chiefly sugar-loaf, the seedsman having deceived me. 1778 [W. MARSHALL] *Minutes Agric.* 28 Apr. 1777 The savoys and sugar-loaves were soon gone. 1842 LANCE *Cottage Farmer* 15 When you plant out your cabbages at the outset, first put a row of early Yorks, then a row of Sugar-loafs.

d. A variety of pine-apple, *Ananas pyramidalis*.

1796 NEMNICH *Polyglot.-Lex.* VI. 910 Sugar-loaf pineapple, *Bromelia ananas*. 1842 LOUDON *Suburban Hort.* 600 The Brown Sugar-loaf. 1885 LADY BRASSEY *The Trades* 343 The sweeter and more juicy 'sugar-loaf' is preferred in England.

e. A species of fossilized sea-urchin.

1862 *Chambers' Encycl.* IV. 578/1 *Galerites*. [The name] popularly given to them..'Sugar-loaves', is descriptive of the elongated and more or less conical shape of their shell.

3. *attrib.* and *Comb.* Shaped like or otherwise resembling a sugar-loaf, as ***sugar-loaf bonnet, button, cabbage*** (see 2 c), ***cap, cornea, crown, eminence, hat*** (see 2 a), ***head, hill*** (see 2 b), ***mountain*** (see 2 b), ***pine*** (see 2 d), ***pippin, rock, -shape, stone, -stump, yew***; used for sugar-loaves or loaf-sugar, as ***sugar-loaf form, mould, paper***; parasynthetic and similative, as ***sugar-loaf-like, -shaped*** adjs.; **sugar-loaf page**, a page wearing sugar-loaf buttons; **sugar-loaf sea**, 'high turbulent waves with little wind' (Smyth *Sailor's Word-bk.*); **sugar-loaf tool**, a tool with an end of conical shape used in seal-engraving to smoothe the surfaces of shields.

1885 DILLON *Fairholt's Cost. in Eng.* I. 403 The high *sugar-loaf bonnet of the French peasants. 1833 T. HOOK *Parson's Dau.* II. vi, A small white-faced boy, who was called 'page' to aunt Eleanor..who..wore..two hundred and forty-eight white *sugar-loaf buttons on his jacket. 1786 ABERCROMBIE *Gard. Assist.* 130 *Sugar-loaf cabbage. 1838 *Penny Cycl.* XI. 75/1 Salads go to market as soon as they are of sufficient size, and sugar-loaf cabbages succeed them. 1809 MALKIN *Gil Blas* XII. i. ¶3 *Sugar-loaf caps of paper. 1885 DILLON *Fairholt's Cost. in Eng.* II. 237 The tall *sugar-loaf crown and broad brim. 1867 *Chambers' Encycl.* IX. 192/1 When it has been sufficiently concentrated..it is run into the *sugar-loaf forms. 1585 HIGINS *Junius' Nomencl.* 165/1 *Apex*,..a *suger-loafe hat: a coppid tanke hat. 1807–8 W. IRVING *Salmag.* xviii. (1860) 402 He usually wore a high sugar-loaf hat with a narrow brim. 1885 DILLON *Fairholt's Cost. in Eng.* I. 402 He wears the high sugar-loaf hat in which the revolutionary heroes..enshrined their evil heads. 1793 HOLCROFT tr. *Lavater's Physiog.* xx. 102 All Indians with flat or *sugar-loaf heads. 1799 MALTHUS *Diary* 9 July (1966) 131 We..saw Doverfield..with his *sugar loaf hills covered with snow. 1808 PIKE *Sources Mississ.* (1810) II. App. 5 A beautiful little sugar loaf hill. 1859 D. BUNCE *Travels with Dr. Leichhardt* iv. 29 There are two lofty sugar-loaf hills..which may be seen from Hobart Town. 1969 Sugar loaf hill [see FAVELA]. 1688 HOLME *Armoury* III. i. 11/1 They wear their Hats higher in the Crown (*Sugar Loafe like)..then Men do. *Ibid.* xxii. (Roxb.) 280/2 A great *Sugar loaf Mould. 1866 *Chambers' Encycl.* VIII. 269/1 The peak called, from its peculiar shape, *Sugar-loaf Mountain. 1837 THACKERAY *Ravenswing* v, The *sugar-loaf page asked whether master was coming home early. 1859 F. A. GRIFFITHS *Artil. Man.* (1862) 96 Blue *sugar-loaf paper.

1796 NEMNICH *Polyglot.-Lex.* VI. 958 *Sugar-loaf pine, *Ananas pyramidalis.* **1842** LOUDON *Suburban Hort.* 533 Dessert apples... *Sugarloaf Pippin, Wormsley Pippin. **1712** E. COOKE *Voy. S. Sea* 384 A *Sugar-Loaf Rock above Water. **1852** BURN *Naval & Milit. Dict.* II. (1863) 276/2 *Sugar-loaf sea, *mer clapoteuse.* **1849** CUPPLES *Green Hand* xiv, The *sugar-loaf shape of the headland. **1885** DILLON *Fairholt's Cost. in Eng.* I. 183 A *sugar-loaf-shaped erection of red cloth. **1789** J. WILLIAMS *Min. Kingd.* II. 129 The.. hard, granulated, *sugar-loaf-stone. **1876** DUNGLISON *Med. Lex.*, **Sugarloaf Stump*, a conical shape assumed by the stump after amputation..due to excessive muscular retraction. **1756** MRS. DELANEY *Autobiog.* (1861) III. 435 The gardens seem to be laid out in the old-fashioned way of mince-pies, arbours, and *sugarloaf yews.

Hence **'sugar-loafed** (†**-loaved**) *ppl. a.*, shaped like a sugar-loaf.

1702 W. J. tr. *Bruyn's Voy. Levant* xl. 156 A sort of Sugar-loaved Hats. **1842** THACKERAY *Fitz-Boodle's Prof.* Wks. 1898 IV. 346 A jacket covered with sugar-loafed buttons. **1872** BAKER *Nile Trib.* ix. 148 A steep sugar-loafed hill. **1875** *Encycl. Brit.* II. 556/1 The *bassinet* was now worn beneath the huge sugar-loafed helm.

†**'sugarly**, *adv. Obs. rare*$^{-1}$. In 6 suggerlie. [f. SUGAR *sb.* + -LY[2].] Pleasantly, agreeably.

1584 D. FENNER *Def. Ministers* (1587) 41 To shew how suggerlie they dealt with manie, and yet in the end did vndermine them.

'sugar-,maple. a. The North American tree *Acer saccharinum*, which yields maple-sugar. Also, the light-coloured wood of this tree.

1731 P. MILLER *Gardeners Dict.* s.v. Acer, There is another Sort of Maple, which is very common in Virginia, and is known by the name of the Sugar Maple. **1753** *Chambers' Cycl.* Suppl. s.v. *Maple*, The sugar maple.. grows to sixty or eighty foot high. **1773** W. LEWIS tr. *Neumann's Chem. Wks.* (ed. 2) II. 72 *note*, A kind of Sugar is prepared from the juice which issues upon wounding or boring certain species of the maple-tree, one of which is named from hence the Sugar-maple. **1851** E. FORBES *Veg. World* in *Art Jrnl. Ill. Catal.* p. vii, The wood of the sugar maple of Canada is the bird's-eye and also curled maple of the cabinet-maker. **1868** *Rep. U.S. Comm. Agric.* (1869) 198 The black sugar maple (*Acer saccharinum*, var. *nigrum*). **1883** *Encycl. Brit.* XV. 524/1. **1936** *Wood Products* Mar. 11/1 During recent years the U.S. Forest Products Laboratory.. has investigated the weight and hardness of sugar maple. **1980** *Family Handyman* Sept. 63/2 A cubic foot of poplar weighs 26 lbs. compared to 39 lbs. for a cubic foot of sugar maple.

b. *attrib.*, as ***sugar-maple land, tree***; **sugar-maple borer** (see quot. 1882).

1792 *Descr. Kentucky* 54 The settlers upon the sugar-maple lands. **1797** *Encycl. Brit.* (ed. 3) XVIII. 63/1 By transplanting the sugar maple-tree into a garden,..the quantity of the sap might be increased. **1882** *Garden* 27 May 370/3 The Sugar Maple borer (Glycobius speciosus), whose grubs are very injurious to Maples.

sugarolly, var. SUGARALLIE.

†**sugar-plate.** *Obs.* [orig. *sucre in plate*, i.e. sugar in the form of a flat cake: see PLATE *sb.* 10.] A dainty kind of sweetmeat. Also applied to a sweet lozenge for medicinal use.

c **1333** *Durham Acc. Rolls* (Surtees) 521 In 3 *li.* zukur in plate et 2 *li.* drages..4*s.* 5*d.* **1390** *Earl Derby's Exp.* (Camden) 19 Pro iiij lb. sucri plat, rouge et blank. **1402–3** *Mem. Ripon* (Surtees) III. 208 Sugur en plate. *c* **1440** *Promp. Parv.* 484/1 Sukyr plate, *sucura crustalis.* **1511–12** *Durham Acc. Rolls* (Surtees) 291 Pro quinque lib. confeccionum et le suggurplatt ad 7*d.* *a* **1536** TINDALE *Expos. Matt.* vi. (*c* 1550) 73 To banket wyth dew (as they saye) of all maner of frutes & confections,..sugreplate wyth malmesaye and romneye burnte with Sugre. **1589** PUTTENHAM *Engl. Poesie* I. xxx. (Arb.) 72 Their banketting dishes of suger plate, or of march paines, and such other dainty meates. **1615** MARKHAM *Eng. Housew.* (1660) 92 To make a kind of Suger plate, take Gum Dragon, and lay it in Rose water two dayes: then take the powder of fair Heppes & Suger, and the juyce of an Orenge. **1630** BRATHWAIT *Eng. Gentlem.* (1641) 153 Physicians [make use] of sugar-plates, which they minister to their patients, to take away the taste of a more bitter potion. **1688** HOLME *Armoury* III. iii. 85/1 *Sugar plate*, is White Sugar sifted, White of Egs, Gum Dragon and Rose Water beaten into a Paste, then moulded into any form, and so Print it.

'sugar-plum. [f. SUGAR *sb.* + PLUM *sb.*]

1. A small round or oval sweetmeat, made of boiled sugar and variously flavoured and coloured; a comfit.

a **1668** DAVENANT *Wits* IV. Wks. (1673) 205 Some Comfits Sir. A mourning Citizen Will never weep without some Sugar-plums. **1673** O. WALKER *Educ.* v. 44 A sensibleness in youth for a gig or a suggar-plum, is the same afterwards for honour or interest. **1709** ADDISON *Tatler* No. 148 ¶11 Little Plates of Sugar-Plumbs, disposed like so many Heaps of Hail-stones. **1712** tr. *Pomet's Hist. Drugs* I. 2 Use it like Caraway seeds for Confects and Sugar-plums. **1828** SCOTT *Jrnl.* 3 May, Compliments flew about like sugar-plums at an Italian carnival. **1840** HOOD *Up Rhine* 197 A little while ago there were proclamations in the papers against poison-coloured sugar-plums. **1859** BOYD *Recr. Country Parson* vi. 199 Sugar-plums..damage the teeth. **1908** [MISS FOWLER] *Betw. Trent & Ancholme* 378, I can see now the sugar-plums, with wire stalks.

2. *fig.* Something very pleasing or agreeable, esp. when given as a sop or bribe.

1608 DEKKER *Lanth. & Candle-Lt.* Wks. (Grosart) III. 270 By stopping the Constables mouth with sugar-plummes (thats to say,) whilst she poisons him with sweete wordes. **1641** J. JACKSON *True Evang. T.* II. 129 With a perfumed Comfite, or a Sugar-plumbe in their mouth, that is, with a word of piety. **1738** tr. *Guazzo's Art Conv.* 70 Thus you leave them with a small sugar-plumb in their mouth. **1789** (*title*) The Sugar Plumb; or, sweet amusements for leisure hours. **1813** MRS. JACKSON in *Sir G. Jackson's Diaries & Lett.* (1873) II. 7 The little sugar-plum, in the shape of a small pension, they have put into your mouth. **1818** SCOTT *Hrt. Midl.* xxxviii, Her zeal for inquiry slaked for the present by the dexterous administration of this sugar plum. **1867** TROLLOPE *Chron. Barset* I. xxiv. 204 An artist..whom the rich English world was beginning to pet and pelt with gilt sugar-plums. **1883** READE *Many a Slip* in *Harper's Mag.* Dec. 136/2 Whilst he delivered these sugar-plums he did not look her in the face.

†**3.** *transf.* **a.** A kind of fossil. *Obs.*

1681 GREW *Musæum* III. §i. v. 296 A Great Tibuline Sugar-Plum. [Cf. *a* **1700** EVELYN *Diary* 20 June 1644, An hard stone, which hangs about like icicles, having many others in the form of comfitures and sugar plums as wee call them.]

†**b.** A kind of knotting. *Obs.*

1750 MRS. DELANY *Life & Corr.* (1861) II. 607, I cannot promise too much for you till I have finished a plain fringe I am knotting..; as soon as that is finished I will do some sugar-plum for you.

4. *attrib.* and *Comb.*, as ***sugar-plum box***; **sugar-plum chalk, land** *dial.*, land having 'a thin, short, chalky surface'.

1750 W. ELLIS *Mod. Husbandm.* VI. ii. 19, iii. 34 (E.D.S.). **1852** THACKERAY *Esmond* I. iii, Her ladyship's snuff-box and her sugar-plum box.

Hence **'sugar-plum** *v. trans.*, to reward or pacify with sweetmeats; hence, to pet, cosset.

1788 H. WALPOLE *Let. to Mrs. H. More* 22 Sept., Instead of being reprimanded (and perhaps immediately after sugar-plum'd) for not learning their Latin..grammar. **1841** *Tait's Mag.* VIII. 7 At present, pretty dear, she is coaxed and sugar-plumbed through life.

sugarro, var. SAGUARO.

sugar-roset: see ROSET *a.* 1 a.

sugar-sop ('ʃʊgəsɒp). Also 8 *Sc.* **succar-sap**, *s.w. dial.* **zugar-zop.** [f. SUGAR *sb.* + SOP *sb.*[1]]

†**1.** *pl.* A dish composed of steeped slices of bread, sweetened and sometimes spiced. Also *fig.* (Earlier †*sugared sops*: see SUGARED *ppl. a.* 1.)

1581 PETTIE tr. *Guazzo's Civ. Conv.* (1586) III. 175 Two drougs..the one of which or both, the Courtier vsing, may long time maintaine himselfe in his Princes fauour: These are abstinence, or else suger soppes. **1592** GREENE *Disput.* Wks. (Grosart) X. 277 A quart of Sugar sops. **1658** ROWLAND tr. *Moufet's Theat. Ins.* 903 You should supply them [bees] with Honey,..give grapes or figs bruised or pounded together, and sugar-sops. **1660** H. MORE *Myst. Godl.* x. xiv. 540 Being poisoned or intoxicated with the unwholsome sugar-sops of Antinomianism and Libertinism. **1663** PEPYS *Diary* 17 April, It being Good Friday, our dinner was only sugar-sopps and fish. **1671** EACHARD *Observ. Answ. Cont. Clergy* 5 Sugar-Sops and Soft Jellies. **1729** [HIPPISLEY] *Flora* I. iv. (ed. 3) 17 Come along Child, and I'll get thee a little Zugar-zops to comfort thy Bowels. *a* **1776** *Wren* in Herd *Coll. Anc. & Mod. Sc. Songs* II. 210 In came Robin Red-breast,..Wi' succar-saps and wyne.

attrib. **1742** J. YARROW *Love at first Sight* Prol., His Mouth b'ing stopt with Sugar-Sop Preferment.

2. The West-Indian Sweet-sop, *Anona squamosa.*

1847 MRS. R. LEE *Afr. Wand.* v. 67 West Indian fruits, such as the delicious cherry, the sugar sop, sour sop, &c.

'sugar-work.

†**1.** Confectionery. *Obs.*

1572 in Feuillerat *Revels Q. Eliz.* (1908) 178 Cullers for the sugerworke. **1653** *Bk. Fruits & Flowers* (title-p.) To make Powders, Civet Bagges, all sorts of sugar-works, turned workes in sugar. **1725** *Fam. Dict.*, *Sultane*, a sort of Sugar-Work.

2. *pl.* (formerly †*sing.*) A sugar factory.

1604 E. G[RIMSTONE] *D'Acosta's Hist. Indies* III. xxii. 187 The wealth of these Ilands, be their sugar-workes and hides. **1681** *Act Parl. Scot., Chas. II.* (1820) VIII. 360/2 The saids Tuo Suggar-works of Glasgow. **1722** DE FOE *Col. Jack* xix, A.. plantation, where they had an ingenio, that is to say, a sugar-house, or sugar-work. **1825** WATERTON *Wand. S. Amer.* I. 2 Higher up stand the sugar-works of Amelia's Waard. **1902** *Encycl. Brit.* XXXII. 116/1 An impetus was given to the sugar industry by the Sugar Works Guarantee Act.

sugary ('ʃʊgərɪ), *sb.* Also 7 **suggarie.** [for **sugarery*, f. SUGAR *sb.* see -ERY and cf. F. *sucrerie.*]

1. A sugar-manufactory. *Obs.* exc. as in b.

1696 *Acts Parl. Scot.*, *Will.* (1823) X. 66/2 The Manufactory of Sugar commonly called the Suggarie.

b. *U.S.* and *Canada.* A place where maple-juice is collected and boiled for the purpose of making sugar; a sugar-camp.

1840 P. H. GOSSE *Canadian Nat.* 67 We will go into the Sugary, where the men are collecting the sap from the maple-trees. **1884** *Allen's New Amer. Farm Bk.* 272 The primitive mode of arranging the sugary, is with large receiving troughs..placed near the fires.

†**2.** Sugar-manufacture. *Obs.*

1747 *State of Sugar-Trade* 6 These Computations are made upon the whole British Sugary.

sugary ('ʃʊgərɪ), *a.* Also 6 **sugerye, sugrie.** [f. SUGAR *sb.* + -Y.]

1. Full of, containing, or impregnated with sugar; pertaining to or resembling (that of) sugar; sweet, sweetened.

1597 A. M. tr. *Guillemeau's Fr. Chirurg.* 49/4 Ther is a sugerye dulcor or sweetnes extracted out of Leade. **1598** FLORIO, *Zuccheroso*,..sugrie. **1707** *Curios. Husb. & Gard.* 72 A sweet and sugary Juice. **1731** MILLER *Gard. Dict.* s.v. *Pyrus*, The Flesh is melting, and if not too ripe, of a sugary Flavour. **1830** LINDLEY *Nat. Syst. Bot.* 118 The sugary sap of Acer saccharinum..from which sugar is extracted. **1844** DISRAELI *Coningsby* I. ix. 37 The baskets of certain vendors of sugary delicacies. **1851** *Jrnl. R. Agric. Soc.* XII. I. 284 A drab-coloured, dry, 'sugary' silt. **1851** RUSKIN *Stones Venice* I. App. xx. 397 Coarse sugary marble. **1870** —— *Lect. Art* vii. 176 A crystalline or sugary frost-work. **1896** A. BEAVAN *Marlboro Ho.* v. 77 Henry..being remarkably fond of all kinds of delicate sugary cates.

2. *fig.* Deliciously or alluringly sweet; honeyed; deceitfully or flatteringly pleasant; also, excessively or offensively sweet. Also *advb.*

1591 SPENSER *M. Hubberd* 819 And with the sugrie sweete thereof allure Chast Ladies eares to fantasies impure. **1834** BECKFORD *Italy* II. 82 As I had just received a sugary epistle from this paragon of piety. **1841** L. HUNT *Seer* (1864) 27 She would not have him, notwithstanding his sugary verses. **1845** DISRAELI *Sybil* (1863) 151 'Is he very violent?' inquired her ladyship, in a sugary tone. **1855** CARLYLE *Let. to J. W. Carlyle* 2 Sept., The Dragon herself is all civility and sugary smiles. **1879** F. HARRISON *Choice of Bks.* (1886) i. 14 Sugary stanzas of ladylike prettiness. **1881** MISS BRADDON *Asphodel* II. 268 Twenty couples were revolving to the last sugary-sweet German waltz.

†**3.** Fond of sugar or sweet things. *rare.*

1664 BEALE in *Evelyn's Pomona* 22, I did once prefer the Gennet-moyl Cider, but had only the Ladies on my side, as gentler for their sugary palats.

suge(n, obs. forms of SAY *v.*[1]

sugeorne, obs. form of SOJOURN *sb.*

sugescent (s(j)uː'dʒɛsənt), *a. rare.* [f. L. *sūgĕre* to suck + -ESCENT.] Misused for: Pertaining to or adapted for sucking.

1802 PALEY *Nat. Theol.* xviii. 340 The sugescent parts of animals. **1844** PLUMMER in *Amer. Jrnl. Sci. & Arts* XLVI. 243 The pig [appeared] to be master of the sugescent art.

suget, obs. form of SUBJECT.

†**sugetable**, *a. Obs. rare.* In 4 soietable. [f. *suget*, SUBJECT *v.* + -ABLE. Cf. SUBJECTABLE.] Subject.

1382 WYCLIF *Bar.* i. 18 We wer not soietable [Vulg. *subjectibiles*] to hym.

†**sugetly**, *adv. Obs. rare.* In 5 sogetly. [f. *suget*, SUBJECT *a.* + -LY[2].] Inherently.

c **1400** *Apol. Loll.* 88 Many trowen þat ymage to be God, & many trowen Goddis vertu sogetly to be þer in.

suggan ('sʌgən, 'suːgən). Also 8 **suggin**, 9 **soo-, s(o)ugan, suggaun, -awn.** [a. Ir. *súgán.*] **a.** *Anglo-Irish.* A straw rope; a saddle. Also *attrib.* in ***suggan chair.***

1722 BP. DOWNES in Nicolson *Epist. Corr.* 556 Instead of saddles perhaps something not better than an Irish suggan. **1789** J. WHITE *Earl Strongbow* II. 89 Cadows, and brogues, and swords, and suggins. **1841** S. C. HALE *Ireland* II. 401 A stout little pig had a sougan fixed to his leg to prepare him for the road. **1888** YEATS *Fairy & Folk Tales* 133 She lulls them to rest in the low *suggaun* chair. **1922** JOYCE *Ulysses* 489 Bloom..leading a black bogoak pig by a sugaun. **1957** E. E. EVANS *Irish Folk Ways* xv. 207 When..the load is placed directly on the ass a simple 'sugan' is sometimes made—a ring of straw some fifteen inches in diameter bound with a fine straw rope. **1977** C. ROCKS in *Winter's Tales 23* 128 My da goes to his own sugan chair inside the hearth.

Comb. **1861** CLINGTON *Frank o' Donnell* 117 Two suggaun-bottomed chairs.

b. *N. Amer.* (Usu. in form **soogan, sugan** ('suːgən).) A thick blanket or padded quilt suitable for camping out.

For evidence of earlier but limited currency of this sense in Scotland see *S.N.D.*

1907 S. E. WHITE *Arizona Nights* 72 Sitting cross-legged on his 'so-gun' in the middle of the floor. **1914** *Chamb. Jrnl.* Oct. 697/2 Alvin had come into camp without a 'sugan' or blankets of his own. **1915** *Dialect Notes* IV. 245 *Soogan*,.. sheep herder's blanket. 'When they move, they just roll up the soogan and are off.' **1926** *Amer. Speech* I. 653/1 [Hobo lingo.] *Sugan*, a bed comforter. **1955** R. HOBSON *Nothing too Good for Cowboy* vii. 66 [I] saw Jimmy John shove him back into the soogans. **1974** D. SEARS *Lark in Clear Air* ii. 32 No matter how quick I turned out of my soogans I would see him up prowling around.

†**sugge.** *Obs.* [Shortening of HAYSUGGE.] The hedge-sparrow.

c **1440** *Promp. Parv.* 483/2 Sugge, bryd, *curuca, linosa* [read *linofa*]. *a* **1500** *Medulla Gram.*, *Curuca*, a sugge, a dumok [*read* dunok]. **1530** PALSGR. 278/1 Sugge a byrde. [**1847** HALLIWELL, *Segge*,..the hedge-sparrow. *Devon.*]

sugge, obs. form of SAY *v.*[1]

†**'sugger**, *v. Obs. rare.* Also 7 **-yre.** [ad. F. *suggérer*, or L. *suggerĕre* (see SUGGEST).] *trans.* To prompt, suggest.

1502 *Ord. Crysten Men* (W. de W.) IV. xxx, After as the spyryte dyabolycall them suggerneth [*sic*] in the mater of usuryes. **1606** tr. *Rollock's Lect. 2 Thess.* 52 (Jam.) The waies of the deuill that he suggyres to false teachers to deceiue men by are infinite.

†**suggeron**, *a. Sc. Obs.* Also 6 **-eorne, -eroun,** 7 **-oine.** [Cf. F. (n.e. dial.) *soco(u)ran, souc(o)rion*, †*sco(u)rion*, also OF. *secourjon*, mod. *escourgeon*,

écourgeon, †*scourgeon*, Norm. *sugrégeon* kinds of barley or wheat.] A kind of oats.

1563 in *Reg. Mag. Sig. Scot.* (1888) 65/1, 1 firl[ot] lie custume et suggeorne aittis. 1564 *Ibid.* (1886) 604/2, 2 bollas avenarum lie suggeroun aittis. 1608 *Ibid.* (1892) 125/1.

† **su'ggest,** *sb. Obs.* [ad. L. *suggestus* (*u*-stem), f. *suggest-*, *suggerĕre* to SUGGEST.] = SUGGESTION.

16.. in Rushw. *Hist. Coll.* (1659) I. App. 12 The reasons of the suggests are these, [etc.]. 1639 G. DANIEL *Ecclus.* xxvi. 73 Whose vertues countermand The loose Suggests of frailtie. 1652 C. B. STAPYLTON *Herodian* xiv. 113 By thy suggest was Abel kill'd of Cain.

suggest (sə'dʒɛst), *v.* Also 6 sugiest. [f. L. *suggest-*, pa. ppl. stem of *suggerĕre*, f. *sug-* = SUB-2 + *gerĕre* to bear, carry, bring.]

1. a. *trans.* To cause to be present to the mind as an object of thought, an idea to be acted upon, a question or problem to be solved; in early use said *esp.* of insinuating or prompting to evil. In extended application, to propose as an explanation or solution, as a course of action, as a person or thing suitable for a purpose, or the like.

1526 *Pilgr. Perf.* (W. de W. 1531) 124 b, The aungell of sathanas..euer suggestynge & mouynge some vyce, vnder the colour of vertue. 1592 SHAKS. *Ven. & Ad.* 651 Disturbing Jealousy..Gives false alarms, suggesteth mutiny. 1595 DANIEL *Civ. Wars* III. ii, Succession, conquest, and election straight Suggested are. 1603 KNOLLES *Hist. Turks* (1621) 148 These men..ceased not continually to suggest vnto him high conceits of himselfe. 1665 GLANVILL *Def. Van. Dogm.* 34 What the Gentleman himself suggests were answer sufficient. 1671 MILTON *P.R.* I. 355 Why dost thou then suggest to me distrust? 1725 DE FOE *Voy. round World* (1840) 161 A Country most remote from us..and consequently it would be suggested as unprofitable to our Commerce. 1779 *Mirror* No. 24 In the *Allegro*, meaning to excite a cheerful mood, he suggests a variety of objects. 1854 MILMAN *Lat. Christ.* III. vii. (1864) II. 156 Gregory dwells on the advantage of being thus constantly suggested to the prayers of friends. *a* 1859 MACAULAY *Hist. Eng.* xxiii. V. 90, I proposed that King James should retire to Rome or Modena. Then you suggested Avignon; and I assented. 1861 PALEY *Æschylus* (ed. 2) *Supplices* 680 *note*, The MSS. have προμαθεὺς or προμηθεύς. Dobree suggested προμαθής. 1886 BARING-GOULD *Court Royal* v, I would suggest your following me into my sanctum sanctorum. 1901 *Cycl. Tour. Club Gaz.* Oct. 389 It is difficult to suggest a remedy.

b. Said of the conscience, feelings, etc.; hence, of external things, to prompt the execution of, provide a motive for.

1583 STUBBES *Anat. Abus.* II. (1882) 93 He that hath the first diuine calling (his conscience suggesting the same vnto him). 1638 JUNIUS *Paint. Ancients* 31 A great many..have lost also the best endeavours their wit could suggest them. 1749 HARTLEY *Observ. Man* I. iii. §2. 347 The frequent making of Hypotheses..would suggest numerous Phaenomena, that otherwise escape notice. 1776 GIBBON *Decl. & F.* xvi. (1782) I. 655 Prudence suggested the necessity of a temporary retreat. 1833 H. COLERIDGE *Biogr. Borealis* 6 His poem, called 'Flecnoe, an English Priest', which is supposed to have suggested to Dryden his famous satire of McFlecnoe. 1856 STANLEY *Sinai & Pal.* xiv. (1858) 473 The sky, the flowers, the trees, the fields, which suggested the Parables. 1875 JOWETT *Plato* (ed. 2) V. 182 The punishments to be inflicted on slaves are suggested by the cruelty of fear. 1880 L. STEPHEN *Pope* iii. 77 The success of the Iliad naturally suggested an attempt upon the Odyssey.

c. Const. clause or inf.: To put forward the notion, opinion, or proposition (*that*, etc.).

1526 *Pilgr. Perf.* (W. de W. 1531) 124 b, Whan..he suggesteth or moueth to man or woman to do suche thinges that he wolde haue them to do. 1600 J. PORY tr. *Leo's Africa* 415 They suggested vnto him, that Gonsaluo was a Magician, who [etc.]. 1727 DE FOE *Syst. Magic* I. iii. (1840) 82 The honourable person..who I seemed to suggest was not to be believed. 1796 H. HUNTER tr. *St.-Pierre's Study Nat.* (1799) II. 567, I have no need to suggest, that these inscriptions might be conceived in a much happier style than mine. 1798 S. & HT. LEE *Canterb. T.* II. 125 The drawing-master..suggested how irksome it ever is to fill up the outline we delight to throw off the fancy. 1875 JOWETT *Plato* (ed. 2) I. 73 They suggest that Socrates should be invited to take part in the consultation.

d. To utter as a suggestion.

1837 DICKENS *Pickw.* xli, 'Will you take three bob?' 'And a bender', suggested the clerical gentleman. 1881 R. A. KING *Love the Debt* xix, 'I think I'd try giving her notice again, first', hesitatively suggested his feeble fellow-bachelor.

e. *refl.* Of an idea, proposition, etc.: To present itself to the mind.

1751 FIELDING *Amelia* I. III. iii. 187 The thought of going back at first suggested itself. 1801 *Farmer's Mag.* Apr. 221 No wonder the idea of emigration should suggest itself. 1861 PALEY *Æschylus* (ed. 2) *Prometh.* 379 *note*, The danger of approaching the crater in an eruption naturally suggested itself. 1898 'H. S. MERRIMAN' *Roden's Corner* x. 101 It must assuredly suggest itself to any one of us that the best method of doing this is [etc.].

†**2. a.** To prompt (a person) to evil; to tempt *to* or *to do* something; to seduce or tempt away. *Obs.*

a 1586 SIDNEY *Arcadia* III. xiii, Pamela (whom thy Maister most perniciously hath suggested out of my dominion). 1588 SHAKS. *L.L.L.* v. ii. 780 Which partie-coated presence of loose loue..Those heauenlie eies that looke into these faults Suggested vs to make. 1591 —— *Two Gent.* III. i. 34 Knowing that tender youth is soone suggested, I nightly lodge her in an vpper Towre. 1601 —— *All's well* IV. v. 47, I giue thee not this to suggest thee from thy master. 1613 —— *Hen. VIII*, I. i. 164 This holy Foxe.. suggests the King our Master To this last costly Treaty. 1643 SIR T. BROWNE *Relig. Med.* I. §37 The unquiet walkes of Devils, prompting and suggesting us unto mischiefe.

†**b.** To insinuate into (a person's mind) the (false) idea *that*, etc. *Obs.*

1607 SHAKS. *Cor.* II. i. 261 We must suggest the People, in what hatred He still hath held them. 1689 *Col. Rec. Pennsylv.* I. 297 Some persons have indeavored to suggest and insence ye minds of the good people, That the Governor had a designe.

3. To give a hint or inkling of, without plain or direct expression or explanation.

1697 DRYDEN *Virg. Georg., Ess.* Wks. 1721 I. 203 Virgil.. loves to suggest a Truth indirectly. 1858 HAWTHORNE *Fr. & It. Note-bks.* (1871) I. 121 It [*sc.* a statue] suggests far more than it shows. 1900 *Jrnl. Sch. Geog.* (U.S.) Apr. 126 Such a knowledge of society cannot be, with profit, more than suggested in the early years.

4. a. Of things: To call up the thought of by association or natural connexion of ideas.

1709 BERKELEY *Th. Vision* §25 One idea may suggest another to the mind. 1733 —— *Th. Vision Vind.* §39 All signs suggest the things signified. 1764 REID *Inquiry* ii. §7 A certain kind of sound suggests immediately to the mind, a coach passing in the street. 1859 HAWTHORNE *Transform.* xxix. 226 Such silvery ones [*sc.* clouds] as those..have often suggested sculpturesque groups, figures, and attitudes. 1864 BRYCE *Holy Rom. Emp.* xv. (1875) 255 Democratic Athens, oligarchic Rome, suggest to us Pericles and Brutus. 1894 H. DRUMMOND *Ascent of Man* 47 A process of growth suggests to the reason the work of an intelligent Mind.

b. To give the impression of the existence or presence of.

1816 A. KNOX *Rem.* (1834) I. 56 This took place..to such a degree, as to suggest strong wishes for reunion with the Roman Catholic Church. 1898 'H. S. MERRIMAN' *Roden's Corner* i. 2 With an air suggesting a desire to attract as little attention as possible.

5. *Law.* To put forward in a 'suggestion'.

1719 LILLY *Pract. Reg.* II. 537 There ought to be an Affidavit made of the Matter suggested. 1768 BLACKSTONE *Comm.* III. vii. 113 If..the court shall finally be of opinion, that the matter suggested is a good and sufficient ground of prohibition in point of law.

6. In hypnotism, to influence by suggestion.

1895 in *Funk's Stand. Dict.* 1903 F. W. H. MYERS *Human Pers.* I. 175 The man who is 'suggested' into sobriety.

7. *absol.* or *intr.* †To prompt or tempt to evil (*obs.*); to make or offer a suggestion.

1599 SHAKS. *Hen. V*, II. ii. 114 Other diuels that suggest by treasons. 1604 —— *Oth.* II. iii. 358 When diuels will the blackest sinnes put on, They do suggest at first with heauenly shewes. 1635 QUARLES *Embl.* I. i. (1718) 7 The devil may suggest, compel he cannot. 1675 MARQ. WORCESTER in *Essex Papers* (Camden) 38 We beg..that you would suggest if you can think of any other person. *a* 1721 PRIOR *Dial. Dead* (1907) 223 That sprightly way of thinking as wildly as your imagination can suggest. 1855 TENNYSON *Will* 14 Who..ever weaker grows thro' acted crime, Or seeming-genial venial fault, Recurring and suggesting still!

suggestable (sə'dʒɛstəb(ə)l), *a.* [f. SUGGEST *v.* + -ABLE.] = SUGGESTIBLE 2.

1848 *Tait's Mag.* XV. 218 There is not a new and indirect tax suggestable.

su'ggested, *ppl. a.* [f. SUGGEST *v.* + -ED[1].

The first three senses are not represented in the vb. but are derivable from senses of L. *suggere*re.]

†**1.** ? Furnished, supplied. *Obs.*

1592 *Soliman & Pers.* II. iii. 5 Loue, by whose suggested power Erastus vsde such dice, as, being false, Ran not by Fortune, but necessitie.

†**2.** (Falsely) imputed. *Obs.*

1640 G. SANDYS *Christ's Passion* 20 Whom we accuse of no suggested crimes.

†**3.** Suborned. *Obs.*

1647 LILLY *Chr. Astrol.* clxi. 678 He..will..receive Punishment..by meanes of..suggested Witnesses, or sinister Informations.

4. Proposed, prompted, insinuated.

1660 MILTON *Free Commw.* Wks. 1851 V. 424 All those suggested Fears and Difficulties..easily overcome. 1667 —— *P.L.* v. 699 Hee..Tells the suggested cause. *a* 1820 T. BROWN *Philos. Human Mind* (1820) II. xxxiii. 189 In the suggested feelings themselves, there is one striking difference. 1884 tr. *Lotze's Logic* 168 We can yet pronounce with perfect certainty that a suggested name is not the right one. 1896 *Pop. Sci. Jrnl.* L. 220 Suggested hallucinations and ideas do not differ..from spontaneous hallucinations.

Hence **su'ggestedness** (see quot.).

1802-12 BENTHAM *Ration. Judic. Evid.* (1827) I. 293 *Suggestedness*..: the quality of having been assisted by suggestions to every good purpose.

suggester (sə'dʒɛstə(r)). Also 6 -oure, 7 -our. [f. SUGGEST *v.* + -ER[1]. Cf. 16th c. F. *suggesteur*, and cf. SUGGESTOR.]

†**1.** One who imputes crime to, or brings a charge against, another. *Obs.*

1450-1530 *Myrr. our Ladye* II. 183 Consentynge to the enuyful sturrer and suggestoure. *a* 1625 FLETCHER *Bloody Brother* III. i, Some suborn'd suggester of these treasons. 1627 in Rushw. *Hist. Coll.* (1659) I. 438 King James, who.. wanted not some suggesters about him to make the worst of all mens actions whom they could misreport. 1630 BRATHWAIT *Eng. Gentlem.* (1641) 24 Whereby that base suggestour might be duely censured.

2. One who suggests or prompts.

1671 CLARENDON *Dial.* Tracts (1727) 308 If it [*sc.* age] cannot suggest all things which occur to more vigorous conceptions, it can judge better of what is suggested than the suggesters themselves. *a* 1710 BULL *Prim. Christ.* (1713) III. 885 The Spirit of God in Person is not the immediate Suggester of this Conclusion. 1844 MRS. BROWNING *Drama of Exile* 1805 Suggesters to his soul of higher things. 1893 LELAND *Mem.* I. 99, I also was the suggester, father, and founder in London of the Rabelais Club. 1903 F. W. H. MYERS *Human Pers.* I. 206 Some telepathic impact from the suggester's mind.

suggestibility (sədʒɛstɪ'bɪlɪtɪ). [f. next + -ITY.] Quality or condition of being suggestible.

1. Susceptibility to (hypnotic or other) suggestion.

1890 *Open Court* 10 Apr. 2197/2 The suggestibility of crowds. 1890 W. JAMES *Princ. Psychol.* II. xix. 97 This suggestibility is greater in the lower senses than in the higher. 1891 *Contemp. Rev.* Nov. 673 The degree of suggestibility is not necessarily proportioned to the depth of sleep. 1903 F. W. H. MYERS *Human Pers.* I. 162 What we want to effect through suggestion is increased suggestibility. 1908 W. MCDOUGALL *Introd. Social Psychol.* iv. 97 The measure of the suggestibility of any subject is, then, the readiness with which he thus accepts propositions. Of course, the proposition is not necessarily communicated in formal language, it may be implied by a mere gesture or interjection. 1924 W. B. SELBIE *Psychol. Religion* iv. 87 Such cases are generally those of persons in a high condition of suggestibility, and it often happens that suggestions do not become active..until they have..incubated in the unconscious realm. 1962 L. DEIGHTON *Ipcress File* 224 Tricayandamino-propene..can change brain's nerve cells and cells of membrane that sheath the cells... From this change the suggestibility of the subject is increased. 1972 *Jrnl. Social Psychol.* LXXXVI. 11 He demonstrated the importance of motivational and experiential factors in determining suggestibility.

2. Capability of being suggested.

In mod. Dicts.

suggestible (sə'dʒɛstɪb(ə)l), *a.* [f. SUGGEST *v.* + -IBLE.]

1. Capable of being influenced by (hypnotic or other) suggestion.

1890 *Open Court* 10 Apr. 2197/2 Great masses of people are for several reasons extremely suggestible. 1891 *Monist* I. 627 She is..extremely suggestible, and very easily hypnotised. 1898 A. LANG *Making Relig.* iii. 61 Known savages..are more 'suggestible' than educated Europeans. 1903 W. JAMES in *Harvard Monthly* Mar. 6 There is no test ..by which, if a title or decoration, a public badge or mark, were to be won by it, some weakly suggestible or hauntable persons would not feel challenged. 1908 W. MCDOUGALL *Introd. Social Psychol.* iv. 100 Children are..inevitably suggestible..because of their lack of knowledge and lack of systematic organisation of such knowledge as they have. 1921 *Discovery* Nov. 294/1 Children are more suggestible than grown persons, and women are more suggestible than men. 1955 *Times* 17 May 3/3 Orchestras being suggestible by professional training cannot wholly eliminate from their playing the implications of a conductor's gestures. 1981 F. HOYLE *Ice* ii. 39 He is very suggestible; if he is told he is stupid, he thinks he is stupid and behaves accordingly.

2. That can be suggested.

1905 W. H. MALLOCK *Reconstr. Belief* II. vii. 134 That civilised human life loses all meaning without it [*sc.* the religion of theism], and that no suggestible substitute is able to take its place.

su'ggesting, *vbl. sb.* [-ING[1].] The action of the vb. SUGGEST; an instance of this, a suggestion.

1677 GILPIN *Dæmonol.* (1867) 412 The same art of wresting Scripture is observable in his secret suggestings.

b. *attrib.*, as ***suggesting power***.

1828 J. BALLANTYNE *Exam. Human Mind* ii. §2. 91 Ideas may be greatly aided in their suggesting power by others which coexist with them.

su'ggesting, *ppl. a.* [-ING[2].] That suggests; †prompting to evil, tempting.

1591 SHAKS. *Two Gent.* II. vi. 7 O sweet-suggesting Loue, if thou hast sin'd, Teach me (thy tempted subiect) to excuse it. 1828 J. BALLANTYNE *Exam. Human Mind* II. §10. 139 If the suggesting idea be stationary, the one suggested must be stationary.

Hence **su'ggestingly** *adv.*, in a suggesting manner.

1840 *Tait's Mag.* VII. 126 'For which papa has no manner of use'..said Miss Cripps, looking at papa, suggestingly.

suggestio falsi (sə'dʒɛstɪəʊ 'fælsaɪ). Pl. **suggestiones falsi.** [mod.L., = suggestion of what is false.] A misrepresentation of the truth whereby something incorrect is implied to be true; an indirect lie. Often in contexts with SUPPRESSIO VERI.

1815 H. MADDOCK *Princ. & Pract. Chancery* I. 208 Whenever *Suppressio veri* or *Suggestio falsi* occur..they afford a sufficient ground for setting aside any Release or Conveyance. 1855 *Newspaper & Gen. Reader's Pocket Compan.* I. 4 He was bound to say that the *suppressio veri* on that occasion approached very nearly to a positive *suggestio falsi*. 1898 KIPLING *Stalky & Co.* (1899) 36 It seems..that they had held back material facts; that they were guilty both of *suppressio veri* and *suggestio falsi*. 1907 W. DE MORGAN *Alice-for-Short* xxxvi. 389 That's suppressio veri and suggestio falsi! Besides, it's fibs! 1962 J. WILSON *Public Schools & Private Practice* i. 19 It is rare to find a positively verifiable untruth in a school brochure: but it is equally rare not to find a great many *suggestiones falsi*, particularly as regards the material comfort and facilities available. 1980 D. NEWSOME *On Edge of Paradise* 7 There are undoubted cases of *suppressio veri*; on the other hand, he appears to eschew *suggestio falsi*.

suggestion (sə'dʒɛstjən, -tʃən). Forms: 4-5 **suggestyun, -tione, -tioun, soggestioun,** 4-6 **suggestyon,** (4, *Sc.* 6 **sugestioun,** 5 **sugiestion, -tyoun,** 6 **suggesteon**), 4- **suggestion.** See also SUBJESTION (cf. OF. *subjestion*). [a. AF., OF. *suggestioun* (mod.F. *suggestion*), = Pr. *suggestio*,

It. *suggestione*, Sp. *sugestion*, Pg. *suggestão*, ad. L. *suggestio*, *-ōnem*, n. of action f. *suggerĕre* to SUGGEST.]

†**1. a.** Prompting or incitement to evil; an instance of this, a temptation of the evil one. *Obs.*

a **1340** HAMPOLE *Psalter* xxiv. 2 þof þai waite nyght and daye with ill suggestions to till me til syn. *c* **1386** CHAUCER *Pars. T.* ¶331 Deedly synne hath first suggestion of the feend. *c* **1440** *Gesta Rom.* lxvi. 303 (Harl. MS.) Tribulacion of þe wordle, temptacion of flesh, and sugiestion of þe devill. *c* **1460** *Wisdom* 497 in *Macro Plays* 52 *Mynde.* To þis suggestyon a-gre we. *Wndyrstondynge.* Delyght þer-In, I haue truly. *Wyll.* And I consent þer-to frelye. **1526** *Pilgr. Perf.* (W. de W. 1531) 124 b, As longe as the mynde is not moued by yᵉ false suggestyon.. there is the lesse ieopardy: as wele whan he fayneth ony thynge by suggestyon that is good, or [etc.]. **1588** A. KING tr. *Canisius' Catech.* 127 Be thrie degreis men principallie cummis to sinne, be suggestion, delectation, and consent. **1595** SHAKS. *John* III. i. 292 Then arme thy constant and thy nobler parts Against these giddy loose suggestions. **1620** T. GRANGER *Div. Logike* 227 That which is spoken, and done by Satanicall Suggestion. **1667** MILTON *P.L.* III. 129 The first sort by thir own suggestion fell, Self-tempted, self-deprav'd.

†**b.** In extended sense: A prompting from within, (hence) intention. *Obs.*

1362 LANGL. *P. Pl.* A. VIII. 69, Bidders and Beggers Beoþ not in þe Bulle, Bote þe suggestion be soþ þat schapeþ hem to Begge. *c* **1550** BALE *K. Johan* (Manly) 963 His suggesteon was to subdew the Yrysh men.

2. a. The action of prompting one to a particular action or course of action; the putting into the mind of an idea, an object of thought, a plan, or the like; an instance of this, an idea or thought suggested, a proposal.

1382 WYCLIF *Gen.* xl. 14 That thow make suggestioun to Pharao, that he lede me out of this prisoun. *c* **1400** LOVE *Bonavent. Mirr.* xlvii, At this suggestioun of John, oure lady ..wolde no lenger letten his buryinge. *c* **1450** *Godstow Reg.* 400 Brefis were directed to hym at the suggestion of the abbesse of Godestowe. **1522** SKELTON *Why not to Court* 1200 Some men myght aske a question, By whose suggestyon I toke on hand this warke, Thus boldly for to barke? **1590** SWINBURNE *Test.* 264 The later testament doth not take away the former, the later being made at the interrogation or suggestion of some other person. **1611** *Bible* 2 Macc. vi. 8 There went out a decree.., by the suggestion of Ptolomee, against the Iewes. **1646** SIR T. BROWNE *Pseud. Ep.* I. v. 18 We are unready to put in execution the suggestions or dictates of reason. **1671** MILTON *Samson* 599 Believe not these suggestions which proceed From anguish of the mind. **1728** CHAMBERS *Cycl.* s.v., A Testament is said to be made by Suggestion, when 'tis made by Surprize, and contrary to the Intention of the Testator. **1736** FRANKLIN *Ess.* Wks. 1840 II. 74 America was not heard of, nor so much as a suggestion in the minds of men that any part of the world lay that way. **1748** MELMOTH *Fitzosborne Lett.* lvi. (1749) II. 78 The wild suggestions of an heated imagination. **1838** JAMES *Robber* ii, Did you not solemnly swear to her to follow my suggestions? **1842** MISS MITFORD in L'Estrange *Life* (1870) III. ix. 169 At the suggestion of friends a subscription was raised. **1876** J. PARKER *Paracl.* II. xviii. 342 Any suggestion to the effect that theology is hostile to science is a lie. **1886** G. ALLEN *Darwin* ii. 25 Erasmus Darwin gave us brilliant suggestions rather than cumulative proof.

†**b.** A foreboding, apprehension. *Obs. rare.*

1748 *Anson's Voy.* II. xi. 257 These gloomy suggestions were soon happily ended.

c. *Hypnotism.* The insinuation of a belief or impulse into the mind of a subject by words, gestures, or the like; the impulse or idea thus suggested.

1887 *Brit. Med. Jrnl.* 12 Mar. 595/2 MM. Fontan and Segard communicated several cases of cure by suggestion. **1892** *19th Cent.* Jan. 24 Proceedings by which Sarchas.. gave sight to the blind..were essentially methods of what we should now call 'suggestion'. **1903** F. W. H. MYERS *Human Pers.* I. p. xxxv, I define suggestion as 'successful appeal to the subliminal self'.

†**3.** The act of making a false or suborned statement or supplying underhand information; an instance of this, a false representation or charge. Often *false suggestion* (= AF. *fause suggestioun*, Britton). *Obs.*

c **1375** *Sc. Leg. Saints* xxxi. (*Eugenia*) 408 þe wikit wyf of putefere,..gert hyme be tane falsely & haldine lang in-to preson thru hyr wikit suggestione. *c* **1380** WYCLIF *Sel. Wks.* III. 216 þis appropringe is geten bi fals suggestion maad to Anticrist. *c* **1386** CHAUCER *Monk's T.* 427 Roger, which þat Bisshope was of Pize, Hadde on hym maad a fals suggestion. **1387** TREVISA *Higden* (Rolls) III. 153 þe Samaritans..lette hire work with sugestiouns and wiþ ȝiftes. **1460** CAPGRAVE *Chron.* (Rolls) 289 Fals suggestiones, by whech many men were disherid of her londis. *a* **1548** HALL *Chron., Hen. VIII*, 194 b, This Cardinall [*sc.* Wolsey]..by craftye suggestion gatte into his handes innumerable treasure. **1552** EDW. VI *Jrnl.* (Roxb. Club) II. 423 Whalley..confessed..how in his accoumptes he had made many false suggestions. **1576** FLEMING *Panopl. Epist.* 235 Thou diddest vse all the suggestions that euer thou couldest inuent..to make them take weapon in hande againste mee. **1592** KYD *Sp. Trag.* III. i. 46 So am I free from this suggestion [of murder]. *Ibid.* 84 The hopeles life which thou..sought By thy suggestions to have massacred. [**1620** J. WILKINSON *Coroners & Sherifes* 2 If any of these causes be untrue, and the Coroner therby discharged of his office by a false suggestion.]

4. *Law.* An information not upon oath.

suggestion upon record: an information drawn in writing showing cause for a prohibition to a suit.

1485 *Rolls of Parlt.* VI. 292/2 The said Thomas..was committed to the Tower..by the comaundement of Edward the IIIIth..uppon a Suggestion and Ympeachment made to hym, that [etc.]. **1548** *Act 2 & 3 Edw. VI*, c. 13 §14 Under the Copie of the saide lybell shalbe written the Suggestyon wherefore the partie soe demaundeth the saide Prohibicion. **1651** tr. *Kitchin's Courts Leet* (1653) 297 Where a Grant of the King is not only of his meere motion, but also of suggestion, there, if any part of the suggestion bee not true, the whole Grant is voyd. **1768** BLACKSTONE *Comm.* III. 113 The party..applies to the superior court, setting forth in a suggestion upon record the nature and cause of his complaint. **1769** *Ibid.* IV. xxiii. 305 This mode of prosecution, by information (or suggestion) filed on record by the king's attorney general. **1835** *Tomlins' Law-Dict.* s.v., There are suggestions in replevin for a *returno habendo*, which, it is said, are not traversable. **1852** *Act 15 & 16 Vict.* c. 76 §191 In case the Right of the deceased Claimant shall survive to another Claimant, a Suggestion may be made of the Death, which Suggestion shall not be traversable.

5. The process by which an idea brings to the mind another idea by association or natural connexion.

For the specific uses in the philosophical terminology of Reid and T. Brown, see quots. 1764, *a* 1820, 1875.

1605 BACON *Adv. Learn.* II. 52 b, The other part of Invention, which I terme Svggestion, doth assigne and direct vs to certaine Markes or Places, which may excite our Minde to returne and produce such Knowledge, as it hath formerly collected. **1764** REID *Inquiry* ii. §7, I beg leave to make use of the word *suggestion*, because I know not one more proper, to express a power of the mind..to which we owe many of our simple notions which are neither impressions nor ideas, as well as many original principles of belief. *a* **1820** T. BROWN *Philos. Human Mind* (1820) II. xxxiii. 190 There is..in the mind, a capacity of association; or as..I would rather term it,—the capacity of Simple Suggestion,—by which feelings, formerly existing, are revived,..as there is also a capacity of feeling resemblance, ..or relation in general,..which mental capacity, in distinction from the former, I would term the capacity of Relative Suggestion. **1868** LOWELL *Among my Bks., Shaks. once more* Ser. I. (1870) 177 It is by suggestion, not cumulation, that profound impressions are made upon the imagination. **1875** *Encycl. Brit.* II. 732/1 [Brown] preferred the word Suggestion to Association, which seemed to him to imply some prior connecting process, whereof there was no evidence in many of the most important cases of suggestion.

6. An indication of the presence or existence (*of* something); a hint, an inkling.

1863 GEO. ELIOT *Romola* I. v, A faint suggestion of weariness struggling with habitual patience. **1879** ROOD *Mod. Chrom.* v. 60 Pure grey or bluish-grey without any suggestion of green. **1898** 'H. S. MERRIMAN' *Roden's Corner* iv. 36 His presence had no suggestion of strength.

¶**7.** Misused for SUBJECTION (sense 1 b). For the reverse see SUBJECTION ¶12.

a **1400** *Ipomedon* (Kölbing) 323 All the lordes aboute him were vndre his suggestion and did him homage.

8. *attrib.*: **suggestion-book, box**, a book, box in which are put written suggestions containing proposals for the alteration or improvement of the administration of an establishment, or the like.

1882 Suggestion Book (Bodleian Library). **1907** *Daily Chron.* 20 July 6/7 A 'suggestion box,' into which any worker may drop a suggestion for the increased comfort of the staff. **1931** W. HOLTBY *Poor Caroline* iv. 113, I put it down in the suggestion-book six weeks ago. **1967** V. GIELGUD *Conduct of Member* i. 11 The Suggestion Book of the Fonthill Club was much like others of its kind. Its contents..dealt with the apparent shortcomings of the House Committee.

su'ggestionable, *a. rare.* [f. prec. + -ABLE.] = SUGGESTIBLE 1. Hence **su,ggestiona'bility** = SUGGESTIBILITY 1.

1890 *Pall Mall Gaz.* 13 May 6/3 The rotation of brilliant surfaces produces in predisposed subjects a particular state of the retina..accompanied with anæsthesia, immobility of the muscles, 'suggestionability'. **1892** *Ibid.* 15 Dec. 2/1 The subject was no longer suggestionable.

su'ggestionism. [f. SUGGESTION + -ISM.] The doctrine or practice of hypnotic suggestion. Hence **su'ggestionist**, one who advocates or practises suggestion; one who treats disease by suggestion; also *attrib.*; **su'ggestionize** *v. trans.*, to influence or treat by suggestion.

1892 *Athenæum* 2 July 17/3 In order to combat materialism it calls to its aid hypnotism, '*suggestionism', or even spiritualism. **1896** *Cosmopolitan* XX. 369/1 Doctor Liebault has good claims to be regarded as the founder of the '*suggestionist school'. **1903** F. W. H. MYERS *Human Pers.* I. 206 To the pure suggestionist, monotonous stimulation and mesmeric passes are alike—mere facilitations of suggestion. **1896** *Daily News* 17 Feb. 6/5 A yelling mob, *suggestionised to the pitch of frenzy.

suggestive (sə'dʒɛstɪv), *a.* [ad. L. **suggestīvus*, f. *suggest-*: see SUGGEST *v.* and -IVE. Cf. It. *soggestivo*, Pg. *suggestivo*; F. *suggestif* is from Eng.]

†**1.** *Law.* Resting upon a 'suggestion' or information: see SUGGESTION 4. *Obs.*

16.. in W. Prynne *Abridgem. Rec. Tower London* (1657) 15 That no pardon be granted to any outlawed by any suggestive means, but only by Parliament. [See *Rolls of Parlt.* II. 376/1.]

2. a. Calculated or fitted to suggest thoughts, ideas, a course of action, etc.; conveying a suggestion or hint; implying something that is not directly expressed.

1631 WEEVER *Anc. Funeral Mon.* 501 A Nunne..by sundrie suggestiue reuelations gaue out, that..he should not raigne. **1828** WHATELY *Rhetoric* in *Encycl. Metrop.* (1845) I. 284/1 The Suggestive kind of writing we are speaking of. **1856** *N. Brit. Rev.* XXVI. 208 Some thoughtful and suggestive chapters by M. de Remusat. **1856** FROUDE *Hist. Eng.* II. 35 It is a living language, pregnant and suggestive. **1884** *Christ. Commw.* 21 Feb. 448/2 It is a suggestive fact that the first thing the Apostle Peter commands us to add to our faith, is courage.

b. Const. *of* that which is suggested.

1850 T. T. LYNCH *Theoph. Trinal* vii. 134 Beautiful things are suggestive of a higher and purer life. **1878** BOSW. SMITH *Carthage* 413 Rough grass, acres of beans and barley, and ploughed fields do not delight the eye, they are not naturally suggestive of anything beyond themselves. **1880** GEIKIE *Phys. Geog.* iv. 165 An observant eye cannot fail to notice much that is suggestive of inquiry.

c. Of a thinker or writer.

1846 DICKENS *Let.* 5 Oct. (1977) IV. 629, I shall have the greatest satisfaction..in putting you in communication with two or three gentlemen who I am sure will be most valuable, willing, and suggestive advisers. **1857** SMILES *Stephenson* (1859) 49 He was a good talker..and a very suggestive thinker. **1875** E. WHITE *Life in Christ* III. xxii. (1878) 324 The critical basis on which this suggestive author builds his hope of the 'Destiny of the Race'.

d. *euphem.* Apt to suggest something indecent.

1888 [implied at SUGGESTIVENESS]. **1889** GUNTER *That Frenchman* xi. 128 Her incomparable drolleries and naughtinesses, in some suggestive opera bouffe, some musical debauch. **1895** C. D. WARNER *Golden House* iii. 24 Her judges were cosmopolitans who had seen the most suggestive dancing in all parts of the world. **1924** R. MACAULAY *Orphan Island* xiv. 182 There were complaints, too, of fashions in dress, which, on the part of the younger females, were becoming immodest and suggestive. **1926** T. DREISER *Amer. Tragedy* I. xviii. 132 They..lay there laughing and yet in a most suggestive position. **1978** L. MEYNELL *Papersnake* iii. 51 Mabel, archpriestess of the art of suggestive repartee.

3. Of a method, plan, etc.: That suggests itself.

1806 P. COLQUHOUN (*title*) Treatise on the Police of the Metropolis, containing a Detail of the various Crimes and Misdemeanours, and Suggestive Remedies. **1863** COWDEN CLARKE *Shaks. Char.* vii. 190 No plan was so suggestive as that of quenching his sight.

4. Pertaining to hypnotic suggestion.

1903 F. W. H. MYERS *Human Pers.* I. 154 The suggestive or hypnotic induction of supernormal powers.

Hence **su'ggestively** *adv.*, in a suggestive manner; in the way of suggestion; so as to suggest something.

1859 RUSKIN *Two Paths* v. §141 The subject is..too wide to be more than suggestively treated. **1884** *Harper's Mag.* Oct. 744/2 'If there *was* any one that hed money to spare,' one added, suggestively. **1891** W. CLARK RUSSELL *Curatica* 20 My old schoolmaster..with his right arm suggestively withdrawn behind his back, as though he were hiding some deadly weapon of offence.

suggestiveness (sə'dʒɛstɪvnɪs). [f. prec. + -NESS.] The quality of being suggestive.

1846 RUSKIN *Mod. Paint.* II. III. II. iii. §15 There is not the commonest subject to which he will not attach a range of suggestiveness almost limitless. **1875** WHITNEY *Life Lang.* viii. 141 The etymological suggestiveness of a term. **1880** H. JAMES *Madonna of Future* 17 Think..of the mother's face and its ineffable suggestiveness. **1888** M. S. VAN DE VELDE *Random Recollections of Courts & Society* x. 252 Some foreigners..wondered at the excessive licence she permitted herself on the English stage, and the marked suggestiveness of her looks and gestures. **1913** MRS. BELLOC LOWNDES *Diary* 7 Jan. (1971) 42 We talked of English prudery, and.. of *The Rosary* and its wonderful success, and I said I felt sure this was owing to the suggestiveness of certain scenes. **1963** L. DEIGHTON *Horse under Water* xxiii. 100, I noticed Singleton's lip curl..at H. K.'s suggestiveness.

So **sugge'stivity**. *rare.*

1842 THACKERAY *Miss Tickletoby's Lect.* i, Taking down rather the heads and the suggestivity (if we may use the phrase) of Miss Tickletoby's discourse.

suggestment (sə'dʒɛstmənt). *rare.* [f. SUGGEST *v.* + -MENT.] Suggestion.

1827 HARE *Guesses* (1859) 54 They fancy that every thought must needs have an immediate outward suggestment.

suggestology (sʌdʒɛ'stɒlədʒɪ). [f. SUGGEST *v.* + -OLOGY.] The study of suggestion, a branch of parapsychology originated by a Bulgarian, Dr. Georgi Lozanov. Similarly **suggesto'paedia**, **sugge'stopedy** [Gr. παιδεία education], the application of suggestology to education, teaching by suggestion.

1970 OSTRANDER & SCHROEDER *Psychic Discoveries behind Iron Curtain* xxii. 293 With suggestopaedia the Bulgarians have expanded time in a very real sense, teaching you in a minute what usually takes many weeks to learn. **1970** *New Society* 31 Dec. 1155/1 This conference is called an 'International Symposium on the Problems of Suggestology'... Among the listed attractions is a visit to the research centre of suggestology in Sofia. **1973** OSTRANDER & SCHROEDER *Psi* xxii. 293 Suggestology is *not* hypnosis. With suggestology you are always in the waking state and aware of everything around you. **1978** HALL-POZHARLIEVA & PASHMAKOVA tr. *Lozanov's Suggestology & Outl. of Suggestopedy* i. 1 Suggestology, the science of suggestion, and its concomitant penetration into pedagogy, suggestopedy, is a newly developing science. **1980** *San Francisco Bay Guardian* 16–23 Oct. 30 (Advt.), Hypnosis/Self-Hypnosis with Dr. Leonard Elkind. Weight. Smoking. Autogenics. Suggestology. Self-Improvement.

su'ggestor. [f. SUGGEST *v.* + -OR. Cf. med.L. *suggestor*.] **a.** = SUGGESTER. ? *Obs.*

1591 LAMBARDE *Archeion* (1635) 114 That such false Suggestors should be imprisoned onely. **1609** T. MORTON *Answ. to Higgons* 27 This opinion..had some suggestors. **1678** CUDWORTH *Intell. Syst.* 137 As this is a mere.. hypothesis,..so the suggestors of it are but mere novices in atheism. **1796** MORSE *Amer. Geog.* I. 332 *note*, Having been ..a principal suggestor of the terms to be offered to France. **1818** HALLAM *Mid. Ages* viii. III. (1819) III. 249 *note*, It is enacted that in every charter of pardon, granted at any one's suggestion, the suggestor's name, and the grounds of his suggestion shall be expressed.

b. *spec.* An employee who submits a practical suggestion for improving working methods, increasing productivity, or the like. *U.S.*

1957 J. L. LUNDY *Effective Industr. Managem.* xii. 198 The suggestors..keep their numbered stubs and use them to claim the awards, which..are posted according to the suggestion number. **1977** *Washington Post* 27 Jan. B2/2 In the suggestion, duly made out on GSA Form 405..the suggestor lists the job title and says: 'Position is unnecessary [etc.].' **1980** *Amer. Banker* 20 Oct. 26/2 A minicomputer.. prepares a status report every 30 days for the suggestor,.. and sends evaluators letters reminding them to act on the suggestions. **1984** *N.Y. Times* 4 Mar. Sect. 22WC. 3/3 What we want..is to create a reservoir of thinkers and suggestors.

suggestour(e, obs. ff. SUGGESTER.

suggestress (səˈdʒɛstrɪs). [f. SUGGESTER + -ESS.] A female suggester.

1845 DE QUINCEY *Suspiria de Profundis* Wks. 1871 XVI. 30 The mother of lunacies, and the suggestress of suicides.

‖**suggestum** (səˈdʒɛstəm). Pl. **-a** (**-ums**). [L. *suggestum*, f. *suggest-*, *suggerĕre* to SUGGEST.] A platform, stage, tribune.

1705 ADDISON *Italy* 127 The ancient Suggestums, as I have often observ'd on Medals, as well as on Constantine's Arch, were made of Wood, like a little kind of Stage. **1772** GRAVES *Spir. Quix.* (1783) III. 91 Wildgoose..took the opportunity of mounting the suggestum (or horse-block) once more. **1859** J. C. HOBHOUSE *Italy* II. 112 Not far from the base of the still remaining suggestum, by the Arch of Severus.

'**sugging,** *ppl. a. dial.* [f. SUG *v.*] Soaking.

1733 W. ELLIS *Chiltern & Vale Farm.* 314 The Land.. thereby can better discharge the sugging Wets.

†**sugh,** *v. Obs.* Forms: 3 **suhhȝhenn** (*Ormin*), **sugge, suwie,** 4 **soghe,** 5 **sugh, sewe.** [Prob. an onomatopœic formation; cf. SOUGH *v.*[1]]

1. *intr.* To sigh.

c **1200** ORMIN 7924 Forr iwhillc mann birrþ wepenn her, & sikenn sare & suhhȝhenn. *c* **1220** *Bestiary* in *Rel. Ant.* I. 224 He suggeden and sorȝeden. **14..** *R. Glouc. Chron.* 6966 (MS. β) He sewede [*MS.* γ sighede] ful sore. *c* **1475** *Partenay* 5024 Raymounde..At the departson sughed sore in breste. [Cf. 1944 sowghid, 6164 sogheth.]

2. *impers.* To be distressing.

a **1225** *Ancr. R.* 306, & hat þet seoruwe þreosche him wiðinne þe heorte mid sore bireousunge, so þet him [*MS. Vernon* hire] suwie, & pinie þet flesch..mid festen. **13..** *E.E. Allit. P.* C. 391 He..Sesez childer of her sok, soghe hem so neuer.

Hence †**sughend** (**suwinde**) *ppl. a.*, distressing, painful.

a **1225** *Ancr. R.* 428 More of þe softe eolie þen of þe bitinde wine; þet is, more of liðe wordes þen of suwinde.

sugh: see SEE *v.*, SHEUGH, SOUGH.

sugi (ˈsuːgɪ). Also 8 **ssugi, suggi.** [Jap.] = CRYPTOMERIA.

1727 [see HINOKI]. **1795** tr. *C. P. Thunberg's Trav.* (ed. 2) III. 123 Ssugi signifies Cedar wood. **1876** *Trans. Asiatic Soc. Japan* IV. 53 One piece of *sugi* of 6 by 3 by 0·4 ft. **1916** E. H. WILSON *Conifers & Taxads of Japan* 69 The Cryptomeria, or Sugi as it is called in Japan, is the noblest of the Japanese conifers. **1954** [see *Japanese cedar* s.v. JAPANESE *a.* b]. **1970** J. KIRKUP *Japan behind Fan* iv. 137 A bus took me on the long winding road, through groves of immense *sugi* or Japanese cedar.

†'**sugill,** '**suggill,** *v. Obs. rare.* [ad. L. *sūgillāre*, *suggillāre*, of doubtful etym. Cf. F. *sugiller.*]

1. *trans.* To beat black and blue, bruise.

1663 BUTLER *Hud.* I. iii. 1039 Though we with blacks and blews are suggil'd.

2. To defame, revile.

1539–40 ABP. PARKER in Strype *Life* (1711) App. 7 To allure the Peoples Minds..to ourselves, with depraving, sugilling, and noting the other. **1561** *Ibid.* 30 This contemptible flock, that wil not shrink to offer their Blood for the defence of Christ's verity, if it be openly impugned, or secretly suggilled.

sugillate, suggillate (ˈs(j)uːdʒɪleɪt, ˈsʌdʒ-), *v.* Now *rare* or *Obs.* [f. L. *sūgillāt-*, *sugg-*, pa. ppl. stem of *sūgillāre* (see prec.).]

1. *trans.* = prec. 1. Chiefly *Med.* in *pa. pple.*, marked with livid spots or patches, bruised.

1623 COCKERAM, *Sugillate*, to beat blacke and blew. **1676** WISEMAN *Chirurg. Treat.* VII. iv. 485 The head of the *Os humeri* was bruised, and remained sugillated long after. **1684** tr. *Bonet's Merc. Compit.* x. 368, I found all whole, onely about the podex all was sugillated. **1859** MAYNE *Expos. Lex.*, *Sugillatus*, having or pertaining to sugillation: sugillated.

†**2.** = prec. 2. *Obs.*

1647 TRAPP *Comm. Acts* xxi. 28 Arminius paved his way first by aspersing and sugillating the fame and authority of Calvin.

†**sugi'llation**[1]. *Obs.* [f. L. *sūgĕre* to suck, with termination from *sūgillātio* (see next).] = SUCKING *vbl. sb.* 1 b, SUCTION 1 c.

1528 PAYNELL *Salerne's Regim.* (1541) D iij b, By sugillation [orig. L. *suctione*] of the membres nedynge meate.

sugillation[2], **suggillation** (s(j)uːdʒɪˈleɪʃən, sʌdʒ-). [ad. L. *sūgillātio*, *-ōnem*, *sugg-*, n. of action f. *sūgillāre* (see SUGILL). So F.]

1. †Beating black and blue (*obs.*); *Med.* a livid or black-and-blue mark; a bruise; ecchymosis.

1623 COCKERAM, *Sugillation*, a beating blacke and blew. **1634** T. JOHNSON *Parey's Chirurg.* XII. i. (1678) 293 There are divers sorts of these Sugillations or blacknesses. **1656** BLOUNT *Glossogr.*, *Sugillation*,..the blood-shot of an eye. **1684** tr. *Bonet's Merc. Compit.* v. 139 A Cataplasm, often in one night, takes away the Sugillation. **1743** tr. *Heister's Surg.* (1768) 105 Red, black, and livid Spots, which we call a Sugillation. **1836–7** *Lancet* II. 181/2 Sugillation coming on after death is always confined to a dependent part. **1859** MAYNE *Expos. Lex.*, *Sugillation*, term for the mark left by a leech, or cupping-glass; also, for those livid spots of various size noticed on dead bodies.

†**2.** Defamation. *Obs. rare*[−1].

1654 WARREN *Unbelievers* c ij b, In this suggillation of his, to make his brethren odious. **1656** BLOUNT *Glossogr.*, *Sugillation*,..reproach, slander.

sugke, obs. form of SUCK *v.*

†**sugratife,** *a. Obs. rare.* [app. f. med.L. *suguratus* (see next) + -IVE.] = next.

1509 HAWES *Past. Pleas.* VIII. iii, They were so wyse and so inventife, Theyr obscure reason, fayre and sugratife.

†**sugurat,** *a. Sc. Obs.* Also 6 **suggurait, sugarat.** [ad. med. Anglo-L. *suguratus*: see SUGAR and -ATE[2].] Sweet, 'honeyed': = SUGARED 2.

1501 DOUGLAS *Pal. Hon.* I. xxxi, Quhat sweit vocis? Quhat wordis suggurait? **1508** DUNBAR *Tua Mariit Wemen* 7 The sugarat sound of hir sang glaid. **1513** DOUGLAS *Æneis* I. Prol. 29 Thi scharp sugurat sang Virgiliane.

sugyner, obs. form of SOJOURNER.

c **1460** *Promp. Parv.* (Winch. MS.) 449 Sugyner, or a comynere, *commensalis.*

suh (sʌ), chiefly *U.S. Southern* and *Black* pronunc. of SIR *sb.* Cf. SAH.

1894 KIPLING *Day's Work* (1898) 50 Most of your prominent siahs, suh, are impo'ted from Kentucky. **1901** W. CHURCHILL *Crisis* I. iv. 38 'T'ank you, Mistah Cantah,' wailed the poor woman, 't'ank you, suh... De Lawd Jesus'll rewa'd you, suh.' **1911** [see HIDE *v.*[1] 2 c]. **1929** W. FAULKNER *Sartoris* II. 117 'Come on here and get in,' he commanded. 'Naw, suh. I'll walk.' **1940** H. G. WELLS *Babes in Darkling Wood* III. ii. 252 Cutting facts dead unless they wear the old school tie! 'Don't know you, suh.' **1971** *Black Scholar* Sept. 38/2 'Yes suh, officer,' she replied.

Suhaili, -eli, variants of SWAHILI.

Sui (sweɪ). Also **Suy, Swi.** [Chinese *sui.*] The name of a dynasty which ruled in China from 581 to 618 A.D. and re-unified the country after the divisions of the Northern and Southern Dynasties period. Freq. *attrib.*

1738 J. B. DU HALDE *Descript. China & Chinese Tartary* I. 194 Thus ended the Dynasty nam'd Swi, the last of five petty ones. **1797** *Encycl. Brit.* IV. 653/1 The whole of their [*sc.* China's] emperors..are comprehended in 22 dynasties, mentioned in the following table..Chin..Swi..Twang [etc.]. **1845** *Encycl. Metrop.* XVI. 550/1 The tower of Kao-ming-chi, with its gardens, temple and pavilions, erected by Kao-tsu of the Swi dynasty. **1897** J. MACGOWAN *Hist. China* xix. 261 Yang-Kien was forty-eight years old when he became Emperor... He gave his dynasty the name of Sui. **1910** *Encycl. Brit.* VI. 195/2 This period of disorder was brought to a close by the establishment of the Suy dynasty. **1958** W. WILLETTS *Chinese Art* I. v. 310 We are concerned only with the Sui and the first four reigns of the T'ang... The Sui Emperors were great patrons of Buddhism. **1969** *Guardian* 2 July 3/2 A 15-inch terra cotta horse of the Sui period (seventh century AD), is offered for £6,000. **1972** *Trans. Oriental Ceramics Soc.* XXXVIII. 29 Much that is ascribed to Sui..should be placed in the opening generations of T'ang. **1979** A. HENNING tr. *Myrdal's Silk Road* (1980) i. 11 Tashkent was known during the Sui dynasty.

‖**suiboku** (ˈsuibokuː). [Jap., lit. 'liquefied ink', f. *sui* water + *boku* ink stick.] A style of Japanese painting in black ink on a white surface characterized by bold brush-work and subtle gradations of tone (see quot. 1970).

1912 E. F. FENOLLOSA *Epochs Chinese & Jap. Art* II. xi. 43 Kakei..made a decided change in Chinese landscape style: the 'In' style..in that he introduced the utmost decorative splendour of *notan*, or dark and light beauty. He made the strong shapes of his touches of glowing ink 'look as if they were falling in drops'. This is 'suiboku', or wet ink. **1959** R. SAITO *Jap. Ink Painting* 13 Because of the value of the light and dark color of the sumi, and the taste and interest which come from each variation of the brush, suiboku painting really reveals the true spirit of the Oriental people. **1959** *Times Lit. Suppl.* 17 Apr. 218/4 The distinction is most apparent, and most interesting, in the field of *suiboku*—the monochrome painting practised by the *bunjin-ga*. **1970** *Oxf. Compan. Art* 1114/1 The essentials of *suiboku* were bold composition in the Chinese style, strength of brush-work, and nuance in the tone of the ink.

suicidal (s(j)uːɪˈsaɪdəl), *a.* [f. SUICIDE *sb.*[2] + -AL[1].]

1. Of, pertaining to, or involving suicide or self-slaughter; (of persons) having a tendency to suicide.

1837 CARLYLE *Fr. Rev.* I. III. iv, With such weapons, homicidal and suicidal. **1849** J. W. WARTER *Southey's Comm.-pl. Bk.* 252 A Suicidal Maniac through Religious Melancholy. **1855** DUNGLISON *Med. Lex.*, Suicidal Insanity. **1886** FAGGE *Princ. Med.* I. 741 Patients affected with this form of melancholia show suicidal tendencies.

2. *fig.* Leading to or involving self-destruction; destructive or fatal to those engaged.

1777 HAMILTON *Wks.* (1886) VII. 529 'Tis only.. misapplying men to employ them in a suicidal parade against New York. **1804** *Ann. Rev.* II. 234 The Rockingham administration, in every thing a suicidal party, had set aside this right. **1855** KINGSLEY *Westw. Ho!* xx, The Spaniards, by some suicidal pedantry, had allowed their navy to be crippled. **1875** JOWETT *Plato* (ed. 2) V. 35 Though victory makes men insolent and is often suicidal to the victors, education is never suicidal.

Hence **sui'cidalism** = SUICIDISM; **sui'cidally** *adv.*, in a suicidal manner; so as to bring destruction or ruin on the actor; **sui'cidalwise** *adv.*, suicidally.

1833 LYTTON *England* I. iii. 48 This gaiety of *suicidalism is not the death *à la mode* with us. **1837** CARLYLE *Fr. Rev.* III. I. vii, A Soldiery, which we saw long since fallen all *suicidally out of square. **1841** EMERSON *Misc.* (1855) 245 Whatever they attempt..reacts suicidally on the actor himself. **1891** *Times* 21 Dec. 9/4 To reside in Italy meant to run almost suicidally the risk of a malarial attack. **1859** W. ANDERSON *Disc.* Ser. II. (1860) 73 You..will not permit its aspirations to have scope and expression; but *suicidalwise, suffocate them.

suicide (ˈs(j)uːɪsaɪd), *sb.*[1] [ad. mod.L. *suīcīda*, f. *suī* of oneself + *-cīda* -CIDE 1. Cf. F. *suicide*, It., Sp., Pg. *suicida.*]

Not in Johnson 1755. For earlier synonyms see SELF-DESTROYER, -KILLER, -MURDERER, -SLAYER.

One who dies by his own hand; one who commits self-murder. Also, one who attempts or has a tendency to commit suicide.

1732 *Lond. Mag.* I. 252 The Suicide owns himself.. unequal to the Troubles of Life. **1769** BLACKSTONE *Comm.* IV. xiv. 189 The suicide is guilty of a double offence: one spiritual, in invading the prerogative of the Almighty..: the other temporal, against the king. **1838** W. BELL *Dict. Law Scot.* 953 The wounds inflicted by a suicide upon himself are usually in the front, and in an oblique direction. **1861** FLOR. NIGHTINGALE *Nursing* (ed. 2) 77 A fourth [patient], who is a depressed suicide, requires a little cheering. **1870** R. C. JEBB *Sophocles' Electra* (ed. 2) 47/1 Suicides used to be interred with a stake through the body, 'to lay the ghost'.

b. *fig.*

1728 YOUNG *Love Fame* (1741) 89 If fate forbears us, fancy strikes the blow We make misfortune, Suicides in woe. **1824–9** LANDOR *Imag. Conv.* Wks. 1853 I. 28/2 Those are the worst of suicides, who voluntarily and propensely stab or suffocate their fame.

c. *attrib.* or as *adj.* (= suicidal).

1817 LADY MORGAN *France* I. (1818) I. 38 The chateau of the suicide husband. **1895** F. M. CRAWFORD *Casa Braccio* xl, The lonely grave of the outcast and suicide woman.

suicide (ˈs(j)uːɪsaɪd), *sb.*[2] Also 7 **sui-cide.** [ad. mod.L. *suicīdium*, f. *suī* of oneself + *-cīdium* -CIDE 2. Cf. F. *suicide*, It., Sp., Pg. *suicidio.*]

For earlier synonyms see SELF-DESTRUCTION, -HOMICIDE, -KILLING, -MURDER, -SLAUGHTER.

a. The or an act of taking one's own life, self-murder. Phr. ***to commit suicide.***

1651 CHARLETON *Ephes. & Cimm. Matrons* (1668) 73 To vindicate ones self from..inevitable Calamity, by Sui-cide is not..a Crime. **1656** BLOUNT *Glossogr.*, *Suicide*, the slaying or murdering of himself; self-murder. **1732** *Lond. Mag.* I. 251 Love and Jealousy, the old unfashionable causes of Suicide. **1765–8** ERSKINE *Inst. Law Scot.* IV. iv. §46 Suicide, which is a species of murder, ought to be governed by the common rules of murder. **1781** COWPER *Truth* 20 Charge not..Your wilful suicide on God's decree. **1817** SELWYN *Law Nisi Prius* (ed. 4) II. 970 A proviso..declaring the policy to be void in case the insured should..commit suicide. **1891** FARRAR *Darkn. & Dawn* lxvi, The terrible disillusionment and suicides of Gallio and of Seneca.

b. *fig.*

1793 V. KNOX *Pers. Nobility* liv. Wks. 1824 V. 125 There should be no war, much less intestine war, which may be justly called political suicide. **1817** D'ISRAELI *Curios. Lit.* III. 189 Men of genius..voluntarily committing a literary suicide in their own manuscripts. **1884** tr. *Lotze's Logic* 468 The rejection of it [*sc.* a theory] could only be arrived at by a very curious sort of logical suicide. **1886** RUSKIN *Præterita* I. 389 The central tragedy of all the world, the suicide of Greece.

c. *attrib.*, esp. as ***suicide letter, note, pact.*** Also *spec.* in *Mil.* use, designating highly dangerous or deliberately suicidal operations and persons, etc., involved in them, as ***suicide aircraft, mission, squad,*** etc.

1773 FOOTE *Bankrupt* III. Wks. 1799 II. 129 November, the suicide season. **1821** BENTHAM *Liberty Press* Wks. 1843 II. 282/1 The rash and ill-judged—the suicide letter of the constitution. **1882** STEVENSON *New Arab. Nts.* 26 The smoking-room of the Suicide Club. **1897** 'MARK TWAIN' *Following Equator* lvii. 546 In India, the annual man-killings by snakes are..as forecastable as are the tiger-average and the suicide-average. **1909** *Westm. Gaz.* 28 Aug. 15/2 The suicide rate per 100,000 persons under twenty..was 8·26. **1911** *Daily Colonist* (Victoria, B.C.) 19 Apr. 4/3 Before he shot himself..he shot Miss Bovee three times, they having previously entered into a suicide pact. **1916** 'BOYD CABLE' *Doing their Bit* iii. 47 You bombers of the 'Suicide Clubs' might note this. **1923** KIPLING *Irish Guards in Gt. War* I. 67 There seemed no meaning or reason in the affair, unless it was a suicide-party of Germans who had run from the attack of the day before and had been ordered thus to die. **1928** A. C. HAVLIN *Hist. Company A, 102nd Machine Gun Battalion* 3 We were to serve as 'suicide squads' in the..26th Division. **1929** D. HAMMETT *Dain Curse* vii. 65 Your husband's letter sounded enough like a suicide letter..so you murdered him. **1938** 'E. QUEEN' *Four of Hearts* xxii. 293 Park left a suicide note to efface his trail and vanished. **1942** *R.A.F. Jrnl.* 13 June 15 If a 'suicide squad' job came along..it would be assumed that every man was ready for that sort of thing. **1945** *News Chron.* 1 June 4/5 Conferences..are believed to have included plans to counter the..suicide plane. According to a Tokio statement, these suicide attacks..are being developed by the..Japanese Naval Command. **1946** *Jrnl. R. Aeronaut. Soc.* L. 293 As with the pages devoted to German aircraft, so with those given to Japanese. They are full and informative, and end with brief interesting notes on suicide aircraft and the Baka flying bomb. **1954, 1956** [see KAMIKAZE *a.* 1]. **1963** 'D. CORY' *Hammerhead* x. 123 Fedora brushed what was left of the suicide pill on to the palm of his hand. **1969** R. RENDELL *Best Man to Die* xv. 147 It's the seat on the driver's left that's called the suicide seat. **1971** *New Scientist* 11 Mar. 531/2 No civil defence measure would improve this state of affairs except perhaps the issue of suicide pills. **1974** 'S. WOODS' *Done to Death* 127, I haven't told him about the suicide note. *Ibid.* 129 Mr Maitland's theory about the suicide letter is right. **1976** A. WHITE *Long Silence* xviii. 158 'And the third objective?'..'Obviously to flee..and eventually return to England. None of you strikes me as the kind of fool who would accept a suicide mission.' **1977** A. GIDDENS *Stud. in Social & Polit. Theory* ix. 308 Her husband left her seven months later, and this precipitated her suicide attempt. **1978** *Times* 21 Nov. 6/4 Mr Jones had forced his followers to make a suicide pact with him. He predicted..all 1,200 members of the sect would die. **1979** T. SHARPE *Wilt Alternative* xvi. 149 Could have left a suicide squad to cover their retreat.

d. *Comb.*, as **suicide blonde** *slang*, a woman with hair dyed blonde (esp. rather amateurishly), a peroxide blonde; **suicide clause**, a clause in a life insurance policy which releases the insurer from liability if the insured commits suicide within a specified period; **suicide squeeze** *Baseball*, the action of a runner on third base in running for home as the ball is pitched (cf. SQUEEZE PLAY).

1942 BERREY & VAN DEN BARK *Amer. Thes. Slang* §430/4 Bottle baby,..peroxide, *suicide blonde, an artificial blonde. **1959** J. BRAINE *Vodi* vii. 104 'You don't have to whitter on about one little suicide blonde.' 'She's a real blonde,' Tom said. **1973** A. SILLITOE *Men, Women & Children* 174 The snow-white hair of a suicide-blonde flashed around: 'Hey up, Margaret!' **1902** C. L. GREENE *Medical Examination for Life Insurance* 357 There can be little doubt that in the case of persons insured under policies containing a *suicide clause, such deaths are very generally reported as accidental. **1976** 'L. BLACK' *Healthy Way to Die* x. 112 Eddie asks her if there is a suicide clause in the life policy. **1955** P. RICHARDS *Mod. Baseball Strategy* xi. 129 The '*suicide-squeeze', which has the runner going home on the pitch, is absolutely certain to work—*if* the batter bunts the ball on the ground. **1974** *Los Angeles Times* 13 Oct. III. 9/5 It is properly called a 'suicide squeeze' because it calls for the runner to arrive at home plate at the same time as the ball.

'suicide, *v.* [f. prec. Cf. F. *se suicider.*]

1. *intr.* and *refl.* To commit suicide.

1841 LEVER *O'Malley* xxxii. 171 Here was I enacting Romeo for three mortal days—soliloquizing, half-suiciding. **1847** MRS. CARLYLE *Lett. & Mem.* (1883) II. 18 The expediency..of suiciding myself is no longer a question with me. **1881** *Philad. Rec.* No. 3443. 1 Isaiah McNeal, aged 60, suicided at Conyngham on Wednesday. *a* **1890** SIR R. BURTON in Lady Burton *Life* (1893) I. 45 There is hardly a place in Italy..where some Englishman has not suicided himself. **1893** *Athenæum* 24 June 794/2 The principal character, after behaving like a cad, suicides 'beautifully'. **1898** 'R. BOLDREWOOD' *Rom. Canvass Town* 133, I don't wonder that they suicide now and then.

2. *trans.* (*euphemistically*) To do to death.

1876 *Spectator* 12 Aug. 997 (*N. & Q.*) As the Divan cannot pass over the next heir..and as it is difficult to suicide him [etc.]. **1898** *Daily News* 17 Oct. 4/5 The actual forger was, to use a convenient piece of French slang, 'suicided' in gaol. **1899** H. WRIGHT *Depopulation* 129 By suiciding the rest of the population. **1900** *Spectator* 2 June 769 It might be safer than suiciding him.

†sui'cidical, *a.* *Obs. rare.* [f. SUICIDE *sb.*[2] + -ICAL.] = SUICIDAL.

1755 H. WALPOLE *Let. to R. Bentley* 19 Oct., The invasion ..begins..to swallow other news, both political and *suicidical.* **1835** *Blackw. Mag.* XXXVII. 107 The ghastly suicidical smile, last relic of the laughter of despair.

suicidism ('sjuːɪsaɪdɪz(ə)m). *rare.* [f. SUICIDE *sb.*[2] + -ISM.] The doctrine or practice of suicide.

1807 *Monthly Mag.* XXIII. 361 Suicidism the doctrine of self-slaughter. **1842** J. STERLING *Ess.*, etc. (1848) I. 385 No doubt the Feudalism of the one, and the Suicidism of the other, are more fully developed in them than in any foreigners.

So **'suicidist**, one who commits suicide.

1880 *Daily Tel.* 24 Sept., In only one..calling did the female suicidists outnumber the male.

suicidology (s(j)uːɪsaɪ'dɒlədʒɪ). [f. SUICIDE *sb.*[2] + -OLOGY.] The study of suicide and its prevention. Hence **suici'dologist**.

[**1929** W. A. BONGER in *Psychiatrisch-Juridisch Geselschap* 9 Feb. 3 De wetenschap van de zelfmoord, the *suicidologie* (cursivering van mij) zou men haar kunnen noemen, is ruim een eeuw oud.] **1964** E. S. SHNEIDMAN in *Contemp. Psychol.* IX. 371/2, I thank Louis Dublin, the Grand Old Man of Suicidology, for this book because in it he..has given us all new clues to suicide. **1967** —— *Bull. Suicidology* July 7/2 The 10-point program for suicide prevention here outlined is a mutual enterprise whose successful development depends on the active interest, support, and activities of 'suicidologists'. **1969** *Nature* 4 Oct. 12/2 The Johns Hopkins University in collaboration with the National Institutes of Mental Health has established a course in 'suicidology'. **1970** L. LASAGNA in O. G. Brim et al. *Dying Patient* 96 The 'suicidology' program concept. **1976** E. S. SHNEIDMAN *Suicidology* 7 Suicidology is defined as the scientific study of suicidal phenomena. **1976** R. K. MCGEE in *Ibid.* 482 The volunteer suicidologist has become a vital component of the suicide prevention scene.

†'suicism. *Obs.* [In sense 1, app. f. L. *sui* of oneself + -ISM, with intercalated *c*; in sense 2, f. SUIC-IDE + -ISM.]

1. = SELFISHNESS.

1654 WHITLOCK *Zootomia* 363 This Peece, or Schisme of Suicisme, and Selfishnesse, hath spawned most of the Heresies and Schismes, that are abroad in the World.

2. = SUICIDE *sb.*[2]

1751 EARL ORRERY *Rem. Swift* (1752) 275 Those rash actions, that often end in dreadful murders.., parricide, and suicism [*ed.* 5. 1752 suicide]. **1772** *Every Man's Mag.* Jan. 295/1 On Suicism, or Self Murder. *Ibid.*, Allow me to use the word Suicism, for the action of Self-murder; and the word Suicide for the Self-murderer. **1773** C. FLEMING *Diss. Self-Murder* Dedic., A remonstrance I had drawn up against suicism.

suid ('s(j)uːɪd), *sb.* and *a.* *Zool.* [f. mod.L. *Suidæ*: see SUIDIAN *a.* and *sb.*] = SUIDIAN *a.* and *sb.*

1957 P. J. DARLINGTON *Zoogeogr.* vi. 403 Fossil suids..are known only from the main part of the Old World. **1969** [see BUNODONT *a.* and *sb.*]. **1970** B. G. F. WEITZ in H. W. Mulligan *African Trypanosomiases* xviii. 419 Table 18.1 shows the results obtained by the Haemagglutination-Inhibition Test on ten suid feeds. **1976** D. PILBEAM in C. J. Jolly *Early Hominids of Africa* 509 Most workers can..sort ..bovids from suids. **1980** *S. Afr. Med. Jrnl.* LVII. 333 *G. brevipalpis* fed mostly on suids.

suide, obs. pa. t. of SUE *v.*

suidian (s(j)uː'ɪdɪən), *a.* and *sb.* *Zool.* [f. mod.L. *Suidæ*, f. *sūs*, *su-* swine: see -ID[3] and -IAN.] Pertaining to, an animal of, the family *Suidæ* or swine.

1880 *Libr. Univ. Knowl.* (N.Y.) VII. 474 The suidians, having long but not at all prehensile snouts.

suift, obs. form of SWIFT.

‖sui generis ('s(j)uːaɪ 'dʒɛnərɪs). [L.] *lit.* Of one's or its own kind; peculiar. Also used *attrib.* †Also illiterately as *sb.*, a thing apart, an isolated specimen.

1787 M. CUTLER in *Life*, etc. (1888) I. 268 The Doctor.. thinks it must be a *sui generis* of that class of animals. **1794** KIRWAN *Elem. Min.* (ed. 2) I. 126 Against the existence of the sparry [fluor], as of an acid *sui generis*, many difficulties were started. **1828** J. P. SMITH *Four Disc.* (1842) 63 The transcendent case before us is absolutely *sui generis*. **1854** *Poultry Chron.* II. 324 The history of this show is 'sui generis'. **1870** NEWMAN *Gram. Assent* II. vi. 197 Certitude is united to a sentiment *sui generis* in which it lives and is manifested. **1944** S. PUTNAM tr. *E. da Cunha's Rebellion in Backlands* ii. 60 Such a climate tends to create a *sui generis* pathology throughout the whole of the northern coastal strip. **1963** J. LYONS *Structural Semantics* i. 2 In this theory meaning is defined as a *sui generis* 'reciprocal relation between name and sense, which enables them to call up one another'. **1977** *Time* 4 Apr. 41/3 The superlative interpretations by the *sui generis* Budapest Quartet come from tapes of live performances at the Library of Congress in 1959 and 1961.

‖sui juris ('s(j)uːaɪ 'dʒʊərɪs). *Law.* [L. = of one's own right.]

a. *Anc. Roman Law.* Of the status of one who was not subject to the *patria potestas*.

a **1614** DONNE *Βιαθανατος* (1644) 105 If a sonne which had not beene *Sui juris* had beene made Consul, he might have emancipated himselfe. **1867** *Chambers' Encycl.* IX. 194/2 A son did not become *sui juris* by marriage. *Ibid.* 195/1 *Connubium* being the foundation of the *patria potestas*, a bastard was *sui juris*.

b. *Modern Law.* Of full age and capacity, legally competent to manage one's own affairs.

1675 MARQ. WORCESTER in *Essex Papers* (Camden) 38 Shee is of an age not only of consent and dissent but to be sui juris. **1749** FIELDING *Tom Jones* I. xii, The woman is..*sui juris*, and of a proper age to be entirely answerable only to herself. **1821** SCOTT *Pirate* iv, Miss Babie..had been *major* and *sui juris*, (as the writer who drew the contract assured her,) for full twenty years.

c. *transf.* One's own master.

1655 FULLER *Ch. Hist.* v. (1837) II. 18 The pope at this time was not *sui juris*, being a prisoner to the emperor.

suike, obs. variant of SWIKE.

suikerbos (‖'sœykərbɔs). *S. Afr.* Also **suikerbosch, -bossie, zuikerbosch.** [Afrikaans, f. *suiker* SUGAR *sb.* + *bos* BUSH *sb.*[1]] = SUGAR-BUSH 2.

[**1793** tr. *C. P. Thunberg's Trav. Europe, Africa, & Asia* I. 292 The *Protea mellifera* (*Tulp-boom* and *zuyker-boom*) contains in its calyx a sweet juice.] **1822** W. J. BURCHELL *Trav. S. Afr.* I. ii. 18 The delicate Humming birds..are, in Southern Africa,..called by the Dutch colonists *Suiker-vogels* (sugar birds), from having been observed..to feed principally on the honey of the flowers of the *Suiker-bosch* (sugar-bush). **1852** C. BARTER *Dorp & Veld* vii. 74 We came upon knolls covered with the evergreen *Suiker bos* a graceful shrub. **1887** A. A. ANDERSON *Twenty-Five Years in Waggon* I. 210 The fine flat-topped Kameel doorn is very common, palms, baobab,..zuiker-bosch, acacia. **1937** S. CLOETE *Turning Wheels* 104 As he rode past a clump of soikerbos [*sic*] a duiker sprang out. **1950** M. M. KIDD *Flowering Plants Cape Peninsula* Pl. 34 June–Aug. Sugar Bush, Suikerbossie. **1952** *Cape Times* 4 Sept. 5/4 The five dozen selected proteas include..two varieties of the furry suikerbos type. **1971** *Cape Argus* 10 July 5 Now is the time to see all those lovely Proteas and suikerbossies in full bloom.

suilk, -kin, -kyn, var. SWILK, SWILKIN.

suillage, obs. form of SULLAGE.

†suillary, *a.* *Obs. rare*[−1]. [f. L. *suillus* (f. *sūs*, *su-* swine) + -ARY.] Of swine.

1762 tr. *Busching's Syst. Geog.* III. 581 The marmouset.. is a kind of badger, but both are most properly classed among the suillary species.

suilline ('s(j)uːɪlaɪn), *a.* and *sb.* [ad. med.L. *suillīnus*, f. *suillus*: see prec. and -INE.] = SUIDIAN.

1880 DANA *Man. Geol.* (ed. 3) 504 New species and genera of Suillines.

suilyie, variant of SULYE *Sc. Obs.*, soil.

sui-mate ('s(j)uːaɪ,meɪt, 's(j)uːiː-). *Chess.* [f. L. *suī* of oneself + MATE *sb.*[1]] = SELF-MATE *sb.* Also *ellipt.* (**sui**) and as *v. intr.*

1870 *Dubuque Chess Jrnl.* 1 Nov. 7 White sui-mates in ten moves. **1890** [see RETRACTIVE *a.* 3]. **1907** S. S. BLACKBURNE *Terms & Themes Chess Problems* 21 Sui-mate Problem. One in which one player..compels the other to mate him. **1965** *New Statesman* 16 Apr. 625 This one is a 'sui in 5', and.. what matters is for White to commit suicide..by forcing Black to mate him in five moves. **1966** *Ibid.* 11 Nov. 718/3 Many readers have let me know their gradual addiction to sui-mates.

suin, dial. form of SOON *adv.*

suine ('s(j)uːɪn), *sb.* [f. L. *sūs*, *su-* swine + -INE[5].] A fatty substance made from pig's lard, used as a butter-substitute.

1881 *Times* 2 Apr. 9/3 Another product—suine—was made from the lard of pigs. **1881** *Chicago Times* 4 June, No person shall mix..suine..with any butter or cheese.

suine ('s(j)uːaɪn), *a.* *nonce-wd.* [f. L. *sūs*, *su-* pig + -INE[1]: cf. L. *suīnus* (see SWINE).] Pig-like, porcine.

1922 JOYCE *Ulysses* 554 The suine scions of the house of Lambert.

suing ('s(j)uːɪŋ), *vbl. sb.* [f. SUE *v.* + -ING[1].]

†1. a. The following of a person or thing; the pursuance of a course of action; the carrying out or execution of something. *Obs.*

1297 R. GLOUC. (Rolls) 10323, & to sywi þis mansinge,.. We asigneþ þe bissop of winchestre þer to,..[and] Of roucetre & of salesburi þe siwinge to do. *c* **1380** WYCLIF *Serm.* Sel. Wks. I. 375 Bi manere of suynge of Crist in perfit weie of vertues. **1382** —— *2 Macc.* iii. 32 For to eschewe out suyngus of thingus [orig. *executiones rerum vitare*]. *c* **1440** *Promp. Parv.* 483/2 Suwynge, or folowynge yn maners and condycyons, *imitacio*. *Ibid.*, Suwynge, of [? or] folowynge of steppys. *c* **1465** *Eng. Chron.* (Camden) 50 The presence of bothe kyngis moste nedis be had, what for settyng to of thair selis, what for the mariage sewyng.

†b. A course, direction. *Obs.*

c **1410** *Master of Game* (MS. Digby 182) xxx, He muste loke þat he take not þe longe of þe wayes, for it is þe werste sewynge þat is.

†2. Succession in time or order of events, etc. ***by suing***: in consequence, consequently. *Obs.*

a **1425** tr. *Arderne's Treat. Fistula* etc. 63 Þe same sekenez þat comeþ of þe vice of menstruez, comeþ also of þe emoroid, & econverso; and so by sewyng þat þai acorde in cure. *Ibid.* 88 Wherfor þe bolnyng in þe wounde is augmented and, by sewyng, þe ake; for þe tone is occasion of þe toþer. *c* **1440** *Promp. Parv.* 483/2 Svynge, or folwynge a sundry tymys (..*P.* suynge of tyme), *successus*.

†3. ? Proportion. (Cf. SUING *ppl. a.* 3.)

1393 LANGL. *P. Pl.* C. XIX. 63 Men may seo on an appultreo meny tyme and ofte, Of o kynne apples aren nat yliche grete, Ne of sewynge smale ne of o swetnesse swete.

4. a. 'Pursuing' at law; legal prosecution or suit; application for a writ. Also ***suing forth***.

c **1440** *Promp. Parv.* 485/1 Sute, or suynge yn maters and cawsys, *prosecucio*. **1563** *Homilies* II. *Rogation Week* iv, Saint Paule blamed the Corinthians, for suche contentious suyng amonge them selues. **1570–6** LAMBARDE *Peramb. Kent* (1826) 144 They fell to suing, provoking, and brawling. **1589** NASHE *Martins Months Minde* Wks. (Grosart) I. 146 The Suing of Martin Senior his liuerie. **1607** COWELL *Interpr.* s.v. *Parson*, He..representeth the church, and susteineth the person thereof, as well in siewing, as being siewed in any action. **1633** STAFFORD *Pac. Hib.* I. xvi. 97 To be at the charge of suing foorth of their pardons. **1668** *Ormonde MSS.* in *10th Rep. Hist. MSS. Comm.* App. v. 78 Your order for the sueing of the said John Baxter. **1712** PRIDEAUX *Direct. Ch.-wardens* (ed. 4) 32 They are a Corporation, and capable of Suing and being Sued. **1946** *Law Rep.* (King's Bench Division) 18 Sept. (1947) 93 The plaintiff was incapable of suing. **1983** *Weekly Law Rep.* 22 July 884 By the grant of a stay the plaintiffs would be deprived of the juridical advantage of suing as plaintiffs in the Admiralty Court.

b. ***suing and labouring clause***: = sue and labour clause (see SUE *v.* 21 d).

1899 R. G. MARSDEN *Digest Cases Shipping* 580 General average and salvage do not come within either the words or the object of the suing and labouring clause of a policy of marine assurance.

5. The action of a suitor; paying court; entreaty, supplication.

1591 SPENSER *M. Hubberd* 896 Full little knowest thou that hast not tride, What hell it is, in suing long to bide. **1598** GRENEWEY *Tacitus, Ann.* XIII. vii. (1622) 189 Great suings preuailed so much for Eprius Marcellus,..that some of the accusers were banished. **1741** MIDDLETON *Cicero* (1742) II.

vi. 151 When Milo offered to drop his suit for the Consulship..he answered, that he would not concern himself with any man's suing or desisting. **1820** BYRON *Mar. Fal.* v. i. 392 Thy suing to these men were but the bleating Of the lamb to the butcher. **1847** CLOUGH *Quest. Spirit* 10 Poems (1862) 32 This answer gave they still unto his suing, We know not, let us do as we are doing.

suing ('s(j)uːɪŋ), *ppl. a.* [f. SUE *v.* + -ING². Cf. SUANT *a.*] That sues.

†**1.** Following. *Obs. rare.*

1388 WYCLIF *Gen.* xxix. 30 He..settide the loue of the wiif suynge [*v.r.* later wijf] bifore the former.

†**2.** Fitting, according to. *Obs.*

c **1380** WYCLIF *Serm.* Sel. Wks. I. 76 It is beter and more suynge þis gospel to seie [etc.].

†**3.** Regular, proportionate; even, uniform. *Obs.*

c **1369** CHAUCER *Dethe Blaunche* 959, I knewe on hir noon other lakke That al hir lymmes nere pure sywynge. **1442** *Rolls of Parlt.* V. 60/2 That every pece of Worsted be suyng thurghoute the Clothe. **1467–8** *Ibid.* 620/1.

4. In *absol.* or *advb.* constr.: (*a*) In succession, one after another; (*b*) afterwards, after.

c **1400** MAUNDEV. (1839) xviii. 191 He takethe on o nyght, and another another nyght, and so forthe contynuelle sewyng. **1412–20** LYDG. *Chron. Troy* IV. 1658 And sevene dayes, suynge by and by, þis lif he ladde. **1430–40** —— *Bochas* v. iii. (1554) 125 b, Milo..slough hymself suyng the twelue day. **1433** —— *St. Fremund* 751 Thre sondry tymes swynge nyht be nyht. **1450–80** tr. *Secr. Secr.* 5 As ye shalle se more pleynlier sewyng bi ordre. *c* **1500** *Melusine* 73 They ..made to the kinge reuerence, after siewyng salewed the barons & lordes. **1519** HORMAN *Vulg.* 15 Moses wrytte, what was done, in the begynnynge of the worlde, and suynge after.

5. Preferring a suit; entreating, supplicating.

1581 A. HALL *Iliad* VI. 109 Meaning by force to rauish me, when as preuailed not His fawning toyes and sewing tales. *a* **1586** SIDNEY *Ps.* XXVIII. ii, To thy self those wordes apply, Which from suing voice do fly. *a* **1704** T. BROWN *Sat. agst. Woman* Wks. 1730 I. 56 Fools of all sorts with pleasure they admit, While they palm vertue on the sueing wit.

6. Bringing an action at law.

1883 *Daily News* 3 July 2/3 His Honour appointed Mr. H. L...as receiver of the estate, and restrained two suing creditors.

Suinglian, obs. form of ZWINGLIAN.

†'**suingly**, *adv. Obs.* [f. SUING *ppl. a.* + -LY².]

1. Accordingly, consequently.

c **1380** WYCLIF *Serm.* Sel. Wks. II. 106 þus seiþ Crist suyngli, Y and my fadir ben al oon; for þei ben oo God, oo substance, and oo kynde. **1382** —— *Gen.* xliii. 7 We answerden to hym sewyngly [Vulg. *consequenter*], aftir that that he askide. **1450–1530** *Myrr. our Ladye* III. 295 *Consequenter*, Sewyngly after couenaunte & accorde. **1493** [H. PARKER] *Dives & Pauper* (W. de W.) ii. Int. 22/2 Lordshyppe perteyneth by kynde unto man, and so suynly to be riche.

2. In order, in due sequence; hence, subsequently, afterwards, later.

c **1400** MAUNDEV. (1839) xxvi. 263 Now schalle I seye zou sewyngly of Contrees and Yles. *c* **1400** *Pilgr. Sowle* (Caxton) II. lviii. (1859) 56 Euery bone went to other, ioynynge them self in theyr propre places, and sewingly the spyrites repayred to the bones. *a* **1425** tr. *Arderne's Treat. Fistula* etc. 55 Many maners of curacions; Of whiche some more profitable..bene sewyngly to be noted vnder compendiousnez to þe vtilite of helyng. *c* **1449** PECOCK *Repr.* IV. i. 417 These textis whiche schulen now suyngli be tretid in this present chapiter. *c* **1510** MORE *Picus* Wks. 20/1 Then suyngly the prophete sheweth what is the roote of this priuacion.

3. Consecutively, in succession.

1453 *Rolls of Parlt.* V. 270/1 Thre dayes suyngly eche after other.

suink(e, obs. forms of SWINK.

suint (swɪnt). [ad. F. *suint*, earlier †*suing*, f. *suer* to sweat, with an indeterminate suffix.] The natural greasy substance in the wool of sheep, consisting of fatty matter combined with potash salts: called also *yolk*.

1791 HAMILTON *Berthollet's Dyeing* I. I. II. i. 125 Wool is naturally covered with a kind of grease called suint. **1874** CROOKES *Dyeing & Calico-Printing* 84. **1875** KNIGHT *Dict. Mech.* 1549/2 In cleansing wool from the *suint*. **1885** BOWMAN *Struct. Wool Fibre* 179 Formerly this suint was looked upon as a kind of soap, because it was soluble in water.

Suiogothic (swiːəʊ'gɒθɪk), *a.* and *sb.* Also 8 Sue(o-)gothic. [ad. mod.L. *Suio-*, *Sueogothicus*, serving as adj. to *Suiones* (*Sueones*) *Gothīque*, which was used to denote the *Sviar*, *Svear* Swedes, and *Götar* (*Göthar*), older *Gautar*, the inhabitants of Götland (the southern portion of Sweden).] Swedish; the (Old and Middle) Swedish language.

1759 B. STILLINGFL. tr. *Linnæus' Orat. Trav.* in *Misc. Tracts* (1762) 16 Its name, still used among the Suegothic vulgar. **1797** *Encycl. Brit.* (ed. 3) VIII. 23/1 Of this Woden many wonderful things are related in the Sueo-gothic chronicles. **1814** JAMIESON *Hermes Scythicus* I. 12 Alemannic *ostar*, Suio-Gothic *öster*, Islandic *austr*, oriens. *Ibid.* II. 4 To the Islandic, the Suio-Gothic, including the ancient language of Sweden, is very nearly allied.

suiorne, obs. f. SOJOURN *sb.* and *v.*

suipte, obs. past t. SWIPE.

suir, obs. form of SURE.

suisection ('s(j)uːɪsɛkʃən). *nonce-word.* [f. L. *suī* of oneself + SECTION.] Self-dissection, self-analysis.

1894 BLACKMORE *Perlycross* 88 The time was not come yet, and..shall never—in spite of all morbid suisection.

suiseki (sui'seːki). [Jap., *sui* water + *seki* stone(s).] The Japanese art of arranging stones on a tray, often one containing shallow water.

1929 *Encycl. Brit.* III. 855/2 Some stones are placed on a tray with low-growing grass or bamboo... Another way of enjoying them, which has been for centuries and is still popular among the Japanese, is known as *sui-seki*... A natural stone of desirable shape is placed in a porcelain or bronze tray or dish with sand and water. **1972** *Islander* (Victoria, B.C.) 2 Dec. 7/2 Very short sections [of a yew log], an inch or two in thickness, could be used as bases for viewing stones after the Japanese suiseki fashion... The art of suiseki is popular in Japan. **1976** *N.Y. Times* 8 Aug. 24 As with all suiseki, the stones must be as found in nature, though they may be cleaned with a soft cloth or brush. However, they are never polished or sculpted.

'**sui-**,**similar**, *a. nonce-word.* [f. L. *suī* of itself + SIMILAR.] Like itself.

1902 BELLOC *Path to Rome* 375 This very repetitive and sui-similar world.

‖**suisse** (swɪs, ‖sɥis). [F. = Swiss.]

1. The porter of a large house; the beadle of a church (in France).

1837 CARLYLE *Fr. Rev.* II. VI. vii, The red Porters of Hôtels are shot at, be they *Suisse* by nature, or *Suisse* only in name. **1888** *Athenæum* 24 Mar. 378/1 A *suisse* enchanting a little choir-boy in a red frock by the cup and ball trick. **1900** CORELLI *Master Christian* vi, The *Suisse* swore at us for having gone in [to the Church]. **1908** A. KINROSS *Joan of Garioch* xxx. 199, I gave my card and half a rouble to the *suisse*.

2. A soft French white cheese resembling NEUFCHÂTEL. Usu. in the form *petit suisse*: see PETIT *a.* (*sb.*) 5.

1892 STEVENSON & OSBOURNE *Wreckers* v. 70 When I called for a *suisse*..I was bluntly told there were no more.

†'**suist.** *Obs.* [f. L. *suī* of oneself or *suus* one's own + -IST.] One who follows his own inclinations; a self-pleaser.

1648 N. STRANGE in *Carier's Motives Convers. Cath. Relig.* (1649) 17 A Suist, one that followes his own dreams or fancy in choice of Scripture. **1654** WHITLOCK *Zootomia* 357 The Grand Schismatick, or Suist, Anatomiz'd. **1656** BLOUNT *Glossogr.*

suit (s(j)uːt), *sb.* Forms: 3–4 **sywte**, 3–8 **sute**, 4–6 **seute, sewte, suyt**, 4–8 **suyte**, 4–9 **suite**, 5–6 **suete, sewt**, (3, 5 **sowte**, 3–5 **soyte**, 4 **sivte, swete, sywete, sywyte, sout(e**, 4–5 **swte, suytte**, 5 **sevte, siewte, sutte, swtte, suytt**, 5, 7 **suet**, 5–6 **sut**, *Sc.* **soit(e**, 5–7 *Sc.* **soyt**, 6 **sueyt, sewet, -it, sutt, swt, shutte, soote**, *Sc.* **soitt, soytt, soyite**, 6–7 *Sc.* **suitt**, 6–8 **shute**, 7 **suett, seut, shuite, shuett**, *dial.* **zuit**, *illiterate* **shoot**), 5– **suit.** [a. AF. *siwte* (12th c.), *siute, sute, seute, suite* = OF. *sieute*, later *suitte*, etc. (mod.F. *suite*, see SUITE):—pop.L. **sequita*, ppl. sb. f. **sequĕre* to follow, SUE.

The med.L. equivalent of *suit* in various senses was *secta* (see SECT *sb.*¹, SET *sb.*²); the French word was also latinized as *seuta, suita*.]

I. *Feudal Law.*

1. **a.** In full, ***suit of court***: Attendance by a tenant at the court of his lord. **b.** In full, ***suit real*** (***royal, regal***), Sc. ***common suit***: Attendance of a person at the sheriff's court or tourn, attendance at the court-leet.

Phr. *to do, give, owe suit.*

1297 R. GLOUC. (Rolls) 11154 Hii clupede sir Ion giffard þat siwte ssolde þer to To come oþer he ssolde in þe merci be ido. *c* **1450** *Godstow Reg.* 42 Vpon homage, relefe, warde and sute of courte. *Ibid.* 152 Makyng sute to the courte of Eton at the wille of the abbesse. *c* **1460** *Oseney Reg.* 10 *Soc* is sute of your homage in your courte, after the custome of þᵉ Reame. **1473–4** *Acc. Ld. High Treas. Scot.* I. 5 A new infeodacione of his landis of Barnagehane..to be haldin of the King in warde and relef and commoune soyt. **1495** *Act 11 Hen. VII*, c. 26 §1 Such inhabitauntes..as owe suyte to the same Tourne. **1502** *Reg. Privy Seal Scotl.* I. 118/2 The calling of smal portionaris and landit men to commune soyite to schiref courtis. **1579** [RASTELL] *Expos. Termes Lawes* 175 Suit riall is when men come to the shirifes tourne or leete, to which court al men shal be compelled to come to know the lawes... And it is called rial suit because of their allegeance. **1597** SKENE *De Verb. Sign.* s.v. *Sok*, Hee quha is oblished to giue Soyte in the Court of his Over-lorde. **1607** COWELL *Interpreter* s.v. *Sectis non faciendis*, Women that for their dower ought not to performe suite of Court. **1618** J. WILKINSON *Treat. Off. Coroners* etc. II. 77 b, All manner of persons which..owe suit royall to this court Leet. **1651** tr. *Kitchin's Courts Leet* (1657) 291 By Tremail it is said, that suit reall is due by reason of the Body. **1704** J. HARRIS *Lex. Techn.* I, *Suit-real* or *regal.* **1766** BLACKSTONE *Comm.* II. 54 To follow, or do suit to, the lord in his courts in time of peace. **1863** H. COX *Instit.* I. viii. 104 The suitors or persons owing suit in the county courts or courts-baron of the King.

c. An instance of this, an attendance at such a court.

14.. *Customs of Malton* in *Surtees Misc.* (1890) 59 Þᵉ.. Burgese schall make bott ij suttes by þᵉ ȝer' to þᵉ sayd cowrtt. *c* **1450** *Godstow Reg.* 205 All maner of sutes of her Courtes. *c* **1460** *Oseney Reg.* 37 All maner sutes of Shires and Hundredes. **1508** *Reg. Privy Seal Scotl.* I. 233 Dischargis him and his saidis landis of all soyttis, comperingis in justice-aris. **1543** tr. *Act 52 Hen. III*, c. 9 For doyng suites vnto the courtes of great lordes. **1592** in *Reg. Mag. Sig. Scot.* (1892) 91/1 With thrie swtis at thrie heid schireff courtis yeirlie.

†**d.** ***to call the suits*** (Sc.): to call over the names of those who were bound to give suit at a court. *Obs.*

1459 in A. Laing *Lindores Abbey* (1876) xvi. 158 Ye quhylk day ye soytts callit ye curt affirmyt ye absens ar patent. **1535** STEWART *Cron. Scot.* III. 489 Judgis war sett and suittis callit sone. **1541** in *Rec. Earld. Orkney* (S.H.S.) I. 62 With power..Soittis to mak be callit. *c* **1550** ROLLAND *Crt. Venus* III. 11 Sutis was callit ilk ane in thair estait. Cheisit ane assyis. *a* **1578** LINDESAY (Pitscottie) *Chron. Scot.* II. 252 The regent causit feild the parliament and call the suittis. **1609** SKENE *Reg. Maj.*, *Crimes* ix. xxviii. 168 b, The soytes suld be first called, with their Lords, and maisters.

2. **a.** ***suit and service***: attendance at court and personal service (see SERVICE *sb.* 8) due from a tenant to his lord; hence used as a formula in describing certain forms of tenure. Also ***homage and suit***; in Sc. usage, ***presence and suit***.

[*c* **1350** *Will. Palerne* 1080 To lasse & to more, þat ouȝten him omage or ani seute elles.] *c* **1380** *Antecrist* in Todd *Three Treat. Wyclif* (1851) 147 Bi sute and servyse þat þei [*sc.* priests] owen to seynes & to chapitres. ? *a* **1400** *Morte Arth.* 3139 He wolde..make hyme seruece and suytte for his sere londes. *c* **1449** PECOCK *Repr.* III. iv. 299 He [*sc.* a priest] muste nedis comaunde and regne upon hise tenauntis, and thei muste needis obeie and do sewtis and seruicis to him. *a* **1500** *Brome Bk.* 157 They may do homage and sewte to my lord. **1504** *Munim. de Melros* (Bann. Club) 601 That thaj aw na presence nor sute in the serref court of Hadingtoune for the said landis. **1605** *Order Keeping Court Leet* 21 Let euery man remember his oath and dutie, and doe his suit and seruices according to the same. **1654** BRAMHALL *Just Vind.* iv. (1661) 77 All Ecclesiasticall persons who held any possessions from the King in capite, were to do suit and service for the same as other Barons did. **1773** T. PERCIVAL *Ess.* (1776) III. 14 Little Bolton, a suburb of Bolton,.. extending into the country as far as the inhabitants are subject to suit and service. **1776** DALRYMPLE *Ann. Scotland* 294 As a freeholder of Annandale, Bruce was bound to give suite and presence in the King's court held at Dumfries. **1820** GIFFORD *Compl. Engl. Lawyer* 31 For homage, fealty, or suit and service, as also for parliamentary wages, it is said that no distress can be excessive. **1824** SCOTT *Redgauntlet* ch. xviii, At a table above the rest..sat enthroned the youthful Sovereign himself,..receiving the suit and homage of his subjects. **1872** E. W. ROBERTSON *Hist. Ess.* 138 Every man of lawful age holding lands in capite of the crown..was bound to give suit and presence in Parliament.

b. *fig.* (Phr. ***to do, owe,*** †***follow suit and service.***)

c **1585** [R. BROWNE] *Answ. Cartwright* 55 Hee shoulde rather loose his righte, then doe suite and homage to a Traytour. **1589** GREENE *Menaphon* Wks. (Grosart) VI. 106 For all she hath let you flie like a Hawke that hath lost hir tyre; yet you meane to follow sute and seruice, though you get but a handfull of smoake to the bargaine. **1596** SPENSER *F.Q.* VI. vii. 34 Then found he many missing of his crew, Which wont doe suit and seruice to his might. **1598** YONG *Diana* 33 By being fauoured in some other place, where thy sutes & seruices may be more esteemed. **1834** DE QUINCEY *Autob. Sk.* Wks. 1853 I. 52, I, being a cadet of my house, owed suit and service to him who was its head. **1861** *Sat. Rev.* 30 Nov. 553 A metropolitan member must, we suppose, do suit and service for his seat. **1881** *Manch. Guard.* 14 Feb. 5 Like many others who have done suit and service to this city.

3. The resort of tenants to a certain mill to have their corn ground; the obligation of such resort. (Cf. SUCKEN¹.) *Hist.*

c **1450** *Godstow Reg.* 138 With þe seute of grindinge, & all oþer pertinences. *Ibid.* 206 Quiet of scuage & sute of here myllys. **1545** in Leadam *Sel. Cases Crt. Requests* (Selden Soc.) 183 The complaynaunt..hath..prevely withedrawen his sute from the said milles & ground his Corne away from thence. **1591** *Knaresb. Wills* (Surtees) I. 175 Dareley mylne, with the soken and suite there to belonginge. **1622** [E. MISSELDEN] *Free Trade* 58 That restraint of the common liberty, which we call Suit of Mill. **1768** BLACKSTONE *Comm.* III. 235 Such is that of doing suit to another's mill. **1903** DOWDEN *Chart. Lindores* Introd. p. lxxxvi, Suit and multure which the abbot claimed from tenants of the nuns on their lands of Kynhard.

†**4.** A due paid in lieu of attendance at the court of a lord. (Cf. *suit-groat, -silver.*) *Obs.*

1523 FITZHERB. *Surv.* 14 b, I shall..truely do and pay the sutes, customes, rentes, and seruyces that longeth thereto. **1527** *MS. Acc. St. John's Hosp., Canterb.*, Paid to Hoth Court for rent sute & loke vs. iiijd. **1577** LEIGH *Surv.* G, Suites of Courte, or annuall fine, for suite and seruice of Courte, to any other Courte. *Ibid.*, A Rente, or a Suite, maie bee sometymes paied out of a Mannour to a Hundred or Sheriues Tourne. **1660** *Act. 12 Chas. II*, c. 24 §5 Any Rents certaine Herriots or Suites of Court belonging or incident to any former Tenure.

II. Pursuit; prosecution, legal process.

†**5.** **a.** Pursuit, chase; also, a pursuit. Phr. ***to follow, make suit. fresh suit*** (see FRESH *a.* 2 c), pursuit made without delay. *Obs.*

c **1325** *MS. Rawl. B 520* lf. 32 Be imad so uers siute [orig. Stat. Winch. c. 1 *Si fresche sute*] þer oppe fram toune to toune. *c* **1350** *Will. Palerne* 2392 Lest þe segges wold haue sesed here seute to folwe. *Ibid.* 2615, & þo þe seute sesed after þe swete bestes. **1390** GOWER *Conf.* III. 373 Thou miht noght make suite and chace, Wher that the game is nought pernable. **1398** TREVISA *Barth. De P.R.* XVIII. xxiv. (Bodl. MS.) Houndes..findeþ here..dennes and warneþ þereof bi sute and bi berkinge. **1486** *Bk. St. Albans* e. v, When he after foode makyth any sute. **1489** *N. Riding Rec.* N.S. (1894) I. 123 To have shot, sute, or course at any of our game. **1534** *Act 26 Hen. VIII*, c. 5 Any outcrie, hute, or fresshe suite of or for any felonye. **1575** GASCOIGNE *Kenelworth* Wks. 1910 II. 93 Though haste say on, let sute obtaine some stay. **1579** RASTELL *Expos. Termes Lawes* 95 b, Freshsuit, is when a man is robbed, and the partye so robbed, followeth the felon immediatlye. **1590** SPENSER *F.Q.* III. xi. 5 He soone resinde His former suit. **1609** SKENE *Reg. Maj., Stat. Dav. II*, 40 Gif the suet, or bruit of three baronies follow any man for reif, theift, or any other trespas. **1760–72** H. BROOKE *Fool of Qual.* (1809) III. 68 He was spied..stealing a bay horse. Fresh suit was made.

†**b.** *transf.* That which is pursued; (in hunting) the scent or (?) quarry. *Obs.*

1593 LODGE *Phillis* (Hunter. Club) 48 Like hungrie houndes that lately lost their suite. **1644** DIGBY *Nat. Bodies* xxxvii. §1. 319 Our howndes that follow a suite of bloud.

†**6.** The pursuit *of* an object or quest. *Obs.*

c **1380** WYCLIF *Wks.* (1880) 409 Man shulde not fayle in þis suyt for god ne for ony creature. *c* **1450** *Godstow Reg.* 1 [To be excommunicated] al þat ben ordened to enquere þer-on, ȝif þei leue the sute þerof. **1590** SPENSER *F.Q.* II. vii. 10 In der-doing armes, And honours suit. **1596** *Ibid.* v. viii. 3 Suite of his auowed quest.

7. The action of suing in a court of law; legal prosecution; hence, †litigation. Phr. ***to go to suit***, to go to law; ***at suit***, at law, engaged in litigation.

This sense perhaps arises partly from a shortening of *suit of court* (see quot. *a* 1400 and cf. sense 1); but it was fully developed in AF., e.g. *a nostre sute, par cutri sute* (Britton).

[*a* **1400** *Old Usages Winch.* in *Eng. Gilds* (1870) 362 And ȝif myd þan ne may hys tenement riȝt, ne oþer dystresse fynde, by sewte of þe court. *Ibid.* 363 A ȝer and a day y-fuld of þe furste day of sewte.] **1477** *Rolls of Parlt.* VI. 187/2 That.. no Styward..hold plee uppon any Action, atte sute of any persone. **1512** *Act 4 Hen. VIII*, c. 4 Preamble, Outlawries had ageynst theym..at the suyt of dyverse maliciouse persones. *a* **1513** FABYAN *Chron.* VII. (1811) 299 All prysoners that lay in any pryson about London, at the Kynges sute. **1558** T. WATSON *Seven Sacr.* xxviii. 178 Grudge, hatred, and sute betwene the parties and theyr frendes. **1583** STUBBES *Anat. Abus.* II. (1882) 10 If one giue neuer so small occasion to another, sute must straight be commenced. **1590** SHAKS. *Com. Err.* IV. iv. 134 Whose suite is he arrested at? *a* **1676** HALE *Hist. Pleas Crown* (1736) II. 280 Tho A. be convict at the king's suit. **1688** HOLME *Armoury* III. xix. (Roxb.) 173/2 If..the parties were at suite in the ciuill courts of justice. **1690** W. WALKER *Idiomat. Anglo-Lat.* 455, I haue a great mind to go to suit. **1766** BLACKSTONE *Comm.* II. 437 Till after suit commenced and judgment obtained in a court of law. **1768** *Ibid.* III. 22 The redress of injuries by suit in courts. **1817** JAS. MILL *Brit. India* v. ii. II. 379 At the suit of a native, he was taken up on a charge of forgery.

†**8.** The prosecution *of* a cause; also, the suing for a writ. ***suit of the king's peace***: see quot. 1607. *Obs.*

1444 *Rolls of Parlt.* V. 110/1 Without any sute of Writte of errour. **1472** *Cov. Leet Bk.* 376 What demene should be taken ffor the mater betwen the Cite and Will. Briscowe, And for the Costes and expenses of the suyt þerof. **1538** STARKEY *England* 191 The longe sute of causys in the Court at Westmonastere. **1544** in Leadam *Sel. Cases Crt. Requests* (Selden Soc.) 96 Duryng the suete of ther case. **1563** *Reg. Privy Council Scot.* I. 251 Compellit to leif the soit of thair saidis caussis. **1607** COWELL *Interpr.*, *Suyte of the Kings peace* is the persiewing of a man for breach of the K. peace, by treasons, insurrections, rebellions, or trespasses.

†**9.** ***in suit.***

a. Engaged in a legal prosecution or lawsuit. *Obs.*

a **1513** FABYAN *Chron.* VII. (1811) 339 Atwene the Londoners and the abbot of the Holy Crosse of Waltham, the whiche hadde bene in suyte many yerys before. **1581** in *Buccleuch MSS.* (Hist. MSS. Comm.) I. 225, I am in such great suits with the Lord Crumwell for that little living which my father left me. **1598** R. BERNARD tr. *Terence, Andria* IV. v, He is alwaies in suite with some man. He is neuer out of the court. *a* **1677** BARROW *Serm.* Wks. 1687 I. 75 He that doth not wave the prosecution of his cause..is deemed still to be in suit. **1688** HOLME *Armoury* III. xv. (Roxb.) 23/2 A docket, the catalogue of the person[s] in suite one with another.

†**b.** Of a person: Being prosecuted. ***to have, put in suit***, to prosecute, take legal action against. *Obs.*

1544 in Leadam *Sel. Cases Crt. Requests* (Selden Soc.) 79 For the which Olyuer Seynt John Esquyer hayth Stokeley in sewt at this present tyme. *a* **1548** HALL *Chron., Hen. VIII*, 1 The kynges grace..pardoned all suche persones, as was then in suite. **1579** TOMSON *Calvin's Serm. Tim.* 223/1 We shall not..want an aduersarie to accuse us, we shall lacke no Eschequer man to put us in shute. **1638** HEYWOOD *Wise Wom.* III. i, If they put mee in suite,..they are poore, and cannot follow it.

†**c.** Of a matter: That is *sub judice* or in dispute. *Obs.*

1538 STARKEY *England* (1878) 118, I see many mennys materys heng in sute ii, iij, or iiij yere and more. **1559** AYLMER *Harborowe* G j b, To put that out of doubte which was in sute. **1664** *Comenius' Janua Ling.* 656 A third man must needs come in (between) to part the fray (to take up the matter in sute).

†**d.** ***to put in suit***(*s*): to put (an instrument) in force in a court of law; also, to set the law in motion concerning (a matter).

c **1618** in *Elsing's Debates Ho. Lords* (Camden) App. 140 The said S[r] Giles putt the said bonds in suite in the Exchequer. *a* **1680** CHARNOCK *Attrib. God* (1834) II. 684 Who hath laid by his bond so many years, without putting it in suits against us. **1760–72** H. BROOKE *Fool of Qual.* (1809) III. 140, I will have that matter put directly in suit, and, as soon as it is recovered, it shall be laid out on a commission for your son. **1845** STEPHEN *Comm. Laws Eng.* (1874) II. 48 The executor..of the donor..bound to put such instrument in suit, for the benefit of the donee.

10. a. A process instituted in a court of justice for the recovery or protection of a right, the enforcement of a claim, or the redress of a wrong; a prosecution before a legal tribunal.

'Suit' is a term of wider signification than action; it may include proceedings on a petition. (*Encycl. Laws Eng.*)

c **1412** HOCCLEVE *De Reg. Princ.* 1521 Whan þe mater is to ende I-broght Of þe straunger, for whom þe suyte haþ be. **1444** *Rolls of Parlt.* V. 109/2 Many dyvers persones bi singuler veniance and nothing of right..been by dyvers Suets sued. **1562** *Child-Marriages* 71 She comensid a sute, and sekid for a divorce to be had bie the lawe betwixe them. **1611** COTGR. s.v. *Guerre, Qui a terre, si, a guerre*: Prov., He that hath soyle hath suits. **1676–7** MARVELL *Corr.* Wks. (Grosart) II. 530 The Bill against the Multiplicity of Atturnyes, and for preventing vexatious Suits. **1768** BLACKSTONE *Comm.* III. 406 The courts..will allow of amendments at any time while the suit is depending. **1844** H. H. WILSON *Brit. India* II. 517 To hear and determine summary suits for the rent and occupancy of land. **1888** BRYCE *Amer. Commw.* xliv. II. 154 Ordinary private law.. upon which nine-tenths of the suits between man and man are founded.

b. More fully, ***suit in law*** (†*of* or †*at law*, †*at the law*) = LAWSUIT. Similarly ***suit in chancery, equity***.

1530 PALSGR. 278/2 Sute at the lawe or court, *sieute*. **1576** FLEMING *Panopl. Epist.* 252 Busily occupied in matters of suites of lawe. *c* **1610** *Women Saints* 182 This woman had a suite in law against a principall man of the Cittie of Cæsarea. **1726** *Mist's Weekly Jrnl.* 3 Sept. in *N. & Q.* (1905) 10th Ser. IV. 95/2 On Monday is to be determined a Suit of Law. **1728** LAW *Serious C.* iii. (1732) 40 These at Suits at Law, those at Gaming Tables. **1817** SELWYN *Law Nisi Prius* (ed. 4) II. 1089 A suit in chancery. **1844** WILLIAMS *Real Prop.* (1877) 93 Actions at law and suits in equity.

†**c.** ***to follow a suit***: to prosecute a legal action. Also *fig. Obs.*

1577 tr. *Bullinger's Decades* 705/2 That hee [Jesus] should alwaies appeare there in the presence of God, to followe all our suites faithfully. **1598** R. BERNARD tr. *Terence, Andria* IV. v, For me a stranger to go follow sutes & brabbles in law. *a* **1624** M. SMITH *Serm.* (1632) 68 The Law containeth matter of inditement against vs, the Deuill followeth the suite. **1631** *Rep. Cases Star Chamb. & High Comm.* (Camden) 187 That they would graunt her alimonie and charges to follow the suit against him.

11. a. The action or an act of suing, supplicating, or petitioning; (a) petition, supplication, or entreaty; *esp.* a petition made to a prince or other high personage. Now *poet.*

1449 *Rolls of Parlt.* V. 148/2 Savyng alwey to the same Erle of Devonshire, his lawfull suete to the Kyng. *c* **1460** FORTESCUE *Abs. & Lim. Mon.* xi. (1885) 136 To some men he hath done in lyke wyse aboff thair merites, through ymportunite off thair suyttes. **1491** *Act 7 Hen VII*, c. 24 An acte was made at the suite of a particuler personne for his particuler cause. **1549–62** STERNHOLD & H. *Ps.*, *Lam.* (1566) 23 For mercy Lord is all my sute. **1554** *Act 1 & 2 Phil. & M.* c. 8 §1 This our supplicacion directed to yo[r] Majesties withe most humble sute, that it may..be exhibited to..the Lorde Cardinall Poole. **1592** KYD *Sp. Trag.* III. xii. 2 The King sees me, and faine would heare my sute. **1605** SHAKS. *Lear* II. ii. 68 This ancient Ruffian..whose life I haue spar'd at sute of his gray-beard. **1625** BACON *Ess.*, *Sutours* (Arb.) 41 Priuate Sutes doe Putrifie the Publique Good. **1657** SPARROW *Rationale* 76 When the Priest makes their suits, and they..say, Amen. **1668** R. STEELE *Husbandm. Calling* v. (1672) 90 Frozen suits meet with cold answers from God. **1741** MIDDLETON *Cicero* (1742) II. vi. 151 When Milo offered to drop his suit for the Consulship. **1814** SCOTT *Ld. Isles* I. xxx, Rest ye here..Till to our Lord your suit is said. **1838** ARNOLD *Hist. Rome* I. 78 They had no jurisdiction, but referred all their suits to the king. **1859** TENNYSON *Elaine* 774 Lightly, her suit allow'd, she slipt away.

†**b.** ***to make*** (*one's*) ***suit***: to supplicate, petition; to sue *to* a person *for* a thing; also const. inf., to petition for something to be done. *Obs.*

c **1430** LYDG. *Min. Poems* (Percy Soc.) 34 Now no man to me makethe ony sute! *c* **1513** MORE *Rich. III* Wks. 53/1 While some for their busines made sute to them that had the doing. *Ibid.* 58/2 This pore Lady made humble suite vnto y[e] king, y[t] she might be restored vnto such smal landes as [etc.]. **1530** PALSGR. 716/2, I sewe, I make sute for a thing, *je pourchasse*. **1556** CHEKE in *Lett. Lit. Men* (Camden) 19 To favor such poore suts for my Libertie as M[r] Dean shall make to your Ma[tie] in my behalfe. **1601** [BP. W. BARLOW] *Serm. Paules Crosse* 2 As I neuer made suite to preach anywhere. **1649** DAVENANT *Love & Hon.* v. iii. 70 My desires make sute, that those who shall Hereafter write the businesse of this day May not beleeve I suffer for the hope Of glorious fame. **1738** WESLEY *Ps.* xlv. xvi. Kings at his Feet shall cast their crown, And humble Suit for Mercy make.

†**c.** *transf.* Earnest search for or endeavour to obtain something. *Obs.*

a **1568** ASCHAM *Scholem.* I. (Arb.) 77 They make great hast to cum to her: they make great sute to serue her. **1613** PURCHAS *Pilgrimage* VII. i. 552 Corrivall vnto..Sennacherib, in sute for the Monarchie of the world. *a* **1627** SIR J. BEAUMONT in Farr *S.P. Jas. I* (1848) 155 The fiends..Make suite to seaze him as their lawfull prey.

12. Wooing or courting of a woman; solicitation for a woman's hand. Also, an instance of this, a courtship.

[**1580** LYLY *Euphues* (Arb.) 342 When the Gods coulde not obtaine their desires by suite, they turned them-selues into newe shapes.] **1590** GREENE *Never too late* (1600) P, Reueale any more his sute hee durst not, because when he began to chat of loue, she shakt him off. *c* **1610** *Women Saints* 73 Offa receyuing that message, did more willinglie giue ouer his suite, ceasing to molest the virgin. *a* **1711** BURNET *Autobiog.* in H. C. Foxcroft *Suppl. Burnet's Hist.* (1902) 480 After two years sute we were married. **1726** POPE *Odyss.* XIX. 164 Rebate your loves, each rival suit suspend. **1775** SHERIDAN *Duenna* II. iii, Doubtless, that agreeable figure of his must have help'd his suit surprizingly. **1823** SCOTT *Peveril* xii, If I come to you with my parents' consent to my suit, will you again say..Julian, we must part? **1864** TENNYSON *Aylmer's Field* 493 Sullen, defiant, pitying, wroth, return'd Leolin's rejected rivals from their suit.

III. Livery, garb; sort, class.

†**13. a.** A livery or uniform; also, in wider use, a dress, garb: chiefly in phr. ***in*** or ***of*** (***a***) ***suit*** = clothed in the same garb or colour, as the members of a retinue or fraternity; also, ***in suit with***, in the same dress or uniform as. *Obs.*

1297 R. GLOUC. (Rolls) 3950 A þousend kniȝtes..Of noble men ycloþed in ermine echon Of o sywte. **13..** *K. Alis.* 182 (Laud MS.) Forþ she ferde, myd her route, A þousande lefdyes of riche soute. **1389** in *Eng. Gilds* (1870) 3 þe brethren and sustren..shul be cloþed in suyt. **1390** GOWER *Conf.* II. 2 That I mai stonde upon his rowe, As I that am clad of his suite. **14..** in *Eng. Gilds* (1870) 446 Alle the bretheren schul be cladde in swte of gownes o ȝere and another ȝere in o swte of hodes. *c* **1450** *Godstow Reg.* 23 Edmunde of Pounteney, now in ȝoure sute I wold þat I were ..Wheþer hit were..whyte, rede, or blewe. *c* **1460** *Wisdom* in *Macro Plays* 60 Here entreth vi women, in sut. *c* **1470** HENRY *Wallace* IX. 293 He gert graith him in soit with his awin men. *a* **1548** HALL *Chron., Hen. IV* (1550) 22 b, Three other appareled in the kynges suite and clothyng. **1588** LAMBARDE *Eiren.* IV. iv. 439 If any company of men..haue made any one generall sute of cloth..to be knowen by. *a* **1633** AUSTIN *Medit.* (1635) 104 These Sisters goe all in a Suite..: They are all in Greene.

†**b.** ***in*** or ***of suit*** (***of a*** or ***the same suit***): (of clothes, etc.) of one or the same colour or material; uniform, to match. ***in suit of*** or ***with***: uniform with, matching. *Obs.*

13.. *E.E. Allit. P.* A 203 Her cortel of self sute schene. *Ibid.* 1108 Alle in sute her liurez wasse. **13..** *Gaw. & Gr. Knt.* 191 þe tayl & his toppyng twynnen of a sute. *c* **1386** CHAUCER *Miller's T.* 56 The tapes of hir white voluper Were of the same suyte of hir coler. **1389** in *Eng. Gilds* (1870) 43 Alle ye bretheren and systeren han a lyuere of sute. **1395** *E.E. Wills* (1882) 5 With docere, costers and bankers, of sute of that forseyde bed. **1431** *Rec. St. Mary at Hill* (1904) 26 A white vestement of o sewte. **1433** *Rolls of Parlt.* IV. 477/1 And the Styward..have..a Robe in sute of the Baylyffs. **1452** in Willis and Clark *Cambridge* (1886) I. 337 A gownecloth in sute with his gentilmen. **1558** in Feuillerat *Revels Q. Eliz.* (1908) 45, vi payer of undersleves of the same stuff and sute.

†**c.** *fig.* (in quot. 1377 said of the human flesh or humanity). Phr. ***to follow suit with***, to do the same as (cf. 20 b). *Obs.*

1377 LANGL. *P. Pl.* B. v. 495 God..þat..in owre sute deydest On godefryday for mannes sake. **1565** T. STAPLETON *Fortr. Faith* 92 Any protestant of what so euer cote or sute he be. **1655** FULLER *Church Hist.* II. 152 Though men had Surnames, yet their Sons did not, as I may say, follow suit with their Fathers. *a* **1661** —— *Worthies, Lond.* (1662) II. 205 Many Clergy-men,..born in this City, did not follow suit with others of their Coat.

†**d.** ***in suit with***: in company with. ***out of suits with***: ? lit. not in the uniform of, hence, out of favour with. *Obs.*

? *a* **1400** *Morte Arth.* 3931 Seuene score knyghtes In soyte with theire soueraynе. **1600** SHAKS. *A. Y. L.* I. ii. 258 One out of suites with fortune.

†**e.** Condition, state. *Obs. rare.*

1350 *Will. Palerne* 1250 þou seidest me ȝer-while þou schuldest me do quelle,..but, sire, in þe same seute sett artow nouȝ.

14. Of various objects (chiefly in phr. with preps. *of, in*): Pattern, style of workmanship or design; *occas.* colour; hence = set (see V).

? *a* **1400** *Morte Arth.* 210 Sexty cowpes of suyte. *c* **1400** *Destr. Troy* 3410 A sadill..With a bridell full bright, bothe of a sewte. **1406** *E.E. Wills* (1882) 13 Ylk man & woman of hem in sute a rynge of xl d. *a* **1423** in *Archaeologia* LXI. 171, ij Fiols of on sute of siluer and gild. **1424–5** *E.E. Wills* (1882) 56 A doseyn spones of too suites. **1444** *Test. Ebor.* (Surtees) II. 112, ij standing cuppis of a sute. **1525** *Ibid.* VI. 11, iiij stottes, iij of on sutie [? suite], with on browne stotte.

†**15.** Kind, sort, class. *Obs.*

Common in the 16th c.

1548 GESTE *Agst. Priv. Masse* A v, It is a stelth of holye thinges, not of the basest sute..but of the holyest and chiefeste kynde. **1570** LEVINS *Manip.* 178/28 A Soote, of things, *genus*. **1573** TUSSER *Husb.* (1878) 46 Now gather vp fruite, of euerie suite. **1586** T. BRIGHT *Treat. Mel.* iv. 13 The particular nourishment containeth not so many sutes, as the earth the nourisher of all things doth. **1594** HOOKER *Eccl. Pol.* III. iii. §2 Touching matters belonging vnto the Church of Christ this wee conceiue, that they are not of one sute. **1642** D. ROGERS *Naaman* 138 Of this sute also is the carriage of such, as upbraid God.

IV. Following, train, suite.

16. a. A company of followers; a train, retinue, SUITE. Also, a company of disciples. Now *arch.* or *dial.* (superseded by *suite*).

1297 R. GLOUC. (Rolls) 3743 Hii of sute were Of king arthures hous. **13..** *Cursor M.* 25668 (Gött.) Leuedi mari! ..helpe þi suite. *c* **1380** WYCLIF *Serm.* Sel. Wks. II. 225 Crist biddiþ men of his suyt þat þei shulden not have two cootis. *c* **1400** *Destr. Troy* 546 In sound for to saile home & your sute all. *Ibid.* 12995 The Cite he assailet with a sewte ofte. *a* **1586** SIDNEY *Arcadia* II. x. (1912) 211 Had there not come in Tydeus & Telenor, with fortie or fiftie in their suit, to the defence of Plexirtus. **1612** T. TAYLOR *Comm. Titus* i. 6 They were so farre from the suit of Saints and good men, that they were vnfit companie for honest ciuill men. **1781** J. MOORE *View Soc. It.* (1790) I. i. 17 Till the Archduke and his suit had passed. **1799** COLERIDGE *Let. to Wife* 14 Jan., Any but married women, or in the suit of married women. **1862** WHYTE-MELVILLE *Inside Bar!* 345 Servant?..didn't bring one; don't want a 'shoot' when I'm driving Crafty Kate. **1865** BARING-GOULD *Werewolves* x. 185 A numerous suit of pages, esquires, chaplains.

†**b.** (*a*) A leash of hounds. (*b*) A flight of mallards. *Obs.*

c **1470** *Hors, Shepe & G.* (Roxb.) ad fin., A Sute of a lyhm. **1486** *Bk. St. Albans.* f vi, A Sorde or a sute of malardis.

c. The witnesses or followers of a plaintiff in an action at law. Now *Hist.*

1647 N. BACON *Disc. Govt. Eng.* I. lxvii, The plaintiffs sect or suit of witnesses. **1768** BLACKSTONE *Comm.* III. 295. **1865** NICHOLS tr. *Britton* I. xxxii, Let the suit be examined..by taking their acknowledgments whether they are villains to the plaintiff. *Ibid.* v. viii. 270 *marg.*, Proof by suit of witnesses.

†**17.** Offspring, progeny; *spec.* the offspring of a villein. *Obs.*

1338 R. BRUNNE *Chron.* (1810) 95 Of þat douhter sute com Malde, þat was of pris. *c* **1450** *Godstow Reg.* 559 The bodies of [5 serfs], with all ther catell, sewtis, and sequelis. *c* **1460** *Oseney Reg.* 10 Your bonde men, with here sute and catell.

V. Set, series.

18. A number of objects of the same kind or pattern intended to be used together or forming a definite set or series.

†**a.** A group. **b.** A set of tools, plate, furniture, locks, etc. **c.** The whole of the sails required for a ship or for a set of spars. †**d.** A set of musical pieces, pictures, etc. **e.** A suite of rooms. **f.** 'A batch of biscuits, weighing 1 cwt., or one charge of the oven' (Simmonds *Dict. Trade*). **g.** *U.S.* The whole complement of hair, whiskers, etc. that a person has. †**h.** A gold watch, usu. with seals, case, etc. *Criminals' slang. Obs.*

a. *c* **1402** LYDG. *Compl. Bl. Knt.* 82 The sute of trees aboute compassing Hir shadowe caste.

b. **1424** *E.E. Wills* (1882) 57 An oþer flat pece [of plate] of þe suit þat were my faders. **1577** HARRISON *England* II. x. 85 b, A siluer salte, a bowle for wine..and a dussen of spoones, to furnishe vp the sute. **1615** in W. M. Williams *Ann. Founders' Co.* (1867) 92 Pd for on Sute of Bell Waights compleat 5 12 0. **1622** MABBE tr. *Aleman's Guzman d'Alf.* II. III. v. 298 A handsome sute of chaires. **1623** in Ellis *Orig. Lett.* Ser. I. III. 143 A rich suite of hangings. **1654** GAYTON *Pleas. Notes* III. v. 100 A Missale, six Crucifixes, a sute of Beads. **1686** PLOT *Staffordsh.* 376 They make them [*sc.* locks] in Sutes, six, eight, or more in a sute. **1712** ADDISON *Spect.* No. 323 ¶21 In Conference with my Mantua-Maker. Sorted a Suit of Ribbands. **1737** *Salmon's Cy. Bldr.'s Estimator* (ed. 2) 111 These [Locks] are likewise sold in Sute. **1762–71** H. WALPOLE *Vertue's Anecd. Paint.* (1786) I. 247 A suit of tapestry. **1778** [W. MARSHALL] *Minutes Agric.* 8 Jan. 1776, A suit of pasturing paddocks are convenient about Home. **1782** [T. VAUGHAN] *Fash. Follies* I. 145 A.. complete suit of diamonds. *a* **1817** T. DWIGHT *Trav. New Eng.*, etc. (1821) II. 196 A suit of oars. **1821** SCOTT *Kenilw.* viii, A woman..changes her lovers like her suit of ribands. **1845** S. JUDD *Margaret* I. ii, There were no suits of knives and forks.

c. **1626** CAPT. J. SMITH *Accid. Yng. Seamen* 17 A suit of sayles. **1635** in Foster *Crt. Min. E. Ind. Comp.* (1907) 114 [To make new sails for his ship, she having only one new] suyte. **1748** *Anson's Voy.* II. ii. 135 With all the..remnants of old sails that could be mustered, we could only make up one compleat suit. **1851** KIPPING *Sailmaking* (ed. 2) 91 Making a suit of Sails for a Barque of 300 Tons. *c* **1860** H. STUART *Seaman's Catech.* 62 The third suit of sails forms the ground tier. **1912** J. MASEFIELD *Dauber* IV. v. in *Engl. Rev.* Oct. 365 He had once worked aloft, Shifting her suits one summer afternoon.

d. **1682** *Lond. Gaz.* No. 1726/4 A Suit of Vocal and Instrumental Musick from the Odeum or Musick Gallery. ?**17..** J. LOEILLET (*title*) Six Suits of Lessons for the Harpsichord or Spinnet. **1779** J. MOORE *View Soc. Fr.* (1789) I. xxxviii. 330 The most admired of all Holben's works is a suit of small pieces.

e. **1741** WARBURTON *Div. Legat.* II. 280 A magnificent Palace..with all its Suits of Apartments. **1789** MRS. PIOZZI *Journ. France* I. 283 The apartments..run in suits like Wanstead house in Essex. **1848** DICKENS *Dombey* iii, A whole suit of drawing-rooms. **1858** *Eng. Cycl., Biog.* s.v. *Usher*, He took up his residence in a suit of apartments provided for him in the inn.

f. **1845** *Encycl. Metrop.* VIII. 802/2 The quantity baked each time, which is called a *suit*, is about 112 pounds weight before being placed in the oven.

g. **1845** S. JUDD *Margaret* II. i, A suit of enormous black whiskers. **1867** AUGUSTA WILSON *Vashti* xxxiii, Leaving a few lines written in pencil on a handkerchief, in which she had wrapped her superb suit of hair. **1893** 'MARK TWAIN' *Pudd'nhead Wilson* ii, She had a heavy suit of fine soft hair, which was also brown.

h. **1718** C. HITCHING *Regulator* 13 They [*sc.* pickpockets] greatly benefit; either by a Suit, *alias* Gold-watch,..or by a Wedge Lobb, *alias* Gold or Silver Snuff-Box. **1839** H. AINSWORTH *Jack Sheppard* II. xiv. 40 A fence, or receiver, ..bargaining with a..pickpocket, for a *suit*,—or to speak in more intelligible language, a watch and seals.

19. A set of garments or habiliments intended to be worn together at the same time. (Cf. 13.)

a. of church vestments, esp. chasuble and dalmatics, cope, etc. of the same colour and material.

1495 in *Somerset Med. Wills* (1901) 330 My sewte of blew velwet vestimentes. **1552–3** *Inv. Church Goods, Stafford* 2, iiij shutes of vestements to minester withall. **1558** *N. Country Wills* (Surtees) II. 6 My suyte of red vestementes. *a* **1700** EVELYN *Diary* 18 Jan. 1645 One priestly cope, with the whole suite. *c* **1716** in J. O. Payne *Rec. Eng. Cath.* 1715 (1889) 105 Vestment suites 12, albs 8, amices 10. **1874** MICKLETHWAITE *Mod. Par. Churches* 163 So that each suit of vestments may have its own drawer.

b. of men's or boys' outer garments; in full, *suit of apparel, of clothes.* Now usually, a jacket and trousers of the same material, sometimes with matching waistcoat, and esp. for formal or office use.

c **1420** *Sir Amadace* (Camden) lvi, Say him my sute is quite. **1552–3** in Feuillerat *Revels Edw. VI* (1914) 89 Five suetes of apparrell. **1553** T. WILSON *Rhet.* 51 He hath his chaunge of sutes, yea, he spareth not to go in his silkes and veluet. **1584** in Feuillerat *Revels Q. Eliz.* (1908) 365, xxxtie ells of sarcenet for fower matachyne sutes. **1625** BACON *Ess., Masques* (Arb.) 540 Let the Sutes of the Masquers, be Gracefull. **1641** SYMONDS *Serm. bef. Ho. Comm.* B ij b, If a man order his Taylor to make him a sute. **1642** in *Decl. Commons Rebell. Irel.* (1643) 29 The six hundred suits of clothes were for the Souldiers in Ireland. **1683** WOOD *Life* (O.H.S.) III. 74 To Mr. Spencer the tayler for turning and altering my gray suite..14*s.* **1738** *Gentl. Mag.* VIII. 4/1 One that..doth not put off his Religion with his Sunday's Suit. **1840** R. H. DANA *Bef. Mast* x, We had on oil-cloth suits and southwester caps. **1877** SPURGEON *Serm.* XXIII. 486 You cannot force that little heart to be anxious about the next suit of clothes. **1892** GUNTER *Miss Dividends* (1893) 93 His light travelling suit. **1897** [see *pyjama suit*, PYJAMAS b]. **1932** G. GREENE *Stamboul Train* I. i. 7 He..required no longer..his suit from Savile Row..to hearten him. *a* **1953** E. O'NEILL *Hughie* (1959) 8 He wears an ill-fitting blue serge suit. **1960** C. DAY LEWIS *Buried Day* ii. 43, I am standing..in a white suit and holding my broad-brimmed round straw hat.

c. of women's attire: in earlier use, an entire set of garments for wear at one time; in recent use, a costume (i.e. coat and skirt). Cf. *trouser suit.*

1761 *Brit. Mag.* II. 444 A suit of cloaths is weaving for a lady of quality, which will amount to 36 l. per yard. **1770** LANGHORNE *Plutarch* (1879) I. 103/2 The bride was to bring with her only three suits of clothes. **1778** MISS BURNEY *Evelina* x, They have promised me a compleat suit of linen against the evening. **1848** THACKERAY *Van. Fair* xiv, Her smartest evening suit. **1913** *Play Pictorial* No. 132. p. vi/3 A great variety of linen suits and frocks in exclusive styles.

d. of armour.

1821 SCOTT *Kenilw.* xxxix. Their suits of leathern and paper armour. **1859** TENNYSON *Geraint & Enid* 95 The three gay suits of armour. **1880** [see ARMOUR *sb.* 1].

e. *transf., fig.*, and *allusively.*

birthday suit (humorous): the bare skin; see also s.v. BIRTHDAY 3.

1593 DRAYTON *Heroic. Ep.* iii. 125 In her Masking Sute, the spangled Skie, Come forth to bride it in her Revelrie. **1607** ROWLANDS *Diogines Lanthorne* 33 A gallant groue, That wore greene Sommers sute. **1697** COLLIER *Ess. Mor. Subj.* II. (1709) 105 Like Cloath ill made, he looks better in the Shop, than he wears in the Sute. *a* **1700** B. E. *Dict. Cant. Crew, Suit and Cloak*, good store of Brandy or any agreable Liquor, let down Gutter-lane. **1804** J. GRAHAME *Sabbath* (1839) 8/2 The redbreast's sober suit. **1809** MALKIN *Gil Blas* I. viii. ¶2, I will strip this holy father to his birthday suit. **1858** W. ARNOT *Laws fr. Heaven* Ser. II. xlix. 403 If honour be your clothing, the suit will last a life-time.

†**f.** Grew's name for the tubular florets (florets of the disk) in composite (and similar) flowers. *Obs.*

1671 GREW *Anat. Pl.* I. v. (1682) 38 The several Thrums or rather Suits, whereof the Attire is made up,..are ever consistent of more than one, sometimes of Two, and for the most part of Three Pieces (for which I call them Suits).

g. = *bathing-suit* s.v. BATHING *vbl. sb.* 2, *swim-suit* s.v. SWIM *sb.* 10 b.

1883 L. TROUBRIDGE *Life amongst Troubridges* (1966) 165 Walked along..meaning to bathe... Ran down in our suits. **1949** D. SMITH *I capture Castle* x. 162 We didn't bathe because none of us had brought suits. **1977** *Times* 16 June 13/6 The suit in our picture..is the first suit for ages..to cover up the spare tyre.

20. **a.** Any of the four sets (distinguished by their several marks, as spades, clubs, hearts, diamonds) of which a pack of playing-cards consists. Also, the whole number of cards belonging to such a set held in a player's hand at one time. Often in fig. context and allusively. *long suit*: see LONG *a.*[1] 5 b, 5 c.

1529 LATIMER *2nd Serm. Card* in Foxe *A. & M.* (1563) 1304/1, I purpose agayne to deale vnto you an other card, almost of the same sute. **1589** *Martins Months Minde* Ep. to Rdr., Leauing the auncient game of England (Trumpe) where euerie coate, and sute are sorted in their degree, [they] are running to their Ruffe where the greatest sorte of the sute carrieth away the game. **1622** PEACHAM *Compl. Gentl.* vii. 65, I haue seene French Cards to play withall, the foure suites changed into Maps of seuerall Countries. **1688** HOLME *Armoury* III. xvi. (Roxb.) 73 Five cards of a shute. **1742** HOYLE *Whist* 12 You need seldom return your Partner's Lead, if you have good Suits of your own to play. *Ibid.* 22 If you have Ace, King, and four small Trumps, with a good Suit, you must play three Rounds of Trumps, otherwise you may have your strong Suit trumped. **1755** YOUNG *Centaur* iii. 144 If there are no Fools to be taken in, he makes a pretty good hand of it with a Knave of the right suit. **1816** SINGER *Hist. Cards* 61 Each Suit consists of nine Cards; the backs are black. **1876** *Encycl. Brit.* V. 100/1 A pack of tarots consists of seventy-eight cards, four suits of numeral cards and twenty-two emblematic cards. **1876** CAMPBELL-WALKER *Correct Card* (1880) Gloss. p. xiii, Beginning with the lowest card but one of the suit you lead originally, if it contains more than four cards. **1884** *Bath Herald* 26 Jan. 3/1 The Government are determined to meet Parliament with a strong suit of trumps in the hand. **1885** PROCTOR *Whist* iv. 69 Keep the command of an adversary's suit. **1898** *Daily News* 4 Jan. 3/1 The police and detectives are the New York reporter's strong suit.

b. *to follow suit* (earlier †*in suit*): to play a card of the same suit as the leading card; hence often *fig.*, to do the same thing as somebody or something else. (Cf. 13 c.)

1680 COTTON *Compl. Gamester* (ed. 2) 61 The elder begins and younger follows in suit as at Whisk. *Ibid.* 82 Not following suit when you have it in your hand. **1788** J. BEAUFORT *Hoyle's Games Impr.* 15 Having but two or three small trumps, he should never force his partner to trump, if he finds he cannot follow suit. **1849** *Chambers's Inform. People* II. 663/2 If a person happens not to follow suite, or trump a suite. **1851** H. MELVILLE *Moby Dick* I. v. 47, I quickly followed suit, and descending into the bar-room accosted the grinning landlord. **1859** DICKENS *T. Two Cities* I. ii, The three other horses followed suit. **1865** —— *Mut. Fr.* III. xv, You can't get beforehand with me... You can only follow suit. You can't deprive me of the lead. **1885** W. E. NORRIS *Adrian Vidal* xvi, The 'Monday Review' happened to be the first to notice 'Two Lovers'; but other journals speedily followed suit.

VI. Sequence; agreement.

†**21.** A succession, sequence. *Obs. rare.*

1412–20 LYDG. *Chron. Troy* II. 6797 Euery day þe blomys wer renewed; And þe blosmys, with many sondri swt. **1589** PUTTENHAM *Engl. Poesie* III. xix. (Arb.) 208 When we make one word begin, and..lead the daunce to many verses in sute. **1625** BACON *Ess., Viciss. Things* (Arb.) 571 Euery Fiue and Thirtie years, The same Kinde and Sute of Years and Weathers, comes about againe.

†**22.** *for suit of*: on account of. *in suit of*: in consequence of. *Obs.*

1451 *Yatton Church-w. Acc.* (Som. Rec. Soc.) 94 Yn costage to Well for sowte of the churche gods yn two tymes, xviijd. *a* **1652** I. JONES in Leoni *Palladio's Archit.* (1742) I. 72 It is a hard thing in suit of the Difficulty to accommodate the Chambers and other Places.

23. *in suit with*: in agreement or harmony with. *of a suit with*: of a piece with.

1797 MRS. A. M. BENNETT *Beggar Girl* (1813) II. 2 A Cerberus in human form whose manual strength was in suit with the ferocity of his manners. *Ibid.* 116 Books, music, maps, papers..totally out of suite with the part of the cabin and its furniture yet remaining. **1806** JEFFERSON *Mem.* etc. (1829) IV. 56 The legislature had sanctioned that idea... It seemed, therefore, that the Governor should be in suit with them. **1899** HARDY *A Changed Man, Enter a Dragoon* (1913) 166 A life whose incidents were precisely of a suit with those which had preceded the soldier's return.

VII. Combinations.

24. *attrib.* and *Comb.*, as (senses 19 b, c) *suit coat, -jacket*; **suit bag**, (*a*) a protective covering for a suit which is not being worn; (*b*) a travelling bag designed to contain a suit of clothes; †**suit-breeder**, a promoter of legal prosecutions; †**suit-broker**, one who made a business of procuring a favourable hearing for suits; †**suit-court** (see quot.); **suit-covenant, -custom** *Feudal Law* (see quots.); **suit-duty**, obligation to give suit at a mill; †**suit-groat**, a due paid in lieu of suit at court; **suit-hold** (see HOLD *sb.*[1] 1 b), tenure by suit and service to the superior; †**suit-jogger**, a promoter of lawsuits; **suit length**, a piece of material of the right size for making into a suit; also *fig.*; †**suit-maker**, one who institutes a suit; **suit-mark**, any of the marks distinguishing suits of cards; **suit-roll** *Hist.*, the roll of persons bound to give suit at a particular court; **suit-service** *Feudal Law*, service rendered by attendance at a lord's court; also *fig.*; †**suit-shape**, a fashion of clothes; †**suit-silver**, a local name for a due paid in lieu of suit at a court; **suit-weight**, used *attrib.* of fabrics of an appropriate thickness for making up into suits; †**suit-worth** *a.*, worthy of imitation.

1966 *Olney Amsden & Sons Ltd. Price List* 5 *Suit bag zipped 51/9 doz. **1978** W. STOVALL *Presidential Emergency* i. 1 He set down his suit bag, underseater and attaché case. **1691** SHADWELL *Scowrers* II. i, Attornys, those *Suit-breeders, those Litigious Rogues. **1632** MASSINGER *Maid of Hon.* II. ii, A *suit-broker in court. **1971** D. E. WESTLAKE *I gave at the Office* (1972) 15 A guy..whose *suitcoat collar was turned up indoors. **1972** *National Observer* (U.S.) 27 May 1/4 Wallace removed his suit coat, handed it to an aide, and moved forward to greet well-wishers. **1755** JOHNSON, **Suit Court*, is the court in which tenants owe attendance to their lord. *Bailey.* **1579** [RASTELL] *Expos. Termes Lawes* 174 b, *Suit couenaunt is when your auncestor haue couenanted with my auncestours to sue to the court of my auncestors. *Ibid.*, *Suit custome is when I and my auncestours haue beene seised of your owne suite and your auncestours, time out of minde. *c* **1460** *Oseney Reg.* 75 Of no *Sute Dewte, by such maner, we shall axe or chalenge of þe forsaide maynye or men. **1556** in *Archaeologia* XXXIV. 53 Paid for a *suitt groat at the same time. **1615** *MS. Acc. St. John's Hosp., Canterb.*, Payd Lordis Rentis..and seut grote. **1864** WHARTON *Law-Lex.* (ed. 3) 868/2 **Suithold*, a tenure in consideration of certain services to the superior lord. **1965** M. SHADBOLT *Among Cinders* x. 79 The crumpled..*suit-jacket with sleeves too short. **1977** *Transatlantic Rev.* LX. 69 She had taken off her suitjacket. **1630** J. TAYLOR (Water P.) *Gt. Eater Kent* Wks. 143/1 Proiect-mongers, *Suit-ioggers, and Stargazers. **1924** J. JOYCE *Let.* 30 Sept. (1957) II. 221 There is now a special cheap edition..about 1/11½ per normal novel *suitlength real continental. **1971** D. LEES *Rainbow Conspiracy* ii. 24 The foreman weaver in most mills is allowed to take any end pieces as part of his perks... More often than not he finds himself with a suit length. **1469–70** in *10th Rep. Hist. MSS. Comm.* App. v. 307 Lasse [= unless] the *suete makere will sue him that hath done the offence, after the course of the commene lawe. **1905** *Athenæum* 18 Nov. 683/3 The *suit-marks were possibly coins, cups, bells, and birds. **1532** *Acc. Ld. High Treas. Scot.* VI. 116 Bringand with thame the *sute roll of thair Sherefdome. **1541** *Records of Elgin* (New Spald. Club) I. 55 Quhilk day was assingit to the saidis personis to produce thair instrumentis and to be enterit in the soit roll. **1914** CLOUSTON *Rec. Earld. Orkney* Introd. p. lxxxv, The suit-rolls containing their names making a practically complete list of the county gentry. **1579** [RASTELL] *Expos. Termes Lawes* 211 b, *Suit seruice is to come to the Court from iij. weekes to iij. weekes by the whole yeare. **1651** tr. *Kitchin's Courts Leet* (1657) 291 Suit-service is by reason of Free-hold, that is, by reason of their tenure, that is, for that they hold of their Lord by suit to his Court. **1870** D. G. ROSSETTI *Youth's Spring-tribute* 13 For this Is even the hour of Love's sworn suitservice. **1598** MARSTON *Sco. Villanie* x. 164 This fashion-mounger..Contemplates *sute shapes. **1672** MANLEY *Cowel's Interpr.*, *Sute-silver, is a small Rent, or sum of Money, which, if paid, does excuse the Freeholders from the appearance at the Court-Barons within the Honor of Clun in Shropshire. **1955** *Archit. Rev.* CXVII. 351 (*caption*) Light *suit-weight Cheviot tweed by Michal Illan. **1963** *Guardian* 10 May 8/4 Tweed, flannel or other suit-weight woollen. **1594** R. CAREW *Tasso* v. 211 If any may *sutewoorth example finde.

b. In *Bridge*, freq. as opp. to NO TRUMP(s) *phr.*, as ***suit-bid, -break, call, contract, declaration, double, game, -jump***; **suit preference signal**, a play of a card of a certain rank to indicate which suit one wishes one's partner to return.

1917 E. BERGHOLT *Royal Auction Bridge* I. 90 In some circles, the practice of raising partner's *suit-bid, when no other bid has intervened, is considerably overdone. **1962** *Times* 24 Oct. 3/7 Why be forced into a higher contract which may be in jeopardy through unlucky *suit-breaks? **1907** *Westm. Gaz.* 18 May 14/1 As to a *suit call, the original lead must never be from a suit that contains a probable trick. **1977** *Homes & Gardens* Feb. 14 Presumably he also appreciates the point I made above about playing unbalanced hands in a *suit contract. **1910** W. DALTON *Saturday Bridge* iv. 65 (*heading*) Defensive *suit declarations by the dealer. **1927** *Observer* 13 Mar. 27 The *suit double..has several interesting aspects. **1910** W. DALTON *Saturday Bridge* vii. 89 There are two distinct games at Bridge, the No Trump game and the *suit game. **1929** M. C. WORK *Compl. Contract Bridge* 52 When determining whether to make a *suit-jump of two or three.. do not be influenced..by Queens or Jacks of other suits. **1934** H. LAVINTHAL in *Bridge World* June 5/1, I am offering a new convention for the defense. I call this convention the High-Low *Suit Preference Signal. **1981** *Times* 14 Nov. 17/6 Where there is any risk of confusion, suit preference signals should not be applied to the first trick.

suit (s(j)u:t), *v.* Forms: 5–6 suyt, 6 sewt, shute, *Sc.* su(i)tt, soute, 6–8 sute, suite, 6– suit. [f. prec.]

†**1.** *intr.* To 'do suit' to a court; hence, to have recourse *to*. *Obs.*

c **1450** *St. Cuthbert* (Surtees) 3575 Shrewes þan on happ sall' suyt To my body for refuyt. *c* **1540** [see SUITING *vbl. sb.* 1].

†**2.** To prefer a suit; to sue *to* a person *for* something. *Obs.*

1526 *Pilgr. Perf.* (W. de W. 1531) 67 These holy fathers knowyng theyr owne conscyence clere..hauynge no record of man to declare them..sewted to almyghty god. **1536** *St. Papers Hen. VIII*, V. 61, I will never soute..of the King of Scottes, but by the Kinges Highnes meanes here. **1567** in Tytler *Hist. Scot.* (1864) III. 247, I am so suited to for to enterprise the revenge. **1641** *Cheke's Hurt Sedit.* Life b iv b, Three powerfull competitors all suiting for it. **1679** C. NESSE *Antid. agst. Popery* 90 God loves to be suited unto by saints and angels. **1719** *Caldwell Pap.* (Maitl. Club) I. 238 I'm ready to think that your lordship's friendship may give it to either of the gentlemen who now suit for it.

†**3.** *trans.* To make an application or appeal for, to solicit; to sue for in a court of law. *Sc. Obs.*

1567 in Tytler *Hist. Scot.* (1864) III. 248 The nobility are of mind to suit assistance of the queen. **1573–4** *Reg. Privy Council Scot.* Ser. I. II. 330 The coistis..and interes sustenit ..aucht to be suitt and persewit alsua befoir the saidis Judgeis. **1575** in *Maitl. Cl. Misc.* (1840) I. 121 He..had humblie suittit..to haue bene admittit to the said celebratioun. **1598** in Row *Hist. Kirk* (Wodrow Soc.) 190 It is caried..that the Kirk..should sute vote in Parliament. **1616** W. HAIG in J. Russell *Haigs* (1881) vii. 162 Never the boldness..to..suit recompence from your Majesty. **1633** W. STRUTHER *True Happiness* 49 If we had merite to deserve it, we needed not Suit it of God. **1710** in *Nairne Peerage Evidence* (1874) 44 What else he may suite ask claim and crave. **1717** *Ibid.* 146 To suit execution hereon.

†**4.** To make one's suit to, petition; to bring a suit against; to sue. *Obs.*

1559–60 *MS. Cott. Calig.* B. IX, Then sall they not fayle to sute zow in zour awne countrey. **1566–7** *Reg. Privy Council Scot.* Ser. I. I. 503 The Quenis Majestie, being ernistlie suitit be the Quene of Inglandis ambassatouris..for payment. *c* **1610** SIR J. MELVIL *Mem.* (1735) 348 The King of Scotland was suiting her Majesty for an Alliance. *a* **1653** BINNING *Serm.* (1845) 272 Let Wisdom have but a patient hearing,..and she will carry it off from all that suit you.

†**5.** *intr.* To pay court *to* a woman. *Obs.*

c **1590** MONTGOMERIE *Wks.* (S.T.S.) Suppl. Vol. 221 First serve, syne sute,..gif thow intend to win thy ladyis grace. **1639** N. N. tr. *Du Bosq's Compl. Woman* II. 58 Iberina..who had a mind to as many men as suited unto her. **1749** FIELDING *Tom Jones* v. v, If the greatest Squire in all the Country would come a suiting to me to-morrow.

†**6.** *trans.* To pursue, follow. *Sc. Obs.*

1582 *Reg. Privy Council Scot.* Ser. I. III. 525 The saidis personis..in lyke maner sutit Johnne Blak,..and wald have brokin up his durris. *c* **1590** J. STEWART *Poems* (S.T.S.) II. 69 The precelling Paladeine.. In sutting him with diligence did tend Quhair thair occurs sic cursit canckerd cair.

†**7. a.** To pursue, aim at; to seek to obtain. *Sc.*

1559–60 *MS. Cott. Calig.* B. IX, Gif by zour frendly support.. ze sall declare that not only sute ze not the ruyne off our country, but will [etc.]. **1587** *Reg. Privy Council Scot.* Ser. I. IV. 197 Minassing and avowing to sute the lyveis of his tennentis. *c* **1590** J. STEWART *Poems* (S.T.S.) II. 218 His mercie great..Quhilk gif ȝe sute..Ȝit he vill led ȝow from that haples place. **1686** J. RENWICK in *Life* (Biogr. Presbyt. 1827) II. 270 He [*sc.* Christ] suites the Creatures Affection, as if it were of some Worth.

†**b.** To seek *in marriage*; to woo. Chiefly *Sc.*

1615 BRATHWAIT *Loves Labyrinth* (1878) 274 Sewing, and suting Thysbe for his bride. **1630** RUTHERFORD *Lett.* (1862) I. vii. 53 The Lord, who is suiting you in marriage. *a* **1639** SPOTTISWOOD *Hist. Ch. Scot.* II. (1677) 105 He was..sent Ambassador to..the Emperor, to suit his daughter Margaret in marriage. **1676** ROW *Contin. Blair's Autobiog.* xii. (1848) 527 Lady Margaret Kennedy had lived a virgin unmarried, (though suited by severals).

†**8. a.** To arrange in a set, sequence, or series; to set in due order, sort out. Also with *forth*. *Obs.*

1552 in *Archæol. Cant.* (1872) VIII. 104 Item iij bells in the steple suted. **1554** in Feuillerat *Revels Q. Mary* (1914) 159 Svting performynge and puttinge the same in aredynes to be engrosed. **1571** —— *Revels Q. Eliz.* (1908) 129 Ffowlding, suting, putting in order and bestowing of the Garmentes. **1586** A. DAY *Eng. Secretorie* I. (1595) 22 All which I referre to their peculiar places each one, as they are suted foorth to be in their kindes deliuered. *Ibid.* 100 There are Letters also might be suted vnder this forme. **1608** TOPSELL *Serpents* 270 As for separating,..carding, or suting their stuffe, they are very Bunglers. **1655** E. TERRY *Voy. East-India* 385 The Company sent the Mogol..an able Coach-man, to sute and mannage some of his excellent Horses. **1695** BLACKMORE *Pr. Arth.* II. 74 He..suits and ranges Natures that agree.

†**b.** *intr.* To range oneself. *Obs. rare.*

1591 SAVILE *Tacitus, Hist.* I. lxiv. 36 As the rest of the souldiers suted on sides.

9. a. *trans.* To provide with a suit of clothes; to clothe, attire, dress. Chiefly *pass. arch.*

1577 STANYHURST *Hist. Ireland* in *Holinshed* 105/2 He woulde not..buy a sute of apparell for himselfe, but hee woulde sute hir [*sc.* his wife] with the same stuffe. **1591** LODGE *Catharos* Wks. (Hunter. Club) 11 Shall I sute thee Cosmosophos?.. I wil haue thee apparailed according to discipline and order. **1596** SHAKS. *Merch. V.* I. ii. 79 How odly he is suited, I thinke he bought his doublet in Italie. **1600** HEYWOOD *1st Pt. Edw. IV*, I. i, Birchin Lane shall suit us. **1604** B. JONSON *King Jas. Entert.* A iij, Whereof the one ..was suted in blacke and purple. *c* **1661** FULLER *Worthies, Cambr.* (1662) 161, I will suit you (if so pleased,) with a light habit. **1662** *St. George's Day* (1685) 10 All suted in..Satin Gowns, and Velvet Caps. **1829** J. STERLING *Ess.*, etc. (1848) I. 85 More solemnly suited with black, he was placed in a room hung round with faded green. **1887** *Pall Mall Gaz.* 12 Feb. 4/1 No caparisoned beasts..suited in burnished mail ..but sturdy steeds.

b. *refl.* To dress or attire oneself. *Obs.* or *arch.*

1594 [R. BARNFIELD] *Affect. Sheph.* II. li, The learned Sisters sute themselues in blacke. **1594** MARLOWE & NASHE *Dido* I. i, It is the vse for Turen maides to..suite themselues in purple. **1600** SHAKS. *A.Y.L.* I. iii 118 Were it not better ..That I did suite me all points like a man? **1607** ROWLANDS *Fam. Hist.* 23 My Armour shall be black! I'le suit me in a mournful Iron-shell. **1624** HEYWOOD *Gunaik.* I. 25 Any man that hath bought cloath to suite himself. **1822** W. JAMESON in *Mem. & Lett.* (1845) 80 One who suits himself only once a year.

c. *transf.* and *fig.*

1589 NASHE *Anat. Absura.* Ep. Ded., Fortune..suted poore Flaunders and Fraunce in her frownes, and saluted Englands soule with a smoothed forehead. **1594** J. DICKENSON *Arisbas* (1878) 30 His Fame..suted in robes of immortalitie,..towres to the clouds. *c* **1600** SHAKS. *Sonn.* cxxvii, My Mistresse eyes [*conj.* brows] are Rauen blacke, Her eyes so suted, and they mourners seeme. **1628** WITHER *Brit. Rememb.* II. 55 Yea, many times he suites His Deity in our poore attributes. **1633** BP. HALL *Hard T., N.T.* 363 Wherefore then, O Saviour, art thou thus suited in crimson and dyed red with blood?

d. To fit (someone) *up* with a specific type of clothing, as for sport, protection, etc. Cf. KIT *v.*[1] 2. *U.S.*

1945 M. H. ALLEE *Smoke Jumper* iii. 24 A man suited up for smoke jumping would almost as soon fall into the fire itself as into deep water. **1970** *New Yorker* 24 Oct. 140/3 Yale suited up sixty men, including four quarterbacks. **1976** *Daily Tel.* 1 Sept. 3/3 Only when everyone [*sc.* U.S. policemen] is suited up is the order given to tackle a disorderly crowd. **1979** *Tucson Mag.* Apr. 66 (Advt.), Dave Bloom and Sons will suit you up for all your active sport needs.

10. a. To make appropriate or agreeable *to*; to adapt or accommodate in style, manner, or proportion *to*; to make consonant or accordant *with*; to render suitable. Also *refl.*

1600 SHAKS. *A.Y.L.* II. vii. 81 He..That..therein suites His folly to the mettle of my speech. **1602** —— *Ham.* III. ii. 19 Sute the Action to the Word, the Word to the Action. **1610** HEYWOOD *Gold. Age* II. i, Oh sute your pitty with your Angell-beauty. **1621** QUARLES *Div. Poems, Esther* (1630) 121 The King commands the servants of his State, To suite respect to Hamans high estate. **1711** SHAFTESB. *Charac.* (1737) I. 200 He..sutes himself..to the fancy of his reader. **1781** COWPER *Charity* 153 To suit His manners with his fate, [he] puts on the brute. **1787** BEST *Angling* (ed. 2) 90 When you make the palmer-fly suit the colour of the silk to the hackle you dub with. **1831** SCOTT *Cast. Dang.* viii, [They] took care to suit their answers to the questions put to them. **1844** KINGLAKE *Eothen* xvii, The peculiar way in which you are obliged to suit yourself to the movements of the beast [*sc.* a camel]. **1865** DICKENS *Mut. Fr.* IV. xiv, 'I mean to knock your head against the wall,' returned John Harmon, suiting his action to his words, with the heartiest good-will. **1874** MAHAFFY *Soc. Life Greece* viii. 261 Try..to perform as well as possible what the gods have suited to your nature.

b. *freq.* in *pass.* (*to be suited to* = 13, 14.)

1596 SHAKS. *Merch. V.* III. v. 70 O deare discretion, how his words are suted. *c* **1605** ROWLEY *Birth Merl.* I. i, Provided My Daughters love be suited with my grant. *c* **1611** CHAPMAN *Iliad* XXIII. 417 Your words are suited to your eyes. **1771** *Junius Lett.* lxi i. (1788) 334 Both the law and the language are well suited to a Barrister! **1821** SCOTT *Kenilw.* xxxviii, I ceased to cons der either courts, or court-intrigues, as suited to my temper or genius. **1837** GORING & PRITCHARD *Microgr.* 210 They will soon..thrust themselves into situations of restraint well suited for the purpose. **1874** GREEN *Short Hist.* vii. §3. (1882) 364 It [*sc.* a policy] was one eminently suited to Elizabeth's peculiar powers.

11. To provide, furnish. Chiefly *pass.* (or *refl.*), to be provided (or provide oneself) *with* something desired and in such a manner as to please one.

1607 TOURNEUR *Rev. Trag.* III. v, Hee's suted for a Lady. **1642** D. ROGERS *Naaman* 45 God..sutes the one with willingnesse to be holpen, and the other with readinesse to helpe. **1782** COWPER *Gilpin* 58 'Twas long before the customers Were suited to their mind. **1837** HOOD *Hymen. Retrosp.* ii. 26 Cook, by the way, came up to-day To bid me suit myself. **1848** DICKENS *Dombey* ii, I hope you are suited, my dear. **1852** THACKERAY *Esmond* III. iii, I am thinking of retiring into the plantations, and..if I want company, suiting myself with a squaw.

†**12.** To find a parallel to, match. *Obs. rare.*

1589 ? LYLY *Pappe w. Hatchet* Wks. 1902 III. 409, I haue taken an inuentorie of al thy..rakehell tearmes, and could sute them in no place but in Bedlam and Bridewell.

13. a. To be agreeable or convenient to (a person, his inclinations, etc.); to fall in with the views or wishes of.

a **1578** LINDESAY (Pitscottie) *Chron. Scot.* (S.T.S.) II. 254 The lordis of Edinburgh..thocht to have taine the same and suitted nocht my lord of Mortounis men of weir. *a* **1595** *Satir. Poems Reform.* xvii. 22 Quhat plesis them, the same the pepill suittis. **1719** *Caldwell Papers* (Maitl. Club) I. 238 Either to answer or not, as best suits your conveniency. **1779** *Mirror* No. 34 That sort of promise which a man keeps when the thing suits his inclination. **1786** JEFFERSON *Writ.* (1859) II. 3 It is only to keep alive pretensions which may authorize the commencement of hostilities when it shall suit them. **1812** BYRON *Ch. Har.* I. iii, But whence his name And lineage long, it suits me not to say. **1889** JEROME *Three Men in Boat* 17 Harris said that the river would suit him to a 'T'. **1894** HALL CAINE *Manxman* III. xix. 190 Then came the change of the day to suit his supposed convenience.

b. ***suit yourself***: do (or think) as you please, please yourself.

1897 KIPLING *Captains Courageous* i. 21 'You stole it.' 'Suit yourself. We stole it ef it's any comfort to you.' **1932** W. FAULKNER *Light in August* xxi. 478 'I reckon I'll ride back here,' she says... 'Suit yourself,' I says. And we drove off. **1953** K. TENNANT *Joyful Condemned* xiii. 120 'Just suit yourself.' Miss Pilcher shrugged her broad shoulders. **1977** 'M. UNDERWOOD' *Murder with Malice* xiii. 118 'I'll probably call back later.' 'Suit yourself,' the woman said, indifferently.

14. a. To be fitted or adapted to, be suitable for, answer the requirements of.

1603 J. DAVIES *Microcosmos* Wks. (Grosart) I. 77/2 What is't On Earth that shee thinks (be'ng so superfine) Worthie to suite her, but alone to reigne? **1650** SIR W. MURE *Cry Blood* 509 Tears sute the season. **1692** LOCKE *3rd Let. Toler.* x. 264 There being..no necessity of Miracles for any other end, but to supply the want of the Magistrate's Assistance, they must, to sute that end, be constant. **1733** POPE *Ess. Man* III. 80 All enjoy that pow'r which suits them best. **1784** COWPER *Task* I. 106 The Sofa suits The gouty limb. **1815** J. SMITH *Panorama Sci. & Art* II. 650 The sort which he knows will suit the soil and situation of his land. **1855** MACAULAY *Hist. Eng.* xx. IV. 453 One poet is the eagle: another is the swan: a third modestly compares himself to the bee. But none of these types would have suited Montague. **1875** JOWETT *Plato* (ed. 2) III. 591 His own explanation did not suit all phenomena. **1891** *Speaker* 11 July 37/1 The error of supposing that what suits a small country could be readily transplanted to large European States.

b. To be good for, 'agree with'; *esp.* to be favourable to the health of (a person).

1814 SCOTT *Diary* 16 Aug. in *Lockhart*, The wet and boggy walk not suiting his gout. **1861** B'NESS BUNSEN in Hare *Life* (1879) II. v. 289 It does not suit my eyes to employ them by candlelight. **1882** *Med. Temp. Jrnl.* I. 128 What suits us we think ought to suit..other people.

c. To be becoming to.

1819 SCOTT *Ivanhoe* xxxv, It suits not our condition to hold with thee long communication. **1872** GEO. ELIOT *Middlem.* i, Souls have complexions too; what will suit one will not suit another. **1884** G. ALLEN *Philistia* II. 5 It suits your complexion admirably.

†**15.** *intr.* To agree *together*. *Obs.*

1630 PRYNNE *Anti-Armin.* 182 They all accord and fitly suite together in one intiretie.

16. To be suitable, fitting, or convenient; to match or be in accord.

1816 JANE AUSTEN *Emma* III. ii. 20 Frank Churchill is a capital dancer, I understand—We shall see if our styles suit. *a* **1817** —— *Persuasion* (1818) IV. v. 91 Mr. Elliot is an exceedingly agreeable man..but we should not suit. **1821** SCOTT *Kenilw.* xiv, If opportunity suits. **1825** T. HOOK *Sayings* Ser. II. *Passion & Princ.* ii, That's well, Sir,..that will suit well. **1847** TENNYSON *Princ.* Concl. 9 What style could suit? **1865** MRS. CARLYLE *Lett.* III. 269 Say Saturday; if that does not suit there will be time to tell me. **1971** 'D. HALLIDAY' *Dolly & Doctor Bird* xiii. 193 I've done an Eysenck personality inventory on you both... You wouldn't suit.

17. Const. preps. **a.** ***to suit with***: to agree, harmonize, or fit in with; to be suitable to; *occas.* to match in colour, etc. *Obs.* or *arch.*

1605 SHAKS. *Macb.* II. i. 60 For feare Thy very stones prate of my where-about, And take the present horror from the time, Which now suites with it. **1611** A. STAFFORD *Niobe* 108 He..sees that the Court is not a place suting with his disposition. **1655** STANLEY *Hist. Philos.* (1701) 59/1 Tzetzes affirms he was Master to Thales, but that suits not with their times. **1677** MOXON *Mech. Exerc.* i. 15 But of that in its proper place, because it suits not with this Section of Filing. **1681** DRYDEN *Abs. & Achit.* 478 This Advice above the rest With Absalom's Mild Nature suited best. **1719** DE FOE *Crusoe* II. (Globe) 509, I have a Project to communicate to you, which, as it suits with my Thoughts, may..suit with yours also. **1751** ELIZA HEYWOOD *Betsy Thoughtless* I. 213 That she should be glad to see him, whenever it suited with his convenience. **1785** CRABBE *Newspaper* 2 A busy, bustling time, Suits ill with writers, very ill with rhyme. **1815** SCOTT *Guy M.* xxviii, His walking-dress..had so much of a military character as suited not amiss with his having such a weapon. **1853** MISS YONGE *Heir of Redclyffe* v, 'A man ought to be six foot one, person and mind, to suit with that grand, sedate, gracious way of Philip's,' said Guy. **1859** *Habits of*

Gd. Society iv. 174 The shawl is affronted with the gown; the bonnet is made to suit with both.

†**b.** *to suit to*: = 13, 14, 17 a. *Obs.*

1632 Sir T. Hawkins tr. *Mathieu's Unhappy Prosp.* 241 Time cooperateth with his industry, and fortune sutes to his vigilance. **1634** Sir T. Herbert *Trav.* 211 Her [*sc.* the dodo's] legs suting to her body. **1653** H. More *Antid. Ath.* II. xii. §1 If I should pursue all that suits to my purpose it would amount to an intire Volume. **1690** T. Burnet *Review Theory Earth* 29 *note*, A Text, that does not suit to their own Notions. *a* **1700** Dryden *Sigism. & Guisc.* 44 She cast her Eyes around the Court, to find A worthy Subject suiting to her Mind. **1802–12** Bentham *Ration. Judic. Evid.* (1827) II. 136 Such solicitations as it suited not to him to make.

†**c.** To be fitted or adapted *for*. *Obs.*

1793 [Earl Dundonald] *Descr. Estate Culross* 5 The bands of Iron Stone are numerous,..suiting partly for Forge and partly for Melting Iron.

†**d.** To act in accordance *with*, conform *to*. *Obs. rare.*

1647 N. Bacon *Disc. Govt. Eng.* I. xvi. (1739) 32 In matters of Action, [they] would suit with the occasion. *Ibid.* lxiv. 136 Two Ordinances made by the King, and such Lords as suted to the King's way. *a* **1660** *Contemp. Hist. Irel.* (Ir. Archæol. Soc.) I. 176 Taaffe was comaunded by the Councell, (as..sutinge to theire factious principles) to marche with his armie.

e. To dress oneself *up* in clothing designed for a specific task or purpose.

1959 J. Blish *Clash of Cymbals* viii. 191 We should suit up at the half-hour. **1967** *Boston Sunday Herald* 30 Apr. I. 22/2 Jim Lyle headed for the flight line to suit up for a routine mission aboard one of the giant radar picket planes. **1975** 'A. Hall' *Mandarin Cypher* xi. 170 'Time to suit up, isn't it?'.. I got into the wet-suit. **1978** G. A. Sheehan *Running & Being* xv. 206 He will suit up and get out on the roads.

suitability (s(j)uːtəˈbɪlɪtɪ). [f. next + -ity.] The quality or condition of being suitable; an instance of this. Const. *to*, *for*, or inf.

1681–6 J. Scott *Chr. Life* II. iv. §2 Wks. 1718 I. 273 If.. we can discover a World of mutual Suitabilities of this to that,..it will be a sufficient Argument that they all proceed from some wise Cause. **1718** De Foe *Fam. Instruct.* (1841) II. I. i. 15 What suitability can there be in two tempers so extremely opposite? **1853** F. W. Newman *Odes of Horace* I Its suitability as a first piece is our excuse for presenting it quite out of chronological order. **1865** Dickens *Mut. Fr.* II. xvi, It was a marriage of pure inclination and suitability. **1867** Mill *Subj. Women* (1869) 170 The suitability of the individuals to give each other a happy life. **1912** *Times* 19 Dec. 19/2 The suitability of the greater proportion of Rhodesia for the breeding of stock.

suitable (ˈs(j)uːtəb(ə)l), *a.* (*adv.*) Also 6–8 **sut(e)able**, 7–8 **suiteable**. [f. suit *v.* + -able, after *agreeable*. Earlier synonyms were *suit-like*, *suitly*.

In the following passage *seuthable* may be an early example of this word, or may haye arisen from a misreading of *semable* as *seutable*:—

1513 Douglas *Æneid* I. Prol. 394 Rycht so, by about speche oft in tymes, And seuthable [*Camb. MS.* semabill] wordis we compile our rymes.]

†**1.** Of furniture, dress, features, etc.: Conforming or agreeing in shape, colour, pattern, or style; matching, to match. Const. *to*, *with*. *Obs.*

1582 N. Lichefield tr. *Castanheda's Conq. E. Ind.* I. lxxvi. 155 His Shooes..were all beset with Aglets of golde, and his Cap couered ouer with Buttons sutable to the same. **1584** in *Scott's Kenilw.* Note K, A crymson sattin counter-pointe,.. A chaise of crymson sattin, suteable. **1594** Plat *Jewell-ho.* I. 21, I had an old wainescot window, that was peeced out with new wainscot by a good workeman, and both becam verie suteable and of one colour. **1614** Markham *Cheap Husb.* II. 110 The colour being sutable with the colour of the feathers on his head. **1625** in *Rymer's Fœdera* (1726) XVIII. 237/2 The Bason enamelled..and the Layer [= ewer] sutable, haveing forty eighte small Dyamonds in the Bason. **1634–5** Brereton *Trav.* (Chetham Soc.) 49 Four dainty suitable quarters in the court. **1635** Stafford *Fem. Glory* 3 Her visage long, and her nose sutable. **1656** Heylin *Surv. France* 98 The beds are all sutable one to the other. *c* **1710** Celia Fiennes *Diary* (1888) 300 The doores to them [*sc.* cupboards] made suiteable to ye wanscoate.

†**2.** Of persons, actions, qualities, conditions, institutions: Conforming or agreeing in nature, condition, or action; accordant; corresponding; analogous; *occas.* congenial. *Obs.*

1592 Greene *Upst. Courtier* Dj, Euery seruile drudge must ruffle in his silkes, or else hee is not suteable. **1617** Moryson *Itin.* II. 88 This is a pleasant towne for seate if the inhabitants were sutable. **1647** N. Bacon *Disc. Govt. Eng.* I. viii. 25 Had not Bishops been somewhat sutable the Roman Clergy had not been like it self. **1649** Bp. Reynolds *Hosea* iii. 19 God sets every blessing upon our score, and expects an answer and returne suteable. **1667** Milton *P.L.* III. 639 In his face Youth smil'd Celestial, and to every Limb Sutable grace diffus'd. **1718** Steele *Fish-pool* 193 The.. painful way, in which fish..are conveyed in Well-boats, must have suitable unhealthy effects. **1748** Melmoth *Fitzosb. Lett.* xlvii, Certain suitable feelings which the objects that present themselves to his consideration instantly occasion in his mind.

†**b.** Const. *to*, *with*. *Obs.*

a **1586** Sidney *Arcadia* III. xi. §5 The matter of your letters so fit for a worthy minde, and the maner so sutable to the noblenesse of the matter. **1597** Hooker *Eccl. Pol.* v. xlix. §1 A worke most suteable with his purpose—who gaue himselfe to be the price of redemption for all. **1620** T. Granger *Div. Logike* 42 Ouid describeth the figure of mans body sutable to his reasonable soule. **1638** Slingsby *Diary* (1836) 6 His disposition is not sutable wi[th] ye rest of his fellow servants. **1646** Sir T. Browne *Pseud. Ep.* I. viii. §11. 33 They have left us relations suitable to those of Ælian. **1711** Shaftesb. *Charac.* I. 33 Those Measures of Offence and Indignation, which we vulgarly suppose in God, are sutable to those original Ideas of Goodness which [He]..has implanted in us.

†**c.** Of two or more things: That are in agreement or accord. *Obs.*

1605 Camden *Rem.*, *Names* (1623) 45 Destinies were superstitiously by *Onomantia* desciphered out of names, as though the names and natures of men were sutable. **1640** F. Roberts *Clavis Bibl.* 303 The suitable wickednesse of Priests and people. **1684** Bunyan *Pilgr.* II. 135 Gaius and they were such sutable Company, that they could not tell how to part.

3. That is fitted for, adapted or appropriate to a person's character, condition, needs, etc., a purpose, object, occasion, or the like. Const. *to*, *for*.

1607 Shaks. *Timon* III. vi. 92 What is amisse in them, you Gods, make suteable for destruction. **1621** Sanderson *Serm.*, *Ad Pop.* iv. (1632) 364 Worthy of all..civill respects sutable to his place and person. **1653** Holcroft *Procopius, Goth. Wars* I. 10 Senseless fears not sutable to the occasion. **1672** Petty *Pol. Anat.* (1691) 78 There are 750,000 in Ireland who could earn 2s. a week..if they had sutable employment. **1711** Steele *Spect.* No. 113 ¶4 As soon as I thought my Retinue suitable to the Character of my Fortune and Youth. **1798** S. & Ht. Lee *Canterb. T.* II. 120 A suitable match for their daughter. **1812** *New Botanic Gard.* I. 59 The most suitable season for transplanting the roots. **1815** Elphinstone *Acc. Caubul* (1842) II. 215 As it was always a distinct government,..it seemed more suitable to treat of it separately. **1822** Scott *Nigel* vi, A dress..more suitable to his age and quality than he had formerly worn. **1860** Tyndall *Glac.* II. iii. 246 A suitable atmosphere enveloping the most distant planet might render it..perfectly habitable. **1893** J. A. Hodges *Elem. Photogr.* vii. 54 To make several experimental exposures on suitable subjects.

†**4.** = suable *a. Obs. rare.*

a **1555** Bradford in Foxe *A. & M.* (1570) III. 1838/1 The wife is no sutable person but the husband.

5. *Comb.*, as ***suitable-sized*** adj.

1892 E. Reeves *Homeward Bound* 337 A fixed price for five years for all the suitable-sized mutton they can grow.

B. as *adv.* = suitably. Const. *to*.

1584 in *Scott's Kenilw.* Note K, A square stoole and a foote stoole, of crimson velvet, fringed and garnished suteable. **1631** May tr. *Barclay's Mirr. Mindes* I. 189 Italy ..is now bounded, (more suitable farre to the intention of Nature,) by the enclosure of those lofty Alpes. **1655** *Theophania* 16 He..ever framed his discourse suitable to his company. **1664** in *Extr. State Papers rel. Friends* (1912) III. 224 That soe wee may steare our Course suitable to your Commands. **1748** Hartley *Observ. Man* I. ii. §5. 235 Where a Person mis-spells suitable to a Mispronunciation. **1796** Mrs. E. Parsons *Myst. Warning* I. 31 To see her dear children cloathed, and attended suitable to their father's birth.

ˈsuitableness. [-ness.] The quality or condition of being suitable; suitability; †conformity.

1613 Purchas *Pilgrimage* (1614) 425 That sutablenesse of their Law to their lawlesse lusts of Rapine and Poligamie. **1668** Wilkins *Real Char.* IV. i. 388 These Grammatical Particles are here contrived to such a kind of distinct sutableness, as each of the several kinds of them, hath a several kind of Character assigned to them. **1748** Hartley *Observ. Man* I. iv. §6. 496 The great Suitableness of all the Virtues to each other. **1839** Hallam *Hist. Lit.* III. vi. §95. 614 The superiority of the original, except in suitableness for representation, has long been acknowledged. **1875** Jowett *Plato* (ed. 2) III. 691 The suitableness of its pastures to every sort of animal.

b. With *a* and *pl.*

a **1586** Sidney *Arcadia* II. xxix. ¶5 For a testimonie of constancie, and a sutablenes to his word. **1658** Baxter *Saving Faith* 12 The men..trie not their acts by a sutableness to the object. **1664** South *Twelve Serm.* ii. (1697) II. 91 He, who creates those Sympathies, and sutablenesses of Nature,..and..brings Persons so affected together. **1709** T. Robinson *Vindic. Mosaick System* 55 Bearing such a Suitableness and Harmony with the more refined Sense..of the Soul of Man. **1880** Mrs. Whitney *Odd or Even?* ii. 17 It was no use to try to carry out a fancy or a suitableness.

suitably (ˈs(j)uːtəblɪ), *adv.* Also 6 **sutetably**, 7 **sutably**. [f. suitable *a.* + -ly.]

†**1.** Chiefly const. *to*: In agreement, conformity, or correspondence; agreeably, correspondingly, according. *Obs.*

1577 Stanyhurst *Descr. Irel.* 1/2 in *Holinshed*, My course pack threede coulde not haue beene sutetably knit with his fine silcke. **1654** Whitlock *Zootomia* 9 In Life Hee is a true Actor..that lives his part Sutably, to strut in Rags, or Crawle in Robes, equally transgresse Decorum. **1686** Horneck *Crucif. Jesus* xxiii. 785 They should perform the task suitably to their leisure. **1729** Butler *Serm.* Wks. 1874 II. Pref. 14 Brutes..act suitably to their whole nature. **1749** *Power Numbers in Poet. Compos.* 52 *note*, Diversifying the Harmony of the Numbers, by a judicious Mixture of them, suitably to the Nature of the Subject.

2. In a suitable or fitting manner; appropriately, fitly.

1681 S. Fell in *Jrnl. Friends' Hist. Soc.* (1912) July 136 Words will rise most suitably to answer the matter in hand. **1709** Steele *Tatler* No. 4 ¶2 These different Perfections are suitably represented by the last great Painter Italy has sent us. **1770** *Boston Gaz.* 26 Nov. 3/1 These..may suitably employ our minds at the approaching solemnity. **1828** Scott *F.M. Perth* v, Never was kiss so well bestowed, and meet it is that it should be suitably returned. **1875** Jowett *Plato* (ed. 2) V. 241 Every melody is right when suitably accompanied.

†**ˈsuitage.** *Obs.* [f. suit *sb.* or *v.* + -age.] The performance of suit by a tenant.

1610 W. Folkingham *Art of Survey* III. v. 72 The Confinage shewes to what Lord,..&c. the Seruice and Suitage..is due.

suitcase (ˈs(j)uːtkeɪs). [f. suit *sb.* + case *sb.*[2]]

1. A small portmanteau designed to contain a suit of clothes. Hence more generally, a piece of luggage in the form of an oblong case, usu. with a hinged side and a handle, for carrying clothes and other belongings.

1902 *Times* 8 May 15/1 Captain Clive..sent on his suit-case and other luggage by another train. **1942** W. Faulkner *Go Down, Moses* 235 The boy waked him at last and got him and the suitcase off the train. **1981** D. M. Thomas *White Hotel* IV. i. 133 She realized they were travellers, for they were weighed down by rucksacks and suitcases.

2. Phr. ***to live out of*** (or ***from***) ***a suitcase*** (or ***suitcases***): to move between temporary accommodation, esp. hotels and boarding houses; to be a wanderer, to have no fixed abode.

1946 L. Durrell *Let.* 25 Sept. in Durrell & Miller *Private Corr.* (1963) 229, I can't tell you what wonderful peace and quiet it is, having a house of your own after so many years living from suitcases in hotels. **1960** J. Weightman tr. *H. de Montherlant's Sel. Essays* 181 To live for years on end out of a small suitcase..seemed so much part and parcel of my everyday life. **1969** *Photoplay* Jan. 69/1 'It never occurred to me it would take ten years to settle down,' Audrey said recently, after ten years of living out of suitcases. **1975** C. Egleton *Skirmish* xiii. 132 He had spent the greater part of his life living out of a suitcase.

3. a. *attrib.* Designating devices small or compact enough to be fitted into a suitcase, usu. in connection with secret or criminal activities, as ***suitcase bomb***, ***radio***, etc.

1954 *Richmond* (Va.) *Times-Dispatch* 25 Mar. 16 (*heading*) Now the 'suitcase A-bomb'. *Ibid.* 16/2 All of which means that a 'suitcase atom bomb' is no longer a figment of the imagination. **1972** T. Ardies *This Suitcase is going to Explode* xiii. 134 Suitcase bombs have been discussed..in public. *Ibid.* xvii. 188 Very damning stuff—such as the plans for constructing a suitcase nuclear bomb. **1974** L. Deighton *Spy Story* xix. 207 Our boy with the suitcase radio set came in five by five. A powerful signal.

b. *Comb.*, as **suitcase farmer** *N. Amer.*, a farmer who is resident on his farm for only a small part of the year (see quots.).

1941 R. Diller *Farm Ownership, Tenancy, & Land Use* 2 'Suitcase farmer' is a term used of farmers on the Great Plains who put in a crop of wheat in the fall and come back to harvest it the next summer, after having spent the winter in their permanent homes elsewhere. **1956** *Saturday Night* (Toronto) 13 Oct. 15/1 The wheat-marketing problem means the end of the 'suitcase farmer', who has been accustomed to spend only a few weeks on his land each spring and summer for seeding and harvesting. **1970** Duckham & Mansfield *Farming Syst. World* II. ii. 114 A 'suit-case' farmer moves seasonally between his several farms.

ˈsuitcaseful. [f. prec. + -ful.] As much as a suitcase will hold.

1928 *Daily Express* 11 Aug. 5/1 Sand tray with which the little ones can play by an open window. If it is possible to persuade a friend to bring back a suitcaseful of shore sand.., so much the better. **1965** J. Fleming *Nothing is Number* II. v. 83 He..brought back a suitcaseful of these books. **1979** J. Sherwood *Hour of Hyenas* xvi. 189 If you'll let me have that suitcaseful of guns that madam lent you.

suite (swiːt). Also 7 **suitte**. [a. F. *suite*: see suit *sb.*]

1. A train of followers, attendants, or servants; a retinue. Also *ellipt.* (*colloq.*) = members of a suite.

1673 Dryden *Marr. à la Mode* v. i, A person who makes so grand a figure in the Court, without the Suitte of a Princess. **1752** Chesterf. *Lett.* (1792) III. 261, I have.. secured you a place in the *Suite* of the King's electoral Embassador. **1766** G. Williams in Jesse *Selwyn & Contemp.* (1843) II. 32 Lord Lincoln..set out immediately with his whole suite for Jack Shelley's. **1788** Pasquin *Childr. Thespis* (1792) 80 Like the suite of the morning, which Guido drew dancing. **1817** M. Cutler in *Life*, etc. (1888) II. 353 Breakfasted..in company with the President and suite. **1877** Froude *Short Stud.* (1883) IV. I. ix. 104 Turning..to the young lords in the archbishop's suite. **1889** Lady Dufferin *Viceregal Life India* I. 205 He and his wife and two 'suite' came to breakfast.

2. a. A succession or series; in earlier use often applied to a series of publications; now chiefly said of series of specimens.

1722 Richardson *Statues in Italy* 151 Here is a *Suite* of Emperors; Busts, Antique. **1761** T. Warton *Life Bathurst* 94 The following suite of letters, written by himself, while Vice-chancellor. **1770** Earl Malmesbury *Diaries & Corr.* I. 53 A continued suite of childish amusements. **1779** Gibbon in *Life & Lett.* (1880) 262 Another reason, which must..pin me to Bentinck-street, is the Decline and Fall. I have resolved to bring out the *suite* in the course of next year. **1805–17** R. Jameson *Charac. Min.* (ed. 3) 127 The suite of crystals of a mineral species. **1824** W. Irving in *Life & Lett.* (1862) II. 152 Mr. Galignani calls..about my editing suite of English authors. **1833** Lyell *Princ. Geol.* III. Pref. p. viii, Suites of shells common to the Sub-apennine beds and to the Mediterranean. **1845** S. Judd *Margaret* I. ii, His laughter exposed a suite of fair white teeth. **1858** Thackeray *Virgin.* xxx, There is nothing so flattering in the world as a good suite of trumps. **1864** J. C. Atkinson *Stanton Grange* 295 A suite of tree-sparrow's eggs, not less than 20 in number. **1874** Westropp *Prec. Stones* 3 The colour suite [of diamonds] is, however, extensive.

b. A number of rooms forming a set used together by a person, a family or company of persons. Also *in a suite* = 5 b (below).

1716 LADY M. W. MONTAGU *Let. to C'tess Mar* 8 Sept., A *suite* of eight or ten large rooms. **1794** MRS. RADCLIFFE *Myst. Udolpho* xliv, A room that opens beyond the saloon, and terminates the suite. **1809** MISS MITFORD in L'Estrange *Life* (1870) I. iii. 80 Five splendid rooms open in a suite. **1824** W. IRVING *T. Trav.* I. 103 My suite of apartments were in a proud melancholy palace. **1885** MABEL COLLINS *Prettiest Woman* i, Her home was a pretty little suite on the second floor.

c. A set of furniture of the same pattern. Now freq. with reference to a three-piece suite of two armchairs and a sofa.

1805 *Times* 7 Nov. 4/2 An elegant drawing-room suite of 5 curtains, chairs, &c... suites of chairs, sofas. **1851** *Catal. Gt. Exhib.* III. 824/1 Suite of sculptured decorative furniture. **1883** MISS BROUGHTON *Belinda* II. 286 The early English suite of rush-bottomed chairs. **1920** 'O. DOUGLAS' *Penny Plain* v. 47 Can you imagine it furnished with a 'suite' ..and a grand piano? **1974** I. MURDOCH *Sacred & Profane Love Machine* 244 She had chosen.. the maroon armchairs of corded velvet (they could not afford a 'suite').

d. *Mus.* † (*a*) A set or series of lessons, etc. (cf. SUIT *sb.* 18 c); (*b*) a set of instrumental compositions (orig. of movements in dance style) to be played in succession; also, an assemblage of movements from opera or ballet scores.

1760 J. MAINWARING *Mem. Life G. F. Handel* 68 The two first movements of Handel's seventh suite in the 1st Vol. of his Lessons formerly stood for the Overture in his famous opera of Agrippina. **1801** BUSBY *Dict. Mus.*, *Suite*, (French) The name formerly given to a set, or course, of lessons, sonatas, concertos, &c. [**1811** *adds* Also applied to a single piece when consisting of several movements.] **1886** A. WEIR *Hist. Basis Mod. Europe* (1889) 548 The grand cyclic forms of modern art, the offspring of the suites. **1887** H. C. BANISTER *Mus. Anal.* 15 The Suites and Partitas of Bach. **1893** G. B. SHAW *Music in London 1890–94* (1932) III. 1 The usual two or three concertos.. selection of overtures, suite from the latest 'incidental music' composed for the theatres. **1902** *Encycl. Brit.* XXXI. 42/1 Edward Alexander MacDowell.. has written.. symphonic poems, overtures, and suites for orchestra. **1928** *Grove's Dict. Mus.* (ed. 3) V. 184/2 The composer.. accepts the term 'suite' as one which allows him a freer hand than symphony and one which indicates more definiteness of design than symphonic poem. **1977** *Zigzag* June 39/4 Only in the lengthy 'Rangers At Midnight' suite do the band really go over the top into arty cleverness.

e. *Geol.* A group of related minerals, rocks, or the like, esp. ones from the same place.

1845 J. PHILLIPS *Geol.* in *Encycl. Metrop.* VI. 678/2 Some of these marls contain beds of gypsum and fossils resembling the suite of Gosau. **1882** A. GEIKIE *Text-bk. Geol.* 648 The earliest system or connected suite of deposits in the Palæozoic series has received the name of Cambrian. **1934** *Bull. Amer. Paleont.* XXI. No. 71. 18 It is sometimes ..convenient to bracket several intimately related members together into what are here called formational suites or in common speech 'suites'. **1937** HATCH & WELLS *Petrol. Igneous Rocks* (ed. 9) v. ii. 273 As it is difficult to speak of a suite of associated rocks of one age and derived from a common magmatic source as a 'province', the term comagmatic assemblage is preferred. **1951** [see NOVÁČEKITE]. **1963**, etc. [see *ophiolite suite* s.v. OPHIOLITE b]. **1972** *Sci. Amer.* Mar. 34/2 Delta and river deposits sweep back across the continent, covering the miogeocline with a suite of continental shales and conglomerates. **1974** *Nature* 15 Nov. 219/2 X-ray diffraction analysis of residue in specimens from the eastern United States showed the mineral suite: chlorite, gibbsite, illite, kaolinite, [etc.]. **1978** *Sci. Amer.* Sept. 85/2 Boundaries between such layers, where one characteristic suite of fossils gives way to another, provide the basis for dividing geologic time into eras, periods and epochs. **1980** *Encounter* May 16/1 Those rocks (second sample though they might be from a suite already sampled by Shackleton) were.. among the most precious data which could possibly have been obtained for geology.

f. A set of jewellery, esp. one containing matching pieces.

1869 S. R. HOLE *Bk. about Roses* viii. 109 Let him display ..casket after casket of lustrous gems. Then invite her to select her *suite*. **1888** *J. Simmons Illustr. Trade Catal.* 25 (*heading*) Coloured bright gold brooches and earrings. Separately, or in suites to match. **1936** *Watchmaker & Jeweller* Feb. 187/2 (*caption*) A costume suite of gilt jewellery. **1981** M. BABSON *Bejewelled Death* i. 14 The Orpington Bequest.. was the last of the monumental suites ..to have survived.

g. The set of components which forms a lavatory; hence also, (matching) bathroom furniture or fittings.

1926–7 *Army & Navy Stores Catal.* 325 The 'Colonial' Closet Suite, comprising strong Vulcanware closet-pan and trap.. polished mahogany seat.. cistern, cover and brackets, brass chain pull and pottery handle. **1951** *Catal. of Exhibits, South Bank Exhibition, Festival of Britain* 125/1 W. C. suite. **1966** *Guardian* 5 July 8/5 A tiled bathroom, with or without a coloured 'suite'. **1973** J. THOMSON *Death Cap* i. 15 Pale green bathroom suite, fitted carpets, the lot.

h. *Computers.* A collection of related programs which can be run one after the other without interruption.

1967 *Oxford Computer Explained* 9 This Suite is run twice a day. **1980** R. MCCRUM *In Secret State* xi. 98 It was just a suite of programmes that wasn't in Lister's index.

3. A sequel, result. *rare.*

c **1800** H. K. WHITE *My own Character* 27 And so in the suite, by these laudable ends, I've a great many foes. **1862** THACKERAY *Philip* xxiv, In case the battle of the previous night should have any suite.

4. A sequel to a literary work. *rare.*

1839 W. IRVING in Ticknor *Prescott* (1864) 181, I had always intended to write an account of the 'Conquest of Mexico', as a suite to my 'Columbus'.

5. en suite (ɑ̃ 'swiːt, Fr. ɑ̃ sɥit). **a.** In agreement or harmony (*with*).

1797 MRS. A. M. BENNETT *Beggar Girl* (1813) II. 79 The decorations.. were not even *en suite* with the polish of the owner's mind. **1860** *Once a Week* 3 Nov. 520/1 She was an antique gem, was this concierge, and we thought if everything in the establishment were *en suite* [etc.].

b. Of rooms: In a series leading from one to the other; so as to form a suite or set. Also as one word and as adj.

1818 MRS. OPIE *New Tales* I. 24 Elegant rooms thrown open *en suite*. **1837** J. F. COOPER *Europe* I. 321 The state apartments lie *en suite*, in the main body of the building. **1968** *Globe & Mail* (Toronto) 13 Feb. 31/3 (Advt.), Large and formal dining room, ensuite a roomy bright kitchen. *Ibid.* 17 Feb. 45 Main floor laundry. Ensuite bath to every bedroom.

suited ('s(j)uːtɪd), *ppl. a.* [f. SUIT *sb.* or *v.* + -ED.]

†**1.** ? Belonging to a group or set. *Obs. rare.*

1621 G. SANDYS *Ovid's Met.* VI. (1626) 109 Twice six Cœlestialls.. Ioue in the midst. The suted figures tooke Their liuely formes: Ioue had a regall looke.

2. With qualifying word: Wearing a suit or attire of a specified kind.

1632 MILTON *Penseroso* 122 Till civil-suited Morn appeer. **1638** FORD *Fancies* I. iii, Enter Livio, fresh suited. **1842** TENNYSON *You ask me why* ii, It is the land that.. sober-suited Freedom chose. **1901** *Westm. Gaz.* 12 Nov. 9/2 The grey-suited brigade.

suiter, shooter ('sjuːtə(r), 'ʃuːtə(r)). *local.* Forms: 6 shewter, 7, 9 shooter, 9 suiter, -or. [f. SUIT *v.* + -ER[1]. Cf. FOLLOWER 5 a (VOLLER), and *suity-board* s.v. SUITY *a.* 3; *suitel* is a variant in Northamptonshire (Baker *N'hampton Gloss.*).] **a.** A round board placed between two cheeses in the press. **b.** A square board in a cider-press placed on the top of the pile of must or 'cheese'. More fully, *suiter-board*.

1586 *Shuttleworths' Acc.* (Chetham Soc.) 29 Fiyffe chef-fates [*i.e.* cheese-vats].. and one shewter vj[s] viij[d]. **1625** in Miss Jackson *Shropsh. Word-bk.* s.v., Eleven chefats, five shooters. **1833** LOUDON *Encycl. Archit.* §1316 [In a cider-press] A square board, termed a shooter. **1870** in Miss Jackson *Shropsh. Word-bk.* s.v. *Follower* Cheese-vats, followers, and suitors. **1886** *Cheshire Gloss.*, *Shooter boards* or *suiter boards*.

suiter, obs. or dial. f. SUITOR.

'suiterer. *rare* [? f. SUITOR *v.* + -ER[1].] One who 'goes after' another: applied to a sodomite.

1720 J. JOHNSON *Collect. Eccl. Laws Ch. Eng.* I. *Excerp. Ecgb.* lxvii, A Suiterer of young Boys [orig. *adolescentium consectctor*].

suith, Sc. form of SOOTH.

suiþe, variant of SWITHE.

suiting ('s(j)uːtɪŋ), *vbl. sb.* [f. SUIT *v.* + -ING[1].]

†**1.** The action of doing suit at a court. *Obs.*

c **1540** in J. R. Boyle *Hedon* (1875) App. 71 Yf anye tenante make defaulte of sewtinge of the said courte at two tymes in the yere.

†**2.** The action of suing for something; suing out a writ; petitioning, supplication; paying court to a woman. *Obs.*

1561 *Reg. Privy Council Scot.* Ser. I. I. 163 To charge.. all utheris personis fra all suting or persewing of the saidis confirmationis. **1572** KNOX in *Calderwood's Hist. Kirk* (Wodrow Soc.) III. App. 767 For suting of justice of the kirk's actions in the session. **1579–80** *Reg. Privy Council Scot.* Ser. I. III. 269 The suitting of redres. **1591** R. BRUCE *Serm.* (Ps. xl.) V vij b, Our suddantie is so greate.. that wee cannot continue in suting. **1631** BRATHWAIT *Eng. Gentlew.* 130 There is no time that exacts more modesty of any woman, than in her time of suiting.

attrib. **1690** C. NESSE *Hist. & Myst. O. & N.T.* I. 158 Mark well who carrieth it in this suiting work.

3. Fitting or adaptation of one thing *to* another.

1707 MORTIMER *Husb.* (1721) I. 89 In the suiting of the Land and Marle together, lies the chief advantage. *Ibid.* II. 276 The third occasion of Unfruitfulness is the not suiting of your Fruit and Soil together. **1898** *Westm. Gaz.* 3 Feb. 3/1 The suiting of one thing to another.

†**4.** The action of clothing or attiring. *Obs.*

a **1637** B. JONSON *Discov.* (1641) 92 That though the nakednesse would shew deform'd and odious, the suiting of it [*sc.* a lie] might draw their Readers.

5. *concr.* Trade name for: Material for making suits of clothes; formerly freq. *pl.* Also applied to the finished garments.

1883 *Daily News* 10 Sept. 2/5 The.. demand for.. fancy tweed suitings continues good. **1923** A. HUXLEY *Antic Hay* iii. 34 A very small man.. popped out from a canyon.. between two stratified precipices of mid-season suitings. **1930** *Daily Express* 8 Sept. 11/5 This cardigan type of tailored suit is made of a soft suiting tweed. **1957** L. DURRELL *Bitter Lemons* 44 His rusty, moth-bedevilled business suiting and wrinkled dicky suggested extremes of dreadful indigence. **1980** J. B. HILTON *Anathema Stone* iii. 28 [He] left the farm with a sample of his suiting in the jaws of a bull-mastiff.

†**'suiting,** *ppl. a. Obs.* [f. SUIT *v.* + -ING[2].] Fitting, suitable.

1642 *Declar. Lords & Comm.* 9 Jan. 3 Some suting course how to have the want of Armes.. to be supplyed. **1708** J. PHILIPS *Cyder* II. 415 Now sportive Youth Carol incondite Rhythms, with suiting Notes. **1801** ELIZ. HELME *St. Marg. Cave* (1819) IV. vii. 95 For my honour and her own it is necessary that all should be suiting. **1821** CLARE *Vill. Minstr.* (1823) I. 113 Wildness is my suiting scene.

Hence †**'suitingly** *adv.*, fittingly.

1540 PALSGR. *Acolastus* I. i. D j, Lyke as it is in maner sutyngly or throughly agreinge betwene vs, so must it nedes cause mutuall loue betwene vs.

†**'suit-like,** *a. Obs.* [f. SUIT *sb.* + -LIKE. Cf. next.] = SUITABLE 1, 2.

1570 FOXE *A. & M.* (ed. 2) II. 1126/1 Being sute like to his glorious life. **1579–80** NORTH *Plutarch* (1595) 54 She put her into mans apparell, and gaue her all thinges sute like to the same. **1583** GOLDING *Calvin on Deut.* xxviii. 59–64 We must vnderstande that all the bodie must be sutelike.

†**'suitly,** *a. Obs.* [f. SUIT *sb.* + -LY[1].] = SUITABLE 1, 2, 3.

1459 *Paston Lett.* I. 477, j. pece of skarlot for trappars.. with rede crossis and rosys. Item, ij. stripis of the same trappuris sutly. *Ibid.* 479 Item, iij. curtaynys sutely. *Ibid.* 480 Item, iij. clothis of grene and whyte, withe braunchis sutely to the other wreten before. **1532** MORE *Confut. Tindale* Wks. 342/2 Frythes Prologue.. is ryght sutely, and a verye mete couer for suche a cuppe. **1595** SOUTHWELL *Mæoniæ* 29 All pangs and heauie passions here may find A thousand motiues suitly to their griefes.

†**'suitly,** *adv. Obs.* [f. SUIT *sb.* + -LY[2].] Fittingly, suitably.

1388 WYCLIF *1 Kings* vi. 18 Al the hows.. hadde hise smethenessis, and hise ioynyngis maad suteli. **1422** YONGE tr. *Secr. Secr.* 209 Thow shalt sutely and besely auise the, whych of ham beste consaill yewyth to the. **1533** MORE *Apol.* xxxiii. Wks. 896/2 If this pacifier.. wil say that we be not sewtly the temporalti and spiritualty of this realme.

suitor ('s(j)uːtə(r)), *sb.* Forms: 3 syutor, 4 sewtour, suytour, 4–5 sutere, 4–7 -er, -our, 5–6 sewter, 5–7 sutor, (5 sutoure, sutter, 6 sueter, sutar, swttar, shu-, shewter, suitour, -ore; *Sc.* 6 soytor(e, 6–7 soytour, 7 swotar), 6–8 suiter, 6– suitor. [a. AF. *seutor*, *suitour*, *sut(i)er*, *-or*, ad. late L. *secūtor*, *-ōrem* (f. *secūt-*, *sequī* to follow, SUE), with assimilation to *suite* SUIT *sb.*]

†**1.** A frequenter (*of* a place). *Obs. rare.*

c **1290** *S. Eng. Leg.* 413 He wax a syutor of tauernes.

†**2.** One of a retinue or suite; hence, an adherent, follower, disciple. *Obs.*

c **1380** WYCLIF *Serm.* Sel. Wks. II. 141 Þat Crist is every-where.. wiþ his apostlis and her suters. *c* **1380** —— *Wks.* (1880) 292 He þat hatiþ blamynge is sutere of þe fend. **1398** TREVISA *Barth. De P.R.* IX. iii. (Bodl. MS.), Plato and his suytors. *c* **1450** *Cov. Myst.* (Shaks. Soc.) 201 Oure Lorde God, that comyth me to, Hese pore servaunt and his sutere. *a* **1483** *Liber Niger* in *Househ. Ord.* (1790) 23 Lordes & gentyls & other comyn sutors. **1509** BARCLAY *Shyp of Folys* (1874) I. 262 Yet dyvers suters suche folysshe wytches have. **1517** in Ellis *Orig. Lett.* Ser. I. II. 4 *note*, So that who shall be a suitour to him may have no other busynesse but give attendaunce upon his plesure. **1586** *Holinshed's Chron.* III. 920/2 Other officers, seruants, reteiners, and suters, that most commonlie dined in the hall. **1601** F. TATE *Househ. Ord. Edw. II* (1876) §94. 56 None of the kinges meignee,.. Knight or clarke serjant, esquier,.. page or sutor. **1830** TENNYSON *How & Why* 1, I am any man's suitor, If any will be my tutor.

3. One who owed suit (see SUIT *sb.* 1) to a court, and in that capacity acted as an assessor or elector. Now only *Hist.*

14.. *Customs of Malton* in *Surtees Misc.* (1890) 60 All maner of playnttes.. schall be.. jugyd be y[e] sutterys of y[e] sayd cowrte. **1506** in *Exch. Rolls Scotl.* XII. 704 All officeris and ministeris of court sic as baillie and juge,.. soutur, dempstar. **1541** *Act 33 Hen. VIII*, c. 24 §3 Any Mayres Sheriffes Recorders, Stewardes Bayliffes Sewters or other officers.. within any Cittie Boroughe or Towne. *c* **1550** ROLLAND *Crt. Venus* III. 4 Great members of Court baith mair & les All is Sutour, to gif finall sentence. **1597** SKENE *De Verb. Signif.* s.v. *Sok*, Na judge aucht of law, or of reason, to accept ony man in court as Soytour, bot gif he can make sufficient and lauchfull reporte of processe. **1609** —— *Reg. Maj.* 79 Ilke soytour before the Schiref represents the person of ane Baron, for quhom he was soytour in that court. *Ibid.* 93 That the court (the soytours of court) be lawfull. **1846** M[c]CULLOCH *Acc. Brit. Emp.* (1854) II. 87 By directing the election to be made by *all* the suitors,.. this statute secured the constituency from undue practices. **1863** [see SUIT *sb.* 1].

†**b.** A tenant who owes suit to a mill. *Obs.*

1602 CAREW *Cornwall* 13 This casualtie may be worth the owner some ten pound, by the yeere, or better if his mil have store of sutors.

4. One who sues or petitions; a petitioner, suppliant. *arch.*

? **1402** QUIXLEY *Ball.* in *Yorksh. Arch. Jrnl.* (1908) XX. 48 Se, lo! How sche [*sc.* Fortune] tourneth þe face hir sutoure fro. *c* **1460** FORTESCUE *Abs. & Lim. Mon.* xx. (1885) 157 The kyng shal.. be wele defended ageyn suche importune suters. **1533–4** *Act 25 Hen. VIII*, c. 21 §6 All Suters for dispensacions, faculties, licences and other wrytynges. **1576** GASCOIGNE *Kenelworth Castle* Wks. 1910 II. 131 That you would.. be a suter for him unto the heavenly powers. **1581** H. WALPOLE in Allen *Martyrdom Campion* (1908) 56 He stands before the throne with harmonie, And is a glorious suter for our sinne. **1607** HIERON *Wks.* I. 178 The apostle is a suter to God on the behalfe of the Ephesians. **1651** WALTON *Life Wotton* in *Reliq. Wotton.* c4b, The Provostship of.. Eton became Void.., for which there were ..many.. powerfull suiters to the King. **1718** *Free-thinker*

No. 147. 310 The frank Philosopher shall be the favourite Suiter. **1822** Scott *Nigel* iii, Those suitors who shall be so bold as to approach the Court. **1878** C. Gibbon *For the King* xvii, The officers stared in amazement at the importunate suitor. **1892** A. E. Lee *Hist. Columbus* I. 195 The colonies of Worthington and Franklinton became rival suitors for the location of the Capital of the State.

†**b.** One who seeks earnestly. *Obs.*

1548 Udall *Erasmus Par.* Pref. 18 Studentes and suters to atteigne to the philosophye of the gospell.

5. A petitioner or plaintiff in a suit.

1503–4 *Act 19 Hen. VII*, c. 28 Preamb., The seid sueters & peticioners were..in dispayre of expedicion of ther suetes. **1560** Daus tr. *Sleidane's Comm.* 108 b, Lawes, whiche concerned partly the judges, partly the advocates, and partly the suters. *a* **1577** Sir T. Smith *Commw. Eng.* II. viii. (1584) 50 In all iudgements necessarily being two parties, the first we call the impleader, suiter, demaunder or demaundaunt and plaintiffe. *a* **1660** *Contemp. Hist. Irel.* (Ir. Archæol. Soc.) II. 108 Amonge sutors in love and in lawe money is a comoun medler. **1856** Emerson *Eng. Traits, Ability*, In the courts, the independence of the judges and the loyalty of the suitors are equally excellent. **1883** *Law Times* 20 Oct. 410/2 The effect of the rule will be to deprive the suitor of the right of conducting his case as he thinks most conducive to his own interest.

6. One who seeks a woman in marriage; a wooer.

a **1586** Sidney *Arcadia* I. xi, My court quickly swarmed full of suiters; some perchaunce loving my state, others my person. **1588** Kyd *Househ. Philos.* Wks. (1901) 273 That noble Grecian dame that bated in the night As much as she had wouen by day, to bleare her sutors sight. **1637** T. Heywood *Emblem. Dial.* xxxvii, Merry Suiters, make mad Husbands. **1781** Cowper *Retirem.* 237 The suitor's air indeed he soon improves, And forms it to the taste of her he loves. **1870** L'Estrange *Life Miss Mitford* I. i. 5 She was rich—her fortune was at her own command—of course she had suitors. **1888** Fergus Hume *Madame Midas* I. i, Miss Curtis soon brought crowds of suitors around her.

7. *attrib.*, as (sense 6) ***suitor-crowd***, etc.; †**suitor-fee**, a fine paid in lieu of suit at court.

1725 Pope *Odyss.* I. 353 To their own districts drive the *suitor-crowd. **1601** *Reg. Mag. Sig. Scot.* 425/1 Necnon 6s. 8d. pro sectis curie de Rescobie vulgo *lie *swotar-fie*.

suitor ('s(j)uːtə(r)), *v.* Now chiefly *dial.* Also 7 **suter, souter,** 9 **suiter, sooter.** [f. prec.]

1. *trans.* To court, woo.

1672 Shadwell *Miser* I, How did you go to work to suitor my Mother? **1706** Phillips (ed. Kersey) s.v., He Suitor'd her in vain several Years. **1824** Scott *Redgauntlet* ch. v, The miller's son..suitored me.

2. *intr.* To be a suitor or wooer (*to*): chiefly in gerund (***to come*** or ***go a suitoring***). Also *fig.*

1668 Sir C. Sedley *Mulberry Gard.* II. ii, You are over-serious For a man that comes a Sutering. **1730** Fielding *Tom Thumb* II. v, In vain to me a suitoring you come, For I'm already promised to Tom Thumb. **1777** Franklin *Lett.* Wks. 1889 VI. 83 A virgin State should preserve the virgin character, and not go about suitoring for alliances. **1817** Scott *Let. to Terry* 12 Mar. in *Lockhart*, A daughter, suitored unto by the conceited young parson. **1838** Barham *Ingol. Leg.* Ser. I. *St. Nich.* vii, Counts a many, and Dukes a few, A suitoring came to my father's Hall.

Hence '**suitoring** *vbl. sb.*, wooing, courtship; also *attrib.*

1671 Mrs. Behn *Amorous Prince* IV. iv, Well, I see there is nothing but soutering I' this Town; wo'd our Lucia were here too for me. **1746** (*title*) Exmoor Courtship, or A Suitoring Discourse, in the Devonshire Dialect and Mode. **1847** Halliwell, *Sootering*... Devon. **1886** Elworthy *W. Somerset Word-bk.*, *Suitering.* **1889** *Athenæum* 14 Dec. 816/3 The usual 'suitorings', sulkings, makings-up, of various couples.

suitor, var. SUITER.

'**suitorcide**, *a.* *nonce-word.* [Badly f. SUITOR *sb.* + -CIDE[1].] Fatal to suitors.

1839 Syd. Smith *Wks.* (1859) Pref. p. vii, To say a word against the suitorcide delays of the Court of Chancery..was treason against the Plousiocracy.

suitorship ('s(j)uːtəʃɪp). [f. SUITOR *sb.* + -SHIP.] The state or condition of being a suitor.

c **1800** R. Cumberland *John De Lancaster* (1809) I. 6 This distinguished personage was now in the fifth year of his suitorship. **1878** Morley *Diderot* I. 125 They revolted..against the old system of suitorship and protection. **1886** T. Hardy *Mayor Casterbr.* II. iii. 33 The sense of occult rivalry in suitorship was..superadded.

suitress ('s(j)uːtrɪs). *rare.* [f. SUITOR *sb.* + -ESS[1].] A female suitor.

1714 Rowe *Jane Shore* III, 'Twere Pity of his Heart, That could refuse a Boon to such a Suitress. **1791** Cowper *Iliad* I. 686, I noticed her a suitress at thy knees. **1894** *Daily Tel.* 1 Dec. 5/4 Both suitresses are of some position and worldly prospects.

suity ('s(j)uːtɪ), *a.* [f. SUIT *sb.* or *v.* + -Y[1].]

†**1.** Appropriate, fitting. *Obs.*

1609 J. Davies *Holy Roode* F ij, In loue, in care, in diligence and dutie, Be thou Her Sonne, sith this to Sonnes is sutie.

2. Of hounds: Matching those of a pack.

1856 'Stonehenge' *Brit. Sports* I. II. iv. ¶344. 124/2 Many men draft young hounds from their looks not pleasing the eye, or from their being too high or too low, or not being 'suity', as it is called.

3. ***suity-board***, in cheese-making: = SUITER a.

c **1830** *Glouc. Farm Rep.* 30 in *Husbandry* (L.U.K.) III, Round boards, called 'suity boards',..are occasionally necessary to place on the cheeses.

Suitzer, obs. form of SWITZER.

‖**suivante** (sɥivɑ̃t). *Obs.* [F., pres. pple. fem. of *suivre* to follow.] A confidential maid.

1698 Vanbrugh *Short Vindic.* 51 Mademoiselle brings to mind what may often be expected from a *Suivante* of her Countrey. **1782** [T. Vaughan] *Fashionable Follies* I. xci. 139 The more secrets Madame had to keep, the better for her suivante. **1812** Scott *Let.* in *Lockhart* (1837) III. i. 17 Lady Douglas's *suivante.*

suiymme, sujee, sujet, sujorn(e: see SWIM, SOOJEE, SUBJECT, SOJOURN.

Suk (suːk), *sb.* and *a.* **A.** *sb.* **a.** An East African people who inhabit an area on the Uganda-Kenya border; a member of this people. **b.** The Nilotic language spoken by the Suk. **B.** *adj.* Of or pertaining to this people or their language.

1902 H. Johnston *Uganda Protectorate* II. xix. 847 The Sūk, like the Turkana, pierce the lower lip... The Sūk women sometimes shave the head. **1902** *Encycl. Brit.* XXXIII. 541/2 The languages spoken in the Uganda Protectorate belong to the following stocks..*Masai* (Bari, Masai, Elgumi, Turkana, Sūk, &c.). **1930** [see Nandi *sb.*[2] and *a.*]. **1936** *Discovery* June 171/2 The Nandi, Masai, Turkana, and Sūk are perhaps the best-known tribes of this group. **1947** [see Kipsigis]. **1953**, etc. [see Sebei]. **1963** *Times* 6 May 19/6 Mr. Jomo Kenyatta, president of the Kenya African National Union, today reminded a crowd already nursed to a happy pitch of electoral enthusiasm by the chanting and dancing of Suk and Kalenjin tribesmen. **1974** *Encycl. Brit. Micropædia* VII. 347/2 Linguists often divide the Nilotic languages into a western group..and a southern group, including Nandi and Suk.

suk, var. SOUK, SUCK.

sukcade, sukces, suke(n: see SUCCADE, SUCCESS, SUCK.

sukebind ('s(j)uːkbaɪnd). [Arbitrary formation: cf. BIND *sb.* 2, 3.] Name given by Stella Gibbons (see quot. 1932) to an imaginary plant associated with superstition and fertility, hence used allusively with reference to intense rustic passions.

1932 S. Gibbons *Cold Comfort Farm* v. 75 In the fulness of summer, when the sukebind hangs heavy from the wains ..'tes the same. **1968** *Listener* 19 Sept. 379/3 The sukebind twines lushly over the grave of Mary Webb, another esteemed pre-war novelist, and since Stella Gibbons planted the fatal seed, nobody has bothered to hack away the undergrowth to discover what lies beneath. **1975** *Times* 15 July 14/3 A Country Sports Fair conjures images of..young couples competing among the sukebind. **1982** W. Golding *Moving Target* 106 Mr Trevelyan's fascinating book... He climbed one or two family trees where the Sukebind was a-blowing.

sukere, sukett: see SUCCOUR, SOCKET.

sukey ('suːkɪ). *dial* and *colloq.* Also with capital initial and **suckey, sukie, suky.** [Dim. of *Susan, Susanna*, fem. name.] A tea-kettle.

The nursery rhyme 'Polly put the kettle on' (see quot. 1981) is known from 1841: *Oxf. Dict. Nursery Rhymes.*

1823 'J. Bee' *Slang* 167 Sukey, a tea kettle. **1875** E. Tweddell *Rhymes Cleveland Dial.* 40 Suckey was bolin' a gud un when we gat there. An' Ah..helpt to fettle t'tea. **1877** E. Peacock *N.W. Lincs. Gloss.* 244/2 *Suky*, a child's name for a tea-kettle. **1898** J. D. Brayshaw *Slum Silhouettes* 182 Now, Sukey boils; fill the teapot, Dick. **1919** 'W. N. P. Barbellion' *Diary* 13 Feb. (1920) 95 Our sukie is an old copper one, and sings sometimes in splendid imitation of an orchestra tuning up. **1952** M. Laski *Village* i. 13 I'll just get the sukey going, and then we'll have a nice cup of tea. **1981** *Jrnl. Lancs. Dial. Soc.* Jan. 46 Many people remember *sukey* as a name for the kettle. 'Sukey's boiling,' they would say. This must originate in the nursery rhyme 'Polly put the kettle on'.

sukh, var. SOUK.

sukiyaki (suːkɪ'jɑːkɪ, ‖su'kijaki). Also **suki-yaki.** [Jap.] A Japanese dish, consisting of very thin slices of beef fried with vegetables in sugar and soy sauce, and often served with rice.

1920 *Japan Advertiser* 22 Aug. 5/1 Another name by which this dish [*sc.* nabe] is usually known outside of Tokyo, is suki-yaki. This is derived from suki, which means a spade, and yaki, to cook. **1932** H. A. Phillips *Meet Japanese* xvii. 185 Beef *sukiyaki* tasted good after a long day's jaunt. **1935** B. Woon *San Francisco & Golden Empire* v. 62 The best *suki-yaki* restaurant is not in the Japanese quarter but in a Japanese hotel near the corner of California Street and Grant Avenue. Here tasteful *suki-yaki* dishes are cooked in chafing-dishes, Japanese style. **1943** H. Mears *Year of Wild Boar* iii. 51 The Japanese who patronized this place..did so only to sample American culture, as in New York the American might dine in a Japanese *sukiyaki* restaurant. **1952** R. Cutforth *Korean Reporter* xvi. 147 There are other famous meals—*Sukiyaki*—a fry of chicken or beef with vegetables and soya. **1964** I. Fleming *You only live Twice* xxii. 253 A highly spiced dish of *sukiyaki*, the national dish of beef stew. **1970** P. & J. Martin *Jap. Cooking* 72 Put a sukiyaki pan or a large, heavy frying pan over a portable cooking stove. **1977** *Time* 19 Dec. 43/1 (*caption*) Drama Coach Lee Strasberg cooks sukiyaki in Manhattan.

sukkah, var. SUCCAH.

†**sukkarke.** *Obs. rare*[−1]. [prob. AFr.] app. = SURCHARGE 1, SURCHARGE *sb.*[1]

c **1400** Maundev. (1839) xxxi. 310 He ȝevethe of the Flesche to his most specyalle Frendes, in stede of Entre Messe, or a Sukkarke [*Roxb.* for a dayntee].

suk-kegh, variant of SOCKEYE, salmon.

sukkelyng, sukkenye, sukkett, sukkin, Sukkot(h, sukle, suklinge, -lynge, sukour, sukudry, sul: see SUCKLING, SUCKENY, SUCKET, SUCKEN[1], SUCCOTH, SUCKLE, SUCKLING, SUCCOUR, SUCCUDRY, SHALL.

‖**Sula** ('sjuːlə). [mod.L. (Willughby, 1676), a. ON. *sūla.*] Applied by Hoier and others to a supposed variety of sea-fowl; in modern *Ornith.* a genus of gannets (family *Sulidæ*).

1678 Ray *Willughby's Ornith.* III. 331 The Sula of Hoier, ..near of kin to, if not the same with the Soland-goose. **1688** Holme *Armoury* II. xii. 262 The Sula is like the Soland Goose for Bodily shape. **1766** Pennant *Brit. Zool.* 162.

sulayne, variant of SOLEIN *Obs.*

sulcal ('sʌlkəl), *a.* *Anat.* [f. SULCUS + -AL[1].] Belonging to or connected with a sulcus.

1889 *Buck's Handbk. Med. Sci.* VII. 300 (Cent. Suppl.). **1901** Dorland *Med. Dict.*, *Sulcal artery*, a branch of the anterior spinal artery in the anterior median fissure, or sulcus, of the spinal cord.

So '**sulcar** *a.*

1900 *Trans. Linn. Soc., Zool.*, March 527 The zooids so oriented that their sulcar (ventral) aspects are abaxial, their asulcar (dorsal) aspects axial.

sulcate ('sʌlkeɪt), *a.* *Nat. Hist.* [ad. L. *sulcātus*, pa. pple. of *sulcāre* (see next).] Marked with (parallel) furrows or grooves.

1760 J. Lee *Introd. Bot.* II. xxxiii. (1765) 160 *Cucurbita*, with a sulcate Fruit. **1828** Stark *Elem. Nat. Hist.* II. 15 Shell thin, hyaline, transversely sulcate. **1872** Coues *N. Amer. Birds* 187 The bill is more or less depressed with smooth, rounded or sulcate, culmen.

†**sulcate**, *v.* *Obs.* [f. L. *sulcāt-*, pa. ppl. stem of *sulcāre* to plough, f. SULCUS. Cf. SULK *v.*[1]] *trans.* To plough (*esp.* the seas).

1577 Hanmer *Anc. Eccl. Hist.* 327 A mightie Easterne winde, which draue the ship with violence, swiftely for to sulcate the seas. *a* **1604** —— *Chron. Irel.* (1633) 85 The Irish nation..would not sulcate the seas, neither give themselves to merchandise. **1656** Blount *Glossogr.*

sulcated ('sʌlkeɪtɪd), *ppl. a.* *Nat. Hist.* [f. L. *sulcātus* SULCATE + -ED.] Sulcate.

1694 *Phil. Trans.* XVIII. 178 The sides of the Astroites are always sulcated, or a little furrow'd. **1753** *Chambers' Cycl.* Suppl. s.v. *Leaf*, *Sulcated Leaf*, one which has a great number of ridges all round it, with obtuse sinuses. **1768** Pennant *Brit. Zool.* I. 39 Their lower part is sulcated lengthways. **1828** Stark *Elem. Nat. Hist.* II. 41 The plaits distant, black, transversely sulcated with white. **1897** W. F. Kirby in Mary Kingsley *W. Africa* 722 All the tibiæ sulcated, front tibiæ with conspicuously open foramina.

sulcation (sʌl'keɪʃən). *rare.* [f. L. *sulcāre* SULCATE *v.*: see -ATION.]

1. Furrowing, grooving.

1658 Phillips, *Sulcation*, a making furrows.

2. A sulcus or set of sulci.

1852 Dana *Crust.* II. 856 The sculpturing of the male being represented in the female by merely a few faint sulcations.

sulcato-, used as comb. form (see -O[1]) of L. *sulcātus* SULCATE *a.* in the sense 'sulcate and...', as ***sul,cato-'areolate, -'costate, -'rimose*** adjs.

1852 Dana *Crust.* II. 855 Epimerals and coxæ of six posterior legs slightly sulcato-areolate. **1866** *Treas. Bot.* 1110/2 *Sulcato-rimose*, furrowed and cracked like the cotyledons of a Spanish chestnut. **1887** W. Phillips *Brit. Discomycetes* 11 Stem..sulcato-costate, and lacunose.

sulch, obs. form of SUCH.

sulciform ('sʌlsɪfɔːm), *a.* [ad. mod.L. *sulciformis*: see SULCUS and -FORM.] Having the form of a sulcus or groove.

1822 J. Parkinson *Outl. Oryctol.* 222 Hinge very broad, furrowed with numerous long sulciform teeth. **1836–9** *Todd's Cycl. Anat.* II. 533/1 The sulciform depression..in the vestibule [of the ear].

†'**sulcous**, *a.* *Obs. rare*[−1]. [f. SULCUS + -OUS.] Sulcate.

1750 G. Hughes *Barbados* 116 The bark..is rough and shagged, if not sulcous.

‖**sulculus** ('sʌlkjʊləs). *Anat.* and *Zool.* [mod.L., dim. of SULCUS. Cf. F. *sulcule.*] A small sulcus or groove. Hence '**sulculate** *a.*, having small grooves.

1848 *Proc. Berw. Nat. Club* II. 338 Longitudinally striate or sulculate. **1859** Mayne *Expos. Lex.* 1226/1. **1900** *Trans. Linn. Soc., Zool.*, March 533 One cannot speak of a sulcus and sulculus in this case.

‖**sulcus** ('sʌlkəs). Pl. **sulci** ('sʌlsaɪ). [L. = furrow, trench, ditch, wrinkle.] **1. a.** A groove made with an engraving tool. **b.** A trench. **c.** A hollow or depression in the land. *rare.*

1662 Evelyn *Sculptura* 126 Monsieur Bosse's invention of the *Eschoppe*, does render the making of this *Sulcus*, much more facile. **1675** —— *Terra* (1729) 14 The *Sulcus* or Trench be made to run from North to South. **1901** A. Trotter *East Galloway Sk.* 158/2 The house..is situated in a sulcus of fertile land.

2. *Anat.* A groove or furrow in a body, organ, or tissue.

1744 tr. *Boerhaave's Inst.* III. 297 The sensible Papillæ lie concealed in the Sulci formed by the Cuticle. **1766** *Complete Farmer* s.v. *Shoeing*, The sulcus of the inner surface of the hoof. **1822–7** GOOD *Study Med.* (1829) V. 252 Hydatids have found the means of forming a nidus in some one of the sulci of the womb. **1872** COUES *N. Amer. Birds* 27 Sulci, like carinæ, are of all shapes, sizes and positions. **1897** *Allbutt's Syst. Med.* IV. 227 A distinct sulcus between the liver and gall bladder is nearly always perceptible to the touch.

b. *spec.* A fissure between two convolutions of the brain.

1833 *Cycl. Pract. Med.* I. 286/2 The sulci which separate the convolutions. **1840** G. V. ELLIS *Anat.* 15 On its under surface, near the median fissure of the brain, is a sulcus, which lodges the olfactory nerve. **1899** *Allbutt's Syst. Med.* VII. 273 That portion of the cerebral hemisphere which lies anterior to the precentral sulcus.

3. *Bot.* The lamella in some fungi.

1856 HENSLOW *Dict. Bot. Terms* 90.

sulcuþ, suld, suldan, suld(e)art, sulder: see SELCOUTH, SHALL, SOLDAN, SUDDART, SHOULDER.

† **sule** *sb.*, var. of SOIL *sb.*[1]; cf. SULYE.

c **1440** *Promp. Parv.* 484/1 Sule erthe.., *solum, tellus.*

† **sule,** *v. Obs.* [OE. *sylian* (also *besylian*), f. *sul-*, related to *sol-*: see SOLE *sb.*[4], SOL *a.*, SOLE *v.*[3], SOLL *v.*, SOLWE *v.*, SOWL *v.*[1], and cf. OFris. *sulenge* soiling, MHG. *süln* to sully.] **a.** *trans.* To soil, sully.

c **897** K. ÆLFRED *Gregory's Past. C.* liv. 419 Sio suȝu hi wille sylian on hire sole æfterðæmðe hio aðwæȝen bið. *a* **1000** *Boeth. Metr.* ix. 60 He on unscyldȝum eorla blode his sweord selede swiðe ȝelome. *a* **1225** *Ancr. R.* 396 þet weren so sike of sunne, & so isuled þer mide. *c* **1230** *Hali Meid.* 35 þis is sunne,..& unwurðcheð þi bodi, Suleð þi sawle.

b. *intr.* To be defiled.

a **1250** *Owl & Night.* 1240 Sum blynd mon..To þare diche his dwele voleweþ, & falleþ, & þar-onne sulieþ.

sulement, variant of SOULEMENT *adv. Obs.*

† **sulf.** *Obs.* ? Toadflax, *Linaria vulgaris.*

c **1450** *Alphita* (Anecd. Oxon.) 104/1 *Linguarium*, assimulatur herbe Sti. I[ohannis] in foliis et in stipite sed fetat. gall. lignarie, angl. sulf [*v.r.* gulf].

sulf, obs. form of SELF.

sulf-: see SULPH-.

sulfa-, altered and U.S. form of SULPHA-, used to form the name of certain drugs (in British English *sulpha-* also occurs): **sulfa'merazine** (also **-izine**) [-MER + AZINE], the readily absorbed sulphonamide $CH_3{\cdot}C_4H_2N_2{\cdot}NH{\cdot}SO_2{\cdot}C_6H_4{\cdot}NH_2$, now rarely used except in Sulphatriad; N[1]-(4-methylpyrimidin-2-yl)sulphanilamide; **,sulfaqui'noxaline** [QUINOXALINE], the sulphonamide $C_8H_5N_2{\cdot}NH{\cdot}SO_2{\cdot}C_6H_4{\cdot}NH_2$, used as a coccidiostat in the treatment of cæcal coccidiosis in poultry; *N*[1]-quinoxalin-2-ylsulphanilamide.

1943 A. D. WELCH et al. in *Jrnl. Pharmacol. & Exper. Therapeutics* LXXVII. 357 The chemistry of this compound, which will be referred to as sulfamerizine, has been described in the publications of several groups. **1945** *Brit. Med. Jrnl.* 3 Feb. 155/1 One new compound—sulphamerazine (or sulphamerizine)—has been the subject of much work in America. **1961** A. GOTH *Med. Pharmacol.* xli. 444 Sulfamerazine and sulfamethazine resemble sulfadiazine in most respects, except for the fact that they are excreted more slowly by the kidney. **1962** H. BURN *Drugs, Med. & Man* xx. 200 Various new substances were prepared in this way, among them sulphathiazole, sulphadiazine and sulphamerazine. These compounds were not only different from sulphanilamide, but were much more potent. **1977** *Approved Names 1977* (Brit. Pharmacopœia Commission) 81 Sulfamerazine. **1944** *Jrnl. Biol. Chem.* CLVI. 343 Recently, a new sulfonamide, sulfaquinoxaline, was introduced. **1961** *New Scientist* 21 Dec. 742/1 Sulfaquinoxaline and sulfadimidine were administered to turkeys either in their food or by intramuscular injection. **1976** *Nature* 17 June 621/2 The number of antagonists is now large, some of the best-known being.., sulphaquinoxaline and actinomycin D. **1977** *Approved Names 1977* (Brit. Pharmacopoeia Commission) 81 Sulfaquinoxaline.

Sulfasuxidine (sʌlfə'sʌksidi:n). *Pharm.* [f. SULFA- + SUX- + -IDINE.] A proprietary name for the drug succinylsulphathiazole.

1942 *Official Gaz.* (U.S. Patent Office) 6 Jan. 9/2 Sharp & Dohme, Incorporated, Philadelphia... *Sulfasuxidine* for pharmaceutical preparations useful as bactericides and as antiseptics. **1943** *Trade Marks Jrnl.* 26 May 223/1 *Sulfasuxidine*... Pharmaceutical substances for human use and for veterinary use..consisting wholly of sulphur compounds... Sharp & Dohms Ltd... 1st April, 1942. **1976** A. I. BRAUDE *Antimicrobial Drug Therapy* i. 11 Succinylsulfathiazole (Sulfasuxidine) is a good example of how the para-NH_2 group becomes free after slow hydrolysis from its inactive form to the active sulfathiazole.

sulfatara, variant form of SOLFATARA.

1884 *Pall Mall Gaz.* 23 Feb. 4/2 The internal fires that still spurt and hiss in the sulfataras.

sulfer, obs. form of SILVER.

† **'sulȝart,** *a. Sc. Obs. rare*[−1]. [prob. f. Gaelic *soilleir* bright.] app. Bright, dazzling.

1513 DOUGLAS *Æneis* XII. Prol. 64 Lusty Flora did hyr blomis spreid Vnder the feit of Phebus sulȝart steid.

sulham ('sʊlhɑ:m). Also †**silham, sulam; selham.** [a. Arab. *zulḥam.*] A large Arab hooded cloak (properly distinguished from the burnous).

1791 W. LEMPRIERE *Tour from Gibraltar to Morocco* ix. 229 They then were obliged to uncover their cap or turban ..and to wear instead of the *haick* the *sulam*, which is a cloak made of white or blue woollen cloth. **1809** J. G. JACKSON *Acct. Empire of Marocco* 138 The Berebbers wear drawers, and a cloak of dark blue cloth, called a Silham. **1817** J. RILEY *Narr. Loss Amer. Brig 'Commerce'* 198 The cloak, or sulam, is made of coarse black cloth. **1891** HALL CAINE *Scapegoat* (ed. 2) viii. 172 He drew forth from the folds of his selham a long knife. **1903** *Westm. Gaz.* 15 Jan. 5/1 The ladies..all wearing Moorish sulhams. **1907** F. CAMPBELL *Shepherd of Stars* vi. 72 Strange faces look out from the jellab and sulham hoods. **1921** *Chambers's Jrnl.* Jan. 22/2 A 'warm man' of merchandise, with robes of a surpassing whiteness, rich cloth selham or burnous, and brilliant lemon-coloured slippers. **1951** W. BLUNT *Black Sunrise* xvii 201 After two or three courses Ismail took off his *selham* and *haik.* **1975** C. CALASIBETTA *Fairchild's Dict. Fashion* 64/1 *Burnoose*.., travelling cape..worn by Moors and Arabs in northern Africa. Also called a *selham.*

suling ('sʊlɪŋ). *Hist.* Forms: 1 **swulung, sulung** (*rare* sulong), *Domesday Bk.* **solin, 2 solling,** (also 7 *Hist.*) **swuling,** (also 9 *Hist.*) **swilling, 2–3** (also 7–9 *Hist.*) **sulling, suling, 4 swol(l)ing, -yng, swyling, suyling, 4–5 swylling, 9** *Hist.* **sullung.** [OE. *swulung, sulung*, probably vbl. sb. of an unrecorded vb. **swul(h)ian*, **sul(h)ian* to plough, f. **swulh, sulh* plough, SULLOW. The generally accepted view that *sulung* is f. *sulh* + *lang, long* long (Sweet in *Anglia* III. 151) and that it is therefore parallel to *furlong* (f. *furh* furrow + *long*) cannot be maintained in face of the divergent form-history and meaning of the two words.] In Kent, the fiscal unit corresponding to the hide (see HIDE *sb.*[2]) and the *carucata* (see CARUCATE) of other counties.

In Latin documents relating to Kent it is called *aratrum*: cf. PLOUGH *sb.* 3 a.

A term that has been erron. identified with this word is *solanda, scolanda, scotlanda* in *Domesday of St. Paul's* (Camden Soc.) 58, 93, 99, 142, 145, 151: see J. H. Round in *Eng. Hist. Rev.* VII. 708 foll.

805 in Birch *Cart. Sax.* (1885) I. 449 Aliquam in Cantia partiunculam terræ hoc est duorum manentium, ubi Sueordhlincas vocitantur Iuxta distributionem suarum utique terrarum ritu saxonica *án sulung* seu in alia loco mediam partem unius mansiunculæ id est *án geocled* ubi ab incolis Ecgheanng lond appellatur. **805** *Charter* in *O.E. Texts* 442 þisses londes earan ðrie sulong æt hæȝyðe ðorne. **805–31** *Ibid.* 443 Ðæt lond æt stanhamstede, xx swulunga. **835** *Will* in Thorpe *Dipl. Angl. Sax.* (1865) 470, & him man sælle an half swulung an Ciollandene. **973** in Birch *Cart. Sax.* (1893) III. 610 Decem mansas, quod Cantigene dicunt, *x. sulunga.* **1086** *Domesday Book* (1783) I. 2 De communitate Sancti Martini habent simul iii. canonici unum solin & xvi. acras. *c* **1140** *Inst. Cnuti* (Liebermann) 295 (MS. H) Scotum ad luminaria..ter in anno uno detur de unaquaque hyda (id est suling, *c* **1160** *Colbert MS.* sulinghida). **11..** *Bk. Battle Abbey* in Selden *Titles Honor* (1631) 636 Cum omnibus apenditijs suis septem Swillingarum id est, Hidarum. **1196** in *Archaeol. Cant.* I. 234 De una sollinga terræ et dimidia, cum pertinenciis, in Estretling. **1209–10** in *Archæol. Cant.* V. 284 De medietate unius sullinge terre. **12..** *MS. Cott. Vesp.* A. xx. 69 b, Svthflict defendit se per v sulingos cum dimidio sulingi de pole. **1364** W. THORNE *Chron.* in Twysden *Hist. Angl. Script.* (1652) 2140 Et debent pro quelibet Swollinga xiv d. per annum pro Schippeshere, timberlode, & bordlode.

a **1667** SKINNER *Etymol. Ling. Angl.* (1671), *Swuling* vel *Suling.* **1706** PHILLIPS (ed. Kersey), *Swoling* or *Suling of Land.* **1867** C. J. ELTON *Tenures of Kent* vi. 124 Opinions have been much divided on this point, viz. whether the Kentish suling corresponded in size to the Norman carucate. **1897** MAITLAND *Domesday & Beyond* 124 At Peckham the Archbishop had an estate which had been rated at six sullungs.

b. *attrib.*: †**suling-land** = PLOUGH-GATE; †**suling-man,** (*a*) a man chosen from the tenants of a suling to collect the dues belonging thereto; (*b*) a service due from tenants of a suling.

1364 W. THORNE *Chron.* xxvii. §1 in Twysden *Hist. Angl. Script.* (1652) 2140 Quae servicia & consuetudines ipsi tenantes annuatim faciunt & solummodo præter corporale servicium quod vocatur *Swollyngman. Ibid.*, iij. rodas dimidiam de terra vocata *Swollyngland* quæ tenentur per diversa servicia subsequentia. **1440–1** in Twysden *Hist. Angl. Script.* (1652) Gloss. s.v. *Sulinga*, Singuli tenentes omnium & singularum prædictarum *Swyllingarum*, & 38. acrar. terræ de *Swyllingland*..eligent & eligere debent de qualibet *Swyllinga*, unum de seipsis qui nominetur *Swyllingmannus.* [**1887** PARISH & SHAW *Dict. Kent. Dial.*, *Swilling-land*, a plough land.]

Suliote ('s(j)u:lɪəʊt), *sb.* (and *a.*) Also **Souliot(e), Suliot.** [ad. Gr. *Σουλιώτης*: see -OTE.] An inhabitant of the Suli mountains in Epirus, of mixed Greek and Albanian origin. Also *attrib.* or as *adj.*

1812 BYRON *Ch. Har.* II. lxxii, Oh! who is more brave than a dark Suliote? **1827** F. G. HALLECK *Alnwick Castle & Other Poems* 10 Bozzaris ranged his Suliote band. **1832** T. GORDON *Hist. Greek Revol.* I. I. i. 76 The Souliotes, the flower of Albanian warriors, were driven from Epirus. **1852** G. F. BOWEN *Mount Athos, Thesaly, & Epirus* viii. 214 The Suliote hamlet of Kiafa. **1897** W. A. PHILLIPS *War of Greek Independence* vii. 127 Marko Botzares, the Suliot hero. **1900** 'ODYSSEUS' *Turkey in Europe* ix. 404 The Suliots have somehow acquired in popular estimation the reputation of being Greeks. As a matter of fact they were a tribe of Christian Albanians. **1910** *Encycl. Brit.* XI. 494/2 On the night of the 21st of August [1823] occurred the celebrated exploit of Marko Botzaris and his Suliotes: a successful surprise attack on the camp of the Ottoman vanguard, in which the Suliote leader fell. **1914** D. J. CASSAVETTI *Hellas & Balkan Wars* xv. 188 Old people would shake their heads sadly and ask if these empty-headed dolls could possibly belong to the same country as the grand Souliot women. **1952** C. M. WOODHOUSE *Greek War of Independence* i. 13 Parts of Crete remained..independent of all foreign rule. So to some extent did Souli, a wild precipitous district above the River Akheron in Epirus (Southern Albania): but the Souliotes were not strictly Greeks. **1973** D. DAKIN *Greek Struggle for Independence* i. 31 The wily Souliots, hoping to find out what Ali was really up to, sent a token force only. *Ibid.*, Back in Souli, Tzavellas and the chief of Souliot chiefs, Georgios Botsaris, decided to defy Ali.

† **sulk,** *sb.*[1] *Obs. rare*[−1]. [ad. L. *sulcus* furrow. Cf. SULK *v.*[1]] A hollow or trough of the sea.

1578 SIDNEY *Wanstead Play* in *Arcadia* (1629) 619 When he soiourned in the surging sulkes of the sandiferous seas.

sulk (sʌlk), *sb.*[2] [f. SULK *v.*[2]]

1. a. *pl.* A state of ill-humour or resentment marked by obstinate silence or aloofness from society. Often with *the* and in phr. ***in the sulks*** (occas. ***in one's sulks***); also ***to take* (*the*) *sulks*** (Sc.), to turn sulky.

1804 J. GRAHAME *Sabbath* (1839) 15/2 A child of about ten months old took sulks, and would not eat. **1818** TODD s.v., We use also, as a colloquial term, to be in *the sulks*; which formerly was, in *the sullens.* **1824** MISS L. M. HAWKINS *Annaline* I. 177 A fit of the sulks. **1831** GREVILLE *Mem.* 8 Dec. (1874) II. 224, I never had the advantage of seeing the Chancellor before in his sulks. **1839** DICKENS *Nickleby* xxvii, Her pretty sulks and peevishness. **1885** SPURGEON *Treas. Dav.* Ps. cxxxi. 2 The child..frets and worries,..or sinks into sulks. **1890** D. DAVIDSON *Mem. Long Life* iv. 93 Ram Bukhs took the sulks. **1894** W. E. NORRIS *St. Ann's* II. 208 When you are tired of being in the sulks, let me know.

b. *sing.* A fit of sulking; the action of sulking.

1792 W. B. STEVENS *Jrnl.* 8 Oct. (1965) I. 48 The strange Sulk of a Day and a half, during our Northern Tour. **1836** J. ROMILLY *Diary* 21 Oct. (1967) 104 Much discussion (in wch the V.Ch. never joined, he being in a grand sulk). **1837** DISRAELI *Venetia* I. xiii, Mrs. Cadurcis remained alone in a savage sulk. **1888** *Contemp. Rev.* LIV. 383 Rodbertus had lived for a quarter of a century in a political sulk against the Hohenzollerns. **1898** *Daily News* 20 June 4/7 To try and force those proposals by a policy of sulk.

2. A person who sulks (*rare*); an obstinate horse (*dial.*)

1883 LORD R. GOWER *Reminisc.* II. xxiv. 125 If one reads away from the others, one appears to avoid the rest and is considered a sulk. **1888** *Berks. Gloss.*, *Zulk*, a term applied to a horse that will not try to do what is required of him.

† **sulk,** *v.*[1] *Obs. rare.* Also 6 **sulke, sulck.** [ad. L. *sulcāre* to plough, furrow, f. *sulcus* furrow.] *trans.* To plough (the seas). Also *intr.*, sometimes with *it.*

1579 *Poor Knight's Palace*, etc. K iv b, To sulke the seas and furrow foming floods. *Ibid.* L ij b, While saylers sulke upon the seas. **1582** STANYHURST *Æneis* II. (Arb.) 50 Two serpents monsterus ouglye Plasht the water sulcking to the shoare moste hastelye swinging. **1612** DRAYTON *Poly-olb.* i. 422 They..keep Upon the lee-ward still, and (sulking up the deep) For Mauritania make. **1682** EARL ARGYLE *To Lady Lindsay* in *Law's Mem.* (1818) 213 Our admirall, though tide and wind say nay, He'll row and work, and sulk it all the way.

Hence † **'sulking** *ppl. a.*, ploughing (the land).

1582 STANYHURST *Æneis* I. 1 (I) forced Thee sulcking swincker thee soyle, thoghe craggie, to sunder.

sulk (sʌlk), *v.*[2] [Source uncertain; perhaps related to SULKE *a.* Cf. NFris. (Sylt) *sulke.*] *intr.* To keep aloof from others in moody silence; to indulge in sullen ill-humour; to be sulky.

1781 MME. D'ARBLAY *Diary* May, I still sulked on, vexed to be teased. **1794** W. BLAKE *Songs Exp.*, *Inf. Sorrow* 8, I thought best To sulk upon my mother's breast. **1852** W. JERDAN *Autobiog.* I. xi. 82 My uncle..sulked a little at my not having made myself celebrated. **1861** READE *Cloister & H.* lxv, He sulked with his old landlady for thrusting gentle advice and warning on him. **1880** *Daily Tel.* 4 Oct., It is now thirteen years that we have been sulking with the Republic of Mexico.

b. *transf.* and *fig.* Of a fish: To remain in hiding and motionless when hooked. Of tea-plants: see quot. 1891. In quot. 1860 *refl.* with *out*: to go out 'sulkily'.

1860 O. W. HOLMES *Elsie V.* (1887) 75 The lamps.. sulked themselves out. **1873** BROWNING *Red Cott. Nt.-cap* 154 Sorrowful Sulked field and pasture with persistent rain. **1873** W. C. PRIME *I go a-fishing* ii. 21 He started down stream, over a low fall and into a deep hole, where he sulked like a salmon. **1884** *Sat. Rev.* 12 July 61/1 [He] was occupied two hours and twenty minutes in landing an eight-pound trout which sulked. **1891** T. C. OWEN *Tea Planting in Ceylon*, When the foliage becomes too luxuriant, and they [*sc.* tea-bushes] sulk and no longer send out vigorous flushes. **1905** SIR F. TREVES *Oth. Side Lant.* II. ii. (1906) 33 Sluggish streams, sulking through a gully of sand and stones.

Hence **'sulker,** one who sulks; **'sulkery** (*nonce-wd.*), = BOUDOIR; **'sulking** *vbl. sb.* (also *attrib.* in **sulking-room** = BOUDOIR) and *ppl. a.*

1888 *Library Mag.* June 313 He called upon the *sulkers to come to the front. **1906** *Month* July 72 *Sulkery, as they translated *boudoir.* **1816** LADY BYRON in *Ld. Broughton's Recoll. Long Life* (1909) II. 203 Such a sitting-room or *sulking-room, all to yourself. **1880** *Daily Tel.* 4 Oct., Not all the sulking of which diplomacy is capable can restore Maximilian to life. **1778** FOOTE *Trip Calais* II. Wks. 1799 IV. 58 You sullen, *sulking, stomachful slut!

sulk(e, variants of SUCK, SWILK.

Sulka ('sʊlkə). The name of *Sulka* & Co., shirtmakers and hosiers (est. 1895), of London and New York, used *attrib.* to designate exclusive fabrics (esp. silk) and garments made, designed, or sold by them. Freq. as ***Sulka tie.***

1925 *Trade Marks Jrnl.* 21 Oct. 2307 *Sulka*... Shirtings and handkerchiefs, being linen piece goods. A. Sulka & Company.., New York City, New York, United States of America; merchants and manufacturers. **1944** A. HUXLEY *Time must have Stop* (1945) vi. 69 The beautifully fitting pearl-grey suit, the Sulka tie. **1963** E. LININGTON *Death of Busybody* x. 126 Mendoza's custom-tailored gray Italian silk and Sulka tie. **1981** 'E. LATHEN' *Going for Gold* ix. 99 Brad, wrapped in yards of Sulka silk, was pacing the floor.

†**sulke**, *a. Obs. rare*$^{-1}$. [? Related to SULK *v.*, SULKY *a.*] Hard to sell; slow in going off.

1636 HEYWOOD *Challenge Beautie* III. i, Never was thrifty trader more willing to put of a sulke commodity, than she was to truck for her maydenhead.

sulkene, obs. form of SILKEN *a.*

sulkily ('sʌlkɪlɪ), *adv.* [f. SULKY *a.* + -LY².] In a sulky manner; with silent or moody ill-humour.

1796 COLMAN *Iron Chest* Pref. p. ii, Here is a scowling, sullen, black Bull,..he stands sulkily before. **1855** MACAULAY *Hist. Eng.* xv. III. 560 Anne, who, when in good humour, was meekly stupid, and, when in bad humour, was sulkily stupid. **1865** FLO. MARRYAT *Love's Confl.* I. xviii. 317 Agnes took the sulkily-granted leave joyfully. **1874** GREEN *Short Hist.* viii. §9 (1882) 560 The stricter Covenanters retired sulkily from the Royal army.

fig. **1823** BYRON *Juan* XIV. xxviii, When..sulkily the river's ripple's flowing. **1839** KEMBLE *Resid. in Georgia* (1863) 69 The eagle..hovered sulkily a while over the river.

sulkiness ('sʌlkɪnɪs). [f. SULKY *a.* + -NESS.] The state or quality of being sulky.

1760 GRAY *Let. to Dr. Clarke* 12 Aug., Three women that laughed from morning to night, and would allow nothing to the sulkiness of my disposition. **1818** SCOTT *Hrt. Midl.* xix, Driven into pettish sulkiness by the persecution of the interrogators. **1885** *Manch. Even. News* 2 Feb. 2/4 Their sulkiness manifests itself in the most peevish manner.

sulkuþ, variant form of SELCOUTH. *Obs.*

sulky ('sʌlkɪ), *sb.* Also 8–9 **sulkey**, 9 **sulkee, sulkie.** [subst. use of SULKY *a.*]

1. A light two-wheeled carriage or chaise (sometimes without a body), seated for one person: now used principally in America for trials of speed between trotting-horses. (So called because it admits only one person. Cf. DÉSOBLIGEANT.)

1756 *Connoisseur* No. 112 ¶4 A formal female seated in a Sulky, foolishly pleased with having the whole vehicle to herself. **1775** J. ADAMS in *Fam. Lett.* (1876) 55 My mare.. ran and dashed the body of the sulky all to pieces. **1796** SOUTHEY *Lett. fr. Spain* (1799) 118 Many sulkies drawn by three mules abreast. **1860** O. W. HOLMES *Elsie V.* xi, The doctor turned and looked through the little round glass in the back of the sulky. **1882** *Standard* 1 Dec. 5/4 (*Canada*) The din and noise of waggons,..buggies, sulkees, and ox teams. **1884** *B'ham Daily Post* 23 Feb. 2/5 American Trotting Sulkie, weighs 56 lb.; to carry 180 lb.

2. *transf.* **a.** A bathing-machine for one. *jocular.*

1806–7 J. BERESFORD *Miseries Hum. Life* (1807) XIV. vi, On re-entering your Sulky in your new character,..you discover, for the first time, that your own towel is safely locked up at home.

b. (See quot.)

1862 MRS. SPEID *Last Years India* 129 A little silver 'sulky',..a small spherical box, pierced all over with small holes [etc.]. This pretty apparatus is intended for brewing a single cup of tea, by the morosely inclined.

3. Short for *sulky-plough* (see 4).

1891 C. ROBERTS *Adrift Amer.* 37 Two single-furrow sulkies with three horses each.

4. *attrib.* passing into *adj.*, applied to (*a*) a set of articles for the use of a single person, (*b*) an agricultural implement having a seat for the driver (*U.S.*).

1786 MACKENZIE *Lounger* No. 89 ¶7 A dispute about the age of a sulky set of China. **1867** *Trans. Ill. Agric. Soc.* VI. 49 Driving a sulky plow, and plowing his one-fourth acre. **1868** *Rep. Iowa Agric. Soc. 1867* 154 It is then plowed with double-shovel, or sulky cultivators. **1875** KNIGHT *Dict. Mech.* 2452 *Sulky-cultivator*, one having a seat for the rider, who manages the plows, moving them to the right or left as the plants in the rows may require. *Ibid.*, *Sulky-rake*, a horse-rake having an elevated seat for the driver. **1879** *Scribner's Mag.* Nov. 137/1 Next spring I..bought me a sulky-plow.

sulky ('sʌlkɪ), *a.* [app. f. SULK *v.*² Cf. NFris. (Sylt) *sulkig.*]

1. Of persons and their actions: Silently and obstinately ill-humoured; showing a tendency to keep aloof from others and repel their advances by refusing to speak or act.

1744 M. BISHOP *Life & Adv.* vi. 45 It is often seen in press'd Men that they are stubborn and sulky. **1790** BURNS *Tam o' Shanter* 10 Our hame, Whare sits our sulky sullen dame, Gathering her brows like gathering storm. **1821** SCOTT *Kenilw.* iii, He has sulky ways too, breaking off intercourse with all that are of the place. **1834** JAMES *J. Marston Hall* xi, My companion generally rode on in sulky silence. **1856** RUSKIN *Elem. Drawing* ii. (1857) 134 The true zeal and patience of a quarter of an hour are better than the sulky and inattentive labour of a whole day. **1880** W. HARRIS *Serm. Boys & Girls* (1881) 40 They were like..sulky children who would be pleased with nothing.

b. Of animals; *spec.* of a fish (cf. SULK *v.*² b).

1810 SCOTT *Lady of L.* I. x, Back limp'd..The sulky leaders of the chase. **1822** LAMB *Elia* I. *Dream children*, A great sulky pike hanging midway down the water. **1828** DAVY *Salmonia* 30, I thought after a fish had been hooked, he remained sick and sulky for some time.

2. Of inanimate natural objects, the weather, etc.: Gloomy, dismal. Of things, with respect to their growth, progress, or movement: Sluggish. Also, *dial.* difficult to work.

1817 W. IRVING in *Life & Lett.* (1864) I. 380 The weather is still sulky and threatening. **1825** SCOTT 11 Oct. in *Fam. Let.* (1894) II. xxiii. 350 One's friends are not so easily entertained on such a sulky day as this. **1849** CUPPLES *Green Hand* ix. (1856) 85 A sulky patch of dark-gray sky. **1867** F. FRANCIS *Angling* vii. 223 Some, again, are termed 'sulky lakes', and are very hard to get fish from at all. **1886** *Cheshire Gloss.*, *Sulky*,..applied to..rock which has no cleavage and is difficult to quarry, very cross-grained timber, &c. **1889** E. E. GREEN in *Ceylon Indep.* (Cent. Dict.), The condition called sulky as applied to a tea-bush is unfortunately only too common on many estates. **1890** CLARK RUSSELL *Marriage at Sea* viii, The sulky undulations of the water. **1905** *Daily News* 31 Aug. 6 The cream..gets 'sulky', or it 'goes to sleep', and then you may churn all day and get no result.

3. *Comb.*, as ***sulky-looking*** adj.

1828 LYTTON *Pelham* II. xxv, A few dull and sulky-looking fir-trees. **1844** H. STEPHENS *Bk. Farm* II. 692 The dull sulky-looking colt.

sull, *sb.* Chiefly *w.* and *s.w. dial.* Also 7, 9 **sul**, 9 **zull**; 7 **soule**, 8 **sewl**, 9 **sole**, **sowle**, **zowl**, **zarl.** [repr. the stem of the oblique cases (*sule*, *sulum*, etc.) of OE. *sulh* SULLOW, or the later nom. *sul*, *sūl.* Somerset *zill* repr. OE. oblique *syl(l* for *sylh* (cf. *sillow*, etc. s.v. SULLOW).] A plough.

1607 J. CARPENTER *Plaine Mans Plough* 109 The Soule.. that Instrument wherewith being fastened to the Oxen, the Husbandman rippeth up his land. **1669** WORLIDGE *Syst. Agric.* (1681) 36 The Sun and the Sull are some Husbandmens Soil. *Ibid.* 332 A *Sull*, a term used for a Plow in the Western parts. **1766** WILLY in *Complete Farmer* s.v. *Turnep*, Ploughing the intervals with a small sull, drawn by one horse. **1791** W. H. MARSHALL *W. England* (1796) II. 276 The plowman carries, in the body of his sewl, a parcel of small rods. **1825** JENNINGS *Observ. Dial. W. Eng.* 86 *Zull*,.. a plough. **1883** *Hampsh. Gloss.*, *Zarl* (zaal), a plough.

b. *attrib.* and *Comb.*, as ***sull-breaking***; **sull-paddle** = PLOUGH-STAFF.

1669 WORLIDGE *Syst. Agric.* (1681) 331 *A Sulpaddle*, a small Spade-staff or Instrument to cleanse the Plough from the clogging Earth. **1766** *Compl. Farmer*, *Sull-paddle*, a plough paddle. **1791** W. H. MARSHALL *W. England* (1796) II. 276 A field..which has long been noted for sewl-breaking.

sull (sʌl), *v. U.S.* [Back-formation from SULLEN *a.*, *adv.* and *sb.*] *intr.* Of an animal, to balk; of a person, to become sullen or to sulk.

1869 *Overland Monthly* III. 127 A mustang..will both 'sull', (have the sulks) and 'buck'. **1891** 'O. THANET' *Otto the Knight* 29 The ox, he sulled,..an' Jim jes' guv 'im one on the head. **1902** *Dialect Notes* II. 246 *Sull*,..to hold a position with imperturbable obstinacy and a total disregard of surroundings, as a possum, or a hog in a corner. **1903** *Ibid.* 332 *Sull*,..to sulk; to balk. 'My oxens sull whenever they get hot.' 'She is a quare child and sulls whenever she is contrairied.' **1929** W. FAULKNER *Sound & Fury* 87 'She sulling again, is she,' Roskus said. **1938** M. K. RAWLINGS *Yearling* xxv. 327 Do he ever come here drunk, remember he ain't human when he gits to sullin'. **1949** *10 Story Western* May 11/2 Tell them slow motion sons to keep them cattle comin' before this drive balks and sulls. **1959** W. FAULKNER *Mansion* 10 All Frenchman's Bend knew Houston: sulking and sulling in his house all alone by himself since the stallion killed his wife four years ago.

Hence (rarely) as *sb.*, a sulky fit, a 'sulk'.

1972 E. WELTY *Optimist's Daughter* II. iv. 97 He's been in a sull ever since you married Judge McKelva and didn't send him a special engraved invitation to the wedding.

‖**sulla** ('sʌlə). [Sp. *sulla.*] A leguminous plant, *Hedysarum coronarium* (also called French honeysuckle), with flowers resembling those of the red clover, found in some Mediterranean countries. Also *attrib.*

1787 JEFFERSON *Writ.* (1859) II. 202 The sulla of Malta, or Spanish St. Foin. **1818** MRS. ILIFF *Poems* (ed. 2) 129 Lovely May Wreathing the sulla-flowers of brightest red, With ears of barley. **1895** *Atlantic Monthly* Mar. 340 The *sulla*, a sort of pink vetch.

sullabub, obs. form of SILLABUB.

sullage ('sʌlɪdʒ). Forms: 6 **sollage**, 7 **sulledge**, 7–8 **suillage**, 8 **sulli(d)ge**, **swillage**, 7– **sullage.** [Of uncertain origin. ? a. AF. **souillage*, **soullage*, **suillage*, f. *souiller* SOIL *v.*¹, SULLY *v.*: see -AGE. The synonymous SOILAGE is perhaps due to a variant **soillage.* In the 17th and 18th cent. the spelling was influenced by SULLY: see SULLIAGE.]

1. Filth, refuse, *esp.* such as is carried off by drains from a house, farmyard, or the like; sewage.

1553 in *Vicary's Anat.* (1888) App. iii. 176 To caraye awaye the Sollage of the Clensinge of the saide Stretes. **1609** in *Sussex Archæol. Coll.* (1867) XIX. 199 Annoying the Bowrne wth the sulledge of his hoggs by a dyke. **1624** WOTTON *Elem. Archit.* (1672) 18 Under-conducts and Conveyances, for the Suillage of the House. **1748** DODSLEY *Preceptor* (1763) I. 180 The Apertures..are either Doors.. or conduits for the Suillage. **1750** W. ELLIS *Mod. Husbandm.* I. I. 39 (E.D.S.) If..highway sullidge and dung are mixed together. **1879** FLOR. NIGHTINGALE in *Jrnl. Indian Assoc. Art Educ.* Oct., The people themselves feel the misery of having no channels to remove sullage away clear from every habitation.

†**2.** *fig.* Filth, filthiness, defilement, pollution.

1641 S. HINDE in W. Hinde *J. Bruen* To Rdr., Free from the sullage of Envie, and detraction. **1673** *Lady's Call.* II. i. §7. 59 The lightest act of dalliance leaves somthing of stain and sullage behind it. **1697** EVELYN *Numismata* ix. 309 The Soul contracts no sullage from the deformity of the Body.

3. The silt washed down and deposited by a stream or flood.

1691 T. H[ALE] *Acc. New Inv.* p. lxi, Such Shelfes arising in our River from the Gravel and Sullage that are wash'd into it. **1725** HENLEY tr. *Montfaucon's Antiq. Italy* (ed. 2) 28 Several Strata of this Kind were form'd by the Suillage of Rivers and Torrents. **1733** W. ELLIS *Chiltern & Vale Farm.* 236 Sullidge which the Waters leaves on the Ground. **1755** *Gentl. Mag.* XXV. 396 The swillage of rivers. **1800** W. CHAPMAN *Witham & Welland* 62 The bottom was found quite hard, and without sullage, from the Grand Sluice to Fishtoft-jetties. **1867** SMYTH *Sailor's Word-bk.* 665.

4. *Founding.* Metal scoria or slag.

1843 HOLTZAPFFEL *Turning* I. 349 The metal is..free from the scoria or sullage, which sometimes renders the upper surface very rough.

5. *Comb.*: **sullage-piece** (see quot. 1875); **sullage-pipe**, a drain-pipe.

1852 BURN *Naval & Milit. Dict.* II. 276/2 *Sullage piece, or dead head, *masselotte.* **1875** KNIGHT *Dict. Mech.* 2452/2 *Sullage-piece*,..a dead-head, or feeding-head. A piece of metal on a casting which occupies the ingate at which the metal entered the mold... In this piece the sullage rises, hence its name. **1907** 'J. HALSHAM' *Lonewood Corner* 214 He reckons it's better for a man to be on the top of a stack than down a *sullage-pipe.

Sullan ('sʌlən), *a.* (and *sb.*). [f. the name of Roman general and dictator Lucius Cornelius *Sulla* (*c* 138–78 B.C.) + -AN.] Of or pertaining to Sulla or his party, or the laws and political reforms instituted by him. Also as *sb.*, a supporter of Sulla.

1866 W. P. DICKSON tr. *Mommsen's Hist. Rome* IV. v. iii. 90 The young Gaius Caesar..brought to trial.. another Sullan officer Gaius Antonius. *Ibid.* v. 167 Antonius, originally a Sullan like Catilina. **1892** W. W. FOWLER *Julius Caesar* ii. 29 Caesar..fled in disguise into the mountains of Samnium. Here he was pursued and captured by the Sullan bloodhounds, who were everywhere. **1905** G. S. GORDON *Let.* 15 Nov. (1943) 10, I *cannot* get out of my head even now the Ontological proofs of the existence of God, the Sullan Constitution, Pericles and Athenian finance, and why Pleasure cannot be an ultimate Ethical end. **1923** T. R. HOLMES *Roman Republic* I. i. 59 The Sullan reign of terror was never forgotten by the Romans. **1949** L. R. TAYLOR *Party Politics in Age of Caesar* i. 21 The *optimates*, who were determined to save what they could of their Sullan prerogatives. **1974** A. WATSON *Law Making in Later Roman Republic* vi. 95 It is not proved that all these *leges* are Sullan. **1976** *Classical Q.* XXVI. 105 The Sullan reforms tell us a little about this.

†**sullayne**, ? erron. form of SEWIN.

1570 LEVINS *Manip.* Q iv, A sullayne, fishe, *salmo paruus.*

sulle, obs. f. SELL *v.*, SHALL *v.*, SILL *sb.*¹

sulledge, obs. form of SULLAGE.

sullen ('sʌlən), *a.*, *adv.*, and *sb.* Also 6 **solen**, **sulleyne**, 6–7 **sollen**, 7 **sull(a)in**, **sulen.** [Later form of SOLEIN.] **A.** *adj.*

1. a. Of persons, their attributes, aspect, actions: Characterized by, or indicative of, gloomy ill-humour or moody silence.

In early use there is often implication of obstinacy or stubbornness.

1573–80 TUSSER *Husb.* (1878) 180 Be lowly not sollen, if ought go amisse. **1592** *Arden of Feversham* I. i. 510 Who would haue thought the ciuill sir so sollen? **1641** 'SMECTYMNUUS' *Vind. Answ.* To Rdr., Wee are called.. sullen and crabbed peices. **1668** *Extr. St. Papers rel. Friends* Ser. III. (1912) 279 Their Saint Penn..is divelishly cryed vp amongest that pervers sullen Faction. **1680** C. NESSE *Church Hist.* 55 Because they might not have what they would, grew sullain, and would have nothing. **1713** STEELE *Guard.* No. 18 ¶2 These contemplations have made me serious but not sullen. **1718** *Free-thinker* No. 149. 323 In the Middle sits Cato, with a sullen Brow. **1795** BURKE *Corr.* (1844) IV. 315 If the better part lies by, in a sullen silence, they still cannot hinder the more factious part both from speaking and from writing. **1814** WORDSW. *Excurs.* VI. 459 Here..they met,.. flaming Jacobite And sullen Hanoverian! **1849** MACAULAY *Hist. Eng.* vi. II. 28 The answer of James was a cold and sullen reprimand. **1879** FROUDE *Cæsar* xxvi. 438 Some were still sullen, and refused to sue for a forgiveness.

b. *transf.* Of animals and inanimate things: Obstinate, refractory; stubborn, unyielding.

1577 B. GOOGE *Heresbach's Husb.* III. 128 b, Which being well punished with hunger, and thyrst, wyll teache him [*sc.* a plough-ox] to leaue that sullen tricke. **1648** GAGE *West Ind.* 89, I got up againe and spurred my sullen jade. **1678** CUDWORTH *Intell. Syst.* I. v. 888 Things are Sullen, and will be as they are, what ever we Think them, or Wish them to be. **1691** RAY *Creation* I. (1692) 38 The stupid Matter.. would be as sullen as the Mountain was that Mahomet commanded to come down to him. **1725** DE FOE *Voy. round World* (1840) 339 The other [bull] proved untractable, sullen, and outrageous. **1859** TENNYSON *Geraint & Enid* 862 As sullen as a beast new-caged.

†**c.** Holding aloof. *Obs.*

1628 EARLE *Microcosm., Acquaintance* (Arb.) 86 Friendship is a sullener thing, as a contracter and taker vp of our affections to some few.

†**d.** *fig.* Baleful, malignant. *Obs.*

1676 DRYDEN *Aurengz.* I. i. 360 Such sullen Planets at my Birth did shine, They threaten every Fortune mixt with mine. **1679** DRYDEN & LEE *Œdipus* III, Ye sullen Pow'rs below. **1703** ROWE *Fair Penit.* II. i, Some sullen Influence, a Foe to both.

†**2.** Solemn, serious. *Obs.*

1583 MELBANCKE *Philotimus* M iij b, So was he free from sulleyne sterne seuerity. *a* **1586** SIDNEY *Apol. Poetrie* (Arb.) 30 Morrall Philosophers, whom me thinketh, I see comming towards me with a sullen grauity. **1640** BP. REYNOLDS *Passions* iv, Some plausible Fancy doth more prevail with tender Wills than a severe and sullen argument. **1719** YOUNG *Busiris* I. i, In sullen Majesty they stalk along, With Eyes of Indignation, and Despair.

3. a. Of immaterial things, actions, conditions: Gloomy, dismal, melancholy; sometimes with the notion of 'passing heavily, moving sluggishly'.

1593 SHAKS. *Rich. II*, I. iii. 265 The sullen passage of thy weary steppes. **1604** —— *Oth.* III. iv. 51 (Q[1]), A salt and sullen rhume. **1605** DANIEL *Philotas* Ep. 59 To sound The deepe reports of sullen Tragedies. **1648** MILTON *Sonn.* xvii, Where shall we sometimes meet, and by the fire Help wast a sullen day. **1712–14** POPE *Rape Lock* IV. 19 No cheerful breeze this sullen region knows. **1775** JOHNSON *Let. to Mrs. Thrale* 1 Aug., The place [*sc.* Oxford] is now a sullen solitude. **1816** BYRON *Pris. Chillon* xiv, With spiders I had friendship made, And watch'd them in their sullen trade. **1858** KINGSLEY *Lett.* (1878) I. 21 It was an afternoon of sullen Autumn rain. *a* **1864** HAWTHORNE *Amer. Note-bks.* (1879) II. 52 A bleak, sullen day.

b. Of a sound or an object producing a sound: Of a deep, dull, or mournful tone. Chiefly *poet.*

1592 SHAKS. *Rom. & Jul.* IV. v. 88 Our solemne Hymnes, to sullen Dyrges change. **1632** MILTON *Penseroso* 76, I hear the far-off Curfeu sound,..Swinging slow with sullen roar. **1742** COLLINS *Ode* ix. 12 Where the beetle winds His small but sullen horn. **1819** SCOTT *Ivanhoe* xliv, The heavy bell.. broke short their argument. One by one the sullen sounds fell successively on the ear. **1849** KINGSLEY *North Devon* in *Misc.* (1859) II. 264 The sullen thunder of the unseen surge.

4. a. Of sombre hue; of a dull colour; hence, of gloomy or dismal aspect. (Also qualifying an adj. of colour = dull-.) Cf. SAD *a.* 8.

a **1586** [implied in SULLENLY 2]. **1592** *Arden of Feversham* III. i. 45 Now will he shake his care oppressed head, Then fix his sad eis on the sollen earth. **1596** SHAKS. *1 Hen. IV*, I. ii. 236 Like bright Mettall on a sullen ground. **1647** HARVEY *Sch. of Heart* XXI. i, Take sullen lead for silver, sounding brass Instead of solid gold. **1665** J. REA *Flora* 130 A dark sullen violet purple colour. **1710** STEELE *Tatler* No. 266 ⁋3 Two apples that were roasting by a sullen sea coal fire. **1713** *Phil. Trans.* XXVIII. 224 A sort of sullen greenish Woodlike rust. **1784** COWPER *Task* II. 212, I would not yet exchange thy sullen skies..for warmer France With all her vines. **1811** SCOTT *Don Roderick* II. i, All sleeps in sullen shade, or silver glow. **1818** KEATS *Sonn. Ben Nevis* 6, I look o'erhead, And there is sullen mist. **1855** TENNYSON *Maud* I. x. i, The sullen-purple moor. **1894** HALL CAINE *Manxman* v. iii. 286 The sky to the north-west was dark and sullen.

†**b. sullen lady**, ? *Fritillaria nigra. Obs.*

1688 HOLME *Armoury* II. iv. 74/1 The sullen Lady, hangeth her head down..and is of an umberish dark hair colour, without any checker or spots. Some call it the black Fritillary.

5. Of water, etc.: Flowing sluggishly. *poet.*

1622 DRAYTON *Poly-olb.* xxviii. 91 Small Cock, a sullen Brook, comes to her succour then. **1628** MILTON *Vac. Exerc.* 95 Sullen Mole that runneth underneath. **1814** SCOTT *Wav.* xxii, The larger [stream] was placid, and even sullen in its course. **1818** SHELLEY *Rosal. & Helen* 398 Each one lay Sucking the sullen milk away About my frozen heart.

6. *Comb.*: parasynthetic adjs., as ***sullen-browed, -eyed, -faced, -hearted***; complementary, as ***sullen-blooming, -looking, -seeming, -smiling***; with other adjs., as ***sullen-sour, -wise***.

1879 O. WILDE in *Time* July 402 No *sullen-blooming poppies stain thy hair. **1831** SCOTT *Cast. Dang.* ii, This *sullen-browed Thomas Dickson. **1961** R. S. THOMAS *Tares* 47 And given to watching, *sullen-eyed, Love still-born, as it was then. **1914** JOYCE *Dubliners* 117 A very *sullen-faced man. **1909** R. BRIDGES *Par. Virg. Æn. VI*, 434 The *sullen-hearted, who..Their own life did-away. **1855** TENNYSON *Maud* I. XVIII. vi, *Sullen-seeming Death. **1849** J. A. CARLYLE tr. *Dante's Inf.* p. xliv, The *Sullen-sour or Gloomy-sluggish. **1919** J. MASEFIELD *Reynard the Fox* I. 29 Surly, Tall, shifty, *sullen-smiling. **1710** STEELE *Tatler* No. 149 ⁋5 A *sullen-wise Man is as bad as a good-natured Fool.

B. *adv.* = SULLENLY. *rare.*

1718 PRIOR *Solomon* II. 201 Sullen I forsook th' Imperfect Feast. **1810** SCOTT *Lady of L.* II. xxxiv, Sullen and slowly they unclasp.

C. *sb.* **a.** (in *pl.*, usually ***the sullens***; rarely *sing.*) A state of gloomy ill-humour; sullenness, sulks. Phr. ***in the sullens, sick of the sullens.***

1580 LYLY *Euphues* (Arb.) 285 She was solitaryly walking, with hir frowning cloth, as sick lately of the solens. **1631** R. H. *Arraignm. Whole Creature* xvi. 280 So long he is sicke in the suds, and diseas'd in the sullens. **1633** MARMION *Fine Comp.* I. iii. B 2, They can doe no more good upon me, then a young pittifull Lover upon a Mistresse, that has the sullens. **1662** HIBBERT *Body Divinity* I. 142 Its a dangerous thing to sit sick of the sullens, or be discontented. *a* **1670** HACKET *Abp. Williams* I. (1692) 84 If his Majesty were moody..he would fetch him out of that Sullen with a pleasant Jest. **1671** WOOD *Life* (O.H.S.) II. 215 When William Lenthall was troubled with the sullins. **1679** DRYDEN *Troil. & Cress.* IV. ii, I'll e'en go home, and shut up my doors, and die o' the sullens, like an old bird in a cage. **1747** RICHARDSON *Clarissa* (1811) I. xviii. 134 No sullens, my Mamma; no perverseness. **1819** SCOTT *Leg. Montrose* xxiii, Annot Lyle could always charm Allan out of the sullens. **1864** CARLYLE *Fredk. Gr.* XVI. viii. IV. 362 Russian Czarina evidently in the sullens against Friedrich. **1868** 'HOLME LEE' *B. Godfrey* xxxvi, Gerrard was in a fit of sullens.

b. *Comb.*, †**sullen-sick** *a.*, 'sick of the sullens', ill from ill-humour.

1614 T. ADAMS *Sinners Passing Bell* Wks. (1629) 247 If the state..lie sullen-sicke of Naboths vineyard. **1650** FULLER *Pisgah* II. vii. §7. 158 On the denyall Ahab falls sullen-sick.

sullen ('sʌlən), *v. rare.* [f. SULLEN *a.*]

1. *trans.* To make sullen or sluggish.

1628 FELTHAM *Resolves* II. xlviii, The Idle man..like a member out of joynt, sullens the whole Body, with an ill disturbing lazinesse. **1894** AMYAND *Only a Drummer Boy* iv. 47 [They] prevented Douglas's happy nature getting completely crushed and sullened.

†**2.** *intr.* To be sullen; to sulk. *Obs.*

a **1652** BROME *Covent Gard.* I. i, Keeping her chamber whole weeks together, sullenning upon her Samplery breechwork.

sullen, obs. form of SELL *v.*, SHALL *v.*

sullenly ('sʌlənlɪ), *adv.* [f. SULLEN *a.* + -LY[2].] In a sullen manner.

1. With gloomy or morose ill-humour.

1650 FULLER *Pisgah* III. xi §15. 434 If any..sullenly say, with Judas Iscariot, *To what purpose is this wast?* **1668** DRYDEN *Secr. Love* III, While jealous pow'r does sullenly o're spy. **1784** COWPER *Task* III. 393 His book, Well chosen, and not sullenly perus'd In selfish silence, but imparted oft. **1841** DICKENS *Barn. Rudge* xvii, 'Give me meat and drink', he answered sullenly. **1879** *Spectator* 13 Sept. 1148 That if the Viceroy were only sufficiently persistent, Afghans, like Turks, would sullenly give way.

2. With sombre or gloomy aspect; with a dull or dismal sound.

a **1586** SIDNEY *Arcadia* III. x. (1912) 402 The colours for the grounde were so well chosen, neither sullenly darke, nor glaringly lightsome. **1794** MRS. RADCLIFFE *Myst. Udolpho* li, The wind..groaned sullenly among the lofty branches above. **1841** W. SPALDING *Italy & It. Isl.* I. 295 The volcanic fires..smoulder sullenly at the present day. **1860** TYNDALL *Glac.* I. xiv. 93 The clouds..sailed sullenly from the west. **1898** H. NEWBOLT *He fell among Thieves* iv, The ravine where the Yassîn river sullenly flows.

sullenness ('sʌlənnɪs). Also 7 solennesse, sulliness, 8 sulleness. [f. SULLEN *a.* + -NESS.]

1. The condition or quality of being sullen in behaviour, aspect, or temper. Also, an instance of this.

a **1586** SIDNEY *Arcadia* III. (1912) 379 Fearing least silence would offend her sullennes. **1644** MILTON *Educ.* Wks. 1851 IV. 392 When the air is calm and pleasant, it were an injury and sullennesse against nature not to go out. **1663** PATRICK *Parab. Pilgr.* xxxii. (1687) 399 His seriousness gives no disgust, his silence is without sullenness. *a* **1721** PRIOR *Cromwell & his Porter* 20 Wks. 1907 II. 262 By..the sulleness of his brow it should be my old Porter. **1784** *Cook's 3rd Voy.* I. viii. I. 154 The countenance..has..sometimes a sullenness or reserve. **1825** SCOTT *Betrothed* iii, They are.. a mixed breed, having much of your German sullenness. **1879** FROUDE *Cæsar* xiv. 205 After a few vicious efforts, they subsided into sullenness.

†**2.** Slowness, reluctance. *Obs.*

1619 LUSHINGTON *Resurrection* I. (1659) 34 No removing of the Tombestone; that besides its weight & sullenness to give way, was rib'd and clasped down with Iron barrs and bonds.

3. Dismalness, gloom.

1885 PATER *Marius* IV. xxiii, The long winter had been a season of unvarying sullenness.

†'**sullenwood.** *Obs.* Altered f. SOUTHERNWOOD, with play on *sullen.*

1632 W. ROWLEY *New Wonder* III, I'l make you eate Sorrill to your supper, though I eate Sullenwood my selfe.

sullepe, variant of SERELEPY *Obs.*

a **1400–50** *Wars Alex.* 4305 Þat sullepe sire at sett all þe werde.

sullepsis, variant of SYLLEPSIS.

sullerⁱ(e, obs. forms of SELLER[1].

'**sullerye.** ? Misprint for *sullinge* = SULING.

1628 COKE *On Litt.* 5 *Vna Hida seu carucata terræ*, which is all one as a plow-land,..su lerye also signifieth a plowland.

'**sullevate**, var. SOLLEVATE *v.* (Cf. SUBLEVATE.)

1595 DANIEL *Civ. Wars* I. xlviii, How he his subiectes sought to sulleuate.

sulle'vation, var. SOLLEVATION *Obs.* (Cf. SUBLEVATION.)

1611 SIR D. CARLETON in *10th Rep. Hist. MSS. Comm.* App. I. 533 To furnish the Albanesi with weapons for a suddaine sullevation. **1623** COCKERAM, *Sullevation*, a murderous intent. **1637** EARL MONM. tr. *Malvezzi's Romulus & Tarquin* 97 To suffocat sullevations in their cradle.

sulli, variant form of SELLY *Obs.*

a **1290** *Pains of Hell* 213 in Herrig's *Archiv* LXII. 403 Neren ncwiȝt hoe þerof adrad: ffor-þi hoe slepeþ in sulli bed.

sulliage ('sʌlɪɪdʒ). Variant of SULLAGE influenced by SULLY *v.*

1667 *Decay Chr. Piety* xi. §2 Though we wipe away with never so much care the dirt thrown at us, there will be left some sulliage behind. **1793** W. H. MARSHALL *Rural Econ. W. Eng.* (1796) II. 358 The sulliage which such places are ever accumulating. **1853** *Bill to establish Metrop. Board Sewers* Preamble 2 The Sewage, Filth, Soil, and Sulliage issuing from the Sewers and Drains. **1879** R. FLETCHER *Dickens* xv. 13 No taint or sulliage falls on all he writ. **188.** R. G. H[ILL] *Voices in Solit.* 111 Oft have I watched and proved her perfidy, And chid with bitter words her sulliage.

sullibib, -bub, obs. forms of SILLABUB.

sullic, -ich(e, var. forms of SELLY *Obs.*

sullidge, var. SULLAGE.

sullied ('sʌlɪd), *ppl. a.* Also 6 solyed, 7 sully'd. [f. SULLY *v.* + -ED[1].] Soiled, polluted (*lit.* and *fig.*); †made gloomy or dull.

1571 [implied in SULLIEDNESS]. *c* **1600** SHAKS. *Sonn.* xv, To change your day of youth to sullied night. **1612** DRAYTON *Poly-olb.* x. 194 Her sullied face. **1683** TRYON *Way to Health* 320 A loathsomely sullied Soul, and an indisposed distempered Body. **1695** A. TELFAIR *New Confut. Sadd.* (1696) 7 Seven small Bones..wrapp'd up in a piece of old sullied Paper. **1734** tr. *Rollin's Anc. Hist.* XV. viii. (1827) VI. 132 The moon..appeared afterwards quite sullied and as it were tinged with blood. **1824** SCOTT *Redgauntlet* ch. xiii, He wore a smart hanger and a pair of pistols in a sullied sword-belt. **1870** DICKENS *E. Drood* i, The choir are getting on their sullied white robes. **1889** R. BRIDGES *Growth of Love* lii, Let the true Muse rewrite her sullied page.

b. ***sullied white***, dirty white.

1681 *Lond. Gaz.* No. 1676/4 A very large Irish Greyhound being of a sullied White, with some pale yellowish spots. **1817** STEPHENS in *Shaw's Gen. Zool.* X. II. 493 The under parts of the body sullied white: the tail greenish black.

Hence †'**sulliedness**, defilement.

1571 GOLDING *Calvin on Ps.* lxviii. 15 Although the land were covered with solyednesse throughe the troublous invasion of the enemies: yit..it recovered hir whitenesse, so as it became as whyte as snowe.

sulli'vation, variant of SOLLEVATION *Obs.*

1605 DANIEL *Philotas* II. i, How can that be donne, Without some sulliuation to insue?

'**sullow.** Chiefly *w.* and *s.w. dial.* Forms: 1 sulh, 1, 3 suluh, 3 solh, (sul(c)h-, sulȝ-, solȝ-, solw-), 4 soluȝ, -ou, *Kent.* zuolȝ, 4–5 solouȝ, -ow, 5 -ouh, -owe, -oȝ, 6 zolow, 7– sullow (9 zullow, sillow, silla, zilla). [OE. *sulh* str. fem., for **swulh*, the *w* being preserved in Kentish ME. *zuolȝ* and OE. *swulung*, ME. *swoling*, etc. (see SULING); ultimately cogn. with L. *sulcus* furrow.

The local variant *sillow* represents OE. dat. sing. or nom. pl. *sylh, sylȝ*. The oblique forms without umlaut (*sule*, etc.) are represented by forms s.v. SULL *sb.*]

1. A plough. (Also in *fig.* context.)

c **897** K. ÆLFRED *Gregory's Past C.* li. 403 Ðæt nan mon ne scyle don his hond to ðære sylȝ, & hawian underbæc. *c* **900** tr. *Baeda's Hist.* v. ix. (1899) 594 Forþon þe heora sylh unrihte gangað. *c* **950** *Lindisf. Gosp.* Luke ix. 62 Ne æniȝ sende hond his on sulh [*Rushw.* suluh] & behaldas on bæcg. *c* **1000** *Sax. Leechd.* I. 404 Þonne man þa sulh forð drife. *c* **1205** LAY. 4260 Þe[t] ælc cheorl æt his sulche hæfde grið al swa þe king sulf. *Ibid.* 31811 Þer cheorl draf his sulȝe i-oxned swiðe fæire. *a* **1225** *Ancr. R.* 384 Ȝif eax ne kurue, ne þe spade ne dulue, ne þe suluh [*MS. T.* ploh] ne erede. **1340** *Ayenb.* 242 Þe ilke þet zet þe hand aþe zuolȝ and lokeþ behinde him. **1340–70** *Alex. & Dind.* 295 Hit is no leue in oure lawe þat we..sette solow on þe feld ne sowe none erþe. **1387** TREVISA *Higden* (Rolls) VII. 445 Þe solouȝ of holy cherche schal nouȝt goo aryȝt. **14..** *Ibid.* App. 535 (Harl. MS. 1900) This day is my solowe y-come to the laste forowe. **1535** in F. W. Weaver *Wells Wills* (1890) 178 A zolow with all other apparell for vj oxen. **1636** H. SYDENHAM *Serm. Sol. Occ.* (1637) 265 The spirituall Plough is not halfe so well manag'd by any, as one that was yesterday conversant with the Goade and the Sullow. *c* **1640** J. SMYTH *Lives Berkeleys* (1883) I. 303 What waynes, carts, sullows, harrows.. remained. **1893** *Wilts. Gloss.*, *Sillow, Sullow,..Sylla*, a plough, was used at Bratton within the memory of persons still living.

†**b.** A plot of land is described as being 'of so many sullows'; hence *sullow* = PLOUGH *sb.*[1] 3 a, PLOUGH-LAND 1. *Obs.*

c **1205** LAY. 13176 Twenti sulhene [*c* **1275** solȝene] lond. *Ibid.* 18779 Þritti solh of londe. *Ibid.* 18789.

2. *attrib.* and *Comb.*, as ***sullow-beam, -board, -handle, -share*** (all *Obs.*).

a **1000** in Wr.-Wülcker 196/1 *Burris, curuamentum aratri*, *sulhbeam. **14..** *Metr. Voc.*, *Ibid.* 628/5 *Buris*, solowbeme. *Ibid.* 628/7 *Barcha*, *solowborde. *c* **1000** ÆLFRIC *Gloss.*, *Ibid.* 104/11 *Stiba*, *sulhhandla. **14..** *Metr. Voc.*, *Ibid.* 628/5 *Stiua*, solowhanddul. **14..** *Trevisa's Higden* (Rolls) VII. App. 527 (Harl. MS. 1900) Heo wole go barfot..uppon nyne *solow schares brennyng and fuyre hote.

†'**sully**, *sb. Obs.* Also 7 sulley. [f. SULLY *v.*] An act of sullying, soiling, or polluting (*lit.* and *fig.*); a stain, blemish.

1602 SHAKS. *Ham.* II. i. 39 You laying these slight sulleyes on my Sonne, As 'twere a thing a little soil'd i' th' working. **1683** MOXON *Mech. Exerc., Printing* xxiv. ⁋19 The Gold or Silver will stick to the least Sully that the Varnish may chance to make. **1711** ADDISON *Spect.* No. 256 ⁋4 These little Spots and Sullies in its Reputation. **1742** FIELDING *J. Andrews* I. iv, Without the least sully of their virtue. **1762** FRANKLIN *Lett.*, etc. Wks. 1840 V. 393 After the explosion, I could find neither any moisture nor any sully from the ink.

sully ('sʌlɪ), *v.* Also 6, 8 sulley, 7 sullie. [app. ad. F. *souiller*: see SOIL *v.*[1]]

1. *trans.* To pollute, defile; to soil, stain, tarnish.

a. in material sense. Now *rare* or *poet.*

1611 SHAKS. *Wint. T.* I. ii. 327 Sully the puritie and whitenesse of my Sheetes? **1615** G. SANDYS *Trav.* 295 The roofe and sides are..sullied..with the smoke of torches. **1756** C. LUCAS *Ess. Waters* II. 164 A sky colored pellicule, sullied with dark spots. **1818** WORDSW. *Near Spring of Hermitage* 12 Rains, that make each rill a torrent, Neither sully it nor swell. **1885** *Manch. Exam.* 25 Mar. 3/2 The delicate white of the vellum cover which a careless touch might sully.

absol. **1601** HOLLAND *Pliny* II. 473 [How] that if one rule paper..therewith [*sc.* silver], it will draw blacke lines, and sullie as it doth.

b. in immaterial sense.

1591 SHAKS. *1 Hen. VI*, IV. iv. 6 The ouer-daring Talbot Hath sullied all his glosse of former Honor By this vnheedfull..aduenture. **1612** *Two Noble K.* I. ii. 5 Before we furthur Sully our glosse of youth. **1657** SPARROW *Bk. Com. Prayer* (1661) 33 Christmas and Epiphany..holy Church held for such high times of joy and Festivity, that they would not have one day among them sullied by.. sorrow and fasting. **1706** PHILLIPS (ed. Kersey) s.v., To *Sully the Fancy*, to fill it with nasty, filthy, or impure Thoughts. **1729** SHELVOCKE *Artillery* v. 355, I will not sully my Page with any Rehearsal of them. **1781** GIBBON *Decl. & F.* xxiv. II. 475 The purity of his virtue was sullied by excessive vanity. **1849** MACAULAY *Hist. Eng.* v. I. 529 His life had been sullied by a great domestic crime. **1874** GREEN *Short Hist.* v. §2 (1882) 226 A merciless massacre sullied the fame of his earlier exploits.

†**2.** *intr.* To become soiled or tarnished. *Obs.*

1596 SHAKS. *1 Hen. IV*, II. iv. 84 Looke you Francis, your white Canuas doublet will sulley. **1654** Z. COKE *Logick* Pref., The Enamel of these Gayeties and Gauds, Sully and soon grow Dusky. **1670** SIR SACKVILLE CROW in *12th Rep. Hist. MSS. Comm.* App. v. 15 The silke sleizie and not Naples, which will soone grown rough, gather dust and sullie.

Hence **'sullying** *vbl. sb.* and *ppl. a.*

1628 FORD *Lover's Mel.* II. ii, The purest whitenesse is no such defence Against the sullying foulenesse of that fury. **1659** C. NOBLE *Mod. Answ. to Immod. Queries* To Rdr., They are also sullyings and discolorings of the sacred memory of the dead. **1707** MORTIMER *Husb.* (1721) I. 337 The sullying and foulness of the Floor. **1715** GAY *Trivia* II. 32 Three sullying trades avoid with equal care. **1842** MANNING *Serm.* vi. (1848) I. 84 He that leaves upon driven snow a dark and sullying touch. **1871** TENNYSON *Last Tourn.* 679 Thro' that sullying of our Queen.

sullybub, obs. form of SILLABUB.

1663 PEPYS *Diary* 12 July, Then to Commissioner Pett's and had a good sullybub.

†**sulp**, *v.* *Obs.* Also 4–5 solp. [Etym. obscure. Possibly related to G. dial. *sulper*, *solper* bog, mud, (? orig.) brine, pickle, *sölpern* to soil, sully.]

trans. To defile, pollute. Hence **'sulping** *vbl. sb.* (= defilement) and *ppl. a.*

a **1350** *St. Laurence* 210 in Horstm. *Altengl. Leg.* (1881) 110 [He] makes it clene, þat no solping þaron es sene. **13..** *E.E. Allit. P.* A. 726 With-outen..mascle of sulpande synne. *Ibid.* B. 550 If he be sulped in synne. *Ibid.* 1135 Sulp no more þenne in synne þy saule. *a* **1400–50** *Wars Alex.* 4292 All þe syn at solp may þe saule. **1412** *26 Pol. Poems* 49 Sulpid in synne derk as nyȝt.

sulph- (sʌlf). *Chem.* Variant of SULPHO- before a vowel, as in ***sulphacetic** (-ate), -acetone, -amic (-ate), -amidate, -amide, -amine, -aminic, -amylic (-ate), -anilic (-ate), -antimonic (-ate, -iate), -ious (-ite), -arsenic (-ate, -iate), -ious (-ite), -arsin, -ethamic (-ate), -ethylic (-ate), -imide, -iodide*: see quots. and the second elements; **sul'pharsenite**, any compound containing the elements sulphur, arsenic, and oxygen.

1843 *Chem. Gaz.* I. 598 *Sulphacetate of silver. *Ibid.* 597 On decomposing the lead salt [*sc.* carbonate of lead]..with sulphuretted hydrogen, an acid is obtained, to which the author [*sc.* M. Melsens] has applied the name of *sulphacetic acid. **1879** WATTS *Dict. Chem.*, Suppl. 1047 **Sulphacetone*..is formed by the action of 1 mol. phosphorus trisulphide on 6 mol. acetone. **1868** *Ibid.* V. 476 Neutral *Sulphamate of Ammonium. **1857** MILLER *Elem. Chem.*, *Org.* iv. §1. 244 *Sulphamic Acid. **1868** WATTS *Dict. Chem.* V. 477 Sulphamic ethers. **1844** *Chem. Gaz.* II. 461 The *sulphamidate of ammonia is prepared by leaving the corresponding *sulphammonate in cold water for some hours. **1868** WATTS *Dict. Chem.* V. 482 Sulphamidate.. formed from the sulphammonate by the action of water. **1838** T. THOMSON *Chem. Org. Bodies* 601 We may represent the compound thus:—$SO^2 + H^2Az + HO$, or an atom of sulphurous acid, an atom of amide, and an atom of water, and distinguish it by the name of **sulphamide*. **1888** MORLEY & MUIR *Watts' Dict. Chem.* I. 186/2 Toluene *sulphamine ..got by heating *p* amido-toluene sulphinic acid with conc. HCl. **1902** *Encycl. Brit.* XXVI. 728/2 Acetanilide..when cautiously dissolved in moderately strong fuming sulphuric acid..is..converted into the *sulphaminic acid $C_6H_5.N(C_2H_3O)(SO_3H)$. **1862** MILLER *Elem. Chem.*, *Org.* (ed. 2) iii. §1. 164 Both the *sulphamylates of baryta. **1852** W. GREGORY *Handbk. Org. Chem.* 233 **Sulphamylic Acid*... This compound is formed exactly like sulphovinic acid. **1856** *Q. Jrnl. Chem. Soc.* IX. 260 *Sulphanilate of Silver. *Ibid.*, M. Gerhardt's well-known *sulphanilic acid. **1896** *Allbutt's Syst. Med.* I. 825 A saturated solution of sulphanilic acid. **1863** WATTS *Dict. Chem.* I. 335 The soluble *sulphantimonates are decomposed by all acids. **1856** MILLER *Elem. Chem.*, *Inorg.* xv. §7. 956 The tribasic *sulphantimoniate of sodium.., or Schlippe's salt. **1878** ABNEY *Photogr.* 72 A scarlet deposit..of silver sulphantimoniate. **1849** D. CAMPBELL *Inorg. Chem.* 290 Pentasulphide of antimony; *sulphantimonic acid, SbS_5. **1859** MAYNE *Expos. Lex.* 1226/2 **Sulphantimonite*, term for a genus of sulphosalts resulting from the combination of antimonious sulphide with the sulphobases. **1868** WATTS *Dict. Chem.* V. 643 *Sulpharsenate of potassium. **1858** GRAHAM & WATTS *Elem. Chem.* II. 548 Monobasic *sulpharseniate of potassium. **1841** BRANDE *Chem.* (ed. 5) 893 Persulphuret of Arsenic. *Sulpharsenic Acid. *Ibid.* 892 Sesquisulphuret of Arsenic..*Sulpharsenious Acid. **1859** MAYNE *Expos. Lex.* 1226/2 **Sulpharsenite*, term for a genus of sulphosalts formed by combination with sulphobases of a degree of sulphuration of the arsenic, corresponding to arsenious acid in its composition. **1868** J. D. DANA *Syst. Min.* (ed. 5) ii. 84 (*heading*) Sulpharsenites, sulphantimonites, sulphobismuthites. **1905** *Nature* 6 Apr. 534/1 To these minerals a third must now be added in hutchinsonite, a new sulpharsenite from the Binnenthal, which also contains thallium as an important constituent. **1954** Sulpharsenite [see HUTCHINSONITE]. **1961** *Brit. Med. Jrnl.* 21 Jan. 5220/2 Sulphasalazine ('salazopyrin', 'asulfidine') has been used extensively in Sweden and America since 1941 in the treatment of colitis. **1977** *Lancet* 29 Oct. 931/1 Inflammatory bowel disease was diagnosed and the patient was put on intramuscular corticotrophin, sulphasalazine, and codeine phosphate. **1868** WATTS *Dict. Chem.* V. 481 *Sulpharsin. *Ibid.* 625 *Sulphethamate of ammonium. **1852** W. GREGORY *Handbk. Org. Chem.* 199 When neutral sulphate of oxide of ethyle is acted on by dry ammonia, there is formed the ammonia salt of a new acid, *sulphethamic acid. **1857** MILLER *Elem. Chem.*, *Org.* iii. §3. 143 *Sulphethylate of potash. *Ibid.* i. 28 Sulpho-vinic or *sulph-ethylic acid. **1841** BRANDE *Chem.* (ed. 5) 463 Exposed to the air, *sulfimide becomes white and deliquesces. **1863** WATTS *Dict. Chem.* I. 338 *Sulphiodide of Antimony.

sulpha ('sʌlfə). *Pharm.* Also (chiefly *U.S.*) **sulfa**. [f. SULPHA(NILAMIDE.] Any of the drugs derived from sulphanilamide. Usu. *attrib.*, as *sulpha drug*.

1942 B. BLIVEN *Men who make Future* i. 11 Within the past year or two, the magical effects of sulfanilamide in curing a whole series of diseases have been supplemented by..the other 'sulfa' drugs. **1951** E. A. MCCOURT *Home is Stranger* xiv. 211 She had asked Weary to get a prescription of some kind from Dr Harrington—sulpha, perhaps. **1956** *Sci. News* XLI. 18 Modifications of sulphanilamide have led to the extensive sulphonamide or sulpha group of drugs. **1967** *New Scientist* 16 Feb. 384/2 A fatal type of malaria..is now being effectively controlled by a new sulpha drug. **1973** E. ARNOLD *Proving Ground* (1974) xiv. 169 The nurses.. applied sulfa powder and repacked and rebandaged the wound. **1975** B. WOOD *Killing Gift* (1976) III. ii. 94 I've given her some sulfa and a shot of codeine so she'll sleep.

sulpha- ('sʌlfə). *Pharm.* Also (chiefly *U.S.*) **sulfa-**, (before a vowel) **sulph-**. [f. SULPHA(NILAMIDE.] Formative element in the names of drugs derived from sulphanilamide, as **sulpha'cetamide** [ACETAMIDE], the sulphonamide $CH_3CO{\cdot}NH{\cdot}SO_2{\cdot}C_6H_4{\cdot}NH_2$, which is used in the form of the sodium salt in the treatment of eye infections; N^1-acetylsulphanilamide; **sulpha'diazine** [AZINE b], the readily absorbed sulphonamide $C_4H_3N_2{\cdot}NH{\cdot}SO_2{\cdot}C_6H_4{\cdot}NH_2$, which is used in the treatment of meningococcal meningitis; N^1-pyrimidin-2-ylsulphanilamide; **sulpha'dimidine** [DI- + PYRI)-MIDINE], the readily absorbed sulphonamide $(CH_3)_2C_4H_2N_2{\cdot}NH{\cdot}SO_2{\cdot}C_6H_4{\cdot}NH_2$, used in the treatment of a wide range of systemic and urinary tract infections; N^1-(4,6-dimethylpyrimidin-2-yl)sulphanilamide; **sulpha'furazole** [FUR(AN + PYR)AZOLE], the readily absorbed sulphonamide $(CH_3)_2C_3NO{\cdot}NH{\cdot}SO_2{\cdot}C_6H_4{\cdot}NH_2$, which is used in the treatment of infections of the urinary tract; N^1-(3,4-dimethyliosoxazol-5-yl)sulphanilamide = *sulphisoxazole* below; **sulpha'guanidine** [GUANIDINE], the poorly absorbed sulphonamide $HN{:}C(NH_2){\cdot}NH{\cdot}SO_2{\cdot}C_6H_4{\cdot}NH_2$, formerly used in the treatment of intestinal infections; N^1-guanidinylsulphanilamide; **sulpha'methazine** [METH(YL + AZINE] = *sulphadimidine* above; **sulpha'methizole** [ME(THYL + THI(O- + *dia*)*zole* (f. DIAZO- + -OLE)], the readily absorbed sulphonamide $CH_3{\cdot}C_2N_2S_2{\cdot}NH{\cdot}SO_2{\cdot}C_6H_4{\cdot}NH_2$, which is used in treating coliform infections of the urinary tract; N^1-(5-methyl-1,3,4-thiadiazol-2-yl)sulphanilamide; **,sulphame'thoxazole** [METH(YL + *is*)*oxazole* s.v. ISO- b], the sulphonamide $CH_3{\cdot}C_3HNO{\cdot}NH{\cdot}SO_2{\cdot}C_6H_4{\cdot}NH_2$, used in the treatment of respiratory and urinary tract infections, and as a component of the preparation co-trimoxazole; N^1-(5-methylisoxazol-3-yl)sulphanilamide; **,sulphame,thoxypy'ridazine** [METHOXY- + PYRIDAZINE], the long-acting sulphonamide $CH_3O{\cdot}C_4N_2H_2{\cdot}NH{\cdot}SO_2{\cdot}C_6H_4{\cdot}NH_2$, used in the treatment of systemic and urinary tract infections; N^1-(6-methoxypyridazin-3-yl) sulphanilamide; **Sulpha'mezathine**, a proprietary name for sulphadimidine (sulphamethazine); **sulpha'pyridine** [PYRIDINE], the readily absorbed sulphonamide $C_5H_4N{\cdot}NH{\cdot}SO_2{\cdot}C_6H_4{\cdot}NH_2$, which is used chiefly in the treatment of dermatitis herpetiformis; N^1-pyridin-2-ylsulphanilamide; **sulpha'salazine** [SAL(ICYL + AZINE], the sulphonamide $C_5H_4N{\cdot}NH{\cdot}SO_2{\cdot}C_6H_4{\cdot}N{:}N{\cdot}C_6H(OH)COOH$, which is used in conjunction with corticosteroids in the treatment of ulcerative colitis; 4-hydroxy-4′-(2-pyridylsulphamoyl) azobenzene-3-carboxylic acid; **Sulpha'triad**, a proprietary name for a mixed sulphonamide drug containing sulphadiazine, sulphamerazine, and sulphathiazole, used in the treatment of acute infections; **sulphi'soxazole** *Pharm.* [*isoxazole* s.v. ISO- b] = *sulphafurazole* above.

1941 *Pharm. Jrnl.* 29 Nov. 188/3 Sulphacetamide is a name which it has been proposed should be adopted for the preparation now known under the trade mark 'Albucid'. **1975** *Prescribers' Jrnl.* XV. 139 Sulphacetamide in the form of eye drops and ointment can produce sensitivity reactions on the skin around the eyes. **1940** R. O. ROBLIN et al. in *Jrnl. Amer. Chem. Soc.* LXII. 2002/2 In order to avoid possible confusion between sulfapyridine and sulfapyrimidine, the term sulfadiazines is suggested for these [pyrimidine] compounds. **1943** [see SULPHATHIAZOLE]. **1956** I. L. FINAR *Org. Chem.* II. xviii. 668 Sulphadiazine..is less toxic than Sulphathiazole; it is the most widely used of the 'sulpha' drugs, its main use being for mild infections. **1980** *Jrnl. Med. Microbiol.* XIII. 131 At therapeutic levels in blood, trimethoprim and sulphadiazine singly produced mainly a bactericidal action on pathogens responsible for urinary-tract infections. **1950** *Brit. Med. Jrnl.* 12 Aug. 409/1 Sulphadimidine ('sulphamezathine') and Sulphamerazine (U.S.P.) have almost identical qualities. **1961** [see *sulfaquinoxaline* s.v. SULFA-]. **1977** *Martindale's Extra Pharmacopoeia* (ed. 27) 1479/2 Sulphadimidine penetrates into cerebrospinal fluid less readily than sulphadiazine and is usually less effective than sulphadiazine in meningeal infections. **1961** *Lancet* 22 July 178/1 Rebollo..claimed a cure [for meningitis due to *Pseudomonas pyocyanea*] with sulphafurazole, given orally. **1976** *Ibid.* 11 Dec. 1276/1, 91 men with nongonococcal urethritis (N.G.U.) were randomly treated with..sulphafurazole (sulfisoxazole). **1941** *Jrnl. Amer. Med. Assoc.* 3 May 2019/2 For 2-sulfanilamidopyrimidine it [*sc.* the Council on Pharmacy and Chemistry of the American Medical Association] adopted the term sulfadiazine and for sulfanilylguanidine the term sulfaguanidine. **1943** *Listener* 16 Sept. 321/2 A quite new drug, sulphaguanidine, shows promise for the treatment of bacillary dysentery; it succeeds here..because much of it is not absorbed, and it therefore remains to act in the intestine. **1958** E. NEWBY *Short Walk in Hindu Kush* xviii. 220 Everyone..was now suffering from dysentery. We all munched sulphaguanadine tablets but even these failed. **1977** *Martindale's Extra Pharmacopoeia* (ed. 27) 1483/1 Sulphaguanidine has been employed for the treatment of local intestinal infections..though it has now been largely superseded by the less toxic sulphonamides, phthalylsulphathiazole and succinylsulphathiazole. **1942** *Lancet* 30 May 639/1 In the summer of 1941 our attention was drawn by Drs. Martin and Rose of the research laboratories of Imperial Chemical (Pharmaceuticals) Ltd. to a near relation of sulphadiazine..to which the name sulphamethazine has been given. **1951** A. GROLLMAN *Pharmacol. & Therapeutics* xxi. 434 Sulfamethazine.., the methyl derivative of sulfamerazine resembles the latter in action and is used for the same purposes as sulfamerazine and sulfadiazine. **1965** *Pharmacopeia U.S.A.* (ed. 17) 785 U.S.P. XVII Title..Sulfamethazine. Other Designation(s)... Sulphadimidine (*BP*). **1978** SPINELLI & ENOS *Drugs in Vet. Pract.* x. 135/1 Foot rot... The following can be used: 1. Sulfamethazine, starting with one intravenous injection [etc.]. **1952** *Chem. Abstr.* XLVI. 686 Sulfathiazole, sulfadiazine, and sulfamethizole have been detd. by this method in various pharm. prepns. **1977** *Lancet* 16 Apr. 863/2 Sulphamethizole and alkali were prescribed pending a culture report. **1960** *Antibiotics & Chemotherapy* (N.Y.) X. 572 A new sulfonamide compound, sulfamethoxazole, is identified chemically as 5-methyl-3-sulfanilamidoisoxazole. **1977** *Lancet* 2 July 4/1 Much of the shigellosis could be successfully treated with ampicillin trihydrate and closely related antibiotics, or with co-trimoxazole (trimethoprim and sulphamethoxazole). **1981** H. J. ROGERS et al. *Textbk. Clin. Pharmacol.* xix. 653 Sulphamethoxazole is about 50% metabolised so that much reaches the urine in an inactive form. **1956** *Antibiotic Med. & Clin. Therapy* III. 386 A new antibacterial sulfonamide, sulfamethoxypyridazine, has been studied in 67 patients. **1980** *Biochem. Pharmacol.* XXIX. 984/1 Kidney weight/body weight ratio, DNA and protein concentrations of kidney cortex were determined in 55-day-old rats repeatedly pretreated with saline, PAH, sulfamethoxypyridazine, cyclopenthiazide and phenobarbital, respectively. **1943** *Trade Marks Jrnl.* 6 Oct. 421/2 *Sulphamezathine*... Pharmaceutical organic substances being sulphanilamido compounds for veterinary use. Imperial Chemical (Pharmaceuticals) Ltd. **1944** *Pharmaceutical Jrnl.* 8 Apr. 154A/3 Imperial Chemicals (Pharmaceuticals), Ltd., now offer their 'Sulphamezathine' brand of sulphadimethylpyrimidine in the form of a stable solution of the sodium salt. **1970** *Country Life* 26 Feb. 491/1 The drinking water should be dosed with sulphamezathine to prevent coccidiosis. **1939** *Jrnl. Amer. Med. Assoc.* 7 Jan. 49/2 Recent reports from investigators indicate that a pyridine derivative of sulfanilamide..is apparently more promising in the treatment of certain types of pneumonia than sulfanilamide itself... The Council has therefore adopted the term 'sulfapyridine'. **1942** *Times* 30 Nov. 2/3 In 1939, by skilled use of the new drug sulphapyridine, it [*sc.* the fatality rate in spotted fever] was brought down to 33 per cent. **1957** [see M AND B]. **1967** [see SULPHANILAMIDE]. **1981** H. J. ROGERS et al. *Textbk. Clin. Pharmacol.* xix. 649 Sulphapyridine in low doses over prolonged periods may control dermatitis herpetiformis. **1948** *Trade Marks Jrnl.* 12 May 348/2 Sulphatriad... Pharmaceutical preparations of sulphonamides... May & Baker Limited... Manufacturing chemists. **1950** 'N. SHUTE' *Town like Alice* vi. 184 The flies would probably result in dysentery but she knew what to do about that; she had plenty of sulphatriad. **1968** J. H. BURN *Lect. Notes Pharmacol.* (ed. 9) 101 If three sulphonamides are used together, as in Sulphatriad, only one-third of the amount of each need be used. **1965** *Pharmacopeia U.S.A.* (ed. 17) 785 U.S.P. XVII Title... Sulfisoxazole. Other Designation(s)... Sulphafurazole (*BP*). **1976** [see *sulphafurazole* above]. **1977** *Lancet* 2 July 4/1 Most of the *S. flexneri* strains were resistant to tetracycline, streptomycin, and sulphafurazole diethanolamine (sulfisoxazole dialomine). **1952** H. Beckman *Pharmacol. in Clin. Pract.* 648 The principal ones [*sc.* sulphonamides] in current use are sulfadiazine, sulfamerazine, Sulfamethazine..and sulfisoxazole.

'sulphacid. [See SULPH-. Cf. F. *sulfacide.*] = SULPHO-ACID.

a **1859** Betton in Worc.

sulphæmoglobin (ˌsʌlfhiːməʊˈgləʊbɪn). *Biochem.* and *Med.* Also **sulph-hæmoglobin, -hemoglobin,** (*U.S.*) **sulfhemo-.** [f. SULP(H- + HÆMOGLOBIN.] A sulphur-containing derivative of hæmoglobin, produced by its reaction with soluble sulphides or sulphides absorbed from the alimentary tract, and giving rise to the greenish discoloration found in putrefying cadavers.

1896 A. Bruce tr. *Thoma's Text-bk. Gen. Path.* I. iii. 43 In poisoning by charcoal fumes, carbonic-oxide-hæmoglobin is formed, and in poisoning by sulphuretted hydrogen, sulph-hæmoglobin or sulph-hæmatin. **1908** Hall & Defren tr. *Abderhalden's Text-bk. Physiol. Chem.* xxiv. 561 This green shade is due to the formation of sulph-hemoglobin, which, however, has never been prepared in a pure state. **1947** K. Simpson *Forensic Med.* xxviii. 314 Sulphaemoglobin forms naturally as post-mortem decomposition sets in. **1980** *Amer. Jrnl. Physiol.* CCXXXVIII. H745/2 This report concerns a method for 'labeling' red blood cells..by the formation of sulfhemoglobin.

Hence **ˌsulphæmoglobiˈnæmia** [Gr. αἷμα blood], the presence of sulphæmoglobin in the blood, caused by drug-potentiated absorption of hydrogen sulphide from the alimentary tract, or direct assimilation of the sulpha group from any sulphonamide.

1910 *Jrnl. Amer. Med. Assoc.* 17 Dec. 2181/2 The patient was observed for some weeks, and as the ordinary blood examination failed to reveal any polycythemia or other abnormality to account for the condition, a tentative diagnosis of sulphemoglobinemia was made. **1961** A. S. MacNalty *Brit. Med. Dict.* 1373/2 It [*sc.* sulphæmoglobin] is produced under the influence of many substances such as nitrates, chlorates, nitrites..etc., causing enterogenous cyanosis or sulphaemoglobinaemia. **1980** *Amer. Jrnl. Clin. Path.* LXXIII. 245/1 In one specimen, marked methemoglobinemia and sulfhemoglobinemia were also demonstrated.

sulphane (ˈsʌlfeɪn). *Chem.* Also (*U.S.*) **sulf-.** [a. G. *sulfane* (Fehér & Laue 1953, in *Zeitschr. für Naturforschung* VIIIb. 687/1): see -ANE.] Any of the hydrides of sulphur, H_2S_x.

1955 *Chem. Abstr.* XLIX. 15590 The results reported in this series, on compds. of the form H_2S_n, M_2S_n, and X_2S_n (M = alkali metal, X = halogen), indicate that they have a paraffin-like chain structure. The generic name *sulfanes* is suggested. **1968** Burton & Machmer in G. Nickless *Inorg. Sulphur Chem.* x. 340 The sulphanes are extremely sensitive compounds and hence are very difficult to prepare in the pure state. **1979** *Geophysical Research Lett.* VI. 807/1 We discuss the possible importance of gaseous elemental sulfur (particularly S_2, S_3..and S_4) and sulfanes (H_2S_n) in the lower atmosphere of Venus.

sulphanilamide (sʌlfəˈnɪləmaɪd). *Pharm.* Also (*U.S.*) **sulf-.** [f. *sulphanilic* s.v. SULPH- (f. ANIL(INE + -IC) + AMIDE.] **a.** The amide of sulphanilic acid, which has wide bacteriostatic activity, has been used, esp. topically, in the treatment of infections due to hæmolytic streptococci, and is the parent compound of the sulphonamides; *p*-aminobenzenesulphonamide, $H_2N{\cdot}C_6H_4{\cdot}SO_2{\cdot}NH_2$.

1937 *Jrnl. Amer. Med. Assoc.* 17 Apr. 1340/2 The Council [on Pharmacy and Chemistry] has therefore formally adopted the nonproprietary name 'Sulfanilamide' for para-aminobenzenesulfonamide. **1942** *Times* 9 Oct. 2/4 A further long list of requirements was sent back from Moscow... The articles dispatched..have included:—530,000 blankets, ..10,000 kilos sulphanilamide. **1953** M. Lowry *Let.* 31 Oct. (1967) 345 The chief engineer has an ulcerated throat, and the ship itself is running on sulfanilamide. **1962** J. Heller *Catch-22* xli. 428 Snowden..shifted the position of his hips a bit so that Yossarian could begin salting the wound with sulfanilamide. **1967** *Martindale's Extra Pharmacopoeia* (ed. 25) 1376/1 Sulfphanilamide,..together with the earlier derivatives, sulphapyridine and sulphathiazole, has been largely superseded by more effective and less toxic compounds. **1974** R. M. Kirk et al. *Surgery* ii. 27 Sulphanilamide powder is sometimes used topically on raw surfaces, in abscess cavities and body spaces such as the peritoneal and pleural cavities.

b. Any substituted derivative of this compound.

1961 in Webster. **1962** H. A. Krebs in A. Pirie *Lens Metabolism Rel. Cataract* 351 The effects..of sulphanilamides on the metabolism of *p*-aminobenzoic acid.

sulphatase (ˈsʌlfəteɪz). *Biochem.* Also (*U.S.*) **sulf-.** [a. G. *sulfatase* (C. Neuberg 1924, in *Naturwissenschaften* XII. 799/2), f. *sulfat* SULPHATE *sb.*: see -ASE.] Any of a group of enzymes found chiefly in mammalian tissues which catalyse the hydrolysis of sulphuric acid esters.

1924 *Chem. Abstr.* XVIII. 3600 The new enzyme sulfatase. **1952** *Biochem. Jrnl.* LI. 585/1 The sulphatases differ with respect to the type of sulphuric acid ester upon which they act. **1964** A. White et al. *Princ. Biochem.* (ed. 3) xl. 775 No sulfatase capable of effecting hydrolysis of sulfate esters of carbohydrates is known to be present in animal tissues. **1980** *Jrnl. Path.* CXXX. 243 The giant lysosomes contained both acid phosphatase and aryl sulphatase.

sulphate (ˈsʌlfeɪt, -ət), *sb. Chem.* Also **sulfate, sulphat.** [ad. F. *sulphate* (De Morveau, etc. *Nomenclature chimique*, 1787), ad. mod.L. *sulphātum* (sc. *acidum* ACID), f. *sulphur*: see SULPHUR, -ATE[1] 1 c.]

1. A salt of sulphuric acid: usually with term indicating the base, as ***sulphate of ammonia, of lime, potassium sulphate.***

1790 Kerr tr. *Lavoisier's Elem. Chem.* 224 Hence the neutral salt in which the metal is least oxydated must be named *sulphite*, and that in which it is fully oxydated must be called *sulphat.* **1791** W. Hamilton *Berthollet's Dyeing* I. i. i. iii. 63 Sulphat of copper. **1794** *Phil. Trans.* LXXXIV. 395 Sulphate of iron (green vitriol). **1799** *Med. Jrnl.* I. 87 Epsom salts, or sulphat of Magnesia. **1809** *Phil. Trans.* XCIX. 151 The sulfate of potass decomposes the phosphate of barita. **1815** J. Smith *Panorama Sci. & Art* II. 470 The sulphates are in general crystallizable. **1831** Davies *Mat. Med.* 331 The sulphates of zinc and copper..are occasionally used as powerful emetics. **1866** Roscoe *Elem. Chem.* ix. 89 Hydrocyanic acid mixed with water distils over, leaving potassium sulphate in the retort. **1877** Huxley *Physiogr.* 120 Such permanent hardness [of water] is due to the presence of sulphate of lime. **1890** F. Taylor *Man. Pract. Med.* 747 Sulphates.—These are precipitable by barium chloride.

attrib. **1803** *Med. Jrnl.* X. 499, I have tried the sulphat of soda poultice. **1856** *Orr's Circ. Sci., Pract. Chem.* 76 The sulphate solution. **1884** Knight *Dict. Mech.* Suppl. 874/1 Sulphate of Mercury Battery.

2. *ellipt.* = Sodium sulphate. Also *attrib.*

[**1879** *Cassell's Techn. Educ.* IV. 355/1 The manufacture of soda ash,..the..sulphate, sulphite, and others.] **1900** *Westm. Gaz.* 29 Dec. 9/2 A fire at the sulphate works of the West Hartlepool Gas Company.

3. sulphate ion, the ion SO_4^{2-}; **sulphate process** *Paper-making*, a method of manufacturing a tough brown paper involving the digestion of wood chips by sodium hydroxide and sodium sulphate to form the pulp; so **sulphate pulp**; cf. KRAFT; **sulphate-reducing** *a. Biol.*, (of a process or micro-organism) bringing about the reduction of sulphate ions to sulphur; *spec.* applied to bacteria of the genera *Desulphovibrio* and *Desulphatomaculum*, which do this as part of their respiratory metabolism.

1902 G. S. Newth *Text-bk. Inorg. Chem.* (ed. 9) xi. 105 SO''$_4$, in the same way, stands for the *sulphate ion, with its two negative charges. **1978** J. R. Holum *Org. & Biol. Chem.* xix. 421 The sulfur dioxide is then oxidized to sulfate ion, which is excreted by the kidneys. **1894** G. Clapperton *Pract. Paper-Making* iv. 32 The former [process]..employs a solution of sodium compounds containing a large percentage of sulphate of soda, and is known as the *sulphate process. **1963** R. R. A. Higham *Handbk. Papermaking* v. 98 There are three basic alkaline processes, which are: Soda process, Sulphate (Kraft) process, Pomilio process. **1974** *Sci. Amer.* Apr. 55/1 Most soda pulp mills changed over to the kraft process (which is also often called the sulfate process). **1907** G. Clapperton *Pract. Paper-Making* (ed. 2) iv. 36 During recent years the demand for '*sulphate' pulp has increased largely, owing to the development of 'Kraft' brown paper. **1962** F. T. Day *Introd. Paper* ii. 19 The wood chips are cooked in digesters in a solution of caustic soda to produce soda pulp, or with a mixture of caustic soda and sulphate of soda to produce sulphate pulp. **1966** F. E. Dean *Paper* ii. 36 Unbleached sulphate or 'kraft'..pulp..is used mainly for tough wrapping paper. **1926** *Science* 1 Jan. 24/1 The oil-field waters in which the *sulphate-reducing bacteria occur are similar in general composition to seawater. **1954** *New Biol.* XVII. 67 Vastly greater amounts of sulphide are formed in nature by a single group of micro-organisms called the sulphate-reducing bacteria... Their sulphate-reducing process corresponds to the respiration of more normal organisms. **1979** *Arch. Microbiol.* CXXI. 261/1 Some sulfate-reducing bacteria are able to utilize colloidal sulfur as respiratory substrate.

Hence **ˈsulphate** *v. intr.*, to become sulphated.

1888 D. Salomons *Managem. Accumulators* (ed. 3) v. 58 If the positives sulphate the surface becomes very hard. **1898** A. Treadwell *Storage Battery* 240 The plates will be found to sulphate more rapidly, and the sulphate will be harder to reduce.

sulphated (ˈsʌlfeɪtɪd), *ppl. a.* [f. mod.L. *sulphātus* or F. *sulfaté*: see SULPHUR, -ATE[1] 1 c.] Combined or impregnated with sulphur or sulphuric acid; charged with or containing sulphates.

1802 *Med. Jrnl.* VIII. 551 Sulphated black iron,—or sulphat of black iron. **1805** Saunders *Min. Waters* 218 Vitriolated or sulphated magnesia. **1896** *Allbutt's Syst. Med.* I. 322 These springs [at Leamington and Cheltenham] may be placed in the group of sulphated waters. **1902** *Encycl. Brit.* XXVII. 562/1 The cotton is impregnated with this sulphated-oil solution.

sulphathiazole (sʌlfəˈθaɪəzəʊl). *Pharm.* Also (*U.S.*) **sulf-.** [f. SULPHA- + *thiazole* s.v. THIO- 1.] The readily absorbed sulphonamide $C_3H_2NS{\cdot}NH{\cdot}SO_2{\cdot}C_6H_4{\cdot}NH_2$, now rarely used; thiazol-2-ylsulphanilamide.

1939 *Jrnl. Amer. Chem. Soc.* LXI. 3593/2 The potentiometric titration curves for the acidification of 2% solution of the sodium salts of 2(*p*-aminobenzene sulfonamido)thiazole (Sulfathiazole) and sulfapyridine are submitted in Fig. 1. **1943** *Endeavour* Apr. 42/1 Sulphathiazole and sulphaciazine are now among the physician's sheet anchors in the treatment of meningitis, gonorrhoea and pneumonia. **1967** [see SULPHANILAMIDE]. **1978** J. Irving *World according to Garp* i. 7 Sulfathiazole was for the clap—with lots of water recommended.

†sulphatic (sʌlˈfætɪk), *a. Chem. Obs.* [f. SULPHATE + -IC.] Pertaining to a sulphate, sulphuric.

1828–32 Webster *Dict.*, *Sulphatic*, pertaining to sulphate. **1836** Brande *Chem.* (ed. 4) 1092 Oil of Wine..Sulphatic Ether; Sulphate of Hydrocarbon.

sulphatide (ˈsʌlfətaɪd). *Biochem.* Also (*U.S.*) **sulf-.** [SULPHAT(E *sb.* + -IDE.] Any of the group of lipids consisting of the sulphuric acid ester of a cerebroside.

1884 J. L. W. Thudichum *Treat. Chem. Constitution of Brain* i. 22 The albuminous substances of the brain may be considered as nitrogenised sulphatides, inasmuch as sulphur is an essential constituent. **1954** A. White et al. *Princ. Biochem.* xxxii. 801 A number of less clearly defined lipids have also been recognized [in the brain], such as sulfatides. .. Only one sulfatide has been isolated and studied, cerebron sulfuric acid. **1966** *Lancet* 24 Dec. 1421/2 The predominance of sulphatide in the white matter of the brain in this disease has been noted by Lees. **1978** *Nature* 7 Dec. 625/1 The negative charge imparted by the sulphate group of the sulphatide does not seem to be the direct cause of its strong adhesion capacity, as other negatively charged lipids, such as ganglioside or phosphatidyl inositol, did not adhere strongly.

sulphating (ˈsʌlfeɪtɪŋ), *vbl. sb.* [f. SULPHATE + -ING[1].] The formation of a sulphate, *esp.* of a deposit of lead sulphate on the plates of a battery.

1890 *Philos. Mag.* 5th Ser. XXX. 162 The chief benefit.. is stated to be that the sodium salt diminishes the chance of objectionable sulphating in the cell. **1902** *Encycl. Brit.* XXV. 29/2 The chief faults are buckling, growth, sulphating, and disintegration.

So **sulˈphation,** conversion into a sulphate; incorporation of a sulphate ion, SO_4^{2-}, into a molecule.

1904 *U.S. Geol. Surv., Monogr.* XLVII. 205 Sulphation is the union of sulphuric acid with base or the substitution of sulphuric acid for another combined acid. **1957** *New Biol.* XXIV. 52 There is an informed opinion which asserts that sulphation is not necessary for metachromasia and that mucopolysaccharides without sulphur are also metachromatic. **1971, 1972** [see SOMATOMEDIN]. **1975** *Nature* 24 Jan. 269/2 Somatomedin, previously known as 'sulphation factor',..stimulates the incorporation of $^{35}SO_4$ into costal cartilage. **1977** *Lancet* 22 Jan. 168/1 The mammary gland itself may be the site of sulphation [of vitamin D].

sulphatite (ˈsʌlfətaɪt). *Min.* [f. SULPHATE + -ITE[1].] Native sulphuric acid.

1868 Dana *Syst. Min.* (ed. 5) 614 *Sulphatite.* Sulphuric Acid... This acid, in a dilute state, has been found in the neighborhood of several volcanoes.

sulphato- (sʌlˈfeɪtəʊ) *Chem.*, before a vowel sometimes **sulphat-** (ˈsʌlfət), a prefix in the name of a compound denoting that it contains a sulphate as an ingredient, as ***sulphato acetic, -carbonate***; **sulphaˈtoxide** (see quot.); **sulphaˈtoxygen**, an old name for the radical SO_4.

1868 Watts *Dict. Chem.* V. 571 *Sulphato-acetic Oxide or Anhydride. **1836** T. Thomson *Min., Geol.*, etc. 106 *Sulphato-carbonate of Barytes. **1855** *Orr's Circ. Sci., Geol.*, etc. 553 Connellite, *Sulphato-chloride of Copper. **1844** Hoblyn *Dict. Terms Med.* (ed. 2), *Sulphatoxygen.* According to the new view of compound radicals, this body is the sulphate radical of sulphate of soda, the oxygen of the soda being referred to the acid; its compounds are termed *sulphatoxides. **1839–47** *Todd's Cycl. Anat.* III. 151/2 A new compound radical, *sulphatoxygen, consisting of 1 part of sulphur with 4 of oxygen.

sulphazin (ˈsʌlfəzɪn). *Pharm.* Also (chiefly *U.S.*) **sulfazin.** [Russ.] A drug consisting of a suspension of one per cent purified sulphur in peach oil, given intramuscularly to induce fever.

1970 *Time* 29 June 30/3 A Soviet drug called Sulfazin, which induces fever and temperature, is administered as a punishment. **1977** *Lancet* 23 July 185/1 There are reports of the use of sulphazin to produce a painful fever. **1979** H. Fireside *Soviet Psychoprisons* iv. 82 If a patient speaks out against such brutality, he is subjected to punishment by overdoses of drugs or injections of sulfazin that make it 'painful for him even to stir'. **1981** M. C. Smith *Gorky Park* I. xii. 185 Sulfazin was one of the favorite narcotics of the KGB.

sulpherous, obs. form of SULPHUROUS.

sulphetrone (ˈsʌlfətrəʊn). *Pharm.* [f. SULPHONE with insertion of *t)etr(asodium* (f. TETRA- + SODIUM).] A trade name for the drug SOLAPSONE.

1947 *Lancet* 20 Dec. 897/2 Two studies were made—(1) to assess the efficacy of streptomycin; and (2) to evaluate the possible synergic action of streptomycin and sulphetrone. **1959, 1974** [see SOLAPSONE].

sulph-hæmoglobin, var. SULPHÆMOGLOBIN.

sulphide (ˈsʌlfaɪd), *sb. Chem.* Also -id. [f. SULPHUR- + -IDE.]

1. A compound of sulphur with another element (usually denoted by a qualifying term).

1836 T. THOMSON *Min., Geol.*, etc. I. 81 Sulphide of arsenic. **1856** MILLER *Elem. Chem., Inorg.* VII. §1. 584 An insoluble metallic sulphide. **1875** A. S. TAYLOR *Poisons* (ed. 3) 51 The alkaline sulphides (sodium and ammonium). **1880** J. W. LEGG *Bile* 30 Sulphide of carbon and benzol are.. good solvents.

b. ***hydrogen sulphide, sulphide of hydrogen***, sulphuretted hydrogen, H_2S. (Also *attrib.*)

1849 D. CAMPBELL *Inorg. Chem.* 264 Sulphide of hydrogen gas. **1873** [see HYDROGEN 2 b]. **1881** *Nature* 6 Oct. 550/2 This sulphide of hydrogen tube.

2. *attrib.*, chiefly with reference to the treatment of metallic sulphides in manufacturing processes.

1893 *Westm. Gaz.* 14 July 6/1 The hitherto intractable sulphide ore. **1899** *Daily News* 22 Apr. 2/7 This company's sulphide plant. **1900** *Ibid.* 10 May 2/7 The sulphide mill.

Hence **ˈsulphide** *v. trans.*, to convert into or impregnate with a sulphide; also **sulphiˈdation**, impregnation with a sulphide; **ˈsulphiding** *vbl. sb.*

1904 *U.S. Geol. Surv., Monogr.* XLVII. 205 Sulphidation is the union of sulphur with a metal forming sulphides. **1950** R. W. MONCRIEFF *Artificial Fibres* viii. 105 The yarn was wound into skeins, and these were washed, sulphided, bleached and washed. **1955** E. E. LOENING et al. in R. S. Schultze *Sci. & Applic. Photogr.* 62 In the case of sulphiding, the left part of the curves is.. absent. **1982** *Photogr. Sci. & Engin.* XXVI. 223/1 Sulfiding of the cathode can be minimized by poising the potential of the cathode more positive than −0·55 v.

sulphidic (sʌlˈfɪdɪk), *a. Chem.* [f. SULPHID(E *sb.* + -IC.] Of or containing sulphides.

1929 H. SCHNEIDERHÖHN in P. A. Wagner *Platinum Deposits & Mines S. Afr.* xvii. 208 (*heading*) The sulphidic ore minerals of the felspathic Harzburgite and Merensky 'reef'. **1959** *Times* 23 Sept. 19/6 Sulphidic minerals, mainly pyrites. **1978** *Metals* (Shell Internat. Petroleum Co.) 4 Rich sulphidic ores, such as those in the massive copper belt of Zambia/Zaire.., have been recovered by underground mining for many years.

sulphinate (ˈsʌlfɪnət). *Chem.* [f. SULPHINIC + -ATE[4].] A salt of sulphinic acid.

1877 *Jrnl. Chem. Soc.* II. 735 It was converted into zinc sulphinate by treatment with zinc-dust under water. **1894** MUIR & MORLEY *Watts' Dict. Chem.* s.v. *Sulphinic Acids*, The ethers are not formed by the action of alkyl halogenides upon sulphinates.

sulphindigotic (sʌlfɪndɪˈgɒtɪk), *a. Chem.* [SULPH-.] ***sulphindigotic acid***: an acid formed by the action of sulphuric acid on indigo. Hence **sulˈphindigotate**, a salt of sulphindigotic acid. (Also SULPHO-INDIGOTIC, -ATE.)

1857 MILLER *Elem. Chem., Org.* viii. 530 Sulphuric acid appears to form several compounds with indigo; two of them have been analysed, viz., the sulphindylic, or sulphindigotic acid, and the sulphopurpuric. **1876** tr. *Schützenberger's Ferment.* 110 Sodium sulphindigotate. **1896** *Allbutt's Syst. Med.* I. 514 Formate and sulphindigotate of sodium.

sulphindylic (sʌlfɪnˈdɪlɪk), *a. Chem.* Also -indilic. [ad. F. *sulfindylique* (Dumas, 1836): see SULPH-, IND(IGO), -YL(E), -IC.] Old synonym of SULPHINDIGOTIC. Hence **sulˈphindylate**, a salt of sulphindylic acid.

1838 T. THOMSON *Chem. Org. Bodies* 378 M. Dumas has lately examined this solution of indigo in sulphuric acid.. and has given it the name of *sulphindilic acid*. *Ibid.*, The sulphindilate of barytes. **1857** MILLER *Elem. Chem., Org.* viii. 530 [see prec.]. *Ibid.*, Sulphindylate of ammonia.

sulphine (ˈsʌlfaɪn). *Chem.* [f. SULPH- + -INE[5].] Any of a group of compounds containing sulphur united to hydrocarbon radicals; also, the hypothetical radical SH_3 from which these are derived.

1880 *Miller's Elem. Chem.* (ed. 5) III. 814 Sulphines and Sulphones. These compounds bear a similar relation to sulphurous and sulphuric acid respectively that the ketones bear to carbonic acid. **1881** ROSCOE & SCHORLEMMER *Treat. Chem.* III. I. 158 Sulphine Compounds. The sulphides unite with the iodides and bromides of the alcohol radicals to form crystallisable salts such as triethylsulphine iodide, $S(C_2H_5)_3I$.

sulphinic (sʌlˈfɪnɪk), *a. Chem.* [f. prec. + -IC.] Applied to acids containing the group SO.OH united to carbon, obtained by reducing the chlorides of the sulphonic acids.

1877 *Jrnl. Chem. Soc.* II. 734 Formation of Sulphinic Acids of the Fatty Group from the Chloranhydrides of the Sulphonic Acids. **1880** *Miller's Elem. Chem.* (ed. 5) III. 57 A few acids have been obtained.. derived from sulphurous acid in the same way that the sulphonic acids are derived from sulphuric acid. They may be termed sulphinic acids.

sulphinpyrazone (sʌlfɪnˈpɪrəzəʊn). *Pharm.* Also (*U.S.*) sulf-. [f. SULPHIN(IC *a.* + PYRAZ(OLE + -ONE.] The uricosuric drug $C_6H_5{\cdot}SO{\cdot}(CH_3)CH{\cdot}C_3HN_2O_2(C_6H_5)_2$, which promotes excretion of urates by inhibiting their reabsorption by kidneys; 1,2-diphenyl-4-(2-phenylsulphinylethyl)pyrazolidine-3, 5-dione.

1958 *Arthritis & Rheumatism* I. 532 The present communication is concerned with G-28315 (4-[phenyl sulfoxyethyl]-1,2-diphenyl-3,5-pyrazolidinedione). [*Note*] The generic name of this compound is sulfinpyrazone. **1961** *Lancet* 30 Sept. 763/2 Aspirin.. could within a few days overcome the effects for which probenecid, sulfinpyrazone, or zoxazolamine had been prescribed. **1978** *Times* 2 Mar. 16/6 The American research project was set up to test the theory that the risk of this further thrombosis might be reduced by treatment with a drug, sulfinpyrazone, which acts on the blood platelets, the small cells that start the process of thrombosis. **1981** H. J. ROGERS et al. *Textbk. Clin. Pharmacol.* xvii. 569 Sulphinpyrazone (Anturan).. is a uricosuric drug related to phenylbutazone which prolongs platelet survival.. without prolonging the bleeding time.

sulphion (ˈsʌlfɪɒn). *Chem.* [f. SULPH- + ION.] The hypothetical radical consisting of one equivalent of sulphur and four of oxygen (SO_4).

1868 MILLER *Elem. Chem.* (ed. 4) II. 186. **1876** HARLEY *Royle's Mat. Med.* 54 The more oxydisable metals, zinc, iron,.. and manganese are dissolved by the dilute acid, hydrogen being liberated, while the Sulphion (SO_4) unites with the metal to form a sulphate. **1909** J. W. JENKINSON *Experim. Embryology* 143 The sulphuric acid radicle (sulphion) is thus necessary for the proper development of the gut.

sulphite (ˈsʌlfaɪt). *Chem.* Also 8 **sulfite**. [ad. F. *sulphite* (*Nomencl. chimique*, 1787), arbitrary alteration of *sulphate*: see -ITE[1] 4 b.]

1. A salt of sulphurous acid: usually with a qualifying term indicating the base.

1790 [see SULPHATE 1]. **1790, 1794** [see SULPHUREOUS *a.* 5]. **1800** tr. *Lagrange's Chem.* I. 219 Sulphite of barytes. **1853** GREGORY *Inorg. Chem.* 270 The sulphites are recognised by their giving off the suffocating smell of sulphurous acid when acted on by a stronger acid. **1867** *Ure's Dict. Arts* (ed. 6) III. 719 *Soda, Sulphite*.. is prepared largely for removing the last traces of chlorine from the bleached pulp obtained in the manufacture of paper. **1893** J. A. HODGES *Elem. Photogr.* 29 Sulphite of soda.

2. *attrib.*, chiefly with reference to the use of sulphite of soda or of lime in certain processes.

1892 *Photogr. Ann.* II. 46 Fill up the forty ounce bottle with the hot ten per cent sulphite solution. **1902** *Encycl. Brit.* XXXI. 457 Two methods.. known respectively as the soda or alkaline process and the sulphite or acid process. **1908** *Westm. Gaz.* 15 Aug. 14/2 The Canadian Pacific Sulphite Pulp Company. **1910** *Encycl. Brit.* (ed. 11) X. 310/2 These cellulose pulps are known in commerce as 'sulphite pulps' and 'soda pulps' respectively. **1911** *Ibid.* XXVI. 67/1 The manufacture of 'sulphite cellulose' from wood.

sulpho- (ˈsʌlfəʊ), before a vowel also SULPH- (q.v.), used as combining form of SULPHUR, in names of chemical compounds containing sulphur, or (in modern use) produced by the substitution of sulphur for oxygen (etc.) in a compound: in this sense now superseded extensively by THIO-, q.v. (Many of the names originated with French chemists.) E.g. SULPHOCYANIC, SULPHOVINIC, with derivatives; ***ˌsulphoantiˈmonic, -arˈsenic*** = *sulphantimonic, -arsenic* (see SULPH-); ***sulphoˈbenzoate***, a salt of ***sulphobenˈzoic acid***, formed by the combination of sulphuric acid with benzoic acid; so ***sulphoˈbenzamate, -benˈzamic, -ˈbenzamide, -ˈbenzide***, etc.; ***sulphoˈcarbonate, -carˈbonic***, etc. = THIOCARBONATE, -CARBONIC; ***ˌsulphocarˈbolic*** = phenolsulphonic. Also SULPHO-ACID, SULPHO-SALT; ***sulpho-compound, -group***. In mod. use often repr. SULPHONYL, as in *sulpho-chlorination, -lipid* below. **ˌsulphobromoˈphthalein** *Pharm.* [BROMO- + PHTHALEIN] = *bromosulphthalein* s.v. BROMO-; **ˌsulphochloriˈnation** *Chem.*, the introduction of the chlorosulphonyl group, $ClSO_2-$, into a molecule; **ˈsulpholipid** *Biochem.*, any of a class of lipids whose structures terminate with the sulphonate group, $-SO_3^-$.

1855 SCOFFERN *Orr's Circ. Sci., Chem.* 473 Pentasulphuret of antimony, otherwise called *sulpho-antimonic acid. **1836** T. THOMSON *Min., Geol.*, etc. 530 *Sulpho-Antimonite of Nickel. **1833** REES tr. *Berzelius' Anal. Inorg. Bodies* 135 *Sulpho-arseniates. *Ibid.* 137 *Sulpho-arsenites. **1842** GRAHAM *Elem. Chem.* 101 *Sulpho-arsenious and *sulpho-arsenic acids, which resemble arsenious and arsenic acids respectively in composition, but contain sulphur instead of oxygen. **1864** WEBSTER, *Sulpho-arsenic*,.. said of an acid consisting of five equivalents of sulphur and one of arsenic. **1836** T. THOMSON *Min., Geol.*, etc. 537 *Sulpho-Arsenide of Cobalt. **1868** WATTS *Dict. Chem.* V. 486 Ethylic *Sulphobenzamate, or *Sulphobenzamic Ether. *Ibid.* 484 Sulphobenzamic acid .. the amic acid of sulphobenzoic acid. **1835** *R. D. & T. Thomson's Rec. Gen. Sci.* I. 206 *Sulpho-benzide. **1854** *Q. Jrnl. Chem. Soc.* VI. 195 *note*, Sulphophenylamide, the amide of Mitscherlich's *sulphobenzidic acid. **1843** *Chem. Gaz.* I. 598 The existence of *sulphobenzine, $C^{24}H^5SO^2$, and of *sulphobenzinic acid. **1835** *R. D. & T. Thomson's Rec. Gen. Sci.* I. 129 The *sulpho-benzoates of zinc. *Ibid.* 128 **Sulphobenzoic Acid.*—This acid is formed by adding benzoin to sulphuric acid as long as any of it is taken up. **1868** WATTS *Dict. Chem.* V. 489 *Sulphobenzol, C^7H^6S. Syn. with Sulphide of Benzylene. **1856** *Fownes' Man. Elem. Chem.* (ed. 6) 489 *Sulphobenzolate of baryta. **1857** MILLER *Elem. Chem., Org.* v. §1. 305 *Sulpho-benzolic and sulphanilic acid, have actually been obtained. **1945** *Jrnl. Amer. Med. Assoc.* 4 Aug. 1001/2 A positive Hanger test or a strong *sulfobromophthalein dye retention also provides valuable evidence [of hepatitis]. **1974** M. C. GERALD *Pharmacol.* ii. 34 Frequently employed diagnostic agents include.. sulfobromophthalein for liver function tests. **1856** *Q. Jrnl. Chem. Soc.* VIII. 271 *Sulphobutylic Acid may be separated from its baryta-salt by sulphuric acid. *Ibid.* IX. 253 *Sulphobutyrate of barium. *Ibid.*, The preparation of disulphopropiolic and *sulphobutyric acid. **1868** WATTS *Dict. Chem.* V. 490 *Sulphocarbamate of Ammonium.. crystallises in long lemon-yellow prisms. *Ibid.*, *Sulphocarbamic acid is obtained in the free state by decomposing the ammonium-salt with dilute sulphuric or hydrochloric acid. *Ibid.* 493 *Sulphocarbamide.. has not yet been obtained. It contains the elements of sulphocyanate of ammonium. **1876** DUNGLISON *Med. Lex.*, **Sulphocarbolates*,.. a class of salts prepared by heating together pure carbolic and sulphuric acids, diluting with water, and saturating with the base, as soda, zinc, &c. *Ibid.*, **Sulphocarbolic Acid*,.. a compound soluble crystalline acid, resulting from the union of hydrated sulphuric acid and pure carbolic acid. **1833** REES tr. *Berzelius' Anal. Inorg. Bodies* 132 The *sulphocarbonates of alkaline earths and metals, when heated, yield a residue of sulphuret, and disengage sulphuret of carbon. **1857** MILLER *Elem. Chem., Org.* iii. §3. 146 *Sulphocarbonic acid (bisulphide of carbon). **1868** WATTS *Dict. Chem.* V. 494 *Sulphocarbonic ethers.* These are bodies having the composition of carbonic ethers, in which the oxygen is replaced, wholly or partly, by sulphur. **1838** T. THOMSON *Chem. Org. Bodies* 196 When ethal is placed in contact with common sulphuric acid, without the application of heat, there is no action. But, when we apply the heat of the water-bath,.. *sulphocetic acid is formed. The *sulphocetate of potash is neutral. **1931** *Jrnl. Amer. Chem. Soc.* LIII. 2648 Phenols can be converted in phenolpolysulfonylchlorides by the action of chlorosulfonic acid. It also was noticed that the reagent caused four distinct types of reaction: namely, sulfonation, *sulfochlorination, chlorination, oxidation. **1980** *Chem. in Brit.* XVI. 466/1 The sulphochlorination of paraffins to alkane sulphonyl chlorides is conducted in the presence of uv light. **1857** MILLER *Elem. Chem., Org.* vi. §1. 374 The sulpholeic acid is more permanent than the *sulpho-compounds of the solid fatty acids. **1838** T. THOMSON *Chem. Org. Bodies* 196 *Sulphoglycerate of lime. **1838** R. D. THOMSON in *Brit. Annual* 313 *Sulpho-glyceric acid. **1871** *Jrnl. Chem. Soc.* N.S. IX. 378 Therefore sulphanilic acid holds the *sulpho- and amide-groups in the positions 1 : 4. **1880** *Jrnl. Soc. Arts* XXVIII. 446 They.. introduced both the sulpho-groups into one side of the molecule. **1930** M. BODANSKY *Introd. Physiol. Chem.* (ed. 2) iii. 70 Aminolipids, *sulfolipids, etc. —groups which are at present not sufficiently well characterized for classification. **1977** D. E. METZLER *Biochem.* ii. 112/2 Chloroplasts contain a large amount of a special sulfolipid. **1838** T. THOMSON *Chem. Org. Bodies* 179 Sulphomethylic acid [is obtained] from *sulphomethylate of barytes. **1836** BRANDE *Chem.* (ed. 4) 1127 *Sulpho-methylic acid. **1826** *Phil. Trans.* CXVI. Index, *Sulphonaphthalates. **1826** FARADAY *ibid.* II. 162, I may.. suggest [the name] *sulpho-naphthalic acid, which sufficiently indicates its source and nature without the inconvenience of involving theoretical views. **1844** *Chem. Gaz.* II. 509 The *sulphonitrite is transformed into *sulphonitrate under the influence of sulphurous acid. *Ibid.* 508 When the sulphonitrite of potash is treated with a fresh quantity of sulphurous acid in presence of an excess of potash, it is completely transformed into another salt, which contains a new acid, which I have named *sulphonitric. *Ibid.*, *Sulphonitrous acid is formed of four elements, which represent sulphuric acid, sulphurous acid, nitrous acid and water. **1837** R. D. THOMSON in *Brit. Annual* 348 *Sulpho-oleic acid. **1845** TODD & BOWMAN *Phys. Anat.* I. 207 The compound of sulphuric acid and elaine, or sulph-oleic acid. **1881** *Encycl. Brit.* XII. 844/1 *Sulphophœnicic acid, sulphopurpuric acid, or indigo purple. **1896** *Allbutt's Syst. Med.* I. 744 *Sulphoricinic phenol. **1841** BRANDE *Chem.* (ed. 5) 1082 *Sulphosaccharate of lead falls. *Ibid.*, Peligot prepared *sulphosaccharic acid by carefully adding 3 parts of sulphuric acid to 1 of grape sugar fused on a water-bath. **1836** *Ibid.* (ed. 4) 956 *Sulphosinapic acid was found by Henry and Garot (*Jour. de Chim. Med.* [1825] I.) in mustard, radish, and turnip-seed... The *Sulphosinapates of the alkaline bases are crystallizable. **1838** T. THOMSON *Chem. Org. Bodies* 903 There exists in it [*sc.* mustard] a peculiar crystallizable body, to which they gave the name of *sulphosinapisin; but which has been shortened by Berzelius into sinapin. **1868** *Fownes' Man. Elem. Chem.* (ed. 10) 224 Tellurium Sulphides.. are brown or black substances, which unite with metallic sulphides, forming salts called sulphotellurites and *sulphotellurates. **1844** FOWNES *Chem.* 310 *Sulpho-telluret [*ed.* **1852** *sulpho-telluride] of bismuth. **1900** *Daily News* 19 Feb. 8/6 A plant capable of treating fifty tons of sulpho-telluride ore. **1868** WATTS *Dict. Chem.* V. 718 Tellurous sulphide combines with the sulphides of basylous metals, forming the *sulphotellurites. **1878** KINGZETT *Anim. Chem.* 197 Compound *sulpho-ureas.

b. *occas.* in other technical uses = 'sulphur': **ˌsulphobacˈteria** *sb. pl.* (see quot.); **sulphoˈchromic** *a.*, sulphur-coloured.

1890 BILLINGS *Nat. Med. Dict.*, *Sulphobacteria*,.. bacterial organisms which grow in sulphurated waters, and which contain sulphur. **1895** *Arnold & Sons' Catal. Surg. Instrum.* 57 Suture or Ligature Sulpho-Chromic Catgut.

ˈsulpho-ˌacid. *Chem.* [f. SULPHO- + ACID.]

a. An acid obtained from another acid by substituting sulphur for oxygen; as sulphocyanic acid, CNHS, from cyanic acid, CNHO: now called THIO-ACID. **b.** An acid which contains the group SO_2.OH united to carbon. (See SULPHONIC.)

1857 *Q. Jrnl. Chem. Soc.* IX. 248 A method is thus indicated by which probably all the hydrocarbons, $C_{n2-2}H_{n2}$, may be prepared from the corresponding sulpho-acids. **1857** MILLER *Elem. Chem., Org.* iii. §3. 141 The hydrates of these sulpho-acids are more unstable than their metallic salts.

sulphocyanic (ˌsʌlfəʊsaɪˈænɪk), *a. Chem.* [f. SULPHO- + CYANIC.] Designating the sulpho-acid related to cyanic acid, occurring in cruciferous plants and in human saliva, and obtainable as a colourless liquid: now THIOCYANIC.

1819 J. G. CHILDREN *Chem. Anal.* 326 Mr. Porrett concludes the composition of sulphocyanic acid to be.. Sulphur..100, Hydrocyanic acid..53. **1830–1** *Lancet* I. 33/2 It has long since been discovered, that the sulphocyanic acid and its salts possess the same action with the persalts of iron as the meconic acid. **1868** WATTS *Dict. Chem.* V. 515 Sulphocyanic anhydride..is formed by the action of cyanic iodide on argentic sulphocyanate.

Hence **sulpho'cyanate**, **-'cyanide** (in *Photography*, short for ammonium sulphocyanide), †**-cy'anodide**, †**-cy'anuret**, a salt of sulphocyanic acid.

1830–1 *Lancet* I. 33/2 No attempt has been made to ascertain whether the *sulphocyanate of iron might be formed at all during the process for detecting opium. **1897** *Naturalist* 42 Sulphides and sulphocyanates of an alcoholic body termed allyl. **1841** *Penny Cycl.* XX. 358/1 The saliva ..is composed of a great proportion of water,..holding in solution..a very minute quantity of *sulpho-cyanide of potassium. **1890** *Anthony's Photogr. Bull.* III. 221 Sulphocyanide of silver is substituted for bromide. **1907** *Westm. Gaz.* 13 Apr. 14/2 A toning-bath in very common use is the sulphocyanide bath. **1838** T. THOMSON *Chem. Org. Bodies* 768 *Sulpho-cyanodide of mercury gives the same products as sulphuret of cyanogen; but instead of sulphur, we obtain sulphuret of mercury. **1833** REES tr. *Berzelius' Anal. Inorg. Bodies* 135 When the hydrogen of the acid unites with the sulphur of the base to form sulphuretted hydrogen, a metallic *sulphocyanuret remains.

sulphocyan(o)- (ˌsʌlfəʊsaɪən, -ənəʊ), *Chem.*, used as the first element in certain names of compounds of sulphur with a cyano-compound, or of compounds of sulphocyanogen: see quots.

1841 BRANDE *Chem.* (ed. 5) 572 Sulphocyanhydric Acid.. is obtained by decomposing basic sulphocyanuret of lead by dilute sulphuric acid. **1859** MAYNE *Expos. Lex.* 1227/1 *Sulphocyanhydrate*, term for a genus of sulphosalts resulting from the combination of cyanhydric sulphide with the sulphobases. **1868** WATTS *Dict. Chem.* V. 509 The sulphocyanates of platinum form two series of double salts, called sulphocyanoplatinites and sulphocyanoplatinates. *Ibid.* 510 Sulphocyanoplatinic Acid.

sulphocyanogen (ˌsʌlfəʊsaɪˈænədʒən). *Chem.* [f. SULPHO- + CYANOGEN.] A compound of sulphur and cyanogen, $(CN)_2S$, obtained as a yellow amorphous powder.

1841 BRANDE *Chem.* (ed. 5) 572. **1878** KINGZETT *Anim. Chem.* 49 The presence of sulphocyanogen in saliva is peculiar to man.

attrib. **1861** *Q. Jrnl. Chem. Soc.* XIII. 319 If we remember in how many respects..the sulphocyanogen-compounds of ethyl and its homologues differ from those of allyl and phenyl.

sulphohydrate, -ic, var. SULPHYDRATE, -IC.

1833 REES tr. *Berzelius' Anal. Inorg. Bodies* 130 The sulphohydrates are decomposed by air. **1838** T. THOMSON *Chem. Org. Bodies* 329 Sulphohydric ether is lighter than water.

ˌ**sulpho-indi'gotic**, *a. Chem.* [ad. F. *sulfo-indigotique* (1832): see SULPHO- and INDIGOTIC.] = SULPHINDIGOTIC. Hence ˌ**sulpho-'indigotate**. So ˌ**sulphoin'dylic** *acid*.

1838 T. THOMSON *Chem. Org. Bodies* 198 To obtain the sulpho-indigotic acid we dissolve the sulpho-indigotate of ammonia in water, and precipitate by acetate of lead. **1855** OGILVIE *Dict.* Suppl., *Sulphoindilic acid*, a blue acid formed by the action of sulphuric acid upon indigo. **1881** CLELAND *Evol.*, etc. v. 132 Sulpho-indigotate of soda.

sulphonal ('sʌlfənəl). *Chem.* Also sulf-. [ad. G. *sulfonal* (*Berichte der chem. Gesellsch.*, 1886, p. 2806), f. *sulfon* SULPHONE.] Diethyl-sulphone-dimethyl-methane, a white crystalline substance, used as a hypnotic.

1889 *Pall Mall Gaz.* 26 Apr. 2/3 Sulfonal is a 'hypnotic,' which is free from the incalculable dangers of the 'narcotic' remedies such as the opiates and chloral. It is obtained.. from the combination of ethyl mercaptan and acetone by the process of oxidation. **1890** *Daily News* 16 Dec. 3/5[A doctor] deposed that he saw deceased at that place, when he said he had been taking sulphonal.

attrib. **1892** ZANGWILL *Bow Mystery* 175, I pocketed the razor and the empty sulfonal phial. **1898** *Allbutt's Syst. Med.* V. 454 Some..fatal cases of sulphonal poisoning.

sulphonamide (sʌlˈfɒnəmaɪd). *Chem.* and *Pharm.* Also (*U.S.*) sulf-. [f. SULPHONE + AMIDE.] **a.** Any organic compound that is an amide of a sulphonic acid, characterized by the group $-SO_2N=$; *spec.* any of the drugs derived from sulphanilamide (and so containing this group).

1881 *Jrnl. Chem. Soc.* XL. 602 The [1:4:3] acid..is converted by ammonia into a sulphonamide crystallising in needles. **1947** *Sci. News* IV. 60 When new drugs like the sulphonamides or D.D.T. are developed, their chemical properties have been reported for thirty years or so, and it is their biological effects which are the true modern discoveries. **1959** *Times* 7 Dec. (Agric. Suppl.) p. vii/4 To prevent coccidiosis in chickens, nitrophenol, a sulfonamide ..is added to the feed. **1964** N. G. CLARK *Mod. Org. Chem.* xx. 414 In most cases, the sulphonamides have convenient melting-points, and are admirably suitable for characterizing both sulphonic acids and amines. **1974** [see POTENTIATED *ppl. a.*]. **1977** *Martindale's Extra Pharmacopoeia* (ed. 27) 1468/1 Because they are similar in chemical structure to *p*-aminobenzoic acid, sulphonamides interfere with the synthesis by micro-organisms of folic acid from *p*-aminobenzoic acid... The sulphonamides have been largely replaced by antibiotics in the treatment of infections.

b. *attrib.* and *Comb.*, as ***sulphonamide drug***, ***group*** (of atoms or of drugs); ***sulphonamide-resistant*** adj.

1943 *Times* 16 June 5/7 Recent American figures suggest that one death occurs from the Sulphonamide drugs in every 2,571 deaths from all causes. **1959** *Sci. News* LI. 96 Antithyroid activity was first observed in some of the sulphonamide drugs, but the first compound used clinically, in 1943 by Astwood in America, was thiourea. **1979** DAVIES & LITTLEWOOD *Elementary Biochem.* iv. 83 Sulfonamide drugs are not effective in open, suppurating wounds; such wounds contain pus and other materials that are a source of *p*-aminobenzoic acid, which antagonizes the action of the sulfonamide drugs. **1939** *Brit. Med. Jrnl.* 5 Aug. 269/2 Sulphanilamide consists of a benzene ring to opposite ends of which are attached an amino group and a sulphonamide group. **1942** *Times* 21 Sept. 5/7 Another most important factor in saving life has been the series of new drugs, of which the sulphonamide group is the most important. **1942** *Proc. Soc. Exper. Biol. & Med.* L. 336 The present report is concerned with the *in vitro* and *in vivo* production of sulfonamide resistant strains of staphylococci. **1968** *Times* 12 Oct. 18/8 One of the organisms sometimes responsible for travellers' diarrhoea is now sulphonamide-resistant. **1981** H. J. ROGERS et al. *Textbk. Clin. Pharmacol.* xix. 649 Sulphadiazine is now only rarely used (with benzylpenicillin) in the treatment of meningococcal meningitis since sulphonamide-resistant meningococci are common.

sulphonate ('sʌlfənət), *sb. Chem.* [See SULPHONIC and -ATE[4].] A salt of sulphonic acid.

1876 *Jrnl. Chem. Soc.* I. 726 Sulphates almost entirely disappeared from the urine, their place being taken by sulphonates. **1883** *Athenæum* 10 Feb. 188/3 By the action of caustic potash on the potassium sulphonate a trihydroxydiphenyl was formed.

sulphonate ('sʌlfəneɪt), *v.* [f. the sb.] To convert into a sulphonate, as by the action of sulphuric acid. Hence **'sulphonated** *ppl. a.*, **'sulphonating** *vbl. sb.*, **sulpho'nation**.

1882 *Jrnl. Chem. Soc.* XLII. 196 The author could not obtain the salt 'A'..by sulphonating pure cymene. **1890** *Athenæum* 27 Dec. 893/1 Sulphonation with its concomitant hydrolysis. **1902** *Encycl. Brit.* XXVI. 720/2 A sulphonating agent. *Ibid.* 728/2 Compounds such as dimethylaniline..are chlorinated, sulphonated, &c., without difficulty. *Ibid.*, That sulphonation involves a similar series of changes there can be little if any doubt, as acetanilide behaves towards sulphonating agents just as it does on chlorination. **1936**, **1966** [see SOAPLESS *a.* b]. **1972** *Materials & Technol.* V. 302 By the use of energetic sulphonating agents such as sulphur trioxide.., fatty acids can be sulphonated at the alpha carbon atom. The sulphonated acids have useful surface-active properties.

sulphone ('sʌlfəʊn). *Chem.* Also -on. [ad. G. *sulfon*, f. *sulfur*: see -ONE a.

The formation is on the analogy of KETONE, the sulphones bearing the same relation to sulphuric acid, $SO_2(OH)_2$, as the ketones to carbonic acid, $CO(OH)_2$.]

Any of a group of compounds containing the radical SO_2 united to two hydrocarbon radicals

1872 *Chem. News* XXVI. 252/2 Action of Phosphoric Perchloride upon Sulphon Acids. **1876** *Encycl. Brit.* V. 506/1. **1877** *Jrnl. Chem. Soc.* II. 613 All of which yield sulphones when heated with phosphoric anhydride. **1880** *Miller's Elem. Chem., Org.* (ed. 5) 814 The sulphones resist oxidation

sulphonic (sʌlˈfɒnɪk), *a. Chem.* [f. SULPHONE + -IC.] Containing the radical $SO_2.OH$ (called the ***sulphonic group*** or ***radical***).

1873 *Jrnl. Chem. Soc.* N.S. XI. 277 Action of Phosphorus Pentachloride on Sulphonic Acids. **1881** *Athenæum* 12 Nov. 634/3 Sulphonic Acids derived from Isodinaphthyl. **1902** *Encycl. Brit.* XXVI. 728/2 The introduction..of the sulphonic group into the aminic group.

sulphonium (sʌlˈfəʊnɪəm). *Chem.* Also (*U.S.*) sulf-. [f. SULPH(UR *sb.* + -ONIUM.] A hypothetical monovalent complex cation having a central sulphur atom bonded to three hydrogen atoms; also, any derivative of this in which one or more of the hydrogen atoms is replaced by organic radicals. Usu. *attrib.*

1894 [see IODONIUM]. **1942** *Jrnl. Amer. Chem. Soc.* LXIV. 1165/1 The ability of dialkyl sulfides to react with ω-halogenated ketones with the subsequent formation of sulfonium halides has been known for some time. **1975** R. F. BROWN *Org. Chem.* xxix. 945 The sulfonium ions (R_3S^+) are much more stable than are the analogous oxonium ions (R_3O^+).

sulphonyl ('sʌlfənaɪl). *Chem.* Also (*U.S.*) sulf-. [f. SULPHONE + -YL.] The divalent radical $-SO_2-$, derived from a sulphonic acid group by removal of the $-OH$ group. Usu. *attrib.*

1920 *Chem. Abstr.* XIV. 1947 Place 3 g. of pulverized sulfonyl chloride in a round-bottomed flask. **1953** *Chem. & Engin. News* 5 Jan. 91/3 The inorganic name of the radical SO_2 is sulfuryl, while its organic name is sulfonyl. **1975** R. F. BROWN *Org. Chem.* xxix. 956 Some of the sulfonyl chlorides and esters have been used so often that trivial names have been coined.

Hence ˌ**sulphony'lation**, conversion into a sulphonyl compound; (as a back-formation) **sul'phonylate** *v. trans.*

1956 *Chem. Abstr.* L. 10677/1 (*heading*) Friedel-Crafts acylation and sulfonylation reactions. **1979** *Tetrahedron Lett.* Sept. 3790 The mild conditions used in this sulphonylation provide some advantages over the more usual preparative methods for unsymmetrical sulphones. **1980** *Chem. Abstr.* XCIII. 843/2 Thiazole hydrobromide was sulfonylated with..arsenesulfonyl chlorides to give the corresponding 7-sulfonylthiazolium chlorides.

sulphonylurea (ˌsʌlfənaɪljʊəˈriːə). *Pharm.* Also (*U.S.*) sulf-. [f. SULPHONYL + UREA.] Any of the group of hypoglycæmic drugs containing the active grouping $-SO_2 \cdot NH \cdot CO \cdot NH-$, which are used orally in the treatment of diabetes.

1956 *Science* 6 Apr. 583/2 A statistically highly significant hypoglycemic response occurred in 34 of the patients with diabetes who were given the sulfonylurea. **1966** *New Scientist* 24 Nov. 433/1 The longing of diabetics for a hypoglycaemic drug which could be taken orally..was realized ten years ago when the sulphonylureas and diguanides were introduced. **1974** M. C. GERALD *Pharmacol.* xxv. 442 The oral hypoglycemic agents, the sulfonylureas such as tolbutamide and the biguanide phenformin, are useful agents for the treatment of the stable maturity-onset diabetes.

sulphopurpuric (ˌsʌlfəʊpɜːˈpjʊərɪk), *a. Chem.* [ad. F. *sulfo-purpurique* (Dumas, 1836): see SULPHO- and PURPURIC.] Applied to an acid obtained by the action of sulphuric acid on indigo. Hence **sulpho'purpurate**.

1838 T. THOMSON *Chem. Org. Bodies* 378. **1857** MILLER *Elem. Chem., Org.* viii. 531 Sulphopurpuric Acid..forms a blue solution in pure water. When acetate of potash is added to this liquid it gives a purple precipitate of sulphopurpurate of potash. **1881** *Encycl. Brit.* XII. 844/1.

sulpho-salt ('sʌlfəʊsɒlt, -sɔːlt). *Chem.* [f. SULPHO- + SALT *sb.*[1] Cf. F. *sulfosel* (Berzelius).] A salt of a sulpho-acid.

1833 REES tr. *Berzelius' Anal. Inorg. Bodies* 126 Sulpho-salts. A small number only of these salts are as yet known. *Ibid.* 128 Sulpho-salts are obtained, in which the radicals of the acid and the base are combined with sulphur, in volumes equal to those of the oxygen which they have lost. **1839** URE *Dict. Arts* 1215 The oxisalt is transformed into a sulphosalt, by the sulphur of the compound gas. **1871** ROSCOE *Elem. Chem.* xvii. 189 Other sulphides correspond to the acid-forming oxides and form compounds with the basic sulphides termed sulpho-salts.

sulphovinic (sʌlfəʊˈvɪnɪk), *a. Chem.* [ad. F. *sulfovinique*, f. *sulfo-* SULPHO- + *vin* wine.] ***sulphovinic acid***: an acid produced by the action of sulphuric acid on alcohol or spirit of wine; ethyl hydrogen sulphate or ethyl sulphuric acid. Hence **sulphovinate** (-ˈvaɪnət).

1826 HENNELL in *Phil. Trans.* CXVI. III. 245 Sulphovinate of potash. *Ibid.* 248 Oil of wine..is resolvable ..into sulphovinic acid. **1844** FOWNES *Man. Elem. Chem.* 388 A solution of sulphovinic acid, or, what is equivalent to it, a mixture, in due proportions, of oil of vitriol and strong alcohol. **1907** J. B. COHEN *Org. Chem.* i. 9.

sulphoxide (sʌlˈfɒksaɪd). *Chem.* [f. SULPH- + OXIDE.] Any compound containing a hydrocarbon radical combined with the group SO.

1894 MUIR & MORLEY *Watts' Dict. Chem.*, *Sulphoxides*, organic compounds R.SO.R′ formed by the action of conc. HNO_3 on sulphides. *Ibid.* s.v., Sulphoxides containing monovalent alcohol radicles form unstable compounds with HNO_3.

sulphur ('sʌlfə(r)), *sb.* Forms: 4–7 **sulphre**, 5–7 **sulphure**, 5, 7, 9 (now *U.S.*) **sulfur**, 6–7 **sulpher**, (4 **sou(l)fre**, **soulphre**, 5 **solfre**, 6 **sulfure**, **sulfre**, **sulphyr**, 7 **sulfer**), 5– **sulphur**. [a. AF. *sulf(e)re* (12th c.), OF. (mod.F.) *soufre* (from 13th c.) = Pr. *solfre solpre*, *sulpre*, It. *solfo*, *zolfo*, OSp. *çufre*, Pg. *xofre* (also, with Arabic article prefixed, OSp. *açufre*, Sp. *azufre*, Pg. *enxofre*):—L. *sulfur(em)*, *sulphur(em)*, whence also Du. *sulfer*, *solfer*.]

1. a. A greenish-yellow non-metallic substance, found abundantly in volcanic regions, and occurring free in nature as a brittle crystalline solid, and widely distributed in combination with metals and other substances. In popular and commercial language it is otherwise known as BRIMSTONE. (See also SULPHUR VIVUM.) In *Chemistry*, one of the non-metallic elements: atomic weight 32, symbol S.

Sulphur exists in two distinct crystalline forms and in an amorphous form. It is manufactured largely from native sulphides of copper and iron; when refined and cast into moulds, it is the ***roll*** or ***stick sulphur*** of commerce. It is highly inflammable, and is used in the manufacture of matches, gunpowder, and sulphuric acid, for vulcanizing rubber, in bleaching, and as a disinfectant.

In popular belief sulphur has been associated with the fires of hell, with devils, and with thunder and lightning.

13.. *E.E. Allit. P.* B. 954 Þe rayn..Of felle flaunkes of fyr & flakes of soufre. *Ibid.* 1036 Alum & alkaran..Soufre sour, & saundyuer. **1390** GOWER *Conf.* II. 264 Eft with water.. Sche made a cercle aboute him thries, And eft with fyr of sulphre twyes. *c* **1420** ? LYDG. *Assembly of Gods* 314 Of fyre and sulphure all hys [*sc.* Pluto's] odour wase. **1549** THOMAS *Hist. Italie* 113 b, The veyne of sulfure in the earth, receiuyng sometymes through the extreme heate of the sonne, a certaine kynde of fyre, kendleth. **1595** *Locrine* III. vi. 51 Through burning sulphur of the Limbo-lake. **1604** SHAKS. *Oth.* III. iii. 329 The Mines of Sulphure. **1638–56** COWLEY *Davideis* III. Note xxx, Thunder hath sulphur in it. **1667** MILTON *P.L.* I. 69 A fiery Deluge, fed With ever-burning Sulphur unconsum'd. **1764** GRAINGER *Sugar Cane*

II. 241 Sulphur's suffocating steam. **1790** KERR tr. *Lavoisier's Elem. Chem.* 221 They do not sufficiently disoxygenate the decomposed part of the acid to reconvert it into sulphur. **1846** G. BIRD *Urin. Deposits* (ed. 2) 27 The sulphur existing in the blood. **1871** TENNYSON *Last Tourn.* 614 Near me stood, In fuming sulphur blue and green, a fiend. **1881** *Med. Temp. Jrnl.* XLVIII. 194 Sulphur combines with carbon, in two proportions of the former with one of the latter. **1891** F. TAYLOR *Man. Pract. Med.* (ed. 2) 72 Good results have been got by burning sulphur in the rooms inhabited by the child.

b. In a refined state, e.g. as flowers of sulphur, it is used medicinally as a laxative, a resolvent, and a sudorific, and as an ingredient of various ointments, esp. for skin diseases.

c **1400** *Lanfranc's Cirurg.* 216 Anointing of oile of camomille & solfre grounden togidere. *a* **1425** tr. *Arderne's Treat. Fistula*, etc. 46 Ane enoyntment made of sope and sulphure. **1578** LYTE *Dodoens* III. xx[x]iv. 365 The iuyce of the roote [of Thapsia]..mingled with sulfre, dissolueth al swellinges being layd vpon. **1789** W. BUCHAN *Dom. Med.* (1790) 641 What stimulants are more active than salt and sulphur? **1897** H. ALDERSMITH *Ringworm* (ed. 4) 185 Sulphur in some form is one of the best applications for ringworm. **1908** W. J. COURTHOPE in *Blackw. Mag.* Sept. 298 The blood impure Sulphur's sharp grains alone have strength to cure.

c. With qualification indicating colour, form, state, origin, etc.: see the qualifying words, and quots. below.

virgin sulphur, native sulphur in the form of transparent amber-coloured crystals. ***volcanic sulphur***, native sulphur in opaque, lemon-yellow, crystalline masses. ***sulphur of ivy***, corruption of SULPHUR VIVUM.

1559, 1590 [see QUICK *a.* 14]. **1668** CHARLETON *Onomast.* 235 *Sulphur Virgineum*..Virgin Sulphur. **1725** *Fam. Dict.* s.v., There are two sorts, one of which is call'd Live Sulphur, and the other Common or Yellow Sulphur. Live or Quick Sulphur is a grey, fat, clayey, inflammable Matter. **1728** CHAMBERS *Cycl.*, Sulphur..is particularly call'd Fossil, or Mineral Sulphur, to distinguish it from the Sulphur of Metals, or of the Philosophers. **1753** *Chambers' Cycl.* Suppl. s.v., The green native sulphur. *Ibid.*, The red native sulphur. **1867** *Chambers' Encycl.* IX. 199/1 Under the names of Black Sulphur, or Sulphur vivum (commonly inquired for at the chemist's under the title of Sulphur of Ivy). **1911** *Encycl. Brit.* XXVI. 62/1 Such pyrites sulphur is usually contaminated with arsenic. *Ibid.* 62/2 Commercial sulphur forms yellow crystals.

d. †***acid of sulphur***, sulphuric acid; †***balm***, †***magistery of sulphur***, milk of sulphur; †***oil of sulphur***, ? sulphuric acid; †***salt of sulphur***, ? potassium sulphate 'impregnated' with sulphuric oxide; †***spirit of sulphur***, sulphuric oxide.

See also ALCOHOL 2, BALSAM *sb.* 2 b, FLOWER *sb.* 2 c, LIVER *sb.*[1] 4, MILK *sb.* 4, RUBY *sb.* 6 b.

1696 PHILLIPS (ed. 5) s.v., *Flower of Sulphur*, the purest of the Sulphur, that sticks to the Head of the Alembic, in sublimation by Fire. **1704** J. HARRIS *Lex. Techn.* I, *Salt of Sulphur*, a Preparation in Chymistry, improperly so called, since it is only a *Sal Polychrestum* impregnated with Spirit of Sulphur, and then reduced to an Acid Salt by Evaporation of all the Moisture. **1706** PHILLIPS (ed. Kersey), *Spirit of Sulphur*..is commonly call'd *Oil of Sulphur per Campanam*, from the Vessel's Shape, being like a Glass-bell, in which it is usually drawn. **1728** CHAMBERS *Cycl.* s.v., Magistery, or Balm..of Sulphur is..called Milk of Sulphur from its Whiteness. **1744** *Phil. Trans.* XLIII. 1 The volatile Acid of Sulphur.

†**e.** *pl.* Masses or deposits of native sulphur.

1697 DRYDEN *Virg. Georg.* III. 684 The Founts where living Sulphurs boil. **1771** *Ann. Reg.* II. 78/1 The inside of the crater, which is incrusted with salts and sulphurs like that of Vesuvius.

f. The colour of sulphur, a greenish-yellow.

1924 R. CAMPBELL *Flaming Terrapin* ii. 32 Panthers' eyes ..Flashed their pale sulphur on the sunless air. **1963** *Listener* 10 Jan. 84/2, I don't like the colours, especially the Ribena, pillarbox, scrofula, and sulphur.

2. a. *Alch.* One of the supposed ultimate elements of all material substances.

1390 GOWER *Conf.* II. 85 The quikselver..Is ferst of thilke fowre named Of Spiritz,..And the spirit which is secounde In Sal Armoniak is founde: The thridde spirit Sulphur is. ? *c* **1480** *Pater Sapientiæ* in Ashm. (1652) 197 Some say that of Sulphur and Mercury all Bodyes minerall are made. ? *c* **1585** etc. [see SALT *sb.*[1] 4]. **1610** B. JONSON *Alch.* II. iii. 153 Where it [*sc.* matter] retaines more of the humid fatnesse, It turnes to sulphur, or to quicksiluer. **1671** J. WEBSTER *Metallogr.* iv. 73 Sulpher is nothing else than pure fire hid in the Mercury. **1683** PETTUS *Fleta Min.* II. 121 All things do consist of Salt, Sulphur and Mercury. **1719** QUINCY *Compl. Disp.* 8 Sulphur or Oil is very soft and unctuous, and the lightest part of Bodies next to Spirit. **1729** [see MERCURY *sb.* 8]. **1894** MUIR *Alch. Ess. & Chem. El.* 12.

b. *fig.*

1591 SYLVESTER *Du Bartas* I. i. 577 He that,..swelting at the Furnace, fineth bright Our soules dire sulphur. **1599** T. M[OUFET] *Silkwormes* 45 Melt not the golden Sulphur of your hart In following stil this fond and fruitlesse art. **1612** CHAPMAN *Rev. Bussy d'Ambois* v. iii. 11 Her vnmatched spirit Can iudge of spirits, that haue her sulphure in them.

†**3.** A compound of sulphur; *esp.* a sulphide. *Obs.*

1471 RIPLEY *Comp. Alch.* Ep., in Ashm. (1652) 111 If it please your Highnes for to reade, Of divers Sulphurs. **1670** CABLE tr. *Valent. Nat. & Supernat. Things* 113 The Sulphur of Iron is found in the Ruby, the Sulphur of Venus in the Emerald. **1683** *Digby's Chym. Secr.* 33 Make also a Sulphur of the said Metals. **1704** J. HARRIS *Lex. Techn.* I, *Golden Sulphur of Antimony*, is made by boiling the Dross arising in the making of Regulus of Antimony in a little more than its weight of common Water..for about half an Hour, and then straining the Liquor, there is Vinegar poured upon it; on which a Reddish or Gold-colour Powder will precipitate. **1849–50** WEALE *Dict. Terms*, *Golden sulphur of antimony*, golden yellow, is the hydro-sulphuret of antimony. **1853** MAYNE *Expos. Lex.* 39/1 The white sulphur of the alchemists.

4. †**a.** Applied to thunder and lightning, a discharge of gunpowder, etc. *Obs.*

1607 SHAKS. *Cor.* v. iii. 152 To teare with Thunder the wide Cheekes a' th' Ayre, And yet to change [? *read* charge] thy Sulphure with a Boult That should but riue an Oake. **1611** —— *Cymb.* v. v. 240 The Gods throw stones of sulpher on me. *c* **1611** CHAPMAN *Iliad* XIV. 346 His [*sc.* Jove's] sulphure casting with the blow, a strong, vnsauoury smoke. **1616** DRUMM. OF HAWTH. *Madrigals* xviii. Wks. (S.T.S.) I. 107 When first the Canon..Against the Heauen her roaring Sulphure shote.

b. Applied popularly to minerals containing sulphur or supposed to be sulphurous.

1799 MUSHET in *Phil. Mag.* IV. 381 *note*, When supercarbonated crude iron is run from the furnace, it is frequently covered with a scurf, which..is found to be a coating of plumbago..: this substance is universally denominated sulphur and..we say that the iron is sulphury. **1872** S. DE VERE *Americanisms* 424 The term sulphur is altogether erroneously given to bituminous rocks occurring in Kentucky and Tennessee, even when no sulphur is present. **1881** RAYMOND *Mining Gloss.*, *Sulphur*, iron pyrites.

†**c.** A volcano. *Obs. rare.*

1764 GRAINGER *Sugar Cane* II. 392 *note*, Volcanoes are called sulphurs or solfaterres in the West Indies.

d. *Mining* (*local*). Carburetted hydrogen, firedamp.

1851 GREENWELL *Coal-Trade Terms Northumb. & Durh.* 53. **1869** *Eng. Mech.* 3 Dec. 276/1.

e. ***vegetable sulphur***: see VEGETABLE *a.* 7.

5. *ellipt.* **a.** = *sulphur butterfly* (see 9).

1832 J. RENNIE *Consp. Butterfl. & M.* 2 The Clouded Sulphur (*Colias Euprome*, Stephens). *Ibid.* 223 The Sulphur (*Tinea sulphurella*, Haworth) appears in November. **1891** B. G. JOHNS *Among Butterfl.* 111 A yellow butterfly which he at first took to be a common Sulphur. **1902** W. J. HOLLAND *Butterfly Bk.* 285 Genus *Catopsilia* ..(The Great Sulphurs). *Ibid.* 289 Genus *Colias*..(The Sulphurs). *Ibid.* 294 Genus *Terias*..(The Small Sulphurs).

b. = *sulphur-headed cauliflower* (see 9).

1842 LOUDON *Suburban Hort.* 626 The late sulphur, sown at the same time, will come into use during April and May.

c. = *sulphur-cast*, *-impression* (see 8).

1801 M. EDGEWORTH *Belinda* I. viii. 240 Helena and her young companions now came into the room, bringing with them the sulphurs at which they had been looking. **1867** *Ure's Dict. Arts* (ed. 6) III. 857 *Sulphurs*, impressions taken by the goldsmiths of the sixteenth century from the engravings executed on plate, paxes, &c., and which they obtained by spreading a layer of melted sulphur on the face of the plate.

6. *colloq.* or *slang.* Pungent talk, 'sulphurous' language.

1897 *Daily News* 31 Aug. 5/7 Doing nothing but sit round and talk sulphur about the new tariff. **1906** *Pall Mall Gaz.* 11 Jan. 1 By putting as much sulphur as possible into his notorious election address.

7. *attrib.* and *Comb.* **a.** Simple attrib. = Of, pertaining to, consisting of, or containing sulphur, as ***sulphur ball, bed, cure, deposit, dust, flake, flame, fume, fumigation, hill, mine, ore, salt, soap, spa, stick, vein, water, well***; in medicinal preparations, as ***sulphur electuary, lotion, lozenge, ointment, tablet***.

1590 MARLOWE *2nd Pt. Tamburl.* III. ii. 41 As if Bellona, Goddesse of the war Threw naked swords and *sulphurbals of fire. **1878** *Times* 10 May 4/3 There are..three great *sulphur beds [in the land of Midian]. **1868** *Rep. U.S. Comm. Agric.* (1869) 571 The *sulphur-cure for the oïdium, the most formidable disease that attacks the vine. **1911** *Encycl. Brit.* XXVI. 61/1 The *sulphur-deposits of Sicily. **1688** HOLME *Armoury* III. xvi. (Roxb.) 92/1 Little balls made vp of powder wett, and rowled in *sulphur dust. **1728** CHAMBERS *Cycl.* s.v., Sulphur-Dust well sifted. **1843** R. J. GRAVES *Syst. Clin. Med.* xxx. 420, I have..seen very good effects from a perseverance in the use of the *sulphur electuary. **1820** SHELLEY *Vis. Sea* 21 Like *sulphur-flakes hurled from a mine of pale fire. **1592** KYD *Sp. Trag.* III. xi. 76 Vpon a *sulpher flame, Your selues shall finde Lorenzo bathing him In boyling lead. **1856** BUCKTON & HOFMANN in *Q. Jrnl. Chem. Soc.* IX. 251 The black residue burns with a sulphur-flame. **1868** *Chambers' Encycl.* X. 744/1 There is.. nothing new in applying *sulphur-fumes..as a disinfectant. **1895** *Arnold & Sons' Catal. Surg. Instrum.* 287 Sulphur Fumes Apparatus (Adams's), for diphtheria. **1886** FAGGE *Princ. Med.* II. 665 *Sulphur lotions or *sulphur fumigations may be substituted. **1632** LITHGOW *Trav.* IX. 403 This Grotto..standeth on the side and root of a *sulphure hill. **1844** HOBLYN *Dict. Terms Med.* (ed. 2) 377/1 *Sulphur lozenges..used in asthma and in hæmorrhoids. **1591** SYLVESTER *Du Bartas* I. iii. 320 Streams, distilling through the *Sulphur-Mines. **1656** J. HARRINGTON *Oceana* (1658) 116 Grotta di cane..is nothing else but such a damp (continued by the neighbourhood of certain Sulphurmines). **1828** DUPPA *Trav. Italy*, etc. 143 The town [of Siculiana] derives considerable advantages from sulphur mines. **1822–7** GOOD *Study Med.* (1829) V. 653 The simplest..cure is to be obtained by the *sulphur ointment. **1675** W. SIMPSON *Sulphur-Bath Knarsb.* 4 The Salt separated from the Sulphur-water, being put into boyling Milk, will make it shil into Curds and Whey;..we..found the *Sulphur Salt to cause a speedy separation. **1899** *Allbutt's Syst. Med.* VIII. 610 The patient may be washed with *sulphur soap, or with sulphur and tar soap. **1709** T. ROBINSON *Nat. Hist. Westmd. & Cumbd.* vii. 45 Towards the Borders of Northumberland, is a *Sulphur-Spaw. **1868** *Chambers' Encycl.* X. 744/1 A piece of *sulphur-stick. **1723** BLACKMORE *Alfred* v. 150 Naphtha and *Sulphur-Veins, that kindled rage. **1665** in *Verney Mem.* (1907) II. 243 The first inst we arrived att the nasty Spaw, and have now began to drinke the horid *sulfer watter. **1854** J. L. STEPHENS *Centr. Amer.* 258 A stream of sulphur-water. **1652** J. FRENCH *Yorkshire Spaw* (title-p.) The Stinking, or *Sulphur Well. **1675** W. SIMPSON *Sulphur-Bath Knarsb.* 1 The Sulphur-Well at Knarsbrough. **1873** *Jrnl. Chem. Soc.* XXVI. 1090 Two of the most noted Harrogate Spas, viz., the 'Old Sulphur Well' and the 'Chloride of Iron Spa'.

b. in chemical terms, as ***sulphur atom, base, compound, dioxide, group, pyrites, series, trioxide, vapour***.

1911 *Encycl. Brit.* XXVI. 64/1 The junction of one ethyl group with a *sulphur atom in the second salt. **1857** MILLER *Elem. Chem., Org.* i. 36 *Sulphur Compound. **1869** ROSCOE *Elem. Chem.* xii. 126 *Sulphur [*ed.* 1866 Sulphuric] Dioxide, or Sulphurous Acid. **1884** OGILVIE s.v., **Sulphur group*, the elementary substances sulphur, selenium, and tellurium; all having a strong attraction for oxygen. **1856** MILLER *Elem. Chem., Inorg.* 565 Sulphurous acid is..regarded as the starting point of several combinations belonging to the *sulphur series. **1869** ROSCOE *Elem. Chem.* xiii. 129 *Sulphur [*ed.* 1866 Sulphuric] Trioxide, or Sulphuric Anhydride. **1844** FOWNES *Man. Elem. Chem.* 164 The density of..*sulphur-vapour.

c. Objective and instrumental, as ***sulphur-bearing, -containing, -flaming, -headed, -impregnated, -scented, -smoking, -tipped*** ppl. adjs.; ***sulphur-roast*** vb.

1911 *Encycl. Brit.* XXVI. 61/2 *Sulphur-bearing Miocene rocks. *Ibid.* 64/2 A group of *sulphur-containing acids of general formula $H_2S_nO_6$. **1601** WEEVER *Mirr. Mart.* (Roxb.) 198 On flintie Etnaes *sulphur-flaming mountaines. **1898** 'MERRIMAN' *Roden's Corner* xvii. 178 The wooden, *sulphur-headed matches supplied by the *café*. **1891** FARRAR *Darkn. & Dawn* lvii, The pale *sulphur-impregnated waters of the river Albula. **1802** COLERIDGE *Let. to Southey* 25 Dec., The Devil *sulphur-roast them! **1867** AUGUSTA WILSON *Vashti* vi, Some red-liveried, *sulphur-scented imp of Abaddon. **1628** MURE *Doomesday* 128 Wks. (S.T.S.) I. 167 Hell's *sulphure-smoking throat. **1728** POPE *Dunc.* I. 235 Ye shall not..*sulphur-tipt, emblaze an Ale-house fire.

8. Special combs.: **sulphur acid**, an old name for sulphides of electronegative metals, as arsenic, antimony; **sulphur alcohol**, a compound of the nature of an alcohol in which sulphur replaces oxygen; **sulphur bacterium** *Biol.*, any of the bacteria which derive their energy from the oxidation of sulphur or inorganic compounds of sulphur; **sulphur bath**, †(*a*) a sulphur-spring; (*b*) a bath to which flowers of sulphur have been added, used in the treatment of skin diseases; **sulphur-cast** = *sulphur-impression*; **sulphur-colour, -coloured** *a.* = *sulphur-yellow* sb. and adj.; also ***sulphur-hued, -tinted***; **sulphur cone** (see quot.); **sulphur cycle** *Ecol.*, the cycle of changes whereby sulphur compounds are interconverted between sulphates and hydrogen sulphide in the air and sulphates, sulphides, and sulphur in organisms and the soil; **sulphur ether**, a compound analogous to ether in which sulphur replaces oxygen; **sulphur-impression**, an impression taken of a seal, medallion, etc. in a composition consisting of sulphur and wax; **sulphur-match**, a lucifer match tipped with sulphur; **sulphur-ore**, an ore which yields sulphur, e.g. iron pyrites; so **sulphur-pyrites**; **sulphur print** *Metallurgy*, a print on photographic bromide paper showing the distribution of sulphur as sulphides in a steel surface with which it has been placed in contact; **sulphur rain** (see quot.); **sulphur salt**, an old name for a salt produced by the combination of a 'sulphur acid' with another metallic base; **sulphur shower** = *sulphur rain*; **sulphur soap**, a medicinal soap containing elemental sulphur for use in treating skin complaints; **sulphur-spring**, a spring containing compounds of sulphur or impregnated with sulphurous gases; **sulphur-tree**, a hardwooded tree, *Morinda lucida*, found in West Central Africa and used for building purposes; **sulphur-weed** = SULPHURWORT; **sulphur-work(s**, a sulphur manufactory; **sulphur-yellow** *sb.* and *a.*, (of) the pale-yellow colour characteristic of sulphur.

1836 T. THOMSON *Min., Geol.*, etc. II. 507 The compounds which it [*sc.* sulphur] forms with arsenic and antimony..constitute *sulphur acids. **1868** WATTS *Dict. Chem.* V. 643 Sulphur-acids, or Sulphanhydrides. **1876** *Encycl. Brit.* V. 553/1 *Sulphur, Selenium, and Tellurium Alcohols and Ethers. **1891** A. B. GRIFFITHS *Res. on Micro-Organisms* viii. 179 All belong to the class of '*sulphur-bacteria'..—that is, bacteria which in the presence of free hydrogen-sulphide oxidize sulphur, forming sulphuric acid. **1939** CLEMENTS & SHELFORD *Bio-Ecol.* iii. 101 Hydrogen sulphide is also acted upon by a remarkable group of sulphur bacteria. **1962** W. W. UMBREIT *Mod. Microbiol.* xv. 276/2 There are three major types of photosynthetic bacteria. The first two of them, the thiorhodaceae and the chlorobacteriaceae, are sulfur bacteria. **1979** ARMS & CAMP *Biology* x. 165 Purple and green sulfur bacteria (Thiorhodaceae) use hydrogen gas and hydrogen sulfide (H_2S) as hydrogen donors. **1675** W. SIMPSON (*title*) A Discourse of the *Sulphur-Bath at Knarsbrough in York-Shire. **1843** R. J. GRAVES *Syst. Clin. Med.* xxviii. 355 By the use of sulphur baths,..all were greatly improved. **1891** FARRAR *Darkn. & Dawn* iii, The sulphur baths of Sinuessa. **1909** LE QUEUX *House of Whispers* xxviii. (1913) 195 *Sulphur-casts of seals recently acquired by that institution. **1866** *Treas. Bot.*, *Sulphureus*, *sulphur-colour; a pale bright-yellow, with a mixture of white. **1897** *Daily News* 24

Apr. 6/4 Sulphur-colour goes admirably with tan. **1811** Shaw *Gen. Zool.* VIII. II. 480 A *sulphur-coloured spot beneath each eye. **1899** *Allbutt's Syst. Med.* VIII. 863 Sulphur-coloured scabs. **1842** Francis *Dict. Arts*, **Sulphur Cone*, an electrical experiment and apparatus to prove the effect of separation of the contact of two bodies, occasioning them to show signs of electricity. **1967** *New Scientist* 9 Nov. 333/1 The continuation and evolution of life depends upon a stable eco-system. A characteristic of such a system is that cyclical transformations of the major biological elements take place within it—the carbon cycle, the nitrogen cycle, the *sulphur cycle and so on. **1973** R. G. Krueger et al. *Introd. Microbiol.* xxx. 745/2 Bacteria can carry out each of the processes in the sulfur cycle; bacteria and certain colorless blue-green algae are the only known living agents of the steps involving interconversions of inorganic forms of sulfur. **1977** I. M. Campbell *Energy & Atmosphere* viii. 289 More efficient dispersal of sulphur dioxide at source cannot be regarded as an acceptable long term solution, since that merely transfers the problem to another region or country, the problem intensified by the fact that the anthropogenic term in the sulphur cycle is of the same order of magnitude as the natural terms. **1857** Gosse *Omphalos* vii. 172 Delicate *sulphur-hued flowers. **1840** R. Ellis *Customs* IV. 154 Duties on..*Sulphur Impressions, for every 100*l* value £5 0*s.* 0*d.* **1830** M. Donovan *Dom. Econ.* I. 281 By means of burning *sulphur matches in the casks. **1879** Farrar *St. Paul* (1883) 568 They sold sulphur matches, and old clothes, and broken glass. **1681** Grew *Musæum* III. III. ii. 345 *Sulphur-Ore..if burnt..hath the scent of Brimstone. **1871** *Jrnl. Chem. Soc.* XXIV. 449 On the Roasting of Sulphur Ores, with a New Roasting Oven. **1912** *Jrnl. Iron & Steel Inst.* LXXXV. 380, I have adopted a method which is virtually a modification of the well known method of obtaining a '*sulphur print'. **1977** R. B. Ross *Handbk. Metal Treatments & Testing* 373 Chemical analysis and micro-examination..require laboratory equipment and skilled personnel, whereas the Sulphur print may be used in relatively unsophisticated conditions. **1796** Kirwan *Elem. Min.* (ed. 2) II. 75 The compound of Sulphur and Iron, called Martial Pyrites, or, *Sulphur Pyrites and often simply Pyrites. **1882** H. Edmonds *Elem. Bot.* 132 Often in Fir forests the pollen is given off into the air in such enormous quantities that it is washed down by the rain as a yellow powder, and is popularly known as *sulphur rain. **1836** T. Thomson *Min., Geol.*, etc. II. 507 Sulphur acids..have the property of combining with other metallic sulphurets as bases, and thus of forming what are called *sulphur salts. **1854** Thoreau *Walden* 340 The sulphur-like pollen of the pitch pine soon covered the pond and the stones and rotten wood... This is the '*sulphur showers' we hear of. **1883** *Evang. Mag.* July 311 The so-called 'sulphur-showers' often seen in pine forests. **1894** A. Watt *Art of Soap-Making* xxi. 172 Sir H. Marsh's *Sulphur Soap... A few drops of otto of roses are added to give the soap an agreeable fragrance. **1925** G. Martin *Mod. Soap & Detergent Industr.* II. II. iv. 34 Sulphur soaps, when dissolved in water, slowly evolve sulphuretted hydrogen, which gives them an unpleasant smell. **1953** J. Davidsohn et al. *Soap Manuf.* I. xxii. 505 Sulfur soaps are frequently prepared in combination with beta-naphthol, tar, glycerine and camphor. **1785** T. Jefferson *Notes on Virginia* vi. 59 We are told of a *Sulphur-spring on Howard's creek of Greenbriar. **1811** W. J. Hooker *Jrnl. Tour in Iceland in 1809* 195 We could not resist the present temptation of alighting from our horses, to visit one of the sulphur-springs that lay in our route. **1874** *Jrnl. Chem. Soc.* XXVII. 881 The Sulphur Springs of Trentschin-Teplitz. **1895** *Daily News* 2 Aug. 6/6 *Sulphur-tinted nasturtiums. **1863** R. F. Burton *Abeok. & Camaroons* II. 77 The *sulphur-tree..also called brimstone-tree. **1850** Miss Pratt *Comm. Things Sea-side* i. 67 The Sea *Sulphur-weed. **1870** Kingsley *At Last* ii, In 1836, two gentlemen of Antigua..set up *sulphur works at the Souffrière of St. Lucia. **1816** Stephens in *Shaw's Gen. Zool.* IX. II. 381 Bunting of a blood-coloured rufous; beneath *sulphur-yellow. **1896** W. F. Kirby *Handbk. Order Lepid.* II. 209 Of a yellow colour, varying from light sulphur-yellow to deep orange.

9. a. *attrib.* passing into *adj.* = 'Of the colour of sulphur, sulphur-coloured, sulphur-yellow', chiefly in specific names of animals having sulphur-yellow colouring, as ***sulphur butterfly, cockatoo, parrakeet, pearl***; esp. in parasynthetic comb., as ***sulphur-bellied, -breasted, -crested, -headed*** adjs.; **sulphur-bottom** (whale), Sibbald's rorqual (see Sibbald); **sulphur (-crested) cockatoo**, a white cockatoo, *Kakatoe galerita*, with a yellow crest, native to Australia; **sulphur tuft**, a toadstool, *Hypholoma fasciculare*, with a yellow cap tinged with brown.

1884 Coues *N. Amer. Birds* 431 *Myiodynastes luteiventris*, *Sulphur-bellied Striped Flycatcher. **1782** Crevecœur *Lett. Amer. Farmer* vi. (1783) 111 The *sulphur-bottom, river St. Lawrence, ninety feet long. **1851** H. Melville *Moby Dick* I. xxxi. 221 Adieu, Sulphur-Bottom! **1904** F. T. Bullen *Creat. Sea* xiv. 177 A huge sulphur-bottom whale.. which..attains a maximum length of one hundred and fifty feet. **1934** R. Campbell *Broken Record* iv. 94 These blue whales are the great sulphur-bottoms. **1959** A. C. Hardy *Open Sea* II. xv. 280 It [*sc.* Sibbald's rorqual] has also been called the sulphur-bottom whale on account of a yellowish scum of diatoms which these whales usually carry when they first return to polar waters again after visiting warmer latitudes for breeding. **1909** *Daily Chron.* 6 Feb. 3/3 The *sulphur-breasted toucan. **1879** Jefferies *Wild Life in S. Co.* 207 *Sulphur butterflies hover here early in the spring. **1891** B. G. Johns *Among Butterfl.* 98 The Brimstone or Sulphur butterfly. **1899** *Daily News* 7 Oct. 8/5 White or *sulphur-chain-stitch. **1811** Shaw *Gen. Zool.* VIII. II. 480 Smaller *Sulphur-crested Cockatoo, *Psittacus sulphureus.* **1893** F. F. Moore *I forbid Banns* 73 Did you ever hear a real sulphur cockatoo in its own woods, mister? **1908** E. J. Banfield *Confessions of Beachcomber* I. i. 17 Sulphur-crested cockatoos sail down upon the red raiment of the tree. **1963** *Times* 8 June 14/3 Probably the most talkative..is one of the four sulphur-crested cockatoos. **1842** Loudon *Suburban Hort.* 626 *Sulphur-headed [cauliflower], of which the best variety is the Portsmouth. **1811** Shaw *Gen. Zool.* VIII. II. 428 *Sulphur Parrakeet. **1832** J. Rennie *Butterfl. & M.* 152 The *Sulphur Pearl (*Margaritia palealis*, Stephens). **1909** E. W. Swanton *Fungi* 115 '*Sulphur-tuft'... Taste intensely bitter. Poisonous. **1979** *Country Life* 25 Oct. 1423/1 The fruiting bodies of sulphur tuft..also grow on tree stumps. **1829** T. C. Haliburton *Hist. & Statistical Acct. Nova Scotia* II. ix. 404 Fish-Whale Species. *Sulphur Whale. *a* **1860** J. W. Dawson in *Borthwick's Br. Amer. Rar.* 221 Another rorqual..is known from its yellow belly as the sulphur-whale.

†**b.** as *adj.* Sulphureous, sulphurous. *Obs*

1594 Marlowe & Nashe *Dido* II. i, Came Hector's ghost, With ashy visage, blueish sulphur eyes. **1596** *Edward III*, III. i. 121 Stir, angry Nemesis, the happie helme, That, with the sulphur battels of your rage, The English Fleete may be disperst and sunke.

sulphur ('sʌlfə(r)), *v.* [f. sulphur *sb.* Cf. F. *soufrer*, Du. *solferen, sulferen.*]

In Urquhart's *Rabelais* (1653) I. xvii. 'sulfured, hopary-mated, moiled and bepist' renders *folfré et habaliné* of the original. Urquhart's copy of the French no doubt had *solfré*, the reading of the first ed. and app. the source also of Cotgrave's *solfié* (glossed 'solfaed; also, distempered'). Modern editors explain *folfré* as = made mad.

1. *trans.* To fumigate with burning sulphur, e.g. for the purpose of bleaching goods, disinfecting, preventing fermentation in casks; to sprinkle (plants) with flowers of sulphur to prevent mould or the like; also, to put (wine) into casks that have been fumigated with sulphur.

1759 *Phil. Trans.* LI. 363 *note*, When the stockings were perfectly new, or the black dipt afresh, and the white newly cleaned and sulphured. **1830** M. Donovan *Dom. Econ.* I. 281 For the purpose of sulphuring wines. **1867** Bloxam *Chem.* 198 Casks for wine or beer are sulphured in order to prevent the action of any substance contained in the pores of the wood. **1883** Stratton *Hops & Hop-pickers* 24 Sulphuring the hop is frequently used to destroy mould insects. **1888** *Encycl. Brit.* XXIV. 608/1 Immediately after ..they blossom the vines are sulphured, to keep off the *Oidium*.

2. To treat with sulphur waters. *rare.*

1837 Ht. Martineau *Soc. Amer.* I. 255 The season had not begun, few having been yet sufficiently sulphured and bathed elsewhere to come here to be braced.

3. To fasten firmly with molten sulphur. *rare.*

1867 *Chambers' Jrnl.* Sept. 624/1 An iron hook sulphured into a small glass flask.

sulphur-. In words in the Dict. beginning thus the second 'u' when unstressed is marked with the pronunc. (-jʊə-); this is now often pronounced (-ə-).

'**sulphurage.** *rare.* [f. sulphur *sb.* + -age.] = sulphuring 2.

1851 *Butler, Wine-dealer*, etc. 28 This *muet* never ferments, or if it show the slightest sign of doing so, the sulphurage is renewed.

†'**sulphurate**, *a. Obs. rare.* [ad. late L. *sulphurātus*, f. *sulphur*: see -ate². Cf. It. *solforato.*] Made or consisting of, or resembling, sulphur; containing sulphurous gases.

1660 H. More *Myst. Godl.* v. xvi. 189 A pale sulphurate colour. **1662** Charleton *Myst. Vintners* (1675) 182 A fresh Cask, newly fumed with a Sulphurate Match. **1666** W. Boghurst *Loimogr.* (1894) 28 Taking..strong waters, sulphurate, and Plague waters.

sulphurate ('sʌlfjʊəreɪt), *v. rare.* [f. sulphur + -ate³, or back-formation from next.] *trans.* To combine with, or convert into, sulphur; to impregnate with, or subject to the action of, sulphur.

1757 tr. *Henckel's Pyritologia* xiii. 248 When I would try to make ores from metals..I am obliged to use metallic earths, or formal metals, also real sulphur and arsenic, in order either to arsenicate, or sulphurate the former. **1852** Burn *Naval & Milit. Dict.* II. (1863) 277/1 Sulphurate, *soufrer, ensoufrer; convertir en sulfure.*

sulphurated ('sʌlfjʊəreɪtɪd), *ppl. a.* [f. late L. *sulphurātus* sulphurate *a.* + -ed¹.]

†**1.** Sulphurous. (In fig. context.) *Obs.*

1609 [Bp. W. Barlow] *Answ. Nameless Cath.* 165 The sulphurated fuell of all disloyaltie.

2. Chiefly *Chem.* Combined or impregnated with sulphur: applied chiefly to sulphides. †***sulphurated hydrogen gas***: hydrogen sulphide, sulphuretted hydrogen. (Survives chiefly in terms of the Materia Medica.)

1747 tr. *Astruc's Fevers* 269 The sulphurated oil of juniper. **1757** tr. *Henckel's Pyritologia* ix. 133 Sulphurated ores. **1790** Kerr tr. *Lavoisier's Elem. Chem.* I. 111 The sulphurated hydrogen gas. **1825** J. Nicholson *Oper. Mech.* 768 The sulphurated mass being brought into fusion. **1868** Royle & Headland *Mat. Med.* (ed. 5) 89 *Potassa sulphurata* ..Sulphurated Potash. Sulphuret (or Sulphide) of Potassium... The Sulphuret of Potassium was formerly known by the name of Liver of Sulphur. **1890** Billings *Nat. Med. Dict.*, *Sulphurated bath*,..Sulphurated potassa 2, water 100 parts; dissolve. *Ibid.*, *Sulphurated oil*, balsam of sulphur. *Ibid.*, *Sulphurated water*,..a solution of sodium mono-sulphide and sodium chloride.

†**3.** = sulphured 2. *Obs.*

1752 *Chambers' Cycl.*, Sulphurated Wine.

sulphuration (sʌlfjʊə'reɪʃən). Now *rare* or *Obs.* [f. sulphur *v.* or sulphurate *v.*: see -ation. Cf. F. *sulfuration.* (L. *sulfurātio* = vein of sulphur.)]

1. Anointing with sulphur. *rare.*

1713 Bentley *Rem. Freethinking* §50 Charms, sulphurations, dippings in the sea.

2. Fumigation with sulphur; = sulphuring 2.

1791 Hamilton *Berthollet's Dyeing* I. I. III. x. 294 Sulphuration [is] exposure to the vapour of sulphur. **1839** Ure *Dict. Arts* 1218 *Sulphuration*, is the process by which woollen, silk, and cotton goods are exposed to the vapours of burning sulphur, or to sulphurous acid gas. **1853** R. Hunt *Man. Photogr.* 93 When the paper is nearly..dry, it must be exposed in a closed vessel to sulphuretted hydrogen gas... It is then a second time submitted to sulphuration. **1858** [see sulphuring *vbl. sb.* 2].

3. Combination with sulphur.

1796 Kirwan *Elem. Min.* (ed. 2) II. 511 Pelletier says 100 parts Tin weigh after Sulphuration 116,5. **1826** Henry *Elem. Chem.* I. 531 A sulphuret of the first degree of sulphuration. **1834** Turner *Chem.* (1847) 425 The two lowest degrees of sulphuration, the tetrasulphuret and disulphuret.

4. Treating with sulphur, vulcanization.

1853 Ure *Dict. Arts* (ed. 4) I. 366 The sulphuration of caoutchouc, a valuable invention.

sulphurator ('sʌlfjʊəreɪtə(r)). [See sulphurate *v.* and -or.] An apparatus for sprinkling plants with flowers of sulphur, fumigating with sulphur, or the like.

1851 *Catal. Great Exhib.* IX. I. 366/2 Sulphurator and fumigator, to diffuse powdered sulphur for destroying mildew. **1884** Ogilvie, *Sulphurator*,..an apparatus for fumigating or bleaching by means of the fumes of burning sulphur. **1913** Dorland *Med. Dict.* 921/1 *Sulphurator*, an apparatus for applying sulphur fumes, as in disinfecting.

†'**sulphure.** *Chem. Obs.* [a. F. *sulphure, sulfure* (*Nomencl. Chimique*, 1787): see -ure.] = sulphide *sb.*

1794 Pearson tr. *Morveau's Chem. Nomencl.* 35-6 Sulphurets, or Sulphures; which were formerly called Hepars or Livers. **1806** S. Parkes *Chem. Catech.* (1819) 544 *Sulphures*, or *Sulphurets*, combinations of alkalies, or metals, with sulphur.

†**sul'phureal**, *a. Obs. rare*⁻¹. [f. L. *sulphureus* sulphureous + -al¹.] Sulphurous. So †**sul'phurean**, †**sul'phureate** *adjs.*

a **1604** Hanmer *Chron. Irel.* (1633) 65 They..sent such a number of damned soules into the sulphureall pits, [etc.]. **1607** R. C[arew] tr. *Estienne's World of Wonders* A 2, Those tartarean woods, and sulphurean lakes. *c* **1620** T. Robinson *Mary Magd.* 758 Though vnto yᵉ poyson'd lake shee went, Vncapable shee was of yᵉ sulphurean sent. **1632** Lithgow *Trav.* I. 21 The Sulphurean mountaine. *Ibid.* IX. 391 A sulphureat Riuer.

sulphured ('sʌlfəd), *ppl. a.* [f. sulphur *sb.* + -ed, after late L. *sulphurātus.*]

1. Full of, or charged with, sulphur; sulphurous.

1605 *Gunpowder Plot* in *Harl. Misc.* (Malh.) III. 15 Sulphured smoke, furious flames, and fearful thunder. **1692** J. Salter *Triumphs Holy Jesus* 22 A fury..Toss'd..a sulphur'd Brand. **1796** R. Polwhele *Influence Local Attachm.* II. xvii, A myriad that escap'd the doom, Cling to the sulphur'd spot. **1801** Moore *Ring* 211 A sulphured smoke Came burning in his breath! **1807** J. Barlow *Columb.* III. 358 Storm, thunder, fire, against the mountains driven, Rake deep their sulphur'd sides.

2. Of wine (see quot.).

1728 Chambers *Cycl.* s.v. *Wine*, Sulphur'd Wine, is that put in Casks wherein Sulphur has been burnt; in order to fit it for keeping, or for Carriage by Sea.

3. Bleached by exposure to the fumes of sulphur.

1908 *Anim. Managem.* (Vet. Departm., War Office) Index, Sulphured oats.

†**sulphu'reity.** *Obs.* [ad. mod.L. *sulphureitās*, f. L. *sulphureus* sulphureous: see -ity.] Sulphureous quality or nature.

1610 B. Jonson *Alch.* II. v. 85 The Aqueitie, Terreitie, and Sulphureitie Shall runne together againe. **1651** French *Distill.* vi. 176 He saith that imperfect bodies have superfluous humidities, and sulphureity generating a combustible blacknesse in them. **1676** *Phil. Trans.* XI. 613 By its sulphureity it will mix it self with the sulphureous salt of calcined Tartar.

sulphureo- (sʌl'fjʊərɪəʊ), used as combining form of L. *sulphureus* sulphureous in the sense of 'sulphureous and...'.

1677 E. Browne *Trav. Germany*, etc. 161 Baths.. esteemed to be Sulphureo-nitrous. **1693** *Phil. Trans.* XVII. 1004 A Sulphureo-saline Spring. **1731** Miller *Gard. Dict.* Y yyy, These sulphureo-aërial Particles in the Leaves. **1754** *Phil. Trans.* XLVIII. 853 The sulphureo-reguline substance. **1871** W. A. Leighton *Lichen-flora* 46 C[*oniocybe*] *furfuracea*, Ach. sulphureous or sulphureo-virescent, apothecia sulphureo-suffused, or with flavo-virescent, naked, elongate stipites.

sulphureous (sʌl'fjʊərɪəs), *a.* Also 6 sulphureus, 8 sulfureous. [f. L. *sulphureus*, f. *sulphur*: see sulphur *sb.* and -eous. Cf. It., Sp., Pg. *sulfureo.*]

1. Of or pertaining to sulphur; full of, containing, or consisting of sulphur.

In the first two quots. the reference is to sulphur *sb.* 2.

1626 Bacon *Sylva* §354 There bee two Great Families of Things..Sulphureous and Mercuriall. **1646** Sir T. Browne *Pseud. Ep.* VI. xii. 335 So doth fire cleanse and purifie bodies, because it consumes the sulphureous parts, which before did make them foule. *a* **1691** BOYLE *Hist. Air* (1692) 60 A very sulphureous Soil. **1731** in *10th Rep. Hist. MSS. Comm.* App. I. 270 The Millypedes or Wood-lice have a sulphureous spirit in them wch I have known do wonders on weak constitutions. **1774** GOLDSM. *Nat. Hist.* (1862) I. viii. 36 Any sulphureous substance, mixed with iron, produces a very great heat by the admission of water. **1807** BYRON *Elegy on Newstead Abbey* xv, War's dread machines.. dart destruction in sulphureous showers. **1842** LOUDON *Suburban Hort.* 217 Where the air is heated by smoke-flues or by fermenting stable dung, it may be charged with sulphureous or other noxious gases. **1875** E. WHITE *Life in Christ* IV. xxiv. (1878) 386 The sulphureous rain [fire and brimstone] destroyed them all!

b. Of sulphur springs or waters.

1608 TOPSELL *Serpents* 34 Those sulphureous Bathes which were neere vnto Cameriacum. *a* **1700** EVELYN *Diary* 4 Nov. 1644, Neere the towne is a sulphureous fountaine which continualy boils. **1792** A. YOUNG *Trav. France* I. 25 The patients lie up to their chins in hot sulphureous water. **1797** UNDERWOOD *Dis. Childhood* I. 99 The Harrowgate, or any other sulphureous water will have a good effect. **1835** *Cycl. Pract. Med.* IV. 479/1 Sulphureous mineral waters have been so named from the sulphuretted hydrogen gas with which they are impregnated. **1911** *Encycl. Brit.* XXVI. 61/1 Natural sulphureous waters, especially hot springs, readily deposit sulphur.

†**c.** *Old Path.* Consisting of 'sulphur' as one of the principles of matter; (of disease) arising from 'sulphurous' matter.

1625 HART *Anat. Ur.* II. x. 120 Such diseases as haue their originall from this Sulphureous and salt matter. *Ibid.*, Some sulphureous, Mercuriall, or saltish and tartareous disease. **1688** HOLME *Armoury* III. xii. 439/2 *Cholagoga*, medicines that purge Sulphureous and Bilious humours. **1702** J. PURCELL *Cholick* (1714) 141 The Curative Indications in this Cause are, to divide and break asunder the Sulphureous Filaments, and ill digested Particles of the Aliments.

2. Derived or emanating from sulphur; hence, having the qualities associated with (burning) sulphur; applied chiefly to cloud, smoke, odour.

a **1552** LELAND *Itin.* (1907) II. 142 The water of the baynes ..having sumwhat a sulphureus and sumwhat onpleasant savor. **1594** NASHE *Terrors Night* Wks. 1904 I. 360 A sulphureous stinking smoak. *a* **1700** EVELYN *Diary* 7 Feb. 1645, Gaping..chasms, out of which issued such sulphureous blasts and smoke [etc.]. **1700** DRYDEN *Ovid's Met.* xv. 509 Ætna vomiting sulphureous Fire. **1725** POPE *Odyss.* XII. 492 Sulphureous odours rose, and smould'ring smoke. *a* **1774** GOLDSM. *Surv. Exp. Philos.* (1776) I. 56 The flash is sudden, the noise is loud, a sulphureous smell ensues. **1842** LOUDON *Suburban Hort.* 201 No sulphureous or other disagreeable effluvium is ever given out by hot-water pipes when they become leaky, as is the case with flues when they are not air-tight. **1866** HERSCHEL *Fam. Lect. Sci.* 22 The dense sulphureous vapour that swept down from the mountain.

b. Thundery. *rare.* (Cf. SULPHUROUS 2 b.)

1751 EARL ORRERY *Rem. Swift* (1752) 58 King William in hopes to dispel this sulphureous body of clouds [etc.].

3. *allusively* and *fig.* †**a.** Hellish, satanic. *Obs.*

[**1624** T. TAYLOR *2 Serm.* ii. 24 We..remember not that they digged a sulphureous pit in 1605, wide enough to swallow three whole kingdomes.] **1644** VICARS *God in Mount* 202 The sulphureous and sanguineous or bloody order and fraternity of Romish Jesuites.

b. Full of the 'sulphur' of hell.

1791 HAMPSON *Mem. J. Wesley* II. 69 Hell and damnation has been denounced..in a stile so horribly sulphureous, that [etc.]. **1865** *Pall Mall Gaz.* 22 Apr. 1 They would be under the absolute sway of the most sulphureous preacher of the neighbourhood.

4. Sulphur-coloured; sulphur-yellow. Also, of the bluish colour of the flame with which sulphur burns.

1656 BLOUNT *Glossogr.*, *Sulphureous*,..of the colour of Sulphur or Brimston. **1794** MRS. RADCLIFFE *Myst. Udolpho* xxix, The accumulating clouds..assumed a red sulphureous tinge that foretold a violent storm. **1796** SOUTHEY *Donica* xxvi, The hallow'd tapers dimly stream'd A pale sulphureous light. **1821** JOANNA BAILLIE *Metr. Leg.*, *Ghost of Fadon* xxix, Till the flame..burn'd Of clear sulphureous blue. **1826** KIRBY & SP. *Entomol.* IV. xlvi. 279 Sulphureous (*Sulphureus*). Yellow with a tint of green. **1865** LIVINGSTONE *Zambesi* xii. 258 The evening sun imparts a sulphureous hue.

†**5.** *Chem.* ***sulphureous acid*** (*gas*): sulphurous acid (gas). ***sulphureous hydrogen***: sulphuretted hydrogen. ***sulphureous salt*** (see quot. 1790). ***sulphureous spirit***: ? sulphur dioxide. *Obs.*

1704 J. HARRIS *Lex. Techn.* s.v:, After the Spirit and Oil of Vitriol are in distillation of that Mineral, driven out by a most Violent Fire..into the Receiver. They commonly Rectifie the Matter in a Glass Body; and the first Spirit that rises then with a very gentle degree of Fire, is called the Sulphureous Spirit of Vitriol. **1789** J. K[EIR] *1st Pt. Dict. Chem.* 6/2 The sulphureous acid, and the marine dephlogisticated acid destroy vegetable colours, and change them to white. **1790** KERR tr. *Lavoisier's Elem. Chem.* 222 *note*, The only one of these salts known to the old chemists was the sulphite of potash, under the name of Stahl's sulphureous salt. **1794** PEARSON tr. *Morveau's Chem. Nomencl.* 4 The word Sulfite denotes compounds consisting of the Sulphureous Acid and each of the above twenty-six different kinds of substances. *Ibid.* 30 Sulphur, which by combining with Oxygen and Caloric produces sulphureous Acid Gaz. **1806** *Gazetteer Scot.* (ed. 2) 297/2 Springs, one of which is impregnated with sulphureous hydrogen gas. **1812** SIR H. DAVY *Chem. Philos.* Wks. 1840 IV. 23 He [*sc.* Stahl] discovered..the nature of sulphureous acid.

Hence **sul'phureously** *adv.*, **sul'phureousness.**

1677 [see SULPHURIOUSLY *adv.* quot. 1638]. **1690** T. BURNET *Th. Earth* III. x. II. 83 Sulphureousness of the Soil. *a* **1701** MAUNDRELL *Journ. Jerus.* (1721) 84 The Sulphureousness of its Smell and Taste. **1727** S. HALES *Statical Ess.* (1731) I. 311 In proportion to the sulphureousness and thickness of those fumes. **1906** *Westm. Gaz.* 7 Sept. 2/1 The air still smelt sulphureously.

sulphuret ('sʌlfjʊərɛt). *Chem.* [ad. mod.L. *sulphurētum*: see SULPHUR *sb.* and -URET. Cf. SULPHURE.] = SULPHIDE *sb.* (Now only in Materia Medica and Mining.)

1790 KERR tr. *Lavoisier's Elem. Chem.* 249 One part ore of molybdena, which is a natural sulphuret of that metal, is put into a retort. **1791** HAMILTON *Berthollet's Dyeing* II. II. II. i. 65 Sulphuret of alkali. **1794** PEARSON in *Phil. Trans.* LXXXIV. 395 Sulphuret of lime (calcareous liver of sulphur). **1811** A. T. THOMSON *Lond. Disp.* (1818) 499 The potash combines with the sulphur of the sulphuret of antimony, and forms sulphuret of potash. **1825** J. NICHOLSON *Oper. Mech.* 629 Lead is obtained from ore, and, from its being generally combined with sulphur, it has been denominated 'sulphuret'. **1839** DE LA BECHE *Rep. Geol. Cornwall*, etc. x. 287 The sulphuret of zinc (the Black Jack of the Cornish miners). **1852** ROYLE *Mat. Med.* (ed. 2) 87 *Potassii Sulphuretum*..Sulphuret of Potassium. **1881** RAYMOND *Mining Gloss.*, *Sulphurets*, in miners' phrase, the undecomposed metallic ores, usually sulphides. Chiefly applied to auriferous pyrites. **1895** *Daily News* 25 June 9/5 Tons of sulphurets treated, 398.

attrib. **1877** RAYMOND *Statist. Mines & Mining* 75 Sulphuret-concentration... Sulphuret-reduction. **1882** *Rep. Ho. Repr. Prec. Met. U.S.* 261 A strong vein of sulphuret ore.

sulphuretted ('sʌlfjʊərɛtɪd), *a.* *Chem.* Also †**-eted.** [f. prec. + -ED[2].] Combined chemically with sulphur; impregnated with sulphur.

sulphuretted hydrogen: hydrogen sulphide, H_2S, a colourless gas with a very offensive odour, prepared by the action of diluted hydrochloric or sulphuric acid upon iron (ferrous) sulphide.

1805 W. NISBET *Dict. Chem.* 373 [New name] Sulphuretted Hydrogen Gas, [old name] Hepatic air. **1818** HENRY *Elem. Chem.* (ed. 8) I. 155 Hydrogen gas,..when procured from zinc and dilute sulphuric acid,..is contaminated with sulphureted hydrogen and carbonic acid. **1842** FRANCIS *Dict. Arts*, *Sulphuretted Alcohol*, a solution of sulphur in alcohol; obtained by boiling them together. *Ibid.*, *Sulphuretted Spirit*, a compound of sulphuretted hydrogen and ammonia. **1845** BALLARD & GARROD *Mat. Med.* 396 Sulphuretted Waters. All these contain hydro-sulphuric acid (sulphuretted hydrogen). **1880** BESSEY *Bot.* 63 The sulphuretted essences contain sulphur. To this class belong the essential oils in mustard,..garlic, asafœtida, etc.

sulphuretum (sʌlfə'riːtəm). *Ecol.* Also (*U.S.*) **sulf-.** Pl. **sulphureta, -tums.** [mod.L., f. SULPHUR *sb.* + -ETUM.] An ecological community of organisms, mainly consisting of sulphur bacteria, which metabolizes sulphur compounds in a closed subcycle of the larger environmental sulphur cycle.

1925 L. G. M. BAAS-BECKING in *Ann. Bot.* XXXIX. 615 The natural ecological community of these [sulphur] bacteria is a miniature cycle in itself, and will be called a sulphuretum. **1967** *New Scientist* 9 Nov. 333/2 One such ecosystem is known as the sulfuretum, based primarily on the sulphur bacteria and essentially anaerobic. *Ibid.*, Palaeochemical evidence, based on fractionation of the sulphur isotopes, has shown that sulfureta were active at least 2×10^9 years ago.

sulphuric (sʌl'fjʊərɪk), *a.* [ad. F. *sulfurique* (*Nomencl. Chimique*, 1787): see SULPHUR *sb.* and -IC I.]

1. *Chem.* ***sulphuric acid***, a highly corrosive oily fluid (hydrogen sulphate, H_2SO_4), also called *oil of vitriol*, in its pure state a dense liquid without colour or smell; prepared on a large scale for use in arts and trades by burning iron pyrites or sulphur and leading the fumes, together with oxides of nitrogen and air, over into chambers into which jets of steam are forced.

Formerly used also for sulphur trioxide, ***sulphuric acid gas***, SO_3; also called ***anhydrous sulphuric acid***.

1790 KERR tr. *Lavoisier's Elem. Chem.* 355 Fluid substances, such as sulphuric and nitric acids. **1791** HAMILTON *Berthollet's Dyeing* I. I. I. i. 5 The solution of indigo in the sulphuric (vitriolic) acid. **1794** PEARSON tr. *Morveau's Chem. Nomencl.* 3 These three species are named the Sulphureous, the Sulphuric, and the Oxygenated Sulphuric Acids. **1815** J. SMITH *Panorama Sci. & Art* II. 420 Sulphuric acid is the union of oxygen and sulphur. **1866** ROSCOE *Elem. Chem.* 169 Salt-cake process. This process consists in the decomposition of salt by means of sulphuric acid.

attrib. **1827** FARADAY *Chem. Manip.* xv. (1842) 393 A sulphuric acid bath..may be used with great advantage in the desiccation of particular gases. **1843** R. J. GRAVES *Syst. Clin. Med.* xxvii. 339 Sulphuric acid baths exerted a favourable influence on the eruptions. **1851** *Catal. Great Exhib.* IV. 1077 Sulphuric acid clay, known in trade under the denomination of aluminas. **1876** DUNGLISON *Med. Lex.* s.v. *Sulphuric Acid*, *Sulphuric Acid Lemonade*..is made by adding together sulphuric acid, water, and syrup.

b. With qualifying word, as *concentrated*, *dilute*, *glacial*, *Nordhausen* (see these words).

anhydrous sulphuric acid, sulphur trioxide. ***fuming sulphuric acid***, a mixture of sulphuric acid and sulphur trioxide. ***German sulphuric acid*** = NORDHAUSEN.

1790 KERR tr. *Lavoisier's Elem. Chem.* 272 Concentrated sulphuric acid. **1800** [see GLACIAL 2 b]. **1842** FRANCIS *Dict. Arts* s.v., Nordhausen or German sulphuric acid. **1867** *Chambers' Encycl.* IX. 203/1 *Sulphuric Anhydride*, formerly known as Anhydrous Sulphuric Acid.

c. Related to or derived from sulphuric acid.

sulphuric anhydride: sulphur trioxide. ***sulphuric ether***, ethylic or vinic ether, a compound formed by the action of sulphuric acid upon spirits of wine. ***sulphuric oxide***: sulphur trioxide.

1815 J. SMITH *Panorama Sci. & Art* III. 96 Ether, sulphuric. **1862** MILLER *Elem. Chem.*, *Org.* (ed. 2) iii. §6. 245 The hydrocarbons of this class combine readily with sulphuric anhydride [*ed.* 1857 anhydrous sulphuric acid]. **1868** WATTS *Dict. Chem.* V. 569 Sulphuric Oxide or Anhydride, SO³. Anhydrous Sulphuric Acid. *Ibid.* 576 Sulphuric Chloride, SO²Cl². **1871** TYNDALL *Fragm. Sci.* (1879) I. xvii. 449 For barely visible redness formic aether is more opaque than sulphuric.

†**2.** Consisting of or containing sulphur. *Obs. rare.*

1794 HUTTON *Philos. Light*, etc. 205 In the deflagration of sulphur, while the phlogistic part escapes in light, the proper sulphuric matter is oxigenated. **1811** PINKERTON *Petral.* II. 62 The rocks of common salt, with the bituminous, sulphuric, and metallic.

sulphuriferous (sʌlfjʊə'rɪfərəs), *a.* *rare.* [f. SULPHUR *sb.* + -(I)FEROUS.] Containing sulphur; sulphurous.

1830 *Fraser's Mag.* II. 275 Beelzebub,..a song!..Give ear While Beelzy breathes his sulphuriferous strain. **1859** MAYNE *Expos. Lex.* 1229/1 *Sulphuriferus*, sulphuriferous.

†'**sulphurine,** *a.* *Obs. rare*[−0]. [f. SULPHUR *sb.* + -INE[2]. Cf. OF. *sulfurin*, *sulphurin*, Pg. *sulfurino*.] Sulphurous.

1731 BAILEY vol. II, *Sulphurine*, of or pertaining to, like or of the quality of sulphur.

sulphuring ('sʌlfərɪŋ), *vbl. sb.* [f. SULPHUR *sb.* or *v.* + -ING[1].]

†**1.** The action of dipping in sulphur. *Obs. rare*[−0].

1648 HEXHAM II, *Een besolfferinge*, A Sulphering, or a Dipping in brim-stone.

2. Exposure to the fumes arising from burning sulphur, to produce whiteness in fabrics, to prevent fermentation in casks, to disinfect, etc.

1800 tr. *Lagrange's Chem.* II. 273 Sulphuring serves to give to silk destined for white stuffs, as well as to woollen cloth, the highest degree of whiteness to be obtained. **1830** M. DONOVAN *Dom. Econ.* I. 281 Whatever care is taken in the racking of wines, they will again ferment, unless they undergo the operation of sulphuring. **1858** HOBLYN *Dict. Terms Med.* (ed. 8), *Sulphuration*, *Sulphuring*, the subjection of woollen and other articles to the fumes of burning sulphur, or sulphurous acid, for decolouring or bleaching purposes. **1860** O'NEILL *Chem. Calico Print.* 63 The effect of sulphuring upon woollen goods is not simply that of whitening, it gives also lustre and brilliancy. **1885** HUMMEL *Dyeing Textile Fabrics* 112 Gas Bleaching, Stoving, or Sulphuring.

3. The sprinkling of plants with flowers of sulphur to prevent or destroy mildew.

1891 *Daily News* 28 July 6/6 The only thing which planters have to all appearance to fear is mould, judging from the free application of the process of sulphuring.

4. (See quot.)

1880 J. LOMAS *Alkali Trade* 57 The *bête noire* of sulphuric acid making is 'sulphuring', or 'subliming'. This is caused by the admission of an insufficient amount of air below the grates of the burners, free sulphur being sublimed and carried forward into the chambers, where it floats upon the surface of the acid.

5. *attrib.*

1839 URE *Dict. Arts* 1218 Sulphuring-rooms are sometimes constructed upon a great scale. **1851** *Catal. Great Exhib.* VI. I. 275/2 Sulphuring apparatus. **1860** O'NEILL *Chem. Calico Print.* 64 A sulphuring stove was in constant work within fifty yards of it. **1875** *Encycl. Brit.* III. 822/2 Thom's sulphuring process [of bleaching wool].

†**sul'phurious,** *a.* *Obs.* Also 5 **sulphuryose,** 6 **sulph-, sulfurius,** 8 **sulphrious.** [ad. OF. *sulphurieux* or L. **sulphuriōsus*: see SULPHUR *sb.* and -IOUS.] = SULPHUREOUS, SULPHUROUS.

1471 RIPLEY *Comp. Alch.* VIII. vii. in Ashm. (1652) 172 [That] hys fatnys sulphuryose Be mynyshyd in hym whych ys infectuose. *c* **1550** ROLLAND *Crt. Venus* I. 833 Ouirset with slicht sulphurious, And suddant mort. **1560** —— *Seven Sages* 38 O suttell Serpent sulphurius. **1599** B. JONSON *Ev. Man out of Hum.* v. iii. (Qo. 1600), Spare no sulphurious [*ed.* 1616 sulphurous] jeast that may come out of that sweatie Forge of thine. **1621** BURTON *Anat. Mel.* I. iii. III. i. 268 At Lypara and those sulphurious Isles. **1627** H. BURTON *Baiting Pope's Bull* 13 That Canon of Trent, which dischargeth a sulphurious Anathema against the doctrine. **1631** GOUGE *God's Arrows* I. §23. 30 Even on a sudden was that faire skie turned into a sulphurious and most dismall skie. **1683** *Digby's Chym. Secr.* 46 Filter and evaporate, and you shall have a Sulphurious Salt. **1698** FRYER *Acc. E. India & P.* 235 Through kindled Fires from sulphurious Caverns. **1701** WARWICK *Mem. Chas. I*, 18 A sulphurious vapour flew from an unadvised mouth of Mr. Clement Cooke. **1727** W. MATHER *Yng. Man's Comp.* 390 A remarkable Well, which being emptied, there presently breaks out a Sulphrious Vapour.

Hence †**sul'phuriously** *adv.*

1638 SIR T. HERBERT *Trav.* (ed. 2) 31 Aden is seated low, sulphuriously [*ed.* 1677 sulphureously] shaded by a high barren Mountaine; whose brazen front scorching the miserable Towne, yeelds a perfect character of Turkish basenesse.

sulphurity (sʌl'fjʊərɪtɪ). *rare.* [f. SULPHUR *sb.* + -ITY.] Sulphurousness. ***His Sulphurity***, Satan.

1650 ASHMOLE tr. *A. Dee's Fasc. Chem.* in *Chym. Collect.* ii. 22 Fire extracts that which exists in the interiours of things, and feeds on the sulphurity [orig. *sulphureitatem*] of them. **1915** *Spectator* 14 Aug. 213/1 His Sulphurity stirs supine mankind into fruitful hustling.

sulphurize ('sʌlfjʊəraɪz), *v.* [a. F. *sulfuriser* (Lavoisier, 1789): see SULPHUR *sb.* and -IZE.]

1. *trans.* To cause to combine chemically with, or to be impregnated by, sulphur; to convert into a sulphur compound.

1794 [see SULPHURIZED]. **1815** HENRY *Elem. Chem.* (ed. 7) I. 314 Sulphurized alcohol. **1870** *Eng. Mech.* 4 Mar. 597/2 Re-agents, either oxidising or sulphurising. **1873** HAYNE in Tristram *Moab* 397 Some stumps [of palm-trees] remain not petrified, but, if I may be allowed the expression, 'sulphurised'. **1892** *Photogr. Ann.* II. 173 To further sulphurise bitumen, M. Valenta dissolves 10 grammes of sulphur..in a sufficient quantity of bisulphide of carbon.

2. To treat or dress with sulphur; to vulcanize (rubber).

1846 *Mech. Mag.* 4 July 2/2 Gutta percha either sulphurised or unsulphurised. **1901** *Lancet* 26 Jan. 252/1 Sulphurised catgut.

3. To fumigate with burning sulphur.

1856 MORTON *Cycl. Agric.* I. 466/2 *Sulphurizing.*—The common process by which fermentation is checked..is called sulphuring or stumming. **1868** *Chambers' Encycl.* X. 222/1 Sulphurising is a process which is especially applied to sweet white wines. **1883** HALDANE *Workshop Rec.* Ser. II. 205/2 Large commercial packages..cannot efficiently be sulphurized without..spreading out the contents. *Ibid.*, Tightly-closed sulphurizing chambers.

Hence **'sulphurized** *ppl. a.* (†*sulphurized hydrogen gas* = sulphuretted hydrogen), **'sulphurizing** *vbl. sb.* and *ppl. a.* (see quots. above); **sulphuri'zation**, the action of sulphurizing.

1794 PEARSON in *Phil. Trans.* LXXXIV. 395 The smell of sulphurized hydrogen gaz, (hepatic air). **1796** KIRWAN *Elem. Min.* (ed. 2) II. 455 These [expedients] were Torrefaction, Sulphurization. **1852** *Fraser's Mag.* XLVI. 502 Finally came vulcanization—i.e. sulphurization. **1883** J. ELLIS in *Nat. Temp. Advocate* Sept., Preserved from fermentation..by sulphurization.

sulphurous ('sʌlfjʊərəs, *in Chem. use* sʌl'fjʊərəs), *a.* Also 6 **sulpherus, -urus,** 6–7 **-erous,** 7 **sulferous,** 7–8 **sulph'rous,** 7, 9 (*U.S.*) **sulfurous.** [ad. L. *sulphurōsus* (whence OF. *sulphureux*, from 14th cent.), or f. SULPHUR *sb.* + -OUS. In sense 5 ad. mod.F. *sulfureux* (*Nomencl. Chimique*, 1787).]

1. = SULPHUREOUS 1.

1530 PALSGR. 326/2 Sulpherus, of the nature of brimston, *sulphureux*. **1582** STANYHURST *Æneis* II. (Arb.) 66 Eech path was fulsoom with sent of sulphurus orpyn. **1612** WOODALL *Surg. Mate* Wks. (1653) 221 *Aqua vitæ* is the Sulphurous part of Wine. **1635** SWAN *Spec. Mundi* v. §2 (1643) 122 Lightning..cometh from sulfurous and other poysonous metallick substances. **1686** *Lond. Gaz.* No. 2163/2 Fire-balls, and other Sulphurous Fire-works. **1825** SCOTT *Talism.* i, The slimy and sulphurous substance called naphtha. **1872** CROOKES tr. *Wagner's Handbk. Chem. Technol.* 257 Alum-shale or schist is a sulphurous iron pyrites. **1879** FARRAR *St. Paul* (1883) 484 Amid the sulphurous storm, she gazed back on the voluptuous ease of the City of the Plain.

b. = SULPHUREOUS 1 b.

1815 J. SMITH *Panorama Sci. & Art* II. 489 The waters called sulphurous, contain sulphuretted hydrogen. **1856** PAGE *Adv. Text-bk. Geol.* iii. 34 Sulphurous mud-springs.

2. = SULPHUREOUS 2.

1607 DEKKER *Knt.'s Conjur.* v. G iij, A Sulphurous stench. **1625** tr. *Camden's Hist. Eliz.* II. 420 The Ile of Folgo, which casteth out sulphurous [*ed.* 1630 sulphury] flames. **1683** TRYON *Way to Health* 68 The sulpherous moist Vapours, which are of a fierce and sharp Nature are evaporated. **1748** *Anson's Voy.* I. x. 104 A strong sulphurous stench. **1868** MISS BRADDON *Dead-sea Fruit* ii. I. 18 The sulphurous odours of a brickfield.

b. Applied to thunder and lightning (*poet.*), †hence to thundery or sultry weather. Also *occas.* volcanic. Cf. SULPHUREOUS 2 b.

1603 SHAKS. *Meas. for M.* II. ii. 115 Mercifull heauen, Thou rather with thy sharpe and sulpherous bolt Splits the ..gnarled Oke, Then the soft Mertill. **1610** —— *Temp.* I. ii. 204 Cracks Of sulphurous roaring. **1634** SIR T. HERBERT *Trav.* 7 The weather was very sulphurous and raging hot. **1660** HICKERINGILL *Jamaica* (1661) 4, I have found the Aire as sulferous and hot in England..as in the hottest seasons at Iamaica. **1667** MILTON *P.L.* I. 171 The Sulphurous Hail Shot after us in storm. **1817** SHELLEY *Rev. Islam* II. xiv, A sulphurous hill. **1820** WORDSW. *San Salvador* 5 Sink (if thou must) as heretofore, To sulphurous bolts a sacrifice.

c. Of or belonging to (the smoke of) gunpowder.

1620 DEKKER *Dreame* 6 The Canons Sulphurous thundering. **1622** DRAYTON *Poly-olb.* xxix. 264 When Edenbrough and Leeth, into the air were blown With powder's sulphurous smoke. **1801** CAMPBELL *Hohenlinden* 24 Where furious Frank and fiery Hun Shout in their sulphurous canopy. **1816** BYRON *Siege of Corinth* xxix, From every crevice comes the shot; From every shatter'd window pour The volleys of the sulphurous shower.

3. *allusively* and *fig.* **a.** Pertaining to sulphur or brimstone as an adjunct of hell or the infernal regions; hellish, satanic. Also, pertaining to or dealing with hell-fire.

1602 SHAKS. *Ham.* I. v. 3 When I to sulphurous and tormenting Flames Must render vp my selfe. **1605** —— *Lear* IV. vi. 130 There's hell, there's darkenes, there is the sulphurous pit. **1682** CREECH tr. *Lucretius* III. 26 No Hell, no sulphurous Lakes. **1812** SHELLEY *Devil's Walk* 138 His sulphurous Majesty. **1816** SOUTHEY *Poet's Pilgr.* I. i. 4 Like Satan rising from the sulphurous flood. **1886** H. W. BEECHER in *Christ. World Pulpit* XXIX. 761 Their hands [*sc.* pirates'] are red with blood; their hearts are sulphurous. **1903** J. C. SMITH *R. Wallace* 126 The sulphurous theology of the North of Scotland.

b. In immaterial sense: Fiery, heated.

1611 B. JONSON *Catiline* III. G 3, She ha's a sulphurous spirit, and will take Light at a sparke. *a* **1628** SIR J. BEAUMONT *Agst. Abused Love* 87 And with a pandar's sulph'rous breath inflam'd, Became a meteor, for destruction fram'd. **1650** HUBBERT *Pill Formality* 138 Quenching his sulphurous lust in dirty puddles. **1858** CARLYLE *Fredk. Gt.* x. ii. II. 583 Duc de Rohan rose, in a sulphurous frame of mind.

c. Of language, expression: Characterized by heat; in recent use, blasphemous, profane.

[**1616**: see SULPHURIOUS quot. 1599.] **1828** CARLYLE *Misc.* (1857) I. 78 And so on through many other sulphurous pages. **1865** HOLLAND *Plain Talk* ii. 69 The sulphurous satire which he points with such deadly fire at the very Society which makes him fashionable. **1879** [see SULPHUROUSLY]. **1897** C. MORLEY *Stud. Board Schools* 3 He used strong language..sulphurous words, and the very biggest D's, I was assured.

4. = SULPHUREOUS 4. Also *advb.*

1837 CARLYLE *Fr. Rev.* I. II. viii, Burning sulphurous-blue,..it still shines. **1899** W. T. GREENE *Cage-Birds* 50 The Sulphurous Finch. **1908** *Daily Chron.* 17 June 6/5 Her dress of sulphurous green cloth.

5. *Chem.* Designating compounds in which sulphur is present in a larger proportion than in sulphuric compounds. ***sulphurous acid***: (*a*) more fully, ***sulphurous acid gas*** (†*air*), an old name for sulphur dioxide; (*b*) the acid (H_2SO_3) resulting from the combination of sulphur dioxide with water. ***sulphurous oxide*** or ***anhydride***: sulphur dioxide, SO_2, a transparent colourless gas with a pungent and suffocating smell, obtained by burning sulphur in dry air or oxygen. Hence, designating compounds derived from sulphurous acid, as ***sulphurous chloride, ether***.

1790 KERR tr. *Lavoisier's Elem. Chem.* Pref. p. xxviii, The sulphurous combinations. *Ibid.* 223 The sulphurous acid is formed by the union of oxygen with sulphur by a lesser degree of oxygenation than the sulphuric acid. **1812** SIR H. DAVY *Chem. Philos.* Wks. 1840 IV. 25 Sulphureous acid air. **1823** FARADAY *Exp. Res.* xx. 89 Mercury, and concentrated sulphuric acid were sealed up in a bent tube and..heat was carefully applied. Sulphurous acid gas was produced where the heat acted. **1848** FOWNES *Man. Elem. Chem.* (ed. 2) 392 Sulphurous ether; AeO,SO_2. **1868** WATTS *Dict. Chem.* V. 540 Sulphurous Oxide, or Sulphurous Anhydride, SO^2. *Ibid.* 542 Sulphurous Chloride, $SOCl^2$. Chloride of Thionyl. Sulphurous Chloraldehyde. **1897** H. ALDERSMITH *Ringworm* (ed. 4) 185 Sulphurous acid..is an excellent parasiticide.

Hence **'sulphurously** *adv.*, in a sulphurous manner; *esp.* with 'sulphurous' language.

1879 FRANCES H. BURNETT *Haworth's* II. vii. 81 Haworth stopped him by swearing again, something more sulphurously than before. **1891** FARRAR *Darkness & Dawn* II. 218 The morning dawned sulphurously hot. **1897** ANNE PAGE *Afternoon Ride* 73 Dr. Browne sulphurously insisting on his wife receiving this 'lady' with cordiality.

†**sulphur vif, vive.** *Obs.* [a. OF. *sou(l)fre vif*: see SULPHUR *sb.* and VIVE.] = next.

c **1400** MAUNDEV. (Roxb.) vii. 25 þe preste..lays þerapon diuerse spiceries and sulphure viue [*ed.* 1839, v. 48 Sulphur vif]. **1471** RIPLEY *Comp. Alch.* IV. vi. in Ashm. (1652) 145 Mercury and Sulphure vive. **1540** tr. *Vigo's Lyt. Pract.* A viij b, Take a quantytie of Sulpher vyfe. **1601** HOLLAND *Pliny* II. 556 The sulphur-vif is digged out of the mine such as we see, that is to say, transparent cleere, and greenish. **1683** *Digby's Chym. Secr.* 5 Sulphur-vive, which is clear and transparent in pieces.

‖**sulphur vivum** ('sʌlfə 'vaɪvəm). [L., = living sulphur.] Native or virgin sulphur; also, in a fused, partly purified form (see quot. 1855).

1651 FRENCH *Distill.* iii. 69 Take of Sulphur vivum as much as you please. **1728** CHAMBERS *Cycl.* s.v. *Sulphur*, *Sulphur Vivum* is thus called, as being such as it is taken out of the Mine. **1855** J. SCOFFERN in *Orr's Circ. Sci., Elem. Chem.* 337 The first rough process of purification consists in exposing the sulphureous materials to a temperature above the fusing point of sulphur... The fused sulphur, brought to this condition, is poured off and allowed to consolidate. It is still far from pure, and is known in commerce under the name of sulphur vivum.

sulphurwort ('sʌlfəwɜːt). [f. SULPHUR *sb.* + WORT. Cf. G. *schwefelwurz*.] An umbelliferous plant, *Peucedanum officinale*, having pale-yellow flowers; hog's fennel.

marsh sulphurwort, *P. palustre*.

1578 LYTE *Dodoens* 298 Of Horestrange or Sulphurwort. **1597** GERARDE *Herbal* II. ccccx. 896 Sulphurwoort or Hogs Fennell, hath a stiffe and hard stalke full of knees or knots. **1627** MAY *Lucan* IX. 1049 Sicilian Thapsos burn'd with Sulphurwort. **1777** JACOB *Cat. Plants* 83. **1858** IRVINE *Illustr. Handbk. Brit. Plants* 596. **1906** *Essex Rev.* XV. 167 The rare sulphur-wort..is still abundant at Landermere.

sulphury ('sʌlfərɪ), *a.* Also 6 **sulfery, sulpherie,** 6–7 **sulphrie, sulph'ry,** 7 **sulfrie, sulphory,** 7, 9 (*U.S.*) **sulfury.** [f. SULPHUR *sb.* + -Y.]

1. Consisting of, containing, or impregnated with sulphur; = SULPHUROUS 1.

1580 FRAMPTON *Dial. Yron & Steele* 154 The yron hath more force, bycause it is not cleane of the sulpherie partes. **1612** DRAYTON *Poly-olb.* iii. 200 That Bathonian Spring, Which from the sulphury mines her med'cinal force doth bring. **1683** PETTUS *Fleta Min.* I. (1686) 34 The gross Sulphury oars. **1686** GOAD *Celest. Bodies* III. ii. 429 Planetary Warmth..may stir the Nitrous Spirit, as well as enflame the Sulfury Particle. **1799** [see SULPHUR 4 b]. **1861** GEIKIE *Edward Forbes* x. 289 The *Statice* clustered along the banks of a sulphury pool. **1892** *Daily News* 23 Sept. 3/2 Sulphury iron.

2. = SULPHUREOUS 2 a.

1614 GORGES *Lucan* VII. 267 The sulfrie aire rusts murdring steele. **1630** [see SULPHUROUS *a.* 2, quot. 1625]. **1697** DRYDEN *Æneid* IV. 555 Dido shall come, in a black Sulph'ry flame. **1812** H. & J. SMITH *Rej. Addr.* viii. 51 Sulphury stench and boiling drench. **1823** PRAED *Troubadour* II. 553 What a villanous, odious, sulphury smell!

b. = SULPHUROUS 2 b.

c **1611** CHAPMAN *Iliad* XIII. 225 A fierie Meteor, with which, Ioues sulphrie hand Opes heauen. *c* **1620** Z. BOYD *Zion's Flowers* (1855) 50 High mountains..have..shops for sulphr'y thunder. **1648** J. BEAUMONT *Psyche* XII. xxxvii. Wks. (Grosart) II. 3 Had Sicily Her Etna lost, this sulphury Region Would shew it her in multiplicity. **1812** BYRON *Ch. Har.* I. xxxviii, Death rides upon the sulphury Siroc. **1854** B. TAYLOR *Lands Saracen* 77 (Cent.), A hot, sulphury haze.

c. Pertaining to gunpowder.

1823 BYRON *Island* III. i, The fight was o'er,..and sulphury vapours upward driven Had left the earth, and but polluted heaven. **1881** PALGRAVE *Vis. Eng.* 274 Iron hailing of pitiless death from the sulphury smoke.

3. a. = SULPHUROUS 3 a.

1630 J. TAYLOR (Water P.) *Jacke-a-Lent* Wks. I. 115/1 The sulphory Necromanticke Cookes. **1648** J. BEAUMONT *Psyche* VIII. ccxii, His [*sc.* Lucifer's] sulphury face. *Ibid.* xv. xlvii, Mighty Terror stopp'd the sulphury road Of their rank breath [*sc.* of the peers of hell]. [**1751** WARBURTON *Pope's Donne Sat.* iv. 184 *note*, They both call out as if they were half stifled by the sulphury air of the place.]

b. = SULPHUROUS 3 b.

1593 MARLOWE & DEKKER *Lust's Dominion* II. v, Sulphury wrath Having..entred into Royall brests: Mark how it burns.

4. = SULPHUREOUS 4.

1900 B. D. JACKSON *Gloss. Bot. Terms* 260/2 *Sulphurinus*, sulphury in tint. **1903** *19th Cent.* Dec. 971 The common Dutch black and sulphury grapes. **1905** E. CHANDLER *Unveiling of Lhasa* xiv. 266 The willows were mostly a sulphury yellow.

sulphuryl ('sʌlfjʊərɪl). *Chem.* Also **-yle.** [f. SULPHUR *sb.* + -YL.] The radical SO_2.

1867 BLOXAM *Chem.* 198 SO_2Cl... It is sometimes called chlorosulphuric acid... It is also known as chloride of sulphuryle. **1880** CLEMINSHAW *Würtz' Atom. The.* 199 That the substituting value of sulphuryl is twice that of acetyl.

attrib. **1869** ROSCOE *Elem. Chem.* 135 Sulphur dioxide unites with chlorine to form sulphuryl chloride, Cl_2SO_2.

sulphydrate (sʌlf'(h)aɪdreɪt). *Chem.* Also **sulf-, sulph-hydrate.** [f. SULPH- + HYDRATE *sb.*, after F. *sulfhydrate*.] A salt of sulphydric acid or hydrogen sulphide; a compound of a metallic atom or radical with the group SH; a hydrosulphide.

1852 tr. *Regnault's Elem. Chem.* II. 539 Sulfhydrate of sulphide of potassium KS, HS. **1859** MAYNE *Expos. Lex.* 1226/2 *Sulphhydrate*, term for a genus of salts resulting from the combination of hydric sulphide with sulphobases. **1868** *Fownes' Elem. Chem.* (ed. 10) 223 Alkaline sulph-hydrates. **1881** *Athenæum* 29 Jan. 169/1 Sulphydrate of Potassium.

sulphydric (sʌlf'(h)aɪdrɪk), *a. Chem.* Also **sulf-, sulph-hydric.** [f. SULPH- + HYDRIC, after F. *sulfhydrique*.] = SULPHURETTED. ***sulphydric acid (gas)***: hydrogen sulphide, sulphuretted hydrogen. ***sulphydric ether*** (see quot. 1852).

1838 *Proc. Amer. Philos. Soc.* I. 84 Sulphydric acid produced a slight discoloration. **1842** *Civil Eng. & Arch. Jrnl.* V. 137/2 He had succeeded in depriving gas..of its ammonia and its sulph-hydric acid. **1852** tr. *Regnault's Elem. Chem.* II. 538 Sulfhydric Ether C_4H_5S..is prepared by passing chlorohydric ether through an alcoholic solution of monosulphide of potassium.

sulphydryl (sʌlf'(h)aɪdrɪl). *Chem.* Also (*U.S.*) **sulfhydryl.** [f. SULPHYDRIC + -YL.] The radical SH; = MERCAPTO(-) b, THIOL b.

1901 DORLAND *Med. Dict.* 653/1. **1924** *Biochem. Jrnl.* XVIII. 1020 The sulphydryl compounds are apparently incapable of combining directly with molecular oxygen. **1946** *Nature* 3 Aug. 155/2 Manganese dioxide is reduced with great ease to form divalent manganese ion by sulphydryl compounds, for example, thioglycollic acid. **1978** *Bull. Amer. Acad. Arts & Sci.* Feb. 10 Elwood Jensen had already made important contributions to..our understanding of the role of sulfhydryl groups in protein structure.

Sulpician (sʌl'pɪʃ(ɪ)ən), *sb.* (*a.*) *Eccl.* [ad. F. *sulpicien*, f. (*St.*) *Sulpice* (see def.).] One of a congregation of secular priests founded in Paris in 1642 by the Abbé Olier, priest of the parish of St. Sulpice, mainly for the training of candidates for holy orders; as *adj.*, belonging to this congregation.

1786 tr. *Dulaure's Pogonologia* p. iii. *note*, The Sulpicians alone have withstood this fashion with a laudable resolution. **1850** NEWMAN *Diffic. Anglic.* I. x. (1891) I. 322 A school of opinion..withstood by the Society of Jesus and the Sulpicians. **1892** *Month* Nov. 312 The Sulpician seminary at Issy. **1904** *Q. Rev.* Jan. 289 A text-book written by a Sulpician and published under the *imprimatur* of the Archbishop of New York.

sulpiride ('sʌlpɪraɪd). *Pharm.* [a. F. *sulpiride*, prob. f. *sul(f-* SULPH- + *pir-*, alteration of *pyr-* PYR(O-: see -IDE.] An anti-emetic and neuroleptic drug used in the treatment of gastro-intestinal disorders, vertigo, and psychiatric conditions; *N*-(1-ethylpyrrolidin-2-ylmethyl)-2-methoxy-5-sulphamoylbenzamide, $(C_2H_5)C_4H_6N(CH_3)\cdot NH\cdot SO_2\cdot C_6H_3(OCH_3)\cdot CO\cdot NH_2$.

1970 *Jrnl. Amer. Med. Assoc.* 10 Aug. 1076/1 The new drug sulpiride was tested to determine its effectiveness in the treatment of ulcerative colitis. **1976** *Lancet* 18 Dec. 1358/1 We concluded that sulpiride should be prescribed with care in hypertensive patients. **1979** *Nature* 11 Jan. 94/2 The antipsychotic drugs, molindone and sulpiride, and the antiemetic drug, metoclopramide, are dopamine antagonists when tested in the anterior pituitary or the brain.

sul ponticello: see PONTICELLO b.

sulse: see SUFF *note*.

sultan (ˈsʌltən), *sb.* Also 6 **soltane, 6–7 soltan, sultane, 7 soultan, sultain(e, sulthan, 8–9 sultaun.** [a. F. *sultan* (from 16th c.) or ad. med.L. *sultānus*, ad. Arab. *sulṭān* king, sovereign, queen, power, dominion; cf. med.Gr. σουλτάνος, Pr., Sp. *sultan*, It. *sultano*, Pg. *sultão*. See also the doublet SOLDAN.]

1. The sovereign or chief ruler of a Muslim country; *spec.* (*Hist.*) the sovereign of Turkey. Also formerly, a prince or king's son, a high officer.

1555 EDEN *Decades* (Arb.) 63 *marg.*, The Soltane of Alcayr in Egypte. *Ibid.* 329 Amonge the Tartars,..Chan, signifieth a kynge, Soltan, the soonne of a kynge. **1596** SHAKS. *Merch. V.* II. i. 26 A Persian Prince That won three fields of Sultan Solyman. **1617** MORYSON *Itin.* I. 66 Vpon that side the Sultan of the Turkes incamped. **1634** SIR T. HERBERT *Trav.* 36 Most of [the Mogul of Surat's] Sultans and Captaines are by birth Persians. **1667** MILTON *P.L.* XI. 395 Where The Persian in Ecbatan sate,..or the Sultan in Bizance. **1703** *Lond. Gaz.* No. 3942/1 Sultan Mahomet, eldest Son of the Grand Signior. **1765** BLACKSTONE *Comm.* I. vii. 260 In Turkey, where every thing is centered in the sultan or his ministers. **1844** H. H. WILSON *Brit. India* I. 365 Among these chiefs, one of the most powerful was the Sultan of Yodhyakarta. **1884** *Pall Mall Gaz.* 29 Feb. 1/2 The Sultan of Turkey is the best hated man throughout his dominions.

b. Taken as a type of magnificence; also *attrib.*

1864 ALLINGHAM *Lawrence Bloomfield* xii. 648 The billowy hills, cloud-shadow'd, roll'd Like spotted sultan-serpent, fold on fold. **1901** *Westm. Gaz.* 16 Dec. 12/1 Tennyson..said he considered Norfolk turkeys the very Sultans of their breed.

c. Used with allusion to an Eastern ruler's harem; also *attrib.*

1872 COUES *N. Amer. Birds* 229 The sultan of the dunghill with his disciplined harem. **1887** BOWEN *Virg. Ecl.* VII. 7 Our sultan goat [L. *vir gregis ipse caper*].

2. An absolute ruler; *gen.* a despot, tyrant.

1648 J. BEAUMONT *Psyche* VIII. ccxii, The rouzėd Grot its awful Sultan [*sc.* Lucifer] knew. **1662** WINSTANLEY *Loyal Martyrol.* (1665) 38 Their Sultan Cromwell. **1719** YOUNG *Revenge* II. i, Love reigns a sultan with unrival'd sway. **1848** THACKERAY *Van. Fair* xx, He would be generous-minded, Sultan as he was, and raise up this kneeling Esther. **1855** TENNYSON *Maud* I. xx. i, The Sultan, as we name him.

3. (orig. †*sultan('s) flower*.) Either of two species of sweet-scented annuals, brought originally from the East, usually distinguished as the purple or white sweet sultan, *Centaurea* (*Amberboa*) *moschata*, and the yellow (sweet) sultan, *C.* (*A.*) *suaveolens*.

1629 PARKINSON *Parad.* 327 Cyanus floridus Turcicus. The Sultans flower. **1688** HOLME *Armoury* II. iv. 64/2 The Sultans flower is purple, and the Thrume almost white. **1753** *Chambers' Cycl.* Suppl., App., *Sultan-flower*, a name sometimes used for the *cyanus*, or blue bottle.

1664 EVELYN *Kal. Hort.* June 69 Flowers, in Prime, or yet lasting,..Sultans. **1731** MILLER *Gard. Dict.* s.v. *Cyanus*, The yellow sweet Sultan. **1786** ABERCROMBIE *Gard. Assist.* 116 Many different sorts [of annuals]: such as..sweet sultan. **1871** MORRIS in Mackail *Life* (1899) I. 238 Those sweet sultans are run very much to leaf.

4. A small white-crested species of domestic fowl, originally brought from Turkey. Also *attrib.*

1855 *Poultry Chron.* II. 526 Sultan Cockerel and Two Pullets, quite new, £5. **1885** *Encycl. Brit.* XIX. 645/2.

5. In full ***sultan hen***, etc. (F. *poule sultane*): = SULTANA 6.

1882 'OUIDA' *Maremma* I. 149 The innumerable pools and streams..which are..known only to the sultan-hen and the wild duck. **1884** COUES *N. Amer. Birds* 675 *Ionornis*, Sultan Gallinules.

6. *attrib.* and *Comb.*, as ***sultan-like*** adj. and adv.; **sultan-bird** (see quot.); **sultan pink, red,** a rich dull pink, red; †**sultan('s) flower** (see 3). (See also senses above.)

1899 A. H. EVANS *Birds* 539 *Parus* may be glossy greenish-black and yellow, as in the *Sultan-bird (*P. sultaneus*). **1697** H. ST. JOHN *To Dryden* in *D.'s Virg.*, So, *Sultan-like in your Seraglio stand. **1821** SCOTT *Pirate* xxxix, An arrogant pretender to the favour of the sisters of Burgh-Westra, who only hesitated, sultan-like, on whom he should bestow the handkerchief. **1837** *Lett. fr. Madras* (1843) 48 A turbaned sultan-like creature. **1899** *Daily News* 21 Oct. 7/7 Some such colour as *Sultan pink or tapestry blue. *Mod. Advt.* The World's Classics..Published in..*Sultan-red Leather.

Hence **ˈsultan** *v. intr.*, to rule as a sultan, play the despot, tyrannize.

1886 BURTON *Arab. Nts.* (abr. ed.) III. 409 Here Janshah abode, Sultaning over them for a year and a half.

sultan, variant of SULTANE *Obs.*

sultana (səlˈtɑːnə, sʌl-). Also 7 **sultanna, 9 sultanah**; *pl.* 7 **sultanaes, 7–8 -a's.** [a. It. (Sp., Pg.) *sultana* fem. of *sultano* SULTAN.]

1. a. The wife (or a concubine) of a sultan; also, the queen-mother or some other woman of a sultan's family.

1585 T. WASHINGTON tr. *Nicholay's Voy.* II. xviii. 51 The Sarail of Sultana, wife to the great Turke. **1599** DALLAM in *Early Voy. Levant* (Hakluyt Soc.) 60 One houre after him [*sc.* the Grand Sinyor] came the Sultana his mother. **1625** PURCHAS *Pilgrims* II. IX. xv. §1. 1581 The Queene, the other Sultanaes, and all the Kings women. **1686** *Lond. Gaz.* No. 2198/1 The Grand Signior offers all his Treasure to be employed in the War. The Sultana 4000 Purses, of 500 Crowns each. **1735** SOMERVILLE *Chase* II. 509 The bright Sultanas of his Court Appear. **1736** *Gentl. Mag.* VI. 467/1 A Sultana, inclosed in a Seraglio, shall govern the whole Ottoman Empire. **1822** BYRON *Juan* VI. lxxxix, Rose the sultana from a bed of splendour. **1879** FARRAR *St. Paul* (1883) 231 Had not Hadassah been a sultana in the seraglio of Xerxes?

b. *transf.* and *fig.*

1838 MOORE *Mem.* (1856) VII. 232 Took my place in the front of Nell's box, between two very pretty sultanas she had provided for me, Georgiana O'Kelly and Miss Burne. **1848** THACKERAY *Van. Fair* xlviii, The elderly sultanas of our Vanity Fair. **1850** —— *Pendennis* vii, It was hard..that the matron should be deposed to give place to such a Sultana. **1864** RAWLINSON *Anc. Mon.*, *Assyria* vii. II. 168 The monarch and his sultana.

2. A mistress, concubine.

1702 FARQUHAR *Twin-Rivals* V. i, I'll visit my Sultana in state. **1796** CHARLOTTE SMITH *Marchmont* I. 78 A person who in youth only was superior to his reigning Sultana. **1818** SCOTT *Hrt. Midl.* xxvi, The favourite sultana of the last Laird, as scandal went—the housekeeper of the present. **1885** MOLLOY *Royalty Restored* II. 83 Her card tables were thronged by courtiers eager to squander large sums for the honour of playing with the reigning sultana.

fig. **1813** BYRON *Giaour* 22 The Rose,..Sultana of the Nightingale. **1826** DISRAELI *Viv. Grey* III. vi, Shine on, (bright moon) sultana of the soul!

†3. = SULTANIN. *Obs. rare*$^{-0}$.

1656 BLOUNT *Glossogr.*, *Sultanin*, or *Sultana*, a Turkish coin of gold worth about Seven shillings six pence.

†4. = SULTANE 3. *Obs.*

a **1693** *Urquhart's Rabelais* III. xlvi, Those great Ladies..with their Flandan, Top-knots and Sultana's. **1693** SOUTHERNE *Maid's last Prayer* II. i, [It] wou'd as ill become me, as a Sultana does a fat body.

†5. A Turkish war-vessel. (Cf. SULTANE 4.) *Obs.* exc. *Hist.*

1728 CHAMBERS *Cycl.* s.v., Sultana is also a Turkish Vessel. **1733** BUDGELL *Bee* I. 74 The Grand Seignior is equipping a Squadron of Ten Sultana's. **1738** *Gentl. Mag.* VIII. 167/2 The Fleet for the Black Sea will be reinforc'd by several Sultanas. [**1810** *Naval Chron.* XXIV. 377 The term *Sultana* is a nonentity.] **1935** P. P. ARGENTI *Occupation of Chios by Venetians* (*1694*) p. xxxix, The enemy fleet..consisted of twenty great sultanas, and thirty galleys and galliots, all under the command of the *Capoudàn Pasha*.

6. Any bird belonging to either of the genera *Porphyrio* and *Ionornis*, found chiefly in the W. Indies, southern U.S.A., and Australia; the purple gallinule or porphyrio. Also *attrib.*

1837 *Partington's Brit. Cycl.*, *Nat. Hist.* II. 609/2 Sultana Hen (*Gallinula porphyrio*). **1840** *Cuvier's Anim. Kingd.* 249 The Common Sultana (*Fulica porphyrio*, Lin.), a beautiful African species. **1870** GILLMORE tr. *Figuier's Reptiles & Birds* 297 The Hyacinthine Gallinule..or Sultana Fowl, is ..an exaggeration of the Water Hen. **1872** DOMETT *Ranolf* XIV. iv, Black Sultana-birds.

7. In full ***sultana raisin***: A kind of small seedless raisin produced in the neighbourhood of Smyrna and other parts of Turkey, Greece, and Australia.

1841 *Penny Cycl.* XIX. 274/1 Muscatels, blooms, sultanas, raisins of the sun, and lexias. **1855** E. ACTON *Mod. Cookery* (rev. ed.) xxi. 442 Sultana raisins are well adapted to these puddings, as they contain no pips. **1873** *Punch* 27 Dec. 262/1 Oysters, forcemeat balls, plovers' eggs, and Sultana raisins. **1886** *Encycl. Brit.* XX. 258/2 Sultana seedless raisins are the produce of a small variety of yellow grape. **1920** C. L. T. BEECHING *Mod. Grocer & Provision Dealer* III. viii. 163 The sultana raisin may be said to share in the good qualities of both the currant and the Valencia. **1938** C. J. ELLIOTT *Retail Grocery Trade* xii. 108 The Australian sultana is a little larger than the Turkey and Smyrna variety. **1966** A. UTTLEY *Recipes from Old Farmhouse* 58 Add one ounce of sugar and one ounce of sultanas.

8. A confection of sugar.

[**1706** PHILLIPS (ed. Kersey), *Sultane* (Fr.),..among Confectioners, a kind of Sugar-work made of Eggs, Powder-sugar, and fine Flower.] **1862** FRANCATELLI *Royal Eng. & For. Confect.* 282 A Sultana made of Spun Sugar in the form of a Summer Bower.

9. (See quot.)

1875 STAINER & BARRETT *Dict. Mus. Terms*, *Sultana*, a violin with strings of wire in pairs, like the cither or cittern. It was similar to the *Streichzither*.

10. = *busy Lizzie* s.v. BUSY *a.* 11; *patient Lucy* s.v. PATIENT *a.* 5.

1938 M. K. RAWLINGS *Yearling* xxvi. 360 The church was decorated with..donations of house plants; sultanas and geraniums, aspidistras and coleas [*sic*]. **1977** [see PATIENT *a.* 5].

11. *attrib.* and *Comb.*: **sultana grape**, the white seedless grape from which sultanas are made; **sultana mother**, the mother of the reigning sultan; **sultana queen**, the favourite concubine of a sultan; hence, a favourite mistress; also *fig.* (See also 6 and 7.)

1861 MRS. BEETON *Bk. Househ. Managem.* 666 *Sultana Grape... The white or yellow grape..produces the Sultana raisin. **1931** C. L. T. BEECHING *Law's Grocer's Man.* (ed. 3) 513/2 The vine which grows the sultana grape is vigorous and upright. **1979** *Illustr. London News* Jan. 66/3 The sultana grape vineyards start a few kilometres to the east of Ayios Nikolaos. **1695** *Lond. Gaz.* No. 3088/2 Who was advanced to that Station by the Interest of the *Sultana Mother. **1753** HANWAY *Trav.* (1762) II. XIII. vii. 326 The greatest part..he sent to the sultan, the sultana mother, and the kislar aga. **1668** DRYDEN *Secret Love* III. i, You are my *Sultana Queen, the rest are but in the nature of your Slaves. **1845** DISRAELI *Sybil* V. i, The victim of sauntering, his sultana queen.

Hence **sulˈtanaship**, the position of a sultana.

1847 JAMES *Russell* vi, 'Very well, then,' he rejoined, with a bitter sneer, 'you will soon be one of a harem! I wish you joy of your sultanaship!'

sultanate (ˈsʌltəneɪt). [f. SULTAN *sb.* + -ATE[1]. Cf. F. *sultanat*.]

1. A state or country subject to a sultan; the territory ruled over by a sultan.

1822 tr. *Malte-Brun's Universal Geogr.* I. xxii. 590 It would be rather interesting to enumerate the various denominations which designate the different states. The use of the terms empire, kingdom, sultanat, khonet, and others, will be learnt in the descriptive part of this work. **1879** A. R. WALLACE *Australasia* xvii. 337 The independent sultanate of Achin. **1880** K. JOHNSTON *Lond. Geogr.* 392 The island of Zanzibar, which forms a central point of the Sultanate.

2. The office or power of a sultan.

1884 *Pall Mall Gaz.* 29 Dec. 1/1 The shadow of the Sultanate is not favourable to the growth of capable successors. **1896** MARQ. SALISBURY in *Times* 10 Nov. 5/1 Through the channel of the Sultanate.

†**sultane.** *Obs.* Also 7 **sultain(e, 7–8 sultan.** [ad. F. *sultane* (Cotgr., 1611), fem. of *sultan* (see SULTAN). Cf. SULTANA.]

1. = SULTANA 1.

1660 F. BROOKE tr. *Le Blanc's Trav.* 79 The King..gave them great commands in his Army,..one of them married the Sultane of Bisnegar. **1694** *Lond. Gaz.* No. 2986/2 The Grand Signior and all the Sultanes coming to the Wedding.

2. = SULTANIN.

1612 JAS. I *Proclam. conc. Bringing of Gold* etc. *into the Realm* 14 May, For Sultaines being xxiij. Carrots, i. graine fine, at least the ounce. iij.li. viij.s. viij.d. **1613** T. MILLES tr. *Mexia's* etc. *Treas. Anc. & Mod. T.* I. 768/2 A Sultain of Gold. **1632** LITHGOW *Trav.* VII. 301 Fiue Sultans of gold..amounting to thirty fiue shillings sterling. **1704** J. PITTS *Acc. Moham.* vii. 91 A Sultane, *i.e.* nine or ten Shilling.

3. A rich gown trimmed with buttons and loops, fashionable in the late seventeenth and the eighteenth centuries.

1689 *Lond. Gaz.* No. 2498/4 A black Sultan with gold buttons and loops. **1690** EVELYN *Mund. Mul.* 2 Nor demy Sultane, Spagnolet, Nor Fringe to sweep the Mall forget. **1732** GAY *Distress'd Wife* V. vii, My Lady will travel in her Sultane, I suppose. **1798** CHARLOTTE SMITH *Yng. Philos.* I. 183 Her muslin Sultane.

4. A Turkish war-vessel.

1695 *Lond. Gaz.* No. 3128/1 Two of the Enemies Ships, called *Sultanes*, were sunk. **1711** *Ibid.* No. 4940/1 All the Fleet is return'd'..., except six Sultans and two Gallies remaining with the Captain-Basha.

5. A sofa, settee. (Cf. OTTOMAN *sb.*[2])

1803 JANE PORTER *Thaddeus* xxvi, I shall have an excuse to squeeze into the *Sultane* which is so 'happy as to bear the weight of Beaufort.'

sultane, obs. form of SULTAN.

sultanesque (sʌltəˈnɛsk), *a.* [f. SULTAN *sb.* + -ESQUE.] Characteristic of a sultan.

1862 G. A. LAWRENCE *Barren Honour* I. vii. 147 After a superb and sultanesque fashion. **1872** *Routledge's Ev. Boy's Ann.* 303/2 His Sultan-esque proposal [of marriage].

sultaness (ˈsʌltənɪs). Now *rare*. Also 7 **sultan(n)esse.** [f. SULTAN *sb.* + -ESS[1].]

1. = SULTANA 1.

1611 COTGR., *Sultane*,..a Sultannesse; or soueraigne Princesse. **1613** PURCHAS *Pilgrimage* III. ix. 240 *marg.*, The Letters of the Great Turke to the Queene, and of the Sultannesse. **1670** *Lond. Gaz.* No. 546/3 The differences between him and the Sultaness his Mother. **1776** *Chron.* in *Ann. Reg.* 114/1 The first and favourite sultaness of the Grand Signior. **1837** HOOD *Desert-Born* 111, I begg'd the turban'd Sultaness the issue to forbear.

b. *attrib.*: **sultaness mother** = *sultana-mother*.

1682 WHELER *Journ. Greece* II. 208 A Royal Mosque, built, and endowed by the Sultaness-Mother. **1796** MORSE *Amer. Geog.* II. 475 She is called asaki sultaness, that is to say sultaness-mother.

†2. = SULTANIN. *Obs.*

1643 HOWELL *Twelve Treat.* (1661) 286 They know the bottom of their servitude by paying so many Sultanesses for every head.

sultanic (sʌlˈtænɪk), *a.* [f. SULTAN *sb.* + -IC.] Of, belonging to, or characteristic of a sultan; hence, despotic, tyrannical.

1827 CARLYLE *Germ. Rom.* I. 208 Princess Melechsala terminated the long series of the Sultanic progeny. **1847** *Blackw. Mag.* LXI. 738 The representative of sultanic dignity. **1878** J. MORLEY *Stud. Lit.* (1891) 301 Those who did not choose to submit to his Sultanic despotism. **1894** *Daily Tel.* 27 Jan. 3/4 Living under conditions of Sultanic luxury.

†**ˈsultanin.** *Obs.* Also 7 **sultanine, -een, -on(e.** [ad. It. *sultanino*, or F. *sultanin* (cf. Pg.

sultanim), ad. Arab. *sulṭānī* SULTANY.] A former Turkish gold coin valued at about 8*s*.

1612 BREREWOOD *Lang. & Relig.* xxv. (1614) 175 The Maronites..pay the Turke large tribute: Namely, for euery one aboue 12 yeares old 17 Sultanines by the yeare. **1617** MORYSON *Itin.* I. 276 In Turkey the gold zechines of Venice are..preferred euen before their owne Sultanones of gold. **1690** DRYDEN *Don Sebastian* I. i, He paid me down for her upon the nail a thousand golden Sultanins. **1694** *Lond. Gaz.* No. 3002/2, 1100 Sultaneens in Gold. **1749** SMOLLETT *Gil Blas* v. i. (1782) II. 182 A present of jewels worth two thousand sultanins of gold.

sultanism (ˈsʌltənɪz(ə)m). [f. SULTAN *sb.* + -ISM.] Rule like that of a sultan; absolute government; despotism, tyranny.

1821 *New Monthly Mag.* II. 354 Our admiration of chivalry and sultanism. **1851** H. MELVILLE *Whale* xxxiii. 161 That certain sultanism of his brain, which had otherwise in a good degree remained unmanifested. **1869** SEELEY *Ess. & Lect.* (1870) 88 Asiatic sultanism was set up, and all public functions fell into the hands of military officials. **1884** —— *Short Hist. Nap. I* (1886) iii. §4. 113 The rising sultanism [of Napoleon in 1804].

sultanist (ˈsʌltənɪst). *rare.* [f. SULTAN *sb.* + -IST.] One who rules as a sultan; an absolute ruler; a despot, tyrant, autocrat.

1659 *Quaeries Prop. Officers Armie to Parl.* 2 The late Sultanist [Oliver Cromwell]..by the assistance of his Mamalukes..assumed the stile of Protector.

sultanize (ˈsʌltənaɪz), *v. rare.* [f. SULTAN *sb.* + -IZE.] **1.** *intr.* To rule as a sultan or despot.

1772 H. WALPOLE *Let. to Mann* 5 Mar., Fifty grand signors have lost their heads for one Charles I., and he might have kept his, if he had not sultanised.

2. *trans.* To make sultan-like or despotic.

1804 J. MACKINTOSH *Let.* 14 Aug. in *Mem.* (1835) I. v. 212 The Governor..is..an..intelligent man; but every Englishman who resides here very long, has..his mind either emasculated by submission, or corrupted by despotic power. Mr. Duncan may represent one genus, the Braminised Englishman; Lord W—— is indisputably at the head of the other, the Sultanised Englishman. **1876** *Hansard Commons* 16 Mar. 103 It was not a wise thing to endeavour even in India to Sultanize the Crown. **1901** *Q. Rev.* Jan. 73 The orientalised, in this case the somewhat sultanised, Englishman.

sultanry (ˈsʌltənrɪ). *rare.* [f. SULTAN *sb.* + -RY.] = SULTANATE 2.

1622 BACON *Adv. touching Holy War* (1629) 129 The Sultanry of the Mamaluches. **1853** *Blackw. Mag.* LXXIII. 732 The first shaking of the Sultanry.

sultanship (ˈsʌltənʃɪp). [Formed as prec. + -SHIP.]

1. = SULTANATE 2. *rare.*

1613 PURCHAS *Pilgrimage* III. ii. 197 The Sultanship of the Chalipha. **1779** FORREST *Voy. N. Guinea* 218 When he resigned the Sultanship to his brother. **1832** *Examiner* 505/1 Pleading for the importation of a Turkish Sultanship.

2. The personality of a sultan; ***his sultanship***, applied as a mock-title to a despot or tyrant.

1822 BYRON *Juan* VIII. cix, They fell..Upon his angry sultanship. **1859** H. KINGSLEY *G. Hamlyn* xxvii, The idea of his having a rival..never entered his Sultanship's head. **1862** MISS BRADDON *Lady Audley* vii, If all the divinities upon earth were ranged before him, waiting for his sultanship to throw the handkerchief.

†**sultany.** *Obs.* Also 7 sultanie, -ee. [ad. Arab. *sulṭānī* adj. imperial, sb. kingdom, sultanin, f. *sulṭān* SULTAN *sb.* Cf. med.L. *soltania.*]

1. = SULTANATE.

1639 FULLER *Holy War* II. xxxv. 89 Two great Lords..fell out about the Sultanie or Vice-royship of that land. **1660** H. MORE *Myst. Godl.* v. xvi. 189 The four Sultanies of the Turkish dominion, Bagdad, Cæsarea, Aleppo, Damascus. **1806** G. S. FABER *Diss. Prophecies* (1814) I. 355 The Euphratean horsemen of the four Turkish Sultanies. **1855** M. BRIDGES *Pop. Mod. Hist.* 205 Bajazet..received from him a patent of sultany.

2. = SULTANIN.

1612 BREREWOOD *Lang. & Relig.* x. (1614) 68 A Sultanie for euery poll. **1615** W. BEDWELL *Arab. Trudg.*, A *Sultanee* is a peece of gold of the value of 7ˢ. 6ᵈ. **1630** *R. Johnson's Kingd. & Commw.* 522 A Sultany is equall to the Chechini of Venice, and sixscore Aspers amount to a Sultanie. **1674** JEAKE *Arithm.* (1696) 134 At..Aleppo, the Exchange is made by Sultanies of 120 Aspers.

sul tasto: see TASTO b.

†ˈ**sulter**, *sb. Obs. rare*⁻¹. In 7 sultre. [f. SULTER *v.*] A spell of sultry weather; in quot. *fig.*

1667 WATERHOUSE *Narr. Fire in London* 116 This Rain of Fertility after Englands Sultre of war and dissension.

†ˈ**sulter**, *v. Obs.* Also 6 sowlter, soulther, 6–7 soulter. [Perhaps for **swulter*, cogn. with SWALTER, SWELTER.] = SWELTER *v.*

1581 [see SULTERING]. **1594** *Sec. Rep. Dr. Faustus* vi. D 3 b, A place..so soultring with hote burning furnaces. **1628** CLAVELL *Recantation* 16 Thus to be furnish'd then, is iust as tho A man should thatch his dwelling house with snow, Which melts, drops, soulters, and consumes away Euen the time of one sun-shining day. **1636** FEATLY *Clavis Myst.* ii. 14 Envy and malice soultred within them, but brake not out into an open flame. **1654** GAYTON *Pleas. Notes* III. i. 64 Horse and Asses tir'd, and soultred with the heat of the day. **1695** BLACKMORE *Pr. Arth.* III. 719 Soultring within, it [*sc.* a mount] casts up Pitchy Smoke.

Hence †ˈ**sultering** *ppl. a.*, sweltering, sultry.

1581 STUDLEY *Seneca's Hercules* IV. 210 Euen now Appolloës sowltring car did fume about my face. *Ibid.* II. Chor., Soulthring fyre. **1594** *Selimus* K 2 When soultring heat the earth's green children spoiles. **1600** HOLLAND *Livy* XXXIV. xlvii. 880 Tedious travaile and soultering heat. **1613** JACKSON *Creed* I. xxiv. 150 All that valley was sultring hotte, and the tops of the mountaines sunke downe. **1628** F. FLETCHER *World Encomp. by Sir F. Drake* 12 We felt the effects of sultring heat.

sulthan, obs. form of SULTAN.

sultrily (ˈsʌltrɪlɪ), *adv.* [f. SULTRY *a.* + -LY².] With sultry or oppressive heat.

1855 BROWNING *Serenade at Villa* 12 Earth turned in her sleep with pain, Sultrily suspired for proof. **1856** MISS WARNER *Hills Shatemuc* xxiv, The day grew sultrily warm.

sultriness (ˈsʌltrɪnɪs). [f. SULTRY *a.* + -NESS.] The quality or condition of being sultry; sultry heat.

1662 J. DAVIES tr. *Olearius' Voy. Ambass.* 8 Yet had they then made a fire, never considering the sultriness of the weather. **1698** FRYER *Acc. E. India & P.* 125, I staid here till Four in the Afternoon to avoid the Sultriness of the Weather. **1748** *Anson's Voy.* II. v. 183 An idea of sultriness and suffocating warmth. **1813** BYRON *Giaour* 300 'Twas sweet of yore to see it [*sc.* the stream] play And chase the sultriness of day. **1886** STEVENSON *Kidnapped* xx, Somewhat sleepy with the sultriness of the afternoon.

fig. **1827** DISRAELI *Viv. Grey* v. vii, My youth flourished in the unwholesome sultriness of a blighted atmosphere. **1886** 'M. FIELD' *Brutus Ultor* I. v, The sultriness of lust is in the air.

sultrome, variant form of SHELTRON¹ *Obs.*

sultry (ˈsʌltrɪ), *a.* Also 6–7 sultrie, 7 soultry, -ie, sowltry. [f. SULTER *v.* + -Y. Cf. SWELTERY.]

1. a. Of the weather, the atmosphere, etc.: Oppressively hot and moist; sweltering.

1594 KYD *Cornelia* II. i. 133 The spring, Whom Sommers pride (with sultrie heate) pursues. **1602** SHAKS. *Ham.* v. ii. 101 *Ham.* The winde is Northerly... Mee thinkes it is very soultry, and hot for my Complexion. **1671** R. BOHUN *Wind* 65 The complexion of the Air is generally more silent..in Soultry Weather. **1748** *Anson's Voy.* II. vii. 213 We had now for several days together close and sultry weather. **1845** J. COULTER *Adv. in Pacific* viii. 102 In this valley it is much more sultry than on the outside of the hilly range. **1871** MISS BRADDON *Fenton's Quest* i, A warm summer evening, with a sultry haze brooding over the level landscape.

b. Of places, seasons of the year, etc.: Characterized by such weather.

1620–6 QUARLES *Feast for Worms* 473 Wks. (Grosart) II. 13 A sowltry Summer's euentide. **1704** POPE *Summer* 65 When weary reapers quit the sultry field. **1748** *Anson's Voy.* II. v. 181 The coast of Brazil is extremely sultry. **1794** MRS. RADCLIFFE *Myst. Udolpho* xxxii, A beautiful evening, that had succeeded to a sultry day. **1836** W. IRVING *Astoria* II. 274 The rigorous winters and sultry summers. **1865** PARKMAN *Huguenots* i. (1875) 6 They..pierced the sultry intricacies of tropical forests.

c. Of the sun, etc.: Producing oppressive heat. *poet.*

1697 DRYDEN *Æneid* VII. 309 Such as born beneath the burning Sky, And sultry Sun betwixt the Tropicks lye. **1704** POPE *Summer* 21 The sultry Sirius burns the thirsty plains. **1784** COWPER *Task* VI. 297 Neither mist, Nor freezing sky nor sultry, checking me. **1804** CAMPBELL *Turkish Lady* 5 Day her sultry fires had wasted. **1817** MOORE *Lalla Rookh, Nourmahal* 50 When Day had hid his sultry flame Behind the palms of Baramoule.

2. Figurative and allusive uses.

a. Chiefly *poet.* (*a*) Associated with oppressive heat; characterized by the overpowering heat of toil; hot with toil.

1637 MILTON *Lycidas* 28 What time the Gray-fly winds her sultry horn. **1682** SOUTHERNE *Loyal Brother* III. i, You were not form'd to run in natures herd, Sultry, and elbow'd in the crowd of slaves. ?**1824** COLERIDGE *First Adv. Love* 5 The sultry hind..stays his reaping. **1833** TENNYSON *Palace Art* 77 The reapers at their sultry toil.

(*b*) Characterized by the heat of temper or passion; hot with anger or lust.

1671 MILTON *Samson* 1246 Stalking..in a sultrie chafe. **1704** POPE *Windsor For.* 195 His [*sc.* Pan's] shorter breath, with sultry air, Pants on her neck. **1784** COWPER *Task* VI. 741 The clouds [are] The dust that waits upon his sultry march, When sin hath mov'd him, and his wrath is hot. **1893** F. ADAMS *New Egypt* 78 Sultry and imperious, brutally and pettily tyrannical to his own immediate *entourage*. **1893** F. THOMPSON *Poems, Poppy* iii, With mouth wide a-pout for a sultry kiss.

b. *colloq.* or *slang.* (*a*) 'Spicy', 'smutty'.

1887 KIPLING *Tales fr. Hills* (1888) 175 Clean-built, careless men in the Army..told sultry stories till Riley got up and left the room. **1900** *Westm. Gaz.* 30 Jan. 4/3 A comedy of exceedingly sultry complexion.

(*b*) Of language: Lurid, 'sulphurous'.

1891 *Pall Mall Gaz.* 9 Oct. 1/2 Certainly no bishop ever heard more sultry or variegated language in his time. **1909** *Westm. Gaz.* 1 Oct. 3/3 She makes the mission ladies' flesh creep, she's that sultry with 'er tongue.

(*c*) 'Hot', 'warm', lively.

1880 'MARK TWAIN' *Tramp Abroad* xxv. 250 It was getting pretty sultry for me. I said to myself, 'Is it possible she is going to stop there, and wait for me to speak? If she does, the conversation is blocked.' **1899** CONAN DOYLE *Duet* xviii, I shall make it pretty sultry for you down at Woking. **1905** H. A. VACHELL *Hill* iv. 76 The Caterpillar would have made things very sultry for him.

(*d*) Of a woman: lascivious or sensual, arousing sexual desire; also *transf.* and in *Comb.* orig. *U.S.*

1940 *Time* 7 Oct. 63/2 He watches..another become a sultry, sirenic dancer. **1946** *Sun* (Baltimore) 25 Apr. 12/1 There is also a ballet touch to Miss Horne's sultry song number, 'Love'. **1949** R. HARVEY *Curtain Time* xvi. 160 Miss Nethersole specialized in sultry rôles and her performance in Daudet's *Sapho* was considered scandalous. **1956** *People* 13 May 4/4 Certainly none of the sultry Continental sirens stood a chance when Diana strolled on to the beach. **1977** C. STORR *Tales Psychiatrist's Couch* i. 6 She exuded an air of unsatisfied sexuality... She was what I'd call sultry. **1978** *Times* 30 Nov. 16/8 A trip to Rio to see the real thing—*real* sultry-eyed temptresses.

c. In book-names of some birds, indicating a reddish tinge.

1783 LATHAM *Gen. Syn. Birds* II. II. 455 Sultry W[arbler]... The edges of the feathers rufous. **1815** STEPHENS in *Shaw's Gen. Zool.* IX. II. 544 Sultry Finch, *Fringilla calida*..upper parts of the body pale rufous brown.

Hence ˈ**sultry** *v. trans.*, to make hot.

1897 F. THOMPSON *New Poems, Ode Setting Sun* x, Cold as the new-sprung girlhood of the moon Ere Autumn's kiss sultry her cheek with flame.

Sulu¹ (ˈsuːluː). [Prob. ad. Sama-Bajaw dial. f. Tau Sug *sulúg* current.] = TAU SUG.

1816 [see MACASSAR 2]. **1898** D. C. WORCESTER *Philippine Islands & their People* viii. 201, I had made numerous attempts in Mindanao, Basilan, and Sulu to get an explanation of the Moro aversion to pork. **1908** N. M. SALEEBY *Hist. Sulu* i. 133 Jolo is the Spanish representation ..of the word Sulu... The complete form of the word is Sulug... The Sulus pronounce it and write it Sūg. *Sūg* means a sea current. *Ibid.* iii. 155 The ancient Sulus..had many myths relating to the marriages and heroic deeds of their gods. **1923** S. Y. OROSA *Sulu Archipelago & its People* v. 67 The people of the Sulu Province number over 170,000, roughly grouped as Sulus and Samals. The dominating and most advanced people are the Sulus or *Tao-Sug*, 'people of the current'. *Ibid.* vi. 72 The Sulu is of the brown or Malay race. **1936** G. A. MALCOLM *Commonwealth of Philippines* iii. 39 The Sulus of whom I would speak..are Moros living in the Sulu Archipelago in the Philippine Islands. **1977** C. F. & F. M. VOEGELIN *Classification & Index World's Lang.* 41 Taw Sug = Tausug = Sulu = Joloano Sulu. Palawan, Philippines, northeast coast of Borneo. Closely related to Maranao.

‖**sulu²** (ˈsulu). [Fijian.] In Fiji: a length of cotton cloth wrapped about the body to form a sarong; hence, a type of sarong worn by both sexes (typically from the waist to the knee by men, and to the ankle by women). Also, a similar fashion garment worn by women.

1850 D. HAZLEWOOD *Feejeean & English Dict.* 129/1 *Sulu-ma*, v. to put on a sulu, or dress... The difference between malo and sulu seems to be in the way in which it is worn: malo is sulu when put round the body and not between the legs. **1897** 'SUNDOWNER' *Rambles in Polynesia* 7 For many years yet..the Polynesian islander will continue to wear his *sulu* or lava-lava, as the case may be. **1921** W. A. CHAPPLE *Fiji—its Problems & Resources* ii. 22 His [*sc.* the Fijian's] sulu is his only garment,..a rectangular piece of cotton cloth that he folds round his loins and tucks in upon itself. **1926** *Glasgow Herald* 25 Sept. 4/5 Clad only in their sulus (or kilts). **1944** W. E. HARNEY *Taboo* (ed. 2) 135, I had only a loincloth—a sulu, as it is called. **1970** *Honey* June 86 Vivid multicoloured patchwork slit sulu 11 gns, and tie top, 84s. **1977** *Times* 20 July 1/7 The staff of the Fijian High Commission had turned out in pinstripe *sulu* skirts and morning jackets.

sulvanite (ˈsʌlvənaɪt). *Min.* [f. SUL(PHUR *sb.* + VAN(ADIUM + -ITE¹.] A bronze-coloured sulphide of copper and vanadium, Cu_3VS_4, that usu. occurs massive, rarely as crystals having cubic symmetry, and is often chemically altered.

1900 G. A. GOYDER in *Jrnl. Chem. Soc.* LXXVII. 1094 (*heading*) Sulvanite, a new mineral. **1974** *Amer. Mineralogist* LIX. 307/2 In all occurrences, sulvanite is coated with alteration minerals consisting of malachite, volborthite, and azurite.

sulve, obs. form of SELF.

sulver, obs. form of SILVER *a.* and *sb.*

sulwe, sulwines: see SOLWE, SOLWINESS.

†**sulye.** *Sc. Obs.* Forms: α. 5 soilie, 7 soilzie; β. 5–6 soulȝe, sulȝe, 5 suilye, 6 sulze, suilȝ(i)e. [Sc. var. of SOIL *sb.*¹] Soil, ground; land, earth.

α. **1434** *St. Andrews Reg.* (Bann. Club) 424 To brek stanys and away leid thru þe landes..withoutyn..spillyng of his soilie. **1609** SKENE *Reg. Maj., Baron Courts* c. 65 §1 Gif any beast..be founden within the Lordship, and the soilzie of any man.

β. **1483** *Acts Parl. Scot., Jas. III* (1814) II. 161/2 þe ground & sulȝe of þe samyn lands. **1493** *Reg. Aberdon.* (Maitl. Club) I. 334 þe soulȝe ande manss of Innernothy. **1513** DOUGLAS *Æneis* IV. i. 76 The riche sulȝe trivmphall Of Aphrik boundis. **1546** *Reg. Mag. Sig. Scot.* 11 Infra solum, territorium et lie suilȝe ejusdem. **1592** *Ibid.* 719/2 Terras husbandias..infra villam, territorium et lie suilȝie de Reidpeth.

sum (sʌm), *sb.*¹ Forms: 3–8 summe, sume, 4–5 soumme, 4–6 somme, chiefly *Sc.* sowm, 4–8 chiefly *Sc.* soume, sowme, 5–6 som, 5–7 some, 5–8 summ (6 soom(e, soomme, *Sc.* soum, sowmme, 7 somm), 4– sum. [a. AF., OF. *summe*, *somme*, from 13th cent. = Pr. *soma*, *somma*, It. *somma*, Pg. *summa*, Sp. *suma*:—L. *summa* fem. (sc. *res*, *pars*) of *summus* highest, for **supmus*, superl. of stem *sup-* of *super* above, *superus* higher (see SUPERIOR). Cf. MDu. *somme* (Du. *som*), MLG., MHG., G. *summe*.]

1. A quantity or amount of money.

a. ***sum of money, gold, silver,*** **†*pence*, etc.**

c **1290** *Beket* 386 in *S. Eng. Leg.* 117 Þe king nam fro ȝer to ȝere..ane summe of panes i-deld bi eche side. *a* **1300** *Cursor M.* 21423 A summe [*Gött.* sume, *Fairf.* soume] o monee. **13..** *Evang. Nicod.* 853 in Herrig's *Archiv* LIII. 407 A sowme of tresore haue þai tane. *c* **1375** *Sc. Leg. Saints* xxvi. (*Nycholas*) 108 With syk a sowme of gold. *c* **1400** MAUNDEV. (1839) ii. 13 To whom the Emperour had leyde hem to wedde, for a gret summe of Sylvre. **1477** EARL RIVERS (Caxton) *Dictes* 67 Yvory or vnicorne bone Is bought for a grete somme of gold. **1500–20** DUNBAR *Poems* lxxix. 12, I tuik fra my Lord Thesaurair Ane soume of money for to wair. **1596** DALRYMPLE tr. *Leslie's Hist. Scot.* II. 296 Quhill thame selfes thay redeimed with a soum of siluer. **1632** *Galway Arch.* in *10th Rep. Hist. MSS. Comm.* App. v. 484 What some or somes of money is due. **1718** *Freethinker* No. 109. 32 He supply'd her..with a convenient Summ of Money. **1797** S. & HT. LEE *Canterb. T.* (1799) I. 329 My father..had long ago vested large sums of money in foreign banks. **1839–41** LANE *Arabian Nts.* I. 71 The servant receives presents of small sums of money. **1875** *Encycl. Brit.* II. 534/1 Suppose that several sums of money are added, and the farthings amount to 29 [etc.].

b. *absol.* = 'sum of money'.

principal sum: see PRINCIPAL *a.* 6.

c **1374** CHAUCER *Troylus* IV. 60 They gonnen trete, Hir prisoneres to chaungen..And for the surplus yeven sommes grete. *c* **1386** —— *Frankl. T.* 492 What somme sholde this Maistres gerdon be? *c* **1400** MAUNDEV. (Roxb.) xxii. 104 Þe somme þat þis citee ȝeldez ȝerely commez to fyue hundreth thowsand florenez. **1496–7** *Act 12 Hen. VII*, c. 12 §4 Yf any of the Collectours..reare more somme than..owe to be areared in or upon any Toun. **1535** COVERDALE *Acts* xxii. 28 With a greate summe optayned I this fredome. **1596** SHAKS. *Tam. Shr.* III. ii. 137 He shall..make assurance heere in Padua Of greater summes then I haue promised. **1690** in *Nairne Peerage Evidence* (1874) 27 That the said soume is only to be payed to the collaterall aires of the said Lord William. **1709** J. WARD *Introd. Math.* (1713) 245 Any Principal or Sum put to Interest. **1794** MRS. RADCLIFFE *Myst. Udolpho* xxxiv, Montoni had lost large sums to Verezzi. **1848** THACKERAY *Van. Fair* xlvii, Such moneys as he required beyond the very moderate sums which his father was disposed to allow him. **1891** KIPLING *Light that Failed* iii, The Central Southern Syndicate had paid Dick a certain sum on account for work done.

c. A quantity of money *of* a specified amount.

c **1386** CHAUCER *Can. Yeom. Prol. & T.* 811 The somme of fourty pound. **1450** in *Exch. Rolls Scotl.* V. 425 *note*, The said sowm of five markis. **1560** DAUS tr. *Sleidane's Comm.* 173 He kept to hymselfe the money that his brother lefte..to the some of LX thousande crownes. **1679–88** *Moneys Secr. Serv. Chas. II & Jas. II.* (Camden) 2 Six other sumes of 150[li] each. **1710** in *Nairne Peerage Evidence* (1874) 151 All & haill the sowme of ten thousand merks Scots money. **1836** *Penny Cycl.* V. 165/2 The above sum of 758*l.* 16*s.* *a* **1901** BESANT *Five Years' Tryst* (1902) 38 The sum of £178. 4s. 10d.

d. ***gross sum,*** **†*sum in great* or *gross, lump sum*.**

1421 in Rymer *Fœdera* (1710) X. 162/2 The said Ambassiatours shall cast to what Some the Wages aboveseid wole drawe to for every of hem..and profre hym that Some in grete. **1523**, etc. [see GROSS *a.* 6]. **1612** HIERON *Life & Death Dorcas* 8, I am forced..in stead of a bill of particulars, which in this case would be very comfortable, to present all in one grosse summe. **1642** COKE *Instit.* II. 659 The rent was paid as a summe in grosse. **1821–2** SHELLEY *Chas. I*, ii. 272 The expenses..Have swallowed up the gross sum of the imposts. **1867**, etc. [see LUMP *sb.*[1] 9].

†e. *transf.* A quantity *of* goods regarded as worth so much. *Obs.* (Cf. SUM *sb.*[2])

c **1400** *Destr. Troy* 11866 Þan payet kyng Priam all the pure sowmes Of gold, & of gay syluer, & of goode whete. **1422** YONGE tr. *Secr. Secr.* 172 A grete Some of catele to charlys appertenynge. **1528** *Star Chamber Cases* (Selden Soc.) II. 175 Newby sold..a serten sum of malte. **1680** *Acts Assembly Nevis* (1740) 6 The Sum of One hundred Pounds of Muscovado Sugar for every such Offence. **1872** SCHELE DE VERE *Americanisms* 64 The term *Sums of Tobacco*, which is still occasionally met with in official papers, has its origin in the fact that for many generations, in old Virginia times, all taxes raised for the support of government officers, ministers, etc., were assessed in so many pounds of tobacco.

†f. A unit of coinage; a money of account. *Obs.*

1634 PEACHAM *Compl. Gent.* (ed. 2) xii. 117 The Greeke summes were a Mina and a Talent.

†2. A number, company, or body (*of* people); a host, band. *Obs.*

Frequent in ME. alliterative poetry.

13.. *E.E. Allit. P.* C. 509 Of þat soumme ȝet arn summe such sottez..As lyttel barnez on barme þat neuer bale wroȝt. ?*a* **1400** *Morte Arth.* 606 Thus they semble in sortes, summes fulle huge. *c* **1400** *Destr. Troy* 1136 A soume of soudiours. *c* **1450** *Mirk's Festial* 89 Þay gedyrt a grete some of men ynto þe castell. **1570** DEE *Math. Pref.* aj, The best Rules..for ordring of all Companies, summes and Numbers of men. **1601** BRETON *Rauisht Soule* Wks. (Grosart) I. 7/1 By Him Who should both Death and Hell destroy, And be the Sauiour of His chosen summe.

†3. *Arith.* A number; *occas.* a whole number as distinguished from a fraction. *Obs.*

1390 GOWER *Conf.* III. 90 Be which [*sc.* algorism] multiplicacioun Is mad and diminucioun Of sommes be thexperience Of this Art and of this science. **1543** RECORDE *Gr. Artes* 118 (E.E.T.S.) 2 For example I wyll set downe this summe 287965. *Ibid.* 118b, When you wyll adde two summes, you shall fyrst set downe one of them..And afterward set downe the other summe. **1655** MARQ. WORCESTER *Cent. Inv.* (1663) 58 Numerations and Substractions of all Summes and Fractions. **1657** HOBBES *Absurd Geom.* Wks. 1845 VII. 370 A third of the sum below is 12, the sum above is 14. **1709** J. WARD *Introd. Math.* (1713) 11 The Number (or Sum) out of which Substraction is required to be made.

4. a. The total number (*of* individual persons or things capable of, or regarded as capable of, numeration). Now only as transf. use of sense 6. **†*by sum***: in all. ***in sum*** (obs. or arch.): all together.

c **1374** CHAUCER *Boeth.* v. met. iii. (1868) 160 Þan knoweþ it to-gidre þe somme and þe singularites, þat is to seyn þe principles and eueryche by hym self. **1377** LANGL. *P. Pl.* B. XVII. 29 [He] hath saued þat bileued so and sory for her synnes, He can nouȝte segge þe somme. ?*a* **1400** *Morte Arth.* 448 Sexty myle on a daye, the somme es bott lyttille! *c* **1400** tr. *Secr. Secr., Gov. Lordsh.* 109 Þes makyn in somme tene thowsand ffyghtynge men. *c* **1400** *Destr. Troy* 1291 He..assemblit his sad men..Seuyn thousand be sowme all of sure knightes. *c* **1425** WYNTOUN *Cron.* IX. ii. 108 Of his folk war mony slayn,..þe sowme [*v.r.* nomer] of þaim I couythe noucht say. **1535** COVERDALE *Ps.* cxxxviii. 17 How deare are thy councels vnto me o God? O how greate is the summe of them? **1667** MILTON *P.L.* XII. 338 Whose foul Idolatries, and other faults Heapt to the popular summe. **1699** BENTLEY *Phal.* ii. 29 Allowing the Summ of xxviii Years. **1718** PRIOR *Solomon* III. 110 By one countless Sum of Woes opprest. **1766** GOLDSM. *Vic. W.* xxviii, 'Now', cried I, 'the sum of my miseries is made up'. **1840** WHEWELL *Philos. Induct. Sci.* I. p. xxxix, An Induction is not the mere sum of the Facts which are colligated. **1868** M. PATTISON *Academ. Org.* v. 307 Human nature considered as one great whole, —i.e. in the sum of its phenomena. **1874** RUSKIN *Val D'Arno* ix. (1886) 115 The victories of Charles, and the massacres, taken in sum, would not give a muster-roll of more than twenty thousand dead. **1877** HUXLEY *Physiogr.* 228 The solid animal fabric returns to swell the sum of the fluids and gases from which..it has been derived.

†b. With reference to accounts of money or arithmetical addition; in full ***whole sum, total sum***: = SUM-TOTAL. Also *fig. Obs.*

c **1400** *Brut* ccv. 234 Þai lete fille v barelles ferers wiþ siluer —þe somme amontede v M[l] li. **1512** *Croscombe Church-w. Acc.* (Som. Rec. Soc.) 32 The holle sum of all the coste xxij[li]. xj[s]. vij[d]. **1543** RECORDE *Gr. Artes* 122 (E.E.T.S.) 2 The hole summe, that amounteth of the addytion. **1573** in Feuillerat *Revels Q. Eliz.* (1908) 227 It was entred after the Totall soomme. **1623** COCKERAM II, The whole summe, *totall.* **1640–1** *Kirkcudbr. War-Comm. Min. Bk.* (1855) 38 Soume of the Valuatioun of the Toun of Kirkcudbryt, iij[m] iij[c] libs. **1781** COWPER *Conv.* 143 His ambiguities his total sum.

5. The total amount or quantity, the totality, aggregate, or whole (*of* something immaterial).

a **1300** *Cursor M.* 11577 It was a mikel sume o quain O þaa childer þat war slain. **1546** J. HEYWOOD *Prov.* (1867) 26 Of the cause, for whiche I com, I pray you paciently here the hole som. **1576** GASCOIGNE *Steele Gl.* 646 Wks. 1910 II. 160 To write, the summe of my conceit, I do not meane. **1600** SHAKS. *A.Y.L.* III. ii. 140 The stretching of a span, buckles in his summe of age. **1718** PRIOR *Solomon* III. 873 Thy Sum of Duty let Two Words contain;..Be Humble, and be Just. **1719** DE FOE *Crusoe* II. (Globe) 330 Sighs, Tears, Groans,..make up the Sum of its Variety. **1772** PRIESTLEY *Inst. Relig.* (1782) I. 43 A greater sum of happiness can exist in a greater number. **1827** MACAULAY *Ess.*, *Macchiavelli* (1897) 48 Public events had produced an immense sum of misery to private citizens. **1946** *R.A.F. Jrnl.* May 152 The *Bulletin* slowly built up a sum of good will among contributors. **1967** G. STEINER *Lang. & Silence* 31 Literature, philosophy, theology, law, the arts of history, are endeavours to enclose within the bounds of rational discourse the sum of human experience.

6. *Math.* **a.** The number, quantity, or magnitude resulting from the addition of two or more numbers, quantities, or magnitudes. †In early use also, the result of multiplication, a product.

c **1430** *Art Nombryng* (E.E.T.S.) viii. 14 Multiplie .3. by hym-selfe, and þe some of alle wolle be .9. **1570** DEE *Math. Pref.* *ij, Number, we define, to be, a certayne Mathematicall Summe, of Vnits. **1685** WALLIS *Treat. Alg.* lxxix. 306 The Sum of an Arithmetical Progression. **1709** J. WARD *Introd. Math.* (1713) 322 The Sum of the two Sides of any plain Triangle. **1715** tr. *Gregory's Astron.* (1726) I. 79 The right Lines *SP, PF* taken together, are equal to the greater Axis: Wherefore half their Sum (that is, *EP*) is equal to half the greater Axis *CA*. **1836** *Penny Cycl.* VI. 388/1 The perpendiculars at these points are in arithmetical progression, 0, *a*, 2*a*, &c...*na*: the sum of all of which is $\frac{1}{2}n(n+1)a$. **1840** LARDNER *Geom.* 83 The figure ABDE, having no angle greater than 180° will have the sum of its external angles equal to four right angles. **1878** CAYLEY *Math. Papers* (1896) X. 186, I use the expression *a sum of squares* to denote the sum of all or any of the squares each multiplied by an arbitrary coefficient.

b. In the calculus of finite differences, the quantity resulting from addition of the values of a function obtained by giving to the variable successive values differing by unity; denoted by the symbol Σ.

†Formerly also applied to an integral (INTEGRAL B. 4 a), considered as the sum of an infinite number of consecutive values of the function.

1696 HALLEY in *Phil. Trans.* XIX. 202 An Easie Demonstration of the Analogy of the Logarithmick Tangents to the Meridian Line or sum of the Secants.

†c. The aggregate of the terms of an equation when all on one side, i.e. equated to zero. *Obs.*

1704 J. HARRIS *Lex. Techn.* I, *Sum of an Equation*, is when the absolute Number being brought over to the other side with a contrary Sign, the whole becomes equal to 0. And this Descartes calls the Sum of the Equation proposed.

d. = *logical sum* s.v. LOGICAL *a.* 7.

1918 C. I. LEWIS *Survey of Symbolic Logic* iii. 185 The 'sum', $a + b$, denotes the class of those things which are either members of *a* or members of *b* (or members of both). **1934** W. V. QUINE *System of Logistic* xvii. 171, $\epsilon' a$ may be called the sum of the class of classes a. **1968** P. A. P. MORAN *Introd. Probability Theory* iv. 185 The advantage of using half-open intervals is that if two of them abut, their sum is again a half-open interval. **1981** W. MARCISZEWSKI *Dict. Logic* 53 The union (sum) of sets: $x \in X \cup Y \equiv (x \in X) \vee (x \in Y)$.

7. A series of numbers to be added or cast up.

1579 GOSSON *Sch. Abuse* (Arb.) 27 They might cast the summe without pen, or counters. *c* **1600** SHAKS. *Sonn.* xlix. 3 When as thy loue hath cast his vtmost summe. **1641** R. MARRIOT *Serm. Commem. Mrs. Dering* 12 He that goes about to cast an account must know his rules... Else, when he hath cast up his summes, he cannot tell whether they be done right or wrong. **1698** FRYER *Acc. E. India & P.* 191 They will in a trice,..cast up the difficultest Sums. **1804–6** SYD. SMITH *Mor. Philos.* (1850) 404 An expert arithmetician adds up the longest sum with the most unerring precision.

8. An arithmetical problem in the solution of which some particular rule is applied; also, such a problem worked out. *colloq.*

1803 *Man in Moon* 24 Dec. (1804) 100 To add up a sum of addition. *a* **1825** FORBY *Voc. E. Anglia* s.v. *Summing*, Solving any question in arithmetic, is doing a sum. **1838** DICKENS *Nich. Nick.* i, Sums in simple interest. **1862** DRAPER *Intell. Devel. Eur.* xvi. (1865) 361 A common multiplication or division sum. **1881** W. HARRIS *Serm. Boys & Girls* 96 Some of you boys and girls are very clever at working sums.

9. a. That which a statement, discourse, writing, or a system of laws, etc. amounts to, or is in essence; an abridged statement containing the substance of a matter; a summary, epitome. *Obs.* or *arch.*

c **1374** CHAUCER *Boeth.* III. pr. viii. (1868) 81 Of alle whiche forseide þinges I may reducen þis shortly in a somme. *c* **1450** *Merlin* 84 Of her wordes this was the somme. **1533** GAU *Richt Vay* 45 This is the soume of the wangel that our lord Iesus christ godis sone is giffine to vsz..and he and al his is owris. **1535** COVERDALE *Ezra* vii. 11 This is the summe of the letter, that kynge Artaxerses gaue vnto Eszdras the prest. **1541** —— *Old Faith* (1547) D vj b, He wolde brynge in to a shorte summe and set in wrytynge, all the lawe that the feathers had. **1560** DAUS tr. *Sleidane's Comm.* Pref. 3, I haue set before the beginnyng of euery boke, the somme or argument. **1626** GOUGE *Serm. Dignity Chivalry* §1 The Summe of this Chapter is A Declaration of the Magnificence of Salomon. **1671** MILTON *Samson* 1557 Tell us the sum, the circumstance defer. *a* **1703** BURKITT *On N.T.* Mark xii. 34 This is the sum of the duties of the first table [of the Commandments]. **1837** SIR F. PALGRAVE *Merch. & Friar* Ded. p. vi, The sum of the objections was this. **1842** BORROW *Bible in Spain* xxiv, He..gave me the history of his life, the sum of which was, that [etc.].

†b. A summary treatise or manual; = SUMMA 3.

a **1325** *MS. Rawl. B. 520* lf. 54b, Here..biginnez þe summe þat is icleped Cadit Assisa. **1474** CAXTON *Chesse* III. iii. (1883) 97 Varro rehereth in his sommes that y[e] riche men ben alle louyd by this loue. **1531** *Dial. on Laws Eng.* II. xxxv. 71 In the said summe called summa Rosella in the said title alienatio, the xiii. article is asked this question. **1541** COVERDALE *Old Faith* (1547) E v, He [*sc.* Moses] made yet an Enchiridion and Summe of all the Actes of hys tyme and of the lawe of God, whyche is called Deuteronomium. *c* **1643** LD. HERBERT *Autobiog.* (1824) 42 Some good sum of Philosophy may be learned. **1680** H. DODWELL *Two Lett.* (1691) 232 For Aquinas, you need hardly read anything but his Sums. *a* **1770** JORTIN *Life Erasmus* (1788) I. 85 The Collectors of Sums, that is, of Common-places of Philosophy and Divinity.

10. ***in sum*** [F. *en somme*, L. *in summa*].

a. (Expressed) in a few words, briefly or summarily. Also **†*in a sum*.** Now *arch.* and *rare.*

c **1374** CHAUCER *Boeth.* I. pr. iv. (1868) 17 Axest þou in somme of what gilt I am accused? **1382** WYCLIF *Dan.* vii. 1 In sum [*gloss* or litil wordis; 1388 schortli; Vulg. *summatim*]. **1526** *Pilgr. Perf.* (W. de W. 1531) 1 b, A treatyse..that sholde conteyne in somme the sentences of illumyned doctours, concernynge perfeccyon. **1555** PHILPOT *Exam.* (1559) 47 The declaration of these thinges more at large, which nowe I wryte in somme. **1561** NORTON & SACKV. *Gorboduc* I. i, This is in somme what I would haue ye wey. **1651** HOBBES *Leviath.* I. iv. 13 To Register, what by cogitation, wee find to be the cause of any thing..and what we find things..may produce, or effect: which in summe, is acquiring of Arts. **1862** F. HALL *Hindu Philos. Syst.* 112 My meaning, in sum, is, that, whereas [etc.].

(*b*) **1537** tr. *Latimer's Serm. Convoc.* ii. B vij b, This alone I can say grossly, and as in a sum. *a* **1699** J. FRASER *Polichron.* (S.H.S.) 418 [They] interrogat him if he appointed not his sone Richard, replyed in a sume, Yea.

b. Used *absol.* as an illative phr.: To conclude in few words; to sum up; in brief, in short.

1562 PILKINGTON *Expos. Abdyas* Pref. 9 In summe, no violent thinge can longe endure. **1597** HOOKER *Eccl. Pol.* v. xlvi. §1 In summe, [they] taught the world no lesse vertuously how to dye, then they had done before how to liue. **1647** MAY *Hist. Parl.* I. ii. 25 They hold that the Church of Rome is a true Church;..That it is lawfull to pray for soules departed [etc.]; in summe they believe all that is taught by the Church, but not by the Court of Rome. *a* **1700** EVELYN *Diary* 6 July 1679, He was also dextrous in Chronology, Antiquities, Mathematics. In sum, an *Intellectus universalis*. **1700** DRYDEN *Fables* Pref., Wks. (1910) 276 In sum, I seriously protest, that no Man ever had ..a greater Veneration for Chaucer than my self. **1761** H. WALPOLE *Let. to G. Montagu* 5 May, We have lost a young genius... He was shot very unnecessarily, riding too near a battery: in sum, he is a sacrifice to his own rashness—and to ours. **1876** DOUSE *Grimm's L.* 107 Hence, in sum, we arrive at simple and symmetrical expressions of all the cases of irregularity.

11. ***sum and substance***: the essence (*of* anything); the gist or pith (*of* a matter).

In quot. 1591, by a twist of the phr., used as = one's all.

1591 SHAKS. *Two Gent.* IV. i. 15 My riches, are these poore habiliments, Of which, if you should here disfurnish me, You take the sum and substance that I haue. **1594** HOOKER *Eccl. Pol.* IV. iii. §2 This in effect is the summe and substance of that which they bring by way of opposition against those orders. **1657** SANDERSON *Serm.* Pref. §5 (1681) A 3 b, This is the sum and substance of the usual Censures and Objections of our Anti-Ceremonian Brethren. **1732** BERKELEY *Alciphr.* v. §15 What is the Sum and Substance, Scope and End of Christ's Religion, but the Love of God and Man? **1852** ROBERTSON *Serm.* Ser. III. xii. 144 That the Sermon on the Mount contains the sum and substance of Christianity. **1889** JESSOPP *Coming of Friars* iv. 168 If any of us were to write down the sum and substance of his knowledge.

†**12.** The upshot, issue, conclusion. *Obs.*

c **1385** CHAUCER *L.G.W.* 1559 *Hypsipyle*, The somme [4 *other MSS.* soth(e]] is this that Iason weddit was Vn-to this queen. *a* **1578** LINDESAY (Pitscottie) *Chron. Scot.* (S.T.S.) I. 402 This was concludit amangis themselffis, and declairit into the king the sowme of the consall. **1654** Z. COKE *Logick* 8 That whatsoever is conceivable of a thing, may be drawn to a right summe. **1670** DRYDEN *2nd Pt. Conq. Granada* IV. ii, On this assault.. Depends the sum and fortune of the war.

13. a. The ultimate end or goal; the highest attainable point. *Obs.* or *arch.*

1340 *Ayenb.* 260 He ssolde him resti ine god þet is þe ende and þe uoluellinge and þe somme of his wylninges. **1565** COOPER *Thesaurus* s.v. *Summus*, The summe & knot of all his glorie was, that he wente into the prouince of Asia, &c. **1631** R. BOLTON *Comf. Affl. Consc.* ii. (1635) 9 Death the end and summ of all feared evils. **1667** MILTON *P.L.* VIII. 522 Thus I have.. brought My Storie to the sum of earthly bliss Which I enjoy. *Ibid.* XII. 575 Thou hast attained the summe Of wisdom; hope no higher. **1706** STANHOPE *Paraphr.* III. 513 He is.. the summe and ultimate End of all we can hope for. **1866** NEALE *Sequences & Hymns* 124 Thee, our wishes' full and perfect sum.

b. *the sum of things* [tr. L. *summa rerum*: see SUMMA 5 a]: the highest public interest, the public good, the common weal; also (by reference to sense 5), the totality of being, the universe.

1667 MILTON *P.L.* VI. 673 Had not th' Almightie Father .. Consulting on the sum of things, foreseen This tumult. **1704** SWIFT *Batt. Bks.* Misc. (1711) 257 The Modern Chiefs were holding a Consult upon the Sum of Things. **1771** *Junius Lett.* lix. (1788) 322 Concessions, such as these, are of little moment to the sum of things. **1850** TENNYSON *In Mem.* lxxxviii, The glory of the sum of things Will flash along the chords and go.

†**c.** *the sum of sums*: = SUMMA 5 b. *Obs.*

1592 NASHE *Str. Newes* H 2 b, The summe of summes is this.

14. *Comb.*, as **sum check** *Computers*, a check on the accuracy of a group of digits in which they are added together and the result compared with a previously computed sum (which may accompany the group as a check digit); also applied to similar checks in which a quantity other than a sum is employed; = *summation check* s.v. SUMMATION[2] 6; so **sum-checked** *a.*

1962 R. V. OAKFORD *Introd. Electronic Data Processing Equipment* ii. 31 If a single *R* check bit is changed, the sum check will fail.. in that row, but not in the four columns. **1972** *Computer Jrnl.* XV. 196/2 A similar routine deals with sum-checked binary input.

†**sum,** *sb.*[2] *Obs.* In 5 summe, 6 som(m)e, 8 summ. [a. AF. *sum(m)e* = OF. (mod.F.) *somme* :—Romanic *sauma* horse-load, for late L. *sagma* packsaddle, a. Gr. σάγμα (whence also ultimately SEAM *sb.*[2]). Cf. SOUM *sb.*[1]

The med.L. and F. words were assimilated in spelling to *summa*, *somme*, SUM *sb.*[1]; med.L. has *sauma*, *sama*, *somma*, *summa* (also *salmata*, *saumata* = OF. *somee*) *bladi*, *olei*, *vini*, denoting definite measures of these commodities.]

A unit of measure or weight of certain commodities: see quots. and cf. SEAM *sb.*[2] 1 b.

In 1314, in Neath, S. Wales, a sum of iron contained 9 pieces (Rogers *Agric. & Prices* I. 472, II. 463).

c **1450** *Godstow Reg.* 424 The mynded luke yaf to the mynded William at the entrying vij. mark and ij. summys of barly. **1480–1** *Acc. Exch. K.R.* 496. No. 23 (P.R.O.), j summe clavorum voc. Sprignaill. **1539–40** in *Archæol. Cant.* (1893) XX. 243, 2 'some' of 'sprygg' 10s. **1545** *Rates Custome House* b viij b, Nidels the some conteinynge, xii. M, x. s. **1570** FOXE *A. & M.* (ed. 2) I. 411/2 A somme of corne was then [A.D. 1257] sold for 26 shillings. [**1711** MADOX *Hist. & Antiq. Exchequer* xiii. 325 Leave to carry DC Summs of Corn [tr. *summas Frumenti*] whither he would.]

sum, *sb.*[3] *Sc.* and *Irish.* Variant of SOUM *sb.*[2]; see also quots. 1744, 1780.

[**1526** in Sir A. Agnew *Hist. Hered. Sheriffs Galloway* (1864) 158 The pertinents—viz., eight *sums* of cows, one mare,.. with their sequels.] **1621** *Sc. Acts, Jas. VI* (1816) IV. 612/2 Act declairing summes Grasse gevin to þe Ministeris for þ^r gleibis to be teyndfrie. **1744** SMITH & HARRIS *County of Down* 134 *note*, A Sum of Cattle in these Parts is what they call a Collop in other Parts of Ireland, consisting of one full grown Cow or Bullock, of three Years old, or a Horse of that Age;.. in some Places a Horse is reckoned a Sum and half. Eight Sheep make a Sum. **1780** A. YOUNG *Tour Irel.* I. 284 Keeping a cow is a sum; a horse a sum and an half;.. a barrel of potatoe setting.. all these are sums.

sum (sʌm), *v.*[1] Forms: 4–6 somme, 4–7 summe (4 sume, *pa. pple.* isommed, 5 some, soume, sowme), 7–8 summ, 6– sum. [a. OF. *sommer*, *summer* (13–14th cent.), or ad. its source, med.L. *summāre* (whence Pr. *somar*, It. *sommare*, Sp. *sumar*, Pg. *sommar*), f. *summa* SUM *sb.*[1]]

1. a. *trans.* To find the sum or total number or amount of; to add *together*; to reckon or count up; to cast up (a column of figures, an account).

a **1300** *Cursor M.* 2345 Folk sua selcut mani brede þat naman suld cun sume ne neuen. **1387** TREVISA *Higden* (Rolls) III. 261 Alle þese ȝeres i-sommed to gidres makeþ foure hondred ȝeres. *a* **1400–50** *Wars Alex.* 1986 Here a gloue full of graynes.. may þou sowme me þire sedis surely þou trowe, þou miȝt a-count all oure kniȝtis. **1511** FABYAN *Will* in *Chron.* (1811) Pref. p. vii, My stuff of household and quyke catall.. beyng praysic, engrossid, and summyd. **1530** PALSGR. 725/1 Tarye tyll I have sommed this accompte. **1570** DEE *Math. Pref.* d iij b, By Arithmetike, the charges of Buildinges are summed together. **1611** *Bible* 2 Kings xxii. 4 That he may summe the siluer which is brought into the house of the Lord. **1641** (Sept.) *Terrier of Plesheybury Manor, Essex* lf. 6 (MS.) The smythes rent is not summed into the rent or valueacion aforesaide. **1655** STANLEY *Hist. Philos.* III. 67 Bring my account-book hither, That I may summe my debts and interest. **1785** GIBEON *Let. to Ld. Sheffield* 13 Mar., A balance neatly cyphered and summed by Gosling. **1816** SCOTT *Antiq.* vi, The banker's clerk, who was directed to sum my cash-account, blundered it three times. **1880** HAUGHTON *Phys. Geog.* iii. 158 *note*, This value must be summed through the time that the sun does not set. **1905** R. GARNETT *Shaks.* 18 Drooping sad eyes toward the sod, as though Summing its blades. **1935** *Lancet* 11 May 1123/1 For the pig,.. the combination of virus plus hæmophilic organism is much more potent than was to be expected from summing the mild diseases caused by the two agents acting separately. **1947** *Electronic Engin.* June 179/1 Suppose.. that it is desired to sum the voltages from *n* sources. **1962** F. I. ORDWAY et al. *Basic Astronautics* vii. 325 The average lifetime.. may be easily determined by summing all lifetimes and dividing by 100. **1971** *Nature* 24 Dec. 485/2 He summed data of six previous studies.. and demonstrated in the total sample an over-representation of the last-but-one position. **1977** J. G. GRAEME *Designing with Operational Amplifiers* vii. 177 The number of signals that can be summed is limited only by increasing circuit errors.

(*b*) With *up*. *c* **1450** *Bk. Curtasye* 540 in *Babees Bk.*, Tyl countes also þer-on ben cast, And somet vp holy at þo last. **1592** SHAKS. *Rom. & Jul.* II. vi. 34, I cannot sum vp some of halfe my wealth. **1651** HOBBES *Leviath.* I. v. 19 Not regarding how each bill is summed up. **1684–5** SOUTH *Serm.* 22 Feb. (1842) I. 172 He.. may as well undertake to count the sands, or to sum up infinity. **1792** D. STEWART *Elem. Philos. Human Mind* I. ii. 112 An expert accountant.. can sum up, almost with a single glance of his eye, a long column of figures. **1798** *Monthly Mag.* VI. 111 Let the speaker of the house sum up the county-polls. **1837** CARLYLE *Fr. Rev.* III. II. vii, When the Voting is done, and Secretaries are summing it up.

b. †*pass.*, and *intr.* for *pass.* To amount *to.*

c **1425** WYNTOUN *Cron.* V. xii. 3638 Þat sowmyt was in multitude V. thousande men, bathe barne and wiff. *a* **1600** G. WHYATT *Life Anne Boleyn* in *Cavendish's Wks.* (1825) II. 207 In three quarters of a year her alms was summed to fourteen or fifteen thousand pounds. **1803** SOUTHEY *Let. to Coleridge* 3 Aug., Those little units of interruption and preventions, which sum up to as ugly an aggregate as the items in a lawyer's bill. **1865** DE MORGAN in *Athenæum* 23 Dec. 889/2 Take those Greek words of which the letters sum into 666. **1966** G. C. HEMMENS *Structure of Urban Activity Linkages* i. 6 The matrix of linkage coefficients is a stochastic matrix where each row sums to one.

c. *trans.* To bring *up* to a certain total. *rare.*

1597 BACON *Coulers Good & Evill* Ess. (Arb.) 144 The howre doth rather summe vp the moments then deuide the daye. **1883** *Century Mag.* July 429/2 Two hundred and eighty three deaths summed up an official record that was confessedly incomplete.

d. *Math.* To find the sum of (a series); in the calculus of finite differences, to find the aggregate of the successive values of a function (SUM *sb.*[1] 6 b).

1776 HUTTON in *Phil. Trans.* LXVI. 479 The former series is summed, with rather more ease than the latter. **1838** *Penny Cycl.* XII. 500/1 It is required to sum the series $\phi x + \phi(x + \Delta x) + \phi(x + 2\Delta x) + \ldots + \phi(x + \overline{n-1}\Delta x)$.

e. *intr.* To do sums in arithmetic.

1825 JENNINGS *Observ. Dial. W. Eng.*, To *Summy* v.n., to work by arithmetical rules. **1838** D. W. JERROLD *Men of Character* I. 260 They tries Narkin, and finds he can read, and write, and sum. **1870** KINGSLEY *At Last* x, She sat summing away on her slate.

f. *trans.* In transf. and fig. uses: To reckon, count, or total *up*.

1597 SHAKS. *2 Hen. IV*, I. i. 167 You cast th' euent of Warre.. And summ'd the accompt of Chance. *a* **1628** PRESTON *Effect. Faith* (1631) 90 When thou hast summed and reckoned all all together, all reasons and all objections to and fro. **1644** VICARS *God in Mount* 105 *marg.*, A briefe recitall of all these foresaid premises summ'd up together. **1687** DRYDEN *Hind & P.* III. 656 An old fanatick Author.. Who summ'd their Scandals up by Centuries. **1784** COWPER *Task* III. 130, I sum up half mankind, And add two thirds of the remaining half. **1820** SCOTT *Monast.* xviii, 'And various other perquisites..', said the Abbot, summing.. the advantages attached to the office of conventual bow-bearer. **1828** CAMPBELL *Lines Depart. Emigr. N.S. Wales* 53 The grey-haired swain.. Shall.. summing all the blessings God has given, Put up his patriarchal prayer to Heaven.

†**2.** To collect into a company. *Obs.*

c **1400** *Destr. Troy* 13356 He.. sowmet his pepull. *c* **1425** WYNTOUN *Cron.* VI. xii. 1070 Bathe men, barnys and women, þar sowmyt war al be ten.

3. To collect into or embrace in a small compass; also with *up*. Chiefly *pass.*

1606 SHAKS. *Tr. & Cr.* I. iii. 325 The purpose is perspicuous euen as substance, Whose grossenesse little charracters summe vp. **1667** MILTON *P.L.* VIII. 473 What seemd fair in all the World, seemd.. in her summd up, in her containd. *Ibid.* IX. 454 She.. in her looks summs all Delight. **1731–8** SWIFT *Pol. Conversat.* Introd. 9 The whole Genius, Humour, Politeness and Eloquence of England are summed up in it. **1832** L. HUNT *Gentle Armour* II. 68 In that last blow his strength must have been summ'd. **1842** TENNYSON *Gard. Dau.* 13 A miniature of loveliness, all grace Summ'd up and closed in little. **1869** BROWNING *Ring & Bk.* x. *Pope* 343 Show me thy fruit, the latest act of thine! For in the last is summed the first and all.

4. To give the substance of in a few words or a brief statement; to summarize, epitomize. Said also of the statement made, or, by extension, of a principle, condition, or the like. (Usually with, now rarely without, *up*.)

1621 MOUNTAGU *Diatribæ* 416 Those many Writers that Photius read, and summed in his *Bibliotheca*. **1677** tr. *Groeneveldt's Treat. Stone* 12 To sum the various and different opinions of Authors. **1825** SCOTT *Talism.* x, To sum the whole, I am aware [etc.]. **1861** READE *Cloister & H.* lxxi, The phase, through which this remarkable mind now passed, may be summed in a word—Penitence. **1875** RUSKIN *Fors Clav.* lx. V. 337 It sums much of what I may have too vaguely and figuratively stated in my letters.

(*b*) With *up*. **1692** R. L'ESTRANGE *Fables* I. ccxvii. 190 Go to the Ant, thou Sluggard; (says the Wise-man) which in Few Words Summs up the Moral of This Fable. **1711** STEELE *Spect.* No. 158 ¶ 2, I have a great deal more to say to you, but I shall sum it up all in this one Remark. **1859** C. BARKER *Assoc. Princ.* i. 9 From these fragments we may thus sum up the general characteristics of Benedictine life. **1871** L. STEPHEN *Playgr. Eur.* (1894) i. 14 The simple statements .. pretty well sum up the reflections of the.. guide-books. **1880** E. KIRKE *Life Garfield* 64 To sum it all up: he is true, kind, manly, honest.

absol. **1899** *Allbutt's Syst. Med.* VII. 667 To sum up; in the treatment of a case of intracranial tumour, the first object [etc.].

5. a. *to sum up*: (of the judge in a trial, or of counsel concluding his case for his client) to recapitulate (the evidence) to the jury before they retire to consider their verdict, giving an exposition of points of law when necessary.

a **1700** EVELYN *Diary* 6 Dec. 1680, Sir Wm. Jones summ'd up the evidence. **1768** BLACKSTONE *Comm.* III. 375 When the evidence is gone through on both sides, the judge in the presence of the parties, the counsel, and all others, sums up the whole to the jury. **1874** *Nairne Peerage Evidence* 171 Mr. Pearson stated.. that he should be prepared, after the evidence now given was printed, to sum up the case on an early day.

b. *absol.* or *intr.*

1805 JAMES *Milit. Dict.* (ed. 2), To *Sum* up.. in a judicial sense. **1849** MACAULAY *Hist. Eng.* v. I. 642 He summed up in the same style,.. and reminded the jury that the prisoner's husband had borne a part in the death of Charles the First. **1884** *Times* (weekly ed.) 12 Sept. 8/2 The judge summed up dead against the claim.

c. *trans.* To form an estimate of, summarize the qualities or character of; to take the measure of.

1889 GRANT ALLEN *Terrible Inher.* viii, The old barrister .. summed him up from head to foot with his keen, critical Old Bailey stare. **1895** 'H. S. MERRIMAN' *Grey Lady* I. viii. (1899) 90 She stood.. looking back at him over her shoulder, summing him up with a little introspective nod.

†**6. a.** To bring to completion or perfection; to consummate; also with *up*. *Obs.*

c **1592** MARLOWE *Jew of Malta* I. i. 3 And of the third part of the Persian ships, There was the venture summ'd and satisfied. **1607** HEYWOOD *Fayre Mayde Exch.* K 2, If yong Franke Golding were come back, To summe our wish. **1636** MASSINGER *Bashful Lover* V. iii, That there might be nothing wanting to Sum up my numerous engagements. *a* **1644** QUARLES *Sol. Recant.* Sol. xi. 36 One good is wanting still To summe a full Perfection. **1667** MILTON *P.L.* IX. 113 Creatures animate with gradual life Of Growth, Sense, Reason, all summ'd up in Man.

†**b.** Of a bird: To complete (its plumage): see SUMMED *ppl. a.* 2. *Obs. nonce-use.*

1667 MILTON *P.L.* VII. 421 They summ'd thir Penns.

†**sum,** *v.*[2] *Obs. rare*$^{-1}$. In 5 summe. [Echoic. Cf. late MHG., G. *summen*, NFris. *summi*; also BUM *v.*[2], HUM *v.*[1]] *intr.* To hum softly.

c **1440** *Pallad. on Husb.* VII. 123 Al subtilly and smale yf that they summe, Al hugely and haske yf that they humme.

†**sum,** *rel. adv.* and *conj. north. Obs.* Forms: 3–4 sume, sim, 3–5 sum (3 summ, 5 sam), 4–5 som(e. [a. Scand. *som*, *sum* rel. adv. and pron. (MSw. *som*, *sum*, *sym*, Sw., Norw., Da. *som*), related to Icel. *sem*. Cf. OE. *swá same* (*some*), OHG. *sô sama*, *sama sô*, OS. *samo sô* likewise, as: see SAME *a.*]

1. orig. after *swa* so, *swilk*, *sli* such, *all* quite, just (cf. MSw. *sva som*, *sliker som*, *alsom*): As.

c **1200** ORMIN Ded. 11 Icc hafe don swa summ þu badd. *Ibid.* 3499 He chæs himm sone kinness menn All swillke summ he wollde. *Ibid.* 5447 Þatt het forrȝife uss all rihht swa, Summ we forrȝifenn oþre All þatt teȝȝ gilltenn uss onnȝæn. *a* **1300** *Cursor M.* 259 Sli word and werc sum we til heild. *Ibid.* 6348 Water bitter sum [*Fairf.* sim] ani brin. *Ibid.* 16386 Sacles es he sa feir se sum i can. *c* **1420** *Avow. Arth.* x, Boudewynne turnes to toune, Sum that his gate lay. *c* **1420** *Sir Amadace* (Camden) lxix, My lenging is no lengur her, With tunge sum I the telle.

2. As a connecting particle with rel. prons., adjs., and advs., becoming a kind of separable suffix equivalent to -EVER, which was itself afterward added to it tautologically to form the separable suffix *-somever* (Cursor M. 21999), now dial. and superseded in literary use by *-soever*. See also WHOSOME, WHATSOME, etc.

c **1200** ORMIN 1827 Whær summ we findenn o þe boc Enngell bi name nemmnedd. *Ibid.* 11404 Ure Laferrd Jesu Crist, Forrþrihht summ he wass fullhtnedd, Wass ledd ut inntill wessteland. *a* **1300** *Cursor M.* 1149 To quat contre sum [*later MSS.* so] þat þou wend. *Ibid.* 20632 In quatkin sinn sim þat þai be. **13..** *Ibid.* 11015 (Gött.) Sone sum [*Cott.* son quen] vr leuedi was mett wid þe angel.. Scho went hir vte of nazareth. *c* **1400** *Ywaine & Gaw.* 1507 That ye be her

This day twelmoth, how som it be. *c* **1400** *Rule St. Benet* (Prose) 14 In what dede sam ye be, loke þat yure þoht and ȝure herte be to god almihten.

sum, obs. form of SOME *pron.*, *a.*[1], and *adv.*

Sumac, var. SOUMAK.

sumach, sumac ('sjuːmæk, 'ʃuːmæk), *sb.* Forms: (4 asimac), 5 **sumak, [symak]**, 6 **sumache, shomacke**, 6–7 **shoemake, shooma(c)ke, shewmake**, 6–7, 9 **sumack**, 7 **schomache, shommacken, showmack, shumach, -ack**, *Sc.* **shoomak**, 7–8 **shoemack**, 8 **shomach**, 9 **shumac(h**, 4 **sumac**, 6– **sumach**. [a. OF. *sumac*, from 13th cent. (= Pr. *simac*, *sumac*, It. *sommaco*, Sp. *zumaque*, Pg. *sumagre*) or med.L. *sumac(h*, a. Arabic *summāq*.

The form *asimac* in the first quot. represents Arab. *as-summāq* (with prefixed article).]

1. a. A preparation of the dried and chopped leaves and shoots of plants of the genus *Rhus*, esp. *R. Coriaria* (see 2), much used in tanning, also for dyeing and staining leather black (cf. *sumach black* in 3) and medicinally as an astringent.

13.. *Sloane MS.* 5 lf. 12/1 Sumac fructus est cuiusdam arboris.. G[allice] & A[nglice] asimac. *c* **1400** *Lanfranc's Cirurg.* 218 Make him a gargarisme wiþ a decoccioun of ro[sin], sumac, balaustiarum. [**1419** *Liber Albus* (Rolls) I. 224 Karke de symak, xii d.] *a* **1425** tr. *Arderne's Treat. Fistula* etc. 63 Medicynez restrictyuez bene þise; Camphore, accacia.. sumak, mirtell. **1580–1** *Act 23 Eliz.* c. 9 §2 Unless the Madder be put in with Shomacke or Gallys. **1600** HAKLUYT *Voy.* (1810) III. 328 Shoemake.. vsed in England for blacke. **1611** COTGR., *Sumach de cuisine*, the berrie, or fruit of that shrub, vsed heretofore in stead of salt, especially in sawces; whence, as it seemes, we call it, meat Sumacke, and sawce Sumacke. **1612** *Sc. Bk. Rates* in *Halyburton's Ledger* (1867) 326 Shoomak or blacking the hundreth weght viii li. **1666** *Lond. Gaz.* No. 71/4 Two Prizes, one laden with Deal, the other with Shommacken. **1728** CHAMBERS *Cycl.*, *Sumac*, a Drug used to die in Green; as also in the Preparation of Black Morocco, and other Leather. **1812** J. SMYTH *Pract. Customs* (1821) 210 The Sicilian Shumack is imported in bags. **1838** T. THOMSON *Chem. Org. Bodies* 422 Sumac, called also young fustic by the British dyers. **1852** MORFIT *Tanning & Currying* (1853) 92 Sicily sumach is in high repute. **1864** *Chamb. Encycl.* VI. 68/1 The tanning of goat-skins.. is done by sewing up the skins, and filling the bag with a decoction of shumac in a warm state.

b. The leaves of the sumach used as a substitute for tobacco.

1823 H. RAVELIN *Lucubr.* 351 The fragrance of the Shumach from their [*sc.* the Sieue Indians'] pipes. **1835** W. IRVING *Tour Prairies* 207 He had scented the smoke of mingled sumach and tobacco.

2. a. Any of the shrubs or small trees of the genus *Rhus* (N.O. *Terebinthaceæ*), esp. *R. Coriaria*, indigenous in southern Europe, which is the chief source of the material used in tanning (see 1).

The most important species are:—*R. Coriaria*, ***tanner's sumach***; called also ***currier's***, †***dyer's***, ***elm-leaved***, ***hide***, †***leather sumach***; *R. typhina* (fever rhus), ***stag('s)-horn sumach***, a picturesque shrub or small tree of North America, with irregular branches and pinnate leaves, frequently cultivated in England as an ornamental tree; called also ***American***, ***Indian***, ***myrtle***, ***myrtle-leaved***, †***red***, ***Virginia(n***, †***wild sumach***; *R. glabra*, ***smooth sumach***; called also ***New England***, ***Pennsylvania***, ***smooth-leaved sumach***; *R. copallina* (gum copal), ***mountain*** or ***narrow-leaved sumach***; *R. venenata* (poison-ash or -elder), ***poison*** or ***swamp sumach***; *R. vernicifera* (lacquer tree), ***Japan*** or ***varnish sumach***; *R. Cotinus*, the ***Venetian***, ***Venice***, or (corruptly) ***Venus*** (see VENUS[2]) ***sumach***; *R. canadensis* (*aromatica*), ***Canadian*** or ***fragrant sumach***; *R. Metopium*, ***coral*** or ***Jamaica sumach***.

1548 TURNER *Names Herbes* (E.D.S.) 67 Plinie maketh three kyndes of Rhois, of the whiche kyndes I knowe one certaynly, whiche is called of the Poticaries Sumache. **1562** —— *Herbal* II. 115 The Sumach which is vsed for a sauce vnto meates, which som call rede: is the fruyte of the lether Sumach. **1597** GERARDE *Herbal* III. cv. 1291 *Rhus Myrtifolius.* Wilde, or Myrtill Sumach. *Ibid.* 1292 This is called in Greeke ῥοῦς.. in English Sumach, Coriars Sumach, and leather Sumach. *Ibid.*, The seede is named.. in Latine *Rhoë culinaria*, and *Rhoë obsoniorum*: in English Meate Sumach, and Sauce Sumach. *Ibid.* 1293 *Coggygria Theophrasti.* Venice Sumach. *Ibid.*, *Cotinus Coriarius Plinij.* Red Sumach. **1629** PARKINSON *Parad.* 611 *Rhus Virginiana.* The Virginia Sumach, or Buckes horne tree of Virginia. **1634** W. WOOD *New Eng. Prosp.* (1865) 18 The Diars Shumach, with more trees there be. **1715** *Phil. Trans.* XXIX. 364 All these Trifoliate Sumachs grow spontaneously about the fertile Cape of Good Hope. **1728** R. BRADLEY *Dict. Bot.* s.v. *Rhus*, The *Rhus Myrtifolia*, or Myrtle-leaved Sumach... The Venice Sumach, or *Coggygria*. **1753** *Chambers' Cycl.* Suppl., App. s.v., Coriars Sumach, or myrtle Sumach... Venetian Sumach. **1760** J. LEE *Introd. Bot.* App. 328 Sumach, Tanner's or Currier's, *Coriaria*. **1797** *Encycl. Brit.* (ed. 3) XVI. 228/2 The glabrum, with winged leaves, grows naturally in many parts of North America; this is commonly titled by the gardeners New England sumach. **1806** MOORE *Ballad Stanzas* iv, Yon sumach, whose red berry dips In the gush of the fountain. **1817** J. BRADBURY *Trav. Amer.* 91 The leaves of *Rhus glabra*, or smooth sumach. **1831** DAVIES *Man. Mat. Med.* 82 The Narrow-leaved Sumach, *Rhus copallinum*, Willd.; the Pennsylvania Sumach, *R. glabrum*, Willd., and the Virginian Sumach, *R. typhinum*, Willd., are all native plants of North America. **1841** *Penny Cycl.* XIX. 485/1 *Rhus venenata* (Poison Sumach, or Swamp Sumach)... *Rhus coriaria* (Hide or Elm-leaved Sumach). **1869** LOWELL *Pict. from Appledore* 53 And on the whole island never a tree Save a score of sumachs, high as your knee. **1884** ALLEN *New Amer. Farm Bk.* 288 The *Rhus Glabrum* is the common sumach of the United States. **1936** W. FAULKNER *Absalom, Absalom!* vi. 214 The old street of the slave quarters—a jungle of sumach and persimmon. **1965** A. LURIE *Nowhere City* (1966) xv. 162 The sumac held them back with its woolly, awkward stems. **1980** *Hunting Ann. 1981* 42/2 Here, the berries of black haw, sumac, bittersweet and greenbrier are important even in winter.

b. Applied to plants of other genera. †***wild sumach***, the bog-myrtle or sweet gale, *Myrica Gale*. ***Chinese sumach***, the ailanto, *Ailanthus glandulosa*. ***West Indian sumach***, *Brunellia comocladifolia* (Treas. Bot. 1866).

1578 LYTE *Dodoens* VI. xii. 672 *Rhus syluestris Plinij.* Plinies wilde Sumac. **1860** DARLINGTON *Amer. Weeds*, etc. 76 Glandular Ailanthus. Chinese Sumach. Tree of Heaven. Tillow or Tallow Tree.

3. *attrib.* and *Comb.*, as ***sumach berry***, ***bush***, ***leaf***, ***root***, ***-tan***, ***tree***, ***tribe***, ***tub***; † **sumach black**, a black dye obtained from sumach; **sumach-tanned** *a.*, tanned with sumach; so **sumach-tanning**.

1655 G. S. *Let. to S. Hartlib* in *Ref. Comm.-W. Bees* 24, I examined *Shoomake Berries which have a red outside. **1580–1** *Act 23 Eliz.* c. 9 §2 A Couloure commonlye called a *Shoomacke and mathered Blacke. **1877** BLACK *Green Past.* xlii, The lake-red of those *sumach bushes. **1857** MILLER *Elem. Chem., Org.* xi. §2. 673 A portion of *sumach leaves and of a stronger infusion is poured into the bag. **1897** BEATRICE HARRADEN *Hilda Strafford* 29 He brought in some logs of wood and some *sumac-roots. **1845** G. DODD *Brit. Manuf.* Ser. v. 196 The skins, shortly before being placed in the *sumach-tan, are subjected to the action of a hydrostatic press. **1906** *Athenæum* 24 Feb. 241/2 *Sumach-tanned leathers seem to be by far the best. **1845** G. DODD *Brit. Manuf.* Ser. v. 196 Both kinds are prepared by *sumach-tanning. **1688** HOLME *Armoury* II. v. 80/1 The *Sumack Tree of Virginia, nicked with nine, or ten leaves on a side like an ash. **1833** SIR J. E. SMITH *Study Bot.* (ed. 7) 316 *Sumachineæ.* *Sumach Tribe. **1845** G. DODD *Brit. Manuf.* Ser. v. 192 The *sumach-tubs present a singular appearance when three or four dozen inflated goat-skins are floating about in the contained liquor.

Hence **'sumac(h)** *v. trans.*, to tan with sumach; chiefly in **'sumaching** *vbl. sb.*

1845 G. DODD *Brit. Manuf.* Ser. v. 192 Once during the process of sumaching the skins are removed from the tub. *Ibid.* 200 The principal difference between sumached leather and alumed leather. **1860** TOMLINSON *Arts & Manuf.* Ser. II. *Leather* 27 The divided skins, or skivers, are sumached in a short time. **1870** *Eng. Mech.* 11 Feb. 534/2 The skins should be well shaved, scoured, and sumaced.

sumack ('s(j)uːmæk). *rare.* [ad. Pg. *sumaca*: see SMACK *sb.*[3]] A two-masted coasting-vessel.

1805 T. LINDLEY *Voy. Brazil* 2 They departed on board a sumack which brought them from Bahia.

sumage, obs. form of SUMMAGE.

sumation, obs. form of SUMMATION.

Sumatra (s(j)uː'mɑːtrə), the name of a large island of the Malay archipelago; used *attrib.* in specific names of animals or products of the island, as ***Sumatra benzoin***, ***cat***, ***dog***, ***monkey*** (cf. SUMATRAN); **Sumatra camphor**, a kind of camphor found in the fissures and cavities of the tree *Dryobalanops Camphora* (*aromatica*), Borneo or Malay camphor; also *attrib.*

1875 *Encycl. Brit.* III. 581/1 In some specimens of *Sumatra benzoin cinnamic acid has been found entirely replacing benzoic acid. **1849** BALFOUR *Man. Bot.* §789 *Dipterocarpaceæ*, the *Sumatra-Camphor Family. **1858** BAIRD *Cycl. Nat. Sci.* s.v. *Camphora*, Sumatra or Malay camphor. **1837** *Partington's Brit. Cycl. Nat. Hist.* I. 744/1 The *Sumatra Cat. It does not appear that this species differs in any material degree from the former [*sc.* Java cat]. **1822** HARDWICKE in *Trans. Linn. Soc.* XIII. 236 The ears of the *Sumatra Dog are more rounded. **1871** *Cassell's Nat. Hist.* I. 92 The *Sumatra monkey.

b. (with capital or lower-case initial). A violent squall in the Straits of Malacca and the Malay peninsula, blowing from the direction of Sumatra.

1842 *Penny Cycl.* XXIII. 272/2 In this season [*sc.* March to September] the Sumatras.. blow, especially in the first part of the night. **1887** *Encycl. Brit.* XXII. 93/2 Rapid squalls (sumatras) also occur during the south-west monsoon.

c. A variety of tobacco yielding a light-coloured leaf.

1911 B. MIALL tr. *Cabaton's Java, Sumatra, & other Islands of Dutch East Indies* xi. 229 The Manilla variety [of tobacco].. has been.. less largely used than the Deli (Sumatra) tobacco. **1912** A. E. TANKER *Tobacco* xii. 85 Leaf used for making British cigars consists of Sumatra, Borneo, and Havana. **1969** *Times* 24 Nov. (Congo Suppl.) p. vi/6 The main varieties [of tobacco] grown are Kentucky, White Burley, Sumatra and heavy Dark Western. **1975** N. FREELING *What are Bugles blowing For?* xiv. 84 He sat.. smoking a small Dutch cigar as a treat: rather heavy—they had mixed some dark Brazilian leaf in with the light Sumatra tobacco.

Sumatran (s(j)uː'mɑːtrən), *a.* and *sb.* [f. prec. + -AN.]

A. *adj.* **a.** Of or pertaining to the island of Sumatra or its inhabitants or language.

1783 W. MARSDEN *Sumatra* 36 The genuine Sumatran character. **1850** LATHAM *Nat. Hist. Man* 140 The wildest varieties of the Sumatran tribes. **1887** *Encycl. Brit.* XXII. 639/2 A remarkable feature of the Sumatran flora is the great variety of trees that vie with each other in stature and beauty.

b. In names of animals indigenous to Sumatra, as ***Sumatran antelope***, ***ape***, ***broadbill***, ***grosbeak***, ***hare***, ***rhinoceros***, ***tapir***; **Sumatran monkey**, one of the sacred monkeys, *Semnopithecus melalophus*; **Sumatran pheasant**, the Argus pheasant (see ARGUS 2); **Sumatran tiger**, a small tiger belonging to the subspecies *Panthera tigris sumatræ*.

1793 PENNANT *Hist. Quad.* (ed. 3) II. 321 *Sumatran Antelope,.. *Cambing ootan*, or Goat of the Woods. **1838** *Penny Cycl.* XII. 408/1 These *Sumatran Apes.. exhibit strong maternal affection. **1880** *Cassell's Nat. Hist.* IV. 119 The same author [*sc.* Davison] writes of the *Sumatran Broadbill. **1801** LATHAM *Gen. Synopsis Birds* Suppl. II. 194 *Sumatran Gr[osbeak] Loxia hypoxantha... Inhabits the rice fields of the island of Sumatra. **1887** *Encycl. Brit.* XXII. 640/1 The *Sumatran hare (*Lepus netscheri*), discovered in 1880. **1871** *Cassell's Nat. Hist.* I. 95 The *Sumatran Monkey, in which the female is light brown and the male is a most extraordinary-looking yellow. **1783** W. MARSDEN *Sumatra* 97 The *coo-ow*, or famous *Sumatran or Argos pheasant. **1834** *Penny Cycl.* II. 483/2 The *Sumatran rhinoceros (*R. Sumatrensis*) resembles the African species. **1849** PICKERING *Races of Man* (1851) 314 The *Sumatran Tapir. **1908** *Proc. Zool. Soc.* 890 Mr. R. I. Pocock.. exhibited photographs of a *Sumatran Tiger, recently purchased by the Society. **1945** F. HARPER *Extinct & Vanishing Mammals of Old World* 310 The Sumatran Tiger .., although less common than formerly, is still numerous in various districts. **1976** *Guardian* 19 Apr. 7/6 Six Sumatran tiger cubs were born at Whipsnade last year.

B. *sb.* A native or inhabitant of the island of Sumatra; also, the Sumatran language.

1688 HOLME *Armoury* III. v. 233/1 The Sumatrans do wear Turbuts on their heads. **1783** W. MARSDEN *Sumatra* 56 The Sumatrans live, in a great measure, upon vegetable food. **1796** MORSE *Amer. Geog.* II. 593 The original clothing of the Sumatrans is the same with that of the inhabitants of the South Sea islands. **1813** *Q. Rev.* Oct. 257 Languages and Dialects.. Cingalese, Malayan, Sumatran. **1850** LATHAM *Nat. Hist. Man* 151 The Malaccan origin of the earlier Sumatrans.

sumbitch ('sʌmbɪtʃ). *U.S. slang.* Contraction of SON OF A BITCH.

1975 O. SELA *Bengali Inheritance* xiii. 108 That sumbitch Winston would go far in Russia. **1976** M. MACHLIN *Pipeline* liii. 533 Play that 'I'm Dreaming of a Fat Paycheck'. That's a sumbitch! **1977** *Time* 7 Mar. 34/2 Strauss, you are a rich sumbitch. **1981** P. MALLORY *Killing Matter* iv. 53 The sumbitch has sure got him a way with the womenfolk.

sumbul ('sʌmbʌl, 'sʊmbʊl). Also **sumbal, sambul**. [a. F. *sumbul*, a. Arab. *sunbul*.] Applied to the roots of certain plants (and to the plants themselves) which are used medicinally: *esp.* (*a*) the spikenard, *Nardostachys Jatamansi*, (*b*) the musk-root, *Ferula* (*Euryangium*) *sumbul*, (*c*) valerian.

East Indian, West African sumbul: see quot. 1887.

1790 SIR W. JONES *Spikenard Ancients* in *Asiat. Res.* II. 408 The true name of the Indian Sumbul was not Cétaca, but Jatámánsi. *Ibid.* 409 The sweet Sumbul is only another denomination of nard. **1839** ROYLE *Bot. Himal. Mts.* I. 242 *Polianthes tuberosa* is described as being one of the kinds of Persian Sumbul. **1861** BENTLEY *Man. Bot.* 562 *Sumbul* is the root of a supposed Umbelliferous plant, which is imported into this country from Bombay and Russia. **1864** *Chamb. Encycl.* VI. 634/1 The drug called Musk Root or Sambul. **1876** *Trans. Clinical Soc.* IX. 97 Valerian and sumbul did him some good. **1887** *Encycl. Brit.* XXII. 641/1 Under the name of East Indian sumbal, the root of *Dorema ammoniacum*, Don., has occasionally been offered in English commerce. *Ibid.*, West African sumbal is the root of a species of *Cyperus*. **1899** *Allbutt's Syst. Med.* VII. 750 Tincture of sumbul.

b. *attrib.*: **sumbul balsam**, the balsamic extract of sumbul-root; **sumbul-oil**, a mixture of volatile oils derived from sumbul; **sumbul-root**, the root of any of the above plants used medicinally as a tonic and anti-spasmodic.

1844 *Chem. Gaz.* II. 240 The oily portion of the *Sumbul balsam. **1868** WATTS *Dict. Chem.* V. 644 **Sumbul-oil*, a mixture of volatile oils obtained by the distillation of sumbul-balsam. **1899** E. J. PARRY *Chem. Essential Oils* 262 Sumbul Oil or Musk-root Oil is obtained from the dried root of *Ferula sumbul*... It has a distinct musk-like odour, and in India the root of *Dorema ammoniacum* is often substituted for it. **1855** DUNGLISON *Med. Lex.*, *Sumbuli radix*, *Sumbul root. **1868** GARROD *Mat. Med.* (ed. 3) 241 Tincture of Sumbul. (Sumbul root, in powder, two and a half ounces; proof spirit, a pint.)

Hence **sumbu'lamic, sum'bulic, sumbu'lolic** *acid*, **'sumbuline** (see quots.).

1844 *Chem. Gaz.* II. 240 The author [Reinsch] calls the acid separated from the oily portion of the Sumbul balsam, Sumbulolic acid, and the previously-obtained balsamic acid, Sumbulamic acid. **1855** GARROD *Mat. Med.* 163 Sumbul.. yields, on distillation,.. an acid capable of crystallisation, named Sumbulic acid. **1868** WATTS *Dict. Chem.* V. 644 *Sumbuline*, the name given by Murawieff to an alkaloid supposed to exist in sumbul-root. *Ibid.*, *Sumbulolic acid.* Syn. with Sumbulic or Angelic Acid. **1874** *Treas. Bot.* Suppl. 1344/2 Sumbul-root.. contains a peculiar acid, called sumbulic acid.

sumd, obs. form of SUMMED.

sumdel, etc., obs. variant of SOMEDEAL.

sume, obs. var. SOAM, chain for draught-animal.

1489 in *Acta Audit.* (1839) 137/1 A pleuch with Irnis ȝokis sume & vper graith belanging to hir.

sume, obs. form of SOME, SWIM.

‖**sumen** (ˈs(j)uːmɛn). [L. *sūmen*:—**sūgmen*, f. *sūgĕre* to suck.] A sow's udder, the dugs of a sow; formerly *Anat.*, the hypogastrium. †Also *transf.*, the fat or rich portion of a thing; also *attrib.* in ***sumen-soil.***

1662 J. CHANDLER *Van Helmont's Oriat.* 239 The undunged fields of Bohemia do yield lesse tartarous fruits than those which were fattened..with the dung of living Creatures, wherein..this earthy Sumen or fattening juyce doth voluntarily melt: Because this Sumen-soil should produce a Tartar in Herbs. *a* **1716** SOUTH *Serm.* Prov. i. 32 (1727) IV. 79 They could not have had Leisure to think upon their Sumens, their Mullets,..and the like..had the Gauls been beseiging their Capitol. **1753** *Chambers' Cycl.* Suppl., *Sumen*, a word used by some anatomical writers to express the hypogastrium. **1788** WOLCOT (P. Pindar) *Peter's Proph.* Wks. 1816 I. 453 Who sent you once the *sumen* of a sow.

sumer, obs. form of SUMMER *sb.*[1]

Sumerian (s(j)uːˈmɪərɪən), *a.* and *sb.* Also **Sumirian, Shumerian.** [ad. F. *sumérien* (Oppert, 1872, in *Journal Asiatique* Ser. VII. I. 114), f. *Sumer* (see def.).]

A. *adj.* Pertaining to Sumer or Sumir, one of the districts of ancient Babylonia, or to its population; *spec.* belonging to the language of the people that created the non-Semitic element in the civilization of Babylonia.

The Sumerian language was formerly co-ordinated with *Akkadian* as a related dialect, but the latter term is now applied to Semitic Babylonian.

1875 SAYCE in *Encycl. Brit.* III. 192/1 The language of the primitive Sumirian and Accadian population of Assyria and Babylonia belonged to the Turanian or Ural-Altaic family of speech. **1882–3** F. BROWN in *Schaff's Encycl. Relig. Knowl.* III. 2174 The old Shumerian king Gudêa. **1887** SAYCE *Lect. Relig. Anc. Babyl.* App. I. 422 Most of the religious and other texts were composed in the Sumerian language. **1895** BOSCAWEN *Bible & Monum.* iii. (1896) 105 We find in the Sumirian Version 'female and male' the order: while in the Semitic texts it is 'male and female.' **1908** BUDGE *Babyl. & Assyr. Antiq. Brit. Mus.* (ed. 2) 4 The beginning of Sumerian civilization may date from a period even as remote as B.C. 4000, or earlier.

B. *sb.* **1.** A non-Semitic inhabitant of Sumer.

[**1872** SAYCE *Assyrian Gram.* 179 The Cassi, I now find, were not identical with the Sumiri or people 'of the dog's language'.] **1878** —— *Babyl. Lit.* 24 It is probable that it was the Accadians rather than the Sumerians to whom was due the invention of the picture writing. **1884** BIRCH *Kouyunjik Gallery Brit. Mus.* 4 The entry of these people (afterwards known as Akkadians and Sumerians) into Babylonia.

2. The language spoken by the inhabitants of Sumer.

1887 SAYCE *Lect. Relig. Anc. Babyl.* App. I. 421 Semitic wives would not have spoken Sumerian with the same purity as their non-Semitic husbands. **1908** BUDGE *Babyl. & Assyr. Antiq. Brit. Mus.* (ed. 2) 53 Grammatical examples in Sumerian, with Assyrian translations.

Hence **Sumero-** (ˈs(j)uːmərəʊ), used as the combining form of *Sumerian* in various formations, = Sumerian and...; so **Su'merogram**, a character or group of characters representing a Sumerian word, used in written Hittite (Akkadian, etc.) as a substitute for the equivalent (longer) word in that language; **Sume'rology**, the study of the Sumerian language and antiquities.

1897 *Expositor* Sept. 162 The first-fruits of his studies in Sumerology. **1906** PINCHES *Relig. Babyl. & Assyria* ii. 10 The Sumero-Akkadians were non-Semites. **1913** S. LANGDON in *Scientia* (1914) XV. 223 There is no trace whatever of these primitive ideas in Sumero-Babylonian religion. **1952** O. R. GURNEY *Hittites* vi. 121 Hittite texts are liberally interspersed with purely Akkadian and Sumerian words, the latter usually written by single signs, the use of which as 'ideograms' (or better, 'Sumerograms') can often be recognized only by means of the context, for they may be the same signs that are normally used for mere syllables. **1965** J. PUHVEL in W. Winter *Evidence for Laryngeals* 83 The Sumerogram used for *Ḫattusa-* reveals its meaning of 'Silver City'. **1983** *Trans. Philol. Soc.* 102 The increasing tendency to make use of Sumerograms and Akkadograms in place of syllabically written Hittite words.

sumetime, -tym(e, obs. ff. SOMETIME *a.*

‖**sumi** (ˈsuːmi). [Jap., = ink, blacking.] (See quot. 1958); = INDIAN INK. Cf. next.

1911 [see *dry brush* s.v. DRY *a.* C. 3]. **1958** M. L. WOLF *Dict. Painting* 285 *Sumi*, Japanese ink or blacking, composed of a mixture of carbon and glue molded into sticks or cakes. When rubbed into water on an inkstone, it becomes the common medium of the painter and writer. **1970** *Globe & Mail* (Toronto) 26 Sept. 26/4 There's another show close to sellout in Kazuo Hamasaki's Japanese sumi paintings.

‖**sumi-e** (ˈsuːmie). Also **sumi-ee, sumiye, sumi-ye.** [Jap.] Japanese ink painting; also *collect.*, sumi pictures. Cf. prec.

1938 D. T. SUZUKI *Zen Buddhism & its Influence on Jap. Culture* I. ii. 24 Calligraphy in the Far East is an art just as much as *sumiye* painting. **1960** H. HAYWARD *Antique Coll.* 271/1 *Sumi-ye*, Japanese ink-pictures, i.e. painted in black only. **1965** W. SWAAN *Jap. Lantern* xiii. 146 Lessons in *sumi-e* (Japanese style, ink painting). **1977** *Time* 17 Jan. 34/3 Every cut of the chisel seems to possess the final, unlaboured rightness of a brush stroke by a master of *sumi-e* (ink painting). **1981** G. MACBETH *Kind of Treason* xx. 196 On the wall he'd hung the *kakemono*.., a thin scroll in *sumi-ee* with a house under a mountain.

sumkyn, obs. variant of SOMEKIN.

sumless (ˈsʌmlɪs), *a.* Chiefly *poet.* [f. SUM *sb.*[1] or *v.*[1] + -LESS.] Without number; that cannot be 'summed' or counted; incalculable.

1599 SHAKS. *Hen. V*, I. ii. 165 To..make their Chronicle as rich with prayse, As is the Owse and bottome of the Sea With sunken Wrack, and sum-lesse Treasuries. **1667** MILTON *P.L.* VIII. 36 While the sedentarie Earth..receaves, As Tribute such a sumless journey brought Of incorporeal speed.., Speed, to describe whose swiftness Number failes. **1725** POPE *Odyss.* IV. 86 Around the Palace shines The sumless treasure of exhausted mines. **1769** FALCONER *Shipwr.* III. 207 Xerxes..Advanc'd with Persia's sumless troops to war. **1823** CAMPBELL *Last Man* 53 Test of all sumless agonies. **1823** DE QUINCEY *Herder* Wks. 1859 XIII. 131 From the abyss of distance and of sumless elevation. **1876** C. L. SMITH tr. *Tasso* XI. xxxvii, Its huge machines and beams of sumless power.

sumleyr, variant of SOMLER *Obs.*, butler.

1565 *Aberd. Reg.* (Jam.), William Grysse sumleyr to..the king & quenis maiesteis.

‖**summa** (ˈsʌmə). Pl. †**summa(e)s.** Also 5 **somma.** [L.: see SUM *sb.*[1]]

†**1.** An amount; = SUM *sb.*[1] 1. *Obs.*

1475 *Paston Lett.* III. 135 The somma off money that I have receyvyd off Wylliam Pecok. **1484** *Ibid.* 313 The summa of *Cli.* **1523–4** *Rec. St. Mary at Hill* (1904) 325 All summaes of Money the whiche the said Thomas had in the custody of the chirch.

†**2.** A sum-total; = SUM *sb.*[1] 4 b. *Obs.*

1442 *Rolls of Parlt.* V. 59/2 Summa of the men MMCCLX men. **1550** W. LYNNE *Carion's Chron.* 29 Summa of the yeares is Cxci. **1596** in *Abst. Protocols Town Clerks of Glasgow* (1897) V. Pref. 14 Summa of this charge and oneratioun extending in haill to the sowme of jm iiijc 1 lib xiijs. iiijd. **1682** *Compt* in *Thanes of Cawdor* (Spalding Club) 359 Summa of the hingings in Scots money as the cost in Flanders is £441, 10s. **1784** in *Nairne Peerage Evidence* (1874) 72 Summa of the inventary iij. c. lxxv.lib viij.s.

3. A summary treatise; = SUM *sb.*[1] 9 b; e.g. the *Summa Theologiæ* of St. Thomas Aquinas.

1725 J. HOWE *Wks.* (1834) 597/2 Such summas of Christian doctrine and practice, as we have pointed to us. **1845** *Encycl. Metrop.* XI. 810/2 To judge adequately of the nature of this Theology, we have only to take a survey of the celebrated *Summa* of Aquinas. **1887** HUXLEY in *19th Cent.* Apr. 491 The second chapter of the work in question, which is entitled 'Law; its definitions', is, from my point of view, a sort of 'summa' of pseudo-scientific philosophy.

†**4.** *advb.* [L. abl. *summā*.] In sum (see SUM *sb.*[1] 10). *Obs.*

1535 COVERDALE *Bible* Ep. Ded., Summa, in all godly regimentes of olde tyme the kynge and temporall iudge was obeyed of euery man. [**1550** —— *Spir. Perle* xviii. 139 In summa to be short, after trouble and aduersite foloweth almaner of goodnes and felicite.] *a* **1560** —— *Bk. Death* I. xx. 76 Summa, he is oure hope, our safegarde, oure triumph, our crowne.

5. Phrases. **a. summa rerum** (ˈrɪərəm) [L. *rērum* of things or affairs]: the highest public interest. Cf. SUM *sb.*[1] 13 b.

1715 SWIFT *Inq. Behaviour Queen's Last Minist.* ¶25 Wks. 1841 I. 503/2, I believe no minister of any party would.. have scrupled to take the same step when the *summa rerum* was at stake. **1837** DE QUINCEY *Revolt Tartars* Wks. 1890 VII. 396 They easily understood that too capital an interest (the *summa rerum*) was now at stake.

b. summa summarum (sʌˈmɛərəm): the grand total; *fig.* the consummation, the ultimate result.

1567 JEWEL *Def. Apol.* I. ix. 65 This is, *Summa Summarum*: whiche thinge beinge graunted, what should a man seeke any farther? **1631** in *Crt. & Times Chas. I* (1848) II. 162 It is thought that, in *summa summarum*, he will be called to be the king's solicitor. **1941** SWENSON & LOWRIE tr. *Kierkegaard's Concluding Unscientific Postscript* II. ii. v. 528 If it is postulated and granted that it is easy to understand that God becomes a particular man, so that the difficulty first emerges in the next fact that He becomes a lowly and despised man—then in *summa summarum* Christianity is humor.

c. summa totalis (təʊˈteɪlɪs): = SUM-TOTAL. Abbreviated *summ' tot'*.

1471 *Paston Lett.* III. 26 Summa totalis, lvjs. iiijd. **1529** MORE *Suppl. Soulys* Wks. 294/1 Summa totalis, xliii. thowsand. li. iii. hundred & xxxiii. li. vi. s. viii. d. **1596** NASHE *Saffron Walden* Wks. 1905 III. 108 Master Spencer, whom I do not thrust in the lowest place because I make the lowest valuation of, but as wee vse to set the *Summ' tot'* alway vnderneath or at the bottome, he being the *Sum' tot'* of whatsoeuer can be said of sharpe inuention and schollership. **1606** *Sir G. Goosecappe* I. i. A 3 b, This is your *Summa totalis* of both their virtues. *a* **1670** HACKET *Abp. Williams* II. (1693) 172 The *summa totalis* of the Civil Magistracy.

summability (sʌməˈbɪlɪtɪ). [f. SUMMABLE *a.*: see -BILITY.] The property of being summable.

1904 *Q. Jrnl. Pure & Appl. Math.* XXXV. 43 In the treatment of certain questions fundamental in the theory we gained nothing by the introduction of the idea of absolute summability. **1968** P. A. P. MORAN *Introd. Probability Theory* viii. 351 The study of the relative strengths of various methods of summability of series.

summable (ˈsʌməb(ə)l), *a.* [f. SUM *v.*[1] + -ABLE.] Capable of being summed.

1784 *Phil. Trans.* LXXIV. 395 Mr. James Bernouilli found summable serieses by assuming a series V. **1841** J. R. YOUNG *Math. Dissert.* iii. 125 None of the series belonging to the class referred to..are summable in finite numbers.

‖**summa cum laude** (ˈsʌmə kʌm ˈlɔːdiː, ˈsʊmə kʊm ˈlaʊdiː, -eɪ), *adv.* (*adj.*, *sb.*,) *phr.* Chiefly *U.S.* [L., 'with highest praise'.] With highest distinction: designating a degree, diploma, etc., of the highest standard. Also *transf.* and *fig.* Occas. *ellipt.* as **summa.** Cf. MAGNA CUM LAUDE.

1900 [see MAGNA CUM LAUDE]. **1951** S. F. NADEL *Found. Social Anthropol.* i. 18 You may be said to have accomplished assimilation *summa cum laude.* **1962** *Listener* 16 Aug. 242/1 He was psychoanalyzed..presumably by what Buddy calls one of those '*summa-cum-laude* thinkers and intellectual men's-room attendants'. **1970** G. GREER *Female Eunuch* 295 Mrs Friedan is a *summa cum laude* graduate of Smith College. **1976** *N.Y. Rev. Bks.* 24 June 4/2 When Commencement Day arrived, Mrs. Plath..[came] to watch her daughter being awarded her *summa cum laude* certificate. **1976** *Time* 20 Dec. 18/2 James R. Schlesinger ..*summa cum laude* and Ph.D in economics at Harvard. **1977** *New Yorker* 19 Sept. 47/3 She had just graduated summa cum laude from the University of Washington, in Seattle. **1978** F. MACLEAN *Take Nine Spies* iv. 132 At Hamburg Sorge had taken his doctor's degree in political science *summa cum laude.* **1980** M. BABSON *Dangerous to Know* vi. 40 An interview with one of the graduates, *summa cum laude*, of the Fat Farm. **1980** *Sci. Amer.* Aug. 35/1 He left Harvard three years later with a most irregular but steadily brilliant record, graduating in three years with an A.B. summa in chemistry.

summage (ˈsʌmɪdʒ). *Obs.* exc. *Hist.* Also 7 **sumage.** [Only as an artificial rendering of med.L. *summagium* (1249 in Gross *Gild Merch.*), ad. OF. *somage*:—med.L. **sagmaticum* (cf. *summaticum*, 1214 in Du C.), f. L. *sagma* (see SUM *sb.*[2]).]

1. A toll payable for carriage on horseback.

c **1450** *Godstow Reg.* 665 Vtterly quyte fro shires and hundredis,..and workes of Castels and howses,..of summage and cariage. **1607** COWELL *Interpr.*, *Sumage* (*Sumagium*) seemeth to be tolle for cariage on horseback. **1867** HART *Hist. & Cartul. S. Petri Glouc.* (Rolls) III. Introd. p. xxii, Their land was to be free from toll, carriage, summage [etc.].

2. A load. (Cf. SOMMAGE.)

c **1660** SIR T. WIDDRINGTON *Anal. Ebor.* (1897) 251 To receive..of every summage of horse carrying fish, a pennyworth of fish.

summand (ˈsʌmænd). [ad. med.L. *summandus* (sc. *numerus*), gerundive of *summāre* to SUM.] One of two or more magnitudes to be summed or added together.

1893 W. B. SMITH *Introd. Mod. Geom.* 146 The areas apposed are called parts or summands of the sum. **1943** *Mind* LII. 243 Even in logic, 'all' means something more... It means..completeness of the logical summands. **1964** E. A. POWER *Introd. Quantum Electrodynamics* iv. 53 Suppose then $n_j \geq 1$, and then in each of the N summands on the right one gets a contribution of $\lambda_\alpha = j$ for that particular summand. **1979** *Proc. London Math. Soc.* XXXVIII. 213 If (G,H) is a countably generated pair with $cd_R G \leq 1$, and $I_H G$ a direct summand of I_G, then $H_\vee G$.

summar (ˈsʌmər), *a.* and *sb. Sc.* Chiefly *Law.* Also 6 **summair, sommair, sumare,** 7–8 **summer.** [a. F. *sommaire*, with subsequent assimilation to its source, L. *summārius* SUMMARY.]

A. *adj.* = SUMMARY *a.*

1585 JAS. I *Ess. Poesie* (Arb.) 56 Ane rype ingyne,..With sommair reasons, suddenlie applyit. **1593** J. NAPIER *Discov. Rev. St. John, Orac.* T 4 b, In summar conclusion, if thou O Rome alledges thy self reformed [etc.]. **1617** *Acts Parl. Scot., Jas. VI*, (1816) IV. 550/1 Quhairby goode and summer Justice may be done. **1628** MURE *Doomesday* 83 A summar processe shall ensew. **1678** G. MACKENZIE *Crim. Laws Scot.* II. viii. §7 (1699) 196 The Pursuer, or Defender, being convict..without any Probation, except summar Cognition. **1693** STAIR *Inst. Law Scot.* IV. iii. §25 A Summar Action is of two sorts. **1838** W. BELL *Dict. Law Scotl.* s.v. *Rolls of Court*, The Summar roll is appropriated to such causes as require dispatch. **1868** *Act 31 & 32 Vict.* c. 100 §63 The Court..shall hear Parties in the Summar Roll.

†**B.** *sb.* = SUMMARY *sb.* 1. *Obs.*

1570 BUCHANAN *Admonit.* Wks. (1892) 22 The summar is this. **1595** in *Cath. Rec. Soc. Publ.* V. 360 The sumare of a letter sent by Mr. Freeman.

summarily (ˈsʌmərɪlɪ), *adv.* [f. SUMMARY *a.* + -LY[2].]

1. In a summary or compendious manner; chiefly of statement, in few words, compendiously, briefly.

1528 MORE *Dyaloge* II. Wks. 178/1 This is of you verye well remembred and well and sommarily rehersed. **1561** T. NORTON *Calvin's Inst.* III. 301 That which is summarily comprehended in this prayer. **1614** RALEIGH *Hist. World* III. ix. (1634) 89 Of the warre betweene these brethren, and summarily of Artaxerxes, we shall haue occasion to speake. **1690** C. NESSE *Hist. & Myst. O. & N. Test.* I. 10 The idæa ..of the great world..was..briefly and summarily expressed..in Man. **1726** LEONI *Alberti's Archit.* I. 10/2 When we come to treat of that Subject..particularly, and not summarily. **1825** JEFFERSON *Autobiog.* Wks. 1859 I. 105 The Marquis introduced the objects of the conference, by summarily reminding them of the state of things in the Assembly. **1873** FARRAR *Fam. Speech* i. 7 It is..my purpose ..summarily to sketch the broadest..results.

†**b.** *ellipt.* To put it shortly, in sum. *Obs.*

1577 tr. *Bullinger's Decades* (1592) 319 Now summarilie this precept doth commaunde vs, to vse our tongues well. **1586** *Let. Earle Leycester* 20 The reasons whereof, were summarily these that follow. **1638** ROUSE *Heav. Acad.* ii. 17 The naturall understanding doth perceive them no better than the eare doth the reason of sounds, or the nose the reason of smels; and summarily, than the senses do the things of the second intention.

2. By summary legal procedure.

1530 PALSGR. 842/1 Sommaryly and playnly, as judgementes somtyme be gyven, *sommairement et de playn.* **1540** *Act 32 Hen. VIII*, c. 7 §1 The..Judge..shall..procede..ordinarily or summarily according to..the said ecclesiasticall lawes. **1572–3** *Reg. Privy Council Scot.* Ser. I. II. 195 That letters be direct be the Lordis of Counsale and Sessioun summarilie without ony calling. **1617** MORYSON *Itin.* III. 241 In Iudgements they..vse to iudge summarily vpon oath. *a* **1722** FOUNTAINHALL *Decis.* (1759) I. 10 The Lords ordained an agent to be summarily examined upon a bill. **1726** AYLIFFE *Parergon* 152 When the Parties may proceed summarily, and they chuse the ordinary Way of Proceeding, the Cause is made Plenary. **1764** BURN *Poor Laws* 289 He may be committed summarily to prison until he shall find sureties. **1826** BELL *Comm. Laws Scot.* (ed. 5) II. 481 It has been held..that restitution of goods in the hands of the trustee may be claimed summarily. **1896** *Daily Graphic* 10 Feb. 7/3 Every dog that is not..provided with a muzzle will be summarily dealt with by the law.

3. Without (unnecessary) formality or delay; without hesitation.

1621 *First & Sec. Bk. Discipl. Ch. Scot.* Pref., Others..summarily deny, that ever this Kirk had any approved discipline. **1794** R. J. SULIVAN *View Nat.* I. 48 Le Cat differed from his contemporary Voltaire, who very summarily gave these heaps of fossil shells to a less powerful cause. **1838** DICKENS *Nich. Nick.* xv, Miss Morleena..was summarily caught up and kissed by Mr. Lillyvick. **1879** BEERBOHM *Patagonia* 3 While the captain was yet doubtful what course to take, the matter was summarily decided by the weather itself. **1886** *Manch. Exam.* 2 Jan. 5/2 He summarily refused all redress.

summariness ('sʌmərɪnɪs). [f. SUMMARY *a.* + -NESS.] The quality or condition of being summary.

1802–12 BENTHAM *Ration. Judic. Evid.* (1827) V. 386 A mode that by its summariness forms the most striking contrast to the regular equity mode. **1890** *Spectator* 26 Apr. 584/2 The summariness which has always characterised English criminal jurisprudence.

summarist ('sʌmərɪst). [f. SUMMARY *sb.* + -IST.] One who compiles a summary.

1873 F. HALL *Mod. Eng.* 311 Among our myriad of substantives like the foregoing are..*socialist, somnambulist, summarist.* **1883** *Pall Mall Gaz.* 25 Sept. 4/2 The summarist of literary history.

summarizable ('sʌməraɪzəb(ə)l), *a.* [f. SUMMARIZ(E *v.* + -ABLE.] Capable of being summarized.

1970 *Nature* 23 May 774/2 In the last 18 pages chairmen attempt to summarize their sessions, but this is disappointing; it is not summarizable material. **1977** M. COHEN *Sensible Words* 139 Conventional intellectual historians who read merely for summarizable ideas.

summarization (ˌsʌməraɪ'zeɪʃən). [f. next + -ATION.] The action or process of summarizing; an instance of this.

1865 J. GROTE *Explor. Philos.* I. 35 There are all kinds of abbreviations and summarizations by the help of language. **1884** tr. *Lotze's Logic* 125 Classifications would belong entirely to applied logic if they aimed at nothing more than complete summarisation. **1900** *Pall Mall Gaz.* 13 Oct. 12 A concise summarization of the present state of things in China.

summarize ('sʌməraɪz), *v.* [f. SUMMARY + -IZE.] *trans.* To make (or constitute) a summary of; to sum up; to state briefly or succinctly.

1871 EARLE *Philol. Eng. Tongue* 5 These, and all such illustrations, may be summarised for convenience sake in the following mnemonic formula. **1881** SIR W. THOMSON in *Nature* XXIV. 434/1 We may summarise the natural sources of energy as Tides, Food, Fuel, Wind, and Rain. **1882** FARRAR *Early Chr.* I. xiii. 276 The four words of St. John, 'The Word became flesh',..summarise and concentrate the inmost meaning of the Old Testament revelation. **1885** *Phillips' Man. Geol.* I. xxv. 526 If we endeavour to summarise the conclusions.

absol. **1889** *Daily News* 10 Dec. 7/6 Assistant Sub-Editor. —— Smart young fellow who can summarise attractively.

Hence **'summarized** *ppl. a.*, **'summarizing** *vbl. sb.* and *ppl. a.*; **'summarizer** = SUMMARIST.

1883 *Athenæum* 7 Apr. 441/3 An admirable piece of summarized history. **1886** *Ibid.* 5 June 739/3 Then follow two pages of rapid summarizing of the mediæval narrative. **1894** *Sat. Rev.* 17 Mar. 287 Mr. Ward is quite a model summarizer. **1910** *19th Cent.* Oct. 682 Nothing..comes amiss to his summarising genius.

†**'summarly**, *adv. Sc. Obs.* [f. SUMMAR *a.* + -LY[2].] = SUMMARILY.

c **1550** ROLLAND *Crt. Venus* III. 119 Mair summarlie we sall cum to the end. **1564** *Reg. Privy Council Scot.* Ser. I. I. 291 To ansuer uther befoir the Lordis of Counsall and Sessioun, summarlie, but diet or tabill upon summondis. **1588** A. KING tr. *Canisius' Catech.* g vij b, I sall pen summairlie ye occasion and ressones. **1633** STRUTHER *True Happiness* 1 The first thing then is his choice, summarly described in the word (*one thing*). **1678** G. MACKENZIE *Crim. Laws Scot.* I. xxvi. §2. (1699) 130 The Commissioners of the Thesaury did summarly..ordain the Sea-men to be whipt. **1689** in *Acts Parlt. Scot.* (1875) XII. 61/1 Many of the Leidges were put to death summarlie without legall tryall Jury or record. **1693** STAIR *Inst. Law Scot.* IV. iii. §25 Heretors of a Paroch are summarly charged to..Stent themselves for Building..Kirks. **1710** in *Nairne Peerage Evidence* (1874) 45 To the effect the said Mr. Robert Nairn may be the more summerly infeft in the said annual rent.

summary ('sʌmərɪ), *sb.* [ad. L. *summārium*, neut. sing. of *summārius* (see next).]

1. A summary account or statement.

1509 in Leadam *Sel. Cases Star Chamber* (Selden Soc.) I. 200 To make a breuiat wodurwise called a summary of al his charteris. **1539** TONSTALL *Serm. Palm Sund.* (1823) 48 This confession conteyneth the hole summarye of our faythe. **1542–3** *Act 34 & 35 Hen. VIII*, c. 1 §4 The..cutting out of any quotacion or summaryes of chapiters expressed..in any suche Bybles. **1596** SHAKS. *Merch. V.* III. ii. 131 Here's the scroule, The continent, and summarie of my fortune. **1638** CHILLINGW. *Relig. Prot.* I. iv. §26 205 The Apostles Creed is the Summary and Abridgment of that faith which is necessary for a Christian. **1724** WATERLAND *Athanas. Creed* iv. 63 Closing This Chapter..with a Table representing a Summary, or short Sketch of what hath been done in it. **1865** PUSEY *Truth Engl. Ch.* 237 What he draws out at length is stated in summary..by Divines or Canonists in the Roman Communion. **1878** R. W. DALE *Lect. Preach.* viii. 231 Sometimes when I have finished a book I give a summary of the whole of it. **1880** HAUGHTON *Phys. Geog.* v. 219 The following summary of the North American lakes.

Comb. **1884** E. YATES *Recoll.* II. iv. 144 The important office of summary-writer in the House of Commons.

†**2.** The sum and substance *of. Obs. rare.*

a **1548** HALL *Chron., Hen. VII*, 11 The summarye of their commyssion was to conclude a truce for a tyme. **1621** T. WILLIAMSON tr. *Goulart's Wise Vieillard* 126 An aduise to wise old men, conteining the summarie and substance of their dutie.

3. The highest point or summit; also, the ultimate outcome. *rare.*

1851 CARLYLE *Sterling* II. ii, This battle..of 'all old things passing away' against 'all things becoming new', has its summary and animating heart in that of Radicalism against Church. **1858** —— *Fredk. Gt.* x. i. (1872) III. 198 A pleasant Lake..: the summary, or outfall, of which..is called the Rhein. **1866** —— *Inaug. Addr.* 176 Valour..the crown and summary of all that is ennobling for a man.

4. Special Comb.: **summary punch**, a card punch that automatically punches the results obtained by a tabulator from a number of other cards; hence as *v. intr.*; **summary-punched** *a.*, **summary punching** *vbl. sb.*

1935 *Astron. Jrnl.* XLIV. 180/1 The wiring for the tabulator and summary punch is changed very little during the cycle. **1949** E. C. BERKELEY *Giant Brains* iv. 50 The reproducer..can..summary punch, or copy totals or summaries obtained in the tabulator into blank cards in the reproducer. **1956** G. A. MONTGOMERIE *Digital Calculating Machines* viii. 154 Automatic punches can also be connected to the tabulator to act as summary punches. **1957** N. CHAPLIN *Introd. Automatic Computers* xv. 341 Summary punching produces, by machine, cards that may contain variable and modified information derived from other cards. *Ibid.* 342 A summary punch machine..usually does not produce more than one hundred summary punched cards per minute. **1970** O. DOPPING *Computers & Data Processing* iv. 75 The summary punch can punch information coming from the registers of the tabulator.

summary ('sʌmərɪ), *a.* [ad. med.L. *summārius* (recorded in class. L. only in neut. sb., see prec.), e.g. in *cognitio summaria* (Grosseteste), *inquisitio summaria* (Bracton); f. *summa* SUM *sb.*[1]: see -ARY[1]. Cf. OF. *sommier*, F. *sommaire* (see SUMMAR), Pr. *sommari*, It. *sommario*, Sp. *sumario*, Pg. *summario.*]

1. Of a statement or account (†*occas.* a term): Containing or comprising the chief points or the sum and substance of a matter; compendious (now usually with implication of brevity).

1432–50 tr. *Higden* (Rolls) I. 29, xv. chapitres bene contexte, not as summary, but as conteynenge necessarily the knowlege of the yle of Bryteyne. **1534** MORE *Comf. agst. Trib.* I. Wks. 1168/1 A summarye commendacion of tribulacion. **1570** FOXE *A. & M.* (ed. 2) I. 1/2 To declare as in a summary table, the misguiding of that church. **1590** GREENWOOD *Answ. Gifford* 19 Yt [*sc.* the Lord's Prayer] being the most summary forme of prayer. **1651** BAXTER *Inf. Bapt.* 321 Most of his summary Aphorisms, I have answered before. **1693** DRYDEN *Juvenal* (1697) Argt. 2 A summary and general view of the Vices and Follies reigning in his time. **1788** REID *Aristotle's Logic* iv. §1. 67 We have given a summary view of the theory of pure syllogisms. **1836** *Penny Cycl.* V. 165/1 (*Book-keeping*) The summary journal, in registering these same purposes, throws away all consideration of particular persons..by raising a single account comprehending them all under the general name of 'bought ledger'. **1879** FARRAR *St. Paul* I. 9 A summary sketch of what he had done and suffered.

†**b.** General, not detailed. *Obs.*

1529 MORE *Suppl. Soulys* Wks. 309/2 The summary effecte of hys boke. **1532** —— *Confut. Tindale* ibid. 395/1 The summarye purpose and effect of Tyndales doctrine. **1719** DE FOE *Crusoe* II. (Globe) 445 A Man..having nothing but a summary Notion of Religion himself.

c. *transf.* Characterized by or involving conciseness and brevity.

1582 STANYHURST *Æneis* I. (Arb.) 28 Chief poyncts I purpose too touche with summarye shortnesse. **1610** *North's Plutarch* 1206 Pouertie is a kind of temperance, and need may be called a summarie obseruation of the lawes. **1783** BURKE *Rep. Indian Committee* Wks. 1808 II. 133 The matter which appears before them, is in a summary manner, this: The Decca merchants [etc.].

2. *Law.* Applied to proceedings in a court of law carried out rapidly by the omission of certain formalities required by the common law. Similarly of a court-martial. (The corresp. use of SUMMARILY is recorded much earlier.)

summary jurisdiction: the determination of cases expeditiously without reference to the ordinary requirements of the common law.

In Scottish law, ***summary application***: an application to a court or a judge without the formality of a summons or full procedure. So ***summary action, cause, diligence.***

1765–8 ERSKINE *Inst. Law Scot.* IV. i. §9 Bills of complaint..may be all tried by a summary action. **1798** *Bay's Rep.* (1809) I. 49 Trials in a summary way deprive the subject of the inestimable trial by jury. **1826** BELL *Comm. Laws Scot.* (ed. 5) II. 480 All those acts of statutory jurisdiction are declared to be competent on summary application. *Ibid.* 481 That one acting as agent for the trustee..though not by the Act expressly subject to summary jurisdiction, is..held to be liable to the same summary proceedings for recovery of..documents. **1835** TOMLINS *Law Dict.* s.v. *Conviction*, The process of these summary convictions is extremely speedy. **1845** MCCULLOCH *Taxation* II. vi. (1852) 240 In cases of summary jurisdiction, or those adjudged by the commissioners and justices, there is little or no delay and little or no expense. **1861** BROUGHAM *Brit. Const.* xv. 220 A member arrested for debt was liberated by a summary application to the Crown. **1867** *Chamb. Encycl.* IX. 206/1 *Summary Diligence*, in the practice of the law of Scotland, means issuing execution without the formality of an action. **1877–81** VOYLE & STEVENSON *Milit. Dict.* Suppl. s.v., When a person subject to military law and being on active service with any body of force is charged with an offence, a summary court-martial may be convened, and shall have jurisdiction to try such offence.

3. Performed or effected by a short method; done without delay. (Cf. SUMMARILY 3, which is earlier.)

1713 SWIFT *Cadenus & Vanessa* Wks. 1841 I. 681/2 The judge..Directed them to mind their brief; Nor spend their time to show their reading: She'd have a summary proceeding. **1771** *Junius Lett.* lxiv. (1788) 336 The mode of trial..and kind of evidence necessary to convict..are..too summary. **1775** SHERIDAN *Rivals* III. i, He has too summary a method of proceeding in these matters. **1833** HT. MARTINEAU *Loom & Lugger* I. iii. 34 It put into their heads the idea of summary vengeance. **1844** DICKENS *Mart. Chuz.* xiii, He cleared the table by the summary process of tilting everything upon it into the fire-place. **1874** GREEN *Short Hist.* viii. §2 (1882) 476 The new weapon was put to a summary use.

†**4.** Consisting of or relating to a mathematical sum or summation. (Cf. SUMMATORY.) *Obs. rare.*

1588 KYD *Househ. Philos.* Wks. (1901) 280 Materiall number is a summarie collection of things numbred. **1805** JAMES *Milit. Dict.* (ed. 2), *Summary arithmetic*, the art of finding the flowing from the fluxion.

†**b.** *transf.* Cumulative. *Obs. rare.*

1816 ACCUM *Chem. Tests* (1818) 55 The united effects produced by the summary action of several tests.

†**5.** Highest; supreme. *Obs. rare.*

1587 GREENE *Euphues his Censure* Wks. (Grosart) VI. 203 Sith Nestor..had..attayned to the summary perfection of wisedome. **1605** BACON *Adv. Learn.* I. i. §3 Hee doth insinuate that the supreame or summarie law of Nature..is not possible to be found out by Man. *Ibid.* I. vi. §6 The two summarye parts of knowledge. **1733** P. SHAW tr. *Bacon's De Sap. Vet.* I. ix. Expl., Philos. Wks. I. 569 There is one summary or capital Law in which Nature meets, subordinate to God.

summat, dial. variant of SOMEWHAT.

summate ('sʌmeɪt), *v.* [f. med.L. *summāt-*, *summāre* to SUM.] **1.** *trans.* To add together or combine; *spec.* in *Physiol.*, with reference to nerve impulses, etc. Also *intr.* and *fig.*

1900 *Nature* LXII. 290/2 The excitatory electrical change in the whole organ..causes merely a change in one direction, which is summated in proportion to the number of discs in the pile. **1922** *Jrnl. Optical Soc. Amer.* VI. 550 When quite differently weighted, in terms of the relative powers of the three elementary processes to generate brilliance, the three chromatic curves should summate to yield the visibility curve. **1932** P. BLOOMFIELD *Imaginary Worlds* xiv. 246 Happiness does not summate. The happiness of ten million individuals is not a millionfold the happiness of ten. **1935** *Discovery* May 140/1 In order to see more clearly in a bad light, we instinctively keep on blinking and peering so that the recurring slight pressures by the eyelids are, when summated, capable of evoking phosphenes. **1935** WINTON & BAYLISS *Human Physiol.* (ed. 2) ix. 349 Responses which are partially or completely super-imposed are said to summate. **1951** G. HUMPHREY *Thinking* i. 17 The implication that stimuli may be linearly summated is accepted by representative objective psychologists. **1957** *Encycl. Brit.* III. 866/1 Similar documents may be assembled and summated before they are journalized. **1962** W. NOWOTTNY *Lang. Poets Use* iv. 78 The particulars which inhabit these schemes, though extraordinarily difficult to summate, permit themselves to be assimilated to a common ideogram of decline. **1970** *Jrnl. Gen. Psychol.* LXXXIII. 144 According to the second principle, two responses having the same form summate. **1971** A. C. GUYTON *Basic Human Physiol.* vi. 63/2 Not only can discharges from separate presynaptic terminals summate with each other, but rapidly successive discharges from the same presynaptic terminal can also summate.

2. *trans.* To summarize.

1955 G. GORER *Exploring Eng. Character* xiv. 269 If the 25 per cent of the population who say that they are influenced either regularly or occasionally by the advice of horoscopes are summated, one finds that there are very few categories where there is a variation of more than 3 per cent from the national norm. **1976** J. BAYLEY *Uses of Division* I. i. 24 It remained for Proust to summate the retrospective social novel.

Hence **su'mmated** *ppl. a.*

1938 J. NEWTON *Introd. Metallurgy* xiii. 406 In slag calculations use is sometimes made of 'summated' percentages by means of which oxides of similar chemical properties are grouped together and treated as a single constituent.

† **summation**[1]. *Obs.* Also 5 somac(i)on. [a. OF. *som(m)acion*, f. *sommer* to summon.] Summons.

1471 CAXTON *Recuyell* (Sommer) 222 Perseus..sente danus vnto the kynge prycus to somene hym that he shold yelde the royame vnto kynge Acrisius. Danus wente to Arges. And accomplisshed the somacion. *c* **1477** —— *Jason* 57 b, Whan Iason vnderstode the somacon that the two damoiselles made he was sore abasshid. **1864** D. G. MITCHELL *Sev. Stor.* 7 The admiring spirit with which..I yielded my pence to his impetuous summation.

summation[2] (sʌˈmeɪʃən). [ad. mod.L. *summātio, -ōnem*, n. of action f. med.L. *summāre* to SUM. Cf. F. *sommation*.]

1. *Math.* The process of finding the sum of a series. Also in fig. context.

1760 *Phil. Trans.* LI. 553 Any branch of it [*sc.* the analytic art] that relates to the summation of series. **1842** *Penny Cycl.* XXIII. 267/1 The summation of a finite number of terms of a series. **1860** SYLVESTER *Math. Papers* (1908) II. 228 The $(\Sigma)^r$ meaning merely the sign of summation *r* times repeated. **1874** STUBBS *Const. Hist.* I. i. 4 The constitutional history of France is thus the summation of the series of feudal development in a logical sequence. **1885** WATSON & BURBURY *Math. Th. Electr.* I. 167 If the system consist only of conductors on which the charges are e_1, e_2, &c., we have $E = \frac{1}{2}\Sigma Ve$, Σ denoting summation for all the conductors.

2. The adding up of numbers; casting up an account; an addition sum.

1816 SCOTT *Antiq.* xxii, It amounts..to eleven hundred and thirteen pounds, seven shillings, five pennies, and three-fourths of a penny sterling—But look over the summation yourself. **1854** H. MILLER *Sch. & Schm.* xxiii. (1858) 512, I never acquired the facility, in running up columns of summations, of the early-taught accountant. **1883** *Nonconf. & Indep.* 28 Dec. 1168/3 A summation made up by me to the end of last year.

3. a. The addition of mensurable quantities (distance, time, etc.), now *esp.* such addition in an electronic device.

1860 TYNDALL *Glac.* I. xi. 81 The summation of distances twenty paces each must finally place us at the top. **1914** PETRIE in *Anc. Egypt* 32 A summation of years. **1962** M. G. HARTLEY *Introd. Electronic Analogue Computers* iii. 23 An arrangement for the summation of three voltages. **1977** J. G. GRAEME *Designing with Operational Amplifiers* vii. 175 This characteristic makes possible signal summation and subtraction through the simple connection of summing or differencing resistors to the amplifier inputs. **1981** F. W. HUGHES *Op Amp Handbk.* viii. 206 The output signal may be a direct mathematical summation of the input signals or may include a determined amount of gain.

b. The process or effect by which repeated or multiple nerve impulses can produce a response that each impulse alone would fail to produce.

1877 M. FOSTER *Physiol.* III. v. (1878) 471 The central mechanism..being thrown into activity through a summation of the afferent impulses reaching it. **1883** *Nature* XXVII. 439 This relation of the contractile tissue to stimuli is usually expressed by saying that the tissue has the power of summation. **1889** *Lancet* 3 Aug. 203/1 A summation of the stimuli appears to go on in the cells. **1956** A. C. GUYTON *Textbk. Med. Physiol.* v. 45/1 If impulses occur too far apart in time..temporal summation will not occur. **1979** SPENCE & MASON *Human Anat. & Physiol.* xi. 293 During spatial summation, nerve impulses in many different stimulatory presynaptic cells travelling to a single postsynaptic cell may all arrive at the postsynaptic cell very close together in time.

c. *Psychol.* Cumulative action or effect (see quots.).

1921 E. J. KEMPF *Psychopathol.* i. 62 The tendency to suppress our affections may accumulate; that is, a summation of the repressing or suppressing egoistic wishes may occur. **1924** J. RIVIERE et al. tr. *Freud's Coll. Papers* I. 95 An assumption which is not improbable in itself—namely, that a *noxia* such as coitus interruptus attains its effect by summation. According to the disposition of the person..a longer or shorter time will be required before the effect of this summation becomes evident. **1955** J. STRACHEY et al. tr. *Freud's Compl. Psychol. Wks.* II. ii. 174 Even a hysteric can retain a certain amount of affect that has not been dealt with; if, owing to the occurrence of similar provoking causes, that amount is increased by summation to a point beyond the subject's tolerance, the impetus to conversion is given.

4. The computation of the aggregate value of conditions, qualities, etc.; summing-up.

1836 LYTTON *Athens* (1837) I. 455 Valour seems to have been for his [Miltiades'] profound intellect but the summation of chances. **1856** DOVE *Logic Chr. Faith* v. i. 262 Our conception of duty is either 'Yea', or 'Nay' without..summations of advantages. **1908** *Daily Chron.* 26 Feb. 3/3 Such is Mr. Wyndham's summation of Scott.

5. The aggregate or sum-total; the resultant or product.

1840 CARLYLE *Heroes* i. (1872) 20 They are not one coherent System of Thought; but properly the summation of several successive systems. **1879** *19th Cent.* Sept. 500 He is the summation of Hebraism and Hellenism. **1885** *Manch. Exam.* 13 July 6/1 Mr. Harrison..regards God as the summation of Humanity.

6. *attrib.* and *Comb.*, as ***summation network, theory***; **summation check** *Computers* = *sum check* s.v. SUM *sb.*[1] 14; **summation tone**, *Acoustics* [G. *summationston* (Helmholtz)] = *summational tone* (see TONE *sb.* 2).

1954 *Computers & Automation* Dec. 22/1 Summation check. **1969** JORDAIN & BRESLAU *Condensed Computer Encycl.* 498 One weakness of the summation check is its inability to detect transposed digits. **1968** D. EADIE *Introd. Basic Computer* xv. 347 In most analog computers the summation network is combined with an operational amplifier. **1901** E. B. TITCHENER *Exper. Psychol.* I. II. 90 If we are not satisfied with this 'summation' theory, we may..suppose that the gaps in sensation are filled out by association. **1867** TYNDALL *Sound* vii. 285 Resultant tones are of two kinds... The former are called difference tones, the latter summation tones. **1875** *Encycl. Brit.* I. 118/2 [Helmholtz] was led..to surmise the formation of summation-tones by the interference of two loud primaries.

summational (sʌˈmeɪʃənəl), *a.* [f. SUMMATION + -AL[1].] Produced by summation or addition. ***summational tone***: see TONE *sb.* 2.

1873 A. J. ELLIS in Atkinson tr. *Helmholtz' Pop. Lect. Sci. Subj.* iii. 102 *note*, These [combinational tones] are of two kinds, differential and summational, according as their pitch is the difference or sum of the pitches of the two generating tones. **1881** *Nature* XXIV. 100, I tried in vain..to obtain resonance for a differential and summational tone.

summative (ˈsʌmətɪv), *a.* [f. med.L. *summāt-* (see SUMMATE) + -IVE.] Operating by means of addition; additive; cumulative, pertaining to accumulation.

1881 G. S. HALL *German Culture* 235 Relatively large and strongly-acting motor cells whose connections with each other are mainly summative. **1891** G. S. WOODHEAD *Bacteria* 379 Both the antagonistic action and this summative action. ?**1930** W. C. WILLIAMS *Sel. Essays* (1954) 103 We've got to experiment with technique long before the final summative artist arrives. **1931** *Brit. Jrnl. Psychol.* July 25 All such views of perception may be distinguished from summative or integrative theories by being called 'response' theories of perception. **1936** *Jrnl. Psychol.* II. 80 (*caption*) The summative efficiency of the samples. **1938** W. BENARY in W. D. Ellis *Sourcebk. Gestalt Psychol.* viii. 105 In these examples brightness differences are the *reverse* of what a summative theory would have demanded. **1968** W. A. SCOTT in Lindzey & Aronson *Handbk. Social Psychol.* (ed. 2) II. xi. 218 We shall use the term *summative* to designate a scale that is scored by adding the response scores on its component items.

summatively (sʌˈmeɪtɪvlɪ), *adv.* [f. SUMMATIVE *a.* + -LY[2].] Additively, cumulatively.

1936 *Mind* XLV. 270 Everything that can be described 'organically' can also be described 'summatively'. It is simply a question of convenience. **1951** G. HUMPHREY *Thinking* iii. 103 Watt professes to hold..a contributory theory of mental energetics, one which derives motive power in the kind of experiment which he performed,.. summatively from task and reproductive tendency. **1976** *Nature* 4 Mar. 59/1 Baylor *et al.* showed that the cones of the red-eared turtle, *Pseudemys scripta elegans*, are summatively and reciprocally coupled over distances up to 50 μm.

summator (sʌˈmeɪtə(r)). [f. SUMMATE *v.* + -OR.] **1.** *Electr. Engin.* That which sums; *spec.* a device which sums the analogue or digital information it receives. Cf. INTEGRATOR.

1930 *Engineering* 11 Apr. 482/1 The summator proper consists of two parts, a series of small dials giving the total kilowatt hours recorded by all the individual meters and larger dials, on which the maximum demand in kilowatts is aggregated. **1953** *Proc. Inst. Electr. Engineers* C. I. 44/1 The summator operates on the same principle of current balance as the telemeter and its error term is the same. **1974** *Jrnl. Appl. Physiol.* XXXVII. 748/1 A problem..is the inherently slow response time of the continuous discharge integrators (usually called analog summators, or merely integrators) used to supply this running average.

2. *Psychol.* In full, ***verbal summator***: (see quots.).

1936 B. F. SKINNER in *Jrnl. Psychol.* II. 71 The verbal summator is a device for repeating arbitrary samples of speech obtained by permuting and combining certain elemental speech-sounds. *Ibid.*, Apart from its use as a test, the summator is valuable in the study of other aspects of verbal behavior. *Ibid.* 73 The verbal summator..evokes latent verbal responses through summation with imitative responses to skeletal samples of speech. **1957** C. E. OSGOOD et al. in Saporta & Bastian *Psycholinguistics* (1961) 293/1 Skinner (1936) has devised a 'verbal summator' technique for studying language behavior... Samples of meaningless speech sounds are repeated until the subject perceives some meaningful form—a kind of verbal inkblot. **1970** *Jrnl. Gen. Psychol.* Oct. 143 Skinner hoped to measure the strength and relative importance of verbal responses and intended that the verbal summator, or Tautophone, as it was subsequently named, should become the instrument for doing so.

†**ˈsummatory**, *a.* *Obs. rare.* [ad. mod.L. *summātōrius*, f. med.L. *summāt-*: see SUMMATE and -ORY.] ***summatory arithmetic, calculus***: see quots.

1704 C. HAYES *Treat. Fluxions* 60 The fundamental Rule in Summatory Arithmetick, to find the Flowing Quantity of a given Fluxion. **1710** J. HARRIS *Lex. Techn.* II, *Summatory Calculus*, according to some, is the same with the *Calculus Differentialis of Leibnitz*; but more properly *Summatory Arithmetick*, is the Art of finding the flowing Quantity, from the Fluxion.

summed (sʌmd), *ppl. a.* Forms: 5 **ysomed, sommyd, summyd, 6 sommed, 6 soom'd, 6–7 somed, 7 somm'd, sum(m)d, summ'd, 5– summed;** *erron.* 6 **soomned, sumned, 7 sumn'd.** [In branch I, f. OF. *som(m)é*, pa. pple. of *sommer* to sum, complete, ad. med.L. *summāre* to SUM. In branch II, f. SUM *v.*[1] + -ED[1].]

I. 1. Of a stag: Having a complement of antlers. Said also of the antlers. Often ***full summed***.

c **1410** *Master of Game* (MS. Digby 182) ii, Þei be halfe in greece or þere aboute þe tyme of mydel Iuny, whan her heed is ysomed. **1486** *Bk. St. Albans, Hunting* e j b, And afterwarde in the toppe when ther .iiii. bene Then shall ye call hym sommyd an hert of .xvi. **1576** TURBERV. *Venerie* xiv, When his head is full sommed. *Ibid.* xviii, By the middest of Iune, their heades will be somed of as much as they will beare all that yeare. **1590** COCKAINE *Treat. Hunting* D, It is then..hard to knowe him by his head, before it be full Soomned. **1623** COCKERAM I. s.v. *Pollard*, Sumn'd or full, is when a Stags head is fully hardned. **1637** B. JONSON *Sad Shepherd* I. ii, [The deer] beares a head, Large, and well beam'd; with all rights somm'd and spred.

2. Of a hawk: Having the feathers full grown. Said also of the plumage. Often ***full summed***.

c **1450** *Bk. Hawking* in *Rel. Ant.* I. 298 If he take colde ore he be full sommyd. **1486** *Bk. St. Albans, Hawking* a viij b, Thos same barris shall telle yow whan she is full summed or full fermyd. **1526** *Pilgr. Perf.* (W. de W. 1531) 79 The yonge byrde whan she is full sumned & hath all her fethers redy to flye. **1575** TURBERV. *Falconrie* 117 When..that hir principal feathers be ful sommed. **1616** SURFL. & MARKH. *Country Farm* VII. xliv. 713 A cleere and bright plume, with ful summed feathers. **1649** G. DANIEL *Trinarch., Hen. IV*, ccxxxiv, Like a young Eagle summ'd..Disdaines a shoale of Dawes. **1688** HOLME *Armoury* II. xi. 237/1. **1852** R. F. BURTON *Falconry Valley Indus* iii. 21.

b. *fig.* and in fig. context: Equipped.

1588 LAMBARDE *Eiren.* IV. xiv. 565 How each of these began at the first and grew in time to be full summed. **1600** W. WATSON *Decacordon* (1602) 358 [Demosthenes was] a full sumd or consumate Orator. *a* **1616** BEAUM. & FL. *Wit without M.* III. i, Till you be summed again. **1649** G. DANIEL *Trinarch., Hen. V*, ccxc, The first Summd Quill Of England. **1671** MILTON *P.R.* I. 14 Inspire..my prompted Song else mute, And bear through highth or depth of natures bounds With prosperous wing full summ'd to tell of deeds Above Heroic.

II. †**3.** Summarized, summary. *Obs.*

a **1653** G. DANIEL *Idyll, Designe* 4 One Obiect in varietie, One Summ'd draught doth before yoᵘ Stand.

4. Summed up; collected into one sum, forming a sum-total. Also with *up*.

1607 CHAPMAN *Bussy d'Ambois* I. i. 19 Man is a torch borne in the wind; a dream But of a shadow, summ'd with all his substance. **1858** HAWTHORNE *Fr. & It. Note-bks.* II. 20 The wholeness and summed-up beauty of woman. **1875** MCLAREN *Serm.* Ser. II. ix. 164 Our summed and collective brightness. **1892** E. REEVES *Homeward Bound* 37 The summed-up impression of Sydney suburbs and harbour is ..picturesqueness.

summeler, arch. form of SOMLER, butler.

1841 JAMES *Corse de Leon* xli, I will make your cook and your summeler to give me some refreshment.

summer (ˈsʌmə(r)), *sb.*[1] Forms: 1 **sumor, (-ur), 1–4 sumer, 3–6 somer, 4–5 somere,** *Sc.* **-yr(e, 4–6** *Sc.* **somir, 4–7 sommer, (3** *Ormin* **sumerr, 4** *Kent.* **zomer, 5 somare, -or, sommyr, sommure,** *Sc.* **swmyr, 6 sommar), 6– summer.** *β. Sc.* **6 symmer, 8–9 simmer.** [OE. *sumor* masc. = OFris. *sumur, -er* (Fris. *sommer, simmer*), MLG. *sommer*, MDu. *somer* (Du. *zomer*), OHG. *sumar* (MHG. *sumer*, G. *sommer*), ON. *sumar* neut. (Sw. *sommar*, Da. *sommer*).

Generally recognized cognates outside Germanic are Arm. *amarn* summer, Skr. *samā* half-year, year, Zend *hama* in summer, OIr. *sam*, W. *haf* summer.]

1. a. The second and warmest season of the year, coming between spring and autumn; reckoned astronomically from the summer solstice (21 June) to the autumnal equinox (22 or 23 Sept.); in popular use comprising in the northern hemisphere the period from mid-May to mid-August; also often, *esp.* as in (*c*) below, in contradistinction to *winter*, the warmer half of the year (cf. MIDSUMMER). (Often with initial capital.)

(*a*) In general use. (Also personified.) Often in ***in summer*** (OE. *on sumera*, ME. *o, a* or *in sumere*).

c **825** *Vesp. Psalter* lxxiii. 17 Aestatem & ver, sumur & lenten. *c* **888** ÆLFRED *Boeth.* iv. §1 Þu þe þam winterdagum selest scorte tida & þæs sumeres dahum langran. *Ibid.* xxi. §1 On sumera hit biþ wearm, and on wintra ceald. *a* **1000** *Gnomic Verses* 7 in Grein I. 338 Winter byð cealdost,.. sumor sunwlitegost. *c* **1200** ORMIN 11254 O sumerr, & onn herrfesstid, O winnterr, & o lenntenn. *a* **1225** *Ancr. R.* 20 Euerich on sigge..vhtsong bi nihte ine winter, ine sumer iþe dawunge. **12..** *Song on Passion* 1 in *O.E. Misc.*, Somer is comen and winter gon. *c* **1375** *Sc. Leg. Saints* xi. (*Simon & Jude*) 454 In þat houre quhen sik clernes suld be as in-to somyre wes. **1390** GOWER *Conf.* II. 38 In Wynter doth he noght for cold, In Somer mai he noght for hete. *a* **1400** *Pistill of Susan* 66 In þe seson of somere..Heo greiþed hire til hire gardin. **1528** MORE *Dyaloge* I. Wks. 135/2, I had leuer shyuer & shake for cold in yᵉ middes of somer, than be burned in the middes of winter. **1594** KYD *Cornelia* II. 89 T' haue made thy name be farre more fam'd and feard Then Summers thunder to the silly Heard. *a* **1599** SPENSER *F.Q.* VII. vii. 29 Then came the iolly Sommer..And on his head a girlond well beseene He wore. *c* **1600** SHAKS. *Sonn.* xciv, The sommers flowre is to the sommer sweet. **1671** MILTON *P.R.* IV. 246 Where the Attic Bird Trills her thick-warbl'd notes the summer long. **1719** DE FOE *Crusoe* I. (Globe) 107 The Seasons of the Year might generally be divided, not into Summer and Winter, as in Europe; but into the Rainy Seasons, and the Dry Seasons. **1786** BURNS *Twa Dogs* 192 It's true, they need na starve or sweat, Thro' Winter's cauld, or Summer's heat. **1868** MORRIS *Earthly Par.* (1890) 61/1 When Summer brings the lily and the rose.

β. **1500–20** DUNBAR *Poems* lxix. 49 Cum, lustie symmer! with thy flouris. **1583** *Leg. Bp. St. Androis* 46 The plesant plane-trie will the leavs vnfauld With fairest schaddow to save the sone in symmer. **1806** TANNAHILL *Braes o Gleniffer* iii. Poems (1900) 152 Oh, gin I saw my bonnie Scots callan, The dark days o winter war simmer to me!

(*b*) In particularized use, *esp.* with qualification or contextually, denoting this season in a certain year.

c **900** *O.E. Chron.* (Parker MS.) an. 897 þy ilcan sumera forwearð nolæs þonne .xx. scipa mid monnum. *c* **1330** R. Brunne *Chron. Wace* (Rolls) 7123 On vs þey wyle þis somer haste. **1393** Langl. *P. Pl.* C. xix. 242 In a somer ich seyh hym,..as ich sat in my porche. *c* **1450** *Brut* ii. 304 In þe xxvij. ȝere of his regne was þe grete derþe of vitailes, þe wiche was clepid þe dere somer. **1530** Palsgr. 814/1 This sommer that commeth. **1594** Kyd *Cornelia* Ded., I will assure your Ladiship my next Sommers better trauell with the Tragedy of Portia. **1599** Hakluyt *Voy.* II. i. Ep. Ded., When it pleased your Honour in sommer was two yeeres to haue some conference with me. *a* **1631** Donne *Poems* (1650) 208 The Springs and Summers which we see. **1842** J. Aiton *Dom. Econ.* (1857) 303 Our [Scotch] summers are said to consist of 3 hot days and a thunder-storm. **1885** W. W. Story *Fiammetta* 19 You will find me there all summer. **1906** R. Bayne *Butler's Anal.* Introd. p. xi, He came to England in the summer of 1720.

(*c*) Phr. ***summer and winter, winter and summer***, OE., ME. (advb. gen.) *sumeres and wintres*, all the year round.

a **1000** *Phœnix* 37 (Gr.) Wintres & sumeres wudu bið ȝelice bledum ȝehongen. *c* **1205** Lay. 2861 Enne blase of fure, þe neuer ne aþeostrede wintres ne sumeres. *c* **1375** *Sc. Leg. Saints* xxii. (*Laurence*) 3 A fare tre callit lawrane, þat wyntyre & somir ay is grene. **1473** *Rental Bk. Cupar-Angus* (1879) I. 189 That ged eyls and fyscis..ma be conseruyt..bath swmyr and wyntir. **1547** *Test. Ebor.* (Surtees) VI. 265 My suster..to have foure kie founde wynter and sommer. **1816** Scott *Antiq.* xxi, A bit bonny drapping well that popples that self-same gate simmer and winter. **1886** C. E. Pascoe *Lond. of To-day* xliii. (ed. 3) 378 Winter and summer, steamboats leave Westminster for Greenwich and Woolwich half-hourly.

b. Applied, with qualification, to a period of fine dry weather in late autumn; see All-Hallow(s 7, Indian summer, Martin[3] 3 c; ***St. Luke's*** (***little***) ***summer, little summer of St. Luke***, such a period occurring about St. Luke's Day, 18 Oct. (Cf. Ger. *altweibersommer*.)

1828 T. Forster *Circle Seasons* 293 Fair, warm, and dry weather, often occurs about this time, and is called St. Luke's Little Summer. **1855** *N. & Q.* 1st Ser. XII. 366/1 A few fine days about this time, called St. Luke's little summer; which the good folks of Hants and Dorset always expect about the 18th of this month. **1881** G. Milner *Country Pleas.* xli. 232 As autumn proceeds, we watch anxiously for that season of respite which..is known..as the Little Summer of St. Luke.

c. *transf.* Summer weather; a season resembling summer; summery or warm weather.

a **1240** *Ureisun* in *O.E. Hom.* I. 193 þer bloweð inne blisse blostmen... þer ne mei non uluwen, uor þer is eche sumer. *a* **1529** Skelton *Bouge of Court* 355 His gowne so shorte that it ne couer myghte His rumpe, he wente so all for somer lyghte. **1634** Milton *Comus* 988 There eternal Summer dwels. *a* **1700** Evelyn *Diary* 24 June 1693, A very wet hay harvest, and little Summer as yet. **1855** Tennyson *Daisy* 92 Lands of summer across the sea. **1892** E. Reeves *Homeward Bound* 140 Here is an everlasting summer of 70° to 80°.

d. In fig. and allusive use.

c **1535** Nisbet *N.T., Prol. Rom.* Wks. (S.T.S.) III. 334 Quhair the spret is, thair is alwayis symmer, ande thair is allwayis gude fructes. **1591** Greene *Farew. Folly* Wks. (Grosart) IX. 323 Beeing as intemperate in the frostie winter of their age, as we in the glowing summer of our youth. **1679** Dryden & Lee *Œdipus* iv. i, She, tho' in full-blown flow'r of glorious beauty, Grow's cold, ev'n in the Summer of her Age. **1811** W. R. Spencer *Poems* 75 The summer of her smile. **1859** Tennyson *Marr. Geraint* 398 For now the wine made summer in his veins. **1874** Lisle Carr *Jud. Gwynne* I. iii. 72 This sudden change from winter to summer.

2. In *pl.* with numeral, put for 'year'. Now only *poet.* or in speaking of a young person's age.

13.. *E.E. Allit. P.* B. 1686 þus he countes hym a kow, þat was a kyng ryche, Quyle seuen syþez were ouer-seyed someres I trawe. **1590** Shaks. *Com. Err.* i. i. 133 Fiue Sommers haue I spent in farthest Greece. **1631** Milton *Ep. March. Winch.* 7 Summers three times eight save one She had told. **1782** Miss Burney *Cecilia* viii. v, Fifteen summers had she bloomed. **1820** Byron *Mar. Fal.* iv. ii. 157 Doge Dandolo survived to ninety summers. **1842** Tennyson *Godiva* 11 The woman of a thousand summers back, Godiva. **1896** *Westm. Gaz.* 18 July 8/2 A good-looking young lady of apparently twenty summers.

3. = *summer-herring* (see 6 b). ? *Obs.*

1682 J. Collins *Salt & Fish.* 106 Of Herrings. Summers are such as the Dutch Chasers or Divers catch from June to the 15th of July.

4. *attrib.* passing into *adj.* **a.** = Of or pertaining to summer, characteristic of summer, summer-like, summery; suitable or appropriate to, used or occupied in, summer; existing, appearing, active, performed, or produced in summer.

As the number of these attrib. uses is unlimited, in most cases only the earliest and most important examples are given here.

(*a*) of natural phenomena, animals, plants, etc. (Cf. OE. *sumorhǽte* summer-heat.)

a **1300** *Siriz* 294 ȝus, bi the somer blome, Hethen nulli ben bi-nomen. **1390** Gower *Conf.* I. 35 Now be the lusti somer floures. **14..** *Nom.* in Wr.-Wülcker 707 *Hec polemita*, a somerboyde [see boud]. *c* **1450** tr. *Giraldus Cambrensis' Hist. Irel.* (1896) 28 Storkes & swalewes, & oþer somer foules. **1500–20** Dunbar *Poems* xi. 26 Thy lustye bewte and thy ȝouth Sall feid as dois the somer flouris. **1588** Shaks. *L.L.L.* v. ii. 293 Blow like sweet Roses, in this summer aire. *Ibid.* 408 These summer flies, Haue blowne me full of maggot ostentation. **1590** —— *Mids. N.* ii. i. 110 An odorous Chaplet of sweet Sommer buds. **1633** Ford *Love's Sacr.* ii. i, Tears, and vows, and words, Moves her no more than summer-winds a rock. **1634** Milton *Comus* 928 Summer drouth, or singed air Never scorch thy tresses fair. **1680** H. More *Apocal. Apoc.* Pref. 26 The Papacy would melt away like a bank of snow in the summer-sun. **1688** Holme *Armoury* ii. xviii. 467/1 These are the true shapes both of the Summer Butter-fly, and the Wood-louse. **1728** Chambers *Cycl.* s.v. *Silk*, The Warmth of the Summer Weather. **1748** Gray *Alliance* 101 Nile redundant o'er his Summer-bed. **1754** —— *Poesy* 83 Far from the sun and summer-gale. **1781** Cowper *Conversat.* 705 But Conversation..Should flow, like waters after summer show'rs. **1790** —— *J. Thornton* 38 The summer rill Refreshes, where it winds, the faded green. **1817** Shelley *Marianne's Dream* 25 The sky was blue as the summer sea. **1820** —— *Witch Atl.* xl, The busy dreams, as thick as summer flies. **1820** Keats *Isabella* ix, Lady! thou leadest me to summer clime. **1834** Mrs. Hemans *Happy Hour* 5 Early-blighted leaves, which o'er their way Dark summer-storms had heaped. **1842** Loudon *Suburban Hort.* 566 The greater part of the summer shoots ought to be stopt. **1848** Dickens *Dombey* iii, The summer sun was never on the street. **1850** Miss Pratt *Comm. Things of Sea-side* iii. 171 The insects of our summer pools. **1879** F. W. Robinson *Coward Consc.* i. i, Without cap or bonnet, as if in fair summer-weather trim.

(*b*) of clothing, food, etc.

1363–4 *Durham Acc. Rolls* (Surtees) 566 In uno panno.. pro somersercortes [*sic*] pro armigeris Prioris. **1393** Langl. *P. Pl.* C. x. 119 He hem forth seluerles in a somer garnement. *a* **1400–50** *Wars Alex.* 4343 Make we na salues for na sares ne na somir-bathis. *c* **1480** Henryson *Mor. Fab.* xi. (*Fox & Wolf*) xviii, It is somer cheis, baith fresche and fair. **1481** *Cely Papers* (Camden) 71, j pack lyeth upprest and sum of that packe ys somer felles. **1530** *Acc. Ld. High Treas. Scot.* VI. 280 Ane pair symmir buttis to the Kingis grace. **1585** T. Washington tr. *Nicholay's Voy.* i. xvi. 17 Sommer cloathing of the women of Malta. **1588** Shaks. *L.L.L.* v. ii. 916 When..Maidens bleach their summer smockes. *c* **1620** *Hatton Corr.* (Camden) 3 At my returne I will make you a sommer sute. **1693** Dryden *Juvenal* i. 40 Charg'd with light Summer-rings his fingers sweat. **1697** —— *Virg. Georg.* iii. 665 A Snake..in his Summer Liv'ry rouls along. **1765** *Museum Rust.* IV. 367 It lies extremely convenient for my summer-pasture. **1797** *Encycl. Brit.* (ed. 3) XVIII. 63/2 The melasses may..compose the basis of a pleasant summer beer. **1801** *Farmer's Mag.* Aug. 325 The summer cheese, which is the best, is made of the evening milk. **1834** *Encycl. Metrop.* (1845) XXII. 366/1 Such is its Summer coat, and..we distinguish it by the name Stoat. **1881** Besant & Rice *Chapl. Fleet* I. 33 Sir Robert is calling every day for a summer sallet to cool his blood.

(*c*) of places or buildings. (Cf. OE. *sumerselde*, summer-house.)

1382 Wyclif *Judg.* iii. 20 Forsothe he sat in the somer sowpynge place [Vulg. *in æstivo cœnaculo*] alone. **1596** *Edw. III*, ii. i. 61 Then in the sommer arber sit by me. **1611** *Bible* Judg. iii. 24 Surely he coureth his feet in his Summer chamber. **1611** —— Dan. ii. 35 [They] became like the chaffe of the summer threshing floores. **1612** Webster *White Devil* i. ii, Tis iust like a summer bird-cage in a garden. **1708** *Lond. Gaz.* No. 4447/1 The Heat of the Weather obliges both sides to retire..into their Summer Quarters. **1783** Cowper *Faithf. Friend* i The green-house is my summer seat. **1837** Lockhart *Scott* I. ix. 307 To establish his summer residence in Lanarkshire. **1847** Tennyson *Princ.* i. 146 A certain summer-palace which I have.

(*d*) of times and seasons. (See also summer-day, -tide, -time.)

c **1440** *Alphabet of Tales* 170 Sho wolde gar hur maydyns gader þe dew on sommer mornyngis. *a* **1578** Lindesay (Pitscottie) *Chron. Scot.* I. 228 Wpoun ane summar morning ..ane of the Inglishe scheipis persaueit tua schipis command wnder saill. **1586** W. Webbe *Eng. Poetrie* Ep. Ded. (Arb.) 15 A sleight somewhat compyled for recreation, in the intermyssions of my daylie businesse, (euen thys Summer Eueninges). **1592** *Arden of Feversham* i. i. 58 Sommer nights are short, and yet you ryse ere day. **1599** Shaks., etc. *Pass. Pilgr.* 159 Youth like summer morn, age like winter weather. **1626** Bacon *Sylva* §606, I left once, by chance, a Citron cut, in a close Roome, for three Summer-Moneths. **1632** Milton *L'Allegro* 130 Such sights as youthfull Poets dream On Summer eeves by haunted stream. **1725** Pope *Odyss.* iv. 55 The dazzling roofs,.. Resplendent as the blaze of summer noon. **1785** Burns *Holy Fair* i Upon a simmer Sunday morn. **1815** Scott *Guy M.* xlv, All the tints of a summer-evening sky. **1821** Shelley *Hellas* 13 Sweet as a summer night without a breath. **1833** Tennyson *Pal. of Art* 62 A gaudy summer-morn. **1892** *Photogr. Ann.* II. 621 Excursions are made during the summer months.

(*e*) of conditions, qualities, or actions.

1594 Shaks. *Rich. III*, iv. iii. 13 Their lips were foure red Roses on a stalke, And in their Summer Beauty kist each other. **1617** Wither *Abuses* ii. iv. 275 Their ancient drunken-summer-reuelings Are out of date. **1636** H. Burton *Div. Trag.* 22 One in Glocestershire being very forward to advance a solemne sommer-meeting [for sports]. **1641** Brome *Joviall Crew* i, After so many Sommer vagaries. **1684** T. Burnet *Th. Earth* i. ix. 123 This reason is a Summer-reason, and would pass very ill in Winter. **1707** Mortimer *Husb.* (1721) I. 194 Towards the end of May, you must give your Ground the Summer-Digging. **1726–46** Thomson *Winter* 644 A gay insect in his summer shine.. spreads his mealy wings. **1787** Burns *Petit. Bruar Water* i, Saucy Phœbus' scorching beams, In flaming summer-pride. **1798** J. Woodforde *Diary* 11 June (1931) V. 121 Master Neville Custance called on us..being very lately come home from School for the Summer Vacation. **1813** Scott *Rokeby* i. i, The Moon is in her summer glow. **1819** Keats *Indolence* ii, The blissful cloud of summer-indolence Benumb'd my eyes. **1826** Lamb *Pop. Fallacies* xii, [The talk] is not of toys, of nursery books, of summer holidays. **1836–9** *Todd's Cycl. Anat.* II. 768/2 The summer-sleep of hibernating animals. **1854** *Poultry Chron.* I. 34/2 Birds that have taken prizes at London Summer Meeting. **1868** *Rep. U.S. Commissioner Agric.* (1869) 255 During this interval of rest..is the best time for summer trimming. **1875** Trollope *Prime Minister* (1876) I. xv. 237 The lawyer's regular summer vacation had not yet commenced. **1878** B. Taylor *Deukalion* iii. i, My bed of long delight and summershine. **1942** O. Nash *Good Intentions* 179 A summer cold Is to have and to hold. **1970** J. Creasey *Part for Policeman* vi. 53 What's the matter with him? Summer 'flu? **1975** *Times* 19 Apr. 9/2 Kathy had been in bed with a so-called summer cold..sniffling and sneezing. **1980** P. Harcourt *Tomorrow's Treason* i. i. 23 What with leave and summer flu, we're already short of staff. **1982** R. Timperley *Face in Leaves* i. 11 The long summer vacation was stretching out ahead of me.

(*f*) with descriptive designations.

1611 Beaum. & Fl. *King & No K.* v. i, *Lyg.* I know you dare lie. *Bes.* With none but Summer Whores.., my means and manners never could attempt above a hedge or haycock. **1645** G. Daniel *Scattered Fancies* xxiii. iv, You are but weake, Meere summer Chanters. **1888** *Encycl. Brit.* XXIII. 45/1 Three if not four species are common summer immigrants to some part or other of the United States.

(*g*) in superlative ***summerest*** (*rare* or *nonce* uses).

1772 H. Walpole *Let. to Mann* 3 Aug., The summerest summer that I have known these hundred years. **1873** H. James *Let.* 24 Mar. (1974) I. 355, I walk abroad in my summerest clothes and am warm. **1979** *Times of India* 17 Aug. 3/4 A wag remarks that half the city's population migrates to cooler climes during the 'summerest' month of May.

b. The possessive *summer's* is similarly used, but now chiefly with *morning, evening*, and *night*. (See also summer's day, summer's tide.)

c **1369** Chaucer *Dethe Blaunche* 821 As the somerys sonne bryghte. **14..** *Sir Beues* 4138 (Pynson) M iv, And so lasted that cruel fyght, Al that longe somers nyght. **1513** Douglas *Æneis* x. vii. 109 In the symmeris drouth, Quhen wyndis risis of the north or south. **1592** *Soliman & Pers.* i. v. 64 The humming of a gnat in Summers night. **1596** Shaks. *1 Hen. IV*, iii. i. 210 Ditties highly penn'd, Sung by a faire Queene in a Summers Bowre. **1601** —— *Jul. C.* iii. ii. 176 'Twas on a Summer's Euening. **1613** Jackson *Creed* i. xxiii. 136 Diseases, neuer perceiued in their Summers growth, vntill they be ripe of death in the Autumne. **1654** Warren *Unbelievers* 22 The Sodomites..shall have a Summers parlour in hell over that soule. **1667** Milton *P.L.* iii. 43 The..sight of vernal bloom, or Summers Rose. *Ibid.* ix. 447 As one..Forth issuing on a Summers Morn. **1721** Ramsay *Keitha* 45 Her presence, like a simmer's morning ray. **1780–2** Cowper *Cricket* 21 Their's is but a summer's song. **1808** J. Mayne *Siller Gun* i. i, Ae Simmer's morning. **1855** Miller *Elem. Chem., Chem. Phys.* iii. §4. 112 If the right rhombic crystals [of sulphate of nickel] be placed in the summer's sun for a few days they become opaque.

c. Applied to crops, etc. that ripen in summer, as ***summer fruit***, more particularly to such as ripen in the summer of the year in which they are sown, as ***summer barley, corn, grain, rye, seed, vetch, wheat***; also *spec.* in popular names of early-ripening apples and pears, as ***summer apple, pearmain, poppering***, etc. (cf. also 6 b).

1398 Trevisa *Barth. De P.R.* xvii. lxv. (Bodl. MS.) Winter seede is sone isowe and somer sede is late isowe. **1535** Coverdale *Amos* viii. 1 Beholde, there was a maunde with sommer frute. **1577** B. Googe *Heresbach's Husb.* 26 Sommer seedes, whiche are sowed before the risyng of the seuen starres, and in the Spring, as Beanes. *Ibid.*, Sommer Barley..and suche other, are sowed in the Spring time. *Ibid.* 27 b, Rye..is sowed..in Februarie, and called Sommer Wheate. *Ibid.* 34 Pease..are sowed among Sommer Corne. **1578** Lyte *Dodoens* iv. i. 453 A sommer wheate or grayne. *Ibid.*, Men sow their winter corne in September, or October, & the sommer corne in March, but they are ripe altogither in July. **1676** Worlidge *Cyder* (1691) 214 The Denny-pear, Prussia-pear, Summer-Poppering..are all very good table-fruit. **1681** Grew *Musæum* ii. iii. iii. 235 Summer Wheat of New England. *a* **1722** Lisle *Husb.* (1757) 174, I spoke..of the husbandry of sowing goar or summer-vetches. **1722** *Phil. Trans.* XXXII. 231 The Apple, that produces the Molosses, is a Summer-Sweeting. **1764** *Ann. Reg.* ii. 2 Several trials of summer-corn..in which both barley and oats have succeeded. **1765** *Museum Rust.* IV. 435 He was..obliged to wait till Mr. Rocque's summer-seed was reaped. **1795** J. Jay *Let.* 12 Dec. in *Columbia Lit. Columns* (1970) XIX. iii. 43 Ten are Summer Pippins, a very large fair Yellow apple. **1812** Sir J. Sinclair *Syst. Husb. Scot.* i. 244 The real spring or summer wheat, has been of late introduced in various districts in Scotland. **1834** *Penny Cycl.* II. 190/1 Summer golden pippin. Summer Thorle. **1854** Mayne *Expos. Lex.* 352/1 Summer-fruits; as cherries, currants, gooseberries, raspberries, strawberries, etc. **1870** J. W. McClung *Minnesota* xi. 154 Among the varieties [of apples]..are.. Summer Pairmain, [etc.]. **1930** J. Dos Passos *42nd Parallel* ii. 145 They ate sweet summerapples.

†**d.** = Having a sunny or southerly aspect; so ***summer-east, -west*** = south-east, -west. *Obs.*

c **1440** *Pallad. on Husb.* i. 491 Thyn oilcelar sette on the somer side. **1555** Eden *Decades W. Ind.* (Arb.) 328 Towarde the sommer East, it confineth with the Tartars. **1604** E. G[rimstone] *D' Acosta's Hist. Indies* iii. v. 135 They do call lower windes those..which blowe from the South to the summer-weast. **1676** *Phil. Trans.* XI. 585 A kind of Solar stove, made in a Summer-wall.

e. *fig.* with reference to prosperous, pleasant, or genial conditions; said *esp.* of friendship that lasts only in times of prosperity, = fair-weather 2.

1592 Nashe *Strange Newes* Wks. 1904 I. 291 His low-flighted affection (fortunes summer folower). **1611** Shaks. *Cymb.* iii. iv. 12 If't be Summer Newes Smile too't before. **1624** Quarles *Job Militant, Digestion* iv, If Winter fortunes nip thy Summer Friends,..despaire not, but be wise. **1632** Massinger *Maid of Hon.* iii. i, Summer-friendship, Whose flattering leaves, that shadowed us in our Prosperity..drop off In the Autumn of adversity! **1727–46** Thomson *Summer* 347 Luxurious Men, unheeding, pass An idle summer-life in fortune's shine. *c* **1800** R. Cumberland *John De Lancaster* (1809) III. 93 We are but summer soldiers. **1805** *Ann. Rev.* III. 584 He was in the Fleet.. deserted by his three Summer friends. **1818** *Ibid.* XIX. 42 He was the frequent visitor of Clarendon, when that admirable man was abandoned by the swarm of summer followers. **1842** TENNYSON *Locksley Hall* 164 Summer isles of Eden.

f. *U.S.* Designating tourists or those who visit a place for a summer holiday. Cf. ***summer boarder***, sense 6 a below.

1886 *Leslie's Monthly* Feb. 203/1 Old Sampson don't like the Summer gentry. **1889** W. D. HOWELLS *Hazard of New Fortunes* I. 135 She frankly gave up her house to the summer-folks (as they call them in the country). **1892** *Rep. Vermont Board Agric.* XII. 139 To these more prominent places may be added a multitude of.. attractive homes to the summer guest. **1898** E. N. WESTCOTT *David Harum* 286 Our friend had met quite a number of the 'summer people'. **1938** *Sun* (Baltimore) 24 Mar. 10/2 New England has been declining. Her rural areas are given over to a sort of subsistence farming or to the entertainment of 'summer people'. **1971** H. T. WALDEN *Anchorage Northeast* 19 So few 'summer people' are here that the term has little or no usage. **1977** *New Yorker* 10 Oct. 112/3 He is the native by the side of the road who, having been called stupid by the summer person exasperated at his inability to provide directions to Portland, says, 'Mebbee, but at least I ain't lost.' **1980** J. COATES *Sentimental Education* 124 She belonged to the town—she was not one of the summer people.

5. *Comb.*: objective, as ***summer-breathing***, ***loving*** ppl. adjs.; indirect objective, ***summer-going*** adj.; instrumental, as ***summer-blanched***, ***-dried***, ***-painted***, ***-shrunk***, ***-soothed***, ***-stricken***, ***-tranced***, pples. and ppl. adjs.; similative, as ***summer-happy***, ***-kind***, ***-merry***, ***-seeming***, ***-sweet*** adjs.; 'in or during summer', as ***summer-basking***, ***-born***, ***-brewed***, ***-felled***, ***-flowering***, ***-green***, ***-idle***, ***-leaping***, †***-lived***, ***-made***, ***-opened***, ***-ripening***, ***-running***, ***-shaded***, ***-staying***, ***-still***, ***-swelling***, ***-threshed***, ***white***, pples. and ppl. adjs.; ***summer-feed***, ***-graze***, ***-till***, ***-yard*** vbs.; ***summer-curer***.

1931 R. GRAVES *Poems 1926–30* 69 You are no more than weather, The year's unsteadfastness To which, now *summer-basking,.. The mind pays no honour. **1864** TENNYSON *Aylmer's F.* 152 One [*sc.* hut] that, *summer-blanch'd, Was parcel-bearded with the traveller's-joy. **1975** *Language for Life* (Dept. Educ. & Sci.) xviii. 267 Many children.. are likely to continue to need special help in the junior school, particularly those *summer-born children who may have had only two years of early schooling. **1806** M. A. SHEE *Rhymes on Art* 68 In calmer seas, and *summer-breathing gales. **1826** *Art of Brewing* (ed. 2) 32 Imperfect fermentation.. causes acidity and other faults in *summer-brewed beers. **1881** *Chicago Times* 14 May, It is to the interest now of the leading *summer-curers [*sc.* of pork] to get values down. **1810** SCOTT *Lady of L.* III. xvi, A *summer-dried fountain. **1799** A. YOUNG *Agric. Linc.* 190, 13 acres of marsh at Grimsby, that *summer-feeds 14 bullocks. **1838** HOLLOWAY *Prov. Dict.*, To *skeer*, to mow lightly over, applied to pastures, which have been summer fed. **1804** *Phil. Trans.* XCV. 92 Proper marks were put to distinguish the winter-felled from the *summer-felled poles. **1897** MRS. VOYNICH *Gadfly* i, In one corner stood a huge *summer-flowering magnolia. **1900** *Daily News* 5 May 4/5 Summer-flowering chrysanthemums. **1954** J. BETJEMAN *Few Late Chrysanthemums* 43 Oh sun upon the *summer-going by-pass Where ev'rything is speeding to the sea. **1799** A. YOUNG *Agric. Linc.* 354 He.. in April *summer-grazed them, taking the wool. **1930** J. DOS PASSOS *42nd Parallel* 137 There was a blue haze at the end of every street of brick houses and dark *summergreen trees. **1917** D. H. LAWRENCE *Look! We have come Through!* 104 And we're going to be *summer-happy And summer-kind. **1955** E. BOWEN *World of Love* iv. 67 The *summer-idle water dawdled in shallows. **1917** *Summer-kind [see *summer-happy* above]. **1596** *Edw. III*, II. i. 107 To musicke euery *sommer leaping swaine Compares his sunburnt louer when shee speakes. **1594** NASHE *Unfort. Trav.* Wks. 1904 II. 275 *Summer liude grashoppers gaping after deaw. **1875** *Zoologist* Ser. II. X. 4693 They [*sc.* starlings] fly into the air with swallows, &c., and catch insects similar to that *summer-loving tribe. **1842** J. AITON *Dom. Econ.* (1857) 206 This.. increases the quantity of your *summer-made manure. **1957** E. BLUNDEN *Poems of Many Years* 279 By the arched grey bridge of *summer-merry streams. **1887** J. R. LOWELL in *Atlantic Monthly* Feb. 250 And listen while Old Hundred pours Forth through *summer-opened doors. **1937** E. MUIR *Coll. Poems* (1960) 80 The lint-white stubble plain From which the *summer-painted birds have flown A year's life on. **1840** J. BUEL *Farmer's Companion* 44 They are cropped with small grains or *summer-ripening crops. **1972** *Trout & Salmon* Feb. 10/2 Clearly the nets are taking an excessive proportion of *summer-running salmon. **1605** SHAKS. *Macb.* IV. iii. 86 This Auarice.. growes with more pernicious roote Then *Summer-seeming Lust. **1850** J. G. WHITTIER *Poet. Wks.* (1898) 340/1 Down the *summer-shaded street A wasted female figure.. Came rushing. **1825** SCOTT *Betrothed* ii, A maiden smiles at the *summer-shrunk brook while she crosses it. **1883** R. BRIDGES *Prometheus the Firegiver* 37 Piloting over the wind-dappled blue Of the *summer-soothed Aegean. **1868** LYNCH *Rivulet* CLX. iii, Can.. The *summer-staying birds forget The winter's force to shun? **1925** A. HUXLEY *Sel. Poems* 38, I am a pool of waters, *summer-still. **1827** SCOTT *Highl. Widow* v, You do but resemble the *summer-stricken stream, which is turned aside by the rushes. **1945** W. DE LA MARE *Burning-Glass* 42 *Summer-sweet as that wild rose. **1591** SHAKS. *Two Gent.* II. iv. 162 Lest the base earth Should.. Disdaine to roote the *Sommer-swelling flowre. **1812** SIR J. SINCLAIR *Syst. Husb. Scot.* I. 346 It enables the farmer to make his *summer-threshed straw into dung. **1847** HALLIWELL s.v., 'That field was *summer-tilled last year', i.e. lay fallow. **1881** O. WILDE *Poems* 66 We too might waste the *summer-trancèd day. **1918** D. H. LAWRENCE *New Poems* 9 The flagged, clean pavement *summer-white. **1840** J. BUEL *Farmer's Comp.* 198 Feeding these crops with the long manure of the yards and stables, instead of *summer-yarding it.

6. a. Special combs.: †**summer-ale**, (*a*) ale brewed in summer, new or heady ale; (*b*) a summer festival (see ALE 3); **summer-barm** *v. intr.*, to ferment in warm weather; †**summer-blink**, a short spell of sunshine in dull weather; **summer boarder** *U.S.*, one who lives at a boarding-house in the country in summer; hence **summer-board** *v. trans.*, to take (someone) as a summer boarder; **summer-boarding**; †**summer-broach**, a maypole decked; **summer camp** orig. and chiefly *U.S.*, a camp providing recreational and sporting facilities during the summer holiday period, usu. for children; **summer catarrh** = HAY-FEVER; **summer cholera** = CHOLERA 2; **summer-colt** (usually *pl.*) *local*, the undulating appearance of the air near the ground on a hot day; see also quot. 1825; **summer complaint** *U.S.*, summer diarrhœa of children; also, infantile cholera and dysentery; **summer cottage** *N. Amer.*, a cottage, usu. at a holiday resort or in the country, occupied during the summer; hence **summer cottager**, one who occupies a summer cottage; **summer country** *N.Z.* (see quot. 1898); **summer diarrhœa** = *summer cholera*; **summer-dream**, a pleasant or happy dream; **summer-eat** *v. trans. dial.*, to use as summer pasture; **summer eggs** = *summer ova* (Cassell, 1887); **summer fever**, hay-fever; **summer-field**, † (*a*) rendering L. *æstiva area* = *summer floor*; (*b*) a field with the summer crop; (*c*) *dial.* a summer-fallow; †**summer floor** [FLOOR *sb.*^{1} 6], a thrashing-floor; **summer-fold** (now *dial.*), a freckle; **summer-gauze**, **-goose** *local*, gossamer; †**summer hall**, (*a*) rendering L. *æstiva area* = *summer floor*; (*b*) = SUMMER-HOUSE 2, 2 b; **summer-heat** [OE. *sumorhǽte*], the heat of summer; *spec.* an arbitrary maximum summer temperature commonly marked on thermometers; **summer kitchen** *N. Amer.*, an extra kitchen, adjoining a house or separate from it, used for cooking in hot weather; †**summer lady**, the queen of the 'summer-game'; **summerlay** *sb. dial.*, land lying fallow in summer; in East Anglia, a turnip fallow; **summerlay** *v. trans. dial.*, to lay fallow; †**summer lea-land** = SUMMER-FALLOW; **summer-lease** *dial.* (see quots.); **summer-leding** *pseudo-arch.* [f. OE. *sumorlida* summer expedition (*O.E. Chron.* an. 871)], see quot.; **summer lightning**, sheet lightning without audible thunder, often seen in hot weather; also allusively and *attrib.*; **summer-long** *adv.* and *a.*, (lasting) throughout the summer; †**summer-lord**, a youth chosen as president of the 'summer-game'; cf. MAY-LORD; **summer master** *Canad. Hist.*, a person in charge of a trading post for the summer only; **summer mastitis**, a severe inflammation of the udder of cows usu. associated with the bacteria *Corynebacterium pyogenes* or *Peptococcus indolicus*; **summer meal** *Sc.*, meal for use until harvest; **summer number**, a summer issue of a periodical, with special features; **summer-ova**, eggs produced by certain freshwater invertebrates in spring and summer; **summer parlour** *Obs.* or *arch.*, an apartment for summer use; †**summer-pole**, a pole decked with flowers erected during the 'summer-games'; **summer pruning**, the selective cutting back of branches of trees or shrubs during the growing season; hence **summer prune** *v.*; **summer-pruned** *ppl. a.*; **summer pudding**, a pudding made of stewed fruit (freq. raspberries and red currants) and bread; †**summer('s) queen** = *summer lady*; **summer rash**, prickly heat, *Lichen tropicus*; **summer resort**, a popular place of resort in the summer, esp. a summer holiday resort; also, the act of visiting such a place; **summer resorter** *U.S.*, one who frequents summer resorts; †**summer-ripe** *a.*, fully ripe; **summer road** *Canad.*, a road suitable for use all year round, as opp. to one used in winter only by sleighs; †**summer-room** = SUMMER-HOUSE 2; **summer sale**, a sale of merchandise at reduced prices in the summer, esp. by shops wishing to clear their seasonal stock; **summer sausage** *U.S.*, a type of dried or smoked sausage which can be made in winter and kept until summer; **summer school**, a school or course of education conducted by a university, etc., in the summer, esp. during the long vacation; **summer-sob** *Sc.*, a summer shower; **summer spot**, a freckle; †**summer-stirring**, summer ploughing; hence †**summer-stir** *v. trans.*; **summer stock** *U.S.*, theatrical productions by a repertory company organized for the summer season, esp. at holiday resorts, freq. *attrib.*; **summer term**, that term of an academic year or of legal sessions which occurs before the summer vacation; **summer theatre**, a theatre operating only in summer; **summer-tilth** *dial.*, fallow land; the cultivation of such land; †**summer top** *v. trans.*, to cut off as in summer pruning; †**summer tree** *Sc.* = *summer-pole*; **summer-weight** *a.*, of clothes: light, suitable for wear in summer; also *transf.*; **summer wood** = *late wood* s.v. LATE *a.*^{1} 4; **summer-work** *sb.* and *v.*, **-working** = SUMMER-FALLOW *sb.* and *v.*; **summer-yellow**, a variety of cotton-seed oil.

1586 A. DAY *Eng. Secretary* I. (1625) 109 The superfluities of *summer-ale, that hath wrought in his giddie braine. **1636** H. BURTON *Div. Trag.* 21 The people.. prepared for a solemne summer-ale. **1828** *Craven Gloss.* (ed. 2) s.v., When malt liquor begins to ferment, in warm weather, before the application of the barm, it is said to be *summer-barm'd. **1637** RUTHERFORD *Let. to R. Gordon* 1 Jan., Yet I am in this hot *summer-blink, with the tear in my eye. **1903** K. D. WIGGIN *Rebecca* x. 107 Mother has *summer-boarded a lot o' the school-marms. **1847** H. N. MOORE *Fitzgerald & Hopkins* 73 And stated also that there were several *summer boarders from the city present. **1879** *Harper's Mag.* July 164 A few quiet summer boarders took shelter for a season's rest. **1897** *Appleton's Ann. Cycl.* 808/1 The statistics of the summer-boarder industry are very incomplete. **1949** *Sat. Even. Post* 25 June 47/2 At the end of one unusually arduous summer he put an ad in a Portland paper for summer boarders. **1880** *Harper's Mag.* Sept. 536/1 *Summer boarding here can be had for one dollar per week. **1619** *Pasquil's Palin.* B 3, A *Sommer-broach, Ycleap'd a May-pole. **1893** *McClure's Mag.* I. 242/2 The camp was founded by Mr. Ernest Berkeley Balch as a *summer camp for boys. **1948** *Sat. Even. Post* 23 Oct. 87/2 He wants to send every youngster in Lawrence to summer camp for at least two weeks. **1958** R. LIDDELL *Morea* III. ii. 238 There [Cerigo] monasteries are, regrettably, regarded merely as summer camps for visitors. **1979** *Country Life* 24 May 1640/1 At the age of 14.. I was packed off to a summer camp in the Welsh hills. **1828** *Medico-Chirurg. Trans.* XIV. 437 Of the Catarrhus Æstivus, or *Summer Catarrh. **1862** *Chamb. Encycl.* III. 6/1 The milder forms of C[holera].. termed by some.. British or *Summer C[holera]. **1685** *Phil. Trans.* XV. 993 An undulating motion [which] our Countrie People call by the name of *Summer Colts in the Air. **1768** ROSS *Helenore* 21 The summer cauts [*mispr.* cauls] were dancing here an' there. **1796** W. H. MARSHALL *Rural Econ. Yorks.* (ed. 2) II. 349 When the air is seen in a calm hot day to undulate,.. the phænomenon is expressed by saying, 'the summer colt rides'. **1825** JAMIESON, *Summer-couts*,.. the gnats which dance in clusters on a summer evening. **1847** E. HALLOWELL in *Amer. Jrnl. Med. Sci.* XIV. 40 On the endemic gastro-follicular enteritis, or '*summer complaint' of children. **1855** DUNGLISON *Med. Lex.*, *Summer complaint*,.. is often.. made to include dysentery and cholera infantum. **1840** *Montreal Transcript* 22 Dec. 402/2 Some owners of lots also propose putting up *summer cottages. **1902** W. D. HOWELLS *Literature & Life* 49 A few houses of the past remain, but the type of the summer cottage has impressed itself upon all the later building, and the native is passing architecturally, if not personally, into abeyance. **1958** *Edmonton Jrnl.* 28 June 25/1 Schools and universities are closing their doors for the next few months and many Canadian households will begin the annual exodus to summer cottage or camp. **1948** *Chicago Tribune* 20 June VII. 12/5 Many *summer cottagers will be happy to know that the same house makes a similar type of cream that repels chiggers. **1971** *Islander* (Victoria, B.C.) 2 May 6/1 In this strange fantasyland live 300 permanent residents and another 3,200 summer cottagers. **1898** MORRIS *Austral Eng.* 444/2 **Summer country*, *n.*, in New Zealand (South Island), country which can be used in summer only; mountain land in Otago and Canterbury, above a certain level. **1922** W. PERRY et al. *Sheep Farming in N.Z.* vii. 88 The higher country.. which is likely to hold snow to some depth in the winter months, is termed 'summer country'. **1947** P. NEWTON *Wayleggo* (1949) 14 A large proportion of the country [in the South Island]—the shady and hindermost areas—is suitable for summer grazing [of sheep] only... Such country is known as 'summer country'. **1883** F. T. ROBERTS *Th. & Pract. Med.* (ed. 5) 196 The so-called sporadic, bilious, or English cholera, or *summer diarrhœa, the symptoms of which sometimes closely resemble those of true cholera. **1820** CLARE *Poems Rural Life* (ed. 3) 60 Ye gently dimpled, curling streams, Rilling as smooth as *summer-dreams. **1905** *Westm. Gaz.* 1 July 14/2 Delighting in the summer-dream of love. **1788** W. H. MARSHALL *Rural Econ. Yorks.* II. 357 **Summer-eat*, to use as pasture. **1870** *Zoologist* Ser. II. V. 2335 A field of summer-eaten clover, from which the sheep had a few days been removed. **1884** A. SEDGWICK tr. *Claus's Elem. Text-bk. Zool.* x. 418 The so-called *summer eggs.. produce generations containing no males. **1952** J. CLEGG *Freshwater Life Brit. Isles* xii. 169 These so-called 'summer eggs' are laid, perhaps twenty or more at a time. **1867** PIRRIE *Hay Asthma* 25 It appears to us, that in many instances, *Summer Fever or Summer Illness, would be more applicable than Hay Fever. **1382** WYCLIF *Dan.* ii. 35 The yren,.. syluer, and gold, ben.. dryuen as in to a qwenchid brond of *somer feeld [1388 somer halle; Vulg. *æstivæ areæ*]. **1594** SHAKS. *Rich. III*, v. ii. 8 The wretched, bloody, and vsurping Boare, (That spoyl'd your Summer Fields, and fruitfull Vines). **1794** T. DAVIS *Agric. Wilts* 59 In the four-field husbandry, where the clover is sown the second year, and mowed the third, the field becomes in the fourth year what is called in Wiltshire 'a summer field'. **1535** COVERDALE *Dan.* ii. 35 Like the chaffe off corne, that the wynde bloweth awaye from y^e *somer floores. **1668** *Lond. Gaz.* No. 282/4 With some Freakles, or *Summer foldes in the Face. **1876** *Whitby Gloss.*, **Summer-gauze*, gossamer; quantities of which, blown from the land to the sea, adheres to the rigging of ships. *a* **1800** PEGGE *Suppl. Grose*, **Summer-goos*, the gossamer. *North.* **1388** *Somer halle [see *summer field*, 1382]. *a* **1400–50** *Wars Alex.* 2922 So silis he furth.. in-to a somere-hall, þare sesonde was a soper. **1429** in *Munim. Magd. Coll. Oxf.* (1882) 16, j somerhalle cum iij cameris ibidem annexis. **1583** STUBBES *Anat. Abuses* M 3 b, They straw the ground rounde about, binde green boughes about it [*sc.* the Maypole], set vp sommer haules, bowers, and arbors. **1781** Cowper *Retirem.* 196 Her [*sc.* Nature's] *summer heats, her fruits, and her perfumes. **1815** J. Smith *Panorama Sci. & Art* II. 319 If the instrument is..intended chiefly to measure the higher degrees of heat, as from a summer-heat to that of boiling water. **1853** M. Arnold *Scholar Gypsy* vii, In my boat I lie Moor'd to the cool bank in the summer heats. **1877** Huxley *Physiogr.* 64 The Summer-heat may never be strong enough to melt all the ice. **1874** *Southern Mag.* XIV. 124 There was Charley's wife..flitting about from house to *summer-kitchen. **1939** H. M. Miner *St. Denis* ii. 25 Airy summer kitchens, which do not retain the heat of the stove, are built onto the sides of the houses. Too exposed to be warm, these annex kitchens are evacuated in winter. **1571** *Summer lady [see *summer lord*]. **1782** W. H. Marshall *Rural Econ. Norfolk* (1795) II. 320 Lambs..bought up by the East Norfolk 'graziers' in order to pick among their *summerlies, and their stubbles, after harvest. **1467** *Paston Lett.* II. 302 He wolde *somerlay and tylle the londe, otherwise then it is. *c* **1503** *Ibid.* III. 402 The seide x. acres londe, sowen with barly and peson, wherof v. acres were weel somerlayde to the seid barly. *c* **1440** *Promp. Parv.* 464/1 *Somyr lay-lond, *novale.* **1863** W. Barnes *Dorset Gloss.*, *Leäze*, or **Zummer leäze*, a field stocked through the summer, in distinction from a mead which is mown. **1886** *W. Som. Gloss.*, *Summerleys, summerleaze*, pasture fed only in summer. **1865** Kingsley *Herew.* iii, A certain amount of '*summer-leding' (*i.e.* piracy between seed-time and harvest). **1833** Tennyson *Miller's Daughter* 13 Gray eyes lit up With *summer lightnings of a soul So full of summer warmth. **1856** Mrs. Gore *Life's Lessons* xxiv, Like summer lightning gleaming from a thunder-cloud. **1872** *Daily News* 7 Nov., When a pheasant is flushed you only catch a summer-lightning glimpse of him. **1888** *Encycl. Brit.* XXIII. 330/1 What is called 'summer lightning' or 'wild-fire'... In the majority of cases it is merely the effect of a distant thunder-storm. It is also often due to a thunderstorm in the higher strata of the atmosphere overhead. **1924** E. Sitwell *Sleeping Beauty* xxvi. 95 When the thickest gold will thrive *Summer-long in the combs of the honey-hive. **1960** C. Day Lewis *Buried Day* ii. 31 On and on droned the voices, blending slumbrously with..the summer-long hum of insects. **1980** *Beautiful Brit. Columbia* Summer 39 In the summer, you may examine thousands of items at the summer-long Crafts Centre. **1571** Grindal *Injunc.* ii. §19 That the Minister and churchwardens shall not suffer any Lordes of misrule, or *sommer Lordes, or Ladies..to come vnreuerently into any Church, or Chapel. **1589** *Marprel., Hay any Work* 3 The sommer Lord with his Maie game. **1913** I. Cowie *Company of Adventurers* 228 Many of these journals were kept by a '*summer master', who was quite often a very illiterate laborer, who could barely scrawl phonetics in the book during the real master's absence on the annual voyage to and from headquarters with the furs and for the outfit. **1967** A. M. Johnson in *Saskatchewan Jrnls.* (Hudson's Bay Rec. Soc.) p. xxviii, He sent Bird to Buckingham House with instructions to leave the summer master in charge there. **1934** R. G. Linton *Vet. Hygiene* (ed. 2) vi. 446 The well-known suppurative form of mastitis..is especially prone to attack dry cows and virgin heifers during the summer months... This form is often referred to as epidemic mastitis or *summer mastitis. **1970** W. H. Parker *Health & Dis. Farm Animals* xv. 212 Infection of a dry cow or unbred heifer with..summer mastitis, is as common in beef as in dairy breeds. **1500–20** Dunbar *Poems* xxxix. 30 Lairdis in silk harlis to the eill, For quhilk thair tennentis sald *somer meill. **1877** Huxley *Anat. Inv. Anim.* 190 In some Rotifers, the eggs are distinguishable, as in certain *Turbellaria*, into *summer and winter ova. **1388** Wyclif *Judg.* iii. 20 He sat aloone in a *somer parlour. **1684** Bunyan *Pilgr.* ii. 26 So he left them a while in a Summer Parler below. **1732** Berkeley *Alciphron* I. 95 As we sate round the Tea-table, in a Summer-Parlour which looks into the Garden. **1829** Scott *Guy M.* Introd., The old man led the way into a summer parlour. **1617** Wither *Abuses* ii. iv. 277 They know how to discommend A May-game, or a *Summer-pole defie. **1619** *Pasquil's Palin.* B 3 b, Since the Sommer-poles were ouerthrowne, And all good sports and merryments decayd. **1786** Abercrombie *Gard. Assist.* 174 *Summer prune by displacing all fore-right productions. **1980** V. Canning *Fall from Grace* vii. 118 They summer pruned the wistaria. **1960** *News Chron.* 6 Aug. 6/4 The *summer-pruned laterals are further shortened. **1707** J. Mortimer *Whole Art of Husbandry* xvii. 396 To the Boughs that put out in Spring, give a *Summer pruning a little after Midsummer. **1725** *Fam. Dict.* s.v. *July*, Vines..will be satisfy'd with a single winter and one summer Pruning. **1806** W. Pontey *Forest Pruner* 235 As a general rule, we think summer is preferable to winter-pruning. **1895** *Meehan's Monthly* May 87/1 Summer pruning is especially effective with coniferous trees... One who understands this business of summer pruning an evergreen can so manage that the tree forms an absolutely perfect specimen. **1972** G. E. Brown *Pruning Trees, Shrubs & Conifers* iii. 50 Summer pruning.. promotes spur formation. **1933** E. C. Carver *Pract. Catering* vi. 114 *Summer pudding. Thin slices of stale bread, stewed fruit... Serve with cream or custard. **1974** P. Haines *Tea at Gunter's* xx. 206 Heaping my plate with summer pudding..I looked at the bread on my plate, oozing deep crimson juice. *c* **1400** *Destr. Troy* 1627 *Somur qwenes, and qwaintans, & oþer qwaint gaumes. **1590** Greene *Mourning Garm.* C 3 b, Faire she was as faire might be..Beautious, like a Sommers Queene. **1820** Good *Nosology* 466 Lichen..Tropicus..Attacks new settlers in the West Indies, and other warm regions... Prickly heat. *Summer-rash. **1832** *Louisville* (Kentucky) *Public Advertiser* 12 July 3/5 He has prepared his House and Garden at the lower end of Jefferson Street, for the purpose of making it a general **Summer Resort.* **1846** *Chambers's Miscellany* XIV. cxxi. 32 Musselburgh,..another pleasing summer resort, is situated two miles eastward. **1853** E. T. Turnerelli *Kazan* II. i. 4 This village is a favourite place of summer-resort for the inhabitants. **1873** J. H. Beadle *Undevel. West* xv. 257 For a summer resort one can spend weeks very pleasantly there. **1882** G. W. Peck *Peck's Sunshine* (1883) 125 He said he should at once begin..by boarding at a summer resort hotel. **1974** *Times* 12 Nov. 14/1 Mr and Mrs Ronald Heywood own a 56-bedroom two star hotel in a summer resort on the east coast. **1889** *Advance* (Chicago) 19 Sept. 673/3 At Astoria the *summer resorters distribute themselves to the various beaches. **1907** 'Mark Twain' in *N. Amer. Rev.* Nov. 327 They respected these elegant summer-resorters. *a* **1670** Hacket *Abp. Williams* ii. (1693) 228 It is an Injury..upon Corn, when it is *Summer-ripe, not to be cut down with the Sickle. **1820** S. H. Wilcocke in L. F. R. Masson *Les Bourgeois de la Compagnie du Nord-Ouest* (1890) II. 224 With the *summer road they were acquainted and that, therefore, they followed. **1909** *Gow Ganda* (Ontario) *Tribune* 17 Apr. 6/2 What will be the cry on the summer roads when we reach those points where the dense forest and rocks obstructs the view ahead? **1974** E. C. Stacey *Peace Country Heritage* i. 7 A few farmers used the..summer road. **1748** *De Foe's Tour Gt. Brit.* (1753) I. 307 On the Summit of this Hill his Lordship built a *Summer-room. **1797** Jane Austen *Sense & Sens.* xiii, One of the pleasantest Summer-rooms in England. **1899** J. F. Fraser *Round World on Bicycle* xxvi. 324 All the millinery shops in Oxford Street begin their early *summer sales or spring-clearance sales. **1923** A. Huxley *Antic Hay* xvi. 223 If I wait till the summer sale, the crêpe de Chine will be reduced by at least two shillings. **1976** *Times* 2 Aug. 16/3 The usual summer sales hiatus. **1893** F. E. Rhorer *Meat Man's Friend* 33 By making *summer sausage the same as above, but allowing the meat to be very coarse, it is called Salami. **1965** *House & Garden* Jan. 60 Summer sausage or Thüringer. These terms are interchangeable with dried cervelas. In fact, all dried sausages of this type are called summer sausage. **1976** T. Gifford *Cavanaugh Quest* (1977) x. 181 She sliced thick chunks of summer sausage. **1860** J. C. Patteson *Jrnl.* Sept. in C. M. Yonge *Life J. C. Patteson* (1874) I. ix. 473 In taking away natives to the *summer school, it must be understood that some..are taken.. merely to teach us their languages. **1871** E. Eggleston *Hoosier Schoolmaster* 1 You might teach a summer school. **1919** M. Beer *Hist. Brit. Socialism* II. iv. xiv. 294 In 1906 a Fabian Summer School was established. **1967** B. Jefferis *One Black Summer* (1968) i. 1 The grounds and buildings would be full of summer school students: doctors who longed to pot; dressmakers who yearned to try their hands at sculpture. **1971** *Daily Tel.* (Colour Suppl.) 3 Dec. 9/2 The lecturer..led his summer school audience down the howling avenues of Joycean puns. **1981** V. Glendinning *Edith Sitwell* xvi. 205 In August Edith had lectured..at a summer school in Cambridge. **1768** Ross *Helenore* 69 Yon *summer sob is out, This night looks well,.. The morn, I hope, will better prove. **1876** Dunglison *Med. Lex.*, **Summer Spots*, Ephelides. **1669** Worlidge *Syst. Agric.* (1681) 332 To **Summer-stir*, to Fallow Land in the Summer. **1766** *Complete Farmer, To Summer-land*, or *To Summer-Stir*, to fallow land in the summer. **1616** Surfl. & Markh. *Country Farm* 555 At mid-May you shall manure it, and in Iune you shall giue it the second earing, which is called *Sommer-stirring. **1942** Berrey & Van den Bark *Amer. Thes. Slang* §587/4 *Straw hat*, a *summer stock theater, in which plays are tried out. **1955** J. P. Donleavy *Ginger Man* vii. 64, I was once approached by a talent scout in summer stock. **1965** *New Statesman* 2 July 20/1 There is a very funny story about Maury Stein, a Summer Stock actor at Indian Lake. **1977** I. Shaw *Beggarman, Thief* iii. vi. 262 'Where've you acted before?'..'Well..noplace.'..'Not even summer stock?' **1853** Root & Lombard *Songs of Yale* 4 Presentation Day is the sixth Wednesday of the *Summer Term, when the graduating Class..are presented to the President as qualified for the first degree, or the A.B. **1859** J. A. Symonds *Let.* Feb. (1967) I. 181, I always connect it in my mind with that interminable Harrow Summer Term. **1922** *Times* 11 Oct. 11/5 During the last weeks of the Summer Term, at the request of the Lord Chancellor, I undertook the trial of undefended suits for divorce, and heard about four hundred cases. **1980** C. Fremlin *With no Crying* ii. 8 It looked like being the best summer term ever. .. O-levels were still a full year away. **1801** *Monthly Mirror* June 414 'Make hay while the sun shines,' has been found a most salutary maxim at the *summer theatres. **1938** L. Bemelmans *Life Class* ii. vii. 189 They were..Bavaria's greatest peasant actors... Their theater, part of the inn, was not the usual..summer theater, a converted old barn, but a real theater. **1981** N. Crisp *Festival* i. 15 Who in their right mind..would have dreamed of a summer theatre at..a somewhat shabby would-be genteel spa. **1818** in Thirsk & Imray *Suffolk Farming 19th Cent.* (1958) 104 To leave all the muck, dung and compost made the last year and all hay, clover hay and *summertilths. **1903** in G. E. Evans *Farm & Village* (1969) 160 Beans and Peas to be twice clean hoed or a clean summertilth. **1970** in —— *Where Beards wag All* viii. 89 Ploughing a long fallow or summer-tilth was a very hard and slow job for the man and his horses. *a* **1548** Hall *Chron., Hen. VII*, 49 The head of thys sedicion was *sommer topped, that it coulde haue no tyme to spryngе any higher. **1555** *Acts Parl. Scot., Mary* (1814) II. 500/1 Gif ony wemen or vthers about *simmer treis singand makis perturbatioun to the Quenis liegis in the passage throw Burrowis. **1883** *Graphic* 14 Apr. (Advt., rear cover), Youth's overcoat, *summer weight. **1931** *Daily Tel.* 22 May 9/6 Summer-weight weaves in hopsack, tweed, and knitted mixtures. **1968** A. Diment *Bang Bang Birds* v. 66 It's hell trying to keep a crease in bottle green, summer-weight cavalry twill. **1977** *Time* 27 June 46/2 The story also has some pretty serious problems, or perhaps more accurately, some puzzling aspects for what is intended as summer-weight entertainment. **1896** W. R. Fisher in W. Schlich *Man. Forestry* V. i. 6 It [*sc.* spring-wood] contains less woody substance than the *summer- or autumn-wood of the same annual zone. **1930** *Forestry* IV. 10 The greater length of the summer wood tracheids of the Sitka spruce is in accordance with the observations of Lee and Smith. **1982** *Sci. Amer.* July 35/2 These make the directly visible springwood ring, followed once the tree is great with leaf by a wider, denser, darker ring of mixed fibrous growth and small summerwood vessels. **1886** *Cheshire Gloss.*, **Summer-work*, a summer fallow. **1682** Martindale in Houghton *Coll. Lett. Impr. Husb.* No. 11. 125 If it [*sc.* land] grow weedy or grassie, we sometimes Fallow or *Summer-work it. **1793** J. H. Campbell in *Young's Annals Agric.* XX. 124 The fallows (or **Summer-workings*) are tumbled over by the plough, and jingled over by harrows. **1801** *Farmer's Mag.* Aug. 263 Rotation of different crops, fallowing, summer-working. **1912** *Standard* 20 Sept. 8/7 Cottonseed oil irregular, *summer yellow spot 10 up, October option 9 points down.

b. In names of animals and plants which are active or flourish in summer (often rendering L. *æstivus, æstivalis* as a specific name): **summer cock** *dial.*, see quots.; **summer crookneck**, a small yellow or orange summer squash with a curved neck; **summer cypress** = belvedere 2; **summer duck**, a North American duck, *Æx sponsa*, the wood-duck; **summer finch** *U.S.*, a popular name for birds of the genus *Peucæa*; † **summer fool**, a species of *Leucojum*; **summer grape**, a North American wild grape, *Vitis æstivalis*; **summer grass**, (*a*) the grass of summer; (*b*) the Australian hairy finger-grass, *Panicum sanguinale*; **summer haw**, *Cratægus flava*; **summer hemp** = fimble *sb.*[1] 1; **summer-herring**, (*a*) a herring taken in summer; (*b*) *U.S.* applied to some fishes resembling the herring, as the alewife, *Clupea serrata*; **summer rape**, *Brassica campestris* (*Treas. Bot.* 1866); **summer red-bird**, the rose tanager, *Pyranga æstiva*, which summers in N. America; **summer rose**, (*a*) a rose of summer; (*b*) an early kind of pear; **summer savory** (see savory 1); **summer snake** = green snake 1; **summer snipe**, the common sandpiper, *Tringoides hypoleucus*; **summer snowflake** (see snowflake 3); **summer squash**, any of several varieties of the gourd *Cucurbita pepo* whose fruits are eaten young; **summer tanager** = *summer redbird*; **summer teal**, the garganey; † **summer-whiting** = pelamyd 1; **summer-worm**, a worm or maggot that breeds in summer; **summer yellowbird**, a N. American wood-warbler, *Dendrœca æstiva*.

1790 Grose *Provinc. Gloss.* (ed. 2) Suppl., **Summer-cock*, a young salmon at that time. York City. **1882** Day *Fishes Gt. Brit.* II. 69 In Northumberland a 'milter' or spawning male is known as a summer-cock or gib-fish. **1890** *Amer. Naturalist* XXIV. 731 *Summer crooknecks appeared in our garden catalogues in 1828. **1969** *Oxf. Bk. Food Plants* 122/1 'Summer Crookneck'..has bright yellow or orange, warty fruits, shaped like a crooked club. **1767** Abercrombie *Ev. Man his own Gardener* (1803) 735/2 Belvidere or *Summer Cypress. **1829** Loudon *Encycl. Plants* (1836) 206 *Kochia scoparia*..summer Cypress. **1732** *Phil. Trans.* XXXVII. 449 The *Summer Duck..is one of the most beautiful of Birds. **1743** M. Catesby *Nat. Hist. Carolina* (1754) I. 97 The Summer Duck..is of a mean size, between the common Wild Duck and Teal. **1860** Gosse *Rom. Nat. Hist.* 199 The Summer-duck of America..delights in woods. **1884** Coues *N. Amer. Birds* 373 *Peucæa æstivalis illinoensis*, Illinois *Summer Finch. **1597** Gerarde *Herbal* i. lxxviii. 121 *Leucoium Bulbosum præcox.* Timely flowring Bulbus violet... In English we may call it..after the Dutch name *Somer sottekens*, that is, *Sommer fooles. **1629** Parkinson *Parad.* (1904) 16 Diuers sorts of Crocus or Saffron flower will appeare, the little early Summer foole or Leucoium bulbosum. **1814** Pursh *Flora Amer. Septentr.* I. 169 *Vitis æstivalis sinuata*..is known by the name of *Summer-grape. **1834** J. J. Audubon *Ornith. Biogr.* II. 92 The Summer Grape..occurs in all the barren lands of the Western Country. **1949** *Amer. Photography* Apr. 244/3 The summer grape is somewhat similar to the blue grape. **1599** Shaks. *Hen. V*, i. i. 65 Which..Grew like the *Summer Grasse, fastest by Night. **1882** 'Ouida' *Maremma* I. 3 The rich loads of summer-grass or grain. **1889** Maiden *Usef. Pl. Australia* 102 *Panicum sanguinale*,..Summer Grass. **1856** A. Gray *Man. Bot.* (1860) 124 *C[ratægus] fláva*, Ait. (*Summer Haw). **1707** Mortimer *Husb.* 118 The light *Summer-hemp, that bears no Seed, is called Fimble hemp. **1614** T. Gentleman *England's Way* 20 A barrell of *Summer-herrings, worth 20 or 30 shillings. **1883** Wallem *Fish Supply Norway* 17 The catch of Summer-herring and Sprat in the Fisheries of the years 1876–1881. **1743** M. Catesby *Nat. Hist. Carolina* (1754) I. 56 *Muscicapa rubra.* The *Summer Red-Bird. This is about the size of a Sparrow ..and..is of a bright red. **1872** Coues *N. Amer. Birds* 111 Summer Red-bird, rich rose-red, or vermilion, including wings and tail. **1727–46** Thomson *Summer* 354 Full as the *summer-rose Blown by prevailing suns, the ruddy maid. **1841** Whittier *Lucy Hooper* 3 All of thee we loved and cherished Has with thy summer roses perished. **1860** Hogg *Fruit Manual* 214 Pears..Summer Rose (Epine Rose; Ognonet; Rose; Thorny Rose). **1802** Shaw *Gen. Zool.* III. ii. 551 *Summer Snake. *Coluber Æstivus*... Native of many parts of North America, residing on trees. **1802** Montagu *Ornith. Dict., Sandpiper—Common*... It is known in some places by the name of *Summer Snipe. **1849** Kingsley *Misc.* (1859) II. 251 The summer snipes flitted whistling up the shallow. **1815** W. Bentley *Jrnl.* 14 Aug. (1914) IV. 346 A more free use has been made of the *summer squash than ever before known. **1902** *Harper's Bazaar* Sept. 766 There was nothing in her larder except a summer-squash pie. **1981** *Farmstead Mag.* Winter 37/1 Winter squash, of course, shares space in seed catalogs with its sister vegetable—the summer squash. **1783** Latham *Gen. Synop. Birds* II. i. 220 *Summer Tanager. A little bigger than an House Sparrow. **1884** Coues *N. Amer. Birds* 317. **1668** Charleton *Onomast.* 101 *Querquedula Cristata..ab aucupibus dicta*, the *Summer-Teal. **1766** [see garganey]. **1879** *Encycl. Brit.* X. 80/1 *n.* **1624** Middleton *Game Chess* v. iii, The pelamis Which some call *summer-whiting, from Chalcedon. **1658** Rowland tr. *Moufet's Theat. Ins.* 1130 The English call them [*sc.* water-worms] *Summer-worms, either because they are seen only in Summer, or they die in Winter. **1668** Charleton *Onomast.* 59 *Lumbrici aquatici*, Summer-Worms. **1820** Shelley *Prometh. Unb.* iv. 313 The jagged alligator, and the..behemoth..multiplied like summer worms On an abandoned corpse. **1872** Coues *N. Amer. Birds* 97 Blue-eyed Yellow Warbler. Golden Warbler. *Summer Yellow-bird.

summer (ˈsʌmə(r)), *sb.*[2] Also 4 sumer, 4–5 swmmer, somere, 4–8 somer, (6 somor), 5 sommere, 6–9 sommer; *Sc.* 6–7 (9) symmer, 9 simmer, (shimmer). See also sommier[2]. [a. AF. *sumer, somer*, = OF. *somier* (mod.F. *sommier*) pack-horse, beam = Pr. *saumier*, It. *somaro*, *somiere*:—pop.L. *saumāriu-s*, for *sagmārius*, f. *sagma* (see SUM *sb.*^{2}). For the sense-development cf. *horse* and F. *cheval*.

The OF. word was adopted in MLG. *somer* long thin pole or tree.]

I. †**1.** A pack-horse. (Cf. SOMER 1, SOUMER.)

1375 BARBOUR *Bruce* XIX. 746 [They] tynt bot litill of thar ger, Bot gif it war ony swmmer [*v.r.* summer] That in the moss wes left liand. **14..** *Guy Warw.* (ed. Copland ? 1560) Ccj b, His neck is great as any sommere; he renneth as swifte as any Distrere [*MS. Auch.* l. 7163 As a somer it is brested bifore in þe brede & swifter ernend þan ani stede]. *c* **1470** *Love's Bonavent. Mirr.* xiv. (Sherard MS.), ȝoure.. knyghtes,.. horses and herneyes, charyotes and summeres.

II. 2. †**a.** *gen.* A main beam in a structure. *Sc.* (in genuine use). *Obs.*

1324 *Acc. Exch. K.R.* Bd. 165 No. 1. m. 4 (P.R.O.), Pro iiij^{xx} xvij. somers pro springaldis.. xij li. xviij.s. viij.d. **1375** BARBOUR *Bruce* XVII. 696 The stane.. hyt the sow in sic maner, That it that wes the mast summer.. In-swndir with that dusche he brak. **1533** in Pitcairn *Crim. Trials* (1833) I. *163 [Breaking their] dooks, [and Fishing in the water of Dee,.. and destruction of the] symmeris [and] hekkis [thereof].

1654 EARL MONM. tr. *Bentivoglio's Wars Flanders* 219 That they might place their Summers in the parts nearest the banks.. and in the middle where it was deepest their boats. **1658** tr. *Porta's Nat. Magick* IV. i. 113 Binde [the vines].. fast to the summers or beams with the sprigs of Broom. **1715** LEONI *Palladio's Archit.* (1742) I. 85 These summers were join'd with other summers across them.

b. A horizontal bearing beam in a building; *spec.* the main beam supporting the girders or joists of a floor (or *occas.* the rafters of a roof). (When on the face of a building it is properly called BREAST-SUMMER.)

1359-60 *Sacrist Rolls Ely* (1907) II. 193 In xij lapidibus pro pendauntz postes portandis iij someres et xx linteles. **1448** in Willis & Clark *Cambridge* (1886) II. 8 The Someres of the seid hows shall be one side xij inch squar and on the other part xiiij inch squar. **1532** in Bayley *Tower Lond.* (1821) App. I. p. xviii, A roffe of tymber, and a bourde made complete, w^{t} a somer and joystes. **1594** T. B. *La Primaud. Fr. Acad.* II. To Rdr. b 3, The saide roome beganne to shake againe, so that one of the sommers of the chamber sprang out of the mortesse, and bowed downeward two feete, but fell not. **1623** *Something Written Occ. Accid. Blacke Friers* 25 At an instant the maine Summer or beame brake in sunder. **1663** GERBIER *Counsel* 42 Double Mortises, which doe but weaken the Summers. **1733** W. ELLIS *Chiltern & Vale Farm.* 96 Mortaises made ready for Plates, Chimney Pieces, and also for Somer and Joysts. **1836** PARKER *Gloss. Archit.* (1850) I. 431 In a framed floor the summers were the main beams, the girders were framed into the summers, and the joists into the girders.

¶The senses 'large stone laid over a column in beginning a cross vault' and 'lintel of a door, window, etc.', which are given in Dicts., do not appear to be in genuine English use, but are from French: see **1728** CHAMBERS *Cycl.* (copying *Dict. de Trévoux*) and **1842** GWILT *Archit.* Gloss.

3. In various other technical applications.

a. *pl.* The framework of stout bars fitted with cross rails or staves, which is added to a cart or wagon to extend its capacity. **b.** A beam in the bed or body of a cart or wagon. †**c.** The sound-board of an organ. *Obs.* **d.** *Sc.* (see quot. 1825). **e.** In the old hand-press, a rail or cross-bar mortised into the cheeks of the press, to prevent them from spreading. **f.** *Tanning.* A horse or block on which skins are pared, scraped, or worked smooth. †**g.** In the spinet, any of the ribs supporting the board holding the tuning-pins. *Obs.* **h.** In a lapidary's mill, each of two opposite bars supporting the bearings of the wheels. **i.** 'The large beam on the top of a cider-press.. which sustains all the pressure' (*W. Som. Gloss.* 1886).

a. **1510** STANBRIDGE *Vocabula* (W. de W.) C iij, *Epyredia*, the somors or the rauys [*mispr.* rauye]. **1530** PALSGR. 272/2 Somers or rathes of a wayne or carte. **1802** JAMES *Milit. Dict.*, *Sommers*, in an ammunition waggon, are the upper sides, supported by the staves entered into them with one of their ends, and the other into the side pieces.

b. **1523** FITZHERB. *Husb.* §5 The bodye of the wayne of oke, the staues, the nether rathes, the ouer rathes, the crosse somer. **1886** *West Som. Gloss.*, *Summer*,.. (tech.) the longitudinal parts of the bottom of a wagon.

c. **1659** LEAK *Waterwks.* 29 The 12 holes that are in the Summer serves to conveigh the wind of the said Summer.. to the Organ Pipes. **1728** CHAMBERS *Cycl.* s.v. *Sound-board*, The Sound-board, or Summer, is a Reservoir, into which the Wind.. is conducted.

d. **1662** LAMONT *Diary* 15 Jan. (1810) 179 The whole roofe and symmers of that said kill were consumed, and only about 3 bolls oatts saffe. **1809** *Edinb. Even. Courant* 21 Dec. (Jam.) As some servants.. were.. drying a quantity of oats on the kiln, the mid shimmer gave way, when three of them were precipitated into the killogy. **1825** JAMIESON, *Simmer, Symmer*,.. one of the supports laid across a kiln, formerly made of wood, now pretty generally of cast metal, with notches in them for receiving the ribs, on which the grain is spread for being kiln-dried; a hair cloth, or fine covering of wire, being interposed between the ribs and the grain.

e. **1662** EVELYN *Sculptura* II. (1906) 13 Upon the Summer or head of the Press marked C let the paper prepared and moistned for the impression lye ready. **1683** MOXON *Mech. Exerc.*, *Printing* x. ¶4 This Summer is only a Rail Tennanted, and let into Mortesses made in the inside of the Cheeks.

f. **1728** CHAMBERS *Cycl.* s.v. *Parchment*, The Skin, thus far prepared by the Skinner, is taken.. by the Parchment-Maker; who first scrapes or pares it dry on the Summer. **1837** WHITTOCK, etc. *Bk. Trades* (1842) 370 (*Parchment-maker*) The workman then stretches the skin to dry in the sun,.. being done enough, it is.. placed on the *summer*, or horse, to be again pared and smoothed with the stone. **1860** TOMLINSON *Cycl. Useful Arts*, *Parchment Making* (1867) II. 275/2 The parchment maker.. stretches it tail downwards upon a machine, called the sumner, consisting of a calf-skin mounted on a frame.

g. **1797** *Encycl. Brit.* (ed. 3) XVII. 692/2 [The spinet] consists of a chest or belly.. and a table of fir glued on slips of wood called summers, which bear on the sides.

h. **1839** URE *Dict. Arts* 739 In each of these summers a square hole is cut out.. which receives the two ends of the arbor [of the cutting wheel]. **1882** *Encycl. Brit.* XIV. 299/1.

4. *attrib.*, as (sense 1) †*summer-saddle*; (sense 2); **summer bar**, the upper summer of a lapidary's wheel; **summer-beam**, **-tree** = sense 2 b; †**summer-piece**, **summer-stone** (see quot. 1833); †**summer-trestle**, ? a railed rack on a trestle-like stand.

1839 URE *Dict. Arts* 739 Every thing that stands above the upper *summer-bar has been suppressed in this representation. **1519** HORMAN *Vulg.* 241 b, The carpenter or wryght hath leyde the *summer bemys [*trabes*] from wall to wall, and the ioystis a crosse. **1766** *Complete Farmer* s.v. *Balk*, The summer-beam or dorman of a house. **1859** PARKER *Dom. Archit.* III. II. vii. 322 The summer-beam well moulded. *c* **1429** in Willis & Clark *Cambridge* (1886) II. 445 Et iij *somerpecys xij^{d}. **1398-9** *Durham Acc. Rolls* (Surtees) 215 Uno *sumersadill et 2 hakenaysadilles. **1792** J. WOOD *Cottages* (1806) 9 The *summer stone.. becomes an abutment.. and support to the rest of the tabling. **1833** LOUDON *Encycl. Archit.* §209 Summer stones (stones placed on a wall, or on piers, for the support of beams, or on the lower angle of gable ends,.. as an abutment of the large stones). *Ibid.* §1368 Ridge-tiles, gutter tiles valley-tiles, and barge and summer-stone tiles. **1452** in Willis & Clark *Cambridge* (1886) I. 282 Principalls with *somere trees conuenient vnto the werk. **1623** *Nottingham Rec.* IV. 388 For takinge vp two summertrees. **1706** PHILLIPS (ed. Kersey), *Summer-Tree*, (among Carpenters) a Beam full of Mortises, for the ends of Joists to lie in. **1875** KNIGHT *Dict. Mech.* 2453/2. **1605** *Shuttleworths' Acc.* (Chetham Soc.) 170 A waller, iiij days fillinge the holles aboute the endes of the *somer trisle in the cowhowse, xij^{d}.

summer ('sʌmə(r)), *sb.*^{3} [f. SUM *v.*^{1} + -ER^{1}.]

1. One who sums or adds; esp. in ***summer-up***, one who or that which sums up; *colloq.* or *dial.* one who does sums, an arithmetician.

1611 COTGR., *Nombreur*, a numberer, reckoner, teller, summer, counter. **1643** DIGBY *Observ. Relig. Med.* (1644) 50 This last great day (the summer up of all past dayes). **1828** D'ISRAELI *Chas. I*, I. iii. 29 That aptitude.. which made him so skilful a summer-up of arguments. **1830** *Blackw. Mag.* XXVIII. 140 A summer-up of the tottle of the whole. **1863-5** STATON *Rays Loominary* (1867) 68 Awm but a bad summer at th' best o toimes. **1960** J. BAYLEY *Characters of Love* iii. 130 Here the confident summer-up of Othello might become a little uneasy.

2. *Electronics.* A circuit or device that produces an output dependent on the sum of two or more inputs or of multiples of them.

1958 W. J. KARPLUS *Analog Simulation* ix. 234 Since the output voltage is proportional to the sum of the input voltages, this circuit is termed 'summer'. **1968** PASSMORE & ROBSON *Compan. Med. Stud.* I. ii. 5 The summer would have many input voltages, each one representing the factors for heat gain.. or the heat loss. **1981** R. G. IRVINE *Operational Amplifier Characteristics* vii. 176 The gain of this circuit may be changed from unity by modifying the value of the feedback resistor on the inverting summer.

summer ('sʌmə(r)), *v.*^{1} Forms: 5-7 somer, 6-7 sommer, (5 someryn, somoryn, 6 soommer, *Sc.* 6 symmer, 9 simmer), 5- summer. [f. SUMMER *sb.*^{1} Cf. MLG. *som(m)eren*, LG. *sommern*, MHG. *sumer(e)n*, *summern*, G. *sommern* and *sömmern*, ON. *sumra*.]

1. *intr.* To pass or spend the summer, to dwell or reside during the summer (now chiefly *Sc.* and *U.S.*); (of cattle, etc.) to be pastured in summer.

c **1440** *Promp. Parv.* 464/2 Somoron [*Winch. MS.* someryn], or a-bydyn' yn' somyr, *estivo.* **1560** *Bible* (Geneva) Isa. xviii. 6 The foule shal sommer vpon it, and euerie beast of the earth shal winter vpon it. **1610** HOLLAND *Camden's Brit.* I. 806 The Ancient Nomades,.. who from the moneth of Aprill unto August, ly out skattering and sommering.. with their cattaile. **1819** SOUTHEY *Let. to N. White* 14 Oct., A great many Cantabs have been summering here. **1842** E. FITZGERALD *Lett.* (1889) I. 100 He is summering at Castellamare. **1880** *E. Cornw. Gloss.* s.v. *Summering*, Store cattle.. are sent summering under the care of the moorland herdsmen. **1895** ANNA M. STODDART *J.S. Blackie* II. 154 A short stay with Dr and Mrs Kennedy, who were summering at Aberfeldy. **1899** MARK TWAIN *Man corr. Hadleyb.*, etc. (1900) 93 A lady from Boston was summering in that village.

†**b.** *transf.* To pass one's time pleasantly. *rare*$^{-1}$.

1568 C. WATSON *Polyb.* 82 After they had ben vexed with long warres in Scicilie, & concluded a league with the Romans, they hoped to soommer and keepe holydaie.

2. *trans.* To keep or maintain during summer; *esp.* to provide summer pasture for (cattle, etc.): said of the land or the grazier. Also *transf.*

Cf. SUMMERING *vbl. sb.*^{1} 1.

1599 SHAKS. *Hen. V*, v. ii. 335 Maides well Summer'd, and warme kept, are like Flyes at Bartholomew-tyde, blinde, though they haue their eyes. **1601** *Account Bk. W. Wray* in *Antiquary* XXXII. 119 For somering ii stirkes, xs. **1610** FOLKINGHAM *Feudigr.* II. x. 63 How many Cattells such a Plot will Winter and Sommer, feed or keepe. **1707** MORTIMER *Husb.* (1721) I. 208 If your Colts be not well weaned, well summered and wintered. **1765** *Museum Rust.* IV. xliv. 190, I am obliged to allow three acres to summer a cow. **1810** J. T. in *Risdon's Surv. Devon* p. ix, Dartmoor summers an immense number of.. sheep. **1883** *Standard* 3 Apr. 3/5 It should be the aim of the grass-land farmer to summer as many and winter as few animals as possible.

b. *spec.* in the management of hunters.

1825 *Sporting Mag.* N.S. XV. 343 Now for summering the hunter. **1862** WHYTE-MELVILLE *Inside Bar* v, The fascinating pursuit for which they [*sc.* hunters] have been bought, and summered, and got into condition. **1879** FEARNLEY *Less. Horse Judging* 114 Our present plan of summering hunters in boxes instead of out in the open.

†**c.** *fig.* To give (a person) a 'sunny' or happy time. *Obs.*

1622 J. TAYLOR (Water P.) *Sir Greg. Nonsence* Wks. (1630) II. 3/2 Time now that summers him, wil one day winter him.

d. *refl.* or *intr.* To sun oneself, bask. Chiefly *fig.*

1837 C. LOFFT *Self-form.* II. 133 Summer house indeed:—and truly my best feelings.. summered themselves there most complacently. **1848** AIRD *Devil's Dream* xxx, Thou shalt summer high in bliss upon the hills of God. **1906** J. HUIE *Singing Pilgr.* 18 To sun and summer in the smile of God.

3. *to summer and winter*: **a.** To spend the whole year; also *transf.* to remain or continue permanently (*with*).

1650 ELDERFIELD *Civ. Right Tythes* 210 The best and usefullest Constitutions of State are those experienced firm ones, that have lived, summered and wintered with us, as we say. **1809** W. IRVING *Knickerb.* (1861) 276 Grey-headed negroes, who had wintered and summered in the household of their departed master for the greater part of a century. **1832** —— *Alhambra* II. 209 The ruined tower of the bridge in Old Castile, where I have now wintered and summered for many hundred years.

b. *trans.* To maintain one's attitude to or relations with at all seasons; to associate with, be faithful to, or adhere to constantly; hence, to be intimately acquainted with; also, to consider or discuss (a subject) constantly or thoroughly; †*occas.* to continue (a practice) for a whole year. Chiefly *Sc.*

a **1626** BRETON *Packet Mad Lett.* I. §15 Wks. (Grosart) II. 10 Shake of such acquaintance as gaine you nothing but discredit, and make much of him that must as well winter as summer you. **1644** RUTHERFORD *Serm. bef. H. of Comm.* 31 *Jan.* 1643 To Chr. Rdr. A 2 b, Whatever they had of Religion, it was never their mind both to summer and winter Jesus Christ. *a* **1670** HACKET *Abp. Williams* II. (1693) 197 [Presbyterianism] was not suitable to the eternal gospel, for the fautors of it did scarce summer and winter the same form of discipline. **1726-8** P. WALKER *Life Peden* To Rdr. (1827) p. xxxv, These have been my Views and digested Thoughts, that I have summer'd and winter'd these many Years. **1816** SCOTT *Antiq.* xliv, We couldna think o' a better way to fling the gear in his gate, though we simmered it and wintered it e'er sae lang. **1849** LONGF. *Kavanagh* xx. Prose Wks. 1886 II. 370, I know the critics root and branch,—out and out,—have summered them, and wintered them,—in fact, am one of them myself. **1865** MRS. STOWE *Little Foxes* (1866) 29 Mrs. Crowfield, who.. has summered and wintered me so many years, and knows all my airs and cuts and crinkles so well. **1891** MRS. LYNN LINTON *Let. to H. Spencer* 28 Mar., I am always afraid of 'summering and wintering' a subject too much.

c. *intr.* To consider or discuss a matter at great length; to be tediously long in discourse. *Sc.*

1822 GALT *Sir A. Wylie* xcviii, I'm no for summering and wintering about the matter. **1832** *Blackw. Mag.* XXXII. 651 The Provost was thus summering and wintering to me. **1833** GALT *Gudewife* in *Fraser's Mag.* VIII. 654/1 What would you be at, summering and wintering on nothing?

4. *trans.* To make summer-like, summery, balmy, or genial.

1863 S. DOBELL *An Autumn Mood* Poet. Wks. 1875 II. 332 Myself a morning, summer'd through and lit With light and summer. **1868** G. MACDONALD *Ann. Q. Neighb.* xi. (1878) 228 His rough worn face, summered over with his child-like smile. **1896** A. AUSTIN *England's Parting* I. iii, Till your name Soared into space and summered all the air.

Hence **'summered** (with adv. prefixed), **'summering** *ppl. adjs.*

1804 ANNA SEWARD *Mem. Darwin* 337 The seas of glass, the noble rocks, the ever-summered gales. **1836** *Fraser's Mag.* XIII. 233 Regularly Nimrodded, as the term for a well summered hunter now is. **1887** SWINBURNE *Locrine* I. i. 10 Seas that feel the summering skies.

†**summer**, *v.*^{2} *Archit. Obs. rare.* In 8 sommer. [Back-formation from SUMMERING *vbl. sb.*^{2}] *intr.* To radiate from or converge towards a centre, like the joints of an arch.

1703 MOXON *Mech. Exerc.* 279 Let the breadth of the upper part of the Keystone be the height of the Arch, *viz.* 14 Inches, and Sommer, from the Centre at I. **1703** T. N. *City & C. Purchaser* 9 The Key-stone.. ought to.. Sommer (or point with its 2 edges) to the Centre.

summer bird.

1. A bird that makes its appearance in summer, a summer migrant; locally applied *spec.* (see quots.). Also *fig.* (cf. SUMMER *sb.*^{1} 4 e).

1597 SHAKS. *2 Hen. IV*, IV. iv. 91 O Westmerland, thou art a Summer Bird, Which euer in the haunch of Winter sings The lifting vp of day. **1607** —— *Timon* III. vi. 34, 2 [*Att.*] The Swallow followes not Summer more willing, then we your Lordship. *Tim.* Nor more willingly leaues Winter, such Summer Birds are men. **1784** COWPER *Task* VI. 921 He cannot skim the ground like summer birds Pursuing gilded flies. **1821** SHELLEY *Epipsych.* 208 The singing of the summer-birds. **1885** SWAINSON *Prov. Names Birds* 103 Wryneck.. Summer bird (Northumberland). **1895** MORRIS *Austral Engl.*, *Summer-bird*, the Old-Colonists' name for the Wood-swallows [*Artamus sordidus*, Lath.]. In Tasmania it is applied to a species of Shrike, *Graucalus melanops*, Lath. **1913** *Melbourne Argus* 27 Dec. 5 The bee martin or summer bird.

†**2.** With allusion to the cuckoo as the 'summer bird': A cuckold. Also ***summer's bird.*** *Obs.*

Cf. SHAKS. *Merry W.* II. i. 127, *L.L.L.* v. ii. 911.

1560 *Scholeh. Women* (1572) B ij, Some other knaue Shall dub her husband a summer bird. ? *a* **1600** *Sack-full of Newes* (1864) 171 The poore man was cruelly beaten, and made a Summers Bird.

†**summer-castle.** *Obs.* In 4–6 somer-, 5 -yr, 6 sommer-. [? f. SUMMER *sb.*[2] + CASTLE *sb.*]

1. A movable tower used in sieges. (Also SUMMER-TOWER.)

? *a* **1400** *Morte Arth.* 3033 The kynge than to assawte he sembles his knyghtez, With somercastelle and sowe appone sere halfes. **1408** CLIFTON tr. *Vegetius' De Re Milit.* IV. viii. (Digby MS. 233) lf. 219 b, 3if þyn enemye sette to þy walles a somercastel oþere a bastyle þat be muche herre þan þe walles. *c* **1440** *Promp. Parv.* 464/1 Somyr castell, *fala*.

2. An elevated structure on a ship. (Also SUMMER-HUTCH.)

1346 *Acc. Exch., K.R.* Bundle 25. No. 7. m. 2 (P.R.O.) In ij haucers emptis..pro j castello vocato somercastell eadem naui. **1496** *Naval Acc. Hen. VII*, (1896) 176 Forcastell the overloppe the somercastell the dekke ovyr the somercastell & the pope. *c* **1500** *Three Kings' Sons* 44 They that were in the somer Castells & toppis of the shippis, that might easely se alle them that were a londe. **1530** PALSGR. 272/2 Sommer castell of a shyppe.

summer-cloud. (Also summer's cloud.) A cloud such as is seen on a summer day, *esp.* one that is fleeting or does not spoil the fine weather. Also *allusively*.

1605 SHAKS. *Macb.* III. iv. 111 Can such things.. ouercome vs like a Summers Clowd, Without our speciall wonder? **1671** MILTON *P.R.* III. 222 A shelter and a kind of shading cool Interposition, as a summers cloud. **1727** WATTS *Hope in Darkness* i. in *Horæ Lyricæ* I. (1743) 133 What tho' a short Eclipse his [*sc.* God's] Beauties shrowd 'Tis but a Morning Vapour, or a Summer-Cloud. **1792** S. ROGERS *Pleas. Mem.* Poems (1839) 3 As summer-clouds flash forth electric fire. **1820** SCOTT *Abbot* xxxvi, Floating in the wind, as lightly as summer clouds. **1893** E. PHILLPOTTS *Summer Clouds* 54 There are people in the world..who would say that we had had a row to-day... I should describe the matter myself as—well, merely a passing summer-cloud.

summer-day. [Cf. WFris. *simmerdei*, (M)LG. *sommerdach*, MHG. *sum(m)ertac* (G. *sommertag*).] = SUMMER'S DAY.

a **1300** *Cursor M.* 9946 A tron of iuor..þat es o gretter light and leme þan somer dai es son bem. **1390** GOWER *Conf.* I. 184 This was upon a Somer dai. *c* **1450** *St. Cuthbert* (Surtees) 5634 In þe hete of somyr day. *a* **1578** LINDESAY (Pitscottie) *Chron. Scot.* (S.T.S.) I. 229 Frome the sone ryssing quhill the sone zeid to in ane lang sommer day. **1608** SHAKS. *Per.* IV. i. 18 While Sommer dayes doth last. **1711** ADDISON *Spect.* No. 128 ¶ 10 The Lady..hates your tedious Summer Days. *a* **1774** GOLDSM. *Surv. Exp. Philos.* (1776) I. 329 He calculated that it [*sc.* the Mediterranean sea] would lose by evaporation, every summer day, fifty-two thousand and eighty millions of tons. **1823** SCOTT *Quentin D.* v, To spend summer-day and winter-night up in yonder battlements. **1848** LYTTON *K. Arthur* I. 6 This soft summer-day.

b. *fig.* and *allusively*. Also *attrib.*

1605 ERONDELL (*title*) The French Garden:..Or, A Sommer dayes labour. Being an instruction for the attayning vnto the knowledge of the French Tongue. **1806** *Ann. Rev.* IV. 466 The summer days of Naples were over. **1833** TENNYSON *May Queen* vi, There's many a bolder lad 'ill woo me any summer day. **1867** AUGUSTA WILSON *Vashti* xxii, No mere gala barge..was his religion; no fair summer-day toy.

ˈsummer-ˌfallow, *sb.* [See FALLOW *sb.* 2.] A lying or laying fallow during the summer; also, land that lies fallow during the summer.

1733 TULL *Horse-hoeing Husb.* vii. 78 This sort of Hoeing has..every Year the Effect of a Summer-fallow. **1765** *Museum Rust.* IV. 143 The ill consequence of not giving it a summer-fallow to clean the ground thoroughly. **1801** *Farmer's Mag.* Jan. 85 The quantity of ground under Summer-fallow this year. **1844** H. STEPHENS *Bk. Farm* III. 990 The sowing of the fallow-crop on the summer-fallow is delayed to autumn. **1875** *Encycl. Brit.* I. 340/1 That prolonged form of it [*sc.* the fallowing process] called a summer or naked fallow.

b. as *adj.* Lying fallow during the summer.

1801 *Farmer's Mag.* Jan. 105 The months of November and December were very favourable for getting the Summer-fallow land seed-furrowed. **1844** H. STEPHENS *Bk. Farm* III. 999, I..trenched 13 acres of my summer-fallow break in the months of June and July.

ˈsummer-ˌfallow, *v.* [See FALLOW *v.*[2]] *trans.* To lay (land) fallow during summer. Also *absol.* Hence **summer-fallowing** *vbl. sb.* and *ppl. a.*

1669 WORLIDGE *Syst. Agric.* (1681) 9 For the same reason are the Summer-Fallowings advantageous to the Husbandman. **1760** BROWN *Compl. Farmer* II. 11 In Staffordshire, they often give their lands a winter-fallowing, besides the three summer-fallowings. **1765** A. DICKSON *Treat. Agric.* (ed. 2) 271 The English writers on agriculture, when giving directions about the opening up of grass-ground, always suppose that the land is to be summer-fallowed. **1778** [W. MARSHALL] *Minutes Agric.* 6 Feb. 1776, The summer-fallowing Farmer. **1813** VANCOUVER *Agric. Devon* 158 In the division of Meshaw, it is common to plough clean before Christmas, and summer-fallow for wheat. **1844** H. STEPHENS *Bk. Farm* III. 990 That part of the fallow-break which is summer-fallowed.

†**ˈsummerful,** *a.* *Obs. rare*[−1]. [f. SUMMER *sb.*[1] + -FUL.] Having the summer development or quality.

1614 T. GENTLEMAN *England's Way* (1660) 5 They do sell them for Sprats, the which, if that they were let live, would all be, at Midsummer, a Fat Summerfull Herring.

summer-game. (Also 4 somere(s) gamen.)

†**1. a.** A festival held at Midsummer, celebrated with dancing, games, dramatic performances, etc.

1303 R. BRUNNE *Handl. Synne* 4681 Daunces, karols, somour games, Of many swych come many shames. *a* **1340** HAMPOLE *Psalter* xvi. 12 þai haf vmgifen me in þe crosse hyngand, as foles þat gedirs til a somere gamen. *c* **1380** WYCLIF *Wks.* (1880) 246 A wilde pleiere of someres gamenes. *c* **1440** *Promp. Parv.* 404/1 Pley, or somyr game, *spectaculum*. **1469** *Test. Ebor.* (Surtees) V. 103 *note*, Accessit cum Thoma Barker..et Margareta More, in regem et reginam ipsius villæ in ludo suo æstivali, Anglice Somer-game, forte electis. **1583** BABINGTON *Commandm.* (1590) 166 Whether carding,..stage plaies, and summer games..be exercises commanded of God for the sabaoth day or no. *a* **1629** HINDE *J. Bruen* xxxiii. (1641) 104 Profane exercises of May-games, and Summer-games [*mispr.* greenes].

†**b.** *attrib.* **summer-game light**: a light burnt in church on the feast of the Nativity of St. John Baptist (Midsummer Day, June 24). *Obs.*

[**1438** *Test. Ebor.* (Surtees) V. 103 *note*, Lumini Æstival in eadem ecclesia v s.] **1464** *Ibid.*, Lumini vocato Somer-game light. **1519** *Ibid.* 103 To the Somer-game lyght in my parishe chirche ij s.

2. *U.S. slang.* (See quots.)

1859 G. W. MATSELL *Vocabulum* 117 *Summer game*, playing merely for amusement. *Summer game*, playing a game for the benefit of another person with his money. **1890** BARRÈRE & LELAND *Slang Dict.* (1897), *Summer game* (American gamblers), playing merely for amusement or benefit of another person, but with his money.

summerhead, Anglo-Indian corruption of SOMBRERO, sun-umbrella.

1797 S. JAMES *Narr. Voy.* 88 Not one European was able to stir outside his door without his summerhead. **1886** YULE & BURNELL *Hobson-Jobson* Suppl. s.v. *Sombrero*, *Summerhead* is a name in the Bombay Arsenal (as M.-General Keatinge tells me) for a great umbrella.

ˈsummer-ˌhouse. [Cf. WFris. *simmerhûs*, MDu. *somerhuys* (Du. *zomerhuis*), MHG. *sum(m)erhaus* (G. *sommerhaus*).]

1. A summer residence in the country. Now *rare*.

1... *Cust. of Newington by Sittingbourne* in *Cowel's Interpr.* (1701), *Homines quoque de walda debent unam domum æstivalem quæ Anglice dicitur* Sumer-hus *invenire, aut viginti solidos dare*. **1382** WYCLIF *Amos* iii. 15 Y shal smyte the wyntyr hous with the somer hous [Vulg. *domo æstiva*]. **1596** SHAKS. *1 Hen. IV*, III. i. 164, I had rather liue With Cheese and Garlick in a Windmill farre, Than feede on Cates, and haue him talke to me, In any Summer-House in Christendome. **1654** GATAKER *Disc. Apol.* 50 The Doctor making onelie a Summer-House of it. **1688** HOLME *Armoury* III. xii. 453/1 *Summer Houses, Bowers*, Places to which the Gentry resort, and abide there dureing the Summer season, for their Recreation and pastime. *a* **1709** J. LISTER *Autobiog.* (1842) 35 At present her summer-house is in Highgate. **1797** W. JOHNSTON tr. *Beckmann's Invent.* II. 38 [Privies] are at present considered to be so indispensably necessary, that few summer-houses are constructed without them. **1881** *Daily News* 26 Sept. 5/2 Its very nearness to London perhaps has made it less of an actual residence and more of a holiday summer-house than it would otherwise have been.

fig. **1754** FIELDING *Voy. Lisbon* Wks. 1882 VII. 82 The wind..slyly slipped back again to his summer-house in the south-west.

2. A building in a garden or park, usually of very simple and often rustic character, designed to provide a cool shady place in the heat of summer.

c **1440** *Pallad. on Husb.* I. 347 Lest the sonne in somer do hit harm, Thi somer hous northest & west let wrie. **1577** B. GOOGE *Heresbach's Husb.* 34 b, Frenche Beanes..climeth aloft,..seruyng well for the shadowyng of Herbers and Summer houses. **1585** HIGINS *Junius' Nomencl.* 389/2 *Horti adonidis*,..a banketting summer house made of trees, herbs, flowers, &c. **1624** WOTTON *Archit.* II. 100 [Paintings of] Land-schips, and Boscage..in open Tarraces, or in Summer houses. **1721** MORTIMER *Husb.* II. 206 Summer-Houses may..be erected at each Corner [of the garden], and made so as to let in the Air on all sides, or to exclude it. **1762–71** H. WALPOLE *Vertue's Anecd. Paint.* (1786) IV. 275 At the end of the terras-walk are two summer-houses. **1824** SCOTT *St. Ronan's* xxxvii, One of her gloves lay on the small rustic table in the summer-house. **1888** MISS BRADDON *Fatal Three* I. vi, There was an old stone summer-house in each angle of that end wall.

†**b.** An arbour or the like used in connexion with the 'summer-game'. *Obs.*

1519 *Test. Ebor.* (Surtees) V. 103 In quo..horreo..loco adtunc vulgariter dicto Somer-house, prædicta Margareta More,..permansit..jocundam se faciendo in eodem.

†**summer-hutch.** *Obs.* In 5 -hoche, -wiche, -wyche. = SUMMER-CASTLE 2.

1417 in *For. Acc. 8 Hen. V*, D/1 *dorso* (P.R.O.), In..ij batellis pro eadem Naui j grapnelle j Somerwyche. *Ibid.* G/1 De..iiij cordis paruis..j Grapnelle j Somerwiche. **1420** in *For. Acc. 3 Hen. VI*, H *dorso* (P.R.O.), j. pompe pro aqua haurienda..j Grapnelle j. somerhoche.

summering (ˈsʌmərɪŋ), *vbl. sb.*[1] [f. SUMMER *v.*[1] or *sb.*[1] + -ING[1].]

1. a. The pasturing of cattle in summer. †Also *attrib.*, as ***summering ground, place, plain***.

1477 *Churchw. Acc. Tintinhull* (Somerset Rec. Soc.) 193 For wynteryng and summering of the chyrche cowe, iij[s]. **1580** *Records of Elgin* (New Spald. Club) I. 156 Fyve s. for the symmering of tua ky to him in symmer last wes. **1595** *Wills & Inv. N.C.* (Surtees 1860) 254, I will that my wiffe be fre to all my sommering places. **1607** TOPSELL *Four-f. Beasts* 605 The Romans had a speciall regard to chuse some places for the summering of their sheepe, and some place for their wintering. **1615** G. SANDYS *Trav.* I. 45 Aladin.. assigned him this village to winter in, and the mountaines adioyning for the sommering of his cattell. **1664** in *Northumb. Gloss.* s.v. *Summering*, All my summering grounds in the parish of Symonburne. **1688** WALTER SCOT *Hist. Name Scot* (repr. 1776) 33 All our south-parts was wood and forrest, Except here and there a summering plain. **1801** *Farmer's Mag.* Apr. 197 Summering on grass, being the customary payment for a cow, L. 3 10 0. **1888** DOUGHTY *Trav. Arabia Deserta* I. 24 When nearly all the villagers lie encamped..for the summering of their cattle.

b. Spending the summer, summer residence. †Also *attrib.*, as ***summering-house, place***. Now *U.S.*

1565 COOPER *Thesaurus* s.v. *Confectus*, When they had done restinge in their summering places. **1675** COVEL in *Early Voy. Levant* (Hakluyt Soc.) 238 The G. Sr. nourishes severall [English mastiffs], and hath here hard by our house a sommering-house for them. **1817–18** COBBETT *Resid. U.S.* (1822) 272 After a long summering upon wild flesh. **1856** MISS WARNER *Hills Shatemuc* x, 'The young ladies' summering in the country had begun with good promise. **1883** *Harper's Mag.* Aug. 331/2 Altoona..is a summering place. **1892** KIPLING in *Times* (weekly ed.) 25 Nov. 13/2 You in England have no idea of what Summering means in the States.

c. The summer treatment of hunters.

1856 'STONEHENGE' *Brit. Rural Sports* II. III. ii. §2. 404/2 In the middle of September the training for the hunting season begins, and at that time the summering may be considered at an end. **1881** *Encycl. Brit.* XII. 194/1 It will probably be nearly a month after the last hunting day before the summering treatment is adopted.

†**2.** A summer excursion, festivity, or revelling.

1606 JAS. VI in *Reg. Privy Council Scot.* VII. 489 Thair forbearing ony suche lyke sommering heirefter. **1630** BRATHWAIT *Eng. Gentlem.* 166 Both Southward in their Wakes, and Northward in their Summerings, the very same Recreations are to this day continued. **1631** —— *Whimzies, Ruffian* 82 His soveraignty is showne highest at May-games, wakes, summerings, and rush-bearings. **1781** J. HUTTON *Tour to Caves* Gloss. (E.D.S.), *Summering*, a rush-bearing.

3. *dial.* **a.** *pl.* Summer apples or pears.

1847 HALLIWELL, *Summerings*,..very early apples and pears. **1877** *N.W. Linc. Gloss.*

b. Summer pasture or feed.

1894 *Morning Post* 3 Feb. 2/1 If the meadow land which belonged to the farm was cut off, leaving only the summering. **1894** *Northumb. Gloss.* s.v., *Summerings, Sommerings*, pastures on the moors; so-called from their being occupied only in the summer months.

c. *pl.* Cattle of one year old.

Cf. ON. *sumrungr*.

1828 *Farm. Jrnl.* 9 June (E.D.D.). **1847** in HALLIWELL.

summering (ˈsʌmərɪŋ), *vbl. sb.*[2] *Archit.* Also 8 som(m)ering. [app. f. SUMMER *sb.*[2] + -ING[1].]

a. *collect.* The beds of the stones or bricks of an arch considered with reference to their direction. **b.** The radial direction of the joints of an arch. **c.** The degree of curvature of an arch.

The term perhaps originally indicated the support given by the impost from which the arch springs (cf. F. *sommier*) and which by its mould determines the curve of the arch, but there is no evidence for a sense (given in some recent Dicts.) 'the first mass of masonry laid upon a pier, column, etc. when it begins an arched construction'.

1703 T. N. *City & C. Purchaser* 9 The Centre for the Skew-back or Sommering to point to... By Sommering, is to be understood the level Joints betwixt the Courses of Bricks in the Arch. **1703** MOXON *Mech. Exerc.* 279 According to the breadth of the Piers between the Windows, so ought the Skew-back or Sommering of the Arch to be. **1751** HALFPENNY *New Des. Chinese Bridges* II. 8 The middle Pieces are taper, according to the somering of the Arch. **1823** P. NICHOLSON *Pract. Builder* 329 In arching, the beds are, by some, called summerings. *Ibid.* 593 *Sommering*, the continuation of the joints of arches towards a centre.

attrib. **1703** MOXON *Mech. Exerc.* 275 Divide the upper Hanse from the centre O, making a right Angle from each sommering Line to the Ellipsis.., this will be the Sommering Mould for the Hanse;..then make another Sommering Mould to fit between two of these Lines. **1725** W. HALFPENNY *Sound Building* 55 Cut the Arch on the End of the Brick, as also the Summering Joint.

summerish (ˈsʌmərɪʃ), *a.* [f. SUMMER *sb.*[1] + -ISH[1].] Somewhat summer-like.

1726 LEONI *Alberti's Archit.* I. 15/1 In Places subject to much Snow, the Coverings shou'd have a very steep Slope ..; but in more Summerish Climates (to use such an Expression) they laid their Coverings less oblique. **1754** H. WALPOLE *Let. to J. Chute* 30 Apr., To-day looks summerish, but we have no rain yet. **1847** JEFFREY *Let. to Mrs. A. Rutherfurd* 21 June, Our weather has been summerish of late, but never quite summer. **1856** HAWTHORNE *Eng. Note-Bks.* (1870) II. 80 In wide-awake hats and loose, blouse-like, summerish garments.

summerize (ˈsʌməraɪz), *v.* [f. SUMMER *sb.*[1] + -IZE.] **1.** *intr.* To spend the summer. *nonce-uses.*

1797 *Monthly Mag.* III. 460 A Series of Familiar Poetical Epistles, from Mr. Simkin Slenderwit, summerising at Ramsgate, to his dear Mother in Town. **1799** *Monthly Rev.* XXX. 350 In this summerising tour from Wisbech to Scarborough. **1891** H. JAMES *Let.* 7 June (1981) III. 342 The Curtises go to India—or believe they do—in the autumn; so I suppose they summerize at the Barbaro.

2. *trans.* To prepare (something) for summer. Also *intr.* for *refl.* *U.S. colloq.*

1935 *Evening Sun* (Baltimore) 3 Apr. 9 Let Hutzler's summerize your home. **1949** *Sun* (Baltimore) 2 June 4 Come to K. Katz and 'summerize'! **1962** *Harper Motors, Inc.* (Charlottesville, Va.) *Advertising Let.*, This time of year you're probably deluged with offers from service stations to 'summerize' your car—that is, drain the antifreeze, check the motor, and get ready for summer driving.

Hence **summeri'zation**, the act or process of preparing a thing for summer.

1974 *Old Times* (Upper Canada College) Autumn 8 With ..the summerization of the Patrick Johnson rink..the quality of extracurricular programs..is greatly enhanced.

'summer-land, 'summerland, *sb.* Also 8 somerland.

1. A summer-fallow. *dial.*

1695 Kennett *Par. Antiq.* Gloss. s.v. *Warectare.* **1723** Lewis *Hist. Tenet* 8 The tilth for this grain is either Somerland, Bean- or Pease grotten, or Clover, or Trefoil-lay. **1765** *Museum Rust.* IV. 145, I make no summer-land on this light land, but plough sufficiently to get out the grass. **1846** *Jrnl. R. Agric. Soc.* VII. II. 589 To make a summerland only for swede turnips.

2. A land where it is always summer; in the language of spiritualists applied to the intermediate state of the departed.

1861 *Herald of Progress* (N.Y.) 13 July 3/4 (*heading*) Tidings from the summer land. A plea in behalf of little children. **1869** *Spiritualist* 17 Dec. 19/3 He found that he could pass through the upper air with ease, and at last they reached what the Spiritualists call the 'Summer Land', but in reality the compound essence of seventeen summers distilled into one, would not equal it in loveliness. **1890** W. James *Princ. Psychol.* I. x. 394 The odd thing is that persons unexposed to spiritualist traditions will so often act in the same way when they become entranced, speak in the name of the departed, ..send messages about their happy home in the summer-land, and describe the ailments of those present. **1895** Workman *Algerian Mem.* 44 The summer-land of oranges, lemons and figs. **1896** Mrs. Besant in *Daily News* 31 Oct. 6/3 The purgatory of the Roman Catholics, the summerland of the spiritualists, the intermediate states of the Hindus and Buddhists. **1901** 'Lux Aurea' (*title*) Light from the Summerland. Being a Series of Articles illustrating the Truth and Teachings of Spiritualism.

Hence **summerland** *v. trans.*, to lay fallow.

1674 Ray *S. & E.C. Words*, To *Summerland* a ground; to lay it fallow a year, *Suff.* **1723** Lewis *Hist. Tenet* 10 They are forc'd to Somerland or lay fallow their ground.

'summerless, *a.* [f. summer *sb.*[1] + -less.] Having no summer; not summery.

1879 *Mem. G. S. Arnold* 104 A summerless tomorrow. **1882** Morris in Mackail *Life* (1899) II. 77 The summerless season.

summer-like ('sʌməlaɪk), *a.* [f. summer *sb.*[1] + -like.] Like, or like that of, summer; summery. †Also = summerly *a.* 1.

1530 Palsgr. 325/1 Sommerlyke, belongyng to the sommer season, *estiual.* **1610** Holland *Camden's Brit.* (1637) 220 In summer time it is a right summer-like Country. **1772** T. Smith *Jrnl.* (1849) 278 Several summer-like days this month [Dec.] **1842** Longfellow in *Life* (1891) I. 413 The weather for ten days past has been delicious and summer-like. **1912** *World* 7 May 681/1 The King..attended the races on Thursday, when the weather was almost summer-like.

'summerling. [f. summer *sb.*[1] + -ling.] A beast put out to graze in summer.

1829 *Glover's Hist. Derby* I. 204 Large pasture fields, for the taking in of summerlings or ley cattle, at fixed prices per week.

summerly ('sʌməlɪ), *a.* [OE. *sumerlic* = OHG. *sumarlîh* (MHG. *sumerlich*, G. *sommerlich*), ON. *sumarligr*; see summer *sb.*[1] and -ly[1].]

†**1.** Of or pertaining to summer; taking place in summer. *Obs.*

c **1000** *Sax. Leechd.* III. 250 Se sumerlica sunnstede. *Ibid.* 252 þære sumerlican hætan. *c* **1050** *Suppl. Ælfric's Gloss.* in Wr.-Wülcker 176/18 *Æstiuus dies*, sumorlic dæȝ. **1559** W. Cunningham *Cosmogr. Glasse* 34 After this somerly reuerting, the Sonne is not perceiued to decline farther North. **1576** Fleming *Panopl. Epist.* 227 The grassehopper ..leapt and chirpte..among the greene herbes and summerlie plantes. **1749** H. Walpole *Let. to Mann* 4 June, As summerly as June and Strawberry Hill may sound, I assure you I am writing to you by the fire-side. **1771** —— *Let. to J. Chute* 9 July, The weather is but lukewarm, and I should choose to have all the windows shut, if my smelling was not much more summerly than my feeling.

2. Having the qualities of summer; summer-like, summery.

a **1225** *Leg. Kath.* 1678 Euch strete..bute sloh & slec, euer iliche sumerlich. *a* **1661** [implied in summerliness]. **1850** T. T. Lynch *Theoph. Trinal* xi. 210 A quiet, most summerly, September day. **1858** *Times* 15 Dec. 6/1 Whenever the season is summerly and the weather is damp and mild. **1894** Jeaffreson *Bk. Recoll.* I. iv. 57, I journeyed in summerly weather..to Oxford.

Hence **'summerliness**, summeriness.

a **1661** Fuller *Worthies, Somerset.* (1662) 17 Some will have it [*sc.* Somersetshire] so called from the Summerlinesse, or temperate pleasantnesse thereof.

summerly ('sʌməlɪ), *adv. rare.* [f. summer *sb.*[1] + -ly[2].] In a manner or condition befitting summer.

1600 Nashe *Summer's Last Will* Wks. 1905 III. 247 Let the prodigall childe come out in his dublet and hose all greasy, his shirt hanging forth, and ne're a penny in his purse, and talke what a fine thing it is to walke summerly. **1839** Ld. Houghton *Treasure-Ship* i, The wind is blowing summerly. **1902** *Rime* in *Daily Chron.* 3 Jan. 5/2 If the January calends be summerly gay, It will be winterly weather till the calends of May.

summers ('sʌməz), *adv. U.S.* [f. summer *sb.*[1] + -s.] During the summer; each summer (for a number of years).

1907 'Mark Twain' *Christian Sci.* II. viii. 235 It [*sc.* a local Christian Science church] can appoint its own far-distributors, summers. **1936** H. W. Horwill *S.P.E. Tract* xlv. 192 A peculiar use of the plural form is illustrated in ..'A niece of theirs had earned her way through College by waiting on the Atkins-Smythes' table, summers'. This usage is said to be a relic of the old adverbial genitive. **1976** *National Observer* (U.S.) 1 May 8/2 The limits have riled Pevsner since college days, when he worked summers in Europe.

summersault, -saut, var. of somersault.

summer's day. [Cf. OFris. *sumersdey* Mid-summer day.] A day in summer: often put typically for a very long day.

a **1300** *K. Horn* 29 Hit was vpon a scmeres day. **1340** Hampole *Pr. Consc.* 715 Als a shadu on þe somers day. **1426** Lydg. *De Guil. Pilgr.* 11613 Vp-on the glade somerys dayes. *a* **1536** *Songs, Carols*, etc. (E.E.T.S.) 117 Lyke a meyny of bullokkis..on a whot somers day, whan they be mad all. **1588** Shaks. *Tit. A.* v. i. 14 Like stinging Bees in hottest Sommers day. **1667** Milton *P.L.* I. 449 To lament his fate In amorous dittyes all a Summers day. **1743** Blair *Grave* 107 Oh! then the longest summer's day Seemed too too much in haste. **1853** M. Arnold *Scholar Gypsy* ii, All the live murmur of a summer's day.

b. Phr. *in* (†*upon*) *a summer's day*, used in various commendatory phrases; *some summer's day*, some day or other, 'one of these fine days'.

1590 Shaks. *Mids. N.* I. ii. 89 A sweet-fac'd man, a proper man as one shall see in a summers day. **1594** Lyly *Mother Bombie* I. iii, As goodly a youth as one shall see in a Summers daie. **1697** H. Wanley in *Bodl. Q. Rec.* (1915) Jan. 112 [The] Vice-Chancellor..with the other Curators, upon some Somers day, might call them all over. **1742** Fielding *J. Andrews* IV. xv, As fine a fat thriving Child as you shall see in a Summer's Day. **1823** Byron *Juan* XIV. lxxxii, There's another little thing..Which you should perpetrate some summer's day. **1848** Thackeray *Van. Fair* xxxvii, You won't see a prettier pair, I think, *this* summer's day, sir.

summer season. 1. The season of summer. Now *rare.*

1362 Langl. *P. Pl.* A. Prol. 1 In A somer sesun whon softe was þe sonne. *a* **1400** *Stockholm Med. MS.* i. 107 in *Anglia* XVIII. 297 Late take a gres in somer-sesoun. **1530** Palsgr. 703/1 In the sommer season I love to shyfte me often. **1588** A. King tr. *Canisius' Catech.* i vij, Giff he [*sc.* the sun] be in ony of ye sowth signes in ye simmer sessone. **1688** Holme *Armoury* III. xii. 453/1 Places to which the Gentry resort, and abide there dureing the Summer season. **1712** Addison *Spect.* No. 477 ¶1 In the Summer-Season the whole Country blooms. **1811** Shelley *'She was an aged woman'* 66 When the time of summer season smiled. **1812** *New Bot. Gard.* I. 88 The cuttings should be made in the summer season.

2. A period in summer for which people are employed in connection with seasonal or holiday entertainment, trade, etc.

1952 W. Granville *Dict. Theatrical Terms* 159 *Seasonal shop*, an engagement for the summer season in, say, a concert party or in a touring company that visits theatres which open only in the summer months. **1973** *Melody Maker* 4 Aug. 50/6 The Teign Valley Stompers from Teignmouth, Devon, who are at present enjoying a summer season on Pontin's Holiday Camps' Devon circuit, have engaged a new trombonist.

summerset, var. form of somerset.

summer solstice. The time at which the sun reaches the summer tropic, *i.e.* in the northern hemisphere, the tropic of Cancer, in the southern hemisphere, the tropic of Capricorn; †*occas.* applied to the tropic itself.

1549 *Compl. Scot.* vi. 37 Distant fiue degreis fra oure symmyr solstice, callit the borial tropic of cancer. **1601** Holland *Pliny* II. 245 About the Summer solstice it sheweth a red floure. **1698** Fryer *Acc. E. Ind. & P.* 23 Five days after our Summer Solstice we had soundings 14 Fathom. **1837** Brewster *Magnet.* 217 The declination has never diminished between the vernal equinox and the summer solstice. **1868** Lockyer *Guillemin's Heavens* (ed. 3) 119 From the 21st of June to the 22d of September, the Earth passes from the Summer solstice to the autumnal equinox.

†**summer's tide.** *Obs.* [Cf. G. *sommerszeit.*] = next.

a **1000** *Phœnix* 209 (Gr.) On sumeres tid sunne hatost ofer sceadu scineð. *a* **1250** *Owl & Night.* 489 Sumerestyde is al wlonk. **1303** R. Brunne *Handl. Synne* 2127 Hyt was yn þe somerys tyde, whan þe hete ys al yn pryde. *a* **1352** Minot *Poems* (ed. Hall) x. 7 Þai sailed furth in þe Swin in a somers tyde. *c* **1465** *Pol. Rel. & L. Poems* (1903) 1 Erly in a sommeristide. **1513** Douglas *Æneis* VI. xi. 57 The byssy beis in schene symmeris tyde.

'summer-tide. Now chiefly *poet.* [Cf. WFris. *simmertiid*, NFris. *sumartidj*, MLG. *sommertyd*, LG. *sommertît*, OHG. *sumarzît* (MHG. *sumerzît*, G. *sommerzeit*).] = summer-time 1.

c **1250** *Gen. & Ex.* 1224 He flemede agar and ysmael In sumertid. **1303** R. Brunne *Handl. Synne* 903 Whan hyt come to somer tyde,..Here vynys florshede feyre & weyl. **1390** Gower *Conf.* II. 328 Whan the world is woxe grene And comen is the Somertide. *c* **1420** ? Lydg. *Assembly of Gods* 334 Grene as any gresse in the somertyde. *a* **1513** Fabyan *Chron.* VII. (1811) 482 In this yere, folowynge the somertyde in Guyan. **1566** Sternhold & H. *Ps.*, *Benedicite*, Ye winter and the sommer tyde.

1800 Wordsw. *Hart-leap Well* 150 Asleep he sank, Lulled by the fountain in the summer-tide. **1873** Geikie *Gt. Ice Age* x. 125 The arctic sun, which shines day and night during the whole summertide. **1891** Morris *Poems by the Way* 123 Ask the Summer-tide to prove The abundance of my love.

'summer-time. Also †summer's time.

1. The season of summer; the time that summer lasts.

1377 Langl. *P. Pl.* B. xv. 94 In somer tyme on trowes, þere somme bowes ben leued and somme bereth none. *c* **1380** Wyclif *Sel. Wks.* II. 400 Hete of somer tyme. *c* **1440** *Pallad. on Husb.* x. 153 In somer tyme hym liketh wel to glade. **1596** Dalrymple tr. *Leslie's Hist. Scot.* II. 345 To Dondei, and S. Johnestoune quhair al that selfe seasone of the ȝeir and sommer tyme he consumet. *c* **1600** Shaks. *Sonn.* xcvii, And yet this time remou'd was sommers time. *a* **1660** *Contemp. Hist. Irel.* (Ir. Archæol. Soc.) I. 87 About 8 o'clock in the afternoone (somer time) he comaunded the horse to come home and make readie. **1778** Miss Burney *Evelina* xl, I thought my cousin would not..have come to town in the summer-time. **1800** Wordsw. *Hart-leap Well* 69 In the summer-time, when days are long, I will come hither. **1846** Dickens *Battle of Life* III, The withered leaves of many summer-times had rustled there. **1885** 'Mrs. Alexander' *At Bay* xi, We've lots of 'em sketching about Denham woods in summer time.

2. The standard time (in advance of ordinary time) adopted in some countries during the summer months (in the British Isles, in 1916, from 21 May to 30 September). Subsequently adopted in the U.K. for daylight saving from March to October (see quot. 1982). Cf. *British Summer Time* s.v. British *a.* 5; *double summer-time* s.v. double *a.* 6.

1916 *Act 6 & 7 Geo. V*, c. 14 An Act to provide for the Time in Great Britain and Ireland being in advance of Greenwich and Dublin mean time respectively in the summer months..This Act may be cited as the Summer Time Act, 1916. **1916** *Times* 26 Aug. 7/2 Of the changes which have already proved themselves to be changes for the better, that which immediately affects the greatest number of people is the introduction of 'summer time'. **1937** D. L. Sayers *Busman's Honeymoon* vii. 158 October 2nd—sun would be setting about half-past five. No, it was Summer Time. Say half-past six. **1967** [see *British Standard Time* s.v. British *a.* 5]. **1982** *Whitaker's Almanack 1983* 142 In the United Kingdom, Summer Time, one hour in advance of G.M.T. will be kept between 01h G.M.T. on the last Sunday in March and 01h G.M.T. on the day following the fourth Saturday in October. Thus, in 1983, Summer Time will be in force between March 27 and October 23.

†**summer-tower.** *Obs.* [See tower *sb.*[1] 5 a.] = summer-castle 1.

1408 tr. *Vegetius' De Re Milit.* (MS. Digby 233) lf. 223/1 Scalus lederrus & somertoures & alle suche gynnes þat ben Iordeyned to clymbe of walles & toures.

'summerward(s, *adv.* [f. summer *sb.*[1]: see -ward(s.] Towards summer.

1889 *Century Mag.* Sept. 774/2 The world seemed to float summerwards in the glimmering haze that wrapped the hills in the afternoons. **1891** *Advance* (Chicago) 9 Apr., The procession of the seasons appears as if in some doubt which way to go, winterward or summerward.

summery ('sʌmərɪ), *a.* [f. summer *sb.*[1] + -y.] Resembling or pertaining to summer; characteristic of or appropriate to summer; summer-like.

1824 Lamb *Let. to B. Barton* Apr., Let me congratulate with you the return of Spring: what a summery Spring too! **1839** Bailey *Festus* 237 Golden fruit grown in the summery suns. **1847** R. W. Church in *Life & Lett.* (1894) I. 76 Their white sails, and the white houses and towers..gave a summery look to the whole. **1859** W. H. Gregory *Egypt* I. 359 The garment is decidedly summery, but is the only article of attire worn by young girls. **1889** Gunter *That Frenchman!* x, For this summery day she is dressed in white muslin. **1889** *Pall Mall Gaz.* 25 May 4/2 The ladies.. donned their prettiest gowns and their summeriest bonnets.

Hence **'summeriness**, summery character or quality.

1840 *Blackw. Mag.* XLVII. 702 The summeriness of the day, or the dewiness of the evening.

summet, obs. form of summit *sb.*

summier, var. of sommier *Obs.*, beam.

summing ('sʌmɪŋ), *vbl. sb.* [f. sum *v.*[1] or *sb.*[1] + -ing[1].]

1. The calculation of a total amount; computation. (occas. *summing up.*)

1387 Trevisa *Higden* (Rolls) II. 91 Eyþer manere summynge is as vnredy as oþer. *c* **1537** De Benese *Meas. Lande* A iiij b, Diuerse rules of summynge of measures. **1611** Cotgr., *Sommation*, a summe, or, the summing, of money. **1836** *Penny Cycl.* V. 164/2 (*Book-keeping*) At the annual summing up it is of great importance to distinguish them in the accounts. **1863** Trevelyan *Compet. Wallah* (1866) 132 Will you ne'er have ceased apocalyptic summing, And left the number of the beast to puzzle Dr. Cumming? **1880** *Plain Hints Needlework* 10 The judges have nothing to do with the ..'summing up' of the marks given.

2. With (rarely without) *up.* The stating of the sum and substance of a matter; summarizing; a summary account or statement.

1546 J. Heywood *Prov.* (1867) 26, I pray you paciently here the hole som. In fayth (quoth he) without any more summyng, I know to beg of me is thy commyng. **1800** Gilpin *Serm.* (1803) II. xlii. 270 This is..the conclusion

—the summing up of the whole work of redemption. **1858** HAWTHORNE *Fr. & It. Note-bks.* I. 215 Michael Angelo's summing up of the world's history and destinies in his 'Last Judgment'. **1883** *Athenæum* 15 Dec. 771/3 The author's summing-up on the subject. **1889** JESSOPP *Coming of Friars* iv. 168 If any of us were to..attempt to discover..the intensity of any great plague..what would his summing-up amount to? **1898** *Daily News* 10 Mar. 6/1 Such is Mr. Decle's summing of Khama.

3. With (rarely without) *up*. A judge's address to a jury, in which he reviews and comments upon the evidence adduced in the case before him: see SUM *v.*[1] 5.

1790 MME. D'ARBLAY *Diary* June, The Queen sent me.. to hear the summing up of Mr. Fox. **1814** J. BOSWELL *Justic. Opera* 71 The proof is strong, a verdict bring,.. And so I end my summing. **1822** SHELLEY *Chas. I*, ii. 391 A jury of children, who found him guilty without waiting for the summing-up. **1883** *Manch. Exam.* 22 Dec. 5/3 A luminous and unimpeachably fair summing up by Lord Justice Clerk Moncrieff.

4. Doing 'sums' or arithmetical problems; the act of performing arithmetical operations.

1825 JENNINGS *Observ. Dial. W. Eng.*, *Summin*, arithmetic. **1828** MISS MITFORD *Village* Ser. III. (1863) 11 Miss Mowbray, who was..too particular about summing. **1860** GEO. ELIOT *Mill on Fl.* II. vii, There were no maps, and not enough 'summing'.

attrib. *a* **1825** FORBY *Vocab. E. Anglia* 333 We have summing-schools, summing-books, and summing-masters.

'summing, *ppl. a.* [f. SUM *v.*[1] + -ING[2].] **1.** That sums or sums up; summarizing.

1860 I. BURNS *Pastor of Kilsyth* 248 The great and summing evil..is just 'the quenching the spirit'. **1887** *Homeop. World* 1 Nov. 501 The president made a few summing-up remarks.

2. *Electronics.* That performs summation; producing an output dependent on the sum of the inputs.

1948 *Electronics* Apr. 124/3 The summing amplifier..is widely used in d-c and a-c servomechanisms. **1960** ROGERS & CONNOLLY *Analog Computation in Engin. Design* ii. 13 When used in this manner, the operational amplifier is known as a summing amplifier. **1963** B. FOZARD *Instrumentation Nucl. Reactors* ix. 107 The point *b* corresponds to the summing junction in a computing amplifier. **1967** *Electronics* 6 Mar. 120/2 A network between the output of a_1 and the summing junction of a_3 can be set to bring the total loop phase shift to 360°. **1981** F. W. HUGHES *Op Amp Handbk.* viii. 208 The inverting AC summing amplifier is similar to the inverting DC summing amplifier, except for the input capacitors.

†**summise,** *v. Obs. rare.* In 5 **-yse**. Variant of SUBMISE *v.*, to submit.

c **1450** *Pol. Poems* (Rolls) II. 227 These made ther enmyes thenne to summyse.

†**summiss,** *a. Obs. rare.* [ad. L. *summissus*, pa. pple. of *summittĕre* SUMMIT *v.*[1]] = SUBMISS *a.* 2.

a **1734** NORTH *Lives* (1890) I. 224 With a summiss voice and aspect, 'My lord,' said he, 'will your lordship be pleased to give me this under your hand?'

†**su'mmission.** *Obs. rare.* [ad. L. *summissio*, *-ōnem*, n. of action f. *summiss-*, *summittĕre* SUMMIT *v.*[1]] = SUBMISSION.

1563 FOXE *A. & M.* 815 To requyre his conformitie and subscription to the sayde summission.

Summist ('sʌmɪst). [ad. med.L. *summista*, f. *summa* SUM *sb.*[1] + *-ista* -IST. Cf. F. *sommiste*, It. *sommista*, Sp. *sumista*, Pg. *summista*.]

1. The author of a summa of religious doctrine, etc., e.g. Thomas Aquinas, author of *Summa theologiæ*, *Summa contra gentiles*; often used *gen.* of the schoolmen.

1545 BALE *Image Both Ch.* I. (East) 117 b, An infinite rable of Sophisters & schoole doctours,..of sentencioners and summistes. **1610** DONNE *Pseudo-m.* 229 Those examples, which Carbo a good Summist alleages. **1679** T. BARLOW *Popery* 38 The Canonists, Casuists, Schoolmen, Summists, Iesuits, &c. are generally, if not universally of this opinion. **1819** M^cCRIE *Life A. Melville* I. iii. 99 The barbarous latin of summists and commentators. **1886** *Encycl. Brit.* XXI. 425/2 Hugo [of St. Victor], by the composition of his *Summa Sententiarum*, endeavoured to give a methodical.. presentation of the content of faith, and was thus the first of the so-called Summists. **1891** T. E. BRIDGETT *Life Sir T. More* 93 Summists and Masters of Sentences.

†**b.** An epitomizer, abridger; *transf.* an epitome, summary. *Obs.*

1600 W. WATSON *Decacordon* (1602) 110 An od conceit I haue of the Iesuits perfection..moues me to place the Generall *loco summi generis* as a Summist of all the rest. **1705** G. BULL *Corrupt. Ch. Rome* iii. in *Lett.* etc. 281 A Book.. entituled, *The Tax of the Apostolical Chamber or Chancery*, whereby may be learned more sorts of Wickedness, than from all the Summists and the Summaries of all Vices. *a* **1734** NORTH *Exam.* III. viii. §17. (1740) 594 The Author is but a Summist of the Libel upon this Head.

2. [It. *sommista*.] In the Roman Curia, an official of the Apostolic Camera who had charge of the issuing of bulls. *Hist.*

1686 J. S[ERGEANT] *Hist. Monast. Convent.* 154 The Office of Summist is of a great value, and is generally possessed by a Cardinal. **1694** MOTTEUX *Rabelais* v. *Lett.* xv. 29 That Apartment where the Summists reside.

†**'summister.** *Obs.* [f. med.L. *summista*: see prec. and -ER[1].] = prec. 1, 1 b.

1586 STANYHURST in *J. Hooker's Hist. Irel.* in *Holinshed* II. 80 If the historian be long, he is accompted a trifler: if he be short, he is taken for a summister. **1598** *Meane in Spending* G 2 b, And thus, though rudely, haue I plaid the Summister.

summit ('sʌmɪt), *sb.* Forms: 5 **somette, sommet(te, -ete,** 6, 8 **summet,** (7 *erron.* **somnet,**) 7– **summit.** [a. OF. *sommette*, *somete* fem. (AF. *sumette*), also *somet*, *sumet* masc. (mod.F. *sommet*), dim. of *som*, *sum*:—L. *summum*, neut. sing. of *summus* (see SUM *sb.*[1]). The modern spelling with *-it* is due to assimilation to SUMMITY, q.v.]

1. a. The topmost part, top; the vertex, apex; †the crown (of the head), boss (of a shield), umbo (of a shell).

1470–85 MALORY *Arthur* v. viii. 174 It clefte his hede fro the somette of his hede. **1471** CAXTON *Recuyell* (Sommer) 414 Vpon the somette or toppe of the tour, he maad an ymage of copre. *Ibid.* 615 The maystres had sette on the sommet or toppe of the hede of hector,..a vessell. *c* **1477** —— *Jason* 16 Iason smote hym on the sommette of his shelde. *a* **1513** FABYAN *Chron.* II. xxxi. (1811) 23 He buylded an Hauen w^t a gate ther ouer... In the summet or pynacle wheron was set a vessell of Brasse. **1706** PRIOR *Ode to the Queen* xxviii, Let Europe sav'd the Column high erect... Sublime the Queen shall on the Summit stand. **1784** COWPER *Task* III. 536 Golden flow'rs, Blown on the summit of th' apparent fruit. **1828** STARK *Elem. Nat. Hist.* II. 63 Shell thin,..with the summit pointed. **1859** TENNYSON *Elaine* 482 A wild wave..Green-glimmering toward the summit. **1866** R. TATE *Brit. Mollusks* iv. 92 The tentacles.. bear the eyes at their summits.

†**b.** *Bot.* By an etymologizing alteration of Grew's SEMET, used for 'anther'; and hence for 'stigma'. *Obs.*

1731 MILLER *Gard. Dict.*, *Summits* or *Apices* are those Bodies which contain the Prolifick Powder. **1753** *Chambers' Cycl.* Suppl., App., *Summits of flowers*, the same with the antheræ, or tops of the stamina. **1796** WITHERING *Brit. Plants* (ed. 3) I. 5 The Germen, the Summit, and the Anthers, are all that are essentially necessary.

c. *Geom.* A point of a polyhedron where three or more faces meet, forming a solid angle.

1805–17 [see *summit angle* in 4]. **1823** BROOKE *Crystallog.* 6 The regular tetrahedron,..contained within four equilateral triangular planes. The solid angle at *a*, is sometimes called its summit.

2. The topmost point or ridge of a mountain or hill. Also, the highest elevation of a road, railway, or canal.

1481 CAXTON *Godfrey* clxx. 251 Syon is toward the weste, on the sommete or toppe theron stondeth the chirche which is named Syon. **1602** SHAKS. *Ham.* III. iii. 18 It is a massie wheele Fixt on the Somnet of the highest Mount. **1697** DRYDEN *Æneis* x. 984 He, like a solid Rock by Seas inclos'd, ..From his proud Summit looking down. *a* **1700** EVELYN *Diary* (1850) I. 3 Leith Hill, one of the most eminent in England for the prodigious prospect to be seen from its summit. **1736** GRAY *Statius* II. 18 Ætna's smoking summit. **1774** GOLDSM. *Nat. Hist.* (1776) I. 155 Some of the summits of the Alps have never yet been visited by man. **1859** DICKENS *T. Two Cities* I. ii, The last burst carried the mail to the summit of the hill. **1860** TYNDALL *Glac.* I. iii. 30 To witness the scene from the summit of the pass. **1891** E. ROPER *By Track & Trail* x. 148 Summit, in railway parlance, means the highest point attained by the line in crossing a mountain.

3. *fig.* **a.** The highest point or degree; the acme.

1711 LADY M. W. MONTAGU *Let. to Montagu* 29 Mar., Wks. 1803 I. 223 Supposing I was at the very summit of this sort of happiness. **1758** J. KENNEDY *Curios. Wilton Ho.* (1786) p. xxvii, Literature had then attained its summit. **1848** PUSEY *Paroch. Serm.* v. (1873) I. 90 If love be the summit of all virtue, humility is the foundation. **1867** H. MACMILLAN *Bible Teach.* vi. (1870) 108 The year has reached its golden summit.

b. The highest level, *spec.* with reference to politics and international relations; also *ellipt.* for *summit conference, meeting*, etc., sense 4 below.

1950 W. S. CHURCHILL in *Times* 15 Feb. 4/2 It is not easy to see how things could be worsened by a parley at the summit, if such a thing were possible. **1955** *Newsweek* 11 Apr. 44/1 Only if the Big Four Foreign Ministers reached 'a substantial measure of agreement' would a further conference be convened—at the summit. **1957** P. FRANK *Seven Days to Never* i. 33 We haven't knuckled under, not at the Summit or anywhere else, and..the alliance stands. **1958** *Listener* 14 Aug. 220/2 Then came the Czestochowa raid; the decision for this must have been taken at the summit. **1959** *Economist* 11 July 92/2 While an agreement not to mention time limits may be enough to get from the foreign ministers' level to the summit, to reach a settlement there will require something more. **1967** *Spectator* 30 June 757/1 The most certain result of the Glassboro summit, in fact, is no more than that Mr. Johnson's standing at home is now rather higher. **1978** R. LUDLUM *Holcroft Covenant* xxxi. 365 Since I left Brazil, I've not owned a weapon... I should like to have one now. Only for the duration of the summit.

4. *attrib.*, as ***summit altar, crater, hill, line, pine, rib, ridge***; **summit angle** = *summit quoin*; **summit level,** (*a*) the highest level reached by a canal, watercourse, railway, or the like; (*b*) a level place in a railway or stretch of water in a canal, with descending planes on either side; **summit meeting,** a meeting between heads of government, etc., to discuss matters of international significance (cf. sense 3 b above); also *transf.*; similarly ***summit conference, talks***; **summit quoin,** the solid angle at a summit of a polyhedron.

1866 J. B. ROSE tr. *Ovid's Met.* 326 A beacon tower with *summit altars stood. **1805–17** R. JAMESON *Char. Min.* (ed. 3) 121 The angle of the acumination, or the *summit angle. **1955** *Times* 23 June 8/3 The senator's resolution demanding that the United States should refuse to attend the '*summit' conference. **1959** *Encounter* Aug. 33/2, I was running out of pennies, and had to have a summit conference with the [telephone] operator. **1977** *Whitaker's Almanack 1978* 590/1 A unified political command for Egypt, Syria, and the Sudan was agreed at the end of the two-day tripartite summit conference in Khartoum. **1880** MISS BIRD *Japan* II. 152 The flank and *summit craters of Monna Loa. **1718** PRIOR *Solomon* I. 375 Higher than er'st had stood the *Summit-Hill. **1810** J. T. in *Risdon's Surv. Devon* p. xxxii, Its *summit level would be 300 feet above the sea. **1845** DARWIN *Voy. Nat.* xix. (ed. 2) 439 Nor does the drainage from the summit-level always fall..into the head of these valleys. **1877** HUXLEY *Physiogr.* 37 The summit-level of the Thames and Severn canal. **1901** C. G. HARPER *Gt. North Road* II. 249 The summit-level of this railway route. **1842** GWILT *Archit.* App. 838 These inter-sections form a curved *summit line. **1955** *N.Y. Times* 5 May 2/5, I say at this moment I see no reason for that *summit meeting. **1963** *Ann. Reg. 1962* 208 Krushchev suggested a Summit meeting. **1977** Summit meeting [see SSRC s.v. S 4 a]. **1882** B. HARTE *Flip* v, The *summit pines..rocked in the blast. **1895** STORY-MASKELYNE *Crystallogr.* ii. §246. 296 The *summit-quoins are symmetrical ditrigonally on the axis. **1842** GWILT *Archit.* App. 838 In Germany the *summit ribs [of a vault] are more frequently omitted than introduced. **1897** *Daily News* 15 Nov. 5/5 The *summit ridge occupied by the enemy. **1955** *Times* 7 May 8/7 There are certainly no indications that Washington has modified its resistance to '*summit talks' with Russia in advance of preparatory soundings.

†**summit,** *v.*[1] *Obs.* In 4–5 **summyt(te,** 5 **summitte.** [ad. L. *summittĕre*, assimilated f. *submittĕre* to SUBMIT.] *trans.* To submit, subject.

c **1374** CHAUCER *Boeth.* II. pr. v. (1868) 49 þanne summytten ȝe and putten ȝoure self vndir þo fouleste þinges. *Ibid.* III. pr. x. 88 For þat veyne ymaginacioun of þouȝt ne desceiue vs nat and putte vs oute of þe soþefastnesse of þilke þinge þat is summyttid to vs. **1401** *Pol. Poems* (Rolls) II. 91, I summitte me to hem. **1432–50** tr. *Higden* (Rolls) III. 125 Then the other vij. kynges schalle summytte theyme to hym. **1483** *Cath. Angl.* 371/2 To Submytte (*A.* to Summyt, *summittere*).

summit, *v.*[2] [f. SUMMIT *sb.* 3 b.] *intr.* To take part in summit meetings.

1972 *Time* 5 June 40 Prime Minister Indira Gandhi is willing to summit with the chap (probably at the end of the month). **1973** *New Scientist* 5 July 30 Nixon the President, summiting and clowning with the visiting Brezhnev, and Nixon, the suspect, seeking to elude the Watergate noose. **1979** *Daily Mail* 23 Jan. 5/2 When he is not summiting in the sunshine there is apparently nothing like All Creatures Great and Small..to help him forget crumbling pay norms and secondary picketing.

summi'teer. [f. SUMMIT *sb.* 3 b + -EER.] One who takes part in summit meetings. Hence **summi'teering.**

1957 *Time* 16 Dec. 21/2 The man who..must lead NATO along the course the summiteers lay down. **1958** *Daily Mail* 31 July 4/3 Macmillan has emerged as a worthy Summiteer. **1962** *Observer* 18 Feb. 11/7 No one knows either what the country thinks about the pay pause or Mr. Macmillan's summiteering. **1978** *Guardian Weekly* 23 July 6 Hot from their discussions on how to save the world from an energy crisis, the six summiteers repaired to the 14th century Gymnich Castle, near Bonn, for dinner. **1982** *Economist* 20 Mar. 12/1 This month's summiteers are likely to turn a blind eye to the subject.

'summitless, *a.* [f. SUMMIT *sb.* + -LESS.] Having no summit.

a **1834** in Sir H. Taylor *Artevelde* Note to I. IV. i, Vast outlines, mountains summitless, grey wastes. **1856** RUSKIN *Mod. Paint.* IV. v. §4 Watching the cloud still march before them with its summitless pillar. **1877** W. R. COOPER *Egypt. Obelisks* i. (1878) 3 The mutilated and summitless fragments [of obelisks].

'summitry. [f. SUMMIT *sb.* 3 b + -RY.] The practice of convening or holding summit meetings, or of using them as a diplomatic device.

1958 *Economist* 8 Feb. 479/1 The Western dislike of time-wasting summitry is due..to a feeling that even an inconclusive get-together would fill the democracies with a false sense of security. **1967** *Spectator* 28 July 97/1 Mr. Macmillan likened the preliminaries to the summitry so dear to his heart to a stately minuet. **1972** LD. GLADWYN *Mem.* xvi. 276 The so-called science of 'Summitry' was now being pursued with zeal and intelligence by the Foreign Office. **1979** *Time* 2 Apr. 26/1 Jimmy Carter initiated his most stimulating success as President six months ago: his summitry that broke 30 years of bloodshed and stalemate to make possible a peace treaty between Egypt and Israel.

†**'summity.** *Obs.* or *arch.* Forms: 5–7 **summitie,** (5 **summite(e, -yt(i)e, sumite,** 6 **sumitie, summitye, sommitie,** 8 *erron.* **sumnity),** 7–9 **summity.** [a. OF. *sommet(t)e*, *summite* (mod.F. *sommité*) = It. *sommità*, Sp. *sumidad*, Pg. *summidade*, ad. late L. *summitās*, *-ātem*, f. *summus* highest, the top of (see SUM *sb.*[1]).]

1. The topmost part, top; = SUMMIT *sb.* 1.

1375 BARBOUR *Bruce* III. 706 Quhilum sum wald be Rycht on the wawys summite [*edd.* **1620, 1670** summitie]. *c* **1440** *Pallad. on Husb.* IV. 240 Sette hem [*sc.* seeds] myddel depe in drie Lond and in weet lond in the summyte [*v.r.* summitee] Aboue. **1571** DIGGES *Pantom.* I. xiv. Ej, The very summitie or vpmost parte of the thing to be measured. **1574** NEWTON *Health Mag.* 31 The Creame or thicke Summitie of

Milke. **1585** Daniel *Paulus Iouius* To Rdr., Wks. (Grosart) IV. 3 On the sommitie of some high Piller. **1599** A. M. tr. *Gabelhouer's Bk. Physicke* 132/2 A qu. of an ownce of redd Roses of the supernalle summityes therof. **1602** Plat *Delightes for Ladies* II. xi, The oyle..fleeting on the top or summity of your water. **1699** Evelyn *Acetaria* (1729) 165 St. John the Baptist and other religious Ascetics were Feeders on the Summities and Tops of Plants. **1703** T. N. *City & C. Purchaser* 9 The Key-stone, is that which is the very sumnity, or top of the Arch. **1725** *Fam. Dict.* s.v. *Baroscope*, The Summity of the Tube is for a Space void of Quicksilver.

2. The topmost point or ridge of a mountain or hill; = summit *sb.* 2.

c **1400** *Sc. Trojan War* II. 1665 Frome hicht of þe sumiteis Descendand amongis þe waleis. *c* **1425** Wyntoun *Cron.* I. (Wemyss) xi. 972 One est half fra þe Egipt se, Sa rynnand in till summytie. **1598** Barret *Theor. Warres* III. ii. 90 The summities..and other places of aduantage. **1631** May tr. *Barclay's Mirr. Mindes* I. 37 Vpon the summity of the high hill, is a flat of great circuit. **1697** Potter *Antiq. Greece* II. ii. (1715) 185 Cyrus..sacrificeth..upon the Summities of Mountains. **1704** Swift *Batt. Bks.* 237 The War..between the Learned, about the higher Summity of Parnassus. **1718** Ozell tr. *Tournefort's Voy.* I. 62 When we reach'd the Summities where we hoped to find very uncommon things, we were forc'd to give over our design by the Fog and Snow.

transf. **1635** A. Stafford *Fem. Glory* 95 Whither should this Eagle flie, but to the summity of the world?

3. *fig.* The highest point or degree; = summit *sb.* 3: also in particularized use.

In quot. 1862 prob. after F. *sommités sociales*.

1588 J. Harvey *Disc. Probl.* 92 Plato and Aristotle in the Summitie of their Ethicall..and Metaphysicall Idees, haue displaied some such philosophicall quiddities. **1600** G. Abbot *Jonah* 125 When a man groweth to the summitie of such malice against himselfe as that natural affection..is quite exiled out of memory. **1660** Jer. Taylor *Duct. Dubit.* I. iv. rule 2 §34 There are summities and principalities of probation proportionable to the ages and capacities of men and women. **1678** Cudworth *Intell. Syst.* I. i. §18. 18 Immaterial or Incorporeal Substance; the Head and Summity whereof is a Deity distinct from the World. **1709** J. Johnson *Clerg. Vade M.* II. p. lxix, They are not in the summity of the Priesthood. **1862** T. A. Trollope *Marietta* I. iv. 80 In making his approaches towards the social summities.

b. A person or thing that is at the head of a body, line, series, etc.

1624 Heywood *Gunaik.* I. 2 Lysis and Philolaus, call it [*sc.* the supreme deity]..a summity of the greatest or smallest number. **1655** M. Casaubon *Treat. Enthus.* iii. (1656) 153 When once ascended to the Summities, or Originall Firsts, we can go no further. **1680** H. More *Apocal. Apoc.* 130 The two chief summities of this Sacerdotal Hierarchy, the two Patriarchates of Rome and Constantinople. **1685** —— *Paralip. Prophet.* xlii. 361 So soon as they were two Summities or Preeminences Ecclesiastical.

† **ˈsummon**, *sb. Obs.* Forms: 4 somun, sumun, sommoun, 4–5 somoun, 5 somoune, -own, summoun(e, 6 somon, 6–7 sommon, 4–8 summon. [f. summon *v.*] = summons.

a **1300** *Cursor M.* 23821 Ilk dai we se somun For to graid and mak us bun. *c* **1320** *Sir Tristr.* 171 He bad his kniȝtes lele Com to his somoun Wiþ hors and wepenes fele. **13..** *E.E. Allit. P.* A. 539 To take her hyre he mad sumoun. ? *a* **1400** *Morte Arth.* 104 Ȝiff thow theis somouns wythsytte, he sendes thie thies wordes. *c* **1470** *Gol. & Gaw.* 10 Dukis and digne lordis,..Sembillit to his summovne. **1581** A. Hall *Iliad* IX. 151 The Heraults they obayed, And when yᵉ kings the sommon heard, from him no whit they stayed. **1596** Bacon *Max. & Use Com. Law* II. (1630) 9 The Kings writs of Processe, be they Sommons, Attachments [etc.]. **1599** Thynne *Animadv.* (1875) 66, I haue not my booke of somons of Barons to parliamente in my handes. **1629** T. Adams *Medit. Creed* Wks. 1231 Esther durst not come into the Presence, till the Scepter had giuen her admission; a summon of that embolden her. **1749** Fielding *Tom Jones* II. ix, Mr. Allworthy..gave orders that the bell should be rung without the doors... All these summons proving ineffectual [etc.]. **1800** Bloomfield *Spring* Poems (1845) 12 Heedlessly they graze, Or hear the summon with an idle gaze.

b. *attrib.*: **summon-master**, one who directs the issue of summonses (*fig.*).

1618 Brathwait *Descr. Death* 3 in *Good Wife*, etc. E 7, Death is..The Summon-maister of mortalitie.

summon (ˈsʌmən), *v.* Forms: α. 3–4 somoune, 3–5 somony, 3–6 somon(e, 4–5 somoun, sommone, sowmoun, -own, (3 sumune(n, 4 somun(e, -own, summone, 5 sumoun, somowne, 6 sumon, -own, sowmon), 6–7 sommon, 4– summon. See also summond *v.* β. 3 someni, sumen, 3–4 someny, 3–5 somene, 3–6 somen, 4–5 somyn, somn-; 4–5 sompne, -y. (See somne *v.*², sompne.) γ. 3–4 sumni, -y, 4–5 sumne. [a. AF., OF. *sumun-, somun-, somon-*, pres. stem of *somondre, semondre* (see summond *v.*) = Pr. *somon(d)re, semondre*:—pop.L. **summonēre* for *summonēre*, in earlier L., to give a hint, suggest, in med.L., to call, cite, summon, f. *sub-* (see sub- 25) + *monēre* to warn (see monition).

The ME. forms with weak vowel in the second syllable (*somene, sumene*) underwent contraction when inflected for the pa. t., pples., and vbl. sb. (*somned, somning*, etc.): cf. somner, sumner¹.

The earliest examples show assimilation in meaning, and partly in form, to ME. *somni*, OE. *somnian*, somne *v.*¹, to assemble.]

1. *trans.* To call together by authority for action or deliberation. †Occas. with *up.* (See summons *sb.* 1, 1 b.)

c **1205** Lay. 424 He heihte his folc sumunen & cumen to him seoluen. *Ibid.* 1482 þa ferde wes isumned & heo forð fusden. *Ibid.* 19183 Ah nu ich wulle fusen & sumnien mine ferde. *c* **1250** *Kent. Serm.* in *O.E. Misc.* 26 þo dede he somoni alle þo wyse clerekes þet kuþe þe laghe. **1297** R. Glouc. (Rolls) 10379 þe pope..alle þe bissops of engelond let someni to rome. **1303** R. Brunne *Handl. Synne* 1800 Do sumne þe folk astyte, þat þey come alle hedyr. *c* **1330** —— *Chron. Wace* (Rolls) 3265 Belyn dide somone his Bretons. **1390** Gower *Conf.* III. 327 He let somoune a parlement, To which the lordes were asent. **1472–3** *Rolls of Parlt.* VI. 42/1 The Lordes..of this Reame, in this present Parlement somoned and holden at Westm'. **1560** Daus tr. *Sleidane's Comm.* 112 Pope Paule by his legate Vergerius sommoneth the counsell of Mantua. **1605** Shaks. *Lear* II. iv. 35 They summon'd vp their meiney, straight tooke Horse. **1647** Clarendon *Hist. Reb.* I. §12 If they had been frequently summoned, and seasonably dissolved. **1677–8** Marvell *Corr.* Wks. (Grosart) II. 603 The Shrieues haue order to summon up all absent Parliament-men. **1711** in *10th Rep. Hist. MSS. Comm.* App. v. 137 He might have called to his assistance..15,000 good men..by summoning the voluntiers. **1748** *Anson's Voy.* III. vii, Thereupon the Governor had summoned his Council. **1758** J. Dalrymple *Ess. Feudal Property* (ed. 2) 266 A distinction was made in the form of summoning the greater and the smaller vassals. **1769** Blackstone *Comm.* IV. xx. 281 Those [contempts] committed by jurymen,..such as making default, when summoned. **1777** Watson *Philip II* (1839) 357 That he should summon the general assembly of the States to meet at least once a year. **1819** Scott *Ivanhoe* xxxviii, The Grand Master had summoned a chapter. **1820** Gifford *Compl. Engl. Lawyer* (ed. 5) 73 A commission from the bishop, directed usually to his chancellor and others of competent learning; who are to summon a jury of six clergymen and six laymen. **1855** Macaulay *Hist. Eng.* xi. III. 23 No royal writ had summoned the Convention which recalled Charles the Second. **1877** Froude *Short Stud.* (1883) IV. I. iv. 44 The king once more summoned a great Council to meet him at Northampton.

b. To call (a peer) to parliament by writ of summons; hence, to call to a peerage. (See summons *sb.* 1 b.)

1375 Barbour *Bruce* I. 592 Thiddir somownys he in hy The barownys of his reawte. **1610** Holland *Camden's Brit.* (1637) 635 William Beauchamp who was summoned afterward to Parliament. **1885** Freeman in *Encycl. Brit.* XVIII. 462/2 One may certainly doubt whether Edward [I], when he summoned a baron to parliament, meant positively to..summon that baron's heirs for ever and ever. **1888** *N. & Q.* 7th Ser. V. 391/2 Thomas Fane married Mary, daughter of Henry, Lord Abergavenny, 1574... She was summoned to the barony of Le Despenser,..1604.

2. To cite by authority to attend at a place named, *esp.* to appear before a court or judge to answer a charge or to give evidence; to issue a summons against. (See summons *sb.* 2.)

c **1290** *S. Eng. Leg.* 74 He liet him somoune al-so To westmunstre, to answerien him of þat he him hadde mis-do. **1303** R. Brunne *Handl. Synne* 510 Al þe godemen of þe toune, Byfore þe bysshop dyden here somoune. *c* **1380** Wyclif *Wks.* (1880) 146 þei..somonen men to chapitre & bi fors taken here goodis. *c* **1380** —— *Serm.* Sel. Wks. I. 205 þei ben somynned and reprovyd many weies, and after put in prison. *Ibid.* III. 320 þei somenen and aresten men wrongfully to gete þe money out of his purse. *c* **1430** Lydg. *Min. Poems* (Percy Soc.) 241 Oon of his bedellys..Cam with his potent instede of a maas, Somowned me. *c* **1460** *Oseney Reg.* 80 Sumne hym by a goode sumnyng that he be afore vs. *c* **1480** Henryson *Mor. Fables, Sheep & Dog* 18 Schir Corbie Rauin..hes..Summonit the Scheip befoir the Uolf. *c* **1532** Du Wes *Introd. Fr.* in *Palsgr.* 938 To somen, *adjourner*. *a* **1578** Lindesay (Pitscottie) *Chron. Scot.* (S.T.S.) I. 100 James Hammelltoun..was sowmond..to wnderly the law. **1655** Fuller *Ch. Hist.* III. xii. §59 It is unfit that Ministers should be summoned, before each proud..under-officer. **1769** Blackstone *Comm.* IV. xx. 279 The courts of common law..making it necessary to summon the party accused before he is condemned. **1774** Warton *Hist. Eng. Poetry* I. xvii. 445 To summon uncanonical offenders into the archdeacon's court. **1875** Jowett *Plato* (ed. 2) V. 167 A witness who will not come of himself may be summoned. **1887** *Courier* 23 June, George Champneys..was summoned for wilfully assaulting Mr. Smeadon.

absol. **1615** Chapman *Odyss.* II. 11 The Heralds then, he strait charg'd to consort The curld-head Greekes, with lowd calls to a Court. They summon'd; th' other came.

†**b.** To call (a plea) into court. *Obs.*

c **1460** *Oseney Reg.* 104 Whereoff 'assisa of the deth of aunceturs' whas i-sumned bitwene them In the forsaide Courte. *Ibid.* 115 Whereof þe plee of 'conuencion' whas i-summonyd bitwene them in þe same courte.

†**c.** *transf.* To call to account. *Obs. rare.*

1654–66 Earl Orrery *Parthen.* (1676) 610 The two Princes summoned Callimachus of his promise.

3. *gen.* To require the presence or attendance of; to bid (a person) to approach by a call, ringing a bell, knocking, or the like; with adv., to call (to a person) to go in a specified direction.

a **1400** *Robt. Cicyle* (MS. Harl. 525) in Parker *Dom. Archit.* (1853) II. 73 [He] somowned him a Barbour before, That as a fole he should be shore. *a* **1536** *Songs, Carols*, etc. (E.E.T.S.) 97 Whan deth commyth,..Obey we must, þer ys no remedye; He hath me somond. **1566** Painter *Pal. Pleas.* I. To Rdr., Their great Graundmother Eue when she was somoned from Paradise ioye. **1592** *Soliman & Pers.* v. ii. 68 Ere we could summon him a land, His ships were past a kenning from the shoare. **1593** Shaks. *3 Hen. VI*, IV. vii. 16 Ile knocke once more, to summon them. **1683** J. Kettlewell *Help Worthy Commun.* III. v. 376 We are summon'd in to profess Repentance. *a* **1700** Evelyn *Diary* an. 1635, When near her death, she summoned all her children then living. **1797** Mrs. Radcliffe *Italian* xii, The matin-bell strikes!.. I am summoned. **1832** Brewster *Nat. Magic* vi. 132 The family was then summoned to the spot, and the phenomena were seen alike by them all. **1885** 'Mrs. Alexander' *At Bay* i, They were soon summoned to table.

4. *fig.* with immaterial or inanimate subject: To call, bid come or go. Often with adv.

1549 *Compl. Scot.* Ep. 6, I beand summond be institutione of ane gude zeil. **1592** Kyd *Sp. Trag.* II. ii. 46 When Vesper ginnes to rise, That summons home distresfull trauellers. **1592** *Arden of Feversham* III. iii. 11 A gentle slumber tooke me, And sommond all my parts to sweete repose. **1608** D. T[uvill] *Ess. Pol. & Mor.* 38 b, Heerein may their practice serue like a seuerer Censor,..and summoning the blood into our faces, make vs ashamed. **1629** Wadsworth *Pilgr.* iii. 14 Euery morning the fift houre summons the vp. **1731** Pope *Ep. Burlington* 142 The Chapel's silver bell you hear, That summons you to all the Pride of Pray'r. **1750** Johnson in *Boswell*, The business of life summons us away from useless grief. **1816** Scott *Old Mort.* xxxv, The attention of Morton was summoned to the window by a great noise. **1818** —— *Rob Roy* i, If my father were suddenly summoned from life.

absol. **1604** Shaks. *Oth.* IV. ii. 169 Hearke how these Instruments summon to supper. **1891** 'Q.' (Quiller-Couch) *Noughts & Cr., Cott. Troy* iv, Its [*sc.* the sea's] voice in his ears, calling, summoning all the way.

5. To call upon (a person) *to do* something.

c **1380** Wyclif *Wks.* (1880) 462 Ȝif crist haue sumnyd hem for to come not to hym. ? *a* **1400** *Morte Arth.* 1212 He somond than the schippemene..To schake furthe with the schyre mene to schifte the gudez. *c* **1400** *Destr. Troy* 1702 He somond all þe Cite..To a counsell to come for a cause hegh. *c* **1450** *Merlin* 249 This squyer hadde ofte Carados somoned to be a knyght. **1592** Shaks. *Ven. & Ad.* 534 Coleblack clouds..Do summon vs to part. **1671** Milton *P.R.* II. 143, I summon all..to be in readiness..to assist. **1781** Cowper *Expost.* 179 That moving signal summoning.. Their host to move. **1825** Scott *Betrothed* ii, He called..on a young..bard,..and summoned him to sing something which might command the applause of his sovereign. **1859** Tennyson *Guinev.* 566 They summon me their King to lead mine hosts.

b. To call upon to surrender.

[**1471** Caxton *Recuyell* (Sommer) 73, J the somone as legat..that thou yelde this cyte vnto his fader kyng saturne. *a* **1548** Hall *Chron., Hen. VIII*, 36 The kyng..sent an heraulde to somon vs to rendre to hym this cytee. **1560** Daus tr. *Sleidane's Comm.* 252 Donauerde, whiche being sommoned to render, had refused. **1643** Baker *Chron.* (1653) 248 The Duke of Exeter was sent..to summon the Citizens to surrender the Town. **1842** Borrow *Bible in Spain* xxxiv, A man advanced and summoned us to surrender.]

1603 [see summoning *vbl. sb.*]. **1607** Shaks. *Cor.* I. iv. 7 Summon the Towne. **1773** Goldsm. *Stoops to Conq.* II. i, He first summoned the garrison. **1810** Wellington in Gurw. *Desp.* (1838) VI. 120 General Mermet summoned the place on the 12th. **1853** Stocqueler *Milit. Encycl.* 271/2.

†**6.** To give warning or notice of, proclaim, call.

c **1400** *Destr. Troy* 205 He cast hym..In a Cite be-syde to somyn a fest. **1591** Shaks. *1 Hen. VI*, III. iii. 35 Summon a Parley, we will talke with him. **1611** —— *Wint. T.* II. iii. 202 Prepare you Lords, Summon a Session.

7. Often with *up*: To 'call' (a faculty, etc.) to one's aid; to bring (one's courage, energy) into action; to call up.

1582 Stanyhurst *Æneis* I. (Arb.) 24 With food they summond theyre force [L. *victu revocant viris*]. **1588** Shaks. *L.L.L.* II. i. 1 Now Madam summon vp your dearest spirits. **1667** Milton *P.L.* IX. 374 Relie On what thou hast of vertue, summon all. **1751** Johnson *Rambler* No. 87 ¶8 We ..summon our powers to oppose it. **1780** *Mirror* No. 87 ¶7 Being obliged to summon up his resolution. **1802** Maria Edgeworth *Moral T.* (1816) I. xviii. 149 He summoned all his fortitude. **1865** Trollope *Belton Est.* xxvi. 317 She had been driven to summon up all her courage to enable her to do so. **1886** Ruskin *Præterita* II. 157 You paused to summon courage to enter.

b. *refl.* To 'pull oneself together'. *rare.*

1821 Scott *Kenilw.* xvi, He summoned himself hastily.

8. To call *into* existence; to call forth.

1742 Young *Nt. Th.* IX. 1558 He summons into being, with like ease, A whole creation, and a single grain. **1837** Carlyle *Fr. Rev.* I. III. iii, M. de Calonne has stretched out an Aaron's Rod over France..and is summoning.. unexpected things. **1841** Whittier *Lucy Hooper* 28 Pain and weariness, which here Summoned the sigh or wrung the tear.

summonable (ˈsʌmənəb(ə)l), *a.* [f. summon *v.* + -able. In AF. *somounable*, OF. *semonnable.*] That can be or is liable to be summoned.

1711 Ld. Molesworth tr. *F. Hotman's Franco-Gallia* (1721) 147 This Meeting of the Court of Judicature was.. summonable by the King's Writs. **1796** Bentham *Panopt.* Corr. Wks. 1843 XI. 115 The strength..of the Barracks distant not above half-a-mile, summonable by signals. **1865** Nichols *Britton* II. 13 That in pleas of trespass..sokemen be summonable and answerable as well as others. **1872** *Pall Mall Gaz.* 5 Aug. 10 The court..was summonable..by himself as lessee of the duchy.

†**ˈsummonance.** *Obs.* In 4 somonaunce, 5 sommonance. [a. AF. **somo(u)naunce*, f. *somo(u)n-* to summon: see -ance.] A summons.

c **1386** Chaucer *Friar's T.* 288 (Harl. MS.), I haue..a somonaunce [*v.rr.* somons, somonce] of a bille,..loke þat þou be..biforn our erchedeknes kne, To answer to þe court of certeyn þinges. **1499** in *Lett. Rich III & Hen. VII* (Rolls) I. 131 They shal make their sommonance in the presence of the deputie. **1616** J. Lane *Contn. Sqr.'s T.* XI. 186 After the lcre of Faerie Landes sommance [*v.r.* sumonance].

†**ˈsummonary**, *a. Obs. rare*⁻¹. [f. summon + -ary.] That deals with summonses.

1762 [P. Murdoch] tr. *Busching's Syst. Geog.* V. 5 That the chancery of Worms..should open the writings addressed to the summonary office of the Circle [orig. *Kreis-Ausschreibamt*].

†**'summond**, *sb. Sc.* and *north. Obs.* Also 5 somond, summound. [f. next.] = SUMMONS.

14.. *Customs of Malton* in *Surtees Misc.* (1890) 58 Noo othyr Balyffe schal make no tachement nor somond. *c* **1480** HENRYSON *Mor. Fab., Sheep & Dog* iv, This summond is maid before witnes anew. **1500-20** DUNBAR *Poems* xiii. 29 Sum castis summondis, and sum exceptis. *c* **1680** DALLAS *Stiles* (1688) 192 The Summond of Adjudication.

†**'summond**, *v. Sc.* and *north. Obs.* Also 4 somend, sumund, 4-5 somond(e, 6 sumond, sowmmond. [a. AF., OF. *somondre, sumundre, semondre*: see SUMMON *v.*] To summon. Hence **'summonding** *vbl. sb.*

a **1300** *Cursor M.* 5324 Þe king þan did his lettres writte To somond al. *a* **1340** HAMPOLE *Psalter* vii. 12 He somondis þaim till penaunce. *Ibid.* cxlviii. 12 Here sumundis he men and women..to loue þe name of oure lord. **1425** *Munim. de Melros* (Bann. Cl.) 544 We gert somond..Johne..abbot of Melrosse..on þe ta part and..Johne hag of bemersyde on þe thoþer part. *a* **1450** *Ratis Raving* III. 383 Bere þow wytnes but somondynge, þow may be set fra wytnesinge. *c* **1575** BALFOUR *Practicks* (1754) 303 Summounding is ane declaratioun of ane certane lauchful day and place, maid befoir sufficient witnessis, to ane partie, to compeir in judgment. *Ibid.* 305 To summound ony persounis to pas upon ony assise or inqueist. *a* **1578** LINDESAY (Pitscottie) *Chron. Scot.* (S.T.S.) I. 67 Thair come ane thunderand woyce out of heawin cryand and sowmmondand him to the extreme iudgement of god. **1639** DRUMM. OF HAWTH. *Hist. Jas. IV*, Wks. (1711) 74 A proclamation..summonding a great many burgesses..to appear..before the tribunal of one Plot-Cock. *c* **1680** DALLAS *Stiles* (1688) 185 That ye lawfully summond, warn and charge the forenamed persons. **1711** in *Nairne Peerage Evidence* (1874) 143 [To] call and convein parties and witnesses summond inquests and asysses.

†**'summonder**. *Sc.* and *north. Obs.* In 5 summunder, somundare, -onder, 7 summondour. Variant of SUMMONER, assimilated to prec.

c **1425** *Eng. Voc.* in Wr.-Wülcker 652 *Hic sitator*, A[e] somundare. **14..** *Nom., Ibid.* 681 *Hic citator, Hic aparator*, a summunder. **1483** *Cath. Angl.* 348/2 A Somonder, *citator*. *c* **1575** BALFOUR *Practicks* (1754) 303 The executioun of summoundis sould be maid be ane lauchful summounder befoir sufficient witnessis. **1609** SKENE *Reg. Maj., Quon. Attach.* 76 The summondour and witnes with him, sould come to the dwelling house of the defender, and summon him to compeir.

†**'summonds**. *Sc.* and *north. Obs.* Forms: 5 so(w)moundis, 5-6 summondis, 6 summoundis, s(o)umondis, 7 summonds. Variant of SUMMONS assimilated to SUMMOND *v.*

14.. in *Surtees Misc.* (1890) 60 The fyrst day of somondes or atachement. *c* **1450** HOLLAND *Howlat* 134 For all statis of kirk that wnder Crist standis, To semble to his summondis. *c* **1470** HENRY *Wallace* IX. 1872 Sowmoundis thai maid, and chargyt Bruce be nayme. **1564-5** *Reg. Privy Council Scot.* Ser. I. I. 321 The copy of the summondis of transferring. *a* **1578** LINDESAY (Pitscottie) *Chron. Scot.* (S.T.S.) I. 150 Than was send ane summondis of foirfaltour. *a* **1649** DRUMM. OF HAWTH. *Hist. Jas. III*, Wks. (1711) 57 Some rent his summonds, and beat shamefully his heraulds. **1672** *Rec. Proc. Justic. Crt. Edinb.* (S.H.S.) II. 77 A Messenger executing a Summonds must shew his Warrand. *c* **1680** DALLAS *Stiles* (1688) 188 Here follow furth the second Dyet as in the first Summonds.

summoned ('sʌmənd), *ppl. a.* [f. SUMMON *v.* + -ED.] In senses of the verb. Also in comb. with adv., as ***summoned-up***.

1697 DRYDEN *Æneid* IV. 977 Thy summon'd Sister, and thy Friend had come. **1812** HOR. SMITH *Rej. Addr., Tale of Drury Lane* 77 The summon'd firemen woke at call. **1820** BYRON *Juan* IV. lix, Her summon'd handmaids bore Their lady to her couch. **1821** JOANNA BAILLIE *Met. Leg., Wallace* xxviii, A summon'd court should there have been. **1977** *New Yorker* 19 Sept. 108/2 Calling beautiful coaches for the harshly summoned-up emergency.

summoner ('sʌmənə(r)). Forms: 4 somunur, -on(o)ur, 6 -oner, 6-7 sommoner, 6- summoner. See also SOMNER, SOMPNOUR, SUMNER[1], and SUMMONDER. [a. AF. *so-, sumenour*, = OF. *somoneor, semoneor* (mod. arch. F. *semonneur*) :—med.L. *summonitōrem*: see SUMMONITOR.]

1. A petty officer who cites and warns persons to appear in court. Now *Hist.*

a **1325** *MS. Rawl. B.* 520 lf. 55 That he be þanne þer to heren þe reconisaunce and that thou habbe þere þe somunurs and this writ. **1389** in *Eng. Gilds* (1870) 30 And viij. men..schulen chesen..a somono[r], for ye nexte yer. **1529-30** *Rec. St. Mary at Hill* 349 Paid to a Somoner for Somenyng of M[r] hiltons, preist ij d. **1530** PALSGR. 725/1, I sommon, as a sommoner dothe one to the courte. **1581** [A. GILBY] *Pleas. Dial. Soldier & Chapl.* L 7 b, The Summoner or Apparitor. **1609** SKENE *Reg. Maj.* I. 7 It is necessare that everie summoner (executer of summons) sall lawfullie verifie his summons. **1651** tr. *Kitchin's Courts Leet* (1657) 561 The Defendant avers, That the summoners now returned were not the summoners in *Precipe*. **1768** BLACKSTONE *Comm.* III. 279 Two of the sheriff's messengers called summoners. **1824** SCOTT *Redgauntlet* let. xi, The Bishop's summoner, that they called the Deil's Rattle-bag. **1865** NICHOLS *Britton* II. 87 Let the summoners [of a jury] be charged to be there. **1865** KINGSLEY *Herew.* xx, Neither summoner nor sheriff of the king..could enter there.

Comb. *c* **1645** HOWELL *Lett.* (1650) I. 432 An inchanted staff, which the devil, summoner like, was used to deliver some mercat-women to ride upon.

2. One who summons another to a place. Often *fig.* of immaterial or inanimate agents.

1580 *Ord. Prayer* in *Liturg. Serv. Q. Eliz.* (1847) 572 A messenger and summoner of us to the dreadful Judgment-seat. **1597** MIDDLETON *Wisd. Solomon* xvii. 3 The darkesome clouds are summoners of raine. **1605** SHAKS. *Lear* III. ii. 59 Close pent-vp guilts..cry These dreadfull Summoners grace. **1808** SCOTT *Marm.* V. xxvi, The summoner was gone. **1820** KEATS *Lamia* I. 11 From high Olympus had he stolen light..to escape the sight Of his great summoner. **1836** BRAY *Descr. Tamar & Tavy* (1879) I. x. 174 The Summoner appeared to be a strange, squint eyed,..old fellow. **1897** E. W. B. NICHOLSON *Golspie* 31 The minister..followed his summoner to the basement of the castle.

3. One who takes out a summons.

1865 *Pall Mall Gaz.* 3 Aug. 10/1 If he will not appear.. the summoner can bring an action against the doctor, should he lose his cause.

summoning ('sʌmənɪŋ), *vbl. sb.* [f. SUMMON *v.* + -ING[1].] The action of the vb. SUMMON; the issue of a summons; †calling to arms; calling to surrender.

c **1330** R. BRUNNE *Chron. Wace* (Rolls) 15349 Made þey somonynge, Of southe & northe, ilka kyng. *c* **1380** WYCLIF *Wks.* (1880) 31 Siche somonynge of prelatis is not groundid in cristis lif ne his apostelis ne reson. *c* **1380** —— *Sel. Wks.* III. 166 By hor feyned sommenyng þei drawen hom fro hor laboure. *c* **1460** *Oseney Reg.* 168 Hugh of Hyngton And moolde his wiffe, the which nowe come By summenyng. **1582** ALLEN *Martyrdom Campion* (1908) 86 This good fellow Havard was somewhat amased at this sodaine sommoning. **1595** in *Buccleuch MSS.* (Hist. MSS. Comm.) I. 228 Let Presgrave make as many warrants as he can against that time for the summoning of the country. **1603** KNOLLES *Hist. Turks* (1638) 66 They..had slaine such messengers as hee had sent vnto them for the summoning of the city. *a* **1693** *Urquhart's Rabelais* III. xxxix. 325 Summonings, Comparitions, Appearances. **1810** SCOTT *Lady of L.* II. xxi, The maid The unwelcome summoning obey'd. **1870** MORRIS *Earthly Par., Hill of Venus* 1552 That might have been the bright archangel's wand, Who brought to Mary that fair summoning. **1875** STUBBS *Const. Hist.* II. xv. §190. 183 The hereditary summoning of a large proportion of great vassals was a middle course. **1891** *Athenæum* 25 Apr. 529/2 A crude *creationism*—or doctrine of the direct summoning into existence of each soul at earthly birth.

'summoning, *ppl. a.* [-ING[2].] That summons.

summoning officer: one whose function is to summon jurors.

1667 MILTON *P.L.* III. 325 When thou..Shalt..from thee send The summoning Arch-Angels to proclaime Thy dread Tribunal. **1778** *Chron.* in *Ann. Reg.* 167 Summoning officer of the juries for the city..of Westminster. *a* **1851** MOIR *Lines Isle of Bute* iii, When flew the fiery cross, with summoning blaze. **1896** *Daily News* 18 Mar. 7/5 The summoning officer who represented the sheriff. **1900** *Ibid.* 21 Dec. 6/3 Highly intelligent dogs will wait for their summoning owner.

†**'summonister**. *Obs.* [f. SUMMON *v.* + -ISTER.] = SUMMONITOR.

1811 J. POLLOCK in *2nd Rep. Comm. Public Rec. Irel.* (1815) 141 The Process which issues from the Summonister to the different Sheriffs. **1835** *Act 5 & 6 Will. IV*, c. 55 §18 The following Offices of the said Court of Exchequer in Ireland..are hereby abolished;..Summonister and Clerk of the Estreats.

†**summo'nition**. *Obs.* Also 5 somon-, 6 sommon-; 5 -ycion, 6 -icion, -ycon, -itioun. [ad. med.L. *summonitio, -ōnem*, n. of action f. *summonēre* to SUMMON.] A summons.

c **1450** *Godstow Reg.* 598 To somon hem, by good somonyciouns, that thei be than before the forsaid Iames and Iohn. **1502** ARNOLDE *Chron.* 82 b/2 Our letters patentis of our Sommonicion of the dett. **1531** in W. H. Turner *Select. Rec. Oxford* (1880) 99 After lawfull summonycon made by the bedylls or other offycers. *c* **1575** BALFOUR *Practicks* (1754) 305 Ane persoun beand summoundit..gif he, the time of the making of the said summonitioun,..do require ane copie fra the persewar [etc.]. **1593** BILSON *Govt. Christ's Ch.* 364 The plea of *Quare impedit*, when the Bishop refuseth the Patrones Clearke as well for the summonitions, as for the returne, is mentioned in the Statute of Marlebridge. **1765-8** ERSKINE *Inst. Law Scot.* IV. i. §4 Where mention is made of the word *summons*, or *summonition*, in the old books of our law..that term is to be understood, not of the warrant of citation, but of the citation given upon the warrant.

b. *attrib.* (see quot.).

a **1816** BENTHAM *Offic. Apt. Maximized, Introd. View* (1830) 18 *Summonition mandate* will accordingly be seen taking place of *sub-pœna*.

†**su'mmonitor**. *Obs.* Also 7 somoniter. [a. med.L. *summonitor*, agent-n. f. *summonit-, -monēre* to SUMMON.] An officer of the Court of Exchequer in Ireland who assisted in collecting the royal revenues by citing defaulters.

1617 MORYSON *Itin.* II. 29 [Irish Court of Exchequer] The Somoniter one hundred sixe shillings eight pence. *a* **1726** GILBERT *Hist. View Crt. Exch.* v. (1738) 109 An Officer, who makes out the first Process, whom they call the Summonitor.

summons ('sʌmənz), *sb.* Forms: 3-5 somouns, -ounce, 3-6 somons, 4-5 somonce, 5-6 sommaunce, (3 somunce, -ounz, 4 -unse, -ones, -aunce, 5 sommonz, -ones, somance, somnes, somounnys, 6 summaunce, 7 sommance, 8 sommons), 6- summons. [a. AF., OF. *sumunse, somo(u)nse* (mod.F. *semonce*) = Pr. *somonsa, -ossa*:—pop.L. **summonsa* (for *summonita*), pa. pple. fem., (used subst.) of *summonēre* to SUMMON.]

1. An authoritative call to attend at a specified place for a specified purpose.

c **1290** *S. Eng. Leg.* I Ich wene þat ich wot ȝwat þis somunce a-mounti schal. *a* **1325** *MS. Rawl. B.* 520 lf. 54 Somune þoru gode somunse .xii. fre men ant trewe of vesinage of .N. **13..** *E.E. Allit. P.* B. 1498 Soberly in his sacrafyce summe wer anoynted, þurȝ þe somones of him selfe þat syttes so hyȝe. *a* **1400** in *Eng. Gilds* (1870) 349 Weche foure and twenty [heuedes of þe Cite] sholde, to þe comenable somaunse of þe forseyde meyre, come. *a* **1483** *Ibid.* 317 Ye shall not..disobaey þ[e] somnes of þ[e] Master and Wardens. *a* **1500** *Gough Chron.* in *Six Town Chron.* (1911) 155 The comons of london wente to yelde hall by cause of a sommaunce made by a commission. *a* **1513** FABYAN *Chron.* VII. (1811) 494 Sir Godfrey de Harecourt, which..wold nat apere after certayn sommaunces, was nowe openly banysshed. **1667** MILTON *P.L.* I. 757 Thir summons call'd From every Band and squared Regiment By place or choice the worthiest. **1781** GIBBON *Decl. & F.* xxvii. (1787) III. 31 He obeyed the summons with the respect of a faithful subject. **1823** SCOTT *Quentin D.* xxi, The great bell was tolled, as summons to a military council. **1878** J. GAIRDNER *Rich. III*, ii. 74 Summonses were issued to fifty gentlemen to receive knighthood.

b. The royal act of calling to the national council or parliament the bishops, earls, and barons by special writ, and the knights and freeholders by a general writ addressed to the sheriffs; hence *spec.* the call to a barony (cf. SUMMON *v.* 1 b).

'The personal right of summons is the essence of the peerage' (Gardiner in *Encycl. Brit.*, 1878, VIII. 297/1).

13.. *Coer de L.* 1255 The kyng comaundyd..At London to make a parlement... To Londoun, to hys somouns, Come erl, bysschop, and barouns, Abbotes, pryests, knyghtes, squyers, Burgeyses, and manye bachelers, Serjaunts, and every freeholdande. **1338** R. BRUNNE *Chron.* (1810) 16 Withouten any somons, & withouten askyng of Erles or barons. **1647** CLARENDON *Hist. Reb.* II. §66 The Parliament met according to summons upon the 13th of April in the year 1640. **1660** R. COKE *Power & Subj.* 109 In every Writ of Summons to the Bishops, there is a clause requiring them to summon these persons to appear personally at the Parliament. **1765** BLACKSTONE *Comm.* I. ii. 189 After the expiration of which [three years], reckoning from the return of the first summons, the parliament was to have no longer continuance. **1818** CRUISE *Digest* (ed. 2) III. 177 It has been a very ancient practice to call up the eldest sons of earls to the House of Lords by writ of summons, by the name or title of a barony vested in their fathers. **1845** DISRAELI *Sybil* IV. vii, That was a barony by writ of summons which had been claimed a century before. **1874** GREEN *Short Hist.* viii. §6. 520 The summons of a Parliament at once woke the kingdom to a fresh life. **1878** STUBBS *Const. Hist.* III. xx. §751. 437 The point of time from which the regularity of the baronial summons is held to involve the creation of an hereditary dignity.

2. A call or citation by authority to appear before a court or judicial officer; also (in full *writ of summons*), the writ by which the citation is made.

a. A citation or writ apprising a defendant that an action has been begun against him and citing him to appear to the action, in default of which the court may proceed to give judgement and award execution against him.

summons and severance: see SEVERANCE 2 c.

a **1300** *Cursor M.* 29519 Þat cursing tald vn-laghful es þat ordir wantes and right-settnes O lagh, bot giuen it es ouer-tite, Wit-vten somons and right respite. *c* **1325** *Poem temp. Edw. II* (Percy) lxvi, The pore men shul to London To somons and to syse. **1429** *Rolls of Parlt.* IV. 346/1 Havyng processe..by somounces, attachmentz and distresse. **1497-8** in *Archaeol. Jrnl.* (1886) XLIII. 167 A fyne lost by Robt Wells for somannce. **1502** ARNOLDE *Chron.* 10 b/2 And y[t] none summaunce attachment nor execuceon by don,.. but by mynystirs of the same cite. **1618** J. WILKINSON *Treat. Off. Coroners* etc. II. 6 The like proces or precepts as are made out of a hundred Court, *mutatis mutandis*, are to be made out of this Court, viz. summons attachment, and distresse infinite. **1764** BURN *Poor Laws* 288 For the executing a summons, where the person to be summoned.. is..out of the way; that a copy thereof left at his dwelling house,..should be enacted to be effectual, as if personally served upon himself. **1810** MISS MITFORD in L'Estrange *Life* (1870) I. iv. 94 We have received a summons from the under-sheriff, which was given over the pale to William this morning. **1869** *Act 32 & 33 Vict.* c. 71 §7 A debtor's summons may be granted by the Court on a creditor proving ..that a debt sufficient to support a petition in bankruptcy is due to him from the person against whom the summons is sought. **1875** *Act 38 & 39 Vict.* c. 77 Ord. II. §1 Every action in the High Court shall be commenced by a writ of summons. **1892** [see TAKE *v.* 85 g].

attrib. and *Comb.* **1881** J. HATTON *New Ceylon* vii. 184 Summons cases for debt. **1886** in Maurice *Lett. fr. Donegal* 72 The summons-server of the Bunbeg district.

b. *Sc. Law.* A citation or writ issuing from the Court of Session under the royal signet, or, if in a sheriff court, in the name of the sheriff.

It consists of three parts: the *libel*, which sets forth the grounds and circumstances on which the action is founded, the *conclusion* or *decerniture*, which declares the terms on which the pursuer desires judgement in his favour, and the *citation* or *will*, which is a warrant for summoning the defender to court.

1609 SKENE *Reg. Maj., Quon. Attach.* 75 b, Summons is ane warning (and declaration) of ane certaine day and place, betwix parties, to ane lawfull day. **1693** STAIR *Instit.* IV. iii. §27 Ordinar Actions proceed not by Brieves, but by larger Summons, which therefore are called Libells. **1718** *Acts of Sederunt* 26 Feb., The first calling, which is to be marked by the under-clerk on the summons. **1765-8** ERSKINE *Inst. Law Scot.* IV. i. §8 All executions of summonses must express the day of appearance, which however is commonly left blank, till the summons be called in court. **1814** *Act 54 Geo. III*, c. 137 §2 Letters or Precepts of Arrestment upon any depending Action may be granted summarily, upon Production of the libelled Summons. **1885** *Encycl. Brit.* XIX. 220/1 In Scotland an action in the Court of Session begins by a summons on the part of the pursuer to which is annexed a condescendence, containing the allegations in fact on which the action is founded.

c. In full, ***summons ad warrantizandum, to warrant*** (law L. *summoneas ad warrantizandum*): the process by which the vouchee in a common recovery was called.

[**1580–1** *Act 23 Eliz.* c. 3 §1 The Returnes of the said Originals and Writtes of Summon. ad Warrantizandum.] **1607** COWELL *Interpr.*, Summons ad Warrantizandum. **1818** CRUISE *Digest* (ed. 2) V. 390 Earl Cowper, the vouchee, had acknowledged the warrants of attorney to appear to the summons. **1835** TOMLINS *Law Dict.*, Summons to Warrant.

d. 'In judges' or masters' chambers, the means by which one party brings the other before a judge (or a master) to settle matters of detail in the procedure of a suit' (Wharton *Law-Lex.*).

1820 *Act 1 Geo. IV*, c. 55 §5 It shall..be lawful for the Justices of the Courts of King's Bench and Common Pleas ..during their..Circuits..to grant such and the like Summonses,..in all Actions and Prosecutions which are or shall be depending [etc.]. **1882** C. SWEET *Dict. Eng. Law* s.v., Summonses are..only used on applications which are either of subsidiary importance, or can be conveniently disposed of in chambers. *Ibid.*, In the Queen's Bench Division some summonses must be heard in the first instance by a master, and others by a judge.

3. *gen.* A peremptory or urgent call or command; a summoning sound, knock, or the like.

1567 FENTON *Trag. Disc.* i. 7b, He suffred himselfe at the first to be subiect to the somonce of loue. *c* **1586** C'TESS PEMBROKE *Ps.* XLIX. iii, Sure at his [*sc.* death's] summons wise and fooles appeare. **1593** SHAKS. *Rich. II*, I. iii. 4 The Duke of Norfolke..Stayes but the summons of the Appealants Trumpet. **1634** MILTON *Comus* 888 Bridle in thy headlong wave, Till thou our summons answered have. **1676** GLANVILL *Season. Refl.* 167 The Dead shall be raised by a General Summons. **1727** SWIFT *Further Acc. E. Curll* Wks. 1751 III. I. 156 He had a lucid interval, that enabled him to send a general summons to all his authors. **1784** COWPER *Task* III. 587 As if conven'd By magic summons of th' Orphean lyre. **1813** SCOTT *Rokeby* IV. vii, The hour was late, When a loud summons shook the gate. **1814** —— *Wav.* xxii, 'Tis the pibroch's shrill summons. **1888** A. K. GREEN *Behind Closed Doors* I. ii, I was requested to call upon—Mrs. A., let us say, on business... Such summonses come frequently. **1889** TENNYSON *Forlorn* iv, You that lie with wasted lungs Waiting for your summons.

b. with qualifying inf. or adv.

1784 COWPER *Task* VI. 336 The total herd receiving.. from one That leads the dance a summons to be gay. **1844** THIRLWALL *Greece* lxii. VIII. 181 Antigonus..was waiting on his southern frontier for the summons to march. ? *c* **1860** *Househ. Words* (Flügel) A horn blowing..was the summons home.

4. *Mil.* The act of summoning a place to surrender. Also, now only, with inf. (cf. 3b).

1617 MORYSON *Itin.* II. 167 Vpon our summons of the Towne, after martiall manner. *a* **1671** LD. FAIRFAX *Mem.* (1699) 15 We..sent a trumpet with a summons to deliver up the town to me. **1682** BUNYAN *Holy War* (1905) 236 The Captains..did send..a summons to Mansoul to yield up her self to the King. **1700** DRYDEN *Cymon & Iph.* 276 Or strike your Sails at Summons, or prepare To prove the last Extremities of War. **1744** M. BISHOP *Life & Adv.* 8 We Pioneers were ordered to go to St. Catherine's Castle, but we were preceded by a Summons, upon which it surrendered. **1802** JAMES *Milit. Dict.* **1844** H. H. WILSON *Brit. India* II. 350 The Kiladar refused to comply with the summons to surrender.

summons ('sʌmənz), *v.* [f. prec. Cf. obs. F. *semoncer, -ser.*]

1. *trans.* = SUMMON *v.* 1, 3, 4, 5, 5b. Now *rare.*

1658 FRANCK *North. Mem.* (1821) 34, I know not except he's come to summons us home. **1728** CHAMBERS *Cycl.* s.v., To *summons* a Place, is to send a Drum, or Trumpet, to command the Governor to surrender. **1772** FLETCHER *Appeal* Wks. 1795 I. 62 The bait of pleasure appears, corrupt nature summonses all her powers. **1802** MARIAN MOORE *Lascelles* II. 75 She was obliged to summons all her fortitude. **1830** W. TAYLOR *Hist. Surv. Germ. Poetry* II. 309 His attendants..came to summons him for the journey.

2. To cite before a court or a judge or magistrate; to take out a summons against.

1780 M. MADAN *Thelyphthora* I. ii. 52 A woman had but to summons her seducer before the judges. **1838** DICKENS *Nich. Nick.* xxxviii, Say another word and I'll summons you. **1904** MARIE CORELLI *God's Good Man* xxv, You can summons me..if you feel so inclined.

Hence '**summonsable** *a.*, rendering one liable to a summons, actionable; '**summonser**, one who summonses; '**summonsing** *vbl. sb.*

1877 R. W. THOM *Jock o' Knowe* 31 (E.D.D.) The sommonser's ca' Wad sound through the grand rooms o' Corby Ha'. **1891** *Sat. Rev.* 25 July 100/1 The fervent exhortations in the streets to apply summonsable language to him. **1893** STEVENSON *Catriona* ix, The purpose..being that..the summonsing be something other than a form.

†**su'mmoperous,** *a. Obs. nonce-wd.* In 7 sumo-. [f. L. *summopere* = *summō opere* with the greatest labour + -OUS.] Highest, utmost.

1647 WARD *Simple Cobler* 9 If the States of the World would make it their summoperous Care to preserve this One Truth in its purity.

summot, obs. form of SOMEWHAT.

†**su'mmotion.** *Obs. rare*⁻¹. [ad. med.L. *summōtio, -ōnem*, f. *summovēre* to remove, f. *sum-* = SUB- 26 + *movēre* to MOVE.] Removal.

1653 R. G. tr. *Bacon's Hist. Winds* 32 In every simple Protrusion..there is no summotion or locall carriage, before the parts of the body doe preternaturally..suffer, and be compressed by the driver.

†'**summulary.** *Obs. rare.* [ad. med.L *summulārius*, f. *summula* dim. of *summa* SUM *sb.*[1] see -ARY[1].]

1. = SUMMULIST.

1581 J. BELL *Haddon's Answ. Osor.* 358b, Wherein reygneth..For Evangelistes,..Decretaries, Summularyes, seditious Sententioners.

2. A summary, compendium.

1643 PRYNNE *Sov. Power Parl.* I. To Rdr., My..Intention was, to have Collected the chiefe Heads..of this and the ensuing Members, into one compendious Summulary.

summulist ('sʌmjʊlɪst). [ad. med.L. *summulista*, f. *summula*: see prec. and -IST.] **a.** A writer of a *summula* or small compendious treatise of a science; an abridger. **b.** A commentator on the *Summulæ Logicales* of Petrus Hispanus (13th cent.).

1652 URQUHART *Jewel* Wks. (1834) 200 The allegation of Bliteri by the Summulists will be of small validity. **1656** [? J. SERGEANT] tr. *T. White's Peripat. Inst.* Author's Des a vj, We only act the part of Abridgers or Summulists. **1694** BURTHOGGE *Reason* 50 Common Logicians and Summulists. **1865** F. G. LEE *C. Davenport's Paraphrast. Expos.* 15 Which ..is a term of diminution (as the Summulists say).

‖**summum bonum** ('sʌməm 'bəʊnəm, 'sʊməm 'bɒnəm). Pl. 'summa 'bona. [L. (Cicero), *summum* neut. sing. of *summus* highest, *bonum* neut. sing. of *bonus* good, used subst.] The chief or supreme good: properly a term of *Ethics*; often *transf.* and in trivial or jocular use.

1563 T. GALE *Inst. Chirurg.* 11 As one myght thynke hymselfe ryght happye, though he neuer dyd attayne to Aristoteles *summum bonum*, or Plato his *Idæa*. **1591** GREENE *Farew. Folly* Wks. (Grosart) IX. 289 The Cyrinaike Philosophers..founded their *summum borum* in pleasure. **1605** A. WARREN *Poor Man's Pass.* etc. H4b, With Plago placing his felicity And summum Bonum in his gluttony. **1690** LOCKE *Hum. Und.* II. xxi. §55 The Philosophers of old did in vain enquire, whether *Summum bonum* consisted in Riches, or bodily Delights, or Virtue, or Contemplation. **1710** NORRIS *Chr. Prud.* iii. 114 Some last End or *Summum Bonum* as 'tis called, some good or other which he looks upon as desirable for itself. **1768** TUCKER *Lt. Nat.* (1834) I. 208 When a glutton sits down to a well-spread table with a good appetite, he possesses as much of the *summum bonum* as can be obtained within the time. **1811** COLERIDGE *Ess. Own Times* (1850) III. 929 Hobbes, who..considered absolute tranquillity and implicit obedience as the *summum bonum* of a State. **1861** H. C. PENNELL *Puck on Pegasus* 152 When.. pap was the *summum bonum* of life, To a mouth in perpetual pucker. **1862** THACKERAY *Philip* vi, To be a painter,..I hold to be one of life's *summa bona*. **1878** *Encycl. Brit.* VIII. 594/1 The *summum bonum* for man [according to Thomas Aquinas] is objectively God, subjectively the happiness to be derived from loving vision of His perfections.

So ‖'**summum 'pulchrum** ('pʌlkrəm) [L. *pulchrum*, neut. of *pulcher* beautiful, used subst.], the highest beauty.

1841 CLOUGH *Τὸ καλόν* v, The Summum Pulchrum rests in heaven above.

‖**summum genus** ('sʌməm 'dʒiːnəs). Pl. 'summa 'genera. [L., *summum* (see prec.), *genus* kind.] The highest or most comprehensive division in a classification; in *Logic*, a genus that is not considered as a species of a higher genus.

1592 NASHE *P. Penilesse* Wks. 1904 I. 235 The diuell, which is the *Summum genus* to vs all. **1593** —— *Christ's T.* ibid. II. 41, I my selfe haue no enemy but Pryde, which is the *Summum genus* of sinne. **1843** DE QUINCEY *Ceylon* Wks. 1890 VII. 455 In the running over hastily the *summa genera* of products by which Ceylon will soon make her name known to the ends of the earth. **1870** MCCOSH *Laws Disc. Thought* I. §35. 28 If we take all things, the Summum Genus is Being; if we take merely an order of things, the Summum Genus is the highest in that order; thus Plant is the Summum Genus in Botany.

‖**summum jus** ('sʌməm dʒʌs). [L., *summum* (see SUMMUM BONUM), *jūs* right, law.] The utmost rigour of the law, extreme severity.

1588 J. UDALL *Diotrephes* (Arb.) 29 Summum ius, must be your best help in this case. **1609** J. DAVIES *Humour's Heaven* I. ccxii, To rule them with the Rod of *Summumius*. **1668** WILKINS *Real Char.* II. viii. §3. 207 Summum Jus, Rigidness, sourness, unreasonableness, iniquity. **1692** T. WATSON *Body Divin.* 50 God doth not go according to the *summum jus*, or rigour of the Law. **1774** BURKE *Corr.* (1844) I. 485 The strict letter and *summum jus* of decorum and propriety.

summure, obs. form of SUMMER[1].

†**summyn(g,** in *all and summyn(g*, a perversion of *all and sum* (see ALL *a.* 12) on some supposed ME. analogy.

1513 DOUGLAS *Æneis* IV. iii. 42 Or list appreif thai peplis all and summyng [*v.r.* summyn] Togiddir middle.

sumne, obs. variant of SUMMON *v.*

sumned, erron. form of SUMMED.

sumner[1] ('sʌmnə(r)). Also 4 sumnor, 5 -ere, 6 -ar, (*erron.* summer, sunner); 4–5 sumpnour(e, 6 sumpner. [a. AF. *sum(e)nour*, f. *sumen-, sumon-*: see SUMMON *v.* and -ER[1]. Cf. SOMNER, SOMPNOUR.] One who is employed to summon persons to appear in court; *esp.* a summoning officer in an ecclesiastical court. Most recently surviving in the Isle of Man.

1362 *P. Pl.* A. II. 46 For Sisours, for Sumnors [B. II. 58 sompnours, *v.r.* sumpnoures; C. III. 59 somners], for Sullers, for Buggers. *c* **1475** *Pict. Voc.* in Wr.-Wülcker 781 *Hic sitarius*, a sumner. **1558** in Feuillerat *Revels Q. Eliz.* (1908) 24 In paninge of two Sumpners cotes .10. *a* **1596** *Sir T. More* IV. v. 149 Thou art reseru'de To be my sumner to yond spirituall courte. **1599** THYNNE *Animadv.* (1875) 85 The bisshop is not her, his sunner, the officiall, ner yet his chansler. **1600** *1st Pt. Sir J. Oldcastle* II. i. 66, I am my lord of Rochesters Sumner. **1602** *2nd Pt. Return fr. Parnass.* IV. ii. 1694 You that liue like a sumner vpon the sinnes of the people. **1612** DEKKER *If it be not Good* I. i, Two of thy Summers dead-drunke here too. **1726–31** WALDRON *Descr. Isle of Man* (1744) 77 An Officer.., called a Sumner, lays a Straw over his, or her Shoulder, and says, By virtue of this, you are Yarded for the Service of the Lord of Man. **1868** MILMAN *St. Paul's* 121 The sumner, and the bellringer of the Cathedral. **1887** HALL CAINE *Deemster* xii, Next day the Bishop sent his sumner round the parish.

fig. *a* **1591** H. SMITH *Serm.* (1637) 349 Age, sicknesse, and Death, the three Sumners. *a* **1612** HARINGTON *Epigr.* II. lxii, An Abbot..cited now, by deaths sharpe Sumner, sicknesse. **1891** HALL CAINE *Scapegoat* i, What the sumner of the Lord of Hosts had not done, the sumner of the Lord Sultan very speedily brought to pass.

Sumner[2] ('sʌmnə(r)). The name of Thomas H. *Sumner* (1807–76), U.S. shipmaster, used *attrib.*, in the possessive, and *absol.*, with reference to a method devised by him in 1837 of finding one's position on the surface of the earth, employing an approximate value of latitude or longitude based on dead reckoning, in conjunction with an astronomical observation, to calculate a number of positions that define a line that must contain the true position; so ***Sumner line*** = *position line* s.v. POSITION *sb.* 7b.

1849 H. RAPER *Pract. of Navigation & Naut. Astron.* (ed. 3) 345 (*heading*) Position on a line of bearing. [*Note*] Or 'Sumner's Method'. **1881** S. T. S. LECKY *'Wrinkles' in Pract. Navig.* II. viii. 201 Unless the error of the latitude is greater than that assumed, the ship must be somewhere on this 'Line of position', which, for convenience, will henceforth in these pages be termed a 'Sumner line', after the American seaman who first brought this useful problem prominently to the notice of the profession. **1901** J. R. WALKER *Explanation of 'New Navigation'* 8 The straight line is called the Sumner Line, or Line of Position. **1919** [see POSITION *sb.* 7b]. **1924** R. CLEMENTS *Gipsy of Horn* xii. 228, I worked a Sumner, or position by double altitude. **1976** *Oxf. Compan. Ships & Sea* 845 *Sumner's position line*, a systemized method of finding a ship's position by means of a sight.

sumnien, obs. form of SUMMON *v.*

sumo ('suːməʊ). [Jap.] In Japan, a form of wrestling in which a wrestler wins a bout by forcing his opponent outside a circle or making him touch the ground with any part of his body except the soles of his feet. Freq. *attrib.*, esp. as ***sumo wrestler, wrestling***; also *absol.*, a sumo wrestler.

1880 W. E. L. KEELING *Tourists' Guide Yokohama* 23 The wrestlers (*sumô*)..will not fail to interest him. **1893** *Jap. Soc. Trans. & Proc.* I. 19, I have seen English wrestling, and found it similar to Japanese *wrestling* (*Sumō*, not *Ju-jitsu*). **1923** J. STREET *Mysterious Japan* ix. 103 The kind of wrestling known as *sumo* still maintains its ancient prestige as the national sport. **1934** [see ALL-IN 2]. **1936** K. NOHARA *True Face of Japan* v. 220 Our taste for prodigies..is gratified by the corpulence of the *Sumo*. **1938** BUSH & KAGAMI *Japanalia* 156/1 *Sumō* wrestlers are huge fellows. **1958** *Times* 27 Dec. 7/6 Such are the advance preliminaries of a bout of *sumo*, the national sport of Japan. **1964** I. FLEMING *You only live Twice* i. 17 It is only the *sumo* wrestlers who drink *saké* in these quantities without showing it. **1966** *New Scientist* 28 July 182/3 Sumo wrestling, in which two monstrous men charge one another, clinch briefly and separate, with one the winner, usually in the space of a few seconds. **1974** *Daily Tel.* (Colour Suppl.) 22 Feb. 39/3 If one is to understand Japan in any depth, a realisation of the significance and the enjoyment of Sumo is as important as it is to appreciate the influence of soccer if one is to understand Britain. **1977** *Time* 4 July 52/2 Surpassing even such traditional Japanese sports as sumo wrestling, *bēsubōru* has become Japan's favorite sport. **1978** M. KENYON *Deep Pocket* x. 125 This character was a sumo-wrestler, hewn from a cliff-face.

sumoom, obs. form of SIMOOM.

sumotori (suːməʊ'tɔːrɪ). [Jap., f. SUMO + *tori* active partner in the performance of techniques.] A sumo wrestler.

1973 *Newsweek* 13 Aug. 92 Anyone who [tries] socking a sumotori in the stomach will gladly go back to brick walls. **1974** *Daily Tel.* (Colour Suppl.) 22 Feb. 39/3 The mature *sumotori* (as Sumo wrestlers are called) is about six feet tall and will weigh anything from 16 to 24 stone.

sump (sʌmp), *sb.* Also 5 sompe, 7 sumpe, 8–9 sumph, 9 sumpt. [a. (M)LG. *sump* (*sumpt*) or MDu. *somp, sump*, Flem. *zompe* (WFris. *sompe*), or ad. (in the mining sense) the related MHG.,

G. *sumpf* marsh, water-level or lodge, sump in metal-working (whence Sw., Da. *sump*); f. *swump-*, related by ablaut to *swamp-* (see SWAMP *sb.*).]

1. A marsh, swamp, morass; (now *dial.*) a dirty pool or puddle.

c **1425** *Cast. Persev.* 427 in *Macro Plays* 90 Myth I ryde be sompe & syke. **1825** BROCKETT *N.C. Gloss.*, *Sump, Sumph*, a bog, a swamp, a miry pool. **1851** *Cumbld. Gloss.*, *Sump*, a puddle. **1905** MCCARTHY *Dryad* 265 Swift Spanish soldiers came..picking their way easily over the sump in which the Athenians wallowed.

2. a. A pit or well for collecting water or other fluid; *spec.* a cesspool; a pond or well from which sea-water is collected for salt-manufacture. Also *fig.*

1680 *Tynemouth Par. Reg.* in *Archaeol. Æliana* XIX. 211 He was drowned in Mr. Lawson's sumpe. **1682** J. COLLINS *Salt & Fish.* 10 The Sea-water they commonly at Spring-Tide let into Ponds called Sumps, from whence 'tis pumpt into their Pans. **1748** BROWNRIGG *Art of Making Salt* 55 They..make a little pond in the rocks, or with stones on the sand, which they call their sump. **1862** SMILES *Engineers* III. 45 He had a wooden box or boot made, twelve feet high, which he placed in the sump or well, and into this he inserted the lower end of the pump. **1884** *Contemp. Rev.* June 798 The experience of the fen system of working by conveyance into sumps. **1893** *Newcastle Daily Jrnl.* 11 July 6/2 It was not true that there were three or four houses with 'sumps' in them, giving off offensive odours. **1963** T. & P. MORRIS *Pentonville* iii. 69 Pentonville represents one of the sumps of the English prison system; a receptacle into which the sludge is continuously drained. **1969** *Gloss. Terms Water Cooling Towers* (*B.S.I.*) 6 *Sump*, a lowered portion of the cold water basin floor for draining down purposes. **1975** *Sci. Amer.* Oct. 23/3 As fast as the heavy water leaked out it was collected in a sump and pumped directly back into the reactor.

b. *Mining.* A pit or well sunk at the bottom of an engine shaft to collect the water of the mine.

1653 MANLOVE *Cust. Lead-mines* 159 They may cause open'd, Drifts, and Sumps, to see If any one by other wronged be. **1700** MACKWORTH *Disc. Mine-Adv.*, *2nd Abstr.* 13 We were not able to sink down our Sumps till the Weather grows Warmer. **1778** PRYCE *Min. Cornub.* 144 A whym Shaft to draw the Deads and Ore from the Sump of the Mine. **1866** *Morning Star* 18 Dec. 6/2 The break-down of a portion of the winding machinery..has prevented the sumph being emptied of its water. **1895** *Times* 16 Jan. 10/1 The obstructions which had been brought to the sump by the rush of water, such as pit-props, tubs.

c. A depression in the bottom of the crankcase of an internal-combustion engine, which serves as a reservoir of lubricating oil.

1907 *Westm. Gaz.* 9 Nov. 14/3 The oil is forced by a gear-driven pump from a sump in the crank-chamber. **1929** [see *skew gear* s.v. SKEW *a.* 2]. **1950** *Brit. Repair Man.*: *Cars* 38/2 The oil filling orifice is housed in the valve top cover, and the sump, which is a steel pressing, has a capacity of 7½ pints. **1980** J. MCCLURE *Blood of Englishman* i. 9 Droopy was removing the sump... He..extended a hand for a No. 8 ring spanner.

3. *Metallurgy.* A pit of stone or metal at a furnace to collect the metal at the first fusion.

1674 RAY *Coll. Words* 114 The mine when melted runs down into the Sump. **1884** LOCK *Workshop Rec.* Ser. III. 424/2 The metal is tapped off into an iron sump.

4. *Mining.* Applied locally to various kinds of drifts or pits (see quots.); also, 'the part of a judd of coal first brought down' (*Eng. & For. Mining Gloss.* 1860).

1747 HOOSON *Miner's Dict.* s.v., The second is so proportioned to supply the first and third Sump, to supply the second, and so on. **1796** *Statist. Acc. Scot.* XVIII. 142 A shaft or sump, as the miners term it, was made to the depth of several fathoms, immediately below the bottom of the waste. **1828** *Craven Gloss.*, *Sump*, a hole sunk below the levels or drifts of a mine at a proper distance to divide the ground, and communicate air to the different works or branches. **1846** BROCKETT *N.C. Words* (ed. 3), *Sumph*..also means a secondary shaft in a mine. **1851** GREENWELL *Coal-trade Terms Northumb. & Durh.* 54 Sump..in driving a stone drift, or in sinking a pit, that portion kept a yard or more in advance of the drift or pit, to enable the gunpowder to act to greater advantage upon the parts left. **1866** *Durham Mining Lang.*, *Sump*, a pit sunk from one level in a mine to a lower level.

5. *attrib.*, as ***sump-head***; **sump drift**, a drift for the construction of a sump; **sump-fuse**, a waterproof fuse used for blasting under water (Smyth *Sailor's Word-bk.*, 1867); **sump guard**, a cowling for protecting the sump of a motor vehicle from perforation on poor roads; **sump-hole**, = 2 a, b; **sump-man**, a pitman's assistant, one who attends to the machinery in an engine-shaft; **sump-plank** (see quot.); **sump-shaft**, an engine-shaft.

1882 *Rep. Ho. Repr. Prec. Met. U.S.* 147 This shaft..was sunk 33 feet below the 2,500-foot level. A *sump drift was run out 50 feet from the bottom. **1968** *Guardian* 6 May 5/5 The 1800 I was driving was standard except for a *sump guard, essential on East African roads. **1980** J. BARNETT *Palmprint* vii. 62 A heavy stone clanged against the sumpguard. **1747** HOOSON *Miner's Dict.*, *Spurfork*, a small sort of Fork..sometimes used to hold Doorsteds in Drifts, or at *Sumpheads asunder. **1847** HALLIWELL, **Sump-hole*, a cesspool. Yorksh. **1897** *Westm. Gaz.* 15 Nov. 2/1 Mr. Goschen..braved the sulphurous fumes..as far as the sump-hole. **1903** *Ibid.* 28 Nov. 6/2 Water pumped..from a sumpt-hole..adjacent to one of the most polluted branches of the Lea. **1839** DE LA BECHE *Rep. Geol. Cornwall*, etc. xv. 605 *Sumpmen. **1866** THORNBURY *Greatheart* III. 211 Then they helped me into the sumpman's house. **1860** *Eng. & For. Mining Gloss.* (ed. 2) 80 **Sump-planks*, strong balks of timber bolted together, forming a temporary bottom, or scaffolding, for the shaft. **1778** W. PRYCE *Min. Cornub.* 171 *Sumph shaft western bottoms.

Hence **sump** *v. intr.*, to dig a sump or (small or temporary) shaft; **ˈsumping** *vbl. sb.*, also *attrib.* (see quots. 1860).

1700 MACKWORTH *Disc. Mine-Adv.*, *2nd Abstr.* 12 We are Sumping and driving in the new Work in good firm..Oar. **1789** J. WILLIAMS *Min. Kingd.* I. 277 Many [miners]..were sumping, driving, and roofing in other parts of the work. **1860** *Eng. & For. Mining Gloss.* (ed. 2) 65 *Sumping-shot*, a charge of powder for bringing down the sump, or for blowing the stone up in a sinking pit. *Ibid.* 80 *Sumping*, a small square shaft, generally made in the air-headings, when crossing faults, &c., or made to prove the thickness of coal, &c. **1886** J. BARROWMAN *Sc. Mining Terms* 65 *Sumping*, cutting down into the floor, or, in sinking, cutting down at the lowest part of the shaft.

sumpathy, obs. form of SYMPATHY.

sumper (ˈsʌmpə(r)). *Mining.* [f. SUMP *sb.* + -ER[1].] A sumping-shot.

1883 GRESLEY *Gloss. Coal-m.* 246 *Sumper*, a shot placed in or very near to the centre of the bottom of a sinking pit.

sumph (sʌmf), *sb.*[1] *Sc.* and *north. dial.* [Origin unascertained.] A soft stupid fellow; a simpleton, blockhead. Also, a surly or sullen man.

1719 RAMSAY *2nd Answ. to Hamilton* vii, Thrawn-gabbit sumphs that snarl At our frank lines. **1789** SHIRREFS *Poems* (1790) 289 When noble souls ly in the dirt, While sumphs jump up so high. **1818** SCOTT *Br. Lamm.* xii, It's doing him an honour him or his never deserved at our hand, the ungracious sumph. **1831** J. WILSON *Noctes Ambr.* Nov., Wks. 1856 III. 282 A Sumph..is a chiel to whom Natur has denied ony considerable share o' understaunin, without ha'in chose to mak him just a'thegither an indisputable idiot. **1871** BLACK *Daughter of Heth* (1872) 73 'Dinna be a sumph!' said the Whaup.

Hence **ˈsumphish** *a.*, stupid; also, sullen; whence **ˈsumphishly** *adv.*, **ˈsumphishness**.

1728 RAMSAY *General Mistake* 65 The sumphish mob. **1802** J. STRUTHERS *Poor Man's Sabbath* xc. *note* Wks. 1850 I. 53 These audacious,..sumphishly selfish assumptions. **1846** C. BRONTE in Mrs. Gaskell *Life* (1857) II. 16 Indiscriminating irony and fault-finding are just *sumphishness*. **1858–61** RAMSAY *Remin.* vi. (1870) 182 A sumphish weather-beaten man.

sumph (sʌmf), *sb.*[2] [Echoic.] The sound of something heavy and limp falling.

1844 LEVER *T. Burke* II. 167 With a heavy sumph the body fell from their hands.

sumph (sʌmf), *v. Sc.* [Cf. SUMPH *sb.*[1]] *intr.* To be stupid; now chiefly, to be sulky.

a **1689** CLELAND *Poems* (1697) 113 (Jam.) They're skant of wit, Who..Will sumph and vote they wot not what. **1867** GREGOR *Banffsh. Gloss.*, *Sumph*, to show sour, sulky temper. **1894** CROCKETT *Lilac Sunbonnet* 73 Liein' sumphin' an' sleepin' i' the middle o' the forenicht.

sumph, variant of SUMP *sb.*

†**ˈsumphion.** *Obs. rare*[−1]. Altered form of SYMPHAN.

c **1590** J. BURELL *Queen's Entry* in Sibbald *Chron. S.P.* (1802) III. 468 With instruments melodious: The seistar and the sumphion.

sumping: see after SUMP *sb.*

sumpit (ˈsʌmpɪt). [a. Malay *sumpit* (*sempit*), blowpipe, properly = narrow.] = SUMPITAN; also *erron.* one of the darts blown from the sumpitan.

1831 DALTON in J. H. Moor *Notices Ind. Archip.* (1837) 50 Hunting parties..amuse themselves with shooting at the children in the trees with the sumpit. **1846** MUNDY *Jrnl.* in *Narr. Events in Borneo* (1848) II. 226 The inhabitants blew showers of sumpits into our boats.

sumpitan (ˈsʌmpɪtən). Forms: 7 **sempitan, zampatan**, 9 **sumputan, sumpitan**. [a. Malay *sumpītan*, f. *sumpit* (see prec.); in Du. *soempitan*. The possibility of connexion between the Malay *sumpītan* and Arabic *sabaṭāna* (see CEBRATANE, SARBACANE) has been suggested.]

A blow-gun made by the Malays from a hollowed cane, from which poisoned arrows are shot.

1634 SIR T. HERBERT *Trav.* 199 They [of Celebes] all vse long Canes (they call them *Sempitans*)..out of which they can blow a little pricking-piercing quill. *a* **1680** BUTLER *Charac.*, *Glutton* (1908) 192 His Entrails are like the Sarcophagus, that devours dead Bodies in a small Space, or the Indian Zampatan, that consumes Flesh in a Moment. **1837** NEWBOLD in *Phil. Trans.* CXXVII. 427 The slender arrows propelled from the Súmpitan, or blow-pipe. **1844** J. TOMLIN *Miss. Jrnls.* 84 A sumputan, or blow-pipe, and a quiver of arrows. **1882** DE WINDT *Equator* 88 A hollow tube eight feet long called by the Poonans 'sumpitan', the chief weapon of this tribe.

sump'n (ˈsʌm(p)(ə)n). Also **somepin, sumpin**, etc. Repr. colloq. (chiefly U.S., esp. Blacks') pronunc. of SOMETHING *sb.*, (*adj.*,) and *adv.*

1880 [see KIN var. CAN *v.*[1]]. **1882** *Indianapolis Jrnl.* 5 Aug. 4/6 They's somepin kindo' hearty-like about the atmosphere. **1929** *Amer. Mercury* Sept. 50/2 Done sumpin' to fine captain one time didn't aim to do. **1938** C. HIMES *Black on Black* (1973) 167 Ef'n yo' is God, den gimme somp'n tuh eat. **1951** X. HERBERT in Murdoch & Drake-Brockman *Austral. Short Stories* 298 Git to jiggery out of it, you stinkin' rottin' black sumpen. **1961** WODEHOUSE *Ice in Bedroom* v. 41 Why not Heels Incorporated or Doublecrossers Limited or sump'n? **1976** *National Observer* (U.S.) 17 Apr. 17/1, I just want to tell him sump'n!

sumpner, -our, variants of SUMNER[1].

‖**sumpsimus** (ˈsʌmpsɪməs). [L., 1st pers. pl. perf. ind. of *sūmĕre* to take.] A correct expression taking the place of an incorrect but popular one (*mumpsimus*).

1545 HEN. VIII *Sp. Parl.* 24 Dec. in Hall *Chron.*, *Hen. VIII* (1548) 261 b, Some be to stiffe in their old Mumpsimus, other be to busy and curious, in their newe Sumpsimus. **1621** MOUNTAGU *Diatribæ* 115 Some very few, too much giuen vp vnto their old *Mumpsimus*, which they would not leaue for the new *Sumpsimus*. **1653** Z. BOGAN *Mirth Chr. Life* 124 One that hath been long in another way ..will not easily be brought to change his old *mumsimus* (as they say) for a new *sumpsimus*. **1818** BENTHAM *Ch. Eng.* Introd. 34 The insufficiency and inaptitude of the old *mumpsimus*, on the back of which they thus clap this their new *sumpsimus*. **1828** SCOTT *Aunt Margaret's Mirr.* (ad init.), The clergyman, who, without vindicating his false reading, preferred, from habit's sake, his old *mumpsimus* to the modern *sumpsimus*. **1882** *Contemp. Rev.* Mar. 372 Did they want a correct *sumpsimus*, or their erroneous but pleasing *mumpsimus*?

†**sumpt.** *Obs. rare.* [ad. L. *sumptus*, f. *sumpt-*, *sūmĕre* to consume, spend.]

a. Expenditure. **b.** Sumptuousness.

a **1560** R. HALL *Life Fisher* in *Wks.* (E.E.T.S.) p. xlvii, His owne great sumpt & expenses in wearing of silke and other costly apparrell. **1548** PATTEN *Exped. Scot.* Pref. d j, They spake drylie, more too tant the sumpt of oure show, then to seme [etc.].

sumpt, variant of SUMP *sb.*

sumpter (ˈsʌm(p)tə(r)), *sb. arch.* Forms: 4–7 **sompter**, 4, 8 **sumter**, 5 **sometour**, 6 **sumtar**, 7 **som(e)ter**, 4– **sumpter**. See also SUMPTURE[2]. [a. OF. *som(m)etier* = Pr. *saumatier* (cf. med.L. *saumaterius*):—pop.L. **sagmatārius*, f. *sagmat-*, *sagma* SUM *sb.*[2]: see -ER[2].]

†**1.** The driver of a pack-horse. *Obs.*

c **1320** *Brasenose Coll. Muniments* 52. 49 (MS.) Robert the Sumpter. **13..** *K. Alis.* 6007 (Laud MS.) Dryuers Gyoures, & Sumters [*v.r.* sumpteris]. *c* **1420** *Sir Amadace* (Camden) xxx, His sometour and his palfray mon bothe. **1523** LD. BERNERS *Froiss.* I. xviii. 21 Incontinent were sent thither horses and sompters, to fetche thens some purueyance. **1601** F. TATE *Househ. Ord. Edw. II* §87 (1876) 52 Al palfreours & somters of the kinges house.

2. A pack or baggage horse; a beast of burden.

1570 FOXE *A. & M.* (ed. 2) I. 302/1 Thus the Byshop.. prouideth out of euery Citie in England ij. palfreys and ij. sumpters. **1577** HOLINSHED *Chron.* II. 718/2 He gaue right great..giftes, lading his sumpters with plate and threasure. *a* **1625** FLETCHER *Noble Gent.* v. i, You should have had a Sumpter..where now you are fain, To hire a Rippers mare. **1697** COLLIER *Ess. Mor. Subj.* II. (1703) 147 He may, like a sumpter, carry things of value, but he never wears them. **1700** DRYDEN *Iliad* I. 74 Then..he..Feather'd Fates among the Mules and Sumpters sent. **1849** ALFORD *Gk. Test.* Matt. xxi. 6, 7 The Lord sat on the foal,..and the mother accompanied, apparently after the manner of a sumpter.

fig. **1605** SHAKS. *Lear* II. iv. 219 Returne with her? Perswade me rather to be slaue and sumpter To this detested groome.

3. A pack, saddle-bag. Now *rare.*

1570 LEVINS *Manip.* 76 A Sumpter, *sarcina.* ?**1611** BEAUM. & FL. *Cupid's Rev.* v. i, I'll have a horse to leap thee, and thy base issue shall carry Sumpters. **1652** COTTERELL tr. *Calprenède's Cassandra* III. (1676) 54 [He] commanded Cloaths of the Macedonian fashion to be taken out of his Sumpter. **1666** *Lond. Gaz.* No. 106/4 His Mules with their Sumpters covered with Scarlet, Embroidered with Gold. **1681** W. ROBERTSON *Phraseol. Gen.* (1693) 198. **1958** L. DURRELL *Balthazar* ii. 32 A liquid-eyed camel..humped down the narrow street threatening to knock us down with its bulging sumpters of *bercim*.

4. *attrib.* (often equivalent to *pack-*; see PACK *sb.*[1] 15). **a.** in sense 1, as ***sumpter boy, man.***

1392–3 *Earl Derby's Exp.* (Camden) 255 Pro expensis de somptermen. *c* **1420** *Sir Amadace* (Camden) xxviii, Thenne his sometour-mon before was dyȝte. **14..** *Lat.-Eng. Voc.* in Wr.-Wülcker 586 *Gerolotista*, a sompturman. **1588** KYD *Househ. Philos.* Wks. (1901) 270 He must needs be chargde with sompter men. **1601** F. TATE *Househ. Ord. Edw. II* §96 (1876) 56 That none of the kinges meignee..charetters or sompter boy..keepe his wife at the court. **1627** J. TAYLOR (Water P.) *Armado* C 4 b, Sumptermen, Littermen and Coachmen. **1725** *MSS. Dk. Portland* (Hist. MSS. Comm.) VI. 81 Saml. Jackson, the sumpter man.

b. in sense 2, as ***sumpter animal, ass, beast, camel, dog, horse, mule, pony***; hence (= baggage-) ***sumpter canoe, car.***

14.. *Lat.-Eng. Voc.* in Wr.-Wülcker 582 *Falerarius*, a sompterhors. **1502** *Privy Purse Exp. Eliz. York* (1830) 14 Six tapettes for the sompter horses. **1577** HARRISON *Descr. Brit.* III. viii, The auncient vse of sommers and sumpter horses is in a maner vtterly relinquished. **1579–80** NORTH *Plutarch* (1676) 430 They overthrew their carriages and sumpter Moyls. **1602** ? DONNE *To Sir N. Smyth* 133 That Scot..who, at his coming up, had not A Sumpter-dog. **1707** MORTIMER *Husb.* (1721) I. 225 Two Mules that were Sumpter-Mules to a Colonel in Flanders. **1758** MRS. DELANY *Let. to Mrs. Dewes* 1 Oct., A train of two chaises and two cars with us..and our sumpter-car. *c* **1760** SMOLLETT *Ode to Indep.* 95 So moves the sumpter-mule, in harness'd pride. **1764** HARMER *Observ.* XI. v. 222 A sumpter camel, which carries his treasure. **1821** SOUTHEY *Exped. Orsua* 191 The sumpter beasts, who were partly laden with powder. **1832** R. & J. LANDER *Exped. Niger* III. xix. 159 Besides our convoy, we had a sumpter-canoe in company. **1863** BARING-GOULD *Iceland* 166 The horses tripped over swamps which would have engulphed the sumpter pony. **1873** TRISTRAM *Moab* iii. 45 The rest..kept a sharp look-out on the sumpter animals. **1879** WALFORD *Londoniana* II. 33 From the knightly charger to the humble sumpter-horse.

c. = Covering or carried by a sumpter animal, as ***sumpter cloth, saddle, trunk.***

1569 *Wills & Inv. Richmond* (Surtees) 219, iiij^or hackney sadles..One sumtar sadle. *c* **1575** J. HOOKER *Life Sir P. Carew* (1857) 177, ij sompter clothes. *c* **1653** in *Verney Mem.* (1907) I. 535 Yalowe haire sumpter trunkes. **1666** *Lond. Gaz.* No. 97/2 Thirty seven Mules with their Sumpter-Cloaths nobly embroidered with Gold. **1715** *Lady G. Baillie's Househ. Bk.* (S.H.S.) 187 For 2 sumter trunks £4 0 0. **1760–72** H. BROOKE *Fool of Qual.* (1809) II. 52, I have seen an ass clothed in a very gorgeous sumpter-cloth. **1818** SCOTT *Br. Lamm.* ix, Without the saddle being decored wi' the broidered sumpter-cloth. **1852** BURN *Naval & Milit. Dict.* II. (1863) 277/1 Sumpter-saddle, *bât, selle de somme.*

Hence †'**sumpter** *v. trans.*, to put on one's back; to wear.

c **1590** *Trag. Rich. II* (1870) 7 For your sakes..For once Ile sumpter a gawdye wardropp.

†'**sumptery,** *a.* and *sb. Obs. rare.* Also 7 **sumptry.** [f. prec. sb. + -Y.] **A.** *adj.* Of or pertaining to sumpter animals.

1546 in *Archæol. Cant.* VII. 192 Y^e sumptery stable w^t y^e Carter's hall.

B. *sb.* Baggage.

1620 SHELTON *2nd Pt. Quix.* lix. 398 They alighted, and Sancho retired with his Sumptry [Sp. *reposteria*] into a Chamber of which the Oast gaue him the Key.

†'**sumptify,** *v. Obs. rare*$^{-0}$. [ad. L. *sumptifacĕre*, f. *sumptus* expense: see -FY.]

1656 BLOUNT *Glossogr.*, *Sumptifie*, to make expences or cost.

sumption ('sʌm(p)ʃən). Also 5 **sumpcion.** [ad. L. *sumptio, -ōnem*, n. of action f. *sumpt-, sūmĕre* to take. Cf. OF. *sumpcion, somption.*]

† **1.** The reception (of the Sacrament, of Christ in the Sacrament). *Obs.*

c **1440** *Alphabet of Tales* 463 When..he had said mes, befor his sumpcions, þe same duffe come agayn. **1624** F. WHITE *Repl. Fisher* 443 By reall sumption of Christs body into the mouth..of the receiuer. **1654** JER. TAYLOR *Real Pres.* iii. 30 The places are exactly parallel;..both of them [are meant] of spiritual sumption of Christ. **1664** OWEN *Vindic. Animad. Fiat Lux* xix. 461 Others think that the Sacrifice consists in three actions of the Priest, Consecration, Oblation and Sumption, or receiving of the Host.

2. †**a.** The taking of a thing as true without proof; hence, an assumption, premiss. **b.** The major premiss of a syllogism. (Cf. SUBSUMPTION 1.)

1572 R. T. *Disc.* 44 The Sumption or assumption the Pope affirmeth..and the conclusion is manifest. **1656** STANLEY *Hist. Philos.* v. 17 Analysis..is a sumption of the thing sought, by the consequents, (as if it were already known) to find out the truth. *Ibid.* 62 Of Syllogismes some are Categoricall..: Categoricall are those whose sumptions and conclusions are simple propositions. **1837–8** SIR W. HAMILTON *Logic* xvi. (1866) I. 295 The proposition in which the relation of the major term to the middle is expressed, is the Sumption or Major Premise. **1874** ELIZ. S. PHELPS in *Sex & Educ.* 132 Sumption.—All women ought to be incapable of sustained activity.

sumptious, -ly, obs. ff. SUMPTUOUS, -LY.

sumptuary ('sʌm(p)tju:ərɪ), *a.* (*sb.*) Also 7 **somptuarie.** [ad. L. *sumptuārius*, f. *sumptus*: see SUMPT and -ARY. Cf. F. *somptuaire*, It., Sp. *suntuario*, Pg. *sumptuario.*] Pertaining to or regulating expenditure.

sumptuary law, a law regulating expenditure, esp. with a view to restraining excess in food, dress, equipage, etc.

1600 E. BLOUNT tr. *Conestaggio* 9 They made sumptuarie lawes, and especially vpon victuals. **1650** BULWER *Anthropomet.* 262 The prodigious and ridiculous vanity of these Times, (if ever) calling for Sumptuary Laws. **1716** LADY M. W. MONTAGU *Let. to C'tess Bristol* 22 Aug., They have sumptuary laws in this town, which distinguish their rank by their dress. **1766** GOLDSM. *Vic. W.* iv, When Sunday came, it was indeed a day of finery, which all my sumptuary edicts could not restrain. **1850** MERIVALE *Rom. Emp.* xiv. (1865) II. 134 The money-lenders were dissatisfied with the sumptuary reforms which Pompeius had encouraged. **1850** HAWTHORNE *Scarlet L.* ii, Of a splendour..beyond what was allowed by the sumptuary regulations of the colony. **1875** STUBBS *Const. Hist.* II. xvi. 413 Sumptuary laws, prescribing the minutiae of diet and dress. **1888** *Encycl. Brit.* XXIV. 642/1 Numerous ancient laws dealt with trade and sumptuary matters.

†**b.** *sb.* One responsible for expenditure. *Obs.*

1789 P. SMYTH tr. *Aldrich's Archit.* (1818) 77 The sumptuary, who furnishes the expence of a building.

sumptuosity (sʌm(p)tju:'ɒsɪtɪ). [ad. late L. *sumptuōsitās*, f. *sumptuōsus* SUMPTUOUS. Cf. F. *somptuosité*, etc.] Lavishness or extravagance of expenditure; magnificence or luxuriousness of living, equipment, decoration, or the like.

1559 BERCHER *Nobylytye Wymen* (Roxb.) 127 Simonides namyd a woman to be..the poyson of lyffe..the battell off Sumptuosytie, the beaste of ffamylyaritie. **1562** J. SHUTE tr. *Cambini's Turk. Wars* 27 A certaine chapell whiche he had buylded with great sumptuositie. **1601** HOLLAND *Pliny* II. 584 No man ever after him was able to match that sumptuositie of his Theatre. **1653** tr. *Carmini's Nissena* 155 The chief Commanders..being treated with such sumptuositie as belonged unto them. **1836** *New Monthly Mag.* XLVIII. 461 This is displayed in an excess of sumptuosity and decoration. **1848** THACKERAY *Van. Fair* xxviii, He was rather a favourite with the regiment, treating the young officers with sumptuosity. **1865** DICKENS *Mut. Fr.* II. xvi, A dinner on the desired scale of sumptuosity cannot be achieved. **1891** FARRAR *Darkness & Dawn* ii. 241 It was called the Golden House, and exceeded in sumptuosity every thing which the world had hitherto seen.

b. An instance of this; a sumptuous thing.

1601 HOLLAND *Pliny* I. 168 To speake of his sumptuosities, of his largesses. **1652** HEYLIN *Cosmogr.* Introd. 18 Alexander..found more Cities and sumptuosities in that little Kingdome of Porus..than in all his other travells. **1843** CARLYLE *Past & Pr.* I. vi. 47 Turn away from their lackered sumptuosities. **1856** T. A. TROLLOPE *Girlh. Cath. de Medici* 56 These and other such sumptuosities of Rome.

sumptuous ('sʌm(p)tju:əs), *a.* Also 5 **somptuouse,** 5–6 **sumptuouse,** 6 **somptious, sumpte(u)ous, -uus, summptuus,** 6–7 **sumptious, sumtuous,** 7 **sumtuose, sumtious.** [a. OF. *somptueux, sumptueux* = Pr. *sumptuos*, It. *sontuoso*, Sp. *suntuoso*, Pg. *sumptuoso*, ad. L. *sumptuōsus*, f. *sumptu-s* expense, f. *sūmĕre* to take, consume, spend.]

1. Of buildings, apparel, repasts, and the like: Made or produced at great cost; costly and (hence) magnificent in workmanship, construction, decoration, etc.

1485 CAXTON *Paris & V.* (1868) 15 The feste whyche was moste sumptuous and noble. **1490** —— *Eneydos* xxii. 80 [He] made it [*sc.* the sacraire] to be welle ornated..& crowned..with crownes of golde..& of other somptuouse thynges. **1515** BARCLAY *Egloges* iv. (1570) Cv/1 No bec of state, of rayment sumptuous. **1532–3** *Act 24 Hen. VIII*, c. 13 §1 The..excesse..used in the sumptuous and costly araye and apparell. **1549** *Compl. Scot.* xvii. 145 No sumpteous clethyng of fine claytht. **1550** T. HOBY *Trav.* 57 A sumptious aqueduct, with dyverse other antiquities. *a* **1586** SIDNEY *Arcadia* III. xxii. (1912) 483 To builde a sumptuous monument for her sister. **1593** SHAKS. *2 Hen. VI*, IV. vii. 106 Is my Apparrell sumptuous to behold? **1639** S. DU VERGER tr. *Camus' Admir. Events* 61 One of the sumptuousest parts of his Pallace. **1671** MILTON *P.R.* IV. 114 Thir sumptuous gluttonies, and gorgeous feasts. **1709** STEELE *Tatler* No. 45 ⁋1 A fine Lady dressed in the most sumptuous Habit. **1721** *New Gen. Atlas* 120 Here is also a sumptuous Foundery for Cannon. **1764** GOLDSM. *Trav.* 181 He sees..No costly lord the sumptuous banquet deal To make him loath his vegetable meal. **1824** DIBDIN *Libr. Comp.* 767 He assumes a yet more majestic aspect in the three sumptuous folios. **1879** S. C. BARTLETT *Egypt to Pal.* iv. 68 In death their greatness followed them to their sumptuous tombs.

adv. *a* **1721** PRIOR *Colin's Mistakes* v. Wks. 1907 II. 81 With Pearl and Jewels was she sumptuous deckt.

b. of conditions, functions, etc.

1590 H. R. *Defiance to Fortune* L 2, He sommoneth his nobles and estates, commanding them to be ready to accompanie him..in the most sumtuous sort they might. **1597** HOOKER *Eccl. Pol.* v. xv. §3 The sumptuous statelines of houses built vnto Gods glory. **1611** CORYAT *Crudities* 88 It is celebrated with very pompous and sumptuous solemnity. **1711** ADDISON *Spect.* No. 108 ⁋5 The Gentleman..had the Pleasure of seeing the huge Jack..served up..in a most sumptuous Manner. **1839** HALLAM *Lit. Eur.* II. 256 That stately and sumptuous architecture which distinguishes this period. **1841** JAMES *Corse de Leon* xv, She was dressed in the most sumptuous mode of the Court. **1891** FARRAR *Darkn. & Dawn* xx, His father had received a sumptuous Cæsarean funeral.

c. Of natural objects: Splendid or magnificent in appearance.

1594 T. B. *La Primaud. Fr. Acad.* II. 7 This..face of heauen so sumptuous to beholc. **1598** DRAYTON *Heroic. Ep.* xx. 88 In beautie sumptuous, as the Northerne waine. **1809** W. IRVING *Knickerb.* II. iv. (1849) 105 The sumptuous prospect of rich unsettled country. **1847** TENNYSON *Princess* IV. 134 She spoke and turn'd her sumptuous head.

†**2.** Of charges, expenses, etc.: Involving a great outlay of money. *Obs.*

1485 *York Memo. Bk.* (Surtees) I. 186 Ther povertie and sumptuouse charges which they dud bere. **1533** ELYOT *Cast. Helth* (1541) 43 Provision agaynste vayne and sumptuous expenses of the meane people. **1541** *Test. Ebor* (Surtees) VI. 139, I will that no sumptuous coste..be mayde at my buriall. **1576** FLEMING *Panopl. Epist.* 384 The trade of merchandise, except it bee sumptuous and costly [etc.]. **1616** R. C. *Times' Whistle* ii. (1871) 22 The..Mausolian monument,..Whose sumptuous cost..Noe poet ..is able to dilate.

†**b.** Costly or expensive to practise or maintain. Chiefly *Sc. Obs.*

1551–2 *Reg. Privy Council Scot.* Ser. I. I. 119 The samyn is sumptuous to his Majesty and nocht necessar to be kepit now. **1608** TOPSELL *Serpents* 76 No creature is so profitable, none lesse sumptuous [than the bee]. **1609** SKENE *Reg. Maj.*, *Forme of Proces* 112 b, The Lords hes abrogat that langsome, tedious, and sumptuous forme of proces. **1632** LITHGOW *Trav.* III. 114 This tributary, tedious, and sumptuous peregrination.

†**3.** Of persons, etc.: Spending largely; (hence) magnificent in equipment or way of living. *Obs.*

1538 STARKEY *England* (1878) 96 Thoughe you found a faute before in the yl byldyng of our cytes..yet, me semyth, gentylmen and the nobylyte are in that behalfe ouer sumptuouse. **1555** EDEN *Decades* III. VII. (Arb.) 166 The sumptuous queene Cleopatra. **1586** A. DAY *Eng. Secretorie* I. (1625) 26 Plaine are their habites for the most part, and nothing sumptuous. **1651** HOBBES *Leviath.* III. xlii. 294 The bishops..were sumptuous in their fare and apparell. **1671** MILTON *Samson* 1072 When first I saw The sumptuous Dalila floating this way. **1762–71** H. WALPOLE *Vertue's Anecd. Paint.* (1786) I. 89 The accession of this sumptuous prince brought along with it the establishment of the arts. **1781** COWPER *Truth* 59 The peacock, see—Mark what a sumptuous Pharisee is he!

'**sumptuously,** *adv.* [f. prec. + -LY².] In a sumptuous manner; at great cost, with great expenditure of money; with magnificence or pomp of living, equipment, decoration, entertainment, etc.

1536 *Act 28 Hen. VIII*, c. 12 §1 The Kynges Highnes..moste sumptuously..hath buylded..many..mansions. *a* **1548** HALL *Chron.*, *Hen. V*, 41 The Frenche kyng..sumpteously banquetted theim. **1551** ROBINSON tr. *More's Utopia* II. (1895) 264 Thither they sende furth some of their citezeins..to lyue theire sumptuously. **1580–1** *Reg. Privy Council Scot.* Ser. I. III. 347 The said wardane hes bene verie suumptuuslie superexpendit in the office of wardanrie. **1611** *Bible* Luke xvi. 19 There was a certaine rich man, which..fared sumptuously euery day. **1617** MORYSON *Itin.* I. 145 A building all of Marble..couered with lead very sumptiously. **1662** J. DAVIES tr. *Mandelslo's Trav.* 225 The women are very sumptuously clad. **1784** COWPER *Task* IV. 251 Not sumptuously adorn'd, nor needing aid, Like homely featur'd night, of clust'ring gems. **1870** F. R. WILSON *Ch. Lindisf.* 76 The whole has been sumptuously coloured. **1894** H. NISBET *Bush Girl's Rom.* 216 The sumptuously-attired Timothy.

b. *transf.* Splendidly, nobly. *rare.*

1750 H. WALPOLE *Let. to Mann* 18 Oct., Why, child, you will find yourself as sumptuously descended as—'All the blood of all the Howards'.

'**sumptuousness.** [f. SUMPTUOUS + -NESS.] The condition or quality of being sumptuous; costliness and magnificence of living, production, equipment, construction, or maintenance.

c **1530** L. COX *Rhet.* (1899) 67 The sumptuousnes of the women of Rome. **1553** EDEN *Treat. Newe Ind.* (Arb.) 13 The Turke..commaunded a greate nauie of shippes with greate sumptuousnes to bee furnished. **1573** BRIDGES *Suprem. Chr. Princes* 479 Many carued Images..with great sumptuousnesse and coste, were sette vp. *a* **1628** F. GREVIL *Sidney* (1652) 208 The sloth or sumptuousnesse of her great Steward, and white staves. **1676** ROW *Contn. Blair's Autobiogr.* xi. (1848) 335 There was most superfluous sumptuousness used at his burial. **1684** *Contempl. St. Man* I. vi. (1699) 62 The sumptuousness of his Palaces. **1758** JOHNSON *Idler* No. 99 ⁋5 He raised a house, equal in sumptuousness to that of the vizier. **1868** E. EDWARDS *Ralegh* I. iv. 58 The royal progresses..were..pageants of no small sumptuousness.

†'**sumpture**¹. *Obs. rare.* Also 8 **sumture.** [f. L. *sumptus* (see SUMPTUOUS) + -URE.]

1. Sumptuousness.

1616 CHAPMAN *Homer's Hymn Hermes* 127 Celebrating all Her traine of seruants; and collaterall Sumpture of Houses.

2. Expense; *attrib.* in ***sumpture law*** = sumptuary law.

1727 A. HAMILTON *New Acc. E. Indies* II. xlvii. 164 For want of sumture Laws among them, it was hard to know the Gentleman from the Beggar.

†'**sumpture**². *Obs.* Altered form of SUMPTER after words in -URE.

1608 CHAPMAN *Byron's Conspir.* III. i, Endure this, and be turnd into his Moile To beare his sumptures. **1648** J. BEAUMONT *Psyche* VII. cclviii, Their sumptures now they hastily provide, Though yet uncertain which way they should tend. **1649** JER. TAYLOR *Gt. Exemp.* II. Disc. xi. §7 To..load their sumptures stil the more by how much their way is shorter. **1706** J. STEVENS *Sp. Dict.*, *Repostéro*..a Sumpture cloth. **1707** —— tr. *Quevedo's Com. Wks.* (1709) 383 We have no Tidings of our Sumptures and Carriages.

sumpy ('sʌmpɪ), *a. dial.* [f. SUMP *sb.* + -Y¹. Cf. Du. *sompig*, G. *sumpfig*, Sw. *sumpig.*] Boggy, swampy.

1829 BROCKETT *N.C. Gloss.*, *Sumpy*, miry, dirty. **1892** J. LUCAS *Kalm's England* 305 There should be no sumpy places.

sum-total (ˌsʌm'təʊtəl). Pl. **sums-total, sum-totals.** [ad. med.L. *summa tōtālis*: see SUM *sb.*¹ and TOTAL *a.* Cf. F. *somme totale.*] The aggregate of all the items in an account; the total amount (of things capable of numeration).

c **1395** *Plowman's Tale* I. 418 The hye goodes frendship hem makes, They toteth on hir somme totall. *c* **1430** *Art of Nombryng* vi. 9 Ioyne the produccioun, and þere wol be the some totalle. **1497** *Naval Acc. Hen. VII* (1896) 325 Somme Totell of almaner Costes Charges & Expences. *Ibid.* 330 Somme Totall of all Stuff Takle & Apparell ordinance Artillarie & Abillamentes of warre. **1523** FITZHERB. *Surv.* 30 To knowe the hole charge of all the partyculers, what they be at the first syght, in the sommes totall. **1533** MORE *Debell. Salem* Wks. 1024/1 He bringeth forth here a fewe amountyng in a some totall to the infinite number of fower. **1675** COCKER *Morals* 4 Compute your Sins Sum-Total for a Year. **1743** BULKELEY & CUMMINS *Voy. S. Seas* Pref. p. xx, The Sum Total we shall ever receive for our Voyage to the South-Seas. **1856** *N. Brit. Rev.* XXVI. 91 In the terms of peace made with France, a sum-total was agreed on for the whole debt. **1864** *Intell. Observ.* VI. 273 The Mint is each day engaged in adding to the sums total. **1865** MRS. GASKELL *Wives & Dau.* xxii, Every time the sum-totals came to different amounts.

b. *gen.* The aggregate or totality *of.*

1660 JER. TAYLOR *Worthy Commun.* i. §2. 38 There are two great Sermons of the Gospel which are the summe total and abreviature of the whole word of God. **1729** BUTLER *Serm.* Wks. 1874 II. 145 These particular enjoyments make up the sum total of our happiness. **1837** CARLYLE *Fr. Rev.* II. III. ii, The diseased things that were spoken, done, the sum-total whereof is the French Revolution. **1875** *Punch* 22 May 215/1 The session will have done something to lessen the sum-total of human suffering. **1878** *N. Amer. Rev.* CXXVI. 35 Throughout the world the sum-total of motion is ever the same. **1906** ANWYL *Celtic Relig.* i. 5 To the sum-total of these religious ideas contributions have been made from many sources.

Hence **sum-'totalize** *v. trans.* and *intr.*, to reckon or state the sum-total, to sum up; whence **,sum-totali'zation**, summing up.

1840 HALIBURTON *Clockm.* Ser. III. ii. 26 But to sum-totalize my story: the next time [etc.]. **1855** —— *Nat. & Hum. Nat.* I. 18 Maxims and saws are the sumtotalization of a thing. **1865** W. G. PALGRAVE *Arabia* I. 29 To decide on the value of each separate coin, and after that to sum-totalize.

sum-up. *rare.* [f. phr. *sum up* (see SUM *v.*[1] 4).] A summing-up, summary.

1894 O'CONNOR in *Romanism & Ritualism* (1895) 257 The truth of Mr. Gladstone's sum-up cannot be questioned.

sumwhat, obs. form of SOMEWHAT.

sumyter, obs. form of SCIMITAR.

1530 PALSGR. 278/2 Sumyter a fauchon, *sumiterre*.

sun (sʌn), *sb.*[1] Forms: 1–7 **sunne**, (1 **sunna**), 3–7 **sonne**, 4–5 (6 *Sc.*) **sune**, 4–7 **sone** (chiefly *Sc.*), **sunn**, 5–6 **son**, (3 **seonne**, 4 **sonn**, *Kentish* **zonne**, *Sc.* **sowne**, **swn**, 5 **soen**, **swne**, *Sc.* **soune**, 6 *Sc.* **soun**), 4– **sun**. *β. Sc.* 4 **sene**, 6 **syn**, 7–8 **sin**, 8 **sinn**. [Com. Teut. wk. fem.: OE. *sunne* = OFris. *sunne*, *sonne* (WFris. *sinne*, dial. *sonne*, *son*, NFris. *sen*), OS. *sunna* (MLG., LG. *sunne*), MDu. *zonne* (Du. *zon*), OHG. *sunnô* (MHG. *sunne*, *sun*, MG. *sonne*, *son*, G. *sonne*), ON. *sunna* (poet.), Goth. *sunnô*; also wk. masc. OE. *sunna*, = OFris. *sonna*, OS. *sunno*, OHG. *sunna*, Goth. *sunna*:—OTeut. **sunnōn-*, *-on-*, f. *sun-*, *s(u)wen-*, whence also Zend (gen.) *χvə̄ng* sun, Gr. ἦν-οψ glittering, OIr. *fur-sunnud* lighting-up.

From the same root *sau-* (*sŭ-*) with *l-* instead of *n*-formative, *sāw(e)l-*, *s(u)wel-* (*sūl-*), are Skr. *súar* (*svàr*), *sūra*, *sūrya* sun, Zend *hvarə* (gen. *hūrō*), Gr. ἥλιος, ἠέλιος, Doric ἀέλιος, Cretan ἀβέλιος, Alb. *üλ* star, L. *sōl* sun, W. *haul*, Ir. *súil* eye, Lith. *sáulė*, Goth. *sauil*, ON. *sól*.]

I. 1. a. The brightest (as seen from the earth) of the heavenly bodies, the luminary or orb of day; the central body of the solar system, around which the earth and other planets revolve, being kept in their orbits by its attraction and supplied with light and heat by its radiation; in the Ptolemaic system reckoned as a planet, in modern astronomy as one of the stars.

The ordinary language as to the sun's course, its rising and setting, etc., is based upon the old view of the sun as a body moving through the zodiac, rising above, passing across the heavens, and sinking below the horizon, etc.

Beowulf 606 Sunne sweȝlwered suþan scineð. *c* **888** ÆLFRED *Boeth.* ix, Đonne seo sunne on hadrum heofone beorhtost scineð, þonne aðeostriaþ ealle steorran. **971** *Blickl. Hom.* 51 þære sunnan hæto. *a* **1000** *Riddles* lxvii. 3 (Gr.) Leohtre þonne mona, swiftre þonne sunne. *c* **1000** ÆLFRIC *Gen.* xxxii. 31 And sona eode sunna upp. *c* **1200** ORMIN 7273 Æst, tær þe sunne riseþþ. *Ibid.* 9400 þe sunness brihhte leome. *c* **1205** LAY. 27805 Ær þe sunne eode to grunde. *a* **1300** *Cursor M.* 291 In þe sune þat schines clere Es a thing and thre thinges sere; A bodi rond, and hete and light. *Ibid.* 388 þe ferth [day]..Bath ware made sun and mon. **1340** *Ayenb.* 27 þe briȝtnesse of þe zonne. **1390** GOWER *Conf.* III. 313 The Sonne arist, the weder cliereth. *c* **1420** in *Rel. Ant.* I. 232 *C.* Wherefore is the son rede at even? *M.* For he gothe toward hell. **1526** TINDALE *Eph.* iv. 26 Lett nott the sonne goo doune apon youre wrathe. *a* **1569** KINGESMYLL *Confl. Satan* (1578) 14 Gods words remaine beyond the days of the Sunne. **1570** *Satir. Poems Reform.* xv. 7 Ȝe Mariguildis, forbid the sune To oppin ȝow euerie morrow! **1634** MILTON *Comus* 374 Though Sun and Moon Were in the flat Sea sunk. **1785** BURNS *3rd Ep. to J. Lapraik* ix, Now the sinn keeks in the west. **1844** H. STEPHENS *Bk. Farm* I. 292 When the sun rises red, wind and rain may be expected during the day. **1873** DAWSON *Earth & Man* i. 9 The sun is..an incandescent globe surrounded by an immense luminous envelope of vapours.

b. In conformity with the gender of OE. *sunne*, the feminine pronoun was used until the 16th c. in referring to the sun; since then the masculine has been commonly used, without necessarily implying personification; the neuter is somewhat less frequent.

a **900** *O.E. Martyrol.* 21 Mar., On domes dæȝe..þonne scineð seo sunne seofon siðum beorhtor þonne heo nu do. *c* **1275** *Passion our Lord* 479 in *O.E. Misc.*, þe sonne bileuede hire lyht. **1377** LANGL. *P. Pl.* B XVIII. 243 How þe sonne gan louke her liȝte in her-self, Whan she seye hym suffre þat sonne & se made. **1535** COVERDALE *Isa.* xxxviii. 8 So the Sonne turned ten degrees bacward, the which he was descended afore. **1552** BP. LATIMER *Serm. St. Stephen's Day* Serm. (1584) 276 Not that the sunne it selfe of her [*ed.* 1607 his] substance shalbe darckened. **1590** SHAKS. *Com. Err.* II. ii. 30 When the sunne shines, let foolish gnats make sport, But creepe in crannies, when he hides his beames. **1662** STILLINGFL. *Orig. Sacræ* III. i. §17 How much bigger the Sun may bee then hee seems. **1667** MILTON *P.L.* VII. 247 For yet the Sun Was not; shee in a cloudie Tabernacle Sojourn'd the while. **1727–46** THOMSON *Summer* 432 'Tis raging noon; and, vertical, the Sun Darts on the head direct his forceful rays. **1798** COLERIDGE *Anc. Mar.* I. vii, The Sun came up upon the left, Out of the sea came he! **1845** DE QUINCEY *Dau. Lebanon* Wks. 1856 V. 280 Up rose the sun on the thirtieth morning in all his pomp.

c. As an object of worship in various religions, and thus (and hence generally) personified as a male being, sometimes identified with various gods, esp. Apollo (cf. SUN-GOD); also in classical mythology said to be drawn in a chariot.

c **1205** LAY. 13934 Saturnus heo ȝiuen sætterdæi, þene Sunne heo ȝiuen sonedæi. *c* **1375** *Sc. Leg. Saints* vi. (*Thomas*) 605 Gere hym mak som offeringe til oure gret god, þe sene. *c* **1560** A. SCOTT *Poems* (S.T.S.) ii. 81 Thir vowis maid to syn and mone. **1599** NASHE *Lenten Stuffe* 45 The sunne was so in his mumps vppon it, that it was almost noone before hee could goe to cart that day. **1610** HEYWOOD *Gold. Age* I. i, I plac'd diuine Apollo Within the Sunnes bright Chariot. **1632** E. BLOUNT *Lyly's Sixe Crt. Com.* Ep. Ded., This Poet, sat at the Sunnes Table: Apollo gaue him a wreath of his owne Bayes. **1634** MILTON *Comus* 51 Who knows not Circe The daughter of the Sun? **1674** S. VINCENT *Young Gall. Acad.* 26 Till the Suns Car-horses stand prancing on the very top of highest Noon. **1727** GAY *Fables* I. xxviii, Parent of light, all-seeing Sun. **1781** COWPER *Conversat.* 67 A Persian, humble servant of the sun. **1868** TENNYSON *Lucretius* 124 Another of our Gods, the Sun, Apollo, Delius, or of older use All-seeing Hyperion. **1887** A. LANG *Myth*, etc. (1899) I. 125 In Samoa the sun had a child by a Samoan woman.

d. As a type of brightness or clearness.

c **950** *Lindisf. Gosp.* Matt. xvii. 2 *Resplenduit facies eius sicut sol*, eft-ȝescean onsione his suæ sunna. *a* **1225** *Leg. Kath.* 1681 Seouen siðes brihtre þen beo þe sunne. *a* **1300** *Cursor M.* 17866 Briȝter þenne þe sonnes beme. *Ibid.* 24648 Bird o blis, na sun sa bright. *c* **1375** *Sc. Leg. Saints* xxv. (*Julian*) 446 Fere mare clere þane is þe sowne in myd-ȝere. **1412** *26 Pol. Poems* 49 Now are þey fayre angels pere, As shynyng sune in goddis syȝt. **1582** ALLEN *Martyrdom Campion* (1908) 19 As every of the rest..did..prove and declare as cleare as the sunne. **1644** JESSOP *Angel of Ephesus* 32 It is as cleare as the Sunne,..that a Bishop and a Presbyter are..the same. **1859** TENNYSON *Marr. Geraint* 231, I..Will clothe her for her bridals like the sun.

e. Phrases and proverbial expressions. (*a*) ***under*** (or ***beneath***) ***the sun***, †***under sun***: on earth, in the world. (*b*) (***as...***) ***as the sun shines on***: = as lives or exists; used in commendatory phrases. (*c*) ***to get the sun of***: (in fighting) to get on the sunward side of (an enemy) so that the sun shines into his eyes. (*d*) ***on which the sun never sets***: an expression applied in the 17th c. to the Spanish dominions, later to the British Empire. (*e*) ***to make the sun shine through***: to make a hole in, 'let daylight into'; so ***to let the sun shine through*** (one), to get wounded. (*f*) ***with the sun***: in the direction of the sun's apparent diurnal movement in the northern hemisphere, i.e. from left to right; similarly ***against the sun*** (= WITHERSHINS). Chiefly *Naut.* (*g*) ***to take the sun***: to make an observation of the meridian altitude of the sun; also ***to shoot the sun*** (see SHOOT *v.* 32 c). (*h*) ***the sun is over the foreyard*** (*Naut.*): it is noon (the time at which the first drink of the day is taken). (*i*) Proverbial or allusive phrases (see quots.).

to hold (etc.) ***a candle to the sun***: see CANDLE *sb.* 5 h. ***crown of the sun***: see CROWN *sb.* 8. ***to make hay while the sun shines***: see HAY *sb.*[1] 3. ***raisins of the sun***: see RAISIN 2 c.

(*a*) *a* **1000** *Andreas* 1013 (Gr.) Gode þancade, þæs ðe hie onsunde æfre moston ȝeseon under sunnan. *c* **1250** LAY. 108 þar Rome nou on stondeð, fele ȝer under sunnan nas ȝet Rome bi-wonnen. *a* **1250** *Owl & Night.* 912 þar beoþ men þat litel kunne of songe þat is vnder sunne. **1303** R. BRUNNE *Handl. Synne* 57 To alle crystyn men vndir sunne. **1382** WYCLIF *Eccl.* i. 10 No thing vnder the sunne newe. *a* **1400–50** *Wars Alex.* 4300 Na supowell vndire son seke we vs neuire. **1508** DUNBAR *Poems* vii. 43 Moste aunterus and able, Wndir the soun that beris helme or scheild. ? **1618** FLETCHER *Hum. Lieut.* I. i, There fights no braver souldier under Sun, Gentlemen. **1638** JUNIUS *Paint. Ancients* 123 Their worke remaineth in the finest place under the Sunne. **1711** STEELE *Spect.* No. 6 ¶ 1, I know no Evil under the Sun so great. **1850** TENNYSON *In Mem.* lxxv, While we breathe beneath the sun. *a* **1862** THOREAU *Yankee in Canada* ii. (1866) 22 What under the sun they were placed there for.. was not apparent.

(*b*) [*c* **1205** LAY. 31087 Nis nan feirure wifmon þa whit sunne scineð on.] *a* **1692** SHADWELL *Volunteers* I. ii, He is as fine a Gentleman as the Sun shines upon.

(*c*) **1588** SHAKS. *L.L.L.* IV. iii. 369 Be first aduis'd, In conflict that you get the Sunne of them.

(*d*) **1630** CAPT. SMITH *Advert.* Wks. (Arb.) II. 962 Why should the brave Spanish Souldiers brag; The Sunne never sets in the Spanish dominions, but ever shineth on one part or other we have conquered for our King. **1640** HOWELL *Dodona's Gr.* 15 Her dominions are very spacious, that the Sun never forsakes her quite. *c* **1645** —— *Lett.* (1650) I. 358 The catholic King..wears the sun for his helmet, because it never sets upon all his dominions, in regard some part of them lies on the other side of the hemisphere among the Antipodes. **1648** GAGE *New Survey W. Indies* Ep. Ded., Our Neighbors the Hollanders..have conquered so much Land in the East and West-Indies, that it may be said of them, as of the Spaniards, That the Sunn never sets upon their Dominions.

1827 SCOTT *Napoleon* VI. v. 141 [Napoleon loq.] The stake I play for is immense—I will continue in my own dynasty the family system of the Bourbons, and unite Spain for ever to the destinies of France. Remember that the sun never sets on the immense Empire of Charles V. **1846** THACKERAY in *Punch* X. 101/2 Snobs are..recognised throughout an Empire on which I am given to understand the Sun never sets. **1857** HUGHES *Tom Brown* I. i, The great army of Browns, who are scattered over the whole empire on which the sun never sets.

(*e*) **1697** COLLIER *Ess. Mor. Subj.* I. (1703) 145 If he draws upon me in the streets, I will not..let the sun shine through me, if I can help it. **1744** M. BISHOP *Life & Adv.* 185 We made the Sun shine through some of the Walls.

(*f*) **1769** FALCONER *Dict. Marine* (1780) 11, *Rouer à tour*, to coil a rope with the sun. *Ibid.*, *Rouer à contre*, to coil a rope against the sun. *c* **1860** H. STUART *Seaman's Catech.* 55 The starboard cable should be bitted with the sun, and the port cable against the sun. **1875** BEDFORD *Sailor's Pocket Bk.* iv. (ed. 2) 90 When the wind shifts against the sun, Trust it not, for back it will run.

(*g*) **1555** TOWRSON in Hakluyt *Voy.* (1589) 100 They tooke y[e] sunne & after iudged themselues to be 24 leagues past the riuer de Sestos. **1869** 'MARK TWAIN' *Innoc. Abr.* ii. (1887) 20, I..found a sextant... Now, I said, they 'take the sun' through this thing. **1895** *Mem. J. Anderson* ii. 21 They watched the Captain daily 'take the sun'.

(*h*) **1844** [see FORE-YARD[2] 1]. **1862** 'VANDERDECKEN' *Yacht Sailor* ix. 123 It will be a favourable time to 'make the sun over the foreyard', and serve out grog in moderation to all hands. **1903** H. HOLMES *Life & Adventures* 11 The sun's over the fore yard; no doubt they have spliced the main brace. **1962** W. GRANVILLE *Dict. Sailors' Slang* 115/2 *Sun over the foreyard*, time for drinking in the ward-room. Eight bells in the forenoon watch: mid-day. It is a traditional Naval convention never to drink before the sun clears the foreyard.

(*i*) **1377** LANGL. *P. Pl.* B. XVIII. 409 After sharpe shoures ..moste shene is þe sonne. **1535** COVERDALE *Matt.* v. 45 He maketh his sonne to aryse on the euel and on the good. **1598** MARSTON *Sco. Villanie* I. iii. 179 It's good be warie, whilst the sunne shines cleer. **1598** SHAKS. *Merry W.* I. iii. 70 Then did the Sun on dung-hill shine.

†**f.** ***line***, ***mount of the sun*** (*Palmistry*): see quot. 1653. ***sun and moon***, a kind of tug-of-war (see quot. 1615). *Obs.*

1615 T. THOMAS *Dict.*, *Dielcystinda*, a kinde of plaie, wherein two companies of boyes holding hands all in a rowe, do pull with hard hold one another till one be ouercome: it is called Sunne and Moone. **1653** R. SANDERS *Physiogn.* 53 The line of the Sun takes its beginning out of the line of Fortune, and ascends, dividing the mount of the Sun, straight to the ring-finger.

2. a. With qualifying word, or in *pl.*, with reference to its position in the sky (or occas. the zodiac), or its aspect or visibility at a particular time or times; †hence sometimes = direction or aspect with respect to the incident rays of the sun; so (*poet.*) ***rising sun*** = east, ***setting sun*** = west. Also in fig. context.

c **1386** CHAUCER *Prol.* 7 Whan..the yonge sonne Hath in the Ram his halfe cours yronne. **1588** SHAKS. *L.L.L.* IV. iii. 91 *Dum.* As faire as day. *Ber.* I as some daies, but then no sunne must shine. **1601** HOLLAND *Pliny* I. 84 Some have set them just in the mids betweene both Sunnes, to wit the setting of it with the Antipodes, and the rising of it with us. **1617** MORYSON *Itin.* III. 110 So that the ground lye vpon the South Sunne, and fenced from cold windes. **1697** DRYDEN *Virg. Georg.* III. 436 Nor to the North, nor to the Rising Sun, Nor Southward..But..to the West. **1709** POPE *Autumn* 100 And the low sun had lengthen'd ev'ry shade. **1721** MORTIMER *Husb.* II. 221 They must be..not too much exposed to the Noon-sun; the Morning-sun being esteemed the best for them. **1726** LEONI *Alberti's Archit.* I. 16/1 We shou'd also observe what Suns our House stands to. **1788** COWPER *Stanzas Bill Mort.* 16 Told that his setting sun would rise no more. **1818** BYRON *Mazeppa* xvii, With just enough of life to see My last of suns go down on me. **1841** J. F. COOPER *Deerslayer* II. xii. 206 You are a man whose fathers came from beyond the rising sun; we are children of the setting sun. **1847** TENNYSON *Princ.* IV. 552 The midsummer, midnight, Norway sun. **1860** PUSEY *Min. Proph.* 367 The fiery empire of Assyrian conquerors sank like a tropic sun. **1865** KINGSLEY *Herew.* iii, A glen which sloped towards the southern sun.

(*b*) ***rising-sun*** (*transf.*): (i) as a decorative motif; (ii) as the emblem of Japan (with ref. to the literal meaning of the country's name in Japanese: see NIPPON).

1840 J. MADISON *Papers* III. 1624 [At the Constitutional Convention, 1787] Doctor Franklin, looking towards the President's chair, at the back of which a rising sun happened to be painted, observed..that painters had found it difficult to distinguish in their art, a rising, from a setting, sun. **1863** *Chambers's Encycl.* V. 683/1 *Japan* (native name, *Nipon*.. i.e., the Land of the Rising Sun). **1895** 'C. E. CRADDOCK' *Mystery Witch-Face Mountain* 185 Some [quilts] were of the 'log cabin' and 'rising sun' variety. **1897** *Far East* 20 Mar. 83/2 The children of the Rising Sun. **1935** J. C. LINCOLN *Cape Cod Yesterdays* 109, I ducked my tousled head under the..'rising-sun comforter' and fell asleep in spite of the racket. **1942** *R.A.F. Jrnl.* 2 May 1 It is difficult to form an exact picture of the air strength of the land of the Rising Sun. **1983** *Jewish Chron.* 27 May 15/3 The cupped-hand emblem replaces the now familiar rising sun logo [of the Jewish Welfare Board].

b. With reference to the heat produced by the sun; hence (*poet.*) = climate, clime.

c **1400** *Destr. Troy* 339 With voiders vnder vines for violent sonnes. **1706** E. WARD *Wooden World Diss.* (1708) 99 A Mediterranean-Sun makes him as dry and huskish in one Summer, as a toasted Bisket. **1757** W. THOMPSON *R.N. Adv.* 8 In strong Winds and Suns the Casks shrink. **1847** C. BRONTE *J. Eyre* xxxiv, I would..toil under Eastern suns, in Asian deserts. **1852** TENNYSON *Ode Wellington* 101 Underneath another sun.

†**c.** In adverbial expressions referring to the time of the rising and setting of the sun, e.g. ***at the sun uprising***, (***a***)***rising***, ***setting***, ***going down***, ***toganging***. *Obs.* See also SUNRISE (-RIST), SUNRISING, SUNSET, SUNSETTING.

The ME. *sonne*, *sunne* is orig. genitive sing.

c **1300** *K. Horn* 847 (Laud), At þe sonne op rysyng [*MS. Harl.* vpspringe]. **1382** WYCLIF *Josh.* xii. 1 At the sonne arisynge [Vulg. *ad solis ortum*]. **1530** PALSGR. 805/2 At the sonne goyng downe, *sur le soleil couchant*. **1540–1** ELYOT *Image Gov.* 67 That no vitailyng house..should..receiue any person, either before the soonne risen, or after the sonne set. **1596** Dalrymple tr. *Leslie's Hist. Scot.* II. 286 About the sone togangeng.

3. *fig.* In allusion to the splendour of the sun or to its being a source of light and heat.

a. Applied to God and to persons. ***Sun of righteousness***, a title of Jesus Christ (after *Malachi* iv. 2).

a **1000** *Phœnix* 587 (Gr.) þær seo soþfæste sunne lihteð wlitiʒ ofer weoredum in wuldres byriʒ. *c* **1200** Ormin 16779 He nass nohht.. full Off all þe rihhte trowwþe, Noff Godess laress brihhte lem, Noff rihhtwisnessess sunne. **1382** Wyclif *Mal.* iv. 2 And to ȝou dredynge my name the sunne of riȝtwisnesse shal springe. **1387–8** T. Usk *Test. Love* II. ii. (Skeat) l. 15 The clips of me, that shulde be his shynande sonne. **1450–1530** *Myrr. our Ladye* III. 306 Heyle vyrgyn mother of god, thow arte the sonne of the day aboue and the mone of the nighte of the worlde. **1521** Fisher *Serm. agst. Luther* Wks. (1876) 312 The lyght of fayth (that shyneth from the spyrytuall sonne almyghty god). **1593** M. Roydon *Elegie* 132 in *Spenser's Astrophel*, Tis likely they acquainted soone, He was a Sun, and she a Moone. **1611** *Bible* Ps. lxxxiv. 11 The Lord God is a sunne and shield [Coverd. a light and defence]. *c* **1611** Chapman *Homer's Iliads* Anagram, Henrye Prince of Wales ovr Svnn, Heyr, Peace, Life. **1704** Norris *Ideal World* II. xii. 473 That eternal Word,..the great intelligible Sun of the whole Rational World. **1827** Keble *Chr. Y.*, *Evening Hymn*, Sun of my soul, thou Saviour dear, It is not night if thou be near. **1864** Tennyson *En. Ard.* 500 He is singing Hosanna in the highest: yonder shines The Sun of Righteousness. **1888** 'J. S. Winter' *Bootle's Childr.* xi, Any one of the Lizas and Pollies and Susies, the suns who had..lighted his heart's firmament.

b. Applied to things or conditions; esp. in expressions referring to prosperity or gladness.

1579 Spenser *Sheph. Cal.* Nov. 67 The sonne of all the world is dimme and darke. **1596** Dalrymple tr. *Leslie's Hist. Scot.* II. 306 Sa bricht a sone began to shine, that al Jnglismen was dung out of hail Scotland. *c* **1600** Shaks. *Sonn.* xlix. 6 When thou shalt strangely passe, And scarcely greete me with that sunne thine eye. **1601** —— *Jul. C.* v. iii. 63 The Sunne of Rome is set. **1612** Bacon *Ess.*, *Deformity* (Arb.) 250 The starres of naturall inclination, are sometimes obscured by the sunne of discipline and vertue. **1792** S. Rogers *Pleas. Mem.* II. 21 When joy's bright sun has shed his evening ray. **1818** Scott *Br. Lamm.* xxi, When the sun of my prosperity began to arise. **1878** Stubbs *Const. Hist.* III. xxi. 613 The sun of the Plantagenets went down in clouds and thick darkness.

4. a. The direct rays of the sun; sunlight; sunshine: orig. and chiefly in advb. phr. ***in the sun*** (OE. *on sunnan*), †***with, against, fornent the sun*** (OE. *wið sunnan*), †***under the sun***.

a **900** *O.E. Martyrol.* 7 March 36 He sæt ute on sunnan. *c* **1000** *Sax. Leechd.* III. 2 Ðelicge upweard wið hatre sunnan. *c* **1250** *Gen. & Ex.* 4075 Ben ðese hangen ðe sunne agen. *c* **1290** *S. Eng. Leg.* 193 þe sonne schon In at one hole. *c* **1375** *Sc. Leg. Saints* xviii. (*Egipciane*) 223 Brynt with þe sone, blak scho vas. **1390** Gower *Conf.* I. 323 Quod he, 'Thanne hove out of mi Sonne, And let it schyne into mi Tonne'. *c* **1400** Maundev. (Roxb.) iii. 10 On þe schire Thursday make þai þat breed..and dries it at þe sonne. **1542** Boorde *Dyetary* viii. (1870) 249 In sommer, kepe your necke and face from the sonne. **1573** Tusser *Husb.* (1878) 117 Wash sheepe..where water doth run, and let him go cleanly and drie in the sun. **1592** Shaks. *Ven. & Ad.* 800 Lusts effect is tempest after sunne. **1607** Topsell *Four-f. Beasts* 624 Some do sheare them within doores, and some in the open sunne abroad. **1659** *Caldwell Papers* (Maitland Club) I. 92 Sett it under the sone in the Caniculare dayes. **1671** Milton *Samson* 3 Yonder bank hath choice of Sun or shade. **16..** *Bessy Bell & Mary Gray* in Child *Ballads* (1890) IV. 77 To biek forenent the sin. **1775** Earl Carlisle in Jesse *Selwyn & Contemp.* (1844) III. 113 Clear frosty days, with a great deal of sun. **1812** *New Bot. Gard.* I. 78 Exposed to the full sun in some dry airy situation. **1853** M. Arnold *Scholar Gypsy* ii, Where the reaper..in the sun all morning binds the sheaves. **1854** *Poultry Chron.* II. 88 Putting trellis-work to admit the sun and air. **1860** Hogg *Fruit Man.* 145 Skin yellow, deep purplish next the sun. **1893** Selous *Trav. S.E. Africa* 98 There was still an hour's sun when we got here. **1898** P. Manson *Trop. Dis.* Introd. p. xi, Extreme cold may cause frost-bite; exposure to the sun, sun erythema.

b. *fig.*, chiefly in phr. ***in the sun***, †(*a*) free from care or sorrow; (*b*) exposed to public view.

out of God's blessing into the warm sun: see god *sb.* 5 c.

1600 Shaks. *A.Y.L.* II. v. 41 Who doth ambition shunne, and loues to liue i' th Sunne. **1602** —— *Ham.* I. ii. 67 *King.* How is it that the Clouds still hang on you? *Ham.* Not so my Lord, I am too much i' th' Sun. **1657** Owen *Schism* i. §13 It is ludicrously said of Physitians, the Effects of their skill lye in the Sunne, but their mistakes are covered in the Church-yard. *a* **1764** Lloyd *Poet* Poet. Wks. (1774) II. 31 Which seeks the sun of approbation. **1859** Tennyson *Marr. Geraint* 714 Since our fortune swerved from sun to shade.

(*c*) ***to have been in the sun*** (slang), to be intoxicated; also ***to have the sun in one's eyes***.

The origin of this phr. is not ascertained, but cf.:—

1619 R. Harris *Drunkard's Cup* 21 They bee buckt [*i.e.* soaked] with drinke, and then laid out to bee Sunn'd and scornd.

1770 *Gentl. Mag.* XL. 559 To express the Condition of an Honest Fellow, and no Flincher, under the Effects of good Fellowship, it is said that he [has]..Been in the Sun. **1840** Dickens *Old C. Shop* ii, Last night he had had 'the sun very strong in his eyes'.

(*d*) ***one's place in the sun***: an individual share in those things to which all have a right; hence, a position giving scope for the development of personal or national life.

The phrase is traceable to Pascal *Pensées* §73 (of autograph MS.) 'Ce chien est à moi, disaient ces pauvres enfants; c'est là ma place au soleil; voilà le commencement et l'image de l'usurpation de la terre.' This is rendered as follows in the earliest Engl. transl.:—

1688 J. Walker tr. *Pascal's Thoughts* xxxi. 246 This Dog is mine, said those poor Children; That's my place in the Sun: This is the beginning and Image of the Usurpation of all the Earth.

Quot. 1897 comes from a speech by Bernhard von Bülow, Chancellor of Germany.

[**1897** *Times* 7 Dec. 5/5 We desire to throw no one into the shade, but we also demand our own place in the sun-light.] **1901** *Times* 20 June 5/4 We have..fought for our place in the sun and have won it. It will be my business to see that we retain this place in the sun unchallenged, so that the rays of that sun may exert a fructifying influence upon our foreign trade and traffic. **1911** *Times* 28 Aug. 6/3 (Wilhelm II's Sp. at Hamburg, 27 Aug.) So that we may be sure that no one can dispute with us the place in the sun that is our due [*den uns zustehenden Platz an der Sonne*]. **1926** Galsworthy *Silver Spoon* I. iii. 22 Five million pounds spent on the organised travel of a hundred thousand working men.. would infect the working class with a feverish desire for a place in the sun. The world is their children's for the taking. **1928** C. R. Longwell in *Theory Continental Drift* (Amer. Assoc. Petroleum Geologists) 145 Perhaps the very completeness of this iconoclasm, this rebellion against the established order, has served to gain for the new hypothesis a place in the sun. **1939** L. MacNeice *Autumn Jrnl.* viii. 35 Sun shines easy, but I no longer Docket a place in the sun. **1951** 'J. Tey' *Daughter of Time* vii. 96, I sure would hate a brother who took my credit and my women and my place in the sun. **1967** V. Lincoln *Private Disgrace* (1968) iii. 37 Lizzie longed for a place in the sun. But..her longing for popularity was self-defeating.

5. With qualification or in phr. **a.** Sunrise or sunset as determining the period of a day. †***from sun to sun***: from sunrise to sunset; so †***between sun and sun***. *Obs.* or *arch.*

a **1400–50** *Wars Alex.* 2303 þe secund day before þe son he at þe cite wildid. **14..** in *Rel. Ant.* I. 319 And so the xix. day ys xiiij. owres long and half, fro son to son. *c* **1470** Henry *Wallace* IV. 281 Eftir the sone Wallas walkit about Vpon Tetht side. **1611** Shaks. *Cymb.* III. ii. 70 One score 'twixt Sun, and Sun, Madam's enough for you. **1631** Byfield *Doctr. Sabb.* 141 Take here day for the day-light betweene sunne and sunne. **1636** R. Skinner in Spurgeon *Treas. Dav.* Ps. xxvii. 11 If a man, travelling in the King's highway, be robbed between sun and sun. **1839** Pusey in Liddon *Life* (1893) II. xxii. 100 By to-morrow's sun she will be, by God's mercy.., where there is no need of the sun.

b. A (particular) day, as being determined by the rising of the sun. *poet.* or *rhet.*

1606 Shaks. *Tr. & Cr.* II. i. 134 By the fift houre of the Sunne. **1611** Beaum. & Fl. *Philaster* III. ii, Your vows are frosts, Fast for a night, and with the next sun gone. **1827** Scott *Highl. Widow* iv, He might count the days which could bring Hamish back to Breadalbane, and number those of his life within three suns more. **1844** Mrs. Browning *Drama of Exile* 1282 But one sun's length off from my happiness. **1855** Browning *Statue & Bust* 150 She turned from the picture at night to scheme Of tearing it out for herself next sun.

c. The time of the sun's apparent revolution in the zodiac, a year. *poet.*

1742 Young *Nt. Th.* v. 772 Virtue, not rolling suns, the mind matures. **1842** Tennyson *Locksley Hall* 138 The thoughts of men are widen'd with the process of the suns.

6. *gen.* A luminary; *esp.* a star as the centre of a system of worlds.

1390 Gower *Conf.* I. 275 A liht, as thogh it were a Sunne. **1623** Drumm. of Hawth. *Flowers of Sion, Hymn Fairest Fair* 229 The Moone moues lowest, siluer Sunne of Night. **1667** Milton *P.L.* VIII. 148 Other Suns perhaps With thir attendant Moons thou wilt descrie. **1847** Tennyson *Princ.* IV. 195 Till the Bear had wheel'd Thro' a great arc his seven slow suns. **1884** A. Giberne in *Sunday Mag.* Nov. 713/2 Stars of all colours,..white suns and red suns blue suns and purple suns, green suns and golden suns.

7. An appearance in the sky like the sun; a mock-sun, parhelion.

1377 Langl. *P. Pl.* B. III. 324 By syx sonnes and a schippe and half a shef of arwes. **1556** *Chron. Grey Friars* (Camden) 69 Abowte Ester was sene..three sonnes shenynge at one tyme in the eyer, that thei cowde not dysserne wych shulde be the very sonne. **1643** Baker *Chron.* (1653) 131 In the seventeenth year of his reign, were seen five Suns at one time together. **1665–6** etc. [see *mock-sun*, mock *a.* 2].

8. a. A figure or image of, or an ornament or vessel made to resemble, the sun (*e.g.* a monstrance with rays); *Her.* a representation of the sun, surrounded with rays and usually charged with the features of a human face; also freq. as the sign of an inn; hence, the name of an inn or of a room in an inn.

c **1450** *Brut* 463 All clothed in white,..with sonnys of golde on theire garmentes. **1593** Shaks. *3 Hen. VI*, II. i. 40 Henceforward will I beare Vpon my Targuet three faire shining Sunnes. **1613** Chapman *Maske Inns Court* A 2, Betwixt euery set of feathers..shin'd Sunnes of golde plate, sprinkled with pearle. **1625** B. Jonson *Staple of N.* IV. iv. 15 He beares In a field Azure, a Sunne proper, beamy. **1636** J. Taylor (Water P.) *Trav. Signes Zodiack* D 7 The Sun at Saint Mary Hill. **1768** *Ann. Reg.* I. 63/2 A magnificent sun of gold, ornamented with diamonds..was placed in the chapel of the palace. **1837** Dickens *Pickw.* li, 'Lights in the Sun, John; make up the fire'. **1837** Carlyle *Fr. Rev.* III. v. iv, Ciboriums, suns, candelabras. **1845** *Encycl. Metrop.* XIV. 243/1 A superb vessel of gold, called the Sun of the Holy Sacrament. **1859** Tennyson *Merlin & V.* 474 The Sun In dexter chief.

b. A kind of circular firework: see quot. 1875.

1749 [see cascade *sb.* 2 b]. **1852** Burn *Naval & Milit. Dict.* I. (1863), *Gloire*, fixed sun in fireworks of very large dimension. **1875** Knight *Dict. Mech.* 874 *Fixed Sun* (Pyrotechnics), a device composed of a certain number of jets of fire distributed circularly like the spokes of a wheel. All the fuses take fire at once... *Glories* are large suns with several rows of fusees. *Ibid.* 1933 *Revolving-sun*, a pyrotechnic device, consisting of a wheel upon whose periphery rockets of different styles are fixed,..one is lighted in succession after another.

†**9. a.** *Her.* In blazoning by the names of heavenly bodies, the name for the tincture Or. **b.** *Alch.* Gold. *Obs.*

1572 Bossewell *Armorie* II. 108 The Garbe is of the Sonne royally supported with two Lyons. **1610** B. Jonson *Alch.* II. i, The great med'cine! Of which one part proiected on a hundred Of Mercurie, or Venus, or the Moone, Shall turne it to as many of the Sunne. **1651** French *Distill.* vi. 197 It will resolve the bodies of the Sunne, and Moone.

10. = sun-fish 1 b.

1807 P. Gass *Jrnl.* 29 The fish here are generally pike, cat, sun, perch, and other common fish. **1896** P. A. Bruce *Econ. Hist. Virginia* I. 113 There were in the waters of Virginia when first explored, grampus,..perch, tailor, sun.

II. Attributive uses and combinations.

11. Simple attrib. **a.** = Of, belonging, or relating to the sun, sunlight, or sunshine, as ***sun-blaze, -fire, -flame, -flush, -glare, -glaze, -glimpse, -glint, -glory, -mote, -tide, -warmth***; with reference to the worship of the sun, etc. (see 1 c), as ***sun-chariot, -child, -deity*** (= sun-god), ***-hero, -horse, -maiden, -man, -sign, -spirit, -temple***.

1837 Carlyle *Fr. Rev.* III. v. iii, Lyons, which we saw in dread *sunblaze, that Autumn night. *Ibid.* II. IV. v, Dawn on us, thou *Sun-Chariot of a new Berline. **1839** T. Mitchell *Frogs of Aristoph.* Introd. 16 That Colchis, from which came the *sun-children. **1872** Calverley *Lovers & Refl.* in *Fly Leaves* (1903) 107 And O the *sundazzle on bark and bight! **1899** *Eng. Hist. Rev.* Apr. 219 The great Sky-shining female deity who mounts to heaven by a ladder and becomes the *Sun-deity. **1867** Pearson *Hist. Eng.* I. 20 The Sulevæ appear, from their name, to have been *sun-elves. **1820** Shelley *Ode to Liberty* v, Each head Within its cloudy wings with *sun-fire garlanded. **1892** J. Tait *Mind in Matter* (ed. 3) 324 Like other fires, the sun-fires need to be stirred. **1857** Thornbury *Songs Caval.* 255 To quench the *sun-flame in the west. **1880** Le Conte *Sight* 27 In the shade of a very thick tree-top the *sun-flecks are circular like the sun. **1924** G. B. Shaw *St. Joan* ii. 27 Joan (rising, with a *sunflush of reckless happiness irradiating her face). **1883** *American* VII. 169 The *sun-glare of such worldly joys. **1890** 'R. Boldrewood' *Col. Reformer* (1891) 356 This.. country, all sand and sun-glare. **1958** C. Tomlinson *Seeing is Believing* (1960) 1 A quick gold, dyeing the uncovering beach With *sunglaze. **1813** Scott *Rokeby* IV. xvii, Like a *sun-glimpse through a shower. **1880** J. E. Watt *Poet. Sk.* 85 Oor *sun-glints o' glory are followed by gloom. **1883** Stevenson *Silverado Sq.* 200 The deep shaft, with the sun-glints and the water-drops. **1929** D. H. Lawrence *Pansies* 117 Men should group themselves into a new order Of sun-men..walking each in his own sun-glory. **1911** F. H. Woods in *Encycl. Relig. & Ethics* IV. 355/1 Cúchulainn as a *sun-hero..was directly connected with Lug, the sun-god. **1898** *Westm. Rev.* May 513 The worship of the *sun-horse. **1611** *Bible* 2 Chron. xiv. 5 He tooke away out of all the cities of Iudah, the high places and the images [*marg. Heb.* and *R.V.* *sun-images]. **1898** *Westm. Rev.* May 513 The car in which the Ashvins drew the *sun-maiden to be married to the moon-god. **1929** *Sun-man [see *sun-glory* above]. **1933** W. de la Mare *Fleeting* 96 The *sun-motes where the mosses drowse. **1893** Addy *Hall of Waltheof* 93 The sign of the cross was itself a *sun-sign amongst the heathen Northmen. **1877** J. E. Carpenter tr. *Tiele's Hist. Relig.* 22 The *sun-spirit was called simply *teotl*, 'the spirit' *par excellence*. **1833** Mrs. Hemans *And I too in Arcadia* 20 Insect-wings in *sun-streaks dancing. **1865** J. H. Ingraham *Pillar of Fire* (1872) 167 The city of Baalbec is famous for its *sun-temple. **1850** Mrs. Browning *Early Rose* xii, Singing gladly all the moontide, Never waiting for the *suntide. **1886** A. Winchell *Walks Geol. Field* 245 The slanting *sun-warmth of the early morning.

b. = Caused by exposure to the sun, induced by the heat of the sun, as ***sun-blister, -film, -haze, -headache, -pain, -rash, -scorch, -thaw, -weariness***, etc. See also *sun-blight*, *-fever* in 13, sunburn, sunstroke, suntan *sb.* (and *a.*).

1883 *Good Words* Aug. 543/2 Paint..of doors and window-frames..'picked out' by irregular touches of *sun-blister. **1910** *Blackw. Mag.* Dec. 829 The smooth *sun-bubbles in the worn green paint Upon the doors. **1898** P. Manson *Trop. Diseases* xii. 204 The phenomena of *sun-erythema. **1930** E. Pound *XXX Cantos* ii. 11 Snipe come for their bath, bend out their wing-joints, Spread wet wings to the *sun-film. **1860** Tyndall *Glac.* I. ii. 9 The pines, gleaming through the *sunhaze. **1898** P. Manson *Trop. Diseases* Introd. p. xi, Exposure to the sun..[may cause] *sun headache. **1855** Dunglison *Med. Lex.*, *Hemicrania*.., pain, confined to one half the head. It is almost always of an intermittent character;—at times, continuing only as long as the sun is above the horizon; and hence sometimes called **Sun-pain. Ibid.*, **Sun Rash*, Lichen. **1907** W. De Morgan *Alice-for-Short* xix. 208 With her hair shaken out and only the least little shade of *sun-scorch from long exposure on the inexhaustible sands. **1798** Coleridge *Frost at Midnight* 70 The nigh thatch Smokes in the *sun-thaw. **1898** P. Manson *Trop. Diseases* xii. 201 These cases might be classified under the term **Sun-traumatism*. **1897** 'H. S. Merriman' *In Kedar's Tents* xxvii. 299 Likely to fall from sheer fatigue and *sun-weariness.

c. = Serving for protection against the sun, used to keep the sunlight off or out, as ***sun-awning, -blind, -canopy, -curtain, -filter, -lotion, -shield, -shutter, -umbrella***: see also *sun-bonnet, -hat, -helmet* in 13, sunshade.

1883 Moloney *W. African Fisheries* 19 These clothes wound around the head of their owners, act as a *sun-awning. **1847** *Zoologist* V. 1643 The shutter-blind (or *sun-blind) of the sitting-room. **1852** Dickens *Bleak Ho.* xix, A shop with a sun-blind. **1598** Hakluyt *Voy.* I. 69 A certaine *Sun Canopie, or small tent (which was to bee caried ouer the Emperours head). **1923** *Heal & Son Catal.: Kitchen Furnit. & Garden Furnit.* 10 Hammock..with sun canopy and fittings complete. **1906** *Westm. Gaz.* 14 July 4/2 White linen *sun-covers embroidered in white. **1893** *Scribner's Mag.* June 746/2 A dingy red *sun-curtain. **1970** *Cape Times* 28 Oct. 18/4 You can select your material from our large range of fabrics in tweed, *sun-filter, satin, taffeta, shantung and parchment. **1979** P. NIESEWAND *Member of Club* vi. 40 The sun filter curtains were..green, yellow and orange stripes. **1967** H. PINTER *Tea Party* 49 You're off to Spain... What *sun lotion do you use, Lois? **1974** W. GARNER *Big enough Wreath* ix. 118 One of the two guards stepped out of the gate-house, *sun-shields hiding his eyes. **1977** G. SCOTT *Hot Pursuit* iii. 29 The driver had my wrist. .. His other hand had to stay on the wheel and his knife was behind the sunshield. **1909** LE QUEUX *House of Whispers* xxii, That..white house with the green *sun-shutters. **1831** *Boston* (Mass.) *Transcript* 31 May 3/2 Light *Sun Umbrellas..are offered at low prices. **1867** A. D. WHITNEY *Summer in Leslie Goldthwaite's Life* viii. 173 Miss Craydocke appeared..under her great brown sun-umbrella. **1904** *Daily Chron.* 21 June 8/3 Votaries of the abolition of head-gear..trusting to a sun-umbrella for shelter.

d. = affording maximum access to the sun; used, worn, etc., for sun-bathing; as ***sun balcony, loggia, parlour, porch, room; sun-dress, -suit, -top; sun-chair.***

1971 'D. HALLIDAY' *Dolly & Doctor Bird* vii. 90 A sun balcony..ran round the..side of the villa. **1976** 'W. TREVOR' *Children of Dynmouth* i. 19 Mrs Dass was reclining on a sun-chair in the bow-window. **1942** R. GODDEN *Breakfast with Nikolides* vi. 138 Her spotted sun-dress, her sun hat and sandals. **1976** I. MURDOCH *Henry & Cato* II. 319 Gerda was wearing a sun dress with shoulder straps. **1965** Sun loggia [see *pram-park* s.v. PRAM[2] 3]. **1911** Sun-parlour [see SOLARIUM 2 a]. **1940** AUDEN *Another Time* 92 The poor old fat banker in the sun-parlour car. **1918** M. B. COOKE *Threshold* 53 Joan went in search of Mr. Farwell and found him reading in the sun porch. **1955** Sun-porch [see MAKE *sb.*[2] 13]. **1977** *Stornoway Gaz.* 27 Aug. 7/5 (Advt.), For Sale. Detached stone-built house..containing living room, bedroom, kitchen, bathroom, sun porch. **1907** E. WHARTON *Fruit of Tree* III. xxiv. 349 A glazed 'sun-room', mosaic pavements, a marble fountain. **1935** *Archit. Rev.* LXXVIII. 167 It contains nine different types of flat, each with an open balcony and a glass-enclosed sun-room that can be thrown open in fine weather. **1977** *Age* (Melbourne) 18 Jan. 9/6 (Advt.), Comp. an imposing ent. hall, a large and charming sittingroom,..mod. kitchen opens to an excellent sunroom. **1929** *Punch* 17 July p. xxxv/2 (Advt.), If preparing for a sun-bath, a swim, or both, slip into the Jantzen Sun-suit! **1971** 'D. HALLIDAY' *Dolly & Doctor Bird* xi. 147, I got out into the garden in my sunsuit. **1937** *Night & Day* 29 July 22/2 Deeply to be deplored are such things as..sun-top dresses. **1972** W. ELLIS *Knife Edge* vi. 114 Emma..innocently seductive in her shorts and sun-top.

12. *Comb.* **a.** Objective and objective genitive, as ***sun-worshipper, -worshipping; sun-cult, -worship; sun-affronting, clouding, -confronting, -creating, -defying, -disdaining, -eclipsing, -enticing, -expelling, -loving, -outshining, -resembling, -screening, -shunning, -staining***, etc., adjs.

1648 J. BEAUMONT *Psyche* VI. ccii, Sharp was their sight, and further could descry Than any Eagle's *Sun-affronting eye. **1835** *Court Mag.* VI. 205 *Sun-bringing May! **1930** R. CAMPBELL *Adamastor* 91 Stripped are the great *sun-clouding planes. **1658** E. PHILLIPS *Myst. Love* Gen. Lud. (1685) 32 Rainbow. Chequer'd,..eye pleasing, *sun-confronting. *a* **1894** CHRISTINA ROSSETTI *Out of the Deep* vii, A handful of *sun-courting heliotrope. **1847** EMERSON *Poems* 84 None so backward in the troop,..But knows the *sun-creating sound. **1911** *Nation* 23 Dec. 510/2 The *sun-cult of Mithras. **1879** LONGFELLOW *Poet. Wks.* (1910) 137 There is a mountain in the distant West That, *sun-defying, in its deep ravines Displays a cross of snow upon its side. **1904** W. DE LA MARE *Henry Brocken* xiii. 150 The *sun-disdaining eagle. **1612** J. DAVIES *Muse's Sacrifice* (Grosart) II. 13/1 Thy *Sunne-ecclipsing glorious face. **1904** W. DE LA MARE *Henry Brocken* vii. 79 His *sun-enticing thatch of hair. **1810** E. MOOR *Hindu Pantheon* 142 A low *sun-excluding viranda. **1591** SHAKS. *Two Gent.* IV. iv. 158 Since she..threw her *Sun-expelling Masque away, The ayre hath staru'd the roses in her cheekes. **1562** *Sun-following [see *Sun spurge*, 13 b]. **1607** J. DAY *Parl. Bees* i. (1888) 218 *Sun-loving marigolds. **1872** CHRISTINA ROSSETTI *Sing Song* 81 Fly away, Sun-loving swallow. **1648** J. BEAUMONT *Psyche* IX. cxxvi, That *Sun-outshining Crown. *a* **1774** TUCKER *Lt. Nat.* (1834) II. 414 The scarlet poppy, and *sun-resembling marigold. **1958** *Which?* I. IV. 17/2 CR had a number of the preparations tested for their *sunscreening quality. **1602** HERING *Anatomyes* 4 *Sun-shunning night-birds. *a* **1586** SIR P. SIDNEY *Arcadia* I. i. (1912) 7 Not able to beare her *sun-stayning excellencie. **1813** *Monthly Rev.* LXXI. 477 The *sun-worship of the Persians, and the manicheism of the Zend-Avesta..are classed with the monotheism of the Jews. **1861** PALEY *Æschylus* (ed. 2) *Pers.* 234 *note*, The sun is called *ἄναξ* in reference to the Persian doctrine of sun-worship. **1867** BRANDE & COX *Dict. Sci.*, etc. s.v., The evidence of language..tends to show the general.. existence of sun worship among the various tribes of men in the earliest ages. *a* **1901** W. BRIGHT *Age Fathers* (1903) I. xi. 204 Terrifying the Christians by such a proof that mere persistency in Christianity, or in rejection of sun-worship, was a capital crime. **1884** OGILVIE, *Sun-worshipper. **1903** *Daily Chron.* 24 Oct. 6/2 The Sun Worshippers were also obliged to go about naked. **1904** BUDGE *3rd & 4th Egypt. Rooms Brit. Mus.* 122 When the first sun-worshippers entered Egypt. **1966** B. H. DEAL *Fancy's Knell* v. 77 Her red bathing suit [was] brilliant against her white skin. Evidently she wasn't the sun worshiper the others were. **1617** PURCHAS *Pilgrimage* v. vii. §6 (ed. 3) 608 Wee haue..spoken of the Bulloches,..*Sunne-worshipping, Giantly bignesse, and Inhumane humanitie, in eating mans-flesh.

b. Instrumental = by or with the sun, as ***sun-alight, -ambered, -awakened, -bedazzled, -begotten, -bemused, -bitten, -black, -blanched, -blazoned, -bleached, -blown, -bred, -brown, -browned, -bruised, -caught, -charged, -coloured, -compelled, -cracked, -dappled, -dark, -darkened, -dazed, -delighted, -desired, -detested, -dimmed, -dozed, -drawn, -driven, -eaten, -faded, -fed, -flaked, -flecked*** (also *fig.*), ***-flooded, -flushed, -fondled, -forgotten, -freckled, -fringed, -gilded, -gilt, -glazed, -graced, -heated, -illumined, -kissed*** (also *spec.* of fruit, freq. with commercial spelling *-kist*), ***-lashed, -licked, -loved, -mellowed*** (*fig.*), ***-parched, -ripened, -scarred, -scorched, -scorching, -scrubbed, -sculptured, -shafted, -shot, -shy, -soaked*** (also *fig.*), ***-stained, -strewn, -struck, -swart, -swung, -warm, -warmed, -whitened, -withered***, etc., adjs. See also *sun-beaten* in 13, SUN-BRIGHT 2, SUNBURNT, SUN-DRIED, SUNLIT, SUN-STRICKEN, SUNSTRUCK.

1904 HARDY *Dynasts* I. I. v. 32 Till we sight Famed Milan's aisles of marble, *sun-alight. **1951** W. DE LA MARE *Winged Chariot* 23 *Sun-ambered, weathered, sweet as new-mown hay. **1820** SHELLEY *Prometh. Unb.* II. iii. 37 The *sun-awakened avalanche! **1946** W. DE LA MARE *Traveller* 18 A dwindling, *sun-bedazzled moon. **1687** DRYDEN *Hind & P.* I. 311 A slimy-born and *sun-begotten Tribe. **1912** W. DE LA MARE *Listeners* 24 A sea Of sun-begotten grain. **1957** L. DURRELL *Bitter Lemons* 118 We'll all subside into *sun-bemused tranquillity. **1920** H. G. WELLS *Mr. Britling sees it Through* I. iii. 72 It was a tall, lean, *sun-bitten youngish man of forty perhaps. **1923** D. H. LAWRENCE *Birds, Beasts & Flowers* 46 Columns dark and soft, *Sunblack men, Soft shafts, sunbreathing mouths. **1947** DYLAN THOMAS *Let.* 3 Aug. (1966) 318 Sunblack webfooted waterboys..bleed from the heat. **1905** *Century Mag.* Aug. 489/1 These stern-faced, *sun-blackened young men. **1840** BROWNING *Sordello* VI. 871 The few fine locks Stained like pale honey oozed from topmost rocks, *Sunblanched the live-long summer. **1919** V. WOOLF *Night & Day* xx. 275 The *sun-blazoned windows. **1835** J. E. ALEXANDER *Sketches in Portugal* xi. 267 Peasants with long and *sun-bleached hair floating about their shoulders..stood behind fruit and vegetable baskets. **1979** *Arizona Daily Star* 5 Aug. A10/3 The approaching slick has not hurt business at the long strip of sun-bleached sand. **1899** KIPLING *Stalky* iii. 67 They reached the *sun-blistered pavilion..just before roll-call. **1595** B. BARNES *Sonnets* lxxx, A *sunne-blowne rose. **1601–11** CHESTER *Poems* (1878) 17 My *Sunne-bred lookes. **1648** J. BEAUMONT *Psyche* x. cccxcv, He..reach'd not his designed Bethany Till two days more their Sun-bred lives had spent. **1844** *Penny Mag.* 17 Aug. 314/2 These half-clad *sun-bronzed fellows..are Arabs. **1861** A. J. MUNBY *Diary* 19 May in D. Hudson *Munby* (1972) 93 His frank intelligent face..has a pure rich *sunbrown tint. **1871** PALGRAVE *Lyr. Poems* 88 Thy sun-brown cheek. **1827** SCOTT *Highl. Widow* i, Donald's *sun-browned countenance. **1957** L. DURRELL *Bitter Lemons* 138 How could such a *sun-bruised world be transformed? **1932** D. GASCOYNE *Roman Balcony* 9 A rusty and serrated leaf, Alive with *sun-caught moisture. **1942** E. BOWEN *Seven Winters* 32 A pinkish *suncharged gauze. **1926** D. H. LAWRENCE *Sun* iv. 13 She stood a few steps, erect, in front of the *sun-coloured woman. **1922** JOYCE *Ulysses* 712 He would hear and somehow reluctantly, *sun-compelled, obey the summons of recall. **1859** R. F. BURTON *Centr. Afr.* in *Jrnl. Geog. Soc.* XXIX. 154 A grassy plain of ..*suncracked earth. **1792** R. CUMBERLAND *Calvary* VIII. 15 The rays, That from the Savior's *sun-crown'd temples beam'd. **1924** R. CAMPBELL *Flaming Terrapin* v. 80 The *sun-dappled herds a-skipping to the song. **1983** A. PRICE *Gunner Kelly* II. 77 The *sun-dappled pools where the stream idled between the trees. **1924** GALSWORTHY *Forest* IV. i, (*stage direction*) Franks comes in. Very *sun-dark and thin. **1926** D. H. LAWRENCE *Sun* iii. 11 The child too was another creature, with a peculiar quiet, *sun-darkened absorption. *Ibid.* i. 6 She went home, only half-seeing, sun-blinded and *sun-dazed. **1942** J. MASEFIELD *Generation Risen* 70 *Sun-delighted earth. **1925** BLUNDEN *English Poems* 55 It glittered mist and fire amain, *Sun-desired, desiring. **1931** R. CAMPBELL *Georgiad* i. 25 Shame to show your *sun-detested sight Among the sons of valour and delight. **1917** D. H. LAWRENCE *Look! We have come Through!* 101 The stars, in their *sun-dimmed closes. *a* **1918** W. OWEN *Poems* (1920) 18 So we drowse, *sun-dozed. **1845** BAILEY *Festus* (ed. 2) 304 The foam-bubble, *Sun-drawn out of the sea into the clouds. **1909** E. POUND *Personae* 48 The stars of heaven sheathe their glory And *sun-driven forth-goeth Settentrion. **1926** D. H. LAWRENCE *Plumed Serpent* xx. 343 She stepped across the *sun-eaten plaza. **1887** KIPLING *From Sea to Sea* (1899) I. 34 The maroon cloth..is..neither strained nor meagre nor *sunfaded. **1926** D. H. LAWRENCE *Sun* iv. 13 Her sun-faded fair hair in a little cloud. **1917** E. POUND *Lustra* 184 The air is solid sunlight, *apricus*. *Sun-fed we dwell there. **1887** HISSEY *Holiday on Road* 260 A *sun-filled atmosphere. **1770** J. ROSS *Contempl.* (MS. Wks.) 226 Fragrant Gales refresh the *Sun-flagged Flow'rs. **1934** S. SPENDER *Vienna* iii. 30 The once *sun-flaked walls. **1844** J. R. LOWELL *Poems* 17 Dim vistas, sprinkled o'er with *sun-flecked green, Wound through the thickset trunks. *a* **1950** J. CLEARY in Murdoch & Drake-Brockman *Austral. Short Stories* (1951) 438 Her laugh is a warm, tumbling sound, sun-flecked and musical. **1904** M. A. VON ARNIM *Adventures of Elizabeth in Rügen* 156 Up there in the *sun-flooded space among the shimmering bracken. **1862** G. M. HOPKINS *Poems* (1967) 10 So those Mermaidens crowded to my rock, And thicken'd, like that drifted bloom, the flock *Sun-flushed. *a* **1960** M. TRIST in 'B. JAMES' *Austral. Short Stories* (1963) 258 He was a nice baby, blue-eyed, fair-haired and with sun-flushed skin. **1935** L. MACNEICE *Poems* 42 The light on the *sun-fondled trees. **1881** O. WILDE *Poems* 219 Bare to *sun-forgotten fields the fire of the sun! **1925** S. O'CASEY *Let.* 7 Feb. (1975) I. 131 One can hardly look for the blossoming of roses in these sun-forgotten places. **1916** W. B. YEATS *Eight Poems*, Imagining a man, And his *sun-freckled face. **1830** TENNYSON *Madeline* ii, Like little clouds *sun-fringed. **1892** STEVENSON & OSBOURNE *Wrecker* xii. 190 Day after day, in the *sun-gilded cabin, the whiskey-dealer's thermometer stood at 84°. **1960** J. BETJEMAN *Summoned by Bells* iii. 26 Only one harbinger of future woe Came to me in those far, sun-gilded days. **1807** W. IRVING *Salmag.* v. (1824) 83 Along Ausonia's *sun-gilt shore. **1837–42** HAWTHORNE *Twice-told T.* (1851) II. xi. 162 The sun-gilt spire of the church. **1915** W. J. LOCKE *Jaffery* iii. 36 A fair-bearded.. giant..ran up and laid a couple of great *sun-glazed hands on my shoulders. **1600** TOURNEUR *Transf. Metam.* viii, Wks. 1878 II. 192 No *sun-grac'd mount? how can the sun mounts grace When mountaines seeke his count'nance to deface? **1856** KANE *Arctic Explor.* I. xx. 242 *Sun-heated snow-surfaces. **1799** T. CAMPBELL *Pleas. Hope* I. 507 His *sun-illumined zone. **1873** E. BRENNAN *Witch of Nemi*, etc. 249 Upon those *sun-kissed hills. **1920** Sunkist [see *Sunshine State* s.v. SUNSHINE *sb.* 6]. **1979** N. & I. LYONS *Champagne Blues* 172 I'll have a nice glass of tomato juice with a quarter of a Sunkist lemon. **1891** O. WILDE *Picture of Dorian Gray* ix. 161 The green, flickering, *sun-lashed garden. **1926** D. H. LAWRENCE *David* ii. 18 He beats himself against the *sun-licked pebbles. *c* **1611** CHAPMAN *Iliad* v. 177 In the *Sun-lou'd Lycian greenes. **1894** H. NISBET *Bush Girl's Rom.* 12 Sun-loved,..but not shallow streams. **1849** C. BRONTË *Shirley* xxxvi. 625 My intention was then formed, but not mature for communication; now it is ripe, *sun-mellowed, perfect. **1848** J. R. LOWELL *Poems* 2nd Ser. 65 The next heart-beat, the wind-hurled pile,..Bursts rattling over the *sun-parched roof. **1915** G. FRANKAU *Tid'apa* i. 7 Do you know our churchyard at Aden; lone tombs on a sun-parched plain. **1935** *Discovery* June 162/2 The fruit is fully *sun-ripened and canned immediately after gathering. **1897** J. L. ALLEN *Choir Invisible* xv. 159 Frenzied fightings and awful deaths had left but the *sun-scarred dust. **1753** *Chambers' Cycl.* Suppl., **Sun-scorched*, a term used by our gardners..to express a distemperature of fruit trees. **1897** MARY KINGSLEY *W. Africa* 358 His march over the sun-scorched plateau. **1633** C. FAREWELL *East-Ind. Colation* 52 Their *sunschorching dayes. **1955** P. LARKIN *Less Deceived* 19 And how remote that bare and *sunscrubbed room. **1955** S. SPENDER *Coll. Poems 1928–53* 159 Already you are beginning to become Fallen tree-trunk with *sun-sculptured limbs. **1910** W. DE LA MARE *Three Mulla-Mulgars* xiv. 193 Nod lifted his face and saw..the vast *sun-shafted precipices. **1890** R. BRIDGES *Shorter Poems* IV. xiv. 75 I'll sit with my love in the scented hay: And watch the *sunshot palaces high. **1936** C. DAY LEWIS *Noah & Waters* 52 Then plunge out of heaven upon his prey, Slanting and swiftsure as a sun-shot ray. *a* **1973** J. R. R. TOLKIEN *Silmarillion* (1977) xvi. 135 What errand have you, Dark Elf, in my lands? An urgent matter, perhaps, that keeps one so *sun-shy abroad by day. **1910** H. G. WELLS *Hist. Mr. Polly* vii. 212 He..dreamt..of the East and West Indies until his heart ached to see those *sun-soaked lands before he died. **1960** *Times* 29 Feb. 15/1 Falla's four sun-soaked dances of Spain. **1916** D. H. LAWRENCE *Twilight in Italy* 36 Her hands and her face were all sun-bleached and *sun-stained. **1916** BLUNDEN *Harbingers* 3, I still can watch the purple-slumbrous main Fretting the *sun-strewn air. **1794** T. DWIGHT *Greenfield Hill* VII. 154 Idolatry fans off the vernal breeze, And *sun-struck Labour, phrenzied, sinks to peace. **1896** A. E. HOUSMAN *Shropshire Lad* xlii. 62 By blowing realms of woodland With sunstruck vanes afield ..Content at heart I followed With my delightful guide. **1963** A. LUBBOCK *Austral. Roundabout* 14 Grey salt-bush, tufts of coarse brownish grass, and stony soil merge into the sun-struck distance. **1867** JEAN INGELOW *Christ's Resurr.* xiii, Indian glades, Where kneel the *sun-swart maids. **1876** 'OUIDA' *Winter City* vi, Blown by a fresh breeze on a *sun-swept moorland. **1874** J. R. LOWELL in *Atlantic Monthly* May 588 Indifferent as the figures on a slate Are to the planet's *sun-swung curve Whose bright returns they calculate. **1957** T. HUGHES *Hawk in Rain* 39 He smiles in a mirror, shrinking the whole Sun-swung zodiac of light to a trinket shape On the rise of his eye. **1856** KANE *Arctic Expl.* II. xxvii. 271 The varied glitter of *sun-tipped crystal. **1819** SHELLEY in Dowden *Life* (1886) II. 247 The soil which is stirring in the *sun-warm earth. **1884** *Expositor* Feb. 129 The physical and chemical forces of the *sun-warmed earth. **1848** J. R. LOWELL *Poems* 2nd Ser. 64 A great cloud edged with *sun-whitened spray. **1844** FABER *Sir Lancelot* xii, *Sun-withered wreaths.

c. Similative and parasynthetic, as ***sun-broad, -clear*** (fig. after G. *sonnenklar*), ***-dazzling, -gold, -heavy, red, -round, -sweet*** adjs.; ***sun-eyed, -faced, feathered, -gloved, -haired, -leaved*** adjs. See also SUN-BRIGHT 1.

1590 SPENSER *F.Q.* II. ii. 21 His *sunbroad shield. **1847** EMERSON *Poems* (1857) 57 Make the aged eye *sun-clear. **1885** *Daily News* 10 Nov. (Ware *Passing Eng.*), It is sun-clear that [etc.]. **1945** W. DE LA MARE *Burning-Glass* 36 The grass takes on a shade Of paradisal green, sun-clear. **1630** J. TAYLOR (Water P.) *Whore* Wks. II. 111/1 Your eyes *sun-dazeling coruscancy will exile all the cloudie vapours of.. melancholly. **1845** BAILEY *Festus* (ed. 2) 222 The *sun-eyed angels. **1602** *Narcissus* (1893) 220 Tell our *Sunnfac't sonne his fortune. **1852** 'NIGHTLARK' *Meanderings of Mem.* I. 196 Sunfaced choristers. **1649** G. DANIEL *Trinarch., Hen. IV*, cccxxxv, The faire *Sun-feather'd Birds. **1939** DYLAN THOMAS *Map of Love* 6 Comes love's anatomist with *sun-gloved hand Who picks the live heart on a diamond. **1911** E. POUND *Canzoni* 5 Guerdoned by thy *sun-gold traces. **1938** S. SPENDER *Trial of Judge* I. 18 Let the nordic *Sunhaired head be matched against cloud drifts. **1918** D. H. LAWRENCE *New Poems* 9 The glimmer of the limes, *sun-heavy sleeping, Goes trembling past me up the College wall. **1939** DYLAN THOMAS in *Poetry* Feb. 26 The *sun-leaved holy candlewoods. **1861** L. L. NOBLE *Icebergs* 176 The *sun-red blushes of beauty. **1918** E. SITWELL *Clown's Houses* 14 Like wooden bumpkins' *sun-round stare. **1937** W. DE LA MARE *This Year, Next Year* 50 Came the woodman with his axe into the *sun-sweet glade.

d. In various advb. relations, = in, to, from (etc.) the sun, as ***sun-arrayed, -born, -delighting, -descended, -drunk, -fast, -flashed, -gazing, -glittering, -glowing, -honeyed, -peering, -shading, -sodden, -steeped***, etc. adjs.; ***sun-exposure; sunbask*** vb. intr. See also SUN-PROOF.

1593 NASHE *Christ's T.* Wks. (Grosart) IV. 249 A bright *sunne-arraied Angell. **1967** C. B. CHRISTESEN in *Coast to Coast 1965–6* 29 When..taxed on this subject while *sun-basking by herself on the top deck. **1656** COWLEY *Pindar. Odes, Plagues of Egypt* vi, They mount up higher, Where never *Sun-born Frog durst to aspire. **1819** NEWMAN *Spring* Poems (1906) 52 Spring! fairest season of the sunborn four. **1883** J. COLBORNE *With Hicks Pasha* (1884) 157 The sun-born fellah soldier, who works stripped under the burning rays. **1632** QUARLES *Div. Fancies* II. xcviii. 110 The *Sun-delighting Flye. **1807** J. BARLOW *Columb.* I. 244 The *sun-descended race. **1925** A. HUXLEY *Selected Poems* 16 The *sun-drunk petals. **1898** P. MANSON *Trop. Diseases* xii. 204 Sequelæ..attributable to *sun exposure. **1962** *Economist* 21 Apr. 250/1 The French have produced a [plastic] geranium which is guaranteed to be *sunfast. **1611** BEAUM. & FL. *Maid's Trag.* I. ii, The day breaks here, and yon *sun-flaring stream Shot from the south. **1905** *Sun-flashed [see IRIDESCE *v.*]. **1876** WHITNEY *Sights & Insights* xxxii. 305 The sweet, *sunfull heaven. **1611** W. BARKSTED *Hiren* (1876) 99 The *sunne-gaz'd Eagle. **1802** SHAW *Gen. Zool.* III. I. 245 *Sun-gazing Lizard, *Lacerta Helioscopa*. **1916** BLUNDEN *Harbingers* 11 Odysseus came..And called without my strong *sun-glittering gates. **1926** D. H. LAWRENCE *Sun* iv. 14 Like a blot of ink on the pale, *sun-glowing slope. **1953** DYLAN THOMAS *Under Milk Wood* (1954) 44 There's the clip clop of horses on the *sun-honeyed cobbles of the humming streets. **1923** D. H. LAWRENCE *Birds, Beasts & Flowers* 84 John, oh John, Thou honourable bird *Sun-peering eagle. **1626** J. GRESHAM *Pict. Incest* (1876) 26 Her dainty fingers..Into *sun-shading litle boughes doe turne. **1822** BYRON *Juan* VIII. lxxxii, The Nile's *sun-sodden slime. **1833** TENNYSON *Lotos Eaters* 74 *Sun-steep'd at noon, and in the moon Nightly dew-fed.

13. a. Special Combs.: **sun arc** *Cinematogr.*, an arc lamp used to simulate sunlight in film production; †**sun-arising**, = SUNRISING; **sun-back**, a low-cut back of a garment; also *attrib.*; **sunbaking** *vbl. sb. Austral.*, sunbathing; **sun-bath**, an exposure to the direct rays of the sun, orig. as a method of medical treatment; basking in the sun; so ***sun-bathing*** sb. and adj.; **sun-bathed** *a.*, bathed in sunshine; **sun-bather**, one who takes a sun-bath; hence (as back-formation) **sun-bathe** *v. intr.*; **sun-beat, -beaten** *adjs.*, upon which the sun beats; **sun bed**, (*a*) a lightweight bed or couch for sun-bathing; (*b*) a bed designed for artificial sun-bathing in ultraviolet light; **Sunbelt** *U.S.* (also as two words) [BELT *sb.*[1] 5 a], a zone consisting of the most southerly states of the U.S., extending from California in the west to the Carolinas in the east; **sun-blast** (now *dial.*), a sudden emission or burst of sunshine (also *fig.*); **sun-blight** (*Australia*), an inflammatory affection of the eyes caused by exposure to sunshine; **sun-bonnet**, a light bonnet with a projection in front and a cape behind to protect the head and neck from the sun; hence **sun-bonneted** *a.*; **sun-break**, (*a*) a burst of sunshine; (*b*) sunrise (cf. *daybreak*); (*c*) = BRISE-SOLEIL; **sun-case** *Pyrotechny*, a case containing a slow-burning composition, forming part of a 'sun': see 8 b above; **sun-charm**, a fire-festival to propitiate the god of the sun; **sun-circle**, a circle of stones supposed to be connected with sun-worship; **sun-clad** *a. poet.*, (*a*) clothed in radiance like the sun; (*b*) clothed in sunshine; **sun-clock**, (*a*) a clock constructed to show solar time; (*b*) *poet.* a sundial; **sun club**, a club for sun-bathers or naturists (NATURIST 2); **sun compass**, a navigational device for finding true north from the observed direction of the sun, allowing for the time of day; also *fig.* and *attrib.*; **sun-crack** *Geol.*, a crack produced by the heat of the sun during the consolidation of a rock; **sun-cream**, a creamy preparation rubbed on the skin to protect it from sunburn or to promote sun-tanning; **sun-cure** *sb.*, a cure involving exposure to the sun's rays; **sun-cure** *v.*, to 'cure' or preserve by exposure to the sun; also **sun-cured** *ppl. a.*; **sun-dance**, a religious dance in honour of the sun, accompanied with rites of self-torture, practised by certain North American Indian peoples; **sun-dart** *poet.*, a ray of sunlight figured as a dart; **sun-dawn**, *poet.*, dawn, daybreak; **sun-deck**, (*a*) the upper deck of a steamer; (*b*) *N. Amer.*, a terrace or balcony situated so as to catch the sun; **sun-disk, -disc**, the disk of the sun, or a figure or image of this, esp. in religious symbolism; **sun-drenched** *a.*, soaked with sunshine; having (typically) very sunny weather; **sun-dry** *a.* = SUN-DRIED *a.*; **sun-dust**, the motes in a sunbeam; hence **sun-dusted** *a.*; **sun-extinct** *a. poet. nonce-wd.*, inwardly dead; **sun-eye** *poet.*, the sun; **sun-fever** (see quots.); **sun-figure** *Biol.*, a radiating figure formed in the protoplasm of a cell during karyokinesis; **sun-flag**, the Japanese flag, bearing an image of the sun; **sun flash**, a flash of sunlight; a device or pattern resembling this (see quots.); **sun-fly**, an artificial fly used by anglers in bright weather; **sun-force**, the force or energy emanating from the sun in the form of heat, light, etc.; **sun furnace**, an apparatus constructed of mirrors designed to concentrate solar energy for use in high-temperature experiments and research; †**sun-gate-down**, sunset; **sun gear** *Mech.* = *sun wheel* (*a*); **sun-glade**, a beam or track of sunlight, *esp.* the track of reflected sunlight on water (cf. *moon-glade*, MOON *sb.*[1] 16); **sun-glass**, (*a*) a lens for concentrating the rays of the sun, a burning-glass; (*b*) a screen of coloured glass attached to a sextant for moderating the light of the sun, a shade-glass (*Cent. Dict. Suppl.* 1909); (*c*) *pl.*, spectacles with tinted lenses for protecting the eyes from sunlight; = *dark glasses* (*b*) s.v. DARK *a.* 14 c; hence **sun-glassed** *a.*, wearing sun-glasses; **sun-glow**, (*a*) a glow or glare of sunlight; also, the colour of this; (*b*) a hazy diffused light seen around the sun, due to fine solid particles in the atmosphere, as after a volcanic eruption; **sun-go-down** *Obs.* or *dial.* sunset; †also app. used advb. = till sunset; so †**sun-going-down**; **sun-gold**, (*a*) an orange dye obtained from coal-tar, also called *heliochrysin*; (*b*) bright sunlight likened to gold (*poet.* and *rhet.*); **sun-grazer** *Astr.* (see quot. 1982); so **sun-grazing** *a.*; **sun-groat** (see quot. 1861); **Sun Gun** *Cinemat.*, a proprietary term for a portable incandescent lamp; †**sun half** = *sunny half* (see SUNNY *a.* 2 b); **sun-hat**, a broad-brimmed hat worn in hot climates to protect the head from the sun; so **sun-helmet** (whence **sun-helmeted** *a.*, wearing a sun-helmet); **sun-heat**, (*a*) heat emanating from the sun; (*b*) a heat-stroke; **sun hot** (see quot. 1961); **sun kiln**, a vat in which potters' clay is exposed to the action of the sun and air; **Sun King** [see ROI SOLEIL], a sobriquet of Louis XIV of France; also *transf.* and *attrib.*; **sun-lamp**, an electric lamp designed to emit radiation of a similar type to that of sunlight; now esp. one that produces ultraviolet light for therapeutic purposes or to produce an artificial sun-tan; hence **sun-lamped** *a.*; **sun-land**, a land of sunshine, a country or region with a sunny climate; **sun-leistering** = SUNNING *vbl. sb.* 3; **sun-line**, (*a*) in Palmistry = *line of the sun* (see 1 f above); (*b*) a line drawn on a card sun-dial, along which a ray of sunlight falls after passing through a slit; **sun lounge**, (*a*) a room built largely of glass to admit the maximum amount of sunlight; (*b*) *U.S.* = *sun-bed* (*a*) above; **sun-lounger** = *sun-bed* (*a*) above; **sun-motor**, a machine which converts solar energy to another form of energy, such as electrical or mechanical energy; **sun-myth**, a myth relating to the sun, a solar myth; **sun-oil**, (*a*) oil rubbed on the skin to prevent sunburn or promote tanning; (*b*) = *sunflower oil* s.v. SUNFLOWER 4; **sun-opal**, = FIRE-*opal*; **sun-painting** = *sun-printing* below; **sun-pan**, a pan in which some substance is exposed to the sun (as brine in salt-making, or clay in pottery manufacture); **sun-path**, the course of the sun; also, the path followed by a ray of sunlight; chiefly *fig.*; **sun-picture**, a picture made by means of sunlight, a photograph; **sun-pillar**, a vertical column of light appearing to extend upwards from the sun; **sun-plane**, a plane with a curved stock, used for levelling the ends of the staves of a cask; †**sun-pond**, ? = *sun-pan*; **sun-power**, (*a*) = *sun-force*; (*b*) (after *candle-power*), the relative intrinsic brightness of a star as measured by that of the sun; **sun-print** *Photogr.*, a print made from a negative by means of sunlight; a daylight print; so **sun-print** *v.*, **-printing** *vbl. sb.*; **sun-quake**, a solar disturbance comparable to an earthquake; †**sun-rest**, sunset; **sun-roof**, (*a*) = *sunshine roof* s.v. SUNSHINE *sb.* 6; (*b*) a part of the roof of a house which is suitable for sunbathing; **sun-scald** [SCALD *sb.*[2]], (*a*) 'scald' produced by the sun's heat; esp. damage to trees caused by the bark being dried by excessive heat and wind; (*b*) a patch of bright sunlight on the surface of water; **sun-scorch**, the burning of leaves by sunlight when a plant lacks sufficient water; also = *sun-scald*; **sunscreen**, (*a*) a screen which gives protection against the sun; (*b*) a preparation intended to screen the skin from ultraviolet rays and thereby prevent sunburn; **sun-seeker**, (*a*) *Astronautics*, a photoelectric device used in satellites and spacecraft which maintains its orientation with respect to the sun and can be used to direct instruments and provide navigational information; (*b*) one seeking a sunny place for a holiday or to live in; **sun-shaft** orig. *U.S.*, a shaft of sunlight, a sunbeam; also *fig.*; **sunship** [-SHIP], a mock title for the sun; **sun-shooter** *Naut. slang*, one who takes an observation of the sun (see SHOOT *v.* 32 c); **sun-side** (now *rare*), the side facing the sun, the sunny side (also *attrib.*); **sun-signalling**, = HELIOGRAPHY 4; †**sun-sitting**, sunset; **sun-smile**, a sunny or gracious smile; **sun-smitten** *a.*, struck by the sun's rays; *spec.* affected with sunstroke; **sun-spark** *U.S.*, the glint of sunlight on an object; **sun-spear**, an eel-spear used in the Irish lakes (see quot.); so **sun-spearer, -spearing**; **sunspecs** *colloq.* = *sun-glass* (*c*); **sun-spell**, = *sun-charm*; **sun-spring** *Obs.* or *arch.*, sunrise (in quot. *a* 1300 *transf.* = east; in quot. 1900 *fig.*); †**sun-still** (see quot.); **sun-telegraphy**, = HELIOGRAPHY 4; **sun-thickened oil**, a polymerized oil of a honey-like consistency, produced from linseed oil by action of the sun and used as a base in oil-painting; **sun-tight** *a.* (after *water-tight*), impervious to the rays of the sun; **sun-time**, (*a*) a time of brightness or joy; (*b*) solar time; **sun-trap**, a place adapted for catching sunshine; **sun valve**, a mechanical device which used the heat of the sun as it appeared or disappeared to turn a lighthouse light off or on; **sun visor**, a projecting shield on a cap, or a hinged screen mounted inside (formerly also outside) a motor vehicle, to shade the eyes from bright sunshine; **sun-wheel**, (*a*) the wheel around which a planet-wheel turns (see *sun-and-planet wheels*, 13 d); (*b*) a figure resembling a wheel, with radiating arms or spokes, supposed to be a symbol of the sun; (*c*) *pl.* the wheels of the mythical chariot of the sun; **sun-yellow**, name for a pale yellow dye obtained from coal-tar, also called *maize*.

1928 *Amer. Speech* III. 366 'Back-spot'.., 'baby-spots', '*sunarcs', 'twins', 'floods' and others. **1930** *Sel. Gloss. Motion Pict. Technician* (Acad. Motion Pict. Arts & Sci., Hollywood), *Sun lamps*, a large lamp (*Sun Arc* or *Sun Spot*) reflecting its light by means of a parabolic mirror. *c* **1440** *Astron. Cal.* (MS. Ashm. 361) fol. 1 b, Boþe of dawyng and of *sonne arysing & also for þe sonne goyng downe. **1633** *Campion's Hist. Irel.* II. vii. 96 They are forced..to keepe them [*sc.* their gates] shut..from sunne set, to sunne arising. **1933** *Sun* (Baltimore) 11 Aug. 8/7 Her *sunback suit she casts aside, She is a nudist—off go things. **1934** *Times* 22 June 17/6 Many swimming and bathing suits now have a 'sun-back' and a high throat line. **1955** J. POTTS *Death of Stray Cat* ii. 18 Summer people..in..their sunback dresses. **1935** E. DARK *Return to Coolami* xxiv. 262 He had wondered..if Susan liked surfing, if she liked *sun-baking. **1977** *Best of Austral. Angler* 63/1 The middle of the day is mostly for sunbaking and dreaming. **1866** *Galaxy* 15 July 544 What you want..is a *sun-bath daily. **1875** *Encycl. Brit.* III. 439/1 A sun bath (*insolatio* or *heliosis*), exposing the body to the sun, the head being covered, was a favourite practice among the Greeks and Romans. **1893** KATE SANBORN *Truthful Woman S. California* 21, I sat on the veranda,..taking a sun-bath, in a happy dream or doze. **1902** H. BEGBIE *Sir J. Sparrow* 127 Captain Chivvy..vowed and declared that sun-baths were the only possible means of dispersing the cholers of the body..and begged his dear friend Sparrow to stick to sun-baths all the days of his life. **1941** A. CHRISTIE *Evil under Sun* vi. 107, I oiled myself and *sunbathed. **1978** 'A. YORK' *Tallant for Disaster* i. 17 Supposing the *Gazette* did learn that Mistress Castanos does sunbathe in the altogether? **1895** K. GRAHAME *Golden Age* (1904) 9 Out into the brimming *sun-bathed world I sped. **1929** *Daily Express* 14 Jan. 19/3 The groups of Lido *sun-bathers. **1973** H. NIELSEN *Severed Key* xviii. 189 Sunny walked on the beach... The sun-bathers and surfers were far behind her. **1600** NASHE *Summer's Last Will* Wks. 1905 III. 274 *Sun-bathing beggers. **1900** *Westm. Gaz.* 31 July 3/2 [Walt Whitman] was convinced that sun-bathing was a fine tonic. **1636** G. SANDYS *Paraphr. Ps. lviii.* Poems (1648) 100 As *Sun-beat Snow, so let them thaw. **1693** DRYDEN *Juvenal* x. 239 Nilus, to convey His Sun-beat Waters by so long a way. **1891** *Cent. Dict.*, Sun-beat, *sun-beaten. **1894** SAFAR *Persian Pict.* 115 The sun-beaten pavement. **1967** *Punch* 11 Jan. p. viii/2 The optimistic can snap up adjustable folding *sun beds. **1979** *Sunday Express* 28 Jan. 16/6 Ever sat down on a foreign beach for a bit of blissful solitude only to find your local pub bore a couple of sunbeds away? **1980** *West Lancs. Even. Gaz.* 9 July 14 (Advt.), 'Mermaid Sontegra' Canopy Sun Beds £2 per half-hour session or course of 6 £10. **1983** *Daily Tel.* 31 Jan. 15/8 Sunbed lamps are designed to cut down ultraviolet B light, which burns before it tans. **1969** K. P. PHILLIPS *Emerging Republican Majority* v. 438 Chart 134 illustrates how the electoral votes of the *Sun Belt will have almost tripled in the half-century between 1920 and 1970. **1976** *National Observer* (U.S.) 24 Apr. 12/1 The movement is away from the noise, dirt, crime, and congestion of the oldest urban centers and to the so-called Sunbelt. **1980** *Christian Sci. Monitor* (Midwestern ed.) 4 Dec. 2/2 In some of the wooded parts of this bustling Sun-belt city, white-tailed deer have been spotted. **1674** FLAVEL *Husb. Spir.* ix. 83 The rain is most beneficial..when there come sweet warm *Sun-blasts with it or after it. *Ibid.* App. 265 The Sun-blasts of prosperity. **1894** H. NISBET *Bush Girl's Rom.* 215 Your eyes bad? A touch of *sun-blight. Wear a pair of blue glasses until the inflammation goes. **1837** *Southern Lit. Messenger* III. 332 She had on a deep *sun-bonnet. **1860** MISS YONGE *Stokesley Secr.* ii, Bessie had put on her lilac-spotted sun-bonnet. **1941** J. MASEFIELD *In Mill* 130 All the horses were wearing sun-bonnets and ear-flappers. **1981** M. BYRD *California Thriller* (1984) x. 82 She wore a sun-bonnet..and carried a clipboard. **1839** *Southern Lit. Messenger* V. 113/2 The bevy of *sun-bonnetted lasses, who gave us of their pies and apples. **1826** CARRINGTON *Dartmoor* 75 O Plym, beloved, to thee I owe the few bright *sun-breaks, that have cheer'd My toilsome pilgrimage. **1850** S. DOBELL *Roman* vi. 79, I, who..Since sunbreak upon one same broken column Sat like a Caryatid. **1881** SHORTHOUSE *John Inglesant* Pref. 9 The sunbreak upon the stainless peaks. **1947** *Archit. Rev.*

CII. 148/1 Covering one-third of it is a key pattern of loggia-like sun-breaks, the scale of which is exactly double that of the rest of the elevation. **1969** J. Elliot *Duel* III. iv. 275 The other creatures on the beach..sat under sun-breaks, walked in and out of the water, tinkered with boats. **1875** Knight *Dict. Mech.* 2454/1 **Sun-case*,..a strong paper case filled with a composition which does not burn so fast as rocket-composition. **1897** D. Butler *Ch. Abernethy* v. 79 Dr. Frazer regards the fire-festivals of November and December as *sun-charms intended to ensure a proper supply of sunshine. **1911** MacCulloch *Relig. Anc. Celts* xviii. 266 The bonfire was a sun-charm, representing and assisting the sun. **1877** E. G. Squier *Peru* xx. 383 The *sun-circles, or Druidical circles of England. **1634** Milton *Comus* 782 The *Sun-clad power of Chastity. **1825** Longf. *Sunrise on the Hills* 4 The sun-clad vales. **1737** *Gentl. Mag.* VII. 68/2 [Joseph Williamson's] Clocks, thus framed, would keep Time to Admiration with the Sun, and therefore he called them his *Sun-Clocks. **1876** H. Gardner *Sunfl., Dream of Noon* 51 The mossy sun-clock. **1936** *Sun Bathing Rev.* June–July 43/2 (*heading*) Non-nudist *sun clubs. **1950** *Sun Bather* Spring 23/1 That's my ideal sun-club. In the National Trust Land, on reserved beaches. In our own gardens, where suitable. **1978** *Lancashire Life* July 31/3 Although Lancashire has four Sun Clubs (naturist terminology for nudist camps), none is on the coast. **1925** *Nat. Geogr. Mag.* Nov. 523/2 In clear weather the *sun compass enabled us to do accurate navigation... Mr. Albert H. Bumstead..invented it for our trip and I consider it a great contribution to science. **1947** *New Biol.* III. 14 The sun may be either to the left or to the right of a marching hopper and it appears that the hopper while marching keeps its direction with reference to the sun. That such 'sun-compass orientation' exists was proved by ingenious experiments in the field. **1967** J. Grierson *Heroes of Polar Skies* iv. 65 Byrd..expected to maintain his heading by the sun compass. **1852** R. F. Burton *Falconry Valley Indus* viii. 80 The ground is gashed with gigantic *sun-cracks. **1858** H. D. Rogers *Geol. Pennsylv.* II. II. 831 A locality where the sun-cracks..are exposed in a roadside quarry. **1966** L. Cohen *Beautiful Losers* I. 91 There is a tube of *sun cream in the glove compartment. **1863** L. M. Alcott *Hospital Sketches* v. 70 Very soon after leaving the care of my ward, I discovered that I had no appetite, and cut the bread and butter interests almost entirely, trying the exercise and *sun cure instead. **1902** *Daily Chron.* 8 Dec. 4/5 Sun-cures for all the depression and ill-humours to which English people are supposed to be peculiarly subject. **1912** *Nation* 8 June 376/1 All that they did not eat to-day they smoked or *sun-cured for to-morrow. **1877** (*Advt.*) Old Judge *Sun cured Virginia Smoking Tobacco. **1849** M. H. Eastman *Dahcotah* p. xxii, The Sioux worship the sun. The **sun dance* is performed by young warriors who dance, at intervals of five minutes, for several days. **1890** *Century Mag.* Mar. 753/2 Ordinarily each tribe..has its own celebration of the sun-dance. **1894** *Outing* (U.S.) XXIV. 88/1 Those dreadful cicatrices left by the sun-dance. *a* **1835** Mrs. Hemans *Storm of Delphi* xiv, And the lightnings in their play Flash'd forth ..Like *sun-darts wing'd from the silver bow. **1835** Browning *Paracelsus* I. 104 We paced..the cheerful town At *sun-dawn. **1885** Swinburne *Mar. Fal.* Ded. vii, One heart whose heat was as the sundawn's fire. **1897** M. Kingsley *Trav. W. Afr.* 130 The captain is on top of the *sun deck most of the time. **1909** *Daily Chron.* 16 Apr. 4/4 On the sun-deck of a steamer. **1950** J. D. MacDonald *Brass Cupcake* (1955) ii. 15 The apartment has a big bedroom, sun deck, living room. **1970** R. Lowell *Notebk.* 111 Thirty raspberry bushes stacked on my sundeck. **1877** J. E. Carpenter tr. *Tiele's Hist. Relig.* 54 An attempt..to substitute the exclusive worship of Aten-Ra, the *sun-disc, for that of Amun-Râ. **1883** V. Stuart *Egypt* 381 The ovals right and left of the sundisk which sheds down its rays upon the royal pair are the solar cartouches. **1924** A. J. Small *Frozen Gold* ii. 47 He was no longer in the *sun-drenched Spring. He had flung himself back..into the winter. **1929** *Radio Times* 8 Nov. 421/3 Honey..from sun-drenched meadows. **1979** R. Gillespie *Crossword Mystery* i. 27 The sun-drenched sidewalk. **1885** W. B. Yeats in *Dublin Univ. Rev.* June 110/2 And with a *sun-dry weed He wrote it on the sands. **1909** H. G. Wells *Tono-Bungay* I. ii. 51 The seaports of the sun-dry Levant. **1849** Thoreau *Week Concord Riv.* 373 The particles of golden light, the *sun-dust, have..fallen like seeds on the earth. **1964** W. Golding *Spire* i. 10 Those two men posed so centrally in the sundust. **1946** R. S. Thomas *Stones of Field* 42 The breeze could bring..songs to his ear from the *sun-dusted moor. **1929** D. H. Lawrence *Pansies* 120 It is only immoral to be dead-alive, *Sun-extinct And busy putting out the sun In other people. **1931** C. Day Lewis *From Feathers to Iron* 23 That golden seed extends Beneath the *sun-eye, the father, To ear at the earth's ends. **1855** Dunglison *Med. Lex.* (1857), *Dengue*,..Solar or *Sun Fever. **1876** *Ibid.*, *Sun Fever*, a fever of tropical regions, which is probably a severe form of febricula or simple fever. **1904** *Brit. Med. Jrnl.* 17 Sept. 638 These 'touches of fever' being either sun-fever or malaria. **1889** *Jrnl. Microsc. Sci.* N.S. XXX. 163 Certain peculiar radiating appearances in the protoplasm are seen..—stars, 'asters', or '*sunfigures'. Cell-division then follows. **1905** J. Fox (*title*) Following the *Sun-Flag: a Vain Pursuit Through Manchuria. **1960** H. Hayward *Antique Coll.* 272/1 **Sun flash horse brass*, a face piece, extremely popular in Kent,..originally a disc of latten..with its centre hand-raised into a high dome or boss and encircled with a wide, flat rim. **1971** J. S. Gunn *Opal Terminol.* 46 *Sunflash*, pattern exhibiting flashes of colour, usually weak, in a dark potch background. **1902** *Encycl. Brit.* XXV. 446/1 For very bright weather and clear water, lightly dressed flies, which are mainly light yellow in colour, are standard favourites, such as the *Sun-fly and the Mystery. **1866** Odling *Anim. Chem.* 78 Either by a direct application of *sun-force or, indirectly, by the aid of those terrestrial transformations of sun-force which are so abundantly at his disposal. **1873** B. Stewart *Conserv. Force* (U.S.) vii. 182 The plant during the day stores up sun-force sufficient to do its work during the night. **1949** *Sun* (Baltimore) 25 Feb. 17/3 A *sun furnace which..can concentrate the temperature of the sun's surface on a space about three inches in diameter. **1955** *Sci. News Let.* 21 May 328/2 French scientists are using the sun furnace to produce and study some minerals which are made at temperatures too high for ordinary furnaces. *c* **1440** *Promp. Parv.* 484/1 Sunne settynge, or *sunne gate downe. **1530** Palsgr. 805/2 At the sonne gate downe, *sur le soleil couchant.* **1935** R. Trautschold *Standard Gear Bk.* xi. 173 The relative speed of the driven internal gear in terms of the speed of the driving *sun gears. **1975** *Sci. Amer.* Dec. 120/2 When the motor drives the cylinder, the idler gear and its companion rotate as a planetary system around the sun gear that is fixed to the base. **1849** H. Melville *Mardi* I. xxxix. 152 He would not be able to perceive us, owing to our being in what mariners denominate the *sun-glade, or that part of the ocean upon which the sun's rays flash with peculiar intensity. **1876** *Forest & Stream* 13 July 368/2 The.. mosquitoes hovered, like flies in a sun-glade. **1906** *Blackw. Mag.* Mar. 394/1 The sun-glade was glittering and twinkling on the water. **1804** M. Lewis *Jrnl.* 19 Aug. in *Orig. Jrnls. Lewis & Clark Expedition* (1904) I. ii. 112 The main chief Brack fast with us & beged for a *Sun glass. **1806** W. Clark *Jrnl.* 2 Apr. in *Ibid.* (1905) IV. xxiv. 236 An Indian whome I hired for a Sun glass. **1837–42** Hawthorne *Twice-told T.* (1851) I. vii. 129 After lighting a cigar with a sunglass. **1927** A. Conan Doyle *Case-Bk. of Sherlock Holmes* xii. 306 He *had* grey-tinted sun-glasses. **1976** 'B. Shelby' *Great Pebble Affair* 119 My sunglasses fell from my hand, cracking one of the hand-ground lenses. **1961** *John o' London's* 6 July 25/1 The *sun-glassed eyes of the vacation-bound. **1972** K. Bonfiglioli *Don't point that Thing at Me* x. 86 Hatted and sun-glassed to the point of anonymity. **1845** Mrs. Norton *Child Islands, Winter* lxviii, Didst Thou ..Never lie dreaming—shut from winter skies,—While the warm shadow of remembered eyes, Like a hot *sun-glow, all thy frame oppress? **1884** *Chamb. Jrnl.* Nov. 707/1 Remarkable coronal appearances and sunglows were noticed in different parts of the world. **1977** *Western Morning News* 30 Aug. 4 (Advt.), 1976 Vauxhall Chevette 4-door Saloon. Sunglow. Low mileage, family saloon. **1595** T. Edwards *Narcissus* (Roxb.) 52 Talke *Sun-go downe. **1715** Pennecuik *To Pr. Orange in Tweeddale* etc. II. 4 For we that live within this Town, Our Sight grows Dim, by Sun go Down. *c* **1440** *Sonne goyng downe [see *sun arising* above]. **1530** Palsgr. 272/2 Sonne goyng downe, *le soleil couchant.* **1885** Hummel *Dyeing Textile Fabrics* 401 *Heliochrysin*..—This colouring matter is the sodium salt of tetra-nitro-naphthol, it is also known as *Sun Gold. **1897** *Outing* (U.S.) XXIX. 554/1 The water..flashed with untold brilliance under the flooding sun gold. **1965** *Observer* 17 Oct. 13/4 The comet may herald the return of a family of '*sun-grazing' comets..which produced some spectacular effects in the last century. *Ibid.*, One theory has suggested that this group of '*sun-grazers' may have been formed in the wake of the sun after it passed through a cosmic dust cloud. **1982** *New Scientist* 21 Oct. 158/3 Comets that pass near the Sun are called 'sungrazers'. **1861** *Gentl. Mag.* CCX. 532 *note*, In the Irish coinage of Edward IV, there are groats with the sun and rose in centre, which were called *sun-groats. **1961** *Official Gaz.* (U.S. Patent Office) 14 Nov. TM 49/1 Sylvania Electrical Products, Inc... **Sun Gun*, for motion picture camera lamps and reflectors. **1969** J. Whale *Half-Shut Eye* iii. 30 The battery-powered hand-lights which cameramen call sun-guns. **1976** *Listener* 12 Feb. 171/2 By shooting a gun numerous times and flashing a sun-gun, we persuaded hordes of bats to fly round the cave. **1565** in *Reg. Mag. Sig. Scot.* 1574 583/1 Dimedietatem terrarum de Westir Gurdie vocat. *the* **sone half*. **1615** in J. Davidson *Inverurie* vi. (1878) 198 The..possessors..of the sun half of the Cruik, finding them-selves to have the better part,..granted..to the shaddow half of the said Cruik ane piece of land, to make the shaddow half so good as the sun half. **1879** Mrs. A. E. James *Ind. Househ. Managem.* 18 A..regular Indian *sun-hat, made of pith. **1898** P. Manson *Trop. Diseases* v. 103 The old resident is very chary about going out without his sun-hat and white umbrella. **1842** Loudon *Suburban Hort.* 489 When the air of the frame is at a high temperature from *sun-heat. **1873** J. Le Conte *Relig. & Sci.* xvi. (1874) 275 Sun-heat, falling upon water, disappears as heat, to reappear as mechanical force which lifts that water into the clouds. **1904** *New Hebrides Mag.* Apr. 10 Cases..of slight sun-stroke, or sun-heat. **1912** *Contemp. Rev.* Apr. 559 Hatless and indifferent to sun-heat that would have killed Europeans. **1879** *Cornh. Mag.* XXXIX. 516 Saint-Luc wore a *sun-helmet. **1883** V. Stuart *Egypt* 3 Up came a British full private of the gallant West Kent..with..a sun-helmet, and a red jacket. **1896** Conan Doyle in *Westm. Gaz.* 7 Apr. 2/1 A crowd of red-fezzed Egyptians and *sun-helmeted Europeans. **1873** C. I. G. Rampini *Lett. from Jamaica* 179 Rockatone (stone) at ribber-bottom (bottom of the river) no know *sun hot. **1961** F. G. Cassidy *Jamaica Talk* vi. 109 The oldest, and still current expression [for *noon*] is *sun hot.* *a* **1822** J. Aiken in S. Shaw *Hist. Staff Potteries* iv. (1829) 98 The fluid mass is next poured into a sieve, thro' which it runs into the largest vat, or *Sun Kiln, until the whole surface is covered..which is left to be evaporated by solar action. **1939** O. Lancaster *Homes Sweet Homes* 26 Few of his fellow-sovereigns enjoyed the robust health of the *Sun King. **1976** N. Thornburg *Cutter & Bone* xi. 258 The women were heavy and overdressed, with elaborate Sun King coiffeurs [*sic*]. **1977** *Time* 8 Aug. 37/1 Yves Saint Laurent, the Sun King of fashion. **1885** *List of Subscribers, Classified* (United Telephone Co.) (ed. 6) 87 Electric *Sun Lamp & Power Co., Limited. **1934** L. Mumford *Metropolitan Milieu in City Devel.* (1946) ii. 34 Finally the sun lamps..overcame the lack of real sunlight in these misplanned domestic quarters. **1957** C. MacInnes *City of Spades* II. v. 141 You're getting so pale... You must have some sun-lamp treatment. **1980** J. Hone *Flowers of Forest* I. 61 An unreal tan... Something assumed..with lotions or sun-lamps. **1976** 'Trevanian' *Main* (1977) xi. 219 There is a lighter tone to his *sun-lamped bronze around the ears, indicating that his haircut is fresh. **1861** Paley *Æschylus* (ed. 2) *Choeph.* 365 *note*, The Hyperboreans, a race supposed to have inhabited the mild *sun-lands beyond the regions from which the north wind blows. **1847** Stoddard *Angler's Comp.* 253 A party who were *sun-leistering or spearing from a boat. **1653** R. Sanders *Physiogn.* 68 The lines which issue from the *Sun-line, and go to the Table-line signifie Children. **1877** *Encycl. Brit.* VII. 161/1 Draw the sun-line at the top of the card. **1910** *Bradshaw's Railway Guide* Apr. 1020 Linden Hall Hydro... Splendid winter garden and *sun-lounge. **1971** [see *double-glazing* s.v. double *a.* A. 6]. **1979** M. Babson *So soon done For* xiv. 103 The sun lounges, the chairs, the cushions..all belonged to the Norrises... She was reclining in one of the sunlounges. **1972** D. Lees *Zodiac* 191 We found ourselves side by side on one of the *sun loungers. **1980** *Daily Tel.* 10 Dec. 3/7 A morning on your sun-lounger on one of Tobago's deserted beaches. **1884** *Cassell's Family Mag.* Mar. 252/1 The *Sun-Motor. Our illustration gives a general view of the machine constructed by Captain J. Ericsson of New York, for utilising the sun's heat in producing mechanical power. *Ibid.* 252/2 The sun-motor may be very useful in some hot parts of the globe. **1952** 'J. Wyndham' in 'E. Crispin' *Best SF* (1955) The main batteries charged by the sun-motor. **1865** Tylor *Early Hist. Man.* xii. 354 St. George, the favourite mediæval bearer of the great *Sun-myth. **1945** 'L. Lewis' *Birthday Murder* (1951) x. 151 Her face bare of lipstick and shining with *sun oil. **1981** *Sci. Amer.* Feb. 62/3 The production of 'sunoil' amounted to 5.6 million tons in 1979–80. **1851** Mantell *Petrifactions* iv. §1. 364 Opaline substances,—the noble opal; *sun-opal; common opal; [etc.]. **1876** C. M. Yonge *Three Brides* I. ix. 142 The likeness of a young man..where the hard verities of *sun-painting had refused to veil the haggard trace of early dissipation. **1971** *Country Life* 8 July 104/1 In the 1840s, before artists reacted violently against the threat posed by the new so-called sun paintings. **1723** *Phil. Trans.* XXXII. 353 The Sea Water is let into their feeding Ponds,..from hence is conveyed into small square Pans, and..from these ..into larger Pans,..which they call Brine, or *Sun Pans. **1831–3** P. Barlow in *Encycl. Metrop.* (1845) VIII. 449/2 The materials for coarse pottery are prepared by a very rude ..method. The place is technically named a sun pan. **1598–9** E. Forde *Parismus* II. (1661) 128 In the *Sun-path of sweet delight. **1847** Emerson *Poems* (1857) 177 The mill-round of our fate appears A sun-path in thy worth. **1876** Morris *Æneid* VI. 796 Beyond the stars,..Beyond the sun-path lies the land, where Atlas heaven upbears. **1846** *Literary Gaz.* 433/2 Genuine *sun-pictures, un-aided by art. **1856** Geo. Eliot *Ess.* (1884) 237 The delicate accuracy of a sun-picture. **1902** *Times* 10 Mar. 15/1 At 6.25 p.m., a very brilliant but narrow *sun pillar appeared, extending from a bank of clouds..to about 35°. **1846** Holtzapffel *Turning* II. 488 The ends of the staves have been levelled by a tool called a *sun plane. **1708** *Lond. Gaz.* No. 4453/3 Large Store-ponds, and *Sun-Ponds for making of Brine. **1877** *Queen's Printers' Bible-Aids* 33/2 Land suffering from an excess of *sun-power. **1905** *Nature* 28 Sept. 532/1 In Fig. 2 the relative distances of..stars..are shown.., the 'sun-powers' of the various stars being represented by a system of symbols. **1858** *Lake Price Man. Photogr. Manip.* 218 Such a negative would suffer considerably by being *sun-printed. *Ibid.*, Injured by sun-printing. **1928** Blunden *Undertones of War* viii. 78 A large sunprint on view at headquarters suspected many enemy mine-shafts. **1791** E. Darwin *Bot. Gard.* I. 29 *notes*, If..the planets were originally thrown out of the sun by larger *sun-quakes. *c* **1400** Love *Bonavent. Mirr.* (1907) 260 They were bounden to kepe the sabboth day, fro the *sonne rest of the day bifore vnto the sonne rest of the self day. *a* **1500** *St. Patrick's Purgatory* 214 in *Brome Bk.* 89 Sweche was hys lyght.. As yt ys in wentyr at the sunne rest. **1966** T. Pynchon *Crying of Lot 49* ii. 38 A small automobile with a *sun roof. **1972** *Country Life* 15 June (Suppl.) 22/2, 5 bedrooms, bathroom, 2 w.c.'s, flat sun-roof. **1980** *Daily Tel.* 23 Jan. 14/4 Electrically operated sunroof and windows and central locking system are included as standard. **1855** *Trans. Mich. Agric. Soc.* VI. 158 The tree has received a *sun scald, and the sap soured in consequence. **1881** *Gard. Chron.* 12 Nov. 621/1 The spots.. look more like the sun-scalds one sees upon the leaves of plants grown under glass. **1896** Lodeman *Spray. Plants* 274 Sun-scald (*Cercospora Apii*). **1897** Kipling *Capt. Cour.* v. 111 It seemed a sin to do anything but loaf over the hand-lines and spank the drifting 'sunscalds' with an oar. **1932** Felt & Rankin *Insects & Diseases of Ornamental Trees & Shrubs* iv. 116 Beech, spruce and pines are subject to sun-scald. **1967** *New Scientist* 30 Nov. 546/2 The temperature of the fruit [*sc.* tomatoes] directly exposed to the sun is at least 5 to 10 deg C higher than the surrounding air, and this high temperature frequently causes sunscald. **1928** B. D. Jackson *Gloss. Bot. Terms* (ed. 4) 469/1 *Sun scorch. The burning of foliage when the soil is parched. **1932** Felt & Rankin *Insects & Diseases of Ornamental Trees & Shrubs* iv. 115 The leaves may transpire more water than the roots can take up in a given length of time. This condition will cause sun-scorch of the leaves. **1950** *N.Z. Jrnl. Agric.* Jan. 5/2 Do not place them [*sc.* unripe tomatoes] at a window exposed to strong sunlight, as this will induce sun scorch and render the skin tough. **1969** *Gloss. Landscape Work* (*B.S.I.*) v. 28 Sun scorch (sunscald), damage caused to bark by unaccustomed exposure to the sun, for example, following the sudden removal of shade. **1738** [G. Smith] *Cur. Relat.* II. 285 They carried forty *Sun-Screens, cover'd with fine Callico, which belonged to the Life-Guard of Dairo. **1845** C. H. Smith in Kitto *Cycl. Bibl. Lit.* (1849) I. 226/2 The royal band of relatives who surrounded the Pharaoh,..bearing his standards, ensign-fans, and sun-screens. **1958** *Which?* I. iv. 17/2 Some sunscreens are lotions, some oils, some creams, others aerosols. **1980** *Daily Tel.* 22 Feb. 15/2 Any exposed area of skin should always be protected, either by a moisturiser or—in hot sun—by a sunscreen. **1956** *Nature* 7 Apr. 645/1 The Royal Aircraft Establishment..is also studying the design of a *sun-seeker for carriage in the rocket. The sun-seeker would be used for measurements of solar radiations and for obtaining ultra-violet pictures of the sun at high altitude. **1963** M. Caidin *Man-in-Space Dict.* 198 As used in manned spacecraft or robot satellites, the sunseeker 'seeks out' the sun by its brightness. An automatic pilot notes the position and angle of the sunseeker, and fires reaction jets to keep the spacecraft oriented on the basis of the position of the sun. **1970** *Times* 31 Dec. (Rev. of Year) p. vii./5 Sunseekers are beginning to look farther afield than the popular Spanish mainland. **1975** D. Francis *High Stakes* ix. 141 Selling dream retirement homes to elderly sun-seekers. **1868** Mrs. Whitney *Patience Strong's Outings* xiii, The maples were splendid in the *sunshafts that shot through. **1908** W. Churchill *Mr. Crewe's Career* xiii. 191 He had but to beckon a shining Pegasus from out a sun-shaft in the sky. *a* **1918** W. Owen *Poems* (1963) 64 Who's prejudiced Against a grimed hand when his own's quite dust, Less live than specks that in the sun-shafts turn. **1941** Blunden *Thomas Hardy* iv. 67 The secret of that apparent indifference was his lifelong purpose ..of striking for truth under the intense sunshafts of philosophic poetry. **1974** F. Warner *Meeting Ends* I. i A sunshaft strikes the steeple by my room. **1836** Poe *Four Beasts in One* II. 206 You need not look up at the heavens; his Sunship is not there—at least not the *Sunship adored by the Syrians. *That* deity..is worshipped under the figure of a large stone pillar. **1886** *Tinsley's Mag.* Oct. 373 The group of *sunshooters on the quarter-deck. **1393** Langl. *P. Pl.* C. xix. 64 Tho þat sitten in þe *sonne-syde sonner aren rype. **1608** WILLET *Hexapla Exod.* 651 The colour of the rine or barke on the sunside is purple. **1719** RAMSAY *To Arbuckle* 116 My ain house..stands on Edinburgh's street, the sun-side. **1852** 'NIGHTLARK' *Meand. Mem.* I. 128 And Sun-side Alps all tortuously slip. **1889** *Encycl. Brit.* Index, *Sun-Signalling. *c* **1460** *Promp. Parv.* (Winch. MS.) 448 *Sunne syttyng, or sunne gate downe, *occasus.* **1837** CARLYLE *Fr. Rev.* II. I. xi, Rewarded by a *sun-smile, and such melodious glad words. **1852** BAILEY *Festus* (ed. 5) 500 The sunsmile of Salvation beamed. **1833** TENNYSON *Pal. Art* xii, Below *sunsmitten icy spires Rose..the scornful crags. **1886** STEVENSON *Kidnapped* xx. 197 It was only by God's blessing that we were neither of us sun-smitten. **1847** EMERSON *Poems* (1857) 110 The *sun-spark on the sea. **1896** *Idler* Mar. 172/1 The burning sun-spark in the bright brass binnacle hood. **1885** *Sat. Rev.* 21 Nov. 673/1 '*Sun-spearing'..is much sought after in the Irish loughs during ..June and July. In the early sunny mornings..the *sun-spearer sallies forth in a..boat... Anguilla comes up writhing on the twelve close set teeth of the *sun-spear. **1975** *Observer* (Colour Suppl.) 20 June 13/4 The Reactolite 90/20 lenses..capable of withstanding the impact of a 1½ oz. steel ball dropped from a height of 50 in., more than double the requirement of the United States' stringent *sunspec regulations. **1976** *Punch* 11 Aug. 234/1 Choose a chair and pull up a glass, push up the sunspecs and just drink in this room. **1907** *Folk-Lore* June 222 The nocturnal festival of Sais..shows signs of being a *sun spell. *a* **1300** *E.E. Psalter* xlix. 2 Fra *sonne springe to setelgange. **1900** *Westm. Gaz.* 14 June 2/3 The sun-spring of love! **1688** HOLME *Armoury* III. xx. (Roxb.) 230 The Italian distillary, or *Sun Still: this is formed of two round bodied glass bottles, one..set with the mouth of it downwards into an other with it mouth vpwards. **1876** VOYLE & STEVENSON *Milit. Dict.* (ed. 3) s.v. *Telegraphy*, *Sun telegraphy is a system of correspondence by means of the sun's rays. **1935** E. NEUHAUS tr. *Doerner's Materials of Artist* iii. 105 *Sun-thickened oil is to be preferred to boiled oils, as also to the resin-oil varnishes. **1975** U. DIX tr. *Wehlte's Materials & Techniques of Painting* 389 Sun-thickened oil darkens rapidly when stored in tin canisters. **1861** BERESF. HOPE *Eng. Cath. 19th C.* iii. 88 To make his building light and well ventilated, and yet *sun-tight. **1844** MRS. BROWNING *Duchess May* li, Her hopes will spring again By the *suntime of her years. **1855** *Lardner's Mus. Sci. & Art* VII. 33 Clock time and sun time. **1883** A. KNOX *New Playground* 66 Secure for him a little 'box'..a sort of '*sun-trap,' don't you know? **1896** *Q. Rev.* July 59 These small, beautifully kept gardens..—sun-traps they must have been with their big, high walls. **1910** *Chambers's Jrnl.* Sept. 620/2 One great feature of this beacon is the *sun-valve, whereby the light is ignited and extinguished automatically at varying periods, according to the time of year. **1936** W. H. MCCORMICK *Mod. Bk. Lighthouses* xi. 92 The light is automatically turned on and off..by placing the light in charge of an 'AGA' Sunvalve. **1975** HAGUE & CHRISTIE *Lighthouses* v. 159 Early in the present century the ..operation of unattended lighthouses..was revolutionised by the invention of the sun- or light-valve. This..consists of an arrangement of reflective gold-plated bars supporting a suspended absorbent black rod; when lit by the sun this rod absorbs the direct heat and that reflected from the other bars and expands downwards thereby cutting off the supply of gas. The first sun-valve was put into operation..near Stockholm in 1907. **1926** *Daily Colonist* (Victoria, B.C.) 8 July 2/1 Bright Sunshine is fine—enjoy it all the more by wearing a *sun visor... A necessity to campers, sportsmen, etc. **1936** *Times* 19 Oct. 8/2 The inside fittings include..sun visors, footrests, etc. **1978** L. HEREN *Growing up on The Times* ii. 30, I..had a large American Ford V8 car fitted with a sun visor projecting over the windscreen. **1827** *Sun-wheel [see *planet-wheel* s.v. PLANET *sb.*[1] 5]. **1891** *Cent. Dict.*, Sun-wheel [sense (*b*)]. **1910** J. MACINTOSH in *Poets of Ayrshire* 138 The horsemen were ready the Sun-wheels to move And carry thee hence to the Kingdom of Love. **1965** *Daily Mail* 28 Oct. 7/3 If we convert the reverse wheel into a sun wheel (stationary wheel) by introducing a brake band, we'll get an intermediate gear ratio and three speeds. **1973** T. PYNCHON *Gravity's Rainbow* I. 100 The symbol used is a rude mandala, a red circle with a thick black cross inside, recognizable as the ancient sun-wheel from which tradition says the swastika was broken. **1890** *Sun yellow [see MAIZE 3].

b. In names of animals and plants: **sun-animalcule**, a microscopic protozoan of the group *Heliozoa*, esp. the common species *Actinophrys sol*, of a spherical form with numerous long, slender, straight, radiating filaments; **sun-bear**, (*a*) a small Malayan species of bear (*Helarctos malayanus*), the *bruang*, having close black fur and a white patch on the breast; (*b*) the Tibetan bear (*Ursus thibetanus*); **sun-beetle**, any one of various scarabæid beetles of the subfamily *Cetoniinæ*, which appear in sunshine; **sun-bittern**, a South American bird, *Eurypyga helias*, with brilliantly coloured plumage, also called *peacock-bittern*; also, any bird of the family *Eurypygidæ*; **sun-cress**, a S. African cruciferous herb, *Heliophila pectinata*; **sun-fern** (see quot.); **sun-fruit**, a shrub or tree of the genus *Heliocarpus*, found in Central America, bearing flat round capsules with radiating bristles; **sun gem**, a brilliantly coloured Brazilian species of humming-bird, *Heliactin cornuta*, distinguished by tufts of feathers on either side of the head; **sun-grass**, = DOOB (*Cynodon Dactylon*); **sun-grebe**, = SUNBIRD 1 c (*Cent. Dict.* 1891); **sun-perch**, = SUN-FISH 1 b; **sun plant**, (*a*) a small, half-hardy, annual herb belonging to one of several varieties of *Portulaca grandiflora*, native to Brazil and bearing single or clustered terminal flowers which open in sun; (*b*) a plant that grows best in full sunlight; **sun-rose**, a name for the genus *Helianthemum*, of which the flowers expand in sunshine: also called *rock-rose*; cf. HELIANTHEMUM; † **sun shell-fish**, a kind of starfish; **sun-spider** = SOLPUGID; **sun spurge**, a common species of spurge, *Euphorbia Helioscopia*, whose flowers follow the sun; **sun-squall, -squawl** *U.S.*, a jelly-fish; **sun-star, sun-starfish**, a starfish having numerous rays, as those of the genus *Solaster*; † **sun tithymal**, sun spurge; **sun-trout** *local U.S.*, the squeteague. † **sun-turning spurge**, sun spurge.

1867 J. HOGG *Microsc.* II. ii. 372 Actinophrys sol, '*sun-animalcule.' **1842** *Penny Cycl.* XXIII. 275/1 Bears are numerous [in Sumatra], and among them is the *sun-bear. **1881** *Encycl. Brit.* XII. 741/2 The Himalayan or Tibetan sun bear. **1894** N. B. DENYS in W. W. Skeat *Malay Magic* (1900) v. 183 The Malayan Sun-bear, the only animal of the bear species in the Peninsula... It is black in colour, with the exception of a semi-lunar-shaped patch of white on the breast, and a yellowish-white patch on the snout and upper jaw. **1931** *Times Educ. Suppl.* 19 Sept. (Home & Classroom Suppl.) p. iv/3 Mr. Charles Tonge has presented a young Malay sun-bear. **1965** R. MCKIE *Company of Animals* ix. 146 Sun bears can become dangerous as their power increases with age. **1836–9** *Todd's Cycl. Anat.* II. 886/2 In the *sun-beetles..the eyes are very protuberant. **1870** GILLMORE tr. *Figuier's Reptiles & Birds* 343 Its brilliant hues have obtained for it in Guinea the name of the Little Peacock or *Sun Bittern. **1876** A. R. WALLACE *Geogr. Distrib. Anim.* II. 358 The Eurypygidæ, or Sun-bitterns, are small heron-like birds with beautifully-coloured wings, which frequent the muddy and wooded river-banks of tropical America. **1884** MILLER *Plant-n.*, *Heliophila pectinata*, *Sun Cress. **1824** LOUDON *Encycl. Gard.* (ed. 2) 1225/2 *Sun-fern, polypodium phegopteris. **1852** G. W. JOHNSON *Cottage Gard. Dict.*, *Sun-fruit, *Heliocarpus.* **1861** J. GOULD *Monogr. Trochilidæ* IV. 212 (*heading*) *Sun Gem. **1912** BRABOURNE & CHUBB *Birds S. Amer.* 144 *Heliactin.. bilophum*..Sun-Gem. **1879** SIR G. CAMPBELL *Black & White* 19 In the South [of the U.S.] an East-Indian grass, known as 'Dhoop' or *Sun-grass, has been introduced. **1897** J. A. GRAHAM *Three Closed Lands* ix. 108 During the cold season the planter has had to pitch his tent in the forest or tall sun-grass. **1804** LEWIS & CLARK *Orig. Jrnls. Lewis & Clark Exped.* (1905) VI. 174 In this lake there is also ..*Sunperch. **1826** AUDUBON *Jrnls.* (1898) I. 162 Roasting the orange-fleshed Ibis, and a few sun-perch. **1835** — *Ornith. Biog.* III. 47 The American Sun Perch. *Ibid.* 50 The Sun Perch..seems to give a decided preference to sandy, gravelly, or rocky beds of streams. **1876** 'MARK TWAIN' *Tom Sawyer* xiv. 123 They were back again with some handsome bass, a couple of sun-perch and a small catfish. **1902** W. S. GORDON *Recoll. Old Quarter* 177 How full were the holes of craw-fish, turtles, sun-perch, grincles, and of daring, voracious pike. **1887** G. NICHOLSON *Illustr. Dict. Gardening* III. 202/2 *Sun-plant. Fl[owers] yellow, purple,..terminal. **1900** B. D. JACKSON *Gloss. Bot. Terms* 260/2 Sun-plants, plants which prefer full sun-light: their stems are often short, the leaves have the palisade cells well developed. **1963** *Oxf. Bk. Garden Flowers* 140/2 Sun Plant. The yellow, pink, scarlet or purple cup-shaped flowers of this little plant from Brazil open in direct sunshine and close in shadow. **1979** W. M. M. BARON *Organization in Plants* (ed. 3) iii. 42 Shade plants can utilize low light intensities more efficiently than sun plants. **1822** *Sun-rose [see HELIANTHEMUM]. **1824** LOUDON *Encycl. Gard.* (ed. 2) 1195/2 Helianthemum, sun-rose. **1884** *Gardening Illust.* 8 Nov. 425/3 The best kinds of Rock Roses and Sun Roses are beginning to reappear in our gardens. **1688** HOLME *Armoury* II. xv. 349/2 The Sea Sun, or the *Sun shell fish.. differs from the Star-fish in this, that all the rays which are five..come out of the sides of the round shell. **1959** *Southwest Rev.* XLIV. 137/1 An arachnid frequently, and naturally, confused with the true vinegarone is the solpugid —or wind-scorpion, wind-spider, or *sun-spider. **1974** *Stand. Encycl. S. Afr.* X. 217/1 The sun-spider can easily be distinguished from all other arachnids by the two immense jaws at the front of the head. **1562** TURNER *Herbal* II. 154 b, This kinde is called in diuerse partes of England Wartwurt; it maye also be called *son spourge, or son folowyrge spourge. **1796** WITHERING *Brit. Plants* (ed. 3) II. 449 *Euphorbia helioscopia*,..Wart-wort... Cats-milk. Sun Spurge. **1850** MISS PRATT *Comm. Things Seaside* i. 84 Almost every one knows the common Sun Spurge, often growing as a weed in gardens. **1865** THOREAU *Cape Cod* v. 79 The *sun-squawl was poisonous to handle. **1897** SHUFELDT *Ch. Nat. Hist. U.S.* 452 Jellyfish, or Sunsqualls. **1843** *Proc. Berw. Nat. Club* II. xi. 50 *S*[*olaster*] *Endeca.*—Purple *Sun Star. *S. Papposa.*—Common Sun Star. **1855** KINGSLEY *Glaucus* 125 The twelve-rayed sun-star (*Solaster papposa*), ..dressed in rich scarlet livery. **1876** *Nature* June 121/2 *Sun Starfish (*Solaster papposa*). **1597** GERARDE *Herbal* II. cxxxii. 406 With leaues like the *sunne Tithymale. **1884** G. B. GOODE *Fisheries U.S.: Nat. Hist. Aquatic Animals* I. 362 In the Southern Atlantic States it [*sc.* the squeteague] is called 'Grey Trout', '*Sun Trout', and 'Shad Trout'. **1888** GOODE *Amer. Fishes* 111 In the Southern Atlantic States it is called..'*Sun Trout.' **1640** PARKINSON *Theatr. Bot.* II. xvi. 188 *Tithymalus Helioscopius.* *Sunne turning Spurge or Wartwort.

c. Combinations of the genitive *sun's*: † **sun's brow**, a kind of bulrush; † **sun's day**, Sunday; † **sun's flower**, applied to the marigold (cf. SUNFLOWER 3 a); † **sun's gem** (tr. L. *solis gemma*), some kind of precious stone (see quot., and cf. SUNSTONE); † **sun's night**, = SUNNIGHT.

1567 MAPLET *Gr. Forest* 35 The Bulrush hath one kinde, which of some is called *Sonnes brow. **12..** in E. M. Thompson *Cust. St. Aug. Cant.* (1904) II. 314 In nocte vero ad matutinos, in primo motu, pulsetur '*Sunnesdeies belle', deinde major Absalon. [**1891** HARDY *Tess* xxiii, On this day of vanity, this Sun's-day..they could hear the church-bell calling.] **1563** HYLL *Art Garden.* (1593) 93 It [*sc.* marigold] is named the *sunnes floure. **1601** HOLLAND *Pliny* XXXVII. x. II. 629 The *Sunnes gem is white. *a* **1300** *Cursor M.* 11280 In august time, þe Imparour, Was vs born vr saueour,.. On *sunnes night.

d. **sun-and-planet wheels**, a form of gearing (invented by James Watt) consisting of a central wheel or *sun-wheel* and an outer wheel or *planet-wheel* (of which there may be more than one) geared together so that the axis of the latter moves round that of the former like a planet round the sun; also extended to other forms of gearing on a similar principle. So ***sun-and-planet gear, motion***, etc.

1816 R. BUCHANAN *Propelling Vessels by Steam* 20 For many years, instead of the crank, Mr. Watt used what are called sun and planet wheels, the one working round the other. **1869** RANKINE *Machinery & Millwork* 246 The Sun-and-Planet Motion is a sort of epicyclic train with periodic action. **1884** F. J. BRITTEN *Watch & Clockm.* 35 A modification of the old bolt and shutter introduced by Sir E. Beckett..is inferior to the 'Sun and Planet' and other maintainers. **1896** *Westm. Gaz.* 5 Dec. 4/2 The gear itself is arranged on the 'sun-and-planet' principle. **1904** G. B. SHAW *Comm. Sense Munic. Trading* 9 Committees of directors who do not know the difference between a piston rod and a sun-and-planets gear.

‖**sun** (sun), *sb.*[2] Pl. sun. [Jap.] A Japanese unit of length, equivalent to approximately 1·19 inches (3·03 centimetres).

1727 [see SHAKU 1]. **1888** *Encycl. Brit.* XXIV. 490/2 Japan. .. Sun, 10 = shaku (11·948 inches = 10/33 metre), 6 = ken, 60 = cho. **1956** K. TOMIKI *Judo* i. 22 Regulations require that the surrounding mats be all 5 *sun* (about 6 inches) lower than the contest area.

sun, *v.* [f. SUN *sb.*[1] Cf. G. *sonnen*.]

1. a. *trans.* To place in or expose to the sun; to subject to the action of the sun's rays; to warm, dry, etc. in sunshine.

[**1519**: see SUNNING *vbl. sb.* 1]. **1558** PHAER *Æneid* v. M ij b, Mewes and birds of seas..sonne their fethers. **1578** LYTE *Dodoens* 739 It doth redily draw vnto it the qualities..of those herbes..with which it is set to be sonned. **1646** SIR T. BROWNE *Pseud. Ep.* 97 Cinnamon..if it be sunned too long ..suffereth a torrefaction. **1802** WORDSW. *To the Daisy* ii, Spring parts the clouds with softest airs, That she may sun thee. **1807** P. GASS *Jrnl.* 239 We remained here all day airing and sunning our baggage and stores. **1898** 'MERRIMAN' *Roden's Corner* ii. 15 My..uncle is sure to be sunning his waistcoat in Piccadilly.

fig. **1807** J. BARLOW *Columb.* IV. 450 Prometheus..from the floods of day Sunn'd his clear soul with heaven's internal ray. **1815** BYRON *Hebrew Mel.*, *All is Vanity* i, I sunn'd my heart in beauty's eyes.

b. *to sun salmon*: see SUNNING *vbl. sb.* 3.

1844 W. H. MAXWELL *Sports & Adv. Scotl.* xxix. (1855) 235, I observed a fellow, in the parlance of the border, *sunning* salmon.

2. a. *refl.* To expose oneself to or bask in the sun.

1610 HOLLAND *Camden's Brit.* (1637) 720 Seales..meete together in droves to sleepe and sunne themselves. **1697** DRYDEN *Virg. Georg.* III. 635 To roofy Houses they repair, Or sun themselves abroad in open air. **1710** ADDISON *Tatler* No. 155 ¶4 These..used to sun themselves in that place.. about dinner-time. **1849** THACKERAY *Pendennis* xlii, He suns himself there after his breakfast when the day is suitable. **1885** E. ARNOLD *Secret of Death* 6 While the snake sunned himself at ease, And monkeys chattered in the trees.

fig. **1841** MIALL in *Nonconf.* I. 9 A privileged class suns itself in the beams of majesty. **1868** FREEMAN *Norm. Conq.* II. ix. 330 The Frenchmen..who had sunned themselves in the smiles of the court.

b. *intr.* for *refl.* or *pass.* Now esp. = *sun-bathe* vb. s.v. SUN *sb.* 13 a. Also *fig.*

Orig. in gerundial phr. *a sunning*: see SUNNING *vbl. sb.* 1 b.

1592 *Nobody & Someb.* in Simpson *Sch. Shaks.* (1878) I. 348 Let me be hangd up sunning in the ayre, And made a scarcrow. **1611** *Second Maiden's Tragedy* (Malone Soc.) 13 Vsurpers svnnynge in their glories like Adders in warme beames. **1622** WITHER *Mistr. Philar.* Wks. (1633) 653 The while he lies Sunning in his Mistresse Eyes. **1871** L. STEPHEN *Playgr. Eur.* (1894) ii. 63 He loves the clouds, and watches them folding and sunning. **1933** V. WOOLF *Jrnl.* 13 Apr. in *Writer's Diary* (1953) 197 But we go today and I shall sun, with only a few books. **1968** *Sat. Rev.* (U.S.) 23 Nov. 48/1 Three beaches where you can swim and sun stark naked. **1976** E. DEWHURST *After Bail* vii. 90 The sun never does anything to my lily-white skin... Alan doesn't let me sun for too long.

3. *intr.* To shine as or like the sun. *rare.*

1611 COTGR., *Soleillant*, Sunning, Sunnie. **1845** MRS. NORTON *Child of Islands* (1846) 42 Man's heart hath buds and leaves Which, sunned upon, put forth immortal bloom. **1855** TENNYSON *Maud* I. XXII. ix, Shine out, little head, sunning over with curls, To the flowers, and be their sun. **1888** T. WATTS in *Athenæum* 17 Mar. 341 A look of joy went sunning over his worn face.

4. *trans.* To shine upon or illumine as or like the sun. Chiefly *poet.*

1637 N. W[HITING] *Albino & Bellama* 123 To make Bellama smile, And with one ray sun her Albino's heart. **1722** W. HAMILTON *Wallace* 78 His Arm no longer could.. Shine in fulgent Arms, and Sun the Field. *c* **1820** S. ROGERS *Italy, Pilgrim* 22 A glade Far, far within, sunned only at noonday. **1867** H. MACMILLAN *Bible Teach.* ii. (1870) 30 Snowed on and sunned in the same hour, these flowers were yet..among the loveliest of nature's productions.

5. with advb. extension: To bring or get into a specified condition by exposure to, or illumination by, the sun. Chiefly *fig.*

1836 SIR H. TAYLOR *Statesman* xv. 103 A disposition [such] that he may sun out all the good in men's natures. **1845** BAILEY *Festus* (ed. 2) 240 But his heart ripened most 'neath southern eyes, Which sunned their sweets into him all day long. **1894** *Brit. Jrnl. Photog.* XLI. 44 Prints were often improved by sunning down the blank sky space. **1896**

A. Austin *England's Darling* III. i, Sunning grey wrinkles into golden smiles.

sun: see SON, SOON, SUNN.

sun-, var. SYN-[1].

ˈsun-baked, *a.*

1. Baked by exposure to the sun, as bricks, pottery, etc.

a **1700** Evelyn *Diary* 19 Aug. an. 1641, A kind of white sun-bak'd brick. **1888** E. Clodd *Story Creation* xi. 217 The sun-baked clay hut. **1897** Mary Kingsley *W. Africa* 322 Fan pottery, although rough and sunbaked, is artistic in form.

2. Excessively heated by the sun; dried up, parched, or hardened by the heat of the sun.

1628 Feltham *Resolves* II. [I.] xxviii. 88 When the Sun-bak'd Peasant goes to feast it with a Gentleman. **1841–4** Emerson *Ess., Art* Wks. (Bohn) I. 145 Let spouting fountains cool the air, Singing in the sun-baked square. **1891** Kipling *Light that Failed* xiii. 243 A sun-baked rose below nodded its head.

sunbeam (ˈsʌnbiːm). [OE. *sun(n)béam*, also *sunne béam*: see SUN *sb.*[1] and BEAM *sb.*[1] The form *sunnëbeme* was current until *c* 1430; *sunbeme* became frequent from 1300, first in northern texts.]

1. a. A beam of sunlight.

c **1000** Ælfric *Saints' Lives* iv. 275 Hwæt fremað þam blindan seo beorhta sun-beam? *c* **1121** *O.E. Chron.* an. 678 (Laud MS.) Her ateowede cometa se steorra on Auguste, & scan .iii. monðas ælce morȝen swilce sunne beam. *c* **1200** Ormin 18979 All all swa summ þe sunebæm Bishineþþ all þe blinde. *c* **1290** *S. Eng. Leg.* I. 480 He saiȝh hire neb, and turnde aȝein so briȝht so sonne-bem. *a* **1300** *Cursor M.* 11228 þe sun beme Gais thoru þe glas. *c* **1300** *Havelok* 592 Of hise mouth it stod a stem, Als it were a sunne-bem. **1426** Lydg. *De Guil. Pilgr.* 16212 Lyke vn-to the Sonne Bemys, Shynynge most hoote, the Sommerys day. **1540–1** Elyot *Image Gov.* 69 High trees..did cast..a pleasant..shadowe, and defended theim..from the vehement heate of the sunne beames. **1589** Greene *Menaphon* (Arb.) 23 The Mermaides ..drying their waterie tresses in the Sunne beames. **1625** N. Carpenter *Geog. Del.* I. ii. (1635) 39 The quiuering light which is spread by the refraction of the Sun-beames in the water. **1632** Milton *Penseroso* 8 The gay motes that people the Sun Beams. **1706** Pope *Let. to Wycherley* 10 Apr., Some [verses] I have contracted, as we do Sun-beams, to improve their..Force. **1840** Dickens *Old C. Shop* xv, Sparkling sunbeams dancing on chamber windows. **1843** Ruskin *Mod. Paint.* I. II. III. i. §13 Where a sunbeam enters, every particle of dust becomes visible.

b. *fig.*

c **1200** Ormin 7278 Crist iss ec soþ sunnebæm þatt all þiss werelld lihhteþþ. *c* **1450** *Godstow Reg.* 16 Now helpe us, good lady!.. Of the blessid sonne-beem ȝeue us summe light. **1624** Sir J. Davies *Ps.* xxi, The sunn-beames of Thy face will cheare his hart. **1807–8** W. Irving *Salmag.* xv. (1824) 278 [They] were delighted to see the sun-beams once more play in his Countenance.

c. (*written*) *with a sunbeam* or *in sunbeams*: in bright conspicuous characters.

a **1770** Jortin *Serm.* (1771) I. i. 12 The great duties of life are written with a Sun-beam. **1891** Farrar *Darkn. & Dawn* xlvi, Such words fall too often on our cold and careless ears with the triteness of long familiarity; but to Octavia..they seemed to be written in sunbeams.

d. Someone, esp. a woman or girl, who enlivens or cheers another. Cf. (*little*) *ray of sunshine* s.v. RAY sb.[1] 1 a.

1886 C. M. Yonge *Chantry House* II. xxi. 190 She was always a sunbeam, with her ever ready attention. **1900** C. H. Chambers *Tyranny of Tears* IV. 128 We're all very sorry you're going—particularly cook. Cook's very strong in her attachments... Cook's words was, 'This'll be a dull 'ouse when the little sunbeam's gone.' **1943** F. Thompson *Candleford Green* viii. 133 Girls..of the type then called 'sunbeams in the home': good, affectionate, home-loving girls. **1970** G. Heyer *Charity Girl* x. 150 She couldn't conceive how she had ever contrived to exist without 'our sweet little sunbeam'.

2. Used as a literal rendering of a native word applied to a radiant-coloured humming-bird.

1613 Purchas *Pilgrimage* VIII. ii. 615 The Brasilians called it *Ourissia*, which signifieth the Sun-beame. **1681** Grew *Musæum* I. IV. i. 61 The Huming Bird. By the Brasilians, called Guanumbi. By Clusius, Ourissia, i.e. a Sun-beam. **1688** R. Holme *Armoury* II. xiii. 297/1 This [Humming] Bird by the Brasilians is also called..*Guara-cyaba*, that is a Sun-beam Bird, and *Guara-cigaba*, the hair of the Sun. **1870** Gillmore tr. *Figuier's Reptiles & Birds* 466 The Indians call these darlings Sun-beams.

3. *Comb.*, as ***sunbeam-proof*** adj.

1820 Shelley *Cloud* 65 Over a torrent sea, Sunbeam-proof, I hang like a roof.

Hence †ˈ**sunbeamed**, ˈ**sunbeamy** (? *U.S.*) *adjs.*, bright as a sunbeam; genial.

1588 Shaks. *L.L.L.* v. ii. 168 To behold with your *Sunne beamed eyes. *a* **1849** Mangan *Poems* (1859) 292 That *sunbeamy standard that shone..To illumine our way. **1890** 'Annie Thomas' *Love of Lady* I. ix. 160 Her sunbeamy nature. **1897** *Pall Mall Mag.* Dec. 444 [Her hair hung] in soft, golden, sunbeamy masses down her back.

ˈsunbird, ˈsun-bird.

1. a. = DARTER 4 a (*Plotus anhinga*).

1796 Nemnich *Polygl.-Lex., Sun bird*, the Surinam darter.

b. Any bird of the passerine family *Nectariniidæ*, which comprises small birds with brilliant and variegated plumage, found in tropical and subtropical regions of Africa, Asia, and Australia; also applied to similar birds of other families.

1826 Stephens *Shaw's Gen. Zool.* XIV. 229 *Cinnyris*,.. Sun-bird. **1859** Tennent *Ceylon* I. II. ii. 168 Beneath our windows the Sun Birds (known as the Humming Birds of Ceylon) hover all day long. **1879** E. P. Wright *Anim. Life* 254 The Sun Birds, or *Nectariniadæ*, are to the Old World what the Humming Birds are to the New World... One species is met so far north as the Jordan valley..called the Jericho Sun Bird (*Cinnyris osea*). **1906** *Westm. Gaz.* 9 Feb. 8/2 A malachite sun bird.

c. The sun-bittern, *Eurypyga helias*.

1825 Waterton *Wand. S. Amer.* iii. 220 Here,..I saw the Sun-bird, called Tirana by the Spaniards in the Oroonoque. **1871** Kingsley *At Last* v, His name is Sun-bird,.. according to..Stedman, 'because, when it extends its wings,..there appears on the interior part of each wing a most beautiful representation of a sun'.

d. Any bird of the family *Heliornithidæ*, which comprises swimming birds found in tropical regions of America, Africa, and Asia; also called *sungrebes* or *finfoots*.

1872 Coues *N. Amer. Birds* 242 The sun-birds, *Heliornithidæ*, are a small but remarkable family.

2. (With hyphen.) **a.** A bird sacred to the sun or connected with sun-worship. **b.** A mythical 'bird of the sun', or the sun regarded as a bird.

1871 Tylor *Prim. Cult.* xvi. II. 262 When at mid-day the sunlight poured down upon the altar,..the sun-birds, the tonatzuli, were let fly up sunward as messengers. **1877** Carpenter tr. *Tiele's Outlines Hist. Relig.* 144 By the infinite world-serpent..he [*sc.* Vishnu] is drawn over the waves of the primeval ocean, or by the sun-bird *Garuḍa* through the sky. **1904** Budge *3rd & 4th Egypt. Rooms Brit. Mus.* 122 The Sun-god Rā was depicted..in the form of a hawk-headed man, because the hawk was regarded as a sun-bird.

ˈsun-blink. *Sc.* [BLINK *sb.*[2]] A gleam of sunshine. Also *attrib.*

1635 Rutherford *Lett.* 22 Apr. (1675) III. 174 There shall be a fair Sun-blink on Christ's old Spouse, and a clear Skie. **1728** P. Walker *Life of Peden* in *Biog. Presbyt.* (1827) I. 136 In our Sun-blink Days of the Gospel. **1728** Ramsay *Robt., Richy, & Sandy* 36 Like sun-blinks on a cloudy winter's day. **1818** Scott *Hrt. Midl.* xiv, The midges that the sun-blink brings out, and the evening wind sweeps away! **1832–53** J. Murray in *Whistle-binkie* Ser. III. 44 Now, simmer, ye maun use us weel, Wi' shower and sun-blink at its heel. **1880** A. B. Todd *Circling Year, Oct.* xiii, The mild sunblinks smile down on the scene.

sunbow (ˈsʌnbəʊ). Chiefly *poet.* [f. SUN *sb.*[1] + BOW *sb.*[1], after *rainbow.*] An arch of prismatic colours like a rainbow, formed by refraction of sunlight in spray or vapour.

1816 Shelley *Let. to Peacock* 22 July, Spray..in the midst of which hung a multitude of sunbows. **1817** Byron *Manfred* II. ii. 1 The sunbow's rays still arch The torrent with the many hues of heaven. **1831** James *Phil. Augustus* I. ii, The thousand colours of the sunbow that hung above its fall. **1847** Whittier *To Delaware* 13 The great lakes..Shall weave new sun-bows in their tossing spray.

ˈsun-bright, *a.* Chiefly *poet.* [OE. *sunbeorht* occurs in sense 2.]

1. Bright as the sun; supremely bright. (Often in hyperbolical use; also *fig.*)

1579 Spenser *Sheph. Cal.* Oct. 72 Sonnebright honour pend in shamefull coupe. **1591** Shaks. *Two Gent.* III. i. 88 How, and which way I may bestow my selfe To be regarded in her sun-bright eye. **1642** H. More *Song of Soul* I. i. 3 The fulvid Eagle with her sun-bright eye. **1667** Milton *P.L.* VI. 100 High in the midst exalted as a God Th' Apostat in his Sun-bright Chariot sate. **1747** D. Mallet *Amyntor & Theodora* Wks. 1759 I. 153 As reason thus the mental storm seren'd And thro the darkness sent her sun-bright ray. **1883** W. Arthur *Fernley Lect.* 73 The sunbright thoughts of man themselves.

2. Bright with sunshine; illumined by the sun.

1744 Akenside *Pleas. Imag.* III. 360 For not the expanse Of living lakes in Summer's noontide calm, Reflects the..sun-bright heavens With fairer semblance. **1827** Keble *Chr. Y., St. James' Day*, Tabor's sunbright steep. *a* **1835** Mrs. Hemans *Maremma* xxiv, A sun-bright waste of beauty. **1894** Stevenson & L. Osbourne *Ebb Tide* iii, The green of sunbright foliage.

sunburn (ˈsʌnbɜːn), *sb.* [f. SUNBURN *v.* OE. had *sunbryne.*] **1. a.** The condition of being sunburnt; discoloration or superficial inflammation of the skin caused by exposure to the sun; the brown colour or tan thus produced.

1652 Cotterell tr. *Calprenède's Cassandra* I. ii. (1676) 2 The sunburn and toil of a long journey had..taken off the lustre of his former beauty. **1820** Good *Nosology* 505 Ephelis. Cuticle tawny by exposure to the sun; often spotted with dark freckles,..Sun-burn. **1852** Hawthorne *Blithedale Rom.* viii, Our faces took the sunburn kindly. **1895** *Pall Mall Mag.* 291 A big..man, with a..crooked line of sunburn across his forehead. **1896** Baden-Powell *Matabele Campaign* xvi, I found that my right knee and thigh have their beautiful..surface marred by eight.. blotches of ruddy sunburn.

transf. **1891** Miss Dowie *Girl in Karp.* 134 He was incapacitated three days with sunburn in his muscles. **1893** Kate Sanborn *Truthful Woman S. California* 93 Another morning you may stumble out trying to rub yesterday's sunburn from your eyes.

b. In plants: = HELIOSIS 2.

1866 *Treas. Bot.* **1896** Lodeman *Spray. Plants* 364 Leaf Blight; Rust; Sunburn (*Sphærella Fragariæ*).

2. The name of a fashion colour.

1923 *Daily Mail* 11 Sept. 11 Nude, Sunburn, Mulatto, and all shades. **1932** *Barker's Sales Catal.* 27 Poplin tennis shirts... Guaranteed fast self colours of blue, champagne, helio, ivory, sunburn, white and light grey.

ˈsunburn, *v.* [Back-formation from SUNBURNING, SUNBURNT.]

1. *trans.* To 'burn', scorch, or discolour (usually the skin) by exposure to the sun; to affect with sunburn; to tan. Also *fig.*

1530 Palsgr. 725/1, I sonne burne, as ones face, or their handes do that the sonne shyneth moche apon, *je hasle.* **1611** Cotgr., *Haler*, to Sunne-burne or scorch in the Sunne. **1634** Sir T. Herbert *Trav.* 1 Hot dayes, which haue Sun-burnt my lines, aswell as face. **1667** Dryden & Dk. Newcastle *Sir M. Mar-all* II. i, My aunt charged me not to pull off my glove for fear of sun-burning my hand. **1805** Emily Clark *Banks of Douro* III. 68 The scorching rays had sun-burnt his face. **1860** Ruskin *Mod. Paint.* V. IX. iii. §2. 218 The Venetians..sunburn all their hermits into splendid russet brown. **1909** Miss G. Guinness *Peru* v. 45 The dry season has sunburnt the hillsides.

2. *intr.* for *pass.* To be discoloured or tanned by exposure to the sun; also of a plant (cf. prec. b).

1832 J. Wilson in *Trans. Hortic. Soc.* (1835) I. 211 If the sun be bright, the leaves would sun-burn in a short time. **1873** J. H. Beadle *Undevel. West* xxix. 640 An Indian will 'sunburn' as much or even more than a white man. **1928** *Daily Mail* 6 Aug. 12/6 One girl tells me she 'doesn't sunburn easily'. **1962** L. Deighton *Ipcress File* i. 14 He had a clear complexion that sunburnt easily.

ˈsun-ˌburner. [f. SUN *sb.*[1] + BURNER 4.] A group of gas-burners with reflectors, circularly arranged so as to suggest the sun, placed near the ceiling of a large room for lighting and (often) for ventilation through an opening above.

1858 Simmonds *Dict. Trade.* **1862** *Catal. Internat. Exhib., Brit.* II. No. 6349 Improved sun burner, with valve. **1881** Miss Braddon *Asphodel* II. 257 The hall was lighted by a.. central chandelier, and two sun-burners in the ceiling.

b. A burner for an oil lamp, kept in position by a thin circular metal plate indented round the edge.

1884 Knight *Dict. Mech.* Suppl.

ˈsunˌburning, *sb.* [f. as prec. + BURNING *vbl. sb.*] 'Burning' by exposure to the sun; sunburn.

1530 Palsgr. 272/2 Sonne burnyng, *hasle.* **1535** Coverdale *Isa.* iii. 24 In steade of a stomacher, a sack cloth, and for their bewty wythrednesse and sonneburnynge. **1599** Shaks. *Hen. V*, v. ii. 154 If thou canst loue a fellow of this temper, Kate, whose face is not worth Sunne-burning.. take me. **1642** Milton *Apol. Smect.* xi. Wks. 1851 III. 314 Those thanks in the womans Churching for her delivery from Sun-burning and Moonblasting. **1680** T. K. *Kitchin-Physician* 10 This Pomade takes away Sun-burning. **1822–7** Good *Study Med.* (1829) V. 699 Blemishes which have no connexion with sun-burning. **1900** D. S. Margoliouth in *Expositor* Jan. 34 Swarthiness produced by sunburning.

So ˈ**sunˌburning** *a. rare*[−1].

1555 Latimer in Strype *Eccl. Mem.* (1721) III. App. xxxvi. 99 A little heate or sun-burning wether.

ˈsunburnt, ˈsunburned, *a.* Forms: see BURN *v.*[1] [f. SUN *sb.*[1] + *burnt, burned*, pa. pple. of BURN *v.*[1] Cf. G. *sonn(en)verbrannt.*]

1. Discoloured, tanned, or superficially inflamed by exposure to sunshine; chiefly of the skin or complexion.

α. c **1400** *Plowman's Tale* 18 Our hoste..saw this man was sunne y-brent. *c* **1530** *Judic. Urines* II. ii. 11 b, Men of Ethyoppe, that are sonne breent. *a* **1550** *Peebles to the Play* in *Pop. Scot. Poems* 6, I dar not come yon mercat to, I am so ill sun-brynt. **1553** T. Wilson *Rhet.* (1580) 5 Thei that walke muche in the Sonne..are..for the moste part Sonne burnt. *a* **1649** Drumm. of Hawth. *Irene* Wks. (1711) 170 The sun-burnt nations of the south. **1676** *Lond. Gaz.* No. 1105/4 A short fat Man with a reddish face, his hair sun burnt. **1705** *Ibid.* No. 4155/4 A black Gelding.., with a short whisk Tail, and Sun-burnt upon it. **1818** Byron *Beppo* xxvi, He was a man as dusky as a Spaniard, Sunburnt with travel. **1825** Scott *Betrothed* xxxi, His swarthy and sunburnt hair. **1858** Longf. *M. Standish* IX. 50 Great was the people's amazement,..Thus to behold once more the sunburnt face of their Captain.

β. ? c **1500** *How the Plowman lerned his Pater-Noster* 130 in Hazl. *E.P.P.* (1864) I. 214 The one [was] sonburned, another black as a pan. **1530** Palsgr. 429/1, I am sonne brunde with sonne. *Ibid.* 725/1 Howe you be sonne burned for one dayes rydynge. **1622** Peacham *Compl. Gentl.* vi. (1906) 52, I would..have done him as much honour, as ever ..the Sun-burnd Ægyptians their Æsculapius. **1813** Scott *Trierm.* II. xxi, The sun-burn'd maid. **1885** 'Mrs. Alexander' *At Bay* i, A broad sunburned face.

†**b.** *fig.* Superficially learned. *Obs. nonce-use.*

a **1568** Ascham *Scholem.* II. (Arb.) 111 So many seeming, and sonburnt ministers..whose learning is gotten in a sommer heat, and washed away, with a Christmas snow againe.

c. *transf.* Of a brown colour, as if sunburnt.

1893 *Lady* 10 Aug. 146/2 Sunburnt straw will be immensely popular for country wear. **1915** *Truth* 25 Aug. 317/1 Pastry and cakes, which may be of a sunburned brown.

2. Scorched, parched, or dried up by the heat of the sun, as land or vegetation; also *fig.*

a. c **1586** C'tess Pembroke *Ps.* LXXVIII. xi, As thick as dust on sun-burnt field. **1597** Drayton *Mortimeriad* Ded. 2 Whilst they boast but of their sun-burnt brayns. **1631** Knevet *Rhodon & Iris* III. iii. F 3, On the sun-burnt brinke of warme Hydaspes. *a* **1658** Cleveland *Content* 80 Whither wilt thou bear My Sun-burnt hope to Loss? *a* **1721** Prior *Amaryllis* 29 On sun-burnt mountain-tops, and parched sands. **1801** *Farmer's Mag.* Aug. 351 The rains..have given a fresh verdure to the sun-burnt grass. **1880** L. Wallace *Ben-Hur* 7 The sunburnt ways of the wilderness.

β. *a*1586 SIDNEY *Arcadia* III. ii. (1590) 249b, The pleasantest fruites, that Sunburnd Autumne could deliuer. **1632** RUTHERFORD *Lett.* 9 Mar. (1675) III. 164 In the same Garden..grow the Saints, God's fair and beautiful Lillies, under wind and rain and all sun-burned.

3. Baked by the heat of the sun, as bricks: = SUN-BAKED 1.

1634 SIR T. HERBERT *Trav.* 61 The Houses are of Sun-burnt bricks. **1686** HEDGES *Diary* 14 Apr., I went to see a great Tower called Nimrod, built of Sun-burnt bricks. **1820** BELZONI *Egypt & Nubia* III. 385 A high wall of sun-burnt bricks. **1862** BEVERIDGE *Hist. India* III. VII. vi. 184 A thick and lofty wall of sun-burned clay.

Hence 'sunburntness *rare*.

1692 O. WALKER *Grk. & Rom. Hist.* 233 C. Pescennius Niger Justus..was called Niger, because of the Sun-burntness of his Neck and Face.

'sunburst. [See BURST *sb.* 3.]

1. A burst of sunlight; a sudden shining of the sun from behind a cloud.

1816 SCOTT *Return to Ulster* iii, And the standard of Fion flash'd fierce from on high, Like a burst of the sun when the tempest is nigh. [*Note*] In ancient Irish poetry, the standard of Fion, or Fingal, is called the *Sun-burst.* **1828** MOORE *'Tis gone, & for ever* ii, When Truth,..like a Sun-burst, her banner unfurl'd. **1841** *Florist's Jrnl.* (1846) II. 33 The offsets..are removed to a temporary stage, fixed to a wall with a north aspect, the better to shade them from sunbursts. **1888** M. GRAY *Reproach Annesley* III. i, A Sun-burst fell upon the violet pall.

fig. **1870** LOWELL *Study Wind., Chaucer* (1871) 177 The invocation of Venus,..by Lucretius, seems to me the one sunburst of purely poetic inspiration which the Latin language can show. **1886** H. M. POSNETT *Compar. Lit.* 185 That sunburst of creative power.

2. a. A firework, a piece of jewellery, etc., constructed so as to imitate the sun with its rays.

1902 GREENOUGH & KITTREDGE *Words & Ways* 260 It would be more logical to arrange the whole article in the form of a sunburst or a star-fish. **1903** *Smart Set* IX. 110/1 A diaphanous white gown, caught at the throat by a diamond sunburst.

b. *attrib.* of things designed or arranged as conventional or stylized representations of the sun and its rays; esp. ***sunburst clock***, a clock framed by radiating arms; ***sunburst pleat*** = *sun-ray pleat* s.v. SUN-RAY 2b.

1908 *Sears, Roebuck Catal.* 362/2 Salt and pepper shakers. In beautiful sunburst pattern. **1920** *Glasgow Herald* 29 Apr. 6 Her bouquet was of 'sunburst' roses. **1927** A. E. W. MASON *No Other Tiger* xxiii. 260 They sold the lot—the emerald ring, the diamond sunburst ear-rings and all. **1939** M. B. PICKEN *Lang. of Fashion* 113/2 *Sunburst p[laits]*, accordion-like plaits that are narrow at top and wider at the bottom, thus producing a flare. Fabric plaited on bias so that plaits radiate from a center. **1949** M. STEEN *Twilight on Floods* III. iv. 426 The gilt sunburst clock over the fireplace. **1962** M. KELLY *Due to a Death* ix. 152 There was a sunburst window over the hairdresser's door. **1969** M. TRIPP *Malice & Maternal Instinct* i. 6 A sunburst clock on one of the blue walls in the main room. **1980** *News & Observer* (Raleigh, N. Carolina) 28 Oct. 17/7 The sun set Sunday on the familiar sunburst insignia.

‖**sunck.** Also 7 sunke, 8 sunk. [N. American Indian; *sunck squaw* app. represents Natick *sonksq*, *sonkusq* queen, mistress (f. *sonqhuau* he overcomes, has the mastery) = Narragansett *saunks*, pl. *saunckssquuaog* (Roger Williams).] In full ***sunck squaw***: The female chief or queen of an American Indian people.

1676 *Connect. Col. Rec.* (1852) II. 458 That ould peice of venum, Sunck squaw Magnus. **1677** HUBBARD *Indian Wars* I. 105 The same Indians..and their Sunke Squaw, or chief Woman of that Indian Plantation. **1797** J. TRUMBULL *Hist. Connect.* I. 347 The six Narraganset sachems, and the sunk squaw or old queen of Narraganset. **1804** J. HAUGHTON in *Mass. Hist. Coll.* IX. 83 *note*, Awaking one night,..and finding his sunck (queen) lying near another Indian, he.. took his knife, and cut three strokes on each of her cheeks.

sund, obs. form of SOUND.

Sunda ('sʌndə). The name of the group of islands in the Malay Archipelago (including Sumatra, Java, Borneo, Celebes, the Moluccas, etc.), used attrib. to specify certain animals, as ***Sunda grosbeak, ox.***

1802 LATHAM *Gen. Synopsis Birds* Suppl. II. 196 Sunda Grosbeak, *Loxia Javensis.* **1883** *Encycl. Brit.* XV. 322/1 Here [in the Malay Peninsula] is..the Sunda ox of Java.

Hence **Sunda'nese**, **Sunda'nesian** *a.*, belonging or native to the Sunda Islands; also *sb.* of the natives or their language.

1876 tr. *Haeckel's Hist. Creation* II. 327 All the Polynesian and Sundanesian dialects and languages can be derived from a common, long since extinct primeval language. **1878** Sundanese [see MADURESE *a.* and *sb.*]. **1880** *Encycl. Brit.* XII. 818/1 The most cultivated of the native tongues is the Javanese... To it Sundanese stands in the relation that Low German holds to High German. *Ibid.* XIII. 607/1 The Javanese are generally darker than the Sundanese... The Sundanese is less than the Javanese proper.

sundae ('sʌndeɪ). orig. *U.S.* Also (*rarely*) sundi. [Origin uncertain. There exist a number of differing accounts both of the invention of the dish and of the coinage of its name.

The name is generally explained as an alteration of *Sunday*, either because the dish originally included leftover ice-cream sold cheaply on Monday, or because it was at first sold only on Sunday, having, according to some accounts, been devised to circumvent Sunday legislation. The alteration of the spelling is sometimes said to be out of deference to religious people's feelings about the word *Sunday*. For several accounts see H. L. Mencken, *The American Language* Suppl. I. (1945), pp. 376–7.]

A confection of ice-cream topped or mixed with crushed fruit, nuts, syrup, whipped cream, etc. locally also called *college ice.*

1897 W. A. BONHAM *Mod. Guide for Soda Dispensers* 126 Peach Sundae. Ice cream, vanilla or peach..5 ounces. Crushed or sliced peaches..2 ounces. Serve with a spoon. Pear, orange, raspberry and other fruit sundaes are made by adding the syrup or fruit to the ice cream. **1904** *N.Y. Evening Post* 21 May (Sat. Suppl.) 4/7 The Sundi, so popular at the confectioner's, can be prepared at home. Make a rich vanilla ice cream and over it pour the juice of your preserved fruits. **1904** *Minneapolis Times* 15 June 6 In one of the Jersey City churches fans and lemonade are distributed. Some brands of 'sundae' might be added with propriety. **1910** *Chambers's Jrnl.* July 431/1 A sundae—a mixture of ice-cream, soda-water, and raspberry juice. **1927** A. P. HERBERT *Plain Jane* 88 I'm fizzy and fiery and fruity and tense, So let's have a sundae and hang the expense. **1951** T. STERLING *House without Door* ii. 22 Year after year.. Schrafft's had been serving lamb and mint jelly and hot fudge sundaes to others. **1970** *Kay & Co.* (Worcester) *Catal.* 1970/71, 896 Six Bohemian sundae glasses in the Zorka design... Perfect for all sweets.

‖**sundang** (sun'daŋ). [Malay.] A heavy two-edged sword used in Malaysia.

1902 *Encycl. Brit.* XXX. 497/1 Malays use...short broad swords called *sûndang.* **1936** G. B. GARDNER *Keris* i. 30 The *sundang* is two edged and may be straight or sinuous. **1947** R. WINSTEDT *Malays* 165 The type..is closer to the Bugis *sundang* or short sword. **1972** M. SHEPPARD *Taman Indera* 133 The largest member of the kris family is the *Sundang*, the sword kris. It originated in the Celebes... The Sundang is a cutting and slashing weapon and is not intended for thrusting.

sundari, variant of SUNDRI.

Sunday ('sʌndeɪ, -dɪ), *sb.* Forms: see below. [OE. *sunnandæȝ*, = OFris. *sunnan-*, *sunnen-*, *sonnendei*, *-di* (NFris. *sanndai*, *senndei*, *sönndei*, EFris. *sendei*, *-di*, etc.), OS. *sunnun-*, *sunnondag*, MLG. *sunnen-*, *sun-*, *sondach*, (MDu. *sonnendach*, *sondagh*, Du. *zondag*), OHG. *sunnûn* or *sunnon dag* or *tag* (MHG. *sunnen* or *sonnen tag*, *sunnetac*, *suntac*, etc., G. *sonntag*), ON. *sunnudagr* (Sw., Da. *søndag*); transl. of late L. *diēs sōlis* = late Gr. ἡμέρα ἡλίου 'day of the sun'.

Now (like the other names of days of the week) with initial capital, which is frequent in early texts, but does not become regular till the 17th.]

1. a. The first day of the week, observed by Christians as a day of rest and worship, in commemoration of Christ's resurrection; the Lord's Day.

α. **1 sunnandæȝ, 2 sunnen dæi, sunnondæȝ, 2–5 sonenday, 3 sunen-, 3–4 sonnen-, 4 sonun-, 4–5 sonnon-, sonon(n)-, 5 sonoun-, sunun-.**

*a*700 *Laws of Ine* c. 3 Ȝif ðeowmon wyrce on Sunnandæȝ. **971** *Blickl. Hom.* 47 þæt hi Sunnandagum.. Godes cyrican ȝeorne secan. *c*1154 *O.E. Chron.* an. 1154 On þe sunnen dæi be foren midwinter dæi. *c*1250 *Gen. & Ex.* 261 Ihesus..Ros fro ded on ðe sunenday. *a*1300–1400 *Cursor M.* 17288 + 1 (Cott.) On sonondai in þe daghyng, he ros fro ded to liue. **1357** *Lay Folks Catech.* (T.) 49 Openly on Inglis oþon sononndaies Teche and preche thaim, that thai haue cure of. **1375** BARBOUR *Bruce* v. 335 The folk apon the sononday Held to Sanct Brydis kirk thar way. *a*1400 *Relig. Pieces fr. Thornton MS.* 5 The thirde commandement es þat we halde and halowe oure haly day, þe sonondaye. *c*1400 MAUNDEV. (Roxb.) iii. 10 On þe Setirday and on þe Sonounday.

β. **1** *Northumb.* **sunnadæȝ, (-doeȝ), sunnedæ, 2 sunne-dei, 2–3 sunedai, 3 sune-day, sonedæi, -dai, 3–4 soneday, (4 sonneday(e).**

*c*950 *Lindisf. Gosp.* Matt. xii. 1 *Sabbato*, in sunnadæȝ. *Ibid.* John v. 16–18 *In sabbato*, in symbeldæȝ... *Sabbatum*, ðone sunnedae. *c*1175 *Lamb. Hom.* 45 Amansed beo þe mon þe sunne-dei nulle iloken. *c*1205 LAY. 13934 Þene Sunne heo ȝiuen sonedæi. **1297** R. GLOUC. (Rolls) 8724 Þe soneday he was ycrouned. **13..** *St. Alexius* (Laud 108) 338 Vpon þe holy soneday. **1393** LANGL. *P. Pl.* C. x. 227 Vp-on sonedayes to cesse godes seruyce to huyre.

γ. **3–4 sundai, 4 sounday, sondai, -dey, zonday, *Sc.* sownday, 4–6 *Sc.* sounday, 4–7 sonday, (5 sondaw, *Sc.* sonda), 5–6 sondaye, 6 sunnedaye, 6–7 sundaie, 4– sunday, Sunday.**

*a*1300 *X Commandm.* 25 in *E.E.P.* (1862) 16 Þe secunde so is þis sundai wel þat ȝe holde. **1303** R. BRUNNE *Handl. Synne* 306 Of al þe festys þat yn holy chyrche are, Holy sunday men oght to spare. **1340** *Ayenb.* 7 Oure lhord aros uram dyaþe to lyue þane zonday. *c*1375 *Sc. Leg. Saints* xxv. (*Julian*) 128 A housband..telyt his land one sownday. **1387** TREVISA *Higden* (Rolls) V. 199 Þe credo þat is i-songe þe Sondayes [*v.r.* Sondawes]. **1456** *Paston Lett.* I. 386 The King hathe ley in London Friday, Saterday, Sonday. **1526** TINDALE *Rev.* i. 10, I was in the sprete on a sondaye. **1561** WINȜET *Four Scoir Thre Quest.* To Rdr., Wks. (S.T.S.) I. 53 At Pasche and certane Soundays efter. **1596** SHAKS. *Tam. Shr.* II. i. 397 Now on the sonday following, shall Bianca Be Bride to you. **1633** G. HERBERT *Temple, Sunday* iv, Sundaies the pillars are, On which heav'ns palace arched lies. **1750** JOHNSON *Rambler* No. 10 ¶7, I seldom frequent card-tables on Sundays. **1839** LONGF. *Vill. Blacksmith* v, He goes on Sunday to the church, And sits among his boys. **1887** RUSKIN *Præterita* II. vi. 198 It was thirteen years later before I made a sketch on Sunday.

b. With specific epithet, as *Advent, Midlent, Mothering, Trinity* (q.v.). † ***the Sunday of the Passion***: Passion Sunday.

1297 R. GLOUC. (Rolls) 10178 Þe sonenday of þe passion.

c. colloq. phr. ***when two Sundays come together (meet)***, never. ***a month of Sundays***, a very long time. ***(one's) Sunday out***, the monthly or other Sunday on which a domestic servant is free; hence ***Sunday outer***. ***Sunday-go-to-meeting clothes, suit***, a humorous expansion of *Sunday clothes*, etc. (cf. *go-to-meeting*, GO *v.* VIII); also *ellipt.* as ***Sunday-go-to-meetings.***

1670 RAY *Collect. Prov.* 194 When two Sundays meet. **1677** COLES *Eng.-Lat. Dict.* s.v., When two Sundays come together. **1831** Sunday-go-to-meetings [see GO-TO-MEETING *sb.*]. **1831** J. R. MOTTE *Diary* 28 Aug. in A. H. Cole *Charleston goes to Harvard* (1940) 100 Rose at 7, and having shaved and dressed myself,—in Sunday-go-to-meeting clothes, started for a walk to Boston. **1841** *Punch* 21 Aug. 65/1 A veritable footman,..upon the occasion of his 'Sunday out'. **1846** D. CORCORAN *Pickings from Picayune* 49 The hoosier asked him if he thought him 'darn'd fool enough to dirty his Sunday-go-to-meetin' clothes'? **1847** J. CODMAN *Sailor's Life & Sailor's Yarns* 25 He..dressed himself in his 'Sunday-go-to-meetings'..and bade adieu to home. **1849** G. E. JEWSBURY *Let.* 29 Mar. (1892) 286 If I don't get a better letter from you, or at least a letter with something in it, you may pass 'a month of Sundays' at breakfast without any letter from me. **1850** KINGSLEY *Alt. Locke* xxvii, I haven't heard more fluent or passionate English this month of Sundays. **1858** [see OUT *adv.* 15b]. **1864** F. LOCKER *Housemaid* i. 6 Thou canst not stir, because 'tis not Thy Sunday out. **1879** DICKENS *Life Charles James Mathews* I. i. 30 A couple advanced who evidently did not belong to the usual class of 'Sunday outers'. **1888** 'R. BOLDREWOOD' *Robbery under Arms* xliv, I ain't been out of this blessed hole..for a month of Sundays. **1894** BARING-GOULD *Queen of Love* I. ii. 15 All in your Sunday-go-to-meeting togs. **1896** HOUSMAN *Shropshire Lad* xxv, Rose Harland on her Sundays out Walked with the better man. **1900** ELIZ. GLYN *Visits Elizabeth* (1906) 15 Such funny, grand, best smart Sunday-go-to-meeting looking clothes.

d. *pl. ellipt.* for: (*a*) Sunday clothes or best; (*b*) Sunday newspapers.

(*a*) **1901** 'MARK TWAIN' in *Century Mag.* Nov. 26/2 Tommy was..not in his Sundays, but in his dreadful work-clothes. **1933** *Punch* 14 June 663/1 Tom was busy brushing up his Sundays to go a-calling at the stationmaster's house. **1944** E. CARR *House of All Sorts* 89 Neither of them noticed the dust on his 'Sundays' as they smiled off down the street.

(*b*) **1949** E. BENN *Happier Days* x. 116 The Sundays and Weeklies were outside the squabbles of the Dailies. **1963** *Listener* 24 Jan. 175/3 An English reviewer, writing in one of the 'posh Sundays'..recently claimed that only Dubliners are now writing outstanding prose. **1976** T. STOPPARD *Dirty Linen* 9 They each carry several newspapers, a whole crop of the day's papers and the Sundays. **1983** *Listener* 27 Jan. 18/3 There are the smart Sundays, the *Guardian's* Agenda page on Monday mornings, and pieces such as this in the literate weeklies.

2. ***Saint Sunday***, a rendering of *Sanctus Dominicus* = St. Dominic, due to confusion with L. *dies dominica* (see DOMINICAL *a.* 2, DOMINICAN) = Sunday. *local.*

St. Dominic's Abbey, Cork, is called St. Sunday's Abbey in an inquisition about the end of Elizabeth's reign (*N. & Q.* 5th Ser. IX. 254), and the Dominican friary in Drogheda was situated near Sunday's Gate (D'Alton *Hist. Drogheda*, 1844, I. 120).

1490 *Yatton Churchw. Acc.* (Som. Rec. Soc.) 117 Payd for Sint Sunday xij[s] ix[d]. **1530** *Test. Ebor.* (Surtees) V. 299, I gyff a hyeff of beis to keip the lyght afore Seynt Sonday and Seynt Erasmus. **1532** in Weaver *Wells Wills* (1890) 70 Our lady a shepe and a kyrtell..St. Katerine a shepe—S. Antony iiij[d]—Saint Sonday iiij[d]. **1539** *Will T. Milnay, of Doncaster*, To be buried in the church of St. George in Doncaster afor Sanct Sonday. **1842** FABER *Styrian Lake* 168 Far to the right St. Sunday's quiet shade Stoops o'er the dell where Grisedale Tarn is laid.

3. *attrib.* and *Comb.* = Of or pertaining to, taking place on or characteristic of Sunday, as ***Sunday audience, book, chime, concert, dinner, drink, evening, excursion, face*** (also ***-faced*** *adj.*), ***morn(ing), paper, pastime, sabbath, trading, train, travelling***; worn on Sunday (also occasionally with possessive ***Sunday's***), as ***Sunday beaver, clothes, coat, garb, garment, hat, suit***; carrying out an activity only on Sundays or for pleasure (on the analogy of *Sunday driver, Sunday painter*), as ***Sunday architect, artist, golfer, novelist, poet, sailor***; objective, as ***Sunday-breaker***; also ***Sunday-like, -seeming*** adjs.; **Sunday best**, one's best attire, worn on Sunday; also **Sunday's best** and *transf.* and *attrib.*; **Sunday** or **Sunday's child** [cf. MLG. *sundageskint*, G. *sonntagskind*], a child born on Sunday, hence, one (according to popular belief) greatly blessed or favoured (so †**Sunday's daughter**); †**Sunday citizen**, a citizen in Sunday clothes; **Sunday closing**, the closing on Sundays of shops, except for the sale of certain commodities, or of public houses, etc.; **Sunday driver**, one who drives chiefly at week-ends, freq. an unpractised, slow, or unskilful driver; **Sunday face**, (orig. *Sc.*) a sanctimonious expression; also (*Irish*) a festive countenance; **Sunday-going** *adj.*, (of clothing, etc.) that one goes out in on Sunday; **Sunday joint**, a roasted joint of meat traditionally served for Sunday lunch; **Sunday letter**, the dominical letter; **Sunday lunch**, the traditional large meal served at midday on Sunday; **Sunday man**, one who goes out only on Sunday; **Sunday observance**, the keeping of Sunday as a day of rest and worship; **Sunday painter**, an amateur painter, one who paints purely for pleasure; often applied to a naïve painter (NAÏVE *a.* 1 c), esp. Henri Rousseau; **Sunday punch** *U.S. slang*, a knock-out blow (of the fist); also *transf.*; **Sunday salt**: see quot. 1808; **Sunday supplement**, an illustrated section issued with a Sunday newspaper, sometimes characterized by the portrayal of voguish living. See also SUNDAY-SCHOOL.

1783 R. RAIKES *Let.* 25 Nov. in *Gentl. Mag.* (1784) LIV. I. 411/1 Upon the *Sunday afternoon, the mistresses take their scholars to church. **1978** *Listener* 6 Apr. 439/1 A small temple of individualism..by a *Sunday architect. **1978** *Times* 12 Apr. 16/5 Those who think the Berlin Wall was built..for *Sunday artists to exhibit their wares on. **1856** *N. Brit. Rev.* XXVI. 30 The preacher should abstain from addressing to a promiscuous *Sunday audience the themes of abstract science. **1840** HOOD *An Open Question* iii, The beaver..So different from other *Sunday beavers! **1794** *Sunday's best [see BEST *a.* 8 d]. [**1844** G. E. JEWSBURY *Let.* 17 Sept. (1892) 143 So, on the whole, you may set it down as one of the best good deeds you ever did—quite a 'Sunday best.'] **1846** *Amulet* 12 Some urchins, dressed out 'in their Sunday's best', all neatly clean. **1846** *Godey's Mag.* July 8/2 Like most of the nobility he dresses with the utmost plainness, hardly above the substantial Yankee 'squire' in his Sunday best. **1849** N. P. WILLIS *Rural Lett.* iii. 325 It was that kind of Sabbath weather in which Nature seems dressed and resting—every tree looking its 'Sunday best'. **1859** [see BEST *a.* 8 d]. **1866** MRS. GASKELL *Wives & Dau.* xlv, Mrs. Gibson was off, all in her Sunday best (to use the servant's expression). **1969** R. BLYTHE *Akenfield* ii. 59 Sunday-best suits. **1811** L. M. HAWKINS *C'tess & Gertr.* xxvii. II. 86, I tell you I have a *Sunday-book; that which at present occupies with me the chief place next the Scriptures, is Klopstock's Messiah. **1855** *Amy Carlton* 89 'Miss Jones will..give out the Sunday books'..a number of histories of good people, Bible stories, parables, allegories, and other books of the same sort. **1885** *Manch. Exam.* 6 July 5/4 He let the fashionable *Sunday-breakers have a piece of his mind. **1886** C. M. YONGE *Chantry House* I. i. 8 He was punished for 'telling fibs', though the housemaid used to speak..of his being a '*Sunday child'. **1888** E. GERARD *Land beyond Forest* xxix. II. 41 Sunday children are lucky, and can discover hidden treasures. —— *Popular Rime*, Sunday's child is full of grace. **1818** SCOTT *Hrt. Midl.* xxxi, The parish church, ..from which at present was heard the *Sunday chime of bells. **1596** SHAKS. *1 Hen. IV*, III. i. 261 Leaue..such protest ..To Veluet-Guards, and *Sunday-Citizens. **1850** *Punch* 31 Aug. 92/2 The *Sunday closing of the country Post was considered no other than an unmeaning rant of a party. **1863** *Punch* 28 Mar. 130 (*caption*) Probable effect of Mr. Somes's Sunday Closing Bill. **1881** *Act* 44 & 45 *Vict.* c. 61 s. 5 This Act may be cited as the Sunday Closing (Wales) Act, 1881. **1932** U. SINCLAIR *Candid Remin.* II. ix. 60 He would join the church, sign pledges, vote for Sunday closing. **1971** *Reader's Digest Family Guide to Law* 660/2 Some areas—parts of Wales and Monmouthshire—have Sunday closing [of public houses] by law. **1642** H. MORE *Song of Soul* I. i. 20 Such as their Phyllis would, when as she plains Their *Sunday-cloths. *a* **1774** FERGUSSON *Hallow-fair* iii. Poems 1789 II. 26 Country John in bannet blue, An' eke his Sunday's claes on. **1779** WARNER in Jesse *Selwyn & Contemp.* (1844) IV. 311 The clod-pated yeoman's son in his Sunday clothes. **1831** CARLYLE *Sart. Res.* III. ii, The mere haberdasher Sunday Clothes that men go to Church in. **17..** *Song, 'There's nae luck about the house'* iii, Gie..Jock his *Sunday coat. **1779** *Mirror* No. 25 ⁋7 One of the best-looking plow-boys had a yellow cape clapped to his Sunday's coat to make him pass for a servant in livery. **1818** SCOTT *Hrt. Midl.* xlii, His best light-blue Sunday's coat, with broad metal-buttons. ?*a* **1150-1259** in *Gest. Abb. S. Albani* (Rolls) I. 99 Cœpit flere præ gaudio; ita dicens,—'Lætare mecum,' ait sermone vulgari,—'Myn gode *Sonendayes doȝhter.' **1670** EACHARD *Cont. Clergy* 110 There is great danger, not only of losing his *sunday-dinner, but [etc.]. **1819** KEATS *Otho* II. i, Serv'd with harsh food, with scum for *Sunday-drink. **1925** *New Yorker* 11 July 11/1 The Sunday painter is to the art-artist what the *Sunday driver is to the owner of the Hispano or Rolls-Royce. **1942** *Sun* (Baltimore) 26 Jan. 18/3 Sunday drivers and sightseers accounted for more than seventy per cent of the total number of cars passing along the Eastern avenue road. **1975** L. DEIGHTON *Yesterday's Spy* xx. 161 The Sunday drivers creeping along the promenade. **1817** LADY MORGAN *France* III. (1818) I. 303 *Sunday evening assemblies. **1825** T. HOOK *Sayings* Ser. II. *Passion & Princ.* xiv. III. 338 A *Sunday excursion to Richmond in a steam-boat. **1756** MRS. CALDERWOOD in *Coltness Collect.* (Maitl. Cl.) 147 You would take them for so many seceders, they put on such a *Sunday face, and walk as if they would not look up. *a* **1779** D. GRAHAM *Writings* (1883) II. 51 Put on a Sunday's face, and sign as ye were a saint. **1786** BURNS *What ails ye Now* in *Poems ascribed to R. Burns* (1801) 29 Wi' pinch I put a Sunday's face on, An' snoov'd awa' before the Session. **1906** E. DYSON *Fact'ry 'Ands* xiii. 165 His Trowsis had er slitherin' chin, 'n' ther Sunday face iv er sick sheep. **1910** T. S. ELIOT in *Harvard Advocate* 26 Jan. 114 Sunday: this satisfied procession Of definite Sunday faces. **1934** DYLAN THOMAS 18 *Poems* 25 For, *sunday faced, with dusters in my glove, Chaste and the chaser, man with the cockshut eye. **1852** E. W. BENSON in *Life* (1899) I. iii. 110, I have all the while I am there a perfect *Sunday-feel. **1822** GALT *Provost* xxxii, The town-officers in their *Sunday garbs. **1679** COLES *Eng.-Lat. Dict.* (ed. 2) s.v., A *Sunday's Garment, *Vestis festa.* **1846** KEBLE *Lyra Innoc.* IV. *Fine Clothes* v, The Sunday garment glittering gay. **1840** *P. Parley's Ann.* I. 270 A band-box containing Miss Mainwaring's *Sunday-going bonnet. **1928** J. BUCHAN *Runagates Club* xii. 319 His clothes..were workman-like, and looked as if they belonged to him—no more the uneasy knickerbockers of the *Sunday golfer. *c* **1921** D. H. LAWRENCE *Mr. Noon* in *Mod. Lover* (1934) 172 They were socialists and vegetarians... None of the horrors of *Sunday joints. **1980** 'M. HEBDEN' *Pel under Pressure* v. 47 He was lying on the floor, trussed up like a Sunday joint. **1430** in Halliwell *Rara Mathem.* (1841) 91 þen schal E be ȝour *sonday letter to þe ȝerus ynde. **1698** *Phil. Trans.* XX. 187 B, the Sunday Letter for this Year. **1834** *Tracts for Times* No. 22. 5 The morning is so lovely, so *Sunday-like. **1840** *Florist's Jrnl.* (1846) I. 99 This was perhaps no great loss to the majority of the *Sunday loungers. **1932** E. M. DELAFIELD *Thank Heaven Fasting* III. ii. 263 Mr. Pelham was sleeping, after *Sunday lunch. **1973** 'M. UNDERWOOD' *Reward for Defector* viii. 63 They sat down to roast lamb, roast potatoes, cauliflower with a cheese sauce and brussel sprouts... 'Mrs Tidmarsh enjoys cooking a proper Sunday lunch.' **1785** GROSE *Dict. Vulgar T.*, **Sunday man*, one who goes abroad on that day only, for fear of arrests. **1819** F. MACDONOGH *Hermit in Lond.* (1820) IV. 120 These hebdomadal loungers are what are called Sunday men. **1786** BURNS *Holy Fair* i, Upon a simmer *Sunday morn. **1629** WADSWORTH *Pilgr.* iii. 18 On *Sunday morning at six of the clocke they hye to their studies. **1841** A. DALLAS *Past. Superintendence* III. i. 431 The Sunday morning congregation consisting of about three hundred persons. **1821** *Acc. Peculations in Coal Trade* 18 The daily or *Sunday newspapers. **1788** WOLCOT (P. Pindar) *Bro. Peter to Bro. Tom* x, Who..Made up a concert every *Sunday night. **1598** BP. HALL *Sat.* IV. ii, Byes he rost for *sunday-noone. **1960** *News Chron.* 9 Mar. 6 Mr. Bratby may be a professional painter, but he is a *Sunday novelist. [**1785**: see OBSERVANCE 1 a.] **1857** *Punch* 4 July 4/2 Having put down the Sabbatarians and secured rational liberty to the millions in respect to *Sunday observance. **1973** J. WAINWRIGHT *High-Class Kill* 209 Pornographic literature—and blue films—and illegal gambling—and anything else the Sunday Observance crowd can think up. **1925** *Sunday painter [see *Sunday driver* above]. **1948** R. O. DUNLOP *Understanding Pictures* iv. 26 Chief of these 'Sunday' painters was the *Douanier* Rousseau—so-called because he was for long a customs official. **1961** M. LEAKE tr. *Bouret's Henri Rousseau* 170 After the publication of this text [*sc.* R. Grey's *Henri Rousseau*] in 1922, the label 'Sunday-painters' became attached to the naïf and primitive painters and to the popular realist masters, and still survives. **1980** B. BAINBRIDGE *Winter Garden* xii. 88 He gathered there were few actual artists in the room. A General was pointed out to him and an Admiral, both retired. He supposed they were Sunday painters, rather like Churchill and Roosevelt. **1812** BYRON *Let. to Ld. Holland* 14 Oct., I have seen no paper but Perry's, and two *Sunday ones. **1848** THACKERAY *Van. Fair* liv, He would by no means permit the introduction of Sunday papers into his household. **1874** GREEN *Short Hist.* viii. §4. 495 The Parliament..had forbidden *Sunday pastimes by statute. **1979** M. MCCARTHY *Cannibals & Missionaries* iii. 73 The Senator..calls himself a '*Sunday poet', so he doesn't publish. **1929** D. RUNYON in *Cosmopolitan* Oct. 64/1 If you argue with Dave the Dude too much he is apt to reach over and lay his *Sunday punch on your snoot. **1944** W. W. ELTON et al. *Guide Naval Aviation* iv. 71 The real 'Sunday punch' of naval aviation is the torpedo bomber. **1979** E. NEWMAN (*title*) Sunday punch. **1645** PAGITT *Heresiogr.* (1661) 189 The keeping of *Sunday-sabbath as strictly as the Jews. **1973** H. NIELSEN *Severed Key* iii. 27 As the day cleared, a few hardy *Sunday sailors took out their boats. **1756** F. HOME *Exper. Bleaching* 238 A particular kind..only made on Sunday; and therefore called *Sunday-salt, or great salt, from the largeness of its grains. **1808** HOLLAND *View Agric. Chesh.* i. 55 The large grained flaky salt..made by slackening the fires betwixt Saturday and Monday, and allowing the crystallization to proceed more slowly on the intermediate day..has got the name of Sunday salt. **1786** BURNS *Holy Fair* vi, I'll get my *Sunday's sark on. **1821** CLARE *Vill. Minstr.* I. 175 A *Sunday scene looks brighter to the eye. **1850** CLOUGH *Dipsychus* II. vi. 69 Good books, good friends..That lent rough life sweet *Sunday-seeming rests. **1738** *Sunday's suit [see SUIT *sb.* 19 b]. **1830** in M. R. Mitford *Stories Amer. Life* I. 280 Sampson stood, in his Sunday suit, showing with his teeth an air of joyous satisfaction. **1888** RIDER HAGGARD *Col. Quaritch* xxxiv, Arrayed in his pepper-and-salt Sunday suit. **1574-5** G. HARVEY *Story of Mercy Harvey* Wks. (Grosart) III. 75 A *Sundaie supper at Mr. S. **1905** E. WHARTON *House of Mirth* II. ix. 429 The photographer whose portraits of her formed the recurring ornament of '*Sunday Supplements'. **1913** [see RINKY-DINK a.]. **1958** J. BLISH *Case of Conscience* I. iii. 36 Stop sounding like a Sunday supplement. You underestimate your own intelligence. **1979** M. TABOR *Baker's Daughter* i. 13 A basement in a Sunday supplement conversion. **1856** *Brit. Alm. & Comp.* 228 [July 2 1855] Lord Grosvenor..withdraws his *Sunday-Trading Bill in the House of Commons. **1883** MISS BROUGHTON *Belinda* III. 122 The *Sunday trains are so awkward that I cannot get on till late in the afternoon. *c* **1815** JANE AUSTEN *Persuas.* xvii, She saw..that *Sunday-travelling had been a common thing.

Hence (chiefly *colloq.*) **Sunday** *v. intr.* (*U.S.*), to spend Sunday; **Sundayed** ('sʌndeɪd, -dɪd) **'Sundayfied** *adjs.* [cf. FRENCHIFIED, etc.], appropriate to Sunday, in Sunday clothes; **'Sundayish** *a.*, somewhat like, or like that of, Sunday; **'Sundayism**, practice or conduct characteristic of the observance of Sunday; †**'Sundayly** *adv.*, every Sunday.

1884 *Lisbon* (Dakota) *Clipper* 13 Mar., H. R. Turner *Sundayed in Fargo. **1884** *My Ducats & My Daughter* III. xxiv. 53 Dick had assumed a tight-fitting suit of glossy black, which gave him the aspect of a *Sunday'd butcher. **1870** *Bazar Bk. Decorum* 164 We are apt to be, as the French say, *endimanchés*, which we may translate by the coined word **Sundayfied*. **1899** C. G. HARPER *Exeter Road* 123 A village ..of a Sundayfied stillness. **1797** R. GURNEY in A. J. C. Hare *Gurneys of Earlham* (1895) I. 70 [The day] was flat, stupid, unimproving, and *Sundayish. **1911** W. W. JACOBS *Ship's Company* 1 Mr. Jobson awoke with a Sundayish feeling, probably due to the fact that it was Bank Holiday. **1850** T. MCCRIE *Mem. Sir H. Agnew* ix. 239 Their own genial and jaunty *Sundayism. **1479-81** *Rec. St. Mary at Hill* 110 Item, payd *sondayly to iij poore almysmen to pray,..&c.

'Sunday-school. 1. a. A school in which instruction is given on Sunday: *esp.* such a school for children held in connexion with a parish or a congregation; such schools are now intended only for religious instruction, but originally instruction in secular subjects was also given.

Robert Raikes, of Gloucester, was the originator in England of the Sunday-school as an adjunct of a church congregation.

1783 *Gloucester Jrnl.* 3 Nov., Some of the clergy,..bent upon attempting a reform among the children of the lower class, are establishing Sunday schools, for rendering the Lord's day subservient to the ends of instruction, which has hitherto been prostituted to bad purposes. **1783** R. RAIKES *Let.* 25 Nov. in *Gentl. Mag.* (1784) LIV. I. 411/2 The success..has induced one or two of my friends to..set up Sunday schools in other parts of the city, and now a whole parish has taken up the object. **1784** WESLEY *Wks.* (1872) IV. 284 Before Service I stepped into the Sunday-school which contains two hundred and forty children, taught every Sunday by several masters. **1791** J. LEARMONT *Poems* 53 'Tis nae i' power o' Sunday Schools..To fleg Vice out o' her strang holes. **1820** *Gentl. Mag.* XC. I. 430/2 Sunday Schools, instruments of disaffection. **1848** THACKERAY *Van. Fair* li, I would rather be a parson's wife, and teach a Sunday School than this. **1885** W. H. WHITE *M. Rutherford's Deliv.* iii, He taught in the Sunday-school, and afterwards, as he got older, he was encouraged to open his lips at a prayer-meeting.

attrib. **1792** *Looker-On* 24 Mar. 36, I really once detected her knitting stockings, for prizes to the Sunday-school girls. **1836** *Partington's Brit. Cycl. Lit.*, etc., III. 855 A Sunday school society was formed in 1785... In 1803, the first Sunday school union was formed in London. **1841** *Penny Cycl.* XXI. 44/1 Sunday-school teachers as a class possess many excellent points of character. **1901** W. R. H. TROWBRIDGE *Lett. her Mother to Eliz.* xx. 96 There was a Sunday-school feast at Braxome.

b. *transf.* A school in which instruction in Socialist principles is given on a Sunday.

1901 *Young Socialist* Apr. 2 We ought to..muster as large an army as possible of young soldiers of our cause... This is already being done in our Socialist Sunday Schools. **1922** J. BUCHAN *Huntingtower* x. 198 Wee Jaikie went to a Socialist Sunday School last winter. **1930** A. P. HERBERT *Water Gipsies* xv. 217 Ernest assumed that it would be a treat for Jane to spend her Sunday afternoon at a proletarian Sunday School. **1978** *Times* 5 May 15/5 As long ago as 1918 to 1925 I attended a William Morris Sunday School in an English industrial city.

2. Used *attrib.* or as *adj.* with allusion to the sanctimoniousness, sentimentality, or strict morals held to be inculcated by Sunday-schools: primly moral.

1843 DICKENS *Mart. Chuz.* (1844) xxvii. 333 'Not the truth?' cried Tigg... 'Don't use that Sunday-school expression, please!' **1894** G. B. SHAW *Let.* 4 July (1965) I. 448 Ober Ammergau was a miserable, genteelified, Sir Noel Patonesque Sunday School piece of illustrated Bibleism: Bayreuth is very different. **1931** *Amer. Mercury* Nov. 352/2 *Gone Sunday-School*, said of a circus that has abolished the grift. *Ibid.* 354/2 *Sunday-school show*, a show on which gambling games for the public have been prohibited. **1952** S. KAUFFMANN *Philanderer* (1953) iii. 54 No, it doesn't matter how good he *is*; how good he tries to be, human good, not Sunday-school good. That's what matters. **1973** *Time* 25 June 6/2 Like the circus before it, the carnival is today largely a 'Sunday school' operation.

Hence **'Sunday-,schooling** *rare*, Sunday-school teaching.

1847 HELPS *Friends in C.* I. viii. 158 In such a thing as this Sunday schooling,..a judicious man..would endeavour to connect it with something interesting.

sunde, obs. form of SOUND.

sunder ('sʌndə(r)), *a.* and *adv.* Forms: see below. [(1) The adj. use in A. 1 is restricted to ME. compounds formed on the model of OE. compounds in *sundor-* (= OS. *sundar-*, OHG. *suntar-*, *sunder-*), as *sundorriht* special right, *sundorspræc* private speech; the use in A. 2 is prob. developed from the predicative use of *sunder* adv. = asunder: see C. (2) Under B. are grouped the phrases derived from ME. advb. phr. *o(n)sunder*, *o(n)sundre*, OE. *onsundran (-um)* ASUNDER, q.v., by substitution of prep. *in* for *on*, *o*, *a*; cf. OS. *an sundran* and ON. *í sundr*, OHG., MHG. *in sunder*. (3) The advb. use in C. arose prob. in an aphetic form of ASUNDER, but form and meaning correspond to OE. *sundor* adv., separately, apart = WFris. *sonder*, *sunder*, NFris. *sanner* prep., without, OS. *sundar* adv., MLG. *sunder* adv., prep., conj., MDu., Du. *zonder* prep., OHG. *suntar*, *-ur*, *-ir*, MHG. *sunder*, *sonder* adj., adv., prep., conj. (= but), G. *sonder* adj. and adv. (arch.), ON. *sundr* adv. (Da. *sønder*), Goth. *sundrô* adv.]

A. *adj.* (Also 3 *Ormin* **sunnderr**, 4 *Sc.* **syndir**, 5 **sonder**, **-ir**.)

†**1.** In compounds formed after OE. compounds of *sundor-* = separate, peculiar, private, as *sundorcræft* special power, *sundorspræc* private conversation: **sunderred**, private advice; **sunderrune**, private conversation or counsel; also **sunder-ble** *a.*, vari-coloured, in quot. subst. *Obs.*

c **1200** *Trin. Coll. Hom.* 29 Al swo cumeð þe deuel in to þe mannes herte þan he wile healde sunderrune wið him. *c* **1200** Ormin 16978 He ne durrste nohht þatt aniȝ mann itt wisste, þatt he wiþþ Crist i sunnderrrun Himm awihht haffde kiþþedd. *c* **1205** Lay. 31414 Ich þe suggen wulle ane sunder rune. *c* **1250** *Gen. & Ex.* 1729 Laban.. bi-taȝte him ðo ðe sunder bles, And it him boren ones bles [Cf. *Genesis* xxx. 32–42]. *Ibid.* 3808 Ðoȝ ðis folc miðe a stund for-dred, Ðoȝ he ben get in sunder red.

†**2.** Separate; various, sundry. *Obs.*

13.. *Cursor M.* 8038 (Gött) þair stouyn was on þat stod þaim vnder, Bot þair croppis ware all sunder [*Cott.* in sunder]. **1375** Barbour *Bruce* v. 506 Bot I herd syndir men oft say Forsuth that his ane e ves out. *a* **1390** *Wyclif's Bible, Judg.* xxi. 21 Whan ȝe seen the douȝtris of Sylo.. goth out sodeynly out of the vines, and takith hem, eche sondry [*MS. C.* sunder] wyues. *c* **1436** *Pol. Poems* (Rolls) II. 151 Tres, levys, and herbis grene, Wyth many sonder colowris.

B. in sunder. (Also 4–6 in sonder, sondre, 3–4 in-synder, 3 in sundre, 4 in sundere, sondire, sondyr(e, 4–5 esondre, 5 in sondir, sondere, sundur, ensundre, ysondur, 6 insundre, -der, in soonder; *Sc.* 4 in-swndir, 5–6 in schunder, 6 in schundyr, -ir, schounder, sounder, sownder, -ir, into sondir.) = asunder *adv.* Now *poet.* or *rhet.*

1. Apart or separate from another or from one another.

a **1300** *Cursor M.* 8038 þair stouen was an þat stod þam vnder, Bot þair croppes war all in sunder. **1387** Trevisa *Higden* (Rolls) I. 73 3if Paradys were so hiȝe, and departed in sonder from euery oþer lond and erþe. *a* **1400** *Minor Poems fr. Vernon MS.* 716/31 Whyl Schip and Roþur togeder was knit, þei dredde nouþer tempest, druyȝe nor wete: Nou be þei boþe In-synder flit. **1470–85** Malory *Arthur* iii. xiv. 116 They departed in sonder. **1513** Douglas *Æneis* xi. xvii. 87 And na lang space thar ostis war in sowndir. **1523** in Ellis *Orig. Lett.* Ser. i. I. 227 Sory I am that the Kingis Highnes and your Grace be nowe so fer in sondre. **1551** Recorde *Pathw. Knowl.* i. Defin., That.. the whole figures may the better bee iudged, and distincte in sonder. **1570–6** Lambarde *Peramb. Kent* (1826) 255 Such as differeth no more from that which we at this day attribute to our Prince, than *Principalis Dominus*, and *Supremus Gubernator* do varie in sunder. **1607** Bp. Andrewes *96 Serm.* (1629) 20 So taking our nature, as. His, and it are growen into one person, never to be.. taken in sunder any more. **1661** Boyle *Examen* (1662) 91 These Scales.. if.. they are pluckt in sunder,.. make a noise equal to the report of a Musquet. **1760–72** H. Brooke *Fool of Qual.* (1809) IV. 33 Let us be united, past the power of parents, rivals, potentates of the world, to tear us in sunder.

2. Of a single object (or of objects singly considered): Into separate parts or pieces. *lit.* and *fig.* Chiefly with vbs. like *break, cleave, cut, tear.*

a **1300** *Cursor M.* 26011 Als þof his hert him brest in sunder. *a* **1375** *Lay Folks Mass Bk.* App. iv. 350 Wiþ his teth a-non He logged, þat al in synder gon lasch. **1375** Barbour *Bruce* xvii. 698 The mast summer.. In-swndir with that dusche he brak. *c* **1400** *Destr. Troy* 5829 He.. hurt hym full sore; The gret vayne of his gorge gird vne ysondur. *c* **1440** *Gesta Rom.* lxi. 253 (Harl. MS.) He kutte ensundre alle his clothis. *c* **1470** Henryson *Mor. Fab.* viii. (*Lion & Mouse*) xxxv, Thay.. schuir the raipis of the net in schunder. **1508** Dunbar *Tua Mariit Wemen* 350, I gert the renȝeis rak, et rif into sondir [*v.r.* schundyr]. **1535** Coverdale *Ps.* cvi[i]. 14 He.. brake their bondes in sonder. **1598** Hakluyt *Voy.* I. 54 Some of these Tabernacles may quickely be taken asunder and set together againe... Other some cannot be taken insunder. **1666** Bunyan *Grace Ab.* §164, I was.. as if my breast bone would have split in sunder. **1709** Hearne *Collect.* 17 Aug. (O.H.S.) II. 236 He was.. cut in sunder by his Father. **1820** Shelley *Ode Lib.* xiii, Vesuvius wakens Aetna, and the cold Snow-crags by its reply are cloven in sunder. **1855** Kingsley *Heroes, Theseus* ii. 210 Their bodies are torn in sunder. **1907** *Verney Mem.* I. 222 Her husband .. torn in sunder by political and religious sympathies.

†**3.** *from (fra) sunder*, in sense 1. *Obs.*

c **1375** *Cursor M.* 14687 (Fairf.) Fra sundre may we neuer twin. **1558** Phaer *Æneid* iii. G iv b, These places two sometime,.. From sonder fel.

†**C.** *adv.* Apart, asunder. *Obs. rare.*

a **1300** *Cursor M.* 20385 Yee þat sa wide war sunder spred. *c* **1400** Maundev. (Roxb.) Pref. 2 A flokk of schepe þat has na schepehird, þe whilk departes sunder. *c* **1400** *Destr. Troy* 11062 The prese of the pepull partid hom sonder. **1539** Tonstall *Serm. Palm Sund.* (1823) 90 Teare sunder your hartes, and not your clothes.

sunder ('sʌndə(r)), *v.* Now *poet.* or rhet. Forms: 1 sundrian, syndrian, *Northumb.* suindria, 3 sundren, -in, 3–5 sundre, 4 *north.* sundir, 4–5 sondre, 4–6 sonder, 5 sondir(e, sundur, -yre, sounder, *Sc.* swndre, 6 soonder, (scinder), *Sc.* sindre, sindir, synder, 6–9 *Sc.* sinder, 4– sunder. [late OE. *syndrian, sundrian*, for earlier *ásyndrian, ásundrian* (see asunder *v.*), *ȝe-, on-, tósundrian* = WFris. *sonderje*, LG. *sundern*, OHG. *sunt(a)rôn, sund(e)rôn*, (MHG. *sunteren, sundern*, G. *sondern*), ON. *sundra*; f. prec.

The rare 16th c. form *scinder*, if not a misprint, is prob. due to association with L. *scindĕre* to cleave.]

1. *trans.* To dissolve connexion between two or more persons or things; to separate or part one *from* another. †Also, to set (a person) apart from a state of life; to remove (something) from a person.

c **950** *Lindisf. Gosp.* Matt. xix. 6 *Quod ergo deus coniunxit, homo non separet*, þæt forðon god ȝe-geadrade monn ne.. suindria. *a* **1050** *Liber Scintill.* i. (1889) 5 Eorþena langnyss na syndrað þa þe soð lufu ȝeþeod. *a* **1067** *Charter of Eadweard* in Kemble *Cod. Dipl.* IV. 209 Ȝif æni man hit awuniȝe mid æfræniȝe þinge.., si he ȝesyndred fram Criste and fram eallen his halȝar. *c* **1200** *Trin. Coll. Hom.* 169 þe licame senegeð, and sundreð hire [*sc.* the soul] fram rihtwisnesse. *a* **1225** *Ancr. R.* 426 Hwon þet fur is wel o brune, & me wule þet hit go ut, me sundreð þe brondes. *c* **1250** *Gen. & Ex.* 468 Of irin. of golde, siluer, and bras To sundren and mengen wis he was. *a* **1300** *Cursor M.* 24616 þan com mi cosin sant iohan,.. Mi soru fra me to sunder. *c* **1325** *Metr. Hom.* 48 Pharisenes.. Thai war sundered of comoun lif. **1338** R. Brunne *Chron.* (1810) 170 þei telc fiueten hundred Sarazins, þat drenkled were, Fourti & sex wer sundred, & alle þo were saued þere. **1375** in Horstmann *Altengl. Leg.* (1878) 130/1, I drede me he shel him sle þerfore sondred shel þeȝ be. *c* **1470** Henry *Wallace* iv. 626 Schir Jhon Butler.. Swndryt the Scottis and did thaim mekill payn. **1525** *St. Papers Hen. VIII*, IV. 297 Ye Lordis .. under colour wald begin new usis to synder me and ye King my son. *a* **1578** Lindesay (Pitscottie) *Chron. Scot.* (S.T.S.) I. 235 The king.. caussit the iudges and men of armes to sinder and red thame [*sc.* combatants]. **1592** Kyd *Sp. Trag.* i. ii. 59 Heere falles a body scindred [*later edd.* sundred] from his head. **1628** Ford *Lover's Mel.* i. i, Twelue monthes we haue been sundred, but henceforth We neuer more will part. **1634** Heywood *Lancs Witches* iv. G iij, The Gentile fashion sometimes we observe To sunder beds. **1697** Dryden *Virg. Georg.* iv. 133 When both the Chiefs are sund'red from the Fight. **1812** Cary *Dante, Purg.* xxxii. 14 That excess of sensible, whence late I had perforce been sunder'd. **1818** Scott *Hrt. Midl.* xxviii, We that are sindered in sorrow may meet again in joy. **1865** Geikie *Scen. & Geol. Scot.* iii. 43 A mass, once evidently connected with the main cliff.. has been sundered by the roof of the tunnel falling in. **1885** Finlayson *Biol. Relig.* 86 Atoms may be so sundered, and forces so transmuted, that the human personality, as such, may cease to be.

refl. *c* **1200** *Trin. Coll. Hom.* 209 þe deuel.. sundrede him seluen fro gode. *a* **1300** *Cursor M.* 22242 Bot all kingrikes þat rome was vnder Fra lauerd-hed o rome þam sundre. **1401** *Pol. Poems* (Rolls) II. 91 He.. that sundrith him from Crist and his chirche. **1591** Spenser *Vis. Worlds Van.* 64 A sword-fish small him from the rest did sunder. **1605** Camden *Rem., Languages* (1623) 22 Holy religious men, which had sundred and seuered themselues from other. **1612** Brerewood *Lang. & Relig.* xxvi. (1614) 185 Before the Apostles left Syria, and sundred themselues to preach the Gospell abroad in the world.

†**b.** To separate in thought, distinguish. *Obs.*

a **1225** *Ancr. R.* 270 þe ȝeteward—þet is wittes skile—þet ouh forto winden hweate, & scheaden þe eilen & tet chef urom þe clene cornes, þet is,.. sundren god from vuele. **1357** *Lay Folks Catech.* (T.) 427 It kennes us to knaw the gode fra the yvel, And als-so to sundir the tane fra the tothir. **1550** Coverdale *Spir. Perle* vii. 65 To sonder and to know the one from the other, the faythfull from the vnfaythfull.

†**c.** To dissolve, put an end to (a state or condition). *Obs.*

a **1300** *Cursor M.* 26054 Reuth.. sundres felauschipe þat was Bituix þe saul and sathanas. **1338** R. Brunne *Chron.* (1810) 28 Whan dede his lyfe sundred, þe folk for him was wo. **1548** Geste *Agst. Priv. Masse* A vj, Thee Pryuee Masse .. sondereth and diuorseth the marriage betwene christ & vs.

2. To divide into two or more parts; to split, break up, cleave.

a **1225** *Ancr. R.* 412 Nu is þeos laste dole.. to-deled and i-sundred o lutle seoue stucchenes. *c* **1330** R. Brunne *Chron. Wace* (Rolls) 13154 þey dide sondre þer route. **1340** Hampole *Pr. Consc.* 4789 Ilka stan, on divers wyse, Sal sonder other in thre partyse. *c* **1400** *Destr. Troy* 7276 He.. Swynget out a sword,.. Sundret the sercle of his sure helme. *a* **1400–50** *Wars Alex.* 4268 Ne nauthire sondire we þe soile ne na sede sawis. **1570–6** Lambarde *Peramb. Kent* (1826) 334 The whole Realme was sundred into particular kingdomes. **1614** Raleigh *Hist. World* iii. vi. §2 Xerxes most barbarously caused the young man.. to be sundered into two parts. **1887** Morris *Odyss.* iii. 449 The beast's neck-tendons he sundered with the blade.

3. To keep apart, separate by an intervening space or barrier, *from* something. *rare.* (Chiefly *pass.*)

1606 Shaks. *Tr. & Cr.* v. x. 27 No space of Earth shall sunder our two hates. **1611** Coryat *Crudities* 54 Which Alpes are sundred by the space of many miles the one from the other. **1876** J. Parker *Paracl.* i. vii. 106 Can any two spheres be much more widely sundered than those of the preacher of the gospel and the artificer in iron and brass? **1887** Morris *Odyss.* i. 58 The long-wrought pillars that sunder the heavens from the earthly land.

4. *intr.* To become separated or severed *from* something; *esp.* of a number of persons, to part.

c **1220** *Bestiary* 703 Wo so seit he [*sc.* turtle-doves] sundren ovt, i seie ðat he leȝeð. *a* **1225** *Leg. Kath.* 1794 Swa þæt nan ne mei sundrin from oðere. *a* **1300** *Cursor M.* 13951 Fra him sal i sundre neuer. *c* **1330** R. Brunne *Chron. Wace* (Rolls) 4454 Of alle þe fighters.. þer was manyon doun leyd, .. & wel mo scholde ȝit þat nyght, Had þey nought sondred for faute of lyght. ? *a* **1400** *Morte Arth.* 7 Whene oure saules schalle parte and sundyre ffra the body. **1570** *Satir. Poems Reform.* xviii. 99 Sinder not now that ar assemblit togidder, Quhill ane be chosin the commoun weill to auance. *a* **1650** Calderwood *Hist. Kirk* (1843) II. 234 They sindered, and were not so familiar after. **1725** Ramsay *Gentle Sheph.* iv. ii, Pate must from his Peggy sunder. **1827** Hood *Hero & Leander* xvi, So brave Leander sunders from his bride. **1867** G. Macdonald *Poems* 116 Its branches sunder not in any wind.

†**b.** To part *with*. *Sc. Obs.*

a **1575** *Diurn. Occurr.* (Bannatyne Cl.) 333 He wald rather byd the will of God nor sinder with the same castell. **1722** Ramsay *Three Bonnets* i. 60 Ye shall hear.. How Joukum sinder'd wi' his bonnet.

5. To be torn, break, or split in pieces.

[**1390** Gower *Conf.* I. 312 The firy welkne gan to thondre, As thogh the world scholde al to sondre.] *c* **1400–50** *Wars Alex.* 3003 Alexander.. rydis To þe grete flode of Granton & in on a glace fyndis. Or he was soȝt to þe side, ȝit sondird þe qweryns. **1593** Shaks. *2 Hen. VI*, iii. ii. 411 Euen as a splitted Barke, so sunder we. **1614** Raleigh *Hist. World* iv. ii. §4 He commanded that this poore Græcian should bee presently slaine: who while hee was a sundring in the Tormentors hand, [etc.]. **1839** *Times* 26 Apr., Let them crack, split and sunder of themselves. **1881** Rossetti *White Ship* 151 The White Ship sundered on the mid-main.

Hence **'sunderable** *a.*, that may be sundered, separable; **'sunderer**, one who sunders or severs.

1885 J. E. Harrison *Stud. Gk. Art* v. 227 In Plato's ideal philosophy, truth, beauty, and goodness are scarcely sunderable. **1888** Meredith *A Reading of Earth* Poems 1898 II. 144 We may cry to the Sunderer, spare That dearest!

sunderance ('sʌndərəns). *rare.* Also 5 sondyrans; *Sc.* sindrance. [f. sunder *v.* + -ance.] Severance, separation.

1435 Misyn *Fire of Love* ii. ix. 91 God forbede þat bodily sondyrans make partynge of sawlis. **1884** *American* VIII. 343 Any sunderance of sympathy with the Mother Country. **1885** J. Payn *Luck of Darrells* I. v. 87 Lest.. your affections should become entangled where of necessity they could not be permanently placed, and cause you pain in the sunderance.

sundered ('sʌndəd), *ppl. a.* [f. sunder *v.* + -ed[1].] Set or kept apart; separated, separate. Also, divided into parts, severed, scattered.

c **1325** *Metr. Hom.* 48 Pharisenes, That sundered men on Englys menes. **1594** Shaks. *Rich. III*, v. iii. 100 Ample enterchange of sweet Discourse, Which so long sundred Friends should dwell vpon. **1678** Dryden *All for Love* iv. i, Set all the Earth And all the Seas, betwixt your sunder'd Loves. **1796** Coleridge *Destiny of Nations* 473 The white bear, drifting on a field of ice, Howls to her sundered cubs. **1871** Rossetti *Poems, Dante at Verona* xix, When the dust Cleared from the sundered press of Knights Ere yet again it swoops and smites. **1876** Tennyson *Harold* iii. i, He.. brought the sunder'd tree again, and set it Straight on the trunk.

sundering ('sʌndərɪŋ), *vbl. sb.* [f. sunder *v.* + -ing[1].] The action of the verb sunder; parting, separation.

c **1250** *Gen. & Ex.* 458 Of merke, and kinde, and helde, & ble, sundring and samening taȝte he. **1401** *Pol. Poems* (Rolls) II. 91 Heresie.. in oure langage meneth sunderyng and partyng. **1435** Misyn *Fire of Love* ii. ix. 91 þe knot vnlousyd of drawynge frenschyp sal comforth heuynes of bodily sondyrynge. **1530** Palsgr. 272/2 Sondring of a thyng, *remotion*. **1582–8** *Hist. James VI* (1804) 126 That was the caus of thair suddaine sindering. **1674** N. Fairfax *Bulk & Selv.* 99 That would partake of sundering, if it were not the least that can be. **1838** Sir W. Hamilton *Logic* xxv. (1866) II. 22 Under Division.. we understand in general the sundering of a whole into its parts. **1863** W. Phillips *Sp.* vi. 121 The sundering of the Methodist and Baptist denominations. **1865** Geikie *Scen. & Geol. Scot.* vi. 121 The profound concavity of these valleys cannot.. arise from the sundering of the sides of a fissure.

So **'sundering** *ppl. a.*, that sunders.

1870 Morris *Earthly Par.* II. iii. 332 A new lonely pain, Like sundering death, smote on her. **1876** Mrs. Whitney *Sights & Insights* xxx. 292 Myriad sparkles of ever sundering atoms. **1885** E. Arnold *Secr. Death* 23 Wide asunder stand Wisdom and ignorance, in sundering ways They lead mankind!

'Sunderland. The name of a town in Tyne and Wear, England, used *attrib.* to designate (*a*) a type of coarse cream-coloured ware, usu. decorated with a pink lustre and transfers, made there in the late eighteenth and nineteenth centuries; also similar ware made elsewhere; (*b*) less frequently, a type of coarse brown earthenware made in Sunderland in the nineteenth century.

1870 W. Chaffers *Marks Pott. & Porc.* (ed. 3) 587 The ware made here was.. decorated with the pink metallic lustre so usual on the Sunderland jugs. **1874** [see *Newcastle pottery* s.v. Newcastle[1] 2]. **1911** J. F. Blacker *19th-Cent. Eng. Ceramic Art* 396 The purple and pink lustre.. decorated the white ware, which must be distinguished from 'Sunderland ware', the brown earthenware, resembling what is known in the trade as 'rockingham'. **1920** [see Pratt]. **1937** J. R. Hodgdon *Collecting Old Eng. Lustre* v. 34 There are many large bowls, mostly of the late Sunderland ware... Mrs Harpur.. is an authority on Sunderland lustre. **1951** John & Baker *Old Eng. Lustre Pott.* xvi. 97 *Sunderland Ware* has always been reserved for a robust glazed brown earthenware lined with a white glaze and suitable for cooking. **1975** P. D. James *Black Tower* iii. 87 A splendid Sunderland lustreware jug commemorating Trafalgar. **1979** 'J. Gash' *Grail Tree* xvi. 165 Dull pink lustres, universally known as 'Sunderland' ware, don't always come from Sunderland.

†**'sunderlepes**, *adv.* (*a.*) *Obs.* Forms: α. 1–2 sunderlipes (1 -as), (2 sunderlipe), 3 sunderlepes, 3–4 sunderlupes, 4 sunderleps, sonderlypes, sondrilepes; β. 1 sindorlipes, senderlipes, 3 synderlepes. [OE. *sunder-, synderlípes*, f. *sundor* (see sunder *a.*) + *-hliep-* (as in onlepy) + gen. *-es*. Cf. serelepes. An OE. *synderlípe* adj. occurs in glosses.]

1. Separately, apart from the rest, severally.

c **1020** *Rule St. Benet* (Logeman) 47 *Psalmi tres singillatim*, þreo sealmas sindorlipes. *a* **1100** *Aldhelm Gloss.* i. 206 (Napier) 7/1 *Sequestratim, i. diuise, i. seorsum*, sunderlipes. *Ibid.* i. 1362, 37/1 *Seperatim, i. singulariter*, synderlipes. *c* **1175** *Lamb. Hom.* 11 Nu weren þas þreo laȝe ȝe-writen inne þa oðre table breode sunderlipes. *c* **1200** *Trin. Coll. Hom.* 5 He cumeð to elch man sunderlupes. *a* **1225** *Ancr. R.* Pref. p. xxiii, þis destinciun aren chapitres fiue.. & spekeð of euch hwet sunder lepes o rawe. *c* **1330** R. Brunne *Chron. Wace* (Rolls) 3879 þus sonderlypes [*v.r.* sunder leps] he dide þem swere, Tyl Argayl schulde þey faiþ bere. **13..** *E.E. Allit. P.*

C. 12 A3t happes he hem hy3t & vche on a mede, Sunderlupes for hit dissert vpon a ser wyse.

2. Especially, particularly.

c **1175** *Lamb. Hom.* 137 Al ðe almisse þe mon deð sunderliþe for to quemen ure drihten, alle þeo cwencheð sunnen. *c* **1200** *Trin. Coll. Hom.* 25 Ac sunderlepes he is here fader mid wisse, þe on rihte bileue and on soðe luue understant his holie fles and his holie blod.

3. predicatively as *adj.* Separate, distinct.

1393 LANGL. *P. Pl.* C. XIX. 193 Siþthen thei ben surlepes [*v.r.* sondrilipes], .. thei han sondry names.

† **'sunderling,** *adv. Obs. rare*⁻¹. [Alteration of SUNDERLY *adv.* by substitution of suffix -LING². But cf. LG. *sunderlinc, -linge(n.]* Severally.

c **1320** *Cast. Love* 290 Foure douhtren hedde þe kyng, And to vchone sunderlyng He 3af a dole of his fulnesse.

† **'sunderly,** *a. Obs.* Forms: 1 sundorlic, synderlic, 2–3 sunderlich, 4 sunderly, 5 sonderly, sondrely. [OE. *sundorlic* (also *synderlic*), f. *sundor*: see SUNDER *a.* + *-lic* -LY¹. Cf. (M)LG. *sunderlik*, OHG. *suntarlîh* (MHG., G. *sonderlich*), ON. *sundrligr*. Cf. SUNDRILY *a.*]

1. Peculiar, special, private.

c **888** ÆLFRED *Boeth.* xxxiii. §5 Seo ʒesceadwisnes .. is synderlic cræft þære saule. *c* **897** —— *Gregory's Past. C.* lii. 409 Ðæm is sundorlic sang to singanne. *c* **1175** *Lamb. Hom.* 91 Ne heore nan nefden sunderlich ehte.

2. Separate, several: distinct, diverse, different.

a **1225** *Ancr. R.* 14 Euerich dole wiðute moncglunge spekeð al bi himsulf of sunderliche þinges. *a* **1400** *Gloss.* in *Rel. Ant.* I. 9 *Singulus, i. unus per se*, sunderly. *c* **1425** *Found. St. Bartholomew's* (E.E.T.S.) 16 Three men .. sonderly went to sonderly Bishops of the See of Rome. **1481** CAXTON *Myrr.* II. ix. 88 The meruayllous trees that growe in ynde .. ben many dyuerse and bere sondrely fruyt.

† **'sunderly,** *adv. Obs.* Forms: 1 suundor-, sundurlice, synderlice, 2–3 sunderliche, (4 sinderliche, sundirly, 5 sondir-, sondre-, 6 sonder-, soondre-, sundur-, sundrely), 5–8 sunderly. [OE. *sundorlice* and *synderlice*: see SUNDER *a.* and -LY². Cf. NFris. *sannerlik* especially, MLG. *sunderliken, -likes*, OHG. *suntarlîhho, sunterlîcho* (MHG. *sunter-, sunderlîche(n)*, G. *sonderlich*). Cf. SUNDRILY *adv.*]

1. Separately, apart; individually; singly.

c **888** ÆLFRED *Boeth.* xli. §5 He hine onʒit þurh þa eaʒan synderlice, .. þurh ʒescead wisnesse synderlice [etc.]. *c* **950** *Lindisf. Gosp.* Mark vii. 33 *Seorsum*, sundurlice. *Ibid.* xiii. 3 *Separatim*, suundorlice. *c* **1000** ÆLFRIC *Saints' Lives* xxiii. 625 þa hine synderlice ælc man beheold. *c* **1175** *Lamb. Hom.* 11 þer weren in þer oðres tables sunderliche .iii. ibode. *a* **1225** *Ancr. R.* 90 Nu ich habbe sunderliche ispeken of þeos þreo limes—of eien, & of muðe, & of earen. *c* **1320** *Cast. Love* 1508 þau3 vche nome of þise þre Be sinderliche seyd. **1490** in Arnolde *Chron.* (1811) 111 In wytnesse wherof the partyes aforsayde to this endenturs, sunderly hath sett ther seales. **1528** MORE *Dyaloge* III. Wks. 355/2, I .. haue also dyuers and manye times sunderlye talked with almost all such. **1542–3** *Act 34 & 35 Hen. VIII*, c. 17 §3 Our .. Soveraigne Lorde .. hathe soondrelye and severallye giuen and graunted unto the saide Bisshopps, divers and soondrye Manoures. *a* **1631** SIR R. COTTON *Abridgm. Rec. Tower* (1657) 362 The King .. declared, that they [*sc.* the Commons] were sunderly bound to him. **1635** SWAN *Spec. Mundi* vii. §3 (1643) 347 Seeing they be laid downe severally, it is fit they be explained sunderly. **1674** N. FAIRFAX *Bulk & Selv.* 108 Every whole being greater than its parts, taken sunderly.

2. Singularly, specially. *rare.*

c **900** tr. *Bæda's Hist.* IV. xxiv. (1899) 480/1 On þysse abbudissan mynstre wæs sum broðor synderlice mid godcundre ʒyfe ʒemæred. **1481** CAXTON *Reynard* xxviii. (Arb.) 70 My wyf his sondrely wyse.

3. Diversely, differently, variously. *rare.*

a **1513** FABYAN *Chron.* VII. (1811) 640 Of this Charlys sundrye wryters sunderly wryte.

4. Dispersedly, widely. *rare.*

1541 *St. Papers Hen. VIII*, I. 681 Commen brutes and rumours, which be sunderly spred here. **1570** FOXE *A. & M.* (ed. 2) 364 b/1 That good thing which by yᵉ almighty God is sonderly dispensed to diuers.

sunderment ('sʌndəmənt). *rare.* [f. SUNDER *v.* + -MENT.] Separation.

1818 MME. D'ARBLAY *Diary* 17 Nov., I saw him ill, .. I felt myself well; it was therefore apparent who must be the survivor in case of sunderment. **1895** *Westm. Gaz.* 17 June 2/3 On both sides of him were other canine brothers and sisters condemned .. to a similar sunderment from home.

† **'sunderness.** *Obs. rare.* In 4 sondernesse, 5 syndernes. [f. SUNDER *a.* + -NESS.] Diversity, variety. (Cf. SUNDRINESS.)

a **1400** *Minor Poems fr. Vernon MS.* xxiv. 339 Heil þat stondest .. On riht half of vr lord; Whom sondernesse vmbigoþ Of vertuwes in a-Cord. *a* **1450** *Ratis Raving* I. 216 Gif þow this sex pontis seis, þow may find sindry qualiteis .. Quha takis kep to this syndernes It is a wertew maist of price.

† **'sunderwise,** *adv. Obs. rare.* In 5 sondirwise, 6 sondre wyse. [f. SUNDER *a.* + -WISE.] Asunder; separately. (Cf. *sundriwise* s.v. SUNDRY 6 c.)

? *a* **1400** *Morte Arth.* 3529 He .. Dubbede of þe Danmarkes, dukes and erlles, Disseueride þem sondirwise, and cites dystroyede. *a* **1536** *Songs, Carols* etc. (E.E.T.S.) 98 Accompte my sorow fyrst & my distres Sondre wyse.

sundew ('sʌndju:). Forms: see SUN *sb.*¹ and DEW *sb.* [ad. early mod.Du. *son-, sundauw*, = G. *sonnentau*, transl. of L. *rōs sōlis* (see ROS SOLIS).

It has been suggested that OE. *sundéaw* (glossing 'rosmarina') is for *sunddéaw, i.e. 'sea-dew', a literal rendering of L. *rōsmarīnus*.]

Any plant of the genus *Drosera*, which comprises small herbs growing in bogs, with leaves covered with glandular hairs secreting viscid drops which glitter in the sun like dew; esp. *D. rotundifolia* (round-leaved or common sundew).

1578 LYTE *Dodoens* III. lxxi. 412 Although that the Sonne do shine hoate .. thereon, yet you shall finde it alwayes moyst .. and for that cause it was called *Ros Solis* in Latine, whiche is to say in Englishe The dewe of the Sonne, or Sonnedewe. **1597** GERARDE *Herbal* III. clv. 1366 It is called in English Sunne deaw, Ros Solis, Youth woort; in the North parts Red rot, bicause it rotteth sheepe, and in Yorkeshire Moore grasse. **1698** *Phil. Trans.* XX. 328 Hairs like those on the Leaves of Sundew. **1757** A. COOPER *Distiller* III. l. (1760) 215 The Ros-Solis or Sundew, from whence this Cordial water has its name. **1840** HODGSON *Hist. Northumb.* III. ii. 360/2 *Drosera anglica*, Greater Sundew. **1870** KINGSLEY *At Last* xii, The long-leaved Sundew, with its clammy-haired paws full of dead flies. *a* **1887** R. JEFFERIES *Field & Hedgerow* (1889) 275 The 'sog', or peaty place where the spring rises, and where the sundew grows.

attrib. **1837** *Partington's Brit. Cycl. Nat. Hist.* II. 330/1 *Droseraceæ*, the Sundew family. **1887** BENTLEY *Man. Bot.* (ed. 5) 550 The Sundew Order.

'sun-,dial. [f. SUN *sb.*¹ + DIAL *sb.*¹] A contrivance for showing the time of day by means of a shadow cast by the sun upon a surface marked with a diagram indicating the hours. (Earlier called simply *dial.*)

Usually a fixed structure of stone, metal, or other hard substance; sometimes a portable object, as a card, requiring adjustment by means of a compass or otherwise.

1599 MINSHEU, *Relox del sol*, a sunne diall. *c* **1629** in *Maitl. Club Misc.* III. 375 Ane Sone dyall and ane piller to set it on. **1665** BOYLE *Occas. Refl.* IV. xv. (1848) 254 The Boat-man took out of his Pocket a little Sun-Dyal, furnished with an excited Needle to direct how to Set it. **1727** POPE *Thoughts Var. Subj.* Swift's Wks. 1751 IV. 292 Like a Sun-dial on the front of a house, to inform the Neighbours and Passengers, but not the Owner within. **1764** J. FERGUSON *Lect.* 221 How to make sun-dials by the assistance of a good globe. **1861** HUGHES *Tom Brown at Oxf.* Introd. (1889) 2 The great college sun-dial, over the lodge. **1874** MICKLETHWAITE *Mod. Par. Churches* 183 A good terse motto is a desirable addition to a sun-dial.

'sun-dog. [Of obscure origin.] A mock sun, parhelion; also, a fragment of a rainbow.

1635 L. FOXE *North-West Fox* (Hakl.) II. 291 This evening Sun dog, I hope may bring some change to our good. **1698** S. SEWALL *Diary* 15 Feb. (1878) I. 471 Remarkable Sun-dogs and a Rainbow were seen. **1840** F. D. BENNETT *Whaling Voy.* I. 3 We noticed the phenomenon named by nautical men a 'wind-gall,' .. or sun-dog. **1896** KIPLING *Seven Seas, Three Sealers* 68 And they saw the sun-dogs in the haze and the seal upon the shore.

sundown, sun-down ('sʌndaʊn). [Perh. a shortening of *sun-go-down* or *sun-gate-down* (see SUN *sb.*¹ 13).]

1. The going down of the sun; the time when the sun goes down; also, the glow of sunset; = SUNSET 1, 1 b; the west. Chiefly *U.S., Eng. dial.*, and *S. Afr., Austral.*, etc.; occas. *poet.* or *rhetorical.*

1620 *Depos. Bk. Archdeaconries Essex & Colch.* 24 Nov. lf. 174 (MS.), Aboute two howers before sunne downe. **1744** W. BLACK *Jrnl.* 1 June in *Pennsylvania Mag. Hist.* (1877) I. 408 We staid till near Sun-down at Mr. Strettell's Villa. **1813** in *Spirit Publ. Jrnls.* XVII. 168 Solid dames of Boston, go to bed at sun-down, And never lose your way, like the loggerheads of London! **1827** J. F. COOPER *Prairie* ii, Have you been far towards the sun-down, friend? **1850** TENNYSON *In Mem.* xli, Oft when sundown skirts the moor. **1853** M. ARNOLD *Scholar Gypsy* iii, Screen'd is this nook .. And here till sun-down, Shepherd, will I be. **1858** O. W. HOLMES *Aut. Breakf.-t.* ix. (1891) 212 The Puritan 'Sabbath' .. began at 'sundown' on Saturday evening. **1873** MORLEY *Rousseau* II. 315 A mournful sombre figure, looming shadowily in the dark glow of sundown. **1896** BADEN-POWELL *Matabele Campaign* xi, I signed his warrant, directing that he should be shot at sundown.

2. A hat with a wide brim. *U.S.*

1873 *Kansas Mag.* Sept. 207/2 A flaring sun-down dangled by its strings. **1888** *Century Mag.* Sept. 769/1 Young faces of those days seemed as sweet and winning under wide-brimmed 'sun-downs' or old-time 'pokes' as [etc.].

3. *U.S. colloq.* Used *attrib.* to designate one who practises as a doctor or lawyer, etc., outside normal working hours or in addition to his principal occupation. Cf. SUNDOWNER 3.

1897 *Boston Transcript* 5 Aug. 5/1 There are sundown doctors, sundown lawyers and sundown ministers. **1904** L. DERVILLE *Other Side of Story* 42 A sundown doctor .. [is] a doctor who practices his vocation after four o'clock, when he can leave his desk in some Government office. **1949** *Sun* (Baltimore) 29 June 8/3 Attorneys practising in the county without maintaining offices there have come to be known as 'sundown' lawyers.

'sundowner. [f. SUNDOWN + -ER¹.]

1. *Australian colloq.* A tramp who makes a practice of arriving at a station about sundown under the pretence of seeking work, so as to obtain food and a night's lodging.

[**1846** C. P. HODGSON *Reminisc. Austral.* 302 A 'Sundowner' (? a task requiring no great exertion which lasts until sundown).] **1868** *Sydney Punch* 14 Nov. 198 (*heading*) The song of the sundowner. **1875** MISS BIRD *Sandwich Isl.* 216 As I rode up to the door, certain obnoxious colonial words, such as 'sun-downers,' and 'bummers,' occurred to me, and I felt myself a 'sundowner' when the host came out and asked me to dismount. **1883** J. BRADSHAW *New Zealand* iv. 26 Another class of labourers .. known by the name of .. Sundowners, because they never approach a habitable place before sun-down, lest they should be requested to take a further stroll. **1894** H. NISBET *Bush Girl's Rom.* 26 Never a tramp was turned away empty-handed unless he was a well-known sundowner.

2. orig. *Colonial* (esp. *S. Afr.*). **a.** An alcoholic drink taken at sunset. Also *transf.* and *attrib.*

1909 *Daily Chron.* 20 Oct. 6/7 The 'sundowner' refreshment of the West African late afternoon. **1921** *Chambers's Jrnl.* Jan. 43/1 Surely you are not going to refuse a solitary sundowner. **1932** E. WAUGH *Black Mischief* viii. 298, I said we'd drop into the Brethertons for a sundowner. **1947** W. S. MAUGHAM *Creatures of Circumstance* 37 See you again at six for a sun-downer. **1966** D. VARADAY *Gara-Yaka's Domain* x. 113 We had a good notion the herd would return for a 'sundowner'. **1978** G. GREENE *Human Factor* II. iv. 86 He sits there on a hot evening swilling his sundowners without a care in the world.

b. An evening drinks party.

1962 *Pretoria News* 9 Nov. 9/3 The war raged on, much to the delight of our sundowner guests. **1971** D. CREED *Trial of Lobo Icheka* xv. 149 I'll throw a Sundowner at your place tonight... Invite anyone you feel I might like to meet. **1973** J. J. MCKELVEY *Man against Tsetse* ii. 73 At the 'sundowners', or cocktail hours, heavy white socks seem safer and more comfortable than black ones.

3. *U.S. colloq.* One who practises as a doctor, etc., outside normal working hours or in addition to his principal occupation. Cf. SUNDOWN, SUN-DOWN 3 and MOONLIGHTER 3.

1886 *Turf, Field & Farm* 10 May 399/3 The night doctors gather the 'stiffs' and the 'sundowners' flourish around them with scalping knives. **1904** *Sun* (N.Y.) 14 Aug. 17 The Washington sundowner is so called because he practises a profession, usually medicine or dentistry, after the close of Government office hours, or after sundown.

Hence **'sundowning,** the practice of a sundowner.

1891 E. KINGLAKE *Australian at H.* 133 A certain gang of bushrangers .. caused it to be known that tramps and such like were under their special protection... The effect of this was to make sundowning an intolerable nuisance within the district.

‖**sundri** ('sʌndrɪ). *East Indian.* Also sundari, soondry, -ee, -ie. [Bengalī *sundarī* (f. *sundar* = Skr. *sundara* beautiful, handsome).] A tree abundant in the Ganges delta, *Heritiera minor*, yielding a tough and durable timber. Also applied to *H. littoralis*, the looking-glass tree. Also ***sundra-, sunder-tree*** (Cent. Dict.).

1831 *Encycl. Brit.* (ed. 7) IV. 241/1 The soondry, so much esteemed in Hindostan for the toughness and hardness of its wood. **1889** MAIDEN *Usef. Pl. Australia* 555 *Heritiera littoralis* .. 'Sundri' of India. **1907** *Blackw. Mag.* Aug. 252/1 The dying and stag-headed *sundri* puts out branches covered with fungi.

sun-dried ('sʌndraɪd), *a.* [f. SUN *sb.*¹ + *dried*, pa. pple. of DRY *v.*]

1. Dried by exposure to the sun, as clay, bricks, or articles of food, etc.

1600 J. PORY tr. *Leo's Africa* VI. 268 Castles .. enuironed with walles made of sunne-dried brickes. **1634** SIR T. HERBERT *Trav.* 35 Houses of sun-dried mud. **1741** BOYSE *Patience* 184 Nor wanted he for fowl or sun-dried fish. **1858** BIRCH *Anc. Pottery* I. 158 Sun-dried clay was used by the Greeks for modelling objects intended for internal decorations.

2. Dried up or parched by the sun, as vegetation, etc.

1638 SANDYS *Paraphr. Div. Poems, Exod. xv*, As Fire the Sun-dri'd Stubble burnes. **1842** *Dumfries Herald* Oct., Where you hear the whins, with their opening capsules, crackling on the sun-dried braes. **1889** CONAN DOYLE *Micah Clarke* 231 Their dark sun-dried faces .. marked them as fishermen or seamen. **1901** 'G. PASTON' *Little Mem. 18th C.* 238 A tuft of sun-dried heather.

sundries ('sʌndrɪz), *sb. pl.* [pl. of SUNDRY *a.* used subst.: cf. ODDS.] **1. a.** Small articles of a miscellaneous kind; *esp.* small items lumped together in an account as not needing individual mention.

1755 FIELDING *Voy. to Lisbon* 182 The whole pitiful 30 l. came pure and neat into the captain's pocket, .. attended with the value of 10 l. more in sundries, into the bargain. **1794** A. YOUNG *Trav. France* II. xix. 421 Live Stock .. Corn .. Tobacco .. Sundries. **1815** W. H. IRELAND *Scribbleomania* 16 The vender of sundries. **1836** *Penny Cycl.* V. 164/2 The word 'sundries' being an abbreviation for 'sundry accounts'. **1838** DICKENS *O. Twist* xxviii, Mr. Giles, Brittles, and the tinker were recruiting themselves .. with tea and sundries. **1866** ROGERS *Agric. & Prices* I. xxi. 547 A few of these [*sc.* ladders] are given in the table of Sundries. **1912** *Times* 19 Dec. 20/3, 6,885 bales, made up as follows:—New South Wales, 387 bales; Queensland, 328; .. British East African, ten; and sundries, five bales.

b. *spec.* (chiefly *Austral.*), in *Cricket*, the extras, or runs scored otherwise than off the bat.

1867 *Australasian* 16 Mar. 332/1 With sundries forty-five, the innings closed for the very long score of 211. **1976** *0–10 Cricket Scene* (Austral.) 13/1 That 104 was seven runs more than the 11 New Zealanders could muster between them.. excluding the 15 sundries.

2. *attrib.* and *Comb.* (***sundries-*** or ***sundry-***), as ***sundry ledger***; **sundries-** or **sundry-man**, a dealer in sundries.

1885 *List of Subscribers, Classified* (United Telephone Co.) (ed. 6) 84 (*heading*) Druggists' sundriesmen. **1888** *Cassell's Encycl. Dict.*, Sundry-man. **1892** *Garden* 27 Aug. 191 Wasp-killers, as supplied by most horticultural sundriesmen. **1894** *Times* 4 June 13/6 Druggists' sundry-men. **1898** *Westm. Gaz.* 2 Nov. 8/1 One of the ledgers, the cash-book, and the sundry ledger.

†**'sundrily,** *a. Obs. rare.* Forms: 1 syndri(ȝ)lic, 4 *Sc.* syndryly, 6 sondrilie. [OE. *syndriȝlic*: see SUNDRY and -LY[1]. Cf. SUNDERLY *a.*] **a.** Separate, individual, special. **b.** Diverse.

a **900** tr. *Bæda's Hist.* IV. xviii. [xvi.] (1899) 426 Tweȝen cynelice cnihtas þa mid syndriȝlicre [*v.rr.* syndrilicre, synderlicre] Godes ȝyfe wæron ȝesiȝefæste. *c* **1375** *Sc. Leg. Saints* xxxvi. (*Baptista*) 386 þane Iohnne criste commendit gretly of uertuise fare & syndryly. [**1556** J. HEYWOOD *Spider & F.* lxx. 94 After recitall so sondrilie, The termes but namd, where memorie is most base: Remembraunce of the whole, these termes bring to place.]

†**'sundrily,** *adv. Obs.* Forms: 1 **syndriȝlice,** *Sc.* 4 **syndryly, 4–5 syndrely, 5 sindrely, syndryli; 4–6 sondrily, 6 -lie, 4 sundrylyche, 7 sundrily.** [OE. *syndriȝlice*: see SUNDRY and -LY[2]. Cf. SUNDERLY *adv.*]

1. Separately, severally, individually.

a **900** tr. *Bæda's Hist.* II. x. [xiii.] (1890) 164 He.. syndriȝlice [*v.r.* synderlice] wæs fram him eallum friȝnende, hwylc [etc.]. **1375** BARBOUR *Bruce* XII. 138 [They] held thair way in full gret hy, Nocht all to-gidder bot syndrely. **1390** GOWER *Conf.* III. 129 Sondrily to everich on [*sc.* star] A gras belongeth and a Ston. *c* **1425** WYNTOUN *Cron.* II. i. 127 Succedit to þat heretage Fourteyn ayris syndrely [*v.r.* sindrely]. **1539** *Act 31 Hen. VIII*, c. 13 §25 The same duke and lorde Cobham.. shall.. enjoye the premisses by them sundrily purchased.

2. Diversely, variously.

c **1425** WYNTOUN *Cron.* VIII. vii. 1453 Off Murrawe and of þe Dowglasse.. Sen syndry spekis syndryli [*v.r* syndrely] I can noucht put þaim in story. **1576** T. NEWTON *Lemnie's Complex.* (1633) 136 These humours being of great force divers wayes, and sundrily affecting the body.

'sundriness. *Obs.* or *rare.* Forms: *Sc.* 4–5 **syndrynes, sindrynes(s; 6 sondrinesse, soundry-, sundrynes.** [f. SUNDRY *a.* + -NESS. Cf. SUNDERNESS.] Diversity, variety; *occas.* a variety of things.

c **1375** *Sc. Leg. Saints* xli. (*Agnes*) 27 Of fele vertuse with syndrynes he clethis þame. *c* **1425** WYNTOUN *Cron.* VIII. xvi. 2443 Qwha skalis his thoucht in syndrynes [*v.r.* sindrynes], In althynge it is þe les. *a* **1450** *Ratis Raving* I. 835 Misknawlege of ȝouthed, The quhilk has mekle syndrynes Tyll wnderstand. **1548** GESTE *Agst. Priv. Masse* E iv b, They were dyuersly respected of god in consyderation of the soundrynes betwixt ye offerers. **1563** BALDWIN in *Mirr. Mag.* II. To Rdr. Lij b, The dyuersytye of braynes in divisyng, is lyke the sundrynes of beastes in engendryng. **1878** W. BARNES *Outl. Eng. Speech-Craft* 86 The goodness of a speech should be sought in.. its fulness of words for all things and time-takings which come, with all their sundrinesses, under the minds of men of the speech, in their common life.

'sundrop(s. [f. SUN *sb.*[1] + DROP *sb.*] Any of the species of *Œnothera* (evening primrose) which open in sunlight.

1796 NEMNICH *Polygl.-Lex.*, Sundrop, *Oenothera.* **1845–50** MRS. LINCOLN *Lect. Bot.* App. 132 *Œnothera.. fruticosa* (shrubby œnothera, sun-drop). **1856** A. GRAY *Man. Bot.* (1860) 131 Sundrops.

sundry ('sʌndrɪ), *a.* Forms: α. 1 **syndriȝ, (syndryȝ,** *Northumb.* **suindriȝ), 1–2 sindriȝ, 2–3 sindri, 4–5 sindre, syndre;** *Sc.* and *north.* **4– sindry, syndry, 5–7 sindri, 5–8 sindrie (5 sendri, 6 sin-, syndrye, -ie, syndery, 8 sendry);** β. **3–4 sundri, 4–6 sondri, -dry(e, (4 sundrii, -dre, sum-dri, sondree), 5–6 sondre, sundery, soundry, 5–7 sundrie, soundrie, 6–7 sondrie, (6 so(u)ndery, -ie, soondrie, 7 sondrey), 4– sundry.** [OE. *syndriȝ* separate, special, private, exceptional, corresp. to MLG. *sunder(i)ch* single, special, LG. *sunderig*, OHG. *sunt(a)rîc, sund(i)rîc, -erîg* special (MHG. *sunderig, -ic*); f. *sunder* SUNDER *a.*: see -Y[1].]

1. Having an existence, position, or status apart; separate, distinct. *Obs.* exc. *dial.*

c **1000** ÆLFRIC *Judg.* Epil. (Gr.) 263 þa senatores.. dæȝ-hwanlice smeadon on anum sindrian huse embe ealles folces þearfe. *c* **1000** *Ags. Ps.* cxl. 12 (Gr.) Ic me syndriȝ eom. *c* **1250** *Gen. & Ex.* 1985 Ðor was in helle a sundri stede, wor ðe seli folc reste dede. *a* **1300** *Cursor M.* 332 þis wright [*sc.* God].. Fra al oþer, sundri [*Fairf.* ys sundre] and sere. *Ibid.* 16094 þe pretori, þat was a sundri stede. **1393** LANGL. *P. Pl.* C. XIX. 192 þre persones in o pensel.. departable from oþer .. And sondry to seo vpon. **1533** N. UDALL *Coronat. Anne Boleyn* in Arb. *Garner* II. 58 The fourth Lady.. peerless in riches, wit, and beauty; Which are but sundry qualities in yon three [*sc.* Juno, Pallas, and Venus]. **1549** COVERDALE, etc. *Erasm. Par.* 1 *Pet.* 9 Let not age, estate, condicion or sondry being in diuerse countres disseuer you a sondre. **1790** MRS. WHEELER *Westmld. Dial.* (1802) 114 She ligs in a sendry kaw boose.

†**2.** Belonging or assigned distributively to certain individuals; distinct or different for each respectively. *Obs.*

a **900** tr. *Bæda's Hist.* IV. xxiii. [xxii.] (1890) 328 þurh syndriȝe þine ondsware [orig. *per singula tua responsa*] ic onȝet & oncneow, þæt [etc.]. *Ibid.* v. xxiii. (1899) 697/1 On septem Epistolas Canonicas [ic sette] syndrie bec. *c* **1000** ÆLFRIC *Deut.* xxxiii. 5 Moyses þa ȝebletsode.. þa twelf mæȝða ælce mid sindriȝre bletsunge. *c* **1205** LAY. 2688 He hefde on liue tuenti sunen and alc hefde sindri moder *a* **1300** *Cursor M.* 9533 Ilkan sum-dri gift he gaue. **1375** BARBOUR *Bruce* x. 731 His men, in-to syndry plas, Clam our the wall. **1430–40** LYDG. *Bochas* I. ii. (MS. Bodl. 263) 17/1 The contre off Sennar thei forsook And ech off hem a sondri contre took. *a* **1548** HALL *Chron., Hen. VIII* 70, iiii hed peces called Armites, euery pece beyng of a sundery deuice. **1549** *Compl. Scot.* vi. 65 Ilk ane of them hed ane syndry instrament to play to the laif, the fyrst hed ane drone bag pipe, the nyxt hed ane pipe maid of ane bleddir and of ane reid, the thrid playit on ane trump [etc.]. **1592** GREENE *Conny Catching* Wks. (Grosart) XI. 84 Those *Amarosos* here in England.. that.. wil haue in euery shire in England a sundry wife. *a* **1700** DRYDEN *Ovid's Art Love* I. 863 Experience finds That sundry Women are of sundry Minds. **1715** PENNECUIK *Truth's Trav.* 114 Ilk an ran a sindrie gait. **1738** WESLEY *Ps.* CIV. iv, His Ministers Heav'n's Palace fill, To have their sundry Tasks assign'd.

†**3.** Individually separate; that is one of a number of individuals of a class or group. Usually with pl. sb. or sing. sb. in pl. sense: Various, (many) different. *Obs.* (or merged in 5).

c **1250** *Gen. & Ex.* 665 Al was on speche ðor bi-foren, ðor woren sundri speches boren. **1375** BARBOUR *Bruce* v. 7 For to mak in thair synging Syndry notis, and soundis sere. **14..** *Sir Beues* (MS. E.) 4313 + 46 He hadde wunnen in to hys hond Many a batayle in sundry lond. *c* **1470** HENRY *Wallace* I. 29 Elrisle.. Auchinbothe, and othir syndry place. **1551** RECORDE *Pathw. Knowl.* I. xvii, Diligently behold how these sundry figures be turned into triangles. **1561** T. HOBY tr. *Castiglione's Courtyer* I. (1577) D vij b, In learning to handle sundrie kinde of weapons. **1596** *Edw. III*, III. i. 69 Like to a meddow full of sundry flowers. **1603** OWEN *Pembrokeshire* (1892) 269 The seuerall sortes of fowle.. and .. the sondrey kindes of takeinge of them. **1677** in *Verney Mem.* (1907) II. 327 There are sundry sorts of Habits becomming Souldiers in particular. **1754** SHERLOCK *Disc.* vii. (1759) I. 215 The Prophets of old were.. destroyed by sundry Kinds of Death.

†**b.** Preceded (rarely followed) by an adj. of number or plurality (esp. *many*). See also 6 e. *Obs.*

1377 LANGL. *P. Pl.* B. XIII 38 þanne cam scripture And serued hem.. of sondry metes manye. **1390** GOWER *Conf.* II. 359 Thei bede.. Tuo sondri beddes to be dyht. **1474** CAXTON *Chesse* IV. v. (1883) 176 Whan he is in the myddes of the tabler he may goo in to viii. places sondry. **1500–20** DUNBAR *Poems* xxvi. 26 Heilie harlottis.. Come in with mony sindrie gyiss. **15..** *Adam Bel* 470 in Hazl. *E.P.P.* II. 158 We haue slaie your fat falow der In many a sondry place. **1570** FOXE *A. & M.* (ed. 2) 1352/2 In those dayes there were ij. sundry Bibles in Englishe. **1570** *Satir. Poems Reform.* xiii. 17 And this he vsis mony sindrie sortis. **1570–6** LAMBARDE *Peramb. Kent* (1826) 198 The third Brooke.. being crossed in the way by seven other sundry bridges. **1617** MORYSON *Itin.* I. 231 Nine sundry Sects of Christians haue their Monasteries within this City. **1678** R. BARCLAY *Apol. Quakers* v. §20. 157 This Parable, repeated in three sundry Evangelists.

†**c.** Comb., as ***sundry-coloured, -shaped*** adjs.

1587 GOLDING *De Mornay* vi. (1592) 62 Afore making this sundrishaped world, God had conceiued an incorruptible paterne thereof. **1593** DRAYTON *Ecl.* i. 14 His sundrie colourec Coat. *a* **1700** EVELYN *Diary* June 1645, The quire, wall'd.. with sundry colour'd stone halfe relievo.

†**4.** Different, other. (Const. *from.*) With pl. sb. or sing. sb. in pl. sense: Diverse, manifold. *Obs.*

13.. *Cursor M.* 4246 (Gött.) Putyfar.. held ioseph in mensk and lare Al þou þair treuthes sundri ware. *c* **1400** *Rom. Rose* 5184 If I may lere Of sondry loves the manere. *c* **1470** HENRY *Wallace* x. 708 The king changyt on syndry hors off Spayn. **1509** HAWES *Past. Pleas.* IV. (Percy Soc.) 19 A venemous beast of sundry likenes. **1535** COVERDALE *Bible* Prol. to Rdr. ¶2 Euery church allmost had ye Byble of a sondrye translacion. **1548** TURNER *Names Herbes* (E.D.S.) 23 Carduus.. is a sundry herbe from Cinara. **1551** —— *Herbal* I. E iij, Dioscorides descrybeth thes herbes seuerally, & so maketh them sondry herbes. **1586** DAY *Engl. Secretorie* I. (1625) 132 How many, and how sundry are the euils wherewith our mortall state is endangered. **1614** W. B *Philos. Banquet* (ed. 2) 113 The sundryest kindes of extremities. **1639** FULLER *Holy War* IV. vi. (1647) 176 A sundry dialect maketh not a severall language. **1668** CULPEPPER & COLE *Barthol. Anat.* III. xi. 152 The external parts about the mouth are sundry.

b. †(*a*) Consisting of different elements, of mixed composition. *Obs. rare.*

1594 HOOKER *Eccl. Pol.* IV. vi. §3 Forbidding them [*sc.* the Jews] to put on garments of sundry stuffe. **1600** SHAKS. *A.Y.L.* IV. i. 17 A melancholy of mine owne, compounded of many simples, extracted from many obiects, and indeed the sundrie contemplation of my trauells, in which my often rumination, wraps me in a most humorous sadnesse.

(*b*) Consisting of miscellaneous items: cf. SUNDRIES.

1790 BEATSON *Nav. & Mil. Mem.* II. 187, 75 tons of sundry wood. **1870** RAYMOND *Statist. Mines & Mining* (1872) 98 The assets of the company [include] Cash in Bank of California $119,609.... Sundry open accounts $2,863. **1913** *Times* 9 Aug. 19/2 Yield, including sundry revenue, £4,855.

5. As an indefinite numeral: A number of, several. (The prevailing use.)

†Occas. with poss. as *sundry his* = several of his.

c **1375** *Sc. Leg. Saints* ii. (*Paulus*) 26 In parelis wes he stad sindry. **1390** GOWER *Conf.* I. 209 This Emperour.. Withinne a ten mile environ.. Hath sondry places forto reste. **1456** SIR G. HAYE *Law Arms* (S.T.S.) 107 And ȝit is thare sindry othir realmes that obeyis nocht to the Emperoure. **1542** UDALL *Erasm. Apoph.* 321 Whom Cicero veray often tymes citeth in soondrie his werkes. **1552** *Bk. Com. Prayer, Morn. Prayer, Exh.*, The scripture moueth vs in sondrye places, to acknowledge and confesse our manyfolde synnes and wyckednesse. **1605** SHAKS. *Macb.* IV. iii. 158 Sundry Blessings hang about his Throne, That speake him full of Grace. **1630** PRYNNE *Anti-Armin.* 118 Subiecting it to sundry alterations, periods, and changes at our pleasure. **1782** MISS BURNEY *Cecilia* II. ii, [She] was then ushered with great pomp through sundry apartments. **1794** *Bloomfield's Reports* 13 The Court having heard.. sundry affidavits read. **1843** JAMES *Forest Days* i, These benches formed the favourite resting-place of sundry old men. **1870** A. R. HOPE *My Schoolboy Fr.* xi. 149 Disturbing the placid repast of sundry forlorn cows. **1913** *Oxf. Univ. Gaz.* 19 Feb. 493/2 Having built some proper out-houses to replace sundry untidy wooden hen-roosts.

†**b.** In collocations, as ***sundry*** (***and***) ***divers***, ***divers*** (***and***) ***sundry***, ***sundry*** (***and***) ***several***. *Obs.*

c **1420** ? LYDG. *Assembly of Gods* 321 Chaungeable of sondry dyuerse colowres. **1483** *Rolls of Parlt.* VI. 245/1 Sundrie and diverse false and traiterous proclamacions. **1495** *Naval Acc. Hen. VII* (1896) 138 Diverse & soundrie shippes. *a* **1548** HALL *Chron., Edw. IV* 222 At sondry and seuerall tymes (and not all at one tyme). **1574** in *10th Rep. Hist. MSS. Comm.* App. v. 424 For dyverse and sondrye good occations. **1590** L. LLOYD *Diall Daies* 76 At sundrie severall times.

c. *ellipt.* and (chiefly Sc.) *absol.* (Cf. SEVERAL *a.* 4 c.)

c **1470** HENRY *Wallace* I. 199 Syndry wayntyt, bot nane wyst be quhat way. **1575** in *Maitl. Club Misc.* I. 115 Syndery boyith of the citie and gentillmen upaland. *a* **1629** HINDE *J. Bruen* xlvi. (1641) 146 Divers and sundry of the workes of the Lord. **1680** H. MORE *Apocal. Apoc.* 123 The not understanding of which has made sundry in vain attempt to predict events foretold in the Apocalypse. *a* **1796** BURNS *Katherine Jaffray* iii, He's tell'd her father and mother baith, As I hear sindry say, O. **1825** T. HOOK *Sayings* Ser. II. *Doubts & F.* i. II. 84 Sundry of those little hemmings and coughings. **1875** WHITNEY *Life Lang.* vii. 115 Sundry of the modern European languages.

6. Phr. †**a.** ***on, in, a sundry***: alteration of *on-*, *in-sunder* (see SUNDER B), ASUNDER. †**b.** ***by sundries***: individually. †**c.** ***in*** or ***on sundry wise*** (occas. ***wises***), later ***sundry wise***: in various or different ways; variously, diversely. **d.** (***in***) ***sundry ways*** (in the same sense). **e.** ***all and sundry***, occas. †***all sundry***: every individual, every single; now only *absol.* (occas. †***all and sundries***) = everybody of all classes, one and all. (orig. and chiefly Sc. = L. *omnes et singuli.*)

a. *c* **1250** *Gen. & Ex.* 393 On sundri ðhenken he to ben. **13..** *Cursor M.* 14665 (Gött.) We er all ane,.. Sua þat we thoru nane-kin art Ne man be made in sundri [*Cott.* in sundre] part. *c* **1330** *Amis & Amil.* 309 Now we asondri schal wende. *a* **1400** *Parlt. 3 Ages* (Roxb.) 90, I.. choppede of the nekke And þ^e hede and the haulse homelyde in sondree. *c* **1420** ? LYDG. *Assembly of Gods* 1765 Whyche iii tymes, a sondry deuydyd, Mayst thow here see.

b. *a* **1400–50** *Wars Alex.* 3909 þai seke out be sundres sexti to-gedire.

c. *c* **1375** *Sc. Leg. Saints* v. (*Johannes*) 558 He taucht þam in syndry vyis. **1375** BARBOUR *Bruce* IX. 441 The laif.. Sesit .. Men, armyng, and marchandiss, And othir gudis on syndri viss. **14..** *Chaucer's Friar's T.* 172 (Harl. MS. 7334) Why.. ryde ȝe þan or goon, In sondry wyse [*v.r.* shape] and nouȝt alway in oon? **1484** in *Lett. Rich. III & Hen. VII* (Rolls) I. 88 Feithful services to us in sundry wises doon. **1549** COVERDALE, etc. *Erasm. Par. Rom.* 33 God doeth in sondry wyse bestow his giftes. **1577** B. GOOGE *Heresbach's Husb.* I. (1586) 3 b, The fruitefull Earth that tyld in sundry wyse, Vnto the eye her goodly fruites dooth yeelde. **1591** R. TURNBULL *St. James* 149 b, Men fall and sinne.. three waies .. and there is no man which doeth not fall through euerie one of these, sundriwise. **1818** SCOTT *Hrt. Midl.* xli, Twa precious saints might pu' sundry wise, like twa cows riving at the same hay-band.

d. *a* **1578** LINDESAY (Pitscottie) *Chron. Scot.* (S.T.S.) I. 3 Ingyne of man be Inclinatioun in sindrie wayes is giwin. **1592** TIMME *Ten Engl. Lepers* E 4 b, This leprosie of pride dooth sundrie waies lay holde upon men. **1605** SHAKS. *Macb.* IV. iii. 48 Yet my poore Country Shall.. More suffer, and more sundry wayes then euer. **1609** SKENE *Reg. Maj.* Table 61 He quha being lawfullie summoned, is absent,.. is sindrie wayes vnlawed according to the diversitie of the courts. **1697** DRYDEN *Virg. Georg.* III. 187 To breed him, break him, back him, are requir'd Experienc'd Masters; and in sundry Ways: Their Labours equal, and alike their Praise. **1743** BULKELEY & CUMMINS *Voy. S. Seas* 36 There have died sundry ways since the Ship first struck forty-five Men.

e. **1389** in Sir W. Fraser *Wemyss of W.* (1888) II. 24 Til there thyngys al and syndry lelily and fermly to be fulfyllyt and yhemmyt. **1480** in *Exch. Rolls Scot.* IX. 120 *note*, All and sendri oure liegis and subditis. **1552** ABP. HAMILTON *Catech.* (1884) 3 Till all and sindry personis. **1562** A. SCOTT *Poems* (S.T.S.) i. 95 To ceis all sindrye sectis of hereseis. **1597** *Reg. Mag. Sig. Scot.* 303/2 Togidder with all and sindrie the teindscheves. **1682** *Lond. Gaz.* No. 1682/1 To have forfault.. all and sundry his Lands, Heretages, Liffrents, and Rents.

absol. **1428** *Munim. de Melros* (Bann.) 519 Till all & syndry to quham þe knawlage of þir presentz lettris sall to cum. **1442** in *Reg. Mag. Sig. Scot.* 63/2 Till al and sindri that thir presentez lettrez sall here or see. **1783** W. GORDON tr. *Livy's Rom. Hist.* IV. ii. 310 Sedition never failed to procure honour and respect to all and sundries, its authors and abettors. **1818** SCOTT *Hrt. Midl.* lii, Join wi' Rob Roy.. and revenge Donacha's death on all and sundry. **1837–42** HAWTHORNE *Twice-told T.* (1851) I. x. 171, I cry aloud to all and sundry, in my plainest accents. **1901** *Scotsman* 13 Mar. 12/2 The city must advertise for estimates from all and sundry.

†**7.** That sunders or separates; dividing; discriminating. *Obs. rare.*

1564 HARDING *Answ. to Jewel's Chalenge* 133 b, They must vse a discretion, and a sundry iudgement betwen the thinges they write agonisticōs, ..and the thinges they vtter dogmaticōs. **1593** A. CHUTE *Beautie Dishonoured* (1908) 111 Thus life, and death, in unitie agreeing Dated the tenor of their sonderie strife.

Hence †**'sundryfold** *a.*, manifold; †**'sundry-head**, diversity, variety; †**'sundrywhere** *adv.*, in various places.

c **1430** LYDG. *Minor Poems* (Percy Soc.) 194 Complexionat of *sondryfold coloures. **1557** PHAER *Æneid* v. M iv b, Skant yemen twayn.. the same coud beare, So sondriefolde it was. **1395** HYLTON *Scala Perf.* (W. de W. 1494) II. xlvi, þe *soundryhede of orders [of angels]. **1548** PATTEN *Exped. Scot.* M vij b, His valiaunce *sundry whear tried. **1568** T. HOWELL *Arb. Amitie* Poems (1879) 35 The fethred foule.. sundrie where his fostring foode, With chirping bill he peekes.

'sundry, *adv. Obs.* exc. *Sc.* Forms: 1 *Northumb.* **syndriȝe, suindriȝe, swyndria**; chiefly *Sc.* and *north.* 4 **syndri**, 4–6 **syndry**, 5 **sindrie**, 6 **sindri**, (9 **sinry, sinnery,**) 5– **sindry**; 3–5 **sundri**, 4 **sondry**, 6–7 **sundrie**, 4–9 **sundry**. [OE. *syndriȝe*, = OHG. *sunt(a)rîgo* (MHG. *sunderige*, LG. *sonderig*, *sünderig*); f. prec.]

1. Separately, apart; severally, individually.

c **950** *Lindisf. Gosp.* Mark iv. 34 *Seorsum*, syndriȝe. *Ibid.* xiv. 19 *Singillatim*, swyndria. *c* **1205** LAY. 24577 Alle þa wepmen at heore mete seten sund[r]i bi heom seoluen. *c* **1250** *Gen. & Ex.* 2354 In lond gersen sulen ȝe sundri riche ben. *a* **1300** *Cursor M.* 20202, I sal to þe a-postles weind onan, And sceu þam sundri an and an, þat tai be her þe thrid dai. **1375** BARBOUR *Bruce* XVII. 297 He.. till gret lordis, ilkane syndri, Ordanit ane felde for thar herbry. *c* **1475** *Rauf Coilȝear* 29 Be thay disseuerit sindrie, midmorne was past. **1524** *St. Papers Hen. VIII*, IV. 129 It may doo gret ewel to Me, and pwt the Kyng my son and Me syndry. **1538** STARKEY *England* (1878) 85 The fautys wych we schal fynde sundry in the partys. **1589** ALEX. HUME *Poems* (S.T.S.) 60 They.. sundrie through the earth were driuen. **1590** SPENSER *F.Q.* II. ix. 48 These three in these three roomes did sundry dwell. **1829** HOGG *Sheph. Cal.* I. i. 20 The herds, wha lived about three miles sindry.

†**b.** In detail. *Obs. rare.*

a **1300** *Cursor M.* 26609 Scrift agh be scire and sundri [*v.r.* sundre] tald.

2. Of a single object (or anything so considered): In or into pieces; to pieces; = ASUNDER *adv.* 4.

1533 BELLENDEN *Livy* I. xi. (S.T.S.) I. 63 How þe Veanis and fidenatis war discomfist, & mecius dictator drawin sindri for his demeritis. **1536** —— *Cron. Scot.* (1821) I. 231 Drawin sindry with wild hors. **1882** *Jamieson's Sc. Dict.* s.v., The thing fell sindry in my han'. **1893** F. MACKENZIE *Cruisie Sk.* ii. (1894) 20 It will be an unco hard hoast that shak's ye sindry.

sun-dry ('sʌndraɪ), *v.* Chiefly in infl. forms **sun-dried, sun-drying.** [Back-formation from SUN-DRIED.] To dry in the sun. **a.** *trans.*

1695 *Disc. Duties on Sugars* 4 Muscovado's, not improv'd by Straining, Sundrying, or the like. **1825** SOUTHEY *Tale Paraguay* II. iv, In turtle shells they hoard the scanty rain, And eat its flesh, sun-dried for lack of fire. **1859** R. F. BURTON *Centr. Afr.* in *Jrnl. Geog. Soc.* XXIX. 405 [Tobacco] is prepared for sale in different forms. Everywhere, however, a simple sundrying supplies the place of cocking and sweating. **1893** D. J. RANKIN *Zambesi Basin* xiv. 244 The meat.. is cut into strips, sun-dried and smoked.

b. *intr.*

1883 STEVENSON *Treas. Isl.* xxix, We'll all swing and sun-dry for your bungling. **1886** —— *Kidnapped* iii. 24, I must have the bed and bedclothes aired and put to sun-dry.

sundry-man: see SUNDRIES 2.

sune, obs. f. SHUN, SON, SOON, SOUND *v.*[1]

suneful, obs. form of SINFUL.

sunegen, -eghen, -egi, obs. forms of SIN *v.*

†**sunegild.** *Obs. rare*$^{-1}$. Also **-ilt.** [f. *sunegen*, SIN *v.* + *-ild* fem. suffix (see GRUCCHILD).] A female sinner.

c **1230** *Hali Meid.* (MS. Titus) 43 As te eadi sunegild [*MS. Bodl.* sunegilt] marie Magdalene.. bireowseð hare gultes.

sunen, obs. form of SHUN.

suneniht, -niȝt, var. SUNNIGHT *Obs.*

'sunfall. Chiefly *poet.* or *rhet.* [See FALL *v.* 7 e.] Sunset.

1600 TOURNEUR *Transf. Metam.* lxxiii, Heauen.. but eu'n now lamented The sun-fall of thy selfe. **1605** *1st Pt. Jeronimo* 895 Many a bleeding hart, which, eare Sunne fall, Shall pay deere trybute. **1870** R. S. HAWKER *Cornish Ball., Aurora* i, Sunfall, and yet no night! **1890** CRAWFURD *Round Cal. Portugal* 33 From early dawn to sunfall.

'sun-fish, *sb.* Also **sunfish.**

1. A name for various fishes, of rounded form or brilliant appearance, or that bask in the sun.

a. Any fish of the genus *Mola* (also called *Orthagoriscus* or *Cephalus*), comprising large fishes of singularly rounded and ungainly form, found in various seas. **b.** Any one of the various species of *Lepomis*, *Pomotis*, and related genera, small fresh-water fishes abundant in N. America. **c.** A name for the basking shark: see BASKING *ppl. a.* 2. **d.** The OPAH, *Lampris luna* or *guttatus*. **e.** A local name for fishes of the genus *Selene*; = MOON-FISH c.

a. 1629 HIGGINSON *Jrnl.* in *Hutchinson Papers* (Prince Soc.) I. 43 A large round fish sayling by the ship's side, about a yard in length and roundness [*printed* rounders] every way. The mariners called it a sunne fish; it spreadeth out the finnes like beames on every side 4 or 5. **1686** RAY *Willughby's Hist. Piscium* 151–2. **1734** *Phil. Trans.* XLI. 343 A Sun-fish weighing about 500 Pound Weight. **1804** SHAW *Gen. Zool.* V. II. 438 The Short Sun-Fish is a native of the European seas..: its general appearance rather represents the head of some large fish than a complete animal. *Ibid.* 439 Oblong Sun-Fish... Variegated Sun-Fish. *Ibid.* 440 Pallasian Sun-Fish. **1839** T. BEALE *Nat. Hist. Sperm Whale* 212 The ugly sun-fish now and then came floating by. **1879** E. P. WRIGHT *Anim. Life* 456 The Short Sun Fish (*Orthagoriscus mola*) is not rare on the west coast of Ireland.

b. 1685 PENN *Furth. Acc. Pennsylv.* 9 There is the Catfish, or Flathead.. Perch, black and white, Smelt, Sunfish, &c. **1796** MORSE *Amer. Geog.* I. 482 In the lakes, yellow-perch, sun-fish, salmon-trout. **1888** GOODE *Amer. Fishes* 67 The Blue Sun-fish, *Lepomis pallidus*, is also known as the 'Blue Bream'.

c. 1746 C. SMITH *State of Waterford* xi. 271 This coast is pretty much frequented by Porpoises, Sun-fish, Seals, &c. **1797** *Encycl. Brit.* (ed. 3) XVII. 714/2 *Squalus*... The *maximus*, basking shark, or the sun-fish of the Irish. **1886** *Ibid.* XXI. 777/2 The Basking Shark (*Selache maxima*), sometimes erroneously called 'Sun-Fish'.. may be seen in calm weather.. motionless, with the upper part of the back raised above the surface of the water, a habit which it has in common with the true sun-fish (*Orthagoriscus*).

d. 1884 *Encycl. Brit.* XVII. 777/1 *Opah* (*Lampris luna*)... From its habit of coming to the surface in calm weather, showing its high dorsal fin above the water, it has also received the name of 'sun-fish'.

e. 1884 GOOGE *Nat. Hist. Aquatic Anim.* 322 *Selene setipinnis*.. known.. in North Carolina as the 'Moonfish' or 'Sunfish'.

†**2.** A kind of starfish with numerous rays: cf. *sun-starfish* s.v. SUN *sb.*[1] 13 b. *Obs.*

1681 GREW *Musæum* I. v. iv. 124 A Star-Fish with Twelve Rays; by some called Sun-Fish.

3. *U.S. colloq.* A manner of bucking. Cf. SUNFISH *v.*

1903 *Wide World Mag.* Mar. 548 A broncho named 'E.A.'.. used a combination of 'sunfish' and 'twister'. **1939** P. A. ROLLINS *Gone Haywire* 260 One prodigious forward jump, then a 'sunfish', and the beast raced into a 'circle buck'.

Hence **'sun,fishery**, the occupation of fishing for sun-fish.

1848 BRABAZON *Fisheries Irel.* v. 51 The Sun Fishery is not confined to the Sun Fish bank of Clew Bay.

'sunfish, *v. colloq.* (orig. and chiefly *U.S.*) [f. the *sb.*] *intr.* To act like a sun-fish, *spec.* of a 'bucking' horse (see quot. 1888). Also *transf.*

1888 ROOSEVELT in *Century Mag.* Apr. 854/2 He may buck steadily in one place, or 'sunfish',—that is, bring first one shoulder down almost to the ground and then the other. **1923** *Century Mag.* CVI. 831/2 Down across Texas it went sunfishin', back-flippin', side-windin'... The Staked Plains used to be heavily timbered until that big wind swiped the trees off. **1971** A. P. MCINNES *Dunlevy* 86 Sometimes the mare sunfished, but the girl stuck solidly. **1979** D. ANTHONY *Long Hard Cure* xxv. 195 He'd ducked.. and gone to one knee, sunfishing a little. His right arm moved.. and his pistol boomed loud.

Hence **'sunfisher**, a horse that sunfishes; **'sunfishing** *ppl. a.* and *vbl. sb.*

1913 in *Dialect Notes* IV. 28 Sunfisher. **1923** *N.Y. Times* 16 Aug. 10/1 As Yak went by the sun-fishing longhorn sort o' sheered. **1924** W. M. RAINE *Troubled Waters* v. 47 Rocking chair [an outlaw horse].. was a noted fence rower, weaver, and sunfisher. *Ibid.* 52 Neither sidebucking nor pitching, sunfishing nor weaving could shake the lean-loined, broad-shouldered figure from his seat. **1961** R. F. ADAMS *Old-time Cowhand* 298 A 'sunfisher' was a hoss that twisted his body into a crescent, or, in other words, when he seemed to try to touch the ground with first one shoulder and then the other, lettin' the sunlight hit his belly. **1967** *Sunday Mail Mag.* (Brisbane) 12 Feb. 3/1 In the flash of a second, he'd switched from 'sunfishing' to 'corkscrewing'.

'sunflower. [tr. mod.L. *flōs sōlis*.]

†**1. a.** The heliotrope (*Heliotropium*). *Obs. rare*$^{-1}$.

1562 TURNER *Herbal* II. 13 b, Because it turneth the leaues about wyth the sonne, it is called Heliotropion, that is, turned wyth the sonne, or sonne flower.

b. Used vaguely or allusively for any flower that turns so as to follow the sun: cf. HELIOTROPE 1.

1652 BENLOWES *Theoph.* IV. xv, Ye Twins of Light, as Sunflow'rs be enclin'd To th' Sun of Righteousnes. **1794** W. BLAKE *Songs Exper., Ah! Sun-Flower* 1 Ah, Sunflower! weary of time, Who countest the steps of the sun. **1852** ROBERTSON *Serm.* Ser. IV. xl. 305 Christian life is as the turning of the sunflower to the Sun.

2. a. Any species of the genus *Helianthus*, N.O. *Compositæ*, chiefly natives of N. America, having conspicuous yellow flower-heads with disk and ray suggesting a figure of the sun; esp. *H. annuus*, a tall-growing plant commonly cultivated for its very large showy flowers.

1597 GERARDE *Herbal* II. ccxlvii. 612 *Flos Solis maior*. The greater Sunne flower. [**1613** PURCHAS *Pilgrimage* VIII. ii. 616 The flower of the Sunne is now no longer the Marigold of Peru, but growth in many places with vs in England.] **1705** TATE tr. *Cowley's Plants* IV. C.'s Wks. 1711 III. 395 The Sun-Flow'r, thinking 'twas for him foul Shame To nap by Day-light, strove t' excuse the Blame; It was not Sleep that made him nod, he said, But too great Weight and Largeness of his Head. **1785** MARTYN *Lett. Bot* xxvi. (1794) 399 The annual Sun-flower.. is a flower of wonderful magnificence. **1824** W. IRVING *T. Trav.* (1849) 395 The family garden, where.. gigantic sunflowers lolled their broad jolly faces over the fences. **1872** OLIVER *Elem. Bot.* II. 197 Sunflower (*Helianthus annuus*), the seeds of which yield a valuable oil.

b. Applied (usually with defining word) to various other composite plants with radiant yellow flower-heads: see quots.

1731 MILLER *Gard. Dict.* s.v. *Corona Solis*, Another Plant or two.. very nearly ally'd to the Sun-Flower... 19. Chrysanthemum; Helenii folio... Dwarf American Sun-Flower... 20. Chrysanthemum,.. Doronici folio,.. Dwarf-Peach-colour'd American Sun-flower. **1753** CHAMBERS *Cycl.* Suppl., App., *Rudbeckia*,.. a genus of plants, called.. in English the Dwarf-sun-flower. **1760** J. LEE *Introd. Bot.* App. 328 Sun-flower, Tickseeded, *Coreopsis*. *Ibid.*, Sun-flower, Willow-leaved, *Helenia*. **1845–50** MRS. LINCOLN *Lect. Bot.* App. 109 *Helenium autumnale* (false sun-flower). *a* **1850** W. A. BROMFIELD *Flora Vectensis* (1856) 253 *I[nula] Helenium*.. Velvet Dock. Wild Sun-flower. **1854** MISS BAKER *Northampt. Gloss.*, Sun-flower. Corn marigold. *Chrysanthemum segetum.*

c. *fig.* Applied to a person of resplendent beauty.

1823 BYRON *Island* II. x, Neuha, the sun-flower of the island daughters.

3. Applied to various plants whose flowers open only in sunshine or in daylight.

†**a.** The marigold: cf. quot. 1563 for *sun's flower* s.v. SUN *sb.*[1] 13 c. *Obs.* †**b.** The genus *Helianthemum* (N.O. *Cistaceæ*), commonly called *rock-rose* (also *sun-rose*: see SUN *sb.*[1] 13 b): usually ***little*** or ***small sunflower***. *Obs.* **c.** The pimpernel. *local.* **d.** The star-of-Bethlehem. *local.*

1670 RAY *Catal. Plant. Angliæ* F j b, *Helianthemum Anglicum luteum* Ger[arde]. Dwarf-Cistus, Little Sun-flower. **1753** *Chambers' Cycl.* Suppl., *Helianthemum*, small Sun-flower. **1866** *Treas. Bot* 1110/2 Sunflower, *Helianthus*; also.. *Calendula officinalis.*

4. *attrib.* and *Comb.*, as ***sunflower-plant, -seed***; ***sunflower-leaved*** adj.; **sunflower oil**, an oil obtained from the seeds of the sunflower; **Sunflower State** *U.S.*, a nickname for Kansas.

1822 *Hortus Anglicus* II. 411 B[uphthalmum] Helianthoides. *Sun Flower-leaved Ox Eye. **1768** *Pennsylvania Gaz.* 6 Oct. 2/3 The *sun-flower oil may prove equally valuable with the best Florence oil, for diet or medicine. **1860** *Ure's Dict. Arts*, etc. (ed. 5) III. 843 Sunflower oil. **1857** A. GRAY *First Less. Bot.* (1866) 156 A *Sunflower-plant.. has been found to exhale twenty or thirty ounces.. of water in a day. **1789** *Trans. Soc. Arts* II. 113 Fifteen bushels of *Sun Flower Seed. **1848** THACKERAY *Van. Fair* xii, There are garden-ornaments, as big as brass warming-pans, that are fit to stare the sun itself out of countenance. Miss Sedley was not of the *sunflower sort. **1888** *Harper's Mag.* June 39/1 Her citizens affectionately speak of Kansas as the '*Sunflower State'. **1904** *Minneapolis Times* 7 June 6 The floods in Kansas are subsiding. There was danger for a time that the Sunflower state would grow a crop of pond lilies. **1965** MRS. L. B. JOHNSON *White House Diary* 2 Sept. (1970) 315 It was a pleasant journey back to the Ranch, flying over the flat, rich lands of Kansas.. sunflowers everywhere, as big as salad plates. You can see why it's called the Sunflower State.

sunfol(e, -ful(l)e, obs. forms of SINFUL.

sung (sʌŋ), *ppl. a.* [pa. pple. of SING *v.*[1]] Uttered in musical tones (*Liturg.* as distinguished from being said without note).

1526 *Cartul. S. Nicholai Aberdon.* (New Spald. Cl.) I. 154 We sall sing.. placebo and dirige one ye vigill of his decess with ane soung mess one ye said day. **1848** R. S. HAWKER in *Life & Lett.* (1905) ix. 137, I do not like sung Psalms. **1906** ALICE WERNER *Natives Brit. Central Africa* x. 231 Most of them [*sc.* stories] contain short pieces which are sung... Steere points out that these sung parts are very common in the Swahili tales.

Sung (sʊŋ), *sb.* Also 7 **Sunga**, 8 and Pinyin **Song.** [Chinese *sòng*.] **a.** The name of a dynasty which ruled in China from 960 to 1279; a member of this dynasty. Also *attrib.*

1673 J. OGILBY *Nieuhoff's Embassy from East-India Co.* I. 249 The Tartars, after a long and tedious destructive War with this Family Sunga for seventy three years, conquer'd the whole Empire, extirpating the whole Family, and set up a new one call'd Ivena. **1738** J. B. DU HALDE *Descr. Empire of China & Chinese Tartary* I. 206 (*heading*) The Nineteenth Dynasty, call'd Song. **1745** tr. J. F. Gemelli Careri in A. & J. Churchill *Coll. Voy. & Trav.* (ed. 3) IV. II. iv. 313/1 When China was rul'd by the family of Sung. **1831** *Canton Miscellany* I. 28 Hwuytsung, an Emperor of the Sung Dynasty. **1893** D. C. BOULGER *Short Hist. China* v. 57 The folly of the Sungs had completed the discomfiture of the Kins. **1925** B. RACKHAM in R. Fry et al. *Chinese Art* 16 A further wide expansion of craftsmanship is shown by the manifold variety of wares of the Sung period. **1958** W. WILLETTS *Chinese Art* I. iii. 133 The Sung Emperors wanted to surround themselves with examples of ancient high art. **1977** *N.Y. Rev. Bks.* 26 May 21/2 (Advt.), To the Sung, poetry was a part of everyday life. **1979** *China Now* Mar./Apr. 9/2 For many practising potters the heights of Chinese ceramics were achieved during the Song Dynasty.

b. Used *attrib.* and *absol.* of the arts, design, and porcelain of the Sung period.

1885 *Trans. Asiatic Soc. Japan* XII. 171 The angular forms.. of the Sung dynasty, usually called the *Sung-pan*.. or '*Sung-block*' printing. **1906** R. FRY *Let.* 2 Dec. (1972) I. 275 He's got.. some first-rate early Chinese Sung pieces. **1933** *Burlington Mag.* Nov. 204/1 It is obviously a copy of a

Sung or Yüan celadon dish. **1937** E. LINKLATER *Juan in China* xii. 222 I've plenty of things to show you, Ming, Sung, pictures, anything you like. **1943** D. WELCH *Maiden Voyage* xviii. 149 This is another type of Sung porcelain called Ying-Ching or 'shadow blue'. **1961** *Guardian* 19 May 9/7 The European eye cannot fail to respond to what it would call the romanticism of Sung landscapes. **1976** M. DELVING *China Expert* ii. 36, I shall hope that whoever stole the Sung vase will make his little slip.

‖**sunga, sanga** (ˈsʌŋgə). [Kulū *sanga.*] A bridge made of beams, used in the Himalayas.

1832 G. E. MUNDY *Pen. & Pencil Sk. Ind.* I. iv. 241 Across a deep ravine..his Lordship erected a neat Sangah, or mountain-bridge, of pines. *Ibid.* v. 280 We crossed [the river] by a sangah loosely formed of pines. **1871** HARCOURT *Himalayan Distr. Kooloo* etc. iii. 67 A *sungha* bridge is formed as follows:—On either side the river piers of rubble masonry, laced with cross-beams of timber, are built up [etc.].

sungar, var. SANGAR.

sungates, *adv. Sc.* (and *arch.*) In 6 sonegatis. Also **singates, sungaets.** [f. SUN *sb.*[1] + *gates*, gen. of GATE *sb.*[2] (cf. 9 b). Cf. OE. *sunganges.*] = SUNWAYS.

1597 *Trials Witchcraft* in *Spalding Misc.* (1841) I. 96 It wilbe ane deir yeir; the bled of the corne growis withersones; and quhan it growis sonegatis about, it wilbe ane gude chaip yeir. **1879** *Shetland Times* 20 Sept. 3/5 They paired and proceeded to the house, walking once round it 'singates', *i.e.* sun ways, or from left to right; that was to secure luck to the pair. **1890** J. SERVICE *Notandums* 100 She was tell't to tak her withershins nine times through a heap o' unwatered yarn, to tak the cat through't sungates aboot as many times again. **1916** A. HUXLEY *Burning Wheel* 49 Though they turn sungates to its widdershins. **1931** [see NOUST].

sunge, obs. form of SIN *v.*

sunȝie, variant of SONYIE *Sc. Obs.*, excuse.

ˈsun-gleam. [GLEAM *sb.* 1.] †**a.** Sunlight. *Obs.* **b.** A gleam of sunshine.

a **1240** *Sawles Warde* in *O.E. Hom.* I. 259 Aȝein þe brihtnesse ant te liht of his leor þe sunne-gleam is dosc. **1813** SHELLEY *Q. Mab* III. 232 One faint April sun-gleam. **1826** MISS MITFORD *Village* Ser. II. (1863) 447 The bright sun-gleams and lengthening shadows of a most brilliant autumn. **1885** *Athenæum* 23 May 669/1 A foreground of whitish..clay reflects a strong sungleam falling there.

ˈsun-god. [Cf. MHG. *sunnengot*, G. *sonnengott.*] The sun regarded or personified as a god; a god identified or specially associated with the sun.

1592 *Soliman & Pers.* I. iii. 86 There happened a sore drought..that the iucie grasse Was seared with the Sunne Gods Element. **1831** KEIGHTLEY *Myth. Gr. & It.* I. v. 57 The ambitious youth instantly demanded permission to guide the solar chariot for one day, to prove himself thereby the undoubted progeny of the Sun-god. **1880** *Encycl. Brit.* XI. 749/2 Hermes is the sun-god as hidden during the night away among the souls of the dead.

So **ˈsun-ˌgoddess.**

1861 BP. G. SMITH *Ten Weeks in Japan* iv. 46 The great 'Sun-goddess'..seems to be the principal object of divine adoration to the multitude.

sungylle, obs. form of SWINGLE.

sunie, obs. Sc. form of SUNNY *a.*

sunk (sʌŋk), *sb. Sc.* and *north. dial.* Also 6–9 **sonk.** [Origin unknown.]

1. A seat of turf.

1513 DOUGLAS *Æneis* III. iv. 30 Syne efter, endlang the see costis bay, Wp sonkis [we] set, and desis did array. *Ibid.* v. vii. 44 Tho gan the grave Acest with wordis chyde Entellus, sat on the greyn sonk hym besyde. **1768** ROSS *Helenore* III. 221 Gang in an' seat you o' the sunks a' round. **17..** *Lizie Lindsay* xxix. in Child *Ballads* IV. 262/2 She sawna a seat to sit down on, But only some sunks o green feall.

2. A straw pad used as a cushion or saddle. (Usually *pl.*) Cf. SOD *sb.*[1] 2.

1787 GROSE *Provinc. Gloss.* (1790), *Sunk*, a canvas pack-saddle stuffed with straw. North. **1807** STAGG *Poems* 7 Wheyle some wi' pillion seats an' sonks To gear their naigs are fussin. **1816** SCOTT *Old Mort.* i, A hair tether, or halter, and a *sunk*, or cushion of straw, instead of bridle and saddle. *a* **1860** J. YOUNGER *Autobiog.* ix. (1881) 90 Now, John,..lay the sunks on your yellow mare.

3. A bank or dyke. Also *attrib.*, as *sunk-dyke.*

1842 A. LAING in *Whistle-binkie* Ser. IV. 72 Wi' rough divot sunks haudin' up the mud wa's. **1866** GREGOR *Banffsh. Gloss.*, *Sunk-dyke*, a dyke built of stone or sods on the one side, and filled with earth on the other. **1875** ALEX. SMITH *New Hist. Aberdeen* II. 925 The larger farms are enclosed.. with earthen sunks and hedgerows.

†**sunk**, *v. Obs.* Also 8 sonk. [Origin unknown.] *intr.* To be sullen; to sulk. Hence **ˈsunkan** *ppl. a.*, sulking, sullen.

1728 RAMSAY *Monk & Miller's Wife* 127 [He] ask'd his sunkan gloomy Spouse, What Supper had she in the House. **1737** —— *To Duncan Forbes* 64 For which they'll now have nae relief, But sonk at hame, and cleck mischief. **1788** PICKEN *Poems* Gloss., *Sunkan*, sullen, sour, ill-natured.

sunk (sʌŋk), *ppl. a.* [pa. pple. of SINK *v.*]

In present usage this form of the pa. pple. in adj. use tends to be restricted to senses implying deliberate human agency; e.g., *sunk fence*; contrast *sunken cheeks, sunken rocks.* (Cf. *shrunk* and *shrunken.*)

1. = SUNKEN 2. Now *rare.*

1398 TREVISA *Barth. De P. R.* IV. iii. (1495) e vj b, Soo the vtter partyes ben vneuyn wyth holownes sonke and had partes areryd. **1601** B. JONSON *Poetaster* Sec. Sounding 4 This is it, That our sunke eyes haue wak't for. **1611** COTGR. s.v. *Elevatoire*, The broken, and sunk-in parts of the scull. *Ibid.* s.v. *Have*, Hollow, sad, or sunke-in eyes. **1682** DRYDEN *Abs. & Achit.* 646 Sunk were his Eyes, his Voice was harsh and loud. *a* **1734** NORTH *Lives* (1826) II. 131 He went about as a ghost, with the visage of death upon him. Such a sunk, spiritless countenance he had. **1766** GOLDSM. *Vic. W.* xxviii, Her temples were sunk, her forehead was tense. **1823** SCOTT *Quentin D.* ii, His strong features, sunk cheeks, and hollow eyes. **1833** J. DAVIDSON *Embalming* 14 Many of their Mummies..are of a dark tanned colour,..the features distinct, the belly sunk. **1891** HARDY *Tess* xxxvi, The sunk corners of her mouth.

Comb. *a* **1601** ? MARSTON *Pasquil & Kath.* (1878) I. 5 The yellow tooth'd, sunck-eyed, gowtie shankt Vsurer. **1624** MASSINGER *Parl. Love* IV. ii, We'll show these shallow fools sunk-eyed despair.

2. Lowered in character, intensity, value, etc. **a.** Depraved, degenerate. Now *rare* or *Obs.*

1680 H. MORE *Apocal. Apoc.* 97 A thing that sunk flesh and blood are too incredulous of. **1681** —— in *Glanvill's Sadducismus* Postscr. 38 The vilest reproach against the God of Israel..that..the dulness of any sunk Soul can stumble upon. **1868** W. R. GREG *Lit. & Soc. Judgm.* 132 She is punished..as the most sunk of sinners.

b. Degraded or reduced in status or value. Now *rare* or *Obs.*

1686 PLOT *Staffordsh.* 274 Who raised again their sunk ancient Family..by their valour only. **1731** SWIFT *Presbyt. Plea of Merit* Wks. 1841 II. 241/2 A sunk, discarded party. **1893** *Daily News* 10 May 5/2 The Bank of New Zealand, some time ago, cut adrift its sunk investments.

c. Of the spirits: Depressed, low. Now *rare* or *Obs.*

1719 DE FOE *Crusoe* II. (Globe) 471, I was exceedingly sunk in my Spirits. **1818** SCOTT *Rob Roy* xxxviii, I saw his daughter's form once more before me in flesh and blood, though with diminished beauty and sunk spirits.

d. *colloq.* Of a person: in a hopeless position, in trouble, in a mess. Freq. *hyperbolical.*

1922 [see SPURLOS VERSENKT]. **1934** A. P. HERBERT *Holy Deadlock* 103 'Hell!' thought Mr. Ransom, 'we're sunk!' **1941** M. ALLINGHAM *Traitor's Purse* xx. 231 You can't say you're afraid we're sunk... Everyone's relying on you. **1951** J. FRAME *Lagoon* 56 If visitors come tonight I am sunk. **1960** G. SANDERS *Mem. Professional Cad* II. v. 136 If you go to a party with the impedimenta of a date, an overcoat or a hat, you are sunk.

3. a. = SUNKEN 1.

1799 KIRWAN *Geol. Ess.* 40 Arresting by their initial softness the various sunk woods and such other vegetable or animal substances. **1806** *Gazetteer Scot.* (ed. 2) 20 It has a sandy shore, with sunk rocks. **1828** J. MACDONALD in Tweedie *Life* ii. (1849) 93 Here is the sunk rock of legalism. **1829** T. CASTLE *Introd. Bot.* III. §i. 56 Nomenclature of the leaf... Sunk—submerged or immersed, entirely under water. **1837** CARLYLE *Fr. Rev.* III. v. vi, So has History written..of the sunk *Vengeur.* **1898** NEWBOLT *Isl. Race* 14 The sunk torpedoes lying in treacherous rank.

b. *spec.* applied to submerged tracts of land.

1830 *Act 11 Geo. IV & 1 Will. IV*, c. 59 §20 A certain Estate called Sunk Island, situate in the River Humber. **1849** LYELL *2nd Visit U.S.* II. 236 The 'sunk country'.. extends along the course of the White Water and its tributaries. **1867** SMYTH *Sailor's Word-bk.*, *Sunk Land*, shallows and swamps. **1915** *Contemp. Rev.* Dec. 770 Wide areas..collapsed into sunklands and inland seas.

4. a. Placed on a lower level than that of the surroundings.

1633 STAFFORD *Pac. Hib.* I. iv. 30 Captaine Iohn Bostocke ..espied the Morians of some of the suncke ambush in the Glinn.

b. In modern technical use, applied to a surface or area lowered, or to an object let in, so as to lie below the general surface, or to work of which depression of level is a principal feature; as *sunk carving, cistern, panel*, etc.

sunk band, cord, a strip of cloth or string on which a binding is constructed, fitted in to furrows across the spine of the book. ***sunk cell***, a cavity in a microscopic slide, to receive the object examined. ***sunk coak***, a groove in the face of a timber, into which a coak or tenon is fitted to form a joint (Knight *Dict. Mech.* 1875). ***sunk-enamel***, champlevé. ***sunk fence***, = HA-HA *sb.*[2] ***sunk garden***, a (portion of a) garden created below the natural level of the surrounding land, a sunken garden (SUNKEN *ppl. a.* 4). ***sunk-head***, (Typogr.) the blank space at the head of a chapter (Knight). ***sunk key***, a pin or cotter fitting into a groove on the shaft in which it is used. ***sunk shelf***, a shelf with a groove to prevent plates or dishes slipping off when stood on their edges (Gwilt *Archit.* Gloss. 1842). ***sunk storey***, a storey below ground level, a basement. ***sunk work*** (Masonry): see quot.

1889 W. MATTHEWS *Mod. Bookbinding* 27 [Raised-band sewing] is three or four times the cost of the ordinary, or *sunk-band, sewing... Sunk-band is the ordinary style of the book sewing of our time. Here the sheets are sawed with three or five furrows to admit the bands of twine. **1959** L. M. HARROD *Librarians' Gloss.* (ed. 2) 258 Sunk Bands (Cords).. Cords or bands..placed in grooves sawn into the backs of sections of a book. **1875** SIR T. SEATON *Fret Carving* 143 It may be called *Sunk Carving; for, contrary to the usual method, the carving is sunk, whilst the ground is left at its original level. **1890** *Science-Gossip* XXVI. 163 The object may be placed..in a watch-glass, or a *sunk cell. **1839** URE *Dict. Arts*, etc. 1203 The earthen floor is excavated to form the molasses reservoir... The bottom holes..allow the molasses to drain slowly downwards into the *sunk cistern. **1959** [see *sunk-band*]. **1965** L. S. DARLEY *Introd. Bookbinding* 61 (*caption*) Sawing for *sunk cords. **1929** *Times* 2 Nov. 10/4 The coral inlay, and red *sunk-enamel (champlevé) on the handle. **1762–71** H. WALPOLE *Vertue's Anecd. Paint.* (1786) IV. 288 The contiguous ground of the park without the *sunk fence was to be harmonized with the lawn within. **1803** [see HA-HA *sb.*[2]]. **1845** DICKENS *Chimes* iii. 119 You may see the cottage from the sunk fence over yonder. **1922** J. BUCHAN *Huntingtower* v. 93 A path which wound down to the *sunk garden. **1973** *Country Life* 15 Nov. 1591/1, I bask on a stone seat in the sunk garden. **1835** R. WILLIS *Archit. Mid. Ages* vi. 65 A row of small *sunk pannels upon the space between the dripstone and window head. *a* **1835** RICKMAN *Styles Archit.* (1848) 127 The interior is..ornamented with *sunk panelling. **1884** F. J. BRITTEN *Watch & Clockm.* 254 With a *sunk seconds the hour hand may be closer to the dial than it otherwise could. **1791** BENTHAM *Panopt.* I. 89 Staircases..from the *sunk story below the Cells to the upper story of the Cells. **1840** MRS. CARLYLE *Let. to J. Forster* Aug., The sunk-story of this respectable, æsthetic house. **1833** LOUDON *Encycl. Archit.* §1104 The door..to have a *sunk thumb sneck. **1823** P. NICHOLSON *Pract. Builder* 316 *Sunk-work is that which has been partly chiselled away, as the tops of window-cills, &c.

5. Of the sun: = SUNKEN 3 b. *rare.*

1908 RIDER HAGGARD *Ghost Kings* xvii. 239 The light from the sunk sun.

sunken (ˈsʌŋkən), *ppl. a.* [pa. pple. of SINK *v.* See note on prec.]

1. That has sunk in water; submerged in, or situated beneath the surface of, water or other liquid.

1375 BARBOUR *Bruce* III. 417 Iamys of Dowglas..Fand a litill sonkyn bate. **1599** SHAKS. *Hen. V*, I. ii. 165 As rich.. As is the Owse and bottome of the Sea With sunken Wrack, and sum-lesse Treasuries. **1743** BULKELEY & CUMMINS *Voy. S. Seas* 118 The Tide running rampant, and in a great Swell, every where surrounded with sunken Rocks. **1830** LYELL *Princ. Geol.* I. xv. 264 The Bell Rock is a sunken reef, consisting of red sandstone. **1842** *Civil Eng. & Arch. Jrnl.* V. (Contents), Sunken vessels, new mode of raising. **1859** DARWIN *Orig. Spec.* xi. 357 In the coral-producing oceans such sunken islands are now marked..by rings of coral or atolls standing over them.

2. Of the eyes, cheeks, etc.: Abnormally depressed or hollow; fallen in. *Comb.*, as ***sunken-eyed.***

1600 SHAKS. *A.Y.L.* III. ii. 393 A leane cheeke..: a blew eie and sunken. **1825** SCOTT *Betrothed* xxx, Her eyes were sunken, and had lost much of their bold and roguish lustre. **1844** MRS. BROWNING *Cry Childr.* iii, They look up with their pale and sunken faces. **1851** H. MELVILLE *Moby Dick* I. xxxiv. 253 Your whales must be seen before they are killed; and this sunken-eyed Platonist will tow you ten wakes round the world, and never make you one pint of sperm the richer. *c* **1853** KINGSLEY *Misc.* (1859) I. i. 38 When he forgets the grey hair and the sunken cheek. **1910** *Westm. Gaz.* 1 Jan. 2/3 A horse..with sunken-in flanks and a bony, bent head. **1971** S. HILL *Strange Meeting* 191 The men glanced up apprehensively as they passed along, and their faces had the sunken-eyed look of suppressed fear.

3. a. That has sunk below the usual or general level; subsided.

1832 G. DOWNES *Lett. Cont. Countries* I. 418 The Arch of Constantine..stands on a sunken area, enclosed by a wall. **1841** DICKENS *Barn. Rudge* i, Its floors were sunken and uneven. **1857** —— *Dorrit* II. x, He..ascended the unevenly sunken steps and knocked.

b. Of the sun: Gone down below the horizon.

1816 SCOTT *Old Mort.* xxxiv, The long train of light that follows the sunken sun. **1820** SHELLEY *Skylark* iii, In the golden lightning Of the sunken sun.

c. Drooping.

1890 CONAN DOYLE *White Company* xxxviii, With crossed ankles and sunken head, he sat as though all his life had passed out of him.

d. *fig.* Depressed, reduced.

1854 LOWELL *Fireside Trav.* Pr. Wks. 1890 I. 180 So gathered the hoarse Northern swarms to descend upon sunken Italy.

4. In technical use: = SUNK *ppl. a.* 4 b, as ***sunken bath, garden, living-room, story***, etc.

sunken battery (Milit.): a battery in which the platform is sunk below the level of the ground.

1808 FORSYTH *Beauties Scot.* V. 421 The enclosures are of various kinds: stone dikes, earthen dikes, ditches, hedges, and half-dikes or sunken-fences. **1831–3** P. BARLOW in *Encycl. Metrop.* (1845) VIII. 613/1 The Ancients employed a sunken die. **1844** H. H. WILSON *Brit. India* II. 340 The rocky nature of the soil..rendered it necessary to carry up earth for the formation of an elevated, instead of a sunken battery. **1860** *Illustr. Lond. News* 25 Feb. 187/3 Unless the window be on the sunken story. **1882** *Garden* 1 Apr. 213/2 The sunken garden is a delightful sight. **1892** G. PHILIPS *Text Bk. Fortif.*, etc. (ed. 5) §569 A sunken caponier tambour. **1925** F. SCOTT FITZGERALD *Great Gatsby* (1926) v. 110 Through dressing-rooms and poolrooms, and bathrooms with sunken baths. **1970** *Globe & Mail* (Toronto) 26 Sept. 42/3 (Advt.), 3 Bedrooms, 3 Washrooms, Electric Light Fixtures, Sunken Living Rooms. **1976** M. MACHLIN *Pipeline* xxxvii. 408 The entrance hall, which gave onto a white-carpeted, sunken living-room, looked as though a regiment of cavalry had galloped through it. **1979** J. MELVILLE *Wages of Zen* xi. 110 The tiled sunken bath was drained and clean.

sunker (ˈsʌŋkə(r)). *Newfoundland.* [f. SUNK *ppl. a.* + -ER[1].] A submerged rock. Also *fig.*

c **1880** in G. S. Doyle *Old Time Songs & Poetry of Newfoundland* (1927) 29 We'll rant and we'll roar on deck and below, Until we see bottom inside the two sunkers. **1896** *Jrnl. Amer. Folklore* IX. 33 Among the peculiar words connected with the fishing I note the following:..*sunker*, a breaker. **1951** *Newfoundland & Labrador Pilot* I. 134 Duck Road shoal, about 4 cables north-eastward of Eastern head and Anchor Cove Sunkers. **1966** A. R. SCAMMELL *My Newfoundland* 63 The words don't seem to have a clear channel from me brain to me lips. Too many sunkers for 'em to ground on, I spose. **1973** *Maclean's Mag.* Jan. 16/1 At dusk, the Nordfjeld slammed onto a 'sunker', a rock that's awash at high tide, one mile off Flowers Cove.

sunket (ˈsʌŋkɪt), *sb.*[1] and *adv. Sc.* and *north. dial.* Also 7–9 sunckat, 8 sunkot, 9 suncket, sunkit. [prob. derived from the strongly aspirated Sc. form of SOMEWHAT represented e.g. by the spelling *sumquhat*. With sense 2 cf. the etymological meaning of KICKSHAWS = F. *quelque chose* something.]

A. *sb.* (chiefly *pl.*)

1. Something, *esp.* something to eat.

1721 RAMSAY *Lucky Spence* iii, Lay sunkets [*v.r.* sunkots] up for a sair leg. *a* **1722** PENNECUIK *Merry Wives of Musselburgh* xlix, I came unco' bravely hame, Whan I gat sunkets in my wame. **1810** STAGG *Minst. of N., Panic* xxi. (E.D.D.) 'Twas mete that sunkets they devised This pestment to destroy.

2. A dainty, tit-bit. Also *fig.*

1788 in *Standard* (1868) 21 Dec., It is resolved to meet at three o'clock to eat sunkets and drink to the glorious Revolution. **1815** SCOTT *Guy M.* viii, There's thirty hearts there that wad hae wanted bread ere ye had wanted sunkets. **1818** —— *Hrt. Midl.* xviii, When they..harle us to the Correction-house..and pettle us up wi' bread and water, and siclike sunkets. *a* **1825** FORBY *Voc. E. Anglia, Sunkets*.., dainty bits; nice feeding. **1857** GEN. P. THOMPSON *Audi Alt.* I. xxiv. 92 Fancy an army landing in England, and holding out such sunkets to tempt submission.

†B. *adv.* To some extent, somewhat. *Obs.*

1686 G. STUART *Joco-ser. Disc.* 2, I's sunckat beuk-learn'd. **1790** JAS. FISHER *Poems* 73 An hour, I trow, an' sunket mair.

sunket (ˈsʌŋkɪt), *sb.*[2] *dial.* [Origin obscure.] A simpleton, a silly fellow.

1823 E. MOOR *Suffolk Words & Phrases* 409 Sunket. A child sickly and unpromising is so called—'Ah! 'tis a poor sunketing thing.' **1895** W. RYE *Gloss. Words E. Anglia* 219 *Sunket*,..a contemptuous appellation of a silly fellow. **1940** C. P. SNOW *Strangers & Brothers* 21 'You can't take sides with those sunkets against me,' said George. His voice had risen. We were used to the odd Suffolk words as his temper got up.

ˈsunkie. *Sc.* [f. SUNK *sb.* + -IE.] A little seat.

1815 SCOTT *Guy M.* xxii, Mony a day hae I wrought my stocking, and sat on my sunkie under that saugh.

sunkland: see SUNK *ppl. a.* 3 b.

sunless (ˈsʌnlɪs), *a.* [f. SUN *sb.*[1] + -LESS.] Destitute of the sun or of the sun's rays; not illumined by the sun; dark or dull through absence of sunlight.

1589 FLEMING *Virg. Georg.* I. 6 Vnlesse thou wilt cut or plash away with bill The shadie boughs of sunlesse soile. **1697** DRYDEN *Æneid* III. 267 Three starless Nights the doubtful Navy strays Without Distinction, and three Sunless Days. **1788** COWPER *Let. to W. Bagot* 19 Mar., Sunless skies and freezing blasts. **1829** SCOTT *Anne of G.* xv, The sunless waves appeared murmuring for their victim. **1842** MACAULAY *Armada* 42 The rugged miners poured to war from Mendip's sunless caves. **1876** R. BRIDGES *Growth of Love* lxvii, A sunless and half-hearted summer. **1880** MEREDITH *Tragic Com.* vi. (1892) 86 Sunless rose the morning.

fig. **1850** BLACKIE *Æschylus* I. 37 Ofttimes we sorrowed from a sunless soul. **1864** TENNYSON *Aylmer's F.* 357, I lived for years a stunted sunless life.

b. *nonce-use.* Existing without the sun.

1633 P. FLETCHER *Purple Isl.* VI. ix, The Sunne lesse starres, these lights the Sunne distain.

Hence **ˈsunlessness**, the condition of being sunless; absence of the sun.

1856 *Chamb. Jrnl.* 20 Dec. 390/1 Their blood scurvy-filled by the four months' sunlessness. **1898** G. W. STEEVENS *With Kitchener to Khartum* 137 Another twelve hours of sunlessness.

sunlet (ˈsʌnlɪt). [f. as prec. + -LET.] A little sun. Also *transf.* (see quot. 1880).

1840 E. FORBES in Wilson & Geikie *Mem.* (1861) ix. 257 One solitary star Shining..—for dark clouds hid Its sister sunlets. **1880** L. WALLACE *Ben-Hur* IV. viii, She wore an open caul upon her head, sprinkled with beads of coral, and strung with coin-pieces called sunlets. **1904** *19th Cent.* Feb. 237 Myriads of little stars, or so-called sunlets.

sunlight (ˈsʌnlaɪt), *sb.* [f. SUN *sb.*[1] + LIGHT *sb.*; cf. WFris. *sinneljacht*, MDu. *sonnelicht*, (Du. *zonlicht*), OHG. *sunnalioht* and *sunnûn lioht* (MHG. *sunnenlieht*, G. *sonnenlicht*).]

1. a. The light of the sun.

c **1205** LAY. 17863 Wel neh al swa brihte swa þe sunne-lihte. *c* **1375** *Cursor M.* 18819 (Fairf.) Angels ar briȝter þen sunneliȝ t. **1390** GOWER *Conf.* II. 220 His wif..Lay with the king the longe nyht, Til that it was hih Sonne lyht. **1535** COVERDALE *2 Sam.* xii. 12, I wyl do this in the sighte of all Israel, and by Sonne lighte. **1667** MILTON *P.L.* IX. 1087 Woods impenetrable To Starr or Sun-light. **1833** TENNYSON *Lady of Shalott* III. iv, His broad clear brow in sunlight glow'd. **1860** TYNDALL *Glac.* I. v. 38 When we pass from open sunlight to a moderately illuminated room. **1893** SIR R. BALL *Story of Sun* 290 To carbon..belongs the distinction of being the main source whence sunlight is dispensed.

b. *fig.*: cf. SUNSHINE 2.

1577 tr. *Bullinger's Decades* (1592) 532 Christ is..the verie sunne light of the preaching of the Gospell. **1863** GEO. ELIOT *Romola* Introd., The faces of the little children, making another sunlight amid the shadows of age. **1864** TENNYSON *Aylmer's F.* 421 In such a sunlight of prosperity. **1891** FARRAR *Darkn. & Dawn* lxvi, The sleek priest..continued to live in the sunlight of Court favour.

c. ***artificial sunlight***: see ARTIFICIAL *a.* 5.

2. (Properly with hyphen.) = SUN-BURNER.

1862–7 *J. Wylde's Circ. Sci.* I. 34/1 The introduction of 'sunlights'..aids in promoting ventilation. **1874** MICKLETHWAITE *Mod. Par. Churches* 192 Sunlights may be ..used in somewhat low and ceiled buildings.

3. *attrib.* and *Comb.*

1863 BOYD *Graver Thts. Country Parson* 192 Who will vivify into sunlight clearness every sound and true belief. **1896** *Spectator* 7 Mar. 339 Living air, and sunlight-gold.

ˈsunlight, *a. poet. rare.* [f. SUN *sb.*[1] + LIGHT *a.*[2] or SUNLIGHT *sb.* after *starlight* adj.] = SUNLIT.

1818 SHELLEY *Euganean Hills* 82 Their [*sc.* rooks'] plumes ..Gleam above the sunlight woods. **1895** R. W. CHAMBERS *King in Yellow, Repairer of Reput.* ii. (1909) 28 The craft which churned the sunlight waters.

ˈsun-ˌlighted, ˈsunˌlighted, *ppl. a.* [f. SUN *sb.*[1] + LIGHTED *ppl. a.*, after *sunlight.*] = SUNLIT.

1787 M. TILGHMAN *Let.* 6 Oct. in *Maryland Hist. Mag.* (1926) XXI. 220 The bright, Sun-lighted Wedding proceedings. **1843** RUSKIN *Mod. Paint.* I. II. III. iii. §18 Melting..into the haziness of the sun-lighted atmosphere. **1861** DICKENS *Let. to Mrs. Watson* 8 July, [The photograph] made me laugh..until I shook again, in open sunlighted Piccadilly. **1890** SIR R. BALL *Star-Land* 74 The earth-lighted side of the moon cannot be compared in brilliancy with the sun-lighted side.

ˈsunlighting, *vbl. sb.* [f. SUNLIGHT *sb.* + -ING[1].]

1. The process, degree, etc., of the illumination of buildings by sunlight.

1961 [see DAYLIGHTING *vbl. sb.* 2]. **1977** *Washington Post* 10 Apr. B5/1 Maximum sunlighting and, therefore, heat capture are assured in the winter when the sun is low.

2. (See quot. 1977.)

1977 D. N. BARON in *Brit. Med. Jrnl.* 22 Oct. 1080/1 If taking on paid outside work during night-time hours is moonlighting then let us call doing outside work (though unpaid) during daytime hours sunlighting. **1978** *Lancet* 14 Jan. 89/2 Then follow 3–4 years of internship or residency training..with opportunities of moonlighting and sunlighting. **1983** *N.Y. Times* 7 Feb. A2/3 Bureaucrats [in Madrid] practiced moonlighting to such an extent it turned into sunlighting.

sunlike (ˈsʌnlaɪk), *a.* and *adv.* [f. SUN *sb.*[1] + -LIKE.]

A. *adj.* Like or resembling the sun, or that of the sun; *esp.* very bright or resplendent.

1596 SHAKS. *1 Hen. IV*, III. ii. 79 No extraordinarie Gaze, Such as is bent on Sunne-like Maiestie. *c* **1611** CHAPMAN *Iliad* XXII. 273 His shield cast a Sun-like radiance. **1642** H. MORE *Song of Soul* II. iii. III. liii, Double Sunlike motion. **1715** CHEYNE *Philos. Princ.* I. 27 These Sun-like Bodies in the Centers of the several Vortices. **1820** SHELLEY *Witch Atl.* lxiv, And she saw princes couched under the glow Of sunlike gems. **1860** TYNDALL *Glac.* II. vii. 260 If the light of an electric lamp be caused to form a clear sunlike disk upon a white screen. **1873** PROCTOR *Expanse of Heaven* 156 That these giant planets are still in the active and sun-like state necessary..for the expulsion of comets.

B. *adv.* Like or in the manner of the sun.

1819 SHELLEY *Cenci* V. iii. 32 That eternal honour which should live Sunlike, above the reek of mortal fame. **1832–5** WILLIS *From the Apennines* 15 Sun-like thou hast power to give Life to the earth.

sunlit (ˈsʌnlɪt), *ppl. a.* [f. as prec. + LIT *ppl. a.*] Lighted or illumined by the sun.

1822 SHELLEY *Triumph of Life* 80 Like the young moon —When on the sunlit limits of the night Her white shell trembles amid crimson air. **1840** WILBERFORCE *Sp. Missions* (1874) 84 Under the sunlit canopy of heaven. **1890** CONAN DOYLE *White Company* xxxvi, Like the shadow of clouds upon a sunlit meadow.

sunly (ˈsʌnlɪ), *a. rare.* [f. as prec. + -LY[1].]

†a. = HELIACAL 1. *Obs.* b. Pertaining or relating to the sun, solar.

1551 RECORDE *Cast. Knowl.* (1556) 274 When Venus doth shyne at euenynge after sonne settinge, she doth rise, as som tearme it, with a sonnely rysinge. **1873** L. WALLACE *Fair God* II. xi. 156 His sunly symbols.

‖**sunn** (sʌn). *Anglo-Ind.* Also 8 son, 8–9 sun, 9 san. [a. Urdū, Hindī *san* (Skr. *çāṇá* hempen).] A branching leguminous shrub, *Crotalaria juncea*, with long narrow leaves and bright yellow flowers, widely cultivated in Southern Asia for its fibre; also, the fibre of this plant used for rope, cordage, sacking, etc.

1774 *Phil. Trans.* LXIV. 99 Of the Culture and Uses of the Son or Sun-plant of Hindostan. **1800** *Ann. Reg., Chron.* 38/1 The new species of hemp called sun, the produce of Bengal..has turned out nearly equal to our own rope. **1813** W. MILBURN *Oriental Comm.* (1825) 289 At Comercolly there are two species of sunn; the best is called phool, the other boggy. **1851** FORBES *Veg. World* in *Art Jrnl. Illust. Cat.* II. p. vj †/2 The Bengal hemp or sunn. **1894** *Times* 17 Aug. 9/4 All binding twine manufactured..from New Zealand hemp, istle or Tampico fibre, sisal grass, or sunn.

b. *transf.* Applied to *Hibiscus cannabinus*, which yields brown or Indian hemp.

1846 LINDLEY *Veget. Kingd.* 369 We know Hibiscus cannabinus, or Sun, is [cultivated] in India, as a substitute for hemp.

c. *attrib.*, as ***sunn-hemp***, ***-plant***, ***-waste***.

1774 [see above]. **1849** BALFOUR *Man. Bot.* §782 *Hibiscus cannabinus* is the source whence sun-hemp is procured in India. **1855** STEPHENS *Bk. Farm* (ed. 2) §3139 *Crotolaria juncea*, the sun hemp. **1887** MOLONEY *Forestry W. Afr.* 186 For Paper-making, the only Indian fibres that seemed hopeful were bamboo.., plantain.., jute, and *sunn* waste.

‖**Sunna** (ˈsʌnə). Also (7 Sunnet), 8 Sonna, 9 Sonnah, Sunnah, -eh, Soonna. [a. Arab. *sunna*[h] (*sunnat*) form, way, course, rule.] The body of traditional sayings and customs attributed to Muhammad and supplementing the Koran. (Cf. SUNNI, SUNNITE.)

[**1687** A. LOVELL tr. *Thevenot's Trav.* I. 48 The difference which they put betwixt that time which God commanded, and the two times of Mahomet, is that they call the first *Fars*, and those of Mahomet, *Sunnet*.] **1728** CHAMBERS *Cycl.*, *Sonna*, a Book of Mahometan Traditions, wherein all the Orthodox Mussulmans are required to believe. **1842** *Penny Cycl.* XXIII. 300/1 Sunnah. **1867** *Chambers' Encycl.* IX. 214/1 The Sunna not only comprises religious doctrines and practice, but also civil and criminal laws, and the usages of common life: the way to eat and to drink, and to dress, and the like. **1883** *Encycl. Brit.* XVI. 553/1 Just as the Torah grew out of the decisions of Moses, so did the Sunna out of those of Mohammed.

†**ˈsunnage.** *Obs. rare*⁻⁰. [f. SUN *sb.*[1] + -AGE, after F. *solage*.]

1611 COTGR., *Solaige*, Sunnage, or Sunninesse.

sunnar, obs. form of *sooner*: see SOON.

sunne, obs. form of SIN, SON, SUN.

sunned (sʌnd, *poet.* ˈsʌnɪd), *ppl. a.* [f. SUN *v.* + -ED[1].] Exposed to, or subjected to the action of, the sun; warmed or dried in the sun; illumined by the sun, sunlit.

1579 SPENSER *Sheph. Cal.* Jan. 77 The pensife boy.. Arose, and homeward droue his sonned sheepe. ? **1605** DRAYTON *Poems Lyr. & Pastoral* Eglog vi. 118 Thou that.. To drink at Auon driuest thy sunned sheep. **1850** T. WOOLNER *My Beautiful Lady* in *Germ.* No. I. 2 The sunned bosom of a humming-bird. **1891** HARDY *Tess* xxvii, Having been lying down in her clothes she was warm as a sunned cat. **1893** *Atlantic Monthly* Feb. 282/1 The sunned but unwarmed sky.

sunner(e, obs. forms of *sooner*: see SOON.

sunne rest: see *sun-rest* (SUN *sb.*[1] 13), SUNRIST.

‖**Sunni** (ˈsʌniː). Also 7–9 Sunnee (7 Sonnj, 8 Sooni, -ey), 9 Sonnee, (Soonee, Soonnee, Suni). [a. Arab. *sunnī* lawful, f. SUNNA.] *collect.* The orthodox Muslims, who accept the Sunna as of equal authority with the Koran. Also *sing.* an orthodox Muslim, a Sunnite.

1626 [see SHIAH 1]. **1634** SIR T. HERBERT *Trav.* 159 The Turkes..call..themselues *Sonnj*, and *Mussulmen*, which is *truly faithfull*. **1753** HANWAY *Trav.* (1762) II. IV. ii. 106 The sect of Sunni comprehends the Turks, the Tartars, the subjects of the Moghol, with some other nations of less note. *Ibid.* V. ii. 134, I am a Sunni, as my ancestors were. **1800** *Asiat. Ann. Reg.* p. xxiii, Two Sects, the one of whom assumed the Title of *Sooney* (or Orthodox), and who branded the opposite Party with the opprobrious Epithet of *Shiah* (or Heterodox). **1836** *Partington's Brit. Cycl. Lit.*, etc. III. 769/2 The Mohammedans [in Sinde] are all Soonees, and most of them of the sect of Haneefee. **1913** *19th Cent.* May 1157 Both Shiahs and Sunnis have been known to lend at usury.

b. *attrib.* or as *adj.*

1827 BUCKINGHAM *Trav. Mesopot.* II. 487 The inhabitants he [*sc.* a Dervish] described as mostly Mohammedans, and of the Soonnee sect. **1833** A. CRICHTON *Hist. Arabia* I. vii. 334 Pillars of the Sonnee faith. **1841** ELPHINSTONE *Hist. India* XII. iii. II. 651 The Sunni religion.

†**sunnight.** *Obs. rare.* Forms: 1 sunnan-niht, 3 suneniht, -niȝt, sonenyht. (See also *sun's night* s.v. SUN *sb.*[1] 13 c.) [OE. *sunnanniht*: see SUN *sb.*[1] and NIGHT *sb.* Cf. OE. *sunnanǽfen* = LG. *sonavend*, OHG. *sunnûn âband* (MHG. *sunnen-*, *sun(r)âbent*, G. *sonnabend*).] The night before Sunday, Saturday night.

c **1000** ÆLFRIC *Hom.* (Th.) I. 216 His lic læȝ on byrȝene ðā sæter-niht and sunnan-niht... And Crist aras of deaðe on ðone easterlican sunnan-dæȝ. *a* **1225** *Ancr. R.* 22 Ȝif ȝe doð þvs eueriche niht, bute a suneniht one. *c* **1250** *Doomsday* 10 in *O.E. Misc.* 162 þat fur schal kumen in þis world On one sune-niȝte [*v.r.* sone-nyhte].

sunnily (ˈsʌnɪlɪ), *adv.* [f. SUNNY *a.* + -LY[2].] In a sunny manner; chiefly *fig.* brightly, cheerfully.

1849 *Tait's Mag.* XVI. 105/1 Faces..beamed sunnily with the light of hope. **1886** DOWDEN *Shelley* II. ii. 45 The time from September 20 to September 24 went sunnily by.

sunniness (ˈsʌnɪnɪs). [f. as prec. + -NESS.]

1. The state of being illumined by the sun, or full of sunshine.

1611 [see SUNNAGE]. **1823** MOORE *Mem.* (1853) IV. 146 In the sweet valley of Chitway, enjoying all the sunniness and leafiness that still lingers around us. **1860** F. GALTON in *Vac. Tour.* 430 The relative sunniness of different places on the calculated path of total eclipse.

†2. Sunburn, tan. *Obs. rare.*

1753 RICHARDSON *Grandison* I. xxxvi. (1754) 254 His face is overspread with a manly sunniness (I want a word) that shews he has been in warmer climates than England.

3. *fig.* Brightness of aspect, feeling, manner, etc.

1837 BEDDOES *Let.* in *Poems* (1851) p. ciii, The chapters in hand requiring a light-hearted sunniness of style. **1880** DISRAELI *Endym.* III. 65 He did not greet her with that mantling sunniness of aspect which was natural to him when they met. **1880** 'VERNON LEE' *Italy* III. i. 68 A certain sincerity and sunniness of nature.

sunning (ˈsʌnɪŋ), *vbl. sb.* [f. SUN *sb.*[1] and *v.* + -ING[1].]

1. Exposure to the sun; basking in the sun.

1519 HORMAN *Vulg.* 169 b, They chaunge the naturall colour of theyr heare with crafty colour and sonnynge [L. *insolatione*]. **1693** SIR T. P. BLOUNT *Nat. Hist.* 42 There are some who affirm, that Cinnamon.. acquires its.. strength by fifteen Days Sunning. **1828** P. CUNNINGHAM *N.S. Wales* (ed. 3) II. 278 Our wo-begone widows are frequently.. scarce permitted to give their mourning weeds the benefit of a second day's sunning before they are entangled in another matrimonial web. **1889** *Anthony's Photogr. Bull.* II. 53 Where it is necessary to degrade the whites of hard prints, that is easily done by sunning. **1894** WALSH *Coffee* (Philad.) 96 Three days' thorough sunning usually suffices to render the coffee quite dry and brittle.

attrib. **1847** STODDART *Angler's Comp.* 308 Pike.. when on the bask, or in sunning humour.

b. In phr. ***a sunning*** (see A *prep.*[1] 12, 13), esp. in ***to set*** (***lay***) ***a sunning***, to expose to the sun, to sun; also ***to sit, hang a sunning***.

1510 STANBRIDGE *Vocabula* (W. de W.) C vj b, *Apricor*, to syt a sonnynge or to sonne. *c* **1518** *Kalender of Sheph.* A v, For & clerkes shewe them bokes of cunnynge, They bydde them lay them vp a sonnynge. **1519** HORMAN *Vulg.* 40 Sette these waters a sonnynge. **1600** NASHE *Summer's Last Will* 198 Old wiues a sunning sit. **1633** T. JAMES *Voy.* 42 They hung a Sunning all day. **1660** F. BROOKE tr. *Le Blanc's Trav.* 67 They gather the cinnamon.. then lay it a fortnight a sunning. **1664** *Comenius' Janua Ling.* 500 Linnen.. is laid a sunning to whiten. **1680** OTWAY *Caius Marius* v. i, When they are set a Sunning upon the Capitol. **1885** JEWETT *Marsh Isl.* xi, The pies were baked, and the pots and pans still a-sunning.

†**2.** Shining like the sun, radiance. *Obs. rare.*

c **1586** C'TESS PEMBROKE *Ps.* LXXXIX. vi, On pathes enlighted by thy faces sunning.

3. *Fishing.* A method of catching salmon by spearing them when dazzled or alarmed by the reflection of sunlight from some bright object.

1843 SCROPE *Salmon Fishing* x. 209 Sunning.. is a mode of taking salmon with a spear by sun light. **1895** *Pall Mall Gaz.* 26 July 9/2 In Norway we have seen the sunning carried on by means of a painted board illuminated by a large lens.

So **'sunning**, *ppl. a.*, basking in the sun.

1902 *Academy* Mar. 225 Where the sunning partridge drums.

†**'sunnish**, *a. Obs.* [f. SUN *sb.*[1] + -ISH[1].] Resembling the sun in colour and brilliancy: applied *poet.* to bright golden hair, etc. Also *advb.*

c **1374** CHAUCER *Troylus* IV. 736 Hire ownded heer that sonnysshe was of hewe. ? *a* **1400** LYDG. *Chorle & Byrde* (Roxb.) 12 Lyke topasion of colour sonnysh bright. **1412–20** —— *Chron. Troy* I. 1977 His sonnysshe here crisped liche gold wyre. *c* **1450** *Mirour Saluacioun* (Roxb.) 126 This womman was alle about closid in sonnysshe clothing.

Sunnism ('sʌnɪz(ə)m). Also **Sunniism.** [f. SUNNA or SUNNI + -ISM.] The doctrines or principles of the Sunnites.

1892 *Chambers's Encycl.* IX. 398/2 The moderate Shîism that has been the national religion of Persia since the native royal line of Safiides ascended the throne in 1499 is more Koranic than Sunnism. **1911** D. S. MARGOLIOUTH *Mohammedanism* v. 174 Nadir Shah attempted to substitute Sunnism. **1953** O. CAROE *Soviet Empire* iv. 50 The Samanids came from Baltch and enforced a rigorous form of Hanafi Sunniism. **1962** G. E. VON GRUNEBAUM *Mod. Islam* 11 The catholicity of Sunnism. **1983** S. AKHAVI in N. R. Keddie *Relig. & Pol. in Iran* viii. 129 His [*sc.* Shariati's] thought has more affinities to Shi'ism than to Sunnism.

Sunnite ('sʌnaɪt). Also 8–9 **Sonnite.** [f. SUNNA or SUNNI + -ITE[1].] A Muslim who accepts the orthodox tradition (*Sunna*) as well as the Koran. (Cf. SHIITE.) Also *attrib.*

1718 [see TRADITION *sb.* 6 c]. **1734** G. SALE tr. *Koran, Prelim. Disc.* iii. (1877) 52 It is the belief of the Sonnites or orthodox that the Korân is uncreated and eternal. **1759, 1847** [see TRADITIONIST 1 b]. **1887** *Encycl. Brit.* XXII. 659/2 *note*, Generally speaking the Sunnites are the more bitter party.

‖**sunnud** ('sʌnʌd). *Anglo-Indian.* Also **sanad.** [Urdū = Arab. *sanad* signature, deed, diploma, seal of magistrate, etc.] A deed of grant; a charter, patent, or warrant.

1759 in J. Long *Sel. Unpub. Rec. Govt.* (*Fort William*) (1869) 184 That your Petitioners.. were permitted by Sunnud from the President and Council to collect daily alms. **1764** *Ann. Reg.* I. 189/2 For all charges.. the lands.. shall be assigned, and sunnuds for that purpose shall be written and granted. **1803** EDMONSTONE in Owen *Wellesley's Desp.* (1877) 317 Shumshere Bahâdur.. has arrived in the province, and assumed the authority over it, under a sunnud from Amrut Rao. **1844** tr. *M. T. Asmar's Mem. Babyl. Princ.* II. 208 The sanad, or certificate of her nobility ran.. as follows. **1876** *Encycl. Brit.* IV. 723/1 The nawab [of Cambay], who is one of the 153 feudatory princes of British India by *Sunnud* or patent. **1896** YOUNGSON *40 Yrs. of Punjab Mission* vi. 58 This proclamation will be as a Sanad for you.

sunny ('sʌnɪ), *sb. U.S. colloq.* [Dim. formation on *sunfish* or *sun-perch*.] = SUN-FISH 1 b.

1835 AUDUBON *Ornith. Biog.* III. 48 To the willow-twig fastened to his waist, a hundred 'sunnies' are already attached. **1888** GOODE *Amer. Fishes* 64 A score of lean, sun-dried perches and Sunnies.

sunny ('sʌnɪ), *a.* Also 4 sunni, 6 sonnye, sunnye, 6–7 sunnie, son(n)y, 7 sonie, *Sc.* sunȝie, sunie, 8 *Sc.* sinny. [f. SUN *sb.*[1] + -Y[1]. Cf. WFris. *sinnich*, LG. *sunnig*, Du. *zonnig*, G. *sonnig* (dial. *sunnig, sönnig*).]

1. Characterized by or full of sunshine; in or during which the sun shines: esp. of a day, weather, or the like.

a **1300** *Cursor M.* 23341 On sunni dai To se fixs in a water plai. **1508** *Pol. Rel. & L. Poems* (1903) 174 Was there neuer sonnye day so cleere. **1592** *Soliman & Pers.* I. ii. 43 Far more welcome.. Then sunny daies to naked Sauages. *c* **1788** BURNS *Fair Eliza* iii, The bee upon the blossom, In the pride o' sunny noon. **1832** LYTTON *Eugene A.* I. v, The fresh yet sunny air stole in. **1851** HELPS *Comp. Solit.* i. (1874) 12 The inhabitants of sunnier climes. **1868** DICKENS *Let. to Miss Dickens* 16 Mar., We have had two brilliant sunny days.

2. a. Exposed to, illumined or warmed by, the rays of the sun; on which the sun shines.

1567 FENTON *Trag. Disc.* xiii. (1898) II. 278 Neither roote of tree, height of rocke, nor sonnye syde of any greene hill. **1587** MASCALL *Cattle* (1596) 58 Cattell.. delight to be in sunnie places in winter.. and in summer to be in thicke shadie woods. **1667** MILTON *P.L.* III. 28 Where the Muses haunt Cleer Spring, or shadie Grove, or Sunnie Hill. **1725** *Fam. Dict.* s.v. *Pears*, Ambrotia, a handsom good siz'd Pear, ..of a smooth, greenish yellow Skin, red of the Sunny Side. **1833** MACAULAY *Ess.*, *H. Walpole* (1897) 275 An entertainment worthy of a Roman epicure, an entertainment consisting of nothing but delicacies, the brains of singing-birds, the roe of mullets, the sunny halves of peaches. **1836** W. IRVING *Astoria* I. x. 158 Those placid streams and sunny lakes stocked with all kinds of fish. **1880** 'OUIDA' *Moths* I. 58 This little gay room was certainly brighter and sunnier.

†**b.** ***sunny half, quarter***: that side of a piece of land which faces the south (opposed to *shadow half*). Cf. *sun half* (SUN *sb.*[1] 13). ***sunny-east***: south-east. Also † ***sunny chamber***, a summer-house. *Sc. Obs.*

1574 in *Reg. Mag. Sig. Scot.* 1587–8. 496/1 Dimidietatem solarem *lie sonnie halff* de Mylntoun de Conen. **1585** *Ibid.* 695/2 Sa mekill of our foirsaid sony halff landis haldin be ws as said is, as lyis outwith the propper designit boundis heirefter following. **1600** *Ibid.* 337/1 Octo bovatas terrarum ..vocatas *the Sonny-quarter*. **1610** *Ibid.* 102/2 Lie sony quarter landis of Tyrie. **1633** *Ibid.* 725/2 *Lie sonie-eist-halff* de Dumbertnit. **1641** *Ibid.* 368/2 Cum claustro et *lie sunȝie-chalmer* cum hortis ejusdem.

c. ***sunny South***: the southern states of the U.S.

1846 *Spirit of Times* (N.Y.) 18 Apr. 96/2 The wish of his heart should always be, peace and prosperity to the 'Sunny South'. **1950** *Chicago Tribune* 11 Mar. 8/3 Eric, the redbird ..flew by, fat 'n' sassy from a sojourn in the sunny South.

3. a. Pertaining to the sun; solar. *rare* (exc. as in b).

1607 TOPSELL *Four-f. Beasts* 465 The Cocke.. is a terror to the Lion.. because they are both partakers of the Sunnes qualities.., and.. there is a more eminent and predominant sunny propertie in the Cocke, then in the Lion.

b. Of light: Of or proceeding from the sun.

1579 SPENSER *Sheph. Cal.* Aug. 81 All as the Sunnye beame so bright. **1590** —— *F.Q.* II. v. 32 There he him found.. In secret shadow from the sunny ray. **1593** BRETON *Daff. & Prim.* Wks. (Grosart) I. 19/1 There was no speach of sonny beame, Nor of the golden silke. **1725** POPE *Odyss.* x. 186 A tall stag.. lay, Stretch'd forth, and panting in the sunny ray. **1880** 'OUIDA' *Moths* I. 74 The sunny daylight seeming to go round her in an amber mist.

fig. **1602** MARSTON *Ant. & Mel.* v. Wks. 1856 I. 61 Your brightest beames Of sunny favour. **1657** F. COCKIN *Div. Blossomes* 47 You bath your souls in this her sunny-shine. **1819** KEATS *Lines to Fanny* 44 O, for some sunny spell To dissipate the shadows of this hell!

4. Resembling the sun in colour or brightness; appearing as if illumined by the sun; (of the hair) bright yellow or golden.

1596 SHAKS. *Merch. V.* I. i. 169 Her sunny locks Hang on her temples like a golden fleece. **1647** COWLEY *Mistr.*, *Vain Love* 8 A rich, and sunny Diamond. **1742** COLLINS *Odes* iv. 45 Truth, in sunny vest array'd. **1810** SCOTT *Lady of L.* I. xxv, His flaxen hair, of sunny hue. **1838** LYTTON *Alice* II. i, Ringlets of darkest yet sunniest auburn. **1887** RIDER HAGGARD *Jess* xxvii, She.. laid her sunny head upon the old man's shoulder.

5. *fig.* **a.** 'Bright', cheerful, joyous; expressing or awakening gladness or happiness.

1545 COVERDALE *Erasm. Enchir.* xiii, To have a clean and sunny mind. **1590** SHAKS. *Com. Err.* II. i. 99 A sunnie looke of his. **1849** DE QUINCEY *Eng. Mail Coach* iii. Wks. 1897 XIII. 325 Again the choir burst forth in sunny grandeur. **1870–2** LIDDON *Elem. Relig.* iv. (1904) 131 Such is Schopenhauer's reply to the sunny Optimism of Leibnitz. **1891** FARRAR *Darkn. & Dawn* xiv, A little boy, whose sweet and sunny face looked the picture of engaging innocence. **1891** E. PEACOCK *N. Brendon* I. 254 Her soul was bright and sunny.

b. ***sunny side*** (*fig.* or in fig. contexts): (*a*) in phrases expressive of cheerfulness or optimism, esp. ***on the sunny side of the wall***; (*b*) ***on the sunny side of*** (an age): on the right side of, i.e. less than (cf. SHADY *a.* 2 b); (*c*) ***sunny side up***: of an egg, fried on one side only; hence ***sunnyside egg***.

(*a*) **1831** E. TRELAWNY *Adventures Younger Son* II. viii. 61 Then, only looking at the sunny side of things, all was bright. **1837** HOWITT *Rur. Life* II. iv. (1862) 138 To present the sunny side of the picture as the reverse of my gloomy one. **1858** TROLLOPE *Doctor Thorne* I. vi. 141 Mary.. was.. of the same age as Frank; but, as I.. have so often said before, 'Women grow on the sunny side of the wall.' **1890** W. S. GILBERT *Gondoliers* II. 119 Live to love and love to live —You will ripen at your ease, Growing on the sunny side —Fate has nothing more to give. **1970** C. MAJOR *Dict. Afro-Amer. Slang* 111 *Sunny side* (*of the street*), the 'good life'; luxury, leisure and comfort.

(*b*) **1865** *Atlantic Monthly* XV. 711 How many of us,.. on the sunny side of thirty, have gone through the 'Paradise Lost'? **1967** *Boston Sunday Globe* 23 Apr. (TV Week) 2/1 That's mighty high flying for a young Negro actor still on the sunny side of 30.

(*c*) **1901** *Dialect Notes* II. 149 *Sunny side up*,.. of eggs, to fry [sic] on only one side. **1948** *Royal Air Force Rev.* Jan. 20/2 It's whizzo when you get a fried egg sunny-side-up for tea. **1953** A. CHRISTIE *After Funeral* xii. 101 Worried, bad-tempered and irritable in the office. *But* since his uncle's death that's all changed. He's like the breakfast eggs (if we had 'em). Sunny side up! **1967** [see ONCE *adv.* B. 8 e]. **1971** H. HOWARD *Murder One* vii. 92 If he's made a funeral in the family he'll fry like a sunny-side egg. **1979** R. FIENNES *Hell on Ice* iii. 32 Ginnie ladled her sunny-side-up eggs' with semolina.

c. ***Sunny Jim***, the name of an energetic character employed as the proprietary name for a brand of breakfast cereal; also used allusively, as a term of address, and as a nickname. Also ***Sonny Jim*** (influenced by SONNY).

'Sunny Jim was the creation of an American schoolgirl called Ficken (not Fincken) and the various jingles which accompanied him were written by Miss Minnie Hanff. It is believed that Sunny Jim was the winning entry in a competition run by the Force Food Company to find a suitable advertising character to promote "Force".'—C. Fincken (A. C. Fincken & Co. Ltd., manufacturers of Force), private let. to ed., 24 June 1983.

1903 *Poster*, High o'er the fence leaps Sunny Jim 'Force' is the food that raises him. **1904** *Trade Marks Jrnl.* 30 Mar. 381 'Sunny Jim'... Cereal Food Products. The firm trading as the 'Force' Food Company, 6, Holborn Viaduct, London, E.C.; Manufacturers. *c* **1904** *Story of Sunny Jim* (Force Food Co.), Jim Dumps was a most unfriendly man, Who lived his life on a hermit plan. He'd never stop for a friendly smile, But trudged along in his moody style. Till 'Force' one day was served to him. Since then they call him Sunny Jim. **1911** CHESTERTON *Innocence of Father Brown* xii. 315 Sir Aaron Armstrong was.. comic... It was like hearing that Sunny Jim had hanged himself. **1911** 'I. HAY' *Safety Match* xii. 187 Mr. Blunt.. cleared the topmost rail... 'Now then, Sunny Jim!' remarked a reproving voice. **1916** *Punch* 5 Apr. 229/1 [He] says he's quite a Sunny Jim, That buoyant health and youthful vim Are sticking out all over him. **1943** *Current Biogr.* (1944) 779/2 Vandegrift—so cheerful that he has earned the nickname 'Sunny Jim'—is.. the toughest Marine Corps leader who ever charged at the head of his troops. **1960** D. STOREY *This Sporting Life* I. v. 127 'All right, all right! Don't preach, sonny. Hey!' she calls to the M.P. 'Hey sonnyjim! What kinda car has Arthur Machin got?' **1962** S. L. GOLDBERG *Joyce* i. 3 What his [*sc.* James Joyce's] early works do not portray.. is the aspect of his character that earned him the family nickname, 'Sunny Jim'. **1967** A. WILSON *No Laughing Matter* II. 127 Does your Mother know you're out, Sonny Jim? **1976** *Times* 6 Apr. 16/1 The new Prime Minister [*sc.* James Callaghan].. enjoys life... He is not called Sunny Jim for nothing.

6. *Comb.* **a.** with other adjs., as ***sunny-clear, golden, -red, -sweet, -warm, -winking***.

1708 J. PHILIPS *Cyder* II. 70 Flames, whose unresisted Force O'er Sand, and Ashes, and the stubborn Flint Prevailing, turns into a fusil Sea, That in his Furnace bubbles sunny-red. **1833** TENNYSON *Palace of Art* xxiv, In tracts of pasture sunny-warm. **1855** —— *Daisy* xii, In bright vignettes.. Of tower or duomo, sunny-sweet. **1858** LEWES *Sea-side Studies* 219 The mystic drama will be sunny clear, and all Nature's processes will be visible to man, as a divine Effluence. **1922** JOYCE *Ulysses* 406 She dare not bear the sunny-golden babe of day. *Ibid.* 216 He walked by the treeshade of sunnywinking leaves.

b. parasynthetic, as ***sunny-coloured, -faced, -hearted, -spirited*** adjs. (with derivatives, as ***sunny-heartedness***); also ***sunny-day*** adj. (*fig.*: cf. SUNSHINE 5 c, SUMMER *sb.*[1] 4 e).

1832 BRYANT *Autumn Woods* vii, Their *sunny-coloured foliage. **1821** SCOTT *Kenilw.* vii, Such *sunny-day courtiers as my noble guest. *a* **1847** ELIZA COOK *Old Mill-stream* xxii, The *sunny-faced child. **1856** MISS YONGE *Daisy Chain* I. xx. (1879) 211 Ethel was brilliantly happy waiting on the children, and so was *sunny-hearted Meta. **1856** J. W. KAYE *Life Sir J. Malcolm* I. iv. 54 The elasticity and *sunny-heartedness of the writer. **1848** FABER *Spir. Confer.* (1870) 143 A *sunny-spirited Christian.

sunnyasee, sunnyasi: see SANNYASI.

sunonima, variant of SYNONYMA.

'sun-proof, *a.* [f. SUN *sb.*[1] + PROOF *a.*] Proof against the sun; through which the sunlight cannot penetrate; unaffected by the rays of the sun.

1606 MARSTON *Sophonisba* IV. i. F j, Thick armes Of darksom Ewe [= yew] (Sun proofe). **1711** GOLDING *Spect.* No. 250 ¶2 The Sun-Proof Eye.. without blinking at the Lustre of Beauty, can distribute an Eye of proper Complaisance to a Room crowded with Company. *c* **1820** S. ROGERS *Italy, Campagna Florence* 24 In the shade Of many a tree sun-proof. **1899** *Daily Tel.* 21 Aug. 7/7 Grey sun-proof vapours.

'sun-ray. [f. SUN *sb.*[1] + RAY *sb.*[1]]

1. A ray proceeding from the sun; a ray of sunlight, a sunbeam. Chiefly *poet.* or *rhet.*

1829 POE *Al Aaraaf* 361 The sun-ray dropp'd in Lemnos. **1886** W. J. TUCKER *E. Europe* 226 Gems.. twinkling like stars, dazzling like the fiercest sun-rays. **1905** 'Q' (Quiller-Couch) *Shining Ferry* vi. 68 The front door had a fanlight through which fell one broken sunray.

2. a. A figure representing this; *pl.* lines radiating from a centre or central disk.

1901 *Westm. Gaz.* 20 Nov. 7/2 The reverse side [of the medal] is surmounted by an impression of the Crown, from which spring sun-rays of the conventional pattern.

b. *attrib.*, denoting a pattern of radiating pleats, as ***sun-ray fashion, pleating***, etc. Also ***sun-ray pleat, sun-ray pleated*** adj.

1897 *Daily News* 2 Jan. 6/3 The skirt being pleated in the sun-ray fashion now so very much in vogue. **1903** *Young Woman* XI. 318/2 For evening dresses accordion pleated —or sun-ray pleated—point d'esprit net is an ideal material. **1904** *Westm. Gaz.* 28 June 4/2 A sunray voile skirt. **1922** JOYCE *Ulysses* 731 The orange petticoat I had on with sunray pleats. **1935** *Times* 4 Nov. 9/3 Sunray pleating gives fullness from the knee. **1959** *Spectator* 2 Jan. 10/2 Short office skirts and dropping Spanish skirts and brisk housewifely sun-ray pleats. **1972** *Country Life* 25 May 1354/2 Sunray pleating is again in fashion. **1978** *Lancashire Life* Apr. 79/2 A tailored jacket which can be teamed with a sunray pleated skirt.

3. An (artificial) ultraviolet ray used for medical or cosmetic treatment. Chiefly *attrib.*, esp. in ***sun-ray lamp***; formerly also *ellipt.* for ***sun-ray treatment***.

1928 *Daily Express* 27 June 3/6 The speedy development of sun-ray clinics all over the country. *Ibid.*, The treatment of disease by artificial sun-rays. **1930** M. KENNEDY *Fool of Family* x. 89, I wonder if sunray treatment would do her good... Sir Ivor knew nothing of sunray, and he had no faith in doctors. **1954** 'N. BLAKE' *Whisper in Gloom* II. xii. 164 Does this young lady..own a sun-ray lamp? **1977** C. FREMLIN *Spider Orchid* xxii. 149 He looked from the bedside table to the sunray lamp.

So **'sun-raying** *a.*, giving forth rays of sunlight.

1850 ALLINGHAM *Poems, Æolian Harp, 'O pale green sea'* i, The sun-raying West.

sunrise ('sʌnraɪz). [app. evolved, through syntactical ambiguity, from clauses such as *forto* (= until), *tofore*, or *before the sun rise*, where orig. *forto*, etc. are conjunctions and *rise* a verb in the subjunctive; cf.:—

13.. *K. Alis.* 5733 (Laud MS.), Men..token hem þer herberewe Forto þe sonne ryse amorowe. **1398** TREVISA *Barth. De P.R.* XIII. xxvi. (1495) D v b/1 They ben huntyd tofore the sonne ryse; *Bodl. MS.* lf. 136/1 Bifore þe sonne riseþ; *orig.* ante ascensum solis.]

a. The rising, or apparent ascent above the horizon, of the sun at the beginning of the day; the time when the sun rises, the opening of day. Also, the display of light or colour in the sky at this time.

c **1440** *Promp. Parv.* 484/1 Sunne ryse [*A.* sunne ryst], or rysynge of þe sunne. **1530** PALSGR. 272/2 Sonne ryse, *solail leuant.* **1603** SHAKS. *Meas. for M.* II. ii. 153 True prayers, That shall be vp at heauen, and enter there Ere Sunne rise. **1671** MILTON *Samson* 1597 The gates I enter'd with Sunrise. **1766** GOLDSM. *Vic. W.* iv, By sunrise we all assembled in our common apartment. **1820** W. SCORESBY *Acc. Arctic Reg.* I. 34 After sun-rise, the surface of the snow is apt to become soft. **1860** TYNDALL *Glac.* I. xxvii. 209 The glory of the sunrise augmented by contrast. **1864** TENNYSON *En. Ard.* 599 The scarlet shafts of sunrise. **1908** [MISS FOWLER] *Betw. Trent & Ancholme* 157, I have never seen so rich and warm a sunrise.

fig. **1823** SCOTT *Quentin D.* x, The first dawn of the arts, which preceded their splendid sunrise.

b. *attrib.*, as ***sunrise flush, -land, path***; **sunrise-gun**, a gun fired at sunrise; **sunrise industry**, a new and expanding industry; cf. *sunset industry* s.v. SUNSET 3. Also quasi-*adj.* = easterly, eastern.

1809 CAMPBELL *Gert. Wyom.* II. v, The sunrise path at morn I see thee trace. **1872** *Routledge's Ev. Boy's Ann.* 367/1 After the sunrise-gun had boomed. **1876** 'OUIDA' *Winter City* ix. 273 With the sunrise flush touching her cheek. **1894** MRS. A. BERLYN (*title*) Sunrise-Land. Rambles in Eastern England. **1980** L. C. THUROW *Zero-Sum Society* (1981) iv. 95 We do need the national equivalent of a corporate investment committee to redirect investment flows from our 'sunset' industries to our 'sunrise' industries. **1980** *Economist* 23 Aug. 16/2 Those who try to shelter dying jobs in sunset industries, and thereby blight the prospects of growth of good jobs in sunrise ones. **1983** *Times* 20 Apr. 21/7 The traditional 'sunset' industries are a pain in the neck for the Industry Secretary. However much he tries to brush them under the carpet in favour of the glamorous 'sunrise' sector of high technology, they persist in creeping back into the public consciousness.

sunrising ('sʌn,raɪzɪŋ). Now *rare* or *arch.* (superseded by SUNRISE). [f. SUN *sb.*[1] + pr. pple. or gerund of RISE *v.*, partly after F. *soleil levant.*] = prec. (In early use often with *the.*)

c **1250** *Kent. Serm.* in *O.E. Misc.* 26 To-janes þo sunne risindde [orig. Fr. *vers le solail levant*]. **13..** *K. Alis.* 2901 Mury hit is in sonne risyng [*Laud MS.* sonnes risynge]. *c* **1330** R. BRUNNE *Chron. Wace* (Rolls) 9237 To morn atte sonne rysyng. **1398** TREVISA *Barth. De P.R.* VIII. xiv. (1495) V v b/2 Venus..warnyth that ye daye comyth anone and the sonne rysynge [*orig.* solis ortum]. **1481** CAXTON *Godfrey* cxxxvii. 205 That alle man shold be in the mornyng to fore the sonne rysynge alle armed. **1565** *Reg. Privy Council Scot.* Ser. I. I. 344 Befoir the sone rysing in the morning. **1594** SHAKS. *Rich. III*, V. iii. 61 Bid him bring his power Before Sun-rising. **1600** DALLAM in *Early Voy. Levant* (Hakluyt Soc.) 96 At the son risinge we paste by Cape Sprott. *a* **1635** NAUNTON *Fragm. Reg.* (Arb.) 31 The most glorious Sun-risings are subject to shadowings and droppings in. **1709** ADDISON *Tatler* No. 20 ¶4 Where he may be seen from Sun-rising to Sun-setting. **1770** LANGHORNE *Plutarch* (1879) I. 169/1 The wind used to blow hard from the mountains at sunrising. **1822–7** GOOD *Study Med.* (1829) IV. 207 The next morning, about sunrising, his sight was restored. **1883** MISS M. BETHAM-EDWARDS *Disarmed* xxx, You are young, and shall greet many a sunrising.

b. *transf.* The quarter or region in which the sun rises; the east; also with defining word indicating the precise quarter in which the sun rises at a specified season, as ***equinoctial, winter sunrising***.

c **1420** *Prose Life Alex.* 76 We seke to ferre towarde þe son rysynge. **1513** DOUGLAS *Æneis* VII. xi. 14 Or for till ettyll into Inde.. Towart the dawing and son rysing to seyk. **1570–6** LAMBARDE *Peramb. Kent* (1826) 3 Nearest to the sunne risinge and furthest from the Northe Pole. **1601** HOLLAND *Pliny* II. xlvii. I. 22 From the equinoctiall sunne-rising bloweth the East wind *Subsolanus*: from the rising therof in Mid-winter, the south-east *Vulturnus*. **1654–66** EARL ORRERY *Parthen.* (1676) 531 We might perceive all those Plains towards the Sun-rising covered with Troops. **1726** LEONI *Alberti's Archit.* I. 98/1 Bed-chambers for summer shou'd look to the South, the Parlours, to the Winter Sunrising. **1868** HOLME LEE *B. Godfrey* xix. 110 The shadowed side towards the sunrising.

c. *attrib.* or quasi-*adj.*

a **1618** RALEIGH *Inv. Shipping* (1650) 13 The French and Spanish called the sun rising winds, East..and the sunne setting winds West. **1725** *Fam. Dict.* s.v. *Hen-House*, The Windows should be on the Sun-Rising side, strongly lathed.

†**'sunrist.** *Obs.* Forms: 4 **sonne rist,** 5 **sunne ryst, rest.** [prob. shortening of *sunne arist* or *uprist*: see ARIST, UPRIST.] The sunrise; the east.

1340–70 *Alisaunder* 791 þis rink, or þe sonne rist,..passes in þe Paleis. *Ibid.* 855 Hee shall fare as farre as any freke dwelles, And right too þe sonne rist his raigne shall last. *c* **1460** *Promp. Parv.* (Winch. MS.) 448 Sunne rest, or rysyng of þe son.

sunset ('sʌnsɛt). Also 4–6 **sonne, sunne set,** 5 **sonsett,** 6 **soonne sette;** 7 **sunnes-set.** [app. f. SUN *sb.*[1] + SET *sb.*[1], but perhaps arising partly (like SUNRISE) from a clause (e.g. *ere the sunne set*).

OE. (Northumb.) *sunset* (Lindisf. Gosp.) was prob. an adoption of ON. *sólarseta, -setr*: see SET *sb.*[1], etym. note.]

1. a. The setting, or apparent descent below the horizon, of the sun at the end of the day; the time when the sun sets, the close of day. Also, the glow of light or display of colour in the sky when the sun sets.

1390 GOWER *Conf.* III. 257 Riht evene upon the Sonne set. *a* **1400–50** *Wars Alex.* 3050 Als sone as þe son vp soȝt þe slaȝtere begynnes, And so to þe son-sett [*Dubl. MS.* And to sett was þe same] slakid þai neuire. **1526** *Pilgr. Perf.* (W. de W. 1531) 257 b, At the houre of complyn, whiche is aboute the sonne set. **1542** UDALL in *Lett. Lit. Men* (Camden) 6 In the evenyng after soonne sette. **1599** SANDYS *Europæ Spec.* (1632) 5 Thrice a day, at sun-rise, at noone, and sun-set. **1623** FLETCHER & ROWLEY *Maid in Mill* IV. ii, It has lasted Too many Sun-sets. **1711** ADDISON *Spect.* No. 110 ¶1 The Butler desired me with a very grave Face not to venture my self in it after Sun-set. **1822** BYRON *Heaven & Earth* I. i, They have kindled all the west, Like a returning sunset. **1858** HAWTHORNE *Fr. & It. Note-bks.* (1872) I. 39 After sunset, the horizon burned and glowed with rich crimson orange lustre. **1873** B. HARTE *What B. Harte Saw* in *Fiddletown*, etc. 98 A flash of water, tremulous and tinted with sunset. **1874** BURNAND *My Time* xi. 90 The Jews begin their Sabbath on Friday at sunset.

b. ***to ride (go, sail, etc.) off into the sunset***, phr. derived from a conventional closing scene of many films used, freq. ironically, to denote a happy ending.

1967 H. HARRISON *Technicolor Time Machine* (1968) iii. 28 He takes the girl with him and together they sail into the sunset to a new life. **1976** W. GOLDMAN *Magic* III. xii. 207, I didn't even bother getting mad at your crack about me going off into the sunset. **1977** *Times* 17 Feb. 6/4 Our black hero..rides off to freedom in the sunset.

2. *fig.* Decline or close, *esp.* of a period of prosperity or the like.

[**1592** SHAKS. *Rom. & Jul.* III. v. 128 When the Sun sets, the Earth doth drizzle daew, But for the Sunset of my Brothers Sonne, It raines downright.] **1613** W. BASSE (*title*) Great Brittaines Sunnes-set, bewailed with a shower of teares. **1621** T. WILLIAMSON tr. *Goulart's Wise Vieillard* 2 Old age..may be called the sunne set of our dayes. **1690** TEMPLE *Misc.* II. iv. 45 So many Ages after the Sun-set of the Roman Learning and Empire together. **1801** CAMPBELL *Lochiel's Warning* 55 'Tis the sunset of life gives me mystical lore, And coming events cast their shadows before. **1898** ILLINGWORTH *Div. Imman.* i. 1 The gloom that darkens, or the hope that glorifies the sunset of our days.

3. a. *attrib.* and *Comb.*, as ***sunset clock, hue, light, mist, ray; sunset-blue, -flushed, -lighted, -purpled, -red*** (also as *sb.*), ***-ripened, -tinted*** adjs.; **sunset-gun**, a gun fired at sunset; **sunset home**, a home (HOME *sb.* 8) for the elderly, a 'twilight' home; **sunset industry**, an old and declining industry. Also quasi-*adj.* = western, westerly, as ***sunset clime***, and quasi-*adv.* = westward, as ***sunset-gazing***.

1874 R. TYRWHITT *Our Sketching Club* 68 Any *sunset-blue tint,—say cobalt and rose-madder. *a* **1853** G. P. MORRIS *Poems* (1860) 155 All this *sunset clime became Familiar with Victoria's name. **1821** CLARE *Vill. Minstr.* II. 7 True to his *sunset-clock he kept, His Goody and his cot to find. **1833** TENNYSON *Lotos Eaters* 17 Far off, three mountain-tops..Stood *sunset-flush'd. **1902** W. WATSON *Coronat. Ode*, Deira with her sea-face to the morn, And Cambria *sunset-gazing. **1840** THOREAU *Jrnl.* 16 June in *Writings* (1906) VII. 141 To hear..the bittern begin to boom from his concealed fort like a *sunset gun! **1861** DICKENS *Gt. Expect.* ii, There was a conwict off last night.. after sunset-gun. **1978** *Dædalus* Spring 220 A society that increasingly emphasizes..singles bars for the young and ..*sunset homes for the elderly. **1899** *Westm. Gaz.* 30 Nov. 2/1 Draperies of silk of *sunset hues. **1980, 1983** *Sunset industry [see *sunrise industry* s.v. SUNRISE b]. **1886** STEVENSON *Kidnapped* viii, I wondered..at the lateness of the *sunset light. **1898** WATTS-DUNTON *Aylwin* XIII. iv, Masses of *sunset mist. **1838** LD. HOUGHTON *Switzerland & Italy* v, The *sunset-purpled ground. **1837** E. B. BROWNING *Epistle to Canary* (1913) 11 A spark of light from highest dawn, Which glows and opens..till *sunset reds are likest to them. **1934** WEBSTER, Sunset-red adj. **1964** *New Yorker* 5 Sept. 86 (Advt.), Slip into the run-about shift... mirage aqua, sunset-red, cactus-green, burnt-clay. **1979** *Arizona Daily Star* 5 Aug. (Parade Suppl.) 24/2 (Advt.), These are handsome..books, smartly bound in sunset red, desert tan and cavalry blue. **1833** TENNYSON *Hesperides* iv. 21 The luscious fruitage..*Sunset-ripened. **1876** J. G. WHITTIER *Mabel Martin* (new ed.) 40 And sad the uncompanioned eves, And sadder *sunset-tinted leaves. **1954** L. MACNEICE *Autumn Sequel* 33 The sunset-tinted Balloons were down.

b. *N. Amer. Pol.* Applied to legislation whereby a government agency or programme is automatically terminated at the end of a fixed period unless formally renewed.

1976 *National Observer* (U.S.) 5 June 1/1 The hottest political idea of the year is something called the sunset bill. *Ibid.* 1/5 Colorado recently became the first state to adopt sunset legislation. **1976** *Wall St. Jrnl.* 25 June 1/1 Colorado's new 'Sunset Law'. The experimental measure would terminate in six years the state's regulatory agencies ..unless they justify their existence. **1978** *Globe & Mail* (Toronto) 15 Feb. 1/3 The Ontario Government is on the verge of embracing sunset law. **1982** *Times* 25 Feb. 7/8 It is not a wilderness protection Bill..but a wilderness sunset Bill, that would end wilderness protection.

Hence (*N. Amer.*) **'sunset** *v.*, (*a*) *intr.*, to decline, sink (*rare*); (*b*) *trans.*, to subject to, or terminate by means of, sunset legislation (see sense 3 b above); **'sunsetty** *a.* (*U.S.*), suggestive of sunset.

1869 MRS. WHITNEY *We Girls* i, 'West over'..We always thought it was a pretty, sunsetty name. **1893** T. N. PAGE *Ole Virginia* 45 Her arms so white, an' her face sort o' sunsetty. **1933** V. MCNABB *Nazareth or Social Chaos* 30 The prodigal's prosperity which sunsets in beggary. **1978** *Canadian Broadcasting Corporation News* 1 June (*oral quot.*), [The] act would be sunsetted out of existence. **1979** *National Jrnl.* 17 Mar. 438/1 In the debate on the sunset bill ..when it was passed by the Senate, we tried to figure out what exactly they thought they were sunsetting. **1982** *N.Y. Times* 28 Sept. B. 10/4 His impatience is also displayed in his plans to 'sunset' the aeronautics board well before it is scheduled to expire.

sunsetting ('sʌn,sɛtɪŋ). Now *rare* or *arch.* (superseded by SUNSET). [f. SUN *sb.*[1] + pr. pple. or gerund of SET *v.*[1], partly after F. *soleil couchant.*]

1. = prec. 1.

c **1440** *Promp. Parv.* 484/1 Sunne settynge, or sunne gate downe, *occasus.* **1565** in Picton *L'pool Munic. Rec.* (1883) I. 113 Eight of the clock after the sunsetting. **1584** COGAN *Haven Health* i. (1636) 10 Antoninus..was wont to come to the wrestling place about Sunne-setting. **1661** GLANVILL *Van. Dogm.* 176 Gassendus saw one [rainbow] at Sun-setting, whose Supreme Arch almost reached our Zenith. **1712** in J. J. Vernon *Parish of Hawick* (1900) 99 John Riddell ..confest yt he brought home ye load of herring upon the Sabbath att the sunsetting. **1815** SIMOND *Tour Gt. Brit.* I. 349 We had another glorious sunsetting. *a* **1854** J. WILSON in *Casquet of Lit.* Ser. II. (1874) I. 164/2 We..used to stalk about..from sunrising to sunsetting. **1868** MORRIS *Earthly Par.* (1870) I. I. 346 When anigh to sunsetting it grew.

2. *transf.* The region in which the sun sets; the west; with defining word indicating the quarter in which the sun sets at a specified season.

1601 HOLLAND *Pliny* II. xlvii. I. 23 Betweene the South and the Southwest..namely, betweene the Noone steed, and the Sunsetting in Winter. **1726** LEONI *Alberti's Archit.* I. 98/1 Bed-chambers for the Winter shou'd look towards the Point at which the Sun rises in Winter, and the Parlour, towards the Equinoctial Sun-setting. **1868** HOLME LEE *B. Godfrey* xix. 110 There were their names on the stone—.. looking towards the sunsetting.

3. *fig.* = prec. 2.

1617 MIDDLETON *Triumphs Honor* Wks. 1840 V. 619 There is no human glory or renown, But have their evening and their sure sun-setting.

4. *attrib.*

a **1618** [see SUNRISING c]. **1797–1803** J. FOSTER in *Life & Corr.* (1846) I. 208 To paint a sun-setting cloud-scene.

sunshade ('sʌnʃeɪd). [See SHADE *sb.* 11. OE. had *sunsceadu*, glossing 'flammeolum' = bridal-veil (cf. SHADOW *sb.* 13 b).]

1. An awning over the outside of a window, to keep the sunlight off. ? *Obs.*

1851 *Catal. Great Exhib.* xxvi. 135 Models of the patent outside sun-shade. **1861** W. H. RUSSELL in *Times* 12 July, Houses of wood, with porticoes, pillars, verandahs, and sun-shades, generally painted white and green. **1875** KNIGHT *Dict. Mech.*

2. A parasol; now usually applied to the larger kinds.

1842 *N.Y. Times* 22 Mar. (Advt.), Umbrellas, parasols and sun-shades manufactured at Newark, N.J. **1852** BAILEY *Festus* (ed. 5) 506 Pavonian canopy of azure held, In manner of a sunshade. **1860** *All Year Round* No. 72. 512 The thousandth, or three thousandth anniversary of the umbrella in India or China, that would be the anniversary of it as a sun-shade. **1895** R. W. CHAMBERS *King in Yellow, Repairer Reput.* ii. (1909) 27 Constance tipped her sunshade to shield her eyes.

3. A hood fixed on the front of a bonnet to keep the sun from the face; also, a broad-brimmed hat.

1872 JEAN INGELOW *Off the Skelligs* viii, I..asked her..to buy me..a sunshade, commonly called an ugly.

4. A device used with a telescope or other observing instrument to diminish the intensity of sunlight, as a darkened glass screen, or a tube projecting beyond the object-glass.

1894 F. M. GIBSON *Amateur Telescopist's Handbk.* 55 Let the student be earnestly admonished to take the best precautions to shield his eyes when engaged in solar observation. The plan commonly adopted is to use the sun-shades which are usually furnished with eye pieces, the colors of which are either neutral-tint, blue, or red.

5. *pl.* = *sun-glass* (*c*) s.v. SUN *sb.*[1] 13 a. Cf. SHADE *sb.* 11 e.

1965 'LAUCHMONEN' *Old Thom's Harvest* ii. 24 The minister took off his sunshades and his naked eyes followed the girl. **1967** *Sunday Times* 28 May 18, I give a lot of speeches with my sunshades on.

sunshine (ˈsʌnʃaɪn), *sb.* Also 3 sunnesin-e, 6 son(ne)shyne, -shine, 6–7 sunneshine, (7 sunschyne, -schene), 6– sun-shine, sunshine. [ME. *sunnesin-e* (which appears very much earlier than SHINE *sb.*) had prob. a similar origin to that of SUNRISE: see quot. *c* 1250. But cf. OFris. *sunna skin*, (M)LG. *sunnenschîn*, MDu. *sonnescijn* (Du. *zonneschijn*), MHG. *sunne(n)-schîn* (early mod.G. *sunnen-*, *sonne-*, *sunschein*, G. *sonnenschein*). OE. had *sunscín*, glossing '*speculum*' = mirror.]

1. a. The shining of the sun; direct sunlight uninterrupted by cloud.

c **1250** *Gen. & Ex.* 3335–7 Ilc man is he bead,..Him gaderen or ðe sunne-sine, Elles he sulden missen hine, For it malt at ðe sunne-sine. **1535** COVERDALE *Job* viii. 16 Oft tymes a thinge doth florish, and men thynke that it maye abyde the Sonneshyne. **1588** LAMBARDE *Eiren.* IV. 372, I shall as the saying is, but set a Candle in the sunne-shine. **1612** WOODALL *Surg. Mate* Wks. (1653) 206 As cleere, as the Sun-shine is at mid-day. **1697** DRYDEN *Virg. Georg.* III. 473 A Cot that opens to the South prepare: Where basking in the Sun-shine they may lye. **1781** COWPER *Let. to J. Newton* 28 May, You seldom complain of too much sunshine..the south walk in our long garden will exactly suit you. **1840** DICKENS *Old C. Shop* xv, Sunshine peeping through some little window. **1842** LOUDON *Suburban Hort.* 566 The gooseberry may be forced in pots... The temperature is never allowed to be high, and abundance of air is given during sunshine. **1860** TYNDALL *Glac.* I. xvii. 119 There was a long fight between mist and sunshine.

†**b.** with *a* and *pl.* A burst or spell of sunshine.

1601 SHAKS. *All's Well* v. iii. 33, I am not a day of season, For thou maist see a sun-shine, and a haile In me at once. **1611** MURE *Misc. Poems* i. 56 Lyk to a fair sunschyne befoir a schoure. **1657** J. WATTS *Scribe, Pharisee*, etc. I. 177 To partake of the benefit of the Sun-shines and Rains. **1747** GOULD *Eng. Ants* 62 They take the Opportunity of a Sun-shine to disperse in the Air.

c. with poss. adj.: cf. LIGHT *sb.* 1 g and quot. 1390 in SUN *sb.*[1] 4.

a **1774** TUCKER *Lt. Nat.* (1834) II. 72 The plain man.. may say..as Diogenes did to Alexander, 'Only please to stand out of my sun-shine'.

d. *to have been in the sunshine* (slang), to be drunk: cf. SUN *sb.*[1] 4 b (*c*).

1857 GEO. ELIOT *Scenes Clerical Life, Janet's Rep.* i. 52 He was in that condition which his groom indicated with poetic ambiguity by saying that 'master had been in the sunshine'.

2. *fig.* (often with literal phraseology retained). **a.** A source of happiness or prosperity. Now freq. as a colloq. form of address to any person. Cf. also (*little*) *ray of sunshine* s.v. RAY *sb.*[1] 1 e.

1595 T. P. GOODWINE *Blanchardyn* liv. 213 Is she gon, the comfort of my youth..the sonshine of my blisse? **1866** B. TAYLOR *Poems, Neighbor* 22 Ye are the sunshine of the earth. **1901** *Harper's Mag.* CII. 798/2 He always used to say, 'Well, how is mamma's little sunshine to-day? **1942** BERREY & VAN DEN BARK *Amer. Thes. Slang* § 184/1 Hap, Happy, Sunshine, a cheerful person. **1972** M. GILBERT *Body of Girl* iv. 43 Hullo, Sunshine. What can we do for you? **1976** P. CAVE *High Flying Birds* ii. 17, I turned back to the ticket man. 'OK now, sunshine?' **1976** *Daily Mirror* 16 Mar. 12/1 Mike Reid's cheery Cockney greeting seems to switch on every girl in the place. 'Hello sunshine,' he says.

b. A favourable or gracious influence.

a **1596** *Sir T. More* IV. v. 98 The rest.. haue had fayre time to growe In sun-shine of my fortunes. **1597** SHAKS. *2 Hen. IV*, IV. ii. 12 That man that sits within a Monarches heart, And ripens in the Sunne-shine of his fauor. **1598** FLORIO *Dict.* Ep. Ded. a 3 b, To me..the glorious and gracious sunne-shine of your Honor hath infused light and life. **1741–2** GRAY *Agrippina* 147 The gilded swarm that wantons in the sunshine Of thy full favour. **1868** FREEMAN *Norm. Conq.* II. ix. (1877) 367 They were to be allowed to bask in the sunshine of the court.

c. A condition or atmosphere of happiness or prosperity.

1593 SHAKS. *3 Hen. VI*, II. ii. 156 Euen then that Sun-shine brew'd a showre for him, That washt his Fathers fortunes forth of France. **1613** PURCHAS *Pilgrimage* VII. xii. 597 Henrie, the Infanta of Portugall, that day-starre, which by his industrie made way to the present Sun-shine of discoueries. **1665** BOYLE *Occas. Refl.* (1848) 67 Those, that during the Sun-shine of prosperity are beset with seeming Friends. **1696** TATE & BRADY *Ps.* xxx. 6 Whilst in my Sun-shine of Success No low'ring Cloud appear'd. **1779** *Mirror* No. 43 ¶8 It would have been inhuman in our philosopher to have clouded, even with a doubt, the sunshine of this belief. **1826** DISRAELI *Viv. Grey* II. iii, In the meantime all was sunshine with Vivian Grey. **1862** MISS BRADDON *Lady Audley* xxxvi, There had never been anything but harmony and sunshine between Lucy Audley and her generous husband.

d. Happiness or cheerfulness of mind or heart; sunny disposition.

1742 GRAY *Eton* 44 The sunshine of the breast. *c* **1836** CARLYLE in *Academy* 17 Sept. (1898) 273/3 Particularly endeavour to keep a good heart... Sunshine in the inside of one is even more important than sunshine without. **1850** W. IRVING *Goldsmith* xxxix. 370 In these genial moments..the sunshine of Goldsmith's nature would break out.

3. *transf.* Light or brightness resembling or suggesting that of the sun; brightness of the eye or the countenance.

1588 SHAKS. *L.L.L.* v. i. 201 Vouchsafe to shew the sun-shine of your face. **1839** LYTTON *Richelieu* IV. i, Deaf to the music of a woman's voice—Blind to the sunshine of a woman's eyes. **1901** W. CLARK RUSSELL *Ship's Adv.* iv. With the stateliness of a frigate she broke into a sunshine of canvas.

4. *attrib.* and *Comb.* Simple attrib. and objective (with reference to indicating or recording sunshine), as ***sunshine map***, ***record***, ***recorder***.

1892 W. A. TAYLOR in *Scott. Geog. Mag.* June 322 The first sunshine recorder was the invention of Mr. John C. Campbell of Islay. **1893** H. N. DICKSON *Ibid.* Aug. (Title on cover), Sunshine Map of the British Isles. *Ibid.* 396 In discussing sunshine records, it is..necessary to distinguish the cases where allowance must be made for latitude from those where the actual duration merely is required. *Ibid.* 400 The general form of the sunshine curve is thus a strong minimum in winter, a steady increase to a maximum in May.

5. *attrib.* passing into *adj.* **a.** Full of or characterized by sunshine; sunshiny, sunny. Now *rare*.

1579 SPENSER *Sheph. Cal.* Jan. 3 All in a sunneshine day, as did befall. **1601** HOLLAND *Pliny* VI. xvi. I. 123 The warme Sunneshine weather. **1632** MILTON *L'Allegro* 98 Young and old come forth to play On a Sunshine Holyday. **1663** S. PATRICK *Parab. Pilgr.* xxvi. (1687) 281 A Fine Sun-shine morning it was. **1715** LEONI *Palladio's Archit.* (1742) II. 75 The Sun-dial..could serve but in Sun-shine Weather. **1765** *Phil. Trans.* LV. 155 In a calm hot sun-shine day,..the air ..appears to have a tremulous motion. **1841** BROWNING *Pippa Passes* [Introd.] 23 Thy fitful sunshine-minutes, coming, going. **1894** 'G. EGERTON' *Keynotes* 155 It is a sunshine Sabbath morning.

b. *fig.* 'Bright', cheerful, cheering; prosperous, happy, joyous.

1593 SHAKS. *Rich. II*, IV. i. 221 God saue King Henry,.. And send him many yeeres of Sunne-shine dayes. **1594** DRAYTON *Amours* ix, Her sun-shine face there chaunsing to espy. **1663** S. PATRICK *Parab. Pilgr.* xxix. (1687) 341 Then were his Sunshine days, and his Heart all in an ardour of Love and Joy. **1833** LONGF. *Outre-mer* (1851) 227 The French have that happy and sunshine temperament. **1834** J. H. NEWMAN *Par. Serm.* (1837) I. xxv. 379 The Bible does not take a pleasant sunshine view of the world.

c. That remains faithful, or subsists, only in prosperity; 'fair-weather'.

1775 BURKE *Let. to Marq. Rockingham* 14 Sept., The worst sort of tories, the sunshine gentlemen of the last reign. **1809** W. IRVING *Knickerb.* VI. vi. (1861) 207 Would you have had me take such sunshine, faint-hearted recreants to my bosom? **1847** WHITTIER *My Soul & I* 25 Summon thy sunshine bravery back. **1876** H. GARDNER *Sunflowers, Leone* I. 108 My sunshine-friends have turned their backs on me.

6. *Comb.*: **sunshine law** *U.S.*, a law making the official meetings and records of certain government agencies accessible to the public; **sunshine roof**, on a motor vehicle, a roof that can be slid open; = *sun-roof* (*a*) s.v. SUN *sb.*[1] 13 a; **sunshine-showery** *a. nonce-wd.*, of a disposition that is cheerful in the midst of trouble; **Sunshine State**, (*a*) *U.S.*, any of several states (see quots.); (*b*) *Austral.*, Queensland; **sunshine-yellow** *a.* and *sb.*, (of) a bright shade of yellow.

1972 *Atlantic Monthly* Sept. 22 The state of Florida has adopted a 'sunshine law' which requires that all official meetings in which public business is transacted be open to the public. **1977** *National Observer* (U.S.) 22 Jan. 16/5 We need an all-inclusive 'sunshine law' in Washington so that special interests will not retain their exclusive access behind closed doors. **1982** *Times Lit. Suppl.* 26 Feb. 225/5 'Sunshine laws' have opened committee hearings to public scrutiny. **1929** *Daily Express* 12 Jan. 4/7 The royal coupé, with a sunshine roof. **1954** J. TRENCH *Dishonoured Bones* II. v. 72 He got out the old Austin..unfastening the sunshine roof. **1977** *Horse & Hound* 14 Jan. 44/3 (Advt.), Land-Rover..sunshine roof. **1830** COLERIDGE *Let. to J. H. Green* 1 June, Mrs. Aders..looks as bright and sunshine-showery as if nothing had ever ailed her. **1893** L. WAGNER *Significance of Names* 36 New Mexico is The Sunshine State. **1918** S. S. VISHER *Geogr. S. Dakota* 60 South Dakota is known as 'the Sunshine State', not because it surpasses in this respect..states..in the southwest, but because of the contrast between South Dakota and the Eastern States and northern European countries from whence most of the persons not born in South Dakota came. **1920** *Monthly Weather Rev.* (U.S. Weather Bureau) Mar. 154/2 In this 'Sunshine State' [*sc.* California] we have 'Sunkist Orange'. **1947** *Time* 17 Mar. 42/2 Employees..are happier in The Sunshine State [*sc.* Florida] where living is so pleasant and healthful. **1962** C. ROHAN *Delinquents* 128 'If you ask me, all Brisbane's full of coppers and all of them bastards,' she said, expressing in one concise sentence the full theory of central government of the sunshine state. **1976** *Daily Record* (Glasgow) 30 Nov. 28/6 And although the Sunshine State has seen a few fancy sights the citizens of Palm Springs are in for an extra special treat next week. **1971** 'A. GILBERT' *Tenant for Tomb* i. 22 The plumber..wanted to install a bright blue bath..and had to be coaxed into substituting a sunshine-yellow one. **1975** A. FRASER *Whistler's Lane* x. 161, I bought myself a blouse in sunshine yellow.

Hence ˈ**sunshine** *v.*, *intr.* to shine as or like the sun (also *impers.*); ˈ**sunshineless** *a.*, dull, gloomy.

1627 J. TAYLOR (Water-P.) *Armado* B 2 b, If it storm'd, rain'd, or blewe, or Sun shinde [*ed.* **1630** Sun-shinde] too hot. **1831** JAMES *Phil. Augustus* I. xvi, The fixed contraction of his brow, and the sunshineless coldness of his lips. **1892** J. LUMSDEN *Sheep-head & Trotters* 278 On the visage of their hero, sunshined for a moment an..answering smile.

ˈ**sunˌshiner.** *local.* A popular name for certain shiny beetles: see quots.

1847 HALLIWELL, *Sun-shiner*, the dark shining beetle. **1866** E. C. RYE *Brit. Beetles* 55 This family [sc. *Feroniides*] comprises several species, the most often seen..being the 'Sunshiners', which are members of the genera *Pterostichus* and *Amara*.

†ˈ**sun-ˌshining,** *sb. Obs. rare.* [f. SUN *sb.*[1] + SHINING *vbl. sb.*] = SUNSHINE *sb.* (*lit.* and *fig.*).

13.. *Coer de L.* 2410 Richard the king, The best under the sun-shining. *a* **1548** HALL *Chron., Edw. IV*, 228 b, All the Constables promises were but fayre sunne shynyng, swetely spoken, and sowerly performed. **1584** COGAN *Haven Health* (1636) 181 By setting Butter..in a platter, open to the Sunne in faire weather..untill it bee sufficiently clarified,.. which will be in twelve or fourteen daies, if there be faire Sunne shining. **1840** *Florist's Jrnl.* (1846) I. 229 Embrace every opportunity of sun-shining, to give air.

b. *to set a sunshining*: to place in the sunshine; *fig.* to expose to view, display.

1601 DENT *Pathw. Heaven* (1617) 35 God hath not giuen such gifts vnto men, to the end they should make sale-ware of them, and set them a sunshining to behold.

ˈ**sunˌshining,** *a.* Now *rare.* [f. SUNSHINE *sb.* + -ING[2].]

1. = SUNSHINY 1, 2. Also *fig.*

1608 TOPSELL *Serpents* 205 A siluer-coloured Lyzard.. liuing in dry and sunne-shining places. *a* **1618** RALEIGH *Prerog. Parl.* 39 When those of the high Countreyes desired raine, and those of the valleyes sunshining dayes. **1657** J. WATTS *Scribe, Pharisee*, etc. III. 51 Those sunshining dayes of Christ Jesus. **1764** *Museum Rust.* II. xxxiii. 108 In fine sun-shining weather. **1819** SHELLEY *Let. to Peacock* 26 Jan., The multitudinous shafts of the sun-shining columns. **1888** *Pall Mall Gaz.* 24 Feb. 2/1 In one place it would be bright and sunshining: in another a snowstorm might be raging.

2. Shining as the sun.

1628 [A. Leighton] *Appeal to Parl.* 207 This cloud being dispersed by the irresistable heat of your Sunshining zeal.

sunshiny (ˈsʌnʃaɪnɪ), *a.* [f. SUNSHINE *sb.* + -Y[1].]

1. Full of or characterized by sunshine: = SUNNY *a.* 1.

1649 N. HARDY *Div. Prosp.* (1654) 15 The wettest Seed-time of a pious Life, shall end in the sun-shiny harvest of a peacefull Death. **1665** BOYLE *Occas. Refl.* (1848) 67 In the Sunshiny months of Summer. **1713** DERHAM *Phys.-Theol.* x. (1798) II. 363 *note*, In warm, sun-shiny weather. **1809** MALKIN *Gil Blas* III. ii. ¶6, I feel disposed..to set out some sunshiny morning for the mountains. **1849** H. MILLER *Footpr. Creat.* i. (1874) 8 The long, clear, sunshiny evenings of the Orkney summer. **1854** —— *Sch. & Schm.* xiv. (1858) 305 A bright sunshiny sky. **1888** DOUGHTY *Trav. Arabia Deserta* I. 542 Every morrow the sun-shiny heat calls them abroad to the easy..labour of their simple lives.

2. Illumined by sunshine: = SUNNY *a.* 2.

1600 FAIRFAX *Tasso* XVI. ix, Sunshinie hils, dales hid from Phœbus raies. **1802** WORDSW. *Stanzas in Copy Cast. Indol.* 26 Retired in that sunshiny shade he lay. **1803** W. TAYLOR in *Monthly Mag.* XIV. 487, I shut my eyes, and call up the idea of a sunshiny landscape. **1880** DISRAELI *Endym.* xlviii, It did not yet occur to Endymion that his garden could not always be sunshiny.

3. Bright as with sunshine: = SUNNY *a.* 4.

1590 SPENSER *F.Q.* I. viii. 20 The fruitfull-headed beast, amaz'd At flashing beames of that sunshiny shield, Became starke blind. *Ibid.* xii. 23 The..glorious light of her sunshyny face. **1824** MISS MITFORD *Village* Ser. I. (1863) 113 The house had still within and without the same sunshiny cleanliness. **1841** BROWNING *Pippa Passes* III. 282 If you killed one Of those sunshiny beetles. **1862** MISS BRADDON *Lady Audley* iii, Her beautiful smile, and sunshiny ringlets!

4. *fig.* 'Bright', joyous: = SUNNY *a.* 5.

1782 MRS. H. COWLEY *Bold Stroke for Husband* II. ii, My dear gloomy cousin, where have you purchased that sunshiny look? **1820** COLERIDGE *Lett., Convers.*, etc. I. vi. 27, I hope that this is a sunshiny spot in the national character. **1857** DUFFERIN *Lett. High Lat.* vi. (ed. 3) 39 His ..daughter—a sunshiny young lady of eighteen. **1863** BOYD *Graver Thoughts C. Parson* viii. 125 Childhood looks sunshiny when we cast back our glance upon it. **1893** LELAND *Mem.* I. 71 A very pleasant and wonderfully polite and sunshiny boy.

ˈ**sunspot.** Also sun-spot.

1. *Path.* A spot or marking on the skin caused by exposure to the sun.

1818–20 E. THOMPSON *Cullen's Nosologia* (ed. 3) 333 Ephelis; Sun Spots. **1872–4** JEFFERIES *Toilers of Field* (1892) 262 Her brown but clear cheek, free from freckles and sun-spots.

2. *Astron.* **a.** A spot or patch on the disk of the sun, appearing dark by contrast with the brighter general surface, and constituted by a cavity in the photosphere filled with cooler vapours.

Sunspots occur only in a zone extending 45° on each side of the sun's equator, often in groups, and last from a few hours to several months; their diameter varies from about 100 to about 100,000 miles; their frequency shows a marked period of about 11 years, corresponding to a periodicity of magnetic and possibly other phenomena on the earth.

1868 LOCKYER *Elem. Astron.* § 121 Its [*sc.* the magnetic needle's] greatest oscillations occurring when there are most sun-spots. **1878** NEWCOMB *Pop. Astron.* III. ii. 248, 1882, 1893, etc., will be years of numerous sun-spots. **1894** W. L. DALLAS in *Indian Meteorol. Mem.* VI. 2 The maximum rainfall agreeing approximately with the maximum sunspots.

b. *attrib.* Also **sunspot cycle**, the recurring increase and decrease in the number of sunspots, with a period averaging just over 11 years.

1883 *Science* I. 462/1 The maximum of auroras corresponds with the minimum sun-spot period. **1884** H. F. BLANFORD in *Indian Meteorol. Mem.* (1894) VI. 2 The epoch of sun-spot maximum approximately coincides with that of minimum pressure. **1913** H. H. TURNER in *Monthly Notices R. Astron. Soc.* Dec. 89 The main Sun-spot swarm was in perihelion in 1816–7. **1922** H. S. JONES *Gen. Astron.* v. 126 There is a remarkable connection between the Sun-spot cycle and the occurrence of magnetic storms on the Earth. **1977** *Jrnl. R. Soc. Arts* CXXV. 157/1 Since the solar output appears to change by a good deal less than 1 per cent, even during solar flares, it is not surprising that weather events show very little correlation with the sunspot cycle.

3. *Cinemat.* A powerful arc lamp used to imitate the light from the sun in colour cinematography; = *sun arc* s.v. SUN *sb.*[1] 13 a.

1930 [see *sun arc* s.v. SUN *sb.* 13 a]. **1976** H. R. F. KEATING *Filmi, Filmi, Inspector Ghote* iii. 29 We are using a great number of different lights for different purposes in filming, Five-Ks, Two-Ks, Sunspots, Solars, Babies.

4. A place that affords plentiful sunshine.

1976 *U.S. News & World Rep.* 2 Feb. 26/1 Most travelers favor sun spots. St. Maarten, in the Netherlands Antilles, leads the parade. **1983** *Listener* 6 Jan. 36/3 (Advt.), First choose your holiday sun-spot, then choose where to stay.

Hence **'sunspottery** [-ERY 2], humorous or contemptuous term for the subject or theory of sunspots, esp. of their connexion with terrestrial phenomena.

1882 R. A. PROCTOR in *Standard* 27 Nov. 2/4, I doubt whether even a twelfth of the astronomers of our time favour 'Sunspottery'.

†**'sunstay.** *Obs. rare.* [f. SUN *sb.*[1] + STAY *sb.*[3]; transl. L. *sōlstitium* SOLSTICE.] = next.

stay of the sun was in use earlier: see STAY *sb.*[3] 3 c.

1577 B. GOOGE *Heresbach's Husb.* I. (1586) 40 b, Varro sayth, that the best tyme for Haruest, is betwixt the Sunne-stay, and the Dogge dayes. **1625** LISLE *Du Bartas, Noe* 177 The Sunne is at highest of this kinde a little after the Sunstay of Summer, and at the lowest soone after the Winter Sunstay.

†**'sun-stead.** *Obs.* Also 7 -steed, -sted. [In OE. *sun(n)stede*, transl. L. *sōlstitium* SOLSTICE: see SUN *sb.*[1] and STEAD *sb.* I.] = SOLSTICE I.

c **1000** *Sax. Leechd.* III. 250 Sumor.. hæfð sunnstede.. winter.. hæfð oþerne sunnstede.

1600 HOLLAND *Livy* XLIV. xxxvi. 1193 Now was it the season of the yeer past sun-stead in summer. **1601** —— *Pliny* II. xix. I. 13 To lengthen the night from the summer sunne-steed. *a* **1636** FITZ-GEFFREY *Holy Transp.* Wks. (Grosart) 169 The season of the yeare wherein our Saviour was borne: namely in the Winter Solstice or Sun-stead. **1638** W. LISLE *Heliodorus* IX. 148 When Summer and Sunsted makes the longest day.

b. The solstitial point (= SOLSTICE 2), or the tropic (TROPIC *sb.* 1 b).

1601 HOLLAND *Pliny* II. lxxvii. I. 36 The position of the Zodiake about the middle parts thereof, is more oblique and crooked, but toward the Sunne-steed more streight and direct. **1601** DOLMAN *La Primaud. Fr. Acad.* (1618) III. 684 The points of the.. Zodiacke, which are the meanes betweene the said Equinoctial points are named Sunsteads or Tropicks. **1662** J. CHANDLER *Van Helmont's Oriat.* 56 If those Instruments [*sc.* hour-glasses and sun-dials] should agree under the Æquinoctial lines, they should varie.. under the Sol-stices or Sun-steads.

'sunstone, 'sun-stone.

†**1.** A rendering of L. *sōlis gemma*, described by Pliny (*N.H.* XXXVII. lxvii) as a white stone which throws out rays like the sun. *Obs.*

1398 TREVISA *Barth. De P.R.* XVI. xc. (Bodl. MS.) lf. 182 b/1 The sonne stone hatte Solis gemma, and is white and schynynge and haþ þ^t name for he schyneþ with bemes as þee sonne doþ.

2. A name given to amber, because the Heliades or daughters of the sun, according to a Greek myth, were changed into poplars and wept amber.

Gr. ἤλεκτρον amber (see ELECTRUM) is related to ἠλέκτωρ, which occurs as an epithet of the sun.

1849 OTTÉ tr. *Humboldt's Cosmos* II. 494 *note*, The electron, the sun-stone of the very ancient mythus of the Eridanus. **1855** BAILEY *Mystic*, etc. 91 Sunstone, which every phantom foul dispels. **1896** W. A. BUFFUM *Tears of Heliades* i. (1897) 7 Trinacria's lustrous and pellucid sun-stone.

3. *Min.* **a.** A name for several varieties of feldspar, showing red or golden-yellow reflexions from minute embedded crystals of mica, oxide of iron, etc. **b.** = CAT'S-EYE 2. (So G. *sonnenstein.*)

1677 PLOT *Oxfordshire* 81, I know not why it [*sc.* the Moonstone] may not as well be called the Sun-stone too. **1794** SCHMEISSER *Syst. Min.* I. 137 Cats Eye... The Sun Stone of the Turks. **1798** [see CAT'S-EYE 2]. **1821** R. JAMESON *Man. Mineral.* 155 Another variety of adularia, found in Siberia, is known to jewellers under the name *Sunstone*. It is of a yellowish-grey colour, and numberless golden spots appear distributed throughout its whole substance. **1884** F. J. BRITTEN *Watch & Clockm.* 216 Moon-Stone, Sun-Stone, Amazon-Stone and Avanturine are forms of felspar.

4. (Always with hyphen.) A stone sacred to the sun, or connected with sun-worship.

1841 *Penny Cycl.* XX. 192/2 The.. relics of Pagan places of worship..; the pillar stone of witness, the tapering sun-stone, [etc.].

5. [tr. ON. *sólarsteinn*.] A stone whose exact properties are uncertain, mentioned in several medieval Icelandic sources.

'A semi-precious stone capable of being used as a burning-glass': P. G. Foote in *ARV: Jrnl. Scandinavian Folklore* (1956), XII. 26–40.

1874 CLEASBY & VIGFUSSON *Icelandic-Eng. Dict.* 579/2 *Sólar-steinn*, m. a sun-stone or loadstone, = leiðarsteinn, used by sailors to find the place of the sun on a cloudy day. **1947** J. E. TURVILLE-PETRE tr. *Story of Rauð & his Sons* 24 The King.. sent a man out to observe the weather, and there was not a patch of clear sky to be seen. The King then asked Sigurd to determine how far the sun had travelled. He gave a precise answer. So the King had the sun-stone held aloft, and observed where it cast out a beam; the altitude it showed was exactly as Sigurd had said. **1968** *Carnegie Mag.* May 152/1 In overcast weather, a 'sunstone' determined the position of the sun. **1970** B. E. GELSINGER in *Mariner's Mirror* LVI. 222 Thorkild Ramskou.. suggested that the sunstone was a crystal such as Iceland spar which polarized light... The sunstone could thus indicate the position of the sun even though the sky was completely overcast. This description.. harmonizes with non-Icelandic references to the sunstone... Pliny the Elder.. described the sunstone or *solis gemma* as a white stone which casts rays of the sun. **1980** M. MAGNUSSON *Vikings!* vii. 191 Unfortunately, today's scholars do not rate the so-called sun-stone as a Viking Age navigational aid..; nothing is sacrosanct in the severe world of scholarship.

'sun-,stricken, *ppl. a.* [f. SUN *sb.*[1] + STRICKEN, after next.] Affected injuriously by the rays or heat of the sun; *spec.* affected with sunstroke. (Often const. as *pa. pple.*)

1844 SIR W. NAPIER *Conq. Scinde* II. vii. (1845) 436 The General.. was suddenly sun-stricken, and.. thirty-three European soldiers fell.. beneath the same malignant ray. **1864** TENNYSON *En. Ard.* 566 Enoch's comrade.. fell Sun-stricken. **1888** DOUGHTY *Trav. Arabia Deserta* II. 180 The heart slenderly nourished, under that sun-stricken climate. **1907** J. H. PATTERSON *Man-Eaters of Tsavo* i. 16 This.. wilderness of whitish and leafless dwarf trees, presented a ghastly and sun-stricken appearance.

'sunstroke. [For the earlier 'stroke of the sun', transl. F. *coup de soleil*. Cf. G. *sonnenstich*.] Collapse or prostration, with or without fever, caused by exposure to excessive heat of the sun.

Also loosely extended to similar effects of heat from other sources, as ***electric sunstroke***: see quot. 1890.

[**1807** J. JOHNSON *Oriental Voy.* 14 Several of the people got sick, with.. what are called 'Coups de Soleil', or strokes of the Sun. **1823** *Gentl. Mag.* XCIII. II. 647/2 He instantly expressed a feeling of having received what is called 'a stroke of the sun'.]

1851 G. W. CURTIS *Nile Notes* xxxvii. 188 Warding off sun-strokes with huge heavy umbrellas of two thicknesses of blue cotton. **1865** DICKENS *Let. to E. Yates* 30 Sept., I got a slight sunstroke last Thursday. **1875** H. C. WOOD *Therap.* (1879) 653 The terrible mortality of sunstroke. **1890** GOULD *New Med. Dict., Sunstroke, Electric*, an illogical term for the symptoms, somewhat similar to those of heat-stroke, produced by too close and unprotected proximity to the intense light emitted in welding metals by electricity.

'sunstruck, *pa. pple.* [f. SUN *sb.*[1] + STRUCK, after prec.] Affected with sunstroke.

1839 BAILEY *Festus* 135 Like a stag, sunstruck, top thy bounds and die. **1893** FORBES-MITCHELL *Remin. Gt. Mutiny* 76, I must go out and get my bonnet for fear I get sunstruck.

‖**sunt** (sʌnt). Also sont. [Arab. *sanṭ*.] A species of acacia, *Acacia nilotica*, of northern Africa, or its wood. Also *attrib.*

1820 BELZONI *Egypt & Nubia* III. 304 We were seated under a dry sunt tree, at a little distance from a small well. **1883** CONDER & KITCHENER *Survey W. Palestine* III. 139 A man who lit a single branch of sunt (acacia), cooked his food for three successive days by it. **1884** J. COLBORNE *Hicks Pasha* 100 Sunt trees grow in great profusion here. **1901** *Knowledge* June 138/2 The timber forming a raft is generally of the 'sont' tree.

'sun-tan, *sb.* (and *a.*). [f. SUN *sb.*[1] + TAN *sb.*[1]]

1. **a.** Tanning or browning of the skin caused by exposure to the sun, esp. that acquired by sun-bathing; the tan obtained by such exposure.

1904 *Westm. Gaz.* 28 Dec. 2/1 It was plain where the brown of sun-tan shaded into the clothes-covered white. **1958** M. K. JOSEPH *I'll soldier no More* xiii. 237 They're just out for a bit of suntan. **1980** *West Lancs. Evening Gaz.* 11 Aug. 10 (Advt.), A guaranteed suntan without sunburn.

b. In *Comb.* designating cosmetics which provide protection against sunburn and promote suntanning, as ***sun-tan lotion, oil***, etc.

1934 *Beautycraft* July 19/1 To acquire a brown, healthy skin.. it must be anointed plentifully with one of the good Sun-tan oils now on the market. **1938** E. AMBLER *Cause for Alarm* vi. 90 The points of his dress collar.. were.. smeared with grease and sun-tan powder. **1951** KOESTLER *Age of Longing* ii. 36 She felt herself go slightly pale under the sun-tan make-up. **1962** 'E. MCBAIN' *Like Love* ix. 132 Contents medicine cabinet.. one tube suntan lotion, one bottle Seconal, one toothbrush. **1976** P. PARISH *Medicines* II. xli. 242 The effectiveness of suntan applications is.. related to their ability to cut out the burning effects of the sun's rays.

2. *pl.* **a.** Lightweight, tan-coloured summer uniform worn by military personnel. **b.** Trousers forming part of this uniform or similar slacks for casual wear. *U.S.*

1937 *Amer. Speech* XII. 75/1 *Suntans*, summer uniform, made of lightweight material with sheen. **1945** E. NEWHOME in *New Yorker* 10 Feb. 22/1 He had removed only his tie and was lying.. in his suntans. **1947** J. BERTRAM *Shadow of War* VIII. v. 279 We stared at the Commodore's drab suntans. **1958** 'E. DUNDY' *Dud Avocado* I. i. 7 The Left Bank uniform of the day, dark wool shirt and a pair of old Army suntans. **1960** J. UPDIKE *Rabbit, Run* 98 He takes clean Jockey pants, T-shirts,.. a pair of laundered suntans.. and a sports shirt from the closet. **1966** *Times* 28 Mar. (Austral. Suppl.) p. viii/4 The streets are full of people in shorts and suntans. **1972** W. MCGIVERN *Caprifoil* (1973) xiii. 217 Admiral Burkholder.. wore suntans, and the collar of his shirt was open.

3. A light-brown fashion colour. Also as *adj.*

1937 [see MIST *sb.*[1] 1 e]. **1976** *Horse & Hound* 3 Dec. 17 (Advt.), Deep pile Borg washable numnah, foam filled. Pony or F.S. general purpose. Cream or suntan.

Hence as *v. trans.* and *intr.*, to expose (oneself) to the sun in order to acquire a tan; **'sun-tanned** *ppl. a.*; **'sun-tanning** *vbl. sb.* and *ppl. a.*

1821 CLARE *Vill. Minstr.* (1823) I. 39 To meet the sun-tann'd lass he dearly loves. **1876** 'MARK TWAIN' *Tom Sawyer* xviii. 185 That swarthy, suntanned skin of his. **1932** *Sun* (Baltimore) 5 Sept. 6/2 The millions busy today suntanning themselves, picnicking in the country. **1938** W. DE LA MARE *Memory* 16 The suntanned soldiers. **1959** *Chambers's Encycl.* III. 762/2 Genetically or environmentally induced melanization (sun-tanning) of the skin may serve a useful function in screening out injurious short-waved fractions of the sunlight from the sensitive underlying tissues. **1961** *Times* 29 Nov. 13/6 Just the right amount of suntanning. **1976** B. SHELBY *Great Pebble Affair* 117 Donnely and I were suntanning on the roof. **1977** N. FAULKS *No Mitigating Circumstances* vii. 99, I had a little lawn tennis at Monfalcone as well as at Trieste, and had an idle, suntanning time.

Suntory (sʌn'tɔːrɪ). Also **Suntori**. The proprietary name of a Japanese whisky.

1959 R. KIRKBRIDE *Tamiko* ii. 11 Here he was.. without even a drink in his hand. 'A double Suntory,' he said to the baaten. **1960** *Trade Marks Jrnl.* 21 Dec. 1659/2 Suntory 809,445. All goods included in Class 33 [*sc.* alcoholic beverages]. Kabushiki Kaisha Kotobukiya (a Corporation duly organised and existing under the laws of Japan).. Osaka, Japan; Manufacturers.—15th Aug. 1960. **1967** 'J. H. ROBERTS' *February Plan* I. i. 17 He.. remembered enough of his long unused Japanese to order a bottle of Suntori. **1975** R. L. DUNCAN *Dragons at Gate* (1976) iii. 99, I have ordered Kobe steaks... I have also requested a bottle of Suntory.

sunuol, -uolliche, obs. ff. SINFUL, -FULLY.

sun-up, sunup ('sʌnʌp). *local U.S.* (chiefly *Midland*), *Caribbean*, and formerly (perh. rendering Afrikaans *sonop*) *S. Afr.* [f. SUN *sb.*[1] + UP *adv.*, after SUNDOWN.] Sunrise. Freq. in phr. ***from sun-up to sun-down***.

1712 T. BANISTER *Let.* 12 Nov. in *Coll. Connecticut Hist. Soc.* (1924) XXI. 377 Wee Set out by or before Sun up, for Wyndham. **1826** J. F. COOPER *Last of Mohicans* I. iv. 69 One would think such a horse as that might get over a good deal of ground atwixt sun-up and sun-down. **1847** LONGFELLOW in *Life* (1891) II. 83 In a letter from Tampico to the N.C. Fayetteville Observer (is the writer a Carolinian?), I find the Anglo-Saxon expression *sun-up*, for sunrise. 'By sun-up, Patterson's regiment had left the encampment.' **1873** J. MILLER *Life among Modocs* viii. 90 Why we should.. toil like gnomes from sun-up to sun-down.. was to them more than a mystery—it was a terror. **1887** RIDER HAGGARD *Jess* xxxii. 305 Will you consent to marry me to-morrow morning at sun up, or am I to be forced to carry the sentence on your old uncle into effect? **1896** *Peterson Mag.* (N.S.) VI. 265/2 On foot from sunup to sundown. **1899** G. H. RUSSELL *Under Sjambok* x. 105 It is a Boer custom to call and drink coffee just after sun-up. **1903** K. D. WIGGIN *Rebecca of Sunnybrook Farm* x. 102, I could teach school from sun-up to sun-down if scholars was all like Rebecca Randall. **1920** [see KLOMP]. **1949** *Caribbean Q.* I. III. 45 Your face turned to sun-up. *a* **1963** S. PLATH *Crossing Water* (1971) 47 The blue hour before sunup. **1965** 'LAUCHMONEN' *Old Thom's Harvest* viii. 99 Another hour and it was sun-up. **1976** A. HALEY *Roots* (1977) cxiii. 646 Twenty-eight wagons were packed and ready to roll on the following sunup.

sunward ('sʌnwəd), *adv.* and *a.* Also 8 *Sc.* sinwart. [f. SUN *sb.*[1] + -WARD.] **A.** *adv.* Orig. †***to the sun-ward*** (in quot. 1611 = on the sunny side): toward the sun; in the direction of the sun.

1611 COTGR., *Avant-pesche*, th' Auant-peach,.. russet on one side, and red to the Sunne-ward. *a* **1711** KEN *Psyche* Poet. Wks. 1721 IV. 252 The Saint, embarking on the Cloud, it rose.. Then faster than it rose, it sunward dropp'd. **1786** BURNS *To Mountain Daisy* v, Thy snawie bosom sun-ward spread. **1788** PICKEN *Poems* 125 A skepp o' Bees,.. Wadg't in atween twa willow trees, An' airtan to the sinwart. **1847** LONGF. *By Fireside, Tegnér's Drapa* i, The mournful cry Of sunward sailing cranes. **1860** TYNDALL *Glac.* I. xi. 82 Clouds.. with their faces turned sunward, shone [etc.].

B. *adj.* Directed toward the sun; moving or facing in the direction of the sun.

1769 FALCONER *Shipwr.* III. 22 As they view His sunward flight. **1795** CAMPBELL *Caroline* II. vi, Shine on her chosen green resort Whose trees the sunward summit crown. **1853** G. JOHNSTON *Nat. Hist. E. Bord.* I. 74 On sunward banks. **1887** SWINBURNE *Locrine* IV. ii. 263 Mightier than the sunward eagle's wing. **1892** BLACK *Wolfenberg* I. 165 Pomegranates.. taking a tinge of crimson on their sunward side.

sunwards ('sʌnwədz), *adv.* [f. SUN *sb.*[1] + -WARDS.]

†**1.** ***from the sunwards***, away from the sun.

1574 W. BOURNE *Regim. Sea* viii. (1577) 31 On the contrary side from the Sunnewardes. **1669** WORLIDGE *Syst. Agric.* (1681) 189 And leave such always down during the Summer that are from the Sun-wards.

2. Towards the sun: = prec. A.

1851 H. MELVILLE *Moby Dick* III. xxx. 189 Here, too, life dies sunwards, full of faith. **1858** CHRISTINA ROSSETTI *From House to Home* l, Each loving face bent Sunwards like a moon. **1873** PROCTOR *Expanse of Heaven* xvii. 189

Supposing such meteoric masses to have travelled sunwards from very great distances.

sunway ('sʌnweɪ), *adv. rare.* [f. SUN *sb.*[1] + -WAY.] = next.

1825 J. NICHOLSON *Oper. Mech.* 143 The running mill-stone is supposed to turn 'sunway,' or as in what is called a right-handed mill. **1852** BURN *Naval & Milit. Dict.*, Sunway, *de gauche à droite.*

sunways ('sʌnweɪz), *adv.* [f. SUN *sb.*[1] + -WAYS; cf. SUNGATES.] In the direction of the apparent daily movement of the sun, i.e. (in the northern hemisphere) from left to right; 'with the sun'.

1774 SHAW in Pennant *Tour Scotl. in 1769* App. ii. 291 At marriages and baptisms they make a procession around the church, *Deasoil*, i.e. sunways. **1828** SCOTT *F.M. Perth* xxvii. *note*, The deasil must be performed sunways, that is, by moving from right to left [*sic*].

sunwise ('sʌnwaɪz), *adv.* (*a.*) [f. SUN *sb.*[1] + -WISE.]

1. = prec.

1865 McLAUCHLAN *Early Scott. Ch.* iv. 33 Everything that is to move prosperously among many of the Celts, must move sunwise. **1885** *Cornh. Mag.* Mar. 271 The brethren made a processional turn round the temple, sunwise.

b. as *adj.*

1881 C. F. GORDON-CUMMING in *Scribner's Mag.* XXII. 738 The old custom of carrying fire in sunwise procession around any given object. **1884** —— in *Macm. Mag.* Feb. 307/2 Pilgrims..walk round the holy city in sun-wise circuit.

2. In the manner of the sun; with brightness like that of the sun. *rare*⁻¹.

1897 F. THOMPSON *Any Saint* xxxix, When He bends down, sun-wise, Intemperable eyes.

sunyasee, -i, variants of SANNYASI.

‖**sunyata** (suː'njataː, ʃ-). *Buddhism.* Also çûnyatâ. [Skr. *śūnyátā* emptiness, non-existence, f. *śūnyá* empty, void.] The concept of the essential emptiness of all things and of ultimate reality as a void beyond worldly phenomena.

1907 D. T. SUZUKI *Outl. Mahâyâna Buddhism* vii. 173 The emptiness of things (*çûnyatâ*) does not mean nothingness..but..conditionality or transitoriness of all phenomenal existences. **1916** A. COOMARASWAMY *Buddha & Gospel of Buddhism* v. 318 The *Prajñāpāramitās* are filled with..texts upon the Emptiness (*Sunyata*) of things. **1938** B. L. SUZUKI *Mahayana Buddhism* i. 15 Sunyata is what is left behind after an endless series of negations, and is therefore the most positive and fundamental of ideas. **1951** E. CONZE *Buddhism* v. 130 We must now make an effort to understand this all-important idea of Emptiness... What we call *emptiness* in English is *sūnyatā* in sanskrit. **1978** C. HUMPHREYS *Both Sides Circle* v. 57 What I call the mystical metaphysics of the *Madhyamika* (Middle Way) School, founded by Nagarjuna and expanded through several centuries into the ultimate concept of *sunyata*, 'no-thing-ness'.

‖**Sun Yat-sen** (sʌn jæt sɛn). Also **Sun Yatsen**. The Cantonese form of the personal name Sun I-xian, adopted by Sun Wen (1866–1925), founder in 1911 of the Republic of China, used *attrib.* to designate a modern style of clothing in China.

1946 O. LANG *Chinese Family & Society* ix. 77 Those who wear long Chinese gowns are usually old-fashioned men... Modern-minded officials wear black coats with high collars, the so-called 'Sun Yat-sen jackets', and tight trousers tucked into black or khaki puttees—a Western garment common in China. **1965** 'HAN SUYIN' *Crippled Tree* I. xvi. 222 Most of us had come to wear the Japanese students' uniform, which later was termed the Sun Yatsen suit, and is now spoken of as the Communist garb. **1977** 'S. LEYS' *Chinese Shadows* (1978) ii. 75 Impeccably cut Sun Yat-sen jackets. (*Note*) Chung-shan chuang, which a silly vogue in the West persists in calling a 'Mao jacket'—as if the present regime had invented it.

Sun Yat-senism (sʌnjæt'sɛnɪz(ə)m). Also as one word. [f. prec. + -ISM.] The political principles of Sun Yat-sen, which included Chinese nationalism, democracy, and the people's livelihood (the 'three principles of the people').

1927 *Observer* 17 July 20/2 The understanding between Chiang Kai-shek and Feng Yu-hsiang is precariously maintained by intermediaries, not by Sun Yat-senism. **1931** tr. *P. M. D'Elia's Triple Demism of Sun Yat-Sen* 41 Some authors have not hesitated to believe that they could make a certain distinction between 'Sunyatsenism' and 'Sunwenism'. **1957** CHIANG KAI-SHEK *Soviet Russia in China* I. i. 36 Officers and cadets at the Academy..formed a rival group named Society for the Study of Sun Yat-senism. **1979** *World Today* June 244 During his long career, Ho Chi Minh made a point of reassuring both Chiang Kai-shek and Mao Tse-tung that he was dedicated, first, to Sun Yat-senism and, later, to Marxism-Leninism-Mao Tse-tung thought.

suoddringe: see SWODDER.

suowe, obs. form of SOUGH *sb.*[1], rushing sound.

1338 R. BRUNNE *Chron.* (1810) 170 Þe kynges owen Galeie ..com þe schip fulle nere. Oþer were þer inowe, þat þer after drouh, Bot he com with a suowe, þat þe schip to rof.

sup (sʌp), *sb.*[1] Forms: α. 6– sup, 6–7 suppe, 7 supp. β. 7 soope, 7–8 (9 *dial.*) soop, soup, (8 *Sc.* soupe, 9 *dial.* sowp, zoop). [f. SUP *v.*[1]

There is no evidence of continuity with OE. *sūpa* (cf. MLG. *sûpe*, early mod.Du. *zuipe*, Du. *zuip*, ON. *súpc*).

The isolated instance of sense 2, unless it be a misprint, is difficult to account for.]

1. A small quantity of liquid such as can be taken into the mouth at one time; a mouthful; a sip. (Also in fig. context.)

α. **1570** LEVINS *Manip.* 189/37 A Suppe, *sorbillum.* **1621** FLETCHER *Pilgrim* IV. i, I'le bring you a sup of Milk shall serve ye. **1657** J. WATTS *Scribe, Pharisee*, etc. III. 71 A sup of wine (as a morsel of bread) may do well enough. **1710** *Brit. Apollo* III. No. 47. 3/1 To see his Brave Army Engage; And to Swallow up, The Allies at a sup. **1719** DE FOE *Crusoe* I. (Globe) 82, I went to my little Store and took a small Sup of Rum. *a* **1764** LLOYD *Fam. Ep. to J. B.* Poet. Wks. 1774 II. 40 With so much wisdom bottled up, Uncork, and give your friends a sup. **1840** THACKERAY *Paris Sk. bk.* v. (1872) 49 Taking a small sup at the brandy-bottle. **1872** CALVERLEY *Fly Leaves, On the Brink* ix, A sup Of barley-water. **1888** W. S. GILBERT *Yeom. Guard* I, Who sipped no sup, and who craved no crumb.

β. **1633** *Orkney Witch Trial* in *Abbotsford Club Miscell.* 152 The powre woman sent in to the said Robertis hous, and got ane soup off milk from his wyff. **1662** TUKE *Adv.* 5 *Hours* I. 10 A soop of Chocolate Is not amiss after a tedious Journey. **1667** DRYDEN *Tempest* II. i, Here's another soop to comfort us. **1719** D'URFEY *Pills* (1872) III. 7 I'll take a full Soop at the merry Milk-pail. **1785** BURNS *Cotter's Sat. Nt.* xi, The soupe their only Hawkie does afford. **1818** SCOTT *Rob Roy* xviii, It's the part o' a kind son to bring her a soup o' something that will keep up her auld heart. **1851** STERNBERG *Northampt. Dial.*, *Soop*, a sup, drop.

b. Phr. (*a*) *bit* (later *bite*) *and* (*a*) *sup*, a little food and drink. So *bit or sup, neither bit nor sup.*

1665 in *Verney Mem.* (1904) II. 244, I save [? have] a bitt and supp bye myselfe 2 owers after them. **1818** LADY MORGAN *Autobiog.* (1859) 148 The moment..we had swallowed our 'bit and our sup,' out we sallied. **1865** G. MACDONALD *Alec Forbes* 15 I ll tak her in wi' my ain bairns, an' she s' hae bit and sup wi' them. **1880** BROWNING *Dram. Idyls* Ser. II. *Pietro* 233 Lodging, bite and sup, with—now and then—a copper..is all my asking. **1902** VIOLET JACOB *Sheep-Stealers* ix, The pleasant offer of a bite and a sup.

c. *transf.* Drink. *dial.*

a **1810** TANNAHILL *Poor Tom* Poems (1846) 109 Poor Tom loves his sup, and poor Tom is despised. **1876** *Whitby Gloss.*, *Sup, Suppings, Sups*, drink of all kinds.

d. *a good sup*: a fair amount, a considerable quantity (of liquid). *dial.*

1601 *Archpriest Controv.* (Camden) II. 173 If a cow give a good soope of milke, she is to be thanked. **1848** A. BRONTË *Agnes Grey* i, [Of a fall of rain] It's comed a good sup last night too. **1872** HARTLEY *Yorksh. Ditties* Ser. I. 97 They reckon to brew a gooid sup o' ale in October.

†**2.** = SOP *sb.*[1] I. *Obs. rare.*

1543 TRAHERON *Vigo's Chirurg.* II. viii. vi. 82 He muste.. eate a sup or shewe made with grated breed & almandes [orig. *panatellam fariolam amigdalatam*...*confectam*].

sup (sʌp), *sb.*[2] *Math.* [f. SUP(REMUM.] Supremum (of).

1940, 1949 [see INFIMUM]. **1968** E. T. COPSON *Metric Spaces* i. 14 The supremum or least upper bound of *A*..is denoted by sup *A*.

sup (sʌp), *v.*[1] Forms: α. 1 supan, 4–5 supe, 4–6 sowp(e, 4–7 soup(e, (4 soupen, 5 sowpon(e, 6 sope, 6–7 soope, 7–8, 9 (*dial.*) soop, 9 *dial.* soup, zoop). β. 1 *Northumb.* suppa, 4–7 suppe, (5 souppe, 6 soppe, 8 supp), 5– sup. *Pa. t. strong* 1 seap (sæp), 4 sop, 4–5 scop; *weak* 1 *Northumb.* -supede, 4 soupede, -ide, sowpide, 6 suppit, supt(e, 6– supped. *Pa. pple. strong* 4 soopen, soupen, 4–5 sopen, -un; *weak* 4 sowpyd, 5 suppyd, 6 suppit, supte, 7 supt, soopt, soop'd, 6– supped. [Three types of formation on the Teutonic root *sūp-* (cf. SOP *sb.*[1], *v.*[1], SOPE, SOWP *sb.*[1]) are represented here: (1) OE. *súpan* str. vb., pa. t. *séap* (**supon*), pa. pple. **sopen* = MLG. *sûpen*, MDu. *zûpen* (Du. *zuipen*), OHG. *sûfan* (MHG. *sûfen*, G. *saufen*, in dial. strong and weak), ON. *súpa*; (2) OE. **suppan*, once in Northumb. pres. ind. pl. *suppas*, corresp. to OHG. *suphjan, supphan, suffan* (MHG., G. dial. *supfen*); (3) OE. **súpian*, once in Northumb. weak pa. t. pl. *ȝesupedon.*

The forms with *pp* in ME. appear first in northern texts.]

1. a. *trans.* To take (liquid) into the mouth in small quantities (as opposed to a draught); †also with *in*. Now chiefly *Sc.* and *north. dial.*; often *spec.* to take (liquid food) with a spoon.

α. *c* **1000** ÆLFRIC *Saints' Lives* iii. 162 He sæp [*v.r.* seap] of ðæm calice eac swylce blod. *c* **1000** *Sax. Leechd.* II. 184 Se þeah þu mid cuclere þæt supe. *Ibid.* 336 Ʒif he þæt broð þonne ær sypð. *a* **1327** *Poem times Edw. II* 238 in *Pol. Songs* (Camden) 334 The best he piketh up himself,...And ȝeveth the gode man soupe the lene broth. *c* **1340** *Nominale* (Skeat) 190 W[oman] mylk and wortis soupith. *c* **1400** MAUNDEV. (Roxb.) xiv. 62 Þai ete bot flesch withouten breed and soupez þe broo. **1470–85** MALORY *Arthur* VII. v. 219 Thou woldest not for alle the brothe that euer thou soupest ones loke hym in the face. **1530** PALSGR. 726/2, I have herde saye that he was dede, but he wyll sowpe as hoote potage as you. **1590** BARROUGH *Meth. Phisick* II. iii. (1639) 105 It is also good for them to soupe the juice of Quinces. **1640** BROME *Sparagus Gard.* II. iii, A Phesants egge soopt with a Peacocks feather. **1643** TRAPP *Comm. Gen.* xxv. 33 As Gideons souldiers, to soop their handful, not to swill their belly-full. **1721** BAILEY, *To Sip*, to soop a little.

β. **13..** *E.E. Allit. P.* B. 108 Þyse ilk renkez..Schul neuer sitte in my sale my soper to fele, Ne suppe on sope of my seve. *a* **1400–50** *Wars Alex.* 3805 Þis solayne sope [= SOPE *sb.*] if I sup. *c* **1450** *Bk. Curtasye* 69 in *Babees Bk.*, Ne suppe not with grete sowndynge Noþer potage ne oþer þynge. **1587** TURBERV. *Trag. Tales* (1837) 143 Who..The poyson supt, and tooke it patientlie. **1615** BRATHWAIT *Strappado* (1878) 193 Which of all these..Could get one bit to eat, or drop suppe? *a* **1682** F. SEMPILL *Blythesome Wedding* 65 And sing'd sheep-heads, and a haggize, And scadlips to sup till ye're fow. **1692** TRYON *Good House-wife* i. 5 You must take nourishing Meats and Drinks, sup good Sack, Old Malago, Tent, or the like. ? **1787** BURNS *Gudeen to you, Kimmer* ii, Kate sits i' the neuk, Suppin' hen-broo. **1818** MISS FERRIER *Marriage* xxvii, Girls that sup their porridge will always cut a good figure. **1841** THACKERAY *Gt. Hoggarty Diam.* xiii, After dinner, it was with difficulty I could get her to sup a little drop of wine-and-water, and dip a toast in it. **1872** HARTLEY *Yorksh. Ditties* Ser. II. 107 Sellin' drink has made mony a chap rich, an suppin it has made thaasands poor. **1889** BARRIE *Window in Thrums* 114 He began to sup his porridge.

b. To drink *up* or *off*, swallow, esp. by mouthfuls or spoonfuls. †Also with *out, in.*

1375 *Creation* 473 in Horstm. *Altengl. Leg.* (1878) 130 Me poȝte Kaym tok Abellis blod And sop it op as he were wod. *c* **1440** *Alphabet of Tales* 463 A white duffe..suppid of all þat was in þe chales with hur neb. *c* **1450** *Mankind* 765 in *Macro Plays* 28 My prepotent father, when ȝe sowpe, sowpe owt yowur messe. *a* **1529** SKELTON *E. Rumming* 380 Ales founde therin no thornes, But supped it [*sc.* ale] vp at ones. **1535** COVERDALE *Isa.* v. 22 Wo vnto them, yᵗ are connynge men to suppe out wyne. **1597** A. M. tr. *Guillemeau's Fr. Chirurg.* 28/1 We must first let him suppe in a soft dressed egge. **1600** J. PORY tr. *Leo's Africa* III. 142 Then will he sup off a cup of cold water as big as a milke-bowle. **1620** VENNER *Via Recta* v. 84 A couple of potched Egges,..supped off warme, eating therewithall a little bread and butter. **1747** WESLEY *Prim. Physick* (1762) 53 Sup it up in the morning fasting. **1870** MRS. JULIE P. SMITH *Widow Goldsmith's Dau.* iii, The contents dealt out into the cracked bowl and tin cup, were immediately distributed; they eagerly supped it up. **1885** 'OUIDA' *Rainy June* 133 To rattle down the Bois in a *milord*, and sup off a *matelote* by the lake with your Romeo.

2. *intr.* To take a sip or sips: to take drink by mouthfuls or spoonfuls; †formerly with partitive *of*. Also const. *up*. Now chiefly *Sc.* and *north. dial.* (or in imitation of this).

c **950** *Lindisf. Gosp.* Matt. xxvii. 34 *Cum gustasset*, mið ðy ȝebirigde *vel* ȝeseap. *c* **1000** *Sax. Leechd.* II. 50 Sup swa ðu hatost mæge. **13..** *Coer de L.* 3085 Lord, we have pork sought; Etes, and soupes off the browys swote. *c* **1325** *Gloss. W. de Bibbesw.* in Wright *Voc.* 150 *Avaunt ke il hume* [*gloss* soupe]. **1377** LANGL. *P. Pl.* B. II. 96 In fastyng-dayes to frete ar ful tyme were And þanne to sitten and soupen til slepe hem assaille. *c* **1475** *Babees Bk.* 144 Whenne your potage to yow shalle be brouhte, Take yow sponys, and soupe by no way. *c* **1500** *Young Childr. Bk.* 127 in *Babees Bk.*, When þou sopys, make no noyse With thi mouth As do boys. **1542** BRINKLOW *Lament.* (1874) 89 We soppe of the broth in which the deuell was soden. **1590** SPENSER *F.Q.* I. iv. 22 A bouzing can, Of which he supt so oft, that on his seat His dronken corse he scarse vpholden can. **1616** B. JONSON *Forest* ix. 7 Might I of Ioue's nectar sup. **1701** GREW *Cosm. Sacra* I. v. §6. 26 Nor therefore could we Supp, or Swallow, without it [*sc.* the tongue]. **1869** *Lonsdale Gloss.*, *Sup up*, to drink off a glass of liquor. **1898** J. MACMANUS *Bend of Road* 94 There wasn't a man ever supped from a noggin in Corradooey he couldn't sweep the floor with! **1952** M. TRIPP *Faith is Windsock* v. 86 Now sup up, as Arthur [a north-countryman] says, and have one on me. **1971** D. LEES *Rainbow Conspiracy* ix. 152 Sup up first—tha's let the beer get cold. **1977** SCOLLINS & TITFORD *Ey up, mi Duck!* III. 30 Men were content just to gossip and 'sup'.

transf. **13..** *E.E. Allit. P.* C. 151 Þe sayl sweyed on þe see, þenne suppe bihoued þe coge of þe colde water.

†**3.** *transf.* and *fig.* **a.** *trans.* Chiefly with *up*: To swallow *up*, consume, absorb. *Obs.*

Frequent as a rendering of L. *absorbere* in biblical versions.

c **897** ÆLFRED *Gregory's Past. C.* lviii. 447 Forðonðe he.. nis nauðer, ne hat, ne ceald, ðeah ic hine supe, ic hine wille eft utaspiwan of minum muðe. *c* **1000** *Ags. Ps.* (Th.) lxviii. 15 Ne me se seað supe mid muðe. *a* **1340** HAMPOLE *Psalter* lxviii. 19 Drown me not þe storme of watire: ne supe me þe grounde. **1382** WYCLIF *Isa.* xxviii. 7 Thei ben sopen awei of wyn, thei erreden in drunkenesse. —— *1 Cor.* xv. 54 Deeth is sopun vp in victorie. —— *Rev.* xii. 16 The erthe openyde his mouth, and soupide [*v.r.* sop vp, soop vp] the flood. *c* **1400** *Psalter* (MS. Bodl. 554) iii. 5 *marg.*, As sopun up for sorewe. **1532** MORE *Confut. Tindale* Wks. 713/1 As for al other sinnes whatsoeuer thei be, faith saith he..suppeth them al vp in a moment. **1566** DRANT *Wail. Hierim.* K iv, The battred wall, prostrate dyd fall,..The earthe supte up the gorgious gates. **1598** BASTARD *Chrestol.* I. xl. 25 Foure lines, which hold me tug an hower or twaine He sups up with a breath and takes no paine. **1621** BURTON *Anat. Mel.* II. ii. III. 319 [A lake] whose waters gush so fast out of the ground, that they will overtake a swift horseman, and by and by with as incredible celerity [are] supped vp. **1652** CULVERWEL *Lt. Nature* I. xvii. (1661) 158 A Ship ready to be split upon a rock, or to be soop'd up of a Wave.

†**b.** Of material objects: To take *in* (water, air). Also *sup out* in the opposite sense. *Obs.*

1513 DOUGLAS *Æneis* VI. vi. 64 The jonit barge, Sa full of riftis, and with lekkis perbraik, Scho suppit huge wattir of the laik. **1566** DRANT *Horace, Sat.* I. iv. B viij, As bellowes sup and beltch out wyndes, to make the yron softe. **1567** GOLDING *Ovid's Met.* VII. (1593) 153 And how Charybdis.. Now sowpeth in, now sowpeth out the sea incessantly. **1644** NYE *Gunnery* II. (1670) 33 Such a peece [of ordnance].. which suppeth and reteineth continually more and more of that wind, which should serve to expell the bullet.

†**c.** *to sup up*: (*a*) to take in, 'swallow' (a story); (*b*) to utter indistinctly, also to retract (one's words). *Obs.*

1579 TOMSON *Calvin's Serm. Tim.*, etc. 518/1 We see that euery man is but too light of credit to sup vp that that shalbee spoken, if there be once any euill report of the

Ministers of Gods worde. **1581** PETTIE tr. *Guazzo's Civ. Conv.* II. (1586) 58 b, We must speak freelie without supping vp our wordes, and bringing them but half forth. **1597** HOOKER *Eccl. Pol.* v. lxii. §14 When.. they haue put vs in hope of agreement, wherefore sup they vp their wordes againe? **1611** COTGR., *Humer le parole*, foolishly to sup, or sucke vp, his owne words; to speake abruptly, or vndistinctly.

†**d.** *absol.* or *intr.* of waters, etc. *Obs.*

In 1382 and 1611 a literalism of translation.

1382 WYCLIF *Isa.* xlii. 14, I shal scateren, and soupen awei togidere. **1513** DOUGLAS *Æneis* III. vi. 128 The large fludis suppis thrise in ane swelth, And wther quhilis spowtis in the air agane. **1611** *Bible* Hab. i. 9 Their faces shall sup vp as the East winde, and they shall gather the captiuitie as the sand.

4. *fig.* To have experience of; to taste; esp. ***to sup sorrow***: cf. L. *haurire dolorem* (Cicero).

c **950** *Lindisf. Gosp.* Matt. xvi. 28 *Qui non gustabunt mortem*, ða ðe ne suppas deað. *Ibid.* Mark, Introd. 4/3 *Gustaturos quosdam mortem*, hia þet gebirigdon *vel* ȝesupedon weron sume oðer þone deað. *c* **1395** *Plowman's Tale* 1096 Holy churche shuld stand full cold, Hir servaunts sitte and soupe sorowe. **1560** A. L. tr. *Calvin's Foure Serm. Songe Ezech.* i, I do nothing but sup up the drink of sorrow. **1599** PEELE *Sir Clyom.* Wks. 1839 III. 123 To sup his dire destruction there for wretched love of me. **1731–8** SWIFT *Pol. Conversat.* 57 I'll make you one Day sup Sorrow for this. **1839** W. CARLETON *Fardorougha* xvi, You'd make him sup sorrow for his harshness. **1901** C. G. HARPER *Gt. North Road* II. 294 Petty delinquents supped sorrow at their hands with a big spoon.

sup (sʌp), *v.*[2] Forms: *α.* 3–6 **soupe**, 4–5 **sope**, 4–6 **sowpe**, (3, 6 *Sc.* **supe**, 4 **soupi**, **sopi**, **souppe**, **sowpy**, **sowppe**, 5 **soope**, **sopye**, 6 *Sc.* **soup**, **sowp**). *β.* 5–7 **suppe**, (5 **suppon**, 6 **soppe**), 6– **sup**. [a. OF. *soper*, *super*, (also mod.F.) *souper* = Pr. *sopar*, of obscure origin.]

1. *intr.* To eat one's supper; to take supper.

α. *c* **1290** *Beket* 697 in *S. Eng. Leg.* I. 126 Heo setten bord and spradden cloth, and bi-gonne to soupe [*other vers.* sopi] faste. *c* **1300** *Havelok* 1765–6 He.. dide greyþe a super riche, ..þat he mithe supe swiþe wel. Also he seten, and sholde soupe, So comes a ladde in a ioupe. **13..** *Sir Beues* (A.) 3088 þat ilche kniȝt, þat sopede wiþ þe ȝerstene niȝt. **1390** GOWER *Conf.* II. 359 Whan thei hadden souped there, Thei schopen hem to gon to reste. **1470–85** MALORY *Arthur* IV. vi. 126 When they had souped at her leyser kyng Arthur was ledde vnto a chamber. **1500–20** DUNBAR *Poems* lxix. 45 How glaid that ever I dyne or sowp. ? **1579** MONTGOMERIE *Misc. Poems* xlviii. 67 My fortun wes to be Ludgit.. with this same companie; Soupit togither; in ane chalmer lay.

β. **14..** *Chaucer's Frankl. T.* 489 (Cambr. MS.) It is al redy thow ȝe wele rygh now. Go we thanne suppe [*v.r.* soupe]. *c* **1440** *Alphabet of Tales* 190 When he had suppid, þer lefte right noght ouer night vnto in þe mornyng. *c* **1440** *Promp. Parv.* 484/2 Suppon, *ceno*. **1538** STARKEY *England* (1878) 26 Hyt ys late and tyme to suppe. **1592** *Arden of Feversham* IV. iii. 13 If this weather would last.. a man should neuer dyne nor sup without candle light. **1620** VENNER *Via Recta* viii. 173 We commonly sup about six houres after we haue dined. **1697** DRYDEN *Virg. Georg.* III. 786 He never supt in solemn State. **1711** SWIFT *Lett.* (1767) III. 221, I.. supped with lord treasurer,.. I staid till two;.. I must sup with him, and he keeps cursed hours. **1777** H. WALPOLE *Let. to H. S. Conway* 10 July, I kept him to sup, sleep.. and breakfast here this morning. **1837** LOCKHART *Scott* I. ix. 286 The officers of the Light Horse.. established a club among themselves, supping once a-week at each other's houses in rotation. **1886** *Pall Mall Gaz.* 27 July 8/1 The Prince and Princess of Wales supped on the Lyceum stage with Mr. Irving and Miss Terry.

b. Const. *on*, *upon*, *off* (†*of*, *with*) the food.

? *a* **1400** *Morte Arth.* 1025 He sowppes.. with seuene knaue childre, Choppid in a chargour. **1535** STEWART *Cron. Scot.* (Rolls) III. 204 Of grene herbis rycht oft [he] did soupe and dyne. **1603** SHAKS. *Meas. for M.* IV. iii. 159, I am faine to dine and sup with water and bran. **1702** YALDEN *Fables* v. 23 He din'd and supp'd upon the best. **1829** SCOTT *Rob Roy* Introd. ad init., They.. took a wedder from the fold, killed it, and supped off the carcass. **1890** DOYLE *White Company* xxvii, They supped on good fare, and slept between lavender-scented sheets.

c. *trans.* To make a supper of; also with cognate object. *rare.*

? *a* **1400** *Morte Arth.* 1208 To sowpe withe þat soueraygne ffulle selcouthe metez. **1809** MALKIN *Gil Blas* VII. xi, After having supped the supper of the damned. **1851** MRS. BROWNING *Casa Guidi Wind.* I. 220 Before the eyes of men, awake at last, Who put away the meats they used to sup.

2. *fig.* (or in fig. context) and *allusively*.

† ***to sup with our Saviour, with Jesus Christ, to sup in heaven*** or ***hell*** (after *Rev.* iii. 20): said of persons who have died or are about to die. Cf. SUPPER *sb.*[1] 1 b.

In quot. 1605 *with* is to be construed with *supt* (cf. quot. 1603 in 1 b), but in modern echoes of the passage *of* is often substituted, and construed with *full*.

[**1382** WYCLIF *Rev.* iii. 20 If ony man shal here my voys, and opene the ȝat, I shal entre to him, and soupe with him. *c* **1386** CHAUCER *Pars. T.* ⁋ 216, I wol entre in-to hym by my grace, and soupe with hym by the goode werkes þat he shal doon, whiche werkes been the foode of god.] ? *a* **1400** *Morte Arth.* 3805 We salle.. Souppe with oure Saueoure solemply in heuene. *a* **1572** KNOX *Hist. Ref.* Wks. 1846 I. 170 My faith is such, that my saule sall sowp with my Saviour this nycht. **1593** SHAKS. *2 Hen. VI*, v. i. 214 You shall sup with Iesu Christ to night. **1605** —— *Macb.* v. v. 13, I haue supt full with horrors. **1607** —— *Cor.* IV. ii. 50 Angers my Meate: I suppe vpon my selfe. **1642** FULLER *Holy & Prof. St.* II. xxi. 137 Dining on Christ in the Sacrament, expecting no other then to sup with him in heaven. **1667** MILTON *P.L.* v. 426 The Sun.. at Even Sups with the Ocean. **1812** SHELLEY *Devil's Walk* x, They sup on the groans of the dying and dead. **1830** SCOTT *Demonol.* vii. 211 The reader may sup full on such wild horrors in the Causes Célèbres. **1873** BURTON *Hist. Scot.* VI. lxxiii. 352 People had supped full of horrors.

3. *trans.* **a.** *Falconry* and *Venery*. To give the last feed of the day to (a hawk, horse, or hound). Also with *up*.

1575 TURBERV. *Faulconrie* 133 Let hir flee but once, and suppe hir vp vpon the pray. *Ibid.* 215 At euening conuey it [*sc.* a casting] into hir gorge, after you haue supt hir. *Ibid.* 310 Supping hir euery night with a ratte or a mouse. **1596** SHAKS. *Tam. Shr.* Ind. i. 28 Huntsman I charge thee, tender wel my hounds... But sup them well, and looke vnto them all. **1622** MABBE tr. *Aleman's Guzman d'Alf.* I. 228 Is it fit.. To feede a horse with sand? To sup a Falcon with straw? **1798** *Trans. Soc. Arts* XVI. 152 At the time of supping the horses up, after they are bedded, give every horse a small armful. **1805** JAMES *Milit. Dict.* (ed. 2), To *sup up*, a term used in the British cavalry, to signify the last duty that is performed.., when the horses are allowed to rest for the night. **1810–** in *Eng. Dial. Dict.*

†**b.** Of food: To furnish a supper for. *Obs. rare.*

1588 SHAKS. *L.L.L.* v. ii. 698 If a haue no more mans blood in's belly, then will sup a Flea. **1653** WALTON *Angler* I. iv, Having caught more fish than will sup myself and my friend.

c. To give a supper to, entertain at supper.

1619 in *Crt. & Times Jas. I* (1848) II. 174 This day, I think, the Lorraine ambassador is supped. **1865** SALA in *Reader* No. 117. 337/1 They will breakfast you, they will sup you. **1907** *Daily Chron.* 20 July 3/2 They lunched her at the Carlton, dined her at the Trocadero, supped her at Prince's.

‖**supari** (suːˈpɑːriː). *East Indian.* Also 7–9 **suparee**, 9 **soopari**, **-ee**. [Hindī *supārī* betel nut.] The areca palm; also, the areca leaf which is chewed with the leaves of the betel palm. Also *attrib.*

1638 SIR T. HERBERT *Trav.* (ed. 2) 28 Sneezing-powder is not more frequent with the Irish, than chawing Arec, (by Arab and Indians call'd *Tauffet* and *Suparee*) is with these Savages. **1849** EASTWICK *Dry Leaves* 214 Is it meant that.. one would.. find.. a high degree of devotion in standing twelve years on one's head, imbedded in supári leaves? **1858** SIMMONDS *Dict. Trade*, Sooparee, Soopari. **1890** D. DAVIDSON *Mem. Long Life* iii. 43 The hamals.. regaling themselves.. by chewing their paun leaf and suparee.

supawn (sʌˈpɔːn). *U.S.* Also 8–9 **suppawn**, 9 **supon** (**supporne**), **sipawn**, **sepon**, **-awn**. [Natick *saupáun* softened, f. *saupáe*, *sabáe* it is softened: cf. Virginian *asapan* (Strachey, 1615), Abenaki *ntsa*ⁿ*ba*ⁿ*n* (Rasles), *nsobon* (Laurent), Narragansett *nasaump* (see SAMP). Cf. Du. *sapaen*, *supaen* (17th c.).] A kind of porridge made of maize flour boiled in water until it thickens. Also *attrib.*

1793 J. BARLOW *Hasty Pudding* (1815) 6 On Hudson's banks while men of Belgic spawn Insult and eat thee by the name Suppawn. *a* **1817** T. DWIGHT *Trav. New Eng.*, etc. (1823) IV. 93 The house contained neither bread nor flour, and we were obliged to sup upon sipawn. **1833** C. F. HOFFMAN *Winter Far West* xii. (1835) I. 141, I helped myself with an iron spoon from a dish of suppawn. **1836** [MRS. TRAILL] *Backw. Canada* 189 A substantial sort of porridge, called by the Americans 'Supporne'. **1868** B. J. LOSSING *Hudson* 122 He went to the church every night at eight o'clock.. to ring the 'suppawn-bell'. This was the signal for the inhabitants to eat their 'suppawn', or hasty-pudding, and prepare for bed.

supe (s(j)uːp). *slang.* Short for SUPER *sb.* Also as *v. intr.*, to act as a supernumerary in a theatre. Cf. SUPER *v.* 1.

1824 in *Spirit Publ. Jrnls.* (1825) 309 A youthful supernumerary compositor, or 'gentleman supe' in a printing establishment. **1885** J. K. JEROME *On the Stage* 59 The other set, the regular bob (sometimes eighteenpence) a-night 'sūps'. **1893** W. K. POST *Harvard Stories* 107 Do you remember the time.. that we saw the old man suping in that spectacular play? **1903** FARMER & HENLEY *Slang*, *Supe*,.. the superintendent of a station. **1915** J. B. RATHBUN *Motion Picture Making* 72 'Westerns' are invariably taken in their proper locale, the 'supes' usually being drawn from the ranches and towns surrounding the studio. **1977** [see SCOFF *v.*[1] 2 c].

†**supellectiˈcarious**, *a. Obs. rare*⁻⁰. [f. late L. *supellecticārius*: see next, -IC, and -ARIOUS.]

1656 BLOUNT *Glossogr.*, *Suppellecticarious*.., that pertains to houshold-stuff.

supellectile (s(j)uːpəˈlɛktaɪl, -tɪl), *a.* and *sb.* Now *rare* or *Obs.* Also 7–8 **supp-**; *erron.* **supellectual**. [ad. L. *supellectilis*, prob. f. *super*, SUPER- 1 + *lectus* couch: see -ILE.]

A. *adj.* Pertaining to or of the nature of household furniture; *transf.* ornamental.

1615 T. ADAMS *Black Devil* 4 Suppellectile Complements instead of substantial Graces. **1800** HURDIS *Fav. Village* 86 To see their supellectile treasures float In playful dance around. **1843** *Blackw. Mag.* LIV. 527 The inhabitants had the choice of being fried or drowned, along with their penates and their supellectile property.

B. *sb.* Furniture (also *fig.*); scientific apparatus or equipment (see next).

1597 A. M. tr. *Guillemeau's Fr. Chirurg.* *iv b, I am not the man which liveth by an other mans mutuated supellectiles. **1657** TOMLINSON *Renou's Disp.* 480 The Shops supellectuals.. are almost innumerable. *a* **1734** NORTH *Lives* (1890) III. 44 To remove all their books.. and such suppellectiles as they esteemed worth the trouble of carrying out. **1793** W. ROBERTS *Looker-on* No. 78 (1794) III. 234 Ideas are the matter, the supellectile of the mind.

‖**supellex** (s(j)uːˈpɛlɛks). *rare.* [L.] *lit.* Household furniture; *fig.* the equipment or apparatus for an experiment or operation.

1553 BRADFORD *Serm. Repent.* To Chr. Rdr., Knowing how short my *supellex* and store is [*ed.* 1574 how slender my store is]. *a* **1697** AUBREY *Lives* (1898) I. 9 The way to make it [*sc.* astrology] perfect is to gett a supellex of true genitures. **1794** KIRWAN *Elem. Min.* (ed. 2) I. 40 This solid therefore should make part of the mineralogical *supellex*. **1885** *Blackw. Mag.* Oct. 523/1 His supellex consisted of the iron pot aforesaid, and a hollow bamboo for water.

super (ˈs(j)uːpə(r)), *sb.*

I. †**1.** [Short for INSUPER.] Something 'standing in super'; a balance remaining over. *Obs.*

1626 BP. H. KING *Serm. Deliverance* 51 If.. you chance to enwrap amongst the common Shoale of gaine.. any thing that belongs to God.. enter it not into your Audit, nor account that amongst your Supers, which is your *Onus*. **1642** C. VERNON *Consid. Exch.* 6 All debts and *Supers* depending in any accounts.

II. [Short for various subst. compounds of SUPER-.] Chiefly *colloq.*, *slang*, or *commercial.*

2. a. = SUPERSALT. **b.** = SUPERPHOSPHATE 2.

1807 T. THOMSON *Chem.* (ed. 3) II. 519 Besides the triple salts and the *subs* and the *supers*. **1900** *Dundee Adv.* 9 June 8/1 The substantial dressing of 4 cwts. supers, 2 cwts. dissolved bones, and 1 cwt. sulphate of ammonia.

3. = SUPERNUMERARY. **a.** *Theatr.* and *Cinematogr.* Cf. EXTRA *sb.* b.

1838 *Actors by Daylight* I. 112/1 Many of the old supers of course remained. **1844** DICKENS *Let.* 3 Jan. (1977) IV. 9 That extraordinary compound of odd scents peculiar to a theatre.. accompanies me, as I meet perspiring supers in the narrow passage. **1853** 'C. BEDE' *Verdant Green* II. iii, If by a super you mean a supernumerary.. then the Pet isn't one. **1859** SALA *Tw. round Clock* (1861) 176 My private belief is that no 'super' could exist long in any atmosphere remote from.. the vicinity of the stage-door of a theatre. **1877** E. W. GOSSE *North. Stud.*, *4 Danish Poets* (1890) 218 The actors gave special performances, and on these occasions Andersen managed to get on the boards and mix with the supers. **1905** J. K. JEROME *Idle Ideas* xv, She sinks down fainting on the stage and is carried off by Supers. **1924** GALSWORTHY *White Monkey* II. ii. 125 The lurid professions—film-super, or mannequin. **1930** E. WAUGH *Vile Bodies* ix. 155 The Colonel's somewhere in that little crowd singing the hymn. .. He was crazy to be allowed to come on as a super.

attrib. **1876** D. COOK *Bk. Play* II. 201 The 'super'.. is under the rule of a 'super-master,' who is in his turn governed by the wavings of the prompter's white flag in the wings.

b. A supernumerary on board ship.

1866 *Daily Tel.* 16 Jan. 7/4 Those were real ships.. and a certain proportion of the 'supers' on board were always sea-sick.

c. *gen.*

1882 *Academy* 14 Jan. 25/3 Th odd four cats are only 'supers'. **1885** G. R. SIMS *Rogues & Vagabonds* lviii. 277 It is the custom when young doctors are anxious to work up a reputation for being fashionable for them to engage a few supers—that is, to give advice gratis to a few selected persons, on condition that they come once or twice a week and help to make a crowd in the waiting-room. **1885** 'MRS. ALEXANDER' *At Bay* i, You ladies will have a cavalier apiece, and one to spare, that's myself; I am only a super now-a-days.

4. = *super-hive* (see SUPER- 3); a box containing a certain number of sections of honey.

1855 *Poultry Chron.* III. 84/2 In the beginning of July the hive was filled with combs, and the bees.. availed themselves of a super, in which they stored some pounds of honey. **1868** *Rep. U.S. Commissioner Agric.* (1869) 275 Honey for market purposes is generally stored in small boxes or supers, about five inches square. **1892** *Garden* 27 Aug. 188 Two and three-quarter supers from each bar frame hive have not been uncommon 'takes,' and the honey is remarkably good.

5. = SUPERINTENDENT.

1857 F. COOPER *Wild Adventures in Austral.* 59 'Scotchy' .. introduced me as a particular friend to Wilder the owner of that run, under the impression that a 'super' was required. **1864** C. R. THATCHER *Songs of War* 12 The Super issued Quite a rabid Proclamation. **1870** GORDON *Bush Ballads, From the Wreck* 23 What's up with our super to-night? **1880** *Blackw. Mag.* Mar. 283, I was 'Super' of a sheep-station up north two years ago. **1916** A. BENNETT *These Twain* iii. 33 The sole lecture of his répertoire, but it had served to raise him ever so slightly out of the ruck of 'Supers'. **1939** 'F. O'BRIEN' *At-Swim-Two-Birds* 80 The policemen were rounded up and marched across the prairies to the Circle N, as fine a body of men as you'd hope to see, myself and the super as proud as be damned at the head of them. **1953** 'N. BLAKE' *Dreadful Hollow* xv. 197 My dear old Super, Pop was always threatening to cut us off with a shilling. **1977** T. BERGER *Who is Teddy Villanova?* i. 1 My apartment, on the door of which the churlish super had posted a notice that tended to humiliate.

6. = SUPERFINE.

1881 *Instr. Census Clerks* (1885) 64 Woollen cloth manufacture.. Super Weaver. **1885** *Times* (weekly ed.) 5 June 7/2 Of the power looms, 1,700 are devoted to the production of extra supers and 3-ply carpets.

7. *Thieves' slang.* A watch. *Comb.* **super-screwing**, watch-stealing.

1859 *Times* 26 Apr. 9/6 The abstraction of the watches (which the thieves term *super-screwing* from the slang of *super*, a watch,.. from the practice of twisting the handles of the watches off). **1903** H. HAPGOOD *Autobiog. of Thief* ii. (1904) 45 The art of 'banging a super', that is, stealing a watch by breaking the ring with the thumb and forefinger, and thus detaching it from the chain.

8. *Bookbinding.* [Origin unknown.] = MULL *sb.*[7] (see quots. 1914, 1970). *U.S.*

1914 J. J. PLEGER *Bookbinding* III. 15 *Super*, a thin, loosely-woven, starched cloth glued on the back of books. **1916** *Rebacking Bks.* (Worcester County, Mass., Law Library) 7 The back had been hand sewed.., a strip of super between the bands pasted on the boards. **1940** PERRY & BAAB *Binding of Bks.* iii. 48 Super cloth (a sized cheese cloth) is too light for reinforcing purposes. **1967** [see MULL *sb.*[7]]. **1970** R. K. KENT *Lang. Journalism* 130 *Super*,..a loose, open-weave cotton material used as reinforcement for the binding of a book: also called *crash*, or in England, *mull*.

9. [Short for SUPERDUPER *a.* or SUPERBOMB.] A colloquial name for the fusion or hydrogen bomb. Now chiefly *Hist.*

1951 W. L. LAURENCE *Hell Bomb* i. 3, I first heard about the hydrogen bomb in the spring of 1945 in Los Alamos... They were already considering preliminary designs for a hydrogen-fusion bomb, which in their lighter moments they called the 'Super-duper' or just the 'Super'. **1958** J. CLEUGH tr. *Jungk's Brighter than Thousand Suns* xvi. 259 In the discussions among those 'in the know' that arose in consequence of the news of the explosion in the Soviet Union one word was continually repeated which outsiders, at that time, would scarcely have understood. It was 'Super'. **1982** *New Scientist* 2 Sept. 642/2 It seems that the realisation of the Super, with its implications of mega-deaths, is not technically out of reach of any power which can produce a fission bomb.

III. [Absol. use of the adj.] **10.** *colloq.* High-octane or top-grade petrol.

[**1965**: see PREMIUM 7b.] **1967** 'G. DOUGLAS' *Death went Hunting* vi. 47 He wanted petrol—four of super, it was. **1978** *Country Life* 25 May 1502/2 French petrol has always been expensive... A gallon of super..costs about £1.37.

Hence '**supering**, (*a*) the action of performing as a 'super' in a theatre; (*b*) the putting of a 'super' on a bee-hive.

1889 *Pall Mall Gaz.* 30 Nov. 7/1 Supering is generally extra time work, done by men who are otherwise engaged in the daytime. **1910** *Daily News* 3 June 4, I advise bee-keepers to find out the needs of the local market before supering.

super ('s(j)uːpə(r)), *a.* [Short for various adj. compounds of SUPER-[1].]

1. *Trade colloq.* = SUPERFICIAL 2. Orig. usu. following the sb., but now also preceding it, as ***super foot***. Cf. *superficial foot* s.v. SUPERFICIAL *a.* 2b.

1833 T. HOOK *Parson's Dau.* III. xii, Hundreds of feet of plinths, at so much per foot, super. **1881** YOUNG *Every Man his own Mechanic* §12 The price of common Belgian glass for ordinary glazing purposes is 3^{d} per foot super. **1909** *Westm. Gaz.* 30 Aug. 2/2 Total cost per super yard per annum.. 11·0 d. **1949** *Gloss Terms Timber* (*B.S.I.*) 23 Super. foot, a square foot of timber of the thickness stated, e.g. 'per super. foot of $1\frac{1}{2}$ in'. **1953** *Brit. Commonw. Forest Terminol.* I. 57 Foot, superficial... A unit of volume equal to 1/12th of a cubic foot. In Australia and New Zealand, applied to standing trees, logs and sawn timber of any thickness, usually under the synonym *Super foot*. **1971** *Sunday Australian* 8 Aug. 4/3 A brick veneer home of this size contains 11,000 superfeet of timber.

2. *Trade colloq.* = SUPERFINE 4.

1842 BISCHOFF *Woollen Manuf.* II. 187 Long wool of the best class that is grown in Kent, which we term super matching, or long drawing. **1850** DICKENS *Dav. Copp.* ix, Showing me a roll of cloth which he said was extra super. **1888** *Daily News* 27 Aug. 7/2 A fair amount of business is doing in wefts, especially in super lustres. **1888** *Ibid.* 5 Nov. 7/1 Half-bred and super wools..; fine and super wethers.

3. *slang.* Very good or pleasant, first-rate, excellent, 'smashing'. Also as *int.*

This sense has developed from and overlaps with sense 2.

[**1837** DICKENS *Pickw.* xli. 445 I'll be upon the wery best extra-super behaviour!] **1895** *Army & Navy Co-op. Soc. Price List* 15 Sept. 1079 White or black super opera bodice. **1923** [see CABARET[1] 2b]. **1932** *Daily Express* 25 June 7/4 We have race meetings here, and super bathing. **1946** J. B. PRIESTLEY *Bright Day* xi. 327 This is jolly good, though. Super. **1954** 'R. CROMPTON' *William & Moon Rocket* i. 27 'Wizard,' said William. 'Super,' said Ginger. **1968** *Sunday Times* 25 Aug. 4/6 Doesn't almost everyone describe something mildly nice as 'super'. **1976** *Evening Post* (Nottingham) 13 Dec. 7/2 His wife Lee, said: 'Isn't it super? We can't get over it.'

super ('suːpə(r)), *v.* **I. 1.** [f. SUPER *sb.* 3a.] *intr.* To appear in a play or film as an extra or supernumerary. *Theatr. slang.*

1889 [implied in *supering* s.v. SUPER *sb.*]. **1920** J. FERGUSON in *Northern Numbers* 98 In Town she 'supered' and would just 'walk on'. **1938** G. B. SHAW *Let.* 20 Sept. in *B. Shaw & Mrs. Campbell* (1952) 323 All the élite of the profession over forty rushed down to Pinewood to super in it [*sc.* a film]. **1976** *New Yorker* 16 Feb. 26/1 Chance for man to super in new Met production of Aida.

2. [f. SUPER *sb.* 8.] *trans.* To back (a book) with super. *U.S.*

1914 J. J. PLEGER *Bookbinding* III. 125 After enough books have been head-banded and supered.., put the backs together.

II. 3. [Short for SUPERANNUATE *v.*] *trans.* To remove (a pupil) from a school or form on account of age. Chiefly *pass.* Cf. SUPERANNUATE *v.* 3a. *School slang.*

1902 'C. TURLEY' *Godfrey Marten, Schoolboy* xi. 135 'I have been in the Lower Fourth exactly four terms,' he went on, 'and my people are getting sick, and Sandy says I shall be 'supered' in a term or two.' **1923** E. W. HORNUNG *Old Offenders & Few Old Scores* 239 He was in our house, and super'd, poor beast! **1937** R. A. KNOX *Double Cross Purposes* v. 84 He always was a scug, till the day he was super'd. **1945** T. RATTIGAN *Love in Idleness* I. 8 He was super'd from Eton. .. Removed for not being in a high enough form.

4. [Short for SUPERIMPOSE *v.*] *trans.* To superimpose (a caption, etc.) on a film. *Television slang.*

1964 [see CUE *v.*[2] a]. **1964** [see CAPTION *sb.* 4]. **1966** G. N. LEECH *Eng. in Advertising* vi. 60 In the transcription [of a television commercial], italicised portions are 'supered' and capitalised portions are in the spoken commentary. **1975** *Listener* 9 Jan. 38/2 Why not super the characters' names towards the end of a play?

super- ('s(j)uːpə(r), -ər), *prefix*, repr. L. *super-* = the adv. and prep. *super* above, on the top (of), beyond, besides, in addition, used in composition with the various meanings detailed below. (Cf. the related Skr. *upari-*, Gr. ὑπερ- HYPER-, OE. *ofer-*, etc. OVER-.)

A certain number of important Latin compounds, chiefly verbs, belong to the classical period, but the great majority are of later date, and many are recorded first from Christian writers. As a living prefix in English, *super-* first appears about the middle of the 15th c.; it became frequent in Elizabethan times, and in the 17th c. it was very widely used. In more recent times it has been extensively introduced into the nomenclature of chemistry and other sciences as a correlative to SUB-. In technical language it sometimes varies with SUPRA- (of which the strict correlative is INFRA-), e.g. *super-local* and *supra-local*, *superorbital* and *supra-orbital*, *superlapsarian* and *supralapsarian*. It continues to be an important formative element in English, especially in senses of branches II and III.

The more important and permanent compounds are entered in this Dictionary as main words; the present article includes such compounds of a general character as have not a permanent status, and scientific terms of which the meaning may (for the most part) be gathered from the meaning of the prefix and that of the radical element.

A considerable number of Latin compounds were adopted in 'learned' form in OF., as *superabonder*, *supereminent*, *supererogation*, *superflu*, *superintendance*, *superscription*, *superseder*; a few of such compounds became permanently established, as *superficie*, *superlctif*, *superstition*, but the majority have been superseded by forms with the 'popular' representative of L. *super-*, viz. *sur-*; e.g. *surabonder*, *suréminent*, *surérogation*, *surintendance*; cf. the parallel forms *superfin*, *surfin* in mod.F.

Pronunciation. The general rule is that the first syllable of the prefix carries the secondary stress of the compound, e.g. *ˌsuper'add*, *ˌsuperero'gation*, *ˌsuper'numerary*, *ˌsuper'phosphate*, *ˌsupersesqui'alteral*, *ˌsupersub'stantial*. But this syllable carries the main stress where there is a contrast, implicit or explicit, with the radical element as a simple word or with some other compound of it, e.g. *'superclass*, *'superflux*, *'superhive*, *'superman*, *'superˌnature*, *'supersalt*, *'superˌsolid*, *'superˌstructure*; *the 'subordinate court and the 'superordinate* In two words and their immediate derivatives (in which the etymological meaning has been obscured), the stress is on the second syllable of the prefix, viz. *su'perfluous*, *su'perlative*.

I. Over, above, at the top (of); on, upon.

1. Forming adjs. in which *super-* is in prepositional relation to the sb. implied in the second element, as in late L. *supercælestis* that is *super cælum* above the heavens, SUPERCELESTIAL, *superterrēnus* that is *super terram* above the earth, SUPERTERRENE, -TERRESTRIAL.

a. Compounds of a general character (chiefly nonce-wds.) and miscellaneous scientific and technical terms.

ˌsuper'aerial, situated above the air or atmosphere. **super'aqueous**, situated above the surface of water. **ˌsuperau'ricular**, situated above the ears. **ˌsupercre'taceous** *Geol.*, lying above the Cretaceous series (cf. *supracretaceous*). **ˌsuperempy'real**, above the empyrean or firmament. **super'glacial**, situated or occurring upon the surface of ice, esp. of a glacier. **super'labial**, placed over or upon the lip. **super'lineal, -'linear**, written above the line. **ˌsuperma'rine**, occurring or performed above or upon the surface of the sea. **super'planetary**, above the surface of a planet; in quot. as *sb.* a superplanetary being. **super'spatial**, above the limits of space. **ˌsuperte'lluric**, 'situated above the earth and its atmosphere' (*Century Dict.* 1891).

1660 INGELO *Bentiv. & Ur.* II (1682) 62 They confine him to the *super-aerial Regions. **1664** POWER *Exp. Philos.* II 118 If there be a Superaerial region of Æther. **1822** P. BEAUCHAMP (Geo. Grote) *Anal. Infl. Nat. Relig.* (1875) 103 Incomprehensible phenomena are ascribed..to the incomprehensible person above. They call forth..the deepest horror..as being sudden eruptions of the super-aërial volcano. **1886** R. MUNRO in *Jrnl. Anthrop. Inst.* May 459 A wooden gangway, probably submerged, stretched to the shore..there has been no evidence to show that the uprights supported a *superaqueous platform. **1845** S. JUDD *Margaret* II. i. (1871) 168 Those *super-auricular capillary appendages, hardened with pomatum. **1832** DE LA BECHE *Geol. Man.* 181 *Supercretaceous Group. (Syn. Superior Order, *Conyb.*; Tertiary Rocks, *Engl. Authors*). *Ibid.* 186 The supercretaceous deposits of London and the Isle of Wight. *a* **1711** KEN *Hymnotheo* Poet. Wks. 1721 III. 90 As *super-Empyreal Waves unsluc'd, With Ocean mix[t], the gen'ral Flood produc'd. **1886** A. WINCHELL *Walks Geol. Field* 274 The summer sun gave origin to *superglacial streams. **1888** *Standard* 13 Dec. 3 Deprived of their *superlabial ornaments. **1877** *Athenæum* 1 Dec. 701/1 MSS. with the so-called Assyrian punctuation or *superlineal vowel points. **1887** *Ibid.* 24 Sept. 401/3 Dr. Wickes..tries to prove that it is a misnomer to style the *superlinear punctuation Assyrian or Babylonian. **1816–18** *Tuckey's Narr. Exped. R. Zaire* i. 29 Few of them [*sc.* the African Atlantic islands] seem to have had *super-marine eruptions. **1845** THACKERAY *Picture-Gossip* ¶ 12 A stout gentleman.. who..believed that he could walk upon the water, and set off in the presence of a great concourse of people upon his supermarine journey. **1827** COLERIDGE in *Blackw. Mag.* (1882) Jan. 117 A bright fire is the apotheosis of coal; and Mary, as fire-maker, a maker of black angels, and other beatified *superplanetaries! **1882–3** *Schaff's Encycl. Relig. Knowl.* II. 950 This *superspatial heaven, above the cloudy and the stellar heavens.

b. *Anat.* and *Zool.* = Situated above, or on the dorsal side of, the part or organ denoted by the second element, as in mod.L. *supergenuālis* that is *super genu* above or upon the knee, applied to the knee-pan. (Cf. SUPRA-.)

ˌsupera'cromial, ***ˌsuperambu'lacral***, ***super-ca'llosal*** (the corpus callosum), ***super-'central*** (the central sulcus of the brain), ***ˌsuper-eth'moidal***, ***super'glottal***, ***ˌsuperla'ryngeal***, ***super'marginal***, ***super'medial***, ***super'orbital*** (also as *sb.*), ***super'sphenoid***, ***supersphe'noidal***, ***ˌsupersqua'mosal*** (a bone of the skull in ichthyosaurs).

1839–47 *Todd's Cycl. Anat.* III. 572/1 Superficial nerves. .. The supra-clavicular and *super-acromial. **1877** HUXLEY *Anat. Inv. Anim.* ix. 563 Each of these ossicles [in the Ophiuridea]..is surrounded by four plates; one median and antambulacral.., two lateral..and one median and *super-ambulacral. **1903** *Amer. Anthropologist* Oct.–Dec. 623 The *supercallosal fissure [in the brain of J. W. Powell] is separated into two pieces. *Ibid.*, The *supercentral is of the usual zygal shape, freely continuous cephalad with the superfrontal. **1870** ROLLESTON *Anim. Life* 25 *Superethmoidal and interorbital vacuities. **1877** SWEET *Phonetics* 10 A vowel..voice (voiced breath) modified by some definite configuration of the *super-glottal passages, but without audible friction. **1910** *Mod. Lang. Rev.* V. 91 A glide with no definite *superlaryngeal articulation. **1852** DANA *Crust.* I. 544 [The hairs] become *super-marginal. **1846** WORCESTER, **Supermedial*, being above the middle. *De la Beche.* **1849** NOAD *Electricity* (ed. 3) 238 The *super-orbital nerve was laid bare in the forehead, as it issues through the supraciliary foramen in the eyebrow. **1854** OWEN in *Orr's Circ. Sci., Org. Nat.* I. 212 Both the lacrymal and superorbital bones answer to a series of bones found commonly in fishes, and called 'suborbitals' and 'superorbitals'. **1884** COUES *N. Amer. Birds* 178 The nasal gland, sometimes called the superorbital gland, from its position in many birds. **1901** DORLAND *Med. Dict.*, **Supersphenoid*, above the sphenoid bone. **1891** *Century Dict.*, *Supersphenoidal. **1866** OWEN *Anat. Vert.* I. 158 The two supplemental bones of the skull [in the Ichthyopterygia] ..are the postorbital and *super-squamosal.

c. *Bot.* in same sense as b (varying with SUPRA-), as ***super'axillary*** (mod.L. *superaxillāris*), ***ˌsuperfoli'aceous***; also in terms relating to the geographical distribution of plants, as ***ˌsupera'grarian***, ***super'arctic*** (see quots.).

1900 B. D. JACKSON *Gloss. Bot. Terms*, **Superagrarian*.. applied to a zone which includes the region of vegetation in Great Britain above the limits of cultivation. **1852** HENFREY *Veget. Eur.* iv. 163 The *Super-arctic [zone], bounded below by the limit of the heather (*Calluna vulgaris*) at an elevation of about 3000 feet. **1802** R. HALL *Elem. Bot.* 183 *Superaxillary Flowers. **1900** B. D. JACKSON *Gloss. Bot. Terms*, **Superfoliaceous* = suprafoliaceous.

d. Forming sbs. denoting something placed over or upon that which is denoted by the radical element, as in eccl. L. *superaltāre* SUPERALTAR, *superfrontāle* SUPERFRONTAL, *superhumerāle* SUPERHUMERAL, *superpelliceum* SURPLICE.

2. With advb. force, = Above, over, on, *occas.* from above (in material or non-material sense), prefixed to verbs, pples., adjs., and nouns of action or state, as in L. *superappārēre* to appear above, *supercrescĕre* to grow over, *superædificāre* to build upon, *superfluĕre* to overflow (see SUPERFLUOUS), *super(im)pendens* overhanging, *superincurvātus* bent over, *superinduĕre* (see INDUE), *super(in)undāre* to overflow, *supermeāre* to flow over, *superscrībĕre* to write above, *superscriptio* (see SUPERSCRIBE, -SCRIPTION), *superstruĕre* to erect above (see SUPERSTRUCT, -STRUCTURE), *supervestīre* to clothe upon.

(*a*) Forming intransitive vbs. and other parts of speech of cognate meaning; e.g. † ***supermeate*** vb.; ***supergravitating***, ***-impending***, ***-inflected***,

-lying, *-situated*, *-standing* pples. and ppl. adjs.; ***superambient***, ***-ponderant*** adjs.; ***superflation***, ***-gravitation***, ***-(in)undation***, †***-meation*** sbs. **super'crescent** *a.*, growing over or on the top of something; so **super'crescence**, a parasitic growth. **super'saliency**, the leaping of the male for the act of copulation; so **super'salient** *a.*

1693 J. Beaumont *Burnet's Th. Earth* II. 106 By what agitation..of the *superambient Air can Waters be driven.. for 450 Miles ascent? *c* **1900** *Buck's Handbk. Med. Sci.* III. 265 (Cent. Dict. Suppl.) Damp soil serves to keep the superambient atmosphere damp. **1646** Sir T. Browne *Pseud. Ep.* II. vi. 98 Like other *supercrescenses, and such as living upon the stock of others, are termed Parasiticall plants. **1638** A. Read *Chirurg.* ix. 66 The *supercrescent flesh doth require a stronger cathereticall medicament. **1746** *Phil. Trans.* XLIV. 223 The concreted Salts..found..candying the supercrescent Furze. **1690** C. Nesse *Hist. & Myst. O. & N. Test.* I. 21 God gave this spirit..by way of infusion, *superflation or breathing upon. **1664** Power *Exp. Philos.* II. 112 According to the weight of the *Supergravitating Water. *Ibid.* 108 The *Supergravitation of the high parts of the water upon the lower. *a* **1711** Ken *Edmund* Poet. Wks. 1721 II. 83 As Divers at the Bottom of the Deep Feel not the vast *superimpending Heap. **1804** Mitford *Inquiry* 86 Pillars..connected by the even pavement on which they stand, and by the superimpending intablature. **1885** R. L. & F. Stevenson *Dynamiter* 158 The day sparingly filtered through the depth of super-impending wood. **1578** Banister *Hist. Man* I. 10 These two processes meting after a *super-inflected maner, are..knit together by an oblique Suture. **1633** T. Adams *Exp. 2 Peter* iii. 6. 1208 Hee recovered the earth from the *superinundation of waters. **1866** Lawrence tr. *Cotta's Rocks Classified* (1878) 378 What thickness of *superlying strata should be assumed as sufficient. **1656** Blount *Glossogr.*, **Supermeate*.., to go or slip over, to run, or flow over. **1658** Phillips, **Supermeation*, a flowing or passing over. **1664** Power *Exp. Philos.* II. 105 The top of the Mountain..being so much nearer the top of the Atmosphære, a lesser weight of *Superponderant Ayr makes a lesser quantity of Quicksilver arise in the Tube. **1646** Sir T. Browne *Pseud. Ep.* III. i. 107 Their [*sc.* elephants'] coition is made by *supersaliency like that of horses. **1903** *Eng. Dial. Dict.*, *Rig v.*[1], to perform the act of supersaliency only, to back. **1836** Smart *Pron. Dict.*, **Supersalient*. **1597** A. M. tr. *Guillemeau's Fr. Chirurg.* 13 b/2 To bringe the *supersituated places together. **1859** C. Forster *Monum. Assyria*, etc. 87 The *super-standing word. **1769** E. Bancroft *Guiana* 12 Those *superundations ..are the source of this redundant fertility.

(*b*) Forming transitive vbs. and related words of cognate meaning: † **super'act** *v.*, to actuate or impel from above. **supera'ffusion**: see quot. **'supercise** *v.* [after *circumcise*]: see quot. **ˌsupercolumni'ation**, the erection of one order of columns upon another. † **super'devil** *v.*, to set the Devil over. † **super'edificate** *pa. pple.*, built or founded *upon* something. † **ˌsuperedifi'cation**, building upon something; *concr.* a superstructure. † **super'edify** *v.*, to build upon a foundation; to erect as a superstructure (also *absol.*). **ˌsuperex'change** *Physics* [ad. F. *superéchange* (H. A. Kramers 1940, in *Magnétisme* (Centre Nat. de la Recherche Sci. de France) III. 49)], an exchange force that acts between the electrons of two cations through those of an intervening anion, as in some antiferromagnetic materials. **super'fix** *v.*, to fix upon something else. † **super'gurgitate** *v.*, to cause to overflow. **ˌsuperin'due** *v.*, to put on as a garment, esp. over another. **ˌsuperin'scribe** *v.*, (i) to inscribe on the top or at the head, (ii) to inscribe over another inscription. **ˌsuperin'vest** *v.*, to clothe as with an outer garment. **super-'Jesuited** *ppl. a.*, ruled over by Jesuits. **superpro'nation** = SUPINATION. **super'satanize** *v.*, to set Satan over. † **super'vested** *pa. pple.*, covered *with* a garment; also *transf.* Also occas. in formations on a sb., as † **superbody** *v.*, to fit a 'body' upon.

1655 Pierce *God's Decrees* §45. 57 That they might not be betray'd into a yawning reliance upon their being *superacted to the working out of their salvation, he bids them work it out with fear and trembling. **1658** Phillips, **Superaffusion*,..a shedding upon, a pouring on the top. **1552** in J. C. Jeaffreson *Middx. County Rec.* (1886) I. 8 A woman's kertyll of Russell worsted *superbodied with damaske. **1784** *Characters* in *Ann. Reg.* 5/1 The men are all circumcised, or rather *supercised; as the operation consists in cutting off only a small piece of the foreskin, at the upper part. **1838** *Civil Eng. & Arch. Jrnl.* I. 94/1 The writer objects—and so do we—to *super-columniation. **1604** N. D. *3rd Pt. Three Conv. Eng.* 279 They were indeuilled, *superdeuilled, and thorowdeuilled. **1508** Fisher *7 Penit. Ps.* cii. Wks. (1876) 180 We may be *superedyfycate vpon cryst. **1610** Donne *Pseudo-martyr* Pref. B2, If we distinguish not betweene Articles of faith and iurisdiction, but account all those *super-edifications and furnitures, and ornaments..to be equally the Foundation it selfe, there can bee no Church. **1624** F. White *Repl. Fisher* 48 In euery building orderly framed, the foundation hath precedence, then followeth superedification, and lastly consummation. **1638** E. Reynolds *Peace Ch.* 41 To this Foundation..must be joyned a progresse in the Superstruction,..and in this superedification it will be needfull to observe these two things. **1558** *Abst. Protocols Town Clerks of Glasgow* (1896) II. 58 Cuthtbert can nocht haif closure at the sowtht ende of his waist..without he haif tollerance of the said Johne to *superedifie upone his gavile. **1582** *N. T.* (Rhem.) 1 Pet. ii. 5 Vnto whom approching, a liuing stone,..be ye also your selues super-edified as it were liuing stones. **1640** Bp. Hall *Chr. Moder.* (Ward) 29/2 We must distinguish between truths necessary, and truths additional or accessory,..truths fundamental, and truths superedified. **1654** H. L'Estrange *Chas. I* (1655) 124 So vigorous a construction of a little City, not super-edefied upon an old bottom, but upstart and new-emergent from the ground. **1950** *Physical Rev.* LXXIX. 354/1 This indicates that the *superexchange directly through the O⁻⁻ion may be more powerful than that between locations making angles of 90° with the O⁻⁻ions. **1967** J. S. Kouvel in J. H. Westbrook *Intermetallic Compounds* xxvii. 529/2 A remarkable feature of these superexchange interactions in ionic materials is that they almost always give rise to an antiparallel rather than parallel (i.e., ferromagnetic) alignment of moments. **1980** A. S. Chakravarty *Introd. Magnetic Properties Matter* xiv. 458 The superexchange mechanism..becomes the dominant factor if the separations between the magnetic ions are too large for the direct exchange mechanism to be operative. **1774** N. Collier in 'Joel Collier' (J. L. Bicknell) *Mus. Trav.* App. 9 It was an angel, and not a fiend, which Mr. Wagner had *superfixed to that excellent piece of machinery. **1653** Urquhart *Rabelais* II. vi. 32 Mammona doth not *supergurgitate any thing in my loculs. **1678** Cudworth *Intell. Syst.* I. v. 818 The Scripture oracles affirm that the earthly house of this Schenos shall be corrupted or dissolved, but the Schenos it self *superindue or put on a house not made with hands [*2 Cor.* v. 2]. **1858** Sears *Athan.* iv. 27 We shall have our lost bodies again, to be superindued upon these attenuated ones. **1820** T. L. Peacock *Misc.* Wks. 1875 III. 328 Nine books..*superinscribed with their [*sc.* the Muses'] nine names. **1886** *Daily Tel.* 23 Feb. (Cassell) It was put into an envelope addressed to M. Floquet, President of the Chamber, and superinscribed in another envelope to the Secretary-General of the Parliament. **1624** Donne *Devot.* (ed. 2) 340 They who haue made iust use of their former daies, be *superinuested with glory. **1922** *19th Cent.* Oct. 594 Even sordidness itself has put off all its vileness, and is seen superinvested in beauty. *a* **1628** F. Grevil *Sidney* (1652) 111 Only to keep those humble religious souls free from oppression, in that *super-Jesuited soveraignty. **1907** *Practitioner* Apr. 486 The arms are fixed in a position of rigid extension, and frequently *superpronation, so that the palms looked outward. **1857** *Truths Cath. Relig.* (ed. 4) 178 [Luther's] assertion is 'that Zuinglius, and all who adhere to his doctrine, are insatanized, *supersatanized and persatanized.' **1657** W. Rand tr. *Gassendi's Life Peiresc* II. 49 Stones that abide long in the bladder, are *supervested with divers crusts. **1697** J. Sergeant *Solid Philos.* 285 Supervested with an Artificial Dress, thrown over them by our Reflexion.

b. with intransitive verbs and their derivatives: = above (in *fig.* sense); in a higher condition, relation, etc.; in nonce-words, as **ˌ*super-e'xist*** vb., ***-e'xistent*** adj., ***-'sistent*** adj. (after SUBSISTENT), ***-sub'sisting*** ppl. adj.

1844 Emerson *Ess.*, *Poet* (1851) 177 The sea, the mountain ridge, Niagara, and every flower-bed, preexist, or *super-exist, in pre-cantations. **1856** R. A. Vaughan *Mystics* (1860) I. 94 All that exists he regards as a symbolical manifestation of the *super-existent. *a* **1834** Coleridge *Lit. Rem.* (1839) IV. 161 The spirit of man, the spirit subsistent, is deeper than both..the body..[and] the soul; and the Spirit descendent and *supersistent is higher than both. **1613** Purchas *Pilgrimage* I. i. 2 Names, in regard both of author & obiect diuine; sometimes..in the concrete; sometimes in the abstract; the first signifying his perfect subsistence; the other his *supersubsisting perfection.

3. Prefixed to descriptive sbs. with adj. force = Placed or situated above, over, or upon something; forming the upper part of (that which is denoted by the second element); higher, upper: as in L. *superædificium* a superstructure, *superficies* SURFACE, etc.; med.L. *supervestīmentum* upper garment; e.g. ***super-cloth***, ***-crust***, ***-ether***, ***-passage***, ***-soil***, ***-stage***, ***-tower***. **'super-hive**, a removable upper compartment of a bee-hive. † **'super-inˌvestiture**, an outer garment. **'super-ˌmonial**, **super-ˌmullion**, a mullion in the tracery of the upper part of a window; hence **super-mullioned** *a.*, furnished or constructed with super-mullions. † **'super-plant**, a plant growing upon another plant; a parasite or epiphyte. **'superˌvestment**, **-ˌvesture**, an outer garment. † **'super-ˌwriting**, writing on the top of other writing.

1630 W. Scot *Apol. Narr.* (1846) 29 A dead corps.. having his *supercloth upon him. **1902** A. Lang *Hist. Scot.* II. x. 255 The Bishop of Dunkeld..had allowed a corpse with a super-cloth over it to be carried into a church 'in popish manner'. **1880** Dana *Man. Geol.* (ed. 3) 147 The series of rocks..that makes up the earth's *supercrust—the only part..which is within the range of direct investigation. **1670** Golt *Divine Hist. Genesis World* 483 The true System of the World,..that is, the *Superæther, and utmost Circumference therof; and within that Concave Sphere, the Æther, [etc.]. **1855** *Poultry Chron.* II. 514 The cap or *super-hive may be removed once or twice during the summer, with from 20 to 40 lbs. of honey. **1756** Horne *Disc.* xvii. (1793) II. 142 'Clothed upon', with a *superinvestiture of the house from heaven, namely, the divine light [*2 Cor.* v. 2, 4]. **1846** F. A. Paley *Man. Gothic Archit.* 184 The smaller tracery-bars, or *super-monials, divide the tracery into compartments. **1847** R. & J. A. Brandon *Anal. Goth. Archit.* (1849) I. 25 The upper part of the tracery is divided by *super-mullions and transoms. **1912** F. Bond *Cathedrals* 337 The supermullion is just beginning to find its way into the tracery (1349–1362). **1838** *Penny Cycl.* XI. 325/1 We might employ the epithet **super-mullioned*, as indicating that the upper divisions of the windows have mullions rising from the arches of the lower ones. **1890** *Archaeol. Jrnl.* XLVII. 92 With plain fenestrations of five-foiled openings supermullioned. **1893** H. M. Wilson *Irrigation Engineering* xii. (1909) 285 Where the canal is at a lower level than the drainage channel, a *super-passage is employed to carry the latter over the canal. **1626** Bacon *Sylva* §556 We finde no *Super-Plant, that is a Formed Plant, but Misseltoe. **1646** Sir T. Browne *Pseud. Ep.* II. vi. 98 An arboreous excrescence, or rather superplant. **1814** *Time's Telescope* (1822) 333 An unhealthy tree is never without these imperfect superplants [*sc.* mosses]. **1864** R. A. Arnold *Hist. Cotton Famine* 433 As the seams of coal are gotten, and the props are removed..the *supersoil falls in. **1879** *Cassell's Techn. Educ.* I. 170/2 There are two kinds of soil, the *super* and the *sub*. The former term is confined to the layer next the surface. **1906** *Athenæum* 10 Mar. 304/2 A *super-stage can be attached for examining transparent objects. **1884** *Contemp. Rev.* July 104 Placing an octagonal *super-tower, or 'lantern', on a square sub-tower. **1868** Marriott *Vest. Chr.* Introd. iii. p. xxi, The *super-vestment [of heathen priests]..was either bordered (*prætexta*) with rich ornament, or wholly made of purple, [or] of scarlet. *Ibid.* ii. p. viii, The *supervesture..the prevailing form of which was that of a large blanket,..admitted..of the greatest variety in arrangement. **1654** Whitlock *Zootomia* 258 To bring *Rasae Tabulae*, clean Tables to every Author, is the advice of no small Philosopher. *Super-writing (being scribling) maketh neither the old, nor the new legible.

b. *Anat.* (*a*) Designating the upper of two parts or members; superior: e.g. ***supermaxilla*** the upper maxilla or jaw (Dorland), ***superpetrosal***. (*b*) Designating a part overlapping another, or formed by such overlapping: e.g. ***superfissure***, ***supergyre***, ***supersulcus*** (Dorland).

1889 *Buck's Handbk. Med. Sci.* VIII. 160/1 *Superfissures and subfissures. These terms are employed herein to designate the fissures which result from the formation of *supergyres and subgyres... The line of overlapping of a supergyre is a superfissure... A subfissure is one which is concealed by a supergyre. *Ibid.* 242/1 The *superpetrosal sinus starts from the cavernous.

c. *Anat.* Forming adjs. (with *super-* in adj. relation to the sb. or subst. phr. implied in the second element: cf. 1 b): (*a*) derivatives from sbs. in b, as ***supermaxillary*** (= pertaining to the upper jaw); (*b*) = situated in, or forming, the upper part of, e.g. ***superalbal***, ***-cerebellar***, ***-cerebral***, ***-dural*** (see quots.).

1853 R. Dunn in *Jrnl. Ethnol. Soc.* (1856) IV. 35 The ..*super-maxillary bones. **1889** *Buck's Handbk. Med. Sci.* VIII. 237/1 *Superdurals. These appear in part as direct continuations of the preceding [*sc.* medidural], and then are double. *Ibid.* 237/2 Veins of the Pia and Brain Substance... The *supercerebrals, passing to the longitudinal sinus... The supercerebral veins return the blood from the convexity as far as the Sylvian fissure, and from the median surface of the hemispheres as far as the *supercallosal fissure. *Ibid.* 238/1 The *supercerebellar vein..empties into the main vein near its termination, or even directly into the sinus tentorialis. *Ibid.* 239/2 The *superalbals..are commonly two small trunks that appear at the outer border of the cœle, opposite the body of the caudate. **1901** Dorland *Med. Dict.*, *Superalbal*,..situated in the upper part of the white substance of the brain, as superalbal veins. *Ibid.*, **Superaural*, located in the upper part of the dura mater.

II. Above (in various figurative senses); higher in rank, quality, amount, or degree.

4. a. Prefixed to adjectives: = Above or beyond, more or higher than, above the range, scope, capacity, etc. of (what is denoted or expressed by the radical part), after eccl. L. *superessentiālis* SUPERESSENTIAL, *supersubstantīvus* supermaterial; e.g. **ˌ*super-an'gelic***, †***-ical*** (= more than angelic, beyond that of an angel), ***-earthly***, †***-elementary*** (see ELEMENTARY 2), ***-intellectual***, ***-legal***, ***-moral***, ***-muscan*** [L. *musca* fly], ***-regal***, ***secular***, ***-sensational***, ***worldly***, adjs.; **ˌsuperadia'batic** *a. Meteorol.*, being or involving a lapse rate greater than that of dry air when it rises and expands adiabatically (viz. approximately one degree centigrade per 100 metres), or a temperature gradient in any other fluid greater than that of an adiabatic expansion of the fluid during upward motion; **super'luminal** *a.* [L. *lūmen*, *lūmin-* light], having or being a speed greater than that of light; **super'national** *a.* = SUPRANATIONAL *a.*; hence **super'nationalist** *a.*; **super-'real** *a.* = SURREAL *a.*; also as quasi-*sb.*; **super-rea'listic** *a.* = SURREALIST, SURREALISTIC *adjs.*

1925 *Nature* 28 Feb. 301/2 The frequent *superadiabatic lapse-rates which occur in the bottom layer of the atmosphere. **1975** *Ibid.* 30 Oct. 748/1 Within the continental tectosphere..the thermal gradients are superadiabatic, and the dominant mechanism of heat transport is conduction, not advection. **1978** *Ibid.* 26 Oct. 726/2 The theory of corona formation [on the sun] is not well developed, and the computation of acoustic fluxes is critically dependent on the theory of superadiabatic convection. **1804** *Doddridge's Wks.* V. 166 *note*, Whether a *super-angelic spirit is capable of being 'reduced to the condition of an infant'. **1864** Pusey *Lect. Daniel* viii. 470 The super-angelic glory of the Messiah. **1674** Brevint *Saul at Endor* 271 Thus this *Superangelical Doctor in the year 1226 ended his daies. **1690** Baxter *Kingd. Christ* ii. (1691) 25 So that Christ hath three Natures. 1. Divine. 2. Superangelical Created. 3. Humane. **1843** *Zoologist* I. 36 The lion and the eagle are not invested with the..*super-animal bravery and magnanimity with which the older naturalists..loved to clothe them. **1588** J. Harvey *Disc. Probl.* 92 Anie such Superplatonicall Intelligence, or *Superaristotelicall intendiment. **1613** Jackson *Creed* I. xiv. §4. 70 It was.. rather *superartificiall, than naturall and artificiall. **1901** *Edin. Rev.* July 60 Tolstoy pleaded that all great teachers commend the impossible, the *super-attainable ideal. **1864**

E. SARGENT *Peculiar* III. 181 Instances in which dogs would seem to have been the mere instruments of a superhuman and *supercanine sagacity. *a* **1661** FULLER *Worthies, Glouc.* (1662) I. 360 Some pressed *super-Canonical Ceremonies. **1627** DONNE *Serm. Lady Danvers* 61 By which, that particular Church must bee *Super-Catholike and Super-vniuersall, aboue all the Churches in the world. **1677** GALE *Crt. Gentiles* II. IV. 302 The..notion of God..as superessential Essence, superdivine Divinitie, *supercausal cause. **1880** LE CONTE *Sight* 154 We find something superphysical and *superchemical. **1793** MARTYN *Lang. Bot.*, *Supra-decompositum folium*, a *Super-decompound leaf..when a petiole divided several times connects many leaflets; each part forming a decompound leaf. **1802** R. HALL *Elem. Bot.* 183 *Super-decompound*..more than doubly compound. **1890** J. MARTINEAU *Seat Author. Relig.* II. II. 214 Demons..driven off only by Messiah with his *superdemonic power. *a* **1631** DONNE *Serm. Hosea ii. 19* (1634) 3 A strange and *super-devilish invention. **1782** J. BROWN *View Nat. & Rev. Relig.* v. v. (1796) 421 Can a man ..believe that the new nature formed by..the Spirit of Christ..is so very superdevilish? **1610** DONNE *Pseudo-martyr* 185 Whether they will pleade Diuine Law, that is, places of Scripture, or Sub diuine Law, which is interpretation of Fathers, or *super diuine law, which is Decretal of Popes. **1677** [see *supercausal* above]. **1876** L. STEPHEN *Eng. Th. 18th C.* I. v. §19. 299 Necessity..belongs to the super-divine sphere—if the phrase may be used. **1872** W. R. GREG *Enigmas of Life* vi. 238 Capable of being moved to exert their *super-earthly powers for the benefit of those who..trust them. **1607** WALKINGTON *Optic Glass* 4 Those ..who..præfer..the regard of the body before the welfare of the *Super-elementary soule. *a* **1744** BOLINGBROKE *Auth. Matters Relig.* vi. Wks. 1754 IV. 292 Moral theology.. contains a *super-ethical doctrine, as some grave divines have ridiculously called it. **1913** *Contemp. Rev.* Oct. 496 The prelude of the superethical Gospel of Humanity. **1871** MEREDITH *H. Richmond* II. 112 She would require *superfeminine power of decision. *a* **1834** COLERIDGE *Lit. Rem.* (1839) IV. 433 The reason is *super-finite. **1887** F. R. STOCKTON *Borrowed Month*, etc. 200 One act..of what might be termed *super-friendly kindness. **1831** CARLYLE *Sart. Res.* II. ii, Swallows..with animated..chirpings, and activity almost *super-hirundine. **1870** LOWELL *Among my Bks.* Ser. I. 199 Such propriety of costume..as shall satisfy the *superhistoric sense, to which..the higher drama appeals. **1880** N. SMYTH *Old Faiths in New Light* v. (1882) 175 The creative Spirit that was in Christ is the *super-historical and divine principle of Christianity. **1660** INGELO *Bentiv. & Ur.* I. (1682) 90 Which he commanded them to behold with the Eye of *Superintellectual Faith. **1794** T. TAYLOR *Pausanias' Descr. Greece* III. 356 The gods..are superintellectual natures. **1840** GLADSTONE *Ch. Princ.* 76 That primary super-intellectual work. **1920** H. G. WELLS *Outl. Hist.* 478/2 He was a real monarch, *super-legal. **1841** NEWMAN *Tracts for Times* No. 90 §8. 61 The doctrine..of a real *super-local presence in the Holy Sacrament. **1891** T. K. CHEYNE *Origin & Relig. Contents Ps.* Introd. p. xxix, The imaginative Biblical symbols of *superlogical phenomena. **1959** K. R. POPPER *Logic Sci. Discovery* ix. 236 Saying that they are 'spread with *super-luminal velocity' is about as helpful as saying that twice two turns with super-luminal velocity into four. **1975** *Physics Bull.* Jan 13/1 The prospect of discovering super-luminal particles is so appealing that the search is started afresh whenever there is an improvement or extension of experimental technique. **1980** Superluminal [see *subluminal* adj. s.v. SUB- 14a]. **1867** DK. ARGYLL *Reign of Law* i. 22 To believe in the existence of miracles, we must..believe.. in the *Supermaterial. **1588** J. HARVEY *Disc. Probl.* 51 Altogether supernaturall, *super-mathematicall, and true myracles. **1657** J. GOODWIN *Triers Tried* 25 So should the grandure of their authority..have been somewhat more competent..and not so hyper-arch-episcopall, so *super-metropolitan. **1922** W. R. INGE *Outspoken Ess.* II. 131 It would be too absurd to suppose that our own State is the only specimen of these superhuman and *supermoral individualities. **1960** K. AMIS *New Maps of Hell* (1961) iii. 84 Religious or quasi-religious feelings.. attach themselves to the super-intelligent or super-moral alien power. *a* **1902** S. BUTLER *Way of All Flesh* (1903) lxxx. 370, I..saw a fly alight on..hot coffee on which the milk had formed a thin skin... I noted with what..almost *supermuscan effort he..made for the edge of the cup. **1929** S. LESLIE *Anglo-Catholic* xv. 208 The Bees which buzzed.. throughout the Papal City, resembling super-muscan flies perched on the walls. **1898** F. W. MAITLAND *Roman Canon Law in Church of England* i. 8 The cosmopolitan, the 'extra-national', or '*super-national' tone of the work of these two English canonists. **1928** G. B. SHAW *Intelligent Woman's Guide Socialism* lxxxiii. 450 Substitute supernational morality, law, and action, for the present international anarchism. **1977** *Irish Democrat* Mar. 3/1 The process of merging the national Governments of western Europe into one supernational administration. **1979** *Dædalus* Winter 190 Andreas Papandreou and his Panhellenic Socialist Movement (PASOK) have been able to capitalize on a *supernationalist stand. **1676** *Doctrine of Devils* 31 Such as are parallel..and *Super-paramount to it. **1810** BENTHAM *Packing* (1821) 255 Parliamentary and *super-parliamentary lawyer-craft. **1588** *Superplatonical [see *superaristotelical* above]. **1659** BAXTER *Key Cath.* xxxiii. 207 Our new *superprelatical Brethren that degrade others that want their Ordination. **1885** A. STEWART *'Twixt Ben Nevis & Glencoe* i. 7 This extraordinary and really *super-quadrupedal *nous* and intelligence. **1935** S. BECKETT *Echo's Bones*, The sphincter..Potwalloping now through the promenaders This trusty all-steel this *super-real Bound for home like a good boy. **1942** *Horizon* July 41 The best Winchester pictures..possess the quality of super-real mystery. **1952** R. CAMPBELL *Lorca* iv. 63 There are also curious nonsensical excursions into the super-real. **1926** A. HUXLEY *Essays New & Old* 185 The adventures of Felix the Cat are *super-realistic in the highest degree. **1955** S. SPENDER *Making of Poem* vi. 103 The golden Romanticism has..claims to set up a super-realistic reality. **1723** WATERLAND *2nd Vind. Christ's Div.* xvi. Wks. 1823 III. 348 You may consider him as King, and so you may present him with regal worship; or as King of kings, and then it will be *super-regal. **1867** O. SHIPLEY *Priestly Absolution* 25 Under the elder Dispensation, the Prophet stood in an almost *super-sacerdotal position. **1881** ROMANES in *Nature* 5 May 2/1 It matters not to science what views her individual cultivators may hold on *super-scientific questions. *a* **1656** BP. HALL *Rem. Wks.* (1660) 302 Let us celebrate this feast, ..not in a worldly but *supersecular manner. **1888** *Supersensational [see *non-spatial* s.v. NON- 3]. **1943** H. READ *Educ. through Art* ii. 28 As for the mental activity called intuition, by which we do not mean any super-sensational faculty of the mind, but the apprehension of abstract quantities and relations..it is the basis of a fourth type of art. **1686** *Spec. B Virginis* 21 Her sacred body is endowed with a *super-seraphical activity, whereby she can render her self present..to all her votaries. **1847** EMERSON *Poems, Merlin* Wks. (Bohn) I. 466 Sparks of the *supersolar blaze. *a* **1704** T. BROWN *Lett. fr. Dead* I. (1707) 163 Since he was got clear of his *Super-Tartarian Concern. **1627** *Superuniversal [see *supercatholic* above]. **1890** *Academy* 12 July 28/2, I heard it asserted..that a sense..of remote natural aspects..was impossible; but..such an abnormally acute *super-visual perception is by no means impossible. **1789** T. TAYLOR *Proclus* II. 385 Every god is super-essential, *supervital, and super-intellectual. **1785** ANNA SEWARD *Lett.* (1811) I. 86 Freedoms, not much calculated to the meridian of *super-worldly refinement. **1874** DYKES *Relat. Kingd. to World* 7 The effort..to attain..super-worldly purity.

(*b*) In corresponding advs., as ***super-'adequately, -artificially, -cathedrically, -diabolically, luminally.***

1830 *Fraser's Mag.* II. 422 The manufacturers affirm that agriculture..is *superadequately, and therefore unfairly protected. **1588** J. HARVEY *Disc. Probl.* 35 Either supernaturally inspired, or *superartificially instructed. **1869** E. W. BENSON in A. C. Benson *Life* (1899) I. vii. 262 Lincoln Cathedral (with its long ridge *super-cathedrically long..) is most grandest. **1782** J. BROWN *View Nat. & Rev. Relig.* v. ii. (1796) 350 So *superdiabolically wicked, as to sin because experienced grace doth abound. **1979** *Nature* 18 Jan. 282/1 (*heading*) *Superluminally expanding radio sources and the radio-quiet QSOs.

(*c*) In related sbs., as ***supernationalism, -nationalist, -nationality***; **super-'realism** = SURREALISM; **super-'realist** = SURREALIST *sb.*; **super-re'ality** = SURREALITY.

1917 G. B. SHAW *Platform & Pulpit* (1962) 106 *Super-nationalism will be limited by general psychological homogeneity. **1980** *Encounter* May 94/1 It thus seems natural to expect an author such as Fleming..to endow his heroes with patriotism and his villains with a super-nationalism of the nastier kind. **1941** L. B. NAMIER in *Time & Tide* 5 July 558/1 The outlook and ideas of the modern *super-nationalists..are very largely of German origin. **1916** E. HOLMES *Nemesis of Docility* i. 16 The nations cling tenaciously to their respective nationalities, as against the *supernationality of Germany. **1933** *Bull. Mus. Mod. Art* Oct. 2/1 *Superrealism is the most conspicuous movement. **1952** R. CAMPBELL *Lorca* iv. 65 The dream region of 'super-realism'. **1931** 'WYNDHAM LEWIS' *Diabolical Principle* 54 The cultural message of *Transition* is still further defined by the incorporation of the *dreamaesthetic* of the *Super-realists into a body already reeking with 'romance'—indeed putrid with the excessive decomposition of that condition. *Ibid.* 65 The *infantile* is the link between the Super-realists and Miss Stein, as it is between Miss Stein and Miss Loos. **1934** H. READ in *Cinema Q.* III. I. 17 Some painters call it a *super-reality (*surréalité*). **1935** D. GASCOYNE *Short Survey Surrealism* v. 109 The more recent ideas of surrealism, which conceive super-reality as existing in the material world, objectively, as well as subjectively in the automatic thought of the unconscious. **1945** H. READ *Coat of Many Colours* xxxix. 198, I believe that in general the plastic arts will tend towards rationality and the poetic arts towards superreality.

b. Prefixed to sbs., forming adjs. in the same sense as above: e.g. ***supergraduate, -seaman, -standard.*** **'super-head,** epithet of a quality of wool (see quot.).

1888 *Rep. Centen. Confer. Missions* II. 426 A *super-graduate course of training. **1839** *Compl. Grazier* (1846) IV. ix. 254 *Head* or *chief*, either because it is derived partly or chiefly from the head, or because it stands at the head of the inferior wools. **Super-head*.—An advance upon the preceding kind, but the sorter not having yet arrived at the best part of the fleece. **1898** *Century Mag.* July 371 After almost *superseaman efforts, they reached the vessel. **1909** *Century Dict.* Suppl. s.v. *Risk*, **Superstandard risk* insurance on the life of one whose habits or heredity or the state of whose health increases his expectancy of life.

5. Prefixed to sbs., forming sbs. denoting something above, beyond, greater or higher than what is expressed by the radical part.

In some cases this use tends to blend with 6b.

a. *gen.*, chiefly in nonce-words, as ***'super-Christ, -Erastian, -septuagenarian.***

1850 *Fraser's Mag.* XLII. 479 The adhesion of one noble lord to the Italian *Superchrist. **1711** G. HICKES *Two Treat. Chr. Priesth.* (1847) II. 393 The *Super-Erastians, Hobbes, Selden, and other such writers. **1915** *Observer* 10 Oct. 7/3 As a *super-septuagenarian I am debarred from active participation.

b. *Mus.* Designating a note next above some principal note, as SUPERDOMINANT, SUPERTONIC.

c. *Nat. Hist.* In classification, denoting a group or division next higher than, or including a number of, those denoted by the radical part, as ***'super-family, -order, -species, -suborder.*** So **'supergalaxy** *Astr.*, a supercluster; *spec.* = *local supercluster* s.v. LOCAL *a.* 2d; hence **superga'lactic** *a.*; **'super-,molecule,** *Chem.*, a complex molecule formed by the combination of molecules of different substances.

1899 G. H. CARPENTER *Insects* iii. 155 Some naturalists.. classing Pararge and its allies as a sub-family of Nymphalidæ... Others, allowing them family rank, would group them together with the Nymphalidæ and other allied families into a *super-family. **1953** E. MAYR et al. *Methods & Princ. Syst. Zool.* iii. 52 The age of specialization has resulted in a general pushing upward of the categories, subfamilies becoming families, and families becoming superfamilies. **1978** *Nature* 16 Nov. 264/2 All three families of humans and apes are included in the superfamily Hominoidea. **1971** *New Scientist* 29 July 245/1 His final choice of *supergalactic equator gave highly positive concentration indices for galaxies in the northern galactic hemisphere. **1982** *Nature* 2 Dec. 409/1 At high supergalactic z coordinates the galaxy density is much lower than near the supergalactic plane $z = 0$. **1946** G. GAMOW in *Nature* 19 Oct. 549/1 The realm of galaxies as seen through Mt. Wilson telescope represents only a small part of a much larger system (a '*supergalaxy' in the super-Shapley sense) rotating round a distant centre. **1955** *Sci. Amer.* Mar. 42/1 One source of radio emission, extending over a long path across the sky, coincides with the plane of the supergalaxy of which the Milky Way is a part. **1971** *New Scientist* 29 July 245/1 The Supergalaxy is, in turn, composed of smaller clusters of galaxies, including the local cluster of about a dozen members, our Galaxy being one of them. **1834** W. PROUT *Chem.* 149 We suppose, that the two molecules of carbon..are associated together into one symmetrical *super-molecule. **1899** G. H. CARPENTER *Insects* iv. 164 Various groupings of these orders into larger divisions ('*super-orders' or 'sub-classes') have been proposed. **1900** B. D. JACKSON *Gloss. Bot. Terms*, **Superspecies*, a group of sub-species or new species regarded as an entity. **1931** E. MAYR in *Amer. Mus. Novitates* No. 469. 2, I propose for *Artenkreis* the more convenient term, Superspecies. I define superspecies as a systematic unit containing geographically representative species that have developed characters too distinct to permit the birds to be regarded as subspecies of one species. **1976** E. DELSON in C. J. Jolly *Early Hominids of Africa* 535 The reliance on superspecies is perhaps..a recognition of our own uncertainties. **1903** R. W. SHUFELDT in *Amer. Nat.* Jan. 34 Order Saururæ. *Supersuborder Archornithiformes. Suborder Archornithes. Family Archæopteridæ.

d. *Geom.* In geometry of more than three dimensions, designating a locus or figure having one more dimension than that denoted by the simple word: e.g. ***'supercube, -curve, -line, -solid, -surface.***

1873 CAYLEY *Math. Papers* (1896) IX. 79 *note*, In 5 dimensional geometry we have: space, surface, subsurface, supercurve, curve, and point-system, according as we have between the six coordinates 0, 1, 2, 3, 4, or 5 equations: and so when the equations are linear, we have: space, plane, subplane, superline, line, and point. **1904** C. E. BENHAM in *Knowledge* Mar. 45/2 (*title*) The Super-Solid. Hints towards a Conception of the 4th Dimension. **1904** G. H. BRYAN *ibid.* May 92/1 A much better idea of the regular character of the 'super-cube' or 'eight-cell', as it is called by most writers, and of its connection with four-dimensional space.

e. Prefixed to the name of a person, forming a vb. in sense 'to excel, surpass, or outdo (the person named) in his characteristic quality or action' (= OUT- 22): as ***'supercæsar.*** *rare.*

1846 LANDOR *Imag. Conv., Jas. I & Casaubon*, Even Caesars are supercaesared by their tenants of the Vatican.

f. *Biol.* **super'female**, a female with a higher ratio of X chromosomes to autosomes than normal females; **'supermale**, a male in which this ratio is lower than in normal males, or the ratio of Y chromosomes to autosomes is higher.

1922 *Amer. Naturalist* LVI. 63 If the intersexes result from an intermediate ratio of X [chromosomes] to autosomes because the X has a net female tendency, then it might be expected that by increasing the ratio of X to autosomes a superfemale would be produced, and conversely, a supermale by increasing the relative number of autosomes. **1955** [see INTERSEX]. **1959** *Lancet* 12 Dec. 1088/1 The inappropriateness of the term 'superfemale' is emphasised by the discovery of a human 3X 2A individual whose primary and secondary sex characters are underdeveloped. **1969** *Guardian* 8 Mar. 3/1 The theory that so-called supermales—men with an extra male chromosome—might be born criminals has lost its first test in a United States court.

6. Prefixed to sbs. with adj. force: Higher in rank, quality, degree, or amount; of a higher kind or nature; superior.

a. With names of officials or persons in authority, forming titles designating one superior to the official denoted by the simple word, as in late or med.L. *supercoquus* head cook, *superjudex* chief judge, *supertextor* chief weaver; e.g. ***'super-arbiter, -attendant*** (= SUPERINTENDENT 2b), ***-doctor, -minister, -quæstor, -sovereign***; also in the names of the corresponding offices or functions, as ***'super-ministry, -sovereignty.***

1673 H. STUBBE *Further Justif. War Neth.* To Rdr. 13 To decide emergent differences a new expedient of Arbiters and *Super-arbiters was found out. **1550** COVERDALE *Order Ch. Denmark* in *Treat. Sacrament* etc. Eiij b, The *super-attendent or chyefe curate commeth in to the pulpyt. **1675** TULLY *Let. Baxter* 30 He had need to have a very competent measure of abilities himselfe, who is to give his verdict of anothers, even so farr as to make him his *super-Doctor of the Chaire. **1946** *Nature* 24 Aug. 247/2 What the Haldane Report recommended, however, was, not placing responsible ministers under a *super-minister, but the consolidation or grouping of departments into a small number of super-ministries with one responsible minister for each. *a* **1974** R. CROSSMAN *Diaries* (1977) III. 666 Benn and Crosland are now super-Ministers of industry and planning, the same level as Barbara and me. **1937** L. HART *Europe in Arms* xv. 191 Ideas of possible organization range from a *super-Ministry which should..absorb the.. existing departments to a small Ministry, superimposed, which should guide the Government. **1975** *Globe & Mail* (Toronto) 25 Nov. 5/3 Liberal leader Robert Nixon also pledged to end the three super-ministries if his party were elected. **1709** MRS. MANLEY *Secret Mem.* (1720) IV. 38 As long as Cajus Æmilius is *Super-Questor. **1625** DONNE *Serm. 3 Apr.* 38 Where there is an inducing of a *super-Soueraigne, and a super-Supremacie,..this is..an vndermining, a destroying of Foundations. **1627** —— *Serm. 6 May* (1649) II. 381 Those that fix a *super-Soveraignty in the people, or in a Presbytery.

b. with nouns of action or condition, etc.; e.g. *'super-agency, -canonization, -comprehension, -division, -good, -one, -organism, -priority, -proportion, -quality, -system, -truth*; **super'gravity** *Physics*, (a theory of) gravity as described or predicted by a supersymmetric quantum field theory; **super'symmetry** *Physics*, a very general type of mathematical symmetry which relates fermions and bosons; hence **,supersy'mmetric** *a.*

This use tends to blend with 5; thus *supercomprehension* = higher comprehension, or comprehension above ordinary comprehension.

1891 *Century Dict.*, **Superagency*, a higher or superior agency. **1628** DONNE *Serm.* xlviii. (1640) 476 This *super-canonization, (for, it was not of a Saint, but of a God). **1887** F. WINTERTON in *Mind* Apr. 268 Molina said..that God saw the future possible acts of man through His '*supercomprehension' of human nature. **1633** AMES *Fresh Suit agst. Cerem.* II. 174 The reason which he bringeth, is onely from the subdivision of true worship. But that doeth not hinder a *superdivision or æquidivision into common and speciall. *a* **1619** FOTHERBY *Atheom.* II. x. §3 (1622) 304 He is..a *Super-good, a Super-truth, a Super-one,..as surpassing all other Bonitie, and Veritie, and Vnitie. **1976** *Physics Lett.* B. LXII. 335/1 The first order formulation with torsion is closely related to the description of *supergravity in superspace. **1980** *Nature* 21 Feb. 717/3 Known as supergravity, the new theory attempts to treat the familiar gravitational field as only a component part of a more elaborate network of forces and fields. *a* **1619** *Super-one [see *super-good* above]. *a* **1899** D. G. BRINTON *Basis Soc. Relat.* I. ii. (1902) 39 Many writers..have spoken of the social unit, the group or the nation, as an 'organism'. Some have further defined it as a '*super-organism'. **1971** E. O. WILSON *Insect Societies* (1972) i. 1/2 The giant of all such 'superorganisms' is a colony of the African driver ant *Anomma wilverthi*. **1973** P. A. COLINVAUX *Introd. Ecol.* xl. 551 The ideas of the superorganism and the social entity no doubt acquired much of their plausibility from the prevalence of the phenomenon of ecological dominance in plant communities of the temperate zones. **1917** W. S. CHURCHILL *Let.* 19 Aug. in M. Gilbert *W. S. Churchill* (1977) IV. Compan. I. 141 At present the Admiralty claim a *super priority upon all supplies. **1952** *Times* 30 June 6/7 Lord De L'Isle and Dudley, V.C...announced on June 7 that the R.A.F. was to be equipped with the GA5 as an all-weather fighter and that it would have 'superpriority'. **1644** DIGBY *Nat. Bodies* ix. § 3. 64 That velocity is the effect of the *superproportion of the one Agent ouer a certaine medium, in respect of the proportion which an other Agent hath to the same medium. **1922** JOYCE *Ulysses* 312 His superb highclass vocalism, which by its *superquality greatly enhanced his already international reputation. **1960** *Times* 3 Oct. (John Harvey Advt. Suppl.) p. ii/3 Super-quality surgical steel. **1974** *Proc. 17th Internat. Conf. High Energy Physics* I. 254/1 A *supersymmetric theory. **1982** *Nature* 26 Aug. 801/1 During the past year there has also emerged a growing interest in particle physics theories that not only unify the description of the three basic interactions (strong, weak and electromagnetic) but which are also supersymmetric. **1974** B. ZUMINO in *Proc. 17th Internat. Conf. High Energy Physics* I. 254/1 Fermi-Bose *supersymmetry was introduced by Wess and the author. It connects Bosons with Fermions. Its existence was suggested by dual models (when formulated as two-dimensional field theories) and the name supergauge symmetry in four dimensions seemed a natural choice. The supergauge algebra having only a finite number of generators in four dimensions, it seems now reasonable to avoid the word gauge and adopt the expression Fermi-Bose supersymmetry, or simply supersymmetry, suggested recently by Salam and Strathdee. **1977** *Physics Today* Apr. 49/3 As far as I know, the only natural way to keep a scalar boson massless is to have a 'supersymmetry',..which puts scalar fields in the same multiplet as massless fermion fields. **1978** *McGraw-Hill Yearbk. Sci. & Technol.* 356/1 Gauge supersymmetry treats all fundamental particles..on the same basis, accomplishes a fusion of spacetime symmetries and internal symmetries.., and promises new types of renormalizable field theories as possible models for unified interactions, perhaps even including gravitation. **1934** WEBSTER, *Supersystem. **1940** BRYANT & AIKEN *Psychol. Eng.* ii. 8 'Universal grammar', a norm or super-system which will comprehend all the various local systems. **1975** *Bio Systems* VII. 15/2 Having pure chemical systems for each of the three subsystems, we connect them to form a chemical supersystem. *a* **1619** *Super-truth [see *super-good* above].

c. In recent (often nonce) formations after SUPERMAN, used to designate a person, animal, or thing which markedly surpasses all others, or the generality, of its class: e.g. *'super-being, block* [BLOCK *sb.* 14], *-boss* [BOSS *sb.*[6]], *-brain, -brute, -car, -carrier* [CARRIER 1 m], *-cinema, -city, -computer, -critic, -crook* [CROOK *sb.* 13], *-dramatist, -goddess, -grid* [GRID 8 a], *-gun, -hero, -heroine, -journalist, -liner* [LINER[2] 8 a], *-magic, -male* (see also sense 5 f), *-nation, -patriot, -port* [PORT *sb.*[1] 1], *-profit, -race, rich* [RICH *sb.* 11], *-salesman, -salesmanship, -ship, -sleuth, speed, -spy, -stud* [STUD *sb.*[2] 4 d], *-tanker* [TANKER[1] 1 a], *-tramp*; **'superalloy** *Metallurgy*, an alloy capable of withstanding high temperatures, high stresses, and often highly oxidizing atmospheres; **'superbike**, (*a*) a motor cycle with a nominal engine capacity of 750 cc. or more; (*b*) a de luxe (often expensive) model of bicycle; **Super Bowl** *U.S. Football* [after ROSE BOWL 2], the final of the National Football League championship, contested annually since 1967 (from 1970, a play-off between the winners of the two sections of the League, the National and the American conferences); **'superchurch**, (*a*) a church formed by the amalgamation of separate churches; (*b*) a very large church; **'supercrat** *N. Amer.*, a powerful bureaucrat; **'super-,Dreadnought**, an all-big-gun ship with an armament superior to that of the Dreadnought class; **Super Glue**, the proprietary name of a strong adhesive; also **superglue**; **'supergrass** [GRASS *sb.*[1] 12] (see quot. 1979); **super-'highway** *N. Amer.*, a road designed for high-speed traffic, a motorway; also *fig.*; **'superjet** a very large or fast jet aeroplane; also *attrib.* and *fig.*; **'superloo** *colloq.*, a public convenience on certain British railway stations which offers a range of washing facilities, including showers; **'super-rat**, a rat that is resistant to the action of the usual rat poisons; **superset** *Math.*, *Linguistics*, etc., a set (SET *sb.*[2] 10 c) which includes another set or sets; **'supersound** sound which is too intense to be endured, or of too high a frequency to be perceived (cf. ULTRASOUND); **'superstate**, a dominant political community, esp. one formed from an alliance or union of several nations; *spec.* = SUPERPOWER 3; **'superstore**, a large store selling a variety of goods and typically situated away from a town's main shopping area; a small hypermarket; **'superwoman**, the female counterpart to a SUPERMAN; in recent use, a woman who fills successfully concurrent roles as career-woman, wife, and mother.

1953 C. L. CLARK *High-Temperature Alloys* xvi. 269 Up to the time of the introduction of these *superalloys it was generally agreed that any alloy intended for high-temperature service should be processed and heat treated. **1981** *McGraw-Hill Yearbk. Sci. & Technol.* 325/1 Superalloys can operate for extended periods of time at temperatures about 1200°F (650° C), and provide resistance to hot corrosion and erosion. **1930** *Daily Express* 8 Sept. 2/4 A patient imagines—quite seriously—that he is a kind of *super-being. **1980** I. WATSON *Gardens of Delight* iv. 28 Who's this 'God' you were telling my people about? An alien superbeing—is that it? **1970** *Cycle World* Oct. 34 Suzuki's entry in the '*Superbike' field just happens to be an excellent touring bike. **1976** *Good Motoring* Nov. 5/2 A strong quota of 'superbikes' in the 750cc-plus category. **1978** WATSON & GRAY *Penguin Bk. Bicycle* i. 39 In 1976 a long-established Austrian cycle firm introduced a top market superbike. **1979** R. BALLANTINE *Richard's Bicycle Bk.* I. ii. 61 It is grand fun to have a superbike, but I would advise leaving this until you are an experienced cyclist. **1928** *Survey* (N.Y.) 1 Mar. 696/1 It is necessary to examine more closely the structure and use of these *superblocks. **1975** *New Society* 14 Aug. 375/3 A whole superblock in front of the museum, including many publishers offices and landmarks.., would have gone. **1916** *Blackw. Mag.* June 813/2 The German *super-bosses. **1977** *Listener* 12 May 608/2 The man..he most admires in Italian public life today, the Fiat superboss. **1966** *Los Angeles Times* 22 Oct. III. 1/5 The capacity of the Coliseum for the *Super Bowl will be 90,000. **1979** *Arizona Daily Star* 1 Apr. H 4/1 One would think the question of desirability of rising profits was of the same genre as who should win the Super Bowl. **1928** G. CAMPBELL *My Mystery Ships* xi. 208 To find out what its [*sc.* the name's] origin is or what it means, we shall have to wait till the person with the *super-brain who thought of it appears before the Invention Board. **1975** *Pix* (Austral.) 13 Nov. 42/5 Futurologist and 'super brain' Dr. Kahn..on a recent visit said the world would be better off if Australians worked harder. **1911** E. UNDERHILL *Mysticism* I. vi. 176 As the angel to the man, so was the dragon to the world of beasts; a creature of splendour and terror, a *super-brute. **1920** *Motor* 3 Nov. 113 (Advt.), The Supreme development of the British *super-car. **1977** *Belfast Tel.* 17 Jan. 9/4 There is everything from the family saloon to the specialised super-cars. **1969** D. ACHESON *Present at Creation* xxii. 195 We urged sending a powerful naval force, including the newly commissioned *supercarrier *Franklin D. Roosevelt*. **1978** *Times* 28 Jan. 4/8 Mr Brown was seeking to make optimum use of the Navy's power in face of the strengthened Soviet Navy, which is making supercarriers increasingly vulnerable. **1970** *Time* 25 May 76 Episcopalians are potential participants in the proposed multichurch Protestant merger, the Church of Christ Uniting. Should the Episcopal Church join the new *super-church, [etc.]. **1977** *Time* 26 Dec. 41/2 The faithful throng to gaudy superchurches with 5,000 to 10,000 seats, green shag wall-to-wall carpeting, pit orchestras and Jesus rock bands. **1923** *Gramophone* Apr. 7/1 A terrace opposite Holland House (now I believe about to be pulled down for a *super-cinema). **1931** *Ann. Reg. 1930* 48 Of the existing cinemas 85 per cent are now wired, and there has been a great advance in the building of new super-cinemas. **1955** *Times* 9 May 3/1 One of Madrid's super-cinemas, the Coliseum. **1958** A. TOYNBEE *East to West* 103 You find yourself interned in one of the standardized *super-cities of the modern world. **1971** *Americana Ann.* 103 Paolo Soleri..planned..gigantic supercities towering high in the air or floating on water. **1968** N. WALFORD tr. *O. Johannesson's Great Computer* IV. 108 The generating of controlling computers must be entirely computer-controlled. This task..was performed.. by linking together about a hundred computers..and combining them..to form a unit known as the *supercomputer. Such a unit had sufficient capacity to breed new computers of its own type. **1982** *Times* 30 Apr. 17/2 The market for supercomputers, as they are generally known, is also set for rapid growth. **1972** *Newsweek* 11 Dec. 25 A slimmed-down, tidied-up..Nixon Inc. with..four or so White House-level *supercrats. **1978** *Globe & Mail* (Toronto) 17 July 2/4 [The Ottawa] system has fewer than a dozen super-powerful bureaucrats who dominate the policy-making process. They are the supercrats, and Mr. Gotlieb is one of the more successful ones. **1903** *Westm. Gaz.* 19 Aug. 2/1 The ideas which the super-dramatist would convey to a *super-critic. **1934** S. G. HEDGES *Plague Panic* xxvi. 211 The organized police systems of the world had failed so utterly to bring this *super-crook to book. **1979** *Daily Mail* 29 Jan. 6/3 The other gel was a super-crook. **1903** *Super-dramatist [see *super-critic* above]. **1909** *Westm. Gaz.* 23 Aug. 2/2 The two *super-*Dreadnoughts* which are to be added to the United States fleet. **1910** *Ibid.* 18 June 14/3 In general dimensions the super-'Dreadnought' of to-day is a battleship of from 500ft. b.p. to, say, 536ft. over all, with a beam of 84ft. to 86ft., and with a draught of 27ft. **1911** R. A. FLETCHER *Warships* 324 The name-ship has been so much improved upon in recent designs that she is as inferior to the last of the super-*Dreadnought* battleships as the displaced pre-*Dreadnoughts* were to her. **1977** *Drive* May–June 91/3 One of the latest *superglue products..is a two-part, metal-to-glass adhesive. **1911** *Contemp. Rev.* June *Lit. Suppl.* 3 One is almost afraid to laugh when Spenser treats Elizabeth as a *super-goddess. **1978** R. MARK *Office of Constable* xiii. 163 The age of the *supergrass had arrived. **1979** *Observer* 8 Apr. 1/3 Twomey and Carpenter claim they were framed by a 'supergrass'—a police informer hoping for lenient treatment in return for turning in other villains. **1983** *Listener* 19 May 7/1 Following information from a supergrass, dozens of people alleged to be members of it had been arrested. **1950** *Times Rev. Industry* May 32/1 The projected 275/300k V British *super-grid transmission system. **1979** *Nature* 8 Nov. 123/2 The extension of the Union-wide 'supergrid' of 1500 V DC transmission lines should, theoretically, allow power stations to be sited anywhere. **1915** *Chambers's Jrnl.* Oct. 661/2 The journalistic words '*superguns' [etc.]. **1929** *Encycl. Brit.* III. 367/1 As fast as the Liége forts fell to the super-guns. **1972** *Village Voice* (N.Y.) 1 June 53/2 Lee and Harry are inclined to put him down for killing the hawk with his supergun. **1917** 'CONTACT' *Airman's Outings* 211 The *super-heroes of the war. **1980** *Dædalus* Spring 119 The only people foolish enough to believe in fairy tales and superheroes (the last survivals in the mythology of atheism). **1970** *Times* 22 Dec. 8 Miss Comic Strip will be..selected for her..desirability as an imaginary *superheroine. **1925** *Amer. City Mag.* Apr. 373/1 The *Super-Highway is unique... It will furnish an express motor traffic highway. **1949** *Word Study* May 1/2 A superhighway toward..success. **1978** J. A. MICHENER *Chesapeake* xiii. 799 She found Route 2, which took her to Route 695, the superhighway circumnavigating Baltimore. **1958** *Daily Herald* 3 Mar. 1/1 They [*sc.* aircraft firms] are talking in terms of a *super jet liner capable of crossing the Atlantic in four hours with 150 passengers. **1964** S. BELLOW *Herzog* (1965) 241 The superjet carried him to Chicago in ninety minutes. **1978** *Detroit Free Press* 16 Apr. (Parade Suppl.) 20/3 Except for her, however, not a single person arrested fits the image usually associated with the superjet, 'fast lane' set. **1916** L. CURTIS *Let.* 13 Nov. in *Let. People India* (1917) 27 As a sort of *super-journalist much of my information has been derived from pumping people with first-hand knowledge. **1976** *Listener* 6 May 554/1 The superjournalists have evidently conquered the supermarket, for the rise of Mr Bob Woodward and Mr Carl Bernstein is now being presented as almost as spectacular a saga as the fall of President Nixon. **1928** *Manch. Guardian Weekly* 31 Aug. 180/3 To enlarge their docks for the building of a *super-liner. **1963** *Economist* 27 July 322 Cunard is still chasing its ambition of a new super-liner. **1969** *Daily Tel.* 17 Dec. 1/4 The charge for using the '*superloo' at Euston and Victoria will go up from 6d to 1s. **1972** *Travelling* Autumn 43/3 Edinburgh's Waverley Station..will provide superloos, catering facilities. **1921** T. R. GLOVER *Jesus in Exper. Men* i. 8 The early Christian..really used the Gospel as a sort of *super-magic. **1972** D. KENNEDY *Recoll. Assiniboine Chief* 156 The old witch saw that she was thwarted by super-magic. **1970** G. GREER *Female Eunuch* 194 Her sister, killed because of the maleficent *supermale. **1907** *Westm. Gaz.* 24 Oct. 6/3 Dr. F. W. Andrewes read a paper on 'Medicine and *Super-Medicine.' **1914** E. BARKER *Nietzche & Treitschke* 25 Treitschke looks to war as the expression of an exclusively national *supernation. **1977** P. JOHNSON *Enemies of Society* xix. 248 Is there to be a huge African super-nation, based only on colour, but with immense racial differences within it? **1917** *N.Y. World* 7 Mar. 10/1 At a Carnegie Hall meeting of..*super-patriots, Irving T. Bush was hissed because he defended the President of the United States. **1945** [see SALISBURY STEAK]. **1977** *Private Eye* 13 May 16/1 That super-patriot the late Lord Beaverbrook. **1969** *Sunday Times* 16 Feb. 30/4 In addition to the container ship, another ship of the future is the LASH vessel (lighter-aboard-ship) that will cruise at high speeds, pausing only briefly at *super-port gathering points to pick up or discharge its fleet. **1970** *Daily Colonist* (Victoria, B.C.) 9 Aug. 5/3 A second superport, providing modern bulk handling facilities. **1946** *Sun* (Baltimore) 9 July 2/2 He declares that Mr. Norton is trying to..swell employers' '*super-profits'. **1974** B. PEARCE tr. *Amin's Accumulation on World Scale* II. ii. 392 The origin and dynamics of the superprofits of monopolies. **1912** C. SAROLEA *Anglo-German Problem* i. 59 The German is convinced that he belongs to a *super-race. **1979** *Jrnl. R. Soc. Arts* CXXVII. 324/2 A single pathogen genotype able to attack all of the components, the so called 'super-race'. **1974** *N.Y. Times* 13 Nov. 47/8 Armed with a new toxic rodent killer, the City Health Department opened a campaign yesterday to destroy a strain of '*super rats' breeding in the South Bronx. **1977** *New Scientist* 28 Apr. 200 This company has developed an anti-coagulant which is particularly effective against super rats..which are already prevalent in the United States and are now being reported in Europe and Asia. **1981** *Oxford Jrnl.* 27 Feb. 6 Pest controllers are battling against a breed of 'super-rats' which are immune to normal poisons. **1969** *Times* 5 May (Wall St. Suppl.) p. xii/2 Many of the *super-rich of the United States live in Texas. **1982** *Country Life* 11 Mar. 666/2 This brilliant..novel about the super-rich in France. **1934** WEBSTER, *Supersalesman. **1936** O. NASH *Primrose Path* 127 And a bright super-salesman Has sold you a pup. **1978** M. PUZO *Fools Die* xvi. 172 A very soft-selling supersalesman. **1933** *Sat. Even. Post* 7 Jan. 21 *Super-salesmanship—1932 model. **1968** Supersalesmanship [see SELL *v.* 3 j]. **1970** *Psychonomic Sci.* XXI (4) 235/3 There is no predetermined hierarchy of *supersets and subsets. **1976** J. S. GRUBER *Lexical Structures in Syntax & Semantics* II. ii. 278 In this case we cannot allow the derived tree to be a subset of that in the lexical environment. The only alternative is to require that the derived tree be a superset of that in the lexical environment. **1937** *Sun* (Baltimore) 16 Nov. 12/1 The reasons that prompted the commission to advise against construction by this country of *superships to rival the Queen Mary. **1974** *National Rev.* (U.S.) 1 Mar. 261 New sources of competitive coal have opened up in Australia, Canada, and South Africa, and again the specter of superships rises to plague us. **1974** *Aiken* (S. Carolina) *Standard* 24 Apr. 4-A/5 It's doubtful if the FBI will long retain, or ever again seek, the *super-sleuth. **1942** *Pop. Sci. Monthly* Feb. 49/2 Sound waves too powerful for the human system to bear, and others too high in pitch for the human ear to hear, are new miracle-working tools in science and industry. In dozens of laboratories, scientists are perfecting sound-generating devices, and discovering new uses for *supersound and ultrasound. **1952** *Chambers's Jrnl.* 1 June 363 Scientists have been having the time of their lives exploring super sound. **1927** *Glasgow Herald* 1 June 15 If we cleaved our way above the ocean at the *superspeeds now contemplated. **1961** *Times* 17 Nov. 17/5 (Advt.), Current Ferranti activities include..Atlas (most advanced super-speed computer in the world). **1937** KOESTLER *Spanish Testament* i. 24 If one had taken them seriously, one might have imagined that half Esturil consisted of *super-spies. **1980** R. HILL *Spy's Wife* viii. 53 Is she another Kremlin super-spy? **1918** O. GREGORY *Meccania* iv. 91 The *Super-State must borrow from the Socialists the conception of an all-embracing power and activity. **1929** B. RUSSELL *Marriage & Morals* xv. 173 The control of the super-State over education would be a positive safeguard against war. *Ibid.*, Loyalty to the international super-State should everywhere be fought. **1935** J. E. C. WELLDON *Forty Years On* ii. 76, I have felt that the Darwinian theory of the survival of the fittest..was responsible for the German doctrine of the super-state, which, as the Germans conceived it, could only be Germany. **1941** A. HUXLEY *Let.* 27 Nov. (1969) 471 The super-states based on the three centres of heavy industry and advanced technology—Europe, North America and East Asia. **1959** N. MAILER *Advts. for Myself* (1961) 272 The iron commisars of the Soviet superstate. **1974** M. B. BROWN *Econ. Imperialism* ix. 225 The nation states, apart from the super-states—USA, EEC, Japan and the USSR—are forced into a client relationship with the giant companies. **1978** *New York* 3 Apr. 45/3 Loyalty to the superstate as a substitute for the supernatural. **1965** *Punch* 7 July 1/2 Why bother with exports when the *superstore will take anything you care to make? **1980** *Times* 13 Feb. 3/2 Comparing superstores with local supermarkets is like comparing apples with oranges. **1975** *Time Out* 19 Sept. 25/1 Petersen, the latest in the 'Alvin Purple' brigade of Australian *superstuds. **1921** *Mex Fuel Oil* (Anglo-Mexican Petroleum Co.) 7 These losses are being made good by the building of several *supertankers, commencing with the *San Florentino*..18,000 tons. **1953** *Wall St. Jrnl.* 1 July 4/2 The S.S. New Jersey Sun, second of four super-tankers being built for Sun Oil Co. **1977** *Whitaker's Almanack 1978* 1035/2 A serious problem would be the shipping and supertankers passing round Cape Horn. **1908** W. H. DAVIES (*title*) The Autobiography of a *Super-Tramp. **1906** *Westm. Gaz.* 22 Jan. 2/2 We middle-aged folk, Supermen and *Superwomen, and 'Men-and-Women-in-the-Street'. **1958** *Listener* 18 Dec. 1040/1 A picture of a girl maybe, fantastically beautiful, a blonde superwoman. **1975** S. CONRAN (*title*) Superwoman. **1976** *National Observer* (U.S.) 11 Sept. 20/5 The superwoman image ignores the reality of the average working woman or housewife.

d. *Mus.* = Next higher in pitch: in SUPEROCTAVE, q.v.

7. Beyond in time, later; as in L. *supervīvĕre* to outlive, SUPERVIVE, SURVIVE; †**super'last** *v. trans.*, to last beyond, outlast.

1648 HERRICK *Hesper., To his Booke* vii. 14 Nor thinke these Ages..Shall live, and thou not superlast all times.

b. With prepositional force, in med.L. *superannātus*, f. *super annum* beyond a year: see SUPERANNATE, SUPERANNUATE.

8. (*a*) Before in time, prior to; as in SUPERLAPSARIAN; e.g. ***super-creation*** (used as adj.), decreed before the Creation.

a **1679** T. GOODWIN *Of Election* I. i, The necessity of an election or super-creation grace, if either angels or men..be certainly..saved.

(*b*) So in nonce-vbs. formed by Heylin after H. L'Estrange's use of SUPERANNUATE *v.* (sense 5), in reference to dating events (so much) too early.

1656 HEYLIN *Extraneus Vapulans* 102 We have here a super-semi-annuating (a fine word of our Authors new fashion) in making Doctor Laud Bishop of Bathe and Wells, seven moneths at least before his time: a superannuating in the great rout given to Tilly by the King of Sweden placed by our Author in the year 1630 whereas that battle was not fought till the year next following; a super-triennuating in placing the Synod of Dort..in the year 1615, that Synod not being holden untill three years after, and if I do not finde a super-superannuating [*sic*; *read* super-sexannuating] (that is to say, a lapse of six years) either in the Pamphlet or the History, I am content, our Author shall enjoy..a publick triumph.

III. In or to the highest or a very high degree; hence, in excess of what is usual, or of what ought to be; superabundant(ly); excessive(ly).

9. a. Prefixed in advb. relation to adjs.: Exceedingly, very highly, extremely, supremely, extraordinarily; over-; as in late or med.L. *supergloriōsus* (Vulgate) exceedingly glorious, *superillustris* very illustrious (see *superillustrious* below), *superlaudābilis* (Vulgate) greatly to be praised; e.g. ***superactive*** (= highly active), ***-ceremonious*** (= over-ceremonious), ***-dainty***, ***-dense***, ***-fast***, ***-glorious***, ***-ingenious***, ***-luminous***, ***-sufficient***, ***-sumptuous***, ***-sweet***, ***-zealous***. †**super'benedict** [L. *benedictus* blessed], supremely blessed; '**superco,lossal** *a. U.S. colloq.*, very large, very good, stupendous; **super-'cool** *a. slang* (orig. and chiefly *U.S.*), very cool (COOL *a.* 4 e), relaxed, fine, etc.; also *absol.* as *sb.*; **super-'extra**, applied to commodities, esp. to a style of bookbinding, of the very best quality (cf. *extra super*, s.v. SUPER *a.* 2); **super'fatted**, (*a*) (of soap), containing an excess of fat, i.e. more than can combine with the alkali; (*b*) *slang*, of persons: overweight, fat; **-'fatty** *a.* = *superfatted* (*a*); **superfidel**, *nonce-wd.* [after *infidel*: cf. SEMI-FIDEL], believing too much; †**superi'llustrious**, honorific title of certain kings and other exalted personages; ,**superine'narrable** [ad. late L. *superinēnarrābilis* (St. Augustine): see INENARRABLE], supremely indescribable; **superi'onic** *a. Physics*, having a high ionic electrical conductivity; also as *sb.*, a superionic substance; **super'massive** *a. Astr.*, having a mass many (i.e. typically between 10^6 and 10^9) times that of the sun; †,**superom'nivalent** [OMNIVALENT], supremely omnipotent; †**super'passing**, surpassing (in quot. as *adv.*); †**superpro'portioned**, of excessive proportions; †**super'sufferable** [SUFFERABLE 1], extremely long-suffering; **super'weak** *a. Particle Physics*, pertaining to or being a proposed interaction several orders of magnitude weaker than the weak interaction which would not be invariant under charge conjugation and space inversion jointly.

1654 tr. *Scudery's Curia Pol.* 87 Hee who is too slow may equally be quickened by him who is *superactive and vigorous. **1873** M. ARNOLD *Lit. & Dogma* ix. 276 St. Augustine prays: 'Holy Trinity, *superadmirable Trinity, and superinenerrable, and superinscrutable, and superinaccessible, superincomprehensible. **1880** W. S. GILBERT *Patience* II, An ultra-poetical, *super-æsthetical, out-of-the-way young man. **1683** E. HOOKER in Pordage *Mystic Div.* Pref. Ep. 107 The ony True,..ever-adorabl and *super-benedict Triune Deitie. **1575** G. HARVEY *Letter-bk.* (Camden) 92 O my soverayne goodman, howe can your owne soverayne joye..but shape a benigne answer to so benigne and *superbenigne a replye? **1601** in Farr *S.P. Eliz.* (1845) II. 431 The *super-blessed Trinity. **1659** GAUDEN *Tears Ch.* IV. xxiii. 625 Superstitious and *Super-ceremonious Prelates. **1833** LAMB *Elia* Ser. II. *Product. Mod. Art*, Those high aspirations of a *super-chivalrous gallantry. **1934** WEBSTER, *Supercolossal. **1937** *Amer. Speech* XII. 241/1 Supercolossal is an adjective heard several times orally in Colorado. **1938** WODEHOUSE *Code of Woosters* v. 130 Big is right, though perhaps 'super-colossal' would be more the *mot juste*. **1947** —— *Full Moon* v. 92 'Her profile. Lovely, don't you think?' 'Yup.' 'And her eyes. Super-colossal.' **1976** *National Observer* (U.S.) 17 July 6/3 The brand-new National Air and Space Museum here is a supercolossal mixture of show biz and science. **1970** T. WOLFE *Radical Chic & Mau-Mauing Flak Catchers* 131 The pimp style was a *supercool style that was much admired or envied. **1975** *Radio Times* 23–29 Aug. 11/4 James Coburn was the nicest of all those Bond-type supercools. **1978** *Hot Car* July 91/3 They were super-cool amongst the sixties surfing set in the USA. **1981** *Times* 22 July 11/2 That style had itself been borrowed from younger Jamaicans, and the super cool they affected. **1699** EVELYN *Acetaria* 105 Eighthly, (according to the *super-curious) that the Knife, with which the Sallet Herbs are cut..be of Silver. **1596** SHAKS. *Tam. Shr.* II. i. 189 Kate of Kate-hall, my *super-daintie Kate. **1596** NASHE *Saffron Walden* Wks. (Grosart) III. 134 Her *super-delicate bastard daughter ceremonious dissembling Italy. **1888** E. GERARD *Land beyond Forest* II. xliv. 220 Some people..there are, of super-delicate digestions. **1967** *Listener* 27 Apr. 545/1 These observations ..imply an origin [of the Universe] from a *superdense state 10,000 million years ago. **1977** *Time* 19 Sept. 50/1 The whole principle of diesel ignition is to raise the temperature of the fuel mixture by compressing it into a superdense mass in the cylinder. **1593** G. HARVEY *Pierce's Super.* ** iv b, Spare me, o *super-dominering Elfe. **1851** MAYNE REID *Scalp-Hunters* ii. 17 His dress will be more gaudy and *super-elegant. **1593** G. HARVEY *Pierce's Super.* 163 Mercury..the most nimble, and *supereloquent God. *c* **1860** B. HARTE *My Other Self* in *Fiddletown*, etc. (1873) 121 Looking in her eyes, and carrying on a conversation in their supereloquent language. **1699** R. L'ESTRANGE *Erasm. Colloq.* (1725) 275 But a Man should rather die, than violate so *super-Evangelical a Rule. **1619** W. SCLATER *Exp. 1 Thess.* (1630) 225 To attaine the *superexcedent end [*sc.* eternal happiness]. **1807** SOUTHEY *Espriella's Lett.* II. 212 Who would be content..to put up with the second best, instead of ordering at once the *super-extra-double-superfine? **1835** *J. R. Smith's Catal. Bks.* May 4/2 New and very elegant calf super extra. **1980** *Lok Sabha Deb.* (Delhi) 5 Aug. 264 A *superfast train like the K.K. Express runs late by 5 to 6 hours. **1982** *Economist* 3 Apr. 120/3 It is at the frontiers of R and D now being done into superfast computers. **1891** C. L. FIELD *Patent Specif.* No. 21438 An Improved Manufacture of *Superfatted Soap. **1892** *Jrnl. Soc. Chem. Industry* 31 May 446/1 This improvement in the manufacture of superfatted soaps consists in adding to soap, made by the cold process, milk, cream, or butter in such quantities that any alkali in excess is saturated and an excess of cream is left. **1927** WODEHOUSE *Small Bachelor* iii. 48 'Important people!' Mr. Waddington snorted sternly, 'A bunch of super-fatted bits of bad news.' **1947** L. HASTINGS *Dragons are Extra* ix. 212 A bald, double-chinned type who looked very like a super-fatted edition of ex-President Hoover. **1834** *Super-fidel [see SEMI-FIDEL]. **1550** R. HUTCHINSON *Image of God* xx. (1560) 100 b, I wil..shew.. that there be thre persons in ye *superglorious deitie. **1648** J. BEAUMONT *Psyche* XVIII. xcix His superglorious most refined Nature. **1593** G. HARVEY *Pierce's Super.* 102 *Superhappy Creatures, that haue illuminate vnderstanding. **1579** SPENSER *Let. to Harvey* Poet. Wks. (1912) 638/2 With many *superhartie Commendations, and Recommendations to your selfe, and all my friendes. **1630** tr. *Camden's Hist. Eliz.* IV. 154 Amongst the Kings which they termed *Superillustrious, the King of England was accompted the third, and the Spaniard the fourth. **1633** LD. WARISTON *Diary* (S.H.S.) 31 Gods *super-incomprehensible goodnes, kyndnes, and merciful tendernes to me. **1873** *Superinenarrable [see *superadmirable* above]. **1594** NASHE *Unfort. Trav.* Wks. (Grosart) V. 65 That abundant and *superingenious clarke Erasmus. **1885** HUXLEY in L. Huxley *Life & Lett.* (1900) II. vi. 95, I shall be curious to see what defence the superingenious Premier has to offer for himself in Parliament. **1628** FELTHAM *Resolves* II. [I.] lxxix. 229 It were a *superinsaniated folly, to struggle with a Power, which I know is all in vaine contended with. **1665** GADBURY *London's Deliv. Predicted* v. 28 It is an Argument of super-insaniated folly. **1972** W. L. ROTH in *Jrnl. Solid State Chem.* IV. 60/1 Such solids, which may be called *super ionic conductors, exhibit ionic conductivities that can be as large as inverse ohm-centimeters at temperatures ranging from near room temperature to 1200°C. **1972** *New Scientist* 11 May 321 A small and hardly known group of compounds called 'superionics' reveal exceptional electrical conductivity in the solid state. **1980** *Jrnl. Physics & Chem. Solids* XLI. 1323/1 The superionic conductors are characterized by their high ionic but very low electronic conductivity at room temperature. **1661** J. DAVIES *Civil Warres* 109 He..applies..to the faithful Montrose..a *super-loyal soul. **1968** D. MOORE tr. *Schatzman's Struct. Universe* i. 15 If our present interpretations are correct, quasars are very remote and *super-luminous. **1977** *Jrnl. R. Soc. Arts* CXXV. 215/1 The enigmatical 'quasars'..are thought to be immensely remote and super-luminous. **1614** B. JONSON *Barth. Fair* v. vi, Thou *superlunaticall hypocrite. **1787** BECKFORD *Italy* (1834) II. xxx. 208 To all these *super-marvellous narrations, the missionary appeared to listen with implicit faith. **1967** *Supermassive [see RELATIVISTIC *a.* 2 b]. **1981** *Economist* 24 Jan. 97/1 Still higher output would result from the collision of super-massive black holes containing, say, a mass equivalent to a million of earth's suns. **1579** G. HARVEY *Letter-bk.* (Camden) 78 Out of Aggrippaes *super-notable fourthe booke. **1650** B. *Discolliminium* 18 They are dextrously pragmatick..*Super-officious. **1602** J. DAVIES *Mirum in Modum* Wks. (Grosart) I. 22/2 God by powre, *super-omnivalent. **1608** J. DAY *Law Trickes* I. i, Thanks:—*superpassing good! **1657** J. SERGEANT *Schism Dispach't* 648 He excepts against the *super proportion'd multitude of members out of one province, which hee says never lawfull Parliament had. **1768** TUCKER *Lt. Nat.* (1834) I. 460 Sentimental *super-refined ladies. **1888** *Pall Mall Gaz.* 24 Oct. 3/2 The distinction is, perhaps, super-refined. **1887** LECKY *Hist. Eng.* VI. xxiii. 299 The combination of mean action and *supersaintly profession. **1633** FORD *Broken H.* IV. ii, 'Tis wonderful, 'Tis *super-singular, not to be match'd. **1656** *Artif. Handsom.* 56 Such a *super-stoicall piece of Philosophy. **1844** HOOD *Forge* I. 70 Walking, leaping, striding along, As none can do but the *super-strong. *c* **1450** *Mirour Saluacioun* (Roxb.) 150 Alle this tholid thow Jhū in paciens *supersuffrable. **1648** JENKYN *Blind Guide* i. 3 The..foolish pamphlets..are a *supersufficient testimony. **1864** DK. MANCH. *Crt. & Soc. Eliz. to Anne* I. xiv. 280 Superabundant pride born of supersufficient wealth. **1922** JOYCE *Ulysses* 497 It is immense, *supersumptuous. **1840** HALIBURTON *Clockm.* Ser. III. (1862) 518 A most *super-superior gall. **1625** GILL *Sacr. Philos.* i. 8 Whatsoever is *supersupreme, or highest in all degrees of perfection. **1593** BRETON *Phoenix Nest* Wks. (Grosart) I. 4/1 Sundrie flowres so *super sweete of smell. **1592** G. HARVEY *Four Lett.* iii. 31 Those Miracles, which some round liberality, and thy *super-thankfull minde, would hugelie enhable thee to worke. **1817** COLERIDGE *Biog. Lit.* xxiii. (Bohn) 290 A series of *super-tragic starts, pauses, screams. **1649** PRYNNE *Vind. Lib. Eng.* 13 More then Regall, ..*Super-transcendent Arbitrary power. **1902** *Encycl. Brit.* XXVI. 66/2 This '*super-virulent' character [of bacillus-cultures]. **1970** *Physical Rev.* D. II. 257 (*heading*) Unitarity and the phase of the mixing parameter in *superweak theories. **1979** CHENG & O'NEILL *Elem. Particle Physics* ix. 206 If the Wolfenstein model is correct, there exists a 'superweak' fifth force in nature. **1627** DONNE *Serm. Easter-day* (1640) 217 A *super-zealous, an over-vehement animosity.

(*b*) In corresponding adverbs, as ***super-colossally***, †***-effluently***, ***-infinitely***, etc.

1966 *New Yorker* 1 Oct. 184 Both *supercolossally ambitious and energetic men. *a* **1711** KEN *Sion* Poet. Wks. 1721 III. 380 O may kind Heav'n on good Macario's Head Grace and Truth *super-effluently shed. **1628** DONNE *Serm. 15 Apr.* (1640) 765 We were still short of numbring the benefits of God, as God; But then, of God in Christ, infinitely, *Super-infinitely short. **1908** *Westm. Gaz.* 5 Aug. 12/1 A prize in books, *super-magnificently bound. **1607** *Barley-Breake* (1877) 9 A little tilt..Whereunto *super-solemnly they goe. *a* **1665** J. GOODWIN *Being filled with the Spirit* (1867) 125 The things promised..are so above measure desirable and *super-transcendently glorious.

b. Prefixed to verbs or participles (with derivatives), in same senses as in a.: as in late L. *superabundāre* to SUPERABOUND, *supereffluĕre* (in the same sense), *superextendĕre* to stretch excessively, *superincendĕre* to inflame greatly; e.g. ,***supera'ccumulate*** (= to accumulate beyond measure), ***-exceed***, ***-extol***, ***-please***, ***-praise***, ***-reward*** vbs.; ,***supera'cidulated*** (= acidulated to excess), ***-civilized*** (also *absol.* as *sb.*), ***-elated***, ***-excited***, ***-faced*** (FACED *ppl. a.*[2] 2), ***-peopled*** pples. and ppl. adjs.; sometimes = 'more than', as in ,***super'neutralized***, '***super'satisfy***. **supera'llowed** *a. Nucl. Physics*, (of a beta decay) having an exceptionally high probability of occurrence as measured by the product of the half-life of the initial state and a emitted electron. **'supercool** *v. trans.*, to cool (a liquid) below its freezing-point without solidifying it. **super'osculate** *v.*, *Geom.*, *trans.* to osculate at more coincident points than usually suffice for determining the locus; so **,superoscu'lation**.

*a***1709** ATKYNS *Parl. & Polit. Tracts* (1734) 215 A smart Epistle.. wherein he does cry out upon the Pope, for that the Pope's Bulls did *superaccumulate (as he terms it) the Words (*Non obstante*). **1828–32** WEBSTER, **Superacidulated*. **1950** *Rev. Mod. Physics* XXII. 397/2 The very lowest $\log_{10} ft \sim 3$ to 4 are allowed transitions between nuclei having similar nuclear wave functions. These transitions are called the *superallowed transitions, while allowed transitions between nuclei not having very similar wave functions have log *ft* ranging from 4 to 6. **1964** *Physical Rev. Lett.* XII. 301/1 The transition from the ground state of ^{37}Cl to the 5·1-MeV excited state of ^{37}Ar is superallowed and has a large matrix element for neutrino absorption. **1975** *Nature* 18 Sept. 179/2 They start.. from basic input experimental data —the lifetimes and energy release of certain particularly simple nuclear β decays known as superallowed transitions. **1865** E. S. FFOULKES *Christ. Div.* 2 The New World..is becoming super-peopled and *super-civilised. **1929** 'R. CROMPTON' *William* i. 12 The Outlaws never made the pretence affected by the super-civilised, of indifference to their neighbours' affairs. **1818** BENTHAM *Ch. Eng.* 174 Suppose the Archbishop of Canterbury..with his own *super-consecrated hands, washing the feet of a dozen of the inhabitants. **1907** *Jrnl. Phys. Chem.* XI. 425 The freezing point curve had been determined.. and there is considerable evidence of the effects of *supercooling. **1652** URQUHART *Jewel* Wks. (1834) 231 Through the too intensive stretching of the already *super-elated strings of their imagination. **1622** MALYNES *Anc. Law-Merch.* Ded., Being confident of your most gratious benignitie and *super-exceeding grace. **1635** HEYWOOD *Hierarchy* II. 78 This great Nature Naturant ..Which All things Holds,..Super-exceedes, Sustaines. *a***1665** J. GOODWIN *Being filled with the Spirit* (1867) 109 Those degrees of [righteousness and holiness] which in persons highly qualified with them do super-exceed that measure or degree of them which are found in Christians of a lower pitch and stature. **1862** LYTTON *Str. Story* xxxiii, A brain *super-excited by the fumes of a vapour. **1696** LORIMER *Goodwin's Disc.* vii. 83 It was necessary that the Decrees..should be *superextended, (i.e. should be enlarged above what they were before). **1865** PUSEY *Eiren.* 369 Who *superextol reason and its discoveries. **1894** C. VICKERMAN *Woollen Spinning* x. 243 In addition to a *super-faced cloth..an immeasurably superior class of tweeds could be produced. **1822–7** GOOD *Study Med.* (1829) V. 12 The stoutest tree, if *superfructified, is impaired for bearing fruit the next year. **1881** TYNDALL *Ess. Floating Matter Air* 90 The same infusions slightly *superneutralized by caustic potash. **1891** *Century Dict.* s.v., A conic having six consecutive points in common with a cubic is said to *super-osculate it. **1902** *Science* 18 Apr. 625/2 On the *Superosculation of Surfaces. **1632** B. JONSON *Magn. Lady* Induct., He is confident it shall *super-please judicious Spectators. **1590** SHAKS. *Mids. N.* III. ii. 153 To vow, and sweare, and *superpraise my parts. **1622** BACON *Let. to Jas. I* in Spedding *Lett. & Life* (1874) VII. 383 They were from time to time far above my merit over and *super-rewarded by your Majesty's benefits. **1853** MRS. GORE *Dean's Dau.* II. x. 253 The..wife and nurse of a *superrheumatised D.D. **1629** DONNE *Serm. 22 Nov.* (1649) II. 417 To merit, and over-merit; To satisfie, and *super-satisfie the justice of God. **1818** T. L. PEACOCK *Nightmare Abbey* x, Like a shuttlecock between two battledores,..flying from point to point on the feathers of a *super-sublimated head. **1832** L. HUNT *Redi Bacchus in Tuscany* 139, I love my wine iced through and through, If I will have it ..*Superultrafrostified.

10. Prefixed with adjectival force to abstract sbs.: Very great, or too great; surpassing; excessive, extreme; after late L. *superabundantia* SUPERABUNDANCE; e.g. ***,superac'tivity***, ***-conformity*** (= overpreciseness in conforming to ecclesiastical rules), ***-effluence***, ***-exiguity***, ***-infirmity***, ***-treason***, ***-vexation***; hence occas. agent-nouns, as ***,super-con'formist***, ***-individualist***. **,superintro'mission** *Sc. Law*, intromission beyond one's legal rights.

1553 BRADFORD *Serm. Repentance* (1574) C iij, Workes of supererogation (yea *superabomination). **1895** *Pop. Sci. Monthly* July 398 A *superactivity of nutrition. **1638** LD. WARISTON *Diary* (S.H.S.) 342 Rayning doune the *super-afluence of his blessings. **1880** *Academy* 28 Feb. 153/3 Its superaffluence of splendour. **1801** W. TAYLOR in *Monthly Mag.* XII. 575/2 The *super-civilization..of Europe. **1684** BAXTER *Par. Congreg.* 22 The writings of *superconformists and subverters, or changers of the church government. **1659** GAUDEN *Tears Ch.* I. xiii. 113 Either to a peevish nonconformity, or to a pragmatick *super-conformity. **1644** DIGBY *Nat. Soul* Concl. 463 His liberall *supereffluence of Being vpon me. **1660** HAMMOND *Χάρις καὶ Εἰρήνη* 41 That the super-effluence of Grace may be resisted. *a***1711** KEN *Lett.* Wks. (1838) 39, I beseech God..to give you a super-effluence of his H. Spirit. **1856** DOVE *Logic Chr. Faith* VI. §5. 369 The *super-excitation of the devotional faculty. **1664** POWER *Exp. Philos.* I. xxxviii. 47 The *super-exiguity of this farinaceous Seed of Wort. **1641** HACKET *Sp. Parl.* in Plume *Life* (1865) 49 The *superexquisiteness of the music. **1802** PALEY *Nat. Theol.* xxvi, The system of animal destruction ought always to be considered in strict connexion with another property of animal nature, viz. *superfecundity. *a***1835** F. W. HOPE in Kirby *Hab. & Inst. Anim.* II. xx. 334 A Superintending Power which ordains checks and counterchecks to remedy the superfecundity of the insect world. **1912** *Engl. Rev.* Mar. 638 Mystical *super-individualism. *Ibid.*, The art of world-forsakers and hermits, of *super-individualists. **1581** J. BELL *Haddon's Answ. Osor.* 375b, Is this..the super-abundance of your eloquence? or..*superinfirmity of your slippery braynes? **1678** FOUNTAINHALL *Decis.* (1759) I. 1 The Ordinary found the pursuer could not reply on *super-intromission, unless she had taken a dative *ad omissa*. *a***1768** ERSKINE *Inst. Law Scot.* III. ix. §52 Where an executor confirmed,.. intermeddles with subjects not given up by him in inventory, after being cited by a creditor, such superintromission makes him liable as a vitious intromitter. **1871** J. BROWN *Lett., to Lady Minto* 31 Dec. (1907) 208 There are too many big words and hints of *superknowledge. **1599** NASHE *Lenten Stuffe* Wks. 1905 III. 186 Not the dimunutiuest nooke or creuise of them but is parturient of the like *superofficiousnes. **1662** HIBBERT *Body of Div.* I. 327 They can do works of supererrogation; therefore they may challenge..a *superperfection to themselves. **1670** H. STUBBE *Plus Ultra* 164 What we experiment here is not the weight of the Air properly, but the *super-ponderancy or over-weight of it. **1805** EUGENIA DI ACTON *Nuns of Desert* I. 238 People being in those times more superstitious than in our present day of *super-refinement. **1654** GAYTON *Pleas. Notes* III. xii. 157 In case of extreme calidity, and *supersufficiency. **1651** CLEVELAND *Scots Apostasy* 19 The infamie this *super-treason brings. **1626** B. JONSON *Staple of News* 3rd Interm. 56 Not teach 'hem to speake Playes, and Act Fables of false newes..to the *superuexation of Towne and Countrey.

b. (Chiefly *Phys.* and *Path.*) Denoting processes or conditions in excess of the normal; as in mod.L. *superfētātio* SUPERFETATION, *supernutrītio* excessive nutrition; e.g. ***,super-alka'linity***, ***-fecundation***, ***-irritation***, ***-salinity***, ***-secretion***. †**,superfoli'ation**, excessive growth of foliage; **'supervoltage** *Physics* and *Med.*, a higher than usual voltage; *spec.* a voltage in excess of 200 kilovolts; usu. *attrib.* with reference to the use of X-rays generated using such voltages.

*c***1865** *J. Wylde's Circ. Sci.* I. 151/1 The *super-alkalinity of the bath. **1822–7** GOOD *Study Med.* (1829) V. 129 The imperfect emission proceeding from *super-erection or priapism. **1855** DUNGLISON *Med. Lex.*, **Superfecundation*, see *Superfoetation*. **1901** DORLAND *Med. Dict.*, *Superfecundation*, the successive fecundation of two ova formed at the same menstrual period. **1857** DUNGLISON *Med. Lex.*, **Superfibrination*, Hyperinosis. *a***1682** SIR T. BROWNE *Tracts* (1683) 76 The Disease of φυλλομανία, ἐμφυλλισμός, or *superfoliation, mention'd by Theophrastus; whereby the fructifying Juice is starved by the excess of Leaves. **1872** T. G. THOMAS *Dis. Women* (ed. 3) 571 *Superinvolution can be confounded with no other condition than undeveloped uterus. **1890** BILLINGS *Nat. Med. Dict.*, **Super-lactation*, excessive secretion of milk. **1648** BAILLIE *Let. to W. Spang* 26 June, I was forced to keep my chamber ten days with a dangerous *superpurgation. **1751** STACK in *Phil. Trans.* XLVII. 274 These two doses.. might cause a superpurgation. **1845** SPOONER *Veterinary Art* (1851) 58 Superpurgation from actual inflammation is extremely dangerous. **1882** J. C. BURNETT (*title*) *Supersalinity of the Blood. **1843** R. J. GRAVES *Syst. Clin. Med.* xx. 233, I often diminish *supersecretion from the lungs by strong hydragogue cathartics. **1934** *Illinois Med. Jrnl.* LXVI. 286/2 Much of the improvement claimed for *super-voltage is available at 200 kilovolts. **1956** A. H. COMPTON *Atomic Quest* i. 14 The new physics laboratory.. would include space for supervoltage equipment. **1976** *Lancet* 6 Nov. 992/2 Patients who received T.N.I. were all treated with supervoltage or megacurie equipment.

11. In prepositional relation with the radical element, as in late L. *supernumerārius*, that is *super numerum* beyond the (normal) number, SUPERNUMERARY.

12. *Chem.* †**a.** Prefixed to vbs., pa. pples., and cognate nouns of action, denoting a high proportion of the ingredient indicated by the radical element; e.g. ***,superazo'tation*** (= the condition of being highly charged with nitrogen), ***-carbonate*** vb., ***-carburetted***, ***-oxidated***, ***-oxygenated***, ***-oxygenation***, ***-phlogistication***.

1783 PRIESTLEY in *Phil. Trans.* LXXIII. 405 By *super-phlogisticating iron with nitrous air. **1789** *Ibid.* LXXIX. 289 What we have called the phlogistication of them, ought rather to have been called their *super-phlogistication. **1793** BEDDOES *Calculus* p. x, Easy extemporaneous way to *supercarbonate alkali to a certain degree. **1794** HUTTON *Philos. Light*, etc. 297 The *super-oxigenated marine acid. **1796** HATCHETT in *Phil. Trans.* LXXXVI. 285 A peculiar metallic substance, which..was liable by *superoxygenation to be converted into a metallic acid. **1799** MUSHET in *Phil. Mag.* IV. 381 *note*, When supercarbonated crude iron is run from the furnace, it is frequently covered with a scurf, which..is found to be a coating of plumbago. **1799** *Monthly Rev.* XXX. 498 Water with the addition of about one-fourth part of the *super-oxydated acid. **1802** *Edin. Rev.* I. 243 Their grand energy.. in a word..depends upon a real *superazotation. **1816** S. PARKES *Chem. Catech.* ix. (ed. 7) 257 *note*, A gas..called *super-carburetted hydrogen and also olefiant gas. *Ibid.* 255 *note*, Sulphuretted hydrogen is capable of combining with an additional portion of sulphur, forming a compound which may be called *super-sulphuretted hydrogen. **1829** *Nat. Philos.* I. *Optics* xviii. 64 (Usef. Knowl. Soc.) Super-oxygenated muriate of potash.

b. In names of compounds, indicating that the ingredient denoted by the radical is in the highest proportion: e.g. ***superacetate*** (= a salt containing the highest proportion of acetic acid); ***superoxide*** orig. = PEROXIDE; in mod. use distinguished from peroxide, and restricted to the anion O_2-; †***supersulphuret*** (= a binary compound containing the highest proportion of sulphur, a persulphide). Otherwise surviving in the names of certain salts used in manufactures or the arts, e.g. SUPERPHOSPHATE.

[**1839**: see SUB- 24.]

1811 A. T. THOMSON *Lond. Disp.* (1818) 555 The dose of *superacetate of lead. **1807** T. THOMSON *Chem.* (ed. 3) II. 396 *Superarseniate of potash. **1826** HENRY *Elem. Chem.* II. 226 The neutral malate of lime..may be obtained by adding lime water to a solution of the *super-malate. **1797** PEARSON in *Phil. Trans.* LXXXVIII. 44 *Super-oxalate of potash. **1847** WEBSTER, **Super-oxyd*, an oxyd containing more equivalents of oxygen than of the base with which it is combined; a hyperoxyd. **1853** W. GREGORY *Inorg. Chem.* 51 Deutoxide (binoxide, peroxide, or superoxide) of manganese. **1950** *Chambers's Jrnl.* Apr. 255/2 It [*sc.* a new lifesaving apparatus] has depended upon finding a method for fairly large-scale production of the chemical used, namely potassium superoxide. **1965** PHILLIPS & WILLIAMS *Inorg. Chem.* I. xiii. 491 The metal oxides so far discussed contain the anion O_2- only. There are also two other series of oxides, the peroxides and superoxides which contain the anions O_2- and O_2- respectively. **1979** *Experientia* XXXV. 245/2 The explanation for such action is the hypothesis that vitamin C can act as an antioxidant as well as oxidant, by generating superoxide. **1807** T. THOMSON *Chem.* (ed. 3) II. 616 *Supersulphate of alumina-and-potash. **1812** SIR H. DAVY *Chem. Philos.* 383 The other sulphuret of tin, or the *supersulphuret is made by heating together the peroxide of tin and sulphur. **1815** J. SMITH *Panorama Sci. & Art* II. 296 *Super-tartrate of potass. **1843** *Penny Cycl.* XXVII. 458/2 Malate of lime and super-tartrate of lime [in the juice of the grape]. **1891** *Science-Gossip* XXVII. 32 The colour is fixed by a mordant of alumina and oxide of tin, and the colour is intensified by super-tartrate of potash.

IV. Expressing addition.

13. In advb. or adj. relation to a vb., sb., or adj.: Over and above, in addition, additional(ly), extra; as in (late) L. *superaddĕre* to add over and above, SUPERADD, *superērogāre* to spend over and above, SUPEREROGATE, *superfētāre* to conceive again while already with young, *supernōmināre* to give an additional name to, SURNAME, *superordināre* to appoint in addition; (late or med.) L. *superaugmentum* further increase, *superindictio* [see INDICTION 2], *supernōmen* SURNAME, *superplūs* SURPLUS: e.g. †***super-assume***, ***-elect***, ***-illustrate***, ***-ordain*** vbs.; ***super-accession***, ***-conception***, ***-dying***, †***-graffing***, ***-illustration***, ***-injustice***, ***-ornament***, ***-sanction***, ***-straining***, ***-stuff*** sbs. and vbl. sbs.; †***super-accessory*** adj. †**,superad'venient** *a.*, coming upon or after something as an addition. †**super-bibe** *v.* [late L. *superbibĕre*] *trans.*, to drink in addition. **super-'calender** *v. trans.*, to subject (paper) to additional calendering, so as to produce a highly glazed surface; chiefly in *ppl. adj.* and *vbl. sb.*; hence **super-'calender** *sb.*, a roller used for supercalendering. **,superfeu'dation**, **,superinfeu'dation**, creation of a new feudal estate out of one already established. **,superinsta'llation**, installation into an office or dignity already held by another (cf. SUPERINSTITUTION). **'super-tax** *sb.*, an additional duty of income tax levied upon incomes above a certain value: abolished as an official term in the U.K. in 1929, but still in common (esp. *attrib.*) use; cf. SURTAX *sb.*

1701 NORRIS *Ideal World* I. vii. 410 One is conceived as a *super-accession to the other. **1698** —— *Treat. Sev. Subj.* 392 The Divine Light..*Superaccessory to the Natural Light. **1647** H. MORE *Song of Soul* Notes 160/1 By the powerfull appulse of some *superadvenient form. **1664** —— *Myst. Iniq.* xx. 77 Which will again be hugely increased by another superadvenient Incertainty. **1620** VENNER *Via Recta* viii. 190 Vpon meats taken againe, let there be assumed a draught of ordinarie Beere, and therewith, or a litle meat *super-assumed. **1691** SANCROFT *Let. to Sir H. North* in D'Oyly *Life* (1821) xi. II. 10, I sometimes eat bread and butter in a morning, and *superbibe my second dish of coffee after it. **1888** *Daily News* 10 Dec. 3/2 The choice *super-calendered paper with which the American magazines have made us familiar. **1894** *Super-calender sb. [see SHEAVE *sb.*[2] 3]. **1902** *Encycl. Brit.* XXXII. 6/1 Super-calendered paper, which is still largely used for the printing of ordinary illustrations. **1911** *Ibid.* (ed. 11) XX. 734/2 For the better class or very highly-glazed papers..a subsequent glazing process is required; this is effected by sheet or plate-glazing and by *super-calendering or web-glazing... The super-calender is used to imitate the plate-glazed surface. **1646** SIR T. BROWNE *Pseud. Ep.* III. xvii. 150 In those *superconceptions where one childe was like the father, the other like the adulterer. **1855** DUNGLISON *Med. Lex.* s.v. *Superfœtation*, Twin cases may be of this kind of superconception. **1627** DONNE *Serm. Lady Danvers* 159 When there was a *Super-dying, a death vpon the death,.. a Spirituall death after the bodily. *a***1734** NORTH *Lives* (1826) I. 360 How can you *super-elect and set up anti-sheriffs to oust them before their title is tried? **1627** DONNE *Serm. 25 Dec.* (1640) 44 That God would *super-endow him with parts, and faculties, fit for that service. **1861** MAINE *Anc. Law* iv. (1870) 107 To mount up, through narrowing circles of *super-feudation, till we approximate to the apex of the system. **1664** EVELYN *Sylva* (1679) 4 *Super-graffing, or the repetition of Graffing, for the inlargement, and melioration of Fruit. **1629** DONNE *Serm., Acts xxiii. 6, 7* (1640) 496 At thy death thou shalt be *super-illustrated, with a Meridionall light. *a***1631** —— *2nd Serm. Gen. i. 26* (1634) 23 Those *super-illustrations, which the blessed shall have in Glorie. **1781** GIBBON *Decl. & F.* xxxvi. (1787) III. 455 The provincials, oppressed by the accumulated weight of indictions and *superindictions. *a***1626** BACON *Consid. Warre w. Spaine* (1629) 5 The Raishing whereof was a meere Excursion of the first Wrong, and a *Super-Iniustice. **1642** FULLER *Holy & Prof. St.* IV. xi. 285 Such a *superinstallation seems an unlawfull bigamy, marrying two husbands at the same time to the same Church. **1590** GREENWOOD *Answ. to Giffard* 32 Christ pronounceth them accursed that add or *superordeyne any thing to his worde.

1709 MRS. MANLEY *Secret Mem.* (1720) I. 114 The *super-Ornaments of the Mind..were not necessary. **1657** in *Burton's Diary* (1828) I. 407 The frequent *super-sanction of Magna Charta. **1626** BACON *Sylva* §182 In the Straining of a String, the further it is strained, the lesse *Superstraining goeth to a Note. **1792** D. LLOYD *Voy. Life* III. 51 If you in works of merit prove too light, They'll add their *super-stuff into the scale. **1906** *Westm. Gaz.* 5 July 2/2 The powers that would..be necessary to obtain a full disclosure of income..under a system of *super-tax. **1908** *Daily Chron.* 23 Nov. 1/6 A graduated super tax on incomes over £5,000 a year. **1931** *Times Lit. Suppl.* 16 July 556/4 The incidence of income-tax and supertax on business profits. **1972** *Daily Tel.* 14 Jan. 13 Our friends, on hearing that we own two houses, put us in the super-tax class. **1978** F. OLBRICH *Desouza pays Price* v. 21 The Taj Mahal Hotel['s]..clientele consisted exclusively of those in the super-tax bracket. **1905** *Ibid.* 23 June 5/7 Only those *super-values would be taxed which are due to the growth of a town [etc.].

†**14.** *Math.* In adjs. denoting ratios expressible by unity (or some other integer) with some number of aliquot parts over; as in late L. *superdīmidius* (sc. *numerus* number) 'that is a half more', i.e. $1\frac{1}{2}$, denoting a ratio of 3:2, *supertertius* 'that is a third over', i.e. $1\frac{1}{3} = 4:3$, *supersesquialter* 'that is $1\frac{1}{2}$ over', i.e. $2\frac{1}{2} = 5:2$; also, with less precise indication of the denominator of the fraction, after *superpartiens* SUPERPARTIENT (cf. *superparticulāris* SUPERPARTICULAR), *superbipartiens* 'that is two parts over', i.e. $1\frac{2}{3} = 5:3$, *superquadripartiens*, 'that is four parts over', i.e. $1\frac{4}{5} = 9:5$. *Obs.*

[**1570** BILLINGSLEY *Euclid* v. 127b, If the antecedent containe aboue the consequent two partes, it is called *Superbipartiens*, as 7. to 5. If 3 partes *Supertripartiens* as 7. to 4.] **1678** PHILLIPS (ed. 4), Superbipartient number. *Ibid.*, Supertripartient number. *a* **1696** SCARBURGH *Euclid* (1705) 180 As 8 to 3 is..$2\frac{2}{3}$..: therefore this proportion is named Duple superbitertial. **1709–29** V. MANDEY *Sys. Math., Arith.* 36 Proportion Superpartient, is the Habitude of a greater Number to a lesser, when the greater contains the lesser once, and moreover some Aliquot parts... The Denominators of it are, $1\frac{2}{3}$, Superbipartient. $1\frac{3}{4}$, Supertripartient. $1\frac{4}{5}$, Superquadrupartient,..etc. ad Infinitum. **1737** E. MANWARING *Stichology* 16 Supertertian Ratio is, when the Arsis and Thesis is as 4 to 3 or 3 to 4.

15. Upon something of the same kind, in a secondary relation; secondary, secondarily: e.g. ***supercommentary*** (= a commentary on a commentary), ***-commentator***, †***-consequency*** (= a consequence of a consequence), ***-heresy***, ***-parasite***, ***-parasitic*** (= HYPERPARASITE, -ITIC), ***-reflection***, ***-reformation***; ***super-crown*** vb.

1876 SCHILLER-SZINESSY *Catal. Hebr. MSS.* 137 This *supercommentary has been printed twice. *Ibid.* 139 Our author as well as other *supercommentators..commented on the short commentary. **1646** SIR T. BROWNE *Pseud. Ep.* I. iii. 9 Not attaining the deuteroscopy, or second intention of the words, they are faine to omit their *superconsequencies, coherencies, figures, or tropologies. **1633** T. ADAMS *Exp. 2 Peter* iii. 18. 1564 Crowned with his [*sc.* Job's] patience, which is *supercrowned with everlasting blessednesse. **1846** *Proc. Philol. Soc.* III. 14 This principle of *super-formation. **1643** SIR T. BROWNE *Relig. Med.* I. §8 Even in Doctrines hereticall there will be *super-heresies. **1891** *Century Dict.*, *Superparasite. **1877** *Encycl. Brit.* VI. 647/2 Another parasite..had become parasitic upon the parasite. The most curious part of this *super-parasitic history is [etc.]. **1626** BACON *Sylva* §241 There be three Kindes of Reflexions of Sounds; A Reflexion Concurrent; A Reflexion Iterant, which we call Eccho; And a *Super-reflexion, or an Eccho of an Eccho. **1622** DONNE *Serm. Easter-Monday* (1660) III. 372 We shall not need any such re-Reformation, or *super-Reformation. **1670** WALTON *Lives* III. 185 Men of the slightest Learning, and the most ignorant of the Common People were mad for a new, or, Super, or Re-reformation of Religion.

V. †**16.** Representing Gr. ὑπερ-, ἐπι-, in nonce-renderings of words in the N.T.: ***superexpostulate*** = Gr. ὑπερεντυγχάνειν to intercede on behalf of; ***superintroduction*** = Gr. ἐπεισαγωγή a bringing in besides. *Obs.* See also SUPERSUBSTANTIAL I.

1647 TRAPP *Comm. Rom.* viii. 26 The Spirit..doth super-expostulate for us. *Ibid.*, *Heb.* vii. 19 The Law is a super-introduction to Christ our hope.

VI. With reduplication of the prefix.

17. Used as an intensifier Cf. Branch III.

1871 W. G. WARD *Ess. Philos. Theism* (1884) II. 259 The super-superabundance..of evidence. *Ibid.*, II. 258 All men have access to super-superabundant evidence for the truth of Theism. *Ibid.*, II. 256 Evidence super-superabundantly sufficient. **1934** 'J. SPENSER' *Limey breaks In* ix. 158 This warder was another of the variety known amongst prison populations as super-super bastards. **1937** A. CALDER-MARSHALL in C. Day Lewis *Mind in Chains* 60 The second stage was reached, where super- and super-super-films were made. **1963** *Supermarket & Self Service* (Johannesburg) Aug. 16/1 A further 'super-supermarket' of American-style dimensions, is under contemplation. **1974** T. P. WHITNEY tr. *Solzhenitsyn's Gulag Archipelago* I. II. iv. 590 Things were neat and clean, they said, and it was always warm, and the only work was mental work—and all of it super-supersecret.

18. Used to denote a further increase in rank or degree. Cf. Branch II.

1971 *Nature* 26 Nov. 182/1 The observations would therefore seem to exclude super-clusters or the still greater hierarchy of super-super-clusters as the source of X-ray background. **1979** *Ibid.* 12 Apr. 615/1 Since nuclear shell theory predicts a further island of stability at Z = 164–184 ..we must consider whether the three peaks originate from decay of super-superheavy elements. **1980** *Sci. Amer.* July 112/1 In this way super-supercoiled molecules can be created, molecules that have many more super-helical twists than are usually present.

superable ('s(j)uːpərəb(ə)l), *a.* [ad. L. *superābilis*, f. *superāre*: see SUPERATE and -ABLE. Cf. OF. *superable*, It. *superabile*, etc.] Capable of being overcome or vanquished; surmountable: the opposite of *insuperable*.

1629 HOBBES *Thucyd.* (1822) 104 If he be superable by money. **1685** BOYLE *Enq. Notion Nat.* 32, I must take leave to complain..of the scarce superable Difficulty of the Task. **1751** JOHNSON *Rambler* No. 126 ¶9 Antipathies are generally superable by a single effort. **1815** JEBB in *Corr. Knox & Jebb* (1834) II. 208 Nothing fairly superable should prevent my forthwith obeying the welcome summons to B——. **1899** *Allbutt's Syst. Med.* VIII. 139 The physician must be on his guard not to be put off from urging change of scene or places of cure, by protestations of hindrances which in health would have been superable enough.

Hence ˌ**supera'bility**, '**superableness**, the quality of being superable; '**superably** *adv.*, so as to be superable.

1727 BAILEY (vol. II), Superableness. **1818** TODD, *Superably*, so as may be overcome. **1889** *Chr. Union* (N.Y.) 10 Jan., The superability of all obstacles.

superabound (ˌs(j)uːpərə'baʊnd), *v.* Also 5 **-habounde**, 7 **suprabound**. [ad. late L. *superabundāre*: see SUPER- 9 b and ABOUND *v.* Cf. obs. F. *superabonder* (OF., F. *surabonder*), It. *soprabbondare*, Sp. *sobreabundar*, Pg. *sobreabundar*, *superabundar*.]

1. *intr.* To abound beyond something else; to be more abundant. (Always with allusion to *Rom.* v. 20.)

1447 BOKENHAM *Seyntys* (Roxb.) 154 Wher wrechydly Synne regnyd grace doth superhabounde. **1579** LYLY *Euphues* (Arb.) 140 What shame is this..that where grace doth abounde, sinne shoulde so superabound? **1647** CLARENDON *Hist. Reb.* VI. §175 If the Mercy, Favour, and Blessing of Almighty God, had not superabounded. **1749** HARTLEY *Observ. Man* II. i. 15 Though Disorder, Pain, and Death do very much abound..yet Beauty, Order, Pleasure, Life, and Happiness, seem to superabound. **1879** FARRAR *St. Paul* II. 219 An apparent paradox—If grace superabounds over sin, why should we not continue in sin? **1907** *Month* Nov. 535 Where distress abounds devotedness will superabound.

†**b.** *trans.* To abound beyond, be more abundant than, exceed greatly. *Obs. rare.*

a **1670** HACKET *Cent. Serm.* (1675) 149 Nothing was defective in him, but did exceedingly super-abound all which could be required in any Priest or Prophet.

2. *intr.* To abound excessively; to be very, or too, abundant.

c **1520** NISBET *N.T.* 1 Tim. i. 14 The grace of our Lord superaboundit [*Wycl.* ouer habounde], with faith and lufe that is in Crist Jesu. **1590** SIR J. SMYTH *Disc. Weapons* Ded 1 The vanitie and ouerweening of yong men..haue so exceeded and superabounded. **1601** DENT *Pathw. Heaven* 155 Lying and dissembling are most rife,..but especially it doth ouerflow and superabound in shopkeepers and seruants. **1623** T. SCOT *Tongue-Combat* 89 This Sect doth suprabound with you. **1638** JUNIUS *Paint. Ancients* 227 Whatsoever doth superabound, issueth out of a full brest. **1827** STEUART *Planter's Guide* (1828) 461 Though no..fermentation can take place without moisture, yet moisture may superabound. **1834** HT. MARTINEAU *Moral* II. 50 The capitalists do not need to combine when labour superabounds.

b. with *in* or *with*: To abound excessively in; to possess or contain in great abundance.

1632 SIR T. HAWKINS tr. *Mathieu's Unhappy Prosp.* 12 Ægypt,..super-abounded in pratteling, and artificyes to calumniate gouernors. **1638** SIR T. HERBERT *Trav.* (ed. 2) 13 Cony Ile..also superabounds with Seales. *Ibid.* 25 They [sea tortoises] superabound in eggs. **1749** HARTLEY *Observ. Man* II. ii. 101 We do not find that forged or false Accounts of Things superabound in Particularities. **1802** W. TAYLOR in *Monthly Mag.* XIII. 10 The English language superabounds with hissings. **1864** BURTON *Scot Abr.* I. iii. 119 To supply the country with that commodity in which it superabounded.

Hence **superabounding** *vbl. sb.* and *ppl. a.*

1560–1 *First Bk. Discipl. Ch. Scot.* in *Knox's Wks.* (1848) II. 186 Yit for ane uniformitie to be keipit, we have thocht gude to adde this as superabondand. **1594** CAREW *Huarte's Exam. Witz* (1616) 65 How many differences of wits grow by meanes of the superabounding of each of these three qualities. **1598** DELONEY *Jacke Newb.* i. (1630) Bjb, Maidens ficklenesse proceedes of vaine fancies, but old womens iealousie of superabounding loue. **1613** PURCHAS *Pilgrimage* II. ii. 93 The superabounding grace of God. **1757** J. EDWARDS *Orig. Sin* II. iv. §1 That superabounding of grace. **1883** *American* VII. 20 Nor are we so superabounding in capital that [etc.]. **1884** J. PARKER *Apost. Life* II. 197 A superabounding religious spirit and activity.

superabundance (ˌs(j)uːpərə'bʌndəns). Also 5–6 **-habundaunce**, 6 **-haboundaunce**, 6–7 **-aboundance**. [ad. late L. *superabundantia*, f. pres. pple. of *superabundāre* to SUPERABOUND: see -ANCE. Cf. obs. F. *superabondance* (OF., F. *sur-*).]

1. The quality of being superabundant; the fact or condition of superabounding; excessive abundance or plentifulness; redundance.

1432–50 tr. *Higden* (Rolls) IV. 37 Puttenge signes þer callede obeli, to betokyn superhabundaunce. **1526** *Pilgr. Perf.* (W. de W. 1531) 263 b, Superhaboundaunce or lacke of some humour, whiche disordereth the body. **1593** NASHE *Christ's T.* Wks. 1904 II. 124 It is the superaboundance of witte that makes Atheists. **1695** WOODWARD *Nat. Hist. Earth* v. (1723) 262 The Luxury and Superabundance of the Productions of the Earth. **1783** JUSTAMOND tr. *Raynal's Hist. Indies* II. 3 The superabundance of population in islands. **1831** BREWSTER *Nat. Magic* i. (1833) 7 The task of selection is rendered extremely difficult, by the superabundance of materials. **1860** PUSEY *Min. Proph.* 225 Such shall be the abundance and superabundance of blessing, that it shall be as though the hills dissolved themselves in the rich streams which they poured down.

2. That which superabounds; a superabundant quantity or amount; a surplus (*of* something).

c **1410** HOCCLEVE *Min. Poems* in *De Reg. Princ.* (1897) p. lx, I pray you..Of youre merites superhabundaunce, As grauntith me of almesse some pietaunce. **1576** NEWTON *Lemnie's Complex.* (1633) 77 That the stomacke be not overcloyed and charged with superabundance or excesse. **1603** HOLLAND *Plutarch's Mor.* 59 For a man to adorne another is an excellent ornament proceeding from a superabundance (as it were) of glorie and honor which is in himselfe. **1785** PHILLIPS *Treat. Inland Nav.* p. v, Navigation..conveys the superabundance of the productions and manufactures of one country..to another. **1827** HARE *Guesses* Ser. I. (1859) 1 A mother should desire to give her children a superabundance of enthusiasm. **1879** *Cassell's Techn. Educ.* I. 219/2 To relieve it of its super-abundance of water.

†**supera'bundancy.** *Obs.* [ad. late L. *superabundantia*: see prec. and -ANCY.] = prec.

1627 J. DOUGHTY *Serm. Div. Myst.* (1628) Ep. Ded., I knowe..the superabundancy of this kinde of writing. *a* **1649** DRUMM. OF HAWTH. *Fam. Ep.* Wks. (1711) 143, I write often unto you, for that..I had rather be charged for superabundancy than defect. **1727** [DORRINGTON] *Philip Quarll* 106 This Gentlewoman wants for no manner of Necessaries..but has rather a Superabundancy. **1754** H. WALPOLE *Let. to R. Bentley* 3 Nov., My chief employ..is planting at Mrs. Clive's, whither I remove all my superabundancies. **1765** in *10th Rep. Hist. MSS. Comm.* App. I. 387 Making amends for the want of Knowledge by the superabundancy of Zeal. **1786** ABERCROMBIE *Gard. Assist.* 15 Pruning out the superabundancy.

superabundant (ˌs(j)uːpərə'bʌndənt), *a.* Also 5–6 **-habunda(u)nt**, **-habounda(u)nt**, 6–7 **-aboundant**; 7 **sup'rabundant**. [ad. late L. *superabundant-*, *-ans*, pres. pple. of *superabundāre* to SUPERABOUND: see -ANT. (Cf. F. *surabondant*.)]

1. Abounding above something else, or above measure; more than (barely) sufficient, enough and to spare; exceedingly abundant or plentiful. Now *rare* or merged in 2 (but cf. next, 1).

c **1410** HOCCLEVE *Min. Poems* in *De Reg. Princ.* (1897) p. xlix, To þat only was thi talent & thi chiere So suffisaunt, lo, —that oure raunsoum were Superhabundaunt over þat was due. **1508** FISHER *7 Penit. Ps.* cxxx. Wks. (1876) 207 Of the whiche superhaboundaunt mercy we haue..spoken. **1592** NASHE *Strange Newes* (1593) 69, I wish vnto thee all superabundant increase. *a* **1633** AUSTIN *Medit.* (1635) 112 The Passion of Christ..was not onely a sufficient, but a superabundant satisfaction for the sinne, of all Mankind. **1683** *Brit. Spec.* 249 Out of their superabundant Loyalty. **1728** MORGAN *Algiers* II. ii. 234 Every Nation has its Peculiarities; nor has Ours abundance of Reason to brag of its super-abundant Regularity. **1830** MACKINTOSH *Eth. Philos.* Wks. 1846 I. 215 His gratitude and native modesty dictated a superabundant care in softening and excusing his dissent from those who had been his own instructors.

2. Abounding above what is fitting or needful; exceeding the normal or required amount; too abundant; more than sufficient (in a bad sense).

[**1432–50**: cf. SUPERABUNDANTLY 2]. **1531** ELYOT *Gov.* III. xxi, Whan the bloode is corrupted, and eyther fleame or Colere..is superhabundaunt, than in the body be ingendred sores and diseases. **1636** in *Collect.* (Oxf. Hist. Soc.) I. 281 Out of a superaboundant caution. **1753** *Chambers' Cycl. Suppl.* s.v. *Wine*, Vinegar which has once thrown off the super-abundant earthy parts, and many of the oily ones. **1815** J. SMITH *Panorama Sci. & Art* II. 363 This forces the superabundant mercury from the amalgam, and renders it solid. **1835** THIRLWALL *Greece* viii. I. 324 A superabundant population might have been easily discharged by the ordinary expedient of a colony. **1871** H. MACMILLAN *True Vine* v. 216 The leaves..need sometimes to be taken away, as super-abundant foliage would shade the fruit.

†**b.** Abounding overmuch *in*, having or containing too much (of something). *Obs. rare.*

1644 DIGBY *Nat. Bodies* xxiv. §8. 222 Vnlesse the mothers seede, do supply or temper, what the fathers was defectiue or superaboundant in.

ˌ**supera'bundantly**, *adv.* [f. prec. + -LY².] In a superabundant degree.

1. Abundantly beyond something else, or above measure; very abundantly or plentifully.

1530 PALSGR. 852/1 Superhabundantly, *superhabundamment*. **1593** NASHE *Christ's T.* Wks. 1904 II. 171 He could haue beene reuenged on thee superaboundantly. **1638** CHILLINGW. *Relig. Prot.* I. vi. §38. 357, I conceive it sufficiently, abundantly, superabundantly proved to be divine Revelation. *a* **1665** J. GOODWIN *Being filled with the Spirit* (1867) 253 Those that shall be superabundantly blessed. **1780** H. WALPOLE *Let. to W. Mason* 9 June, We have now, superabundantly, to fear robbery: 300 desperate villains were released from Newgate. **1860** MILL *Repr. Govt.* (1865) 48/2 These things are superabundantly evident. **1885** *Spectator* 8 Aug. 1045/2 She discovers his character, and then husband and wife reproach each other superabundantly.

2. More than enough (in a bad sense); too abundantly; to or in excess, superfluously.

1432–50 tr. *Higden* (Rolls) IV. 313 This Tiberius, callede Nero, was namede..of disporters Biberius Mero, for cause he 3afe hym to drynke superhabundantely wyne. **1654** tr. *Scudery's Curia Pol.* 185 Those who will be superabundantly and tediously wise. **1755** MAGENS *Insurances* I. 443 The King, super-abundantly, ordered the Treaties..to be examined. **1844** EMERSON *Ess.* Ser. II. Experience (1876) 72 My reception has been so large, that I am not annoyed by receiving this or that superabundantly. **1891** *Leeds Mercury* 25 May 5/3 The assertion that Italian art is superabundantly represented in the National Gallery.

'super-acid, *a.* and *sb.* Also **super acid.** [SUPER- 12 b.]

A. *adj.* **1.** *Chem. **superacid salt*** = SUPERSALT.

1808 WOLLASTON in *Phil. Trans.* XCVIII. 96 Other instances of super-acid and sub-acid salts. **1857** MILLER *Elem. Chem., Org.* vi. §3. 425 A remarkable superacid salt (KO, 2HO, $2(C_8H_4O_6)$ 3Aq).

2. Excessively acid.

1901 in DORLAND *Med. Dict.*

3. Of, pertaining to, or designating a non-aqueous solution having very great protonating power.

1927 CONANT & HALL in *Jrnl. Amer. Chem. Soc.* XLIX. 3047 We investigate certain of the properties of these solutions in which salt formation is exceptionally complete, and we propose to call such solutions 'superacid solutions'. **1940** GLASSTONE *Textbk. Physical Chem.* xii. 959 On account of the very marked tendency of the $CH_3 \cdot CO_2H_2{}^+$ ions to lose the proton they have taken up from the acid, the solutions exhibit acidic properties, e.g., in catalysis, of an exceptionally strong nature and so they have been called super-acid. **1968** *Accts. Chem. Res.* I. 202/1 The acidity of fluorosulfuric acid can be considerably increased by the addition of SbF_5 and SbF_5–SO_3, and the resulting solutions are the most highly acidic media known... These systems may therefore be justifiably called superacid media. **1979** *Science* 5 Oct. 14/3 Two superacid systems used very frequently are HSO_3F-SbF_5 (Magic Acid)..and HF-SbF_5 (fluoroantimonic acid).

B. *sb.* A solution of a strong acid in a very acidic solution, which is an extremely effective protonating agent; any acid stronger than some standard acid in either Brönsted acid (i.e., proton-donor) or Lewis acid (electron-acceptor) systems.

1968 *Jrnl. Amer. Chem. Soc.* XC. 2726/1 (*caption*) Chemistry in super acids. **1979** *Science* 5 Oct. 13/3 All protic acids stronger than 100 percent sulfuric acid should be classified as superacids. *Ibid.* 14/2 It is suggested that those [Lewis acids] stronger than anhydrous aluminum chloride ..should be categorized as superacids. *Ibid.* 16/3 The astonishing acidity of Magic Acid and related superacids allows protonation of exceedingly weak bases.

Hence **supera'cidic** *a.* = SUPER-ACID *a.* 3.

1979 *Science* 5 Oct. 14/3 These superacidic systems can be 10^{16} times stronger than 100 per cent sulfuric acid.

,supera'cidity. [f. SUPER-ACID *a.*, after ACIDITY.] **a.** *Med.* (See quot.)

1900 DORLAND *Med. Dict.* 653/2 *Superacidity*, increase of the normal acidity of the gastric secretion.

b. *Chem.* The quality or state of being superacid.

1927 *Jrnl. Amer. Chem. Soc.* XLIX. 3061 Our work indicates that the proximate cause of superacidity in a solution is an abnormally high value of the hydrogen-ion activity. **1979** *Science* 5 Oct. 14/2 It should always be kept in mind that superacidity encompasses both Bronsted and Lewis acid systems.

'supera'cute, *a.* and *sb.* [In A., f. SUPER- 9 + ACUTE *a.* In B., ad. med.L. *superacūta* (sc. *nota*).]

A. *adj.* Excessively acute.

1679 ALSOP *Melius Inq.* II. v. 307 As if some Superacute Philosopher should undertake to prove that because eating and sleeping are subordinate to Health and Life, therefore we ought to lay very little stress on them. **1912** D. CRAWFORD *Thinking Black* xix. 388 These superacute senses of the raw bush negro.

†**B.** *sb. Mus.* The highest note of the gamut.

1504 W. CORNYSSHE *Treat. Inform. & Mus.* xix. in Herrig's *Archiv* (1908) CXX. 425 Enformacione will steteche [*sic*] a doctor hys game, from superacute to the doble diaspason.

superadd (s(j)uːpər'æd), *v.* [ad. L. *superaddĕre*: see SUPER- 13 and ADD *v.*]

1. *trans.* To add over and above; to add to what has been added; to put as a further addition. Often a mere strengthening of *add*: To add besides; 'to join any thing extrinsick' (Johnson).

1641 MAISTERTON *Serm.* 14 That which it superaddeth is a power to reflect upon it self. **1642** *Reg. Privy Council Scot.* Ser. II. VII. 329 His wrath will be turned away and all temporall blessings of prosperitie and peace will be abundantlie supperaddit. **1681** *Whole Duty Nations* 21 If any thing was wanting in the former Revelation..to superadd what might render it most complete. **1760–72** H. BROOKE *Fool of Qual.* (1809) III. 43 Our Gothic ancestors either adopted what they judged excellent in the British constitution, or rather superadded what was deemed to be excellent in their own. **1776** JOHNSON *Let. to Wetherell* 12 Mar. in *Boswell*, We must set the copies at fourteen shillings each, and superadd what is called the quarterly-book. **1817** JAS. MILL *Brit. India* v. v. II. 530 Famine now raged in all his horrors; and the multitude of the dead and the dying threatened to superadd the evils of pestilence. **1860** TYNDALL *Glac.* I. xi. 80 Loss of two nights' sleep, with two days' toil superadded. **1897** *Allbutt's Syst. Med.* IV. 379 Fibroid thickening and hypernucleation are superadded in process of time.

b. Const. *to* (*unto*).

a **1458** GASCOIGNE *Life St. Bridget* in *New Leg. Eng.* (1516) 124 b, She nat oonly kepe þe fastyngs..þt holy churche commaundeth but she superadded therto many other. *a* **1552** LELAND *Itin.* (1768) I. p. xxiii, To superadde a Worke as an Ornament..to the Enterprises afore saide. **1692** BENTLEY *Boyle Lect.* ii. 16 Motion in general superadded to Matter cannot produce any Sense and Perception. **1700** DRYDEN *Fables* Pref., Poems (1910) 269 The Manners of Æneas are those of Hector superadded to those which Homer gave him. **1768** STERNE *Sent. Journ.*, *Moulines*, She had, super-added likewise to her jacket, a pale green ribband. **1778** BURKE *Corr.* (1844) II. 249 A French war is added to the American; and there is all the reason in the world to expect a Spanish war to be superadded to the French. **1874** CARPENTER *Mental Phys.* I. i. (1879) 23 The Cerebrum..is superadded to this Axial Cord. **1899** *Allbutt's Syst. Med.* VII. 272 Irritative phenomena..are superadded to the paralytic symptoms.

c. *absol.* To make a further addition *to*.

1660 R. BURNEY Κέρδιστον Δῶρον Ep. Ded. 3 All the people ought to..superadde to the honour of his Majestie, not limit it at all. *a* **1769** JOHNSON in Boswell 26 Oct. 1769, A man who is converted from Protestantism to Popery..parts with nothing: he is only superadding to what he already had.

2. *spec.* To add as a further statement; to say, state, or mention in addition. (With simple obj. or obj. clause.)

1640 BP. HALL *Humb. Remonstr.* 20 To this commentary, we shall super-adde the unquestionable glosse of the clear practice of their immediate successors. **1651** N. BACON *Disc. Govt. Eng.* II. i. (1739) 8 The King..superadded, that it should be treason for any man to endeavour to repeal any of their determinations. *a* **1734** NORTH *Lives* (1826) II. 100 There was an odd passage at the council board which..shall be superadded. **1781** COWPER *Hope* 434, I superadd a few essentials more. **1857** DICKENS *Dorrit* II. xv, Here Mrs. General stopped, and added internally..'Papa, potatoes, poultry, prunes, and prism'. 'Mr. Dorrit', she superadded aloud, 'is ever most obliging'.

Hence **super'added** *ppl. a.*, **super'adding** *vbl. sb.* Also **super'addible** *a.*, capable of being superadded; †**,supera'dditament** = next, 2.

a **1628** PRESTON *Serm.* (1630) 2 They can shew no ground ..for their..*superadded opinions. **1650** in Ellis *Orig. Lett.* Ser. II. III. 361 A superadded mercy to all the rest. **1756** BURKE *Subl. & Beaut.* v. i, Painting affects in the same manner, but with the superadded pleasure of imitation. **1843** PUSEY *Serm. Holy Euch.* 10 The remains of original corruption and our own superadded sins. **1854** OWEN in *Orr's Circ. Sci., Org. Nat.* I. 166 The broken parts may be cemented together by newly superadded shell-substance. **1812–29** COLERIDGE *Lit. Rem.* (1838) III. 108 A finite divided from, and *superaddible to, the infinite. **1655** SANDERSON *Serm.* (1681) II. Pref. 7 The *superadding of examples to commands. **1628** C. POTTER *Consecr. Serm.* (1629) 44 The Church of Rome hath adulterated and obscured her Catholique verities with intolerable *superadditaments. **1647** M. HUDSON *Div. Right Govt.* I. iv. 19 All those relative Entities which are placed in the other seven predicaments are but onely circumstantial superadditaments grounded upon one of these three.

superaddition (,s(j)uːpərə'dɪʃən). [f. SUPERADD, after *addition*.]

1. The action (or an act) of superadding, or the condition of being superadded; further addition. Often a mere strengthening of *addition*: cf. SUPERADD 1.

1609 *Bible* (Douay) Ezek. iii. *comm.*, More grace added to the former which was sufficient before, and by this superaddition is made effectual. **1664** POWER *Exp. Philos.* I. 74 By a super-addition of the oyl of Vitriol, you may re-tincture as before. **1753** JOHNSON *Adventurer* No. 115 ¶15 If his topics be probable and persuasory, that he be able to recommend them by the superaddition of elegance and imagery. **1807** G. CHALMERS *Caledonia* I. III. vii. 408 With all these powers, in superaddition to his own character. **1897** *Allbutt's Syst. Med.* IV. 364 With a further increase of vascular tension and the superaddition of hypertrophy of the heart, the dropsy will lessen or cease.

2. Something superadded; a further addition.

1649 JER. TAYLOR *Gt. Exemp.* Disc. i. §12 Virtue being superaddition to Nature. **1662** GUNNING *Lent Fast* 63 One part of the Aerians superaddition to the Arrian heresie. **1714** STEELE *Lover* No. 29 (1723) 170 He hath so clogg'd it, and sophisticated it with Superadditions, that it may be he hath altered the Nature..of it. *a* **1866** J. GROTE *Exam. Utilit. Philos.* xv. (1870) 226 A superaddition to, not a constituent of, man's moral existence. **1897** *Allbutt's Syst. Med.* III. 256 The ultimate composition of the lardaceous superaddition is that of the protein bodies.

So **,supera'dditional,** †**,supera'dditionary** *adjs.*, of the nature of a superaddition.

1637 BASTWICK *Litany* IV. Title-p., More Articles superadditionall vpon superadditionall. **1669** W. SIMPSON *Hydrol. Chym.* 35 A simple mineral salt..without any superadditionary additaments. **1847** P. FAIRBAIRN *Typol. Script.* I. i. 3 What might now be regarded as fundamental, ..must have been, to a considerable extent, super-additional.

superadiabatic: see SUPER- 4 a (*a*).

,superaerody'namics, *sb. pl.* [f. SUPER-, with reference to the *upper* atmosphere.] The study of motion of and in a gas so rarefied that it has to be treated as a collection of individual particles rather than a continuous fluid. Hence **,superaerody'namic** *a.*

1934 A. F. ZAHM in *Jrnl. Franklin Inst.* CCXVII. 153 (*heading*) Superaerodynamics. **1952** W. F. HILTON *High-Speed Aerodynamics* xiii. 351 The Mach number should be greater than the Reynolds number for superaerodynamic conditions to prevail. *Ibid.* 353 There is no reason why *M* should not be less than unity; i.e., a subsonic superaerodynamic flow could exist. **1957** *Jrnl. Aeronaut. Sci.* XXIV. 527/1 The mechanics of the kinetic theory of gases is employed to describe the drag force on the nose of a missile moving in the superaerodynamic region of the atmosphere. **1960** *McGraw-Hill Encycl. Sci. & Technol.* XIII. 293/2 It is convenient to divide superaerodynamics into three flow regimes.

superallowed, -alloy: see SUPER- 9 b, 6 c.

superaltar ('s(j)uːpər,ɔːltə(r)). *Eccl.* Also 4–6 **superaltare,** 5–7 **-altarie, -y,** (5 **-altarye, -altori**), 6 **-alter.** [ad. med.L. *superaltāre*: see SUPER- 1 d and ALTAR.]

1. A portable stone slab consecrated for use upon an unconsecrated altar, a table, etc. Also *attrib.*

c **1380** *Antecrist* in Todd *Three Treat. Wyclif* (1851) 146 þei suspenden men and chirches, boþe auters and super-altares. **14..** *Voc.* in Wr.-Wülcker 614/35 *Superaltare*, a superaltarye. *c* **1475** *Pict. Voc.* ibid. 753/25 *Hoc superaltare*, a superaltori. **1493–4** *Rec. St. Mary at Hill* (1904) 198 For makyng of the crossys on þe superaltarys, iiij d. **1530** PALSGR. 494/2 Thynke you this superaltare is consecrate. **1551** SIR J. WILLIAMS *Acc. Monastic Treas.* (Abbotsf. Club) 24 A superaltare, garnished with siluer and gilte, and parte golde, called the greate saphure of Glasconbury. **1568** GRAFTON *Chron.* II. 383 They ordeyned a Superaltare of Siluer, and guilt, and therein the storye of Saint Edwarde was grauen most curiously. **1578** in Kempe *Losely MSS.* (1836) 248 Anie masse bookes, superaltaries, or anie other suche thing belonging to the masse. **1609** SIR E. HOBY *Let. to T. H*[*iggons*] 91 Your Schismatical positions, your merits, satisfactions, perfections, supererogations, Masses, Vigils, superaltaries. **1849** ROCK *Ch. Fathers* I. iii. 252 Another super-altar of jasper, circular in shape, and mounted in silver, upon which St. Austin was said to have celebrated, was once in the possession of our great abbey of St. Alban's. **1908** *Athenæum* 12 Sept. 298/1 No relic was necessary for a side altar or one of occasional use, provided a duly consecrated small portable super-altar stone or slab was used by the celebrant.

2. A structure erected above an altar (at the back): **a.** a reredos; **b.** a retable or gradine.

1848 B. WEBB *Cont. Ecclesiol.* 156 There is a stone super-altar of twelve small niches, filled by figures. **1858** *Direct. Anglic.* (ed. J. Purchas) 6 Along the back of the *mensa* extends a ledge..called the super-Altar; upon it are placed two Lights, and between these a cross of metal. **1860** [W. L. COLLINS] *Luck of Ladysmede* I. 151 Here is the great super-altar, of the twelve Apostles, in silver tricked out with gold. **1867** *Church & State Rev.* 16 Feb. 164 He removed a Cross, and a pair of candlesticks, together with the superaltar upon which they were placed. **1870** F. R. WILSON *Ch. Lindisf.* 132 Over the communion table there is a marble super-altar.

†**superancy.** *Obs. rare*^−1^. [ad. late L. *superantia*, f. pres. pple. of *superāre*: see SUPERATE and -ANCY.] The quality of exceeding or surpassing; superiority.

1578 SIDNEY *Wanstead Play* in *Arcadia* etc. (1605) 574 Either according to the penetrancie of their singing, or the melioritie of their functions, or lastly the superancy of their merits.

†**superannate,** *a. Obs. rare.* [ad. med.L. *superannātus* (of cattle) more than a year old, f. *super annum* beyond a year: see SUPER- 7 b and -ATE[2]. Cf. F. *suranné*, It. *soprannato*.] = SUPERANNUATED.

1608 J. KING *Serm.* 5 Nov. 15 It is not so auncient & superannate as the story of Pope Ione. **1629** MAXWELL tr. *Herodian* (1635) 268 He alledging he was super-annate, refuses the Empire. [**1652** C. B. STAPYLTON *Herodian* XIV. 121 Audentius therefore safely shall them Guard, If he be pleas'd..But he replies (with Modesty) I cannot, You see, quoth he, my time is super-ann'ate.]

†**superannate,** *v. Obs. rare.* [f. med.L. *superannātus*: see prec. and -ATE[3].]

1. *intr.* To live beyond the year; to survive till the next year.

1626 BACON *Sylva* §448 The Dying, in the winter, of the Roots of Plants, that are Annuall, seemeth to be partly caused by the Over-Expence of the Sap into Stalke, and Leaves; which being prevented, they will super-annate, if they stand warme.

Cf. **1656** BLOUNT *Glossogr.*, *Superannate*, *Superannuate*, to out-wear with years, to out-live, or exceed in years, to grow old, or out of date, to live longer. *Bac*[*on*].

2. *trans.* ? To be too ancient for.

1658 SIR T. BROWNE *Hydriot.* iii. 42 These crumbling reliques..superannate such expectations.

†**superannated,** *pa. pple.* and *ppl. a. Obs.* [f. med.L. *superannātus* (see above) + -ED[1].] = SUPERANNUATED.

1605 CHAPMAN *All Fools* III. i. 267 Spent poets, super-annated bachelers. **1610** DONNE *Pseudo-martyr* 124, I neuer found..that a Saint..may be superannated, and grow too old to bee Canoniz'd. **1651** BP. HALL *Confirm.* 3 Can the Doctrine of the Resurrection..and of the last Judgment, be ever unseasonable, and super annated? **1654** GATAKER *Disc. Apol.* 42, I returned, That I was now superannated, and having waived the Degree, when I might have had it at thirtie five, would not now..seek..it at three score.

supe'rannuable, *a.* [f. SUPERANNU(ATE *v.* + -ABLE.] (Of a post or salary) that entitles the holder to superannuation (sense 2).

1950 *Times* 27 Apr. 1/4 (Advt.), The above appointments are superannuable under the British Electricity Authority and Area Boards Scheme. **1960** *Times Lit. Suppl.* 18 Nov. 748/2 The appointment is superannuable. **1971** *Daily Tel.* 13 Apr. 6/6 (Advt.), A permanent superannuable post paying up to £2,691 per annum. **1978** *Nature* 18 May p. xxvii/1 (Advt.), Annual salary (superannuable) will be within the professional range which has a minimum of HK$131,640.

super'annuate, *a.* and *sb.* Now *rare.* [ad. mod.L. **superannuātus*, altered f. *superannātus* SUPERANNATE.] **A.** *adj.* = SUPERANNUATED.

1647 WARD *Simple Cobler* 21 As if former Truths were grown superannuate and saplesse, if not altogether antiquate. **1654** GAYTON *Pleas. Notes* I. iv. 13, I believe Rosinante was a Gelding, or else a Stallion super-annuate. **1765** BLACKSTONE *Comm.* I. xiii. 421 Sailors,..when maimed, or wounded, or superannuate. **1866** MANSFIELD *School Life Winchester Coll.* (1870) 237 *Superannuate*—a boy who was obliged [*c* 1840] to leave at Election, owing to his being past eighteen years of age. 'Founders' were not 'Superannuate' till they were twenty-five. **1869** LOWELL *Cathedral* 647 Superannuate forms and mumping shams.

B. *sb.* A superannuated person; *spec.* at Winchester School (see quot. 1866 in A.).

1816 *Hist. Colleges Winchester, Eton & Westminster* 46 Boys between eighteen and nineteen years old, called superannuates. **1822** JEFFERSON *Writ.* (1830) IV. 351 Two ancient servants, who..have a reasonable claim to repose.. in the sanctuary of invalids and superannuates. **1855** POTTS *Liber Cantabr.* I. 416 Funds out of which exhibitions..are given to superannuates of the foundation [of Winchester College]. **1901** *Westm. Gaz.* 25 July 2/2 The prison service is no longer a refuge for the superannuates of the Army and the Navy.

superannuate (s(j)uːpə'rænjuːeɪt), *v.* [Back-formation from next.]

†**1.** *trans.* To render antiquated or obsolete: said of the lapse of time, etc. Also, to set aside or reject as antiquated or out-of-date. *Obs.*

1649 E. MARBURY in Spurgeon *Treas. David* xxxiv. 22 No age shall ever superannuate them [*sc.* God's promises], or put them out of full force and virtue. **1660** H. MORE *Myst. Godl.* To Rdr. 10 That bold Enthusiast..who seems to endeavour to superannuate Christianity..and to introduce another Evangelie. **1680** —— *Apocal. Apoc.* 220 Nor does this season, being Regnum Spiritus, superannuate this Sacrament, but rather call for it. **1691** NORRIS *Pract. Disc.* 119 None shall be thought worthy to be retained in it but only these Two, Praise and Love; all the rest shall be superannuated and cease. **1830** MACKINTOSH *Eth. Philos.* Wks. 1846 I. 59 Two centuries have not superannuated probably more than a dozen of his [Hobbes's] words. **1865** *Spectator* 18 Feb. 176 The Railway companies..have killed the coaches, superannuated the barges.

†**b.** To put off for a time. *Obs. rare*$^{-1}$.

1654 H. L'ESTRANGE *Chas. I* (1655) 125 Not to delay and super-annuate longer this expectation.

2. To dismiss or discharge from office on account of age; *esp.* to cause to retire from service on a pension; to pension off.

1692 LUTTRELL *Brief Rel.* (1857) II. 557 Collonel Murray ..is superannuated, and a pension given him of 250£ for life. **1758** *Case of Authors by Prof. Stated* 57 Being superannuated with a lucrative Sine-Cure. **1835** MARRYAT *Jacob Faithful* xlvi, The governors..thought it necessary to superannuate him with a pension. **1838** DICKENS *Nich. Nick.* xxxv, This isn't the first time you've talked about super-annuating me. **1885** MISS BRADDON *Wyllard's Weird* I. vii. 196 Why do you not superannuate poor old Gretton, and let Bothwell be your steward?

3. *pass.* and *intr.* To become too old for a position or office; to reach the age at which one leaves a school, retires from an office, etc.

1814 G. HARDINGE *Let.* in Nichols *Lit. Anecd. 18th C.* (1814) VIII. 543 He was educated at Eton school,..but superannuated, and became a member of St. John's College in Cambridge. **1817** J. EVANS *Excurs. Windsor*, etc. 352 At nineteen years of age the scholars [at Eton] are superannuated, when they pass off some to Cambridge, and others to Oxford. **1904** *Daily News* 18 Apr. 3 [He] will superannuate at the forthcoming Wesleyan Conference, and retire from the editorship of the Connexional publications.

b. *trans.* To cause to be too old. *rare.*

1893 W. G. COLLINGWOOD *Life Ruskin* I. ix. 96 Ruskin could not now go in for honours, for his lost year had superannuated him.

4. To outlast, outwear. *rare.*

1820 HAZLITT *Lect. Dram. Lit.* 294 The passion of curiosity had in him [*sc.* Sir T. Browne] survived to old age, and had superannuated his other faculties.

†**5.** *intr.* To be a year out in date. *Obs. nonce-use.*

1655 H. L'ESTRANGE *Chas. I* Pref. A4, In assigning all both Things and Actions their proper times, no one of which ..is so in these Annals misdaid, as to super-annuate, and not many to vary from the very day of their prime existence. [Cf. SUPER- 8 (*b*).].

¶The alleged sense 'to last beyond the year', copied in mod. Dicts. from Johnson, is founded on an alteration, in later editions of Bacon, of SUPERANNATE (q.v., sense 1).

superannuated (s(j)uːpə'rænjuːeɪtɪd), *pa. pple.* and *ppl. a.* [f. mod.L. **superannuātus*, altered from med.L. *superannātus* SUPERANNATE, after L. *annuus* (see ANNUAL).]

1. Of persons (or animals): Disqualified or incapacitated by age; old and infirm.

†Formerly const. *to* with inf. = too old to be or to do something; also const. *from* = not subject to or capable of something, on account of old age.

pa. pple. **1639** FULLER *Holy War* I. xxii. 34 Barzillai, super-annuated to be a courtier. **1643** SIR T. BROWNE *Relig. Med.* I. §42 Were there any hopes to out-live vice, or a point to be super-annuated from sin. **1648** T. HILL *Strength Saints* Ep. Ded. A iij, If you omit to elect them, they must (being superannuated) bee most disgracefully throwne off. **1658** SIR T. BROWNE *Hydriot.* iv. 65 Old age, which..makes men..superannuated from the bold and couragious thoughts of youth. **1665** SIR T. HERBERT *Trav.* (1677) 212 When any are super-annuated,..seeing they can do no more Work they are to expect no more Wages. **1757** H. WALPOLE *Let. to Mann* 17 Jan., I trust he [*sc.* the Pope] was superannuated when they drew from him the late Bull enjoining the admission of the Unigenitus on pain of damnation. **1787** *Minor* 59 The horses, being likewise superannuated, were exchanged for others. **1851** MAYHEW *Lond. Labour* I. 342, I subscribed regularly to Society, and knew that if I got superannuated I should be comfortably maintained by the trade. **1873** HAMERTON *Intell. Life* I. vii. 36 We shall be either superannuated or dead.

ppl. a. *c* **1645** HOWELL *Lett.* (1650) I. 20 This goodly antient city..looks like..some superannuated virgin that hath lost her lover. *a* **1694** SOUTH *Serm., Rom. i. 32* II. 247 Old Age..the proper Season for a super-annuated Sinner to enjoy the Delights of Sin in the Rebound. **1714** WATERLAND *Lett. Lay-Baptism* II. iii. (1892) 231 We may fairly suppose there might be about a thousand [Levites] fifty years old, and consequently superannuated. *a* **1791** WESLEY *Minutes Sev. Convers.* Wks. 1830 VIII. 326 How can we provide for superannuated and supernumerary Preachers? **1819** A. CLARKE in *Life* (1840) ix. 331 A superannuated cock whose muscles were impenetrable to the teeth. **1836–7** DICKENS *Sk. Boz, Boarding-House* i, Mr. Calton was a superannuated beau—an old boy. **1886** W. J. TUCKER *E. Europe* 110 A giggle from a withered superannuated governess.

absol. **1726** LEONI *Alberti's Archit.* I. 86/2 Those whom you take in..are the Superannuated, and those who want their Senses.

b. *transf.* of personal actions or attributes.

1707 *Reflex. upon Ridicule* 301 Her superannuated Charms. **1852** THACKERAY *Esmond* I. xi, With a fascinating, superannuated smile she complimented him on his wit. **1860** MOTLEY *Netherl.* vii. I. 436 In all this there was much of superannuated coquetry.

2. Of things: Impaired by age, worn out; antiquated, obsolete, out of date.

pa. pple. *a* **1633** AUSTIN *Medit.* (1635) 280 The pleasure I tooke in them [*sc.* worldly things]..being taken off, they wither, grow uselesse, and are super-annuated, like an old tent. **1728** CHAMBERS *Cycl.* s.v. *Wine*, In France, the Wines that keep best,..are reckon'd superannuated at five or six Leaves old. **1883** H. JUTA tr. *Van der Linden's Instit. Holland* 283 The judgments of the High Court become superannuated after a lapse of five years... The judgments of Amsterdam, however, do not become superannuated.

ppl. a. **1654** GAYTON *Pleas. Notes* III. xi. 148 From rags, Snattocks, Snips,..super-annuated Smocks and Shirts, come very faire Sheets. **1665** GLANVILL *Scepsis Sci.* vi 25 This superannuated Conceit deserves no more of our remembrance. **1689** *Dial. betw. Timothy & Titus* 3 Thy threadbare Cassock and superannuated Beaver. **1832** tr. *Sismondi's Ital. Rep.* v. 115 Vieri de Cerchi..proposed to substitute equal laws, for superannuated proscriptions. **1856** *N. Brit. Rev.* XXVI. 67 The three Theologies, which now stand in view of our British Christianity—namely, the superannuated Logical, the modern Philosophical, and the future Biblical.

absol. **1876** GEO. ELIOT *Dan. Der.* xlii, Obstinate adherence to the superannuated.

b. *loosely.* That has lasted a very long time; inveterate; very old. *rare.*

1644 QUARLES *Barnabas & B.* 36 Hath Gilead balm enough to heal thy superannuated sores? **1839** DE QUINCEY *Recoll. Lakes* Wks. 1862 II. 6 No more than the sun fails to gladden the heart, because it is that same old superannuated sun that has gladdened it for thousands of years.

3. Discharged from service on a pension after attaining a certain age. Also said of the pension.

1740 CIBBER *Apol.* (1756) I. 116 He dy'd soon after, a superannuated pensioner. **1771** SMOLLETT *Humphry Cl.* 13 July, A superannuated lieutenant on half-pay. **1802** JAMES *Milit. Dict.* s.v., To be placed upon the super-annuated list is to be recommended to the board at Chelsea. **1817** *Jrnl. Ho. Commons* LXXII. 97/1 Superannuated or retired Allowances, to Persons late belonging to the Office of Ordinance. **1848** DICKENS *Haunted Man* i. 13 There's my father,..superannuated keeper and custodian of this Institution, eigh-ty-seven year old.

superannuation (ˈs(j)uːpərænjuːˈeɪʃən). [f. SUPERANNUATE or prec.: see -ATION.]

1. The condition of being superannuated; impairment of the powers or faculties by old age; the state of having outlived one's vigour; senile infirmity or decay. *Obs.* or *rare.*

1755 JOHNSON, *Superannuation*, the state of being disqualified by years. **1772** MRS. DELANY *Life & Corr.* Ser. II. (1862) I. 449, I feel so old y^t its impossible to stir from home. Sorry I am you sh^d be affected by my superannuation. **1782** T. POWNALL *Treat. Antiq.* 54 The mere doating of super-annuation. **1824** HOGG *Conf. Sinner* 85 In his last ravings, he uttered some incoherent words... These..were the words of superannuation. **1827** SCOTT *Chron. Canongate* i, To dribble away life in exchanging bits of painted pasteboard round a green table, for the piddling concern of a few shillings, can only be excused in folly or superannuation.

†**b.** The condition of being out of date; antiquated or obsolete state or character.

1658 PHILLIPS, *Superannuation*, an out-living, or growing out of date. *a* **1834** COLERIDGE *Church & State* (1839) 277, I..doubt, whether the superannuation of sundry superstitious fancies be the result of any real diffusion of sound thinking. **1845** DE QUINCEY *John Foster* Wks. 1890 XI. 337 A monk he seemed by..the superannuation of his knowledge.

2. The action of superannuating an official; also, the allowance or pension granted to one who is discharged on account of age.

a **1704** T. BROWN *Walk round Lond., Coffee-Houses* (1709) 39 Their [*sc.* the lieutenants'] only hopes were now Half-Pay, or Superannuation. **1820** *Edin. Rev.* XXXIII. 485 Superannuations in the Foreign Office. **1834** *Act 4 & 5 Will. IV*, c. 24 §10 In no Case..shall any Superannuation or Allowance exceeding Two Thirds of the Salary and Emoluments of any such Officer, Clerk, or Person, be granted. **1863** P. BARRY *Dockyard Econ.* 3 Buildings..in which wretched labourers wear out soul and body for 13s. weekly and contingent superannuation. **1887** RUSKIN *Præterita* II. §92. 163 The superannuation, according to law, in his sixtieth year of Joseph Couttet, the Captain of Mont Blanc.

b. At certain schools, the attainment of the specified age at which a boy is required to leave.

1831 W. L. BOWLES *Life Ken* II. Introd. p. xiv, After his superannuation at [Winchester] School, he has another year's grace. **1865** *Reader* 9 Sept. 285/3 Nineteen years..is ..the age prescribed by King Henry's Statutes for the superannuation of his scholars [at Eton].

3. *attrib.* (in sense 2), as ***superannuation allowance, fund, scheme.***

1817 *Jrnl. Ho. Commons* LXXII. 276/2 To defray the charge of the Superannuation Allowances or Compensations. **1821** in *Parl. Papers Eng.* (1828) V. 492 That the Individuals who may hereafter enjoy the benefit of Superannuation Allowances, should be called upon to contribute to a Superannuation Fund. **1891** *Pall Mall Gaz.* 20 Oct. 2/3 Recent inquiries into superannuation schemes. **1911** *Act 1 & 2 Geo. V*, c. 55 §25 A superannuation or other provident fund.

supera'nnuity. *rare.* [f. prec., after *annuity.*]

1. Superannuated condition.

1781 COWPER *Let. to J. Hill* 3 Feb., A writer..might construct a plausible argument to prove that the world itself is in a state of superannuation, if there be such a word. If not, there must be such a one as superannuity.

2. A superannuation allowance.

1893 *Daily News* 4 Dec. 5/3 He was superannuated upon his full pay, and upon this superannuity..he lived for more than fifty years.

So ˌ**supera'nnuitant**, one who is superannuated or receives a superannuation allowance.

1830 CASSAN *Bishops of Bath & Wells* II. 271 Let the surplus proceeds be appropriated to the use of superannuitants.

†ˌ**supera'pparent**, *a.* *Obs.* *rare*$^{-1}$. [ad. L. *superappārens*, *-ent-*, pres. pple. of *superappārēre*: see SUPER- 2 and APPEAR *v.*] Appearing above the rest; prominent, conspicuous.

1432–50 tr. *Higden* (Rolls) IV. 109 He was callede Epiphanes, as noble other superapparente [L. *super apparens*].

†**super'arrogancy.** *Obs.* [ad. mod.L. *superaroganciа*, suggested by Tindale (*Wicked Mammon*, 1528, 26 b) as 'a meter terme' for 'opera supererogationis'. See SUPER- 9, ARROGANCY.] Extreme arrogance, with allusion to *supererogation.* So †**super'arrogant** *a.*; †**super'arrogate** *v. trans.*, to claim or assume with great arrogance; *intr.* to behave with great arrogance; †ˌ**superarro'gation.**

1593 G. HARVEY *Pierce's Super.* 13 Hee hath builded towers of Superarrogation in his owne head. **1599** LINCHE *Fount. Anc. Fiction* E iij, Foiled and disgraced in such their superarrogating challenges. **1601** DEACON & WALKER *Answ. to Darel* 118 Howsoeuer the pride of mans nature might superarrogate some thing vnto it selfe. **1614–15** BOYS *Exp. Fest. Ep. & Gosp.* Wks. (1630) 607 They be works of supererrogation, or, if you will haply of superarrogation. **1615** T. ADAMS *Black Devil* 16 To cure spirituall impotencies, leprosies, & possessions..is not in his power, though in his pride, and super-arrogant glory. **1633** STRUTHER *True Happiness* 55 The old blinde cyclopick superarrogancie. **1634** HEYWOOD & BROME *Witches of Lanc.* II. Dj b, You seeme to me to super-arrogate, Supplying the defects of all your kindred To innoble your own name. **1651** H. L'ESTRANGE *Answ. Marq. Worcester* 21 Supererogation (or Superarrogancy rather).

†**superate**, *pa. pple.* *Obs.* [ad. L. *superātus*, pa. pple. of *superāre*, f. *super* over, above.] Overcome, conquered.

c **1450** *Mankind* 306 in *Macro Plays* 12 The rebellyn of my flesch, now yt ys superatt. **1515** BARCLAY *Egloges* iv. (1570) C vj b, Hercules..Was by this monster ouercome and superate.

†**superate**, *v.* *Obs. rare.* [f. L. *superāt-*, pa. ppl. stem of *superāre*: see prec. and -ATE³.]

1. *trans.* To rise above, overtop.

1599 A. M. tr. *Gabelhouer's Bk. Physicke* 113/2 Take the flowers of Verwene,..infuse heeron oyle Olive, that the flowers may be superatede & covered the depth of thre fingers. *Ibid.* 200/1 Burye both these pots..that the earth may superate the superior pot, the altitude of a qv[arter] of a yarde.

2. To surpass, exceed.

1596 J. TRUSSELL in Southwell *Triumphs over Death* To Rdr., That when a tempest comes their Barke to tosse, Their passions shall not superate their losse. **1656** BLOUNT *Glossogr., Superate*,..to exceed, to excel. **1657** TOMLINSON *Renou's Disp.* I. vi. xxvi. 387 A Physician..who being accustomed to eat bitter almonds would superate all in drinking [orig. *omnes potando superabat*].

3. To overcome, conquer; to get over, surmount.

1597 A. M. tr. *Guillemeau's Fr. Chirurg.* 49/2 The Patient might be wholy superated and overcome, and fall downe dead. **1653** GAUDEN *Hierasp.* 364 Unexpected enchantments,..which salve all inconveniences, superate all hyperbolies, and transcend all difficulties. **1691** W. NICHOLLS *Answ. Naked Gospel* 18 He does not enumerate all the difficulties their Faith was to superate. **1788** *Trifler* No. 25. 325, I..can superate a mortification in any part of the body without amputation.

superation (s(j)uːpəˈreɪʃən). *rare.* [ad. L. *superātio, -ōnem*, n. of action f. *superāre* (see prec.).]

1. Overcoming, surmounting, conquest.

1866 HOWELLS *Venetian Life* ii. 29 This superb and artistic superation of the intrinsic difficulties of dancing.

2. *Astron.* 'The apparent passing of one planet by another, in consequence of the more rapid movement in longitude of the latter' (*Cent. Dict.*).

superˈaudible, *a.* **1.** [SUPER- 9 a.] Very loud. *nonce-use.*

1921 D. H. LAWRENCE *Tortoises* 47 That fragile yell, that scream, Super-audible.

2. [SUPER- 4 a.] Of a frequency: greater than the highest audible frequency; ultrasonic. Of a sound: too high-pitched to be audible. Now *rare.*

1922 [see SUBAUDIBLE *a.* 2]. **1926** R. W. HUTCHINSON *Wireless* 237 The resultant wave is anything from 2,000 metres to, say, 12,000 metres in length (super-audible frequency). **1944** *Proc. IRE* XXXII. 735/2 Superaudible noise impulses which may be present.

superb (s(j)uːˈpɜːb), *a.* [ad. L. *superbus* proud, superior, distinguished, magnificent. Cf. F. *superbe*, It. *superbo.*]

1. Of buildings, monuments, and the like: Of noble and magnificent proportions or aspect.

1549 *Compl. Scot.* iii. 25 The kyng anchises lamentit the distructione of the superb troy. **1683** *Brit. Spec.* 111 Their humble Cottages he changed into fair Houses and stately Palaces, superb Porticoes, and sumptuous Baths. *a* **1700** EVELYN *Diary* 23 May 1645, Behind the quire is the superb chapell of Ferdinand I. **1756–7** tr. *Keysler's Trav.* (1760) II. 398 This superb obelisk was, by order of Sixtus V... removed. **1821** SCOTT *Kenilw.* xxxviii, In this mood, the vindictive and ambitious Earl entered the superb precincts of the Pleasance. **1868** FREEMAN *Norm. Conq.* II. x. 508 The church itself..gradually gave way to the superb structure with which we are all familiar.

2. Grandly and sumptuously equipped, arrayed, or decorated.

a **1700** EVELYN *Diary* 22 Oct. 1658, Saw the superb funerall of the Protector. **1717** PRIOR *Alma* I. 382 Thus, if You Dine with my Lord May'r,..painted Flags, superb and neat, Proclaim You welcome to the Treat. **1763** CHURCHILL *Ghost* IV. 639 A superb and feather'd hearse, Bescutcheon'd and betagg'd with Verse. **1795** *Gentl. Mag.* July 607/1 A superb watch, set with brilliants. **1814** SCOTT *Wav.* xvi, He fired his piece accordingly, but missed the superb monarch of the feathered tribes. **1894** P. PINKERTON *Adriatica, On Asolan Hills*, I survey The procession superb of the clouds.

b. in specific appellations of many gorgeously coloured birds, plants, etc.; see quots.

superb bird of paradise, *Lophorhina* (*Paradisea*) *superba*, a species of which the male is violet-black with green iridescence, having a gorget of metallic green feathers, and an erectile hood or mantle of velvet-black plumes on the shoulders; **superb lily**, a plant of the genus *Gloriosa* (*Methonica*), esp. *G. superba*; **superb warbler**, the blue wren of Australia, *Malurus cyaneus*. (See Shaw's *Zool.* for many other names of birds.)

1760 J. LEE *Introd. Bot.* (1788) App., Superb Lily, *Gloriosa*. **1783** LATHAM *Gen. Synopsis Birds* II. II. 709 Superb Pheasant, *Phasianus superbus*. **1796** NEMNICH *Polygl.-Lex.*, Superb warbler, *Motacilla cyanea*. **1802** SHAW *Gen. Zool.* III. II. 433 Superb Snake. *Coluber Elegantissimus* ..appears to be a beautiful species, measuring about two feet in length. **1809** *Ibid.* VII. II. 494 Superb Paradise-bird. *Paradisea Superba*... This species is about the size of a Thrush, and is a bird of great singularity of plumage. **1847** L. LEICHHARDT *Overland Exped.* iii. 80 We also observed the superb warbler, Malurus cyaneus of Sydney. **1902** *Encycl. Brit.* XXV. 795/1 The death adder, the brown, the black, the superb, and the tiger snakes [of Australia].

3. Of conditions, language, thought, etc.: Grand, stately, majestic.

1784 COWPER *Tiroc.* 751 Or is thine house, though less superb thy rank, If not a scene of pleasure, a mere blank. **1825** J. NEAL *Bro. Jonathan* I. 90 The superb language of Job. *a* **1834** COLERIDGE *Notes & Lect. Shaks.* (1875) 220 The lines, as epic narrative, are superb. **1851** RUSKIN *Stones Venice* I. vii. §17 A superb breadth of proportion.

4. Expressing emphatic approval: Very fine; splendid; magnificent.

a **1729** CONGREVE *An Impossible Thing* 190 Not all the Wiles that Hell could hatch Could conquer that Superb Mustach. **1753** MRS. DELANY *Let. to Mrs. Dewes* 3 Dec., It is one of the finest things I ever read in my life; was ever a superb family better described! **1827** DISRAELI *Viv. Grey* v. ix, The dinner was sumptuous, the wines superb. **1872** JENKINSON *Engl. Lake Distr.* (1879) 181 During the descent there are superb views of a portion of the higher reach of Ullswater. **1908** [MISS FOWLER] *Betw. Trent & Ancholme* 160 One of the most superb singers of our century.

†**5.** Proud, haughty. *Obs.*

1654 tr. *Scudery's Curia Pol.* 166 If they be too superb and haughty their pride is to be punished with severity. *a* **1697** AUBREY *Lives, W. Oughtred* (1898) II. 111 Before he dyed he burned a world of papers, and sayd that the world was not worthy of them; he was so superb.

†**suˈperbiate**, *v. Obs. rare.* [f. L. *superbia* pride, or *superbīre* to be proud: see -ATE³. Cf. It. *superbire, superbiare.*]

1. *trans.* To render haughty. In quot. *absol.*

1628 FELTHAM *Resolves* II. [I.] lxix. 196 Italie builds a Villaine: Spaine superbiates: Germanie makes a Drunkard.

2. *intr.* To be proud (*to do* something).

1785 TRUSLER *Mod. Times* III. 144, I was introduced to him as one of the literati, whom he must superbiate to receive.

†**suˈperbience.** *Obs. rare.* [f. L. *superbientem*: see next and -ENCE.] 'Proud' or luxuriant growth.

1671 GREW *Anat. Pl.* I. vi. §2 As the Pilling is but the Continuation of the utmost part of the Barque; so is this, but ..the swelth and superbience of the Inner Part thereof.

†**suˈperbient,** *a. Obs. rare.* [ad. L. *superbientem*, pres. pple. of *superbīre* to be proud, f. *superbus* proud, SUPERB. Cf. It. *superbiente.*] Insolent, overbearing.

1647 N. BACON *Disc. Govt. Eng.* I. xxxviii. 93 The wise Saxon King, espying the danger in entrusting the lives and estates of the poorest sort unto the dictate of these superbient humours. **1651** *Ibid.* II. lxiv. 218 He wanted his Fathers sence, and had too much of his Grandfather's superbient humour.

†**superˈbifical,** *a. Obs. rare*$^{-0}$. [f. L. *superbificus*, f. *superbus* SUPERB: see -FIC and -AL¹.] So †**superˈbiloquence** [L. *superbiloquentia*], †**superˈbiloquent** *a.*

1656 BLOUNT *Glossogr.*, *Superbifical*,..that doth a thing proudly, that makes proud. *Ibid.*, *Superbiloquence*,.. arrogant speeking, proud, and haughty words. **1658** PHILLIPS, *Superbiloquent*, speaking proudly or haughtily.

super-bike: see SUPER- 6 c.

†**suˈperbious,** *a. Obs. rare.* [a. OF. *superbieus* (= obs. It. *superbioso*) or ad. med.L. **superbiōsus*, f. *superbia* pride, f. *superbus* SUPERB.]

1. Proud, overbearing, insolent.

c **1510** *Kalendar of Sheph.* E iv, Yᵉ moyste rayne of dethe which..causeth them to tomble by the strength of theyr superbyous blastes into the fourneys euerlastynge. **1595** *Locrine* II. iv. 25 Superbious Brittaine, thou shalt know too soone The force of Humber and his Scithians. **1603** HARSNET *Pop. Impost.* xxiii. 162 That addition, in scorne and superbious contempt annexed by you, vnto our publique prayer, God saue the Queene. ? *a* **1700** in D'Israeli *Cur. Lit., Hist. Theatre during Suppr.*, Those proud parroting players..a sort of superbious ruffians.

2. Stately, grand, superb.

1588 PARKE tr. *Mendoza's Hist. China* 17 In all such cities that bee the heads of the prouinces, is resident a vizroy,.. and dwelleth in the house that (in euery such citie) the king hath ordeined..all the which..are superbious and admirable. **1650** J. REYNOLDS *Flower Fidel.* 5 Beholding the Zephyr-Gale fairly blow the Swanlike Sails from the superbious Mast. **1657** TOMLINSON *Renou's Disp.* Pref., Here you may view the superbious Trees. **1714** MRS. MANLEY *Adv. Rivella* 79 The superbious chief Seat of the Doubles.

Hence †**suˈperbiously** *adv.*, superbly; †**suˈperbiousness**, superbness.

1632 LITHGOW *Trav.* VIII. 369 Mosquees..are well benefited and superbiously decored within and without. *c* **1650** *Don Bellianis* 78 The Prince Don Gallaneo..did superbiously adorn himself. **1654** COKAINE *Dianea* IV. 367 The superbiousnesse of Asia, and the rarities of Africa here demonstrated the extreames of their power.

superbity (s(j)uːˈpɜːbɪtɪ). In 6 **superbite.** [a. OF. *superbité* or ad. med.L. **superbitās*, f. *superbus* SUPERB: see -ITY.] Pride, arrogance. Also *concr.* an embodiment of pride, a proud person.

a **1550** *Image Hypocr.* II. 81 in *Skelton's Wks.* (1843) II. 423 And eke it is forbode That he no novice be, Lest with superbite He do presume to hye. **1653** R. SANDERS *Physiogn., Moles* 7 In a woman, it denotes superbity, and an elated minde. **1686** tr. *Chardin's Trav. Persia* 117 In all his Actions and Discourse [he] manifested a most insupportable Superbity. **1903** *Sat. Rev.* 22 Aug. 234 The unimaginative superbities find themselves confronted by a force they have always striven to ignore. **1924** G. B. SHAW *St. Joan* p. ix, She went to the stake without a stain on her character except the overweening presumption, the superbity as they called it, that led her thither. *a* **1945** E. R. EDDISON *Mezentian Gate* (1958) xxix. 141 In her nose, a critical outward-regarding superbity that judged without appeal. **1979** C. P. SNOW *Coat of Varnish* xxxviii. 297 In spite of his superbity, he might possess a kind of self-protective cunning.

superbly (s(j)uːˈpɜːblɪ), *adv.* [f. SUPERB *a.* + -LY².] In a superb manner.

1. With a magnificent or majestic aspect or demeanour.

1762–3 CHURCHILL *Ghost* IV. 1174 With labour'd visible design Art strove to be superbly fine. **1812** J. WILSON *Isle of Palms* III. 825 He calmly views The gallant vessel toss Her prow superbly up and down. **1865** 'E. C. CLAYTON' *Cruel Fortune* I. 172 The Countess swept superbly from the room. **1870** LOWELL *Among my Bks.* Ser. I. (1873) 184 A mountain seen from different sides by many lands, itself superbly solitary.

2. With sumptuous provision, equipment, adornment, or decoration.

1761 CHURCHILL *Apology* 151 For me let hoary Fielding bite the ground, So nobler Pickle stand superbly bound. **1772** WILKES *Corr.* (1805) IV. 138, I went to Deptford; and dined most agreeably, as well as superbly, on board an East Indian ship. **1784** tr. *Beckford's Vathek* (1868) 73 Vathek came close after, superbly robed. **1835** LYTTON *Rienzi* I. i, Their steeds caparisoned superbly.

3. Very finely, splendidly.

1828 LYTTON *Pelham* I. xi, She supplied the place of the dilapidated baronet with a most superbly mustachioed German. **1863** 'E. C. CLAYTON' *Queens of Song* II. 145 She was equally grand as Semiramide and as Arsace, and sang the music of both parts superbly. **1892** *Photogr. Ann.* II. p. lxvii, The most fascinating of all paper Printing Methods. Gives the most superbly finished pictures.

suˈperbness. *rare.* [f. as prec. + -NESS.] Superb character or quality.

1696 PHILLIPS (ed. 5), *Superbness*, Pride, Haughty Disdain. **1898** G. W. CABLE *Grandissimes* xiv. 76 It was a femininity without humanity—something that made her, with all her superbness, a creature that one would want to find chained.

ˈsuperbomb. [SUPER- 6 c.] **a.** Also **super bomb.** A fission bomb. *Obs.* exc. *Hist.*

1940 O. R. FRISCH in *Ann. Rep. Progr. Chem.* XXXVI. 16 Since the energy release in this reaction would be about 10^5 times larger than in ordinary chemical reactions..it has been feared that it might form the basis for the construction of a super-bomb exceeding the action of ordinary bombs by a factor of 10^6 or more. **1941** in H. D. Smyth *Gen. Acct. Devel. Atomic Energy Mil. Purposes* (1945) iv. 38 In such a reaction the energy would be released at an explosive rate which might be described as a 'super bomb'. **1964** M. GOWING *Britain & Atomic Energy 1939–45* i. 34 A chain fission reaction was a possibility, the inevitable question had arisen. Could this energy be harnessed for making a super bomb?

b. A fusion or hydrogen bomb. Cf. SUPER *sb.* 9.

1951 W. L. LAURENCE *Hell Bomb* i. 3 'Is it true about the superbomb?' I asked him. 'Will it really be as much as fifty times as powerful as the uranium or plutonium bomb?' **1961** *New Statesman* 15 Sept. 330/1 For this interpretation not least among the exhibits in evidence is Krushchev's grim emphasis on his 100-megaton superbomb, which American experts regard as militarily poor but incredibly dirty. **1975** *Sci. Amer.* Oct. 106/2 It called for the fastest possible development of the hydrogen bomb, which was widely referred to at the time as the superbomb (or simply the Super).

†**superˈbound,** *v.*, obs. contr. f. SUPERABOUND.

1561 EDEN *Arte Nauig.* Pref., Suche as..superbounde in all notorious vyces. **1640** SANDERSON *Serm.* (1681) II. 150 As his sufferings encreased, his comforts had..such a proportionable rise, that where those abounded, these did rather superbound.

†**suˈperbous,** *a. Obs. rare.* [f. L. *superbus*: see SUPERB and -OUS.] = SUPERBIOUS.

1584 SOUTHERNE in Puttenham *Eng. Poesie* III. xxii. (Arb.) 259. **1601** W. PARRY *Trav. Sir A. Sherley* 10 A most insolent superbous and insulting people. **1652** KIRKMAN *Clerio & Lozia* 156 The General made two superbous Triumphs of vanquisher and vanquished. **1653** A. WILSON *Jas. I*, 251 A house of that Superbous and elegant Structure. **1660** F. BROOKE tr. *Le Blanc's Trav.* 72 He esteemes himself very potent, and assumes very superbous and high Titles. **1709** MRS. MANLEY *Secret Mem.* (1720) IV. 107 They..lodg'd him at a finer Palace, more superbous than the former.

Super-Bowl: see SUPER- 6 c.

super-calender: see SUPER- 13.

ˌsupercaliˌfragilisticˌexpialiˈdocious, *a.* Also **supercalifragilistic;** formerly also other varr. [Fanciful: cf. SUPER *a.* 3.] A nonsense-word used esp. by children, now chiefly expressing excited approbation: fantastic, fabulous.

Made popular by the Walt Disney film 'Mary Poppins' in 1964. The song containing the word was the subject of a copyright infringement suit brought in 1965 against the makers of the film by Life Music Co. and two song-writers: cf. quots. 1949, 1951. In view of earlier oral uses of the word sworn to in affidavits and dissimilarity between the songs the judge ruled against the plaintiffs.

1949 PARKER & YOUNG (*unpublished song-title*) Supercalafajalistickespialadojus. **1951** —— (*song-title*) Supercalafajalistickespeealadojus; or, The super song. **1964** R. M. & R. B. SHERMAN (*song-title*) Supercalifragilisticexpialidocious! **1967** *Decisions U.S. Courts involving Copyright 1965–66* 488 The complaint alleges copyright infringement of plaintiff's song '*Supercalafajalistickespeealadojus*' by defendants' song '*Supercalifragilisticexpialidocious*'. (All variants of this tongue twister will hereinafter be referred to collectively as 'the word'.) **1971** *Daily Tel.* 6 Nov. 13/5 If you can stand more than a day of Supercalifragilisticexpialidocious entertainment you can settle in at the concrete Contemporary Resort Hotel. **1972** *Atlanta Constitution* 9 Apr. 20A/1 Disney World, the new supercalifragilistic-expialidocious tourist attraction created by the folks who brought you Mickey Mouse, is packing them into Orlando. **1980** *Amer. Speech* LV. 266 Whatever the ancestry of *supercalifragilisticexpialidocious*, it entered the general public consciousness as a result of the wonderful world of Disney. **1982** *N.Y. Post* 29 July 64/3 His eyes are willing unspoken words to life as though they were part of one of those supercalafragilistic electronic scoreboards.

supercargo (s(j)uːpəˈkɑːgəʊ). [Alteration of SUPRACARGO by prefix-substitution.] An officer on board a merchant ship whose business it is to superintend the cargo and the commercial transactions of the voyage. †Also formerly, an agent who superintended a merchant's business in a foreign country.

1697 DAMPIER *Voy.* (1729) I. 511 One Mr. Moody, who was Supercargo of the Ship. **1719** DE FOE *Crusoe* I. (Globe) 39 The Question was, whether I would go their Super-Cargo in the Ship to manage the Trading Part upon the Coast of Guinea? **1732** FIELDING *Lottery* ii. 14 A Man of the first Quality, and one of the best Estates in the Kingdom: Why, he's as rich as a Supercargo. **1782** *Phil. Trans.* LXXII. 48 The Directors of the East India Company, to give proper orders to their factors and super-cargoes in China, to procure some of the best seed that can be obtained. **1800** *Asiat. Ann. Reg., Hist. Ind.* 32/2 With the port of Rangoon..they carried on a very considerable trade, and had supercargoes stationed there. **1828–43** TYTLER *Hist. Scot.* (1864) I. 272 Richard le Furbur, a trader of the inland town of Roxburgh, had sent factors or supercargoes to manage his business in foreign countries. **1836** MARRYAT *Pirate* ix, The pirate had been questioning the supercargo as to the contents of the vessel. *c* **1870** GLADSTONE in Morley *Life* (1903) I. I. i. 9 My father.. went in one of these ships at a very early age as a supercargo.

transf. **1713** *Guardian* No. 95 ¶1 Mr. Purville was Supercargo to the great Hamper, in which were the following Goods.

Hence **super'cargoship**, the office or occupation of supercargo.

1809 P. IRVING in *W. Irving's Life & Lett.* (1864) I. 222, I am averse to any supercargoship, or anything that may bear you to distant or unfriendly climates. **1879** HILL *Life Irving* 55 He seems even to have considered a supercargoship.

supercede, var. (now erron.) of SUPERSEDE.

supercelestial (ˌs(j)uːpəsɪˈlɛstɪəl), *a.* (*sb.*) [f. late L. *supercælestis* = Gr. ὑπερουράνιος: see SUPER- 1 a, 4, and CELESTIAL. Cf. obs. F. *superceleste*; It. *sopracceleste*, Pg. *sobreceleste*; Sp., Pg. *sobrecelestial*.]

1. That is above the heavens; situated or existing above the firmament.

1559 W. CUNNINGHAM *Cosmogr. Glasse* 2 Ptolomæus, Atlas, and Alphonsus.. founde out the maruelous course and sondry motions, of the supercelestiall bodies. **1561** [see SUBCELESTIAL A.]. **1635** SWAN *Spec. Mundi* (1670) 31 How can it therefore be that these should be those supercelestial waters separated from all other waters by the firmament, seeing the firmament is above them? **1660** INGELO *Bentiv. & Ur.* II. (1682) Index Hh ij b, *Hyperuranic*,.. Supercelestial things, which the Gnosticks bragg'd that they were able to see. **1684** T. BURNET *Th. Earth* I. 16 Some have thought those to be waters plac'd above the highest heavens, or super-celestial waters. **1744** BERKELEY *Siris* §366 What this philosopher in his Phædrus speaketh of the super-celestial region, and the divinity resident therein. **1847** LEWES *Hist. Philos.* (1867) I. VI. iv. 250 No poet has ever celebrated these supercelestial things, nor ever will celebrate them, as they deserve.

2. More than heavenly; of a nature or character higher than celestial.

1561 DAUS tr. *Bullinger on Apoc.* (1573) 19 The augmentation of the supercelestiall grace and lyght. **1578** J. JONES *Preserv. Bodie & Soule* Ep. Ded., The supercelestiall or not to be seene graces in God are very manifestly knowen by his most wonderful workes. **1644** SIR E. DERING *Prop. Sacr.* ii. 17 A.. supercelestiall,.. life-giving mystery. **1672** STERRY *Freed. Will* (1675) 239 Jesus Christ is a supernatural, supercælestial Spirit, far above the nature of Souls or Angels in the first Creation. *a* **1711** KEN *Hymns Evang.* Poet. Wks. 1721 I. 97 Discourse salvifick, he at Meals instill'd, And Souls with Food supercelestial fill'd. **1826** G. S. FABER *Diffic. Romanism* (1853) 263 That they might learn the flesh which he would give them to be supercelestial and spiritual food. **1856** R. A. VAUGHAN *Mystics* (1860) II. IX. iii. 138 To the higher faculty, then, there are already visible.. gleams of a super-celestial dawn. **1902** W. M. ALEXANDER *Demon. Possess. N.T.* viii. 227 These evil powers.. drag them down from God and super-celestial things to those below.

†**b.** In ironical or trivial use. *Obs.*

1566 W. P. tr. *Curio's Pasquine in Traunce* 110 b, They are altogether idle questions of vayne things, crooked, more than supercelestiall, crabbed, and Seraphicall. **1576** KNEWSTUB *Confut.*, etc. (1579) 39 Hee hath.. ouerthrowen all H.N. his spiritual constructions, and supercelestiall [*sic*] interpretations. **1603** FLORIO *Montaigne* III. xiii. (1632) 630 Super-celestiall opinions, and under-terrestriall manners, are things, that amongst us, I have ever seene to bee of singular accord.

†**B.** *sb.* A supercelestial being. *Obs. rare*$^{-1}$.

1652 BENLOWES *Theoph.* Pref., This spiritual Poem, which treateth on Sub-cælestials, Cælestials and Super-cælestials.

†**super'celical**, *a. Obs. rare*$^{-1}$. [See SUPER- 1 a and CELICAL.] Supercelestial.

1654 VILVAIN *Theorem. Theol.* i. 28 Mans Soul for excellence hath a far sublimer supercelical efficient.

supercession, var. (now erron.) of SUPERSESSION.

'supercharge, *sb.* [SUPER-[1] 3, 10.]

1. *Her.* A charge borne upon another charge. *rare.*

1766 PORNY *Elem. Her.* (1777) T viij b/2. **1780** EDMONDSON *Heraldry* II. Gloss., *Super-charge*, is a term that hath been applied by some to express one figure borne on another... N. B. This word, *Super-charge*, is now seldom or ever used, *surmounted* being a better term.

2. An excessive charge; an overcharge. *rare.*

1826 DISRAELI in Monypenny *Life* (1910) I. vii. 95, I generally detect the *aubergiste* in a super-charge.

3. *Engin.* An explosive charge of higher than usual pressure in the cylinders of an internal-combustion engine; increased pressure of the charge.

1912 E. BUTLER *Evol. Internal Combustion Engine* vi. 69 It has been proposed by Clerk and others to employ super-compression of the charge.., the combustion cylinder thereby receiving a super-charge of air. **1948** *Petroleum Handbk.* (Shell Petroleum Co. Ltd.) (ed. 3) xxv. 356 The extra fuel has a certain cooling effect, and this permits an increase in boost (degree of supercharge). **1971** L. J. K. SETRIGHT *Power to Fly* v. 120 The immediate effect of the new fuel was to allow a greater degree of supercharge.

'supercharge, *v. Engin.* [SUPER- 9 b.] *trans.* To increase the pressure of the fuel-air mixture in (an internal-combustion engine).

1919 W. J. WALKER tr. *Devillers's Automobile & Aero Engines* xxiv. 384 Each compressor, having two compression strokes per revolution, can supercharge two cylinders. **1924** *Glasgow Herald* 6 May 4 The proposition of super-charging engines for sea-going and for road as well as for air service. **1966** *McGraw-Hill Encycl. Sci. & Technol.* VII. 208/2 Supercharging a two-cycle diesel engine requires some means of restricting or throttling the exhaust in order to build up cylinder pressure.

supercharged, *pa. pple.* and *ppl. a.* [SUPER-[1] 9 b.] **1.** (*super'charged.*) Charged to excess; overcharged.

1876 PAGE *Adv. Text-bk. Geol.* xv. 283 Shallow seas super-charged with saline matter. **1889** *Athenæum* 12 Oct. 499/1 The story is supercharged with the frolicsome spirit and delicate humour that [etc.]. **1909** *Q. Rev.* Oct. 463 Our supercharged imagination.

2. *Engin.* (*'supercharged.*)

a. Of the fuel-air mixture in an internal-combustion engine: increased in pressure by mechanical means. **b.** Of a vehicle or its engine: equipped with a supercharger.

1919 W. J. WALKER tr. *Devillers's Automobile & Aero Engines* xxiv. 387 The volume of the supercharged mixture remains sensibly constant during injection. **1943** J. B. PRIESTLEY *Daylight on Saturday* vii. 41 Where did Germany get her first super-charged aero engines from? **1955** *Times* 5 May 16/5 The newest of our engines to be publicly announced is a supercharged turboprop of 4 000 h.p. **1980** *Daily Tel.* 21 May 14/3 The preview of super-charged prototype models in Turin.

'supercharger. *Engin.* [f. SUPERCHARGE *v.* + -ER[1].] A compressor that increases the pressure of the fuel-air mixture supplied to the cylinders of an internal-combustion engine. Cf. BLOWER[1] 3 d.

1921 A. W. JUDGE *Automobile & Aircraft Engines* x. 452 The power required to drive the supercharger is about 6 per cent. **1946** *Happy Landings* July 3/1 The supercharger control.. should be operated smartly. **1960** G. MAXWELL *Ring of Bright Water* II. x. 144 The supercharger screamed, dial needles moved with incredible rapidity towards red zones: I had a glimpse of the speedometer hovering at 125 m.p.h. **1980** *Daily Tel.* 21 May 14/3 Manufacturers have been increasingly attracted to the turbocharger because it is driven by waste gases from the exhaust, while the supercharger is driven by a power take-off from the engine.

'supercharging, *vbl. sb. Engin.* [f. SUPERCHARGE *v.* + -ING[1].] The action or use of a supercharger.

1922 *Encycl. Brit.* XXX. 41/1 Supercharging for high flying. **1937** *Discovery* Dec. 386 (caption) The McClelland two-stroke petrol turbine engine. The unfinned cylinders are pumps providing a supercharging effect. **1980** *Daily Tel.* 21 May 14/3 Fiat officials indicated that the ultimate intention was to apply super-charging to its small and medium volume production models.

†**superchery** (s(j)ʊˈpɜːtʃərɪ). *Obs.* exc. in F. form **supercherie** (sypɛrʃəri). Also 6 -chierie, 7 -chiery, 7–8 -cherie. [a. F. *supercherie*, ad. It. *superchieria* (var. *soverchieria*), f. *superchio* (var *soverchio*) superfluous, excessive, = OSp., Pg. *sobejo*:—pop.L. **superculu-s*, f. *super* over, above.]

1. An attack made upon one at a disadvantage; (a piece of) foul play.

1598 FLORIO *Ital. Dict.*, *Soperchiaria*, a superchierie, a wrong or iniury offred with ods or aduantage, also superfluitie, an affront. **1603** —— *Montaigne* II. xxvii. 400 It is a Superchiery,.. as being wel armed, to charge a man who hath but a piece of a sword, or being sound and strong, to set vpon a man sore hurt. **1639** CHAS. I *Declar. Tumults Scot.* 380 By their supercherie violence and terrifications. **1656** EARL MONM. tr. *Boccalini's Advts. fr. Parnass.* I. lxxi. (1674) 90 [The] swaggering companions, which he was accustomed to make use of in his supercheries and foul play to men of honour.

2. Trickery, deceit. Also with *a* and *pl.*

1650 EARL MONM. tr. *Senault's Man bec. Guilty* 168 All men know these Messengers [*sc.* the senses] are unfaithfull, .. and that Nature hath given her [*sc.* the soul] an inward light, to free herself from their Superchery. **1716** M. DAVIES *Athen. Brit.* III. *Arianism* 3 He was not likely to succeed in that Supercherie, by Reason of.. almost unavoidable Certainty of being discover'd immediately. **1781** H. WALPOLE *Let. to Mann* 13 July, That I might not contribute .. to any legal supercherie, I insisted [etc.]. [**1811** GIFFORD in *M. Napier's Corr.* (1879) 3 A little *supercherie* of which I have been guilty in filching a couple of lines from one of your quotations.]

superchurch: see SUPER- 5 c.

†**supercile.** *Obs. rare*$^{-1}$. [ad. L. *supercilium*: see SUPERCILIUM.] Superciliousness.

1679 J. GOODMAN *Penit. Pard.* I. ii. 24 He.. did not use such branded persons with the same supercile and disdain that their great men were wont to do.

†**super'cilian.** *Obs. rare*$^{-1}$. [f. SUPERCILIOUS + -AN.] A supercilious person.

1689 T. PLUNKET *Char. Gd. Commander* 20 Any supercilian in fine clothes.

superciliary (s(j)uːpəˈsɪlɪərɪ), *a.* (*sb.*) [ad. mod.L. *superciliāris*, f. *supercilium*: see SUPERCILIUM and -ARY[2]. Cf. F. *sourcilier.*] Of or pertaining to the eyebrow, or to the region of the eyebrow; supra-orbital.

superciliary arch or *ridge*, a prominence of the frontal bone, over the eye, produced by the development of the frontal sinuses; also, in various animals, a prominence consisting of the projecting upper edge of the orbit itself.

1732 MONRO *Anat. Bones* II. (ed. 2) 86 The Foramina, or Holes,.. of the frontal Bone,.. one in each superciliary Ridge [etc.]. *Ibid.*, The superciliary Foramina,.. often instead of a Hole, a Notch only is to be seen. **1733** G. DOUGLAS tr. *Winslow's Anat.* (1756) I. 22 On the Outside [of the Os Frontis] we observe the following Eminences; two superciliary Arches, which form the upper Edge of each Orbit, or the Supercilia. **1813** PRICHARD *Phys. Hist. Man* 57 The superciliary arches scarcely to be perceived. **1831** R. KNOX *Cloquet's Anat.* 667 The Supra-orbitar or Superciliary Artery... Arrived at the base of the orbit, after furnishing some minute ramifications to the periosteum and the two muscles above mentioned, it issues from that cavity by the superciliary notch. **1871** DARWIN *Desc. Man* II. xix. 316 The superciliary ridge is generally more strongly marked in man than in woman.

b. Situated over the eye; also *transf.* having a marking over the eye (cf. SUPERCILIOUS 3 b).

1872 COUES *N. Amer. Birds* 19 Forehead,.. middle head or crown,.. hind head, or occiput. The lateral border of all three together constitutes the 'superciliary line,' that is, line over the eye. **1888** P. L. SCLATER *Argentine Ornith.* I. 51 Above grey, slight superciliary mark whitish.

B. *sb.* A superciliary ridge or marking.

1864 THURNAM in *Mem. Anthrop. Soc.* I. 144 The superciliaries are well marked, the orbits rather small. **1888** P. L. SCLATER *Argentine Ornith.* I. 97 Distinct superciliaries white.

†**superci'liosity.** *Obs. rare.* [f. next + -ITY.] Superciliousness.

1606 BIRNIE *Kirk-Buriall* (1833) 13 As if such superciliosity could sweeten the bitter swarfes of their sowre death. **1637** BASTWICK *Litany* I. 6 The Statelinesse, severity, pride of their carriage and superciliosity. **1652** URQUHART *Jewel* 58 They, with a Pharisaical Superciliosity, would always rebuke the.. Sectaries as Publicans and sinners.

supercilious (s(j)uːpəˈsɪlɪəs), *a.* [ad. late L. *superciliōsus*, f. *supercilium*: see SUPERCILIUM and -OUS. Cf. F. *sourcilleux.*]

1. Haughtily contemptuous in character or demeanour; having or marked by an air of contemptuous superiority or disdain.

a **1529** [implied in SUPERCILIOUSLY]. **1614** PURCHAS *Pilgrimage* II. viii. (ed. 2) 137 There was small reckoning had of the Galilæans by their supercilious and superstitious brethren of Iudæa. **1638** SIR T. HERBERT *Trav.* (ed. 2) 19 Let me advise our Men to.. not contemne them from their indefensive nakednesse, or by a supercilious conceit of their owne weapons and field practises. **1771** SMOLLETT *Humphry Cl.* 26 June, His mother eyed me in silence with a supercilious air. **1799** J. ROBERTSON *Agric. Perth* 38 The supercilious landlord, who, with an air of disdain, keeps his tenants at a distance. **1845** DISRAELI *Sybil* v. vi, Sybil had made the enquiry and received only a supercilious stare from the shop-man. **1876** GEO. ELIOT *Dan. Der.* I. ii, Smiling at her ironically, and taking the air of a supercilious mentor.

†**2.** 'Dictatorial, arbitrary, despotic, overbearing' (J.), exacting or severe in judgement, censorious.

1598 B. JONSON *Ev. Man in Hum.* Ded. to Camden, There are, no doubt, a supercilious race in the world who will esteeme all office, done you in this kind, an injurie. **1616** CHAPMAN tr. *Homer's Wks.*, *Concl. Verses* 27 To see our supercilious wizerds frowne. **1625** B. JONSON *Staple of N.* IV. i, *Fit.* I ha' mark'd him all this meale, he has done nothing But mocke, with scuruy faces, all wee said. *Alm.* A supercilious Rogue! **1644** MILTON *Divorce* To Parl. Eng. A 3 b, In the Gospel we shall read a supercilious crew of masters, whose holinesse.. was to set straiter limits to obedience, then God had set. **1725** DE FOE *Voy. round World* (1840) 96 This.. was neither more nor less than trading and bartering, though from supercilious punctilio, we had in a manner been denied it. **1758** JOHNSON *Idler* No. 12 ¶2 Hopeless as the claim of vulgar characters may appear to the supercilious and severe. **1791** BOSWELL *Johnson* an. 1745, His pamphlet.. was fortunate enough to obtain the approbation even of the supercilious Warburton himself.

†**3. a.** Pertaining to the eyebrows. *Obs. rare*$^{-0}$.

1656 BLOUNT *Glossogr.*, *Supercilious*.. pertaining to the eyebrowes. **1658** PHILLIPS, *Supercilious*,.. having great eyebrows.

†**b.** *Zool.* In names of various animals distinguished by a conspicuous stripe, process, etc. over the eye: rendering L. *superciliosus* or *superciliaris* of the systematic name. *Obs.*

1782 LATHAM *Gen. Synopsis Birds* I. II. 643 *Alcedo superciliosa*.. Supercilious K[ingfisher]... From the bill, over the eyes, passes a narrow orange stripe. *Ibid.* 673 *Merops superciliosus*.. Supercilious B[ee-eater]. **1802** SHAW *Gen. Zool.* III. I. 220 Supercilious Lizard. *Lacerta Superciliosa*... This Lizard.. having.. the appearance of a pair of sharp-pointed, horn-like processes above and beyond each eye. **1803** *Ibid.* IV. I. 169 Supercilious Blenny. *Blennius Superciliosus*.. immediately over each eye is situated a small palmated crest or appendage. **1824** STEPHENS *Shaw's Gen. Zool.* XII. I. 266 Supercilious Jacana (*Parra superciliosa*).. Dark shining green Jacana, with white superciliary lines.

super'ciliously, *adv.* [f. SUPERCILIOUS + -LY[2].] In a supercilious manner; with haughty contempt; disdainfully; †dictatorially, dogmatically, censoriously.

a **1529** SKELTON *Replyc.* Wks. 1843 I. 208 Whan they haue ones superciliusly caught A lytell ragge of rethorike. **1609** B. JONSON *Sil. Wom.* v. iii, Set your faces, and looke superciliously, while I present you. **1627** DONNE *Serm.*, *Rev. iv. 8* (1640) 434 Some binde themselves exactly, rigidly, superciliously, yea superstitiously to the number of foure. **1647** CLARENDON *Hist. Reb.* II. §43 The Earl.. who was a punctual man in point of Honour, received this Address superciliously enough. **1697** BENTLEY *Phal.* (1699) 198 He talks most superciliously, and with the greatest assurance. **1709** SWIFT *Vindic. Bickerstaff* Wks. 1755 II. I. 169 If men of publick spirit must be superciliously treated for their ingenious attempts, how will true useful knowledge be ever advanced? **1799** HAN. MORE *Fem. Educ.* (ed. 4) Introd. p. xviii, Let it not be suspected..that she superciliously erects herself into the impeccable censor of her sex and of the world. **1862** LYTTON *Str. Story* i, The proprietors [of the shops] were decorously pompous,—the shopmen superciliously polite. **1865** MISS BRADDON *Only a Clod* xl, Harcourt smiled superciliously.

super'ciliousness. [f. as prec. + -NESS.] The quality or character of being supercilious; haughty contemptuousness.

a **1656** HALES *Serm., Rom. xiv. 1* in *Golden Rem.* (1673) 29 It falls out oftentimes, that men offend..as much by familiarity, as by superciliousness and contempt. **1697** COLLIER *Ess. Mor. Subj.* I. (1703) 232 To surrender these privileges up to the superciliousness of every assuming or ignorant pretender. **1751** JOHNSON *Rambler* No. 87 ¶9 He has inflamed the opposition..by arrogance and superciliousness. **1851** GALLENGA *Italy* iv. 239 Excessive spruceness, ermine-like exclusiveness and fastidiousness,.. but nothing like *morgue* and superciliousness. **1881** W. R. SMITH *O.T. in Jewish Ch.* xi. 326 The superciliousness, with which traditionalists declare the labours of the critics to be visionary.

‖**supercilium** (s(j)uːpəˈsɪlɪəm). Pl. -ia (-ɪə). [L., = eyebrow; ridge, summit; haughtiness, etc.]

1. The eyebrow. *Obs.* exc. *Anat.*

1672 MARVELL *Reh. Transp.* I. 200, I marked how your answerer looked when he spoke of the day of judgment. Very gravely..and yet without any depressing or exalting his superciliums.

b. *Zool.* A superciliary streak or marking.

1817 STEPHENS *Shaw's Gen. Zool.* X. I. 34 Chesnut red Manakin..supercilia whitish above, margined with black.

2. *Arch.* †**a.** A narrow fillet above the cymatium of a cornice. *Obs.* **b.** A fillet above and below the scotia of an Attic base. **c.** The lintel or transverse part of a door-case.

1563 SHUTE *Archit.* E iij b, Geue .2. [partes] vnto Cymatium,..the seuenth parte is lefte for Supercilium or Regula. **1664** EVELYN *Acc. Archit.* in *Freart's Archit.* etc. 138 Corona is by some cal'd Supercilium, but rather I conceive Stillicidium the Drip. **1728** CHAMBERS *Cycl.*, *Supercilium*, in the ancient Architecture, the uppermost Member of the Cornice; call'd by the Moderns, Corona, Crown, or Larmier. *Ibid.* s.v., Supercilium, is also used for a square Member under the upper Tore in some Pedestals. Some Authors confound it with the Tore itself. **1828–9** J. NARRIEN *Arch.* in *Encycl. Metrop.* (1845) V. 290 The lintel, or *supercilium*, corresponds with the architrave; above the supercilium is a kind of frize, which he calls *hyperthyrum*, and, over this, a *corona*, or cornice. *Ibid.*, The supercilium extends, right and left, beyond the exterior of the antepagmenta. **1850** LEITCH tr. *C. O. Müller's Anc. Art.* §281 (ed. 2) 311 The supercilium is similar to the architrave, and the hyperthyrum to the cornice.

3. *Anat.* The lip or margin of a bony cavity, esp. of the acetabulum.

1706 PHILLIPS (ed. Kersey), *Supercilium*,..the lip or side of a Cavity or hollow Part at the end of a Bone, particularly a Cartilage or Gristle of the Coxendix or Hip-bone. **1733** G. DOUGLAS tr. *Winslow's Anat.* (1756) I. 72 Besides what has been said of the Acetabulum in general, there are..the Edge called the Supercilium, the Cartilaginous Cavity [etc.]. **1771** *Encycl. Brit.* I. 204/2 A little above the supercilium of the cotyloid cavity or acetabulum.

†**4.** Superciliousness, haughtiness. *Obs. rare*$^{-1}$.

1733 T. STEWARD *Ordin. Charge*, Your general Behaviour should..no way discourage a becoming..Familiarity with you, by a lofty *Supercilium*, or a forbidding Austerity.

'superˌcluster. *Astr.* [SUPER- 5 c.] A cluster of objects that are themselves clusters (in quot. 1930, of stars, but now only of galaxies).

1930 R. J. TRUMPLER in *Lick Observatory Bull.* XIV. 187/2 It seems worth while to examine the hypothesis that our Milky Way system..together with the two Magellanic Clouds and about a hundred globular clusters form a cluster of extra-galactic objects which we may call the 'supercluster'. **1958** *Astron. Jrnl.* LXIII. 260/2 The local super-cluster of galaxies is an irregular assembly of groups, clouds and clusters dominated by the Virgo cluster in its center. **1970** *Nature* 19 Dec. 1137/1 Wolfe and Burbidge argue from these observations that super-clusters of galaxies ..must definitely be ruled out. **1978** PASACHOFF & KUTNER *University Astron.* i. 6 Before we could enlarge our field of view another 100 times we might see a supercluster—a cluster of clusters of galaxies. **1982** *Daily Tel.* 1 Dec. 1/6 The largest-known object in the universe, a supercluster of millions of galaxies, has been discovered.

Hence **'superˌclustering** *vbl. sb.*

1960 *Soviet Astron.* III. 910 We conclude that not only clustering, but also superclustering, is a general characteristic of the distribution of galaxies. **1971** D. W. SCIAMA *Mod. Cosmol.* vii. 96 The suggested scale of their clustering would be much the same in relation to their separation as is the case for the clustering or super-clustering of galaxies.

'supercoil, *sb. Biochem.* [SUPER- 5 c.] A coiled coil; *spec.* a structure sometimes assumed by DNA in which the double helix itself is coiled or looped. Cf. SUPERHELIX.

1965 PEACOCKE & DRYSDALE *Molecular Basis Heredity* IV. 168 In the fibre, these molecules take the form of 'super-coils' in which the axis of the DNA helix is itself coiled with a pitch of 120Å and a diameter of 100Å. **1976** *Nature* 10 June 516/1 Supercoils could be introduced into progeny molecules either before sealing of the closed circular form, or subsequent to an initial closing of the molecule. **1980** *Sci. Amer.* July 100/2 Because the forces that stabilize the double helix are strong the closed circular molecules resist such underwinding, and..they compensate by forming supercoils.

'supercoil, *v. Biochem.* [f. prec. sb.]

a. *trans.* To make (a molecule) into a supercoil. **b.** *intr.* To become a supercoil.

1967 *Jrnl. Molecular Biol.* XXV. 28 Only molecules in which both strands are intact can be supercoiled in either sense. **1971** *Nature* 29 Oct. 591/2 Segrest and Cunningham start with the tropocollagen molecule, a three-strand rope formed by supercoiling two indentical helices termed a_1 and a_2. **1982** *Sci. Amer.* July 87/1 When the ethidium is removed, the ring [of DNA] supercoils.

Hence **'supercoiled** *ppl. a.*, having the structure of a coiled helix; **'supercoiling** *vbl. sb.*, the action or result of forming a supercoil; also *attrib.*

1967 *Jrnl. Molecular Biol.* XXV. 23 It would be desirable to have independent evidence on the direction of supercoiling and to obtain an estimate of the number of supercoiling turns. *Ibid.* 27 The supercoiled form of polyoma DNA can be converted to the unsupercoiled form by one single-strand scission. **1980** *Sci. Amer.* July 100/1 Affecting DNA's in a wide range of sizes and shapes (including some that are not organized into a double helix), supercoiling takes a variety of forms. **1980** *Proc. Nat. Acad. Sciences* LXXVII. 2445/1 A massive tangle of catenated supercoiled molecules.

supercolossal: see SUPER- 9 a (*a*).

supercon'ducting, *ppl. a. Physics.* [f. SUPER- 9 b, tr. Du. *suprageleidend* (H. K. Onnes 1913, in *Versl. van de gewone Vergad. d. Wis- en Natuurk. Afdeeling, K. Akad. v. Wetensch. te Amsterdam* XXI. 1390).] Possessing no electrical resistivity; employing a substance in this state.

1913 H. K. ONNES in *Proc. Sect. Sci. K. Akad. Wetenschap. Amsterdam* XV. 1429 A thread of super-conducting mercury, if an ordinary conducting particle were present anywhere in the current path, could show resistance at that spot. **1935** *Discovery* July 213/2 The fascinating transition of metals into the super-conducting state when near to absolute zero. **1958** *Listener* 11 Dec. 984/1 A current once established in a superconducting lead ring will continue to flow indefinitely. **1966** C. R. TOTTLE *Sci. Engin. Materials* vi. 127 The superconducting state can be destroyed by the application of an external magnetic field. **1978** *Jrnl. R. Soc. Arts* CXXVI. 608/2 The savings from introducing superconducting generators are relatively small.

Hence (as a back-formation) **supercon'duct** *v. intr.*, to conduct electricity without any resistance.

1964 *New Scientist* 20 Aug. 441 (*heading*) USSR field windings that superconduct. **1976** G. K. HAINES *Supercold, Superhot* v. 30 More than twenty-five elements have now been found that will superconduct.

supercon'duction. *Physics.* [SUPER- 10 a.] = SUPERCONDUCTICITY; conduction of electricity without resistance.

1940 E. F. BURTON et al. *Phenomena Temperature Liquid Helium* x. 322 It might be possible to explain the discrepancy..in the apparent number of superconduction electrons. **1959** *Electronic Engin.* XXXI. 589/2 Domains of ferromagnetism alternating with domains of superconduction, the latter having a magnetization antiparallel to the applied field.

ˌsuperconduc'tivity. *Physics.* [SUPER- 10 a.] The property of having zero electrical resistivity exhibited by some substances at temperatures close to absolute zero.

1913 H. K. ONNES in *Proc. Sect. Sci. K. Akad. Wetensch. Amsterdam* XV. 1428 (*heading*) Experiments on the possible influence of contact with an ordinary conductor upon the superconductivity of mercury. **1934** *Times Lit. Suppl.* 26 July 531/3 A similar property of superconductivity, acquired at specific low temperatures, has since been found also in a number of other metals and in certain alloys. **1959** *Sci. News* LI. 21 The idea of loss-free electromagnetic devices was immediately suggested when superconductivity was first discovered, and a number of efforts have since been made to find metals or alloys that would exhibit superconductivity at higher than [liquid] helium temperatures. **1978** *Jrnl. R. Soc. Arts* CXXVI. 608/2 Superconductivity..offers the prospect of lower capital costs and higher efficiencies than conventional generators for large units.

So **supercon'ductive** *a.* = SUPERCONDUCTING *ppl. a.*

1913 H. K. ONNES in *Proc. Sect. Sci. K. Akad. Wetensch. Amsterdam* XVI. 116 The actual degree of conductivity of the superconductive mercury. **1955** H. B. G. CASIMIR in W. Pauli *Niels Bohr* 119 There exist many metals that do not become superconductive in the temperature range in which they have been investigated. **1966** K. MENDELSSOHN *Quest for Absolute Zero* ix. 199 In 1930 de Haas and Voogd had found that wires of lead-bismuth alloy remained superconductive in magnetic fields as high as 20,000 oersted. **1972** *Physics Bull.* Oct. 615/1 The highest transition temperature for superconductive materials reported so far is 21 K in a three element compound, niobium-aluminium-germanium.

supercon'ductor. *Physics.* [f. SUPER- 6 c, tr. Du. *suprageleider* (H. K. Onnes 1913, in *Versl. van de gewone Vergad. d. Wis- en Natuurk. Afdeeling, K. Akad. v. Wetensch. te Amsterdam* XXI. 1390).] A substance that becomes superconducting at sufficiently low temperatures; also, such a substance in the superconducting state.

1913 H. K. ONNESS in *Proc. Sect. Sci. K. Akad. Wetensch. Amsterdam* XV. 1429 A pushing forward of the electrons in the galvanic current through a super-conductor without performance of work. **1931** *Ann. Reg. 1930* 61 Meissner discovered that copper sulphide is a superconductor. *Ibid.*, Niobium carbide becomes a superconductor at 10° A. **1955** H. B. G. CASIMIR in W. Pauli *Niels Bohr* 119 At temperatures above the transition point..superconductors behave in all respects like these normal metals. **1959** *Sci. News* LI. 21 The real difficulty in the use of superconductors in magnetic devices is the fact that superconductivity is destroyed by fields of only a few hundred oersted. **1969** ROSE-INNES & RHODERICK *Introd. Superconductivity* i. 5 About half the metallic elements are known to be superconductors and..a large-number of alloys are superconductors. **1983** *New Scientist* 24 Mar. 802/1 Like most of the organic superconductors already known, the new material loses its resistance only under high pressure.

'superconscious, *a. Psychol.* [SUPER- 4 a.] Transcending human or normal consciousness. Also *absol.*

1884 F. W. H. MYERS in *Proc. Soc. Psychical Res.* II. 219 We shall come, perhaps, to find *super-conscious* as necessary a term as *sub-conscious*. **1904** HARDY *Dynasts* I. v. iv. 166 In that immense unweeting Mind is shown One far above forethinking; purposive, Yet superconscious. **1921** *Public Opinion* 28 Jan. 90/2 What the world needs is a man whose genius will come from the superconscious, the divine. **1940** A. HUXLEY *Let.* 12 Jan. (1969) 449 It looks as though there were a kind of spiral development, from unconscious animal, through conscious human up to what for lack of better words may be called super-conscious spiritual. **1953** R. F. C. HULL tr. *Jung's Psychol. & Alchemy* in *Coll. Wks.* XII. ii. 268 There are people who can never understand the unconscious as anything but a *sub*-conscious, and who therefore feel impelled to put a superconscious alongside or possibly above it.

Hence **super'consciousness.**

1898 *Advance* (Chicago) 27 Jan. 107/2 [Jesus] had now reached the state of mind known to Hindus as samahdo or super-consciousness, and there was no pain for him on the cross. **1901** *Harper's Mag.* CII. 788/1 Since this unpleasant whirl of superconsciousness had swept over him. **1940** *Mind* XLIX. 130 The condition of 'super-consciousness' which most Indian philosophers and mystics agree to be attainable in this life. **1962** M. SADHU *Samadhi* i. 13 The question of the higher aspects of consciousness in man, often called simply the Superconsciousness, is becoming more and more urgent.

'supercontinent. *Geol.* [SUPER- 6 c.] One of the large land masses that are thought to have existed in the geological past and from which two or more of the present continents are thought to be derived; = PROTOCONTINENT. Cf. GONDWANALAND, LAURASIA, PANGÆA.

1963 *Sci. Amer.* Apr. 89/1 According to Wegener all the continents had been joined in a single supercontinent about 200 million years ago. **1969** *Times* 25 Apr. 13/8 Australia and Antarctica are also thought to have been joined together, the land mass they formed being part of the supercontinent of Gondwanaland. **1970** [see PANTHALASSA]. **1977** A. HALLAM *Planet Earth* 210 In the late Permian we thus encounter a single sea-less supercontinent, a phenomenon probably unique in the history of the Earth.

ˌsupercon'traction. [SUPER- 13.] The contraction of a hair or fibre to less than its original length after treatment with heat or chemicals.

1933 ASTBURY & WOODS in *Phil. Trans. R. Soc.* A. CCXXXII. 337 The appearance of the phenomenon of 'super-contraction' just described is perhaps the most striking manifestation of this change. *Ibid.* 359 A general effect to which we have ventured to attach the term 'super-contraction', to distinguish it from the property of a normal stretched hair, when wetted, of returning exactly to its original unstretched length. **1954** ALEXANDER & HUDSON *Wool* iii. 75 Supercontraction of unstrained fibres was first observed by Speakman. **1977** F. KIDD in R. S. Asquith *Chem. Natural Protein Fibers* ix. 394 Woods..recorded 50% supercontraction of Cotswold wool.

So **ˌsupercon'tract** *v. intr.* and *trans.*, to (cause to) undergo supercontraction; **ˌsupercon'tracted, -con'tracting** *ppl. adjs.*

1933 *Phil. Trans. R. Soc.* A. CCXXXII. 365 With respect to the *minimum* (super-contracted) length,..permanent set develops even in hot water. **1953** R. W. MONCRIEFF *Wool Shrinkage* xxv. 352 Fibres..which had not been treated with diepoxybutane in the phosphate buffer did not subsequently supercontract in metabisulphite. **1954** ALEXANDER & HUDSON *Wool* iii. 76 Phenol is a much more effective supercontracting agent than formamide. **1962** W. J. ONIONS *Wool* ii. 38 Steam set fibres are also resistant to boiling 5 per cent sodium bisulphite, which supercontracts untreated fibres. **1977** F. KIDD in R. S. Asquith *Chem. Natural Protein Fibers* ix. 394 White skunk hairs.. supercontract more in sodium metabisulfite than do human hairs.

super'cool, *v.* [SUPER- 9 b.] **a.** *trans.* To subject to supercooling.

1932 F. F. GROUT *Petrogr. & Petrol.* III. 232 In the absence of seeding some magma intrusions may be greatly supercooled. **1959** B. CHALMERS *Physical Metallurgy* vi. 265 The liquid of composition *O* is supercooled until a nucleus in one of the phases forms. **1976** *Nature* 22 July 323/2 The cell contents are readily supercooled.

b. *intr.* To undergo supercooling.

1940 *Lancet* 17 Feb. 303/2 The capacity to supercool may be abolished by soaking the skin in water, and skin which does not supercool may be induced to do so by leaving it unwashed for a week. **1959** B. CHALMERS *Physical*

Metallurgy vi. 244 When a metal sample is sufficiently subdivided into isolated drops, some supercool to the extent of about $0{\cdot}2T_E$ before nucleation occurs. **1975** *Rev. Mod. Physics* XLVII. 454/1 The $A \rightarrow B$ transition [in liquid ³He] strongly supercooled the first time the transition was made from temperatures considerably above T_0.

super-cool, *a.*: see SUPER- 9a (*a*).

super'cooled, *ppl. a.* [SUPER- 9b.] **a.** Liquid though below the freezing point. **b.** Apparently solid, but formed from a liquid without a definite change of phase and having (on the atomic scale) the disorder of a liquid.

1898 *Chem. News* 29 July 59/1 (*heading*) The variation with the temperature of the number of nuclei which are formed in different supercooled liquids. **1937** *Times* 14 Oct. 11/4 Local conditions may cause the moisture in a cloud to become, in the meteorologist's phrase, 'supercooled'. **1947** J. C. RICH *Materials & Methods Sculpture* xi. 329 Glass is sometimes referred to as a supercooled liquid, because the material has no definite melting point. **1966** C. R. TOTTLE *Sci. Engin. Materials* iii. 81 Any material possessing the properties of a supercooled liquid, having failed to crystallize and therefore being amorphous in structure, can be called a glass. **1980** *Jrnl. R. Soc. Arts* May 369/2 Silver iodide smoke particles can also provide 'kernels' on which ice crystals can grow in supercooled cloud.

super'cooling, *vbl. sb.* [SUPER- 9b.] The cooling of a liquid to below its freezing point without solidification or without crystallization occurring; more widely, cooling to below the temperature of a phase transition without the change of phase occurring; reduction in the temperature of a phase transition.

1898 *Chem. News* 29 July 59/1 The number of points increase with strong super-cooling. **1922** GLAZEBROOK *Dict. Appl. Physics* I. 947/2 The supercooling of a vapour without condensation is analogous to the supercooling of a liquid without crystallization. **1963** R. A. FLINN *Fund. Metal Casting* ii. 21 Some supercooling usually ensues before initial crystallization. **1975** *Rev. Mod. Physics* XLVII. 463/2 This would explain..experiments [on ³He] at melting pressure..where *no* superheating of the $B \rightarrow A$ transition is observed while supercooling of the $A \rightarrow B$ transition is common. **1980** S. A. MORSE *Basalts & Phase Diagrams* iii. 28 Supercooling results from the fact that the nucleation of a crystal is a random process, requiring the accidental arrangement..of atoms in the pattern of the crystal structure, after which a crystal nucleus may grow at a great rate.

supercrat: see SUPER- 6c.

super'critical, *a.* [SUPER- 9a.] **1.** Highly critical.

1610 HOLLAND *Camden's Brit.* I. 687 By our Critickes good leave (who..presuming so much of their great wits are supercriticall). **1661** GAUDEN *Consid. Liturgy* 25 These supercritical censors. **1937** *Even. News* 12 Feb. 11/1 Only the super-critical, rather cosmopolitanminded audience of the West End still look coolly on their simple robust brand of humour.

2. Of, pertaining to, or designating a fluid at a temperature and pressure greater than its critical temperature and pressure.

1934 *Econ. Geol.* XXIX. 457 The first work on critical and supercritical phenomena of solutions was done by Hannay and Hogarth in 1879. **1968** *New Scientist* 27 June 697/1 Supercritical boilers probably present more problems. **1972** *Physics Bull.* Apr. 236 The use of supercritical helium for cooling superconducting and other low temperature equipment. **1981** E. CORLETT *Revolution Merchant Shipping* 40/1 Natural gas..at normal temperatures..is supercritical...It cannot be liquefied by pressure unless below −82° C.

3. Of a flow of fluid: faster than the speed at which waves travel in the fluid. Of an aerofoil: giving rise to such a flow over much of its surface when its speed relative to the bulk fluid is subcritical, but in such a way that flow separation is largely avoided.

1941, etc. [see SUBCRITICAL *a.* 2]. **1967** *Aviation Week* 24 July 25/1 Whitcomb describes the shape as a 'supercritical airfoil' because it enables aircraft in subsonic flight to achieve these higher critical Mach numbers before the normal drag rise is experienced in transonic flight. The shape of the upper surface of the transonic wing permits predominantly supersonic air flow to be maintained across the wing. **1969** *Ibid.* 17 Feb. 22/1 Improved version of the National Aeronautics and Space Administration's 'supercritical wing'..will begin test flights in mid-1970. **1977** *McGraw-Hill Yearbk. Sci. & Technol.* 422/1 Supercritical compressor blades. **1979** *Time* 2 Apr. 21/2 With only two engines and a 'supercritical' wing that cuts aerodynamic drag, it is the most fuel-efficient commercial jet flying today.

4. *Nucl. Physics.* Containing or being more than the critical mass (see CRITICAL *a.* 7b).

1950 GLASSTONE *Sourcebk. Atomic Energy* xiv. 394/2 The presence of stray neutrons in the atmosphere makes it impossible to prevent a chain reaction in a supercritical mass. **1958** J. CLEUGH tr. *Jungk's Brighter than Thousand Suns* xii. 191 If he passed the point or was not quite quick enough in breaking contact, the mass might become 'super-critical' and produce a nuclear explosion. **1973** *Nature* 23 Mar. 251/1 Assuming a relative ²³⁵U abundance throughout the [hypothetical] planet equal to the terrestrial crustal abundance, there is just enough energy to disperse the planet if the ²³⁵U could be assembled into a super-critical mass.

Hence **,supercriti'cality,** supercritical state.

1959 *Times* 5 Mar. 2/4 (Advt.), Join a section concerned with the assessment of criticality hazards in the handling and processing of fissile materials and to carry out theoretical research into the factors governing criticality and supercriticality. **1976** L. SANDERS *Hamlet Warning* (1977) I. xi. 95 The blast..would be well into the kiloton range. The trick was..to bring the mass to supercriticality uniformly and at the same instant.

'supercurrent. *Physics.* [f. *super-* in SUPERCONDUCTOR, etc.] An electric current flowing without dissipating energy, as in a superconductor.

[**1936** *Nature* 16 May 824/1 The assumption for the supra-conductor is, that $I = I_c + I_s$... That is to say, there is a third sort of current, I_s, call it the supra-current.] **1940** E. F. BURTON et al. *Phenomena Temperature Liquid Helium* x. 302 We must now recognize three entirely different kinds of electric current..: (1) the displacement current in an insulator..; (2) the ordinary conduction current..; (3) the super-current. **1962** *New Scientist* 22 Nov. 454/3 Superconductivity can also be destroyed by increasing the supercurrent itself beyond a critical value. **1966** K. MENDELSSOHN *Quest for Absolute Zero* x. 242 Superfluid flow, just as a persistent supercurrent, is distinguished by zero entropy. **1980** *Sci. Amer.* May 43/1 In the absence of a magnetic field, and with a current below a critical value, a supercurrent flows through the Josephson junction just as if the superconductor were not interrupted by the insulating barrier.

super'dominant. *Mus.* [SUPER- 5b.] The note next above the dominant; the sixth of the scale: more usually called SUBMEDIANT. Also *attrib.* applied to a chord having this note for its root.

c **1833** J. GWILT *Music* in *Encycl. Metrop.* (1845) V. 777/1 *Superdominant*, the sixth of the key in the descending scale. **1880** STAINER *Composition* §26 The third degree of the minor scale can be part of the tonic, mediant, or super-dominant chords. **1889** E. PROUT *Harmony* i. §13 Some writers..call [the sixth note of the scale] the 'Superdominant'.

†**super'duce,** *v.* *Obs. rare.* [ad. late L. *superdūcĕre*, f. *super-* SUPER- 2 + *dūcĕre* to lead.] *trans.* To superinduce.

1477 NORTON *Ord. Alch.* v. in Ashm. (1652) 64 Twinckling and glittering as in Magnetia is, Light is cause thereof within matter of Cleernes; Which is superduced upon waterly vapour, Before tyme incenced with Heate.

So **super'duct** *v. rare*⁻⁰ [f. L. *superduct-*, pa. ppl. stem of *superdūcĕre*: see above].

1901 DORLAND *Med. Dict.*, *Superduct*, to carry up or elevate.

,super-'duper, *a. colloq.* (orig. *U.S.*). Also **sooper-dooper, super-dooper, super duper.** [A reduplicated extension of SUPER *a.*] Especially splendid, powerful, etc.; exceptional, particularly good.

1940 *N.Y. Times* 27 Sept. 27/7 (Advt.), After seeing this new M-G-M sooper dooper musical smash, our little voice went pattering all over the house. **1942** *Fortune* Feb. 104/3 Joining the Hearst organization he rapidly became what he calls a super-dooper circulator in Milwaukee, Detroit, Boston. **1942** *Sun* (Baltimore) 5 Mar. 8/8 A week ago officers knew before the curtain rose that something super-duper was about to be staged. **1949** *Hansard Commons* 26 May 1490 They are now subsidising the building of a 'super-duper' liner to compete with the Cunard flagships. **1951** *People* 3 June 2/2 British Railways put on a super-duper Pullman car special from Victoria to Epsom. **1958** D. WALLACE *Forty Years On* i. 5 Super-duper rockets with fancy-nancy warheads. **1971** *News-Advocate* (Barbados) 20 Mar. 8/1 Now this promises to be a super duper weekend. **1975** *New Yorker* 24 Mar. 33/ The Colony range from the modest Villa Torino unit..to the superduper Viking Executive units. **1978** M. PUZO *Fools Die* xvi. 181 There was one super-duper bicycle that I was sorry she had bought.

supereffluence: see SUPER- 10.

super-'ego. *Psychoanal.* [SUPER- 5.] A Freudian term for that aspect of the psyche which has internalized parental and social prohibitions or ideals early in life and imposes them as a censor on the wishes of the ego; the agent of self-criticism or self-observation. Also *transf.*

1924, etc. [see ID²]. **1938** *Times Lit. Suppl.* 26 Feb. 132/4 When the moral superego takes charge and the ego is no longer coercive but submissive. **1945** AUDEN *Coll. Poetry* 242 The fatal ease with which Conscience, i.e., the voice of God, is replaced by 'my conscience', i.e., the Super-Ego. **1958** M. ARGYLE *Relig. Behaviour* xii. 157 If religious behaviour is derived from the super-ego in some way, religion should have an irrational 'super-ego' quality about it. **1958** W. J. H. SPROTT *Human Groups* x. 173 The importance of the primary group can be expressed by saying that the group acts as the 'super-ego' of its members. **1965** *Listener* 2 Sept. 337/2 Lord Reith—one of the few twentieth-century Britons who have been willing to cast themselves as the community's superego. **1972** *Jrnl. Social Psychol.* LXXXVI. 157 The less dramatic resolution of the Oedipal complex experienced by females causes them to have a weaker superego than males. **1981** W. EBERSOHN *Divide Night* xi. 153 Freud..had decreed that the human psyche had three parts, the Id, the Ego, and the Super-ego.

,superele'vation. [SUPER- 6b, 13.]

†**1.** Elevation to a higher rank. *Obs. rare*⁻¹.

1654 tr. *Scudery's Curia Pol.* 166 If the Prince intend a super-elevation to any of his subjects.

2. The (amount of) elevation of the outer above the inner rail at a curve on a railway, or of one side of a road above another. Also *transf.* (see quot. 1930.)

1889 G. FINDLAY *Eng. Railway* 54 To balance the centrifugal force of a train running round a curve, it is necessary for the outer rail on a curve to be raised somewhat above the inner rail, and the smaller the radius, and the higher the speed of the trains, the greater must be the super-elevation. **1896** *Westm. Gaz.* 9 Oct. 5/1 The accident was aided..by..the superelevation of the left hand rail being only 2¼ inches instead of 3½, and therefore suitable for a speed of sixteen miles an hour only. **1906** *Daily Chron.* 3 Aug. 5/6 The arch of the road is of too large a character, and the superelevation is on the wrong side of the road. **1930** *Engineering* 14 Feb. 193/3 The spillway channels [of the dam] are curved, requiring large superelevation of the floor toward the outside.

3. Additional elevation.

1900 *19th Cent.* Apr. 641 In one well alone..no less than 8 feet of superelevation..were traversed before the alluvial deposit was reached.

super'eminence, *sb.* [ad. late L. *superēminentia*, f. *superēminent-*: see below and -ENCE. Cf. obs. F. *supereminence*, F. *suréminence.*] The quality or fact of being supereminent; supreme or special eminence; *rarely* in physical sense, supreme height or loftiness.

1616 BULLOKAR *Eng. Expos.*, *Supereminence*, authoritie, or dignitie aboue others. **1626** T. H[AWKINS] *Caussin's Holy Crt.* 99 The same ought to be in God, as in theyr source, with a radiant lustre of supereminence. **1641** MILTON *Reform.* II. 89 In supereminence of beatifick Vision. **1665** SIR T. HERBERT *Trav.* (1677) 3 The Hill called Garachiga [in Teneriffe]..outbraves..all the Earth for supereminence. **1691** BAXTER *Nat. Ch.* xiii. 55 Magistrates represent him [*sc.* God] in his Super-eminence and Ruling Power. **1813** SHELLEY *Q. Mab* VIII. 211–12 *Note*, The supereminence of man is like Satan's, a supereminence of pain. **1819** SCOTT *Leg. Montrose* xvi, Montrose..had expected from that party the supereminence of council and command. **1850** MRS. JAMESON *Leg. Monast. Ord.* (1863) 123 The question of his supereminence as a painter.

Hence †**super'eminence** *v. trans.*, to place in a position of supereminence.

1647 M. HUDSON *Div. Right Govt.* title-p., The Phansyed State-Principles Supereminencing *salutem populi* above the Kings Honour.

super'eminency. Now *rare* or *Obs.* [Formed as prec.: see -ENCY.] = prec.

In quot. 1866–7 with possessive as a fictitious title of rank.

1585–7 T. ROGERS *39 Art.* xxxvi. (1625) 197 The degrees of Ecclesiasticall supereminencie. **1631** GOUGE *God's Arrows* III. §62. 301 Records..which by an excellency and super-eminency [cf. EMINENCE 8c] are called Scriptures. **1638** SIR T. HERBERT *Trav.* (ed. 2) 191 The supereminency of the hill. *a* **1682** SIR T. BROWNE *Tracts* i. (1684) 31 A kind of Sceptre in their hands, denoting their supereminencies. **1691** NORRIS *Pract. Disc.* 223 The ὑπεροχὴ or supereminency of the Divine Nature. **1726** AYLIFFE *Parergon* 95 The Archbishop of Canterbury, as he is Primate over all England ..has a Super-eminency..over the Archbishop of York. **1866–7** BARING-GOULD *Cur. Myths Mid. Ages, Prester John* (1894) 45 The palace in which our Supereminency [*sc.* Prester John] resides.

supereminent (s(j)uːpər'ɛmɪnənt), *a.* [ad. L. *superēminent-*, *-ens*, pres. pple. of *superēminēre* to rise above, f. *super-* SUPER- 2 + *ēminēre*: see EMINENT and cf. SUPER- 9a. Cf. obs. F. *supereminent*, F. *suréminent.*]

1. Lofty above the rest; supremely or specially high. Now *rare.*

1555 EDEN *Decades* I. VI. (Arb.) 90 Paria is the Region which possesseth the supereminente or hyghest parte thereof. **1615** G. SANDYS *Trav.* 221 The uttermost promontory that stretcheth to the West, with the supereminent mountaine, now called Capo Saint Pisano. **1635** HEYWOOD *Hierarchy* 4 The lofty Hils, and super-eminent Mountains. **1653** A. WILSON *Jas. I* Proeme 2 When they [*sc.* Princes] shall so much debase that sublime and supereminent Region they are placed in. **1892** LD. LYTTON *King Poppy* xi. 348 A single supereminent tower.

2. Exalted above others in rank or dignity; supremely exalted.

1583 [W. CECIL] *Exec. Justice in Eng.* C iii b, Be you subiect..to the King, as to him that is supereminent [1 Pet. ii. 13]. **1588** J. HARVEY *Disc. Probl.* 43 What other nation.. may presume to..aduance it selfe unto any such surmounting, and supereminent honor? *a* **1600** HOOKER *Eccl. Pol.* VIII. viii. §1 Touching the king's supereminent authority in commanding. **1640** BP. HALL *Episc.* II. iii. 96 Most manifest it is, that the Apostles of Christ had a supereminent power in Gods Church. **1651** C. CARTWRIGHT *Cert. Relig.* II. 65 The Marquesse saith, that anciently the Church had one Super-eminent (by Divine Law) which was the Pope. **1790** BURKE *Rev. France* 63 Were they then to be awed by the super-eminent authority and awful dignity of a handful of country clowns? **1861** PEARSON *Early & Mid. Ages Eng.* 90 A king of Kent is therefore the first supereminent king of England, and he is succeeded by the kings of Northumbria.

†**b.** Superior *to. Obs. rare*⁻¹.

1657 J. WATTS *Scribe, Pharisee*, etc. I. 47 They are infinitely..supereminent to these, as God is above man.

3. Distinguished *above* others in character or attainment; conspicuous *for* some quality.

1599 NASHE *Lenten Stuffe* B 2 b, This superiminente principall Metropolis of the redde Fish. **1607** WALKINGTON *Optic Glass* 60 And but for this [proneness to venery] they were supereminent aboue all men. **1611** SPEED *Theat. Gt. Brit.* xliii. (1614) 85/1 Kendal..for the..practise of making cloath so excels the rest, that in regard thereof it carryeth a supereminent name above them. **1651** HOWELL *Venice* 203 Som were supereminent for holines, and high virtues. **1875** HELPS *Soc. Press.* x. 142 With these three super-eminent hosts or hostesses, everything was prepared for me that I could possibly want.

4. Of qualities, conditions, etc.: Specially or supremely remarkable in degree; signal or noteworthy above that of others.

1581 Allen *Apologie* 90 b, The high dignitie of Priesthod ..is..commended..for the high supereminent power of doing the vnblouddy sacrifice vpon the altar. **1592** Nashe *Strange Newes* (1593) 65 Thy supereminent gifts. **1651** *Fuller's Abel Rediv., Bradford* 181 The noblest, and most supereminent of all other Sciences. **1668** H. More *Div. Dial.* v. xxviii. (1713) 495 The anointing of our Head and true High-priest the Lord Jesus..in a supereminent manner. **1787** Polwhele *Engl. Orator* III. 376 The Career Of Talents supereminent and vast. **1835** Poe *Adv. Hans Pfall* Wks. 1864 I. 4 A fantastic bow-knot of super-eminent dimensions. **1893** Sir R. Ball *Story of Sun* 320 The Sun would begin to be shorn of those supereminent splendours which at present distinguish it.

super'eminently, *adv.* [f. prec. + -LY^2.] In a supereminent manner or degree; eminently above others; supremely.

1617 Lady Englefield *Let.* in *Slingsby's Diary*, etc. (1836) 297 Christ as man receaved this power supereminently of God. **1625** Gill *Sacr. Philos.* i. 5 Other attributes we give unto God, which signifie perfections supereminently. **1660** R. Burney *Κέρδιστον Δῶρον* (1661) 75 A Prince is exalted by God supereminently next to himself. **1721** R. Keith tr. *T. à Kempis, Vall. Lillies* xxvi. 78 That.. God may be..by thee beloved, blessed, praised, and supereminently exalted to all Eternity. **1825** Scott *Talism.* x, From that commanding height the banner of England was supereminently displayed. **1893** Symonds *Michelangelo* I. v. 206 A style so supereminently noble and so astoundingly original as Michelangelo's.

supererogant (s(j)uːpə'rɛrəgənt), *a. rare.* [ad. late L. *superērogans, -ant-*, pr. pple. of *superērogāre* to SUPEREROGATE.]

= SUPEREROGATORY. Hence **supe'rerogantly** *adv.*, more than is required.

1737 Stackhouse *Hist. Bible* VI. ii. (1749) II. 840/2 Then was this Commission..far from being needless, or supererogant. **1892** *Temple Bar* May 51 They endeavoured to graft on to the natural goodness of man supererogant virtues. **1897** W. Watson *Poems, To S.W. in the Forest* 4 Is our London..so Super-erogantly fair That yourself it well can spare?

†**supe'reroganting**, *a. Obs. rare*$^{-1}$. [Formed as prec. + -ING^2.] Supererogating.

1550 Bale *Apol.* 22 Ricardus de Media villa sayth, that it [*sc.* a vow] is a promyse of a supererrogantinge purpose.

†**supe'rerogate**, *a. Obs. rare.* [ad. L. *superērogātus*, pa. pple. of *superērogāre*: see next.] Supererogatory, superfluous.

1790 *Bystander* 44 This..is surely a superarogate [*sic*] ambition. *Ibid.* 335 [The *World*] in a mighty supererogate way, extols Mr. Sheridan.

supererogate (s(j)uːpə'rɛrəgeɪt), *v.* Also 7 -errogate. [f. L. *superērogāt-*, pa. ppl. stem of *superērogāre*, f. *super-* SUPER- 13 + *ērogāre* to pay out (see EROGATE *v.*). Cf. obs. F. *supereroguer*, obs. It. *soprarogare, superarogare*.]

†**1.** *trans.* To pay over and above; to spend in addition. Also *absol. Obs. rare.*

1582 *N.T.* (Rhem.) Luke x. 35 He tooke forth two pence, and gave to the host, and said, Have care of him: and whatsoever thou shalt supererogate [Vulg. *supererogaveris*] I at my returne wil repay thee. **1613** Purchas *Pilgrimage* II. viii. 118 Besides that which the Law enioyned (which is iust debt) they supererogated, and of their owne free accord disbursed vpon the Temple and Sacrifices.

†**b.** To grant or bestow in addition. *Obs. rare*$^{-1}$.

1644 Bp. Maxwell *Prerog. Chr. Kings* 188 The Lord..in his bounty supererogated what was fit for his more magnificence.

2. *intr.* To do more than is commanded or required; *spec.* to perform a work or works of SUPEREROGATION. ? *Obs.*

1593 Bell *Motives conc. Romish Faith* (1605) 26 The cause that pardons are of force, is the vnity of the mysticall bodie, in which many haue supererogated in the woorkes of penance, to the measure of their owne demerites. **1621** Burton *Anat. Mel.* III. iv. I. i. 714 We cannot..haue any perfection in this life, much lesse supererogate. **1651** Baxter *Inf. Bapt.* 303 Can that be obedience which hath no command for it? Is not this to supererogate? and to be righteous over much? **1661** Glanvill *Van. Dogm.* 164 Aristotle acted his own instructions; and his obsequious Sectators have super-erogated in observance. **1699** Burnet *39 Art.* xiv. 135 Unless it can be supposed that by obeying those Counsels a Man can compensate with Almighty God for his Sins, there is no ground to think that he can supererogate. **1727** J. Richardson *Gt. Folly Pilgr. Irel.* 81 If it should be granted that some have supererogated, that is brought God into Debt to them.

†**b.** Const. *of, with* the person in whose service the works are performed. *Obs.*

1608 Bp. Hall *Pharis. & Chr.* (1609) B vij, Gods Law was too strait for their holinesse: It was nothing, vnlesse they did more then content God, earne him (for these were Popish Iewes) and supererogate of him. **1618** —— *Contempl., O.T.* XIII. *Jonathan's Love*, That good Captaine little imagining, that himselfe was the Philistim, whom Saul maligned, supererogates of his Master, and brings two hundred for one. *a* **1643** J. Shute *Judgem. & Mercy* (1645) 217 But have we brought forth fruit? Oh, some fruits we supererogate with God in. **1644** Bp. Maxwell *Prerog. Chr. Kings* 168 They may supererogate with their Prince, by doing many Acts of bounty, favour and Grace.

†**c.** *trans.* To do (something) beyond what is required; to perform as a work of supererogation. *Obs. rare.*

1621 Mountagu *Diatribæ* 379 They teach..that Tithing *πᾶν λάχανον*, was not commanded, but supererogated to the Law. **1624** —— *Gagg* 100 Workes supererogated by them, when they doe more than God requireth.

†**d.** *intr.* To make up by excess of merit *for* the failing of another. *Obs.*

1625 Jackson *Creed* v. xxxii. §4 Both of them presumed their zealous costs upon Saints monuments, should.. supererogate for their predecessors sins. **1649** Milton *Eikon.* xxiv. 195 The fervencie of one man in prayer cannot supererogate for the coldness of another.

†**e.** *trans.* To deserve and more than deserve. *Obs. rare.*

1639 Fuller *Holy War* v. xvi. (1647) 257 Having super-errogated the gallows..by their several misdemeanours.

Hence **super'erogating** *vbl. sb.* and *ppl. a.*

1603 J. Davies *Microcosmos* Pref., Wks. (Grosart) I. 17/1 These super-supererogating Workes. **1627** W. Sclater *Expos. 2 Thess.* (1629) 3 That euer thought of supererogating should enter the heart of man. *a* **1643** Ld. Falkland, etc. *Infallibility* (1646) 158 It might be but an act of a little supererogating charity, if you would sometimes prove your assertions, even when by strict law you were not bound to it. **1673** Hickeringill *Greg. F. Greyb.* 43 If their merits were never so..supererogating. **1674** Burnet *Subjection* (1675) 2 Not content with the strictest rigors of Justice, our Saviour hath also obliged us to the supererogatings (if I may so speak) of Charity. **1683** E. Hooker *Pref. Pordage's Mystic Div.* 67 Nor any supererogating perfections, or rather præsumptuous.. enthusiasms. **1692** Patrick *Answ. Touchstone* 122 What doth this Discourse prove? But that they shall have a greater reward themselves? but there is not a syllable of their supererogating for others.

supererogation (ˌs(j)uːpərɛrə'geɪʃən). Also 6 **superogacyon, -ation,** 6–8 **supererrogation.** [ad. late L. *superērogātiō*, n. of action f. *superērogāre*: see prec. Cf. obs. F. *supererogation* (mod.F. *surérogation*), It. *supererogazione* (in Florio, *soprarogatione, superarogatione*), etc.] The action (or an act) of 'supererogating' (SUPEREROGATE *v.* 2); chiefly in phr. ***work(s of supererogation.***

1. a. *R. C. Theol.* The performance of good works beyond what God commands or requires, which are held to constitute a store of merit which the Church may dispense to others to make up for their deficiencies.

1526 *Pilgr. Perf.* (W. de W. 1531) 58 b, Not onely where thou oughtest so to do of duty, but also of deuoute perfeccyon & superogacyon [*sic*: cf. OF. *superrogacion*]. **1553** *Articles agreed on by Bishoppes 1552* xiii, Voluntarie woorkes besides, ouer, and aboue Goddes commaundementes, whiche thei cal woorkes of Supererogation, cannot be taught without arrogancie, and iniquitie. **1583** Babington *Commandm.* (1590) 68, I haue no merites or good workes to come before Thee with-all, much lesse am I able to doo workes of super-erogation. **1612** T. Taylor *Comm. Titus* i. 4. (1619) 57 All that Popish doctrine concerning workes of preparation and disposition before grace: and of merit and supererogation after. **1645** Milton *Tetrach.* I. Wks. 1851 IV. 252 The fear is, least this not being a command, would prove an evangelic counsel, and so make way for supererogations. **1650** Fuller *Pisgah* 415 Some will say, this was but a ceremonious super-erogation of Maccabeus, in making such an ordinance. **1874** H. R. Reynolds *John Bapt.* v. §2. 317 The Roman Catholic commentators have generally recognized in the Baptism of Christ by John a part of His work of supererogation.

attrib. **1738** *Oxf. Methodists* 8 They observe strictly the Fasts of the Church; and this has given occasion to such as do not approve of them, abusively to call them supererogation men.

b. *transf.* and *gen.* Performance of more than duty or circumstances require; doing more than is needed.

1592 Nashe *Strange Newes* A 4 b, The strong fayth you haue conceiu'd, that I would do workes of supererrogation in answering the Doctor. **1599** B. Jonson *Cynthia's Rev.* II. i, Then thou hast not altered thy name, with thy disguise? —O, no, that had beene supererogation. **1612** Woodall *Surg. Mate* Wks. (1653) 408 Let not the younger Artist presume, in a work of supererogation..to be too busie. **1643** Drumm. of Hawth. *Decl. agst. Gross Petition* Wks. (1711) 210 Such is the Supererogation of some of the Petitioners, above what His Majesty requires. **1710** Steele *Tatler* No. 54 ¶6 An Act of so great Supererogation, as singing without a Voice. **1756** H. Walpole *Let. to Conway* 24 Jan., I was prepared to be very grateful if you had done just what I desired; but I declare I have no thanks ready for a work of supererogation. **1796** Mme. D'Arblay *Camilla* IX. viii, Reason might have shewn this a tie of supererogation. **1870** Spurgeon *Treas. Dav.* Ps. xlii. 3 It was a supererogation of malice to pump more tears from a heart which already overflowed. **1876** Bartholow *Mat. Med.* (1879) 149 It may appear to be a work of super-erogation to notice the popular fallacy that quinia..remains combined with the textures of the body.

†**2.** See quots. and cf. SUPEREROGATE 1. *Obs. rare*$^{-0}$.

1604 R. Cawdrey *Table Alph., Supererogation*, giuing more then is required. **1616** Bullokar *Expos., Supererogation*, laying out of more then one hath receiued.

supererogative (ˌs(j)uːpərɪ'rɒgətɪv), *a. rare.* [f. late L. *superērogāt-* (see SUPEREROGATE) + -IVE.] = SUPEREROGATORY.

1599 Sandys *Europæ Spec.* xlii. (1605) P j, Their spirituall treasure of super[er]ogative [*ed.* 1629 Supererogatorie] workes. **1611** A. Stafford *Niobe* II. 61 A fellow..who can iustlie brag of nothing of his owne, but liues vpon the supererogatiue deedes of his Ancestours. **1641** Milton *Animadv.* ii. 15 O new and never-heard of Supererogative heighth of wisdome and charity in our Liturgie!

supe'rerogator. *rare.* [f. SUPEREROGATE *v.* + -OR.] One who performs works of supererogation.

1679 *Let. Vind. Ref. Ch.* 9 These horrid Supererogators do seem..to out-act the most Holy Law-giver. **1826** *Westm. Rev.* Jan. 34 Man is not here a mere supererogator, an unbidden counsellor.

supererogatory (ˌs(j)uːpərɪ'rɒgətərɪ, ˌs(j)uːpə'rɛrəgətərɪ), *a.* (*sb.*) Also 7 **-errogatory.** [ad. scholastic L. *superērogātōrius*, f. *superērogāt-*: see SUPEREROGATE and -ORY^2. Cf. Sp. *supererogatorio* and F. *surérogatoire*.] Characterized by, or having the nature of, supererogation; going beyond what is commanded or required; *loosely*, superfluous.

1593 G. Harvey *Pierce's Super.* 18 Were his penne as supererogatory a woorkeman as his harte. **1629** [see SUPEREROGATIVE, quot. 1599]. **1640** Howell *Dodona's Gr.* (1645) 105 The supererogatory services, and too great benefits from subjects to kings are of dangerous consequence. *a* **1653** Gouge *Comm. Heb.* iv. 16 (1655) 468 The folly of those that trust to the supererrogatory works of others, as if any man were able to do more than he is bound to do. **1720** Welton *Suffer. Son of God* II. xv. 406 Too much taken with Supererogatory Fasts..rather than those which are commanded. **1740** Richardson *Pamela* (1824) I. 205 That you could take the faults of others upon yourself; and, by a supposed supererogatory merit, think your interposition sufficient to atone for the faults of others. **1820** Shelley *Prometh. Unb.* Pref., Nothing can be equally well expressed in prose that is not tedious and supererogatory in verse. **1860** Motley *Netherl.* xix. (1868) II. 484 It had now become supererogatory to ask for Alexander's word of honour. **1886** *Punch* 16 Jan. 28/2 Sending..spare books.. and supererogatory newspapers to our Hospitals.

b. *sb.* A supererogatory act; a work of supererogation. *nonce-use.*

1748 Richardson *Clarissa* (1811) VIII. 347 Why may I not proceed in my supererogatories? **1749–50** —— *Let. to Mrs. Belfour* 9 Jan., No supererogatories do I allow of in marriage.

Hence †ˌ**supereroga'torian** *Obs. nonce-wd.*, one who believes in supererogation; ˌ**supere'rogatorily** *adv.*, in a supererogatory manner, beyond the requirements of the case, superfluously.

1753 Richardson *Grandison* (1754) I. vii. 32 With all your relations indeed, their Harriet cannot be in fault... Supererogatorians all of them (I will make words whenever I please) with their attributions to you. **1838** *New Monthly Mag.* LII. 446 Many a dial..most supererogatorily informs us that 'time flies'. *a* **1849** Poe *Cooper* Wks. 1864 III. 397 We are tautologically informed that improvement is a consequence of embellishment and supererogatorily told that the rule holds good only where the embellishment is not accompanied by destruction.

†**super'essence.** *Obs. rare*$^{-1}$. [SUPER- 5.] That which is above, or transcends, essence or being.

a **1706** Evelyn *Hist. Relig.* (1850) I. 176 All essence and super-essence..was always what He is, and always shall be.

ˌ**supere'ssential**, *a.* [ad. late L. *superessentiālis* (cf. Gr. *ὑπερούσιος*), f. *super-* SUPER- 4 a + *essentia* ESSENCE: see -AL^1. Cf. obs. F. *superessentiel*.] That is above essence or being; transcending all that exists; = SUPERSUBSTANTIAL 2.

1587 Golding *De Mornay* iii. (1592) 28 God..is..the superessential Being, (that is to say, a Beeing which farre surmounteth, passeth, and excelleth all Beeings). **1614** Purchas *Pilgrimage* I. ii. (ed. 2) 9 That vncreated superessentiall light, the eternall Trinitie, commanded this light to be. **1683** Tryon *Way to Health* 145 This Internal Super-essential Water sustaineth every Beeing, and is the Radix and Life of the outward Water. **1789** T. Taylor *Proclus* II. 386 If the first deity is super-essential, but every god, so far as a god is of the first series, hence every god will be super-essential. **1856** R. A. Vaughan *Mystics* (1860) I. 96 No man could make an actual God of that super-essential ultimatum. **1902** Fairbairn *Philos. Chr. Relig.* I. iii. 102 God is super-essential, and can be expressed in no category.

Hence ˌ**supere'ssentially** *adv.*, in a manner or mode that transcends all being.

1789 T. Taylor *Proclus* II. 387 All things are contained in the gods, uniformly, and super-essentially. **1856** R. A. Vaughan *Mystics* (1860) I. VI. v. 194 Dionysius writeth how God doth..superessentially surpass all images, modes, forms, or names that can be applied to Him.

supe'ressive, *a.* (and *sb.*) *Gram.* [f. L. *superesse* to be higher than, survive, remain + -IVE.] Designating a case or grammatical relation which expresses position above or on top of. Also *absol.* as *sb.*

1903 [see INTROESSIVE *a.*] **1951** W. K. Matthews *Languages U.S.S.R.* vi. 99 Marr and M. Brière..recognise secondary cases—a locative, an inessive..a superessive, a disjunctive, [etc.]. **1954** Pei & Gaynor *Dict. Linguistics* 207 *Superessive*, in certain languages (notably, languages of the Finno-Ugric family) a declensional case, having the same denotation as the English preposition *on* or *upon*. **1971** D. I. Slobin in W. O. Dingwall *Survey Linguistic Sci.* 310 A variety of Hungarian case endings on nouns indicating such locative relations as illative, elative,..and superessive—that is, in plain English,..the directional notions of *into, out of*, ..and the positional notion of *on top of*.

supe'rette. orig. and chiefly *U.S.* [f. SUPER(MARKET + -ETTE.] A small supermarket.

1938 *Sat. Even. Post* 17 Sept. 85/3 It also developed a store called the 'Super-ette', which is a compact, limited-stock, self-service store. **1956** *Sun* (Baltimore) 10 Feb. 23/1 There were an estimated 67,500 'superettes' in 1953. **1963** *Listener* 10 Jan. 75/1 Supermarkets and superettes (the latter still large by British standards) together took over four-fifths of all American retail food trade in 1958. **1976** *Daily Times* (Lagos) 3 Nov. 12/1 (Advt.), A spacious van for traders, commercial houses,..supermarkets and superettes.

,supere'xalt, *v.* [ad. late L. *superexaltāre*: see SUPER- 9 b and EXALT *v.*]

1. *trans.* To exalt or raise to a higher, or to the highest, position or rank; to exalt supremely.

1625 GILL *Sacr. Philos.* ii. 183 The first order of separate or created beings, is that of the fountaine, which by the meanes of vision is superexalted above all the rest. **1649** JER. TAYLOR *Gt. Exemp.* I. Ad Sect. ii. 21 The holy Maid..was superexalted by an honour greater than the world yet ever saw. *a* **1677** BARROW *Serm. Mark xvi. 19* Wks. 1686 II. 434 God..having super-exalted him, and bestowed on him a name above all names.

2. To extol or magnify exceedingly. *rare.*

1609 BIBLE (Douay) *Dan.* iii. 57 Al workes of our Lord blesse ye our Lord, prayse and superexalt him for euer. **1864** SIR C. F. L. WRAXALL *Historic Bye-Ways* I. iii. 47 We may ..say, that had it not been for Frederick William I., there would hardly have been a Frederick the Great. Still, this must not cause us to super-exalt him.

Hence **supere'xalted** *ppl. a.*

1654 JER. TAYLOR *Real Pres.* 239 So high and separate, superexalted secret, as is that of the holy Trinity.

,superexal'tation. [SUPER- 10; cf. prec.] Exaltation to a higher or the highest degree; supreme or excessive exaltation.

1624 D. CAWDREY *Humilitie* 40 God will haue his will done, onely with reason: The proud man will haue his against all reason; There's his superexaltation of him, aboue all that is called God. **1627** DONNE *Serm. Exod. iv. 13* (1640) 42 The over-bending, and super-exaltation of zeale. *a* **1661** HOLYDAY (J.), In a superexaltation of courage, they seem as greedy of death as of victory. **1880** *Athenæum* 25 Sept. 395/1 The superexaltation of St. Peter in face of the historical evidence which remains as to St. Paul's influence at Rome. **1887** J. HUTCHISON *Lect. Philippians* x. 103 God highly exalted Him. This super-exaltation, then, is described as of God's favour.

,superex'cel, *v.* [ad. L. **superexcellĕre* (cf. obs. F. *superexceller*): see SUPER- 9 b and EXCEL, and cf. SUPEREXCELLENT.] *trans.* and *intr.* To excel highly or supremely. Hence **,superex'celling** (also 6 *Sc.* -and) *ppl. a.*, superexcellent.

c **1450** *Mirour Saluacioun* (Roxb.) 39 Marie superexcellis of all seints the state. **1530** LYNDESAY *Test. Papyngo* 438 Iames the secunde, Roye of gret renoun, Beand in his super-excelland glore. **1552** —— *Monarche* 5019 Superexcelland Sapience. **1613** T. MILLES tr. *Mexia's Treas. Anc. & Mod. T.* 13/1 The Trees [in Paradise] may signifie..the liues of the Saints, their super-excelling fruites [etc.]. **1658** R. FRANCK *North. Mem.* (1821) 129 There's not a rivulet in Scotland..superexcels this Calvin [= Kelvin] for diversion with small trout. **1905** *Westm. Gaz.* 11 Nov. 10/2 Where Barbara excels, and super-excels, is in her dogs.

super'excellence. [f. SUPEREXCELLENT: see -ENCE.] The quality or condition of being superexcellent; superior or supreme excellence.

1652 T. BENLOWES in *Benlowes' Theoph.* Pref. Verses C 1 b, This Original; Whose charming Empire of her Grace does Sense Astonish by a super-Excellence. **1683** PORDAGE *Mystic Div.* 36 The Super-excellence of the Divine Being. **1768** TUCKER *Lt. Nat.* (1834) I. 190 The proud..if they still retain a fondness for reflecting on their superexcellence, it is like the unnatural thirst of a drunkard. **1885** R. L. & F. STEVENSON *Dynamiter* 179 Considering the depth of his demerit and the height of the adored one's super-excellence.

super'excellency. Now *rare.* [f. as prec.: see -ENCY.] = prec. Also, something that is superexcellent.

1587 GOLDING *De Mornay* iii. (1592) 29 Then is it this first simplicitie which is the King; the Soueraignetie and Super-excellencie of all things. **1600** J. PORY tr. *Leo's Africa* III. 205, I could finde no such superexcellencie in him. **1603** BRETON *Dial. Pithe & Pleasure* Wks. (Grosart) II. 15/1 Man ..can effect so rare excellencies in the worlde, and beholde so many superexcellencies in the heauens, as the eye of no creature but man is able to looke after. **1660** R. BURNEY *Κέρδιστον Δῶρον* (1661) 109 Our Parliaments in England and Scotland have a superexcellency above all the councels of the world. **1707** NORRIS *Treat. Humility* i. 38 The superexcellency of his nature. **1870** GILLESPIE *Being & Attrib. God* IV. iii. (1906) 212 The one great Attribute, or Super-Excellency of Holiness.

super'excellent, *a.* (*sb.*) [ad. late L. *superexcellent-*, *-ens*: see SUPER-[1] 9 a and EXCELLENT.] That superexcels; excellent in a high degree; very or supremely excellent.

1561 PRESTON *K. Cambyses* 948 A banquett royall and superexcellent. **1621** BURTON *Anat. Mel.* II. iv. II. i. 452 Tobacco, divine, rare, superexcellent Tobacco. **1660** R. BURNEY *Κέρδιστον Δῶρον* (1661) 108 The King, to whose super-excellent power and facultie God himself gives witnesse to. **1712** STEELE *Spect.* No. 540 ¶6 In Holiness, Temperance, Chastity, and Justice super-excellent. **1844** H. STEPHENS *Bk. Farm* I. 490 The system of *under* or *deep-draining*, being the deepest method of any, is super-excellent. **1874** LISLE CARR *Jud. Gwynne* I. i. 20 A very true woman and no super-excellent heroine.

b. *sb.* A superexcellent person or thing. *nonce-use.*

1816 MOORE *Let. to Power* 24 Sept., Two or three of the Irish [songs] equal to any I have done;..but our plan is to go on till we can select twelve super-excellents.

Hence **super'excellently** *adv.*

1683 E. HOOKER *Pref. Pordage's Mystic Div.* 103 That.. Divinest Mysterie of Love, sciz God made Flesh: which gave (as one superexcellently) the Angels new Anthems. *a* **1687** COTTON *New-Year* 38 And then the next in reason shou'd Be superexcellently good. **1906** *Westm. Gaz.* 15 Mar. 8/1 The atmosphere of the highly cultured..home..is superexcellently achieved.

super-exchange: see SUPER- 2 a (*b*).

†,superex'crescence. *Obs. rare.*

1. [SUPER- 10.] Increase in excess. *Sc.*

1499 *Reg. Privy Seal Scotl.* I. 51/1 To ansuer to the king of the superexcrescence of the proffitis. **1549** D. MONRO *West. Isles* in *Macfarlane's Geogr. Collect.* (S.H.S.) III. (1908) 301 The superexcrescens of the said ky and sheipe.

2. [SUPER- 3.] An excrescence growing over a surface.

Cf. late L. *superexcrescĕre.*

1676 WISEMAN *Chirurg. Treat.* IV. v. 321 After the Escar separated, I rubb'd the remaining Superexcrescence with a Vitriol-stone.

†,superex'pend, *v. Sc. Obs.* Also 6 -exspend. [SUPER- 9 b. In med.L. *superexpendĕre* was applied to supererogatory fasting.]

1. *to be superexpended*: to have spent beyond one's income or means; to be out of pocket or in arrears: often with advb. acc. or phr. expressing the amount.

1473 *Acc. Ld. High Treas. Scot.* I. 75 And sua is the Comptare superexpendit j^m j^c lxxix li. iiij s. x d. **1500–20** DUNBAR *Poems* xiii. 23 Sum super expendit gois to his bed. **1559** *Extr. Aberd. Reg.* (1844) I. 325 Quhat he beis super expendit, the same to be allowit to him. **1591** *Exch. Rolls Scotl.* XXII. 162 The comptar is superexpendit de claro in the sowme of aucht thousand ane hundreth fourtene pundis sevin schillingis fyve pennyis. **1637** RUTHERFORD *Lett.* (1862) I. lxxxv. 219 We shall be..so far from being superexpended..that angels cannot lay our counts nor sum our advantage and incomes. **1676** ROW *Contn. Blair's Autobiogr.* xii. (1848) 453 They were not provided with horses..being superexpended by attending Parliament so long. **1686** BURNET *Trav.* i. 24 The Bailifs..pretend they are so far super-expended, that they discount a great deal of the publick revenue, of which they are the receivers, for their reimbursement.

2. *trans.* To spend (time) wastefully. *rare.*

1513 DOUGLAS *Æneis* Direct. 31 Quhar that I haue my tyme superexpendit, *Mea culpa*, God grant I may amend it.

†,superex'pense. *Sc. Obs.* [SUPER- 10. Cf. prec.] Expenditure above receipts or income; out-of-pocket expenses.

1473 *Acc. Ld. High Treas. Scot.* I. 74 Sum totale of all the parcialis of thir expensis befor wirtin, except the superexpensis of the last compt. **1566** *Reg. Privy Council Scot.* Ser. I. I. 472 For payment of the superexpenssis maid be thame in thair offices. **1567–8** *Ibid.* 611 Takin up be the Laird of Mynto in his superexpenssis. **1607** *Extr. Aberd. Reg.* (1848) II. 288 Thomas Fischer and Willeam Speares superexpenssis in thair negotiatioune.

†superexpone. *v. Sc. Obs. rare.* [f. SUPER- 9 b + EXPONE *v.* 3.] *trans.* = SUPEREXPEND.

1491 *Acta Dom. Conc.* (1839) 230/1 þe quhilk soume he superexponit mare þan þe commoun gudis of þe said toune extendit to.

†superface. *Obs. rare*[−1]. ? Misprint for SUPERFICE, or etymologizing alteration of SURFACE.

1633 T. ADAMS *Exp. 2 Peter* ii. 4. 514 The superface of the earth.

super-fatted: see SUPER- 9 a (*a*).

super'fecta. *U.S.* [f. SUPER- 6 c, after *perfecta.*] A method of betting in horse-racing whereby the bettor must pick the first four finishers of a race in the correct order.

1972 *Compton Yearbk. 1971* 532/2 *Superfecta*, a system of betting on races in which the bettor must pick the first, second, third, and fourth horses in this sequence in a specified race in order to win. **1972** *N.Y. Post* 1 Mar. 63/5 Besides superfectas, seats, TV..the track also plans to improve the lighting. **1973** *Sunday Mirror* 9 Sept. 20/2 The gang went to work on trotting races in New York, fixing 'superfecta' races. **1977** *Time* 21 Nov. 46/3 The growth of exotic betting devices—superfectas and the like—with their huge pay-offs represents an additional impetus to crooked horsemen.

superfemale: see SUPER- 5 f.

superfetally (s(j)uːpəˈfiːtəlɪ), *adv.* Also -foet-. [Formed after SUPERFETATION: see -AL[1] and -LY[2].] By superfetation.

1910 THOMPSON tr. *Aristotle's Hist. Anim.* v. ix, Animals like the hare, where the female can become superfoetally impregnated.

†super'fetant, *a. Obs.* Also 7 -fœt-. [ad. L *superfētant-*, *-ans*, pr. pple. of *superfētāre* to SUPERFETE.] Conceiving by superfetation. So **super'fetate** *v.*, *intr.* to conceive by superfetation; **super'fetate** *a.*, over-productive, superabundant.

1610 HEALEY *St. Aug. Citie of God* (1620) 194 Some creatures are superfoetant, that is, breeding vpon breed. **1623** COCKERAM, *Superfœtate*, after the first young to conceiue another. **1681** GREW *Musæum* I. v. i. 91 The Female brings forth..twice in one month, and so is said to Superfœtate. **1845** R. W. HAMILTON *Pop. Educ.* iii. 55 The refuge for what otherwise would be a superfetate population.

superfetation (ˌs(j)uːpəfiːˈteɪʃən). Also -fœt- (7 -fæt-). [ad. late or mod.L. *superfētātio*, n. of action f. *superfētāre* to SUPERFETE. Cf. F. *superfétation*, It. *superfetazione*, etc.]

1. *Phys.* A second conception occurring after (esp. some time after) a prior one and before the delivery; the formation of a second fetus in a uterus already pregnant: occurring normally in some animals, and believed by some to occur exceptionally in women.

1603 HOLLAND *Plutarch's Mor* 843 Erasistratus attributeth it [*sc.* engendering of twins] unto divers conceptions and superfætations, like as in brute beasts. **1615** CROOKE *Body of Man* 314 This superfætation is..a second conception, when a woman already with child..conceiueth againe. **1661** LOVELL *Hist. Anim. & Min.* Isag. b 2 b, The hare is often troubled with superfetation. **1754–64** SMELLIE *Midwif.* II. 86 What you have writ me seems to favour the notion of superfoetation. **1836–9** *Todd's Cycl. Anat.* II. 469/1 The quadrupeds in which superfœtation..is said to occur possess a uterus with two horns. **1871** A. MEADOWS *Man. Midwifery* (ed. 2) 103 Cases of double or bihorned uteri are probably quite as rare as genuine cases of superfœtation.

b. *Bot.* In early use, applied to processes supposed to be analogous to superfetation in animals, e.g. the growth of a parasite, or an excessive production of ears of corn; in mod. use, the fertilization of the same ovule by two different kinds of pollen.

1626 BACON *Sylva* §556 The Misseltoe..is a Plant, vtterly differing from the Plant, vpon which it groweth. Two things therfore may be certainly set downe: First, that Super-fœtation must be by Abundance of Sap, in the Bough that putteth it forth: Secondly, that that Sap must be such, as the Tree doth excerne, and cannot assimilate. **1651** in *Hartlib's Legacy* (1655) 107 Such a super-fœtation of ears must necessarily proceed from an improvement by the Root. **1707** *Curios. Husb. & Gard.* 156 'Tis a sort of Superfetation, by which one Grain of Corn conceives and brings forth several Young, that in the common Course..ought to be born successively. **1728** CHAMBERS *Cycl.* s.v., We meet with something like a Superfetation in Plants too; there being a kind of Lemon found to grow inclosed in the Body of another. **1816** KEITH *Phys. Bot.* II. 368 The other species of superfetation in which one seed is supposed to be the joint issue of two males. **1885** GOODALE *Physiol. Bot.* (1892) 9 The formation of two or more embryos, occurs occasionally as a kind of superfoetation in some seeds. **1900** B. D. JACKSON *Gloss. Bot. Terms*, *Superfoetation*, the fertilization of an ovary by more than one kind of pollen.

2. *fig.* Additional production; the growth or accretion of one *upon* another; superabundant production or accumulation.

1641 H. L'ESTRANGE *God's Sabbath* 13 Consider the Law it self, and you shall see the positive accrue to the naturall by way of superfœtation. **1675** PLUME *Life Hacket* in *Cent. Serm.* p. v, That one School [*sc.* Westminster] furnishing two entire Colledges of great size in Cambridg and Oxon, besides whom it does send to other places by way of Superfetation. **1684** *Case of Cross in Baptism* 6 The Superfoetation of Ceremonies..began to be very burdensom. *a* **1703** BURKITT *On N.T.* Ded. to Ld. Fitzwalter, Plays and Romances, and such-like Corrupting and Effeminating Trash, which the Superfœtation of the Stage furnishes the Nation with. **1840** DE QUINCEY *Mod. Superst.* Wks. 1854 III. 341 Mark the superfetation of omens—omen supervening upon omen, augury engrafted upon augury. **1882** STALLO *Mod. Physics* 114 In this endless superfetation of ætherial media upon space and ordinary matter.

b. In particularized sense: An instance of this; an additional product; an accretion, excrescence; a superabundant or superfluous addition.

1642 CHAS. I *Answ. 19 Prop.* 4 These humble Desires.. are intended to make way for a Superfetation of a (yet) higher nature. **1654** H. L'ESTRANGE *Chas. I* (1655) 6 Those dismall calamities which befel his son, were doubtlesse ampliated by a superfetation of causes. **1675** V. ALSOP *Anti-Sozzo* III. ii. 257 This Distinction was but the Superfoetation of his own Parturient Brain. **1725** POPE *Shaks. Wks.* I. Pref. 8 The most [of Shakespeare's errors] are such as are not properly Defects, but Superfœtations. **1817** COLERIDGE *Biog. Lit.* xxiii. (1907) II. 206 The play may conclude as it began, viz. in a superfetation of blasphemy upon nonsense. **1820** LAMB *Elia* Ser. I. *South-sea House*, Layers of dust have accumulated (a superfœtation of dirt!) upon the old layers. **1861** M. PATTISON *Ess.* (1889) I. 30 He has thrown this superfetation of his historical work into twelve essays. **1903** *Athenæum* 28 Feb. 275/2 His..edition ..suffered from a superfetation of notes.

Hence **†superfe'tatious** *a.*, of the nature of superfetation.

1673 [R. LEIGH] *Transp. Reh.* 24 The superfetatious Miracles of Art.

†superfete, *v. Obs.* Also -fæte. [ad. L. *superfētāre*, f. *super-* SUPER- 13 + *fētus* FŒTUS.] *intr.* and *trans.* To conceive by superfetation; in quots. *fig.* (in quot. 1654, to add to, reinforce).

c **1645** HOWELL *Lett.* (1753) 125 So is my fancy quickned by the glance of His benign aspect and countenance, It makes me pregnant and to superfæte, Such is the vigor of His beams and heat. **1650** —— *Ep. Ded.* in *Cotgrave's Dict.*, His brain may..raise and superfæte a second thought before the first be uttered. **1654** GAYTON *Pleas. Notes* III. v. 100 That..they [*sc.* nuns] might superfete their vow, and not only forsweare the use, but the very looks of Men-kinde.

†**superfice.** *Obs.* [a. OF. *superfice* or ad. its source, L. SUPERFICIES.]

1. *Geom.* = SUPERFICIES 1.

c **1391** CHAUCER *Astrol.* I. §21 The zodiak in heuene is ymagened to ben a superfice contienyng a latitude of 12 degrees. *c* **1643** LD. HERBERT *Autobiog.* (1824) 44 The knowledge of lines, superfices, and bodies,..is not much useful for a gentleman unless it be to understand Fortifications. **1695** ALINGHAM *Geom. Epit.* 4 The kinds of Magnitude, which are principally Three, to wit, Length, Breadth and Thickness, or a Line, a Superfice, and a Solid. **1823** J. MITCHELL *Dict. Math. & Phys. Sci.*, *Superficies*, or *Superfice*, in Geometry, the outside or exterior surface of any body. This is considered as of two dimensions, viz. length and breadth, but without thickness.

2. The surface of a body or object; = SUPERFICIES 2.

c **1374** CHAUCER *Boeth.* III. pr. viii. (1868) 81 þe body of alcibiades þat was ful fayr in þe superfice wiþ oute. **1549** *Compl. Scot.* vi. 56 The superfice of that roundnes is of mair quantite nor is the space or largenes that is betuix his tua een. **1599** ALEX. HUME *Hymns* iii. 93 The fields, and earthly superfice, With verdure greene is spread. **1636** BRATHWAIT *Rom. Emp.* 276 The whole superfice of the Sea was covered with them. *a* **1684** LEIGHTON *Comm. 1 Pet.* i. 2 (1693) 16 [It] doth not wither as the grasse, or flower lying on the superfice of the earth. **1703** *Phil. Trans.* XXIII. 1401 Hard and perfect Stone..of a Grain and Superfice exactly like those I have seen taken out of the Bladder. **1813** VANCOUVER *Agric. Devon* 117 [It] is discharged with such a hollow or concave superfice downwards, as completely to whelm over and invert every square inch of the lifted furrow.

b. *transf.* That which forms, or is upon, the surface.

1542 BOORDE *Dyetary* xiii. (1870) 265 Euery thyng that is vnctious..doth swymme aboue in the brynkes of the stomacke:..the excesse of suche nawtacyon or superfyce wyll ascende to the or[if]yse of the stomacke.

3. *fig.* Outward show or appearance; = SUPERFICIES 5 c.

1678 R. BARCLAY *Apol. Quakers* ii. §2. 23 The more Serious..satisfie themselves not with the Superfice of Religion. *a* **1684** LEIGHTON *Comm. 1 Pet.* iii. 8 Wks. (1868) 160 This courteousness is not contrary to that evil, only in the superfice and outward behaviour.

superficial (s(j)uːpəˈfɪʃəl), *a.* (*sb.*) Also 5–7 -ficiall, (5 -ficialle, -fyciall, 6 -fi-, -fycyall, -fytial, -fyxcyall). [ad. late L. *superficiālis*, f. SUPERFICIES: see -AL[1]. Cf. F. *superficiel*, It. *superficiale*, Sp., Pg. *superficial*.] **A.** *adj.*

1. Of or pertaining to the surface; that is, lies, or is found at or on the surface; constituting the surface, outermost part, or crust.

Sometimes *spec.* in *Geol.* etc. = pertaining to the surface of the earth, as deposits; not belonging to the consolidated formation.

c **1420** ? LYDGATE *Assembly of Gods* 538 Sodeynly by weet constreynyd..Was the ground to close hys superfyciall face. **1503** HAWES *Examp. Virt.* VII. 145 Mannes humayne partyes superfyxcyall. **1555** EDEN *Decades* I. IV. (Arb.) 82 The myners dygged the superficiall or vppermost parte of the earthe. **1587** GREENE *Penelopes Web* Wks. (Grosart) V. 150 Nature had made her beautifull by a superficiall glorie of well proportioned lineaments. **1692** RAY *Disc.* ii. (1732) 6 Over the superficial Part of the Earth. **1796** KIRWAN *Elem. Min.* (ed. 2) I. 420 Superficial combustions..produce singular effects, which have often been mistaken for those of true volcanos. **1796** C. MARSHALL *Garden.* iv. (1813) 48 An excellent way of manuring, where the superficial soil is much exhausted. **1829** T. CASTLE *Introd. Bot.* 58 With regard to their superficial figure, they are either capillary, linear, gramineous, [etc.]. **1842** *Penny Cycl.* XXIII. 305/1 A more exact appreciation of the causes which have permitted the aggregation of the 'superficial deposits'. **1872** HUXLEY *Physiol.* v. 129 The rise in the temperature of the superficial blood. **1884** BOWER & SCOTT *De Bary's Phaner.* 557 The white superficial periderm of younger stems.

b. Of actions or conditions: Taking place or existing at or on the surface.

1815 J. SMITH *Panorama Sci. & Art* II. 146 The velocity of running water..is generally about nine-tenths of the superficial velocity. **1871** TYNDALL *Fragm. Sci.* (1879) I. iv. 129 An amount of light derived from superficial reflection. **1887** BENTLEY *Man. Bot.* (ed. 5) 283 In the Flowering Rush, ..they [*sc.* the ovules] cover the whole inner surface of the ovary except the midrib; in which case the placentation is sometimes described as superficial.

†**c.** Drawn or delineated upon a (flat) surface. *Obs. rare.*

1603 DANIEL *Def. Ryme* G 4, Historye (which is but a Mappe of men)..dooth no otherwise acquaint vs with the true Substance of Circumstances, than a superficiall Carde dooth the Sea-man with a Coast neuer seene. **1664** POWER *Exp. Philos.* Pref. c iij b, Gloss'd outside Fallacies; like our Stage-scenes, or Perspectives, that shew things inwards, when they are but superficial paintings.

d. *Anat.* Applied to organs or parts situated just beneath the skin; subcutaneous.

1804 ABERNETHY *Surg. Obs.* 21 The superficial veins appear remarkably large. **1835–6** *Todd's Cycl. Anat.* I. 467/2 The subcutaneous or superficial bursæ. **1884** W. PYE *Surg. Handicraft* 14 The line of the superficial femoral artery.

e. Applied to the right to enjoy the surface of land for building or other purposes; also to persons possessing such a right.

1830 SIR C. WETHERELL in Concanen *Trials, Rowe v. Benton* 16 His case is that he, as a superficial occupier, has a right to that which is taken up from under the soil. *Ibid.*, He may have both the superficial right, and the right to the minerals.

2. Of or pertaining to a superficies; relating to or involving two dimensions; *esp.* relating to extent of surface. (Distinguished from *linear*, and from *solid.*) ***superficial measure***, square measure.

1571 DIGGES *Pantom.* II. i. M j, Multiplie one of the equall sides in it selfe, the halfe of the producte is the Area or superficiall Contente. **1656** tr. *Hobbes' Elem. Philos.* (1839) 184 An angle is of two sorts; for, first, it may be made by the concurrence of lines, and then it is a superficial angle; or by the concurrence of superficies, and then it is called a solid angle. **1726** *Dict. Rust.* (ed. 3), *Superficial*, or Square Measure..in a square Mile 640 square Acres [etc.]. **1824** *Act 5 George IV*, c. 74 §1 All other Measures of Extension whatsoever, whether the same be lineal, superficial or solid. **1831** BREWSTER *Optics* xli. 336 The superficial magnifying power is the number of times that it [*sc.* an object] is magnified in surface. **1880** GEIKIE *Phys. Geog.* iv. 172 [Europe] has six times more coast-line in proportion to its superficial extent than Africa has.

b. ***superficial foot, yard***, etc.: a rectangular space measuring a foot, yard, etc. each way, or a space of whatever shape containing the same amount of area; a square foot, etc. (SQUARE *a.* 1 b.).

1597 SKENE *De Verb. Sign.* s.v. *Particata*, Ane superficiall fall of lande, is sa meikle boundis of landes, as squairly conteinis ane lineall fall of bredth, and ane lineall fall of length. **1707** MORTIMER *Husb.* (1721) II. 96 If a Board hold 2 Foot and 3 Inches in breadth, 5 Inches and 3 tenth parts of an Inch in length will make a square superficial Foot of Plank. **1825** J. NICHOLSON *Oper. Mech.* 628 All faced work in slate skirting..is charged by the foot superficial. **1833** LOUDON *Encycl. Archit.* §987 A proper bond stone to be laid through the full thickness of the wall every superficial yard.

†**c.** *Math.* Of a number: Compounded of two prime factors (analogous to the two dimensions of a surface). *Obs.*

1398 TREVISA *Barth. De P.R.* XIX. cxxvi. (1495) mm iv b, The nombre Superficiall is wryten not oonly in lengthe but also in brede and is conteyned in lengthe & in brede. *c* **1430** *Art Nombryng* (E.E.T.S.) 14 Nombre superficial is þat comethe of ledynge [= multiplying] of oo nombre into another, wherfor it is callede superficial, for it hathe .2. nombres notyng or mesurynge hym, as a superficialle thynge hathe .2. dimensions, þat is to sey lengthe and brede. **1704** J. HARRIS *Lex. Techn.* I, *Superficial Numbers*; the same with *Plain Numbers*.

3. Appearing 'on the surface'; external, outward.

1561 T. HOBY tr. *Castiglione's Courtyer* I. (1900) 90 Musicke..ought necessarilye to be learned..not onely for the superficial melodie that is hard, but to be sufficient to bring into us a newe habite that is good. **1711** ADDISON *Spect.* No. 15 ¶3 Smitten with every thing that is showy and superficial. **1773** BURKE *Let. to Marq. Rockingham* 29 Sept., There is a superficial appearance of equity in this tax. **1855** MACAULAY *Hist. Eng.* xxi. IV. 581 Those superficial graces for which the French aristocracy was then renowned throughout Europe. **1883** GILMOUR *Mongols* xviii. 210 The superficial aspects of Buddhism..as embodied in the life and habits of the Mongols.

4. That is only on or near the surface; affecting only the surface, not extending much below the surface; not deep.

1594 NASHE *Christ's T.* To Rdr., Wks. 1904 II. 186 Euen of sands and superficiall bubbles they will make hideous waues and dangerous quicke-sands. **1652** CRASHAW *Carmen Deo Nostro* Wks. (1904) 209 His [*sc.* the sun's] superficiall Beames sun-burn't our skin; But left within The night & winter still of death & sin. **1676** WISEMAN *Chirurg. Treat.* v. i. 348 In small and superficiall Wounds, Nature of her own accord is wont to effect the Cure. **1794** G. ADAMS *Nat. & Exp. Philos.* II. xx. 378 The colours of the eggs of certain birds are entirely superficial, and may be scraped off. **1849** *Sk. Nat. Hist., Mammalia* IV. 104 Their principal food is afforded by the roots of plants, which is the object of their extensive and superficial burrows. **1854** J. S. C. ABBOTT *Napoleon* (1855) I. xi. 201 When the surgeon came..to inspect his wound, it was found that it was only superficial. **1877** HUXLEY *Physiogr.* 176 Compared with the great depths of the ocean, the Gulf Stream is extremely superficial.

5. Concerned only with what is on the surface, and is therefore apparent or obvious; lacking depth or thoroughness; not deep, profound, or thorough; shallow.

a. of perception, feeling.

1533 MORE *Debell. Salem* Wks. 1030/1 There be few partes in hys booke..that shall..appere so good at length, as they seme..at the fyrst sight and at superficyall reading. **1576** FLEMING *Panopl. Epist.* Epit. A j b, Luckie was hee that might haue but a superficiall viewe of his person. *Ibid.* 188 Many..taking but as it were, a superficiall viewe of these thinges, fall into this erronious..opinion. **1683** DRYDEN *Life Plutarch* 114 To vindicate our author's judgment from being superficial. *a* **1688** CUDWORTH *Immut. Mor.* (1731) 95 Sense is but a slight and Superficial Perception of the Outside..of a Corporeal Substance. **1728** WELSTED in J. Henley *Oratory Trans.* No. 1. 10 [John Henley] was admitted to Priest's Orders..: The Examination..was very short and superficial. **1791** MRS. RADCLIFFE *Rom. Forest* viii, Pity and superficial consolation were all that Madame La Motte could offer. **1845** MᶜCULLOCH *Taxation* I. iv. (1852) 111 On a superficial view, nothing seems fairer,..and yet few things would, in reality, be more unfair and mischievous. **1879** HARLAN *Eyesight* i. 9 A superficial and hasty glance at its general outlines.

b. of attainments, knowledge, learning.

1576 FLEMING *Panopl. Epist.* 281 Touching Nature their skill is but superficiall, and like a shadowe destitute of substaunce. **1605** BACON *Adv. Learn.* I. i. §3 A little or superficiall knowledge of Philosophie may encline the minde of man to Atheisme. **1667** PEPYS *Diary* 24 Feb., He speaks well, and hath pretty, slight, superficial parts, I believe. **1791** BOSWELL *Johnson* I. Introd. 7 Men of superficial understanding, and ludicrous fancy. **1836** H. COLERIDGE *North. Worthies* Introd. (1852) p. xxiv, Nothing is more likely to delude and puzzle simple persons..than a superficial acquaintance with the heads of history. **1865** RUSKIN *Sesame* ii. §75 There is a wide difference between elementary knowledge and superficial knowledge.

c. of statement, description, exposition.

1576 FLEMING *Panopl. Epist.* 377, I thinke it more auailable to kepe silence..then by saying litle, and yᵉ same superficiall, to incurre reprehension, for attempting that, which I am not able to compasse. **1591** SHAKS. *1 Hen. VI*, v. v. 10 This superficiall tale, Is but a preface of her worthy praise. **1624** GATAKER *Transubst.* 36 His proofes are tedious, superficiall, and stuffed with impertinent allegations. *a* **1667** COWLEY *Agric.* Wks. 1906 II. 405 To read Pompous and Superficial Lectures out of Virgils Georgickes [etc.]. **1777** ROBERTSON *Hist. Amer.* VII. (1778) II. 270 The accounts.. are superficial, confused and inexplicable. **1855** SINGLETON *Virgil* I. Pref. 18 A florid and superficial style of construing. **1875** JOWETT *Plato* (ed. 2) V. 339 Of the courts of law..a superficial sketch has been given.

d. *transf.* of persons, in respect of their actions, attainments, or character.

1603 SHAKS. *Meas. for M.* III. ii. 147 A very superficiall, ignorant, vnweighing fellow. **1650** BULWER *Anthropomet.* 130 Superficial Philosophers doe much please themselves with this division. **1749** FIELDING *Tom Jones* XVII. v, Nor are Instances of this Kind [of the firmness and constancy of a true friend] so rare, as some superficial and inaccurate Observers have reported. **1853** C. BRONTE *Villette* xviii, Superficial, showy, selfish people. **1867** FREEMAN *Norm. Conq.* I. i. 2 To a superficial observer the English people might seem..to be wiped out of the roll-call of the nations.

6. Of conditions, qualities, actions, occupations: Not involving a profound or serious issue; of insignificant import or influence.

c **1530** *Judic. Urines* III. i. 46 b, Colour of the vryne is a thyng that is but shadowyng and superfycyall, and a thyng that now is and now it is not. **1626** BACON *Sylva* §383 The Generall Opinion is, that Yeares Hot and Moist, are most Pestilent; Vpon the Superficiall Ground, that Heat and Moisture cause Putrefaction. **1655** MARQ. WORCESTER *Cent. Inv.* Ded. p. iv, I made it but for the superficial satisfaction of a friends curiosity. **1805** WORDSW. *Prelude* III. 209 Empty noise And superficial pastimes. *a* **1852** D. WEBSTER *Wks.* (1877) IV. 416 A change superficial and apparent only, not deep and real. **1867** FREEMAN *Norm. Conq.* I. ii. 19 It would seem that the Roman occupation of Britain was, after all, very superficial.

7. That has only the outward appearance of being what is denoted by the sb.; only apparent or on the surface, not real or genuine.

1623 COCKERAM, *Superficiall*, bearing shew only on the outside. **1638** HEYWOOD *Wise Wom.* III. i, All Sutors..being repulst..doe but waste their dayes In thanklesse suites, and superficiall praise. **1664** H. MORE *Myst. Iniq.* I. xvi. 56 All such Ludicrous and Superficial Religion must needs leave the body of sin entire and untouched, and the inward Mind dead and starved. **1875** JOWETT *Plato* (ed. 2) II. 3 The old quarrel has at least a superficial reconcilement.

B. *absol.* or as *sb.*

1. With *the*: That which is superficial (in any sense). †*in the superficial*: on a plane surface.

1579 FENTON *Guicciard.* I. 56 The Cardinall.. admonished them..that they should not consider onely the superficiall and beginning of thinges [orig. *la superficie, e i principii delle cose*], but see deepely that which with time, and in tyme may happen. **1589** PUTTENHAM *Engl. Poesie* III. xxv. (Arb.) 310 The artes of painting and keruing, whereof one represents the naturall by light colour and shadow in the superficiall or flat, the other in a body massife. **1878** BOSW. SMITH *Carthage* 381 When the due distinction has been drawn between the ephemeral and the lasting, the superficial and the essential. **1892** BRYCE in *Daily News* 28 Nov. 3/2 There was all the difference in the world between the elementary and the superficial.

2. With *the*: Those who are superficial; rarely *pl.* superficial persons.

1701 SWIFT *Contests & Diss. in Athens & Rome* iv. Wks. 1841 I. 292/2 The ambitious, the covetous, the superficial, and the ill designing; who are..apt to be bold, and forward. **1828** LYTTON *Pelham* I. xv, It is the young, the light, the superficial who are easily misled by error. **1852** COL. HAWKER *Diary* (1893) II. 337 If my plans are adopted, the Government superficials cannot pass them off as their own suggestions.

3. *pl.* Superficial characteristics or qualities.

1832 R. H. FROUDE *Rem.* (1838) I. 294 They cannot sink us so deep as these people have allowed themselves to fall while retaining all the superficials of a religious country. **1850** *Fraser's Mag.* XLII. 437 Such men..will varnish over a dexterous partizan with the superficials of greatness. **1897** WATTS-DUNTON *Aylwin* II. iv, Excepting in the merest superficials, there is a far greater variety in women than in men.

superˈficialism. [f. prec. + -ISM.] Superficial character, superficiality.

1839 J. P. SMITH *Script. & Geol.* 325 A vicious superficialism is when self-fondness persuades a man..that his knowledge is something great. **1860** SMILES *Self Help* xi. 281 The multiplication of books..tends rather towards superficialism than depth or vigour of thinking.

superˈficialist. [f. SUPERFICIAL + -IST.] One whose knowledge, observation, or treatment is superficial.

1652 BOYLE *Wks.* (1772) I. *Life* p. l, A solid knowledge of that mysterious language..(whatever is given out to the contrary by superficialists..) is, I say, somewhat difficult. **1775** JEKYLL *Let. to Father* 31 May, As to the manners, I am at present but a mere superficialist. **1805** EUGENIA DE ACTON *Nuns of Desert* I. 14 In understanding,..she was her equal, and by superficialists might have been deemed superior.

superficiality (s(j)uːpəfɪʃɪˈælɪtɪ). [f. SUPERFICIAL + -ITY. Cf. F. *superficialité*, It. *-alità*, etc.]

1. The quality of pertaining to, or being situated in or near, the surface.

1530 PALSGR. 278/2 Superficialyte, *superficialité*. **1646** SIR T. BROWNE *Pseud. Ep.* VI. x. 322 By which Salts the colours of bodies are sensibly qualified, and receive degrees of lustre or obscurity, superficiality or profundity. **1869** SPENCER *Princ. Psychol.* (1870) I. 166 The relative superficiality or centrality of these nerves.

†2. Superficial area or content. *Obs. rare.*

1690 LEYBOURN *Curs. Math.* 327 The Dodecaedron is larger than all the other together..in. Superficiality. **1811** *Self Instructor* 150 It is necessary to know how to find the superficiality [of solid bodies].

3. Lack of depth, thoroughness, or solidity; shallowness of learning, character, etc. Also, an instance of this.

1661 H. D. *Disc. Liturgies* 34 The charge of serving God in Prayer with rudeness, unpreparedness, barrenness, superficiality. **1677** GILPIN *Dæmonol.* (1867) 4 A formal superficiality of religion. **1736** BOLINGBROKE *Patriot.* (1749) 58 And hence all that superficiality in speaking, for want of information. **1821** LAMB *Elia* Ser. I. *Mrs. Battle's Opinions on Whist*, She despised superficiality, and looked deeper than the colours of things. **1840** CARLYLE *Heroes* vi. (1858) 359 The strong daring man..has set all manner of Formulas and logical superficialities against him. **1866** GEO. ELIOT *F. Holt* xxiv, Talkers whose noisy superficiality cost them nothing. **1893** LIDDON, etc. *Pusey* I. xi. 254 The superficiality so common a hundred years ago in religion as in other matters.

superˈficialize, *v.* [f. SUPERFICIAL + -IZE.]

†1. *trans.* To make a surface of (paint or colour); also *transf.* to cover (the cheeks) with a surface of paint, to paint. *Obs. rare.*

1593 NASHE *Christ's T.* (1613) 159 That colour on their cheeks you behold superficializ'd, is but sir Iohn whites, or sir Iohn Red-caps liuery. **1633** [see SUPERFICIALIZED].

b. *fig.* To put a surface or gloss upon; to gloss over. *rare.*

1849 WHIPPLE *Lit. & Life* vi. (1851) 98 It is a characteristic weakness of the day to superficialize evil; to spread a little cold cream over Pandemonium.

2. *intr.* To treat a subject or do something superficially.

1656 BLOUNT *Glossogr.*, *Superficialize*, to do any thing on the outside, or not throughly. **1871** *Galaxy* (N.Y.) Mar. 328 (Cent.) Better to elaborate the history of Greece or of Rome or of England than to superficialize in general history.

3. *trans.* To render superficial, give a superficial character to.

1828 PUSEY *Hist. Enq.* I. 138 Morus and Koppe superficialized still further the Christian ideas. **1863** M. PATTISON in *National Rev.* Jan. 217 It is a necessary consequence of the advance of education that every subject becomes vulgarised and superficialised.

Hence **superˈficialized** *ppl. a.*, **superˈficializing** *vbl. sb.*

1633 T. ADAMS *Exp. 2 Peter* ii. 14 (1865) 484/1 Were it not for superficialized Cheeks, and enticing dresses, the most graceless lecher would abhor them. **1828** PUSEY *Hist. Enq.* I. 129 The first theologians..gave occasion to the superficializing or the rejection of Christian doctrine. **1907** *Catholic Weekly* 27 Dec. 1/5 The long school hours to which children are being subjected will soon breed a race of superficialised prigs.

superficially (s(j)uːpəˈfɪʃəlɪ), *adv.* [f. SUPERFICIAL + -LY².]

1. On or at the surface; *Anat.* just beneath the surface. Const. *to*: On or at the surface of.

1570 FOXE *A. & M.* (ed. 2) 2121/1 They..began to refricate and rippe vp the old sore, the skarre wherof, had bene but superficially cured. **1603** HOLLAND *Plutarch's Mor.* 229 This change and transmutation of the said polype or pour-cuttle fish, entreth not deeply in, but appeareth superficially in the skin. **1646** SIR T. BROWNE *Pseud. Ep.* II. i. 52 Ice..will..neither float above like lighter bodies, but being neare, or in equality of weight, lye superficially or almost horizontally unto it. **1737** BRACKEN *Farriery Impr.* (1757) II. 215, I could easily see the Vein pass superficially upon the Out-side of the Tumour. **1767** GOOCH *Treat. Wounds* I. 361 The tent is to be left out, and the wound dressed superficially. **1853** LYELL *Princ. Geol.* xvii. (ed. 9) 257 Beds of turf..precisely similar to those now formed superficially on the extreme borders of the Adriatic. **1870** ROLLESTON *Anim. Life* 3 Another vein, which, from its being placed superficially to the sterno mastoid muscle, we know to be the homologue of the external jugular of anthropotomy.

b. in fig. context.

1638 BAKER tr. *Balzac's Lett.* II. 196 Things that wounded me heretofore at the very heart, doe not now so much as superficially touch me. **1647** H. MORE *Poems* 195 Our soul's not superficially colourd by phantasms. **1735** BOLINGBROKE *On Parties* iv. 36 When the same Opinions revived at the Restoration, They did not sink deep even then into the Minds of Men; but floated so superficially there, that [etc.].

2. Without depth or thoroughness of knowledge, observation, treatment, etc.; not profoundly or thoroughly.

1526 *Pilgr. Perf.* (W. de W. 1531) 61 Dayly to thynke on these v thynges folowynge, not superficially, that is lyghtly passyng ouer them, but with grauite, inwardly. **1576** FLEMING *Panopl. Epist.* 155 Your grace..will take a viewe of the cause, & wey the same, not superficially, but with due consideration. **1606** SHAKS. *Tr. & Cr.* II. ii. 165 You haue both said well: And on the cause and question now in hand, Haue gloz'd, but superficially. **1667** MILTON *P.L.* VI. 476 Whose Eye so superficially surveyes These things, as not to mind from whence they grow. **1712** STEELE *Spect.* No. 432 ¶8 By such early Corrections of Vanity, while Boys are growing into Men, they will gradually learn not to censure superficially. **1821** LAMB *Elia* Ser. I. *Old & New Schoolm.*, The modern schoolmaster..must be superficially, if I may so say, omniscient. **1867** FREEMAN *Norm. Conq.* I. iv. 273 Looked at superficially, there is a certain likeness between the two. **1875** MISS BRADDON *Strange World* I. i. 18, I have studied the subject but superficially in the pages of our friend Cicero.

3. As to outward appearance or form; externally, on the surface.

1570 R. HICHCOCK *Quintess. Wit* (1590) 20 Nobilite and gravitie, wherof men superficially make such estimation. **1571** GOLDING *Calvin on Ps.* lxxi. 22 He will not give thanks unto God feynedly, nor superficially, but..with an earnest zelousnes. **1878** H. S. WILSON *Alpine Ascents* iii. 103 Melchior..looks superficially like an Italian. **1890** *Spectator* 31 May 753/1 The old story over again,..always superficially true, and always substantially false. **1893** *Bookman* June 86/1 Her ambitions superficially so different at different times, and yet substantially the same.

superˈficialness. [f. SUPERFICIAL *a.* + -NESS.]

1. = SUPERFICIALITY 3.

1624 GATAKER *Transubst.* 118 The Superficialnesse of his silly and unlearned Adversarie. **1661** GAUDEN *Consid. Liturgy* 10 That rudenesse and unpreparednesse, that barrennesse and superficialnesse,..to which every private Minister is daily subject. **1711** *Countrey-Man's Lett. to Curate* 95 The Curat in the Answer manifestly Writes with a Superficialness that's below even Table-chat. **1827** HARE *Guesses* Ser. II. (1848) 60 Herder..owing to the superficialness of his metaphysical knowledge, had but vague conceptions with regard to the progress of mankind. **1860** EMERSON *Cond. Life, Fate* Wks. (Bohn) II. 309 Our America has a bad name for superficialness. *a* **1902** A. B. DAVIDSON *Called of God* x. 258 This sterner side usually showed itself, when Christ had to deal with sentiment, or propriety, or superficialness.

2. = SUPERFICIALITY 1.

1899 *Allbutt's Syst. Med.* VI. 72 It [*sc.* mediastinitis] might be suspected from the intensity and superficialness of post-sternal pain.

†**superˈficialty.** *Obs. rare.* [f. SUPERFICIAL + -TY¹.] Surface; extent of surface, area.

c **1400** MAUNDEV. (1839) xvii. 186 Oure Contree ne Irelond ne Wales..ne ben not in the superficyalte cownted aboven the Erthe... For the Superficialtee of the Erthe is departed in 7 parties, for the 7 Planetes: and tho parties ben clept Clymates.

†**superˈficiary**, *a.* (*sb.*) *Obs.* [ad. late L. *superficiārius* (of buildings) situated on another man's land, in mod.L. superficial: see SUPERFICIES and -ARY¹. Cf. F. *superficiaire*, etc.]

A. *adj.*

1. = SUPERFICIAL *a.* 1, 4.

1615 CROOKE *Body of Man* 957 At the sides of the processes it hath superficiary or shallowe bosomes. **1638** A. READ *Chirurg.* xxviii. 205 Wounds of the lungs..are either superficiary and small, or deepe. **1696** WHISTON *Th. Earth* III. (1722) 231 There is a constant and vigorous heat diffused from the Central towards the Superficiary parts.

2. = SUPERFICIAL *a.* 2.

a **1680** GLANVILL *Sadducismus* (1681) 156 A Trinal Distance or solid Amplitude, that is to say, not linear onely and superficiary.

3. = SUPERFICIAL *a.* 5.

1605 TIMME *Quersit.* II. vii. 140 If they be more inwardly and exactly examined than by that superficiary and slight maner of tasting and experimenting. **1642** H. MORE *Song of Soul* To Rdr., The superficiary knowledge of tongues. **1693** *Phil. Trans.* XVII. 618 The Superficiary Proficients would for ever be deterr'd from attempting to grasp at such an Immensity. **1702** C. MATHER *Magn. Chr.* IV. iv. (1852) 74 They used a 'diligent exploration' concerning the faith and repentance of their communicants, lest haply it should be only superficiary.

B. *sb.* (See quot. and SUPERFICIAL *a.* 1 e.) *rare*⁻⁰.

1656 BLOUNT *Glossogr.*, *Superficiary*, he that hath built an house upon another mans ground, and therefore pays Quit-rent.

Hence †**superˈficiarily** *adv.*, superficially.

1634 T. JOHNSON *Parey's Chirurg.* XXI. xxxi. (1678) 481 I divided the skin..with much scarification but only superficiarily.

†**superficie.** *Obs.* Also 6 -ye. [ad. L. *superficiēs*: see next. Cf. F. *superficie*.] = next.

1545 RAYNALDE *Byrth Mankynde* 2 Vpon the outward face & superficye of this skyn, there is yet another thynner skyn. **1567** MAPLET *Gr. Forest* 43 It then ariseth vp againe to the waters top, and so keepeth ouerlie and aboue the waters highest superficie. **1709** V. MANDEY *Syst. Math., Optics* I. vii. (1729) 656 A Figure of Radiation, is that whose Base exists in a visible Superficie. **1726** LEONI *Alberti's Archit.* III. 1/2 A Superficie is that extreme part of a body which we consider, not with regard to..depth, but only with regard to breadth and length.

superficies (s(j)uːpəˈfɪʃiːz). Pl. superficies; also 6–7 -ficiesses. [a. L. *superficiēs*, f. *super-* SUPER- 3 + *faciēs* FACE *sb.*

The pronunciation (s(j)uːpəˈfɪʃiːz) is given as an alternative in most U.S. dictionaries from Worcester, 1846, onwards. Metrical examples of the 17th cent. also point to a quadrisyllabic pronunciation.]

1. *Geom.* A magnitude of two dimensions, having only length and breadth; that which forms the boundary or one of the boundaries of a solid, or separates one part of space from another; a surface.

1530 RASTELL *Bk. Purgat.* II. xx. e 2 b, A superfycyes is that which hath but length and brede & no maner of thyckenes. **1570** BILLINGSLEY *Euclid* I. Def. vi. 2 The extremes or limites of a bodye are superficiesses. **1612** BACON *Ess., Seeming Wise* (Arb.) 214 It is a ridiculous thing ..to see what shifts these formalists haue..to make Superficies to seeme body, that hath depth and bulke. **1662** HOBBES *Seven Prob.* Wks. 1845 VII. 67 Many lines set together make a superficies though their breadth be insensible. **1684** ASH in *Phil. Trans.* XIV. 673, 2 angles or superficies are equal when one being put on the other, it neither exceeds, nor is exceeded. **1690** LOCKE *Hum. Und.* II. xiii. §13 To divide and separate actually is, as I think, by removing the parts one from another, to make two Superficies, where before there was a Continuity. **1815** J. SMITH *Panorama Sci. & Art* II. 703 To know the names of differently shaped superficies and solids, as circles, triangles, parallelograms, cubes, &c. **1831** BREWSTER *Optics* xiv. 114 To allow them [*sc.* rays] to pack into a spherical superficies as they converge to their poles or points of origin.

2. The outer surface of a body, which is apparent to the eye, or is immediately adjacent to the air or to another body.

1577 HANMER *Anc. Eccl. Hist.* II. xvii. 30 So that the externall shewe of wordes, resemble the superficyes of the body. **1590** GREENE *Mourn. Garm.* Wks. (Grosart) IX. 169 The eye..coueteth that euery superficies be faire and pleasing. **1607** TOPSELL *Four-f. Beasts* 500 When the wormes are followed by Molds..they flie to the superficies and very toppe of the earth. **1611** CORYAT *Crudities* 404 Here I haue obserued the people in the bathes feede together vpon a table that hath swimmed vpon the superficies of the water. **1614** GORGES *Lucan* IX. 375 For scarcely now a little boate Can on the superficies flote, Of those drown'd sands where water stayes. **1660** BOYLE *New Exp. Phys. Mech.* 12 The internal superficies of the Receiver. *Ibid.* xxx. 227 Conspicuous waves that appear'd upon the superficies of our agitated smoke. **1789** J. WILLIAMS *Min. Kingd.* I. 135 The river begins to run across the superficies of these coals. **1862** GOULBURN *Pers. Relig.* I. iii. (1864) 29 The difference of colour..is produced by some subtle difference of texture or superficies.

†b. A plane or level surface. *Obs. rare.*

1674 JOSSELYN *Voy. New Eng.* 161 Two hills of equal height.., the one well fortified on the superficies with some Artillery mounted. **1704** SWIFT *T. Tub* ii. Wks. 1760 I. 36 He was shown in the posture of a Persian emperor, sitting on a Superficies.

3. That which constitutes the outermost part of a body; the surface layer. Now *rare.*

1603 HOLLAND *Plutarch's Mor.* 1174 The lakes and rivers ..seeme in their superficies to be some time reddish, and otherwhiles of a violet colour. **1621** BURTON *Anat. Mel.* II. ii. I. i. 306 Crato..admits rost meat, if the burned and scorched *superficies*, the browne we call it, be pared off. **1628** VENNER *Baths of Bathe* 6 Onely the superficies, or vpper part of the Bath is cooled. **1707** MORTIMER *Husb.* (1721) II. 124 To render the Superficies of the Earth loose. **1847** H. MILLER *First Impr. Eng.* iv. (1857) 49 The rubbish of the subterranean workings is scarce at all suffered to encroach.. on the arable superficies.

b. *Rom.* and *Civil Law.* A building or other thing in or on the surface of a piece of land, which is by art or nature so closely connected with as to form part of it; the right possessed by a person over any such building or other thing in or on the surface of another's land.

1850 in BURRILL *Law Dict.* **1853** T. C. SANDARS *Inst. Justinian* II. v. (1859) 215 The right of *superficies* was almost identical with that of *emphyteusis*, but applied only to the *superficies*, that is, things built on the ground, not to the ground itself. It was the right of disposing freely of a building erected on another man's soil without destroying it, subject to the payment of a yearly rent. **1856** BOUVIER *Law Dict. U.S.* (ed. 6), *Superficies*, a Latin word used among civilians. It signifies in the edict of the prætor whatever has been erected on the soil.

4. Superficial area or extent.

1656 HOBBES *Six Lessons* Wks. 1845 VII. 305 The superficies of the conoeides is greater than the superficies of the sphere. **1753** N. TORRIANO *Non-Naturals* 51 The whole Weight of Air, which presses equally upon a Body of about 15 square Feet Superficies. **1798** *Survey Prov. Moray* iii. 171 The whole superficies of the parish contains 21 square miles. **1832** DE LA BECHE *Geol. Man.* (ed. 2) 2 The superficies of the Pacific Ocean alone is estimated as somewhat greater than that of the whole dry land with which we are acquainted. **1847** H. MILLER *First Impr. Eng.* vi. (1857) 92 The slabs, each containing a superficies of about twenty-four feet.

5. †a. The 'surface' (of something immaterial, *esp.* of the mind or soul). *Obs.*

1586 HOBY *Polit. Disc. Truth* xvii. 73 We must not onely consider, the superficies and beginnyng of thinges, but to looke more inwardly what may happen in time. **1607** HEYWOOD *Fayre Mayde Exch.* i. C j b, *Anth...* But what is loue? *Frank.* A voluntary motion of delight, Touching the superficies of the soule. **1638** BAKER tr. *Balzac's Lett.* (vol. II) 25 Greek and Latin make not men valiant, nor are things that descend to the bottom of the soul, they scarce reach to the outermost superficies. *a* **1658** CLEVELAND *Committee* 38 The Type of Flesh and Bloud, the Skeleton And Superficies of a thing that's gone. *a* **1700** KEN *Edmund* Poet. Wks. 1721 II. 287 Those Thoughts..spread the Superficies of my Mind.

†b. The outward form or aspect. *Obs.*

1589 [? NASHE] *Almond for Parrat* E j b, The deuill.. prouided a rustie superficies wherin to wrap him as soone as euer he was separated from his mothers wombe. **1612** N. FIELD *Woman is a Weather cock* III. ii, Could Nature make So faire a superficies, to enclose So false a heart? **1638** FEATLY *Transubst.* 56 You beleeve that Christ's body is contained under the superficies or accidents of bread. **1781** JOHNSON *L.P.*, *Waller* Wks. 1787 II. 260 His images [are] such as the superficies of nature readily supplies.

c. That which is merely superficial; the outward appearance as distinct from the inner or real nature or condition.

1589 [? LYLY] *Pappe w. Hatchet* L.'s Wks. 1902 III. 400 A good honest strippling..askt his sweete sister, whether lecherie in her conscience were a sinne? In faith (quoth she) I thinke it the superficies of sinne. **1593** *Tell-Trothe's N. Y. Gift* (1876) 28 They that only haue entertained the superficies of loue. **1622** MABBE tr. *Aleman's Guzman d'Alf.* III. i. 187, I only lookt vpon the Superficies, I went no farther then the outward appearance. **1752** JOHNSON *Rambler* No. 196 ¶5 He who has seen only the superficies of life believes every thing to be what it appears. **1847** DISRAELI *Tancred* II. xiii, He held that the state of England, notwithstanding the superficies of a material prosperity was one of impending doom. **1888** PATER *Ess. fr. Guardian* (1896) 106 What [his life] really most resembles, different as its superficies may look, is the career of those early mediæval religious artists.

†**d.** An outward show concealing something, a cloak. *Obs. rare.*

1589 GREENE *Orpharion* Wks. (Grosart) XII. 67 Then must we confesse that beauty is..to be esteemed aboue all things, as the very couer and superficies vnder which vertue lyes hid. **1612** WEBSTER *White Devil* I. ii. 19 Her coynesse? thats but the superficies of lust most women have.

†**e.** A superficial account, a sketch. *Obs. rare.*

1670 G. H. *Hist. Cardinals* III. II. 261 But all that I have said yet of the Election of the Pope, has been nothing but a meer superficies of the policies of the Court.

superfine ('s(j)uːpəfaɪn, s(j)uːpə'faɪn), *a.* (*sb.*) [ad. med.L. **superfinus* (implied in *superfinitās*): see SUPER- 9a and FINE *a.* Cf. F. *superfin* (also *surfin*), Sp., Pg. *superfino*, also It. *sopraffino*, Sp. *sobrefino*.]

A. *adj.* †**1.** ? Exceedingly subtle. *Obs. rare.*

c **1440** LYDG. *Hors, Shepe, & G.* 313 This Agnus dei.. Which wessh a-wey all venym superfyne On Calverie.

2. Excessively refined, nice, fastidious, or elegant; over-refined, over-nice.

1575 GASCOIGNE *Making of Verse* Wks. 1907 I. 465 Many inventions are so superfine, that they are *Vix good.* **1589** GREENE *Menaphon* (Arb.) 51 She heard him so superfine, as if Ephæbus had learnd him to refine his mother tongue. **1622** VENNER *Via Recta* (ed. 2) 170 Them that out of a superfine daintinesse cannot liue but by sweete meates. **1695** LOCKE *Reason. Chr.* (1696) 305 The bulk of Mankind have not leisure for Learning and Logick, and superfine distinctions of the Schools. **1825** T. HOOK *Sayings* Ser. II. *Man of Many Fr.* (Colburn) 136 A pair of superfine ladies' footmen. **1830** MISS MITFORD *Village* Ser. IV. 264 (*Two Dolls*) The care of his granddaughter left entirely to a vulgar old nurse and a super-fine housekeeper. **1837** CARLYLE *Fr. Rev.* II. I. iii, Madame..trains up a youthful D'Orléans generation in what super-finest morality one can.

3. †Consisting of very fine particles or threads (*obs.*). Also of a file with extremely fine teeth.

1656 EARL MONM. tr. *Boccalini's Advts. fr. Parnass.* II. lxxi. 348 Princes were now no longer able..to throw dust in their Subjects Eyes, though it were most artificial and superfine. **1706** PHILLIPS (ed. Kersey), *Superfine*, very fine or thin; as Superfine Wire, Thread, Cards, &c. **1728** CHAMBERS *Cycl.*, *Superfine*... The Term is particularly used among Gold Wiar-drawers, for the Gold or Silver-wiar, which after being drawn through an infinite Number of Holes, each less and less, is, at length, brought not to be bigger than a Hair. **1875** KNIGHT *Dict. Mech.* 2455/1 *Superfine File*, a dead-smooth file.

4. Of manufactured goods: Extremely fine in quality; of the very best kind; (of liquid) the purest or clearest.

1682 *Rec. Scott. Cloth Manuf. New Mills* (S.H.S.) 40 John Rae is ordered when he gives out wool..to sett down a letter for a distinction that is C for course M for midleing F for fine and S.F. for super fine. **1707** MORTIMER *Husb.* (1721) II. 332 Till you observe your Cyder to be very transparent, which then may be called Superfine. **1710** *Tatler* No. 245 ¶2 Seven cakes of superfine Spanish wool. **1774** *Chesterfield's Lett.* (1792) I. 238 The very best wool, which we make use of here in manufacturing our superfine cloths. **1818** BYRON *Juan* I. cxcviii, The wax was superfine, its hue vermilion. **1872** L. P. MEREDITH *Teeth* (1878) 12 The bread, pastry, cake, etc., so much in use and made of superfine flour.

5. Superlatively fine or excellent.

1850 E. FITZGERALD *Let. to J. Allen* 9 Mar., I have read but very little of late; indeed my eyes have not been in superfine order. **1885** RUSKIN *Præterita* I. ii. 47 In the fixed purpose of making an ecclesiastical gentleman of me, with the superfinest of manners.

B. *sb. pl.* Goods of superfine quality.

1812 BIGLAND *Beauties Eng. & Wales* XVI. 787 The chief manufacture..is cloth, which was formerly almost wholly of the coarser kinds; but the manufacture of superfines has of late..increased. **1880** J. DUNBAR *Pract. Papermaker* 20 Superfines, ¼; Spanish Esparto, Fine, ¼.

†**'superfine,** *v. Obs. rare*$^{-1}$. [f. prec. adj.] *intr.* To refine too much.

1702 PENN *Maxims* §209 He that superfines upon other Men's Actions, cozens himself, as well as injures them.

'superfinely, *adv.* [f. prec. adj. + -LY².] In a superfine manner or degree.

1693 W. FREKE *Sel. Ess.* xix. 106 Their Picking of Straws, Notions so idle, and yet so particular and superfinely nice. **1884** SPURGEON in *Homiletic Monthly* (U.S.) Aug. 640 A superfinely genteel and affected audience.

'superfineness. *rare.* Also 6 -finesse. [f. prec. adj. + -NESS; in early use after FINESSE.] The quality of being superfine; excessive refinement.

1575 G. HARVEY *Letter-bk.* (Camden) 93 That is another fitt of your mill, violent, celestiall, incomprehensible, peremptorye superfinesse. **1575** GASCOIGNE *Glasse Govt.* I. v. Wks. 1910 II. 23, I could rather content my self to be buryed..then to liue in such a miserable and precise world as this is, Oh what Superfinesse are we now growen unto? **1862** *Fraser's Mag.* July 74 A work of..much subtle sweetness and delicacy, tending, however, to pass into tenuity and superfineness.

'super-'finery. *nonce-wd.* [f. SUPER- 10 + FINERY, after SUPERFINE.] Excessive refinement.

1842 J. STERLING *Ess.*, etc. (1848) I. 444 The delicacies, and subtleties, and super-fineries of so many mysterious passions.

'superfinish, *a. nonce-wd.* [f. SUPERFINE *a.* + -ISH¹.] Somewhat superfine.

1866 CARLYLE *Remin.* (1881) I. 224 Continually preaching a superfinish morality about benevolence, munificence, health, peace.

'superfix. *Phonetics.* [f. SUPER- 2, after *prefix*, *suffix*, etc.] A sequence of stress or other suprasegmental phonemes which is treated as part of the grammatical structure of words and phrases.

1951 TRAGER & SMITH *Outl. Eng. Structure* II. 56 Suprasegmental morphemes consisting of patterns of stress, with the possibility of including plus junctures, are called superfixes. Those consisting of pitches and a terminal juncture are called intonation patterns. *Ibid.*, A morphemic phrase consists of two or more bases, with their suffixes, and a superfix. **1954** [see SIMULFIX]. **1956** H. WHITEHALL in *Kenyon Rev.* XVIII. 415 In their *Outline*, Trager and Smith have..assembled some..linguistic tools. Their exposition of the superfix..throws..light on the distinction between the verse of Wyatt, Donne,..Hopkins, and Eliot in which superfix patterns function freely..as part of the rhythm, and the verse of Surrey, Pope, Tennyson, in which the superfixes are frozen..in the rhythm. **1965** [see *high-tone* s.v. HIGH *a.* 22a]. **1972** HARTMANN & STORK *Dict. Lang. & Linguistics* 226/1 *Superfix*, term used to describe the suprasegmental or prosodic features of a particular word or utterance, e.g. the stress pattern which distinguishes modifier + noun *green house* from the compound noun *greenhouse*.

'superflow. *Physics.* [f. *super-* in SUPERFLUID *sb.* and *a.*] Flow of a superfluid.

1939 *Canad. Jrnl. Res.* XVII A. 163 An ordinary flow of the whole fluid is superposed on the super-flow. **1966** [see LAMBDA 4]. **1975** *Nature* 10 Jan. 93/3 It is superflow in the film which is responsible for the well known and dramatic phenomenon of the beaker of helium which empties itself while remaining upright.

†**superflue,** *a.* (*adv.*, *sb.*) *Obs.* Also 4-6 **superflu,** 5-6 **-fleu,** *Sc.* **-flew.** [a. OF. *superflu* (from 13th cent.) = Pr. *superflu*, It., Sp., Pg. *superfluo*, or ad. their source L. *superfluus*, f. *superfluĕre*, f. *super-* SUPER- 2 + *fluĕre* to flow.]

A. *adj.* **1.** More than sufficient, superabundant; = SUPERFLUOUS 1.

c **1400** *Apol. Loll.* 51 Þat þei geyt þer of superfleu riches, prid of world, and lust of flesch. *a* **1425** tr. *Arderne's Treat. Fistula* etc. 44 If þer growe..any superflue flesshe in þe hole. **1460-70** *Bk. Quinte Essence* 3 It haþ a synguler strenkþe..to drawe awey þe superflue humouris fro þe heed. **1533** BELLENDEN *Livy* II. xix. (S.T.S.) I. 202 The romanis..had superflew nowmer of pepill to abandoun þe rage of vncouth Inemyis. **1566** *Reg. Privy Council Scot.* Ser. I. I. 471 Be interchange of the excrescence and superflew frutis growand in the Laich and Hielandis.

b. Having something in excess.

superflue number, a number the sum of the aliquot parts of which exceeds the number itself.

1398 TREVISA *Barth. De P.R.* XIX. cxxiv. (1495) 445b, Superflue nombres & Diminutif ben vnordynatly disposyd and compownyd of noo certen ende of nombres. *c* **1420** *Wyclif's Bible* Lev. xxii. 23 *margin*, In Ebreu it is, a scheep and an oxe superflu and dymynute, that is, hauynge a membre superflu ether failinge a membre.

2. Not needed or necessary; = SUPERFLUOUS 2.

c **1380** WYCLIF *Serm.* Sel. Wks. II. 76 Þe first part of þis gospel makiþ ende of Cristis ordre;..and whatevere be more in any ordre is superflue. *c* **1400** LOVE *Bonavent. Mirr.* vii. (1908) 53 Gostly circumsicioun, that is kuttynge away fro vs alle superflue thinges that disposen to synne. **1484** CAXTON *Fables of Poge* iv, The superflue cure of them whiche gouerne the dogges and hawkes. **1509** BARCLAY *Shyp of Folys* (1874) I. 17 Som tyme addynge, somtyme detractinge and takinge away suche thinges a[s] semeth me necessary and superflue.

b. Useless, vain; = SUPERFLUOUS 2d.

1388 WYCLIF *Wisd.* xvi. 29 The hope of an vnkynde man ..schal perische as superflu [Vulg. *supervacua*] watir. *c* **1430** *Life St. Kath.* (1884) 27 Þe secte of ȝoure fayth is so superflu and vnresonable þat hit semeþ to be receyued of noon þat hath his ryght mynde. **1483** CAXTON *Gold. Leg.* 184/2 The wordes & menaces that thou hast spoken been but vayne and superflue.

3. Exceeding what is right or normal, immoderate, excessive; = SUPERFLUOUS 3.

1388 WYCLIF *Eccl.* ii. 26 He ȝaf turment, and superflu bisynesse to a synnere. *c* **1412** HOCCLEVE *De Reg. Princ.* 3825 Many a lust superflu mot he lete, And lykerous. *a* **1425** tr. *Arderne's Treat. Fistula*, etc. 34 Þe emplastre remoued, þer appered aboue ȝe emplastre ful putrid quitour in superflue quantite. **1561** in *Exch. Rolls Scotl.* XIX. 477 This chairg is superflew. Charge in the soum of £112 albeit he suld be chargit with £91. **1584** *Reg. Privy Council Scot.* Ser. I. III. 661 Ony superflew or extraordinar panis.

4. Of persons: Extravagant, excessive; = SUPERFLUOUS 4. Const. *in*, *of*.

c **1380** WYCLIF *Serm.* Sel. Wks. I. 200 Freris and preestis þat gadren hem tresure,..and algatis fynden [? are found to be] a peple superflue and charginge. *c* **1425** *St. Mary of Oignies* I. xi. in *Anglia* VIII. 147/31 Ȝee superflue wymmen full of pompe and pryde. *Ibid.* II. iii. 155/33 She hadde be superflue in cloþes. **1509** BARCLAY *Shyp of Folys* (1874) II. 215 He is a fole that his erys wyll inclyne Lyghtly to his wordes..that apereth superflue of langage. **1556** *Aurelio & Isab.* (1608) K v, It sholde be beter to faille a litell in the justice, than to be superflue in crualte.

B. *adv.* In excess, excessively.

c **1400** *Apol. Loll.* 50 It semiþ good..þat þe kirk be honorid, neuerþeles not to mikil nor superflue, ne curiously. **1553** *Acc. Ld. High Treas. Scot.* X. 213 The compositioun of the Courte Buke of Hadingtoun, witht quhilk the comptar wes..superflu chargit..extending to xxiiij li. **1588** *Rot. Scacc. Reg. Scot.* XXI. 352 *marg.*, Vrang calculat and superflue chargit, 10s.

C. *sb.* That which is superfluous.

c **1380** WYCLIF *Sel. Wks.* III. 146 Lordes schulden helpe hom [*sc.* their servants], as kepere of a vyneȝerd schulde helpe þo vynes, and kutt awey supe[r]flu þat growes in hom.

superfluence (s(j)uː'pɜːfluːəns). *arch. rare.* [f. L. *superfluens* SUPERFLUENT: see -ENCE.] Superabundance.

In quot. 1859 perh. an error for *supereffluence*.

c **1530** *Songs, Carols*, etc. (1907) 114 Whan..lekis geve hony in þer superfluens; Than put in a woman your trust & confidens. **1859** PUSEY *Lent. Serm.* (1874) 353 One act of God brought us into this rich and abundant superfluence of grace, by which God would make us saints, if we would.

So †**superfluency,** excess.

1672 MARVELL *Reh. Transp.* I. 57 The Ornaments and Superfluencies of Invention and Satyre.

superfluent (s(j)uː'pɜːfluːənt), *a. rare.* [ad. L. *superfluent-*, *-ens*, pr. pple. of *superfluĕre*: see SUPERFLUE and -ENT.]

1. = SUPERFLUOUS, in various senses.

c **1440** *Pallad. on Husb.* II. 294 In Nouember kitte of the bowes drie, Superfluent & thicke. **1676** WISEMAN *Chirurg. Treat.* I. xxiii. 124, I cut off as much of the Skin as was superfluent, and brought the rest together. **1804** COLERIDGE in *Blackw. Mag.* (1882) CXXXI. 124 The present German philosophers, who are sinking back rapidly into miscellany, and superfluent, and arbitrary. **1822** SCOTT *Let. to A. Constable* 28 May, A sort of historical prayer, in which Lochleven is superfluent enough to remind God Almighty [etc.]. **1882** J. NICHOL *Amer. Lit.* iv. 128 Though superfluent, he never brings in bombast to plaster lack of knowledge.

2. Flowing or floating above. *Obs.* or *arch. rare.*

c **1440** *Pallad. on Husb.* XI. 476 In hondis clene vphent Al that wol swymme & be superfluent. **1871** R. ELLIS tr. *Catullus* xvii. 10 Where the superfluent lake, the spongy putrescence, Sinks most murkily flushed.

3. Superabundant.

a **1711** [implied in SUPERFLUENTLY]. **1848** BAILEY *Festus* xxiii. (ed. 3) 289 Its breast, which burns With all concentrate and superfluent woe. **1885** L. OLIPHANT *Sympneumata* 181 That junction of love-force may reproduce the superfluent quantities that will go forth to succour through the world.

Hence †**su'perfluently** *adv.*, superabundantly.

a **1711** KEN *Hymns Evang.* Poet. Wks. 1721 I. 390 Luke rapt at Jesus Love,..Himself an Holocaust to Jesus gave. Luke superfluently fir'd, Strait from all Worldly Cares retir'd.

superfluid (stress variable), *sb.* and *a. Physics.* [SUPER- 6c, 9a.] **A.** *sb.* (*'superfluid.*) A fluid that exhibits superfluidity.

1938 P. KAPITZA in *Nature* 8 Jan. 74/2 The helium below the λ-point enters a special state which might be called a 'superfluid'. **1950** [see *quantum liquid* s.v. QUANTUM 7a]. **1965** *Economist* 22 May 935/2 Helium itself behaves oddly. If cooled below 2·2 degrees K it becomes a 'superfluid'. **1974** *Nature* 15 Mar. 195/2 With the discovery of the new phases of ³He, the number of known superfluids in nature has been doubled. **1982** *McGraw-Hill Yearbk. Sci. & Technol.* 227/1 The neutrons in a neutron star..are expected to form a *p*-wave-paired superfluid whose properties should be related to those of ³He-A and B.

B. *adj.* (*super'fluid.*) Exhibiting or pertaining to superfluidity.

1941 *Physical Rev.* LX. 357/2 We might regard liquid helium as if it consisted of a 'mixture' of two liquids—one is 'superfluid' without viscosity..and the other is 'normal'. **1947**, etc. [see NORMAL *a.* 2k.] **1968** C. G. KUPER *Introd. Theory Superconductivity* ii. 20 At any temperature $T < T_c$ only a fraction..of the electrons are in the condensate ('superfluid' electrons) and the remainder are 'normal' electrons. **1974** *Nature* 6 Dec. 441/2 Liquid ³He..under its own saturated vapour pressure..was found to undergo a superfluid transition at 0·93 mK.

superflu'idity. *Physics.* [SUPER- 10.] The property of flowing without viscosity or friction which, with other exceptional properties, is exhibited by the isotopes of liquid helium below certain temperatures; an analogous property of other collections of particles (as the electrons in a superconductor) that exhibit quantum effects on a macroscopic scale.

1938 *Physical Rev.* LIV. 952/2 The transport properties ..of liquid helium, when passing the λ-point actually change in a very conspicuous manner; thus one speaks of a 'superfluidity' and of a 'super-heat-conductivity'. **1955** H. B. G. CASIMIR in W. Pauli *Niels Bohr* 131 The Bose-Einstein gas is the only model known at present that leads to macroscopic wave functions at finite temperatures and the super-fluidity of liquid helium has almost certainly something to do with this model. **1967** *New Scientist* 25 May 454/1 In superconductivity, as in its counterpart superfluidity, we are faced with phenomena that are quite outside our ordinary physical experience. **1975** *Rev. Mod. Physics* XLVII. 430/1 Observation of fourth sound [in ³He] proves the existence of superfluidity. **1976** *Sci. Amer.* Dec. 56/1 Under the name of superconductivity, superfluidity is also displayed by the conduction electrons in a great many metals and alloys.

† **super'fluitance.** *Obs. rare.* [f. SUPER- 2 + L. *fluitāre*, frequent. of *fluĕre* to flow + -ANCE.] That which floats on the surface.

Confused by Blount *Glossogr.* with *superfluity*.
1646 SIR T. BROWNE *Pseud Ep.* II. i. 56 *Sperma Cœti* (which is a bituminous superfluitance on the sea). *Ibid.* II. v. 92 Out of the cream or superfluitance, the finest dishes.. are made.

superfluity (s(j)uːpəˈfluːɪtɪ). Also 4–6 **-ite, -yte,** 6–7 **-itie,** (5 **-itee, -ytee, -flovite,** 6 **-flueity,** *Sc.* **-flwitie**). [a. OF. *superfluite* (from 12th c.) = Pr. *superfluitat*, It. *superfluità*, Sp. *superfluidad*, Pg. *-ade*, ad. med.L. *superfluitās*, f. *superfluus*: see SUPERFLUE and -ITY.] The quality of being, or something that is, superfluous.

1. Superabundant supply, superabundance; the condition of there being (or of one's having) more than enough; an instance of this.

c **1380** WYCLIF *Serm.* Sel. Wks. II. 58 þanne shulde man han etun and diffied, and delyvered him of superfluyte. **1387** TREVISA *Higden* (Rolls) VI. 465 Seculer lordes schulde take awey the superfluyte of here possessiouns, and ȝeve it to hem þat nedeþ. *c* **1400** *Pilgr. Sowle* (Caxton 1483) III. ix. 55 Many other myght haue ben fed and fulfylled with theyr superfluytees. **1526** TINDALE *Mark* xii. 44 They all putt in off their superfluite: But she off her poverte cast in all that she had. **1597** SHAKS. *2 Hen. IV*, II. ii. 20 To beare the Inuentorie of thy shirts, as one for superfluity, and one other, for vse. **1642** FULLER *Holy & Prof. St.* III. vi. 165 Some think private mens superfluity is a necessary evill in a State. **1647** N. BACON *Disc. Govt. Eng.* I. iv. (1739) 10 This Island hath from time to time been no other than as a Sewer to empty the superfluity of the German Nations. **1751** JOHNSON *Rambler* No. 104 ¶2 They.. naturally laid out their superfluities upon pleasure. **1781** COWPER *Charity* 455 Her superfluity the poor supplies. **1803** MALTHUS *Popul.* I. vi. 82 The common error of confounding a superfluity of inhabitants with great actual population. **1842** LOUDON *Suburban Hort.* 283 It receives too much sap, and ultimately perishes from superfluity, as the other did from insufficiency. **1876** GEO. ELIOT *Dan. Der.* xxxvi, The distasteful petty empire of her girlhood with its irksome lack of distinction and superfluity of sisters.

† **b.** Jocularly given as the 'proper term' for a company of nuns. *Obs.*

14.. *Porkington MS. 10* in *Trans. Philol. Soc.* (1909) Suppl. 48 A Superflovite of nonnys.

2. The condition or fact of being more abundant or copious than is necessary; excessive quantity or number; *esp.* excess in diet or dress.

c **1386** CHAUCER *Prol.* 436 Of his diete mesurable was he For it was of no superfluitee. *c* **1386** —— *Nun's Pr. T.* 107 This dreem.. Cometh of greet superfluytee Of youre rede Colera. *c* **1450** *Mirk's Festial* 126/2 þe herys of his berd þat comyth of superfluyte of humors of þe stomok. **1483** CAXTON *G. de la Tour* e iv, The grete wast and superfluyte of her gownes. *c* **1532** DU WES *Introd. Fr.* in *Palsgr.* 898 Prolixite is superfluitie of wordes in declaryng a thynge. **1591** SPENSER *Ruines Rome* xxiii, In a vicious bodie, grose disease Soone growes through humours superfluitie. **1671** DRYDEN *Even. Love* Pref. a 2, I think there's no folly so great in any Poet of our Age as the superfluity and wast of wit was in some of our predecessors. **1733** CHEYNE *Engl. Malady* III. iv. (1734) 304 Superfluity will always produce Redundancy, whether it be of Phlegm or Choler. **1820** LAMB *Elia* Ser. I. *South-sea House*, Sums.. set down with formal superfluity of ciphers. **1862** DARWIN *Orchids* vi. 276 Thus the act of fertilization is completed, and there is no superfluity in the means employed.

† **b.** *in, of, to superfluity*: in or to excess. *Obs.*

c **1430** *Wyclif's Bible* 1 Chron., Prol., Siche thingis that weren addid to of superfluyte, he markyde with litil ȝerdis. *c* **1440** *Jacob's Well* 136 ȝif þou haue a coueytous loue to superfluyte of temperall ryches. **1562** BULLEIN *Bulwarke, Bk. Sick Men* 51 If there be twoo humours, equall aboundyng together, extremely in superfluite.

c. Unnecessary action or procedure. *arch.*

Cf. SUPERFLUOUS *a.* 2b.
c **1420** ? LYDG. *Assembly of Gods* 1824 To make exposicion therof, new or olde, Were but superfluyte. **1905** R. GARNETT *Shakespeare* 85 So crammed the Court is with particulars, More to adduce were superfluity.

3. A thing or part that is in excess of what is necessary, or that can be dispensed with. Chiefly *pl.*

c **1400** tr. *Secreta Secret., Gov. Lordsh.* 77 Whenne superfluytes waxen in hem, þes tokenynges sewen. **1474** CAXTON *Chesse* III. i. (1883) 76 A crokyd hachet for to cutte of the superfluytees of the vignes and trees. **1553** EDEN *Treat. Newe Ind.* (Arb.) 37 *marg.*, Ryches and superfluites contemned. **1611** *Bible* Transl. Pref. ¶3 What thanks had he for cutting off the superfluities of the lawes? **1628** T. SPENCER *Logick* 189 The superfluities of a definition are 6. **1650** BULWER *Anthropomet.* 221 Like a superfluity it is every moneth driven forth the wombe. **1773** JOHNSON *Let. to Boswell* 24 [22] Feb., Some superfluities I have expunged, and some faults I have corrected,.. but the main fabrick of the work remains as it was. **1776** ADAM SMITH *W.N.* I. xi. III. I. 239 When we are in want of necessaries we must part with all superfluities. **1860** EMERSON *Cond. Life, Culture* Wks. (Bohn) II. 374 Self-denial.. that saves on superfluities and spends on essentials.

† **4.** Action or conduct characterized by or exhibiting excess or extravagance; immoderate indulgence or expenditure; an instance of this. *Obs.*

c **1386** CHAUCER *Pard. T.* 9 They.. eten also and drynken ouer hir myght, Thurgh which they doon the deuel sacrifise .. By superfluytee abhomynable. *c* **1425** *St. Mary of Oignies* II. iv. in *Anglia* VIII. 161/32 Whan a man fleeþ superfluyte, [he] sumtyme fallith into chynchery. **1432–50** tr. *Higden* (Rolls) IV. 51 He.. ȝafe hym to ydelnes, lecchery, and to superfluites, wastenge nyȝhtes in lechery and synne. **1523** LD. BERNERS *Froiss.* I. ccxi. 252 He shewed many thynges to fall on the prelates of the Churche, for the great superfluitie and pryde that was as than vsed amonge theym. **1541** *Test. Ebor.* (Surtees) VI. 139, I will that.. no superfluyte be mayde at my buriall. **1600** HOLLAND *Livy* XXXIV. iii. 854 That we might not be stinted and gaged in our excessive expenses, in our dissolute profusion, in costly vanities and superfluities. **1651** HOBBES *Leviath.* II. xxx. 179 They,.. whom superfluity, or sloth carrieth after their sensuall pleasures. **1801** *Farmer's Mag.* Jan. 82 A rigid economy of our resources,.. a retrenchment of every superfluity on the part of the opulent.

† **superfluli,** *adv. Obs. rare.* [f. SUPERFLUE *a.* + -LY².] Superfluously.

c **1383** *Concl. Loll.* in *Eng. Hist. Rev.* (1911) Oct. 744/2 It is not leful to swere fals neiþir trewe superfluli oþir in veyn. **1388** WYCLIF *Ps.* xxx. 7 [xxxi. 6] Thou hatist hem that kepen vanytees superfluli. **1395** PURVEY *Remonstr.* (1851) 83 To charge cristene men nedelesli or superfluli with nouelries vnherd, not groundid in holy scripture.

ˌ**superfluoˈrescence.** *Physics.* [SUPER- 6c.] The co-operative emission of radiation by a system of atoms as a result of fluorescence and the spontaneous correlation of excited atomic states; also, superradiance.

1966 *Jrnl. Appl. Physics* XXXVII. 682 (*heading*) Studies of ruby superfluorescence and population inversion. **1974** *Sci. Amer.* June 31/1 Since short-pulse laser systems must store large amounts of energy prior to pulse amplification, high gain coefficients in large-aperture amplifiers present two difficult problems. The first is termed superfluorescence. This is simply the normal fluorescence emitted spontaneously by the excited laser material, amplified by the gain of the material itself. **1975** BONIFACIO & LUGIATO in *Physical Rev.* A. XI. 1507/2 The system spontaneously creates correlations, i.e., a macroscopic dipole which gives rise to a pulse whose maximum intensity is proportional to N^2 and whose time duration is proportional to N^{-1}. We call this phenomenon superfluorescence. **1980** *Nature* 8 May 70/1 Superfluorescence produces radiation pulses which have much larger amplitudes than those which one would obtain in normal incoherent atomic radiation processes.

Hence ˌ**superfluoˈrescent** *a.*

1973 *Appl. Physics Lett.* XXII. 79/2 Figure 1 illustrates the repetitive superfluorescent pulses observed at 3370 Å in N_2. **1977** R. L. BYER in Harper & Wherrett *Nonlinear Optics* ii. 89 For efficient superfluorescent operation the input noise field must be amplified by approximately 10^{16}.

superfluous (s(j)uːˈpɜːfluːəs), *a.* (*sb.*) Also 5–6 **superfluouse,** (6 **-ose,** *Sc.* **-fluus, -fluis, -flowis, -flouis**). [f. L. *superfluus*: see SUPERFLUE and -OUS.]

1. That exceeds what is sufficient; of which there is more than enough; excessively abundant or numerous.

1432–50 tr. *Higden* (Rolls) III. 459 We ȝiffe not attendaunce to superfluous meytes, wherefore we be not seke. **1483** CAXTON *Cato* C vj b, Thou oughtest not to stryue .. wyth them that ben ful of superfluous wordes. **1526** *Pilgr. Perf.* (W. de W. 1531) 54 We .. sholde.. dygge our vyne wele .. & cutte away the superfluous braunches. **1540–1** ELYOT *Image Gov.* 72 For as muche as I suppose that ye call theym superfluouse humours, whiche are more than conuenient to the naturall proporcion and temperature of the body. **1603** SHAKS. *Meas. for M.* III. i. 153, I haue no superfluous leysure, my stay must be stolen out of other affaires. *c* **1655** MILTON *1st Sonn. to Cyriack Skinner* 13 Heav'n.. disapproves that care,.. That with superfluous burden loads the day. **1764** *Museum Rust.* IV. 22 To take off any superfluous or ill-placed shoots. **1772** *Junius Lett.* lxviii. (1788) 347, I shall state.. the several statutes.. omitting superfluous words. **1860** TYNDALL *Glac.* I. ii. 28 Divesting myself of all superfluous clothes. **1880** HAUGHTON *Phys. Geog.* v. 224 Lake Tanganika discharges its superfluous waters into the southern branch of the Congo.

2. a. That is not needed or required; unnecessary, needless, uncalled-for.

c **1450** tr. *De Imitatione* III. xxxi. 101 What art þou made wery wiþ superfluous cures? **1534** MORE *Treat. Passion* Wks. 1281/1 To long for yᵉ knowledge of lesse necessarye learning, or delite in debating of sundrye superfluous problemes. **1581** in D. Digges *Compleat Ambass.* (1655) 420 Your abode there is but superfluous, and more chargeable.. then serviceable. **1597** MORLEY *Introd. Mus.* Annot., Seeing therefore further discourse wil be superfluous, I wil heere make an ende. **1639** SALTMARSHE *Policy* 96 If you have beene neglected by any, and thought superfluous. **1736** BUTLER *Anal.* II. i. Wks. 1874 I. 152 To say revelation is a thing superfluous.. is, I think, to talk quite wildly. **1775** JOHNSON *Let. to Mrs. Thrale* 13 July, Your anxiety about your other babies is, I hope, superfluous. **1824** W. IRVING *T. Trav.* I. I. vi. 80 The forms and ceremonies of marriage began to be considered superfluous bonds. **1855** PRESCOTT *Philip II* II. xiv. I. 299 After the oath of allegiance he had once taken a new one seemed superfluous. **1898** F. D. HOW *Life Bp. W. How* xviii. 253 This warning was not superfluous.

absol. **1831** CARLYLE *Sart. Res.* I. vii, A State of Nature, affecting by its singularity, and Old-Roman contempt of the superfluous.

b. Often in impers. phr. with inf.

1530 PALSGR. 27, I thinke it but superfluous to kepe suche ordre in all other consonantes. **1559** in Strype *Ann. Ref.* (1709) I. App. x. 439 It is a superfluous thinge.. to call into judgment agaíne matters which have ben tried. **1656** COWLEY *Misc.* Pref., Some of them made when I was very young, which it is perhaps superfluous to tell the Reader. **1713** BERKELEY *Hylas & Phil.* I. Wks. 1871 I. 282 It is therefore superfluous to inquire particularly concerning each of them. **1831** LAMB *Elia* Ser. II. *Ellistoniana*, To descant upon his merits as a Comedian would be superfluous. **1873** HAMERTON *Intell. Life* x. vii. 370 It is superfluous to recommend idleness to the unintellectual, but the intellectual too often undervalue it.

c. *transf.* Of a person: Doing more than is necessary. *rare.*

1596 SHAKS. *1 Hen. IV*, I. ii. 12, I see no reason, why thou shouldest bee so superfluous, to demaund the time of the day. **1667** MILTON *P.L.* IV. 832 If ye know, Why ask ye, and superfluous begin Your message, like to end as much in vain? **1880** *Daily News* 3 Jan. 2/2 We will not be so superfluous as to criticise this amusing drawing.

† **d.** Of no account or effect; unprofitable, vain. *Obs. rare.*

a **1533** LD. BERNERS *Gold. Bk. M. Aurel.* (1546) Riv, Damsels.. thinketh all their tyme lost, and superfluous vnto the day of theyr mariage. **1609** *Bible* (Douay) Wisd. xi. 16 Some erring did worshippe dumme serpents, and superfluous beastes. **1654** BRAMHALL *Just Vind.* viii. (1661) 241 This challenge of infallibility diminisheth their authority, discrediteth their definitions, and maketh them to be superfluous things.

† **3. a.** Exceeding what is right, desirable, normal, or usual; immoderate, inordinate. *Obs.*

c **1450** *Mankind* 232 in *Macro Plays* 9 Be-ware of excesse! þe superfluouse gyse I wyll þat ȝe refuse. **1533** GAU *Richt Vay* 95 Al inordinat and superfluis desiris in meittis and drinkkis and slepinge. **1567** MAPLET *Gr. Forest* 36 His stalke or bodie.. is somewhat grosse or superfluous. **1575** in *Maitl. Club Misc.* I. 114 The pompious convoy and superflouis banketting to Margerat Denelstoun the day of hir mariage. **1611** *Bible* Lev. xxi. 18 A blind man, or a lame, or he that hath a flat nose, or any thing superfluous. **1613** SHAKS. *Hen. VIII*, I. i. 99 A proper Title of a Peace, and purchas'd At a superfluous rate.

† **b.** *Mus.* = AUGMENTED *ppl. a.* 2b. *Obs.*

1753 *Chambers' Cycl.* Suppl., *Superfluous* interval, in music, is one that exceeds a true diatonic interval by a semitone minor. Thus the *Superfluous* second, or tone, contains a semitone minor more than a tone, or greater second. **1864** ENGEL *Mus. Anc. Nat.* 361 A superfluous second may, in sound at least, be taken as identical with a minor third. **1866** [see PRIME *sb.*² 4b].

† **4.** Having, consuming, or expending more than enough; superabundantly supplied; extravagant in expenditure. Const. *in, with. Obs.*

1535 COVERDALE *Isa.* v. 11 Wo be vnto them that ryse vp early to vse them selues in dronkynnes, and yet at night are more superfluous with wyne. **1585** T. WASHINGTON tr. *Nicholay's Voy.* III. xi. 90 b, The dressing of their meat.. differeth from ours, being so superfluous, curious, and delicate,.. whereas.. theirs is scant, bare, and grosse. **1605** SHAKS. *Lear* II. iv. 268 Our basest Beggers Are in the poorest thing superfluous. **1667** MILTON *P.L.* VIII. 27 Reasoning I oft admire, How Nature wise and frugal could commit Such disproportions, with superfluous hand So many nobler Bodies to create, Greater so manifold to this one use. **1711** J. GREENWOOD *Engl. Gram.* 233 Our Alphabet is deficient in some respects, and superfluous in others.

5. Special collocations: ***superfluous hair***, bodily hair considered to be unattractive in women, esp. on the face; ***superfluous woman***, a woman unlikely to marry, because of a surplus of women over men in the population; also ***superfluous girl***.

1876 GEO. ELIOT *Dan. Der.* II. III. xxi. 49 The sad faces of the four superfluous girls, each, poor thing.. having her peculiar world which was of no importance to any one else. **1800** in C. W. Cunnington *Feminine Attitudes* (1935) ii. 44, I shall sell a compound to take off all superfluous hair. **1873** *Young Englishwoman* Aug. 414/1 Will you kindly tell us.. whether you know of any depilatory that may be safely used for the removal of superfluous hair? **1933** D. L. SAYERS *Murder must Advertise* iv. 69 Do you suffer from superfluous hair? **1976** CADOGAN & CRAIG *You're a Brick, Angela!* v. 74 Superfluous hair, poor complexions and excessive perspiration preoccupied many readers. **1886** L. M. ALCOTT *Jo's Boys* i. 22 There is a plenty for the 'superfluous women' to do... I.. am very glad.. that my profession will make me a useful.. spinster. **1911** G. B. SHAW *Getting Married* Pref. 140 In our population there are about a million monogamically superfluous women, yet it is quite impossible to say of any given unmarried woman that she is one of the superfluous. **1978** CADOGAN & CRAIG *Women & Children First* vii. 133 The 1921 census showed a 1,700,000 surplus of women over men as a result of the slaughter of the war years.. the so-called superfluous woman.

superfluously (s(j)uːˈpɜːfluːəslɪ), *adv.* [f. prec. + -LY².] In a superfluous manner or degree.

1. More than sufficiently; in excess of what is proper or necessary; superabundantly.

1502 ATKYNSON tr. *De Imitatione* I. xxv. (1893) 178 They labour moche, & speke but lytell superfluously. **1584** COGAN *Haven Health* ccxi. (1636) 215, I advise all men not to linger the time long in eating and drinking superfluously. **1615** W. LAWSON *Country Housew. Garden* (1626) 24 To dresse the roots of trees, to take away the tawes, and tangles, that.. grow superfluously and disorderly. **1751** SMOLLETT *Per. Pickle* (1779) I. iv. 29 Her attention to the guests was superfluously hospitable. **1818** SCOTT *Hrt. Midl.* xxvi, She was now amply or even superfluously provided with the means of encountering the expenses of the road.

2. In addition to what is needed; hence, without necessity, unnecessarily, needlessly.

1557 RECORDE *Whetst.* B4b, Not onely superfluously, but also falsely, should thei bee placed here: seynge thei doe belong to other places of right. **1653** H. MORE *Antid. Ath.* II. x. §6 Discriminative Providence,.. doing nothing superfluously or in vain. **1738** WARBURTON *Div. Legat.* I. I. iv. 40 As making God act unnecessarily and superfluously. **1861** LD. ACTON *Lett.* (1909) 235 Do not superfluously imitate the Cardinal. **1884** tr. *Lotze's Logic* 165 It is difficult .. to prove.. that *Q* also has the predicate *z* which is superfluously added in the definition actually given.

† **3.** Beyond measure, excessively, inordinately, extravagantly. *Obs.*

1528 MORE *Dyaloge* I. Wks. 157/1 Pryde longed superfluously to gete by couetyse and gredynes many folkes lyuynges in his owne handes. **1528** PAYNELL *Salerne's Regim.* Lijb, The wyne..shulde be alayde with moche water..but nat so superfluously alayde..than as in sommer. **1584** COGAN *Haven Health* clxxvi. (1636) 161 Sea fish is of better nourishment, then fresh water fish..because it is not so superfluously moist. **1597** A. M. tr. *Guillemeau's Fr. Chirurg.* 21/1 Immediatlye therafter the water superfluoselye issueth therout. **1603** LD. STIRLING *Darius* IV. ii, Those gorgeous halles, With fourniture superfluouslie faire.

superfluousness (s(j)uːˈpɜːfluːəsnɪs). [f. SUPERFLUOUS + -NESS.] Superfluity.

a **1540** BARNES *Wks.* (1573) 211/1 All onely I spake against the superfluousnes, and the abuse of them [*sc.* possessions]. **1561** T. NORTON *Calvin's Inst.* II. 301 This semeth a weake superfluousnes of wordes. **1567** MAPLET *Gr. Forest* 39 Crowtoe..being drunken..with Wine purgeth the Gall of his superfluousnesse. **1600** SURFLET *Countrie Farme* VI. xxii. 795 Such wines doe not load the bodie with superfluousnes of serous excrements. **1897** *Current Hist.* (Buffalo, U.S.) VII. 380 The superfluousness of royal state. **1899** 'A. HOPE' *King's Mirror* xviii. 192 A state of conscious and wretched superfluousness.

superflux (ˈs(j)uːpəflʌks). [ad. med.L. *superfluxus*, f. *superfluĕre*: see SUPERFLUE and FLUX.]

1. A superfluity, superabundance, or surplus.

1605 SHAKS. *Lear* III. iv. 35 Take Physicke, Pompe, Expose thy selfe to feele what wretches feele, That thou maist shake the superflux to them. **1632** ROWLEY *Woman Never Vexed* I. i. B3, To groane under the superflux of blessings. **1775** S. J. PRATT *Liberal Opin.* cix. (1783) IV. 32 Shall they steal their own necessaries from the superflux of another? **1809** MALKIN *Gil Blas* x. ii. ¶5 Hadst thou but thrown to them the superflux of that abundance, in which..thou rolledst. **1826** LAMB *Elia* Ser. II. *Popular Fallacies* vi, If nothing else could be said for a feast, this is sufficient, that from the superflux there is usually something left for the next day. **1872** BROWNING *Fifine* xliv, Art..discards the superflux, Contributes to defect. **1880** SWINBURNE *Stud. Shaks.* i. 36 In these two there is no flaw, no outbreak, no superflux, and no failure.

2. An overflowing, or excessive flow, of water or other liquid.

1760 S. DERRICK *Lett.* (1767) I. 102 Another very remarkable waterfall is the superflux of a collection of water on the top of the high mountain of Mongerlogh. **1779** G. KEATE *Sketches fr. Nat.* (ed. 2) II. 209 The astonishing supply of water..the superflux of which clears all the drains and sewers. **1897** *Allbutt's Syst. Med.* III. 235 A superflux of the urinary water..without any increase of the urinary solids.

ˈsuperfly, *a.* and *sb. U.S. slang.* [SUPER- 9a: cf. FLY *a.* 1.]

A. *adj.* **a.** Very good, excellent, the best (esp. in the context of drugs). **b.** *spec.* Typical of the film character Super Fly (see quot. 1975[1]). Also with capital initial.

1971 R. WOODLEY in *Esquire* Apr. 79/1 'That,' he said in crisp, sure tones, 'is top-shelf coke. Super-fly.' **1971** —— in *New York* 30 Aug. 29/1 They figure if the cat O.D.'d, it must have been some superfly dope. **1974** *Florida FL Reporter* XIII. 50/2 A kind of Swahili-speaking Superfly image. **1975** *Wentworth & Flexner's Dict. Amer. Slang* Suppl. 747/2 *Superfly*,..very wonderful, desirable, or attractive... Became popular after the 1972 motion picture *Super Fly*, about a cocaine dealer in Harlem. **1975** *Los Angeles Times* 14 July II. 5/3 Last year a ninth-grader impressed the entire student body on several occasions by wearing flashy 'super fly' suits. **1976** *National Observer* (U.S.) 8 May 16/2 Ban outlandish and distracting clothes... No Superfly suits, no platform shoes. **1977** E. LEONARD *Unknown Man No. 89* vii. 67 The beauty parlor... Get his superfly hair fixed up.

B. *sb.* [From the title of the film: see sense b of the adj. above.] One who sells illegal drugs, a 'pusher'.

1973 *Black Panther* 7 July 7/3 The high level dope pushers, the 'Super Flys', were the target. **1974** *Black World* Sept. 25/2 *Long Black Song* tells us, here in the 1970's, that the days of darky entertainers, superflies, sweetbacks, and Melindas, if not over, are numbered.

superfœtation, var. SUPERFETATION.

superfrontal (ˈs(j)uːpəfrʌntəl). [ad. med.L. *superfrontāle*: see SUPER- and FRONTAL *sb.*]

1. [SUPER- 3.] A covering of silk or stuff hanging over the upper edge of an altar frontal.

1858 *Direct. Anglic.* (ed. J. Purchas) 5 The slab of the Altar should be covered with the cere-cloth, which in its turn is covered by the superfrontal, which hangs down about ten inches below. **1903** *Westm. Gaz.* 7 Sept. 10/2 A lady has presented to St. Paul's Cathedral a magnificent frontal and superfrontal.

2. [SUPER- 1d.] A dossal.

[**1844** PUGIN *Gloss. Eccl. Orn.* s.v. *Frontal*, A piece of richly embroidered stuff was also frequently hung above the altar, called a Super-frontale, or upper Frontal, being in fact a low dossell.] **1887** *Hook's Ch. Dict.*, *Super-frontal.* I. Originally a decoration attached to the wall behind and above the altar.

superfusate (s(j)uːpəˈfjuːzeɪt). *Med.* [f. SUPERFUSE *v.* + *-ate*, after *filtrate*, *precipitate*.] Any solution which has been used in the process of superfusion.

1970 *Proc. Soc. Exper. Biol. & Med.* CXXXIII. 1373/2 The presence of a constant concentration of LH in the superfusate in this system furnishes an appropriate control to evaluate the release obtained in response to hypothalamic extracts. **1979** *Experientia* XXXV. 225/2, 5-min fractions of superfusate were collected serially in glass vials.

superfuse (s(j)uːpəˈfjuːz), *v.* [f. L. *superfūs-*, pa. ppl. stem of *superfundĕre*: see SUPER- 2 and FUSE *v.* In sense 3, a new formation on SUPERFUSION 2.]

1. a. *trans.* To pour over or *on* something.

1657 TOMLINSON *Renou's Disp.* 162* Either a Ptisane or decoction..must be superfused. **1677** GALE *Crt. Gentiles* IV. II. viii. §3. II. 449 This Holy Spirit from the beginning of the World is said..to be superfused on the waters. *a* **1700** EVELYN *Diary* 13 Dec. 1685, Pouring first a very cold liquor into a glass, and super-fusing on it another.

b. *Med.* To subject (tissue) to, or employ (fluid) in, the technique of superfusion. Also, of a liquid, to flow over the surface of (tissue) in a thin layer. Cf. PERIFUSE *v.*

1953 *Brit. Jrnl. Pharmacol. & Chemotherapy* VIII. 322/1 Two tissues were suspended one above the other and the same fluid was superfused over them both. **1964** *Ibid.* XXIII. 360 The blood superfused the second tissue and was then returned to the jugular vein by gravity. **1975** *Nature* 25 Dec. 754/2 The exposed suboesophageal ganglia were superfused with continuously flowing snail Ringer. **1978** *Ibid.* 29 June 765/2 Each stream of blood superfused a separate collagen strip which was excised from the Achilles tendon of a rabbit.

2. To sprinkle or affuse; to suffuse in baptism.

1657 J. WATTS *Scribe, Pharisee*, etc. III. 27 A young man of the Hebrews being desperately sick and calling for baptism, in want of water was superfused with sand. *a* **1834** COLERIDGE *Lit. Rem.* (1836) II. 409 'Sprinkled' [with water], or rather affused or superfused.

3. To cool (a liquid) to a temperature below its melting-point without causing it to solidify; to supercool, overcool, undercool.

1902 *Encycl. Brit.* XXVIII. 568/1 It is generally possible to cool a liquid several degrees below its normal freezing-point without a separation of crystals... A liquid in this state is said to be 'undercooled' or 'superfused'.

Hence **superˈfused** *ppl. a.*, subjected to superfusion; **superˈfusing** *ppl. a.*, that superfuses.

1902 [see sense 3 of the vb.]. **1953** *Brit. Jrnl. Pharmacol. & Chemotherapy* VIII. 322/2 Stoppage of the flow may itself cause contraction of superfused muscle. **1977** *Nature* 6 Jan. 85/2 Test solutions were assayed..by their effects on isolated, superfused smooth-muscle organs. **1980** *Ibid.* 3 Jan. 93/1 (*caption*) Potassium chloride was added..to the superfusing fluid for 2-min periods at intervals of 16 min.

superfusion (s(j)uːpəˈfjuːʒən). [ad. late L. *superfūsio*, *-ōnem*, n. of action f. *superfūs-*, *superfundĕre* to SUPERFUSE.]

1. [SUPER- 2.] **a.** The action or operation of pouring liquid, etc. over something. Also *fig.*

1657 J. WATTS *Scribe, Pharisee*, etc. III. 68 Our way of superfusion, or aspersion with water. **1867** J. W. HALES in Farrar *Ess. Lib. Educ.* 307 Is what is called classical instruction at our schools anything better than a more or less copious superfusion of facts? **1871** NAPHEYS *Prev. & Cure Dis.* II. ii. 455 In cases of delirium tremens with high fever, what is called cold superfusion may be used while the patient is held in the warm bath.

b. *Med.* The technique of causing a stream of liquid to run over the surface of a piece of suspended tissue, keeping it viable and allowing the interchange of substances between it and the fluid to be observed.

1953 *Brit. Jrnl. Pharmacol. & Chemotherapy* VIII. 321/1 A piece of intestine may be suspended in air and kept in good condition by a stream of a suitable solution running over its surface... This technique may be called superfusion, since the fluid runs over the tissue, by analogy with perfusion, in which the fluid runs through the tissue. **1970** *Proc. Soc. Exper. Biol. & Med.* CXXXIII. 1373/2 Continuous superfusion of a single pituitary gland might also permit new approaches to the study of mechanisms and dynamics of LH release. **1980** *Nature* 3 Jan. 92/2 Superfusion of these slices for 2 min with Krebs' solution containing added KCl ..increased the tritium overflow.

2. [SUPER- 4.] The cooling of a liquid below its melting-point without solidification taking place.

1866 *Sci. Rev.* Dec. 145/3 There is..a marked difference between the circumstances in which solidification takes place in superfusion and supersaturation. **1880** W. C. ROBERTS *Introd. Metallurgy* 31 The cooling mass of molten metal does not 'flash' or pass through the remarkable state known as 'superfusion.'

supergalactic, -galaxy: see SUPER- 5c.

supergene (ˈs(j)uːpədʒiːn), *a. Min.* [f. SUPER- 1a: see -GEN 3.] Of an ore or mineral: enriched or deposited by a downward-moving solution; involving deposition by a downward-moving solution.

1914 F. L. RANSOME in *Bull. U.S. Geol. Survey* No. 540. 153 The suggestion is offered that minerals deposited by generally downward-moving and initially cold solutions may be termed supergene minerals. **1944** [see *paravauxite* s.v. PARA-[1] 2c]. **1977** A. HALLAM *Planet Earth* 112 Where leaching of sulfide ore deposits occurs, residual red and brown iron hydroxyoxide cappings (gossans) are left, and other elements can be carried down and precipitated in a zone of 'supergene' enrichment near the water table.

ˈsupergene, *sb. Genetics.* [f. SUPER- 6c + GENE[1].] A group of closely linked genes, freq. having related functions.

1949 DARLINGTON & MATHER *Elem. Genetics* ii. 46 Thus the cross between male and female is a back-cross for the X-Y pair of chromosomes or, if you like, the X-Y supergene, and half the offspring are of each sex. *Ibid.* v. 118 The differences could be interpreted as two gene differences so closely linked as never to recombine (two-gene system). Or one of them could be regarded as associated with an inversion inhibiting recombination (one super-gene system). **1978** *Nature* 13 July 164/1 The *t* complex seems to provide an example of a 'supergene'—a large chromosomal segment with multiple genes involved in similar, or closely related functions.

ˈsupergiant, *sb.* and *a.* [SUPER- 6c.]

A. *sb.* **a.** A very large star that is even brighter than a giant, in many cases despite being relatively cool. (The dominant sense.)

1927 H. N. RUSSELL et al. *Astronomy* II. xxi. 725 Certain very bright stars, much more brilliant than the ordinary giants, are sometimes called super-giants. **1959** *Listener* 26 Feb. 370/2 A very brilliant white super-giant such as Rigel. **1978** PASACHOFF & KUTNER *University Astron.* xi. 294 The sun..is only one-millionth as luminous as the most brilliant of the red supergiants.

b. A supergiant galaxy (see sense b of the adj. below).

1975 S. VAN DEN BERGH in A. Sandage et al. *Stars & Stellar Systems* IX. xii. 531 Assuming the brightest stars in the Sc giant galaxy M33 to be similar to those in the Sc supergiant M100.

B. *adj.* **1.** *Astr.* **a.** Designating a star that is a supergiant.

1930 R. H. BAKER *Astronomy* ix. 372 Super-giant stars are extraordinarily luminous giants. **1973** *Daily Tel.* 29 Sept. 13/1 Under the best conditions it might be possible with glasses to glimpse the red supergiant star Antares in Scorpius. **1981** *Nature* 15 Oct. 513/1 Red giant and super-giant stars have long been favourites of professional and amateur astronomers.

b. Of a galaxy: in the brightest of five luminosity classes.

1960 S. VAN DEN BERGH in *Astrophysical Jrnl.* CXXXI. 216 The nomenclature for the luminosity classes has been chosen to agree with that used in the Yerkes system of stellar luminosity classification: (I) supergiant galaxy, (II) bright giant galaxy, (III) normal giant galaxy, (IV) subgiant galaxy, and (V) dwarf galaxy. **1978** *Sci. Amer.* Nov. 103/1 It [*sc.* the Perseus cluster]..harbors a centrally located supergiant elliptical galaxy, which is a strong radio source and is surrounded by an X-ray-emitting cloud and a massive halo of stars.

2. *gen.* Extremely large.

1977 *Time* 1 Aug. 37/1 In June a high-pressure air mass began building up just east of the Rockies. It stayed there, with some up-and-down movement of air, and slowly turned into a supergiant oven. **1981** *Sci. Amer.* Nov. 66/2 Several supergiant natural-gas fields were found north of the Arctic Circle.

ˌsupergranuˈlation. *Astr.* [SUPER- 6b.] A pattern of large convective cells, each thousands of miles across, covering the surface of the sun. So **superˈgranular** *a.*, of or pertaining to supergranulation; **superˈgranule**, an individual cell of this kind.

1962 R. B. LEIGHTON et al. *Astrophysical Lett.* CXXXV. 494 Some of the properties of the large cells suggest that they may be a giant system of convective cells—a supergranulation—analogous to the ordinary granulation but originating in deeper layers where the scale height is relatively great. **1964** *Astrophysical Jrnl.* CXL. 1120 The velocity cells (called 'supergranules')..have an average diameter of 32000 km. **1967** K. O. KIEPENHEUER in J. N. Xanthakis *Solar Physics* xiii. 385 Even large spots, with their strong magnetic fields and complex structures, seem to be tied into the pattern of the supergranular network. **1973** *Nature* 14 Dec. 412/1 Spicules..cluster favourably in regions of enhanced magnetic fields along supergranular boundaries within the chromosphere. **1976** D. F. GRAY *Observation & Analysis Stellar Photospheres* xviii. 442 The gas flow in a supergranule mimics that of the granule, but the size of the convective cell is about 20 times as large..and there is no brightness variation across a supergranule. **1977** *New Scientist* 13 Jan. 77/1 The supergranulation 'cells', unlike the small convective granulations visible on the Sun's surface, are of the order of 15000 to 30000 km across.

supergrass, -gravity: see SUPER- 6c, b.

†**superˈgression.** *Obs. rare.* [ad. late L. *supergressio*, *-ōnem*, n. of action f. *supergredī*, f. *super-* SUPER- 9b + *gradī* to step, walk.] The exceeding of a limit; excess.

1477 NORTON *Ord. Alch.* iv. in Ashm. (1652) 47 For doubt of perrills many moe then one, And for supergression of our stone. *a* **1631** DONNE *Serm., Ps. xxxviii. 4* (1649) 186 Above those exaltations, and supergressions of sin.

ˈsupergroup. a. [SUPER- 5c.] A group composed of a number of other groups.

1943 M. SCHLAUCH *Gift of Tongues* 63 Finno-Ugric and Nenets..together form a super-group. **1969** *Proc. Geol. Soc.* Aug. 145 The following formal lithostratigraphical divisions are recognized: *Supergroup, Group, Formation, Member, Bed. Ibid.*, A supergroup consists of two or more adjacent and naturally related or associated groups. **1972** *Sci. Amer.* Sept. 133/2 In the next step most of these groups are combined, five at a time, to form 'super-groups' of 80 conversations each.

b. [SUPER- 6c.] In rock music: a group formed by star musicians from different bands. Also *loosely*, an exceptionally talented or successful group.

1970 *Times* 7 Jan. 7/1 What the pop world calls a super-group is a group formed by star musicians from ordinary groups. **1976** *Sounds* 11 Dec., I can only hope and pray that ..two supergroups will emerge, but they have one hell of a name to live up to. **1976** *New Musical Express* 17 Apr. 23/3 They're what's already been described as a pub-rock supergroup. **1980** *Washington Post* 4 Dec. D9 Last night,

The Police filled a packed Warner Theater with a lithe, sensual and utterly danceable brand of rock that is going to propel them to supergroup status in the next few years.

'superheat, *v.* [f. SUPER- 9 b + HEAT *v.*] *trans.* To heat to a very high temperature; *esp.* to raise the normal temperature of (steam); more widely, to heat (a substance) above the temperature of a phase transition without the change of phase occurring.

1859 *Times* 23 Apr. 10/4 The various proposed methods of superheating steam. **1861** *Leeds Mercury* 2 Nov., It is found most advantageous to superheat the steam to about 100 degrees above the temperature of plain steam. **1869** *Amer. Jrnl. Sci.* XCVII. 12 To subject the oils to a temperature above their boiling points, or in other words, to super-heat their vapors. **1875** KNIGHT *Dict. Mech.* 2333/1 *Steam-chimney*, an annular chamber around the chimney of a boiler-furnace for superheating steam. **1939** CARPENTER & ROBERTSON *Metals* II. xiv. 1194 Marked changes in the structure of cast iron could be produced by superheating the melt, i.e. heating to a temperature considerably higher than that required to melt the metal.

Hence **'superheat** *sb.*, the state of being superheated; the excess of temperature of a vapour above its temperature of saturation.

1884 *Methodist Mag.* 787 Solubility is increased by heat, superheat, and pressure. **1903** *Engineering Mag.* Feb. 756 A superheat of 100° F., or 55° C.

'super,heated, *ppl. a.* [f. SUPER- 9 b + HEATED *ppl. a.*]

1. a. (Of steam or vapour): Heated above its temperature of saturation. More widely, (of a substance) heated above the temperature of a phase transition without the change of phase occurring.

1857 MILLER *Elem. Chem., Org.* vi. §2. 375 Injecting superheated steam at a temperature of between 500° and 600° into heated fat. **1873** SPON *Workshop Rec.* Ser. I. 377/1 By applying superheated steam both time and fuel are saved. **1915** *Nature* 11 Feb. 662/1 The iodine which is transpired as superheated vapour is condensed there. **1931** G. W. TYRRELL *Volcanoes* vi. 161 Some of the material was melted up by the ascent of a highly super-heated lava.

b. *transf.* Operated by superheated steam.

1883 E. P. RAMSAY *Food Fishes N.S. Wales* 24 The offal.. of fish.. was disintegrated and dried by superheated system. **1911** *Daily News* 25 Jan. 2 The North-Western Company are now constructing.. twenty superheated engines.

2. *gen.* Heated above the ordinary temperature or degree; excessively heated or hot; also *fig.*

1866 *Spectator* 10 Mar. 267/2 This sort of superheated intellectual strain... The peculiar superheated grandeur and magnificence attached by Americans to the idea of the Union. **1880** A. R. WALLACE *Isl. Life* I. ix. 188 An additional reservoir of super-heated water. **1888** FENN *Off to Wilds* xxii. 157 They were up in one of the superheated rifts among the rocks, with the sun pouring down. **1912** *Hibbert Jrnl.* Oct. 30 This gathering of super-heated men.

So **'superheater**, an apparatus for super-heating steam; **'superheating** *vbl. sb.*, (*a*) the process of heating steam or vapour above its temperature of saturation; also more widely (cf. SUPERHEAT *v.*); (*b*) excessive heating, over-heating.

1861 *Leeds Mercury* 2 Nov., The temperature, immediately on leaving the *superheater, was as high as 600 degrees. **1886** *Encycl. Brit.* XXI. 824/1 Engines of large cylinder capacity to admit of great expansion, with surface-condensers and superheaters to the boilers. **1861** *Leeds Mercury* 2 Nov., Some parties entertain the idea that *superheating may be advantageously applied where steam is used for heating purposes. **1897** *Daily News* 16 Sept. 2/2 Other cold water is conveyed into a spiral coil and superheating chamber above the light. **1898** P. MANSON *Trop. Diseases* xii. 207 Super-heating of the blood. **1980** S. A. MORSE *Basalts & Phase Diagrams* iii. 28 Superheating of crystals above their melting temperature is a rare phenomenon.

super'heavy, *a.* (*sb.*). [SUPER- 9 a.]

a. *gen.* Extremely heavy, heavier than the normal. Occas. as *sb.*

1952 *Sci. Amer.* May 44/1 It is a job for accurate balancing and gyroscope controls.. and therefore an ideal spot for Hevimet, super-heavy Carboloy created-metal. **1974** *Physics Bull.* Dec. 578/3 The quarks give way to.. super-heavy mesonic matter and, ultimately, neutrons, protons and the lighter mesons. **1976** *Daily Times* (Lagos) 22 Sept. 30/1 That's how wrestling 'superheavy' Ray Apallon begins the open challenge to 'any of your Nigerian heavy-weight wrestlers'.

b. *Nucl. Physics.* Of, pertaining to, or designating an element with an atomic mass or atomic number greater than those of the naturally occurring elements; *spec.* having an atomic number of 110 or more and belonging to a group having a limited range of proton/neutron ratios which confer enhanced stability against radioactive decay. Also as *sb.*, such an element.

1955 J. A. WHEELER in W. Pauli *Niels Bohr* 183 The superheavy nuclei that are neutron stable. **1962** L. DEIGHTON *Ipcress File* xviii. 107 Tritium is also called super-heavy hydrogen. **1970** *Physics Bull.* Dec. 534/2 The success of this view.. has led to the suggestion that there exists a further 'island' of stability around mass number 300: superheavy nuclei which may have lifetimes from a fraction of a second, up to many years. **1971** *New Scientist* 18 Feb. 344/3 The radioactive counts from the mercury source showed the most promise for a superheavy. **1979** *Nature* 16 Aug. 549/2 There is no convincing evidence that superheavy elements have been discovered. **1980** *Physical Rev.* C. XXI. 1664/2 The recent theoretical estimates of low barriers.. are supported by the failure to detect superheavies in the ^{48}Ca + ^{248}Cm reaction.

super'helical, *a. Biochem.* [f. SUPERHELIX, after HELICAL *a.*] Belonging to or consisting of a superhelix.

1966 *Jrnl. Gen. Physiol.* XXXXIX. 125, I wonder whether you would explain again how you calculated the number of superhelical turns. **1974** *Nature* 5 Apr. 476/3 The superhelical structure imposes upon the DNA molecule a topological restraint. **1980** *Sci. Amer.* July 108/1 It is possible to gain a general understanding of how a left-handed superhelical coil.. is transformed into a right-handed interwound superhelix by considering the linking number.

Hence **super'helically** *adv.*; also **,superhe'licity**, the state of being superhelical.

1974 *Nature* 20 Sept. 248/2 The affinity of the repressor for the operator.. increases with increasing negative superhelicity up to a factor of approximately 14 for the DNA with – 160 superhelical turns. **1978** *Ibid.* 12 Jan. 128/2 Superhelically wound oligonucleosome fibres. **1980** A. KORNBERG *DNA Replication* i. 25 Supertwisting, supercoiling, and superhelicity are terms for the twisting upon itself of the duplex DNA strands.

'superhelix. *Biochem.* Pl. **-helices.** [SUPER- 5 c.] A helix formed from a helix; *spec.* a three-dimensional structure sometimes assumed by polypeptides, in which double protein or DNA helices are themselves coiled into a higher-order helix. Cf. SUPERCOIL *sb.*

1964 G. H. HAGGIS *Introd. Molecular Biol.* iv. 80, α-Helices probably twist together like the strands of a rope, in keratin and myosin, to form super-helices. **1971** *Nature* 5 Nov. 27 (*caption*) Since the normal DNA double helix is right handed, the superhelix is more likely to be left handed. **1980** *Sci. Amer.* July 100/1 In the chromatin.. of higher organisms the DNA is wound around a core of protein to form a left-handed solenoidal superhelix.

'superhet, colloq. abbrev. of next. Also *fig.*

1926 *Glasgow Herald* 12 Jan. 10 The real heart of a superhet set is the first detector. **1926** R. W. HUTCHINSON *Wireless* 236 The multivalve.. 'Super-Het' is scarcely a receiving set.. for a beginner. **1937** [see *direct vision* s.v. DIRECT *a.* 1 b]. **1951** R. HOGGART *Auden* vi. 195 So the scene for a work such as this [sc. *The Age of Anxiety*] must be a time-ridden, newspaper-headline-obsessed, 'superhet' city. **1960** *Practical Wireless* XXXVI. 342/2 The output is fed by a jack into the L.F. portion of a six transistor superhet. **1976** *CB Mag.* June 1/2 (Advt.), This handsomely styled 23-channel solid-state CB two-way radio features a.. dual-conversion superhet receiver with RF stage.

super'heterodyne, *a.* and *sb. Radio.* [f. SUPER(SONIC *a.* (and *sb.*) + HETERODYNE *a.*]

A. *adj.* Employing or involving a method of radio reception (also used in television) in which a signal from a tunable local oscillator is combined with the incoming carrier wave to produce an ultrasonic intermediate frequency whose value is fixed and predetermined, so that it is unnecessary to vary the tuning of the subsequent amplifier and detector and increased selectivity and amplification are possible.

1922 *Wireless World* 1 Apr. 11/1 The Armstrong super-heterodyne principle, in which the incoming signals are heterodyned before the first detector valve. **1934** *Times Rev. Year 1933* 1 Jan p. ix/4 Superheterodyne receivers were especially popular. **1966** *McGraw-Hill Encycl. Sci. & Technol.* XI. 257/1 Frequency-modulation (FM) receivers are almost always superheterodyne. **1976** *Gramophone* July 232/2 The superheterodyne circuit made modern radio possible. **1977** W. TUTE *Cairo Sleeper* vii. 128 'Hafiz the barman has a wireless set.'.. It was a superheterodyne job with valves.

B. *sb.* A superheterodyne receiver.

[**1921** *Q.S.T.* May 16/1 If a good U.S. amateur with such a set and an Armstrong Super could be sent to England, reception of U.S. amateurs would straightway become commonplace.] **1922** *Ibid.* July 7/1 Super-regeneration is.. the method that makes two tubes do all the work that ten used to do in the super-heterodyne. **1933** K. HENNEY *Radio Engin. Handbk.* xvii. 449 The h-f superheterodyne seldom has high sensitivity, unless the first or h-f tube is regenerative. **1940** [see CHASSIS 5]. **1965** *Wireless World* July 336/2 The various oscillators in superheterodynes have all set their own problems.

super-highway: see SUPER- 6 c.

superhuman (s(j)uːpəˈhjuːmən), *a.* (*sb.*) [ad. med.L. *superhūmānus*: see SUPER- 4 and HUMAN *a.* Cf. F. *surhumain*, It. *soprumano*, Sp., Pg. *sobrehumano*.] Above that which is human; more than human.

a. Of a quality, act, etc.: Higher than that of man; beyond the capacity or power of man.

1633 EARL MANCH. *Al Mondo* (1636) 203 This is the state of Loves life in God, which giveth a super-humane being unto man, man being yet on earth. *a* **1711** KEN *Hymns Evang.* Poet. Wks. 1721 I. 127 Bless'd water in the Font.. Though worthless in itself, in Sacred use It Graces super-human can produce. **1797** MRS. RADCLIFFE *Italian* i, There was no necessity for superhuman means to obtain such knowledge. **1864** PUSEY *Lect. Daniel* (1876) 453 The miracle of superhuman knowledge. **1874** H. ROGERS (*title*) The Superhuman Origin of the Bible Inferred from Itself. **1896** DK. ARGYLL *Philos. Belief* 326 Superhuman agencies and powers.

absol. **1876** GLADSTONE *Homeric Synchr.* 198 Such prodigies of valour as may fairly be.. considered to approximate to the superhuman.

b. Of a person or being: Higher than man; having a nature above that of man.

1824 MACAULAY *Misc. Writ.* (1860) I. 64 To describe superhuman beings in the language, and to attribute to them the actions, of humanity may be grotesque, unphilosophical, inconsistent. **1866** LIDDON *Bampton Lect.* vi. (1875) 296 Christ is a superhuman person.

c. In rhetorical or hyperbolical use: Higher or greater than that of any ordinary man; beyond the average human capacity, stature, etc.

1822 SCOTT *Nigel* vi, The superhuman yells which he uttered. **1867** FREEMAN *Norm. Conq.* I. v. 419 Seven months of almost superhuman energy. **1891** FARRAR *Darkn. & Dawn* l, While he was still steeped to the lips in super-human luxury.

d. as *sb.* Used to render G. *übermensch* SUPERMAN.

1896 W. WALLACE in *Academy* 1 Aug. 75/2 [Nietzsche] a hermit of the present, and a man, or rather a more than man, a 'superhuman', of the future.

,superhu'manity. [f. prec. + -ITY.] The character or quality of being superhuman (or a superman).

1797 T. GREEN *Diary Lover of Lit.* (1810) 45 The superhumanity of which scheme is finely exposed by Cicero in the next Book. *c* **1810** COLERIDGE *Lit. Rem.* (1838) III. 250 He meant by the word *Lord* his divinity, or at least essential super-humanity. *c* **1825** WORDSW. in Knight *Life* (1889) II. App. 319 The sublimity, the superhumanity, of his genius. **1892** ZANGWILL *Childr. Ghetto* I. i, Rich people .. radiating an indefinable aroma of superhumanity. **1903** [see SUPERMAN].

super'humanize, *v.* [Formed as prec. + -IZE.] *trans.* To make, or represent as, superhuman.

1854 MILMAN *Lat. Christ.* IV. vii. II. 149 Pure spirit, without any intermediate human, yet superhumanised, form. **1876** MEREDITH *Beauch. Career* xxxiv, There are touches of bliss in anguish that superhumanise bliss. **1894** STOPF. BROOKE *Tennyson* x. 367 Arthur is a little superhuman... Why did Tennyson superhumanise him?

super'humanly, *adv.* [-LY².] In a superhuman manner; to a degree beyond what is human.

1830 DE QUINCEY *R. Bentley* Wks. 1857 VII. 170 An author so superhumanly imaginative as Milton. **1856** R. A. VAUGHAN *Mystics* (1860) II. IX. ii. 295 To live, not humanly, but superhumanly. **1883** *Athenæum* 19 May 627/3 An astonishingly and almost superhumanly clever schoolboy.

So **super'humanness**, superhumanity.

1900 *Speaker* 10 Mar. 611/2 The Bismarckian trampling upon common conventions is part of the Bismarckian superhumanness.

super'humeral. [ad. late L. *superhumerāle* (Vulgate), neut. sing. (sc. *vestīmentum*) of **superhumerālis*: see SUPER 1 a and HUMERAL. Cf. OF. *superhumeral*, It. *superumerale*, etc.] An ecclesiastical vestment worn over the shoulders, as the Jewish ephod, or an amice or pallium; *fig.* a burden carried on the shoulders.

1606 BP. ANDREWES *Serm.* ii. (1631) 13 He.. Endured them; and endured, for them heavie things; a strange Superhumerall, the print whereof was to be seene on his shoulders. [**1688** HOLME *Armoury* III. iv. 187/1 The *Amictus*, or *Superhumerale*, which like the *Ephod* of the Priests and Levites, or Vail covers the Head and Shoulders of the Priest.] **1868** MARRIOTT *Vestiar. Christ.* xxix. 79 The Superhumeral or Ephod. This being so worn as to cover the shoulders, he [*sc.* Bede] regards it as typical of the labour of good works, of 'the easy yoke, and light burden'.

superhumerate, *v.* A spurious word, error in Richardson's *Dict.* for SUBHUMERATE (q.v. quot. 1628).

†**su'perial**, *a.*¹ *Obs.* [ad. med.L. **superiālis*, f. *superus* (see SUPERIOR) or *superius* adv. higher. Cf. *inferial*.] = SUPERIOR *a.* in various senses.

1432–50 tr. *Higden* (Rolls) III. 395 He.. callede certeyne spirittes.. superialle and inferialle. *a* **1545** BOORDE *Pronost.* Prol. in *Introd. Knowl.*, etc. (1870) 25 The son.. i lumynatynge as wel the inferyal planetes as yᵉ superyal planetes. **1547** —— *Brev. Health* lix. 26 b, A Canker, the whiche doth corode.. the superial partes of the body. **1561** *Godly Queene Hester* Prol. 11 Some.. Affirmed honour dewly to pertayne.. to power and superiall raigne. **1591** SPARRY tr. *Cattan's Geomancie* 2 It is the proper and naturall mouing of the bodies superiall and celestial. **1719** JONES in Toland *Hist. Druids* (1814) 240 There were in this land about a hundred superial Kings, that governed this land successively: that were of the British blood.

su'perial, *a.*² *nonce-word.* [f. SUPER *sb.* 3 a + -IAL.] Pertaining to a theatrical 'super'.

1885 J. K. JEROME *On the Stage* 61 His madness did not interfere at all with his superial duties.

superim'posable, *a.* [f. SUPERIMPOSE *v.* + -ABLE.] Capable of being superimposed.

1920 in WEBSTER. **1925** *Rep. Proc. Imperial Bot. Conf.* 1924 41 Repeated examination in the same and different years of families derived from the same matings or selfings ..gave rise to curves so similar as to be in many cases superimposable. **1933** *Jrnl. Theol. Stud.* XXXIV. 97 Private objects, such, e.g., as the different elliptical shapes seen by individuals at different distances, &c., from a circular plate, are often not compatible, congruent, or superimposable. **1971** *Nature* 9 July 106/2 The system is symmetric, for it is superimposable on its mirror image. **1979** *Dædalus* Summer 90 They are both interchangeable and superimposable.

ˌsuperimˈpose, *v.* [f. SUPER- 2 + IMPOSE *v.* after *superimposition*.]

1. *trans.* To impose or place (one object) *on* or *upon* another; to lay above or on the top.

a. *gen.*

1823 H. J. BROOKE *Introd. Crystallogr.* 291 The first plate of molecules which is superimposed on the primary plane. **1851** D. WILSON *Preh. Ann.* (1863) I. ix. 288 An ancient churchyard was superimposed on a still older cemetery. **1867** J. HOGG *Microsc.* I. ii. 142 Producing a mixture of all the colours by superimposing three films one on the other. **1892** *Photogr. Ann.* II. 211 One thickness of ruby paper with one thickness of orange paper superimposed.

b. *spec.* in *Geol.* in reference to stratification: always in pa. pple. (cf. SUPERIMPOSED 1).

1794 KIRWAN *Elem. Min.* (ed. 2) I. 362 These sandstones have been found crystallized in rhomboidal tables superimposed one upon the other. **1802** PLAYFAIR *Illustr. Hutton. The.* 88 The schistus was not super-imposed on the granite, after the formation of this last. **1863** LYELL *Antiq. Man* iii. 43 Four buried forests superimposed one upon the other.

2. *fig.* To cause to follow *upon* something else and to exist side by side with it.

1855 BAIN *Senses & Int.* III. iv. §9, I have the idea of a mountain and the idea of gold, and by superimposing the one upon the other, I can evoke the image of a mountain of gold. **1879** EARLE *Philol. Engl. Tongue* (ed. 3) §334 This diminutival form *-et*, *-ette*, was in old French often superimposed upon the effete diminutival *-el*. **1889** *Spectator* 28 Sept. 395/2 Superimposed on them are the Spaniards, and next to these the Italian, Swedish, English, and German settlers. **1897** *Allbutt's Syst. Med.* IV. 381 The puerperal kidney has a mixed nature; it is one of diffuse nephritis upon which granular contraction is rapidly superimposed.

3. To place (a person) in a position as a superior.

1902 W. L. MATHIESON *Politics & Relig.* xviii. II. 193 Their object had been to superimpose on the Presbyterian organisation certain officials.

4. *intr.* Of two figures or the like: to be capable of being brought into coincidence; to occupy the same positions in relation to their contexts.

1971 *Nature* 2 July 12/2 Counts from the highest polysome fraction superimpose on the zones corresponding to the two major light chains. **1972** *Sci. Amer.* Aug. 95/1 The degree to which the fields do not superimpose can be measured, and in this case there was a range of six degrees of horizontal disparity and two degrees of vertical disparity. **1975** *Nature* 10 Jan. 127/1 The sheets could then superimpose, forming the observed structures. **1978** *Ibid.* 27 July 389/2 (*caption*) Note that the peaks do not superimpose.

ˌsuperimˈposed, *ppl. a.* [f. prec. + -ED[1].]

1. a. Placed or laid upon something else; often *loosely* with pl. sb., laid one upon another.

1805–17 R. JAMESON *Char. Min.* (ed. 3) 123 They [*sc.* alterations of figures] are named superimposed, when they occur in the same part of the fundamental figure, and when the first alteration is modified by a second. **1832** GELL *Pompeiana* I. vi. 109 To bear the superimposed weight. **1834–5** J. PHILLIPS *Geol.* in *Encycl. Metrop.* (1845) VI. 703/1 Basaltic pillars, if permitted to assume their natural shapes, without pressing one against another, would resemble a number of superimposed spheroids. **1849** RUSKIN *Seven Lamps* v. §13. 148 The curious variations in the adjustments of the superimposed shafts. **1879** H. GEORGE *Progr. & Pov.* v. i. (1881) 252 Imagine a pyramid composed of superimposed layers.

b. *Phys. Geog.* Applied to 'a natural system of drainage that has been established on underlying rocks independently of their structure' (*Funk's Stand. Dict.* 1895).

1875 J. W. POWELL *Explor. Colorado Valley* 166 The beds in which the streams had their origin..have been swept away. I propose to call such superimposed valleys. **1898** I. C. RUSSELL *River Developm.* vii. 244 (*heading*) Superimposed streams. *Ibid.* 245 A drainage system inherited in this manner by one geological terrane from another is said to be superimposed. **1977** A. HALLAM *Planet Earth* 76/2 Alternatively, in superimposed drainage, the river courses may have initially developed on a cover of rocks whose structure was different to that of the rocks beneath, the upper beds having since disappeared through erosion.

2. *fig.* Superadded; caused to co-exist.

1850 DENISON *Clock & Watch-m.* 104 A secondary or superimposed motion to the hands. **1891** HARDY *Tess* xlvi, His heated face, which had also a superimposed flush of excitement.

3. Placed over another in rank.

1861 PEARSON *Early & Mid. Ages Eng.* 90 The strong Norman yoke and the superimposed Norman nobility crushed Angle and Dane and Saxon into Englishmen.

ˌsuperimˈposited, *a. rare.* [f. L. *superimpositus*, pa. pple. of *superimpōnĕre* (f. *super-* SUPER- 2 + *impōnĕre* to IMPONE) + -ED[1].] (See quot.)

1826 KIRBY & SP. *Entomol.* IV. xlvi. 350 Superimposited (*Superimpositum*). When the foot-stalk of the abdomen is inserted in the upper part of the postscutellum, so as to leave a considerable space between it and the postpectus.

ˌsuperimpoˈsition. [f. SUPER- 2 + IMPOSITION, after L. *superimpōnĕre* (see prec.).] The action of superimposing, or state of being superimposed; superposition.

1684 *Phil. Trans.* XIV. 674 The side OC = BC, CD = AC, the angle D = A, and OCD = BCA, which is manifest by taking the common angle ACO out of the 2 right angles BCO, ACD, therefore by superimposition the whole triangles are equal. **1851** RUSKIN *Stones Venice* I. i. §28 The arrangement of the nave pier in the form of a cross accompanies the superimposition of the vaulting shaft. **1879** H. GEORGE *Progr. & Pov.* II. ii. (1881) 97 Mexico, as Cortez found it, showed the superimposition of barbarism upon a higher development. **1907** *19th Cent.* Nov. 703 The superimposition of the utilitarian..civilisation of the West on the Indian civilisations.

So **superimˈposure**, something superimposed.

1875 BROWNING *Aristoph. Apol.* 1527 Show the base—The live rock latent under wave and foam: Superimposure these!

ˌsuperimˈpregnate, *v.* ? *Obs.* [SUPER- 13.] *trans.* To impregnate or imbue in addition, as a solution of one substance *with* another substance.

1677 GREW *Anat. Pl.* (1682) Lect. vii. 298 A Solution of above five Drachms of Nitre may be superimpregnated with no less quantity of Sal Armoniac. **1754** LEWIS in *Phil. Trans.* XLVIII. 658 A solution of platina, superimpregnated with as much mercury as it was capable of taking up.

ˌsuperimpregˈnation. [SUPER- 13.]

1. Impregnation with an additional substance.

1677 GREW *Anat. Pl.* (1682) Lect. vii. 296 With what difference of quantity this Superimprægnation would be made, upon the Solution of different Salts? *Ibid.* 298 The ascent of the Water upon a Superimpregnation, is the same, by whatsoever Salt the first Impregnation be made.

2. = SUPERFETATION. *rare*⁻⁰.

1727 BAILEY (vol. II), *Superimprægnation*, a second Conception, after one has conceived before. **1828** in WEBSTER (citing Coxe). **1859** MAYNE *Expos. Lex.*, *Superimpregnatio*..the same as *Superfœtatio*: superimpregnation.

ˌsuperinˈcumbence. *rare.* [f. next: see -ENCE.] The fact of being superincumbent.

a **1837** SIR E. BRYDGES (Worcester, 1860). **1846** LANDOR *Imag. Conv.*, *Odysseus* etc. Wks. I. 397/1 The highest nations are gasping for existence, crushed by the superincumbence of the lowest.

So **superinˈcumbency** (Ogilvie 1850).

ˌsuperinˈcumbent, *a.* [ad. L. *superincumbent-em*, pr. pple. of *superincumbĕre*: see SUPER- 2 and INCUMBENT.] Lying or resting upon, or situated on the top of, something else; overlying. (Chiefly in scientific use.)

1664 POWER *Exp. Philos.* II. 105 The variation of the gravity of the Superincumbent Ayr. **1674** PETTY *Disc. Dupl. Proportion* 117 Water-Divers..the lower they go, do find their stock of Air more and more to shrink; and that according to the Roots of the Quantities of the super-incumbent Water or Weight. **1785** COWPER *Let. to J. Newton* 19 Mar., The round table, which we formerly had in use, was unequal to the pressure of my superincumbent breast and elbows. **1830** LYELL *Princ. Geol.* xv. I. 281 The soft argillaceous sub-stratum..hastens the dilapidation of the superincumbent mass of limestone. **1874** HARTWIG *Aerial W.* i. 2 Air is a very elastic body, and, in consequence of the earth's attraction, each superincumbent stratum presses upon all those below it.

predicative. **1842** LOUDON *Suburban Hort.* 485 The soil is generally light, but superincumbent on a subsoil, which is supplied with water.

b. Situated or suspended above; overhanging.

1835 T. MITCHELL *Acharn. of Aristoph.* 230 *note*, Above this mother earth..was seen stretched the superincumbent heaven. *a* **1845** BARHAM *Ingol. Leg.* Ser. III. *Jerry Jarvis's Wig*, Either side of the superincumbent banks was clothed with a thick mantle of tangled copsewood.

c. Of pressure: Exerted from above.

1854 RONALDS & RICHARDSON *Chem. Technol.* (ed. 2) I. 107 If..coke is prepared under considerable superincumbent pressure the blisters which form in the softened coal are pressed together. **1866** ROSCOE *Elem. Chem.* iv. 40 Water boils when the tension of its vapour is equal to the superincumbent atmospheric pressure.

d. *fig.*

1821 SHELLEY *Adonais* xxxii, A Power Girt round with weakness;—it can scarce uplift The weight of the superincumbent hour. **1848** CLOUGH *Amours de Voy.* I. 35 A tyrannous sense of superincumbent oppression. **1875** E. WHITE *Life in Christ* I. viii. (1878) 81 The superincumbent accumulations of pagan and mediæval thought.

Hence **ˌsuperinˈcumbently** *adv.*

1796 KIRWAN *Elem. Min.* (ed. 2) II. 249 Fracture narrowly and divergingly striated, or superincumbently striated.

ˌsuperindiˈvidual, *a.* (and *sb.*). [SUPER- 4 a.] Of or pertaining to that which is above or greater than the individual. Also as *sb.*

1916 F. VON HÜGEL *German Soul* 92 The moral relation between the individual and the super-individual unity. **1924** W. B. SELBIE *Psychol. Relig.* 150 The crowd will then act and feel, and express itself together. In doing so it becomes an entity or super-individual. **1936** J. KANTOR *Objective Psychol. Gram.* iv. 49 Those who would reject psychology from linguistics because linguistic phenomena are superindividual. **1943** *Mind* LII. 342 His [*sc.* Kant's] phrase *Bewusstsein überhaupt*, 'consciousness in general', though sometimes supposed to stand for a super-individual consciousness, might equally well..be taken to mean a character which all individual consciousnesses have in common.

Hence **ˌsuperindiˈvidualist, -individuaˈlistic** = SUPERINDIVIDUAL *a.*; also [SUPER- 9 a], that favours a high degree of individualism.

1934 WYNDHAM LEWIS *Let.* 2 Nov. (1963) 223 Handicapped as we are under a super-individualist legislation—which allows the utmost licence in criticism of the State, in contradistinction to the Individual. **1943** *Mind* LII. 342 The majority of Kant's followers have, I suppose, adopted what I may call the 'super-individualist' interpretation. **1958** W. STARK *Sociol. Knowledge* i. 19 American society was also super-individualistic.

ˌsuperinˈduce, *v.* [ad. late L. *superindūcĕre* to cover over, bring upon, add, f. *super-* SUPER- 2, 13 + *indūcĕre* to INDUCE.]

1. *trans.* To bring (a person) into some position in addition to, or so as to displace, one who already occupies it. **a.** To take (a second wife) within the lifetime of the first (or, by extension, shortly after her death); also, to bring (the child of another wife) into the inheritance in preference to the former heir. *Obs.* or *arch.*

Cf. med.L. *superinducta* 'mulier extranea, concubina.

c **1555** HARPSFIELD *Divorce Hen. VIII* (Camden) 73 It was plain adultery to superinduce any other wife, his former living. **1626** DONNE *Serm.*, *John xiv. 2* (1640) 740 And when we have *Primogenitum Ecclesiæ*, The eldest son by the Primitive Church, The Creed of the Apostles, they will super-induce another son by another *venter*,..and..make their Trent-Creed larger then the Apostles. **1647** TRAPP *Comm. Matt.* xix. 5 Thou shalt not superinduce one wife to another. **1650** JER. TAYLOR *Funeral Serm. C'tess Carbery* Wks. 1831 IV. 108 When Pompey saw the ghost of his first lady, Julia, who vexed his rest and his conscience, for superinducing Cornelia on her bed within the ten months of mourning. **1855** MILMAN *Lat. Christ.* IX. iv. IV. 65 The King is to be warned that.., as he cannot have legitimate offspring by her whom he has superinduced, his kingdom would pass to strangers.

b. To appoint (a person) to an office over the head of another; = SUPERINDUCT. *Obs.* or *arch.*

1647 CLARENDON *Hist. Reb.* v. §374 When the fleet was commanded by sir John Pennington, before the earl of Warwick was superinduced into that charge against the King's will. **1904** M. HEWLETT *Queen's Quair* II. ix. 307 Upon such a crisis, intending for the best, Mary Beaton superinduced a stout,..gamesome lady, her aunt.

2. To bring in over and above, or 'on the top of', something already present; to introduce in addition (esp. something extraneous). Const. *on*, *upon* (rarely *to*, *into*).

1605 BACON *Adv. Learn.* II. To the King §13 The Anoyntment of God superinduceth a Brotherhood in Kings & Bishops. *Ibid.* II. vii. §6 Whosoeuer knoweth any forme knoweth the vtmost possibilitie of superinducing that Nature vpon any varietie of Matter. **1651** JER. TAYLOR *Serm. for Year* I. iii. 32 Death brought in by sin, was nothing superinduced to man. **1659** H. L'ESTRANGE *Alliance Div. Off.* 174 It is not like that Christ would superinduce any new establishment to former Rights. **1676** GREW *Musæum, Anat. Stomach & Guts* vii. 29 Another Ferment superinduc'd to that of the Stomach. **1767** STERNE *Tr. Shandy* (1802) IX. i. 207 Nor did she superinduce the least heat into her humours. **1791** BOSWELL *Johnson* 26 Mar. 1776, His size, and figure, and countenance, and manner, were that of a hearty English 'Squire, with the parson super-induced. **1814** CHALMERS *Evid. Chr. Revel.* v. (ed. 3) 156 He superinduces his own testimony to that of the original writers. **1854** MILMAN *Lat. Christ.* I. i. I. 30 *note*, Westward the old Punic language prevailed, even where the Roman conquerors had superinduced Latin. **1860** MILL *Repr. Govt.* (1865) 16/1 Their improvement cannot come from themselves, but must be superinduced from without. **1874** LUBBOCK *Mod. Savages* in *Manch. Sci. Lect.* Ser. v. & vi. 248 The savage does not abandon his belief in Fetichism..but he superinduces on it a belief in beings of a higher..material nature. **1877** E. CAIRD *Philos. Kant* II. vi. 295 The form of unity superinduced on the matter of the ideas connected.

3. To bring or cause to come *upon* a person or thing; to bring on, induce; *esp.* to induce (a disease, etc.) in addition to one already existing.

1615 CROOKE *Body of Man* 200 An instinct of lust or desire, not inordinate such as by sinne is super-induced in man, but natural. **1687** RYCAUT *Hist. Turks* II. 223 Opium being taken..in a small quantity, about the bigness of a Tare, superinduces at first a strange chearfulness about the heart. **1749** HARTLEY *Observ. Man* II. ii. 107 That State of our Waters, which was superinduced at the Deluge, may be the Cause of the Rainbow. **1803** *Med. Jrnl.* X. 539 Whether it was merely sufficient to remove the direct debility, or whether in such large doses as to superinduce the indirect. **1822–7** GOOD *Study Med.* (1829) I. 581 It [*sc.* idiopathic cough] has often proved highly dangerous in its results, by superinducing peripneumony. **1859** MEREDITH *R. Feverel* xxiii, A..physician who has..overlooked the change in the disease superinduced by one false dose. **1889** *Science-Gossip* XXV. 208 That the tremendous mechanical energies which ..metamorphosed the archæan gneiss..was [*sic*] quite sufficiently potent to superinduce the semblance of bedding on the bright red Cambrian grit mountains.

b. *loosely* for: To induce.

1816 T. L. PEACOCK *Headlong Hall* i, The alacrity with which he sprang from the vehicle superinduced a distortion of his ankle. **1884** J. COLBORNE *Hicks Pasha* 118 The water of the White Nile is supposed to superinduce dysentery.

4. In physical sense: To bring, draw, deposit, etc. *over* or *upon* a thing as a covering or addition.

1660 F. BROOKE tr. *Le Blanc's Trav.* 262 Superinducing an Apes skin over his humane shape. *a* **1661** FULLER *Worthies*, *Suffolk* (1662) III. 67 For some boggled much thereat as false Heraldry in Devotion, to super-induce a Doctoral hood over a Friers Coul. **1709** T. ROBINSON *Nat. Hist. Westm. & Cumberl.* vii. 46 The West side, or Skirts of these Mountains..seems to be Earth superinduced upon the Mountain-Strata by the general Flood. **1813** VANCOUVER *Agric. Devon* 283 A black peaty stratum, superinduced with morass or red bog. **1865** MILL *Exam. Hamilton* xiii. 239 One [colour] may limit another by being superinduced partially over it.

5. To induce or persuade in addition. *nonce-use.*

1790 *Bystander* 248 He was super-induced to grant it by the many..handsome things Phocion had just been saying of his dear sister.

Hence **superinducing** *vbl. sb.* and *ppl. a.*
1668 WILKINS *Real Char., Dict., Superinducing*, again-marrying of married person. **1822-7** GOOD *Study Med.* (1829) IV. 630 Superinducing tumours and congestions have been found in the neck. **1849** NOAD *Electricity* (ed. 3) 196 The super-inducing influence of the current.

ˌsuperinˈduced, *ppl. a.* [f. prec. + -ED[1].] Brought in or on over and above something; introduced or induced in addition: see the verb.
1649 JER. TAYLOR *Gt. Exemp.* Pref. ¶33 He tooke off those many superinduced rites, which God injoyned to the Jewes. **1660** —— *Worthy Commun.* ii. §2. 124 Our natural needs, or our superinduced calamities may force us to run to God. **1709** STRYPE *Ann. Ref.* I. xix. 219 In shaking off the Pope's fetters, and recovering religion from his superinduced tyranny and superstitions. **1849** RUSKIN *Seven Lamps* vi. §16. 178 The superinduced and accidental beauty is most commonly inconsistent with the preservation of original character. **1866** HERSCHEL *Fam. Lect. Sci.* vi. §38. 254 That colour is not a superinduced but an inherent quality of the luminous rays.

ˌsuperinˈducement. [-MENT.] The action or an act of superinducing; something superinduced.
1637 REYNOLDS *Serm. preached 12 July* 7 Some [Truths] are *de fide*, against those who deny Fundamentals. Others *circa fidem*, against those who by perilous superinducements bruize and wrench the foundation. **1698** LOCKE *3rd Let. to Bp. of Worcester* (1699) 400 In all such Cases the superinducement of greater Perfections..destroys nothing of the Essence or Perfections that were there before. **1704** NORRIS *Ideal World* II. i. 53 The supposition..that the superinducement of any perfection not contained in the idea of matter, should of necessity alter the species of it. **1832** CHALMERS *Pol. Econ.* vi. 177 The foreign trade is a superinducement on the home. **1844** *N. Brit. Rev.* I. 92 To imagine that any such accession of wealth..would accrue to our country by the superinducement of an extrinsic population.

†**ˌsuperinˈduct**, *v. Obs.* [f. late L. *superinduct-*, pa. ppl. stem of *superindūcĕre* to SUPERINDUCE.] *trans.* To bring in over and above, to superinduce; *esp.* to induct or appoint to an office in addition to, or over the head of, another. Hence **superinˈducted** *ppl. a.*
1638 BP. MOUNTAGU *Art. Enq. Visit.* A4b, A superinducted Lecturer in another mans cure. *a* **1641** —— *Acts & Mon.* ii. (1642) 120 Ismael was the sonne of a Concubine, a superinducted wife. **1654** H. L'ESTRANGE *Chas. I* (1655) 90 He was twice repulsed upon his Petition for a Captains place, and others super-inducted over his head. **1659** —— *Alliance Div. Off.* 136 Confirmed..by a ratification superinducted to a former establishment. *a* **1662** HEYLIN *Laud* (1668) 364 Those who had been Superinducted into other Mens Cures (like a Doctor added to the Pastor in Calvin's Plat-form).

ˌsuperinˈduction. [ad. late L. *superinductio, -iōnem*, n. of action f. *superindūcĕre* to SUPERINDUCE.] The action, or an act, of superinducing.
†**1.** (See SUPERINDUCE 1 a, b.) *Obs.*
1626 DONNE *Serm., John xi. 21* (1640) 816 That that spirit might at his will..informe, and inanimate that dead body; God allowes no such Super-inductions, no such second Marriages upon such divorces by death. **1655** FULLER *Ch. Hist.* IV. i. §36 No man in place of power or profit, loves to behold himself buried alive, by seeing his successour assigned unto him, which caused all Clergy-men to hate such superinductions.
2. The action, or an act, of bringing in something additional; introduction over and above.
1641 SYMONDS *Serm. bef. Ho. Comm.* D j b, What super-inductions of evill upon evill have we had? *a* **1662** HEYLIN *Laud* II. (1671) 258 St. Paul must needs be out in the Rules of Logick when he proved the Abrogating of the old Covenant by the superinduction of a new. **1670** CLARENDON *Ess.* Tracts (1727) 140 The Superinduction of others for the Corroboration and Maintenance of Government. **1765** BLACKSTONE *Comm.* I. x. 369 The subject is bound to his prince by an intrinsic allegiance, before the superinduction of those outward bonds of oath, homage and fealty. *a* **1779** WARBURTON *Div. Legat.* IX. Note A, Wks. 1788 III. 736 The futility of Mr. Locke's superinduction of the faculty of thinking to a system of Matter. **1817** COLERIDGE *Biogr. Lit.* xviii. (1907) II. 47 Existence..is distinguished from essence, by the superinduction of reality. **1854** MILMAN *Lat. Christ.* IV. ii. II. 44 The superinduction of an armed aristocracy in numbers comparatively small. **1882** FARRAR *Early Chr.* I. 407 *note*, There takes place a cancelling of the previous commandment and a superinduction of a better hope.
b. *Sc. Law.* Insertion of a word or letter in a document.
1693 STAIR *Inst. Law Scot.* IV. xlii. §19 (ed. 2) 689 If the Writ appear to be Vitiate *in substantialibus*, by Deletion, Razing, or Superinduction of Letters and Words, which may alter the same. *Ibid.* 690.
c. Something superinduced or adventitious; an (extraneous) addition.
1756 J. CLUBBE *Misc. Tracts, Hist. Wheatfield* (1770) I. 78, I mean those superinductions in the progeny, which they derive, not by imitation, but from the very loins of their progenitors. **1792** MARY WOLLSTONECR. *Rights Wom.* vi. 263 To efface the superinductions of art that have smothered nature.
3. The bringing or putting of some material thing over or upon another as a covering or addition.
1650 FULLER *Pisgah* IV. v. 98, I conceive this blackness no superinduction of a dark die on Davids clothes, but rather a dirty hue contracted..from neglect of washing them. **1733** TULL *Horse-hoeing Husb.* xix. 278 Superinductions of Earth are an Addition of more Ground, or changing it. **1785** PHILLIPS *Treat. Inland Nav.* 23 The more easy will be the superinduction of manure upon lands in the vicinage of the Canal. **1827** STEUART *Planter's Guide* (1828) 342 A striking improvement of property is thus made, by the superinduction of a new soil. **1831** T. L. PEACOCK *Crotchet Castle* vii, There was an Italian painter, who obtained the name of *Il Bragatore*, by the superinduction of inexpressibles on the naked Apollos and Bacchuses of his betters.
4. The action of inducing or bringing on. *rare.*
a **1897** in H. L. Gordon *Sir J. Simpson* vii. 111 The superinduction of the anæsthetic state.

superinˈfect, *v. Med.* [Back-formation from next.] *trans.* **a.** To cause (an infected cell) to be further infected *with* an organism of a similar kind. **b.** Of a bacterium or virus: to infect (a cell that already contains organisms of a similar kind).
1954 *Jrnl. Bacteriol.* LXVII. 696/1 Lysogenic cells were superinfected with phages. **1971** *Nature* 23 Apr. 496/3 By superinfecting it with a mixture of cat leukaemia and sarcoma virus the defective human virus might be helped. **1980** *Internat. Jrnl. Radiation Biol.* XXXVII. 120 When cells of *E. coli* are superinfected by phage λ, the phage DNA can appear in three distinct forms.
Hence **superinˈfected**, **superinˈfecting** *ppl. adjs.*
1954 *Jrnl. Bacteriol.* LXVII. 698/2 The superinfected culture produces both the carried type and the super-infecting type of phage. **1961** *Virology* XIV. 220 The genetic incorporation of the superinfecting P2 was studied by examining the progeny of the superinfected cells. **1976** *Path. Ann.* XI. 259 Bacterial and, to a lesser extent, viral infections were also encountered in patients with multiple superinfecting organisms. **1981** *Virology* CIX. 74/1 The same concentration of PAA was also applied to the superinfected Raji cells.

ˌsuperinˈfection. *Med.* [SUPER- 15.]
a. An infection occurring after or on top of an earlier infection, *esp.* as a consequence of treatment of the latter by broad-spectrum antibiotic or other therapy. **b.** The further infection of cells that are already infected with a similar organism, *esp.* as a technique in virology and immunology.
1922 *Stedman's Med. Dict.* (ed. 7) 972/2 *Superinfection*,..a fresh infection added to one of the same nature already present. **1954** *Jrnl. Bacteriol.* LXVII. 702/2 The type of phage produced after superinfection was studied both in mass culture and in single burst experiments. **1961** *Lancet* 12 Aug. 352/2 Bacteræmia developed as a super-infection during antibiotic therapy. **1974** M. C. GERALD *Pharmacol.* xxvi. 459 While the incidence of superinfection is low with narrow-spectrum antibiotics such as penicillin, it is a common occurrence with tetracycline and other broad-spectrum antibiotics. **1981** *Virology* CIX. 72/1 Superinfection of the nonproducer cells with EBV..is known to induce synthesis of EA and MA.

†**superinfund**, *v. Obs. rare*[−1]. [ad. late L. *superinfundĕre*: see SUPER- 2 and INFUND *v.*] *trans.* To pour upon or over something.
1599 A. M. tr. *Gabelhouer's Bk. Physicke* 33/2 Superinfunde heereon iij pintes of fluvial water.

†**ˈsuperinˈfuse**, *v. Obs.* [SUPER- 13.] *trans.* To infuse in addition.
1619 DONNE *Serm.* 16 June (1660) III. (292) To a historical and a moral faith, God super-infuses true faith. **1650** *Vindic. Hammond's Addr.* §71. 34 The Parents begetting of the childe is an argument, that the Soul is not superinfused from God. **1660** JER. TAYLOR *Duct. Dubit.* II. i. rule 6. §3 For a sin to be against Nature..does not always superinfuse a..special malignity..into it, above other sins.
So †**ˌsuperinˈfusion.**
1657 in Southey *Comm.-pl. Bk.* Ser. II. (1849) 382/2 Life is united to death, and Christ to Adam, not without the super-infusion of blood.

ˈsuperinˈspect, *v.* Now *rare* or *Obs.* [f. eccl. L. *superinspect-*, pa. ppl. stem of *superinspicĕre*: see SUPER- 2, 2 b and INSPECT *v.*] *trans.* To inspect as a superior official; to oversee. So **ˌsuperinˈspection**, oversight.
1617 COLLINS *Def. Bp. Ely* II. x. 540 Why the King should haue Iurisdiction..or Superinspection, without administration or execution. **1677** *Govt. Venice* 170 The *Ephori* had..a superinspection upon the Conduct of all Persons who manage it [*sc.* the Commonwealth]. **1691** MAYDMAN *Naval Spec.* 123 He superinspects the whole Affair of Victualling at that Port.

superˈinstitute, *v.* Now *rare* or *Obs.* [SUPER- 13.] *trans.* To institute (a person) to a benefice over the head of another. Also *fig.*
1647 CLEVELAND *Hermaphrodite* 18 His is the Donative, and mine the Cure, Then say, my Muse,..Who 'tis that Fame doth superinstitute. **1647** FULLER *Good Th. in Worse T.* (1841) 101 Heaven will not superinstitute a miracle, where ordinary means were formerly in peaceable possession.
So **ˌsuperinstiˈtution**, institution of a person to a benefice to which another is already instituted; also *transf.*
1643 PRYNNE *Sov. Power Parl.* II. 73 That..divers incumbents were outed of their benefices by superinstitutions upon presentations of the King. **1644** OWEN *Duty of Pastors & People* i. 6 A superinstitution of a new ordinance, doth not overthrow any thing that went before in the same kinde. **1669** GRIMSTON tr. *Croke's Rep.* II. 464 If this sentence should make the admission and institution void *ab initio*, it would destroy the induction of the King, and make the superinstitution (which at the first was meerly void) to be good. **1672** *Cowell's Interpr., Super-institution*.., one Institution upon another; as where A. is admitted and instituted to a Benefice upon one Title, and B. is admitted, instituted, &c. by the Presentment of another. **1767** R. BURN *Eccl. Law* (ed. 2) I. 152 If a second institution is granted to the same church, this is a superinstitution.

superinˈtelligent, *a.* **1.** [SUPER- 4 a.] Above or beyond the range of intelligence.
1960 [see *super-moral* s.v. SUPER- 4 a].
2. [SUPER- 9 a.] Very highly intelligent.
1971 B. DE FERRANTI *Living with Computer* ix. 80 Recent work..demonstrates that by transplanting brain tissues super-intelligent animals can be produced. **1977** *Time Out* 28 Jan.-3 Feb. 60/4 (Advt.), Our labour force..is super-intelligent.

superintend (ˌs(j)uːpərɪnˈtɛnd), *v.* [ad. eccl. L. *superintendĕre*: see SUPER- 2 and INTEND *v.*]
1. *trans.* To have or exercise the charge or direction of (operations or affairs); to look after, oversee, supervise the working or management of (an institution, etc.).
c **1615** BACON *Adv. Sir G. Villiers* Lett. 1872 VI. 22 The King will appoint Commissioners in the nature of a Council, who may superintend the works of this nature, and regulate what concerns the colonies. **1673** S. PARKER *Reproof* 167 To this purpose did our blessed Saviour depute the Apostolical order..to superintend the Affaires of his Holy Catholique Church. **1765** *Museum Rust.* IV. 420 The appointing proper persons to superintend such gardens or nurseries. **1796** MORSE *Amer. Geog.* I. 148 British America is superintended by an officer styled governor general. **1802** MARIA EDGEWORTH *Moral T.* (1816) I. viii. 58 The lady, who superintended the charity-school. **1838** LYTTON *Alice* I. x, He could more often escape from public cares to superintend his private interests. **1859** LD. ACTON *Let.* in Gasquet *Ld. Acton & his Circle* (1906) 64 Newman will want superintending in the matter of foreign tongues. **1891** FARRAR *Darkn. & Dawn* xxiii, The cooks and other slaves who superintended the meals of the imperial family.
b. To exercise supervision over (a person).
1776 *Trial of Nundocomar* 77/1, I was his chief gomastah: I used to superintend his other gomastahs, and sometimes write myself. **1811** SHELLEY *St. Irvyne* viii, I burn with curiosity and solicitude to learn for what thou hast thus superintended me.
c. *intr.* with †*over*, or *absol.*
1663 PATRICK *Parab. Pilgr.* xxxi. (1665) 377 This superintends over all, and issues forth her directions and orders to them. **1678** CUDWORTH *Intell. Syst.* I. iv. §13. 229 They called both the Childbearing of Women, and the Goddesses that superintend over the same Eilithuia or Lucina. **1883** G. MOORE *Mod. Lover* x, She declared that she was ready to superintend.
†**2.** *trans.* To keep a watch upon. *Obs. rare.*
1654 tr. *Scudery's Curia Pol.* 188 The eyes of all the earth observe our motion and superintend our actions.
Hence **superinˈtended** *ppl. a.*, **superinˈtending** *vbl. sb.* and *ppl. a.*
1713 DERHAM *Phys. Theol.* IV. xi. §4 (1727) 189 What hath been said..plainly argues Design, and a super-intending Wisdom. **1765** BLACKSTONE *Comm.* I. 107 The general superintending power of the legislature in the mother country. **1799** S. & HT. LEE *Canterb. T.* (1800) III. 14 In the hall he was stopped by a faithful superintending domestic. **1809** in *Trans. Soc. Arts* (1811) XXVIII. 173 A. Shennan, Superintending-Master of the First Division [of the Fleet]. **1819** W. TAYLOR in *Monthly Rev.* LXXXIX. 79 The antient mischiefs of a superintended press. **1855** MACAULAY *Hist. Eng.* xx. IV. 399 The..coalition..would be..dissolved if his superintending care were withdrawn.

ˌsuperinˈtendence. Also 7–9 -ance. [Formed as next: see -ENCE. Cf. obs. F. *superintendance* (mod.F. *surintendance*), It. *sopr(a)intendenza*, Sp., Pg. *superintendencia*.]
1. The function or occupation of a superintendent; the action or work of superintending.
1603 HOLLAND *Plutarch's Mor.* 1312 Eudoxus..asked the reason, why Ceres had no charge and superintendance over Love matters. *a* **1665** J. GOODWIN *Being filled with the Spirit* (1867) 83 They do it by virtue of a certain superintendence and instigation of the Spirit of God. **1779** *Mirror* No. 25 ¶3, I was just returning from the superintendence of my plows in a field. **1814** SCOTT *Wav.* iii, Had his father placed him under the superintendence of a permanent tutor. **1867** RUSKIN *Time & Tide* ii. §8 To occupy themselves in the superintendence of public institutions. **1876** *Encycl. Brit.* V. 668/2 The..intendant of circuit, who has a direct general superintendence over all the affairs of the circuit.
†**2.** A body of superintendents of the Church of Scotland. *Obs.*
a **1578** LINDESAY (Pitscottie) *Chron. Scot.* II. 232 The maist pairt of the vniuersitie of Sanctandros convenit with the haill ministeris and superintendence in Edinburgh.

ˌsuperinˈtendency. Also 6–7 -encie, 7 -ancie, 7–8 -ancy. [ad. med.L. *superintendentia*, f. *superintendent-*, *-ens* SUPERINTENDENT: see -ENCY.]
1. The office or position of a superintendent; the function, authority, or right of superintending; the exercise of this function, superintendence. Const. *of*, †*above*, *over* (that which is controlled). **a.** in reference to a definite business, institution, etc.
1598 BARRET *Theor. Warres* II. i. 19 The Superintendencie thereof [*sc.* the munitions] resteth in him [*sc.* the Sergeant Major]. **1602** J. CLAPHAM *Hist. Gt. Brit.* II. II. v. (1606) 221 The Britans (imagining that he..would.., being settled in

a superintendency over them,..despise them). *a* **1617** HIERON *Wks.* (1620) II. 441 The Pope and his faction challenge a superintendency aboue Kings, all must be subiect vnto him, and he to no body. **1649** MILTON *Eikon.* xiii. 133 Arch-Presbytery..claiming to it self a Lordly power and Superintendency both over Flocks and Pastors. **1697** COLLIER *Ess. Mor. Subj.* I. v. 193 We find from S. Paul, that one reason of his giving Titus the super-intendency of Crete was, to ordain Elders in every City. **1727** A. HAMILTON *New Acc. E. Ind.* xlvii. II. 176 She was then honoured with the Superintendency of his Majesty's Confectionary. **1768** BLACKSTONE *Comm.* III. vi. 81 The courts at Westminster-hall have a concurrent jurisdiction with these, or else a super-intendency over them. **1845** LD. CAMPBELL *Chancellors* xxiv. (1857) VI. 99 The Court of Chancery, the guardian of all infants, with the superintendency and cognizance of all trusts. **1845** STEPHEN *Comm. Laws Eng.* (1874) I. 67 The courts of common law have the superintendency over these courts. **1882** *Rep. to Ho. Repr. Prec. Met. U.S.* 153 The Santiago mill..had a large..business under the superintendency of Donald McKay.

b. in general sense: often as an attribute of the Divine Being.

1641 EARL MONM. tr. *Biondi's Civil Wars* III. 100 By which actions having..freed himselfe from the superintendencie of others. **1679** J. GOODMAN *Penit. Pard.* III. ii. (1713) 297 The special superintendency, guidance and influence of his Holy Spirit. **1682** HOWE *Self-dedication* Ep. Ded. (1702) A3, It looks like an Artifice and Contrivance of Providence..that it might indear to you its Accurate superintendency over your Life. **1709** STEELE *Tatler* No. 135 ¶3 The Superintendency of Providence. **1882** FARRAR *Early Chr.* 219 The grace of superintendency was at work.

2. A district (*spec.* in the Lutheran Church, a collection of parishes) under the charge of a superintendent; in China, one of the administrative divisions of the country.

1762 tr. *Busching's Syst. Geog.* VI. 340 The ten parishes in it constitute a particular superintendency. **1847** tr. *Bunsen's Ch. Future* vi. 151 The superintendencies..coincide most happily with those minor divisions of the country, established by the Prussian code. **1896** *Westm. Gaz.* 13 Nov. 8/3 Ten millions will be furnished by the Tsung-li-Yamen from the last loan, and the Northern and Southern superintendencies will furnish three millions and seven millions respectively.

superintendent (ˌs(j)uːpərɪnˈtɛndənt), *sb.* and *a.* Also 6–9 **-ant**. [ad. eccl. L. *superintendent-*, *-ens*, pr. pple. of *superintendĕre* to SUPERINTEND. Cf. obs. F. *superintendant* (mod.F. *surintendant*), It. *sopr(a)intendente*, Sp., Pg. *superintendente*.]

A. *sb.* One who superintends.

1. a. An officer or official who has the chief charge, oversight, control, or direction of some business, institution, or works; an overseer. Const. *of*, †*over*.

1588 KYD *Househ. Philos.* Wks. (1901) 264 These [servants] would I deuide into two formes..as the one of superintendents, surueighors, or work-maisters, the other of workmen. **1598** BARRET *Theor. Warres* IV. i. 92 Superintendent of all the Sergeants. **1653** H. COGAN tr. *Pinto's Trav.* xxvii. 103 One of those Super-intendents of Justice, that..are sent throughout the Provinces for to make report unto the King of all that passeth there. *Ibid.* lviii. 226 The Super-intendent over all the other Civil and Criminal Ministers. **1770** LANGHORNE *Plutarch* V. 98 As his family, and particularly his daughters, wanted a proper superintendant. **1801** J. ADAMS *Wks.* (1854) IX. 583 The new superintendent of the commercial relations between France and the United States. **1897** *Punch* 17 July 22 *Servant* (to convalescent Curate, prop of the Sunday School). 'Please, Sir, the Superintendent wants to know how you are.' **1902** *Encycl. Brit.* XXVII. 678/2 The city board of education has as its executive officer a superintendent of schools.

b. *transf.* and *gen.*

1575 TURBERV. *Faulconrie* 371 Spaniels..are superintendantes and necessarie servantes both for the hawke and the falconer. **1603** HOLLAND *Plutarch's Mor.* 1313 He is the superintendant and reformer of mens language as touching the gods. **1624** BURTON *Anat. Mel.* Democr. to Rdr. (ed. 2) 8 'Twas Seneca's fate, that Superintendent of wit. **1688** BOYLE *Final Causes* iv. 234 Without any particular guidance of a most wise Superintendent [*sc.* God].

c. *spec.* A head official who administers the affairs of a district; a governor.

1758 J. DALRYMPLE *Ess. Feudal Property* (ed. 2) 10 The superintendants of Folkland, called Coples. **1770** COOK *Voy. round World* III. xii. (1773) 715 The superintendant of the island of Ourust. **1775** ADAIR *Amer. Ind.* 252 Our first Indian super-intendant. **1847** W. C. L. MARTIN *Ox* 113/2 A tract of coast..divided into islands respectively under the care of superintendents.

d. *U.S.* The conductor of a railway train.

1835 BRECK *Recoll.* (1877) 275 'Make room for the ladies!' bawled out the superintendent.

e. A police officer next above the rank of inspector.

1832 *Observer* 24 June 4/4 Mr. Thomas, the Superintendent of Police, F Division, came before..the presiding Magistrate. **1836** *Act 6 & 7 Will. IV*, c. 13 §2 Inspectors, and Superintendents, Clerks, Chief and other Constables, Sub-Constables, and Officers [of the Royal Irish Constabulary]. **1885** *Encycl. Brit.* XIX. 337/1 All promotions in the [police] service up to the rank of superintendent are made from the next rank below. **1907** G. B. SHAW *Major Barbara* Pref. 171 Those who pester our police superintendents with confessions of murder might very wisely be taken at their word and executed. **1936** G. HEYER *Behold, here's Poison* iv. 71 Things are more serious than I had supposed. This is Superintendent Hannasyde, of Scotland Yard. **1977** 'E. CRISPIN' *Glimpses of Moon* viii. 150 Not at all, Superintendent. Partial deafness must be quite a handicap in your profession.

2. *Eccl.* **a.** Adopted as an etymological rendering of Gr. ἐπίσκοπος 'overseer' (see BISHOP) of the N.T.; used controversially instead of 'bishop' by extreme Protestant reformers of the 16th century, and subsequently by Catholics with reference to bishops of the Church of England. *Obs.* exc. *Hist.*

1554 T. MARTIN *Traictise Marr. Priestes* Giv, He [*sc.* Clement of Rome] speketh of Bishops and Archbishops, whom thei wold haue termed superintendentes and ministers. **1555** POYNET *Apologie* 53 The word superintendent being a very latyn word made English by vse, should in tyme haue taught the peple by the very etymologie and proper signification, what thinge was ment when they hard that name which by this terme busshop, could not so well be donne. **1567** JEWEL *Def. Apol.* VI. ii. 597 Yee mighte easily haue knowen, that a Superintendente, is an Anciente name, and signifieth none other, but a Bishop. **1574** R. BRISTOW *Treat. Motives unto Cath. Faith* xxxix. (1599) 152b, Most ill,..and therefore euery where most despised,..most scorned [are] the Superintendents and Ministers themselues. **1589** [? LYLY] *Pappe w. Hatchet* L.'s Wks. 1902 III. 403 [Martinists] studie to pull downe Bishopps, and set vp Superintendents, which is nothing else, but to raze out good Greeke, & enterline bad Latine. **1613** F. T. *Suppl. Discuss. Barlowes Answ.* v. 206 *heading*, M. Barlow and his fellow-Superintendents proued to be no Bishops. **1649** BP. HALL *Cases Consc.* III. v. (1650) 208 Writing to Titus the great Super-intendent of Crete. **1721** STRYPE *Eccl. Mem.* II. II. xxiii. 444 The very Name of Bishop grew odious among the People, and the Word Superintendent began to be affected. [**1730** C. HAYES tr. *Sarpi's Beneficiary Matters* xv. 46 The Bishop, as Super-Intendant and Pastor-General, might regulate the Distribution of Tythes.]

b. In certain Reformed churches on the Continent, a chief or presiding minister; *spec.* among the Lutherans, a minister who has control of the churches and pastors of a particular district.

Coverdale, 1550, uses *super-attendent* (see SUPER- *prefix* 6a).

1560 DAUS tr. *Sleidane's Comm.* 160 The Senate appointed them a churche [at Strasburg], wherof Iohn Caluine was fyrste for certeine yeres the superintendent. **1564** STAPLETON tr. *Staphylus' Apol.* Pref. 7b, Nicolaus Amsdorfius a famous Superintendent amonge the Lutherans. **1570** FOXE *A. & M.* (ed. 2) III. 1692/1 Henry Bullinger, chief Superintendent in the Citie of Zuricke. **1602** PARSONS *Warn-word* 44b, A great Superintendent in Saxony. **1681** BURNET *Hist. Ref.* II. App. 396 The Zuinglians had no Superintendents, for ought I can find; nor was Hooper ever called Superintendent, but Bishop. **1694** MOLESWORTH *Acc. Denmark* xvi. 253 There are six Superintendents in Denmark, who take it very kindly to be called Bishops, and My Lord. **1706** tr. *Dupin's Eccl. Hist. 16th C.* II. v. 128 The Ministers and Super-Intendants of Hereticks. **1879** *Encycl. Brit.* X. 469/2 A synodal constitution for the Evangelical State Church was introduced in Prussia in 1875... The parishes..are grouped into dioceses.., presided over by superintendents, who are subordinate to the superintendent-general of the province.

c. In the Church of Scotland, a minister chosen to preside over and visit the parochial ministers of a particular district, to direct its administration, and to ordain ministers. Now *Hist.*

1561 *First Bk. Discipl. Ch. Scot.* in *Knox's Wks.* (1848) II. 198 To him that travelleth from place to place, quhom we call Superintendentis, quho remane as it war a moneth or less in one place, for the establishing of the kirk. *Ibid.* 200 It is to be noted, that the Readaris be putt in by the Kirk, and admissioun of the Superintendent. **1561** *Maitl. Club Misc.* III. 267 Superintendent of Fyffe Fothryk & Strathern. **1566** in J. Chamberlayne *St. Gt. Brit.* (1710) 362 The Superintendants, Ministers and Commissioners within the Realm of Scotland, to their Brethren the Bishops and Pastors of England. *c* **1630** SIR T. HOPE *Minor Practicks* (1729) §56 The several Kirks were planted by the Superintendants appointed in every Province, by the General Assembly. *a* **1637** SPOTTISWOODE *Hist. Ch. Scot.* v. (1655) 258 The Superintendents held their office during Life, and their power was Episcopal. *a* **1768** ERSKINE *Inst. Law Scot.* I. v. §5 Parochial presbyters, and over them certain church-officers, styled superintendents. **1885** *Encycl. Brit.* XIX. 679/1 Under Knox's agency Edinburgh, St. Andrews, Aberdeen, Jedburgh, Perth, Dunfermline, and Leith had fixed ministers appointed, whilst wider districts were placed under superintendents or travelling ministers.

d. The name given by John Wesley to men whom he ordained to act as bishops in the United States; now, among Wesleyan Methodists, the presiding minister of a circuit.

1784 WESLEY in Southey *Life* (1820) II. 440, I have this day set apart, as a Superintendent, by the imposition of my hands and prayer,..Thomas Coke,..a Presbyter of the Church of England. **1785** T. COKE *Serm. Godhead Christ* Ded., To the Rev. Francis Asbury, Superintendent, the Elders, Deacons, and Helpers, of the Methodist Episcopal Church in America. **1883** *Encycl. Brit.* XVI. 189/1 The admission of members into the society [of Wesleyans] had, up to 1797, been entirely in the hands of the itinerant preachers,—that is, the 'assistant', henceforth to be styled the 'superintendent', and his 'helpers'. **1885** *Minutes of Wesleyan Conf.* 24 He was a painstaking Superintendent.

3. ***superintendent-general*** [GENERAL *a.* 10], an officer exercising supreme control over a number of superintendents.

1793 in *Encycl. Brit.* (1875) III. 390/2 Superintendent-general of barracks. **1847** tr. *Bunsen's Ch. Future* vi. 143 For the two Churches of the Rhenish provinces and Westphalia, there is a superintendent-general appointed, to whom the title of bishop is also given. **1879** [see 2b].

B. *adj.* Superintending; exercising superintendence or oversight; holding the position of a superintendent. Now (in English use) chiefly in designations of officials.

1597 BEARD *Theatre God's Judgem.* (1612) 12 Their high and superintendent estate is no priuiledge to exempt them from the..obedience which they owe vnto God. **1642** J. M[ARSH] *Argt. conc. Militia* 38 They exercise a superintendent jurisdiction over all other Courts. **1651** HOWELL *Venice* 48 The Decemvirs, who..were created to have the sole and superintendent power of all things. **1653** H. MORE *Antid. Ath.* I. x. §3 It implies that there is a Superintendent Principle over Nature. **1738** CHAMBERS *Cycl.* s.v. *Bishop*, The superintendant bishop of Copenhagen. **1828** J. BALLANTYNE *Exam. Human Mind* iii. §1. 169 An influence that is purely superintendent. **1881** *Instr. Census Clerks* (1885) 23 Superintendent Registrar. **1889** W. WILSON *State* §471 Districts were grouped under a superintendent provincial organization. **1913** *Times* 7 Aug. 3/2 The superintendent visiting officer of the London wards.

superintendential (ˌs(j)uːpərɪntɛnˈdɛnʃəl), *a.* *rare.* [f. SUPERINTENDENT *sb.*, after *presidential*.] Of the nature of, or directed by, a superintendent.

1898 B. GREGORY *Side Lights* 247 Steady-going, sedative Superintendential ministers. **1905** *Q. Reg. Presbyt. Ch.* Apr. 349 The congregations in the three towns of Emden, Leer, and Aurich, form a Diocese or 'Inspection' or 'Superintendential District.'

ˌsuperinˈtendentship. [-SHIP.] The office or position of a superintendent.

1583 STOCKER *Civ. Warres Lowe C.* II. 57b, Diuers deuises were practized, to obtaine & keepe ye authority & superintendentship in his Ma. countries. **1589** [? NASHE] *Almond for Parrat* D4b, G. W. of Wig-house chosen to the ..function of a pastor,..at length seased..on the superintendentship of Sidborough. *a* **1650** CALDERWOOD *Hist. Kirk* (1843) II. 207 The Assemblie nominated in leets for the superintendentship, Mr Alexander Gordoun, intituled Bishop of Galloway, and Mr Robert Pont, minister of Dunkelden. **1693** *Lond. Gaz.* No. 2919/1 The Super-Intendantship of his Catholick Majesties Revenues. **1888** *Pall Mall Gaz.* 8 Oct. 3/2 Promotion to a superintendentship direct from the Criminal Investigation Department is forbidden. **1897** *Westm. Gaz.* 29 Dec. 1/3 The Superintendentship of the Royal Small Arms Factory at Enfield.

†**b.** Used with possessive as a depreciatory title for a bishop of the Church of England (see SUPERINTENDENT *sb.* 2). *Obs.*

1565 HARDING *Confut. Apol.* v. x. 256b, It should haue becomme Scoggin..or Will Sommer, to haue tolde this tale much better, then your superintendentships.

c. A superintendent's period of office.

1614 PURCHAS *Pilgrimage* I. xii. (ed. 2) 64 In which his Superintendentship,..such laudable sciences as might safely be learned, he promoted and furthered.

ˌsuperinˈtender. *rare.* [f. SUPERINTEND *v.* + -ER[1].] A superintendent.

1776 BURROW *Rep.* IV. 2291 A Superintender of Salt-works. **18..** WHEWELL (Ogilvie, 1882), Our relation to the Superintender of our moral being. **1893** *Scott. Leader* 20 Feb. 5 The Town and County Councils, who are to appoint the registration superintenders.

So **ˌsuperinˈtendress**, a female superintendent.

1814 in Southey *Life A. Bell* (1844) II. 689 The conduct of the superintendress.

superionic: see SUPER- 9a(*a*).

superior (s(j)uːˈpɪərɪə(r)), *a.* and *sb.* Also 4–9 -iour, 6 -ioure, -your. [a. OF. *superior*, *-our* (mod.F. *supérieur*) = It. *superiore*, Sp., Pg. *superior*, ad. L. *superior*, *-ōrem*, compar. of *superus* that is above, f. *super* above.] **A.** *adj.*

1. Higher in local position; situated above or further up than something else; upper; †belonging to the upper regions, heavenly, celestial (*obs.*). Now chiefly in technical use: see senses 9–13.

1390 GOWER *Conf.* I. 361 In Ynde the superiour. **1432–50** tr. *Higden* (Rolls) I. 127 Cedar is a region in the superior parte of Palestine. **1553** EDEN *Treat. Newe Ind.* (Arb.) 24 The superiour or high India..is a region excedinge large. **1631** MASSINGER *Emperor East* I. ii, The motion, with the divers operations, Of the superior bodies. **1664** POWER *Exp. Philos.* II. 101 The superiour particles of the Ayr pressing the inferiour. **1709** V. MANDEY *Syst. Math., Arith.* (1729) 21 Numerator, is the superior Term of the Fraction. **1712–14** POPE *Rape Lock* II. 70 Amid the circle, on the gilded mast, Superior by the head, was Ariel plac't. **1799** KIRWAN *Geol. Ess.* 380 All the superior earthy and stony matter having been swept away by floods. **1838** LYELL *Elem. Geol.* xii. 268 The relative age of the superior and inferior portions of the earth's crust. **1839** MURCHISON *Silur. Syst.* I. xxxiii. 441 The sandy flagstone..is, apparently, thrown unconformably against the superior formations. **1879** *Cassell's Techn. Educ.* I. 98/1 The superior course [in building].

b. in predicative use, quasi-adv.: In or into a higher position; higher; upward. *poet.*

1718 PRIOR *Henry & Emma* 113 When Superior now the Bird has flown, And headlong brought the tumbling Quarry down. **1718** POPE *Iliad* XIII. 41 He sits superior, and the chariot flies. **1807** J. BARLOW *Columb.* VI. 271 Tall on the boldest bark superior shone A warrior ensign'd with a various crown.

2. Preceding in time or serial order; earlier, former; †before-mentioned, above.

1534 WHITINTON *Tullyes Offices* III. (1540) 126 To the which selfe questyons and consultacyons of the superior bokes many thinges be suffyciently disputed. **1599** A. M. tr. *Gabelhouer's Bk. Physicke* 132/2 Adde..to the superiour potion a qu[arter] of an ownce of redd Roses.

3. Higher in rank or dignity; more exalted in social or official status.

1485 CAXTON *Chas. Gt.* 203 God hath..made the superyor in worldly puyssaunce aboue al other kynges. **1539** TONSTALL *Serm. Palm Sund.* (1823) 37 For who is superiour? he that sytteth at the table, or he that serueth at the table? is not he superiour that sytteth? **1558** C. GOODMAN (*title*) How Superior Powers oght to be obeyd of their subiects. **1671** MILTON *P.R.* IV. 167 If thou wilt fall down, And worship me as thy superior Lord. **1726** AYLIFFE *Parergon* 72 This kind of an Appeal..transfers the Cognizance of the Cause to the Superiour Judge. **1760** *Caut. & Adv. Off. Army* 149 Putting so palpable an Affront on his superior Officer. **1837** CARLYLE *Fr. Rev.* I. v. ix, He says he obeyed superior orders. **1875** MAINE *Hist. Instit.* iv. 102 Superior ownership has arisen through..purchase from small allodial proprietors.

b. ***Father*** or ***Mother Superior***: = B. 2.

1706 PHILLIPS (ed. Kersey) s.v., The chief Governour or Governess of a Monastery, otherwise call'd Superiour Father, or Superiour Mother. **1846** MRS. A. MARSH *Father Darcy* II. xi. 187 A feeling upon which the Father Superior calculated with security. **1907** [see MOTHER *sb.*[1] 3 b].

4. Higher in ideal or abstract rank, or in a scale or series; of a higher nature or character. Sometimes contextually or by implication: Supernatural, superhuman.

1533 MORE *Answ. Poysoned Bk.* I. xi. 40 b, As we say a man is obedyent vnto his owne reason, and yet is not his owne reason another power superiour aboue hym selfe. **1634** MILTON *Comus* 801, I feel that I do fear Her words set off by some superior power. **1646** CRASHAW *Name above every Name* 95 May it be no wrong, Blest heav'ns, to you, and your superior song, That [etc.]. **1660** R. COKE *Justice Vind.* Ep. Ded. 7 Conscience..supposes some superior law informing men to do, or not do a thing. **1704** in *Pa. Hist. Soc. Mem.* IX. 350 There is a general infatuation, as if by a superior influence, got among us. **1725** DE FOE *Voy. round World* (1840) 154 Those people who have any notion of a God must represent him to themselves as something superior. **1726** BUTLER *Serm. Rolls Chap.* iii. 45 The several Passions being naturally subordinate to the one superior Principle of Reflection and Conscience. **1871** B. STEWART *Heat* (ed. 2) §26 The superior limit of the mercurial thermometer's accurate employment.

†**b.** In theological or religious use, applied to the soul or the spirit. *Obs.*

1638 ROUSE *Heav. Univ.* (1702) 162 While my superior mind breatheth and longeth after Thee. **1663** PATRICK *Parab. Pilgr.* xxxii. (1687) 395 It is an holy, chast and innocent pleasure..which riseth higher than sense, and seeks the superiour part. *a* **1700** in *Cath. Rec. Soc. Publ.* IX. 342 Keeping herself united to him..whome she possessed in her superior wil and soule, in solitude. **1745** A. BUTLER *Lives Saints, S. Jane Frances* (1821) VIII. 296 She laboured ..to gain..an absolute ascendant of the superior part of her soul over the inferior.

c. *Logic.* Having greater extension.

1843 MILL *Logic* I. vii. §3 Biped is a genus with reference to man and bird, but a species with respect to the superior genus, animal. **1864** BOWEN *Logic* iv. 87 Of any two Concepts in such a series, that one is called the Superior, Higher, or Broader, which has the greater Extension.

5. Higher in degree, amount, quality, importance, or other respect; of greater value or consideration.

1579–1642 [see 6 a]. **1702** ROWE *Tamerl.* I. ii, Nations unknown Shall..Bend to his Valour, and Superior Virtue. **1708** SWIFT *Sacram. Test* Wks. 1755 II. I. 127 When they are the superior number in any tract of ground, they are not over patient of mixture. **1756** BURKE *Subl. & Beaut.* Introd., Wks. 1842 I. 27 That the critical taste does not depend upon a superiour principle in men, but upon superiour knowledge. **1798** *Hull Advertiser* 14 Apr. 2/4 She escaped by superior sailing. **1816** SCOTT *Old Mort.* xxxi, It might be easily defended against a very superior force. **1827** FARADAY *Chem. Manip.* xv. (1842) 350 The air will enter into the gasometer, being forced inwards by the superior external pressure. **1883** LD. BLACKBURN in *Law Rep.* 8 *App. Cases* 462 Those who sought to turn the man in possession out must shew a superior legal title to his.

6. Const. *to* (†occas. *with*, *than*). **a.** Higher in status or quality than; hence, greater or better than; †formerly also *advb.* = more or better than, above, beyond.

1526 *Pilgr. Perf.* III. I. x. 32 b, Pride saithe to euery persone..dispyce all other,..thou oughtest to be superiour to them all. **1579** LYLY *Euphues* (Arb.) 190 In the one thou art inferiour to al men, in the other superior to al beasts. *c* **1611** CHAPMAN *Iliad* xx. 383, I..well know, thy strength superiour farre, To that my nerues hold. **1632** LITHGOW *Trav.* VIII. 369 A City..farre superior in greatnesse with Aleppo. **1642** JER. TAYLOR *Episc.* xi. 60 The Apostles..were Superior to the 72. **1757** W. WILKIE *Epigoniad* I. 25 Who arms the first, and first to combat goes, Tho' weaker, seems superior to his foes. **1784** T. COKE *Serm. Ordin. F. Asbury* 27 Dec. (1785) 14 *note*, An Officer of the Church superior to the Presbyters. **1796** MRS. J. WEST *Gossip's Story* I. 218 He behaves to me with yet superiour esteem and respect, than when he was at Stannadine. **1830** SCOTT *Monast.* Introd., A being, however superior to man in length of life. **1857** KINGSLEY *Two Y. Ago* xv, He seems so superior to the people round him. **1907** *Verney Mem.* I. 269 He was.. superior in numbers to the enemy.

advb. **1762** GOLDSM. *Cit. W.* l, It is to this ductility of the laws that an Englishman owes the freedom he enjoys superior to others. **1785** G. A. BELLAMY *Apol.* (ed. 3) I. 45, I loved his Lordship superior to the whole world.

b. Too great or strong to be overcome or affected by; not mastered by; above the influence or reach of.

1647 CLARENDON *Hist. Reb.* I. §88 Jealousy of his Master's honour, (to whom his Fidelity was Superior to any temptation). **1700** PRIOR *Written in Robe's Geogr.* 11 That I may Read, and Ride, and Plant, Superior to Desire, or Want. **1775** J. BRYANT *Mythol.* II. 393 The crocodile, and Hippopotamus, were emblems of the Ark; because during the inundation of the Nile they rose with the waters, and were superior to the flood. **1791** MRS. RADCLIFFE *Rom. Forest* viii, Adeline was superior to the affectation of fear. **1804–5** WORDSW. *Prelude* VI. 137 The one Supreme Existence,..to the boundaries of space and time..Superior. **1821** SCOTT *Kenilw.* xiv, To that foible even she was not superior. **1863** MRS. OLIPHANT *Salem Chapel* ii. 36 So strangely superior to her surroundings, yet not despising or quarrelling with them.

advb. **1804** EUGENIA DE ACTON *Tale without Title* II. 100 If there are any who wish to act superior to that last-mentioned very useful endowment.

c. Transcending, on a higher plane than.

1841 MYERS *Cath. Th.* III. §7. 22 Human thought is always superiour to its expression. **1865** LECKY *Ration.* (1878) II. 29 A bond of unity that is superior to the divisions of nationhood.

7. Characteristic of one who is superior (in senses 3 and 4); also, from sense 6 b, 'free from emotion or concern; unconquered; unaffected' (J.) *poet.* or *rhet.*

1667 MILTON *P.L.* IV. 499 He in delight Both of her Beauty and submissive Charms Smil'd with superior Love. *Ibid.* V. 902 Hostile scorn, which he susteind Superior, nor of violence fear'd aught. *Ibid.* VIII. 532 Here passion first I felt, ..in all enjoyments else Superiour and unmov'd. **1718** POPE *Iliad* XIV. 387 She ceas'd, and smiling with superior Love, Thus answer'd mild the Cloud-compelling Jove. **1742** —— *Dunc.* IV. 105 There mov'd Montalto with superior air. **1746** HERVEY *Medit.* (1818) 40 With a wise indifference, if not with a superior disdain! **1819** SHELLEY *Cenci* II. i. 117 Never again..with fearless eye, And brow superior..Shalt thou strike dumb the meanest of mankind.

b. Applied ironically to persons of lofty, supercilious, or dictatorial manner or behaviour (or to their actions, etc.).

1864 DISRAELI *Sp. Ho. Comm.* 8 July, In private life there is always..some person,..who is regarded as a superior person. They decide on everything, they lecture everybody. .. The right hon. member for Stroud is the 'superior person' of the House of Commons. **1890** *Daily News* 4 Oct. 5/1 He gave himself airs of affectation. He was superior. **1897** A. D. INNES *Macaulay's Ld. Clive* 128 *note*, The 'superior' person who posed as an authority on matters of culture. **1902** WISTER *Virginian* xviii, One or two people I have knowed..never said a superior word to me.

c. *advb.* In a superior style; with a superior air.

1726 POPE *Iliad* V. 517 The Sire of Gods and Men superior smil'd [μείδησεν]. **1815** JANE AUSTEN *Emma* xxvi, Jane Fairfax did look and move superior. **1894** S. FISKE *Holiday Stories* (1900) 129, I no longer smiled superior upon Paddy from Cork.

8. In a positive or absolute sense (admitting comparison with *more* and *most*): Supereminent in degree, amount, or (most commonly) quality; surpassing the generality of its class or kind.

1777 SHERIDAN *Sch. Scand.* I. i, A person of your ladyship's superior accomplishments and understanding. **1812** SIR H. DAVY *Chem. Philos.* 3 A species of air that supports flame in a superior degree. **1854** THACKERAY *Wolves & Lamb* I. (1899) 23 What a woman she was—what a superior creature! **1888** MISS BRADDON *Fatal Three* I. iii, They were altogether superior people for their class. **1888** 'J. S. WINTER' *Bootle's Childr.* x, Sadly in need of a superior needle-woman! **1891** —— *Lumley* i, Let me give you a little more of the mayonnaise,..it's very superior.

9. *Astron.* **a.** Applied to those planets whose orbits lie outside that of the earth (originally, according to the Ptolemaic astronomy, as having their spheres above that of the sun). **b.** ***superior conjunction***: see CONJUNCTION 3. **c.** ***superior meridian***: that part of the celestial meridian which lies above the pole: so ***superior passage*** (of the meridian), etc.

1583 R. HARVEY (*title*) An Astrological Discourse vpon the great and notable Coniunction of the two superiour Planets, Satvrne & Ivpiter. **1690** LEYBOURN *Curs. Math.* 751 The Motion of the Superiour Planets. **1786–7** BONNYCASTLE *Astron.* 435 Superior Planets, are those which move at a farther distance from the sun than the earth, and are Mars, Jupiter, Saturn, and the Georgium Sidus. **1833** HERSCHEL *Astron.* viii. 253 The superior conjunction will happen when the earth arrives at D, and the planet at *d* in the same line prolonged on the other side of the sun. **1834** MRS. SOMERVILLE *Connex. Phys. Sci.* xiv. 112 The rotation of the earth brings the same point twice under the meridian of the moon in [a day], once under the superior, and once under the inferior, meridian. **1839** MOSELEY *Astron.* xvi. 58 Let the altitude of the star be observed when it is on the meridian ..at what is called its superior passage.

10. *Bot.* Growing above some other part or organ: said of the ovary when situated above or free from the (*inferior*) calyx, and of the calyx when adherent to the sides of the (*inferior*) ovary so that the calyx-lobes are above the ovary.

Also occas. applied to those parts of an axillary flower which lie nearest to the axis (= *posterior*) and to a radicle when directed towards the apex of the fruit (= *ascending*).

1785 MARTYN *Lett. Bot.* v. (1794) 52 Such are called superior flowers, as being above the germ. *Ibid.* xvi. 172 Having..a capsule for a seed-vessel, superior or inclosed within the calyx. **1796** WITHERING *Brit. Plants* (ed. 3) II. 396 Chrysosplenium... Calyx superiour. **1845** LINDLEY *Sch. Bot.* (1862) 13 In many cases the calyx is united to the surface of the pistil..and is then called superior or adherent. **1849** BALFOUR *Man. Bot.* §357 If a whorl of the flower consists of four parts, that which is turned towards the floral axis is called superior or posterior. **1861** BENTLEY *Man. Bot.* 318 The Samara is a superior, two or more celled fruit. *Ibid.* 351 The radicle is said to be superior or ascending..when it is directed towards the apex of the pericarp.

11. *Anat.* and *Zool.* Applied to parts or organs situated above, or in a higher position than, others of the same kind (distinguished as *inferior*), or above the usual or normal position.

1733 G. DOUGLAS tr. *Winslow's Anat.* I. ii. §14 (1756) I. 39 The superior Conchæ of the Ethmoidal Bone. *Ibid.* 75 At the superior and anterior part of the Thorax, between the Scapula and the sternum. **1815** STEPHENS in *Shaw's Gen. Zool.* IX. I. 44 All the feathers of the superior parts of the body. **1826** KIRBY & SP. *Entomol.* IV. 314 Eyes..Superior ..when they are placed in the upper part of the head. *Ibid.* 335 *Superior*, the anterior wings are so denominated if when at rest they are placed upon the posterior wings. **1831–2** *Lancet* II. 119/2 The superior angle of the bifurcation of the carotid and subclavian. **1840** W. J. E. WILSON *Anat. Vade M.* (1842) 33 The superior Maxillary are the largest bones of the face, with the exception of the lower jaw. **1881** MIVART *Cat* 72 The superior meatus of the nose.

12. *Printing.* Applied to small letters or figures, or other characters, made to range above the line, at or near the top of the ordinary letters.

1683 MOXON *Mech. Exerc., Printing* 391 Superiour Letters, are often set to Marginal Notes. **1770** LUCKOMBE *Hist. Printing* 257 Superiour Letters, or else Superior Figures ..were originally..intended to be employed in Matter that is explained by Notes. **1847** SIR F. MADDEN *Layamon's Brut* III. 657 Instead of brackets, superior commas should have been used.

13. *Fortif.* ***superior slope***: the inclined upper surface of the parapet.

1852 BURN *Naval & Milit. Dict.* (1863) s.v. **1892** G. PHILIPS *Text Bk. Fortification, etc.* (ed. 5) 60.

B. *sb.*

1. A person of higher rank or dignity; one who is above another or others in social or official station; *esp.* a superior officer or official. (Commonly with possessive pronoun.)

1483 CAXTON *Gold. Leg., Adam* §6 Lyke as they were inobedyent to theyr superyor, ryght soo theyr membres began to meue ayenst theyr superior. **1502** ATKYNSON tr. *De Imitatione* III. xiv. (1893) 209 Lerne thou to obey gladlye to thy superior. **1558** *Extr. Rec. Burgh Peebles* (1872) 252 The difference..was referrit to tuelf burgessis..and my lord Yester..superiour. **1565** HARDING *Confut. Apol. Ch. Eng.* 190 The Bishop of Rome..in spirituall causes can haue no superiour. **1617** MORYSON *Itin.* I. 170 The Archbishop thereof long time challenged the Primacie in the Italian Church, neuer acknowledging the Bishop of Rome for superiour. **1659** HAMMOND *On Ps.* i. 1 The Rebukes and Censures of Superiours. **1760** *Caut. & Adv. Off. Army* 9 A brisk, alert young Man, who makes it his Study to know, and his Pleasure to perform his Duty, cannot fail of attracting the Regard and Recommendation of his Superiors. **1781** COWPER *Charity* 275 While conscience..Owns no superior but the God she fears. **1786** BURKE *Art. agst. W. Hastings* xx. Wks. 1813 XII. 20 For which I was responsible to my King, and the Company my immediate 'superiours'. **1817** PARR *Wks.* (1828) VII. 257 In respectful conformity to the commands of my ecclesiastical superiors. **1844** [G. R. GLEIG] *Light Dragoon* xxv, Our superiors may think as they please,—but we, who fill up the ranks of the British army, know [etc.]. **1876** J. GRANT *Burgh Sch. Scot.* II. ii. 128 It is unpleasant for a teacher to be opposed to his patrons and superiors.

2. The head of a community of religious (a monastery, nunnery, convent, abbey, etc.); also, the head of a religious order or congregation (more fully, ***superior-general***) or of a department of it.

1497 BP. ALCOCK *Mons Perfect.* c iij b/1 But & he be inobedyent to his superyor than he is no monke but a deuyl. **1582** ALLEN *Martyrd. Father Campion* (1908) 6 So making his choise of the societie of the name of Jesus, he went to Rome, where by the superior of that order he was admitted. **1585** T. WASHINGTON tr. *Nicholay's Voy.* III. xvii. 102 b, A generall chapter or assembly, in which their Priour or Superiour is president. **1621** *Eng. Prot. Plea for Eng. Priests & Papists* 61 The supposed guiltines of M. Garnet, superior of the Iesuits here at that time. *a* **1700** EVELYN *Diary* 4 Nov. 1644, A Benedictine monke and Superior of his Order for the English College of Douay. **1775** in C. Butler *Hist. Mem. Engl. Cath.* lxxv. §9 (1821) IV. 353 The society of Jesus, of which I was superior-general. **1844** A. P. DE LISLE in E. Purcell *Life* (1900) I. vii. 118 After dinner the Superior of the Passionist Monks called upon us. **1850** MRS. JAMESON *Leg. Monast. Ord.* (1863) 21 Benedict, being chosen Superior of the monastery near Subiaco. **1883** *Encycl. Brit.* XVI. 709/1 The founder in 1115 entrusted the superior-generalship of the whole institute to the abbess of the nuns. **1897** E. L. TAUNTON *Engl. Black Monks* II. 301 *note*, They were united into one congregation, with the abbess of Fontevraud as superior-general.

†**b.** *gen.* A governor; a superintendent. *Obs.*

1554 W. PRAT *Aphrique* G j b, There is gyuen to theym an other superior by the Cytizens. **1585** T. WASHINGTON tr. *Nicholay's Voy.* III. x. 90 Ouer these two kitchins..are set and ordained foure superiours.

3. *Feudal Law.* One who (or the successor of one who) has granted an estate of heritable property to another (termed the *vassal*) on condition of the annual payment of a certain sum or the performance of certain services.

1538 STARKEY *England* (1878) 114 Yf a man dye..leuyng hys heyre wythin age, hys landys fal in to the handys of the sayd superyor and lord. **1561** *Abst. Protocols Town Clerks Glasgow* (1896) III. 3 David Bruce..resignit,..and ouregaif in the handis of Robert Callendar..his superior, all and haile ane pece of the Mayneis of B. **1567** *Reg. Privy Council Scot.* Ser. I. I. 540 The giftis of wardis..falland..in oure said sonnis handis as superiour thairof. **1689** in *Acts Parlt. Scot.* (1875) XII. 74/1 The forfaultors of vassells and cre[dito]rs..who shall be innocent of þair superiors or debitors crymes. **1710** in *Nairne Peerage Evidence* (1874) 45 Our immediat lawfull superiors of the said lands. **1753** J. DALRYMPLE *Ess. Feudal Property* (ed. 2) 46 In the origin of the feudal law in Europe, the gift which the vassal on his entry gave to the superior, consisted of armour. **1882** *Encycl. Brit.* XIV. 264/1 Each owner who holds of the sovereign may grant a subordinate estate to be held of himself as 'superior' or lord.

b. ***subject superior***: a superior who holds as subject of a sovereign.

1734 *Treat. Orig. & Progress of Fees* 34 Such Charters are granted by the Sovereign only, and by no Subject Superior. *a* **1768** ERSKINE *Inst. Law Scot.* II. vii. §6 (1773) 281 In lands holden of subject-superiors. **1882** *Encycl. Brit.* XIV. 264/1 The means of commuting the services they had bound themselves to pay to the 'subject superior', and of converting themselves into direct vassals of the crown.

4. A person, or (less commonly) a thing, of higher quality or value than another; one that excels another in some respect. (Commonly with genitive pronoun or *of*.)

1634 FORD *Perk. Warbeck* I. ii, I am confident Thou wilt proportion all thy thoughts to side Thy equals, if not equal thy superiors. **1681** J. SCOTT *Chr. Life* I. iii. §3. (1684) 168 To honour those that are our Superiours whether in Place or Virtue. **1715** POPE *Iliad* II. 722 Dorion,..Superiour once of all the tuneful race. **1807** CRABBE *Par. Reg.* III. 444 None his superior, and his equals few. **1875** JOWETT *Plato* (ed. 2) IV. 231 No one is the superior of the invincible Socrates in argument. **1911** PETRIE *Revol. Civilis.* iii. 54 The period of art which is the rival, if not the superior, of the classical age.

†**5.** *Astron.* A superior planet: see A. 9a. *Obs.*

1679 MOXON *Math. Dict.* s.v. *Postventional*, Before or after any great Conjunction of the Superiors. *Ibid.*, *Superiors*, Saturn, Jupiter, and Mars, are called so..because their Orbs are above the Sun.

†**6.** *Arith.* A number or figure standing above another. *Obs. rare.*

1709 V. MANDEY *Syst. Math.*, *Arith.* (1729) 68 Subtract the Multiplied from its Superior.

7. *Printing.* A superior letter or figure: see A. 12.

1726 S. LOWE *Lat. Gram.* Notes 1 The superior letters in parentheses answer to superiors in the grammar. **1770** LUCKOMBE *Hist. Printing* 258 Superiors of the smallest size are..inconvenient to the Reader. **1882** J. SOUTHWARD *Pract. Printing* (1884) 17 For use in algebraic..works small letters are cast upon the upper part of the shank. These are called superiors.

†**su'periorate.** *Obs. rare*⁻¹. [ad. med.L. *superiōrātus*, f. *superior*: see prec. and -ATE¹.] = SUPERIORSHIP 2.

1498 *Reg. Privy Seal Scotl.* I. 32/1 That our soveran lord be the law recover..the superiorate of the said landis.

superioress (s(j)uːˈpɪərɪərɪs). [f. SUPERIOR *sb.* + -ESS.] A female superior; the head of a convent or order of nuns; a mother superior. Also *superioress-general.*

1671 WOODHEAD *St. Teresa* II. iv. 25 The charge of being Superioress. **1745** A. BUTLER *Lives Saints*, *B. Colette* (1821) III. 40 He constituted her superioress-general of the whole Order of St. Clare. *Ibid.*, *S. Frances* 94 Chosen superioress of her congregation. **1827** DOYLE in W. J. Fitz-Patrick *Life* (1880) II. 27 Novices are not permitted to invite any person, unless expressly desired to do so by the superioress. **1890** J. BRENAN in *38th Rep. Dept. Sci. & Art* (1891) 41 The Superioress, Convent of Mercy, Newry.

superiority (s(j)uːpɪərɪˈɒrɪtɪ). Also 6 *Sc.* -atie, supperioritie. [a. OF. *superiorite* (= It. *superiorità*, Sp. *-idad*, Pg. *-idade*) or ad. their source, med.L. *superiōritās*: see SUPERIOR and -ITY.] The quality or condition of being superior.

†**1. a.** Superior rank, dignity, or official status; superior or supreme command; position or authority as a superior. Const. *of*, *over*. *Obs.*

1526 *Pilgr. Perf.* (W. de W. 1531) 48b, None shold be so hardy..to coueyte superiorite, or to commaunde obedyence. **1561** T. NORTON *Calvin's Inst.* IV. xx. (1634) 744 That there bee made prayers..for Kings and for all that be set in superiority. **1577** HOLINSHED *Chron.* II. 580/2 Kyng Iohn hadde resigned the superioritie of hys Kyngdome..vnto the Pope. **1617** MORYSON *Itin.* I. 5 Luneburg..is one of the free Imperiall Cities; but the Duke of Luneburg challengeth a superiority ouer it. **1633** SIR J. BURROUGHS *Sov. Brit. Seas* (1651) 6 Such is his..indubitable right to the Superiority of the Seas of England. **1662** WINSTANLEY *Loy. Martyrol.* (1665) 103 [Cromwell] having..attained to the Superiority over the Three Kingdomes. **1709** STEELE *Tatler* No. 39 ¶1 Superiority is there given in Proportion to Men's Advancement in Wisdom and Learning.

†**b.** *pl.* Prerogatives of a superior; superior ranks. *Obs.*

1558–9 *Act 1 Eliz.* c. 1 §1 Thauncient Jurisdiccions Aucthoritees Superiorities and Preheminencies. **1581** LAMBARDE *Eiren.* I. x. (1588) 61, I doe utterly renounce..all foraine jurisdiction, powers, superiorities and authorities. **1660** H. MORE *Myst. Godl.* v. xvii. 204 Without changing any Temporal Powers and Superiorities. **1705** HICKERINGILL *Priest-cr.* II. iv. 40 They..strive to monopolize..the highest Dignities, Superiorities and Authorities.

†**c.** *transf.* The superior or ruling class, those in authority. *Obs. rare.*

1542 BOORDE *Dyetary* xii. (1870) 263 A general commaundment hath ben sent from the superyoryte to the commonalte.

†**d.** A community governed by one who has the title of 'superior'. *Obs. rare.*

1721 STRYPE *Eccl. Mem* II. II. xxi. 413 The duchy of Milan,..the superiority of Flanders..the kingdom of Navarre.

e. The position or office of superior of a religious community, superiorship. *rare.*

1706 PHILLIPS (ed. Kersey), *Superiority*,..a being Superiour in a Monastery. **1777** W. DALRYMPLE *Trav. Sp. & Port.* 112 To exchange the superiority of Alcantara for the archbishopric of Seville.

2. a. *Feudal Law.* The position or right of the superior (see SUPERIOR B. 3) of an estate; the lordship of an estate.

a **1572** KNOX *Hist. Ref.* Wks. 1846 I. 427 The Laird of Restalrig,..to quhome the superioratie of Leyth appertenit. **1628** *Sc. Acts Chas. I* (1870) V. 189 Superiorities and Teinds. **1678** G. MACKENZIE *Crim. Laws Scot.* II. xi. §3 (1699) 202 No Lands..but such as belong to him, in whose favours that Jurisdiction was granted, either in Property, or Superiority. **1746** BP. SHERLOCK *Let.* 10 June in *10th Rep. Hist. MSS. Comm.* App. I. 292 The North Britains are so attached to the usages of their country, so fond of the superiorities, [etc.]. **1759** ROBERTSON *Hist. Scot.* III. (1851) I. 237 His superiorities and jurisdictions extended over many of the northern counties. *a* **1768** ERSKINE *Inst. Law Scot.* II. iv. §11 (1773) 212 The superior must lose all the casualties of superiority. **1805** FORSYTH *Beauties Scot.* I. 122 The superiority of the Canongate,..and barony of Broughton, were vested in the Earl of Roxburgh. The Town-Council of Edinburgh purchased these superiorities from the earl. **1828–43** TYTLER *Hist. Scot.* (1864) I. 33 John Comyn, lord of Badenoch,..acknowledged the superiority of Edward. **1868** *Act 31 & 32 Vict.* c. 101 §104 The person having right to the superiority of any lands. **1883** F. H. GROOME *Ordn. Gaz. Scot.* IV. 402/1 Under the superiority of the Baillies of Dochfour, Kingussie is a police burgh.

b. Such a position or right as conferring franchise: see quots. *Sc.*

1846 MCCULLOCH *Acc. Brit. Empire* (1854) II. 212 These fictitious votes, or 'superiorities,' as they were called, soon became matter of traffic,..about half these freeholders possessed merely the superiority—the parchment franchise—without having any right to an acre of the ground! **1861** MAY *Const. Hist.* (1863) I. vi. 300 The county franchise [in Scotland] consisted in 'superiorities,' which were bought and sold in the market.

3. The condition of being stronger than or prevailing over another; supremacy. *Obs.* exc. const. *to* in sense of SUPERIOR *a.* 6b.

a **1548** HALL *Chron.*, *Hen. VI*, 171 Studyeng..how to..get the superioritie and ouerhand aboue their euilwillers. **1553** *Respublica* III. v. 823 *Avar.* And howe dyd all frame with our Mounsire Authorytee? *Oppr.* Att length he wonne the full superiorytee. **1607** (*title*) Lingva: Or The Combat of the Tongue, And the fiue Senses For Superiority. **1611** CORYAT *Crudities* 171 These two streetes doe seeme to contend for the superiority, but the first..is the fairest of them. **1653** R. SANDERS *Physiogn.* 119 The Table line prenotes fidelity, and superiority over enemies. **1770** LANGHORNE *Plutarch* VI. 130 (*Artaxerxes*) They lost their superiority in Greece by the ill-fought battle of Leuctra. *a* **1831** A. KNOX *Rem.* (1844) I. 72 His..obvious superiority to the world and the flesh.

4. a. The quality or condition of being higher, greater, or better in some respect, or of having some attribute in a higher degree, than something else. Const. *to*, *over*, *above*.

1694 LUTTRELL *Brief Rel.* (1857) III. 335 Captain Keggins,..said to have differed with the Dutch about superiority of command. **1707** ADDISON *Pres. St. War* Wks. 1766 III. 257 Our superiority to the enemy in numbers of men and horse. **1736** BUTLER *Anal.* I. iii. Wks. 1874 I. 64 Rational animals have not necessarily the superiority over irrational ones. **1765** *Museum Rust.* IV. 88 Hence appears the great superiority of the hoeing culture. **1794** MRS. RADCLIFFE *Myst. Udolpho* xii, Signor Montoni had an air of conscious superiority animated by spirit and strengthened by talents. **1856** EMERSON *Eng. Traits*, *Aristocracy* Wks. (Bohn) II. 77 All nobility in its beginnings was somebody's natural superiority. **1883** MISS M. BETHAM-EDWARDS *Disarmed* i, He tries to crush me with his superiority. But I am his match with the tongue.

b. With *a* and *pl.* An instance of this.

a **1704** T. BROWN *Eng. Sat.* Wks. 1727 I. 26 Horace and Juvenal..challenge with justice a superiority above all the rest. **1755** YOUNG *Centaur* iii. Wks. 1757 IV. 168 Splendid superiorities cannot be neutral, with regard to the characters of those who possess them. **1839** JAMES *Louis XIV*, III. 247 That nation..made vast efforts to obtain a superiority at sea. **1865** M. ARNOLD *Ess. Crit.* vi. 188 A land where every one has some culture and where superiorities are discountenanced.

5. Special Comb.: **superiority complex**, (*a*) *Psychol.*, an attitude of superiority which conceals actual feelings of inferiority and failure; (*b*) *gen.*, an exaggerated sense of personal superiority; (cf. *inferiority complex* s.v. INFERIORITY 2).

1929 A. ADLER *Probl. Neurosis* vi. 87 In his business we find the man with a 'superiority complex': but if he were to lose his position..he would promptly go back to the expression of inferiority and make capital out of it. **1936** H. PREECE in *Crisis* Dec. 364/2 Each expression of this interest in the Negro is the manifestation of a definite superiority complex. **1945** A. L. ROWSE *English Spirit* xxxiii. 232 The English have a singular faculty for depreciating their great men. (Is it perhaps a form of superiority-complex?) **1979** *Nature* 11 Oct. 424/2 The Egyptian scientific community does not like or agree with the Israeli superiority complex.

superiorly (s(j)uːˈpɪərɪəlɪ), *adv.* [f. SUPERIOR *a.* + -LY².] In a superior place, degree, or manner.

1. In a higher position or place; in the upper part, above; to a higher position, upwards.

1556 J. HEYWOOD *Spider & F.* lxxxviii. 109 Spiders are plaste a boue superiorlie, And flies beneth them plaste inferiorlie. **1597** A. M. tr. *Guillemeau's Fr. Chirurg.* 46/2 The third ascendeth superiorlye, from the soule of the foote towardes the knees. **1599** —— tr. *Gabelhouer's Bk. Physicke* 144/2 An externall meanes to provoack stooles for those which nether superiourlye, nor inferiourlye can vse anye Physick. **1836** *Penny Cycl.* V. 260/1 Its belly of a reddish brown superiorly and a dirty grey beneath. **1870** ROLLESTON *Anim. Life* 141 In this central furrow [was] lodged..most superiorly the water-vascular canal.

2. In a higher degree, more highly, better.

1643 SIR J. SPELMAN *Case of Affairs* 15 The superioritie..that is subordinately in the inferiour Courts, is but more superiourly in the House of Lords than them. **1779** W. ALEXANDER *Hist. Women* (1782) I. viii. 280 Where the love of the men is directed more to the sex than the individual, a woman has no motive to excite even a wish of being superiorly beautiful. **1816** BENTHAM *Chrestom.* i. Wks. 1843 VIII. 16/1 The superiorly instructed boy. **1828** P. CUNNINGHAM *N.S. Wales* (ed. 3) II. 327 Superiorly watered to almost any other district in the colony. **1830** MARRYAT *King's Own* xxxi, The launch..firing round and grape..with a rapidity that almost enabled her to return gun for gun to her superiorly-armed antagonist.

3. In positive or absolute sense: In a high degree, highly; more or better than the generality; beyond the average; supereminently.

1728 MORGAN *Algiers* I. Pref. p. xiv, A Person so superiorly capable of giving it. **1755** SHEBBEARE *Lydia* (1769) I. 314 The..dejection..that attends those who chuse mourning for the death of those whom they love superiorly. **1783** H. WALPOLE *Let. to Earl of Strafford* 11 Dec., With regard to letter-writing, I am firmly persuaded that it is a province in which women will always shine superiorly. **1802** MRS. E. PARSONS *Myst. Visit* I. 98 To conceive their woes superiorly great. **1802–12** BENTHAM *Ration. Judic. Evid.* (1827) V. 474 Evidence..of a nature so superiorly trustworthy. **1835** BECKFORD *Recoll.*, etc. 18 This superiorly fine and glowing morning. **1882** STEVENSON *New Arab. Nts.* II. xii. 220 A work of art superiorly composed.

4. With an air or attitude of superiority.

1844 EMERSON *Ess.*, *Nominalist & Realist*, The audience..judge very wisely and superiorly how wrong-headed and unskilful is each of the debaters to his own affair.

So **su'periorness**, superiority.

1796 MME. D'ARBLAY *Camilla* III. vi, I don't see the great superiorness of learning, if it can't keep a man's temper out of a passion.

su'periorship. [f. SUPERIOR *a.* and *sb.* + -SHIP.]

1. The state of being superior, superiority. *nonce-use.*

1709 MRS. MANLEY *Secret Mem.* (1720) III. 267 How do you think we agree about the Point of Superiorship?

2. The position or office of superior.

1874 MRS. H. WOOD *Mast. Greylands* xxxii, You will be sorry, now, that you have resigned the superiorship to me. **1909** J. STARK *Priest Gordon of Aberd.* Introd. p. xxiii. Freed from the Jurisdiction of the English Prelates and Jesuit Superiorship.

superius (s(j)uːˈpɪərɪəs). *Mus.* [a. L. *superius*, neut. (used as *sb.*) of *superior* SUPERIOR *a.*] (See quots. 1801, 1876.) Also *transf.*, a person who sings this part.

[**1519** O. PETRUCCI *Motetti de la Corona* (heading) Libro secundo. (Superius.)] **1776** J. HAWKINS *Gen. Hist. Sci. & Pract. Music* II. I. vii. 86 *Quinible*..may rather mean a high part.., which in general lies above the tenor..and at others between the contretenor and the superius or treble. **1801** T. BUSBY *Dict. Mus.*, *Superius*,..the name by which the contrapuntists of the fifteenth and sixteenth centuries distinguished the *upper part* of any composition. **1876** STAINER & BARRETT *Dict. Mus. Terms* 412/1 *Superius*,..a name given to the upper part in a composition by the writers of the sixteenth century. **1907** *Grove's Dict. Mus.* (ed. 2) III. 631/1 'Le Parangon des Chansons', printed by 'Jaques Moderne'..in nine volumes..and..so arranged that the Superius and Tenor sit facing each other, on opposite sides of the table—the Superius reading from the lower half of the left-hand page, and the Tenor from the upper half. **1954** G. REESE *Music in Renaissance* i. 16 The *texture* in which a vocal top line (or, as this part is interchangeably called, treble, superius, cantus, or discantus) is supported by a subordinate, instrumental tenor and contratenor was much in vogue. **1970** *Proc. R. Mus. Assoc.* 1969–70 95 The fourth and final line of the text..telescopes the beginning and end of Sandrin's superius. **1977** *Early Music* Apr. 243/3 Surely..the superius should cadence on C with the other voices. *Ibid.* July 419/2 The superius of his motet *Sufficiebat*..is closely related to the tenor of Hayne's chanson *Mon souvenir.*

superjacent (s(j)uːpəˈdʒeɪsənt), *a.* [ad. late L. *superjacent-*, *-ens*, pr. pple. of *superjacēre*: see SUPER- 2 and JACENT. Cf. F. *surjacent.*] Lying above or upon something else; overlying, superincumbent. (Now chiefly in technical use.)

1610 GUILLIM *Heraldry* III. xxiii. (1611) 171 Such was the coat before the addition of the superiacent canton. **1664** POWER *Exp. Philos.* II. 108 As 32. foot of Superjacent water would raise up a Mercurial Cylinder of 29. inches. **1831** R. KNOX *Cloquet's Anat.* 314 The muscles of the arm are dissected by removing the superjacent skin [etc.]. **1867** MURCHISON *Siluria* i. (ed. 4) 13 The superjacent crystalline rocks..of Lower Silurian age. **1897** *Allbutt's Syst. Med.* II. 1077 The superjacent skin is freely moveable, but the tumour cannot be slipped over the subjacent tissues.

†**super'jection.** *Obs. rare.* [ad. L. *superjectiōnem*, f. *superject-*, *-jacĕre*, f. *super-* SUPER- 2 + *jacĕre* to throw.]

1. The action of casting over or upon something.

1656 BLOUNT *Glossogr.*, *Superiection*, a laying or casting upon.

2. Exaggeration, hyperbole.

1657 REEVE *God's Plea* 204 His nimieties of expression, his diffluences, redundances, superjections, and transiliences of speech.

superjet: see SUPER- 6 c.

,Superlap'sarian, *sb.* and *a. Theol. rare.* [See SUPER- 8, and cf. SUBLAPSARIAN.] = SUPRALAPSARIAN.

1668 H. MORE *Div. Dial.* III. xv. (1713) 209 The Religion of the Superlapsareans, the Object whereof is Infinite Power unmodified by either Justice or Goodness. *a* **1679** T. GOODWIN *Disc. Election* IV. viii. Wks. 1682 II. 305 Those that are called Superlapsarians, they say, Man came up into God's mind first without the consideration of the Fall. **1807–8** SYD. SMITH *Plymley's Lett.* Wks. 1859 II. 137/1 Every sublapsarian, and superlapsarian, and semi pelagian clergyman.

† **super'lation.** *Obs. rare*$^{-1}$. [ad. L. *superlātio*, *-ōnem*, n. of action f. *superlāt-*: see next.] Exaggeration, hyperbole.

1636 B. JONSON *Discov.*, *Periodi..Superlatio*, There are words, that doe as much raise a style, as others can depresse it. Superlation, and over-muchnesse amplifies.

superlative (s(j)uː'pɜːlətɪv), *a.* and *sb.* Also 4–5 -yf, 5 -yff, -yfe, 5–6 -yve, 7 -if. [a. OF. *superlatif* (13th c.) = Pr. *superlatiu*, It., Sp., Pg. *superlativo*, ad. late L. *superlātīvus*, f. *superlātus* (used as pa. pple. of *superferre*), f. *super-* SUPER- II + *lāt-* (for **tlāt-*), pa. ppl. stem of *tollěre* to take away.] A. *adj.*

1. a. *Gram.* Applied to that inflexional form of an adjective or adverb used, in comparing a number of things, to express the highest degree of the quality or attribute denoted by the simple word, as *sweet-est*, *tru-est*, *often-est* (or to the periphrasis used in the same sense, as *most sweet*, *most true*, *most often*); the adjective or adverb is then said to be in the ***superlative degree***, and is usually preceded by the definite article. Freq. used *allusively*.

The English periphrastic form is also frequently used (with the indefinite article), like the inflexional form in Latin and Greek, in an absolute or intensive sense, to express a very high degree of the quality or attribute, without definite comparison with other objects.

c **1386** CHAUCER *Merch. T.* 131 Ther nys no thyng in gree superlatyf As seith Senek aboue an humble wyf. **1447** BOKENHAM *Seyntys* (Roxb.) 162 In love among these thre To spekyn aftyr degrees of comparysoun Mary stood in the superlatyue degre. **1530** PALSGR. 71 He standeth for the superlatyve degre. **1575** GASCOIGNE *Making of Verse* Wks. 1907 I. 466 If I should undertake to wryte in prayse of a gentlewoman, I would..finde some supernaturall cause wherby my penne might walke in the superlative degree. **1636** B. JONSON *Engl. Gram.* II. iv, These adverbs, *more*, and *most*, are added to the Comparative, and Superlative degrees themselves. **1651** HOBBES *Govt. & Soc.* xv. §14. 249 He.. must use such [titles] as are either Negative, as infinite, eternall, incomprehensible, &c., or superlative, as most good, most great, most powerfull. **1657** TRAPP *Comm. Ezra* v. 8 'God of gods, Lord of lords'— yea He is a degree above the superlative. *a* **1667** COWLEY *Ess.*, *Of Liberty* Wks. (1906) 383 The Positive Parting with a little bow, the Comparative at the middle of the room, the Superlative at the door. **1824** L. MURRAY *Engl. Gram.* (ed. 5) I. 250 Adjectives that have in themselves a superlative signification, do not properly admit of the superlative or comparative form..such as, 'Chief, extreme, perfect'. **1886** KINGTON OLIPHANT *New Engl.* I. 165 The Superlative Adverb *gladlyest*. *Ibid.* II. 189 [Miss Burney] is fond of the French idiom that places the Superlative Adjective after the Substantive; as 'a facility the most happy'. **1910** J. W. HARPER *Social Ideal* xiii. §3. 150 Liberty is the positive, equality the comparative, and brotherhood the superlative agency of social progress.

b. Exaggerative, hyperbolical. (Cf. B. 1 b.)

1588 FRAUNCE *Lawiers Logike* Ded., To disgrace the one, or advance the other in comparison wise, by superlative woordes, and hyperbolicall amplifications. **1828** MISS MITFORD *Village* Ser. III. (1863) 7 To all who knew Nelly's opinion of her own doings, this praise appeared superlative. **1906** CHURCHILL *Sp. Ho. Comm.* 21 Mar., I hope I shall not be drawn..into imitating..the protracted, superlative, and, I think, rather laboured exhibition with which he has occupied the attention of the House.

2. Raised above or surpassing all others; extremely high, great, or excellent; supereminent, supreme. a. Of persons and material things.

c **1410** HOCCLEVE *Mother of God* 9 Modir of mercy,..þat of al vertu art superlatyf. **1423** JAS. I *Kingis Q.* cxcvii, Gowere and chaucere,..Superlatiue as poetis laureate. **1477** EARL RIVERS (Caxton) *Dictes* 123 The viij. leches..whiche were all .viij. superlatyff aboue all other lechis. **1592** NASHE *Strange Newes* I iv, Betweene you and me declare..whether you be not a superlatiue blocke, for al you readd the Philosophie Lecture at Cambridge. *a* **1628** F. GREVIL *Life of Sidney* (1652) 75 A Peer of this Realme,..superlative in the Princes favour. **1630** DEKKER *2nd Pt. Honest Wh.* Wks. 1873 II. 170 O euerlasting, supernaturall superlatiue Villaine! **1657** *North's Plutarch, Add. Lives* (1676) 18 Natural Philosophy, wherein Aristotle was so superlative. **1706** E. WARD *Wooden World Diss.* (1708) 105 He..allows Newcastle Ale and Salmon to be the most superlative Diet in the Universe. **1838** DICKENS *Nich. Nick.* xxxiv, You are the demdest, knowing hand,..the cunningest, rummest, superlativest, old fox. **1868** STANLEY *Westm. Abbey* iii. 124 Its Chapter House, its ornaments..were to be superlative of their kind.

b. Of immaterial things, actions, qualities, etc.

c **1550** ROLLAND *Crt. Venus* I. 760 Thay..Ponderat weill the falt superlatiue. **1610** HOLLAND *Camden's Brit.* (1637) 256 Queene Elizabeth,..worthy of superlative praise. **1625** BACON *Ess.*, *Viciss. Things*, Superlatiue and Admirable Holinesse of Life. **1647** N. BACON *Disc. Govt. Eng.* I. lii. (1739) 93 Reason of State, which as the times then were, was evident and superlative. **1665** WITHER *Lord's Prayer* Preamb., This superlative Form of Prayer. **1762** FALCONER *Shipwr.* III. 115 Thy state..Gain'd, like thine arms, superlative applause. **1798** S. & HT. LEE *Canterb. T.* II. 27 Miss Archer's advice she treated with superlative contempt. **1878** BOSW. SMITH *Carthage* 189 This religious mission he ..carried out to the best of his superlative ability.

c. ***superlative surprise***, the name given to an especially complicated method of change-ringing. Cf. SURPRISE *sb.* 5 b.

1788 W. JONES et al. *Key to Art of Ringing* xi. 179 Superlative Surprise... The above is an original composition of our own on purpose for this work, and has never yet been rung: the principle upon which it is founded, will..give it credit among amateurs of the art, for..it will plainly appear the most even treble bob peal..discovered. **1843** *Cambr. Chron.* 6 Dec. 4/3 The company of change-ringers, of Saffron Walden, performing..upwards of 1,200 changes of Superlative Surprise. **1874** W. BANISTER *Art & Science Change Ringing* 33 (*heading*) Superlative Surprise. **1931** E. MORRIS *Hist. Change Ringing* 458 Harry Withers.. once..conducted a peal of Superlative Surprise at Selly Oak, Birmingham. **1965** W. G. WILSON *Change Ringing* 237/2 Superlative Surprise Major, 1:4.

B. *sb.*

1. a. *Gram.* The superlative degree; an adjective or adverb in the superlative degree.

Also, by extension, applied to any word denoting the highest degree of some quality (quot. 1802).

1530 PALSGR. Introd. p. xxviii, We and the latines forme our comparatives and superlatyves out of our posytives. **1567** SANDERS *Rocke Ch.* ii. 31 According to the Greeke phrase (where the comparatiue standeth for the Superlatiue). **1638** BAKER tr. *Balzac's Lett.* (vol. II) 220, I will now at the end of my letter, add a superlative, and say I am Sir y^{r} most humble, most faithfull. *a* **1721** PRIOR *Dial. Dead, Charles & Clenard* (1907) 218 Your very Titles, Your *Serenissimus* and *Augustissimus* are superlatives created by the Power of us Grammarians. **1802** PALEY *Nat. Theol.* xxiv, 'Omnipotence,' 'omniscience,' 'infinite' power, 'infinite' knowledge, are superlatives; expressing our conception of these attributes in the..most elevated terms. **1824** L. MURRAY *Engl. Gram.* (ed. 5) I. 250 Double comparatives and superlatives should be avoided: such as, 'A worser conduct;'..'The most straitest sect'. **1886** KINGTON OLIPHANT *New Engl.* II. 43 There is the old superlative of the Adverb, 'the rudeliest welcomed'. **1892** KELLNER *Engl. Syntax* §255 *heading*, The Comparative and Superlative used absolutely.

fig. **1583** GREENE *Mamillia* Wks. (Grosart) II. 47 Virginity you say is delightful, yet matrimony more pleasant: Virginity you put in the positiue, but matrimonie in the superlatiue. **1725** WATTS *Logic* II. iii. iii. §6 Some Persons have a violent and turgid Manner both of Talking and Thinking... They..pronounce concerning everything in the Superlative. **1856** EMERSON *Eng. Traits*, *Truth* Wks. (Bohn) II. 53 An Englishman..avoids the superlative, checks himself in compliments.

b. *transf.* An exaggerated or hyperbolical expression; usually *pl.*, exaggerated language or phraseology.

1597 DRAYTON *Heroic. Ep.* x. 64 His birth from heauen thy Tudor not deriues, Nor stands on typ-toes in superlatiues. **1597** BP. HALL *Sat.* I. Prol. 12 [He] Hath made his pen an hyred Parasite, To..pranck base men in Proud Superlatiues. **1697** DRYDEN *Virgil*, *Life* (1721) I. 45 Nor were they under the constraint..of violent Superlatives at the close of their Letter. **1896** *Fam. & Pers. Mem. Ld. Selborne* I. ix. 137 He thought and felt in superlatives.

2. A person or thing surpassing all others of the class or kind; one who or a thing which is supereminent or supreme; the highest example (*of* a quality). Now *rare*, and with allusion to sense 1.

1600 W. WATSON *Decacordon* (1602) 359 Amongst the most famous preachers in Rome..three were..all superlatiues in a different kind. *c* **1645** HOWELL *Lett.* (1688) IV. 433 This..is the best of all, and may be called the Superlatif of the three. **1777** SHERIDAN *Sch. Scandal*, *To Mrs. Crewe* 38 Nature's best and heaven's superlative. **1885** W. F. CRAFTS *Sabbath for Man* (1895) 188 The so-called Christians who sanction these Sunday parties are the superlatives of hypocrisy. **1903** *Westm. Gaz.* 17 Sept. 5/2, I sell bread here made from best 'London whites' and 'superlatives' at 6d. per loaf.

3. The highest or utmost degree of something; the height, acme. Usually with allusion to sense 1.

1583 MELBANCKE *Philotimus* Ff ij, The prince of whome I speake, is in the Positiue degree of her Superlatiue. **1589** PUTTENHAM *Engl. Poesie* I. viii. (Arb.) 29 Monasticall men then raigning al in their superlatiue. **1623** MASSINGER *Dk. Milan* III. iii, Dearest lady,..Make a superlative of excellence In being greatest in your saving mercy. **1653** R. SANDERS *Physiogn. Moles* 4 The superlative of his good fortunes shall be in Merchandizing. *a* **1687** WALLER *On Divine Poesy* I. 24 What mortal can with heav'n pretend to share In the superlatives of wise, and fair? **1837** CARLYLE *Fr. Rev.* I. v. ix, So many highest superlatives achieved by man are followed by new higher; and dwindle into comparatives and positives!

su'perlatively, *adv.* [f. prec. adj. + -LY^{2}.]

1. In a superlative manner; in the highest (or a very high) degree; supereminently, supremely.

1596 WARNER *Alb. Eng.* XII. lxxiv. (1612) 307 What, is she married? Then do yee superlatiuely sinne. **1639** FULLER *Holy War* I. xxiv. (1840) 45 Valour was not wanting in the Turks, but superlatively abundant in the Christians. **1706** E. WARD *Wooden World Diss.* (1708) 68 Channel-Cruizers, ..are superlatively the best for his Purpose. **1796** MORSE *Amer. Geog.* I. 728 There are 35 species of Mexican birds that are superlatively beautiful. **1828** P. CUNNINGHAM *N.S. Wales* (ed. 3) II. 265 The fantastic airs and quavers of others [*sc.* singers] were superlatively ridiculous. **1835** POE *Adv. Hans Pfaall* Wks. 1864 I. 3 A brim superlatively broad. **1868** KINGLAKE *Crimea* (1877) IV. vi. 145 Superlatively important matters.

2. With the use of superlatives; with exaggeration. *rare.*

c **1615** BACON *Adv. Sir G. Villiers* ii. §1, I shall not speak superlatively of them [*sc.* laws of England]; but this I may truly say, they are second to none in the Christian world.

So **su'perlativeness**, the quality of being superlative.

1727 BAILEY (vol. II). **1888** H. W. PARKER *Spir. Beauty* (1891) 70 Variation into all forms of use and loveliness and final superlativeness.

'superlattice. [SUPER- 5.] 1. *Metallurgy.* An ordered arrangement of some of the atoms in a solid solution extending through large parts of it and coexisting with the disorder of the remaining atoms; also, a solid solution possessing this; = SUPERSTRUCTURE 3.

1932 *Proc. R. Soc.* A. CXXXVI. 211 A structure of this kind is usually termed a superlattice (überstruktur). **1951** N. F. M. HENRY et al. *Interpret. X-Ray Diffraction Photographs* xv. 211/1 The use of the word 'superlattice' is unfortunate. The original German word *Uberstruktur* conveyed perfectly the concept of a new type of ordered structure being imposed on the existing disordered phase. This has nothing to do with the type of lattice. **1966** C. R. TOTTLE *Sci. Engin. Materials* viii. 187 Domains form and grow during normal superlattice formation, according to composition, temperature, and time of annealing. **1967** A. H. COTTRELL *Introd. Metallurgy* xiv. 190 When formed from true metals the structure is often an ordered solid solution or superlattice, in which the two species are arranged in some regular alternating pattern. **1978** *Nature* 9 Nov. 168/2 Evidence..that an FeNi $L1_0$ superlattice exists in the taenite of the Cape York and Toluca meteorites. **1979** [see SUPERSTRUCTURE 3].

2. *Physics.* A small-scale periodicity in the composition of a semiconductor.

1970 *IBM Jrnl. Res. & Development* XIV. 61 We consider a one-dimensional periodic potential, or 'super-lattice', in monocrystalline semiconductors formed by a periodic variation of alloy composition or of impurity density during epitaxial growth. **1977** *McGraw-Hill Yearbk. Sci. & Technol.* 380/1 Photocurrent measurements in the superlattice structures have made it possible to observe simultaneously quantum states and associated anomalous conductance.

† **super'liminary**, *a. Obs. rare*$^{-1}$. [f. L. *super* above + *līmin-*, *līmen* threshold + -ARY.] Preliminary, introductory.

1675 V. ALSOP *Anti-Sozzo* i. 6 It has been accounted very ominous to stumble at the Threshold, and whilest he layes it down as a superliminary Maxim that all Errour has some, yet to instance in One which has no, Appearance of Truth.

superloo, -luminal: see SUPER- 6 c, 4 a (*a*).

† **super'lucrate**, *v. Obs. rare.* [f. late L. *superlucrāt-*, pa. ppl. stem of *superlucrārī*, f. *super-* SUPER- 13 + *lucrārī*, f. *lucrum* LUCRE.] *trans.* To gain in addition, make a profit of (so much). So † **,superlu'cration**, additional gain or profit; † **superlucrator**, one who gains a profit.

1652 URQUHART *Jewel* Wks. (1834) 213 For no respect will they depart from so much as one single peny, whose emission doth not..superlucrate beyond all Conscience an additional increase. *a* **1687** PETTY *Pol. Arith.* iv. (1690) 73 The Superlucration will be above Three Millions and Six Hundred thousand Pounds per annum. *Ibid.* 77 There are more Superlucrators in the English, than the French Dominions. *Ibid.* viii. 107 Although..the People of England do thrive, and that it is possible they might Superlucrate twenty five Millions per annum. **1698** C. DAVENANT *Disc. Publick Rev.* I. v. 195 Where the Annual Income exceeds the Expence, there is a Superlucration arising. **1719** W. WOOD *Surv. Trade* 155 The Superlucration from the same Number of Men, over and above their own Nourishment. **1768** *Woman of Honor* II. 177 The scandalous superlucration of pensions and reversions.

super'lunar, *a.* [Formed as next, after *sublunar.*] = next.

1742 POPE *Dunc.* IV. 451 The head that turns at superlunar things, Pois'd with a tail, may steer on Wilkins' wings. **1839** J. STERLING *Ess.*, etc. (1848) I. 292 When he can get a brighter tint..by means of some strange..Carlylism, English, Scotch..Lunar, or altogether Superlunar,..he uses it. **1900** *Daily News* 7 Dec. 6/7 This superior and superlunar attitude.

superlunary (s(j)uːpə'l(j)uːnərɪ), *a.* (*sb.*) [f. L. *super* SUPER- 1 + *lūna* moon + -ARY, after *sublunary.*] Situated above or beyond the moon; belonging to a higher world, celestial; *fig.* extravagant: the opposite of *sublunary*.

1614 PURCHAS *Pilgrimage* I. ii. (ed. 2) 8 Our sense, which thence receiueth Light, and there in the æthereall region seeth new Starres and superlunarie Comets. **1634** T. CAREW *Cœlum Brit.* Wks. (1824) 156 Jupiter hath before a frequent convocation of the superlunary peeres recanted. **1676** MARVELL *Mr. Smirke* 31 This superlunary instance does not serve in the least to confirme his Argument that he makes against the Authors words. **1708** H. DODWELL *Expl. Dial. Justin* 78 Genius, a Dæmon,..a Superlunary Being, whom he supposes to have a Language proper to their own Kind. **1742** YOUNG *Nt. Th.* VI. 756 Other ambition than of crowns in air, And superlunary felicities. **1837** CARLYLE *Misc. Ess.*, *Diam. Necklace* (1872) V. 159 The foolish Cardinal, since no sublunary means..will serve, has taken to the superlunary. **1885** MEREDITH *Diana* xliii, As for her superlunary sphere, it was in fragments.

†**b.** *sb.* A superlunary being. *Obs.*

1708 H. DODWELL *Expl. Dial. Justin* 80 They were not Superlunaries (as Mr. Chishull supposes).

super-male: see SUPER- 5 f (and 6 c).

superman ('s(j)u:pəmæn). [f. SUPER- 6 + MAN *sb.*¹, transl. G. *übermensch* (F. W. Nietzsche, German philosopher, 1844–1900). Cf. F. *surhomme* (Lichtenberger, 1901), occas. *superhomme*. *Overman* and (occas.) *beyond-man* have been used.] **1.** An ideal superior man conceived by Nietzsche as being evolved from the normal human type; *loosely*, a man of extraordinary power or ability; a superior being. Also *transf.* and *allusively*.

1903 G. B. SHAW *Man & Superman* 196 We have been driven to Proletarian Democracy by the failure of all the alternative systems; for these depended on the existence of Supermen acting as despots or oligarchs; and not only were these Supermen not always or even often forthcoming at the right moment and in an eligible social position, but when they were forthcoming they could not..impose superhumanity on those whom they governed. **1903** *Speaker* 17 Oct. 61/1 It is possible by breeding, by education, by social reconstruction, that the Superman may be attained. **1904** G. S. HALL *Adolescence* I. 47 Relatively.. man is now in a recent epoch,..in which a new story has been added to his nature, so that he is now a super-man to his ancient forebears. **1907** *Westm. Gaz.* 20 Mar. 2/1 Christ is now the Spiritual super-man, who has anticipated humanity and reached the goal of its spiritual evolution. **1912** C. SAROLEA *Anglo-German Problem* i. 59 Like Nietzsche, the modern German believes that the world must be ruled by a superman, and that he is the super-man. **1925** H. V. MORTON *Heart of London* 110 Above the kneeling priests is the Pharaoh, that ancient superman. **1942** *R.A.F. Jrnl.* 13 June 15 They are neither freaks nor super-men. *Ibid.* 18 The stories told in the newspapers to emphasise the superman qualities which the Commandos deny possessing. **1959** KOESTLER *Sleepwalkers* v. ii. 471 Both considered themselves supermen and started on a basis of mutual adulation. **1969** G. JACKSON *Let.* 28 Dec. in *Soledad Brother* (1971) 179 How could there be a *benevolent* superman controlling a world like this.

2. (With capital initial.) The name of an invincible hero with superhuman powers, including that of flight, introduced in an American comic strip (1938). Also *transf.* and *allusively*.

1938 *Action Comics* June 1 So was created..Superman! champion of the oppressed, the physical marvel who had sworn to devote his existence to helping those in need! **1940** *Time* 26 Feb. 44/3 Last week Superman took to the air in earnest, as a three-a-week serial. **1942** H. HAYCRAFT *Murder for Pleasure* ix. 191 Converting Strangeway's wife Georgia into what Miriam Allen de Ford calls 'a sort of female Superman'. **1958** *Times Lit. Suppl.* 1 Apr. p. xx/4 The impression remains of a sense of values associated with 'Superman' and American comics. **1968** S. ELLIN *Valentine Estate* III. iv. 142 'How the hell did he come to miss me?'.. 'You're Superman,' the first man answered. 'Bullets bounce off you.' **1976** *Survey* Winter 1 The..*New York Times*..in the past presented Henry Kissinger as a species of diplomatic superman. **1977** *New Scientist* 14 Apr. 59/3 Schlesinger..is riding high at present—pictured in a superman suit on a recent *Time* magazine cover. **1980** F. WELDON *Puffball* 77 'Now it's our turn.' 'I don't want it to be,' she said, as if he, like Superman, could turn the world the other way.

Hence '**supermanhood**; also '**supermanism**, the doctrine of the superman; '**supermanly** *a.* [cf. MANLY *a.* 2], having the qualities of, or befitting, the or a superman; whence **supermanliness**.

1905 CHESTERTON *Heretics* 85 If the Superman..is merely more supermanly [than other men], they may be quite indifferent to him. **1907** MARETT *Threshold Relig., Is Taboo a Negative Magic?* (1914) 97 Lest they be blasted by the superman's supermanliness. **1910** *Dublin Rev.* Oct. 344 Human nature..is likely to remain still exactly the same. Those who believe it to be travelling towards moral supermanhood have obviously not studied it. **1916** SIR J. YOXALL in *19th Cent.* Sept. 467 Perhaps he [*sc.* Nietzsche] got some adumbration of Supermanism in that way. **1924** W. J. LOCKE *Coming of Amos* xix. 254 My vanity was pricked by what seemed to be her lack of confidence in my supermanhood. **1964** *Punch* 1 Apr. 507/3 Convincingly exciting, despite hero's slight leaning towards supermanhood.

'**supermarket**. orig. *U.S.* Also **super market**. [SUPER- 6 c.] **1. a.** A large self-service shop, selling a wide range of groceries and household goods, and freq. one of a chain of stores.

1933 *N.Y. Times* 25 Feb. 28/1 In a move interpreted by the trade as an effort to help both corporate chains and independent wholesale grocers fight the competition of 'super-markets' which have sprung up in the last two years, the Associated Grocery Manufacturers of America, Inc., yesterday drew up a proposed model law for States which may seek to prevent the sale of standard grocery products at or below purchase price. *Ibid.* 5 Mar. 11/4 For three months now a large supermarket in New Jersey has been doing a business reputed to average $100,000 a week. **1933** *Chain Store Age* (Gen. Merchandise ed.) June 95/1 The 'One-stop-drive-in super market' provides free parking, and every kind of food under one roof. **1949** R. GRAVES *Seven Days in New Crete* 121 We buyers..drifted round with our baskets, silently helping ourselves to whatever we wanted... The procedure recalled that of an American super-market. **1959** *Spectator* 25 Sept. 409/1 This applies particularly to supermarkets, whose whole economy depends on people going in to buy a can of beans and coming out with a dazed expression and three pounds' worth of groceries. **1969** *Islander* (Victoria, B.C.) 6 July 8/2 Your supplies..come from a good delicatessen and..your super market. **1978** *Oxford Consumer* Mar. 4/1 The change from counter to self-service stores in Britain only started in the late 1950's/early 1960's, when a supermarket was defined as having a minimum sales area of 2,000 sq. ft. **1979** M. BOYCE *I was There!* 70 The pithead baths is a supermarket now.

b. *transf.* and *fig.*

1962 *Listener* 26 July 127/2 The Marshall Plan and this vast new Supermarket have destroyed the roots of that sickness. **1973** J. W. POLIER in A. E. Wilkerson *Rights of Children* p. xiv, The 1970 White House Conference on Children announced that prepared reports would offer 'a supermarket of proposals'.

2. a. *attrib.*, as ***supermarket chain, company, shopping***, etc.

1933 *N.Y. Times* 26 Feb. 15/8 The independent and corporate chain stores are standing together against the alleged menace of the 'super-market' competition. **1934** *Archit. Rec.* LXXVI. 206 Markets are now built up to the street line and are of the 'super-market' type. **1951** C. W. MILLS *White Collar* I. ii. 25 As supermarkets mushroomed ..the chains began to imitate their supermarket competitors. **1963** *Times Rev. Industry* Aug. 65/2 Premier.. is one of the few supermarket companies proper with a highly developed and well integrated scheme. **1967** G. WILLS in Wills & Yearsley *Handbk. Management Technol.* 192 A product which cannot gain distribution in the major supermarket chains may have a very high direct percentage distribution yet a low percentage sterling distribution. **1975** D. LODGE *Changing Places* iii. 115 We seem to have fixed on the same day for supermarket shopping. **1977** F. PARRISH *Fire in Barley* ii. 24 A lifetime of deep-frozen scampi, supermarket Riesling, [etc.].

b. *Comb.*, as **supermarket trolley**, a wire basket on wheels which a supermarket customer can push around the shop collecting goods for purchase; also (U.S.) ***supermarket cart***.

1972 *Even. Telegram* (St. John's, Newfoundland) 28 June 29/6 (Advt.), 5 supermarket carts. **1970** *Cape Times* 28 Oct. 21/3 (Advt.), Lawn mowers, kitchenware, glassware, 22 supermarket trollies. **1977** *Irish Times* 8 June 8/8, I wandered in to sit with the farmers, and saw a heifer that would fit into a supermarket trolley sell for £60. **1982** BARR & YORK *Official Sloane Ranger Handbk.* 95/1 He and his chums stage a mixed doubles wheelbarrow/piggy-back/supermarket trolley race down the High/the Broad/the Cornmarket.

Hence ,**supermarke'teer** [-EER], a person or company involved in a supermarket business.

1960 *Spectator* 13 May 712 Nor have many of the supermarketeers realised that self-service in itself gets you nowhere. **1964** *Punch* 29 Jan. 174/3 Other supermarketeers include London Grocers. **1973** *Guardian* 17 Feb. 13/6 To ask them to cut their profits still further would, in the view of the supermarketeer, be both unjust and ineffective.

'**supermart.** [SUPER- 6 c.] = prec.

1954 *Archit. Rev.* CXVI. 234 Beneath the two major blocks..the lower floors will house shops, a supermart, a highways terminal, an art museum, [etc.]. **1961** *Guardian* 17 Feb. 8/6 The baby sitting up in the supermart trolley. **1978** P. VAN GREENAWAY *Man called Scavener* xiv. 193 Take any name familiar to our age: a supermart..a refrigerator.

supermassive: see SUPER- 9 a (*a*).

'**supermind. 1.** [SUPER- 6 c.] A mind of exceptional capacity or ability; a person possessing such a mind.

1918 *Daily News* (Chicago) 5 Jan. 10/6 (*heading*) Four super-minds ruling in Loop. **1962** 'S. RANSOME' *Without Trace* v. 50 Loot that wasn't dropping soon enough because ..that high-geared supermind of Lynch's kept hanging fire. **1975** J. TAYLOR *Superminds* (1976) ix. 161 The view of a group of defence workers..who advised their government to liquidate all superminds as being a menace to security.

2. [SUPER- 5 a or 6 b.] An extended or superior mind that is a composite of many individual minds.

1941 L. MACNEICE *Poetry of W. B. Yeats* vi. 126 This mind, for Yeats, is not so much the mind of God as the super-mind of humanity. **1965** *Listener* 1 July 26/1. This civilization exists in a corporate form, the individual thinking units of which have long ago been synthesized into one super-mind.

'**super,multiplet.** *Physics.* [SUPER- 6 b.]

a. A group of transitions in an atom between spectral terms of different multiplicity, all the transitions involving the same change in the orbital quantum number *l* of an electron from the same initial value.

1927 RUSSELL & MEGGERS in *Sci. Papers Bureau of Standards* (U.S.) XX. 331 The five terms first mentioned are evidently closely related, and their combinations with the triad ^3P, $^3D'$, ^3F can be arranged in the form of a 'supermultiplet'. **1935** CONDON & SHORTLEY *Theory Atomic Spectra* ix. 245 The set of all lines arising in transitions between two polyads..having the same parent configuration is known as a supermultiplet. **1972** I. I. SOBEL'MAN *Introd. Theory Atomic Spectra* xxxi. 313 By summing eqn. (31.48) over all transitions $\mathcal{J} \to \mathcal{J}'$ within the given multiplet we obtain the line strength of this multiplet. .. Summing over *LL'*..gives the line strength of the supermultiplet.

b. In particle physics, a multiplet (sense b) in the broader sense, comprising particles of different hypercharge as well those of different charge.

1952 *Ann. Rev. Nucl. Sci.* I. 44 The two states belong to the same supermultiplet (in this case a single charge multiplet with $S = \frac{1}{2}$ and $T = \frac{1}{2}$). **1964** *New Scientist* 27 Feb. 523/3 The discovery of the omega-minus confirms that other groupings of particles into families or 'supermultiplets' are valid. **1972** G. L. WICK *Elementary Particles* v. 82 They thought that all these particles might belong to a larger multiplet, or supermultiplet, which connects both different isotopic spin and different strangeness.

†**super'mundal**, *a. Obs. rare.* Variant of SUPERMUNDIAL.

1577 *Misogonus* III. iii, My heade is so full of the supermundall science.

super'mundane, *a.* [ad. med.L. *supermundānus* (Thomas Aquinas), f. *super-* SUPER- 1 + *mundus* world: cf. MUNDANE.]

1. Elevated in nature or character above what pertains to the earth or world; belonging to a region above the world.

1677 GALE *Crt. Gentiles* II. IV. 448 The Spirit of God is called by these Platonistes..the Supermundane soul of the Universe. **1678** CUDWORTH *Intell. Syst.* I. iv. §36. 546 The Platonists..had..several Distinctions amongst them concerning their Gods, as between..The Supermundane and the Mundane Gods. **1788** T. TAYLOR *Proclus* I. 159 In a distribution of mundane and super-mundane figures, you will always find that the circle is of a diviner nature. **1818** JEFFERSON *Writ.* (1830) IV. 309 Perhaps, in that super-mundane region, we may be amused with seeing the fallacy of our own guesses. **1855** MILMAN *Lat. Christ.* XIV. ii. VI. 405 The triple and novene division ran throughout, and connected,..almost identified the mundane and supermundane Church. **1903** SWETE *Stud. Teaching Our Lord* v. 144 Life in a Divine Kingdom must have a supermundane source.

b. Humorously or ironically applied to what is ideal, fantastic, or chimerical.

1870 H. LONSDALE *Life R. Knox* xiii. 248 He never could give countenance to the supermundane hypotheses of his friend Professor W. Macdonald. **1878** *N. Amer. Rev.* CXXVI. 489 According to this super-mundane argument, the rule of the Southern States was justly given over to the armed minority.

2. Situated above the earth. *rare.*

1882-3 *Schaff's Encycl. Relig. Knowl.* II. 950 Heaven is in this case [*Gen.* viii. 20] supermundane..distinct from the earth.

Hence ,**supermun'danity**, something supermundane.

1843 J. B. ROBERTSON tr. *Moehler's Symbol.* II. 189 Earthly bonds cannot be, without violence,..at once, replaced by super-mundanities.

†**super'mundial**, *a. Obs. rare.* [ad. late L. *supermundiālis*: cf. prec. and -IAL.] = SUPERMUNDANE 1.

1678 CUDWORTH *Intell. Syst.* I. iv. §36. 563 Plato conceiveth, that there are certain Substances, Invisible, Incorporeal, Supermundial, Divine and Eternal; which he calls Ideas.

†**su'pern**, *a. Obs.* Forms: 5–6 superne, 8 supern. [a. OF. *superne* (= It., Sp., Pg. *superno*) or ad. L. *supernus*, f. *super* over, above.]

1. = SUPERNAL 1.

c **1480** HENRYSON *Prayer for Pest* 65 Poems (S.T.S.) III. 167 Superne lucerne, guberne this pestilens. **1500-20** DUNBAR *Poems* lxxxv. 1 Haile, sterne superne! Haile, in eterne. **1508** FISHER *7 Penit. Ps.* cii. Wks. (1876) 177 They semed..very apte..vnto the superne & celestyall Iherusalem. *a* **1568** *The Sterne is Rissin* 30 in *Dunbar's Poems* (S.T.S.) II. 329 To the superne eternall regioun.

2. = SUPERNAL 3 b. *rare.*

1703 T. N. *City & C. Purchaser* 12 Walking-places, whose supern part..is..supported by Columns.

‖**supernaculum** (s(j)u:pə'nækjʊləm), *adv.* and *sb. slang.* Also 6 **-nagulum, -negulum,** 7 **-nagullum, -naculam.** [mod.L. rendering of G. *auf den nagel* on to the nail, in phr. *auf den nagel trinken* to drink off liquor to the last drop.]

A. *adv.* Used in reference to the practice of turning up the emptied cup or glass on one's left thumb-nail, to show that all the liquor has been drunk; hence, to the last drop, to the bottom.

1592 NASHE *P. Penilesse* E 4 *marg.*, Drinking super nagulum, a deuise of drinking new come out of Fraunce; which is, after a man hath turnd up the bottom of the cup, to drop it on his naile, & make a pearle with that is left; which, if it shed, & he cannot make stand on, by reason ther's too much, he must drinke againe for his pennance. *c* **1600** *Timon* II. v. (1842) 38, I drinke this to thee super naculum. **1654** GAYTON *Pleas. Notes* III. vi. 102 The whole school (I mean *Schola Bibendi*)..follow that way to a drop, which is called in the most authentick and emphaticall word they have, *super naculum.* **1678** DRYDEN *Limberham* I. i, He drank thy health five times, *supernaculum*, to my son Brainsick. **1728** RAMSAY *To his Friends In Ireland* 11 Drinking.. bumpers fair out, Supernaculum but spilling. **1827** DISRAELI *Viv. Grey* VI. i, As he withdrew the horn from his mouth, all present..gave a loud cry of 'Supernaculum!' **1835** *Edinb. Rev.* Oct. 41 Personages..drinking *supernaculum* out of grotesque goblets.

b. *ellipt.*

1664 COTTON *Scarron.* I. 108 She set it to her Nose,.. Until that she had supt it all in. Then turning't Topsey on her Thumb Says look, here's *Super-naculum.* **1739** 'R. BULL' tr. *Dedekindus' Grobianus* 180 Yours first turn topsy-turvy on your Thumb, And cry, behold! here's Supernaculum. [*a* **1745** MESTON *Poems* (1767) 194 Sir, pull it off, and on your thumb *Cernamus supernaculum.*]

Comb. **1622** MASSINGER & DEKKER *Virg. Mart.* II. i. C i v b, Bacchus,..grand Patron of rob-pots, vpsie-freesie-tiplers, and super-naculam takers.

c. *transf.* and *fig.*

1598 B. JONSON *Case is Altered* IV. iii. (1609) F 4 b, I confesse Cupids carouse, he plaies super negulum with my liquor of life. **1599** NASHE *Lenten Stuffe* L 1 b, Not the lowsie riddle wherewith fishermen constrayned.. Homer.. to drowne hymselfe,.. but should be dressed and set before you *super-nagulum*, with eight score more galliarde crosse poynts.

B. *sb.* **1.** A liquor to be drunk to the last drop; a wine of the highest quality; hence, anything excellent of its kind.

1704 W. KING *Orpheus & Euridice* 253, I saw some Sparks as they were Drinking, With mighty Mirth, and little thinking Their Jests were *Supernaculum.* **1760** FOOTE *Minor* I. 43 Levant me, but it is supernaculum—Speak when you have enough. **1785** GROSE *Dict. Vulg. T., Supernaculum*, good liquor, of which there is not even a drop left sufficient to wet one's nail. **1804** W. BLAKE *Let. to W. Hayley* 28 Dec., With our good Flaxman's good help, and with your remarks on it [*sc.* a portrait] in addition, I hope to make it a 'supernaculum'. **1822** BYRON *Werner* I. i. 376 'Tis here! the supernaculum! twenty years Of age, if 'tis a day. **1895** H. WATSON in *Chap-Bk.* III. 490, I called for Burgundy—some of the right supernaculum.

2. A draught that empties the cup to the last drop; also, a full cup, a bumper.

1827 DISRAELI *Viv. Grey.* VI. i, One pull—a gasp—another desperate draught—it was done! and followed by a supernaculum almost superior to the exulting Asmanshausen's. **1845** LOWELL *Eurydice* 8 And empty to each radiant comer A supernaculum of summer.

Hence **super'nacular** *a.* (of drink), excellent; also *transf.*

1848 THACKERAY *Bk. Snobs* xxxi, Some white hermitage at the Haws (by the way, the butler only gave me half a glass each time) was supernacular. **1920** G. SAINTSBURY *Notes on Cellar-bk.* 18 Some of the finer kinds [of sherry] are really supernacular—the best 'Tio Pepe', for instance. **1958** [see DEVADASI].

supernal (s(j)uːˈpɜːnəl), *a.* (*sb.*) Also 5–7 -all, 6 -al(l)e. [a. OF. *supernal* (12th c., later *supernel*) = It. *supernale*, Pg. *supernal*, or ad. med.L. **supernālis*, f. *supernus* SUPERN: see -AL[1].]

A. *adj.* **1.** That is above or on high; existing or dwelling in the heavens.

c **1485** *Digby Myst.* II. 422 The hye god supernall. **1500–20** DUNBAR *Poems* lxx. 9 O hie supernale Father of sapience. **1566** GASCOIGNE & KINWELMERSHE *Jocasta* I. i. 38 Desirous still to searche The hidden secrets of supernall powers. **1582** STANYHURST *Æneis* II. (Arb.) 48 Thee do I craue, Priamus, by Gods almightye supernal. *c* **1592** BRETON *C'tess Pembroke's Passion* lxxxv, He.. sits on the supernall throne. **1595** SHAKS. *John* II. i. 112 That supernal Iudge that stirs good thoughts. **1634** BP. HALL *Contempl., N.T.* IV. xxi, Many degrees there are of celestial happiness.. Those supernal mansions are not all of a height. **1649** OGILBY tr. *Virg. Georg.* IV. (1684) 125 *note*, To the Infernal Deities they offer'd Black Beasts, to the Celestial, White; Because (saith Arnobius..) to Supernal Gods,.. the more joyful Colour is acceptable. **1840** K. H. DIGBY *Mores Cath.* x. Epil. (1847) III. 809/1 May the King of Angels lead us to the society of the supernal citizens. **1866** NEALE *Sequences & Hymns* 71 Laud to Him, to Whom Supernal Thrones and Virtues bend the knee. **1869** GLADSTONE *Juv. Mundi* vii. (1870) 199 Not even those deities, who are omnipresent upon earth.. are precisely informed as to what takes place in the supernal region. **1908** *Athenæum* 30 May 662/2 The supernal gods, representing the growing powers of law and order.

2. Belonging to the realm or state above this world or this present life; pertaining to a higher world or state of existence; coming from above.

1483 CAXTON *Gold. Leg.* 303/1 He had mekenes in conuersacion, supernal doctryne in predicacion. **1513** BRADSHAW *St. Werburge* I. 1092 Our lorde hath shewed secretes mystycall To his electe persones by grace supernall. *Ibid.* 3215 The lockes and the barres.. Fell downe.. by power supernall. **1599** SANDYS *Europæ Spec.* (1632) 212 The three-fold plenitude of his [*sc.* the pope's] supernall, terrestriall, and infernall power. *c* **1610** *Women Saints* 70 The supernall pietie of god. **1667** MILTON *P.L.* VII. 573 God.. Thither will send his winged Messengers On errands of supernal Grace. **1685** EVELYN *Mrs. Godolphin* (1888) 219 To possess those Divine and supernall pleasures of doeing good. **1794** COLERIDGE *Religious Musings* 92 By supernal grace Enrobed with Light, and naturalised in Heaven. **1850** W. IRVING *Mahomet* xxxviii. (1853) 189 He had made choice of supernal existence. **1903** F. W. H. MYERS *Human Pers.* I. 5 Supposed communications with a supernal world.

3. a. Situated in, or belonging to, the sky or upper regions; celestial, heavenly. *Obs.* or *arch.*

1503 HAWES *Examp. Virt.* I. 6 With Saturne and Mercury that wer supernall. **1509** —— *Past. Pleas.* xxv. *title*, Of the hye influences of the supernall bodies. **1603** DANIEL *Epistles* Wks. (1717) 360 Like to those Supernal Bodies set Within their Orbs. *a* **1797** MASON *Dufresnoy's Art of Painting* 16 High o'er the stars you take your soaring flight, And rove the regions of supernal light. *c* **1870** LONGF. *Dante's Paradiso* XXIII. 30 Above the myriads of lamps, A Sun that one and all of them enkindled, E'en as our own doth the supernal sights.

b. Situated above or at the top, upper; above ground; high up, lofty in position. *rare.*

1599 A. M. tr. *Gabelhouer's Bk. Physicke* 132/2 Adde.. a qu. of an ownce of redd Roses, of the supernalle summityes therof. **1806** T. MAURICE *Indian Antiq.* I. 106 The great similarity which prevails in the architecture, supernal and subterraneous. **1816** T. L. PEACOCK *Headlong Hall* ii, Picking off the supernal fragments of an egg he had just cracked. **1871** B. TAYLOR *Faust* (1875) II. I. i. 6 The mountain summits, grand, supernal.

4. High in rank or dignity, elevated, exalted.

1549–62 STERNHOLD & H. *Magnificat*, He hath put downe the mightie ones From their supernall seate. **1616** R. C. *Times' Whistle* etc. (1871) 125 Then downe she [*sc.* Fortune] thrustes from their supernall seat Princes & kings. **1845** CARLYLE *Cromwell* IV. I. 402 Dread Phantoms, glaring supernal on you.

5. Supremely great or excellent, 'divine'.

1818 DWIGHT *Theol.* (1830) I. ix. 188 Leaves and blossoms of supernal beauty. **1847** LONGF. *Ev.* I. iii. 5 Glasses.. Sat astride on his nose, with a look of wisdom supernal. **1899** E. MARKHAM *Man with the Hoe*, etc. 123, I know, Supernal Woman, Thou dost seek No song of man. **1907** *Westm. Gaz.* 19 July 2/1 A lordly and supernal cake.

B. *sb.* A supernal being. *rare.*

1755 AMORY *Mem.* (1769) I. 230 Every grove had its deity, or supernal who delighted in it. *Ibid.* 253 St. Nicholas is their third grand supernal. **1861** I. TAYLOR *Spir. Hebrew Poetry* 340 If among the supernals [of Milton] the true sublime is attained, it is in hell, not in heaven.

Hence (*nonce-wds.*) **su'pernalist**, one who believes in the existence of supernal beings (in quot. *attrib.* or as *adj.*); **super'nality**, the quality of being supernal; in quot. with possessive as a humorous title for a celestial being.

1892 *Athenæum* 25 June 829/2 The conception of nature as inclusive of beings of a superhuman character, or the *Supernalist conception. **1599** NASHE *Lenten Stuffe* G 4, Whereof their *supernal ties.. seemed to be something sorie.

su'pernally, *adv. rare.* [f. prec. + -LY[2].]

1. Above; upwards; at the top or highest point.

1597 A. M. tr. *Guillemeau's Fr. Chirurg.* 35/2 They thrust the same alonge the finger supernallye or vpwardes. **1599** —— tr. *Gabelhouer's Bk. Physicke* 4/2 Tye it supernally on the crowne of your heade. **1788** T. TAYLOR *Proclus* I. 159 To survey its whole series, beginning supernally, ending in inferiors.

2. By supernal or heavenly power; celestially.

1630 J. TAYLOR (Water P.) *Superbiæ Flagellum* Wks. I. 36/1 For it with pride can neuer be infected, But humbly is supernally protected.

3. In trivial use: Supremely, 'divinely'.

1895 *Westm. Gaz.* 5 Feb. 2/1 Supernally floury potatoes.

†**super'natancy.** *Obs. rare.* [f. as next: see -ANCY.] That which floats on the surface, scum. (Cf. SUPERFLUITANCE.)

1670 H. STUBBE *Plus Ultra* 150 As is observed in the Serum of the blood sometimes, when the supernatancy is whitish, and not transparent.

supernatant (s(j)uːpəˈneɪtənt), *a.* and *sb.* [ad. L. *supernatant-*, *-ans*, pr. pple. of *supernatāre*: see SUPER- 2 and NATANT.] **A.** *adj.* **a.** Swimming above, floating on the surface (as a lighter liquid on a heavier).

1661 BOYLE *Certain Physiol. Ess.* (1669) 244 Whilst the substance continu'd fluid, I could shake it,.. with the supernatant Menstruum, without making between them any.. lasting Union. **1782** WITHERING in *Phil. Trans.* LXXII. 329 The powdery parts are allowed to subside until the supernatant liquor becomes clear. **1826** HENRY *Elem. Chem.* II. 133 When the silver has entirely precipitated,.. the clear supernatant liquor is to be poured off. **1839** *Penny Cycl.* XV. 217/2 Milk from which the supernatant fluid, or cream, has been removed is termed skim-milk. **1867** J. HOGG *Microsc.* I. iii. 227 After allowing the precipitate to settle for a day, draw off the clear supernatant fluid with a syphon. **1897** *Allbutt's Syst. Med.* IV. 424 A grayish-white deposit of pus with a supernatant cloud of mucus.

b. Said of that part of a floating body that is above the surface.

a **1687** PETTY *Treat. Naval Philos.* I. i, The supernatant part of the Ship. *c* **1850** *Rudim. Navig.* (Weale) 154. **1867** SMYTH *Sailor's Word-bk., Supernatant part of a ship*... This was formerly expressed by the name *dead-work.*

c. *fig.*

1903 F. W. H. MYERS *Human Pers.* I. 351 Certain disintegrated elements in the primary supernatant consciousness.

B. *sb. Biol.* and *Med.* A supernatant substance.

1922 *Brit. Med. Jrnl.* 19 Aug. 297/2 To this high refinement.. Otto, Munter, and Winkler attribute the potency of their products as compared with supernatants obtained by the centrifuge only. **1955** *New Biol.* XIX. 91 The supernatant is decanted and again spun usually at about 10,000 to 20,000 g for twenty minutes. **1977** *Proc. R. Soc. Med.* LXX. 192/2 The supernatants were decanted into plastic counting vials and mixed with 10ml Instagel.

supernatation (ˌs(j)uːpənəˈteɪʃən). Now *rare* or *Obs.* [ad. L. *supernatātiō*, *-ōnem*, n. of action f. *supernatāre* (see prec.).] The action of floating on the surface.

1623 BP. HALL *Contempl., O.T.* XIX. *Elisha raising Iron*, To fetch up the Iron which was heavy, and naturally vncapable of supernatation. **1626** BACON *Sylva* §790 *margin*, Experiment Solitary touching the Super-Natation of Bodies. **1646** SIR T. BROWNE *Pseud. Ep.* II. i. 52 They are differenced by supernatation or floating upon water, for Chrystall will sinke in water.. but Ice will swim. **1668** WILKINS *Real Char., Dict. Supernatation*, upon-swimming.

†**super'nate**, *v. Obs. rare.* [ad. L. *supernatāre*: see SUPERNATANT.] *intr.* To float on the surface. **b.** *trans.* To float upon or above.

1683 SALMON *Doron Med.* I. xxv. 291 Upon which affuse so much.. wine as may supernate them at least four Inches. **1694** —— *Bate's Dispens.* (1713) 491/2 Separate the supernating Liquor.

'supernate, *sb. Biol.* and *Med.* [f. SUPERNATANT *a.* and *sb.*, after *filtrate*, *precipitate.*] = SUPERNATANT *sb.*

1943 *Jrnl. Immunol.* XLVI. 326 After centrifuging these mixtures the supernates were tested for the presence of a sheep-cell hemolysin. **1979** *Experientia* XXXV. 193/2 After decantation of the supernate into counting vials.

supernation, etc.: see SUPER- 4 a (*a*) and (*c*), 6 c.

supernatural (s(j)uːpəˈnætjʊərəl, -tʃərəl), *a.* (*sb.*) [ad. med.L. *supernātūrālis* (Thomas Aquinas), f. *super-* SUPER- 4 a + *nātūra* NATURE: see -AL[1]. Cf. OF. *supernaturel* (16th c.; mod.F. *surnaturel*), It. *soprannaturale*, Sp., Pg. *sobrenatural*.] **A.** *adj.*

1. That is above nature; belonging to a higher realm or system than that of nature; transcending the powers or the ordinary course of nature.

1526 *Pilgr. Perf.* (W. de W. 1531) 190 Fayth is a supernaturall lyght, & therfore it is indiuysyble, as all graces supernaturall be. **1555** BRADFORD in Foxe *A. & M.* (1570) III. 1822/1 If a woman that is natural, can not finally forget the child of her wombe,.. God which is a father supernaturall,.. wyll not forget you. **1561** T. NORTON *Calvin's Inst.* II. 73 Of nature is giltinesse, and sanctification is of supernaturall grace. **1594** HOOKER *Eccl. Pol.* I. xi. §3 Those supernaturall passions of ioy, peace, and delight. **1601** SHAKS. *All's Well* II. iii. 3 They say miracles are past, and we haue our Philosophicall persons, to make moderne and familiar things supernaturall and causelesse. *a* **1619** FOTHERBY *Atheom.* II. v. §3. (1622) 240 Hee flyeth aboue those inferior and naturall concauses, vnto the supreme and supernaturall Cause. **1646** SIR T. BROWNE *Pseud. Ep.* I. xi. 44 Thus hath he also made the ignorant sort beleeve that naturall effects.. proceed from supernaturall powers. **1749** HARTLEY *Observ. Man* I. iii. §7 412 Inspiration.. termed supernatural properly, in Contradistinction to all Knowledge resulting from the common Laws of Nature. **1772** PRIESTLEY *Inst. Relig.* (1782) I. 319 Testimony.. declared in supernatural voices from heaven. **1865** LECKY *Ration.* I. i. 77 The pestilences which desolated nations were deemed supernatural. **1866** LIDDON *Bampton Lect.* vi. (1875) 296 Christianity is a supernatural religion. **1892** J. TAIT *Mind in Matter* (ed. 3) 308 The Apostles considered supernatural power as something resident in Jesus. **1907** J. R. ILLINGWORTH *Doctr. Trinity* ii. 39 When the Word was made Flesh, a supernatural Being entered what we call the order of nature.

b. *transf.* Relating to, dealing with, or characterized by what is above nature.

1569 SANFORD tr. *Agrippa's Van. Arts* i. 4 b, The Supernaturall Philosophers vse the Coniectures of Naturall Philosophers. **1616** R. C. *Times' Whistle* etc. (1871) 148 As well in naturall philosophy As supernaturall theologie. **1832** W. IRVING *Alhambra* I. xi. 146 The Court of the Lions has also its share of supernatural legends. **1834** K. H. DIGBY *Mores Cath.* v. i. 14 During the supernatural ages of which I am attempting the history. **1844** KINGLAKE *Eothen* Pref, Lady Hester Stanhope's conversation on supernatural topics.

2. More than the natural or ordinary; unnaturally or extraordinarily great; abnormal, extraordinary; †*occas.* beyond the normal number, supernumerary. *Obs.* or *arch.*

1533 ELYOT *Cast. Helthe* (1539) 16 Unnaturall or supernaturall heate distroyeth appetite. **1594** NASHE *Unfort. Trav.* E iv b, A precious supernaturall pandor, apparelled in all points like a gentleman. **1597** A. M. tr. *Guillemeau's Fr. Chirurg.* 27/1 Conserninge the supernaturall teeth, it is sometimes daungerous to drawe them. **1656** DUCHESS OF NEWCASTLE in Firth *Life* (1886) 287 My sister.. whom I.. loved with a supernatural affection. **1797** MRS. RADCLIFFE *Italian* xvii, He seemed suddenly animated with supernatural strength. **1814** MRS. J. WEST *Alicia de Lacy* IV. 249 A supernatural share of fortitude appeared communicated to this long-suffering lady. **1874** H. R. REYNOLDS *John Bapt.* i. §1. 5 The figures of some of the heroes of the past.. do assume supernatural dimensions, or at any rate look so colossal as to appear super-human.

B. *absol.* or *sb.*

1. *absol.* with *the.* That which is supernatural.

1830 SCOTT *Monast.* Introd., The introduction of the super-natural and marvellous. **1867** H. MACMILLAN *Bible Teach.* Pref. (1870) p. vi, The supernatural is not antagonistic to the constitution of nature, but is the eternal source of it. **1905** CHESTERTON *Heretics* 99 Take away the supernatural, and what remains is the unnatural.

2. *sb. pl.* Supernatural things.

In quot. 1587 applied to Aristotle's *Metaphysics* (see the etym. of METAPHYSICS).

1587 GOLDING *De Mornay* xx. (1592) 316 Aristotle in his Supernaturals rehearseth.. a certeyne aunswere of Simonides.. that it belongeth to none but onely God, to haue skill of the things that are aboue nature. **1591** SYLVESTER *Du Bartas* I. i. 705 If a Wise-man.. By th' onely power of Plants and Minerals Can work a thousand supernaturals. *a* **1656** HALES *Gold. Rem.* III. (1673) 57 Think we then to dive into supernaturals, and search out those causes which God hath locked up in his secret treasures? **1722** DE FOE *Plague* (1754) 223 The secret Conveyance of Infection.. is more than sufficient to execute the Fierceness of divine Vengeance, without putting it upon Supernaturals and Miracle. **1891** *But How if the Gospels are Historic?* 10 Neither.. can it be said that anything in the primary nature of mind necessarily precludes belief in supernaturals.

3. A supernatural being.

1729 S. JOHNSON (*title*) Hurlothrumbo; or, the Super-Natural. **1801** SOUTHEY in Robberds *Mem. W. Taylor* (1843) I. 386 In Milton and in Klopstock.. the supernaturals are the agents, the figures, not the wires. **1836** [MRS. TRAILL] *Backw. Canada* x. 153 This is too matter-of-fact country for such supernaturals to visit. **1886** C. ROGERS *Soc. Life Scot.* xxi. III. 338 There was a supernatural which had its home in hill centres... This was the 'Urisk'.

Hence **super'naturaldom** (*nonce-wd.*), the realm of supernatural things or beings.

1867 AUG. J. E. WILSON *Vashti* vi, The popular nerve, which closely connected the community with supernaturaldom, thrilled afresh.

super'naturalism. [f. prec. + -ISM.]

1. Supernatural character or quality; a system or collection of supernatural agencies, events, etc. Rarely in *pl.* supernatural agencies or means.

1799 W. TAYLOR in Robberds *Mem.* (1843) I. 285 Stripping the legend of all its supernaturalism. **1853** E. MIALL *Bases Belief* III. ii. (1861) 107 In the case of Jesus of Nazareth,.. Supernaturalism was a necessary feature of his work. **1859** R. F. BURTON *Centr. Afr.* in *Jrnl. Geog. Soc.* XXIX. 346 Charms and spells, exorcisms and talismans.. will be in demand, and wherever supernaturalisms are in requisition, men will be found for a consideration to supply them. **1878** GLADSTONE *Prim. Homer* vi. 87 The really grand figures in this department of the Homeric supernaturalism are the Erinuës.

2. Belief in the supernatural; a theory or doctrine which admits or asserts the reality of supernatural beings, powers, events, etc.

1809 W. TAYLOR in *Crit. Rev.* Ser. III. XVII. 463 He.. mingles superstition with his supernaturalism. **1836** *Partington's Brit. Cycl. Lit.* etc. III. 857/1 Supernaturalism considers the Christian religion as an extraordinary phenomenon, out of the circle of natural events, and as communicating truths above the comprehension of human reason. **1858** J. MARTINEAU *Stud. Christ* 251 The Roman Catholic system.. its ecstatic phenomena, its physical supernaturalism. **1886** *Encycl. Brit.* XX. 289/1 Rationalism had as its antitheses.. supernaturalism, and.. naturalism.

super'naturalist, *sb.* (*a.*) [f. as prec. + -IST.] One who believes in the supernatural; an adherent of supernaturalism. Also *attrib.* or as *adj.* = next.

1650 HOBBES *De Corp. Pol.* 48 The opposition.. of supernaturalists.. to rational and moral Conversation. **1659** HOOLE *Comenius Vis. World* (1672) 207 The Supernaturalist searcheth out the Causes, & Effects of things. **1684** tr. *Agrippa's Van. Arts* i. 8 Supernaturalists use the Conjectures of Naturalists. **1838** *Penny Cycl.* XI. 198/2 The Orthodox or Supernaturalists. **1884** J. R. SEELEY in *Contemp. Rev.* Nov. 671 The supernaturalist theory. **1893** LELAND *Mem.* I. 204 Justinus Kerner, the great German supernaturalist, mystic, and poet.

ˌsupernatura'listic, *a.* [f. prec.: see -ISTIC.] Holding the belief of a supernaturalist; of, belonging to, or characteristic of supernaturalists; pertaining to or involving supernaturalism.

1841 *Penny Cycl.* XIX. 311/2 The so-called Supernaturalistic Rationalists, admitted.. a supernatural revelation, but considered reason as the only means of recognising.. it. **1882** CHEYNE *Isaiah* vi. App. ¶1 Compelling us to a 'supernaturalistic' conception of Old Testament prophecy. **1896** A. W. BENN in *Academy* 18 July 43/2 The 'rationalistic' theory, according to which the so-called miracles were natural occurrences interpreted in a supernaturalistic sense.

ˌsupernatu'rality. [f. SUPERNATURAL + -ITY.]

1. The quality of being supernatural; supernaturalness.

1638 CHILLINGW. *Relig. Prot.* I. vi. §74. 381 If these be certain grounds of supernaturality, our faith may have it as well as yours. **1677** GALE *Crt. Gentiles* II. IV. 75 That Supernaturalitie is a Mode.. included in al virtuose Habits.. because human Nature,.. as now corrupted, cannot reach an end or act supernatural. **1866** *Elgin & Guide to Cath.* 28 The element of wonder or supernaturality.

2. Something that is supernatural; a supernatural object, occurrence, etc.

1665 J. SERGEANT *Sure Footing* 81, I wonder what else is Supernaturality but this which he miscalls Nature. **1849** *Fraser's Mag.* XXXIX. 665 A *catasetum*, full of supernaturalities, startled us. *a* **1856** H. MILLER *Rambles Geol.* vi. (1858) 322 A meal-mill.. once known as the scene of one of those supernaturalities that belong to the times of the witch and the fairy.

super'naturalize, *v.* [f. as prec. + -IZE.] *trans.* To make supernatural; to impart or attribute a supernatural character to.

a **1643** AUG. BAKER *Sancta Sophia* (1857) 270 Without any prejudice.. to the work, yea, to the great improvement and super-naturalizing of it. *a* **1680** CHARNOCK *Attrib. God* (1834) II. 76 His humanity is supernaturalized and elevated by the activity of the Holy Ghost. **1843** *Blackw. Mag.* LIII. 403 No barbarian ever deified, or supernaturalized, every process around him. **1867** W. G. WARD *Ess. Philos. Theism* (1884) II. 193 The office of Grace, in supernaturalizing the soul and human action.

Hence **ˌsupernaturali'zation.**

1933 *Downside Rev.* LI. 729 St Thomas gives no support.. to the original views of Rousselot.. as to the need of a kind of supernaturalization of the (natural) intellectual powers in order to accept and assent to revelation. **1961** E. L. MASCALL *Grace & Glory* i. 15 The sanctification and the supernaturalization of our whole being, body and soul alike—this is the purpose for which the Catholic Church and its whole sacramental equipment exist.

supernaturally (s(j)uːpəˈnætjʊərəlɪ, -tʃərəlɪ), *adv.* [f. as prec. + -LY².] In a supernatural manner.

1. By supernatural agency or means; in a manner transcending the ordinary course of nature.

c **1450** tr. *De Imitatione* III. xxiv. 94 All þat we haue outwarde or inwarde, naturely or supernaturaly, all are þi benefetes. **1526** *Pilgr. Perf.* (W. de W. 1531) 50 b, The vij gyftes of the holy goost directeth man supernaturally. **1577** tr. *Bullinger's Decades* (1592) 834 John Gerson hath defined Ecclesiasticall authoritie to bee a power supernaturallie and spiritually giuen of the Lord to his Disciples. **1651** HOBBES *Govt. & Soc.* xii. §6. 180 It is a common doctrine, That faith and holinesse are not acquired by.. naturall reason, but are.. supernaturally infused. *a* **1768** SECKER *Lect.* (1769) I. xv. 235 God.. may.. subject us to any Difficulties that he pleases, provided he bestows on us, whether naturally or supernaturally, the Power of going through them. **1841** MYERS *Cath. Th.* III. §6. 22 In no case have we any proof.. of Truth having been as supernaturally conveyed by any men to their fellows as it has been conveyed by the Spirit of God to themselves.

†**2.** Abnormally, preternaturally.

1597 A. M. tr. *Guillemeau's Fr. Chirurg.* 28 b/1 The bloode which supernaturallye hath issued out of any parte.. as in those which spitt bloode, or bleede much out of the nose. **1752** LAW *Spir. Love* II. (1816) 106 Nothing.. can be done to any creature supernaturally, or in a way that is without, or contrary to, the powers of nature.

3. More than naturally; to an abnormal extent; extraordinarily. *Obs.* or *arch.*

1589 NASHE *Pref. Greene's Menaphon* (Arb.) 11 Sir Iohn Cheeke, a man of men, supernaturally traded in al tongues. *c* **1590** MARLOWE *Faustus* ix, I'le gul him supernaturally. **1599** B. JONSON *Cynthia's Rev.* II. iv. (Qo. 1601) You neuer skind a new beauty more prosperously in your life, nor more supernaturally [*ed.* 1616 metaphysically]. **1853** G. BRIMLEY *Ess., Bleak Ho.* (1858) 289 So dreadfully amiable and supernaturally benevolent.

super'naturalness. [f. as prec. + -NESS.] The quality of being supernatural; supernatural character.

1730 BAILEY (fol.), Supernaturalness. **1817** COLERIDGE *Biog. Lit.* xxiii. (1907) II. 198 Notwithstanding the supernaturalness of the storm.. the whole of his gang had been saved. **1873** SPENCER *Stud. Sociol.* vii. (1874) 170 Declining monarchical power brings with it decreasing belief in the supernaturalness of the monarch. **1898** T. ADAMSON *Stud. Mind in Christ* iii. 72 The supernaturalness of Christ's knowledge.

supernature (ˈs(j)uːpəˌneɪtjʊə(r), -tʃə(r)). [f. SUPER- + NATURE, after *supernatural.*] That which is above nature; a supernatural realm or system of things; something supernatural.

1844 THACKERAY *May Gambols* Wks. 1902 XIII. 436 A conversation.. which must have been taken from nature, or Mother Bunch's delightful super-nature. **1858** *Chamb. Jrnl.* X. 217 There is a certain mystery and supernature about Wilkinson. **1876** J. WEISS *Wit, Hum. & Shaks.* xi. 369 The eldritch women are the nearest hint of supernature which he had. **1898** CLODD *Tom Tit Tot* Introd. 2 When these [tales] were woven out of old traditions, no sharp lines severed nature from super-nature.

†**su'pernity.** *Obs. rare*⁻⁰. [ad. L. *supernitās*, f. *supernus* SUPERN.]

1721 BAILEY, *Supernity*,.. a being above or aloft.

†**super'nodical,** *a. Obs. humorous nonce-wd.* [f. SUPER- III + NODDY *sb.*¹ + -ICAL.] Extremely silly. So †**super'nodity,** excessive silliness.

1594 *Taming of Shrew* (Shaks. Soc. 1844) 24 O supernodicall foule! **1613** J. TAYLOR (Water P.) *Laugh & be Fat* Wks. (1630) II. 70/2 To giue you titles supernodicall. **1622** BRETON *Strange Newes* Wks. (Grosart) II. 6/2 One greate foole.. willing to shew the greatnesse of his little wit.. to the subiects of his Supernoditie.

super'normal, *a.* [SUPER- 4 a.]

1. Exceeding that which is normal.

1868 W. R. GREG *Lit. & Soc. Judgm.* 356 This vast amount of super-normal celibacy. **1910** G. TYRRELL *Autobiog.* (1912) I. iii. 33 This deafness is covered by the acquired, super-normal acuteness of the other ear.

2. Applied to phenomena of an extraordinary or exceptional kind, involving a higher law or principle than those ordinarily occurring, but not necessarily supernatural. Also *absol.*

1885 MYERS in *Proc. Soc. Psych. Res.* III. 30 *note*, I have ventured to coin the word 'supernormal' to be applied to phenomena which are beyond what usually happens... By a supernormal phenomenon I mean,.. one which exhibits the action of laws higher, in a psychical aspect, than are discerned in action in everyday life. **1886** *Times* 30 Oct. 9/4 The phenomena of mesmerism, of hypnotism, and of other abnormal or supernormal conditions of the human consciousness. **1898** *Month* Sept. 228 Alleged instances of the supernormal.

Hence **super'normally** *adv.*

1895 *Daily News* 22 Nov. 4/7 Knowledge supernormally acquired. **1899** A. LANG *Myth, Rit. & Relig.* xii. II. 23, Morals divinely and supernormally revealed.

ˌsupernor'mality. [f. SUPERNORMAL *a.* + -ITY.] **a.** The quality of exceeding what is normal; an instance of this.

1909 O. J. LODGE *Survival of Man* I. i. 2 Assertions concerning psychological supernormalities have not only excited attention, but have rather notably roused the interest of careful and responsible students. **1922** *19th Cent.* Oct. 600 One of the first indications of potential genius in school children is unusual precocity or mental supernormality. **1955** W. NAYLOR *Silver Birch Anthol.* 8 The faculty of being able to deliver, week after week, words of wisdom.. in this spontaneous fashion, is in itself evidence of supernormality. **1977** D. MORRIS *Manwatching* 277 Having exhausted one line of supernormality, we switch to another, selecting a new element for improvement and dwelling on that until it too has become stale.

b. [SUPER- 9 a.] The quality of being exceedingly normal. *rare.*

1945 *New Yorker* 7 Apr. 74/2 Now that the end [of the war] is practically at hand, the supernormality of the English is surprising.

super'nova. *Astr.* Pl. **-novae, -novas.** [SUPER- 6 c.] **1.** A star that undergoes a sudden and temporary increase in brightness like a nova but to a very much greater degree, as a result of an explosion that disperses most of the stellar material.

1934 BAADE & ZWICKY in *Physical Rev.* XLV. 138/1 Supernovae flare up in every stellar system (nebula) once in several centuries. **1934** —— in *Proc. Nat. Acad. Sci.* 15 May 254 The extensive investigations of extra-galactic systems.. brought to light the.. fact that there exist two well-defined types of.. novae which might be distinguished as common novae and super-novae. **1939** [see NOVA 2]. **1965** *Listener* 20 May 741/1 Only three supernovae, the stars of 1054, 1572, and 1604, have appeared in our Galaxy since records began. **1976** *Sci. Amer.* Dec. 89/1 Some supernovas may leave behind cosmic ashes in the form of a neutron star or black hole. **1977** *Whitaker's Almanack 1978* 155/1 One important source of radio noise is the Crab Nebula, which is known to be the remains of the supernova of A.D. 1054. **1978** PASACHOFF & KUTNER *University Astron.* xi. 296 On the average, Type I supernovae reach an absolute magnitude of − 19 at peak brightness, while that of Type II supernovae is about 2 magnitudes fainter.

2. *fig.*

1965 *Listener* 14 Jan. 84/3 Look at the soft gleam of D major near the start of the development (bar 170)—the distant glow of fiery *supernova*, into the heart of which we are at length to be flung. **1974** *State* (Columbia, S. Carolina) 1 Apr. 10A/1 As far as the networks were concerned, the satiric supernova had burned out. **1979** *Tucson* (Arizona) *Citizen* 20 Sept. 7B/6 (*heading*) 'Buck Rogers' no supernova, but it won't wink out, either.

3. *attrib.*, as ***supernova explosion, remnant.***

1960 *McGraw-Hill Encycl. Sci. & Technol.* XIII. 303/2 The remains of an old supernova explosion. **1975** *Sci. Amer.* Mar. 29/2 The Crab Nebula is the remnant of a supernova explosion. **1960** *McGraw-Hill Encycl. Sci. & Technol.* XIII. 304/1 Unexplained radio sources also may be from supernova remnants. **1978** PASACHOFF & KUTNER *University Astron.* xi. 296 Optical astronomers have photographed two dozen of these stellar shreds, which are known as supernova remnants.

†**super'numeral,** *a. Obs. rare.* [f. L. *super numerum*: see SUPER- II and NUMERAL.] = SUPERNUMERARY *a.* 1.

1603 FLORIO *Montaigne* III. ix. 577 My booke is alwayes one: except that.. I give my selfe law to adde thereto.. some supernumeral [orig. *supernumeraire*] embleme. **1638** FEATLY *Strict. Lyndom.* I. 57, I answer for the Knight, that he created no supernumerall cardinall: for he would not usurpe upon the Popes priviledge.

super'numerariness. *rare.* [f. next + -NESS.] The state of being supernumerary; excess above the regular or required number.

1652 H. L'ESTRANGE *Amer. no Jewes* 68 Reasons.. for Plantation... 1. Expulsion. 2. Supernumerarinesse. **1657** J. SERGEANT *Schism Dispach't* 649 If there were any error in the supernumerarines of Bishops out of some one Province. **1727** in BAILEY vol. II.

supernumerary (s(j)uːpəˈnjuːmərərɪ), *a.* and *sb.* [ad. late L. *supernumerārius* applied to soldiers added to a legion after it is complete, f. *super numerum*: see SUPER- II and -ARY¹. Cf. obs. F. *supernumeraire* (mod.F. *surnuméraire*), It. *soprannumerario*, Sp., Pg. *supernumerario*.]

A. *adj.*

1. a. That is beyond or in excess of the usual, proper, regular, stated, or prescribed number or †quantity; additional, extra, left over. Now *rare* in the general sense.

1605 BACON *Adv. Learn.* II. i. §1 As for that part [of theology], which seemeth supernumerarie, which is Prophecie, it is but Diuine Historie. **1640** BP. HALL *Episc.* II. iii. 96 St. Paul, the Posthumous, and Supernumerary, but no lesse glorious Apostle. **1684** FOUNTAINHALL *Decis.* (1759) I. 258 Only by one vote supernumerary, they repelled the late Magistrates defences. **1694** FALLE *Jersey* ii. 70 To buy up this Supernumerary Cidar, and distill it into Brandy. **1711** ADDISON *Spect.* No. 110 ¶2 When Night heightens the Awfulness of the Place, and pours out her supernumerary Horrors upon every thing in it. **1712** HEARNE *Collect.* (O.H.S.) III. 425 Mr. Burgher's Plate is mightily approv'd of... I have had supernumerary Copies wrought off. **1742** BLAIR *Grave* 19 The sickly taper.. Lets fall a supernumerary horror. **1749** [J. MASON] *Numbers in Poet. Comp.* 61 This Measure consists of all Trochees, with a supernumerary long Syllable at the End of the Line. **1758** JOHNSON *Idler* No. 29 ¶3 The hours which I was obliged to watch.. I considered as supernumerary. **1831** BREWSTER *Optics* xxxii. 265 Within the primary rainbow,.. and without the secondary one, there have been seen supernumerary bows. **1872** O. W. HOLMES *Poet Breakf.-t.* xi. 344 My supernumerary fellow-boarder, whom I would have dispensed with as a cumberer of the table, has proved a ministering angel.

in post-position or predicatively (const. *to*). **1646** SIR T. BROWNE *Pseud. Ep.* IV. xii. 219 The intercalation of one day every fourth yeare,.. or 6 houres supernumerary. **1667** MILTON *P.L.* x. 887 A Rib.. from me drawn, Well if thrown out, as supernumerarie To my just number found. **1670** WALLIS in Rigaud *Corr. Sci. Men* (1841) II. 519, I sent yesterday.. a cut supernumerary to perfect what I sent you before.

b. *spec.* Applied to an official, officer, or employee not formally belonging to the regular body or staff, but associated with it to assist in case of need or emergency. (See B. b, c.)

1624 LD. KPR. WILLIAMS in *Fortescue Papers* (Camden) 203 To make him a supernumeraye Iudge of the Common Pleas, without fee or charge. **1683** W. LLOYD in *Lett. Lit. Men* (Camden) 188 To be a supernumerary Usher in his

Schoole. **1693** LUTTRELL *Brief Rel.* (1857) III. 67 Edward Southwell, esq.,..is supernumerary clerk to the councill. **1726** AYLIFFE *Parergon* 139 In some of the said Churches there are supernumerary Canons (whom we falsely call Prebendaries). **1802** JAMES *Milit. Dict.*, *Supernumerary*... In a strict military sense it means the officers and non-commissioned officers that are attached to a regiment or battalion for the purpose of supplying the places of such as fall in action, and for the better management of the rear ranks when the front is advancing or engaged. **1824** in *Spirit Publ. Jrnls.* (1825) 309 A youthful supernumerary compositor..in a printing establishment.

c. *Bot.* and *Zool.* Applied to structures or organs occurring (either in individuals or in types) in addition to the normal ones.

1733 G. DOUGLAS tr. *Winslow's Anat.* I. ii. §19 (1756) I. 53, I call by the name of supernumerary Bones, several pieces found in some Skulls, chiefly between the Parietal and Occipital Bones. *Ibid.*, The supernumerary Teeth placed out of the Rank of the rest. **1828** STARK *Elem. Nat. Hist.* I. 469 *Dactylopterus..volitans*,..supernumerary pectoral fins very large. **1835** LYELL *Princ. Geol.* III. iii. (ed. 4) II. 438 Those races of dogs which have a supernumerary toe on the hind foot. **1857** A. GRAY *First Less. Bot.* (1866) 26 Accessory or Supernumerary Buds. **1878** T. BRYANT *Pract. Surg.* I. 563 Supernumerary teeth are not infrequently found in the upper incisive region.

d. *Genetics.* Of a chromosome: additional to the normal complement of autosomes and sex chromosomes. Cf. sense f of the sb. below.

1907 E. B. WILSON in *Biol. Bull.* XII. 304 The unpaired chromosome may be either present or absent in either the male or female, and hence is without significance in sex-production. It is in fact a kind of supernumerary chromosome, which I shall designate as the '*s*-chromosome' in order to distinguish it from the odd sex-chromosome of the usual type. **1927** *Jrnl. Agric. Res.* XXXV. 782 The distribution of a supernumerary chromosome to the four daughter cells has been studied and found to be erratic. **1969** BROWN & BERTKE *Textbk. Cytol.* xviii. 380/1 Supernumerary chromosomes are usually much smaller than the autosomes and for that reason have often been termed 'fragment' chromosomes.

2. That is beyond the number needed or desired; superfluous, unnecessary. Now *rare*.

1640 BP. HALL *Chr. Moder.* I. vi. 54 The lavish, and super-numerary carowses of drunkennesse. **1654** H. L'ESTRANGE *Chas. I* (1655) 130 That he might therefore take the better notice of what was supernumerary to his own preservation. **1712** ADDISON *Spect.* No. 413 ¶6 Were it not to add Supernumerary Ornaments to the Universe. **1751** JOHNSON *Rambler* No. 126 ¶5 Nor should it [*sc.* fear] be suffered to..beset life with supernumerary distresses. **1847** DE QUINCEY *Sp. Mil. Nun* i, He had three daughters already... Supernumerary daughters were the very nuisance of Spain.

†**3.** Exceeding or excessive in number; too or more numerous. *Obs. rare.*

1682 *Sec. Plea Nonconf.* 58 Here's a Religious Exercise to a supernumerary Company. **1715** *Wodrow Corr.* (1843) II. 27 We shall have few Tories in. [We] hear,..the Whigs in England are vastly supernumerary.

B. *sb.* A supernumerary person or thing; one beyond the regular, usual, or necessary number; an additional or extra one associated with the regular body or set; *esp.* a supernumerary official or employee. **a.** *gen.*

1639 BAKER tr. *Balzac's Lett.* IV. 206 You may consult with Vida and Eracastorius; and if they be not of the same opinion, Scaliger may be the supernumerary. **1668** H. MORE *Div. Dial.* I. ii. §11. 236 That Divine Providence in the generations of Fishes, Birds and Beasts, cast up in her account the Supernumeraries that were to be meat for the rest. **1670** R. COKE *Disc. Trade* 36 Supernumeraries of Solicitors, Bankers, Scriveners, and Userers. **1691** in *Cal. Treas. Papers* (1868) I. Pref. 52 Your pet' collected the duty of excise..of Endfield..and in bringing to London the money..he and the supervisor & supernumerary were sett upon neare Edmington. **1719** LONDON & WISE *Compl. Gard.* 225 When I Plant two Roots near each other..I..reject both Branches which shoot from the two opposite Ears, to avoid that Confusion of those Supernumeraries which injure the principal Stem. **1737** FIELDING *Tumble-down Dick* Ded., You are too great..a Manager, to keep a needless super-numerary in your house. **1835** W. IRVING *Tour Prairies* ii, Such of our horses as had not been tired out ..were taken with us as pack-horses, or supernumeraries. **1860** EMERSON *Cond. Life, Wealth* Wks. (Bohn) II. 358 The eldest son must inherit the manor; what to do with this supernumerary?

b. On board ship, a sailor, or one of a body of sailors, over and above the ship's complement.

1666 PEPYS *Diary* 23 July, Sixteen ships..certainly might have been manned, and they been serviceable in the fight, and yet the fleete well-manned, according to the excesse of supernumeraries, which we hear they have. **1758** *M.P.'s Let. on Navy* 11 The..Practice of bearing Men upon the Books of his Majesty's Ships..as Supernumeraries; under which Denomination they are intitled to Victuals only..and not to Wages. **1833** M. SCOTT *Tom Cringle* xv, The whole crew with our black supernumeraries.

c. An additional officer attached to a body of men in the army or navy for some special purpose.

1796 *Instr. & Reg. Cavalry* (1813) 35 Each rank in single file (the rear supernumeraries still on the flank). **1811** *Regul. & Orders Army* 109 For the purpose of Instruction, young Officers may be put on Duty as Supernumeraries with senior Officers. **1849** COBDEN *Speeches* 85 Supernumeraries (superintendents from admirals downwards). **1877–81** VOYLE & STEVENSON *Milit. Dict.* Suppl. s.v., An officer shall be retained as a supernumerary on the strength of the regiment or corps:—(*a*) In case of a reduction in the establishment or corps... (*b*) While waiting a vacancy after retiring from the Seconded List.

d. A retired Wesleyan minister.

[*a* **1791** WESLEY *Minute. Sev. Convers.* Wks. 1830 VIII. 326 How can we provide for superannuated and supernumerary Preachers?] *a* **1791** —— in Southey *Comm.-pl. Bk.* Ser. II. (1849) 35 When his strength for labour fails him, he..is made a supernumerary, and derives a small assistance..from a fund to which he paid, during his health, one guinea per annum. **1822** J. MACDONALD *Mem. J. Benson* 437 Mr. Rankin, an old Preacher..who resided in London as a Supernumerary. **1885** *Minutes Wesleyan Conf.* 11 What Supernumeraries now return to the full work?

e. *Theatr.* A person employed in addition to the regular company, who appears on the stage but does not speak. Colloq. abbreviated *super* (see SUPER *sb.* 3).

1755 C. CHARKE *Life* 115 A poor, beggarly Fellow who had been sometimes Supernumerary in Drury-Lane Theatre. **1836** DICKENS *Sk. Boz, Brokers' Shops*, Purchased of some wretched supernumeraries or sixth-rate actors. **1851** MAYHEW *Lond. Labour* I. 383/1, I..sunk to be a supernumerary for 1*s*. a night at one of the theatres. **1886** *Academy* 30 Jan. 83/2 A stage crowded with supernumeraries, flooded with strange lights.

f. *Genetics.* A chromosome which may be absent from normal individuals of either sex, having little or no effect on phenotype and occurring irregularly.

1909 E. B. WILSON in *Jrnl. Exper. Zool.* VI. 150 The chromosomes in question are the ones which in earlier papers I have called the 'supernumeraries'. **1917** E. E. CAROTHERS in *Jrnl. Morphol.* XXVIII. 469 Another variation which has attracted attention in our collection of Acridian material..is the presence in certain individuals of one, or sometimes two, entities which I shall designate as supernumeraries. They possess the staining capacity of chromatin. **1969** BROWN & BERTKE *Textbk. Cytol.* xviii. 381/1 A..peculiarity of supernumeraries which seems to indicate that they have genes for their own survival is preferential fertilization in corn.

Hence **super'numeraryship**, the position of a supernumerary.

1898 B. GREGORY *Side Lights* 548 The second supernumeraryship of Mr. Everett.

†**super'numerate**, *v.* *Obs. rare*$^{-1}$. [f. L. *super numerum* beyond the number + -ATE[3]; cf. SUPER- 11. (Late L. *supernumerāre* = to count in over and above.)] *trans.* To outnumber.

1689 G. HARVEY *Curing Dis. by Expect.* ix. 65 The Injuries of bleeding..do by far supernumerate the benefits received by it.

†**super'numerous**, *a.* *Obs. rare.* [SUPER- 9a.] Excessive in number; too numerous.

a **1661** FULLER *Worthies, Northampt.* (1662) II. 298 The Earl of Oxford was heavily fined for supernumerous attendance. **1756** *Monitor* No. 26. I. 233 To save the expence of keeping up a supernumerous army.

supero- (s(j)uːpərəʊ), modern combining form of L. *superus* that is above, upper (see SUPERIOR), in terms of anatomy and zoology, designating parts situated above or on the upper side. **a.** in adjs., as **supero-an'terior** *a.*, situated above and in front; **supero'dorsal** *a.*, situated above and towards the back; **supero-ex'ternal** *a.*, situated above and on the outside; **supero'frontal** *a.*, situated in the upper part of the forehead, or of the frontal lobe of the brain; **supero-in'ternal** *a.*, situated above and on the inside; **supero'lateral** *a.*, situated above and on one side; **supero-oc'cipital** *a.* = SUPEROCCIPITAL; **superopo'sterior** *a.*, situated above and behind. **b.** in derived advs., as *superodorsally*, *-externally*, *-internally*, *-posteriorly*.

1849 DANA *Geol.* App. I. (1850) 686 *Supero-anterior margin slightly depressed. **1899** *Proc. Zool. Soc. London* 19 Dec. 1029 *Supero-dorsally it [the proötic] is notched to form the inferior border of the floccular fossa. **1903** *Ibid.* 17 Mar. 269 The alisphenoid..is not yet completely ossified... Its *supero-external angle is produced outwards to form the postorbital process. **1899** *Ibid.* 19 Dec. 1029 The exoccipital ..is bounded *supero-internally by the supraoccipital, and *supero-externally by that portion of the proötic cartilage which lodges the floccular fossa. **1875** *Encycl. Brit.* I. 874/1 *note*, The *supero-, mid-, and infero-frontal subdivisions of the frontal area of the skull. **1890** BILLINGS *Med. Dict.* s.v. *Frontal*, The superior frontal or supero-frontal [sulcus]. **1870** ROLLESTON *Anim. Life* 103 Common Crayfish... The *supero-lateral ossicles. **1866** J. A. MEIGS *Cranial Forms Amer. Aborig.* 29 No. 1447..exhibits the *supero-occipital flatness of the Swedish form. **1852** DANA *Crust.* II. 1272 This *supero-posterior portion of the shell. **1849** —— *Geol.* App. i. (1850) 699 *Supero-posteriorly there are four smaller..depressions.

ˌ**superoc'cipital**, *a.* and *sb.* *Anat.* and *Zool.* [SUPER- 1 b.] **A.** *adj.* Situated at the upper part of the occiput or back of the head. **B.** *sb.* The superoccipital bone, an element of the skull usually forming part of the occipital bone, but in some lower vertebrates constituting a distinct bone.

1854 OWEN in *Orr's Circ. Sci.*, *Org. Nat.* I. 205 The neural spine..is the 'superoccipital'. **1858** HOBLYN *Dict. Terms Med.* (ed. 8), Super-occipital Bone. **1875** *Encycl. Brit.* III. 705/2 (Birds), The perfected occipital arch has a pair of super-occipitals..as in man.

'**superoctave.** *Mus.* [SUPER- 6 d.] **a.** An organ-stop sounding two octaves higher than the ordinary pitch, i.e. an octave above that called 'octave' (OCTAVE 3 e); = FIFTEENTH B. 2 b. **b.** 'A coupler pulling down keys one octave above those struck' (Stainer and Barrett *Dict. Mus. T.* 1876).

[**1688** in Hopkins *Organ* (1870) 453 [The fine organ in the Temple Church was built by Father Smith, in 1688... The following is a copy of Father Smith's original disposition of the Stops]..Great Organ...4. Quinta, of mettle...5. Super Octavo.] **1884** *Encycl. Brit.* XVII. 831/2 The 2 [= 2-foot] fifteenth, or superoctave, of the great organ.

†**super'onerate**, *v.* *Obs. rare.* [f. legal L. *superonerāt-*, pa. ppl. stem of *superonerāre* (Bracton), f. *super-* SUPER- 9 b + *onerāre* to ONERATE.] *trans.* To overload; to burden excessively. So †ˌ**superone'ration** [ad. legal L. *superonerātio*], overloading.

1607 COWELL *Interpr.* s.v. *Commissarie*, The Bishop.. doeth by superonerating their circuit with a commissarie.. wrong..the poorer sort of subjects. **1638** RAWLEY tr. *Bacon's Life & Death* (1650) 64 Aire begets new Aire out of watry moisture, yet notwithstanding the old Aire still remains; whence commeth that Super-Oneration of the Aire. **1671** R. BOHUN *Wind* 14 It must needs..crow'd and superonerate the former Spaces. *Ibid.* 16 By the Repletion, or Superoneration of the Atmosphere.

†**supe'rordinanced**, *a.* *Obs. nonce-wd.* [f. SUPER- II + ORDINANCE + -ED[2] (the suffix being irregularly used).] That is or professes to be above, i.e. not subject to, ordinances (see ORDINANCE 8). So †**super'ordinancer**, †**super'ordinancing** *ppl. a.*

1656 S. WINTER *Serm.* 171 Our superordinanc'd men that are above ordinances but below pietie. *a* **1665** J. GOODWIN *Being filled with the Spirit* (1867) 348 Men who suffer themselves to be led by this superordinancing spirit. *Ibid.* 359 The reason..by which the seekers or super-ordinancers do make attempt to justify their..giving over the ministry of the gospel.

super'ordinary, *a.* [SUPER- 4 a.] That is above, beyond, or superior to the ordinary.

1630 *R. Johnson's Kingd. & Commw.* 388 Recommended to that honour, for some superordinary skill at their weapon. **1706** E. WARD *Wooden World Diss.* (1708) 43 When he gets a superordinary Dinner. **1802–12** BENTHAM *Ration. Judic. Evid.* (1827) V. 57 A man of super-ordinary probity. **1903** *Edin. Rev.* Jan. 77 Influences that should rather be defined as superordinary than supernatural.

super'ordinate, *a.* (*sb.*) [f. SUPER- II, after *subordinate.*] **A.** *adj.* Superior in rank: the opposite of SUBORDINATE, esp. in *Logic* and *Gram.* Const. *to.*

1620 T. SCOTT *God & King* (1623) 84 You that are next the lowest, consider the like, and so successiuely as you are superordinate. **1802–12** BENTHAM *Ration. Judic. Evid.* (1827) I. 59 The judge of appeal, superordinate to the judge first spoken of. **1817** JAS. MILL *Brit. India* v. ix. II. 719 Whatsoever patronage is in the hands of the subordinate and obeying body, in reality belongs to the superordinate and commanding. **1864** BOWEN *Logic* iv. 87 Animal is Superior or Superordinate to mammal. **1934** PRIEBSCH & COLLINSON *German Lang.* vi. 318 The older construction is characterized by the precedence of the superordinate infinite, e.g. *lassen tragen.* **1949** C. E. BAZELL in *Travaux du Cercle Linguistique de Copenhague* V. 77 If..the functions of one member (e.g. the substantive) alone are similar to the functions of the whole group, this member is said to be superordinate. **1954** *Theology* LVII. 326 It would not necessarily be apparent which was the subordinate and which the superordinate sex. **1970** T. LUPTON *Managem. & Social Sci.* (ed. 2) iii. 80 The superordinate manager must work hard to create conditions for the subordinate such that the latter will feel that he is being supported and encouraged. **1974** W. REES-MOGG *Reigning Error* i. 21 Only those who appreciate my superordinate quality are fit to live in our new world of Nazism/Fascism/Soviet Communism. **1979** *Trans. Philol. Soc.* 37 In Italian promotion of the subordinate *si* into the superordinate clause..results in the unacceptable sequence *si si.*

B. *sb.* One who is superior in rank; a superior; that which is of a superior order or category.

1802–12 BENTHAM *Ration. Judic. Evid.* (1827) V. 556 *note*, This unlearned judge copying the pattern set him by his learned superordinates. **1816–30** —— *Offic. Apt. Maximized, Extract Const. Code* (1830) 14 Service rendered by a subordinate, the superordinate not having contributed any thing to the performance of it. **1934** PRIEBSCH & COLLINSON *German Lang.* vi. 318 Extensions of the infinitives and participles..sometimes follow their superordinates. **1957** R. W. BROWN in Saporta & Bastian *Psycholinguistics* (1961) 505/1 The concrete noun..is likely to be more picturable than its superordinate. **1969** GREENFIELD & BRUNER in J. S. Bruner *Beyond Information Given* (1974) xxi. 388 An itemized superordinate in labeling form. **1972** *Jrnl. Social Psychol.* LXXXVI. 302 The use of a superordinate..functionally eliminated one element from the set.

supe'rordinate, *v. rare.* [f. as prec.] *trans.* To place in a superior order or rank. Const. *to.*

1853 SIR W. HAMILTON *Logic* App. ii. 443 Two notions are superordinated to a third.

ˌ**superordi'nation.** [ad. eccl. L. *superordinātio*, *-ōnem* choice of a bishop's successor, f. *superordināre*: see SUPER- 13 and ORDINATION.]

1. Ordination of a person, while another still holds an office, to succeed him in that office when it shall become vacant. *rare.*

1655 FULLER *Ch. Hist.* II. ii. §27 After the death of Augustine, Laurentius..succeeded him, whom Augustine, in his Life-time..ordained in that Place... Such a super-Ordination in such cases was Canonicall.

2. a. *Logic.* The action of superordinating or condition of being superordinated; superordinate position or relation.

1864 BOWEN *Logic* viii. 244 The relations of inclusion and exclusion, of subordination and superordination, of Intension and Extension, existing between two Concepts and a Third. **1887** W. L. DAVIDSON in *Mind* Apr. 234 The relations that obtain between groups are those of subordination, superordination and co-ordination.

b. The condition of belonging to a higher or more powerful category or class; opp. *subordination.*

1952 V. O. KEY *Politics, Parties, & Pressure Groups* (ed. 3) i. 4 Politics deals with human relationships of superordination and subordination,..of the governors and the governed. **1959** G. D. MITCHELL *Sociol.* iii. 41 The relationship between father and son is one of super- and sub-ordination. **1975** A. RYLE *Frames & Cages* xiii. 121 The concept of superordination recurs through the book.

ˌsuperor'ganic, *a.* (and *sb.*). *Sociol.* [SUPER- 4 a.] Applied to the social and cultural aspects of life which evolve from and transcend the individuals in society. Also *absol.* as *sb.*; occas. *transf.*

1862 SPENCER *First Princ.* II. xiv. §3. (1875) 316 Phenomena which, for want of a better word, we may term super-organic. **1876** —— *Princ. Sociol.* (1877) I. 3 The four Volumes, that have followed First Principles, have dealt with Organic Evolution... We have now to enter upon the remaining division—Superorganic Evolution. **1917** A. L. KROEBER in *Amer. Anthropol.* XIX. 163 (*title*) The superorganic. **1932** A. RAVEN (*title*) Civilization as divine superman. A superorganic philosophy of history. **1962** E. E. EVANS-PRITCHARD *Ess. Social Anthropol.* ii. 34 Spencer clearly formulated the theory of gradual modification of species or structure..and..extended his evolutionary ideas to include the social or super-organic. **1968** *Internat. Encycl. Social Sci.* XV. 124/2 It was Spencer who coined the term 'superorganic', which, following its use by Kroeber in 1917 in his article 'The Superorganic', has been accepted as designating the unique and distinct elements in human behavior, and therefore as synonymous with 'culture'. **1973** P. A. COLINVAUX *Introd. Ecol.* xl. 550 A first grand generalization was the persuasive philosophy of Clements and his disciples..who likened the climax stage to some super-organic being.

super'ovulate, *v.* *Physiol.* [Back-formation from SUPEROVULATION.] **a.** *intr.* To produce abnormally large numbers of ova at a single ovulation. **b.** *trans.* To cause (an animal) to do this. So **super'ovulated** *ppl. a.*

1956 *Nature* 3 Mar. 429/1 Fallopian tubes from a super-ovulated female, killed approximately 12 hr. after mating to one of these males, were fixed in Bouin. **1961** M. C. CHANG in C. A. Villee *Control of Ovulation* 185 It seems that ovulation can be easily induced in the pregnant rabbits and that about half of the pregnant animals super-ovulate; that is ovulate a larger number of eggs than expected. **1970** *Sci. Jrnl.* May 50/2 Hormonal treatment can be used to get the female to superovulate. **1971** *Nature* 10 Sept. 125/2 Random bred female albino mice..were superovulated with gonadotrophins. **1979** *Ibid.* 25 Jan. 298/2 Two-celled embryos were collected from super-ovulated donor ewes early on day 2 of their oestrous cycle. **1979** *New Scientist* 26 Apr. 269/2 [They] super-ovulated 14 heifer cows up to 10 times in rapid succession—and the cows responded with crops of up to 19 eggs at a single ovulation.

So **ˌsuperovu'lation** [SUPER- 10 b].

1927 *Amer. Jrnl. Anat.* XL. 213 Superovulation, or the liberation of an unusual number of ova invariably occurs. **1981** *Sci. Digest* Aug. 89/1 They were beginning to suspect that superovulation..might be disrupting the internal reproductive environment.

†ˌsuperpar'ticular, *a.* (*sb.*) *Arith. Obs.* [ad. late L. *superparticulāris*: see SUPER- 14 and PARTICULAR.] Applied to a ratio in which the antecedent contains the consequent once with one aliquot part over (e.g. $1\frac{1}{2}$, $1\frac{1}{3}$, $1\frac{1}{4}$ times), i.e. the ratio of any number to the next below it ($\frac{3}{2}$, $\frac{4}{3}$, $\frac{5}{4}$); also (***multiple superparticular***) to one in which the antecedent contains the consequent any number of times with one aliquot part over (e.g. $2\frac{1}{2}$, $2\frac{1}{3}$, $3\frac{1}{2}$, $3\frac{1}{3}$.). Also *sb.*, a superparticular ratio.

1557 RECORDE *Whetst.* B ij, If the greater [number] containe the lesser, and any one parte of hym, that proportion is called Superparticulare. **1570** BILLINGSLEY *Euclid* v. 127 b, Multiplex Superperticular is when the antecedent containeth the consequent more then once, and moreouer onely one parte of the same. **1597** MORLEY *Introd. Mus.* Annot., Proportions of multiplicitie might be..vsed..without great..offence: but those superparticulars and superpartients carry great difficultie. **1621** BURTON *Anat. Mel.* I. iii. I. iv, 'Tis superparticular, *sesquialtera, sesquitertia* ..all those geometrical proportions are too little to express it. *a* **1696** SCARBURGH *Euclid* (1705) 180 In all Superparticulars the Numerator is, or may ever be reduced to an Unite. *Ibid.*, If..there remains..any Quotal part of the Consequent..then the proportion is called Multiple Superparticular. **1776** SIR J. HAWKINS *Gen. Hist. Mus.* I. vi. 83 The sesquioctave tone, as being in a superparticular ratio, is incapable of an equal division. **1842** *Smith's Dict. Gr. & Rom. Antiq.* 624/2 Each of the four ratios..is superparticular; i.e., the two terms of each differ from one another by unity.

Hence **†ˌsuperparticu'larity.**

1597 MORLEY *Introd. Mus.* Annot., Al soundes contained in habitude of multiplicitie, or superparticularity, were of the olde musicians esteemed consonantes.

†super'partient, *a.* (*sb.*) *Arith. Obs.* [ad. late L. *superpartientem, -ens,* f. *super-* SUPER- 14 + *partiens*, pr. pple. of *partīrī* to divide.] Applied to a ratio in which the antecedent contains the consequent once (or, ***multiple superpartient,*** any number of times) with any number (greater than one) of aliquot parts over. Also *sb.*, a superpartient ratio.

1557 RECORDE *Whetst.* B ij b, If the difference be .2. partes .3. partes, or more partes: the proportion is named superpartiente. As 5 to 3. **1570** BILLINGSLEY *Euclid* v. 127 b, Multiplex Superpartient, is when the antecedent contayneth the consequent more then once, and also more partes then one of the consequent. **1597** [see SUPERPARTICULAR]. **1694** *Phil. Trans.* XVIII. 69 The several Denominations of Geometrical Rations, as Multiplex, Superparticular, Superpartient. *a* **1696** SCARBURGH *Euclid* (1705) 180, 8 to 3 is in proportion Multiple Superpartient. **1709–29** [see SUPER- 14]. **1788** T. TAYLOR *Proclus* I. 50 Every kind of reasons [= ratios], multiplex, super-particular, super-partient, and the opposite to these.

super'personal, *a.* [SUPER- 4 a.] Transcending the limits of what is personal. Also *absol.* Hence **'superperson, super'personalism, ˌsuperperso'nality.**

1860 EMERSON *Cond. Life* vi. (1861) 141 The nameless Thought, the nameless Power, the superpersonal Heart. **1899** C. F. D'ARCY *Idealism & Theology* ii. 95 If the conception of personality is not adequate as a final description of Deity, then we must believe in God as ultimately superpersonal unity. **1924** G. B. SHAW *Saint Joan* p. xvii, An appetite for evolution..[is] a super-personal need. **1926** W. D. LIGHTHALL *Superpersonalism* 26 We can proceed a stage further, and call it the Person of Evolution. But its vast and complex personality requires a differentiating term. May we not apply to it the term 'Superperson'? and call its personality a 'superpersonality', its point of view the 'superpersonal', the system of its study, 'Superpersonalism'? **1927** J. S. HUXLEY *Relig. without Revelation* i. 52 Metamorphosed from a divine person into a super-person. **1939** AUDEN in *I Believe* (1940) 20 But this does not warrant ascribing to a culture a super-personality, conscious of its parts as I can be conscious of my hand or liver. **1963** *Observer* 31 Mar. 11/3 The God hypothesis asserts the existence of some kind of supernatural personal or superpersonal being. **1977** *Rolling Stone* 21 Apr. 68/2 A chair is made by a person, so the world has to be made by a superperson.

super'phosphate. [SUPER- 12 b.]

1. *Chem.* A phosphate containing an excess of phosphoric acid; an acid phosphate.

1797 PEARSON in *Phil. Trans.* LXXXVIII. 17 It was..Scheele who discovered, that the urine of healthy persons contains superphosphate, or acidulous phosphate, of lime. **1811** A. T. THOMSON *Lond. Disp.* (1818) 479 By the strong acids it [phosphate of soda] is converted into superphosphate of soda. **1876** HARLEY *Royle's Mat. Med.* (ed. 6) 62 When the superphosphate is heated with charcoal, tribasic phosphate is re-formed, and phosphoric acid set free.

2. In full ***superphosphate of lime***: an impure superphosphate of lime prepared by treating bones, coprolites, etc. with sulphuric acid, and used as a manure.

1843 W. HAY in *Farmer's Mag.* Jan. 42/2 By the action of sulphuric acid on bones a superphosphate of lime is produced. **1861** *Times* 10 Oct., Swedes, manured and sown with guano and superphosphate. **1868** *Rep. U.S. Commissioner Agric.* (1869) 221 A hundred and fifty to a hundred and seventy-five pounds of superphosphate strewn in the furrows to be ridged over. **1879** *Cassell's Techn. Educ.* II. 198/2 Mineral superphosphate is prepared by pouring sulphuric acid..on phosphorite or coprolites.

super'physical, *a.* [SUPER- 4.] That is above, or of a higher order than, the physical; = HYPERPHYSICAL.

a **1603** T. CARTWRIGHT *Confut. Rhem. N.T.* (1618) 228 Supernaturall and Superphisicall Theology. **1865** *Pall Mall Gaz.* 19 Oct. 3 'What causes the motor nerves to pull the trigger?' Is the cause physical or super-physical? **1880** N. SMYTH *Old Faiths in New Light* vii. (1882) 281 Any suggestions, or intimations, which may come to us..of superphysical modes or spheres of existence. **1904** H. A. A. KENNEDY *St. Paul's Concept. Last Things* v. 233 The process of super-physical activity in the existence of the exalted Christ. **1924** W. B. SELBIE *Psychol. Relig.* 277 Various forms of super-physical life.

super'plastic, *a.* and *sb.* *Metallurgy.* [SUPER- 9 a, 10: see SUPERPLASTICITY.] **A.** *adj.* Of, pertaining to, or designating a metal capable of extreme plastic extension under load; involving or characteristic of such materials.

1947 *Chem. Abstr.* XLI. 2375 The superplastic alloy cannot be a mixt. of solid solns. of Al and Zn. **1970** *New Scientist* 12 Mar. 504/2 One of the most suitable titanium alloys—Ti-318—is superplastic at 930°C if correctly worked, and can be made to stretch and flow like plastic. **1978** *Jrnl. R. Soc. Arts* CXXVI. 689/1 It is possible that the single heat cycle combination of superplastic forming and diffusion bonding will revolutionize the fabrication of titanium sheet structures for aircraft applications. **1978** *Nature* 16 Nov. 209/2 The consolidated product can have very fine grain sizes which in turn leads to great ductility at ambient temperature—even to superplastic behaviour.

B. *sb.* A superplastic metal.

1969 *New Scientist* 2 Jan. 22/2 This metal, after treatment which reduces the grain size to about a micrometre, behaves like a superplastic at room temperature—it can be stretched by a factor of about 10 in one direction without breaking. **1971** *Britannica Yearbk. Sci. & Future 1972* 406 While the superplastics are only starting to shed their image as laboratory curiosities, the fiber composites have almost arrived.

Hence **super'plastically** *adv.*; **ˌsuperpla'sticity** [tr. Russ. *sverkhplastichnost'* (Bochvar & Sviderskaya 1945, in *Izvestiya Akad. Nauk SSSR: Otdelenie tekhnicheskikh Nauk* IX. 824)], the state or quality of being superplastic.

1947 *Chem. Abstr.* XLI. 2375 (*heading*) Superplasticity in zinc-aluminum alloys. **1969** *Sci. Jrnl.* June 75/2 At one time, it was considered that superplastic metallic alloys were amorphous-like and for this reason behaved superplastically. **1977** *Jrnl. R. Soc. Arts* CXXV. 348/1 The exploitation of superplasticity in titanium sheet opens the way for shaped components of reduced cost. **1978** *Ibid.* CXXVI. 688/1 When the temperature of the blank reaches 950°C the argon pressure is increased at a programmed rate to expand the blank into the tool superplastically.

†'superplus. Chiefly *Sc. Obs.* [a. med.L. *superplus*: see SUPER- 13 and PLUS.] = SURPLUS.

1561 *Reg. Privy Council Scot.* (1877) I. 193 Samekle thairof to be employit to the Quenis Majestie..., and samekle thairof to the ministeris..; and the excrescence and superplus to be assignit to the auld possessouris. **1584** B. R. tr. *Herodotus* I. 14 Wt a superplus & addition of 24 powndes. **1591** R. BRUCE *Serm.* v. L iij, And when, efter their maner; they haue satisfied him, they make a superplus, quhilk they call workes of supererogatioun. **1641** in *Fasti Aberd.* (1854) 157 They ordene the superplus of the rents of the said bischoprik to be imployed upone the reparatione of the edifices of the said colledges. **1687** [SHIELDS] *Hind let loose* 105 A super-plus of Caution. **1760** C. JOHNSTON *Chrysal* (1822) I. 24 To employ the super-plus in acts of private benevolence. **1762** GOLDSM. *Ess., Female Warriors,* There must be a superplus of the other sex. **1796** ANNA SEWARD *Lett.* (1811) IV. 224 A superplus of time from that which is employed in providing for his natural wants. **1825** J. NICHOLSON *Oper. Mech.* 172 The cold-water pump F keeps up an abundant supply in the cistern EE, and the superplus is discharged at W.

†superplusage. *Obs.* [ad. OF. *superplusage* or med.L. *superplusagium*: see prec. and -AGE.] = SURPLUSAGE.

1450 *Rolls of Parlt.* V. 194/1 Aunsweryng to oure saide Progenitours of the superplusage. **1509–10** *Chr. Coll. Acc.* in Willis & Clark *Cambridge* (1886) II. 196 The superplusage of the last accompt xl *li.* **1543** *Richmond Wills* (Surtees) 48 The superplusage and overplus of my goods, above not bewhethed. **1583** in Feuillerat *Revels Q. Eliz.* (1908) Table iii. 360–1 The Superplusage of his laste Declaratione ended vltimo Octobris. **1621** DONNE *Serm. Christmas Day* (1649) II. 333 Their Doctrine of Supererogation, that a man might do so much more then he was bound to do for God, as that that superplusage might save whom he would. **1661** J. FELL *Hammond* 14 A stock was rais'd..for the apprentising of young Children... And after this there yet remain'd a Superplusage for the assistance of the neighbour Parishes.

†super'politic, *a.* *Obs.* [SUPER- II, III.] **a.** In early use, with reference to the Jesuits: That is above or overrules ordinary politics or policy. **b.** Later, taken in the sense: Over-politic, exceedingly crafty.

1599 SANDYS *Europæ Spec.* (1632) 46 That super-politike and irrefragable order as they compt it, of the Jesuites, who couple in their perswasions, as one God and one Faith, so one Pope and one King. [**1640** HOWELL *Dodona's Gr.* 79 That super-politique and irrefragable Societie of the Loyolists.] **1641** MILTON *Reform.* II. 53 [quoting Sandys]. **1647** JER. TAYLOR *Lib. Proph.* viii. 152 At the Florentine Council the Latins acted their masterpiece of wit and stratagem, the greatest that hath been till the famous and superpolitick design of Trent. **1659** GAUDEN *Slight Healers* (1660) 90 By a super-politick policy.

So **ˌsuperpo'litical** *a.*, that is above or independent of politics.

1667 LOCKE *Ess. conc. Toleration* in Fox Bourne *Life* (1876) I. 182 The private and super-political concernment between God and a man's soul, wherein the magistrate's authority is not to interpose.

superposable (s(j)u:pə'pəʊzəb(ə)l), *a.* [f. next + -ABLE.] Capable of being superposed. Hence **ˌsuperposa'bility,** the property of being superposable.

1870 CHAUVENET *Elem. Geom.* VIII. 265 The triangles..are mutually equilateral, and also isosceles; therefore they are superposable and are equal in area. **1882** MINCHIN *Unipl. Kinemat.* 68 Any two possible acceleration systems in uniplanar motion are superposable in a single acceleration system. **1913** *Jrnl. Chem. Soc.* CIII. 839 There are evidently two vertical planes of symmetry cutting diagonally through the ring carbon atoms, and it might be objected that the presence of these two planes of symmetry are in reality the cause of the superposability. **1963** R. BALLABH *Hydrodynamic Superposability* i. 1 The idea of superposability as regards fluid motions does not seem to have engaged the attention of mathematicians in a formal way until the year 1940. **1973** *Engin. Fracture Mechanics* V. 555 The same is practically true for elastomers also but, in addition, their ultimate properties are well described by a failure envelope which approximates time-temperature superposability.

superpose (s(j)u:pə'pəʊz), *v.* [ad. F. *superposer*, f. *super-* SUPER- 2 + *poser* to POSE, after L. *superpōnĕre* (see SUPERPOSITION).]

1. *trans.* To place above or upon something else. Usually in *pa. pple.*; often loosely of two or more things in a vertical series (= placed one above or upon another).

1823 tr. *Humboldt's Geognost. Ess. Superpos. Rocks* 90 A whitestone, which is superposed on the formation of granite and gneiss. **1843** *Civil Eng. & Arch. Jrnl.* VI. 98/2 The column and trabeation in relief, and superposed upon the frieze and arch. **1867** J. Hogg *Microsc.* I. i. 12 The object-glass was composed of three lenses superposed. **1904** *Brit. Med. Jrnl.* 17 Sept. 656 A few parasites could be seen superposed or underlying a red blood corpuscle.

b. *fig.* (Also *absol.*)

1848 M. Arnold *Sonn. to Republ. Fr. contin.* 10 Bursting through the network superpos'd By selfish occupation. **1855** Lewes *Goethe* (1864) 52 They superpose *ab extra*, instead of trying to develope *ab intra*. *Ibid.* 53 His portraitures carry their moral with them, in them, but have no moral superposed. **1906** Petrie *Relig. Anc. Egypt* xii. 78 Amid all the varieties of idea and bad readings superposed, the task of critical understanding is almost hopeless.

2. *Physics*, etc. To bring into the same position so as to coincide; to cause to occupy or co-exist in the same space without destroying one another, as two or more sets of physical conditions (e.g. undulations, light-rays, etc.), or one such in relation to another.

1831 Brewster *Optics* xii. 105 The rings seen..will consist of all the seven differently coloured systems of rings superposed as it were. **1854** *Pereira's Polarized Light* (ed. 2) 262 The two circularly polarized rays..will emerge superposed, and will compound a single ray polarized in a single plane. **1860** Tyndall *Glac.* I. xiv. 95 Upon the large and general motion of the glacier, smaller motions are superposed. **1881** Broadhouse *Mus. Acoustics* 178 One simple tone is thus superposed upon another.

b. *Geom.* To transfer (one magnitude) ideally to the space occupied by another, esp. so as to show that they coincide.

1870 [implied in superposable]. **1885** [implied in superposed 3].

super'posed, *ppl. a.* [f. prec. + -ed[1].]

1. Placed above or upon something else, or (loosely, of two or more things) one above or upon another.

1823 tr. *Humboldt's Geognost. Ess. Superpos. Rocks* 17 A table in which the superposed rocks succeed each other from below upwards. **1861** Beresf. Hope *Eng. Cathedr. 19th C.* ii. 40 Chartres Cathedral..with the broad triplet and superposed rose of the west end. **1875** tr. Witkowski (*title*) A Movable Atlas showing the positions of the various Organs of Voice, Speech, and Taste, by means of superposed coloured plates. **1896** *Daily News* 2 Mar. 8/3 Roofing the covered drain with three superposed layers of iron girders.

2. *Bot.* Situated directly above another part of the same kind (or one directly above another) as leaves on a stem, etc.: opposed to *alternate*.

1861 Bentley *Man. Bot.* 330 Two ovules..may be placed at different heights, and then..follow the same direction, when they are superposed.

3. *Physics*, *Geom.*, etc. Brought into the same position so as to coincide; occupying, wholly or partly, the same space or place (actually, apparently, or ideally).

1868 Lockyer *Guillemin's Heavens* (ed. 3) 167 To an observer placed on the Sun, the Moon seems projected on the Earth, hiding a portion of the surface, although it is true that the two superposed disks, as they are both luminous, would not permit the darkened part of the surface of the terrestrial globe to be seen from the Sun. **1885** Leudesdorf *Cremona's Proj. Geom.* 169 To construct the self-corresponding elements of two superposed projective forms.

4. *Phys. Geog.* = superimposed 1 b.

1895 W. M. Davis in *Geogr. Jrnl.* (R.G.S.) V. 139 Their drainage is accomplished in great part by subsequent streams..and not by superposed streams imperfectly adjusted to the structures. *Ibid.* 143 Superposed drainage, settling down into unknown structures through an unconformable cover.

†**super'posit**, *v. Obs. rare.* [f. L. *superposit-*, pa. ppl. stem of *superpōnĕre*: see super- III and posit *v.*] *trans.* To place above others; to exalt.

1661 Feltham *Resolves* II. xiv. (ed. 8) 207 Without it [*sc.* power], he were not God: 'tis that which distinguisheth and super-posits him above all.

superposition (ˌs(j)uːpəpəˈzɪʃən). [ad. F. *superposition*, ad. late L. *superpositio*, *-ōnem*, n. of action f. *superpōnĕre*, f. *super-* super- 2, 13 + *pōnĕre* to place (see position).] The action of superposing or condition of being superposed.

1. *gen.* The placing of one thing above or upon another.

1830 Herschel *Study Nat. Phil.* §261 Bergmann.. showed how at least one species of crystal might be built up of thin laminæ ranged in a certain order, and following certain rules of superposition. **1853** Kane *Grinnell Exp.* xlii. (1856) 394 The infraposition and superposition of two fluids of differing densities. **1861** Beresf. Hope *Eng. Cathedr. 19th C.* ii. 43 The massiveness and squareness of its forms, the frequent use of superposition [in Norman architecture]. **1879** Rutley *Study Rocks* x. 153 The superposition of one crystal on another sometimes gives rise to cruciform figures.

b. An instance of this; also, a series of things placed one above another.

1828–32 Webster, *Superposition* 2, that which is situated above or upon something else. **1836** Mrs. Somerville *Connex. Phys. Sci.* xvii. (ed. 3) 161 The resulting figure varying with the number of the superpositions, and the angles at which they are superposed. **1894** M. O'Rell *John Bull & Co.* 295 The land is a succession, a superposition, of plateaus, hills, and mountains.

c. *fig.*

1871 Smiles *Charac.* ii. (1876) 33 The child's character is the nucleus of the man's; all after-education is but superposition. **1872** Bagehot *Physics & Pol.* (1876) 49 The superposition of the more military races over the less military. **1904** *Brit. Med. Jrnl.* 10 Sept. 582 The superposition of doses.

d. *Eccl. Antiq.* Of fasts (see quot.).

After eccl. L. *superpositio (jejunii)*, eccl. Gr. ὑπέρθεσις τῆς νηστείας. Cf. F. *jeûnes de superposition*.

1710–22 Bingham *Antiq.* xxi. i. §25 Victorinus Petavionensis..speaks of several Sorts of Fasts observed among Christians, some of which were only till the Ninth Hour, some till Evening, and some with a Superposition or Addition of one Fasting-Day to another. Though we must note, That the Superposition of a Fast..sometimes denotes a new appointed Fast of any Kind.

2. *Geom.* The action of ideally transferring one figure into the position occupied by another, esp. so as to show that they coincide.

1656 Hobbes *Six Lessons* Wks. 1845 VII. 197 The superposition of quantities, by which they render the word ἐφαρμογή, cannot be understood of bodies, but only of lines and superficies. **1793** Beddoes *Math. Evid.* 36 This measure of the eye would not be sufficiently exact to satisfy us that the angles are equal; we must obtain a measure by real or imagined super-position. **1837** Hallam *Lit. Eur.* III. iii. §77 *note*, Most of plane geometry may be resolved into the super-position of equal triangles. **1882** Proctor *Fam. Sci. Studies* 16 The perfect equality of the triangles might be tested by superposition.

b. *Physics*, etc. The action of causing two or more sets of physical conditions or phenomena (e.g. undulations or other motions) to coincide, or co-exist in the same place; the fact of such coincidence or co-existence.

1830 Herschel *Sound* in *Encycl. Metrop.* (1845) IV. 790 The principle of the superposition of vibrating motions.. must be admitted in Acoustics. **1831** Brewster *Optics* xxii. 195 The superposition of these two systems of rings would reproduce white light. **1879** G. Prescott *Sp. Telephone* 248 A composite curve which represents the effect produced by the superposition of one set of waves upon another.

fig. **1858** J. Martineau *Stud. Christ.* 143 We accept them both (penal redemption and moral redemption), putting them, however, not in succession, but in super-position so that they coalesce.

3. *Geol.* The deposition of one stratum upon another, or the condition of being so deposited.

1799 *Monthly Rev.* XXX. 15 The many turnings and superposition of strata. **1823** tr. *Humboldt's Geogn. Ess. Superp. Rocks* Pref p. v, The most remarkable superpositions of rocks in both hemispheres. **1832** De la Beche *Geol. Man.* 202 This superposition of gravel, in which the rolled fragments are sometimes by no means small. **1870** Yeats *Nat. Hist. Comm.* 27 A correct knowledge of the law of superposition of rocks. **1879** *Encycl. Brit.* X. 295/1 The underlying beds must be older than those which cover them. This simple and obvious truth is termed the law of superposition.

4. *Bot.* The relative position of leaves or other members on an axis, when situated directly above one another, not alternating.

1880 A. Gray *Struct. Bot.* vi. §3. (ed. 6) 179 Non-alternation of the members of contiguous circles: Anteposition or Superposition.

superpository (s(j)uːpəˈpɒzɪtərɪ), *a. Eccl. Antiq. rare.* [ad. L. **superpositōrius* (rendering eccl. Gr. ὑπερθέσιμος), f. *superposit-*, pa. ppl. stem of *superpōnĕre* (see prec.)] Applied to additional fasts: see superposition 1 d.

1710–22 Bingham *Antiq.* xxi. i. §25 Superpository or Additional Fasts.

'superpower. Also super power. [super- 6.]

1. [super- 6 c.] orig. and chiefly *U.S.* Electrical power produced by the co-ordination and interconnection of existing power plants for greater economy and efficiency. Freq. *attrib.* Now *Hist.*

1921 W. S. Murray in *Prof. Papers U.S. Geol. Survey* No. 123. 11 On first presenting the subject considered in this report to the late Secretary of the Interior..I used the word 'superpower' to describe a system that would furnish power to the railroads and the industries within the territory between Boston and Washington that has now become more familiarly known as the superpower zone. **1921** *Independent* CVII. 316/2 The problems certain to arise within the circuit of the super-power zone are like those connected with the interstate and intrastate services of the railroads. *Ibid.* 317/2 The probable issues of super-power seem to make such a body [*sc.* a Federal control agency] inevitable. **1926** *Encycl. Brit.* (ed. 13) 681/2 The basis for a super-power system lies in the economy effected by the interconnection of electric power systems whose peak loads are reached at different times. **1983** T. P. Hughes *Networks of Power* xi. 297 Only one month after World War I ended, William S. Murray, a consulting electrical engineer, urged the secretary of the interior to prepare the ground for this superpower system.

2. [super- 6 b.] Power of a greater kind or degree than the ordinary.

1922 D. H. Lawrence *Aaron's Rod* xviii. 269 Newly flushed with his own male super-power, he was going to have his reward. **1928** G. B. Shaw *Intelligent Woman's Guide* lxxxiii. 454 The more power the people are given the more urgent becomes the need for some rational and well-informed superpower to dominate them. **1931** *Times Lit. Suppl.* 26 Sept. (Home & Classroom Suppl.) p. iv/2 A super-power amplifier with an undistorted output of 125 watts. **1970** *New Society* 5 Feb. 231/3 This is an entity which has recently escaped from the dominance of Europe: and is now shadowed by the dominance of American superpower. **1975** *Microwave Jrnl.* XVIII. 50/3 The power of conventional microwave generating devices can be increased appreciably only through a matched increase of the..electron beam intensity. It is therefore tempting to use intense Relativistic Electron Beams to generate 'super power' microwaves. **1977** *N.Y. Rev. Bks.* 23 June 39/2 We do not, and cannot hope to, have a monopoly of 'superpower' in our world, as Rome had in hers.

3. [super- 6 c.] A nation or state having a dominant position in world politics; one which has the power to act decisively in pursuit of interests which embrace the whole world; *spec.* the United States of America and the Union of Soviet Socialist Republics.

[**1930** *Economist* 12 July 63/2 The most important contributions to the Conference..were descriptions of what has actually taken place in the..control of super-power zones.] **1944** W. T. R. Fox *Super-Powers* ii. 20 There will be 'world powers' and 'regional powers'. These world powers we shall call 'super-powers', in order to distinguish them from the other powers..whose interests are great in only a single theater of power conflict. **1957** *Foreign Affairs* XXXV. 177 Britain is no longer a Super-Power. **1967** *Spectator* 30 June 758/2 Almost by definition superpowers do not have to care about face... America will continue to be a superpower whatever it does about Vietnam. **1971** *Guardian* 9 Dec. 12/1 China has..been drawn into a Super Power type of defence of Pakistan. **1977** E. Heath *Travels* viii. 166 What I saw when I arrived was a laudable achievement, possible only to a military commander with the resources of a superpower. **1978** J. Updike *Coup* (1979) ii. 54 Capital investments cleverly pried from the rivalry between the two super-powers (and that shadowy third, China, that has the size but not as it were the mass, the substance, to be called super).

†**super'principal**, *a.* (*Obs. rare*[−1]), intended for **superprincipial* (see super- II and principial), a rendering of eccl. Gr. ὑπεράρχιος before all beginning.

1677 Gale *Crt. Gentiles* IV. II. iii. §2. 246 Eulogus, in Photius [says] Essence it self is one thing in the superprincipal Trinitie, and another thing in us.

superpronation: see super- 2 a (*b*).

super'radiant, *a. Physics.* [super- 9 a.] Involving or exhibiting superradiance.

1954 R. H. Dicke in *Physical Rev.* XCIII. 102/2 For want of a better term, a gas which is radiating strongly because of coherence will be called 'super-radiant'. **1974** *Sci. Amer.* June 126/1 The optical gain of the rapid discharge is so large that emission becomes superradiant, which means that the unit will lase without an optical cavity. **1978** *Nature* 20 Apr. 742/2 The word superradiant has often been misused..but is now taken to mean either the coherent radiation generated by a system of atoms possessing an externally created macroscopic polarisation rather akin to a phased array of dipoles, or alternatively the incoherent fluctuating radiation produced by a system of excited atoms possessing no initial polarisation but instead developing a cooperative decay behaviour through quantum correlations.

Hence **super'radiantly** *adv.*; also **super'radiance**, the spontaneous emission of coherent radiation by a system of atoms, esp. when the coherence is due to the initial correlation of the atoms by an external macroscopic polarization.

1965 *Physical Rev. Lett.* XIV. 589 (*heading*) Nuclear superradiance in solids. **1974** *Sci. Amer.* June 126/2 If the ultraviolet pulses are focused by a cylindrical lens to a line on the surface of the dye.., the dye will often lase superradiantly in visible light along the direction of the line. **1979** *New Scientist* 8 Mar. 763/2 The wave analogue of this process was called 'super-radiance': incident waves in certain modes would be amplified (rather than absorbed) by a rotating black hole, and would carry away some of the black hole's rotational energy.

†**superrant.** *Obs. rare*[−1]. (Derivation and meaning unknown; perh. an error.)

1597 [see *subtercubant* under subter-].

super-rat: see super- 6 c.

super'rational, *a.* [super- 4.] That is above, or beyond the scope of, reason; higher than what is rational. So **super'rationally** *adv.*

1683 E. Hooker *Pref. Pordage's Mystic Div.* 66 The veri Spirit of the Mind is elevated, supersensualy and super-rationaly sublimed. **1752** Law *Spir. Love* II. (1816) 111 A religion not grounded in the power and nature of things, is unnatural, supernatural, or superrational. **1826** Coleridge in *Lit. Rem.* (1838) III. 38, I should think it more correct to describe the mysteries of faith as *plusquam rationalia* than superrational. **1890** J. Martineau *Seat Author. in Relig.* IV. i. 316 This communicated idea, being super-rational, plants the Supreme Good beyond the range of all philosophy. **1891** Meredith *One of our Conq.* III. x. 192 Reason took a superrational leap.

super-real, etc.: super- 4 a (*a*) and (*c*).

ˌsuperregeneˈration. *Electronics.* [super- 6 b.] Regenerative amplification in which self-oscillation is prevented by repeated quenching of the signal at an ultrasonic frequency.

1922 *Q.S.T.* July 7/1 At a meeting of the Institute of Radio Engineers, Edwin Howard Armstrong on June 7th gave his new invention of super-regeneration to a tense and expectant audience. **1922** E. H. Armstrong in *Proc. IRE* X. 244 This new result is obtained by the extension of regeneration into a field which lies beyond that hitherto considered its theoretical limit, and the process of amplification is therefore termed super-regeneration. **1943** F. E. Terman *Radio Engineers' Handbk.* IX. 664 Receivers employing superregeneration find their chief usefulness in the wavelength range 0·5 to 10 meters. **1975** R. L. Shrader *Electronic Communication* (ed. 3) xviii. 435/2 This type of superregeneration is often produced in RF amplifiers and is characterized by a wide band of spurious signals that it generates.

Hence **superre'generative** *a.*, employing or characterized by superregeneration; **super-re'generatively** *adv.*; **superre'generator**, a superregenerative device.

1922 *Q.S.T.* July 9/2 The super-regenerative amplifier. *Ibid.* 11/1 In the super-regenerator there is periodically sufficient positive resistance to wipe out this oscillation and hence it is not heard. **1934** *Wireless Engineer* XI. 35/1 The receiver may be made to function super-regeneratively by increasing the s.g. voltage to the point of 'squegging'. **1948** SLURZBERG & OSTERHELD *Essent. Radio* v. 232 Superregenerative detector circuits are used in light, compact, portable code receivers. **1959** R. L. SHRADER *Electronic Communication* xvii. 542 When coupled to an antenna, the superregenerator radiates a very broad signal. **1965** *Guardian* 18 Jan. 16/3 The popular super-regenerative receiver..is the simplest and the cheapest on the market. **1975** R. L. SHRADER *Electronic Communication* (ed. 3) xviii. 434/2 A demodulator used in the past in the VHF range is the superregenerative detector.

super regulum, obs. var. SUPERNACULUM.

'super-,royal, *a.* [SUPER- 4.]

1. That is above royal or kingly rank; higher than royal. *rare.*

1612 T. JAMES *Corrupt. Script.* II. 93 Books, that do either impugne, or question the Popes superroiall power. *c* **1662** F. KERBY in *O. Heywood's Diaries* (1883) III. 31 The brats of prelacy presume a super-royal vertue to assume.

2. Designating a size of paper next above that called *royal* (ROYAL *a.* 11), measuring about 19–21 by 27–28 inches.

1681 T. FLATMAN *Heraclitus Ridens* No. 36 (1713) I. 238 He is going to bind up all his Sheets in Super-Royal Paper. **1755** Flyleaf in *Whole Duty of Man*, A large Bible..printed on Super Royal Paper. **1831–3** BARLOW *Manuf.* in *Encycl. Metrop.* (1845) VIII. 768/2 Drawing paper..Super royal..2 ft. 3 in. by 1 ft. 7 in. **1870** J. POWER *Handy-bk. Bks.* 113 *Super-royal*..Name given to a size of paper measuring 27½ in. by 19¼ in. **1885** *Encycl. Brit.* XVIII. 226/2 Book and Drawing Papers... Super royal, 19¼ × 27... Printing Papers... Super royal, 21 × 27... Cartridge Papers... Super royal, 19¼ × 27½. **1888** *Ibid.* XXIII. 700/2 The dimensions of the papers commonly used in book-printing are:—imperial, 22 × 30 inches; super royal, 20½ × 27½; royal, 20 × 25.

supersalt ('s(j)uːpəsɒlt, -ɔː-). *Chem.* [f. SUPER- 12 b + SALT *sb.* 6.] A salt containing an excess of the acid over the base; an acid salt.

1806 *G. Adams' Nat. & Exp. Philos.* (Philad.) I. App. 547 Some salts are formed by an additional dose of their acids, and hence termed super-salts. **1807** T. THOMSON *Chem.* (ed. 3) II. 575 Phosphate of Lime. Of this salt there are two varieties; the first neutral, the other a supersalt. **1844** FOWNES *Man. Elem. Chem.* 207 Many of the compounds called *super*, or *acid salts*..ought strictly to be considered in the light of double salts.

supersalt, variant of SUPERSAULT *Obs.*

super'saturate, *sb.* *rare*⁻¹. [f. next.] A supersaturated state (in quot. *fig.*).

1860 EMERSON *Cond. Life, Power* Wks. (Bohn) II. 338 Success..rarely found in the right state for an article of commerce, but oftener in the supersaturate or excess, which makes it dangerous.

super'saturate, *v.* [SUPER- 9 b; after F. *sursaturer.*] *trans.* To saturate to excess; to add more of some other substance to (a given substance) than is sufficient to saturate it: chiefly in *Chem.* and *Physics* (cf. SATURATE *v.* 3, 4). Const. *with.*

1788 KEIR in *Phil. Trans.* LXXVIII. 325 When the acid has been completely saturated, or perhaps supersaturated, by..alternate evaporation to dryness, and re-dissolution in water. **1794** R. J. SULIVAN *View Nat.* I. 342 We could have no rain, unless the air were supersaturated with water, as it would part only with what it could not retain in solution. **1807** T. THOMSON *Chem.* (ed. 3) II. 333 According to him [*sc.* Macquer], prussian blue is nothing else than iron supersaturated with phlogiston. **1854** F. BAKEWELL *Geol.* 45 The water would become super-saturated, and the salt be deposited. **1857** LIVINGSTONE *Trav.* xxiv. 475 The plains, which in October and November were well moistened,..now become supersaturated. **1863** TYNDALL *Heat* v. 153 The liquid is..supersaturated with sulphate of soda.

refl. **1789** J. PILKINGTON *View Derbysh.* I. vi. 263 Water by a large quantity of calcareous gas will thus in close vessels super-saturate itself with lime.

absol. **1801** *Phil. Trans.* XCI. 197 *note*, That chymist supersaturates by nitric acid. **1839–47** *Todd's Cycl. Anat.* III. 803/2 Supersaturating with nitric acid, and precipitating by a salt of baryta as usual.

b. *fig.*

1802–12 BENTHAM *Ration. Judic. Evid.* (1827) V. 264 Saturated as he [*sc.* Coke] was, and super-saturated, with law learning. **1828** SOUTHEY in *Q. Rev.* XXXVII. 219 Mr. Hallam, supersaturated as he is with malevolence toward the Anglican church. **1863** R. F. BURTON *Abeokuta* II. 95 The members, supersaturated with Exeter Hall influences. **1911** FISHBERG *Jews* xxiii. 551 The Spanish nation of to-day is supersaturated with 'Jewish blood'.

Hence **super'saturating** *vbl. sb.*

1857 MILLER *Elem. Chem., Org.* i. 22 Its amount may be determined by..filtering, supersaturating with ammonia.

super'saturated, *ppl. a.* [f. prec. + -ED¹.] Saturated to excess; having more of some (specified or implied) substance added than is sufficient for saturation.

1794 PEARSON tr. *Morveau's Chem. Nomencl.* 33 Soda combined with a smaller proportion of Boracic Acid in which the Alkali predominates is named supersaturated Borate of Soda [*le borax sursaturé de soude*]. **1871** B. STEWART *Heat* (ed. 2) §107 Experiments on supersaturated saline solutions. **1884** *Harper's Mag.* Mar. 601/1 A catch basin for the super-saturated soil. **1910** *Encycl. Brit.* VIII. 714/1 The super-saturated air having no dust to condense on would condense on our clothes.

,supersatu'ration. [f. SUPERSATURATE *v.*: see -ATION.] The action of supersaturating; the condition or state of being supersaturated; addition of more than is sufficient for saturation (cf. SATURATION 3).

1791 *Phil. Trans.* LXXXI. 400 By a super-saturation of the medium. **1793** BEDDOES *Calculus* 22 A supersaturation of the alkali. **1836** J. M. GULLY *Magendie's Formul.* (ed. 2) 116 The supersaturation of the system with iodine..may be known by..the following symptoms. **1842** PARNELL *Chem. Anal.* (1845) 321 The lead in excess now existing in the solution is precipitated by supersaturation with sulphuretted hydrogen gas. **1876** *Phil. Mag.* II. 216 This is a consequence..of the condition of supersaturation being maintained even in solutions from which crystals of sugar are being deposited. **1902** *Encycl. Brit.* XXVIII. 568/1. **1941** [see KERN *sb.*² 3]. **1983** *Sci. Amer.* June 108/3 The concentration of dissolved nitrogen in the dolphin's muscle tissue was indicative of a degree of supersaturation that in a human diver would have been dangerous.

fig. **1802–12** BENTHAM *Ration. Judic. Evid.* (1827) I. 435 By supersaturation, as well as by inanition, the powers of the mind..may be destroyed.

†**supersault.** *Obs.* Also 6 -salt(e. [Alteration of OF. *soubresaut* (see SOBERSAULT) after L. *super.*] A somersault; also *fig.* hyperbole, exaggeration.

1503 *Acc. Ld. High Treas. Scot.* II. 387 Item, to the Inglis spelair, that playit the supersault, v Franch crounis. **1535** STEWART *Cron. Scot.* (Rolls) III. 474 Sayand of him, with sic ane supersalt, That he wes neuir noittit with ane falt. **1547** *Bk. Marchauntes* f iiij b, He made a supersault and willyngly as a tumbler fell downe as in a sown, feining to be rauished. **1572** SIR T. SMITH in Ellis *Orig. Lett.* Ser. II. III. 20 Vaulting with notable supersaltes & through hoopes.

superscribe (s(j)uːpə'skraɪb, 's(j)uːpəskraɪb), *v.* [ad. late L. *superscrībĕre*, f. *super-* SUPER- 2 + *scrībĕre* to write. Cf. It. *soprascrivere*, Sp. *sobrescribir*, Pg. *sobrescrever*]

1. *trans.* To inscribe or mark *with* writing on the surface or upper part; to write upon; to put an inscription on or over.

What is superscribed is usually denoted by a compl.; but it occas. forms the subject of the vb.

1605 R. CAREW in *Lett. Lit. Men* (Camden) 99 A Booke..which was by the Statyoner superscribed on the backe..to Mr. Camden. **1624** BP. HALL *True Peacemaker* in *Var. Treat.* (1627) 543 He who hath graciously said all this while, '*Da pacem, Domine*' (Give peace in our time, O Lord!) may superscribe at the last his iust trophees with 'Blessed be the Lord which teacheth my hands to warre, and my fingers to fight!' **1651** CLEVELAND *Poems* 24 No Fellon is more letter'd, though the brand Both superscribes his shoulder and his hand. **1705** ADDISON *Italy* (1733) 54 A stone superscrib'd *Lapis Vituperii.* **1712** STEELE *Spect.* No. 423 ¶4 He received a Message..superscribed *With Speed.* *a* **1901** W. BRIGHT *Age Fathers* (1903) I. ii. 19 A sealed packet with a leather covering, superscribed, 'Statement of the Catholic Church [etc.]'.

2. *spec.* To write a name, address, or direction on the outside or cover of; to address (a letter, etc.) *to* a person. (Also with compl.) *arch.*

1598 [see *superscribed* below]. **1617** DONNE *Serm. 2 Nov.* (1661) III. 97 There is Gospel, but not preached to them; there are Epistles, but not superscribed to them. **1665** MANLEY *Grotius' Low C. Wars* 374 The Emperour sent Letters soon after, superscribed to the States of Holland. **1738** in *10th Rep. Hist. MSS. Comm.* App. I. 516 You forgot to superscribe your Letter to me, which puzzled Mr. Waters a little how to send it. **1825** MACAULAY *Ess., Milton* (1897) 1 The whole was wrapped up in an envelope, superscribed *To Mr. Skinner, Merchant.* **1906** E. A. ABBOTT *Silanus* xxxiii. 323 Scaurus usually superscribed his letters to me with his own hand.

b. To write (a name or address) upon a letter.

1728 FIELDING *Love in sev. Masques* IV. iv, This Letter, I did, indeed, write, but not to you... His Name to whom I designed it is erased, and yours superscribed.

3. To write one's name at the head of a document: opposed to SUBSCRIBE 1. **a.** with the name as obj.

1611 SPEED *Hist. Gt. Brit.* IX. xxi. §67 The aforesaid Noble Prince hath superscribed his name; and the witnesses..haue subscribed their names. *a* **1661** FULLER *Worthies, Surrey* (1662) III. 78, I perceive that Princes, when writing to Princes subscribe their names, and generally superscribe them to subjects.

b. with the document as obj. (also with compl.).

1775 L. SHAW *Hist. Moray* IV. 179 Our Kings never did subscribe their charters..and of late they superscribe them. **1826** SCOTT *Woodst.* xxxviii, The lines forwarded by..Dr. Rochecliffe, superscribed in small letters, C.R., and subscribed Louis Kerneguy. **1845** LD. CAMPBELL *Chancellors* I. Introd. 25 This [bill of proposed patent]..is superscribed by the sovereign, and sealed with the Privy Signet. **1863** H. COX *Instit.* III. vi. 669 The King's signet, used in sealing all grants superscribed by the Royal sign-manual.

4. To write (a letter or word) above another, or above the line of writing.

1776 [see *superscribed* below]. **1861** PALEY *Æschylus* (ed. 2) *Pers.* 757 *note*, Hermann has edited ἐξερήμωσεν πέσος... He explains a various reading πεσσὸν by supposing σ was superscribed to correct the final ν. **1887** HORSTMANN *Early S. Eng. Leg.* 93 Soule. *note*¹ superscribed later.

Hence **superscribed** (-'skraɪbd, *poet.* -'skraɪbɪd) *ppl. a.*; **super'scribing** *vbl. sb.*

1598 MARSTON *Pigmal., Sat.* i. 137 Why..Lett'st thou a superscribed letter fall? *a* **1631** DONNE *Valed. my Name* x, In superscribinge, my name flowe Into thy fancy from thy pane. **1776** J. RICHARDSON *Arab. Gram.* iv. 14 They assume..the sound of such superscribed vowels. **1861** PALEY *Æschylus* (ed. 2) *Prometh.* 694 *note*, Κρήνην, with a superscribed α as a variant for κρήναν or κράναν.

superscript ('s(j)uːpəskrɪpt), *sb.* and *a.* [ad. late L. *superscriptus*, pa. pple. of *superscrībĕre*: see prec. and cf. SCRIPT.]

†**A.** *sb.* **1.** = SUPERSCRIPTION 3. *Obs. rare*⁻¹.

1588 SHAKS. *L.L.L.* IV. ii. 135 Was this directed to you?..I will ouerglance the superscript. To the snow-white hand of the most beautious Lady Rosaline.

2. A superscript character.

1901 [see SUBSCRIPT *sb.* 2]. **1927** [see KRONECKER DELTA]. **1945** F. A. FICKEN in F. A. Berry et al. *Handbk. Meteorol.* II. 144 In work with tensors, indices occur as superscripts as well as subscripts. **1970** G. K. WOODGATE *Elem. Atomic Struct.* iv. 67 The notation for a level specifies the value of *j* as a subscript to the letter code for *l*. The superscript gives the..multiplicity of the term.

B. *adj.* Written above a letter, or above the line of writing: opp. to SUBSCRIPT B.

1882 R. C. JEBB *Life Bentley* 119 There is no correction, superscript or marginal. **1900** I. TAYLOR in *N. & Q.* 9th Ser. VI. 485/2, *ü* stands for the diphthong *ue*, the superscript dots being originally..a curtailed form of the German script *e*.

superscription (s(j)uːpə'skrɪpʃən). [a. OF. *superscription* or ad. late L. *superscriptio*, *-ōnem*, n. of action f. *superscrībĕre* to SUPERSCRIBE]

I. That which is superscribed.

1. A piece of writing or an inscription upon or above something. *arch.* (after Matt. xxii. 20, Luke xx. 24).

1388 WYCLIF *Luke* xx. 20 Shewe ȝe to me a peny; whos ymage and superscripcioun [1382 writynge aboue] hath it? *Ibid.* xxiii. 38 And the superscripcioun [1382 wrytinge aboue] was writun ouer hym with Greke lettris, and of Latyn, and of Ebreu, This is the kyng of Jewis. *c* **1400** MAUNDEV. (1839) xxi. 231 The Superscripcioun aboute his lityll Seel is this, *Dei Fortitudo omnium hominum.* *c* **1480** HENRYSON *Test. Cress.* 604 (Skeat) Sum said he maid ane tomb of merbell gray, And wrait hir name and superscriptioun. **1535** COVERDALE *John* xix. 19 Pilate wrote a superscripcion, and set vpon the crosse. **1630** *R. Johnson's Kingd. & Commw.* 292 In the Church of this Castle are interred the bodies of M. Luther, and P. Melancthon, under two faire Marble stones, with superscriptions of copper upon them. *a* **1711** KEN *Hymnotheo* Poet. Wks. 1721 III. 55 John shew'd on each the Superscription grav'd, Which Solomon experienc'd,..Vanity and Vexation there he read. **1860** MANSEL *Proleg. Log.* (ed. 2) 16, I see lying on the table before me a number of shillings of the same coinage. Examined severally, the image and superscription of each is undistinguishable from that of its fellow.

b. *fig.* and *allusively. arch.*

1612 T. TAYLOR *Comm. Titus* iii. 7. (1619) 677 God forbid that I should for this or that sinnefull pleasure,..or whatsoeuer coine hauing Satans superscription vpon it, sell mine inheritance. **1642** MILTON *Apol. Smect.* 21 Finding him thus in disguise without his superscription or Phylactery either of *holy* or *Prelat.* **1671** —— *Samson* 190, I learn..How counterfeit a coin they are who friends Bear in their Superscription. **1782** ABIGAIL ADAMS in *Fam. Lett.* (1876) 409 Your daughter, your image, your superscription, desires to be affectionately remembered to you.

2. *spec.* A piece of writing at the head or beginning of a document; a heading.

a **1390** WYCLIF *Ps.* Prol. iii, Alle the salmys of Dauid..of whiche alle..nyne made Dauid himself, two and thretti han not superscripcioun. **1542–3** [see SUBSCRIPTION 1]. **1790** PALEY *Horæ Paul.* xv, The superscription proves that Timothy was already with St. Paul when he wrote to the Corinthians from Macedonia. **1901** DORLAND *Med. Dict.* (ed. 2), *Superscription*, the sign ℞ before a prescription.

3. The address or direction on a letter. *Obs.* or *arch.*

1518 H. WATSON *Hist. Oliver of Castile* (Roxb.) E i, He apperceyued the lettre, and he sawe euydently that the super scrypcyon was of his felowes hande wrytynge. **1591** SHAKS. *1 Hen. VI*, IV. i. 53 No more but plaine and bluntly? (*To the King.*) Hath he forgot he is his Soueraigne? Or doth this churlish Superscription Pretend some alteration in good will? **1622** PEACHAM *Compl. Gent.* i. 15 Scarce will he open a note..if *Don* be not in the superscription. **1738** in *10th Rep. Hist. MSS. Comm.* App. I. 513, I was extremely pleased to receive your handwriting in the Superscription of a Letter. **1798** S. & HT. LEE *Canterb. T., Yng. Lady's T.* II. 369 When her eye glanced on the superscription, hardly could her trembling fingers break the seal. **1806** J. BERESFORD *Miseries Hum. Life* xii. (ed. 3) I. 293 Eagerly breaking open a letter, which, from the superscription, you conclude to be from a dear..friend. **1840** THACKERAY *Shabby-genteel Story* ii, When the family beheld the name of Lord Viscount Cinqbars upon the superscription.

4. A name signed; a signature. ? *Obs. rare.*

c **1681** in *Verney Mem.* (1904) II. 397 To each clerk that took the poll, being foure, a guinea, to the men that got superscriptions for them, the like. **1856** LEVER *Martins of Cro' M.* lxv, 'Is that in your handwriting, Sir?'.. 'Yes, every word of it, except the superscription of the witnesses.'

II. 5. 'The act of superscribing' (J.). *rare*⁻⁰. Hence in mod. Dicts.

superscrive (-'skraɪv), *v. Sc. arch.* [Alteration of SUPERSCRIBE after *descrive*, *inscrive.*] *trans.* = SUPERSCRIBE.

1639 SIR A. JOHNSTON *Diary* (S.H.S.) 90 The king superscryved the declaration. **1886** STEVENSON *Kidnapped* i,

Here is the testamentary letter itself, superscrived by the own hand of our departed brother.

supersedable (s(j)uːpəˈsiːdəb(ə)l), *a.* Also -sedeable. [f. SUPERSEDE *v.* + -ABLE.] That may be superseded; *spec.* in *Law*: see SUPERSEDE *v.* 4 b.

1779 *Ann. Reg., Chron.* 216/2 Numbers of them had been long supersedable, or intitled to their discharges under insolvent acts. **1831-2** in T. Chitty *Archbold's Pract. Crt. Queen's Bench* (1838) II. 915 All prisoners who have been.. in the custody of the marshal or warden for the space of one calendar month after they are supersedeable, although not superseded, shall be forthwith discharged.

supersedal (s(j)uːpəˈsiːdəl). *rare.* [f. SUPERSEDE *v.* + -AL[1] 5.] Supersession.

1667 WATERHOUSE *Narr. Fire in London* 62 What alas signifies Haman's rage, if God.. bring in Ester his Enemy to his supersedal?

supersede (s(j)uːpəˈsiːd), *v.* Forms: 5-9 supercede, (6 *Sc.* -ceid, 6-7 -sead, -e, *Sc.* 6-7 -seid, 7 -cid, -seed), 6- supersede. [a. OF. *superceder*, later -*seder*, ad. L. *supersedēre* (in med.L. often -*cedere*) to sit above, be superior to, refrain from, omit, in med.L. to succeed to an estate, f. *super-* SUPER- I, II + *sedēre* to SIT. Cf. It. *soprassedere*, Sp. *sobreseer*.]

†**1.** *trans.* To postpone, defer, put off, suspend the execution of. *Sc. Obs.*

1491 *Acta Dom. Conc.* (1839) 196/2 He sall supercede þe payment of þe said v[c] frankis. **1533** BELLENDEN *Livy* II. xxi. (S.T.S.) I. 214 Þe equis and Wolschis wald supersede þare batall na langare bot quhil þe recent doloure of þare last discomfitoure war ourepast. **1580-1** *Reg. Privy Council Scot.* Ser. I. III. 346 His Majestie.. will caus superceid the executioun of rigour of his lawis.. aganis thame for sum reasonable space. **1618** LD. DUNFERMLINE *Let.* in G. Seton *Mem.* vi. (1882) 126, I..am content ye superseid the outredding of the warke, till your leisour and commoditie permitt you to see it donne. **1646** SIR T. HOPE *Let.* in *Misc. Scott. Hist. Soc.* (1893) I. 135, I sall labour.. to supercid the bargen of the land to zour awin coming.

†**b.** To defer taking action with respect to; to put aside (a thing); to put off (a person). *Sc. Obs.*

1533 BELLENDEN *Livy* II. xxi. (S.T.S.) I. 214 Thus mycht nowthir þare weris be supersedit [orig. *omitti*] nor ȝit clerely dantit. *Ibid.* IV. xxii. II. 130 How þe romanis send þare legatis to Veanis to desire reddres..; how þe veanis war supersedit for þe Civil divisioun amang þame. **1591** *Reg. Exch. Rolls Scotl.* XXII. 572 Johne Chalmer.. promest faithfullie to caus him compeir the said day.. and the thesaurar hes superceidit him quhill the said day.

†**c.** *intr.* or *absol.* To defer action, to delay, hesitate. *Sc. Obs.*

c **1550** ROLLAND *Crt. Venus* II. 164 Without mair baid thay wald not superseid. *Ibid.* 624 To clym ȝone Cord faith I will superseid. **1639** SIR T. HOPE *Let.* in *Misc. Scott. Hist. Soc.* (1893) I. 110 If ye resolue to supercid at hir request till Witsonday.

†**d.** *intr.* for *pass.* To be postponed. *Sc. Obs.*

1569 *Reg. Privy Council Scot.* Ser. I. I. 687 His bill of complaint; quhairupoun answer wes to superceid quhill his Graces cuming.

†**2.** *trans.* To desist from, discontinue (a procedure, an attempt, etc.); not to proceed with. *Obs.*

1527 *St. Papers Hen. VIII*, I. 246, I could not see, but Your bothe Majesties must supersede and give place to your ardent appetites, in concluding of the said mariage. **1589** WARNER *Alb. Eng.* VI. xxxiii. (1612) 162 Then beleeue I loue it more Than that for other law than Life to Supersead my Clame. **1661** GLANVILL *Van. Dogm.* 250 But I shall supersede this endless attempt. **1687** in Picton *L'pool Munic. Rec.* (1883) I. 256 Wee doe hereby direct you.. to supersead and forbeare all prosecution. **1709** HEARNE *Collect.* (O.H.S.) II. 165 His warrant for superseding the Execution. **1721** *Col. Rec. Pennsylv.* III. 142 [That] the new road now complained of by the Petitioners be for the present Superseded. **1750** CARTE *Hist. Eng.* II. 361 The king.. superseded all his other preparations for the invasion of Scotland.

†**b.** *intr.* To desist, forbear, refrain. Const. *from* the action, or *inf. Obs.*

a **1578** LINDESAY (Pitscottie) *Chron. Scot.* (S.T.S.) I. 88 The king tuik werie heavie witht this heigh contempt bot superceidit for the tyme. **1596** DALRYMPLE tr. *Leslie's Hist. Scot.* I. 127 Of vthiris Magistratis to make mentione,.. I superseid and pas ouir. **1624** BP. MOUNTAGU in *Cosin's Corr.* (Surtees) I. 24. I have sent for my papers from my Lord Keper, and have them: therefore let your Lord supersede from asking. **1644** [H. PARKER] *Jus Populi* 19, I shall have occasion to be more large hereafter upon this, and therefore I now supersede. **1706** T. LINING in A. Shields *Church-Communion* A 4, Lest I should darken counsel by Words without Knowledge, I shall supersede. **1850** F. W. NEWMAN *Phases of Faith* 177, I therefore quite supersede to name the many other difficulties in detail.

†**c.** *trans.* To cause to forbear, to restrain. *Obs.*

1675 V. ALSOP *Anti-Sozzo* Pref., I was superseded a while by a more weighty Consideration.

†**3.** To refrain from (discourse, disquisition); to omit to mention, refrain from mentioning. *Obs.*

1586 WARNER *Alb. Eng.* III. xviii. 74 Ye Mars-stard Pichtes.. Ye Dardan Brutes,.. I superseade the rest: Ye come to fight. **1607** TOPSELL *Four-f. Beasts* 230, I supersede any further discourse heereof, till we come to the declaration of the greater beast. **1671** R. BOHUN *Wind* 35, I supersede many remarks from our Sea voyages;.. and shall instance only two. **1675** V. ALSOP *Anti-Sozzo* i. 27 Of which supposed Order.. I shall supersede any further Disquisition at present. **1689** T. PLUNKET *Char. Gd. Commander, etc.* Ded. 93 One thing.. I cannot supersede,.. And that is,.. Here to record what should be known to all.

†**4.** To put a stop to (legal proceedings, etc.); to stop, stay. (Cf. SUPERSEDEAS.) *Obs.*

a **1662** HEYLIN *Laud* (1668) 111 Inhibiting all Processes, and Superseding all proceedings against Recusants. **1812** *Examiner* 25 May 324/2 Bankruptcy Superseded. J. Boone, Piccadilly, haberdasher. **1838** W. BELL *Dict. Law Scot.*, *Supersedere*, is.. a private agreement amongst creditors.. that they will supersede or sist diligence, for a certain period.

b. *Law.* To discharge by a writ of supersedeas

1817 W. TIDD *Pract. Crts. King's B. & Com. Pleas* (ed. 6) I. xiv. 371 If the defendant be superseded, or supersedeable for want of proceedings before judgment, the plaintiff may nevertheless take or charge him in execution, at any time after judgment. **1831-2** [see SUPERSEDABLE].

†**5.** To render superfluous or unnecessary; to preclude the necessity of. *Obs.*

1663 *R. Loveday's Lett.* To Rdr., This ingenuous Author, whose blamelesse repute, and fair deportment.. superseded all censure. **1673** *Lady's Call.* II. iii. §1 Widowhood, which tho it supersedes those duties which were terminated merely in the person of the husband, yet it endears those which may be paid to his ashes. **1684** RAY *Let. to H. Sloane* 11 Feb., It is not my intention to supersede the use of any approved botanic authors. *a* **1699** STILLINGFL. *Serm. John* iv. 24 Wks. 1710 I. 609 The Gospel doth not supersede any Reasonable Duties of Divine Worship. **1729** BUTLER *Serm.* Pref., Wks. 1874 II. 21 Resentment cannot supersede the obligation to universal benevolence. **1797** BURKE *Regic. Peace* iii. Wks. 1808 VIII. 289 The mortal animosity of the regicide enemy supersedes all other panegyrick.

†**b.** With dat. of the person: To spare a person (trouble). Hence, to relieve (a person) *from* a task. *Obs.*

1657 SANDERSON *Serm.* Pref. §5 Much of which having.. received its answer beforehand.. might supersede me the labour of adding any more now. **1660** STILLINGFL. *Iren.* II. v. §1 (1662) 200 Three might have been superceded from our former labour, but that [etc.].

6. To make of no effect; to render void, nugatory, or useless; to annul; to override. ? *Obs.*

1654 GAYTON *Pleas. Notes* III. viii. 117 A superannuate Creature, who (notwithstanding that her yeares did supercede her vocation) prudently shifted her Trade into that of a Matron. *a* **1676** HALE *Prim. Orig. Man.* I. ii. (1677) 60 The contrary command of the Will supersedes the command of the Appetite; the Appetite desires it, but the Hand is forbidden by the Will to reach it. **1790** BURKE *Rev. France* 312 The municipalities supersede the orders of the assembly, and the seamen in their turn supersede the orders of the municipalities. **1791** COWPER *Iliad* XV. 128 How vain.. the hope to supersede His purpose. **1817** JAS. MILL *Brit. India* IV. ix. II. 287 A power of superseding the operations and suspending the authority of the Presidents and Councils. **1844** H. H. WILSON *Brit. India* I. vii. I. 417 When in this capacity he superseded all other rights. **1863** D. WILSON *Preh. Ann.* III. vi. (ed. 2) II. 160 The Norman invader superseded Anglo-Saxon institutions.

†**b.** *spec.* To dissolve by writ of supersedeas.

1702 *Lond. Gaz.* No. 3860/4 The said Commission is superceded under the Great Seal of England.

7. *pass.* To be set aside as useless or obsolete; to be replaced *by* something which is regarded as superior.

1642 J. M[ARSH] *Argt. conc. Militia* 16 Our judgement is bound up in, and superseded by theirs [*sc.* the parliament's]. **1678** BUTLER *Hud.* III. i. 964 To that alone the Bridegroom's wedded, The Bride a Flam that's superseded. **1697** C. LESLIE *Snake in Grass* (ed. 2) 205 This whole Chapter of Burrough's Trumpet.. was stifled and superseded by these same Prophets, in the New Edition of Burrough's Works, 1672. **1788** PRIESTLEY *Lect. Hist.* IV. xviii. 155 In this method, the process of the mind, of reducing intervals of time to lines is superseded, and done in a more accurate manner. **1807** G. CHALMERS *Caledonia* I. II. i. 233 This Celtic race was superceded by invading Goths. **1838** ARNOLD *Hist. Rome* I. Pref. p. vi, When this work must be superseded by a more perfect history. **1878** C. STANFORD *Symb. Christ* i. 24 From the necessity of its present perfection it can never be superseded by an arrangement more complete. **1884** F. TEMPLE *Relat. Relig. & Sci.* i. 8 The examination of this fact led to the old rule being superseded.

8. To take the place of (something set aside or abandoned); to succeed to the place occupied by; to serve, be adopted or accepted instead of.

1660 PEPYS *Diary* 3 July, The Officers and Commissioners of the Navy we met.. and agreed upon orders for the Council to supersede the old ones. **1766** BLACKSTONE *Comm.* II. xxiii. 376 The statute of Elizabeth.. supersedes and repeals all former statutes. **1835** MISS MITFORD in L'Estrange *Life* (1870) III. iii. 34 [The *Athenæum*] is the fashionable paper now, having superseded the 'Literary Gazette'. **1857** RUSKIN *Pol. Econ. Art* ii. (1868) 96 The work of living men not superseding, but building itself upon the work of the past. **1861** BROUGHAM *Brit. Const.* x. 138 The services of the crown vassals superseded salary in the civil as well as pay in the military department. **1866** ROGERS *Agric. & Prices* I. xxi. 530 Oxen were superseding horses in farm-work. **1874** GREEN *Short Hist.* vii. §5. 388 Carpets superseded the filthy flooring of rushes. **1913** *Act 3 & 4 Geo. V*, c. 20 §14 In no case shall oaths of verity or credulity supersede production of legal evidence.

9. To supply the place of (a person deprived of or removed from an office or position) *by* another; also to set aside or ignore in promotion, promote another over the head of; *pass.* to be removed from office to make way for another.

1710 SWIFT *Let. to Dr. Sterne* 26 Sept., He is not yet removed, because they say it will be requisite to supersede him by a successor, which the queen has not fixed on. **1760** *Caut. & Adv. Off. Army* 149 His Majesty.. superseded the Ensign, and gave his Commission to another. **1851** HUSSEY *Papal Power* ii. 62 Hilary.. deposed one [bishop], and superseded another who was sick.. by ordaining one in his place. **1868** E. EDWARDS *Ralegh* I. xviii. 362 Whilst he was yet on his journey.. he had been already superseded in his office. **1870** *Pall Mall Gaz.* 23 Sept. 11/2 The lady superintendent has been 'superseded' on account of her inability to account for certain sums of money.

b. To supply the place of (a thing).

1861 PALEY *Æschylus* (ed. 2) *Pers.* 841 *note*, The genuine ῥῆσις has certainly been superseded. **1873** SYMONDS *Grk. Poets* xi. 344 To expurgate the Greek Anthology of Cephalas from impurities and to supersede it by what he considered a more edifying text.

10. Of a person: To take the place of (some one removed from an office or †promoted); to succeed and supplant (a person) in a position of any kind.

1777 ROBERTSON *Hist. Amer.* II. (1783) I. 191 Francis de Bovadilla.. was appointed.. to supersede him, and assume the government of the island. **1799** NELSON 25 Mar. in Nicolas *Disp.* (1845) III. 306 Captain Maling takes his passage to supersede Captain Nisbet in the Bonne Citoyenne. **1828** SIR W. NAPIER *Penins. War* II. iii. (1878) I. 71 Sir Charles Cotton, after superseding Sir Sidney Smith, had blockaded the mouth of the Tagus. **1848** DICKENS *Dombey* lviii, This was the very Mrs. Wickam who had superseded Mrs. Richards as the nurse of little Paul. **1878** LECKY *Eng. in 18th Cent.* I. i. 150 His brilliant and impetuous colleague was in both quarters rapidly superseding him.

Hence **superˈseded** *ppl. a.*

a **1831** A. KNOX *Rem.* (1844) I. 86 Superstition—such as the Jews retained for their superseded law. **1883** *Century Mag.* Sept. 645 The superseded constable's prosecution for 'railing' at the marshal who supplanted him! **1906** PETRIE *Relig. Anc. Egypt* vii. 56 [Seb] was the 'prince of the gods', .. the superseded Saturn of Egyptian theology.

‖**supersedeas** (s(j)uːpəˈsiːdɪæs). Also 5 -sidias, 5-7 -sedias, 6 -sedyas, -sideas, 7 -sedæas, -sedies. [L., = you shall desist, 2nd pers. sing. pres. subj. of *supersedēre* to SUPERSEDE.]

1. *Law.* A writ commanding the stay of legal proceedings which ought otherwise to have proceeded, or suspending the powers of an officer: so called from the occurrence of the word in the writ.

Clerk of the Supersedeas, an official of the court of common pleas who made out writs of supersedeas.

1393 LANGL. *P. Pl.* C. III. 187 Somenours and southdenes þat *supersedeas* takeþ. *Ibid.* x. 263 The tarre is vntydy þat to þyne sheep by-longeþ, Hure salue ys of *supersedeas* in someneres boxes. *c* **1400** *Pride of Life* (Brandl 1898) 380 Þer [in hell] ne fallit ne maynpris, ne supersidias. **1450** *Paston Lett.* I. 146 For in a general oyer and termyner a *supersedeas* may dassh al, and so shall not in a special. **1506** (*title*) The boke of Iustices of peas the charge with all the process of the cessyons, warrantes supersedyas and all that longyth to ony Iustyce to make. **1591** LAMBARDE *Archeion* (1635) 64 His Supersedeas may not stay a Court of Common Iustice from proceeding. **1622** MALYNES *Anc. Law-Merch.* 224 Vntill the Lord Chanceller doe dissolue the said Commission by a Supersedeas. **1656** T. FORSTER *Lay-mans Lawyer* To Rdr., The formes of all Mittimusses,.. Supersediasses, Certioraries. **1658** *Practick Part of Law* (ed. 5) 2 The clark of the Supersedeas, who makes Writs to supersede the Outlawing of persons. **1671** F. PHILLIPS *Reg. Necess.* 339 The Justices allowed a Supersedeas to stay an Assise, where the Defendant was in the service of the King in his Wars beyond the Seas. **1753** *Scots Mag.* XV. 63/2 His Majesty granted.. a supersedeas of the parliament's arret. **1765** BLACKSTONE *Comm.* I. ii. 166 By writ of privilege, in the nature of a *supersedeas*, to deliver the party out of custody when arrested in a civil suit. **1853** T. I. WHARTON *Pennsylv. Digest* (ed. 6) 221 The effect of a supersedeas lawfully ordered is to annihilate a commission of bankruptcy.

b. More fully, ***writ of supersedeas***.

1454 *Rolls of Parlt.* V. 239/2 In suche cases as writtes of Supersedeas of Privelegge of Parlement be brought and delivered. **1566** [see SIGNIFY *v.* 6]. **1634-5** *Irish Act 10 & 11 Chas. I*, c. 10 §2 His Majesties writs of supersedeas are often-times directed to the justices of peace.. requiring them.. to forbeare to arrest or imprison the parties aforesaid. **1772** *Lond. Chron.* 26-28 Mar. 304/1 His Majesty's writ of supersedeas was on Tuesday last served on Joseph Greenleaf, Esq; late a Justice of the Peace for the county of Plymouth, requiring him to surcease all further proceedings in that office. **1885** *Law Rep. 10 Appeal Cases* 226 An averment which required to be proved.. by a writ of supersedeas.

c. *attrib.* and *Comb.*

c **1475** *Plumpton Corr.* (Camden) 30 One which hath bene of old a supersedias mounger. **1710** J. CHAMBERLAYNE *Pres. St. Gt. Brit.* II. 667* Supersedeas Office, is in the Poultry-Compter, London.

†**2.** *fig.* Something which stops, stays, or checks; const. *for*, *of*, *to*, also *from*; phr. ***to give a supersedeas to***, to check. *Obs.*

1555 *Act 2 & 3 Phil. & M.* c. 18 §1 Which Commyssions so bearing a later date have been a Supersedeas & clere discharge unto.. the said former Commissions. **1590** GREENE *Orl. Fur.* (1599) B j b, To set a *Supersedeas* of my wrath. **1592** WARNER *Alb. Eng.* VII. xxxvi. 157 A Supersedias for her loue was euery new-come frend. *a* **1610** BABINGTON *Wks.* (1622) II. 127 Sweet Death is a Supersedeas for all [*sc.* diseases]. **1619** W. Y. *To Rdr.* in *Hieron's Wks.* II. 428 That will be no *Supersedeas* vnto them from death. **1642** D. ROGERS *Naaman* 58 If God had not discharged him from it by a Supersedeas to his ordinary Charge. **1654** HAMMOND *Fundamentals* xii. §10 To intermit our watch, to slacken our diligence, to give a Supersedeas to industrie. **1662** GURNALL *Chr. in Arm.* verse 18. I. i. §1. (1679) 337/1 Neither Gods promise, nor Abrahams faith thereon gave any Supersedeas to his duty in prayer. **1686-7** P. HENRY *Diaries & Lett.* (1882) 354 If your Gown had been burnt, it might have been lookt upon as a tacit *super Sedæas* to your further progress in those studyes. **1737** L. CLARKE *Hist. Bible* (1740) II. 208 Saul with joy receives this

Supersedeas of the Sanhedrim's commission by a divine command.

Hence †**super'sedeate** *v. trans.*, to stop the procedure of, countermand.

1641 PRYNNE *Antipathie* 44 Requiring him to supersedeate his Mandates.

†**super'sedement.** *Sc. Obs. rare.* [f. SUPERSEDE + -MENT, after med.L. *supersedimentum.*] Postponement, adjournment.

1498 *Reg. Privy Seal Scot.* I. 27/1 A Letter to Schir Wilzam Striveling of the Kere,..with a protection..and respitt and supersedement to him, his men,..for al actionis ..movit or to be movit agains him or thaim. **1586** *Reg. Privy Council Scot.* Ser. I. IV. 66 Alwayes with grite lenitie and superseidment of tyme.

supersedence (-'siːdəns). *rare.* Also -cedence. [f. SUPERSEDE + -ENCE; cf. med.L. *supersedentia* (F. *surséance*).] = SUPERSESSION.

1793 HAMILTON *Wks.* (1886) VII. 79 The supersedence of the exercise of those functions..being a measure of great delicacy and magnitude. **1834** H. O'BRIEN *Round Towers Irel.* 363 St. Patrick..having established Christianity here [*sc.* in Ireland], in supercedence of a religion, the most prominent symbols of which were snakes, cockatrices, and serpents. **1882** *Rep. Ho. Repr. Prec. Met. U.S.* 597 The supersedence of Cornish rollers was..a natural sequence of improved mechanism and method.

superseder (s(j)uːpə'siːdə(r)). [f. SUPERSEDE *v.* + -ER[1].] One who or that which supersedes.

1786 MME. D'ARBLAY *Diary* 25 Sept., My presidency was abolished..by the sudden return of its rightful superseder. **1835** BROWNING *Paracelsus* IV. 346 The delights you fain would think The superseders of your nobler aims. **1881** G. ALLEN *Colin Clout's Cal.* v. (1883) 28 The remaining ganoids, sharks, and lampreys all show signs of depending mainly upon smell, their modern superseders show signs of depending mainly upon sight.

‖**supersedere** (ˌs(j)uːpəsɪ'dɪəriː). *Sc. Law.* Also 8 -cedere. [L. (see SUPERSEDE).] A judicial order granting a debtor protection against diligence of creditors (see DILIGENCE[1] 5); also, a private agreement amongst creditors to postpone action against a debtor for a certain time.

1547 *Acc. Ld. High Treas. Scot.* IX. 70 Writtinges to the persoun of Dysart for the laird of Glarettis supersedere fra the air. **1585** *Reg. Privy Council Scot.* Ser. I. III. 758 Gevand him ane supersedere to be unpersewit for certane yeiris nixt to cum for ony dettis. **1630** *Sc. Acts Chas. I* (1814) V. 224/2 Anent the greevance givin in be the burrowes tuicheing protectiounis and Supersedereis. **1714–26** GIDEON GUTHRIE *Monograph* (1900) 60 They racked all their wits to get my Supercedere stopped. **1816** SCOTT *Antiq.* xliii, Mr. Sweepclean, *secede paulisper*, or, in your own language, grant us a supersedere of diligence for five minutes. **1826** G. J. BELL *Comm. Laws Scot.* (ed. 5) II. 501 The creditors generally consent to a supersedere of diligence. **1838** W. BELL *Dict. Law Scot.* s.v., A creditor who commits a breach of supersedere is liable to the debtor in damages.

super'seding, *vbl. sb.* [f. SUPERSEDE *v.* + -ING[1].] The action of the verb SUPERSEDE.

†**1.** Postponement, delay. *Obs.*

1637–50 ROW *Hist. Kirk* (Wodrow Soc.) 92 The King's Commissioner desyred the superseeding of the pronounceing of the finall sentence till first the King should be advertised of it.

2. Supersession. Also *attrib.* (or *ppl. a.*).

1805 JAMES *Milit. Dict.* (ed. 2), *Superseding signal*, a signal hoisted..on board a ship, giving notice that some individual has been deprived of his authority. **1823** CRABB *Technol. Dict.*, *Superseding* (*Polit.*), a term applied to any officer in the army, or navy, who succeeds to the identical situation of another by special appointment. **1908** W. CHURCHILL *Mr. Crewe's Career* xxvii. 441 Hilary had read the superseding orders. **1909** R. LAW *Tests of Life* xvi. 320 An implied correction, a tacit superseding of the popular belief.

supersedure (-'siːdjʊə(r)). *U.S.* [f. SUPERSEDE + -URE.] = SUPERSESSION.

1788 HAMILTON *Federalist* II. 319 An implied supersedure of the trial by jury, in favour of the civil law mode of trial. **1865** *Even. Standard* 12 May, An announcement of the removal or supersedure of Sherman. **1866** ALGER *Solit. Nat. & Man* IV. 211 The supersedure of actual companionship by an ideal one. **1894** *Forum* (U.S.) Feb. 683 The Cabinet which had just come into power, by supersedure of the Wilcox ministry the day before.

†**super'seminate,** *v. Obs.* [f. late L. *supersēmināt-*, pa. ppl. stem of *superséminare*, f. *super-* SUPER- 2 + *sēmināre* to sow, SEMINATE. Cf. It. *soprasseminare*, Sp. *sobresembrar*, Pg. *-semear.*]

1. *trans.* To sow on the top of something previously sown. Also *absol.* Chiefly *fig.* with allusion to the parable of the tares (Matt. xiii. 24, 25). Hence **super'seminated** *ppl. a.*

1620 tr. *Caussin's Ang. Peace* 30 Would..that Charity.. would suffocate these superseminated tares of contentions. **1637** REYNOLDS *Sermon 12 July* (1638) 17 While there is corruption in our Nature,..and an envious man to superseminate, there will still bee..men that will bee differently minded. **1651** JER. TAYLOR *Clerus Domini* 20 That cannot be done with joy, when it shall be indifferent to any man to superseminate what he please. **1690** C. NESSE *Hist. & Myst. O. & N. Test.* I. 67 The envious one comes after to super-seminate and sow his tares.

2. To sprinkle with an additional layer.

1699 EVELYN *Acetaria* 135 Laying of Clean..Wheat-Straw upon the Beds, super-seminating and over-strowing them thick with the Powder of bruised Oyster-Shells.

†ˌ**supersemi'nation.** *Obs.* [ad. late L. *supersēminātio*, *-ōnem*, n. of action f. *supersēmināre*: see prec.] A sowing on the top of something previously sown. So †**super'seminator**, one who 'superseminates'.

1633 T. ADAMS *Exp. 2 Peter* iii. 16 (1865) 789 God did never sow it [*sc.* the seed]; it is the enemy's supersemination of tares. **1640** BASTWICK *Ld. Bishops* v. E 2, No sooner was the wheat of the Gospell sowne, but that wicked one had his Supersemination of Tares of manifold errors. **1657–61** HEYLIN *Hist. Ref.* Ded. (1674) A 2 b, They were no more then Tares... And being of an after sowing (a Supersemination, as the Vulgar reads it). **1679** C. NESSE *Antid. agst. Popery* 140 Satan, that Super-Seminator, sows his tares in the night.

ˌ**supersensi'bility.** *rare.* [SUPER- 10.] Excessive or abnormal sensibility.

1905 *19th Century* Aug. 205 This supersensibility, unless under stern control, is not devoid of danger.

super'sensible, *a.* (*sb.*) [SUPER- 4 a.] **a.** That is above the sensible; beyond what is perceptible by the senses.

1798 A. F. M. WILLICH *Elem. Crit. Philos.* 180 The *supersensible substratum* of nature is that object, of which we can determine nothing in an affirmative sense. **1828–32** WEBSTER (citing Murdock). **1847** EMERSON *Repr. Men, Uses Gt. Men* Wks. (Bohn) I. 280 Genius is the naturalist or geographer of the supersensible regions, and draws their map. **1862** STEPHEN *Ess. Barrister* 325 An apparently necessary relation..between the sensible phenomenon and the supersensible reality. *a* **1881** A. BARRATT *Phys. Metempiric* (1883) 20 It cannot..give any solidity or reality to a supersensible hypothesis.

b. *absol.* or as *sb.* That which is supersensible.

1803 *Edin. Rev.* I. 254 The glory of illuminating his countrymen in purisms and supersensibles. **1856** MASSON *Ess. Biog. & Crit.* 34 In Shakespeare..there was..a tendency towards the supersensible and invisible. **1881** SHAIRP *Asp. Poetry* iii. 69 So far then poetry and religion are akin, that both hold of the unseen, the supersensible.

Hence **super'sensibly** *adv.*

1868 A. B. ALCOTT *Tablets* 16 A creed dealing thus supersensibly with the elements must have fertilizing properties.

super'sensitive, *a.* [SUPER- 9 a.] Extremely or excessively sensitive. Cf. SUPERSENSITIVITY 2. Hence **super'sensitively** *adv.*, **super'sensitiveness.**

In first quot. a mistranslation of G. *übersinnlich* (see SUPERSENSUAL 1 note and quot. 1833).

1839 J. BIRCH tr. *Goethe's Faust* 182 Thou super-sensitive, most sensual wooer!—A girl nose-leads the mighty-doer! **1840** HOOD *Open Quest.* iv, What is the brute profanity that shocks The super-sensitively-serious feeling? **1864** WEBSTER, *Supersensitiveness*, excessive or over-sensitiveness; morbid sensibility. **1880** MISS E. S. PHELPS *Sealed Orders* 300 Her supersensitive ear detects the scratch of her mother's pen. **1891** HARDY *Tess* xxxvi, The self-combating proclivity of the supersensitive. **1895** J. CHAMBERLAIN in *Westm. Gaz.* 22 July 2/3 That sectional supersensitiveness which tends to keep apart the two wings of the great National party. **1949** CANNON & ROSENBLUETH *Supersensitivity of Denervated Structures* ii. 11 They are often quite easily rendered supersensitive to some agent, e.g., adrenaline, by preliminary treatment with one or another chemical substance, e.g., cocaine or thyroxine. **1962** *Nature* 3 Feb. 487/1 The increased secretory activity seen in the supersensitive submaxillary glands. **1978** *Life Sciences* XXIII. 1283 Rats were supersensitive to norepinephrine as well as to dopamine.

ˌ**supersensi'tivity.** [SUPER- 10.]

1. Great or excessive sensitivity.

1934 [see FRAYED *ppl. a.*[2]]

2. *Physiol.* The state or fact of a tissue or organ having an increased sensitivity to stimuli, as manifested by a longer or increased response, a reduced threshold, or increased susceptibility.

1949 CANNON & ROSENBLUETH *Supersensitivity of Denervated Structures* ii. 11 The term supersensitivity covers several possibly different phenomena. **1959** *Jrnl. Physiol.* CXXXXVII. 178 Organs chronically deprived of their motor nerves develop an increased sensitivity to the neurohumoral transmitter and to other chemical agents. This phenomenon is observed in several types of tissue, e.g. striated muscle, smooth muscle, ganglia and glands, and is known as denervation supersensitivity. **1963** *Pharmacol. Rev.* XV. 226 The changes and modifications of dose-response curves of sympathomimetic amines by various drugs or procedures known to cause super- and subsensitivity to this group of substances. **1974** *Sci. Amer.* Jan. 48/3 This partial denervation could conceivably lead to chemical supersensitivity, accessory sprouting of collateral nerve fibers or the formation of new synaptic contacts.

super'sensory, *a.* [SUPER- 4 a.] Above or independent of the organs of sense.

1883 GURNEY & MYERS in *Fortn. Rev.* Mar. 441 The excitement of danger or imminent death has a potent influence in facilitating the transference of supersensory impressions. **1886** MYERS *Phant. Living* I. Introd. p. lxv, Telepathy, the supersensory transference of thoughts and feelings from one mind to another.

super'sensual, *a.*

1. [SUPER- 4 a.] That is above or beyond (the power of) the senses, or higher than what is perceptible by the senses; also, relating to such things as transcend sense; often = spiritual.

In translations and echoes of Goethe's *Faust* (*Martha's Garden*), 'supersensual sensual' renders G. *übersinnlicher sinnlicher* (*Freier*).

1683 E. HOOKER *Pref. Pordage's Mystic Div.* 60 His most agreeabl and supersensual Companion and Fellow-laborer in the Evangelic-angelic Work. *Ibid.* 99 A Diaphanous Manifesto and perspicuous Demonstration..ever from supersensual sight and intellectual Vision. **1816** COLERIDGE *Statesm. Man.* (1817) 360 The paramount gentlemen of Europe..held high converse with Spenser on the idea of supersensual beauty. **1833** tr. *Goethe's Faust* 148 Thou super-sensual, sensual lover, a chit of a girl leads thee by the nose. **1841** MYERS *Cath. Th.* III. §12. 45 The Rationalist.. measuring supersensual objects only by logical and other terrestrial apparatus. **1865** M. ARNOLD *Ess. Crit.* vi. (1875) 248 Supersensual love, having its seat in the soul. **1870** LOWELL *Among my Bks.* Ser. I. (1873) 149 Sensual proof of supersensual things. **1874** TENNYSON *Merlin & V.* 107 Such a supersensual sensual bond As that gray cricket chirpt of at our hearth. **1885** STEVENSON in *Contemp. Rev.* Apr. 550 [The writer's] pattern, which is to please the supersensual ear, is yet addressed..to the demands of logic.

b. *absol.* with *the.*

1858 LYTTON *What will he do?* VII. xxiii, In our inmost hearts there is a sentiment which links the ideal of beauty with the Supersensual. **1869** LECKY *Europ. Mor.* II. iv. 106 [Religion] allures them to the supersensual and the ideal.

2. [SUPER- 9 a.] Extremely sensual. *rare.*

In quot. 1835 a misunderstanding of Goethe's *übersinnlich* (see note on sense 1 and quot. 1833).

1835 R. TALBOT tr. *Goethe's Faust* (1839) 422 Thou sport of super-sensual desire! A little Gypsy leads thee by the nose. **1867** SIR E. B. LYTTON in *Lett. Robt. 1st Earl of Lytton* (1906) I. ix. 207 The 'Gyges and Candaules' have [*sic*] some dangerous supersensual lines which I advise you to reconsider. It will not do for you to be 'Swinburnian'.

Hence **super'sensualism,** supersensual thought or doctrine; ˌ**supersensua'listic** *a.*, of or pertaining to supersensualism; **super'sensually** *adv.*, in a supersensual manner.

1683 E. HOOKER *Pref. Pordage's Mystic Div.* 66 The veri Spirit of the Mind is elevated, supersensually and superrationally sublimed. *a* **1861** CUNNINGHAM *Hist. Theol.* (1864) II. xxiii. 191 The neology of Germany combining easily with a sort of mystical supersensualism was fitted to interest the feelings. **1865** *Reader* 22 July 89/3 All merely supersensualistic theories. **1906** SIR O. LODGE in *Hibbert Jrnl.* Jan. 320 It [*sc.* Christianity] postulates a supersensually visible and tangible vehicle or mode of manifestation.

super'sensuous, *a.* [SUPER- 4 a.]

= SUPERSENSUAL 1. Also *absol.* with *the.*

1809–10 COLERIDGE *Friend* (1837) I. 209 Whatever is conscious self-knowledge is reason; and in this sense it may be safely defined the organ of the supersensuous. **1825** —— *Aids Refl.* (1848) I. 276 Spiritual truths and objects super-sensuous. **1853** MERIVALE *Rom. Emp.* xxix. (1865) III. 372 Their rejection of supersensuous theories went only to the denial of a resurrection of the body. **1872** LIDDON *Elem. Relig.* iii. 91 Man is regarded as composed of a body, and of a single supersensuous nature, which is sometimes called life or soul, and sometimes spirit. **1876** *Athenæum* 16 Dec. 806/2 A remarkable case of supersensuous perception.

Hence **super'sensuousness.**

1865 tr. *Strauss' Life Jesus* II. II. xcvii. 414 On these words ..the whole of the sensuous supersensuousness [cf. SUPERSENSUAL 1, note] of that Gospel is distinctly stamped.

super-service. Nonce-rendering of HYPERDULIA, q.v.

1826 SOUTHEY *Vind. Eccl. Angl.* 470 The *hyperdulia*, super-service, or ultra-devotion to the Virgin.

super'serviceable, *a.* [SUPER- 9 a.] More serviceable than is required or fitting; doing or offering service beyond what is desired; officious.

1605 SHAKS. *Lear* II. ii. 19 A..glasse-gazing super-seruiceable finicall Rogue. **1815** *Monthly Mag.* XXXVIII. 112 A prefix or an adjacent whensoever it is officious or super-serviceable. **1841** EMERSON *Lect., Conserv.* Wks. (Bohn) II. 276 What a compliment we pay to the good Spirit with our super-serviceable zeal! **1883** J. HAWTHORNE *Dust* II. 34 Shop-keepers bowed in their doorways, rubbing superserviceable hands. **1901** W. MORISON *Johnston of Warriston* iv. 21 Even the rashest and most superserviceable of his officials on the spot could do nothing.

Hence **super'serviceableness.**

1881 *Philad. Record* No. 3412. 2 The insolent superserviceableness of professional detectives.

supersession (s(j)uːpə'sɛʃən). Also 8–9 -cession. [ad. med.L. *supersessio* (*-cessio*), *-ōnem*, n. of action f. *supersess-*, *supersedēre* to SUPERSEDE. Cf. F. *supersession.*] The action of superseding or condition of being superseded.

†**1.** Cessation, discontinuance. *Obs. rare*$^{-0}$.

1656 BLOUNT *Glossogr.* [copying Cotgrave], *Supersession*, a surceasing, a leaving off, or giving over.

2. The setting aside, abrogation, or annulment *of* a rule, law, authority, conditions, etc.

1790 PALEY *Horæ Paul.* v. (1809) 167 Our Epistle..avows in direct terms the supersession of the Jewish law, as an instrument of salvation even to the Jews themselves. **1798** *Bay's Amer. Law Rep.* (1809) I. 192 The election of a new sheriff was a supercession of the former's office. **1859** TENNENT *Ceylon* VI. iii. II. 73 Their chiefs and headmen, insulted by the supercession of their authority. **1893** *Times* 3 June 9/4 The supersession of a number of amendments by the application of the closure to a whole clause.

3. The removal of a person from office and substitution of another in his place; also, the passing over or setting aside of a person in promotion.

1801 WELLINGTON in Gurw. *Desp.* (1837) I. 306 My supercession must have been occasioned, either by my own misconduct, or by an alteration of the sentiments of the Governor General. **1809** *Ibid.* IV. 370 These officers are injured by the temporary supercession of themselves by their juniors. **1841** ELPHINSTONE *Hist. India* XII. iv. II. 667 He immediately gave the appointment of commander-in-chief to Ahmed Khán Bangash,..in supersession of Najib u doula. **1894** WOLSELEY *Marlborough* I. 25 Captain Aylmer was made Admiral over his head. This supercession followed soon upon his eldest brother's disgrace. **1912** *Times* 19 Dec. 11/1 The disciplinary action taken by the Board of Admiralty..involved the supersession of one officer and the censure of another.

4. The process of displacing, or condition of being displaced *by* another.

1855 G. B. WOOD *Treat. Pract. Med.* (ed. 4) I. 227 *Supersession.* By this process is meant the displacing or prevention of one affection by the establishment of another in the seat of it. **1865** *Times* 25 Jan. 12/2 That vessel..since her supercession for Her Majesty's personal use by the Victoria and Albert. **1875** M. PATTISON *Casaubon* 487 It is the fate of science that the books, in which it is consigned, are in a constant state of supersession. **1892** LYDEKKER *Phases Anim. Life* 37 The supersession of the Pterodactyles by the Birds as the lords of the air. **1912** W. H. STEVENSON in *Eng. Hist. Rev.* Jan. 22 *note*, The supersession of *aratrum* by *carruca* among the Gauls.

supersessive (s(j)uːpəˈsɛsɪv), *a.* [f. L. *supersess-*, pa. ppl. stem of *supersedēre* to SUPERSEDE + -IVE.] Having the quality or character of superseding; taking the place *of* something or some one displaced.

1817 G. S. FABER *Eight Diss.* (1845) I. 170 The name Russia..instead of being a modern appellation supersessive of Muscovy,..is one of very remote antiquity. **1881** FAIRBAIRN *Life Christ* vii. 117 A new faith supersessive of the old.

So **super'sessor**, = SUPERSEDER; **super'sessory** *a.* = SUPERSESSIVE.

1883 FAIRBAIRN *City of God* II. iii. (1886) 194 Schools that have denied God have had to coin supersessory and substitutive terms, like 'Substance' or 'Force', 'The Unknown' or 'The Unconscious'. **1894** *Q. Rev.* Oct. 567 His supersessor was only known as a youthful nobleman.

super'sexual, *a.* **1.** [SUPER- 4a.] Beyond or outside the sphere of sexuality.

1895 *World* 20 Mar. 15/2 She had resolved from the very outset to maintain her companionship with Lucas on a supersexual basis. **1976** *Encounter* June 51 A pop-star pseudo-Christ has to be at once sexy, bisexual and supersexual, so as to cater simultaneously for all possible needs.

2. [SUPER- 9a.] Having strong sexual appetites, highly sexed.

1970 R. D. ABRAHAMS *Positively Black* v. 112 This is done commonly by picturing men as supersexual animals who cannot control themselves when they see another woman.

'supersign. **1.** [SUPER- 3a.] A diacritical mark written or printed above a letter.

1947 H. JACOB *Planned Auxiliary Lang.* 40 Supersigns were introduced to make Esperanto fully phonetic. **1958** J. BERRY in J. A. Fishman *Readings Sociol. of Lang.* (1968) 745 The supersigns interfere with spacing and involve 'kerning'.

2. [SUPER- 6b] A combination of letters, figures, etc., forming a unit.

1976 J. J. WHITE in *Visible Lang.* X. 81 It is possible to view them as iconic 'supersigns'; i.e., as *collections* or *configurations* of symbolic signs (viz. words). *Ibid.*, Whether iconicity occurs at the sign or supersign level would be something which semiotic analyses would have to consider.

super'sonic, *a.* (and *sb.*) [f. SUPER- 4a + L. *sonus* sound + -IC, as tr. F. *ultra-sonore.*] **1.** Of, pertaining to, or designating sound waves or vibrations with frequencies greater than those audible to the human ear or greater than 20,000 Hz.

This use of *supersonic* is now deprecated in scientific contexts, *ultrasonic* being the preferred term.

1919 *Electrician* 25 Apr. 494/2 The French have experimented with a system in which a continuous wave signal in heterodyned to a supersonic frequency. **1930** *Daily Express* 22 May 6/5 The wireless enthusiast, whether..crystal-set owner or disciple of the supersonic heterodyne, will still have his moments of doubt. **1957** I. MURDOCH *Sandcastle* xiv. 224 The next act was to blow a long blast upon the supersonic whistle. **1975** *Gramophone* Jan. 1412/3 CD-4 employs a carrier tone at supersonic frequency (30,000 Hz). **1980** *Daily Tel.* 5 Mar. 17/4 The Fisheries Agency team is using supersonic waves of 24 kilohertz which ..have proved effective in repelling the dolphins without affecting ordinary fish.

2. a. Involving, pertaining to, capable of, or designating speeds greater than (*spec.* up to five times) the speed of sound. Cf. HYPERSONIC *a.*, SONIC *a.*

1934 *Jrnl. R. Aeronaut. Soc.* XXXVIII. 866 (*heading*) Supersonic wind channel for model tests. **1936** *Aircraft Engineering* Sept. 260/2 The wing shows what the Germans call a 'supersonic profile', because the aeroplane is supposed to fly the greater part of its route at supersonic speeds. **1948** 'N. SHUTE' *No Highway* xii. 313 It [*sc.* an aircraft] was at the speed of sound... He said he'd been through to the supersonic zone several times. **1953** *Hansard Commons* 11 May 881 As for the problem of the supersonic bang, I must tell the hon. Gentleman that there is absolutely no solution in sight. In fact, we are probably in for some rather noisy times. **1972** *Nature* 18 Aug. 379/2 A low density tunnel for simulating supersonic and hypersonic flight at altitudes of 20 to 70 miles. **1978** *Jrnl. R. Soc. Arts* Dec. 37/1 The Concorde is to-day the precursor of much larger supersonic transport aircraft in years to come.

b. *ellipt.* as *sb.* An aeroplane capable of flying at speeds greater than the speed of sound.

1947 *Times* 1 Jan. 3/3 It is generally assumed here that cooperation in research will cover tests now being carried out by both countries in the field of supersonics, guided missiles, and the development of jet aircraft engines. **1962** *Listener* 5 July 36/2 The demand for supersonics came from the aircraft manufacturers. **1968** *Economist* 11 May 71/1 With jumbo jets and the supersonics on the horizon, aviation insurers had enough to worry about already. **1973** *Times* 24 May (Aviation Suppl.) p. vi/5 When supersonics have, by public demand, taken over all long-haul air services ..we may well wonder what all the argument was about.

3. *colloq.* **a.** Very fast. **b.** Excellent, wonderful, exciting, etc. Also as *int.*

1947 *Argus Week-End Mag.* 25 Oct., Isn't he simply supersonic! **1954** C. DAVIES *Let.* 24 Dec. in B. Russell *Autobiogr.* (1969) III. ii. 96 My thoughts were speeding along with yours at a super-sonic rate. **1955** G. DORMAN *Swooping Vengeance* iv. 31 Ginge's eyes gleamed and he said eagerly,..'Gee, Wing! This *is* supersonic! Can I be in it too?' *Ibid.* v. 44 'Absolutely supersonic!' was Ginge's enthusiastic comment. **1963** *Listener* 17 Jan. 109/2 The unique problems with which the continent [*sc.* Africa] is struggling in an age of supersonic speed of change. **1972** R. GODDEN *Diddakoi* iv. 83 Miss Brooke made girdle scones ..'Supersonic!' said Clem. **1980** *Daily Mail* 23 July 33 (Advt.), Young men required for supersonic battle of wits.

Hence **super'sonically** *adv.*

1952 *Chambers's Jrnl.* June 363/2 They [*sc.* rats] are being lured forth by their mating-note, produced supersonically, and trapped as they emerge. **1970** *Daily Tel.* 2 Sept. 26/6 The St David's Civic Society..has launched a national campaign to stop the Concorde flying supersonically over land.

super'sonics, *sb. pl.* (const. as *sing.*). [f. prec.: see -IC 2.] The science of sound waves or vibrations with frequencies greater than those audible to the human ear or greater than 20,000 Hz.

1925 *Nature* 9 May 690/1 The method adopted to measure the vibrational energy in the water at the high frequencies used in supersonics is interesting. **1952** *Chambers's Jrnl.* June 363/1 The urge to explore supersonics afresh arose from the infestation of reservoirs by seagulls.. Scientists have been..studying the artificial application of supersonics, and..have evolved a method of producing a high-intensity beam of sound of any desired frequency. **1977** *Jrnl. R. Soc. Arts* CXXV. 361/1 Supersonics has a place by the end of the century.

supersound: see SUPER- 6c.

'superspace. *Physics.* [SUPER- 5d.] A concept of space-time arising out of the attempt to quantize the gravitational field, in which points are defined by more than the usual four coordinates; also, a space of infinitely many dimensions postulated to contain actual space-time and all possible spaces.

1971 *Daily Tel.* (Colour Suppl.) 7 May 35 Inside superspace there is neither space nor time. **1972** *Nature* 15 Dec. 382/2 This point of view which leads to the notions of 'superspace' and quantum fluctuation of three geometries, was described by Professors K. Kuchar and J. A. Wheeler. **1974** A. BERRY *Next 10,000 Yrs.* 111 All the stars and galaxies that we can see are on the curved, solid part of the doughnut, while the hole in the middle represents the mysterious region of Superspace. **1975** *Physics Lett.* B. LVI. 178/2 The usual supersymmetry transformation is then a linear transformation in the 8 dimensional 'superspace' of z^A. **1976** B. ZUMINO in Arnowitt & Nath *Gauge Theories & Mod. Field Theory* 262 We call superspace a space whose points are labeled by four commuting coordinates x^a and by a number of additional totally anticommuting coordinates θ^a, $\theta^a\theta^b + \theta^b\theta^a = 0$, which also commute with the x^a. **1978** *Sci. Amer.* Feb. 138/3 The superspace theories are elegant but technically complicated. **1980** P. DAVIES *Other Worlds* v. 104 We may construct a different world for each shape of space. Stitching them altogether [*sic*] gives us an infinite-dimensional superspace. Contained in superspace are all the possible spaces... Each space of superspace will contain its own superworld of all possible particle arrangements.

† **super'spend**, *v.* *Sc.* *Obs.* Variant of SUPEREXPEND.

1508 DUNBAR *Tua Mariit Wemen* 397 That super spendit euill spreit, spvlȝeit of all vertu. **15..** —— *Poems* xiii. 23 Sum super expendit [*v.r.* superspendit] gois to his bed. **1558** *Extr. Rec. Burgh Peebles* (1872) 251 To be ansuerit of..the rest of the taxt that he is superspendit. **1560** ROLLAND *Seven Sages* 94 The Knicht..wox sa wonder pure in hand And alwayis superspendit. **1632** LITHGOW *Trav.* x. 450 When their owne Irish Rent masters haue any voyage for Dublin, or peraduenture superspended at home in feasting of strangers.

'superstar. [SUPER- 6c.]

1. An outstanding performer in the theatre, music, sport, etc.; something exceptionally successful, advanced, etc. Freq. *attrib.*

1925 W. DEEPING *Sorrell & Son* 130 You wouldn't expect a couple of cinema super-stars to be running away from publicity. **1936** 'RIFF' & 'RAFF' *They're Off!* v. 40 A.. relation of my own was running a horse with no less a person than our super-star jockey in the saddle. **1969** N. COHN *AWopBopaLooBop* (1970) xx. 188 He became a superstar but he wasn't happy. **1972** *Guardian* 24 Feb. 14/4 [David] Frost's importance is not the super-star status. **1976** *Nature* 8 Apr. 471/1 Superstar technology is the name given by a working party of the Council for Science and Society to highly innovatory, large scale technical projects. **1978** *Detroit Free Press* 5 Mar. c 14 (Advt.), Hertz, the superstar in the Rent-A-Car industry has an immediate vacancy. **1980** M. FONTEYN *Magic of Dance* 32 From the Charleston it was an easy step to the emergence of a male superstar dancer. **1982** *London Rev. Bks.* IV. xxiv. 20/2 Star quality, however, was not at all what was looked for in those who played opposite a superstar like Kean.

2. *Astron.* A very important or powerful heavenly body. *rare.*

1929 S. LESLIE *Anglo-Catholic* iv. 58 He..meditated.. upon sun and moon, whose counter-changes and performances in the sky he followed with deep amaze. These super-stars of heaven never ceased to vary in effects. **1964** [see QSO s.v. Q II. 2b].

Hence **'superstardom.**

1973 *Harper's Mag.* Oct. 111 Apparently, in the eyes of one dazzled by his own celebrity,..superstardom puts a man above the law. **1977** *Times Lit. Suppl.* 22 Apr. 479/2 Hollywood exacts its price for superstardom.

super-state: see SUPER- 6c.

† **superstit**, *a.* *Obs. rare*$^{-1}$. [ad. L. *superstes*, *-stit-*: see SUPERSTITIE.] Surviving.

a **1623** BUCK *Rich. III* (1646) 69 That..charge, to honour Father and Mother, is not to be understood, only of our Parents superstits, and living here with us, but our forefathers.

† **super'stitiate**, *v.* *Obs. rare*$^{-1}$. In 7 -ciate. [f. SUPERSTITIOUS: see -ATE[3].] *trans.* To regard superstitiously.

a **1688** BUNYAN *Saints' Privilege* §68 Wks. 1692 I. 277/2 The Jews, when they supersticiated the Gift, in counting it more Honourable than the Altar.

† **superstitie.** *Obs. rare*$^{-1}$. [f. L. *superstit-*, *-stes* (f. *super-* SUPER- 7 + *stit-*, unaccented f. *stat-*, pa. ppl. stem of *stāre* to stand) + *-ie*, -Y.]

(?) Power of survival.

1654 VAUGHAN *Flores Solit.* II. 76 The people are the many waters, he turn'd their froth and fome into pearls, and wearied all weathers with an unimpaired Superstitie.

superstition (s(j)uːpəˈstɪʃən). Also 5-7 -icion, 6 -icioun, -itioun, -icyon, -ycyon. [a. OF. *superstition* (= It. *superstizione*, Sp. *supersticion*, Pg. *superstição*) or their source L. *superstitio*, *-ōnem*, n. of action f. *superstāre* to stand upon or over, f. *super-* SUPER- 2 + *stāre* to stand.

The etymological meaning of L. *superstitio* is perhaps 'standing over a thing in amazement or awe'. Other interpretations of the literal meaning have been proposed, e.g. '*excess* in devotion, over-scrupulousness or over-ceremoniousness in religion' and 'the *survival* of old religious habits in the midst of a new order of things'; but such ideas are foreign to ancient Roman thought.]

1. Unreasoning awe or fear of something unknown, mysterious, or imaginary, esp. in connexion with religion; religious belief or practice founded upon fear or ignorance.

1538 STARKEY *England* (1878) 189 Theyr [*sc.* monks'] solytary lyfe, wych hath brought forth, wyth lytyl profyt to the publyke state, much superstycyon. **1549** LATIMER *Ploughers* (Arb.) 30 Where the Deuyll is residente..vp wyth al superstition and Idolatrie, sensing,..holye water, and newe seruice of menes inuenting. **1597** HOOKER *Eccl. Pol.* v. iii. §2 Superstition is, when things are either abhord or obserued, with a zealous or fearefull, but erroneous relation to God. **1651** HOBBES *Leviath.* II. xxvii. 155 A man may stand in fear of Spirits..through his own superstition. **1653** JER. TAYLOR *Serm. for Year* I. ix. 116 It is superstition to worship any thing..besides the Creator. **1776** ADAM SMITH *W.N.* v. i. (1904) II. 435 Science is the great antidote to the poison of enthusiasm and superstition. **1777** ROBERTSON *Hist. Amer.* IV. Wks. 1851 V. 372 Wherever superstition is so established as to form a regular system, this desire of penetrating into the secrets of futurity is connected with it. **1808** PIKE *Sources Mississ.* (1810) III. App. 24 The people's superstition is so great that they are running after the holy father in the streets, and endeavoring to kiss the hem of his garment. **1854** MILMAN *Lat. Christ.* IV. vii. (1864) II. 367 A copious list of miracles wrought by certain images.. showing the wretched superstition into which the worship of images had degenerated. **1891** FARRAR *Darkn. & Dawn* li, Nero had fits of superstition.

b. In particularized sense: An irrational religious belief or practice; a tenet, scruple, habit, etc. founded on fear or ignorance.

1402 *Pol. Poems* (Rolls) II. 56 Foure general synnes, sett up bi sir Adam, Jakke, among ȝour maistris, cedicions, supersticions, the glotouns, and the proude. **1432-50** tr. *Higden* (Rolls) II. 283 Diuerse supersticiones began of ydolatry. **1547** *Homilies* I. *Serm. of Good Wks.* III. (1859) 61 Other kinds of papistical superstitions..as of Beads, of Lady Psalters and Rosaries. **1608** SHAKS. *Per.* III. i. 50 *1st Sailor.* The sea workes hie, The Wind is lowd, and will not lie till the Ship Be cleard of the dead. *Per.* That's your superstition. **1660** JER. TAYLOR *Duct. Dubit.* II. iii. rule 13. §23. 465 When they began to say, that..all wine was an abomination, they pass'd into a direct superstition. **1736** BUTLER *Anal.* I. iv. 75 By Religion's being corrupted into Superstitions, which indulge Men in their Vices. **1849** MACAULAY *Hist. Eng.* x. II. 621 The notion would still prevail that the kingly office is the ordinance of God in a sense different from that in which all government is his ordinance. It was plain that, till this superstition was extinct, the constitution could never be secure. **1856** R. A. VAUGHAN *Mystics* (1860) I. VI. ii. 160 The Portuguese have a superstition according to which the soul of a man who has died, leaving some duty unfulfilled..is frequently known to enter into another person.

2. An irrational religious system; a false, pagan, or idolatrous religion. Now *rare* or *Obs.*

1526 TINDALE *Acts* xxv. 19 They..hadde certayne questions agaynst him off their awne supersticion. **1603** KNOLLES *Hist. Turks* (1621) 5 The Turks received the Mahometane superstition. **1613** PURCHAS *Pilgrimage* II. vi. 110 The present Iewish superstition. **1630** *R. Johnson's Kingd. & Commw.* 564 [Mohammed] making him [*sc.* Ali] the head of his superstition, with the title of Caliph. **1671** MILTON *Samson* 15 Unwillingly this rest Thir Superstition yields me. **1771** SMOLLETT *Humphry Cl.* 4 July, A conference with his friend Voltaire, about giving the last blow to the Christian superstition. **1813** PRICHARD *Phys. Hist. Man* viii. §1. 402 These authors regard the latter [*sc.* Buddhism] as the ancient and indigenous superstition of the East.

b. A religious ceremony or observance of a pagan or idolatrous character. Now *rare* or *Obs.*

a **1529** SKELTON *P. Sparowe* 1350 The Phitonesse..by her supersticyons, And wonderfull condityons,..raysed vp..Samuell that was dede. **1604** E. G[RIMSTONE] *D'Acosta's Hist. Indies* IV. xxx. 293 They did assemble there for theyr dances and superstitions. **1608** HEYWOOD *Lucrece* II. i, Our superstition's ended, sacred priest, Since we have had free answer from the gods. **1849** ROCK *Ch. Fathers* I. iii. 294 The heathen Britons made use of balls of crystal in their idle superstitions.

†**c.** Religious observance. *Obs. rare*$^{-1}$.

1513 DOUGLAS *Æneis* XII. xiii. 63, I sweir tharto be the onplesand well Of Stix,..Quhais only dreidfull superstitioun heyr The Goddis kepis, that nane dar it forsweyre.

†**d.** Idolatrous or extravagant devotion. *Obs.*

1625 FLETCHER, etc. *Lover's Progress* III. iii, May I not kiss ye now in superstition? For you appear a thing that I would kneel to.

†**3.** 'Over-nicety; exactness too scrupulous' (J., 1755). (Cf. SUPERSTITIOUS 3.) *Obs. rare*$^{-0}$.

4. *transf.* (from 1). Irrational or unfounded belief in general; an unreasonable or groundless notion.

1794 HUTTON *Philos. Light*, etc. 107, I am afraid there are many men of science..that only believe the theory of heat and cold in prejudice or superstition, i.e. without having seen its evidence. **1851** SPENCER *Social Statics* xix. 209 Of the political superstitions,..none is so universally diffused as the notion that majorities are omnipotent. **1868** M. PATTISON *Academ. Org.* v. 120 The superstition of the law-courts that a man can exercise rights of property after his death to all time.

Hence **super'stitional** *a.*, characterized by superstition, superstitious; **super'stitionist**, one given to superstition, or holding superstitious beliefs; **super'stitionless** *a.*, free from superstition.

1683 E. HOOKER *Pref. Pordage's Mystic Div.* 44 Doctrines Traditional, *Superstitional, and Deductional. *c* **1850** LADY BLANCHE BALFOUR *Prayer* in J. Robertson *Remin.* (1897) 54 From careless or superstitional acquiescence where I should inquire, Good Lord, deliver me. **1651** H. MORE *Second Lash* in *Enthus. Tri.*, etc. (1656) 184 The arbitrarious precepts of supercilious Stoicks, or surly *Superstitionists. **1676** GLANVILL *Seasonable Reflect.* 139 Melancholy Superstitionists or distracted Enthusiasts. **1798** W. TAYLOR in *Monthly Mag.* VI. 549 The disguising reverence with which superstitionists have regarded them [*sc.* the Hebrews]. **1846** WORDSWORTH in Chr. Wordsw. *Mem.* (1851) II. 425 A wretched set of religionists.., superstitionists I ought to say, called Mormonites. **1890** A. J. VOGAN *Black Police* xii. 188 The *superstitionless training Billy had received.

†**superstiti'osity.** *Obs. rare.* In 5 -ciosite, -tie. [a. OF. *supersticiosite* or ad. med.L. *superstitiōsitās*, f. *superstitiōsus* SUPERSTITIOUS: see -ITY.] Superstitiousness; *pl.* superstitious beliefs or observances.

c **1400** *Apol. Loll.* 98 God Almiȝty kepe vs..fro þer supersticiositeis, vanites, errors, and desseytis. **1520** *Caxton's Chron. Eng.* I. fol. vi/1 They were deceyued by deuylles, & great supersticiositie in y^e cytee was made.

superstitious (s(j)uːpəˈstɪʃəs), *a.* Also 4–7 -icious, 5 -ycyus, 5–6 -ycious, 6 -icyous, -ycyous(e, -iciouse, -itiouse, *Sc.* -itius. [a. OF. *superstitieux* (= It. *superstizioso*, Sp., Pg. *-icioso*), ad. L. *superstitiōsus*, f. *superstitio* SUPERSTITION.]

1. Of the nature of, involving, or characterized by superstition.

c **1386** CHAUCER *Frankl. T.* 544 To maken hise Iapes and his wrecchednesse Of swich a superstricious cursednesse. **1426** LYDG. *De Guil. Pilgr.* 20234 That..I may represse Thyn errours and thyn ffolye, Groundyd on Astrologye, Wych ne be nat vertuous, For they be superstycyous. **1538** BALE *Thre Lawes* 865 With rytes superstycyouse. **1561** T. NORTON *Calvin's Inst.* IV. 136 Shall we denie that it is a superstitious worshippyng, when men do throwe themselues downe before bread, to worship Christe therein? **1678** CUDWORTH *Intell. Syst.* I. ii. §8. 68 In their Superstitious Belief, of Ghosts, Spirits, Dæmons, Devils, Fayries and Hob-goblins. **1776** GIBBON *Decl. & F.* xiv. (1782) I. 508 Fear is commonly superstitious. **1866** KINGSLEY *Life & Lett.* (1877) II. 241 The superstitious terror with which that meteor-shower would have been regarded in old times. **1874** GREEN *Short Hist.* ix. §1. 588 [To the Puritans] It was superstitious to keep Christmas, or to deck the house with holly and ivy.

transf. **1588** KYD *Househ. Philos.* Wks. (1901) 258 The Husband commeth not with those prophane and superstitious cleppings as the delicate and wanton Louer doth. **1791** PAINE *Rights of Man* (ed. 4) 104 To unhinge it from the superstitious authority of antiquity.

b. *superstitious uses* (Law): see quot. 1827.

1596 BACON *Max. & Use Com. Law* I. x. (1630) 52 The statute of Chantries that willeth all lands to be forfeited, giuen or imploied to a superstitious vse. **1602–3** in Coke *Reports* (1604) IV. 106 b, Intant que le statute [*viz.* 1 Edw. VI, c. 14] per expres parols abrogate & tolle touts tiels superstitious vses queux fuerent dauer continuance a touts iours. **1715** *Act 1 Geo. I*, Stat. II. c. 50 (*heading*) To enquire of the Estates..of Popish Recusants, and of Estates given to superstitious Uses. **1790–1** *Act 31 Geo. III*, c. 32 §17. **1827** JARMAN *Powell's Devises* II. 13 Superstitious uses..are declared..to be where lands, tenements, or goods, are given for the maintenance of persons to pray for the souls of dead men in purgatory, or to maintain perpetual obits, lamps, &c. **1848** WHARTON *Law Lex.* s.v. *Charities*, The history of the law of charities prior to the 43rd Eliz. c. 4, which is emphatically called the Statute of Charitable Uses, is extremely obscure... It is clear that no superstitious uses are within the purview of the statute.

2. Subject or addicted to superstition; believing or practising superstitions.

1526 TINDALE *Acts* xvii. 22 Ye men of Attens, I perceave that in all thynges ye are somwhat [1534 to] supersticious. **1589** PUTTENHAM *Engl. Poesie* III. xxii. (Arb.) 267 To abuse the superstitious people, and to encomber their busie braynes with vaine hope or vaine feare. **1598** SHAKS. *Merry W.* IV. iv. 36 The superstitious idle-headed-Eld Receiu'd..This tale of Herne the Hunter, for a truth. **1671** MILTON *P.R.* II. 296 It seem'd..to a Superstitious eye the haunt Of Wood-Gods and Wood-Nymphs. **1791** BURKE *Let. to Capt. Woodford* 11 Feb., I am extremely superstitious, and think his coming into it was of evil augury. **1849** MACAULAY *Hist. Eng.* i. I. 88 Prone to the error, common in superstitious men, of mistaking his own peevish..moods for emotions of pious zeal. **1882** PITMAN *Mission Life Greece & Pal.* 251 The Maronite sect, which is a very ignorant and superstitious sect.

absol. (with *the*). **1728** CHAMBERS *Cycl.* s.v. *Superstition*, The Punishment allotted by several Councils for the Superstitious, was to fast a Month in Prison. **1913** *Nature* 14 Aug. 607/2 The omen of blood was viewed with some alarm by the superstitious in the village.

†**b.** Idolatrously or extravagantly devoted. *Obs.*

1582 LYLY in *T. Watson's Poems* (Arb.) 30 Were not men more superstitious in their praises, then women are constant in their passions. **1613** SHAKS. *Hen. VIII*, III. i. 131 Haue I..Lou'd him next Heau'n? Obey'd him? Bin (out of fondnesse) superstitious to him? *a* **1704** T. BROWN *Beauties* Wks. 1730 I. 42 My superstitious love adores them all.

†**3.** Over-scrupulous; punctilious; extremely careful or particular. *Obs.*

1535 [see SUPERSTITIOUSLY 2]. **1553** EDEN *Treat. Newe Ind.* (Arb.) 10 Yf..anye supersticious head shall thinke it a heynous matter in any poynte to contrary Saainct Augustyne. **1590** SWINBURNE *Test.* 5 It is rare if at the last; after long and superstitious reuolution, one man at least among so many subtile heads..doe not espie some defect or excesse in the definition. **1608** TOPSELL *Serpents* 261 They [spiders] haue giuen themselues to curious and superstitious hunting,..watching and espying their prey. **1617** MORYSON *Itin.* III. 221 The Germans are so superstitious in this kind, as a Gentleman may haue an action against him, who saith hee is no Gentleman. **1648** J. BEAUMONT *Psyche* I. ccxxiii, Shall squeamish He my Pleasures harvest by Fond superstitious coyness thus prevent? **1680** OTWAY *Orphan* II. i, The superstitious Statesman has his sneer. **1816** [implied in SUPERSTITIOUSLY 2].

4. Used in or regarded with superstition; venerated, observed, or believed in, in the way of superstition. Now *rare* or *Obs.*

1566 in Peacock *Engl. Ch. Furnit.* (1866) 120 The mass bookes and all other popishe and supersticious bookes. **1595** in *Maitl. Club Misc.* I. 77 To absteyne fra keiping of superstitious dayes. **1599** B. JONSON *Cynthia's Rev.* I. iv, Pulling downe a superstitious crosse. *c* **1618** MORYSON *Itin.* IV. v. i. (1903) 399 The sweating of stones, Nodding of Images, and like supperstitious Miracles. **1665** J. WEBB *Stone-Heng* (1725) 140 To cleanse away the Filth of the superstitious Victims [*sc.* sacrificed oxen]. *a* **1700** B. E. *Dict. Cant. Crew, Superstitious-Pies*, Minc'd, or Christmas-Pies, so Nick-nam'd by the Puritans, or Precisians, tho' they can Eat em. *a* **1700** EVELYN *Diary* 25 Dec. 1657, An ordinance made that none should any longer observe the superstitious time of the Nativity (so esteem'd by them). **1774** PENNANT *Tour Scot. in 1772* 23 An..arch, decorated with a variety of superstitious figures. **1879** S. C. BARTLETT *Egypt to Pal.* xx. 436 The room..contained some superstitious spots.

†**b.** Magical; having or credited with supernatural efficacy. *Obs.*

1412–20 LYDG. *Chron. Troy* I. 363 þer was noon helpe..þat vaille myȝt ageyn þe cursed charmys; þei wer so strong and superstitious. *c* **1450** *Mankind* 313 in *Macro Plays* 12 To defende me from all superstycyus charmys. **1651** HOBBES *Leviathan* III. xxxvi. 225 All those Impostors, that pretend by the helpe of familiar spirits, or by superstitious divination of events past..to foretell the like events in time to come. [**1728** CHAMBERS *Cycl.* s.v. *Magic*, Superstitious Magic consists in the Invocation of Devils.]

†**5.** Extraordinary; excessive; superfluous. *Obs.*

c **1407** LYDG. *Reason & Sens.* 4301 Eke Phedra lovede hyr sone yn lawe, Whos love was superstycious. **1484** CAXTON *Fables of Alfonce* viii, There is folke superstycious or capaxe that they may not be contented with fewe wordes. **1598** HAKLUYT *Voy.* I. 150 Certain sinister reports and superstitious slanders. **1638** SIR T. HERBERT *Trav.* (ed.2) 301 They..have such a superstitious conceit of their owne merit and temper [etc.]. **1640** FULLER *Joseph's Coat* v. 143 Let us take heed wee bee not all condemned by God, for being Fellons, *de se*; for wilfull murthering our owne lives, with our knifes by our superstitious eating.

super'stitiously, *adv.* [f. prec. + -LY^2.] In a superstitious manner.

1. In the way of superstition; with irrational religious belief or observance.

1552 ABP. HAMILTON *Catech.* 21 b, To defend thair self..aganis fyre, watter, swerd,..with certene takinnisor writingis supersticiously. **1561** T. NORTON *Calvin's Inst.* I. xi. (1634) 37 Because God will not be worshipped superstitiouslie, therefore whatsoever is given to idols is taken from him. **1611** SHAKS. *Wint. T.* III. iii. 40 Dreames, are toyes, Yet for this once, yea superstitiously, I will be squar'd by this. **1686** PLOT *Staffordsh.* 207 The common people superstitiously beleive, that tis very dangerous to break a bough from it. **1767** S. PATERSON *Another Trav.* I. 375 The superstitiously-zealous in their own way, they would shew like a company of saints. **1847** C. BRONTË *Jane Eyre* xi, But that neither scene nor season favoured fear, I should have been superstitiously afraid. **1882–3** *Schaff's Encycl. Relig. Knowl.* III. 2268 Friday is superstitiously held to be an unlucky day.

†**2.** Over-scrupulously; punctiliously; with excessive care or exactness. *Obs.*

1535 JOYE *Apol. Tindale* (Arb.) 39 Here thou seist whother Tindale is brought for so supersticyously steking to onely one significacion of this worde *Resurrectio.* **1659** HAMMOND *Annot. Ps.* xxxi. 6 That heathen men..are..wont to apply themselves..to false gods..observing their responses most superstitiously. **1676** HOBBES *Iliad* Pref. (1686) 8 A fault proper to Translators, when they hold themselves too superstitiously to their Authors words. **1725** WATTS *Logic* IV. i, Neither of these two Methods should be too scrupulously and superstitiously pursued. **1791–1823** D'ISRAELI *Cur. Lit., Hist. New Words*, But we have puritans or precisians of English, superstitiously nice! **1816** BENTHAM *Chrestom.* 292 For division, the dichotomous..mode is most to be commended,..but it ought not to be every where hunted out too superstitiously and anxiously.

super'stitiousness. [-NESS.] The quality or character of being superstitious.

1526 *Pilgr. Perf.* (W. de W. 1531) 233 b, The contemplacyon of suche turneth eyther to supersticyousnes, or else to a fantasticall curiosite. **1548** CRANMER *Catech.* ()iij b, Superstitiousnes of beades, and confidence in oure owne merites. **1657** J. WATTS *Scribe, Pharisee*, etc. I. 232 As there is no popishnesse, so, I do not see what superstitiousnesse there can be in it. **1885** RAWLINSON *Egypt & Babylon* v. 83 He showed an equal superstitiousness when..he would not allow himself to commence the work of restoration,..until he had first waited for a 'fortunate month'. **1908** *Q. Rev.* Apr. 483 One trait of the barbaric mind—superstitiousness.

superstore: see SUPER- 6 c.

‖**superstratum** (s(j)uːpəˈstreɪtəm, -ˈstrɑːtəm). Pl. **-strata.** [mod.L., neut. sing. of pa. pple. of L. *supersternĕre* to spread over, f. *super-* SUPER- 2 + *sternĕre* to lay down, strew.] **1.** A stratum or layer deposited over or upon something; an overlying or superficial stratum.

1806 *Amer. State Papers, Ind. Affairs* (1832) I. 737 The superstratum is of a blackish brown color, upon a yellow basis. **1823** BYRON *Juan* IX. xxxvii, First out of, and then back again to chaos, The superstratum which will overlay us. **1840** LYELL *Princ. Geol.* II. vii. (ed. 6) II. 79 The superstrata were precipitated into hollows prepared for them.

2. a. *Linguistics.* A language responsible for linguistic change (esp. in vocabulary) in another upon which it is imposed and over which it is temporarily dominant. Cf. SUBSTRATUM 5 a.

[**1932** E. TAPPOLET in *Archiv für das Studium der neueren Sprachen* CXI. 234 Von ähnlichen Erwägungen geleitet, sprach von Wartburg (Leipzig) über die Wirkung des *Superstratums*.] **1953** J. B. TREND *Lang. & Hist. Spain* xii. 167 Spanish-speaking America offers an exceptionally favourable field for examining the linguistic concepts of substratum and superstratum. **1976** W. F. H. NICOLAISEN *Scottish Place-Names* vi. 84 The place-names created by a certain language form an adstratum to English names in one place, a superstratum in another, and a substratum in most places.

b. *attrib.* and *Comb.*, as ***superstratum influence, language***.

1957 *Publ. Amer. Dial. Soc. 1956* XXVI. 100 A substratum influence is one derived from a dominated language, a superstratum from a dominant language. **1960** *Amer. Speech* XXXV. 234 Substratum languages can affect all features of grammar, whereas superstratum languages tend to affect vocabulary only. **1978** *Canad. Jrnl. Ling. 1977* XXII. 206 After surveying the distribution, function, and status of each Romance language..it discusses the thorny problem of the influence exerted by the so-called substratum and superstratum languages.

superstruct (s(j)uːpəˈstrʌkt), *v.* Now *rare* or *Obs.* [f. L. *superstruct-*, pa. ppl. stem of *superstruĕre*, f. *super-* SUPER- 2 + *struĕre* to build.] *trans.* To build upon something else; to construct upon a foundation; to erect as a superstructure.

a. Usually *fig.* or in fig. context. (Very common in the latter half of the 17th c.)

a **1643** LD. FALKLAND, etc. *Infallibility* (1646) 20 All that Master Chillingworth's large Booke hath superstructed on this foundation. **1646** HAMMOND *Tracts* 87 What small ground it hath..as a foundation to superstruct any other doctrines upon. **1652** H. L'ESTRANGE *Amer. no Jewes* 1 The Author first layes down six Conjectures, upon which he superstructs the maine Fabrique of his Work and Arguments. *a* **1687** PETTY *Pol. Arith.* i. (1691) 21 The effects of their Policy, superstructed upon these natural Advantages, and not as some think upon the excess of their Understandings. *a* **1734** NORTH *Exam.* I. i. §8 (1740) 18 This he lays down for a Foundation whereon to superstruct a wonderful Colossus of Reproach. **1779–81** JOHNSON *L.P., Pope* Wks. 1787 IV. 99 Those..on whose approbation his esteem of himself was superstructed. **1819** T. HOPE *Anastasius* (1820) I. vi. 124 This artificial exterior, this refinement of appearance, were the more remarkable from the simplicity of mind, the singleness of heart, on which they seemed superstructed.

absol. **1642** SIR S. D'EWES *Autobiog.* (1845) II. 294 Lady Win hath laid a foundation of hope for mee, upon which I must beseech you to superstruct. **1661** POWER *Exp. Philos.* Pref. (1664) C 4, Though he have erroneously superstructed upon his Experiments. **1737** L. CLARKE *Hist. Bible* (1740) II. 210 Daily improving and increasing and superstructing upon that foundation.

b. More rarely *lit.*; occas. in reference to natural structures. (Also *absol.*)

1664 EVELYN *Sylva* xviii. 39 Vitruvius tells us, that the Morasses about Ravenna..were pil'd with this Timber [*sc.*

alder], to superstruct upon. *a* **1687** PETTY *Treat. Naval Philos.* I. ii, The Cabbins and what is usually superstructed upon the upper Deck. **1831** T. HOPE *Ess. Orig. Man* II. 28 Former masses inorganic and lifeless superstruct in unbroken cohesion with them other later parts having all the essential attributes of organization, life and growth. **1843** MRS. ROMER *Rhone*, etc. I. 309 Upon which, in latter times, the Moors had superstructed a fortress.

Hence **super'structed** *ppl. a.*; **super'structing** *vbl. sb.*

1654 HAMMOND *Fundamentals* ii. Wks. 1674 I. 278 Doctrines.. apt to obstruct or intercept the superstructing of Christian life. *Ibid.* xii. 300 It were unreasonable.. to.. wonder at this constancy in particular superstructed errors ...., whilst [etc.]. **1826** G. S. FABER *Diffic. Romanism* (1853) 374 *note*, Their superstructed doctrinal decisions. **1831** T. HOPE *Ess. Orig. Man* I. 29, I have cleared away.. all later, more partial and more superstructed attributes not only of mind but even of matter.

†**super'struction.** *Obs.* [ad. L. **superstructio*, *-ōnem*, n. of action f. *superstruĕre*: see prec. Cf. SUBSTRUCTION.]

1. = SUPERSTRUCTURE.

a. *fig.* or in fig. context.

1624 USSHER *Serm.* 22 The unitie of the faith.. here spoken of, hath reference.. to the foundation: as that which followeth of a perfect man.. to the superstruction and perfection. **1638** CHILLINGW. *Relig. Prot.* I. iii. §57. 165 You must.. believe the Church Infallible in all her proposalls, be they foundations, or be they superstructions. **1650** HOBBES *De Corp. Pol.* 125 For the Points of Faith necessary to Salvation, I shall call them Fundamentall, and every other Point a Superstruction. **1683** E. HOOKER *Pref. Pordage's Mystic Div.* 71 Rotten Foundations, superstitious superstructions.

b. *lit.* or in physical sense. *rare.*

1612 SELDEN *Illustr. Drayton's Poly-olb.* x. 165 A great water, which could endure continuance of no heauy superstruction. *a* **1687** PETTY *Treat. Naval Philos.* I. ii, The superstructions upon the upper Deck.

2. The action of building upon something. *rare*$^{-0}$.

1864 in WEBSTER; hence in later Dicts.

superstructive (s(j)uːpə'strʌktɪv), *a.* (*sb.*) Now *rare.* [f. L. *superstruct-*: see SUPERSTRUCT and -IVE.] Belonging to the superstructure; = SUPERSTRUCTURAL: opposed to *fundamental*.

1642 *Fuller Answ. to Dr. Ferne* 8 If it bee written it is superstructive and not fundamentall; written Laws, that were not Lawes before written, are repealeable and alterable. **1654** HAMMOND *Fundamentals* xvii. Wks. 1674 I. 319 Nothing but the removing his Fundamental error can rescue him from the superstructive. **1903** R. BRIDGES *Poems Classical Prosody* Ep. i. 228 Laying foundation of its knowledge in physical law,.. erecting Superstructive of all .... a new Science of Man.

†**B.** *sb.* Something belonging to or constituting the superstructure. *Obs.*

1625 MOUNTAGU *App. Cæsar* 120, I divided also the objects of erring or not erring, two wayes: into Fundamentalls, or superstructives. **1644** HUNTON *Vind. Treat. Monarchy* v. 37 The Common Lawes, which are.. the basis and foundation of this Government, the Statute Lawes being but after superstructives.

So **super'structor**, one who builds a superstructure; **super'structory** *a.*, = next.

1650 R. HOLLINGWORTH *Exerc. Usurped Powers* 16 You subvert all setled Laws, whether fundamentall or superstructory. **1652** R. ROBINSON *Christ all* xxii. (1656) 424 A house whose corners are laid with precious stones, and whose Superstructory stones are all lively stones. *a* **1734** NORTH *Exam.* I. iii. (1740) 193 Was Oates's Narrative a Foundation or a Superstructure, or was he one of the Superstructors or not?

super'structural, *a.* [f. next + -AL^1.] Belonging to or constituting a superstructure.

1884 TRAILL in *Macm. Mag.* Nov. 30/1 The argumentative foundation which has been made to bear so vast a superstructural conclusion. **1893** *Home Missionary* (N.Y.) July 144 Foundational rather than superstructural.

superstructure ('s(j)uːpə,strʌktjʊə(r), -tʃə(r)). [f. SUPER- 3 + STRUCTURE, after *superstruct*, *superstruction*. Cf. F. *superstructure* (from 18th c.).] That which is built upon something else as a foundation; a structure raised upon something.

1. a. *lit.* A building considered in relation to its foundation; an upper part of a building, erected upon a lower supporting part; any material structure resting on something else as a foundation.

c **1645** HOWELL *Lett.* I. II. xv. (1892) 126 In som Places, as in Amsterdam, the Foundation costs more than the Superstructure. **1679** MOXON *Mech. Exerc.* viii. 137 Though the Ground-plates.. be part of the Carcass, yet I thought fit.. they should be laid, before I treated of the superstructure. **1738** *Gentl. Mag.* VIII. 378/2 The City Surveyor.. declared.. that it would be beneficial to the Superstructure to have the Foundation laid early. **1813** VANCOUVER *Agric. Devon* 89 It frequently happens, that the lower part of the building is made of stone, and its superstructure of cob. **1868** LYELL *Princ. Geol.* xli. (ed. 10) II. 404 The accumulation of the subaërial superstructure of the great cone. **1876** *Encycl. Brit.* IV. 284/1 The superstructure of a bridge consists of the roadway and the beam, arch, or chain used to carry the roadway from support to support.

b. *Railway Engineering.* (See quot.)

1864 WEBSTER, *Superstructure*,.. the sleepers, rails, and fastenings, in distinction from the road-bed;—called also *permanent-way*.

c. *Geol.* [tr. G. *oberbau* (C. E. Wegmann 1935, in *Geol. Rundschau* XXVI. 332).] A relatively shallow overlying layer of an orogenic belt that is unaffected by plutonic activity or metamorphism.

1944 *Proc. Geologists' Assoc.* LV. 69 A distinction must be drawn, he [*sc.* Wegmann] maintains, between happenings in the non-migmatitic superstructure (Oberbau) and the migmatitic infrastructure (Unterbau) lying below. **1972** J. G. DENNIS *Structural Geol.* xvii. 394 In many orogenic belts, the superstructure has not been preserved in place: most of it has been eroded or transported to the external zone as allochthons.

d. *Biochem.* The higher-order structure of a protein or enzyme molecule which is superimposed upon the sequence of amino-acids or nucleotide bases.

1962 A. SPECTOR in A. Pirie *Lens Metabolism Rel. Cataract* 334 The *N*-terminal residues of native proteins are probably not readily accessible to the enzyme since such groups are masked or buried in the superstructure of the molecule. **1973** *Nature* 7 Sept. 23/1 The term superstructure will be used to include the secondary and higher order structures that might be super imposed upon the primary base sequence of a nucleic acid. **1981** *Sci. Amer.* Feb. 60/2 (*caption*) Helical superstructures might be formed with increasing salt concentration.

2. a. *fig.* or in fig. context: An immaterial structure, as of thought, action, etc., figured as being built upon something else as a foundation.

1641 J. JACKSON *True Evang. T.* III. 224 Lay a good foundation, and then the superstructure is like to stand. **1646** J. HALL *Horæ Vac.* 20 Thrift.. is.. the Base whereon the Superstructures of all other wisdome lyes. **1698** NORRIS *Pract. Disc.* (1711) III. 2 In Geometry some plain Propositions are laid down,.. in order to further Theory, which, as a Superstructure, is to be rais'd upon those Foundations. **1791** COWPER *Yardley Oak* 122 So stands a kingdom, whose foundation yet Fails not, in virtue and in wisdom laid, Through all the superstructure. **1840** MACAULAY *Ess., Ranke's Hist.* (1897) 549 Every fresh story is as solid a basis for a new superstructure as the original foundation was. **1905** J. B. BURY *Life St. Patrick* App. 276 The visit to Pope Celestine at Rome has no legendary superstructure.

b. *Pol.* and *Econ.* In Marxist theory, the institutions and culture which are considered to result from or reflect the economic system on which a society is based.

[**1903** *Social Democrat* VII. 274 The Greeks attained to a high pitch of civilization, with a slave class as the basis of its economic superstructure.] **1904** N. I. STONE tr. *Marx's Contributions Critique Pol. Econ.* 11 The sum total of these relations.. constitutes the economic structure of society—the real foundation, on which rise legal and political superstructures. **1926** M. EASTMAN *Marx, Lenin & Sci. of Revolution* iv. 50 It is obvious that if the material basis positively *determined* the superstructure, we should not have to *disregard* the superstructure and examine the basis, for the one could be directly inferred from the other. **1943** J. A. SCHUMPETER *Capitalism, Socialism, & Democracy* xi. 121 We now turn to the cultural complement of the capitalist economy—to its socio-psychological superstructure, if we wish to speak the Marxian language—and to the mentality that is characteristic of capitalist society. **1960** E. R. GOODMAN in J. A. Fishman *Readings Sociol. of Lang.* (1968) 729 Man considered language as an element in the Marxist superstructure dependent upon the economic base of society... Just as this base might be changed by force, so Man thought, the linguistic superstructure should be impelled to develop toward its ultimate goal. **1975** *Chinese Econ. Stud.* VIII. IV. 10 The superstructure refers to the national government, army, law, and other political systems and their corresponding ideological forms, such as philosophy, literature, and fine arts. **1977** R. WILLIAMS *Marxism & Lit.* II. vi. 111 Cultural work and activity are not now, in any ordinary sense, a superstructure.

3. *Metallurgy.* = SUPERLATTICE 1.

1932 *Proc. R. Soc.* A. CXXXVI. 216 The type of superstructure represented by FeAl gives other lines [in an X-ray diffraction photograph]. **1979** *Nature* 11 Oct. 469/2 Ordered solid solutions (superstructures or superlattices), in which atoms of one kind segregate into a particular set of lattice positions, are usually obtained by slow cooling at the critical ordering temperature.

supersubstantial (,s(j)uːpəsəb'stænʃəl), *a.* [ad. late L. *supersubstantiālis* (Vulgate), f. *super-* SUPER- 4 a + *substantia* SUBSTANCE: see -AL^1. Cf. F. *sursubstantiel* (†-ciel), It. *soprassustanziale*, Sp., Pg. *supersubstancial*.]

1. In allusion to, or as a rendering of, late L. *supersubstantialis* in the Vulgate version of Matt. vi. 11 (translating Gr. ἐπιούσιος, which is now generally held to mean 'pertaining to the coming day'): Above or transcending material substance; spiritual: esp. in reference to the eucharistic bread.

Cf. *Wycl. Bible* Matt. vi. 11 Oure breed ouer other substaunce.

1534 MORE *Treat. Passion* Wks 1342/2 That heauenlye and supersubstancyall breadde and cuppe, beyng consecrate with that solemne benediction, is profitable to the lyfe and saluacyon of the whole man. **1550** VERON *Godly Sayings* (1846) 78 In ye Lords praier.. we say: give us the supersubstancial bread, not this bread that goeth intoo the body; but that bread of everlastyng life, which upholdeth the substance of our soule. **1555** CRANMER in Strype *Eccl. Mem.* (1721) III. xxx. 236, I have sinned.. against men, whom I have called from this supersubstantial morsel. **1609** *Bible* (Douay) Exod. xvi. *comm.*, It is our way-faring special provision, dailie and supersubstantial bread, til we shal possesse the promised land. **1665** WITHER *Lord's Prayer* 110 By preferring the meat that perisheth before that supersubstantial Bread of Life which came from Heaven. **1852** J. BROWN *Disc. & Say. Our Lord* I. iv. 245 Give us the supersubstantial bread—the bread of life. **1899** FR. DOLLING in C. E. Osborne *Life* x, The Body and Blood of Christ Himself, our daily supersubstantial bread.

2. Above or transcending all substance or being; = SUPERESSENTIAL: chiefly of God.

1534 MORE *Treat. Passion* Wks. 1339/2 Thys.. woorde Godde, signifyeth.. not onelye the vnitie of the Godheadde, but also the trinitie of the three persones, and not onely theyr supersubstaunciall substance, but also euery gracious propertie. **1602** WARNER *Alb. Eng.* XIII. lxxviii. (1612) 321 Locall vnlocally each wheare, super-substantiall, who Knows all that was, is, and is not. *a* **1633** AUSTIN *Medit.* (1635) 90 They saw a Starre, with five Beames... 1. Materiall, the Starre in the East: 2. Spirituall, the Starre of Faith, in their hearts. 3. Intellectuall, an Angel in a Dreame: 4. Rationall; the Virgin Marie; 5. Supersubstantiall; Christ himselfe. **1651** J. F[REAKE] *Agrippa's Occ. Philos.* II. vi. 181 Three persons in the supersubstantiall Divinity. **1855** MILMAN *Lat. Christ.* XIV. ii. (1864) IX. 63 He is the Thearchic Intelligence, the Supersubstantial Being.

Hence **,supersubstanti'ality** (*rare*$^{-0}$); †**,supersub'stantially** *adv.*, in a supersubstantial manner (in quot. in sense 2). So **,supersub'stantiate** *v.* [after *transubstantiate*] *trans.*, to make supersubstantial.

1606 WHETENHALL *Disc. Abuses Ch. Christ* 18 To supersubstantiat the blessed bread of the Lords Supper into the cursed Idoll of the Popes masse. **1611** FLORIO, *Soprasostantialità*, supersubstantiality. **1651** J. F[REAKE] *Agrippa's Occ. Philos.* III. v. 356 Belief which is a true faith, is super-substantially above all science and understanding conjoyning us immediately to God. **1825** COLERIDGE *Aids Refl.* App. C. (1858) I. 382 Fluids and ethers.. to whatever quintessential thinness they may be treble distilled, and (as it were) super-substantiated.

super'subtle, -'subtile, *a.* [SUPER- 9 a.] Extremely or excessively subtle; over-subtle.

1599 SANDYS *Europæ Spec.* (1632) 104 Admiring them in the rest of their super-subtill inventions. **1604** SHAKS. *Oth.* I. iii. 363 A fraile vow, betwixt an erring Barbarian, and a super-subtle Venetian. **1614** PURCHAS *Pilgrimage* II. xii. (ed. 2) 175 The Cabbalist as a super subtile transcendent, mounteth.. from this sensible world vnto that other intellectuall. **1823** LAMB *Elia* Ser. II. *Child Angel*, By reason that Mature Humanity is too gross to breathe the air of that super-subtile region. **1824** MISS MITFORD *Village* Ser. I. (1863) 106–7 Over-informed, super-subtle, too clever for her age. **1856** R. A. VAUGHAN *Mystics* (1860) II. 75 The super-subtile fancies of theosophy. **1879** McCARTHY *Own Times* II. xxiv. 211 A tendency to over-refining and super-subtle argument.

So **super'subtilize** *v. trans.*, to make over-subtle; **super'subtlety**, excessive subtlety.

1858 MASSON *Milton* I. vi. 443 In him [*sc.* Donne] there were gathered up.. all the tips and clippings of super-subtlety among the Elizabethans. **1870** LOWELL *Study Wind.* 245 The filigree of wire-drawn sentiment and supersubtilized conceit.

super-super-: see SUPER- 17, 18.

,super-su'perlative, *a.* (*sb.*) [SUPER- 4 a.] 'More than superlative'; of the very highest quality or degree. Also *sb.*, a degree beyond the superlative.

1607 R. C[AREW] tr. *Estienne's World of Wonders* 65 Supersuperlatiue knauery. **1642** VICARS *God in Mount* (1644) 11 The Archbishops super-superlative power. **1658–9** in *Burton's Diary* (1828) IV. 198 Union is most desirable with brethren Protestants; nay, Protestants of the best profession in the world. This is super-superlative. **1767** S. PATERSON *Another Trav.* I. 422 His highest taste—That super-superlative *gout.* **1801** SOUTHEY *Let. to J. Rickman* 20 Nov., We must create a super-superlative to reach the idea of his magnitude.

Hence **,super-su'perlatively** *adv.*

1641 'SMECTYMNUUS' *Vind. Answ.* Pref. A4b, Men so transcendently perfidious, and so supersuperlatively unfaithfull. **1648** E. SIMMONS in T. Wodenote *Herm. Theol.* Pref. A1xb, The malitious Jews.. were not so super-superlatively vile as to consult his [*sc.* Christ's] death because he was content in their stead.. to be accounted as a sinner.

super-symmetric, -symmetry: see SUPER- 6 b.

,supertechno'logical, *a.* **1.** [SUPER- 9 a.] Involving or employing highly advanced technology.

1968 *Economist* 14 Dec. p. xxv/3 Some sort of middle course will be found, between the super-technological and the purely sociological. **1977** P. JOHNSON *Enemies of Society* xii. 164 The galaxy of star universities which formed the vertebrae of the super-technological East Coast.

2. [SUPER- 4 a.] Beyond or superseding the technological.

1973 *Nature* 6 Apr. 382/1 A branch of this water-drawing and wood-hewing supertechnological fraternity would be preserving health.

super'temporal, *a.*^{1} (*sb.*) [SUPER- 4 a.] That is above time; transcending time. Also *sb.*, a supertemporal thing.

1678 CUDWORTH *Intell. Syst.* I iv. §36. 625 Plotinus and Numenius.. declare him [Plato] to have asserted, Three Super-Temporals or Eternals, Good, Mind or Intellect, and the Soul of the Universe. **1892** N. SMYTH *Chr. Ethics* I. i. §4. 81 Our super-temporal and super-sensible being. **1905** J. C.

Jones in T. Stephens *Child & Relig.* v. 187 They must have sinned—sinned..in a super-temporal state according to Julius Müller.

super'temporal, *a.*² (*sb.*) *Anat.* and *Zool.* [SUPER- 3 c (*b*).] **a.** Situated in the upper part of the temples or temporal region. **b.** *sb.* A supertemporal bone.

1854 OWEN in *Orr's Circ. Sci., Org. Nat.* I. 179 The bones ..that circumscribe the lower part of the orbit... In fishes they are called 'suborbitals'... A similar series of bones sometimes overarches the temporal fossæ, and are called 'supertemporals'. **1889** *Buck's Handbk. Med. Sci.* VIII. 155/2 (Descr. of Figure) Left supertemporal. *Ibid.* 158/2 The great length of the supertemporal fissure, and its dorsal subdivision.

†**ˌsuperte'rraneal**, *a. Obs. rare*⁻¹. [See SUPER- 1 a and cf. SUBTERRANEAL.] = next.

1686 PLOT *Staffordsh.* iii. §42. 133 All which, whether super or subterraneal, I take in general to proceed from stagnations in the subterraneal Vaults of the Earth.

superterranean (ˌs(j)uːpətə'reɪnɪən), *a.* (*sb.*) [f. mod.L. **superterrāneus*, f. *super-* SUPER- 1 a + *terra* earth: see -AN.] That is or dwells above, or on the surface of, the earth; above-ground: opposed to *subterranean*. Also *sb.*, a dweller above ground or on the earth.

1691 R. KIRK *Secret Commw.* i. (1815) 3 A superterranean and a subterranean Inhabitant, perfectly resembling one another. *Ibid.* 6 If any Superterraneans be so subtile, as to practice Slights for procureing a Privacy to any of their Misteries. **1816** G. S. FABER *Orig. Pagan Idol.* III. 268 With numerous chambers both superterranean and subterranean. **1827** *Blackw. Mag.* XXII. 386 The subterranean in fictitious composition must always be subject either to the laws of the superterranean, or of the supernatural. **1846** J. DUDLEY *Naology* 365 In what..may be called their superterranean structures, their temples. **1875** LITTLEDALE in *Contemp. Rev.* Mar. 577 This is all we know about superterranean churches before Constantine.

ˌsuperte'rraneous (-'eɪnɪəs), *a.* [f. mod.L. **superterrāneus*: see prec. and -EOUS.] = prec.

1671 *Phil. Trans.* VI. 2232 The admirable Fabric of the Super-terraneous and Subterraneous complex Globe of Earth, Air and Water. **1686** PLOT *Staffordsh.* 71 There are many Lakes in the World of Salt water, that have no superterraneous Vents into the Sea. **1825** FOSBROOKE *Encycl. Antiq.* (1843) I. 112 The Mandræ, or early monasteries of Ireland, are..mere superterraneous caverns.

superterrene (ˌs(j)uːpətə'riːn), *a.* [ad. late L. *superterrēnus*: see SUPER- 1 a and TERRENE.]

1. = SUPERTERRANEAN.

1709 T. ROBINSON *Nat. Hist. Westmoreld.* iv. 23 The Division of the Waters..was made into Waters subterrene, superterrene, and nubiferous. *a* **1871** DE MORGAN *Budget Parad.* (1872) 137 Gutta percha and Rowland Hill are the great discoveries of our day;..gutta percha being to the submarine post what Rowland Hill is to the super-terrene. **1881** G. MILNER *Country Pleas.* xxi. 105 When your progenitors nested or herded in such a superterrene covert.

2. Existing or dwelling in a region above the earth; belonging to a higher world: = next, 1.

1755 SMOLLETT *Quix.* I. III. xii. 178, I am positive it began with 'subterrene and sublime princess!' It could not be subterrene, said the barber, but superterrene or sovereign. **1866** MILL in *Edin. Rev.* CXXIII. 328 The gods..must live in the perpetual contemplation of these glorious and superterrene existences.

superterrestrial (ˌs(j)uːpətə'rɛstrɪəl), *a.* [See SUPER- 1 a and TERRESTRIAL.]

1. Existing, or belonging to a region, above the earth; celestial: = prec. 2. Also *fig.*

1727 EARBERY tr. *Burnet's St. Dead* (1728) II. 47 Moses.. described the Formation of all super-terrestrial and terrestrial Bodies. **1798** W. TAYLOR in *Monthly Mag.* VI. 554 A confidence in super-terrestrial protection, and a belief in supernatural powers. **1846** DE QUINCEY *Antig. Sophocles* Wks. 1860 XIV. 203 Ever since the restoration of letters there has been a cabal,..for exalting as something superterrestrial, and quite unapproachable by moderns, the monuments of Greek literature. **1865** tr *Strauss' New Life Jesus* I. xlix. I. 422 The change into the superterrestrial state.

2. = SUPERTERRANEAN.

1875 LD. BLACHFORD in *Life Ld. Coleridge* (1904) II. ix. 252 Subterranean and superterrestrial operations.

super'tonic. *Mus.* [SUPER- 5 b.] The note next above the tonic; the second of the scale. Also *attrib.* applied to a chord having this note for its root.

1806 CALLCOTT *Mus. Gram.* II. v. 135 The Supertonic, or second above the Key-note. **1867** MACFARREN *Harmony* (1892) 128 The chromatic raising of the 3rd in the supertonic chord. **1868** OUSELEY *Harmony* xi. (1875) 128 The dominant of a dominant, i.e. the supertonic. **1889** PROUT *Harmony* xiii. 135 The chord of the supertonic seventh. *Ibid.* 144 The dominant seventh resolves on the tonic, submediant, or subdominant chord, or on a supertonic discord.

super'tunic. *Antiq.* Also in L. form. [ad. med.L. *supertunica*: see SUPER- 3 and TUNIC *sb.*] An outer tunic; *spec.* the vestment worn above the dalmatic (or tunicle) by a sovereign at his coronation.

1625-6 *Coronation Chas. I* (1892) 36 The Deane of Westminster goeth on araying yᵉ King. 1. With yᵉ Supertunica, or close Pall. *a* **1700** EVELYN *Diary* 23 Apr. 1661, Then [at the Coronation] was..put on..the cobbium, syndon [*i.e.* colobium sindonis], or dalmatic, and over this a supertunic of cloth of gold. **1843** LYTTON *Last Barons* IV. iii, He looks brave in his gay supertunic. **1860** FAIRHOLT *Costume Eng.* (ed. 2) 83 King John [in his effigy]..wears a supertunic of crimson embroidered with gold. **1891** *Proc. Soc. Antiq.* 15 Jan. 216 The rest of the costume consists of supertunic and kirtle.

†**superva'caneal**, *a. Obs. rare*⁻¹. [f. L. *supervacāneus*: see next and -AL¹.] = next.

c **1555** HARPSFIELD *Divorce Hen. VIII* (Camden) 115 Though it be..with long painted supervacaneall words exorned and set forth.

supervacaneous (ˌs(j)uːpəvə'keɪnɪəs), *a.* Now *rare* or *Obs.* [f. L. *supervacāneus*, f. *super-* SUPER- III + *vacāre* to be empty or void: see -EOUS. Cf. It., Sp., Pg. *supervacaneo.*] Vainly added over and above what is essential; superfluous, redundant.

c **1555** HARPSFIELD *Divorce Hen. VIII* (Camden) 146 For the avoiding of supervacaneous tediousness we will cut off all such endless matters. **1641** J. TRAPPE *Theol. Theol.* viii. 313 Account not any part of this venerable Volume to be superfluous or super-vacaneous. **1684** tr. *Bonet's Merc. Compit.* VI. 217 As much supervacaneous humour as they had lost, so much new strength they had acquired. **1772** NUGENT *Hist. Fr. Gerund* II. 85 Conjectural argument is supervacaneous when the words of the oracle are clear. **1825** BENTHAM *Offic. Apt. Maximized, Indications* Postscr. (1830) 23 Desire is sufficient: accomplishment, or anything like an approach to it, supervacaneous! **1838** BEARD in E. G. Holland *Mem. J. Badger* xvii. (1854) 348 While others contend about the supervacaneous part of religion.

Hence **ˌsuperva'caneously** *adv.*; **ˌsuperva'caneousness**.

1657 W. MORICE *Coena quasi Κοινὴ* xii. 178 They might have..spared supervacaneously to shew us the difference. **1730** BAILEY (fol.), Supervacaneousness.

†**super'vacuous**, *a. Obs.* [f. L. *supervacuus*: see SUPER- III and VACUOUS.] = prec. adj.

1615 CROOKE *Body of Man* 315 If..the wombe should at certaine times open it self to expell that that is superuacuous. **1633** AMES *Fresh Suit agst. Ceremon.* II. 442 Those Ceremonies are supervacuous and vaine. *a* **1706** EVELYN *Hist. Relig.* (1850) II. 285 The Pope..may dispense the supervacuous duties of others (who do more than is required for their salvation) to sinners who have no merit of their own. **1799** E. DU BOIS *Piece Fam. Biog.* I. p. iv, I shall wave my supervacuous honours.

supervene (s(j)uːpə'viːn), *v.* [ad. L. *supervenīre*, f. *super-* SUPER- 13 + *venīre* to come. Cf. OF. *so(u)rvenir* (mod.F. *survenir*), Pr. *sobrevenir*, It. *sopravvenire*, Sp. *sobrevenir*, Pg. *sobrevir.*]

1. *intr.* To come on or occur as something additional or extraneous; to come directly or shortly after something else, either as a consequence of it or in contrast with it; to follow closely upon some other occurrence or condition.

1647-8 COTTERELL *Davila's Hist. Fr.* (1678) 11 Upon a sudden supervened the death of the king. **1664** EXTON *Maritime Dicaeologie* I. iv. 16 New differences and controversies arising and supervening, which they could not judge or determine by the Rhodian Laws. **1804** *Med. Jrnl.* XII. 386 Soon after, a vomiting of an offensive and greenish-coloured fluid supervened. **1849** C. BRONTE *Shirley* ii, A bad harvest supervened. Distress reached its climax. **1867** PEARSON *Hist. Eng.* I. 409 The king was bruised by the pommel of his saddle; fever supervened, and the injury proved fatal. **1883** *Daily Tel.* 10 Nov. 5/2 The marked change which has supervened in the habits and tastes of the junior members of both Universities.

b. Const. *on*, *upon*, rarely *to* (the preceding occurrence, condition, etc.).

1692 BENTLEY *Boyle Lect.* vii. (1693) 29 This power [*sc.* mutual gravitation]..cannot be..essential to Matter. And ..it could never supervene to it, unless..infus'd into it by an immaterial..Power. **1831** CARLYLE *Sart. Res.* III. x, A kind of..Jew's-harping and scrannel-piping..to which the frightfullest species of Magnetic Sleep soon supervened. **1850** GLADSTONE *Glean.* V. cxx. 243 Upon this there supervened..that idea of royal power [etc.]. **1868** —— *Juv. Mundi* ii. (1869) 43 Upon this local name [Argeioi] there had supervened..the paramount and wider name of Achaioi. **1870** *Daily News* 1 Dec., Typhus supervening on a gunshot wound.

†**2.** *trans.* To come directly or soon after, to follow closely (= *supervene upon*, 1 b); occas. to come after so as to take the place of, to supersede.

1725 *Phil. Trans.* XXXIII. 392 The Fever frequently supervening a Surfeit. **1788** T. TAYLOR *Proclus* I. Diss. 17 It first perceives a thing destitute of ornament, and afterwards the operations of the adorning artificer supervening its nature. **1810** in *Dk. Buckingham's Mem. Geo. III* (1855) IV. 430 This triumph..although..it affects the..situation..is not so decisive..as to supervene the necessity of a change.

Hence **super'vener**, something that supervenes; in quot. applied to a substance added to another.

1656 [? J. SERGEANT] tr. *T. White's Peripat. Inst.* 63 When the supervener has aggregated to it self the parts of that humid body wherein the dissolution was made.

supervenience (s(j)uːpə'viːnɪəns). *rare.* [f. SUPERVENIENT: see -ENCE.] The fact of being supervenient, or of supervening; supervention.

1644 DIGBY *Nat. Bodies* xvii. §4. 148 The place..is thus, by the superuenience of a guest of a contrary nature.. purged from the superaboundance of the former ones that annoyed it. **1885** STEVENSON *Prince Otto* I. iv, I would look ..to the natural supervenience of a more able sovereign.

†**super'veniency.** *Obs. rare.* [Formed as prec.: see -ENCY.] = prec.

1647 M. HUDSON *Div. Right Govt.* Introd. p. viii, Through whose superveniencie the meanest gifts and blessings of nature doe become sufficient to make a man Eternally happy. **1659** *Gentl. Calling* viii. §16 The more moderate pains become insensible by the superveniency of the more acute.

b. *Sc. Law.* The fact or condition of being supervenient: said of a right.

1681 STAIR *Inst. Law Scot.* II. xxvii. 136 If they should not be entered before the superveniency. *a* **1712** FOUNTAINHALL *Decis.* (1759) II. 361 *Jus fuit fundatum*, and the superveniency accresces.

supervenient (s(j)uːpə'viːnɪənt), *a.* [ad. L. *supervenient-*, *-ens*, pr. pple. of *supervenīre* to SUPERVENE.] Supervening; coming upon something as an extraneous addition; coming on after (and in connexion or contrast with) something else; occurring or appearing subsequently.

1594 ALEX. HUME *Treat. Consc.* Pref. 46 By reason of the cold supervenient winter, I was tyed to the bed. **1628** WOTTON in *Reliq.* (1672) 557 It shall teach me to reserve myself..for such supervenient temptations. **1644** DIGBY *Nat. Bodies* xv. 135 If then pure water be putt vpon that chalke, the subtilest dry partes of it, do easily ioyne to the superuenient moysture. **1662** STILLINGFL. *Orig. Sacr.* III. iii. §7 The necessity of any supervenient act of grace. **1711** in *Nairne Peerage Evidence* (1874) 137 According to the time prescribed be the Act of Parliament or be any supervenient law. **1713** DERHAM *Phys.-Theol.* VIII. vi. 429 Some other supervenient, additional Insects, laid in after the Apple was grown. **1758** JOHNSON *Let. to Langton* 9 Jan. in *Boswell*, Some supervenient cause of discord may over-power this original amity. **1839** HALLAM *Lit. Eur.* III. iv. §114 III. 412 It is..reasonable..to restrain the terms of a promise, where they clearly appear to go beyond the design of the promiser, or where supervenient circumstances indicate an exception which he would infallibly have made. **1875** E. WHITE *Life in Christ* v. xxxi. (1878) 533 The whole eternal life to follow will be a result not of primeval law but of supervenient grace.

b. Const. *to* (that which precedes).

1654 HAMMOND *Fundamentals* ii. §9. 22 That branch of belief was in him supervenient to Christian practise. **1662** PETTY *Taxes* 71 A tax supervenient to a mans other expences. *c* **1690** *Inform. for Sir T. Dalziel of Binns* 1 Albeit the Debt now acclaimed was by a Law supervenient to the Disposition.

c. *Sc. Law.* Of a right: That is acquired by the disponer subsequently to the act of transmission. Also *allusively*.

1644 MAXWELL *Prerog. Chr. Kings* 55 What he had before by hypostaticall union onely, now he had it by another supervenient Right of merit. **1681** STAIR *Inst. Law Scot.* II. xxiv. §2 A supervenient Right..was found to accresce to the Earl of Lauderdail.

supervening (s(j)uːpə'viːnɪŋ), *vbl. sb.* [f. SUPERVENE + -ING¹.] The action of the verb SUPERVENE; supervention.

1667 BOYLE *Orig. Formes & Qual.* etc. (ed. 2) 345 The supervening of a higher Form. **1685** —— *Effects of Motion* iv. 42 Bottles..being full of the liquor were firmly stopped before the supervening of the Cold. **1737** WATERLAND *Eucharist* x. Wks. 1823 VII. 287 It is not the water that confers this benefit,..but it is the appointment of God, and the supervening of the Spirit. **1826** BELL *Comm. Law Scot.* (ed. 5) II. 7 Although the supervening of an heritable security..makes a moveable debt heritable. **1862** F. HALL *Hindu Philos. Syst.* 241 In the theory of Berkeley, the world, birth, death, [etc.]..are true, and not of such a nature, that they vanish away on the supervening of right apprehension.

super'vening, *ppl. a.* [f. as prec. + -ING².] That supervenes; supervenient.

1653 JER. TAYLOR *Serm. for Year* I. xii. 153 The imperfection of nature where we stand by our creation, and supervening follies. **1681** STAIR *Inst. Law Scot.* II. xxiv. §2 The superveening Right..accresces without any new solemnities. **1721** R. KEITH tr. *T. à Kempis' Valley of Lillies* Pref. p. iv, The supervening Changes that may..befal the Soul. *a* **1768** ERSKINE *Inst. Law Scot.* III. iii. §71 Though he should afterwards have obtained a decree in his favour on a supervening title. **1826** BELL *Comm. Law Scot.* (ed. 5) I. 698 Every supervening right acquired by the disponer after the transmission. **1835** SIR J. ROSS *Narr. 2nd Voy.* xxix. 408 A supervening haze. **1849** RUSKIN *Seven Lamps* iv. §26. 116 That west front is made up of..many unfinished and supervening designs. *a* **1871** GROTE *Eth. Fragm.* iv. (1876) 87 The feeling of a supervening liability to the disesteem of others is interwoven with the idea of wrong doing.

supervention (s(j)uːpə'vɛnʃən). [ad. late L. *superventio*, *-ōnem*, n. of action f. *supervenīre* to SUPERVENE. Cf. Sp. *supervencion*, Pg. *-venção.*] The action or fact of supervening; coming on in addition; subsequent occurrence.

1649 BP. HALL *Cases Consc.* IV. vi. (1654) 352 An espousal contract..may..be broken off..by the supervention of a legall kindred, inexpected. **1721** BAILEY, A *Supervention*,.. a coming upon one suddenly. **1800** *Med. Jrnl.* IV. 314, I had reason to apprehend a supervention of delirium. **1851** H. MAYO *Pop. Superst.* (ed. 2) 38 The only security we..know of, that life has left the body, is the supervention of chemical decomposition. **1858** GLADSTONE *Homer* III. 17 The mere supervention of one race upon another, the change from a Pelasgian to an Hellenic character. **1879** *St. George's Hosp. Rep.* IX. 687 The interval between the accident and the supervention of tetanus.

†**super'vide**, *v. Obs. rare*⁻¹. [ad. med.L. *supervidēre*, f. *super-* SUPER- 2 + *vidēre* to see.] *trans.* To look upon, survey.
c **1430** LYDG. *Min. Poems* (Percy Soc.) 78 As I me lenyd unto a joyful place, Lusty Phebus to supervide [*MS.* supervive], How God Almyghti of his grete grace, Hath florisshed the erthe on every side.

supervisal (s(j)uːpə'vaɪzəl), *sb.* Now *rare.* [f. med.L. *supervīs-*, pa. ppl. stem of *supervidēre*: see prec. and -AL[1] 5.]
1. = SUPERVISION 1.
1652 EVELYN *State France* Misc. Writ. (1805) 60 The High Chamberlain of France..hath the supevisall..of all officers of the King's bedchamber. *a* **1716** SOUTH *Serm.* (1717) IV. 389 The Regulation and Supervisal of the whole Course of a Man's Life. **1763** H. WALPOLE *Let. to G. Montagu* 1 July, I do not love to trust a hammer or a brush without my own supervisal. **1826** *Examiner* 488/1 The new buildings are from the designs of different Architects, but subject..to the supervisal of..Mr. Nash. **1839** CARLYLE *Chartism* iii. 123 Supervisal by the central government.
2. = SUPERVISION 2.
1749 H. WALPOLE *Let. to Mann* 17 May, The supervisal of it [*sc.* the Life of the first Duke of Marlborough]. **1751** WARBURTON in *Pope's Wks.* IV. 42 *note*, A paper wherein he never had the least hand, direction or supervisal. **1762** tr. *Busching's Syst. Geog.* III. 590 [Congresses] annually held for the supervisal of the accounts of the bailiages.

super'visal, *a. rare*⁻¹. [f. med.L. *supervīs-* (see prec.) + -AL[1] 1.] Supervisory.
1838 G. S. FABER *Inquiry* 559 Ignatius,..like Timothy and Titus and Clement and Polycarp, had received his supervisal authority from the immediate hands of an Apostle.

super'visance. *rare*⁻¹. [Formed as prec. + -ANCE.] = SUPERVISION.
1864 BURTON *Scot Abr.* I. i. 25 He had neglected the opportunity which a supervisance of the wretched and ruined finances afforded.

†**supervise**, *sb. Obs. rare*⁻¹. Also 7 -vize. [f. next.] The act of supervising; inspection, perusal.
1602 SHAKS. *Ham.* v. ii. 23 An exact command,..That on the superuize no leasure bated.

supervise (s(j)uːpə'vaɪz), *v.* Also 9 -vize. [f. med.L. *supervīs-*, pa. ppl. stem of *supervidēre*: see SUPERVIDE.]
†**1.** *trans.* To look over, survey, inspect; to read through, peruse. *Obs.*
1588 SHAKS. *L.L.L.* IV. ii. 125 You finde not the apostraphas, and so misse the accent. Let me superuise the cangenet [= canzonet]. **1596** NASHE *Saffron Walden* V 4, In both my bookes I haue obiected some perticular vice more against him than pumps and pantofles, which those that haue not faith inough to beleeue, may toote & superuize. **1629** WADSWORTH *Pilgr.* viii. 78, I superuised the letter of Dr. Hall and Mr. Bedell, which I found in my Father's study. **1700** T. BROWN tr. *Fresny's Amusem.* 10 If any Man ..has an Inclination..to supervise almost all the Conditions of Humane Life. *a* **1711** KEN *Preparatives* Poet. Wks. 1721 IV. 15 All my Omissions supervise, And to what Guilt they all arise To my own self my Vileness shew.
†**b.** To overlook, command a view of. *Obs.*
1658 R. FRANCK *North. Mem.* (1821) 127 Those eminent high Highlands, that supervise those shady valleys below them.
†**c.** *spec.* To read through for correction; to revise. *Obs.*
1655 [see *supervising* below]. **1725** POPE *Shaks. Wks.* I. Pref. p. xv, If any were supervised by himself, I should fancy the two parts of Henry the 4th, and Midsummer-Night's Dream might have been so. **1751** EARL ORRERY *Rem. Swift* xvii. (1752) 131 Two additional volumes, both which were supervised and corrected by the author.
2. To oversee, have the oversight of, superintend the execution or performance of (a thing), the movements or work of (a person).
c **1645** HOWELL *Lett.* I. i. iii, The small time I supervis'd the Glasse-house, I got amongst those Venetians some smatterings of the Italian Toung. **1667** PRIMATT *City & C. Build.* 58 Adde one shilling for every square for the master-Brick-layers super-vising them. **1678** CUDWORTH *Intell. Syst.* I. v. 672 All is supervised by One Understanding and Intending Cause. **1726** LEONI *Alberti's Archit.* II. 97/1 You undertake to supervise and compleat the work. **1856** KANE *Arctic Expl.* II. xv. 166 My own energies just equal to the duty of supervising our final departure. **1869** *Latest News* 5 Sept. 7 The formation of local committees of vigilance to supervise the police. **1914** *Eng. Hist. Rev.* Jan. 183 As Papal Chancellor, Albert of Mora supervized the drafting of papal bulls.
Hence **super'vising** *vbl. sb.* and *ppl. a.*
1655 tr. *Semedo's Hist. China* vi. 35 Every one hath the liberty to print what he pleaseth, without the Supervising, Censure, or Licence, of any one. **1766** ENTICK *London* IV. 188 Who shall have the supervising..of all the physicians. **1845** STOCQUELER *Handbk. Brit. India* (1854) 45 The responsibility of the local administration to the two supervising authorities. **1871** *Figure Training* 110 The foot ..requiring almost as much supervising care as the figure.

supervisee (ˌs(j)uːpəvaɪ'ziː). [f. prec. + -EE.] One who is supervised; *spec.* a person under police supervision.
1880 *Standard* 23 Apr. 2/7 Charged..with not reporting himself to the police, under the Prevention of Crimes Act, he being a 'supervisee' under the Act. **1891** *Law Times* XCI. 204/2 The apprehension of licensees and supervisees.

supervision (s(j)uːpə'vɪʒən). [ad. med.L. *supervīsio, -ōnem*, n. of action f. *supervidēre*: see SUPERVIDE.
The earliest recorded instance of the word is in the 1st Fo. (1623) text of SHAKS. *Othello* III. iii. 395, where the true reading is 'supervisor' (1st Qo.).]
The action or function of supervising.
1. a. General management, direction, or control; oversight, superintendence.
1640 BP. HALL *Episc.* II. vii. 121 Having had the speciall supervision of the whole Asian Church. **1768** BLACKSTONE *Comm.* III. iv. 46 [The chancellor] seems to have had the supervision of..charters, letters, and such other public instruments of the crown, as were authenticated in the most solemn manner. **1781** WARTON *Hist. Kiddington* (1783) 17 An old donation, for the sustenance of a perpetual lamp to burn before the high-altar in the royal chapel at Islip, under the trust and supervision of the abbats of Westminster. **1846** MCCULLOCH *Acc. Brit. Empire* (1854) I. 211 The central office at Somerset House..for..the general supervision and conduct of the business of registration. **1859** *Musketry Instr.* 99 Officers charged with the Supervision of the Musketry Training of the Troops. **1877** J. NORTHCOTE *Catacombs* I. v. 90 The artists..worked under ecclesiastical supervision. **1877** BLACK *Green Past.* vi, The police supervision is very strict.
b. Special Comb.: **supervision order**, a court order placing a child or young person under the supervision of a local authority or a probation officer in cases of delinquency, petty crime, etc.
[**1933** *Act 23 & 24 Geo. V.* c. 12 §62 An order placing him ..under the supervision of a probation officer, or of some other person appointed for the purpose by the court.] **1938** *Act 1 & 2 Geo. VI* c. 40 Supervision order in place of order committing to care of fit person. **1968** J. LOCK *Lady Policeman* xv. 126 The juvenile court placed her under a Supervision Order and she returned home. **1980** *Times Lit. Suppl.* 28 Nov. 1347/3 The usual treatment [in dealing with schoolboy truancy] is to place the child under a supervision order: he is then seen by a social worker or probation officer from time to time.
2. The action of reading through for correction; revision by a superior authority. *Hist.* (Cf. SUPERVISOR 3, quot. 1881.)
1881 *N.T.* (Rev. Vers.) Pref. 8 A final supervision of the whole Bible [of 1611], by selected members from Oxford, Cambridge, and Westminster.

†**super'visit**, *v. Obs. rare.* [f. SUPER- + VISIT *v.*, after *supervise.*] *trans.* To supervise, look after. Only in †**super'visiting** *ppl. a.*
1615 T. ADAMS *Myst. Bedlem* i. 15 Locke vp this vessell with the Key of faith,..guard it with supervisiting diligence. **1616** R. CARPENTER *Past. Charge* 51 This charge of superuisiting diligence.

supervisor (s(j)uːpə'vaɪzə(r), 's(j)uːpəvaɪzə(r)). Also 5-6 -vysour, 5-7 -visour, 7 -viser. [ad. med.L. *supervīsor*, f. *supervīs-* (see SUPERVISE). Cf. OF. *superviseur* (16th c.).] One who supervises.
1. A person who exercises general direction or control over a business, a body of workmen, etc.; one who inspects and directs the work of others.
Supervisor of the Excise: an officer who supervised and inspected the books, etc. of the inferior officers of the department.
1454 in H. Anstey *Epist. Acad. Oxon.* (O.H.S.) I. 326 William Churche, supervisor of þe werks of þe sayd scollis. *c* **1520** SKELTON *Magnyf.* 1808 And here I make the vpon Lyberte To be superuysour. **1579** LYLY *Euphues* (Arb.) 132 Him he sets not as a suruayour and ouerseer of his manors, but a superuisour of hys childrens conditions and manners. **1642** FULLER *Holy & Prof. St.* III. xxi. 212 Bishop Andrews ever placed the picture of Mulcaster his Schoolmaster over the doore of his study..as to be his Tutour and Supervisour. **1667** in Pettus *Fodinæ Reg.* (1670) 38 A Supervisor of the Mills and Works. **1689** *Lond. Gaz.* No. 2428/4 Captain Robert Bathurst, Collector, and John Gilloway, Supervisor, of Excise. **1771** BURKE *Let. to R. Shackleton* 31 July, Mr. Vansittart, and Mr. Ford, and Scraften, were the only supervisors for the company on board the unfortunate Aurora. **1845** FORD *Handbk. Spain* I. 123 The sole supervisor of all the edifices of the Peninsula. **1883** in A. J. Adderley *Fisheries Bahamas* 50 Mr. Gregor Buccich, a telegraph supervisor, in the island of Lesina, in Dalmatia. **1884** *Manch. Exam.* 6 Dec. 5/5 Mr. Constantine, supervisor of excise, seized the plant [of an illicit still].
†**b.** A person appointed by a testator to supervise the executors of the will; = OVERSEER *sb.* 1 b.
1456 *Paston Lett.* I. 372 The said bille to be put up to the Kyng, whiche is chief supervisor of my said Lordis testament. **1496** in *Somerset Med. Wills* (1901) 340, I make John Fitziames the yonger supervysour and I bequethe to him for his laboure 10 s. **1555** EDEN *Decades* (Arb.) 56 Other famous and godly men (as superuisours of his testamente). **1583-93** GREENE *Mamillia* II. Wks. (Grosart) II. 240 For the performance of my will, I leaue the whole Senate as superuisors. **1637** WOTTON in *Reliq.* (1672) 54, I do pray the foresaid Dr. Bargrave, and Mr. Nicholas Pey, together with Mr. John Harrison..to be Supervisors of this my last Will and Testament. **1672** *Cowell's Interpr.* s.v., It was anciently, and still is a Custom among some, especially of the better sort, to make a Supervisor of a Will, but it is to litt e purpose. **1719** D'URFEY *Pills* V. 270 Time..do I make The Supervisor of my Will. **1767** BURN *Eccl. Law* (ed. 2) IV. 97 *marg.*, Supervisors [*text*, Overseers of a will].
c. An inspector of highways; now only *U.S.* a road-master on a railway.
1555 *Act 2 & 3 Ph. & M.* c. 8 §1 Yf the Cariages..shall not be thought nedefull by the Supervisors to bee occupyed upon any of the said days. **1755** *Dict. Arts & Sci.* IV. s.v., Supervisor formerly was used for surveyor of the highways. **1868** Road supervisor [see ROAD *sb.* 10 b]. **1898** *Engineering Mag.* XVI. 65 He is often assisted by..a master carpenter, master mason, and track-supervisors, the latter having charge of the track on a sub-division of the line.
†**d.** A keeper or curator. *Obs. rare.*
1691 WOOD *Ath. Oxon.* II. 431 Cosmo the great Duke of Tuscany..made him Supervisor of his Medals.
e. In some of the United States, An elected officer, or one of a board of such officers, charged with the administration of a township. (Cf. SELECTMAN.)
1882 A. SHAW in *Fortn. Rev.* Oct. 491 The supervisor is both a town and a county officer. He is general manager of town business, and is also a member of the County Board, which is composed of the supervisors of the several towns.
†**2.** An onlooker, spectator, observer. *Obs.*
1604 SHAKS. *Oth.* III. iii. 395 (Qo. 1) Would you the supervisor, grossly gape on? **1610** *Histrio-m.* II. 234 These admirable wits of Italy..Are curious supervisours over strangers.
3. One who reads over, esp. for the purpose of correction; a reviser. Now *rare* or *Obs.*
1624 BEDELL *Lett.* vi. 101 The Superuisors..of the Canon Law,..acknowledge, that..this sentence is not found. **1687** DRYDEN *Hind & P.* Pref. p. iii, I am now inform'd both of the Author and Supervisers of his Pamphlet. **1732** BENTLEY *Milton's P.L.* Pref. a iij, That Edition is without Faults; because He [*sc.* Milton]..had chang'd his old Printer and Supervisor. **1808** W. WILSON *Hist. Diss. Ch.* I. 44 Archbishop Bancroft, who was supervisor of the present translation, altered it in fourteen places. **1881** *N.T.* (Rev. Vers.) Pref. 8 These supervisors [of the 1611 version] are said by one authority to have been six in number, and by another twelve.

super'visorship. [f. prec. + -SHIP.] The office of a supervisor. Also, contextually, the function of a supervisor; a body of supervisors.
1485 *Rolls of Parlt.* VI. 349/1 Th' office of Supervisorship of oure Werkys. **1643** *Three Lett.* 18 Did we ever think it possible both Houses should ever pretend to such a supervisorship over that trust? **1691** T. H[ALE] *Acc. New Invent.* p. cv, The abuses done to those Rivers, may well call for the Supervisorship of some particular Person or Persons. **1772** BURKE *Let. to W. Dowdeswell* 7 Nov., He offered me the first place in a supervisorship of three. **1783** W. F. MARTYN *Geog. Mag.* II. 107 The supervisorship of fourteen grammar-schools. **1895** *Chamb. Jrnl.* XII. 817/1 That January which, had the poet-exciseman lived, would have witnessed his promotion to a supervisorship.

supervisory (s(j)uːpə'vaɪzərɪ), *a.* [f. L. *supervīs-* SUPERVISE + -ORY[2].] Having the function of supervising; of, pertaining to, or exercising supervision.
1847 in WEBSTER. **1848-9** CALHOUN *Disc. Const. & Govt. U.S.* Wks. 1863 I. 180 The Senate, in addition to its legislative, is vested also with supervisory powers in respect to treaties and appointments. **1854** W. R. WILLIAMS *Relig. Progr.* iii. 63 A supervisory and sleepless Providence. **1879** D. J. HILL *Bryant* 147 His introductions to publications upon which his work was mainly supervisory, rather than constructive.
transf. **1902** *Encycl. Brit.* XXXIII. 238/2 (*Telephone*) Two auxiliary incandescent lamps ('supervisory lamps') are introduced in such a way that, so long as the receivers of both subscribers are removed from the hooks, the lights do not glow.

super'visure. *rare*⁻¹. [f. L. *supervis-* SUPERVISE + -URE.] Supervision.
1769 BURKE *Let. to Marq. Rockingham* 13 Aug., The naval force..would not be sent, unless the court should consent to name the commander of that force..one in their commission of supervisure.

†**super'vive**, *v. Obs.* [ad. late L. *supervīvĕre*, f. *super-* SUPER- 7 + *vīvĕre* to live. Cf. F. *survivre* to SURVIVE.] To live beyond or after another person, an event, etc.: = SURVIVE. **a.** *intr.*
a **1552** LELAND *Itin.* (1768) II. 33 William was slayn, and Alice supervivid. **1597** *Reg. Mag. Sig. Scot.* 304/1 The last of the four persones foirsaidis supervivand. **1648** HERRICK *Hesper.* (title of poem) Great Spirits supervive. **1654** EARL MONM. tr. *Bentivoglio's Wars Flanders* 10 Assuring them that they shall always see my father supervive in me, in favouring and protecting them. **1671** BARROW *Serm. Ps. cxii.* 9 Wks. 1687 I. 460 He [*sc.* the bountiful man] supervives in the heart of the afflicted, which still..rejoyces in the ease which he procured him.
b. *trans.* To outlive.
1586 SANDYS in J. J. Cartwright *Chapt. Hist. Yorks.* (1872) 137 Myne eldest sonne..hathe supervived him. **1634** T. JOHNSON *Parey's Chirurg.* II. (1678) 46 Neither doth Death give an end to that hatred, but it supervives their Funeral. **1706** CLARKE *Let. to Mr. Dodwell* (1718) 8, I beseech you, if the Soul be such..what Revolutions in Nature will it not be able to resist and supervive?
So †**super'vivant**, a survivor; †**super'vivency**, survival.
c **1555** HARPSFIELD *Divorce Hen. VIII* (Camden) 281 The strange bloody spectacle wherein the one brother was butcher to the other.., and the supervivant..beheaded not long after. **1659** T. WHITE *Middle State Souls* 10 The Stoicks..acknowledged the soul's supervivency..after the decay of the body.

†**superviver**[1]. *Obs. rare.* [f. prec. + -ER[1].] A survivor.
a **1614** DONNE *Βιαθανατος* (1644) 62 The charity of the Supervivers imputed to them Baptisma fluminis, as they hope, or at least, Sanguinis, for that they saw.

†**superviver**². *Obs. rare.* In 6 -or. [app. f. SUPERVIVE + -ER⁴, as in *trover, user*. For the variant in *-or*, cf. CESSER.] = SURVIVER².

1542 *Richmond Wills* (Surtees) 33 The holl lands ar cumme unto me..by force off supervivor off the saide William Herryson.

supervoltage: see SUPER- 10 b.

supervolute ('s(j)u:pəvəl(j)u:t), *a. Bot.* [ad. L. *supervolūtus*, pa. pple. of *supervolvĕre*, f. *super-* SUPER- 2 + *volvĕre* to roll.] Applied to convolute leaves one of which envelops another in the bud, or to vernation in which this occurs; also to the lobes of a gamopetalous corolla each of which overlaps the next in the bud like convolute petals, or to æstivation in which this occurs.

1832 LINDLEY *Introd. Bot.* 410 *Supervolute* (supervolutiva). **1861** BENTLEY *Man. Bot.* 146 When a convolute leaf encloses another which is rolled up in a like manner,..the vernation is supervolute. **1880** A. GRAY *Struct. Bot.* iv. §2. (ed. 6) 139 In Convolvulus and Datura the narrow plaits in the flower-bud overlap one another in a convolute way, when they are said to be Supervolute.

So '**supervolutive** *a.* [ad. mod.L. *supervolūtīvus*, see above and -IVE], applied to vernation or æstivation in which the leaves or corolla-lobes are supervolute.

1866 *Treas. Bot.* 1111/1.

superweak: see SUPER- 9 a (*a*).

super'weening, *a. nonce-wd.* [Formed by substitution of prefix SUPER- for OVER-.] = OVERWEENING.

1862 LYTTON *Str. Story* xli, The insane have..no attribute more in common than that of superweening self-esteem.

superwoman: see SUPER- 6 c.

superyse, variant of SUPPRISE *Obs.*

†**supet.** *Obs. rare*⁻¹. [app. f. SUP *v.*¹ + -ET¹. Cf. *sippet, soppet*.] = SUPPING *vbl. sb.*¹ 2.

1382 WYCLIF *2 Sam.* xiii. 8 The which takynge meele mengide togidir, and meltynge in his eyen she sethide the supettis [1388 soupyngis].

†**supeter.** *Obs. rare*⁻⁰.

1611 COTGR., *Sollerets*, supeters; foot-peeces of Armour; Armor for the feet. [**1680** HARFORD tr. *Gaya's Traité*.]

suphrosyne: see SOPHROSYNE.

supinate ('s(j)u:pɪneɪt), *v. Physiol.* [f. L. *supīnāt-*, pa. ppl. stem of *supīnāre*, f. *supīnus* SUPINE *a.*] *trans.* To turn (the hand or fore limb) so that the back of it is downward or backward; also, to turn (the leg) outwards. Opposed to PRONATE.

1831 R. KNOX *Cloquet's Anat.* 322 When the hand is in pronation, this muscle supinates it. **1836–9** *Todd's Cycl. Anat.* II. 73/2 The hand was supinated. **1849–52** *Ibid.* IV. 1517/1 The patient is unwilling to pronate or supinate his hand. **1855** HOLDEN *Hum. Osteol.* (1878) 152 The biceps can supinate, as well as bend the fore arm.

supination (s(j)u:pɪ'neɪʃən). [ad. L. *supīnātio, -ōnem*, n. of action f. *supīnāre*: see prec. and -ATION. Cf. F. *supination*, It. *supinazione*, etc.

There is no evidence in support of Johnson's def. 'the act of lying with the face upward'.]

Physiol. The action of turning the hand or fore limb so that the back of it is downward or backward; the position of a limb so turned. Opposed to PRONATION. Also *attrib.*

1666 J. SMITH *Old Age* (1676) 62 They [*sc.* the muscles] can perform..flexion, extension; pronation, supination, the Tonick motion, circumgiration. **1745** *Phil. Trans.* XLIII. 296 A gummatous Swelling upon the upper Head of the Radius on the right Arm, checking the Motion of this Bone in Pronation and Supination. **1835–6** *Todd's Cycl. Anat.* I. 286/1 Bones..so articulated together..as to admit of scarcely any degree of..supination. **1872** HUXLEY *Phys.* vii. 171 When the palm is turned upwards the attitude is called supination. **1887** D. MAGUIRE *Art Massage* iv. (ed. 4) 59 He [*sc.* the masseur] does not use pronation or supination movements till after he has massed the forearm and the articulations of the elbow.

b. *Fencing.* (see quots.)

1805 A. GORDON *Treat. Sci. Defence* 17 Then project the thrust, rolling your hand still more in quarte, or supination. **1890** A. HUTTON *Fixed Bayonets* 152 Gloss., *Supination*, the position of the sword-hand with the nails upwards.

supi,nato-ex'tensor, *a. Anat.* [f. *supinato-* (used as combining form of L. *supīnātus* supinated, in sense of SUPINATOR) + EXTENSOR.] Applied to the mass of supinator and extensor muscles of the fore or hind limb, or their action.

1872 HUMPHRY *Myology* 28 The muscles on the dorsal aspect of the leg and foot form a supinato-extensor mass. *Ibid.* 169 The fibres on the dorsal aspect, having a supinato-extensor action, take a similar direction.

supinator ('s(j)u:pɪneɪtə(r)). *Anat.* [mod.L., f. *supīnāt-*, *supīnāre* to SUPINATE: see -OR. Cf. F. *supinateur* (16th c.).] A muscle by which supination is effected or assisted; *spec.* one of two muscles of the fore-arm or fore limb, *supinator radii brevis* and *supinator radii longus.*

1615 CROOKE *Body of Man* 783 The second supinator which is the shorter..ariseth fleshy. **1770** PENNANT in *Phil. Trans.* LX. 323 The tendinous muscles..have much the same effect on the tail as the supinator and pronators have in turning the hand. **1808** BARCLAY *Muscular Motions* 389 In rolling the arm, the rotators radiad co-operate with the muscles called supinators. **1872** HUMPHRY *Myology* 42 In the dorsal aspect, the short or deep extensor is connected only with the lower edge of the supinator.

attrib. **1826** KIRBY & SP. *Entomol.* xliii. IV. 172 Insects..cannot have the Supinator and Pronator muscles. **1875** *Encycl. Brit.* I. 839/1 The supinator and pronator muscles are all inserted into the radius.

supine ('s(j)u:paɪn), *sb. Gram.* Also 6 supyne, -in. [ad. L. *supīnum*, neut. sing. (sc. *verbum* word) of *supīnus* (see next): cf. F. *supin*. The word was applied by Roman grammarians to the gerund as well as the supine.] In Latin grammar, applied to forms of a verbal noun, the one an accusative singular ending in *-tum* or *-sum*, used with verbs of motion and called the ***first*** or †***former supine***, the other a locative singular ending in *-tū* or *-sū* (varying in early times with a dative singular in *-tuī*, *-suī*), used with adjectives and called the ***second*** or †***latter supine***.

The term is applied by some grammarians to the English infinitive with *to* (OE. *tó scéawienne*, mod. Eng. *to show*).

a **1522** LILY *Gram. Rudim.* in *Colet's Æditio* (1537) D iv, Ther cometh of a verbe deryuied a parte called a supine lyke the participle of the pretertens. These are .ii. The first endeth in *um*,..and his significacion is actiue... The seconde supine endeth in *u*..& his significacion is passiue [*Introd. Gram.* (1549) B iij, Called the fyrste supyne..called the later Supyne]. **1530** PALSGR. Introd. p. xxxvii, I set out all his rotes and tenses..as the latin grammariens have done the preterites and supines of suche verbes as..be of any diffycultye. **1665** R. JOHNSON *Scholars Guide* 1 Observe the Radix of words, and the Supines of Verbs, and they will direct to write right. *a* **1721** PRIOR *Dial. Dead, Chas. & Cl.* (1907) 216 Grammarians,..meer Traders in Gerunds and Retailers of Supines. **1831** SYD. SMITH *Wks.* (1859) II. 220/1 Schoolboys believe that Gerunds and Supines will be abolished, and that Currant Tarts must ultimately come down in price. **1854** ANDREWS & STODDARD *Lat. Gram.* 77 The supine in *um* is called the former supine; that in *u*, the latter. **1894** W. M. LINDSAY *Latin Lang.* §88 The 1st Supine is also found in Umbrian, e.g. *aseriato etu* 'observatum ito'. In the Romance languages the Supines have been lost. **1898** SWEET *New Engl. Gram.* §2314 Of the large number of verbs which take the infinitive in Old-English the greater number are now followed by the supine.

supine ('s(j)u:paɪn, formerly s(j)u:'paɪn), *a.* In 6 *Sc.* suppyne. [ad. L. *supīnus* (whence OF. *souvin*, Pr. *sobi(n)*, *supi(n)*, It., Sp., Pg. *supino*), f. Italic **sup-*, root of *super* above, *superus* higher: see -INE¹.]

1. Lying on one's back, lying with the face or front upward. Also said of the position. Often predicatively or quasi-advb.

Sometimes used loosely for 'lying, recumbent'.

c **1500** KENNEDY *Passion of Christ, At Cumplin Tyme* 1290 Apoun his bak he did ly on suppyne. **1615** CROOKE *Body of Man* 268 The position or manner of lying of the sickeman, eyther prone that is downeward, or supine that is vpward. **1646** SIR T. BROWNE *Pseud. Ep.* IV. vi. 193 That women drowned swim prone but men supine, or upon their backs, are popular affirmations, whereto we cannot assent. **1658** —— *Hydriot.* iv. 21 They buried their dead on their backs, or in a supine position. **1700** DRYDEN *Ceyx and Alcyone* 295 Where lay the God And slept supine, his Limbs display'd abroad. **1715** POPE *Iliad* IV. 603 Supine he tumbles on the crimson sands. *a* **1788** POTT *Chirurg. Wks.* II. 57 When the patient is in a supine posture. *a* **1806** H. K. WHITE '*Ye unseen Spirits*' 4 As by the wood-spring stretch'd supine he lies. **1876** *Trans. Clinical Soc.* IX. 72 Having placed the patient in the supine position. **1881** J. PAYN *Grape from Thorn* xi, The ancient Romans, taking their meals, as they did, supine, and resting on one elbow.

b. Of the hand or arm: With the palm upward; supinated.

1668 CULPEPPER & COLE *Barthol. Anat.* IV. viii. 165 The Radius makes the whole Arm prone or supine. **1865** TYLOR *Early Hist. Man.* iii. 48 The rustic Phidyle should hold out her supine hands. **1868** LIVINGSTONE *Last Jrnls.* 15 Nov. (1873) I. 346 The Africans all beckon with the hand, to call a person, in a different way from what Europeans do. The hand is held, as surgeons say, prone, or palm down, while we beckon with the hand held supine, or palm up.

c. (*a*) Of a part of the body: Situated so as to be upward; upper, superior.

1661 LOVELL *Hist. Anim. & Min.* b 5, Their finns are foure, two in the prone part, two in the supine, & circumvallate round. *Ibid.*, The eyes [of fishes] are in the supine part of their heads. **1826** KIRBY & SP. *Entomol.* xxxiv. III. 415, I have seen a fly turn its head completely round, so that the mouth became supine and the vertex prone. *Ibid.* xlvi. IV. 268 Supine Surface... The upper surface.

(*b*) *Bot.* See quot., and cf. PROCUMBENT *a.* 2.

1853 MACDONALD & ALLAN *Bot. Wordbk.* 32 *Supine*... The face of a leaf is called the supine disc.

d. *transf.* Sloping or inclining backwards. *poet.*

1697 DRYDEN *Virg. Georg.* II. 373 If the Vine On rising Ground be plac'd, or Hills supine, extend thy loose Battalions. **1817** SHELLEY *Rev. Islam* XII. xxi. 4 The prow and stern did curl, Horned on high, like the young moon supine.

2. *fig.* Morally or mentally inactive, inert, or indolent.

1603 [implied in SUPINELY 2]. **1621** BURTON *Anat. Mel.* II. i. IV. ii. 301 Through their..contempte, supine negligence, extenuation, wretchednes & peeuishnesse, they vndoe themselues. **1630** DONNE *Serm. Easter-day* (1640) 246 So also did they fall under the rebuke and increpation of the Angell for another supine inconsideration. **1650** SIR E. NICHOLAS in *N. Papers* (Camden) I. 198 The Pr. of Orange ..died..of the Small Pox thro' the supine negligence or worse of some of his Physicians. **1732** BERKELEY *Alciphr.* IV. §13 The lazy supine airs of a fine gentleman. **1761** HUME *Hist. Eng.* lv. (1806) IV. 225 They lived in the most supine security. **1779** BOSWELL *Let. to Johnson* 17 July, A supine indolence of mind. **1807** JEFFERSON *Writ.* (1830) IV. 72 The first ground of complaint was the supine inattention of the administration. **1819** SHELLEY *Cenci* IV. iv. 181 The supine slaves Of blind authority. **1852** THACKERAY *Esmond* I. v, He wakened up from the listless and supine life which he had been leading.

advb. **1615** G. SANDYS *Trav.* I. 36 So supine negligent are they.

†**b.** ***supine of***: indifferent to, negligent of. (Cf. LISTLESS *a.*) *Obs. rare.*

1724 WELTON *Chr. Faith & Pract.* 195 A profane..mind that is altogether supine of religion.

c. Not active; passive.

1843 RUSKIN *Mod. Paint.* II. v. iii. §21 The stream in their hands looks active, not supine, as if it leaped, not as if it fell. **1878** H. S. WILSON *Alpine Ascents* i. 11 In which the body is supine while the fancy remains active.

supinely (s(j)u:'paɪnlɪ), *adv.* [f. SUPINE *a.* + -LY².] In a supine position or manner.

1. On one's back. Also *transf.* of inanimate things. Chiefly *poet.*

1656 COWLEY *Anacreont.* ix. 2 Underneath this Myrtle shade, On flowry beds supinely laid. **1703** ROWE *Fair Penit.* Epil. 15 Who Snores at Night supinely by her Side. *c* **1706** PRIOR *Cantata* 3 Beneath a verdant Lawrel's ample Shade, ..Horace, immortal Bard, supinely laid. **1759** *Phil. Trans.* LI. 305 The patient being supinely placed upon a steady table,..I caused his hands and feet to be tied together. **1833** MRS. BROWNING *Prometh. Bound* 429 Now, he lies A helpless trunk supinely, at full length. **1871** R. ELLIS tr. *Catullus* xvii. 4 Lest it [*sc.* the bridge] plunge to the deep morass, there supinely to welter. *Ibid.* xxxii. 11 Here I languish alone, supinely dreaming.

2. With lack of exertion or attention; inertly, indolently; †passively.

1603 B. JONSON *Sejanus* II. ii. 382 If hee, for whom it is so strongly labour'd, Shall, out of greatnesse and free spirit, be Supinely negligent. **1647** CLARENDON *Hist. Reb.* III. §54 This doctrine..was most supinely and stupidly submitted to. **1681** DRYDEN *Span. Friar* III. iii, But when long try'd, and found supinely good, Like Æsop's Log, they leapt upon his Back. **1691** RAY *Creation* II. (1704) 296 Neither is the Aqueous Humor, as some may supinely imagine, altogether useless. **1725** DE FOE *Voy. round World* (1840) 301 The Spaniards..who are the most supinely negligent people in the world. **1749** SMOLLETT *Regic.* II. iv, Shall I, alas! Supinely savage, from my ears exclude The cries of youthful woe? **1781** COWPER *Hope* 198 If priest, supinely droning o'er his charge. **1830** HERSCHEL *Study Nat. Phil.* I. iii. §65. 74 Supinely and helplessly carried down the stream of events.

supineness (s(j)u:'paɪnnɪs). Also 7 supiness. [f. SUPINE *a.* + -NESS.]

1. Supine behaviour or state of mind; inertness.

1616 J. EARLE *On Mr. Beaumont* 55 Thy Workes..Nor with that dull supinenesse to be read, To passe a fire, or laugh an houre in bed. **1678** *Lively Oracles* Pref. §2 That irreligion, prepossession, and supiness which the pursuit of sensual plesures certainly produces. **1758** JOHNSON *Idler* No. 60 ¶ 12 He..wonders at the supineness with which their works have been hitherto perused. **1860** MILL *Repr. Govt.* ii. (1865) 11 All the negligences, indolences, and supinenesses of mankind. **1868** PEARD *Water-farm.* viii. 87 If through supineness, or over-confidence, the favorable opportunity is wasted. **1898** R. B. O'BRIEN *Life C. S. Parnell* ix. I. 195 The agitators acted with vigour and ability; the Government with supineness and stupidity.

2. 'Posture with the face upward' (J.). *rare*⁻⁰.

†**su'pinity.** *Obs.* [ad. L. *supīnitās*, f. *supīnus* SUPINE: see -ITY.]

1. = SUPINENESS 1.

1548 UDALL *Erasm. Par.* Pref. a vj b, To liue altogether in a carelesse supinitee. **1646** SIR T. BROWNE *Pseud. Ep.* I. viii. 34 Their relations falling generally upon credulous Readers, they meet with prepared beliefes, whose supinities had rather assent unto all, then adventure the triall of any. **1705** in *Pa. Hist. Soc. Mem.* X. 1 Coasts so ill guarded, by the supinity of the governors and captains of the frigates. **1728** MORGAN *Algiers* II. i. 218 Spanish Passiveness and Supinity. **1750** BEAWES *Lex Mercat.* Pref. (1752) p. vii, To remedy which, and to supply the Supinity of others.

b. Physical inactivity or sluggishness. *rare*⁻¹.

1725 *Fam. Dict.* s.v. *Dropsy*, When the Dropsy proceeds from the real Indisposition..of the Liver, it's known by.. Litherness or Supinity of the Belly.

2. = SUPINENESS 2. *rare.*

1638 JUNIUS *Paint. Ancients* 295 That the breast and belly be not so put forth as to bow the backe, seeing all supinitie is odious. **1755** in JOHNSON.

†**supire,** *v. Sc. Obs.* [a. OF. **supirer*, *sopirer*, var. *souspirer* to SUSPIRE.] *intr.* To sigh.

c **1590** BUREL *Pilgr.* I. in Watson *Coll. Sc. Poems* (1709) II. 34 Than softlie did I suoufe and sleep,..Svpyring, quhils wyring, My tender bodie to. *Ibid.* II. 48 My spreit supirs and sichs maist sair.

supje, variant of SOPIE.

suple, obs. form of SUPPLE, SUPPLY.

supota, obs. form of SAPOTA.

supowail, variant of SUPPOWELL. *Obs.*

supp (sʌp). Colloq. abbrev. of SUPPLEMENT *sb.*[1] 1 b. Usu. *colour supp.*
1968 *Punch* 6 Nov. 646/2, I don't want to..get myself interviewed in a colour-supp series. **1974** *Listener* 17 Jan. 95/1 To decorate a Mini outrageously for a colour supp. **1975** J. SYMONS *Three Pipe Problem* xv. 136, I read this *Observer* colour supp. piece, you see.

suppable (ˈsʌpəb(ə)l), *a. rare.* Now *Sc.* [f. SUP *v.*[1] + -ABLE.] That may be supped.
1483 *Cath. Angl.* 372/1 Suppabylle, *sorbulis, sorbabulis.* **1745** tr. *Columella's Husb.* VIII. xvii, Such victuals as are next to such as are supable, as new cheese, or curds out of the milk-pail. **1825** JAMIESON s.v., Thai kail ar sae saut they're no suppable.

†**ˈsuppage.** *Obs. rare*⁻¹. [f. SUP *v.*[1] + -AGE.] Used to represent Gr. ὄψον relish (Philo Περὶ βίου θεωρητικοῦ, ed. Mangey, p. 477).
1597 HOOKER *Eccl. Pol.* v. lxxii. §6 For foode they had bread, for suppage salt, & for sawce herbes.

†**suppalˈpation.** *Obs. rare.* [f. L. *suppalpāt-, suppalpārī*, f. *sup-* = SUB- 22 + *palpāre* to stroke, coax: see -ATION.] Coaxing, wheedling.
c **1625** BP. HALL *St. Paul's Combat* II. Wks. 1634 II. 450 Let neither buggs of feare, nor suppalpations of favour weaken your hands from laying load upon the beast of error. *a* **1656** —— *Serm. Ps. cvii. 34* Wks. 1662 III. 197 If plausible suppalpations, if restlesse importunities will hoyse thee, thou wilt mount.

†**supparasitate**, *v. Obs. rare.* [f. L. *supparasitāt-, supparasitārī*, f. *sup-* = SUB- 22 + *parasitārī* to play the parasite: see PARASITE and -ATE[3].] *intr.* To fawn, flatter. Hence †**supparasiˈtation**, fawning, flattery.
1623 COCKERAM, *Supperasitate*, to flatter one for a meales meat. **1623** BP. HALL *Best Bargaine* Wks. (1624) 518 At the last, a galling Truth shall haue more thanks, than a smoothing supparasitation. **1634** —— *Fall of Pride* Wks. II. 405 To serve the humors of the great, by grosse supparasitation. **1647** TRAPP *Marrow Gd. Authors* in *Comm. Ep.* 620 Godly men rather heed sound rebukes then smooth supparasitations.

†**suppart**, *v. Obs. rare.* [f. *sup-* = SUB- 9 (*a*) + PART *v.*] *trans.* To subdivide.
1620 T. GRANGER *Div. Logike* 307 Distribution.. deducteth that whole state..into his principall parts, supparting, or diuiding them.

suppawn, variant of SUPAWN.

†**suppeˈdaneous**, *a. Obs. rare.* [f. late L. *suppedāneus*: see next and -EOUS.] Placed under or supporting the feet; of the nature of a footstool, pedestal, or the like; also applied to a mountain lying at the foot of another.
1646 SIR T. BROWNE *Pseud. Ep.* v. xiii. 254 He had slender legs, but encreased them by riding after meales; that is, the humours descending upon their pendulosity, they having no support or suppedaneous stability. **1656** BLOUNT *Glossogr.*, *Suppedaneous*, belonging to a foot-stool, or anything that is set under the feet. **1659** H. L'ESTRANGE *Alliance Div. Off.* 263 Seeing it is suppedaneous, the Pedestal to support nobler truths. *a* **1711** KEN *Hymnotheo* VIII. Poet. Wks. 1721 III. 240 Hymnotheo..Strait to a suppedaneous Mountain went.

‖**suppedaneum** (sʌpɪˈdeɪnɪəm). [late L. *suppedāneum*, neut. sing. used subst. of *suppedāneus*, f. *sup-* = SUB- 1 a + *ped-, pēs* foot.] A support for the feet of a crucified person, projecting from the vertical shaft of the cross.
1863 LADY EASTLAKE in Mrs. Jameson *Hist. Our Lord* II. 142 His feet always separate, and with two nails upon the footboard, or *suppedaneum* (a Greek feature). **1887** J. R. ALLEN *Early Chr. Symbol.* 155 In some cases the feet of the Saviour are supported on a suppedaneum.

†**suppedit**, *v. Obs. rare.* Also 6 *Sc.* supedeit. [ad. med.L. *suppedītāre*: see SUPPEDITATE *v.*[2]] *trans.* To overthrow, subdue.
1483 CAXTON *Cato* f ij b, He may not be surmounted ne suppedyted or ouercomen of al the world. **1491** —— *Vitas Patrum* (W. de W. 1495) I. li. 106 b/2 By the helpe of god, he suppedyted and put vnder fote the deuyll. **1549** *Compl. Scot.* xv. 126 My impaciens suld be supportit be cause that the occasione of it hes suppedit my rason. *Ibid.* xix. 160 The gude exempil of ther gude conuersatione vald extinct and supedeit..al peruerst opinions.

†**suˈppedital.** *Obs. nonce-wd.* [Earlier SUBPEDITAL, f. SUB- 1 a + L. *ped-, pēs* foot, after *suppeditate.*] (See quot. and SUPPEDITARY.)
1596 HARINGTON *Anat. Metam. Ajax* L iij, At Oxford..I gat some quaynt phrases..as namely in steed of praying the Cobler to set two patches on my shoes, I could haue said, set me two semicircles vpon my suppeditals.

†**suˈppeditament.** *Obs. rare.* [ad. L. **suppeditāmentum*, f. L. *suppeditāre* SUPPEDITATE *v.*[1]: see -MENT.] *pl.* Supplies.
1599 R. LINCHE *Fount. Anc. Fiction* M ij, Fed and maintained by the increases, fruits, and suppeditaments thereof. **1661** FELTHAM *Resolves* II. xxi. (ed. 8) 227 Those brave Suppeditaments, that a great Estate allows them to do good withall.

†**suˈppeditary.** *Obs. nonce-wd.* = SUPPEDITAL.
1596 LODGE *Wits Miserie* 23 To the cobler he saith, set me two semicircles on my suppeditaries.

†**suˈppeditate**, *pa. pple. Obs.* [ad. med.L. *suppeditātus*, pa. pple. of *suppeditāre* SUPPEDITATE *v.*[2]] Subdued, overcome.
a **1548** HALL *Chron., Hen. VII*, 10 b, After that kyng Henry had thus..repressed & suppeditate the cyuile dissencion. *Ibid.* 41 b, After that tumult appeased & suppeditate, he would wᵗ all expedicion set vpon Scotland.

†**suˈppeditate**, *v.*[1] *Obs.* Also 7 -at. [f. L. *suppeditāt-*, pa. ppl. stem of *suppeditāre* intr. to be supplied, abound, trans. to supply in abundance.] *trans.* To furnish, supply.
1535 CRANMER *Let. to Crumwell* in *Misc. Writ.* (Parker Soc.) 314 There is not one article of those which I have drawn but would suppeditate sufficient occasion for a whole sermon. **1631** A. B. tr. *Lessius' De Prov. Num.* I. vii. 74 Great hils do suppeditate and minister matter for building, as stones, lyme, wood. **1657** W. MORICE *Coena quasi Κοινὴ* xi. 123 [It] will suppeditate an Argument for proof of this opinion. *a* **1693** *Urquhart's Rabelais* III. xxxi. 261 To suppeditate,..and supply him with store of Spirits. **1754** *Mem. G. Psalmanazar* Pref. 20 The same Divine Providence will suppeditate all the necessary helps.

†**suˈppeditate**, *v.*[2] *Obs. rare.* [f. med.L. *suppeditāt-*, pa. ppl. stem of *suppeditāre*, app. f. *sup-* = SUB- 1 a + L. *ped-, pēs* foot, with assimilation to prec.] *trans.* To overthrow, subdue.
[**1538**: see SUBPEDITATE.] *c* **1545** H. PARKER *Hyst. Massuctio* (Royal MS. 18 A. lxii. lf. 6) Ambicyouse..by batell to suppeditate and spoyle as well the as all thy famylye. *a* **1548** HALL *Chron., Edw. IV*, 248 A malle to destroye, and suppeditate high power and nobilitie. **1656** BLOUNT *Glossogr.*

suppeditation (sʌpɛdɪˈteɪʃən). Now *rare* or *Obs.* [ad. L. *suppeditātio, -ōnem*, n. of action f. *suppeditāre* SUPPEDITATE *v.*[1] Cf. CF. *suppeditation.*] The action of supplying what is needful; supply. In first quot., service, usefulness.
1605 BACON *Adv. Learn.* II. xxii. §4, I cannot sufficiently maruayle that this parte of knowledge..should bee omitted both in Morality and Policy, considering it is of so great Ministery, and Suppeditation to them both. **1652** SCLATER *Civ. Magistracy* (1653) 19 The Suppeditation of wholsom pastures and provisions. **1659** H. MORE *Immort. Soul* III. xiv. §9. 478 How nimble the Soule is to act upon the suppeditation of due Matter. **1884** BLACKMORE *Hist. Sir T. Upmore* II. 268 Prolonging his unjust tenure, by the suppeditation of heirs to his estate.
†**b.** A supplement. *Obs. rare.*
1639 SALTMARSHE *Policy* 219 A Suppeditation to the Former Policies. The Second Booke.

†**suˈppeditator.** *Obs. rare.* In 6 suped-. [f. L. *suppeditāt-, -āre* SUPPEDITATE *v.*[1]: see -ATOR.] One who supplies or furnishes.
1542 BECON *Pathw. Prayer* xxxvi. O viij, Yᵉ gyuer & supeditatour of so great good thinges.

†**suˈppeditor.** *Obs. rare.* [f. *sup-* = SUB- 1 a + L. *ped-, pēs* foot, with ending assimilated to prec. words.] A support.
1728 R. MORRIS *Ess. Anc. Archit.* 26 That single Spire, erected on so seemingly feeble Suppeditors.

suppen, suppende, variants of SHEPPEND *Obs.*

supper (ˈsʌpə(r)), *sb.*[1] Forms: see below. [a. OF. *soper, super*, (also mod.F.) *souper*, subst. use of vb. *souper* SUP *v.*[2]]
1. a. The last meal of the day; (contextually) the hour at which this is taken, supper-time; also, such a meal made the occasion of a social or festive gathering. Often without article, demonstrative, possessive, or the like, esp. when governed by a prep. (***to have supper; at, to, for, after supper***).
Formerly, the last of the three meals of the day (breakfast, dinner, and supper); now applied to the last substantial meal of the day when dinner is taken in the middle of the day, or to a late meal following an early evening dinner. Supper is usually a less formal meal than late dinner.
α. Examples with final stressing. Forms: 3 super(e, 3–5 soper, 4–5 sopere, soupere, (4 sopeer, -iere, sopper, 5 suppere, soupier, *Sc.* suppa(i)r, 8 *local Irish* seppear).
c **1275** *Passion our Lord* 90 in *O.E. Misc.* 40 Þo vre louerd wes isethe to his supere [*rime* ihere]. *c* **1290** *Beket* 1195 in *S. Eng. Leg.* I. 140 A-non after soper, Wel mildeliche he bad is oste for-to comen him ner. *c* **1305** *Land Cokayghe* 20 Þe met is trie, þe drink is clere, To none, russin, and sopper. **1338** R. BRUNNE *Chron.* (1810) 44 Alle was wele, tille euen after þe soupere He ȝede about, & plaied with þo þat were him nere. *c* **1386** CHAUCER *Frankl. T.* 461 He shewed hym er he wente to Sopeer, Forestes, Parkes, ful of wilde deer. *c* **1400** *Anturs of Arth.* xxvi, Dame Gaynour and alle, Went..To þe suppere [*rime* were]. **1425** *Ord. Whittington's Alms-house* in Entick *London* (1766) IV. 354 Both at meet and soupier. *a* **1430** *Stans Puer* 55 in *Babees Book* 31 At mete & at soper kepe þee stille & softe. **1463** *Bury Wills* (Camden) 21 He to prey for my soule at euery meel, mete or sopeer. *c* **1475** *Rauf Coilȝear* 223 The Coilȝear tald Mony sindrie taillis efter Suppair [*rime* bair]. **1788** VALLANCEY *Voc. Bargie* in *Trans. R. Irish Acad.* II. 33 *Seppear*, supper.

β. Examples with initial stressing. (But early prose instances are often ambiguous.) Forms: 3–6 soper, 4–6 souper, 5–6 soupper, sopper, (3–4, 7 super, 4 sopere, 5 sopar, sowper, *Sc.* souppar, 6 *Sc.* suppare), 5– supper.
c **1290** *S. Eng. Leg.* I. 225 Þe monekes wende to bedde & slepe, þo soper was ido. *c* **1300** *Havelok* 1762 Hauelok he gladlike under-stod..And dide greyþe a super riche. **13..** *E.E. Allit. P.* B. 829 Þenne seten þay at þe soper, wern serued by-lyue. **1382** WYCLIF *Luke* xiv. 24 Noone of tho men that ben clepid, schal taaste my souper. *c* **1386** CHAUCER *Prol.* 799 Which of yow that bereth hym best of alle..Shal haue a soper at oure aller cost. *c* **1400** *Rule St. Benet* (verse) 1583 Þat euer-ilkon wil of hir laue þe third part til hir sopper saue. *c* **1440** *Generydes* 141 Anon vpon ther soper was redy. *c* **1470** HENRY *Wallace* VIII. 1180 To souppar went, and tymysly thai slepe. **1470–85** MALORY *Arthur* I. xi. 50 They wente home and vnarmed them and so to euensonge and souper. **1483** *Cath. Angl.* 372/1 A Supper, *cena.* **1542** BOORDE *Dyetary* viii. (1870) 249 After your supper, make a pause or you go to bedde. **1561** WINȜET *Four Scoir Thre Quest.* xviii. Wks. (S.T.S.) I. 84 Quhy mak ȝe ȝour communioun afoir dennar, sen our Saluiour institutit His haly sacrament efter suppare? **1588** SHAKS. *L.L.L.* I. i. 240 When beasts most grase, birds best pecke, and men sit downe to that nourishment which is called supper. **1605** —— *Macb.* III. i. 25 Is't farre you ride? *Ban.* As farre, my Lord, as will fill vp the time 'Twixt this, and Supper. **1606** *Sir Gyles Goosecappe* I. i, Captaine Fowleweather,..whose valours within here at super with the Countes Eugenia. **1606** [see DINNER *sb.* 1]. **1620** VENNER *Via Recta* viii. 178 Our vsuall time..for supper..[is] about six. **1671** T. HUNT *Abeced. Scholast.* 13 After dinner sit a while, after supper walk a mile. **1707** HEARNE *Collect.* 29 Sept. (O.H.S.) II. 54 He would not have Act Suppers any more. **1766** GOLDSM. *Vicar W.* vi, He sat down to supper among us, and my wife was not sparing of her gooseberry-wine. **1853** KINGSLEY *Hypatia* xix, At last hunger sent him home to supper. **1889** *Harper's Mag.* Jan. 294/2 The photographing of evening parties, suppers, and weddings. **1905** R. BAGOT *Passport* x. 90 After a late dinner which was practically merely a supper.
b. *fig.* and *allusively.* Phr. †***to go to supper with the devil***, to go to hell: cf. SUP *v.*[2] 2.
13.. *E.E. Allit. P.* B. 107 Þyse ilk renkez þat me renayed habbe..Schul neuer sitte in my sale my soper to fele. **1382** WYCLIF *Rev.* xix. 9 Blessid thei, that ben clepid to the soper of weddingis of the lomb [**1611** the marriage supper of the Lambe]. *Ibid.* 17 Come ȝe, and be ȝe gederid to gydere to the greet soper of God. **1502** *Ord. Crysten Men* (W. de W.) v. vii, The dyner or the souper of paradyse. ? *a* **1533** FRITH *Antith.* (1829) 307 Notwithstanding it is to be feared that they go to supper with the devil. **1556** *Aurelio & Isab.* (1608) Pv, The Quene & the ladies put them againe together for to geve unto Affranio a verey bitter sopper. **1592** *Arden of Feversham* v. i. 188 But wherefore do you bring him hether now? You haue giuen me my supper with his sight. **1593** SHAKS. *3 Hen. VI*, v. v. 85 To London all in post, and as I guesse, To make a bloody Supper in the Tower. **1891** J. M. DIXON *Dict. Idiom. Eng. Phrases, To set one his supper*, to perform a feat that cannot be imitated or surpassed.
c. *U.S.* Tea: see quots.
1818 H. B. FEARON *Sk. Amer.* 44 A mechanic..has 3 meals a-day, coffee with fish or meat for breakfast; a hot dinner; and tea (called supper) in the evening. **1859** GOSSE *Lett. Alabama* 68 The meal which we are accustomed to call 'tea', is by Americans, universally, I believe, called 'supper', and it is the final meal; there being but three in the day. **1864** C. GEIKIE *Life in Woods* viii. (1874) 153, I chatted..till tea, or as they called it, supper.
2. *spec.* **a.** ***the Last Supper*** (***the Supper***, † ***his last supper***, † ***the holy supper***): the last meal taken by Jesus Christ with the apostles before his crucifixion, at which he instituted the Eucharist (see b). † ***Our Lord's Supper Day***, Maundy Thursday (*Cena Domini*).
[*a* **1300** *Cursor M.* 15281 Quen þis super was all don Iesus ras of his sette.] **13..** *Bonaventura's Medit.* 23 *heading*, Now of þe soper of oure lorde Ihesu. **1340** *Ayenb.* 133 Hueruore he zede to his apostles þe niȝt of þe sopiere, [etc.]. *c* **1375** *Sc. Leg. Saints* iii. (*Andreas*) 362 At his laste super sine sad he ..'ane of ȝou betrese me sall'. *c* **1421** *26 Pol. Poems* 104 Lyueliche quyk bred..Whyche in þe table of þe holy sopere, Wiþ-outen doute was ȝouen oure fay. *c* **1450** *Merlin* iii. 59 The place of Iudas, ther as he satte at the soper. *c* **1450** *Mirk's Festial* 125 Schere þursday..in holy chyrch hit is called our Lordys supperday. *a* **1536** *Songs, Carols*, etc. (1907) 35 Most best belovid & beste be-triste, Which at his last soper did lye on his breste. **1843** *Penny Cycl.* XXVI. 339/2 In 1497 he [*sc.* Leonardo da Vinci] commenced his celebrated painting of the Last Supper, on a wall of the refectory of the Dominican convent of the Madonna delle Grazie. **1913** G. EDMUNDSON *Ch. Rome First Cent.* vi. 152 It was after the Supper on the last night of the Lord's earthly life.
b. ***the Lord's Supper, the Supper of the Lord, the Dominical Supper, the Supper***: the Eucharist or Holy Communion.
(The short form, *the Supper*, has been favoured by extreme Protestants since the 16th century. Cf. *supper-sabbath* in 4.)
The source of this sense is 1 Cor. xi. 20, where the term is by many taken to include the agape and the Eucharist.
1382 WYCLIF *1 Cor.* xi. 20 Therfore ȝou comynge to gidere into oon, now it is not for to ete the Lordis sopere [*Dominicam caenam*, Κυριακὸν δεῖπνον]. **1533** TINDALE (*title*) The supper of the Lorde After the true meanyng of the Sixte of Iohn and the .xi of the fyrst Epistle to the Corhinthians,..incidently in the exposition of the supper: is confuted the letter of master More against Iohn Fryth. **1549** *Bk. Com. Prayer* (*heading*), The Svpper of the Lorde, and the holy Communion, commonly called the Masse. **1553** *Articles agreed on by Bishoppes* 1552 xxix, The Sacramente of the Lordes supper [L. *Sacramentum Eucharistiæ*]. **1560** DAUS tr. *Sleidane's Comm.* 335 b, An open disputation..concerning the Lordes supper, and the presence of Christ his body. **1560** BACON *New Catech.* Wks. 1564 I. 452 b, S. Ihon Chrisostom..hath these wordes. Forasmuch as it is the dominical supper, yᵗ is to say, the

lords, it ought to be common. **1588** *Art. agst. Cartwright* in Fuller *Ch. Hist.* IX. vii. §27 The Censures, and Keyes of the Church, as publick admonition, suspension from the Supper, and from execution of offices ecclesiastical. **1764** Maclaine tr. *Mosheim's Eccl. Hist.* I. iv. §7. (1833) 36/2 Of the bread and wine presented in these offerings, such a quantity was separated from the rest as was required in the administration of the Lord's supper. **1854** H. MILLER *Sch. & Schm.* xxiv. (1858) 533 The sacrament of the Supper is celebrated in most of the parish churches of the north of Scotland only once a year. **1861** W. L. ALEXANDER tr. *Dorner's Person of Christ* I. i. §3. 167 We shall..not say too much if we designate the Supper the climax of the ancient Christian worship. **1878** T. L. CUYLER *Pointed Papers* 148 The Lord's Supper is the monument of the Atonement. **1908** *Expositor* May 423 Baptism and the Supper are perpetually present in the Church.

†**3.** *pl.* Short for *supper-plates. Obs. rare.*

1787 in H. Owen *Two Cent. Ceramic Art Bristol* (1873) 348, 6 doz. Table Plates,..4 doz. Soups,..3 doz. Suppers.

4. *attrib.* and *Comb.*, as ***supper-bell, -board, -box*** (BOX *sb.*[2] 9), ***-dish, -fruit, -hour, -light, -meal, -money, -parlour, -room, -sherry, -table, -things*** (THING *sb.*[1] 12 d), ***-tray***; objective, as ***supper-eater, -lover***; also **supper-bar**, a bar or counter at which suppers are served in a tavern, etc.; †**supper-bed** = *supper-couch*; **supper club**, a restaurant serving suppers and usu. providing entertainment; †**supper-couch**, a couch for reclining on at meals; **supper dance**, (*a*) a dance after which the man escorts his partner into supper; (*b*) a dancing party at which supper is served; **supper house**, an establishment which supplies suppers after the closing of the theatres; **supper-party**, a party assembled at supper, a social gathering of this kind; **supper-quadrille**, the quadrille danced just before supper; **supper-room**, a room in which supper is served; also = *supper-house*; †**supper-sabbath**, a Communion Sunday; **supper-tavern** = *supper-house*; †**supper-while** = SUPPER-TIME.

1881 *Instr. Census Clerks* (1885) 61 Oyster Room, *Supper Bar, Restaurant Keeper. *a* **1661** HOLYDAY *Juvenal* (1673) 215 *Supper-beds,..Whose Brass-Front shew'd an Asse's vile head Crown'd. [*note* p. 222 In the ancient and innocent times, saies the Poet, they did not adorn their *supper-couches with pearls and curious shells.] **1770** P. V. FITHIAN *Let.* 30 Nov. in *Jrnl. & Lett.* (1900) I. 9 About seven the *supper Bell rings. **1825** T. HOOK *Sayings* Ser. II. *Passion & Princ.* v, The boys' supper-bell resounded in the hall. **1940** W. FAULKNER *Hamlet* I. iii. 77 Walking on toward the brazen sound of Mrs. Littlejohn's supper-bell. **1918** G. FRANKAU *One of Them* xx. 154 Gay with a thousand *supper-boards, whose drink Was poured to rag-time tunes by Herman Finck. **1836-7** DICKENS *Sk. Boz, Scenes* xiv, A numerous assemblage of ladies and gentlemen..had rushed from their half-emptied stout mugs in the *supper boxes. **1927** H. CRANE *Let.* 19 Dec. (1965) 313, I don't think I'll dare attend that *supper club again. **1977** *New Yorker* 8 Aug. 66/3 Only after a time of heading a hotel and supper-club trio did he turn his hand to composing and arranging. **1885** F. C. BAYLOR *On Both Sides* 64 'A *supper-dance, then,' he stupidly insisted. **1928** 'BRENT OF BIN BIN' *Up Country* xvi. 284 Thank heaven, here was the supper dance for which he was committed to good old Mrs Mac. **1948** M. LASKI *Tory Heaven* viii. 110 'May I have the supper-dance?' he had said to Penelope. **1979** S. SMITH *Survivor* xxvii. 253 The Christmas Eve supper dance was one of the biggest nights of the year in [hospital] sp9. **1888** DOUGHTY *Trav. Arabia Deserta* I. xxii. 594 A *supper-dish was set before me of mutton and temmn. **1799** MALTHUS *Diary* 29 May (1966) 37 We told him that we were no *supper eaters. **1888** J. PAYN *Myst. Mirbridge* xxiii, Supper-eaters do not live long. **1667** MILTON *P.L.* IV. 331 To thir *Supper Fruits they fell. **1814** JANE AUSTEN *Mansfield Park* II. x. 227 Previous inquiries..about the *supper-hour. *a* **1843** SOUTHEY *Comm.-pl. Bk.* (1849) 557 Eight—the supper hour [*temp.* Charles II]. **1855** TROLLOPE *Warden* xvi. 265 It was a London *supper-house. *a* **1860** ALB. SMITH *Med. Student* (1861) 17 Ruddy chops and steaks are temptingly displayed in the windows of the supper-houses. **1537** *N. Country Wills* (Surtees) 148 Three candelstickes for *soper lightes wrethid. **1829** LYTTON *Disowned* xvi, Miserable *supper-lovers that we are. **1823** SCOTT *Quentin D.* xx, Durward..assigned his former pretext of a headach for not joining the household of the Bishop at the *supper-meal. **1598** R. BERNARD tr. *Terence, Heautontim.* IV. ii, I will conuey into my fingers againe that *supper money that would so faine be gone. **1726** LEONI *Alberti's Archit.* I. 103/2 Baths and *supper Parlours..shou'd be towards the West. **1808** *Monthly Pantheon* I. 684/2 The more gay and fashionable may go to balls or *supper parties. **1822** T. MITCHELL *Com. Aristoph.* II. 75 The conviviality of the Athenians made the torch a very necessary appendage to their supper-parties. **1848** THACKERAY *Van. Fair* liv, He had been at a fast supper-party given the night before. **1835** MARRYAT *Olla Podr.* (1840) III. 131 Just before the *supper-quadrille,..a loud noise below..was heard. *a* **1661** HOLYDAY *Juvenal* (1673) 88/1 Dempster..takes *agger* for some eminent place in the *triclinium*, or *supper-room. **1794** MRS. RADCLIFFE *Myst. Udolpho* xliv, They now returned to the supper-room. **1842** LOVER *Handy Andy* xxi, The laughter of the supper-room, and the inviting clatter of its knives and forks were ringing in his ear. **1858** SIMMONDS *Dict. Trade, Supper-rooms*, shell-fish shops and taverns in London, where suppers and refreshments can be had, after public amusements are terminated. **1902** VIOLET JACOB *Sheep-Stealers* x, The brothers..were watching a quadrille from the door of the supper-room. **1690** C. NESSE *Hist. & Myst. O. & N. Test.* I. 38 Upon the *supper-sabbaths whereon we all eat the same spiritual meat. **1863** TREVELYAN *Compet. Wallah* (1866) 233 A four hours' lounge in a back drawing-room, sweetened by fine *supper-sherry at twenty-eight and six. **1781** R. F. GREVILLE *Diary* 6 Aug. (1930) 12 At this time the distribution of the *Supper Tables was mentioned to Him. **1794** MRS. RADCLIFFE *Myst. Udolpho* lvi, Round the supper-table appeared a group of faces smiling with felicity. **1862** MISS BRADDON *Lady Audley* xxxviii, In one of the principal hotels..sitting at a neatly-ordered supper-table. *a* **1860** ALB. SMITH *Med. Student* (1861) 41 The Toms, Charleses, and Henrys of the *supper-taverns. *c* **1825** MRS. SHERWOOD *Penny Tract* 10 She was putting away the *supper-things. **1847** C. BRONTË *Jane Eyre* I. v. 74 Monitors, fetch the *supper-trays! **1854** MRS. GASKELL *North & S.* xvi, The wardrobe shelf with handles, that served as a supper-tray on grand occasions! **1575** *Brieff Disc. Troub. Franckford* (1846) 63 He had spoken..in *supperwhile, certeine wordes tendinge to the slander off them and their ministery. **1609** W. M. *Man in Moone* (1849) 43 All supper while..he peereth..into the platters to picke out dainty morsels.

supper ('sʌpə(r)), *sb.*[2] [f. SUP *v.*[1] + -ER[1].]

a. One who sups or sips: chiefly with prefixed sb., as †***blood-supper*** = blood-sucker, ***kale-supper, wine-supper***. Also (*north. dial.*), a habitual drinker. **b.** The sucker of a pump.

1524, *a* **1563** [see BLOOD-SUPPER]. **1535** COVERDALE *Joel* i. 5 Wake vp ye dronckardes, & wepe: mourne all ye wyne suppers. **1611** FLORIO, *Sorbitore*, a sipper, a sooper, a swallower. **1611** COTGR., *Buvereau..*, a bibber, supper, or sipper; one that drinks little, and often. *Ibid.*, *Soupape*,..the Supper, or Sucker of a Pumpe. **1816** SCOTT *Antiq.* iv, Aiken was ane o' the kale-suppers o Fife.

'supper, *v.* [f. SUPPER *sb.*[1]]

1. *trans.* **a.** To give supper to, provide with supper; to entertain at supper; = SUP *v.*[2] 3 c.

1622 MABBE tr. *Aleman's Guzman d'Alf.* I. 108 Then did I supper my selfe vpon my bread. **1715** W. SHRIGLEY in *J. Byrom's Jrnl. & Lit. Rem.* (Chetham Soc.) I. 29 We intend to dinner him and supper him round, and by degrees make him our own. **1814** SCOTT *Wav.* lxiv, Winna ye be suppered like princes? **1839** HOOD *Ode St. Swithin* 74 They wish you on your own mud porridge supper'd. **1888** *Pall Mall Gaz.* 23 Apr. 11/1 They were 'suppered' under the presidency of Mr. Bailie Shearer on the Friday night.

b. To give (horses, cattle, etc.) their evening feed and bed them down for the night; also with *up*: cf. SUP *v.*[2] 3 a. Also *fig.* to give (a person) as much as he cares to have of something. Chiefly *Sc.* and *north. dial.*

1805 R. PARKINSON *Tour Amer.* 68 Going to look at the horses after what is called suppering them up at night. **1816** SCOTT *Old Mort.* xxxvii, I ken weel what belangs to suppering a horse. *Ibid.* xxxviii, The horse was properly suppered up. **1816** —— *Bl. Dwarf* xvii, A bonny breakfast the loons gae me the ither morning, and him at the bottom on't; and trow ye I wasna ready to supper him up? **1877** J. HATTON *Bitter Sweets* xx, Harkaway had been duly 'suppered up'. **1888** G. MACDONALD *Elect Lady* 133 Dawtie found Andrew in the stable, suppering his horses.

c. Of food: To serve for the supper of: = SUP *v.*[2] 3 b.

1818 SCOTT *Rob Roy* xxx, Walter Cuming of Guiyock, wha hadna as muckle o' him left thegither as would supper a messan-dog.

2. *intr.* To take one's supper; to sup.

1691 MEEKE *Diary* 27 Aug. (1874) 43 This night we cut down all our corn, and many persons suppered here. **1840** HALIBURTON *Letter Bag* i. 14, [I] Tea'd, suppered, champagned, tidied myself for bed, and I fear—snored. **1891** 'ANNIE THOMAS' *That Affair* III... 19 She has been suppering without intermission since Archie left her.

suppering ('sʌpərɪŋ), *vbl. sb.* [f. SUPPER *v.* + -ING[1].] The providing or eating of supper; the entertainment of guests at supper.

1740 RICHARDSON *Pamela* II. 62 The Breakfasting-time, the Preparations for Dinner,..and the Supperings, will fill up a great Part of the Day. **1784** R. BAGE *Barham Downs* I. 173 Such visiting and dressing, and dinnering, and suppering. **1827** HOOD *Lycus* 25 Once, at my suppering, I pluck'd in the dusk An apple.

b. The evening feeding of cattle, etc.; also with *up*. Also *concr.* the food given.

c **1818** CLARE *Summer Evening* 86 Far and near, the motley group Anxious claim their suppering-up. **1829** LOUDON *Encycl. Plants* (1836) 683 In Scotland..before the introduction of naked fallows and turnips, it [*Cuicus arvensis*] formed the *suppering* of housed cattle, during five or six weeks of every summer. **1899** CROCKETT *Kit Kennedy* 243 Kit must be back at Loch Spellanderie for the suppering of the horses.

supperless ('sʌpəlɪs), *a.* [f. SUPPER *sb.*[1] + -LESS.] Without supper.

1515 BARCLAY *Egloges* ii. (1570) B iv/1, I had leuer Cornix go supperlesse to bed. **1579** GOSSON *Sch. Abuse* (Arb.) 45 Their Wiues and Children cry out for bread, and go to bedde supperlesse ofte in the yeere. **1598** B. JONSON *Ev. Man in Hum.* III. iv, They'le keepe a man devoutly hungrie, all day, and at night send him supperlesse to bed. **1623** BINGHAM *Xenophon* 23 The most part of the Grecians were supperlesse, as also they wanted their dinner that day. **1728** POPE *Dunc.* I. 115 Swearing and supperless the Hero sate. **1822** T. L. PEACOCK *Maid Marian* iii, The baron had passed a supperless and sleepless night. **1866** MISS BRADDON *J. Haggard's Dau.* I. 72 If he had not supped with the minister he might have gone supperless to bed.

'supper-time. The time at which supper is taken.

1362 LANGL. *P. Pl.* A. VII. 250 Keep sum til soper tyme. *cc* **1400** *Destr. Troy* 3398 When yt seyit to Sopertyme he seruyt hir well With all daintes on dese & drynkes ynow. *c* **1420** *Sir Amadas* (Weber) 208 Sir Amadas was com and don lyght, And hit was soper tyme. **1518** H. WATSON *Hist. Oliver of Castile* (Roxb.) M 4, But bycause that the souper tyme approched..he abode not longe there. **1594** SHAKS. Rich. III, v. iii. 47 It's Supper time my Lord, it's nine a clocke. **1677** EARL ESSEX in *Essex Papers* (Camden) II. 134 It being neer supper time we went to supper. **1766** EARL MARCH in Jesse *Selwyn & Contemp.* (1843) II. 17 The letters come here generally about supper-time. **1848** THACKERAY *Van. Fair* li, The greatest triumph of all was at supper-time. She was placed at the grand exclusive table with His Royal Highness. **1902** VIOLET JACOB *Sheep-Stealers* xiv, She yawned, and wondered what she could do to amuse herself until supper-time.

attrib. **1580** TUSSER *Husb.* (1878) 178 *marg.*, Supper time huswiferie.

†**'supperward.** *Obs.* [f. SUPPER *sb.*[1]: see -WARD.] ***to supperward***: to supper; at or about supper-time. Also as *adv.* (*U.S. rare*) = SUPPERWARDS *adv.*

c **1563** *Jack Juggler* 221 She vseth for hir bodylie helth, and safegard To chyd daylie oone fite, too supperward. **1608** GOLDING *Epit. Frossard* I. 15 The English Captaine..in an euening, when the French men were to supperward, brake suddainelie out of a wood. **1932** W. FAULKNER *Light in August* xv. 330 The townspeople began to move supperward.

So **'supperwards** *adv. rare*, to supper.

1887 *Field* 19 Feb. 251/3 Again resuming our way, we proceeded supperwards. **1897** *Animal World* (R.S.P.C.A.) XXVIII. 75/1 The moon's silvery beams, dancing on the waters, warned me to be hastening supperwards.

supping ('sʌpɪŋ), *vbl. sb.*[1] [f. SUP *v.*[1] + -ING[1].]

1. The action of SUP *v.*[1]; drinking by spoonfuls or mouthfuls; †an instance of this, a sup. Also, swallowing up, absorption.

c **1400** tr. *Secr. Secr., Gov. Lordsh.* 81 At morwyn fastyng, to take a soupyng of venegre. *c* **1440** *Promp. Parv.* 466/2 Sowpynge, *sorbicio*. *Ibid.*, Suppynge al vp, or al owte, *absorbicio*. **1591** PERCIVALL *Sp. Dict.*, *Sorvo*, supping vp, *sorbitio*. **1611** FLORIO, *Sorbitione*, a sooping or sipping vp. [**1611** *Bible* Hab. i. 9 Their faces shall sup vp [*marg.* Heb. the supping vp of their faces] as the East winde.]

†**b.** *attrib.*, as ***supping draught***; ***supping meat***, = 2; ***supping medicine***, potable medicine. *Obs.*

1382 WYCLIF *John* xxi. 5 Therfore Ihesu seith to hem, Children, wher ȝe han ony soupynge thing [Vulg. *pulmentarium*]? **1388** —— *2 Sam.* xiii. 8 Sche took mele, and medlide, and made moist bifor hise iȝen, and sethide soupyngis [*v.r.* soupinge metis]. *c* **1400** *Lanfranc's Cirurg.* 225 Make herof a souping medicyn, þat it be as þicke as hony. *c* **1440** *Promp. Parv.* 466/2 Sowpynge mete, or drynke. **1598** FLORIO, *Sorbitello*, a sip or supping draught. **1611** *Ibid.*, *Sorbetto*,..any kind of thin supping broth. **1614** W. B. *Philos. Banq.* (ed. 2) 26 Wee must abstaine from those *Sorbilia*, supping meates. **1651** WITTIE tr. *Primrose's Pop. Err.* III. v. 147 Hippocrates..perswades to nourish the sick with supping meats, rather than with solid meats.

2. Chiefly *pl.* Food (*sing.* a food) that can be supped; liquid food, spoon-meat; *esp.* broth. Now *dial.*

1388 WYCLIF *2 Sam.* xiii. 6 Y biseche, come Thamar, my sistir, that sche make twei soupyngis [1382 two maner of potagis; Vulg. *sorbitiunculas*] bifor my iȝen. **1470-85** MALORY *Arthur* IX. xxi. 370 They bathed hym and wasshed hym and gaf hym hote suppynges til they had brought hym wel to his remembraunce. **1510** STANBRIDGE *Vocabula* (W. de W.) B iij, *Sorbitiuncula*, a suppynge. **1542** BOORDE *Dyetary* xxxvii. (1870) 299 Let them haue .iii. tymes in a daye warme suppynges. **1561** HOLLYBUSH *Hom. Apoth.* 4 Geue him a good broth of a pollet or chycken, or els a supping of yong beafe or veele. **1601** HOLLAND *Pliny* XXII. xxiv. II. 137 Wax taken inwardly in a supping or broth. **1651** FRENCH *Distill.* v. 142 You must give the patient some warme suppings all the time this medicine is working. **1668** CULPEPPER & COLE *Barthol. Anat.* Man. IV. xii. 348 Such as have lost their teeth are fain to content themselves with suppings. **1754-64** SMELLIE *Midwif.* III. 77, I directed some Thebaick drops..with warm suppings. *a* **1825** FORBY *Voc. E. Anglia, Soupings*, any sort of spoon-meat. **1879** MISS JACKSON *Shropsh. Word-bk.*, *Supping*, spoon-meat of any kind, but more especially milk and water boiled and thickened with oatmeal... Calves' supping is food that they can *suck up* made with linseed..in milk and water.

supping ('sʌpɪŋ), *vbl. sb.*[2] [f. SUP *v.*[2] + -ING[1].] The action of taking supper.

a **1400-50** *Wars Alex.* 4439 Ȝoure soure sowping in vnseson, ȝoure surfete of drinkis. *c* **1440** *Promp. Parv.* 484/2 Suppynge, *cenacio, cenatus*. **1620** VENNER *Via Recta* viii. 179 This order of supping being obserued, there will remaine a competent time..before they goe to bed,..for the meats..to concoct. *a* **1721** PRIOR *Dial. Dead, Locke & Montaigne* (1907) 244, I may find what will dress a Supper, but nothing else to the present purpose of my own Supping. **1798** S. & HT. LEE *Canterb. T.* II. 187 Nor would he excuse the party from supping *al fresco* in his gardens. **1891** *Daily News* 6 Mar. 5/3 The public 'suppings' still prevail at Christ's Hospital.

b. *attrib.*, as ***supping-day, -parlour, -place, -room***.

c **1450** in Aungier *Syon* (1840) 372 On *suppynge dayes they may take an egge or two, or any other thynge ordeyned for them by the officers. **1552** HULOET, *Suppyng parlour or place, *cœnatio*. **13..** *Bonaventura's Medit.* 160 To þe *sopyng place aȝen þan þey come. **1382** WYCLIF *Mark* xiv. 15 And he schal shewe to ȝou a greet souping place strewid. **1483** *Cath. Angl.* 350/1 A Sowpynge place, *cenaculum, cenatorium*. **1534** MORE *Treat. Passion* Wks. 1307/1 He shal shewe you a great supping place paued. *a* **1633** AUSTIN *Medit.* (1635) 148 A private *Supping-roome.

'supping, *ppl. a.* [f. SUP *v.*[2] + -ING[2].] Taking supper.

c **1885** MASSON *Mem. London in 'Forties* i. (1908) 32 An elderly gentleman..seemed to take a benevolent interest in all the supping groups.

supplace (sə'pleɪs), *v. rare.* [Formed by the substitution of *place* for the second syllable of SUPPLANT, after *replace.*] *trans.* To take the place of, supersede.

1861 G. MUSGRAVE *By-Roads* 20 A little chapel..was supplaced by a church of large dimensions. **1867** —— *Nooks & Corners Old France* I. 352 Supplaced by a broad sheet of plate glass.

†**su'pplant,** *sb. Obs. rare.* [f. next.] = SUPPLANTATION.

1390 GOWER *Conf.* I. 239 Supplant with his slyhe cast Fulofte happneth forto mowe Thing which an other man hath sowe. *Ibid.* 258 This Bonefas, which can noght hyde The tricherie of his Supplant.

supplant (sə'plɑːnt, -æ-), *v.* Also 4–5 supplaunt(e, 4–7 -plante, 7 suplant. See also SUBPLANT. [a. OF. *supplanter* (= It. *soppiantare*, Sp. *suplantar*, Pg. *supplantar*), or ad. L. *supplantāre* to trip up, overthrow, f. *sup-* = SUB- 26 + *planta* sole of the foot, PLANT *sb.*[2]]

†**1.** *trans.* To trip up, cause to stumble or fall by tripping. *Obs. rare.*

a **1340** HAMPOLE *Psalter* xxxvi. 33 [xxxvii. 31] His gangyngis sall not be supplantid [Vulg. *non supplantabuntur gressus eius*]. *Ibid.* cxxxix. [cxl.] 5 þe whilke thoght forto supplant my gatis. **1604** R. CAWDREY *Table Alph.*, *Supplant*, to trip, or ouerthrowe with the feet. **1667** MILTON *P.L.* x. 513 His Armes clung to his Ribs, his Leggs entwining Each other, till supplanted down he fell A monstrous Serpent.

b. To throw down, overturn. *rare.*

1831 CARLYLE *Sart. Res.* I. v, He..has to straddle out his legs, lest the very wind supplant him.

†**2.** *fig.* To cause to fall from a position of power, superiority, or virtue; to cause the downfall of, bring low. *Obs.*

a **1340** HAMPOLE *Psalter* xvi. 14 [xvii. 13] Rise lord, bifor cum him and supplant him. **1445** in *Anglia* XXVIII. 269 Lechery the dowsett syn..coude nat the supplante. **1447** BOKENHAM *Seyntys* (Roxb.) 46 Oure lord jhesu Supplanted the devyl oure ruggyd enmy. **1522** MORE *De quat. Noviss.* Wks. 85/1 He set vpon our fyrst parentes in paradyse, and by pride supplanted them. *c* **1610** *Women Saints* 81 The diuell enuying these her vertuous studies, thought to supplant her. **1629** MASSINGER *Picture* II. ii, To suplant her ile imploy.. Two noted courtiers of approued cunning In all the windings of lusts labirinthe. **1780** COWPER *Progr. Err.* 59 Nor these alone..Seek to supplant his inexperienc'd youth.

†**b.** To bring to nought, upset (a design, etc.).

1382 WYCLIF *Job* viii. 3 Whether God supplauntith dom, and the Almyȝti turneth vpso doun, that is riȝtwis? *a* **1677** BARROW *Serm. Rom. xi. 33* Wks. 1686 III. 257 Doth it not supplant his own designs, and unravel all that he for so many ages hath been doing?

3. To dispossess and take the place of (another), esp. by treacherous or dishonourable means. Also *absol.* †Const. *of* or *from* (a possession).

a **1300** [implied in SUPPLANTER 1]. **1382** WYCLIF *Jer.* ix. 4 Eche brother supplauntende shal supplaunte, and eche frend gilendely shal go. **1390** GOWER *Conf.* I. 242 Agamenon Supplantede the worthi knyht Achilles of that swete wiht, Which named was Brexeida. *Ibid.* 243 Amphitrion him hath supplanted With sleyhte of love. *c* **1430** *Freemasonry* 203 Ther schal no mayster supplante other. *a* **1513** FABYAN *Chron.* VII. (1811) 436 Lest he for his synguler auauntage wolde supplant hym of that eldam. **1529** in *Vicary's Anat.* (1888) App. xiv. 256 *marg.*, No man to supplant Another yn taking from hym his Cure. **1610** SHAKS. *Temp.* III. iii. 70 You three From Millaine did supplant good Prospero. **1656** in *Verney Mem.* (1907) II. 4. I am not without fear that you may supplant me in hir favor. **1731** BP. T. WILSON in Keble *Life* (1863) xxii. 759 He most unworthily supplanted and turned out the worthy Curate.. out of his own cure of souls. **1838** LYTTON *Calderon* i. 63 It became the object of his life to supplant his father. **1858** LONGF. *M. Standish* IV. 76 You have betrayed me! Me, Miles Standish, your friend! have supplanted, defrauded, betrayed me!

b. *transf.* (Cf. 6.)

1398 TREVISA *Barth. De P.R.* xvii. clxxvii[i]. (Bodl. MS.) lf. 234 b/1 þe left þ[t] is wiþ þe grape schal not be remeued.. but þe oþer leues þat beþ ferre, for þese leues scholde supplante þe grapes.

†**c.** To get or take by supplantation. *Obs. rare.*

1484 CAXTON *Curiall* 4 b, And after..another newe one cometh to the court and shal supplante thy benediction.

†**4.** To take up by the roots; to root out, uproot (a plant or something likened thereto). Often in fig. context in association with PLANT *sb.*[1] or PLANT *v. Obs.*

1570–6 LAMBARDE *Peramb. Kent* (1826) 238 The Normans ..laboured by all means to supplant the English [language], and to plant their owne language amongst us. **1582** STANYHURST *Æneis* III. (Arb.) 71 The tre supplanted, that first fro the roote seat is haled. **1588** SHAKS. *Tit. A.* I. i. 447 Dissemble all your griefes and discontents, You are but newly planted in your Throne, Least then the people.. supplant vs for ingratitude. **1610** —— *Temp.* III. ii. 56 Trinculo, if you trouble him any more in's tale, By this hand, I will supplant some of your teeth. **1624** DARCIE *Birth of Heresies* To Rdr., Weedes, the which if they be not carefully and dayly supplanted, will soone ouergrow the good plants. **1631** R. BOLTON *Comf. Affl. Consc.* xv. (1635) 79 Like a staffe stucke lightly in the ground, which every.. blast of wind [may] supplant, and overthrow. **1644** QUARLES *Barnabas & B.* 326 Foxes destroy it [*sc.* a vineyard], and the wild boar supplants it.

5. To remove from its position, get rid of, oust; occas. to replace or supersede *by* something else. Now *rare.*

1576 FLEMING *Panopl. Epist.* 67, I suppose that al your sorrow cannot with such facilitie be supplanted, but that a few sparkles wil remaine. **1603** OWEN *Pembrokeshire* ii. (1892) 37 The Conqueror haueinge purpose to Supplante the Englishe nation out of England. **1604** DRAYTON *Owle* 614 Supplant the Alpes, and lay them smooth and plaine. **1624** CAPT. J. SMITH *Virginia* IV. 106 This in ten daies more, would haue supplanted vs all with death. **1784** COWPER *Task* I. 609 War follow'd for revenge, or to supplant The envied tenants of some happier spot. **1819** EARL LAUDERDALE *Publ. Wealth* 347 The habits of a man possessed of small fortune..naturally suggest the desire of supplanting the labour he performs. **1862** SPENCER *First Princ.* I. v. §32. (1875) 117 To supplant them by higher ones ..is to set up vague and uninfluential motives for definite and influential ones.

6. Chiefly of things: To take the place of, succeed to the position of, supersede.

1671 TRENCHFIELD *Cap Gray Hairs* (1688) 18 'Tis no hard matter for the talk of Religion, to supplant the practice of it. **1789** MRS. PIOZZI *Journ. France* I. 34 These pantomimes will very soon supplant all poetry. **1828** D'ISRAELI *Chas. I*, II. xii. 311 The genius of commerce was fast supplanting that nobler spirit which had made them a nation. **1857** TOULMIN SMITH *Parish* 100 Fresh Churchwardens can sue those whom they have supplanted. **1871** FREEMAN *Norm. Conq.* IV. xvii. 93 The minster, which has been wholly supplanted by work of later date.

†**7.** (See quots.) *Obs.*

1601 HOLLAND *Pliny* XVII. xxiii. I. 537 Yet is there one manner besides of planting & maintaining Vines..: namely to supplant, that is, lay along upon the ground the whole stocke or maine bodie of a Vine. **1656** BLOUNT *Glossogr.*, *Supplant (supplanto, a sub et planto)*, to plant underneath, to under-plant and set up a thing bending to the ground.

Hence **su'pplanted** *ppl. a.*

1671 MILTON *P.R.* IV. 607 Now thou hast aveng'd Supplanted Adam. **1894** *Nature's Method in Evol. Life* iv. 55 Either..the supplanter is of a higher grade, or..the conditions of existence have become less favourable for the supplanted.

†**su'pplantal.** [-AL[1] 5.] = SUPPLANTING *vbl. sb.*

1891 *Harper's Mag.* June 69/1 The excitements of the day had..withdrawn his mind from..his fear of supplantal.

†**su'pplantarie.** *Obs. rare.* [f. SUPPLANT + *-arie* for -ERY.] Supplantation.

1390 GOWER *Conf.* I. 237 The fifte Which is conceived of Envie, And cleped is Supplantarie. *Ibid.* 241 Yit hadde I levere In my simplesce forto die, Than worche such Supplantarie.

supplantation (ˌsʌplɑːn'teɪʃən, -æ-). Also 5 subplant-. [a. OF. (mod.F.) *supplantation* (= It. *supplantazione*, Sp. *suplantacion*, Pg. *suppiantação*), ad. late L. *supplantātio*, *-ōnem*, n. of action f. *supplantāre* to SUPPLANT.]

1. The dispossession or displacement of a person in a position, esp. by dishonourable means.

1390 GOWER *Conf.* I. 258 The Mitre with the Diademe He hath thurgh Supplantacion. **1430–40** LYDG. *Bochas* III. iv. (MS. Bodl. 263) 155/2 Moordre doon for subplantacioun [*ed.* **1554** supplantacion] Requereth vengaunce. **1592** TIMME *Ten Engl. Lepers* E j, Jacob by supplantation attained to a blessing. **1600** W. WATSON *Decacordon* (1602) 266 No iealousies nor suspitions, no enuie nor supplantations. *a* **1631** DONNE *Serm.*, *1 Cor. xii. 3* (1640) 315 The sinister supplantations of pretenders to places in Court. *a* **1635** NAUNTON *Fragm. Reg.* (Arb.) 49 Those that he relyed on, began..to be sensible of their own supplantation, and to project his. **1646** OWEN *Country Ess.* Wks. 1851 VIII. 66 Tried and proved ineffectual for the supplantation of truth. **1654** WHITELOCKE *Jrnl. Swed. Emb.* (1772) II. 83 The.. losse of their trade in Muscovia, by supplantation of the Dutch. **1751** JOHNSON *Rambler* No. 103 ⁋13 No interest in view, and therefore no design of supplantation.

2. The supersession or displacement *of* one thing *by* another.

1608 HIERON *Defence* III. 122 If the sayd ordinance, after a supplantation or other decay therof, be agayne restored & reestablished. *c* **1819** COLERIDGE *Lit. Rem.* (1836) II. 123 A complete suppression and habitual supplantation of immediate selfishness. **1837** W. A. BUTLER *Serm.* Ser. II. xix. (1856) 283 That Church of perfect holiness shall be not the supplantation of the present, but its continuance.

†**3.** Overthrow, downfall. *Obs.*

1617 *French Jubile* 2 You display your greatnes, by the supplantation of a Tyrannie established in your State.

¶**4.** Illiterate or jocular for *supplication.*

1590 R. WILSON *Three Lords & Ladies Lond.* H iij, Read my supplantation and my suit yee shall know. **1593** LODGE *W. Longbeard* (Hunter. Club) 13 After the councell of some poore Cittizens, [the widow] put vppe a supplication or a supplantation (as the sillier sort of people called it).

supplanter (sə'plɑːntə(r), -æ-). [a. OF. *supplanteor* (mod.F. *supplanteur*), ad. late L. *supplantātōrem*, agent-n. f. *supplantāre* to SUPPLANT: see -ER[1].]

1. One who dispossesses or displaces another in his position, esp. by unworthy practices.

a **1300** *Cursor M.* 3744 Right-wisli es iacob his nam, þat es to sai..Supplanter als of heritage. **1390** GOWER *Conf.* I. 241 If thou understode..In loves cause what it doth, A man to ben a Supplantour. *c* **1614** FLETCHER, etc. *Wit at Sev. Weapons, Persons repr. in Play*, Cunningham, a discreet gen. Sir Gregories comrade and supplanter. **1691** BP. KEN *Let.* 7 June in Plumptre *Life* (1888) II. xx. 52 D[r] Kidder is now said to be my Successour or rather supplanter. **1703** W. HAMILTON *Life Bonnell* II. 167 He was rarely known to speak an Angry word against his Supplanter. **1841** LYTTON *Night & Morn.* I. iii, Those children are our disgrace and your supplanters. **1899** *Daily News* 25 July 6/1 When the prodigal has satisfied poetic justice, and retaliated by nearly killing his supplanter.

†**2.** One who causes the downfall or destruction of a person or thing; an overthrower. *Obs.*

a **1340** HAMPOLE *Psalter* xiii. 11 [xiv. 7] Iacob is als mykill at say as wrestlere or supplantere of syn. **1422** CAPGRAVE *Treat. Rule St. Aug.* in *Life* (1910) 145 So may our blessid fader Augustyn be cleped a supplanter of þe Deuel. **1672** W. DE BRITAINE *Dutch Usurp.* 33 The Hollanders are the great Supplanters of Trade, and obstructers of Commerce. *a* **1716** SOUTH *4th Serm. Isa. v. 20* (1727) VI. 109 A treacherous Supplanter and Underminer of the Peace of all Families and Societies.

3. A thing that displaces or supersedes another.

1865 *Sat. Rev.* 11 Nov. 622/1 Natural Provençal and natural Swabian, as distinguished from their high-polite supplanter. **1905** J. B. FIRTH *Highw. Derbyshire* xi. 172 The old road..is little more than half as long as its modern supplanter.

supplanting (sə'plɑːntɪŋ, -æ-), *vbl. sb.* [f. SUPPLANT *v.* + -ING[1].] The action of the verb SUPPLANT in various senses; supplantation.

a **1325** *Prose Psalter* xl. 10 [xli. 9] Hij þat eten min loues, herieden vp me supplauntynge oþer puttyng out. **1382** WYCLIF *Prov.* xi. 3 Supplaunting of peruertid men shal waste them. *c* **1440** LYDG. *Hors, Shepe & Goos* 604 in *Pol. Rel. & L. Poems* 40 Fals supplantyng, clymbyng vp of foolis, Vnto chaires of wordly dygnyte. **1633** P. FLETCHER *Purple Isl.* XII. lv, For to this end th' Almighty did him frame, And therefore from supplanting gave his ominous name. **1642** FULLER *Holy & Prof. St.* III. xvi. 194 Such a place will thrive the better..when new Colonies come not in with Extirpation of the Natives; for this is rather a Supplanting then a Planting. **1706** STANHOPE *Paraphr.* III. 511 We should be guilty of no Emulation, no Supplanting, no Injury to any other. **1717–18** HOADLY *Serm. 1 Cor. x. 11.* 20 Those Divisions and Supplantings that were among the King's own Friends. **1891** HARDY *Tess* xxiii, Such supplanting was to be.

supplantment (sə'plɑːntmənt, -æ-). *rare.* [f. SUPPLANT *v.* + -MENT.] = prec.

1912 *Blackw. Mag.* Nov. 653/1 The hussar and the lancer have no reason to regard their supplantment by flying corps as a dire calamity.

supple ('sup(ə)l), *sb. Sc.* and *north. dial.* Also **souple, suple, soople.** [app. var. of *swupple*, *swouple*, SWIPPLE, assimilated to *supple.*]

1. The part of a flail that strikes the grain in thrashing.

1634 (8 Dec.) *Rec. Baron Crt. Colstoun* (MS.), Unlawes Pa[k]. Nycolsone in eastmanis in 40*s.* for cutting and transporting tua soupellis furth of the lairds wode & geving tham to Pa[k]. Ormistoun, confest. **1701** LADY GRISELL BAILLIE *Househ. Bk.* (1911) 9 For 2 sives and 2 ridles 1 li. 10*s.* suples 8 *s.*.. I. 18. 0. For expence of selling 20 bolls oats, I. 6. 0. **1789** DAVIDSON *Seasons* 143 The scatter'd ears That frae the swingin supple spread afar. **1807** STAGG *Poems* 14 A lang flail souple full'd his neif. **1844** H. STEPHENS *Bk. Farm* III. 989 The flail consists of two parts, the hand-staff or helve..and the supple or beater. **1893–4** *Northumbld. Gloss.*, *Soople, Souple, Swipple*, the loose, swinging arm of a flail.

2. A cudgel.

1815 SCOTT *Guy M.* xxv, A gude oak souple in his hand. **1827** —— *Two Drovers* i, 'They had their broadswords, and I have this bit supple', shewing a formidable cudgel.

supple ('sʌp(ə)l), *a.* Forms: 3–7, 8–9 *Sc.* and *north. dial.* souple, (6 souble (?), soupil, *Sc.* soupill, sowpil, 6–7 suple, 7, 9 *Sc.* and *north. dial.* soople), 5– supple. [a. OF. *supple*, *sople*, (mod.F.) *souple*:—L. *supplicem*, *supplex* lit. 'bending under', hence, submissive, suppliant, f. *sup-* = SUB- 2 + *plic-*, root of *plicāre* to fold (cf. PLIANT).]

†**1.** Of soft or yielding consistency; not rigid; soft, tender. *Obs.*

1297 R. GLOUC. (Rolls) 4577 þoru hauberc & þoru is coler þat nere noþing souple He smot of is heued. *c* **1395** *Plowman's Tale* 58 Of sondry sedes that ben sewe; It semeth that som ben unsounde. For some be grete growen on grounde, Som ben souple [*ed.* **1542** souble], simple and small. *a* **1400** *Anc. Cookery* in *Househ. Ord.* (1790) 442 Take swynes lire, and sethe hit, and hewe hit smalle,.. ande make hit right souple.

2. a. That is easily bent or folded without breaking or cracking; pliant, flexible.

c **1386** CHAUCER *Prol.* 203 His bootes souple, his hors in greet estaat. *c* **1430** LYDG. *Min. Poems* (Percy Soc.) 201 Hire pylche souple. **1513** DOUGLAS *Æneis* XI. xiii. 7 The sowpill schaftis baldly sche On athir sydis thik sparpellis and leyt fle. **1583** *Leg. Bp. St. Androis* 749 This poysoned preicheor of Godis word Is not vnlyk ane suple suord. *a* **1586** SIDNEY *Arcadia* II. xi. (1912) 220 Her bellie..Like Alablaster faire and sleeke, But soft and supple satten like. **1657** R. LIGON *Barbadoes* 109 They will wash and not shrinke in the wetting, and weare very long and soople. **1697** DRYDEN *Virg. Georg.* III. 266 For his soft Neck, a supple Collar make Of bending Osiers. **1725** *Fam. Dict.* s.v. *Lentise*, Their Ends and middle Veins are reddish, supple, and gluey. **1785** BURNS *Scotch Drink* iv, On thee aft Scotland chows her cood, In souple scones, the wale o' food! **1838** DICKENS *Nich. Nick.* xiii, A fearful instrument of flagellation, strong, supple, wax-ended, and new. **1871** NAPHEYS *Prev. & Cure Dis.* II. vi. 581 The material [of the dress] should be soft and supple. **1872** BLACK *Adv. Phaeton* xxxi. 411 Persistently whipping the stream with his supple fly-rod. **1899** *Allbutt's Syst. Med.* VIII. 670 The remedy should be rubbed in with sufficient frequency and in sufficient quantity to keep the skin supple and unctuous.

†**b.** *transf.* of the internal organs of the body.

c **1400** tr. *Secreta Secret., Gov. Lordsh.* 70 Vse a lytel trauaill yn ridynge.. It dryues out wyndys, comfortys þe body and makys hit souple. **1710** T. Fuller *Pharm. Extemp.* (1719) 1 Middling Ale.. scoureth.. slimy Filth, from off the .. Glands; turns it over the Pylorus, and leaves a balmy, benign Litus instead, to keep all supple and easy.

c. ***souple Tam***, 'a child's toy, which, being pulled by a string, shakes and seems to dance' (Jamieson, 1825). *Sc.*

[**1818** Scott *Rob Roy* xxvii, It [a horse]'s a grand bargain. .. The stringhalt will gae aff when it's gaen a mile; it's a weel-ken'd ganger; they ca' it Souple Tam.] **1870** R. Chambers *Pop. Rhymes Scotl.* 18 And ye'll get a coatie, And a pair o' breekies—Ye'll get a whippie and a supple Tam!

d. *fig.* Adaptable; elastic.

1781 Cowper *Hope* 602 Some wiser rule.. Supple and flexible as Indian cane, To take the bend his appetites ordain. **1879** Farrar *St. Paul* (1883) 219 His supple address and determination saved Rome from a revolution. **1890** Gladstone in *Daily News* 4 June 6/1 To make the human mind a supple, effective, strong, available instrument.

3. a. Of the body, limbs, etc.: Capable of bending easily; moving easily or nimbly.

1530 Palsgr. 325/1 Souple, lythe, *souple*. **1610** Shaks. *Temp.* iii. iii. 107, I doe beseech you (That are of suppler ioynts) follow them swiftly. **1625** Bacon *Ess., Custom & Educ.* (Arb.) 371 The Ioints are more Supple to all Feats of Actiuitie. **1747** Richardson *Clarissa* (1810) I. xviii. 132 Limbs so supple; will so stubborn! **1781** J. Moore *View Soc. It.* xlix. (1790) II. 52 We all bowed to the ground; the supplest of the company had the happiness to touch the sacred slipper. **1827** Scott *Surg. Dau.* iii, If he listed to tak some [dancing-] lessons, I think I could make some hand of his feet, for he is a souple chield. **1833** *Regul. & Instr. Cavalry* i. 40 The Horse.. will be rendered supple, active, and obedient. **1873** Dixon *Two Queens* xix. i. IV. 4 Henry at thirty-five was still a young man in the flower of life: tall, fair, and supple.

b. ***supple knee***: in reference to insincere or obsequious obeisance. Cf. 4.

1593 Shaks. *Rich. II*, i. iv. 33 A brace of Dray-men bid God speed him well, And had the tribute of his supple knee. **1616** R. C. *Times' Whistle* vi. (1871) 89 It cost him nothing but a supple knee, And oyly mouth & much observancie. **1667** Milton *P.L.* v. 788 Will ye submit your necks, and chuse to bend The supple knee? **1742** Young *Nt. Th.* vi. 294 Religion, public order, both exact External homage, and a supple knee. **1781** Cowper *Table Talk* 127 Servility with supple knees, Whose trade it is to smile, to crouch, to please.

c. *transf.* of movements, etc.: Characterized by flexibility of body or limb.

1592 Shaks. *Rom. & Jul.* iv. i. 102 Each part depriu'd of supple gouernment, Shall stiffe and starke, and cold appeare like death. **1778** Earl Pembroke *Equitation* 63, I define the supple trot to be that in which the horse at every motion that he makes, bends and plays all his joints. **1809** Roland *Fencing* 66 Keep a firm, steady, and supple position of the body. **1853** Bronte *Villette* xxv, Her movements had the supple softness, the velvet grace of a kitten.

†**d.** Of wind: Gentle, soft. *Obs. rare.*

1652 Crashaw *Carmen Deo Nostro* Wks. (1904) 194 Be they such As sigh with supple wind Or answer Artfull Touch.

4. *fig.* Yielding readily to persuasion or influence; compliant. Const. *to*.

c **1340** Hampole *Prose Treat.* 20 Forto breke downe the vnbuxomnes of the body.. that itt myght be souple and redy, and not moch contrarious to the spirite in gostely wyrkynge. *c* **1400** *Rom. Rose* 3376 A feloun firste though that he be, Aftir thou shalt hym souple se. *c* **1440** *Jacob's Well* 281 For all þe herte, tunge, and dede, arn so harde as grauell-stonys,.. but it arn supple ynow to þe world, to þe flesch, & to þe deuyll. **1607** Shaks. *Cor.* v. i. 55 When we haue stufft These Pipes.. With Wine and Feeding, we haue suppler Soules Then in our Priest-like Fasts. **1633** G. Herbert *Temple, Holy Bapt.* ii. ii, Let me be soft and supple to thy will. **1668–9** Pepys *Diary* 12 Jan., It being about the matter of paying a little money to Chatham Yard, wherein I find the Treasurers mighty supple. *a* **1674** Clarendon *Hist. Reb.* xiv. §1 Cromwell did not find the Parliament so supple and so much to observe his Orders, as he expected they would have been. **1735** H. Walpole *Let. to Ld. Harrington* 2 Oct. in *10th Rep. Hist. MSS. Comm.* App. i. 261 His Lordship's supple and mild temper. **1807** Crabbe *Par. Reg.* i. 715 Sad, silent, supple; bending to the blow, A slave of slaves. **1861** *Sat. Rev.* 23 Nov. 528 The City Marshal of Baltimore has been arrested, and a suppler instrument fills his place. **1886** Stevenson *Kidnapped* 4 Be soople, Davie, in things immaterial.

5. a. Compliant or accommodating from selfish motives; artfully or servilely complaisant or obsequious.

1607 Shaks. *Cor.* ii. ii. 29 His assent is not by such easie degrees as those, who hauing beene supple and courteous to the People, Bonnetted, without any further deed, to haue them at all into their estimation, and report. *a* **1700** Evelyn *Diary* 27 Nov. 1666, By no means fit for a supple and flattering courtier. **1726** Swift *Paraphr. Hor.* i. Ode xiv. 55 Like supple Patriots of the modern Sort, Who turn with ev'ry Gale that blows from Court. **1812** Crabbe *Tales* v. 366 That servile, supple, shrewd, insidious throng. **1849** Macaulay *Hist. Eng.* ii. I. 246 Cunning, supple, shameless, free from all prejudices, and destitute of all principles. **1884** R. W. Church *Bacon* iii. 61 The shrewd and supple lawyers who hung on to the Tudor and Stuart Courts.

b. *transf.* Characterized by ingratiating or fawning complaisance.

1633 Ford *'Tis Pity* ii. ii, Call me not deare, Nor thinke with supple words to smooth the grosenesse Of my abuses. **1649** Milton *Eikon.* iii. Wks. 1851 III. 354 By smooth and supple words.. to make som beneficial use or other eev'n of his worst miscarriages. **1690** Ld. Lansdowne *Brit. Enchanters* 689 We Britons slight Those supple arts which foreigners delight. **1818** Scott *Br. Lamm.* xxi, The supple arts by which he had risen in the world. **1841** Emerson *Lect., Man the Reformer* Wks. (Bohn) II. 236 The ways of trade are grown selfish to the borders of theft, and supple to the borders.. of fraud.

6. *Sc.* Clever; cunning.

1715 Ramsay *Christ's Kirk Gr.* ii. ix, A souple taylor to his trade. **1824** Scott *Redgauntlet* let. xii, It's Gil Hobson, the souple tailor frae Burgh.

†**7.** Of oil: That renders pliant or flexible; suppling. Also in fig. context. *Obs. rare.*

1579–80 North *Plutarch* (1595) 12 Bring.. sowple oyle, his bodie for to baste. *a* **1593** Marlowe *Ignoto* Wks. 1850 III. 263, I cannot dally, caper, dance, and sing, Oiling my saint with supple sonnetting. **1600** Heywood *2nd Pt. Edw. IV*, Wks. 1874 I. 96 His defiance and his dare to warre, We swallow with the supple oil of peace.

8. *Comb.*: parasynthetic, as ***supple-chapped, -faced, -kneed, -limbed, -minded, -mouthed, -sinewed, -tempered, -thewed, -visaged***; advb., as ***supple-sliding, -working*** adjs.

1602 Marston *Ant. & Mel.* Induct., Wks. 1856 I. 3 A *supple-chapt flatterer. **1931** V. Woolf *Waves* 100 The little men at the next table... *Supple-faced, with rippling skins. **1888** J. Payn *Myst. Mirbridge* vii, This crowd of *supple-kneed dependents. **1844** Kinglake *Eothen* xvii, The grisly old man at the helm.. and the boy, *supple-limbed, yet weather-worn already. **1882** 'Ouida' *Maremma* I. 205 A large, sinewy, supple-limbed man. *a* **1586** Sidney *Arcadia* (1622) 380 A verie gentle and *supple-minded Zelmane. **1598** Marston *Sco. Villanie* 168 Some *supple mouth'd slaue.. striuing to vilefie My dark reproofes. **1842** Tennyson *Locksley Hall* 169 Iron-jointed, *supple-sinew'd, they shall dive. **1860** —— *Sea Dreams* 164 My eyes .. Read rascal in the motions of his back, And scoundrel in the *supple-sliding knee. **1865** J. R. Lowell *Ode Recited at Commemoration* vi. 27 They could not choose but trust In that sure-footed mind's unfaltering skill, And *supple-tempered will. **1959** R. Graves *Coll. Poems* 317 Free from the cramps of yesterday, Clear-eyed and *supple-thewed. **1809** Malkin *Gil Blas* ix. iii. ¶2 The part of a *supple-visaged son-in-law sat upon me to perfection. **1387–8** T. Usk *Test. Love* iii. vii. (Skeat) I. 103–4 The even draught of the wyr-drawer maketh the wyr to ben even and *supple-werchinge.

supple ('sʌp(ə)l), *v.* Forms: 4–7, 8–9 *Sc.* and *north. dial.* **souple**, 7, 8–9 *Sc.* **soople**, (4 **souplen**, 5 **supplyn, -on, -un**, 6 **soupil, sopel, sowple**, 6, 9 **suple**, *Sc.* **sowpel**, 7 **suppel**), 6– **supple**. [f. supple *a.*, after OF. *asoplir* (mod.F. *assouplir*). See also supply *v.*[3]]

1. *trans.* To soften, mollify (the heart or mind); to cause to yield or be submissive; to make compliant or complaisant. *Obs.* or *arch.*

1390 Gower *Conf.* III. 256 Thus this tirannysshe knyht Was soupled. *c* **1400** *Rom. Rose* 2244 And he, that pride hath hym withynne, Ne may his herte, in no wise, Meken ne souplen to servyse. **1532** More *Confut. Tindale* Wks. 437/1 Menne are so supled and made humble in hert, yᵗ they will willingly goe shew themselfe their own sinnes to the priest. **1583** Golding *Calvin on Deut.* xiv. 85 Hee meekeneth and suppleth them as if a wilde beaste were tamed. **1625** Donne *Serm. 24 Feb.* (1626) 45 Men soupled and entendred with Matrimoniall loue. **1655** Fuller *Ch. Hist.* ii. iii. §3 Suppled with Sicknesse, he confessed his Fault. *a* **1703** Burkitt *On N.T.* Luke xxiii. 42 How powerful must that grace be, which suppled that heart in a moment, which had been hardening in sin for so many years. **1760** Sterne *Serm.* III. 212 To mollify the hearts and supple the temper of your race. **1815** Scott *Guy M.* lv, When I conclude my examination of Dirk Hatteraick to-morrow—Gad, I will so supple him!

b. *intr.* and *refl.* To be submissive or compliant *to*. *Obs.* or *arch.*

c **1440** *Jacob's Well* 280 Here hertys arn so harde.. þat it mowe noȝt brestyn ne supplyn to goodnes. **1742** Richardson *Pamela* III. 392 Having a Spirit above suppling himself to an unworthy Mind for sordid Interest sake. **1748** —— *Clarissa* (1810) IV. xxxvi. 241 Then her family, my bitter enemies—to supple to them, or if I do not, to make her as unhappy as she can be from my attempts. **1877** Tennyson *Harold* i. i. 80 And he hath learnt, despite the tiger in him, To sleek and supple himself to the king's hand.

2. To make (skin, leather, and the like) supple, pliant, or flexible.

1530 Palsgr. 726/2, I shall sowple your gloves. **1542** *Acc. Ld. High Treas. Scot.* VIII. 132 For twa barkit hors hidis,.. xv. s. Item for sowpelling and grathing thairof, iiij. s. **1559** Morwyng *Evonym.* 366 Wull vnskoured suppled in wine or vinegar. **1601** Holland *Pliny* xxiii. viii. II. 171 Touching the bitter Almond tree, the decoction of the roots thereof, doth supple the skin and lay it even and smooth without wrinkles. **1638** Davenant *Madagascar* 19 Rude, dull Mariners.. this Oyntment use Not to perfume, but supple their parch'd Shooes. **1721** *Phil. Trans.* XXXI. 168 After they have soaked the Hide for some time, they stretch and supple it. *a* **1722** Lisle *Husb.* (1757) 270 They may stand in some muck-hill, or moist place, in order to supple their claws. **1791** Cowper *Odyss.* xxi. 215 When we have chafed and suppled the tough bow. **1839** Ure *Dict. Arts* 767 When the skins have been sufficiently swelled and suppled by the branning, they may receive the first oil. **1863** *Morn. Star* 1 Jan. 6 A Basle manufacturer, who uses fine silk, which is weighted or 'supled,' as the trade term goes. **1876** in *Textile Colourist* III. 102 [Patent, Périnaud, for] Suppling re-dyed silks. **1915** J. Buchan *Hist. War* iii. 90 Men lame from hard new boots not yet suppled by use.

b. *intr.* for *pass.*

1844 Browning *Garden Fancies* ii. viii, And clasps were cracking and covers suppling!

†**3.** To reduce the hardness of, to soften. Also *absol. Obs.*

1545 Raynalde *Byrth Mankynde* 56 Hote and moyste thinges, whiche haue the properte to lenifye and sople. **1567** Maplet *Gr. Forest* 88 His onely bloud being kept warme suppleth the Adamant stone. *c* **1586** C'tess Pembroke *Ps.* cxlvii. iii, The rayne.. Supples the clods of sommer-scorched fields. **1598** Chapman *Iliad* vi. [x.] 469 She that supples earth with blood. **1659** *Gentl. Calling* (1696) 14 The Earth.. must be mollified and suppled with their sweat, before it will become penetrable. **1710** T. Fuller *Pharm. Extemp.* (1719) 2 The sweeter, softer and thicker Ale is, the more it suppleth, filleth and nourisheth. **1725** *Fam. Dict.* s.v. *Walnut*, The Shells grow tender, especially, if you supple 'em a little in warm Cows Milk. **1728** E. Smith *Compl. Housew.* (1750) 287 This medicine.. will.. soften the asperity of the humours.. relaxing and suppling the solids at the same time.

†**4.** To soften or mollify (a wound, swelling, etc.) by applying an unguent, a fomentation, etc.; to anoint with oil. Also in fig. context. *Obs.*

1526 Tindale *Prologue to N.T.*, The Evangelion,.. whych sowpleth, and swageth the wondes of the conscience. **1541** *Sarum Primer* N iv (*Dirige*), Thou haste soupled myne heed in oyle; and my cup beynge full is ryght goodly. **1545** Raynalde *Byrth Mankynde* 56 Anoyntmentes wherwith ye may sople yᵉ priuy place. **1579** Langham *Gard. Health* (1633) 315 Apply them to supple, mollifie, ripen, and dissolue all kindes of tumours hot or cold. **1590** Spenser *F.Q.* iii. v. 33 She.. Into his wound the iuyce thereof did scruze, And round about.. The flesh therewith she suppled and did steepe. **1644** Milton *Areop.* (Arb.) 77 All the faith and religion that shall be there canoniz'd, is not sufficient.. to supple the least bruise of conscience. *a* **1688** Bunyan *Accept. Sacrif.* Wks. (Offor) I. 711 Wash me, Lord, supple my wounds, pour Thy wine and oil into my sore.

absol. **1578** Lyte *Dodoens* 201 With the floures of Lillies there is made a good Oyle to supple, mollifie & digest. **1612** T. Taylor *Comm. Titus* ii. i. (1619) 336 He seeketh to wound and gall, but he healeth nor suppleth not. **1662** Hibbert *Body Div.* i. 156 Pouring in oyl to supple and heal.

†**b.** *transf.* To rub (oil, etc.) on or into something so as to soften it. *Obs. rare.*

1560 Daus tr. *Sleidane's Comm.* 334 b, He powreth out the oyle and suppleth it in.

5. To make (the limbs, the body, the person) supple or capable of bending easily; *spec.* of the training of saddle-horses (see quot. 1753).

1570 Foxe *A. & M.* (ed. 2) I. 70/1 Contrary to thexpectation of men, his body was in the latter punishment and tormentes soupled and restored. **1613** R. Harcourt *Voy. Guiana* 55 He.. went.. to the Bath, and washed.. his hand.. therein, which soopled his fingers in such manner, that.. hee could stirre and stretch them out. **1638** Mayne *Lucian* (1664) 373, I must think that the best and most proportionable exercise, which both supples the body, and renders it flexible, and pliant. **1652** H. L'Estrange *Amer. no Jewes* 14 Oyle.. such as he carried with him.. to supple his joints and tired Limbs. **1749** Chesterf. *Let. to Son* 15 May, Apply yourself diligently to your exercises of dancing, fencing, and riding,.. to fashion and supple you. **1753** *Chambers' Cycl.* Suppl. s.v., To *supple* a horse, in the manege, is to make him bend his neck, shoulders, and sides, and to render all the parts of his body more pliable. **1765** Chesterf. *Let. to Son* 25 Oct., The hot bath.. supples my stiff rheumatic limbs. **1847** *Infantry Man.* (1854) 3 In order to supple the recruit,.. he will be practised in the.. movements. **1861** J. Brown *Horæ Subs.* II. 256 Old broken-down thorough-breds that did wonders when soopled. **1881** T. A. M'Carthy *Calisth. & Drilling* 17 This exercise is to strengthen the leg and upper arm, supple the shoulders, and expand the chest. **1897** Kipling *Capt. Cour.* ii. 45 Manuel bowed back and forth to supple himself.

b. *fig.* and allusively.

1555 Philpot in Coverdale *Lett. Martyrs* (1564) 240 Christ annoynt vs, that we may be suppled in these euil dayes to runne lyghtly, vnto the glory of the lord. **1638** A. Cant *Serm.* in Kerr *Covenants & Covenanters* (1895) 101 His legs were soupled with consolation, which made him run. **1639** Fuller *Holy War* iii. xviii. (1840) 147 His seven thousand whose knees were not suppled with the Baalism of that age. **1659** Arrowsmith *Chain Princ.* 395 Cheerfulness supples the joynts of our hearts, and so rendereth them nimble and active in holy performances. **1893** Stevenson *Catriona* vii, Ye'll have to soople your back-bone, and think a wee pickle less of your dainty self.

6. *gen.* (from 4 and 5): To make pliant, flexible, or smooth; also, to tone down, modify.

1530–1 Tindale *Jonas* Prol., To sowple thy soule with the oyle of theyr swete blessynges. **1612** Donne *Lett.* (1651) 91 That nothing hath soupled and allayed the D. of Lerma in his violent greatnesse, so much as the often libels made upon him. **1612** T. Taylor *Comm. Titus* i. 4. (1619) 63 Nor all the baulme in Gilead can so supple their positions, that we may ioyne with them. **1614** W. B. *Philos. Banquet* 75 Mint supples the sharpnesse of the Tongue. **1626** Donne *Serm. Easter-day* (1640) 210 Some of them mollifie and souple the impossibility into a difficulty. **1642** R. Harris *Serm. Ho. Commons* 20 There is no temptation so strong, but faith will conquer it: no affliction so great, but faith will supple it. **1742** Young *Nt. Th.* ix. 2183 His balmy bath, That supples .. The various movements of this nice machine. **1867** M. Arnold *Celtic Lit.* 181 The hard unintelligence, which is just now our bane.. must be suppled and reduced by culture. **1887** Lowell *Democracy*, etc. 240 To set free, to supple and to train the faculties. **1901** Mollison *Poems* 180 Come.. souple thou my pen tae screed, A rhymin' line or twa.

supple, obs. and dial. f. supply.

suppleant, supplear, obs. ff. suppliant, supplier.

suppled ('sʌp(ə)ld), *ppl. a.* [f. supple *v.* + -ed[1].] Made supple; softened.

1594 O. B. *Quest. Profit. Concern.* 31*b, When I shall finde that I tooke for suppled honie, to become stiffe darts. **1598** Chapman *Iliad* iii. [vii.] 259 Let vs impart, Some ensignes of our strife to shew, each others suppled hart. **1657** Reeve *God's Plea* Ep. Ded. Relig. Cit. 5 Why should not they prepare an Elixir for her out of their suppled eyes, rent heart-strings,.. to preserve her at an exigent?

supplee, obs. form of SUPPLY.

'supple-jack. [f. SUPPLE *a.* + JACK *sb.*[1] (cf. sense 32).]

1. a. A name for various climbing and twining shrubs with tough pliable stems found in tropical and subtropical forests; applied in the West Indies to various sapindaceous plants, as species of *Paullinia* and *Serjania*, and *Cardiospermum grandiflorum*; in central America, to the rhamnaceous *Berchemia volubilis*, and to a species of *Zizyphus*; in Australasia, to *Ventilago viminalis*, *Ripogonum parviflorum*, *Rubus australis*, and other plants of similar habit.

1725 SLOANE *Jamaica* II. 185 Supple-Jacks. The stalk.. is about the thickness of one's thumb... They grow in woods and are used for walking sticks. **1773** COOK *Voy. S. Pole* I. v. (1777) I. 96 In many parts the woods are so over-run with supple-jacks, that it is scarcely possible to force one's way amongst them. **1814** PURSH *Flora Amer. Septentr.* I. 188 *Zizyphus volubilis*..in the Dismal swamp, near Suffolk in Virginia,..is known there by the name of Supple-Jack. **1820** T. GREEN *Univ. Herbal* II. 260 *Paullinia Polyphylla*; Parsley-leaved Paullinia, or Supple Jack. **1864** GRISEBACH *Flora Brit. W. Ind. Isl.* 788/1 Supple-jack: *Paullinia curassavica*, *barbadensis*, and *Cardiospermum grandiflorum.* **1867** SAUTER tr. *Hochstetter's New Zealand* vi. 135 The so-called 'supple-jack' of the colonists (*Ripogonum parviflorum*). **1884** J. H. KERRY-NICHOLLS *King Country* xxii. 266 The supple-jacks, which we found growing everywhere [in New Zealand] in a perfect network of snakelike coils.

b. The stems of these plants as a material.

1804 A. DUNCAN *Mariner's Chron.* II. 251 Bits of blankets ..sewed together with split supple-jacks. **1865** *Reader* No. 119. 405/2 Lashed together with strips of supple-jack.

2. A walking-stick or cane made of the stem of one of these plants; a tough pliant stick.

1748 SMOLLETT *Rod. Random* xxiv, He bestowed on me several severe stripes, with a supple Jack he had in his hand. **1785** WOLCOT (P. Pindar) *Odes to R.A.'s* I. iii. Wks. 1812 I. 73 Take, take my supple-jack, Play Saint Bartholomew with many a back! **1818** SCOTT *Rob Roy* xxvii, You will never rest till my supple-jack and your shoulders become acquainted. **1891** MEREDITH *One of our Conq.* xxxi, A good knot to grasp; ..there's no break in it, whack as you may. They call it a Demerara supple-jack.

3. *U.S.* A toy representing the human figure, the limbs of which are manipulated by a string. Also *fig.* Cf. SUPPLE *a.* 2 c. ? *Disused.*

1776 M. CUTLER *Jrnl.* 17 June in *Life & Correspondence* (1888) I. 55 They made us several presents of the small affairs in the cabins, such as sweetmeats, cayenne-pepper, supple-jacks, cassada or bread..trinkets etc. **1791** W. MACLAY *Jrnl.* 25 Feb. (1927) xiv. 390 Schuyler is the supple-jack of his son-in-law Hamilton. **1835** A. B. LONGSTREET *Georgia Scenes* 13 Bob Simons danced..like a 'Suple-Jack' ..when the string is pulled with varied force, at intervals of seconds. **1853** P. KENNEDY *Blackwater Chron.* x. 147 His body spread out as usual in his favorite position of a supple-jack distorted to the utmost. **1871** W. WHITMAN *Democr. Vistas* 30 How the millions of sturdy farmers and mechanics are thus the helpless supple-jacks of comparatively few politicians. **1904** *N.Y. Times* 8 July 5 Those political supplejacks who go about with sanctimonious moan, saying: 'The President is wrong, but we must support the President.'

Hence **supple'jackically** *adv.* (*humorous nonce-wd.*), in a manner suggesting the use of a supple-jack.

1844 J. T. HEWLETT *Parsons & W.* liv, My father looked supple-jackically at me.

supplely ('sʌp(ə)llɪ), *adv.* Also 9 **supply.** [f. SUPPLE *a.* + -LY[2].] In a supple manner, with suppleness.

1611 COTGR., *Agilement*,..quickely, promptly, supplely, readily. **1689** HICKERINGILL *Ceremony Monger* i. Wks. 1716 II. 388 Does his Ecclesiastical Don-ship bow and cringe so supplely..to something, or to nothing? **1832** *Examiner* 721/2 Not of strength to bear any pressure without supplely bending. **1890** *Harper's Mag.* Oct. 744/2 Freely and supplely she straightened her back. **1898** G. ALLEN *Incid. Bishop* 54 She was tall..and very supply knit.

supplement ('sʌplɪmənt), *sb.*[1] Also 5-7 **supplyment, 6 suplement, 6-7 suppliment.** [ad. L. *supplēmentum*, f. *supplēre* SUPPLY *v.*[1] Cf. F. *supplément* (from 16th c., superseding OF. *supploiement*, *suppleement*, *suppliement*), It. *supplemento*, Sp. *suplemento*, Pg. *supplemento*.

In sense 4 used as a noun of action to *supple*, SUPPLY *v.*[1]; cf. SUPPLYMENT.]

1. Something added to supply a deficiency; an addition to anything by which its defects are supplied; an auxiliary means, an aid; occas. of a person. (Now *rare* in general sense.)

1382 WYCLIF *Mark* ii. 21 No man seweth a pacche [Vulg. *assumentum*] of rude [*gloss* or newe] clothe to an old clothe, ellis he takith awey the newe supplement [*gloss* or pacche; Vulg. *supplementum*], and a more brekynge is maad. **1398** TREVISA *Barth. De P.R.* VIII. xxi. (Bodl. MS.) lf. 85 b/2 But þeiȝe sterres haue liȝte of here owne. ȝitte to perfectioun of here liȝt þei fongeth supplemente [**1495** supplyment; orig. *complementum*] and help of þe sonne. **1544** *St. Papers Hen. VIII*, I. 764 The Lord Chauncelour..shall..admit and swere..Mr. Cox to be his Aulmoner,..and Mr. Cheke as a suppliment to Mr. Cox. **1594** HOOKER *Eccl. Pol.* III. viii. §10 Vnto the word of God..we do not add reason as a supplement of any maime or defect therin. **1628** FELTHAM *Resolves* II. [I.] xxxvii. 114 Minerva cur'd Vlysses of his wrinkles and baldnesse; not that she tooke them away by supplements. **1664** H. MORE *Myst. Iniq.* 94 God would have afterwards raised other persons of Apostolical purity..to have made a Supplement to the former. **1698** FRYER *Acc. E. India & P.* 250 Fording the River without such a Suppliment [as a bridge]. **1728** YOUNG *Love Fame* I. 12 Instructive Satire,..Thou shining supplement of public laws! **1856** J. RICHARDSON *Recoll.* I. vi. 142 As supplements to this bowl, small cups, brimming with milk punch were placed upon the table. **1861** PALEY *Æschylus* (ed. 2) *Supplices* 154 *note*, Hermann's supplement οὐς completes the anapaestic verse. **1893** G. H. PEMBER *Earth's Earliest Ages* 67 How wonderful a supplement may, in the World to Come, be added to our present scanty information.

b. A part added to complete a literary work or any written account or document; *spec.* a part of a periodical publication issued as an addition to the regular numbers and containing some special item or items.

1568 GRAFTON *Chron.* I. 3 As Iames Philip of Bergamo sayth, in the suppliment of his Chronicles. **1576** FLEMING tr. *Caius' Dogs* (1880) 44 The winding vp of this worke, called the Supplement. **1650** ROW (*title*) A Supplement of the Historie of the Kirk of Scotland. **1683** WOOD *Life* (O.H.S.) III. 35 He died Sunday 21 Jan. (20 Jan., saith the suppliment to his will). **1696** RAY in *Lett. Lit. Men* (Camden) 202 To speed the finishing and fitting my Supplement for the Presse. **1779** JOHNSON *L.P.*, *Cowley* Wks. 1787 II. 22 His work, to which my narration can be considered only as a slender supplement. **1863** LYELL *Antiq. Man* i. 5 In my 'Elements or Manual of Elementary Geology' and in the Supplement to the fifth edition of the same. **1868** FREEMAN *Norm. Conq.* II. App. 577, I accept his account..as a supplement, to the account in the Chronicles. **1887** (Nov. 5) Special Literary Supplement to The Spectator.

c. *Math.* (*a*) †*supplements of a parallelogram* = *complements of a parallelogram* (COMPLEMENT *sb.* 5 b). *Obs.* (*b*) *supplement of an arc* or *angle*, the amount by which an arc is less than a semicircle, or an angle less than two right angles; also *attrib.*, as *supplement-chord*. (*c*) An additional term introduced in certain cases in an equation or expression (abbreviated *supp.*).

1570 BILLINGSLEY *Euclid* I. Theorem xxxii. 53 In euery parallelograme, the supplementes of those parallelogrammes which are about the diameter, are equall the one to the other. *Ibid.* Prop. xliii. 53 b, Supplementes or Complementes are those figures which with the two parallelogrammes accomplish the whole parallelogramme. **1704** J. HARRIS *Lex. Techn.* I, *Supplement* of an Ark, in Geometry or Trigonometry. **1747** T. SIMPSON *Elem. Plane Geom.* 138 If the Measure of the Supplement-chord of any Arch be increased by the Number 2, the Square-root of the Sum will be the Supplement-chord of half that Arch. **1801** *Encycl. Brit.* (ed. 3) Suppl. II. 630/2 The supplement of 50° is 130°; as the complement of it is 40°. **1842** GWILT *Archit.* §1038 ADE being a semicircle BDE is the supplement of the arc AB, which arc, reciprocally, is the supplement of BDE. **1861** FERRERS *Trilinear Co-ordinates* vi. 112 The angle between the asymptotes of the reciprocal hyperbola will be the supplement of that between the tangents. **1868** CAYLEY *Math. Papers* (1893) VI. 263, I introduce into the equation a term called the 'Supplement' (denoted by the abbreviation 'Supp.')... The expression of the Supplement should in every case be furnished by the theory. **1884** tr. *Lotze's Logic* 278, $h. f^2 x. d h.$ is the general term of this second series, and is what we must add as supplement to the general term of the first series.

†**2.** The action of supplying what is wanting; the making good *of* a deficiency or shortcoming.

1483 CAXTON *Gold. Leg.* 345/1 The feeste of all the sayntes was establysshed..Fyrste for the dedycacion of the Temple secondly for supplement of offences done. **1523** SKELTON *Garl. Laurel* 415 Mayster Chaucer to Skelton... Your besy delygence Of that we [*sc.* Chaucer, Gower, and Lydgate] beganne in the supplement. **1575** in *Reg. Mag. Sig. Scot.* 1585. 261/1 Our said kirk..haveand neid and mister of beitment and supplement. **1586** A. DAY *Eng. Secretorie* II. (1625) 76 For better supplement of the learners knowledge. **1591** *Reg. Privy Council Scot.* IV. 611 Ane new gift of the saidis landis grantit with all dew solempniteis and with supplement of all faultis. **1610** DONNE *Pseudo-martyr* 21 Councels submitted their decrees to the Emperours for Authoritie and supplement of defects. **1660** R. COKE *Power & Subj.* 135 Equity is..either a remission or moderation of the laws..or..a supplement of the law in cases wherein things in conscience ought to be done.

b. Sc. Law. *letters* (or *writ*) *of supplement*, a writ issuing from the Court of Session to compel the appearance before an inferior court of a person who resides out of its jurisdiction. *oath in supplement*, an oath of a party on his own behalf, admitted to confirm imperfect evidence, such as the oath of a single witness, so as to constitute sufficient legal proof: cf. *suppletory oath* s.v. SUPPLETORY *a.* b.

1672 in G. J. Bell *Comm. Laws Scot.* (ed. 5) I. 331 *note*, The count-book, with the merchant's oath in supplement, was sufficient to make it a full probation. **1693** STAIR *Inst. Law Scot.* (ed. 2) IV. xlv. §17. 710 Whosoever is cited by a Messenger, to Compear and Depone by an Oath of Calumny, Verity or Supplement, if he do not Depone, he is holden as Confest. **1765-8** ERSKINE *Inst. Law Scot.* I. ii. §17 The pursuer must apply to the court of session..for letters of supplement..containing a warrant to cite the defender to appear before the judge of the territory where the controverted subject lies. **1826** G. J. BELL *Comm. Laws Scot.* (ed. 5) II. 66 *note*, If the original creditor do not live within the jurisdiction in which the arrestee resides,..he must be summoned by a writ of supplement from the Court of Session. **1838** W. BELL *Dict. Law Scot.* 378 s.v. *Evidence*, The oath in supplement is admitted to supply deficiencies in legal evidence, where the party whose oath is allowed has brought what is called a *semiplena probatio*.

†**3.** The reinforcement *of* troops; chiefly *concr.* (*sing.* and *pl.*), reinforcement(s). *Obs.*

a **1548** HALL *Chron., Hen. VI*, 137 Twoo M. archers, and foure hundred speres, was sente into Gascoyne, as a suppliment to the countrey. **1549** *Acts Privy Council* (1890) II. 273, xvj Albanoys horsmen, to him allotted for the suplement of his band. **1600** HOLLAND *Livy* XLII. x. 1121 The Pretors also, which required to have a supplement with them into Spain. **1665** MANLEY *Grotius' Low C. Wars* 421 Souldiers both of Horse and Foot were..drawn together.. as a Supplement to the old exhausted Militia.

†**4.** The action of supplying or providing; that which is supplied; supply, provision. *Obs.*

1544 *St. Papers Hen. VIII*, I. 766 We see manifest occasion of moche greatter charge, then was att the begynnyng consideryd;..and..as We cannot use any other present meanes, for the supplement hereof, thenne [etc.]. **1545** *Ibid.* III. 519 Supposing that they have of His Majestie sufficient supplyment for ther furnyture. *Ibid.* 543 We coulde have no supplement of caske for their victualles, but suche as we had from..Waterforde. **1588** PARKE tr. *Mendoza's Hist. China* 77 Generall puruier and president of the counsell of warre: whose office is..for the suppliment of garrisons. **1615** CHAPMAN *Odyss.* IX. 242 We had not spent Our ruddie wine aship-boord: supplement Of large sort, each man to his vessell drew. **1658** OSBORN *K. James* Wks. (1673) 494 The People, if they denied him supplement or inquired after the disposure of it, were presumptuous peepers into the sacred Ark of the State.

†**supplement,** *sb.*[2] *Obs. rare*⁻¹. [f. SUPPLE *v.* + -MENT.] Suppleness.

1583 STUBBES *Anat. Abus.* I. 54 It [*sc.* whoredom].. consumeth the moysture and supplement of the bodie.

supplement, var. SUPPLIMENT.

supplement ('sʌplɪmɛnt, sʌplɪ'mɛnt), *v.* (First in Sc. writers.) [f. SUPPLEMENT *sb.*[1]] *trans.* To furnish a supplement to, supply the deficiency in; also, to supply (a deficiency). Freq. const. *by* and (more recently) *with.*

In recent story-writing, to add as a supplementary statement or remark.

1829 JAS. MILL *Hum. Mind* (1869) II. 62 Clusters of sensations, supplemented by possibilities of sensation. **1833** CHALMERS *Power of God* I. vi. (1834) I. 224 The strong appetite of hunger supplements the deficiency of the rational principle of self-preservation. **1857** J. W. DONALDSON *Chr. Orthod.* Introd. p. viii, This work is a continuous essay, supplemented by a number of special disquisitions on certain important subjects. **1863** GLADSTONE *Financ. Statem.* 442 The spiritual food is to be supplemented, as Scotchmen say, by something which finds a shorter way to their perceptions and their appetites. **1868** G. DUFF *Pol. Surv.* 23 The two sets of dissimilar conditions supplement and throw light upon each other. **1875** ROSSETTI *Hood's Poet. Wks.* Ser. II. Pref. p. xv, It is now thought desirable to supplement this by a second volume. **1878** MISS BRADDON *Open Verdict* i, If I am a poor creature as a parson, you supplement me so well, Selina, that, between us, I think we do our duty to the parish. **1888** 'J. S. WINTER' *Bootle's Childr.* xi, 'Yes, a disparity,' answered Maud... 'It means age!' 'And not less than twenty years,' supplemented Pearl. **1890** G. GISSING *Emancipated* I. I. v. 151 Then he strolled away and supplemented his meal with a fine bunch of grapes. **1940** H. G. WELLS *Babes in Darkling Wood* III. iii. 270 She realised she had forgotten her lunch, and she supplemented her tea with two boiled eggs. **1946** BIBLE (Rev. Stand. Version) 2 Pet. i. 5 Make every effort to supplement your faith with virtue. **1952** S. KAUFFMANN *Philanderer* (1953) vi. 97 When everyone else was making money, Robert was forced to supplement his insufficient income with his savings. **1977** K. M. E. MURRAY *Caught in Web of Words* vi. 105 He had spare time in which to supplement his income by literary work.

Hence **'supplemented** *ppl. a.*, **'supplementing** *vbl. sb.* and *ppl. a.*

1865 W. KAY *Crisis Hupfeldiana* 80 Their cancellings, supplementings, and arbitrary assumptions. **1901** *Westm. Gaz.* 30 Nov. 2/1 'You love the garden?' she hazarded... 'And everything in it,' was his supplemented answer. **1904** R. SMALL *Hist. Congreg. U.P. Ch.* I. 529 A winding-up was insisted on by the Supplementing Board.

supplemental (sʌplɪ'mɛntəl), *a.* (*sb.*) Also 7-8 **suppli-.** [f. SUPPLEMENT *sb.*[1] + -AL[1].]

a. = SUPPLEMENTARY. Const. *to*, *of*. Now chiefly *U.S.*

supplemental air, the air that remains in the lungs after an ordinary expiration: cf. quot. 1855 s.v. SUPPLEMENTARY *a.* b.

1605 BACON *Adv. Learn.* II. ii. §7 Wee speake nowe of parts of Learning supplementall, and not of supererogation. **1629** GAULE *Holy Madn.* 134 Womens Supplimentall Art, does but the rather bewray Natures Defects. **1668** HALE *Pref. to Rolle's Abridgm.* c j b, An Appendix was intended that might have been supplemental of some Titles. **1768** BLACKSTONE *Comm.* III. xxvii. 448 If new matter arises, which did not exist before, he [*sc.* the plaintiff] must set it forth by a supplemental bill. **1795** MASON *Ch. Mus.* II. 153 All those supplemental graces which really serve to assist musical expression. **1866** LIDDON *Bampton Lect.* v. (1875) 220 Viewed in its historical relation to the first three Gospels it is supplemental to them. **1866** HUXLEY *Physiol.* iv. (1869) 102 About as much more in addition to this remains in the chest after an ordinary expiration, and is called *Supplemental air.* **1872** T. BRYANT *Pract. Surg.* (1878) I. 563 Supplemental teeth are occasionally developed in both temporary and permanent sets. **1952** *Sun* (Baltimore) 28 Aug. 1/3 The supplemental defenses of anti-aircraft artillery and infantry posts. **1958** *Yearbk. Agric. 1957* (U.S. Dept. Agric.) 769/1 *Supplemental irrigation*,..irrigation during dry periods in regions where normal precipitation supplies most of the moisture for crops. **1966** K. AMIS in *New Statesman* 14 Jan. 52/1, I have never before met *supplemental* for *supplementary* except as the term for the second-bite-at-the-cherry examination for pass students at the University College of Swansea. **1969** D. ACHESON *Present at Creation* (1970) xviii. 159 A supplemental budget estimate was prepared. **1976** *Amer. N. & Q.* XV. 2/1 Supplemental to this special number of *AN&Q.* **1980** *Amer. Speech 1976* LI. 202 All of those partial records will be included in the atlas as supplemental evidence.

b. *Math.*

supplemental angle, either (in relation to the other) of two angles which are together equal to two right angles. ***supplemental arc***, either of two arcs which are together equal to a semicircle. ***supplemental chord***, the chord of a supplemental arc. ***supplemental triangle***, either (in relation to the other) of two spherical triangles in which the angular points of the one are the poles of the sides of the other, and each side of the one is the supplement of the corresponding angle of the other.

1798 HUTTON *Course Math.* (1827) I. 315 Let C and D be two angles..standing on the supplemental arc AEB; then will the angle C be equal to the angle D. **1827** AIRY *Trigon.* in *Encycl. Metrop.* (1845) I. 683 Suppose great circles EF, FD, DE..to be described, of which A, B, C are respectively the poles; they will intersect in the points D, E, F, and form a spherical triangle, called the polar or supplemental triangle. **1840** LARDNER *Geom.* vii. 78 If a quadrilateral figure be inscribed in a circle, its opposite angles will be supplemental. **1842** *Penny Cycl.* XXIII. 300/1 Chords or arcs of a circle or other curve which have a common extremity, and together subtend an angle of two right angles at the centre, are sometimes called supplemental chords or arcs.

c. *sb.* A supplementary fact, etc. *rare.*

1670 BLOUNT *Law Dict.* Pref. (1691) (a) ij, In the Supplementals, Bracton, Britton,..and divers other Authors have been my Guides. **1836** SOUTHEY *Lett.* (1856) IV. 454 There are three works which I shall want for our supplementals. **1852** DE MORGAN in Graves *Life Sir W. R. Hamilton* (1889) III. 344 You do not see how I get my supplementals.

Hence **supple'mentally** *adv.*, by way of supplement.

1768 *Woman of Honor* III. 254 Clara, in her turn, or supplementally for her sister, would bless me with her company. **1853** G. S. FABER *Downfall Turkey* 77 The cities of the Medes are only subjoined supplementally.

supplementarity (sʌplɪmɛn'tærɪtɪ). *rare.* [f. SUPPLEMENTARY *a.* + -ITY, after F. *supplémentarité* (J. Derrida).] The condition or quality of being supplementary.

1976 G. C. SPIVAK tr. *Derrida's Of Grammatology* II. iv. 314 In as much as we designate the impossibility of formulating the movement of supplementarity within the classical logos. **1979** C. NORRIS in *PN Rev.* X. 38/1 Writing is the example *par excellence* of a supplementarity which enters into the heart of all intelligible discourse.

supplementary (sʌplɪ'mɛntərɪ), *a.* (*sb.*) [f. SUPPLEMENT *sb.*[1] + -ARY[1]. Cf. F. *supplémentaire.*] **a.** Of the nature of, forming, or serving as, a supplement. Const. *to.*

1667 *Decay Chr. Piety* xviii. 399 Divinity would not then pass the Yard and Loom,..nor Preaching be taken in as an easier supplementary Trade, by those that disliked the pains of their own. **1770** PENNANT *Brit. Zool.* IV. Ded. p. iv, To you therefore I address this little supplementary work. **1793** BEDDOES *Lett. Darwin* 9 These I shall from time to time submit..as supplementary to the knowledge accumulated by former experience. **1823** LAMB *Elia* Ser. II. *Old China*, Competence to age is supplementary youth. **1855** MACAULAY *Hist. Eng.* xiii. III. 287 To this Claim..was added a supplementary paper containing a list of grievances. *a* **1862** BUCKLE *Civiliz.* (1864) II. vi. 437 Each is supplementary to the other; so that in order to understand either, it is necessary to study both. **1908** *Athenæum* 15 Aug. 182/2 A supplementary volume of whose memoirs was published a few years ago.

b. In various technical uses.

Esp. of welfare payments. ***supplementary benefits*** replaced National Assistance in 1966, and were superseded by income support in 1988.

1796 *Act 37 Geo. III*, c. 3 §2 If a sufficient Number of Officers..cannot be found to accept of Commissions in the Supplementary Militia..it shall be lawful for the said Lieutenants..to appoint for that Service, such a Number of the Officers in the Army..as his Majesty shall approve. **1826** G. J. BELL *Comm. Laws Scot.* (ed. 5) II. 214 Of Supplementary Deeds or Acts.—These are certain acts and steps of conveyancing necessary for supplying the links of a defective conveyance. *Ibid.* 409 Of the method of affecting the acquisitions of the bankrupt subsequent to sequestration... The best method..is, that the trustee.. shall apply to the Court for a supplementary sequestration. **1838** W. BELL *Dict. Law Scot.* s.v., When all the parties interested have not been called, or where the original summons requires amendment, and the defender has not appeared, a supplementary or auxiliary summons is necessary. **1841** *Hansard Commons* 5 Mar. 1361 He had.. felt it his duty late in the year, to bring forward a supplementary estimate of 22,000*l.*, to carry into effect the recommendation of the naval and military commission, which increased the estimates for the whole year to 6,185,000*l.* **1842** *Penny Cycl.* XXII. 343/2 The supplementary triangle. [Cf. SUPPLEMENTAL b.] **1848** CAYLEY *Math. Papers* I. 362 The supplementary cone (i.e. the cone generated by lines through the vertex at right angles to the tangent planes of the cone in question). **1855** DUNGLISON *Med. Lex.* (1857) s.v. *Respiration*, The supplementary or reserve air or that which can be expelled by a forcible expiration, after an ordinary outbreathing. **1875** KNIGHT *Dict. Mech.* 2455/1 *Supplementary Engine*, an auxiliary steam-engine, for feeding the boiler when the main engine is at rest. **1891** F. TAYLOR *Man. Pract. Med.* (ed. 2) 347 Increased vesicular murmur happens..over one lung or part of a lung, when another part of the lung is not properly in use. It is then called compensatory or supplementary breathing. **1920** W. S. CHURCHILL *Let.* 3 Mar. in R. S. Churchill *Winston S. Churchill* (1969) II. Compan. II. xiii. 985 The House is now discussing peacefully the supplementary Estimates of the Navy. **1940** *Economist* 27 Jan. 141/2 The direct cost involved in the change over to a new central organisation for the payment of supplementary pensions is..nil. **1966** *Hansard Commons* 7 Mar. 1730/2 Will the right hon. Lady confirm whether supplementary benefits will now be the subject of Parliamentary Questions to her? **1966** *Whitaker's Almanack 1967* 1109/1 The supplementary pension may be claimed by persons over pension age and the supplementary allowance by persons aged 16 or over but under pension age, who are not in full-time work. **1973** B. MATHER *Snowline* vii. 85 He was getting nothing—unemployment pay, supplementary allowance—not a sausage. **1977** in R. Crossman *Diaries* III. 124 The House of Commons must annually debate and pass three Consolidated Fund Bills, authorizing the issue of the supply of funds to cover the civil and defence estimates and supplementary estimates. **1977** *Proc. R. Soc. Med.* LXX. 602/1 That there are five million people in receipt of supplementary benefit is as much a sign of affluence as poverty for of households receiving benefit 96% have television, 68% washing machines, 62% a refrigerator and 23% a car.

c. *sb.* A supplementary person or thing.

In recent parliamentary use, a question supplementary to that put down on the question-paper.

1812 SOUTHEY in *Edinb. Ann. Reg.* III. I. 485/2 Supplementary deputies were then to be chosen, who were to take their seats in case of any vacancy by death; the supplementaries were, as nearly as could be, in the proportion of one to three. **1879** *Scribner's Monthly* Dec. 304 The prayers..are simply preliminaries and supplementaries to the sermon. **1902** ALICE TERTON *Lights & Shadows in Hosp.* i. 3, I was called a 'supplementary', which was a dignified title for a charwoman. **1904** *Westm. Gaz.* 16 May 1/2 Lord Cranborne..did not altogether ignore supplementaries, but he came one or two bad croppers over them.

Hence **supple'mentarily** *adv.*, by way of supplement.

1862 F. HALL *Hindu Philos. Syst.* 205 To indicate, supplementarily, the object denied. **1899** *Pop. Sci. Monthly* Sept. 677 Those we propose to tax supplementarily are mostly wealthy.

supplementation (sʌplɪmɛn'teɪʃən). [f. SUPPLEMENT *v.* + -ATION.] The action of supplementing; also, an instance of this, a supplementary addition.

1854 FERRIER *Inst. Metaph.* 450 To redeem from contradiction a centreless circle or a stick with only one end, two supplementations are required. **1873** A. W. WARD tr. *Curtius' Hist. Greece* I. II. i. 218 The war had made great gaps in the military body itself, and it was in the interest of the state to fill these up... This supplementation miscarried. **1903** G. E. UNDERHILL in *Eng. Hist. Rev.* Oct. 756 The shortest supplementation [of lines in a fragmentary papyrus] is always the most probable.

supplementer (see the *vb.*). Also -or. [f. SUPPLEMENT *v.* + -ER[1].] One who supplements.

1644 FEATLY *Roma Ruens* 12 The author and supplementer of Catalogus testium veritatis. **1697** DRYDEN *Virgil, Life* **j b, Franshemius, the Learn'd Supplementor of Livy, has inserted this Relation into his History. **1869** BONAR *Life J. Milne* xix. 409 Not one minister out of a thousand would have borne such supplementing, however needful, or would have so cordially thanked the supplementer. **1873** G. W. KITCHIN *Hist. France* I. III. x. 380 'Which thing', says the Supplementor to William of Nangis, 'came not to pass'. **1906** ORR *Probl. O.T.* x. 344 So long as the Jehovist was regarded as a mere supplementer of the Elohist.

suppleness ('sʌp(ə)lnɪs). [f. SUPPLE *a.* + -NESS.] The quality or condition of being supple.

1. Flexibility and elasticity: sometimes with implication of nimbleness of movement (cf. 2).

1626 BACON *Sylva* §610 The Supplenesse and Gentlenesse of the Iuyce of that Plant, being that which maketh the Boughes also so Flexible. **1707** *Curios. Husb. & Gard.* 69 There is no part..in which the Subtility and Suppleness of the Sap more claim our Admiration, than in Trees that are grafted. **1782** SIR J. REYNOLDS *Disc.* xi. (1876) 29 That suppleness which is the characteristic of flesh. **1791** HAMILTON *Berthollet's Dyeing* I. I. ii. 134 By scouring, silk acquires its suppleness and whiteness. **1858** O. W. HOLMES *Aut. Breakf.-t.* ix. (1883) 186 Hair like the fibrous covering of a cocoa-nut in..suppleness as well as color. **1858** CARLYLE *Fredk. Gt.* v. ii. (1872) II. 68 You have beaten Louis XIV. to the suppleness of washleather.

2. Of the body or limbs: Capability of bending easily.

1768 TUCKER *Lt. Nat.* I. II. xx. 47 Nature may have prepared one man for a dancer by giving him strength and suppleness in his joints. **1774** GOLDSM. *Nat. Hist.* (1776) VII. 165 Serpents..have the length and the suppleness of the eel. **1838** DICKENS *Nich. Nick.* xiii, Giving his right arm two or three flourishes to try its power and suppleness. **1893** ECCLES *Sciatica* 80 Elderly persons from whom feats of suppleness could not be expected.

3. Flexibility or adaptability of mind, character, etc.

1594 CAREW *Huarte's Exam. Wits* v. (1596) 62 Children.. through the great supplenesse of their braine, abound in memory. **1638** BAKER tr. *Balzac's Lett.* (vol. II.) 160 He hath both the substance and the suppleness which are necessary in dealing with the brains of that country. **1665** BOYLE *Occas. Refl.* (1848) 35 Bringing those that use to write their Thoughts to what may be call'd a certain Suppleness of Style. **1807** KNOX & JEBB *Corr.* (1834) I. 328 A certain suppleness in your mental powers, by virtue of which they will bend to all occasions and subjects, with an ease and readiness [etc.]. **1878** O. W. HOLMES *Motley* xxi. 187 As a diplomatic his great want is suppleness.

4. Yielding disposition or character, compliantness, complaisance. ? *Obs.* exc. as in b.

1629 DONNE *Serm. Whitsunday* (1640) 309 God findes a better disposition, and souplenesse, and maturity, and mellowing, to concurre with his motion in that man. **1671** WOODHEAD *St. Teresa* I. xxv. 172 There never remains any sweetness, or softness, or suppleness in the Soul; but she is, as it were, frighted. **1752** JOHNSON *Rambler* No. 189 ¶11 A governess, whom misfortunes had reduced to suppleness and humility.

b. Servile or obsequious compliance or complaisance.

c **1727** HARTE *Eulogius* 398 He smooth'd his voice to the Bizantine note, With courtly suppleness unfurl'd his face. **1838** LYTTON *Alice* III. i, Naturally dictatorial and presumptuous, his early suppleness to superiors was now exchanged for a self-willed pertinacity. **1855** PRESCOTT *Philip II*, I. ii. I. 13 He had none of the duplicity or of the suppleness which often marks the character of the courtier. **1879** FARRAR *St. Paul* (1883) 207 The ever-rising tide of Roman sensuality and Græco-Syrian suppleness.

suppler ('sʌplə(r)). *rare.* [f. SUPPLE *v.* + -ER[1].] A person or thing that supples.

1620 SHELTON *Quix.* II. I. xiii. 78, I haue suppler [orig. *despegador*] hangs at the pummell of my horse, as good as touch.

†**supplete**, *v. Obs. rare.* In 7 suppleat. [f. L. *supplēt-*, pa. ppl. stem of *supplēre*: see SUPPLY *v.*[1]] *trans.* To supplement.

1664 EXTON *Maritime Dicaeol.* I. iv. 20 Laws..which sprang from the Rhodes, suppleated out of several other titles in the body of the Civil Law.

su'ppletion. Also 4 supplecioun, 5 -plecion, supplexion. [a. OF. *sup(p)letion, supplection*, ad. L. **supplētio, -ōnem*, f. *supplēre* SUPPLY *v.*[1]]

†**1.** Supplementation, supplement. *Obs. rare.*

a **1325** *MS. Rawl. B.* 520 lf. 47 b, Ware fore diuerse supplecicouns of lawe ant newe forlokinges bihouez. **1483** CAXTON *Gold. Leg.* (1892) 33 The quinquagesme..is instituted for supplecion & fulfyllyng. *c* **1485** *Digby Myst.*, *Conversion of St. Paul* 359 The compyler here-of shuld translat veray so holy a story, but with fauorable correccyon of my fauorable masters of þer benygne supplexion.

2. *Linguistics.* The replacement of a form which is missing from a grammatical paradigm by one derived from a different root. Also *attrib.*

1933 L. H. GRAY in *Language* IX. 84 Athematic verbs, as well as their semantic equivalents elsewhere, seem peculiarly liable to suppletion by other verbs to furnish their aorists. **1942** BLOCH & TRAGER *Outl. Linguistic Anal.* iv. 58 Suppletion may be regarded as an extreme kind of internal change, in which the entire base..is replaced by another form. **1951** [see MORPHOLEXICAL *a.*]. **1959** F. W. HOUSEHOLDER in Saporta & Bastian *Psycholinguistics* (1961) 21/1 It is always possible (with due allowance for irregularity and suppletion) to derive a related expression of structure B. **1978** *Language* LIV. 21 Cases of feminine suppletion like *mon amie* are not included.

suppletive (sʌ'pliːtɪv), *a.* (*sb.*) [ad. med.L. *supplētīvus*, f. *supplēt-*: see SUPPLETE and -IVE. Cf. F. *supplétif.*] **1.** Having the attribute of supplying deficiencies. *rare.*

1816–30 BENTHAM *Offic. Apt. Maximized, Extract Const. Code* 52 His functions will be exercised by a depute of his, as per Ch. viii. Prime Minister, §4. Self-suppletive Function. **1862** F. HALL *Hindu Philos. Syst.* 53 Cognition is here denoted by the suppletive expression after 'will'.

2. *Linguistics.* Displaying suppletion. Also as *sb.*, a suppletive form.

1926 L. BLOOMFIELD in *Language* II. 161 If in a construction all the component forms are irregular, the whole form is *suppletive.* If *go* be taken as the stem of the verb, then the past *went* is suppletive. **1933** *Language* IX. 83 'Buy'..appears only in the aorist, serving as suppletive to the present and imperfect of ὠνέομαι. **1934** PRIEBSCH & COLLINSON *German Language* II. ii. 140 For the suppletive comparatives and superlatives cf. the Germanic section. **1957** S. POTTER *Modern Linguistics* iv. 101 *Aller* is suppletive (*aller, vais, irai*). **1964** R. H. ROBINS *Gen. Linguistics* v. 207 Such roots involving total variation among their allomorphs are sometimes called suppletive. **1976** J. S. GRUBER *Lexical Structures in Syntax & Semantics* II. ii. 303 The past tense is not used in those cases in which we have a suppletive form.

So †**su'ppletively** *adv.*, so as to supply deficiencies.

1644 MAXWELL *Prerog. Chr. Kings* x. 104 This tenet, that a King hath his Soveraigne power, *communicativé*, not *privativé*, from the people, that he is so invested with it, that the people have it habitually, suppletively, and may resume it in some exigent cases. [Cf. **1660** BONDE *Scut. Reg.* 71 The people..still retaining the same [government] in the collective body, that is to say, in themselves *suppletive.*]

suppletory ('sʌplɪtərɪ), *a.* and *sb.* [ad. late L. *supplētōrius* (neut. sing. as sb. = supplement), f. *supplēt-*: see SUPPLETE and -ORY[2].]

A. *adj.* Supplying a deficiency; supplementary. Const. *to, of.* †In first quot., expletive. Now *rare.*

1628 DONNE *Serm. Christmas Day* (1640) 52 Many men have..certaine suppletory phrases, which fall often upon their tongue, and..have certaine suppletory Oathes, with which they fill up their Discourse. **1656** BRAMHALL *Replic.* ix. 372 Let him that dare..say that it is a suppletorie Sacrifice, to supply the defects of the Sacrifice of the Cross. **1659** FULLER *App. Inj. Innoc.* I. 42 A Book..which..will be suppletory of all such defects. **1673** *Lady's Call.* I. i. §7 As a suppletory ornament to the deckings of gold and pearl and costly aray. **1778** JOHNSON 15 Apr. in *Boswell*, His hope of salvation must be founded on..obedience; and where obedience has failed, then, as suppletory to it, repentance. **1802** PALEY *Nat. Theol.* xiv. §1 This double or suppletory provision [of teeth]. **1818** CRUISE *Digest* (ed. 2) IV. 305 By suppletory or explanatory evidence. **1856** A. BUTLER *Hist. Anc. Philos.* I. 114 The genus 'pronoun' does not more truly classify the words in a language that are suppletory of nouns. **1874** STEPHEN *New Comm. Laws Eng.* v. viii. (ed. 7) III. 446

Equity..a..portion of our juridical system—distinct from and suppletory to the common law.

b. Law. ***suppletory oath***, an oath (given by a party in his own favour) admitted to supply a deficiency in legal evidence: cf. *oath in supplement* s.v. SUPPLEMENT *sb.*[1] 2 b.

1726 AYLIFFE *Parergon* [305] If I can only prove the Tenor thereof by one Witness, I shall not be admitted to the Suppletory Oath through a Defect of Evidence. **1768** BLACKSTONE *Comm.* III. xxiii. 369 Abroad..a man's own books of accounts..with the suppletory oath of the merchant, amount at all times to full proof. **1802-12** BENTHAM *Ration. Judic. Evid.* (1827) V. 563 The suppletory oath is admitted in default of other sufficient evidence.

†**B.** *sb.* A supplement. *Obs.*

1649 JER. TAYLOR *Gt. Exemp.* II. Disc. viii. §20. 70 The rite of confirmation..is an admirable suppletory of an early Baptisme. **1672-5** COMBER *Comp. Temple* (1702) 475 A Suppletory for any particular omitted. **1698** NORRIS *Pract. Disc.* IV. 86 Force must be made use of as a Suppletory to the defects of Reason. **1707** —— *Treat. Humility* iv. 162, I look upon grace as the suppletory of corrupt nature.

Hence †**'suppletorily** *adv.*, by way of, or as a, supplement.

1622 DONNE *Serm. Christmas Day* (1640) 4 This personall name of the Father (*It pleased the Father*) is but added suppletorily by our Translators, and is not in the Originall.

supplexion, variant of SUPPLETION *Obs.*

†**suppliable**, *a.*[1] *Obs. rare.* [f. SUPPLY *v.*[3] + -ABLE.] Supple.

1599 A. M. tr. *Gabelhouer's Bk. Physicke* 114/2 He causeth the sayede Image to be overdeckede with an Oxehyde..&..glueth on the sayede skinne a suppliable Dogges skinne.

suppliable (sə'plaɪəb(ə)l), *a.*[2] *rare.* Also **supplyable.** [f. SUPPLY *v.*[1] + -ABLE.] Capable of being supplied or supplemented.

1667 WATERHOUSE *Narr. Fire in London* 23 If suppliable elsewhere, yet with more charge. **1681** *Acts Parl. Scot., Chas. II* (1820) VIII. 243/1 That all such writes..wherin the Writer & witnesses are not designed, shall be null, And are not supplyable by condescending upon the Writer. **1754** ERSKINE *Princ. Sc. Law* (1809) 11 Where statutes establish certain solemnities as requisite to deeds, such solemnities are not suppliable by equivalents.

supplial (sə'plaɪəl). Now *rare* or *Obs.* [f. SUPPLY *v.*[1] + -AL[1].] The act of supplying.

1752 WARBURTON *Princ. Nat. & Rev. Relig.* iv. Wks. 1788 V. 58 For the supplial of our imaginary..wants. *a* **1779** —— *Div. Legat.* IV. v. Wks. 1788 II. 560 To form the principal members of his demonstration with an unornamented brevity, and leave the supplial of the small connecting parts to his reader's sagacity. **1801** MASON *Suppl. Johnson's Dict.* Pref. p. iii, The supplial of omissions. **1819** G. S. FABER *Dispensations* (1823) I. 276 The..supplial of all the wants of life.

b. A thing that supplies the place of another.

1837 C. RICHARDSON *Dict.* Pref. iii, It may be deemed a supplial of many books.

suppliance[1] (sə'plaɪəns). Now *rare.* [f. SUPPLY *v.*[1] + -ANCE; cf. SUPPLIANT *a.*[2]] = SUPPLY *sb.*

1598 CHAPMAN *Iliad* IV. [VIII.] 321 When he..lookt vp for helpe to heauen, Which euer at command of Ioue, was by my suppliance geuen. **1604** SHAKS. *Ham.* I. iii. 9 (Q.), A Violet in the youth of Primy Nature;..sweet not lasting The perfume and suppliance of a minute. **1664** POWER *Exper. Philos.* 118 In suppliance of that seeming Vacuity. **1786** ANNA SEWARD *Lett.* (1811) I. 160 To leave something to the suppliance of the heart and the fancy. **1845** TRENCH *Huls. Lect.* Ser. I. v. 95 What a man wins by his labour, be it inward truth, or only some outward suppliance of his need. **1884** BROWNING *Ferishtah, The Sun* 160 To lack is not to gain Our lack's suppliance.

suppliance[2] ('sʌplɪəns). *rare. poet.* [f. SUPPLIANT *a.*[1]: see -ANCE.] The action of a suppliant; supplication.

c **1611** CHAPMAN *Iliad* XVIII. 402 Mightie suppliance, By all their graue men hath bene made. **1615** —— *Odyss.* VI. 211 If..He should..trie with words of grace, In humblest suppliance, if he might..gaine Her grace. **1773** J. ROSS *Fratricide* I. 4 (MS.) Smile on the suppliance of an humbler Bard. **1873** W. S. MAYO *Never Again* xii, The Kaiser smiled, then lifts his child From suppliance at his knee.

So **'suppliancy**, the condition of a suppliant.

1837 *Fraser's Mag.* XVI. 588 The living image of abject suppliancy!

suppliant ('sʌplɪənt), *sb.* and *a.*[1] In mod. use *poet.* or *rhet.* Also 5 **-eant**, 5-6 **-iaunt**, 6-7 **-yant.** [a. F. *suppliant* (superseding older *so(u)pleiant*, *-oiant*), pr. pple. of *supplier* SUPPLY *v.*[2]

In early use sometimes stressed *su'ppliant.*]

A. *sb.* One who supplicates; a humble petitioner.

1429 *Rolls of Parlt.* IV. 346/2 The seide Suppliauntz doubten hem of damage and prejudice. **1480** *Cov. Leet Bk.* 429 Albe-it your pore suppleant to his gret coste & charge hath demaunded the contentacion therof, ȝit he in no wyse can be satisfied. **1549-62** STERNHOLD & H. *Ps.* XXVIII. ii, The voice of thy supplyant heare. **1555** EDEN *Decades* (Arb.) 125 The blessed virgin..with her rodde loosed the bandes of her suppliant. **1594** SHAKS. *Rich. III*, I. i. 74 Heard you not what an humble Suppliant Lord Hastings was, for her deliuery? **1667** MILTON *P.L.* x. 917 Thy suppliant I beg, and clasp thy knees. **1738** WESLEY *Ps.* IV. i, God of my Righteousness Thy humble Suppliant hear. **1814** BYRON *Ode Napoleon* v, The Arbiter of others' fate A Suppliant for his own! **1848** LYTTON *Harold* VIII. iii, The mother is a suppliant to the son for the son.

Comb. **1669** DRYDEN *Tyr. Love* IV. i, She Suppliant-like, e're long, thy succour shall implore.

B. *adj.* Supplicating, humbly petitioning.

a **1586** SIDNEY *Arcadia* III. (1912) 418 One might see by his eyes (humbly lifted up to the window where Philoclea stood) that he was rather suppliaunt, then victorious. **1591** SHAKS. *Two Gent.* III. i. 234 When she for thy repeale was suppliant. **1666** DRYDEN *Ann. Mirab.* ccl, The Rich grow suppliant, and the Poor grow proud. **1781** GIBBON *Decl. & F.* xxvii. (1787) III. 46 The tribunal of the magistrate was besieged by a suppliant crowd. **1818** SCOTT *Rob Roy* xxxiv, I had..seen the followers of this man commit a cruel slaughter on an unarmed and suppliant individual. **1859** TENNYSON *Guinev.* 656 She look'd and saw The novice, weeping, suppliant.

b. *transf.* Expressing or involving supplication.

1667 MILTON *P.L.* I. 112 To bow and sue for grace With suppliant knee. **1697** DRYDEN *Virg. Georg.* IV. 775 With Vows and suppliant Pray'rs. **1767** WILKES *Corr.* (1805) III. 193 Was it possible for me after this to write a suppliant letter to lord Chatham? **1800** WORDSW. *Hart-leap Well* 22 With suppliant gestures. **1870** BRYANT *Iliad* I. VI. 197 Stretched forth their suppliant hands To Pallas.

Hence **'suppliantness** (Bailey, vol. II. 1727).

†**supp'liant**, *a.*[2] *Obs. rare*[−1]. [f. SUPPLY *v.*[1] + -ANT.] Supplying deficiencies; supplementary.

1611 SHAKS. *Cymb.* III. vii. 12 Those Legions..whereunto your leuie Must be suppliant.

†**suppliant**, *a.*[3] *Obs. rare*[−1]. [f. SUPPLY *v.*[3] + -ANT.] Suppling, emollient; = SUPPLE *a.* 7.

1631 R. H. *Arraignm. Whole Creature* xiii. §2. 204 To thinke to heale a green wound with suppliant oyles, and yet the poysoned bullet stick still in the flesh.

suppliantly ('sʌplɪəntlɪ), *adv.* [f. SUPPLIANT *a.*[1] + -LY[2].] In a suppliant manner, or as a suppliant; in the way of supplication; beseechingly.

1565 STAPLETON tr. *Bede's Hist. Ch. Eng.* 158 Entreating as suppliantly as I could to have licence to galloppe my horse ..with the other younge men. **1605** CAMDEN *Rem.* (1637) 255 His brother John..came in..and suppliantly besought Richard, brotherly to pardon his..offences. **1750** *Student* I. 139 Can [he]..not prostrate himself..before the throne of grace, and suppliantly implore the divine mercy for his..sins? **1842** G. S. FABER *Prov. Lett.* (1844) I. 230 Suppliantly invocating the saints. **1895** *Daily News* 10 May 6/3 Two hundred members of the House of Commons called at his private house..suppliantly to ascertain how they stood with him.

‖**suppli'camus.** *Obs. nonce wd.* [L., = 'we supplicate', 1st pers. pl. pres. indic. of *supplicāre* to SUPPLICATE: after legal terms such as *mandamus*, etc.] A petition, entreaty.

1574-5 G. HARVEY *Mercy Harvey* Wks. (Grosart) III. 89 Swearing that she should haue any thing he had at commaundiment, and vse him as familiarly..as her owne brother; with a many sutch goodly supplicamussis.

†**'supplicancy.** *Obs. rare*[−1]. [f. next: see -ANCY.] Suppliant quality, beseechingness.

1728 GORDON *Tacitus, Ann.* xv. 408 The first letter..contain'd nothing of supplicancy or abasement.

supplicant ('sʌplɪkənt), *sb.* and *a.* Now *rare* exc. *arch.* Also 7 **suplicant.** [ad. L. *supplicantem, -ans*, pr. pple. of *supplicāre* to SUPPLICATE. Cf. It., Pg. *supplicante*, Sp. *suplicante.*]

A. *sb.* = SUPPLIANT *sb.*

1597 HOOKER *Eccl. Pol.* v. xxxv. §1 The Prince and people of Nineueh assembling themselues as a maine army of supplicants. **1650** ROW *Hist. Kirk* Suppl. (Wodrow Soc.) 491 The supplicants [in 1638] gave in a Supplication to his Majestie's Commissioners for a free Generall Assemblie and Parliaments. **1693** tr. *Dupin's Hist. Eccl. Writers* II. 109 The Third Rank of Catechumens was, that of those that were present at the Prayers, who were called the *Supplicants* or the *Prostrati.* **1834** K. H. DIGBY *Mores Cath.* v. vi. 184 The pious supplicants, who repair to the churches. **1873** BURTON *Hist. Scot.* VI. lxix. 161 The Supplicants treated the king's person with great reverence.

b. *spec.* One who supplicates for a degree: see SUPPLICATE *v.* 3.

1649 LAMONT *Diary* (Maitl. Club) 6 Ther was 12 [scholars] in euery colledge, and two supplicants laureat. **1901** RASHDALL & RAIT *New College* 220 When a Fellow of New College takes any degree, his name is omitted from the list of supplicants.

B. *adj.* = SUPPLIANT *a.*[1]

1597 SHAKS. *Lover's Compl.* 276 All these hearts that doe on mine depend,..supplicant their sighes to you extend. **1605** CAMDEN *Rem., Epigr.* 16 One did write this supplicant Verse to the Emperour. **1705** HULL *Corrupt. Ch. Rome* iii. 268 [They] offer'd to this Council their Letters supplicant, confessing that they had sinn'd. **1787** *Phil. Trans.* LXXVII. 259 Pricking up the ears when anxious,..depressing them when supplicant. **1807** J. BARLOW *Columb.* II. 338 A sovereign supplicant with lifted hands. **1834** K. H. DIGBY *Mores Cath.* v. iii. 85 The supplicant people.

Hence **'supplicantly** *adv.* = SUPPLIANTLY.

1864 in WEBSTER.

‖**supplicat** ('sʌplɪkæt). Also 7-9 **-ate.** [L., = he supplicates, 3rd pers. sing. pres. ind. of *supplicāre* to SUPPLICATE. Formerly often assimilated in form to abstract nouns in -ATE[1]:—L. *-ātus* (but cf. med.L. *supplicātus*).

In university use arising from its occurrence as the first word in the formula used by the proctor in presenting the petition. In quots. 1660 and 1859[2], perh. an independent formation in -ATE[1].]

A supplication, petition *spec.* (now only) in English universities, a formal petition for a degree or for incorporation (cf. SUPPLICANT b, SUPPLICATE *v.* 3, SUPPLICATION e).

1660 Z. CROFTON *Fastening of St. Peter's Fetters* 153 The servants query..was not a supplicate for an Authoritative Release; but a scrutiny into the Extent of the Oath. **1665** J. BUCK in Peacock *Stat. Cambr.* (1841) App. B. p. xc, There are no supplicats put up for King's College Fellows. **1691** WOOD *Ath. Oxon.* I. *Fasti* 637 This year was a Supplicate made in the venerable Congregation of Regents for one Tho. Dalby to be admitted to a Degree in Decrees. *Ibid.* 641 Supplicat. *Ibid.* 662 This year.. there was a kind of a Supplicate made for one Magnus a Doctor beyond the Sea, to be incorporated here. **1715** M. DAVIES *Athen. Brit.* I. 23 This Supplicat being granted, he was..crown'd..with a Wreath of Lawrel; that is, doctorated in the Arts of Grammar and Rhetorick. **1859** *Cambr. Univ. Cal.* 2 No degree is ever conferred without a Grace for that purpose. The Grace in this instance is termed a Supplicat. **1859** MASSON *Milton* I. vii. 678 The king has hitherto shown his displeasure by leaving the supplicates substantially unanswered. **1906** WELLS *Oxf. Degree Ceremony* 8 One of the Proctors reads out the *supplicat.*

supplicate ('sʌplɪkeɪt), *v.* (Also 7 *pa. pple.* **-ate.**) [f. L. *supplicāt-*, pa. ppl. stem of *supplicāre*, f. *sup-* = SUB- 2 + *plic-*, root of *plicāre* to bend (cf. *supplex, supplic-* SUPPLE). Cf. SUPPLY *v.*[2]]

1. *intr.* To beg, pray, or entreat humbly; to present a humble petition. Const. *to* or *unto* a person (*obs.*), *for* a thing; also with dependent clause introduced by *that*, or inf.

1417 in Ellis *Orig. Lett.* Ser. II. I. 55 Wee..have supplicated unto him..to attend heare. **1625** BACON *Ess., Friendship* (Arb.) 181 A Man cannot sometimes brooke to Supplicate or Beg. **1625** USSHER *Answ. Jesuit* 457 Doe we supplicate vnto these, because by these we supplicate vnto God? **1652** NEEDHAM tr. *Selden's Mare Cl.* 34 Giacomo Croato..was..assailed by an armed Bark of Pirates..and supplicate's that som order might bee taken therein. **1654** in *Verney Mem.* (1907) I. 556, I supplicate to non for there good word. *a* **1700** EVELYN *Diary* 23 Feb. 1645, Supplicating for a victory over the Turks. **1771** tr. *Horstius' Parad. Soul* App. 7 O holy Mary..supplicate for the devout Female Sex. **1791** MRS. RADCLIFFE *Rom. Forest* ix, I supplicated to know what was designed me. **1805** WORDSW. *Ode to Duty* v, I supplicate for thy control. **1862** R. VAUGHAN *Eng. Nonconform.* 44 He urged..that the rubric should not supplicate that the bread and wine might become the body and blood of Christ to the recipient. **1864** TENNYSON *En. Ard.* 163 Annie..Besought him, supplicating, if he cared For her or his dear children, not to go. **1876** MISS BRADDON *J. Haggard's Dau.* II. 19, I have thought of you often..and have supplicated for you in my prayers.

2. *trans.* To petition humbly. **a.** with the person addressed as obj.; also with compl. clause or inf.

1642 *Decl. Lords & Comm. Gen. Assemb. Ch. Scot.* 11 The Assembly has humbly supplicate the Kings Majesty. *a* **1696** in Aubrey *Misc.* 165 They have supplicated the Presbyterie, who judicially appointed publick Prayers to be made. **1835** LYTTON *Rienzi* I. iv, To supplicate Clement VI to remove the Holy See from Avignon to Rome. **1864** TENNYSON *Boadicea* 9 Shall I brook to be supplicated?

b. with the thing sought as obj.

1660 R. COKE *Power & Subj.* 244 The Church..did supplicate protection from the temporall powers. **1779** *Mirror* No. 35 ¶3, The blessings which a fond father should supplicate from Heaven for his offspring. **1791** MRS. RADCLIFFE *Rom. Forest* vi, I supplicate of you a few moments' private discourse. **1838** JAS. GRANT *Sk. Lond.* 242 Supplicating a crust of bread for her famishing children. **1854** MISS M. S. CUMMINS *Lamplighter* xxiii, To supplicate Heaven's blessing upon them.

3. *spec. intr.* In Oxford University, to present a formal petition for a degree or for incorporation. †Also *trans.*, to present such a petition to (Congregation).

1691 WOOD *Ath. Oxon.* I. *Fasti* 638 Thom. Beaumont..did supplicate to be licensed to proceed in Divinity. *Ibid.* 639 John Newland..supplicated for a Degree in Divinity. *Ibid.* 642 James Denton..sometimes Fellow of Kings Coll. in Cambridg, did..supplicate to be incorporated. *Ibid.* 643 Richard Ede,..Scholar in Musick, did supplicate the ven. Congregation to be admitted Bachelaur of that Faculty. *Ibid.* 644 Eight [men] supplicated to oppose. **1830** *Oxf. Univ. Cal.* 16 In the sole instance of supplicating for Graces ..every Member of the House is invested.. with a suspending negative upon each Grace for three times. **1891** *Ibid.* 76 No Graduate in any Faculty can supplicate for incorporation without..having obtained express permission from the Hebdomadal Council.

Hence **'supplicated** *ppl. a.*

1861 WARDLAW *Lect. Romans* (1869) I. ii. 26 Under the supplicated guidance of the Holy Spirit.

supplicating ('sʌplɪkeɪtɪŋ), *ppl. a.* [f. SUPPLICATE *v.* + -ING[2].] That supplicates, or expresses supplication; humbly petitioning or entreating.

1649 MILTON *Eikon.* iv. Wks. 1851 III. 362 As for that supplicating People they did no hurt either to Law or Authority. **1726** SWIFT *Gulliver* III. i, I then put myself into the most supplicating postures, and spoke in the humblest accent. **1797** MRS. RADCLIFFE *Italian* xvi, 'Do not leave me,' said she, in accents the most supplicating. *a* **1859** MACAULAY *Hist. Eng.* xxiv. (1861) V. 177 A request made..in earnest and almost supplicating terms. **1880** MEREDITH *Tragic Com.* (1881) 72 She would not have listened..to a silly supplicating girl.

Hence **'supplicatingly** *adv.*

1865 MEREDITH *Rhoda Fleming* xliv, Rhoda..turned her eyes supplicatingly on Robert. **1884** GOLDSMID *Wright's Pol. Songs* II. 45 *Song of Lewes*, Those whose aid he will ask supplicatingly.

supplication (sʌplɪˈkeɪʃən), *sb.* Also 5 supl-. [a. OF. (mod.F.) *supplication* (= It. *supplicazione*, Sp. *suplicacion*, Pg. *supplicação*), ad. L. *supplicātio*, *-ōnem*, n. of action f. *supplicāre* to SUPPLICATE.] The action, or an act, of supplicating; humble or earnest petition or entreaty.

1384 in Arnolde *Chron.* (1811) 36 At the supplicacion of the Mayre Sherefs and Communalyte of the cite of London to vs mekely Imade. *c* **1399** CHAUCER *Purse* 26 Ye that mowen alle myn harme amende Haue mynde vpon my supplicacion. **1417** in Ellis *Orig. Lett.* Ser. II. I. 58 Hee dayly made suplication to have peace. **1432–50** tr. *Higden* (Rolls) III. 227 His moder and his wife..made a supplicacion to hym for the savegarde of the cite. *a* **1513** FABYAN *Chron.* v. cxxxi. (1811) 114 He..ordeyned such meanes as byllys of supplicacion,..that the causes and matiers of poore men myght come to his knowlege. **1555** EDEN *Decades* (Arb.) 80 They made humble supplication to the Admiral. **1671** MILTON *Samson* 1459, I have attempted..the Lords..With supplication prone and Fathers tears To accept of ransom for my Son. **1781** GIBBON *Decl. & F.* xviii. (1787) II. 94 Peace was at length granted to their humble supplications. **1855** MACAULAY *Hist. Eng.* xiv. III. 475 Pathetic earnestness of supplication. **1856** FROUDE *Hist. Eng.* II. viii. 301 In a moment the noise and bravado..was hushed into a supplication for forgiveness.

b. A written or formal petition. *Obs.* exc. *Hist.*

1390 GOWER *Conf.* III. 352 Whanne I this Supplicacioun ..Hadde after min entente write Unto Cupide and to Venus. *c* **1460** FORTESCUE *Abs. & Lim. Mon.* xiv. (1885) 143 þat all supplicacions wich shalbe made to þe kynge..be sende to þe..counsell. *a* **1578** LINDESAY (Pitscottie) *Chron. Scot.* (S.T.S.) I. 90 Schir patrick gray..passit haistelie with the said wreitting and supplicatioun of the kingis to the erle of douglas. **1592** KYD *Sp. Trag.* III. xiii. 78 Whats heere? 'The humble supplication of Don Bazulto for his murdred Sonne.' **1606** DEKKER *Newes fr. Hell* Wks. (Grosart) II. 91 Great wagers were layd..that when the Supplication was sent, it would not be receyued; or if receyued, it would not be read ouer. **1650** [see SUPPLICANT *sb.*]. **1816** SCOTT *Old Mort.* xxx, A paper, termed a Remonstrance and Supplication. **1822** —— *Nigel* iii, To have the Supplication put into his Majesty's own hands.

c. (A) humble prayer addressed to God (or a deity); chiefly *pl.*, esp. in phr. ***prayers and supplications***; *spec.* the petitions for special blessings in litanies.

1490 CAXTON *Eneydos* xiii. 46 Bifore the aulters thei offred sacrifices with grete supplycacyons and prayers. **1526** TINDALE *Acts* i. 14 These all continued with one acorde in prayer and supplicacion. —— *1 Tim.* ii. 1 That..prayeers, supplicacions, peticions, and gevynge of thankes be had for all men. **1526** *Pilgr. Perf.* (W. de W. 1531) 3 The sayd Moyses..made supplicacyon to God. **1549** *Bk. Com. Prayer, Communion* ad fin., Assist us mercifully, O Lord, in these our supplicacions and praiers. *Ibid.*, *Litany* ad fin., With one accorde to make our comune supplicacions unto thee. **1643** SIR T. BROWNE *Relig. Med.* II. §6. 154, I cannot see one say his Prayers, but in stead of imitating him, I fall into a supplication for him. **1657** SPARROW *Bk. Com. Prayer* 100 These Collects after the Letany, though the matter of them hath been prayed for before particularly in the Supplications foregoing [etc.]. **1663** PATRICK *Parab. Pilgr.* xxv. (1687) 278 In devout supplications to Jesus. **1678** CUDWORTH *Intell. Syst.* I. iv. §27. 455 We conclude, that this *Kyrie Eleeson*, or *Domine Miserere*, in Arrianus, was a Pagan Litany or Supplication to the Supreme God. **1817** SHELLEY *Rev. Islam* x. xxvi, Each among the train To his own Idol lifts his supplications vain. **1837** CARLYLE *Fr. Rev.* I. I. i, The churches resounded with supplications and groans. **1882** *Encycl. Brit.* XIV. 696/1 From an early period the special written litanies of the various churches all showed the common features which are now regarded as essential to a litany, in as far as they consisted of (1) invocations, (2) deprecations, (3) intercessions, (4) supplications.

d. *Rom. Antiq.* A religious solemnity decreed on the occasion of some important public event, esp. in thanksgiving for victory.

1606 HOLLAND *Sueton.* 10 By reason that his affaires sped well..hee obtained in regard thereof solemne Supplications both oftner, and to hold more daies than ever any man did (before himselfe). **1741** MIDDLETON *Cicero* (1742) II. VII. 229 After the contemptible account which Cicero gives of Bibulus's conduct in Syria, it must appear strange to see him honored with a supplication, and aspiring even to a Triumph. **1753** *Chambers' Cycl.* Suppl., App. s.v., On subduing the Sabines, in the year of the city 304, a supplication of one day only was ordained.

e. *spec.* In Oxford University, a formal petition for a degree or for incorporation: cf. SUPPLICAT.

1691 WOOD *Ath. Oxon.* I. *Fasti* 640 This year was a Supplication made in the ven. Congregation of Regents for one Rich. Bere..to be graduated in Divinity. *Ibid.* 670 Richard Brynckley..Dr. of Divinity of Cambridge... His supplication..was granted..and his incorporation..set down..under this year (1524). **1810** *Oxf. Univ. Cal.* 3 In the Congregation degrees are conferred, graces or supplications for them having been there previously proposed and passed. **1895** RASHDALL *Univ. Europe* II. 508 This abstention on the part of Wykehamists from the 'supplications', which had come to be regarded as essential to all other candidates.

Hence **suppliˈcation** *v.*, *trans.* to make supplication to; **suppliˈcationer**, a petitioner.

1585 in *Cath. Rec. Soc. Publ.* V. 106 Against th'untruth of such libellers and supplicationers. **1589** [? NASHE] *Almond for Parrat* N.'s Wks. 1905 III. 365 The Protestationer, Demonstrationer, Supplicationer, Appellationer. **1593** —— *Christ's T.* Wks. (Grosart) IV. 61, I haue..humbly supplicationd you, to accept of my largesse.

†**supplicative**, *a.* *Obs. rare.* [f. L. *supplicāt-*: see SUPPLICATE and -IVE.] Supplicatory.

1600 W. WATSON *Decacordon* (1602) 120 A very formall letter, petitionall or supplicatiue.

supplicator (ˈsʌplɪkeɪtə(r)). [ad. late L. *supplicātor*, agent-n. f. *supplicāre* to SUPPLICATE.] One who supplicates; a suppliant, petitioner.

1634–5 BRERETON *Trav.* (Chetham Soc.) 81 This is a pretty supplicator. **1687** [SHIELDS] *Hind let loose* 57 Our sneaking Supplicators, & Petitioners, & Pardon-mongers. **1794** T. TAYLOR *Pausanias' Descr. Greece* II. 195 Other ambassadors and supplicators were sent to the Romans. **1843** LYTTON *Last Bar.* IV. ii, The supplicators then withdrew from the royal presence.

supplicatory (ˈsʌplɪkətərɪ), *a.* [ad. med.L. *supplicātōrius*, f. *supplicātor*: see prec. and -ORY[2]. Cf. F. *supplicatoire*.] Expressing, consisting of, or containing supplication.

letters supplicatory, ***supplicatory letters*** = F. *lettres supplicatoires*, mod.L. *supplices litteræ*. (*Obs.* exc. *Hist.*)

c **1450** *Mankind* 866 in *Macro Plays* 32 Wyth-owte deserte & menys supplicatorie, ȝe be compacient to my inexcusabyll reprowe. **1550** *Reg. Privy Council Scot.* I. 92 Heraldis with lettres supplicatouris. **1579** STUBBES in *Harington's Nugæ Ant.* (1804) I. 151 To offer this supplicatorye submission and peticion into your Majesties handes. **1583** TRAVERS (*title*) An Answere to a Svpplicatorie Epistle of G. T. for the pretended Catholiqves. **1699** BURNET *39 Art.* xxv. 283 The Pardon that we give in the Name of God, is only declaratory of his Pardon, or supplicatory in a prayer to him for Pardon. **1732** NEAL *Hist. Purit.* I. 205 They framed a supplicatory letter. **1742** RICHARDSON *Pamela* III. 289, I..laid my Hand upon her Ladyship's in a supplicatory Manner. **1820** SOUTHEY *Wesley* II. 553 A supplicatory hymn for his recovery was sung in the church. **1876** BANCROFT *Hist. U.S.* V. xxii. 578 The Vermont council of safety despatched supplicatory letters for aid to the New Hampshire committee.

b. Of persons: Suppliant. *rare.*

1880 MEREDITH *Tragic Com.* (1881) 287 After the manner of supplicatory ladies appealing to lawyers.

Hence **supplicatorily** *adv.*, in a supplicatory manner.

1625 DONNE *Serm. 26 Apr.* (1649) II. 289 Having the dignity of a Parent upon her, she [*sc.* the Church] does not proceed supplicatorily, .. but .. imperatively, authoritatively.

‖**supplicavit** (sʌplɪˈkeɪvɪt). *Law.* [L., = he has supplicated, 3rd pers. sing. perf. ind. of *supplicāre* to SUPPLICATE.] A writ formerly issuing out of the King's Bench or the Court of Chancery for taking surety of the peace against a person: so called from the first word in the writ.

1507 in Leadam *Sel. Cases Star Chamber* (Selden Soc.) 260 By virtue of the kynges writt of supplicauit to them directed. **1518** —— *Sel. Cases Crt. Requests* (Selden Soc.) 14 Robert..sued oute of the kynges chauncry a wrytte of supplicauit ayenst your seid besechour. **1623** BACON *Ordinances* §87 No *Supplicavit* for the good behaviour shall be granted, but upon Articles grounded upon the Oath of two at the least. **1682** LUTTRELL *Brief Rel.* (1857) I. 162 Articles were exhibited, in a speciall supplicavit formerly granted in the court of Kings bench..by the court of arches ..against Edmund Hickeringill, minister, for severall indignities offered to that court. **1769** BLACKSTONE *Comm.* IV. xviii. 250 If the justice is averse to act, it may be granted by a mandatory writ, called a *supplicavit*.

supplice. *rare.* [ad. L. *supplicium*, f. *supplic-*, *supplex* (see SUPPLE *a.*). In quot. 1911 ad. F. *supplice*.] Punishment; torture.

1656 BLOUNT *Glossogr.*, *Supplice*.., punishment, correction, pain, torment; it is also used for Prayer or Supplication, and sometimes for Sacrifice. *Mr. Montagu.* **1911** MRS. OLIPHANT *Salem Chapel* I. 12 It is easier to play the victim under the supplice inflicted by a pretty girl than by two mature matrons.

supplie, obs. form of SUPPLY.

supplied (səˈplaɪd), *ppl. a. rare.* [f. SUPPLY *v.*[1] + -ED[1].] In senses of the verb: usually with prefixed adv., as ***well-supplied***.

1609 CHAPMAN *Tears of Peace, Addr. Death* 31 The river needes the helpfull fountaine ever, More then the fountaine the supplyed river. **1900** *Westm. Gaz.* 29 May 4/1 A well-supplied advance depôt.

supplier (səˈplaɪə(r)). Forms: 5–6 *Sc.* supplear, 7 -yer, 7– supplier. [f. SUPPLY *v.*[1] + -ER[1].]

†**1.** One who takes the place of or acts as substitute for another. *Obs.*

1491 *Cartular. S. Nicholai Aberdon.* (New Spalding Club) I. 255 Ilkane chaplane writin to ye haly blude mess.. falȝeande in þe doinge of þame sal pay iiii d to ye supplear.

†**2.** A helper, supporter; an assistant. *Obs.*

1515 in Pitcairn *Crim. Trials* (1833) I. 232* Makand him and his assignais Keparis ouersearis, correkaris, and suplearis of the Isle of Litill Comeray..becaus Robert Huntare..Forrestar of heretage of þe said Ile, is nocht of power to resist þe personis þat waistis þe samyn, without suplé and help. **1525** *St. Papers Hen. VIII*, IV. 418 Togither with yair part takaris, assistaris, supplearis. **1586** *Reg. Privy Council Scot.* IV. 71 Ressavaris, supplearis and intercommonaris with the Kingis rebellis. **1654** tr. *Scudery's Curia Pol.* 69 His neighbour Princes will censure his ambition, and rather be spectators of his successes, then be supplyers.

3. One who makes up a deficiency.

1607 CHAPMAN *Bussy d'Ambois* II. i. 103 All vaunt themselves Law-menders and suppliers. **1737** STACKHOUSE *Hist. Bible* v. v. (1752) I. 745/2 Saul might set up for..a Supplier of the Default of Joshua.

4. One who (or that which) furnishes something needed; a provider, purveyor.

c **1630** RISDON *Surv. Devon* §202 (1810) 211 Dartmore, our daily supplier. **1796** MORSE *Amer. Geog.* II. 440 Brundusium..was the great supplier of oysters for the Roman tables. **1827** *Examiner* 99/1 The suppliers of intellectual gratification. **1858** GEN. P. THOMPSON *Audi Alt.* lxxvi. II. 28 To reduce Asia to be the supplier of the European slave-market. **1897** MARY KINGSLEY *W. Africa* 665 Van Huytemers and Peters are the two great suppliers of the gin that goes to West Africa. **1907** O'GORMAN *Motor Pocket Bk.* (ed. 2) 463 You cannot have too many spares, though the supplier will tell you the contrary.

b. An apparatus for supplying something; a feeder.

1823 J. BADCOCK *Dom. Amusem.* 147 A kind of funnel-shaped supplier.

ˈ**suppliment.** *dial.* Also -ement. [Corruption of SUBLIMATE.] Corrosive sublimate. Also ***silver suppliment***.

1809 PARKINS *Culpepper's Eng. Phys. Enlarged* 385 How to take away little red pimples from the face. Take two ounces of lemon juice, two ounces of rose water, two drachms of silver suppliment. **1886** *Cheshire Gloss.* s.v., A chemist, if asked for supplement, would perfectly well understand what was wanted.

suppliment, obs. form of SUPPLEMENT *sb.*

suppline, obs. Sc. form of SIPLING.

suppling (ˈsʌplɪŋ), *vbl. sb.* [f. SUPPLE *v.* + -ING[1].] The action of SUPPLE *v.*; making supple.

a. in literal senses.

1577 B. GOOGE *Heresbach's Husb.* II. (1586) 87 b, Of Oyle, some part serueth for meate, and other for the sowpling of the bodie. **1655** MOUFET & BENNET *Health's Improv.* (1746) 221 The Butter..is most thin, liquid, moist and penetrating, whereby such a suppeling is procured, that their Cheeses do rather ripen than dry with long lying. **1668** WILKINS *Real Char.* II. vi. §5. 173 That Cavity or Glandule ..containing an unctuous substance for the suppling of the Feathers. **1676** MACE *Musick's Mon.* 56 That part..will ask good Suppleing with Water and Heat, before it will yield. **1720** W. GIBSON *Diet. Horses* x. (1731) 163 The suppling of the Joints [of a horse], which is generally first practised, is very reasonable. **1802** C. JAMES *Milit. Dict.*, *Siguette*,..a sort of nose-band..which is put on the nose of a horse, to forward the suppling or breaking of him. **1889** BADEN-POWELL *Pigsticking* 124 A few hours of quiet suppling and bending will amply repay the trouble.

b. in fig. senses.

1617 R. FENTON *Treat. Ch. Rome* 64 It cureth by way of suppling, to teach them to be gracious Soveraignes, to establish their royal thrones by mercy. **1625** DONNE *Serm. 3 Apr.* 26 For the suppling of boysterous, and for the becalming of tempestuous humours. **1853** RUSKIN *Stones Venice* II. vi. §59 That quickening and suppling of the dull spirit that cannot be gained for it but by bathing it in blood. **1865** LOWELL *Scotch the Snake* Prose Wks. 1890 V. 245 We doubt if any substantial excellence is lost by this suppling of the intellectual faculties.

suppling (ˈsʌplɪŋ), *ppl. a.* [f. SUPPLE *v.* + -ING[2].] That renders the skin or the joints of the body supple; also, softening, emollient.

1562 TURNER *Herbal* II. 101 The rosin..of the popler is menged oft tymes with softenyng and souplyng emplasters. **1562** *Burnynge of Paules Ch. in Lond.*, Nothinge..does more ease the paines of the sicke bodye than these supplinge oiles. **1638** RAWLEY tr. *Bacon's Life & Death* (1650) 64 Onely three Set Diets: The Opiate Diet, the Diet Malacissant, or Suppling; and the Diet Emaciant, & Renewing. **1639** T. DE GREY *Compl. Horsem.* 272 Mollifie the heeles of the horse with suppling things. **1648** HERRICK *Hesper.*, *To the King to cure Evill*, All those suppling healing herbs and flowers. **1650** VENNER *Via Recta, Baths of Bathe* 356 The Crosse-bath is an excellent temperate soupling bath. **1710** T. FULLER *Pharm. Extemp.* 422 By means of suppleing Oils, those Fibrillae are..lubricated, and relaxed. **1871** *Daily News* 11 Apr. 6 Good marching..tells of weary but necessary hours over the goose step, of laborious and oft-repeated 'suppling' motions.

b. in fig. context or allusively.

1563 *Form Medit.* in *Liturg. Serv. Q. Eliz.* (Parker Soc.) 505 Mollify..O Lord, our flinty hearts with the suppling moisture of thy Holy Spirit. **1595** SOUTHWELL *St. Peter's Compl.* lxxx, Pour suppling showers upon my parchèd ground. **1632** G. HERBERT *Priest to Temple* xviii, Mollifying and suppling words. **1659** W. CHAMBERLAYNE *Pharonnida* II. 154 If ere thy sober Reason did submit To suppling Mirth. **1713** C'TESS WINCHELSEA *Misc. Poems* 382 Employ my Hand, yet warm, to close the Wound, And with my suppling Tears disperse the anguish. **1727** P. WALKER *Life R. Cameron* in *Biogr. Presbyt.* (1827) I. 194 In the 1719, there was a softning, soupling, sweetning Oil, composed and made up by the cunning Art of carnal Wit, and State-policy.

†**suˈpplode**, *v.* *Obs. rare*[−0]. [ad. L. *supplōdĕre*, f. *sup-* = SUB- + *plaudĕre* PLAUD *v.*] *intr.* To stamp with the feet. So †**suˈpplosion** [L. *supplōsio*].

1599 *Broughton's Lett.* xii. 42 It deserueth a supplosion or an hissing. **1623** COCKERAM, *Supplode*, to stampe with the foot. **1656** BLOUNT *Glossogr.*, *Supplosion*.., a stamping or noise with the feet.

†**supplusage.** *Obs.* Variant of SURPLUSAGE.

c **1475** *Pol. Poems* (Rolls) II. 283 With the supplusage of oone of thyse iij. thynges. **1507–8** *Rec. St. Mary at Hill* 262 We haue Resseyuyd of the Supploragiis [? Supplusagis] of the last yere ix li viij s iiij d.

supply (səˈplaɪ), *sb.* Forms: 5 supplye (6–7 *pl.* supplyes), 5–6 *Sc.* supple, 6–8 supplie, 7– supply. [f. SUPPLY *v.*[1] (In early use mainly *Sc.*)]

I. The action of supplying, or condition of being supplied.

†**1.** Assistance, succour, support, relief. Also predicated of a person or thing that is the means of assistance or support. *Obs.*

Phr. *to make* (*a*) *supply*, to give assistance.

1423 JAS. I *Kingis Q.* xv, Ryght as the schip that sailith stereles Vpon the rokkis most to harmes hye, For lak of It that suld bene hir supplye. *Ibid.* cxii, In this case sche [*sc.* Minerva] may be thy supplye. *c* **1480** HENRYSON *Fables, Fox, Wolf, & Cadger* xiv, ȝe man tak trauell and mak vs sum supple. **1513** DOUGLAS *Æn.* III. x. 105, I leis..all supple of our travale and pane. **1549** *Compl. Scot.* Ep. Queen 1 The langorius desolat & affligit pepil, quhilkis ar al mast disparit of mennis supple. **1567** *Gude & Godlie B.* (S.T.S.) 46 Quhair I culd nocht the Law fulfill, My warkis maid me na supplie. *Ibid.* 162 Thow art..My hope, support, and haill supplie. **1587** TURBERV. *Trag. Tales* (1837) 32 When he sawe Nastagio bent For her supplie, whom he would reave of life. **1598** R. BERNARD tr. *Terence, Phormio* I. iv, Heere will I lie in a bush to make a supply, if you shall faile in anything. **1602** SHAKS. *Ham.* II. ii. 24 To expend your time with vs a-while, For the supply and profit of our Hope. *c* **1614** MURE *Dido & Æneas* I. 566 See how Penthesilea leads Her Amazonian trowpes to Troye's supplie! **1697** DRYDEN *Virg. Georg.* II. 597 Apple Trees..Want no Supply, but stand secure alone.

2. The act of making up a deficiency, or of fulfilling a want or demand.

Phr. †*to make* (*a*) *supply*, to fill up a deficiency.

1500–20 DUNBAR *Poems* xxviii. 35 Supportand faltis with ȝour supple. **1596** BACON *Max. & Use Com. Law* II. (1635) 61 The maner of making supply when the part of the heire is not a full third. **1638** QUARLES *Hieroglyph.* I. Epigr. i. 3 Thy wants are far more safe then their supply. **1662** H. MORE *Philos. Writ.* Pref. Gen. (1712) 17, I omitted to set down the Succession of the Pythagorick School..and therefore I will here make a supply out of Diogenes Laertius. **1768** TUCKER *Lt. Nat.* I. xxvii. 186 Why are usefull things good? because they minister to the supply of our wants and desires. **1824** L. MURRAY *Eng. Gram.* (ed. 5) I. 317 The supply of the ellipsis..gives an uncouth appearance to these sentences. **1835** T. MITCHELL *Acharn. of Aristoph.* App. 245 A system..which drew..upon the purses of the tributary states for a supply of those pecuniary demands, which the native resources of Athens were unable to furnish.

†**3. a.** The act of supplying something needed; the filling up *of* a place or position; the provision *of* a person or thing in the place of another; the substitution *of* a thing for something else. *Obs.*

1585 in *Presbyt. Movem. Eliz.* (Camden) 53 Mr. Tay.. desired the brethren to helpe him..for the supplie of his place. **1607** SHAKS. *Timon* II. i. 27 My releefe Must not be tost and turn'd to me in words, But finde supply immediate. **1608** J. KING *Serm. S. Mary's, Oxf.* 5 Two partes, first the cession or decease of the one, secondly the succession and supply of the other. **1667** MILTON *P.L.* XI. 736 The South-wind..all the Clouds together drove..; the Hills to their supplie Vapour..Sent up amain. **1673** TEMPLE *United Prov.* Wks. 1731 I. 34 This Course seems to have been instituted by way of Supply or Imitation of the Chamber of Mechlyn.

b. Now only in reference to persons: The act, or position, of supplying a vacancy, or officiating temporarily instead of another, esp. as a minister or preacher; *on supply* = acting in such a capacity.

1580 CAMPION in Allen *Martyrdom Campion* (1908) 23 Such as..are to be sent for supplie,..let them be well trained for the pulpit. **1896** 'IAN MACLAREN' *Kate Carnegie* 248 A 'probationer', who on Saturdays can be seen at any country junction, bag in hand, on his patient errand of 'supply'. **1905** *Daily Chron.* 1 Sept. 1/6 Wanted, an Assistant School-master, on 'Supply.' **1912** *Universe* 16 Aug. 12/1 Southwark... Father Hallett [stationed] on supply at Melior Street.

4. a. The provision or furnishing *of* a person, etc. with necessaries.

1781 COWPER *Charity* 251 These have an ear for his paternal call, Who makes some rich for the supply of all. **1805** COLLINGWOOD 7 Oct. in Nicolas *Disp. Nelson* (1846) VII. 83 *note*, The active part he takes in everything that relates to the supply of the Fleet. **1848** DICKENS *Dombey* xx, The Native then handed him separately, and with a decent interval between each supply, his wash-leather gloves, his thick stick, and his hat. **1876** VOYLE & STEVENSON *Milit. Dict.* (ed. 3) s.v., In time of peace the method of supply is by contract for the principal articles of sustenance.

b. *in short supply*: see SHORT *a.* 15 a.

II. That which is supplied.

†**5.** *coll. sing.* or *pl.* An additional body of persons, esp. reinforcements of troops. *Obs.*

c **1470** HENRY *Wallace* v. 87 Butleris men so stroyit war that tide, In to the stour he wald na langar bide. To get supple he socht on to the staill. **1591** SHAKS. *1 Hen. VI*, I. i. 159 The Earle of Salisbury craueth supply. **1597** —— *2 Hen. IV*, IV. ii. 45 Though wee here fall downe, Wee haue Supplyes, to second our Attempt. *a* **1624** in *Capt. J. Smith's Virginia* III. vi. 59 There we found the last Supply [of colonists] were all sicke. **1633** T. STAFFORD *Pac. Hib.* III x. (1821) 335 The two thousand supplyes, that were now landed out of England. **1685** STILLINGFL. *Orig. Brit.* v. 297 The Romans..sent them speedy Supplies. **17..** *Outlaw Murray* xliii. in Child *Ballads* V. 196/1 Word is gane to Philiphaugh,..To meet him the morn wi some supply.

†**6. a.** A substitute. Const. *of*. *Obs.* exc. as in b.

1567 FENTON *Trag. Disc.* xiii. (1898) II. 279 Usinge the pointe of a sharppe bodkyn as a supplie of a steeled chezell.

b. One who supplies a vacancy or acts as substitute for another; *esp.* a minister or preacher who temporarily officiates in a vacant charge or pulpit; also, a supply teacher (see 12 a).

1584 in *Presbyt. Movem. Eliz.* (Camden) 36 Mr. Newman moued whether he might get a standing supply for his place. **1697** in W. S. Perry *Hist. Coll. Amer. Col. Ch.* (1870) I. 10 To give notice what number of ministers was wanting, and earnestly to solicit for a suitable Supply. **1718** BP. ROBINSON *Ibid.* 200, I should be glad to hear from you what vacant Churches are in your parts, to the end I may..procure you a supply. **1888** HOWELLS *Annie Kilburn* xxx, Supply after supply filled his pulpit. **1892** *Pall Mall G.* 8 Oct. 7/2 Some servants..will only stay in situations for short periods... These would make excellent supplies. **1957** A. WILSON *Bit off Map & Other Stories* 152 'Why can't they get a Supply in?' 'Supply teachers need notification.' **1974** M. HIGGINS *Changeling* i. 7 Your replacement is only a supply, and.. the Head'd be only too happy to have you back.

†**7. a.** A supplement or appendix *to* a literary work.

1585 BANISTER *Chyrurg.* Title-p., Encreased and enlightened with certaine Annotations, Resolutions, and Supplyes, not impertinent to this Treatise. **1596** DANETT tr. *Comines* (1614) 225 (*heading*) A Supply to the Historie of Philip de Commines from the death of King Lewis the XI. **1638** BAKER tr. *Balzac's Lett.* (vol. III.) 1 A Supply to the Second part; or The Third Part of the Letters of M. de Balzac.

†**b.** *gen.* Something supplementary, additional, or auxiliary; a supplement, adjunct. *Obs.*

1620 [G. BRYDGES] *Horæ Subs.* 21 To make himselfe the encreasing figure, whilst the rest serue but for supplyes. **1625** BURGES *Pers. Tithes* 49 All these Defects are supplyed in this Statute of Edw. the 6. For, (passing ouer the supplies touching Prædiall Tithes) wee may finde these supplies for Personal Tithes. *a* **1626** BP. ANDREWES *96 Serm., Holy Ghost* (1661) 488 To do that was to be done, Christ was enough; needs no supply. **1752** HUME *Ess. & Treat.* (1777) I. 197 Municipal laws are a supply to the wisdom of each individual.

8. a. A quantity or amount *of* something supplied or provided.

1607 SHAKS. *Timon* II. ii. 201, I am proud, say, that my occasions haue found time to vse 'em toward a supply of mony. **1665** MANLEY *Grotius' Low C. Wars* 241 The Queen of England..ordered a supply of mony to the King of France, together, with four thousand English Souldiers. **1703** DAMPIER *Voy.* III. 16 Till..the greatest part of the Salt-water is congeal'd..or til a fresh Supply of it comes in again from the Sea. **1710–11** ATTERBURY *Serm., 1 Cor. x. 13* (1734) I. 102 What is Grace, but an Extraordinary Supply of Ability and Strength to resist Temptations? **1832** HT. MARTINEAU *Life in Wilds* ix. 117 The greatest possible supply of human labour. **1837** DICKENS *Pickw.* ii, The wire was passed, and a fresh supply ordered. **1846** J. BAXTER *Libr. Pract. Agric.* (ed. 4) I. 34 Certain crops..require a particular alkali; the vine, for example,..and sorrel,..must needs have supplies of potash. **1849** MACAULAY *Hist. Eng.* v. I. 592 The duke had brought.. but a scanty supply of pikes and muskets. **1898** G. B. SHAW *Plays* II. *Candida* 95 Carrying..a handbag, and a supply of illustrated papers.

†**b.** *spec.* (*absol.*) A collection of materials to form the basis of an argument or treatise. *Obs.*

1662 MORE *Antid. Ath.* II. xi. heading, A Supply from ordinary and known Examples as convictive..of a discerning Providence. **1714** SWIFT *Pres. St. Aff.* Wks. 1755 II. I. 203 Systems, that..are supplies for pamphlets in the present age.

9. *absol.* (A) provision of funds or food; (a quantity of) money or provisions supplied or to be supplied: now chiefly *spec.* the food and other stores necessary for an armed force.

a. *sing.* (Now *rare*, exc. as *attrib.* of b: see 12.)

1611 *Bible* 2 Cor. viii. 14 That now at this time your abundance may be a supply for their want, that their abundance also may be a supply for your want. **1622** FLETCHER *Span. Cur.* I. i, When this is spent, Seek for supply from me. **1769** FALCONER *Dict. Marine* (1780), *Supply*, a fresh recruit of provisions or stores sent to a ship or fleet. **1825** P. BUCHAN *Gleanings, Willie Wallace* xi, If ye be a captain as good as ye look Ye'll give a poor man some supplie. **1831** SCOTT *Ct. Rob.* xx, Judging that it was full time to carry some supply to Count Robert, who had been left without food the whole day. **1836** W. IRVING *Astoria* xlix. III. 107 The slaughter of so many buffaloes had provided the party with beef for the winter, in case they met with no further supply.

b. *pl.*

?*c* **1650** *Hist. Tom Thumb* III in Hazl. *E.P.P.* II. 244 Finding all retir'd and gone, His hunger to suffice In cautious sort he moves along; Nature wants some Supplies. *a* **1687** PETTY *Pol. Anat.* (1691) 6 England..sent Money and other Supplies into Ireland. **1690** C. NESSE *Hist. & Myst. O. & N. Test.* I. 26 After other losses..there may be found some supplys for repairing them. **1777** ROBERTSON *Hist. Amer.* v. (1783) II. 267 Notwithstanding the supplies which they received from the Tlascalans, they were often in want of provisions. **1875** *Encycl. Brit.* II. 582/1 The Surveyor-General of Ordnance, assisted by a director of supplies and transport, and a director of artillery and stores. **1881** JOWETT *Thucyd.* I. 169 The invaders remained until their supplies were exhausted.

10. a. *coll. sing.* or *pl.* A sum of money granted by a national legislature for expenses of government not provided for by the revenue.

1626 SIR J. ELIOT *Sp. in Ho. Comm.* in *Apol. Socrates* etc. (Grosart) I. 152 Yᵉ extraordinary resort to his sub[jec]ᵗˢ for supplies. **1670** *Hatton Corr.* (Camden) 57 Of this I suppose they waite the parlimᵗˢ results for supplyes. **1689** *Acts Parlt. Scotl.* (1875) XII. 56/2 be collector of the supply in the schyre of Edinburgh. **1735** BOLINGBROKE *On Parties* 77 After these Invasions were over, They voted a Supply. **1817** EARL GREY in *Parl. Deb.* 28 The supplies of last year were 35 millions, and the ways and means did not exceed 20 millions. **1827** HALLAM *Const. Hist.* viii. (1876) II. 19 As the ordinary revenues might prove quite unequal to great exigencies, the constitution has provided another means..parliamentary supply. **1867** *Chambers' Encycl.* IX. 218/1 All bills authorising the expenditure of public money must originate in the House of Commons, and be based on resolutions moved in a Committee of Supply. **1874** GREEN *Short Hist.* viii. §5. 517 The Commons declared..that redress of grievances must precede the grant of supplies.

b. *Commissioners of Supply*: see quots. (*Sc.*)

a **1768** ERSKINE *Inst. Law Scot.* I. iv. §31 The commissioners of supply are the persons appointed by parliament in their yearly acts of supply, to levy the land-tax within the county to which they are named. **1838** W. BELL *Dict. Law Scot.* 184 Under the militia acts the commissioners of supply have also power to assess for failures to make up the *quota* for allowances to the families of militiamen.

11. *Pol. Econ.* The amount of any commodity actually produced and available for purchase: correlative to DEMAND *sb.* 4 b.

1776–1878 [see DEMAND *sb.* 4 b]. **1843** CARLYLE *Past & Present* IV. v. 368 The sixpence a day and supply-and-demand principle. **1878** JEVONS *Prim. Pol. Econ.* 103 The labour which is required to get more of a commodity governs the supply of it. **1900** LD. ALDENHAM *Colloquy on Currency* 82 If the demand exceeds the supply the price will rise. If the supply exceeds the demand the price will fall. **1919** M. BEER *Hist. Brit. Socialism* I. II. iv. 152 We have been dealing with pure theory, leaving out of account such factors as supply and demand. **1936** J. M. KEYNES *Gen. Theory Employment, Interest & Money* v. xxi. 292 Prices are governed by the conditions of supply and demand. **1976** J. SNOW *Cricket Rebel* 19 Most boys wanted to bat and because I could do both I usually found myself caught up with a ball in my hand due to the law of supply and demand.

III. 12. a. *attrib.* and *Comb.*: in sense 9, esp. = having charge of or carrying the supplies of an army, as ***supply column, department, officer, train*** (of wagons), ***wagon***; also (partly with ref. to the supplies of an army and partly *gen.*) ***supply base, depot, line, ship, station, store***; in sense 11, ***supply price***. Also (partly from SUPPLY *v.*¹) ***supply-boat, -shop***; = supplying water or other substance to some mechanism, apparatus, etc., as ***supply-cistern, -dam, -pipe, -pump, -roller*** (supplying ink to other rollers in a printing-press); **supply day**, a day on which the House of Commons debates an Opposition motion criticizing the Government's proposed expenditure (cf. sense 10 a); **supply-driven** *a. Econ.*, propelled by factors on the side of supply such as a lowering of costs or an increase in availability; contr. with *demand-driven* and *market-driven*; **supply drop**, the dropping of supplies by parachute; **supply house**, (*a*) *U.S.*, a commercial establishment selling supplies; (*b*) *Canad.*, a hut, tent, lean-to, or other structure, used as a storehouse; **supply-side** *a. Econ.* (orig. *U.S.*), pertaining to the supply side of the economy; hence, designating a policy designed to increase the incentives to produce and invest, by means of tax cuts; hence **supply-sider**, an advocate of this policy; **supply teacher**, a teacher supplied by the education authority to fill a (temporary) vacancy; hence, one who is regularly employed to do this; hence (as a back-formation) **supply-teach** *v. intr.*, to work as a supply teacher; **supply teaching** *vbl. sb.*

1958 L. URIS *Exodus* I. xviii. 101 It was a fenced-in area containing several acres of trucks and other rolling stock and a dozen enormous warehouses. During the war the depot had been a major *supply base for the Allies in the Middle East. **1840** J. F. COOPER *Pathfinder* II. ix. 73 We shall lie in wait..to intercept their *supply-boats. **1897** *Outing* (U.S.) XXX. 327/1 The steamers upon this route are supply-boats. **1842** LOUDON *Suburban Hort.* 209 The *supply cistern.. must be so placed that its bottom is not lower than the highest point of the pipes. **1899** *Westm. Gaz.* 9 Nov. 2/1 Every day the regimental transport replenishes its supplies from the Brigade *Supply column, which in its turn fills up from the Divisional Supply column. **1875** *Encycl. Brit.* II. 582/1 The Army Service Corps consists of 12 transport companies and 11 *supply companies, officered from the supply and transport sub-department. **1844** STEPHENS *Bk. Farm* II. 266 When water is the power, the sluice of the *supply-dam should be drawn up to the proper height. **1946** *May's Treat. Parliament* (ed. 14) xxv. 686 The House had attempted to counter this tendency [*sc.* the government's postponement of the discussion of estimates] by making one day each week a compulsory *supply day. **1959** *Listener* 12 Mar. 441/1 The time allotted to the opposition for the criticism of policy and administration in supply days and so forth would not need to be curtailed. **1976** H. WILSON *Governance of Britain* i. 19 Defeated on a snap vote on a Supply Day debate on the stocks of cordite in government depots, he threw in his hand. **1876** VOYLE & STEVENSON *Milit. Dict.* (ed. 3), *Supply Department*, a branch of the control department.., now..replaced by the commissariat department. **1918** E. S. FARROW *Dict. Military Terms* 596 Main *supply depots are established at advanced bases or at convenient positions on the railway. **1921** *Daily Colonist* (Victoria) 18 Mar. 3/2 Two all-metal monoplanes have made an initial flight..carrying 1,000 pounds of gasoline each for the supply depot at Hay River. **1984** *Financial Times* 14 Nov. 22/4 The new streamlined structure should switch the group from being a *supply driven company to one which is market-driven. **1985** *Ibid.* 5 Aug. 26/6 The growth is both demand- and supply-driven. On one side are fast-growing companies bursting out of..capital constraints ..On the other side stand investors who are fast shedding their national prejudices in favour of international diversification. **1947** 'N. SHUTE' *Chequer Board* iv. 86 Last job was a Dakota squadron in South-East Asia Command. *Supply drops, I suppose. **1978** T. ALLBEURY *Lantern Network* iii. 33 You have been given details of..suitable areas for supply drops. **1897** *Sears, Roebuck Catal.* 1 Sears, Roebuck & Co., (Incorporated), Cheapest *Supply House on Earth, Chicago. **1905** L. MOTT *Jules of Great Heart* 161 A voyageur showed him to the supply-house, and he got some pemmican, tea and bread, and a blanket. **1957** V. J.

KEHOE *Technique Film & Television Make-Up* xiii. 194 Get a small sized balsa wood head form from a hat supply house. **1975** *New Yorker* 7 July 73/1 While discarded manufactured objects found in the street or in junk shops may be richly charged with poetic and psychological associations..this is not the case with new supply-house items. **1942** *R.A.F. Jrnl.* 3 Oct. 11 We were detailed to attack Jerry's *supply lines. **1956** D. L. LINTON *Sheffield* p. xxiii, It can serve the other towns of the region with wholesale and retail goods, professional and social services only over 'supply lines' that are relatively costly in maintenance, operation, or time. **1899** *Westm. Gaz.* 15 Nov. 5/2 Our *supply officers. **1858** LARDNER *Hand-bk. Nat. Phil.* 150 The *supply pipe EE, descending from the upper reservoir, communicates with the top and bottom of the cylinder by the horizontal pipes F and G. **1890** A. MARSHALL *Princ. Econ.* I. v. iii. 403 When the amount produced..is such that the demand price is greater than the *supply price. **1840** *Civil Engin. & Arch. Jrnl.* III. 77/2 The force or *supply-pump. **1875** KNIGHT *Dict. Mech.* 2455/1 **Supply-roller* (*Printing*), an intermediate working-roller. **1915** J. M. DE ROEBECK in M. Gilbert *Winston S. Churchill* (1972) III. Compan. I. 753 The passage of *supply ships for the Fleet through the Dardanelles with the forts still intact is a problem to which I can see no practical solution. **1975** *BP Shield Internat.* May 6 To enable it to continue operations for several days when supply ships cannot come alongside. **1898** *Daily News* 4 May 7/4 Meat.. leaped up a halfpenny a pound yesterday in the *supply shops just outside Smithfield Market. **1976** *Wall St. Jrnl.* 9 Apr. 8/1 (*heading*) *Supply-side fiscalism. *Ibid.* 15 Nov. 26/4 Supply-side. fiscalists..agree that tax changes do not affect total demand, but they emphasize the effects on supply. **1980** *N.Y. Times* 22 June IV. 20 They recommend capital formation and other supply-side policies that have recently become fashionable. **1980** *Wall St. Jrnl.* 28 Feb. 24/3 Reception to '*supply-siders' was still hostile..when they criticized the economic models being used by the congressional budget committees for assuming that higher government spending was better for the economy than lower tax rates. **1981** *Christian Sci. Monitor* (Weekly Internat. ed.) 7 Sept. 20/3 The supply-siders who persuaded President Reagan to seek a balanced budget by cutting taxes. **1909** F. ASH *Trip to Mars* xxxiv. 262 Airships are of no use without a *supply-station. **1885** *List of Subscribers, Classified* (United Telephone Co.) (ed. 6) 204 *Supply Stores... Army & Navy Auxiliary Co-operative Supply, Limited... Civil Service Supply Associations, Limited. **1946** W. FAULKNER *Portable Faulkner* 752 A pair of offices up a flight of stairs above the supplystore. **1902** *Daily Chron.* 18 Apr. 3/2 It was agreed that '*supply' teachers..should be paid for the week's holiday allowed on account of the Coronation. **1963** S. MARSHALL *Experiment in Education* iii. 115, I happened to be ill..and the only supply teacher the L.E.A. could find at short notice was an Indian teacher. **1969** R. GODDEN *In this House of Brede* xv. 341 Father Gervase has gone as supply teacher for a fortnight to Bishop Palin's Grammar School for Boys. **1976** *Rhyl Jrnl. & Advertiser* 9 Dec. 20/5 (Advt.), Applications are invited from Qualified Teachers..who wish to be included on the Authority's list of Supply Teachers for Primary and/or Secondary Schools. **1957** *Kingston* (Ontario) *Whig-Standard* 24 Jan. 17/6 She told the students something of the practice and *supply teaching possible while at college. **1968** *New Statesman* 22 Mar. 376/1 I am now supply teaching in London. **1976** *Times Lit. Suppl.* 13 Aug. 1006/5 He was a student at the London School of Economics, wanted to be a writer and did supply teaching for a living. **1980** J. BARNES *Metroland* III. i. 138, I was supply teaching in Wandsworth at the time: twenty-five quid a week for the privilege of having your bicycle tyres let down each week by different kids at different schools. **1860** H. GREELEY *Overland Journey* 55 Our route..was no longer encumbered with great army *supply-trains. **1902** *Words of Eye-witness* 228 A person unused to supply-trains. **1866** A. D. RICHARDSON *Secret Service* xix. 241 Their retreat was a stampede, leaving behind great quantities of ammunition ..*supply-wagons and ambulances. **1894** H. GARDENER *Unoff. Patriot* 275 Their supply-wagons had not come up until long after the struggle.

b. Pl. *supplies* (sense 9 b) is occas. used *attrib.*

1898 *Engin. Mag.* XVI. 44 Pay-roll total and supplies-cost total. **1906** *Daily Chron.* 16 Oct. 5/5 The unbusinesslike methods of the Supplies Office at Pretoria.

supply (sə'plaɪ), *v.*[1] Forms: 4–5 sowple, suplie, 4–6 *Sc.* supple, suple, (5 *Sc.* supplee), 4–7 supplye, 5–7 supplie, (6 supploy(e), 6– supply. [a. OF. *so(u)pleer*, earlier *soup(p)leier, -oier*, later *supplier*, mod.F. *suppléer*, ad. (with change of conjugation) L. *supplēre* (whence also Pr. *suplir*, It. *supplire*, Sp. *suplir*, Pg. *supprir*), f. *sup-* = SUB- 26 + *-plēre* to fill (*plē-nus* FULL).]

†**1.** *trans.* To help, aid, assist; to succour, relieve; to support, maintain; *occas.* to deliver *from.*

1375 BARBOUR *Bruce* XI. 627 *rubric*, How gud Iames of Douglass askit at king Robert the Bruce leiff to gang to supple erll Thomas Randall. **1456** SIR G. HAYE *Law Arms* (S.T.S.) 165 Lat man do that in him is, and syne traist in Goddis help, and he sall supplee his gude rycht. **1464–5** *Acts Parlt. Scotl.* (1875) XII. 31/1 þat he nothir supple support nor resett þe saide Alane in þe saide dedis. **1508** DUNBAR *Poems* iv. 43 In medicyne the most practicianis..Thame self fra ded may not supple. **1596** DALRYMPLE tr. *Leslie's Hist. Scot.* I. 340 He supplies king Henrie his gude father sair vexte with rebellis. **1630** CAPT. J. SMITH *Trav. & Adv.* 18 The very Bulwarke and Rampire of a great part of Europe, most fit by all Christians to have beene supplyed and maintained. **17..** *Duke of Athole's Nurse* xiii. in Child *Ballads* IV. 154/2 O can you supply me? For she that was to meet me in friendship..Has sent nine men to slay me.

absol. c **1550** ROLLAND *Crt. Venus* I. 637 O Cupid King.. Attend thir wordis that ar sa pungitiue... Bot ȝe supple, I may not thame sustene.

†**2.** To furnish with (additional) troops; to reinforce. Also *absol. Obs.*

c **1470** HENRY *Wallace* VII. 1119 Agayne Wallace he prewit in mony press, With Inglismen suppleit thaim at his mycht. **1525** *St. Papers Hen. VIII*, IV. 412 To help fortefy and suple our confederat ye King of France. **1579–80** NORTH *Plutarch* (1895) III. 228 Supplying still with a few on either side, at the length they came to a maine battell. **1615** G. SANDYS *Trav.* 105 Where he left his most tired souldiers, and supplied his army with the people of that countrey. **1825** SCOTT *Betrothed* viii, These detachments..supplied by reinforcements which more than recruited their diminished numbers.

3. †**a.** To make up (a whole) by adding something; to fill *up*, complete. *Obs.*

c **1375** *Sc. Leg. Saints* xii. (*Mathias*) 356 Sa tuk þai hyme for þe twelf to be, þe parfyt nowmyre for to suple. *Ibid.* xxxiii. (*George*) 539 His wikit wil ȝet to suple,..he..gert George til hyme be present. **1552** HULOET, Supployе or make vp the full nombre of hundreth souldiers that lacked of that nombre called *centuria, subcenturio.* **1579–80** NORTH *Plutarch, Publicola* (1595) 113 He supplyed vp the number of Senatours that were greatly decayed.

†**b.** To add to (something); to make up a deficiency in; to supplement. *Obs.*

c **1375** *Sc. Leg. Saints* xv. (*Barnabas*) 30 Dyscipilis..þat Criste assignit for to be In helpe his warke to suple. **1591** SPENSER *Teares Muses* 537 Shee wept and waild..And all the rest, her sorrow to supplie, Did throw forth shrieks and cries. **1615** BRATHWAIT *Strappado* (1878) 184 Nature is supplide in him by Art. **1671** tr. *Palafox's Conq. China* xv. 285 That by their valour they might supply the little intelligence they had in this way of fighting. **1730** A. GORDON *Maffei's Amphith.* 195 The Book..was altered and supplied by the hand of a Stranger.

c. To add (something that is wanting).

c **1450** CAPGRAVE *Life St. Aug.* (1910) 41 Augustin supplied swech good werkis which he coude not do him-selue. **1533** MORE *Apol.* xlii. OO j b, The knowledge the party lacketh must be supplyed the more effectually by the iudges. **1546** *Reg. Privy Council Scot.* I. 56 Quhat wantis of the hale soum..to be supleit be thaim for payment of the hale soum. **1567** SANDERS *Rocke of Chvrche* ii. 30 The Particle ὤν, is to be supplied to these woordes, ὁ μείζων. **1697** DRYDEN *Virg. Georg.* Ded., Having said what he thought convenient, he always left somewhat for the Imagination of his Readers to supply. **1824** L. MURRAY *Eng. Gram.* (ed. 5) I. 430 Supply words that are wanting. **1861** PALEY *Æschylus* (ed. 2) *Supplices* 591 *note*, Μὴ is to be supplied from the preceding negative clause. **1862** SPENCER *First Princ.* I. iv. §24 (1875) 79 Another fundamental condition of thought, omitted by Sir W. Hamilton, and not supplied by Mr. Mansel.

4. To make up for, make good, compensate for (a defect, loss, or void); to compensate for (the absence of something) by providing a substitute.

c **1375** *Sc. Leg. Saints* xxxii. (*Justin*) 207, I sal al his fawt supple. **1398** TREVISA *Barth. De P.R.* VI. iv. (Bodl. MS.) lf. 36/1 So that þe vertu of þe norise be instede and suplie [*ed.* **1495** sowple] and fulfille þe defaute of þe child. **1491** *Cartular. S. Nicholai Aberdon.* (New Spalding Club) I. 255 Alss oft as he [a chaplain] falȝes in execucion of his office.. he sal pay i d..to him þat suppleis yat falt. **1526** *Pilgr. Perf.* (W. de W. 1531) 51 These..vertues..supplyeth yᵉ defautes that be lefte in yᵉ powers of the soule by synne. **1563–7** BUCHANAN *Reform. St. Andros* Wks. (S.T.S.) 12 Ane man of ..sufficient doctrine to supple the regentis absens. **1600** E. BLOUNT tr. *Conestaggio* 225 That which most supplied their want of experience. **1653** HOLCROFT *Procopius* Pref. A iv, The knowing Translator hath supplyed the defect out of the Latine copies. **1695** LD. LONSDALE in *Eng. Hist. Rev.* (1915) Jan. 91 That the intermission off my Storie for almost seven years should now..be supplied. **1709** SWIFT *Adv. Relig.* Wks. 1755 II. I. 119 He, that would keep his house in repair, must attend every little breach or flaw, and supply it immediately. **1764** GOLDSM. *Trav.* 145 Yet still the loss of wealth is here supplied By arts. **1780** COWPER *Progr. Error* 172 Cards,..and the polish'd die, The yawning chasm of indolence supply! **1834–47** J. S. MACAULAY *Field Fortif.* (1851) 18 If defended by three ranks, two of them stand on the banquette; the first rank fires, the second loads, and the third rank supplies casualties. **1859** *Once a Week* 2 July 16 The tadpole needs his tail to swim with; and Nature kindly supplies any accident that may deprive him of it.

absol. **1673** *Lady's Call.* I. i. §12 There will not remain many topics of discourse, unless this be called in to supply.

5. To fulfil, satisfy (a need or want) by furnishing what is wanted.

1567 *Gude & Godlie B.* (S.T.S.) 18 Thy nychtbour lufe, and als supplie His neid. **1600** *Chester Pl., Banes* 35 See these pagentes played to the beste of theire skill; wher to supply all wantes, shalbe noe wantes of good will. **1623** MILTON *Ps.* cxxxvi. 86 All living creatures he doth feed, And with full hand supplies their need. **1666** MARVELL *Corr.* Wks. (Grosart) II. 189 Which is not from any want of ardor in the House to supply the publick necessityes. **1784** COWPER *Task* III. 798 Some private purse Supplies his need with an usurious loan. **1817** JAS. MILL *Brit. India* IV. v. II. 165 If [he] withheld the revenues and supplied not the exigencies of the state. **1901** CORDINGLEY *Dict. Stock Exch. T.* 56 When..there are not sufficient shares issued to supply the demands made.

6. To furnish, provide, afford (something needed, desired, or used): orig. with personal subj.; later freq. and now usually with impersonal subj.

c **1520** SKELTON *Magnyf.* (1908) 1663 That he knowe not but that I haue supplyed All that I can his matter for to spede. **1624** WOTTON *Archit.* 69 The reception of light..we must now supplie..by some open Forme of the Fabrique. **1697** DRYDEN *Virg. Georg.* I. 221 Dodonian Oaks no more supply'd Their Mast. **1700** —— *Ovid's Met., Baucis & Philemon* 148 What their tardy feet denied, The trusty staff (their better leg) supplied. **1704** PRIOR *Celia to Damon* 79 Nearer Care..supplies Sighs to my Breast, and Sorrow to my Eyes. **1713** STEELE *Englishman* No. 7. 47 He will tell you, with his Eyes shut, what Province, what Mountain supplied the Liquor. **1816** J. SMITH *Panorama Sci. & Art* II. 387 All the tin used in England is supplied by the mines of Cornwall, which furnish 3000 tons annually. **1827** FARADAY *Chem. Manip.* xvi. (1842) 401 A sound cork, perforated so as to form a ring... Half a dozen of these will supply handles to most tubes. **1835** NEWMAN *Lett.* (1891) II. 109 By way of showing the hopelessness of any of us supplying your desideratum. **1857** MILLER *Elem. Chem., Org.* i. 46 In order to supply the hydrochloric ether, a mixture of hydrochloric acid and alcohol is placed in the retort. **1910** D. G. HOGARTH in *Encycl. Brit.* I. 248/2 The fresco-paintings..of Crete have supplied the clearest proof of it.

†**b.** To put or appoint as a substitute. (Cf. 9, 10, 11.) *Obs. rare.*

a **1618** RALEIGH *Maxims of State* (1651) 72 [He] feared that David would supplie Benagit in his place.

7. To furnish (a thing) *with* what is necessary or desirable; in early use, without constr., to provide for the maintenance of, make provision for.

1529 *Registr. Aberdon.* (Maitland Cl.) I. 396 To sustene supple mentene apperall mend and uphald..þe brig forsaid. **1588** KYD *Househ. Philos.* Ind. 103 Entertainment of guests, how to be supplyed. **1599** SHAKS. *Hen. V*, I. i. 17 A hundred Almes-houses, right well supply'd. **1605** in *Abstr. Protocols Town Clerks of Glasgow* (1896) II. 116 Willing to set fordwart, manteine and supply thair guid and godlie purpois. **1607** SHAKS. *Timon* III. ii. 40 Requesting your Lordship to supply his instant vse with so many Talents. *Ibid.* IV. ii. 47 Nor ha's he with him to supply his life. **1697** DRYDEN *Virg. Georg.* III. 320 Feed him full and high: Indulge his Growth, and his gaunt Sides supply. **1707** *Curios. in Husb. & Gard.* 264 The Salts..contribute very much to the abundantly supplying the Plants with what is requisite. **1784** COWPER *Tiroc.* 27 She..With flow'r and fruit the wilderness supplies. **1799** HAN. MORE *Fem. Educ.* (ed. 4) I. 135 To supply by individual kindness those cases of hardship which laws cannot reach. **1884** H. GIBBES in Thompson *Tumours of Bladder* 59 The growth is well supplied with blood-vessels.

b. *transf.* To furnish with an occupant, tenant, or contents; to fill. *poet.*

1607 SHAKS. *Cor.* III. iii. 35 Keepe the Chaires of Iustice Supplied with worthy men. **1607** —— *Timon* III. i. 18 An empty box..which..I come to intreat your Honor to supply. **1715** POPE *Iliad* III. 64 Thy figure promised with a martial air, But ill thy soul supplies a form so fair.

c. *Anat.* and *Phys.* Of a nerve or blood-vessel: To furnish with energy or nourishment (the part or organ to which it is distributed).

1843 R. J. GRAVES *Syst. Clin. Med.* xxx. 397 The branch given off by the ulnar nerve to supply the little finger. **1899** L. HILL *Man. Hum. Physiol.* xx. 181 The right and left subclavian arteries supply respectively the right and left shoulder and arm.

8. To furnish or provide (a person) *with* something; in early use, without constr., to satisfy the wants of, provide for; now usually, to furnish with regular supplies of a commodity.

1567 *Gude & Godlie B.* (S.T.S.) 8 Honour thy Elderis; and thame supplie, Geue that thair neid of the requyre. **1603** SHAKS. *Meas. for M.* v. i. 212 This is the body That tooke away the march from Isabell, And did supply thee at thy garden-house In her Imagin'd person. **1646** J. HALL *Poems* I. 10 Feathers..Which..might..stitch't into a web, supply anew With annuary cloakes the wandring Jew. **1686** tr. *Chardin's Trav. Persia* 26 He could not subsist if they should refuse to supply him. **1726** SWIFT *Gulliver* I. i, They supplied me as fast as they could, showing..astonishment at my bulk and appetite. **1775** BURKE *Lett., to R. Champion* (1844) II. 31, I am sincerely thankful to you for your care, in supplying us with the earliest intelligence. **1827** LYTTON *Pelham* lxxiii, Can Sir Reginald Glanville's memory.. supply him with no probable cause? **1878** JEVONS *Prim. Pol. Econ.* 30 China supplies us with vast quantities of tea. *Mod.* (e.g. on baker's cart) Families supplied daily.

9. To fill (another's place); *esp.* (now only) to occupy as a substitute.

c **1375** *Sc. Leg. Saints* xii. (*Mathias*) 318 þat we stablyste ane in þe place, þe quhyle to supple of Iudas. **1548** ELYOT s.v. *Fungor, Fungi vice alicuius*,..to be in an other mannes steede, to supply an other mannes roume. **1596** SHAKS. *Tam. Shr.* III. ii. 249 Lucentio, you shall supply the Bride-groomes place. **1667** MILTON *P.L.* II. 834 A race of upstart Creatures, to supply Perhaps our vacant room. **1750** GRAY *Elegy* 82 Their name, their years, spelt by th' unletter'd muse, The place of fame and elegy supply. **1802** C. JAMES *Milit. Dict.* s.v., Covering serjeants supply the places of officers when they step out of the ranks, or are killed in action. **1831** JAMES *Phil. Augustus* I. ii, The place of his casque was supplied by a large brown hood. a **1859** MACAULAY *Hist. Eng.* xxiii. (1861) V. 103 She died; and her place was supplied by a German princess.

†**b.** To serve (a turn). *Obs. rare.*

1602 R. CAREW *Cornwall* 82 These poore instruments for want of better did supplie a turne.

†**10.** To fulfil, discharge, perform (an office or function), *esp.* as a substitute for another. *Obs.*

1432–50 tr. *Higden* (Rolls) VII. 133 This Benedict made pope but symple in connynge, made an oþer pope under hym to supplye his office. **1533** GAU *Richt Vay* 104 Paul sais notht yat it is sufficient to ane bischoip to haiff ane prechour to supple his office. c **1586** C'TESS PEMBROKE *Ps.* LXXVII. iii, My hart in office lame, My tongue as lamely fares, No part his part supplies. **1626** in *10th Rep. Hist. MSS. Comm.* App. v. 328 They may be removeable..and others chosen in his or their place..to supply the residue of the said yeere. **1667** MILTON *P.L.* x. 1001 Let us seek Death, or hee not found, supply With our own hands his Office on our selves. **1680** MOXON *Mech. Exerc.* xii. 203 The Joyners Mallet would supply the Office of this Tool. **1748** *Anson's Voy.* II. ii. 135 Mixed with wood-ashes, to supply the use of tallow.

11. To take the place of; to serve as, or furnish, a substitute for; to make up for the want of; to replace. Now *rare* or *Obs.*

c **1606** ROWLANDS *Terrible Battle* D 3, [They] fall sicke; and die,..and others them supply. **1618** BOLTON *Florus* To Rdr. (1636) A 7, The words which are here and there inserted..are..explanatory of the Author's meaning, supplying marginall notes. **1642** D. ROGERS *Naaman* To Rdr., Thou art worth ten thousand of us; if we dye, wee may be supplied. **1667** MILTON *P.L.* x. 1078 A comfortable heat ..Which might supply the Sun. *a* **1700** EVELYN *Diary* 8 Mar. 1689, The Hearth Tax was remitted for ever, but what was intended to supply it,..is not nam'd. **1770** GOLDSM. *Des. Vill.* 56 A bold peasantry,..When once destroyed, can never be supplied. **1818** CRUISE *Digest* (ed. 2) VI. 332 The Court has no power to strike out the word *such*; and if they did, what are they to supply it with? **1873** L. WALLACE *Fair God* I. xii, Lamplight..ill supplying the perfect sun-shine.

12. Of a preacher or minister: To occupy (a church, pulpit, etc.) as a substitute, or temporarily; to act as 'supply' for (another); also *absol.*

1719 SPOTSWOOD in W. S. Perry *Hist. Coll. Amer. Col. Ch.* (1870) I. 202 When the Church he now supplies, became void by the death of the former incumbent. **1788** M. CUTLER in *Life*, etc. (1888) I. 434 Mr. Dana preached here, who was supplied by Mr. D. Story. **1895** *Cornh. Mag.* Aug. 155 To 'supply the pulpits' of ministers who left home. **1905** HARTING *Sardinian Chapel* 30 The Rev. Thomas Gabb.. for some years..'supplied' at Mrs. Langdale's private chapel.

†**supply**, *v.*² *Obs.* Forms: 4-6 supplie, 5-6 supplye, 6 supple, suply(e, supply. [a. OF. (mod.F.) *supplier*, earlier *soup(p)loier*, *sopleier* :—L. *supplicāre* (whence also Pr. *sopleiar*, *sopliar*, *soplegar*, *soplicar*, It. *supplicare*, Sp. *suplicar*, Pg. *supplicar*): see SUPPLICATE *v.*] = SUPPLICATE *v.*

a. *trans.* with person as obj.

c **1374** CHAUCER *Boeth.* III. pr. viii. (1868) 80 Yif þou wilt shynen wiþ dignites, þou most bysechen and supplien hem þat ȝiuen þo dignitees. **1474** CAXTON *Chesse* Ded., I requyre & supplye your good grace not to desdaygne to resseyue this lityll sayd book. *c* **1520** SKELTON *Magnyf.* (1908) 797 Why dost thou not supplye, And desyre me thy good mayster to be? **1539** *St. Papers Hen. VIII*, I. 604, I supplie Our Blessed Creatour to sende Your Highnes encreace of honour.

b. *intr.* (const. *to*, *unto*).

1489 CAXTON *Faytes of A.* I. i. 2, I supplye humbly to the said right hie offyce. **1491** —— *Vitas Patr.* (W. de W. 1495) I We supplye ryght humbly to our worthy Sauyour Ihesu Cryste that his prompt grace maye be to vs presented. **1533** *St. Papers Hen. VIII*, I. 392 In your moste humble wise, ye supplye unto us, in your said letters, to graunte unto you our lycence [etc.].

c. *trans.* with obj. of cognate meaning: To present (a request). *rare.*

1546 *St. Papers Hen. VIII*, I. 884 To wryte to His Majeste, to supplie my present sute to his Person.

†**supply**, *v.*³ *Obs.* [? Alteration of SUPPLE *v.* by assimilation to SUPPLY *v.*¹, or after *apply*.] = SUPPLE *v.* Hence **supplying** *ppl. a.*²

1535 *Goodly Primer*, A Prayer for the mollifying & supplyeng hard hearts. **1544** PHAER *Regim. Lyfe* (1560) S vj, To supply the gummes and the sinewes. **1656** *T. de Grey's Compl. Horsem.* (ed. 3) 137 By applying supplying, or mollifying Oyles or Unguents. **1660** GAUDEN *God's Gt. Demonstr.* 33 Mercy..oyls the wheels, and supplies the joynts, that Justice goes on with less cry and complaint. **1709** *Temple's Misc., Ess. Gout* (ed. 5) 59 They drew down the Humours, and supplied [*earlier edd.* suppled] the Parts, thereby making the Passages wider.

supplyable, -ant: see SUPPLIABLE, SUPPLIANT.

supplying (sə'plaɪɪŋ), *vbl. sb.*¹ [f. SUPPLY *v.*¹ + -ING¹.] The action of SUPPLY *v.*¹ in various senses; filling of a place or vacancy; substitution; †supplementation; †assistance, reinforcement (*Sc.*); provision, supply.

c **1380** WYCLIF *Wks.* (1880) 453 Hou cristis chirche is disseyued bi suppliyng of vikeris, & þes persouns ben absent þe while. *c* **1470** HENRY *Wallace* I. 105 In that castell the erle gert hald thaim in, At to thar men with out thai mycht nocht wyn; Na thai to thaim suppleyng for to ma. **1499** *Reg. Privy Seal Scot.* I. 46/1 The..suppleing and assistance gevin be him to diuers rebellis. **1570** T. NORTON tr. *Nowel's Catech.* 73 That thys their confirmation should be taken for a certaine supplying [orig. *supplementum*] of Baptisme..as though Baptisme els were vnperfect. **1586** *Acts Privy Council* (N.S.) 166 The said summe..to be by him employed for the supplyinge of the store with the same parcells. **1625** DONNE *Serm., Christmas Day* (1640) 22 A filling of all former vacuities, a supplying of all emptinesses in our soules. **1625-6** in Willis & Clark *Cambr.* (1886) I. 444 To the Glasier..for yᵉ supplyeinge of paynted glasse. **1626** in *10th Rep. Hist. MSS. Comm.* App. v. 474 The supplieing and refreshing of the needefull exigentes of the poore. **1643** BAKER *Chron., Hen. VIII*, 38 The Emperour gave to the Master of Saint Iohns of Hierusalem the Island of Maltas, in supplying of the Island of Rodes, which the Turke..had won from that Order. **1682** in *Scott. Antiq.* (1901) July 3 In the..suppleing of vacant places within the colledge. **1883** *Athenæum* 26 May 661/1 Mysteries..partly solved by the supplying of a date or a name.

So **su'pplying** *ppl. a.*¹, that supplies.

1798 HUTTON *Course Math.* (1807) II. 273 A..vessel.. kept constantly full of water, by a large supplying cock at the top. **1895** *Daily News* 2 Jan. 5/7 The credit system on which the fisheries..are conducted is..perilous to the supplying merchants.

†**supplying**, *ppl. a.*² *Obs.*: see SUPPLY *v.*³

†**supp'lyment.** *Obs. rare.* Also 6 suppliment. [f. SUPPLY *v.*¹ + -MENT.] The act of supplying, or what is supplied.

1589 WARNER *Alb. Eng.* VI. xxix. 129 If wealth be said my want, I say your Grace doth want no wealth: And my suppliment shalbe loue, imployed to your health. **1611** SHAKS. *Cymb.* III. iv. 182 You haue me rich, and I will neuer faile Beginning, nor supplyment.

supplyment, obs. form of SUPPLEMENT.

suppoaille, -ayle, variants of SUPPOWELL *Obs.*

suppois, -oise, -oiss, obs. Sc. ff. SUPPOSE.

suppoist, Sc. form of SUPPOST.

†**suppone**, *v.* Chiefly *Sc. Obs.* [ad. L. *suppōnĕre*: see SUPPOSE *v.* Cf. Pr. *supponer*, It. *sopporre*, Sp. *suponer*, Pg. *suppôr*.]

1. *trans.* To substitute fraudulently = SUPPOSE *v.* 13.

1542 *St. Papers Hen. VIII*, V. 231 Yat ye malefactouris may be punist in yair awn personis, and na uyeris [= others] supponit in yair place.

2. To think or believe to be the case, be of opinion: = SUPPOSE *v.* 1.

c **1500** *Lancelot* 2230 Aduentur is non so gret to pref As I suppone, nor ȝhe sal It esschef. *a* **1578** LINDESAY (Pitscottie) *Chron. Scot.* (S.T.S.) I. 26 It is supponit he thocht seing the cuntrie swa dewydit as said is to haue hac sum reull in the realme. *c* **1587** MONTGOMERIE *Sonn.* lxiv. 1, I am sorie that ȝe suld suppone Me to be one in lucre to delyte. **1597** SKENE *De Verb. Sign.* s.v. *Bastardus*, And (as I suppone) na reasone can be given quhairfore it is so called.

b. With reference to future events: To look for, expect, anticipate: = SUPPOSE *v.* 4.

c **1550** ROLLAND *Crt. Venus* I. 925 For I suppone he will me hald partie. *a* **1578** LINDESAY (Pitscottie) *Chron. Scot.* (S.T.S.) I. 21 To haue support aganis the gouernour.. quhome he supponit schortlie to cum to invaid him. *c* **1614** MURE *Dido & Æneas* I. 976 She..in love suppones A sweeter issue.

3. To assume, take for granted: = SUPPOSE *v.* 6, 9. Also as conj. = SUPPOSE *v.* 7 e.

1536 BELLENDEN *Cron. Scot.* (1821) I. p. lv, First, I suppone, that the thing that I say..be nocht takin in repreif of every man. **1637** GILLESPIE *Eng. Pop. Cerem.* IV. i. 2 Because he could not prove this..he choosed to suppone it. **1650** MURE *Cry of Blood* 157 The Taske in hand, suppone the hazard great, Yet neither case, nor cure are desperate. *a* **1658** DURHAM *Comm. Revelation* i. 5. (1660) 13 It suppones two objects of Worship, and two kinds of Divine Worship: which is false.

4. To place under. *rare*⁻⁰.

1611 COTGR., *Supposement*, a supponing, or putting of a thing vnder another.

support (sə'pɔət), *sb.* Also 5-6 supporte, 6 suport. [f. SUPPORT *v.* Cf. F. *support* (from 15th c.).] **I.** The action of supporting.

1. a. The action, or an act, of preventing a person from giving way, backing him up, or taking his part; assistance, countenance, backing.

1390 GOWER *Conf.* III. 193 To do pite support and grace, The Philosophre..A tale of gret essample tolde. *c* **1430** LYDG. *Min. Poems* (Percy Soc.) 22 Lat no man bost. Of tresoure, riches, nor of sapience, Of wordly support. **1490** CAXTON *Eneydos* xxi. 76 Neuer socours ne comforte by me, nor of my supporte, was gyuen to theym. **1533** BELLENDEN *Livy* II. xiii. (S.T.S.) I. 179 Vetusius consul was send in pare supporte. *c* **1549** *Reg. Aberdon.* (Maitland Cl.) II. 307 Vtheris gratitudis helpis supportis and guid dedis els done to ws. *a* **1578** LINDESAY (Pitscottie) *Chron. Scot.* (S.T.S.) II. 163 They..send to Ingland for suport..; quhilk suport was grantit to thame. **1777** BURKE *Corr.* (1844) II. 195 When you find men that you ought to trust, you must give them support. **1802** NELSON 10 Nov. in Nicolas *Disp.* (1845) V. 30 Your gallant support of me at the Battle of Copenhagen. **1849** MACAULAY *Hist. Eng.* vii. II. 191 That the great plan ..might obtain the approbation and support of his father-in-law. **1874** GREEN *Short Hist.* ix. §3. 622 Clarendon was still strong in the support of the House of Commons.

†**b.** Phr. (see SUPPORTATION 1 b). *Obs.*

c **1430** LYDG. *Lyke the Audience* 127 in *Pol., Rel. & L. Poems* (1903) 55 Vndir support of his [*sc.* Christ's] magnificence. —— *Min. Poems* (Percy Soc.) 48 Under support of your pacyence. **1493** *Petronilla* 41 (Pynson), With humble support of youre audience Peysed youre power and youre holynesse What may this mene? *a* **1500** *Flower & Leaf* 590, I..put al I had seen in wryting, Under support of hem that lust it rede.

c. Spiritual help; also subjectively, mental comfort.

1500-20 DUNBAR *Poems* ix. 37 To ignorantis nocht gaif I my teiching,..Nor to my nychtbouris support of my praying. **1673** FLAVEL *Fount. Life* xxxiii. Wks. 1701 I. 170 When one asked holy Mr. Baynes how the Case stood with his Soul, he answered; 'Supports I have, tho' Suavities I want.' **1793** BURKE *Corr.* (1844) IV. 177, It would be a matter of support and consolation to me. **1794** MRS. RADCLIFFE *Myst. Udolpho* ii, We must ask support from above. **1861** MRS. STOWE *Pearl Orr's Isl.* iv. 26, I hope the Cap'n and Mrs. Pennel'll get some support at the prayer-meetin' this afternoon. **1891** FARRAR *Darkn. & Dawn* xviii, She felt a sense of support in truths which..kindled her imagination and touched her heart.

d. Corroboration or substantiation (*of* a statement, principle, etc.); advocacy (*of* a proposal, motion, etc.): chiefly in phr. *in support of*.

1771 *Junius Lett.* xlvii. (1788) 260, I..feel a considerable pleasure in being able to communicate any thing..in support of his opinions. **1857** J. SCOTT *Common Bench Rep.* N.S.I. 658 Overend, Q.C. and Chandler, in support of the rule. **1875** JOWETT *Plato* (ed. 2) V. 16 Nearly all of [these words]..have the support of some poetical or other authority. **1891** *Law Times* XCII. 105/1 The evidence to be called in support of their statement.

e. *Mil.* The action of supporting other troops. *in support*: acting as a second line. (Cf. 5 b.)

1805 JAMES *Milit. Dict.* (ed. 2) s.v., *Line of support*, the second line in action. **1892** G. PHILIPS *Text Bk. Fortif., etc.* (ed. 5) 115 The whole of these troops, whether firing, or either in support or in reserve.

f. The provision or availability of services that enable something to fulfil its function or help to keep it operational.

1953, etc. [see *ground support* s.v. GROUND *sb.* 17 d]. **1967** [see sense 9 a]. **1968** *Materials Evaluation* Sept. 180/2 Programming and graphics support is essential if one hopes to raise the status of laboratory thermal plotters..to a significant useful tool. **1970** *Wall St. Jrnl.* 20 Mar. 9 Traditionally, support came with the cost of a computer. **1976** *Evening Advertiser* (Swindon) 31 Dec. 8/2 The MBE goes to..Mr Walter Chapman, manager of the ground support team backing Concorde at Fairford. **1977** *Fortune* Jan. 104/2 Customers are unhappy with the software support and service they receive. **1986** *A & B Computing* Nov. 13/1 The software has often been of a poor quality and software support is often patchy at best, being very limited in quality and professionalism.

†**2.** Bearing or defraying *of* charge or expense.

1591 *Exch. Rolls Scot.* XXII. 102 Assignit to the comptar in support of the chairgis and burding of his office. *a* **1700** EVELYN *Diary* 21 Feb. 1666, For support of the next yeares charge.

3. The action of keeping from failing, exhaustion, or perishing; *esp.* the supplying *of* a living thing with what is necessary for subsistence; the maintenance *of* life.

1686 tr. *Chardin's Coronat. Solyman* 98 A very great scarcity..of all things necessary for humane support. **1760** FOOTE *Minor* I. Wks. 1799 I. 239, I will cast him out, as an alien to my blood, and trust for the support of my name and family to a remoter branch. **1774** GOLDSM. *Nat. Hist.* (1776) VI. 169 All fish..stand in need of air for their support. **1781** COWPER *Conv.* 771 She boasts..That while in health, the ground of her support Is madly to forget that life is short. **1802** MARIA EDGEWORTH *Moral T., Forester* xii, She had a large family, that depended upon her labour, and her character, for support. **1829** T. CASTLE *Introd. Bot.* 285 The wonderful provisions for the propagation and support of plants. **1856** FROUDE *Hist. Eng.* I. i. 66 To provide some other means for the support of the impotent poor. **1857** MILLER *Elem. Chem., Org.* ii. 55 Alone, it is insufficient for the support of life. **1915** R. HOLMES *My Police Crt. Friends* v. 152 A youth..being found about the streets without visible means of support.

b. The action of contributing to the success or maintaining the value of something.

1912 *Times* 19 Dec. 18/3 Rio Tinto [shares] touched 71⅞ at one time on French support. *Ibid.* 20/3 Egyptian futures.. relapsed to 9 to 11 points below last night under Continental selling and poor support.

4. a. The action or fact of holding up, keeping from falling, or bearing the weight of something; the condition of being so supported.

1663 PATRICK *Parab. Pilgr.* i. (1687) 2 His Leggs beginning..to fail him, and to deny him so much as their support. **1671** MILTON *Samson* 1634 Those two massie Pillars That to the arched roof gave main support. *a* **1700** EVELYN *Diary* June 1645, Without any support of columns. **1796** *Phil. Trans.* LXXXVI. 47 The pressure of the fluid, by which the solid is supported, acts upward, in the direction of a vertical line (usually called the line of support) which passes through the centre of gravity of the part immersed. **1812** *New Bot. Gard.* I. 94 Slender stems which require support. **1842** GWILT *Archit.* Gloss., *Points of Support*, the points or surfaces on which a building rests.

b. *Sc. Law.* The resting of the whole or part of a building or of a beam on the property of the servient tenement.

1681, **1754** [see SERVIENT *a.* 2]. **1838** W. BELL *Dict. Law Scot.* s.v. *Servitudes*, An urban servitude is in some way connected with houses: to this class belong support, *oneris ferendi*, *tigni immittendi*, stillicide.., light, prospect. *Ibid.* s.v., Where a servitude of support is constituted by writing.

II. One who or that which supports.

5. a. A person or thing that upholds or sustains (in *fig.* senses); a supporter, 'prop', 'stay'.

1594 KYD *Cornelia* IV. ii. 201 High Ioue the heauens among (Their support that suffer wrong). **1649** JER. TAYLOR *Gt. Exemplar* III. 164 It is to us a comfort and support, pleasant to our spirits. **1671** MILTON *Samson* 554 O madness, to think use of..strongest drinks our chief support of health. **1720** OZELL tr. *Vertot's Rom. Rep.* I. VI. 332 Wholesome Terror was the Support of the Sumptuary Laws. **1741** SHENSTONE *Judgem. Hercules* 314 Nor swells the grape..Without the firm supports of industry. **1831** SCOTT *Ct. Rob.* xxx, [Hereward] the most important support of Comnenus during the whole of that eventful day. **1849** MACAULAY *Hist. Eng.* vi. II. 125 Institutions, which..had been considered as the strongest supports of monarchical power.

b. *Mil.* (*pl.*) A supporting body of troops; the second line in a battle. (Cf. 1 e.)

1852 BURN *Naval & Milit. Dict.* II. s.v., Supports to a line of skirmishers. **1875** BEDFORD *Sailor's Pocket Bk.* vii. (ed. 2) 263 The leading boats are to contain skirmishers and supports.

c. *Computing.* Software or peripherals that are available for use with a particular computer.

1984 *Which Micro?* Dec. 20/1 The BBC Micro..has.. software and hardware support. **1985** *Which Computer?* Dec. 92/3 No external memory support is mentioned, and the system doesn't support the 8087 co-processor.

6. a. That which supports life; supply of necessaries; means of livelihood or subsistence; †formerly sometimes simply = food, provisions.

1599 DALLAM in *Early Voy. Levant* (Hakluyt Soc.) 88 We carried our supportes and other Lugedge to the sea-sid.

1611 *Bible, Transl. Pref.* ¶1 Liuelyhood and support fit for their estates. **1613** SHAKS. *Hen. VIII*, II. iii. 64 To which Title, A Thousand pound a yeare, Annuall support,..he addes. **1789** *Massachusetts Spy* 20 Aug. 3/2 We now doubt his acceptance of that place, unless a decent support should be annexed to it. **1791** MRS. RADCLIFFE *Rom. Forest* III. xx. 210 La Luc..tried to take some support; but the convulsions of his throat would not suffer him to swallow. **1823** SCOTT *Quentin D.* xxxv, I trust there is charity enough among the noble friends of my house, to make up some support for the orphan of Croye.

b. One who or that which furnishes means of livelihood, or maintains a person or community.

1745 POCOCKE *Descr. East* II. II. II. xxiii. 114 The support of this place is a great export of white wine. **1825** LAMB *Elia, Barbara S——*, Her slender earnings were the sole support of the family. **1883** GILMOUR *Mongols* xxiii. 285 He was.. the sole support of his father.

7. a. Anything that holds up, or sustains the weight of, a body, or upon which it rests.

1570 LEVINS *Manip.* 173/35 A Supporte, *adminiculum*. **1681** H. KEEPE *Mon. Westm.* 23 That curious Chappell.. built by Henry VII whose battlements, Windows, Supports and adornments speak..the magnificence of the Founder. **1827** FARADAY *Chem. Manip.* xxiv. (1842) 648 A crucible,.. with its cover and a support. **1854** J. L. PETIT *Archit. Stud. France* p. viii, Mark the directions of the several thrusts and supports. **1875** BENNETT & DYER tr. *Sachs' Bot.* III. v. 782 Curvatures caused..by the pressure of supports on tendrils. **1879** R. K. DOUGLAS *Confucianism* iv. 95 A chair which.. stands unevenly on its feet is useless as a support.

†**b.** *Metaph.* = SUBSTRATUM 1. (Cf. SUPPORT *v.* 8 c.) *Obs. rare.*

1690 LOCKE *Hum. Und.* II. xxiii. §4 Because we cannot conceive, how they [*sc.* qualities] should subsist alone, nor one in another, we suppose them to exist in, and supported by some common subject; which Support we denote by the name Substance.

c. *Photogr.* The substance (as glass, paper, etc.) which supports the sensitive film on which the image is produced.

1878 ABNEY *Photogr.* v. 36 In the collodion process,..the support may be of glass, if it be backed with some dark-coloured substance.

d. The solid substance or material on which a painting is executed.

1892 J. G. VIBERT *Sci. of Painting* viii. 96 A picture is composed of three altogether distinct elements:—1. The support, or the material substance painted on, as wood, canvas, stone, paper, etc. **1926** A. P. LAURIE *Painter's Methods & Materials* iv. 53 Well-seasoned panels of wood form an excellent support for pictures. **1958** M. L. WOLF *Dict. Painting* 286 The *support* is covered with the *ground*.. for evenness, and is then ready to receive the actual painting.

8. *Math.* The smallest closed set of elements outside which a given function or mapping is zero.

1964 A. P. & W. ROBERTSON *Topological Vector Spaces* i. 18 Let $K(S)$ be the set of real (or complex) valued functions continuous and of compact support on the separated locally compact space S. **1967** MACLANE & BIRKHOFF *Algebra* iv. 143 Show that the set of all functions f with finite support constitute a ring..under pointwise sum and convolution product. **1980** D. L. COHN *Measure Theory* vii. 200 Define functions g_1 and g_2 by $g_1 = h_1$ and $g_2 = h_2 - (h_1 \wedge h_2)$. Then g_1 and g_2 are non-negative, their supports are included in U_1 and U_2 respectively.

III. 9. *attrib.* **a.** That provides support or acts as a support.

1953 F. P. MAGOUN in *Speculum* XXVIII. 460 At least some of the language of the *Riddles* is traditional, since verses from these appear in the support-evidence. **1962** *Listener* 29 Mar. 549/1 The British..could be fairly allowed to bring back a division [from Germany] to this country and let that division act in a support role. **1964** *Language* XL. 26 Old French developed a 'support vowel'..only where there would have been an unwieldy cluster otherwise. **1967** *Times Rev. Industry* June 20/2 The ratio of 'support staff' to salesmen. **1972** *Guardian* 2 Feb. 1 The dollar sank close to its new 'support floor'. **1975** *Offshore* Sept. 9/1 Now converted into a support ship for the North Sea. **1976** M. MACHLIN *Pipeline* liii. 526 By one p.m. Simon Orloff had climbed the twelve foot support member. **1976** *Spare Rib* Dec. 8/2 Up till now I've always done support gigs. **1977** C. MCFADDEN *Serial* (1978) ix. 24/1 He was uptight about the support money he gave her. **1980** *New Age* (U.S.) Oct. 21/1 How important it is to use your personal support network, and your head, when dealing with illness.

b. *spec.* Designating stockings or tights reinforced with elastic yarn to support the muscles and veins of the legs.

1970 *Vogue* May 64/2 Ours is the *original* support stocking. **1971** *Ibid.* Nov. 26/1 Support tights don't have to be thick and ugly. *a* **1975** R. CROSSMAN *Diaries* (1977) III. 640 These surgeons come and go but they know nothing about support stockings. **1975** *Guardian* 25 Mar. 13/5 Support hose or support tights are supplied through the Hospital Supply Service. **1976** *Times* 26 Mar. 10/3 The support tights market in America has been booming.

10. Special Combs., as **support barge**, a barge providing assistance for offshore oil-drilling; **support buying**, the purchase of a commodity, a currency, or stocks and shares, in order to encourage a price rise; **support cost**, the cost of supporting something; *spec.* the cost of supporting the armed services; **support group**, (*a*) a group of musicians taking a subordinate part in a concert; (*b*) a group of people giving support to a charitable or political organization; **support line** *Mil.*, the second line of troops in a battle; a trench occupied by such troops; **support price**, a minimum price for agricultural produce, maintained by support buying or deficiency payments; **support trench** *Mil.*, a trench forming part of a line of strong points in the rear of the strong points of the firing line.

1976 *Offshore Engineer* Apr. 5/1 Field operator Occidental has given a letter of intent for a long-term charter of the *Bredford*, the first purpose-built semi-submersible *support barge. **1932** *Economist* 9 Jan. 69/2 The time to support prices was opportune. *Support buying of highgrade bonds, particularly in the railroad list, has resulted in improvement of prices and a stronger tone in all security markets. **1969** *Times* 13 Jan. 11/1 There will..be support buying to support the levies in some cases. **1958** *Spectator* 14 Feb. 192/2 To talk about the foreign policy of a small Power would be a little ridiculous if international affairs consisted purely of rocket sites and *support costs. *a* **1974** R. CROSSMAN *Diaries* (1976) II. 208, I went across to the Party meeting on German support costs. **1969** *Listener* 10 July 59/1 After all this and the excellent *support groups, the Rolling Stones were a musical disappointment. **1976** *Spare Rib* Dec. 13/1 Our support group is small so we have very few problems with disagreements on tactics, etc., but have to work harder. **1977** *Lancashire Life* Dec. 75/1 CARE's Wigan support group invited the organisation to inspect the building. **1917** W. OWEN *Let.* 4 Feb. (1967) 430 We worked back through the reserve, & *support lines to the crazy village where the Battalion takes breath. **1918** *Aussie* Aug. 10/1 In that sector of the front..there was a small town... Subsequently, as our Support Line settled down in front of it, it became the object of minute attention on the part of Fritz. **1971** S. HILL *Strange Meeting* ii. 110 Garrett had asked Hilliard to write to the men's relatives, as soon as they got into the support line the following day. **1943** *Sun* (Baltimore) 30 Jan. 18/4 So-called *support prices, the minimum which canners may pay this year to growers who participate in the subsidy program,..are as follows. *Ibid.* 2 Oct. 6/2 The food planners tell us solemnly that this is not a subsidy program; it is a support-price program. **1949** A. MCLINTOCK *Descr. Atlas N.Z.* 44 Since the war 'support schemes' have also been established for wool and export meat, based on the reserve funds built up during the war and post-war periods of stabilisation..[but] in the long run 'support prices' cannot diverge very far from market realisations. **1974** *Times* 15 Jan. 1/7 The Council..had rejected..an immediate 10 per cent rise in the support price for beef paid to farmers. **1915** *Times* 29 Apr. 9/6 From a *support trench, about 600 yards from the German lines, he observed the gas. **1923** KIPLING *Irish Guards in Great War* I. 40 The line of support-trenches was held.

support (sə'pɔət), *v.* Also 4–5 supporte, 5 suppoorte, 6 *Sc.* suport (*pa. pple. contracted* support), 7 subport. [ad. (O)F. *supporter* (= Pr. *supportar*, It. *sopportare*, Sp. *su-*, *soportar*, Pg. *soportar*, *supportar*), ad. L. *supportāre* to convey, f. *sup-* = SUB- 26 + *portāre* to carry (see PORT *v.*[1]).]

1. a. *trans.* To endure without opposition or resistance; to bear with, put up with, tolerate. (In mod. use often a gallicism.)

1382 WYCLIF *2 Cor.* xi. 1, I wolde ȝe schulden susteyne a litil thing of myn vnwysdom, but and supporte me [*gloss* or bere vp me]. **1388** —— *Col.* iii. 13 And support ȝe echon other. **1455** in *Rep. Hist. MSS. Comm., Var. Coll.* IV. 203 All charges and taxes..ye shall supporte and bere to your power. **1549** *Compl. Scot.* xvii. 143 The vice of thy ȝongest brother suld be supportit be rason of his ignorance. **1654** tr. *Scudery's Curia Pol.* 100 How can they support infamy as a matter indifferent? *a* **1700** EVELYN *Diary* 25 July 1673, These things his high spirit could not support. **1731** FIELDING *Mod. Husb.* IV. iv, I know several women of fashion I could not support for a tiring woman. **1773** MRS. CHAPONE *Improv. Mind* (1774) I. iii. 83, I cannot support even the idea of your becoming one of those undone lost creatures! **1848** THACKERAY *Van. Fair* xxv, I respectfully decline to receive Mrs. Rawdon—I can't support *that* quite. **1897** *Allbutt's Syst. Med.* II. 433 Occasionally it [*sc.* milk] is not well supported by the patient in any form. **1901** *Daily Mail* 30 Oct. 4/4 He prefers to support the poacher's intrusion than to risk shooting at him.

†**b.** To endure, undergo, *esp.* with fortitude or without giving way; to bear up against. *Obs.*

1604 SHAKS. *Oth.* I. iii. 259, I a heauie interim shall support By his deere absence. **1605** —— *Lear* v. iii. 197 His flaw'd heart..too weake the conflict to support. **1615** G. SANDYS *Trav.* 146 Wrongs and contumelies, which they support with an invincible patience. **1671** MRS. BEHN *Forc'd Marr.* I. ii, Prethee how does she support this news? *a* **1700** in *Cath. Rec. Soc. Publ.* (1911) IX. 336 A greevious infirmity .. w[ch] she supported wth great patience, and Resignation. **1773** JOHNSON *Let. to Mrs. Thrale* 17 Aug., At supper there was such a conflux of company that I could scarcely support the tumult. **1794** MRS. RADCLIFFE *Myst. Udolpho* xxxviii, If she believed herself well enough to support the interview. **1805** EMILY CLARK *Banks of Douro* II. 40 Neither of them could support being alone.

c. *trans.* To sustain (a contest). *rare.*

1801 S. TURNER *Hist. Anglo-Sax.* III. ix. II. 156 Within two months afterwards, the princes of Wessex supported another battle with the recruited confederates at Merton.

2. a. *trans.* To strengthen the position of (a person or community) by one's assistance, countenance, or adherence; to uphold the rights, claims, authority, or status of; to stand by, back up.

1390 GOWER *Conf.* III. 157 And ek his kinges realte Mot every liege man conforte, With good and bodi to supporte. **1424** in *Cal. Pat. Rolls, 8 Hen. VI*, 30 The xxiiij aldermen.. xal..supporten the mair..in..counsell ghevyng, in walkyng with hym on principal dayes and in procession. *c* **1450** LOVELICH *Grail* xiv. 648 To him ward ful faste he gan to Ride Forto supporten him at that Tyde. **1508** DUNBAR *Poems* vii. 28 Oure indeficient adiutorie,..That neuer saw Scot yit indigent nor sory, Bot thou did hym suport, with thi gud deid. **1568** GRAFTON *Chron.* II. 70 Sending to the King, to..desyre him, that he would not support nor maintaine his enemie within his Realme. **1607** SHAKS. *Cor.* I. i. 84 [They] Make Edicts for Vsurie, to support Vsurers. **1651** HOBBES *Leviath.* II. xxix. 168 So was Thomas Becket..supported against Henry the Second, by the Pope. **1686** tr. *Chardin's Coronat. Solyman* 104 Being supported by the favour of his Prince. **1849** MACAULAY *Hist. Eng.* iii. I. 354 A government, supported and trusted by London. **1884** A. R. PENNINGTON *Wiclif* vii. 240 He had no party in the country to support him.

b. To uphold or maintain the validity or authority of (a thing); also, to give support to (a course of action).

1638 CHILLINGWORTH *Relig. Prot.* iv. §16. 198 The Divels instrument to support errours, and superstitions. **1713** ADDISON *Cato* I. i, To form new battles, and support his crimes. **1742** KAMES *Decis. Crt. Sess. 1730–52* (1799) 45 It is the genius of law to support deeds, as far as they can be supported. **1748** LD. HARDWICKE in *Collect. Juridica* (1791) 383 The recovery suffered by him was before the debts were paid,..and consequently he could not make a good tenant to the *præcipe* to support his recovery. **1800** *Addison's Rep.* 11 The report..did not pursue the sub-mission and so could not be supported. **1882** PEBODY *Eng. Journalism* xx. 148 That he should bring out an evening paper to support the cause of the Throne.

†**c.** To second, corroborate; also, to intensify, as by contrast. *Obs. rare.*

1720 OZELL tr. *Vertot's Rom. Rep.* II. VIII. 28 These Advantages in Tiberius, were supported by a noble Air, an engaging Countenance [etc.]. **1778** SIR J. REYNOLDS *Disc.* viii. (1876) 453 That light is to be supported by sufficient shadow.

†**3. a.** *refl.* To assert, maintain. *Obs. rare*[−1].

1468 *Paston Lett.* II. 314, As I support me to alle the world, I put nevyr maner ne lyfelode of my Maister Fastolf yn trouble.

b. To back up in a statement or an opinion.

1686 W. HOPKINS tr. *Ratramnus* Dissert. iv. (1688) 65 *note*, Bertram..determining the Sacramental change to be Figuratively wrought, not corporally,..and supporting him-self by the Testimony of St. Augustine. **1744** AKENSIDE *Pleas. Imag.* Design ¶7 The authority of Virgil..will best support him in this particular. **1771** *Junius Lett.* xlvi. (1788) 258 But Junius has a great authority to support him; which ..I accidentally met with this morning in the course of my reading.

c. To furnish authority for or corroboration of (a statement, etc.); to bear out, substantiate.

1761 FOOTE *Liar* II. Wks. 1799 I. 298 *Sir Ja.*.. But, for the son, you never—. *M. Gr.* Sat eyes upon him. *Sir Ja.* Really? *M. Gr.* Really. *Sir Ja.* Finely supported. **1782** PRIESTLEY *Corrupt. Chr.* I. II. 212 [This] is not at all supported by fact. **1817** SELWYN *Law Nisi Prius* (ed. 4) II. 962 To support an averment in a declaration on a policy of insurance on goods. **1856** FROUDE *Hist. Eng.* (1858) I. i. 14 The advocates of both [theories] can support their arguments with an appeal to experience. **1885** *Law Times Rep.* LIII. 478/1 The application was supported by an affidavit of the applicant. **1895** *Ibid.* LXXIII. 701/2 The statute..does not seem..to support the assertions for which it was cited.

d. To second or to speak in favour of (a proposition, or one who makes a proposition); to maintain, or contend for the truth of (an opinion, etc.).

1736 *Gentl. Mag.* VI. 718/1 This Proposition was supported and inforced by the D—ke of A—le. **1842** BISCHOFF *Woollen Manuf.* II. 105 Lord Wharncliffe.. promised to support Lord Harewood when he presented the petition to the House of Lords. **1849** MACAULAY *Hist. Eng.* iv. I. 445 Godolphin..had supported the Exclusion Bill. **1860** TYNDALL *Glac.* II. xiii. 296 M. Agassiz supported this theory for a time.

4. a. To provide for the maintenance of, bear the expense of; †also, to provide funds to meet (expenditure). Now only with immaterial obj.

c **1413** [see SUPPORTING *vbl. sb.* 2]. **1439** *E.E. Wills* (1882) 115 She beryng, yeldyng, payng and supportyng þerof þe ferme yerely, and oþer charges duryng her lyf. **1553** *Acc. Ld. High Treas. Scot.* X. 175 To the..wardane of the Myddill Marchis, to support his expensis, xl li. **1585** [see SUPPORTING *vbl. sb.* 2]. **1662** GERBIER *Principles* 15 Ten Thousand Gilders *per annum*, to support and alter what he had Built amisse. **1691** T. H[ALE] *Acc. New Invent.* p. lxvii, No allowance of any Sallary to support their Office. **1705** tr. *Bosman's Guinea* 342 These..eat of the best that is to be gotten as long as they have anything to support it. **1817** *Parl. Deb.* 801 That they supported the expenses out of the interest of the arrears which they withheld. **1818** SCOTT *Hrt. Midl.* li, Allowances for the purpose of..supporting the hospitality of the representative of Majesty. **1849** MACAULAY *Hist. Eng.* iii. I. 336 This luxury was supported by a thriving trade.

b. *Law.* Of an estate: To be such as to provide for (a remainder).

1694 in Salkeld *Reports* (1721) 576 The contingent Remainder to him was not discharged by the vesting in the Crown..because of the Wife's Estate, which is sufficient to support it. **1766** BLACKSTONE *Comm.* II. xi. 166 A lease at will is not held to be such a particular estate, as will support a remainder over. **1772** FEARNE *Contingent Remainders* (1791) 424 It was agreed that such limitation was void as a contingent remainder, because there was no freehold to support it.

5. a. To furnish food or sustenance for; to supply with the necessaries of life.

c **1430** LYDG. *Min. Poems* (Percy Soc.) 212 No Corn up growe nor greyn..Man to suppoorte. *c* **1470** HENRY *Wallace* II. 413 Syluer thai had, all with him has he tayne, Him to support. **1562** *Aberd. Kirk Sess. Rec.* (Spalding Cl.) 7 Gif thai support nocht thair awin fader and moder. **1650** CROMWELL *Let.* 9 Sept. in *Carlyle*, The Ministers in England are supported, and have liberty to preach the Gospel. **1762–71** H. WALPOLE *Vertue's Anecd. Paint.* (1786) V. 227 By which community..he had been supported, after he became incapable of business. **1791** J. LONG *Voy. Indian Interpreter* 106 We had very little food, but fortunately killed three large bears in the middle of the portage, which supported us several days. **1801** *Farmer's Mag.* Apr. 193 The burden of supporting the poor ought to be sustained by all ranks. **1842** Miss Mitford in L'Estrange *Life* (1870) III. ix. 137, I must so far neglect my dear father as to gain time for writing what may support us. **1845** Lingard *Anglo-Saxon Ch.* (1858) II. xii. 204 During the winter they were supported at the expense of the inhabitants.

†**b.** *gen.* To supply. *Sc. Obs. rare.*

a **1508** Dunbar *Tua Mariit Wemen* 467, I have ane secrete serwand..That me supportis of sic nedis. **1632** Lithgow *Trav.* I. 25 This Prouince is mainely watered..with stately Po... The Riuers Ladishe, Montanello, Della Guarda, and other forcible streames supporting the shoulders of it.

c. To sustain (the vital functions); also, to keep up the strength of (a sick person).

1704 Fuller *Med. Gymn.* (1711) 103 A Gentleman.. found that Riding supported him as much as the Change of Air. **1706** E. Ward *Wooden World Diss.* (1708) 56 The poor Souls, to support Nature, are oblig'd..to spend their Pay upon the very Wine that was assign'd to them. **1786** J. Hunter *Treat. Venereal Dis.* vi. iii. (1810) 530 The patient must be supported. **1842** [see nature *sb.* 10 b].

d. *intr.* for *refl.* To live *on. U.S.*

1870 W. M. Baker *New Timothy* 232 (Cent. Dict.) We have plenty of property; he'll have that to support on in his preachin'.

†**6.** To make good, repair (a deficiency). *rare.*

c **1449** [see supporting *vbl. sb.* 3]. **1500–20** Dunbar *Poems* xxviii. 35 3e..Supportand faltis with 3our supple. **1563–7** Buchanan *Reform. St. Andros* Wks. (S.T.S.) 11 The principal sal support the defectis of absens of the public reidar and regentis.

7. a. To bear, hold, or prop up; to keep from falling or sinking; †*occas.* to carry (the train of a robe).

c **1420** ? Lydg. *Assembly of Gods* 1528 Next whom stood Moyses,..Aaron & Vrre, hys armes supportyng. *a* **1548** Hall *Chron., Hen. VII*, 53 b, Next after folowed the lady Cicile suster to yᵉ quene supporting the treyne of the spouse. **1591** Shaks. *1 Hen. VI*, ii. v. 14 These Feet, whose strengthlesse stay is numme, (Vnable to support this Lumpe of Clay). **1600** —— *A.Y.L.* ii. vii. 199 Support him by the arme. **1667** Milton *P.L.* ix. 427 Stooping to support Each Flour of slender stalk, whose head..Hung drooping unsustained. **1786** Abercrombie *Gard. Assist.* 180 Rolling grass, trimming and supporting plants. **1842** Lover *Handy Andy* xxiv, Andy, in his fall, endeavouring to support himself, caught at the suspended articles above him. **1862** Miss Braddon *Lady Audley* xxxii, Her perfect chin supported by her hand. **1885** 'Mrs. Alexander' *At Bay* vi, As he supported his friend's unsteady steps.

†**b.** *refl.* To hold oneself up, keep an erect position. *Obs.*

1593 Shaks. *Rich. II*, ii. ii. 83 Here am I left to vnderprop his Land, Who weake with age, cannot support my selfe. **1727** Gay *Begg. Op.* i. viii, My head swims! I'm distracted! I can't support myself—Oh! (*Faints in a chair.*)

†**c.** To give one's arm to (a lady); to take (a person) on one's arm. *Obs.*

1625 in Ellis *Orig. Lett.* Ser. i. III. 201 The Queen..came out..supported by the Count de Tilliers her Lord Chamberlain. **1632** Massinger *City Madam* i. ii, May I have the honour To support you, lady? **1768** Sterne *Sent. Journ.*, *Sword*, The Marquis..supported his lady;—his eldest son supported his sister. **1816** Scott *Old Mort.* xliv, He offered his arm, and supported her into the small anteroom.

†**d.** (*Mil.*) ***to support arms***, to carry the musket vertically against the left shoulder, with the hammer resting on the left arm held horizontally across the body. *Obs.*

1833 *Regul. Instr. Cavalry* i. 28 Sentries posted with advanced arms may afterwards 'support' them.

e. To sustain (a weight of so much).

1726 Leoni *Alberti's Archit.* viii. vii. II. 69/2 The Wall ought to be allowed a due Thickness for the supporting such a weight. **1815** J. Smith *Panorama Sci. & Art* II. 185 A piece of iron, the weight of which is rather more than a given magnet will support. **1831** Brewster *Optics* x. 93 An artificial horse-shoe loadstone, which carried 13½ oz.,..at last supported 31 oz., by continuing it in the sun's light.

f. *Her.* in *pass.* To be flanked by supporters.

1562 Legh *Armory* 88 b, Supported with a Mantiger Argent..and a wiuerne Or. **1610** Guillim *Heraldry* vi. vii. 280 [A shield] Supported by a Lion Rampand, gardant.. and an Vnicorne. **1864** Boutell *Her. Hist. & Pop.* xix. (ed. 3) 296 Each shield..is supported by figures of angels.

8. a. To constitute the substratum of (a structure); to sustain in position above, have on it or at the top.

1617 Moryson *Itin.* i. 194 The second Bridge..is supported with pillars of wood. **1686** Plot *Staffordsh.* 372 The whole [town-hall] being supported with a curious Portico of arch-work. **1759** Brown *Compl. Farmer* 98 Let the board be a little supported by two ledges. **1796** Withering *Brit. Plants* (ed. 3) II. 337 Spokes of the umbel from 3 to 7, each supporting only 1 flower. **1842** Loudon *Suburban Hort.* 504 The floor of the pit may be supported on arches. **1863** Lyell *Antiq. Man* ii. 17 These [piles] have evidently once supported villages. **1907** *Verney Memoirs* I. 3 'Andirons' in front to support the logs of wood.

†**b.** *Her.* in *pass.* (see quots.). *Obs.*

1562 Legh *Armory* 109 If a Pale be vpon a Lion, or any other beast,..he is debrused with a Pale. But if the beast be on the Pale, then that beast is supported of the same Pale. **1728** Chambers *Cycl.*, *Supported*, in Heraldry, a Term apply'd to the uppermost Quarters of a Shield, when divided into several Quarters; these seeming, as it were, supported or sustain'd by those below... The Chief is also said to be supported when it is of two Colours, and the upper Colour takes up two Thirds of it: In this Case it is supported by the Colour underneath.

†**c.** *Metaph.* To be the subject or substratum of. (Cf. support *sb.* 7 b.) *Obs.*

1656 Jeanes *Fuln. Christ* 154 There is an ability in the person of the word, to suppositate..the manhood, and there was a capacity in the manhood to be assumed, supported, and terminated by the person of the word. **1690** [see support *sb.* 7 b]. **1710** Berkeley *Princ. Hum. Knowl.* i. §68 It must be observed, that it [*sc.* matter] supports nothing at all.

9. a. To keep (a person, his mind, etc.) from failing or giving way; to give courage, confidence, or power of endurance to.

1602 Marston *Antonio's Rev.* Prol., Heere's the prop that doth support our hopes. **1611** *Bible* 1 Esdras viii. 52 That the power of the Lord our God, should be with them that seeke him, to support them in all wayes. *c* **1655** Milton *2nd Sonn. to C. Skinner* 9 What supports me, dost thou ask? The conscience, Friend, to have lost them overply'd In libertyes defence. **1667** —— *P.L.* xii. 496 With inward consolations recompenc't, And oft supported so as shall amaze Thir proudest persecuters. **1719** Watts *Ps.* cxlvi. vi, The Lord supports the sinking mind. **1779** *Mirror* No. 63 ¶9 He was supported by the conscious admiration of those countrymen whom he had left. **1818** Miss Ferrier *Marriage* ii. xxii, They are wonderfully supported and behave with astonishing firmness. **1838** Lytton *Leila* iv. iv, 'Support me O Redeemer,' she murmured.

†**b.** *refl.* (occas. *intr.*) To bear up *under* an infliction or *against* an untoward event. (Cf. 1 b.)

1638 Junius *Paint. Ancients* 192 Though a man bee nev[e]r so shamefaced, yet may he support himselfe by the helpe of a good conscience. **1756** Amory *Buncle* (1770) IV. 88 As to myself..I brought a consumption into the world with me, and by art have supported under it. **1777** Johnson *Let. to Mrs. Thrale* 22 Oct., Against a blow so sudden,..I wonder that she supports herself.

10. a. To maintain unimpaired, preserve from decay or depreciation.

1515 Barclay *Egloges* iv. (1570) C vj b/1 Supporting Iustice, concorde and equitie. **1526** *Pilgr. Perf.* ii. v, Some benefytes supporteth the same [lyfe of grace in our soules]. **1605** Shaks. *Lear* i. iv. 287 Men..That..in the most exact regard, support The worships of their name. **1628** T. Ball *Life Preston* (1885) 163 The Dʳ. used all his friends for to support & keepe in power this statute. **1710** Prideaux *Orig. Tithes* i. 5 His Worship be provided for with such a part of our substance, as may be sufficient to support it. **1802** James *Milit. Dict.* s.v., To support the ancient character of the corps. **1891** Farrar *Darkn. & Dawn* xlv, The brave and honest Corbulo, who had supported the fame of Roman courage on so many a hard-fought field.

b. To preserve from failure, contribute to the success of (an undertaking); also, to maintain (a price).

1779 Sheridan *Critic* i. i, On the first night of a new piece they always fill the house with orders to support it. **1855** *Poultry Chron.* III. 551 For wheat the quotations of Monday were barely supported. **1898** *Westm. Gaz.* 24 Oct. 9/3 Indian gold shares have been supported.

c. To maintain in being or in action; to keep up, keep going; to provide the necessary matter for. (Cf. 4, 5; see also 12.)

1738 Swift *Pol. Conversat.* Introd. 12 The genuine Productions of superior Wits, to embellish and support Conversation. **1766** Goldsm. *Vicar W.* xvii, She had been for some time supporting a fictitious gaiety. **1778** Miss Burney *Evelina* lxiii, I supported no part in the conversation. *Ibid.* lxxvi, I..wished Lord Orville had supported his own reserve, and suffered me to support mine. **1785** Swinburne *Trav.* II. xliv. 307 The conversation..was well supported till mid-night. **1812** Sir H. Davy *Chem. Philos.* 3 A species of air that supports flame in a superior degree. **1826** *Art of Brewing* (ed. 2) 31 Keeping a quantity of this fermentable matter unattenuated, in order to support the natural consumption. **1838** Lytton *Alice* viii. vii, Fear not..support your courage—nothing shall harm you. **1856** Froude *Hist. Eng.* II. viii. 252 The earth will not support human life uncultivated. **1875** Jevons *Money* (1878) 254 A town which is able to support two banks.

absol. **1827** Lytton *Pelham* III. iv, If it can create, can it not also support?

d. Of specie: To guarantee the convertibility of (a paper currency).

1868 Rogers *Pol. Econ.* iv. (1876) 38 Great part of this [specie] is used to support the notes which circulate within the country.

e. *Computing.* Of a computer, operating system, etc.: to allow the use or operation of (a program, language, device, etc.) with it.

1973 W. D. Manville *Microprogramming Support for Programming Languages* (Thesis, U. of Cambridge) iv. 62 Various actual and virtual machine languages are compared to determine how efficiently they support a particular high-level language, BCPL. **1981** *Electronics* 10 Mar. 165/1 Software supported by the operating system will remain compatible across the product line and across time. **1982** *Which Computer?* June 35/2 The Altos will support BASIC, Cobol and Fortran as development languages. **1983** *Austral. Microcomputer Mag.* Aug. 23/2 The motherboard has eight slots to support expansion cards which provide a Z80 processor. **1985** *Which Computer?* Apr. 24/2 The system wouldn't run with more than three or four terminals even though it was supposed to support a minimum of 20. **1985** *Pract. Computing* June 83/3 Alas, the package is not converted to U.K. use and so does not support floating £ signs or European date formats.

11. To sustain (a character) in a dramatic performance; *gen.* to act or play (a part), bear (a character), maintain (a certain behaviour or course of conduct).

1709 Steele *Tatler* No. 48 ¶4 They supported a general Behaviour in the World which could not hurt their Credit or their Purses. *a* **1763** Shenstone *Ess.* Wks. 1765 II. 40 The higher character a person supports, the more he should regard his minutest actions. **1775** Sheridan *St. Patrick's Day* i. ii, I hate militia officers,..clowns in military masquerade, wearing the dress without supporting the character. **1791** *Theatr. Guardian* No. 6. 61 The characters were admirably supported. **1801** Strutt *Sports & Past.* iii. vi. 224 Persons capable of well supporting assumed characters. **1888** Bryce *Amer. Commw.* I. 195 In order to support the *rôle* which they unconsciously fall into when talking to Europeans.

12. a. To give assistance to in a battle, esp. by a second line of troops; to act with, second (a leading actor); to assist as a subordinate in a contest, a musical performance, or the like. (Cf. 2.)

1848 Alison *Hist. Eur.* liv. §69 (ed. 7) XII. 115 As Junot perceived that their attack did not at once prove successful, they were supported in the end by the whole reserve of infantry under Kellerman. **1876** Voyle & Stevenson *Milit. Dict.* s.v. *Skirmishers*, To support them [*sc.* skirmishers] when weakened..is the duty of the supports. **1889** *Harper's Mag.* Nov. 871/1 As Ophelia,..she supported the elder Booth. **1901** *Daily Chron.* 23 Nov. 9/5 Whaley is grandly supported by the two Milburns. **1910–11** A. W. Ward in *Encycl. Brit.* VIII. 534/2 Metropolitan 'stars' travelled.. generally alone, sometimes with one or two subordinates in their train, and were 'supported', as the phrase went, by the stock company of each theatre. **1913** *Times* 14 May 6/2 The battalion had established its firing line on the opposite side of the canal with its machine guns and the Field Artillery section supporting the attack.

b. To occupy a position by the side of, with the object of giving assistance or encouragement; hence, to assist by one's presence or attendance.

[Cf. quot. 1424 in sense 2, and the following:—

1697 Dryden *Virg. Georg.* iv. 316 The servile Rout their careful Cæsar praise..They crowd his Levees, and support his Throne.]

1886 *Manch. Examiner* 14 Jan. 5/6 Mr. Gladstone was supported right and left by Lord Hartington and Sir William Harcourt. **1896** *Pall Mall Mag.* Jan. 105 The Viceroy and Vicereine stand before Tippoo's throne,.. supported on either side by the leading officials. **1913** *Times* 7 Aug. 8/5 Sir W. Watson Cheyne, who presided, was supported by many highly distinguished surgeons.

c. *Sport.* To be a supporter or follower of (a team, etc.). Cf. supporter 5 b.

1952 J. Arlott *Concerning Soccer* viii. 122 The spectator has the loudest word; for the good of football he should support good football. **1962** K. Wolstenholme *Book of World Soccer* 55/2 When you think of all that, what other football club is there worth supporting? **1979** E. John in K. Keegan *Against the World* x. 071 I've always supported England, I've stood on the terraces at Wembley, so what I relish now is the sheer luck of having the privilege to travel with the team.

supportable (sə'pɔətəb(ə)l), *a.* [ad. L. **supportābilis*, f. *supportāre* to support: see -able. Cf. F. *supportable.*]

I. In active sense.

†**1.** Affording support or assistance. *Obs. rare.*

1533 Bellenden *Livy* i. viii. (S.T.S.) I. 49 þe favoure of goddis apperit to þame sa supportabill and helplie in all thare besines.

II. In passive sense.

2. Bearable, tolerable, endurable.

a **1577** Sir T. Smith *Commw. Eng.* iii. iv. (1584) 96 This thing seemed not supportable to the noble prince King Henrie the eight. **1610** Shaks. *Temp.* v. i. 145 Supportable To make the deere losse, haue I meanes much weaker Then you may call to comfort you. **1637** Bastwick *Litany* ii. 18 It is a prodigious wickednes..and a thing not supportable to compare the Creator of all things to the creature. *a* **1691** Boyle *Hist. Air* (1692) 158 The steams of their carcases would make the air so stinking and offensive, that it was scarce supportable. **1711** Addison *Spect.* No. 169 ¶3 Good-nature..makes even Folly and Impertinence supportable. **1784** Cowper *Task* v. 604 The loss of all That can..make frail life, Short as it is, supportable. **1810** Vince *Astron.* xxi. 228 It grew very faint, and was easily supportable to the naked eye. **1894** Stevenson & Osbourne *Ebb Tide* i. i, The thought of death is always the least supportable when it draws near to the merely sensual and selfish.

b. Capable of being successfully resisted.

1711 in *10th Rep. Hist. MSS. Comm.* App. v. 157 Their.. assault with such numbers not being supportable.

3. Capable of being maintained, confirmed, or made good; defensible.

1631 J. Burges *Answ. Rejoined* 54 Some reason supportable by the word of God. **1793** Washington *Lett.* Writ. 1891 XII. 290 To take fair and supportable ground I conceive to be our best policy. **1812** J. J. Henry *Camp. agst. Quebec* 173 These ideas are..supportable by the authority of some of the best physicians. **1885** *Law Times Rep.* LIII. 431/1 Bills containing charges which might not be supportable on taxation.

4. In physical sense: Capable of being held up or sustained. *rare.*

1832–4 De Quincey *Cæsars* Wks. 1859 X. 88 Obliged to cover..each space upon which they trode with parts of their dress, in order to gain any supportable footing.

Hence **supporta'bility, su'pportableness**, the quality or condition of being supportable; **su'pportably** *adv.*, in a supportable manner, endurably.

a **1660** Hammond *Serm. Matt. xi. 30* Wks. 1684 IV. 477 The supportableness of the burthen. **1846** Worcester, Supportably. **1867** Carlyle *Remin.* (1881) II. ii. 239 My new illustrious 'study' was definable as the least inhabitable ..bit of human workmanship in that kind... But, by many and long-continued efforts..I did get it patched together into something of supportability.

†**supportal.** *Obs. rare.* Also 5 -ayle. [f. support *v.* + -al¹ 5 (†-*aile*).] = support *sb.* 1, 5.

14.. in *Tundale's Vis.* (1843) 97 Thou art oure scheld and oure supportayle. **1574** J. Dee in *Lett. Lit. Men* (Camden) 34 Uppon..hope, that som nedefull supportal wold be for me..devysed. *a* **1618** Sylvester *Miracle of Peace* iii, Thou Nurse of Vertues, Muses chief supportall.

† **su'pportance.** *Obs.* [f. SUPPORT *v.* + -ANCE.]

1. Assistance, backing; = SUPPORT *sb.* 1, 1 c.

c **1490** *Plumpton Corr.* (Camden) 74, I..desire..that in such things as my..beloved Cosin, Mary Gascougne, hath to doe with you,..that ye will give unto hir ayde and supportance. **1596** SPENSER *State Irel.* Wks. (Globe) 668/2 He is like to make a fowle stirre there, though of himselfe of noe power, yet through supportaunce of some others. **1601** SHAKS. *Twel. N.* III. iv. 329 He will fight with you for's oath sake:..therefore draw for the supportance of his vowe, he protests he will not hurt you. **1608** HEYWOOD *Lucrece* Wks. 1874 V. 204 We are of our selfe Without supportance, we all fate defie, Aidlesse. **1625** BP. MOUNTAGU *App. Cæsar* 11 Those two Townes and States, next unto God, have stood by supportance of the Crowne of England. **1631** GOUGE *God's Arrows* iii. §44. 264 Christ..returned to prayer againe and againe, and found sufficient supportance. **1638** G. SANDYS *Paraphr. Div. Poems, Ps. cix,* That they may know ..how I by Divine Supportance stand.

transf. **1589** GREENE *Menaphon* (Arb.) 63 [Thou] that earst while wert honoured in euery mans eye through the supportance of thy beautie.

2. Maintenance, sustenance; = SUPPORT *sb.* 3.

1593 NASHE *Christ's T.* (1613) 67 She was constrained (for her liues supportance)..to kill him and roast him. **1595** *Wills & Inv. N.C.* (Surtees 1860) 280 To the releaffe and supportance of such as she shall fynd to be vertuusly disposed. **1615** G. SANDYS *Trav.* 108 For the supportance of his owne estate. **1631** HEYWOOD *London's Jus Hon.* Wks. 1874 IV. 274 By these types and symboles of Honour..all other inferiour Magistracies..receive both being and supportance. **1644** JESSOP *Angel of Ephesus* 31 As if the Church did give supportance and stabilitie to the truth. **1659** *Lady Alimony* II. vi, Th' Court..for supportance, Allots us Alimony. **1830** W. TAYLOR *Hist. Surv. Germ. Poetry* III. 19 Orphan of father betimes, on her I was thrown for supportance.

3. The action of supporting, propping, or holding up; = SUPPORT *sb.* 4.

1593 SHAKS. *Rich. II,* III. iv. 32 Giue some supportance to the bending twigges. **1604** TOOKER *Fabrique Ch.* vi. 116 Chap. 6. Of supportance and keeping the fabrique of the church vpright. **1631** GOUGE *God's Arrows* iii. §48. 273 This ..supportance of Moses hands in regard of his bodily weaknesse. **1664** POWER *Exp. Philos.* I. 5 The other four legs ..by which she [*sc.* the fly] layes hold on the rugosities..of all bodies she walks over, even to the supportance of her self, though with her back downwards. **1804** W. TAYLOR in *Ann. Rev.* II. 351 To estimate our well being by the weight of our burdens and place, like caryatids, our perfection in our supportance.

† **b.** *fig.* Applied to the relation of a subject to an attribute: cf. SUPPORT *sb.* 7 b, *v.* 8 c. *Obs.*

1656 JEANES *Mixt. Schol. Div.* 83 The supportance of the flesh in, and union with the person of the word.

4. That which supports (in various senses).

1597 MIDDLETON *Wisd. Solomon* ix. 4 My crowne doth want supportance for to beare. **1610** HOLLAND *Camden's Brit.* I. 427 A twofold supportance that it had on either side to uphold..the lofty top. **1617** COLLINS *Def. Bp. Ely* I. i. 17 As Peter of the Churche, so these words of Peter, a semblable supportance. **1631** MASSINGER *Believe as You List* II. ii, The tribute Rome receives from Asia, is Her chief supportance. **1638** FORD *Fancies* I. iii, Name and honour: What are they? a mere sound without supportance. **1830** W. TAYLOR *Hist. Surv. Germ. Poetry* I. 313 So Boreas,..The blooming hop, and its supportance, flings.

† **supportasse.** *Obs.* (or *Hist.*) [Obscure formation on SUPPORT *v.*; perh. an error.] = SUPPORTER 3 b.

1583 STUBBES *Anat. Abuses* I. (1879) 52 A certain deuice made of wyers,..whipped ouer either with gold, thred, siluer or silk, and this hee [*sc.* the Devil] calleth a supportasse, or vnderpropper. This is to be applyed round about their necks vnder the ruffe,..to beare vp the whole frame and body of the ruffe from falling and hanging down. **1902** *Athenæum* 2 Aug. 163/3 Plate xlvi. shows a vandyked ruff with its supportasses.

† **suppor'tation.** *Obs.* Also 5 subp-, 6 soportacion. [a. OF. *supportation*, ad. late L. *supportātio, -ōnem*, f. *supportāre* to SUPPORT.]

1. Assistance, countenance; = SUPPORT *sb.* 1.

c **1386** CHAUCER *Melib.* ¶176 They wol yeue yow Audience and lookynge to supportacion in thy presence, and scorne thee in thyn Absence. **1426** LYDG. *De Guil. Pilgr.* 9182 Deff, and also specheles, And off no reputacioun, Ne wer thy supportacioun. **1427** *Rolls of Parlt.* V. 408/2 That no Lorde..receyve..Pilours, Robbours..or eny other open misdoer, so that the parties greved..shal not..pursue ayenst hem lawefully, bycause of such supportation of Lordeship. **1433** LYDG. *St. Edmund* I. 1023 Al envyous supplantacioun Hadde in his siht no supportacioun. **1452** in Ellis *Orig. Lett.* Ser. I. I. 12 With the help and supportation of Almighty God, and of our Lady. **1485** *Rolls of Parlt.* VI. 322/1 The said Morgan..hath greate supportacion, and is mighty in the said Shyre. **1515** BARCLAY *Egloges* iii. (1570) C iij/1 Their theft and fraudes, and their extortion And of misliuers their supportation. **1553** in Ellis *Orig. Lett.* Ser. II. II. 213, I utterly denye to Smyth any supportacion at my handes in any of his misdemenors against my Lorde. **1603** KNOLLES *Hist. Turks* (1621) 453 Purposing by the supportation of his father, to make himselfe lord and Soveraign..of all Latium. **1650** W. D. tr. *Comenius' Gate Lat. Unl.* §660 Let the atturnie..not fail his client (as being one that..relies upon his supportation). **1659** HAMMOND *On Ps.* cxlvi. 9 Shut out from all sorts of humane supportation.

b. Used in formulæ of supplication or submission, esp. ***under*** or ***with supportation of***; = SUPPORT *sb.* 1 b.

1426 *Pol. Poems* (Rolls) II. 133 Undir favoure and supportacioun, Thus I begyn on my translacioun. **1426** LYDG. *De Guil. Pilgr.* 16866 And certys, lady, with Supportacion off your grace [etc.]. *c* **1460** METHAM *Wks.* (1916) 145, I, the endygter in Englysch, haue folowyd the sentens off ther wordys, vndyr the supportacionys off my masterys in this syens. **1519** *Interl. Four Elem.* (Percy Soc.) 3 By your pacyens and supportacyon A lytyll interlude.. here shall be declaryd. *c* **1558** CAVENDISH *Wolsey* (1893) 126 Under your correccion my lord, and supportacion of this noble audyence, ther is no thyng more ontrewe. *a* **1610** HEALEY *Theophrastus* (1616) To Rdr., Be it spoken with the supportation of better iudgements.

c. = SUPPORT *sb.* 1 c.

1502 ATKYNSON tr. *De Imitatione* II. ix. (1893) 187 We be gladde to haue consolacion and supportacion in all our lyfe and labours. **1597** J. T. *Serm. Paules C.* 67 The supportation of vs, wherein God, when wee are weake,..reuiueth vs. **1623** BP. HALL *Contempl., O.T.* XVIII. vi, The strongest faith sometime staggereth, and needeth new acts of heavenly supportation. **1627** DONNE *Serm. Christmas Day* (1640) 45 God shall raise thee with that supportation, Feare not thou worme of Iacob. **1681** FLAVEL *Right. Man's Ref.* 263, I am with you by way of protection, direction, supportation, and salvation.

2. Bearing *of* expense; = SUPPORT *sb.* 2.

1437 *Rolls of Parlt.* IV. 503/2 In relief, confortation and supportation of the grete and importable charges. *a* **1548** HALL *Chron., Hen. VIII,* 229 b, The supportacion of parte of the great and excessiue charges, whiche wee supporte and beare. *c* **1598** BACON *Off. Alienations* Wks. 1831 XIII. 369 The benefited subject should render some small portion of his gain..for the supportation of the king's expense. **1749** *Hist. Windsor* viii. 103 Equal portions, towards their sustentation and maintenance, and the supportation of the burthen of the Chapel.

3. The relief or maintenance *of* a person, institution, office, etc. by a supply of funds; the keeping up *of* a building, etc. (Cf. SUPPORT *sb.* 3.)

1421 *Rolls of Parlt.* IV. 159/2 The whiche vitaille hath be so high supportacion to the Soudeours. **1445** in Willis & Clark *Cambr.* (1886) I. Introd. p. lviii, For to grawnt to your sayd besecher sum supportacyon to relevyng of tho sayd pouer College. **1544** *Supplic. Hen. VIII* (E.E.T.S.) 44 The supportation and mayntenaunce of common scoles. **1547** *Act 1 Edw. VI,* c. 14 §2 All annuall Rents..employed..for the..supportacion..of anny Stipendary Preist. **1625** MARKHAM *Weald of Kent* Ep. Ded. A ij b, Your supportation of the poore. **1628** COKE *On Litt.* 17 For the necessary sustentation, maintenance and supportation of the lord and his household. *Ibid.* 54 b, The law doth fauour the supportation & maintenance of houses of habitation for mankind. **1640** WALTON *Life Donne* in *Serm.* B v, A most dutifull son to his Mother, carefull to provide for her supportation. **1656** HEYLIN *Surv. France* 281 The establishment and supportation of the meanest Oratory dependent on the Church of England. **1704** E. CHAMBERLAYNE *Pres. St. Eng.* II. xv. (ed. 21) 195 Supportation, Aid, or Help of young Tradesmen.

b. Means of support.

1576 FLEMING *Panopl. Epist.* 325 Myne owne industrie.. is my only and alone supportation, the staffe and stay of my children.

c. Relief *of* disease, need, etc.

1527 ANDREW *Brunswyke's Distyll. Waters* A j, To conforte and supportacyon of theyr infyrmytees. **1609** *Bible* (Douay) Exod. xxviii. Comm., Supportation of the peoples infirmitie.

4. The preservation of anything in being; = SUPPORT *sb.* 3.

c **1480** HENRYSON *Fables, Preach. Swallow* viii, All creature he maid for the behufe Of man, and to his supportatioun. **1513** *Life Henry V* (1911) 23 In the defence and supportacion of our Catholique faith. **1536** CROMWELL in Merriman *Life & Lett.* (1902) II. 14 The supportacion and mayntenaunce of..the frenche kinges warres against Themperour. **1547** BALE *2nd Exam. Anne Askewe* 45 It is no newe thynge that Christes doctryne hath supportacyon amonge the counsels of thys worlde. **1581** J. BELL *Haddon's Answ. Osor.* 478 b, What bolsteryng and supportation of lyes was there? **1611** SPEED *Hist. Gt. Brit.* IX. vi. (1623) 518 In supportation of young Henries quarrell. **1618** BOLTON *Florus* (1636) 25 The first armes which the people tooke were for supportation of their freedome. **1662** HIBBERT *Body Div.* II. 108 There is a power derived from the man to the woman..towards the supportation of life and well-being. **1691** I. MATHER in *Andros Tracts* II. 288 Powers necessary for the Supportation of their Government.

5. Endurance. (Cf. SUPPORT *v.* 1 b.)

1502 ATKYNSON tr. *De Imitatione* I. xxiii. (1893) 173 The supportacion of euery trybulacion for the loue of our lorde. **1586** A. DAY *Engl. Secretorie* II. (1625) 57 With what supportation and vnaccustomed griefe I haue retained them. **1751** in *Cath. Rec. Soc. Publ.* (1914) XIV. 134 Her patient Supportation of many Infirmities. [**1875** H. J. COLERIDGE *Preach. Beatitudes* 254 These fruits he [*sc.* St. Bernadine] calls 'supportation', or bearing with one another.]

6. Physical or material holding or propping up: = SUPPORT *sb.* 4. Also in fig. context.

1610 HEALEY *St. Aug. Citie of God* XIII. xviii. (1620) 460 Why may not an earthly body be in heauen as well as the whole earth hang alone without any supportation? **1615** CROOKE *Body of Man* 454 As for supportation and strength it needed no assistance from the other parts. **1625** K. LONG tr. *Barclay's Argenis* I. vi. 16 That Tree, by whose supportation they came to that high growth. **1633** BP. HALL *Occas. Medit.* cxxxiv. 332 The elme yeelds a beneficiall supportation to that weake..plant. *a* **1768** ERSKINE *Inst. Law Scot.* III. viii. §96 If he go on foot, he must not be supported, or lean on any person by the way...if his going thither appear to be done with a special view to give validity to the deed, a more slender proof of supportation will be received as evidence of it.

supportative (sə'pɔətətɪv), *a. rare.* [f. SUPPORT *v.* + -ATIVE.] = SUPPORTIVE *a.*

An unnecessary formation, since the shorter *supportive* is completely established.—R.W.B.

1972 *Nature* 24 Mar. 154/2 These two basically different types of control are complementary and supportative. **1976** *Times* 22 July 14/2 (Advt.), A perceptive, sensitive and intelligent individual capable of organising our president in a supportative manner. **1981** *Spectator* 7 Feb. 19/2 Then follow the supportative words, the substructuration of Belonging.

supportayle, variant of SUPPORTAL *Obs.*

su'pported, *ppl. a.* [f. SUPPORT *v.* + -ED[1].] Upheld, sustained, maintained, etc.: see the verb.

1802 JAMES *Milit. Dict.* s.v., A well supported fire from the batteries; a well supported fire of musquetry. **1833** *Regul. & Instr. Cavalry* I. 29 The men fall in with supported arms. **1876** HARDY *Ethelberta* xxxiii, To appear as the supported and not the supporter. **1901** *J. Black's Carp. & Build., Scaffolding* 52 The hammering necessary to tighten the wedges is often a cause of fractures in the supported wall.

supporter (sə'pɔətə(r)). Also 5 -our. [f. SUPPORT *v.* + -ER[1].] One who or that which supports.

1. a. One who sides with, backs up, assists, or countenances a person, cause, etc.

1432-50 tr. *Higden* (Rolls) IV. 165 Marius and his supporters. *c* **1450** *Brut* II 370 A Squier of Walis þat was a rebell & a ryser, and supporter of Owen of Glyndore. **1526** *Pilgr. Perf.* (W. de W. 1531) 114 b, He was also called a glutton,..a deceyuer of the people, a supporter of synners. **1588** GREENE *Pandosto* (1607) 50, I am accused that I haue been a supporter of Fawnias pride. **1647** CLARENDON *Hist. Reb.* II. §87 The Marquis of Hamilton..was like to stand in need of great Supporters. **1733** SWIFT *Let. to D'chess Queensberry* 20 Mar., You are grown very tetchy since I lost the dear friend who was my supporter. **1836** HOR. SMITH *Tin Trump.* (1876) 255 Staunch supporters of the Church. **1855** MACAULAY *Hist. Eng.* xviii. IV. 209 Some French brandy..part of James's farewell gift to his Highland supporters. **1868** E. EDWARDS *Ralegh* I. xxv. 586 He was the supporter of an English alliance with France.

b. *Mil.* A force that supports another, as in a second line. (Cf. SUPPORT *sb.* 5 b, *v.* 12.)

1796 *Instr. & Reg. Cavalry* (1813) 196 The last one or two squadrons of such a column are always to be considered as the supporters of those that attack. **1902** *Words of Eyewitness* 144 Two companies of the East Surrey were ordered forward..to cover the retreat. Which suffered most, supporters or supported, I do not know.

2. a. One who keeps a person or thing from failing, giving way, or perishing; a sustainer, maintainer.

a **1475** G. ASHBY *Dicta Philos.* 1062 Yf he be iuste, of right a supportour. **1589** NASHE in Greene *Menaphon* Pref. (Arb.) 17 George Peele,..the chiefe supporter of pleasance nowe liuing, the Atlas of Poetrie. **1641** J. JACKSON *True Evang. T.* III. 213 Peace..is the very supporter of Individualls, Families, Churches, Common-wealths. *c* **1650** SOUTH *Serm., John xv. 26* (1744) VIII. 402 Under so many discouragements from without, they must needs have sunk, had they not had some supporter within. **1679** C. NESSE *Antichrist* Ep. Ded., Nobility..wants its true supporter, and soon dwindles into nothing. **1682** DRYDEN *To Duchess of York* 8 Love was no more when Loyalty was gone, The great Supporter of his awful Throne.

b. *Chem.* A substance that maintains some process, esp. combustion.

1806 G. ADAMS *Nat. & Exp. Philos.* I. App. Amer. Ed. 541 Acids may be divided into three classes,..2, supporters of combustion. The acid supporters are the oxymuriatic, and the hyperoxymuriatic. *c* **1865** LETHEBY in *Circ. Sci.* I. 88/2 When coal gas is burnt in atmospheric air.., we call the gas the combustible, and the air..the supporter.

3. a. A thing (or person) that sustains the weight of something, or upon which something rests; a prop; a basis or substratum; = SUPPORT *sb.* 7.

1595 SHAKS. *John* III. i. 72 My greefe's so great, That no supporter but the huge firme earth Can hold it vp. **1601** HOLLAND *Pliny* XVI. xl. I. 489 The foure entire stones which bare up the said Obeliske as supporters. **1650** W. D. tr. *Comenius' Gate Latin Unl.* §439 Hee bear's up (undersetteth) the leavie tendrels with props, or supporters. **1665** SIR T. HERBERT *Trav.* (1677) 136 That noted Aquaduct..the pipes by supporters reaching from Mountain to Mountain. **1703** T. N. *City & C. Purchaser* 10 The Supporters, or Butments of this Arch. **1707** MORTIMER *Husb.* (1721) I. 147 A Building set upon Supporters. **1774** J. BRYANT *Mythol.* II. 334 The priests, and supporters..carry the sacred vehicle. **1809** A. HENRY *Trav.* 98 A pole which might be called the supporter of the building.

† **b.** A wire frame for supporting a large ruff. (Cf. SUPPORTASSE.) *Obs.*

1592 WARNER *Alb. Eng.* IX. xlvii. (1612) 218 Busks, Perrewigs, Maskes, Plumes of feathers fram'd, Supporters. **1599** MINSHEU *Span. Dial.* 15/2 Head rolles, coifes of gold, supporters, gorgets of networke. **1601** DENT *Pathw. Heaven* (1831) 38 It was never good world, since starching and steeling,..supporters and rebatoes..came to be in use.

c. A leg. (Now only *humorous.*)

1601 HOLLAND *Pliny* VII. l. I. 183 The eye-sight decayeth .., the hearing followeth soon after, then faile the supporters. **1625** SHIRLEY *Maid's Rev.* I. ii, These brawny arms, this manly bulk, and these colossian supporters. **1681** DINELEY in *Jrnl. Kilkenny Archæol. Soc.* Ser. II. I. 178 The supporters of the woemen are very large. **1863** SALA in *Temple Bar* VIII. 73, I am feeble on the supporters.

† **d.** Each of the divisions of the calyx, regarded as supporting the corolla or flower; a sepal. *Obs.*

1626 BACON *Sylva* §590 The Sockets, and Supporters of Flowers, are Figured: As in the Five Brethren of the Rose. **1712** tr. *Pomet's Hist. Drugs* I. 51 Each of the Flowers has five or six Purple Supporters.

e. *Naut.* See quot.; also = BIBB.

1815 BURNEY *Falconer's Dict. Marine, Supporters,* in ship building, a name given to the knee-pieces of oak-timber under the cat-heads.

† **f.** *Metaph.* = SUPPORT *sb.* 7 b. *Obs. rare.*

1697 LOCKE *Let. to Bp. Worc.* Wks. 1714 I. 352 A Relation cannot be founded in nothing, or be the Relation of nothing, and the thing here related as a Supporter, or a Support, is not represented to the Mind by any clear and distinct Idea.

g. A jock-strap.

1895 *Montgomery Ward Catal.* Spring & Summer 488/3 The best fitting, most comfortable and effective supporter yet devised. Used by ball players, athletes and the theatrical profession generally. **1978** R. DOLINER *On the Edge* (1979) iv. 66 The Senator pulled on his supporter, made a cup of his hand and laid himself gently to rest in the elastic sling.

4. *Her.* A figure of an animal mythical creature, human being, etc., represented as holding up or standing beside the shield; each of two such figures, one on each side of the shield.

1572 BOSSEWELL *Armorie* II. 112 Of the supporters, the one is a Beuer.. The other assistant is an Harpie. **1599** THYNNE *Animadv.* (1875) 42 The erle of Kent bearethe a wiuer for his Creste and supporters;..the erle of Cumberlande, a wiuer geules for his supporters. **1610** GUILLIM *Heraldry* VI. vi. 271 If the things be huing and sease vpon the Shield, then shall they be called properly Supporters. *a* **1700** EVELYN *Diary* 17 Sept. 1662, A field Argent, with a canton of the armes of England; the supporters two talbots Argent. **1778** PENNANT *Tour in Wales* (1883) I. 41 The dragon and the gre-hound, the Supporters of the arms of England during the reign of Henry VII. **1814** SCOTT *Wav.* viii, Two rampant bears, the supporters of the family of Bradwardine. **1849** MACAULAY *Hist. Eng.* iii. I. 322 He knew the genealogies and coats of arms of all his neighbours, and could tell which of them had assumed supporters without any right. **1868** CUSSANS *Her.* xv. (1882) 194 Double Supporters were not generally adopted until the Fourteenth Century.

allusively, **1615** BRETON *Char. vpon Essaies* Wks. (Grosart) II. 9/1 Her Supporters are Time and Patience, her Mantle Truth.

5. a. One who attends another for the purpose of giving physical or moral support; hence, an attendant, as in a procession: sometimes with allusion to prec. sense.

a **1586** SIDNEY *Arcadia* III. xxi. (1912) 477 The fayre Ladie being come to the scaffold, and then made to kneele downe, and so lefte by her unkinde supporters. **1603** SHAKS. *Meas. for M.* v. i. 18 Come Escalus, You must walke by vs, on our other hand: And good supporters are you. *a* **1616** BEAUM. & FL. *Wit without M.* IV. i, Fie, how I sweat under this Pile of Beef;..give some supporters, or else I perish. **1632** MASSINGER & FIELD *Fatal Dowry* v. i, You have done me a disgrace in giving cause To all the street to think I cannot stand Without these two supporters for my arms. **1642** in Rushw. *Hist. Coll.* III. (1692) I. 783 The Likeness of the Standard was much of the fashion of the City-Streamers used at the Lord-Mayor's Show, having about twenty Supporters. **1675** SOUTH *Serm., Judg. viii. 34–5* (1727) I. 449 Ingratitude..sitting in its Throne, with Pride at its Right-Hand, and Cruelty at its Left; worthy Supporters of ..such a reigning Impiety. **1784** COWPER *Task* I. 479 Others are dragg'd into the crowded room Between supporters. **1825** SCOTT *Betrothed* x, The most gallant knights of the Constable's household..walked as mourners and supporters of the corpse, which was borne upon lances.

b. One who supports a particular form of sport or who makes a practice of following the fortunes of a particular team, by attending matches, etc.

1922 *Glasgow Herald* 30 June 8 An enthusiastic supporter of baseball. **1928** *Daily Mail Year-bk.* 84/2 The supporters of the Chelsea F.C. **1972** T. STOPPARD *Jumpers* I. 40 That he [*sc.* God] should have been taken up by a glorified supporters' club is only a matter of psychological interest. **1973** *Times* 24 Apr. 8/4 You have been wonderful supporters. I think I am very fortunate to play my last match in front of such wonderful people. **1976** *Milton Keynes Express* 2 July 42/6 There was a unanimous vote that a supporters' club be formed to further promote the need for a track in the area as soon as possible. **1980** *Daily Tel.* 19 Sept. 3/3 More than 30 supporters were ejected during the match, eight were still in police custody.

supporter, obs. form of SAPOTA.

†**su'pportful**, *a. Obs. rare.* [f. SUPPORT *sb.* + -FUL.] Affording support.

1610 *Mirr. Mag., Eng. Eliza* cxciii, Vpon th' Eolian gods supportfull wings. **1615** CHAPMAN *Odyss.* XXIII. 182 A Cities most supportfull Lords.

su'pporting, *vbl. sb.* [f. SUPPORT *v.* + -ING[1].]

1. †Assistance, succour (*obs.*); backing.

1421 *Cov. Leet Bk.* 36 To graunt hem a reward..in supportyng of hur honestye. **1436** *Libel Eng. Policy* in *Pol. Poems* (Rolls) II. 163 To Fflaundres passe forth bye, They schulde not be suffrede.. Ffor supportynge of oure cruelle enmyes. **1530** PALSGR. 278/2 Supportyng, *assistence, support.* **1565** ALLEN *Defence Purg.* (1886) 10 For which plain supporting of undoubted wickedness S. Jerome calleth them often Christian epicures, bolsterers of sin. **1869** FREEMAN *Norm. Conq.* III. App. E. 623 The proposing and supporting of opposing candidates.

2. Maintenance (of a person, an institution).

c **1413** *York Memorandum Bk.* (Surtees) I. 63 The forfetes ..shalbe employed..to the craft to the supporting of their pageant and othere chargez. *c* **1470** HARDING *Chron.* CLXXXIX. iii, To the pore supportyng. **1585** T. WASHINGTON tr. *Nicholay's Voy.* III. vi. 79 All other thinges necessary for the supporting of his house & estate.

†**3.** The action of making good a defect; repair.

c **1449** PECOCK *Repr.* III. x. 338 The endewing 3ouun to the brigge of Londoun into the supporting of his contynuel appeiring [= impairing].

4. The action of holding or propping up.

1646 SIR T. BROWNE *Pseud. Ep.* IV. vii. 196 The lifting or supporting of persons inebriated. **1709** T. ROBINSON *Nat. Hist. Westmoreld.* 31 The Roof of the Colliery will not stand without supporting. **1726** LEONI *Alberti's Archit.* I. 35/2 Very improper and unfaithful in supporting of great Weights. **1827** FARADAY *Chem. Manip.* ii. (1842) 42 The tubes..will often require supporting.

†**5.** Taking away, removal. *Obs. rare.*

1608 WILLET *Hexapla Exod.* x. 121 In those daies I will cause the sunne to go downe at noone, and I will darken the earth in the cleare day.. The supporting of the light of the sunne, the priuative cause, and the bringing of darknesse vpon the aire, the positiue cause.

su'pporting, *ppl. a.* [f. as prec. + -ING[2].]

1. That keeps from falling or sinking; that holds or props something up. Now chiefly *technical.*

c **1610** NORDEN *Cornwall* (1728) 91 The force of the water, which depriued them of the earth and other subportinge meanes. **1789** COWPER *Stanzas* 14 Faith's supporting rod. **1825** J. NICHOLSON *Oper. Mech.* 513 They are rivetted fast into the supporting-piece OH. **1834–47** J. S. MACAULAY *Field Fortif.* (1851) 136 The number of supporting bodies necessary to form a bridge. **1880** BESSEY *Bot.* vii. 89 Certain inner cells..become modified into sclerenchyma, or some other supporting tissue. **1883** *Pall Mall G.* 17 Mar. 10/2 The supporting arch underneath it having given way.

2. That preserves from failing or giving way; sustaining.

supporting point: a fortified point or pivot in a line of defence.

1681 FLAVEL *Meth. Grace* xxii. 282 These supporting hopes the Lord sees necessary to encourage industry in the use of means. **1705** STANHOPE *Paraphr.* I. 46 The supporting Expectation of the like Rewards of our Sufferings. **1834** COLERIDGE *Table-t.* (1836) 320 The supporting assurance of a reconciled God, who will not withdraw his spirit from me in the conflict. **1871** 'M. LEGRAND' *Cambr. Freshm.* 25 A remark..to the effect that 'there was something very supporting about a glass of sherry'. **1892** FOX IRWIN *Notes Fortific.* (ed. 2) 82 In preparing a position for defence, certain supporting points or pivots would be selected. **1893** *Westm. Gaz.* 18 Feb. 8/1 A collapse in the entire market was only prevented by some strong supporting orders in such stocks as Milwaukees.

3. That gives assistance or relief; also, confirmatory, corroborative.

1799 *Instr. & Reg. Cavalry* (1813) 283 The supporting detachments, from which the skirmishers are advanced. **1892** *Pall Mall G.* 26 Sept. 5/1 A supporting party was taken as far as the Humboldt Glacier, where they turned back, and Mr. Peary and Mr. Astrup alone went on. **1897** MARY KINGSLEY *W. Africa* 525 This bore out the theory..[but] in the Bantu case I did not hear of such a supporting incident happening.

4. That provides subsistence or maintenance.

1897 MARY KINGSLEY *W. Africa* 51 In Spanish possessions alone is a supporting allowance made to missionaries. **1900** B. D. JACKSON *Gloss. Bot. Terms, Supporting Plant*, a plant upon or in which another grows; a host plant.

5. Of actors or their roles, or of items in a programme of entertainment, usu. at a cinema: subordinate, less important.

1933 P. GODFREY *Back-Stage* v. 62 The fake star can be made to twinkle brightly by absorbing the surrounding light of the 'supporting cast'. **1939** *Chatelaine* Nov. 24/4 Some will continue for a while in minor productions and supporting roles. **1947** M. GILBERT *Close Quarters* vii. 108, I reached the cinema in time for the beginning of the supporting picture. **1953** [see *big stuff* s.v. BIG *a.* B 2]. **1966** *Listener* 23 June 918/1 The supporting performances..are enthusiastically full-blooded. **1977** *Rolling Stone* 21 Apr. 31/3 Blondie begins to seek out that untapped audience with a supporting slot on Iggy Pop's American tour.

Hence **su'pportingly** *adv.*, so as to support; in quot. 1895, with an unshrinking spirit.

1895 MEREDITH *Amazing Marr.* xl, [They] must be either voluble or supportingly proud to keep the skin from shrinking. **1896** F. H. BURNETT *Lady of Quat.* xiii. 196 He gave her his arm and drew her..supportingly away.

supportive (sə'pɔːtɪv), *a.* [f. SUPPORT *v.* + -IVE.] Having the quality of supporting; affording support; sustaining. (*lit.* and *fig.*)

1593 NASHE *Christ's T.* Ep. Ded., To the supportiue perpetuating of your canonized reputation, wholie this booke haue I destined. **1689** *Thoughts Justice Gentl. Undertaking at York* 1 These Laws are not destructive but supportive of one another, and all supportive of Man. **1887** *Amer. Jrnl. Psychol.* Nov. 97 Nor is the collapse of supportive tissue beneath, which has been suggested as a cause of abnormal dermal sensations [etc.]. **1908** *Amer. Jrnl. Sociol.* XIV. 49 The architecture was harmonious, and mutually attractive and supportive. **1954** H. C. SHANDS in *Amer. Jrnl. Orthopsychiatry* XXIV. 84 It is necessary that the anxious individual have available a supportive pattern of relationship to depend upon through the learning period. **1962** HENDERSON & GILLESPIE *Text-bk. Psychiatry* xi. 286 This sort of supportive psychotherapy is relevant in every case. **1965** *Listener* 30 Sept. 501/3 Supportive material, notes by the editor, and letters by other hands are made to fill in the picture. **1972** *Science* 20 Oct. 229/3 She appears to interpret her findings as supportive of a smaller proportion of genetic variance among blacks than among whites. **1973** *Black Panther* 23 June 6/2 She has vein trouble in her legs for which she wears supportive stockings. **1978** G. VIDAL *Kalki* vi. 149 'Senator White says that..he's going to call Mr. Kalki, as a witness... Will Mr. Kalki be supportive?' 'Hopefully, Kalki is supportive of all of us all of the time and for all time.' **1980** *Daily Tel.* 6 Dec. 12/4 Most American psychotherapists now advertise themselves as 'supportive'.

Hence **su'pportiveness**.

1968 A. J. TANNENBAUM in H. L. Foster *Ribbin'* (1974) i. 4 They have worked with the children..in order to win their confidence and provide supportiveness. **1978** *Nature* 17 Aug. 698/1 We have also tried to determine whether there was a dorso-ventral pattern of host supportiveness of tumour growth.

su'pportless, *a.* [f. SUPPORT *sb.* + -LESS.]

†**1.** That cannot be 'supported'; insupportable, intolerable. *Obs. rare.*

1643 MILTON *Divorce* II. xx. Wks. 1851 IV. 118 As if they had a designe by making wedlock a supportlesse yoke, to violate it most.

2. Destitute of support, unsupported.

1681 J. SCOTT *Chr. Life* II. iii. Wks. 1718 I. 240 By giving up the Belief of a God, I..leave my self utterly destitute and supportless. *a* **1717** PARNELL *Battle of Frogs & Mice* III. 92 Full on the leg arrives the crushing wound: The frog, supportless, writhes upon the ground. **1744** WARBURTON *Remarks Sev. Occas. Refl.* 118, I left it not [*sc.* my argument] ..naked and supportless; but..standing strongly on its Conclusion.

Hence **su'pportlessly** *adv.*, without support.

1893 F. THOMPSON *Judgment in Heaven* viii, A sinister chasm,..whose verges soon..Supportlessly congest with fire, and suddenly spit forth the moon.

†**su'pportment.** *Obs.* [f. SUPPORT *v.* + -MENT.] The act or fact of supporting; support.

1623 T. POWELL *Attorn. Acad.* A j, To trve Nobilitie and tryde Learning, beholden To no Mountaine for Eminence, nor Supportment for his Height, Francis, Lord Verulam. **1631** R. H. *Arraignm. Whole Creature* Ep. Ded., It could not walke without such pillers of supportment. **1638** WOTTON *Let. to Sir E. Bacon* 31 Dec., That not taking effect by the supportment of Spain he fell to other Roman arts. **1641** MILTON *Ch. Govt.* II. iii, Prelaty both in her fleshly supportments, in her carnall doctrine of ceremonie and tradition. **1658** OWEN *Tempt.* vii. 151 It [*sc.* the Gospel] gives supportment, relief, refreshment,.. in every condition. **1769** *De Foe's Tour Gt. Brit.* (ed. 7) IV. 257 Two steep Hills..joined by two dry Arches, and a Wall of Supportment.

supportress (sə'pɔːtrɪs). [f. SUPPORTER + -ESS[1]: see -TRESS.] A female supporter. (Applied to a person, or a thing personified.)

1621 T. WILLIAMSON tr. *Goulart's Wise Vieillard* 163 A gracious and stedfast hope, the good nursse and supportresse of his old age. **1637** MASSINGER *Guardian* I. ii, You are my gracious patroness and supportress. **1680** *Seasonable Mem. Hist. Notes Liberties Presse & Pulpit* 36 The City of London..the very Nurse and Support[r]esse of the Rebellion. **1819** KEATS *Lamia* II. 123 A haunting music, sole perhaps and lone Supportress of the faery-roof, made moan.

†**su'pporture.** *Obs.* [f. SUPPORT *v.* + -URE.] = SUPPORTATION.

1609 HEYWOOD *Brit. Troy* XIII. lxxxv, Oh! Thou the awe of Kings, Death to thy Foes, supporture to thy Friends. **1613** —— *Braz. Age* II. ii, Oh father Ioue thou laist vpon thy sonne Torments aboue supporture. **1624** —— *Gunaik.* I. 30 The globe of the earth hangs in the middle of the aire, without supporture. **1661** K. W. *Conf. Charac., Good Old Cause* (1860) 62 It..professeth a Herod's delight in the John Baptists of our time,..but intendeth nothing less then their supporture.

supposable (sə'pəʊzəb(ə)l), *a.* Also 7–8 **supposeable.** [f. SUPPOSE *v.* + -ABLE. Cf. F. *supposable.*] Capable of being supposed; that may be thought to exist or to be true, or assumed for the sake of argument; presumable, imaginable.

1681 *Whole Duty Nations* 26 The Regions not being so united in Government,..the distribution of Churches easily follows the distinction easily supposable in their civil state. **1726** BUTLER *Serm. Hum. Nat.* iii. 47 *note*, Perfection, though plainly intelligible and supposeable, was never attained by any Man. **1748** —— *Serm. 1 Pet. iv. 8*, 11 They are highly to be blamed for not making some Provision against Age and supposeable Disasters. **1781** COWPER *Let. to Newton* 21 May, It..is hardly a supposable case, but..we will endeavour to suppose it for a moment. **1867** BUSHNELL *Mor. Uses Dark Th.* (1869) 273 What..are the supposable ends and uses of God in the appointment of a discipline so appalling? **1882** HAMLEY *Traseaden Hall* III. 53 There was no supposable reason why he should..put a complexion other than the true one upon the duel.

b. Qualifying a clause anticipated by *it.*

1643 SYMMONS *Loyal Subjects Belief* 29 Laws..are the King's..revealed, or written will, and therefore 'tis supposeable that his personall will may..be coordinate with them. **1696** WHISTON *Theory Earth* II. (1722) 91 'Tis very supposable that 'tis our Ignorance..which occasions our lax and general Interpretations. **1736** BUTLER *Anal.* Introd., 'Tis supposeable, there may be Frost in England any given day in January next. **1849** G. M. COOPER in *Sussex Archæol. Coll.* (1850) III. 22 These are sufficient [proofs]..to render it supposable that this sequestered spot is the Dene once dignified by the presence of the great Alfred. **1884** *Law Times Rep.* L. 647/2 And if they can, is it supposable that they may be turned out and afterwards re-enter?

†**c.** That may be presumed *to be* or *to do* something. *Obs.*

1647 HAMMOND *Power of Keys* iv. 76 They being supposeable to understand that unknown tongue. **1659** *Gentl. Calling* iv. §5 This..is the least that is supposeable to be required of them. *a* **1834** LAMB *Misc. Wks.* (1871) 498 The amazing change which is supposable to take place.

d. That may be supposed or presumed to be (what is denoted by the noun).

1891 J. WINSOR *Columbus* xii. 272 This supposable neophyte does not again appear in history.

Hence **su'pposably** *adv.* (chiefly *U.S.*), as may be supposed; presumably.

a **1866** J. GROTE *Exam. Util. Philos.* (1870) vi. 107 The happiness of any supposably actual being. **1881** RUSKIN *Love's Meinie* I. iii. 134 This aesthetic water-hen..lived at Cheadle,..in the rectory moat,..'always how-ever leaving it in the spring,' (for Scotland, supposably?). **1883** *Science* I. 94 Conditions affecting two celestial objects which are supposably near enough to be influenced alike. **1893** 'MARK TWAIN' *Pudd'nhead Wilson* ii, Sitting on a wheelbarrow..at work, supposably, whereas he was in fact only..taking an hour's rest.

supposal (sə'pəʊzəl). Also 4-5 **supposaile**, 4-6 **-ail**, 5-7 **-all**, 6 **-ell**, 7 **-eall**. [a. OF. *supposail(l)e*, f. *supposer* to SUPPOSE: see -AL[1] 5.]

†**1.** The action of supposing, supposition: esp. in phr. ***upon supposal*** (*of* or *that*..); also ***by, upon supposal***, as is (or was) supposed, supposedly.

c **1380** WYCLIF *Sel. Wks.* III. 344 We mai seie bi supposal, þat we gesse þat it is so. **1553** *Act 1 Mary* Sess. II. c. I. §2 Matters of no strengthe or effecte, but onelye by supposall. *a* **1577** SIR T. SMITH *Commw. Eng.* III. ii. (1609) 102 Complaint to the Chancellour vpon supposall of losse, or lacke of euidence. **1589** PUTTENHAM *Engl. Poesie* I. xxvi. (Arb.) 66 Praising and commending (by supposall) the good conformities of them both. **1592** in J. Morris *Troubles Cath. Forefathers* (1877) 29 It pleased God..that this journey turned her to the restoring of her health, whereas by supposal his [*sc.* the magistrate's] sending for her was only of purpose that thereby she might have died. *a* **1619** FOTHERBY *Atheom.* I. vi. §2 (1622) 41 Vpon supposall, that There is a God. **1647** JER. TAYLOR *Lib. Proph.* xx. 250 The supposall and pretence of his personall Prerogatives. **1691** WOOD *Ath. Oxon.* II. 684, I have told you that the said Archb. Williams was, upon supposal, buried at Aberconway. **1692** PATRICK *Answ. Touchstone* 97 God absolves by his Ministers; who cannot see into men's hearts; and therefore can only pronounce, that he absolves them..upon supposal of their unfeigned Repentance. *a* **1734** NORTH *Lives* (1826) II. 396 The magistrate seizes all..upon supposal of the party's having cheated the state. **1802-12** BENTHAM *Ration. Judic. Evid.* (1827) IV. 110 All such relevant articles..as lie within his own custody, power, knowledge, or supposal. **1839** SIR W. HAMILTON *Discuss.* (1852) 202 There is no possible room for the supposal of any change.

2. An act of supposing; something that is supposed; a supposition, hypothesis; an assumption, conjecture. Now *rare*.

†*by supposals*: as may be supposed.

1387-8 T. USK *Test. Love* III. iii. (Skeat) I. 129, I am comforted bee my supposaile in blisse, and in joy to determine after my desires. **1440** in *Wars Eng. in France* (Rolls) II. 459 This supposaille it ne is not greetly to be feered. **1511** in *10th Rep. Hist. MSS. Comm.* App. v. 325 There have bene greate varianñce now of late..and by supposails in likwise to be in tyme commynge. **1593** BILSON *Govt. Chr. Ch.* 239 From this supposall these three conclusions are drawen. **1605** VERSTEGAN *Dec. Intell.* i. (1628) 12 As touching their names, of Germans and Almans sundry supposals haue bin made. **1644** J. GOODWIN *Innoc. Truimph.* (1645) 68 This is but *petitio Principii*, a supposall of that which is the main Question. **1662** J. DAVIES tr. *Mandelslo's Trav.* 162 Upon a false supposal, that between Indus and Ganges there were thirty degrees, whereas there are scarce ten. ? **1710** LADY M. W. MONTAGU *Lett., to Mrs. Hewet* (1887) I. 28, I am..in hopes we shall return..the latter end of the year; but all that is supposals, and I have no ground to believe it. **1730** FIELDING *Rape upon Rape* III. xi, *Mrs. Squeez*.. I cannot say but I have a generous Pity for any one whom I imagine to be accused wrongfully. *Ramble*. I am obliged to you indeed, Madam, for that Supposal. **1757** WARBURTON *Unpubl. Papers* (1841) 315 The supposal of another necessarily existent Being is adding to infinitude. **1885** *Academy* 25 July 61/3 A..division of categorical judgments into those which involve a supposal and those which do not. **1891** HALL CAINE *Scapegoat* xiv, The Kaid.. according to their supposals, had called on him to correct what he had done amiss.

†**3.** A notion, opinion. *Obs.*

1589 FLEMING *Virg. Ecl.* x. Argt. 29 If we may beleeve the supposall of Servius. **1602** SHAKS. *Ham.* I. ii. 18 Holding a weake supposall of our worth; Or thinking..Our State to be disioynt, and out of Frame. **1612** COTTA *Disc. Dang. Pract. Phys.* II. i. 76 Methodians..arrogated this name unto themselves in the best sense, as onely in their owne supposall meriting the title of true art and method.

†**4.** A suggestion, proposal. *Obs.*

1715 M. DAVIES *Athen. Brit.* I. Pref. 27 A Syncronical half-sheet, stil'd, The Proposal,..the primitive Title is much plainer, thus, The Supposal: Or, A New Scheme of Government. **1747** RICHARDSON *Clarissa* I. xxii. 149, I suppose it is the way of this sex to endeavour to entangle the thoughtless of ours, by bold supposals and offers.

†**5.** A statement, allegation (as in a writ or indictment). Cf. SUPPOSE *v.* 11. *Obs.*

1429 *Rolls of Parlt.* IV. 346/1 That..the partie that seweth have juggement to recovere his dette ayeinst the seide Cominaltes, after the supposell of here Writtes. **1531** *Dial. on Laws Eng.* F iv b, Whervpon foloweth a false supposel in the writte, and a false supposell in the declaratyon. **1602** FULBECKE *Pandectes* 14 An attainder.. shal haue relation to the time of the felony done, according to the supposall of the inditement. **1651** tr. *Kitchin's Courts Leet* (1653) 477 He need not take traverse that it is not frank fee, for that, that the Writ is but a Supposall.

suppose (sə'pəʊz), *sb.* [f. SUPPOSE *v.*]

1. An act of supposing; a supposition, hypothesis, conjecture. Often (now always) referring to a supposition expressed or expressible by means of the verb 'suppose'.

1566 GASCOIGNE *Supposes* Prol., I suppose you shoulde have hearde almoste the laste of our Supposes, before you could have supposed anye of them arighte. **1586** A. DAY *Engl. Secretorie* I. (1625) 65 How ill-beseeming it is..that it should so fall out, you by supposes coniecture. **1591** *Troub. Raigne K. John* (1611) 67 If it be true, die for thy tidings price; If false, for fearing me with vaine suppose. **1633** B. JONSON *Tale Tub* III. vii, Fatted with Supposes of fine Hopes. **1672** VILLIERS (Dk. Buckhm.) *Rehearsal* v. (Arb.) 127 Suppos'd! Ay, you are ever at your suppose. **1753** RICHARDSON *Grandison* (1810) II. v. 79, I began with my *roundabouts*, and my *suppose's*. **1791-3** in *Spirit Publ. Jrnls.* (1799) I. 290 Various other supposes have been offered. **1835** MARRYAT *Pacha of Many Tales* III. 103 (*Water-carrier*) Those confounded Moussul merchants! Their supposes always come to pass. **1875** HANNAH W. SMITH *Chr. Secret Happy Life* viii, Nothing else will take all the risks and 'supposes' out of a Christian's life. **1897** FLOR. MARRYAT *Blood of Vampire* xii, Harriet's mind was full of 'Supposes'.

†**b.** In generalized sense: Supposition. *Obs.*

1594 NASHE *Unfort. Trav.* 16 Whether you will part with so much probable friendly suppose or no, Ile haue it in spite of your hearts. **1612** SELDEN *Illustr. Drayton's Poly-olb.* iv. 67 There was, by suppose, a correction of what was faulty in forme or matter. **1719** D'URFEY *Pills* II. 330 He..Must know a Dun, with genuine suppose, As Spannels do their Masters, by the Nose.

†**2.** A belief, notion, opinion. *Obs.*

1587 FLEMING *Contn. Holinshed* III. 1327/2 Alwaies addicted to a maruellous suppose in himselfe of ripe iudgement. **1630** WIDDOWES *Schysmatical Puritan* Pref., He is pure, not really, but in his owne suppose.

†**3.** (An) expectation. *Obs.*

1602 MUNDAY tr. *Palm. Eng.* II. ix, [She] will returne as greatly displeased, as she arrived here with suppose of pleasure. **1606** SHAKS. *Tr. & Cr.* I. iii. 11 We come short of our suppose so farre, That after seuen yeares siege, yet Troy walles stand.

†**4.** Purpose, intention. *Obs.*

1597 MIDDLETON *Wisd. Solomon* xi. 13 Breathlesse in wasting of so vaine a breath, Dumb in performance of their tongues suppose. *c* **1616** CHAPMAN *Homer's Hymn Appollo* 394 Here I entertaine suppose To build a farr-fam'd Temple.

suppose (sə'pəʊz), *v.* Also 4 **sopos**, 4-5 **sopose**, (chiefly *Sc.*) **suppos**, **-oss**, 5 *Sc.* **suppoiss**, 5-6 **supose**, *Sc.* **suppois**, 6 **suppoose**, *Sc.* **suppoise**, **supos**. [a. OF. *sup(p)oser*, (mod.F. *supposer*), f. *sup-* = SUB- 2 + *poser* POSE *v.*[1], to represent L. *supposit-, suppōnĕre* SUPPONE *v.*]

†**1. a.** *trans.* To hold as a belief or opinion; to believe as a fact; to think, be of opinion. Usually const. clause; also with obj. and compl., acc. and inf., rarely with simple obj. *Obs.*

1340 HAMPOLE *Pr. Consc.* 3776 We shuld trow, and suppose ay þat alle er save..þat we se here gude werkes wirk, And has þe sacramentes of halikyrk. **1357** *Lay Folks' Catech.* (L.) 163 Aue Maria. Men gretyþ comunly oure lady ..and we suppose þat þis gretynge sauys many a man. *a* **1400-50** *Wars Alex.* 577 Be many cause at I ken I kan noȝt supose It be consayued of my kynde ne come of my-selfe. *c* **1400** *Destr. Troy* 2317 We might say this for certen, & suppose it in hert. *c* **1400** MAUNDEV. (Roxb.) xiii. 57 Lamech slew Cayn with ane arowe, supposing he had bene a wylde beste. *c* **1450** LOVELICH *Merlin* 1084 (Kölbing), This ne may non child be: It is the devel, ful sykirle;..We supposen, it be a devel of helle! **1470-85** MALORY *Arthur* VII. xviii. 241 It semeth..said kynge Arthur that ye knowe his name, and fro whens he is come..I suppose I doo so said Launcelot or els I wold not haue yeuen hym thordre of knyȝthode. **1483** CAXTON *Cato* b ij b, That euery man may suppose and saye good of the. *c* **1500** *Melusine* 3 Many thinges, which men suposen not to be true. **1509** FISHER *Funeral Serm. C'tess Richmond* Wks. (1876) 297 Suppose not ye..she wolde..as feruently haue mynystred vnto hym as euer dyde Martha? **1526** TINDALE *2 Cor.* xi. 5, I suppose that I was nott be hynde the chefe apostles. *c* **1590** GREENE *Fr. Bacon* ii. 38 Joying that our academy yields A man suppos'd the wonder of the world. **1591** SHAKS. *1 Hen. VI*, II. iv. 29 Let him that is a true-borne Gentleman,..If he suppose that I haue pleaded truth, From off this Bryer pluck a white Rose with me. *Ibid.* v. iii. 110 Would you not suppose Your bondage happy, to be made a Queene? **1658** SIR T. BROWNE *Hydriot.* iii. 48 While we suppose common wormes in graves, 'tis not easie to finde any there.

†**b.** with *as*, ellipt., and in parenthetical phr. Cf. dial. *I suppose* = I understand, believe, or know: see *Eng. Dial. Dict.*

1390 GOWER *Conf.* III. 174 But for al that I schal noght glose Of trouthe als fer as I suppose. *c* **1391** CHAUCER *Astrol.* Prol., Alle the conclusiouns that han ben fownde,..ben vn-knowe perfitly to any mortal man in this regioun, as I suppose. *a* **1400-50** *Wars Alex.* 842* Who am I þat am here, as þou supposez? **1465** *Paston Lett.* II. 233 John Pampyng knowyth hym well jnow I suppose. **1469** in *Somerset Med. Wills* (1901) 216 Two pair of hosis, price I suppose 8s. **1509** FISHER *Funeral Serm. C'tess Richmond* Wks. (1876) 290 In euery of these I suppose this countesse was noble. **1556** in Feuillerat *Revels Q. Mary* (1914) 215, I have made a Comodie..mete as it is supposed to be played before the Quene. **1779-81** JOHNSON *L.P.*, *Mallet* Wks. IV. 283 Glover rejected, I suppose, with disdain the legacy.

†**c.** Const. inf.: To believe that one does or is (so-and-so). *Obs.*

1474 CAXTON *Chesse* III. iii. (1883) 105 They supposid well to haue knowen many other thynges. *c* **1500** *Melusine* 30 Thou hast slayn thy lord..how be it that at that ooure thou supposest not to haue doon it. **1601** DOLMAN *La Primaud. Fr. Acad.* (1618) III. 706 Some suppose to haue a very good foundation for judiciall astrologie. **1681** RYCAUT tr. *Gracian's Critick* 114 One had his eyes so dazled, that he supposed to see that which he never beheld.

†**d.** *intr.* with inverted const.: To seem. *rare*$^{-1}$.

1390 GOWER *Conf.* II. 128 Bot al to lytel him supposeth, Thogh he mihte al the world pourchace.

†**2.** To form an idea of, conceive, imagine; to apprehend, guess. Also *intr.* with *of*. *Obs.*

c **1386** CHAUCER *Wife's Prol.* 786 Who wolde leeue, or who wolde suppose The wo that in myn herte was? **1390** GOWER *Conf.* I. 116 The king supposeth of this wo, And feigneth as he noght ne wiste. *Ibid.* 199 Tho sche supposeth what it mente. *Ibid.* III. 78 This yonge lord..axeth if that he supposeth What deth he schal himselve deie. *c* **1450** *Merlin* ii. 25 When thei herde these words, supposed wele what he ment. **1566** [see SUPPOSE *sb.* 1]. **1591** SHAKS. *1 Hen. VI*, IV. i. 186 More furious raging broyles, Then yet can be imagin'd or suppos'd. *c* **1600** —— *Sonn.* lvii. 10 Nor dare I question..Where you may be, or your affaires suppose. **1781** MRS. INCHBALD *I'll tell you what* v. i, If you cou'd suppose how obstinate Sir George was.

†**3. a.** To have in mind or as an object of thought or speculation; to think of, conceive, imagine; contextually, to suspect. *Obs.*

c **1375** [see SUPPOSING *vbl. sb.* 2]. **1382** WYCLIF *2 Macc.* iii. 32 Lest..the kyng supposide eny malice of Jewis..done aȝeinus Helyodore. **1390** GOWER *Conf.* I. 71 Sche, which al honour supposeth. *Ibid.* III. 72 The queene tolde him al the cas As sche that guile non supposeth. *a* **1400** *Pistill of Susan* 216 þe semblaunt of susan wolde non suppose. **1586** A. DAY *Engl. Secretorie* I. (1625) 78 You must suppose and harpe vpon the end that must succeed vnto your trauaile. **1593** SHAKS. *Lucr.* 133 When great treasure is the meede proposed, Though death be adiunct, ther's no death supposed. **1599** —— *Hen. V*, III. Chor. 3, Suppose, that you haue seene The..King at Douer Peer, Embarke his Royaltie.

†**b.** To attribute (something) *to* a person. *rare.*

13.. *Coer de L.* 1725 Thou art mys-tought, To have on me swylk a thought,..And swylke a treson to me sopos. **1614** SELDEN *Titles Hon.* 155 The ancientest Scepter among the Graecians must forsooth be suppos'd to Iupiter.

†**c.** To suspect (a person). *Obs.*

a **1700** EVELYN *Diary* 12 Feb. 1684, Then were..tried and ..fin'd Mr. Hampden and others for being suppos'd of the late Plot. **1763** JOHNSON *Let.* 29 Sept. in *Misc. Philobib. Soc.* (1860-1) VI. 34 You suppose your housekeeper..of treachery.

†**4.** Const. inf., acc. and inf., or obj. clause referring to the future, rarely with simple obj.: To expect. *Obs.*

1303 R. BRUNNE *Handl. Synne* 6970 Whan Seynt Ihon herde þat seye, þat Troyle supposed for to deye. **1390** GOWER *Conf.* I. 49 If thou wolt my schrifte oppose Fro point to point, thanne I suppose, Ther schal nothing be left. *c* **1400** *Leg. Rood* (1871) 95 þe tre es funden whilk we suppose Sall ger vs all oure pouwer lose. **1426** *Paston Lett.* I. 26, I suppose to see yow on Palm Sunday. **1447** BOKENHAM *Seyntys* (Roxb.) Introd. 5 We dede dryve A cruel tyraunth in to a fen..Wher I supposed to have myschevyd. **1456** *Paston Lett.* I. 374 Yn the ende of thys terme y suppose to be at London. **1474** CAXTON *Chesse* III. iii. (1883) 100 He was ryght seeke And..men supposid hym to dye. **1513** BRADSHAW *St. Werburge* I. 1260 Wofully he went to his bed..Supposynge some dethe withouten any remedy. **1525** LD. BERNERS *Froiss.* II. ccxlviii. 762 It were to suppose, that if the erles of Huntyngton and of Salysbury were alyue..the Frenchmen then wolde soone passe ouer the see. **1596** DANETT tr. *Comines* (1614) 61 The Lord of Hymbercourt marched straight to the City, supposing to enter without resistance. **1671** MILTON *Samson* 1443 Wherefore comes old Manoa in such hast..supposing here to find his Son? **1760** *Impostors Detected* II. v. I. 193, I never supposed..to have had this grant for nothing.

†**5.** Const. inf.: To purpose, intend. *Obs.*

c **1450** [see SUPPOSING *vbl. sb.* 3]. **1474** CAXTON *Chesse* II. i. (1883) 22 Whan he sawe Alixandre he supposid to haue axid his requeste. *c* **1500** *Melusine* 224 It is the kinge of Anssav [etc.] with theire puyssaunce that supposen to goo reyse the siege of praghe.

6. To assume (without reference to truth or falsehood) as a basis of argument, or for the purpose of tracing the consequences; to frame as a hypothesis; to put as an imaginary case; to posit. Chiefly with clause as obj.; also with simple obj., obj. and compl., acc. and inf.

c **1315** [see 7 a]. **1377** LANGL. *P. Pl.* B. XVII. 293, I pose [*v.r.* sopose] I hadde synned so, and shulde now deye. *c* **1380** WYCLIF *Wks.* (1880) 284 Here we schal suppose as Cristen mennes bileue, þat god is cheef lord. *c* **1420** *26 Pol. Poems* 106, I suppose þe prest haue but on ost, Breke it, and parte to twenty and mo: As moche is þe leste cost As in þe grettest pece of þo. **1697** tr. *Burgersdicius' Logic* II. ix. 42 Suppose Aristotle, or the like instead of Man, and make an Expository Syllogism, with it. *Ibid.* xvii. 72 First, supposing the Species, you suppose also the Genus. **1726** SWIFT *Horace, Ode* I. xiv. 7 Let me suppose thee for a ship a-while, And thus address thee in the sailor's style. **1728** LAW *Serious C.* x. (1729) 143 Now do but suppose a man acting unreasonably; do but suppose him extinguishing his reason. **1746** FRANCIS tr. *Horace, Sat.* II. iii. 221 Let us suppose you heard An able doctor [etc.]. **1749** HARTLEY *Observ. Man* I. i. §2. 60 Let us suppose the first Object to impress the Vibrations A, and then to be removed. **1815** SCOTT *Guy M.* xvi, Which..might..do more harm than good in the case supposed. **1818** BYRON *Juan* I. lxxxv, I only say, suppose this supposition. **1823** H. J. BROOKE *Introd. Crystallogr.* 157 If we suppose the octahedron to be placed with its axis horizontally. **1835** J. YOUNG *Lect. Intell. Philos.* xxvii. 273 There is a great difference..between supposing an absurdity and conceiving it. **1875** JEVONS *Money* (1878) 254 As a second case, let us suppose that there is a town which is able to support two banks. **1889** O. FISHER *Phys. Earth's Crust* xx. (ed. 2) 268 The closeness of the folds of a crumpled rock, formed as supposed, would depend upon [etc.]. **1906** A. E. H. LOVE *Math. Th. Elasticity* i. (ed. 2) 33 We suppose that the axis of *x* is the direction in which contraction takes place.

7. Often in imper. or pres. pple. absol., introducing a hypothetical statement or case.

a. (*a*) with clause as obj.

c **1315** SHOREHAM VII. 445 Suppose here hijs [= is] o iustyse, God and truwe. **1593** SHAKS. *3 Hen. VI*, IV. i. 14 Suppose they take offence without a cause. **1667** MILTON *P.L.* II. 237 Suppose he should relent..with what eyes could we Stand in his presence? **1709** J. WARD *Introd. Math.* (1734) 435 Suppose the Length of a Brewer's..Back..be 217,5 Inches. **1721** in *Cath. Rec. Soc. Publ.* VIII. 305 They shall cause to be said thrice thirty Masses for Mother Abbesse, supposing she dyes. **1728** LAW *Serious C.* ix. (1729) 128 Suppose I had pressed an universal temperance, does not religion enough justify such a doctrine? **1862** RUSKIN *Unto this Last* I. §24 Supposing the captain of a frigate saw it right..to place his own son in the position of a common sailor. **1871** BROWNING *Pr. Hohenstiel-Schwangau* 7 Suppose my Œdipus should lurk at last Under a pork-pie hat and crinoline. **1904** W. E. NORRIS *Nature's*

Comedian xi, My objections—supposing I have any—wouldn't give you a sleepless night, I imagine.

(*b*) *colloq.* introducing a suggestion or proposal.

1779 *Mirror* No. 34 ¶9, 'Suppose one of the ladies should give us an English song,' said I. 'Tis a good motion,' said Mr. Bearskin, 'I second it'. **1806** J. BERESFORD *Miseries Hum. Life* (ed. 3) II. xiv, Suppose we pass to some of the less ignoble Miseries of the country. **1844** D. JERROLD *Story of Feather* xxviii. (1873) 191 Suppose you go to sleep, that you may get up in time enough. **1908** R. BAGOT *A. Cuthbert* iii. 24 By the way, supposing you were to drop 'uncle-ing' me?

b. with acc. and inf.

*a***1513** FABYAN *Chron.* I. ix. (1811) 13 It shulde seme y^t Troynouant, or London, was buylded before..Yorke aboute an hondreth and xl. yeres; supposynge the Cytie of London to be begonne in the seconde yere of Brutes reygne. **1590** LUCAR *Lucarsolace* III. xlii. 136 Supposing ABCD to be the assigned square, diuide any one side therof into two equal parts. **1678–9** STILLINGFL. *Serm. 7 Mar.* Wks. 1710 I. 257 Suppose a man to have riches and honours. **1734** J. WARD *Yng. Math. Guide* 305 Suppose the Δ BCD to be an Isosceles Δ. **1861** LUND *J. Wood's Elem. Alg.* 237 Supposing O to be excluded as a value of either *x* or *y*.

c. with obj. and compl.

1698 FRYER *Acc. E. India & P.* 391 Suppose Twenty Mules, Thirty Asses,..more or less committed to their Care. **1766** FORDYCE *Serm. Yng. Women* (1767) I. iii. 85 Suppose me speaking to you as a brother. **1821** SCOTT *Kenilw.* vi, You would have me believe that my noble lord is jealous? Suppose it true, I know a cure for jealousy. **1855** BROWNING *In a Balcony* 280 Suppose her some poor keeper of a school. **1857** RUSKIN *Pol. Econ. Art* i. §32 Supposing them sculptors, will not the same rule hold? **1867** —— *Time & Tide* ii. §7 Even supposing a gradual rise in social rank possible for all well-conducted persons.

d. In imper. parenthetically or ellipt.; often = 'as (for example)', 'say'. Now *rare* or *Obs.*

1577 tr. *Bullinger's Decades* i. (1592) 8 Moses..was borne ..of those fathers whom God appointed to be witnesses of his will,..suppose Amram, Kahad, Iacob, Sem, Methusalem and Adam. **1631** CHAPMAN *Cæsar & Pompey* Plays 1873 III. 175 *Cato.* But is not euery iust man to him selfe The perfect'st law? *Ath.* Suppose. **1736** BUTLER *Anal.* I. i. 12 That we are to exist hereafter in a State as different suppose from our present [etc.]. *Ibid.* II. v. 196 A Person.. breaks his Limbs, suppose. *Ibid.* II. vi. 216 If there be a strong Bias within, suppose from indulged Passion. **1800** SCOTT *Let.* in *Lockhart* x, To treat with the proprietors of some established paper—suppose the Caledonian Mercury. **1831** BREWSTER *Optics* iv. 38 M N is a dense medium (suppose glass).

e. The imperative became equivalent to a hypothetical conjunction = If; *usually*, even if, albeit, though, although. *Sc.*

1375 BARBOUR *Bruce* I. 2 Storyss to rede ar delitabill, Supposs that thai be nocht bot fabill. *c***1375** *Sc. Leg. Saints* xviii. (*Egipciane*) 249 Suppos at I mane synful be, A-byde a lytil & spek with me. *c***1470** HENRY *Wallace* I. 374 It dide him gud, suppos he sufferyt payne. *Ibid.* x. 823 Supposs we murn, ye suld haiff no mer waill. *c***1500** *Lancelot* 1070 His hawbrek helpit, suppos he had no scheld. **1533** GAU *Richt Vay* 51 Thay cuir noth supos God haiff the hewine alen, sua that thay mycht lewe heir sa lang as thay vald. *c***1560** A. SCOTT *Poems* (S.T.S.) ix. 2 Considdir, hairt, my trew intent, Suppois I am no^t eloquent. *Ibid.* xi. 27 To Venus als suppois ȝe wyle thame—Ressoun; Bot be ȝe frawdfull and begyle thame—Tressoun. **1585** JAS. I *Ess. Poesie* (Arb.) 60 Thir indifferent wordis, composit of dyuers syllabes, are rare, suppose in monosyllabes, commoun. **1618** A. SIMSON *Serm. John v. 35* in *Wodrow Soc. Sel. Biog.* (1845) I. 124 He giveth the name of the light to John, suppose the light John had, he had it from Christ. **1775** SHIRREFS *Christmas Feast* xiv. Poems (1790) 213 For John o' pipe-skill wasna scant, Suppose I say 't. **1867** [MRS. E. ALLARDYCE] *Goodwife at Home* xiii, I wyte her squeelin's nae been hain't, Suppose I say't mysel.

8. *trans.* To entertain as an idea or notion sufficiently probable to be practically assumed as true, or to be at least admitted as possibly true, on account of consistency with the known facts of the case; to infer hypothetically; to incline to think: sometimes implying mistaken belief.

Idiomatically: *do you suppose..?* is used to express an indignant rejection of a suggestion or proposal; *you may suppose* = you may be pretty sure.

a. with clause as obj.

[**1526** TINDALE *Luke* vii. 22 Which of them tell me, will love hym moost? Simon answered, and sayde: I suppose that he to whom he forgave moost.] **1601** R. JOHNSON *Kingd. & Commw.* (1603) 2 Neither let any man suppose that from wilines without force, nor force without iudgment, can proceed any proiect of worthy consideration. **1615** G. SANDYS *Trav.* 8 It being supposed that Cicero was there buried. **1710** SWIFT *Jrnl. to Stella* 29 Sept., I drink no aile (I suppose you mean ale). **1766** LD. HOLLAND in Jesse *Selwyn & Contemp.* (1843) II. 19, I suppose Lord March has a horse runs there, as I see he had at Ipswich. **1821** SCOTT *Kenilw.* x, He..darted away from him with the swiftness of the wind, when his pursuer supposed he had nearly run him down. **1852** MRS. STOWE *Uncle Tom's C.* xxii, Where do you suppose New Jerusalem is, Uncle Tom? **1862** MRS. H. WOOD *Mrs. Hallib.* II. xxiii, 'Have any of you seen my microscope?'..Jane looked round. 'My dear, I lent it to Patience to-day. I suppose she forgot to return it.' **1865** LUBBOCK *Preh. Times* 45 It has been supposed that tin was at one time abundant in Spain. **1883** STEVENSON *Treasure Isl.* III. xiii, 'Jim, Jim!' I heard him shouting. But you may suppose I paid no heed. **1908** R. BAGOT *A. Cuthbert* v. 43, I was not thinking of myself, but of you. Do you suppose that I want you to remain unmarried in order to secure my own position?

b. with *as*, *so*, or ellipt. in comparative clause. Also *I suppose*, ellipt. for *I suppose so*, as a hesitant or reluctant affirmative.

1615 W. LAWSON *Country Housew. Garden* (1626) 7 The sap is the life of the tree,..neither doth the tree in winter (as is supposed) want his sap no more then mans body his bloud. **1779** *Mirror* No. 8 ¶4 That Mirror..is of higher value than you suppose. **1885** 'MRS. ALEXANDER' *At Bay* ix, 'His sorrow must have been great.' 'I suppose so.' **1888** 'J. S. WINTER' *Bootle's Childr.* vi, 'Is she pretty?'..'Yes; I suppose so,'..'some people think so, but we never did.' **1902** VIOLET JACOB *Sheep-Stealers* xiv, The roads were no better than the old Squire had supposed. **1959** 'E. MCBAIN' *'Til Death* (1961) v. 67 'I think that's wise, don't you?' 'I suppose.' **1973** S. COHEN *Diane Game* (1974) xii. 103 'Look how much good information is published by..guys at universities.' 'Yes, I suppose.' **1976** 'TREVANIAN' *Main* (1977) x. 206 'Is she a viable?'..'I suppose. She had reason and opportunity.'

c. with obj. and compl. (sb., adj. or adj. phr., †advb. phr.).

1634 MILTON *Comus* 576 Supposing him som neighbour villager. **1651** HOBBES *Leviath.* II. xxvi 142 He that supposeth himself injured. **1671** R. BOHUN *Wind* 302 These Miraculous Emotions of the Atmosphere can hardly be supposed from the agitation of common vapours of Air. **1692** LOCKE *Toleration* III. ix. Wks. 1727 II. 408 The Mass in France is as much suppos'd the Truth, as the Liturgy here. **1779** *Mirror* No. 8 ¶3, I supposed his present of little intrinsic value. *c***1780** COWPER *Jackdaw* i, There is a bird who, by his coat,..Might be suppos'd a crow. **1821** SCOTT *Kenilw.* xxi, Those foibles which are chiefly supposed proper to the female sex. **1837** WILKINSON *Mann. & Cust. Anc. Egypt.* ii. (1841) I. 65 M. Champollion supposes them the Scythians.

d. with acc. and inf. (The passive of this, which is very frequent, expresses the fact of the subject being credited with some action or quality: now esp. = to be expected, intended, or meant; to have as a duty, to be obliged.)

The pronunc. of the pa. t. is often colloquially modified from (sə'pəʊzd) to (sə'pəʊst). The negative is, idiomatically, freq. used to mean 'to have a duty or obligation not (to do something)'.

[**1611** *Bible* John xx. 15 Supposing him to be the gardiner.] **1614** PURCHAS *Pilgrimage* IV. vi. (ed. 2) 368 Zoroaster..a Chaldæan, supposed to liue in the time of Abraham. **1687** A. LOVELL tr. *Thevenot's Trav.* II. 170 He did not do as the rest did, who are all supposed to understand their Trade. **1769** *De Foe's Tour Gt. Brit.* (ed. 7) III. 351 Alderney, supposed by Camden to be the *Arica* of Antoninus. **1831** SCOTT *Ct. Rob.* xviii, He was supposed vigorously to espouse the quarrel of the Varangians. **1856** FROUDE *Hist. Eng.* I. iv. 278 They supposed themselves to have gained a victory. **1859** DICKENS *Tale of Two Cities* III. x. 223 We saw the man, who was supposed to be at the gate, standing silent behind him. **1863** *Proc. Linnean Soc.* VII. p. xxvii, Still less does it seem consistent with that impartiality which every reviewer is supposed to possess. **1864** BRYCE *Holy Rom. Emp.* xvi. (1875) 287 Relics supposed to be those of Bartholomew the Apostle. **1875** JOWETT *Plato* (ed. 2) IV. 130 He may be supposed to have thought more than he said. **1886** GUILLEMARD *Cruise Marchesa* II. 105, I am not aware that this genus [of spider] is avivorous, but the huge Mygale is supposed to be. **1894** J. POPE *Mem. Rt. Hon. Sir John A. Macdonald* I. ii. 24 It appears that Mr. Baldwin considered this notice as sufficient to relieve him of the ordinary obligations which are supposed to govern the actions of Cabinet Ministers. **1902** 'R. CONNOR' *Glengarry Days* ii. 43 Girls are not supposed to be soldiers, are they, Margaret? **1914** G. B. SHAW *Misalliance* 86 Look here, Mr Percival youre not supposed to insult my sister. **1931** *Morning Post* 31 Jan. 6 Officers..were not 'supposed' to keep a scrap log. **1949** E. CALDWELL *This Very Earth* xi. 112 What's a girl supposed to do on Tuesday nights..? Bring her diary up to date? **1953** *N.Y. Herald-Tribune* 29 Apr. 4 They were supposed to address the lecturer as comrade. **1963** E. ALBEE *Who's Afraid of Virginia Woolf?* (1964) 84 When Daddy retired, he'd take over the college... That's the way it was supposed to be. **1969** A. CHRISTIE *Hallowe'en Party* xiii. 141, I brought her in lots of things that she was not supposed to eat. **1976** M. MACHLIN *Pipeline* xi. 134 That's more than the whole job was supposed to cost in the first place. **1976** P. & W. PROCTOR *Women in Pulpit* vi. 106 If that outburst was supposed to shock me because I'm a woman—forget it, brother!

†**e.** with simple obj. *Obs. rare.*

1596 DRAYTON *Legends* I. 153 Telling for truth, what thou canst but suppose.

f. in parenthetical phr. ***I suppose, it is supposed.***

1678 DRYDEN *Kind Keeper* II. i. You mean, I suppose, the peaking creature, the married woman, with a sideling look. **1707** FARQUHAR *Beaux Strat.* I. i, *Bon[iface].* This way, this way, Gentlemen... *Aim[well].* You're my Land-lord, I suppose? **1828** SCOTT *F.M. Perth* xxvi, Tell us how this tale ended—with Conachar's escape to the Highlands, I suppose? **1859** TENNYSON *Idylls of King, Enid* 275 If, as I suppose, your nephew fights In next day's tourney. **1885** 'MRS. ALEXANDER' *At Bay* xi, He fell and it is supposed was instantaneously killed.

g. *absol.*

1865 DICKENS *Mut. Fr.* I. iii, 'Do you suppose there has been much violence..among these cases?' 'I don't suppose at all about it..I ain't one of the supposing sort.'

h. *trans.* To bring by supposing.

1647 WARD *Simple Cobler* 35, I am not without some contrivalls in my patching braines; but I had rather suppose them to powder, than expose them to preregular.. judgements. **1747** RICHARDSON *Clarissa* (1811) I. viii. 48 They ask not for my approbation, intending, as it should seem, to suppose me into their will.

9. a. To lay down or assume as true, take for granted.

*c***1380** WYCLIF *Sel. Wks.* III. 437 Sequestre we al mannes lawe, supposynge Crists ordynaunce. **1688** in *5th Coll. Papers rel. Pres. Juncture Affairs* 18 It supposes Mens Lands to be already butted and bounded, when it forbids removing the Ancient Land-marks. **1799** *Med. Jrnl.* I. 198 'The Italians will always object,' says he, 'that you suppose what requires to be demonstrated.' **1818** CRUISE *Digest* (ed. 2) VI. 273 The law supposes that a man may vary his intent, even while he is writing his will. **1875** JOWETT *Plato* (ed. 2) V. 132 Plato seems to suppose that life should be passed wholly in the enjoyment of divine things.

b. To presume the existence or presence of.

1696 WHISTON *Th. Earth* IV. (1722) 371 A Rain-Bow were seldom or never to be suppos'd before the Deluge. **1860** RUSKIN *Mod. Paint.* V. IX. vi. §23 An adoration of shepherds with nothing to adore,..the Christ being 'supposed' at the side. **1869** GLADSTONE *Juv. Mundi* iii. 89 We have no reason to suppose, among the races actually named, any radical difference of language.

10. Of actions, conditions, facts: To involve as a ground or basis; to require as a condition; to imply, presuppose.

1660 JER. TAYLOR *Worthy Commun.* Introd., Some take it [*sc.* the Holy Communion] to strengthen their faith, others to beget it, and yet many affirm that it does neither, but supposes faith beforehand as a disposition. **1662** STILLINGFL. *Orig. Sacræ* II. i. §1 Mans obligation to obedience unto God, doth necessarily suppose his originall to be from him. **1681** DRYDEN *Abs. & Achit.* 385 Lavish Grants suppose a Monarch tame. **1699** BENTLEY *Phal.* 447 These plainly refer to and suppose one another, as a half Crown English supposes a Crown. **1728** LAW *Serious C.* ix. (1729) 122 Covetousness..supposes a foolish and unreasonable state of mind. **1759** JOHNSON *Rasselas* xxvii, Patience must suppose pain. **1855** BAIN *Senses & Int.* III. iii. §18 Heat supposes cold.

†**11.** To state, allege: esp. formally in an indictment. *Obs.*

1411 *Rolls of Parlt.* III. 650/1 Certein Commune of Pasture..whiche the said Lord..claymes..as it is supposed by the same Bille. **1485** *Ibid.* VI. 295/1 The..Duke affirmed a Bill of Trespass..supposeing by the same Bill, that the said Thomas Thorpe should have taken [= had taken].. divers Goodes. **1544** tr. *Littleton's Tenures* 102 He may haue a wrytte..supposynge by his wryt y^t his aduersary hath entred into the landes or tenementes. **1651** tr. *Kitchin's Courts Leet* (1653) 477 The Demandant shall not answer to the Barr, nor to the Voucher, but ought to maintain his Writ, that they are Tenants, as the Writ supposes.

†**12.** To feign, pretend; *occas.* to forge. *Obs.*

1566 PAINTER *Pal. Pleas.* I. v. 13 The maide..was the doughter of his owne bondwoman, who afterwardes being stolen awaye, was caried to the house of Virginius, and supposed to be his childe. **1622–3** *N. Riding Rec.* (1885) III. II. 161 Ninian Etherington, supposing himself to be a Sheriffes Baliffe, did distreigne and carrie awaie a cow. **1655** tr. *Sorel's Com. Hist. Francion* III. 62 A place where they understood nothing better than supposing of false titles. **1676** WYCHERLEY *Pl. Dealer* I. i, Keep all that ask for me from coming up; suppose you were guarding the Scuttle to the Powder room.

†**13.** To substitute by artifice or fraud: cf. SUPPOSITITIOUS. *Obs.*

1614 SELDEN *Titles Hon.* II. i. 176 That they when the Queen is in child-birth,..warily obserue least the Ladies should priuily counterfeit the enheritable sex, by supposing som other Male when the true birth is female. **1631** MASSINGER *Believe as You List* II. ii, To suppose a bodie; and ..to inter it In a rich monument, and then proclaime 'This is the bodye of Antiochus'. **1641** EARL MONM. tr. *Biondi's Civil Wars* v. 111 Shee..did suppose the sonne of a Iew.. that he might personate the Duke of Yorke. **1767** *Speeches, &c. in Douglas Trial* 48 Persons guilty of supposing children.

†**14.** To put or place under something; to append. *Obs. rare.*

1608 [see SUPPOSED 4]. **1608** CHAPMAN *Byron's Conspir.* IV. Plays 1873 II. 234 Foolish Statuaries, That under little [statues of] Saints, suppose great bases. **1649** JER. TAYLOR *Gt. Exemp.* II. Ad Sect. xii. 101 The three coronets, which themselves..supposed as pendants to the great crown of righteousnesse. **1797** [see SUPPOSED 5].

supposed (sə'pəʊzd), *ppl. a.* [f. prec. + -ED[1].]

1. Believed or thought to exist, or to be what the sb. denotes, but uncertainly or erroneously.

1582 N. LICHEFIELD tr. *Castanheda's Conq. E. Ind.* I. i. 2 b, This supposed Presbiter Ioan. **1593** SHAKS. *Lucr.* 455 The sight which makes supposed terror trew. *a***1653** GOUGE *Comm. Heb.* vii. 15. (1655) 188 When a supposed able man ..faileth in his estate. **1681** FLAVEL *Meth. Grace* xxviii. 401 Hezekiah, upon his supposed death-bed. **1690** LOCKE *Hum. Und.* II. xxiii. §2 The supposed, but unknown, support of those qualities we find existing. **1781** GIBBON *Decl. & F.* xxix. (1787) III. 111 Arcadius was easily persuaded to resent the supposed insult. **1821** SCOTT *Kenilw.* xxxv, Say, that in a moment of infatuation, moved by supposed beauty,..I gave my hand to this Amy Robsart. **1859** MILL *Liberty* i. 12 Those..classes..to whose real or supposed interests democracy is adverse. **1905** R. BAGOT *Passport* vii. 66 The wines were execrable..and the man who poured them out told us their supposed dates.

absol. **1603** SHAKS. *Meas. for M.* II. iv. 97 You must lay downe the treasures of your body, To this suppos'd.

†**b.** Believed (with assurance), admitted. *Obs.*

1643 SIR T. BROWNE *Relig. Med.* I. §21 Curiosities.. discussed by men of most supposed ability.

†**2.** 'Put on', feigned, pretended, counterfeit. *Obs.*

1566 PAINTER *Pal. Pleas.* I. xxiii. 44 b, It is no pure and naturall affection, but rather a supposed and Ciuile loue. **1592** GREENE *Conny Catch.* III. 38 He cuts the ring from the purse, and by his supposed man (rounding him in the eare) sends it to the plot-layer of this knauerie. **1598** SHAKS. *Merry W.* IV. iv. 61 Let the supposed Fairies pinch him. *a***1641** MOUNTAGU *Acts & Mon.* i. (1642) 11 The onely true God,..no supposed, false, subintroducted God or Gods. **1664** JER. TAYLOR *Dissuas. Popery* II. I. §3 The traditions.. were..Apocryphal, forg'd, and suppos'd.

†**b.** Supposititious. *Obs.*

1652 J. WRIGHT tr. *Camus' Nat. Paradox* I. 11 Not well pleased to see that a supposed child should reap, before the season, that which she..desired to preserve in their owne family. **1787** CHARLOTTE SMITH *Romance Real Life* I. 175 To name a guardian for the supposed child.

†3. Assumed as a premiss: in quot. *absol.*
1697 tr. *Burgersdicius' Logic* II. vi. 20 A Syllogism is a Speech in which something being suppos'd, something different from that suppos'd, by Reason of the Suppos'd, does of Necessity follow.

†4. Placed beneath; underlying. *Obs. rare*⁻¹.
1608 TOPSELL *Serpents* 114 The Chamælion..doth not change his owne colour into a supposed colour, but when it is oppressed with feare or griefe.

†5. *Mus.* Applied to a note added or introduced below the notes of a chord, or to an upper note of a chord when used as the lowest note (*supposed bass*) instead of the *fundamental bass* or 'root', i.e. to the lowest note of an 'inversion' of the chord; hence applied to the harmony of an 'inversion'. Also applied to a 'discord' introduced as a passing-note. (Cf. SUPPOSITION 5.) *Obs.*
1797 *Encycl. Brit.* (ed. 3) XVIII. 83/2 s.v. *Supposition*, Concords by supposition are those where the continued bass adds or supposes a new sound below the fundamental bass. .. Of these..there are three sorts,..the first, when the added sound is a third below... The second..when the supposed sound is a fifth below... The third..where the supposed sound is below a concord of the diminished seventh. 1845 *Encycl. Metrop.* V. 734 Every bass note which has a sixth upon it is a supposed bass. *Ibid.* 735 The supposed harmony of the third of the key is..borrowed from the fundamental harmony of the key note. *Ibid.* 755 The supposed discord is on the second accented part of the bar.

supposedly (sə'pəʊzɪdlɪ), *adv.* [f. prec. + -LY².]
1. In the way of supposition; by supposition; as is (or was) supposed.
1611 W. SCLATER *Key* (1629) 293, I..would not easily bee brought to diuulge my conceits supposedly true. 1629 BP. HALL *Reconciler* 33 Little doe these men see the toyles, and anxieties that attend this supposedly-pleasing eminence. 1651 BAXTER *Inf. Bapt.* Apol. 5 So that the Rebaptized husband would not pray with his (supposedly) unbaptized wife. 1717 BERKELEY *Tour Italy* Wks. 1871 IV. 538 Beneventum..Cathedral..built supposedly on the foundation of an old temple. 1805 W. TAYLOR in *Ann. Rev.* III. 544 This supposedly exemplary mother too was the educatress of Caligula. 1865 J. GROTE *Moral Ideals* (1876) 202 'Love your enemies' (it being supposedly your friends that you do love). 1881 *Athenæum* 25 June 848/3 Nor is the supposedly parallel passage at all to the purpose. 1916 *Times* 5 June 8/3 Our three battle cruisers had been blown up, supposedly as the result of gun-fire.

†2. Feignedly, pretendedly. *Obs.*
1618 T. GAINSFORD *Hist. P. Warbeck* 33 By that time.. she verily belieued he was the same she had supposedly contriued: & he quite forgot, that euer his first originall came out of the Dunghill.

supposer (sə'pəʊzə(r)). *rare.* [f. SUPPOSE *v.* + -ER¹.] One who supposes, in various senses; †one who makes a statement or allegation (*obs.*); one who frames a hypothesis or makes an assumption.
1593 MUNDY *Def. Contraries* 10 Some good supposer may say, that riches serve for a pleasant and recreative life. 1678 R. RUSSELL tr. *Geber* II. I. II. iv. 50 Every one of these Supposers is adverse to the other according to his Supposition. 1747 RICHARDSON *Clarissa* (1811) I. xxvi. 185 You never knew so bold a supposer.

supposing (sə'pəʊzɪŋ), *vbl. sb.* [f. SUPPOSE *v.* + -ING¹.] The action of the verb SUPPOSE.
1. †Thinking, opinion (*obs.*); assumption, supposition. Now usually, the expression of opinion by means of the verb 'suppose'.
†*by supposing*, as is (or was) supposed; †*to my supposing*, as I think, in my opinion.
c1386 CHAUCER *Clerk's T.* 985 To my supposynge She koude nat aduersitee endure. 1390 GOWER *Conf.* II. 256 Thei spieke aloud for supposinges Of hem that stoden there aboute. 1448-9 METHAM *Amoryus & Cleopes* 64 Alle thei seyd that yt was, be supposyng, Grwe; but qwat yt ment, thei nyst ryght noght at alle. c1450 LOVELICH *Grail* lvi. 530 More Cler to ȝoure vndirstondyng Thanne Owther Frensch Oþer latyn, to my soppösing. 1530 PALSGR. 278/2 Supposyng, *conjecture*. c1585 [R. BROWNE] *Answ. Cartwright* 24 By his iffs and supposings he will gather against vs what proofes he list. 1613 WITHER *Abuses Stript* I. v, He nought complaines Of Mens opinions; but..Doth both their censures and supposings scorne. 1820 BYRON *To Moore* 25 Dec., We should have some..composing, correcting, supposing. 1857 MRS. GATTY *Parab. Nature* Ser. II. (1868) 97 If it comes to supposing..I shall suppose it won't. 1880 AGNES GIBERNE *Sun, Moon, & Stars* x. 215 But supposings often have to give in to facts.

†2. Suspicion: *to have supposing*, to suspect. *Obs.*
c1375 *Cursor M.* 1089 (Fairf.), Supposinge [*Cott.*, etc. mistrauing] had he sone þat he sum wikketnes had done. 1375 BARBOUR *Bruce* VI. 520 The kyng, that na supposing had That thai war mair than he saw thair. c1450 *St. Cuthbert* (Surtees) 5049 þe Jauelers supposyng had nane þat he wald away gane.

†3. Purpose, intention. *Obs. rare.*
c1450 *St. Cuthbert* (Surtees) 7624 For supposyng full he had, Monkys at cuthbert cors restore.

†4. ? Substitution, replacement. *Obs. rare.*
1591 LODGE *Catharos* (Hunter. Club) 4 Diogenes wisheth infinite good speede to your good proceedinges, and curseth endleslie your ill demeanors: wishing the last to perish without supposing, the first to flourish without supplanting.

†5. Feigning; forgery. *Obs. rare.*
1655 [see SUPPOSE *v.* 12].

So **su'pposing** *ppl. a.*, that supposes; whence **su'pposingness**.
1662 J. CHANDLER *Van Helmont's Oriat.* 311 The sensitive soul liveth in us,..yet because it wants a bruital and specifical supposingness, therefore it rejoyceth only in an undistinct life of light. 1865 [see SUPPOSE *v.* 8 g].

†**supposit.** *Sc. Obs.* [ad. L. *suppositus*: see SUPPOST.] = SUPPOST b.
1532 in *Parl. Papers Eng.* (1837) XXXVII. 181 (Rep. Commiss. Univ. Scotl., St. Andrew's) The rector, studentis, and suppositis of the Universite of Sanctandris. 1547 *Ibid.* 235 (Glasgow) Immuniteis..granted to the said Universite, rectouris, and suppositis tharof.

supposita, pl. of SUPPOSITUM.

†**su'ppositał**, *a. Metaph. Obs.* [ad. mod.L. *suppositālis*, f. *suppositum*: see SUPPOSITUM and -AL¹.] Belonging or relating to a 'supposite': see SUPPOSITE *sb.* 1. So †**supposi'tality** [mod.L. *suppositālitās*], the condition of being 'suppositał', or of being a 'supposite'; †**su'ppositate** *v. trans.*, to be in the relation of a 'supposite' to; to be the subject of.
1656 JEANES *Mixt. Schol. Div.* 81 The second person [of the Trinity]..alone terminates the *suppositall, or personal dependance of the manhood. 1682 H. MORE *Annot. Glanvill's Lux O.* 238 Indiscerpibility maintains their suppositał Unitie, as it does in all Spirits that have to do with Matter. 1545 BALE *Myst. Iniq.* 34 Substancialite, deificalite, ..modalite, *supposytalite, ypostaticalite. 1656 JEANES *Fuln. Christ* 135 If the manhood of Christ subsist any manner of way, then it is [? in] a person, or *suppositum*: for what is subsistence here, but suppositality, and therefore it, and *suppositum* are reciprocated. a1670 SOUTH *Serm. Col. ii. 2* (1727) IV. 318 No Wonder therefore, if these Men..have by their Modalities, Suppositalities, Circumincessions, and twenty such..Chimeras, so misrepresented this..Article of the Trinity to Mens Reason, as to bring them..at length to deny it. 1711 tr. *Werenfels' Logomachys* 101 Then follow.. your greater and lesser Realitys, modal Entitys,..Then the States, Amplications, Principles of Individuation, Suppositalitys,..and whole cartloads of Qualitys. 1627 J. DOUGHTY *Serm. Div. Myst.* (1628) 12 Those queries, whither God be *materia prima*, and, whither Christs divinitie might not *suppositate a fly. 1656 JEANES *Fuln. Christ* 154 There is an ability in the person of the word, to suppositate, and assume the manhood.

suppositary, obs. f. SUPPOSITORY *sb.* and *a.*

supposite, *sb.* Now *rare.* Also -it. [ad. L. SUPPOSITUM, q.v.]
1. *Metaph.* A being that subsists by itself, an individual thing or person (= SUBSTANCE 2); sometimes, a being in relation to its attributes (= SUBSTANCE 3, SUBJECT *sb.* 6); = SUPPOSITUM 1.
1612 SHELDON *Serm. at St. Martin's* 7 A Christ consisting both of God and man; a perfect supposit, a compleat Person. 1675 BURTHOGGE *Causa Dei* 55 Passions, as Actions are of Persons or Supposites. 1678 BP. NICHOLSON *Expos. Catech.* 192 That Christ is in the Sacrament corporally, Substantially, and perhaps Consubstantially, may have a respect to the subject or Supposite of the *Relatum* and *Correlatum*. c1882 G. M. HOPKINS *Sermons & Devotional Writings* (1959) II. iii. 146 A person is defined a rational (that is/intellectual) supposit.
2. *Gram.* = SUBJECT *sb.* 8; also, the antecedent of a relative.
c1620 A. HUME *Brit. Tongue* (1865) 30 We inquyre of that we wald knaw; as, made God man without synne; and in this the supposit of the verb followes the verb. We avoue that quhilk we knaw; as, God made man without sinne; and in this the supposit preceedes the verb. 1677 W. HUGHES *Man of Sin* I. xii. 51 The Relative [whose] referred to the former, not the latter Antecedent..[the Lord] is the only Supposite ..to whom it could relate. 1929 tr. *St. Thomas Aquinas's Summa contra Gentiles* IV. IV. xxxiv. 144 Relative terms, nouns or pronouns, relate to the same supposit.

†**supposite**, *a. Obs. rare.* [ad. L. *suppositus*, pa. pple. of *suppōnĕre* to SUPPONE.]
1. a. Placed or situated below.
1640 BROME *Antipodes* I. vi, The people through the whole world of Antipodes..Resemble those to whom they are supposite.
b. Occupying a lower position or rank; subject.
1677 GALE *Crt. Gentiles* II. IV. 196 Not opposite to God but supposite or subordinate.
2. Supposed, assumed.
1653 R. BAILLIE *Dissuas. Vind.* (1655) 21 The supposite and imaginary causes.

suppositer, variant of SUPPOSITOR *Obs.*

‖**suppositio materialis** (sʌpə'zɪʃɪəʊ mətɪərɪ'eɪlɪs). *Logic.* [med.L.] Reference to a word or phrase used simply as an example within a statement, and devoid of its normal semantic function.
1843 MILL *Logic* I. II. ii. 29 This employment of a word to denote the mere letters and syllables of which it is composed, was termed by the schoolmen the *suppositio materialis* of the word. 1921 W. E. JOHNSON *Logic* I. x. 169 The scholastic logicians introduced the phrase 'suppositio materialis'..but modern logicians have interpreted this phrase as equivalent to what they call the 'universe of discourse'. 1935 H. STRAUMANN *Newspaper Headlines* ii. 67 The two sentences: 1. The first line of Gray's *Elegy* states a proposition, and 2. 'The first line of Gray's *Elegy*' does not state a proposition. Both utterances are true, but in the second case the validity entirely depends on the inverted commas. This phenomenon used to be well known in mediaeval scholasticism under the name of *suppositio materialis*, and it still plays an essential part in semantics. 1961 [see HYPOSTASIS 8].

supposition (sʌpə'zɪʃən). [ad. L. *suppositio*, *-ōnem*, n. of action f. *supposit-*, *suppōnĕre* to SUPPONE. Cf. F. *supposition*, It. *supposizione*, Sp. *suposicion*, Pg. *supposição*.
The current meanings arose from the equation of med.L. *suppositio* to Gr. ὑπόθεσις HYPOTHESIS, of which it is the etymological equivalent. In older L. *suppositio* is recorded only in the senses of 'placing under' and 'substitution'.]
The action of supposing, or what is supposed.
†1. *Scholastic Logic.* Something held to be true and taken as the basis of an argument. *Obs.*
c1449 PECOCK *Repr.* II. viii. 186 Wherfore, alle thingis seen, this..reule or supposicion is trewe. a1529 SKELTON *Replyc.* 112 But ye were *confuse tantum*, Surrendring your supposycions. 1551 ROBINSON tr. *More's Utopia* II. (1895) 185 Those rules of restryctyons, amplyfycatyons, and supposytyons, very wittelye inuented in the small Logycalles. 1588 FRAUNCE *Lawiers Logike* II. iv. 92 b, Suppositions are built rather upon idle supposals of schoolemen, then grounded upon any sure foundation of naturall experience. c1590 MARLOWE *Faustus* vi, Who knowes not the double motion of the plannets? The first is finisht in a naturall day, The second thus, as Saturne in 30. yeares,..the Moone in 28. dayes. Tush, these are fresh mens suppositions.
2. The action of assuming, or, usually, that which is assumed (which may be either true or false), as a basis of argument or a premiss from which a conclusion is drawn.
a1596 *Sir T. More* II. iv. 113 Let me sett vp before your thoughts, good freindes, On [= one] supposytion. 1669 OWEN *Expos. Ps. cxxx.* 338 The due performance of all principal mutual Gospel Duties..depends on this supposition, that [etc.]. 1704 NORRIS *Ideal World* II. xi. 414 The position of this chapter involves a supposition. It is here supposed that there are Divine Ideas. 1706 PRIOR *Ode Queen* Pref., Upon the Supposition of these Facts, Virgil wrote the best Poem that the World ever read. 1725 in *10th Rep. Hist. MSS. Comm.* App. I. 175 Even putting the supposition that nothing can be done from the north this summer. 1736 BUTLER *Anal.* I. i. 24 Upon supposition that they are compounded. 1754 EDWARDS *Freed. Will* I. iii. (1762) 22 All opposition is shut out and denied, in the very supposition of the case. 1765 *Museum Rust.* IV. 358 This calculation goes on the supposition that each mower dispatches three acres. 1798 HUTTON *Course Math.* (1806) I. 45 Making the other number of supposition the 1st term. 1836 H. ROGERS *J. Howe* ii. (1863) 32 On the supposition —a supposition which the whole history of the period amply justifies [etc.]. 1887 *48th Rep. Deputy Kpr. Publ. Rec.* 625 The supposition that the defendant had broken the plaintiff's close.
†b. An assumption made to account for the known facts: = HYPOTHESIS 3. *Obs.*
1603 HOLLAND *Plutarch's Mor.* 1187 One of those suppositions alone was sufficient to make good the reason. 1669 STURMY *Mariner's Mag.* VI. iii. 105 The Copernican supposition of the Earths Motion.
3. A notion or idea that the thing in question is true, held without certainty or assurance, but as sufficiently probable to be assumed or admitted on account of agreement with the facts of the case; a hypothetical inference, or the action of making such inferences; an uncertain (sometimes, by implication, a false or mistaken) belief. †*in supposition*, in uncertainty, uncertain, doubtful (*obs.*).
1596 SHAKS. *Merch. V.* I. iii. 18 My meaning in saying he is a good man, is..that he is sufficient, yet his meanes are in supposition. 1599 —— *Much Ado* IV. i. 240 The supposition of the Ladies death, Will quench the wonder of her infamie. 1613 PURCHAS *Pilgrimage* VIII. ii. 611 A supposition, that there might be some Ilands or Parts of the Continent in times past, which is now swallowed by the mercilesse Ocean. 1667 PEPYS *Diary* 12 July, It is only said to be his [handwriting] by supposition. 1747 FRANKLIN *Ess.* Wks. 1840 III. 9 These are not mere suppositions, for I have heard some talk in this strange manner. 1790 PALEY *Horæ Paul.* xi. Wks. 1825 III. 215 That supposition is inconsistent with the terms and tenor of the epistle. 1832 BREWSTER *Nat. Magic* ii. 34, I..was driven to the extreme supposition that a crystallization was taking place in..the aqueous humour of the eye. 1861 PALEY *Æschylus* (ed. 2) *Choeph.* 659 *note*, Klausen thinks that Clytemnestra must have overheard the remarks of Orestes..but the supposition is hardly necessary.
†b. Used vaguely, with various shades of meaning: Idea, notion; imagination, fancy; *occas.* suspicion, expectation. *Obs.*
1586 A. DAY *Engl. Secretorie* I. (1625) 123 To torment your self by a needlesse supposition. 1590 SHAKS. *Com. Err.* III. ii. 50 Spread ore the siluer waues thy golden haires; And as a bud Ile take thee, and there lie: And in that glorious supposition thinke, He gaines by death, that hath such meanes to die. 1632 LITHGOW *Trav.* II. 69 Songs of Arcadian Sheepheards..did recreate my fatigated corps with many sugred suppositions. 1635 PAGITT *Christianogr.* II. iv. (1636) 59 The Inquisition crusheth not only the beginnings, but the smallest suppositions in being contrarily affected. 1719 DE FOE *Crusoe* I. (Globe) 18, I meditated nothing but my Escape;..but found no Way that had the least Probability in it: Nothing presented to make the Supposition of it rational. 1784 SIR J. REYNOLDS *Disc.* xii. (1876) 39 They proceed upon a false supposition of life.
†4. Fraudulent substitution of another thing or person in place of the genuine one; cf. SUPPOSITITIOUS 1. *Obs.*
1569 J. SANFORD tr. *Agrippa's Van. Artes* 11 b, The deceits of Rhea, and the supposition of the stone. 1641 EARL MONM. tr. *Biondi's Civil Wars* v. 111 If she had a hand in the false supposition of an Edward Plantagenet. 1797 *Monthly Mag.* III. 536 Nothing was so common among the Athenian women as the supposition of children.

†**b.** Insertion of something not genuine in a writing; that which is so inserted, an interpolation, a spurious passage; a spurious writing, a forgery.

1603 HOLLAND *Plutarch's Mor.* 1028 In what verses he useth so to doe, be sure they were of speciall marke, or els suppositions and suspected to be none of his making. **1608** BP. HALL *Epist.* IV. viii, All cary in them manifest brands of falshood and supposition. **1662** OWEN *Liturgies* v. Wks. 1855 XV. 22 Those treatises are justly suspected to be suppositions.

†**5.** *Mus.* **a.** The introduction of passing-notes foreign to the harmony (called ***discords by supposition***). **b.** The introduction of an extra note below the notes of a chord, or the transference of an upper note of a chord to the bass, as in an 'inversion' (cf. SUPPOSED 5). **c.** A bar common to two overlapping sections of rhythm, being the last bar of one and also the first of the other. *Obs.*

1728 CHAMBERS *Cycl.* s.v., There are several Kinds of Supposition: The first is, when the Parts proceed gradually from Concord to Discord, and Discord to Concord; the intervening Discord serving only as a Transition to the following Concord. **1730** *Treat. Harmony* 29 There is a way in Division of making use of Discords, upon the Second accented Part of the Bar, which way is called Supposition. **1752** tr. *Rameau's Treat. Musick* 95 Minor Discords by Supposition may be prepared by another common Discord. **1797** [see SUPPOSED 5]. **1838** G. F. GRAHAM *Mus. Comp.* 19/2 (tr. *Reicha*) The supposition is a measure which.. counts as two; 1. as final measure of the first rhythm; and, 2. as initial measure of the following rhythm. **1845** *Encycl. Metrop.* V. 752 Discords.. may be.. used without.. regular preparation and resolution, though they are then no longer considered in the light of discords but passing.. notes. *margin*, Discords by supposition.

†**6.** *Scholastic Logic.* Any of the different meanings of a term. *Obs.*

1697 tr. *Burgersdicius Logic* I. xxvi. 106 The diverse Acceptions of Words, which the Schoolmen call Suppositions, Effect no Homonymy... When I say Man is an Animal, the Word Animal is taken in the Concrete... This Concrete Acception is by the Schoolmen termed Personal, who dispute very largely of Acceptions, or, as they speak, Suppositions.

†**7.** *Med.* Application of a suppository. *Obs.*

1643 J. STEER tr. *Exp. Chyrurg.* vi. 23 The belly being first emptied by a supposition.

suppositional (sʌpəˈzɪʃənəl), *a.* [f. prec. + -AL[1] 1.] Of the nature of, involving, or based on supposition; hypothetical, conjectural; supposed.

1662 J. CHANDLER *Van Helmont's Oriat.* xxi. §5. 130 Having gotten an example (erroneous and supposi[ti]onall) [orig. *putaticio*] they straightway slide to a generality. **1664** POWER *Exp. Philos.* II. 95 We have the sensible eviction of our own eyes to confute this Suppositional Vacuity. *a* **1716** SOUTH *Serm., 1 John iii. 30* (1744) IX. 327 Men and angels ..have also a certain knowledge of them; but it is not absolute, but only suppositional; that is, upon supposal that such and such things continue in their being. **1865** MOZLEY *Miracles* vii. 152 To say that all this change would have gone on without doctrine, is.. suppositional only. **1901** H. W. HOLDEN *Guidance for Men* 140 The case is not altogether a suppositional one; it is found in fact.

Hence †**suppositioˈnality**, suppositional quality (but in quots. app. used for SUPPOSITALITY); **suppoˈsitionally** *adv.* (in mod. Dicts.), hypothetically.

1650 CHARLETON *Paradoxes* 133 How much the Law and the Soule differ in the suppositionality of Essence. **1662** J. CHANDLER *Van Helmont's Oriat.* xxxv. §33. 268 The amative or loving faculty, which proceeds from that supposi[ti]onality [orig. *suppositionalitate*] of the minde which is substantial love.

suppositionary (sʌpəˈzɪʃənərɪ), *a. rare.* [f. SUPPOSITION + -ARY[1].] = SUPPOSITIONAL.

1808 J. WEBSTER *Nat. Philos.* 152 This.. knowledge is more vague and suppositionary. **1812** SHELLEY *Let.* in Dowden *Life* (1887) I. 282 The manner in which you have reproved my suppositionary errors.

suppositious (sʌpəˈzɪʃəs), *a.* [Partly shortened or illiterate form of SUPPOSITITIOUS, partly directly from SUPPOSITION.]

1. = SUPPOSITITIOUS 1. Now *rare* or *Obs.*

1624 MOUNTAGU *Immed. Addr.* 212 The testimony produced is none of his: It is suppositious, and a counterfeit. **1656** BRAMHALL *Replic.* v. 206, I spake not this to the disparagement of that venerable Saint, but to discredit that suppositious treatise. **1672** MARVELL *Reh. Transp.* I. 138 The only question.. was.. whether it [*sc.* the child] was not spurious or suppositious. **1768** BLACKSTONE *Comm.* III. xxiii. 362 When a widow feigns herself with child, in order to exclude the next heir, and a suppositious birth is suspected to be intended. **1815** MRS. PILKINGTON *Celebrity* III. 130 With the intention of ordering the suppositious Mrs Johnson to quit her roof. **1863** REDDING *Yesterday & Today* III. 275 Suppositious letters between the Rev. James Hackman and Miss Ray.

2. = SUPPOSITITIOUS 2. Now *rare* or *Obs.*

1655 [see SUPPOSITITIOUS 2, quot. *c* 1645]. **1781** WARTON *Hist. Engl. Poetry* III. p. vii, Who.. is often a monarch that never existed, and who seldom, whether real or suppositious, has any concern with the circumstances of the narrative. **1793** ANNA SEWARD *Let. Parr* 3 Feb., The suppositious treasons, forged and alleged.

3. a. Involving or based on supposition; = SUPPOSITIONAL, SUPPOSITIVE 1.

1698 HEARNE *Duct. Hist.* (1714) I. 7 The Julian Period.. is a suppositious Number. **1810** W. WILSON *Hist. Diss. Ch.* III. 362 Their integrity.. appears to us as very suppositious. **1824** J. JOHNSON *Typogr.* II. xii. 457 Although suppositious alphabets of the aboriginal Britons have been produced. **1847** R. W. HAMILTON *Rewards & Punishm.* viii. (1853) 369 With such exception we have nothing to do: it is purely suppositious. **1905** JOYCE *Let.* 12 July (1966) II. 97 We might take a small cottage outside Dublin... Not that I imagine that the atmosphere of our suppositious cottage could.. become more unpleasant to you than the atmosphere you are at present breathing. **1957** G. E. HUTCHINSON *Treat. Limnol.* I. iv. 231 Most of the evidence is purely suppositious. **1978** P. W. J. RILEY *Union of England & Scotland* 4 Although the island comprised more than one kingdom the term 'Great Britain' was already respectable usage... James [VI/I] now contemplated for this suppositious entity not only one king but one kingdom. **1982** *Christian Sci. Monitor* 26 Aug. 9/2 Being at the center of population has some commercial advantage for local inhabitants. The last stop of the suppositious point was at Mascoutah, Ill., in 1970—a town now dethroned by the new centre.

b. ? Addicted to supposition or conjecture. *rare*[−1].

1798 R. P. *Tour Wales* 18 (MS.), The Castle [at Ludlow] on whose early date the suppositious antiquary has many doubts to determine.

Hence **suppoˈsitiously** *adv.*, spuriously; hypothetically.

1693 tr. *Dupin's Hist. Eccl. Writers* II. 30 Books.. that were suppositiously obtruded upon the World by Hereticks. **1862** MASSON in *Macm. Mag.* Aug. 324 The career suppositiously assigned to men of his class in most Art and Culture novels.

†**suppositist.** *Obs. rare*[−1]. [f. L. SUPPOSITUM or *suppositio* SUPPOSITION + -IST.] One who deals in supposition or conjecture.

1634 SIR T. HERBERT *Trav.* 206 The inhabitants are numbred by some presuming Suppositist aboue sixtie millions.

supposititious (səpɒzɪˈtɪʃəs), *a.* [f. L. *suppositītius, -īcius*, f. *supposit-*, pa. ppl. stem of *suppōnĕre*: see SUPPONE and -ITIOUS.]

1. Put by artifice in the place of another; fraudulently substituted for the genuine thing or person; hence, pretended (to be what it is not), not genuine, spurious, counterfeit, false.

a. *gen.* (Now *rare.*)

1615 CROOKE *Body of Man* 244 Aristotles nice conceited vse therefore is but supposititious and not the true vse of Nature. **1646** EARL MONM. tr. *Biondi's Civil Wars* IX. 222 Lambert tooke upon him the person of the Earl of Warwick, by the direction of a Priest; and Ralph Wilford (for so was this second supposititious Earl called) by the direction of an Augustine Frier. **1653** GATAKER *Vind. Annot. Jer.* 85 Who ..hath shrewdly shaken the main foundations of their Supposititious Science. **1700** RYCAUT *Hist. Turks* III 513 He hastned away this supposititious Envoy all he could. **1770** G. WHITE *Selborne, To Barrington* 12 Apr., You wonder.. that the hedge-sparrows, etc., can be induced.. to sit on the egg of the cuckoo without being scandalised at the vast disproportioned size of the supposititious egg. **1828** SCOTT *F.M. Perth* Introd., If any Seneschal.. had by means of paint,.. endeavoured to palm upon posterity supposititious stigmata [*sc.* stains of Rizzio's blood]. **1830** JAMES *Darnley* xxix, Being tall and thin, he had great need of some supposititious contour, to make his height seem less enormous.

b. *spec.* of a child, *esp.* one set up to displace the real heir or successor; sometimes used for 'illegitimate'; also said of the birth of such a child. Also *fig.*

1625 BACON *Ess., Empire* (Arb.) 305 The Succession of the Turks, from Solyman, vntill this day, is suspected to be vntrue, and of strange Bloud; For that Selymus the Second was thought to be Supposititious. *a* **1631** DONNE *Serm., 1 Cor. xv. 50* (1649) II. 126 In abastardizing a race, by supposititious children. **1652** A. ROSS *Hist. World* I. .. 3 [The] King of Cappadocia.. had one son.. who died young, but his two supposititious sons.. contended for the kingdome. **1701** *Lond. Gaz.* No. 3759/5 A Person.., whose Supposititious Birth, and the known Laws of the Land, for ever debar from any Pretence thereto. **1711** ADDISON *Spect.* No. 189 ¶9 They conclude that the reputed Son must have been Illegitimate, Supposititious, or begotten in Adultery. **1765** BLACKSTONE *Comm.* I. xvi. 456 A proceeding at common law, where a widow is suspected to feign herself with child, in order to produce a supposititious heir to the estate. **1849** MACAULAY *Hist. Eng.* ix. II. 411 Not one person in a thousand doubted that the boy was supposititious. **1875** JOWETT *Plato* (ed. 2) III. 97 A supposititious son, who has made the discovery that his reputed parents are not his real ones.

fig. **1641** MILTON *Prel. Episc.* Wks. 1851 III. 79 Imposing upon our belief a supposititious ofspring of some dozen Epistles. **1934** H. G. WELLS *Exper. Autobiogr.* I. v. 255 Russia.. is now no longer a Communism nor a democratic Socialism... It is a novel experimental state capitalism... It is the supposititious child of necessity in the household of theory.

c. of a writing, or passage or word in a writing.

1611 T. JAMES *Corrupt Scripture* I. 36 The 97. Treatise.. Censured To be supposititious. **1626** DONNE *Serm., John xiv. 2* (1640) 743 A supposititious word, which is not in the Text. **1693** DRYDEN *Juvenal* Ded. (1697) p. xlvii, When 'tis made publick, it will easily be seen by any one Sentence, whether it be supposititious, or genuine. **1699** BENTLEY *Phal.* Pref. p. xi, Some Reasons, why I thought Phalaris's Epistles supposititious. **1751** SMOLLETT *Per. Pickle* (1779) I. xiv. 123 A supposititious letter of recommendation. **1778** WARTON *Hist. Engl. Poetry* II. 166 That these distichs are undoubtedly supposititious, and that they could not possibly be written by the very venerable Roman whose name they bear. **1868** MILMAN *St. Paul's* vii. 132 Attempted to be proved by supposititious charters.

†**2.** Pretended or imagined to exist; feigned, fictitious; fabulous; fancied, imaginary. *Obs.*

1620 [G. BRYDGES] *Horæ Subs.* 388 All going in the habit of Schollers, and no sooner come thither, but they take vpon them false and supposititious names. *c* **1645** HOWELL *Lett.* (1650) II. 94, I tearm the gold Mine he went to discover, an ayrie and supposititious [*ed.* 1655 suppositious] Mine. **1652** GAULE *Magastrom.* xi. §10. 108 Seeing the judgement depends upon them, and they upon supposititious circles, and angles. **1702** tr. *Le Clerc's Prim. Fathers* 23 In the time of this Author, whether he be Genuine or Supposititious. **1774** WARTON *Hist. Engl. Poetry* I. Diss. i. i 4 b, The ideal histories of Turpin and Geoffrey of Monmouth, which record the supposititious achievements of Charlemagne.

3. = SUPPOSITIOUS 3.

1674 JEAKE *Arith.* (1696) 334 As in Extraction of Roots and Equations.. in working the Question is called the Supposititious or Quesitious Root. **1682** H. MORE *Annot. Glanvill's Lux O.* 72 To fetch an Argument from the supposititious Supremacy of the Will of God over his Wisdom and Goodness. **1804** *Edin. Rev.* V. 114 The case is not entirely a supposititious one. **1850** GROVE *Corr. Phys. Forces* (ed. 2) 106 As the knowledge of any particular science developes itself,.. hypotheses, or the introduction of supposititious views, are more and more dispensed with. **1865** DICKENS *Mut. Fr.* I. iv, If you were in embarrassed circumstances—this is merely supposititious. **1879** HARLAN *Eyesight* iii. 32 Rays of light.. are merely supposititious lines used.. to bring the effects of an intangible force within the range of mathematical calculations.

Hence **suppoˈsiˈtitiously** *adv.* (in quots., in sense 3); **suppoˈsiˈtitiousness** (in quots., in sense 1).

1623 (*title*) A New and Merrie Prognostication: Being a Metrical Satire, supposititiously assigned to Will Summers. **1654** OWEN *Doctr. Saint's Persev.* Pref. Cj, The supposititiousness of these Epistles. **1665** SIR T. HERBERT *Trav.* (1677) 31 Unable to penetrate so far Southward as.. River Nilus springs: albeit, supposititiously he derives it from the *Lunæ montes.* **1695** *Whether Preserv. Protest. Relig. was Motive Revol.* 39 The Supposititiousness of the Prince of Wales. **1716** M. DAVIES *Athen. Brit.* III. 63 Dr. Raynolds ..discover'd the Supposititiousness of the Book, *De Vita Prophetarum*, Father'd by the Papists upon Epiphanius. **1859** SALA *Gas-light & D.* ix. 108 Some terrible Dartford or Hounslow explosion, by which his limbs were (supposititiously) blown off. **1870** BARING-GOULD *Orig. Relig. Belief* (1871) I. 343 Faculties actually or supposititiously inferior to other faculties.

suppositive (səˈpɒzɪtɪv), *a.* (*sb.*) [ad. late L. *suppositīvus*, f. *supposit-*, pa. ppl. stem of *suppōnĕre* to SUPPONE. Cf. F. *suppositif.*]

1. Of the nature of, implying, or grounded on supposition; suppositional.

†*suppositive necessity* = 'hypothetical necessity' (HYPOTHETICAL 3).

1605 CAMDEN *Rem.* 39 Not out of suppositiue coniectures, but out of Alfricus Grammer. **1621** SANDERSON *Serm.* (1632) 368 Not an absolute and positive, but a conditional and suppositive necessity. **1650** FULLER *Pisgah* III. x. 434 Suppositive was the offence of Saint Paul (onely on their bare surmise) but positive must be his punishment. **1662** J. CHANDLER *Van Helmont's Oriat.* 186 It is a suppositive Aphorisme. **1881** *Scribner's Monthly* Feb. 634, I said we had about one hundred dollars worth. This was a rough guess. .. We were, however, forced to pay twenty-five per cent. on the suppositive one hundred dollars. **1892** J. TAIT *Mind in Matter* IV. (ed. 3) 290 His verdict on a suppositive case of the kind was, 'If they believe not Moses [etc.].'

b. *Gram.* Expressing a supposition, conditional; as *sb.* a conditional conjunction. *rare.*

1751 HARRIS *Hermes* II. ii. (1786) 244 As to Continuatives, they are either Suppositive, such as, *If*; or Positive, such as, *Because*... The Suppositives denote Connection, but assert not actual Existence.

2. = SUPPOSITITIOUS 1 c.

1910 DYSON HAGUE in *The Fundamentals* I. vi. 101 They conjecture that these four suppositive documents were not compiled and written by Moses.

suˈppositively, *adv.* [f. prec. + -LY[2].] In a suppositive manner; in the way of supposition; upon some supposition; hypothetically.

1576 FLEMING *Panopl. Epist.* 269 *marg.*, Not as though vertue could be in extremitie,.. but he meaneth suppositiuely, if it were so that vertue coulde exceede. **1650** in *Athenæum* 13 Dec. (1879) 763/2 He accused Marsys to be an unfaithfull Translator, in positiuely rendring what the King suppositiuely speakes. **1678** R. BARCLAY *Apol. Quakers* vii. §7. 216 It.. signifies *really*, and not *suppositively*, that Excellent Quality.

†**suˈppositor.** *Obs.* Also 6 -ar, -oure, 6–7 -er. [Alteration of next after agent-nouns in -ER, -OR.] = next.

1545 RAYNALDE *Byrth Mankynde* 55 A suppositar tempered with sope, larde, or the yolke of egges. **1547** BOORDE *Brev. Health* xlii. 21 b, A naturall egestion, other by course of nature, or els by suppositors, or.. other easy purgacions. **1564–78** BULLEIN *Dial. agst. Pest.* (1888) 50 The bodie must haue benefite by Purgation with Clister, or Suppositer. **1667** DRYDEN & DK. NEWCASTLE *Sir M. Mar-all* IV. i, Clysters, Suppositers, and a barbarous Pothecary's Bill. **1689** WALKER *Siege Derry* 30 A piece of a Bladder in the shape of a Suppositor.

fig. **1607** MIDDLETON *Fam. Love* III. vi, A plague upon him for a Glister! he has given our loves a suppositor with a recumbentibus. **1638** FORD *Fancies* III. i, Evermore fantastical, As being the suppositor to laughter; It hath sav'd charge in physic.

¶ Used in the sense of 'supporter', 'support': cf. SUPPOSITUM, SUPPOST.

1628 FORD *Lover's Mel.* I. ii, Mountebanks, empirics, quack-salvers,.. are all suppositors to the right worshipful doctor. **1652** GAULE *Magastrom.* xi. §10. 108 May not their twelve Houses of the Zodiack be..called so many Castles in the ayr? what reedish, nay strawy, suppositors doe they stand upon?

suppository (sə'pɒzɪtərɪ), *sb.* Also 6–7 **-ary, -arie.** [ad. late L. *suppositōrium*, neut. sing., used subst., of *suppositōrius* placed underneath or up, f. *supposit-*, *suppōnĕre* to SUPPONE. Cf. F. *suppositoire.*] A plug of conical or cylindrical shape to be introduced into the rectum in order to stimulate the bowels to action (or to reduce hæmorrhoids), or into the vagina or urethra for various purposes.

c **1400** *Lanfranc's Cirurg.* 13 If he may not schite oones a day, helpe him þerto, or with clisterie, or wiþ suppositorie. ? **1485** KNUTSSON *Bk. Pest.* 5 Prouoke a laxe by a suppositorye. **1522** MORE *De Quat. Noviss.* Wks. 100 Pilles, potions, plasters, glisters, and suppositaries. **1533** ELYOT *Cast. Helthe* III. v. (1541) 56 Suppositories ar made somtyme with hony only, sodden, rolled on a bourde, and made rounde, smaller at the one ende than at the other.. they must be put vp in at the fundement, to the great end. **1580** HOLLYBAND *Treas. Fr. Tong*, *Vn Pessaire*, a kinde of suppositories to prouoke a womans flowers. **1597** GERARDE *Herbal* I. xc. 145 Used in maner of a pessarie or mother suppositorie. **1610** MARKHAM *Masterp.* I. xci. 174 Nothing can purge the guts with that gentlenesse which a suppositary doth. **1621** BURTON *Anat. Mel.* II. iv. II. iii, Suppositaries of Castilian sope. *c* **1720** W. GIBSON *Farrier's Dispens.* x. (1734) 249 The common and usual Suppository..is made with Honey and Salt. **1876** *Trans. Clinical Soc.* IX. 103 The extract of belladonna was ordered to be administered in the shape of suppositories.

fig. **1583** MELBANCKE *Philotimus* S iij b, It is not my purginge pilles..but Cornelius his swete suppositorye, that must minister you phisicke.

†**b.** Applied abusively to a person. *nonce-use.*

1610 B. JONSON *Alch.* v. v, Madame Suppository. **1675** COTTON *Scoffer Scoft* 96 This Jack..this Glisterpipe..this vile Suppository.

su'ppository, *a.* Also 6–7 **-ary.** [ad. late L. *suppositōrius* (see prec.).]

†**1.** Used as, or pertaining to, a suppository. *Obs.*

1599 A. M. tr. *Gabelhouer's Bk. Physicke* 145/2 Take Hernes greace,..as bigge as a hasellnutte, administre the same from vnder, like a suppositorye pille. **1607** TOPSELL *Four-f. Beasts* 256 Giue it the patient by svppository meanes for the bloody Flix.

†**2.** = SUPPOSITITIOUS I. *Obs.*

1641 EARL MONM. tr. *Biondi's Civil Wars* v. 142 The robberies, which with suppository beards were done upon the high wayes by his Souldiers.

3. = SUPPOSITIONAL. Now *rare.*

1644 G. PLATTES in Hartlib *Legacy* (1655) 236 Unlesse I should have set a suppository value, upon part of it. **1652** GAULE *Magastrom.* 107 Whether..a bare hypothesis or sole suppositary argument, may not..with the same facility..be denyed, as it is affirmed? **1672** PENN *Spir. Truth Vind.* 49, I am at a stand what he intends with his suppository Introduction. **1780** M. MADAN *Thelyphthora* I. 85 The whole passage is suppository or hypothetical. **1898** *Westm. Gaz.* 15 June 10/1 These recent suppository interviews.

So †**su'ppositorily** *adv.*, as a suppository.

1547 BOORDE *Brev. Health* clxxii. 61 b, Confecte this togyther with the whyte of an egge..and suppositaryly use it.

suppositous (sʌ'pɒzɪtəs), *a. nonce-wd.* [f. L. *suppositus*, pa. ppl. of *suppōnĕre*: see SUPPOSITUM.] Supposed, assumed.

1922 JOYCE *Ulysses* 686 An infinity rendered equally finite by the suppositous probable apposition of one or more bodies equally of the same and of different magnitudes.

‖**suppositum** (sə'pɒzɪtəm). Pl. **supposita.** [Scholastic L., neut. sing., used subst., of *suppositus*, pa. pple. of *suppōnĕre* to SUPPONE.]

†**1.** *Metaph.* = SUPPOSITE *sb.* I. *Obs.*

1646 SIR T. BROWNE *Pseud. Ep.* III. xvii. 148 Some of the Rabbines..conceived the first man an Hermaphrodite; and Marcus Leo..in some sense hath allowed it, affirming that Adam in one suppositum without division, contained both male and female. **1648** ESTWICK *Treat. Holy Ghost* 36 The person is the very *suppositum*, in which the nature subsists. **1651** BAXTER *Inf. Bapt.* 259 Can you know the *suppositum*, even the subject and accident by that Accident alone? **1719** WATERLAND *Vind. Christ's Divinity* xxv. 387 The Father is Creator, but the Son a Creature; and therefore they cannot be One and the same *Hypostasis*, or *Suppositum.*

2. *Logic.* **a.** Something supposed or assumed, an assumption. **b.** *pl.* The things or objects denoted by a given term.

1833 W. H. GILLESPIE *Argt. Being & Attrib. God* I. III. i. (1871) 32 The..fatal objection to such *supposita.* **1889** *Cent. Dict.* s.v. *Extension*, The extension [of a term] is also called the *supposita*, the *subjective parts*,..the *scope*,..and the *breadth.*

suppost (sə'pəʊst). *Obs.* exc. *Hist.* Also 6 *Sc.* **suppoist**, 6–7 **supposte.** [a. OF. *suppost* (mod.F. *suppôt*), ad. L. *suppositus*, pa. pple. of *suppōnĕre* to SUPPONE.] A subordinate; a supporter, follower, adherent. (In first quot. app. a subsidiary set of organs.)

1490 CAXTON *Eneydos* xxvii. 104 The Impression cogytyue of the entendement, wherof she [*sc.* the eyeball] maketh a present to the suppost indicatyf. **1547** *Bk. Marchauntes* a viij, God knoweth by what supposts by what workmen by what croseidiers, such a worke [*sc.* a crusade] was handled. **1559** in Knox *Hist. Ref.* II. Wks. 1846 I. 417 The craft of Sathan and his suppoistis. **1593** in *Spalding Club Misc.* I. 7 All the commound Ennemies of our native cuntrie, Sick as of spain and all thair suppoistis, ieswittis, prestis, and all utheris. **1600** HOLLAND *Livy* XXIV. xxxii. 531 The instruments and supposts of the Tyrant. **1601** J. WHEELER *Treat. Comm.* 25 Controuersies arising betweene ..the brethren, members, and supposts of the said Companie. **1646** R. BAILLIE *Anabaptism* Pref. (1647) A 2, Have the Supposts of Rome (think we) lost all their wonted stomach towards Protestant blood? **1694** MOTTEUX *Rabelais* IV. xlviii. 188 Homenas..attended by his Aposts (as they said) and his Supposts or Officers.

b. *Sc.* A member (of a university).

For earlier examples see SUPPOSIT.

1561 *First Bk. Discipl. Ch. Scot.* in *Knox's Wks.* (1848) II. 217 The hoill Principallis, Regentis, and Suppostis that ar graduat. *Ibid.* 219 The Beddellis stipend shalbe of everie entrant and suppost of the Vniversitie, ii. schillingis. **1597** in Spottiswood *Hist. Ch. Scot.* VI. (1655) 447 Any Suppost having received the degree of a Master of Arts, might be chosen Rector. [**1819** MᶜCRIE *Life Melville* I. v. 212 The University of St Andrews was formed on the model of those of Paris and Bologna. All its members or supposts, as they were called,..were divided into nations.]

†**su'pposure.** *Obs. rare.* [f. SUPPOSE *v.* + -URE: cf. *composure.*] A supposition, hypothesis.

1613 CHAPMAN *Rev. Bussy D'Ambois* Plays 1873 II. 143 There hung a taile Of circumstance so blacke on that supposure That [etc.]. **1663** BUTLER *Hud.* I. iii. 1322 Thy other Arguments are all Supposures, Hypothetical.

†**suppowell**, *sb. Obs.* Forms: 4–5 *Sc.* **suppowale, -aill, -all,** 5 **suppowaile, -aylle, -elle, supowaill, supowel, suppouel(l, suppowle, sow(b)powaylle, -aille, suppoayle, -aille,** *Sc.* **suppouaill, -ele, (sowpowayle, sowpewaille,** 6 **suppoyle),** 5–6 **suppowell.** Also SUBPOUELLE. [a. AF. **suppouail*, **suppoial*, *suppuail*, var. *souspoial*, f. *sou(s)poier*, *-puier*:—pop. L. **sub(tus)podiāre*, f. *sub(tus)* under + *podium* prop, stay: cf. APPUI.

The word has been often misunderstood and altered in early MSS. or prints, and some modern editors have misread *suppouail* as *supponail.*]

Support, assistance, succour.

1375 BARBOUR *Bruce* XVI. 139 Weyn ȝhe ȝon rebaldis durst assale Vs..Bot gif thai had suppowale neir? *a* **1400–50** *Wars Alex.* 4300 Na supowell vndire son seke we vs neuire. **1400** in *Lett. Hen. IV* (Rolls) 23, I, as one of yhour poer kyn.. requere yhow of holp and suppowall. ? **1407** HOCCLEVE *Min. Poems* (1892) 59 Ye wole vs helpe and been our suppoaille. **1426** LYDG. *De Guil. Pilgr.* 24312 For mor suer sowpewaille To the bordoun spiritual A staf is nedful. **1513** DOUGLAS *Æneis* VIII. iii. 176 Wyth succours and suppowell, blythly I Sall ȝow fra hyne hame to ȝour army send.

b. A prop, support.

c **1400** LOVE *Bonavent. Mirr.* vi. (1908) 47 A kusshyne oure lady to sitte on and a suppoayle [*W. de W.* (**1520**) suppoyle] to lene to.

Hence †**suppowell** *v. trans.*, to support, succour; †**suppoweller**, a supporter; †**suppowelling** *vbl. sb.*; †**suppowelment** = SUPPOWELL *sb.*

1391 in Fraser *Lennox* (1874) II. 44 The said Erle..and.. his sone salbe lele helparis, conselleris, suppouailairis, promotouris and furtheraris to the said Erle of the Lenenax. ? *a* **1400** *Morte Arth.* 2818 Walde þow suffire me..With a soppe of thi mene suppowelle theym ones? *c* **1400** MAUNDEV. (Roxb.) xviii. 83 Þai hing so þikk þat, bot if þai ware suppoweld by oþer treesse, þai myght noȝt bere þaire fruyt. **1409** in *Exch. Rolls Scot.* IV. p. ccix, He sal be til him..lele helper and suppouellour. **1426** LYDG. *De Guil. Pilgr.* 3740 Yovr werkys alle I sowbpowaylle, And hem supporte. **1430–40** —— *Bochas* IV. Prol. (MS. Bodl. 263) 207/2 Eek of memorye upholdere and norice And Registreer to suppowaile trouthe. *c* **1440** *York Myst.* xxxiv. 11, I comaunde you..þat noman appere To suppowle þis traytoure. *c* **1470** HARDING *Chron.* LXII. ii. (MS. Arch. Seld. B. 10) lf. 41 Wher nede was he made suppowialment [*ed.* **1543** suppowelment]. *Ibid.* CLXXVIII. xviii. 141 b, And alle were slayne withoute suppowalment. **1513** DOUGLAS *Æneis* IV. x. 32, I hoip it sall proffit, na litill thing, My gret help.. and suppowelling.

suppreme: see SUPPRIME.

suppress (sə'prɛs), *v.* Also 6 **supress**; see also SUBPRESS. [f. L. *suppress-*, pa. ppl. stem of *supprimĕre*, f. *sup-* = SUB- 2 + *premĕre* to PRESS.

See note on SUPPRISE *v.*]

1. *trans.* To put down by force or authority.

a. To cause (a proceeding, an activity) to cease, e.g. to quell (a rebellion); to put a stop to the use or employment of.

c **1380** [see SUPPRESSING *vbl. sb.*]. **1538** STARKEY *England* (1878) 182 The pryncys of our tyme haue thys offyce [*sc.* of Constable] vtturly suppressyd. **1548** UDALL *Erasm. Par.* Ded. to Q. Katerine 17 A cockesure waie to make al obedient people hate the ghospell, and to prouoke the rulers and magistrates to suppresse it. **1575** GASCOIGNE *Kenelworth* Wks. 1910 II. 103 You waters wilde suppresse your waves. **1590** SIR J. SMYTH *Disc. Weapons* 2 Our Long Bowes..no more to be vsed, but to be vtterly suppressed and extinguished. **1601** in Moryson *Itin.* II. (1617) 189 To suppresse the present Rebellion in Mounster, I..haue designed foure thousand foot. **1647** CLARENDON *Hist. Reb.* I. §149 To Discountenance, and Suppress all bold enquiries. **1679–88** *Secr. Serv. Money Chas. II & Jas. II* (Camden) 138 To blow up the houses to suppress the fire. **1699** J. DUNTON *Acc. Convers. Irel.* in *Dublin Scuffle* etc. 337 A Nonconformist Meeting was suppresst at Gallway. **1705** ADDISON *Italy* 18 Their Fleet..is now reduced to Six Gallies. When they had made an Addition of but Four new ones, the King of France sent his Orders to suppress them. **1841** D'ISRAELI *Amen. Lit.* (1867) 63 The Saxons..found that they could not suppress the language of the fugitive people. **1843** PRESCOTT *Mexico* (1850) I. 201 Military expeditions..employed to suppress the insurrections of the natives. **1869** MOZLEY *Univ. Serm.* i. 1 By simple carnage she [*sc.* the Church] suppressed the Reformation in Italy, Spain, and France. **1875** JOWETT *Plato* (ed. 2) III. 30 That blasphemous nonsense..is got at secondhand from the poets and ought to be suppressed.

transf. *a* **1862** BUCKLE *Civiliz.* (1864) II. v. 403 If a man suppresses part of himself, he becomes maimed and shorn. **1879** HARLAN *Eyesight* vi. 87 Persons with squint learn to use only one eye, and the image on the retina of the other is said to be 'suppressed'.

†**b.** To put down or overwhelm by force; to vanquish, subdue. *Obs.* (Cf. SUPPRISE *v.* 4.)

c **1425** WYNTOUN *Cron.* II. 29 (MS. Cott.), Cam..kynge of Baktranys..Fyrst he [*sc.* Nynus] suppressit [*MS. Wemyss* supprisit] wiþe his mycht, And slew hym syne wyþe fors in fycht. **1566** Q. ELIZ. in Ellis *Orig. Lett.* Ser. III. III. 361 Yet this we do not conceave of that rebell as of one whom we cannot correct and suppresse. **1579–80** NORTH *Plutarch* (1595) 47 He caused thirtie of the chiefest men of the cittie ..to come into the market place wel appoynted & furnished, to suppresse those that would attempt to hinder their purpose. **1596** SPENSER *F.Q.* VI. i. 41 In vaine he seeketh others to suppresse, Who hath not learnd him selfe first to subdew. **1614** RALEIGH *Hist. World* IV. iii. §18 With an Armie [he] made great hast toward Cilicia, hoping to suppresse him before hee should bee able to make head. **1647** CLARENDON *Hist. Reb.* IV. §60 The Loss of Rochel, by first Suppressing Their Fleet with His Own Royal Ships. *c* **1720** DE FOE *Mem. Cavalier* II. 253 Messengers were sent to York for a Party to suppress us. **1794** S. WILLIAMS *Vermont* 373 When the war came on, the leaders of mobs, and the mobs which they created, appeared in their true light: The former sunk into contempt, and the latter were soon suppressed.

c. To reduce (a person, a community or corporate body) to impotence or inactivity, as by deprivation of office or dissolution; *occas.* †to prohibit or restrain from doing something.

a **1475** [see SUPPRESSING *vbl. sb.*]. **1539–40** WRIOTHESLEY *Chron.* (Camden) I. 109 The howse of Sion was suppressed into the Kinges handes. **1545** BRINKLOW *Compl.* xxii. (1874) 53 Soch abbeys as thei haue suppressyd. **1573** L. LLOYD *Marrow of Hist.* (1653) 23 Fortune..never advanced any to dignity, but she suppressed the same again unto misery. **1639** FULLER *Holy War* v. vi. (1840) 251 Cardinal Wolsey, by leave from the pope, suppressed certain small houses of little value. **1693** *Col. Rec. Pennsylv.* I. 380 Notwithstanding thereof Wᵐ Powell does ferrie people over the Skuillkill to the petitioner's damage and yrfor [= therefore] requesting the said Wᵐ Powell may be suppresst. **1697** *View Penal Laws* 159 Whosoever shall be lawfully discharged and suppressed touching his making of Mault. **1765** *Museum Rust.* IV. 198 Forestallers certainly raise the price of markets a little, therefore should be suppressed. **1874** GREEN *Short Hist.* iv. §5. 198 The King was strong enough..to suppress the outlaws by rigorous commissions. **1887** *Spectator* 24 Sept. 1265 The Government..issued proclamations suppressing the National League.

transf. **1858** C. W. GOODWIN in *Cambr. Ess.* 271 He exterminated wild beasts and suppressed the crocodiles.

d. To withhold or withdraw from publication (a book or writing); to prevent or prohibit the circulation of.

1560 DAUS tr. *Sleidane's Comm.* 310 Yᵉ wryting was suppressed by your captaines and gouernour of your Realme. **1624** GATAKER *Transubst.* 40 To intercept writings, and seeke to suppresse things published. **1644** MILTON *Areop.* (Arb.) 47 Those books..cannot be suppressed without the fall of learning. **1738** BIRCH *Life Milton* M.'s Wks. I. 46 After the Work was ready for the Press, it was near being suppress'd by the Ignorance or Malice of the Licenser. **1759** *Idler* No. 67 ⁋3, I leave it to you to publish or suppress it. **1867** SMILES *Huguenots Eng.* i. (1880) 9 The government tried to suppress the book [*sc.* Tindale's Bible], and many copies were seized and burnt.

2. To subdue (a feeling, thought, desire, habit).

1526 *Pilgr. Perf.* (W. de W. 1531) 12 b, This gyfte suppresseth and putteth downe all carnalytees. **1598** BARCKLEY *Felic. Man* (1631) 487 Morall vertues are very necessary; for by them our unruly affections and unprofitable desires are bridled or suppressed. **1631** GOUGE *God's Arrows* iii. §47. 271 We ought..if any such [thoughts] ..rise, presently to quash and suppresse them. **1711** SHAFTESB. *Charac.* (1737) II. 70 To the suppressing the very habit and familiar custom of admiring natural beautys. *a* **1721** SHEFFIELD (Dk. Buckhm.) *Wks.* (1753) I. 8 No cold repulses my desires suppress'd. **1862** SPENCER *First Princ.* I. iii. §15 (1875) 49 Our consciousness of Space and Time cannot be suppressed.

3. a. To keep secret; to refrain from disclosing or divulging; to refrain from mentioning or stating (either something that ought to be revealed, or that was formerly stated or included, or that may be understood from the context).

1533 MORE *Debell. Salem* Wks. 1023/1 In the rehearsing againe of hys owne wordes..he is fayne to suppresse and steale awai these his own generall wordes. **1555** BRADFORD in Strype *Eccl. Mem.* (1721) III. App. xlv. 127 Yt wyll not suffer me to suppresse or kepe secret from you suche matters. **1615** G. SANDYS *Trav.* 292 The rest I suppresse, in that offensively immodest. **1667** MILTON *P.L.* VII. 123 Things not reveal'd which th' invisible King, Onely Omniscient hath supprest in Night. **1681** CONSET *Pract. Spir. Crts.* I. iii. §1 (1700) 10 Whether it were surreptitiously obtained, the truth being supprest. **1697** tr. *Burgersdicius' Logic* II. xi. 48 If the Subject of the Consequent be put into the Antecedent, the Major is suppress'd. **1711** [see SUPPRESSING *vbl. sb.*]. **1713** ADDISON *Guardian* No. 109 ⁋2, I shall suppress what has been written to me by those who have reviled me..and only Publish those Letters which approve my Proceedings. **1728** CHAMBERS *Cycl.* s.v. *Suppression*, Words that are necessarily imply'd, may be suppress'd. **1796** H. HUNTER tr. *St. Pierre's Study Nat.* (1799) III. 269 She has pronounced his name but once,.. and he suppresses it altogether. **1828** MACAULAY *Hist. Misc.*

Writ. 1660 I. 241 What is told in the fullest.. annals bears an infinitely small proportion to what is suppressed. **1871** PALGRAVE *Lyr. Poems, Pro Mortuis* viii, Ah, 'tis but little that the best.. Can leave of perfect fruit or flower! Ah, let all else be graciously suppress When man lies down to rest!

b. To leave (something) out in a system or design. *rare.*

1851 PUGIN *Chancel Screens* 39 The monstrous idea.. of suppressing the return stalls, and throwing open the whole choir.

4. To restrain from utterance or manifestation; not to express.

1557 *N.T.* (Genev.) 2 Tim. ii. 16 Suppresse prophane and vayne wordes. **1591** SHAKS. *1 Hen. VI*, IV. i. 182 Well didst thou Richard to suppresse thy voice. **1663** BUTLER *Hud.* I. ii. 683 Talgol, who had long supprest Inflamed Wrath, in glowing Breast. **1709** STEELE *Tatler* No. 114 ¶1 The Husband.. suppressing and keeping down the Swellings of his Grief. *a* **1721** PRIOR *Pastoral Dial.* 66 Suppress thy Sighs. **1746** FRANCIS tr. *Horace, Sat.* II. viii. 83 While Varius with a napkin scarce suppress'd His laughter. **1824** SCOTT *St. Ronan's* xxxvi, Here Mowbray could not suppress a movement of impatience. **1859** DICKENS *T. Two Cities* I. v, Nor compressed lips, white with what they suppressed. **1888** F. HUME *Mme. Midas* I. i, He suppressed his real tastes till he became the husband of Miss Curtis.

refl. **1755** WARBURTON in *W. & Hurd's Lett.* (1809) 201 How superior is it to any thing we have had or are like to have in the polite way!—but I suppress myself.

†**5. a.** To press down; to depress; to press or weigh upon. Also *absol. Obs.*

1542 [see SUBPRESS]. **1547** BOORDE *Brev. Health* cxix, It may come also of a reumatyke humour supressyng the brayne. **1590** SPENSER *F.Q.* I. iii. 19 That disdainfull beast .. Vnder his Lordly foot him proudly hath supprest. **1596** *Ibid.* VI. viii. 18 He staide his hand.. Yet nathemore he him suffred to arize; But still suppressing [etc.]. **1597** A. M. tr. *Guillemeau's Fr. Chirurg.* b iij b/1 The plate layede in the mouth, to keepe downe and suppres the tonge. **1620** [see SUPPRESSED *ppl. a.*].

†**b.** To ravish, violate. *Obs.* (Cf. SUPPRISE *v.* 3.)

1590 SPENSER *F.Q.* I. vi. 40 He it was, that earst would haue supprest Faire Vna.

†**6.** *fig.* To bring or keep low, into or in subjection; to bear heavily upon, weigh down. *Obs.*

1537 *Lett. & Papers Hen. VIII*, XII. I. 16 My being here doth but with thought weaken the body and suppress the heart. **1542-5** BRINKLOW *Lament.* 10 b, The parcialyte of iudges, suppressynge the pore, and aidynge the riche. **1588** GREENE *Pandosto* (1843) 18 Her vital spirits being suppressed with sorrow. **1594** MARLOWE & NASHE *Dido* I. i, Poore Troy so long supprest, From forth her ashes shall aduance her head. *a* **1618** RALEIGH *Prerog. Parl.* (1628) Ep. Ded., Those that are supprest and helpelesse are commonly silent. *a* **1649** DRUMM. OF HAWTH. *Oath Knight* Wks. (1711) 138 Masterful thieves and outlaws, that suppress the poor.

7. To hinder from passage or discharge; to stop or arrest the flow of.

1621 BURTON *Anat. Mel.* II. v. II. 481 If blacke blood issue foorth, bleede on, if it be cleere and good, let it be instantly suppressed. **1716** POPE *Iliad* v. 109 Fate suppress'd his Breath. **1842** LOUDON *Suburban Hort.* 357 Suppressing the direct channel of the sap. **1854** SIR B. BRODIE *Psychol. Inq.* I. iv. 129 Hæmorrhage, which.. it was impossible to suppress.

8. a. To prevent or inhibit (an action or phenomenon); *esp.* to eliminate, partly or wholly (electrical interference or unwanted frequencies).

1929 T. E. SHEA *Transmission Networks & Wave Filters* I. i. 20 For demodulation and recognition of signals the carrier frequency and one sideband may be suppressed. **1933** *Popular Sci.* Jan. 57/2 Interference troubles are present in abundance... To suppress these oscillations, 25,000-ohm resistors are placed in each spark plug lead. **1964** R. F. FICCHI *Electr. Interference* iv. 29 Shielding is the only practical method of suppressing interference which is radiated directly from a source. **1969** J. H. GREEN *Basic Clin. Physiol.* xvi. 91/2 The hormones of the adrenal cortex have an action in suppressing allergic responses. **1977** *Lancet* 5 Nov. 954/2 A 6-day course of oral dexamethasone at a dosage which would completely suppress A.C.T.H. in a person with adrenal insufficiency. **1980** PIERCE & POSNER *Introd. Communication Sci. & Systems* x. 224 A data signal with dc suppressed is sent through.. single-sideband telephone links.

b. To fit with a suppressor.

1948 *Electronic Engin.* XX. 95 Garages and service stations are asked to co-operate in 'suppressing' cars already on the road. **1955** *Times* 31 Aug. 5/1 Everyone, he said, should beware of people who told them that all appliances must now be suppressed, especially if they were trying to sell suppressors. **1970** *AA Bk. Car.* 332 (*heading*) Suppressing the coil and the dynamo.

†**su'ppressable,** *a. Obs. rare*[−1]. [f. prec. + -ABLE.] = SUPPRESSIBLE.

1609 W. M. *Man in Moone* (Percy Soc.) 5 When age beganne to tame that never otherwise suppressable indomitam juventutem.

suppressal (sə'prɛsəl). *rare.* [f. as prec. + -AL[1] 5.] = SUPPRESSION 1 b.

1651 HOWELL *Venice* 107 Nothing could heap more honor upon him then the suppressall of the enemy. **1857** W. R. ALGER *Orat. 4 July* 33 It reflects infamy on our Government, that an iron hand of suppressal was not promptly laid on these marauding parties.

suppressant (sə'prɛsənt). [f. SUPPRESS *v.* + -ANT[1].] An agent that suppresses or restrains; *spec.* (more fully ***appetite suppressant***) a drug which suppresses appetite.

1958 *Jrnl. Amer. Med. Assoc.* 24 May 437/1 We were particularly impressed with the marked reduction in side-effects with the new drug, as compared with our previous experience with other appetite suppressants. **1968** *McGraw-Hill Yearbk. Sci. & Technol.* 189/1 material that is applied directly to the burning fuel to reduce the intensity or rate of burning is termed a suppressant. **1974** M. C. GERALD *Pharmacol.* ii. 28 One group of appetite suppressants is composed of indigestible gums that swell when they come into contact with the stomach's fluids. **1977** P. THEROUX *Consul's File* 73 Ayer Hitam was malarial, and the tablets we took.. were only suppressants.

suppressed (sə'prɛst), *ppl. a.* [f. as SUPPRESSAL + -ED[1].] **a.** In various senses of the verb SUPPRESS.

1620 T. GRANGER *Div. Logike* 155 Earth-creeping sprigge, base bred, of heac suppresst. *c* **1790** COWPER *Comm. Milton's P.L.* Wks. 1837 XV. 298 The author possesses more fire than he shows. There is suppressed force in it. **1791** BURKE *Th. French Aff.* Wks. 1808 VII. 44 The suppressed faction, though suppressed, exists. Under the ashes, the embers of the late commotions are still warm. **1801** *Med. Jrnl.* V. 63 The suppressed perspirable matter. **1810** SCOTT *Lady of L.* I. xxiv, With smile suppressed and shy. **1843** BORROW *Bible in Spain* xv, Recently removed from some of the suppressed convents. **1845** DARWIN *Voy. Nat.* xiv. (1879) 307 The suppressed action of the volcanos. **1863** GEO. ELIOT *Romola* v, A voice.. altered by some suppressed feeling. **1863** HOTTEN *Hand-bk. Topogr.* 103/2 Sm. 8vo, with the rare Suppressed leaf. **1897** *Allbutt's Syst. Med.* IV. 9 Symptoms.. known as.. 'suppressed' 'anomalous' or 'latent gout'.

b. *Bot.* Said of parts normally or typically present, but not found in the particular case in question. (Usually as predicate or pa. pple.)

1849 BALFOUR *Man. Bot.* §647 In Tropæolum pentaphyllum.. there are three petals suppressed, as shown by the position of the two remaining ones; there are two rows of stamens, in each of which one is awanting, and there are two carpels suppressed. **1870** HOOKER *Stud. Flora* 410 Carex Bœnninghauseniana... Bracts sometimes wholly suppressed.

c. *Forestry.* Of a tree: growing in the lower levels of a forest.

1893 [see DOMINANT *a.* 6]. **1938** J. S. BOYCE *Forest Pathol.* xvi. 388 In Germany suppressed trees of artificially infected red beech were found to be more susceptible to decay. **1976** [see OVERTOPPED *ppl. a.*].

d. Fitted with an interference suppressor.

1959 *Which?* Aug. 91/1 All [clothes driers].. were stable .., and suppressed for TV though none was completely suppressed for radio. **1970** *AA Bk. Car.* 332/3 (*caption*) On cars not fitted with suppressed high-tension leads or caps, insert individual line suppressors in each HT lead.

e. **suppressed-carrier** *Telecommunications*, usu. *attrib.* (see quot. 1924).

1924 S. R. ROGET *Dict. Electr. Terms* 251/1 *Suppressed carrier wave telephony*, a system of Carrier Current Telephony in which the excess of unmodulated carrier wave is filtered out and not transmitted, but re-introduced in the receiving apparatus in sufficient quantity to prevent distortion. **1935** [see PILOT *sb.* 6]. **1959** [see PHASING *vbl. sb.* 1]. **1974** HARVEY & BOHLMAN *Stereo F.M. Radio Handbk.* ii. 12 In the Zenith-G.E. system.. a suppressed-carrier or balanced modulator is employed.

Hence **suppressedly** (-ɪdlɪ) *adv.*, in a suppressed tone; with restrained utterance or the like.

1867 C. J. SMITH *Syn. & Antonyms* s.v. *Aloud*, Inaudibly. Suppressedly. **1873** MISS BROUGHTON *Nancy* I. 24, I have.. said 'good-night' in a tone as suppressedly hostile as his own. **1880** —— *Sec. Th.* II. iv, They both laugh low and suppressedly. **1887** HARDY *Woodlanders* III. v. 87 His eyes now suppressedly looked his pleasure.

suppresser (sə'prɛsə(r)). *rare.* [f. as prec. + -ER[1].] = SUPPRESSOR.

1882 in OGILVIE (Annandale). **1895** *Columbus* (Ohio) *Disp.* 22 Oct. 4/4 The president is a great suppresser of news and holds his cabinet severely in check.

suppressible (sə'prɛsɪb(ə)l), *a.* [f. SUPPRESS + -IBLE.] Capable of being suppressed. Hence **suppressi'bility**, capacity for being suppressed.

1837 CARLYLE *Fr. Rev.* I. II. iv, A mere confusion of tongues... Not manageable, suppressible, save by some strongest and wisest man. **1871** R. WILSON (*title*) Prostitution Suppressible. **1973** *Clin. Endocrinol.* II. 369 There was a good correlation between a normal TRH response and normal thyroid suppressibility by T_3. **1977** *Lancet* 5 Nov. 954/2 Inadequate A.C.T.H. suppressibility in patients with Addison's disease while on treatment may be due to the maintenance of a secondary pituitary hyperplasia by inadequate replacement therapy.

suppressing (sə'prɛsɪŋ), *vbl. sb.* [f. SUPPRESS + -ING[1].] = SUPPRESSION (chiefly in sense 1).

c **1380** WYCLIF *Sel. Wks.* III. 460 In suppressing of kynges state and destroyynge of obediens of prestis to lordis. *a* **1475** ASHBY *Active Policy* 417 Ye must subdewe with al suppressyng Euery persoune. Pretendyng right to your coronacion. **1542-5** BRINKLOW *Lament.* (1874) 120 Your euell suppressynge of the pore. **1561** *Reg. Privy Council Scot.* I. 186 For the suppressing of malefactouris. **1591** WEBBE in Wilmot *Tancred & Gismund* *3 b, The suppressing of this Tragedie, so worthy for yᵉ presse. **1635** (*title*) A Proclamation for the Suppressing of profane Swearing and Cursing. *a* **1699** TEMPLE *Ess., Popular Discont.* ii Wks. 1720 I. 265 Some more effectual way.. for preventing or suppressing of common Thefts and Robberies. **1711** ADDISON *Spect.* No. 135 ¶12 The suppressing of several Particles which must be produced in other Tongues to make a Sentence intelligible. **1753** *Scots Mag.* XV. 66/2 The suppressing of this insurrection.

So **suppressing** *ppl. a.*, that suppresses (in quot., ? oppressing: cf. SUPPRESS *v.* 6).

1632 LITHGOW *Trav.* x. 456 O foolish pride, O suppressing ambition!

suppression (sə'prɛʃən). [ad. L. *suppressio*, *-ōnem*, n. of action f. *suppress-*, *supprimĕre* to SUPPRESS. Cf. F. *suppression* (15th c.).]

1. The action of putting down, as by power or authority; **a.** a practice or custom, a proceeding or movement, etc.; *occas.* †the quenching (of fire).

1528 MORE *Dyaloge* IV. Wks. 250/2 He magnifyeth baptisme but to the supression of penance & of al good liuing. **1551** T. WILSON *Logic* (1580) 48 b, The first suppression of the Popes whole power. **1574** *Homilies* II. *Agst. Rebell.* 617 (*heading*) The suppression of the last rebellion. **1607** CHAPMAN *Bussy d'Ambois* IV. i. 168 My love (Like to a fire disdaining his suppression) Rag'd being discourag'd. **1658** T. WALL *Charact. Enemies Ch.* 42 To read their own shame in the suppression of mischief fruitlessly attempted. **1737** in *10th Rep. Hist. MSS. Comm.* App. I. 267 The Suppression of Play-houses. **1776** ADAM SMITH *W.N.* II. ii. I. 392 The suppression of twenty shilling notes, would probably relieve it [*sc.* the scarcity of gold and silver]. **1825** JEFFERSON *Autobiog.* Wks. 1859 I. 71 The result was.. suppression of corvees, reformation of the gabelles. **1828** SCOTT *F.M. Perth* ix, The extension of the dominion and the wealth of the church, and the suppression of heresy.

attrib. **1806** SURR *Winter in Lond.* III. 199 These suppression chaps intend to enforce the penal statute, and compel us to go to church! **1902** *Westm. Gaz.* 2 July 2/1 In favour of a rigorous suppression policy.

b. persons or communities.

1570-6 LAMBARDE *Peramb. Kent* (1826) 225 A Monasterie .. which (in the late.. generall suppression) was found to be of the yeerly value of an hundreth and twenty pounds. **1590** SIR J. SMYTH *Disc. Weapons* 35 b, After that victorie and suppression of the Rebels. **1625** in Ellis *Orig. Lett.* Ser. I. III. 206 A farther suppression of all Popish Recusants and disinheriting of them. **1784** W. STRICKLAND in B. Ward *Dawn Cath. Revival* (1909) I. 78 On the suppression of the Society of Jesus. *c* **1868** G. PRYME *Autobiog. Recoll.* xv. 231 An Irish Act of Parliament for the suppression of 'Rapparees, Tories, and other Robbers.' **1888** GASQUET *Hen. VIII & Eng. Monast.* I. 86 They turned out the agents engaged on the suppression [*sc.* of monasteries], and reinstated the canons.

c. Withholding or withdrawal from publication; prevention or prohibition of the circulation of a book or writing.

a **1700** EVELYN *Diary* 19 Aug. 1674, The noise of this book's suppression made it presently be bought up. **1736** POPE *Let. to Mr. Allen* 5 June, The only use to my own character, as an Author of such a publication, would be the suppression of many things.

2. The action of keeping secret; refusal to disclose or reveal; also, the leaving of something unexpressed.

1728 CHAMBERS *Cycl., Suppression*, in Grammar, an Omission of certain Words in a Sentence, which yet are necessary to a full.. Construction. **1749** *Power & Harmony Prosaic Numbers* 63 A seasonable Silence, or imperfect Speech (a Figure which the Rhetoricians call a Suppression). **1782** MISS BURNEY *Cecilia* VIII. iv, The incident was too extraordinary.. to have any chance of suppression. **1837** MACAULAY *Ess., Bacon* (1843) II. 284 Unpardonable distortions and suppressions of facts. **1878** GLADSTONE *Prim. Homer* 142 Homer, like Shakespeare, is remarkable for the suppression of himself.

3. Restraint or stifling (of utterance or expression).

1706 PHILLIPS (ed. Kersey), *Suppression*, the Act of Suppressing, Smothering, &c. **1751** H. WALPOLE *Let. to Mann* 21 Mar., He [*sc.* a thrush] had dangerous suppressions of breath. **1827-35** WILLIS *Shunammite* 37 His breast Heaving with the suppression of a cry. **1861** GEO. ELIOT *Silas M.* I. i, The self-complacent suppression of inward triumph that lurked in the narrow slanting eyes and compressed lips. **1865** SWINBURNE *Atalanta* 2042 With tears and suppression of sighs.

†**4.** Depression, lowering; pressure of a superincumbent weight. *Obs. rare.*

1709-29 V. MANDEY *Syst. Math., Astron.* 353 Refraction, is the Elevation or Suppression of any Star by reason of.. the Vapors Elevating themselves from the Earthly Globe. **1753** *Chambers' Cycl.* Suppl., *Suppressionis ignis*, a fire of suppression, a term used in chemistry to express such an application of fire to any subject, that it shall at once act upon it above and below... The usual way.. is by covering the vessel.. with sand, and then laying hot coals upon that.

5. *Med.* and *Path.* Stoppage or arrest (of a discharge or secretion).

1601 HOLLAND *Pliny* XXII. xxv. II. 143 It amendeth the suppression or difficultie of voiding urine. **1615** CROOKE *Body of Man* 336 Oftentimes vpon the suppression of their courses their bellies swell and they thinke they are conceiued. **1719** QUINCY *Compl. Disp.* 121 Simon Paule gave it in Suppression of Urine. **1822-7** GOOD *Study Med.* (1829) V. 41 Suppression of the menses. The secretion obstructed in its regular periods of recurrence. **1845** BUDD *Dis. Liver* 222 The disorder of digestion and the suppression of bile. **1877** M. FOSTER *Physiol.* II. iv. (1879) 378 The cessation of renal activity, the so-called suppression of urine.

6. *Bot.* Absence or non-development of some part or organ normally or typically present.

1845 ASA GRAY *Bot. Text-bk.* 191 The non-production (suppression) of one whorl of organs. **1849** BALFOUR *Man. Bot.* §647 Suppression is liable to occur in all the parts of plants, and gives rise to various abnormalities. **1882** VINES *Sachs' Bot.* 363 The protonema differs from the Moss-stem .. in the suppression of those further divisions by which the tissue of the stem is produced from its segments.

7. a. *Psychol.* The restraint or repression of an idea, an activity, or a reaction by something more powerful.

1880 W. James *Coll. Ess. & Rev.* (1920) 197 What is this volition?..the permanent suppression of an idea although it may be immediately and urgently pleasant. *Ibid.*, What do we mean by 'suppression'? Either complete oblivescence, or such presence as to evoke the steady sentiment of aversion or negation. **1894** Creighton & Titchener tr. *Wundt's Human & Animal Psychol.* 206 It may sometimes be observed that these phenomena of suppression do not extend to the entire image. **1951** T. C. Ruch in S. S. Stevens *Handbk. Exper. Psychol.* v. 172/2 Suppression exists in two forms. The first is termed 'suppression of motor activity'.. and the second form is 'suppression of electrical activity'. **1971** K. H. Pribram *Languages of Brain* vii. 138 Thus some sort of suppression of responsiveness must occur when an imbalance in the ordinary mode of excitation is produced, and their suppression exceeds the malfunction produced solely by disuse. **1974** Atkinson & Birch in Atkinson & Raynor *Motivation & Achievement* xv. 274 The impact of some feature of the immediate environment is not so much an instigation to activity as the opposite, suppression of an activity.

b. *Psychoanal.* The action or result of (consciously) inhibiting an unacceptable feeling, desire, or memory. Cf. repression 2 c.

1913 A. A. Brill tr. *Freud's Interpretation of Dreams* v. 199 The theory of repression..asserts that such repressed wishes still exist, contemporaneously with an inhibition weighing them down. Language has hit upon the truth when it speaks of the 'suppression' of such impulses. **1926** J. S. Huxley *Ess. Pop. Sci.* vii. 72 Repression, suppression, sublimation, and the rest are [psychological] realities; and we are finding out how our minds do work. **1955** E. Mosbacher tr. *Ferenczi's Final Contrib. Psycho-anal.* iv. 265 With suppression one does not feel the pain, only the *effort* which is necessary to 'alienate over' the pain. With repression one does not even feel this any longer. **1969** H. Nagera et al. *Basic Psychoanal. Concepts* II. ix. 43 The possibilities range from complete suppression..to an intensity which is greater than the ideational content would lead one to expect. **1977** A. Sheridan tr. *Lacan's Four Fundamental Concepts Psycho-anal.* ii. 27 Is it not possible to see emerging from the text itself..the reality of the disappearance, of the suppression, of the *Unterdrückung*, the passing underneath?

8. *Electr.* Prevention of electrical interference.

1933 *Jrnl. Inst. Electr. Engineers* LXXIII. 543/2 Devices for the suppression of interference from many items of electrical plant, particularly domestic appliances, could be incorporated in future designs. **1964** R. F. Ficchi *Electr. Interference* vii. 110 Capacitors are used when suppression is required on two commutator motors. **1970** *R.A.C. Guide & Handbk.* 56 Radio Interference Suppression. Regulations made by the Postmaster General.

9. *Phonetics.* The lowering of normal stress levels in verse; an instance of this.

1956, 1973 [see promotion 1 f].

Hence **su'ppressionist**, an advocate of suppression.

1886 *Daily Tel.* 11 Nov. (Cassell), Think of it, ye modern suppressionists.

‖**suppressio veri** (sə'prɛʃɪəʊ 'viːəraɪ). [mod.L., = suppression of what is true.] Misrepresentation of the truth by concealing facts which ought to be made known. Cf. suggestio falsi.

1755 Chesterfield in *World* No. 105. 632 Here is not only the *suppressio veri*, which is highly penal, but the *crimen falsi* too. **1815, 1855** [see suggestio falsi]. **1889** *Athenæum* 20 Apr. 500/3 There is an unintentional *suppressio veri* in his assertion. **1905** *Spectator* 25 Feb. 286/2 The English Church Union could hardly subscribe *ex animo* to an interpretation containing an important *suppressio veri*. **1950** M. Hay *Foot of Pride* v. 135 It would not be easy to find a more flagrant case of *suppresio veri* than this omission..of any reference to the notorious Rohling scandal. **1979** J. Melville *Wages of Zen* iii. 28, I told him exactly who I am and, with a touch of *suppressio veri*, what I'm about.

suppressive (sə'prɛsɪv), *a.* [f. L. *suppress-*: see suppress and -ive.] Having the quality or effect of suppressing.

1778 Johnson 25 Apr. in Boswell, I consider it as a very difficult question..whether one should advise a man not to publish a work, if profit be his object... I should scruple much to give a suppressive vote. **1822–7** Good *Study Med.* (1829) II. 232 The miasm it [*sc.* typhus] generates, though more suppressive or exhaustive of sensorial energy, is less volatile, than that of marsh-lands. **1860** Froude *Hist. Eng.* xxxv. VI. 529 The use of strong suppressive measures to keep down the unruly tendencies of uncontrolled fanatics. **1885** W. H. White *Mark Rutherford's Deliv.* ii. (1892) 25 Nor was it even possible for any single family to emerge amidst such altogether suppressive surroundings.

Hence **su'ppressively** *adv.*

1837 Carlyle *Misc. Ess., Mirabeau*, The former set of pangs he..crushes down into his soul suppressively.

suppressor (sə'prɛsə(r)). Also 6–7 -our; see also suppresser. [f. suppress + -or. Late L. had *suppressor*.] **1. a.** One who or that which suppresses.

1560 in *Maitl. Club Misc.* III. 217 The Pape quhai is the verray Antichriste and suppressour of Godis glorie. **1632** Lithgow *Trav.* ix. 388 He was no suppressour of the subiects. **1682** Sir T. Browne *Chr. Mor.* 13 Humility and charity, the great suppressors of envy. **1711** E. Ward *Vulgus Brit.* viii. 91 And so from a Rude Mob became, The fierce Suppressors of the same. **1868** Freeman *Norm. Conq.* II. viii. 194 Rudolf of Ivry..the savage suppressor of the great peasant revolt.

b. *spec.* A device for stopping a machine or part to which it is fitted from causing electrical interference.

1930 *Engineering* 14 Nov. 626/1 A diagram..is given in Fig. 16, the transmitting and receiving suppressors being marked TS_1 and TS_2. **1948** *Electronic Engin.* XX. 95 An ignition suppressor for fitting in the H.T. supply lead from the coil. **1955** [see suppress *v.* 8 b]. **1970** [see suppressed *ppl. a.* d].

2. *Genetics.* A gene in whose presence the effects of some other gene are not expressed. Also ***suppressor gene***.

1928 *Zeitschr. f. Induktive Abstammungs- und Vererbungslehre* XLVI. 85 (*heading*) The genetics of 'black suppressor' in Drosophila melanogaster. **1932** *Amer. Naturalist* LXVI. 323 That the suppressor is a translocated wild-type allelomorph rather than a mutation in another gene has been proved in certain cases. **1960** *Heredity* XV. 91 The phenotypic manifestation of the suppressor gene is hidden by the mutation *en.* **1966** *Ann. Rev. Microbiol.* XX. 409 The best characterized and most intensively studied of the suppressor mutations which affect the translation process are the suppressors of the two classes of mutants, 'amber' and 'ochre'.

3. *Electronics.* = *suppressor grid*, sense 4 below.

1937 F. E. Terman *Radio Engin.* (ed. 2) iv. 128 The virtual cathode in conjunction with the plate and suppressor grid forms the equivalent of a triode tube in which the suppressor is the grid. **1959** [see grid 5 a]. **1968** Romanowitz & Puckett *Introd. Electronics* vi. 237 The suppressor is usually connected to the cathode and is thus at full negative potential with respect to the plate.

4. Special Combs.: **suppressor (T) cell** *Immunol.*, a thymus-dependent lymphocyte which can suppress the stimulation of antibody production in lymphocytes in the presence of antigen; **suppressor grid** *Electronics*, in a thermionic valve, a coarse grid situated between electrodes (usu. the screen grid and the anode) so as to stop secondary electrons emitted by the latter from reaching the former.

1972 *Jrnl. Immunol.* CVIII. 590/1 It is possible that there are separate populations of activator (*x*) and suppressor (*y*) T cells. **1979** *Jrnl. Exper. Med.* CXLIX. 1018 The suppressor T Cells regualted the DH [*sc.* delayed hypersensitivity] in the induction stage. **1981** *Nature* 23 July 357/2 Nonspecific suppressor cells may be one explanation for the severe immunodeficiency and the recurrent infectious complications characteristic of patients with chronic GvHD [*sc.* graft-versus-host disease]. **1931** *Electronics* Nov. 176/2 In order to avoid the effects of secondary emission from the plate..an auxiliary electrode was inserted to suppress this secondary current. The advantages of this same sort of suppressor grid are utilized in the..power pentode design. **1944** *Electronic Engin.* XVII. 163 The suppressor grids are generally operated at cathode potential. **1974** Harvey & Bohlmann *Stereo F.M. Radio Handbk.* ii. 13 If a modulating signal is now applied, the bias on the suppressor grid is alternately raised and lowered in sympathy with the modulating signal.

supprice, -icioun, var. supprise, -ission *Obs.*

†**supprime**, *v. Obs. rare.* In 5 suppryme, 6 suppreme. [ad. L. *supprimĕre* or F. *supprimer* to suppress.] *trans.* = suppress.

1490 Caxton *Eneydos* xiii. 48 The mone obscure.. suppryme th the lyghte of the sonne. **1549** *Compl. Scot.* xix. 158 The prudens and autorite that the lord hes gyffin to the, suld suppreme ther ignorante error & obstination.

†**su'pprior.** *Obs.* Also 4–5 -our(e, 5–6 -er. [a. OF. *suppriour* (14th c.), med.L. *supprior*: see sub- 6 and prior. (Cf. Sp. *suprior.*)] = subprior.

1338 R. Brunne *Chron.* (1810) 208 Þe priour said, 'Þis day þe suppriour chese we'. **1377** Langl. *P. Pl.* B. v. 171 Bothe Prioure an supprioure and owre *pater abbas.* c **1430** Lydg. *Min. Poems* (Percy Soc.) 64 The suppriour beholdyng aboute overalle, As is his office, that non of them were absent. **1485** Caxton *St. Wenefryde* 14 Randolf whiche was Suppryour of the hows. c **1534** [see supprioress]. **1535** in *Lett. Suppr. Monast.* (Camden) 54, I have often commandidd..the supprior..that ther shulld no seculer bois be conversant with ony of the monkes. **1637** Gillespie *Eng. Pop. Cerem.* iii. v. 87 When the Supprior of the Abbey of Saint Andrewes was disputing with John Knox.

So †**su'pprioress** [OF. *supprioresse* (14th c.), med.L. *suppriorissa*], = subprioress.

a **1400** *Relig. Pieces fr. Thornton MS.* (1914) 54 Blyssede þat abbaye..þat hase so haly ane abbas as Charyte, a prioresse as Wysedome, a supprioresse as Mekenes. a **1455** *Lett. Marg. Anjou & Bp. Beckington* (Camden) 164 To the Supprioauresse of None Eton. c **1534** in J. Bacon *Liber Regis* (1786) p. xi, The names of the supprior, supprioresse, sexten, selerer.

†**supprise**, *sb.* Chiefly *Sc. Obs.* Also 5 -ice, -yce, 5–6 -is, -yse, 6 -yss. [a. AF., OF. *suprise*, var. of *surprise* surprise *sb.* Cf. med.L. *subprisia, suppris(i)a* usurpation, extraordinary impost.]

1. Injury, wrong, outrage, oppression.

c **1425** Wyntoun *Cron.* vii. 2132 (MS. Wemyss) Þare he ..lesit all his noble name. Thare fell ane of his floure de lice, To do his fallow sic suppris. *Ibid.* viii. 4902 With his ost, quhare he ourraid, Gret suppris [*MS. Cott.* wastynge] in þe cuntre he maid. **1442** *Extr. Aberd. Reg.* (1844) I. 7 The supprise that Master John of Caydow did in the outtakyn of Adam of Hillis net. c **1470** Harding *Chron.* clxxxix. iii. (MS. Ashm. 34) lf. 147 Wiþ oute suppryce [*v.r.* supprise] or any extorcion Of þe porayle. c **1500** *Lancelot* 691 For to tell ..his gret distresse Of presone and of loues gret suppris, It war to long. **1500–20** Dunbar *Poems* lxxxiv. 49 Substance with honour doing nane suppryss.

2. Surprise, unexpected attack.

c **1470** Henry *Wallace* viii. 694 Yhe wyrk nocht as the wys, Gyff that ye tak the awnter off supprice. c **1500** *Lancelot* 3479 Ws ned no more to dreding of suppris; We se the strenth of al our ennemys.

3. Conquest, defeat.

c **1425** Wyntoun *Cron.* vi. 1749 (MS. Wemyss) He persauit in þat fycht At he wes neire a supprice sone.

†**supprise**, *v.* Chiefly *Sc. Obs.* Also 4 -ice, 4–5 -iss, 4–6 -yse, 5 -is, -yss, (-ese), 5–6 -ys, -eis, 6 -ize, -yis(s; 5 suprise, superyse, 8 suprize. [f. AF., OF. *supris-e*, var. of *sur-, sourpris-e*, or *souspris-e*, pa. pple. of *surprendre* surprise *v.*, *sousprendre* susprise *v.*

Through variants like *suppriss*, this vb. became confused with suppress, of which it has some of the meanings.]

1. *trans.* To come upon or attack unexpectedly; to surprise.

1375 Barbour *Bruce* iii. 11 He assemblyt his men..And come for to suppris the king, That weill wes war of thar cummyng. *Ibid.* vi. 37 Thai thoucht him for to suppris; And gif he fled on ony vis To follow him vith the hunde. c **1375** *Sc. Leg. Saints* xl. (*Ninian*) 876 A gret oste of Ingland, For to supprice hym, var cumand. **1471** Caxton *Recuyell* (Sommer) 676 Aboute the houre of none cam a grete tempeste And supprysed them sodaynly.

b. To ensnare, betray.

c **1450** *St. Cuthbert* (Surtees) 1848 Þe deuel, with his quaynty̆s, Will be aboute ȝow to suppryse, And draw ȝow heyn. a **1600** Montgomerie *Misc. Poems* xliv. 26 Wo to the spyis first did suppryis My hairt within ȝour hald!

2. Of a feeling, etc.: To come upon suddenly and forcibly, seize, overtake, affect violently: usually in pa. pple. (const. *with* the feeling, etc.).

c **1374** Chaucer *Troylus* iii. 1184 This Troilus, with blysse of þat supprised, Put al in goddes hond. **1420–22** Lydg. *Thebes* 2017 It scheweth wel that thow were not wis, But supprised with a manere rage. **1426** —— *De Guil. Pilgr.* 6166 With gret desyr I was supprysed In my thouht & my corage. **1430–40** —— *Bochas* viii. xxvii. (MS. Bodl. 263) 404 Take and supprised he was wt dronknesse. a **1513** Fabyan *Chron.* vi. ccxvi. (1533) 139/1 For thys vyctory Harolde was suppreised [1559 suppressed] wyth pryde. **1523** Skelton *Garl. Laurel* 537 So am I supprysyd with pleasure and delyght To se this howre now. **1592** Breton *C'tess Pembroke's Love* (Grosart) 24/2 A secret ioie that did the soule suprise. **1611** Mure *Misc. Poems* i. 60 ȝouth then, with courage and desyer..assayed My Sences to suppryse.

b. To affect with surprise.

1775 in *Nairne Peerage Evidence* (1874) 123 If departed souls can be supriz'd sure hers would be so to meet in the regines of bliss one she thought was still here in this world of woe.

3. To do violence to, injure, outrage; to oppress; to ravish, violate (a woman).

c **1375** *Sc. Leg. Saints* xlix. (*Tecla*) 157 Scho..Cryit hye: supprice me nocht Na haf nocht foly in to thocht! c **1400** *Apol. Loll.* 75 Austeyn..seiþ þus: Sum supprise wiþ seruil chargis our religioun, þat our Lord Ihu Crist wold to be fre. a **1400–50** *Wars Alex.* 2390 (Ashmole MS.), He wald neuire suprise [*Dublin MS.* sussprise] no sege vndir heuen. c **1425** Wyntoun *Cron.* i. 310 (MS. Wemyss), Sindry spretis.. Slepand women wald suppris..That gat þire gyantis ofgret mycht. **1456** Sir G. Haye *Law Arms* (S.T.S.) 156 The citee sulde be wele punyst that revengis nocht hir burgeis suppresit, or opprest wrangwisly... I lefully defend me agayne othir that wald suppris me wrangwisly. c **1470** Harding *Chron.* cxiv. xiii. (MS. Ashm. 34) lf. 89 b, He..his comons never his tyme supprysed [*v.r.* supprissed]. **1500–20** Dunbar *Poems* xliii. 47 Sic ladyis wyiss, Thay ar to pryis,..Swa can devyiss, And not suppryiss Thame, nor thair honestie.

4. To overpower, overcome, subdue; *occas.* to put down, suppress.

c **1420** *Anturs of Arth.* 306 Þei shullene dye one a day... Suppriset with a surget [*Thornton MS.* Supprysede with a sugette]. c **1425** Wyntoun *Cron.* vi. 1709 (MS. Cott.), Schir Knowt..Dowttyt to be suppryssit son, Or in þe batel al wndoyn. c **1450** *St. Cuthbert* (Surtees) 4468 All þe strenth of ȝour enmys I sall schende and sone supprys. a **1475** Ashby *Dicta Philos.* 396 The kynge hathe the charge theim to supprise, That wolde surmonte, or in vices arise. **1594** Marlowe & Nashe *Dido* i. i, Ay me! the Starres supprisde like Rhesus Steedes, Are drawne by darknes forth Astræus tents. **1601** Chester *K. Arthur* iv, Chaste to her husbands cleare vnspotted bed, Whose honor-bearing Fame none could supprize. c **1614** Mure *Dido & Æneas* i. 157 His kinde she hates, which should the same supprise.

5. a. To undertake. **b.** To uphold. *rare.*

c **1401** Lydg. *Floure Curtesye* 232 Euer as I can supprise in myn herte. c **1430** *Syr Gener.* (Roxb.) 1912 Demean you al wey in such wise Min honour and worship I may supprise.

Hence †**supprised** *ppl. a.*, (*a*) oppressed (in quot. c 1400 *absol.*), (*b*) appearing suddenly; †**suppriser**, ? betrayer; †**supprising** *vbl. sb.*, surprise, unexpected attack; †**supprission** (-icioun), oppression.

1375 Barbour *Bruce* vii. 551 The kyng, That had no dreid of supprising, ȝeid vnarmyt, mery and blith. c **1400** *Apol. Loll.* 79 Goddis law biddiþ help þe supprised, jugiþ to þe fadirles, defendiþ þe wydow. c **1425** Wyntoun *Cron.* iv. 2026 (MS. Wemyss), And vnder gret exactioun Haldin in to suppricioun [*MS. Cott.* 2020 supprission]. a **1547** Surrey *Æneid* iv. 37 She..with supprised teares [orig. *lacrimis obortis*] Bained her brest. **1592** Breton *Pilgr. Parad.* (Grosart) 11/2 Thou wicked witch,..To bring a desperate spirit to defame, And by illusion, first the soules supriser, That heares thy wordes, and wil beleeue the same.

suppryme: see SUPPRIME.

†**su'ppullulate**, *v. Obs. rare.* [f. L. *sup-* = SUB- 27 + *pullulāt-*: see PULLULATE.] *intr.* To sprout forth in place of another.

1601 Bp. W. BARLOW *Defence* 175 These Hydraheaded expositions, one suppullulating after another. **1609** —— *Answ. Nameless Cath.* 236 Such Hydra-headed Treasons, suppullulating one after the other.

†**'suppurable**, *a. Obs. rare.* [ad. mod.L. *suppūrābilis*, f. L. *suppūrāre* to SUPPURATE: see -ABLE.] Liable to suppurate; suppurating.

1684 tr. *Bonet's Merc. Compit.* VIII. 286 The Liver is of little sense;..therefore crude ones [*sc.* tumours] cannot be distinguished from suppurable ones, but in process of time. **1758** J. S. *Le Dran's Observ. Surg.* (1771) 88 A Reflux of suppurable Matter.

suppurant ('sʌpjʊərənt), *a.* and *sb. rare.* [ad. L. *suppūrantem*, pres. pple. of *suppūrāre* to SUPPURATE.] = SUPPURATIVE *a.* 2 and *sb.*

1767 GOOCH *Treat. Wounds* I. 218 Their secret applications, which they termed attrahents, but are to be looked upon only as suppurants. **1889** *Mayne's Med. Vocab.* (ed. 6), *Suppurant*... festering: suppurating.

†**'suppurate**, *ppl. a. Obs. rare.* [ad. L. *suppūrātus*, pa. pple. of *suppūrāre* (see next).] Formed by suppuration.

1601 HOLLAND *Pliny* XXII. xxv. II. 138 In case it be needfull..to cleanse them from suppurat matter therein gathered.

suppurate ('sʌpjʊəreɪt), *v.* Also 7 supurate. [f. L. *suppūrāt-*, pa. ppl. stem of *suppūrāre*, f. *sup-* = SUB- 2 + *pūr-*, *pūs* PUS. Cf. F. *suppurer*.]

†**1.** *trans.* To cause (a sore, tumour, etc.) to form or secrete pus; to bring to a head. Also *absol.* to induce suppuration. *Obs.*

1563 T. GALE *Antidot.* I. vi. 4 When as all hope is paste by other medicines, then we take those in vse whyche doe suppurate. **1600** SURFLET *Country Farm* III. lxxxiv. 626 This oile is singular good for to suppurate and ripen impostumes. **1694** SALMON *Bate's Dispens.* (1713) 696/2 It..dissolves or suppurates Venereal Buboes. **1779** *Gentl. Mag.* Feb. 80/2 When these tumours are suppurated and broke, or opened, they need only to be frequently cleansed.

2. *intr.* To form or secrete pus, come to a head.

1656 RIDGLEY *Pract. Physick* 131 A little swelling..which suppurating is like a Barly-corn. **1732** ARBUTHNOT *Rules of Diet* in *Aliments*, etc. (1735) 348 This Disease..is generally fatal if it suppurates, the Pus is evacuated into the lower Belly. **1794–6** E. DARWIN *Zoon.* (1801) I. 441 If these glands suppurate externally, they gradually heal. **1843** R. J. GRAVES *Syst. Clin. Med.* xxvi. 331 If the ulcer suppurated freely, the dressing was used oftener. **1854** H. MILLER *Sch. & Schm.* vi. (1858) 119 My injured foot..suppurated and discharged great quantities of blood and matter. **1876** *Trans. Clinical Soc.* IX. 136 Although the cyst..had not suppurated.

†**b.** *intr.* (*transf.*) To exude like pus. *Obs. rare.*

1693 EVELYN *De la Quint. Compl. Gard.* II. 38 By reason that the wound cannot soon be clos'd, and that the Gum Supurates through it.

Hence **'suppurated** *ppl. a.*, **'suppurating** *vbl. sb.* (also *attrib.*); also †**'suppurater** = SUPPURATIVE *sb.*

1612 WOODALL *Surg. Mate* Wks. (1653) 1 The incision Knife..for the opening of any Apostume suppurated. **1684** tr. *Bonet's Merc. Compit.* II. 45 If the Bubo give no hope of Suppuration..when you have used Suppuraters a long time [etc.]. **1747** tr. *Astruc's Fevers* 123 Whilst they are simply obstructed, they are called crude; but if they begin to suppurate, they are called suppurated. **1758** J. S. *Le Dran's Observ. Surg.* (1771) 88 Was it a Reflux of suppurated Pus? **1813** J. THOMSON *Lect. Inflam.* 304 These diversities in the appearance and duration of the suppurating process. **1822–7** GOOD *Study Med.* (1829) I. 476 Where it [*sc.* the pancreas] was found suppurated and gangrenous. **1842** ABDY *Water Cure* 13 They remained..nearly two weeks, without suppurating.

suppurating ('sʌpjʊəreɪtɪŋ), *ppl. a.* [f. prec. + -ING².] That suppurates.

1. Promoting suppuration.

1612 WOODALL *Surg. Mate* Wks. (1653) 88 A contused wound..will desire also suppurating medicines. **1876** tr. *von Ziemssen's Cycl. Med.* XI. 92 Mezereon, croton oil..and suppurating ointments of various kinds.

2. Forming or secreting pus; attended or marked by suppuration.

1647 MAY *Hist. Parl.* I. vii. 77 Now we see what the sores are..let us be very carefull to draw out the cores of them, not to skin them over with a slight suppurating festring cure, least they breake out againe. **1803** *Med. Jrnl.* IX. 85 To convert every recent wound into a suppurating sore. **1843** R. J. GRAVES *Syst. Clin. Med.* xxii. 266 Suppurating pneumonia. *Ibid.* xxix. 371 A suppurating tumour resembling a whitlow. **1899** *Allbutt's Syst. Med.* VI. 574 Suppurating corns.

suppuration (sʌpjʊə'reɪʃən). Also 6 -acyon. [ad. L. *suppūrātio*, *-ōnem*, n. of action f. *suppūrāre* to SUPPURATE. Cf. F. *suppuration*.]

1. The process or condition of suppurating; the formation or secretion of pus; the coming to a head of a boil or other eruption.

1541 COPLAND *Galyen's Terap.* 2 Fijb, Yf there be.. vehement pulsacyon, in such wyse that there is no more hope of the curacyon of the sayd partyes without suppuracyon, all the auncyentes apply the sayd suppuratyfe medycynes. **1543** TRAHERON *Vigo's Chirurg.* II. xxi. 23 An aposteme..that commethe to suppuration by the ayde of medicines and nature. **1676** WISEMAN *Chirurg. Treat.* IV. iv. 267, I applied again the *Malagma*, which caused a Suppuration of the remainder. **1732** ARBUTHNOT *Rules of Diet* in *Aliments*, etc. (1735) 342 The Inflammation ends in a Suppuration and an Abscess in the Lungs. **1797** M. BAILLIE *Morb. Anat.* (1807) 79 When inflammation of the lungs terminates in suppuration. **1868** DARWIN *Anim. & Pl.* xii. II. 12 A cow lost a horn by suppuration. **1899** *Allbutt's Syst. Med.* VIII. 762 The suppuration of acne spots.

†**2.** A suppurating or suppurated boil, sore, etc.

1603 HOLLAND *Plutarch's Mor.* 57 One that had a suppuration in his chist. **1607** TOPSELL *Four-f. Beasts* 259 The dung..being applyed to the suppurations. **1658** ROWLAND tr. *Moufet's Theat. Ins.* 1105 They will concoct the Impostumes and suppurations of the breasts.

suppurative ('sʌpjʊərətɪv), *a.* and *sb.* Also 6 -yfe. [ad. mod.L. *suppūrātīvus*, f. *suppūrāt-*: see SUPPURATE *v.* and -IVE. Cf. F. *suppuratif* (from 16th c.), It., Pg. *suppurativo*, Sp. *supurativo*.]

A. *adj.*

1. Having the property of causing suppuration; inducing the formation of pus.

1541 [see SUPPURATION 1]. **1607** TOPSELL *Four-f. Beasts* 705 It is meet to vse a suppuratiue and not a gluttinatiue maner of cure. *c* **1720** W. GIBSON *Farrier's Dispens.* i. (1734) 23 Rye... It's chief Service is in suppurative and discutient Charges or Cataplasms. **1760–72** J. ADAMS tr. *Juan & Ulloa's Voy.* (ed. 3) I. 46 A small suppurative plaister. **1822–7** GOOD *Study Med.* (1829) IV. 404 Those irritant, exulcerant, or suppurative applications, which have been employed by many practitioners.

2. Attended or characterized by suppuration.

1794 J. R. COXE *Ess. Inflamm.* 54 Mr. John Hunter has divided inflammation into the adhesive, the suppurative and the ulcerative. **1835–6** *Todd's Cycl. Anat.* I. 61/2 This suppurative sloughing process had opened a passage..into the..colon. **1879** *St. George's Hosp. Rep.* IX. 621 Suppurative catarrh of the middle ear.

B. *sb.* A medicine or preparation which promotes suppuration.

1568 SKEYNE *The Pest* (1860) 40 Gif the humore be malignant,..suppuratiues most be expede [*sic*]. **1671** SALMON *Syn. Med.* III. xvi. 368 Suppuratives..bring blood, raw, superfluous and undigested humours to matter and ripeness. **1766** *Phil. Trans.* LVI. 93 Strong suppuratives, in the form of cataplasms, were now used. **1822–7** GOOD *Study Med.* (1829) III. 508 Increasing the tone of the vessels, by warm suppuratives and astringents. **1887** MOLONEY *Forestry W. Afr.* 292 *Fagonia arabica*,..this plant has a great reputation in India as a suppurative in the cases of abscess.

†**'suppuratory**, *a.* and *sb. Obs. rare.* [ad. L. *suppūrātōrius*, f. *suppūrāt-*: see SUPPURATE *v.* and -ORY².] = SUPPURATIVE *a.* 2 and *sb.*

1657 TOMLINSON *Renou's Disp.* I. xiv. 30 That [medicament] is called *Διαπυητικόν*, or a suppuratory, which is most congruent and like to our nature. **1730** *Phil. Trans.* XXXVI. 362 Purulent, suppuratory and scrophulous Distempers. **1747** tr. *Astruc's Fevers* 280 At the approach of the suppuratory fever.

†**suppure**, *v. Obs. rare*⁻⁰. [a. F. *suppurer*, ad. L. *suppūrāre* to SUPPURATE.] To suppurate.

1611 COTGR., *Maturer*,..to matter, to suppure.

†**'supputate**, *v. Obs.* (Also *pa. pple.* in 6 -ate.) [f. L. *supputāt-*, pa. ppl. stem of *supputāre*: see SUPPUTE *v.* and -ATE³.] *trans.* To calculate, reckon, compute. Also *absol.* or *intr.*

1559 W. CUNNINGHAM *Cosmogr. Glasse* 107 Adde the degrees, and mi. to the Longitude (for which th' Ephemerides ar supputated, because thy place is East from it). **1571** DIGGES *Pantom.* IV. xxi. Ciijb, Behold the table folowing, where ye shal finde the number of all the sides, diameters and Axes of these inscribed bodyes ready supputate. **1614** SELDEN *Titles Hon.* I. iii. 163 Their Hegira ..is supputated from the flight of Mahumed, out of Mecha. **1680** AUBREY in *Lett. Eminent Persons* (1813) III. 490 He supputated, and found that everything considered 'twas much dearer. **1691** WOOD *Ath. Oxon.* I. 158 Ephemerides.. supputated..for the elevation and meridian of London.

†**suppu'tation**. *Obs.* [ad. L. *supputātio*, *-ōnem*, n. of action f. *supputāre* to SUPPUTE. Cf. F. *supputation* (from 16th c.).]

1. The action (of or an act) of calculating or computing; a method or system of reckoning; calculation, computation, reckoning.

1432–50 tr. *Higden* (Rolls) I. 27 Florentius, monke of Wurcestre, whom y folowe specially with Marianus Scotte in the supputacion of yeres. **1545** JOYE *Exp. Dan.* Bjb, A brife supputation of the ages and yeres of the world. **1555** EDEN *Decades* (Arb.) 65 Euery leaque conteyneth foure myles, after theyr supputations. **1560** BIBLE (Geneva) *Esther* Argt. 218b, The supputation of yeres, wherein the Ebrewes, and the Grecians do varie. **1650** TWYSDEN in Rigaud *Corr. Sci. Men* (1841) I. 67 For the ready supputation of the places of the planets. **1652–62** HEYLIN *Cosmogr.* Introd. (1672) 17/2 Chronologies..are only bare supputations of times, with some brief touch upon the Actions therein hapning. **1696** AUBREY *Misc.* 24 The skill of dealing with difficult supputations of Numbers not then discoverable. **1698** HEARNE *Duct. Hist.* (1714) I. 7 The Julian Period..is a supputation of 7980 years. Invented by Julius Scaliger. **1751** *Act 24 Geo. II*, c. 23 §1 That..the said Supputation, according to which the Year of our Lord beginneth on the twenty-fifth Day of March, shall not be made use of from and after the last Day of December, one thousand seven hundred and fifty-one. **1825** A. CLARKE *Comm. O.T.*, *Ps.* lxxxi. 3 They..sent persons to the top of some hill..about the time which, according to their supputations, the new moon should appear.

b. *transf.* Estimation, reckoning.

1643 SIR T. BROWNE *Relig. Med.* I. §18 In a wise supputation all things begin and end in the Almighty. **1654** TRAPP *Comm. Job* xxxviii. 18 They have their supputations and conjectures. **1677** PLOT *Oxfordsh.* 224 He so disturbed and confounded all his supputations, that [etc.].

2. (See quot.) *rare*⁻⁰.

1656 BLOUNT *Glossogr.*, *Supputation*.., a pruyning or cutting Trees.

†**su'ppute**, *v. Obs.* [ad. L. *supputāre* to cut off below, lop, prune, to count up, f. *sup-* = SUB- 2 + *putāre* to trim, prune, to clear up, settle, reckon. Cf. F. *supputer* (from 16th c.).] = SUPPUTATE. Hence †**su'pputed** *ppl. a.* (*fig.*)

1432–50 tr. *Higden* (Rolls) I. 37 þe Romanes..ascribede theire yeres from the begynnenge of theire cite y-made. But ..Cristen men suppute theire yeres from the Incarnacion of Criste. *Ibid.* V. 453 Men supputenge tymes of kynges. **1622** DRAYTON *Poly-olb.* xxix. 363 Free from this supputed shame. *a* **1727** NEWTON *Chronol. Amended* Introd. (1728) 4 Others supputing the times by the Succession of the Kings of the Lacedæmonians, affirm that he was not a few years older than the first Olympiad.

‖**supra** ('s(j)uːprə), *adv.*, (*a.*), *prep.* [L. *suprā* adv. and prep. (see next).] **A.** *adv.*

1. = ABOVE A. 4; previously, before (in a book or writing). Also in L. phr. ***ut supra*** = as above. (Abbreviated *sup.*)

[*c* **1440** *Promp. Parv.* 355/2 Nyggarde (or muglard, *supra*, or nygun, or pynchar, *infra*), *tenax*.] **1526** in *Exch. Rolls Scot.* XV. 273 *note*, The said pensioun of fourty pundis to the said maister Walter,..quhill he be promovit be ws to benefice ut supra. **1616** R. COCKS *Diary* (Hakl. Soc.) I. 100, 10 cattis tobaco to hym selfe, cost as *supra*. **1668** in *Extr. St. Papers rel. Friends* Ser. III. (1912) 279 The book called The sandy Foundation Shaken, of the same date, ut supra. **1753** *Chambers' Cycl.* Suppl. s.v. *Leaf*, *Villose* Leaf. See *Pilose* Leaf, supra. **1861** PALEY *Æschylus* (ed. 2) *Supplices* 953 *note*, On the metre of this verse see supra 7.

†**2.** = ABOVE A. 7; in addition, further; more.

1592 NASHE *Strange Newes* H2, Was sinne so vtterly abolished with Tarltons play of the seuen deadly sins, that ther could be nothing said *supra* of that argument? **1778** STILES *Diary* 24 Sept. (1901) II. 302 Mr. Beers æt. 60 & supra.

†**B.** *adj.* Additional, extra. *Obs.*

1598 BARRET *Theor. Warres* IV. iv. 115 The which being not aduertised that they be any *supra* Round, he is bound to giue the word to none but only vnto the Sentinell. **1773** *Ann. Reg.*, *Chron.* 89/1 To defray the supra charge of coinage.

C. *prep.* in phr. ***supra protest*** [ad. It. *sopra protesto* 'upon protest']: see quots. and PROTEST *sb.* 2.

1809 R. LANGFORD *Introd. Trade* 22 After a bill has been protested, it is sometimes accepted by a third party, for the purpose of saving the reputation of a drawer or of an endorser. Such an acceptance is called an acceptance 'Supra Protest'. **1847** B. F. FOSTER *Counting-ho. Assist.* 87 Payment supra protest. *Ibid.* 99 The acceptor *supra* protest is bound to notify without delay his acceptance to the person for whose honor it was made.

supra- ('s(j)uːprə), *prefix*, repr. L. *suprā-* = *suprā* (related to *super* and ultimately to *sub*) adv. and prep., above, beyond, in addition (to), before in time, occurring in a few compounds in classical and late Latin; in med. and mod.L. it is mainly restricted to technical terms. Its meanings in English are for the most part parallel to, but in much less vogue than, those of SUPER-; but it is more prevalent than the latter in certain uses, e.g. the scientific uses in 1 a and 1 b, in which it is most commonly employed as a living prefix.

The stressing is as in compounds of SUPER-, q.v.

I. Over, above, higher than; (less commonly) on, upon: in a physical sense.

1. In prepositional relation to the sb. implied in, or constituting, the second element: = SUPER- 1; as in late L. *suprācælestis* SUPRACELESTIAL, mod.L. *suprā-axillāris* (*axilla* AXIL), *suprāfoliāceus* (*folium* leaf).

a. Miscellaneous adjs., chiefly scientific: = SUPER- 1 a, c. ˌ**supra-'aerial**, situated above the air or atmosphere; ˌ**supra-'axillary**, *Bot.*, arising above an axil, as a branch or bud; **supra'coralline**, *Geol.*, lying immediately above the Coralline Oolite; ˌ**supracre'taceous**, *Geol.*, lying above the Cretaceous series, as the Tertiary and more recent formations; **supra'crustal** *a.* and *sb. Geol.*, (a stratum, formation, etc.) lying above the basement rocks of the crust; **supra'facial** *a. Chem.*, (of a concerted reaction undergone by a molecule) involving the formation of two new bonds on the same face of the molecule; ˌ**suprafoli'aceous**, **supra'foliar**, *Bot.*, situated or arising above (or upon) a leaf; **supra'glacial**, occurring upon the surface of ice, esp. of a glacier; **supra'lineal**, written above the line; **supra'littoral** *a. Ecol.*, applied to a biogeographic zone normally taken as extending from mean high tide to the limit of influential sea spray or land vegetation; also *ellipt.* as *sb.*; ˌ**suprama'rine**, situated or occurring above the sea; **supra'medial**, lying above the middle (e.g. of a series of rocks); **supra'tropical**, next 'above', i.e. higher in latitude than, the tropical (see quot.).

1694 HALLEY in *Phil. Trans.* XXXIII. 120 The Firmament, supposed by Moses to sustain a *Supra-aerial Sea. **1760** J. LEE *Introd. Bot.* III. xxi. (1765) 218 *Supra-axillary. **1870** HOOKER *Stud. Flora* 256 Solanum,.. flowers in the forks of the stem, or supra-axillary. **1885** ETHERIDGE *Strat. Geol.* xli. 453 The *Supra-Coralline Beds. **1832** DE LA BECHE *Geol. Man.* (ed. 2) 221 The marine *supracretaceous rocks of the South of France. **1852** LYELL *Man. Elem. Geol.* ix. (ed. 4) 103 Groups of Fossiliferous Strata.. Tertiary, Supracretaceous, or Cainozoic. **1946** *Amer. Jrnl. Sci.* CCXLIV. 851 The *supracrustal formations are subjected to folding, plastic deformation, fractures and thrusts in which the blocks of the basement also take part. **1973** *Nature* 21 Sept. 138/1 The Isua supracrustals may represent a shallow-water shelf facies. **1965** WOODWARD & HOFFMANN in *Jrnl. Amer. Chem. Soc.* LXXXVII. 2512/1 In the first process, here designated *suprafacial, the hydrogen atom is associated at all times with the same face of the π-system. **1980** E. N. MARVELL *Thermal Electrocyclic Reactions* i. 5 Thus for a π bond a suprafacial process forms new connections on the same side of the nodal plane. **1777** S. ROBSON *Brit. Flora* 21 **Supra-foliaceous*, coming out above the leaves, as in Asperifoliæ. **1866** *Treas. Bot.* 1111/1 **Suprafoliar*, growing upon a leaf. **1894** GEIKIE *Gt. Ice Age* (ed. 3) 207 The beds of these *supra-glacial rivers. **1874** T. H. KEY *Language* 61 The fact of its [*sc.* the aspirate's] having passed into a mere *supra-lineal mark in classical Greek suggests the question whether it had not even in those days become an unmeaning symbol. **1909** WARMING & VAHL *Œcol. Plants* IV. xli. 173 Thus arises a kind a *supra-littoral 'region'. **1949** T. A. & A. STEPHENSON in *Jrnl. Ecol.* XXXVII. 298 We therefore formally propose that the three main zones of the shore be called: Supralittoral Fringe, Midlittoral Zone, Infralittoral Fringe. **1967** *Oceanogr. & Marine Biol.* V. 464 The plants and animals living in the supralittoral zone can either tolerate or need a permanent or almost permanent emersion, but with moistening by sprays and waves. **1974** *Nature* 22 Feb. 520/2 The environmental significance of each of these.. seems to reflect various aspects of turbulence, turbidity, and/or desiccation in the littoral or supralittoral. **1832** LYELL *Princ. Geol.* II. 195 The effects.. of subterranean action on *supramarine land. **1863** —— *Antiq. Man* xiii. (ed. 3) 232 Difficulty in distinguishing between the effects of the submarine and supramarine agency of ice. **1855** J. PHILLIPS *Man. Geol.* 157 Millstone grit (*supramedial group). **1826** KIRBY & SP. *Entomol.* IV. xlix. 485 Beginning at 84° N.L. he [*sc.* Latreille] has seven Arctic ones [*sc.* climates], which he names polar, subpolar, superior, intermediate, *supratropical, tropical, and equatorial.

b. *Anat.* and *Zool.* Extensively used to form adjectives (some of which are also used *ellipt.* as sbs.) in the sense 'Situated above, or on the dorsal side of (sometimes, upon the upper surface of) the part or organ denoted by the second element': as in mod.L. *suprācostālis* (*costa* rib), *suprārēnālis* SUPRARENAL. = SUPER- 1 b.

Numerous compounds of this class appear in recent Dicts., general and technical; the following is a selection of the more important. The meaning can usually be inferred from that of the second element; where necessary, a brief explanation or reference is added in parentheses. (Cf. SUB- 1 b.)

supra-ab'dominal, supra-a'cromial, supra-'anal, supra-'angular (the angular bone of the lower jaw in some vertebrates: cf. ANGULAR 2 a, quot. 1855), ***supra-ary'tenoid, supra-'auditory, supra-au'ricular, supra'branchial, supra'buccal, supra'cæcal, supra'caudal, supra'condylar, -'condyloid*** (= above a condyle or condyles of the humerus, femur, etc.), ***supra'costal, supra'coxal, supra'cranial*** (= on the upper surface of the cranium), ***supra'-dorsal, supra'dural*** (= above the dura mater), ***supra-'ethmoid, supra'glottic*** (above the glottis), ***suprahe'patic*** (on the upper surface of the liver), ***supra'hyoid, supra-'iliac*** (= on the upper surface of the ilium), ***supra'marginal*** (*spec.* above the upper edge of the Sylvian fissure), ***supra'mastoid, supra'nasal, supra-'nervian, supra'neural*** (= above a neural axis), ***supra'nuclear*** (NUCLEUS), ***supra-'ocular*** (= above the ocular region, *spec.* of the small scales in reptiles above the superciliaries; also *sb.*), ***supra-œso'phageal*** (= on the dorsal side of the œsophagus, applied to a nervous ganglia in invertebrates), ***suprapa'pillary*** (= above the biliary papilla), ***suprapa'tellar, supra'pedal*** (= above the 'foot' of a mollusc), ***supraphar'yngeal*** (= *supra-œsophageal*), ***supra'pubian, -'pubic*** (hence ***supra'pubically*** adv., above the pubis), ***supra'pygal*** (of plates of the carapace in tortoises; also *sb.*), ***supra'rimal*** (RIMA), ***supra'septal*** (SEPTUM), ***suprasta'pedial, supra'sternal, supra'trochlear*** (TROCHLEA (*a*), (*b*)), ***supratym'panic, supraumbi'lical, supraven'tricular*** (VENTRICLE 1 and 2); **suprameatal** (-miːˈeɪtəl) *a.*, situated above the acoustic meatus; **supra-'optic** *a.* situated above the optic chiasma; **supra'sellar** *a.*, situated or occurring above the sella turcica.

1835–6 *Todd's Cycl. Anat.* I. 114/1 Two *supra-abdominal nervous columns generally extend along the middle of the back. **1840** G. V. ELLIS *Anat.* 130 The *transversalis humeri* artery.. ends by dividing into the *supra-acromial and supra-scapular arteries. **1893** H. MORRIS *Treat. Hum. Anat.* 831 The supra-acromial branches cross the clavicular insertion of the trapezius and the acromion process. **1867** LANKESTER in *Ann. & Mag. Nat. Hist.* Nov. 335 The *supra-anal organ is very small. **1835–6** *Todd's Cycl. Anat.* I. 277/1 The anterior extremities of the angular and *supra-angular pieces are wedged into corresponding grooves of the symphyseal element. **1896** NEWTON *Dict. Birds* 872 The bones forming the right and left Mandibulæ.. namely, the Dentals, Splenials, Supra-angulars, Angulars and Articulars. **1872** COHEN *Dis. Throat* 48 The arytenoid and the *supra-arytenoid cartilages, with their connecting muscle. **1866** HUXLEY *Laing's Preh. Rem. Caithn.* 87 The mastoid processes are large, the *supra-auditory ridges strong. **1890** BILLINGS *Nat. Med. Dict.*, **Supra-auricular diameter*, parietal diameter, inferior. **1916** KEITH in *Man* XVI. 101 Skull of an aged man. Maximum length, 195 mm.; width, 140 mm.;.. height (supra-auricular), 116 mm. **1889** DUNMAN & WINGRAVE *Gloss. Terms*, **Supra-branchial*, applied to the dorsal division of the pallial chamber in the Lamellibranchiata.. above the gills, which separate it from the infra-branchial chamber. **1883** *Encycl. Brit.* XVI. 665/1 Large special ganglia (optic, stellate, and *supra-buccal) are developed in the higher forms (Siphonopoda). **1901** P. C. MITCHELL in *Trans. Linn. Soc., Zool.* Oct. 188 In *Spheniscus* the portion between the supra-duodenal loop and the rectum.. is expanded into a minor fold,.. to which I give the name '*supra-cæcal kink'. **1890** *Proc. Zool. Soc. Lond.* 180 The *supracaudal muscle is the direct continuation backwards of the *spinalis dorsi.* **1881** MIVART *Cat* 91 An elongated opening.. called the *supracondylar foramen which transmits the median nerve and brachial artery. **1899** *Allbutt's Syst. Med.* VI. 659 Supracondylar fracture may readily implicate the nerve. **1866** *Quain's Elem. Nat.* (ed. 7) II. 385 The occasional prominence called the *supracondyloid process. **1884** T. BRYANT *Pract. Surg.* (ed. 4) II. 634 Mr. W. Stokes, of Dublin, advocates.. the supra-condyloid amputation of the thigh. **1855** OGILVIE *Suppl.*, **Supra-costal*,.. the supra-costal muscles, which raise the ribs. **1890** BILLINGS *Nat. Med. Dict.*, *Supracostal groove*, light furrow sometimes found along upper edge of the body of a rib, at its posterior extremity. **1872** HUMPHRY *Myology* 21 The *supra-coxal part of the pelvis. **1848** OWEN *Homol. Vertebrate Skel.* 48 The frontals and parietals, being ossified in *supra-cranial fibrous membrane. **1889** *Nature* 20 June 172/1 The.. details of the mouth-plates, the *supradorsal membrane,.. and other.. portions. **1889** *Buck's Handbk. Med. Sci.* VIII. 232/2 *Supradural branch or *ramus parietalis.* **1888** ROLLESTON & JACKSON *Anim. Life* 96 In the Salmon this region [*sc.* the mesethmoidal cartilage].. is covered by a *supra-ethmoid bony plate. **1890** *Retrospect Med.* CII. 302 The narrowing of the *supraglottic portion of the larynx. **1848** DUNGLISON *Med. Lex.* s.v. *Hepatic*, Hepatic Veinsor *Supra-hepatic veins.. open into the vena cava inferior. **1904** *Brit. Med. Jrnl.* 17 Sept. 672 In suprahepatic abscess the pus occurs between the layers of the coronary ligament. **1882** *Quain's Elem. Anat.* (ed. 9) I. 292 *Suprahyoid muscles. **1870** FLOWER *Osteol. Mammalia* XVII. 285 The ilium is flattened and expanded, and has a greatly extended.. *supra-iliac border. **1872** H. A. NICHOLSON *Palæont.* 109 Ananchytidæ.. anus.. marginal, or *supramarginal. **1899** *Allbutt's Syst. Med.* VII. 433 The left visual word-centre.. is now.. supposed to be situated in the angular and possibly in part of the supramarginal convolution. **1893** H. MORRIS *Treat. Hum. Anat.* 37 A ridge of bone, the *supra-mastoid crest, runs immediately above the external auditory meatus. **1893** W. MACEWEN *Pyogenic Infective Dis. of Brain & Spinal Cord* i. 9 The apex of this triangular depressed area points forward. The author proposes to name this area the *supra-meatal triangle. **1922** *Brit. Med. Jrnl.* 29 July 164/2 Later experience in using this suprameatal angle as a guide has been extensive. **1980** *Gray's Anat.* (ed. 36) iii. 302/2 Immediately above and behind the meatus there is frequently a small depression with a bony spicule (suprameatal spine) in its anterior margin. This lies within the area of the suprameatal triangle. **1865** *Reader* No. 145. 409/1 The *supranasal notch. **1903** *Proc. Zool. Soc. Lond.* II. 125 Nostril pierced in a single nasal; no supranasal. **1888** *Supranervian [see *subnervian*, SUB- 1 b]. **1899** *Allbutt's Syst. Med.* VII. 623 The *supra-nuclear connections of the nerve. **1977** *Lancet* 12 Nov. 1029/2 One [patient] had periodic vertigo due to a supranuclear vestibular lesion. **1979** *Jrnl. Compar. Path.* LXXXIX. 503 The supranuclear cytoplasm of the superficial epithelial cells. **1897** GÜNTHER in Mary Kingsley *W. Africa* 696 Two large *supraoculars on each side. **1835–6** *Todd's Cycl. Anat.* I. 524/1 The.. *supra-œsophageal ganglions are protected by a dense membrane. **1840** *Penny Cycl.* XVI. 112/2 The brain, or supracœsophageal mass. **1921** TILNEY & RILEY *Form & Function Central Nerv. Syst.* xxxi. 550 Situated above the optic chiasm and in communication with the chamber of the third ventricle is a small canal which projects outward over the optic nerve. This is the *supra-optic canal. **1980** K. E. MOYER *Neuroanatomy* xxviii. 70/2 The supra-optic nucleus is located directly over the lateral portion of the optic chiasm. **1897** *Allbutt's Syst. Med.* III. 723 The duodenum is more extensively dilated [in infra-papillary carcinoma] than in *supra-papillary carcinoma. **1902** D. J. CUNNINGHAM *Text-bk. Anat.* 293 The joint-cavity may communicate with bursæ situated in relation to the inner head of the gastrocnemius muscle and the tendon of the semi-membranosus muscle, besides the large *supra-patellar bursa already described. **1975** L. M. ELSON *It's your Body* v. 284 (*caption*) Supra-patellar bursa. **1888** ROLLESTON & JACKSON *Anim. Life* 110 A *supra-pedal gland appears to be present in all *Pulmonata.* **1878** BELL tr. *Gegenbaur's Comp. Anat.* 351 There is but one buccal ganglion in the Dibranchiata, and behind it there is a large *supra-pharyngeal ganglion. **1848** DUNGLISON *Med. Lex.*, **Supra-Pubian Nerve*, is the internal ramus of the inguino-cutaneous branch of the first lumbar nerve. **1835–6** *Todd's Cycl. Anat.* I. 507/1 The shortest route by which the bladder can be reached at this early age is according to the method of the *suprapubic operation. **1847–9** *Ibid.* IV. 280/1 In the turtles.. the supra-pubic muscle divides into two fasciculi. **1887** *Brit. Med. Jrnl.* I. 1098/2 A suprapubic abscess. *Ibid.* 1214/2 Supra-pubic lithotomy in a boy. *Ibid.* 204/2, I.. proceeded to open the bladder *suprapubically upon the point of an ordinary lithotomy-staff. **1889** NICHOLSON & LYDEKKER *Palæont.* II. 1086 While.. the nuchal is a cartilage bone, the pygal and *suprapygals are of purely dermal origin. **1893** H. MORRIS *Treat. Hum. Anat.* 948 The cavity is naturally divided into two portions—*supra- and infra-rimal—divided by the glottis. **1934** J. H. GLOBUS *Neuroanatomy* (ed. 6) I. 15 The diamond shaped somewhat depressed space outlined at the base of the brain is called the interpeduncular space..; and because it overlies the sella turcica in the base of the skull, it is often termed the *suprasellar space. **1977** *Lancet* 9 Apr. 780/1 Air encephalograms were performed on 7 of the 12 patients with prolactin levels between 15 and 30 μg/l and in all 7 suprasellar extension of the tumour was found. **1890** *Q. Jrnl. Micros. Sci.* XXX. 137 The smaller division of the cœlom, the *supraseptal cavity, is continued into the tentacles. **1875** W. K. PARKER in *Encycl. Brit.* III. 710/2 The short, notched *supra-stapedial.. the slender, combined infra-stapedial and stylo-hyal.. are still cartilaginous. **1862** H. W. FULLER *Dis. Lungs* 4 The *supra-sternal is the hollowed space which lies immediately above the notch of the sternum. **1876** *Quain's Elem. Anat.* (ed. 8) I. 27 The occurrence of suprasternal bones in some animals. **1882** *Ibid.* (ed. 9) I. 27 The upper end [of the sternum] is marked by the deep suprasternal notch. **1836–9** *Todd's Cycl. Anat.* II. 280/1 It [*sc.* the frontal nerve].. ascends round the superciliary arch,.. and is thenceforth called by some the external frontal nerve in contradistinction to a branch from itself, the *supra trochlear, or internal frontal. **1870** FLOWER *Osteol. Mammalia* x. 157 The large *supratympanic or mastoid bulla [of *Pedetes caffer*]. **1906** *Practitioner* Dec. 781 Rolleston thinks that, for practical purposes, it is advisable to adopt Oppenheim's division of the reflex into a *supra-umbilical and infra-umbilical zone. **1978** *Acta Path. Japonica* XXVIII. 288 Just after birth.., this female patient showed deep cyanosis and supraumbilical abdominal hernia. **1865** *Reader* 11 Mar. 288 The *supra-ventricular masses of the hemispheres [of the brain]. **1974** *Ciba Symposium* XX. 133 Localization of the infiltrate in the AV node blocks the supraventricular impulses when the atrial rate increases. **1979** *Brit. Med. Jrnl.* 15 Dec. 1553/2 Disopyramide.. has been used to treat supraventricular and ventricular arrhythmias.

c. With sb., denoting a part situated above that denoted by the second element, as mod.L. *suprăclāvicula*, SUPRACLAVICLE.

d. *Phonology.* ***supra'dental*** (also as *sb.*), ***supra'glottal*** (also as *sb.*), ***suprala'ryngeal.***

1926 B. KARLGREN *Philology & Ancient China* iv. 80 No pronouncement is here made about whether these sounds were hard, *supradental ('cerebrals'), *tṣ-*, *tṣ'-*, *ṣ-*, etc., somewhat resembling English heart*sh*aped. **1969** *Language* XLV. 125 To say that the supradentals are merely occurrence phenomena of [r] plus dental leads to undesirable results. **1935** *Amer. Speech* X. 311/2 The quality of vowels depends not only on *supra-glottal resonances, but.. on the complex and variable sound emmitted by the larynx. **1964** CRYSTAL & QUIRK *Prosodic & Paralinguistic Features in Eng.* iii. 39 Supraglottals may be tense or lax. **1979** *Amer. Speech 1978* LIII. 290 The supraglottal articulatory motions and positions used in human language.. are not used by other animals at all. **1964** J. C. CATFORD in D. Abercrombie et al. *Daniel Jones* 29 Phoneticians should be able to classify 'voice qualities' and other phonatory activities in as systematic a way as they classify *supralaryngeal articulation. **1978** *Amer. Speech* LIII. 292 They carefully measured chimpanzee supralaryngeal cavities.

2. In adverbial relation to the second element: = SUPER- 2. † **supra'nominated** *ppl. a.*, above-named. ˌ**suprapo'sition**, the action of placing or state of being placed above or upon something; position above; in quot. 1788 = SUPERPOSITION 2. ˌ**supraso'riferous** *a.*, *Bot.*, bearing sori on the upper surface.

1599 A. M. tr. *Gabelhouer's Bk. Physicke* 344/2 Take.. of the *supra-nominatede poudre 3 qu. of an ownce. **1683** E. HOOKER *Pref. Pordage's Mystic Div.* 105 The Architypous Globe, or Original Beeing is the Basis.. of all other Essences,.. brought forth out of the Womb of pure Nature supra-nominated. **1788** in E. H. Barker *Parriana* (1829) II. 64 Coincidence can only be proved by *supraposition. **1855** T. R. JONES *Aquarian Nat.* 9 Their.. steady supraposition upon each other should ensure.. stability. **1857** T. MOORE *Handbk. Brit. Ferns* (ed. 3) 46 Crenato-lobate above, *suprasoriferous.

3. In adjectival relation to the sb. constituting or implied in the second element: = SUPER- 3.

a. *Anat.* and *Zool.* = Superior, upper; (a structure) situated above some other, or forming or belonging to the upper part of (that denoted by the second element): chiefly in mod.L. terms, as ***supramamma.*** Also **supra'commissure**, a commissure of nerve-fibres above and in front of the pineal body.

1889 *Buck's Handbk. Med. Sci.* VIII. 132/1 The diatela.. is.. continuous with the supracommissure. **1901** DORLAND *Med. Dict.* (ed. 2), Supramaxilla.. Supra-obliquus.. Supra-turbinal. **1902** *Amer. Anthropol.* IV. 172/1 The significance of the 'supramamma' (a sort of rudimentary mamma).

b. *Anat.* and *Zool.* Prefixed to adjs., or forming derivative adjs. from sbs. in a (sometimes used ellipt. as sbs.): = Pertaining to or situated on the upper... or the upper part of (what is expressed by the second element), as ***supralabial*** (the upper lip), ***supramaxillary*** (the upper jaw).

1891 *Cent. Dict.*, *Supralabial. **1904** *Biol. Bulletin* Nov. 293 A black spot, just above the sixth supralabial. *Ibid.*, The supralabials are dusky yellow. **1847–9** *Todd's Cycl. Anat.* IV. 548/1 Its *supra-maxillary part is constituted by one or two large branches. **1872** HUMPHRY *Myology* 46 The supra-maxillary, or second division of the fifth [nerve].

II. Above (in various figurative senses): higher in quality, amount, or degree. (Cf. SUPER- 4, 5, 6.)

4. a. Prefixed to adjectives: = SUPER- 4 a, as ***supra-Christian, -conscious, -decent, -dialectal, -historical, -individual, -intellectual, -legal, literal, -local, -logical, -mechanical, -moral, -normal*** (= SUPERNORMAL), ***-ordinary, -racial, -rational, -regional, -sentential***; **ˌsupramo'lecular**, composed of many molecules; higher in organization than a molecule; **ˌsuprare'lational**, of a postulated being or power that transcends or includes all that is relational; † **supravulgar**, that is above the common or ordinary. Also in derived sbs., as ***supra-rationalism***, and advs., as ***supra-locally***.

1867 SWINBURNE *Blake* (1868) 266 Thus prophesies Blake, in a fury of *supra-Christian dogmatism. **1891** JAS. ORR *Chr. View God & World* ii. (1893) 70 Hartmann.. speaks..of his Absolute..as **supra*-conscious. **1902** *Contemp. Rev.* Mar. 385 Experimental psychical research is throwing great light on..the importance of the subconscious and supraconscious, or the 'Subliminal' self. **1953** J. STRACHEY tr. *Freud's Interpret. of Dreams* in *Compl. Wks* V. vii. 615 We must avoid, too, the distinction between 'supraconscious' and 'subconscious', which has become so popular in the more recent literature of the psychoneuroses, for such a distinction seems precisely calculated to stress the equivalence of what is psychical to what is conscious. **1908** *Hibbert Jrnl.* Jan. 436 The intelligence..tries to apprehend the *supra-corporeal in terms of the corporeal. **1938** S. BECKETT *Murphy* v. 90 As different..as a *voyeur's* from a *voyant's*, though Wylie was no more the one in the indecent sense than Murphy was the other in the *supradecent sense. **1960** P. DORF tr. M. M. Guxman in J. A. Fishman *Readings Sociol. of Lang.* (1968) 768 Even in the formation process of the new written Bashkir national language, the problem of working out a unified, *supradialectal literary norm,..was in the twentieth century just as real as it was in eighteenth- and nineteenth-century Germany or Italy. **1894** N. BUCHANAN tr. *Harnack's Hist. Dogma* I. ii. 97 History and doctrine are surrounded by a bright cloud of the *suprahistorical. **1936** *Mind* XLV. 293, I would fain hold.. that the highest values are, not only *supra-individual, but supra-national. **1885** SETH *Scot. Philos.* vi. 188 The hungering and thirsting of men's hearts after..some *supra-intellectual union..with the source of all. **1875** DIGBY *Real Prop.* vi. (1876) 289 He would..be restrained.. by the extra-legal, or, if the expression may be allowed, *supra-legal power of Chancellor. **1949** *Archivum Linguisticum* I. 164 A mark of palatalization in the shape of a *supraliteral meniscus. **1852** BP. FORBES *Nicene Creed* viii. 146 Immensity..and *supralocal existence, are the qualities of the true God. *Ibid.* xiii. 227 The supra-local Presence of His Body in the Sacrament of the Altar. **1866** *Clerical Jrnl.* 3 May 422/1 Jesus Christ..offers, and..is offered, on all earthly altars supernaturally and *supra-locally. **1896** W. CALDWELL *Schopenhauer's System* i. 42 This fondness of Schopenhauer for the *supra-logical character of intuition and genius has its dangerous side. **1936** *Essays & Studies* XXI. 136 In the case of words like 'spell' and 'Host' the supra-logical connotation and accidental associations reinforce the literal meaning. **1740** CHEYNE *Regimen* 3 Impossible..that an Animal Body could have been.. formed without a *Supra-mechanical Organisation. **1909** *Cent. Dict.* Suppl., **Supramolecular* **1961** *Nature* 8 July 145/1 A supramolecular organization of the enzyme systems. **1976** *Sci. Amer.* July 65/1 One of the major challenges in cell biology today is the mapping of supramolecular structures such as membranes and ribosomes. *a* **1894** ROMANES *Thoughts Relig.* I. ii. (1895) 81 Without being *supra-moral..He may be unmoral. **1897** LANG in *Contemp. Rev.* Dec. 774 *Supranormal phenomena. **1902** W. JAMES *Var. Relig. Exper.* 484 Our supra-normal cognitions, if such there be, and if we are telepathic subjects. **1959** B. WOOTTON *Social Science & Social Pathology* ii. 59 Exceptionally difficult problems, failure to cope adequately with which might well be a sign, ..of their lack of the supra-normal qualities which the situation demands. **1977** J. L. HARPER *Population Biol. of Plants* x. 328 Partial closure of stomata..usually occurs when supra-normal concentrations of CO_2 are applied to leaves. *a* **1623** SWINBURNE *Treat. Spousals* (1686) 22 Yet doth their *supraordinary Understanding..supply that small defect of Age. **1651** N. BACON *Disc. Govt. Eng.* II. xxx. (1739) 136 The Pope had now usurped a power supraordinary over all Appeals. **1922** JOYCE *Ulysses* 717 With what antagonistic sentiments were his subsequent reflections affected?.. Abnegation? In virtue of.. extraracial attraction, intraracial inhibition, *supraracial prerogative. **1894** N. BUCHANAN tr. *Harnack's Hist. Dogma* I. App. iii. 346 The Divine Original Essence is *supra-rational. **1882–3** *Schaff's Encycl. Relig. Knowl.* III. 1995 Their..views were designated as supranaturalism, and not as *suprarationalism or irrationalism. **1973** R. C. VAN CAENEGEM *Birth of Eng. Common Law* i. 14 The justices in eyre or itinerant royal judges..were called *justitiarii totius Angliae*, to indicate that their commission was *supraregional. **1910** W. JAMES *Coll. Ess. & Rev.* (1920) 497 Mr. Bradley tumbles to philosophy's call. Down he slides, to the dry valley of 'absolute' mare's nests and abstractions, the habitation of the fictitious *suprarelational being which his will prefers. **1936** *Mind* XLV. 538 His initially hopeless attempt to make sense..of freedom and individuality in terms of his supra-relational whole. **1961** Y. OLSSON *Syntax Eng. Verb* ii. 34 This constitutes a new kind of intersectional concord, often exceeding the limits of the sentence (**supra-sentential concord*). **1697** COLLIER *Ess. Mor. Subj.* I. (1703) 81 To furnish himself with *supravulgar and noble qualities.

b. Prefixed to a sb., forming an adj., as ***supra-clan, -class, -Elder, -language, -party, -state*** (cf. SUPER- 4 b), ***-village***.

1979 *Social Sci. & Med.* XIII. D. 209/2 Within these dispersed people, there was no *supraclan political system to organize for mutual defense. **1952** C. BARDSLEY *Bishop's Move* viii. 96 A *supra-class Church founded on Life and Love. **1977** M. WALKER *National Front* iv. 84 The NF's supra-class, supra-party appeal. **1958** D. TAIT *Tribes without Rulers* 193 There is no *supra-Elder authority to impose a solution on recalcitrants of a district. **1975** *Amer. Speech 1972* XLVII. 253 Such *supralanguage phenomena as rhyme and assonance in verse. **1914** *Contemp. Rev.* Aug. 200 If there is an inter-State life there is also a *supra-State life. **1974** tr. *Wertheim's Evolution & Revolution* iii. 245 The creation of *supra-village organizations.

5. Prefixed to a sb. = SUPER- 5; as ***supra-entity***.

1647 HERRICK *Noble Numb.*, *Upon God*, God is not onely said to be An Ens, but Supraentitie.

6. = Higher, superior (cf. SUPER- 6 b), as ***supra-body, -burgher, -consciousness, -council, -language, -organism, -parliament***, † ***-passion, -system, -world***.

1967 M. AYUB KHAN *Friends not Masters* xi. 199 There was obviously no place for a *supra-body of religious experts exercising a power of veto over the Legislature and the Judiciary. **1905** JOYCE *Let.* 19 July (1966) II. 99 Also desirables are..a sizeable beefsteak.., and..an intelligent *supra-burgher like yourself to share the meal. **1911** A. MITCHELL tr. *Bergson's Creative Evolution* 275 It is consciousness, or rather *supra-consciousness, that is at the origin of life. **1914** *19th Cent.* July 121 This *supra-consciousness..is seen..to be independent of the material senses. **1974** *Physics Bull.* Mar. 86/1 A formalized *supra-council of scientific institutions. **1980** *Encounter* July 50/1 *Finnegan's Wake*..the project of a *supra-language distinct to the given text. **1949** KOESTLER *Insight & Outlook* II. xi. 167 We must expect the ultimate achievement of a proportionate superiority in the mature human *supra-organism. **1971** *Supra-parliament [see MULTINATIONAL *a.* and *sb.*]. **1624** F. WHITE *Repl. Fisher* 538 The merits and *supra-passions of Saints. **1964** *Language* XL. 274 Modern Greek has two independent and partial phonological *suprasystems. **1907** E. E. FOURNIER D'ALBE (*title*) Two New Worlds. I. The Infra-World. II. The *Supra-World.

7. Above in degree or amount, beyond, more than (what is expressed by the second element): with sbs., as ***ˌsupra-cente'narian*** (so ***ˌsupra-cente'narianism***), or adjs., as ***supra'maximal, supra-'optimal*** (also ellipt. as sbs., *sc.* temperature); **supra'lethal** *a.*, exceeding what is lethal; so **supra'lethally** *adv.*; **supra'maximal** *a. Physiol.*, greater than what is required to produce the maximum response; hence **supra'maximally** *adv.*; **ˌsupraquan'tivalent** *a.*, more than equivalent, higher in ideal than real value; so ***supraquantivalence***; **supra'thermal** *a. Physics*, having greater energy than that associated with thermal excitations; **supra-'threshold** *a. Physiol.*, exceeding the threshold value required for the perception of a stimulus.

1870 SCOFFERN *Stray Leaves Sci. & Folk-lore* 470, I do not find that women figure as *supra-centenarians in any way comparable to men. **1881** W. D. MACRAY *Index Registers Ducklington* Pref., One case of *supra centenarianism is recorded; the 'old widow Knapp' was buried 10 March 1727, at the age of 105. **1957** *Jrnl. Exper. Zool.* CXXXVII. 426 A total continuous dose of 24 kr, referred to as a *supralethal dose, was given to interphase cells at each exposure. **1979** *Nature* 11 Oct. 490/2 Supralethal doses of chemoradiotherapy followed by allogeneic bone marrow transplantation are being used to treat patients with acute leukaemia. **1955** *Jrnl. Exper. Zool.* CXXX. 190 (*heading*) Survival and cell division in *supralethally x-irradiated giant amoebae following injection of nonirradiated protoplasm. **1975** *Nature* 20 Nov. 233/2 (*caption*) Supralethally irradiated rats. **1905** *Science* 23 June 948 Death at the *supramaximal or subminimal may be due to changes of a very definite nature. **1925** LIDDELL & SHERRINGTON in *Proc. R. Soc.* B. XCVII. 497 The reflex mode of employing the motor units is to subject them to an incitement which is 'supra-maximal' in the sense that it is in excess..of that which is necessary to evoke in them individually their 'maximal' response. **1977** *Lancet* 30 Apr. 942/1 Desmedt and Borenstein have modified this test..by first applying a train of supramaximal stimuli at 3 Hz for 4 minutes. **1973** *Nature* 26 Oct. 465/1 The sciatic nerve was stimulated *supramaximally at a rate of 6.4 Hz with square waves of 0.5 ms duration. **1904** *Science* 2 Dec. 751 This reaction is repeated as long as an effective *supraoptimal or suboptimal temperature continues. **1903** *Alien. & Neurol.* Feb. 50 (Cent. D., Suppl.) Occupation is very especially suited to produce a *supraquantivalence of certain ideas. *Ibid.*, We had previously considered as the basis of the *supraquantivalent idea the frequent repetition..of definite trains of thought. **1969** *New Yorker* 12 Apr. 104/3 The three pots are the passive seismic experiment, the solar-wind experiment, and the *suprathermal-ion-detector. **1980** *Nature* 29 May 285/1 Of perhaps even greater interest was an image of the suprathermal X-rays, or bremsstrahlung derived from interactions of the hot electrons with ions from the exploding pusher. **1946** *Ibid.* 27 July 131/2 The strength of the stimulating current was gradually increased to threshold and *supra-threshold values. **1980** VAN BOMMEL & DE BOER *Road Lighting* ii. 35 The supra-threshold level of visibility can be expressed in terms of the visibility level attainable.

8. Before in time; = SUPER- 8; as in SUPRALAPSARIAN; so †**ˌSupra-crea'tarian**, one who believes that in the divine decrees the purpose of election and reprobation was antecedent to that of creation; also as *adj.*

1660 HEYLIN *Hist. Quinquart.* III. 61 According to the Supra-lapsarian, or Supra-creatarian way. *Ibid.* 64 The Supra-lapsarians..(or Supra-creatarians rather, as a late judicious Writer calls them).

III. In the highest or to a very high degree.

9. Very highly, extremely, = SUPER- 9 a, b: as ***supra-censorious, supra-feminine, supra-fine*** (= SUPERFINE), ***supra-sensitive*** (= SUPERSENSITIVE), ***supra-subtle*** (= SUPERSUBTLE), adjs.; ***supragravitate, supra-parasite*** (with *it*, to play the parasite to excess), ***supra-saturate*** (= SUPERSATURATE), vbs.; **supracon'ducting** *ppl. a.* [tr. Du. *suprageleidend*: see SUPERCONDUCTING *ppl. a.*] = SUPERCONDUCTING *ppl. a.*; so **supra-con'duction, -conductive** *a.*, **ˌsupraconduc'tivity, supraconductor**; all now *rare*.

1901 *Westm. Gaz.* 31 Aug. 5/2 This *supra-censorious censorship of minor news. **1932** *Nature* 10 Dec. 880/2 The application of mechanical stresses..raises the transition temperature of a *supraconducting metal. **1937** M. & B. RUHEMANN *Low Temperature Physics* IV. ii. 269 It is by no means clear whether at sufficiently low temperatures all metal become supraconducting. **1932** *Nature* 10 Dec. 879 (*heading*) Electric *supra-conduction in metals. *Ibid.*, Currents of electricity started in a ring of metal in the *supra-conductive state will continue apparently undiminished in intensity. **1941** *Ibid.* 13 Sept. 317/1 It.. appears that, in sufficiently pure and homogeneous samples of tantalum, the changes of electrical resistance..and specific heat accompanying the establishment of the supra-conductive state occur at one and the same temperature. **1930** *Engineering* 16 May 640/3 Some of the discoveries made by the late Professor Kamerlingh Onnes,..as, for instance, *supraconductivity. **1962** P. J. & B. DURRANT *Introd. Adv. Inorg. Chem.* xviii. 591 Graphite does not show supraconductivity. **1976** *Progress in Sci. Culture* (E. Majorana Centre) Spring 90 The most important theoretical items were probably the nuclear analogy of supraconductivity..and the accounting of wave functions for deformed nuclei. **1933** *Nature* 14 Oct. 602/1 The use of a *supra-conductor (therefore completely free from Joule heating) has been more than once suggested for the production of magnetic fields at low temperatures. **1883** *Fortn. Rev.* July 117 A *supra-feminine love of softness and splendour. **1819** SYD. SMITH *Game Laws* Wks. 1859 I. 259/1 The *supra-fine country gentleman. **1672** FLAMSTEED in Rigaud *Corr. Sci. Men* (1841) II. 139 The apogæon part of the system may contain more of matter..and consequently ..may *supragravitate and incline the axis towards the synodical line. **1654** GAYTON *Pleas. Notes* III. vi. 108 The slave Sancho doth *supra-parasite it. **1770** *Phil. Trans.* LXI. 341 Till the fluids are (if I may use that expression) *supra-saturated with the acid. **1893** W. H. HUDSON *Idle Days Patagonia* xii. (1899) 194 *Suprasensitive retinae. **1894** *Athenæum* 13 Jan. 47/2 The same *supra-subtle unraveller of mysteries.

IV. 10. Expressing addition; involving addition or repetition (cf. SUPER- 13, 14, 15): as † ***supra-addition*** (= SUPERADDITION 2), ***supra-compound*** (= a compound of a compound, a compound of more than two elements); †**ˌsuprabi'partient** = *superbipartient* (see SUPER- 14); **ˌsuprade'compound, ˌsuprade'composite** *adjs. Bot.*, additionally decompound; triply or more than triply compound.

a **1706** EVELYN *Hist. Relig.* (1850) II. 46 These..were the doctrines and *supra-additions of the Scribes and Pharisees. **1753** HOGARTH *Anal. Beauty* xi. 136 The length of the foot .., in respect to the breadth, makes a double *suprabipartient, a diapason, and a diatesseron. **1791** HAMILTON tr. *Berthollet's Dyeing* I. I. i. 22 At other times they unite with the salts and form *supracompounds. **1816** J. SMITH *Panorama Sci. & Art* II. 532 Acids, alkalies, [etc.] ..may sometimes form supra-compounds with the cloth, and thereby change its colour. **1753** *Chambers' Cycl.* Suppl. s.v. *Leaf*, **Supradecomposite Leaf*, one which has the common petiole divided more than twice. *Ibid.* s.v. *Leaf (Compound)*, The *supradecompound [leaf]. **1777** S. ROBSON *Brit. Flora* 204 Hemloc Dropwort. Leaves supradecompound. **1874** GARROD & BAXTER *Mat. Med.* 225 The leaves are supra-decompound, the leaflets oblong and ovate.

†**supra'cargo.** *Obs.* Also 7 sopracargo. [ad. Sp. *sobrecargo* (f. *sobre* over + *cargo* CARGO), whence F. *subrécargue*, also †*supercarge* (Voltaire), Pg. *sobrecarga.*] = SUPERCARGO.

1667 DENHAM *Direct. Painter* I. xiii. 12 Though Clifford in the Character appear Of Supra-Cargo to our Fleet and their. **1674** J. COLLINS *Introd. Merchants-Acc.* E 3, Journal of the Sopracargos Accounts. **1719** DE FOE *Crusoe* I. (Globe) 198 What Business had I to..turn Supra Cargo to Guinea, to fetch Negroes? **1813** MILBURN *Oriental Commerce* II. 533 The Company's instructions to the supracargoes of their ships are very particular as to the mode of package and stowage. **1824** *Encycl. Metrop.* (1845) XVI. 589/1 The black [teas],..or boheas, [are brought] from Fŏ-kyen, called the Bohea country by the Supra-cargoes at Canton. **1844** H. H. WILSON *Brit. India* I. 321 The supracargoes..at last counselled acquiescence.

ˌsuprace'lestial, *a. rare.* [f. late L. *suprācælestis*: see SUPRA- 1, 4 a, CELESTIAL.] = SUPERCELESTIAL 1, 2.

1432–50 tr. *Higden* (Rolls) II. 291 Abraham, experte in astronomy,..folowede in erthe that he vnderstode by the disposicion of bodies supracelestialle. **1811** R. HINDMARSH tr. *Swedenborg's Coronis* 110 If I have told you earthly things, and ye believe not, how shall ye believe if I shall tell you supra-celestial things? [Cf. John iii. 12 τὰ ἐπουράνια.]

suprachoroid (s(j)uːprə'kɔərɔɪd), *sb.* and *a. Ophthalm.* Also **-chorioid**, and in L. form **-chor(i)oidea.** [ad. mod.L: see SUPRA- 1 b and CHOROID *a.* (*sb.*).] **A.** *sb.* A layer of loose cellular tissue lying between the choroid and the sclera. **B.** *adj.* Epithet of this layer.

1892 A. DUANE tr. *Fuchs's Text-bk. Ophthalm.* iv. 245 The suprachorioid..consists of numerous fine non-vascular but richly pigmented lamellæ lying between the chorioid proper and the sclera. **1896** W. A. FROST *Fundus Oculi* i. 12 Between the sclerotic and the choroid is some loose cellular tissue —the suprachoroidea. **1959** S. DUKE-ELDER *Parsons' Dis. of Eye* (ed. 13) i. 6 The greater part of the muscle is composed of meridional fibres running antero-posteriorly on the inner aspect of the sclera to find a diffuse insertion into the suprachoroid. **1962** *Gray's Anat.* (ed. 33) 1258 It [*sc.* the sclera] is separated from the outer surface of the chorioid by an extensive perichorioidal space, which is traversed by an exceedingly delicate cellular tissue, termed the suprachorioid lamina. **1971** M. J. HOGAN et al. *Histol. Human Eye* viii. 386 The suprachoroidea lies between the choroid and the sclera and appears to be derived partly from each tissue. **1978** F. W. NEWELL *Ophthalmology* (ed. 4) i. 15/1 The outermost layer, the suprachoroid (*lamina fusca*), is made up of delicate lamellae composed of elastic and collagenous fibers to form a syncytium.

So ˌ**supracho'roidal** *a.*, situated above the choroid.

1887 F. FERGUS tr. *Meyer's Pract. Treat. Dis. Eye* iv. 148 (*caption*) Supra choroidal space. **1918** J. H. PARSONS *Dis. Eye* (ed. 3) xvii. 334 Fuchs.. attributes it to slight separation of the ciliary body, so that the aqueous percolates from the anterior chamber into the suprachoroidal space. **1975** *Symposium on Glaucoma: Trans. New Orleans Acad. Ophthalm.* xix. 304 The surgeon should then confirm that the probe may be introduced with equal facility.. into the space between the ciliary body and sclera which anatomists call the suprachoroidal space.

supraciliary (s(j)uːprə'sɪlɪərɪ), *a.* (*sb.*) *Anat.* and *Zool.* [f. SUPRA- 1 b, after *superciliary*.] = SUPERCILIARY; as *sb.* applied *spec.* to the small scales attached to the eyelids in reptiles, below the supra-oculars.

1828–32 in WEBSTER (citing URE). **1863** HUXLEY *Man's Place Nat.* II. 76 In the Man,.. the supraciliary ridges or brow-prominences usually project but little. **1874** COUES *Birds N.W.* 450 A yellowish suffusion about the head, and especially along the supraciliary stripe. **1903** *Proc. Zool. Soc. Lond.* II. 125 Five supraoculars,.. 10 or 11 supraciliaries.

supraclavicle (-'klævɪk(ə)l). *Anat.* and *Zool.* Also in L. form ˌ**supracla'vicula**. [See SUPRA- 1 c and CLAVICLE[1].] A superior bone of the scapular arch in some fishes, above the clavicle.

1873 MIVART *Elem. Anat.* 162 In bony Fishes, where the clavicles.. may not only be provided with a distinct inter-clavicle, but also each with a distinct portion above—the supra-clavicle. **1880** GÜNTHER *Fishes* iii. 59 The scapular.. arch is suspended from the skull by the (suprascapula) post-temporal.. Then follows the (scapula) supraclavicula. **1888** ROLLESTON & JACKSON *Anim. Life* 416 The *Ganoidei* and *Teleostei* have investing bones known as supra-clavicle, clavicle, inter-clavicle, and post-clavicle.

supraclavicular (-klə'vɪkjʊlə(r)), *a. Anat.* and *Zool.* [In sense 1, ad. mod.L. *suprāclāviculāris*, f. *suprā* SUPRA- 1 b + *clāvicula* CLAVICLE[1]; in sense 2, f. SUPRACLAVICLE: see -AR.]

1. Situated above the clavicle or collar-bone.

1847–9 *Todd's Cycl. Anat.* IV. 753/2 The supra-clavicular and acromial nerves, form the termination of the cervical plexus. **1876** *Trans. Clinical Soc.* IX. 193 Forced breathing called into play the diaphragm far more than the supra-clavicular muscles. **1886** FAGGE *Princ. Med.* I. 755 In one of my cases, these supraclavicular swellings were much larger than hen's eggs.

2. Pertaining to the supraclavicle.

In recent Dicts.

supracleithrum (s(j)uːprə'klaɪθrəm). *Zool.* Pl. **-cleithra**. [SUPRA- 1 c.] A dermal bone dorsal to the cleithrum in the pectoral arch of some fishes and amphibians.

1905 A. SEDGWICK *Student's Text-bk. Zool.* II. vii. 162 These bones are now often called supracleithrum, cleithrum and clavicle respectively. **1949** A. S. ROMER *Vertebr. Body* vii. 179 Above each cleithrum there are usually additional elements—typically a supracleithrum and post-temporal, and sometimes other bones as well—which curve upward and forward above the gill chamber and anchor the dermal girdle to the skull. **1981** PEARSON & BALL *Lect. Notes Vertebr. Zool.* iv. 52/1 Large clavicles occur in paleoniscoids and Polypterus, with large cleithra and smaller postcleithra, supracleithra, and post-temporals above them.

supracoracoid (s(j)uːprə'kɒrəkɔɪd), *sb.* and *a. Zool.* Also in L. form **-coracoideus**. [f. SUPRA- 1 c + CORACOID *a.* and *sb.*] **A.** *sb.* A muscle in some birds, amphibians, and reptiles which passes over the coracoid bone and is attached to the head of the humerus and to part of the sternum. **B.** *adj.* Of, pertaining to, or designating the supracoracoid.

1933 L. A. ADAMS *Introd. Vertebrates* iv. 86 (*in figure*) Supracoracoideus. **1949** SAUNDERS & MANTON *Man. Pract. Vertebr. Morphol.* (ed. 2) ix. 88 The supracoracoideus muscle elevates the wing. **1956** A. S. ROMER *Osteol. of Reptiles* vii. 308 Beneath the anterior end of the glenoid is a supracoracoid foramen (or coracoid foramen), carrying.. the supracoracoid nerve. **1974** ANDREW & HICKMAN *Histol. Vertebr.* vi. 107/2 The powerful muscles of flight (pectoral and supracoracoid) are centrally located on the sternum. **1979** *Nature* 15 Mar. 247/2 It has been argued that the structure of the coracoid of *Archaeopteryx* would not have permitted the supracoracoideus muscle to function as a wing elevator.

supra'human, *a. rare.* [SUPRA- 4 a.] = SUPERHUMAN.

1740 CHEYNE *Regimen* 40 Outward and inward Means may be.. bestow'd, by external Providences, suprahumane ..Aid and Grace. **1809** J. FOSTER *Contrib. Eclectic Rev.* (1844) I. 379 No believer in any supra-human means, in any immediate interposition of the Almighty. **1840** DE QUINCEY *Rhetoric* Wks. 1859 XI. 42 Any supra-human intelligence, divine or angelic.

So ˌ**suprahu'manity** = SUPERHUMANITY.

c **1810** COLERIDGE in *Lit. Rem.* (1838) III. 253 An essential supra-humanity in Christ.

Supralapsarian (ˌs(j)uːprəlæp'sɛərɪən), *sb.* and *a. Theol.* [f. mod.L. *suprālapsārius*, f. *suprā* SUPRA- 8 + L. *lapsus* fall, LAPSE: see -IAN. Cf. F. *supralapsaire*.]

A. *sb.* A name applied to those Calvinists who held the view that, in the divine decrees, the predestination of some to eternal life and of others to eternal death was antecedent to the creation and the fall: opposed to INFRALAPSARIAN.

1633 HOARD *Gods Love to Mankind* 13 The Maintainers of the Absolute Decree do say.. eyther that all actions.. and all events.. are absolutely necessary; so the Supralapsarians: or that all mens ends (at least) are unalterable and indeterminable by the power of their wills; so the Sublapsarians. **1674** HICKMAN *Quinquart. Hist.* (ed. 2) 75, I believe, with the Supralapsarian, that God hath decreed, not to bestow converting Grace upon many whom he could easily (had he so pleased) have converted. **1674** BOYLE *Excell. Theol.* I. i. 50 Some few Theologues.. have got the name of Supra-lapsarians, for venturing to look back beyond the fall of Adam for God's decrees of election and reprobation. **1797** *Encycl. Brit.* (ed. 3) XVIII. 84/1 According to the supralapsarians, the object of predestination is, *homo creabilis et labilis*; and, according to the sublapsarians and infralapsarians, *homo creatus et lapsus*. **1849** MACAULAY *Hist. Eng.* iii. I. 400 The young candidate for academical honours.. was strictly interrogated by a synod of louring Supralapsarians as to the day and hour when he experienced the new birth.

B. *adj.* Of or pertaining to the Supralapsarians or their doctrine; that is a Supralapsarian.

1633 HOARD *Gods Love to Mankind* 2 The rest of that side, thinking to avoyd the great inconveniences, to which that supralapsarian way lyeth open,.. present man to God in his decree of Reprobation, lying in the fall. **1733** NEAL *Hist. Purit.* II. 79 A treatise of Beza's upon the Supralapsarian scheme of Predestination. **1764** MACLAINE tr. *Mosheim's Eccl. Hist.* XVII. (1833) 639/1 The Supralapsarian and Sublapsarian divines forgot their debates and differences. **1831** MACAULAY *Ess., Pilgr. Progr.* (1897) 191 An absurd allegory written by some raving supralapsarian preacher who was dissatisfied with the mild theology of the Pilgrim's Progress. **1839** HALLAM *Lit. Eur.* III. ii. §32 The Supra-lapsarian tenets of Calvin. **1885** *Encycl. Brit.* XIX. 670/2 The supra-lapsarian view was.. adopted by Beza and other Calvinists, as it had been held by some of the Augustinian schoolmen.

Hence ˌ**Supralap'sarianism** [cf. mod.L. *suprālapsāriismus*], the doctrine of the Supralapsarians. So †**Supra'lapsary** *sb.* and *a.* = SUPRALAPSARIAN.

1728 CHAMBERS *Cycl.*, *Supralapsary*, in Theology, a Person who holds, that God, without any Regard to the good or evil Works of Men, has resolv'd, by an eternal Decree, to save some, and damn others. **1755** JOHNSON, *Supralapsary*, antecedent to the fall of man. **1775** ASH, Supralapsarianism. **1841** *J. Evans' Sk. Denom. Chr. World* 80 Recent divines who have gone to the height of Supralapsarianism. **1874** GREEN *Short Hist.* viii. §1. 458 Whitgift strove to force on the Church the supralapsarianism of his Lambeth Articles.

supraliminal (s(j)uːprə'lɪmɪnəl), *a. Psych.* [f. SUPRA- 1 a + L. *limin-*, LIMEN threshold: after *subliminal*.] Above the limen or threshold of sensation or consciousness; belonging to the ordinary or normal consciousness: opp. to SUBLIMINAL.

1892 MYERS in *Proc. Soc. Psychical Res.* Feb. 306, I hold ..that this subliminal consciousness.. may embrace a far wider range.. of.. activity than is open to our supraliminal consciousness. *Ibid.* [see SUBLIMINAL]. **1903** F. W. H. MYERS *Human Personality* I. i. 14 Sensations, thoughts, emotions, which.. by the original constitution of our being, seldom emerge into that *supraliminal* current of consciousness which we habitually identify with ourselves. **1918** [see OVERLEARN *v.*]. **1931** *Brit. Jrnl. Psychol.* Jan. 305 Another series [of observations] was made in which a supraliminal admixture of spectral light was reduced until the field appeared pure white. **1971** *Jrnl. Gen. Psychol.* Jan. 122 Manipulating intensity.. from subliminal to supraliminal luminance results in.. emergence of linear detail.

Hence **supra'liminally** *adv.*

a **1901** MYERS *Hum. Personality* I. 87 We need not postulate any direct or supernormal knowledge,—but merely a subliminal calculation,.. expressing itself supraliminally.

supralunar (s(j)uːprə'l(j)uːnə(r)), *a.* [See SUPRA- 1 a and LUNAR, and cf. SUBLUNAR.] = next: cf. SUPERLUNAR.

1719 STEELE *Old Whig* No. 2. 12 Comets, said he, are Two-fold, Supra-lunar, and Sub-lunar. **1848** KINGSLEY *Yeast* ii, I am.. utterly deficient in that sixth sense of the angelic or supralunar beautiful, which fills your soul with ecstasy. **1856** —— *Misc.* (1859) II. 114 The most supralunar rosepink of piety, devotion, and purity.

supralunary (s(j)uːprə'l(j)uːnərɪ), *a.* [See SUPRA- 1 a and LUNARY, and cf. SUBLUNARY.] = SUPERLUNARY.

1635 SWAN *Spec. Mundi* (1670) 84 The admittance of terrene Exhalations to join their forces towards the effecting of supralunary Comets. *a* **1656** HALES *Gold. Rem.* (1673) 276 Certain strange supralunary arguments, which never fell within the sphere of common action. **1691** NORRIS *Pract. Disc.* 216 If it be once granted that there is a Providence, 'tis an absurd.. conceit, to confine it.. to the Supralunary Regions. **1903** *Blackw. Mag.* Nov. 628/1 His head full of these supralunary matters.

supramundane (s(j)uːprə'mʌndeɪn), *a.* [ad. mod.L. **suprāmundānus*, f. *suprā* SUPRA- 1 a, 4 a + *mundus* world. Cf. F. *supramondain*, It. *soprammondano*.] = SUPERMUNDANE.

1662 STANLEY *Hist. Chaldaick Philos.* (1701) 8/2 The Supramundane Light, an Incorporeal Infinite luminous Space, in which the intellectual Beings reside. **1678** CUDWORTH *Intell. Syst.* I. iv. §14. 243 These Eternal Gods of Plato, called by his Followers θεοὶ ὑπερκόσμιοι, the Supramundane Gods. **1744** HARRIS *Three Treat.* II. (1765) 363 Beings divine, supramundane, and.. unchangeable. **1829** CARLYLE *Misc.* (1857) II. 52 The supramundane, divine nature of Virtue. **1872** LIDDON *Elem. Relig.* iii. 83 Revelation has familiarized Christians with the angels, as supramundane beings. **1884** *Manch. Exam.* 10 Oct. 5/3 Free trade is.. suitable rather for an ideal and supramundane existence than for the present state of society.

supra'national, *a.* [SUPRA- 4 a.] Having power, authority, or influence that overrides or transcends national boundaries, governments, or institutions.

1908 *Dublin Rev.* Oct. 384 One great Supranational body, in which there should be 'neither Jew nor Greek'. **1924** J. C. W. REITH in *Radio Times* 29 Feb. 361/2, I like to think that wireless, as with music, is supra-national, a word coined, I believe, by Lord Cecil to indicate that which is above not only nationality, but something more even than international. **1941** *Burlington Mag.* Feb 38/1 Mediaeval artists shared the common task of glorifying God under the guidance of a supra-national church. **1950** W. S. CHURCHILL in *Hansard Commons* 27 June 2147, I would add, to make my answer quite clear to the right hon. and learned Gentleman, that if he asked me, 'Would you agree to a supranational authority which has the power to tell Great Britain not to cut any more coal or make any more steel, but to grow tomatoes instead?' I should say, without hesitation, the answer is 'No'. **1958** A. J. ZURCHER *Struggle to unite Europe 1940–1958* vii. 80 This first European supranational community set up its administrative offices in Luxembourg on August 10, 1952. **1962** A. SAMPSON *Anat. of Britain* xxvii. 429 The very biggest firms in Britain.. belong more to an international, than a national economy. And in the Common Market they are likely to become much more supra-national. **1973** *Observer* (Colour Suppl.) 12 Aug. 19/3 They were 'intergovernmental' rather than 'supranational' —that is to say based on negotiation between sovereign Governments, not on the principle that the institution itself, operating as a unit, could overrule member Governments. **1977** M. WALKER *National Front* ii. 25 His [*sc.* Mosley's] book *The Alternative*, which advocated a European nationalism, a new supra-national state of Europe.

Hence **supra'nationalism**, ˌ**supranatio'nality**.

1921 *Glasgow Herald* 14 Oct. 10 It was only a developed sense of supra-nationalism that would in the future make war unthinkable. **1930** *Tablet* 16 Aug. 206/2 The Popes held out.. against every threat.. which aimed at lowering the supra-nationality of the Papacy. **1955** A. L. ROWSE *Expansion of Elizabethan England* vii. 241 One sees, as against the supra-nationalism of the Habsburgs.., the nationalist assumption.. that the Low Countries should govern themselves. **1959** *Times Lit. Suppl.* 3 Apr. 187/3 The actual degree of supranationality in these Communities. **1971** *Mod. Law Rev.* XXXI. VI. 607 It is clear that with the elements of supranationality are commingled features of a more typical international organisation. **1980** *Times Lit. Suppl.* 10 Oct. 1134/1 Supranationalism has lost what appeal it had in the 1950s.

supranatural (s(j)uːprə'nætjʊərəl, -tʃərəl), *a.* (*sb.*) *rare.* [See SUPRA- 4 a and NATURAL *a.* Cf. F. *supranaturalisme, -iste*.] = SUPERNATURAL.

1857 P. FREEMAN *Princ. Div. Serv.* II. 32 To express.. their.. conceptions of the divine and supranatural element in the subject. **1874** J. H. BLUNT *Dict. Sects* 125/1 A mechanical Deity that is only so far supra-natural as that Infinite Substance must always stand in antagonism with the finite. **1908** *Hibbert Jrnl.* July 808 We measure the change from the standpoint of the supranatural.

So **supra'naturalism**, **supra'naturalist**, ˌ**supraˌnatura'listic** *a.*, **'supra-ˌnature** (= SUPERNATURALISM, etc.).

1828–32 WEBSTER (citing MURDOCK), Supranaturalism. **1842** BRANDE *Dict. Sci.*, etc., *Supranaturalists*, a name given of late years to the middle party among the divines of Germany, to distinguish them from the Rationalists,.. and from the Evangelical party. **1846** GEO. ELIOT tr. *Strauss' Life Jesus* Introd. §11. I. 46 Those theologians.. who think to unite both parties by this middle course—a vain endeavour which the rigid supranaturalist pronounces heretical, and the rationalist derides. **1846** WORCESTER (citing *P. Cyc.*), Supra-naturalistic. **1856** R. A. VAUGHAN *Mystics* (1860) II. XIII. i. 250 They sought.. for a sign; and in their credulous incredulity, grew greedy of every supranaturalism except the scriptural. **1866** *Chambers' Encycl.* VIII. 120/2 The struggle between Rationalism and Supranaturalism. **1890** J. F. SMITH tr. *Pfleiderer's Developm. Theol.* II. ii. 122 The difficulties of the supranaturalistic theology. **1908** *Hibbert Jrnl.* July 808 It is increased knowledge of nature which has made supra-nature incredible.

ˌ**supra-oc'cipital**, *a.* and *sb. Anat.* and *Zool.* [ad. mod.L. *suprā-occipitālis*: see SUPRA- 1 b and OCCIPITAL.] = SUPEROCCIPITAL.

1846 OWEN in *Rep. Brit. Assoc.* I. 319 The flattening.. of the human supraoccipital, parietal and frontal bones. **1848** —— *Homol. Vertebrate Skel.* 5, I.. regard the supraoccipital as the serial homologue of the parietal and the midfrontal. **1851** MANTELL *Petrifactions* iv. §3. 390 The horns being placed more anteriorly in relation to the supra-occipital ridge. **1880** GÜNTHER *Fishes* 56 The supraoccipital separates the parietals, and forms a suture with the frontals.

supraopticohypophysial (s(j)uːprəˌɒptɪkəʊ haɪpəʊˈfɪzɪəl), *a.* *Anat.* Also -eal. [f. *supraoptic* adj. s.v. SUPRA- 1 b + -O + HYPOPHYSIAL *a.*] Applied to a tract of nerve fibres in the brain running from the supraoptic nucleus to the hypophysis.

[**1937** *Jrnl. Path. & Bacteriol.* XLIV. 310 The fact.. seems to indicate that at this time the lesion was confined to the supraoptic-hypophyseal system.] **1943** STRONG & ELWYN *Human Neuroanat.* xvii. 317/2 They [*sc.* the connections of the hypothalamus with the posterior lobe of the hypophysis] are unmyelinated fibers which arise principally from the supraoptic and paraventricular nuclei and form a well defined bundle, the supraopticohypophysial tract. **1961** *Lancet* 2 Sept. 525/1 A lesion in the tuberal nuclei, with or without damage to the supraopticohypophyseal system, resulted in diabetes insipidus. **1980** K. E. MOYER *Neuroanatomy* xxxiii. 80 The supraopticohypophysial tract..comes principally from the supraoptic nucleus.

supra-ˈorbital, *a.* (*sb.*) *Anat.* and *Zool.* [ad. mod.L. *suprā-orbitālis*: see SUPRA- 1 b and ORBITAL.] Situated or occurring above the orbit of the eye. Also as *sb.* a supra-orbital artery, vein, bone, or nerve.

1828 QUAIN *Elem. Anat.* 648 The external, or supra-orbital branch [of the frontal nerve]. **1846** OWEN in *Rep. Brit. Assoc.* I. 283 The bones of the dermo-skeleton are:—The Supratemporals; The Supraorbitals; The Suborbitals; The Labials. **1868** DARWIN *Anim. & Pl.* I. iv. 117 The supra-orbital plates or processes of the frontal bones are much broader than in the wild rabbit. **1876** TOMES *Dental Anat.* 39 Pain..is often referred to the point of emergence of a nerve, as..in supra-orbital neuralgia.

Also **supra-ˈorbitar**, **supra-ˈorbitary** [mod.L. *suprā-orbitārius*], *adjs.*

1782 MONRO *Anat.* 287 The sight may be lost by an injury done to the supra-orbitar branch. **1814** SIR C. BELL *Anat. Expression* ii. (ed. 3) 49 The prominences over the orbits (the supra-orbitary ridges), which are peculiar to a more advanced age. **1856** TODD & BOWMAN *Phys. Anat.* II. 7 The fissure which bounds the supra-orbitar convolution.

supra-ˈpersonal, *a.* [SUPRA- 4 a.] = SUPERPERSONAL *a.*

1918 J. H. LECKIE *World to Come* II. 322 The notion..of attaining some supra-personal state of being is not an idea that can appear reasonable. **1934** M. BODKIN *Archetypal Patterns in Poetry* 276 The sense of..a supra-personal life present within the group, which is made explicit in the writings of St. Paul. **1949** H. READ *Conc. Hist. Mod. Painting* vii. 249 The 'vibrations of the spirit' that then take place are.. perhaps supra-personal, in that they assume the archetypal patterns into which mankind projects an explanation of its destiny. **1955** J. BURNABY *Christian Words & Christian Meanings* iii. 48 It may sometimes be wholesome for us to tell ourselves that God is not 'a person', but 'supra-personal', or even 'Absolute Being'. **1958** *Times Lit. Suppl.* 23 May 278/3 Its [*sc.* The Warburg Institute's] character is also suprapersonal, and it is never likely to lose its identity and be submerged in some more general apparatus of historical research. **1972** M. KIRKHAM in *Focus on Robert Graves* No. 3 (1973) 40 The feeling might be called impersonal, in the sense that it reflects..everybody's response to a general condition; a better word would be 'suprapersonal', to signify a going-beyond personality.

suprarenal (s(j)uːprəˈriːnəl), *a.* (*sb.*) *Anat.* [ad. mod.L. *suprārēnālis*: see SUPRA- 1 b and RENAL.] **A.** *adj.* **a.** Situated above the kidney; applied to a pair of ductless glands (***suprarenal bodies, capsules, corpuscles, glands***), one immediately above each kidney; also to other structures connected with these.

1828 QUAIN *Elem. Anat.* 500 The kidneys and supra-renal capsules. **1840** W. J. E. WILSON *Anat. Vade M.* (1842) 309 The Supra-renal are sometimes branches of the phrenic or of the renal arteries. *Ibid.* 350 The Supra-renal veins terminate partly in the renal veins, and partly in the inferior vena cava. **1876** tr. *Wagner's Gen. Pathol.* 154 The connective tissue corpuscles of the supra-renal glands. **1883** *Encycl. Brit.* XV. 365/1 The 'suprarenal bodies' or 'adrenals'. **1905** H. D. ROLLESTON *Dis. Liver* 271 The various preparations of suprarenal gland substance.

b. *transf.* Of, pertaining to, or affecting the suprarenal capsules.

1876 BRISTOWE *Theory & Pract. Med.* (1878) 583 There are no lesions..which are constantly associated with the supra-renal affection. *Ibid.* 585 Supra-renal degeneration.

B. *sb.* A suprarenal capsule (in quot. 1841, a suprarenal artery).

1841 R. E. GRANT *Outl. Comp. Anat.* 512 The aorta gives off..the two small phrenic arteries..to the diaphragm; two or more minute supra-renals to the supra-renal capsules. **1895** *Athenæum* 7 Dec. 795/2 The supra-renal bodies of fishes... There was no relation..between the supra-renals and the lymphatic head-kidney. **1897** *Allbutt's Syst. Med.* III. 313 Glands without ducts, such as the..suprarenals.

Hence **supraˈrenalin**, **supraˈrenin**, a substance extracted from suprarenal capsules, used as a hæmostatic.

1904 *Brit. Med. Jrnl.* 17 Sept. 681 The constitution of suprarenin. **1909** *Chem. & Druggist* 20 Feb. 316/2 Novocain-Suprarenin Dental Tablets..contain.. Suprarenin borate. **1909** *Cent. Dict.*, Suppl., Suprarenalin.

‖**suprascapula** (s(j)uːprəˈskæpjʊlə). *Anat.* and *Zool.* Pl. -æ. [mod.L.: see SUPRA- 3 a and SCAPULA.] A bone (or cartilage) in the upper or anterior part of the scapular arch or shoulder-girdle, in fishes, and in some batrachians and reptiles.

1854 OWEN in *Orr's Circ. Sci., Org. Nat.* I. 175 The special names of the above elements of the hæmal arch of the occipital vertebra are, from above downwards, 'supra-scapula',..'scapula',..'coracoid'. **1888** ROLLESTON & JACKSON *Anim. Life* 81 [The dorsal scapular] consists of a broad semicartilaginous supra-scapula and an ossified scapula.

supraˈscapular, *a.* *Anat.* and *Zool.* [ad. mod.L. *suprāscapulāris*: see SUPRA- 1 b, 3 b and SCAPULAR *a.*] Situated above or upon the scapula; belonging to or connected with the upper or anterior part of the scapular arch, or the suprascapula.

1828 QUAIN *Elem. Anat.* 160 A foramen, for the transmission..of the supra-scapular nerve. *Ibid.* 401 The supra-scapular and posterior-scapular arteries. *Ibid.* 416 The nerve passes through the supra-scapular notch, or foramen. **1854** OWEN in *Orr's Circ. Sci., Org. Nat.* I. 190 The suprascapular plate remains long cartilaginous, and always partly so. *Ibid.* 210 The upper or suprascapular piece ..retains..its cartilaginous state. **1878** T. BRYANT *Surg.* I. 479 The suprascapular artery and vein will always be seen behind the clavicle.

Also †**supraˈscapulary** *a.*

1693 tr. *Blancard's Phys. Dict.* (ed. 2), *Infra Spinatus Musculus*, or *Supra Scapularis Secundus*, proceeds under the Spine, from the Basis of the Scapula, with the Second, Supra Scapulary, Carnous and Thick, and runs into the Ligament of the Shoulder. **1828–32** WEBSTER.

suprascript (ˈs(j)uːprəskrɪpt), *a.* [ad. late L. *suprāscriptus*, f. *suprā* above + *scriptus* written.] Written above: = SUPERSCRIPT *a.*

1896 W. M. LINDSAY *Introd. Latin Textual Emend.* 36 In the original the *h* was expressed by this suprascript sign. **1902** *Scotsman* 5 Nov. 11/7 To have one's attention, at the height of a tragic climax, hitched up by a suprascript cipher.

†**supra-sedeas**, error for SUPERSEDEAS.

1615 BRETON *Char. Ess.* Wks. (Grosart) II. 10/1 It is a *supra sedeas* for all diseases.

suprasegmental (ˌs(j)uːprəsɛgˈmɛntəl), *a.* and *sb.* *Linguistics.* [f. SUPRA- 4 a + SEGMENTAL *a.* 2 c.] **A.** *adj.* Designating a feature or features of a sound or sequence of sound other than those constituting the consonantal and vocalic segments, as stress, pitch, and intonation in English.

1941 TRAGER & BLOCH in *Language* XVII. 224 These two kinds of phonemes [*sc.* juncture and prosodic phonemes] are usually recognizable only as modifications of other sound-types; they are suprasegmental. **1942** C. F. HOCKETT in *Language* XVIII. 8 Features..which clearly extend over a series of several segmental groupings are *suprasegmental*. **1942, 1952** [see PROSODIC *a.* 2]. **1953** [see *intrasegmental* s.v. INTRA- 1]. **1968** P. KRATOCHVÍL *Chinese Lang. Today* ii. 35 The most striking suprasegmental feature of MSC syllables is the characteristic contour known as the tone. **1971** [see PROSODEME]. **1975** N. CHOMSKY *Logical Struct. Linguistic Theory* iii. 111 In this study, suprasegmental features (pitch, stress, juncture) have not been seriously considered.

B. *sb.* A suprasegmental feature.

1955 N. CHOMSKY *Logical Struct. Linguistic Theory* (microfilm, Mass. Inst. Technol.) vii. 278 It has often been suggested that constituent structure be determined by considerations involving suprasegmentals. **1965** *Word Study* Feb. 2/2 Structural and contextual meanings are signaled largely by intonational clues, by such suprasegmentals as pitch, stress, and juncture. **1975** *Language* LI. 737 How we perceive duration, pitch, and intensity is an area that seldom receives serious attention in the literature on suprasegmentals. **1981** *Amer. Speech* LVI. 306 A summary of paralanguage, including suprasegmentals, hesitation phenomena, and nonlinguistic sounds.

Hence ˌ**supraseg'mentally** *adv.*, in terms of suprasegmental features.

1957 S. POTTER *Modern Linguistics* v. 105 Sentences may be described *suprasegmentally* in respect of the prosodemes of *length, stress* and *pitch*. **1970** J. W. GAIR *Colloq. Sinhalese Clause Structures* vi. 133 The focus may be marked only suprasegmentally, even if the form of the predicator indicates that the focus is elsewhere in the clause.

supraˈsensible, *a.* (*sb.*) [SUPRA- 4 a. So F.] = SUPERSENSIBLE; also *absol.* with *the*.

1839 *Penny Cycl.* XIII. 177/1 Kant applies the term of *noumenon* to the notion of God, and generally to all supra-sensible objects, which may be conceived of. *Ibid.*, The acceptance of this postulate [of the practical reason] as true and legitimate does not constitute a scientific certainty,.. which indeed does not exist for the supra-sensible. **1855** KINGSLEY *Westw. Ho!* ii, Your Platonical 'eternal world of supra-sensible forms'. **1902** A. M. FAIRBAIRN *Philos. Chr. Relig.* I. vi. 200 Religion is, subjectively, man's consciousness of relation to suprasensible Being.

supraˈsensual, *a.* [SUPRA- 4 a.] = SUPERSENSUAL.

1857 KINGSLEY *Two Y. Ago* I. 10 Of him, too,..I presume, an ideal exists eternally in the supra-sensual Platonic universe. **1868** LIGHTFOOT *Philippians* 198 The star is the suprasensual counterpart, the heavenly representative; the lamp, the earthly realisation. **1889** SKRINE *Mem. E. Thring* 79 The touch of supra-sensual things, the breath of religious mystery.

supraˈsensuous, *a.* (*sb.*) = SUPERSENSUOUS. Also *absol.* with *the*.

1866 WESTCOTT *Ess.* i. (1891) 2 An inherent communion with a divine and suprasensuous world. **1902** *Pop. Sci. Monthly* Apr. 519 The scientist often has recourse to the suprasensuous. **1947** A. EINSTEIN *Music in Romantic Era* III. xviii. 340 An idea which then led to the assertion that true, ideal music is not heard at all, but in non-sensuous and suprasensuous. **1957** J. I. M. STEWART *Use of Riches* 41 He knew why this picture was neither better nor worse than the Maremma or the La Verna... Brilliantly sensuous, it was yet suprasensuous.

supraspecies (ˈs(j)uːprəˌspiːʃiːz, -siːz). [f. SUPRA- 6 + SPECIES *sb.*] (See quot. 1940.) So **supraspeˈcific** *a.*, above the rank of a species.

1940 J. S. HUXLEY *New Systematics* 10 We may substitute the term 'species-group', reserving the term 'supraspecies' for groups of an intermediate nature, in which it is dubious whether the constituent groups are best called subspecies or species. **1942** E. MAYR *Systematics & Origin of Species* vii. 169 The term supraspecies..seems to me to be an unfortunate combination. **1961** Supraspecific [see NOMENCLATURAL *a.*]. **1975** *Nature* 9 Oct. 516/1 Because supraspecific taxa have different numbers of species, their observed linearity is evidence for the ecological reality of supraspecific taxa.

supraˈspective, *a.* *rare*$^{-1}$. [f. L. *suprā* above, after *introspective*.] Surveying from above.

1864 SALA in *Temple Bar* Mar. 483 Tranquilly supraspective of the bustle and clamour.

supraspinal (s(j)uːprəˈspaɪnəl), *a.* *Anat.* [ad. mod.L. *suprāspinālis*: see SUPRA- 1 b and SPINAL.] Situated above or upon a (or the) spine.

a. Situated above the spine of the scapula: opp. to *infraspinal* (see INFRA- B.).

1733 G. DOUGLAS tr. *Winslow's Anat.* III. iv. §7 (1756) I. 183 *Supra-Spinatus*..is a thick narrow Muscle,..filling all the Supra-Spinal Cavity of the Scapula. **1835–6** *Todd's Cycl. Anat.* I. 569/2 The spine is..so placed as to divide the dorsum of the scapula into a supra-spinal and infra-spinal depression. **1847–9** *Ibid.* IV. 435/1 The supra-spinal branch [of the supra-scapular artery]..is distributed to the supra-spinatus muscle.

b. = SUPRASPINOUS b.

1835–6 *Todd's Cycl. Anat.* I. 374/1 On the lips of the spinous processes of the neck some fibres may be shown, to which the name supra-spinal muscles has been given. **1855** DUNGLISON *Med. Lex.*, Supra-spinal ligaments, are..1. The Dorso-lumbo-supra-spinal ligament,..extending above the spinous processes of the dorsal and lumbar vertebræ... 2. Cervical-supra-spinal ligament,..which extends above all the cervical spinous processes.

c. (See quot.)

1836–9 *Todd's Cycl. Anat.* II. 980/1 A distinct vascular canal..is extended along the upper surface of the abdominal portion of the cerebro-spinal cord in perfect Lepidopterous insects... We have designated this structure the *supra-spinal vessel.*

‖**supraspinatus** (ˌs(j)uːprəspaɪˈneɪtəs). *Anat.* [mod.L., f. L. *suprā* SUPRA- 1 b + *spīna* SPINE: see -ATE².] A muscle arising from the supraspinal fossa of the scapula, and inserted into the greater tuberosity of the humerus, serving to raise and adduct the arm.

[**1704** J. HARRIS *Lex. Techn.* I, *Supra Spinatus*, or *Supra Scapularis*, is a Muscle..placed above the Spine of the Shoulder-blade.] **1733** G. DOUGLAS tr. *Winslow's Anat.* (1756) I. 291 The Supra-Spinatus is commonly supposed to join with the Deltoides in lifting up the Arm. **1828** QUAIN *Elem. Anat.* 161 It [*sc.* the capsular ligament] receives additions from the tendons of the supra and infra spinatus muscles. **1875** SIR W. TURNER in *Encycl. Brit.* I. 838/2 The muscles which cause these movements are inserted into the humerus; the supra-spinatus, infra-spinatus, and teres minor into the great tuberosity; the sub scapularis into the small tuberosity.

supraspinous (s(j)uːprəˈspaɪnəs), *a.* *Anat.* [ad. mod.L. *suprāspīnōsus*, f. L. *suprā* SUPRA- 1 b + *spīna* SPINE.] Situated above or upon a spine.

a. = SUPRASPINAL a.

1828 QUAIN *Elem. Anat.* 374 The *supra-spinatus* is placed at the superior part of the shoulder in the supra-spinous fossa of the scapula. **1876** *Trans. Clinical Soc.* IX. 151 On percussion there was absolute dulness in the left sub-clavian and supra-spinous regions.

b. Situated above or upon the spinous processes of the vertebræ.

1828 QUAIN *Elem. Anat.* 152 The supra-spinous ligament consists of small, compressed bundles of longitudinal fibres, which connect the summits of the spinous processes. **1875** SIR W. TURNER in *Encycl. Brit.* I. 835/1 Inter- and supra-spinous ligaments connect adjacent spinous processes, and in the neck the supra-spinous ligament forms a broad band.

suprasterol (s(j)uːprəˈstɛrɒl). *Biochem.* [ad. G. *suprasterin* (A. Windaus et al. 1930, in *Ann. d. Chem.* CCCCLXXIII. 20): see SUPRA- + -STEROL.] Either of two optically active polycyclic isomers (***suprasterol I, II***) of $C_{28}H_{44}O$ produced by prolonged irradiation of vitamin D.

1931 *Chem. Abstr.* XXV. 301 Ergosterol in EtOH, subjected to the action of Hg light at about 75° for 50 hrs., gives a mixt. of suprasterol I..and II. **1943** *Endeavour* Apr. 73/2 Calciferol itself [vitamin D] was also liable to be broken down further to inactive substances—toxisterol and suprasterols I and II. **1976** H. CAMPION et al. in B. E. C. Nordin *Calcium, Phosphate & Mineral Metabolism* xii. 452 Ergocalciferol itself can, under prolonged irradiation, undergo irreversible photoisomerization to compounds known as suprasterol$_2$ I.

supratemporal (s(j)uːprəˈtɛmpərəl), *a.*[1] (*sb.*) *Anat.* and *Zool.* [See SUPRA- 1 b and TEMPORAL *a.*[2]] = SUPERTEMPORAL *a.*[2] (*sb.*).

1846 [see SUPRA-ORBITAL]. **1854** OWEN in *Orr's Circ. Sci., Org. Nat.* I. 187 The suborbital, superorbital, and supra-temporal scale-bones are removed. **1866** HUXLEY *Laing's Preh. Rem. Caithn.* 95 The..supra-temporal ridges are but little marked. **1888** ROLLESTON & JACKSON *Anim. Life* 95 [In the perch] a forked bone, the supra-temporal scale, connects the fore-limb to the skull.

supraˈtemporal, *a.*[2] [See SUPRA- 4 a and TEMPORAL *a.*[1]] = SUPERTEMPORAL *a.*[1]

1882 FARRAR *Early Chr.* II. 404 That life is..eternal, i.e. spiritual, supratemporal, Divine. **1882** WESTCOTT *Hist. Faith* xi. (1883) 144 The 'eternal' does not in essence express the infinite extension of time but the absence of time: not the omni-temporal but the supra-temporal.

ˌsuprateˈrraneous, *a. rare.* [f. L. *suprā* SUPRA- 1 a + *terra* land, earth; after *subterraneous.*] = SUPERTERRANEOUS.

1666 *Phil. Trans.* I. 186 The things, to be observ'd..may be..divided..into Supraterraneous, Terrestrial, and Subterraneous. *a* **1900** SPRUCE in B. D. Jackson *Gloss. Bot. Terms* s.v., Supraterraneous Perianth.

So **ˌsuprateˈrrestrial** *a.* = SUPERTERRESTRIAL 1.

1887 *Andover Rev.* Jan. 42 She might find her first supra-terrestrial experience in some dim subjacency of aromatic spiritual forest, in which she might smoke a spiritual pipe in peace. **1908** ORR *Resurrect. Jesus* vii. 198 That supra-terrestrial sphere to which it [*sc.* Christ's resurrection body] now more properly belonged.

supravaˈginal, *a. Anat.* [See SUPRA- 1 b and VAGINAL.] Situated above or outside a sheath or sheathing membrane; situated, or performed, above the vagina.

1891 in *Cent. Dict.* **1893** H. MORRIS *Treat. Hum. Anat.* 890 The supravaginal space around the optic nerve. *Ibid.* 1083 The cervix..may be divided into..an upper supravaginal zone, a middle zone of vaginal attachment, and a lower intravaginal zone, the os uteri. **1901** *Lancet* 5 Oct. 917 Arguments..in favour of supra-vaginal amputation of the uterus rather than total hysterectomy.

†**supraˈvise**, *v. Obs.* [f. med. or mod.L. *suprāvīs-*, pa. pple. stem of *suprāvidēre* (in med.L. to reconnoitre), f. *suprā* SUPRA- 2 + *vidēre* to see.] *trans.* = SUPERVISE *v.* 2. Also *absol.*

1606 HOLLAND *Sueton.* 231 Surveying and supravising the publick works. **1618** S. WARD *Jethro's Justice* (1627) 7 If God supravise not, Samuell the Seer shall take seuen wrong before one right. **1640** in Carlyle *Misc. Ess.* (1872) VII. 65 No man did supravise all the clerkes.

†**supraˈvision**. *Obs.* [ad. med.L. *suprāvīsio, -ōnem*: cf. prec. and VISION.] = SUPERVISION 1.

1642 JER. TAYLOR *Episc.* (1647) 107 There comes upon me (saith S. Paul) daily the care or Supravision of all the Churches. **1651** —— *Clerus Domini* iii. §15 Taking supravision or oversight of them willingly. **1667** —— *Gt. Exemp.* Disc. xix. §12. (ed. 4) 477 The supravision of a Teacher over him.

†**supraˈvisor**. *Obs.* Also 6 -our. [ad. med.L. *suprāvīsor*: cf. prec.] = SUPERVISOR 1, 1 b, c, 3.

1566 GASCOIGNE *Supposes* v. ii, I make thee supra visour of this supper. **1609** W. M. *Man in Moone* (Percy Soc.) 2 What false orthographie escapeth in the print, impute to the hast of the supravisor of the proofes. **1614** in *Trans. Cumbld. & Westmld. Archaeol. Soc.* III. 116 To take panes as supravisors to see the performinge of all things accordinge to this my will and testament. **1653** JER. TAYLOR *Serm. for Year* I. xxiii. 297 They made Aræus titular [admiral] and Lysander supravisor of him. *a* **1677** BARROW *Serm. Heb. xiii. 17* Wks. 1686 III. 270 The Curators, or Supravisors of the Church. **1694** in Picton *L'pool Munic. Rec.* (1883) I. 320 The Supravis[rs] of the Highway.

supravital (s(j)uːprəˈvaɪtəl), *a. Histology.* [SUPRA-.] Of a stain or the process of staining: involving living tissue, esp. blood, outside the body. Hence **supraˈvitally** *adv.*

1921 *Arch. Internal Med.* XXVIII. 513 Janus green B.., used as a supravital stain in dilute solutions.. stains mitochondria an intense green. *Ibid.* 515 The reticulum present in certain erythrocytes is seen as a delicate network and is best demonstrated by staining supravitally with brilliant cresyl blue or azur II. **1930** *Edin. Med. Jrnl.* XXXVII. 429 Supravital staining.—The process consists of the application of basic dyes to portions of tissues removed during life or immediately after somatic death. **1972** C. GURNEY in C. E. Mengel et al. *Hematology* i. 6 When stained supravitally with a number of special stains, these young cells show small dark granules. **1974** *Nature* 22 Feb. 551/2 The supernatant was then shaken from the wells and supravital stain was added.

supremacist (s(j)uːˈprɛməsɪst), *sb.* and *a.* [f. SUPREMACY + -IST, orig. in *white supremacist.*]

A. *sb.* One who believes in the supremacy of one of the races or of either of the sexes or of any other social group. B. *adj.* That is a supremacist. Orig. and freq. preceded by defining word: see also *male supremacist* s.v. MALE *sb.* 4, *white supremacist* s.v. WHITE *a.* 11 e.

1959, etc. [see *white supremacist* s.v. WHITE *a.* 11 e]. **1961** WEBSTER, *Supremacist*.., an advocate or adherent of some concept of group supremacy; *esp*: *white supremacist*. **1968** in B. & T. Roszak *Masculine/Feminine* (1970) 256 Men.. maintain a dominant position for themselves, and as supremacists, try to perpetuate that position of dominance. **1969** *Manifesto for N.Y. Radical Feminists* in J. Hole & E. Levine *Rebirth of Feminism* (1971) 443 The purpose of the male power group is to fulfill a need. That need is psychological, and derives from the supremacist assumption of the male identity. **1975** *Economist* 1 Feb. 24/1 Weaning the more sensible loyalists away from their Protestant supremacist partners. **1976** P. DRISCOLL *Barboza Credentials* v. iii. 217 An ultra-white brotherhood of supremacist bitter-enders. **1982** *Washington Post* 4 Mar. D 1/1 None of this football nonsense of airy polls full of supremacist blather.

So **suˈpremacism**: see *white supremacism* s.v. WHITE *a.* 11 e.

supremacy (s(j)uːˈprɛməsɪ). Also 6 **supremasie, -isie, 6–7 -acie, -icie, 7 -acye, supreamacie, 8 supreamacy.** [f. SUPREME *a.* + -ACY 2. Hence F. *suprématie*, It. *supremazia*, Sp., Pg. *supremacia.*]

1. The condition of being supreme in authority, rank, or power; position of supreme or highest authority or power.

a. with reference to the position of the sovereign (***royal*** or ***regal supremacy***) as supreme head in earth of the Church of England (as declared in the statute 26 Hen. VIII, c. 1, an. 1534), or as supreme governor of England in spiritual and temporal matters (as in 1 Eliz. c. 1, an. 1558–9). Also used retrospectively of the more indefinite authority claimed by earlier sovereigns.

Act of Supremacy (or ***Supremacy Act***), any of the acts of parliament in which this is laid down. ***Oath of (the King's) Supremacy***, the oath in which this is acknowledged.

1549 *Bk. Com. Prayer, Ord. Deacons*, The Othe of the Kynges Supremacie. I from henceforth shal utterly renounce..the Bysshop of Rome, and his aucthoritie, power, and iurisdiction... And I from hencefoorth wyll.. take the Kynges Maiestie, to be the onely Supreme head in earth, of the Church of Englande. **1554** *Act 1 & 2 Philip & M.* c. 8. §42 Albeit the Title or Stile of Supremacye or Supreme Hedd of the Church of Englande and of Irelande ..never was..lawfully attributed..to any King..of this Realme. **1603** *Const. & Canons Eccles.* ii, Whosoeuer shall hereafter..impeach in any part his [the King's] regal Supremacy in the said causes [ecclesiastical] restored to the Crowne. **1626** in Ellis *Orig. Lett.* Ser. I. III. 243 All three of them have taken the Oath of Allegeance, some say of Supremacy also. **1710** *Managers' Pro & Con* 62 If the Party will allow the Queen her Supreamacy. **1769** BLACKSTONE *Comm.* IV. 53 The statute 1 W. & M. st. 2. c. 18..which exempts all dissenters..from all penal laws relating to religion, provided they take the oaths of allegiance and supremacy. **1839** KEIGHTLEY *Hist. Eng.* I. 103 [William the Conqueror] asserted his royal supremacy over the clergy of England. **1880** *Encycl. Brit.* XI. 664/2 Sir Thomas More and Fisher..were executed for refusing to accept the Supremacy Act (1535). **1884** *Encycl. Brit.* XVII. 701/1 Statutes of Charles II. and George I. enacted that no member should vote or sit in either house of parliament without having taken the several oaths of allegiance, supremacy, and abjuration.

b. with reference to the supreme authority of the see or bishop of Rome (***papal supremacy***).

1560 DAUS tr. *Sleidane's Comm.* 222 Those places of scripture, which the Bishop [of Rome] doeth vsurpe to establyshe hys supremacie [orig. *ad sui primatus confirmationem*]. **1561** T. NORTON *Calvin's Inst.* I. Pref., So that no man lift vp hys fynger agaynst the supremicie of the Apostolike sea. **1624** GATAKER *Transubst.* 132 So long as he acknowledgeth the Popes Supremacie. **1714** FORTESCUE-ALAND *Pref. Fortescue's Abs. & Lim. Mon.* 69 Possibly Rome had not then resolved to derive her Supremacy from St. Peter. **1757** in *Cath. Rec. Soc. Publ.* VII. 189 The learned Bossuett makes it an article of faith, the Supremacy of y[e] pope, as does the Councill of Trent.

c. *gen.* in the relation of one person, sovereign, state, etc. to another, or of God to the universe.

1547 TONSTALL in Burnet *Hist. Ref.* (1681) II. I. *Collect. Rec.* 107, I fortuned to find many Writings for the Supremacy of the King to the Realm of Scotland. **1584** B. R. tr. *Herodotus* I. 31 Determining to atchieue y[e] supremisie. **1596** SHAKS. *Tam. Shr.* v. ii. 109 Peace it boads, and loue, and quiet life, An awfull rule, and right supremicie. **1614** RALEIGH *Hist. World* III. xii. §5. 150 They (who had beene accustomed vnto such a supremacie, as they would in no wise communicate with..Athens..). **1667** MILTON *P.L.* III. 205 Man disobeying..sinns Against the high Supremacie of Heav'n. **1782** PRIESTLEY *Corrupt. Chr.* I. I. 150 The divine being cannot give his own supremacy. **1835** THIRLWALL *Greece* viii. I. 291 The steps by which Sparta rose to a supremacy above the rest of the Dorian states. **1847** PRESCOTT *Peru* (1850) II. 170 The Indian lords then tendered their obeisance..after which the royal notary read aloud the instrument asserting the supremacy of the Castilian Crown. **1848** R. I. WILBERFORCE *Doctr. Incarnation* iv. (1852) 74 A supremacy over them [*sc.* the inferior creatures], had been the result of Adam's likeness to their Creator. **1856** DOVE *Logic Chr. Faith* VI. §4. 354 Revelation exhibits..the Supremacy of God.

d. With possessive as a mock title.

1760–72 H. BROOKE *Fool of Qual.* (1809) II. 14 Truth, so please your supremacy, has been sunk in..a well.

e. *fig.* Said of qualities, influences, etc.

1583 MELBANCKE *Philotimus* G iij, I giue you the supremasie of my soule, vse it as you list. **1663** PATRICK *Parab. Pilgr.* xxxii. (1687) 387 It suffers reason to retain its throne, or rather exalts..its Supremacy..to a greater height. **1809–10** COLERIDGE *Friend* I. vi. (1865) 25 The disbelief of essential wisdom and goodness..prepares the imagination for the supremacy of cunning with malignity. **1874** GREEN *Short Hist.* iii. §4. 133 Abelard claimed for reason the supremacy over faith.

2. Supreme position in achievement, character, or estimation.

1589 GREENE *Menaphon* (Arb.) 35 Iuno for maiestie, Pallas for wisedome, and Venus for beautie had let my Samela haue the supremacie. **1693** DRYDEN *Juvenal* Ded. (1697) p. viii, That your Lordship is form'd by Nature for this Supremacy, I cou'd easily prove..from the distinguishing Character of your Writing. **1836** HOR. SMITH *Tin Trumpet* (1876) 335 The discovery that water would resist being boiled above 212 degrees has conferred upon England its manufacturing supremacy. **1872** YEATS *Techn. Hist. Comm.* 250 To secure the naval supremacy of Athens over the rest of the Greek states. **1879** *Cassell's Techn. Educ.* III. 154 English gunpowder has long held almost undisputed supremacy as to excellence of quality and strength.

Suprematism (s(j)uːˈprɛmətɪz(ə)m). Also **suprematism.** [ad. Russ. *suprematizm.*] An artistic movement initiated by the Russian painter Kazimir Malevich in 1913; the abstract, geometrical style of art produced by this movement. Hence **Suˈprematist**[1] (*a*) *sb.*, an adherent of Suprematism; (*b*) *adj.*, of, pertaining to, or characteristic of Suprematism.

[**1915** K. MALEVICH (*title*) Ot Kubizma do Suprematizma.] **1933** *Times Lit. Suppl.* 2 Feb. 76/3 The various channels in which the Futurist movement has run.. orphism..suprematism. **1936** *Bull. Museum of Mod. Art* Nov.–Dec. 6 Malevich, the Suprematist, passed through a proto-Dada phase in 1914. **1948** H. READ *Art Now* (ed. 3) iv. 104 Malevich and Tatlin revolted against the naturalistic tradition and established a completely geometrical style which they called *Suprematism*. **1955** *Archit. Rev.* CXVII. 226/1 Malevitsch, in *Bauhausbuch* No. 11, hopefully says of his own filleted and rectilinear aesthetic 'thus one may also call Suprematism an aeronautical art'. **1958** *Spectator* 14 Feb. 203/1 His Suprematist work exploiting a simple vocabulary of colours and shapes and rhythms. **1958** *Listener* 31 July 168/3 Malevich and the Suprematists reflected it, in a form so extreme and absolute that it led to the painting of a picture consisting of a white square on a white ground. **1972** [see RAYONISM, RAYONNISM]. **1972** *Times* 13 Apr. 4/8 A Suprematist construction of about 1916 ..by Ivan Puni made £3,200. **1980** I. MURDOCH *Nuns & Soldiers* i. 80 He became a cubist, then a surrealist, then a *fauve*: a futurist, a constructivist, a suprematist.

suprematist[2]: see *white suprematist* s.v. WHITE *a.* 11 e.

supreme (s(j)uːˈpriːm), *a.*[1] and *sb.*[1] Also 6 **suppreme, 6–7 supreame, 7–8 supream.** [ad. L. *suprēmus*, superl. of *superus* that is above, f. *super* above. Cf. F. *suprême*, It., Sp., Pg. *supremo.*

In poetry, esp. when attrib., freq. stressed ˈ*supreme*.]

A. *adj.*

1. Highest (in literal sense), loftiest, topmost. Now only *poet.*

1523 SKELTON *Garl. Laurel* 694 What thynge occasionyd the showris of rayne, Of fyre elementar in his supreme spere. **1653** R. SANDERS *Physiogn.* 115 The supream angle not joyned..predicts loss of the eyes. **1661** LOVELL *Hist. Anim. & Min.* 299 The venters are the inferiour, or abdomen; the middle, or thorax; or the supreame, which is the head. **1695** WOODWARD *Nat. Hist. Earth* I. (1723) 89 The supreme or outmost Stratum of the Globe. **1808** MACAULAY in Trevelyan *Life & Lett.* (1876) I. i. 32 Day set on Cambria's hills supreme. **1878** BROWNING *La Saisiaz* 75 Blanc, supreme above his earth-brood.

2. a. Highest in authority or rank; holding the highest place in authority, government, or power.

Chiefly in technical collocations, and first used in the expressions ***supreme head*** and ***supreme governor*** in the enactments of Henry VIII's and Elizabeth's reigns (respectively) dealing with the position of the sovereign as the paramount authority (as against the bishop of Rome). (Cf. SUPREMACY 1 a.)

Supreme Court of Judicature: (*a*) in India (see quot. 1773); (*b*) in Great Britain and Ireland (see JUDICATURE 1). ***Supreme Soviet***: the national legislature of the U.S.S.R.; also, the national legislature of any of its constituent republics.

1532–3 *Act 24 Hen. VIII*, c. 12 Preamble, Where by dyvers sundrie olde autentike histories and cronicles it is manifestly declared and expressed that this Realme of Englond is an Impire..governed by oon Supreme heede and King. **1534** *Act 26 Hen. VIII*, c. 1, That the Kyng our Soveraign Lorde..shalbe..reputed the onely supreme heed in erthe of the Churche of England callyd Anglicana Ecclesia. **1558–9** *Act 1 Eliz.* c. 1. §19 (Form of Oath), I..doo ..declare in my Conscience, that the Quenes Highnes is thonelye supreme Governour of this Realme..aswell in all Spirituall or Ecclesiasticall Thinges or Causes as Temporall. **1560** DAUS tr. *Sleidane's Comm.* 66 b, Geuyng hym his faythe as to his supreme Magistrate. **1597** SKENE *De Verb. Sign.* s.v. *Scaccarium*, Some callis it [*sc.* the Exchequer] the soveraigne and supreame court. **1611** *Bible* 1 Pet ii. 13 Submit your selues to euery ordinance of man.. whether it be to the King, as supreme, Or vnto gouernours. **1656** J. HAMMOND *Leah & Rachel* Postscr. (1844) 30, I.. will abide such censure..as the supreame power of England shall find me to have merited. **1672–5** COMBER *Comp. Temple* (1702) 119 Such Miscreants..who should thirst so vehemently for the blood of its Supream Governor. **1765** BLACKSTONE *Comm.* I. ii. 146 Of magistrates also some are supreme, in whom the sovereign power of the state resides; others are subordinate, deriving all their authority from the supreme magistrate. **1770** *Junius Lett.* Ded., When we say that the legislature is supreme, we mean, that it is the highest power known to the constitution. **1773** *Act 13 Geo. III*, c. 63 §13 That it shall..be lawful for his Majesty,..to..establish a Supreme Court of Judicature at Fort William [in Bengal]. **1790** A. J. DALLAS (*title*), Reports of Cases adjudged in the Courts of Pennsylvania, namely, the Common Pleas, Supreme Court, and the High Court of Errors and Appeals. **1844** H. H. WILSON *Brit. India* III. ix. III. 535 The Supreme Council..was to consist of six members, of whom four were to be officers of the four Presidencies. **1861** BROUGHAM *Brit. Const.* xvii. 255 The judicial power exercised by the Lords as a supreme Court of Judicature in all matters of law. **1873** *Act 36 & 37 Vict.* c. 66. §4 The said Supreme Court shall consist of two permanent Divisions, one of which, under the name of 'Her Majesty's High Court of Justice', shall have and exercise original jurisdiction..and the other of which, under the name of 'Her Majesty's Court of Appeal', shall have and exercise appellate jurisdiction. **1881** *Encycl. Brit.* XIII. 789/2 In the United States the supreme court consists of a chief justice and eight associate justices. **1936** *Times* 15 June 11/4 The legislative assemblies will consist of one All-Union Parliament called the 'Supreme Council (or Supreme Soviet) of the U.S.S.R.'. **1947** *Ann. Reg. 1946* 218 M. Kalinin, chairman of the Presidium of the Supreme Soviet, resigned for reasons of health. **1957** *Whitaker's Almanack 1958* 950/1 The Union Republics and Autonomous Republics have Supreme Soviets..of their own..although their jurisdiction is severely circumscribed in favour of the central Government. **1974** tr. *Sniečkus's Soviet Lithuania* 67 The Supreme Soviet of the Lithuanian SSR has approved the Five-Year Plan for the economic development of the Republic for 1971–5. **1978** *Ann. Reg. 1977* 490 Article 90 [of the Constitution of the USSR 1977]. The term of the Supreme Soviet of the USSR, the Supreme Soviets of Union Republics, and the Supreme Soviets of Autonomous Republics shall be five years.

†Const. *to*. **1642** JER. TAYLOR *Episc.* §36 The king is supreme to the bishop in impery.

b. Said of the authority, command, etc.

1539 TONSTALL *Serm. Palm Sund.* (1823) 61 Faustinus.. alleged.. that the bysshop of Rome ought to haue the orderynge of all Great Matters..by his supreme auctoritie. **1594** SHAKS. *Rich. III*, III. vii. 118 It is your fault, that you resigne The Supreme Seat, the Throne Maiesticall. **1659** HAMMOND *Dispatcher Disp.* iv. §4 What the rights are, which are peculiar to the Supreme Pastourship. **1667** MILTON *P.L.* III. 659 Uriel,..thou..here art likeliest by supream decree Like honour to obtain. **1726** POPE *Odyss.* XIX. 170 He, long honour'd in supreme command. **1754** ERSKINE *Princ. Sc. Law* (1809) 13 Jurisdiction is either supreme, inferior, or mixed. **1840** THIRLWALL *Greece* lvi. VII. 185 When they had joined their forces, Craterus resigned the supreme command to his colleague. **1863** H. COX *Inst.* I. i. 2 The supreme power of making and abrogating laws.

c. *transf.* and *fig.* (chiefly predicative).

1656 BRAMHALL *Replic.* iv. 159 In a great Family there are several offices, as a Divine, a Physitian, a Schoolmaster, and every one of these is supreme in his own way. **1667** MILTON *P.L.* IV. 91 The lower still I fall, onely Supream In miserie. *a* **1680** BUTLER *Rem.* (1759) I. 238 Man is supreme Lord and Master Of his own Ruin and Disaster. **1726** BUTLER *Serm. Rolls Chap.* ii. 26 Which Principle..being in Nature supream,..ought to preside over and govern all the rest. **1838** DICKENS *Nich. Nick.* xxi, The temple of fashion where Madame Mantalini reigned paramount and supreme. **1878** STUBBS *Const. Hist.* III. xviii. 158 During the session parliament was supreme. **1884** F. TEMPLE *Relat. Relig. & Sci.* ii. (1885) 59 To believe that the rule of duty is supreme over all the universe, is the first stage of Faith. **1892** WESTCOTT *Gospel of Life* 89 Each science is supreme within its own domain.

ellipt. **1718** PRIOR *Solomon* II. 36 The spreading Cedar, that an Age had stood, Supreme of Trees, and Mistress of the Wood. **1774** BRYANT *Mythol.* II. 125 He seems to have been the supreme of those..spirits described above.

3. a. Of the highest quality, degree, or amount. ***the supreme sacrifice***: the laying down of one's life for one's country in battle; also *transf.*

1593 SHAKS. *Lucr.* 780 Let their exhald vnholdsome breaths make sicke The life of puritie, the supreme faire, Ere he arriue his wearie noone-tide pricke. **1609** DANIEL *Civ. Wars* IV. xli, Hee could not meane t' haue peace with those, Who did in that supreame degree offend. *a* **1631** DONNE *Paradoxes* (1652) 17 If these kil themselves, they do it in their best and supream perfection. **1649** E. REYNOLDS *Hosea* vi. 82 The supreame end and happinesse of the soule. **1751** JOHNSON *Rambler* No. 110 ¶1 That to please the Lord and Father of the universe, is the supreme interest of created.. beings. **1847** HELPS *Friends in C.* I. vi. 96, I have a supreme disgust for the man who at the hustings has no opinion beyond..the clamour round him. **1849** MACAULAY *Hist. Eng.* iii. I. 412 In no other mind have the demonstrative faculty and the inductive faculty coexisted in such supreme excellence. **1856** EMERSON *Eng. Traits, Race* Wks. (Bohn) II. 20 They have sound bodies, and supreme endurance in war and in labour. **1872** LIDDON *Elem. Relig.* i. 5 The needs of the human mind, and among them..its supreme need of a religion. **1878** R. W. DALE *Lect. Preach.* vii. 212 The death of Christ, which is the supreme revelation of the Divine love. **1916** W. M. CLOW *Evangel of Strait Gate* xv. 173 These young men..have gone down not only to the horror of the battlefield but to the gates of death as they made the supreme sacrifice. **1935** J. E. C. WELLDON *Forty Years On* i. 46 Citizenship demands at times the supreme sacrifice—as it was called during the Great War of 1914–18. **1955** J. BURNABY *Christian Words & Christian Meanings* vi. 104 The 'supreme sacrifice', in the cliché of the wartime newspaper, does consist in the carrying of disregard of self to the limit. **1965** J. A. MICHENER *Source* (1966) 491 Because He [*sc.* Christ] offered Himself as the supreme sacrifice two things happened. We were saved and He ascended to Godhood. **1981** HINCHLIFF & YOUNG *Human Potential* v. 98 When one speaks of the dead of two world wars as having made the supreme sacrifice, one means that the sacrifice was made for..one's country.

b. Of persons: Highest or greatest in character or achievement.

c **1611** CHAPMAN *Iliad* v. 1 Then Pallas breath'd in Tydeus sonne: to render whom supreame To all the Greekes,..she cast a hoter beame, On his high mind. **1837** CARLYLE *Fr. Rev.* I. I. ii, The Supreme Quack. **1874** CREIGHTON *Hist. Ess.* i. (1902) 1 In..the reflective and analytic class, Lionardo and Dante stand supreme. **1878** GLADSTONE *Prim. Homer* 138 Homer exhibits Odusseus as a supreme master of the bow. **1891** FARRAR *Darkn. & Dawn* xvii, You are a supreme artist.

ellipt. **1814** WORDSW. *Laodamia* ix, Supreme of Heroes —bravest, noblest, best!

c. Of a point or period of time: Of highest or critical importance.

1878 BOSW. SMITH *Carthage* 170 The Carthaginian government managed, even in this supreme hour, to thwart Hamilcar. **1883** *Manch. Examiner* 26 Nov. 5/1 The generals have been at loggerheads at the supreme moment of the battle.

d. *spec.* applied to highly excellent varieties of fruits or vegetables.

1706 LONDON & WISE *Retir'd Gard'ner* I. xi. 48 Summer Pears. The Little Muscat, The Supreme, The Cuisse-Madame. [**1860** HOGG *Fruit Man.* 221 Pears... Windsor (Bell Tongue..Summer Bell; Suprême).] **1882** *Garden* 21 Jan. 38/1 Supreme [a variety of pea]..gives large successional pickings.

4. *spec.* applied to God (or his attributes), as the paramount ruler of the world, or the most exalted being or intelligence; also to the most exalted of heathen deities.

1594 SHAKS. *Rich. III*, I. i. 13 Take heed you daily not before your King, Lest he that is the supreme King of Kings Confound your hidden falshood. **1607** —— *Cor.* v. iii. 71 With the consent of supreame Ioue. **1634** MILTON *Comus* 217 He, the Supreme good, t' whom all things ill Are but as slavish officers of vengeance. **1667** —— *P.L.* x. 70 Mine both in Heav'n and Earth to do thy will Supream. **1672–5** COMBER *Comp. Temple* (1702) 93 That Supream Lord, the Creator of Heaven and Earth. **1699** BURNET *39 Art.* i. 38 The Supream and Increated Being. **1711** SHAFTESB. *Charac.* (1737) II. 274 Whether there be really that Supreme-One we suppose. **1751** HARRIS *Hermes* Wks. (1841) 235 Original truth having the most intimate connexion with the Supreme Intelligence. **1820** SHELLEY *Œd. Tyr.* I. i. 1 Thou supreme Goddess! **1836** THIRLWALL *Greece* xiii. II. 165 When the victim was to be offered to the supreme God, it was taken up to the top of the highest hil. **1854** *Orr's Circ. Sci., Org. Nat.* I. 29 The proposition..that human science is..adverse to the belief in a Supreme Intelligence. **1902** *Encycl. Brit.* XXXII. 824/1 The Festival of the Supreme Being, decreed by the National Convention, designed by David and conducted by Robespierre.

5. Last, final, as belonging to the moment of death. Now only a gallicism: cf. F. *le moment suprême*.

1606 HOLLAND *Sueton.* 56 The supreme iudgments & testimonies of his friends..delivered at their deaths. **1648** [see 6 b]. **1894** SIR E. SULLIVAN *Woman* 57 When Queen Elizabeth was dying she had her band summoned to her ante-chamber..when she felt the supreme moment approaching she told the musicians to strike up her favourite air.

6. In comparative and superlative.

a. Comparative ***supremer***. *rare*.

1683 KENNETT tr. *Erasm. on Folly* (1709) 125 After their reign here they must appear before a supreamer judge. **1748** RICHARDSON *Clarissa* (1811) VIII. xxiv. 109 Having given way to supremer fervours.

b. Superlative ***supremest, most supreme***.

1631 MASSINGER *Emperor East* IV. i, Fate..appointed you To the supremest honour. **1648** HERRICK *Hesper., Upon a Maide* 6 Virgins, come, and in a ring Her supreamest requiem sing. *a* **1674** TRAHERNE *Chr. Ethics* (1675) 11 There are many degrees of blessedness beneath the most supream. **1725** POPE *Odyss.* IV. 325 Throned in omnipotence, supremest Jove Tempers the fates of human race. **1772–84** *Cook's Voy.* (1790) V. 1637 This man felt the most supreme pleasure. **1862** MISS BRADDON *Lady Audley* xxxiv, In her supremest hour of misery.

B. *sb.* †**1.** A person having supreme authority, rank, or power; a supreme authority, ruler, or magistrate; sometimes = superior. *Obs.*

1553 CROME in Strype *Eccl. Mem.* (1721) III. App. x. 24 That they that be prohybyte of the byshops,..ought to cease from preachyng..till they haue purgyd them byfore the supreme of soche suspicion. *a* **1578** LINDESAY (Pitscottie) *Chron. Scot.* (S.T.S.) I. 98 He wald nocht enter his sone into his landis the said Earle being supreme thairof. **1592** SHAKS. *Ven. & Ad.* 996 She clepes him..Imperious supreme of all mortall things. **1631** CHAPMAN *Cæsar & Pompey* II. i. Plays 1873 III. 148 This day had prou'd him the supreame of Cæsar. **1654–66** EARL ORRERY *Parthen.* (1676) 349 There ought to be a Supreme above the Law. **1660** WATERHOUSE *Arms & Arm.* 177, I return to London which I find of great consequence to her Supremes. **1671** MILTON *P.R.* I. 99 Their King, their Leader, and Supream on Earth. **1677** W. HUGHES *Man of Sin* I. vi. 27 Was it not a fine cast of his office, that one of them [*sc.* popes] practised upon one of these Supremes [*sc.* emperors]? **1725** POPE *Odyss.* XIII. 144 Old Ocean's dread Supreme. **1807** E. S. BARRETT *Rising Sun* III. 100 By the act of Reformation, the lord was declared to be the supreme of the church.

2. The highest degree or amount *of* something.

1760–72 H. BROOKE *Fool of Qual.* (1809) II. 20 The qualities that intitle a man to this supreme of denominations. **1817** KEATS *Sleep & Poetry* 235 A drainless shower Of light is poesy; 'tis the supreme of power. **1858** GEN. P. THOMPSON *Audi Alt. Part.* lxv. I. 249 The Native Indian term for the supreme of folly, is 'monkey business'.

3. As a title of God (or an exalted deity). ***the Supreme***: the Supreme Being, God.

[**1667** MILTON *P.L.* VI. 723 O Father, O Supream of heav'nly Thrones. *Ibid.* VIII. 414 To attaine The highth and depth of thy Eternal wayes All human thoughts come short, Supream of things.] **1702** ROWE *Tamerl.* I. i, O thou Supream! **1711** ADDISON *Spect.* No. 257 ¶7 It is the greatest Folly to seek the..Approbation of any Being, besides the Supreme. *a* **1766** MRS. F. SHERIDAN *Nourjahad* (1767) 197 May the Supreme grant thy petition. **1820** SHELLEY *Hymn Merc.* i, Heaven's dread Supreme. **1884** *Contemp. Rev.* Feb. 256 That aboriginal law of self-sacrifice which links the Supreme to His creatures.

†**4.** The highest or topmost part. *Obs. rare*$^{-1}$.

1660 F. BROOKE tr. *Le Blanc's Trav.* Ded. A 2 b, One, who ..took not his information at the shore or Suburbs, but.. visited the intestines and supreme, whence he might the better look below, and round about him.

5. ***supreme of chicken*** = *suprême de volaille* s.v. SUPRÊME *sb.*[2] (*a.*[2]) 2 a.

1939 *Vogue's Cookery Bk.* 81 Supreme of Chicken. 1 chicken 4 eggs 1½ cups cream. **1959** A. CHRISTIE *Cat among Pigeons* xiv. 154 Ann Shapland..was sitting at a table.. eating Supreme of chicken. **1983** *Out of Town* Dec. 72/2 The pastry case on the Supreme of Chicken..was a little too generous.

‖**suprême** (syprɛm), *sb.*[2] (*a.*[2]) [F., f. L. *suprēmus*: see SUPREME *a.*[1] and *sb.*[1]] **1.** A kind of sauce (see quot. 1906). Also ‖***sauce suprême, suprême sauce***.

1813 L. E. UDE *French Cook* viii. 191 (*heading*) Filets of fowls sautés au suprême. **1846** A. SOYER *Gastronomic Regenerator* 342 Fillet three fowls.., sauté the same,..sauce over with a sauce suprême. **1906** *Mrs. Beeton's Bk. Househ. Managem.* lxii. 1671 *Suprême*, a rich, delicately flavoured cream sauce, made from chicken stock, etc. **1936** LUCAS & HUME *Au Petit Cordon Bleu* 73 Pour over the following *suprême* sauce. **1948** *Good Housek. Cookery Bk.* 303 Suprême Sauce. Make as for Velouté sauce, but add up to ¼ pint of cream. **1961** *Harper's Bazaar* Feb. 72/2 There are three kinds of *roux*... Pale—for making *veloutés, suprême* sauces and *allemande* sauce.

2. a. In full, ***suprême de volaille***: a dish consisting of breast of chicken or other poultry usu. served with a white sauce. **b.** The part of the bird used in making *suprême de volaille*.

1850 THACKERAY *Pendennis* II. i. 6 The supreme de volaille was very good. **1864** M. B. CHESNUT *Diary* 31 Jan. in C. V. Woodward *Mary Chesnut's Civil War* (1981) xxii. 551 Gumbo, ducks and olives, suprême de volaille. **1907** [see JARDINIÈRE 2]. **1944** A. SIMON *Conc. Encycl. Gastron.* VI. Birds 111/2 The suprêmes are constituted by the meat on each side of the breast, from the point where the wing originates to the extremity of the stomach. **1975** *Times* 22 Feb. 7/2 Chicken Neptune—a suprême stuffed with prawns and butter and served with a shellfish sauce (£2.20). **1979** J. TOVEY *Entertaining with Tovey* 61 For cream soups I use a chicken..stock. Use..the bones of a bird from which you have cut the suprêmes. **1983** *Sunday Tel.* 17 Apr. 18/5 While they ladle out the mulligatawny or dish out the *suprême de volaille*.

supremely (s(j)uːˈpriːmlɪ), *adv.* [f. SUPREME *a.* + -LY[2].]

1. In a supreme degree, to a supreme extent.

1615 CHAPMAN *Odyss.* XXIV. 24 The supremely strenuous Of all the Greeke hoast. **1696** TATE & BRADY *Ps.* c. iv, For He's the Lord, supreamly good. **1718** PRIOR *Solomon* I. 53 The fair Cedar, on the craggy Brow Of Lebanon nodding supremely tall. **1726** POPE *Odyss.* XXIII. 62 How blest this happy hour, should he appear, Dear to us all, to me supremely dear! **1781** COWPER *Ep. Lady Austen* 34 The hand of the Supremely Wise. **1865** E. C. CLAYTON *Cruel Fortune* I. 123 That young person..was supremely jealous of every new pet her mistress took a fancy to. **1870** LOWELL *Among my Books* Ser. I. (1873) 169 More supremely incapable [of this] than any other man who ever wrote English. **1885** 'MRS. ALEXANDER' *Valerie's Fate* vi, Those [moments]..dwelt forever in the memory of both as supremely blissful.

†**2.** By or with supreme authority or power. *rare*.

1687 A. LOVELL tr. *Thevenot's Trav.* I. 65 All suits are there supreamly decided. **1734** tr. *Rollin's Anc. Hist.* (1827) I. II. iii. 301 The senate decided supremely, and there lay no appeal from it.

So **suˈpremeness**, the quality of being supreme; supreme degree.

1843 POE *Premature Burial* Wks. 1864 I. 331 The supremeness of bodily and of mental distress. **1896** A. WHYTE *Bible Char.* x. I. 112 An amazing elevation, detachment, supremeness, and sweetness of soul.

†**suˈpremist.** *Obs. rare.* [f. SUPREME *a.* + -IST.] One who takes upon himself supreme authority.

1649 HEYLIN *Relat. & Observ.* II. 200 The Junto of Tituler Supremists at Westminster..are very unwilling to quit their long-held Dominion. **1651** C. WALKER *Hist. Independ.* III. 18 Our Self-created Supremists.

supremity (s(j)uːˈprɛmɪtɪ). Now *rare*. [ad. late L. *suprēmitās, -tātem*, f. *suprēmus* SUPREME: see -ITY. Cf. OF. *supremite*.]

1. = SUPREMACY 1. ? *Obs.*

1538 in *Lett. Suppr. Monast.* (Camden) 186 The Welsh rudenes decreasynge, Christian cyvilitye maye be introduced to the famous renowne of the kynges supremytye. **1540–1** ELYOT *Image Gov.* (1549) 146 Whether theyr natures were obstinate or proude, aspiryng vnto supremitee. *a* **1548** HALL *Chron., Rich. III*, 51 Victorie and supremitie ouer his enemies. *a* **1661** FULLER *Worthies* (1662) I. vi. 19 The Pope (whose Supremity he [*sc.* Henry VIII] had suppressed in his Dominions). **1716–20** *Lett. Mist's Jrnl.* (1722) I. 292 You here stand fair for the Supremity; for Men in their Dotage generally yield an implicite Obedience to their Wives.

2. = SUPREMACY 2.

1882 W. SHARP *Rossetti* viii. 408 Such sonnets..and others of like supremity.

†**3.** = SUPREME *sb.* 4. *Obs.*

1584 B. R. tr. *Herodotus* I. 57 In the top or supremity of the highest turret is another Chappell.

supremo (suːˈpriːməʊ, suːˈpreɪməʊ), *sb.* [f. Sp. (*generalissimo*) *supremo* supreme general.]

a. A supreme leader or ruler; one holding the highest military or political authority.

The reference in quot. 1944 is to Earl Mountbatten of Burma, whose nickname this was during his period as Supreme Allied Commander, South-East Asia (cf. quot. 1966).

1937 C. S. FORESTER *Happy Return* iv. 43 No expostulation on his part would override the orders given by el Supremo. *Ibid.* 46 'Supremo,' sighed Hernandez... 'The captain came instantly on hearing your summons.' **1944**

Daily Express 6 July 2/7 Why the Supremo?.. A handsome, romantic figure. Hence the Latin-sounding nickname. **1958** *Ibid.* 11 July 1/1 Now their advice and complaints can reach the Cabinet or the Prime Minister only through their 'supremo'—the chairman of the staff chiefs. **1966** E. H. COOKRIDGE *From Battenberg to Mountbatten* ix. 188 In June 1946 Lord Mountbatten's post as Supremo in South-East Asia came to an end and he returned to England. **1979** A. FOX *Threat Warning Red* ii. 21 Pat Cleary, a two-star British admiral, was the representative in Brussels of the American NATO supremo in Norfolk, Virginia.

b. *transf.* One who has overall charge of some department of government or sphere of activity.

1963 *Daily Express* 21 Oct. 1/4 Some, particularly in the Research Department, may follow the supremos into resignation. **1972** *Observer* 10 Dec. 2/7 The appointment of a Land Release Supremo with regional teams to unclog the machinery which is holding up the release of land. **1976** H. WILSON *Governance of Britain* iv. 97 The successful attack by other ministers to prevent him [*sc.* Herbert Morrison] from becoming an economic supremo. **1983** *Private Eye* 17 June 7/1 A short list of possible replacements.. included.. the ruthless supremo of the Royal Philharmonic Orchestra.

supremum (s(j)uːˈpriːməm). *Math.* [L., = highest, neut. of *suprēmus* (see SUPREME *a.* and *sb.*).] The smallest number that is greater than or equal to each of a given set of real numbers; an analogous quantity for a subset of any other ordered set.

1940, **1949** [see INFIMUM]. **1968** E. T. COPSON *Metric Spaces* i. 13 An ordered field *S* is said to have the supremum property if and only if every non-empty subset of *S*.. has a supremum in *S*. **1971** HADLEY & KEMP *Variational Methods in Economics* ii. 53 We now define U* as the supremum of levels of utility which can be maintained indefinitely.

sup. versed: see SUVERSED *Math.*

suq, var. SOUK.

sur, obs. form of SIR *sb.*

sur- (sə(r)), *prefix*, a. (O)F. *sur-*, earlier *sour-*, *sor-*, *soure-* (repr. L. *super*), used in various senses of SUPER-, as in *surcharger* to burden excessively, overburden, SURCHARGE, *surcot* upper coat, SURCOAT, *surnom* additional name, SURNAME, *surpasser* to pass beyond, SURPASS, *surseoir* (:—L. *supersedēre* to SUPERSEDE) to suspend, delay (cf. SURCEASE), *survivre* to live beyond, SURVIVE. As a living suffix, *sur-* is or has been used in a few compounds, chiefly (*a*) nonce-words formed after existing words, as †*surburdened* [after SURCHARGED], †*surgirdle* [after SURCINGLE]; esp. after the legal terms SURREBUTTER, SURREJOINDER, q.v., as ***surrebend***, ***surrebribe***, †***surrecompounded***, †***surrecountermand*** vbs., †***surregaining***; (*b*) variants of technical terms compounded with SUPER- or SUPRA-, as ***sur'ciliary*** = SUPERCILIARY, ***suroc'cipital*** = SUPEROCCIPITAL, ***su'rrenal*** = SUPRARENAL; also **sur'anal** *a. Zool.* = *supra-anal* adj. s.v. SUPRA- 1 b; also as *sb.*, a suranal plate; †**sura'nnation** = SUPERANNUATION; †**ˌsurazo'tation** *Chem.* = *superazotation* in SUPER- 12 a; †**surclose**, ? a final close; †**sur-'clouded** *pa. pple.*, shaded from above; †**sur'contract**, a contract following upon a previous contract; **sur'current** *a. Bot.*, 'the opposite of decurrent; when a leafy expansion runs up the stem' (*Treas. Bot.* 1866); †**sur'feoff** *v.* [after med.L. *super(af)feudare*] *trans.*, to invest (a person) with an estate which one already holds from another (cf. *super(in)feudation* in SUPER- 13); †**surflux**, overflow, flood; **sur'human** *a. Lit.* = SUPERHUMAN *a.* (cf. F. *surhumain*); **sur-in'vest** *v. trans.*, to provide with outer clothing; †**sur'match** *v. trans.*, to excel, surpass; †**sur'pay** *v. trans.*, to more than compensate for; **surpreci'ation**, enhancement of price or value; †**surre'bound** *v.*, to echo repeatedly; †**sur'saturated** *a. Chem.* = SUPERSATURATED; †**sur'stretching** *ppl. a.*, extending far; **sur'style** *v. trans.*, = SURNAME *v.*

1906 J. B. SMITH *Explan. Terms Entomol.* 135 **Suranal*, supra-anal. **1925** A. D. IMMS *Gen. Textbk. Entomol.* 41 The tergum of the last segment, whatever its numerical designation may be, is frequently referred to as the suranal plate or pygidium. **1962** D. NICHOLS *Echinoderms* v. 66 In the urchin immediately after metamorphosis the whole of the aboral surface is covered by an apical disk of plates, consisting of a central suranal, through which the anus opens, a ring of five basals, [etc.]. **1656** BLOUNT *Glossogr.*, **Surannation*.. a growing old, stale or above a years date. **1802** *Med. Jrnl.* VIII. 534 Their different degree of virulence depends on the different degree of *sur-azotation. **1577** HARRISON *England* I. iii. 3/2 in *Holinshed*, They were not now able to remooue the importable loade of the Normanes from our *surburdened shoulders. **1874** DAWKINS *Cave Hunt.* vi. 219 The *surciliary ridges are strongly marked. **1589** PUTTENHAM *Engl. Poesie* III. xix. (Arb.) 225 The Epigrammatist will vse to conclude.. his Epigram with a verse or two, spoken in such sort, as it may seeme a manner of allowance to all the premisses, and that with a ioyfull approbation, which the Latines call *Acclamatio*, we therefore call this figure the *sur-cloze or consenting close. **1632** LITHGOW *Trav.* x. 494 This Ile of Arrane is.. *sur-clouded with Goatfield Hill. **1584** *Leycesters Commw.* (1641) 30 Hee will alwayes yet keepe a voyd place for a new *surcontract with any other. *c* **1482** in *Cal. Proc. Chanc. Q. Eliz.* (1830) II. Pref. 70 Affermyng that the same Piers Bank shuld have *surfeffed the same Robert Scrop of trust in divers parcells of londes. **1660** F. BROOKE tr. *Le Blanc's Trav.* 217 The *surfluxes and inundations which fertilize all Egypt. **1483** *Cath. Angl.* 372/1 A *Surgyrdylle,.. *succingula*. **1933** T. E. LAWRENCE *Let.* 1 Aug. (1938) 773 He takes figures of to-day and projects their shadows on to clouds, till they grow *surhuman and grotesque. **1952** E. POUND *Personae* 56 Beauty That seems to be some quivering splendour cast By the immortal nature on this quicksand And by surhuman fates. **1819** W. TENNANT *Papistry Storm'd* (1827) 95 The plumes, that *sur-invest her skin. **1636** *Montgomerie's Cherrie & Slae* 76 (Wreittoun's ed.), Poets.. Whose Muse *surmatches mine. **1848** OWEN *Homol. Vertebr. Skel.* 146 His recognition of the '*suroccipital' in both mammals. **1603** FLORIO *Montaigne* III. v. 529 One ill kisse doth *surpay [orig. *surpaye*] one good. **1884** *Manch. Exam.* 1 Nov. 5/2 The tendency to *surpreciation in the value of gold as compared with other commodities. **1893** H. M. DOUGHTY *Our Wherry* 63 We.. unravelled the bends and rebends and *surrebends of the Geeste. *c* **1611** CHAPMAN *Iliad* XXI. 361 Earth resounded; and great heauen, about did *surrebound. **1849** DE QUINCEY *Eng. Mail Coach* i. Wks. 1862 IV. 294 This whole corporation was constantly bribed, rebribed, and often *sur-rebribed. **1683** TRYON *Way to Health* 536 All their Regiments of Compounded, Recompounded, Decompounded and *Surrecompounded Medicines. **1570** FOXE *A. & M.* (ed. 2) I. 121/2 Sabinus.. had geuen forth his letters, rehearsing withal the generall recountermaunde... Last of al now he sendeth downe ageyne an other *Surrecountermaund. **1611** SPEED *Hist. Gt. Brit.* IX. x. §28 The Castle of Dunbarre.. was re-gained by the Scots: for recouery, or *sur-re-gaining whereof, the King sent Iohn Earle of Surrey. **1844** HOBLYN *Dict. Terms Med.* (ed. 2), **Surrenal* [misdefined]. **1806** *G. Adams' Nat. & Exp. Philos.* (Philad.) I. App. 532 The epithet *sur-saturated, or the preposition *sub* is prefixed when the base of the salt is in excess. *a* **1560** PHAER *Æneid* IX. Cciij, Their heads to heauen they lift.. and hie *sur-stretchyng skies they check. **1632** LITHGOW *Trav.* x. 498 The delectable planure of Murray.. may be *surstyled, a second Lombardy. *a* **1661** FULLER *Worthies*, *Somersetshire* III. (1662) 27 Gildas, sirnamed the Wise.. was eight years junior to another Gildas called Albanius... He was also otherwise sur-stiled, Querulus.

‖**sura**[1] (ˈsura). *Anglo-Indian.* Also 7 **sure**, **sury**, **suri**. [a. Skr. *surā* spirituous liquor, wine (*surākara* coco-nut tree). Cf. F. *soure* (17th c.).] The fermented sap of various species of palm, as the wild date, the coco-nut, and the palmyra; = TODDY *sb.* 1. Also *attrib.*, as ***sura-house***, ***-tree***.

1598 W. PHILLIP tr. *Linschoten* I. lvi. 101/2 The pot in short space is full of water, which they call *Sura*, & is very pleasant to drinke, like sweet whay. **1609–10** W. FINCH in Purchas *Pilgrims* (1625) I. IV. iv. §6 436 A goodly Countrey .... abounding with wild Date Trees.. whence they draw a liquor called *Tarrie* or *Sure*. **1623** in Foster *Eng. Factories Ind.* (1908) II. 314 The elephantes hath destroyed many hundreds of coques and sura trees. **1684** tr. *Tavernier's Trav.* II. 86 (Y.) Nor could they drink either Wine, or Sury, or Strong Water. **1700** S. L. tr. *Fryke's Voy. E. Ind.* iii. 47 This [juice from the Coco-Nut Tree] they call *Suri*, which is to be sold at the *Suri*-houses. **1874** *Treas. Bot.* Suppl.

sura[2] (ˈsʊərə). Also 7 **surat**, 9 **surah**, **soura**. [a. Arab. *sūraʰ*. Cf. F. *sura*, *surate*. (The earliest examples represent the word with the def. art. prefixed, *assūraʰ*.)] A chapter or larger section of the Koran.

[**1615** W. BEDWELL *Moham. Impost.* II. §45 Teach me.. out of the law of our Prophet, out of euery Assora of the same, some certaine perfections. *Ibid.* O iij, This booke is deuided into sundry sections or Chapters, which they call Assurats, or Azoara's. **1630** J. TAYLOR (Water P.) *Wks.* II. 89/2 In the third booke of thy Alcaron and in the seuen and thirty Asaria.] **1661** BOYLE *Style Script.* (1675) 160 Mahomet himself was so proud of it [*sc.* the Alkoran], that .... he defy's its opposers to equal one surat or section of it. **1850** W. IRVING *Mahomet* xxxv. (1853) 176 To promulgate before the multitude of pilgrims.. an important *sura*, or chapter of the Koran, just received from heaven. **1886** CONDER *Syrian Stone-Lore* ix. (1896) 337 The earlier Suras are chiefly concerned with the warnings as to the coming day of judgment, and with descriptions of the end of the world.

‖**sura**[3] (ˈsura). Also 9 **soor**. [a. Skr. *sura* (Hindī *sur*) god, deity.] In Hindu demonology, a good angel or genie.

1795 T. MAURICE *Hindostan* (1820) I. I. xii. 417 The superior, or northern hemisphere, is the region of delight,.. and in it Indra presides with an army of Soors, or good genii. **1806** —— *Ind. Antiq.* I. 17 The Indian Soors and Assoors, that is the good and evil Genii. **1834** CAUNTER *Orient. Ann.* ix. 115 It was reported that they had been received into the bosom of Siva, among the suras of the supreme paradise.

†**sura'bound**, *v. Obs. rare.* In 5 **surhabunde**. [a. OF., F. *surabonder*: see SUPERABOUND.] *intr.* To superabound. So †**surabundance**, overflowing; ††**surabundantly** *adv.*, superabundantly.

c **1400** tr. *Secr. Secr.*, *Gov. Lordsh.* 76 Whenne superfluytez ouer mekyll *surhabundys to þe heued. *Ibid.* 81 Yn Iuyn, whenne humours surhabunden. **1471** CAXTON *Recuyell* (Sommer) 275 A.. pestelence. That toke his begynnyng of a *surabondance of the see, wherof yᵉ stretes of troye were full.. of water. *a* **1400** *Pauline Epistles* Eph. iii. 20 To hym.. þat may alle þyng make *surabundauntli.

†**sura'ddition.** *Obs. rare.* [See SUR- and ADDITION; cf. F. *suraddition*.] An additional name or title (see ADDITION 4).

1611 SHAKS. *Cymb.* I. i. 33 His Father Was call'd Sicillius, ... But had his Titles by Tenantius, whom He seru'd with Glory, and admir'd Successe; So gain'd the Sur-addition, Leonatus.

suragat, obs. illit. form of SURROGATE *sb.*

†**surage**. *Sc. Obs.* Also **sureis**, **surriche**. [? a. north-eastern OF. **souriche*, **sourige* = central OF. *sourise* mouse, fem. of *souris* (:—pop.L. **sōricem*, *sorex*) mouse.

The original meaning was perhaps 'mouse-grey cloth'. Dialectal forms with *ch*, *g*, occur in derivatives of *souris* in OF., e.g. *sorigier* mousetrap, *sourichon* young mouse.]

surage gray: name of some textile fabric.

1530–1 *Acc. Ld. High Treas. Scot.* V. 414 For ane eln surage gray to be ane pare of hois to the King, price.. xxiiij.s. **1532** *Ibid.* VI. 76 To be the King ane cloik, ij elnis and ane quarter surage gray. **1533** *Ibid.* 183 To be the King ane pair hois ane elne sureis gray. **1544** *Ibid.* VIII. 280, vj quarteris surriche gray.

surah (ˈs(j)ʊərə). [? repr. a pronunciation of SURAT.] A soft twilled silk fabric used for women's dresses.

1873 *Young Englishwoman* May 234/1 Surah is a kind of twilled Indian silk tissue, extremely soft and brilliant. **1881** *Truth* 19 May 686/2 One [dress] of cream-coloured surah, brocaded in a design of rosebuds. **1883** A. S. HARDY *But yet a Woman* 65 Stéphanie herself in her pale blue surah *robe de chambre*. **1893** [see SLEAZY *a.* 2 β].

surah, variant of SURA[2].

surahee, -hi, surai, suraiee, variants of SERAI[2].

surahwa: see SAOUARI.

sural (ˈs(j)ʊərəl), *a. Anat.* [ad. mod.L. *sūrālis* (cf. F. *sural*, It. *surale*, Sp. *sural*), f. *sūra* calf of the leg.] Of or pertaining to the calf of the leg; esp. in ***sural artery***, ***vein***.

1615 CROOKE *Body of Man* 734 The Surall vaine is disseminated into the muscles of the *Sura* or calfe. **1672** WISEMAN *Wounds* iv. 40 Wounded by a puncture in the Inside of the calf of his leg into the Surall Artery. **1840** G. V. ELLIS *Anat.* 674 The lower or sural branches.. three or four in number. **1878** A. HAMILTON *Nervous Dis.* 259 The case of a ballet-dancer.. in which the sural muscles were affected. **1899** *Allbutt's Syst. Med.* VIII. 59 Spasm of the sural muscles.

suramin (ˈsɜːrəmɪn). *Pharm.* Also **Suramin**. [Etym. unknown: perh. f. SURRA.] A complex symmetric urea used in the treatment of trypanosomiasis and filariasis. Also ***suramin sodium***.

1941 *Brit. Pharmacopœia 1932* Add. IV. 33 Suramin is the symmetrical urea of the sodium salt of *m*-benzoyl-*m*-amino-*p*-methylbenzoyl-1-aminonaphthalene-4:6:8-trisulphonic acid. **1951** A. GROLLMAN *Pharmacol. & Therapeutics* xx. 416 Atoxyl.. was the first drug used successfully in trypanosomiasis. Tryparsamide .... was an improvement and with Suramin.. is effective in the treatment of the early stage of the disease before the organisms appear in the spinal fluid. **1974** *Encycl. Brit. Micropædia* IX. 687/3 Suramin sodium, a white or pinkish powder soluble in water, is administered in an aqueous or saline solution. **1978** *Nature* 22 June 627/1 Three antitrypanosomal drugs are listed by the WHO as essential for the treatment of human sleeping sickness caused by African trypanosomiasis. They are melarsoprol (Mel B), pentamidine (Lomidine) and suramin (Antrypol, Germanin).

†ˈ**surance.** *Obs.* Also 4 **surrawns**, 5 **suraunce**, **-awnce**, **surans(e**, **seuerans**, **sewrawnce**, **-aunce**, 6 **sorance**. [a. OF. *surance*, f. *sur* SURE *a.*, after ASSURANCE, of which it may be sometimes merely an aphetic form. Cf. SOVERANCE.]

1. A pledge, guarantee; = ASSURANCE 1.

c **1300** *Beket* 1910 Ich wole assoilli hem in thisse forme, fawe, That hi do surance forto stonde to holi churche lawe. *cc* **1400** *Destr. Troy* 10238 He said þat his suranse sothely was fals, And done for dissait. **1412–20** LYDG. *Chron. Troy* IV. 4553 Suraunce & oþe of old made to þe toun. *c* **1450** LOVELICH *Merlin* 2212 He mad hem to swere, vppon here Sewraunce, to-forn him there, that be ony weye they scholden me sle. **1532** TINDALE *Expos. Matt. v–vii.* vi. 68 b, To geve vs yet more sensible and surer sacramentes and suraunces of his goodnes. *a* **1557** *Diurn. Occurr.* (Bannatyne Cl.) 40 The laird of Langtoun tane in surance for suffering of the Inglismen. **1588** SHAKS. *Tit. A.* v. ii. 46 Now giue some surance that thou art Reuenge.

2. The insuring of property, etc.; = ASSURANCE 5, INSURANCE 4.

1547 *Insurance Policy* in R. G. Marsden *Sel. Pleas Crt. Admir.* (1897) II. 48 In full payment of this sorance a bove sayd. *c* **1550** *Ibid.*, The beste made.. byll of surance.

3. Security, safety; = ASSURANCE 7.

1426 LYDG. *De Guil. Pilgr.* 23359 And where the gate is kept well,.. that vycis may ha none entrie, that place stant in suerte,.. and ther is suraunce & eke trust. *c* **1470** HARDING *Chron.* XC. xv. (MS. Arch. Seld. B. 10) lf. 70 Thus wedde he hir at yorke in al suraunce. *a* **1475** ASHBY *Active Policy* 549 Gentilmen shuld nat yeve clothyng But to their howshold meyne, for surance That no man be their power excedyng. **1559** *Mirr. Mag.*, *K. James Murdered* xv, He counsayled me for surance of my state. **1603** J. DAVIES *Microcosmos* 155 Put into his hand the awfull Sword Of Iustice; so, the good shall bee assur'd,.. Sith Iustice goodmens surance doth inlarge.

4. Certitude, confidence; = ASSURANCE 8.

c **1450** LOVELICH *Grail* xv. 80 Of that Surawnce Am I.

surangular (sɜːr'æŋgjʊlə(r)), *a. Zool.* [See SUR- and ANGULAR.] = *supra-angular* (SUPRA- 1 b).
1841 *Penny Cycl.* XX. 456/1 The surangular portion.. forms the upper border between the coronoïd apophysis and the articulation. **1873** MIVART *Elem. Anat.* 120 We may find, as in the Sauropsida, an actual lower jaw consisting of several distinct bones, dentary, angular, sur-angular, coronoid, splenial, and articular.

surans, obs. form of SORANCE.
c **1440** *Alphabet of Tales* 64 þer happend a surans for to fall in hys lymbe þat his fute rotid off.

† **surantler.** *Obs.* Also -antlier. [a. OF. *surantoillier* (Gaston de Foix): see SUR- and ANTLER.] The second branch of a deer's horn, next above the brow-antler; = BEZ-ANTLER.
The term was copied from Turbervile by many later compilers, but appears to have had no real currency.
1576 TURBERV. *Venerie* xxi. 53 Antoiller.. the Surantlier neare vnto the Antlier the which ought a little to enlarge it selfe some what more from the beame than the firste [Antlier]. [**1630** J. TAYLOR (Water P.) *Navy Land Ships* Wks. I. 93/1 The hornes haue many dogmaticall Epithites, as a Hart hath the Burs, the Pearles, the Antliers, the Surantlers, the Royals, the Surroyals, and the Croches.]

Surat (s(j)ʊ'ræt, 's(j)ʊəræt, 'sʊræt). Also 7 -att, -et. The name of a town and district in the presidency of Bombay, India, used *attrib.* to designate (*a*) a kind of cotton produced in the neighbourhood, (*b*) coarse cotton goods, usually uncoloured; also *ellipt.* and as *sb.* (with *pl.*) = *Surat cotton*, etc.
1643 in E. B. Sainsbury *Cal. Crt. Min. E. Ind. Co.* (1909) 329 [Calicoes] Suratt narrowes. **1653** *Lading Du. E. Ind. Ships*, 225 pieces Surets. **1842** *Penny Cycl.* XXIII. 277/1 They import salt, dates, and Surat piece-goods. **1846** *Commercial Mag.* Oct. 184 We quote now an advance.. of ⅛d. in all descriptions of Surat. **1861** SIMMONDS *Ure's Philos. Manuf.* 87 (Descr. of Figure), Surat Cotton. **1865** *Pall Mall G.* No. 80 1/1 East Indian cotton, or 'Surats'. **1885** HUMMEL *Dyeing Textile Fabrics* 2 The Madras, Surat, and short-stapled Egyptian cotton.

suray, obs. form of SERAI[1].

surbahar ('sɜːbəhɑː(r)). [Bengali *surbāhār*.] A mellow-toned Indian stringed instrument or esraj, larger than a sitar.
1896 S. M. TAGORE *Universal Hist. Mus.* 88 A distinguished musician Babu Kaly Prosonno Banerji.. plays skilfully on the *Víná, Sur-báhár* and *Setár*. **1914** A. H. F. STRANGWAYS *Music of Hindostan* iii. 88 Next to the expressive *vīnā* comes the dignified *surbahar*. **1927** *Grove's Dict. Mus.* (ed. 3) II. 706/1 The *Surbahar* (Calcutta) has sympathetic strings, a mellow tone, is fatiguing to play and expensive to buy. **1969** R. SHANKAR *My Music* i. 37/1 A cousin of the sitar is the large, deep-toned *surbahar*. **1979** *Radio Times* 6–12 Jan. 54/6 (*heading*) Imrat Khan plays surbahar and sitar.

surbait, variant of SURBATE *v.*[2]

surbase ('sɜːbeɪs). *Arch.* Also 8 sirbace. [f. SUR- + BASE *sb.*[1]]
a. A border or moulding immediately above the base or lower panelling of a wainscoted room; also, = *chair-rail* (CHAIR *sb.*[1] 15).
1678 MOXON *Mech. Exerc.* vi. 106 The Middle Rail hath commonly two bredths of the Margent of the Stile, viz. one breadth above the Sur-base, and the other below the Surbase. **1744** LANGHORNE *Country Justice* I. Poems (1790) 282 Where, round the hall, the oak's high surbase rears The field-day triumphs of two hundred years. **1760** *Phil. Trans.* LI. 798 From the top of the surbase within to the pavement of the cell is 7 feet. **1791** *Oxf. Archd. Papers* MS. Oxon. b. 26, lf. 177b (Bodl. Libr.) Neat Chimney piece.. suitable Hearthstone.. with a Sirbace and Skirting. **1834** M. SCOTT *Cruise Midge* xviii, The whole of the surbases and wooden work about the windows and doors were of well-polished and solid mahogany. **1871** MISS BRADDON *Lovels of Arden* xxxii, As her severe eyes surveyed wall and ceiling, floor and surbase. **1875** *Encycl. Brit.* II. 474/1 *Surbase*.., an upper base is the term applied to what, in the fittings of a room, is familiarly called the chair-rail. **1880** *Cassell's Fam. Mag.* 112 The height of the surbase or chair-rail.
attrib. **1825** J. NICHOLSON *Operative Mech.* 605 Surbase-moulding.
b. A cornice or series of mouldings above the dado of a pedestal, podium, etc.
1815 J. SMITH *Panorama Sci. & Art* I. 171 Each upper portion, as surbase of pedestal, capital of column, cornice of entablature, divides into three parts. **1837** *Civil Engin. & Arch. Jrnl.* I. 352/2 The cornice or surbase of the pedestal on which the statue of the Duke is placed. **1887** *Times* (weekly ed.) 9 Dec. 15/1 The temple rests on a stylobate, having a finely moulded base and surbase.
attrib. **1845** PARKER *Gloss. Archit.* (ed. 4) s.v. *Pedestal*, The cornice, or surbase mouldings, at the top [of a pedestal].

surbased (sɜː'beɪst), *a. Arch.* Also 8 surbast. [repr. F. *surbaissé*, f. *sur-* exceedingly = SUPER- 9b + *baissé* lowered.] ***surbased arch***, an arch whose rise is less than half the span. So ***surbased dome***.
1763 GRAY *Let. to Mason* 8 Feb., Roger's own tomb.. has.. a wide surbased arch with scalloped ornaments. **1793** *Gentl. Mag.* May 422/1 Under each chancel window, nearest the East end, is a surbast arch. **1825** J. NICHOLSON *Oper. Mech.* 540 The semicircular are called perfect arches, and those less than a semicircle, imperfect, surbased, or diminished arches. Arches are also called surmounted, when they are higher than a semicircle.

So **sur'basement** [F. *surbaissement*], the condition of being surbased.
1833 CRABB *Dict. Gen. Knowl.* (ed. 3), *Surbasement*, the trait of any arch.. that describes a portion of an ellipsis.

'surbased, *pa. pple. Arch.* [f. SURBASE + -ED[2].] Provided with a surbase.
1791 *Oxf. Archd. Papers* MS. Oxon. b. 26, lf. 177b (Bodl. Libr.), Two Chambers.. to be Skirted and Sirbaced. **1818** TODD [erroneously citing quot. 1763 s.v. SURBASED *a.*]; hence in mod. dicts.

† **surbate,** *sb. Obs.* Also 6–7 surbat. [f. SURBATE *v.*] Soreness of the feet or hoofs caused by walking; foot-soreness.
1587 MASCALL *Govt. Cattle, Horses* (1627) 118 By that meanes hee may saue his horse often-times from danger of surbat. **1645** 'MARTIN-MARPRIEST' *Martin's Eccho* 16 You remember how the Bishops poasted you furiously too and fro like Iehu.., untill with foundring and surbates they had even wearied you of your lives. **1725** *Fam. Dict.* s.v. *Horse Feeder*, If the Feeder finds his Horse subject to Lameness or Stiffness, to Surbate or Tenderness of Feet. **1805** JAMES *Milit. Dict.* (ed. 2).

† **surbate,** *v.*[1] *Obs. rare.* [ad. OF. *surbatre* (see SURBATED) to beat excessively.] *intr.* ? To bear down heavily *on*.
c **1450** *Merlin* 531 Agravain hadde so chaced and Gaheries xx saisnes that thei surbated on Pignoras that com with an hundred saisnes.

† **surbate,** *v.*[2] *Obs.* Also 6–8 -bait, 7 -beat(e. [Back-formation from SURBATED. Cf. next.]
1. *trans.* To bruise or make sore (the hoofs or feet) with excessive walking; to make (an animal or person) foot-sore.
1590 SPENSER *F.Q.* III iv. 34 Least they.. should.. surbate sore Their tender feet vpon the stony ground. **1607** MARKHAM *Caval.* III. (1617) 7 His own waight beating vpon the hard earth, would both surbate and bring him to an incurable lamenesse. **1611** SPEED *Hist. Gt. Brit.* IX. xx §47 The Rebels.. whom King Henry.. suffered.. to.. surbate themselves with a long march. **1660** BLOUNT *Boscobel* 29 Which contributed much towards the surbating and galling His Majesties Feet. **1707** MORTIMER *Husb.* (1721) I. 232 Chalky Land surbates.. Oxens Feet more than any other Soil.
absol. **1615** JACKSON *Creed* IV. II. i. §4 Softest waies in moist winters surbeate the sorest in dry Summers.
2. *intr.* for *pass.* To become foot-sore.
1590 COCKAINE *Treat. Hunting* C4, Who so hunteth vnbreathed hounds at the Bucke first in hot weather, causeth them to imbost and surbate greatly. **1610** MARKHAM *Masterp.* II. xci. 378 If your horse surbate in your trauell. **1614** —— *Cheap Husb.* II. i. (1668) 70 Horned Cattel in Lincolnshire are.. strong hoved, not apt to surbait. **1725** *Fam. Dict.* s.v. *Hoof*, That Horse.. will not carry a Shoe long, nor travel far, but soon surbate.

† **surbate,** *pa. pple.* and *ppl. a. Obs. rare.* Forms: 5 surbat, 6 surbet, -beate [ad. OF. *surbatu* (see next).] = next.
1496 [see SURBATED b, *a* **1450**]. **1590** SPENSER *F.Q.* II. ii. 22 As when a Beare and Tygre.. Espye a traueiler with feet surbet. **1598** BP. HALL *Sat.* v. ii. 20 Thy right eye gins to leape for vain delight And surbeate toes to tickle at the sight.

† **surbated,** *pa. pple.* and *ppl. a. Obs.* or *dial.* Also 5 surbatted, 5–7 surbatted, 6–8 -baited, 7 *erron.* -boted. [f. OF. *surbatu* (pa. pple. of *surbatre*, f. *sur-* exceedingly = SUPER- 9b + *batre* to beat) + -ED. OF. *surbatu* is not recorded in the sense of the Eng. word, the F. term being *solbatu* (1664 in Hatz.-Darm.), for which see SOLE-BAITING; but Cotgrave (1611) has *surbatture* 'surbating' (as well as *soubattue, soubatture*); cf. also obs. It. *sobattere, sobattuto* 'surbated', *sobattitura* 'surbating'.] **a.** Of the hoofs or feet: Bruised or sore with much walking.
c **1410** *Master of Game* (MS. Digby 182) xii, If þe soles of hir feete be surebated. **1577** B. GOOGE *Heresbach's Husb.* (1586) 132 If the bullockes feete be neare worne, and surbated, washe them in Oxe pysse warmed. **1601** HOLLAND *Pliny* XI. xxxvii, When they see their Oxe hoofes surbatted and worne too neere the quick with overmuch travell. **1607** TOPSELL *Four-f. Beasts* 689 Those members that are surboted or riuen of their skin. **1617** R. FENTON *Treat. Ch. Rome* 142 The feet of our blessed Sauiour: those surbated feet which tred vpon the earth naked and miserable. *a* **1700** EVELYN *Diary* 7 Sept. 1666, My haire was almost sing'd, and my feete unsufferably surbated. **1766** *Compl. Farmer* s.v. *Surbating*, There is nothing better for surbated feet than tar melted into the foot. **1816** *Sporting Mag.* XLVII. 61 We have seen the hoofs of a horse perfectly surbated, from long standing upon the hard.. stones.
b. Of animals or persons: Foot-foundered, foot-sore; weary with excessive travelling on foot.
a **1450** *Fysshynge w. Angle* (1883) 2 The hunter.. cummet home.. reyn beton seyr prykud with thornes and hys clothes torne.. sum of hys howndes lost som surbatted [*ed.* 1496 surbat]. **1576** TURBERV. *Venerie* 123 When you are ouertaken with the night, or that your houndes are surbated and wearie. **1579** LANGHAM *Gard. Health* (1633) 10 The leaues.. are good to be put into the shooes of them that are surbated and wearie, to mitigate the heat and paine. **1612** tr. *Benvenuto's Passenger* A vij, A surbated and weary Passenger. **1639** T. DE GREY *Compl. Horsem.* 111 To be applyed to the feet.. when the horse is.. surbated. **1647** CLARENDON *Hist. Reb.* VIII. §127 They begun their march again; which they continued all that Night;.. they could not but be extremely weary, and surbated. **1670** EVELYN *Sylva* xix. (ed. 2) 84 The fresh Leaves [of the Alder] alone applied to the naked soal of the Foot, infinitely refresh the surbated Traveller. **1737** BRACKEN *Farriery Impr.* (1756) I. 348 He will (if used upon hard Roads) become surbated or beaten of his Feet in a very short Time. **1887** F. T. HAVERGAL *Heref. Gloss.* s.v., As a woman said of her daughter who had walked 30 miles to see her: 'When her came her was fine surbated.'
c. *transf.* and *fig.*
1592 in *Lyly's Wks.* (1902) I. 478 Vertue tying wings to the thoughts of virgins, swiftnes becommeth surbated. **1634** W. TIRWHYT tr. *Balzac's Lett.* 291 Doe you not think my sighes must needes be surbated, in going every day foure hundred leagues? **1661** WEBSTER *Cure for Cuckold* II. iv, We are all.. at a stand,.. the music ceas'd, and dancing surbated.

† **surbater.** *Obs. rare.* [f. SURBATE *v.*[2] + -ER[1].] One who wearies another out by walking.
1633 B. JONSON *Tale Tub* IV. iii, A lackey.. or a foot-man, Who is the Surbater of a Clarke currant.

† **surbating,** *vbl. sb. Obs.* Forms: see SURBATE *v.*; also 6–7 *erron.* surbutting. [f. SURBATED: see -ING[1].] The action of making the hoofs or feet sore by walking; foot-soreness.
The definition in quot. 1607[2] is repeated in later works of reference.
1576 TURBERV. *Venerie* 15 That he [*sc.* a hound] is strong.. and able to endure long without surbaiting of himselfe. **1591** PERCIVALL *Sp. Dict.*, *Despeadura*, surbating. **1600** SURFLET *Country Farm* I. xxiii. 136 For surbutting, boile honie and hogs-grease in white wine. **1607** MARKHAM *Caval.* III. (1617) 7 Not any of these horses but will endure the hard earth without surbating or lamenesse. **1607** TOPSELL *Four-f. Beasts* 413 Surbating.. is a beating of the Hooue against the ground. **1759** BROWN *Compl. Farmer* 11.

surbeat(e, variant of SURBATE *v.*[2]

surbeaten, error for SURBATED.
a **1667** SKINNER *Etymol.* (1671), *Surbeat*, or to be *Surbeaten*.

† **sur'bed,** *v. Obs.* [f. SUR- in the sense of 'up' + BED *sb.* 12b (= under side of a block of stone).] *trans.* To set (a block of stone) edgeways (see quots.); also, to set (coal) edgeways on a fire.
1677 PLOT *Oxfordsh.* 76 They take care to surbed the stone, *i.e.* set it edg-ways, contrary to the posture it had in the bed. *c* **1680** *Enquiries* 2/1 Quarries.. in what order do the beds lie? whether surbedded in work, or laid as they grew in the bed? **1686** PLOT *Staffordsh.* iii. 126 If they would have it [coal] burn quick and flame clear,.. they surbed it, i.e. set it edgways, the cleaving way next the fire. *c* **1700** KENNETT *MS. Lansd. 1033* lf. 377 To surbed coal, to set it edgwaies on the fire that the heat and flame may cleave it and make it burn with greater vehemence. **1712** J. MORTON *Nat. Hist. Northampt.* 116 Let the Stones that are for Oven-Hearths.. be set Edge-ways, or Sur-bedded, as the Masons speak, that is, the Position they had in the Earth inverted. *c* **1767** G. WHITE *Selborne* iv. *To Pennant*, It is a freestone, cutting in all directions; yet has something of a grain parallel with the horizon, and therefore should not be surbedded. *Ibid.*, *note*, Surbedding does not succeed in our dry walls.

† **sur'brave,** *v. Obs.* [f. SUR- + BRAVE *v.*]
1. *trans.* To make very 'brave' or splendid. (Cf. BRAVE *v.* 5.)
1584 HUDSON *Du Bartas' Judith* III. 22 The Persians proud.. With plates of gold, surbraved all their bands [orig. *Fait les escailles d'or de ses armes reluire*].
2. To excel in splendour or beauty.
c **1600** W. FOWLER *Wks.* (S.T.S.) I. 377 He is to me the wight Whose truthe surbraues the best.

surbutting, erron. form of SURBATING.

surcar, rare obs. form of SIRCAR.

† **sur'cark.** *Obs. rare*[−1]. In 4 surkarc. [a. AF. *surcarke*: see SUR- and CARK *sb.*] Excess.
13.. *Cursor M.* 9843 (Gött.), If þu fonde.. A barn.. þat had thre fete, or handis thre,.. And.. siþen anoþer.. þat wantid eyder fote or hand,.. surkarc [*Cott.* ouercark] of kinde had þe tan, And kind was to þat oþer wan.

† **sur'carking,** *vbl. sb. Obs. rare*[−1]. [f. SUR- + CARK *v.* + -ING[1].] Great trouble or distress.
c **1330** *Arth. & Merl.* 3945 (Kölbing), þis ich seuen, saunfail þe cark hadde of þe batayl... Ac in al þis surcarking Merlin com to Ban, þe king.

surceance, -aunce, var. SURSEANCE *Obs.*

† **sur'ceasance.** *Obs.* Forms: 6 sursesance, 7 surcesance, surceasance. [f. SURCEASE *v.*, after SURSEANCE.] = SURSEANCE.
1585 HOLINSHED *Chron.* II. *Hist. Scot.* 323/2 Being at the same time a sursesance made on both sides,.. the Scots ceassed not to make sundre inuasions into our realme. **1611** SPEED *Hist. Gt. Brit.* IX. vii. §39 He was.. perswaded.. not to refuse Saladines offers for a surceasance from hostilitie. *a* **1637** SPOTTISWOOD *Hist. Ch. Scot.* v. (1677) 254 She began to treat with both parties for a surceasance of Arms.

surcease (sɜː'siːs), *sb. arch.* Also 7 -ceasse, -cesse. [f. next.] The action, or an act, of bringing or coming to an end; (a) cessation, stop; *esp.* (a) temporary cessation, suspension, or intermission. **a.** Const. *of* or genitive.
In mod. use often with a reminiscence of quot. 1605.
1586 A. DAY *Eng. Secretorie* II. (1625) 25 My request is for the surcease of all this iarre. **1590** NASHE *1st Pt. Pasquil's Apol.* A 4, Seeking with my hart a surcease of Armes. **1605** SHAKS. *Macb.* I. vii. 4 If th' Assassination Could trammell vp the Consequence, and catch With his surcease, Successe. **1653** H. COGAN tr. *Pinto's Trav.* xlix. (1663) 193 By this surcease of Trade the Custom-houses.. fell much in their

Revenue. **1709** MRS. MANLEY *Secret Mem.* (1720) IV. 237 Nothing but Death can make that Man desist, who sustains almost its Pangs without a Surcease of Diligence. *a* **1768** ERSKINE *Inst. Law Scot.* IV. iii. §24 Creditors sometimes grant voluntarily a surcease of personal execution in behalf of their debtor, which is commonly called a *supersedere*. **1816** SCOTT *Antiq.* xv, The crafty pony availed himself of this surcease of discipline to twitch the rein out of Davie's hands. **1845** POE *Raven* 10 Vainly I had sought to borrow From my books surcease of sorrow. **1855** MOTLEY *Dutch Rep.* II. vi. (1866) 254 They requested her Highness to order a general surcease of the Inquisition. **1916** J. BUCHAN *Hist. War* xciii. XIII. 53 It was carried on in all weathers..with no surcease of keenness.

b. Const. *from*.

1597 HOOKER *Eccl. Pol.* v. lxxi. §8 Surcease from labour is necessarie. **1600** W. WATSON *Decacordon* (1602) 349 A surcease from all state medles. **1643** BAKER *Chron.* (1679) 194/1 The Duke of York..commands a surcease from further hostility. **1879** SALA *Paris Herself Again* II. xviii, Private schools for boys give four days' surcease from lessons.

c. Without construction.

a **1593** MARLOWE *Ovid's Elegies* II. xiv, Fruites ripe will fall, let springing things increase, Life is no light price of a small surcease. **1601** in Farr *S. P. Eliz.* (1845) II. 430 O endlesse ioy without surcease. **1712** in Maclaurin *Argts. & Decis.* (1774) 50 After a long surcease, he renewed the cause. **1873** LONGF. *Wayside Inn, Monk of Casal-Maggiore* 137 All the while he talked without surcease. **1881** *Daily Tel.* 25 Mar. 5/4 There is no surcease in the torrent of Princes..who continue to pour into the capital.

surcease (sɜːˈsiːs), *v. arch.* Forms: α. 5 sursese, 5–6 sursease, 6 surseace. β. 5 surceese, (sourcesse), 5–6 surcese, -cesse, 6 -ces, -ceas, -ceace, 6–7 -ceasse, 8 -cess, 5– surcease. [f. OF. *sursis*, fem. *sursise* (cf. AF. *sursise* sb., omission), pa. pple. of *surseoir* to refrain, delay, suspend:—L. *supersedēre* to SUPERSEDE. The spelling was at an early date assimilated to CEASE (*cesse, ceasse*).]

1. *intr.* To leave off, desist, stop, cease from some action (finally or temporarily). (Cf. SUPERSEDE 2 b.) **a.** const. †*of*, *from*.

1428 *Lett. Marg. Anjou & Bp. Beckington* (Camden) 40 Men sayen hit hadde be muche better for me to have surcesed of my service long or this. **1429** *Rolls of Parlt.* IV. 342/2 The Tresorer.., may have in commaundement by Writt, to sursese of any proces made. **1433** *Ibid.* 425/2 That the seide Collectours..sursease of eny levie to make. *c* **1510** MORE *Picus* Wks. 14/1 Wherfore he counseiled Picus to surceace of study. **1538** CROMWELL in Merriman *Life & Lett.* (1902) II. 159 The kinges pleasure is that..you do Surcese and cause the partie to surces frome any further sute. **1549** *Bk. Com. Prayer, Ord. Deacons*, The Bisshoppe shal surcease from ordering that person. **1597** HOOKER *Eccl. Pol.* v. xlvii. §4 Vnder that pretense to surcease from prayers as bootles or fruitles offices. **1615** BRATHWAIT *Strappado* (1878) 165 Silke-wormes..Who do surcease from labour now and then. **1667** MILTON *P.L.* VI. 258 The great Arch-Angel from his warlike toile Surceas'd. **1812** CARY *Dante, Purg.* xxv. 131 Nor from the task..Surcease they. **1853–8** HAWTHORNE *Engl. Note-bks.* (1879) II. 104, I..thereupon surceased from my labors.

b. without construction (*spec.* to discontinue legal proceedings).

1456 *Paston Lett.* I. 390, I shal be his servaunt and youres unto such tyme as ye woll comande me to sursese and leve of. **1479** *Ibid.* III. 257 My Lord of Ely desyred myn oncle as well as you to surcease. **1544** CRANMER *Let.* in *Misc. Writ.* (Parker Soc.) 411 For the better expedition of the matter, I have sent to the dean of the arches, commanding him to surcease therein. **1586** A. DAY *Engl. Secretorie* I. (1625) 13 Wishing vnto you and yours as much happinesse as myselfe am clogged with carefulnes, I surcease. **1596** SPENSER *F.Q.* IV. ii. 19 In stead of praying them surcease, They did much more their cruelty encrease. **1637–50** ROW *Hist. Kirk* (Wodrow Soc.) 440, I might relate many others,..but I surceasse. *a* **1652** BROME *Covent Gard. Weeded* IV. i, Hector ..held up his brazen lance, In signal that both armies should surcease. **1671** F. PHILLIPS *Reg. Necess.* 114 To stay and Surcease and no further prosecute or proceed against the Complainant. **1859** SINGLETON *Virgil* x. 1260 Surcease. I now am coming, doomed to die.

c. const. *inf.*

1535 CROMWELL in Merriman *Life & Lett.* (1902) I. 420 His graces pleasure is that ye shall surcease any farther to yntermedle with the..landes belongyng to the Busshopriche of Hereford. **1542** UDALL *Erasm. Apoph.* 231 b, Onlesse thei would surceasse so to abuse hym. **1553** T. WILSON *Rhet.* (1580) 193, I will surcesse to talk any further of this matter. **1615** BRATHWAIT *Strappado*, etc. (1878) 254 Beasts to their caues resort, surcease to prey. **1671** MILTON *Samson* 404 She surceas'd not day nor night To storm me over-watch't, and wearied out. **1708** J. PHILIPS *Cyder* I. 364 Prevent the Morning Star Assiduous, nor with the Western Sun Surcease to work. **1802** STRUTHERS *Poor Man's Sabbath* ix, Till yonder orbs surcease t' admeasure nights and days. **1863** W. K. KELLY *Curios. Indo-European Tradit.* i. 7 They could never surcease to feel the liveliest interest in those wonderful meteoric changes.

†**d.** *transf.* To forbear, omit (*to do* something).

1542 UDALL *Erasm. Apoph.* Pref., & so forth of the other writers whiche I surcease by name to speake of. **1577** HARRISON *England* II. xiii. [xvii.] (1877) I. 291, I might take occasion to tell of the..voiages made into strange countries by Englishmen..but..I surcease to speake of them. **1610** HEALEY *St. Aug. Citie of God* (1620) 246 Tertullian..wrote much: which being recorded I surcease to recount.

2. To come to an end, be discontinued; to cease.

1439 in *Antiq. Repertory* (1780) III. 274 That all manere of processe..in the mesne tyme surcese. *a* **1513** FABYAN *Chron.* VI. clxxi. (1811) 167 He..seased that Kyngdom, and ioyned it to his owne of West Saxons, by whiche reason the Kyngdome of Mercia surseased. **1533–4** *Act 25 Hen. VIII*, c. 21 §2 All suche pensiones censes porcions and peterpense,..shall frome hense forthe clerely surcesse and never more be levyed. **1600** HAKLUYT *Voy.* (1810) III. 36 It may ..bee thought that this course of the sea doth sometime surcease..because it is not discerned all along the Coast of America. *a* **1633** T. TAYLOR *God's Judgem.* I. I. xv. (1642) 48 That the cause being taken away, the effect also might surcease. **1675** E. WILSON *Spadacr. Dunelm.* 15 These [*sc.* Rain or Snow] surceasing the Springs also become dry. *c* **1750** SHENSTONE *Ruin'd Abbey* 238 Nor yet surceas'd with John's disastrous fate Pontific fury! **1860** MOTLEY *Netherl.* vi. I. 322 Intrigues and practices..would of necessity surcease. **1898** HARDY *Wessex Poems* 146 When I surcease, Through whom alone lives she, Ceases my Love.

3. *trans.* To desist from, discontinue; to give up, abandon (a course of action, etc.); also, to refrain from. (Cf. SUPERSEDE 2.)

1464–9 *Plumpton Corr.* (Camden) 25 To cause the said Thomas & Richard to surcease & leve theire said threatnings. **1493** *Ibid.* 105, I caused them to surcease ther purpose unto the tyme I had wrytten to you, & known your mynd. **1544** in *Sel. Cases Crt. Requests* (Selden Soc.) 97 Olyuer shall withdrawe & surseace all maner his suettes and accions. **1577–87** HOLINSHED *Chron.* III. 813/2 That it might please him to surcease his cruell kind of warre, in burning of townes and villages. **1590** SPENSER *F.Q.* III. iv. 31 The waues..their rage surceast. **1607** DEKKER *Hist. Sir T. Wyat* Wks. 1873 III. 99 Surcease your armes, discharge your Souldiers. **1621** BURTON *Anat. Mel.* Democr. to Rdr. 49 [If he] prosecute his cause, he is consumed, if he surcease his suite he looseth all. *a* **1648** LD. HERBERT *Hen. VIII* (1683) 40 It was resolved to surcease the War for this Year, Winter now beginning to enter. **1658** W. BURTON *Itin. Anton.* 140 For my part I surcease all farther enquiry. **1720** POPE *Iliad* XXIII. 970 Greece..Bade share the honours and surcease the strife. *a* **1774** TUCKER *Lt. Nat.* (1834) II. 514 Did he surcease the common civilities..would he have better leisure to perform more important services? **1820** SCOTT *Abbot* xiv, The hobby-horse surceased his capering. **1897** F. THOMPSON *New Poems* 219 [She] had surceased her tyranny.

†**b.** To give up, resign (a position or office).

[Cf. quot. *c* 1435 s.v. SURCEASING *vbl. sb.* 1.]

1552 *Lit. Rem. Edw. VI* (Roxb.) II. 432 The chauncellour of th' augmentation was willed to surcease his commission, geven him the third yeare of our raigne.

†**4.** To put a stop to, bring to an end, cause to cease; to stay (legal proceedings.). *Obs.*

c **1435** in Kingsford *Chron. Lond.* (1905) 48 For as much as the Kyng was changid all plees in euery place weren surcesed. **1490** *Act. 4 Hen. VII*, c. 20, No relesse..be.. available or effectuell to lette or to surceace the seid accion. **1594** SPENSER *Amoretti* xi, All paine hath end,..but mine no price nor prayer may surcease. **1594** KYD *Cornelia* I. 220 If gentle Peace Discend not soone, our sorrowes to surcease, Latium..will be destroyd. **1692** tr. *Sallust* 72 'Tis death not torment that surceases all our Miseries. **1695** TEMPLE *Hist. Eng.* (1699) 174 The abrogating or surceasing the Judiciary Power, exercised by the Bishops.

†**b.** To cause to desist *from* some action. *rare*$^{-1}$.

1791 COWPER *Iliad* xv. 311 Ajax me..hath with a stone Surceas'd from fight, smiting me on the breast.

†**5.** To put off, defer; to delay till the end of, overpass (the time for doing something). *Obs. rare.*

1531 *Dial. on Laws Eng.* II. xxxvi. 74 When the ordinarie hathe surcessed his tyme he hathe loste his power. **1560** [see SURCEASING *vbl. sb.* 3]. *a* **1693** *Urquhart's Rabelais* III. xl. 332, I defer, protract,..surcease,..and shift off, the Time of giving a Definitive Sentence.

†**sur'ceasement.** *Obs. rare*$^{-1}$. [f. SURCEASE *v.* + -MENT.] = SURCEASE *sb.*

a **1641** MOUNTAGU *Acts & Mon.* ii. (1642) 145 The surceasement of Cyrus Edict, and the Temples building, during most part of Cambyses reigne.

surceasing (sɜːˈsiːsɪŋ), *vbl. sb. arch.* [f. SURCEASE *v.* + -ING[1].] The action of the verb SURCEASE.

1. The action of leaving off or desisting from some proceeding.

†In quot. *c* 1435, ceasing to occupy a position, resignation.

c **1435** in Kingsford *Chron. Lond.* (1905) 20 A copye to be delyuered to hym off his Resignyng and Surcesyng. **1473** *Rolls of Parlt.* VI. 65/2 So that..there be a perpetuall sursesyng for and of any ferther execution of any such Sentence. **1579** NORTHBROOKE *Dicing* (1843) 38 Sleep is a surceasing of all the sences from trauel. **1579** FENTON *Guicciard.* (1618) 357 That between the Pope and Alphonso d'Este, there should be a surceassing of armes at the least for sixe moneths. **1594** HOOKER *Eccl. Pol.* I. xiv. §3 His surceasing to speake to the world since the publishing of the Gospell. **1600** SURFLET *Country Farm* VII. lxvi. 897 The birde..growing melancholike, as by surceasing and abstaining to sing. **1818** COLEBROOKE *Obligations* 40 Forbearance of a suit for a specific..time, or surceasing of a suit.

†**2.** The action of putting a stop to something.

1553 BRENDE *Q. Curtius* x. 223 It was agreed..that Embassadours should be sent..for the surcessing of all strife. **1579** SPENSER *Let. Harvey* Poet. Wks. (1912) 635/2 They haue proclaimed..a generall surceasing and silence of balde Rymers.

†**3.** The action of putting off or deferring. *Obs.*

1560 DAUS tr. *Sleidane's Comm.* 389 They..wil..maruel at this long delay and surceasing.

So **sur'ceasing** *ppl. a.* (in quot., gradually ceasing, abating, diminishing).

1881 R. BUCHANAN *God & Man* II. 250 The seas came along with slowly surceasing force.

†**surcept**, *v. Obs. rare*$^{-1}$. [f. SUR- + *-cept* in *intercept*, ? after *surcease*.] *trans.* To intercept.

1579 FENTON *Guicciard.* VI. 306 He had iust occasion to doubt of them..by the testimonie of certeine letters..newly surcepted.

surceyance, variant of SURSEANCE *Obs.*

surch, rare obs. form of SEARCH.

1663 G. FOX in *Jrnl. Friends' Hist. Soc.* Oct. (1914) 149 Cornall Kerby sent solgers to surch in boxes..for mee.

†**'surcharge**, *sb.*[1] *Sc. Obs.* Also **sowrcharge.** [Variant (formed by substitution of prefix SUR-) of SUBCHARGE, sense 1, or *sucharge* (see quot. 1489 below, and *Cath. Angl.* 371/1 'A Sucharge, *impomentum*').] An additional or second dish or course. Also *fig.*

1489 *Barbour's Bruce* XVI. 458 (Edinb. MS.) That sowrchargis [*Camb. MS.* sucharge, *ed. Hart* subcharge] to chargand wes. *c* **1500** KENNEDY *Passion of Christ* 258 Till all his sair he soucht na saw bot ane, The quhilk wes ded, as surcharge till his sorrow. **1500–20** DUNBAR *Poems* lxvii. 19 Off quhais subchettis [*v.r.* quhois surcharge] sour is the sals.

surcharge (ˈsɜːtʃɑːdʒ), *sb.*[2] [f. next, or ad. F. *surcharge* (from 16th c.): see SUR- and CHARGE *sb.*]

1. a. A pecuniary charge in excess of the usual or just amount; an additional or excessive pecuniary charge; = OVERCHARGE *sb.* 2.

1601 F. TATE *Househ. Ord. Edw. II.* §67. (1876) 48 So as the cuntry..may not wax deere by surcharge without reson. **1646** W. HUGHES *Mirr. Justices* i. §5 Sherriffs, who too high charge the people, by a surcharge upon the people of horses, or of doggs. **1686** tr. *Chardin's Coronat. Solyman* 95 She besought him to remit the Surcharge which he had laid upon the poor Armenians. **1812** *Sporting Mag.* XXXIX. 101 A surcharge made on him for 10l. **1838** ARNOLD *Hist. Rome* I. xvii. 351 It might happen..that no property tax was levied, and in that case the censor's surcharge, or over valuation, would have been inoperative. **1896** *Allbutt's Syst. Med.* I. 486 A history of fistula..does not call for surcharge [in life assurance].

b. *Equity.* The act of showing an omission in an account, or a statement showing this: cf. SURCHARGE *v.* 1 b.

a **1700** EVELYN *Diary* 8 Apr. 1687, The accompt was at last brought to one article of the surcharge, and referr'd to a Master. **1754** LD. HARDWICKE in Vezey *Reports* (1773) II. 566 The court takes it as a stated account, and establishes it: but if any of the parties can shew an omission, for which credit ought to be, that is a surcharge: or if any thing is inserted, that is a wrong charge, he is at liberty to shew it, and that is falsification. **1884** *Law Rep. 27 Chanc. Div.* 111 The Defendant carried in a complete account, and the Plaintiffs carried in a surcharge.

c. A charge made by an auditor upon a public official in respect of an amount improperly paid by him: cf. SURCHARGE *v.* 1 c.

1879 *Daily News* 25 Mar. 4/6 They charge interest on the advances, and this interest the auditor has disallowed. It would therefore fall on the members of the Board as a surcharge.

2. *Law.* (tr. law-L. *superoneratio.*) The overstocking of a common or forest: see SURCHARGE *v.* 2. *Obs.* exc. *Hist.*

1569 in *S'hampton Crt. Leet Rec.* (1905) I. 53 To y[e] greate Surchardge of y[e] said comon. **1598** MANWOOD *Lawes Forest* xiv. 84 To inquire..what number of Acres, the place of Common, wherein the surcharge is supposed to be made, doth containe. *a* **1634** COKE *Inst.* II. (1642) 370 A writ *de secunda superoneratione* lyeth..onely against them, against whom the writ was brought, and which were particularly charged with surcharge in the writ. *Ibid.* IV. lxxiii. (1648) 293 Surcharge of the Forest [see SURCHARGE *v.* 2]. **1768** BLACKSTONE *Comm.* III. xvi. 239 If, after the admeasurement has thus ascertained the right, the same defendant surcharges the common again, the plaintiff may have a writ of second surcharge, *de secunda superoneratione*, which is given by the statute Westm. 2. 13 Edw. I. c. 8. **1797** JACOB *Law Dict.*, Surcharge of Common.

3. An additional or excessive 'charge', load, burden, or supply (of something material or immaterial); = OVERCHARGE *sb.* 1.

1603 FLORIO *Montaigne* I. ii. (1632) 3 Being otherwise full, and over-plunged in sorrow, the least surcharge brake the bounds and barres of patience. **1603** HOLLAND *Plutarch's Mor.* 200 Adding as it were some olde surcharge to their toils and fooleries. **1605** BACON *Adv. Learn.* II. To the King §14 The great quantitie of Bookes maketh a shewe..of superfluitie.., which surcharge neuerthelesse is not to be remedied by making no more bookes, but by making more good books. **1626** —— *Sylva* §228 The Aire, after it hath receiued a Charge, doth not receiue a Surcharge, or greater Charge, with like Appetite, as it doth the first Charge. *a* **1683** OWEN *Chamber of Imagery* viii. (1870) 34 The sending of missionaries, as they call them, or a surcharge of friars from their over-numerous fraternities. **1683** BURNET tr. *More's Utopia* II. (1684) 125 When Nature is eased of any surcharge that oppresses it. **1746** *Phil. Trans.* XLIV. 712 After the Gun-barrel and Phial have been sufficiently excited,..the Surcharge is dissipated; so that the continuing the Motion..ever so long after the Saturation is complete, does not increase the electrical Force. **1769** BLACKSTONE *Comm.* IV. 323 Any surcharge of punishment on persons adjudged to penance, so as to shorten their lives. **1803** JEFFERSON *Writ.* (1830) IV. 10 The surcharge of the learned, might in time be drawn off to recruit the laboring class of citizens. **1898** P. MANSON *Trop. Diseases* xxii. 339 A surcharge of aliment and alcohol.

4. The action of surcharging or condition of being surcharged; overloading.

1625 BACON *Ess., Plantations* (Arb.) 534 Send Supplies.. so, as the Number may liue well, in the Plantation, and not by Surcharge be in Penury. **1793** BEDDOES *Calculus* 204 Preventing the surcharge of oxygene in the blood. **1799** *Med. Jrnl.* II. 385 Cases of surcharge, retention, or indigestion. **1822–7** GOOD *Study Med.* (1829) IV. 645 Atonic apoplexy..is more a result of vascular debility than of vascular surcharge. **1882** BAIN *Jas. Mill* vi. 304 Mill, whose mind was.. in a state of surcharge upon the question of free enquiry.

5. An additional mark printed on the face of a postage-stamp, esp. for the purpose of changing its face value.

1881 *Stamp-Collector's Ann.* 15 In that of 10 cents the surcharge is found sometimes with and sometimes without the word *cents*. *Ibid.* 24 The V.R. surcharge was also imitated. **1914** F. J. MELVILLE *Postage Stamps* 19 The.. most important of the additions to a stamp is the 'overprint' or 'surcharge'.

6. *Ceramics.* 'A painting in a lighter enamel over a darker one which forms the ground' (Cent. Dict. 1891).

7. *Civil Engin.* **a.** The part of a load that is above the horizontal plane containing the top of a retaining wall. **b.** A load placed upon uncompacted material to compress it.

1881 *Van Nostrand's Mag.* XXV. 336/2 The author found a wall of slag blocks having a batter of ⅙ of the height, and an effective thickness of 1 foot sustained a bank of broken slag 10 feet high, with a surcharge of some 5 feet more. **1930** *Engineering* 30 May 689/3 The heavy 24-in. steel beam.. was intended for applying a surcharge to the filling in the bin. **1967** C. A. O'FLAHERTY *Highways* xii. 597 A surcharge of uncompacted material is added on top [of the embankment] to accelerate the outflow of water and the compaction of the underlying compressible material.

surcharge (sɜːˈtʃɑːdʒ), *v.* [a. OF. *surcharger*: see SUR- and CHARGE *v.* Cf. Pr., Sp. *sobrecargar*, It. *sopraccaricare*, Pg. *sobrecarregar*.]

1. *trans.* To charge (a person) too much as a price or payment; to overburden with expense, exactions, etc.; to subject to an additional or extra charge or payment.

1429 *Rolls of Parlt.* IV. 352/1 Diverse Customers.. standen surcharged, and in weie to be surcharged in hire accomptes. **1475** *Bk. Noblesse* (Roxb.) 75 How that men usurpen.. in surchargeyng them unduelie. **1587** HARRISON *England* II. xiii. (1877) I. 260 To surcharge the rest of the parish, & laie more burden vpon them. **1655** FULLER *Ch. Hist.* IX. vi. §8 John Whitgift succeeding in the Arch-Bishoprick, found it much surcharged in the valuation. *a*1700 EVELYN *Diary* 17 Sept. 1655, The taxes were so intollerable.. surcharged as that county had been.. during our unnatural war. **1798** *Anti-Jacobin* 1 Jan., And sorely to surcharge the Duke I trowe he was ne slack. **1812** *Examiner* 7 Sept. 570/2 The Surveyor.. for Assessed Taxes.. surcharges him. **1845** MᶜCULLOCH *Taxation* I. iv. (1852) 127 On this principle, farmers who are undertaxed should be surcharged.

b. *Equity.* To show an omission in (an account); *absol.* to show that the accounting party ought to have charged himself with more than he has.

1754 LD. HARDWICKE in Vezey *Reports* (1773) II. 566 A liberty to surcharge and falsify these several stated accounts. **1826** WHEATON *Rep. Cases Supreme Crt. U.S.* XI. 256 If.. the defendant plead.. a settled account, the plaintiff may surcharge, by alleging and proving omissions in the account, or may falsify, by showing errors in some of the items stated in it.

c. To make a charge upon (a public official or body) in respect of an amount improperly paid by him; hence, to disallow (an item of expenditure in an account).

1885 *Manch. Exam.* 13 Apr. 5/3 The Auditor had given notice to the Guardians.. of his intention to surcharge them with an amount of £157. **1885** M. STANHOPE *Sp. Ho. Commons* 11 Aug., If any item of expenditure is illegal it is liable to be surcharged by the auditor. **1901** *Westm. Gaz.* 11 Jan. 3/2 The School Board was surcharged by the auditor in 1885 in respect of illegal Science and Art classes.

2. *Law.* To overstock (a common, etc.) by putting more cattle into it than the person has a right to do or than the pasture will sustain. Also *absol. Obs.* exc. *Hist.*

1480 *Cov. Leet Bk.* 456 That the lawe of the lande ys that the lorde of the soyle may surcharge and put þerin what noumber hit lykes. *a*1500 *Brome Bk.* 164 ȝe schall enquere ..ȝef ony mane surchargeth yowre comune. **1598** MANWOOD *Lawes Forest* xiv. 83 If he.. do surcharge the comon with so many beasts, that the wild beasts of the kings Forrest can not haue sufficient feed there. *a*1634 COKE *Inst.* IV. lxxiii. (1648) 293 Surcharge of the Forest. *Superoneratio Forestæ*, is when a Commoner in the Forest putteth on more Beasts than he ought, and so surchargeth the Forest. *a*1776 in Burrow *Reports* IV. 2431 Where a Commoner was intitled to Common for a certain Number of Cattle.. there if he surcharged, another Commoner might distrain.

3. To put an additional or excessive (physical) burden or weight upon; to overload, weigh down.

1582 STANYHURST *Æneis* II. (Arb.) 60 When shee shaw Priamus yoouthlyk surcharged in armoure. **1600** HOLLAND *Livy* VII. xxiii. 265 The Gaules being surcharged with dartes either sticking through their bodies, or fast set in their shields, and so weighing them downe. *c*1600 DAVISON *Ps. xxiii.* in Farr *S. P. Eliz.* (1845) II. 320 Thou my board with messes large Dost surcharge. **1603** KNOLLES *Hist. Turks* (1621) 33 As was the greatest servant of Christ, Peter, surcharged with two chaines. **1667** MILTON *P.L.* v. 58 O fair Plant,.. with fruit surcharg'd, Deigns none to ease thy load and taste thy sweet? **1671** —— *Samson* 728 Like a fair flower surcharg'd with dew. **1706** J. PHILIPS *Cerealia* 125 Whilst black pots walk the round with laughing Ale Surcharg'd. **1753** RICHARDSON *Grandison* (1781) VI. iii. 347 Her eyes.. surcharged, as I may say, with tears of joy. **1811** *Glenbervie Jrnls.* (1910) 138 A round hat surcharged with feathers. **1869** SPURGEON *Treas. Dav.* Ps. xxv. 17 A lake surcharged with water by enormous floods.

b. With reference to surfeit of food or drink. Also *fig.*

1603 KNOLLES *Hist. Turks* (1638) 182 The defendants of the Castle.. surcharged themselues.. with excesse both of meat and drink. **1622** VENNER *Via Recta* viii. (ed. 2) 190 They.. greatly erre.. that.. presse and surcharge their bodies with ouer-much meat. *a*1644 QUARLES *Sol. Recant.* Sol. xi. 79 Thou mayst surcharge as well as sterve The soile; But wise men know what seed will serve. **1784** COWPER *Tiroc.* 20 Still to be fed, and not to be surcharged.

c. To charge to excess *with* moisture, a substance in solution, or the like.

1611 SPEED *Theat. Gt. Brit.* xix. (1614) 37/1 The Fenny [soil] surcharged with waters. **1771** SMOLLETT *Humphry Cl.* 4 July, A gross stagnated air, surcharged with damps from vaults. **1798** *Surv. Prov. Moray* iii. 127 All the water seems surcharged with iron. **1803** MALTHUS *Popul.* II. ii. (1806) I. 339 The seeds with which every wind is surcharged sow the ground thickly with firs. **1815** J. SMITH *Panorama Sci. & Art* II. 261 The whole of the identical electricity that surcharges one side of a phial. **1816** WORDSW. *French Army in Russia* II. 7 Winter's breath surcharged with sleety showers. **1849** CLARIDGE *Cold Water Cure* 109 When the body is surcharged with heat. **1867** LYELL *Princ. Geol.* (ed. 10) I. II. xv. 330 Winds blowing from the sea are generally surcharged with moisture. **1897** *Allbutt's Syst. Med.* III. 163 The blood.. was always found surcharged with urates. *fig.* **1884** *Manch. Exam.* 7 May 4/7 Such words.. are surcharged with a certain amount of invidiousness.

4. In non-physical senses: To weigh down, overburden; to bear heavily upon.

1581 LAMBARDE *Eiren.* I. ix. (1602) 41 The Commission of the peace.. surcharged with vaine recitals. **1592** KYD *Sp. Trag.* III. vii, Mine exclaimes, that haue surcharged the aire With ceasles plaints. **1611** SPEED *Theat. Gt. Brit.* xxxix. (1614) 78/2 Surcharged and over-worne with the troublesome toyles.. of warre. **1635** JACKSON *Creed* VIII. ii. §2 To surcharge our ordinary humane conditions with the extraordinary estate of a servant.. this was that unexpressible humiliation. **1643** MILTON *Divorce* v. 11 When human frailty surcharg'd, is at such a losse. *a*1684 LEIGHTON *Comm. I Pet.* iii. 15 The greatest affairs surcharge him [*sc.* God] not and the very smallest escape him not.

b. To oppress or overwhelm (*with* emotion, sorrow, or suffering).

1566 DRANT *Wail. Hieremie* v. in *Horace* etc. L ij, Our hearte with sadnesse is surcharged. **1588** GREENE *Pandosto* (1843) 23 Surcharged before with extreame joy and now suppressed with heavie sorrowe. **1590** MARLOWE *2nd Pt. Tamburl.* III. i, Ioue surcharg'd with pity of our wrongs. **1647** WARD *Simple Cobler* (1843) 54 My heart is surcharged, I can no longer forbear. *a*1649 DRUMM. OF HAWTH. *Poems* Wks. (1711) 32 Sur-charg'd with grief, fraught with annoy. **1667** MILTON *P.L.* XII. 373 Discerning Adam with such joy Surcharg'd. **1804** WORDSW. *Vaudracour & Julia* 50 Till his spirit sank, Surcharged, within him. **1835** MARRYAT *Jacob Faithful* xviii, My heart was too much surcharged.. my grief found vent. **1904** M. HEWLETT *Queen's Quair* II. x, Had she been less charged with them [*sc.* troubles] she had been warier; but she was indeed surcharged.

c. *pass.* To have an excess of inhabitants, inmates, or members.

1572 *Act. 14 Eliz.* c. 5 §40 Yf it shall chaunce any Cytie.. to have in yt moore poore Folkes then the Inhabitauntes thereof shalbe able to releve.. uppon Certyfycate thereof made, and of the number and names of the persones with which they be so surchardged [etc.]. **1637** EARL STIRLING *Domes-day* v. v, Else th' earth surcharg'd would starve her nurslings soon. **1667** MILTON *P.L.* II. 836 Least Heav'n surcharg'd with potent multitude Might hap to move new broiles. **1793** GOUV. MORRIS in Sparks *Life & Writ.* (1832) II. 370 Already the prisons are surcharged. **1837** P. KEITH *Bot. Lex* 146 This analysis brings him down to the several classes of the first grand group, which, from their number, are prevented from being surcharged with too many tribes or families. **1913** FRAZER *Scapegoat* v. 226 An atmosphere surcharged with devils.

†**5.** To make an overwhelming attack upon see CHARGE *v.* 22. *Obs.*

1588 KYD *Househ. Philos.* Wks. (1901) 239, I beheld a little Kidde surchargd, pursued and anon ouertaken by two swift Grey-hounds. **1596** SPENSER *F.Q.* IV. ix. 30 Foure charged two, and two surcharged one.

6. To print an additional mark on the face of (a postage-stamp), esp. for the purpose of changing its value.

1870 J. E. GRAY *Catal. Postage Stamps* (ed. 5) 169 Value surcharged in coloured ink. **1870** *Routledge's Ev. Boy's Ann.* Feb., Suppl. 3/1 Current adhesives, surcharged with service. **1881** *Stamp-Collector's Ann.* 14 A new value of 8 cents has been created by surcharging the 12 cents with 8 cents in black. *Ibid.* 16 A 50 reis stamp, green,.. surcharged *Guine* in black.

Hence **surˈcharging** *vbl. sb.* (also *attrib.*).

1598 MANWOOD *Lawes Forest* xv. 82 The surcharging of the Forrest with more beasts then they may Common withall. **1602** CAREW *Cornwall* I. 23 b, Let not the owners commendable industrie, turne to their surcharging preiudice. **1622** [E. MISSELDEN] *Free Trade* 130 The Surcharging of the Cloth Trade. **1768** BLACKSTONE *Comm.* III. xvi. 238 This injury by surcharging can properly speaking only happen, where the common is appendant or appurtenent. **1881** *Stamp-Collector's Ann.* 16 By the last mail we are informed that the surcharging has again ceased. **1889** *Spectator* 27 Apr. 568/1 Easements in that direction will only tend to the surcharging of rents.

surcharged (sɜːˈtʃɑːdʒd), *ppl. a.* [f. prec. + -ED¹.] Overburdened, overloaded, charged to excess. Also *fig.* (In quot. 1837 = SUPERHEATED 1.)

1615 BRATHWAIT *Strappado* (1878) 100 Surcharged brests must needs their greefes expresse. *a*1658 SLINGSBY *Diary* (1836) 201, I found no Billows.. to endanger the passage of my late surcharged vessel. **1681** FLAVEL *Right. Man's Ref.* vi. 197 Causing the designs of the wicked, like a surcharged gun, to recoil upon and destroy themselves. **1798** S. & HT. LEE *Canterb. T.* II. 283 The surcharged heart cannot resist.. unmerited kindness. **1822-7** GOOD *Study Med.* (1829) I. 135 [Thirst] is.. intolerable on a surcharged stomach. **1837** *Civil Engin. & Arch. Jrnl.* I. 26/2 The steam being saturated with heat.. this surcharged steam becomes a floating agent. **1849** ALISON *Hist. Eur.* II. viii. §18. 247 Quarries.. employed as a place of deposit for the bones in the surcharged cemeteries of the capital. **1860** MAURY *Phys. Geog.* (Low) xx. §834 Vapour borne by those surcharged winds. **1867** BRANDE & COX *Dict. Sci.*, etc., *Surcharged or Overcharged Mine*, in Military Mining, a mine loaded with a very great charge of powder. It is sometimes called a globe of compression.

b. Of a postage-stamp: see SURCHARGE *v.* 6.

1881 *Stamp-Collector's Ann.* 16 The surcharged sixpennies, doing duty for pennies, are discontinued.

†**surˈchargement.** *Obs. rare.* [f. as prec. + -MENT: cf. F. *surchargement* (16th c.).] = SURCHARGE *sb.*² 1.

1613 DANIEL *Hist. Eng.* II. 76 [It] yeelded that continuall surchargement of people, as they were forced to vnburthen themselues on other Countries.

surcharger (sɜːˈtʃɑːdʒə(r)). [f. SURCHARGE *v.* + -ER¹.] One who surcharges.

1569 in W. H. Turner *Select. Rec. Oxford* (1880) 327 S'chargers Cattell to be impounded. **1598** MANWOOD *Lawes Forest* xiv. 82 (*heading*) Of surchargers of the Forest. **1812** *Examiner* 7 Sept. 570/2 The Surveyor (*i.e.* Surcharger) was the only person who had the power to give any relief! **1863** COWDEN CLARKE *Shaks. Char.* xiv. 363 A distrainer for rent, or a surcharger of taxes.

†**surˈchargure.** *Obs. rare.* [f. SURCHARGE *v.* + -URE.] = Surcharge *sb.*² 1.

1614 J. ROBINSON *Relig. Communion* vi. §7 Wks. 1851 III. 263 Outwardly.. disburdened of such sins, as clogged their consciences, as is the dog by vomiting of his surchargure.

surcingle (ˈsɜːsɪŋ(ə)l), *sb.* Forms: 4-7 sursengle, 5 surcyngylle, sorseynggle, 6 sursyngle, -cyngle, 6-8 sursingle, (7 *erron.* sussingle, 7, 9 circingle), 7- surcingle. [a. OF. *sur-*, *so(u)rcengle*, *-sangle*: see SUR- and CINGLE.]

1. A girth for a horse or other animal; *esp.* a large girth passing over a sheet, pack, etc. and keeping it in place on the animal's back.

1390 *Earl Derby's Exped.* (Camden) 13 Et pro viij burrewez, j sursengle, et j pare raynes. **1470-85** MALORY *Arthur* VII. xvi. 238 And eyther smote other in myddes of their sheldes that the paytrellys sursenglys and crowpers braste. **1553** in Kempe *Losely MSS.* (1836) 139, 7 great horses, with horse cloths, sursyngles, bytts, hed stalls, &c. **1600** SURFLET *Country Farm* I. xxviii. 177 To haue their cloathes put vpon their backes, either the linnen one to keepe the flies away, or else the woollen one to keepe them warme, and that they suffer him to make the same fast with a surcingle. **1668** WORLIDGE *Syst. Agric., Dict. Rust.* 276 A *Sussingle*, a large Girt that Carriers use to binde or fasten their Packs withal. **1695** *Lond. Gaz.* No. 3132/4 One brown Gelding.. some sign of a Sursingle tied across his Back, also a Curb on his near Hock. *c*1720 W. GIBSON *Farrier's Guide* II. lxv. (1738) 220 A Strap may be fixed to the Breast-cloth, which may pass between his Fore-legs and be fastened to his Sursingle. **1816** SCOTT *Bl. Dwarf* x, 'Thou maun do without horse-sheet and surcingle now, lad,' he said, addressing the animal. **1882** *Manchester Weekly Times* 25 Mar. 8/2 A surcingle was drawn over Jumbo's back. **1890** 'R. BOLDREWOOD' *Col. Reformer* I. 151 Have you no cavesson, or breaking-bit, or web surcingle?

b. (See quot.)

1801 FELTON *Carriages* Gloss., *Surcingle*, a leather strap and buckle, sewed to a chaise saddle, the same as a belly band to a housing.

2. A girdle or belt which confines the cassock. Now *rare.*

1672 MARVELL *Reh. Transp.* I. 68 This Gentleman.. stragling by Temple-bar, in a massy Cassock and Surcingle. *a*1683 OLDHAM *Wks.* (1686) 75 Cassock, Sursingle, and shaven Crown. **1728** POPE *Dunc.* II. 350 Each rev'rend Bard arose; And Milbourn chief.. Gave him the cassock, surcingle, and vest. **1837** BARHAM *Ingol. Leg.* Ser. I. *Grey Dolphin*, He drew the buckle of his surcingle.. tighter.

Hence †**surcingled** *pa. pple.*, fastened or girded with a surcingle; †**surcingler** (*nonce-wd.*), one who wears a surcingle, a clergyman; †**surcingling** (*nonce-wd.*), a flogging with a surcingle.

1598 BP. HALL *Sat.* IV. vi, Some pannel.. Sursingled to a galled hackney's hide. **1647** WARD *Simple Cobler* (1843) 27 Comparing the.. splender wherewith our Gentle-women were imbellished.., with the gut-foundred goosdom, wherewith they are now surcingled. **1654** GAYTON *Pleas. Notes* III. i. 67 Indeed dry-bastings, cudgelings, surcinglings were too mean for a Knight. **1662** *Tryal T. Tonge* 6 That there should be never a Lawn-Sleeve, never a Surcingler should have a hole to hide his head in.

surciour, obs. form of SEARCHER.

1647 HAWARD *Crown Revenue* 20 Surciour: Fee, 40. o. o.

†**ˈsurcle.** *Obs.* (Also 7 surcul, 9 surcule.) [ad. L. *surculus*. Cf. F. *surcule*.] A small or young shoot of a plant; a sprout, sprig, twig; also, a small branch of a nerve, blood-vessel, etc.

1578 BANISTER *Hist. Man* v. 71 The left Nerue.. enwrappeth the nether Orifice of the ventricle with some surcles. **1646** SIR T. BROWNE *Pseud. Ep.* II. vi. 98 Misseltoe.. sprouteth not forth in boughs and surcles of the same shape and similary unto the tree that beareth it. *Ibid.* IV. iii. 183 The Azygos, or *vena sine pari*, whose surcles are disposed unto the other lower. **1657** TOMLINSON *Renou's Disp.* 673 They sometimes cut off its tender surcles [*printed* succles]. [**1681** tr. *Willis' Rem. Med. Wks.* Vocab., *Surculs*, little..shoots. **1860** MAYNE *Expos. Lex.*, *Surculus*..a twig: a surcule.]

surcle, obs. form of CIRCLE.

†**surcloy,** *v.* *Obs.* [f. SUR- + CLOY *v.*, after *surfeit.*] *trans.* To cloy excessively, surfeit.

1594 KYD *Cornelia* I. 216 For faire Corne-ground are our fields surcloid With worthles Gorse. *Ibid.* v. 176 Streames of blood like Riuers fill the downes; That being infected with the stench thereof Surcloyes the ground. **1606** SYLVESTER *Du Bartas* II. iv. *Magnificence* 490 With surfeit and with sleep surcloyd. *a* **1618** —— *Quadrains of Pibrac* lxii, A greedy Eater..Who so surcloyes his stomach with his Cates, That [etc.]. *c* **1620** Z. BOYD *Zion's Flowers* (1855) 47 His stomach he surcloyeth not with food.

surcoat ('sɜːkəʊt). Forms: 4 **surkot,** (**sorcot**), 4–7 (9) **surcote,** 5 **surkote, -cotte,** (**ser-, syrcote,** 5–6 **circot(e,** 6 **circotte,** *erron.* **surcourt**), 7 **surcoate,** 8 **-koat,** 7– **surcoat.** [a. OF. *sur-*, *sor-*, *sour-*, *sircot* (also *-cote*): see SUR- and COAT *sb.* Cf. Pr. *sobrecot*, It *sopraccotta*, *sorcotto*.

MLG., MSw. *sorcot*, MDu. *sorcote*, ONorw., MHG. *surkot*, med.L. *sor-*, *surcotium* are from Fr.]

1. An outer coat or garment, commonly of rich material, worn by people of rank of both sexes; often worn by armed men over their armour, and having the heraldic arms depicted on it.

As part of the insignia of orders, etc., the surcoat is now a short sleeveless garment of crimson velvet worn with a mantle.

a **1330** *Syr Degarre* 791 He hadde on a sorcot ouert, I-forred with blaundeuer apert. **13..** *Gaw. & Gr. Knt.* 62 His surkot semed hym wel, þat softe was forred. *c* **1386** CHAUCER *Prol.* 617 A long surcote of pers vpon he hade. ? *a* **1400** *Morte Arth.* 3252 A duches dereworthily dyghte.. In a surcott of sylke fulle selkouthely hewede. **1457** *Cov. Leet Bk.* 299, & there folowed then mony moo ladyes yn her mantels, surcotes & other appareyll to theyre astates acustumed. **1494** in *Househ. Ord.* (1790) 120 On New-Yeares day, the King ought to weare his kirtle, his circote, and his pane of armes. **1562** LEGH *Armory* (1597) 96 Gentlewomen vnder the degree of a countesse, haue armes on Taberts, but the countesse and so vpwards shal haue their Armes in surcotes and mantels. **1603** DRAYTON *Bar. Wars* II. xxiii, Upon his Surcote, valiant Nevil bore A Silver Saltoyre. **1654** H. L'ESTRANGE *Chas. I* (1655) 110 The hole Colledge of Heralds mounted on horse-back, in their rich Surcoats. **1805** SOUTHEY *Madoc.* I. xv, Embroider'd surcoats and emblazon'd shields. **1845** S. AUSTIN *Ranke's Hist. Ref.* v. ix. III. 263 They were all in light armour, with red surcoats. **1885** C. W. C. OMAN *Art of War* 42 The colour of bannerole, crest, and surcoat was that of the regimental standard. **1911** MAX BEERBOHM *Zuleika Dobson* iii. 32 The heavy mantle of blue velvet,..the crimson surcoat [of the Garter].

attrib. *a* **1400** *Octouian* 1180 Sche..yn hys ryght hond left ..Her surkot sleue.

2. An undershirt, vest, semmit. *Sc.*

Perh. associated with *sarkit*, 'a kind of short shirt, or blouse' (*Banffsh. Gloss.* 1866).

1768 *Song* in Ross *Helenore* 132 A surkoat hough side [i.e. reaching to the thigh].

surcom-: see CIRCUM-.

†**surcrease,** *sb.* *Obs.* [a. OF. *surcres*, *-creis*, f. pres. stem of *surcreistre*: see SURCREASE *v.* Cf. *increase* sb.] A growth or addition over and above; an increment, accession; a surplus, excess.

1600 HOLLAND *Livy* VIII. xxix. 302 Over and above all these, the Vestine people, as a surcrease to their troubles, joined and banded with the Samnites. *a* **1603** T. CARTWRIGHT *Confut. Rhem. N.T.* (1618) 98 Not (as the Iesuites make it) to serue for a surcrease or ouerplus of righteousnesse and merite. **1603** FLORIO *Montaigne* I. xxix. (1632) 98 If the..husbandlike affection be..surcharged with that a man oweth to alliance and kindred, there is no doubt, but that surcrease may easily transport a husband beyond the bounds of reason. **1612** DRAYTON *Poly-olb.* i. 515 Their surcrease grew so great, as forced them at last To seek another soyle.

So †**sur'crue** [after ACCRUE *sb.* (OF. *acreue*), CREW *sb.*[1] (OF. *creue*)], †**surcroist** [OF. *surcroist* (mod.F. *surcroît*), later form of *surcrois*, *-creis*, *-cres*: see above], †**surcroitre** ? [OF. *surcroistre* inf. used subst.].

1496–7 *Plumpton Corr.* (Camden) 130 Send to me..a byll of such lands as ye are content to departe with to Kilborne in exchange, & if ye wyll have the surcrortr [*sic*]... **1601** HOLLAND *Pliny* XXI. iv. II. 83 Cæpio..was of opinion, That the hundred-leafe Rose..should not be put into Chaplets, unlesse it were last in manner of a tuft, to make a sur-croist, or about the edges as a border. *c* **1638** WOTTON *Let. to Walton* in *Reliq.* (1672) 361 It [*sc.* the fever] had once left me, as I thought; but it was only to fetch more company, returning with a surcrew of those splenetick vapours. *c* **1825** SCOTT *Let. to Laidlaw* (in *Athenæum* 6 Apr. (1895) 442/3), I have..great resources, and considerable securities, and am confident..to pay every man his own, with a large surcrue.

†**sur'crease,** *v.* *Obs.* [f. OF. *surcreiss-*, present stem of *surcreistre*, *-croistre* (mod.F. *-croître*), f. *sur-* SUR- + *creistre* (:—L. *crēscĕre*) to grow.]

1. *intr.* To grow greater or more numerous; to increase to excess.

1566 DRANT *Wail. Hieremie* i. in *Horace* etc. Kj, In wealthe surcreasyng faste. **1601** HOLLAND *Pliny* XXXIII. ii. II. 460 The companie so surcreased, that..they could not bee contained all within the chamber of Iudges.

2. To grow over.

1632 LITHGOW *Trav.* III. 94 If any..digge deepe holes, the earth of it selfe in a small time will surcrease without any ayde of man.

3. *trans.* To grow greater than; to increase beyond.

1603 HOLLAND *Plutarch's Mor.* 175 In case these.. elements..covet to have more than their just proportion,.. seeking one to surcrease and over-grow another.

†**sur'crescent,** *a.* *Obs.* *rare*$^{-1}$. [f. SUR- = SUPER- 2 + CRESCENT *a.*] Growing upon or over.

1626 J. GRESHAM *Pict. Incest* (1876) 26 She [*sc.* Myrrha] With willing minde her selfe doth subiugate To the surcrescent [*printed* surrescent] barque.

surcroist, surcrue: see under SURCREASE *sb.*

surcudant, surcuidrie, var. SURQUIDANT, SURQUIDRY *Obs.*

surcul(e: see SURCLE.

†**surculate,** *v.* *Obs.* *rare*$^{-0}$. [f. L. *surculāt-*, pa. ppl. stem of *surculāre*, f. *surculus* SURCLE.]

1623 COCKERAM, *Surculate*, to prune trees.

surcu'lation. *rare.* ? *Obs.* [ad. L. **surculātio*, *-ōnem*, n. of action f. *surculāre* (see prec.). Cf. F. *surculation.*] Pruning; the action of cutting off shoots for propagation.

1668 WORLIDGE *Syst. Agric.*, *Dict. Rust.* 276 *Succulation* [sic], a pruning of Trees. *a* **1682** SIR T. BROWNE *Tracts* (1684) 48 The Olive being not successfully propagable by Seed, nor at all by surculation. **1878** W. MACCALL tr. *Letourneau's Biol.* 276 Budding, germination, or surculation.

surculigerous (sɜːkjuː'lɪdʒərəs), *a.* *Bot.* [f. mod.L. *surculigerus*, f. *surculus* SURCLE: see -GEROUS.] Producing suckers.

In recent Dicts.

surculose ('sɜːkjʊləʊs), *a.* *Bot.* *rare.* [ad. L. *surculōsus*, f. *surculus* SURCLE: see -OSE.] Producing shoots or suckers.

1845 ASA GRAY *Bot. Text-bk.* Index, *Surculose*, bearing suckers. **1861** BENTLEY *Man. Bot.* 112.

†'**surculous,** *a.* *Obs.* *rare*$^{-1}$. [ad. L. *surculōsus*: see prec. and -OUS. Cf. F. *surculeux.*] Of the nature of a shoot. Also, = prec.

1597 GERARDE *Herbal* II. cxxxii. 405 This plant..hath.. rootes, couered ouer with a thicke barke, plaited as it were with many surculous sprigs. **1656** BLOUNT *Glossogr.*, *Surculous*.., full of shoots or sprigs.

†**surculus.** *Bot.* *Obs.* Pl. **surculi.** [L., = young twig, branch, shoot.] (See quots. 1775, 1849.)

1775 ASH, *Surculus*, a shoot, a sucker, a slip; a middle branch between the larger and smaller ribs of a leaf. **1826** KIRBY & SPENCE *Introd. Entomol.* III. 227 The cocoon..is fastened by one side to the roots or surculi of Typha latifolia. **1849** J. H. BALFOUR *Man. Bot.* 639 *Surculus*, a sucker proceeding from the neck of a plant, and afterwards rooting, as in the Rose.

surcuydry, variant of SURQUIDRY *Obs.*

surd (sɜːd), *a.* and *sb.* Also 6–7 **surde.** [ad. L. *surdus* (in active sense) deaf, (in pass. sense) silent, mute, dumb, (of sound, etc.) dull, indistinct.

The mathematical sense 'irrational' arises from L. *surdus* being used to render Gr. ἄλογος (Euclid bk. x. Def.), app. through the medium of Arab. *açamm* deaf, as in *jaðr açamm* surd root.]

A. *adj.* **1.** *Math.* Of a number or quantity (esp. a root): That cannot be expressed in finite terms of ordinary numbers or quantities: = IRRATIONAL A. 3. (Cf. INCOMMENSURABLE 1.) (See also quots.)

1551 RECORDE *Pathw. Knowl.* II. Pref., Quantitees partly rationall, and partly surde. **1571** DIGGES *Pantom.* IV. vi. X ij, Tetraedrons side being rationall, the Axis is surde, and it beareth proportion to the side as 1. to $\sqrt{24}$. **1623** BP. ANDREWES *XCVI Serm.* xvi. (1629) 156 Such surd numbers, such fractions we shall meet with, we shall not tell how or when to gett through. **1659** LEYBOURN *Arith.* IV. iv. (1660) 339 There are many sorts of surd roots, some are simple,.. others are compound. **1798** HUTTON *Course Math.* (1806) I. 80 The cube root of 8 is rational, being equal to 2; but the cube root of 9 is surd or irrational. **1861** T. LUND *J. Wood's Elem. Alg.* 97 An equation may be cleared of a surd by transposing the terms so that the surd shall form one side, and the rational quantities the other, and then raising both sides to that power which will rationalize the surd. **1908** G. H. HARDY *Course Pure Math.* i. 7 If a is a rational number, the two numbers $\pm\sqrt{a}$ are either rational or irrational, and ..*generally* the latter. Numbers of this kind, when irrational, are called pure quadratic surds. A number $a \pm \sqrt{b}$..is sometimes called a mixed quadratic surd. **1959** G. & R. C. JAMES *Math. Dict.* 379/2 *Surd*, a sum of one or more irrational indicated roots of numbers. Sometimes used for irrational number. **1962** H. COHN *Second Course in Number Theory* iii. 40 If a, b, c are integers..we define the conjugate surds $\lambda = (a + b\sqrt{D})/c$, $\lambda' = (a - b\sqrt{D})/c$.

†**2.** Deaf. *Obs.* *rare.*

1682 SIR T. BROWNE *Chr. Mor.* III. §6 He..may.. apprehend how all Words fall to the Ground, spent upon such a surd and Earless Generation of Men. **1819** H. BUSK *Vestriad* I. 763 Whistlings, whizzes, strike thy senses surd.

3. *fig.* †**a.** Not endowed with sense or perception; insensate, unintelligent. *Obs.*

In quot. 1668, deficient in perception, dull: cf. c.

1601 HOLLAND *Pliny* XXVII. xiii. II. 292 Those medicinable vertues..bestowed vpon those surd and senslesse hearbs. **1668** H. MORE *Div. Dial.* II. xxvi. (1713) 174 My palate is something more surd and jacent. *a* **1676** HALE *Prim. Orig. Man.* I. ii. (1677) 44 Neither Chance nor surd or inanimate Nature could be the Efficient of such a Being.

b. Irrational, senseless, stupid. (In recent use only as a direct figure from 1.)

1610 A. COOKE *Pope Joan* 60 Rupertus,..commonly called Grosthead. A great Philosopher..though it pleased your Pope Innocentius the fourth, to call him old foole, surd, and absurd companion. **1625** JACKSON *Creed* V. xlvii. §6 Their irrational and surd conceits of scripture's sense. **1642** H. MORE *Song of Soul* II. i. I. vii, And foul blasphemous belch from their surd mouth resounds.

1863 M. PATTISON *Ess.* xvii. (1889) II. 295 The surd and irrational complexion of that party is due to the circumstance that all its best minds went from it. **1891** H. JONES *Browning as Teacher* 24 The problems have a surd or irrational element in them.

†**c.** Not clearly or keenly perceived, dull; stingless. *Obs.*

1597 A. M. tr. *Guillemeau's Fr. Chirurg.* 48/2 The dolour not so pungent and sharp, but somwhat more surde and benumde. **1599** —— tr. *Gabelhouer's Bk. Physicke* 202/2 Take..oyle of Hempeseede and surde nettles.

†**d.** Conveying no sense, meaningless. *Obs.*

1605 BACON *Adv. Learn.* II. xxv. §4 The Ceremonies of Idolatrie and Magicke that are full of Non-significants and surde characters.

4. *Phonetics.* Uttered without vibration of the vocal cords; voiceless, 'breathed': opposed to SONANT. (Cf. F. *sourd.*)

1767 *Ess.* in *Ann. Reg.* 194/1 Mute, surd, and nasal syllables. **1773** KENRICK *Dict.*, *Gram. Eng. Lang.* 27 All our modes of articulation, whether surd or vocal. **1863** MAX MÜLLER *Sci. Lang.* Ser. II. vii. (1868) 297 No longer mere interjections..uncertain between surd, sonant, or aspirated enunciation. **1887** COOK tr. *Sievers' O.E. Gram.* 99 P is a surd labial stop.

5. *Arabic Gram.* (tr. Arab. *açamm* lit. deaf). Applied to verbs in which the second and third letters of the root are the same.

1776 RICHARDSON *Gram. Arab. Lang.* III. v. 97 The Surd verb, so called because the last radical is not heard, coalescing with the second by Teshdid. **1777** —— *Arab.-Pers. Dict.* 138 *el' asammu* The *surd* or *teshdid* conjugation of Arabick verbs. **1823** W. PRICE *Gram. 3 Oriental Langs.* 112 Conjugation of the Surd Verb, *della*, he ogled.

B. *sb.* **1.** *Math.* A surd or irrational number or quantity, esp. root: see A. 1.

1557 RECORDE *Whetst.* L l iij, Those nombers are not Surde nombers properly, but sette like Surdes. As the Square roote of .4. **1571** DIGGES *Pantom.* IV. vii. X ij b, The Hexaedrons comprehending Spheres Dimetiente beeing rationall, his Axis is a surde. **1674** JEAKE *Arith.* (1696) 294 Surdes are Simple or Compound, Integral or Fracted. **1743** EMERSON *Fluxions* 83 Any Power of the Quantity under the Vinculum (in any Binomial or Trinomial Surd). **1869** 'LEWIS CARROLL' *Phantasmagoria* 110 Yet what are all such gaieties to me Whose thoughts are full of indices and surds?

attrib. **1869** J. H. SMITH *Elem. Algebra* 164 Surds of the same order are those for which the root-symbol or surd-index is the same.

fig. **1856** FERRIER *Inst. Metaph.* iv. (ed. 2) 143 It becomes the absolutely incogitable—a surd. **1877** E. CAIRD *Philos. Kant* II. xv. 551 The old difficulty..that reappears always as the inexplicable surd of his philosophy.

2. *Phonetics.* A speech-sound uttered without 'voice'; a 'breath' consonant: see A. 4.

1789 E. DARWIN *Bot. Gard.* II. 60 Weighs with nice ear the vowel, liquid, surd, And breaks in syllables the volant word. **1842** *Proc. Philol. Soc.* I. 7 The tenues (otherwise surds, or whisper-letters). **1871** *Public Sch. Lat. Gram.* 7 The use of C as a surd made K superfluous.

†**surd,** *v.*[1] *Obs.* [Repr. OE. **seordan*: see SARD *v.*] *trans.* To defile.

a **1400** *Leg. Rood* (1871) 143, I sauh my child ben surded and soyled.

surd, *v.*[2] [f. L. *surdus*: see SURD *a.*] *trans.* To deaden or dull the sound of, as by a 'sordine' or mute. Also '**surding** *vbl. sb.* used *attrib.*

1625 LISLE *Du Bartas, Noe* Ded. ¶¶j b, To surd it, as young trompeters are wont. **1885** *Encycl. Brit.* XIX. 70/2 A surding or muting effect produced by impeding the vibration of the strings [of a pianoforte] by contact of small pieces of buff leather.

surd, var. SOURD *v.* *Obs.*, to arise, spring.

1509 HAWES *Past. Pleas.* VIII. i. (Percy Soc.) 29 Invencion, Whiche surdeth of the most noble werke Of v. inward wittes.

surdar, variant of SIRDAR.

surden, obs. form of SORDINE.

1616 A. MUNDAY *Chrysan.* B 3, The Trumpets sound their seuerall Surden flourishes. *Ibid.* B 4 b, The first sound of Surden Trumpets. *Ibid.* C 1, A full flourish without Surdens.

†**surdesolid,** *sb.* (*a.*) *Math.* *Obs.* Also **surdsolid.** [ad. mod.L. *surdesolidus*. Cf. It. *surdesolido*, G. †*surdesolidalisch*.

The origin of mod.L. *surdesolidus* is obscure. In Zedler's *Universal Lexicon*, s.v. *Dignitas*, the term is given as the name of the 5th power 'according to the Arabs', corresponding to *quadratocubus*, the name 'according to Diophantus'; the 7th power is *surdesolidum secundum*, and the 11th *surdesolidum tertium*. If the term is of Arabic origin, it may = **surdē solidum*, lit. deafly solid, i.e. of a power not 'communicating with', i.e. not derivable from, 2 or 3 or their powers (cf. the origin of mathematical L. *surdus*, SURD *a.* note).]

= SURSOLID.

1557 RECORDE *Whetst.* Hiij b, Thei appeare to bee ouersene, that call those .. nombers Surdesolides, seing thei are not any waies Surde nombers. **1579** DIGGES *Stratiot.* II. i. 33 Squares, Cubes, Zenzizenzike, and Surd Solides. **1674** JEAKE *Arith.* (1696) 177 A Squared Cube Number [= *numerus quadrato-cubus*] .. is called a Surdesolide, or Sursolide. **1726** E. STONE *New Math. Dict.* s.v. *Locus*, The antient Geometricians did call Plain Loci, such that are Right Lines or Circles; and Solid Loci, those that are Parabola's, Ellipses, or Hyperbola's; and Surd-Solid Loci, such that are Curves of a superiour Gender than Conick Sections. **1728** CHAMBERS *Cycl.*, *Sursolid*, or *Surdesolid*, in Arithmetic, the Fifth Power of a Number ... 32, the fifth Power, or Sursolid, or Surdesolid Number of 2.

surdi'mutism. = SURDOMUTISM. (Cf. F. *surdimutité*.)

In recent Dicts.

surdine, obs. form of SORDINE.

surdiny, obs. form of SARDINE *sb.*[2]

surdism ('sɜːdɪz(ə)m). *Path.* [f. L. *surdus* deaf: see SURD *a.* and -ISM.] (See quot.)

1898 D. WILLIAMS *Med. Dis. Infancy* xxxvii. 494 The term *surdism* is applied to those degrees of deafness which make 'the acquisition of speech in the very young impossible by ordinary means, or which involve the loss of recently acquired speech'.

surdity ('sɜːdɪtɪ). [ad. L. *surditās*, *-ātem*, n. of quality f. *surdus* deaf: see SURD *a.* and -ITY. Cf. F. *surdité*.] Deafness. (Now *Path.*)

1597 A. M. tr. *Guillemeau's Fr. Chirurg.* 29b/1 Agaynst surditye, payne, and vlceration of the eares. **1678–9** SIR T. BROWNE *Let. Son* 1 Mar., If it fayleth, incurable surditie ensueth. **1880** *Daily Tel.* 23 Feb., Ears long since overtaken by the surdity of death. **1882** tr. *Ribot's Dis. Memory* 152 Sometimes he does not understand the meaning of words, written or spoken, although the senses of hearing and sight are intact (cases of verbal surdity and cecity).

surdomute (sɜːdəʊ'mjuːt), *a.* and *sb. rare*⁻⁰. [f. *surdo-*, taken as comb. form of L. *surdus* SURD *a.* + MUTE *a.* Cf. mod.L. *surdomutitās* (Dunglison).] = DEAF-MUTE. So **surdo'mutism**, deaf-mutism.

1880 *Nature* 11 Mar. 459/1 Surdo-mutism is, in the majority of cases, the immediate result of cerebral lesions. **1890** GOULD *New Med. Dict.*, *Surdomute* .. a deaf and dumb person.

surdon, obs. form of SORDINE.

1630 BRATHWAIT *Eng. Gentlem.* (1641) 193 Here sounds the Surdon of religious sorrow, the awaker of devotion.

sure (ʃʊə(r), ʃɔə(r)), *a.* and *adv.* Forms: 4– sure; also 4–6 sur, seur, (5 sewr, suere, sewir, scewre, suyre, swyr), 5–6 seure, sewre, sewer, 5–7 suer, *Sc.* suir, (6 suar, swer, syuer, shure, sowr, *Sc.* suire, suyr, swuer). [a. OF. *sur-e*, *seur-e* (dial. *segur*; cf. Pr., Cat. *segur*, It. *sicuro*, Sp., Pg. *seguro*, Rum. *sigur*):—L. *sēcūru-s*, f. *sē* without + *cūra* care, CURE *sb.*[1] The OF. var. *sour-e* is represented by Sc. SOVER.]

A. *adj.*

I. Safe, secure.

†**1. a.** Free from or not exposed to danger or risk; not liable to be injured or destroyed; = SAFE *a.* 6, SECURE *a.* 3. Const. *from*. *Obs.* (or merged in other senses).

13.. *Coer de L.* 5908 Kyng Richard dwellyd with honoure, Tyl that Jaffe was made al sure. **1340–70** *Alex. & Dind.* 9 No syte nor no sur stede sojli þei ne hadde. **1399** LANGL. *Rich. Redeles* I. 104 All þat þey moued .. Was to be sure of hem-self and siris to ben y-callid. **1426** LYDG. *De Guil. Pilgr.* 949 He shal .. Make the sur .. From al tempestys of the se. *c* **1440** *Generydes* 4605 Owt of ther enmys handes they were sure. *c* **1450** tr. *De Imitatione* I. xiii. 14 There is no man all sure fro temptacions whiles he lyueþ. **1513** DOUGLAS *Æneis* VII. xii. 114 For defens, to kepe thair hedis suyr, A ȝallo hat [they] woyr of a wolfis skyn. **1573** *Satir. Poems Reform.* xxxix. 165 Sa Grange beleuit the madin Castell suir. **1591** SHAKS. *Two Gent.* v. i. 12 The Forrest is not three leagues off, If we recouer that, we are sure enough. **1607** — *Timon* III. iii. 40 Doores .. must be imploy'd Now to guard sure their Master. **1625** tr. *Gonsalvius' Sp. Inquis.* To Rdr. A iv, If we .. thinke our selues sure and the storme passed. **1648** GAGE *West Ind.* xi. 38 The Mexicans also thought the same [place] to be sure with the trees which were crossed the way.

†**b.** Of a condition, procedure, etc.: Free from risk. *Obs.*

1422 YONGE tr. *Secr. Secr.* xxxii. 183 Hit Is more Sure to euery Prynce to comaunde His Pepill well willynge to hym, than ewill willynge. *a* **1548** HALL *Chron.*, *Edw. IV*, 228b, [He] thought it more surer to heare the fayre wordes of the Constable, .. then to geue credit to theyr vntrew .. doynges. **1599–1600** DALLAM in *Early Voy. Levant* (Hakluyt Soc.) 90, I knew that in her [*sc.* the ship Hector] was a sur passidge. **1608** CHAPMAN *Byron's Consp.* I. ii, To leave a sure pace on continuate earth, And force a gate in jumps from tower to tower.

†**c.** Const. *of*: Free from (a bad quality).

c **1440** *Pallad. on Husb.* XI. 294 Wherof .. so maad is the nature, Of bitternesse or salt that hit is sure.

†**d.** With *from* or *for* and vbl. sb.: 'Safe' from doing something, certain not to—; also with passive sense, certain not to be ——ed. *Obs.*

1586 STAFFORD in *Eng. Hist. Rev.* Jan. (1913) 57, I would keep him there to undo himself, and sure enough from coming home to undo others. **1592** GREENE *Disput.* 8 He had some twentie poundes about him, but hee had planted it so cunningly in his doublet, that it was sure enough for finding. **1633** BP. HALL *Hard Texts, Ezek.* xvi. 458, I .. will make thee sure enough from adding this leudnesse to thine other abominations. *a* **1644** CHILLINGW. *1st Serm. Ps. xiv. 1* §47 A thousand weights, to fasten him on the earth, to make him sure for ever ascending to God.

†**e.** Phr. *the sure* or *surer side*: the safe side. *to be on the sure side* (also *to be sure*): to run no risks. *Obs.*

1528 MORE *Dyaloge* I. Wks. 172/2 As though ye wer sure by your confidence in god, that hys grace had enclined your assent to the surer syde. **1588** SHAKS. *Tit. A.* IV. ii. 126 He is your brother by the surer side. **1633** T. ADAMS *Exp. 2 Peter* i. 10. 218 Have you said your prayers? .. say them againe .. you know it is good to be sure. **1667** DRYDEN & DK. NEWCASTLE *Sir M. Mar-all* v. i, I'm resolv'd to be on the sure side; I will have certain proof of his wit, before I marry him. **1677** HORNECK *Gt. Law Consid.* iii. (1704) 70 It would become a wise man .. to endeavour to be on the sure side of the hedge.

†**2. a.** Of a place or receptacle: Affording security or safety; = SAFE *a.* 7, SECURE *a.* 4. *Obs.*

c **1400** *Destr. Troy* 687 þen suet þai with solas into a sure chamber. **1471** CAXTON *Recuyell* (Sommer) 108 Acrisyus .. was well eased that his doughter was in so seur a place. **1506** *Kal. Sheph.* Hij, Our shyppe may not enter into no sewer hauen. **1653** H. COGAN tr. *Pinto's Trav.* xliv. 172 The Chinese Necoda disembarqued all his commodities, .. and put them into sure rooms.

†**b.** *transf.*, with *keeping* or other sb. of similar meaning; = SAFE *a.* 8. *Obs.*

1431 *Acts Privy Council* IV. 95 Ordeint for þe defense seure and saufgarde of þe saide lande. *c* **1450** *Brut* ccxlii. 359 þe Duk brouȝt King Richard .. to London, and put hym yn the Tour, vndir sure kepyng as a prisoner. **1481** CAXTON *Godfrey* xviii. 48 He delyuerd to them good conduyte and sewr tyl they cam to constantynoble. **1539** in *Abstr. Protocols Town Clerks Glasgow* (1897) IV. 119 To put it [*sc.* 10s. yearly] in suyr kepyng. **1544** *Extr. Aberd. Reg.* (1844) I. 199 The consell ordanis thair chartour keyst .. to be put in suir fermans for keping in secreit manir. **1572** HULOET s.v., To put yᵉ prysoners or captiues in sure ward.

†**3.** Safe in one's possession or keeping; not liable to be lost or to escape; hence, unable or unlikely to do harm or cause disturbance; = SAFE *a.* 10, SECURE *a.* 5. *to make* (a person or thing) *sure*: to get into one's possession or power, to secure: = *make sure of*, 13 a (*b*); to put beyond the power of doing harm; (contextually) to make away with, kill. *Obs.*

1462 in Sharp *Illustr. Trin. Ch. Coventry* (1818) 41 To se þat .. þe boks be lokkyd sure in þe vestre. **1472–3** *Rolls of Parlt.* VI. 36/2 When he was dede they kutte of oon of his legges .. and his hede from his body, to make him sure. *Ibid.* 45/1 That the seid Sir Humfrey haue and hold .. the maner .. sure from the said Johane and hir heires. *c* **1489** CAXTON *Sonnes of Aymon* xiii. 311 See that he be kepte sure. **1588** SHAKS. *Tit. A.* II. ii. 187 Farewell my Sonnes, see that you make her sure. **1590** *Cobler Canterb.* 20 Seeing the olde beldame was sure [*i.e.* soundly asleep], he began to reueale vnto hir how long hee had loued hir. **1596** SHAKS. *1 Hen. IV.* v. iii. 48, I haue paid Percy, I haue made him sure. **1601** HOLLAND *Pliny* VIII. vii. I. 195 To cut his throat, so making him sure for telling tales. **1633** T. STAFFORD *Pac. Hib.* I. viii. (1821) 106 And his sonnes bound very safe and sure. **1713** ADDISON *Cato* II. vi, Make Cato sure, and give up Utica. *a* **1715** BURNET *Own Time* (1823) II. III. 77 an. 1675, He reckoned he would make the next session sure. **1718** HICKES & NELSON *J. Kettlewell* II. §55. 172 Upon pretence of making all Sure, and saving the King's Honour.

II. Trustworthy, firm, steadfast.

4. a. That can be depended or relied on; not liable to fail or disappoint expectation; trustworthy, reliable. Now *arch.* or *dial.*

1340–70 *Alisaunder* 266 þat citie wer sure men sett for too keepe. **14..** *Why I can't be a Nun* 361 in *E.E.P.* (1862) 147 A fayre garlond of yve grene Whyche hangeth at a taverne dore, Hyt ys a false token, .. But yf there be wyne gode and sewer. *c* **1440** *Generydes* 4575, 'I wold', quod he, 'this hors were cherisshid wele, For he is sure and good'. **1506** *Kal. Sheph.* H ij, We must haue .iii. suer maryners that may kepe our shyp fro the daunger of these .iii. rockes. **1596** HARINGTON *Metam. Ajax* 39 Thou hast a Iury of sure free-holders, that gaue a uerdite against them. **1624** CAPT. J. SMITH *Virginia* III. 73 The President .. resolved with Captaine Waldo (whom he knew to be sure in time of need) to surprise Powhatan. **1667** MILTON *P.L.* XI. 852 From out the Arke a Raven flies, And after him, the surer messenger, A Dove. **1837** CARLYLE *Fr. Rev.* II. III. iv, Bouillé is at Metz, and could find forty-thousand sure Germans. **1846** MRS. A. MARSH *Father Darcy* II. i. 18 Did I not send this by a sure hand, .. I would not venture to go thus far with you. **1883** STEVENSON *Treas. Isl.* III. xiii, Loaded pistols were served out to all the sure men.

b. Applied to agents or their actions, this sense (by admixture of sense 8) tends to become subjective: Steady, steadfast, unfaltering; †constant, faithful; †(of conduct) steady, well-ordered.

a **1450** *Knt. de la Tour* (1868) 16 The yonggest doughter .. was most .. goodly in her behauing countenaunce, and manere most seure and ferme. **1471** CAXTON *Recuyell* (Sommer) 319 Their was none than so seure but he was aferde. *a* **1475** ASHBY *Active Policy* 130 Vertuos dedys & condutes seure. **1483** CAXTON *Cato* hj, Thou oughtest to .. desyre oueral to lede good lyf and sure in this worlde. **1483** — *G. de la Tour* g v j b, For the sure trouthe that euer she bare vnto her lord. *c* **1485** *Digby Myst.*, *Convers. St. Paul* 100 Your felow was not suer of foote. **1523** LD. BERNERS *Froiss.* I. xviii. 24 The englisshe oste made good and sure watche. *c* **1610** *Women Saints* 145 Treasures .. which he hath promised me .. if I will remayne sure to him. **1628** FELTHAM *Resolves* II. [I.] lxxxix. 258 Sometimes a failing and returne, is a prompter to a surer hold. **1638** JUNIUS *Paint. Ancients* 324 Such archers .. as have the surest hand. **1696** TATE & BRADY *Ps.* xciii. 5 Thy Promise, Lord, is ever sure. **1743** FRANCIS tr. *Horace, Odes* III. ii. 31 With sure steps, .. Vengeance o'ertakes the trembling villain's speed. **1855** MACAULAY *Hist. Eng.* xix. IV. 276 His judgment was clearest and surest when responsibility pressed heaviest on him. **1860** TYNDALL *Glac.* I. xi. 84 In order to get surer footing in the snow. *Ibid.* xxiii. 162 Found myself by no means so sure a climber as usual. **1908** *Animal Managem.* 271 The animal [*sc.* mule] is a proverbially sure stepper.

5. Of material objects (in early use esp. of weapons or armour): Not liable to break or give way, sound, 'trusty'; not liable to be displaced, firm, firmly fixed, immovable. † *sure land*, the mainland, terra firma. (Cf. SECURE *a.* 3 e.) *arch.*

sure foundation, *sure ground*, and the like, are often used in fig. context: cf. 9 b.

13.. *Gaw. & Gr. Knt.* 588 Gurde wyth a bront ful sure. *c* **1440** *Generydes* 2732 The helme was sure, or ellys he had hym slayn. **1463** *Bury Wills* (Camden) 20 And the stoon werk be made sewr. *a* **1470** TIPTOFT *Cæsar* xii. (1530) 15 Carpenters to be brought from the sure lande to repayre the navey. *c* **1470** HENRY *Wallace* XI. 1060 A courch .. apon his handys thai laid, And wndyr syn with seuir cordys thai braid. **1523** FITZHERB. *Husb.* §135 Make a good and a sure hedge. **1534** TINDALE *2 Tim.* ii. 19 The sure grounde of God remayneth. **1535** COVERDALE *Ps.* xcii[i]. 1 He hath made the rounde worlde so sure, that it can not be moued. —— *Isa.* xxviii. 16, I wil laye a stone in Sion, .. for a sure foundacion. **1596** MASCALL *Cattle* 120 Thy .. cartbodie strong and sure to beare a burthen. *a* **1634** CHAPMAN (Webster 1864), Which put in good sure leather sacks. **1648** MARKHAM *Housew. Gard.* III. x. (1668) 75 A sure dry wall. **1832** HT. MARTINEAU *Homes Abroad* ii. 32, I am anxious to go on sure ground. **1865** SWINBURNE *Poems & Ball.*, *Triumph Time* 41 We had stood as the sure stars stand. *Ibid.*, *Phædra* 38 Make thy sword sure inside thine hand and smite.

6. Firmly established or settled; steadfast, stable; not liable to be destroyed or overthrown.

†**a.** Of states of mind, or of persons in respect of these. (Cf. 8.)

13.. *E.E. Allit. P.* A. 1089 For I dar say, with consciens sure, Hade bodyly burne abiden þat bone [etc.]. **1413** HOCCLEVE *Min. Poems* viii. 14 Seur confort haue I. *a* **1425** *Cursor M.* 18712 (Trin.), He bad his disciplis .. Ouer al þe world þe gospel preche .. to vche creature For þei shulde in trouþe be sure. **1549** *Bk. Com. Prayer*, *Burial*, In sure and certayne hope of resurreccion to eternall lyfe. **1582** ALLEN *Martyrdom Campion* (1908) 114 He had a sure confidence that all should goe well with him. **1596** DALRYMPLE tr. *Leslie's Hist. Scot.* I. 287 Throw a certane suspicioune and suir opinioun.

b. Of immaterial things and states considered objectively. *arch.*

c **1520** NISBET *N.T.* (S.T.S.) I. 15 To mak thair vocatiounn suir be gud werkis. **1535** COVERDALE *1 Chron.* xviii. 12, I wyl make his seate sure for euer. **1560** DAUS tr. *Sleidane's Comm.* 41 Yᵗ eyther a suer peace, or els a long treuce may be taken. **1697** DRYDEN *Virg. Georg.* IV. 303 Th' immortal Line in sure Succession reigns. **1746** HERVEY *Medit.* (1767) I. 81 A Decree, much surer than the Law of the Medes and Persians, has irrevocably determined the Doom. **1787** JEFFERSON *Writ.* (1859) II. 206, I know of no mercantile house in France of surer bottom. **1867** MORRIS *Jason* I. 32 He may wish to make quite sure his throne By slaying me and mine.

†**c.** Of possessions, etc.: That may be counted on to be received or held (cf. 9). *to make sure*: to secure *to* or settle upon a person. *Obs.*

c **1450** *Godstow Reg.* 276 He willed and graunted hit to be sure for hym and his heires. **1467–8** *Rolls of Parlt.* V. 579/1 To be made sure ayenst us and oure Heires. **1482** *Ibid.* VI. 204/1 Oure seid Soverayn Lord shuld cause the same Due, to be made sure to hym and to his seid heires masles. **1515** BARCLAY *Egloges* II. (1570) B iv/1 Better .. a small handfull with rest and sure pleasaunce, Then twenty dishes with wrathfull countenaunce. **1533** GAU *Richt Vay* 65 His marcie is maid swuer to wsz. **1628** [see *chequer-pay*, CHEQUER *sb.*[1] 16]. **1669** R. MONTAGU in *Buccleuch MSS.* (Hist. MSS. Comm.) I. 436 If I thought this would be sure money. **1670** RAY *Proverbs* 207 As sure as Check, or Exchequer pay.

†**7. a.** Engaged to be married, betrothed, affianced (*to make sure*, to betroth); also, joined in wedlock, married. *Obs.*

1470 *Paston Lett.* II. 393 Mestresse Gryseacresse is sure to Selenger. *c* **1536** *Songs, Carols*, etc. (1907) 154 Lady Mary, þe Kyngis dowghter, was mad sure .. to þe yong Kyng of Castile. **1592** *Arden of Feversham* I. 151 The Painter .. Hath made reporte that he and Sue is sure. [**1598** SHAKS. *Merry W.* v. v. 237 She and I (long since contracted) Are now so sure that nothing can dissolue vs.] **1608** MIDDLETON *Trick to Catch Old One* III. i, I am but newly sure yet to the widow. **1632** BROME *North. Lass* II. ii, I presum'd .. you had beene sure, as fast as faith could bind you, man and wife. **1665** P. HENRY *Diaries & Lett.* (1882) 175 My man william Griffith was marryd .. to one of Baschurch, to whom hee had been sure since before hee came to mee.

†**b.** Engaged or bound by allegiance or devotion (*to* a person or party). *to make sure*, to bind by allegiance, or secure the allegiance of. *Obs.*

1567 *Gude & Godlie Ball.* (S.T.S.) 209 Sen we ar all to Sin maid sure, Throw Adamis Inobedience. **1591** SAVILE *Tacitus, Hist.* I. lxiv. 36 The next city, was that of the Lingones, sure to their side. **1643** BAKER *Chron.* (1660) 77 Though King John had entred upon Normandy, and made that Province sure unto him, yet the Province of Anjou stood firm for Arthur. *a* **1715** BURNET *Own Time* (1724) I. II. 201 To make all that party sure to himself.

III. Subjectively certain.

8. Certain in mind; having no doubt; assured, confident; = CERTAIN *a.* 4, SECURE *a.* 2. Also, convinced, persuaded, morally certain.

In the former sense *I am sure* is commonly used colloq. to give asseverative force to a statement; e.g. *I'm sure I don't know*; *I don't know, I'm sure*.

In the latter sense ***I am sure*** sometimes becomes equivalent in force to SURELY *adv.* 4 b; e.g. quot. 1818 in c (*b*).

a. Const. *of*; rarely, by ellipsis, without const.

c **1450** LOVELICH *Merlin* 9740 We wolden preyen the.. of on thyng vs sewr forto make. *a* **1500** *Chaucer's Dreme* 855 For of one thing ye may be sure He wil be yours, while he may dure. **1591** SHAKS. *Two Gent.* v. ii. 40 He.. guesd that it was she, But being mask'd, he was not sure of it. **1686** tr. *Chardin's Trav. Persia* 158, I was sure of one thing, that [etc.]. **1709** POPE *Ess. Crit.* 567 Be silent always when you doubt your sense; And speak, tho' sure, with seeming diffidence. **1732** BERKELEY *Alciphr.* IV. §3 Whatever we can perceive by any sense we may be sure of. **1791** BOSWELL *Johnson* May an. 1776, We are surer of the odiousness of the one, than of the errour of the other. **1818** J. W. CROKER in *C. Papers* 8 Dec. (1884) I. 124 He never could distinguish Buonaparte, or his staff, to be sure of them. **1867** RUSKIN *Time & Tide* xvi. §99 Never teach a child anything of which you are not yourself sure. **1908** R. BAGOT *A. Cuthbert* xxviii. 373 Anthony understands, and forgives—I am sure of it.

b. Const. clause. Also with ellipsis of clause (mod. colloq. ***well, I'm sure!*** is used as an exclamation of surprise: cf. e).

a **1330** *Syr Degarre* 761 Par fai, (he saide,) Ich am al sure, He that bette that fure Wil comen hom ȝit to niȝt. *c* **1350** *Will. Palerne* 973 Be þou sur.. holliche al min help þou schalt haue sone. *c* **1386** CHAUCER *Melib.* ⁋796, I knowe wel, and am right seur, that he shal nothyng doon in this nede with-outen my conseil. *c* **1420** ? LYDG. *Assembly of Gods* 524 So may ye be sewre he shall yow nat escape. **1474** CAXTON *Chesse* III. viii. (1883) 152 He was sewr that he had wonne. **1535** COVERDALE *Ps.* cxxxix. [cxl.] 12 Sure I am that the Lorde wil auenge the poore. **1596** SHAKS. *Merch. V.* III. i. 53, I am sure if he forfaite, thou wilt not take his flesh. **1602** —— *Merry W.* (Qo.) 742 [III. i. 60], I am shure you know him. **1670** in *12th Rep. Hist. MSS. Comm.* App. v. 22, I am suere you would bee with us if wishes could bring you. **1709** BERKELEY *Th. Vision* §51 Sure I am, it is worth some attention. **1778** MISS BURNEY *Evelina* (1791) II. xxxii. 202 I'm sure I can't recollect. **1779** *Mirror* No. 16. ⁋7, I am not sure if the disposition to reflections of this sort be.. a proper one. **1832** HT. MARTINEAU *Demerara* i. 19 You might have been sure that I should remember you when you told me your name. **1840** THACKERAY *Shabby-genteel Story* ix, 'Well, I'm sure!' said Becky; and that was all she said. **1885** 'MRS. ALEXANDER' *At Bay* i, Look in on us now and again. I am sure my daughter will be delighted. **1885** —— *Valerie's Fate* iv, 'Are you going?' 'I am not sure.'

c. † (*a*) With inversion of the two clauses, ***be ye sure, you may be sure*** (etc.) thus coming at the end of the sentence.

a **1400** *Octouian* 1038 Hys fomen myghte of hym be agast, We mowe be sure. **1513** BRADSHAW *St. Werburge* I. 707 Thus was her maner in youthe, be ye sure. **1560** DAUS tr. *Sleidane's Comm.* 292 b *marg.*, An holy box sent down from heauen you may be sure.

(*b*) In parenthetical use, ***be sure, you may be sure, I am sure***, to which the main sentence is virtually subordinate.

1340–70 *Alex. & Dind.* 991 We ne sain noukt, king, be þou sur, for sake of our pride. *c* **1350** *Will. Palerne* 74 It wanted nouȝt.. þat þei ne fond him as faire as for here state longed, & þe beter, be ye sure, for [etc.]. **1565** *MS. Cott. Cal. B. ix.* lf. 218 Your lordship, I am sure, is partaken of such letters as I write to Mr. Secretary. *c* **1680** BEVERIDGE *Serm. I Cor. xv. 58* Wks. 1729 I. 423 You will be uncertain whether they .. be lawfully called.. as be sure many of them are not. **1710** —— *Def. Bk. Psalms* 29 The Company had this Privilege granted them from the King; who, be sure, would never grant them the Privilege of printing any Book, but what he .. had first allowed of. **1818** SCOTT *Br. Lamm.* xxxiii, The Master of Ravenswood cannot, I am sure, object to your presence.

(*c*) In colloq. asseverative use these phrases are often placed at the end of the sentence: cf. (*a*).

1830 N. S. WHEATON *Jrnl.* 42 To all my inquiries who he was? I only received for answer—'I don't know, I'm sure'. **1837** DICKENS *Pickw.* ii, It will give me great pleasure, I am sure. **1848** THACKERAY *Van. Fair* xli, 'Don't know, I'm shaw,' replied the Colonel.

d. Const. inf.: see 12.

e. In phr. ***to be sure*** = as one may be sure, for a certainty, certainly, undoubtedly, of course; now colloq. and often concessive = it must be admitted, indeed; also absol. ***well, to be sure!*** as an exclamation of surprise (cf. b).

1657 SPARROW *Bk. Com. Prayer* (1661) 4 Morning and Evening, to be sure, God expects from us.. a publick worship. **1657** W. RAND tr. *Gassendi's Life Peiresc* II. 3 He proved at last so happy, as to recover the greatest part of such things as he most respected. To be sure, he obtained his precious stones. **1682** BUNYAN *Holy War* 150 If he heard his neighbour tell his tale, to be sure he would tell the quite contrary. **1718** HICKES & NELSON *J. Kettlewell* II. §23. 125 At Christmas, if he invited no Body else, to be sure he Entertained the Poorer Sort of his Neighbours. **1731–8** SWIFT *Pol. Conversat.* i. 47 *Neverout.* Miss, I'll tell you a Secret, if you'll promise never to tell it again. *Miss.* No, to be sure. **1778** WARNER in Jesse *Selwyn & Contemp.* (1844) III. 354 Yes! war we shall have to be sure. **1795** *Hist. Ned Evans* I. 183 The wind is contrary, to be sure, but it is far from a storm. **1847** MRS. SHERWOOD *Fairchild Family* (1854) III. iii. 32 Well, to be sure, this is a large room. **1853** MRS. GASKELL *Ruth* xxxiii, Ruth.. told him she wanted to speak to him for a few minutes. 'To be sure, my dear! Sit down!' said he. **1863** S. WILBERFORCE *Sp. Missions* (1874) 275 'You would have been snugger if you had stayed at home.' Why to be sure they would. **1875** JOWETT *Plato* (ed. 2) I. 18 There you are in the right, Socrates, he replied. To be sure, I said. **1902** VIOLET JACOB *Sheep-Stealers* viii, 'Well, well, to be sure!' exclaimed the Pig-driver. **1913** C. READ in *Eng. Hist. Rev.* Jan. 55 They had, to be sure, patched up their differences, but their sentiments towards each other.. were far from cordial.

f. Colloq. phr. ***don't (you) be too sure***, do not depend too confidently (upon something).

1866 MAYNE REID *Headless Horseman* iii. 16 'Don't be too sure, all of ye,' said the surly nephew. **1916** G. B. SHAW *Pygmalion* v. 189 But dont you be too sure that you have me under your feet to be trampled on and talked down. **1942** T. BAILEY *Pink Camellia* xviii. 98 Don't be too sure. You're the girl I want, and I'm going to have you.

IV. Objectively certain.

9. a. That one may count on as about to be; certain to come or happen; also, certain to become what is denoted by the noun; = CERTAIN *a.* 2 b.

1565 ALLEN *Defence Purg.* xvii. 283 One.. frameth (as he supposethe) his negatiue argument, to the more sure shake of oure faithe herein. **1615** SIR W. MURE *Misc. Poems* xiii. 16 Bewar such schame becum thy suirest hap. **1692** PRIOR *Ode Horace* xiii, Sure and sudden be their just Remorse. **1746** FRANCIS tr. *Horace, Sat.* II. iii. 21 Unhappy bard! to sure contempt you run. **1781** COWPER *Retirem.* 263 To make thee but a surer prey. **1858** SEARS *Athan.* ix. 78 Confusion is the pretty sure result. **1896** HOUSMAN *Shropshire Lad* lxii, Luck's a chance, but trouble's sure.

b. That one may rely on as true; undoubted, indisputable; = CERTAIN *a.* 3. Now *rare*.

1470 *Paston Lett.* Suppl. (1901) 133, I pray yow send me swyr tydyngis of the world. **1556** *Chron. Gr. Friars* (Camden) 32 A pele was comandyd to be ronge.. for sewer worde and tydynges that Richard de la Pole was slayne. *a* **1578** LINDESAY (Pitscottie) *Chron. Scot.* I. 31 He haid suire knawledg quhair the king was at his pastyme. *a* **1620** J. DYKE *Sel. Serm.* (1640) 2 It is a sure thing that a Christian so demeaning himselfe.. may live the most comfortable life of any man in the world. **1667** MILTON *P.L.* II. 154 How he can Is doubtful; that he never will is sure. **1849** JAMES *Woodman* iii, The news was too sure, the tale too sad to be false. **1867** RUSKIN *Time & Tide* xvi. §93 And very sternly I say to you—and say from sure knowledge—that [etc.].

c. ***for sure***: as or for a certainty, undoubtedly: = *for certain* (CERTAIN *a.* 7). Now *colloq.*, and often in phr. ***that's for sure***, placed at the end of the sentence.

a **1586** SIDNEY *Ps.* XXVI. i, I held for sure, that I should never slide. **1671** MILTON *P.R.* II. 35 Now, now, for sure, deliverance is at hand. *a* **1850** ROSSETTI *Dante & Circle* I. (1874) 60 He makes oath: 'Forsure, This is a creature of God till now unknown'. **1883** STEVENSON *Treas. Isl.* I. vi, These fellows who attacked the inn to night—bold, desperate blades, for sure. **1897** MARY KINGSLEY *W. Africa* 305, I have promised the Fans to pay off in whatever they choose, and I know for sure they want powder. **1971** C. BONINGTON *Annapurna South Face* xiii. 156 We can't do it in the next two days..—that's for sure. **1981** C. ROSS *Scaffold* 106 Well, who's telling? Not me, that's for sure.

d. ***sure thing***, a certainty, a secure prospect; freq. as asseverative affirmation: Yes, indeed! Also as *attrib. phr. colloq.* (orig. *U.S.*).

1836 J. HILDRETH *Dragoon Campaigns Rocky Mts.* 24, I say, stranger, didn't I say that old 'Slow and Easy' was a sure thing, in the end? **1848** *Sporting Life* 22 Jan. 269/1 Teetotum had the call for the July in the betting, and it was booked a sure thing for her. **1896** ADE *Artie* ii. 9 You never see such a sure-thing crowd in your life. *Ibid.* xvi. 147 'Sure thing,' says he. **1908** J. M. SULLIVAN *Criminal Slang* 2 *Sure thing gambler*, character who bets with suckers at race tracks. **1933** D. L. SAYERS *Murder must Advertise* v. 91 'Should you care to make one in our next dope-raid?' 'Sure thing. When do you expect it?' **1943** *Sun* (Baltimore) 22 Apr. 18/1 Ralph Root apparently thought Overlin was a sure thing. Roberts drew his whip. **1953** W. BURROUGHS *Junkie* iii. 38, I had one of his sure-thing croakers reach for a telephone on me. **1962** P. GREGORY *Like Tigress at Bay* v. 63 'Sure thing, boss,' she said lightly. **1963** N. MARSH *Dead Water* (1964) vi. 158, I appreciate your reluctance to form a theory too soon.. But ..it looks a sure thing to me. **1979** C. MACLEOD *Family Vault* xxiii. 150 'Would you mind getting this box for us?' 'Sure thing, Mr Verplanck.'

10. a. Of methods or means: That may be relied on to attain its end or to produce the desired or stated result; unfailing, unerring: = CERTAIN *a.* 2 c.

sure card: see CARD *sb.*[2] 2 b.

1530 in Strype *Eccl. Mem.* (1721) III. App. x. 21 The moost sewryst waye that Scripture doth teache to worshipe sayntts withall, ys to lyve the lyffe that they lyvid. **1592** *Arden of Feversham* v. i. 90 It is vnpossible; but here comes he That will, I hope, inuent some surer meanes. **1653** RAMESEY *Astrol. Restored* 218 To.. impart unto them the truth and surest rules for the judging thereof. **1665** BOYLE *Occas. Refl.* III. vi. (1848) 158 These that are concern'd for the.. saving of Souls, think it a less good sign of a sure Sermon, that [etc.]. **1697** DRYDEN *Virg. Georg.* I. 122 Long Practice has a sure Improvement found. **1762** in *10th Rep. Hist. MSS. Comm.* App. I. 342, I hope that will be the surest Way of bringing about a General Peace so necessary to Europe. **1812** CRABBE *Tales* xv. 179 Every point enforce By quoting much, the scholar's sure resource. **1865** M. ARNOLD *Ess. Crit.* ii. (1875) 74 A perfectly sound and sure style. **1879** R. K. DOUGLAS *Confucianism* iv. 94 His surest way of acquiring a trace of the divine afflatus must be by studying ..their careers.

b. Of signs or signals: Giving trustworthy indication; producing or leading to certainty; infallible.

1559 W. CUNNINGHAM *Cosmogr. Glasse* 75 Everye Climate hathe a proper name, for the surer difference of one from an other. **1667** MILTON *P.L.* I. 278 In all assaults Their surest signal. **1697** DRYDEN *Virg. Georg.* III. 119 The Colt that for a Stallion is design'd, By sure Presages shows his generous Kind. **1780** *Mirror* No. 93. ⁋3 The surest mark of a weak mind. **1830** HERSCHEL *Study Nat. Phil.* §386 There is no surer criterion of the state of science in any age. **1886** *Tip Cat* xxi. 289 He became more irritable and impatient —a sure sign, Dr. Lee declared, of approaching convalescence.

c. ***sure-fire*** adj. phr., certain to succeed or attain the desired end (occas. in predicative use). *colloq.* (orig. *U.S.*). Less frequently, ***sure-shot*** (chiefly *U.S.*).

[**1901** 'H. MCHUGH' *Down Line* 93 Swift often told himself that he could give Marshall P. Wilder six sure-fires and beat him down to the wire.] **1909** P. G. WILLIAMS in *Sat. Even. Post* 5 June 17/2 *Sure fire*, certain of success. **1912** *Variety* 18 May 8/2 The Rev. William Sunday (Billy) the evangelist or sure-fire evangelist, has done one of the worst 'financial flops' in the history of his travels. **1914** [see FIXER 1]. **1926** WHITEMAN & MCBRIDE *Jazz* viii. 171 In the old days, it took six months to spread even the most sure-fire song over the United States. **1933** D. L. SAYERS *Murder must Advertise* iii. 41 He thought it was a sure-fire mascot. **1941** B. SCHULBERG *What makes Sammy Run?* ii. 28 The most surefire story sale that's come to Hollywood in years. **1952** J. STEINBECK *East of Eden* 79 The preacher turned over his hole-card, the sure-fire card. **1960** G. E. EVANS *Horse in Furrow* vi. 82 You could get a *sure-shot* cigar for tuppence in those days. **1967** N. FREELING *Strike out if not Applicable* 14 He had certain surefire jokes that were repeated all over Holland. **1974** G. F. NEWMAN *Price* vii. 238 Buy into Nu-Schoenberg... They're sure-fire, I promise you. **1983** *Listener* 16 June 8/1 The search for a sure-fire hit in American network television engages thousands of minds and millions of dollars every year.

V. Senses combining III and IV.

11. With *of*: †Having (the thing mentioned) secured to one (***to make*** a person ***sure of*** a thing = ***to make*** a thing ***sure to*** a person, in 6 c); †holding securely in one's possession or power; certain to receive, get, attain, find, have, or keep. Also with gerund, as ***sure of getting*** = certain to get. (See also 13.)

Here the certainty may be subjective or objective, or both combined: e.g. *he is sure of* = 'he is confident of getting', or 'it is certain that he will get'.

13.. *Seuyn Sages* (W.) 2033 The king hem made seur Of warisoun and gret honour. *c* **1386** CHAUCER *Melib.* ⁋486 Whan thow trowest to be moost seur and siker of hire helpe she wol faille thee. **14..** *Sir Beues* (M.) 499 Beues was sure of no wepyn.. That he myght deffend hym with all. *c* **1412** HOCCLEVE *De Reg. Princ.* 306 He schulde of his lif seure ben & certeyne. *c* **1450** *Mirk's Festial* 56 Who so lyueth a fowle lyfe, he may be sure of a foule ende. **1518** *Sel. Pleas Star Chamber* (Selden) II. 132 Yf he gave hym one strype he shalbe suer of an other strype. **1572–3** *Reg. Privy Council Scot.* II. 177 Thay offerit to.. discharge the half of thair.. wageis, being maid sure of the uther half.. to be payit at sum competent day. *a* **1580** J. HEYWOOD *Dial. Wit & Folly* (Percy Soc.) 15 The wyttles ys sewer of salvashyon. **1587** in *Cath. Rec. Soc. Publ.* V. 140 The young king of Scotland remaineth still amongst his.. ennemies, who suffer him to take his pastime.. under a shew of liberty, but they think themselves sure ynough of him. **1653** MIDDLETON & ROWLEY *Sp. Gipsy* II. i, English Gipsies, in whose companie a man's not sure of the eares of his head they so pilfer. *a* **1718** PRIOR *Solomon* III. 290 Sure of the Toil, uncertain of the Prize. **1719** DE FOE *Crusoe* II. (Globe) 571 We are sure of Sea there. **1766** GOLDSM. *Vicar W.* xvi, They who had warm fortunes were always sure of getting good husbands. **1825** COBBETT *Rur. Rides* 458 This is a crop of which a man may always be sure, if he take proper pains. **1847** MARRYAT *Childr. New Forest* viii, I feel sure of his permission. **1893** *Law Times* XCV. 305/2 If she wished to be sure of her income she should.. avoid dabbling in the shares of new companies.

12. With inf. (act. or pass.): Certain to do or to be something: = CERTAIN *a.* 6.

Properly a constructional use of 8, this sense was orig. subjective, but came subsequently to express, and now always expresses, objective certainty, and therefore *transf.* became applicable to things. *he is sure to return*, now = 'it is certain that he will return', could formerly mean 'he is certain that he will return', now expressed by *of* with the gerund (see 11).

c **1400** *Laud Troy Bk.* 15612 Thei myȝt ther-fore be sur & bold To scle the kyng & brenne Ilyoun. **1530** TINDALE *Answ. More* II. xii. Wks. (1573) 300/1 The Apostles, Patriarkes and Prophetes were sure to be folowed. **1556** J. HEYWOOD *Spider & F.* D iv, He makth him sewre to wyn, who ever leeses. **1563** *Homilies* II. *Sacrament* I. I iij b, Thus much he must be sure to hold, that in the Supper of the Lorde, there is no vayne ceremonie. **1616** SHELDON *Mirr. Antichr.* Pref. ¶¶ j b, Such Conuerts.. are sure to bee beset with diuerse sorts of Aduersaries. **1662** J. DAVIES tr. *Olearius' Voy. Ambass.* 400 The Governour, who many times is not sure to return again, takes his leave of the City. **1713** ADDISON *Guard.* No. 101 ⁋9 If they have any Wit or Sense, they are sure to show it. **1821** LAMB *Elia* Ser. I. *Mackery End*, Whatever heat of opposition.. I set out with, I am sure always, in the long-run, to be brought over to her way of thinking. **1841** HELPS *Ess., Trans. Business* (1842) 95 You may save time by not labouring much, beforehand, at parts of the subject which are nearly sure to be worked out in discussion. **1885** *Manch. Exam.* 13 July 5/2 The.. oration .. was sure to be full of pungent criticism.

13. Phr. ***to make sure*** (intr. or with clause).

a. (*a*) *absol.*, or with *of* followed by a noun of action: To make something certain as an end or result (cf. 9 a); to preclude risk of failure.

1565 ALLEN *Def. Purg.* To Rdr. 6 b, And therefore to make sure, I humbly submit my selfe to the iudgement of suche.. as.. are made the lawful pastors of our soules. **1698** FRYER *Acc. E. India & P.* 176 To make sure, he made another Shot at her. **1890** *Chamb. Jrnl.* 3 May 287/2 This allows the man.. to make sure of a good grip. **1891** *Ibid.* 21 Feb. 119/2 It is difficult to make sure of finding the birds.

(*b*) with *of* followed by a sb.: To act so as to be certain of getting or winning; to secure.

1673 TEMPLE *To Dk. Ormond Conjunct. Affairs* Misc. (1680) 164 A Peace.. cannot fail us here provided we make sure of Spain. **1726** ATTERBURY *Serm., Isa. lx. 22* I. 102 It hath ever had the warmest, and ablest.. Heads employ'd in its defence; and hath taken care to make sure of them, by Bountiful Rewards. **1844** BROWNING *Colombe's Birthday* II. 9 Let me hasten to make sure Of one true thanker. **1878**

Bosw. Smith *Carthage* 293 After making sure of the country to the north of the Ebro.

b. (*a*) with clause or *of*: To make something certain as a fact (cf. 9 b); to preclude risk of error; to ascertain.

1876 Bristowe *Theory & Pract. Med.* (1878) 825 To make sure that all the copper has been precipitated. **1888** Mrs. Notley *Power of Hand* I. iii. 36 That fellow rode up to the house to make sure Tristram was away. **1889** F. C. Philips *Ainslie's Courtsh.* I. vii. 87 He just waited for a few hours to make sure of his position.

(*b*) *loosely*. To feel certain, be convinced.

1886 Stevenson *Kidnapped* xxi, He stormed at me all through the lessons..and would push me so close that I made sure he must run me through the body. **1887** Westall *Capt. Trafalgar* iv. 49 He suspected nothing, and made quite sure of succeeding. **1893** Selous *Trav. S.E. Africa* 158, I made sure I should get finer specimens later on.

14. Phr. *be sure* (*to do* something, or *that*..., also mod. colloq. *and*: see and B. 10) = take care, don't fail (only in imper. or inf.): *sure* thus becoming contextually equivalent to 'careful'.

1573 Tusser *Husb.* v. (1878) 14 Then dailie be suer to looke. **1625** Bacon *Ess., Discourse* (Arb.) 19 Let him be sure, to leaue other Men their Turnes to speak. **1674** N. Cox *Gentl. Recreat.* (1677) 180 Be sure you Seel her not too hard. **1680** Moxon *Mech. Exerc.* xii. 208 You must be sure to screw it hard up. **1780** *Mirror* No. 98. ¶ 15 Be sure to put on your great coat, and to take a chair in coming home. **1865** Ruskin *Sesame* i. §13 At least be sure that you go to the author to get at his meaning. **1892** *Photogr. Ann.* II. 335 Be sure and button the lid.

B. *adv.*

1. Securely, safely: = surely *adv.* 1. *Obs.* or *arch.*

14.. *Sir Beues* (Pynson) 3573 They were armed sure and wel. **1500–20** Dunbar *Poems* ix. 76 With the Foure Vertewis Cardenall, Aganis vycis seure enarming me. **1555** Cranmer *Let.* in *Misc. Writ.* (Parker Soc.) 446, I might have sent them by the carrier sooner, but not surer. **1591** Shaks. *1 Hen. VI*, v. i. 16 The sooner to effect, And surer binde this knot of amitie. **1596** Bacon *Max. & Use Com. Law* II. (1635) 46 The land being so sure tyed upon the heire as that his father could not put it from him. **1600** W. Cornwallis *Ess.* I. i. B iij I would not..do any thing more then stand the surer vpon my guard to resist fortune. **1667** Milton *P.L.* iv. 897 Let him surer barr His Iron Gates.

2. Certainly, with certainty; without risk of failure: = surely *adv.* 2, 3. Now *dial.* = 'for certain, without fail'; otherwise *Obs.* exc. as in b and c.

c **1400** *Destr. Troy* 277 Sum sayn full sure & for sothe holdyn, Hit was þe formast on flete þat on flode past. **1479** in *Eng. Gilds* (1870) 413 So that..they may the better, sewrer, and more diligenter,..ministre their said Officez. **1556** Lauder *Tractate of Kyngis* 298 3e suld not..promoue thame To that..cure, Except 3e vnderstude, moste sure, Thame apt. **1586** Marlowe *1st Pt. Tamburl.* II. iii, These are the wings shall make it flie as swift, As dooth the lightening:..And kill as sure as it swiftly flies. **1693** Locke *Educ.* § 13 Children would..lay the Foundations of an healthy..Constitution much surer, if they..were kept wholly from Flesh. **1797** Mrs. M. Robinson *Walsingham* III. 257 The higher the objects of contempt are placed, the surer they become marks for the observing multitude. **1820** Lamb *Elia* Ser. I. *Christ's Hosp.*, Woe to the school, when he made his morning appearance in his passy, or passionate wig. No comet expounded surer. **1902** Banks *Newspaper Girl* 156, I'll pay you the five dollars a week then, sure.

3. a. Qualifying a statement: Assuredly, undoubtedly, for a certainty. Now *poet.* and, in asseverative expressions, *Irish* and *N. Amer. colloq.* (freq. introduced between subj. and vb., as a mere intensive).

a **1425** *Cursor M.* 21887 (Trin.), Euery creatoure sure Aftir þe state of Bettre her makere knowe þen mon. *c* **1460** *Wisdom* 50 in *Macro Plays* 37 The prerogatyff of my loue ys so grett, þat wo tastyt þerof þe lest droppe, sure, All lustis & lykyngis worldly xall lett. **1568** *Satir. Poems Reform.* xlviii. 31 Seure, be my witting, not brunt in the litting. *a* **1586** Sidney *Ps.* xxv. ii, Sure, sure, who hope in thee, Shall never suffer shame. **1599** *George a Greene* E j, Were he as good as G. a Green, I would strike him sure. **1653** Milton *Hirelings* (1659) 27 He took not sure his whole estate with him to that warr. **1681** Dryden *Abs. & Achit.* 360 His Mercy ev'n th' Offending Croud will find, For sure he comes of a Forgiving Kind. **1715** De Foe *Fam. Instruct.* I. i. (1841) I. 6 Sure it is a fine place. **1791** Cowper *Iliad* xxii. 86 Of all ills that wait On miserable man, that sure is worst. **1842** Lover *Handy Andy* v, Och sure, my heart's broke with you. **1848** Kingsley *Saint's Trag.* II. v, That name speaks pardon, sure. **1861** *Trans. Illinois Agric. Soc.* IV. 460 Once successfully transplanted it will live sure. **1876** 'Mark Twain' *Tom Sawyer* iv. 83 They're coming, sure. **1896** Housman *Shropsh. Lad* xxxiii, Sure, sure,..If single thought could save,..You should not see the grave. **1897** *Punch* 3 Apr. 166/1 'That's a drop of good Whiskey—eh, Pat?' *Pat.* 'Faith, ye may well say that, Sorr. Shure, it wint down my T'roat loike a Torchlight Procession!' **1908** 'Yeslah' *Tenderfoot S. Calif.* i. 14 It sure was a cold night. **1933** J. Cozzens *Cure of Flesh* i. 20 Sure, the truck came. Is anything wrong? **1953** *Manch. Guardian Weekly* 22 Jan. 7 You sure left an awful mess in Washington. **1969** A. Lurie *Real People* 106 Parts of it were pretty, sure. In a phony way, like this place. **1975** R. Davies *World of Wonders* (1977) I. vii. 83 You didn't need feet to fly a plane, but you sure needed brains.

b. With weakened emphasis, it (*a*) becomes concessive = One must admit, admittedly, of course, (*b*) is used to guard against over-statement = At any rate, to say the least, or (*c*) = surely *adv.* 4 b. Now *dial.*

1552–3 in Feuillerat *Revels Edw. VI* (1914) 89, I know not howe ye be provided to furnish me but suer methinkes I sholde haue nolesse then five suetes of apparrell. **1583** Greene *Mamillia* Wks. (Grosart) II. 14 Whether hee were better lyked for his calling, or loued for his courtesie: but sure whether it were, he had gayned the heartes of all the people. **1587** Fleming *Contn. Holinshed* III. 1981/1 The spoile was not rich sure, but of white bread, oten cakes, and Scotish ale. **1616** B. Jonson *Devil an Ass* II. v, Hell! why is shee so braue? It cannot be to please Duke Dottrel, sure. **1658** *Whole Duty Man* xv. §15 That all under his charge be taught all necessary things of this kind, and then sure more especially his wife. **1713** Pope *Let. to Swift* 8 Dec., Sure no clergyman ever offered so much out of his own purse for the sake of any religion. **1722** De Foe *Plague* (1754) 23, I shall Name but a few of these Things; but sure they were so many. **1766** Goldsm. *Vicar W.* xxviii, Sure it cannot be! **1797** Jane Austen *Sense & Sens.* xxxv, Sure, you an't well. **1851** Thackeray *Engl. Hum.* vi. (1853) 314 He would have talked of his great friends of the Club..sure he knew them intimately.

c. Used to emphasize *yes* or *no*; also alone = Certainly *colloq.* and *dial.* (chiefly *N. Amer.*).

1803 G. Colman *John Bull* I. 4 *Den.* Troth, and myself, Mr. Dennis Brulgruddery, was brought up to the church. *Dan.* Why, zure! **1813** *Sk. Char.* (ed. 2) I. 83 'What, was Mad Ross there?'.. 'Oh yes, sure'. **1861** Waugh *Birtle Carter's Tale* 6 A glass ov ale. Ay, sure; yo'st have it in a minute. **1862** Miss Braddon *Lady Audley* xix, 'You say a blacksmith has been here?' 'Sure and I did, sir.' **1914** Wodehouse *Man Upstairs* 133 'Is that a fact?' 'Sure,' murmured Archibald. **1963** Mrs. L. B. Johnson *White House Diary* 26 Nov. (1970) 11 If it had been a request to chop off one's right hand one would have said, 'Sure'. **1975** R. Stout *Family Affair* xi. 130 I'm under arrest. I asked if you could finish your lunch, and they said sure, no hurry.

4. a. In similative phr. (*as*) *sure as*, followed by a clause, or by various sbs., as *death, fate, a gun*: see also these words, and egg *sb.* 4 b. ***sure as hell*** (U.S. slang), most certainly; (*as*) ***sure as God made little apples***, etc.: see apple *sb.* 1 b.

c **1374** Chaucer *Troylus* III. 1633 Also seur as red is euery fir, As gret a craft is kep wel as wynne. **1573** Tusser *Husb.* lxxvii. (1878) 170 Take runagate Robin, to pitie his neede, And looke to be filched, as sure as thy creede. **1618** Bolton *Florus* I. xviii. (1636) 58, I see, as sure as can be, that I am borne under the constellation of Hercules. *c* **1650** *Robin Hood & Tanner's Dau.* viii. in Child *Ball.* (1882) I. 109/2 As sure as they were borne. **1660** Shirley *Merch. Wife* iv. viii, As sure as death, this is one Of the rogues. **1676** Hobbes *Iliad* II. 32 [He] thought To take Troy now as sure as any thing. **1701** Farquhar *Sir H. Wildair* v. v, *Stand.*... You'll be serious when I tell you that her Ghost appears. *Wild.* Her Ghost! Ha, ha, ha... *Stand.* As sure as Fate, it walks in my House. **1731–8** Swift *Pol. Conversat.* i. 4 *Lady Smart.* Oh! Colonel, are you here? *Col.* As sure as you're there, Madam. **1742** Fielding *J. Andrews* iv. xiv, That's true, as sure as Sixpence, you have hit on the very thing. **1824** Scott in *Edin. Weekly Jrnl.* 9 June 181/3 As sure as ever ye sit there, She'll tell the Bailie. **1828** J. Neal *Rachel Dyer* xix. 238 He will get away if you turn your head... That he will! if you don't look sharp, as sure as my name is Peter P. **1833** Ht. Martineau *Loom & Lugger* II. iii. 44 As sure as the year came round. **1856** C. M. Yonge *Daisy Chain* I. ii. 13 Madam, said I, you'll have to answer for your mother's death, as sure as my name's Dick May. **1859** Meredith *R. Feverel* ix, I'll transpoort Tom Bakewell, sure as a gun. **1944** E. S. Gardner *Case of Black-Eyed Blonde* xx. 194 I'm telling you just as sure as you're sitting there, that if you don't get men out to Jason Bartsler's place, a murder is going to be committed. **1976** *Listener* 6 May 562/3 Wayne.. introduces me to Commemorativo Tequilla. 'It doesn't hurt your head, but it may hurt your back, as you sure as hell fall over a lot.'

b. In phr. ***sure enough***.

a **1545** Sir E. Howard in Ellis *Orig. Lett.* Ser. III. I. 150 Sewre inough Sir therys moche vitall at Sandwich, and they have no vessels to bryng it to us. **1641** J. Shute *Sarah & Hagar* (1649) 178 The Sin of Oppression, sure enough, will be payed home. **1773** C. Dibdin *Deserter* I. ii. (1775) 12 Ah, indeed, the soldiers make sad work with young women's hearts sure enough. **1848** Thackeray *Van. Fair* lxiii, The number came up sure enough. **1891** 'J. S. Winter' *Lumley* v, And you were so angry with me when you went off—I saw it, sure enough.

C. *Comb.* (chiefly adverbial or parasynthetic), as ***sure-aimed, -founded, -grounded, -handed, -nosed, -presaging, -seeing, -set, -settled, -slow, -steeled*** adjs.; **sure-enough** *a. U.S. colloq.* [cf. B. 4 b], genuine, real; †**sure-hold**, something affording a secure hold.

1776 Mickle tr. *Camoens' Lusiad* 150 The *sure-aim'd vengeance of the Lusian steel. **1884** 'Mark Twain' *Huck. Finn* xxii, They all come riding in..looking just like a gang of real *sure-enough queens. **1897** Flandrau *Harvard Episodes* 172 It is n't given to many of us to have real, sure-enough feelings around here in college. **1725** Pope *Odyss.* I. 278, I build my claim *Sure-founded on a fair Maternal fame. **1708** Sewel II, *Vastgegrond*, *sure-grounded. **1930** M. Mead *Growing up in New Guinea* iii. 23 The decisive, angry gesture..had taught him to be alert and *sure-handed. **1962** *Times* 26 Feb. 4/1 [The French rugby team] were able to start attacks..and surehanded, to develop them. **1647** Trapp *Comm. Rom.* ix. 6 That word of promise ..which is *sure-hold, Yea and Amen. **1650** —— *Comm. Exod.* xii. 41 His promises are good sure-hold. **1607** Topsell *Four-f. Beasts* 151 The White Houndes are said to be the quickest-sented and *surest nosed. **1651** Davenant *Gondibert* I. II. xlv, Sure nos'd as fasting Tygers. **1610** Holland *Camden's Brit.* I. 109 Lucky *sure-presaging auguries. **1794** Coleridge *Relig. Musings* iv, Fear,..*Sure-refuged hears his hot pursuing fiends Yell at vain distance. **1866** Whipple *Char. & Charact. Men* 309 Shakespeare, the *sure-seeing poet of human nature. **1648** J. Beaumont *Psyche* xx. lii, Peace had trode all Perils under Her *sure-set feet. **1896** Housman *Shropsh. Lad* xxxiii, This long and sure-set liking. **1587** Golding *De Mornay* xxxiv. (1592) 551 Nature..is a steady and *suresettled Lawe. **1603** J. Davies (Heref.) *Microcosmos* Pref., With a *sure-slow winge. *a* **1616** Beaum. & Fl. *Bonduca* III. i, Thou *sure-steel'd sternness, Give us this day good hearts, good enemies, Good blowes o' both sides.

sure, *v. Obs.* exc. *dial.* (see Eng. Dial. Dict.). Forms: see prec.; also 5 **suyr, sewyr**; 6 *pa. pple.* (*Sc.*) **suirit, sewarit, -at, sewarat, severit.** [Aphetic f. assure *v.* Cf. sover *v.*]

†**1.** *trans.* To make or keep safe, to secure; = assure 1. *Obs.*

c **1380** Wyclif *Wks.* (1880) 14 Whanne þei..suren hem of al perel. *c* **1470** Harding *Chron.* clxxvii. vi. (MS. Arch. Seld. B. 10) lf. 139 b, þey myht nat passen oute But thorou3th a mosse þat al men trowed was sured. **1535** Stewart *Cron. Scot.* (Rolls) III. 412 That halie place wes suirit..Fra fyre, bot nocht fra spul3e and fra reif. **1567** *Gude & Godlie B.* (S.T.S.) 108 And with thair handis thay sall the sure, That thow hurt nocht aganis ane craig Thy fute.

†**2.** To give an assurance or promise to (a person); to secure (a thing) to a person *by* a pledge or promise. *Obs.*

1377 Langl. *P. Pl.* B. v. 547 Conscience and kynde witte ..deden me suren hym sikerly to serue hym for euere. *c* **1450** Lovelich *Merlin* 12386 And also anothir thing sche schold hym Sure: that harm to his body scholde sche neuere do. *c* **1460** *Play Sacram.* 279, I wolle sure yow be thys lyght Neuer dystrie yow daye nor nyght.

†**3.** To bind by promise, plight, pledge (one's faith or troth). *Obs.*

c **1400** *Beryn* 1486, I suyr 3ew my trowith..That I shall do my devoir. *c* **1450** *Merlin* xxxi. 628 Than thei sured theire feithes be-twene hem two to holde these covenauntes. *c* **1450** *Godstow Reg.* 170 Henry, than stywarde of Godestowe, suryd hys trowthe for the Abbas & couent þys couenant to be kepyd.

†**4.** *pass.* To be bound by a promise or pledge; *spec.* to be engaged to marry, to be betrothed (cf. sure *a.* 7 a). *Obs.*

1420–22 Lydg. *Thebes* 2234 He sured was and sworn To Tydeus. *c* **1475** *Partenay* 5087 In noble Bretain gan he to mary, Affyed and sured to A gret lady. **1484** Caxton *Fables of Poge* xi, A wydower wowed a wydowe for to..Wedde her to his wyf And at the last they were agreed and sured to gyder. *a* **1578** Lindesay (Pitscottie) *Chron. Scot.* (S.T.S.) II. 38 All the bordairis..quho war sewarat witht thame. *Ibid.* 42 Quho had bene constranit..to be severit [*v.r.* suirit] and tak on the reid crose and obey thame selfis to be trew subiectis to king Harrie.

5. To make (a person) sure or certain; = assure 9, 10. Now *dial.*

c **1400** *Beryn* 1886, I suyr þe be my fey That þow art much I-bound to me. *c* **1430** Lydg. *Min. Poems* (Percy Soc.) 112 Fyrst I wyll be sewyred, That ower cownselle ye wylle kepe. *a* **1536** *Songs, Carols*, etc. (E.E.T.S.) 9 He was born of a virgyn pure,..as I you sure. [**1667** Dryden & Dk. Newcastle *Sir M. Mar-all* iv. i, How shall I be 'sur'd 'tis so?]

sure: see sewer *sb.*[1], sir *sb.*, sour *a.*, sura[1].

sureal, obs. form of surroyal.

sureby: see suresby.

†**sured**, *ppl. a. Obs. rare.* Aphetic f. assured. (Cf. sure *v.*)

a **1542** Wyatt *Penit. Ps.* cxliii. Prol. iv, Then will I crave with sured confidence. **1549** *MSS. Dk. Rutland* (Hist. MSS. Comm.) IV. 355 To a Ducheman, for that my Lord causyd him to gyve a suryd Scotyshman his nagge agayne, vs. **1567** Painter *Pal. Pleas.* II. *ad fin.*, A plot founded on sured ground. *a* **1586** Sidney *Arcadia* iv. (1622) 443 For euer lamed of our sured might.

Hence †**suredly** *adv.*, assuredly.

1630 Lennard tr. *Charron's Wisd.* II. ii. §10. 263 He that walks moderately..directeth his businesse..more suredly and cheerefully.

†**surefast**, *a. Obs. rare*[−1]. [f. sure *a.* after *steadfast*.] Stable, fixed.

1583 Melbancke *Philotimus* Dd iij b, A perfect plat..of surges that embrace the earth with winding waues, & of the surefast centrie ground.

sure-footed (stress variable), *a.* [sure *a.* 4 b.]

1. Sure of foot; treading securely or firmly; not liable to slip, stumble, or fall.

1707 [implied in *surefootedness*]. **1764** Smollett *Trav.* xx. (1766) I. 313 The mules of Piedmont..are the only carriage that can be used in crossing the mountains, being very sure-footed. **1834** Caunter *Orient. Ann.* xv. 207 The elephant is remarkably surefooted, seldom stumbling, and much more rarely falling. **1845** S. Austin *Ranke's Hist. Ref.* II. 425 A few sure-footed landsknechts..guarded the steps of their veteran leader; and thus..he traversed the terrific pass. **1884** *Times* (weekly ed.) 12 Sept. 7/2 Hills..so steep that even the sure-footed hill cattle could not tread them.

2. *fig.* Not liable to make a 'slip' or error; proceeding surely; unerring.

1633 Herbert *Temple, Dotage* ii, True earnest sorrows, rooted miseries,..Sure footed griefs, solid calamities. **1678** Cudworth *Intell. Syst.* 170 Thus that safe and sure-footed Interpreter, Alex. Aphrodisius, expounds his Masters Meaning. **1849** Macaulay *Hist. Eng.* vii. II. 257 The one human being who was able to mislead that farsighted and surefooted judgment. **1864** Lowell *Lincoln* Wks. 1890 V. 199 Worthy of his cautious but sure-footed understanding.

Hence ˌ**sure'footedly** *adv.*, ˌ**sure'footedness**; so †**sure-footing**.

1665 J. Sergeant (*title*) Sure-footing in Christianity, or Rational Discourses on The Rule of Faith. **1702** Penn *Maxims* Wks. 1726 I. 847 The Wise Man..has in every Thing an Eye to Sure-Footing. **1707** Mortimer *Husb.* (1721) I. 224 [Mules] are the best sort of Creatures..for Burden and Surefootedness. **1869** W. B. Rands *Chaucer's Eng.* I. i. 8 Logical sure-footedness. **1869** *Pall Mall G.* 14 July 7 It is said..that the sturdy old mountaineer's eyesight was failing, and that he had lost of late some of the sure-footedness for which he has been famous. **1936** *Discovery* Aug. 242/1 Clambering sure-footedly about the larger.. trunks. **1977** *Times Lit. Suppl.* 15 Apr. 449/2 Walks surefootedly through the minefield that separates fulsome idolatry from condescending anecdotal chit-chat.

†**surefully**, *adv. Obs. rare*⁻¹. [irreg. f. SURE *a.* + *-fully*, adv. to -FUL 1.] In security.

1495 *Act 11 Hen. VII*, c. 2 Preamble, The Kyngis grace.. desireth.. his subgettis.. to leve quietly and surefully to the plesure of God and according to his lawes.

suregene, obs. form of SURGEON.

†**sureguard.** *Obs. rare*⁻¹. In 7 -gard. [f. SURE *a.* after *safeguard*.] = SAFEGUARD *sb.* 4.

1604 E. G[RIMSTONE] *D'Acosta's Hist. Indies* v. xv. 367 They tooke them from thence,.. sending them to the Court with suregards.

sureis: see SURAGE *Obs.*

surely ('ʃʊəlɪ, 'ʃɔəlɪ), *adv.* Forms: see SURE *a.*; also 4 surliche, surlych, *comp.* surlokere, 4–6 surly, -lie, 6 shorly, showrly, suuerlie. [f. SURE *a.* + -LY².] In a sure manner.

I. Expressing the manner of an action, etc.

1. a. Without danger, or risk of injury, loss, or displacement; securely, safely; firmly. *arch.*

13.. *Sir Beues* (A.) 2559 Hii þouȝten.. He wolde hem surliche lede. *c* **1400** MAUNDEV. (Roxb.) ix. 34 He myght seurly dwell in þat citee withouten.. any harme takyng. *c* **1400** *Destr. Troy* 1236 The souerayn hym-seluon was surly enarmyt. **1464** *Paston Lett.* Suppl. (1901) 85, I charge you ..ye suffer noon of thayme to passe oute of your garde, but suerle to kepe thaym. **1523** FITZHERB. *Husb.* §32 The husband may set shepe.. vnder the same scaffold.. if it be well and surely made. *a* **1533** LD. BERNERS *Huon* cxxiv. 449 Grauell to balayse his shyp withal that it myght sayle the more suerlyer. **1615** W. LAWSON *Country Housew. Garden* (1626) 22 Your stakes.. would be so surely put.. that they breake not, if any thing happen to leane vpon them. **1648** GAGE *West Ind.* xix. 140 The Indian must be.. surely tied to a post by his hands. **1697** DRYDEN *Virg. Georg.* IV. 585 Thus surely bound, yet.. The slipp'ry God will try to loose his hold. **1834** LYTE *Hymn*, '*Praise, Lord, for Thee in Zion waits*' iii, How blest Thy saints! how safely led! How surely kept!

†**b.** With security or stability of obligation or loyalty; steadfastly. *Obs.*

c **1380** *Sir Ferumb.* 1281 Ac arst þow schalt sykery me, & þy treuþe surly plyȝte, þat þou for me schalt don a þyng þat y schal the saye. *c* **1450** *Godstow Reg.* 660 Wherfor he willed and comaunded surely that the forsaid mynchons shold haue and holde all ther almesse and possessions. **1465** *Paston Lett.* II. 209, I shall have the maner sewrlyer to me ..than the Dewk shall have Cossey. **1561** WINȜET *Four Scoir Thre Quest.* §9 Wks. (S.T.S.) I. 78 Keipand suirlie the articulis of our beleif. **1596** SHAKS. *Tam. Shr.* IV. ii. 36 That I may surely keepe mine oath. **1596** SPENSER *F.Q.* V. xii. 2 Whom all the bands, Which may a Knight assure, had surely bound. **1612** T. TAYLOR *Comm. Titus* ii. 14. (1619) 513 Whose bonds are.. binding them euery day surelier then other ouer to destruction.

2. With certainty, assurance, or confidence; for certain; undoubtingly, confidently. *arch.*

13.. *E.E. Allit. P.* C. 315 Ȝet surely I hope, Efte to trede on þy temple. *c* **1380** *Sir Ferumb.* 520 Wanne þy hert ys hol & fer þe surlokere þou miȝt fiȝte. *c* **1420** *Chron. Vilod.* 1561 Ȝet þis we mow wyton & know seurly þat god [etc.]. **1483** CAXTON *Gold. Leg.* 255/2 The bisshop.. wente oute ageynst the enemyes surely and the peple folowed hym. **1529** MORE *Dyaloge* III. v. 76/2 And than yᵗ case onys graunted, ye deduce your conclusyon very surely. *a* **1530** in Ellis *Orig. Lett.* Ser. I. I. 304, I trowst showrly to come vp to Londone. **1533** GAU *Richt Vay* 8 To traist suuerlie al time guid of hime as of thair maist tender fader. *a* **1548** HALL *Chron., Edw. IV*, 232 b, Spekyng these wordes (thinking surely much to please the kyng). *a* **1578** LINDESAY (Pitscottie) *Chron. Scot.* (S.T.S.) I. 115 He beleivit suirelie that the king had beine thair. **1629** MILTON *Hymn Nativ.* iv, As if they surely knew their sovran Lord was by. **1820** KEATS *Lamia* II. 113 Knowing surely she could never win His foolish heart from its mad pompousness.

3. a. So as to be certain to achieve or reach a result or end; without risk of failure; infallibly.

Now chiefly in *slowly but surely*.

c **1400** *Destr. Troy* 2456 Serche it full suerly, and se to þe ende. *c* **1460** FORTESCUE *Abs. & Lim. Mon.* ii. (1885) 113 The prince.. mey therby þe more surely do justice than bi is owne arbitrment. **1495** *Trevisa's Barth. De P.R.* v. xxviii. (W. de W.) iij/2 Noo party of the body towchyth and gropyth so surely as the honde. *c* **1520** *Everyman* 147 Yf I sholde this pylgrymage take, And my rekenynge suerly make,.. Sholde I not come agayne shortly? **1612** BRINSLEY *Lud. Lit.* xiii. (1627) 181 The most excellent patterns.. doe most auaile, to teach the soonest and sureliest. **1653** BAXTER *Chr. Concord* 13 That.. their duties.. may be the surelier performed. **1754** SHERLOCK *Disc.* (1759) I. i. 3 The best Religion is that which will most surely direct us to eternal Life. **1873** SPON *Workshop Rec.* Ser. I. 3/2 If a drawing could be.. surely made without mistake.. it might be made in ink. **1912** W. B. SELBIE *Nonconformity* xii. 228 These things are slowly but surely coming about.

†**b.** Soundly, thoroughly. *Obs. rare.*

App. confused with SORELY.

c **1450** tr. *Higden, Harl. Contin.* (Rolls) VIII. 479 The Lollardes bytoke that Frere and trode hym under theire feete and bete hym surely. **1513** *Life Hen. V* (1911) 17 At such enterprises both he and his Companie weare surelie beaten.

II. Qualifying a statement.

4. a. (*a*) Certainly, assuredly, undoubtedly. Often with less emphasis, as a mere intensive: Truly, verily, indeed.

13.. *E.E. Allit. P.* B. 1643 Hit is surely soth, þe souerayn of heuen Fylsened euer þy fader. *c* **1375** *Cursor M.* 23031 (Fairf.), þaire penaunce sal be seurely To loke on þa deuels witerli. *c* **1400** *Beryn* 2316 And ȝit suyrly I mervell nat þouȝ þat it be so. *c* **1450** LOVELICH *Grail* lv. 116 'How May I this beleve?' quod Aleyn, 'ȝis sewrly', quod the kyng, 'In Certeyn'. **1530** PALSGR. 866/2 Ye suerly, *voyre certes.* **1592** *Arden of Feversham* IV. iv. 26 As surely as I liue, Ile banish pittie if thou vse me thus. **1596** DALRYMPLE tr. *Leslie's Hist. Scot.* I. 22 The principal amang the tounes is halden (surlie) Edinburgh. **1599** SHAKS. *Hen. V.* III. ii. 126 Ile pay't as valorously as I may, that sal I suerly do. **1641** J. JACKSON *True Evang. T.* III. 171 Abimelech.. seeing Isaac sporting with Rebecca, concluded thereupon that she was surely his Wife. **1831** SCOTT *Ct. Rob.* xx, Alas! they seem but too surely to be here. **1845** FORD *Handbk. Spain* I. 16 Money makes the mare and its driver to go as surely in Spain as in all other countries. **1850** TENNYSON *In Mem.* xxx, Surely rest is meet. **1867** H. MACMILLAN *Bible Teach.* x. (1870) 208 As surely as the leaf fades, so surely shall we fade. **1907** GRANDGENT *Introd. Vulgar Latin* §251 Initial *h* was surely very feeble.. during the Republic.

(*b*) As an affirmative answer: cf. SURE *adv.* 3 c.

1821 SCOTT *Kenilw.* xii, 'Know you Cumnor-place, near Oxford?' 'Surely,' said the clergyman. **1876** C. M. YONGE *Three Brides* II. viii. 152 'I must go. Can I?' 'Surely, as soon as there is a train.' **1922** E. RAYMOND *Tell England* II. i. 166 'Surely,' answered my companion, which was a new way he had acquired of saying 'yes'. **1975** M. RUSSELL *Murder by Mile* iii. 19 'Like to follow me along?' 'Surely.'

b. Used to express a strong belief in the statement, on the basis of experience or probability, but without absolute proof, or as implying a readiness to maintain it against imaginary or possible denial: = as may be confidently supposed; as must be the case; may not one be sure that...? (The chief current sense.)

1588 SHAKS. *L.L.L.* I. ii. 93 Greene indeed is the colour of Louers: but to haue a Loue of that colour, methinkes Sampson had small reason for it. He surely affected her for her wit. **1667** MILTON *P.L.* IV. 923 Had'st thou alleg'd To thy deserted host this cause of flight, Thou surely hadst not come sole fugitive. **1712** STEELE *Spect.* No. 302 ¶7 Surely never did such a Philosophic Soul inhabit such a beauteous Form! **1732** BERKELEY *Alciphr.* I. §16 You will not surely deny the conclusion, when you admit the premises? **1794** MRS. RADCLIFFE *Myst. Udolpho* xxxiii, 'Surely, Annette,' said Emily, starting, 'I heard a noise: listen.' **1832** HT. MARTINEAU *Elia of Gar.* ii. 21 Twelve! it cannot be so much surely. **1846** DICKENS *Cricket on Hearth* i, They might know better than to leave their clocks so very lank and unprotected, surely. **1870** FREEMAN *Norm. Conq.* (ed. 2) I. App. 679 This incident is surely an essential part of the story. **1891** FARRAR *Darkn. & Dawn* xxxvi, Surely it could not fail! **1908** R. BAGOT *A. Cuthbert* xxviii. 373 If Anthony will forgive me, surely God will!

c. With the second syllable stressed and lengthened (ʃʊə'laɪ), in prec. sense, or as a mere intensive. *dial.* or *vulgar colloq.*

1837 DICKENS *Pickw.* vi, 'Reg'lar good land that,' interposed another fat man. 'And so it is, sure-ly,' said a third fat man. **1859** LANG *Wand. India* 253 He did love her, sure*ly*, sir. **1864** TENNYSON *Northern Farmer, O.S.* xiv, What a man a beä sewer-loy!

†**surement.** *Obs.* Also seure-, surment. [a. AF. **surement*, aphetic f. *assurement* ASSUREMENT. Sometimes confused with *serement* SERMENT, oath; cf. SOREMENT.] An assurance, pledge.

c **1386** CHAUCER *Frankl. T.* 806, I yow relesse madame in to youre hond Quyt euery surement [*Ellesm.* (*or* ? sirement), *Cambr., Corp., Petw., Lansd.* surement, *Harl.* seurement, *Heng.* serement] That ye han maad to me. *c* **1400** *Laud Troy Bk.* 13022 Ther-to made he his surment To holde hem stable. *a* **1400–50** *Wars Alex.* 2748 Loke to þi-selfe, For sekire & on my surement I seke ȝow agayns. **1497–8** *N. Riding Rec.* (1894) I. 194 The which.. seyth upon our concience and surment that [etc.].

sureness ('ʃʊənɪs, 'ʃɔə-). Forms: see SURE *a.* [f. SURE *a.* + -NESS.] The quality or condition of being sure.

†**1.** Security, safety; steadfastness, stability. *Obs.*

c **1412** HOCCLEVE *De Reg. Princ.* 5031, & hym sueth gladnesse Which þat of pees conseilith þe suernesse. **1412–20** LYDG. *Chron. Troy* III. 5526 Far-wel oure hele, now Hector is goon, In whom þe surnes of vs eurychon Was wont to reste. *c* **1430** *Pilgr. Lyf Manhode* I. cxxvi. (1869) 67 The surenesse of the armure. *c* **1430** LYDG. *Min. Poems* (Percy Soc.) 123 That han betymes passid this thurghfare, And kowde therin fynde no surenesse. *c* **1460** *Oseney Reg.* 13 With þe surenesse [orig. *sanctione*] of þⁱˢ present letters we make sure [etc.]. *a* **1500–34** *Cov. Corpus Chr. Pl.* II. 238 That in this lande here he schuld make surenes, And he to be cawlid the King of Pes. *a* **1548** HALL *Chron., Hen. VI*, 129 Admonishyng hym.. not to myngle.. his safetie and surenesse, with the vnstablenesse and vnsuretie of his newe alye. **1573** *Satir. Poems Reform.* xl. 30 Quhat surenes fand the Bischopis halynes Into Dumbartane? **1650** T. B[AYLEY] *Worcester's Apoph.* To Rdr., [Like] the man who went to search after the surenesse of the foundation when his house was all on fire. **1666** T. WATSON *Godly mans Pict.* 96 The Promises are comfortable: 1 For their sureness... 2 For their suitableness.

†**b.** *to the more* or *for* (*more*) *sureness*: to make sure, to be on the safe side, so that there shall be no doubt. *Obs.*

c **1450** *Godstow Reg.* 192 To the more surenesse, this charter is made endented. **1612** T. TAYLOR *Comm. Titus* iii. 2. (1619) 575 How often for surenes hath the Lord threatned [etc.]. **1668** MARVELL *Corr.* Wks. (Grosart) II. 253, I write these few words in the Post-house, for surenesse that my letter be not too late. **1679** *Hist. Jetzer* 10 M. Magdalene, who devoutly gather'd the Blood that dropt from his wounds as he hung there, and for sureness took up the Earth with it. *a* **1714** SHARP *Serm. Exod. xx. 8* Wks. 1754 IV. 220 They were in doubt which was the right day.. and therefore, for sureness, they would keep both. *a* **1728** WOODWARD *Nat. Hist. Fossils* (1729) I. 118 He diverted himself.. with the Speculation of the Seed of Coral; and, as for more sureness he repeats it, the Sperme of Coral.

2. a. Objective certainty. †Phr. *in* or *for sureness*, for certain, surely, certainly.

c **1485** *Digby Myst., Convers. St. Paul* 31, I schall aske of them in suernes, To persue. *a* **1500** *Ratis Raving* 3013 For suernes thai wald neuer wyrk. *c* **1530** *Judic. Urines* II. ii. 13 b, Yet is ther no suernys of amendyng. **1674** N. FAIRFAX *Bulk & Selv.* Contents, A time beyond which the world shall not hold out, may be fastned on, from the sureness of the bodies rising again. **1849** M. ARNOLD *Poems, To Gipsy Child by Sea-shore* 42 That sure pain Whose sureness grey-haired scholars hardly learn! **1871** BURR *Ad Fidem* xii. 228 Does it follow that they [*sc.* miracles] have never occurred, or even that they cannot be known with scientific sureness to have occurred?

b. Subjective certainty.

a **1572** KNOX *Hist. Ref.* Wks. 1846 I. 26 Faith is a suirness. **1584** LODGE *Hist. Forbonius & Prisceria* in *Alarum* etc. G iij, I shall ouerpasse the sorrow by surenesse. **1641** SMECTYMNUUS *Vind. Answ.* §13. 129 You give us no ground of your surenesse. **1890** *Spectator* 8 Mar., A strong affection and sureness of faith. **1908** *Edin. Rev.* Apr. 345 Memoranda collected.. gave him the sureness needed for his gigantic undertaking.

3. The quality of being unfailing or unerring; trustworthiness or accuracy of aim, perception, etc.

1837 W. IRVING *Capt. Bonneville* xli. III. 128 The detection of this blunder in the two veterans, who prided themselves on the sureness and quickness of their sight. **1860** TYNDALL *Glac.* II. xvii. 316 The chamois.. with its.. admirable sureness of foot. **1883** *Manch. Guard.* 3 Nov. 7/4 That network of agencies which in England is, with characteristic slowness, but we hope also with characteristic sureness, developing into a real system of national education. **1912** J. L. MYRES *Dawn Hist.* viii. 181 An artistic style.. able to draw inspiration from other styles.. without losing the sureness of its own touch.

†**surepel.** *Obs. rare*⁻¹. [? a. AF. **surepel*, f. *sure* SUR- + *pel* PELL *sb.*¹] A cover for a book.

? *a* **1400** *Morte Arth.* 3317 A sawtere semliche bowndene, With a surepel of silke sewede fulle faire.

surereall, obs. form of SURROYAL.

†**suresby, sureby.** *Obs.* Also suers-. [f. SURE *a.* + -BY 2.] An appellation for a person (and hence for a thing) that is 'sure' or may be depended upon.

[*a* **1553** UDALL *Royster D.* IV. i. (Arb.) 59 Is there any man but I Sym Suresby alone, That would haue taken such an enterprise him vpon?] **1553** BRADFORD *Serm. Repent.* (1574) E vj b, Remedy now know I none. What said I none?.. Yes, there is one which is suresby, as they say, to serue, if any thyng wyl serue. **1588** *Marprel. Epist.* 4, I am olde suersbie at the proofe of such matters. **1588** J. HARVEY *Disc. Probl.* 98 Sundry like ancient surebies and old sokers. **1598** R. BERNARD tr. *Terence, Andria* IV. v, You are the same man that you were: old suresbie [*ed.* **1607** surebie]: no flinsher. **1602** F. HERING *Anat.* 14 He flieth to those old Suresbies and Trudge blew-coats, Antimony and Mercury Precipitate. **1603** HARSNET *Pop. Impost.* xii. 63 This was the traynd sent, he knew his dogges were old suers-by at this. **1634** *Withals' Dict.* 562 *Lyaius sive Heracleus lapis*, hee is old suresby. **1643** TRAPP *Comm. Gen.* xxix. 13 Look rather unto the Lord,.. he is the onely Suresby, as they say; and will never fail us.

attrib. **1612** T. JAMES *Corrupt. Scripture* II. 13 All the printed and written copies haue forsaken him, saue only the old suresby Cambron copie. **1675** J. SMITH *Chr. Relig. Appeal* II. 83 Dealing with every man at his own suresby-weapon.

‖**Sûreté** (syrte). [Fr., = SURETY *sb.*, security.] In full, *Sûreté nationale*, the French police department of criminal investigation, controlled by the Ministry of the Interior. Also *transf.* of similar forces elsewhere.

Since 1966 amalgamated with the Prefecture of Police of Paris in the *Police Nationale.* The department was previously known as the *Sûreté générale* and the *Service de la Sûreté*, and was latterly also responsible for policing the provincial towns of France.

1871 *Observer* 9 Apr. 6/4 M. Ranc.. was the chief of the Sûreté Generale under Gambetta. **1885** *Encycl. Brit.* XIX. 343/2 The *service de sûreté*, or detective department (out of uniform).. comprises a commissary, principal inspectors, brigadiers, and 211 inspectors. **1917** J. F. MACDONALD *Two Towns—One City* III. i. 192 This foreign gentleman.. represents the *Sûreté* (or Criminal Investigation Department) of Paris. **1926** D. L. SAYERS *Clouds of Witness* iii. 94, I have written to the Sûreté and the Crédit Lyonnais to produce his papers. **1935** A. CHRISTIE *Death in Clouds* xi. 115 At the Sûreté Poirot renewed acquaintance with the Chief of the Detective Force. **1955** *Times* 9 May 8/3 The Binh Xuyen garrison which has been occupying the headquarters of the Sûreté in Saigon. **1963** A. ORLOV *Handbk. Intelligence & Guerrilla Warfare* xii. 143 An old Soviet informant who was an officer of the French Sûreté Générale (Secret Police). **1973** 'M. INNES' *Appleby's Answer* x. 97 The great Vidocq, who transformed the efficiency of the Paris Sûreté by.. insisting that his detectives should never forget a face. **1980** R. GRAYSON *Monterant Affair* xi. 94 The hotel was.. within easy walking distance of Sûreté headquarters.

surety ('ʃʊətɪ, 'ʃʊərɪtɪ), *sb.* Forms: 4–5 suretee, surte, seur(e)te, -tee, sewrte, 4–6 suerte, 5 seuerte, sewerte(e, (swer-, suyrte, -tee, -tie, surtey), 5–6 surete, suertee, -ty, sewertie, surtee, 5–7 sure-, suertie, (6 suer-, soertye, seurtie, sew(e)rtye, surtie, -ty, *Sc.* swir-, suirtie), 6–7

suretye, surtye, 6– **surety**. [a. OF. *surte, -tey, seurte,* later *seurete* (mod.F. *sûreté*):—L. *sēcūritātem, -tās,* f. *sēcūrus* SURE *a.*: see -TY[1].]

I. Condition of being (or something that is) sure.

†**1.** Safety, security *from* danger, an enemy, etc.

13.. *E.E. Allit. P.* C. 58 Did not Ionas in Iude suche Iape sum-whyle, To sette hym to sewrte, vnsounde he hym feches? *c* **1374** CHAUCER *Former Age* 46 In surte they slepte. *c* **1425** *Cast. Persev.* 1546 in *Macro Plays* 123, I prey ȝou putte me In-to sum place of surete, þat þei may not harmyn me. **1432** *Paston Lett.* I. 31 For the goode reule, demesnyng and seuretee of the Kynges persone. *a* **1450** *Knt. de la Tour* (1868) 36 It is good that ye do so for the suerte of youre good name. *a* **1533** LD. BERNERS *Huon* cxxi. 432 He sate downe to reste hym, and layd his sword by hym, thynkynge then to be in a suerty. **1572** *Form Com. Prayer* B iv b, That by thy ayde ..we may obtayne suertie from our enimies. **1585** T. WASHINGTON tr. *Nicholay's Voy.* I. i. 1 b, That for the more suretie of his voyage, he shoulde returne by Sea. **1604** E. G[RIMSTONE] *D'Acosta's Hist. Indies* IV. ii. 206 For the conservation, reparation, suretie, ornament and exaltation of his workes. **1620** [G. BRYDGES] *Horæ Subs.* 268 It much concerned the surety of Augustus his gouernment, to haue ..them content.

†**b.** Security of contract, right, or possession.

c **1400** *Destr. Troy* 641, I hoope þu will holde þat þu here said: More suerty, for sothe, yet I sue fore. **1422** YONGE tr. *Secr. Secr.* xxxiii. 186 For more grettyr Surte thay bounde ham in grete Somes by dyvers Instrumentes. **1442** *Rolls of Parlt.* V. 57/2 Ye myght not have ..the seide possessions in enheritaunce to youre availle and suerte. *a* **1475** ASHBY *Active Policy* 183 How may any estate be in seurtee Of his welthe.. If couetous folke be in his favour? **1545** *Test. Ebor.* (Surtees) VI. 227 For the more sewrtie I have setto my seal.

†**c.** *transf.* A means of safety, a safeguard. *Obs.*

c **1386** CHAUCER *Pard. T.* 609 Looke which a seuretee is it to yow alle That I am in youre felaweshipe yfalle. *c* **1400** tr. *Secr. Secr., Gov. Lordsh.* viii. 53 And y trist þat þis techinge shall be ..surtee and sufficiante to þy gouernaille. **1540** *Act 32 Hen. VIII,* c. 14 §1 The nauy .. is ..a greate defence and suerty of this realme.

2. †**a.** Trustworthiness, reliability. *Obs. rare.*

1470–85 MALORY *Arthur* XIII. v. 617 For the suerte of this swerd I brought none with me. *c* **1530** L. COX *Rhet.* (1899) 56 Cato was honored for his ernestnes and surete. **1591** *Troub. Raigne K. John* II. (1611) 90, I need not doubt the suretie of your wills.

b. Accuracy; = SURENESS 3. *rare.*

1422 YONGE tr. *Secr. Secr.* 132 Sotylte and Vndyrstondynge, seurte of connynge. **1799** STUART in Owen *Wellesley's Desp.* (1877) 114 The enemy pierced through the jungles with such surety and expedition. **1892** *Sat. Rev.* 17 Dec. 705/1 He handled French..with neatness of movement and surety of touch.

3. †**a.** Freedom from care or anxiety; feeling of safety; confidence; = SECURITY 3. *Obs.*

c **1374** CHAUCER *Troylus* II. 833 Myn lif to lede In al Ioyȝe & seurte out of drede. *c* **1450** tr. *De Imitatione* I. xx. 24 þe surete of holy men was neuere wiþoute drede of god... The surete of shrewes growiþ of pride & presumpcion. **1481** CAXTON *Godfrey* xxvi. 58 His vyctorye brought Solyman in in grete pryde, and in grete sewrte he smote in to the lodgis of the Cristen men. **1523** LD. BERNERS *Froiss.* I. cclvi. 380 Sir Perducas Dallreth ..turned ..Englisshe ..whereof the duke of Aniou ..thought than the lasse surete in the sayd Sir Perducas. *c* **1598** DELONEY *Thomas of Reading* Wks. (1912) 222 Pouerty with suretie, is better than honour mixed with feare.

b. Certain knowledge; = SECURITY 2, SURENESS 2 b. *arch.*

1509 FISHER *Funeral Serm. C'tess Richmond* Wks. (1876) 307 Veray suerte can not be had but only by the reuelacyon of god almighty. **1577** *St. Aug. Manual* (Longman) 29 So as I might reioice in suretie of the incorruptiblenesse of the everlastyng immortalitie. **1870** RUSKIN *Lect. Art* iii. (1875) 81 Doing what the hand finds to do, in surety that.. whatsoever is right the Master will give.

4. †**a.** Certainty of an end or result aimed at; certainty of obtaining something. *for surety* (*of*), in order to make sure (of) or ensure. *Obs.*

1387–8 T. USK *Test. Love* I. v. (Skeat) l. 9 Acrisius shette Dane his doughter in a tour, for suertee that no wight shulde of her have no maistry. **1454** *Rolls of Parlt.* V. 263/2 If he .. myght be putte in suerte of payment therof. **1509–10** *Act 1 Hen. VIII,* c. 16 Preamble, Divers actis of Parliament have been made for suerty of Payment of the expensez. **1526** *Pilgr. Perf.* (W. de W. 1531) 26 Whiche putteth hym in surety of as moche lawfull money to be delyuered to hym in an other countre. **1607** MARKHAM *Caval.* II. xiv. 139 You must obserue that his head and necke stand streight ..for suretie wherof you shal euer carry the outmost reine euer a litle straiter then the inmoste.

†**b.** Certainty of a fact or event. *Obs.*

1412–20 LYDG. *Chron. Troy* II. 2253 It is wel bet by-tymes to abstene þan put in doute þat stant in surete. *c* **1449** PECOCK *Repr.* I. xiv. 78 Probabilite a this side suerte [i.e. short of certainty]. **1594** PLAT *Jewell-ho.* II. 5 For the most parte you shall have all the oiles of your hearbs ..to ascend with the first pottle of water, neverthelesse for the more surety you may draw of a gallon, and prove what you can gather out of the last pottle. **1604** SHAKS. *Oth.* I. iii. 396, I know not if 't be true, But I .. Will do, as if for Surety.

c. A certainty, fact: esp. in phr. *for* or *of a surety* = for certain. *arch.*

c **1460** SIR R. ROS *La Belle Dame* 675 But þis is the seurte, I must suffre, which way þat euer hit go! *c* **1475** *Harl. Contin. Higden* (Rolls) VIII. 446 A man wolde have thouȝhte as for a suerte that he scholde have spedde welle. **1523** LD. BERNERS *Froiss.* I. clvii. 190 The kyng ..rode to Charters to have the better of surety what thenglysshmen dyd. **1535** COVERDALE *Gen.* xv. 13 Knowe this of a suertye, that thy sede shalbe a straunger, in a londe that is not theirs. **1598** R. BERNARD tr. *Terence, Andria* Argt. 2 As soone as hee knewe for a suretie his loue. **1816** SCOTT *Old Mort.* xxx, He was of a surety lawfully redeemed from death. **1886** STEVENSON *Kidnapped* i, 'Nay,' said Mr. Campbell, 'who can tell that for a surety?'

II. Means of being sure. (See also 1 c.)

5. A formal engagement entered into, a pledge, bond, guarantee, or security given for the fulfilment of an undertaking. Chiefly in phr. *to do, make, find, give, put in, take surety* or *sureties*; *in, to, under, upon surety.* Now superseded by SECURITY 8.

13.. *Sir Beues* (A.) 73 Maseger, do me surte þat þow nelt nouȝt discure me To no wiȝt. *c* **1386** CHAUCER *Knt.'s T.* 746, I defye the seurete and the bond Which that thou seist þat I haue maad to thee. —— *Man of Law's T.* 145 He shal han Custance in mariage, And certein gold,.. And heer to founden sufficient suretee. —— *Wife's T.* 55 And suretee wel I han er þat thou pace Thy body for to yelden in this place. —— *Frankl. T.* 853 But wolde ye vouche sauf vp on seuretee Two yeer or thre for to respiten me. *c* **1400** *Destr. Troy* 11494 Þai depely desyret.. To haue suertie full sad of a syker pes. **1424** *Cov. Leet Bk.* 83 The Costis that John Leeder spendithe ..in getyng Suertie of C li. þat was lent vnto kyng Henry the vj^{te}. *c* **1440** *Engl. Conq. Irel.* 75 Thay toke Surtey, and othis Sware. **1447** *Rolls of Parlt.* V. 129/2 Money by hir receyved, and in suretees remaynyng in the kepyng of the saide Katerine. **1470–85** MALORY *Arthur* XV. ii. 557 Thenne was there pees betwyxe the Erle and this Aguarus, & grete seurte that the erle shold neuer werre ageynst hym. **1495** *Cov. Leet Bk.* 569 þat they be putte vnder suertie ..vnto such tyme þat þe Maire .. may be suerly acerteyned of their good behauyng. **1530–1** *Act 22 Hen. VIII,* c. 12 §3 He shall be kepte in the Stockes till he hathe founde suertie to goo to servyce or ellse to laboure. **1536** CROMWELL in Merriman *Life & Lett.* (1902) II. 7 Ye shall ..put hym to Sewrtye to appere before the kinges Cownsayle. **1588** SHAKS. *L.L.L.* II. i. 135 There remaines vnpaid A hundred thousand [crowns] more: in surety of the which, One part of Aquitaine is bound to vs. *a* **1628** F. GREVIL *Cœlica* lxxi, Find suerties, or at Honour's Sessions dye. **1632** LITHGOW *Trav.* VIII. 358 Hauing obtayned my pasport ..and surety taken for my life and moneyes. **1752** HUME *Ess. & Treat.* (1777) I. 338 A man may find surety nearly to the amount of his substance. **1762** —— *Hist. Eng.* I. viii. 282 He agreed to pay the sum; and immediately gave sureties for it. **1848** MRS. JAMESON *Sacr. & Leg. Art* (1850) 469 [He] prevailed upon the jailer by large bribes, and by giving sureties for his return, to permit him to visit his wife.

†**b.** A document embodying such an agreement or pledge. *Obs.*

1425 *Rolls of Parlt.* IV. 289/1 For as muche as the seurtees of yis said somme .. may not have beene engrossed. **1430–40** LYDG. *Bochas* I. vi. (MS. Bodl. 263) 23/2 Atween the which bi surete off hond In mariage there was maad a bond. *c* **1500** *Three Kings' Sons* 187 The trews was taken bytwene them .. and whan the surtees were made, sworne, and ensealed [etc.].

c. *surety of* (*the*) *peace*, a bond entered into for the maintenance of peace between parties; *spec.* in *Law*, a security entered into to the king by the offending party and taken by a justice for keeping the peace; so *surety for* (*the*) *good behaviour*: see quot. 1808.

c **1400** MAUNDEV. (Roxb.) xxxii. 145 He graunt þam suertee of peess. **1444** *Rolls of Parlt.* V. 110/1 Persons that be .. in thair Wardes by condempnation, execution,.. suertee of pees. **1479** in *10th Rep. Hist. MSS. Comm.* App. v. 313 What so ever parson ..be bounde in suertie of the peace. **1507** in Leadam *Sel. Cases Star Chamber* (Selden) 259 Suertie of peas was taken afore the Justice of peas .. ayenst John Sawyer. **1581** LAMBARDE *Eiren.* II. ii. (1588) 82, I will (at this day) call Suertie of the Peace, an acknowledging of a bond to the Prince, taken by a competent Iudge of Record, for the keeping of the Peace. **1769** BLACKSTONE *Comm.* IV. 252 Wherever any private man hath just cause to fear, that another will burn his house, or do him a corporal injury,.. he may demand surety of the peace against such person. **1808** HUTCHESON *Treat. Just. Peace Scot.* II. ii. §3. I. 391 Any justice of peace may command this surety of the peace, and grant his warrant for it upon the complaint of any person 'threatened, or fearing to be wronged'. *Ibid.* §4. 399 Surety for good behaviour, is a recognizance entered into to the king for being of good behaviour. The good behaviour including the peace, he that is bound to the former, is therein bound to the latter also.

6. *gen.* Ground of certainty or safety, guarantee: = SECURITY 7. Now *rare.*

c **1400** *Destr. Troy* 9241 Þou shall .. say hym vpon sewertie thy-seluyn with mouthe,.. I shall filsyn þis forward, in faith, þat I can. *c* **1500** *Lancelot* 2388 What suerte schal I have for to gone At libertee out of this danger free? *a* **1548** HALL *Chron., Edw. V,* 6 On the suretie of his owne conscience he determined to goo to them. **1556** *Aurelio & Isab.* (1608) D viij, The Quene with suche suerties and with many other thinges,.. withoute fearinge more daenger nor the deathe of hir doughter she confortede hir. **1667** MILTON *P.L.* v. 538 My self and all th' Angelic Host .. our happie state Hold, as you yours, while our obedience holds; On other surety none. **1838** LYTTON *Leila* II. i, Thou didst ask me for a surety of my faith. **1855** PRESCOTT *Philip II,* II. x. I. 254 Their character and position .. were sufficient sureties that they meditated no violence to the state.

7. A person who undertakes some specific responsibility on behalf of another who remains primarily liable; one who makes himself liable for the default or miscarriage of another, or for the performance of some act on his part (e.g. payment of a debt, appearance in court for trial, etc.); a bail: = SECURITY 9.

Formerly also applied collectively to a number of persons.

1428 in *Surtees Misc.* (1888) 3 Yt was awarded yat John Lyllyng suld fynd seurte of v^{c} marke ..and apon yis John Gascoigne and William Bedale become pleges and seurte for ye sayd John Lyllyng. **1451** *Paston Lett.* I. 194 He proferyd me suerte, men of the seid town of Routon. **1535** COVERDALE *Ecclus.* xxix. 14 A good honest man is suertye for his neghboure. **1538** in R. G. Marsden *Sel. Pleas Crt. Adm.* (Selden) II. 67 And for your more suertye I have geven youe for my soertye in this case William Parkar merchaunt. **1596** SHAKS. *Merch. V.* v. i. 254 Then you shall be his suretie. **1660** JER. TAYLOR *Duct. Dubit.* III. ii. rule 7. §2 Persons conjunct in Contract; such as are Pledges in War, Sureties for Debt, Undertakers for appearance, and the like. **1765** BLACKSTONE *Comm.* I. Introd. iv. 110 Ten freeholders .. were sureties or free pledges to the king for the good behaviour of each other. **1805** C. JAMES *Milit. Dict.* (ed. 2) s.v., Every paymaster in the British service is obliged to find two sureties, who bind themselves in given sums, for the security of monies entrusted to him by government. **1847** TENNYSON *Princess* v. 24 King, you are free! We did but keep you surety for our son. **1875** JOWETT *Plato* (ed. 2) V. 525 When a man becomes surety, let him give the security in a distinct form.

Comb. *c* **1600** SHAKS. *Sonn.* cxxxiv. 7 He learnd but suretie-like to write for me, Vnder that bond that him as fast doth binde.

b. A sponsor at baptism. *Obs.* or *arch.*

1548–9 (Mar.) *Bk. Com. Prayer, Public Baptism,* These infantes muste ..promise by you, that be theyr suerties. **1575** *Reg. St. Olave's Ch., Hart St.* 14 Apr., Baptism of Henry Deaveraux third Sonne to the Earle of Essex... The Earle of Northumberland and the Lord Burrowes and the Lady Rich weare Sewerties. **1704** NELSON *Fest. & Fasts* ix. (1739) 585 Those who promised by their Sureties in Baptism do renew ..that Contract. **1803** GILPIN *Serm.* III. xxiii. 259 You know ..how many come as sureties for children, who are themselves .. ignorant of all the duties of religion.

c. *fig.* Applied to Christ (after Heb. vii. 22).

[**1535** COVERDALE *Ps.* cxviii[i]. 122 Be thou suertie for thy seruaunt to do him good, that the proude do me no wronge.] **1557** *N.T.* (Genev.) Heb. vii. 22 By so muche is Iesus made a suretie of a better Couenant. **1709** WATTS *Hymns* I. cl. 7 To this dear Surety's Hand Will I commit my Cause. **1781** COWPER *Convers.* 506 Soon after He that was our Surety died. **1869** SPURGEON *Treas. David* Ps. xv. 4 Our blessed Surety swore to his own hurt, but how gloriously he stood to his suretyship.

attrib. **1645** RUTHERFORD *Tryal & Tri. Faith* (1845) 235 It is only the cautionary, the surety-righteousness of Christ-God, that is made ours. **1782** J. BROWN *Nat. & Rev. Relig.* III. ii. (1796) 222 What .. reward of his surety-service, Christ should have from God the Father. **1868** H. LAW *Beacons of Bible* 77 The sin-bearer, and His surety-agony.

†**d.** phr. *to call to surety.*

1601 SHAKS. *All's Well* v. iii. 108 She call'd the Saints to suretie, That [etc.].

Hence †**surety** *v. trans.*, to be surety for.

1601 SHAKS. *All's Well* v. iii. 298 Good mother fetch my bayle. Stay Royall sir, The Ieweller that owes the Ring is sent for, And he shall surety me. **1607** —— *Cor.* III. i. 178 Wee'l Surety him.

suretyship ('ʃʊətɪʃɪp, 'ʃʊərɪtɪʃɪp). Forms: see prec.: also 6 **suertishipe, -shyp, surtishipp, suretishippe,** 7–9 **suretiship**. [f. prec. sb. + -SHIP.] The position or function of a surety (see prec. 7); responsibility or obligation undertaken by one person on behalf of another, as for payment of a debt, performance of some act, etc.

1535 COVERDALE *Prov.* xi. 15 He that is suertye for a straunger, hurteth himself: but he that medleth not with suerteshippe, is sure. **1562** *Act 5 Eliz.* c. 21 §5 To releas .. the said suertieshippe of good Abearing. **1612** W. PARKES *Curtaine-Dr.* To Rdr. (1876) 4 Beware of Suretiship. **1659** *Gentl. Calling* (1696) 103 To rook him at Play, entangle him in Suretiship. **1745** *De Foe's Eng. Tradesman* xi. (1841) I. 86 Suretiship for the debt. **1762** STERNE *Tr. Shandy* V. i, A poor man undone by shipwreck, by suretyship, by fire. **1870** BURTON *Hist. Scot.* liii. (1873) V. 6 The regent was not satisfied with this suretiship. **1880** *Encycl. Brit.* XIII. 161/2 Private suretyship is attended by many evils.

b. Said of Christ.

1642 T. GOODWIN *Christ set forth* 148 He is not quit of this Surety-ship and engagement. **1681–6** J. SCOTT *Chr. Life* II. vii. §6 Wks. 1718 I. 420 We have not only God's Word, but also the Suretyship of our Saviour to depend on.

ˌsurexci'tation (sɜːr-). [ad. F. *surexcitation*: see SUR- and EXCITATION.] Excessive excitation.

1873 MORLEY *Rousseau* I. vii. 279 The product of intellectual sur-excitation. **1880** EARL OF DUFFERIN in *Times* (1881) 4 Jan. 4/5 Had the Government been supported by a united public opinion in Great Britain, the present surexcitation in Ireland could never have been generated. **1896** *Pop. Sci. Monthly* Apr. 779 A surexcitation of the kidneys.

So **surex'cited** *a.*, over-excited.

1864 MEREDITH *Emilia* l, Sur-excited Sentiment. **1885** —— *Diana* xi, In a sharp-strung mood, bitterly surexcited.

surf (sɜːf), *sb.* Also 8 **surff**. [Continues SUFF *sb.* in chronology and meaning, but the relation between the forms is not clear. (Not in general Dicts. before Todd, 1818.)

Both *suff* and *surf* are used particularly in reference to the coast of India, a circumstance which makes a native origin for the words probable.]

1. a. The swell of the sea which breaks upon a shore, esp. a shallow shore. (In recent use usually with implication of sense 2.)

1685 W. HEDGES *Diary* (Hakl. Soc.) I. 182 [At Fort St. George, Madras] This unhappy accident, together with ye greatness of ye Sea and Surf ashore, caused us to come aboard again. **1719** DE FOE *Crusoe* I. (Globe) 50 My Raft was now strong enough to bear any reasonable Weight; my next Care was .. how to preserve what I laid upon it from the Surf of the Sea. **1745** P. THOMAS *Jrnl. Anson's Voy.* 35 The Landing is bad by reason of pretty much Surf, and great Stones like Rocks. **1774** GOLDSM. *Nat. Hist.* (1862) I. xvii. 97 This rising of the waves against the shore, is called by mariners the surf of the sea. **1783** W. MARSDEN *Hist. Sumatra* (1811) 34 The surf..is used in India, and by navigators in general, to express a peculiar swell and breaking of the sea upon the shore. **1836** W. Irving *Astoria* II. 100 Low bellowings..like the hoarse murmurs of the surf on a distant shore. **1840** E. E. Napier *Scenes & Sports For. Lands* I. p. xii, The progress of the neophyte..in that far land, from the moment when having crossed the 'surf'. [*Note.* An expression equivalent to entering or leaving India, as a person is never supposed to venture across this tremendous barrier of the Coromandel coast, unless on such momentous occasions.] **1886** Ruskin *Præterita* I. 379 Half-a-mile of dangerous surf between the ship and the shore. **1906** Max Pemberton *My Sword for Lafayette* xxiv, The distant thunder of the sea surf upon an angry shore.

b. with *a*. Also *transf.* (in first quot.).

1698 Fryer *Acc. E. India & P.* 14 A notable Fish..It might be in length forty Feet.. bolting out of the Water with a great Surf. **1748** *Anson's Voy.* II. ii. 134 The wind.. occasioned such a surf, that it was impossible for the boat to land. **1763** Thompson *Temple of Venus* i. 14 A dull promiscuous sound a-far..like..southern surffs upon an iron shore. **1803** Wittman *Trav. Turkey* 3 A military artificer was unfortunately washed off the vessel by a surf. **1840** Macaulay *Ess., Clive* ¶8 Fort St. George had arisen on a barren spot beaten by a raging surf. **1879** *A. R. Wallace's Australasia* xvi. 303 The southern coast..is exposed to a heavy and dangerous surf, which rolls in upon the shore at all seasons.

2. a. The mass or line of white foamy water caused by the sea breaking upon a shore or a rock.

1757 tr. *Keysler's Trav.* IV. 141 *note*, Salt..was not produced here as in other countries by a desiccation of the surf of the sea [tr. Tacitus *Ann.* XIII. lvii. *non ut alias apud gentis eluvie maris arescente unda*]. **1784** Cowper *Task* VI. 155 Light as the foamy surf That the wind severs from the broken wave. **1833** Tennyson *Dream Fair Wom.* viii, White surf wind-scatter'd over sails and masts. **1882** 'Ouida' *Maremma* I. 78 She played with the sails, with the surf, and with the crystals of the salt.

b. *transf.* and *fig.*

1847 Longf. *Ev.* II. iii. 24 Just where the woodlands met the flowery surf of the prairie. **1873** Lowell *Above & Below* II. i, To behold The first long surf of climbing light Flood all the thirsty east with gold.

3. *attrib.* and *Comb.*: Simple attrib., 'of or pertaining to surf', as ***surf barrier***, ***-beach***, ***-beat***, ***-billow***, ***line***, ***-rock***, ***-sound***, ***-thunder***; locative, as ***surf-bathe*** vb., ***-bather***, ***-bathing***, ***-fish*** vb., ***-fisherman***, ***-fishing***, ***lifesaver***, ***lifesaving***, ***-rider***, ***-riding***, ***-swimmer***, ***-swimming***; ***surf-sunk*** adj.; instrumental, as ***surf-battered***, ***-beaten***, ***-bound***, ***-showered***, ***-tormented***, ***-vexed***, ***-washed***, ***-wasted***, ***-worn*** adjs.; similative, as ***surf-white*** adj.; also **surf-bird**, a small, plover-like bird, *Aphriza virgata*, found on the Pacific coast of America; **surfboard**, a long narrow board on which one rides over a heavy surf to shore; hence as *v. intr.*, to ride on a surfboard (also *fig.*); **surfboarder**, **surfboarding** *vbl. sb.*; **surf-boat**, a boat specially constructed for passing through surf; hence **surf-boatman** = *surfman*; **surf-bum** *slang*, a surfing enthusiast who frequents beaches suitable for surf-riding; cf. *ski bum* s.v. SKI *sb.* 2 b; **surf-casting** *vbl. sb.*, fishing by casting a line into the sea from the shore; so (as a back-formation) **surf-cast** *v. intr.*, **surf-caster**; **surf-clam**, a large clam, esp. *Mactra* (or *Spisula*) *solidissima*, found on the Atlantic coast of the United States (*Funk's Standard Dict.* 1895); **surf-coot** = *surf-duck*; **surf day**, a day marked by rough surf along the shore (see quot. 1854); **surf-duck**, a North American species of sea-duck of the genus *Œdemia*, esp. *O. perspicillata*, found sometimes in Great Britain; **surf-fish**, any one of the numerous species of the family *Embiotocidæ*, abundant on the coast of California; **surf-grass**, any of several species of marine grass of the genus *Phyllospadix* (family Zosteraceæ), having thickened rootstocks and slender stems and growing underwater on rocky shores in temperate regions; **surf-man** *U.S.*, a member of the crew of a surf-boat; hence **surfmanship**; **surf music**, a variety of rock music which celebrates the sport of surf-riding; **surf-perch** = *surf-fish*; **surf-ride** *v. intr.* [back-formation from *surf-riding* above] = *surfboard* vb. above; also *fig.* and as *v. trans.* and *sb.*; **surf safari** = SURFARI; **surf-scoter** = *surf-duck*; **surf-shiner**, a small California fish, *Cymatogaster aggregatus* (Webster 1911); **surf-smelt**, a species of smelt, *Hypomesus olidus*, found on the Pacific coast of the United States; **surf-whiting**, the silver whiting, *Menticirrus littoralis*.

1940 V. Brittain *Testament of Friendship* xii. 192 You'll look at the Rhodes Memorial and the Union Buildings..; you'll..*surf-bathe at Durban.., and then you'll begin to think you know everything. **1893** Kate Sanborn *S. California* 163 *Surf bathers go in every month of the year. **1884** *Encycl. Brit.* XVII. 461/1 Conveniences for *surf-bathing. **1902** *Temple Bar* May 579 Like *surf-battered swimmers. **1932** N. Palmer *Talking it Over* 137 *Surf-beaches of any size are rare in the world. **1966** *Weekly News* (N.Z.) 19 Jan. 11/1 Mt. Maunganui is probably one of New Zealand's best-known surf beaches. **1977** *Herald* (Melbourne) 17 Jan. 14/4 Within 16 km of Wollongong are 17 superb surf beaches. **1873** 'Mark Twain' *Gilded Age* lx. 543 A receding of tides, a quieting of the storm-wash to a murmurous *surf-beat. **1974** *Encycl. Brit. Micropædia* IX. 689/2 Surf beat, ocean waves of uncertain origin, with the relatively long periods of 1 to 5 minutes. These low-frequency waves appear to be related to the interaction of normal wind waves and swell. Surf beat is believed responsible for the generation of seiches in bays. **1801** Campbell *Lochiel's Warning* 82 Like ocean-weeds heaped on the *surf-beaten shore. **1890** 'R. Boldrewood' *Col. Reformer* (1891) 154 The deep-toned ceaseless roll of the *surf-billows. **1872** Coues *N. Amer. Birds* 245 *Aphriza*, *Surf Bird. *c* **1826** Richards in Gosse *Ocean* vi. (1849) 285 Those who were standing on the beach saw the *surf-board ..floating on the water. **1931** T. E. Lawrence *Let.* 14 July (1938) 729 Here is a final report..on the little surf-board target. **1934** Webster, *Surfboard, v.i.*, to ride the surf on a surfboard.—*surfboarding, n.* **1938** E. Hemingway *Fifth Column* (1939) III. iv. 103 Or what about Malindi where you can surfboard on the beach. **1962** *Coast to Coast 1961–62* 63 He wished he could stand up and walk away from Pammie and go out with the surf-board riders. **1962** M. McLuhan *Gutenberg Galaxy* 248 (*heading*) Heidegger surf-boards along on the electronic wave as triumphantly as Descartes rode the mechanical wave. **1953** *Pop. Mechanics* July 157 Hitching a ride on a beach-bound ocean wave with a featherlight surf-board is rated tops in water sports by practiced *surf-boarders. **1969** *Britannica Bk. of Year 1968* 801/1 *Surfari*, a group of surfboarders who travel together in search of good surfing areas. **1964** *Sunday Mail Mag.* (Brisbane) 17 May 1 *Surfboarding was virtually forgotten until the late 1930's. **1856** Dickens *Wreck Golden Mary* (1898) 22, I gave..the word to lower the Long-boat and the *Surf-boat. **1883** J. D. Campbell *Fisheries China* 5 (Fish. Exhib. Publ.) The catamarans or surf-boats of South Formosa. **1886** *Encycl. Brit.* XXI. 804/2 The Madras surf boats. **1880** *Scribner's Mag.* Jan. 323 It is an erroneous notion that the experience of the sailor qualifies him for a *surf-boatman. **1884** *19th Cent.* Feb. 239 The noisy tumult of a *surf-bound shore. **1958** *Surf-bum [see PETITE *a.* 2]. **1971** Surf-bum [see PIPE-LINE *sb.* c]. **1975** *Country Life* 16 Jan. 131/2 *Surf-cast for corvina..on a California beach and you will probably have to show your California fishing licence. **1968** 'S. Jay' *Sleepers can Kill* xxiv. 248 When you've walked through to the beach, you'll see a *surfcaster, fishing by himself. **1928** *N.Y. Times* 8 Oct. 21/4 Charles Vollum of Philadelphia became *surf casting champion of the United States today at the annual tournament of the Dover Fishing Club of Philadelphia. **1963** *Weekly News* (Auckland, N.Z.) 8 May 56/6 Pukehina surfcasting beach. Near Te Puke, Bay of Plenty, one of the best surfcasting beaches in New Zealand. **1979** *Angling* July 45/3 As a contemporary guide to the basics of general shorefishing it gives excellent surfcasting instruction. **1884** *Bull. U.S. Nat. Museum* No. 27. 260 Hen Clam, *Surf Clam, or Sea Clam. Florida and Gulf of Mexico to Labrador. **1949** [see SKIMMER *sb.* 1 c]. **1978** *Times* 29 July 3/6 More than two weeks after the wreck..we saw millions of dead molluscs, urchins, razor and surf clams. **1885** Seebohm *Brit. Birds* III. 610 To the hunters on Long Island it [the Surf-scoter] is known as the 'Spectacled Coot' and '*Surf-Coot'. **1854** G. W. Peck *Melbourne & Chincha Islands* 187 Often when the mornings are still, and the surface of the sea undisturbed by a ripple, the surf will be rolling tremendously on the narrow beaches. .. These are called '*surf-days', and special allowance is made for them in the charter parties of vessels loading at the islands. **1950** J. S. Learmont *Master in Sail* 60 Surf days did not count as working days. These surf days are peculiar to the northern part of the coast of Chile. **1808–13** A. Wilson & Bonaparte *Amer. Ornith.* (1832) III. 70 Black, or *Surf Duck, *Anas perspicillata*... This duck is peculiar to America, and..confined to the shores and bays of the sea. **1882** Jordan & Gilbert *Fishes N. Amer.* 585 Embiotocidæ. The *Surf-fishes... Fishes of the Pacific coast of North America, inhabiting bays and the surf on sandy beaches. **1940** O. H. P. Rodman *Handbk. Salt-Water Fishing* iii. 99 We will make a definite statement in regard to wetting down your cutty hunk line before you really start surf fishing. **1979** 'A. Blaisdell' *No Villain need Be* vii. 120 They like to surf-fish, and they claim rain.. drives 'em in toward the beach. **1920** Heilner & Stick *Call of Surf* i. 5 Those great and goodly fish which so frequently take into their capacious jaws the bait of the *surf fisherman. **1967** O. E. Middleton in *Coast to Coast 1965–66* 123 The surf-fishermen leaned out over the shallows. **1920** Heilner & Stick *Call of Surf* i. 4 *Surf fishing is by no means a new development of the angler's art..but only of late years has it begun to achieve real popularity. **1949** S. K. Farrington *Fishing the Atlantic* iv. 82 Surf fishing at Narragansett should be a revelation. **1923** L. Abrams *Illustr. Flora Pacific States* I. 94 *Phyllospadix torreyi* S. Wats. Torrey's *Surf-grass. **1981** *Sci. Amer.* Mar. 92/1 The sea grasses number 12 genera and ..about 50 species... Eelgrass and surfgrass are familiar examples in temperate regions. **1977** *N.Z. Herald* 8 Jan. 1–6/4, I have been talking to the wife of a *surf lifesaver, and she spoke of the apparent indifference people show on being saved from drowning. **1968** W. Warwick *Surfriding in N.Z.* 1 It is difficult to imagine how closely it was once associated with the *surf lifesaving movement. **1887** O. J. Humphrey *Wreck of Rainier* 33 When the *surf line was hauled tight the boat would run on the line and be kept head to the sea. **1923** H. Belloc *Sonnets & Verse* I. 28 Above the surf-line, into the night-breeze; Eastward above the ever-whispering trees. **1965** P. L. Dixon *Compl. Bk. Surfing* 142 If the dory broaches in the surf line and turns over, bail out and get clear of oars and falling boat. **1880** *Scribner's Mag.* Jan. 322/2 The keeper [of the surf-boat] commands the crew of six *surfmen. *Ibid.* 334 Until 1871..*surfmanship was not a standard of qualification. **1965** *N.Z. Listener* 17 Dec. 4/1 The million-dollar industry of *surf music, surf movies and surf-wear. **1977** *Sounds* 9 July 28/2 The Turtles started out playing surf music at High School hops in LA. **1889** *Amer. Naturalist* Oct. 923 *Micrometrus aggregatus*, one of the viviparous *surf-perches. **1953** 'S. Rattray' *Bishop in Check* 101 One-half per cent of them play tennis—or swim, or *surf-ride. **1958** *Listener* 2 Oct. 494/1 This motorization wave is not something on which the rich alone can surf-ride. **1973** *Times* 1 June (Australia Suppl.) p. i/3 The Whitlam Government has been in office just six months tomorrow. For the Prime Minister it has been 'a surf ride so far'. **1976** *National Observer* (U.S.) 19 June 1/3 Now, surf-riding his victory in the California Presidential primary last week, he's racing to a showdown with Gerald Ford. **1882** *Hawaiian Almanac* 52 At one time they sent their champion *surf-rider to compete with chiefs in the sport at Hawaii. **1981** L. Leamer *Assignment* iii. 43 They take this drug. They have learned this from these hippie surf-riders. **1882** *Hawaiian Almanac* 52 Among the various sports and pastimes of the ancient Hawaiians..the principal one..is that of surf-bathing, or more properly speaking, *surf-riding. **1898** Jean A. Owen *Hawaii* iii. 81 Surf-riding on boards is still much practised. **1800** Coleridge *Piccolom.* I. xii, The *surf rocks of the Baltic. **1962** *Austral. Women's Weekly* 24 Oct. (Suppl.) 3/4 **Surf safari*, a trip around different beaches to find a good surf. **1835** Jenyns *Man. Brit. Vertebr. Anim.* 240 *O*[*idemia*] *perspicillata*, Steph. (*Surf Scoter.) **1882** Jordan & Gilbert *Fishes N. Amer.* 294 Hypomesus, Gill. *Surf Smelts... H[ypomesus] pretiosus... Surf Smelt... Pacific coast, from California northward; abundant, spawning in the surf. **1828** Campbell *Death-boat Heligoland* 22 Now *surf-sunk for minutes, again they uptossed. **1845** Gosse *Ocean* vi. (1849) 283 The cry of 'A Shark!' among the *surf swimmers will instantly set them in the utmost terror. **1858** R. M. Ballantyne *Coral Island* xxv. 305 'What sort of amusement is this *surf swimming?'.. 'Each man..has got a short board or plank, with which he swims a mile or more to Sea, and then, gettin' on the top o' yon thunderin' breaker, they come to shore on the top of it.' **1890** 'R. Boldrewood' *Col. Reformer* (1891) 150 The wind is..from the south, we shall have the *surf-thunder in perfection. **1829** Poe *Dream within a Dream* ii, I stand amid the roar Of a *surf-tormented shore. **1852** Mundy *Antipodes* (1857) 24 Green turfy knolls sloping abruptly to the *surf-vexed beach. **1861** L. L. Noble *Icebergs* 180 The bleak, *surf-washed rocks. **1854** H. Miller *Sch. & Schm.* xxiv. (1858) 532 The picturesque *surf-wasted stacks of the granitic wall of rock. **1897** Mary Kingsley *W. Africa* 391 The young women..with their soft dusky skins,..pretty brown eyes, and *surf-white teeth. **1882** Jordan & Gilbert *Fishes N. Amer.* 933 M[enticirrus] littoralis... *Surf Whiting... South Atlantic and Gulf coast. **1878** Geikie *Geol. Sketches* ii. (1882) 34 Weather-beaten or *surf-worn sheets of rock.

surf (sɜːf), *v.* [f. the sb.] **1.** *intr.* To form surf. *rare.*

1831 J. Wilson in *Blackw. Mag.* XXIX. 141 The breakers surfing on a lee-shore. **1832** *Ibid.* XXXII. 131.

2. To go surf-riding; to surf-ride. Also *transf.* and *fig.*

1917 *Chambers's Jrnl.* Apr. 280/2 The depth of the lagoon is trifling.., and this it is which makes surfing there so safe and enjoyable. **1932** *Ibid.* Aug. 462/2, I had snaps, too, of the children, riding or surfing, and of the whole family in their ocean-going yacht. *a* **1957** R. Campbell *Coll. Poems* (1960) III. 83 Over its surge in red tornadoes rolling My heart goes surfing on the waves of fire. **1965** *N.Z. Listener* 17 Dec. 4/5 Once a person is bitten by this surfing bug he seems to become insatiable. He surfs every day he can, the whole year round. **1970** *Motor Boat & Yachting* 16 Oct. 29/1 *La Russhe* surfed handsomely down the backs of the heavy swell and buried herself into the short steep seas on the way. **1976** M. Birmingham *Heat of Sun* iv. 51 Biriwa has..a comparatively safe beach..where you can surf when the tide is right.

3. *trans.* **a.** To ride (a boat) on the surf. **b.** To surf-ride at (a specified place).

1965 P. L. Dixon *Compl. Bk. Surfing* 18 Dories, canoes, sailing catamarans, and a few special motorboats can be surfed by experts. Where waves break far from shore and spill gradually forward. **1967** W. Murray *Sweet Ride* vi. 85 Ten years ago..no one surfed this place but him. **1968** *Surfer Mag.* Jan. 56/1 Paulo surfed a beach break off the famous Rio Copacabana called Posto Six Pier.

Hence ˈ**surfing** *vbl. sb.*, surf-riding, surfboarding.

1955 A. Ross *Australia 55* xv. 214 The essential art of surfing is timing. **1959** H. Hobson *Mission House Murder* xviii. 119 When they'd had enough surfing, they brought the boards back up the beach. **1963** *Wall St. Jrnl.* 22 July 1 Surfin' music is characterized by a heavy echo guitar sound, supposed to simulate the roar of the surf. **1971** 'D. Halliday' *Dolly & Doctor Bird* i. 2 Skin diving, rum punches, calypso night-clubs, surfing, dancing, gambling.

surf, var. *suff*, SOUGH *sb.*[2], SOUGH *v.*[2]

1794 *Trans. Soc. Arts* XII. 237 Length of the drains, three hundred and ten yards,..the whole surfed with stone.

surface (ˈsɜːfəs), *sb.* [ad. F. *surface* (from 16th c.), f. *sur-* SUR- + *face* FACE *sb.*, after L. *superficiēs*: cf. obs. Sp. *sobrehaz*, Sp. *sobrefaz*, Pg. *sobreface*, and SUPERFICE, SUPERFICIE, SUPERFICIES.]

1. a. The outermost boundary (or one of the boundaries) of any material body, immediately adjacent to the air or empty space, or to another body.

1611 Cotgr., *Surface*, the surface; the superficies or vpper part. **1662** Evelyn *Sculptura* II. (1906) 8 The Rollers doe universally touch the imediate surfaces of the Table. **1715** tr. *Gregory's Astron.* (1726) I. 158 If the contiguous Surfaces were perfectly smooth, there would be no impression of the Bodies upon one another. **1800** tr. *Lagrange's Chem.* II. 16 The matter must be calcined till it becomes of an orange yellow colour at the surface. **1831** Brewster *Optics* iv. 27 An optical prism..is a solid having two plane surfaces..which are called its refracting surfaces. **1889** Welch *Text Bk. Naval Archit.* i. 5 The submerged part of a vessel at rest in still water is subjected to fluid pressure, which acts, at each point, in a direction perpendicular to the surface of the ship at that point.

b. *fig.*, usually denoting that part or aspect of anything which presents itself to a slight or casual mental view, or which is perceived without examination; outward appearance; often in such phrases as ***on the surface*** = superficial(ly. Also, ***to scratch the surface*** (*of*): see SCRATCH *v.* 3 a.

1725 Watts *Logic* I. v, There are some Persons who never arrive at any deep..Knowledge..because they are perpetually fluttering over the Surface of Things. **1781** COWPER *Ep. Lady Austen* 8 Prose answers.. all the floating thoughts we find Upon the surface of the mind. **1847** TENNYSON *Princess* IV. 234 These flashes on the surface are not he. **1855** PALEY *Æschylus* Pref. (1861) p. xiii, In such passages.. there is.. scarcely a word that does not involve.. a meaning that lies below the surface. **1871** FREEMAN *Norm. Conq.* IV. xvii. 75 They may have seen through the real motives of the invitation, but on the surface everything was.. honourable. **1888** BURGON *Lives 12 Gd. Men* II. v. 2 No name more readily rose to the surface of conversation than his.

2. *Geom.* A magnitude or continuous extent having only two dimensions (length and breadth, without thickness), such as constitutes the boundary of a material body (sense 1) or that between two adjacent portions of space; a superficies.

1658 PHILLIPS, *Surface*, the same as *Superficies*. **1704** J. HARRIS *Lex. Techn.* I. s.v., There are Plane Surfaces, and there are Crooked or Curved ones. **1830** KATER & LARDNER *Mech.* i. 4 The external limits of the magnitude of a body are lines and surfaces. **1842** *Penny Cycl.* XXIII. 303/2 *Surfaces of the second degree.* This name is given to all those surfaces of which the equation is of the second degree. **1869** RANKINE *Machinery & Millwork* 569 A ruled surface is one in which every point is traversed by a straight line lying wholly in the surface. **1887** CAYLEY in *Encycl. Brit.* XXII. 668/1 A surface may be regarded as the locus of a doubly infinite system of points.

3. a. The outermost part of a material body, considered with respect to its form, texture, or extent; the uppermost layer; *esp.* in art or manufacture, an exterior of a particular form or 'finish'.

1698 KEILL *Exam. Th. Earth* (1734) 119 It is plain that but one half of the Rays which fall upon the first Surface, would fall upon the second, but one fourth of them upon the third. **1800** tr. *Lagrange's Chem.* II. 408 It.. forms the external coating of calculi, and may be distinguished by its unequal surface. **1831** BREWSTER *Optics* iv. 35 Then R b will be the ray as refracted by the first surface of the sphere. **1846** ELLIS *Elgin Marb.* II. 76 A thin surface has been carried away from the whole bas-relief. **1873** E. SPON *Workshop Receipts* Ser. I. 2/1 Take the surface off the paper with fine glass-paper. **1879** *Cassell's Techn. Educ.* II. 122 Such matt or dead surfaces. **1880** *Academy* 23 Oct. 299 We find in the work of this artist a finish and a perfection of surface rare [etc.].

b. *spec.* The upper boundary or top of ground or soil, exposed to the air (in *Mining*, as distinct from underground workings and shafts); the outer (according to ancient ideas, the upper) boundary of the earth.

1612 DRAYTON *Poly-olb.* ix. 140 With sterne Eolus blasts, ..Shee onely ouer-swells the surface of her bank. **1629** MILTON *Hymn Nativ.* xvii, The aged Earth agast.. Shall from the surface to the center shake. **1697** DRYDEN *Virg. Georg.* IV. 182 Cucumers along the Surface creep. **1719** in *10th Rep. Hist. MSS. Comm.* App. I. 197 The surface of the quarry. **1796** W. H. MARSHALL *Rural Econ. W. Eng.* II. 4 The surface is exceedingly broken, into sharp ridges. **1832** DE LA BECHE *Geol. Man.* (ed. 2) 9 If waters descend from the surface into a mine. **1868** LOCKYER *Elem. Astron.* ix. §50. (1879) 313 On the Earth's surface, *i.e.* at 4,000 miles from its centre. **1878** *Argosy* XXV. 430 We parted at surface—he went down the shaft.

c. The upper boundary or top of a body of water or other liquid.

1625 N. CARPENTER *Geogr. Delin.* I. ii. (1635) 40 Euery surface of the water is either only plaine, or only round. **1641** J. JACKSON *True Evang. T.* III. 209 Two pots floting upon a pond, or surface of a water with this word, 'If we knock together, we sink together.' *a* **1700** EVELYN *Diary* 8 Feb. 1645, The water of it is fresh and swete on the surface, but salt at botome. **1781** COWPER *Hope* 184 The wat'ry stores that sleep Beneath the smiling surface of the deep. **1835** MARRYAT *Jacob Faithful* xxxix, Tom.. dived after me, brought me up again to the surface. **1858** LARDNER *Hand-bk. Nat. Phil.* 26 When a liquid contained in any vessel is in a state of rest, its surface will be horizontal. **1877** HUXLEY *Physiogr.* 69 The vapour is derived only from the exposed surface of the liquid.

d. The outside of an animal or plant body, or of any part of it; the outer boundary of the integument; also, the inner boundary of a hollow or tubular part.

1748 *Anson's Voy.* I. x. 101 Discoloured spots dispersed over the whole surface of the body. **1796** WITHERING *Brit. Plants* (ed. 3) III. 771 Polypodium. Capsules disposed in distinct circular dots on the under surface of the leaf. **1822–7** GOOD *Study Med.* (1829) V. 366 Diseases affecting internal surfaces. **1851** CARPENTER *Man. Phys.* (ed. 2) 198 The Teeth are formed.. upon the surface of the Mucous membrane of the mouth. **1861** BENTLEY *Man. Bot.* 290 The surface of the style may be either smooth, or covered in various ways with glands and hairs.

e. *Fortif.* (See quot.)

1702 *Milit. Dict.* (1704), *Surface*, is that part of the Exterior side, which is terminated by the Flank, prolong'd or extended, and the Angle of the nearest Bastion.

f. *Aeronautics.* An aerofoil, considered as something whose intended effects arise superficially.

1843 *Mechanics' Mag.* 8 Apr. 277/2 The main surfaces.. are here placed one above the other, and each pair are connected together by strong shafts. **1912** W. WRIGHT in C. C. Turner *Romance of Aeronautics* xvii. 178 A smaller surface set at a negative angle in front of the main bearing surfaces or wings will largely counteract the effect of the fore-and-aft travel of the centre of pressure. **1930** P. H. SUMNER *Marine Aircraft* ii. 104 The larger the aeroplane the larger the control surfaces become and the loads necessary to move elevators, rudder and ailerons may become too heavy for the pilot to operate their surfaces. **1974** *Encycl. Brit. Macropædia* I. 377/1 The essential components of an airplane are a wing system to sustain it in flight, tail surfaces to stabilize the wing, movable surfaces (ailerons, elevators, and rudders) to control the attitude of the machine in flight, [etc.].

g. ***surface-to-air, surface-to-surface*** adj. phrs., of, pertaining to, or designating a guided missile designed to be launched from the ground or at sea, and directed respectively at a target either in the air, or elsewhere on the earth's surface. Cf. *air-to-air* adj s.v. AIR *sb.*[1] B. III. 1; *ground-to-air*, *ground-to-ground* s.v. GROUND *sb.* 17 d; *SAM* s.v. S. 4 a.

1950 *Sun* (Baltimore) 7 Feb. 1/2 Research continues on these surface-to-air missiles. **1951** D. C. COOKE *Jets, Rockets & Guided Missiles* 146 This is a Surface-to-Surface Missile, Air Force, Third Model, Second Modification. **1954** *Jrnl. Brit. Interplanetary Soc.* XIII. 164 One of the first G.E.C. missiles, the Hermes A-1 is a development of the German Wasserfall in a surface-to-surface rôle. **1959** *Listener* 4 June 984/3 A British Thunderbird surface-to-air guided missile. **1962** *Times* 11 Aug. 6/1 The Government yesterday made their expected announcement that Blue Water, the surface-to-surface guided missile.. is to be cancelled. **1978** R. MCCUTCHAN *Blackmail North* vi. 69 Russia's been supplying Libya with a big range of surface-to-surface and surface-to-air missiles.

4. An extent or area of material considered as a subject for operations.

1662 EVELYN *Sculptura* I. v. (1906) 123 A much larger discourse.. treating of the practise of Perspective upon irregular Surfaces. **1718** *Free-thinker* No. 63. 52 The Canvass is no longer a level, Lifeless Surface. **1762–71** H. WALPOLE *Vertue's Anecd. Paint.* (1786) III. 59 His exuberant pencil was ready at pouring out gods, goddesses, [etc.] over those public surfaces on which the eye never rests long enough to criticize. **1867–72** BURGH *Mod. Marine Engin.* 360 To calculate the area of the frictional surfaces. **1869** RANKINE *Machinery & Millwork* 571 When the highest.. degree of accuracy is required in a plane surface, its form may.. be given approximately by the planing machine.

5. Superficial area or extent. †Also in fig. phr. (quot. *a* 1640).

a **1640** JACKSON *Creed* XI. iv. §15. (1657) 3341 This Doctrine is so necessarie for manifesting the just measure of their unthankfulnesse which perish, that without This we cannot take so much as a true Surface of it; not so much as the least Dimension of Sin. **1798** HUTTON *Course Math.* (1807) II. 51 To find the Solidity of a Sphere.. Multiply the surface by the diameter, and take ⅙ of the product for the content. **1825** J. NICHOLSON *Oper. Mech.* 706 To find the Surface of a Cylindrical Ring. **1871** C. DAVIES *Metric Syst.* I. 12 The unit of surface is a square whose side is ten metres. **1909** *Westm. Gaz.* 18 Mar. 4/1 After the 'pitch' [of a propeller] the most important detail of design is the 'surface,' which is usually taken to be the combined area of all the blades when laid out flat.

6. *attrib.* and *Comb.* **a.** *attrib.* in lit. sense, chiefly locative = pertaining to, existing or occurring on, the surface of something, as ***surface-action, -crevice, -crust, -deposit, -dressing, film*** (also *spec.* in sense (*b*)), ***friction, layer, -light, ornament, -temperature***, etc.; *spec.* (*a*) in reference to the surface of the ground (3 b), esp. in *Mining*, occurring, carried on, etc. at or near the surface, as ***surface break, cut, dirt, mine, mining, movement, ore, working, works*** (see also *surface-damage* in d); of persons, employed in, or in connexion with, work at the surface, as ***surface captain, hand, labourer, people***; also in various connexions (*Geol.*, *Agric.*, etc.), as ***surface bed, earth, exploration, find*** (both *Archæol.*), ***heat, manuring, mould, peat, product, production, sod, soil, spring, stone, trap, wind, worker***; (*b*) in reference to the surface of water or other fluid (3 c), as ***surface current, drift, energy, food, motion, ripple, towing*** (TOWING *vbl. sb.*[1]), ***velocity***.

1844 FOWNES *Man. Elem. Chem.* 104 Coal-gas.. may be made to exhibit the phenomenon of quiet oxidation under the influence of this remarkable *surface-action [of platinum, etc.]. **1879** *Encycl. Brit.* X. 240/1 Epigene or Surface Action—the changes produced on the superficial parts of the earth. **1850** ANSTED *Elem. Geol., Min.* etc. 582 *Surface beds and deposits. **1886** J. BARROWMAN *Sc. Mining Terms* 66 **Surface break*, the.. sinking of the strata reaching to the surface which is consequent on the working of coal by longwall. **1832** BABBAGE *Econ. Manuf.* xx. (ed. 3) 202 A *Surface-captain, with assistants, receives the ores raised. **1850** ANSTED *Elem. Geol., Min.* etc. 456 Rain, penetrating the minute *surface-crevices of an exposed rock. **1849** J. GRAY *Earth's Antiquity* ii. 53 The *surface-crust of the Earth. **1860** MAURY *Phys. Geog. Sea* (Low) viii. §391 A *surface current flows north from Behring's Strait into the Arctic Sea. **1867** SMYTH *Sailor's Word-bk.*, *Surface Current* ..Also, fresh water running over salt at the mouths of great rivers. **1877** RAYMOND *Statist. Mines & Mining* 215 Little work.. has been done except *surface-cuts and holes dug to trace the lode. **1858** HOBLYN *Dict. Terms Med.* (ed. 8), **Surface-deposit*, in Electro-plating. The operation of depositing a surface of gold or silver upon a foundation of cheaper metal. **1877** RAYMOND *Statist. Mines & Mining* 215 The *surface-dirt all contains gold.. but no rich silver-ore is found on the surface. **1812** SIR J. SINCLAIR *Syst. Husb. Scot.* I. 163 When dung is lodged near the surface, it promotes too rapid a vegetation in the foliage.. a circumstance that.. circumscribes *surface-dressing very much. **1880** A. R. WALLACE *Isl. Life* 279 Ocean-currents and *surface-drifts are.. efficient carriers of plants. **1664** EVELYN *Kal. Hort.* (1729) 204 Take off the *Surface-earth about an Inch or two deep. **1876** *Ibid.* V. 59/1 That part of the energy which depends on the area of the bounding surface of the liquid. We may call this the *surface energy. **1949** W. F. ALBRIGHT *Archaeol. of Palestine* iii. 49 The great increase of *surface exploration in Palestine in the middle decades of the nineteenth century. **1903** *Proc. R. Soc.* LXXII. 222 The influence of the stroking is therefore limited to a very thin *surface film. **1981** O. N. BISHOP *Physics* xvii. 161/2 The liquid closest to the surface of the object may show adhesion with it; there is often a surface film of liquid which is carried along with the object. **1917** *Surface find [see IROQUOIAN *a.* and *sb.*]. **1977** *Antiquaries Jrnl.* LVII. 324 The seal-matrices ..derive either from excavations or from surface-finds at known sites. **1847** STODDART *Angler's Comp.* 85 March-browns.. create, on their appearance, the earliest natural cravings in the fish for *surface food. **1846** HOLTZAPFFEL *Turning* II. 658 The *surface-friction against the thread of the screw. **1842** LOUDON *Suburban Hort.* 681 The roots of the celeriac may be taken up on the approach of frost, and preserved in sand or soil out of the reach of *surface-heat. **1838** *Jrnl. Statist. Soc.* June 73 *Surface Labourers.. £2. 6. 0. Per Month. **1875** DAWSON *Dawn of Life* iv. 85 To deposit the final *surface-layer of its shell. **1879** ROOD *Chromatics* vii. 79 In velvet the attempt is made to suppress all *surface-light, and to display only those rays which have penetrated deeply among the fibres, and have become highly coloured. **1887** MOLONEY *Forestry W. Afr.* 105 We find *surface-manuring best for the coffee-tree. **1877** RAYMOND *Statist. Mines & Mining* 124 The branches of Rock Creek.. have furnished paying *surface-mines. **1805** R. W. DICKSON *Pract. Agric.* II. 596 The harrow.. renders the baked *surface-mould fine and powdery. **1886** A. WINCHELL *Walks Geol. Field* 103 The *surface-movement of earthquake-waves. **1877** RAYMOND *Statist. Mines & Mining* 146 The *surface-ore was so favorable and the vein so perfect. *a* **1878** SIR G. SCOTT *Lect. Archit.* (1879) II. 86 Ornaments in very slight relief usually known as *surface ornaments. **1854** RONALDS & RICHARDSON *Chem. Technol.* (ed. 2) I. 23 Light spongy *surface-peat. **1839** DE LA BECHE *Rep. Geol. Cornwall*, etc. xv. 565 Two captains or agents, with a few miners and *surface-people. **1897** GEIKIE *Anc. Volcanoes Gt. Brit.* I. 27 The *surface-products of volcanic action. **1709** T. ROBINSON *Nat. Hist. Westmoreld.* vii. 48 The *Surface-Productions.. peculiar to the Mountains, Heaths, or Dales. **1877** HUXLEY *Physiogr.* I The *surface ripples raised by the passing breeze. **1805** R. W. DICKSON *Pract. Agric.* I. 160 The *surface sods should be carefully pared off. **1709** T. ROBINSON *Nat. Hist. Westmoreld.* xii. 70 The greatest Rains seldom moisten the Earth deeper than the *Surface-Soil. **1856** MORTON *Cycl. Agric.* II. 649 To unite the stirring of the subsoil with the turning of the surface soil. **1832** DE LA BECHE *Geol. Man.* (ed. 2) 13 The temperature of *surface-springs. **1851** MANTELL *Petrifactions* iii. §5. 289 Chiselling away the *surface stone. **1875** *Encycl. Brit.* II. 337/2 The.. Neolithic Period, or, as it has been sometimes called, the Surface-Stone Period. **1893** A. S. ECCLES *Sciatica* 19 The *surface-temperature of the affected limb. **1885** *Science* 15 Mar. 213 A steam launch, in which to make *surface towings. **1887** [see TOWING *vbl. sb.*[1]]. **1886** *Encycl. Brit.* XXI. 715/2 A *surface-trap or gully outside the house. **1850** W. R. BIRT *Hurricane Guide* 13 Which to the various countries over which they pass appear as *surface-winds. **1839** DE LA BECHE *Rep. Geol. Cornwall*, etc. xv. 564 There are few regularly-planned *surface-works. **1963** *Times* 2 Mar. 8/5 The miners' demands include pensions at 50 for underground workers and at 55 for *surface workers.

(*c*) *Electr.*, as ***surface conduction, density, electrification, winding***.

1873 F. JENKIN *Electr. & Magn.* Index, *Surface conduction, or creeping on insulators. **1878** *Encycl. Brit.* VIII. 17/2 Electrical '*surface density'.. means quantity of electricity on an element of surface divided by the element of surface. **1878** *Encycl. Brit.* VIII. 66/1 *Surface electrification on insulators. **1902** *Encycl. Brit.* XXVII. 583/2 For multipolar armatures with two or more layers of inductors, '*surface' or 'barrel' winding is now extensively used.

(*d*) *Naut.* Designating ships which move on the surface of the water as opp. to submarine vessels, as ***surface craft, ship, vessel, warship***, etc.; also *Comb.*, as ***surface-borne, -sailing*** adjs.

1905 *Trans. Inst. Naval Archit.* XLVII. 407 Misconceptions exist.. as to the relative chances of accidents happening to boats compared with surface craft. **1910** C. W. DOMVILLE-FIFE *Submarines of World's Navies* II. 101 This is if the surface warship was steaming in an erratic course. **1915** W. E. DOMMETT *Submarine Vessels* 5 The term 'submersible vessels' should.. be reserved for those which, whilst mainly surface vessels, can be brought to an awash or submerged condition. **1928** C. F. S. GAMBLE *Story North Sea Air Station* xiii. 224 A pilot might sight.. a submarine and a surface-borne craft like a cruiser or destroyer. **1939** *Sun* (Baltimore) 17 Apr. 9/1 The North Haven surface ship to be used in transporting supplies, will carry 314,000 separate items. **1945** *Army & Navy Jrnl.* 18 Aug. 1534 *ASV, Airborne Surface Vessel Detection*, airborne radar devices used to locate surface vessels and surfacing submarines. **1954** *Ann. Reg. 1953* 337 *The Tirpitz*.. a well-documented account of the career and sinking of the war-time surface raider. **1975** *Listener* 17 June 77/2 The 'Bismarck'.. was later sunk by surface vessels. **1982** A. MELVILLE-ROSS *Trigger* ii. 33 You don't have enough surface ships left for you to hoist your admiral's flag.

(*e*) In reference to (chiefly, public) transportation at ground- or sea-level, as opp. to underground or air carriage (orig. *U.S.*); cf. *surface car*, sense 6 d. Also, *spec.* applied to mail or post, as ***surface letter, parcel***, etc.; cf. *surface mail*, sense 6 d below.

1906 'MARK TWAIN' *Let.* 5 May in C. Clemens *Mark Twain* (1932) 156 My daughters are frequently robbed by conductors on the surface lines. **1909** *N.Y. Even. Post* (Semi-weekly ed.) 4 Mar. 1 On streets leading to these ferries surface travel was blocked by heavily laden vehicles stalled. **1927** *New Republic* 12 Oct. 208/2 Chicago, alas! despite the fact that it could undoubtedly solve its transportation difficulties by surface carriage,.. has decided to go in for subways. **1933** *Jrnl. R. Central Asian Soc.* Jan. 81 Surface transport conditions for the necessary stores and spares are bad. **1934** *Air Mail Service* (G.P.O. Green Paper 1), The actual cost incurred for handling, surface transmission, and air conveyance. **1951** *Overseas Air Mails* (G.P.O.) Feb. 1/2 The general regulations applicable to ordinary surface parcels..apply to air parcels. **1956** L. Zilliacus *From Pillar to Post* xiii. 163 An ordinary surface letter..takes a week or more... By air it takes two or three days. **1977** *National Observer* (U.S.) 1 Jan 2 Adams is also a critic of several leading schemes for deregulation of airlines and surface carriers.

(*f*) *Linguistics.* Of or pertaining to the level of language at which normal communication exists, as opposed to the underlying level revealed by 'deep' semantic and syntactic analysis, esp. as ***surface grammar***. See also *surface structure*, sense 6 d below.

1953 G. E. M. Anscombe tr. *L. Wittgenstein's Philos. Investigations* I. 168e In the use of words one might distinguish 'surface grammar' from 'depth grammar'. What immediately impresses itself upon us about the use of a word is the way it is used in the construction of the sentence, the part of its use..that can be taken in by the ear.—And now compare the depth grammar, say of the word 'to mean', with what its surface grammar would lead us to suspect. **1958** C. F. Hockett *Course in Mod. Linguistics* xxix. 249 This most apparent layer constitutes, we shall say, *surface grammar*. Beneath it lie various layers of *deep grammar*, which have much to do with how we speak and understand but which are still largely unexplored, in any systematic way, by grammarians. **1965** N. Chomsky *Aspects of Theory of Syntax* 199 In place of the terms 'deep structure' and 'surface structure', one might use the corresponding Humboldtian notions 'inner form' of a sentence and 'outer form' of a sentence... The terms 'depth grammar' and 'surface grammar' are familiar in modern philosophy in something roughly like the sense here intended. **1967** D. G. Hays *Introd. Computational Linguistics* viii. 155 Their system begins with a surface parser. **1972** *Language* XLVIII. 678 His general discussion of what syntax is all about deals exclusively with surface phenomena, chiefly the order of elements in a sentence. **1977** *Word 1972* XXVIII. 92 Yet the simplest solution superficially is not necessarily the best, and a surface-oriented approach to *tá* predicates is faced with problems, too. **1981** A. C. Thiselton in *Believing in Church* iii. 51 Language is said to determine the scope and limits of thought on the basis of vocabulary-stock or even surface-grammar.

b. *attrib.* in fig. sense (see 1 b), often equivalent to an adj. = superficial.

1828 Carlyle *Misc.* (1857) I. 207 No vain surface-logic detains him. **1859** W. Collins *Q. of Hearts* i, With a quaint surface-sourness of address, and a tone of dry sarcasm in his talk. **1860** O. W. Holmes *Prof. Breakf.-t.* vi. (Paterson) 122 Good-breeding is Surface-Christianity. **1864** Pusey *Lect. Daniel* i. 43 The slight variations between the Aramaic of Daniel and Ezra are in conformity with their slight difference in age. But these are petty surface-questions. **1866** G. Macdonald *Ann. Q. Neighb.* viii. (1878) 129, I had only a certain surface-knowledge. **1875** Whitney *Life Lang.* vi. 102 Skimming a mere surface comprehension off that which has a profound meaning. **1905** F. Young *Sands of Pleasure* II. iv, I always keep to mere acquaintance and surface friendships with such people.

c. *Comb.* with pples., adjs., vbs., agent-nouns, and nouns of action: (*a*) locative (= 'on the surface'), as ***surface-deposited***, ***-dressed***, ***-dry***, ***-dwelling***, ***-feeding***, ***-scratched*** adjs.; ***surface-feed***, ***-grip*** (grip *v.*[2]), ***-hoe***, ***sow*** (chiefly *N.Z.*) vbs.; ***surface-dweller***, ***-feeder***; ***surface-sowing***, ***-sown*** (chiefly *N.Z.*), ***-swimming*** adjs. and sbs.; (*b*) objective, as ***surface-skimmer***; ***surface sterilization*** (hence ***surface-sterilize*** vb., ***-sterilized*** ppl. adj.), ***-tapping***.

1898 F. Davis *Romano-Brit. City of Silchester* 16 The subsidence..of the *surface-deposited material. **1892** J. Anderson in J. R. Allen *Early Chr. Monum. Scot.* (1903) I. p. vi, The stone..is not squared or *surface-dressed. **1878** Abney *Photogr.* xxi. 151 This prevents the chance of any of the prints getting *surface-dry. **1880** A. R. Wallace *Isl. Life* 89 It was long thought that they were *surface-dwellers only. **1888** H. Woodward *Guide Fossil Fishes Brit. Mus.* (ed. 2) 43 The living *surface-dwelling genera *Myripristis* and *Holocentrum*. **1907** *Westm. Gaz.* 5 Jan. 3/3 Widgeons are entirely surface-feeding ducks, and like most *surface-feeders they sleep out at sea by day. **1902** Millais (*title*) The Natural History of the British *Surface-Feeding Ducks. **1851** *Jrnl. R. Agric. Soc.* XII. II. 293 The fields are regularly *surface-gripped as soon as the wheat is sown. **1885** *Garden* June 572 *Surface-hoed and heeled up latest Potatoes. **1868** *Rep. U.S. Commissioner Agric.* (1869) 17 Undrained, *surface-scratched fields, so numerous in the defective cultivation of the present day. **1748** Richardson *Clarissa* III. 145, I love to plague thee, who are..a *surface-skimmer in learning, with out-of-the-way words and phrases. **1841** Miall in *Nonconf.* I. 9 The summer day politicians.., the ephemeral surface skimmers. **1868** *Eclectic Rev.* Aug. 114 The mere surface-skimmer of books. *a* **1911** D. G. Phillips *Susan Lenox* (1917) I. xiii. 213 We shallow surface-skimmers make such a..fuss. **1921** H. Guthrie-Smith *Tutira* xix. 163 The land is *surface-sown with grass and clover seed. **1882** W. D. Hay *Brighter Britain!* I. viii. 197 In spite of..the rough ground, and the mere *surface-sowing, our grass will carry four sheep per acre. **1950** *N.Z. Jrnl. Agric.* Apr. 309/2 The uncertain establishment of plants from the surface sowing of clover seeds. *Ibid.* Feb. 121/1 The more fertile *surface-sown hill country of the North Island. **1954** Kirk & Othmer *Encycl. Chem. Technol.* XII. 914 Ultraviolet radiation exhibits extremely low penetration. Because of this the major applications have been in air sanitation and *surface sterilization of food products, packaging materials.., and working spaces. **1978** *Canad. Jrnl. Bot.* LVI. 226/1 Close the open end of the syringe with a syringe nose cap to keep the seeds and sterilizing solution from being ejected during surface sterilization. **1956** *Nature* 17 Mar. 534/2 The adult female mosquito was *surface-sterilized by immersion for 2 min. in a 0·5 per cent solution of mercuric chloride in 50 per cent ethyl alcohol. The surface-sterilized insect was transferred to insect Ringer solution. **1967** K. M. Smith *Insect Virol.* ix. 165 Pupae were surface-sterilized in 70% ethanol for 5 minutes. **1978** *Canad. Jrnl. Bot.* LVI. 225 (*heading*) Rapid, contamination-free sowing of surface-sterilized seeds and spores. *Ibid.* 226/1 After the seed is surface sterilized, remove the nose cap and affix a sterile 18-gauge needle to the syringe. **1925** J. T. Jenkins *Fishes Brit. Isles* 73 The coryphænidæ are tropical and sub-tropical fish of pelagic or *surface-swimming habits. **1970** *Commercial Fisheries Rev.* Apr. 4/1 The government of American Samoa seeks to broaden the islands' economic base by harvesting surface-swimming tunas. **1855** Dickens *Dorrit* II. xx, A knocker produced a dead flat *surface-tapping.

d. Special comb.: **surface-active** *a. Physical Chem.*, (of a substance) able to affect the wetting or surface tension properties of a liquid; hence **surface-activity**; **surface blow** *Engin.*, a device by which the surface water and scum in a steam boiler may be blown off; hence **surface blow-off**, the act of discharging this scum; **surface-car** *U.S.*, a tramcar running on a track level with the surface of the ground, as distinct from an elevated or underground track; **surface casing** *Oil Industry*, the length of casing in a bore-hole which is nearest the surface; **surface caterpillar** = *surface-grub*; **surface chemistry**, the study of the chemical processes occurring at the boundaries between different phases; **surface-chuck** (see quot.); **surface-coated** *a.*, (of paper or cardboard) having a specially finished surface; **surface-colour**, colour exhibited, in the case of certain substances, by the light reflected from the surface; **surface condensation**, condensation of steam by a *surface-condenser*; **surface-condenser**, in a steam-engine, a condenser in which exhaust-steam is condensed by contact with cold metallic surfaces; **surface-contact**, (*a*) contact of surfaces; (*b*) applied *attrib.* to a system of electric traction in which the current is conveyed to the cars through conductors on the surface of the roadway; **surface couching** *Embroidery*, a form of couching (couch *v.*[1] 4 b) in which the couched thread is held flat on the surface of the fabric by stitches looped over it (cf. *underside couching* s.v. underside b); so **surface couched** *pa. pple.*; **surface-crossing**, a level crossing on a railway; **surface-damage**, damage done to the surface of the ground by mining operations; *pl.* compensation payable for this; see also quot. 1886; **surface-drain** *Agric.*, a drain cut in the surface of the ground; so **surface-drainage**, **-draining**; **surface effect**, any effect associated with, or only encountered near, a surface; also *attrib.*, esp. designating an air-cushion vehicle in which the cushion is sealed by rigid sidewalls and flexible seals fore and aft (cf. sidewall 3 b); **surface-gauge** (see quot.); **surface-grinder**, **surface-grinding machine**, a machine for grinding something to a perfectly plane surface; **surface-grub**, the larva of various moths, which live just beneath the surface of the soil; a cutworm; **surface-integral** *Math.*, an integral taken over the whole area of a surface; **surface mail**, a postal service for conveying mail by land or sea, contrasted with airmail; the mail conveyed; **surface noise**, a background hiss heard on reproduction of a gramophone record owing to irregularities in the surface of the groove walls; **surface paper**, (photographic or printing) paper made with a special surface on one side; **surface-plane**, a form of machine for planing timber; also, a carpenter's plane for planing a flat surface; **surface-planer** = *surface plane*; so **surface planing** (also *attrib.*); **surface-plate**, (*a*) a plate or flat bar of iron fixed on the upper surface of a rail on a railway; (*b*) an iron plate for testing the accuracy of a flat surface; **surface-printing**, printing from a raised surface (as distinguished from an incised plate), as from ordinary type, or (in calico-printing) from wooden rollers cut in relief; so **surface-printed** *a.*; **surface process**, a process of surface-printing; **surface-rib** *Arch.*, a rib applied to the surface of vaulting merely for ornament; **surface-road** *U.S.*, a railroad on the surface of the ground, as distinct from an elevated or underground railroad; **surface-roller** (see quot., and cf. *surface-printing* above); **surface shelter**: in the war of 1939–45, an air-raid shelter at ground-level; **surface speed**, the speed of which a submarine is capable when moving on the surface; **surface structure** *Linguistics* (esp. in *Generative Grammar*), the syntactic elements forming an utterance or sentence, contrasted with the 'hidden' or not immediately recognizable logical form underlying such elements (the *deep structure*: see deep *a.* IV. c); a string of such elements arranged with labels and brackets to show the relationship of the constituent parts; **surface-tension** *Physics*, the tension of the surface-film of a liquid, due to the cohesion of its particles; **surface-water**, (*a*) water that collects on the surface of the ground; (*b*) the surface layer of a body of water; **surface-worm** = *surface-grub*. See also surfaceman.

1920 *Chem. Abstr.* XIV. 3256 The changes in the surface tension brought about by acid and alkali are so slight the titration with *surface active substances as indicators cannot be significantly disturbing. **1978** P. W. Atkins *Physical Chem.* viii. 240 The material described in this section is put to use in the study of surface-active agents (or surfactants). These agents include long chain molecules, such as soaps and detergents, which accumulate at the water-air interface and lower the surface tension. **1925** *Chem. Abstr.* XIX. 3094 It was proved that in certain diseases the *surface activity of the urine not only deviates from its normal value in the quant. sense, but that in conditions such as *morbus meculosis* it suffers qual. changes. **1972** *Materials & Technol.* V. x. 273 (*heading*) Principles of surface-activity. **1859** W. J. M. Rankine *Man. Steam Engine* III. iv. 453 Another blow-off cock is sometimes so placed as to discharge occasionally the scum, consisting of crystals of salt, which collects on the surface of the water: this is called the '*surface blow'. **1888** R. H. Thurston *Man. Steam Boilers* xii. 446 When using sea-water in the boilers, frequently blowing off from the bottom or a continuous discharge from the 'surface-blow' or 'scum pipes' is essential to keeping the water so fresh as not to produce deposits or incrustation. **1888** *Lockwood's Dict. Mech. Engin.* 361 **Surface blow-off*, the blowing off of the scum which collects on the top of the water in a boiler. **1977** Woodruff & Lammers *Steam-Plant Operation* (ed. 4) v. 254 Surface blowoff is advantageous in skimming or removing oil from the boiler water. **1890** *N.Y. Tribune* 11 May (Cent. Dict.) The Americanisms one hears upon the front platforms of New-York *surface cars. **1909** Eliz. L. Banks *Myst. F. Farrington* 103 She took a surface car to help her on her way. **1946** L. C. Uren *Petroleum Production Engineering* (ed. 3) I. xi. 388 Some varieties of *surface casing are made of galvanized sheet steel. **1977** *Offshore Engineer* Aug. 28/2 A widely used drilling programme..using 30″ conductor pipe, 20″ surface casing. **1852** *Surface caterpillar [see *surface-grub* below]. **1926** E. K. Rideal (*title*) An introduction to *surface chemistry. **1951** A. E. Alexander *Surface Chem.* p. v, The study of surface chemistry gives an unusually clear insight into the real existence and behaviour of molecules. **1975** *McGraw-Hill Yearbk. Sci. & Technol.* 174/2 Conductance monitoring of thin-film electrodes constitutes a powerful new approach to the study of surface chemistry and physics. **1842** Francis *Dict. Arts*, **Surface Chuck*, a chuck used for the purpose of holding any flat material, while the surface of it is turned flat and even. **1908** *Westm. Gaz.* 23 Jan. 1/3 A firm interested in '*surface-coated boards'. **1899** W. Watson *Text-bk. Physics* §387. 556 In the case of the bodies referred to..as showing *surface colour, light of a particular colour seems unable to penetrate at all, and is therefore reflected, so that the transmitted light will be without this colour. **1867–72** Burgh *Mod. Marine Engin.* 253 As far back as the year 1832 Mr. Hall..proved..that *surface condensation was..economical. **1863** J. Jack in *Proc. Inst. Mech. Engin.* 150 (*title*) Effects of *Surface Condensers on Steam Boilers. **1846** Holtzapffel *Turning* II. 663 Those nuts..which are..used..for the regulating screws of slides and general machinery, are made much thicker..; this greatly increases their *surface-contact, and durability. **1898** S. P. Thompson in *Westm. Gaz.* 13 Oct. 2/3 Surface-contact systems..are much less costly than the underground conduit, and equally dispense with the unsightly overhead wires. **1938** A. G. I. Christie *Eng. Medieval Embroidery* 25 **Surface Couching*. The method of couching familiar to modern workers, that of securing one or more threads by passing another across them.., although well known in the Middle Ages, does not appear to have been extensively used. *Ibid.*, The medieval English embroidery, preserved in the Musée de Cluny,..is surface-couched throughout. **1963** *Opus Anglicanum* (V. & A. Mus. Exhib. Catal.) 14/1 Silver-gilt and silk thread in underside and surface couching and stem stitch. *Ibid.* 44/2 In the band with butterflies the metal threads are surface couched. **1841** *Penny Cycl.* XIX. 251/1 When the Liverpool and Manchester line was projected,..no danger was anticipated from such intersections, which are called *surface-crossings. **1801** *Farmer's Mag.* Apr. 202 Liberty of working minerals..upon paying *surface-damages. **1838** W. Bell *Dict. Law Scot.*, *Surface-damage*, damage done to the surface of the ground in consequence of mining operations. **1886** J. Barrowman *Sc. Mining Terms* 66 *Surface damages*, ground occupied and damaged by colliery operations. **1833** *Ridgemont Farm Rep.* 132 in *Libr. Usef. Kn.*, *Husb.* III, Forming the *surface-drains ('grips') across the ridges. **1833** Loudon *Encycl. Archit.* §824 *Surface Drainage. **1799** *View Agric. Lincoln.* 72 A *surface-draining plough. **1805** R. W. Dickson *Pract. Agric.* I. 13 In the surface-draining of land, different sorts of ploughs are in use in different places. **1905** R. C. H. Heck *Steam-Engine & Other Steam-Motors* I. iv. 109 The *surface-effect.—Of the total interior surface of the cylinder, that part which may be called the clearance-surface—including the cylinder head and the piston-face, with the steam-passages. **1945** [see *mass effect* s.v. mass *sb.*[2] 10 d]. **1962** *Marine Engin./Log* Oct. 72/2 A surface-effect ship is being developed under a $370,000 MarAd contract. **1979** *Canad. Jrnl. Biochem.* LVII. 106/1 This preference [for phosphatidylcholine] is manifested in the ethereal system, in which surface effects are absent. **1875** Knight *Dict. Mech.*, **Surface-gage*, an implement for testing the accuracy of plane surfaces. **1884** *Ibid.* Suppl. 875 Thomson's *surface grinder..has..driving arrangements, constructed to grind and buff the surfaces of work too large or heavy to be taken to the ordinary grinding machines. *Ibid.*, Thomson, Sterne, & Co.'s..*Surface Grinding Machine. **1852** G. W. Johnson *Cottage Gard. Dict.*, **Surface Grubs*, or caterpillars, are the larvæ of several species of..Night Moths. **1875** Cayley *Math. Papers* IX. 321 On the Prepotential *Surface-integral. **1878** W. K. Clifford *Dynamic* III. 201 The surface-integral of the spin over any closed surface is zero. **1935** *Post Office Mag.* Jan. 2/2 1928, new services introduced and direct air or combined air and *surface mails to half the countries of the world. **1946** R. ALLEN *Home Made Banners* xii. 156 Pop's reply was so long that it came by surface mail. **1956** *B.B.C. Handbk. 1957* 247 It is published in a surface mail edition at an annual rate of 25 *s.* **1977** P. MOYES *To Kill Coconut* vi. 82 Look at the date. Three weeks old. Just arrived by surface mail. **1921** *Daily-Colonist* (Victoria) 17 Mar. 7/7 The Sonora plays with a total absence of that '*surface noise' or record scratching which you had believed could not be eliminated. **1981** *Hi-Fi Answers* Sept. 87/1 The general idea was to boost high frequencies on recording, so that when an equal and opposite act was applied on play-back it cut out a lot of the surface noise. **1892** *Photogr. Ann.* II. 60 Use a paper which is white on one side... This paper can be bought at a stationer's under the name of *surface paper. **1875** KNIGHT *Dict. Mech.*, **Surface-plane* (Wood-working), a form of planing-machine for truing and smoothing the surface of an object run beneath the rotary cutter on the bed of the planer. **1873** J. RICHARDS *Wood-working Factories* 131 *Surface planers, that cut away a constant amount of wood, gauged from the surface that is planed. *Ibid.*, The under cylinder of a double surfacing machine, or bottom cylinders generally, are examples of *surface planing. **1875** KNIGHT *Dict. Mech.* 2457 A surface-planing machine. **1825** J. NICHOLSON *Oper. Mech.* 652 At every eighteen inches or two feet of the length of this *surface-plate, a tenon is firmly welded or riveted. **1846** HOLTZAPFFEL *Turning* II. 865 The operator must be provided with the means of testing the progressive advance of the work, he should therefore possess a true straight-edge, and a true surface-plate. **1875** KNIGHT *Dict. Mech.* 2457 Books, newspapers, woodcuts, and lithographs are all *surface-printed. **1838** *Civil Eng. & Arch. Jrnl.* I. 266/1 The Production of coloured Impressions on Paper,.. by *Surface Printing. **1839** URE *Dict. Arts* 219 Another modification of cylinder printing, is that with wooden rollers cut in relief: it is called surface printing. **1875** KNIGHT *Dict. Mech.* 2458 The rose-engine work around the portrait, if printed from by the *surface-process [etc.]. **1835** R. WILLIS *Archit. Mid. Ages* vii. 82 These three classes of ribs may be designated as Groin Ribs, Ridge Ribs, and *Surface Ribs. **1889** *Cent. Dict.*, *Surface-road. **1903** *N.Y. Evening Post* 3 Sept. 6/4 The short-haul business is well provided for by the existing surface roads. **1875** KNIGHT *Dict. Mech.*, **Surface-roller*, the engraved cylinder used in calico-printing. **1940** *New Statesman* 19 Oct. 375 He is getting worried about his wife and children in their *surface shelters. **1902** *Encycl. Brit.* XXXII. 576/2 With her original machinery the *Plunger* was to have had a *surface speed of 15 knots. **1976** G. COOK *Silent Marauder* i. 58 The K-class steam-driven submarine..could produce a surface speed of twenty-four knots. **1964** N. CHOMSKY *Current Issues in Linguistic Theory* i. 10 Thus the syntactic component must provide for each sentence (actually, for each interpretation of each sentence) a semantically interpretable *deep structure* and phonetically interpretable **surface structure*, and, in the event that these are distinct, a statement of the relation between these structures. **1969** *Neuphilologische Mitteilungen* LXX. 203 The distinction between 'surface' and 'deep' structures should be given up, since no such contrast exists: there are only structures and their meanings. **1971** *Archivum Linguisticum* II. 131, I shall use the traditional term *Article* to refer to *the*, *a*, *this*, etc. when I am characterizing them as surface-structure elements. **1975** *Ibid.* VI. 23 Even mutations which are determined by a lexical environment are not all triggered by the surface structure. **1977** E. VON GLASERFELD in D. M. Rumbaugh *Language Learning by Chimpanzee* v. 103 In this context it must be said that Chomsky's introduction of the terms 'surface structure' and 'deep structure'..seemed a step in the right direction. **1876** *Encycl. Brit.* V. 57/1 In 1804 Thomas Young founded the theory of capillary phenomena on the principle of *surface-tension. **1793** [EARL DUNDONALD] *Descr. Estate of Culross* 21 Blue clay, forming a..barrier against *surface water. **1850** ANSTED *Elem. Geol., Min.* etc. 461 The surface-water, when in excess, penetrates into the sub-soil. **1860** MAURY *Phys. Geog. Sea* (Low) ix. §430 The surface-water of Loch Lomond. **1894** BARING-GOULD *Deserts S. France* I. 7 The wells are mere reservoirs of surface water.

'surface, *v.* [f. prec. sb.]

1. *trans.* To give a (particular kind of) surface, esp. a smooth or even surface, to; to smooth or polish the surface of; also, to cover the surface of (*with* something).

1778 [W. MARSHALL] *Minutes Agric.* 12 Apr. 1776, The soil had two plowings, was harrowed, rolled,..and afterward surfaced as level as a table. **1837** *Blackw. Mag.* XLI. 186 Soft-cushioned and aerated ground, surfaced and inlaid with thinnest mother-of-pearl. **1869** RANKINE *Machine & Hand-tools* Pl. H 8, This lathe is..adapted..for surfacing..the general class of work to be met with in engineering establishments. **1875** KNIGHT *Dict. Mech.*, *Marble-scourer*, a rubber for surfacing marble slabs. **1897** *Outing* (U.S.) XXX. 233/1 The track is surfaced with cement.

2. *intr.* To mine near the surface; to wash the surface deposit or 'dirt' for gold or other valuable mineral.

1860 MRS. MEREDITH *Over the Straits* iv. 133 I've been surfacing this good while; but quartz-reefin's the payinest game now.

3. a. *trans.* To bring or raise to the surface.

1885 *Money Market Review* 29 Aug. (Cassell's Encycl. Dict.) To surface the tinstuff now accumulated.

b. *fig.* To bring to public notice; *spec.* to produce or expose (a defector, spy, etc.). *U.S. colloq.*

1955 *N.Y. Times* 6 Mar. IV. 2/6 In Moscow last week the authorities 'surfaced' a brilliant British atomic scientist who had disappeared behind the Iron Curtain five years ago. **1963** J. JOESTEN *They call it Intelligence* I. iv. 45 Now and then secret agents are purposely 'surfaced'. **1973** *N.Y. Times* 20 May I. 64/1 Martin Tolchin, another Times reporter, surfaced one of the stories last October. **1974** *Anderson* (S. Carolina) *Independent* 23 Apr. 1B/2 Rep. Dan Marrett..surfaced the controversial issue.

4. a. *intr.* To rise to the surface of the water. Also *fig.*

1898 *Pall Mall Mag.* Nov. 358 [The fish] surfaced within a few feet of me. **1935** *Jrnl. R. United Services Inst.* LXXX. 126 Diving and surfacing were carried out by filling or employing a number of goatskins. **1955** *Times* 18 Aug. 8/3 [The officer]..had an under-water swimming suit with breathing equipment. He failed to surface. **1959** *Listener* 9 Apr. 635/2 The *Skate* surfaced ten times during the voyage. **1965** M. SHADBOLT *Among Cinders* xxvi. 276, I swam down a gloomy passage..and surfaced in a gently lighted room. **1974** L. DEIGHTON *Spy Story* xviii. 192 Nuclear subs go faster submerged... When we surfaced they did the usual tests.

b. *fig.* Of persons: to become fully conscious or alert, esp. after sleep. Also, to come to general notice (after a period of seclusion), to appear in public view.

1959 H. HAMILTON *Answer in Negative* ii. 33 He was rather silent over the meal... It was only when they had returned to the drawing-room that he really surfaced and returned to the case. **1963** *Times* 11 Jan. 3/7 He went to bed early last night and did not feel well enough to surface today. **1968** 'R. SIMONS' *Death on Display* xii. 180 'Has there been any sign of that damned Tebaugh woman yet?' 'Afraid not. .. She still hasn't surfaced.' **1971** 'A. GILBERT' *Tenant for Tomb* v. 73 If there wasn't a reason he'd have—what's the word?—surfaced before this. **1975** *New Yorker* 21 Apr. 133/1 Members of revolutionary committees that were created by the Communists over the past several years in all South Vietnamese provinces have now surfaced.

c. Similarly, of something newly presented to public attention, esp. after being concealed.

1971 *Nature* 26 Feb. 590/1 The proposal surfaced last December with the report of a panel of consultants commissioned by Senator Ralph Yarborough. **1973** *Time* 5 Feb. 51/1 The dispute soon surfaced in the press. **1978** R. LUDLUM *Holcroft Covenant* xxvii. 318 She wanted me to be prepared if it ever surfaced, if anyone for any reason ever remembered and tried to use the information.

surfaced ('sɜːfəst), *a.* [f. prec. sb. or vb. + -ED.]

1. Having a surface of a specified kind (with adv., or in comb.)

1668 H. MORE *Div. Dial.* II. xxi. (1713) 154 It is unnatural for the Beams of the Sun to be reverberated to our eyes from several Bodies variously surfaced in the same form of Light. **1804** *Med. Jrnl.* XII. 412 Somewhat knotty, or unequally surfaced. **1831** T. L. PEACOCK *Crotchet Castle* i, A bold round-surfaced lawn. **1875** LOWELL *Among my Bks.* Ser. II. 187 That delicately surfaced nature of his [*sc.* Spenser's]. **1890** *Photogr. Jrnl.* 24 Jan. 60 Matt-surfaced Glass.

2. Provided with a (special) surface or surfaces. Esp. of paper treated on one side to receive a sharp printed impression. (Usu. without qualifying word.)

1888 *Paper & Printing Trades Jrnl.* Mar. 29/1 The use of highly surfaced super-calendered paper..is extending to this country. **1967** M. A. KHAN *Friends not Masters* iii. 23 The only good stretch of surfaced road that existed, to my knowledge, was somewhere in Pabna district. **1971** D. POTTER *Brit. Eliz. Stamps* vi. 68 All these stamps were issued on surfaced paper.

3. Of a submarine: that is afloat but not submerged.

1943 *Times* 6 Dec. 4/5 On the sixth day a Liberator attacked a surfaced U-boat near this convoy. **1974** L. DEIGHTON *Spy Story* xviii. 193 If London's reception is poor, surfaced subs in transit monitor for them.

surfacely ('sɜːfəslɪ), *adv. rare.* [f. SURFACE *sb.* 7 b + -LY[2].] 'On the surface'; superficially.

1885 L. OLIPHANT *Sympneumata* 106 The change from the trueness of man's dual nature, to the falseness of a nature surfacely admixed with base ingredients. **1893** J. PULSFORD *Loyalty to Christ* II. 420 Ordinary friends may know you surfacely.

surfaceman ('sɜːfəsmən). Pl. **-men.** [f. SURFACE *sb.* 3 b + MAN *sb.*[1]] A miner or other labourer who works at the surface, or in the open air; on a railway, a workman who keeps the permanent way in repair.

1878 (*title*) Songs of the Rail. By Alexander Anderson, Railway Surfaceman,..Dumfriesshire. **1900** *Yorkshire Post* 8 Jan. 6/6 South Yorkshire Surfacemen's Wages.

surfacer ('sɜːfəsə(r)). [f. SURFACE *v.* + -ER[1].]

1. a. A person or an instrument that produces a smooth or even surface.

1778 [W. MARSHALL] *Minutes Agric.* 20 May 1775 *Observ.*, These waves, which the Surfacer had left as smooth as gravel-walks, were then raised into flutes.

b. *spec.* A woodworking machine for cutting and planing the surface of wooden boards.

1884 J. KANE *Shavings & Sawdust* xviii. 81 Small surfacers..used by cabinet and piano factories..should have all the four rolls driven. **1937** H. HJORTH *Machine Woodworking* v. 139 A single planer or surfacer planes only one side of a board at a time, while a double surfacer planes both sides at the same time.

2. One who mines near the surface.

1882 in OGILVIE (Annandale).

3. A paint used to smooth any slight unevennesses of a surface before another coat is applied.

1927 *Automotive Manufacturer* July 13/2 For the first coat, use primer and surfacer, half and half, spraying on a medium coat... No sanding will be needed prior to spraying the coat of surfacer. **1954** A. ST. J. MASTERS *Do your own Spray Painting* viii. 75 For amateur use there is no doubt that the best plan is to continue with the cellulose surfacer as previously described. **1979** *Guardian* 30 May 5/3 (Advt.), The body is then given a surfacer, sprayed with a sealer and oven-hardened.

surface wave. [SURFACE *sb.*] **a.** A wave of displacements propagated along the surface of a solid or a liquid.

1887 LD. RAYLEIGH in *Proc. Lond. Math. Soc.* XVII. 11 It is not improbable that the surface waves here investigated play an important part in earthquakes, and in the collision of elastic solids. **1900** *Nature* 4 Oct. 562/1 The earthquake wave takes about 110 minutes to travel from its origin to the opposite end of the earth's diameter, but whether it is propagated through the centre of the earth or as a surface wave cannot at present be decided. **1953** H. KOLSKY *Stress Waves in Solids* ii. 16 Where there is a bounding surface.. elastic surface waves may also occur. These waves..are similar to gravitational surface waves in liquids. **1973** *IEEE Trans. Microwave Theory & Techniques* XXI. 176/1 Their size, design flexibility, and reproducibility make acoustic surface-wave devices excellent candidates for many important applications in radar and communication systems.

b. *Radio.* [tr. G. *oberflächenwelle* (A. Sommerfeld 1911, in *Jahrb. d. drahtl. Telegr.* IV. 166).] A radio wave propagated along the surface of the earth.

1913 [see *space wave* s.v. SPACE *sb.*[1] 20]. **1943** [see *ground wave* s.v. GROUND *sb.* 18]. **1971** [see *sky wave* s.v. SKY *sb.*[1] 9].

surfacing ('sɜːfəsɪŋ), *vbl. sb.* [f. SURFACE *v.* + -ING[1].]

1. The action or process of giving a (smooth or even) surface to something; *concr.* the coating with which a body (*spec.* a road) is surfaced.

1859 F. A. GRIFFITHS *Artil. Man.* (1862) 205 The surfacing [of the copper rings in an Armstrong gun] should be performed after every 100 rounds. **1882** *Garden* 18 Mar. 186/1 Walks..should..have received surfacings of fresh gravel. **1890** *Science-Gossip* XXVI. 89 Mr. S. E. Peal.. sends a copy of his paper, 'A Theory of Lunar Surfacing by Glaciation.' **1897** *Catal. Maiolica Ashm. Mus. Oxf.* 4 Certain of the Greek, Etruscan, and Roman..wares, on which a thin surfacing or semi-glazing seems to have been applied. **1908** C. E. MORRISON *Highway Engin.* iii. 46 Gravel roads seem to occupy an intermediate place between those of earth and broken stone, in the tractive force required, character of surfacing, and cost of construction. **1937** *Times* 13 Apr. p. iii/2 Much that can make for safety lies in the expert designing, surfacing and lighting of the highways. **1954** *Gloss. Highway Engin. Terms* (*B.S.I.*) 31 *Surfacing*, the top layer or layers, comprising the wearing course and/or base course but not the base.

attrib. **1846** HOLTZAPFFEL *Turning* II. 477 The ordinary surfacing planes. **1869** RANKINE *Machine & Hand-tools* Pl. H 7, A sliding and surfacing motion. **1873** J. RICHARDS *Wood-working Factories* 131 The under cylinder of a double surfacing machine.

2. Mining for gold, etc. by washing the surface deposit; *concr.* the deposit so treated.

1853 E. CLACY *Lady's Visit to Gold Diggings Austral.* vi. 85 The riches of Peg Leg Gully were brought to light through the surfacing of three men with wooden legs, who were unable to sink a hole in the regular way. **1861** T. M'COMBIE *Australian Sk.* 133 What is termed 'surfacing' consists of simply washing the soil on the surface of the ground, which is occasionally auriferous. **1890** 'R. BOLDREWOOD' *Miner's Right* xv, It seems they have been mopping up some rich surfacing.

3. Of a submarine: rising to the surface of the water. Also *fig.* Cf. SURFACE *v.* 4 a.

1922 *Glasgow Herald* 27 Apr. 7 Submarine H 42 rose to the surface some 30 yards right ahead of the Versatile... The reason for her surfacing was not known. **1958** *Times* 18 Dec. 11/4 Surfacing is an effective word to indicate those friends who suddenly appear on the doorstep after touch has been lost with them for months. **1970** *Wall St. Jrnl.* 6 Nov. 1/1 The surfacing of high-school students' demands is relatively recent in its own right.

surfactant (sə'fæktənt). *Chem.* [f. initial elements of *surf*ace-*act*ive adj. s.v. SURFACE *sb.* 6 d + -ANT[1].] A surface-active agent. Also *attrib.*

1950 *American Dyestuff Reporter* XXXIX. 379/3 A new word, Surfactants, has been coined by Antara Products, General Aniline & Film Corporation, and has been presented to the chemical industry to cover all materials that have surface activity, including wetting agents, dispersants, emulsifiers, detergents and foaming agents. **1959** *Times* 7 Dec. (Agric. Suppl.) p. vii/1 Since the war, various growth supplements have been recommended, including arsenic acid supplements, surfactants..hormones and antibiotics. **1967** *New Scientist* 28 Sept. 686/2 They propose that a process of solubilization takes place under the influence of a surfactant—a substance which lowers the surface tension of water. **1968** *Gloss. Formwork Terms* (*B.S.I.*) 25 *Surfactant* (surface-active agent, activating agent, deprecated), a chemical which lowers the surface tension of water. *Note.* Surfactants are used in mould oils to reduce the occurrence of blowholes in the concrete face. **1972** *Daily Colonist* (Victoria, B.C.) 27 Feb. 24/7 Doctors believe hyaline membrane..is an unwanted substitute for a totally or partially missing 'surfactant' membrane that in normal babies keeps the lungs from collapsing. **1979** *Enhanced Oil Recovery* (Shell Internat. Petroleum Co.) 5 Injection of water containing surfactants (soap-like chemicals) into the reservoir can lower the oil/water interfacial tension very substantially..and therefore mobilize the oil held by capillary forces.

surfacy ('sɜːfəsɪ), *a.* Also **surfacey.** [f. SURFACE *sb.* 1 b + -Y[1].] 'On the surface', without depth; superficial.

1887 W. ARMSTRONG in *Art Jrnl.* June 167/1 Titian fails to give the substance of flesh. His flesh is surfacy and without the variety of truth; it is, in fact, without texture. **1957** *Psychol. Rev.* LXIV. 139/1 When we are fixated upon the vase in the Rubin reversible figure, the background recedes, is less surfacy, and..seems to provide a less centrally adequate form of sensory input. **1975** *Citizen* (Ottawa) 3

Nov. 57/3 Neither he nor Dame Peggy wish to deliver glib, surfacy imitations. **1979** *Rydge's* (Sydney) Apr. 105/2, I would still be trying to select the one that had the fine edge, but I wouldn't be as surfacey as to select it on that one aspect.

surfari (sɜːˈfɑːrɪ). [Blend of SURF *sb.* and SAFARI *sb.*: cf. *surf safari* s.v. SURF *sb.* 3.] A journey made by surfers in search of good conditions for surfboarding; a group of surfers travelling to or around suitable beaches. Phr. ***on surfari*** (S. Afr.): cf *on safari* s.v. SAFARI *sb.* 1 a.

1963 *Pix* 28 Sept. 63 Driving in a surfari to the beach is just one point better than travelling 'Robinson Crusoe' (alone). **1965** J. POLLARD *Surfrider* ii. 21 Soon it will be too crowded, other 'surfaris', groups of surfers looking for a surf, are already on the beach. **1965** *S. Afr. Surfer* I. III. 27 Takkies has made it to the beach at Zinkwazi where he meets three stokies who are on surfari. **1968** *Surfer* IX. IV. 69 Ever since Endless Summer, surfers visiting Cape St. Francis have been disappointed, day after day, by fast unrideable, rock-riddled waves where Bruce found the best surf of his world surfari.

surfeit (ˈsɜːfɪt), *sb.* Forms: 4 **surfeyte, sorfait,** 4–5 **surfaite, -feet, sorfete,** 4–6 **surfait,** 4–8 **surfet,** 5 **-fayte, -fett, -ffete, -phette,** 5–6 **-fete, -fette,** 6 **-fayt, -ffet, -fyt, -fecte,** *Sc.* **-phat,** 6–7 **surfit,** 7 **-ffett,** 6– **surfeit.** [a. OF. *sor-, surfait, -fet* excess, surplus, = Pr. *sobrefach*:—pop.L. **superfactum*, n. of action f. **superficĕre* (cf. late L. *superficiens* excessive, OF. *sorfaisant* intemperate, immoderate), f. *super-* SUPER- 9 b + *facĕre* to do, act.]

1. Excess, superfluity; excessive amount or supply *of* something. (In later use only as *fig.* from 4.)

a **1300** *Cursor M.* 22884 (Cott.) Agh we þer-on to seke resun Hu he dos alkin thing to nait, Certes þat war bot surfait. **13..** *Ibid.* 23566 (Gött.) For if þai a-noþer heuen wroght, It war sur-fait [*Cott.* vnnait] and all for noght. *c* **1400** tr. *Secr. Secr., Gov. Lordsh.* 52 What kyng þat wille continue giftys yn surfaytes ouer þat his kyngdom wyl suffyse to hym. **1634** SIR T. HERBERT *Trav.* 224 Surfeit of presuming ignorance. **1663** COWLEY *Ode His Majesties Restor.* v, 'Tis Happy, which no Bleeding does indure A Surfet of such Blood to cure.

1844 GLADSTONE *Glean.* V. lvii. 125 Nor is he..to be reproached either with want of charity or with surfeit of pride. **1847** PRESCOTT *Peru* III. viii. (1850) II. 168 The effect of such a surfeit of the precious metals was instantly felt on prices. **1889** *Spectator* 26 Oct., An abundance, nay, a surfeit, of works treating..of Scotland..have been printed.

†**2.** Action that exceeds the limits of law or right; (*a*) transgression, trespass, fault. *Obs.*

13.. *Gaw. & Gr. Knt.* 2433 In syngne of my surfet I schal se hit ofte. *c* **1430** LYDG. *Min. Poems* (Percy Soc.) 145 He took noon heed his surfetys to redresse. *Ibid.* 177 To do no surfet in woord nor in language. *c* **1450** *Pol. Rel. & L. Poems* (1903) 142 O ihesu, grant..That..thy .v. wowndis..May wach in vs all surfetis reproueable.

3. (An) excessive indulgence, (an) excess. (In later use only as *fig.* from 4, 4 b.)

1387–8 T. USK *Test. Love* II. xiv. (Skeat) l. 58 This is the sorinesse of fayned love; nedes of these surfettes sicknesse mote folowe. **1422** YONGE tr. *Secr. Secr.* xxxiv. 186 Put away euery Surfete, and restrayne thy desyres. *Ibid.* lxix. 246 Trauaill of body, and company of women, a man may vse wyth-out surfaite. **1612** *Two Noble K.* IV. iii, That intemprat surfeit of her eye hath distemperd the other sences. **1635** A. STAFFORD *Fem. Glory* (1869) 20 [She] kept her soule from the surfets to which carnall delights invite all things humane. *a* **1680** BUTLER *Rem.* (1759) II. 73 Perpetual Surfeits of Pleasure have filled his Mind with bad and vicious Humours.

1847 DISRAELI *Tancred* II. xvi, All ends in a crash of iconoclastic surfeit. *a* **1865** in TYLOR *Early Hist. Man.* iv. 74 She..would..shut herself up and 'indulge herself in a surfeit of sounds'.

4. Excessive taking *of* food or drink; gluttonous indulgence in eating or drinking. Also in fig. context.

1338 R. BRUNNE *Chron.* (1810) 311 Feyntise, liþt duellyng, on mornes long to lie, Surfeyte in euenyng, & luf of licchorie. **1387** TREVISA *Higden* (Rolls) IV. 329 þese lyved lengest..for þey..dede noon surfeet of mete and of drynke. **1446** LYDG. *Nightingale Poems* ii. 266 Agenst glotenye he drank eysel and galle, To oppresse surfayte of vicious folkes alle. *c* **1470** *Lydgate's Hors, Shepe, & G.* (Roxb.) 27 In mete and drynke be thou mesurable, Beware of surfete and misgouernance. **1528** MORE *Dyaloge* I. Wks. 1147/2 The sykenes that foloweth our intemperate surfayt. *c* **1530** H. RHODES *Bk. Nurture* in *Babees Bk.* (1868) 105 Eate without surfet. **1671** MILTON *Samson* 1562 Feed on that first, there may in grief be surfet. **1684** *Foxe's A. & M.* III. 404/1 Fasting is only to avoid surfet.

b. In particularized sense: An excessive indulgence in food or drink that overloads the stomach and disorders the system. Also in fig. context.

1362 LANGL. *P. Pl.* A. v. 210 After al þis surfet an Accesse he hedde. **1377** *Ibid.* B. XIII. 405, [I] more mete ete and dronke þen kende miȝt defie—And kauȝte seknesse sumtyme for my sorfetes ofte. *c* **1430** LYDG. *Min. Poems* (Percy Soc.) 68 Suffre no surfetis in thy house at nyght, Ware of reresoupers. **1513** MORE *Rich. III* (1883) 34 With which disease nature being..weaked, waxeth the lesse able to beare out a new surfet. **1580** LYLY *Euphues* (Arb.) 252 Age seeketh rather a Modicum for sustenaunce, then feastes for surfets. **1647** COWLEY *Mistr., Agst. Fruition* 29 Of very Hopes a surfeit he'll sustain, Unless by Fears he cast them up again. **1649** in *Verney Mem.* (1907) I. 447 It's possible to have a surfeit of water as well as wine. **1732** ARBUTHNOT *Rules of Diet* in *Aliments* etc. 269 The best Remedy after a Surfeit of Fruit. **1747** WESLEY *Prim. Physick* (1762) p. xx, Strong Liquors do not prevent the Mischiefs of a Surfeit. **1851** THACKERAY *Engl. Hum., Swift* (1853) 23 He was half-killed with a surfeit of Shene pippins.

†**c.** The excessive amount eaten. Also in fig. context. *Obs.*

c **1400** tr. *Secr. Secr., Gov. Lordsh.* 67 Many þat withdrew hem froo etynges of surfaytz. *c* **1550** LLOYD *Treas. Health* a v, If it chance a dronken man sodenly to fal spechlesse, he shall..dye..excepte eyther he fall to an agew, or els he receyue his spech agayne at the houre when the surfyt is digestyd. **1582** STANYHURST *Æneis* II. (Arb.) 54 Theire steed hath vpvomited from gorge a surfet of armdmen. **1601** BP. W. BARLOW *Serm. Paules Crosse* 62 Himselfe a surfet to the realme, to be spewed out iustly. **1640** G. SANDYS *Christ's Passion* III. 29 Let melting Stars their sulphrous surfet shed. **1700** BLACKMORE *Job* 87 His loathing stomach..Shall cast the precious surfeit up again.

5. The morbid condition caused by excessive eating or drinking; sickness or derangement of the system arising from intemperance; †also applied more widely to fevers or fits arising from other causes. Also in fig. context.

a **1513** FABYAN *Chron.* VII. ccxxix. 260 Kynge Henry..toke a surfet by etynge of a lamprey, & therof dyed. **1589** NASHE *Anat. Absurd.* D ij b, More perrish with the surfet then with the sworde. **1589** [? LYLY] *Pappe w. Hatchet* in L.'s Wks. 1902 III. 398 Bastard Senior was with them at supper, and I thinke tooke a surfet of colde and raw quipps. **1606** G. W[OODCOCKE] *Hist. Ivstine* XXXVI. 115 He caught a surfet by the heat of the sun. **1631** R. BOLTON *Comf. Affl. Consc.* (1635) 302 Hee drank not so indiscreetly..of that immeasurable sea as..to fall into a surfeit of security. **1655** CULPEPPER, etc. *Riverius* I. ii. 10 A surfet going before, with crude and sharp belchings. **1693** LOCKE *Educ.* §17 More Fevers and Surfeits are got by People's Drinking when they are hot, than by any one Thing I know. **1760–2** GOLDSM. *Cit. W.* xv, He died of a surfeit caused by intemperance. **1837** *Brit. Husb.* II. 530 (Libr. Usef. Knowl.) They [*sc.* pigs] are..not uncommonly seized with surfeit and indigestion. **1871** NAPHEYS *Prev. & Cure Dis.* I. i. 44 He died of a surfeit.

b. An eruptive disease in horses and other animals, arising from immoderate feeding and other causes.

c **1720** W. GIBSON *Farrier's Guide* II. xii. (1738) 49 By a Surfeit is principally understood all such Maladies as proceed from immoderate feeding. **1753** J. BARTLET *Gentl. Farriery* 173 The wet surfeit..appears on different parts of the body of a horse. **1841** DICK *Man. Vet. Sci.* (1862) 148 An eruption which is called a *Surfeit*, or the Nettle-rash. **1846** J. BAXTER *Libr. Pract. Agric.* (ed. 4) I. 454 When the coat of a horse stares, he is said to labour under a surfeit. The skin is covered with scurf and scabs... Sometimes the surfeit appears on the skin in small lumps. **1894** ARMATAGE *Horse in Health & Disease* xxiv.

6. Disgust arising from excess; nausea, satiety. ***to (a) surfeit***: to satiety, *ad nauseam*.

1644 HOWELL *Engl. Teares* (1645) 175 God grant that people do not take at last a surfet of that most divine Ordinance of preaching. **1672** MARVELL *Reh. Transp.* I. 116 He discourseth it at large, even to surfeit. **1683** BURNET tr. *More's Utopia* (1685) 99 They think the doing of it so often should give one a Surfeit of it. **1796** BURKE *Regic. Peace* i. Wks. 1808 VIII. 148 Matter and argument have been supplied abundantly, and even to surfeit. **1822** HAZLITT *Table-t.* Ser. II. xvi. (1869) 331 Do not make a surfeit of friendship, through over-sanguine enthusiasm. **1855** R. A. WILSON *Mexico* 51 He enjoys to a surfeit these bounties of nature. **1878** BROWNING *Poets Croisic* vii, Swords, scrolls, harps, that fill The vulgar eye to surfeit.

7. *Mining.* = CHOKE-DAMP.

1708 J. C. *Compl. Collier* (1845) 45 Some Collieries are very subject to this fatal Surfeit. **1812** J. HODGSON in J. Raine *Mem.* (1857) I. 97 This after-damp is called..surfeit by the colliers. **1883** GRESLEY *Gloss. Coal-mining.*

8. *attrib.* and *Comb.*, as ***surfeit suffocation***; ***surfeit-gorged, -slain, -swelled, -swollen, -taking*** adjs.; †**surfeit-water**, a 'water' or medicinal drink for the cure of surfeit.

1693 TATE *Dryden's Juvenal* II. 5 A Sot,..*surfeit-gorg'd, and reeking from the Stews. **1682** OTWAY *Venice Preserved* I. i, *Surfeit-slain fools. **1823** LAMB *Elia* Ser. II. *Amicus Redivivus*, A case of common *surfeit suffocation. **1597** SHAKS. *2 Hen. IV*, v. v. 54 Such a kinde of man, So *surfeit-swell'd, so old, and so prophane. **1592** NASHE *P. Penilesse* Wks. (Grosart) II. 72 *Surfit-swolne Churles. **1746** FRANCIS tr. *Hor., Sat.* II. ii. 30 The pale, Surfeit-swoln guest. **1593** SHAKS. *Lucr.* 698 So *surfeit-taking Tarqvin fares. **1633** FORD *'Tis Pity* III. iv, Did you give her aught? An easy *surfeit-water, nothing else. **1757** A. COOPER *Distiller* III. xvii. (1760) 173 There are two Kinds of Surfeit-water, one made by Distillation and the other by Infusion. **1801** *Sporting Mag.* XVIII. 22, I was obliged to take a little surfeit-water before I went to bed.

ˈ**surfeit**, *a.* *Obs.* or *arch.* Also 6 **surfett, -fat, sirfoot** (?). [In sense 1, a. OF. *surfet, -fait*:—pop. L. **superfactu-s*, pa. pple. of **superficĕre* (see prec.). In sense 2, app. contracted from *surfeited*, ? after FORFEIT *a.*]

†**1.** Excessive; immoderate, intemperate. *Sc. Obs.*

1502 [implied in SURFEITLY]. **1533** BELLENDEN *Livy* I. xxii. (S.T.S.) I. 122 þe said pepill..war movit aganis him for þe surfett spending of þare laubouris. **1535** STEWART *Cron. Scot.* (Rolls) II. 429 Surfat Drinking. **1542** *Records of Elgin* (New Spald. Cl. 1903) I. 73 The entres siluer dischargit to the said James for the surfet expensis maid be him in the Kingis servece. *a* **1578** LINDESAY (Pitscottie) *Chron. Scot.* (S.T.S.) I. 102 Wexit and irkit..throw frequent heirschipis and surfeit raidis. **1597** *Reg. Privy Council Scot.* V. Introd. 67 Wine drunk in abundance,..sirfootfeats [? = surfeit feasts] casten abroad on the causey.

†**b.** Of a horse: Suffering from surfeit. *Obs.* In quot. app. confused with *scurvy*.

1624 L. W. C. *Disc. Age Horse* C j b, For a Scurfet Horse. Take a quart of Beere or Ale..and give it him.

2. Satiated, surfeited.

1699 LOCKE *Educ.* (ed. 4) §108 Childish Play..which they should be weaned from, by being made Surfeit of it. **1877** L. MORRIS *Epic Hades* I. 54, I hid my face within my hands, and fled, Surfeit with horror.

ˈ**surfeit**, *v.* Forms: see the sb. [f. SURFEIT *sb.*: cf. FORFEIT *v.*]

1. *trans.* To feed to excess or satiety; to sicken or disorder by overfeeding (†or by unwholesome food). Also *absol.*

1393 LANGL. *P. Pl.* C. XIV. 188 Ich see noone so ofte sorfeten soþliche so mankynde; In mete out of mesure and meny tymes in drynke. *a* **1578** LINDESAY (Pitscottie) *Chron. Scot.* (S.T.S.) I. 13 Thay that ar maist furthie in the ingyring and surffetting thame sellffis. *c* **1645** HOWELL *Lett.* v. 30 The Fannian Law..allowes a chirping cup to satiet, not to surffet. **1747–96** MRS. GLASSE *Cookery* iii. 17 Pork must be well done, or it is apt to surfeit. **1748** *Anson's Voy.* III. ii. 311 The few [fish] we caught..having surfeited those who eat of them.

†**b.** With *away*: To dissipate by excessive indulgence. *nonce-use.*

1607 MIDDLETON *Michaelm. Term* II. ii. 23, I..surfeited away my name and state In swinish riots.

2. *fig.* or *gen.* To fill or supply to excess; to oppress or disgust with over-abundance of something.

1592 NASHE *P. Penilesse* (ed. 2) 4 Hauing..surfetted my minde with vanitie. **1600** W. CORNWALLIS *Ess.* I. xxi. M v, Vpon occasion I would speake, but niggardly, and rather starue then surfet my Auditory. **1615** CHAPMAN *Odyss.* II. 582 When sleepe so surfeted Their leaden ey-lids. **1668–9** PEPYS *Diary* 6 Mar., He is weary and surfeited of business. **1683** *Apol. Prot. France* Pref. p. ii, By over-stocking those populous Manufactures,..and by surfeiting the Land with people. **1742** YOUNG *Nt. Th.* v. 260 With mixt manure she surfeits the rank soil. **1821** LAMB *Elia* Ser. I. *My Relations*, If you are not already surfeited with cousins. **1882** B. D. W. RAMSAY *Recoll. Mil. Serv.* II. xvi. 140, I..had been surfeited with office-work. **1882** MISS BRADDON *Mt. Royal* II. xi. 246 My wife surfeits herself with poetry.

3. *intr.* To eat or drink to excess *of*; to feast gluttonously or over-abundantly *upon*. (In early use more widely, including sensual indulgence in general.)

1422 YONGE tr. *Secr. Secr.* xxxiv. 186 Temporance, by the wiche a man kepyth and holdyth mesure in ettynge and drynkynge, and surfetyth not, as in women. *Ibid.* lxi. 237 Yf a man do surfete of mette and drynke, the kyndely hette shal be enfebelit. **1559** *Mirr. Mag., Owen Glendour* xxvii, Such ..as fysh before the net Shal seldome surfyt of the pray they take. **1575** LANEHAM *Let.* (1871) 59, I haue seen him..so..surfit, az he hath pluct of hiz napkin, wyept his knife, & eat not a morsell more. **1632** SANDERSON *Serm.* 443 Surfetting vpon the delicatest fishes. **1665** BOYLE *Occas. Refl.* v. x. (1848) 338 Ev'n the wholesomest Meats may be surfeited on. **1697** DRYDEN *Virg. Georg.* III. 789 He never supt in solemn State,..Nor surfeited on rich Campanian Wine. **1819** SHELLEY *Masque of Anarchy* xliii, Such diet As the rich man in his riot Casts to the fat dogs that lie Surfeiting beneath his eye. **1856** KANE *Arctic Expl.* II. xxvi, A merrier set of gourmands..never surfeited in genial diet.

b. *fig.* To indulge in something to excess; to take one's fill, 'feast', 'revel'. Now *rare* or *Obs.*

1586 WARNER *Alb. Eng.* IV. xx. (1612) 98 Sweetely surfeiting in ioy. **1594** DRAYTON *Ideas* xxxiii, Whilst yet mine eyes doe surfet with delight. **1601** SHAKS. *Twel. N.* I. i. 2 If Musicke be the food of Loue,..Giue me excesse of it; that surfetting, The appetite may sicken, and so dye. **1633** BP. HALL *Hard Texts* Eccles. xi. 8 He shall have no lust to surfet of these things. **1655** FULLER *Ch. Hist.* II. ii. §26 Piety is most healthful..where it can least surfeit of Earthly Pleasures. **1658** DEKKER, etc. *Witch of Edmonton* I. i. Wks. 1873 IV. 355 We will surfeit in our embraces, Wench. **1707** PRIOR *Satire Poets* 153 Starving for Meat, not surfeiting on Praise. **1832** *Examiner* 673/2 The laity have done much wrong to the clergy in allowing it to cram, and surfeit, and pall, and hebetate, with forbidden wealth.

4. To suffer the effects of over-feeding; to fall sick in consequence of excess (†or by eating unwholesome food). Now *rare* or *Obs.*

1585 SANDYS *Serm.* x. §7. 156 Let vs returne no more to the flesh pots of Egypt, let vs not lust after quailes: for if wee feede vpon them, we shall surfet of them to our destruction. **1596** SHAKS. *Merch. V.* I. ii. 6 They are as sicke that surfet with too much, as they that starue with nothing. **1624** CAPT. J. SMITH *Virginia* IV. 148 They spared no vncleane..beast, ..but eat them vp also..; and by this meanes their whole Colony well-neere surfeted, sickned and died. **1700** LOCKE *Hum. Und.* (ed. 4) II. xxxiii. §7 A grown Person surfeiting with Honey, no sooner hears the Name of it, but his Phancy ..carries Sickness..to his Stomach. **1760–2** GOLDSM. *Cit. W.* xv, If an epicure..shall happen to surfeit on his last night's feast.

b. *fig.* or *gen.* To suffer from over-abundance; to become disgusted or nauseated by excess of something; to grow sick *of*. Now *rare* or *Obs.*

1605 A. WARREN *Poore Mans Passion* cxiii. E iij, Some Vsurer..Whose gorged chests surfet with cramming gold. **1607** CHAPMAN *Bussy D'Ambois* II. i. 15 The slenderest pittance of commended vertue, She surfets of it. **1640** QUARLES *Enchirid.* III. 2 Be not too fond, lest she surfeit. *a* **1668** LASSELS *Voy. Italy* (1670) I. Pref., Traveling preserves my yong nobleman from surfeiting of his parents. *a* **1700** EVELYN *Diary* 4 Oct. 1683, Surfeiting of this, I..went contented home to my poor, but quiet villa. **1719** DE FOE *Crusoe* (Globe) 321 The Man of Pleasure..surfeited of his Vice. **1814** CARY *Dante, Inf.* XIX. 57 So early dost thou surfeit with the wealth.

†**5.** To trespass, transgress. (Cf. SURFEIT *sb.* 2.)

c **1440** *Promp. Parv.* 484/2 Surfetyn, or forfetyn yn trespace, *forefacio, delinquo.*

'surfeited, *ppl. a.* [f. SURFEIT *sb.* or *v.* + -ED.]

1. Fed or filled to excess; oppressed or disordered by or as by over-feeding.

1605 SHAKS. *Macb.* II. ii. 5 The surfeted Groomes doe mock their charge With Snores. **1610** —— *Temp.* III. iii. 55 The neuer surfeited Sea. **1784** COWPER *Task* III. 758 They that feed th' o'er-charg'd And surfeited lewd town with her fair dues. **1842** MANNING *Serm.* (1848) I. 22 Take a watchful, self-denying man..and compare him with the heavy, surfeited man. **1886** H. F. LESTER *Under two Fig Trees* 182 And then divide the morsel among these already surfeited gluttons.

2. Of a horse: Affected with the 'surfeit'. ? *Obs.*

1667 DRYDEN & DK. NEWCASTLE *Sir M. Mar-all* II. ii, His folly's like a sore in a surfeited horse, cure it in one place, and it breaks out in another. **1753** J. BARTLET *Gentl. Farriery* 170 A horse is said to be surfeited, when his coat stares.

surfeiter ('sɜːfɪtə(r)). Forms: 5 **surfetour**, 6 **surfeter, surffetter**, 6–7 **surfetter**, 7– **surfeiter**. [f. SURFEIT *v.* + -ER[1].] One who surfeits; a glutton, gormandizer; †formerly also in wider sense: One given to sensual excess, a profligate, libertine.

1413 *Pilgr. Sowle* (Caxton 1483) III. ix. 55 Bollers of wyn and ale, dronkelewe surfetours. **1547–64** BAULDWIN *Mor. Philos.* (Palfr.) 45 A lecher, a rioter, a surfetter, a brauler. **1606** SHAKS. *Ant. & Cl.* II. i. 33 This amorous Surfetter. **1657** RUMSEY *Org. Salutis* iv. (1659) 17 That..there remains part of the meat undigested..is too well known to moderate Surfeiters. **1756** W. DODD *Fasting* (ed. 2) 11 Religious duties, which how can the sleepy surfeiter ever perform? **1866** *Pall Mall G.* 2 Oct. 3 The royal surfeiter *par eminence*..Henry I.

'surfeiting, *vbl. sb.* Now *rare.* Forms: see SURFEIT *v.*; also 6 *Sc.* **surfesting**. [f. SURFEIT *v.* + -ING[1].] = SURFEIT *sb.* 4, 5.

1526 TINDALE *Luke* xxi. 34 Take hede to youre selves, lest youre hertes be overcome, with surfettynge and dronkennes. **1533** ELYOT *Cast. Helthe* (1539) 23 Some doo suppose, if they be eaten rawe with vyneger, before meate, it shall preserue the stomake from surfettynge. **1551** T. WILSON *Logic* (1580) 38 b, If dronkennesse be deulishe, then surffectyng is deulishe. **1583** *Leg. Bp. St. Androis* 287 Surfesting of sundrie spyces. **1604** E. G[RIMSTONE] *D'Acosta's Hist. Indies* IV. xvii. 257 They might eate much, without any feare of surfetting. **1632** tr. *Bruel's Praxis Med.* 79 Such as are much addicted to surfettings..are subiect to the apoplexy. **1650** W. D. tr. *Comenius' Gate Lat. Unl.* §823 Hee that is drunk..hath for his punishment surfetting (an heavie head). **1821** LAMB *Elia* Ser. I. *Grace before Meat*, Gluttony and surfeiting are no proper occasions of thanksgiving.

'surfeiting, *ppl. a.* [f. SURFEIT *v.* + -ING[2].]

1. Given to excessive eating or drinking; gluttonous.

1588 KYD *Househ. Philos.* Wks. (1901) 258 The most incontinent and surfeiting companion. **1621** BURTON *Anat. Mel.* II. iv. I. i. 431 Surfetting courtiers and staulfed Gentlemen lubbers.

2. Producing a state of surfeit or satiety.

1715 NELSON *Addr. Pers. Qual.* 77 The surfeiting Draught Solomon took of Pleasure. **1722** DE FOE *Col. Jack* (1840) 258 It is a subject too surfeiting to entertain people with the beauty of a person they will never see. **1753** RICHARDSON *Grandison* IV. xxxvi. 246 A fond husband is a surfeiting thing. **1809** MALKIN *Gil Blas* VII. xv. ¶9 Unbounded prodigality in our..table, even to a surfeiting degree.

† **'surfeitly**, *adv. Obs.* In 6 **-etly**. [f. SURFEIT *a.* + -LY[2].] Immoderately, intemperately.

1502 ARNOLDE *Chron.* (1811) 171 Theis thyngis make clene blod so thei be not surfetly taken. **1536** BELLENDEN *Cron. Scot.* (1821) II. 15 New tribute sa surfetly tane.

† **'surfeitness**. *Sc. Obs. rare.* In 5 **surfastnes** (?), 6 **sirffeitnes**. [f. SURFEIT *a.* + -NESS.] = SURFEIT *sb.* 4.

a **1500** *Ratis Raving* etc. 270 Se surfastnes [*sic*] the nocht assailȝhe Vitht slep. **1535** STEWART *Cron. Scot.* (Rolls) III. 545 Sic sirffeitnes alway to be refusit, And sufficience of meit and drink be vsit.

surfel, -fet, etc., obs. or var. ff. SURFLE, SURFEIT.

surfer ('sɜːfə(r)). [f. SURF *sb.* or *v.* + -ER[1].] One who rides a surfboard; a surfboarder. Also *fig.*

1955 A. ROSS *Australia 55* xv. 214 The heads of the surfers bob over several ignored undulations. **1962** M. MCLUHAN *Gutenberg Galaxy* 144 (*heading*) Peter Ramus and John Dewey were the two educational *surfers* or wave-riders of antithetic period. **1966** T. PYNCHON *Crying of Lot 49* vi. 147 What chance has a lonely surfer boy For the love of a surfer chick? **1970** A. TOFFLER *Future Shock* xiii. 255 Surfers display sores and nodules on their knees and feet as proud proof of their involvement. **1978** G. A. SHEEHAN *Running & Being* vi. 75 'Surfing is a spiritual experience,' says Michael Hynson, one of the world's top surfers.

† **surfetous**, *a.* (*adv.*) *Obs.* Forms: 4–6 **-ouse**, 5 **surf(f)etus**, 6 **surfettouse**. [a. AF. *surfetous*, f. *surfet* SURFEIT *sb.*: see -OUS.] Immoderate, intemperate; surfeited with food or drink.

a **1400** *Minor Poems fr. Vernon MS.* xlix. 382 Large table and plentyuouse Makeþ men of Ianglyng surfetouse. **1422** YONGE tr. *Secr. Secr.* lxv. 242 To kepe covstoume is moche wourth to mayntene hele, so that hit be not surfetouse. **1552** HULOET, Surfetouse, *crapulosus.*

b. *adv.* Excessively, superabundantly.

c **1400** *Destr. Troy* 4219 Hyt semys not surfetus harde No vnpossibill. *Ibid.* 9352 Surffetus mony, Bothe of kynges, & knightes & kid men of armes.

So **'surfetry** (also 5 **serfetrie**) [after *surquidry*], (*a*) presumption, (*b*) surfeit; † **'surfeture** [cf. OF. *surfeiture* arrogance], † **'surfety**, surfeiting.

c **1400** *Laud Troy Bk.* 13133 Hit was open *surfetrie, And on gret pride & folye. **1303** R. BRUNNE *Handl. Synne* 339 Sum men dremyn for *surfeture þat etyn or drynkyn ouer mesure. *a* **1450** *Pol. Rel. & L. Poems* (1903) 286 So þe seek wol do wysely, And kepe him-self fro *surfety [*v.r.* serfetrie]. **1561** HOLLYBUSH *Hom. Apoth.* 20 b, Then must the harte nedes waxe faynte, as well as of excesse of fyllinge or surffetty.

surficial (sə'fɪʃəl), *a. Geol.* [f. SURFACE *sb.*, after *superficial.*] Of or pertaining to the surface of the earth. Cf. SUPERFICIAL *a.* 1 a.

1892 J. D. DANA in *Amer. Jrnl. Sci.* CXLIV. 166 The outflow retains a thickness of 250 feet quite to its extreme western limit, which it could not have done if it had been a subaerial, or, using a much needed new word, a surficial flow. **1926** [see HYPABYSSAL *a.*]. **1981** COSTA & BAKER *Surficial Geol.* ii. 25/2 Both surficial and bedrock geologic maps can be used to identify and classify materials, hazards, and resources.

Hence **sur'ficially** *adv.*, on the surface (esp. of the earth).

1895 J. D. DANA *Man. Geol.* (ed. 4) IV. 806 The trap was poured out surficially from fissures along the eastern margin of the area. **1918** [see CREEP *v.* 10]. **1944** C. PALACHE et al. *Dana's Syst. Min.* (ed. 7) I. 799 The crystals..are often surficially bounded by a yellow or brown alteration shell. **1971** *Nature* 2 July 41/1 In the theory of plate tectonics convergent plate junctures are the loci of orogeny, marked surficially by arc-trench systems.

surfie ('sɜːfɪ). *slang* (chiefly *Austral.*). [f. SURF *sb.* + -IE.] A surfer or surfboarding enthusiast, *spec.* characterized as one of a set of long-haired, sun-tanned young people on a beach. Also *attrib.*

1962 *Austral. Women's Weekly* 24 Oct. (Suppl.) 3/4 *Surfie*, a fond term for a good and keen surfer. **1963** *Sunday Mail* (Brisbane) 10 Nov. 23 He talk surfie talk..'cowabunga, wipe-out, I'm get stoked..yay gremmies'. **1967** *Coast to Coast 1965–66* 254 In one coffee-bar doorway stood the hoodlums..glowering at the pink and orange and green of the surfies going by. **1972** *Sunday Mail* (Brisbane) 26 Mar. 8/2 They have peddled the mushrooms to all-night trippers, located through surfie contacts. **1981** *Times Lit. Suppl.* 30 Jan. 110/5 He agrees to deliver a deal for this scruffy surfie and the plot is primed.

† **surfle**, *sb. Obs.* [f. next.]

1. An embroidered border or hem; also, one of the pleats made in hemming.

c **1532** DU WES *Introd. Fr.* in *Palsgr.* 906 The surfyls, *les ourletz.* **1615** CROOKE *Body of Man* III. v. 110 That the same Chylus might the better bee sucked vp by the Veynes, these transuerse foulds make this coate longer,..for this cause also it was..gathered into Plights; and these foulds or surphles are moueable..as the surphles of a hemme gathered vpon a thred. [**1846** FAIRHOLT *Costume Eng.* (1860) 593 *Surple*, a border or embroidered edge to a garment.]

2. A face-wash, cosmetic. Also ***surfle water***.

1593 NASHE *Christ's T.* V j b, At twenty their liuely colour is lost, theyr faces are soddin & perboyld with French surfets [? surfels]. **1611** RAVENSCROFT *Melismata* D ij b, Red Leather and Surflet [*sic*] water, Scarlet colour or Stauesaker, Will yee buy any fair complection?

† **surfle**, *v. Obs.* Forms: 4–6 **surful**, 5 **-fel, -fyle**, 6 **-fyl, -fyll, -ffill, -ffyll, -full, -pheul**, 6–7 **-fle, -phul**, 7 **-fell, -phle, -phal**, ? *erron.* **-ple**. [a. AF. **surfiler* = med.L. *superfīlāre*, f. *super-* SUPER- 2 + *fīlāre*, f. *fīlum* thread, FILE *sb.*[2]; after *perfīlāre* to PURFLE.]

1. *trans.* To embroider. Hence **surfled** *ppl. a.*, **surfling** *vbl. sb.*

1399 *Mem. Ripon* (Surtees) III. 133 Et in salario j mulieris surfuland prædictum baner 4*d.* **14..** *Voc.* in Wr.-Wülcker 614/38 *Superfilo*, to surfyle. **1481–90** *Howard Househ. Bks.* (Roxb.) 516 Payd to Iohn Peryman for the surfelyng of nappre ware..vj. d. **1523** SKELTON *Garl. Laurel* 803 With burris rowth and bottons surffillyng [*v.r.* surfullinge], In nedill wark raysyng byrdis in bowris. *a* **1529** —— *Col. Cloute* 220 Vnder her surfled [*v.r* surfuld] smocke.

2. *transf.* To paint or wash (the face, etc.) with a cosmetic. Hence **surfled** *ppl. a.*, **surfling** *vbl. sb.* (occas. *concr.* a face-wash or cosmetic); also *attrib.* in **surfling water**.

c **1550** *Dice-Play* (Percy Soc.) 35 This mother baud.. having at home a well painted mannerly harlot,..went, in the morning, to the apothecaries for half-a-pint of sweet water that commonly is called surfulyng water. **1575** GASCOIGNE *Ferd. Ieron.* Wks 228 Thy painted pale, and wrinckles surfled vp. **1596** LODGE *Wits Miserie* (Hunter. Cl.) 44 Shee had learnt al the subtilties of painting, dying, and surfling, some three yeares in Venice. **1598** MARSTON *Sco. Villanie* I. i. 57 Smugge Lesbia Hath..A muddy inside, though a surphul'd face. —— *Pygmal.*, *Sat.* ii. 144 What hether do'st thou bring? But surpheulings, new paints, and poysoning? **1604** —— *Malcontent* II. iv, Doctor Plaster-face ..the most exquisite in forging of veines,..dying of haire, sleeking of skinnes,..surphleing of breastes, blanching and bleaching of teeth. *a* **1644** QUARLES *Virgin Widow* II. i, For one ounce and a half of surfling water, 0 .7. 6. **1650** BULWER *Anthropomet.* 222 Our Court Ladies, with whom Surpling and Court holy-water are a little too frequent. *a* **1652** BROME *City Wit* IV. i, Her Eye artificially spirited, her Cheek surphuled, her Teeth blanch'd.

surflewe, erron. form of SUFFLUE.

† **surfoil**. *Obs.* In 7 **-foyl**. [f. SUR- (= SUPER- 3) + FOIL *sb.*[1]] Used by Grew for a structure serving to cover and protect the leaves, as a bud-scale or a cotyledon.

1671 GREW *Anat. Plants* I. i. §46 The Plume, in Corn, is trussed up within a membranous Sheath: and that of a Bean, cooped up betwixt a pair of Surfoyls. *Ibid.* I. iv. §17 Every Bud, besides its proper Leaves, is covered with divers Leafy Pannicles or Surfoyls.

† **'surfoot**, *a. Obs. rare.* [Formed after SURBATE by substitution of *foot* in the second syllable, with reminiscence of *sore-footed.*] Footsore.

1631 BRATHWAIT *Whimzies, Char. Corranto-coiner* 25 His inventing genius, wearied and surfoote with raunging over so many unknowne regions. **1638** —— *Barnabees Jrnl.* II. (1818) 61 Thence at Meredin appeare I, Where growne surfoot and sore weary, I repos'd.

surful, variant of SURFLE *Obs.*

surfuse (sɜː'fjuːz), *v. Physics.* [f. SUR- + FUSE *v.*] = SUPERFUSE 3. Hence **surfused** (-'fjuːzd) *ppl. a.* So **surfusion** (-'fjuːʒən) = SUPERFUSION 2.

1883 *Nature* 4 Jan. 235/2 Researches on the duration of solidification of surfused substances. **1898** *Ibid.* 27 Oct. 620/1 A very minute quantity of a solid will cause a mass of the same substance to pass from the surfused to the solid state. *Ibid.* 620/2 Surfusion..is not confined to pure metals, ..the eutectic alloy in the bismuth-copper series presents a marked case of surfusion.

surfy ('sɜːfɪ), *a.* [f. SURF *sb.* + -Y.] Abounding in surf; consisting of or resembling surf.

1738 A. HILL *Let.* 11 May in G. Sherburn *Corr. Alexander Pope* (1956) IV. 98 The rushing of a watery sound—a kind of hollow, washy murmur, like the workings of a surfy tide. *a* **1814** *Apostate* II. iv. in *New Brit. Theatre* III. 320 The surfy shore. **1824** *New Monthly Mag.* X. 501 The surfy billows broke across the bow. **1878** STEVENSON *Edinburgh* (1889) 164 When the gulls desert their surfy forelands. **1889** RUSKIN *Præterita* III. iv. 156 The countless ranks of surfy breakers.

surfyl(e, -fyll, var. SURFLE *Obs.*

† **sur'gain**, *v. Obs. rare*$^{-1}$. [f. SUR- + GAIN *v.*, ? after *overwin.*] *trans.* To overcome.

1586 BRIGHT *Melanch.* xxxv. 200 Your crased body surgained with melancholy.

surgant, erron. form of SURGENT.

† **sur'gation**. *Obs. rare*$^{-1}$. [irreg. f. SURGE *v.* + -ATION, ? after *purgation.*] Erection.

1688 HOLME *Armoury* II. xvii. 388/2 The Surgation, or rising of the instrument of Procreation.

surge (sɜːdʒ), *sb.* Forms: 5–7 **sourge**, (6 **sowrge, shourge**, *pl.* **surgies**, 7 **surdge, syrge**), 6– **surge**. [Of obscure origin. In the earliest examples (sense 1 a, b) transl. OF. *sourgeon* (mod.F. *surgeon*), f. *sourge-*, pres. stem of *sourdre*:—L. *surgĕre* to rise. In senses 3, 4 f. SURGE *v.*]

† **1. a.** A fountain, stream. *Obs.*

1490 CAXTON *Eneydos* iv. 18 The whiche trees, soo cutte.. yssued oute..a sourge [orig. *vne sourgon*] of blacke bloode droppynge doun to the erthe. *Ibid.* vi. 26 [Her eyes] seemed two grete sourges [orig. *sourions*] wellynge vp grete affluence of teerys. **1538** ELYOT *Scatebræ*, the bollynge or rysynge vppe of water out of a spryng or sourges of water. **1567** TURBERV. *Epit.* etc., *Louer to his carefull Bed* 24 Thus with a surge of teares bedewde (O bed) I thee forsake.

† **b.** The source of a river or other water. Also *fig. Obs.*

1523 LD. BERNERS *Froiss.* I. i. 1 All great ryuers are.. assemblede of diuers surges [orig. *surgeons*] and sprynges of water. **1587** HARRISON *England* I. xi. in *Holinshed* I. 48/1 Charwell..issueth so fast at the verie surge, that it groweth into a pretie streame, in maner out of hand. *Ibid.* II. xxi. 211/1 Yet is the surge of that water alwaies seuen foot from the salt sea. **1588** ALLEN *Admon.* 4 The nexte immediate surge of our sores.

2. a. A high rolling swell of water, esp. on the sea; a large, heavy, or violent wave; a billow.

In this use and in b, chiefly *poetic* or *rhetorical.*

1530 PALSGR. 278/2 Surge of the see, *uague.* **1533** ELYOT *Cast. Helthe* II. xiv. (1539) 31 b, The beste fyshe..is tossed and lyfte vp with wyndes and sourges. **1555** EDEN *Decades* (Arb.) 277 The sea was..vnquieted with surgies and monsters. **1558** BP. WATSON *Seven Sacram.* xiv. 87 To haue a mans shyppe drowned at once wyth one greate sourge and waue of the sea. **1625** N. CARPENTER *Geogr. Delin.* II. ii. (1635) 20 The Sea is euerywhere plaine and like it selfe, except the rising of the waues and surges. **1673** DRYDEN *Marr. à la Mode* II. i, As open to the gusts of passion, As the bare shore to every beating surge. **1726–46** THOMSON *Winter* 162 The mountain-billows..surge above surge, Burst into chaos with tremendous roar. **1840** R. H. DANA *Bef. Mast* xxv, All this time the sea was rolling in immense surges. **1861** TENNYSON *Sailor Boy* 9 The sands and yeasty surges mix In caves about the dreary bay. **1885** *Athenæum* 23 May 669/3 A noble sea view..where grand surges move in ranks..till they beat furiously on the shore.

b. Such waves or billows collectively; the rising or driving swell of the sea.

1567 TURBERV. *Epit.*, etc., *To the rayling Rout of Sycophants* 7 Such as earst in cutting of the Surge..Bode bitter blast and scornefull Neptunes scurge. **1624** CAPT. J. SMITH *Virginia* I. 2 The very surge of the Sea sometimes overflowed them. **1702** *Lond. Gaz.* No. 3845/2 Some Boats were overset by the Surge of the Sea, it blowing them very fresh. **1749** SMOLLETT *Regicide* IV. iii, Thy specious words Shall sooner lull the sounding surge. **1771** FRANKLIN *Autobiog.* Wks. 1840 I. 30 It was in a place where there could be no landing, there being a great surge on the beach. **1855** KINGSLEY *Westw. Ho!* vi, Laced with white foam from the eternal surge. **1871** TYNDALL *Fragm. Sci.* (1879) I. vii. 238

As we were just clearing the rock, the bow came obliquely to the surge.

c. *fig.* (or, more freq., in fig. context) in reference to feelings, influences, actions, events, etc.: Impetuous onset or agitated movement. Also, a rapid increase in price, activity, etc., esp. over a short period.

1520 WHITINTON *Vulg.* (1527) 21 He is moost moderate and studyous to auoyde surges of his passyon. **1534** MORE *Comf. agst. Trib.* I. Wks. 1140/1 To..strength the walles of our heartes agaynst the gret sourges of this tempesteous sea. **1540** MORYSINE *Vives' Introd. Wysd.* Pref. A v, Men assauted with the surges of sower fortune. **1550** BALE *Engl. Votaries* II. K viij, Peters litle ship..was very like..to be ouer rowne & drouned, the shourges of scismatikes & of heretikes wer so great. **1583** H. HOWARD *Defensative* R ij, Sometyme floting in the surges of mishap. **1602** MARSTON *Antonio's Rev.* IV. ii, They have opened all his rotten parts Unto the vaunting surge of base contempt. **1682** TATE *Abs. & Achit.* II. 1132 This year did Ziloah Rule Jerusalem, And boldly all Sedition's Syrges stem. **1807** BYRON *Hours Idleness, Medea of Euripides* i, What mind can stem the stormy surge Which rolls the tide of human woe? **1834** H. MILLER *Scenes & Leg.* v. (1857) 55 The observances of the old system were effaced..by the hasty surges of popular resentment. **1841–4** EMERSON *Ess., Over-Soul* Wks. (Bohn) I. 117 It is an ebb of the individual rivulet before the flowing surges of the sea of life. **1890** *Spectator* 29 Mar., No surge of public opinion would have saved them from the gallows. **1964** *Ann. Reg. 1963* 191 The final deficit for the fiscal year which ended on 30 June 1963 was $6,200 million, largely because of the surge in business spending and improved tax collection. **1976** *Yellowstone Explorer* July 7/2 The surge in the use of back-country areas is certainly as true here in Yellowstone as it is in other wild places across the country. **1980** *N.Y. Times* 18 Nov. B7/3 The population surge in the Sun Belt has been even greater than expected.

d. *transf.* in reference to various physical things, as fire, wind, sound; also to 'rolling' or undulating hills or the like.

In *Physics*, a sudden or irregular change of pressure; a sudden or violent oscillation of electric current.

1667 MILTON *P.L.* I. 173 The fiery Surge, that from the Precipice Of Heav'n receiv'd us falling. **1810** SOUTHEY *Kehama* XXIII. x, The smoke and vapours of all Padalon.. were spread, With surge and swell, and everlasting motion. **1863** J. R. GREEN *Lett.* (1901) 117 On the low surge of hills that close the horizon, is the house. **1865** BARING-GOULD *Werewolves* xiii. 233 The surge of the old Gregorian tone. **1869** LOWELL *Cathedral* 69 The surges of the warm south-west. **1887** ABERCROMBY *Weather* v. 167 When we look at a series of these surges [of atmospheric pressure] we find a decided tendency of the motion to travel from west to east, or from south-west to north-east. **1908** *Times* 3 Oct. 12/6 The 'surge' of the high-tension current caused some control switches to fuse. **1911** W. N. SHAW *Forecasting Weather* iii. 72 The last of the charts to represent the classification of isobars..are selected to show what Abercromby calls 'surge' —that is to say, a general alteration of pressure that seems to be superposed upon the changes related to a low pressure centre. **1936** *Discovery* Sept. 289/2 It is thus possible to study the passage of 'surges' travelling along the mission line at 186,000 miles a second. **1973** *Physics Bull.* Mar. 148/3 The high voltage cathode-ray oscillograph..was used to detect lightning discharges and other electrical surges in high voltage transmission lines. **1979** *Time* 8 Jan. 80/3 That includes..keeping a weather-eye on cold surges (masses of low-temperature air moving rapidly down from Siberia).

3. *Naut.*, etc. The slipping back of a rope or chain wound round a capstan, etc.; more generally, a sudden jerk or strain.

1748 *Anson's Voy.* II. i. 112 With our utmost efforts, and with many surges and some purchases we made use of to encrease our power. **1805** A. DUNCAN *Mariner's Chron.* IV. 109 At eleven o'clock, a fatal swell gave the ship a sudden shock: she gave a surge, and sunk almost instantaneously. **1849** CUPPLES *Green Hand* viii. (1856) 76 Till the 'cleets' brought him up with a 'surge' fit to have parted the line. **1860** *Merc. Marine Mag.* VII. 180 They might have seen or heard a surge of the cable. **1869** RANKINE *Machine & Hand-tools* Pl. O 2, Jerks or surges are entirely avoided.

4. *Naut.* The part of a capstan or windlass upon which the rope surges.

1664 E. BUSHNELL *Compl. Shipwright* 67 A..Windless, with a Surdge in the middle, as is the Surdge of a Crab, or Capstane. *c* **1850** *Rudim. Navig.* (Weale) 154 *Surge*, the tapered part of the whelps, between the chocks of the capstan, upon which..the messenger may surge itself without any incumbrance.

5. *Naut.* A rhythmic motion forward and aft that is in addition to any steady speed of the vessel.

1949 K. C. BARNABY *Basic Naval Archit.* xvii. 255 A very uneven drive, such as that given by a single-cylinder paddle-wheel engine, will cause a perceptible surge. **1968** F. N. SPIESS in J. F. Brahtz *Ocean Engin.* xv. 566 Stability against horizontal oscillatory motion (surge and sway) and against roll and pitch can chiefly be achieved by providing horizontal extent comparable to or greater than a wavelength. **1977** *Offshore Engineer* May 44/3 During these tests, the data acquisition system recorded..surge, sway and yaw of the lay barge.

6. *attrib.* and *Comb.*, as ***surge-crest***, ***-voice***; ***surge-beat(en*** adj.; **surge chamber**, **tank** *Civil Engin.*, a chamber (often open to the air) connected by a T-junction to a water pipe so as to absorb surges of pressure by filling and drops in pressure by emptying; **surge voltage** *Electr.*, the peak voltage produced in a transmission line by an electrical surge.

1852 M. ARNOLD *Tristram & Iseult* I. 104 The *surge-beat Cornish strand. *a* **1810** SHELLEY *M. Nicholson's Fragm., Ravaillac* 16 The *surge-beaten mould. **1928** *Daily Express* 10 Oct. 12 The pent-up waters sweep through a narrow tunnel to the *surge chamber of a newly built power-house, driving the turbo-generators. **1974** *Encycl. Brit. Macropædia* XVIII. 770/2 To assist regulation with long pipelines, a surge chamber is often connected to the pipeline as near as possible to the turbine, thus enabling part of the water in the pipeline to pass into the surge chamber as the turbine is closed. **1839–52** BAILEY *Festus* 91 In vain they urge their armies to the fight: Their *surge-crests crumble 'neath our stroke of might. **1909** *Trans. Amer. Soc. Mech. Engineers* XXX. 443 '*Surge tank' is a term applied to a stand pipe or storage reservoir placed at the down-stream end of a closed aqueduct to prevent undue rise of pressure in case of a sudden diminution of draft, and to furnish water quickly when the gates are opened, without having to wait for the velocity in the long feeder to pick up. **1930** *Engineering* 3 Jan. 19/2 Each divided tunnel is provided with a separate surge tank. **1975** *North Sea Background Notes* (Brit. Petroleum Co.) 27 Injection water surge tanks, filters and pumps are located on this deck. **1890** 'R. BOLDREWOOD' *Miner's Right* (1899) 163/2 The whispering *surge-voices. **1904** E. B. RAYMOND *Alternating Current Engin.* ii. 76 The *surge voltage is an entirely separate phenomenon from that of resonance. **1979** C. A. GROSS *Power System Analysis* iv. 118 Surge voltages provide the most stringent test and supply the rationale for the standard impulse voltage waveform.

surge (sɜːdʒ), *v.* Also 6–7 **sourge**. [Partly f. OF. *sourge-* (see prec.), or a. early mod.F. *sorgir* (F. *surgir*), = Pr. *sorzer*, *sorgir*, It. *sorgere*, Sp., Pg. *surgir*, ad. L. *surgĕre* to rise; partly f. SURGE *sb.*]

1. *intr.* To rise and fall or toss on the waves; to ride (at anchor, or along over the waves). †In earliest use, ? to come to anchor; cf. F. *surgir*, to come to land.

1511 *Guylforde's Pilgr.* (Camden) 71 The same Tewsdaye at nyghte late we surged in ye Rode. **1585** T. WASHINGTON tr. *Nicholay's Voy.* I. vii. 7 By force of oares we came surging along..beyond the cape of Matafus. **1588** GREENE *Pandosto* (1607) 13 Since thou must goe to surge in the gastfull waues. **1611** *Admiralty Crt. Exam.* 8 June 41 The..lighter..made faste to the shippe surging at an anker in the Thames. **1850** B. TAYLOR *Eldorado* i. (1862) 2 The mass of spars and rigging drifted at her side, surging drearily on the heavy sea. **1867** SMYTH *Sailor's Word-bk.* s.v., A ship is said to surge on a reef when she rises and falls with the heave of the sea, so as to strike heavily.

†**b.** *pass.* ? To be cast up by the surge. *Obs.*

1581 T. HOWELL *Deuises* F iiij b, Twixte death and doubt, still surgde vpon the sande, Stayde vp by hope to light on fyrmer lande.

†**2.** To rise, spring, issue, as a stream from its source, or from underground. *Obs.*

1549 THOMAS *Hist. Italie* 27 It [*sc.* the Fontana da Trevi] sourgeth vnder the hille called Monte degli hortuli. **1632** LITHGOW *Trav.* IX. 403 The Sulphatara..after an excessiue raine surgeth sixe foote high with blacke boyling water. *a* **1661** FULLER *Worthies, Surrey* (1662) III. 79 A River.. which at a place called the Swallow, sinketh unto the Earth and surgeth again some two miles off nigh Letherhead. *Ibid., Warwick.* 125 The river Anas in Spain,..having run many miles under ground, surgeth a greater channell then before.

†**b.** *gen.* To rise, ascend, mount. *Obs. rare.*

a **1591** H. SMITH *Wks.* (1867) II. 480 Till lust, as lighter, up doth surge. **1665** SIR T. HERBERT *Trav.* (1677) 196 The Mountains Imaus, which towards the North surge more and more to an incomprehensible height.

3. To rise in great waves or billows, as the sea; to swell or heave with great force, as a large wave; to move tempestuously.

1566 [see SURGING *ppl. a.*]. **1570** LEVINS *Manip.* 224/25 To sourge, *fluctuare*. **1586** FERNE *Blaz. Gentrie* 298 The waues of the sea..either surged tempestuouslye or calmed quietlye according to his pleasure. **1851** 'WRANGLER' (J. B. Hume) *Poems early Years, Diver* vi, It [*sc.* the abyss] seethes and it surges and hisses and raves, As when water by fire is cross'd. **1862** M. HOPKINS *Hawaii* 12 Giddy precipices..against whose walls the waves beat, and surge. **1865** KINGSLEY *Herew.* vi, The sea boiled past them, surged into the waist, blinded them with spray. **1869** PHILLIPS *Vesuv.* iv. 115 The lava surged, not flowed, over, as angry waves do over a sandy bar.

b. *transf.* of a crowd of people, a wind, etc.

In *Physics*, to vary or oscillate suddenly or violently, as a pressure or an electric current.

1845 HIRST *Com. Mammoth* etc. 14 Their forms had gone O'er the far forests, surging on. **1853** KINGSLEY *Hypatia* xxvi, The mob pressed onward from behind, surged up almost to the barrier. **1859** DICKENS *T. Two Cities* II. i, He ..began to roll and surge in bed. **1860** TYNDALL *Glac.* I. xvi. 115 The wind surging with the full deep boom of the distant sea against the precipice. *a* **1862** BUCKLE *Civiliz.* (1864) II. v. 409 To hear of such things is enough to make one's blood surge again. **1887** ABERCROMBY *Weather* v. 166 Sometimes filling up of a cyclone is tolerably local; other times surging is on an enormous scale. **1891** CONAN DOYLE *White Company* xxxv, From below there surged up the buzz of voices. **1894** LD. WOLSELEY *Life Marlborough* I. 4 The civil wars, which about 1642, began to surge westward into Somerset and Devon.

c. *fig.*, chiefly ***surge up***, of feelings, thoughts, etc.

1853 C. BRONTE *Villette* x, Something..that brought surging up into the mind all one's foibles and weak points. **1877** MRS. OLIPHANT *Makers Flor.* xv. 375 All the enthusiasm of old surged up to answer this appeal. **1883** *Contemp. Rev.* June 768 What rival claims and pretensions have already surged up. **1908** R. BAGOT *A. Cuthbert* xxiii. 309 Her mind was working rapidly, and, indeed, she was scarcely able to disentangle ideas which surged through it.

4. *trans.* To cause to move in, or as in, swelling waves or billows; to drive with waves.

1607 WALKINGTON *Optic Glass* iv. (1664) 50 Wine..calms the roughest tempest of whatsoever more vehement Imagination sourgeth in any man. **1862** THORNBURY *Turner* I. 313 The..monster..hurls rocks at the departing vessel that..surge it back again towards the shore. **1873** LOWELL *Parable, 'Said Christ Our Lord'* iv, Great organs surged through arches dim Their jubilant floods in praise of Him.

5. *Naut.*, etc. **a.** *intr.* To slip back accidentally, as a rope or chain round a capstan, windlass, etc.; to slip round without moving onwards, as a wheel.

a **1625** *Nomenclator Navalis* (Harl. MS. 2301) 139 When they heave at the Capstaine and the Caboll slips back againe they say the Cabell surges. **1627** CAPT. J. SMITH *Sea Gram.* ix. 44 If it [*sc.* the cable] be..slimie with ose, it surges or slips backe vnlesse they keep it close to the whelps. **1840** R. H. DANA *Bef. Mast* xxiv, The chain surged so as almost to unship the barrel of the windlass. **1862** NARES *Seamanship* 87 *Surging*, the hawser slipping up the barrel of a capstan, or veering out the cable suddenly. **1882** HEDLEY *Inventor Railw. Locomotion* 59 It had been always thought that engine-wheels on a smooth surface would 'surge' or slip round without advancing.

b. *trans.* To let go or slacken suddenly (a rope wound round a capstan, etc.); also with the capstan, etc. as obj. Also *absol.*

1769 FALCONER *Dict. Marine* (1780), *Choquer la tournevire*, to surge the capstern. *Ibid., Dévirer le cable*, to surge the cable about the capstern or windlass, in order to prevent it from riding, with one part over another. **1850** SCORESBY *Cheever's Whalem. Adv.* ix. (1858) 120 The line would be 'surged', or slacked out. **1853** in Kane *Arctic Expl.* (1856) I. vii. 70 It's blowing the devil himself, and I am afraid to surge. **1862** NARES *Seamanship* 146 Secure the hawser for surging the topmast to start the crosstrees off the mast-head. **1867** SMYTH *Sailor's Word-bk., Surge Ho!*, the notice given when a rope or cable is to be surged.

c. *intr.* Of a ship: To sweep, pull, or jerk in a certain direction. Also *transf.*

1839 DARWIN *Voy. Nat.* x. (1852) 212 Every now and then, a puff from the mountains, which made the ship surge at her anchors. **1849** CUPPLES *Green Hand* xiv. (1856) 144 Jove! how she [the ship] surged to it. **1856** KANE *Arctic Expl.* I. xxvi. 338 The brig surged and righted. **1895** *Outing* (U.S.) XXVI. 358/1 The fish surges and the rod bends alarmingly.

surge, obs. form of CIERGE, SERGE.

surgeand, -ant, obs. forms of SURGEON.

surgeant, obs. form of SERGEANT.

1596 RALEIGH *Discov. Guiana* 17 A Surgeant or Alferez.

surged, *ppl. a. rare.* ? *Obs.* [f. SURGE *sb.* or *v.* + -ED.] **a.** Raised or moved as in swelling waves. **b.** *Her.* = UNDÉ, WAVY.

1635 SWAN *Spec. Mundi* (1670) 314 The harmless choristers of the ecchoing groves do then begin to tune again their surged throats. **1688** HOLME *Armoury* I. 19/1 Wavee, or Wavey, or Waved, or Unde, or Surged.

surgeful ('sɜːdʒfʊl), *a. poet. rare.* [f. SURGE *sb.* + -FUL.] Full of surges or billows.

1612 DRAYTON *Poly-olb.* i. 212 Her soveraigne when shee sees t'approach the surgefull deepe. *Ibid.* xiv. 214 Upon her spacious breast tossing the surgefull tides. **1877** BLACKIE *Wise Men* 192 Upon that surgeful sea where you are launched.

surgeless ('sɜːdʒlɪs), *a. rare.* [f. as prec. + -LESS.] Free from surges.

1578 *Mirr. Mag., Compl. Crassus* xliv, In surgelesse Seas of quiet rest. **1903** A. SMELLIE *Men of Covt.* iv. 67 The surgeless calm.

surgent ('sɜːdʒənt), *a.* and *sb.* [ad. L. *surgentem*, *surgens*, pr. pple. of *surgĕre* to rise: see SURGE *v.*]

A. *adj.* **1. a.** Rising or swelling in waves, or as a flood or spring; surging. *lit.* and *fig.*

a **1592** GREENE *Alphonsus* I. Wks. (Rtldg.) 226/1 When the surgent seas Have ebb'd their fill, then waves do rise again. **1854** SALA *Dutch Pict.* vii, Her voice is melancholy and tristfully surgant [*sic*]. **1887** MEREDITH *Ballads & P.* 151 The surgent springs Of recollections. **1896** G. A. SMITH *Twelve Proph.* (1900) I. 105 A Deity who is not only manifest Character, but surgent and importunate Feeling.

b. *gen.* Rising, ascending.

1885 G. MACDONALD *Diary Old Soul* Oct. 31 My surgent thought shoots lark-like up to thee.

c. *Psychol.* A term used by the psychologist R. B. Cattell (b. 1905), in his factorial analysis of personality, to designate a type characterized by resourcefulness and responsiveness considered as a distinct source trait.

1933 R. B. CATTELL in *Brit. Jrnl. Psychol.* Jan. 326 The essence of the temperament is expressible by some term conveying the idea of 'leaping' or 'rising up' with facility. 'Repressed' and 'Unrepressed' convey more than we are entitled to infer at present... The word 'Surgent', from the Latin *surgo*, seems most aptly to express the quality which the tests reveal. **1940** J. BOWLBY *Personality & Mental Illness* v. 71 This division corresponds roughly to the division of surgent personalities into good- and bad-tempered. **1968** *Psychol. Abstr.* XLII. 68/2 Findings..gave more significance to the covariances between 'surgent' character traits and inventive factors.

2. *Geol.* Applied by H. D. Rogers to the fifth of his fifteen divisions of the palæozoic formations in the Appalachian chain, synonymous with the Clinton group of N. America, and partly corresponding to the Middle Silurian of Europe.

1858 H. D. ROGERS *Geol. Pennsylv.* I. 106.

†**B.** *sb.* One who (or that which) rises in rebellion or opposition; cf. *insurgent*. *Obs. rare*$^{-1}$.

1657 F. COCKIN *Div. Blossomes* 107 If thou art spoused unto Christ, O soul, each surgent I'll controule.

Hence '**surgency**, the attribute possessed by the surgent personality (see sense 1 c of the adj.).

1933 R. B. CATTELL in *Brit. Jrnl. Psychol.* Jan. 327 The amount of [trait] '*c*' possessed by any individual could be referred to as the degree of Surgency. 1940 J. BOWLBY *Personality & Mental Illness* v. 70 The hypomanic personality has much surgency. 1952 *Brit. Jrnl. Psychol.* May 153 The range covered is very comprehensive, including such recent words as..narcoanalysis, surgency and tele. 1973 R. B. CATTELL *Personality & Mood* i. 10 Intelligence, ego strength, surgency, and characterological anxiety..are source traits.

surgeon ('sɜːdʒən), *sb.* Forms: α. 4 **sorgien, surgeyn,** 4–5 **surgyen, -yne,** 4–6 **surgien, surgen,** 5 **-ene,** 5–6 **-yn,** 5–7 **-ian, -ean,** 6 **-in,** (7 **shirgian**). β. 5 **surgeoun, surion, -oune, serion, sorg(e)on,** 5–6 **surgyon,** 5–7 **-ion,** 6 **-ione, sowrgeon,** 7 **surgon,** 5– **surgeon.** γ. 5 **surgeand,** 6 **-ea(u)nt, -iant, -ynte.** δ. 5 **suregene,** 6 *Sc.* **sur(r)igian(e, -ine, -eane, surrugin, -yȝen.** [a. AF. *surgien* (13th c.), also *sirogen, sur(r)igien*, contracted form of OF. *serurgien, cirurgien*, mod.F. *chirurgien*: see CHIRURGEON. Cf. OPg. *surgião* (beside mod.Pg. *cirurgião*). MDu. *surgien, -ijn, surisien* were also from OF.]

1. a. One who practises the art of healing by manual operation; a practitioner who treats wounds, fractures, deformities, or disorders by surgical means. In early use often more widely, a medical man, doctor. Now *spec.* one who holds a licence or diploma from the Royal College of Surgeons or any other body, legally qualifying him to practise in surgery; hence (now *rare*) = general practitioner.

For the relation between *surgeon* and *physician* see note and quots. under PHYSICIAN *sb.* 2 b. See also *barber surgeon* s.v. BARBER *sb.*, *house surgeon* s.v. HOUSE *sb.*[1] 24. ***Surgeons' Hall***: see HALL[1] 6.

α. 13.. *Guy Warw.* (A.) 1659 þilke monk sorgien [*Caius MS.* a phisician] was, þe vertu he knewe of mani a gras; þe wounde he biheld stedefastliche. 1338 R. BRUNNE *Chron.* (1810) 229 His surgien him tolde, if he suld him saue, & his lif holde, reste behoued him haue. *c*1350 *Will. Palerne* 964 Alle the surgens of salerne. *c*1386 CHAUCER *Melib.* ¶45 A Surgien by licence and assent of swiche as weren wise. 1426 LYDG. *De Guil. Pilgr.* 1535 Swych be no goode surgyens, Lechys, nor physycyens. 1551 T. WILSON *Logic* (1580) 42 b, The Surgean can not heale a wound, except the dead fleshe bee cut out. 1567 HARMAN *Caveat* xii, The Surgien made hym gape, and we could see but halfe a toung. *c*1618 MORYSON *Itin.* IV. v. i. (1903) 424 The vniversities..haue yealded famous Phisitians, who in Italy are also Shirgians.

β. *c*1400 *Melayne* 1343 If any Surgeoun myghte helpe thee. 14.. *Chaucer's Melib.* ¶39 (Camb. MS.), Surgeons Phisiciens olde folk And ȝynge. *c*1440 *Promp. Parv.* 485/1 Surion, or surgen. 1470–85 MALORY *Arthur* VIII. ix. 285 She was a noble surgeon. 1471 *Paston Lett.* III. 3, I have sent hym a serjon, whyche hathe dressid hym. 1511–12 *Act 3 Hen. VIII*, c. 11 Schedule (1817) III. 31 *note*, Memorandum that Sowrgeons be comprised in this Acte like as Phisicions. 1596 NASHE *Saffron Walden* F j b, No lecture at Surgeons Hall vppon an Anatomie may compare with them in longitude. *c*1610 *Women Saints* 120 A Surgeons iron. 1653 in *Verney Mem.* (1907) I. 576, I must ..have the opinnion of a surgon and a doctor both. 1726 SWIFT *Gulliver* IV. iv, I was bred a Surgeon, whose trade it is to cure wounds and hurts in the body. 1843 BETHUNE *Sc. Fireside Stor.* 27 To the young surgeon these invitations were highly gratifying. 1858 *Act 21 & 22 Vict.* c. 90 §40 Any person who shall..falsely..use the..Title of a Physician, Doctor of Medicine,..Surgeon [etc.]..shall..pay a Sum not exceeding Twenty Pounds. 1877 *Encycl. Brit.* VII. 665/1 The museum and lecture rooms of the Royal College of Surgeons. 1880–5 SIR J. PAGET *Mem. & Lett.* ii. (1901) 19 It was decided that I should be a 'Surgeon'—meaning a general practitioner.

γ. 1537 in *Vicary's Anat.* (1888) App. ii. 112 [Thomas Vicary] surgiant [to the King]. *c*1550 *Knight Curtesy* 274 in Hazl. *E.P.P.* II. 78 A surgeand by his arte Heled his woundes. 1583 MELBANCKE *Philotimus* E j b, He..may.. wishe for a surgeaunt to sette his necke bone. 1592 *Extracts Munic. Acc. Newcastle* (1848) 24 Paid to John Colson, surgynte, for his accustomed fee for helping to cure the mamed poore folke, 40*s*.

δ. *c*1460 *Promp. Parv.* (Winch.) 449 Surion, or suregene. *c*1500 *Lancelot* 2724 He..al the surryȝenis socht, Wich for to cum was reddy at his neid. 1524 *Acc. Ld. High Treas. Scot.* V. 238 Robert Kynnard, Surrigeane to the King. 1553 *Douglas' Æneis* XII. vii. *heading*, No mannis cure, nor craft of surrigine Mycht heill Eneas, bot Venus medycyne.

b. A medical officer in the army, navy, or air force (on board ship = 'ship's doctor').

† ***surgeon's mate***: an assistant to a ship's doctor. ***surgeon-assistant*** = assistant surgeon (see ASSISTANT *a.* 3). ***surgeon-general***: see GENERAL *a.* 10; also (*U.S.*), the senior medical officer of the Bureau of Public Health or similar state authority; hence ***surgeon-generalship***. ***surgeon-major***: see MAJOR *a.* 7.

1591 *Garrard's Art Warre* 51 Other meane offices, as Drums, Fifes, Surgeans, and the Clarke of the Band. 1599 DALLAM in *Early Voy. Levant* (Hakl. Soc.) 13 Mr. Chancie ..was our fysition and surgin for the seae. 1612 WOODALL *Surg. Mate* Pref., Wks. (1653) 8 The..trust for.. appointing fit..Surgeons, and Surgeons Mates for their ships and services. *Ibid.* 19 A Surgeons Chest, or..Surgery provisions for Military uses. 1706 G. FARQUHAR *Recruiting Officer* (ed. 2) IV. ii. 49 In short, the Operation will be perform'd with so much Dexterity, that with general Applause you will be made Surgeon General of the whole Army. 1758 J. S. tr. *Le Dran's Observ. Surg.* (1771) 67 Mr. Terrier,..Surgeon-Major to his Majesty's Regiment. 1777 *Jrnls. Continental Congress U.S.* (1907) VII. 162 There [shall] be a physician and Surgeon General with the main army. 1802 JAMES *Milit. Dict.*, *Surgeon*,..a staff officer, who is chief of the medical department in each regiment or hospital, &c. *Ibid.*, *Surgeon-General*, the first or senior surgeon of the army. 1805 *Ibid.* (ed. 2) s.v., *Navy Surgeon*, one who is obliged to act in the three capacities of physician, surgeon, and apothecary, on board a ship of war. 1836 MARRYAT *Midsh. Easy* xxxix, Will you send an assistant-surgeon on board to look after two of my men who are hurt? 1837 DICKENS *Pickw.* ii, Doctor Slammer, surgeon to the 97th. 1837 LOCKHART *Scott* I. x. 324 It was discovered that the patronage of the season had been exhausted, with the exception of one surgeon-assistant's commission. 1867 BRANDE & COX *Dict. Sci.*, etc. III. 666 In the Army, the officers of the medical department are classed as follows: Director-general, who ranks as a major general,..surgeon, as major; assistant-surgeon, as lieutenant. *Ibid.*, In the Royal Navy there are the following grades: inspector-general of hospitals and fleets, deputy-inspector, staff-surgeon, surgeon, assistant-surgeon. 1869 *Boyd's Business Directory* 111 Governor's Staff [N.Y. State]—..Surgeon-General, Jacob S. Mosher, of Albany. 1876 VOYLE & STEVENSON *Milit. Dict.* (ed. 3), *Surgeon-Major*, a medical officer who is attached to and in medical charge of a regiment. 1886 *New York Tribune* 16 Aug. (Cent. Dict.), Surgeon-generalship. 1887 *Brit. Med. Jrnl.* 12 Mar. 604/1 Whether an Admiralty surgeon..can wear uniform, or not. 1894 *Outing* (U.S.) XXIV. 234/1 In addition to the brigade-surgeon..there are also one surgeon with rank of major and one assistant surgeon with rank of captain for each of the five regiments. 1917 *Rep. Surgeon General, U.S. Navy* 16 The Surgeon General, as a member of the General Medicine Board, has participated in the work [for the Council of National Defense]. 1973 *Philadelphia Inquirer* (Today Suppl.) 7 Oct. 4 (Advt.), Warning: the Surgeon General has determined that cigarette smoking is dangerous to your health.

c. *fig.*

1535 COVERDALE *Exod.* xv. 26 Then wyl I laye vpon ye none of the sicknesses, that I layed vpon Egipte, for I am the Lorde thy surgione. 1557 *Tottel's Misc.* (Arb.) 255 So should not loue so work my wo, To make death surgeant for my sore. 1567 ALLEN *Def. Priesthood* 220 He..also maketh priestes to be as well the iudges as surgeons of our soules. 1628 EARLE *Microcosm.*, *Critic* (Arb.) 56 A Criticke..is the Surgeon of old Authors, and heales the wounds of dust and ignorance. 1711 SHAFTESB. *Charac.* (1737) II. 84 The 'solutio continui', which bodily surgeons talk of, is never apply'd in this case, by surgeons of another sort. 1940 L. MACNEICE *Last Ditch* 22 Here she stands who was twenty and is thirty. The same but different and he found the difference A surgeon's knife without an anaesthetic. 1962 *Daily Tel.* 13 Sept. 1/1 Sir Alexander Bustamante said that the Treaty of Rome was a 'surgeon's knife thrust into the Commonwealth body'.

2. = *surgeon-bird, -fish*: see 3 b.

1855 *Orr's Circ. Sci.*, *Org. Nat.* III. 182 In the common Jacana..the claw of the hind toe is excessively elongated and acute, from which circumstance the name of the *surgeon* has been applied to it. 1880 GUNTHER *Study Fishes* 439 'Surgeons' occur in all tropical seas.

3. a. *attrib.*: appositive, as ***surgeon-apothecary, -aurist, -dentist, -masseur, -oculist, -radiographer; surgeon-colonel, -lieutenant.***

1776 *Pennsylv. Even. Post* 16 Mar. 138/1 Dr. L. Butte and Co. Surgeon-Dentists. 1848 DUNGLISON *Med. Lex.* (ed. 7), *Surgeon-apothecary*, one who unites the practice of surgery with that of the apothecary. A general practitioner. 1854 MAYNE *Expos. Lex.* 369/2 They [*sc.* general practitioners] are also called Surgeon-Apothecaries, because..they are Members of a College of Surgeons, besides being Licentiates of the Apothecaries Company. 1872 GEO. ELIOT *Middlem.* xlv, Lydgate did not dispense drugs. This was offensive both to the physicians whose exclusive distinction seemed infringed on, and to the surgeon-apothecaries with whom he ranged himself. 1881 *Instr. Census Clerks* (1885) 27 Surgeon-Aurist. *Ibid.*, Surgeon-Oculist. 1885 *Crt. Jrnl* 27 Mar., A surgeon-masseur of considerable repute. 1898 *Lond. Gaz.* 26 Aug. 5142/1 Whereas We have deemed it expedient to alter the Ranks of the Officers of Our Indian Medical Service: Our Will..is that the following alterations shall be made:—Present Ranks. Surgeon-Colonel... Surgeon-Lieutenant-Colonel. New Ranks. Colonel. Lieutenant-Colonel. 1901 *Nature* 5 Sept. 454/1 Surgeon-radiographer to the Imperial Yeomanry Hospital, South Africa.

b. *Comb.*, as ***surgeon-like*** adv.; **surgeon-bird**, the jacana; **surgeon-fish**, a herbivorous, tropical, marine fish of the family Acanthuridæ, distinguished by sharp spines on either side of the tail; **surgeon's knot** (see quot. 1968).

1870 GILLMORE tr. *Figuier's Reptiles & Birds* 302 Called *Surgeon Birds, from the resemblance the claw on their back toe bears to a lancet. 1871 *Harper's Mag.* July 191/2 The terror of all, the *surgeon-fish,..boldly swims in every quarter, opening and shutting his lancet. 1931 J. R. NORMAN *Hist. Fishes* v. 97 The Surgeon-fishes..of tropical seas derive their name from the presence of a lancet-like spine on either side of the fleshy part of the tail. 1974 *Environmental Conservation* I. 72 (*caption*) A Surgeon-fish.. is prominent on right below. 1733 *Med. Ess. & Obs. Soc. in Edin.* I. 108 By the help of a needle, or a flexible eye'd probe, the *surgeons knot is made with the thread. 1945 *Ann. Surg.* CXXI. 440 The artery was secured to the tube..by a No. 3 Deknatel ligature tied tightly behind the holding ridge, using a surgeon's knot. 1968 E. FRANKLIN *Dict. Knots* 27 *Surgeon's knot.* This is a variation of the reef knot in which an extra turn is taken at the start to help prevent the knot from tending to loosen while being completed. Used by surgeons for tying a ligature and by us [*sc.* Scouts] for parcels, etc. 1602 *2nd Pt. Return fr. Parnass* I. i. 5 *Surgean-like thou dost with cutting heale.

Hence '**surgeon** *v. trans.*, to cure as by surgical art; '**surgeoncy**, surgeonship; '**surgeoness**, a female surgeon; '**surgeoning**, surgery; '**surgeonless** *a.*, without a surgeon; '**surgeonship**, the office or position of a surgeon.

1850 BLACKIE *Æschylus* I. 13, I chaunt some dolorous ditty, making song, Sleep's substitute, *surgeon my nightly care. 1869 LD. LYTTON *Orval* 249 Who will surgeon me This gash? 1792 *Dublin Even. Post* 18 Feb. 1/2 (Advt.), Wanted, a *surgeoncy in a regiment of infantry. 1804 W. TAYLOR in Robberds *Mem.* (1843) I. 477 Having accepted a surgeoncy and an ensigncy in the militia. 1893 *Times* 3 Oct. 7/3 A discussion at St. George's Hospital about a contested election to a vacant surgeoncy. 1729 *Indenture of Apprenticeship* (Hammersmith Archives: PAF/1/272, Ref. 70), Mary Webb, daughter of John Webb, a poor child of the said parish, apprentice to Anne Saint of St. Leonard's Shoreditch in the County of Middlesex—*surgeoness. 1815 MRS. PILKINGTON *Celebrity* II. 213 He pronounced the marchioness a very skilful surgeon or surgeoness. 1869 LD. LYTTON *Orval* 79 Silly lancet, all Thy simple *surgeoning cures nothing. 1889 *Blackw. Mag.* CXLV. 555/1 Long voyages in *surgeonless ships. 1885 *American* X. 291 Who has given 1400 *surgeonships to the Democrats in the Pension Bureau. 1887 *Pall Mall G.* 17 Sept. 10/1 The surgeonship of some local clubs.

†'**surgeoner.** Chiefly *Sc. Obs.* Forms: 6 **sor-, surugenar, surriginare, surigeoner,** (**suringer**). [f. SURGEON *sb.* + -ER[1].] = SURGEON.

1526 *Sc. Acts Jas. V* (1874) II. 320 The yerlie fee..gevin be oure souerane lorde to..George Leithe his surriginare. *a*1578 LINDESAY (Pitscottie) *Chron. Scot.* (S.T.S.) I. 235 Weill leirnit in the art of mediecein and also ane cuning sorugenar. 1596 DALRYMPLE tr. *Leslie's Hist. Scot.* I. 142 *marg.*, Medicineris & Surigeoneris or Barbouris. 1599 *Sir Clyom.* xvi. 86 Cham but vather Corin the shepherd, cham no suringer I.

†**surgeonrer.** *Obs. rare*$^{-0}$. In 5 **surionrer.** [f. SURGEON *sb.*, after next.] A surgeon.

1483 *Cath. Angl.* 372/1 A Surgen (*A.* Surionrer), *aliptes*.

†'**surgeonry.** *Obs.* Forms: 4–5 **surgenrie,** 5 **surgeonry,** 6 *Sc.* **surgenary, surigeonrie.** [f. SURGEON *sb.* + -RY, after OF. *ser-, cirurgiennerie* (f. *cirurgien* CHIRURGEON + *-erie*, -ERY).] Surgery.

14.. *Langland's P. Pl.* B. XVI. 106 [He] did him assaye his surgerye [*v.r.* surgenrie] on hem þat syke were. *a*1500 in *Archæologia* LIX. 10 Yf she wolde goo to a surgeon namyd Sabastian, he shuld releyff hir with his conyng of surgeonry. 1505 *Seal of Cause, Edin.* 59 (Jam.) We..grant the samen to the forsaids crafts of surgenary and Barbars. 1596 DALRYMPLE tr. *Leslie's Hist. Scot.* I. 140 The mysterie of medicine and surigeonrie. 1730 in BAILEY (fol.); hence in JOHNSON.

†**surger.** *Obs.* [a. OF. *surgier*, rare by-form of *surgien* SURGEON.] A surgeon.

*a*1400–50 *Wars Alex.* 3132 (Dubl.), He gart seke þair sarys & þaim salue with surgers [*Ashm.* surgens] noble.

surgeraunt, variant of SOJOURANT *Obs.*

*c*1475 *Promp. Parv.* 484/2 (MSS. K. & H.) Surgeraunt, *S.* sugyner, or a comyner, *commensalis, conviva*.

surgery ('sɜːdʒərɪ). Also 4 **sirgirie,** 4–6 **surgerye,** 4–7 **surgerie,** 6 **sowrgerie, surregerie.** [ad. OF. *surgerie*, contracted f. *ser-, cirurgerie* CHIRURGERY. (For another form of contraction cf. OF. *surgie*, whence MDu. *surgie*, OPg. *surgia* (beside mod.Pg. *cirurgia*), med.L. *surgia*.)]

1. a. The art or practice of treating injuries, deformities, and other disorders by manual operation or instrumental appliances; surgical treatment.

13.. *Sir Beues* (A.) 3672 Boþe fysik and sirgirie ȝhe hadde lerned of meisters grete. *c*1386 CHAUCER *Prol.* 413 In al this world ne was ther noon hym lik To speke of phisik and of Surgerye. *c*1450 *Mankind* 850 in *Macro Plays* 32 Whyll a wond ys fresch, yt ys prowyd curabyll be surgery. 1505 in Marwick *Edinb. Guilds* (1909) 59 That na..person..vse ony poyntis of saidis craftis of surregerie or barbour craft within this burgh bott gif [etc.]. 1600 SHAKS. *A.Y.L.* III. ii. 64 And they [*sc.* our hands] are often tarr'd ouer, with the surgery of our sheepe. 1604 —— *Oth.* II. iii. 260 *Iago.* What are you hurt Lieutenant? *Cas.* I, past all Surgery. 1667 DAVENANT & DRYDEN *Tempest* v. i. (1670) 77 Henceforward let your Surgery alone, for I had Rather he should dye, than you should cure his wound. 1777 COOK *Voy. Pacific* III. ix. (1784) II. 152 They perform cures in surgery, which our extensive knowledge..has not..enabled us to imitate. 1861 FLOR. NIGHTINGALE *Nursing* (ed. 2) 94 Surgery removes the bullet out of the limb, which is an obstruction to cure, but nature heals the wound. 1887 *Brit. Med. Jrnl.* 22 Jan. 166/2 Dental Surgery. 1897 W. ANDERSON *Surg. Treatm. Lupus* 2 A bold and skilful surgery is usually exercised in the one case, and only half-hearted measures in the other.

†**b.** Phr. (*to take, go*) *to surgery*, for or to surgical treatment; (*to lie, be*) *at surgery*, under surgical treatment, in the doctor's hands. *Obs.*

1398 TREVISA *Barth. De P.R.* VII. lv. (1495) r iv/1 They [that haue the stone] shall be take to surgery. 1535 COVERDALE *Jer.* xlvi. 11 In vayne shalt thou go to surgery, for thy wounde shall not be stopped. 1555 in Strype *Eccl. Mem.* (1721) III. App. xlv. 137 How manye mens wyves and doughters in Flaunders lye at surgerye. 1565 STAPLETON tr. *Bede's Hist. Ch. Eng.* 146 While he was at surgerie in curing he dyed. 1586 J. HOOKER *Hist. Irel.* in Holinshed II. 93/1 Taking his waie to Downemore..where he laie at surgerie.

c. *fig.*

1628 WITHER *Brit. Rememb.* IV. 1428 God shend us from the harm Of such like Surgery. 1643 MILTON *Divorce* II. xvii. Wks. 1851 IV. 109 A..creature,..to whose ease you cannot adde the tithe of one small atome, but by letting alone your unhelpfull surgery. 1845 CARLYLE *Cromwell* v. (1871) II. 143 Terrible Surgery this: but *is* it Surgery and Judgment, or atrocious Murder merely? 1913 H. W. CLARK *Hist. Engl. Nonconf.* III. i. II. 69 Nonconformity had entered far too deeply into the nation's life to be eradicated by the severest surgery of law.

d. *Math.* The topological alteration of manifolds by conceptually removing a neighbourhood and replacing it by another having the same boundary; an instance of this.

1961 J. MILNOR in *Proc. Symp. Pure Math.* III. 39 Given any imbedding of $S^p \times D^{q+1}$ in a manifold W of dimension $n = p + q + 1$, a new manifold W' can be formed by removing the interior of $S^p \times D^{q+1}$ and replacing it by the interior of $D^{p+1} \times S^q$. This procedure will be called surgery. *Ibid.* 40 A surgery of type $(o, n + 1)$ replaces W by the disjoint sum $W + S^n$. **1974** *Encycl. Brit. Macropædia* XVIII. 503/1 If M is an oriented manifold of dimension $n \geq 4$, one can, by a succession of surgeries of index 1, kill the whole fundamental group π_1 of M. **1979** M. A. ARMSTRONG *Basic Topology* vii. 162 The result is a surface homeomorphic to the torus. A further surgery will give us the sphere.

2. a. The room or office in a general practitioner's house or a health centre where patients are seen and treatment is prescribed; the regular session at which a doctor receives patients for consultation in his surgery.

1846 *Bentley's Misc.* June 549 A small den [Dr. Faunce] called 'the surgery'. **1862** MISS BRADDON *Lady Audley* xxxix, The door of the little surgery was ajar... The surgeon was standing at the mahogany counter, mixing a draught in a glass measure. **1872** L. P. MEREDITH *Teeth* (1878) 252 In some localities, the dentists.. crowd their surgeries together in the same building. **1938** F. B. YOUNG *Dr. Bradley Remembers* i. 1 Between six and eight.. Dr. Bradley 'took' his evening surgery as usual. **1944** J. D. CARR *Till Death do Us Part* xi. 113 I've got to be back.. for surgery at half-past ten. **1964** D. FRANCIS *Nerve* v. 73 I'm late for surgery... Those pills ought to keep him quiet. **1975** 'J. BELL' *Victim* ii. 23 Dr. Swallow was dealing with his morning surgery.

b. Hence, a session at which a Member of Parliament, local councillor, etc., is available to be consulted locally by his constituents, usu. on regular occasions. Also, the room or office at which this occurs.

1951 *Hansard* (Commons) 19 Feb. 966 It is a practice of mine.. to call personally upon as many of my constituents as I can, and I find that by doing this a different set of problems is presented to me from those which my post-bag or even my weekly 'surgery' bring. **1957** *Times* 22 Apr. 7/7 On the question of surgeries, they are largely a self-imposed task about which MP's cannot complain since they are so often the chosen method of getting votes at the next election. **1964** G. E. NOEL *Harold Wilson & 'New Britain'* xiv. 111 As Prime Minister he intends, whenever humanly possible, to retain the system initiated in Ormskirk of personally visiting constituents who have reported problems instead of obliging them to attend 'surgeries'. **1968** *Times* 7 Nov. 11/5, I was at my 'surgery' near the hall when constituents called to complain that they could not gain admittance to the meeting. *a* **1974** R. CROSSMAN *Diaries* (1975) I. 258, I am going to have three successive days sitting on the front bench, followed on Friday by a full day of official visitations and a surgery in Coventry. **1982** P. TURNBULL *Dead Knock* vii. 126 Councillor Floyd.. was holding a surgery in the Council Chambers.

c. A similar occasion when free advice is provided by lawyers, accountants, or others.

1973 *Observer* (Colour Suppl.) 18 Nov. 39/1 The law surgery.. run by the Sheffield Free Legal Information Service. **1980** *Daily Tel.* 7 June 19/3 An increasing number of Citizens' Advice Bureaux have regular 'surgeries' chaired by volunteer local accountants. **1981** *Times* 4 Apr. 2/5 The Asian community is.. providing census 'surgeries' for householders.

3. *attrib.*

1612 WOODALL *Surg. Mate* Pref., Wks. (1653) 8 The fitting and furnishing their Surgerie Chests with medicines. *Ibid.* 19 Severall proportions or explainings.. of Surgery provisions. **1848** THACKERAY *Van. Fair* xxxviii, He would abstract lozenges.. from the surgery-drawers. **1872** TENNYSON *In Childr. Hosp.* i, Fresh from the surgery-schools of France. **1881** *Instr. Census Clerks* (1885) 31 Hospital and Surgery Officer.

surgiant ('sɜːdʒɪənt), *a. Her.* [irreg. f. F. *surgir* to rise + -ANT.] = ROUSANT.

1688 HOLME *Armoury* II. xi. 230/2 An Eagle displaid, Surgiaunt. *Ibid.* 478/2 A Stork surgiant, Argent.

surgiant, obs. form of SURGEON.

surgical ('sɜːdʒɪkəl), *a.* (*sb.*) [Alteration of CHIRURGICAL after *surgeon, surgery*. Cf. med.L. *surgicus*.] **1. a.** Pertaining to, dealing with, or employed in surgery or the surgeon's art.

1770 COOK *Voy. round World* II. ix. (1773) 461 The vulnerary herbs and surgical art of the country. **1800** *Med. Jrnl.* IV. 280 A Course of Lectures on Select Surgical Cases in the Hospital. ? *c* **1800** SYD. SMITH in Lady Holland *Mem.* (1855) I. 15 'It requires', he used to say, 'a surgical operation to get a joke well into a Scotch understanding.' **1846** HOLTZAPFFEL *Turning* II. 911 Surgical scissors are of many forms. **1884** THOMPSON *Tumours of Bladder* 39 The dusty pages of old surgical writers. **1899** *Allbutt's Syst. Med.* VII. 585 The drainage.. of the tympano-antral cavities by a surgical opening into the antrum.

b. *Path.* Resulting from surgical treatment.

1859 SIMPSON in *Nat. Encycl.* I. 150 Not unfrequently followed by Surgical fever. **1890** BILLINGS *Nat. Med. Dict.*, *S[urgical] kidney*, diseased kidney, resulting from.. operations on the genito-urinary tract.

c. Of garments: worn to cure, correct, or relieve an illness or deformity.

1896 *Woman's Life* 10 Oct. 200/2 (Advt.), Surgical hosiery, belts, etc. **1910** *Bradshaw's Railway Guide* May (Advt. facing p. xv), Bailey's surgical hose. **1955** W. GADDIS *Recognitions* I. i. 24 Her mother.. done in by a surgical belt salesman from New York. **1974** D. RAMSAY *No Cause to Kill* I. 7 Painfully swollen legs encased in surgical stockings.

d. *fig.* or in fig. contexts.

1939 C. ISHERWOOD *Goodbye to Berlin* 68 The afternoon he came to say good-bye there was a positively surgical atmosphere in the flat. **1962** *Listener* 8 Mar. 400/2 Purchase tax—deliberately uneven and at times deliberately surgical in its effect.

e. Designating swift and precise military attack, esp. from the air. orig. *U.S.*

1965 T. C. SORENSEN *Kennedy* xxiv. 684 The idea of.. a so-called 'surgical' strike.. had appeal to almost everyone first considering the matter, including President Kennedy. **1971** *Harper's Mag.* Nov. 55 Even the language of the bureaucracy—the diminutive 'nukes' for instruments that kill and mutilate millions of human beings, the 'surgical strike' for chasing and mowing down peasants from the air by spraying them with 8,000 bullets a minute—takes the mystery, awe, and pain out of violence. **1974** E. NEWMAN *Strictly Speaking* ii. 63 The war in Indochina produced a host of terms that media folks accepted at their peril: protective reaction strike, surgical bombing, free-fire zone. **1978** *Guardian Weekly* 5 Mar. 9/3 Moscow might be ready to undertake a surgical strike to take out China's nuclear installations.

2. *ellipt.* as *sb.* A surgical case or ward; †a surgical operation. *colloq.*

1828 W. SEWALL *Diary* 1 July (1930) 121/2 Sat off for home, accompanied by Reed's son, for the purpose of having a surgical on his foot. **1961** [see KNIFE *sb.* 1 f]. **1976** C. STORR *Unnatural Fathers* i. 11 I'm awfully muddled, the way surgicals and medicals are mixed up here.

Hence '**surgically** *adv.*, by the application of, or in relation to, surgical treatment; also *fig.*

1805 J. TAYLOR *Let.* 25 Jan. in *Minutes of Evidence* 200 in *Parl. Papers 1809* II. 1, The lad was brought to Dublin.. and was surgically rejected and dismissed before I received the letter. **1879** *St. George's Hosp. Rep.* IX. 96 The patient.. was treated surgically for a left inguinal hernia. **1880** BARWELL *Aneurism* 32 All these forms of disease are surgically somewhat peculiar. **1965** *Economist* 18 Sept. 1074/2 More surgically still, General de Gaulle calls for an 'interpretation' of the common market treaty which in fact violates it.

Surgicenter ('sɜːdʒɪˌsɛntə(r)). *U.S.* Also **surgicenter.** [f. SURGI(CAL *a.* + CENTRE *sb.*] The proprietary name for a surgical unit where minor operations are performed on out-patients.

1969 FORD & REED in *Arizona Medicine* Oct. 801/2 The building to house the Surgicenter is under construction at 1040 East McDowell Road, Phoenix. *Ibid.* 804/2 The Surgicenter.. is designed to provide quality surgical care to the patient whose operation is too demanding for the doctor's office, yet not of such proportion as to require hospitalization. **1971** *Official Gaz.* (U.S. Patent Office) 15 June TM183 Surgicenter, Inc., Phoenix, Ariz... *Surgicenter.* For providing facilities for doctors to perform surgical operations on patients... First use Feb. 12, 1970. **1973** *Americana Annual* 450 A trend toward development of more outpatient or ambulatory care services by hospitals was also evident in 1972. A noteworthy development was the emergence of 'surgicenters' where minor surgery can be performed on an out-patient basis. **1977** *Washington Post* 7 Nov. C7/4 The new facility will have 16 operation rooms, plus two 'surgicenters' for patients needing minor surgery that does not require hospitalization. **1981** *National Jrnl.* (U.S. Govt. Research Corp.) 20 June 1113/1 Surgicenters and other new services and programs that will be cultivated in a pro-competitive environment.

surginess ('sɜːdʒɪnɪs). [f. SURGY + -NESS.] The quality or condition of being surgy.

1799 COLERIDGE in *New Monthly Mag.* (1835) XLV. 221 Rising in a frolic surginess.

surging ('sɜːrdʒɪŋ), *vbl. sb.* [f. SURGE *v.* + -ING[1].] The action of the verb SURGE.

1. Rising, swelling, or rolling of great waves; impetuous movement of the sea or any body of water; also *transf.* and *fig.* (see SURGE *v.* 3 b, c).

1585 T. WASHINGTON tr. *Nicholay's Voy.* I. iv. 3 b, Thinges cast vp by the sourging of the Sea. **1594** BLUNDEVIL *Exerc.* VII. xxxi. (1636) 702 Driven by force of contrary Winds, by surging of the Sea, or by overthwart Tides. **1853** KANE *Grinnell Exp.* xxii. (1856) 172 The masses.. by the surging of the sea have been rubbed as round as pebbles. **1853** SIR H. DOUGLAS *Milit. Bridges* 257 Surgings of the water, by which waves are thrown over the sides of the vessel. **1883** *Law Times* 20 Oct. 410/2 The surging up of those Teutonic instincts of freedom.

2. *Naut.* The action of suddenly slackening a rope or chain wound round a capstan, etc. Also *attrib.*, as ***surging-drum***.

1839 *Civil Engin. & Arch. Jrnl.* II. 158/1 An Improved Capstan and Winch for Purchasing.. Ship's Anchors, without the application of a Messenger, in which there is no Fleeting or Surging. **1886** J. M. CAULFEILD *Seamanship Notes* 4 Seeing enough cable up for surging to the cat. **1902** A. ALCOCK *Nat. Indian Seas* 52 The dredge was slowly hauled in, the rope being reeled over a surging-drum attached to the ship's steam-winch.

3. *Electr.* The occurrence of surges in a current; also, a surge.

1904 E. B. RAYMOND *Alternating Current Engin.* ii. 75 On underground cables, where the ratio of l to c is much lower than in overhead wires, the tendency to puncture, due to surging, is much less. **1926** R. W. HUTCHINSON *First Course Wireless* vii. 105 The discharge consists, not of a steady flow, but of a number of rapid oscillations or surgings of electricity to and fro. **1966** *McGraw-Hill Encycl. Sci. & Technol.* XIII. 323/2 Surging in electric circuits corresponds to overshooting.

4. *Mech.* An increased action in a valve spring of an internal-combustion engine owing to its natural frequency of oscillation coinciding with the frequency of operation of the valve.

1931 H. R. RICHARD *High-Speed Internal-Combustion Engine* (ed. 2) viii. 227 Periodic vibrations in the spring itself ('surging'). **1975** M. J. NUNNEY *Automotive Engine* ii. 80 To lessen any tendency towards surging within the operating speed range of the engine, the valve springs are designed to have a high natural frequency of vibration.

'**surging**, *ppl. a.* [f. as prec. + -ING[2].] Rising, swelling, rolling, or tossing heavily, as waves.

1566 STUDLEY tr. *Seneca's Agam.* [1.] 624 The surging seas. **1590** SPENSER *F.Q.* I. v. 38 Fom surging gulf two Monsters streight were brought. **1610** HOLLAND *Camden's Brit.* (1637) 634 With surging billowes it came rolling and in-rushing amaine. **1634** SIR T. HERBERT *Trav.* 19 [One] surging waue aboue the rest, hit our broad-side. **1671** MILTON *P.R.* IV. 18 Surging waves against a solid rock. **1793** BURNS *Behold the Hour* i, I'll often greet the surging swell. **1869** TOZER *Highl. Turkey* I. 381 [The boats] are borne down through the surging current.

b. *fig.* or in fig. context, of feeling, action, etc.

1576 FLEMING *Panopl. Epist.* 78 Swallowed vppe in surgeinge seas of sorrowe. **1633** G. HERBERT *Temple, Glance* ii, Surging griefs. **1834** DE QUINCEY in *Tait's Mag.* I. 30/2 This moving, surging, billowing, world of ours. **1876** GEO. ELIOT *Dan. Der.* li. (Poem) Surging visions of her destiny.

c. *transf.* Moving in or as in large waves, undulating heavily or forcibly, heaving (as sound, wind, a crowd, etc.); also, of broadly undulating form, 'rolling' (as hills).

1603 H. PETOWE *Eliza's Funeral* B j b, My heauie lookes and all my surdging mones. **1667** MILTON *P.L.* II. 928 The surging smoak. *Ibid.* IX. 499 Rising foulds, that tour'd Fould above fould a surging Maze. **1728–46** THOMSON *Spring* 745 The surging air receives The plumy burden. **1831** SCOTT *Ct. Rob.* xxix, Hid from view in the surging volumes of darkness. **1847** EMERSON *Poems, Monadnoc*, Where the airy citadel O'erlooks the surging landscape's swell. **1868** *Daily News* 22 July, The surging, shouting, yelling crowd. **1876** GEO. ELIOT *Dan. Der.* iii, The gradual rise of surging woods. **1891** FARRAR *Darkn. & Dawn* l, Two days afterwards Rome was in a sea of surging flame.

surgion(e, obs. form of SURGEON.

surgy ('sɜːdʒɪ), *a.* [f. SURGE *sb.* + -Y.] Full of or abounding in surges; pertaining to or characteristic of surges; billowy, tempestuous. Also *fig.*

1582 STANYHURST *Æneis* II. (Arb.) 69 Throgh surgye waters with mee too seek ther auenturs. **1602** MARSTON *Ant. & Mel.* IV. Wks. 1856 I. 46 Was ever prince.. With louder shouts of tryumph launched out Into the surgy maine of government? **1658** E. PHILLIPS *Myst. Love* Gen. Lud. 37 Streames rumbling, surgy, chiding. **1773** BEATTIE *Triumph Melancholy* xlvii, We roll With headlong haste along life's surgy stream. **1818** KEATS *Endym.* I. 121 The surgy murmurs of the lonely sea. **1820** WAINEWRIGHT *Ess. & Crit.* (1880) 45 By them eight white soft-sliding hours.. ride with surgy velocity on a trail of volleying clouds.

surgyen, -yn, -yon, obs. forms of SURGEON.

surgyon, error for SOJOURNER. (Cf. *surgeraunt*.)

14.. *Voc.* in Wr.-Wülcker 602/4 *Perendinator*, a surgyon.

surhound, obs. form of SURROUND *v.*

Surian, obs. form of SYRIAN.

suric, obs. form of SARK.

suricate ('s(j)ʊərɪkeɪt). Also **-kate, -cat.** [a. F. *surikate*, ? of native African origin.

Schreber, *Die Säugethiere*, 1778, p. 435, points out (*a*) that Buffon's statement (see quot. 1781–5) as to the native home of this animal is wrong, and (*b*) that Du. *surikat* or *surikatje* is applied not to it, but to the tailed makis, esp. the macaco (as Pallas remarks, *Misc. Zool.*, 1778, p. 60 *n*.).]

An animal of the genus *Suricata*, esp. *S. zenik* or *S. tetradactyla*, a viverrine burrowing carnivore of Cape Province; the meerkat or zenick.

1781–5 SMELLIE tr. *Buffon's Nat. Hist.* (1791) VII. 166 The Surikate, or Four-toed Weasel.. is a native of Surinam, and other provinces of South America. **1800** SHAW *Gen. Zool.* I. II. 384 The Surikate is distinguished by a long sharp-pointed nose. **1875** *Zoologist* X. 4511 The suricate is nearly allied to the civet.

surigian, obs. Sc. form of SURGEON.

‖**surimono** (suri'moːno). Pl. unchanged; (anglicized) -s. [Jap.] A print; *spec.* a small-sized Japanese colour print used to convey greetings or to mark a special occasion.

1899 C. J. HOLMES *Hokusai* 9 He.. designed many *surimono*—the dainty cards used for festive occasions. *Ibid.* 15 The celebrated designer of *surimonos*. **1910** *Daily News* 16 May 4/5 It is worth while knowing what a surimono is. **1961** *Times* 7 Mar. 22/6 Two fine surimono by Kunisada. **1977** *Times* 18 July 10/3 The Japanese *surimono* was a wood-block print.

Surinam (s(j)ʊərɪ'næm). **a.** The name of the country in S. America formerly called Dutch Guiana; used *attrib.* in specific names of animals, plants, and products, as ***Surinam bunting, darter, falcon, grass, medlar, quassia, rat, shrew, sprat, tern***; also, in names of pidgin or creole languages spoken in Surinam, as ***Surinam Negro-English, Taki-Taki***; cf. SRANAN; **Surinam bark**, the bark of species of *Andira*, or that of *Cinchona magnifolia*, used in medicine; **Surinam cherry**, (*a*) a South American tree, *Malpighia glabra*, or its edible aromatic fruit; (*b*) an evergreen shrub or small tree, *Eugenia uniflora*, native to tropical America; also, its edible red fruit; **Surinam poison**, a tropical leguminous plant, *Tophrosia toxicaria*, or the poison derived from the leaves; **Surinam (water) toad**, a large flat toad, the PIPA.

1844 HOBLYN *Dict. Terms Med.*, *Surinam Bark, worm bark. The bark of the *Andira inermis*, or Cabbage-bark tree. **1858** SIMMONDS *Dict. Trade*, *Surinam-bark*, a cinchona bark of indifferent quality, the produce of *Cinchona magnifolia*. **1783** LATHAM *Gen. Synopsis Birds* III. 212 *Surinam B[unting]... Bigger than a Lark, but like it in colour... Inhabits Surinam. **1895** 'F. FRANCESCHI' *Santa Barbara Exotic Flora* 33 The *Surinam Cherry..[is] growing too in Montecito. **1920** BRITTON & MILLSPAUGH *Bahama Flora* 304 *Eugenia uniflora*... Native of South America. Surinam Cherry. **1972** C. D. ADAMS *Flowering Plants Jamaica* 522 Surinam Cherry. Shrub to 2·5 m. high;..berries red, edible. **1785** LATHAM *Gen. Synopsis Birds* VI. 626 *Surinam D[arter]... It is often domesticated by the inhabitants, and known to them by the name of the *Sun Bird*. **1781** *Ibid.* I. 84 *Surinam F[alcon]. *Falco sufflator*, Lin. **1756** P. BROWNE *Jamaica* 300 *Surinam Grass. This plant was lately introduced to Jamaica. **1857** HENFREY *Bot.* §506 The *Surinam Medlar (*Mimusops Elengi*). **1934** *Amer. Speech* IX. 181 (*heading*) *Surinam Negro-English. **1964** Surinam Negro-English [see NEGRO 1 d]. **1756** P. BROWNE *Jamaica* 296 *Surinam Poison. This plant has been introduced into Jamaica..on account of its intoxicating qualities. **1876** HARLEY *Mat. Med.* (ed. 6) 675 *Surinam Quassia Tree is the representative of a genus very closely allied to Picræna. **1774** GOLDSM. *Nat. Hist.* (1824) III. 447 *Surinam rat, the phalanger, a small monkey. **1800** SHAW *Gen. Zool.* I. II. 536 *Surinam Shrew. *Sorex Surinamensis*. **1854** *Orr's Circ. Sci., Org. Nat.* I. 101 The most singular situation of the eyeball ..is that of the *Surinam sprat. **1967** R. I. MCDAVID in G. V. Bobrinskoy *Lang. & Areas* 86 A viable language in its own right—like *Surinam Taki-taki. **1776** P. BROWN *Illustr. Zool.* 98 Pl. 39, The *Surinam Tern... Size of a black bird. **1774** GOLDSM. *Nat. Hist.* (1824) III. 145 The Pipal, or the *Surinam Toad. **1896** *Proc. Zool. Soc.* 5 May 595 One of the females of the *Surinam Water-Toad..with her back covered with eggs.

b. Epithet of a variety of potato. ? *Obs.*

1796 NEMNICH *Polygl.-Lex.*, *Red and white Surinam*, a sort of potatoes. **1815** J. SMITH *Panorama Sci. & Art* II. 635 The ox-noble, Surinam, Irish purple, Howard or clustered, and red potatoes, are for fodder.

Hence **Suri'namer** [-ER[1]], a native or inhabitant of Surinam; **surinamine** (also **-ina**), *Chem.* an alkaloid supposed to be contained in Surinam bark.

1838 T. THOMSON *Chem. Org. Bodies* 290 Of Surinamina. This alkali was discovered in 1824, by M. Overduin, in the bark of the *Geoffroya Surinamensis*. **1852** W. GREGORY *Handbk. Org. Chem.* 366 Surinamine and Jamaicine are two alkaloids, found in *Geoffræa Surinamensis* and *G. inermis*. ?**1943** *Holland carries On* (Netherlands Information Bureau, N.Y.) 27/1 The Surinamers are..far from being moulded..into a real national community. **1963** H. MITCHELL *Europe in Caribbean* xii. 119 Instruction is modelled on that of the Netherlands, where many Surinamers complete their studies. **1969** *Atlantic Monthly* Nov. 48/3 The border confrontation gave the Surinamers something new to talk about. **1976** *Daily Times* (Lagos) 26 Aug. 24/3 The black Surinamers (the former Dutch Guyanese in South America) could live with, and tolerate, the Indians, Japanese, Lebanese Jews, Ameri-Indians, Caribs, Arowaks and a salad of cultures over the century.

Surinamese (s(j)ʊərɪnæ'miːz), *sb.* and *a.* [f. SURINAM + -ESE.] **A.** *adj.* Of or pertaining to Surinam or its people. **B.** *sb.* A native or inhabitant of Surinam; *pl.*, the people of Surinam.

?**1964** *Final Rep. Surinam-American Technical Cooperative Service* 37/2 Its objective was to supplement.. training facilities provided for Surinamese technicians. **1972** *Guardian* 25 Mar. 12/6 The West Indians and Surinamese who have the luck to find a modern flat, cram it with friends and relations. **1979** *Dictionaries* I. 147 There are native speakers of Surinamese Dutch, and there is indigenous transmission of the language form from generation to generation. **1980** *Times* 18 Mar. 7/4 When it was announced that Mr Bruma would form the new Cabinet, many Surinamese were astonished.

†**suring**, *vbl. sb. Obs.* [f. SURE *v.* + -ING[1].] Betrothal.

1530 PALSGR. 278/2 Suryng in maryage, *fianceailles*.

suringer: see SURGEONER.

†**surintendent**, *sb.* and *a. Obs.* Also 8 -ant. [ad. F. *surintendant*: see SUR- and INTENDANT.] = SUPERINTENDENT *sb.* and *a.*

1663 GERBIER *Counsel* a4, Your Surintendents of Buildings. **1690** TEMPLE *Ess.*, *Heroic Virtue* ii. Wks. 1720 I. 203 A Surintendent, sent more immediately from Court to inspect the Course of Affairs. **1709** MRS. MANLEY *Secret Mem.* (1720) III. 165 Another Sur-Intendant of the royal Revenue. *a* **1721** PRIOR *Dial. betw. Charles & Clenard* Wks. 1907 II. 216 The Surintendants and Customers that keep the Register.
c **1645** HOWELL *Lett.* I. xxxv. (1650) 57 There is a surintendent Counsell of ten.

So †**surin'tendence** (only in Fr. form **-ance**), †**surin'tendency** = SUPERINTENDENCE, -ENCY.

1650 COWLEY *Let.* 28 May, Wks. (Grosart) II. 347 In this distress of the Finances Monsieur Demery is dead, and Monsieur D'avaux, who was joined with him in the Surintendency has quitted the Charge. **1692** C. O'K[ELLY] *Macariæ Excidium* in *Narratives Contests Irel.* (Camden) 77 The surintendency of all affairs, both civil and military. **1744** LADY M. W. MONTAGU *Let. to W. Montagu* 12 June, The *surintendance* of all public diversions.

surion, -oune, obs. forms of SURGEON.

surjection (sɜː'dʒɛkʃən). *Math.* [f. SUR-, after INJECTION 5.] An onto mapping.

1964 W. J. PERVIN *Found. Algebraic Topology* i. 11, *f* is a surjection or epimorphism. **1979** *Q. Jrnl. Math.* XXX. 358 The well-known surjection from tensor powers of P_{ab} to lower central factors of F.

Hence **sur'jective** *a.*, that is a surjection.

1964 S.-T. HU *Elem. Gen. Topology* i. 7, $f: X \to Y$ is surjective if, for every point *y* in *Y*, there exists at least one point *x* in *X* such that $f(x) = y$. **1968** D. L. CLARKE *Analytical Archaeol.* ix. 360 The taxa of one aspect are related to the taxa of the other aspects as elaborate injective and surjective mappings. **1979** *Proc. London Math. Soc.* XXXVIII. 209 We recall some facts..about the abelian group *A*(*G*)... If *F* is a finite subgroup of *G*, then $A(G) \to A(F)$ is surjective.

surkney: see SUCKENY, smock.

surkot, -kote, obs. forms of SURCOAT.

surlepes, variant of SERELEPES *Obs.*

surlily ('sɜːlɪlɪ), *adv.* [f. SURLY + -LY[2].] In a surly manner. †**a.** Imperiously, haughtily. *Obs.* **b.** With gloomy ill-humour or churlish moroseness.

1611 COTGR., *Orgueilleusement*, proudly, surlily, scornefully, arrogantly. **1651** H. MORE *2nd Lash* in *Enthus. Tri.*, etc. (1656) To Rdr. 8 *Quando ego non curo tuum, nè cura meum*, is but surlily said of the old man in the Comedy. **1659** GAUDEN *Slight Healers* (1660) 67 It is superciliously yea very surlily spoken, to persons much better every way then themselves, Stand by, we are holier than you. *a* **1700** EVELYN *Diary* 29 June 1688, [The Seven Bishops] denied to pay the Lieutenant of the Tower (Hales, who us'd them very surlily) any fees. **1711** *Vind. Sacheverell* 81 The good Man ..sat very surlily pious. *a* **1774** GOLDSM. tr *Scarron's Com. Romance* (1775) II. 77, I immediately demanded of the slave where he was: he surlily answered, that wherever he was, it was not for me. **1837** LYTTON *E. Maltrav.* I. i, 'You can't miss your way well,' said the man, surlily: 'the lights will direct you.' **1875** HAYWARD *Love agst. World* 16 'Come, Florence,' said Tollemache, surlily, 'let us get home.'

surliness ('sɜːlɪnɪs). [f. as prec. + -NESS.] Surly character, condition, or manner.

†**a.** Imperiousness, haughtiness, arrogance. *Obs.* **b.** Gloomy ill-humour, churlish moroseness.

1587 T. NORTON *Calvin's Inst.* IV. i. §16 *margin*, The surlinesse of some by reason of pride, and a vaine opinion of their owne holines. **1593** BILSON *Govt. Chr. Ch.* 389 To ouer-rule Christian princes and Churches with greater surlines than euer did Patriarke or Pope. **1603** HOLLAND *Plutarch's Mor.* 128 A kinde of froward surlinesse hardly to be pleased. **1644** MILTON *Areop.* (Arb.) 36 To..mollifie the Spartan surlinesse with his smooth songs and odes. **1691** HARTCLIFFE *Virtues* 164 That we fall not upon either of the extremes, base Submission, or Surliness. **1700** DRYDEN *Pal. & Arc.* II. 192 None greets; for none the Greeting will return; But in dumb Surliness, each arm'd with Care His Foe profest, as Brother of the War. **1747** RICHARDSON *Clarissa* (1810) I. xliii. 328 How shall I stand the questions of some, the set surliness of others? **1831** SCOTT *Cast. Dang.* xix, The surliness which has replaced their wonted courtesy of manners. **1879** SEGUIN *Black For.* ii. 38 This independence of character does not produce any surliness of manner in the Black Forest peasantry.

†**surling**. *Obs. nonce-wd.* [app. f. SURLY, on the (false) analogy of *lordly*, *lordling*.] A surly fellow.

1605 CAMDEN *Rem.*, *Anagr.* 157 As for these sowre surlings, they are to be commended to Sieur Gaulard.

surloin: see SIRLOIN.

surly ('sɜːlɪ), *a.* Also 6 -li, 7 -lie, -ley. [Altered spelling of SIRLY *a.*]

†**1.** ? Lordly, majestic. *Obs. rare.*

1566 DRANT tr. *Horace*, *Sat.* I. ii. Bjb, How he doth decke, and dighte His surlye corps in rytche aray.

†**2. a.** Masterful, imperious; haughty, arrogant, supercilious. *Obs.*

c **1572** I. B. in Gascoigne *Posies* (1575), The sauerie sappes in Gascoignes Flowers that are,..Could not content the surly for their share, Ne cause them once to yeeld him thankes therefore. **1573** G. HARVEY *Letter-bk.* (Camden) 4, I have not shoun mi self so surli towards mi inferiors. **1579** SPENSER *Sheph. Cal.* July 203 Sike syrlye shepheards. [*Glosse*] *Surly*, stately and prowde. **1589** PUTTENHAM *Engl. Poesie* III. xxiv. (Arb.) 299 With the great personages his egals to be solemne and surly, with meaner men pleasant and popular. **1601** SHAKS. *Twel. N.* II. v. 163 Be opposite with a kinsman, surly with seruants. **1682** DRYDEN *Medal* 311 The surly Commons shall respect deny. **1697** —— *Virg. Past.* IX. 6 When the grim Captain in a surly Tone Cries out, pack up ye Rascals, and be gone. **1726** POPE *Odyss.* XXIII. 50 Stern as the surly lion o'er his prey.

†**b.** as *adv. Obs.*

1601 SHAKS. *Jul. C.* I. iii. 21 Against the Capitoll I met a Lyon, Who glaz'd vpon me, and went surly by, Without annoying me. **1693** R. LYDE *Acc. Retaking 'Friend's Adv.'* 10 Those that carried themselves most surly towards me.

3. a. Churlishly ill-humoured; rude and cross; 'gloomily morose' (J.). Said of persons (or animals), or their actions or attributes.

1670 RAY *Prov.* 208 As surly as a butchers dog. **1677** OTWAY *Cheats of Scapin* I. i, Thou art as surly as if thou really couldst do me no good. **1722** DE FOE *Col. Jack* (1840) 7 Captain Jack..a surly, ill-looked rough boy, had not a word in his mouth that savoured either of good manners, or good humour. **1757** SMOLLETT *Reprisal* I. i, Commend me to the blunt sincerity of the true surly British mastiff. **1770** GOLDSM. *Des. Vill.* 105 Nor surly porter stands in guilty state. **1807** CRABBE *Par. Reg.* III. 245 And surly beggars cursed the ever-bolted door. **1840** DICKENS *Old C. Shop* xvi, A surly, grumbling manner. **1865** KINGSLEY *Herew.* xix, A surly voice asked who was there. **1884** F. M. CRAWFORD *Rom. Singer* ix. I. 187 Dry throats make surly answers, as the proverb says.

b. as *sb.* (*quasi* proper name). *nonce-use.*

1748 SMOLLETT *Rod. Random* v, Well, well, old surly,.. thou art an honest fellow.

4. *fig.* from 2 and 3: †'Imperious', stern and rough (*obs.*); (of soil, etc.) obstinate, refractory, intractable; (of weather, etc.) rough and gloomy, threatening and dismal.

c **1600** SHAKS. *Sonn.* lxxi, You shall heare the surly sullen bell Giue warning to the world that I am fled From this vile world. **1646** G. DANIEL *Poems* Wks. (Grosart) I. 69 The Lawes Of Surly fate. **1654** TUCKNEY *Death Disarmed* 24 Seneca according to his surly stoical principle would persuade himself..that it is ill to desire death. **1662** R. MATHEW *Unl. Alch.* §86. 120 Surly griefs, as Sciatica and Gout in the feet. *a* **1668** LASSELS *Voy. Italy* (1698) I. 46 Our horses eased us, the ascent not being so surly as we expected. **1693** EVELYN *De la Quint. Compl. Gard.* II. 195 In a surly Season. **1696** PRIOR *To the King after Discov. Conspiracy* 70 By sounding Trumpets, mark, and surly Drums, When William to the open Vengeance comes. **1697** DRYDEN *Virg. Georg.* I. 154 Before the surly Clod resists the Rake. **1733** W. ELLIS *Chiltern & Vale Farm.* 11 Their surly Clay Grounds. **1784** BURNS *Man made to Mourn* i, Chill November's surly blast. **1871** R. ELLIS *Catullus* lxiii. 16 The surly salt seas. **1881** C. WHITEHEAD *Hops* 19 Where the marls on the chalk are somewhat less surly and intractable. **1901** *Munsey's Mag.* (U.S.) XXIV. 796/1 The straight, flat, surly clouds.

5. *Comb.*, as *surly-browed*, *-looking*, *-sounding* adjs.; **surly-boots** [cf. *lazy-boots*, *sly-boots*], an appellation for a surly person; †**surly-borne** *a.*, haughty in bearing or demeanour.

1710 *Fanatick Feast* 12 Old *Surly-Boots..threw off his Cloak. **1812** COMBE *Syntax*, *Picturesque* xxii, When Surly-boots yawn'd wide, and spoke. **1606** SHAKS. *Tr. & Cr.* II. iii. 249 *Vliss.* If he were proud. *Diom.* Or couetous of praise. *Vliss.* I, or *surley borne. *a* **1618** SYLVESTER *Panaretus* 1373 So swelling-proud; so *surly-brow'd the while. **1904** W. H. HUDSON *Green Mansions* vii. 97 Two dogs..They were *surly-looking brutes. **1954** W. FAULKNER *Fable* 141 Followed by a thin wiry surly-looking private. **1833** T. HOOK *Parson's Dau.* III. i, The *surly-sounding mandate.

surly, obs. form of SURELY.

‖**surma, soorma** ('sʊəmə). *E. Ind.* Also [7 surmee,] 9 -meh, -mè, soorma, -ee. [a. Urdū = Pers. *surma(h)*.] A black powder consisting of sulphide of antimony or of lead, used by Indian women for staining the eyebrows and eyelids.

[**1687** A. LOVELL tr. *Thevenot's Trav.* I. 56 They [*sc.* Turkish women] paint their Eye-brows and Eye-lids with a blackish colour, which they call *Surmee*.] **1819** T. HOPE *Anastasius* (1820) II. iii. 59 A pair of eyes..were not deemed to possess all their requisite powers, until framed in two black cases of surmeh. **1820** T. S. HUGHES *Trav. Sicily* I. ix. 255 Their eyebrows..tinged with surmè. **1837** ROYLE *Antiq. Hindoo Med.* 100 With it [*sc.* sulphuret of antimony], I believe, is frequently confounded the sulphuret of lead, which, in Northern India, is called *soormee*..and used as a substitute for the former. **1896** *Month* May 33 Henna for her nails, kohl and soorma for her eyes. **1913** *19th Cent.* May 996 Shams-ud-Din blackened the edges of my eyelids with surma (antimony).

surmaia, surmark, var. SYRMÆA, SIRMARK.

surmaster ('sɜːˌmɑːstə(r)). [f. SUR- = SUPER- 6 a + MASTER *sb.*[1]] The title of the second master at St. Paul's School, London.

c **1512** COLET in *Archaeologia* LXII. 230 Twoo techers perpetuall oon callid the Maister, and that other callid the Ussher or surmaister. **1744** *Gen. Even. Post* No. 1658, Mr. Thickness, Chaplain of St. Pauls School was chosen Sur-Master of the said School. **1886** *Athenæum* 17 Apr. 521/2 The Rev. J. H. Lupton, sur-master of St. Paul's School. **1889** *Pauline* VIII. 8 The Surmaster, on behalf of his colleagues and the school, accepted the gift.

surmatch: see SUR-.

surmè, -mee, -meh: see SURMA.

surment, surmet, var. SUREMENT, SUMMIT.

surmia, var. SYRMÆA.

surmisable (sɜː'maɪzəb(ə)l), *a.* Also surmiseable. [f. SURMISE *v.* + -ABLE.] That may be surmised; conjecturable, supposable.

1817 KEATINGE *Trav.* I. 186 The name *argali*, besides the importance of its surmiseable radical, gives much scope for important deductions in its affinity..with the *arayal*. **1862** CARLYLE *Fredk. Gt.* XIV. viii, Should Prince Karl, as is surmisable, make new attempts there. **1875** POSTE *Gaius* I. Introd. 21 All systems of law..contain many provisions which are hardly surmisable by any but professional lawyers.

surmisal (sɜː'maɪzəl). Now *rare.* [f. as prec. + -AL[1] 5.] = SURMISE *sb.*

1641 MILTON *Ch. Govt.* II. Introd., From this needlesse surmisall I shall hope to disswade the intelligent..auditor. **1657** *North's Plutarch* (1676) Add. Lives 40 All the aforesaid cavils..are..founded on bare surmisals and forged stories.

1676 Glanvill *Ess. Philos. & Relig.* iv. 1 Those unkind surmisals concerning natural Wisdom. **1894** *Westm. Gaz.* 27 Dec. 7/2 If this surmisal be erroneous.

surmisant (sɜːˈmaɪzənt). *nonce-wd.* [f. as prec. + -ANT[1], after *informant*.] A surmiser.
1748 Richardson *Clarissa* VI. xlv. 62 He meant no reflection upon her Ladyship's informants, or rather *surmisants* (as he might call them).

surmise (sɜːˈmaɪz, ˈsɜːmaɪz), *sb.* Also 5–6 **-myse**, (6 **-mies**, 7 *Anglo-Ir.* **-mishe**), 6–8 **-mize**. [a. AF., OF. *surmise*, vbl. sb. f. *surmettre*: see next.]

†**1.** *Law.* A formal allegation or information; *spec.* in *Eccl. Law*, the allegation in the libel. *Obs.*
1451 *Rolls of Parlt.* V. 218/2 That averment..may be hadde..for every partie..to have or enjoye any of the premisses, by theire surmyse that the seid Londes..were yeven or graunted for other Londes [etc.]. **1455** *Ibid.* 334/1 That al suche persones..uppon whom any suche surmyse is made, so that it be thought by the Justicez..afore whome suche surmyses is hadde, that suche surmyse is trewe and not doon of malice, remayne and abyde yn youre prisone. **1481** *Cov. Leet Bk.* 473 A surmyse made to my lorde prynce of diuerse Iniuryes don by hym & oþer persones. **1485** *Rolls of Parlt.* VI. 327/1 The said John Calcote the Fader, by an untrue surmyse made unto King Edward the fourth..was appeched of high Treason. **1534** *Star Chamber Cases* (Selden) II. 317 That the seid henry..exhybyt one other byll of surmyse for the premyssez in to the kynges Courte of Chauncery. **1595** *Expos. Terms Law* s.v. *Ley*, In cases of secrecie where the plaintife cannot proue the surmise of his suit by any deed or open acte. **1713** Gibson *Codex* 1071/2 Prohibition may be granted upon a Collateral Surmise: That is, upon a Surmise of some Fact or Matter not appearing in the Libel.

†**2.** An allegation, charge, imputation; *esp.* a false, unfounded, or unproved charge or allegation. *Obs.* (in later use merged in 4).
1531 Elyot *Gov.* ii. xi, In them that be constante is neuer mistrust or suspition, nor any surmise or iuell reporte can withdrawe then from their affection. c**1540** tr. *Pol. Verg. Eng. Hist.* (Camden No. 29) 38 After being reserved ix. monthes for that cause, and her surmise founde false, she was burned. **1563** *Homilies* ii. *Almsdeeds* iii. (1640) 166 It is the crafty surmize of the divell to perswade us it. **1577** Harrison *England* ii. xi. [xviii.] (1877) i. 296 They wage one poore man or other, to become a bodger, and thereto get him a licence vpon some forged surmise. **1582** T. Cartwright in Nicolas *Mem. Sir C. Hatton* (1847) 304 The slanderous surmise of my disloyalty to her Majesty's estate. **1600** Holland *Livy* xxviii. xl. 699, I shall incurre the sinister opinion and surmise of two things. a**1660** *Contemp. Hist. Irel.* (Ir. Archæol. Soc.) II. 180 The subdellegation of the provinciall councell of Vlster by the surmishes of My Lord Primat.

3. (A) suspicion. *Obs.* or merged in 4.
1509 Hawes *Past. Pleas.* xx. (Percy Soc.) 94 Demeane you so that in no wyse No man perceyve of your love surmyse. **1567** Maplet *Gr. Forest* 105 Without any surmise or suspect had of his part of any such kind of deceipt. **1643** Milton *Divorce* 16 Let him not put her away for the meer surmise of Judaicall uncleannes. **1719** Young *Busiris* iv. i, Was ever man thus left to dreadful thought, And all the horrors of a black surmise! **1794** Mrs. Radcliffe *Myst. Udolpho* xxx, There was something so extraordinary in her being at this castle,..that a very painful surmise arose concerning her character. [**1862** Ld. Brougham *Brit. Const.* iv. 62, I never even have heard a surmise against the purity of members.]

†**b.** A 'suspicion', slight trace (*of* something).
1586 A. Day *Engl. Secretorie* i. (1625) 141 So much as any surmize of that whereof I haue beene thereby aduertised. **1595** Daniel *Civ. Wars* iii. lviii, Glad to finde the least surmise of rest. **1736** *Col. Rec. Pennsylv.* IV. 141 Avoid every Surmise of acting otherwise than the most dutiful Subjects. **1837** Carlyle *Fr. Rev.* iii. ii. vii, Some faintest ineffectual surmise of mercy.

4. An idea formed in the mind (and, often, expressed) that something may be true, but without certainty and on very slight evidence, or with no evidence; a conjecture.
1594 Hooker *Eccl. Pol.* i. viii. §3 Surmises and sleight probabilities will not serue. **1670** Milton *Hist. Eng.* i. 5 The rest, as his giving name to the Ile or ever landing heer, depends altogether upon late surmises. **1748** *Anson's Voy.* ii. xiii. 270 This appeared, by the event, to be an ill-grounded surmise. **1817** Keats *Sonn., Chapman's Homer* 13 All his men Look'd at each other with a wild surmise. **1860** Tyndall *Glac.* ii. xiii. 296 Another early surmise was..that the glacier slid along its bed. **1878** Earle *Philol. Eng. Tongue* v. Postscr. (1879) 253 Horne Tooke was, I believe, the first to throw out this surmise.

b. in generalized use.
1590 H. R. *Defiance to Fortune* G 4, He was not assured whether he spake vpon surmise, or that he had some secret knowledge of his loue to Susania. **1597** Shaks. *2 Hen. IV*, i. iii. 23 Coniecture, Expectation, and Surmise Of Aydes incertaine, should not be admitted. **1700** Dryden *Pal. & Arc.* ii. 486 Suspicions, and Fantastical Surmise. **1817** Jas. Mill *Brit. India* v. iv. II. 453 Allegations which, if they had general surmise..in their favour, were unsupported by particular facts. **1878** Browning *La Saisiaz* 262 The knowledge that I am, and, since I am, can recognize What to me is pain and pleasure: this is sure, the rest—surmise. **1912** *Eng. Hist. Rev.* Oct. 821 Surmise has often to supply the lack of knowledge.

†**5.** The formation of an idea in the mind; conception, imagination. *Obs.*
1592 Warner *Alb. Eng.* vii. xxxvii. (1612) 180 That Vermen that hath reason, and his owne defects espies, Doth seeme to haue a soule, at least doth thriue by such surmies. **1593** Shaks. *Lucr.* 1579 Being from the feeling of her own griefe brought, By deep surmise of others detriment. **1597** Hooker *Eccl. Pol.* v. lxv. §15 Pretending that the crosse..is not by them apprehended alone, but hath in their secret surmise or conceipt a reference to the person of our Lord Iesus Christ. **1637** Milton *Lycidas* 153 For so to interpose a little ease, Let our frail thoughts dally with false surmise.

surmise (sɜːˈmaɪz), *v.* Also 5–6 **surmyse**, (5 **sirmyse, sormyse**, 6 **sormise**), 6–7 **surmyze**, 6–8 **surmize**. [f. AF., OF. *surmis-e*, pa. pple. of *surmettre* to accuse: see SURMIT and cf. prec. and SURPRISE *v.*]

†**1.** *trans.* To put upon some one as a charge or accusation; to charge *on* or *upon*, allege *against* a person; *spec.* in *Law*, to submit as a charge or information, allege formally. *Obs.*
c**1400** *Beryn* 3665 His owne fawte, & his owne wrong, On beryn he hath surmysid. **1473** Warkw. *Chron.* (Camden) 5 Humfrey Haward and other aldermen were arested, and treasoune surmysed uppon them. **1526** *Pilgr. Perf.* (W. de W. 1531) 98 Care not what ony persone sayth, suspecteth, surmiseth, whyspereth or rowneth of ye here in erth. a**1548** Hall *Chron., Hen. VIII*, 59 b, The straungiers..surmysed a complaynt againste the poore carpenter. a**1557** Mrs. M. Basset tr. *More's Treat. Passion* M.'s Wks. 1354/1 That he should..haue heynous crimes surmysed against him.

†**b.** const. clause or acc. and inf.
1467–8 in *Oxf. Stud. Soc. & Legal Hist.* (1914) IV. 217 Where it is surmysed by the seid bill that the seid William [etc.]. **1480** *Cov. Leet Bk.* 439 These be þe names of the ffeldes þat þe seid Laurens surmysed shuld be Comien þat were kept seuerell. **1495** P. Warbeck *Declar.* in Bacon *Hen. VII* (1622) 151 My mortall Enemie hath..falsely surmised mee to bee a fayned Person, giuing mee Nick-names. **1509–10** *Act 1 Hen. VIII*, c. 4 Preamble, Enditementes for offenses surmysed to be doone contrarye to the same Statutes. c**1589** in *Horsey's Trav.* (Hakl. Soc.) App. 318 Hierom Horssey and one Anthony Marshe surmised to the Counsaill that the agent had written treason against the State.

†**c.** after *as*.
1464 *Cov. Leet Bk.* 323 We..maruayllyng gretely..of your suffrance..yf it be as is surmysid. **1528** More *Dyaloge* i. Wks. 110/1 Thinkinge..that..Luther saied not so euyll as is surmised vpon him. **1565** Jewel *Repl. Harding* i. 4 Neyther dooe wee refuse your fantasies bicause they be Catholike, as you surmise. **1623** in *N. Shaks. Soc. Trans.* (1885) 507 As in the said Bill is falsely surmised.

†**d.** *absol.* To make allegations.
1528 Roy *Rede me* (Arb.) 32 Wherfor agaynst vs they will nowe surmyse Seynge that gone is the masse.

†**e.** *pregnantly.* To allege falsely or groundlessly. *Obs.*
1477 Hen. VII in Ellis *Orig. Lett.* Ser. i. I. 20 The grete malice..as she shewed lately in sending hider of a fayned boye, surmising him to have been the son of the Duc of Clarence. **1530** in W. H. Turner *Sel. Rec. Oxford* (1880) 88 M. Burton saithe the article is surmysed and nothyng trew.

†**f.** To accuse, charge (a person) *with*. *Obs. rare*$^{-1}$.
a**1485** Fortescue *Wks.* (1869) 499 Sir James of Audeley..which was surmised with the gettinge of the said Phillipe.

†**g.** ? To impugn. *Obs. rare*$^{-1}$.
1609 Alex. Hume *Admon.* Wks. (S.T.S.) 180 Persuading them that it wes the..defence of treu religioun (then surmysed by the Earles of Huntlie, Errol, and Angous) that he intended.

†**2.** To devise, plan, contrive, *esp.* falsely or maliciously. Chiefly const. inf. *Obs.*
1509 Hawes *Past. Pleas.* (Percy Soc.) 3 As was the guyse..Of the poetes olde, a tale to surmyse, To cloke the truthe of their infirmitie. **1549–62** Sternhold & H. *Ps.* xxvii. 14 They surmise against me still false witnesse to depose. **1567** *Gude & Godlie B.* (S.T.S.) 152 The Jewis did..euer mair surmyse, With vnkyndnes to keill me. **1632** Lithgow *Trav.* v. 198 All I surmise Is shrewdly stopt.

†**3.** To suppose, imagine (*that* a thing is so); to expect. *Obs.*
1509 Barclay *Shyp of Folys* (1570) 104 Alexander..all the worlde subdued as I surmise. **1572** *Act 14 Eliz.* c. 12 §2 The said Acte hathe not..brought the good Effecte that then was hoped and surmysed. **1578** H. Wotton *Courtlie Controv.* 135, I..thinke it meere folly for a man to breake hys necke wilfullye, surmising happily to please his maistresse therby. **1624** Quarles *Job* Poems (1717) 187, I'm scorned of my Friends, whose prosp'rous state Surmises me..to be cast away From Heaven's regard. **1667** Milton *P.L.* xi. 340 Surmise not then His presence to these narrow bounds confin'd Of Paradise or Eden. **1725** Pope *Odyss.* iv. 995 'Tis impious to surmize, the pow'rs divine To ruin doom the Jove-descended line.

†**b.** To form an idea of, conceive, imagine. Also *absol.* *Obs.*
1586 A. Day *Engl. Secretorie* i. (1625) 43 It is incredible to thinke, and vnpossible to bee surmised..how detestable hath beene the originall progression..of his most wicked..life. **1593** Shaks. *2 Hen. VI*, iii. ii. 347 So get thee gone, that I may know my greefe, 'Tis but surmiz'd, whiles thou art standing by. **1602** —— *Ham.* ii. ii. 108, I haue a daughter..Who in her Dutie and Obedience, marke, Hath giuen me this: now gather, and surmise.

†**4.** To suspect. *Obs.*
1571 Campion *Hist. Irel.* ii. ix. (1633) 108 Him they surmized to keepe a Kalender of all their doings. **1617** Moryson *Itin.* i. 236 If this discourse makes any surmise that we did some things against our conscience while wee liued in this Monastery.

b. To give an inkling of, hint. *rare*$^{-1}$.
1820 Ranken *Hist. France* VIII. i. vi. 250 There were state secrets which he never surmised to them.

5. To form a notion that the thing in question may be so, on slight grounds or without proof; to infer conjecturally. Const. obj. cl. or simple obj.
1700 Dryden *Sigismonda & Guisc.* 171 What Thoughts he had beseems not me to say, Though some surmise he went to fast and pray. **1768** H. Walpole *Hist. Doubts* 59 Such omissions cannot but induce us to surmise that Henry had never been certain of the deaths of the princes. **1817** Jas. Mill *Brit. India* v. viii. II. 629 The Governor-General surmised a circumstance, which always seems to have animated him to peculiar severity. **1835** I. Taylor *Spir. Despot.* iii. 94 Whatever the Jewish nation might surmise or know concerning a future life. **1871** Freeman *Norm. Conq.* IV. xvii. 83 Is it going too far to surmise that during William's Lenten pilgrimage to Caen, it was fully arranged who should be the next to fill the throne of Augustine?

b. *absol.* or *intr.*
1820 Keats *Cap & Bells* vii, Show him a garden, and with speed no less, He'll surmise sagely of a dwelling house. **1878** Browning *La Saisiaz* 160 Can I know, who but surmise? **1906** Beatrice Harraden *Scholar's Dau.* xi. 220 We were only surmising. It was stupid of me to begin it.

†**6.** ? To take up into itself. *Obs. rare*$^{-1}$.
1578 Banister *Hist. Man* v. 70 This coate [of the ventricle] first receiueth and surmiseth, all the Veynes, Arteries, and sinewes that are reached to the ventricle.

surmised (sɜːˈmaɪzd), *ppl. a.* [f. prec. + -ED[1].]
†**1.** Submitted as a charge or information to a court of law; charged upon or alleged against some one; more generally, alleged, supposed. *Obs.*
1530 *Sel. Cases Star Chamber* (Selden) II. 49 Thanswere of Elys abbott of Croxston to the surmysed byll of compleynt of John Molshoo. **1531** in W. H. Turner *Select. Rec. Oxford* (1880) 102 Under the pretence of that surmysyd new graunt. **1571** Golding *Calvin on Ps.* vi. 1 He was charged with the slaunder of a surmysed crime. **1633** Heywood *Eng. Trav.* iv. Wks. 1874 IV. 73, I shall doubtlesse acquit my selfe Of this surmised murder. **1649** in *Def. Rights & Priviledges Univ. Oxf.* (1690) 17 Before the time of the grant of those surmised charters to the City of Oxford.

†**2.** Devised falsely, feigned. *Obs.*
1514 Barclay *Cyt. & Uplondyshm.* (Percy Soc.) 16 This is trewe hystory, & no surmysed fable.

†**3.** Imagined, supposed, fancied. *Obs.*
1578 H. Wotton *Courtlie Controv.* 237 Some surmised contentation receyued in dreaming. **1597** Hooker *Eccl. Pol.* v. lxvii. §1 That his Flesh is meate, and his Bloud drinke, not by surmised imagination, but truely. **1602** J. Manningham *Diary* (Camden) 63 He..entreated the surmised assured gent. to hold his cardes till he returned.

4. Inferred conjecturally.
1860 Gen. P. Thompson *Audi Alt.* cii. III. 5 We are not to sit down under surmised dishonour. **1879** Todhunter *Alcestis* 109 Beckoning me From the bare known to a surmised beyond. **1899** Garvie *Ritschlian Theol.* viii. §6. 257 Love is directed for the furtherance of the recognised or surmised purpose which another sets himself.

surmiser (sɜːˈmaɪzə(r)). Also 6 **surmowser**, **-mysar**, 7 *Anglo-Ir.* **-misher**. [f. as prec. + -ER[1].] One who surmises.
†**1.** One who makes allegations or charges (esp. ill-founded or malicious) against some one; a (false) accuser. *Obs.*
c**1515** *Cock Lorell's B.* (Percy Soc.) 11 Surmowsers, yll thynkers, and make brasers. **1542** Udall *Erasm. Apoph.* 248 He made & autorised suche surmisers & piekers of quereles to bee his deputies. **1588–9** *Reg. Privy Council Scot.* IV. 358 Surmysaris and forgearis of leyis. **1619** in *Fortescue Papers* (Camden) 78 The burden would lye upon them as upon partiall surmisers and promoters. a**1660** *Contemp. Hist. Irel.* (Ir. Archæol. Soc.) I. 142 Not well understandinge the fetch and groundes of the surmishers.

2. One who makes a surmise or conjecture (esp. ill-founded); *spec.* (with qualifying word, as *evil*) one who suspects evil of another.
1591 Greene *Maiden's Dr.* Wks. (Grosart) XIV. 313 The brainsicke and illiterate surmisers, That like to Saints would holy be in lookes. **1632** Lithgow *Trav.* viii. 339 Let not surmisers thinke, ambition led My second toyles, more flash-flowne praise to wed. **1678** *Lively Oracles* ii. §39, I should first desire these surmisers to point out the time when, and the persons who began this design. **1710** Palmer *Proverbs* 39 Evil surmisers. **1843** Newman *Lett.* (1891) II. 423 Tom may suspect it and Copeland, so may Church and Marriott. Indeed, I cannot name the limit of surmisers. **1883** G. Macdonald *Castle Warlock* III. iii. 49 There is something here that wants looking into—if not by an old surmiser, yet by the young women themselves!

surmishe, etc., obs. Anglo-Ir. f. SURMISE, etc.

surmising (sɜːˈmaɪzɪŋ), *vbl. sb.* [f. as prec. + -ING[1].] The action of the verb SURMISE; the framing of conjectures; suspicion, esp. of evil.
1526 Tindale *1 Tim.* vi. 4 Envie, stryfe, realinges, evyll surmysinges, superfluus disputynges. a**1586** Sidney *Arcadia* iii. (1629) 340 By surmizings of his owne minding to marre their fortunes. a**1653** Binning *Useful Case Consc.* i. (1693) 9 Surmisings, whisperings and reports of others. **1828–43** Tytler *Hist. Scot.* (1864) II. 184 James's late unjustifiable proceedings..had occasioned some unquiet surmisings in the minds of his nobility.

So **surˈmising** *ppl. a.*, that surmises; suspecting, suspicious; †accusing; aiming at (*obs.*).
1535 Tindale *Tracy's Test.* Wks. (1573) 435/1 A blynd monster and a surmisyng beast, fearyng at the fall of euery leafe. **1601** Weever *Mirr. Mart.* D iij, My life-surmising Bishops swolne in rage,..Went to the king. c**1862** E. Dickinson *Poems* (1955) I. 348 Sweeter—the Surmising Robins—Never gladdened Tree—Than a Solid Dawn.

†**surˈmit**, *v. Obs.* Also 5 **-met(te**, 5–6 **-myt(te**. [a. AF., OF. *surmetre*:—late L. *supermittĕre* (also *suprā-*), in med.L. to accuse, f. *super-* SUPER 2 + *mittĕre* to put.]
1. *trans.* To charge, impute; to allege, suggest (often falsely); = SURMISE *v.* 1.

1411 *Rolls of Parlt.* III. 650/1 The..Lord the Roos.. compleyneth hym by a Bille, surmettyng on the same Robert, that he..dyd assemble greet noumbre of men. *Ibid.* 650/2 The matier on hym surmetted by the sayd Bille. **1447** *Ibid.* V. 137/2 Certein trespass and offens, or dettes surmitted to be don or due to theim. **1447** *Shillingford Lett.* (Camden) 96 Such Mayer Baillyffs and Comminalte as thei surmytten where yn the saide Citee. *c* **1450–5** in *Oxf. Stud. Soc. & Legal Hist.* (1914) IV. 202 As the seid suppliaunt hath surmitted by his bill. **1490** *Plumpton Corr.* (Camden) 101 The same Margrett sayth, that..John Scargill..made such wyll of the same..tenements, & other premyses,..as is surmytted by the same byll. **1503** *Act 19 Hen. VII*, c. 17 Divers persones..surmytted a Byll in the parlement holden at Westminster. **1533–4** *Act 25 Hen. VIII*, c. 12 Sondry bokes..Surmyttyng and puttyng fourthe the same false and feyned practyses..to be..true myracles. **1537** CROMWELL in Merriman *Life & Lett.* (1902) II. 104 You may..declare vnto him, howe thinformacion..was vntruly surmytted vnto him, as they haue themselfes confessed.

b. = SURMISE *v.* 1 f (const. *of*). *rare*$^{-1}$.

c **1470** HARDING *Chron.* CLII. ii. (MS. Arch. Seld. B. 10) lf. 127 Kyng Philip..Somonde Edward afore him to appere Surmittyng him of Robry.

2. = SURMISE *v.* 3 b. *rare*$^{-1}$.

c **1570** *Pride & Lowl.* (Shaks. Soc.) 67 They were fantasticall, imagined; Onely as in my dreame I dyd surmit.

†**surmontant**, *a.* *Obs. rare*$^{-1}$. [a. OF. *surmontant*, pr. pple. of *surmonter* to SURMOUNT.] Dominant, superior.

c **1400** tr. *Secr. Secr., Gov. Lordsh.* 112 Whenne [the soul] ys surmontant, and holdys lordschipe vpon þe body.

†**surmouncy.** *Obs. rare*$^{-1}$. In 4 sourmouncye. [irreg. f. SURMOUNT + -CY.] Dominance, superiority.

13.. *K. Alis.* 595 (Linc. Inn MS.) Þe ay is round and signefieþ He schal haue þe sourmouncye [*Laud MS.* seignorye] Þat is round þe myddallerd.

surmount (sɜːˈmaʊnt), *v.* Also 4–6 sour-, sor-, 5 sirmount(e, 5–6 surmont(e, 6 -mownt, *Sc.* -munt. [a. AF., OF. *surmunter*, *so(u)rmonter*, mod.F. *surmonter* (= Pr. *sobremontar*, It. *sormontare*), ad. med.L. *supermontāre*: see SUR-, SUPER- 2 and MOUNT *v.*]

†**1.** *trans.* To rise above, go beyond, surpass. **a.** in quality, attainment, etc.: To excel, be superior to. *Obs.*

c **1369** CHAUCER *Dethe Blaunche* 826 So had she Surmountede hem al of beaute. *c* **1385** —— *L.G.W.* Prol. 123 Comparison may noon y-maked bee For yt surmounteth pleynly alle odoures. **1412–20** LYDG. *Chron. Troy* I. 3344 A stoon..þe whiche..of colour surmounteth euery grene. *c* **1430** —— *Min. Poems* (Percy Soc.) 232 Holsom and glad is the memorye Of Crist Jhesu! surmountyng al swetnesse. **1508** DUNBAR *Gold. Targe* 260 O reuerend Chaucere,..Surmounting ewiry tong terrestriall, Alls fer as Mayes morow dois mydnycht. **1531** ELYOT *Gov.* Proheme, Whome, I beseche god, ye may surmount in longe life and perfect felicitie. **1590** SPENSER *F.Q.* II. x. 1 The famous auncestryes Of my most dreaded Soueraigne..By which all earthly Princes she doth farre surmount. **1613** PURCHAS *Pilgrimage* VIII. ii. 735 In Siluer, Potozi seemes to haue surmounted any one Mine of the World, besides those of new Spaine. **1624** QUARLES *Sion's Sonn.* Poems (1717) 347 See how Kings Courts surmount poor Shepherds Cells, So this, the pride of Solomon excels. **1667** DAVENANT & DRYDEN *Tempest* Pref., We may satisfie our selves with surmounting them in the Scene, and safely leave them those Trappings of Writing,..with which they adorn the Borders of their Plays.

†**b.** in amount or magnitude: To exceed, amount to more than, be greater than. Also, to pass beyond (a specified point or amount); e.g. to live beyond (a certain age); to spend more than (one's income). *Obs.*

c **1374** CHAUCER *Troylus* III. 1038 Som so ful of furye is and despit, That it sourmounteth his repressyoun. *c* **1374** —— *Boeth.* III. pr. viii. (1868) 80 Mayst þou sourmounten þise olifuntz in gretnesse or weyȝt of body? *c* **1489** CAXTON *Sonnes of Aymon* i. 37 How hath yᵉ euyl thys daye surmounted yᵉ goode. **1526** *Pilgr. Perf.* (W. de W. 1531) 228 b, Aged persones that hath surmounted and passed that age. **1546** in Dugdale *Monast. Anglic.* (1821) III. 283/2 The kinges maiesties landes doe surmount the lands of the said John Norris by the yearly value of xlj s. xj d. ob. **1570** *Act 13 Eliz.* c. 4 §8 Yf the Landes..solde..do surmount, after the Rate and Value aforesaid, the Debt and Arrearages. **1570** BUCHANAN *Admonitioun* Wks. (S.T.S.) 21 To incur the cryme of surmonting my priuat estait. **1581** LAMBARDE *Eiren.* II. vii. (1588) 276 If two or moe persons, do ioyne in the stealing of goods that do surmount xii d. **1591** —— *Archeion* (1635) 50 Where the Mischiefe doth surmount the common growth. **1600** HOLLAND *Livy* XXI. lviii. 426 There arose so terrible a..tempest..that it surmounted well near the foule trouble..endured in the Alpes. *a* **1674** TRAHERNE *Chr. Ethics* (1675) 471 Many charitable and pious works, perhaps surmounting his estate. *a* **1676** HALE *Prim. Orig. Man.* II. i. (1677) 131 The Inhabitants of the World do daily increase, and their increment surmounts daily their decrease. **1776** *Conn. Col. Rec.* (1890) XV. 357 That the debts..due from the estate..surmount the inventoried part of said estate the sum of £46. 3. 1½.

†**c.** To be above the reach or capacity of, to transcend: = SURPASS 4. *Obs.*

1502 *Ord. Crysten Men* (W. de W. 1506) I. vii. 69 Thynges yᵉ whiche surmounteth the puyssaunce and capacyte of natural understandynge. **1553** *Respublica* III. ii. 626 Theye ferre sormounte all praise that my tong can expresse. **1671** MILTON *Samson* 1380 How thou wilt here come off surmounts my reach. **1686** *Oldham's Wks.* Pref. 5 Nothing can be said so choice and curious which his Deserts do not surmount. **1738** WESLEY *Ps.* CXXXIX. xiii, Thy Thoughts of Love to me surmount The Power of Number to recount.

†**2.** *absol.* or *intr.* **a.** (from 1 a). To be superior, to excel. *Obs.*

1447 BOKENHAM *Seyntys* (Roxb.) 156 Not oonly this Marye..surmountyd in dygnyte But also..She of naturys yiftys had the sovereynte. **1509** HAWES *Past. Pleas.* L (Percy Soc.) 11 O ye estates surmountynge in noblenesse. **1517** TORKINGTON *Pilgr.* (1884) 12 The Richesse, the sumptuous buyldyng,..with all other thynges that makyth a Cite glorius Surmownteth in Venys a bove all places that ever I Sawe. **1577** HARRISON *England* II. xv. (1877) I. 271 The noble men and gentlemen doo surmount in this behalfe. *a* **1641** BP. MOUNTAGU *Acts & Mon.* iv. (1642) 256 She was a woman, as in birth royall, so in all naturall graces surmounting. **1687** tr. *Sallust* 85 There were two Great Men of different..Manners of Living, yet in Vertue both surmounting.

b. (from 1 b.) To exceed, be greater or more numerous; to be in excess, predominate, preponderate; also, to remain over as a surplus. *Obs.*

a **1533** LD. BERNERS *Gold. Bk. M. Aurel.* (1546) B iij b, This our age..is not called of yron, for faute of sages, but bycause the malycious people surmounte. **1534** WHITINTON *Tullyes Offices* I. (1540) 27 That we maye..se bothe in addycion and subtraction what somme may surmounte of the remaynes. **1541** COPLAND *Galyen's Terap.* 2 G iv, Somtyme ye shal vse detraction of blode, yᵗ is when the blode surmounteth. **1560** DAUS tr. *Sleidane's Comm.* 393 The cleargy, which in the consistory of the Empire surmounte in nombre. **1621** ELSING *Debates Ho. Lords* (Camden) 83 My mysery doth more surmount that his Majesty is drawen in to be a party.

3. *trans.* To prevail over, get the better of, overcome. **a.** a person; †also said of an emotion or desire. Now *rare.*

1390 GOWER *Conf.* I. 217 He his fader in desdeign Hath.. set of non acompte, As he which thoghte him to surmonte. *c* **1400** *Laud Troy Bk.* 6161 His hert gret angur surmounted. *a* **1400–50** *Wars Alex.* 2361 (Ashm.), Sexes [= Xerxes] in sum time surmountid all kyngis. *a* **1450** *Knt. de la Tour* 117 Seint Katerine, that by her witte..surmounted the grettest philosophers in Grece. **1509** HAWES *Past. Pleas.* XVI. (Percy Soc.) 73 Thus covetyse shal nothyng surmount Your yonge ladyes herte. **1525** LD. BERNERS *Froiss.* II. xcv 284 He feared leste they wolde surmounte hym, and take awaye his realme from hym. *a* **1530** WOLSEY in Cavendish *Life* (1893) 153 The sodden joy surmounted my memory. **1849** MACAULAY *Hist. Eng.* ii. I. 275 The attempts of the rival ministers to surmount and supplant each other.

b. temptation, hostility, (now usually) a difficulty or obstacle; by association with sense 7 = to rise superior to, get over.

1483 CAXTON *G. de la Tour* f iij, They surmounted many grete temptacions. **1600** HOLLAND *Livy* XXXVIII. I. 1015 The very indignation and shame of this example surmounted the malice of his adversaries. **1683** TEMPLE *Mem.* Wks. 1720 I. 403 About which, the Swedes could not surmount the Difficulties during the Course of their Mediation. **1706** E. WARD *Wooden World Diss.* (1708) 19 His Aversion is not so invincible, but it may be surmounted by a weighty Present. **1748** *Anson's Voy.* III. ix. 398 He saw it would be impossible for him to surmount the embarassment he was under. **1780** JOHNSON *Let. to Mrs. Thrale* 11 Apr., We have had very cold weather; bad riding weather for my master, but he will surmount it all. **1828** D'ISRAELI *Chas. I*, I. ii. 23 Thus early Charles surmounted the obstacles which nature had cast in his way. **1844** H. H. WILSON *Brit. India* III. 118 After surmounting the embarrassment and delays inseparable from a deficient supply of conveyance.

†**c.** *absol.* or *intr.* To overcome, prevail. *Obs.*

1400 tr. *Secr. Secr., Gov. Lordsh.* cxi. 111 Sweche er of þe nombre of hem þat surmounten and ouercomen. *c* **1477** CAXTON *Jason* 78 b, The whiche assemblid in thys maner by grete pryde that surmounted on them.

4. *trans.* To mount, rise, or ascend above (also *fig.*); also, to reach or extend above, surpass in height, be higher than, overtop. Now *rare.*

c **1374** CHAUCER *Boeth.* IV. met. i. (1868) 110, I haue.. swifte feþeres þat surmounten þe heyȝt of þe heuene. **1423** JAS. I *Kingis Q.* lxxxvii, Sum for desyre, surmounting thaire degree. **1489** CAXTON *Faytes of A.* II. xxxv. 147 There ben so highe [engyns] that not onely they surmonten the walles but also the highest towres. **1578** LYTE *Dodoens* I The great Sothrenwood doth..surmount the heigth or stature of a tal man. **1633** P. FLETCHER *Pisc. Ecl.* III. iii, She the highest height in worth surmounts. **1664** POWER *Exp. Philos.* II. 91 Any time of the year it [*sc.* the quicksilver] will not much surmount the..height..of 29 inches. **1688** HOLME *Armoury* III. xiii. 479/2 Mounts gradually surmounting each other. **1794** R. J. SULIVAN *View Nat.* I. 57 It is clear that the waters never surmounted those high summits, or at least remained but a short time upon them.

†**b.** To go back in date beyond. *Obs. rare.*

a **1647** HABINGTON *Surv. Worc.* (Worc. Hist. Soc.) I. 77 A family whose ancestors surmounted for tyme of continewance theare the Conquest.

†**5.** *intr.* To mount, rise, ascend (above something); to extend in height; *fig.* to exalt oneself; to arise, spring up. *Obs.*

1430–40 LYDG. *Bochas* I. ii. (MS. Bodl. 263) 15/2 So hih a tour..Which that sholde surmounte aboue the skie. *a* **1475** ASHBY *Dicta Philos.* 397 Theim to supprise That wolde surmonte, or in vices arise. *c* **1475** *Partenay* 2510 Ful gret ioy of hert in hym gan surmount. **1483** CAXTON *G. de la Tour* d viij, The waters..surmounted by heyght of ten cubites upon the hyghest montayn. **1539** TONSTALL *Serm. Palm Sund.* (1823) 27 Disobedience of the deuyll, not kepynge the order of his creation, but surmountynge farre aboue it. **1563** SHUTE *Archit.* F ij, If the piller surmount from 25 to 30. the height of the pillor must be deuided into 12 partes.

†**b.** To amount *to* (so much). *Obs.*

In quot. 1551 a loose translation.

1551 ROBINSON tr. *More's Utop.* II. (1895) 116 Betwene thys two corners the sea runneth in,..and there surmounteth into a large and wyde sea [orig. *per ingens inane diffusum*]. **1576** FOXE *A. & M.* (ed. 3) 102/1 The whole summe was founde to surmount to 294. yeares. **1599** HAKLUYT *Voy.* II. I. 293 Presents to the Viceroy and Bassas, which are said to surmount to twentie thousand dollars. *a* **1656** USSHER *Ann.* VI. (1658) 439 The custom which in former times was farmed for ten hundred thousand drachma's, scarce now surmounts to a hundred and fifty thousand.

†**c.** To result from addition; to arise or be produced *from* something. *Obs.*

1571 DIGGES *Pantom.* II. v. M ij b, Adde all the sides of that Triangle together, taking halfe of the number which surmounteth. **1572** *Will of W. Lyly* (P. Prob. Reg., Bodfelde 4) All my goodes I will be solde, and the money that shal surmount of the same [etc.]. **1654** VILVAIN *Enchir. Epigr.* I. xxvi, From which, they say, all mixtils doe surmount [orig. *existunt*].

6. *trans.* To mount upon, get on the top of; *usually*, to mount and cross to the other side of, climb across, get over; *occas.* to round or weather (a cape); also, to extend over and across.

a **1533** LD. BERNERS *Gold. Bk. M. Aurel.* Prol. (1535) A j, [They] surmounted the hyghe mounte of Olympius, there to contemplate..the influences of the planettes in the heuen. **1585** T. WASHINGTON tr. *Nicholay's Voy.* I. i. 1 Hauing.. surmounted the height and sharpnesse of the mount Rhodope. *Ibid.* II. i. 31 b, The sea which..casteth against [Cape] Malee, is such that without great labour..she is not to be recouered or surmounted. **1765** *Museum Rust.* IV. 250 The difficulty of surmounting obstacles by their shorter radii. **1819** J. FOSTER *Contrib. Eclectic Rev.* (1844) I. 505 He would sometimes leap over the wall at a spring, in preference to taking the trouble to open the gate or surmount a stile just at hand. **1825** SCOTT *Talism.* xii, The surmounting one crag only lifts the climber to points yet more dangerous. **1829** *Chapters Phys. Sci.* 357 Telescopes enable the eye to surmount immense distances. **1860** TYNDALL *Glac.* I. xii. 89 Simond surmounted the next ridge.

absol. **1843** WORDSW. *Grace Darling* 53 Each grasps an oar, and struggling on they go— ..alike intent Here to elude and there surmount.

7. To stand, lie, or be situated above; to rest on the top of; to top, crown. Orig. in *Heraldry*, said of a crest above a shield, also of a charge represented as laid upon another so as to extend across and beyond it. Chiefly in pa. pple.: ***surmounted by*** = having above or on the top.

1610 GUILLIM *Heraldry* VI. vii. 280 A rich Mantle of cloth of Gold, doubled Ermine,..surmounted by a Lion passant, gardant. **1634** PEACHAM *Compl. Gentl.* xv. 192 A fesse engrailed Argent surmounted by another not engraild Gules. **1688** HOLME *Armoury* II. vii. 148/1 Two Reynards or Foxes counter saliant, the dexter surmounted of the sinister Gules. *Ibid.* 198/1 A Serpent Imbowed, the head debrused (or surmounted) of the tail. *Ibid.* xix. 479/1 Thre Swans Necks..surmounting (or debrusing) each other. **1820** W. IRVING *Sketch Bk.* II. 58 (*Christmas Eve*) The huge square columns that supported the gate were surmounted by the family crest. **1856** STANLEY *Sinai & Pal.* iii. 167 The two domes..which surmount the Holy Sepulchre and the Basilica of Constantine. **1864** BOUTELL *Her. Hist. & Pop.* vii. (ed. 3) 33 When a Canton and Bordure are blazoned upon the same shield, the Canton surmounts the Bordure. **1869** TOZER *Highl. Turkey* I. 36 An artificial mound..with some indications of a wall having surmounted it. **1882** CUSSANS *Her.* vi. (ed. 3) 86 In the case of one Ordinary lying on another, *Surmounted by*, or *Over all* is always used, and never *Debruised by*.

Hence **surmount** *sb.* (*rare*$^{-1}$), something that surmounts, something placed on the top; **surˈmountal** (*rare*$^{-1}$) [-AL[1] 5], the act of surmounting or getting over.

1879 P. R. DRUMMOND *Perth. Bygone Days* v. 24 Leaping a gate where there was a surmount of spikes. **1886** J. W. GRAHAM *Neæra* (1887) II. xvi. 292 It was too lofty to afford any hope of surmountal.

surmountable (səˈmaʊntəb(ə)l), *a.* [f. prec. + -ABLE. Cf. F. *surmontable.*] That may be surmounted; conquerable, superable.

1611 COTGR., *Surmontable*, surmountable, surpassable. **1669** TEMPLE *Let. to Ld. Arlington* Wks. 1720 II. 191 He saw there would be another Difficulty less surmountable than all the rest. **1745** YOUNG in *Richardson's Corr.* (1804) II. 12 Evils they are, but surmountable ones. *a* **1806** HORSLEY *Serm., Luke iv. 18–19* (1816) I. 218 The temptations of all situations are equally surmountable. **1904** W. M. RAMSAY *Lett. Seven Churches* iv. 49 The difficulties of cultivation are no longer surmountable by a passive and uninventive population.

Hence **surˈmountableness**.

1847 in WEBSTER.

surˈmounted, *ppl. a.* [f. SURMOUNT *v.* + -ED[1].]

1. *Arch.* Applied to an arch or vault whose rise is greater than half the span: opp. to SURBASED.

1728 CHAMBERS *Cycl.* s.v. *Vault*, All above Hemispheres are call'd..surmounted Vaults. **1825** [see SURBASED *a.*]. **1836** PARKER *Gloss. Archit.* (1850) 40 Surmounted arches.

2. Overcome, vanquished.

1824 WIFFEN *Tasso* IX. xxviii, Honour..itself is base, Which no surmounted toils of jeopardy aggrace!

surˈmounter. Also 6 -our. [f. as prec. + -ER[1].] One who or that which surmounts; †one who or that which excels (*obs.*); an overcomer, vanquisher.

c **1500** *Three Kings' Sons* 177 A man that hight Le Surnome, whiche was the floure and surmountour of alle othir. **1589** PUTTENHAM *Engl. Poesie* III. xxv. (Arb.) 309 Arte is not only an aide..to nature in all her actions, but..in some sort a surmounter of her skill. *a* **1610** HEALEY *Epictetus* (1636) 2 Surmounters of all lets and impediments.

sur'mounting, *vbl. sb.* [-ING¹.] The action of the verb SURMOUNT; also, something that surmounts.

14.. *Voc.* in Wr.-Wülcker 581/24 *Excessus*, excesse, passynge oute, or surmountynge. **1812** *Examiner* 5 Oct. 635/1 On the entablature is an unadorned parapet, or surmounting of the front. **1860** TYNDALL *Glac.* I. viii. 60 The steady surmounting of difficulties.

sur'mounting, *ppl. a.* [-ING².] That surmounts.

†**1.** Surpassing, excelling, exceeding. *Obs.*

c **1407** LYDG. *Reson & Sens.* 5102 So excellent and so notable, Surmountyng and delytable. **1412–20** —— *Chron. Troy* I. 4352 Be-cause sche was surmountyng of bewte. *c* **1500** *Proverb* in *Antiq. Rep.* (1809) IV. 393 The sermountynge pleasure, who can expresse, Whiche is in armony of songe? **1583** STUBBES *Anat. Abus.* I. (1879) 76 Taking a singular felicity & surmounting pleasure in seeing them to go plumed and decked in the Feathers of deceiptfull vanity. **1593** G. HARVEY *Pierce's Super.* 18 Exceeding Aretine himselfe; that bestowed the surmountingest amplifications at his pleasure. **1627** *Lisander & Cal.* x. 215 The admirable attractions of her surmounting beauty. **1685** OTWAY *Windsor Castle* 137 That good Angel whose surmounting Power Waited Great Charles in each emergent hour. **1752** R. SHIRRA in *Rem.* (1850) 188 The absolute freedom and surmounting sovereignty of his grace.

†**2.** Arising or resulting from addition. *Obs.*

1571 DIGGES *Pantom.* II. xvii. O ij, Square the sides..and the productes seuerally multiplie in the number of perches to bee taken away, the surmountyng summes diuide by the Area of the whole triangle.

3. Situated above or on the top of something.

1661 MORGAN *Sph. Gentry* I. iv. 52 A Surmounting Star, is a bearing, denoting Sons of such a father who was advanced by Vertue. **1688** HOLME *Armoury* II. xix. 472/2 Schepsen of Silisia hath for his Crest seven such [*viz.* blades of grass], each surmounting and imbowed to the sinister. **1902** *Academy* 12 Apr. 379/1 His bookcases with their surmounting busts.

surmullet (sɜːˈmʌlɪt). Also 7 sir-. [ad. F. *surmulet.*] The red mullet; a name comprising species of *Mullus*, esp. *M. surmuletus*, the Striped Surmullet, red with three longitudinal yellow stripes, highly prized from ancient times as a food-fish, and *M. barbatus*, the Plain Surmullet, of a plain red.

a **1672** WILLUGHBY *Ichthyogr.* (1686) Tab. S. 7 *Mullus major Salv[iani]*, a Sirmullet. **1674** RAY *Coll. Words, Sea Fishes* 103 Sur-Mullet, *Mullus Antiquorum*. **1738** *MSS. Dk. Portland* (Hist. MSS. Comm.) VI. 175 We had a very good dinner, and a fish which is much prized and valued called a surmullet. **1769** PENNANT *Brit. Zoo.* III. 227 The Red Surmullet..*Mullus barbatus*. *Ibid.* 229 The Striped Surmullet, *Mullus major*. **1776** ADAM SMITH *W.N.* I. xi. I. 273 Asinius Celer purchased a surmullet at the price of eight thousand sestertii. **1899** *Contemp. Rev.* Aug. 202, I have seen surmullets, when going from the brown sand to the dark rocks, quickly change from one colour to the other.

surn (sɜːn). [ad. mod.L. *Surnia.*] An owl of the genus *Surnia*; a hawk-owl.

1840 *Cuvier's Anim. Kingd.* 175 The Rayed Surn..is about the size of the Sparrow-hawk.

‖**surnai** (ˈsʊrnaɪ). Also surná, surnay. [a. Urdū *surnā, surnāe* = *Pers. surnā*, also *sūrnā*.] An Oriental variety of oboe.

[**1662** J. DAVIES tr. *Olearius' Voy. Ambass.* 208 There were also common Hawboyes, which they [*sc.* Persians] call *Surnatzi*.] **1905** *Daily Chron.* 24 Feb. 8/5 An instrument called surná, that bears a resemblance..to a Scotch bagpipe. **1907** *Blackw. Mag.* June 819/1 Moving to the thunder of tom-toms and to the squeal of the *surnais* (native pipes).

surname (ˈsɜːneɪm), *sb.* Forms: α. 4–6 **sorname**, (4 surnome, *Sc.* swrname, suorname, -nome, 5 surnam, surename, 6 sur(r)e name, *Sc.* sourname, surnawm, 7–8 sur-name), 4– **surname**. β. 4–5 **sire name**, **sirename**, (6 sirnome, syrname, syr name), 6–8 **sir-name**, 6–9 **sirname** (8 sir name). [f. SUR- + NAME *sb.*, after AF., OF. *surnum, sornom*: see SURNOUN.

The spellings *sirname, sirename* are due to etymologizing alteration on SIR *sb.*, SIRE *sb.*, quasi 'father's name'.]

1. A name, title, or epithet added to a person's name or names, esp. one derived from his birthplace or from some quality or achievement. *Obs.* or *arch.*

c **1330** *Arth. & Merl.* 5488 (Kölbing), Þe .xxxix. Osoman, cert, His surname was: hardi of hert. *c* **1375** *Sc. Leg. Saints* vii. (*Jacobus Minor*) 15 Þis haly manne [*sc.* James the Less], þat foure swrnamys had. *c* **1375** *Cursor M.* 15218 (Fairf.) Ivdas of þa xij. was an his surnome scariot hiȝt. *c* **1400** MAUNDEV. (1839) 104 Fro thens gon men to Nazarethe, of the whiche oure lord berethe the surname. **1526** TINDALE *Acts* i. 23 Barsabas (whose syrname was Iustus). **1577–87** HOLINSHED *Chron.* I. 58/2 Which sitting still in Rome had triumphs and surnames appointed them of such nations as their capteins did vanquish. **1589** R. HARVEY *Pl. Perc.* (1860) 13 My sirnome is *Peace-Maker* one that is but poorely regarded in England. **1607** SHAKS. *Cor.* v. iii. 170 To his sur-name Coriolanus longs more pride Then pitty to our Prayers. **1683** KENNETT tr. *Erasm. on Folly* 118 If they did but practice their Sirname of Most Holy. **1702** C. MATHER *Magn. Chr.* III. II. i. (1852) 355 They gave Janus the sir-name of *Pater*. **1837** CARLYLE *Fr. Rev.* I. I. i, President Hénault, remarking on royal Surnames of Honour [etc.]. **1842** TENNYSON *St. Sim. Styl.* 159, I, Simeon of the pillar, by surname Stylites.

†**b.** A second, or an alternative, name or title given to a person, place, edifice, etc. *Obs.*

1388 WYCLIF *Gen.* xxxv. 6 Therfor Jacob cam to Lusa,..bi sire name Bethel. **1388** —— *Ecclus.* xlvii. 19 In the name of the Lord, to whom the surname [1382 toname] is God of Israel. ? *a* **1500** *Chester Pl.* (1906) 16 The church is called St. Mary The surname Ara Cœli. **1513** DOUGLAS *Æneis* VIII. x. 12 The Grekis ancyane, Quhilk clepit bene to surname Pelasgane. **1531** ELYOT *Gov.* II. iv, Nobilitie, whiche is the commendation, and as it were, the surname of vertue. **1567** FENTON *Trag. Disc.* ii. (1898) I. 88 With what title or sorname of constancy the fond philosophers of olde time do baptyse those accions of meare fury. **1632** LITHGOW *Trav.* IV. 150 They will not be content with the bare name of Images, but they impose a surname or epithite of sanctity, tearming them holy Images. **1638–56** COWLEY *Davideis* IV. Note 1, I have before declared that Baal was the Sun, and Baal Peor, a sirname, from a particular place of his worship. **1646** LLUELYN *Men-Miracles* etc. 66 Peter is Sirname to his Salt [*sc.* saltpetre].

2. The name which a person bears in common with the other members of his family, as distinguished from his *Christian* or *given name*; a family name.

1375 BARBOUR *Bruce* III. 99 Twa brethir..Thar surname wes Makyne-drosser; That is al-so mekill to say her As the durwarth sonnys. **1393** LANGL. *P. Pl.* C. IV. 369 þat is noȝt reisonable..to refusy my syres sorname [*v.rr.* surname, sirename]. **1465** *Irish Act 5 Edw. IV*, c. 16 Qe chescun irroys home..preigne a luy surname englois de vne vile come Sutton Chestr..ou color come White Blake. **1565** *Child-Marriages* 65 Sir Edmound (what his syrname was, this deponent knoweth not), a priest that syrved at Balderston Chappell. **1595** MAUNSELL *Catal.* 3 They make their Alphabet by the Christen name, I by the Sir name. **1605** CAMDEN *Rem.* (1637) 48 In late yeares Sirnames have beene given for Christian names among us, and no where else in Christendome. **1691** WOOD *Ath. Oxon.* I. 224, I find seven of his Sirname to be Students in the said College. **1749** FIELDING *Tom Jones* VII. xii, But the lieutenant..was not contented with Sophia only. He said he must have her sir-name. **1818** HALLAM *Mid. Ages* (1819) I. ii. II. 205 Two innovations devised in the eleventh and twelfth centuries; the adoption of sirnames, and of armorial bearings. **1875** W. S. HAYWARD *Love agst. World* 72, I shall not sign my surname. **1876** FREEMAN *Norm. Conq.* V. xxv. 563 The Norman Conquest..brought with it the novelty of family nomenclature, that is to say, the use of hereditary surnames.

b. *transf.*, esp. = COGNOMEN 1 (*a*), e.g. Publius Cornelius *Scipio*.

c **1375** *Sc. Leg. Saints* xxxvi. (*Baptista*) 928 Þe thred herrod had alsua til his suornome agrippa. **1481** CAXTON *Godfrey* xxxiv. 71 In this tyme was Emperour a greke,..and was named alexes, and to his surname Conius [i.e. Alexius Comnenus I]. **1598** GRENEWEY *Tacitus, Ann.* II. vii. (1622) 42 That none of the Scribonian familie should take vpon him the surname of *Drusus*. **1654** tr. *Martini's Conq. China* 106 Adding to his name (as usually they do) the Sirname of *Pingsi*. **1657** *North's Plutarch* Note 91 *Albus* was the sirname of the Posthumians.

†**3.** A family, clan. *Sc. Obs.*

1455 in *Charters &c. Edinb.* (1871) 79 The surnam and nerrest of blude to the said Williame. **1508** KENNEDIE *Flyting w. Dunbar* 416 Hang Dunbar, Quarter and draw, and mak that surname thin. **1553–4** *Reg. Privy Council Scot.* I. 152 Thame, their kyn, freyndis, servandis, allya, assisteris and surname. **1565** *Ibid.* 361 To resset ony rebellis and surname of Clangregour.

surname (ˈsɜːneɪm, sɜːˈneɪm), *v.* Also 6 syr-, 6–9 sir-. [f. prec. Cf. OF. *sournommer* (mod.F. *surnommer*).] To give a surname to: chiefly *pass.*

1. *trans.* To give an additional name, title, or epithet to (a person).

a. with descriptive adj., sb., or phr.

a **1548** HALL *Chron., Hen. VI* 100 b, He gathered so muche treasure, that no man in maner had money but he, and so was he surnamed the riche Cardinall of Winchester. **1560** DAUS tr. *Sleidane's Comm.* 59 b, That seing we professe the name of Christ, we may rightly chalenge that to our selues, that we may be surnamed Christians. **1588** SHAKS. *L.L.L.* v. ii. 553, I Pompey am, Pompey surnam'd the big. **1601** HOLLAND *Pliny* v. xxix. I. 108 The renowmed cittie Magnesia, surnamed, Vpon Mæander. **1607** R. JOHNSON (*title*) The Most Pleasant History of Tom a Lincolne,..the Red Rose Knight, who for his valour..was surnamed the Boast of England. **1634** SIR T. HERBERT *Trav.* 30 Tamberlaine (sirnamed the Scourge of God). **1671** MILTON *P.R.* II. 199 How hee sirnam'd of Africa dismiss'd..the fair Iberian maid. **1769** ROBERTSON *Chas. V*, XII. III. 454 His successor Cosmo, sirnamed the Great. **1807** G. CHALMERS *Caledonia* I. III. vii. 396 Kenneth IV..was sirnamed *Grim*, from the strength of his body, rather than the force of his character. **1871** SMILES *Charac.* i. (1876) 20 William of Orange, surnamed the Silent. **1908** [MISS FOWLER] *Betw. Trent & Ancholme* 73 We surnamed our young friend 'Orpheus with his Flute'.

b. with a recognized proper name.

1539 *Bible* (Great) Acts x. 18 Symon which was syrnamed Peter. **1576** GASCOIGNE *Steele Gl.* 490 Paulus he, (Æmilius surnamed). **1611** *Bible* Isa. xliv. 5 Another shall subscribe with his hand vnto the Lord, and surname himselfe by the name of Israel. **1613** PURCHAS *Pilgrimage* I. xvi. 73 Antiochus his sonne, surnamed *Epiphanes*. **1756–7** tr. *Keysler's Trav.* (1760) I. 64 The famous Switzer, Theophrastus Bompast, sirnamed Paracelsus. **1818** CRUISE *Digest* (ed. 2) V. 69 Roger, sirnamed Vacarius,..read public lectures at Oxford on the Roman law. **1868** FREEMAN *Norm. Conq.* II. viii. 205 The commander of the district was Thurstan surnamed Goz.

2. To give such-and-such a surname to; to call (a person) by his surname or family name.

1512 *Act 4 Hen. VIII*, c. 9. §1 By what soever name or names surname or surnames the same William be named or surnamed in the said acte. **1605** VERSTEGAN *Dec. Intell.* vi. (1628) 181 [They] began to surname themselues after such places as they properly possessed. *c* **1630** RISDON *Surv. Devon* §60 Rockbeare..had..lords sirnamed thereof. **1682** PIERS *Descr. W. Meath* (1770) 108 Thus you have Mac Gowne surname himself Smith [*marg.* Irish now change their names into English].

†**3.** To call by another or additional name; to attach another appellation or designation to; more widely, to designate, entitle. *Obs.*

1561 in Heath *Grocers' Comp.* (1869) 96 Evil pepper syrnamed gynger. **1599** NASHE *Lenten Stuffe* 35 The Scotish Iockies or Red-shanks (so surnamed of their immoderate raunching vp the red shanks or red herrings). **1601** HOLLAND *Pliny* v. xxvii. I. 105 Seleucia upon the river Calicadmus, surnamed also Trachiotis. **1606** G. W[OODCOCKE] *Hist. Ivstine* xx. 76 Al that part of Italy (surnamed the greater Greece). **1632** LITHGOW *Trav.* VII. 311 The great Pyramides, surnamed the Worlds wonders. **1671** MILTON *P.R.* IV. 279 All the schools Of Academics old and new, with those Sirnam'd Peripatetics. **1697** POTTER *Antiq. Greece* I. viii. (1715) 31 The other Part of the Temple..Sirnam'd *Πολιάς*.

Hence †**surnamed** *ppl. a.*, having such-and-such a designation.

1659 MILTON *Civil Power* Wks. 1851 V. 317 The papist..by the church,..understands the pope, the general councels prelatical only and the surnam'd fathers.

surnamer. *nonce-wd.* [f. SURNAME *v.* + -ER¹.] Puttenham's englishing of ANTONOMASIA.

1589 PUTTENHAM *Engl. Poesie* III. xvii. (Arb.) 192 Not *metonimia*, but *antonomasia*, or the Surnamer, (not the misnamer, which might extend to any other thing aswell as to a person) as he that would say: not king Philip of Spaine, but the Westerne king.

surnap. *Obs.* exc. *Hist.* Also **-nape**. [a. AF., OF. *sur-, sournap(p)e*, f. *sur-* SUR- + *nape* table-cloth, NAPE *sb.*²] A towel or napkin provided at table for use when washing the hands.

1381–2 *Durham Acc. Rolls* (Surtees) 592 Pro surnape pro tabul. d'ni Prioris. **1478** in *Illustr. Anc. State & Chivalry* (Roxb.) 31 After the surnapp made. **1554** *Ibid.* 54 The surnape wᵗ drawen, then the[y] whashed. *a* **1548** HALL *Chron., Hen. VIII*, 4 b, After the Surnap laied, and that the kynges grace, & the Quene had wasshed.

[**1802** MRS. RADCLIFFE *Gaston de Blondeville* Posth. Wks. 1826 II. 31 The King's sewer having laid the end of the surnap and a towel on the board. **1859** PARKER *Dom. Archit.* III. iii. 75 *note*, The surnape appears to have answered the purpose of the modern table napkin.]

surnominal (sɜːˈnɒmɪnəl), *a.* [f. SURNAME *sb.*, after *name, nominal.*] Of or pertaining to surnames.

1875 LOWER *Eng. Surnames* (ed. 4) II. viii. 83 The surnominal characteristics of that province. **1914** E. WEEKLEY *Romance of Names* (ed. 2) 186 The first element is Anglo-Sax. hengest, stallion, and its most usual surnominal forms are Hensman and Hinxman.

†**surnoun.** *Obs.* Forms: 4 sournoun, 4–5 surnoun(e, 5 sewrnown, surnon. [a. AF. *surnoun* = OF. *sornom*, f. *sur-* SUR- + *nom* name, after med.L. *supernōmen, suprānōmen* (cf. late L. *supernōmināre* to surname): cf. Pr. *sobrenom*, It. *soprannome*, Sp. *sobrenombre*, Pg. *sobrenome.*] = SURNAME *sb.* 1, 1 b, 2.

c **1325** *Chron. Eng.* 982 in Ritson *Metr. Rom.* II. 311 Richard queor de lyoun, That was his sournoun. **1375** BARBOUR *Bruce* XVII. 152 Of Keth, and of Gawlistoune He hecht, throu differens of sur-noune. *c* **1450** LOVELICH *Merlin* 10208 Whanne thus amended was þat town, thanne wolde he ȝeven hit a Sewrnown, and after Logryvs Logres cald hit he. **1457** HARDING *Chron.* i. in *Eng. Hist. Rev.* Oct. (1912) 741 Of kynge Edward with longshankes by surnoun. **1472–3** *Rolls of Parlt.* VI. 37/2 As if they were named by name of Baptisme, surnon and addition.

suroccipital: see SUR-.

†**surot.** *Obs.* [a. OF. *surot*, var. of *suros*: see SEREW.] A swelling on a horse's shank.

1601 HOLLAND *Pliny* XXVIII. xv. II. 332 The surots or rugged werts [orig. F. *surotz*] in horse legs.

suround, surow, surpage, -paich, -paish: see SURROUND, SEROW, SURPEACH.

surpass (sɜːˈpɑːs, -æ-), *v.* [ad. F. *surpasser* (= obs. It. *sorpassare*), f. *sur-* = SUPER- 2 + *passer* to PASS.]

1. *trans.* To pass over, go beyond, overstep (a limit): often in fig. context; also, to go beyond (a certain period of time). *Obs.* or *arch.*

1588 KYD *Househ. Philos.* Wks. (1901) 240 The Ryuer..was swoln so high as it farre surpast the wonted limmits. **1652** C. B. STAPYLTON *Herodian* I. 3 Infamous was the Life of Ptolomy, Surpassing bounds of Civill Modesty. **1667** MILTON *P.L.* XI. 894 Nor let the Sea Surpass his bounds. **1706** E. WARD *Wooden World Diss.* (1708) 82 He cooks by the Hour-Glass..; and will no more surpass one Puncto of Time, than a scrupulous Virtuoso in the Concoction of his Stomach. **1788** V. KNOX *Winter Even.* II. v. viii. 173 In poetical excellence..he cannot be said to have often surpassed the line of mediocrity. **1799** J. ROBERTSON *Agric. Perth.* 237 If they are left to surpass the ordinary period, the succeeding growth suffers. **1839** THACKERAY *Leg. St. Sophia of Kioff* xix, Nor cared they to surpass the river's bank.

2. †**a.** To pass or mount above; to surmount. *Obs.*

1639 DRUMM. OF HAWTH. *Conv. w. B. Jonson* Wks. (1711) 226 The one flying swift, but low; the other, like the eagle, surpassing the clouds. **1769** PENNANT *Brit. Zool.* III. 241 Salmon..gain the sources of the Lapland rivers..., and surpass the perpendicular falls of Leixslip [etc.].

b. To extend above or beyond. Now *rare*.

1601 HOLLAND *Pliny* XXVII. i. II. 269 High mountains also and the cliffes surpassing the verie clouds. **1687** A. LOVELL tr. *Thevenot's Trav.* II. 80 This frontispiece hath a Minaret on each side which surpass it above three fathom in height. **1852** MACGILLIVRAY *Brit. Birds* V. 474 Tarsus two inches long; wings surpassing the tail by two inches. **1880** *Nature* 1 Jan. 212 Where mountain masses..surpassed the level of perpetual snow.

3. To go beyond (another) in degree, amount, or quality; to be or do more or better than; to be greater than, to exceed; to be superior to, to excel.

1555 BRADFORD in Strype *Eccl. Mem.* (1721) III. App. xlv. 127 The natural love that I beare to my natyve countreye, surpassing all daungers that maye chaunce to my bodye and goods. *a* **1586** SIDNEY *Arcadia* I. xiii, Philoclea..muche resembling (though I must say much surpassing) the Ladie Zelmane. **1590** SPENSER *F.Q.* I. x. 58 This great Citie that does far surpas. **1625** MEADE in Ellis *Orig. Lett.* Ser. I. III. 209 You may see..how much this Plague, for the time and number, surpasses that of 1603. **1667** MILTON *P.L.* I. 778 They..who seemd In bigness to surpass Earths Giant Sons. *Ibid.* II. 370 This would surpass Common revenge. *a* **1700** EVELYN *Diary* 5 May 1645, A villa..surpassing..the most delicious places I ever beheld. **1802** PALEY *Nat. Theol.* xxvi. (1819) 449 The gifts of nature always surpass the gifts of fortune. **1819** KEATS *Fall Hyperion* I. 337 The Goddess,.. Surpassing wan Moneta by the head. **1827** FARADAY *Chem. Manip.* v. (1842) 165 The silica will be in a state of division far surpassing any which can be obtained merely by mechanical means. **1860** TYNDALL *Glac.* I. xviii. 133 The heat surpassed anything of the kind I had ever felt. **1874** GREEN *Short Hist.* iii. §2. 118 In the rapidity and breadth of his political combinations he far surpassed the statesmen of his time.

b. To exceed (a specified measure, as weight, speed, etc.). *rare.*

1591 in Picton *L'pool Munic. Rec.* (1883) I. 83 That anie one townes man..shall..buie anie rendred tallowe not surpassing one cwt of roughe tallowe. **1898** *Daily News* 21 Sept. 3/1 The Boa was not put to her highest speed, but.. she surpassed 24 knots an hour.

c. To go beyond (something done or existing) in action or achievement; to do something that is more or better than.

1592 SHAKS. *Ven. & Ad.* 289 When a Painter would surpasse the life, In limming out a well proportioned steed. **1728** YOUNG *Love Fame* III. 120 The plenteous harvest calls me forward still, Till I surpass in length my lawyer's bill. **1841** D'ISRAELI *Amen. Lit.* xv. (1867) 176 Johnson surpassed all his preceding labours in his last work. **1842** LOUDON *Suburban Hort.* 249 These seeds not only germinated well, but in rapidity surpassed my expectations.

4. To be beyond the range, reach, or capacity of; to be more than can be attained, achieved, or apprehended by; to be too much or too great for; to transcend.

1592 *Sol. & Pers.* III. i. 101 The least of these surpasse my best desart. **1611** SHAKS. *Wint. T.* III. i. 2 The Temple much surpassing The common prayse it beares. **1642** H. MORE *Song of Soul* II. iii. II. viii, Not multiplying beings to surpasse Their use. **1671** MILTON *Samson* 1313 Thy strength they know surpassing human rate. **1784** COWPER *Task* IV. 710 His Paradise surpass'd The struggling efforts of my boyish tongue To speak its excellence. *Ibid.* VI. 759 Oh scenes surpassing fable, and yet true. **1850** MCCOSH *Div. Govt.* IV. ii. (1874) 488 This surpasses the utmost exertions of human ingenuity. **1861** BUCKLE *Civiliz.* (1873) II. viii. 504 The poverty and wretchedness of the people surpass all description. **1897** GLADSTONE *E. Crisis* 2 The Armenian massacres have surpassed in their wickedness all modern experience.

surpassable (sə'pɑːsəb(ə)l, -æ-), *a. rare.* [f. prec. + -ABLE.] Capable of being surpassed, exceeded, or excelled; †surmountable (*obs.*).

1611 [see SURMOUNTABLE]. **1698** NORRIS *Pract. Disc.* IV. 28 A very Vincible and Surpassable Discouragement.

†**sur'passant,** *a. Obs. rare.* [ad. F. *surpassant*, pr. pple. of *surpasser* to SURPASS.] Surpassing.

1654 tr. *Scudery's Curia Pol.* 70 Other Kings will behold us far more eminent for our fortune or more surpassant for our vertue and valour.

†**sur'passed,** *ppl. a. Obs. nonce-wd.* [f. SUR- + *passed*, PAST *ppl. a.*, after *overpassed*.] Bygone.

1620–55 I. JONES *Stone-Heng* (1725) 21 The Customs of surpassed Ages.

surpasser (sə'pɑːsə(r), -æ-). [f. SURPASS *v.* + -ER[1].] One who surpasses or excels.

1805 W. TAYLOR in *Ann. Rev.* III. 240 Rowe, often the model, and oftener the surpasser of Voltaire. **1838** *New Monthly Mag.* LIII. 554 The surpassers of Columbus, who, by means of the telescope, have revealed to us new worlds in the heavens. **1897** in *Advance* (Chicago) 22 Apr. 507/1 To surpass his surpasser.

sur'passing, *vbl. sb.* [f. as prec. + -ING[1].] The action of the verb SURPASS.

1736 AINSWORTH, A surpassing, *præstantia, eminentia, præcellentia.* *a* **1774** TUCKER *Lt. Nat.* (1834) II. 139 The frequency of them transfers satisfaction from the advantage gained by surpassing to the surpassing itself.

sur'passing, *ppl. a.* (*adv.*) [f. as prec. + -ING[2].] That surpasses what is ordinary; greatly exceeding or excelling others; of very high degree.

c **1580** JEFFERIE *Bugbears* IV. ii. 24 A surpassinge longing on the sodayne is bred. **1582** T. WATSON *Centurie of Love* xxix. (Arb.) 65 The Authour in this Sonnet..setteth forth the surpassinge worthines of his Ladie. *c* **1595** CAPT. WYATT *R. Dudley's Voy. W. Ind.* (Hakl. Soc.) 14 Such a laborynth of surpassing troubles. **1610** HOLLAND *Camden's Brit.* (1637) 203 An Emperour surpassing in all..Christian piety. **1667** MILTON *P.L.* IV. 32 O thou..with surpassing Glory crownd. **1815** SHELLEY *Alastor* 288 Wasting these surpassing powers In the deaf air, to the blind earth. *a* **1859** MACAULAY *Hist. Eng.* xxiii. V. 112 The surpassing beauty of his horses, and the multitude of his running footmen. **1884** *Manch. Exam.* 14 May 5/1 To the transcendent meanness and surpassing untruthfulness which lie at the basis of such an insinuation.

b. *adv.* = next. (Cf. PASSING *adv.*) *Obs.* exc. *poet.*

1598 MARSTON *Pygmal.* 136 Ends not my Poem then surpassing ill? **1653** URQUHART *Rabelais* II. ix. 59 A young man..surpassing handsome in all the lineaments of his body. **1808** FOSTER in *Life & Corr.* (1846) I. 266 A large and surpassing ugly town. **1839–52** BAILEY *Festus* 381 Surely sin Must be surpassing lovely when for her Men forfeit God's reward.

sur'passingly, *adv.* [f. prec. + -LY[2].] In a surpassing degree; exceedingly, supereminently.

1658 ROWLAND tr. *Moufet's Theat. Ins.* 908 Johan. Bauhinus a very learned Physician, and surpassingly well seen in the knowledge of simples. **1698** W. CHILCOT *Evil Thoughts* vii. (1851) 84 His radiant likeness is stamped upon every glorified soul, which makes it surpassingly fair and beautiful. **1834** L. RITCHIE *Wand. Seine* 103 Surpassingly fair and good. **1847** HELPS *Friends in C.* I. vi. 88 How surpassingly interesting is real life, when we get an insight into it. **1891** MEREDITH *One of our Conq.* III. xii. 245 His Idea had been surpassingly luminous.

So **sur'passingness.** *rare.*

1879 MEREDITH *Egoist* xxii, The effect of the luckless comparison was to produce an image of surpassingness in the features of Clara that gave him the final, or mace-blow.

surpay: see SUR-.

†**'surpcloth.** *north. Obs.* Also 6–7 sirpe, syrpe-, 6–8 sirp- (6 serp-, syrpt(e)-, 7 sirpt-, sirpluth); see also CLOTH, CLOTHES. [Alteration of SURPLICE by substitution of *cloth* for the second half of the word.] A surplice.

1525 *Churchw. Acc. St. Michael, Spurriergate, York,* Payd for a syrpe clothe mendyng ij d. ob. **1557** *Richmond Wills* (Surtees) 97 Item I gyffe unto Sir John Dyxson my surpclothe. **1557–75** *Diurn. Occur.* (Bannatyne Cl.) 104 And als assistit with rockattis and huidis, the bischope of Ross, the pryour of Quhitherne, and sindrie vthers with serpclaithes and huidis. **1596** *Vestry Bks.* (Surtees) 271 To Roberte Waytsones wyfe for washyng the syrpte cloys. **1615** BRATHWAIT *Strappado* (1878) 110 A Church-man..his Syrpe-cloth..discarded quite Resoluing fully now to be a Knight. **1665** *Vestry Bks.* (Surtees) 219 For weshing the sirpluths, 8 s. **1698** *Ibid.* 26: For altering the clerk's surpcloth, 1 s. **1778** *Finghall Churchw. Acc.* (MS.) For mending Sirpcloth, 9d.

†**surpeach.** *Obs.* Forms: 8 sirpeach, surpage, -peach, 9 -paich, -peych, -paish, sirpesh. [a. Urdū *sarpēch*, = Pers. *serpēsh*.] An ornament of gold, silver, or jewels, on the turban.

1753 HANWAY *Trav.* IV. 191 *note*, A sirpeach, which is wore round the turbant. **1759** in Long *Select. Unpubl. Rec. Fort William* (1869) I. 193, 1 Culgah..1200. o. o. 1 Surpage ..600. o. o. **1776** *Francis Lett.* (1901) I. 321 Betsey is charmed with the surpeach and flatters herself it is diamond. **1811** KIRKPATRICK tr. *Lett Tippoo Sultan* 263 Three Kulgies, three Surpaishes, and three Puduks. [*Note.*] *Surpaich*, or *Surpaish*, that is the *Aigrette.*

surpegue, anglicized form of SERPIGO. (Cf. *suppeago* in Shaks. *Tr. & Cr.* II. iii. 82, 1st Folio.)

a **1632** T. TAYLOR *God's Judgem.* II. iv. (1642) 57 Aches . surpegues..rheumes.

surphal, -ph(e)ul, -phle, -ple: see SURFLE.

‖**sur place** (syr plas), *adv.* [Fr.] **1.** At the place in question; 'on the spot'.

1915 LADY R. CHURCHILL *Let.* 21 Nov. in M. Gilbert *Winston S. Churchill* (1972) III. Compan. II. 1284, I can understand that you want to study *sur place* this new phase of warfare. **1939** 'A. BRIDGE' *Four-Part Setting* xii. 157 You didn't stay and face the situation and the pain *sur place*, did you? **1976** *Listener* 28 Oct. 533/2 It is..exciting to read a regional novel *sur place.*

2. *Ballet.* Without leaving the place where one has been standing.

1930 CRASKE & BEAUMONT *Theory & Pract. Allegro in Classical Ballet* 87 *Relevez* sharply *sur place* on the *left pointe.* **1947** *Ballet Annual* I. 28 Her *fouettés* were *sur place*, and one never doubted her ability to complete the thirty-two. **1950** FRENCH & DEMERY *Advanced Steps in Ballet* 37 *Petits battements sautés.* These should be *sur place.*

surplice ('sɜːplɪs). Forms: 3–7 surplis, 4–6 surples, -plys, 4–7 -plesse, -plise, (4 surplees, 5 sarplys, serples, sorplise, sourples, suplice; sorplers, solepers, sullipers), 5–6 surplyse, -plese, (6 sorplys, syrplys, -plis, -plasse, -pleys, surplyce, -plasse, -plusse, -plois, surpelis, sirplis, -pleys, cirples, scherples; serppelys, shorpells surpells, -peles, syrpeles), 6–7 surpless, -plisse, 5–8 -plus, (7 syrplesse, surpliss, sirplus, cirploise, serpils), 4– surplice. [a. AF. *surpliz*, OF. *sourpeliz*, *sor-*, *sur-*, also *supelis*, *souplis* (mod.F. *surplis*), = Pr. *sobrepelitz*, It. *superpellicio*, Sp., Pg. *sobrepelliz*, ad. med.L. *superpellicium*, *-eum* (sc. *vestimentum* garment), neut. of adj. f. *super-* SUPER- 1 a + *pellicia* fur garment (f. *pellis* skin: see PELISSE).]

A loose vestment of white linen having wide sleeves and, in its amplest form, reaching to the feet, worn (usually over a cassock) by clerics, choristers, and others taking part in church services.

'Its name is derived..from the fact that it was formerly put on over the fur garments which used to be worn in church..as a protection against the cold' (*Encycl. Brit.*, 1911, XXVI. 137/1).

c **1290** *All Souls' Day* 345 in *S. Eng. Leg.* 430 His cope oþur is surplis þe preost he seith it isse. *c* **1325** *Metr. Hom.* 161 Tua clerkes..In surplices wit serges berande. **13..** *Adultery* 89 in Horstm. *Altengl. Leg.* (1881) 369 There come one in a whyte surples [*v.r.* surplyse]. *c* **1386** CHAUCER *Miller's T.* 137 A gay surplys As whit as is the blosme vp on the rys. **1429–30** *Rec. St. Mary at Hill* (1904) 74 For wasshyng..of aubes & sarplys..ij s. **1491–2** *Ibid.* 173 A sourples for the clarke..ij s. **1506–7** *Ibid.* 260 j surplus for boll the sexton xij d. **1509** BARCLAY *Shyp of Folys* (1570) 9 With your shirtes brodered and displayed In fourme of surplois. **1548–9** (Mar.) *Bk. Com. Prayer, Communion* (Rubr. at end), The Priest shall put upon him a playn Albe or surplesse, with a cope, and say al thinges at the Altar.. untill after the offertory. **1553** in Daniel-Tyssen *Surrey Ch.-Goods* (1869) 102 For newe collering of a scherples. **1553** MACHYN *Diary* 8 Aug. (Camden) 39 A grett company of chylderyn in ther surples. *a* **1592** GREENE *Alphonsus* III. Wks. (Grosart) XIII. 368 Rise Calchas vp, in a white Cirples and a Cardinals Myter, and say [etc.]. **1601** SHAKS. *All's Well* I. iii. 99 Though honestie be no Puritan, yet it will doe no hurt, it will weare the Surplis of humilitie ouer the blacke-Gowne of a bigge heart. **1617** ASSHETON *Jrnl.* (Chetham Soc.) 88 Some argument ab[t] Mr. Leighs ministring y[e] Sacrament with the Cirploise. **1633** ROWLEY *Match Midn.* I. B4, Has turn'd his stomacke, for all the World like a Puritanes, at the sight of a surplesse. **1641** *Impeachm. Bp. Wren* in Rushw. *Hist. Coll.* III. (1692) I. 352 He [*sc.* Bp. Wren]..in the said Year 1636. commanded..all Ministers to Preach constantly in their Hood and Surplice, a thing not used before in that Diocess. **1678** WANLEY *Wond. Lit. World* v. iii. §8. 474/1 Sixtus [I]..ordered..that Priests should minister in Linnen Surplices. **1753** CHALLONER *Cath. Chr. Instr.* 153 The Bishop..invests them with a Surplice, and so receives them into the Clergy. **1807** CRABBE *Par. Reg.* III. 816 He fill'd the sevenfold surplice fairly out. **1820** W. IRVING *Sketch Bk.* II. 14 (*Westm. Abb.*) The choristers, in their white surplices, crossing the aisle and entering the choir. **1866** G. MACDONALD *Ann. Q. Neighb.* v, Is it a point of conscience with you to wear the surplice when you preach?

1440–1 *Norwich Sacrist's Roll* (MS.), In factura alb. amict. sulliperes. **1492–3** *Ibid.*, Pro xxij ulnis panni linei cum factura de le Solepers, xj s. **1478** *Croscombe Churchw. Acc.* (Som. Rec. Soc.) 8 Wasscheng of vestments and Sorplers. **1509** *Ibid.* 30 Of Alys Vaysse a rynge of sylver and a serppelys. **1511** *Pilton Churchw. Acc.* (ibid.) 60 For mendyng of the shorpells..iiij *d.* **1566** *Engl. Ch. Furniture* (Peacock 1866) 85 A alb—wherof ys mayd a surpells for the preste. **1606** *Burford Reg.* in *Var. Coll.* (Hist. MSS. Comm.) I. 78 Mr. Segwick hath not worne the serpils sence the tyme he hath ben vicar of Ockborne Saint Andrew.

b. *transf.* Applied to various ample or enveloping garments.

1382 WYCLIF *1 Sam.* ii. 18 Samuel seruede before the face of the Lord, a child gird with a surplesse [1388 lynnun clooth; Vulg. *ephod lineo*]. **1382** —— *2 Chron.* v. 12 Sonis and bretheren of hem, clothid with surples [1388 white lynun clothis; Vulg. *byssinis*]. **1488–92** *Acc. Ld. High Treas. Scot.* I. 85 The surples of the robe riall. **1558** PHAER *Æneid* VIII. (1562) Cc iij, Some trayling mantels loose, or syrpleys wyndie wyde of skyrts. **1635** R. N. tr. *Camden's Hist. Eliz.* I. 48 Shan O'Neal came out of Ireland with a Guard of Axbearing Galloglasses with..yellow surplises. **1756** MRS. CALDERWOOD in *Coltness Collect.* (Maitl. Cl.) 184 Above this, fine muslin surpluses with point, which makes a very genteel dress. **1898** MISS YONGE *J. Keble's Parishes* xv. 175 *Surplice*, smock-frock. 'Ah! sir, the white surplice covers a great deal of dirt'—said by a tidy woman of her old father.

c. *attrib.* and *Comb.*, as *surplice brabble, closet, coat, fashion*; **surplice-backed** *a.*, wearing a surplice; **surplice day**, a holy day or its eve, when members of a college wear surplices in chapel; **surplice duty**, that part of an incumbent's duties which consists in the recital of public prayer; **surplice fees**, the dues received by an incumbent for the performance of marriages, burials, and other ministerial offices; **surpliceman** *nonce-wd.*, a clergyman; **surplice pin**, properly, a peg to hang a surplice on; hence, a hat-peg; **surplice-wise** *adv.*, like a surplice.

a **1845** HOOD *Dean & Chapter* i, Hail to each *surplice-back'd adapter. **1641** MILTON *Reform.* II. Wks. 1851 III. 54 To make a Nationall Warre of a *Surplice Brabble, a Tippet-scuffle. **1874** MICKLETHWAITE *Mod. Par. Churches* 61 Besides the *surplice-closets, and a cupboard..there need be no other furniture in the choir-vestry. **1902** *Daily Chron.* 24 May 8/3 Supposing a bottle-green length were chosen for a costume, it might have a short *surplice coat. **1663** WOOD *Life* (O.H.S.) I. 511 To come on *surplice dayes to Merton College prayers. **1824** HITCHINS & DREW *Cornwall* II. 633 The *surplice duty of this parish is now performed by the rector of Blisland. **1845** HOOD *Surplice Question* 3 A very pretty public stir Is making down at Exeter, About the *surplice fashion. **1725** T. THOMAS in *MSS. Dk. Portland* (Hist. MSS. Comm.) VI. 129 The allowance of the Curate here..is twenty marks a year, and the *surplice fees. **1768** BLACKSTONE *Comm.* III. vii. 89 Whatsoever falls under the denomination of surplice-fees, for marriages or other ministerial offices of the church. **1818** BENTHAM *Ch. Eng.* 49 Surplice fees are unknown in Scotland. **1814** BYRON in *Lett. & Jrnls.* (1898) II. 395 There be some strange phrases in the prologue (the exhortation), which made me turn away, not to laugh in the face of the *surpliceman. **1833** LOUDON *Encycl. Archit.* §691 Five hat pins, or *surplice pins, as they are called by upholsterers. **1459** *Paston Lett.* I. 475 A goune of clothe of golde, with side slevis, *surplices wise. **1565** SPARKE *Hawkins' 2nd Voy.* (Hakl.

Soc.) 54 Gownes of mosse..which they sowe together artificially, and make the same surpleswise.

surpliced ('sɜːplɪst), *a.* [f. prec. + -ED².] Wearing or vested in a surplice.

a **1765** MALLET *Funeral Hymn* ii, As the surplic'd train draw near To this last mansion of mankind. **1835** I. TAYLOR *Spir. Despot.* VI. 262 The hundreds of surpliced idlers that swelled the episcopal pageant. **1852** ROCK *Ch. Fathers* III. I. 371 Headed by coped and surpliced choristers. **1871** *Echo* 6 Jan., In 180 [churches] the surplice is used in the pulpit, in 151 there are surpliced choirs.

b. *fig.* Clothed in white.

1845 KINGSLEY in *Macm. Mag.* No. 246. 520 Frozen fields that surpliced lie.

surpling: see SURFLE.

surplus ('sɜːpləs), *sb.* and *a.* Pl. **-uses** (†**-usses**). Also 4–6 **-pluis**, 5 **-ples**, **-plice**, 5–6 **-pluse**. [a. AF., OF. *surplus*, *so(u)rplus* (whence med.L. *surplus*) = Pr. *sobreplus*, ad. med.L. *superplūs*, f. *super* SUPER- IV + *plūs* more.]

A. *sb.*

1. a. What remains over and above what has been taken or used; an amount remaining in excess. †Also, (a) superfluity, superabundance.

c **1374** CHAUCER *Troylus* IV. 60 þey gonnen trete Here prisoneres to chaungen most and leste, And for the surplus, yeue sommes grete. *c* **1407** LYDG. *Reson & Sens.* 5859 Oonly for to han victoire With-oute surplus of wynnyng. **1511–12** *Act 3 Hen. VIII*, c. 6 §1 The Wever..shall..restore to the same Clothier the surpluis of the same yerne. **1607** SHAKS. *Cor.* I. i. 46 He hath faults (with surplus) to tyre in repetition. **1611** —— *Wint. T.* v. iii. 7 It is a surplus of your Grace, which neuer My life may last to answere. **1663** BUTLER *Hud.* I. i. 391 In th' Holsters..Two aged Pistols he did stow, Among the surplus of such meat As in his Hose he could not get. **1736** *Gentl. Mag.* VI. 585/1 In Case the future Produce of those Duties should amount to more than 800,000*l.* a Year, those Surplusses were by them.. appropriated to the Civil List. **1790** BURKE *Fr. Rev.* 236 In every prosperous community something more is produced than goes to the immediate support of the producer. This surplus forms the income of the landed capitalist. **1821** CRAIG *Lect. Drawing* etc. vii. 400 Pour the surplus of this liquid immediately away. **1827** JARMAN *Powell's Devises* (ed. 3) II. 85 That where there was a direction to sell land for a particular purpose, the surplus did not form 'part of the personal estate, so as to pass by the residuary bequest.' **1835** LYTTON *Rienzi* VI. i, A brief, sheeted stream bore its surplus into the lake. **1878** JEVONS *Prim. Pol. Econ.* 95 The rent of better land will consist of the surplus of its produce over that of the poorest cultivated land. **1879** LUBBOCK *Addr. Pol. & Educ.* vi. 125 We are slightly diminishing our Debt in two ways, by accidental surpluses and by terminable annuities. **1892** *Photogr. Ann.* II. 194 Fold the paper over the edge of frame and double down the surplus on the side. **1905** *Act 5 Edw. VII*, c. 17 §5 Any surpluses..which may be effected by the saving of expenditure upon votes within the same department.

b. *Polit.* In some systems of election by transferable vote: the votes which are transferred from a candidate who has attained the quota necessary for election to one who has not.

1926 HOAG & HALLETT *Proportional Representation* 345 The particular ballots of a candidate to be transferred as his surplus shall be those which have received certain serial numbers. **1950** THEIMER & CAMPBELL *Encycl. World Politics* 353/1 In successive counts by the electoral officials the candidates with most preferences are elected and their surpluses over the minimum quota necessary for election transferred according to the voters' preferences until all the seats are filled. **1973** *Irish Times* 2 Mar. 1/1 This was also the first striking example of Fine Gael votes transferring to Labour: Mr. Kyne was elected on the surplus of Mr. Eddie Collins.

†**2.** What remains to make up a whole; the remainder, the rest. *Obs.*

c **1400** *Rom. Rose* 3675 Who therto may wynnen, ywisse, He of the surplus of the praye May lyfe in hoope to gette some daye. **1430–40** LYDG. *Bochas* II. ii. (MS. Bodl. 263) 97/2 Touchyng the surplus off his gouernaunce..In Iosephus his story ye may reede. *c* **1489** CAXTON *Sonnes of Aymon* x. 272 There are com agayn but thre hundred, and the surplus is all slayn or taken. *a* **1500** *Ratis Raving* 1812 And al the surplice of the schame Scho wyll bere bauldly with the blam. **1502** *Ord. Crysten Men* (W. de W. 1506) IV. xxvii. 323 To knowe the tokens of deth to the ende that he may denounce as well vnto the pacyente as vnto his frendes that they puruaye of the surplus. **1518** H. WATSON *Hist. Oliver of Castile* (Roxb.) C 3 b, Yf that thou haue not compassyon vpon me the surplus of my dayes shal be in anguyssh. **1597** BEARD *Theatre God's Judgem.* (1612) 539 Whatsoeuer punishments the wicked suffer before they die, they..must descend into the appointed place to receiue the surplus of their paiments which is due vnto them. **1759** MILLS tr. *Duhamel's Husb.* II. ii. 166, I left for the luserne, nine beds,..and destined the surplus to be sowed with wheat.

B. *attrib.* passing into *adj.* **1.** That is in excess of what is taken, used, or needed.

1641 *Jrnls. Ho. Comm.* II. 177 What is fit to be done with the surplus Money. **1776** ADAM SMITH *W.N.* I. xi. I. 203 They now exchange their surplus peltry, for blankets, firearms, and brandy. **1795** VANCOUVER *Agric. Essex* 181 To relieve the wet heavy woodlands of their surplus water. **1812** G. CHALMERS *Dom. Econ. Gt. Brit.* 66 The annual value of the surplus produce of the land, and labour of England, which was then exported to foreign countries, amounted only to 4,086,087*l.* **1879** H. GEORGE *Progr. & Pov.* II. i. (1881) 88 The natural law gets rid of surplus population. **1893** J. A. HODGES *Elem. Photogr.* (1907) 109 Until all the surplus gelatine is expelled.

2. ***surplus value*** (Econ., esp. in Marxism), that part of the value of the results of human labour which accrues beyond the amount needed to reproduce the initial labour power.

1816 S. T. COLERIDGE in D. P. Calleo *Coleridge & Idea of Modern State* (1966) i. 12 The nearest approach to the realization of such a state is a colony, composed of 100 wealthy Planters, and a 100,000 Slaves, the surplus value of whose labor above the price of the scanty food and cloathing centers in the 100. **1887** *Encycl. Brit.* XXII. 211/1 The fundamental principle of the Marx school..is the theory of 'surplus value,'—the doctrine..that, after the labourer has been paid the wage necessary for the subsistence of himself and family, the surplus produce of his labour is appropriated by the capitalist who exploits it. **1904** W. T. MILLS *Struggle for Existence* xxv. 325 Labor produces more than the cost of its own reproduction. This product of labor in excess of the labor cost of producing labor is the 'surplus value' of Karl Marx. **1933** H. G. WELLS *Shape of Things to Come* I. §4.51 The entrepreneur, the capitalist, became the villain of his [*sc.* Marx's] piece, using the prior advantage of his capital to appropriate the 'surplus value' of production. **1944** G. B. SHAW *Everybody's Political What's What?* i. 1 He [*sc.* Marx] proved up to the hilt that capital in its pursuit of what he called Mehrwerth, which we translate as Surplus Value (it includes rent, interest, and commercial profit), is ruthless. **1966** T. PYNCHON *Crying of Lot 49* iv. 89 How can you be against a corporation that wants a worker to waive his patent rights. That sounds like the surplus value theory to me, fella, and you sound like a Marxist. **1975** *Chinese Econ. Stud.* VIII. IV. 60 Capitalist production is commodity production aimed at reaping surplus value.

3. Of a shop: that sells goods which are surplus to (chiefly, military) requirements.

1951 R. SENHOUSE tr. *Colette's Last of Chéri* 208 Jean de Touzac—is in the surplus store racket. What a set! **1970** A. FOWLES *Dupe Negative* xi. 140, I found a surplus store and bought a duffel bag. **1978** S. WILSON *Dealer's Move* iii. 40, I..drove down to a surplus shop in Hampstead Road, and bought a down-filled sleeping-bag.

Hence as *v. trans.* (U.S. Mil. colloq.), to dispose of (property which is surplus to requirements); also with *out*. Chiefly in *pass.*

1963 D. BROUN *Egypt's Choice* (1964) i. 12 The helicopter ..used to belong to the United States Marine Corps. It was surplussed out a year ago. **1968** R. WEST *Sk. from Vietnam* i. 18 Many were 'surplused' during the following month.

surplusage ('sɜːpləsɪdʒ). Also 5 **-plausage**, 6 **-plesage**, (**-plushach**), 6–9 **-plussage**, 7 **-plus(s)adge**. Also SUPPLUSAGE. [ad. med.L. *surplusagium*, f. *surplus*: see prec. and -AGE. Cf. AF. *superplusage*, med.L. *superplusagium.*]

1. = SURPLUS 1.

c **1407** LYDG. *Reson & Sens.* 6341 To refuse and voyde clene Of excesse all surplusage. **1430–40** —— *Bochas* v. xvi. (MS. Bodl. 263) 279/1 He took non heed of al the surplusage Of ther tresours. *c* **1470** HARDING *Chron.* Proem xl. (MS. Arch. Seld. B. 10) lf. 8 b, How of this Reame þe noble gouernours Haue kepte it..In victorie triumphe and surplausage. **1527** *Lanc. Wills* (Chetham Soc.) I. 28 The surplushach of the said money to dispose for my soule. *c* **1530** *Songs, Carols*, etc. (E.E.T.S.) 77 Of this pore secte it is the vsage, Only to take þat nature may susteyn; Banysshyng clen all oþer surplusage. **1531** ELYOT *Gov.* III. viii, Fortitude..is a..meane betwene two extremities, the one in surplusage, the other in lacke. **1553** *Act 7 Edw. VI*, c. 1 §11 Delyvering to the partie distreigned the surplusage and overplus of the valew of every such distres. **1579–80** NORTH *Plutarch* (1595) 497 (*Sylla*) Catulus campe being plentifully victualed, they sent their store & surplusage vnto Marius souldiers. **1607** WALKINGTON *Optic Glass* 115 Any ..cause that generates a surplussage of blood. **1637** HEYWOOD *Royall King* I. Wks. 1874 VI. 6 You load me with a surplussadge Of comptlesse debt to this thrice valiant Lord. **1670–1** *Act 22 & 23 Chas. II*, c. 10. §5 To make distribution of the Surplusage of the Estate of any person dying intestate. **1696** in *Col. Rec. Pennsylv.* I. 494 The Surplusage for defraying the debts of the government. **1715** tr. *Pancirollus' Rerum Mem.* II. xiii. 353 [They] tie them close..winding the Surplusage of the String about them. **1775** JOHNSON *West. Isl.* Wks. X. 410 The cattle to live wholly on the surplusage of the summer. **1840** CARLYLE *Heroes* iii. (1858) 255 The gifted man is he who sees the essential point, and leaves all the rest aside as surplusage. **1882** J. H. BLUNT *Ref. Ch. Eng.* II. 36 The documents were mere surplusage, the bishops exercising jurisdiction without them. **1888** *Times* (weekly ed.) 30 Mar. 5/3 Any other question might seem merely surplusage.

b. An excess or superabundance (*of* words); *spec.* in *Law*, a word, clause, or statement in an indictment or a plea which is not necessary to its adequacy.

a **1530** J. HEYWOOD *Love* (Brandl) 137 To abreueate the tyme and to exclude Surplusage of wordes. **1589** PUTTENHAM *Engl. Poesie* III. xxii. (Arb.) 264 The Poet or makers speech becomes vicious..by nothing more than by vsing too much surplusage. **1649** C. WALKER *Hist. Independ.* II. 245 The word..was a surplusage, for which no Indictment could lie. **1651** tr. *Kitchin's Courts Leet* (1657) 420 Formedon of a house, and in the perclose of the Writ there is a house and meadow; and after view the Tenant cannot shew that in abatement, for that it is but a Surplusage. **1708** *Term Rep.* VIII. 497 The word 'feloniously' in this declaration is impertinent, and may be rejected as surplusage. **1851** SIR F. PALGRAVE *Norm. & Eng.* I. 353 Nor is it surplussage to reiterate the same thought or fact. **1880** MUIRHEAD *Gaius* Introd. p. xii, Omissions and surplusages in the MS. **1884** *Law Rep. 25 Chanc. Div.* 685 The reference to widowhood could not..be treated as surplusage, but was the principal part of the condition. **1908** *Pitman's 'How to take Minutes'* 33 Many minute books contain a surplusage of words.

2. = SURPLUS 2.

c **1407** LYDG. *Reson & Sens.* 4768 Thou gest of me no more langage, I put al the surplusage In thyn ovne eleccion After thy discrecion. **1430–40** —— *Bochas* VIII. xxiv. (MS. Bodl. 263) 400/2 To conclude & leue the surplusage In that bataile ded was many a kniht. **1472–3** *Rolls of Parlt.* VI. 49/2 The surplusage of the price therof..to be delyvered to the owner. *a* **1513** FABYAN *Chron.* VI. clviii. (1811) 147 Of the holynes of this martyr..the legende of Sayntes reportith the surplusage.

†**sur'poose.** *Obs.* Also **surposh.** [a. Urdū *sarpōsh* = Pers. *serpūsh* veil, f. *ser* head + *pūsh* covering.] A cover of a (silver) vessel.

1698 FRYER *Acc. E. India & P.* 130 A Service in Plate covered with Embroidered Velvet over Noble Surpooses or Covers. **1828** *Asiatic Costumes* 29 The tobacco..is put into the chillum..covered with a massive and richly-chased silver surposh, or cover. **1829** SHIPP *Mem. Milit. Career* II. vi. 159 Tugging away at your hookah, find no smoke; a thief having purloined your silver chelam and surpoose.

†**surprend,** *v. Obs. rare*⁻¹. [ad. F. *surprendre* to SURPRISE.] *trans.* To surprise.

1549 EDW. VI *Lit. Rem.* (Roxb.) 227 The French King.. sent..certain shippes to surprend our shippes.

†**surpress,** *v. Obs.* [Altered form of SUPPRESS, after *surprise* (beside *supprise*).] *trans.* = SUPPRESS *v.* 6.

1566 GASCOIGNE *Jocasta* Epil. 22 Thambitious sonne doth oft surpresse his sire. **1577–82** BRETON *Toyes Idle Head* Wks. (Grosart) I. 51/1 Some sayd, that Children should surpressed be by feare. **1607** WALKINGTON *Optic Glass* 31 Not molested by this terrestrial masse, which otherwise will bee a burthen ready to surpress the soul.

surprisable (sə'praɪzəb(ə)l), *a.* [f. SURPRISE *v.* + -ABLE.]

1. That may be surprised; liable to surprise or unexpected attack.

a **1639** SPOTTISWOOD *Hist. Ch. Scot.* VI. (1677) 415 Upon intelligence that the Castle of Carlile..was surprisable. **1654–66** EARL ORRERY *Parthen.* (1676) 52 Rendring us..the more secure, and consequently the more surprizable. **1865** SWINBURNE *Chastelard* IV. i. 150 Is not your spirit surprisable in sleep? Have you no evil dreams?

¶ **2.** Causing surprise, surprising. (*illiterate.*)

1782 MISS BURNEY *Cecilia* v. xii, A little mean-looking man..whispered,..'It's surprizeable to me..you can behave so out of the way!'

surprisal (sə'praɪzəl). Now *rare* or *Obs.* Also 6 **-ysall**, 6–7 **-isall**, 7 **-izall**, 7–8 **-izal**. [f. SURPRISE *v.* + -AL¹.] The act of surprising or state of being surprised; something that surprises.

1. = SURPRISE *sb.* 1.

1591 SPENSER *Virg. Gnat* 536 Laërtes sonne..boasts his good euent In working of Strymonian Rhæsus fall, And efte in Dolons subtile surprysall. **1611** SPEED *Hist. Gt. Brit.* VII. xvii. §4. 289 The surprizal of these three Cities, Glocester, Bathe, and Cirencester. **1620** in Foster *Eng. Factories Ind.* (1906) 222 Their to land our masters monies and goods, for whose surprizall the Portingalls fought. **1627** W. SCLATER *Exp. 2 Thess.* (1629) 111 The siege and surprisall of Ierusalem by Titus and Vespatian. **1634** MILTON *Comus* 618 How to secure the Lady from surprisal. **1648** *Eikon Bas.* xxvi. 223 (*heading*) The Armies Surprisall of the King at Holmeby. **1757** HUME *Hist. Gt. Brit.* II. ii. 192 (an. 1668) An insurrection was projected, together with a surprizal of the castle of Dublin. **1820** W. IRVING *Sketch Bk.* (1859) 213 Surrounded by hostile tribes, whose mode of warfare is by ambush and surprisal. **1865** CARLYLE *Fredk. Gt.* XVIII. iii. (1872) VII. 144 The Prussians..had nearly got into the place by surprisal.

2. = SURPRISE *sb.* 2; *occas.* sudden lapse (*into*).

1613 PURCHAS *Pilgrimage* IX. xiv. 745 One..who by the Sunnes surprisall, was turned into a Nightingale. *a* **1631** DONNE *Serm., Gen. iii. 24* (1649) II. 442 Though the belly, the bowels of sin, in sudden surprisals, and ebullitions..of our concupiscencies, be subject to him [*sc.* the devil]. *a* **1639** [see SUDDEN *sb.* 2]. **1647** SPRIGGE *Anglia Rediv.* II. ii. (1854) 76 A sudden surprisal of the tide called the Eager, where he very narrowly escaped drowning. **1667** MILTON *P.L.* v. 245 Least wilfully transgressing he pretend Surprisal, unadmonisht, unforewarnd. **1675** OWEN *Indwelling Sin* iii. (1732) 27 His [*sc.* David's] great surprizal into Sin was after ..manifold Experiences of God. **1683** KENNETT tr. *Erasm. on Folly* (1709) 125 They will divert them with sport and mirth, lest they should..be damped with the surprizal of sober thoughts.

3. = SURPRISE *sb.* 3.

1660 *Trial Regic.* 18, I do desire some time to consider of it: for it is a great Surprisal. **1679** J. GOODMAN *Penit. Pard.* III. vi. (1713) 388 It can be no surprisal to Almighty God who foreknows all things from the beginning. **1799** MRS. J. WEST *Tale of Times* I. 89 My lady stopped his exordium.. by one of those sweet surprisals in which..she abounded. **1843** *Tait's Mag.* X. 188 It is usually a rather melancholy surprisal.

†**4.** = SURPRISE *sb.* 4. *Obs.*

1652 LOVEDAY tr. *Calprenede's Cassandra* II. 96 In a rapture of joy, surprisall, and astonishment. **1674** in *Phenix* (1721) I. 297 It is easy to imagine how great the surprizal of our Embassador was, when they receiv'd this Answer. *a* **1814** *Witness* II. iii. in *New Brit. Theatre* I. 22 In the sad surprisal to behold, A thing so miserable human still.

surprise (sə'praɪz), *sb.* Forms: see the verb; also 6 *Sc.* **surpryis**, 9 *Sc.* **seerpreese**. [a. AF., OF. *surprise* (= It., Sp. *sorpresa*, Pg. *surpresa*), pa. pple. fem., used subst., of *surprendre*: see next. Cf. the earlier SURPRISE *sb.*]

1. *Mil.* The (or an) act of assailing or attacking unexpectedly or without warning, or of taking by this means; sudden attack or capture of a fort, a body of troops, etc. that is unprepared; †formerly also in more general sense, seizure (of a person, a place, or spoil).

1457 HARDING *Chron.* in *Eng. Hist. Rev.* Oct. (1912) 747 The wynners had it all withoute surpryse. **1583** *Reg. Mag. Sig. Scot.* 196/2 Odiosissime et innaturalis surreptionis lie surpryis, captivitatis, restrictionis lie restraint regie persone. **1617** MORYSON *Itin.* II. 159 Carefull watches against sallies or surprises of the Enemy. **1635** HEYWOOD *Hierarchy* II. 81 Æneas caried his..houshold gods into Italy, after the surprise and combustion of Troy. **1645** PAGITT *Heresiogr.* i. 11 The surprise of Munster [which had been besieged 18 months]. **1648** *Eikon Bas.* xxi. 193 Nor doe I think, that by the surprize of my Letters, I have lost any more then so many papers. **1704** SWIFT *Batt. Bks.* Misc. (1711) 259 Resolving by Policy or Surprize, to attempt some neglected Quarter of the Antients Army. **1772** *Chron.* in *Ann. Reg.* 129/1 Those taken prisoners in the surprize of the baggage. **1802** JAMES *Milit. Dict.* s.v., When it is found expedient to attempt a surprize in the field, a sufficient number of men must be collected for the purpose. **1879** FROUDE *Cæsar* xiv. 203 A fortified camp..capable of resisting surprises. *Ibid.* 220 The surprise was complete: the Roman army was in confusion.

2. a. *gen.* The (or an) act of coming *upon* one unexpectedly, or of taking unawares; a sudden attack. Now *rare* or *Obs.* exc. as in b.

1598 SHAKS. *Merry W.* v. v. 131 The guiltinesse of my minde, the sodaine surprize of my powers. **1609** TOURNEUR *Funeral Poem* 439 Where sodaine dangers with a fierce access Have made surprise upon him. **1622** R. HAWKINS *Voy. S. Sea* (1847) 135 Neither packe nor chest is free from their [*sc.* insects'] surprises. **1796** BURKE *Corr.* (1844) IV. 394 This is no casual error, no lapse, no sudden surprise. **1894** H. DRUMMOND *Ascent of Man* 198 What deer have to arm themselves most against is surprise.

b. *to take by surprise* († *at a surprise*): to come upon unexpectedly, take unawares; hence, to astonish by unexpectedness: = SURPRISE *v.* 3, 5.

[**1687** T. BROWN *Saints in Uproar* Wks. 1730 I. 78 To hinder the wicked from attacking you by surprize.] **1691** tr. *Emilianne's Observ. Journ. Naples* 305 He might always be sure of his Blow, and could never be taken at a Surprize. **1806** J. BERESFORD *Miseries Hum. Life* (ed. 3) II. vii, A rushy pool, which takes you by surprise. **1849** MACAULAY *Hist. Eng.* viii. II. 365 That he was taken by surprise is true. But he had twelve hours to make his arrangements. **1860** TYNDALL *Glac.* II. xx. 338 This statement, I confess, took me by surprise. **1875** STUBBS *Const. Hist.* II. xvi. 482 Richard took the kingdom by surprise.

†c. An attack of illness; a sudden access *of* emotion. *Obs.*

1670 W. MONTAGU in *Buccleuch MSS.* (Hist. MSS. Comm.) I. 480 She..was at the time of her surprise actually intending the proposal. **1697** COLLIER *Ess. Mor. Subj.* I. (1709) 120 In the Heat and Surprize of Passion. **1719** DE FOE *Crusoe* II. (Globe) 330 An Excess of Joy, a Surprize of Joy.

3. a. Something that takes one by surprise; an unexpected occurrence or event; anything unexpected or astonishing.

1592 *Arden of Feversham* III. iii. 30 Such great impression tooke this fond surprise. God graunt this vision bedeeme me any good. **1670** COTTON *Espernon* III. XII. 639 He was in Bed, ..when this news came to him; and doubtless it was convenient for him, that it should find him in that posture, the better to resist so strange a surprize. **1770** FOOTE *Lame Lover* III. 69 My being here was as much a surprize upon Miss Charlot as ——. **1772** PRIESTLEY *Inst. Relig.* (1782) I. 278 They are never any surprize to us. **1870** MOZLEY *Univ. Serm.* iv. (1876) 91 Surprises of this kind here..look like auguries of a greater surprise in the next world. **1879** S. C. BARTLETT *Egypt to Pal.* iv. 97 Egypt, it has been well said, is the land of surprises.

b. *spec.* A fancy dish, or an ingredient of a dish, a present, or the like, designed to take one by surprise.

1708 W. KING *Cookery* v, A Surprize is..a dish..which promising little from its first appearance, when open abounds with all sorts of variety. **1888** *Harper's Mag.* Jan. 240/1 One lady..worked day and night..to achieve her various 'surprises'. **1888** 'J. S. WINTER' *Bootle's Childr.* xi, We want you to make us a surprise to put Father's Christmas present in. **1893** EARL DUNMORE *Pamirs* II. 233 Plates of hot dough, with all sorts of juicy surprises inside them.

4. The feeling or emotion excited by something unexpected, or for which one is unprepared. **†a.** Alarm, terror, or perplexity, caused by a sudden attack, calamity, or the like. *Obs.*

1608 SHAKS *Per.* III. ii. 17 Our lodgings..Shooke as the earth did quake:..Pure surprize and feare, made me to quite the house. **1722** DE FOE *Plague* (1754) 221, I have seen them in strange Agitations and Surprises on this Account. **1758** S. HAYWARD *Serm.* xvi. 496 Every thing..conspires to fill the soul with gloom and melancholy, nay with the greatest surprize and consternation. **1816** SCOTT *Antiq.* xxvii, My lord has been in sic a distress, and sic seerpreese, as I ne'er saw man in my life.

b. The feeling or mental state, akin to astonishment and wonder, caused by an unexpected occurrence or circumstance. Also, in phr. *the surprise of one's life*(*time*); cf. *of one's life* s.v. LIFE *sb.* 8 a.

1686 tr. *Chardin's Trav. Persia* 20 The Vizier, faigning a kind of surprise, And what, said he, Are those Gentlemen still here? **1743** POCOCKE *Descr. East* I. II. v. 122 We went on to the north, the Nile running through the rocks... I ask'd them when we should come to the cataract, and to my great surprize they told me, that was the cataract. *a* **1763** SHENSTONE *Ess.* Wks. 1765 II. 214 Surprise quickens enjoyment, and expectation banishes surprise. **1822** SCOTT *Nigel* x, Lord Dalgarno expressed much surprise at understanding that Nigel proposed an instant return to Scotland. **1908** G. K. CHESTERTON *Orthodoxy* iii. (1909) 52 By asking for pleasure, he lost the chief pleasure; for the chief pleasure is surprise.

with *a.* **1712** ADDISON *Spect.* No. 357 ¶8 Circumstances which give a delightful Surprize to the Reader. **1794** MRS. RADCLIFFE *Myst. Udolpho* xxvii, She looked with a surprise on Annette. **1898** 'H. S. MERRIMAN' *Roden's Corner* xiii. 138 Cornish..looked at the printed words with a vague surprise.

phr. **1927** W. E. COLLINSON *Contemp. Eng.* 117 The surprise of his lifetime. **1931** *Daily Express* 15 Oct. 10/3 You will have the surprise of your life.

c. As *int.*: *surprise, surprise*: an exclamation indicating surprise. Sometimes parenthetically. Freq. in irony or sarcasm.

1953 B. GLEMSER *Dove on his Shoulder* vi. 111 'Roger!' Miss Marsh laughed. 'Surprise! Surprise!' **1962** *Times* 24 Nov. 4/6 The plum Monday spot finally went—surprise, surprise—to our old friend *Naked City.* **1970** A. PRICE *Labyrinth Makers* xiv. 178 Surprise, surprise! I didn't expect to see you. **1978** I. MURDOCH *Sea* 106, I gather you didn't even know Lizzie was living with Gilbert. Surprise, surprise. Everybody knew that. **1982** N. PAINTING *Reluctant Archer* vii. 124 At the end of the programme the identity of the 'mystery accompanist' was divulged. It was of course (surprise, surprise!) me!

5. a. *attrib.* and *Comb.*, as *surprise attack, target, turn, visit, weapon*; *surprise-free* adj.; **surprise packet**, a sealed packet with contents designed to surprise, sold at a trivial price; also *fig.*; **surprise-party**, (*a*) a body of troops for an unexpected attack; (*b*) orig. *U.S.*, a party who meet by agreement at a friend's house without invitation, bringing provisions with them; also, the celebration or function itself; **surprise-piece**, a part of the mechanism of a repeating watch (see quot.).

1900 *Daily News* 4 Aug. 6/1 Our *surprise attacks only surprised ourselves by the thoroughness of the enemy's preparation for them. **1968** *Listener* 20 June 791/1 Kahn and Wiener flatly deny that they're making 'predictions': they are merely sketching 'possible scenarios' for the future, based on what they call '*surprise-free projections'. **1900** *Westm. Gaz.* 15 Sept. 3/2 There is a dash of the '*surprise packet'—if the expression may pass—about this bulky volume. **1841** LEVER *C. O'Malley* xlv. 235 Three cavalry regiments..intended for a *surprise party. **1858** H. D. THOREAU *Jrnl.* 9 Aug. (1906) XI. 86 There are also regattas and fireworks and 'surprise parties' and horse-shows. **1860** O. W. HOLMES *Prof. Breakf.-t.* iv, Now, then, for a surprise-party! **1872** SCHELE DE VERE *Americanisms* 236 On such an occasion friends and parishioners appear suddenly—for it is generally a surprise-party at the same time—at the parsonage. **1909** E. NESBIT *Daphne in Fitzroy St.* xvii. 272, I thought you'd like the surprise party. Was I wrong? **1969** N. W. PARSONS *Sagebrush Harp* xxi. 118 A vogue for surprise parties began among the English families in our community. **1884** F. J. BRITTEN *Watch & Clockm.* 254 **Surprise Piece*.., a loose plate under the quarter snail of a repeating watch which prevents the quarter rack reaching the snail if the mechanism is set going at the hour. **1894** *United Service Mag.* Oct. 39 Practice at *surprise targets appearing suddenly at unknown ranges. **1891** CONST. MACEWEN *Three Wom. in One Boat* 72 *Surprise-turns and crooked bends make you, if you know your river, as crafty as any old fox. **1891** BP. W. How in F. D. How *Mem.* xxiii. (1898) 323, I..paid them a *surprise visit. **1946** *Rep. Internat. Control Atomic Energy* (Dept. of State, Washington) I. 4 This danger is accentuated by the unusual characteristics of atomic bombs, namely their devastating effect as a *surprise weapon, that is, a weapon secretly developed and used without warning.

b. *Bell-ringing.* Applied to certain complicated methods of change-ringing.

1874 BANISTER *Change Ringing* 16 New Doubles..may be rung by a system generally accepted by experienced ringers in surprise methods. *Ibid.* 58 London Surprise Major. **1902** *Encycl. Brit.* XXVI. 521/2 A variety of 'plain methods' and 'Treble Bob methods', among the latter being the so-called 'Surprise' methods, the most complicated and difficult of all.

surprise (sə'praɪz), *v.* Also 5–6 surpryse, 6–9 surprize, (7 -pryze, -price). [f. AF., OF. *surpris-e*, pa. pple. of *surprendre* (= Pr. *sobre-*, *sorprendre*, It. *sorprendere*, Sp. *sorprender*, Pg. *surprender*) :—med.L. *superprendĕre* *-*præhendĕre*: see SUR- and PREHEND, and cf. the composition of *overtake*. See also the earlier SUPPRISE and SUSPRISE.]

1. *trans.* To 'take hold of' or affect suddenly or unexpectedly.

†a. Chiefly *pass.* To be seized *with* (or *of*) a desire, emotion, etc., a disease or illness. *Obs.*

1485 CAXTON *Chas. Gt.* 231 Thenne ganellon was surprysed wyth thys fals auarye. **1490** —— *Eneydos* vi. 28 He shall be soo surprysed wyth angre and furyouse woodnes. *c* **1500** *Melusine* i. 10 He was so surprysed of her loue that he coude nat holde contenaunce. **1570** FOXE *A. & M.* (ed. 2) II. 995/2 The rule..who surprised with lyke pride and disdaine..caused hys cappe to be hanged vp vpon a pole, chargyng..all..to do obeysance to the cappe. **1576** FLEMING *Panopl. Epist.* 315 My mynde being surprised with sorrow. **1594** PLAT *Jewell-ho.* III. 17 [They] were suddenly surprised with a great loosenesse. **1611** *Bible* Isa. xxxiii. 14 The sinners in Zion are afraid, fearefulnesse hath surprised the hypocrites. **1617** MORYSON *Itin.* II. 296 He was surprised with a burning Feuer. **1667** MILTON *P.L.* II. 753 All on a sudden miserable pain Surpris'd thee. *Ibid.* VI. 774 Them unexpected joy surpriz'd. *a* **1700** EVELYN *Diary* 10 Apr. 1666, Visited Sir William D'Oylie, surprized with a fit of apoplexie. *c* **1720** DE FOE *Mem. Cavalier* (1840) 39 Surprised with joy at the motion.

†b. To overcome, overpower (the mind, will, heart); to captivate. *Obs.*

1474 CAXTON *Chesse* III. vi. (1883) 132 So that ye wyn or drynke surpryse hym and ouercome his brayn. **1481** —— *Myrrour* I. v. 26 The moneye hath so surprysed them that they may extende to none other thinge. **1611** SHAKS. *Wint. T.* III. i. 10 The eare-deaff'ning Voyce o th' Oracle,..so surpriz'd my Sence, That I was nothing. **1621** ELSING *Debates Ho. Lords* (Camden) 84, I may be surprised with errour, but not corrupted. **1633** T. ADAMS *Exp. 2 Peter* ii. 14 A fair skin surpriseth a fleshly heart. **1676** DRYDEN *Aurengz.* IV. i, Pow'r, like new Wine, does your weak Brain surprize. *a* **1700** EVELYN *Diary* (Chandos Classics) 17 So..temperate, that I have heard he had never been surprised by excess.

c. *absol.* or *intr.*

a **1700** EVELYN *Diary* 8 Feb. 1645, The vapours ascend so hot that entring with the body erect you will even faint with excessive perspiration, but stooping lower as suddaine a cold surprizes.

2. a. *Mil.*, etc. To assail or attack suddenly and without warning; to make an unexpected assault upon (a place, body of troops, person, etc. that is unprepared); †to take or capture in this way.

a **1548** HALL *Chron., Edw. IV*, 222 b, By some gyle or engyne sodaynly to trap and surprise the erle. **1611** *Bible* Jer. xlviii. 41 Kerioth is taken, and the strong holds are surprised. **1687** A. LOVELL tr. *Thevenot's Trav.* III. 29 His march was secret enough, though he hastened it to surprise Surrat. **1688** HOLME *Armoury* III. xv. (Roxb.) 27/1 Lowe built boates..which..will strike to the sides of great shippes, and with their guns..either suddenly surprice the same or sinke it. **1709** STEELE *Tatler* No. 1 ¶8 The Enemy had formed a Design to surprize two Battalions of the Allies. **1803** JANE PORTER *Thaddeus* ii. (1831) 16 A plan was laid for surprising and taking the royal person. **1808** SCOTT *Life Dryden* D.'s Wks. 1882 I. 173 A man, surprised in the dark and beaten by ruffians, loses no honour by such a misfortune. **1867** FREEMAN *Norm. Conq.* (1877) I. vi. 459 Every effort to take or surprise the Norman outpost was rendered hopeless. **1888** J. F. MAURICE *Milit. Hist. Camp. 1882* xii. 73 An army suddenly attacked within the lines which it had reckoned upon to ward off its enemy is in a military sense surprised.

†b. *gen.* To capture, seize; to take possession of by force; to take prisoner. *Obs.*

1588 SHAKS. *Tit. A.* I. i. 284 Treason my Lord, Lauinia is surpris'd. **1593** —— *2 Hen. VI*, IV. ix. 8 Is the Traitor Cade surpris'd? **1606** G. W[OODCOCKE] *Hist. Ivstine* IX. 41 Some he beheaded, others banisht, and all their goods were surprised. *Ibid.* xv. 65 Surprizing the kingdome to himself. **1632** LITHGOW *Trav.* III. 94 When Nigropont, and diuerse other Iles were surprised from the Venetians. **1661** *Act 13 Chas. II* c. 9 §6 Ships which shall be surprised or seized as prize. **1667** MILTON *P.L.* XII. 453 He [*sc.* Messiah]..there shall surprise The Serpent, Prince of aire, and drag in Chaines Through all his realme. **1799** SHERIDAN *Pizarro* II. i, A servant of mine, I hear is missing, whether surprised or treacherous I know not.

fig. **1592** KYD *Sp. Trag.* III. x. 90 Thy tresses, Ariadnes twines, Wherewith my libertie thou hast surprisde.

†c. To hold in one's power, occupy. *Obs.*

1540 *Act 32 Hen. VIII*, c. 24 Consideryng..that the Isle of Rhoodes..is surprised by the Turke. **1607** DEKKER & WEBSTER *Sir T. Wyat* A 2 b, With me, that in my handes, Surprise the Soueraigntie.

†d. To rescue or deliver as by force, 'snatch' (*from* something). *Obs. rare*$^{-1}$.

1687 *Lond. Gaz.* No. 2258/2 As also in your unparalell'd Clemency, by which you have surprized your distressed Subjects from the jaws of Ruine.

3. a. To come upon unexpectedly; to take unawares; to take or catch in the act; hence *fig.* to find or discover (something) suddenly, to detect.

1592 *Soliman & Pers.* II. ii. 264 If the Gouernour Surprise me heere, I die by marshall law. **1655** tr. *Sorel's Com. Hist. Francion* XII. 22 The Italian seeing himself surprized did.. intreat him to give him leave to be gone. **1662** J. DAVIES tr. *Mandelslo's Trav.* 244 We were surprized by a calm, which kept us in the same place all that day. **1665** P. HENRY *Diaries & Lett.* (1882) 168 A meeting at Wrexham surprisd,..some payd 5[lb] some went to prison for 3 months accord. to the Act. *a* **1700** EVELYN *Diary* 2 Feb. 1665, I saw a masq perform'd at Court by 6 gentlemen and 6 ladys, surprizing his Majesty, it being Candlemas-day. **1726** POPE *Odyss.* XIX. 686 Ulysses will surprize the unfinish'd game. **1803–6** WORDSW. *Ode Intim. Immort.* 148 High instincts before which our mortal Nature Did tremble like a guilty Thing surprised. **1879** J. GRANT in *Cassell's Techn. Educ.* IV. 96/1 In order to surprise Nature in her wonders, he was wont to perambulate the garden..lantern in hand. **1880** GROVE *Dict. Mus.* I. 202/1 *note*, In the Finale..we almost surprise the change of style in the act of being made. **1886** RUSKIN *Præterita* II. vi. 193, I never travelled in bad weather unless surprised by it. **1890** MAARTENS *Sir J. Avelingh* xv, He had surprised an ugly secret about a Government tender.

†b. ? To 'overtake', anticipate. *Obs. rare*$^{-1}$.

1591 NASHE *Prognost.* A 4, The effects cannot surprise the cause.

†c. *causatively.* To introduce unexpectedly, 'spring' *upon* some one. *Obs. rare*$^{-1}$.

1769 *Chron.* in *Ann. Reg.* 75/1 To support the re-election, lest any candidate in the opposite interest should have been ..attempted to be surprized upon the county.

4. † a. To implicate or ensnare (a person) as by a sudden proposal or disclosure. *Obs.*

1642 SLINGSBY *Diary* (1836) 91 Not willing to use his old friendship..in a way to surprize his judgments. **1667** MILTON *P.L.* IX. 354 Least by some faire appeering good surpris'd She [*sc.* Reason] dictate false, and missinforme the Will. **1702** VANBRUGH *False Friend* v. i, If I did not know he was in love with Leonora, I could be easily surprized with what he has told me.

b. To lead unawares, betray *into* doing something not intended.

1696 PHILLIPS (ed. 5), To *Surprise*,..to lead a Man into an Error, by causing him to do a thing over hastily. **1711** ADDISON *Spect.* No. 112 ¶3 If by chance he has been surprized into a short Nap at Sermon. **1742** *Act 15 Geo. II* c. 30 Persons who have the Misfortune to become Lunaticks, may..be liable to be surprised into unsuitable

Marriages. **1818** SCOTT *Hrt. Midl.* ii, Many..whose feelings surprised them into a very natural interest in his behalf. **1873** BLACK *Pr. Thule* xvii, He had never yet met any woman who had so surprised him into admiration.

5. a. To affect with the characteristic emotion caused by something unexpected; to excite to wonder by being unlooked-for. †Formerly also in stronger sense (cf. SURPRISE *sb.* 4a), to astonish or alarm; also, to excite to admiration. Often *pass.*, const. *at* (†*with*) or inf.; colloq. ***to be surprised at*** = to be scandalized or shocked at; also as a retort: ***you'd be surprised***, the facts are not as you would think.

1655 *Theophania* 103 Alexandro acquainted him with the occasion of their coming thither, with which he was exceedingly surprised at first. **1687** A. LOVELL tr. *Thevenot's Trav.* I. 248 They..have Secrets which surprize the most knowing, many thinking them to be knacks of Magick. **1692** L'ESTRANGE *Fables* lxxi, People were not so much Frighted, as they were Surpriz'd at the Bigness, and Uncouth Deformity of the Camel. **1719** DE FOE *Crusoe* I. (Globe) 156, I was exceedingly surpriz'd with the Print of a Man's naked Foot on the Shore. **1768** GOLDSM. *Good-n. Man* III. i, You'll be surpriz'd, Sir, with this visit. **1794** MRS. RADCLIFFE *Myst. Udolpho* xlvii, The apparition of the dead comes not ..to terrify or to surprise the timid. **1816** SCOTT *Old Mort.* xxx, Macbriar..was surprised at the degree of agitation which Balfour displayed. **1833** T. HOOK *Parson's Dau.* III. vi, 'You surprise me.' 'I tell you truth,' said George. **1860** TYNDALL *Glac.* I. xii. 88, I was surprised..to find some veins of white ice. **1908** R. BAGOT *A. Cuthbert* xxi. 256 And yet you talk our language well—really very well. I am agreeably surprised. **1926** MAINES & GRANT *Wise-Crack Dict.* 16/2 *You'd be surprised*, admitting entire satisfaction with results. **1948** 'J. TEY' *Franchise Affair* x. 102 'What else could she have been doing?'..Robert bit back a 'You'd be surprised!' **1964** 'E. MCBAIN' *Ax* v. 82 'I don't think the boys would know without *your* knowing too.'..'Sometimes. .. You'd be surprised.' **1971** 'D. HALLIDAY' *Dolly & Doctor Bird* ii. 19 'The emergency situation is perhaps more frequent in medicine than in portrait-painting.' 'You'd be surprised,' said the man Johnson gently.

absol. **1684** EARL ROSCOM. *Ess. Transl. Verse* 146 On sure Foundations let your Fabrick Rise, And with inviting Majesty surprise. **1781** COWPER *Charity* 544 The turns are quick, the polish'd points surprise. **1845** R. W. HAMILTON *Pop. Educ.* ii. (1846) 30 It is..to be doubted, whether any class of Society be so strictly moral [as the poor]. The statement may at first surprise.

b. *intr.* for *pass.*

1943 *Mod. Lang. Notes* LVIII. 14 They wanted to surprise me, but I don't surprise so easy. **1978** *Guardian Weekly* 1 Jan. 20/4 You don't drive cabs in Harlem if you surprise easily.

†6. *Cookery.* To dress or serve in the manner of a 'surprise'. *Obs.*

1769 MRS. RAFFALD *Eng. Housekpr.* (1778) 103 A Shoulder of Mutton surprized.

surprised (sə'praɪzd), *ppl. a.* [f. prec. + -ED¹.]

1. Attacked or come upon unexpectedly; captured by sudden attack; taken by surprise or unawares. Also *absol.*

1620 in Foster *Eng. Factories Ind.* (1906) 210 Through the Decans campe and lately surprized cuntries. **1668** WILKINS *Real Char.* III. ii. §6. 308 The result..of a surprized Judgment. **1697** DRYDEN *Æneid* II. 514 So, from our arms, surpris'd Androgeos flies. **1779** *Collins' Peerage* II. 74 The Earl..recovered the town, and revenged the death of the surprised. **1819** SCOTT *Ivanhoe* xlv, A dignity which.. inspired courage into his surprised and dismayed followers. **1901** 'LINESMAN' *Words Eye-witness* (1902) 311 The confusion, terror, and indignation of the surprised gives little scope or will to take prisoners those of the beaten surprisers whom it is impossible to shoot.

2. Excited to wonder by something unexpected; affected or characterized by surprise.

1882 *Little Folks* 3/1 She had a bright colour, and large surprised blue eyes. **1885** 'MRS. ALEXANDER' *At Bay* iv, The surprised admiration which Elsie and her home had excited on his first visit. **1897** MARY KINGSLEY *W. Africa* 48 San Thomé..was discovered by its surprised neighbours to be amassing great wealth by growing coffee.

Hence **sur'prisedly** (-zɪdlɪ) *adv.*, †(*a*) by surprise or sudden attack; (*b*) in a manner expressing surprise, with surprise; **sur'prisedness** (-zɪdnɪs), state of being surprised (in quot. *transf.*, quality of being caused by surprise).

1672 H. MORE *Brief Reply* 65 The invincibleness of the mistake, the sudden surprisedness..of the mistake may be a ground..of excusing the person as to the severity of punishment. **1680** —— *Apocal. Apoc.* 188 'For in one hour is she made desolate'; that is, surprizedly and unexpectedly. **1867** MISS BROUGHTON *Cometh up as Flower* x, Nothing could be more surprisedly pitifully penitent than the expression of his..eyes.

†sur'prisement. *Obs. rare*⁻¹. [f. SURPRISE *v.* + -MENT.] = SURPRISE *sb.* I.

1613–18 DANIEL *Coll. Hist. Eng.* (1626) 47 Many skirmishes interpassed, with surprizements of Castles.

surpriser (sə'praɪzər). [f. SURPRISE *v.* + -ER¹.] One who or that which surprises; † a capturer.

1584 *Reg. Privy Council Scot.* III. 659 Taikeris and surprisers of the said burgh and castell. **1643** BAKER *Chron., Eliz.* 56 The Surprizers of the King. **1648** E. SYMMONS *Vind. Chas. I* 15 These Papers might have been Evidences of Truth and of Loyalty too had the Surprizers of them been guilty of these Vertues. **1665** EARL OF SANDWICH in *Pepys' Diary*, etc. (1870) 596 Prizes taken on the 3rd and 4th of September:—Surprizers,..Assurance, Anthelope, Adventure, Mary. *a* **1674** CLARENDON *Hist. Reb.* XI. §120 The surprisers were to be ready upon such a part of the Wall. **1712** ADDISON *Spect.* No. 538 ¶3 The Subject of Antipathies was a proper Field wherein such false Surprizers might expatiate. **1865** CARLYLE *Fredk. Gt.* XVIII. xiv. (1872) VIII. 73 Our Cavalry, cutting-in upon the disordered surprisers. **1901** [see SURPRISED I].

surprising (sə'praɪzɪŋ), *vbl. sb.*¹ [f. SURPRISE *v.* + -ING¹.] The action of the verb SURPRISE.

1589 *(title)* The Protestatyon of Martin Marprelat. Wherin not with standing the surprizing of the printer, he maketh it known vnto the world that he feareth, neither proud priest,..nor godlesse catercap. **1603** KNOLLES *Hist. Turks* (1638) 89 To take occasion for the surprising of the Christians. **1615** in *Buccleuch MSS.* (Hist. MSS. Comm.) I. 168 Surprising and taking of forts. **1688** HOLME *Armoury* III. xvi. (Roxb.) 97/1 To hinder an enimyes surprizeing of a gate, or stop him in his passage. **1889** *Athenæum* 20 Apr. 498/3 Abductions and forced marriages,..stratagems and surprisings.

† surprising, *vbl. sb.*² *Obs. rare*⁻¹. [f. SUR- + *prising*, PRIZING *vbl. sb.*¹] The action of setting an excessive price on something.

1583 STUBBES *Anat. Abus.* II. (1882) 36 In the surprising of their hides, they are worthy of reprehension. For that which they buy for ten shillings, they will hardly sell for twentie shillings.

sur'prising, *ppl. a.* [f. SURPRISE *v.* + -ING².]

1. Coming upon one unexpectedly; taking unawares; capturing by sudden attack; also, †overpowering.

1645 WALLER *Apol. for having Loved before* 2 They that never had the use Of the Grapes surprizing juyce. **1655** VAUGHAN *Silex Scint., Day of Judgem.* ii, When all shall streame and lighten round, And with surprizing flames Both Stars and Elements Confound. **1665** BOYLE *Occas. Refl.* V. x. (1848) 335 The unwary Bird, while she is gazing upon that glittering Light..heedlessly gives into the Reach of the surprizing Nets.

2. Causing surprise or wonder by its unexpectedness; astonishingly wonderful.

1663 PATRICK *Parab. Pilgr.* xiii. (1687) 91 They can present you with a thousand Abrahams, and as many Josephs, whose adventures were so strange, that fiction is not able to invent any thing so surprising. **1687** A. LOVELL tr. *Thevenot's Trav.* I. b ij, It is a surprizing thing, that at the same time he could pursue his other Observations of the Countrey, and study the Languages. *a* **1700** EVELYN *Diary* 25 Oct. 1644, One of the lions leaped to a surprising height. **1726** BUTLER *Serm. Rolls* vii. 125 There is a more surprizing Piece of Iniquity yet behind. **1850** SCORESBY *Cheever's Whalem. Adv.* Pref. (1858) 6 Certain surprising incidents herein recorded. **1908** R. BAGOT *A. Cuthbert* vi. 49 It was not..surprising if she had, comparatively early in life, developed a certain love of authority.

†b. Exciting admiration, admirable; occas. *advb. Obs.*

1580 G. HARVEY *Let. to Spenser* in *Spenser's Poet. Wks.* (1912) 627/1 The renowned, and surprizing, Archpoet Homer. **1648** BOYLE *Seraph. Love* (1660) 125 The neat and surprizing Characters and Flourishes of a Greek and Hebrew Bible curiously Printed. **1687** MRS. BEHN *Lucky Chance* I. i, Rise Cloris, charming Maid arise! And baffle breaking Day, Show the adoring World thy Eyes Are more surprizing Gay. *a* **1700** EVELYN *Diary* 3 Aug. 1654, The river running so delightfully under it, that it may passe for one of the most surprizing seates one should meete with. **1831** D. E. WILLIAMS *Life Sir T. Lawrence* I. 343 It is really a surprising portrait.

sur'prisingly, *adv.* [f. prec. + -LY².] In a surprising manner or degree.

†1. By, or in the way of, surprise; unexpectedly.

1667 WATERHOUSE *Narr. Fire Lond.* 167 Generosity abhors to take an advantage poorly and surprisingly against any man. **1730** *Phil. Trans.* XXXVI. 444 There broke such a violent Clap of Thunder,..that she and three of her Children were very surprizingly struck down. **1742** H. BAKER *Microsc.* II. vii. 108 Changes are produced in Fluids surprizingly and suddenly.

2. So as to cause surprise; astonishingly, wonderfully; †admirably.

1661 BOYLE *Style of Script.* (1675) 169 Maimed and abrupt sentences, words surprisingly misplaced. **1681** FLAVEL *Meth. Grace* xix. 343 How surprizingly glorious the sight of Jesus Christ will be to them. **1743** EMERSON *Fluxions* 285 The Forces exerted on these small Bodies must be surprizingly great. **1756** NUGENT *Gr. Tour, Italy* III. 52 The church of St. Mark is..surprizingly enriched with marble and mosaic work. **1825** COBBETT *Rur. Rides* 62 That wood breeds maggots surprisingly. **1866** GEO. ELIOT *F. Holt* ii, Surprisingly little altered by the fifteen years.

So **sur'prisingness**, surprising character, unexpectedness.

1686 J. SCOTT *Chr. Life* I. II. iii. 100 The life of Wit consists in the Surprisingness of its Conceits and Expressions. **1737** L. CLARKE *Hist. Bible* VIII. (1740) 509 The surprizingness of this discovery. **1962** N. STREATFEILD *Apple Bough* vi. 83 What never wore off was the surprisingness of Grandfather.

surquayne. *pseudo-arch.* [a. OF. *surquanie*, var. *sou(s)canie*: see SUCKENY.] Used vaguely or typically for an upper garment.

1887 ASHBY STERRY *Lazy Minstrel* (1892) 21 What surquayne or partlet could look better than My saint's curly jacket of black Astracan?

†surquidance. *Obs. rare*⁻¹. In 5 -cuydaunce. [a. OF. *surcuidance*, f. *surcuidant*: see next and -ANCE.] = SURQUIDRY.

1481 *Cov. Leet Bk.* 476 The seid Scottes, of their Custumable pryde and surcuydaunce ramaynyng obstinatly in their first purpose.

†surquidant, *a. Obs. rare*⁻¹. In 6 surcudant. [a. OF. *surcuidant*, pr. pple. of *surcuidier*:—pop. L. **supercōgitāre*, f. *super-* SUPER- + *cōgitāre* to think, COGITATE.] = SURQUIDOUS.

a **1529** SKELTON *Replyc.* Wks. 1843 I. 209 Puffed..full of vaynglorious pompe and surcudant elacyon.

†surquidour. *Obs. rare*⁻¹. In 4 sour-. [a. OF. **surcuidour*, f. *surcuidier* (see prec.), if *sourquidours* be not an error for *sourquidous* (see next): cf. first quot. s.v. SURQUIDROUS.] A haughty or arrogant person.

1393 LANGL. *P. Pl.* C. XXII. 341 Pruyde sente forþ sourquidours [B. XIX. 335 surquydous] hus seriauns of armes.

†'surquidous, 'surquedous, *a. Obs.* Also 4–5 -quydous, 6 -quidus. [a. AF. **surcuidous*, f. *surcuidier* (see SURQUIDANT).] Overweening, arrogant, presumptuous, overbearing.

1377 LANGL. *P. Pl.* B. XIX. 335 Pruyde..sente forth surquydous [C. XXII. 341 sourquidours] his seriaunt of armes. **1390** GOWER *Conf.* I. 118 With low herte humblesce suie, So that thou be noght surquidous. *c* **1407** LYDG. *Reason & Sens.* 6694 An vnycourne..Which is a beste Surquedous. **1420–22** —— *Thebes* II. 2018 It scheweth wel that thow were not wis..To take on the this surquedous massage. **1483** CAXTON *G. de la Tour* f v b, Grete folye is to a man come from lowe degree..to become..prowde and surquydous. *c* **1500** *Melusine* 96 Ye were therof surquydous, & it is wel right yf euyl is comme to you therof. *c* **1540** *Pilgryms T.* 377 in *Thynne's Animadv.* (1875) 87 Sum.. wher fraurd, disobedient, & surquidus.

†surquidrous, surquedrous, *a. Obs.* Also 5 -quy-. See also SUCCUDROUS. [f. next + -OUS, after prec.] = prec.

The first quot. is doubtful: cf. SURQUIDOUR.

c **1430** *Pilgr. Lyf Manhode* I. xxvi. (1869) 17 Michel is he of foolhardiment and surquidoures [F. *de foul & oultrecuide hardiement*]. **1481** CAXTON *Myrr.* III. xvi. 172 They be of the nature of proud foles that ben surquydrous. *a* **1550** *Image Hypocr.* II. 459 in *Skelton's Wks.* (1843) II. 428 Thou arte so monstrous..Proude and surquedrous. **1593** G. HARVEY *Pierce's Super.* 52 More surquidrous then Anaxius.

†'surquidry, 'surquedry. *Obs.* Forms: 3–4 surquiderie, 4–7 surquidrie, -quedrie, (8–9 *arch.*) surquedry, 5–6 surquidry, (4 so(u)rquydrye, -yȝe, surquidre, 4–5 -drye; 4 -quydrie, -dery, 5 -dry(e, 5–6 -quedrye, 7 -dree); 4 -quy-, 5 -qui-, 7 -quetry (5 -quitery); 4 -cudry, 6 -cuydry(e, 6–7 -cuidrie; 4 cirquytrie, 5 -cudrie. See also SUCCUDRY. [a. OF. *s(o)urcuiderie*, f. *s(o)urcuidier*: see SURQUIDANT and -ERY.]

1. Arrogance, haughty pride, presumption. (In first quot. app. personified.)

a **1225** *Ancr. R.* 56 Me surqⁱderie [*v.rr.* Me surqⁱde sire, Me sire], ne iherest tu þet Dauid [etc.]. *c* **1315** SHOREHAM IV. 282 Ho yst þat neuer nas yblent Wyþ non surquydery? **13..** *E.E. Allit. P.* A. 309 Þat is a poynt o sorquydryȝe, þat vche god mon may euel byseme. *c* **1375** *Sc. Leg. Saints* xxviii. (*Margaret*) 46 Scho had symply hyre fud & clath, to cleth hyre honestly, for-out pryd and surcudry. ?*a* **1400** *Morte Arth.* 3399 Thow has schedde myche blode, and schalkes distroyede, Sakeles, in cirquytrie. **1412–20** LYDG. *Chron. Troy* I. 452 (MS. Digby 230) lf. 31b/2 Alle þo..That.. wolde..rebelle in any maner weye Of surquidrie or pride to werreye. **1576** GASCOIGNE *Steele Gl.* (Arb.) 54 Such Surcuydry, such weening ouer well. **1591** SPENSER *World's Vanitie* 105 He..Was puffed vp with passing surquedrie, And shortly gan all other beasts to scorne. **1602** CAREW *Cornwall* 58 He held Aristotle superiour to Moses and Christ, and yet but equall to himselfe. But this extreame Surquedry forfeyted his wittes. **1657** EARL MONM. tr. *Paruta's Pol. Disc.* 195 The War was..undertaken with great surquedrie, and with great hopes of victory and glory. **1713** CROXALL *Orig. Canto Spencer* xxxix. (1714) 26 She past in haughty Surquedry, Like some great Queen thus richly garnished. **1793** I. WILLIAMS *Mem. Warren Hastings* 47 We cannot become illustrious by fury or surquedry. **1825** SCOTT *Betrothed* xviii, A judgment specially calculated to abate and bend that spirit of surquedry.

fig. **1642** H. MORE *Song of Soul* I. II. lxi, To an inward sucking whirlpools close They change this swelling torrents surquedry.

b. with *a* and *pl.* A piece of arrogance.

1602 MARSTON *Ant. & Mel.* III. Wks. 1856 I. 34 O, had it eyes, and eares, and tongues, it might See sport, heare speach of most strange surquedries. **1609** [BP. W. BARLOW] *Answ. Nameless Cath.* 341 Citing it for a proofe, and not confuting it for a surquedrie. **1647** WARD *Simple Cobler* (1843) 31 Fashions..are the surquedryes of pride.

c. *transf.*: cf. PRIDE *sb.*¹ 5.

1607 WALKINGTON *Optic Glass* 32 That heavenly worke of works, natures surquedry and pride.

¶2. Misused for: Excess (esp. of indulgence), surfeit.

1594 *Selimus* in *Greene's Wks.* (Grosart) XIV. 220, I haue ..surfeted with pleasures surquidrie. **1598** *Pilgr. Parnass.* IV. 486 Theile..make you melte in Venus' surque[d]rie. **1598** MARSTON *Sat.* iv. 49 Poems (1879) 49 In strength of lust and Venus surquedry. **1612** *Pasquil's Night-cap* (1877) 2147 Diseases hidden, Which doe proceed from lust and surquedrie. **1623** COCKERAM II, The *Ouerplusse*, Surquedrie, Surplusage. **1647** TRAPP *Comm. Eph.* v. 18 This is called by Luther, *Crapula sacra*, a spirituall surquedry or surfet. **1656** HEYLIN *Extraneus Vapulans* 315 Their stomacks not well cleared from the Surquedries of that Mighty Feast.

†'surquidy, 'surquedy. *Obs.* Also 5 -quidie, -quydy, -quedye, 5–6 -quedie, (6 syrcuyte). [a. OF. *surquidee*, **sourcuidee*, f. *s(o)urcuidier*: see SURQUIDANT and -Y.] = prec.

c **1407** LYDG. *Reason & Sens.* 2581 Pompe, pride, and surquedye. **14..** *Chaucer's Pars. T.* ¶993 (Harl. MS.) þe Surquidie þat he haþ in cristes mercy. **1430–40** LYDG. *Bochas* Prol. (MS. Bodl. 263) 3/1 Thei.. Supposyng in ther surquedie Ther estatis sholde be durable. **1540** *St. Papers Hen. VIII*, III. 187 Ther grete pryde and surquedy ys partely swaged. **1560** T. H. tr. *Ovid's Fable Narcissus* Dij, Syrcuyte and pride. **1595** T. EDWARDS *Cephalus & Procris* (Roxb.) 29 Pale death Lay with his surquedie to draw her breath. **1819** SCOTT *Ivanhoe* xxviii, Are ye yet aware what your surquedy and outrecuidance merit, for scoffing at the entertainment of a prince of the House of Anjou?

‖**surra** ('suːrə, 'sʌrə). [Marathi *sūra* air breathed through the nostrils.] A disease of horses and other domestic animals in India, China, and other countries, caused by the flagellate *Trypanosoma evansi* and characterized by periods of increasingly severe fever and loss of weight, usually leading to death.

1883 W. ROBERTSON *Textbk. Practice Equine Med.* xi. 235 Surra may be conveniently defined as a specific blood disease of the horse. **1890** BILLINGS *Nat. Med. Dict.* **1904** *Brit. Med. Jrnl.* 20 Aug. 368 Tabanus can carry the trypanosome of Surra. **1932** RILEY & JOHANNSEN *Med. Entomol.* xviii. 300 They [*sc.* tabanids] transfer by direct inoculation certain trypanosomes of animals, such as *Trypanosoma evansi*, which causes the highly fatal surra of horses. **1962** GORDON & LAVOIPIERRE *Entomol. for Students of Med.* xxiv. 155 There are a number of species [of tabanid] which are vectors of diseases to domestic animals, such as surra.

surrah, obs. variant of SIRRAH.

1602 [see VAY(E].

†su'rreach, *v.* *Obs.* *rare*⁻¹. [f. SUR- + REACH *v.*¹] *trans.* To extend beyond.

1606 B. BARNES *Offices* I. 1 If.. I should presume to talke of things surreaching the scope of my apprehension.

surreal (sə'riːəl), *a.* [Back-formation from SURREALISM, SURREALIST *a.* and *sb.* Poss. coined (as *surréel*) in Fr. Cf. *super-real* adj. s.v. SUPER- 4 a (*a*).] Having the qualities of surrealist art; bizarre, dreamlike. So **surre'ality, su'rreally** *adv.*

1936 D. GASCOYNE tr. *Breton's What is Surrealism?* vi. 66 As I said in the *Manifesto*: 'I believe in the future transmutation of those two seemingly contradictory states, dream and reality, into a sort of absolute reality, of surreality, so to speak.' **1937** *Burlington Mag.* Jan. p. xiv/1 Some 'surreal' influence haunts the regions of the Black Forest. **1952** *N.Y. Times Bk. Rev.* 4 May 26/5 I'll agree with that; however I didn't select the surrealism, the distortion, the intensity, as an experimental technique but because reality is surreal. **1956** *Time* 18 June 109/1 Author Gascar's power to evoke disgust, which he does by combining familiar objects in unfamiliar ways, until they become surreal and emetic. **1968** *New Yorker* 25 May 87/1 A surreally funny hour of film.. which is goonish, rude, and altogether relieving. **1968** P. OLIVER *Screening Blues* vi. 199 A startling flight of sexual fantasy, it [*sc.* 'Coffee Blues'].. extends to surreal associations which imply the sexual virtuosity of the singer. **1974** *Encycl. Brit. Micropædia* IX. 693/2 The world of dream and fantasy would be joined to the everyday rational world in 'an absolute reality, a surreality'. **1976** S. HYNES *Auden Generation* vii. 227 As the 'thirties moved on toward the end, there was only the surreal... Even the agents of order were surreal and terrifying. **1980** J. O'FAOLAIN *No Country for Young Men* xv. 319 Scale impresses him. He calls it 'art'. 'Surreality', if you please. **1982** *Times Lit. Suppl.* 21 May 549/1 Surreally hard-edged, the world *Child's Play* projects is one where details have a hallucinatory vividness.

surrealism (sə'riːəlɪz(ə)m). Also †in F. form ‖**surréalisme**, and with capital initial. [ad. F. *surréalisme*, f. *sur-* super- + *réalisme* realism; the precise English equivalent would be *super-realism* (see SUPER- 4 a (*b*)).] A movement in art and literature seeking to express the subconscious mind by any of a number of different techniques, including the irrational juxtaposition of realistic images, the creation of mysterious symbols, and automatism (q.v., sense 5); art or literature produced by or reminiscent of this movement.

The term *surréalisme*, coined by Guillaume Apollinaire (see quot. 1917), was taken over by the poet André Breton as the name of the movement, which he launched with his *Manifeste du Surréalisme* in 1924; his statement there of the term's meaning is given in quot. 1935.

[**1917** 'G. APOLLINAIRE' *Notes to 'Parade'* in *Table Ronde* (1952) Sept. 45 De cette alliance nouvelle, car jusqu'ici les décors et les costumes d'une part, la chorégraphie d'autre part, n'avaient entre eux qu'un lien factice, il este résulté, dans 'Parade', une sorte de surréalisme.] **1927** C. CONNOLLY *Let.* 21 Apr. in *Romantic Friendship* (1975) 294 His [*sc.* Brueghel's] realism with people, 'surrealisme' with places, is like Crabbe. **1931** [see POPULISM b]. **1934** C. LAMBERT *Music Ho!* II. 78 Surrealism may conveniently be defined as the free grouping together of incongruous and non-associated images. **1935** D. GASCOYNE tr. A. Breton in *Short Survey Surrealism* iv. 61 *Surrealism*, pure psychic automatism, by which it is intended to express, verbally, in writing, or by other means, the real process of thought. **1952** R. BRYDEN in *Granta* 29 Nov. 8/1 Sometimes we find that neither subject suffers from juxtaposition, but that together they form a new kind of experience to Surrealism, which we rather admire. **1970** *Oxf. Compan. Art* 1115/1 Surrealism sought to explore the frontiers of experience and to broaden the logical and matter-of-fact view of reality by fusing it with instinctual, subconscious, and dream experience in order to achieve an absolute or 'super' reality. **1978** *Amer. Scholar* Summer 357 It is clear, from what people say about contemporary surrealism.., that such poetry is supposed to be terribly mysterious, profound stuff.

surrealist (sə'riːəlɪst), *a.* and *sb.* Also †in F. form ‖**surréaliste** and with capital initial. [ad. F. *surréaliste*, f. *sur-* super- + *réaliste* realist.]

A. *adj.* Of, pertaining to, or characteristic of, surrealism. **B.** *sb.* An adherent of surrealism. Also *transf.*

The adjective was coined by Guillaume Apollinaire (see quot. 1918), perhaps (according to Robert) in the sense of F. *surnaturaliste*, and was taken over by the movement founded by André Breton (see prec.).

[**1918** 'G. APOLLINAIRE' *Les Mamelles de Tirésias* (1946) 9 Pour caractériser mon drame, je me suis servi d'un néologisme qu'on me pardonnera car cela m'arrive rarement et j'ai forgé l'adjectif surréaliste qui.. définit.. une tendance de l'art.] **1918** *Egoist* Apr. 56/1 Surréaliste is the denomination M. Guillaume Apollinaire.. has attached to his play, *Les Mamelles de Tirésias*... Thus he must be credited with the foundation of a successor to the *Unanimiste* and *Simultaneiste* schools. **1925** R. FRY *Let.* 1 May (1972) II. 567, I went yesterday.. to see the works of the two great Sure-realist [*sic*] painters Miro and Masson. **1925** —— *Let.* 11 Nov. (1972) II. 584 That beastly young Surrealist Masson. **1929** A. HUXLEY *Do what you Will* i. 16 The Surréalistes.. have presented us.. with the dream-like incoherencies which creative thought uses as its raw material. **1934** *Sun* (Baltimore) 25 Oct. 12/2 The Senator is the *surrealist* of politics—for surely he is above reality—or below it or to the right or left of it. **1936** D. GASCOYNE *Man's Life is this Meat* (verso title-page), With the exception of Nos. 1–6, the poems in this collection are Surrealist poems. **1940** L. TRILLING in *Kenyon Rev.* Spring 157 The Surrealists have, with a certain inconsistency, taken from Freud a kind of scientific sanction for their program. **1942** E. WAUGH *Put out More Flags* i. 39, I should have thought an air raid was just the thing for a surréaliste.. limbs and things lying about in odd places. **1958** *Sunday Times* 26 Jan. 13/4 Behind the Empress, entirely dominating her.. was the surrealist figure of Rasputin. **1964** M. MCLUHAN *Understanding Media* (1967) II. xvii. 180 The elders of the tribe.. had never noticed that the ordinary newspaper was as frantic as a surrealist art exhibition. **1978** K. J. DOVER *Greek Homosexuality* III. 133 'Surrealist' elements are very rare in Greek art, but an exception is the 'phallos-bird' which has the legs, body and wings of a bird but a neck and head in the form of a curved penis.

Hence **surrea'listic** *a.*, characteristic or suggestive of surrealism; **surrea'listically** *adv.*

1930 *Nation* 6 Dec. 326/1 The sheer absurdity of the characters' behaviour produced a sort of *surréalistic* poetry. **1934** WEBSTER, Surrealistically. **1958** *Spectator* 20 June 813/1 He produced Hauptmann's *Hannele* surrealistically as early as 1895. **1959** M. PUGH *Chancer* 36 Your eyes are so bloody bloodshot that they look like surrealistic marbles. **1979** *United States 1980/81* (Penguin Travel Guides) 129 You might hear along the way that Cleveland isn't the town it used to be, but surrealistically speaking, what place is? **1980** *N. & Q.* Dec. 505/2 As usual in De Quincey's surrealistic dream prose, several ideas coalesce in a single image.

surrebend, -rebound, -rebribe: see SUR-.

surrebutter (sʌrɪ'bʌtə(r)). *Law.* [f. SUR- + REBUTTER, after *surrejoinder*.] In old common-law pleading, a plaintiff's reply to a defendant's rebutter. Also *transf.*, a further rejoinder.

a **1601** SIR T. FANSHAWE *Pract. Exch.* (1658) 146 They must proceed with Rebutter, and sur-rebutter, untill every point materiall be put in perfect issue. **1770** FOOTE *Lame Lover* II. Wks. 1782 III. 34 Rejoinders, sur-rejoinders, rebutters, sur-rebutters, replications. **1866** LOWELL *Biglow P.* Introd., Poems (1912) 279/2 Mr. Bartlett (in his dictionary above cited) adds a surrebutter in a verse from Ford's 'Broken Heart'. **1888** MORLEY in *Daily News* 17 Oct. 6/1 Controversy is seldom profitable after it gets down to the stage of sur-rebutter and sur-rejoinder. **1893** LELAND *Mem.* I. 295 Then came the attack on the impropriety of the whole thing, and finally Mr. Barnum's triumphant surrebutter.

So **†surrebut** *sb.*, shortening of or error for SURREBUTTER; **surre'but** *v.* [cf. REBUT] *intr.* to reply to a rebutter (also *transf.*); *trans.* to repel as by a surrebutter; **surre'buttal** [cf. REBUTTAL], surrebutter.

1587 HARRISON *England* II. ix. (1877) I. 202 The parties plaintiffe & defendant.. proceed.. by plaint or declaration, barre or answer, replication, reioinder, and so by rebut, surrebut to issue and triall. **1726** T. MADOX *Firma Burgi* x. §21. 198 To this William Cokenage Surrebutteth. He saith, That [etc.]. **1845** DE QUINCEY *Wordsw. Poetry* Wks. 1857 VI. 258 A smart reciprocation.. of asserting and denying,.. butting, rebutting, and 'surrebutting'. **1866** BLACKMORE *Cradock Nowell* iv, To revive their efficacy, and so surrebut all let and hindrance. **1889** *Times* 25 Nov. 5/4 The State's rebuttal and surrebuttal of the defence. **1895** *Q. Rev.* July 264 The members of the majority.. not unnaturally surrebut on this interpretation. **1909** ELIZ. BANKS *Myst. Fr. Farrington* 311 There were witnesses to come in rebuttal, but he.. could call witnesses in surrebuttal.

surrecompounded, -countermand: see SUR-.

†surrect, *a.* *Obs.* *rare*⁻¹. [ad. L. *surrectus*, pa. pple. of *surgĕre* to rise, stand up.] Upright.

1692 PLUKENETT *Let. Mr. Ray* 17 July (1718) 249 The *Paronychic Hispanica Clus*... is a more surrect Plant.

surrection (sə'rɛkʃən). *rare.* Also 5 surreccioun, -ecion, 6 -eccyon, -eccion, -exyon. [ad. late L. *surrectio*, *-ōnem*, n. of action f. *surrect-*, *surgĕre* to rise. Cf. OF. *surrection*.]

†1. A rising in rebellion, insurrection. *Obs.*

c **1418** *Pol. Poems* (Rolls) II. 247 To shape sodeyn surreccioun Agaynst oure liege lord kynge. **1516** in Arnolde *Chron.* (1811) p. l, Yᵉ surrexyon of vacabondis, and prentysys.. agaynst straungers. **1528** LD. SANDYS *Let. Wolsey* 9 Mar. (Publ. Rec. Off.), If there be eny such surreccion.. I shall doo the best may lye in me to pacifie theym.

2. Rising (in general). *Obs.* exc. as *nonce-wd.* after *resurrection*.

1509 HAWES *Past. Pleas.* (Percy Soc.) 191 The mornyng was past, But Afrycus Auster made surreccion, Blowyng his bellowes. **1599** A. M. tr. *Gabelhouer's Bk. Physicke* 55/2 Sepulte the same.. agaynste the surrection of the Sunne. **1845** BROWNSON *Wks.* V. 342 It would not be a *re*-surrection, but a simple *surrection*.

surreine ('sʌreɪn). Also 7 -ein, -ine. [? f. SUR- + F. *reine* queen. (Cf. †*sur-belheur*, a variety of apple.)] A variety of pear.

1629 PARKINSON *Parad.* (1904) 593 The Surrine is no very good peare. **1664** EVELYN *Kal. Hort.* (1679) 36 Pears.. Squib, Surrein, Dagobert. **1873** *J. Scott's Orchardist* 409 (*Pears*) Rameau (*Sur Reine, Surpasse Reine*)... It was raised by Van Mons about 1825.

†surreined, *ppl. a.* *Obs. rare.* [Of uncertain formation: generally taken to be f. SUR- + REINED *ppl. a.*¹] Of a horse: Over-ridden, overworked.

1599 SHAKS. *Hen. V*, III. v. 19 A Drench for sur-reyn'd Iades. **1601** [? MARSTON] *Pasquil & Kath.* IV. 44 A surreinde Iaded wit, but a rubbes on.

surrejoin (sʌrɪ'dʒɔɪn), *v.* *Law.* [Back-formation f. next, after *rejoin*.] *intr.* (or with *obj. cl.*) To reply, as a plaintiff, to the defendant's rejoinder; to make a surrejoinder. Also *transf.*

1594 WEST *2nd Pt. Symbol., Chancerie* §75 Then may the plaintife surreioyne to the second rejoinder. *c* **1640** J. SMYTH *Lives Berkeleys* (1883) I. 108 Salisbury surreioynes and saith, That hee never tooke the Earle Marischall for his dettor. **1855** MACAULAY *Hist. Eng.* xi. III. 64 Instead of acquiescing in his first thoughts, he replied on himself, rejoined on himself, and surrejoined on himself. **1883** *Law Rep. 11 Q.B. Div.* 583 The plaintiff surrejoined that the 35*l.* was not a reasonable fine. **1890** *Pall Mall G.* 2 July 3/1 Mr. Arthur Palmer surrejoins about 'What I saw at Tel-el-Kebir',.. generally returning the compliment of mendacity all round.

surrejoinder (sʌrɪ'dʒɔɪndə(r)). *Law.* [f. SUR- + REJOINDER.] In old common-law pleading, a plaintiff's reply to the defendant's rejoinder. Also *transf.* an answer to a rejoinder or reply (in general).

The order of the pleadings is: plaintiff's *declaration*, defendant's *plea*, plaintiff's *replication*, defendant's *rejoinder*, plaintiff's *surrejoinder*, defendant's *rebutter*, plaintiff's *surrebutter*.

1542–3 *Act 34 & 35 Hen. VIII*, c. 27 §50 The Prenotarye to have for the.. replicacion, rejoyndre, surrejoyndre, for everye of them if they be enrolled.. xijd. **1644** PRYNNE & WALKER *Fiennes's Trial* 47 The whole three dayes first defence being made intirely together, and then the Reply, Rejoinder, and Surrejoinder thereunto. **1682** LUTTRELL *Brief Rel.* (1857) I. 236 The atturney generall hath pleaded in surrejoinder to the citty of Londons rejoinder to the quo warranto against their charter. **1770** [see SURREBUTTER]. **1886** W. E. NORRIS *My Friend Jim* I. 70 To make such a rejoinder as that would only have been to expose myself to a surrejoinder which it would have been.. futile to attempt to rebut. **1903** MORLEY *Gladstone* II. v. iii. 49 Mr. Gladstone.. was too much in earnest to forego rejoinder and even surrejoinder.

†surrend, *v.* *Obs. rare.* [ad. OF. *surrendre* to SURRENDER.] *trans.* = SURRENDER *v.*; in quot. *c* 1475 used = give back, restore (cf. RENDER *v.* 3).

1450 *Rolls of Parlt.* V. 184/2 If ony persone.. hadde estate.. of the yifte or graunte by Letters Patentes of ony of youre Progenitours, and hafe surrendid [? *error for* surrenderid] the said Letters Patentes in to youre Chauncery.. to be cancelled. *c* **1475** *Partenay* 4986, I can noght.. werke ne labour soo As tho mortall ded ther lif to surrend.

surrender (sə'rɛndə(r)), *sb.* Also 5 sure render, 6 surrendre. [a. AF. *surrender*, = OF. *surrendre*, inf. used as sb.: see next.] The action or an act of surrendering.

1. *Law.* **a.** The giving up of an estate to the person who has it in reversion or remainder, so as to merge it in the larger estate; *e.g.* the giving up of a lease before its expiration; *spec.* the yielding up of a tenancy in a copyhold estate to the lord of the manor for a specified purpose; *transf.* a deed by which such surrender is made.

1487 *Rolls of Parlt.* VI. 394/1 Determynation of the States.. by Deth,.. or by ony other wise then by Surrender. **1512** *Knaresb. Wills* (Surtees) I. 4, I will that my feoffees maike a sufficiente and lawful estaite, by surrender or otherwais. **1523** FITZHERB. *Surv.* 14 Surrenders of landes holden by the yerde. **1535** *Act 27 Hen. VIII*, c. 27 §7 The said Chauncellour shall have power.. to take surrendre of any leases. **1583** MELBANCKE *Philotimus* X iv b, I haue wastfully spente.. the surrender of my fathers landes. **1590** WEST *Symbol.* I. II. §311 An Instrument of Surrender is an instrument testifiyng.. that the particuler tenant of landes.. doth.. agree, that he which hath the next immediate remainder or reuersion thereof shall also haue the particuler estate of the same in possession. **1628** COKE *On Litt.* 338 If a man make a Lease for yeares to begin at Michaelmasse next, this future interest cannot bee surrendred, because there is no Reuersion wherein it may drowne, but by a Surrender in Law it may be drowned. As if the Lessee before Michaelmasse take a new Lease for yeares..this is a Surrender in Law of the former Lease. **1679–88** *Moneys Secr. Serv. Chas. II & Jas. II* (Camden) 69 For the charge of a surrender made by Lord Arundell of Trerice, and inrolling the same, 3 0 0. **1766** BLACKSTONE *Comm.* II. 365 Surrender,..the yielding up of the estate by the tenant into the hands of the lord, for such purposes as in the surrender are expressed. **1818** CRUISE *Digest* (ed. 2) I. 277 A term cannot be merged by surrender till the tenant has entered. **1825** *Act 6 Geo. IV*, c. 16 §3 If any such Trader shall..make ..any fraudulent Surrender of any of his Copyhold Lands.

b. The giving up of letters patent granting an estate or office; *Hist.* the yielding up of tithes in Scotland to the Crown.

1557 *Test. Ebor.* (Surtees) VI. 261 Upon dewe surrender mayde to my handes of the other sayde severall patentes. **1628** *Sc. Acts Chas. I* (1870) V. 189/1 Such of his Majesties Subjects as had right to whatsoever erection of..Teinds and others forsaids who should make surrender thereof in his Majesties hands. **1654** H. L'ESTRANGE *Chas. I* (1655) 126 His..Commission of Surrender of Superiorities and Tithes, by which the Ministers and Land-owners were bought out..from the Clientele and Vassallage of the Nobility and Laique Patrons. **1662** HUGHES *Abridgm. Law* III. 1904/2 Of Surrender of the King's Letters Patents, what shall be said a good Surrender of them, and what not. **1729** JACOB *Law Dict.* s.v., A Surrender may be made of Letters Patent to the King, to the End he may grant the Estate to whom he pleases.

c. The action of surrendering to bail.

1710 PALMER *Proverbs* 10 The Bail has a sort of Custody and Command of the Prisoner. A Surrender is our Discharge.

d. The giving up by a bankrupt of his property to his creditors or their assignees; also, his due appearance in the bankruptcy court for examination, as formerly required by the bankruptcy acts.

1745 *De Foe's Eng. Tradesman* vii. (1841) I. 48 Upon his honest and faithful surrender of his affairs, he shall be set at liberty. **1766** BLACKSTONE *Comm.* II. 481 In case the bankrupt absconds..between the time of the commission issued, and the last day of surrender, he may by warrant.. be committed to the county goal. **1825** *Act 6 Geo. IV*, c. 16 §112 If any Person..declared Bankrupt, shall not.. surrender himself to them [*sc.* Commissioners], and sign or subscribe such Surrender, and submit to be examined before them..[he] shall be deemed guilty of Felony.

e. †(*a*) See quot. 1755. (*b*) The abandonment of an insurance policy by the party assured on receiving part of the premiums.

surrender value, the amount payable to an insured person on his surrendering his policy.

1755 MAGENS *Insurances* II. 92 When any Goods or Ships that are insured, happen to be lost,..then the Assured is obliged to abandon such Goods or Ship to the Benefit of the Assurers, before he can demand any Satisfaction from them. The Surrender must be made by Notice in writing, by the Messenger of the maritime Court. **1880** *Encycl. Brit.* XIII. 179/1 The surrender value to be allowed for a policy which is to be given up should be less than the reserve value. **1887** J. HENRY *Handbk. Life Assurers* (ed. 2) 51 The value to be offered by the office for a surrender of the policy.

2. The giving up of something (or of oneself) into the possession or power of another who has or is held to have a claim to it; *esp.* (*Mil.*, etc.) of combatants, a town, territory, etc. *to* an enemy or a superior. In wider sense: Giving up, resignation, abandonment.

c **1485** *Digby Myst., Christ's Burial* 301 To his fadere, for vs he made a sure render. **1560** DAUS tr. *Sleidane's Comm.* 354 The Senate refused to make surrender or to receiue a power into the citie. *Ibid.* 400 Albeit they were layde at with many weapons, yet toke they it by surrender. **1588** SHAKS. *L.L.L.* I. i. 138 To speake..About surrender vp of Aquitaine. **1633** T. STAFFORD *Pac. Hib.* II. xxv. (1821) 452 Which they did not deliver unto him as a Surrender, but to shew and manifest their Dutys. **1667** MILTON *P.L.* IV. 494 With eyes Of conjugal attraction unreprov'd, And meek surrender. **1689** *Sc. Acts Will. & M.* (1875) XII. 54/2 That at the surrender of the castle þe avenews be gaurded be the town gaurds. **1790** BURKE *Rev. France* 88 That he may secure some liberty, he makes a surrender in trust of the whole of it. **1792** ALMON *Anecd. W. Pitt* II. xxx. 145 That a repeal of the Stamp Act would be a surrender of the authority of the British Legislature over the Colonies. **1856** KANE *Arctic Expl.* I. xxvii. 353 Nothing depresses..so much as a surrender of the approved and habitual forms of life. **1862** STANLEY *Jew. Ch.* (1877) I. xx. 386 Sacrifice.. consists..in the perfect surrender of a perfect Will and Life. **1871** FREEMAN *Norm. Conq.* (1876) IV. xviii. 206 [The terms of peace] did not involve the surrender or driving out of the English exiles. **1911** E. BEVERIDGE *North Uist* iv. 58 Although offering surrender, all were slain.

b. *Cards.* In the game of ombre, the act of throwing up one's hand and paying one's forfeit to the pool instead of to an adversary.

1874 H. H. GIBBS *Ombre* (1878) 32 Surrender was formerly not allowed in English play.

†**3.** An act of rendering (thanks). *Obs. rare*$^{-1}$.

1594 in *Cath. Rec. Soc. Publ.* V. 283 To give to his temporal benefactors a sweet surrender of thanks.

surrender (səˈrɛndə(r)), *v.* Also 5 sorendre, 6 surrendre, *Sc.* surrander. [a. AF. *surrender* = OF. *surrendre* (13th c.), f. *sur-* SUR- + *rendre* to RENDER. The Anglo-L. equivalents were *superreddere* (*c* 1400) and *sursum reddere* (13th c.).

In the retention of the inflexion of the AF. inf. this word follows RENDER *v.*; cf. TENDER *v.*[1]]

1. *Law.* **a.** *trans.* To give up (an estate) to one who has it in reversion or remainder; *spec.* to give up (a copyhold estate) to the lord of the manor, either by way of relinquishing it or of conveying it to another.

1466 *Mann. & Househ. Exp.* (Roxb.) 348 Thomas Edmunde of Douercorte sorendryd into Iohn Sparre..alle the londe..that he hathe. **1544** tr. *Littleton's Tenures* I. ix. 16 b, Yf he wyll alyen hys lande to another, him behoueth after some custome to surrendre the tenementes in some court &c into the lordes handes. **1606** *Munim. de Melros* (Bann.) 658 To..surrander vpgeif and ouergeif All and haill þe maner place of Melrose... In the handis of oure said souerane lord. **1766** BLACKSTONE *Comm.* II. 144 If I grant a lease to A for the term of three years, and after the expiration of the said term to B for six years, and A surrenders or forfeits his lease at the end of one year, B's interest shall immediately take effect. **1800** *Addison's Rep.* 12 The award was..that a lease should be surrendered. **1875** DIGBY *Real Prop.* (1876) 378 He may at common law surrender his estate to the remainderman or reversioner by simple deed.

absol. **1628** COKE *On Litt.* I. 59 Euerie Copiholder may surrender in Court and need not alleadge any custome therefore. **1818** CRUISE *Digest* (ed. 2) VI. 54 If a person devises a copyhold for the benefit of persons of this kind, without surrendering to the use of his will. **1845** STEPHEN *Comm. Laws Eng.* (1874) I. 524 The under-lessees (by refusing to surrender, in their turn, notwithstanding they had covenanted to do so).

b. To give up (letters patent, tithes) into the hands of the sovereign. (Cf. SURRENDER *sb.* 1 b.)

1473 *Rolls of Parlt.* VI. 82/1 He to surrender uppe unto us his seid Letters Patentes. **1628** *Sc. Acts Chas. I* (1870) V. 189/2 That all superiorities of Erections should be freely resigned and surrendered in his Majesties hands without any composition. **1662** HUGHES *Abridgm. Law* III. 1906/1 It was found..That G. did Surrender and Restore the said Letters Patents, in Chancery, to be cancelled.

c. *refl.* or *intr.* of a bankrupt: To appear in the bankruptcy court for examination.

1707 *Lond. Gaz.* No. 4318/4 He being declared a Bankrupt, is required to surrender himself. **1766** BLACKSTONE *Comm.* II. 481 At the third meeting, at farthest, ..the bankrupt..must surrender himself personally to the commissioners. **1825** *Act 6 Geo. IV*, c. 16 §117 The Bankrupt shall be free from Arrest or Imprisonment by any Creditor in coming to surrender. **1845** POLSON in *Encycl. Metrop.* II. 835/1 If he fails..to surrender himself, and submit to be examined before the court, or upon examination does not discover all his..estate.

d. *trans.* Of a bail: To produce (the principal) in court at the appointed time. Also *intr.* or *refl.* of the principal, usually in phr. ***to surrender to one's bail***.

1747 VINER *Abridgm. Law & Equity* III. 499 An Action of Debt was brought on the Recognizance against the Bail,.. and the Principal was surrender'd. *Ibid.*, On a Suggestion that the Defendant had surrender'd himself in Discharge of his Bail. **1835** *Penny Cycl.* III. 288/1 Unless they, the bail, pay the costs and money recovered for him, or surrender him to custody. **1848** *Act 11 & 12 Vict.* c. 42 §23 Such Justice of the Peace may..admit such Person to Bail..and ..shall take the Recognizance of the said accused Person and his Surety..that he will then surrender and take his Trial. **1883** *Law Times* 29 Sept. 363/1 Magistrates should in all cases grant bail unless they have good reason to suppose that the prisoner will not surrender.

2. To give up (something) out of one's own possession or power into that of another who has or asserts a claim to it; to yield on demand or compulsion; *esp.* (*Mil.*) to give up the possession of (a fortress, town, territory, etc.) to an enemy or assailant. Also *fig.* Const. *to*.

Formerly also with *up* (now *rare* or *obs.*).

1509 HAWES *Past. Pleas.* XLII. (Percy Soc.) 207 The body ..wyll not remember Howe erth to erth must his strength surrender. **1561** T. HOBY tr. *Castiglione's Courtyer* II. (1577) L iij b, What offices has thou to surrender into my handes? quoth the Pope. **1585** T. WASHINGTON tr. *Nicholay's Voy.* I. xix. 23 b, If they..did surrender the place he would exempt out of them two hundreth. **1590** SPENSER *F.Q.* II. x. 45 Till he surrendred Realme and life to fate. **1613** SHAKS. *Hen. VIII*, I. iv. 81 One..More worthy this place then my selfe, to whom..I would surrender it. **1651** HOBBES *Leviath.* II. xxvii. 160 Though he have surrendred his Power to the Civill Law. *a* **1700** EVELYN *Diary* 26 May 1684, Luxembergh was surrendered to the French. **1782** COWPER *Friendship* 117 Plebeians must surrender And yield so much to noble folk. **1784** —— *Task* VI. 102 Some to the fascination of a name Surrender judgment. **1832** BREWSTER *Nat. Magic* xii. 299 The diamond and the gems have surrendered to science their adamantine strength. **1850** ROBERTSON *Serm.* Ser. III. iii. (1872) 41 There are others, who..would surrender the conscience of each man to the conscience of the Church. **1874** A. B. DAVIDSON *Introd. Hebr. Gram.* 29 In words with the Art[icle] the weak *he* usually surrenders its vowel to the prep[osition] and disappears.

with *up*. *c* **1590** MARLOWE *Faustus* iii, Say, he surrenders vp to him his soule. **1592** KYD *Sp. Trag.* III. xii. 76 Ile make a pick-axe of my poniard, And heere surrender vp my Marshalship. **1610** HOLLAND *Camden's Brit.* (1637) 394 They surrendred up this Manour unto King Henry the Eight. **1673** RAY *Journ. Low C.* 3 Ostend was surrendred up to Arch-Duke Albert. *a* **1715** BURNET *Own Time* (1823) II. 310 To surrender up some of those great jurisdictions over the Highlands that were in his family. *a* **1774** HARTE *Vision Death* 256 Surrender up to me thy captive-breath.

b. More widely: To give up, resign, abandon, relinquish possession of, esp. in favour of or for the sake of another.

1509 HAWES *Past. Pleas.* xx. (Percy Soc.) 96 Ryght so let wysdome your sorowe surrendre. **1565** HARDING *Confutation* IV. vii. 187 b, His sonne tooke vpon him forthwith the administration of the Empire,..would not surrender the state which he liked well. **1594** KYD *Cornelia* V. 463 Afterward..I will surrender my surcharged life. **1779** *Mirror* No. 35, He must surrender his own character, and assume the hue of every company he enters. **1833** HT. MARTINEAU *Fr. Wines & Pol.* iv. 62 Sounds reached her which gave her back a little of the hope which she had wholly surrendered. **1871** R. W. DALE *Commandm.* x. 253 For those whom we love we gladly surrender our personal comfort and ease.

3. *refl.* To give oneself up into the power of another, esp. as a prisoner.

1585 T. WASHINGTON tr. *Nicholay's Voy.* I. xix. 23 Fainte heartedlie to surrender themselues to the mercie of those, at whose hands was nothing to be looked for, but miserable seruitude. **1693** *Mem. Cnt. Teckely* I. 82 That [*sc.* garrison] of Licowa surrendred it self the next day. **1760** *Cautions & Adv. Officers Army* 30 The French fired all their Arms into the Air; then threw them down, and surrendered themselves Prisoners of War. **1823** SCOTT *Quentin D.* xxiii, It is the banner of the Count of Crèvecœur,..to him I will surrender myself. **1828** LYTTON *Pelham* III. xix, His..desire to appease his mind, by surrendering himself to justice. **1891** FARRAR *Darkn. & Dawn* lv, They were..informed that the Apostle..had thought it right to..surrender himself as a prisoner.

b. *fig.* To give oneself up *to* some influence, course of action, etc.; to abandon oneself or devote oneself entirely *to*.

1713 ATTERBURY *Serm.* (1734) II. 48 Those..who do not surrender themselves up to the Methods it prescribes. **1833** HT. MARTINEAU *Manch. Strike* viii. 88 We must surrender ourselves..to our duties.

4. *intr.* for *refl.* = 3; chiefly *Mil.* (said of a body of men, a town or fortress, etc.); also *fig.*

1560 DAUS tr. *Sleidane's Comm.* 286 b, Whan they had surrendred [orig. *facta deditione*]. **1593** SHAKS. *Rich. II*, IV. i. 156 Fetch hither Richard, that in common view He may surrender. **1676** EARL ORRERY in *Essex Papers* (Camden) 58, I lay before it [*sc.* Limerick]..untill the Plague and Famine made it surrender, we could not take it. **1691** [see DISCRETION 5 b]. *a* **1721** PRIOR *Songs* vi. 25 Nothing's proof against those eyes, Best resolves and strictest ties To their force must soon surrender. **1790** BEATSON *Nav. & Mil. Mem.* II. 239 The Commodore was determined that the place should surrender at discretion. **1845** DISRAELI *Sybil* VI. xii, 'Surrender,' said the commander of the yeomanry. 'Resistance is useless.' **1890** *Spectator* 1 Nov. 595/1 They only sent fifteen hundred men, who accomplished nothing, and were finally compelled to surrender at discretion.

†**5.** To render, return (thanks, etc.). *Obs.*

1542 BOORDE *Dyetary* viii. E j, Surrendrynge thankes to hym for his manyfolde goodnes. **1578** H. WOTTON *Courtlie Controv.* 125 To surrender their accustomed honor vsed yearely vnto the..mistresse. **1588** PARKE tr. *Mendoza's Hist. China* 180 They had surrendred vnto him thankes. *Ibid.* 195 Hee tooke his leaue of vs with great friendship and curtesie: who did surrender the same after our custome.

Hence **suˈrrendered** (-əd) *ppl. a.*, **suˈrrendering** *vbl. sb.* and *ppl. a.*

1648 (*title*), The Demands..of The Earle of Norwich..to Generall Fairfax, concerning the surrendering of the said City. **1711** in *10th Rep. Hist. MSS. Comm.* App. v. 174 Articles of agreement for the surrendering of Lymerick. **1837** CARLYLE *Fr. Rev.* I. v. vi, The Hôtel de Ville 'invites' him to admit National Soldiers, which is a soft name for surrendering. **1876** LOWELL *Among my Bks.* Ser. II. 119 Dante..believed that..his [*sc.* the Lord's] kingdom would be established in the surrendered will. **1901** *Westm. Gaz.* 20 May 7/1 Parties of the latter returned into the town and searched the place for surrendering burghers. **1911** SIR H. CRAIK *Life Clarendon* I. xii. 323 Fairfax..had..accepted the others as surrendered prisoners.

surrenderee (sərɛndəˈriː). *Law.* [f. prec. vb. + -EE.] The person to whom an estate, etc. is surrendered: correlative to *surrenderor*.

1662 HUGHES *Abridgm. Law* III. 1907/1 A Copyholder doth Surrender unto the use of a Stranger, for ever, and the Lord admits the Surrenderee to hold to him and his heirs. **1741** T. ROBINSON *Gavelkind* I. vi. 98 The Surrenderee died before Admittance. **1766** BLACKSTONE *Comm.* II. 326 The surrenderor must be in possession; and the surrenderee must have a higher estate, in which the estate surrendered may merge. **1843** *Penny Cycl.* XXVII. 390/1 A devisee or surrenderee of copyholds. **1875** POSTE *Gaius* I. §169 The surrenderee of a guardianship is called a cessionary guardian.

surrenderer (səˈrɛndərə(r)). [f. as prec. + -ER[1].] One who surrenders, in any sense.

1628 *Sc. Acts Chas. I* (1870) V. 191/2 The Teinds of whatsoever Lands and Barronies perteining to the saids Persons Surrenderers in property.

surrenderor (səˈrɛndərɔː(r)). *Law.* [f. as prec. + -OR 2 d.] One who surrenders an estate, etc. to another: correlative to *surrenderee*.

a **1683** SCROGGS *Courts-leet* (1714) 148 When a Surrender is made to the Use of a Will, the Fee-Simple remains in the Surrenderor. **1766** BLACKSTONE *Comm.* II. 368 Till admittance of *cestuy que use*, the lord taketh notice of the surrenderor as his tenant. **1818** CRUISE *Digest* (ed. 2) VI. 45 A surrender to the use of a will must be presented: but by special custom such presentment may be made at the next court, after the death of the surrenderor. **1875** POSTE *Gaius* I. §170 On his death..the guardianship reverts to the surrenderor.

surrendry (səˈrɛndrɪ). Now *rare*. Also 6 **surendrie, 6–7 surrendrie, 6–8 surrendery.** [f. SURRENDER: see -RY.] = SURRENDER *sb.*

1547 *Acts Privy Council* (N.S.) II. 504 The Commissioners appoynted for the surrendery of the College of Kyrkeswold. **1560** DAUS tr. *Sleidane's Comm.* 274 He wynneth partly by force, partly by surendrie, he fireth the castell, and spareth the people. **1597** J. PAYNE *Royal Exch.*

38 Let vs be ready to say.. at the surrendrie of our last gaspe: I have fought a good fyght. **1610** HOLLAND *Camden's Brit.* I. 37 Cassivellaunus.. sent Embassadour to Cæsar by Conius of Arras, tendring unto him a Surrendry. **1657** FARINDON *Serm.* Pref. (1672) c 1 b, When they have made a surrendry of themselves to such a Church. **1685** CROWNE *Sir C. Nice* v. Dram. Wks. 1874 III. 345 Did not I stipulate upon the surrend'ry of myself to this house, to be kept from women? **1695** KENNETT *Par. Antiq.* viii. 39 He frighted the City.. into a surrendry to him. **1781** *Connecticut Gaz.* 7 Sept., Immediately on the surrendry, the valiant Col. Ledyard.. and 70 other officers and men were murdered. **1796** MORSE *Amer. Geog.* I. 465 Upon the forced surrendry of the Plymouth Company's patent to the crown, in 1735. **1877** SPARROW *Serm.* vi. 82 That entire surrendry of the whole soul.

Surrentine (sʌ'rɛntaɪn), *a.* [ad. L. *Surrentīnus*, f. *Surrentum*, a maritime town of Campania, now Sorrento.] Belonging to Surrentum or the neighbouring hills, anciently famous for an excellent wine.

1601 HOLLAND *Pliny* XIV. vi. I. 414 That the Physicians had laid their heads togither, and agreed to give the Surrentine wine so great a name. **1833** REDDING *Mod. Wines* (1851) 8 Surrentine was a wine commended by the Emperor Caligula. **1845** *Encycl. Metrop.* XXV. 1271/1 The Falernian,.. Gauran, and Surrentine hills.. towered above the rich plains and cities below.

†**surrepent**, *a. Obs.* [ad. L. *surrēpentem*, *-ens*, pr. pple. of *surrēpĕre*: see SURREPTION².] Creeping beneath or stealthily. So †**surrepency**, the quality of creeping stealthily or stealing upon one.

1608 J. KING *Serm.* 5 *Nov.* 27 This serpent surrepent generation, with their mentall reseruations, their amphibolous, amphibious propositions. *a* **1678** WOODHEAD *Holy Living* (1688) 160 Taking heed.. of the surrepency of some degree of unbelief.

†**surre'ply**, *sb. Obs. rare.* [f. SUR- + REPLY, after *surrejoinder.*] An answer to a reply. So †**surre'ply** *v.*, to answer to a reply.

1605 Z. JONES tr. *Loyer's Specters 46 marg.*, A surreply to the former answered. **1650** WELDON *Crt. Chas. I* (1651) 187 Buckingham sur-replyed, Its false. **1683** E. HOOKER *Pref. Pordage's Mystic Div.* 84 So haply you mai repli. But then, I fear, you may com with a surreplie, as hee did.

†**su'rrept**, *v. Obs. rare.* [f. L. *surrept-*, pa. ppl. stem of *surripĕre*: see SURREPTION¹.] *trans.* To snatch or take away stealthily; to steal, filch. Hence †**su'rrepted** *ppl. a.*

a **1548** HALL *Chron., Hen. VII*, 20 b, [He] onely studyed and watched how to surrept and steale thys turtle out of her mewe and lodgynge. **1600** W. WATSON *Decacordon* (1602) 34 Cardinall Caietans surrepted letter of authoritie. **1603** OWEN *Pembrokeshire* (1892) 229 Without archedignitie, wch longe since hath ben surrepted. **1643** QUARLES *Loyall Convert* Wks. (Grosart) I. 142/1 It is no offensive War for a King to endeavour the Recovery of his surrepted right. **1657** BILLINGSLY *Brachy-Martyrol.* xxi. 72 Yet was my life by strangers Surrepted not.

surreption¹ (sə'rɛpʃən). Also 5 **-tyon**, 5-7 **-cion**, etc. [ad. L. *surreptio*, *-ōnem*, n. of action f. *surripĕre* to seize or take away secretly, purloin, (in the Vulgate) to make false suggestions, f. *sur-* = SUB- 25 + *rapĕre* to seize. Cf. OF. *surreption*, and SUBREPTION¹.]

†**1.** Suppression of truth or fact for the purpose of obtaining something, or the action of obtaining something in this way (cf. SUBREPTION 1); more generally, fraudulent misrepresentation, or other underhand or stealthy proceeding. *Obs.*

c **1400** *Pilgr. Sowle* (Caxton) I. xxxvi. (1859) 40 This lady Misericord.. hath caused in this Courte grete annoye.. by cause of purchacyng of this letter... But, me semyth.. that somme poyntes conteyned therynne ben not to be receyued, for they semyn geten and purchacyd by surreptyon. *c* **1450** *Godstow Reg.* 676 He charged that none sholde be made abbesse there by violence or wylynesse of surrepcion. *c* **1555** HARPSFIELD *Divorce Hen. VIII* (Camden) 148 Marvel it is.. the Pope should be abused.. by any surreption. **1600** W. WATSON *Decacordon* (1602) 252 The excommunication of Pius 5. [against Q. Elizabeth was] procured vpon false suggestions, and so by surreption. **1609** *Bible* (Douay) Dan. vi. 6 Then the princes, and governers by surreption suggested to the king [Vulg. *surripuerunt regi*], and spake unto him. *a* **1616** B. JONSON *Pr. Henry's Barriers* 109 Fame by surreption got May stead us for the time, but lasteth not. **1624** BEDELL *Lett.* iii. 71 It occasioned the Arch-Priest here ..to thinke those letters forged, or gotten by surreption. **1649** BP. HALL *Cases Consc.* (1650) 369 The surreption of secretly-mis-gotten dispensations. **1662** *Jesuits' Reasons* (1675) 121 You, by Grace or Surreption, have purloyn'd a Command from that Court. **1720** J. JOHNSON *Coll. Eccl. Laws Ch. Eng.* I. P vj, We do.. forbid the Charter.. to be of any Validity, because gotten by Surreption, and unsincere Suggestions.

2. The action of seizing or taking away by stealth; stealing, theft. *by surreption*: by stealth, stealthily (cf. next). Now *rare* or *Obs.*

1603 OWEN *Pembrokeshire* (1892) 274 Leaste by surrepcion the Knappan should be snatched by a borderer of the game. **1610** CARLETON *Jurisd.* 47 Which power in Bishops the Pope hath by surreption drawen to himselfe. **1641** H. L'ESTRANGE *God's Sabbath* 28 To distinguish truth from fables, which had by surreption intruded. **1651** HOBBES *Leviath.* II. xxx. 179 Fraudulent surreption of one anothers goods. *a* **1656** HALES *Gold. Rem.* (1673) I. 82 He which otherwise dies, comes by surreption and stealth, and not warrantably unto his end. **1661** GODOLPHIN *View Adm. Jurisd.* Introd., Rendring Ship or Lading liable.. to a seizure or surreption. *a* **1680** BUTLER *Rem.* (1759) I. 407 The Dr. was so impatient to try the Experiment solitary, that.. he adventured.. to invade it by Surreption and Involation. **1860** G. GROVE in W. Smith *Dict. Bible* I. 370 Four soldiers, ..whose express office was to prevent the surreption of the body.

†**3.** Something introduced by stealth, an interpolation. *Obs. rare*$^{-1}$.

c **1637** JER. TAYLOR *Reverence due to Altar* (1848) 43 The *Missa latina Antiqua*.. was set forth by protestants to be a redargution of the surreptions, and innovations in the later Missals.

†**surreption**² (sə'rɛpʃən). *Obs.* Also 6 **-cion**, **-cyon**, etc. [ad. patristic L. **surreptio*, *-ōnem*, n. of action f. *surrēpĕre*, f. *sur-* = SUB- 2, 25 + *rēpĕre* to creep.] An unperceived creeping or stealing upon one or into one's mind (of evil thoughts or suggestions); hence, a sudden or surprise attack (of temptation, sin): freq. used to describe either the kind of sin or the subjective state of the sinner.

The ultimate source of this use appears to be *Deut.* xv. 9 (Vulg.) 'Cave ne forte subrepat tibi impia cogitatio'.

1502 *Ord. Crysten Men* (W. de W. 1506) IV. xxii, Yf by precypytacyon or surrepcyon in worde without consentynge of wyll a man swereth false. **1529** MORE *Suppl. Soulys* Wks. 321/2 Some sodayne waueryng of the mynd in time of prayer, or some surrepcion & crepyng in of vain glory. **1557** EDGEWORTH *Serm.* 285 Surreption or priuy creping of matters into mens mindes **1624** GEE *Hold Fast* 20 The Deuill gaineth ground of vs onely by Surreption. **1625** USSHER *Answ. Jesuit* 142 The Church.. sometimes judgeth by surreption and ignorance, whereas God doth alwayes judge according to the truth. **1645** HAMMOND *Sinnes* 4 Satan ..assaulting me.. on the suddaine, when I have not time, to use those meanes which I might otherwise use, which we call suddaine surreption. *c* **1650** JER. TAYLOR *Devotions Occas. Sacram.* iii, All surreptions and sudden incursions of temptation. **1680** H. DODWELL *Two Lett.* (1691) 80 Hypocrisy by Surreption.. is both less dangerous, and less imputable than Hypocrisy by design. *a* **1711** KEN *Man. Prayers* Wks. (1838) 427 Even the just man falls seven times a day, through sins of ignorance, or sudden surreption, or inadvertency.

b. A lapse due to such an attack.

1536 *St. Papers Hen. VIII*, I. 509 A lightnes gyven in a maner by a naughtye nature to a commonaltie, and a wonderous sodayne surreption of gentilmen. **1641** M. FRANK *Serm.* (1672) 82 That it was but a slip, or weakness or surreption. **1649** JER. TAYLOR *Gt. Exemp.* I. Disc. ii. 68 Sometimes such surreptions and smaller undecencies are pardoned.

†**su'rreptious**, *a. Obs* [Shortened form of SURREPTITIOUS *a.*¹, or directly f. SURREPTION¹: cf. *suppositious.*] Surreptitious. So †**su'rreptiously** *adv.*, surreptitiously.

1573 *Reg. Privy Council Scot.* II. 318 The said signature ..is.. impetrat surreptiouslie. **1587** *Ibid.* IV. 173 [The said Bishop] hes of lait.. surreptiouslie purchast letters of discharge. **1630** USSHER *Lett.* (1686) 430 Whether it carrieth not with it a powerful *Non obstante* to that surreptious Grant. **1642** CHAS. I. *Answ. Proposals Ho. Parl.* 19 Any surreptiously gotten Command of the King.

†**surrep'titial**, *a. Obs. rare.* [f. L. *surreptītius*: see next and -IAL.] = next.

1600 W. WATSON *Decacordon* (1602) 264 The Iesuiticall plots for restoring religion in this land by surreptitial excommunications, depositions, inuasions. *Ibid.* 327 Surreptitiall suggestions of some euill and factious persons.

surreptitious (sʌrɪp'tɪʃəs), *a.*¹ Also 5-6 **-cious**. [f. L. *surreptītius*, *-icius* = *subrepticius* (see SUBREPTITIOUS) + -OUS. Cf. OF. *surreptice*, It. *surrettizio*, OPg. *sorr-*, *surre(p)ticio*.]

1. Obtained by 'surreption', suppression of the truth, or fraudulent misrepresentation: = SUBREPTITIOUS a.

1443 *Proc. Privy Council* V. 297 þt þei see þe patentes þt þe Kyng hath graunted and see which be surrepticious. *a* **1712** FOUNTAINHALL *Decis.* (1759) II. 419 That it was surreptitious and obreptitious, containing a plain falsity. **1719** *Ld. Herbert's Hen. VIII* 108/1 If it shall.. appear, that any such Apostolical Dispensations shall be.. invalid, ineffectual, unsufficient, surreptitious or arreptitious. **1728** CHAMBERS *Cycl.*, *Subreptitious* or *Surreptitious*, a Term applied to a Letter, Licence, Patent or other Act, fraudulently obtain'd of a Superior, by concealing some Truth, which had it been known, would have prevented the Concession or Grant. **1855** MILMAN *Lat. Chr.* XIV. i. *note* f, The Parliament declared the ordinance surreptitious, and contrary to the rights of the Bishops.

2. Taken, obtained, used, done, etc. by stealth, secretly, or 'on the sly'; secret and unauthorized; clandestine.

c **1645** HOWELL *Lett.* I. III. xxx. The Hollander hath done him [*sc.* the King of Spain] more mischief by counterfeiting his Copper Coyns,.. bringing it in by strange surreptitious wayes, as in.. hollow Masts. **1661** *Sir H. Vane's Politics* 7 The Pagentry of his [*sc.* Oliver Cromwell's] surreptitious state. **1768** BLACKSTONE *Comm.* III. 130 In order to prevent the surreptitious discharge of prisoners. **1817** COLERIDGE *Biog. Lit.* I. 265 A surreptitious act of the imagination, which.. likewise supplies by a sort of *subintelligitur* the one central power, which renders the movement harmonious and cyclical. **1848** THACKERAY *Van. Fair* xlviii, O ladies! how many of you have surreptitious milliners' bills? **1866** MRS. H. WOOD *St. Martin's Eve* xvi, Stealing surreptitious glances at him through her veil. **1885** RUSKIN *Præterita* I. iv. 13 The surreptitious enjoyments they devised.

b. Of a passage or writing: Spurious, forged. Of an edition or copy of a book: Issued without authority, 'pirated'.

1615 CROOKE *Body of Man* 316 Wee conclude that the place aboue vrged is surreptitious. **1648** BOYLE *Seraph. Love* Ep. Ded. (1700) 3 To run the risk of a surreptitious Edition of a Discourse. **1728** POPE *Dunc.* Let. Publisher, A correct copy of the Dunciad, which the many surreptitious ones have rendered so necessary. **1858** *Times* 29 Nov. 6/4 When they give their word that a publication is surreptitious. **1870** LOWELL *Among my Bks.* Ser. I. (1873) 167 Plays which they reprinted from stolen and surreptitious copies.

c. *transf.* Acting by stealth or secretly; †taking by stealth, appropriating secretly (*obs.*); stealthy, crafty, sly.

1615 CHAPMAN *Odyss.* XXI. 296 To take, or touch with surreptitious Or violent hand, what there was left for vse. **1635** BRATHWAIT *Arcadian Princ.* 19 Only some surreptitious proctours were there fishing, who knew no.. Law-Intergatory, but the demand of their undeserved fees. **1683** BARNARD *Heylin* 12, I have not been surreptitious of whole pages together out of the Doctors printed volumnes, and appropriated them to my self without any Mark or Asterism. **1856** MISS MULOCK *John Halifax* xxx, The old man's look,.. betraying his surreptitious curiosity. **1868** E. EDWARDS *Ralegh* I. ii. 31 He organized a new expedition.. with the same surreptitious countenance which had been shown to him. **1898** 'H. S. MERRIMAN' *Roden's Corner* xxi. 223 Glancing at the clock with a surreptitious eye.

†**surrep'titious**, *a.*² *Obs. rare.* [f. SURREPTION², after prec.] Characterized by or of the nature of 'surreption'; stealthily suggested to or introduced into the mind.

1534 MORE *Treat. Passion* Wks. 1276/2 A soden surrepticious delyte, cast by the diuel into the sensual parte, is no sinne at all,.. except the will.. consent.

surrep'titiously, *adv.* [f. SURREPTITIOUS *a.*¹ + -LY².] In a surreptitious manner.

a. By 'surreption': see SURREPTITIOUS *a.*¹ 1.

1587-8 *Reg. Privy Council Scot.* IV. 260 [Having been] previlie and surreptitiouslie [obtained]. **1655** FULLER *Ch. Hist.* IX. ii. §25 The reasons.. were falsely, and surreptitiously suggested to his Holiness. **1689** *Col. Rec. Pennsylv.* I. 258 Certain decrees and Orders surreptitiously obtained by Thomas Wollaston. **1823** LINGARD *Hist. Eng.* VI. 179 The dispensation.. was said.. to have been surreptitiously obtained. **1876** BANCROFT *Hist. U.S.* I. x. 323 All charters and patents which had been surreptitiously obtained.

b. In an underhand way; secretly and without authority; clandestinely, by stealth, 'on the sly'.

1643 SIR T. BROWNE (*title*) A true and full coppy of that which was most imperfectly and Surreptitiously printed before vnder the name of Religio Medici. **1648** D. JENKINS *Wks.* 45 Which confutes their saying that the King got the Seale away surreptitiously. **1656** COWLEY *Misc.* Pref., Either surreptitiously before, or avowedly after my death. **1710** STEELE & ADDISON *Tatler* No. 259 ¶1 Surreptitiously taking away the Hassock from under Lady Grave-Airs. **1865** *Athenæum* 28 June 124/2 James Duke begins the world as an anonymous infant, laid surreptitiously in a basket of clean linen. **1871** SMILES *Charac.* x. (1876) 272 She carried it to church.. in the guise of a missal, and read it surreptitiously during the service. **1879** FROUDE *Cæsar* viii. 87 The proscription was over, and the list had been closed; but Roscius's name was surreptitiously entered upon it. **1898** 'H. S. MERRIMAN' *Roden's Corner* xvi. 174 She surreptitiously touched the animal with her heel.

†**c.** Spuriously. *Obs.*

1680 *Lond. Gaz.* No. 1556/4 That the Book.. is falsly, and surreptitiously Ascrib'd to that worthy Person.

So **surrep'titiousness**.

1902 'H. S. MERRIMAN' *Vultures* xxix. 258 The quietness of the streets had a suggestion of surreptitiousness.

†**su'rreptive**, *a. Obs. rare*$^{-1}$. [ad. late L. *surreptīvus* = *subreptīvus*: see SUBREPTIVE.] = SURREPTITIOUS *a.*¹ 1.

1633 T. STAFFORD *Pac. Hib.* III. i. 286 How may it then bee, that those [Apostolicall] Letters were surreptiue?

†**su'rreverence**. *Obs.* Also 7 **sur-reverence**, **surreverance**. [Variant of SIR-REVERENCE.]

1. = SIR-REVERENCE 1, 1 b.

1586 WARNER *Alb. Eng.* II. x. 27 All for loue (surreuerence Loue). **1600** NASHE *Summers Last Will* E iij b, Surreuerence of their worships, they feed at my stable, table, euery day. **1625** tr. *Gonsalvius' Sp. Inquis.* To Rdr. B j b, Whose very name should not be spoken of without Surreuerence and great contempt.

b. By association with SUR- *prefix*, used for: Great reverence.

1592 NASHE *Strange Newes* C j b, Wherein mee thinks (the surreuerence of his works not impaired) he hath verie highly ouershotte himselfe. **1622** FLETCHER *Prophetess* I. iii, *Dio...* So great a reverence, and so stai'd a knowledge—*Max.* Surreverence, you would say.

2. = SIR-REVERENCE 2, 2 b.

[**1599** NASHE *Lenten Stuffe* 75, I might as well haue writte of a dogges turde (in his teeth surreuerence).] **1655** tr. *Sorel's Com. Hist. Francion* III. 73 Flinging Squibs, Crakkers, Dirt, and sometimes stinking Surreverences. **1663** HEATH *Flagellum* (1672) 18 Having besmeared his own Cloths and hands with Surreverence. **1710** HEARNE *Collect.* (O.H.S.) III. 20 Some Persons abus'd the Statue of the late K. William.. leaving a Surreverence upon the Back of his Horse.

†**su'rreverently**, *adv. Obs. nonce-wd.* [f. SUR- + REVERENTLY, after prec.] Very reverently: *ironically* with reference to SURREVERENCE 2.

1632 B. JONSON *Magn. Lady* I. i, A reverend youth, You use him most surreverently me thinkes!

surrexyon, obs. form of SURRECTION.

surrey[1] ('sʌrɪ). An American four-wheeled two-seated pleasure carriage, the seats being of similar design and facing forwards; also, a motor-carriage of similar structure.

Originally applied to an adaptation of the Surrey cart (an English pleasure cart with an open spindle seat first built in the county of Surrey) introduced into the U.S.A. by J. B. Brewster & Co. of New York in 1872. (*The Hub* March 1882.)

1896 HOWELLS *Idyls in Drab* 34 Hacks and barouches, and light, wood-coloured surreys and phaetons. **1896** *Cosmopolitan* XX. 420/1 The Hill locomotor... In design the vehicle is a canopy-top surrey with two seats.

Surrey[2] ('sʌrɪ). The name of a county in southern England, used *attrib.* in **Surrey capon, chicken, fowl**, to designate a fowl specially fattened before being killed and prepared for cooking.

1874 L. WRIGHT *Bk. Poultry* xxii. 319 We have often been asked to describe the large 'Surrey' or 'Sussex' fowls which are so largely reared for the London market. **1910** J. T. BROWN *Encycl. Poultry* II. 459/1 'Surrey Fowls'. A trade description for the best produce of the Sussex fattening coops. **1938** [see *Light Sussex* s.v. LIGHT *a.*[2] 3]. **1971** *Selfridge Xmas Food Catal.* 6/1 Surrey capons.. Plump full-breasted succulent birds. **1971** *Guardian* 27 Nov. 3/8 You tuck the quail into a poulet de bresse (a Surrey fowl would do).

surriall, obs. form of SURROYAL.

surrigeane, -ian, -ine, obs. Sc. ff. SURGEON.

surripe, obs. form of SYRUP.

surrogacy ('sʌrəgəsɪ). *rare.* [f. next: see -ACY.] The office of a surrogate; surrogateship.

1811 J. CECIL *Mem. R. Cecil* in *Wks.* (1827) I. 19 He had before recommended him.. for the Surrogacy annexed to.. his Living. **1829** *18th Rep. Comm. Crts. Justice Irel.* 77 Copy Commission of Surrogacy to Sir Henry Meredyth.

surrogate ('sʌrəgət), *sb.* (*a.*) Also 7 *Sc.* **surragat**, 8 *illit.* **suragat**. [ad. L. *surrogātus*, assimilated f. *subrogātus* SUBROGATE *pa. pple.* Cf. It. *surrogato*, OF. *surrogué*.]

A. *sb.* **1.** A person appointed by authority to act in place of another; a deputy. **a.** *gen.*

1604 R. CAWDREY *Table Alph.*, *Surrogate*, a deputie in anothers place. *c* **1616** CHAPMAN *Homer's Hymn to Mars* 6 Ioint surrogate of Iustice [orig. συναρωγὲ Θέμιστος]. **1618** in *T. Pont's Topogr. Acc. Cunningham* (Maitl. Club) 202 Patrik Huntar,.. executour-dative surragat, in place of the Procuratour-fischall. **1642** JER. TAYLOR *Episc.* (1647) 57 A helper, or a Surrogate in Government. **1657** HAWKE *Killing is M.* 24 Princes make others Surrogates, and Executioners of their Judicial Acts.

b. The deputy of an ecclesiastical judge, of a bishop or bishop's chancellor, esp. one who grants licences to marry without banns.

1603 *Const. & Canons Eccl.* xciii, Any Iudge of the Prerogatiue Court, or any his Surrogate or his Register or Apparitor. **1631** *Star Chamber Cases* (Camden) 76 The said Dunsterfeild.. persuaded the said Skinner to goe with him to the Court to gett a licence for the marriage of the said parties. They came before the Surrogate. **1694** E. CHAMBERLAYNE *Pres. St. Eng.* III. (ed. 18) 359 If he be found duly qualified, the Bishop or his Surrogate, institutes him. **1753** *Act 26 Geo. II*, c. 33 §7 That.. no Surrogate deputed by any Ecclesiastical Judge, who hath Power to grant Licences of Marriage, shall [etc.]. **1885** *Times* 12 Dec. 6/1 The president of the court [*sc.* the York Chancery Court] was represented by a surrogate. **1890** W. CLARK RUSSELL *Marriage at Sea* xv. Postscr., The Rev. Thomas Moore, Rector of All-hallows-the-Great, late Surrogate in the Diocese of Canterbury. **1912** G. W. E. RUSSELL *Edw. King* iv. 140 The Sentence of Consecration was read by the Surrogate.

c. *Hist.* In the former British colonies, one appointed to act as judge in the vice-admiralty court in place of a regular judge; in New York and some other States, a judge having jurisdiction over the probate of wills and settlement of estates of deceased persons.

1816 *Act 56 Geo. III*, c. 82 The judicial Acts of Surrogates who have executed the Offices of Judges in the Courts of Vice Admiralty established in His Majesty's Plantations and Colonies. **1858** KENT *Comm. Amer. Law* (ed. 9) II. v. xxxvii. 530 The first judge of the county acts in cases in which the surrogate is disqualified to act. **1867** SMYTH *Sailor's Word-bk.*, *Surrogates*,.. naval captains formerly acting for judges in Newfoundland. **1887** *Encycl. Brit.* XXII. 695/2 In New Jersey the surrogate is an official of the orphans' court, grants unopposed probates, &c.

2. a. *fig.* and *gen.* A person or (usually) a thing that acts for or takes the place of another; a substitute. Const. *for*, *of*. Also as the second element of a Comb., chiefly in *father-surrogate* s.v. FATHER *sb.* 12, *mother-surrogate* s.v. MOTHER *sb.*[1] 17 a.

1644 BULWER *Chirol.* 15 The Hand was instituted Surrogate and Vicar of the Heart. **1650** FULLER *Pisgah* III. xii. 343 Hereupon a substitute or surrogate was provided for him to bear his Cross. **1830** *Blackw. Mag.* XXVIII. 267 What corresponding force can be devised..? Certainly no absolute one; but, as the best surrogate, Kant proposes a Federal Union of States. **1845** *Foreign Q. Rev.* XXXIV. 274 Fixedness of purpose and of principle was to him a surrogate for alacrity. **1869** CARLYLE in *Mrs. Carlyle's Lett.* III. 26 Getting up at six, and riding to Clapham Common.. by way of surrogate for sleep. **1950** A. HUXLEY *Themes & Variations* 46 Not a trace of the divine or the eternal remains, and the notions of State, Nation and Party are therefore free to expand into vast and monstrous caricatures of God. In the service of this God-surrogate and of his prophet, Efficiency, totalitarian dictators find it right and proper to behave with systematic savagery. **1970** MASTERS & JOHNSON *Human Sexual Inadequacy* v. 147 *Partner surrogate* has been reserved to indicate the partner provided by the cotherapists for an unmarried man referred for treatment who has no one to provide psychological and physiological support during the acute phase of the therapy. **1979** [see *sex surrogate* s.v. SEX *sb.* 5].

b. *spec.* = SUBSTITUTE *sb.* 6 b.

1887 *Pall Mall G.* 25 Nov. 5/1 That the word 'butter' shall be expunged from the trade name of all surrogates for butter. **1891** F. L. OSWALD in *Voice* (N.Y.) 5 Feb., Ground pepper, ground coffee, mustard and tea, are mixed with surrogates too numerous to mention. **1897** *Allbutt's Syst. Med.* II. 896 Many other drugs are recommended.. as surrogates for morphine.

c. *spec.* A surrogate partner in sex therapy.

1975 M. COLE in S. Jacobson *Sexual Problems* 103 The use of male surrogates for the treatment of vaginismus and frigidity of various types has proved to be even more successful. **1976** T. SHARPE *Wilt* xii. 119 'I was a surrogate,' said Sally. 'A surrogate?' 'Like a sex counsellor.'

d. A woman whose pregnancy arises from the implantation in her womb of a fertilized egg or embryo from another woman.

1978 *Time* 5 June 59 The demand for surrogates remained strong... Despite potential legal problems, some have already opted for surrogate mothers. **1982** *New Scientist* 7 Oct. 16 This slippery slope would begin to steepen if the same technical procedure were to be applied to a non-donor who was not sterile but who acted as a surrogate ('foster mother') for the donor.

B. *attrib.* or *adj.* That is a surrogate; taking the place of or standing for something else; representative. Now esp. in contexts where the substitute is intended to fulfil the emotional needs of a person. Also used in sense 2 d above.

a **1638** MEDE *Wks.* (1672) 604 The Virgin-Christians of the Gentiles, (who are the Surrogate Israel). **1829** *18th Rep. Comm. Crts. Justice Irel.* 77 *margin*, Commission appointing Sir H. Meredyth Surrogate Judge. **1840** J. WILSON *Lect. Anc. Israel* vi. 119 These Christian nations.. being the spiritual, or surrogate Israel. **1910** F. C. CONYBEARE in *Encycl. Brit.* (ed. 11) IX. 873/1 An ἀντίτυπον or surrogate body. **1955** *Times Lit. Suppl.* 25 Feb. p. ix/1 Poe lived riotously in Dupin... Dupin was to him what Jim Hawkins was to Stevenson or Hadrian VII to Frederick Rolfe, a surrogate self living the life denied to the writer. **1977** *Time* 15 Aug. 50/3 In the life of the mind, Saville lives a surrogate boyhood. **1977** C. MCFADDEN *Serial* (1978) xliii. 92/2 His Surrogate Parent for the session made him drink a lot of lemon-grass tea. **1978** Surrogate mother [see sense 2 d above]. **1979** *Sci. Amer.* June 36/3 Will this research lead.. to the use of 'surrogate parents', where, for example, rich women might pay poor women to carry their children? **1979** W. STYRON *Sophie's Choice* xi. 316 Sophie found herself acting as a kind of surrogate kin, a younger sister or daughter.

surrogate ('sʌrəgeɪt), *v.* Now *rare* or *Obs.* Also 7 (*Sc.*) **-at**; 6 (*Sc.*) *pa. t.* **-ate**, *pa. pple.* **-at, -aitt, suregat**, 6–7 *pa. pple.* **-ate**. [f. L. *surrogāt-*, pa. ppl. stem of *surrogāre*, assimilated f. *subrogāre* to SUBROGATE.]

1. *trans.* To appoint as a successor, substitute, or deputy: = SUBROGATE *v.* 1.

1533 BELLENDEN *Livy* II. iv. (S.T.S.) I. 140 þai belevit þat he wald vsurpe þe crovn, becaus he surrogate nocht haistelie ane new consul in þe place of brutus. *Ibid.* 142 He sett ane counsell to surrogate ane colleig in þe place of brutus. *Ibid.* III. vii. I. 270 The consull denyit to do ony thing concernyng þe said law, quhil he had surrogate ane colleig in þe place of Valerius þat was deceissit. **1611** SPEED *Hist. Gt. Brit.* IX. xxiv. §10 The Oath of Supremacie.. was offered vnto them, the refusers whereof were.. depriued, and others surrogated that were more loyally affected. **1637** GILLESPIE *Engl. Pop. Cerem.* II. i. 7 Those conforming Ministers, who are surrogate in their stead. **1662** H. MORE *Philos. Writ.* Pref. Gen. (1712) 25 This earthly Adam failing in his office, the Heavenly was surrogated in his room. **1679** C. NESSE *Antichrist* 162 The Pope of Rome.. did surrogate the kings of France. **1705** HICKERINGILL *Priest-cr.* I. (1721) 62 Solomon is surrogated by God, in his stead, to the holy Work. **1853** LD. CAMPBELL in Ellis & Blackburn *Rep.* I. 614 Chancellor.. with power of surrogating a fit person for his substitute with the Bishop's approbation.

b. To substitute in respect of a right or claim: = SUBROGATE *v.* 3.

1536 BELLENDEN *Cron. Scot.* (1821) II. 451 William, Erle of Douglas,.. clamit the croun, be richt of Edward Balliol and the Cumin; saying he wes surrogat to baith thair richtis. **1652** Z. BOYD in *Zion's Flowers* (1855) App. 24/2 Quhome I .. surrogat substitute and imputte in my full richt tytill and place of the samyne. **1710** in *Nairne Peerage Evid.* (1874) 153 We.. surrogate & substitute the said master James Nairne.. in our full right and place therof pro tanto.

2. To put instead of another; to substitute: = SUBROGATE *v.* 2.

1586 FERNE *Blaz. Gentrie* 302 Least that strange and base stocks should presume to be surrogated in the place.. of the noble and free borne. **1596** BACON *Max. Com. Law* xix. (1630) 69 This act.. was repealed, and a new law surrogate in place thereof. **1609** SKENE *Reg. Maj.*, *Stat. Robt. I*, 34 And the tyme of the birth, three lichts or candels salbe in the house, because darknesse is meet and convenient to surrogat ane false birth, as gif it were the trew birth. *a* **1638** MEDE *Wks.* (1672) 750 That the Jews should be rejected, and the Gentiles surrogated in their stead. **1654** VILVAIN *Theorem. Theol.* viii. 209 The Earth.. shal be renewed or a new surrogated. **1664** H. MORE *Myst. Iniq.* 322 How punctually they have surrogated the Blessed Virgin into the place of Venus. **1681** HICKERINGILL *Vind. Naked Truth* II. 14 How do they wrest the holy Scriptures to surrogate their preposterous Hierarchy. *a* **1768** ERSKINE *Inst. Law Scot.* III. vi. §7 That subject which is surrogated in the place of the first. **1827** SCOTT *Napoleon* lxxxiii, They had.. a title to the price which had been surrogated in place of the property.

†**3.** *intr.* To act for another as a surrogate or substitute; *fig.* to minister *to*. *Obs. rare.*

1681 HICKERINGILL *Black Non-Conf.* iii. Wks. 1716 II. 44 When decrepit old Age cannot surrogate to their Lust. **1681** —— *Vind. Naked Truth* II. 1 Whose Pens were glad to Surrogate to their Pencels, and write—This is a Cock, and This a Bull.

Hence '**surrogated** *ppl. a.*, '**surrogating** *vbl. sb.*

a **1679** T. GOODWIN *Election* III. iii. Wks. 1683 II. 138 Deut. 9. 14. I will make of thee a Nation greater and mightier than they: And to be in their room a Surrogated People to him, as they by Election had been. **1679** C. NESSE *Antichrist* 163 In usurping his authority of surrogating and deputing of Caesars.

surrogateship ('sʌrəgət-ʃɪp). [f. SURROGATE *sb.* + -SHIP.] The office of a surrogate.

1846 WORCESTER cites *Ed. Rev.*

surrogation (sʌrə'geɪʃən). Now *rare.* [ad. med.L. *surrogātio*, *-ōnem*, assimilated f. *subrogātio* SUBROGATION. Cf. OF. *surrogation*, It. *surrogazione*.]

1. Appointment of a person to some office in place of another.

1533 BELLENDEN *Livy* V. xiv. (S.T.S.) II. 195 Becaus sa grete myscheif fell to romanis eftir þe surrogatioun of the said censore. **1600** HOLLAND *Livy* XLI. xvi. 1105 The surrogation of a colleague unto him. **1608** BP. HALL *Epist.* IV. x, Ye magistrates.. whom God hath on purpose, in a wise surrogation, set vpon earth. **1642** JER. TAYLOR *Episc.* (1647) 15 The prediction of the Apostacy of Iudas, and Surrogation of S. Matthias. **1717** KILLINGBECK *Serm.* vi. 120 A Surrogation and new Choice of an Apostle to succeed into the Room of Judas.

2. *gen.* Substitution: = SUBROGATION 1.

a **1638** MEDE *Wks.* (1672) 736 The calling of the Gentiles, .. by way of surrogation to the Jews. *a* **1653** GOUGE *Comm. Heb.* x. 10 This surrogation had been in vain, if Christs Sacrifice had not made perfect. *a* **1711** KEN *Hymns Evang.* Poet. Wks. 1721 I. 40 Thou a full Freedom to Thyself hast kept, A Surrogation for us to accept. **1911** W. W. FOWLER *Relig. Exper. Roman People* xiv. 322 Even if we were to grant the human sacrifice, the surrogation of [straw] puppets is a most unlikely thing to have happened.

‖**surrogatum** (sʌrə'geɪtəm). *Sc. Law.* [L., neut. sing. of *surrogātus*, pa. pple. of *surrogāre* to SURROGATE.] A thing put *in the place of* another; a substitute.

1766 KAMES *Princ. Equity* (1767) 224 This new bond, being a *surrogatum* in place of the former. *a* **1768** ERSKINE *Inst. Law Scot.* II. x. §29 Its value is the fifth of the rent payable for both stock and tithe; which is accounted a reasonable *surrogatum*, in place of a tenth of the increase.

surroie, obs. form of SERAI[1].

su'rround, *sb.* [f. the vb.]

1. An act of surrounding; *spec.* (orig. and chiefly *U.S.*) the process of hunting certain wild animals by surrounding them and driving them into a place from which they cannot escape.

1825 in *N. Dakota Hist. Q.* (1929) IV. 35 The Mandans went out to kill Buffalo, by making whats called a surround, at 8 miles distant from fence. **1837** W. IRVING *Capt. Bonneville* xlvi. III. 220 It was at length proclaimed, that all who were able to lift a club.. should muster for the 'surround'. **1851** MAYNE REID *Scalp Hunters* xxxii. 247 The hunters were getting forward with the 'surround'. **1903** SIR M. G. GERARD *Leaves fr. Diaries* viii. 250 Allowing time for the surround to be accomplished, he then strolled off with the remaining.. sepoys.

2. A border or edging of a particular material, nearly or quite surrounding the central piece, as of linoleum or felt round a carpet.

1893 *Ludgate Monthly Mag.* Jan. 328/2 Central bordered carpets are now most in vogue, with a surround of linoleum. **1896** MRS. J. E. PANTON *Suburban Resid.* 29, I have covered the gaping stained 'surround' with felt. **1912** *Sphere* 28 Dec. p. ii, A large cameo brooch set in a surround of finely-chased gold.

3. The area or substance surrounding something; the vicinity, surroundings, or environment (*of* something).

1922 *Daily Mail* 11 Nov. 15/4 The inflammation often extends to the surround of the eye and to the wattles and throat [of poultry]. **1937** *Nature* 3 July 12/2 Large thermal inertia in the optical parts and small and slow changes in the surround of each instrument were required. **1939** *Country Life* 11 Feb. p. xxi/1 (Advt.), All types of Fencing and Tennis Court Surrounds are described in Catalogue 495. **1943** H. J. MASSINGHAM *Men of Earth* ii. 10 A country building.. in relation to its matrix or surround. **1959** *Listener* 1 Jan. 13/1 It was the country, the flat agricultural surround, that so ravished me. **1962** *Which? Car Suppl.* Oct. 139/1 [There was] creaking noise from steering column surround. **1976** L. VAN DER POST *Jung & Story of Our Time* (1978) iii. 70 My own isolation in a great natural surround. **1978** *Nature* 14 Sept. 141/2 Bipolar cell responses to illumination of the surround have been thought to be mediated by horizontal cells.

surround (sə'raʊnd), *v.* Forms: 5 **sourround**, 5–6 **suround**, 5–7 **surund**, 6 **surrownd, surrunde**, 7 **sorround, sur-round, surhound**, (*pa. pple.* **surround**), 6– **surround**. [a. AF. *sur(o)under*, OF. *soronder*, *s(o)uronder* to overflow (trans. and intr.), *fig.* to abound, to surpass, also, to dominate, overlook = Pr. *sobrondar*:—late L. *superundāre* to overflow (fig.), f. *super* SUPER- 2 + *undāre* to rise in waves, f. *unda* wave.

The modern spelling was established before 1600; association of the word with *round* (quasi *sur-* + *round*) no doubt helped to fix the spelling with *rr*.]

I. 1. a. *trans.* To overflow, inundate, flood, submerge. *Obs.* exc. *dial.*

1444 *Rolls of Parlt.* V. 109/2 By grete creteyns of water, many Townes and Londes to grete quantite beth sourrounded. **1587** HOLINSHED *Chron.* III. 1537/2 The said pent being surrounded at euerie high water. **1609–10** *Act 7 Jas. I*, c. 20 §1 The Sea hath broken in..and hath decayed surrounded and drowned vp much hard Grounde. **1622** CALLIS *Stat. Sewers* (1647) 57 For suffering a Sewer..to be unrepaired, by reason whereof his grounds..were surrounded. **1631** *Star Chamber Cases* (Camden) 48 One complaining against another for letting downe a sea wall soe that not onely his but diverse other men's grounds were surrounded. **1877** S. B. J. SKERTCHLEY *Geol. of Fenland* ii. 17 In winter nearly all the peat-land was drowned, or as the old fen-men say 'surrounded'.

fig. **1624** SIR J. DAVIES *Psalm xviii*, Wks. (1869) I. 382 When..floods of wickednes did mee surhound. **1628** P. M. *Life Sejanus* 51 Seianus saw himselfe surrounded with a storme, in one of the fairest daies of his fortune. **1633** P. FLETCHER *Elisa* II. xxii, My heart, surround with grief, is swoln so high. **1634** W. TIRWHYT tr. *Balzac's Lett.* a 3 b, So surunded with the torrent of his Witt.

†**b.** *intr.* To overflow. *Obs. rare.*

1572 HULOET s.v., Nilus doth surrunde, ouerflowe or runne ouer. **1592** WARNER *Alb. Eng.* VIII. xli. (1612) 197 Streams, if stopt, surrownd. ?**1598** MARLOWE *Ovid's Elegies* III. v. 86 The waters more abounded: And from the channell all abroad surrounded. **1599** T. M[OUFET] *Silkwormes* 64 Lest outward moisture innly being got Surrounding, drownes the little infant-flye.

II. 2. a. To enclose, encompass, or beset on all sides; to stand, lie, or be situated around; also, to form the entourage of; often *pass.* const. *with* or *by* = to have on all sides or all round.

1616 BULLOKAR *Eng. Expos.*, *Surround*, to compasse round about. **1629** MILTON *Hymn Nativ.* xi, At last surrounds their sight A Globe of circular light. **1653** —— *Ps. vii.* 26 Th' assemblies of each Nation Will surround thee, seeking right. **1700** R. PEARSON *Naaman Vind.* 87 Thou wilt ..when thou awakest, find thy self sur-rounded with Devils and everlasting burnings. **1725** DE FOE *Voy. round World* (1840) 291 Stupendous precipices which surrounded us. **1726** SWIFT *Gulliver* III. ii, At my alighting, I was surrounded by a croud of people. **1771** *Junius Lett.* xlix. (1788) 267 He saw the throne already surrounded by men of virtue and abilities. **1794** MRS. RADCLIFFE *Myst. Udolpho* xxxi, The thick woods which surrounded them excluding all view of the country beyond. **1827** HALLAM *Const. Hist.* (1842) I. iii. 159 This neither suited the inclination of Elizabeth, nor of some among those who surrounded her. **1860** TYNDALL *Glac.* II. iii. 246 If the planet Neptune..be surrounded by an atmosphere. **1868** LOCKYER *Elem. Astron.* Introd. (1870) 1 The earth on which we live is..surrounded by stars on all sides.

b. Said of immaterial things, as conditions.

1639 G. DANIEL *Ecclus.* ix. 47 Thinke, without defence, Thou art Surround in danger. **1682** TATE *Abs. & Achit.* II. 188 A monarch's crown with fate surrounded lies. *a* **1771** GRAY *Amatory Lines* 1 With beauty, with pleasure surrounded. **1791** MRS. RADCLIFFE *Rom. Forest* ix, Recollect the dangers that surround you. **1891** FARRAR *Darkn. & Dawn* x, The dignities which surrounded her exalted rank. **1900** *Jrnl. Sch. Geog.* (U.S.) Apr. 126 The social conditions surrounding the individual.

c. *Mil.* To enclose (a place, or a body of troops) on all sides so as to cut off communication or retreat; to invest.

a **1649** WINTHROP *New Eng.* (1853) I. 279 Our men surrounded the swamp, being a mile about, and shot at the Indians. **1799** SHERIDAN *Pizarro* v. iv, Well! if surrounded, we must perish in the centre of them. **1802** JAMES *Milit. Dict.* s.v., A town is said to be surrounded when its principal outlets are blocked up.

3. To go or extend round (an object or body, a room, or the like); to encircle, as a frame, border, etc.

1688 HOLME *Armoury* II. iii. 57/1 He beareth Gules, a Garbe, Or, with an Adder..his head aloft, and the tail surrounding it. **1697** DRYDEN *Virg. Georg.* IV. 410 With sev'n-fold Horns mysterious Nile Surrounds the Skirts of Egypt's fruitful Isle. **1700** —— *Pygmalion* 48 An embroider'd Zone surrounds her slender Waste. **1774** GOLDSM. *Nat. Hist.* (1776) III. 81 A white list..at the bottom of the neck, which it entirely surrounds. **1821** SCOTT *Kenilw.* iv, Large oaken presses, filled with shelves of the same wood, surrounded the room. **1829** in *Encycl. Metrop.* (1845) VI. 237 A complete frame surrounding the aperture. **1886** C. E. PASCOE *Lond. To-day* xxv. (ed. 3) 237 The massive tomb of the Duke of Wellington,..with the names of his victories surrounding the base.

†**4.** To go or travel around; to make the circuit of, *esp.* to circumnavigate. *Obs.*

1638 SIR T. HERBERT *Trav.* (ed. 2) 16 Pharao Necho.. incouraged the Phœnicians (then, proud of their Art in Navigation) to surround Afrique. **1655** FULLER *Ch. Hist.* XI. vii. Ded., The ship called the Desire, wherein Captain Cavendish surrounded the world. **1719** DE FOE *Crusoe* II. (Globe) 375 When I was driven out to Sea..in my Attempt to surround the Island. **1727** —— *Syst. Magic* I. iv. (1840) 107 He surrounds the tree fifteen times. **1751** R. PALTOCK *P. Wilkins* (1884) I. 130 Though I had surrounded the whole lake, yet I had not traced the out-bounds of the wood next the rock. **1825** SCOTT *Talism.* iv, As a second time, in surrounding the chapel, they passed the spot on which he kneeled.

5. To cause to be encircled or enclosed *with* something.

1635 VALENTINE *Foure Sea-Serm.* 8 We that inhabite the Islands, which God hath moated about, and surrounded with a girdle of waters. **1653** MILTON *Ps. v.* 39 As with a shield thou wilt surround Him with thy lasting favour. **1847** C. BRONTË *J. Eyre* xxxv, He surrounded me with his arm, almost as if he loved me. **1848** W. K. KELLY tr. *L. Blanc's Hist. Ten Y.* II. 344 Was it possible that true republicans should ask of their party..to surround itself with all the appearances of fear? **1908** R. BAGOT *A. Cuthbert* ii. 9 Those mental and moral barriers with which the average Englishman surrounds himself.

III. 6. The verb-stem in Comb., as **surround sound, surround-sound,** any of various systems of stereophony involving three or more speakers surrounding the listener so as to give a more realistic effect; *esp.* a four-, five-, or six-speaker system employing signal matrixing, with the aim of reproducing the original front-to-back floor-to-ceiling, and side-to-side sound distribution. Also *attrib.*

1969 *High Fidelity Mag.* Sept. 63/1 Vanguard's initial offering in what it has termed 'Surround Sound' will include the Berlioz Requiem, which calls for four brass bands to be spread around the cardinal points of the hall. **1974** *Nature* 13 Dec. 535/2 The present upsurge of interest in surround-sound was in some measure triggered by engineers and producers playing back such four-track material directly into four amplifiers and loudspeakers distributed approximately in a square near to the corners of the monitor room. **1978** *Broadcast* 6 Mar. 18/3 In radio, engineers are experimenting with surround sound systems as the next step forward from stereophonic sound. **1981** *Hi-Fi Answers* May 58/1 Efforts were made in the mid seventies to market a system of surround sound which went by the name of quadraphonics. **1983** *Listener* 19 May 34/1 It can create a remarkable surround-sound effect.

surrounded (səˈraʊndɪd), *ppl. a.* [f. SURROUND *v.* + -ED[1].]

†**1.** Overflowed, flooded. *Obs.*

c **1586** C'TESS PEMBROKE *Ps.* LXXVIII. xvii, Those surrounded lands, Saw watry clearnes chang'd to bloudy gore. **1610** FOLKINGHAM *Feudigr.* I. ix. 20 Surrounded grounds may be won by Sewing them with competent Draines. *c* **1682** J. COLLINS *Salt & Fishery* 23 The surrounded Level at Erith hath been..commended for its fertility.

2. Encompassed, encircled: chiefly in *comb.*

1891 HARDY *Tess* xxv, His father's hill-surrounded little town.

†**surrounder**[1]. *Obs. rare*$^{-1}$. [a. AF. *surounder*, inf. used subst.; see SURROUND *v.* and -ER[4].] Overflow, inundation.

1622 CALLIS *Stat. Sewers* (1647) 83 What grounds lye within the..danger of waters either within the surrounder by the sea, or the inundation of the fresh waters.

surrounder[2] (səˈraʊndə(r)). [f. SURROUND *v.* + -ER[1].] One who or that which surrounds.

1683 KENNETT tr. *Erasm. on Folly* 92 They fence themselves in with so many surrounders [orig. *tanto agmine*] of Magisterial Definitions. **1789** MME. D'ARBLAY *Diary* 18 Jan., I had no plan but to save appearances to the surrounders. **1829** NAPIER *Penins. War* VII. iii. (Rtldg.) I. 345 The troops to be surrounded were more..numerous than the surrounders. **1830** W. TAYLOR *Hist. Surv. Germ. Poetry* II. 1 Some poets may learn of their ordinary surrounders. **1890** GUNTER *Miss Nobody* ii. (1891) 23 'Not play in it!' cry several of his surrounders.

surrounding (səˈraʊndɪŋ), *vbl. sb.* [-ING[1].]

I. The action of the verb SURROUND.

†**1.** Overflowing, inundation. *Obs.*

1449 in Fulman *Rerum Anglic. Script. Vett.* (1684) I. 524 Because of surundyng of waters. **1572** HULOET, Surrunding, or ouerflowing of water.

2. The fact of being around or encompassing *rare*$^{-0}$.

1775 in ASH.

II. That which surrounds.

3. *pl.* Those things which surround a person or thing, or in the midst of which he or it (habitually) is; things around (collectively); environment.

1861 *Q. Rev.* Oct. 471 We know more about Plutarch's personal history and surroundings [etc.]. **1861** SMILES *Engineers* VI. i. II. 6 The place remained comparatively rural in point of size and surroundings. **1873** HAMERTON *Intell. Life* XII. i (1876) 431 That which we are, is due to the accidents of our surroundings. **1884** F. TEMPLE *Relat. Relig. & Sci.* iii. (1885) 81 My character..has not come out of the antecedents and surroundings according to any fixed law. **1891** FARRAR *Darkn. & Dawn* lxii, We cannot blame him too severely if, in such an age and such surroundings, he had been stained by the vices in the midst of which he lived.

4. A number of persons standing around; a body of attendants; entourage.

1877 FROUDE *Short Stud.* (1883) IV. I. ii. 22 The wealthiest peer in England did not..appear in public with a more princely surrounding. **1891** *Daily News* 22 Jan. 3/4 Their games were watched with much interest by a surrounding of Southerns.

b. *pl.* Persons surrounding or attending upon a person.

1894 *Daily News* 31 Dec., I have now received particulars of the death from the immediate surroundings of the King. **1907** *Verney Mem.* I. 118 They lived on their estates and did their duty by their surroundings.

suˈrrounding, *ppl. a.* [-ING[2].] That surrounds.

1. That is (or are) around; encompassing, circumjacent.

1634 MILTON *Comus* 403 And let a single helpless maiden pass Uninjur'd in this wilde surrounding wast. **1667** —— *P.L.* I. 346 Twixt upper, nether, and surrounding Fires. **1704** POPE *Windsor For.* 262 The bow'ry mazes, and surrounding greens. **1781** COWPER *Hope* 305 Lord paramount of the surrounding plains. **1794** MRS. RADCLIFFE *Myst. Udolpho* i, The beauty of the surrounding scene. **1806** A. HUNTER *Culina* (ed. 3) 197 Serve up in a deep dish, with the surrounding sauce. **1828–43** TYTLER *Hist. Scot.* (1864) I. 138 They ravaged the surrounding country with merciless execution. **1845** STOCQUELER *Handbk Brit. India* (1854) 3 Venice..raised herself..to an eminence that excited the jealousy..of surrounding nations. **1890** *Science-Gossip* XXVI. 209 The ammonia is rapidly oxidised in the soil into nitric acid, which at once combines with the surrounding bases to form nitrates.

†**2.** Moving round, circling. *Obs. rare*$^{-1}$.

1657 S. PURCHAS *Pol. Flying-Ins.* 16 They will expatiate and dance the Hay in circling motions, and surrounding vagaries.

†**suˈrroundry.** *Obs. rare.* [f. SURROUND *v.* + -RY.] Surrounding boundary, circuit, compass.

1621 BP. MOUNTAGU *Diatribæ* 128 Doe wee not know he cannot trauell ouer all this Iland, within the surroundry of the foure Seas? *a* **1641** —— *Acts & Mon.* i. (1642) 71 Shut up within surroundry of no one Country.

†**Surroy.** *Obs.* [Assimilated f. *suthroy (see SOUTH and ROY *sb.*[1]), after *norroy*.] The second King-of-Arms in England, having jurisdiction south of the Trent; also (now only) called CLARENCEUX.

1671 E. CHAMBERLAYNE *Pres. St. Eng.* II. (ed. 5) 268 Clarencieux..His Office is to marshal and dispose the Funerals of all the lower Nobility, as Baronets, Knights, Esquires, and Gentlemen on the South-side of Trent, and therefore sometimes called *Surroy* or *Southroy*.

surroy, obs. form of SERAI[1].

1612 COVERTE *True Rep.* 32 The City of Gorra, where are many Surroyes, or Innes. **1615** tr. *De Monfart's Surv. E. Indies* 8 Huge lodgings (like hamlets) called Caravan-sara, or Surroyes, for the benefit of Caravanes.

surroyal (ˈsɜːrɔɪəl). *Venery.* Forms: 4 **surryal,** 5 **surereall, sureale, surriall,** 7 **surroyall, surroial,** 7– **surroyal, sur-royal.** [f. SUR- + ROYAL *sb.* (REAL *sb.*[1]).] An upper or terminal branch of a stag's antler, above that called 'royal' (ROYAL B. 3). Also *attrib.*

a **1400** *Parlt. 3 Ages* 30 The ryalls full richely raughten frome the myddes With surryals full semely appon sydes twayne. *c* **1410** *Master of Game* (MS. Digby 182) xxiv, Auntelere and ryall and surereall. *Ibid.* xxxiii, Bitwene þe sureale and þe fourche or troche. **1576** TURBERVILE *Venery* xxi. 54 The Burre..Antlier..Surantlier... All the rest which growe afterwardes, vntill you come to the crowne, palme, or croche, are called Royals & Surroyals. **1630** J. TAYLOR (Water P.) *Navy Land Ships* Wks. I. 93/1. **1638** GUILLIM *Heraldry* III. xiv. (ed. 3) 179 Skilfull Wood-men describing the head of a Hart, doe call the..Vpper part of all The..Surroyall Toppe. **1883** *Science* I. 181/2 The 'royal' and 'sur-royal' of the Wapiti. **1893** LYDEKKER *Horns & Hoofs* 271 The portion above the trez-tine..carrying the surroyals.

surrugin, -yen, obs. Sc. ff. SURGEON.

surrunde, obs. form of SURROUND.

surryph, variant of SERIF.

surs, obs. form of SOURCE.

†**sursanure.** *Obs. rare.* [a. AF., OF. *sursanure* cicatrice, f. *sur-* (= SUPER- 3) + *sanure, seneure, or OF. *soursané* pa. pple. healed over: see SUR-, SANE *v.*, -URE, and cf. Pr. *sobresanar* to form a scar.] The healing over of a wound; a wound healed outwardly or superficially.

c **1386** CHAUCER *Frankl. T.* 385 Wel ye knowe that of a Sursanure In Surgerye is perilous the cure But men myghte touche the Arwe or come thereby. *c* **1400** LYDG. *Flower of Curtesye* 75 My wounde abydeth lyk a sursanure.

sursarara, obs. corruption of CERTIORARI: see SISERARY.

1617 J. TAYLOR (Water P.) *Trav. Hamburgh* Wks. 1630 I. 84/1 Sursararaes, Procedendoes.

sursassite (ˈsɜːsəsaɪt). *Min.* [ad. G. *sursassit* (J. Jakob 1926, in *Schweiz. Min. und Petrogr. Mitt.* VI. 376), f. *Sursass*, name of the Oberhalbstein region in the Rhaeto-Romance dialect: see -ITE[1].] A hydrated silicate of manganese and aluminium, found as tufts and radial aggregates of reddish brown or yellow monoclinic crystals.

1928 *Chem. Abstr.* XXII. 45 (*heading*) Sursassite, a manganese silicate from Val d'Err. **1964** *Amer. Mineralogist* XLIX. 168 Various chemical formulae have been proposed for sursassite. **1973** *Mineral. Rec.* IV. 290/1 Recently braunite..and sursassite..have been found in Palos Verdes Hills, Los Angeles County, California... The only other occurrence of sursassite known in North America is in New Brunswick..Maine.

†**sursault,** *sb. Obs. rare.* Also 4 **sursaute,** 5 **soursaut.** [a. AF. *sursaut*, OF. *soursaut, -sault*, f. *sur-* = SUPER- 2 + *saut* leap (:—L. *saltu-s*).]

a. *a sursaut*: of a sudden.

1338 R. BRUNNE *Chron.* (1810) 337 Sursante [? *read* A sursaute; LANGTOFT *A sursaut*] he þam mette, als þei fro kirke cam. *c* **1430** *Pilgr. Lyf Manhode* IV. lxii. (1869) 205 Whan..j..hadde leyn þere a while, sodeynliche and a soursaut j sigh an old oon þat was clumben anhy vp on my bed.

b. A start.

1598 YONG *Diana* 71 With a sudden sursault she awaked. Hence † **sur'sault** *v. trans.*, to attack suddenly. **1598** YONG *Diana* 81 An enamoured hart may be as well sursaulted with a sudden ioy, as with an vnexpected sorrow. **1600** —— in *Eng. Helicon* T j b, My hart, sursaulted with the fill Of thousand great vnrests, and thousand feares.

surseace, -sease, obs. forms of SURCEASE.

† **surseance.** *Obs.* Also 6 -seaunce, -ceaunce, -ceyance, 6–7 -ceance. [a. OF. *surseance*, *-ceance*, *-coyance* (mod.F. *surséance*), f. *surseoir*: see SURCEASE and -ANCE.] (A) cessation or suspension (*of* hostilities).

1523 *St. Papers Hen. VIII*, IV. 72 If he woll not accept the surseaunce of warre. *a* **1548** HALL *Chron., Hen. VIII*, 249 Beyng at the same tyme a surceaunce made on bothe sides. **1579** FENTON *Guicciard.* XVIII. 1037 A surseance of armes to thend to giue sufferance and tyme to treate a peace. *a* **1648** LD. HERBERT *Hen. VIII* (1683) 601 A Surseance of War for five or six days was concluded.

sursengle, surserare, sursese, obs. ff. SURCINGLE, SISERARY, SURCEASE.

† **sur-sharp.** *Mus. Obs.* [f. SUR- + SHARP, rendering med.L. *superacūta*: see SUPERACUTE.] The highest note of the gamut.

1801 BUSBY *Dict. Mus.* s.v. *System*, A fifth tetrachord above, or tetrachord of the sur-sharp.

sursingle, obs. form of SURCINGLE.

† **sursise.** *Obs.* Also 9 (*Hist.*) sursize. [a. AF. *sursise* (cf. med.L. *sursisa*, *supersisa*) negligence, delay, ? hence, penalty for this, vbl. sb. fem. f. *surseoir*:—L. *supersedēre* to SUPERSEDE.] A penalty formerly exacted at Dover for failure to pay the castle-guard rent.

1540 *Act 32 Hen. VIII*, c. 48 §1 Greate penalities and forfaictures comonlye callid in the said Castell of Dovorr Sursises. **1570–6** LAMBARDE *Peramb. Kent* (1826) 141. **1876** *Encycl. Brit.* V. 198/2.

† **sursolid**, *sb.* and *a.* *Math. Obs.* [app. etymologizing alteration of SURDESOLID, by reference to SUR- *prefix*; *surd-solid* was app. an intermediate form. Cf. F. *sursolide*, It. *soprasolido*.]

A. *sb.* The fifth power of a number or quantity; also, an equation of the fifth degree.

Also extended to higher uneven powers, not being multiples of 2 or 3: see quot. 1700.

1557 RECORDE *Whetst.* G iij b, .4. multiplications doe yelde a sursolide. **1613** TAPP *Pathw. Knowledge* 295 If the quantity be sursolids and the number 1024, then is the sursolid roote thereof 4. **1672** GREGORY in Rigaud *Corr. Sci. Men* (1841) II. 230 One which will serve for all cubic equations, another for all biquadratics, another for all sursolids. **1695** J. WALLIS in *Phil. Trans.* XIX. 3 If we would Extract the Root of an imperfect Sursolid. **1700** MOXON *Math. Dict.* (1701) s.v., 32 is the 5th power of 2, and is called the Sursolid..128 the 7th power, or the second Sursolid. **1806** ROBERTSON in *Phil. Trans.* XCVI. 310 A sursolid, or an equation of five dimensions. **1817** H. T. COLEBROOKE *Algebra*, etc. 140 First the highest power, for example the sursolid; then the next, the biquadrate; after it the cube, &c.

B. *adj.* Of the fifth degree; that is a fifth power or root; involving the fifth power of a quantity.

Also applied to a problem, etc. involving expressions or magnitudes of higher degree than that called 'solid' (cf. quot. 1704 s.v. SOLID *a.* 2 c), and to loci of a higher degree than those termed 'solid' (see quot. 1726 s.v. SURDESOLID).

1557 RECORDE *Whetst.* G iv, That roote is a Sursolide roote, that yeldeth a Sursolide nomber. **1672** GREGORY in Rigaud *Corr. Sci. Men* (1841) II. 230 A sursolid equation. **1704** J. HARRIS *Lex. Techn.* I, *Sursolid-Problem*..is that which cannot be resolved, but by Curves of a higher nature than Conick-Sections. *Ibid.*, *Place Sursolid*, is when the Point is in the Circumference of a Curve of an higher Gender than the Conick Sections. [Cf. PLACE *sb.* 8 b.] **1706** J. WARD *Introd. Math.* I. xi. (1713) 135 To Extract the Sursolid Root.

sursum- (sɜːsəm-), formative element [f. L. *sursum* from below, up] used in terms in *Ophthalm.*, as **sursum'duction** [a. F. *sursumduction* (G. T. Stevens 1886, in *Arch. d'Ophtalm.* VI. 545): see DUCTION], vertical movement upwards of one eye alone; the degree to which this action occurs; **sursum'vergence** [L. *vergentia* (f. *vergere* to bend, turn): see -ENCE], the simultaneous movement of one eye upwards and the other downwards, classified as *left* or *right* according to which eye moves upward; the degree to which this motion occurs; **sursum'version** [L. *version-em*, f. *vertere* to turn: see -ION], the parallel upward movement of both eyes.

1893 G. E. DE SCHWEINITZ *Dis. Eye* ii. 76 *Sursumduction, or the power of uniting the image of the candle flame, seen through a prism placed with its base downward before one eye, with the image of the same object as seen by the other eye, is ascertained by beginning the trial with a weak prism..and gradually increasing its strength. **1949** W. S. DUKE-ELDER *Text-bk. Ophthalm.* IV. xlv. 3814 Depending on whether the [eye] movement is in, out, up or down, the terms adduction, abduction, supraduction (sursumduction) and infraduction (deorsumduction) are employed. **1975** M. M. PARKS *Ocular Motility & Strabismus* xviii. 149/1 Dissociated double hyper-deviation is synonymous with alternating sursumduction which describes the upturning movement of each eye as the cover-uncover test is performed. **1897** A. DUANE *New Classification of Motor Anomalies of Eye* 38 The *sursumvergence, i.e., the amount by which the eyes can diverge in a vertical plane, is determined by the strength of prism placed up or down before the eyes, which the latter can overcome when looking at a distant object. **1962** H. W. BROWN in G. M. Haik *Strabismus* (Symposium N. Orleans Acad. Ophthalm.) xii. 243 The normal limits of sursumvergence are small. **1974** BURIAN & VON NOORDEN *Binocular Vision & Ocular Motility* xiii. 207/2 In some texts the normal limits for distance fixation are given as..3Δ to 4Δ for sursumvergence and deorsumvergence. **1897** A. DUANE *New Classification of Motor Anomalies of Eye* 68 Explanation of the conditions..may be had by assuming a weakness of deorsumversion in the former case and of *sursumversion in the latter. **1975** M. M. PARKS *Ocular Motility & Strabismus* ii. 14/2 Vertical versions are supraversion (sursumversion) and infraversion (deorsumversion).

Sursum corda ('sɜːsəm kɔːdə). [L. *sursum* upwards + *corda*, pl. of *cor* heart.] In Latin Eucharistic liturgies, the words addressed by the celebrant to the congregation at the beginning of the Eucharistic Prayer; in English rites, the corresponding versicle, 'Lift up your hearts'. Also *transf.* and *attrib.*

1559 T. BECON *Displaying of Popishe Masse* in *Works* (1563) III. 41 b Before it was *Sursum Corda*, Lift vp your hearts vnto the Lord, but now is *Sursum Capita*, come in, Lift up your heads. **1744** [see ANAPHORA 2]. **1837** J. ROMILLY *Diary* 2 Nov. (1967) 133 Crick made a long dull oration ending with 'Sursum corda'. **1889** H. M. LUCKOCK *Div. Liturgy* xxi. 176 The Gallican was almost alone among the ancient Liturgies in placing the prayers for the Church before the *Sursum Corda* ('Lift up your hearts'), which commenced the more sacred part, the Anaphora in the East, the Canon in the West. **1917** *Daily Chron.* 2 July 2/6 A fine speech ended finely on the sursum corda note. **1934** S. BECKETT *More Pricks than Kicks* 31 That..is where I have sursum corda. **1955** W. GADDIS *Recognitions* II. i. 332 Thus called upon, he took courage: the sursum corda of an extravagant belch straightened him upright. **1971** N. FREELING *Over High Side* I. 6 Oranges..smelt, like everything else, of plastic... Sursum corda, thought Van der Valk; get up off the floor.

sursurrara, obs. corruption of CERTIORARI: see SISERARY.

sursyngle, obs. form of SURCINGLE.

surtax ('sɜːtæks), *sb.* [ad. F. *surtaxe*: see SUR- and TAX *sb.*] An additional or extra tax on something already taxed. *spec.*, an additional income tax at higher rates charged on personal incomes above a certain value; = *super-tax* sb. s.v. SUPER- 13. Also *attrib.*

A surtax on personal income was introduced in the U.S. in 1913. In the U.K. the designation *surtax* officially replaced *super-tax* in 1929; this tax was abolished in 1973 when a new graduated system of income tax was established.

1881 *Leeds Mercury* 6 Apr., The reduction of the surtax on foreign spirits. **1888** *Pall Mall G.* 24 Apr. 12/1 Champagne wine in the ordinary magnums, bottles, pints, and half pints will pay with duty and surtax 3*s.* 6*d.* per gallon. **1902** *Spectator* 2 Aug. 137/1 The local Treasuries are to receive a surtax upon the Customs. **1916** *Yale Law Jrnl.* Apr. 427 The Tariff Act of 1913..provides for levying, assessing and collecting an additional income tax. This additional tax is commonly known as a 'surtax'. **1927** *Rep. Comm. Nat. Debt & Taxation* 416 in *Parl. Papers* (Cmd. 2800) XI. 371 In view..of the already complicated character of the present Income Tax and Super-tax,..we think it might be found convenient to raise the additional revenue..by the introduction of a special graduated Sur-tax applicable to investment income alone. **1940** *Economist* 20 Apr. 718/2 The average surtax-payer will have about £2,650 left. **1954** *U.S. News & World Rep.* 19 Mar. 102/3 Other changes..are provided in the massive tax bill. The normal tax and the surtax on personal income are combined. **1970** *Money Which?* Mar. 4/1 The Surtax Office will work out how much surtax you have to pay, on the basis of the information you give your Tax Inspector for income tax. **1978** *Daily Tel.* 12 May 2/4 The amendment..raised the point at which 'surtax' starts from £7,000 to £8,000 of taxable income.

So '**surtax** *v. trans.*, to tax additionally, charge with a surtax.

1906 C. BIGG *Wayside Sk. Eccl. Hist.* v. 126 *note*, What we call Socialism now appears to be merely the right of the poor to surtax the rich. **1934** G. B. SHAW *On Rocks* II. 237, I shall get three and a half per cent..and on that..I shall be income-taxed and surtaxed. **1950** —— *Farfetched Fables* 96 To substitute cost-of-production prices..for prices loaded with enormous rents for the proprietors of London land and Seaham mines, not equivalently surtaxed.

surte, -tee, -tey, -tie, obs. forms of SURETY.

surtout (sɜː'tuːt, sɜː'tuː). Also 7 sur-toute, 7–8 sur-tout, (8 surtoot, -toit (?), sourtoot, suttout (?), 9 surtoo). [a. F. *surtout*, f. *sur* above + *tout* everything.] A man's great-coat or overcoat.

Applied *c* 1870 to a kind of single-breasted frock-coat with pockets cut diagonally in front.

1686 *Lond. Gaz.* No. 2108/4 A white Surtout lin'd with black. **1693** DRYDEN *Juvenal* iii. 250 The torn Surtout and the tatter'd Vest. *a* **1700** B. E. *Dict. Cant. Crew*, *Surtout*, a loose, great, or riding Coat. **1712** ARBUTHNOT *John Bull* II. iv, He was forced constantly to wear a surtout of oiled cloth, by which means he came home pretty clean. **1731** SWIFT *Answ. Simile* 140 And since we find you walk a-foot, We'll soundly souce your frize surtout. **1788** BURNS *Extempore on W. Smellie* 2 The old cock'd hat, the grey surtout. **1800** WEEMS *Washington* x. (1877) 113 With a surtout over his regimentals. **1840** BARHAM *Ingol. Leg.* Ser. I. *Tragedy*, He put on his *surtout*, And went to a man with a beard like a Jew. **1840** DICKENS *Old C. Shop* xi, He wore a long black surtout reaching nearly to his ancles. **1843** LYTTON *Last Bar.* IV. v, A green surtout of broad cloth over a tight vest of the same colour. **1858** MRS. OLIPHANT *Laird of Norlaw* II. 39 The new coat which his mother called a surtoo. **1870** DICKENS *E. Drood* xviii, Being buttoned up in a tightish blue surtout, with a buff waistcoat and gray trousers. **1894** CROCKETT *Raiders* (ed. 3) 160 He was wont to take off his loose surtout and travel in his sleeved waistcoat.

attrib. **1686** *Lond. Gaz.* No. 2106/4 A new Red Coat lin'd with a Buff-colour'd lining, surtout Sleeves. **1687** *Ibid.* No. 2236/4 A light-colour'd..Sur-toute Coat. **1703** *Ibid.* No. 3957/4 A Cynnamon-colour Surtoit Coat with black Buttons. **1710** *Ibid.* No. 4739/4 A dark Suttout Coat. **1759** *Phil. Trans.* LI. 289 The velvet cape of a surtout coat.

† **b.** A hood (with a mantle), worn by women.

1690 EVELYN *Mundus Muliebris* 130 Pins..By which the curls are fastened, In radiant firmament set-out, And over all the hood sur-tout. **1694** N. H. *Ladies Dict.* 11/2 A *Surtout*, is a Night-Hood, which goes over, or covers the rest of the head geer. **1721** RAMSAY *Tartana* 124 The Hood and Mantle make the tender faint; I'm pain'd to see them moving like a tent..But know each fair who shall this Surtout use, You're no more Scots. **1785** G. A. BELLAMY *Apol.* (ed. 3) I. 109 My mother had prudently provided herself with a good surtout.

† **c.** *fig.* An outer covering or integument. *Obs.*

1732 *Hist. Litteraria* IV. 167 The different sorts of Fruit, ..some having a Surtout of a harder Texture, and some softer. **1771** BARRINGTON in *Phil. Trans.* LXV. 13 This upper..coat is composed also of hairs which are white from the top to the root, and form the winter surtout for the animal.

† **d.** *Cookery.* Applied to various fancy dishes.

1706 PHILLIPS (ed. Kersey), *Surtout*, a Term in the Confectioners Art; as Pistachoes in Surtout... Also a Term in Cookery, as Pigeons dress'd in Surtout. **1743** *Lady's Companion* (ed. 4) I. 183 A Surtout of Soals.

† **sur'tray**, *v.* *Obs.* *rare*$^{-1}$. [a. AF. **surtraire*, (cf. OF. *sourtraire* to seduce), used for *s(o)ustraire*, ad. L. *substrahēre* to SUBSTRACT.] *trans.* To draw off, take away, subtract. So † **surtrete** *v.*

c **1440** *Pallad. on Husb.* III. 1097 A skep of palm thenne after to surtray is This wyn. *Ibid.* IV. 460 Heer & ther the drie awey surtrete. *Ibid.* X. 208 Surtrete hem first and after multiplie.

‖ **surturbrand** ('sɜːtɜːbrænd). Also 8 *erron.* sutur-, sortebrand. [a. G. *surturbrand*, ad. Icel. *surtarbrandr*, f. *Surtar*, gen. of *Surtr* (related to *svartr* SWART *a.*) name of a fire-giant + *brandr* BRAND *sb.*] A name for lignite as occurring in Iceland.

1760 MILLES in *Phil. Trans.* LI. 545 An extraordinary sort of wood, which they call sortebrand, or black brand. **1780** VON TROIL *Iceland* 42, I have seen tea-cups, plates, &c. in Copenhagen made of suturbrand, which takes a fine polish. **1804** *Phil. Trans.* XCIV. 397 The Bovey coal is found in strata, corresponding in almost every particular with those of the surturbrand in Iceland. **1863** BARING-GOULD *Iceland* p. xxiv, The alternation of basalt and surturbrand.

surty, obs. form of SURETY.

‖ **surucucu** (suruku'ku). Also **sirocucu**, **surukuku.** [a. Tupi *surucucú*.] A large, venomous pit viper, *Lachesis muta*, native to tropical America and distinguished by black bands and blotches on a reddish-yellow skin; = *bush-master* s.v. BUSH *sb.*[1] 11.

1845 *Encycl. Metrop.* XXV. 775/2 *Surukuku*,..probably the *Boschmeester*, or *Coenicoussi*, of the inhabitants of Surinam. **1910** R. L. DITMARS *Reptiles of World* IV. 339 This terrible creature is known under several titles—the Sirocucu, the Mapepire and the Bushmaster. **1967** *Times* 23 Nov. 10/7 The Indian girl..heard a surucucu coming through the undergrowth. It's the biggest poisonous snake in Brazil, and really very dangerous because it's aggressive.

† **surundacion.** *Obs.* *rare*$^{-0}$. [f. *surund*, SURROUND + -ATION, after *inundation*.] Flooding.

1552 HULOET, Surundacion, *alluuies*,..*inundatio*.

survear, -veior, etc., obs. ff. SURVEYOR.

surveigh, obs. form of SURVEY.

surveil (sə'veɪl), *v.* Also **surveille.** [Back-formation from SURVEILLANCE.] *trans.* To exercise surveillance over (someone), subject (someone) to surveillance. Also with a place or area as obj., and *absol.* Hence **sur'veilled** *ppl. a.*, **sur'veilling** *vbl. sb.*

1960 *Federal Suppl.* (U.S.) CLXXXII. 750/1 The plaintiff also stresses that the store as a whole, and the customer exits especially, were closely surveilled. **1966** *Harper's Mag.* Oct. 37/1 If the U.S. Central Intelligence Agency is as adroit in surveilling others as it is in escaping surveillance of itself, the Republic can relax. **1968** *Guardian* 6 Aug. 4/1 It was some time before I was being surveilled..with the full courtesy of a Home Office warrant. **1969** *New Scientist* 10 July 10/1 Night surveilling systems for railway marshalling yards. **1972** B. F. CONNERS *Don't embarrass Bureau* II. 123 'You'll have to conduct the surveillance.' ..'I'm supposed to surveil her?' 'That's right.' **1975** O. SELA *Bengali Inheritance* xix. 169 'Where the hell is everybody?'..'Out... Surveilling. Big emergency.' **1980** N. FREELING *Castang's City* xvii. 111 A few hints are conveyed by the word 'light'. Not around twenty-four hours: that's 'intense' and needs three separate shifts... Light means not leaning on people: the surveilled aren't supposed to notice.

surveillance, (sɜːˈveɪləns, -ljəns, səˈveɪ(j)əns, F. syrvɛjɑ̃s). [ad. F. *surveillance*, n. of action f. *surveiller*: see next and -ANCE.] **a.** Watch or guard kept over a person, etc., esp. over a suspected person, a prisoner, or the like; often, spying, supervision; less commonly, supervision for the purpose of direction or control, superintendence.

[**1799** *Monthly Rev.* XXX. 578 Vast *depôts* of..property ..in the rooms belonging to the office of the committee of *Surveillance.*] **1802** LEMAISTRE *Rough Sk. Mod. Paris* xxix. 236 They are kept under the constant 'surveillance of the police.' [*Note, Surveillance*, Watch, or special care.] **1815** J. W. CROKER in *Croker Papers* 19 July (1884) I. 67 General Becker—the officer who was charged with the surveillance of Buonaparte. **1825** T. HOOK *Sayings* Ser. II. *Man Many Fr.* (Colburn) 84 A tour under the *surveillance* of a tutor. **1834** MARRYAT *P. Simple* xx, Not to allow parole or permission to leave the fortress, even under surveillance. **1853** HUMPHREYS *Coin-coll. Man.* xxii. (1876) 301 The copper [coinage] remained under the surveillance of the Senate. **1882** J. C. MORISON *Macaulay* i. 6 No Puritanic surveillance directed his choice of books. **1884** *Manch. Exam.* 2 May 4/7 He says that Portugal will carry out the provisions of the Treaty under the surveillance of England.

b. *attrib.*, esp. of devices, vessels, etc., used in military or police surveillance.

1947 *Aviation* Feb. 83/3 It recommended that surveillance radar be developed as an adjunct to airport traffic control... Surveillance radar could be used by control tower personnel to..locate planes [etc.]. **1958** *Times* 24 July 9/6 New methods of detection by surveillance drones, airborne and ground radar, [etc.]. **1960** *Signal* Mar. 41/1 BMEWS will have a long-range surveillance radar system which reportedly will detect ICBM's as they rise over the horizon at distances of several thousand miles. **1966** M. WOODHOUSE *Tree Frog* viii. 63 The Americans are putting up about one new surveillance satellite every fifteen days or so. **1968** *Globe & Mail* (Toronto) 3 Feb. 9/6 The USS Pueblo, the electronic surveillance ship seized by North Korea. **1975** D. PITTS *Target Manhattan* (1976) ii. 262 He switched on the surveillance cameras and looked at the street. **1976** *Honolulu Star-Bull.* 21 Dec. B-6/1 He was on a surveillance team which saw Scanlan and Maiava meet with the informer on different occasions. **1980** *Globe & Laurel* July/Aug. 199/2 Its initial appearance took E Coy —on surveillance duty—completely by surprise.

surveillant (sɜːˈveɪlənt, -ljənt, səˈveɪ(j)ənt, F. syrvɛjɑ̃), *sb.* [ad. F. *surveillant*, pr. pple. (used subst.) of *surveiller*, f. *sur-* above, over + *veiller* (:—L. *vigilāre*) to watch.] One who exercises surveillance; a person who keeps watch over another or others; a superintendent, e.g. of a prison.

1819 B. E. O'MEARA *Exp. Trans. St. Helena* 76 Lieutenant Jackson of the Staff corps, who had been previously employed as the surveillant of General Gourgaud. **1837** DE QUINCEY *Rev. Tartars* Wks. 1854 IV. 134 His mixed character of ambassador and of political *surveillant*..gave him a real weight in the Tartar councils. **1901** *Daily Express* 18 Mar. 7/1, I got through the day..yarning with the surveillants and the convicts. **1905** MRS. C. N. WILLIAMSON *Castle of Shadows* vii. 161 White-clad surveillants with revolvers on their hips.

surˈveillant, *a. rare.* [ad. F. *surveillant* (see prec.).] Exercising surveillance.

1841 *Fraser's Mag.* XXIV. 29 At Whiggery's kibes sneaks the surveillant tail-er. **1882** in OGILVIE.

†**survenant.** *Obs. rare*⁻¹. [a. OF. *survenant*, pr. pple. of *survenir*: see next.] One who comes up, or to a place; a comer.

c **1400** tr. *Secr. Secr., Gov. Lordsh.* 103 Þat his court be opyn to all suruenantz.

†**survene**, *v. Obs.* [f. after SUPERVENE by substitution of prefix SUR-. Cf. F. *survenir*.]

1. *intr.* = SUPERVENE 1.

1666 G. HARVEY *Morb. Angl.* xxx. (1672) 87 Such a sputation survening upon it proves more perilous than otherwise. **1678** —— (*title*) Casus Medico-Chirurgicus: Or, A most Memorable Case of a Noble-Man, Deceased. Wherein is shewed, His Lordship's Wound, the various Diseases survening, &c.

b. To come upon some one, arrive suddenly or unexpectedly. *nonce-use.*

1716 M. DAVIES *Athen. Brit.* III. 77 Their Master Blondel survening, and subunderstanding it.

2. *trans.* = SUPERVENE 2.

1665 G. HARVEY *Advice agst. Plague* 1 Plagues do ordinarily survene great Inundations. **1666** —— *Morb. Angl.* iv. 42 Those evil accidents, that survene an Hypochondriack Melancholy.

So †**surˈvenient** *a.* = SUPERVENIENT.

1677 CARY *Palæol. Chron.* Pref. p. iv, The which Design ..came in process of time to be quickned by a sur-venient occasion from some Learned Gentlemen of my Acquaintance.

†**survenue.** *Obs. rare*⁻¹. [ad. F. *survenue*, n. of action f. *survenir*: see SUPERVENE and cf. VENUE.] A later or subsequent arrival.

1651 N. BACON *Disc. Govt. Eng.* II. xlii. 110 Nor did the fundamentals alter..by the..mixture of people of severall Nations in the first entrance, nor from the Danes or Normans in their survenue.

survew, -vewe, obs. forms of SURVIEW.

survey (ˈsɜːveɪ, səˈveɪ), *sb.* Also 6–7 **-vay, -veigh,** 7 **servey.** [f. next.] The action, or an act, of surveying; the object or result of this.

1. a. The act of viewing, examining, or inspecting in detail, esp. for some specific purpose; usually *spec.* a formal or official inspection of the particulars of something, *e.g.* of an estate, of a ship or its stores, of the administration of an office, etc.

1548 in *Eng. Gilds* (1870) 203 The Certyfycath of the Suruey of alle the late Colagys, Chauntryes, [etc.]. *a* **1570** in Feuillerat *Revels Q. Eliz.* (1908) 407 Vpon which survey it will appere where and in whome the abuse is. **1596** BACON *Max. & Use Com. Law* II (1630) 7 A Court, whereunto the people of euery Hundred should be assembled twice a yeare for surueigh of Pledges. **1719** DE FOE *Crusoe* I. (Globe) 83 Having perceiv'd my Bread had been low a great while, now I took a Survey of it, and reduc'd myself to one Bisket-cake a Day. **1763** *Brit. Mag.* IV. 175 Compounders neglecting to ..pay their composition-money, shall be charged with the duty, and become liable to a survey. **1769** FALCONER *Dict. Marine* (1780), *Survey*, an examination made by several naval officers into the state or condition of the provisions, or stores belonging to a ship, or fleet of men of war. **1772** *Jacob's Law Dict.* (ed. 9) s.v., On the falling of an estate to a new lord,..a court of survey is generally held. **1800** COLQUHOUN *Comm. Thames* vi. 237 The Regular Perambulations of the Police Boats in their daily and nightly surveys of the River. **1802** in East *Rep. Cases Crt. K.B* (1808) IV. 590 He had had a survey on her [*sc.* the ship] on account of her bad character. **1855** LEIFCHILD *Cornwall* 145 Each gang of men accustomed to work together, selects one of their number to represent and act for them on the day appointed for the 'setting or 'survey'. **1868** E. EDWARDS *Ralegh* I. xxv. 597 James now directed a minute survey of that portion of Ralegh's fleet.

b. *transf.* A written statement or description embodying the result of such examination.

1613 in *Scott. Hist. Rev.* Oct. (1910) 12 One ancient survey..which..Denton restored againe, but the same is since embezelled. *c* **1645** HOWELL *Lett.* II 18, I had spare hours to couch in writing a survay of these Countreys. **1652** NEDHAM tr. *Selden's Mare Cl.* 82 In the survey or Breviarie of the dignities of the East onely three Provinces are reckoned under the Proconsul of Asia. **1801** *Farmer's Mag.* Apr. 192 Not above thirty lines of the Survey are occupied upon this subject. **1808** EAST *Rep. Cases Crt. K.B.* IV. 590 *margin*, The survey which accompanied the letter gave the ship a good character. **1876** FREEMAN *Norm. Conq.* V. xxii. 6 As an historical monument, the value of the Domesday Survey cannot be overrated.

c. A kind of auction for the sale of farms: see quot. 1796. *local.* (*s.w.*)

1725 *Farley's Exeter Jrnl.* 28 May 4 On Thursday..will be held a Survey at the House of William Haydon..for sale of the Inheritance of divers Messuages **1796** W. H. MARSHALL *Rural Econ. W. Eng.* I. 71 The disposal of farms for three lives is generally by what are provincially termed *surveys*; a species of auction; at which candidates bid for the priority of refusal, rather than for the thing itself.

d. 'A district for the collection of the customs, under the inspection and authority of a particular officer. *U.S.*' (Cent. Dict. 1891).

†**2.** Oversight, supervision, superintendence.

1535 *Act 27 Hen. VIII*, c. 27 § 5 All hereditamentes apperteynyng..to any the said Monasteries..shalbe in the order survey and gouernaunce of the said Courte. **1647** N. BACON *Disc. Govt. Eng.* I. xxiii. (1739) 41 He regulated the Courts of Justice under his Survey. **1654** G. GODDARD *Introd. Burton's Diary* (1828) I. p. lxv, They had the survey, and, perhaps, advice in all.

3. a. The, or an, act of looking at something as a whole, or from a commanding position; a general or comprehensive view or look.

1589 GREENE *Menaphon* (Arb.) 46 Taking her eye from one particular obiect, she sent it abroad to make generall suruey of their countrey demeanours. **1601** SHAKS. *All's Well* v. iii. 16 He lost a wife, Whose beauty did astonish the suruey Of richest eies. **1666** DRYDEN *Ann. Mirab.* ccxxii, He ..O'relooks the Neighbours with a wide survey. **1718** POPE *Iliad* xv. 492 Great Hector view'd him with a sad survey, As stretch'd in dust before the stern he lay. **1840** HOOD *Up Rhine* 44, I had time now to look round, and, on taking a survey of the company, was not sorry to recognise our old acquaintance. **1848** DICKENS *Dombey* liii, After a moment's survey of her face. **1871** CALVERLEY *Charades* I. xi. in *Verses & Transl.* 74 Then to my whole [*sc.* pier-glass] he made his way; Took one long lingering survey; And softly, as he stole away, Remarked, 'By Jove, a bird!'

b. *concr.* That which is thus viewed; a view, prospect, scene; †a delineation of this, a 'view', picture (*obs.*).

a **1700** EVELYN *Diary* 13 Sept. 1666, I presented his Majesty with a survey of the ruines. **1821** JOANNA BAILLIE *Metr. Leg., Lady G.B.* 8 Delighted with the fair survey. **1844** MRS. BROWNING *Lost Bower* x, In childhood, little prized I That fair walk and far survey. **1853** PHILLIPS *Rivers Yorks.* i. 17 Overlooking with a magnificent survey the vale of Eden.

4. *fig.* A comprehensive mental view, or (usually) literary examination, discussion, or description, *of* something.

a **1568** ASCHAM *Scholem.* II. (Arb.) 131 Sturmius is he, out of whom, the trew suruey and whole workemanship is..to be learned. **1593** BANCROFT (*title*) A Svrvay of the Pretended Holy Discipline. **1598** STOW (*title*) A Svrvay of London. Contayning the Originall, Antiquity, Increase, Moderne estate, and description of that Citie. **1599** HAKLUYT *Voy.* I. Pref. *5 b, Let vs take a sleight suruey of our traffiques and negotiations in former ages. **1635** PERSON (*title*) Varieties: or, A Svrveigh of rare and excellent matters, necessary and delectable for all sorts of persons. **1729** BUTLER *Serm.* Wks. 1874 II. 123 It may set us upon a more frequent and strict survey and review of our own character. **1780** BENTHAM *Princ. Legisl.* xvii. §26 Upon taking a survey of the various possible modes of punishment. **1836** THIRLWALL *Greece* II. xi. 1 We have already taken a survey of the legends relating to the origin of the people of Attica. **1871** BLACKIE *Four Phases* I. 125 The most critical questions, which require comprehensive survey, cool decision, and impartial judgment.

5. a. The process (†or art) of surveying a tract of ground, coast-line, or any part of the earth's surface; the determination of its form, extent, and other particulars, so as to be able to delineate or describe it accurately and in detail; also, a plan or description thus obtained; a body of persons or a department engaged in such work.

ordnance survey: see ORDNANCE 5.

1610 FOLKINGHAM *Feudigr.* I. i. 1 Suruey in generall is an Art wherby the view and trutinate intimation of a subiect, from Center to Circumference is rectified. The Suruey of Possessions..is the Arts by which their Graphicall Description is particularized. **1654** WHITLOCK *Zootomia* 201 Geometry, it may be, teacheth me Wisdome, not to lose a Pearch of my many Acres, through imperfect Survey. **1765** *Museum Rust.* V. 101 To any person..who shall make an accurate survey of any county, upon the scale of one inch to a mile. **1774** M. MACKENZIE *Marit. Surv.* p. xxii, Thence it is, that so few Surveys have been continued beyond the Extent of a large Bay, or River. **1841** *Civil Eng. & Arch. Jrnl.* IV. 402/1 The accurate survey of the river Thames, from Staines to Yanklet-creek..has been just completed. **1856** *Orr's Circ. Sci., Mech. Philos.* 260 For drawings of land-surveys, it is usual to employ chains as units of measurement. **1876** VOYLE & STEVENSON *Milit. Dict.* s.v., Such surveys or military sketches are furnished by the topographical branch of the intelligence department. **1879** C. C. KING in *Cassell's Techn. Educ.* IV. 92/1 How, with very portable instruments, the survey of a small area is conducted.

transf. **1849** MRS. SOMERVILLE *Connex. Phys. Sci.* xxxvii. 434 Before he went to the Cape of Good Hope, in order to complete the survey of the heavens.

b. A systematic collection and analysis of data relating to the attitudes, living conditions, opinions, etc., of a population, usu. taken from a representative sample of the latter; freq. = POLL *sb.*¹ 7 d. Also preceded by a defining word, as (*public*) *opinion survey*, *social survey*: see under the first element.

1927 [see *social survey* s.v. SOCIAL *a.* 12]. **1935** *Fortune* July 65 (*heading*) Fortune applies to factual journalism the technique of the commercial survey. *Ibid.* 66/2 Fortune will present the results of independent surveys of national scope scientifically conducted. *Ibid.* 66/1 It seems obvious that the survey technique is not only as well adapted to journalistic use as to other uses but considerably better adapted. **1959** J. W. KRUTCH *Human Nature & Human Condition* vii. 127 One survey made by the Gallup Poll may reveal that 61 per cent of all adults could not remember having read one book during the year just passed. **1965** M. FRAYN *Tin Men* xiii. 69 The crash survey showed that people were not interested in reading about road crashes unless there were at least ten dead. **1969** *Times* 7 Jan. 8/6 Both science and arts students believe in magic to an equal extent, according to a survey carried out at Ghana University. **1979** [see SAMPLE *sb.* 2 d].

6. *attrib.* (chiefly in senses 4 and 5). **survey course** *U.S.*, an introductory academic course in which the significant features of a wide subject area are studied.

1610 HOLLAND *Camden's Brit.* 205 We find in the said survey-booke of his [*sc.* Domesday], the King had in this Citie three hundred houses. **1772** *Regul. H.M. Service at Sea* 19 He [*sc.* a Captain or Commander] is to demand from the Clerk of the Survey, a Survey-Book, with an Inventory of the Stores. **1800** *Proc. Parl.* in *Asiat. Ann. Reg.* 16/2 A reduction of survey charges. **1845** STOCQUELER *Handbk. Brit. India* (1854) 59 Great..service has been rendered in the survey department by officers of the Indian navy. **1890** L. C. D'OYLE *Notches* 52, I saw that it was a survey-party by their instruments. **1911** *Daily Colonist* (Victoria, B.C.) 13 Apr. 14/2 An advertisement was published yesterday.. calling for tenders for the purchase of the old survey ship, which formerly served in the war fleets. **1930** L. G. D. ACLAND *Early Canterbury Runs* 1st Ser. ix. 224 This was in 1852 when a few wooden buildings..were all there was of Christchurch, except survey pegs. **1941** C. FADIMAN *Reading I've Liked* (1946) p. xxii, My brother, five years my senior and a student at Columbia College, was at the time taking a conventional survey course that used a sound standard anthology. **1951** M. MCLUHAN *Mech. Bride* (1967) 47/1 Survey techniques inevitably throw up images of normalcy. **1964** P. MEADOWS in I. L. Horowitz *New Sociol.* 450 Others exploited survey-questionnaire methods. Indeed, industrial society became in the 'thirties the land of the Gallup Poll—'Galluputia'. **1967** M. ARGYLE *Psychol. Interpersonal Behaviour* ix. 151 In fact the reliability of survey interviews is not very high. **1978** *N. & Q.* Feb. 82/1 Brief or survey treatment of major authors.

survey (səˈveɪ), *v.* Also 6 **servey, survaye,** 6–7 **survay, surveigh,** 7 **survei,** *pa. t.* **survaid.** [a. AF. *surveier, -veir,* = OF. *so(u)rv(e)eir* (pres. stem *sorvey-*):—med.L. *supervidēre* SUPERVIDE.]

1. *trans.* To examine and ascertain the condition, situation, or value of, formally or officially, e.g. the boundaries, tenure, value, etc. of an estate, a building or structure, accounts, or the like; more widely, to have the oversight of, supervise. *spec.*, to examine the condition of a property on behalf of its prospective buyer.

1467–8 [see SURVEYING *vbl. sb.* 1]. **1472–5** *Rolls of Parlt.* VI. 159/1 To survey and kepe the Waters and grete Ryvers there,..and to doo due execution by the said Statutes,.. aswell by their survew,..as by enquestes therof to be taken. **1512** *Act 4 Hen. VIII*, c. 13 §3 Accomptes..to be taken veyed surveyede & comtrolled by [etc.]. **1523** FITZHERB. *Surv.* Prol., Howe all these maners..& tenementes shulde be extended, surueyed, butted, bounded, and valued. *a* **1570** in Feuillerat *Revels Q. Eliz.* (1908) 407 Suche.. surveiours..as..will survey the office and the whole charge therof. **1591** SHAKS. *1 Hen. VI*, I. iii. 1, I am come to suruey the Tower this day; Since Henries death, I feare there is Conueyance. **1601** F. TATE *Househ. Ord. Edw. II*, §14. (1876) 13 The fruit which the purveiour..shal provide.. shalbe surveied bi the same clarke before any be spent. **1625** *Impeachm. Dk. Buckhm.* (Camden) 31 To survey al the bils of lading and to compare al the merchants marks. **1709** *Act 8 Anne* c. 5 §18 All Makers of Candles shall..keep all the Candles..which shall not have been surveyed..separate.. from all other their Candles which shall have been surveyed. **1860** GEO. ELIOT *Let.* 5 Sept. (1954) III. 342 It is a better house than I care to have..moreover, the place must be surveyed by a builder before we can come to a final decision. **1880** *Times* 17 Dec. 5/6 The Persian Monarch, st., is reported..to be leaking slightly... She will be surveyed.

2. To determine the form, extent, and situation of the parts of (a tract of ground, or any portion of the earth's surface) by linear and angular measurements, so as to construct a map, plan, or detailed description of it. Also *absol.*

1550 CROWLEY *Epigr.* 1371 A manne that had landes.. surueyed the same, and lette it out deare. **1587** LADY STAFFORD in *Collect.* (O.H.S.) I. 208 The woods were seen and surveighed by him.., so that he knew the number of acres. **1796** MORSE *Amer. Geog.* I. 22 The Romans measured or surveyed all these places with the greatest care. **1846** *Blackw. Mag.* Apr. 506/1, I was out surveying the whole morning. **1879** C. C. KING in *Cassell's Techn. Educ.* IV. 93/2 Let us assume..that the surveyor having walked over the area he intends to survey..has..selected..a somewhat central position, on which to measure his base.

3. To look carefully into or through; to view in detail; to examine, inspect, scrutinize; to explore (a country). Now *rare* or *Obs.*

1592 NASHE *P. Penniless Supplic* I 2 b, When he comes in to seruey his wares. **1613** CAMPION *El. Pr. Henry* 51 His care had beene Suruaying India, and implanting there The knowledge of that God which hee did feare. *a* **1631** DONNE *Poems, Dampe* i, When I am dead..my friends curiositie Will have me cut up to survay each part. **1658** in *Verney Mem.* (1907) II. 82 To survey all my letters and actions.. with a most rigid and censorious eye. *a* **1700** EVELYN *Diary* 17 Aug. 1669, To London, spending almost the intire day in surveying what progresse was made in rebuilding the ruinous Citty. **1725** DE FOE *Voy. round World* (1840) 241 The whole of this time my landlord and I spent in surveying the country, and viewing his plantation. **1798** S. & HT. LEE *Canterb. T.* II. 134 He took the piece he was drawing, and, holding it behind the light, to survey it, [etc.]. **1871** JOWETT *Plato* IV. 279 At all seasons of the year..let them [*sc.* wardens] survey minutely the whole country,..acquiring a perfect knowledge of every locality.

4. a. To look at from, or as from, a height or commanding position; to take a broad, general, or comprehensive view of; to view or examine in its whole extent.

c **1586** C'TESS PEMBROKE *Ps.* LXXII. iii, From sea to sea He shall survey All kingdoms as his own. **1615** CHAPMAN *Odyss.* x. 128, I..thence suruaid From out a loftie watch towre.. The Countrie round about. **1667** MILTON *P.L.* VIII. 268 My self I then perus'd, and Limb by Limb Survey'd. **1697** DRYDEN *Virg. Georg.* III. 354 Often he turns his Eyes, and, with a Groan, Surveys the pleasing Kingdoms, once his own. **1782** COWPER *Alex. Selkirk* i, I am monarch of all I survey, My right there is none to dispute. **1811** LAMB *Guy Faux* Misc. Wks. (1871) 374 Two persons..are intently surveying a sort of speculum..which stands upon a pedestal. **1832** HT. MARTINEAU *Hill & Valley* iii. 38 You.. like to survey the ranks of slaves under you. **1873** HALE *In His Name* vi. 48 He surveyed the whole figure of the rider.

absol. **1667** MILTON *P.L.* III. 555 Round he surveys, and well might, where he stood So high above the circling Canopie Of Nights extended shade.

b. *fig.* To take a comprehensive mental view of; to consider or contemplate as a whole.

a **1596** *Sir T. More* IV. v. 65 Lets now suruaye our state. **1630** PRYNNE *Anti-Armin.* 126 Suruay we all the internall, all the externall meanes of grace. *a* **1656** HALES *Gold. Rem.* I. (1673) 253 If we surveigh and sum up all the forces which the Divil, Flesh, World, are able to raise. **1712** ADDISON *Hymn* in *Spectator* No. 453 ¶7 When all thy Mercies, O my God, My rising Soul surveys. **1749** JOHNSON *Van. Human Wishes* 2 Let observation with extensive view, Survey mankind from China to Peru. **1875** JOWETT *Plato* (ed. 2) IV. 259 He surveyed the elements of mythology,..which lay before him. **1888** F. HUME *Mme. Midas* I. Prol., In a short time they were able to rise to their feet and survey the situation.

absol. **1859** CORNWALLIS *Panorama New World* I. 121 Here was a scene that spoke a history. Let me survey.

†**c.** To observe, perceive, see. *Obs. rare*⁻¹.

1605 SHAKS. *Macb.* I. ii. 31 The Norweyan Lord, surueying vantage, With..new supplyes of men, Began a fresh assault. **1615** BRATHWAIT *Strappado* (1878) 178 Bid them haue recourse vnto their glasse, And there surueigh how swiftly time doth passe.

5. Also ('sɜːveɪ). To carry out a survey (sense 5 b) of (a group of people, or its beliefs, living conditions, etc.).

1953 POHL & KORNBLUTH *Space Merchants* (1955) iii. 34 Survey the book-buyers, the repeat-viewers. **1958** M. ARGYLE *Relig. Behaviour* iv. 31 Beliefs have also been repeatedly surveyed by one or two investigators. *Ibid.* vi. 63 Kuhlen and Arnold..surveyed over 500 children grouped around the ages of 12, 15 and 18.

Hence **surveyed** (-'veɪd), *ppl. a.*

1890 'R. BOLDREWOOD' *Col. Reformer* (1891) 251 A surveyed township. **1895** *Daily News* 4 Oct. 7/3 The only surveyed block now obtainable in that mine.

surveyable (sə'veɪəb(ə)l), *a. rare.* [f. SURVEY *v.* + -ABLE.] Capable of being surveyed.

1658 OSBORN *Q. Eliz.* Ep., More of London being surveyable in a minute from Pauls Steeple, than can be seen in an age out of Cheap-side. **1837** in *Fraser's Mag.* XV. 654 Now the explosion becomes a thing visible, surveyable. **1858** CARLYLE *Fredk. Gt.* VII. iii. (1872) II. 265 From which the whole ground..is surveyable to spectators of rank. **1882** *Fraser's Mag.* XXVI. 434 The [Philological] Society is going to deal..with the recoverable, the surveyable English of the printing-press.

surveyal (sə'veɪəl), *rare.* [f. as prec. + -AL¹.] The act of surveying; survey.

a **1677** BARROW *1st Serm. 1 Tim. iv. 10* Wks. 1686 III. 451 The truth of this doctrine will farther appear by the declaration and surveyal of those respects according to which Christ is represented the Saviour of men. **1891** MEREDITH *One of our Conq.* I. xiv. 262 Taken by the brain to shoot up to terrific heights of surveyal.

surveyance (sə'veɪəns). *rare.* Also 5 **surve(i)aunce**, 6 **surveyaunce**. [a. OF. **surve(i)ance*, f. *surveeir* to SURVEY. In mod. use directly f. SURVEY *v.* + -ANCE.] Survey; superintendence, oversight; inspection.

(Sometimes app. confused with SURVEILLANCE.)

c **1386** CHAUCER *Doctor's T.* 95 (Ellesm.) Youre is the charge of al hir surueiaunce [*Hengw.* surueaunce; *other MSS.* sufferaunce, suffra(u)nce] Whil þat they been vnder youre gouernaunce. *c* **1520** SKELTON *Magnyf.* (1906) 1787 In Pleasure and Surueyaunce..I haue set my hole Felycyte. **1531** *Act 23 Hen. VIII*, c. 18 §1 Within .xl daies after suche surveiaunce made and monycion to the said owners gyven. **1597** MIDDLETON *Wisd. Solomon* To Gentl. Rdrs. Bj, I giue you the surueyaunce of my new-bought grounde.

1880 *Times* 19 Aug. 4 We must expect to find such objects in the excavations if proper surveyance of the workmen be exercised. **1883** *American* VI. 118 The price of lands reduced to a sum which would pay the expenses of surveyance and sale.

surveying (sə'veɪɪŋ), *vbl. sb.* [f. SURVEY *v.* + -ING¹.] The action of the verb SURVEY.

1. The action of viewing or examining in detail (esp. officially); †the exploration (of a country).

1467–8 *Rolls of Parlt.* V. 598/2 The surveying aswell of the Veerte as of the Venyson of oure Forest. **1577** V. LEIGH (*title*) The..science of Surueying of Landes, Tenementes, and Hereditamentes. **1596** BACON *Max. & Use Com. Law* II. (1630) 10 Besides surueying of the Pledges of Freemen, and giuing the oath of Allegeance, and making Constables. **1607** in *Hist. Wakefield Gram. Sch.* (1892) 74 If great occasion shall be for the surveyinge of the whole..of the howses or landes to the schole belonginge. **1622** CALLIS *Stat. Sewers* (1647) 5 Commissions for the surveying and repairing of Walls, Banks and Rivers. **1632** LITHGOW (*title*) The Totall Discourse, Of the Rare Aduentures..of long nineteene Yeares Trauayles..in Surueighing of Forty eight Kingdomes.

2. The process or art of making surveys of land: see SURVEY *sb.* 5, *v.* 2, and LAND-SURVEYING.

1551 RECORDE *Pathw. Knowl.* Ep. King, In suruaiyng & measuring of landes. **1639** *Boston Rec.* (1877) II. 41 A great lott..twelve acrs, paying for the same..three shillings an acr upon the entrance of the platform or bounders thereof, after the Surveying of it. **1682** WHELER *Journ. Greece* Pref. a ij, I..reduced their Positions into Triangles;..an ordinary rule in surveighing. *a* **1727** NEWTON *Chronol. Amended* ii. (1728) 248 This King wrote a book of surveying, which gave a beginning to Geometry. **1867** BRANDE & COX *Dict. Sci.*, etc. s.v., *Naval Surveying*, the science of determining the lines on which seas may be safely navigated.

†**3.** Oversight, superintendence. *Obs.*

1538 ELYOT, *Libitinarius*, he that hath the suruayeng and charge aboute burienges.

4. *attrib.*: †**a. surveying-board, -place**, a sideboard or hatch on which the dishes were placed ready for serving at a meal under the direction of the 'surveyor' (SURVEYOR 1 d). *Obs.*

a **1483** *Liber Niger* in *Househ. Ord.* (1790) 45, xx squires attendaunt uppon the King's person..to help serve his table from the surveying bourde, and from other places, as the assewer woll assigne. *c* **1543** in Parker *Dom. Archit.* III. 78 A new halle, with a squillery, saucery, & surveyng place. *c* **1600** in *Archaeologia* LXIV. 392 The surveying place by the kitchin dore. **1608** in Willis & Clark *Cambridge* (1886) II. 494 Yᵉ kitchen, butry, surveying place.

b. Applied to instruments or appliances used for, and to ships employed in, surveying.

1641 MILTON *Ch. Govt.* I. i. Wks. 1851 III. 98 Discipline, whose golden surveying reed..measures every quarter and circuit of new Jerusalem. **1669** STURMY *Mariner's Mag.* v. i. 2 In that socket you put the head of your three legged Surveying-Staff. *a* **1691** BOYLE *Hist. Air* (1692) 134 Having gotten together all the surveighing chains the city afforded ..we went into the Church. **1701** MOXON *Math. Instr.* 17 *Reducing scale*,..Sometimes 'tis called a Surveying Scale. **1728** CHAMBERS *Cycl.* s.v., [The] Surveying Cross..in France..serves in lieu of a Theodolite. *Ibid.* s.v. *Quadrant*, The Common, or Surveying Quadrant. *Ibid.*, *Perambulator*, ..an Instrument for the measuring of Distances, call'd also Pedometer, Way-wiser, and Surveying Wheel. **1840** *Civil Eng. & Arch. Jrnl.* III. 108/2 A very useful..addition to the ordinary Surveying Poles. **1846** HUXLEY in L. Huxley *Life & Lett.* (1900) I. ii. 26 Surveying ships are totally different from the ordinary run of men-of-war. **1883** SIMMONDS *Dict. Trade* Suppl., *Surveying Chain*, a measuring chain 66 feet long, with iron rings and links. **1905** A. R. WALLACE *Life* I. vi. 86 My strong surveying boots cost 14*s.* a pair.

sur'veying, *ppl. a.* [f. as prec. + -ING².] That surveys: see the verb.

1592 R. D. *Hypnerotomachia* 21 Hir [*sc.* an Eagle's] suruaighing spreding traine. **1599** B. JONSON *Cynthia's Rev.* v. ix, Whose courtly habite is the grace of the presence, and delight of the surueying eye. *a* **1644** QUARLES *Sol. Recant.* ch. vi. 5 The worlds surveighing Lamp. **1697** DRYDEN *Æneid* XI. 796 A steepy Mountain..Whence the surveying Sight the neather Ground commands.

survey line. Also with hyphen. [f. SURVEY *sb.* + LINE *sb.*²] **a.** A line along which the measurements and observations are made in a survey.

1889 G. W. USILL *Pract. Surveying* v. 139 The accuracy of a survey..will best be assured by arranging the survey-lines so that the offsets shall be as short as possible. **1930** S. W. PERROTT *Surveying for Schools* i. 3 It frequently happens that the group or groups of survey lines..do not form triangles. **1981** J. PETTET *Site Surveying & Levelling* 9 Measurements can then be carried out between these points, or from the survey lines joining them, to complete the survey.

b. *Dentistry.* A line scribed on a cast of a tooth marking the place of greatest diameter with respect to the chosen line of insertion of the denture.

1949 V. R. TRAPOZZANO *Comprehensive Rev. Dentistry* xx. 565 Draw the labial of a mandibular molar and indicate a typical survey line. **1954** OSBORNE & LAMMIE *Partial Dentures* vii. 80 If a carbon marking rod is substituted for the vertical plane and a tooth takes the place of the curved surface, then an actual line will be produced at the level of the maximum tooth bulge. This is known as the survey line. **1980** R. W. BLAKESLEE et al. *Dental Technol.* xi. 271 The resultant survey line shows those hard and soft tissues over which the removeable partial denture must pass when it is placed and withdrawn by the patient. The survey line also shows the height of contour of each tooth.

surveyor (sə'veɪə(r)). Forms: α. 5–6 **surveyoure**, 5–7 **surveyour, surveior**, 6–7 **surveiour**, (6 **survayour, -ore, -er, survoier, serveiour, -veyar, surveighor, -our**, 7 **surveigher, surveier, surveyer**), 5– **surveyor**. β. 5 **surveour(e, surviour(e, survyour, -owre**, 5–6 **survear**, 6 **surveor**. [a. AF., OF. *surve(i)our*, f. *surveeir* to SURVEY: see -OR.] One who surveys.

1. One who has the oversight or superintendence of a person or thing; an overseer, supervisor.

a. *gen.* (also *fig.*)

c **1440** CAPGRAVE *Life St. Kath.* I. 263 He was suruyour to all þat þer wer, And..he payed her hyer. *c* **1440** *Promp. Parv.* 485/1 Survyowre, *supervisor*. *c* **1520** SKELTON *Magnyf.* (1906) 1862 Your Suruayour, Crafty Conueyaunce. **1552** HULOET, Surueiour of a bridall, *pronubus*. **1593** SHAKS. *2 Hen. VI*, III. i. 253 Wer 't not madnesse then, To make the Fox surueyor of the Fold? **1616** BRETON *Good & Badde, Worthy Judge* Wks. (Grosart) II. 7/2 Hee is a surueier of rights and reuenger of wrongs. *a* **1631** DONNE *Serm., Matt. v. 8* (1640) 112 Men who are so severe..may..become Surveyors, and Controllers upon Christ himself.

b. As a title of officials in various departments, offices, or works; e.g. one who superintends the construction of a building, the administration of an office or department, the collection of taxes, the keeping of a structure in good order or repair.

Usually (except where the context is explanatory), with a defining phr., as ***surveyor of highways, of taxes***, †***of wards and liveries***, or with prefixed sb., as ***borough, district, forest, road, timber surveyor***.

surveyor of the navy: formerly, an official whose duty was 'to know the State of all Stores, and see the Wants supplied; to survey the Hulls, Masts, and Yards, and estimate the Value of Repairs by Indenture; to charge all Boatswains and Carpenters of his Majesty's Navy with what Stores they received; and at the End of each Voyage, to state and audite their Accompts' (Chamberlayne's *Pres. St. Gt. Brit.*).

1442 *Rolls of Parlt.* V. 54/2 Sercheours, Countrollours, and Surveyours of Serchis. **1472–3** *Ibid.* VI. 58/1 Controller and Surveyour of the Kynges werkes there. **1518** in Lupton *Life Colet* (1887) App. A. 278 The Maisters and surveyors of the scole. **1540–1** ELYOT *Image Gov.* xix. 35 b, Surueyours and other that..gathered the reuenues of his crowne. **1543** tr. *Act 9 Hen. V*, Stat. II. c. 4 Wardeyns and surueyours and minysters of the eschaunges out of the tower. **1553** in *Archaeologia* XII. 382 Surveiors of the Stable. **1555** *Act 2 & 3 Ph. & Mary*, c. 8 §1 The Constables & Churche-wardens of every parishe..shall..electe..twoo honest persons..to bee Surveyours & orderers..of the worckes for Amendement of the Highewais. **1555** EDEN *Decades* (Arb.) 185 There is..appointed to euery man by the suruoiers of the mynes, a square plotte of grounde. **1631** WEEVER *Anc. Funeral Mon.* 582 This man..was the master Mason or Surueior of the kings stone-works. **1660** in *Pepys' Diary* (1870) 43 His Royal Highness James, Duke of York, Lord High Admiral..Sir William Batten, Surveyor. **1666** *Ibid.* 7 Oct., He dreads the reports he is to receive from the Surveyors of its [*sc.* the fleet's] defects. **1670** PETTUS *Fodinæ Reg.* 41 The Surveyor of the Melting, who is to see the Silver cast out. **1698** T. SAVERY *Navig. Improv.* 8 The Commissioners of the Navy..told me, that the Model must be survey'd by Mr. Dummer the Surveyor of the Navy. **1708** J. CHAMBERLAYNE *Pres. St. Gt. Brit.* II. III. 618 Surveyor of the High-ways. **1709** *Brit. Apollo* II. No. 67. 4/1 [In the Customs] a Surveyor and 16 Tidewaiters. **1793–4** *Matthews's Bristol Directory* 37 Surveyor of the Distilleries,..Surveyor of the Salt duties. **1872** DE VERE *Americanisms* 264 *Surveyor*, an official who surveys all the inspectors, weighers, gaugers,..in a United States Customs-House.

†**c.** (of a will) = OVERSEER 1 b, SUPERVISOR 1 b.

1420 *E.E. Wills* (1882) 54 The surveiors of my testament. *c* **1430** LYDG. *Min. Poems* (Percy Soc.) 240 To make Jhesu to be cheef surveyour, Of my laste wyl set in my Testament. **1463** in *Bury Wills* (Camden) 43 Be yᵉ avys and supportacion of yᵉ surviour and my executours.

†**d.** An officer of the royal or other great household who superintended the preparation and serving of the food. *Obs.*

c **1450** *Bk. Curtasye* 545 in *Babees Bk.* (1868) 317 Surueour and stuarde also. *a* **1483** *Liber Niger* in *Househ. Ord.* (1790) 37 A Surveyour for the Kyng, to oversee, with the maister cooke for the mowthe, all maner of stuffe of vytayle which is best and moste holsom, and the conveyaunce and sauf guarde of it. *a* **1513** FABYAN *Chron.* VII. 586 Ye shall vnderstande yᵗ this feest was all of fysshe. And for yᵉ orderyng of yᵉ seruyce therof, were dyuers lordes appoynted..as stewarde, controller, surueyour. **1601** F. TATE *Househ. Ord. Edw. II*, §36. (1876) 22 A serjant surveiour of the dressor for the hall.

†**e.** One who had the oversight of the lands and boundaries of an estate and its appurtenances. *Obs.*

1485 *Rolls of Parlt.* VI. 349/1 That this Acte of Resumption..be [not] prejudicial..to John Huse..for any Graunte made to hym, of the Office of Survearship of all the Lands and Tenements of Richemonde fee..or to be Survear of the same in any maner fourme. **1523** FITZHERB. *Surv.* Prol., It is necessary that euery great estate..shulde haue a Surueyour that can extende, but, and bounde, and value them. **1574** in *10th Rep. Hist. MSS. Comm.* App. v. 335 Fowre Aldermen shalbe elected surveighours yearely..to determyne all mischaunces and variaunces of mearing betwixt thinhabitaunts. **1577** HOLINSHED *Chron.* I. *Hist. Scot.* 10/1 Men..were apointed to be Surueyours of the whole countrey, and to deuide the same..into a set number of equal portions. **1583** STUBBES *Anat. Abus.* II. (1882) 29 When a gentleman..hath a farme..to let..he causeth a surueior to make strict inquirie what may be made of it. **1647** CLARENDON *Hist. Reb.* I. §208 He employed his own Surveyor..to treat with the Owners, many whereof were his own Tenants. **1782** MISS BURNEY *Cecilia* IX. i, She sent for the surveyor who had the superintendance of her estates. *fig.* **1621** QUARLES *Argalus & P.* I. (1629) 24 Thrice had the bright surueyour of the heauen Diuided out the dayes and nights by euen And equall houres. **1624** FORD *Sun's Darling* III. iii. (1656) 25 What land soe're, the worlds surveyor, the Sun, Can measure in a day.

†**f.** The or a principal magistrate of a town or district. *Obs.*

1548 *Acts Privy Council* II. 555 The Survayore of Bolloyne. **1679** *Providence Rec.* (1895) VIII. 44 Ye Surveyor of ye Towne..shall see to ye retaineing..a suitable..prievelledge..not with standing.

†**g.** A censor or licenser of books for the press.

1663 *Cal. St. Papers* 240 Order for a warrant for..appointing Roger L'Estrange surveyor of all books.

2. One who designs, and superintends the construction of, a building; a practical architect.

The duties are now usually divided between the architect, who prepares the design, and the *quantity surveyor*, who estimates the labour and the amounts of materials necessary for carrying out the design.

1460 CAPGRAVE *Chron.* (Rolls) 219 The kyng began the newe edifiyng of Wyndesore, and mad Maystir William Wikham survioure of the same werk. **1593** FALE *Horologiographia* Title-p., Of speciall vse..for diuers Artificers, Architects, Surueyours of buildings, free-Masons. **1603** DEKKER *Wonderfull Yeare* Wks. (Grosart) I. 120, [I] bespake one [*sc.* a coffin], and (like the Surueyours of deaths buildings) gaue direction how this little Tenement should be framed. **1663** GERBIER *Counsel* 4 A skilful Surveyor, from whose Directions the several Master-workmen may receive Instructions by way of Draughts, Models, Frames, &c. *a* **1700** EVELYN *Diary* 23 Sept. 1683, The surveior has already begun the foundation for a palace. **1703** MOXON *Mech. Exerc.* 253 The drawing of Draughts is most commonly the work of a Surveyor. **1843** *Civil Eng. & Arch. Jrnl.* VI. 19/2 Several surveyors were called for the defendant, who stated it was the custom of the profession to charge 2½ per cent for rejected plans. *fig.* **1662** GERBIER *Princ.* 2 The great Architect and Surveyor of Heaven and Earth.

3. a. One whose business it is to survey land, etc.; one who makes surveys, or practices surveying: see SURVEY *sb.* 5, *v.* 2, SURVEYING *vbl. sb.* 2.

See also LAND-SURVEYOR 2. *surveyor's chain* = Gunter's chain: see GUNTER I.

1551 RECORDE *Pathw. Knowl.* Pref., Suruayers haue cause to make muche of me [*sc.* geometry]. **1608** A. NORTON tr. *Stevin's Disme* B4, The Surueyor or Land-meater. **1652** NEDHAM tr. *Selden's Mare Cl.* 135 Things used by Surveyors in the bounding of Lands. **1794** S. WILLIAMS *Vermont* 378 The magnetic needle can never give to the surveyor a straight and accurate line. **1840** *Buel's Farmer's Companion* 285 A surveyor's chain is 4 poles, or 66 feet, divided into 100 links of 7·92 inches. **1879** C. C. KING in *Cassell's Techn. Educ.* IV. 92/2 In many cases the pace of the surveyor is used for determining distances.

b. A name for certain caterpillars: = GEOMETER 4, LOOPER[1] I.

1682 LISTER *Gœdart Of Insects* 24 Our Country-people call these kinds of Catterpillars, Surveyours (Geometræ) because of their Gate, which is like a Pole turned over and over, when one measures Land. **1816** KIRBY & SP. *Entomol.* xxii. (1818) II. 289 The true geometers or surveyors.

c. One whose business it is to inspect and examine land, houses, or other property and to calculate and report upon its actual or prospective value or productiveness for certain purposes.

1795 VANCOUVER *Agric. Essex* 186 The Surveyor cannot close this report without expressing..his warmest acknowledgements to the following gentlemen. **1812** in *Civil Eng. & Arch. Jrnl.* (1842) V. 253/2 Towards the support..of some worthy character bred a surveyor and architect. **1847** SMEATON *Builder's Man.* 168 The business of the surveyor is to measure and value the work executed by the builder. **1858** SIMMONDS *Dict. Trade*, *Surveyor*,..an inspector of shipping, tonnage, &c. for Lloyds; an examiner of buildings for a fire-insurance office. **1867** SMYTH *Sailor's Word-bk.*, *Lloyd's Surveyors*, practical persons specially appointed in London..to investigate the state and condition of merchant-ships for the underwriters. **1881** *Instr. Census Clerks* (1885) 28 Insurance Surveyor.

4. a. One who views or looks at something; a beholder. *rare.*

1558 PHAER *Æneid* VII. Sivb, On euery syde they seeke, and send Surveiours through the coast. **1590** GREENE *Mourn. Garm.* (1616) 30 The eye beeing the surueyour of all exteriour obiects. **1829** LANDOR *Imag. Conv.* Ser. II. *Diogenes & Plato* I. 496 The brightest of stars appear the most..tremulous in their light..from the vapours that float below, and from the imperfection of vision in the surveyor.

b. *fig.* One who takes a mental view of something; an examiner, contemplator.

1606 FORD *Honor Tri.* (1843) 29 If a curious surveior will upon this approve that louers have beene witty. **1640** BP. HALL *Episc.* III. v. 245 These which I have abstracted from our judicious surveyer. **1905** J. B. BURY *Life St. Patrick* iii. 45 To the surveyor of the history of humanity this is the interest which Pelagius possesses.

5. surveyor-general, †*general surveyor* (see GENERAL *a.* 10): a principal or head surveyor; one who has the control of a body of surveyors, or the general oversight of some business. Hence *surveyor-generalship*.

Applied esp. to the chief supervisor of crown or public lands, of the customs and other administrative departments. *surveyor-general of the ordnance*: see ORDNANCE 3.

In *U.S.* a government officer who supervises the surveys of public lands.

1515 *Act 7 Hen. VIII*, c. 7 §37 Surveyour generall of all and singler our Castellis Lordeshippes Manours londes called Richemond [etc.] in the shire of Yorke. **1541-2** *Act 33 Hen. VIII*, c. 39 §1 A certeyne Court commonly to be called the Court of the generall Surveyors of the Kingis landis. **1575** *Nottingham Rec.* IV. 157 The Quen's Maiesty's Generall Serveyar. **1665** PEPYS *Diary* 31 Oct., Surveyor-Generall of the Victualling. **1693** LUTTRELL *Brief Rel.* (1857) III. 8 Sir Joseph Tredenham has kist the Kings hand for the place of surveyor generall of England. **1708** J. CHAMBERLAYNE *St. Gt. Brit.* II. III. 560 Surveyor-General of the Riding Officers appointed for the Guard of Kent and Sussex. **1728** CHAMBERS *Cycl.* s.v., The Surveyor General of the King's Manors;..Surveyor General of the Works. **1754** (*title*) An east prospect of the city of Philadelphia: taken by George Heap..under the Direction of Nicholas Skull, Surveyor General of the Province of Pennsylvania. **1780** *Chron.* in *Ann. Reg.* 217/1 A surveyor-general of the excise. **1809** MALKIN *Gil Blas* VII. xv. ¶5, I was proclaimed principal manager and surveyor-general of the family. **1831** in R. Ellis *Customs* (1840) IV. 273 The Board cannot admit the absence of an officer on leave, to be a sufficient ground for delaying an investigation before the Surveyors-general. **1882** *Standard* 9 Dec. 5/4 The Surveyor Generalship of the Ordnance.

6. *Dentistry.* An instrument used to survey the casts of teeth, esp. to determine parallelism between surfaces on different teeth.

1928 W. E. CUMMER in Turner & Anthony *Amer. Textbk. Prosthetic Dentistry* (ed. 5) ix. 326 The Ney surveyor, in addition to the vertical marking member, includes a tilting table to which the cast is attached. **1939** J. OSBORNE *Dental Mechanics for Students* ix. 97 A clasp surveyor is a useful instrument for determining the exact position of the clasps. **1980** R. W. BLAKESLEE et al. *Dental Technol.* xi. 267/2 A dental surveyor consists of a platform to which an adjustable vertical tool holder is attached so that it is perpendicular to the platform.

surveyorship (səˈveɪəʃɪp). [f. prec. + -SHIP.] The office of surveyor.

1485 [see SURVEYOR 1 e]. **1539** POLLARD in *Lett. Suppr. Monast.* (Camden) 261 That he myght have the surveorshype of Glastonbery. **1591** PERCIVALL *Sp. Dict.*, *Alarifadgo*, surueiorship of buildings. **1774** FOOTE *Cozeners* I. Wks. 1799 II. 150 The surveyorship of the woods there is vacant. **1850** HAWTHORNE *Scarlet L.* Introd. (1852) 37 It was my chief trouble..that I was likely to grow gray and decrepit in the Surveyorship.

surview (səˈvjuː, ˈsɜː-), *sb.* Forms: 5 surveu, 5-6 -vewe, 5-7 -vew, 6 -viewe, 6- **surview**. [a. AF., OF. *surveu(e*, f. *surveer* to SURVEY; cf. *view*.]

†**1.** Inspection: = SURVEY *sb.* 1. *Obs.*

1432 *Rolls of Parlt.* IV. 406/1 Yat no Vessell of wyn pas fro the place of thair makyng,..on lesse yat it be..marked..be a knowe signe..of the saide persones yat are assigned to ye survewe and ye assay therof. **1472-5** [see SURVEY *v.* 1].

†**2.** Supervision; = SURVEY *sb.* 2. *Obs.*

c **1421** *Proc. Privy Council* II. 366 It be ordeinede whenne yat any souldeours deye..yat he yat shall be taken in his stede be receyved be ye survewe of ye tresourer. **1431** *E.E. Wills* (1882) 90, I woll that sir Nicholl Dixon..have the suruewe of my..Executours.

3. A view (esp. mental) of something as a whole, or in its details; the action of taking such a view; consideration, contemplation; = SURVEY *sb.* 3, 4.

1576 FLEMING tr. *Caius' Dogs* (1880) 42 Leauing the seruiewe of hunting and hauking dogs. **1579** G. HARVEY *Let. to Spenser* S.'s Wks. (1912) 640/2 Vppon the suruiewe of them, and farther conference. **1612** J. CARTWRIGHT (*title*) The Preachers Travels... Containing a full suruew of the Kingdom of Persia. **1619** SANDERSON *Serm.* (1657) I. 14 If you will please to take a second surview of the four severall particulars, wherein the Cases seemed to agree. **1633** HEYWOOD *Eng. Trav.* IV. Wks. 1874 IV. 63 Your seruant tels me, you haue great desire To take suruiew of this my house within. **1710** *Now or Never* 13, I shall take a short Surview, and then put an End to your Lordship's trouble. **1817** COLERIDGE *Biog. Lit.* xviii. (1882) 172 That prospectiveness of mind, that surview, which enables a man to foresee the whole of what he is to convey. **1889** BROWNING *Asolando, Reverie* x, Mind, in surview of things, Now soared, anon alit, To treasure its gatherings. **1903** *Records of Elgin* (New Spalding Cl.) I. 7 To take a calm surview of the whole case. **1958** *Medical World* LXXXIX. 9 (*heading*) Surview of the National Health Service 1948–58. **1961** K. TYNAN *Curtains* I. 118 Mr. Dallas' play, a scathing surview of the Trojan War, is acted with notable assurance. **1977** *Times Lit. Suppl.* 23 Dec. 1508/5 Dickens's imaginative achievement in creating a whole surview of the chaos that can be unleashed in a riot is masterly.

†**4.** *concr.* = SURVEY *sb.* 1 b. *Obs.*

1570-6 LAMBARDE *Peramb. Kent* (1826) 191 In the auncient rentals and surviewes of the possessions of Christes Church in Canterburie.

surview (səˈvjuː), *v.* Forms: see prec. [f. prec.]

1. *trans.* To take a general view of, to view as a whole (with the eyes or mind); = SURVEY *v.* 4, 4 b; also, to command a view of, overlook; in weakened sense, to look upon, behold (cf. SURVEY *v.* 4 c). *Obs.* or *arch.*

1567 DRANT *Horace, Ep. Arte Poet.* B ij, If that the matter in the mynde thou wilte before surview. *Ibid.* xvi. E vij, The declining sonne that doth the fieldes surview. **1579** SPENSER *Sheph. Cal.* Feb. 145 Yt chaunced..The Husbandman selfe to come that way, Of custome for to seruewe his grownd. **1590** —— *F.Q.* II. ix. 45 That Turrets frame..lifted high aboue this earthly masse, Which it surview'd. **1592** GREENE *Disput.* 21, I spared no glaunces to suruiew all with a curious eye-fauour. **1621** G. SANDYS *Ovid's Met.* XI. (1626) 238 All done in Heauen, Earth, Ocean, Fame suruiews. **1628** *World Encomp. by Sir F. Drake* 9 The people..gaue vs leaue..to take our pleasure in suruewing the Iland. **1855** BAILEY *Mystic* 21 The dragon king, world-lifed, who saw The first, and will the last of gods surview.

†**2.** To examine, inspect; = SURVEY *v.* 1, 3.

1601 R. JOHNSON *Kingd. & Commw.* (1603) 53 When these yong lads are brought to Constantinople, they are surviewed by the captaine of the Ianizars. **1625** in *Cosin's Corr.* (Surtees) I. 51 The College of Enquisitors..that must be for surviewing books.

Hence †**surˈviewer**, a surveyor, supervisor.

1783 WALDRON *Contn. B. Jonson's Sad Sheph.* v. 106 The maid I'll wed; make Lorel o'er my flocks..Surviewer.

survioure, obs. form of SURVEYOR.

†**survise**, *v.* *Obs. nonce-wd.* [Formed by substitution of prefix SUR- in SUPERVISE.] *trans.* To look upon, behold.

1599 B. JONSON *Ev. Man out of Hum.* III. iv. (1600) H iij b, It is the most vile, foolish, absurd, palpable, and ridiculous Escutcheon that euer this eye suruisde.

†**survisor.** *Obs. rare*$^{-1}$. By-form (see SUR-) of SUPERVISOR (1 b).

1449 in *Wars Eng. in France* (Rolls) I. 495 Youre said uncle..desired you..to be in his said testament principal survis[o]ure therof.

survivable (səˈvaɪvəb(ə)l), *a.* [f. SURVIVE + -ABLE.] **1.** Capable of surviving.

1879 *19th Cent.* Oct. 597 Conditions upon which..[we] can continue to live and to leave a survivable posterity. **1973** *Washington Post* 13 Jan. A23/3 The only survivable..nuclear deterrent forces. **1982** *Daily Tel.* 17 Nov. 5/1 The sinking of the destroyer Sheffield, 3,500 tons, and of the Atlantic Conveyor, 14,946 tons, by Exocet missiles was seen by some as evidence 'that large surface ships are not survivable, or at least not in a cost effective manner'.

2. Capable of being survived (esp. of an accident); not fatal.

1961 in WEBSTER. **1967** *Times Rev. Industry* Feb. 38/3 The attitude to safety in survivable accidents, while officially condoned, is indefensible. **1981** *Brit. Med. Jrnl.* 10 Oct. 963/1 The suggestion that a nuclear war may be survivable. **1982** *Observer* 14 Mar. 5/1 The report..published by the United States Transportation Safety Board in Washington ..defines a 'survivable' accident as one in which the forces exerted on passengers do not exceed the limits of human tolerance and in which the aircraft structure remains substantially intact.

Hence **survivaˈbility**, capability of surviving; now esp., ability to survive military attack.

18.. *N.Y. Reports* XCIX. 260 (Cent. Dict.) It must be held that these rules still determine the survivability of actions for tort. **1964** *Financial Times* (Defence Survey) 23 Mar. 21/4 The solid fuel missile..which, when widely dispersed in underground silos.., offers reasonable survivability against any first strike. **1972** *Sci. Amer.* July 14/2 Methods of anti-submarine warfare that might eventually threaten the survivability of missile-launching submarines. **1976** *Ibid.* July 64/1 (Advt.), Computer-aided design is used to model..helicopter 'survivability' under the most turbulent conditions. **1980** D. BLOODWORTH *Trapdoor* xi. 62 This..Airborne Command Post is designed to improve communications and so increase survivability in case of sudden nuclear attack. **1981** *Times* 28 Feb. 15/3, I suggest that..the overriding problem is the flammability of aircraft fuel. If we can reduce this, many of the survivability problems will diminish.

survival (səˈvaɪvəl). Also 6-7 -all. [f. SURVIVE + -AL[1] 5.]

1. a. The continuing to live after some event (*spec.* of the soul after death); remaining alive, living on.

1598 CHAPMAN *Iliad* III. [VII.] 42, I promise thee that yet thy soule shall not descend to fates, So hearde I thy suruiuall cast, by the celestiall states. **1615** —— *Odyss.* I. 638 The returne of my lou'd Sire, Is past all hope; and should rude Fame inspire..a flattring messenger, With newes of his suruiuall [etc.]. **1743** FRANCIS tr. *Hor., Odes* IV. xiii. 27 Ah! tragical survival! She glorious died in beauty's bloom, While cruel Fate defers thy doom To be the raven's rival. **1812** COLERIDGE *Lett., to Wordsworth* (1895) 601 More cheerful illustrations of our survival, I have never received, than from the recent study of the instincts of animals. **1818** COLEBROOKE *Obligations* 88 An assurance of a ship lost or unlost; or benefit of survival of an absent person. **1872** DARWIN *Orig. Spec.* iv. (ed. 6) 71 If a single individual were born, which varied in some manner, giving it twice as good a chance of life as that of the other individuals, yet the chances would be strongly against its survival. **1908** J. ORR

Resurrect. Jesus viii. 229 The survival of the soul is not resurrection.

b. ***survival of the fittest*** (Biol.): a phrase used to describe the process of *natural selection* (q.v., s.v. SELECTION 3 b), expressing the fact that those organisms which are best adapted to their environment continue to live and produce offspring, while those of the same or related species which are less adapted perish.

1864 SPENCER *Princ. Biol.* §164 This survival of the fittest, implies multiplication of the fittest. *Ibid.* §165 This survival of the fittest..is that which Mr. Darwin has called 'natural selection, or the preservation of favoured races in the struggle for life'. **1875** BENNETT & DYER tr. *Sachs' Bot.* 843 The theory of descent explains intelligibly how plants have obtained their extraordinarily perfect adaptations for resisting the struggle for existence; this struggle has itself been the means of their obtaining them by the 'Survival of the Fittest'. **1877** HUXLEY *Anat. Inv. Anim.* 40 The result of the struggle for existence would be the survival of the fittest among an indefinite number of varieties.

2. *transf.* Continuance after the end or cessation of something else, or after some event; *spec.* continuance of a custom, observance, etc. after the circumstances or conditions in which it originated or which gave significance to it have passed away.

1820 COLERIDGE in *Lit. Rem.* (1839) IV. 79 The evidence of a future state and the survival of individual consciousness. **1860** A. L. WINDSOR *Ethica* vii. 359 Though oratory at Rome was naturally more prolific and its chances of survival greater [than in Greece]. **1870** LUBBOCK *Orig. Civiliz.* i. (1875) 2 The use of stone knives in certain ceremonies is evidently a case of survival. **1871** TYLOR *Prim. Cult.* I. 60 We do not hear of it [*sc.* the spear-thrower] as in practical use at the Conquest, when it had apparently fallen into survival. **1875** WHITNEY *Life Lang.* IX. 156 Cases of survival from former good usage.

attrib. **1897** MARY KINGSLEY *W. Africa* 487 This custom is now getting into the survival form in Libreville and Glass. **1906** *Fortn. Rev.* Apr. 746 It is the true belief that has the greatest survival-value.

3. (with *a* and *pl.*) Something that continues to exist after the cessation of something else, or of other things of the kind; a surviving remnant; *spec.* applied to a surviving custom, observance, belief, etc. (see 2). Also, used *spec.* in *Anthrop.* with ref. to a theory that from such surviving customs and observances the earlier stages in the evolution of a culture can be reconstructed.

1716 M. DAVIES *Athen. Brit.* II. 164 The..survivals of such old Manuscript-Publications. **1867** E. B. TYLOR in *Proc. R. Inst.* V. 91 Their remnants have lingered on into a period of higher mental culture, and have become survivals. **1873** —— *Primitive Culture* (ed. 2) I. i. 16 Among evidence aiding us to trace the course which the civilization of the world has actually followed, is that great class of facts to denote which I have found it convenient to introduce the term 'survivals'. **1874** L. MORRIS *Serm. in Stones* iii, What are they But names for that which has no name, Survivals of a vanished day? **1874** CARPENTER *Mental Phys.* I. ii. (1879) 98 Instincts..which may be presumed to be survivals of those which characterized some lower grade. **1875** MAINE *Hist. Instit.* i. 14 This ancient written verse is what is now called a survival, descending to the first ages of written composition from the ages when measured rhythm was absolutely essential. **1883** J. HATTON & M. HARVEY *Newfoundland* 202 The Esquimaux are looked upon by some recent ethnologists as the 'survivals' of the Cave Men of Europe. **1908** R. BAGOT *A. Cuthbert* vi. 49 Jane Cuthbert was..a late survival of a type by no means uncommon..in the earlier half of her century. **1920** R. R. MARETT *Psychol. & Folk-lore* v. 99 Folk-lore, usually defined as the study of survivals, needs to conceive its object in a dynamic, not a static way. **1937** R. H. LOWIE *Hist. Ethnol. Theory* v. 41 Applying the principle of survivals, the author interprets mythological references to outstanding women as relics of a one-time gynaecocracy. **1944** B. MALINOWSKI *Sci. Theory of Culture* iii. 29 The real harm done by the concept of survivals in anthropology consists in that it functions on the one hand as a spurious methodological device in the reconstruction of evolutionary series; and, worse than that, it is an effective means of short-circuiting observation in field-work. **1965** L. MAIR *Introd. Social Anthrop.* ii. 26 Rivers was the last British field anthropologist to interpret usages that he actually observed as survivals of an earlier stage of society.

4. *attrib.* and *Comb.*, as ***survival capsule, car, course, kit, machine, pack, rate, skill, suit, training***; **survival bag**, a large plastic bag used by climbers as a protection against exposure; **survival curve**, a curve showing how the number of survivors varies with the size of a radiation dose or with the length of time after a dose; **survival time** *Biol.*, the time for which a biological system survives after a given dose of a chemical or ionizing radiation; **survival value** *Biol.*, the property of any heritable or other character that renders the individuals possessing it more likely to survive and reproduce; also *transf.*; also, the ability to survive.

1971 *Guardian* 22 Feb. 10/2 Cheap, light plastic or plasticised '*survival bags' can be bought for a few shillings. **1977** *Navy News* Aug. 21/3 The party spent the night practically underwater in polythene survival bags. **1960** *Britannica Bk. of Year* 557/2 The phrase **survival capsule* was used to mean the pilot's detachable compartment in a manned rocket. **1962** *Amer. Speech* XXXVII. 272 **Survival car*,..a traffic patrol car equipped with all sorts of strapping and cushioning devices to insure survival of the driver in case of a high-speed collision or roll-over. **1961** D. HUFF *Score* (1962) i. 2 Sometimes I wonder why my high school didn't give me a course in how to take tests. These days it would be a *survival course. **1936** E. C. SMITH in B. M. Duggar *Biol. Effects of Radiation* II. xxvii. 893 It has already been mentioned that deviations from the logarithmic type in the S-shaped *survival curves have been attributed by many to other varying factors. **1947** *Radiology* XLIX. 322/2 Since the survival curves for the two radiations are very similar, it is possible to establish a standard base curve which represents the expected survival for any combination of added doses of beta rays and gamma rays. **1980** *Genetics* XCV. 281 After UV treatment, [mutant] *pso1-1* in stationary phase is very sensitive and demonstrates an exponential survival curve. **1944** *Yank* 21 July 2/1 A plastic-boxed *survival kit (fishhooks, dextrose tablets, first-aid materials and other stuff). **1962** D. SLAYTON in *Into Orbit* 24 He would have a survival kit attached to the raft, which included a mirror he could use to signal airplanes overhead, some packages of shark repellant and a knife for cleaning fish. **1973** *Times* 17 May 12/6 Compiled a kind of survival-kit beginning with instructions on how to write out a cheque. **1976** R. DAWKINS *Selfish Gene* ii. 21 The replicators which survived were the ones which built *survival machines for themselves to live in. **1970** 'B. MATHER' *Break in Line* ix. 116 Compressed rations that had probably been stolen from American Air Force *survival packs. **1953** E. SMITH *Guide to Eng. Traditions & Public Life* 240 The increase of population was largely due not so much to a higher birth-rate as to a higher *survival-rate. **1976** *National Observer* (U.S.) 6 Nov. 17/2 Such '*survival skills' as filling out a job application and using a telephone book. **1980** *Christian Sci. Monitor* (Midwestern ed.) 4 Dec. B32/1 *Survival suits and inflatable life rafts must now be provided by the shipping companies. **1947** *Radiology* XLIX. 359/1 *Survival time, which was one of the most sensitive responses, showed effects following daily exposures in the range of 0·1n of fast neutrons and 1r of gamma rays. **1980** *Amer. Jrnl. Hematol.* VIII. 290 The gamma model is so far the best among the nine recommended methods for calculating the mean survival time in ^{51}Cr-labeled platelet survival study. **1972** *National Observer* (U.S.) 27 May 1/1 Bondurant's school is one of a handful that offer this '*survival' training. **1912** J. S. HUXLEY *Individual in Animal Kingdom* i. 16 This..view of the individual, as a whole whose diverse parts all work together in such a way as to ensure the whole's continuance, or, as the evolutionist would say, whose structure and working have '*survival-value', cannot stand without some qualification. **1924** J. A. THOMSON *Sci. Old & New* xlvii. 280 The notable musical talent of birds..has its survival-value in connection with mating and as an expression of very vital emotion. **1944** A. L. ROWSE *Eng. Spirit* xvii. 142 The survival-value of the College must be rated extraordinarily high. **1965** J. D. CHAMBERS in Glass & Eversley *Population in Hist.* xiii. 313 The survival-value of the small man under the impact of enclosures should not be under-estimated. **1966** *Listener* 17 Mar. 385/2 This behaviour has great survival value. So long as the troop sticks together, the prospects of a predator getting a meal are slim.

survivalism (sə'vaɪvəlɪz(ə)m). *rare.* [f. SURVIVAL + -ISM.] **1.** A theory of survival (see SURVIVAL 3).

1892 F. W. MAITLAND *Let.* 4 Sept. (1965) 104, I am putting into the L.Q.R. a protest against Mr. Gomme's 'survivalism'.

2. A policy of trying to ensure one's own survival or that of one's social or national group.

1952 *Round Table* Dec. 26 The persistence of the unceasing attack on 'survivalism'..argues that the Soviet critics recognize..the existence of a national pride. **1953** O. CAROE *Soviet Empire* xiii. 223 The minstrels sang of heroes of the resistance, and their original work is therefore banned as tainted with 'survivalism'. **1982** *New Musical Express* 30 Oct. 19/1 The survivalism of Jamaica's sufferers.

survivalist (sə'vaɪvəlɪst). *rare.* [f. SURVIVAL + -IST.] **1.** One who holds a theory of survival.

1882 GOLDW. SMITH in *Pop. Sci. Monthly* XX. 776 When you give a man a lower seat at table, the survivalist sees in the act a desire to have the force of gravity on your side. **1893** F. W. MAITLAND in *Law Q. Rev.* IX. 44 Had the manner in which Coton Field was occupied in 1835 been brought to the notice of some of our 'survivalists', they would have pronounced it to be an interesting relic of archaic times. **1968** *Encycl. Brit.* IX. 519/2 The controversy between the diffusionists, who believed culture contacts to be the main explanation of peasant beliefs and customs, and the survivalists, who attributed them to the processes of folk memory and to oral tradition handed down through the ages.

2. One who succeeds in surviving; one who makes a policy of aiming to survive. Also *attrib.*

1922 *Glasgow Herald* 6 May 9/2 They cannot deprive the London Scot of his reputation as a dancer and his fame as the survivalist of an institution so noteworthy as the Royal Caledonian Ball. **1953** O. CAROE *Soviet Empire* xi. 177 That, however, is what Communists would nowadays call a feudal survivalist deviation. **1978** *Time* 17 Apr. 2/2, I admire politicians... They're the best of the survivalists. **1980** *Times Lit. Suppl.* 25 Apr. 476/2 As historians come to appreciate the strength of 'survivalist' Catholicism, so Protestantism seems to be less and less a pre-ordained and natural consummation, England's manifest destiny.

survivance (sə'vaɪvəns). [ad. early mod.F. *survivance*, f. *survivant*: see next and -ANCE.]

1. = SURVIVAL 1. Now *rare.*

a **1623** BUCK *Rich. III*, III. (1646) 87 Our best Chroniclers make it doubtfull whether those two Princes were so lost.. or no, and infer that one of them was thought to be living many years after his death;..which opinion I like the better, because it mentioneth the survivance but of one of them. **1644** DIGBY *Nat. Soul* Concl. 448, I see, that all this huge product of Algebraicall multiplication, appeareth as nothing, in respect of thy remayning, and neuer ending suruiuance. *a* **1706** EVELYN *Hist. Relig.* (1850) I. 192 So fixed was this good man in the belief of the soul's survivance. **1773** JOHNSON *Let. to Mrs. Thrale* 27 Apr., I am reasoning upon a principle very far from certain, a confidence of survivance. **1819** SCOTT in Lockhart *Life* xlvi, That two of them should die without any rational possibility of the survivance of the third. **1836** I. TAYLOR *Phys. Theory* (1857) 11 That which Christianity requires us to believe is the actual survivance of our personal consciousness embodied. **1874** *Act 37 & 38 Vict.* c. 94 §9 A personal right..shall.. vest..in the heir..by his survivance of the person to whom he is entitled to succeed.

b. *fig.* = SURVIVAL 2.

1838 *Blackw. Mag.* XLIII. 34 The chances are much against the survivance..of any work..which has early attained to a very great celebrity. **1867** DK. ARGYLL *Reign of Law* vii. 382 The survivance of the ancient domestic industries of so many centuries was no longer possible.

2. The succession to an estate, office, etc. of a survivor nominated before the death of the existing occupier or holder; the right of such succession in case of survival.

c **1674** *Acc. Scot. Grievances under Lauderdale* 22 The abuse of gifts of the reversions or survivances of places to children and boys. **1714** BURNET *Hist. Ref.* III. I. 3 *Gratias Expectativas*, or the Survivances of Bishopricks. *a* **1715** —— *Own Time* (1766) I. 443 His son had the survivance of the Stadtholdership. **1791** LD. AUCKLAND *Corr.* 12 Dec. (1861) II. 396 Ewart..is discontented with his pension, which, however, is very high, I believe 1500*l.* a year, paying nett above 1000*l.*, with the survivance of half to Mrs. Ewart. **1820** *Ann. Reg.* II. 1189 The Emperor..created him..a baron of the Roman empire, with survivance to his heirs male. **1884** *Edin. Rev.* Oct. 427 William II., who had already been elected to the survivance of his offices.

So †**sur'vivancy.**

1659 TORRIANO, A surviving, or survivancie, *sopravivimento, sorvivimento.* **1662** J. DAVIES tr. *Olearius' Voy. Ambass.* 96 The best Politicians..are so far from allowing a survivancy in Governments, that they would have a Sovereign to change the Governours from three years to three years. **1753** *Scots Mag.* May 252/2 That survivancy of all the said offices be in the longest liver of the two.

sur'vivant, *a. rare.* [ad. F. *survivant*, pr. pple. of *survivre* to SURVIVE.] Surviving.

c **1555** HARPSFIELD *Divorce Hen. VIII* (Camden) 236 To marry the brother's wife if he died without children, the brother survivant. **1635** J. HAYWARD tr. *Biondi's Banish'd Virg.* To Rdr., In respect many of them..are to this day survivant. **1654** tr. *Scudery's Curia Pol.* 116 The remainder and survivant party. **1934** F. SCOTT FITZGERALD *Tender is Night* I. xix. 107 But they were frightened at his survivant will.

absol. **1677** GALE *Crt. Gentiles* III. 190 To animate the survivant, and to encourage them to the like exploits.

survive (sə'vaɪv), *v.* Also 6 **survyve**, 7 *Anglo-Irish* **surveywe**. [a. AF. *survivre*, OF. *so(u)rvivre* (mod.F. *survivre*), = Pr. *sobreviure*, It. *sorvivere*, Sp. *sobrevivir*, Pg. *-viver*:—late L. *supervīvĕre*, f. *super-* SUPER- 2 + *vīvĕre* to live.]

1. a. *intr.* To continue to live after the death of another, or after the end or cessation of some thing or condition or the occurrence of some event (expressed or implied); to remain alive, live on.

1473 *Rolls of Parlt.* VI. 95/2 To have and perceyve the said cs yerely, to the said Mary and Robert, for the terme of their lyfes, and either of [them] survivyng. **1503–4** *Act 19 Hen. VII*, c. 25 Preamble, Lyfe [is] as uncertayne to suche as survyve as was to them now departed. *a* **1513** FABYAN *Chron.* I. xxv. 18 They testyfye that Porrex was slayne and Ferrex suruyuyd. **1591** SHAKS. *Two Gent.* IV. ii. 110, I did loue a Lady, But she is dead... *Sil.* Say that she be: yet Valentine thy friend Suruiues. **1615** CROOKE *Body of Man* 335 Many children borne the seuenth month suruiue and do well. *a* **1660** *Contemp. Hist. Irel.* (Ir. Archæol. Soc.) II. 26 Wee..will in open fielde fight with as many of those our disparagers as longe as any of us will surveywe. **1697** DRYDEN *Æneid* II. 814 Look if your helpless Father yet survive; Or if Ascanius, or Creusa live. **1771** *Junius Lett.* lxi. (1788) 330 The son of that unfortunate prince survives. **1808** SCOTT in Lockhart *Life* i. (1839) I. 33 He survived a few days, but becoming delirious before his dissolution, [etc.]. **1894** H. DRUMMOND *Ascent of Man* 278 There are vastly more creatures born than can ever survive. **1911** MARETT *Anthropology* iii. 70 To survive is to survive to breed. If you live to eighty, and have no children, you do not survive in the biological sense.

b. *transf.* To continue to exist after some person, thing, or event; to last on.

1593 SHAKS. *Lucr.* 204 Yea though I die the scandale will suruiue. **1654** tr. *Scudery's Curia Pol.* Ded., They survive to future Ages by their Actions. **1671** MILTON *Samson* 1706 Though her body die, her fame survives. *a* **1721** PRIOR *To C'tess Dowager of Devonshire* 53 Thro' circling Years thy Labours would survive. **1830** SCOTT *Hrt. Midl.* Introd., A late amiable and ingenious lady, whose wit and power of remarking and judging of character still survive in the memory of her friends. **1850** TENNYSON *In Mem.* xxxviii, If any care for what is here Survive in spirits render'd free. **1885** *Law Times* 9 May 22/2 The mortgagor can inspect the title deeds while his right to redeem survives. **1907** BP. ROBERTSON in *Trans. Devon Assoc.* 50 A Norman family whose name survives in place-names all over Devon.

c. *Law.* Of an estate, etc.: To pass *to* the survivor or survivors of two or more joint-tenants or persons who have a joint interest.

1648 *Bury Wills* (Camden) 205 Whereas by the death of the sayd Isabell my daughter the estate and interest in the said mortgaged premises..is survived and come to the sayd Catherine and Anne my daughters. **1818** CRUISE *Digest* (ed. 2) VI. 425 If one died under age, his or her part would not descend, but survive to the others.

2. *trans.* To continue to live after, outlive. **a.** To remain alive after the death of (another).

1572 HULOET s.v., To the entent that he may suruiue thee. **1596** SHAKS. *Tam. Shr.* II. i. 125 And, for that dowrie, Ile assure her of Her widdow-hood, be it that she suruiue me In all my Lands and Leases whatsoeuer. ***a*1680** GLANVILL *Sadducismus* II. (1681) 166 Thinking they had Souls surviving their bodies. **1772** *Gentl. Mag.* XLII. 245/1 The Lord Chancellor made an order for two issues at law to be tried, whether General Stanwix survived his Lady, or whether Mrs. Stanwix survived the General. **1849** MACAULAY *Hist. Eng.* v. I. 568 Argyle, who survived Rumbold a few hours, left a dying testimony to the virtues of the gallant Englishman. **1880** MUIRHEAD *Gaius* III. §16 If he..is survived by children of brothers predeceased, the inheritance belongs to all of them.

b. To continue to live after (an event, point of time, etc.), or after the end or cessation of (a condition, etc.).

1588 SHAKS. *Tit. A.* v. iii. 41 Because the Girle, should not suruiue her shame. **1591** —— *1 Hen. VI*, III. ii. 37 France, thou shalt rue this Treason with thy teares, If Talbot but suruiue thy Trecherie. ***a*1610** PARSONS *Leicester's Ghost* (1641) 34 What others wrot before I doe survive. **1717** LADY M. W. MONTAGU *Let. to C'tess Mar* 16 Jan., If I survive my journey, you shall hear from me again. **1777** PRIESTLEY *Matter & Sp.* (1782) I. xxii. 286 Whether brutes will survive the grave we cannot tell. **1849** MACAULAY *Hist. Eng.* v. I. 631 When Swift had survived his faculties many years, the Irish populace still continued to light bonfires on his birthday. **1852** H. ROGERS *Ecl. Faith* (1853) 193, I see few of my youthful contemporaries who have not survived their infidelity. **1883** E. P. ROE in *Harper's Mag.* Dec. 52/2 I've known peach buds to survive fifteen below zero.

c. *transf.* To continue to exist after the death or cessation of (a person, condition, etc.), or after the occurrence of (an event); to outlast.

1633 P. FLETCHER *Poet. Misc., Ps. i.* ii, The soul..Still springs, buds, grows, and dying time survives. **1694** ADDISON *St. Cecilia's Day* iv, Musick shall then exert its pow'r, And sound survive the ruins of the world. **1788** GIBBON *Decl. & F.* xlix. V. 139 In his [*sc.* Charlemagne's] institutions I can seldom discover the general views and the immortal spirit of a legislator, who survives himself for the benefit of posterity. **1847** EMERSON *Repr. Men, Napoleon* Wks. (Bohn) I. 374 The principal works that have survived him are his magnificent roads. **1885** 'MRS. ALEXANDER' *At Bay* iii, It is pleasant to find that so much faith in your fellow-creatures survives the experience.

3. *intr.* and *trans.* In trivial use. Freq. in phr. *I'll survive.*

1902 KIPLING *Traffics & Discoveries* (1904) 30 'But it'll bore you to death,' he says... 'I'll survive,' I says, 'I ain't British. I can think,' I says. **1928** M. ARLEN *Lily Christine* xiii. 240 'All this trouble your silly husband has brought on you!' 'Oh, we'll survive that,' she said lightly. **1949** 'J. TEY' *Brat Farrar* xxxi. 278 The fact that we are making him part of the family..will take a lot of the fun out of it for the scandal-mongers. We'll survive, Nell. And so will he. **1958** C. S. FORESTER *Hornblower in W. Indies* 184 'I don't envy you, frankly.' 'No doubt I'll survive, sir.' **1971** 'F. CLIFFORD' *Blind Side* IV. ii. 157 'It's nice... Cosy.' 'No *fados*, I'm afraid.' 'I'll survive.'

Hence **sur'viving** *vbl. sb.*, survival.

1818 CRUISE *Digest* (ed. 2) IV. 173 Her surviving was a continuing act. **1900** MARY KINGSLEY *Notes* 203 No amount of experience in her husband's habit of surviving ever made her feel he was safe.

sur'viver[1]. Now *rare* or *Obs.* [f. prec. + -ER[1].] = SURVIVOR.

1602 SHAKS. *Ham.* I. ii. 90 The Suruiuer bound In filiall Obligation..To do obsequious Sorrow. **1634** T. JOHNSON *Parey's Wks.* II. 62 There is the like mutuall bond of love betweene Turtles, for if one of them die, the surviver never solicites Hymen more. **1726** in *Nairne Peerage Evidence* (1874) 35 Nor shall any part of the deceasers patrimonies accress to the survivers. **1825** J. NEAL *Bro. Jonathan* xxxii. III. 201 The surviver is George.

Hence †**sur'vivership** = SURVIVORSHIP; †**sur'vivery**, survivors collectively.

1638 SIR T. HERBERT *Trav.* (ed. 2) 271 Seleuchus Callynicus sonne to Antiochus Theos by survivership (after long stormes) seeming to steare in that unruly Ocean. **1680** RICH *Ep. Seven Ch.* 90 When the Irish had murdered two hundred thousand, they little thought that they had but excited the Survivery to a terrible Revenge.

†**sur'viver**[2]. *Obs.* In 6 -oure, 6–7 -or. [f. SURVIVE + -ER[4]. Cf. SUPERVIVER[2].] = SURVIVORSHIP.

1544 tr. *Littleton's Tenures* III. iii. 63 b, They shall haue this by discent & nat by the suruyuour as ioyntenauntes haue. **1583** in *East Anglian* Apr. (1910) 249 By survivor sole seysed of and in the said Mannor. **1602** WARNER *Alb. Eng.* Epit. (1612) 381 Iohn of Gaunt, by birth the fourth, by suruiuor the second Sonne of Edward the third.

surviving (sə'vaɪvɪŋ), *ppl. a.* [f. as prec. + -ING[2].] That survives. **a.** Still living after another's death.

1593 SHAKS. *Lucr.* 519 Thy suruiuing husband. **1660** R. COKE *Power & Subj.* 144 We find the sentence of the Pope and Wilfrids restitution still opposed by the surviving Bishops in Alfreds sons reign. **1780** *Mirror* No. 81 ¶5 After the first transports of my mother's grief were subsided, she began to apply herself to the care of her surviving child. **1855** MACAULAY *Hist. Eng.* xv. III. 576 The surviving members of the High Court of Justice which had sate on Charles the First. **1861** PALEY *Æschylus* (ed. 2) *Choeph.* 817 *note*, The dead Agamemnon and the surviving Electra.

b. Still remaining after the cessation of something else.

1593 SHAKS. *Lucr.* 223 This dying virtue, this suruiuing shame. **1820** SHELLEY *Witch Atl.* xxiv, If I must weep when the surviving Sun Shall smile on your decay. **1837** CARLYLE *Fr. Rev.* I. II. viii, The surviving Literature of the Period.

survivor (sə'vaɪvə(r)). Also 6–7 -our. [f. SURVIVE + -OR.] One who (or that which) survives.

1. a. A person, animal, or plant that outlives another or others; one remaining alive after another's death, or after some disaster in which others perish.

1624 DONNE *Devot.* (ed. 2) 27 As though that one were the suruiuour of all the sonns of men, to whom God had giuen the world. **1683** DRYDEN *Life Plutarch* 59 That he was at Rome either in the joynt reign of the two Vespasians, or at least in that of the survivour Titus. **1765** *Museum Rust.* IV. 361, I am now sorry that I counted not the plants,..I should then have known what proportion the deceased bore to the survivors. **1791** COWPER *Yardley Oak* 1 Survivor sole, and hardly such, of all That once liv'd here. **1856** KANE *Arctic Expl.* I. xiv. 163 My dogs..had perished; there were only six survivors of the whole pack. **1874** GREEN *Short Hist.* viii. §6. 518 Of the band of patriots..he [Pym] was the sole survivor.

fig. **1859** *Sporting Mag.* Dec. 393 In the last half-hour there were only six [hunting men] up, over a very severe bit of country; Jack Morgan [the huntsman]..one of the survivors.

b. *attrib.* or *appos.* Surviving. *rare*$^{-1}$.

1602 WARNER *Alb. Eng.* Epit. (1612) 371 Edward yongest, but Suruiuor Sonne of the aforesaid Egelred.

c. Special *Comb.*: **survivor syndrome**, the (freq. delayed) symptoms, such as disintegration of personality, nightmares, tension, and guilt, which are classed as a syndrome and can afflict someone who has survived a dehumanizing and degrading experience of terror.

1968 W. G. NIEDERLAND in H. Krystal *Massive Psychic Trauma* iv. 63 Only in this way can we understand, in our appraisal of these people, the mental condition from which they suffer today: this survivor syndrome which I have described as a clinical entity. **1979** B. BETTELHEIM *Surviving* 29 Unable to embark on the strenuous and hazardous task of integrating their personalities, such survivors suffer from a psychiatric disorder which has been named the concentration camp survivor syndrome.

2. *spec.* in *Law.* One of two or more designated persons, esp. joint-tenants or other persons having a joint interest, who outlives the other or others; a longer or the longest liver.

1503–4 *Act 19 Hen. VII*, c. 25 §1 As yf the seid persones ..hade be jointly named with the seid Survivours. **1592** WEST *1st Pt. Symbol.* §103 A. Within one yeare next after the decease of the suruiuor of them. **1607** SHAKS. *Cor.* v. vi. 19 The fall of either Makes the Suruiuor heyre of all. **1759** *Ir. Act 33 Geo. II*, c. 4 §17 Any two of them, or the survivors or survivor of them, or the heirs of such survivor, may sell.. any part of the estate. **1766** BLACKSTONE *Comm.* II. xii. 183 The entire tenancy upon the decease of any of them remains to the survivors, and at length to the last survivor. **1818** CRUISE *Digest* (ed. 2) II. 434 A. devised lands to B. and C., and the survivor of them. **1855** MACAULAY *Hist. Eng.* xix. IV. 326 As the annuitants dropped off, their annuities were to be divided among the survivors, till the number of survivors was reduced to seven.

3. *colloq.* One who has the knack of surviving afflictions unscathed.

1971 P. D. JAMES *Shroud for Nightingale* ix. 295 She would be earning a good living somewhere... The Mary Taylors of the world were natural survivors. **1978** J. ANDERSON *Angel of Death* xiv. 167 You're a survivor, Paul. People like you always come through.

Hence **sur'vivoress** (-vress), a female survivor.

***a*1711** KEN *Sion* Poet. Wks. 1721 IV. 414 The Survivress in soft mournful Tones The Death of Sister Philomel bemoans.

survivor, -oure, var. SURVIVER[2].

survivorship (sə'vaɪvəʃɪp). [f. SURVIVOR + -SHIP.]

1. *Law*, etc. **a.** The condition of a survivor, or the fact of one person surviving another or others, considered in relation to some right or privilege depending on such survival or the period of it.

presumption of survivorship, the presumption of the momentary or brief survival of one of a number of persons who have perished by the same calamity, as affecting rights of inheritance.

1697 *Lond. Gaz.* No. 3315/4 An Order, Nº 3179, Sir John Burgoyne..for 100l. on Survivorships, on the Life of Lucy Burgoyne. **1772** R. PRICE *Observ. Reversionary Payments* (ed. 2) 75 Since the duration of survivorship is in the present case..equal to the duration of marriage. **1815** J. MILNE (*title*) A treatise on the valuation of annuities and assurances on lives and survivorships. **1825** *Beck's Elem. Med. Jurispr.* 209 Of the presumption of survivorship of mother or child, when both die during delivery. *Ibid.* 211 Of the presumption of survivorship of persons of different ages, destroyed by a common accident. **1834** HT. MARTINEAU *Farrers* vii. 114 Jane ought to have given the largest proportion, not only because she had no claims upon her, but because her survivorship enriched her by means of this very death. **1842** *Penny Cycl.* XXIII. 330/2 The chance of survivorship is that of one individual, now of a given age, surviving another, also now of a given age. **1872** *Hist. Broughton Place Church* 56 The Rev. Andrew Thomson was inducted as colleague and, in case of survivorship, successor to the Rev. Dr. Brown.

b. A right depending on survival; *e.g.* the right of the survivor or survivors of a number of joint-tenants or other persons having a joint interest, to take the whole on the death of the other or others; the right of future succession, in case of survival, to some office not vacant at the time of the grant.

***a*1625** SIR H. FINCH *Law* (1636) 60 Two Abbots cannot bee Ioyntenants..for they cannot haue the effect of it, which is suruiuorship. **1647** N. BACON *Disc. Govt. Eng.* I. xiii. (1739) 24 The Clergy..turned both King and Lords out, and shut the doors after them, and so possessed themselves of the whole by Survivorship. **1691** T. H[ALE] *Acc. New Invent.* p. lvii, The Conservatorship..may by survivorship accrue to a Colour-man in the Strand. **1726** AYLIFFE *Parergon* 163 Where the Grant has been by Survivorship. **1827** JARMAN *Powell's Devises* II. 317 That each annuitant should receive a proportionable share of his fortune, with benefit of survivorship and right of accruer. **1860** *Commercial Handbk* 70 *Survivorship in Life Assurance*, a reversionary benefit, contingent upon certain lives being survivors. **1860** FREER *Hen. IV*, II. II. iv. 89 He offered the government of Burgundy, with the survivorship for his son. **1867** BRANDE & COX *Dict. Sci.* etc. s.v., The values of annuities and assurances in every order of survivorship, where there are only three lives. **1888** *Encycl. Brit.* XXIII. 598/1 On the death of one trustee there is survivorship.

†**c.** *concr.* That which comes to a person by survivorship. *Obs. rare.*

1633 SIR J. BOROUGHS *Sov. Brit. Seas* (1651) 23 Canutus the Dane, coming not long after to be King first of halfe the Realme..and after the death of Edmond of the whole Survivorshippe.

d. *attrib.*: **survivorship annuity** (see quot.).

1838 DE MORGAN *Ess. Probab.* 206 To find..the value of an annuity on the life of B, aged *n*, the first payment of which is to be made at the end of the year in which the life of A, aged *m*, fails. This is called a survivorship annuity, since it can never be paid unless B survive A.

2. a. *gen.* The state or condition of being a survivor; survival.

1709 STEELE *Tatler* No. 53 ¶2 We are now going into the Country together, with only one Hope for making this Life agreeable, Survivorship. **1711** —— *Spect.* No. 192 ¶2 The Survivorship of a worthy Man in his Son. **1748** RICHARDSON *Clarissa* VI. 334 In case of survivorship, I most cheer-fully accept of the sacred office you are pleased to offer me. **1837** DE QUINCEY *Rev. Tartars* Wks. 1854 IV. 132 As old men, we reap nothing from our sufferings, nor benefit by our survivorship. **1865** GROTE *Plato* II. xxiii. 203 The Epikureans denied altogether the survivorship of soul over body. **1877** J. MARTINEAU in Drummond & Upton *Life & Lett.* (1902) viii. II. 38 It is better to have, than to give, the grief of survivorship.

b. The probability of surviving to a given age; the proportion of a population that does this.

1949 L. I. DUBLIN et al. *Length of Life* (ed. 2) ix. 178 With information available regarding the actual mortality and survivorship of the cohort born in 1890, it becomes possible to compute..the average years of life lived after any attained age. **1954** *Q. Rev. Biol.* XXIX. 105/1 These quantities are nicely summed up by the familiar life-table function, survivorship (l_x)..and by the age-specific birth rate. **1978** *Nature* 5 Oct. 466/1 In higher forms life span and survivorship can be expressed in terms of allometric and Gompertz equations.

3. A body of survivors.

1867 WOOLRYCH *Bar & Serjeant-at-Law* 7 The Bar will survive, and the survivorship will consist of the Queen's Counsel and the Barristers-at-Law.

4. Special Comb.: **survivorship curve**, a curve showing the proportion of a population surviving at different ages.

1953 E. P. ODUM *Fund. Ecol.* vi. 108 The resulting curve is called a survivorship curve. **1976** *Nature* 1–8 Jan. 12/2 Van Valen..has made a notable contribution in this respect by applying the survivorship curve technique of population biologists to the study of extinction rates for numerous fossil taxa.

survyour, -owre, obs. ff. SURVEYOR.

surwan ('sɜːwɑːn). *India.* Also -aun, ser-, sirwan. [a. Urdū = Pers. *sārbān*, f. *sār* camel + *-bān* keeper.] A camel-driver.

1821 [M. SHERER] *Sk. India* 242 To..hire good camels, and to engage surwans for them. **1828** MUNDY *Pen & Pencil Sketches* (1832) II. i. 1 Camels..resisting every effort..of their serwâns to induce them to embark. **1884** F. BOYLE *Borderland* 289 The sirwans were mustering at earliest dawn.

sury, variant of SURA[1].

sus, suss (sʌs), *sb. slang.* **1.** [Abbrev. of SUSPICION or SUSPICIOUS *a.*] Suspicion of having committed a crime; suspicious behaviour, esp. loitering; the sus law. Freq. in phr. *on sus.*

1936 'J. CURTIS' *Gilt Kid* xxv. 248 What you nick me for? Sus? **1963** T. & P. MORRIS *Pentonville* xv. 312 Men who are, in the prison idiom, 'done for sus', that is to say, prosecuted as 'suspected persons or reputed thieves loitering with intent to commit a felony'. **1970** G. F. NEWMAN *Sir, You Bastard* ii. 74 Chance nickings in the street, from anything on sus, to indecent exposure. **1978** G. WILLIAMS *Textbk. Criminal Law* xxxvii. 817 Another provision of the Vagrancy Act s.4 (as amended) allows the punishment on summary conviction of 'suspected persons' and 'reputed thieves' who 'frequent and loiter' in certain public places with intent to commit an arrestable offence. Persons 'found' committing the offence can be arrested. In police jargon, the man is 'picked up on sus'. **1981** *Times* 24 Aug. 3/8 The delight at the passing of 'sus' is, however, mitigated by a degree of apprehension about its replacement, the newly created offence of 'interference with vehicles'.

2. [Abbrev. of SUSPECT *sb.*[2] or SUSPECTED *ppl. a.*] A suspected person, a police suspect.

1936 'J. CURTIS' *Gilt Kid* xxix. 281 Yes, there was a bit of a scoring match when they claimed me. Picked me up as a sus and then hung a screwing rap on me. **1967** K. GILES *Death in Diamonds* vi. 110 Sorry, old man, they found your chief sus. with his neck broken. **1970** R. BUSBY *Frighteners* viii. 80

He's going to go running to the law, because if he don't, he's the number one suss. **1977** *Evening Standard* 8 Mar. 8/2 'Sus' is an ugly word whose meaning is now known to nearly every young West Indian living in London. It is short for 'suspected person'. Its widespread and growing use by the police against black youngsters is coming to be regarded by many lawyers . . as a major scandal.

3. *attrib.* and *Comb.*, as ***sus book, case, charge, offence***; **sus law**: until 1981, the law by which a person could be arrested on suspicion of committing a crime; effective since the Vagrancy Act (5 *Geo. IV* c. 83) of 1824.

1970 J. Boland *Big Job* xv. 124 The Sus book . . was where lists of Suspected Persons were kept. **1977** *Morning Star* 19 Jan. 2/4 These limitations have serious impact in 'sus' (being a suspected person) and 'enclosed premises' charges. **1977** *Evening Standard* 8 Mar. 8/3 A study of a number of 'sus' cases shows that they all conform to a remarkably similar pattern. **1981** *New Statesman* 13 Feb. 3/1 The government is proposing to keep the 'Sus' laws in Scotland, even though they are being repealed in England and Wales. *Ibid.* The 'useful and necessary' provisions of the Vagrancy Act 1824 and the Burgh Police (Scotland) Act 1892 which define sus offences in Scotland. **1981** *Times* 24 Aug. 318 The controversial 'sus' law, under which people can be arrested on suspicion that an offence is likely to be committed, is no more. The Criminal Attempts Act, which comes into force today, abolishes section 4 of the Vagrancy Act 1824.

sus, suss (sʌs), *v. slang.* [Abbrev. of suspect *v.*; cf. prec.

Participles of the verb are usu. formed with a double final consonant in the stem. The form with final double *s* has now spread to the infinitive. The substantive, however, is still most commonly encountered with a single final consonant (*sus*).]

1. a. *trans.* To suspect (a person) of a crime (cf. sus *sb.* 1). Also in general use.

1953 D. Webb *Crime is my Business* x. 202 He turned to Hodge and said, 'Who's sussed for this job?' **1959** *Observer* 11 Oct. 21/4 Commercial artist . . pursued by beat blonde he has never seen. . . Later heavily sus-ed of her murder at the beach house. **1960** [see lot *sb.* 2 d]. **1966** C. Rougvie *Gredos Reckoning* iii. 49, I sussed a weirdie and asked: 'You queer or something?' **1970** R. Busby *Frighteners* ii. 25 You'll get sussed right off. The club boys'll mark you down for a copper the minute you walk through the door.

b. With obj. clause: to suspect, to imagine or fancy (something) as likely; hence, to feel or surmise.

1958 [see get *v.* 27 d]. **1960** *Punch* 24 Feb. 284/2, I sussed that all the dodgy bookshops would soon be skint. **1969** *It* 4–17 July 14/1 It wasn't a situation too conducive to free, relaxed chat and one could suss that Mick was a bit fed up with having to reel out witty and intelligent quips for the voracious appetites of the human media. **1977** *Transatlantic Rev.* lx. 192 Mercurially sussing that the largest ingredient of the briefcase was dollar bills, [he] added: 'Were you aware . . that the largest ingredient of bank-note paper was Indian Hemp?'

2. To work or figure *out*; to investigate, to discover the truth about (a person or thing). Also with obj. clause and without const.

1966 *Queen* 28 Sept. 28/3 Youth susses things out on its own. **1969** Fabian & Byrne *Groupie* xxix. 207 When chicks came round I enjoyed sussing them out, and trying to guess which one would last and which one would be dropped. **1971** *It* 2–16 June 18/2 Everybody seems to have at least two nicknames plus their birth-signs so every little chickie can think they've got it sussed. **1971** N. Saunders *Alternative London* xxvii. 256 Talk to him to sus him out—if you're not sure of him, don't leave him out of your sight. **1975** *Daily Tel.* 20 Jan. 7/1 'If ever my members sussed out that I can't read, I'd be a gonner,' he said. **1976** P. Cave *High Flying Birds* x. 105 Stay there a minute. I'll go and suss it out. **1977** *Daily Mirror* 10 May 17/1 It took me about half a day to suss out the industry and realise how easy it would be to move in. **1977** *Sounds* 9 July 30/5 Here we have a stylish axe/singer who's sussed the factors that made Benson such a universally popular guitarist. **1980** *Times Lit. Suppl.* 26 Sept. 1064/3 A morning's browsing in a book shop will suffice for you to suss out the market.

susannite (s(j)uːˈzænaɪt). *Min.* Also **suzannite**. [ad. Ger. *suzannit* (Haidinger, 1845), f. proper name *Susanna* (see below): see -ite[1] 2 b.] A mineral found in the Susanna mine at Leadhills in Scotland, chemically identical with lead-hillite, but crystallizing in the rhombohedral system.

1845 *Encycl. Metrop.* VI. 501/1 *Suzannite*, sulphato-tri-carbonate of Lead. **1868** Dana *Min.* (ed. 5) 626 Susannite . . Lustre resinous—adamantine. Color white, green, yellow, brownish-black. Streak uncolored.

susceptance (səˈsɛptəns). *Electr.* [f. suscept(ible *a.* + -ance.] In an alternating current circuit, the imaginary part of the admittance, as opposed to the real part or conductance.

1894 Steinmetz & Bedell in *Trans. Amer. Inst. Electr. Engineers* XI. 648 Admittance, conductance and susceptance are thus used as the inverse correspondents of impedance, resistance and reactance, and may be added as vector quantities. **1960** H. W. Jackson *Introd. Electric Circuits* xiv. 307 Susceptance is the ability of an inductance or capacitance to pass alternating current. *Ibid.*, Capacitive susceptance is a + *j* quantity. **1966** *McGraw-Hill Encycl. Sci. & Technol.* XIII. 330/1 Susceptance is a function involving both resistance and reactance. If resistance is negligible, the *B* = . . the reciprocal of the reactance.

susceptibility (səsɛptɪˈbɪlɪtɪ). [f. next: see -ity. Cf. med.L. *susceptibilitas* (Abelard), F. *susceptibilité* (from 18th c.).] The quality or condition of being susceptible; capability of receiving, being affected by, or undergoing something.

1. Const. *of* (now rare) or *to*.

a. Capability of undergoing a specified action or process.

The action is mostly, now always, denoted by a noun (occas. by a passive infinitive), which is usually equivalent to a passive gerund: e.g. *susceptibility of application* = capability of being applied; *s. to reflection* = capability of being reflected.

1644 Bp. Maxwell *Prerog. Chr. Kings* viii. 91 *Potestas passiva regiminis*, a capacity or susceptibility to be governed. **1794** G. Adams *Nat. & Exp. Philos.* I. x. 399 In proportion to its susceptibility of liquifaction in a low degree of temperature. **1823** Coleridge *Table-t.* 3 Jan., A visible substance without susceptibility of impact, I maintain to be an absurdity. **1850** Robertson *Serm.* Ser. iii. iii. (1872) 35 Its susceptibility of application to the purpose. **1891** Meredith *One of our Conq.* xxviii, A certain face close on handsome, had a fatal susceptibility to caricature.

b. Capability of being, or disposition to be, affected by something; sensibility or sensitiveness to something specified: (*a*) external influences, impressions, etc.

a **1676** Hale *Prim. Orig. Man.* i. i. (1677) 35 The susceptibility of those influences, and the effects thereof. **1833** I. Taylor *Fanat.* i. 20 The susceptibility to the opinions of those around us. **1855** J. H. Newman *Callista* (1890) 328 A sense of relations and aims, and a susceptibility of arguments, to which before she was an utter stranger. *a* **1862** Buckle *Civiliz.* (1864) II. vi. 570 Sympathy, being a susceptibility to impression, is also a principle of action.

(*b*) feelings or emotions.

1751 Johnson *Rambler* No. 112 ⁋2 The same laxity of regimen is equally necessary to intellectual health, and to a perpetual susceptibility of occasional pleasure. **1755** Young *Centaur* iv. Wks. 1757 IV. 209 A tenderness of heart, and a susceptibility of awe, with regard to God. **1846** Grote *Greece* i. i, Susceptibility of pleasure and pain.

(*c*) physical agents or agencies, disease, etc.

1803 Beddoes *Hygëia* ix. 171 When young persons . . begin to have too great susceptibility of cold. **1820** Faraday *Exp. Res.* xvi. (1859) 66 The difference between these two alloys as to susceptibility to oxygen. **1882** *Med. Temp. Jrnl.* L. 67 My studies . . have pointed to childhood as a period of extreme susceptibility to this disorder. **1890** *Science-Gossip* XXVI. 218/2 The period of maximum susceptibility of the larva to the colour.

2. Without const.

a. (*a*) Capacity for feeling or emotion; disposition or tendency to be emotionally affected; sensibility.

1753 Richardson *Grandison* V. xxi. 123 Yet was her susceptibility her only inducement; for the man was neither handsome . . nor genteel. **1805** James *Milit. Dict.* (ed. 2) s.v. *Susceptible*, Men of extreme susceptibility are not calculated for command. **1849** Macaulay *Hist. Eng.* i. I. 66 The susceptibility, the vivacity, the natural turn for acting and rhetoric, which are indigenous on the shores of the Mediterranean Sea. **1879** McCarthy *Own Times* II. xx. 78 There was something about the time and manner of the papal bull calculated to offend the susceptibility of a great and independent nation.

(*b*) *pl.* Capacities of emotion, esp. such as may be hurt or offended; sensitive feelings; sensibilities.

1754 Richardson *Sir Charles Grandison* IV. xxxiii. 228 Emily is a good girl; but she has susceptibilities already. **1846** Grote *Greece* i. i. II. 39 The women, whose religious susceptibilities were often found extremely unmanageable. **1871** Macduff *Mem. Patmos* i. 6, It was the 'another King, one Jesus' which had roused the susceptibilities—kindled the jealous fury—of the minions of Cæsar. **1884** Gladstone in *Daily News* 23 Oct. 5/7, I have not knowingly wounded the susceptibilities or assailed the opinions of any one who may read them. **1896** *Daily Graphic* 10 Feb. 7/1 Nobody wants to offend French susceptibilities by the suggestion that our neighbours have jockeyed us in Siam.

b. Capacity for receiving mental or moral impressions.

1782 V. Knox *Ess. Moral & Lit.* ii. I. 7 Furnished with a natural susceptibility, and free from any acquired impediment, the mind is then [*sc.* in youth] in the most favourable state for the admission of instruction. **1852** H. Rogers *Ecl. Faith* 298 The same 'susceptibilities' and 'potentialities' are in each human mind.

c. Capability of being, or disposition to be, physically affected (as a living body, or an inanimate thing); *spec.* the capacity of a substance (e.g. iron) for being magnetized, measured by the ratio of the magnetization to the magnetizing force.

1816 J. Smith *Panorama Sci. & Art* II. 283 Different animals are susceptible of galvanism in very different degrees. In cold-blooded animals, this susceptibility sometimes continues for several days after death. **1817** J. Scott *Paris Revisit.* (ed. 4) 287 An inhabitant of these islands, who has constitutional susceptibilities that are unpleasantly affected by a humid . . atmosphere. **1883** *Encycl. Brit.* XV. 267/1 The earlier experimenters arrived for the most part at the conclusion that the susceptibility κ of weakly magnetic bodies is constant. **1903** *Lancet* 4 Apr. 945/2 Susceptibility is very nearly allied to predisposition; it may perhaps be defined as acquired predisposition.

susceptible (səˈsɛptɪb(ə)l), *a.* and *sb.* [ad. med.L. *susceptibilis* (Boethius, Thomas Aquinas), f. *suscept-*: see susception and -ible. Cf. F. *susceptible*.]

A. *adj.* **1.** Const. *of* or *to*: Capable of taking, receiving, being affected by, or undergoing something.

a. with *of*: Capable of undergoing, admitting of (some action or process).

The following noun of action may usually be paraphrased by a passive gerund, as *susceptible of proof* = capable of being proved. A passive gerund sometimes occurs, as *susceptible* (= capable) *of being exercised*.

1605 Bacon *Adv. Learn.* ii. x. § 1 This subject of man's body is of all other things in nature most susceptible of remedy. **1657** Purchas *Pol. Flying-Ins.* i. iii. 5 Their [*sc.* bees'] leggs are not susceptible of a sting. **1663** J. H. tr. *Selden's Mare Cl.* (title-p.), The Sea is proved by the Law Of Nature and Nations, not to be Common to all men, but to be Susceptible of Private Dominion and Propriety. **1665** Evelyn *Let. to C. Wren* 4 Apr., My little boy . . is now susceptible of instruction. **1796** Morse *Amer. Geog.* II. 47 The provinces most susceptible of those improvements . . which are essential to the subsistance of man. **1817** Jas. Mill *Brit. India* v. ix. II. 710 The following propositions are susceptible of strict and invincible proof. **1821** Shelley *Hellas* 815 *note*, A sort of natural magic, susceptible of being exercised . . by any one who [etc.]. **1824** L. Murray *Engl. Gram.* (ed. 5) I. iii. xix. 314 The word . . was often susceptible of both uses. **1867** F. Harrison *Quest. Ref. Parlt.* 236 Scarcely susceptible of any criticism but contempt. **1871** B. Stewart *Heat* (ed. 2) § 86 The diamond . . is not susceptible of fusion even at a very high temperature.

b. with *of*: Capable of taking or admitting (a form or other attribute).

a **1639** Wotton *Parallel Essex & Buckhm.* (1641) 2 He . . moulded him . . to his owne Idea, delighting . . in the choyse of the Materialls; because he found him susceptible of good forme. **1725** Pope *Pref. to Shaks.* ⁋8 It is hard to imagine that . . so enlightened a mind could ever have been susceptible of them [*sc.* defects]. **1760–2** Goldsm. *Cit. W.* xci, Perhaps no qualities in the world are more susceptible of a finer polish than these. **1796** Kirwan *Elem Min.* (ed. 2) I. 20 This operation is susceptible of various stages and degrees of perfection. **1879** *Cassell's Techn. Educ.* I. 169/2 Nor does it admit of that beauty of decoration of which they are susceptible.

c. with *of*, now more commonly *to*: Capable of receiving and being affected by (external impressions, influences, etc., esp. something injurious); sensitive to; liable or open to (attack, injury, etc.).

1647 Clarendon *Hist. Reb.* ii. § 52 All which . . made him susceptible of some Impressions . . which otherwise would not have found such easy admission. *a* **1734** North *Exam.* i. ii. § 45. (1740) 52 Being very susceptible of Offence. **1791** Mrs Radcliffe *Rom. Forest* (1820) III. 132 He was peculiarly susceptible of the beautiful and sublime in nature. **1814** D'Israeli *Quarrels Auth.* I. 172 Hill . . was infinitely too susceptible of criticism. **1830** —— *Chas. I*, III. x. 223 Men of their ardent temper were susceptible of the contagion of his genius. *a* **1867** J. Bryce in Brodrick *Ess. Reform* (1867) 245 Susceptible from their very excess of acuteness to every transient impression. **1869** F. W. Newman *Misc.* 128 Early poets are not susceptible to the ridiculous as we are. **1876** *Q. Rev.* CXLI. 78 Swift, like Goethe, was exceedingly susceptible of female influences. **1883** *Manch. Guard.* 12 Oct. 4/5 In a period of uncertainty stocks which are quoted far above their face value are more susceptible to attack. **1915** *Eng. Hist. Rev.* Jan. 168 It is curious to find him susceptible to the beginning of the Gothic Revival.

d. with *of* (rarely *to*): Capable of receiving into the mind, conceiving, or being inwardly affected by (a thought, feeling or emotion); capable of; disposed to; †disposed to take up or adopt; †able to take in or comprehend.

1646 J. Hall *Horæ Vac.* 10 The multitude is susceptible of any opinions. **1699** Locke *Educ.* (ed. 4) § 167 Childrens Minds are narrow, and weak, and usually susceptible but of one Thought at once. **1744** Harris *Three Treat.* Wks. (1841) 99 As the rational only are susceptible of a happiness truly excellent. **1760–72** H. Brooke *Fool of Qual.* (1809) II. 33 That capital secret, of which you are not yet susceptible. **1776** Gibbon *Decl. & F.* xvi. (1782) I. 676 His temper was not very susceptible of zeal or enthusiasm. **1784** Cowper *Task* iii. 323 A heart Susceptible of pity. **1838** Lytton *Alice* i. iv, Her young heart was susceptible only of pleasure and curiosity. **1871** R. W. Dale *Commandm.* x. 257 It was God who made us susceptible to hope and to fear.

e. with *of* or *to*: Capable of being physically affected by; *esp.* liable to take, subject to (a disease or other affection).

1793 Beddoes *Catarrh* 155 Children are so susceptible of inflammations. **1802** —— *Hygëia* vii. 50 The young of the dog kind are less susceptible of this particular . . disease. **1816** [see susceptibility 2 c]. **1887** *Encycl. Brit.* XXII. 162/2 An increasing number of individuals who have become susceptible to smallpox.

†**f.** with *of* (rarely *to*) and gerund or noun of action: Capable of, or in fit condition for (doing something). *Obs.*

1829 *Chapters Phys. Sci.* 350 Transparent carbonate of lime susceptible of doubling the images of objects. **1838** Buckstone *Shocking Events* (French's ed.) 9 *Spo.* (To Dorothy). Are you susceptible of a promenade? *Dor.* I shall be delighted. ? *c* **1850** Thackeray (in *W. Brown's Catal.* No. 159, Aug. (1905) 71), I am getting better and am susceptible to seeing ladies.

2. Without const. **a.** Capable of being affected by, or easily moved to, feeling; subject to emotional (or mental) impression; impressionable.

1709 Prior *Henry & Emma* 519 With Him, who next should tempt her easie Fame; And blow with empty Words the susceptible Flame. *a* **1821** V. Knox *Lib. Educ.* xlvi. Wks. 1824 IV. 179 In the most susceptible periods of their lives. **1838** T. Mitchell *Clouds of Aristoph.* 188 The moral influences which particular . . modes of music were apt to exert over the minds of their susceptible countrymen. **1849** Macaulay *Hist. Eng.* ix. II. 455 The tidings were eagerly welcomed by the sanguine and susceptible people of France.

1875 Jowett *Plato* (ed. 2) V. 70 We must remember also the susceptible nature of the Greek.

b. Subject to some physical affection, as infection, etc.

1875 H. C. Wood *Therap.* (1879) 149 Tartar emetic is an irritant, acting upon some .. susceptible skins in a very short time. 1899 *Allbutt's Syst. Med.* VII. 549 By cultures and by inoculations into susceptible animals.

†**3.** Capable of being taken in by the mind; comprehensible, intelligible. Const. *to*. *Obs. rare*$^{-1}$.

1694 Salmon *Bate's Dispens.* (1713) 439/1 To make it susceptible to every mean Understanding, we will give you it .. in the following Words.

B. *sb. Med.* An individual capable of getting a disease because not immune.

1923 *Jrnl. Exper. Med.* XXXVII. 255 The massive lethal dose of a 1:200 dilution or less selects a relatively constant number of susceptibles. 1944 L. E. H. Whitby *Med. Bacteriol.* (ed. 4) iii. 30 When the proportion of susceptibles is high the disease becomes epidemic until the endemic level of susceptibles is again reached. 1980 *Sci. Amer.* July 26/3 A graph shows the cases reported from 1950 on; there are peaks every four to seven years, time to accumulate a pool of new susceptibles 'following the high birth rate' in densely populated areas.

Hence **su'sceptibleness** = susceptibility; **su'sceptibly** *adv.*, in a susceptible manner.

a 1631 Donne *Serm., Ps. xxxii. 8* (1640) 611 Grace finds out mans naturall faculties, and exalts them to .. a susceptiblenesse of the working thereof. 1785 G. A. Bellamy *Apol.* II. 111, I heard a voice uttering somewhat aloud; but what it was I could not distinguish, from being so susceptibly interested in my part.

susception (sə'sɛpʃən). [ad. L. *susceptio*, *-ōnem*, n. of action f. *suscept-*, pa. ppl. stem of *suscipĕre*, f. *sus-* (see sub- ad init. and 25) + *capĕre* to take. Cf. F. *susception*.]

†**1.** The action of taking up, or taking upon oneself (in various senses): taking, assumption, reception, acceptance, undertaking.

1610 Marcelline *Triumphs Jas. I*, 6c The susception of Christianity, and profession of the Catholique Faith. 1624 Bp. Hall *Contempl., N.T.* ii. *Christ Tempted*, I see the susception of our humane nature, laies thee open to this condition. 1642 H. More *Song of Soul* ii. ii. iii. xxiv, Nor is she chang'd by the susception Of any forms. 1651 Jer. Taylor *Holy Dying* v. §3 The Jews .. confessed their sins to John in the susception of baptism. 1675 Brooks *Gold. Key* Wks. 1867 V. 256 Christ's susception of the sinner's guilt. *a* 1677 Barrow *Serm. Phil. ii. 8* Wks. 1687 I. 486 The willing susception and the chearfull sustenance of the Cross. *a* 1714 M. Henry *Treat. Baptism* ii. Wks. 1853 I. 510/1 The children's right to baptism [hath] been built so much upon their susception by sponsors, that [etc.]. 1726 Ayliffe *Parergon* 140 Before he is of a Lawful Age for the Susception of Orders. 1738 E. Erskine *Serm.* Wks. 1871 II. 497 It comes about by his own voluntary susception and undertaking.

†**2.** Susceptibility *of*; also *transf.* an attribute of which something is susceptible. *Obs. rare.*

1656 Hobbes *Six Lessons* Wks. 1845 VII. 239, I may as well conclude from the not susception of greater and less, that a right angle is not quantity. *a* 1687 Petty *Pol. Anat.* (1691) 48 By the Coelum .. I understand the .. Weight and Susceptions of Air, and the Impressions made upon it.

3. The action or capacity of taking something into the mind, or what is so taken; passive mental reception (distinguished from *perception*). *rare.*

1756 Toldervy *Hist. 2 Orphans* IV. 189 None can exhibit nature in her most striking attitudes, but those whose susceptions are adequate to their task! 1877 Conder *Basis Faith* iv. 164 *note*, 'Susception' would be a better term for 'all states of consciousness which are simply presentative, not representative' (Mansel).

susceptive (sə'sɛptɪv), *a.* [ad. med.L. *susceptīvus* (Thomas Aquinas), f. *suscept-*, *suscipĕre*: see prec. and -ive. Cf. It. *suscettivo*, Sp. *susceptivo*.]

1. Having the quality of taking or receiving, receptive; in later use *esp.* disposed to receive and be affected by impressions (= susceptible 2 a).

1548–77 Vicary *Anat.* ix. (1888) 77 The Matrix in woman .. is an instrument susceptiue, that is to say, a thing recey[u]ing or taking. 1641 Sir E. Dering *Sp. on Relig.* 22 Oct. xii. 41 We neither had a decisive voyce .. nor a deliberative voyce .. nor lastly .. a susceptive voice, in a body of our own to receive their resolutions. 1674 Petty *Disc. Dupl. Proportion* 130, I might suppose .. that Atoms are also Male and Female, and the Active and Susceptive Principles of all things. 1788 D. Gilson *Serm.* viii. 223 All the tender workings of the susceptive breast of Mary. 1802 Corry *Mem. A. Berkeley* 47 This accidental interview made a still deeper impression on the susceptive heart of Lucy. 1863 J. G. Murphy *Comm. Gen.* xi. 21–2 The susceptive and conceptive powers of the understanding. 1874 Motley *John of Barneveld* II. xxii. 404 Impressible, emotional, and susceptive. 1887 Sir A. de Vere *Ess. Poetry* I. 105 He will listen, with the susceptive faith of youth.

2. With *of*: Having the quality of receiving, disposed or ready to receive (something specified); receptive of; admitting of; affected by, sensitive to: = susceptible 1.

1637 Gillespie *Engl. Pop. Cerem.* iii. iv. 68 They belong to the substance of the worship, and withall are susceptive of coadoration. *a* 1676 Hale *Prim. Orig. Man.* iv. viii. (1677) 367 He becomes a Creature properly susceptive of a Law, and capable of Rewards and Punishments. *a* 1677 Barrow *Serm. Rom. xii. 18* Wks. 1687 I. 399 It incenses the people (hugely susceptive of provocation) with a sense of notable injury done. —— *Serm. Eph. i. 13* ibid. II. 201 As mankind is naturally susceptive of religious impressions. 1722 Wollaston *Relig. Nat.* v. (1724) 78 [Matter] is passive .. to the impressions of motion, and susceptive of it. 1822–7 Good *Study Med.* (1829) II. 588 Rendering the body more susceptive of the ordinary causes of this disease. 1872 Morley *Voltaire* 95 The nature that is susceptive of passion. 1901 G. Tyrrell in *Life* (1912) II. iii. 95 Like a wheelbarrow, I am not susceptive of sustained impetus.

†**b.** Taking or including within its scope; relative to. *Obs. rare*$^{-1}$.

1681 J. Owen *Enq. Evang. Ch.* xi. 221 The Object of it [*sc.* discipline], as it is Susceptive of Members, is professed Believers; and as it is corrective, it is those who stubbornly deviate from the Rule of Christ.

Hence **su'sceptiveness** = next.

1873 M. Arnold *Lit. & Dogma* (1876) 157 Men raised by a truer moral susceptiveness above their countrymen. 1907 *Edin. Rev.* Jan. 204 Our insular susceptiveness.

susceptivity (sʌsɛp'tɪvɪtɪ). [f. prec. + -ity.] The quality of being susceptive; susceptibility.

1722 Wollaston *Relig. Nat.* v. (1724) 74 A natural discerpibility and susceptivity of various shapes and modifications. 1851 Carlyle *Sterling* iii. vii, A man of infinite susceptivity; who caught everywhere .. the colour of the element he lived in. 1871 Forster *Dickens* I. iii. 52 A stern .. isolation of self-reliance side by side with a susceptivity almost feminine.

†**su'sceptor.** *Obs.* [a. late L. *susceptor*, f. *suscept-*: see susception and -or. Cf. OF. *suscepteur*.]

1. A godfather or sponsor at baptism.

1655 Fuller *Ch. Hist.* ii. ii. §103 Such Susceptors were thought to put an Obligation on the Credits (and by reflection on the Consciences) of new Christians (whereof too many in those dayes were baptized out of civile Designes) to walk worthy of their Profession. 1680 H. Dodwell *Two Lett.* (1691) To Rdr. §11 Even adults were not admitted without the Testimony of Susceptors or God-fathers. *a* 1700 Evelyn *Diary* (1850) I. 4, I had given me the name of my grandfather, .. who, together with a sister of Sir Thomas Evelyn .. and Mr. Comber, .. were my susceptors. 1743 Stukeley *Abury* II. 76 They had susceptors, sponsors, or what we call godfathers.

2. A supporter, maintainer. *rare*

1652 N. Culverwel *Lt. Nature* Ep. Ded. (1661) 2 You, who .. were sometimes ear-witnesses of it, will now become its Susceptours. 1680 V. Alsop *Mischief Impositions* Ep. Ded., The height of my ambition was to provide my self of a Right Worshipful Susceptor.

suscipiency (sə'sɪpɪənsɪ). *rare*$^{-1}$. [Formed as next + -ency.] Receptiveness; capacity of receiving impressions.

1885 *Jrnl. Spec. Philos.* Jan. 88 The assumed chasm .. between power to conceive and mere suscipiency to perceive.

suscipient (sə'sɪpɪənt), *a.* and *sb.* Now *rare* or *Obs.* [ad. L. *suscipient-*, *-ens*, pr. pple. of *suscipĕre*: see susception.]

A. *adj.* **1.** Receiving, recipient.

1649 Jer. Taylor *Gt. Exemp.* ii. Disc. x. 139 Nothing is required in the person suscipient, and capable of alms, but that he be in .. want. *a* 1677 Barrow *Serm. Acts iv. 24* Wks. 1686 II. 178 [God] effecting miracles .. without any preparatory dispositions induced into the suscipient matter. 1684 tr. *Bonet's Merc. Compit.* xv. 528 Care must be taken .. of the Lungs, as suscipient, and sometimes constantly productive of the Matter.

b. Disposed to receive, receptive. *rare*$^{-1}$.

1815 *Zeluca* I. 13 She instructed her daughter's suscipent youth in the prevalent system [etc.].

2. With *of*: That takes into its scope.

1655 Stanley *Hist. Philos.* i. (1687) 7/1 These which are the first motions, and suscipient of the second corporal, bring all things into augmentation, and decrease.

B. *sb.* One who receives, a recipient (esp. of a sacrament).

1611 W. Sclater *Key* (1629) 236 To confer grace by force of the very Sacramentall action .., not by the merit .. of the suscipient. *Ibid.* 258 Iudas ministred baptisme sufficient in it selfe, I doubt not also but effectual to the beleeuing suscipient. 1651–3 Jer. Taylor *Serm. for Year* (1678) 359 Men cannot be worthy suscipients [of the sacraments] unless they do many excellent acts of Vertue. 1660 —— *Duct. Dubit.* i. iv. rule 5 §3 The stronger efficient upon the same suscipient should produce the more certain .. effect.

†**suscita'bility.** *Obs. rare*$^{-1}$. [f. L. *suscitāre* + *-ability* (see -able and -ity).] Excitability.

1610 B. Jonson *Alch.* ii. v, *Sub.* How know you him [*sc.* mercury]? *Fac.* By his viscositie, His oleositie, and his suscitabilitie.

suscitate ('sʌsɪteɪt), *v.* Now *rare.* Also 6 **sussitate**, 6–7 **suscitat**; 6 *pa. pple.* **suscitat(e**. [f. L. *suscitāt-*, pa. ppl. stem of *suscitāre*, f. *sus-* = sub- 26 + *citāre* to excite (see cite *v.*).] *trans.* To stir up, excite (rebellion, dispute, a feeling, etc.).

1528 *Impeachm. Wolsey* 140 in Furniv. *Ballads fr. MSS.* I. 356 þou haste suscitate suche A wonderfull dyssencion. 1531 Elyot *Gov.* ii. iii. (1883) II. 26 That they which do eate or drinke .. may sussitate some disputation or reasonynge. *Ibid.* iii. xxvi. 414 He shall .. suscitate or raise the courage of all men inclined to vertue. 1536 *St. Papers Hen. VIII*, II. 298 The disturbance and rebellion suscitate by the said persons. 1557 Edgeworth *Serm.* 73 When the Germaynes suscitated and raysed vp all maner of heresies by Luther and that rable. 1597 A. M. tr. *Guillemeau's Fr. Chirurg.* 12b/1 We apply the boxes to suscitate the menstrualles of woemen. *a* 1631 Donne *Serm., 1 Thess. v. 16* (1649) II. 471 Such a joy a man must suscitate and awaken in himselfe. *a* 1693 *Urquhart's Rabelais* iii. xlv. 368 By the approved Doctrine of the ancient Philosophers, .. such a brangling Agitation .. should .. be judged to .. be quickned and suscitated by the .. Inspiration of the Prophetizing .. Spirit. 1876 *World* V. No. 108. 18, I am not .. wantonly suscitating one more unsatisfied curiosity by proclaiming one more unfathomable mystery. 1893 *Scribner's Mag.* XIII. 343/1 Suggestions that the soul of inanimate things can .. suscitate in the realms of psychological revery.

b. To raise (a person) out of inactivity; to exalt the condition of.

1597 A. M. tr. *Guillemeau's Fr. Chirurg.* *vj, As one erectede and suscitatede out of a swound. 1650 Howell *Giraffi's Rev. Naples* i. 24 Masaniello .. began more then ever by sound of Drum to suscitat the peeple. 1675 Baxter *Cath. Theol.* ii. v. 90 It is Action that God doth suscitate the Soul to. 1876 J. Ellis *Cæsar in Egypt* 158 Thou that dost .. Subdue the stern, and suscitate the meek.

†**c.** To call into being or activity, 'raise up'.

1532 More *Confut. Tindale* Wks. 824/1 A prophet .. shal your Lord god suscitate and reyse vp for you. 1657 *North's Plutarch, Constantine Gt.* 3 The enemy of mankinde .. did suscitate and stir up the Heretick Arius. 1885 M. E. Martin tr. *Lasserre's Mirac. Episodes Lourdes* 356 The obstacles suscitated by the Evil One.

†**d.** To promote (an action at law). Only in *pa. pple. Sc. Obs.*

1560 in *Maitl. Club Misc.* III. 223 The caus being suscitate at the actes in presence of parties to preif as said is in the actioun be Williame. 1562 *Ibid.* 304 The .. caus of diuorce .. being suscitat at desyr of Archebald in presens of Anne.

e. To impart life or activity to; to quicken, vivify, animate. ? *Obs.*

1646 Sir T. Browne *Pseud. Ep.* vi. vii. 308 The Sunne [in Ireland] onely suscitates those formes, whose determinations are seminall. 1813 T. Busby *Lucretius* I. iii. 632 And human atoms suscitate the sky. 1830 W. Phillips *Mt. Sinai* i. 148 Soul so suscitates his frame With quicker spark celestial.

Hence **'suscitated**, **'suscitating** *ppl. adjs.*

1811 Shelley *St. Irvyne* Prose Wks. 1888 I. 218 Wildered by the suscitated energies of his soul almost to madness. 1840 *New Monthly Mag.* LIX. 202 The suscitating juices with which the occidental luxury is presented to us.

suscitation (sʌsɪ'teɪʃən). Now *rare.* [ad. late L. *suscitātio*, *-ōnem*, n. of action f. *suscitāt-*, *-āre*: see prec. and -ation. Cf. F. *suscitation*, in OF. = resurrection.] The action of suscitating or condition of being suscitated; stirring up, rousing, excitement; quickening; incitement.

1646 Sir T. Browne *Pseud. Ep.* vii. xvii. 379 Such [seminals] as in other earths by suscitation of the Sunne may arise unto animation. 1653 H. Cogan tr. *Pinto's Trav.* xliv. 259 To quit their beliefe, .. to imbrace another new one by the suscitation of the Farazes. 1659 Pearson *Creed* v. (1816) I. 387 The temple is supposed here to be dissolved, and being so to be raised again; therefore the suscitation must answer to the dissolution. 1742 Fielding *J. Andrews* i. xiii, If the malign concoction of his humours should cause a suscitation of his fever. 1771 Fletcher *Checks* iii. Wks 1795 II. 33 A spiritual seed of light sown in the soul of every son of man, whose kindly suscitations whoever follows, [etc.]. 1806 R. Cumberland *Mem.* 386 His spirit was alive in every feature; it did not need the aid of suscitation. 1870 *Daily Tel.* 5 Oct., One of the journals which contribute to the suscitation of our spirits and the elevation of our courage.

†**suscite**, *v. Obs. rare.* Also 5 **sussite**. [a. (O)F. *susciter*, ad. L. *suscitāre* to suscitate.] *trans.* To raise up (from or as from death); to resuscitate.

c 1430 *Pilgr. Lyf Manhode* i. xcv. (1869) 52 In the sixte [article of the Creed] descended doun in to helle; .. In the seventhe sussited. *Ibid.* ii. cxxxiv. 128 Seint nicolas that suscited the thre dede. 1483 Caxton *G. de la Tour* e vij b, Alle this is very trouth as wytnesseth many that ben suscited ageyne. *c* 1500 *Melusine* 151 Of whom we .. are all suscited of the cruel .. boundage of thenemyes of our lord Jhu Cryst.

‖**sushi** ('suʃi, 'suːʃɪ). [Jap.] A Japanese dish consisting of small balls of cold boiled rice flavoured with vinegar and commonly garnished with slices of fish or cooked egg. Also *attrib.* Hence **sushiya** (su'ʃija), in Japan, a shop which serves *sushi*.

1893 A. M. Bacon *Jap. Interior* xi. 180 Domestics served us with tea and sushi or rice sandwiches. 1910 J. Inouye *Home Life in Tokyo* vi. 77 The most common food taken on such an occasion is *sushi*, which is a lump of rice which has been pressed with the hand into a roundish form with a slight mixture of vinegar and covered on the top with a slice of fish or lobster, or a strip of fried egg, or rolled in a piece of laver. 1928 K. Yamato *Shoji* vi. 77 His *sushi*, to afford the acme of succulence, had to be eaten at the stall. 1936 K. Tezuka *Jap. Food* 74 *Sushi* has been made in many ways since olden times and is prized by rich and poor alike. 1967 D. & E. T. Riesman *Conversations in Japan* 282 We were standing at the *sushi* buffet of the train. 1968 P. S. Buck *People of Japan* xiii. 158 Since sushi is nothing more than the equivalent of a sandwich, or fishy snack, the sushi bar can hardly be described as a den of iniquity. 1970 P. & J. Martin *Jap. Cooking* 53 The *sushiya*, or sushi shop, plays in Japan a role curiously similar to that of the pub in England.

susi, variant of soosy.

Susian ('suːzɪən), *a.* and *sb.* [ad. L. *Sūsiānus*, Gr. *Σούσιος* *Σουσιανή* Susian, f. the name (*τά*) *Σοῦσα* Susa (cf. OPers. *Shush*): see -ian.]

A. *adj.* Of or pertaining to (Susa, the ancient capital of) Susiana (modern Khuzistan in Iran), its natives or inhabitants, or the language spoken by them. **B.** *sb.* **a.** A native or inhabitant of Susiana or its capital, Susa. **b.** The language of the Susians, known from inscriptions of the third millenium B.C., also known as Elamite (see ELAMITE *sb.* and *a.*). Also **Susi'anian** *a.* and *sb.*

? **1552** W. BARKAR tr. *Xenophon's Cyropædia* IV. sig. Qiv, They had selected a moste goodly tente for Cyrus, and a Seusian woman. **1601** P. HOLLAND tr. *Pliny's Nat. Hist.* VI. xxvii. 138 It receiveth..the river Hedypnus..and one more out of the Susianes countrey. **1857** W. K. LOFTUS *Trav. Chaldæa & Susiana* xxviii. 372 The details of the Susian and Persepolitan structures. *Ibid.* xxx. 408 A much-defaced and weathered inscription, written in a language which M. Oppert terms 'late Susanian'. *Ibid.* 426 Pliny, referring to Susa, says that 'the Eulæus surrounded the citadel of the Susians'. **1874** A. H. SAYCE in *Trans. Soc. Bibl. Archaeol.* III. 466 The Susians, or Susianians proper, who had their seat at Shushan. *Ibid.* 474 This plural in *-ib* (or *-be* after a consonant) meets us again in Susian. *Ibid.* 476 Susian or southern Susianian. *Ibid.* 484 The Susian and Accadian genitive follows the substantive which governs it. **1877** G. RAWLINSON *Orig. of Nations* II. iv. 213 The primitive Babylonians and their neighbors and kinsmen, the Susianians. *Ibid.*, Babylonian and Susianian royal names. **1915** P. M. SYKES *Hist. Persia* I. iv. 57 In Elam there are found..proper names..which belong to a language..known among scholars as Anzanite, Susian, or simply Elamite. *Ibid.* 58 The chief deity..was referred to as..the 'Susian'. *Ibid.* 54 There was a very ancient occupation of the Susian plain. **1948** W. W. TARN *Alexander the Great* II. II. 311 It remains to consider the Susian satrapy mentioned above. **1965** W. CULICAN *Medes & Persians* v. 98 Besides Medes, Persians and Susians, R. D. Barnett has listed..Haraiva [*etc.*]. *Ibid.* 102 The tablets..are file-copies kept by the Susian scribes.

Susie-Q ('suːzɪ kjuː). Also Suzie-Q, Suzi-Q, and without hyphen. [Origin unknown.] A modern dance of Negro origin; the step characteristic of this dance (see quots.).

1936 DAVIS & COOTS (*song-title*) Doin' the Suzi-Q. *Ibid.* 4 A new dance hit the town, It's really gettin' 'round, It's lots of fun, I found, Doin' the Suzi-Q. **1937** L. SHOMER *How to Dance* 37 The Suzi-Q is the latest and most intricate of Fox Trot Steps. To begin with, it combines the features of the tap-dance with the nimble Off-Beat Syncopated Running Steps and Turns. **1938** A. MURRAY *How to become Good Dancer* 188 Neither truckin' nor the Susie-Q is a complete dance in itself. Both are skylarking steps that add variety. *Ibid.* 190 The Susie-Q is a solo dance. It is not danced with a partner. **1946** MEZZROW & WOLFE *Really Blues* xiii. 235 And from the old folks' shuffle to the Suzie Q and Sand, wasn't none of them steps new to grandpa—just the names were different. **1956** G. P. KURATH in A. Dundes *Mother Wit* (1973) 106/2 The Susie-Q and Truckin' are said to have developed in New York's Negro quarter, Harlem. **1963** *N.Y. Times Mag.* 27 Oct. 104/2 [The Negroes'] body rhythm and frank sensuality turned the formal European waltz into the closely clutched two-step and one-step,..the Susie Q. and the big Apple.

suskin, -kyn: see SESKYN.

1423 [see SESKYN]. **1543** tr. *Act 3 Hen. V*, A j, Galyhalpens, & the money called Suskyne & Dotkyne [cf. 1413 s.v. SESKYN]. *Ibid.*, Any galyhalfpens, suskyns, or dotkyns. [There are numerous later references to this Act, e.g., **1544** *Fitzherbert's Bk. Justice of Peace* 9 Galyhalfpens, soskyns, dodkyns. **1581** LAMBARDE *Eiren.* II. vii. (1588) 233 Those Felonies of Gallyhalfpence, Suskins, and Dodkins.]

‖**suslik** ('sʌslɪk). Also souslik, -lic, suslic. [a. Russ. *suslik*. *Cf. F. souslic, -lik.*] A species of ground-squirrel, *Spermophilus citillus* (or other related species), found in Europe and Asia.

1774 tr. *Stæhlin's Acc. North. Archipelago* 32 The speckled field-mouse (*Mus Citellus*), which they call *Jewraschki* or *Suslik*. **1833** *Penny Cycl.* I. 441/2 The zizel or souslic marmot. **1842** *Ibid.* XXII. 270/1 The sousliks are very quarrelsome among themselves. **1896** LYDEKKE *Brit. Mammals* 300 Voles,..Picas,..and Susliks.

suspeccion, -oun, var. SUSPECTION *Obs.*

suspecion, -oun, -ous, obs. ff. SUSPICION, SUSPICIOUS.

suspect (sə'spɛkt), *sb.*[1] *Obs.* or *arch.* Also 4 *Sc.* -ec, 5–6 -ecte, 6 -eckte, *Sc.* -ek. [ad. L. *suspectus*, in class L. looking up, a height, esteem, respect, in med.L. suspicion (after *suspectus* pa. pple., and *suspicĕre*), f. *suspect-, suspicĕre*: see SUSPECT *a.* and *v.* Cf. It. *sospetto.*]

1. The or an act of suspecting, or the condition of being suspected; = SUSPICION I.

In earliest use chiefly in phraseological expressions: see esp. b, and cf. RESPECT *sb.*

c **1386** CHAUCER *Doctor's T.* 263 The peple anon hath suspect of this thyng,..That it was by the assent of Apius. *c* **1440** *Alphabet of Tales* 49 þat no suspecte rise betwix vs þat myght hurte þi gude name. *a* **1542** WYATT *Poems*, '*And if an lye*' 22 My suspect is without blame, For..othr moo have denyd the same; Then it is not Jelowsye. *c* **1560** A. SCOTT *Poems* (S.T.S.) xxxiv. 141 Thairfor fle fra suspek. **1577** HOLINSHED *Chron.* II. 1777/2 If any of you be in suspect, that..my meaning is to do..any thing where-with the realme may haue iust cause to be discontented. **1590** SHAKS. *Com. Err.* III. i. 87 You..draw within the compasse of suspect Th' vnuiolated honor of your wife. **1595** DANIEL *Civ. Wars* III. xxxiii, They might hold sure intelligence Among themselues without suspect t' offend. *c* **1600** CHALKHILL *Thealma & Cl.* (1683) 121 Without suspect they fell into the Trap Anaxocles had laid. **1620** QUARLES *Feast for Wormes* iv. 1 When a Thiefe's appre'ended on suspect. **1628** FELTHAM *Resolves* II. [I.] xciii. 271 By this meanes, they often bring goodnesse, into suspect. **1649** JER. TAYLOR *Gt. Exemp.* I. Ad Sect. ii. §9 If the Holy Jesus did suffer his Mother to fall into misinterpretation and suspect. **1881** SWINBURNE *Mary Stuart* II. i. 71 She..avows By silence and suspect of jealous heart Her manifest foul conscience.

†**b.** *to have* (or *hold*) *in suspect*: to be suspicious of, suspect: cf. SUSPICION 2 f. *Obs.*

c **1386** CHAUCER *Melib.* ¶230 Thou shalt also haue in suspect the conseillyng of wikked folk. **1493** *Festivall* (W. de W. 1515) 30 b, By counseyle of the people he had the lyon in suspecte. **1523** LD. BERNERS *Froiss.* I. cclxii. 388 The vycount of Rochechourt..was had in suspect to haue tourned frenche. **1533** J. HEYWOOD *Johan* A iij, Well husbande, nowe I do coniect That thou hast me somwhat in suspect. **1593** SHAKS. *3 Hen. VI*, IV. i. 142 Giue me assurance with some friendly Vow, That I may neuer haue you in suspect. **1615** DANIEL *Hymen's Tri.* II. i, Held ever in Restraint, and in Suspect.

†**c.** Const. *in*, *of*, *to* (the person or thing about whom or which something is suspected). *Obs.*

c **1386** CHAUCER *Clerk's T.* 905 This olde poure man Was euere in suspect of hir mariage. **1523** LD. BERNERS *Froiss.* I. xlvii. 68 Wherof all the Countrey..had great suspect of treason to the Captayne. *a* **1533** —— *Gold. Bk. M. Aurel.* (1546) R v, Ther fel on him an other malady..which put..his frendes in great suspect of his helthe. **1535** in *Lett. Suppr. Monast.* (Camden) 74 Not for any defaut or suspect that I have in doctour Lee. **1638** NABBES *Bride* I. iii. (1640) B iv, Thou art base In thy suspect of her. **1660** F. BROOKE tr. *Le Blanc's Trav.* 264 That you may have no suspect of these my words.

d. Const. *of* (the evil suspected).

1523 [see c]. **1555** PHILPOT in Foxe *A. & M.* (1563) 1388/2, I haue bene in prison thus long..upon suspecte of setting foorth the reporte thereof. **1567** MAPLET *Gr. Forest* 105 She..slinketh into his companie without any surmise or suspect had of his part of any such kind of deceipt. **1596** SPENSER *F.Q.* VI. iii. 23 The faire Serena..Wandred about the fields..Without suspect of ill or daungers hidden dred. *a* **1639** WEBSTER *Appius & Virginia* I. i, Arraign'd before the Senate For some suspect of treason.

e. with *a* and *pl.* = SUSPICION I b.

1541 WYATT *Def.* Poet. Wks. (1831) p. lviii, Neither God's law, nor man's law..condemneth a man for suspects: but for such a suspect..that may be so apparent..that it may be a grievous matter. **1594** SHAKS. *Rich. III*, I. iii. 89 You do me shamefull iniurie, Falsely to draw me in these vile suspects. **1598** YONG *Diana* 145 Behold then..how much he was giuen to false suspects and wrongfull iealousie. **1657** J. SERGEANT *Schism Dispach't* 457 The former manner of proceeding..makes..the Writer..fall under a just suspect. **1768** GOLDSM. *Goodn. Man* v. i, Have I had my hand to addresses, and my head in the print-shops; and talk to me of suspects?

†**f.** Ground of suspicion; = SUSPICION I c.

1586 A. DAY *Engl. Secretorie* II. (1625) 17 Seeing..you also doe grant, that in all his behauiour you neuer saw so much as one suspect.

†**2.** Expectation; *esp.* apprehensive expectation; = SUSPICION 4. *Obs.*

c **1375** *Sc. Leg. Saints* xxxvi. (*Baptista*) 1013 Suspec had he þat þai for his iniquite Suld sla hyme. *c* **1400** *Rule St. Benet* (Prose) 126 Hauynge euer suspect for to be brought to the ferefull Iugement of god. **1620** QUARLES *Feast for Wormes* xi. 11 Was there, O was there not a iust suspect, My preaching would procuer this effect?

suspect ('sʌspɛkt, sə'spɛkt), *a.* and *sb.*[2] Also 4 suspette, 4–7 suspecte, 6 *Sc.* suspek. [ad. L. *suspectus*, pa. pple. of *suspicĕre* (see next): partly after OF. *sospet*, later (and mod.F.) *suspect* = Pr. *sospech*, It. *sospetto*, OSp. *suspecto*, Pg. *suspeito*.

The present currency of this word is chiefly due to its revived use in connexion with the events of the French Revolution (cf. *la loi des suspects* of 1793).]

A. *adj.* Suspected; regarded with suspicion or distrust; that is an object of suspicion; in early use also, exciting or deserving suspicion, suspicious.

1340 *Ayenb.* 205 Behoueþ him beuly þe encheysones of zenne ase speke prineliche to wyfman in stede suspect on wyþ one. *c* **1386** CHAUCER *Clerk's T.* 485 Suspecious was the diffame of this man, Suspect his face, suspect his word also. **1401** *Pol. Poems* (Rolls) II. 87 Who is oonis suspect, he is half honged. **1433** *Rolls of Parlt.* IV. 447/1 Duellyng in a suspect and wycked place. **1525** tr. *Brunswyke's Handywork Surg.* xv. Dj, Yf ye woundyd persone haue any of these chaunches..it is a suspecte tokyn or sygne. **1525** *Extr. Aberd. Reg.* (1844) I. 113 Quhat sumeuer personis that beis suspekit to have ony suspek person within thaim. **1576** GASCOIGNE *Steele Gl.* 242 An age suspect, bycause of youthes misdeedes. **1605** BACON *Adv. Learn.* II. xxv. §13 As for..compleatnes in diuinitie it is not to be sought, which makes this course of artificiall diuinitie the more suspecte. **1671** MILTON *P.R.* II. 399, I see What I can do or offer is suspect. **1702** *Guide for Constables* 111 If a scholar in the university..begin to be suspect.

1817 BYRON *Beppo* xvii, Shakspeare described the sex in Desdemona As very fair, but yet suspect in fame. **1837** CARLYLE *Fr. Rev.* III. II. v. (1872) 77 We have him..lying safe in the Prison of Grenoble, since September last, for he had long been suspect! **1880** *Fortn. Rev.* May 677 Every doctrine..which claimed an *à priori* or intuitive character, was therefore suspect. **1897** *Allbutt's Syst. Med.* II. 431 In tropical regions,..all water should be looked upon as suspect and treated accordingly.

†**b.** *to have* or *hold* (a person or thing) *suspect*: to be suspicious of, suspect. *Obs.*

c **1380** WYCLIF *Wks.* (1880) 291 ȝif þou seie þat popis lawe spekiþ oþer wise of jugement, haue þe popis lawe more suspette. *c* **1380** —— *Sel. Wks.* II. 388 If þei failen in þis point, have hem suspect as fendis children. *c* **1412** HOCCLEVE *De Reg. Princ.* 1517 Hard is be holden suspect with þe grete: His tale schal be leeued but nat ourys. *c* **1430** LYDG. *Min. Poems* (Percy Soc.) 185 Have me not suspecte, I mene no tresone. **1500–20** DUNBAR *Poems* xx. 34 Be thow not ane roundar in the nwke, For, gif thow be, men will hald the suspect. *c* **1530** L. COX *Rhet.* (1899) 71 We haue one suspecte that of very lykelyhode it shulde be he that hathe commytted the cryme. *a* **1533** LD. BERNERS *Gold. Bk. M. Aurel.* (1546) G iij, Wise men haue hym as suspecte that the commons desyre.

†**c.** Const. *to* (north. dial. *till*) the person suspecting. (Cf. SUSPECT *v.* I b.) *Obs.*

a **1300** *Cursor M.* 27325 þat sco hir saul be sauuand, And noght suspect til hir husband. **1580–1** *Reg. Privy Council Scot.* III. 347 Quhairthrow he may be suspect judge to thame. **1635** R. N. tr. *Camden's Hist. Eliz.* I. 127 This sounded not very pleasingly in the Spaniard's eares, to whom the power of the French was suspect. **1663** HEATH *Flagellum* (1672) 6 Stealing the young Pidgeons,..and that so publiquely, that he became dreadfully suspect to all the adjacent Country.

d. Const. *of* the evil, etc. suspected.

c **1380** WYCLIF *Wks.* (1880) 2 Al þis nouelrie of ordris is suspect of ypocrisie. **1423** JAS. I *Kingis Q.* cxxxvii, The remanant..For otheris gilt ar suspect of vntreuth. **1432** *Paston Lett.* I. 32 Eny persone..suspect of mysgovernance. **1556** J. HEYWOOD *Spider & F.* x. 54 Ye may detaine A flie: suspect of crime, not proued plaine. **1591** SYLVESTER *Du Bartas* I. iii. 317, I fear, of Envie I should be suspect.

1837 CARLYLE *Fr. Rev.* III. IV. vi, If Suspect of nothing else, you may grow, as came to be a saying, 'Suspect of being Suspect!' **1912** W. WARD *Life Newman* I. ii. 73 The members of the party were suspect of Romanism.

†**e.** Const. *inf.* *Obs. rare.*

1523 LD. BERNERS *Froiss.* I. viii. 6 He held them suspect to be ageynst hym. **1553** T. WILSON *Rhet.* (1580) 102 Many often tymes are suspecte to speake thynges of malice, or for hope of gaine.

B. *sb.* **1.** A suspected person; one suspected of some offence, evil intention, or the like; a suspicious character, esp. one under surveillance as such.

1591 LAMBARDE *Eiren.* I. iii. 16 A Constable might at the common lawe, haue bailed a suspect of felonie by Obligation. **1592** WARNER *Alb. Eng.* IX. xlix. (1612) 226 Recusants and Suspects of note. **1602** LAMBARDE *Eiren.* II. vii. 196 If such Suspect shall refuse to be so bound, then may such Iustice send such Suspect to the next Gaole.

1802 C. JAMES *Milit. Dict.*, *Suspect*, a term adopted by the modern French to signify any person suspected of being an enemy, or indifferent to the cause of the Revolution. **1838** SIR J. STEPHEN *Eccl. Biogr.* (1849) II. 210 'Relations of peace and amity' were established between the Intendant and the suspects. **1852** GLADSTONE *Glean.* (1879) IV. 97 If they are in search of a political suspect, and conceive he has absconded. **1881** *Daily Tel.* 18 June, Arrested as a suspect under the Coercion Act. **1899** R. P. WATSON *Mem.* 131 Landing here I was treated as a suspect.

†**2.** A thing regarded with suspicion. *Obs. rare.*

1625 BACON *Ess.*, *Innovations* (Arb.) 527 That the Nouelty, though it be not reiected, yet be held for a Suspect.

suspect (sə'spɛkt), *v.* Also 6 *Sc.* -ek, -eck, 6–7 *contr. pa. pple.* suspect. [f. L. *suspect-*, pa. ppl. stem of *suspicĕre* to look up, look up to, admire, esteem, (chiefly in pa. pple.) to suspect, f. *su(b)-* (see SUB- ad init. and 24, 25) + *specĕre* to look, cognate with Skr. *spaç* to see, OHG. *spehôn* (see ESPY).]

1. *trans.* To imagine something evil, wrong, or undesirable in (a person or thing) on slight or no evidence; to believe or fancy to be guilty or faulty, with insufficient proof or knowledge; to have suspicions or doubts about, be suspicious of.

c **1500** *Lancelot* 1632 But he the Iug, that no man may susspek, Euery thing ful Iustly sal correk. **1515** SAMPSON in Strype *Eccl. Mem.* (1721) I. i. 16 As they heard the tenor of the breve, one of them with a quick mind suspected the breve in three places. **1560** DAUS tr. *Sleidane's Comm.* 71 Zwynglius dred bad measure suspecting bothe the men and the place. *Ibid.* 239 Bothe Fraunce & Englande leuie great force of men, whiche is greatly to be suspected. **1596** SHAKS. *Merch. V.* I. iii. 162 Whose owne hard dealings teaches them suspect The thoughts of others. **1615** G. SANDYS *Trav.* 53 The disunitie of the professors made many to suspect the profession. **1649** LOVELACE *Poems* 38 Souldiers suspected of their courage. **1691** RAY *Creation* I. (1692) 74, I suspect all those Relations concerning Trees growing at the bottom of the Sea. **1776** *Trial of Nundocomar* 97/2 Did you see upon the face of the bond any thing to make you suspect it? **1781** COWPER *Table-T.* 141 To be suspected, thwarted, and withstood, E'en when he labours for his country's good. **1858** FROUDE *Hist. Eng.* III. xiii. 170 The people suspected the gentlemen, the gentlemen feared the people. **1879** 'E. GARRETT' *House by Works* I. 82 Jacob gave Paul no reason to suspect the effect of a wider scope of life and happiness. **1897** 'G. ALLEN' *Typewriter Girl* vi. 60 The meat and bread were wholesome; but I suspected their cleanliness.

†**b.** *suspected to* (a person): mistrusted by; = *suspect to*, SUSPECT *a.* c. *Obs.*

After L. *suspectus* with the dative.

1570 BUCHANAN *Admon.* Wks. (S.T.S.) 25 Not suspectit to ane king and assurit of his awin estait. **1579** FENTON *Guicciard.* (1618) 268 The licentious bahauiour of the Commons was suspected to him. **1667** MILTON *P.L.* XII. 165 He..leaves his Race Growing into a Nation, and now grown Suspected to a sequent King. **1692** DRYDEN *St. Euremont's Ess.* 212 A Science which was already suspected to me appeared too vain to enslave my self to it any longer. **1769** *Junius Lett.* i. (1788) 38 Behold..the administration of justice become..suspected to the whole body of the people. **1807** ROBINSON *Archæol. Græca* III. ix. 240 To the more sagacious..the answers of the oracle were suspected.

†**c.** Const. clause: To doubt *whether*... *rare.*

1698 FRYER *Acc. E. India & P.* 337, I shrewdly suspect whether ever this were the Hecatompylos of Ortellius.

2. To imagine or fancy something, esp. something wrong, about (a person or thing) with slight or no proof: with various const.

expressing that which is so imagined. **a.** const. *of*, †*with*, †*for*.

1483-4 *Act 1 Rich. III*, c. 3 (*heading*) An Act for baylyng of persons suspected of Felony. **1502** *Acc. Ld. High Treas. Scot.* II. 348 Certane personis that wer suspeckit of murthur. **1598** SHAKS. *Merry W.* IV. iv. 7, I rather will suspect the Sunne with cold Then thee with wantonnes. *a* **1623** BUCK *Rich. III*, I. (1646) 4 Philippe le Grosse.. suspected him for too familiar commerce with his bed. **1641** PRYNNE *Antipathie* I. i. 29 Many suspected for doing it, were committed to prison. **1727** SWIFT *Circumcis. E. Curll* Wks. 1755 III. I. 165 Most of the children of Israel are suspected for holding the same doctrine. **1802** MARIA EDGEWORTH *Moral T.* (1816) I. iii. 17 At least tell me, that you do not really suspect me of any hand in her death. **1863** LYELL *Antiq. Man* iii. 36 Those who are too well acquainted with the sagacity..of Hekekyan Bey to suspect him of having been deceived. **1897** WATTS-DUNTON *Aylwin* I. i, I half began to suspect myself of secret impulses of a savage kind.

b. with obj. and compl. (sometimes introduced by *as* or *for*), and in corresp. passive use. Now *rare* or *Obs.*

1515 BARCLAY *Egloges* II. (1570) B iij b/2 Thou mayst suspect and trowe Him more in fauour..then thou. **1593** SHAKS. *2 Hen. VI*, III. ii. 186 Than you, belike, suspect these Noblemen, As guilty of Duke Humphrie's timelesse death. **1594** —— *Rich. III*, I. iii. 223 Thy Friends suspect for Traytors. **1611** —— *Wint. T.* II. iii. 107 Least she suspect, as he do's, Her Children, not her Husbands. **1667** MILTON *P.L.* IX. 337 Let us not then suspect our happie State Left so imperfet by the Maker wise. **1689** in *Acts Parlt. Scotl.* (1875) XII. 58/2 A warrant to cite such as are suspect guilty to compeir. **1706** E. WARD *Wooden World Diss.* (1708) 72 One would not suspect him by his Phiz, for a Politician. **1742** YOUNG *Nt. Th.* I. 418 At thirty man suspects himself a fool; Knows it at forty, and reforms his plan.

c. with obj. and inf., and in corresp. passive use.

1525 [see SUSPECT *a.* 1]. *a* **1548** HALL *Chron., Hen. VI* 176 The citezens of the citie..they sore suspected, rather to fauour then to hate, the erles of Marche, & Warwycke. **1604** SHAKS. *Oth.* V. i. 85, I do suspect this Trash To be a party in this Iniury. **1647** FULLER *Good Th. in Worse T.* (1841) 120 His gracious majesty hath been suspected to be popishly inclined. **1691** RAY *Creation* Pref. (1692) A v, By Virtue of my Function, I suspect my self to be obliged to Write something in Divinity. **1798** FERRIAR *Illustr. Sterne*, etc. 68 Who would suspect this heroic strain to be a plagiarism? **1872** GEO. ELIOT *Middlem.* lxxi, He believed that Lydgate suspected his orders to have been intentionally disobeyed. **1899** *Allbutt's Syst. Med.* VIII. 486 [They] have recorded cases of hæmatemesis suspected to own a similar cause.

†**d.** with obj. and clause introduced by *that* (cf. 3 b). *Obs. rare.*

1551 T. WILSON *Logic* (1580) 47 We suspect suche a one that he is not altogether cleare. **1594** SHAKS. *Rich. III*, III. vii. 89 Sorry I am, my Noble Cousin should Suspect me, that I meane no good to him.

3. To imagine or fancy (something) to be possible or likely; to have a faint notion or inkling of; to surmise. **a.** with simple object.

c **1550** LLOYD *Treas. Health* T j, Geue the same vnto the pacient to drinke in the houre suspectid of the feuers approching. **1563** FOXE *A. & M.* 1714/2 Much suspected by mee, Nothing proued can be. Quod Elizabeth the prisoner. *c* **1590** GREENE *Fr. Bacon* ii. 13 We hear, that long we haue suspect, That thou art read in Magicks mysterie. **1625** BACON *Ess., Suspicion* (Arb.) 528 There is Nothing makes a Man Suspect much, more then to Know little. **1646** SIR T. BROWNE *Pseud. Ep.* I. iii. 11 If all be true that is suspected, or halfe what is related, there have not wanted, many strange deceptions. **1647** CLARENDON *Hist. Reb.* I. §23 They had thought of an expedient..and that it should be Executed before it should be Suspected. **1777** BURKE *Corr.* (1844) II. 147 You do not..suspect half enough the villany of others. **1827** SCOTT *Chron. Canongate* iv, Whether the..old woman did, or did not, suspect the identity of her guest with [etc.]. **1862** CARLYLE *Fredk. Gt.* XII. iii. (1872) IV. 145 Who dared suspect our King's indifference to Protestantism? **1879** HARLAN *Eyesight* ii. 17 This is the first symptom looked for when opium poisoning is suspected.

b. with obj. clause; also parenthetically, with *as* or *so*, or ellipt.

1549 *Compl. Scot.* xii. 100 Pontius his sone suspekit that his father dottit in folie throcht his grit aige. **1638** JUNIUS *Paint. Ancients* 182 Suspecting that there was some unknowne verture in that picture, he called it backe. **1654-66** EARL ORRERY *Parthen.* (1676) 495 He read something in my Face which made him..suspect who I was. **1687** A. LOVELL tr. *Thevenot's Trav.* I. 77 They have strangled..Sultan Osman, because (as they suspected) he had a mind to rid himself of them. **1788** M. CUTLER in *Life*, etc. (1888) I. 415, I..suspected it was too late for any kind of medicine to produce any valuable effect. **1815** SCOTT *Guy M.* l, I believe I may have some wrongs to repair towards you—I have often suspected so. **1849** MACAULAY *Hist. Eng.* viii. II. 348 *note*, The late Alexander Knox..learned, I suspect, much of his theological system from Fowler's writings. **1866** G. MACDONALD *Ann. Q. Neighb.* xxxiii. (1878) 558, I did not even suspect how ill she would be. **1871** BLACKIE *Four Phases Morals* i. 82 The young Examinee is pleasantly surprised at finding that he knows more than he suspected.

4. *absol.* (from 1 or 3) or *intr.* To imagine something, esp. some evil, as possible or likely; to have or feel suspicion.

1592 SHAKS. *Ven. & Ad.* 1153 It shall suspect where is no cause of feare, It shall not feare where it should most mistrust. **1604** —— *Oth.* III. iii. 170 Oh, what damned minutes tels he ore, Who dotes, yet doubts: Suspects, yet soundly loues? **1691** NORRIS *Pract. Disc.* 55 It will then be as lawful for me to Suspect as to Judge more absolutely. **1819** SHELLEY *Cenci* v. ii. 43 Some..slave.., bade to answer, not as he believes, But as those may suspect or do desire Whose questions thence suggest their own reply. **1849** JAMES *Woodman* ix, Iola was too young and simple to suspect or to doubt.

†**5.** *trans.* With reference to a future possibility: To expect; *esp.* to expect with dread or apprehension. (With simple obj. or obj. cl.; rarely with inf.) *Obs.* or merged in 3.

1509 HAWES *Past. Pleas.* XXXIII. (Percy Soc.) 162, I dyde suspecte That the great gyaunte unto me wolde hast. **1650** FULLER *Pisgah* III. vi. 330 When the siege of Jerusalem was suspected from Rezin king of Syria and Pekah king of Israel. **1660** —— *Mixt Contempl.* (1841) 257 The innocent child whose precipice they suspected. **1787** *William of Normandy* I. 131 He rather suspected to receive a reward for his pretended fidelity. **1794** PALEY *Evid.* III. iv. (1817) 300 One might have suspected, that at least all those who stood by the sepulchre when Lazarus was raised, would have believed in Jesus.

†**6.** To regard, take note of, care for; to respect.

1590 GREENE *Never too late* (1600) 70 Tush the Lord regardeth not the way of sinners, nor suspecteth the misdeeds of men. **1605** TIMME *Quersit.* I. ii. 8 They were.. continued in theyr being by that diuine power, perpetually maintaining and suspecting them. **1649** DAVENANT *Love & Hon.* V. iii. 22 It shall be openly perform'd, to shew I not suspect men's censure or dislike. **1656** *North's Plutarch* 927 (*Epaminondas*) Not suspecting [*edd.* 1612, 1631 respecting] the dignity of an Ambassador, nor of his Country.

†**7.** With *inf.* To think in the least, have any idea of (doing something). *Obs. rare*$^{-1}$.

1628 GAULE *Pract. The.* (1629) 179 Farre be it from vs, wee should once suspect to chide him.

Hence **su'specting** *vbl. sb.* and *ppl. a.*

1691 NORRIS *Pract. Disc* 54 Not that we think Suspecting to be in itself unlawful. **1732** SWIFT *Advant. by Repealing Test* ¶24 If I had not known it already to have gotten ground in many suspecting heads.

suspectable (sə'spɛktəb(ə)l), *a.* Also 8 *erron.* -ible. [f. prec. + -ABLE.] That may or should be suspected; open to suspicion.

1748 RICHARDSON *Clarissa* V. lviii. 363 Evermore is parade and obsequiousness suspectable. *a* **1761** *Ibid.* (1768) III. lxii. 318 As poverty is generally suspectible, the Widow must be got handsomely aforehand. **1802-12** BENTHAM *Ration. Judic. Evid.* (1827) V. 730 Infirm and suspectable evidence. **1859** W. ANDERSON *Disc.* Ser. II. (1860) 198 You ..might show yourself..of suspectable profession, if you were complaisant. **1887** *Yorksh. Post* 23 Feb. 5/7 It is only in this direction that Europe is suspectable.

su'spectant, *a. Her.* [ad. L. *suspectantem*, *-ans*, pr. pple. of *suspectāre*, f. *suspect-*: see SUSPECT *v.* and -ANT.] (See quot.)

1688 HOLME *Armoury* II. vii. 144/1 *Suspectant*, *Spectant*, looking upwards, the Nose Bendwise.

su'spected, *ppl. a.* [f. SUSPECT *v.* + -ED[1].]

1. That one suspects of something evil or wrong; regarded with suspicion; imagined guilty or faulty; suspect.

1559 in Strype *Ann. Ref.* (1709) I. App. xi. 35 If any.. disagreed from his forefathers, he is..to be judged suspected. **1560** DAUS tr. *Sleidane's Comm.* 150 That all thynges myght be decided by mete and no suspected persones. **1562** TURNER *Herbal* II. 51 Noble men..that are bydden to dynner of theyr enemies or suspected frendes. **1563** HYLL *Art Garden.* (1593) 138 By eating of Garlike, a man may the safelier goe into a suspected aire, and by stinking places. **1610** HEYWOOD *Gold. Age* II. i, The Iron bar'd dores and the suspected vaults, The Barricadoed gates. **1615** MANWOOD *Lawes Forest* xxiv. §5 241 All others found in the Forest searching and going after a suspected maner. **1662** STILLINGFL. *Orig. Sacræ* I. iv. §1 Their eldest Historians are of suspected credit even among themselves. *a* **1700** EVELYN *Diary* 16 July 1649, To..walke..with our guns ready in all suspected places. **1794** VANCOUVER *Agric. Cambr.* 125, I became here a suspected person, and could obtain no information whatever. **1826** G. J. BELL *Comm. Laws Scot.* (ed. 5) I. 553 She must have..a bill of health when she sails from a suspected port. **1855** MACAULAY *Hist. Eng.* xviii. IV. 234 Whether the danger of trusting the suspected persons or the danger of removing them were the greater. **1861** *Chambers' Encycl.* II. 95/1 A suspected bill [of health], commonly called a touched patent or bill, imports that there were rumours of an infectious disorder. **1924** *Times* 30 Dec. 10/1 The search and detention of suspected ships.

2. That one suspects to exist, or to be such; imagined possible or likely.

1706 STANHOPE *Paraphr.* III. 495 Defamation does not use to stop at manifest, no, nor at suspected Vice. **1831** SCOTT *Ct. Rob.* xxvii, In the character of a more than suspected traitor. **1904** *Verney Mem.* II. 11 Sir Ralph was suddenly arrested,..by the Lord Protector's soldiers, as a suspected Royalist.

3. *the suspected*, a moth, *Parastichtis suspecta*, which has reddish-brown fore-wings and is found in Europe and northern Asia.

1908 R. SOUTH *Moths Brit. Isles* II. 7 The Suspected.. Of this species there are two groups of forms—plain and variegated. **1948** W. J. STOKOE *Caterpillars Brit. Moths* I. 323 The Suspected... The chief British quarters of this species appear to be in Yorkshire. **1973** *Times* 5 May 12/8 The men who christen moths must be poets. Consider some of the enchanting names of those recorded in the garden.. Heart and Dart, Flame Shoulder, Nutmeg, Common Quaker, The Suspected, [etc.].

Hence **su'spectedly** *adv.*, so as to be suspected; **su'spectedness**, state of being suspected.

1609 [see SUSPECTLY, quot. *a* 1577]. **1656** *Artif. Handsom.* 93 Those, who..have..either undiscernibly..or suspectedly..or declaredly..used such additaments. **1658** J. ROBINSON *Stone* 96 Some of Hipocrates Aphorisms..by losing their lustre, contract a suspectednesse. **1654** H. MORE *Myst. Iniq.* 311 A many Pseudo-Cabbalists have brought the very name of Cabbala into a suspectedness.

suspecter (sə'spɛktə(r)). [f. SUSPECT *v.* + -ER[1].] One who suspects; = SUSPECTOR.

a **1625** FLETCHER *Hum. Lieut.* IV. viii, A base suspecter of a virgins honour. **1662** H. MORE *Philos. Writ.* Pref. Gen. §10 The jealous Suspecters or Opposers of new Truths. **1895** F. T. ELWORTHY *Evil Eye* 436 The countercharm is worked by the suspecter's turning the largest coal upside down.

suspectful (sə'spɛktfʊl), *a.* Now *rare* or *Obs.* [f. SUSPECT *sb.*[1] + -FUL.]

†**1.** Having regard or respect for something; mindful *of*. *Obs. rare*$^{-1}$.

1570 FOXE *A. & M.* (ed. 2) I. 159/2 He willeth him..to be sollicitous for his soule, and suspectfull of the houre of his death.

2. Full of suspicion; inclined to suspect; mistrustful; = SUSPICIOUS 2.

a **1586** SIDNEY *Arcadia* II. (1912) 317 In whom the innate meanes will bring forth ravenous covetousnes, and the newnes of his estate, suspectfull cruelty. **1611** *Second Maiden's Trag.* I. i, Thei'd lyu'de suspectfull still, warnde by their feares. **1640** HOWELL *Dodona's Gr.* 21 Alwaies emulous and suspectfull of her. **1644** MILTON *Areop.* (Arb.) 59 To include the whole Nation..under such a diffident and suspectfull prohibition. **1682** OTWAY *Venice Preserved* III. ii, Our good Fortune Has..Strengthen'd the fearful'st, charm'd the most suspectful. **1856** LEVER *Martins of Cro' M.* xiv, The most suspectful, unimpulsive, and ungenerously-disposed of all natures.

†**3.** Exciting or deserving suspicion; = SUSPICIOUS 1. *Obs. rare.*

1603 FLORIO *Montaigne* I. xxiii. (1632) 59 Spare no powder, which would serve as a gratification toward these suspect-full troupes. **1641** MILTON *Reform.* I. Wks. 1851 III. 30 The dangerous and suspectfull translations of the Apostat Aquila. **1642** HOWELL *For. Trav.* (Arb.) 47 Nothing could make France more suspectfull to England than the addition of those Countreyes.

Hence **su'spectfulness**, proneness to suspicion.

1872 LEVER *Ld. Kilgobbin* v. (1875) 37 The half-suspectfulness of one not fully assured of what he was listening to.

suspectible: see SUSPECTABLE.

†**su'spection.** *Obs.* Also 4 suspectioun, -eccioun, 4-5 -eccyon, 5-6 -eccion, -ectyon, 6 *Sc.* -ectione. [a. OF. *s(o)uspection*, ad. L. *suspectio*, *-ōnem*, in med.L. suspicion, f. *suspect-*, *suspicĕre* to SUSPECT: see -TION.] = SUSPICION.

13.. *Coer de L.* 965, I took hem, thorwe suspeccyon,..to my prisoun. *a* **1340** HAMPOLE *Psalter* xxx. 9 To..haf ill susspeccioun of a trew frend. *c* **1374** CHAUCER *Boeth.* I. pr. iv. (1868) 20 My wijf and þe compaignie of myn honeste frendis,..defenden me of al suspeccioun [*v.r.* suspecion] of syche blame. *c* **1430** *Pilgr. Lyf Manhode* I. lvi. (1869) 34 Ther mihte be gret suspeccion that in sum..cornere the filthe were heled or heped. **1487** *Act 3 Hen. VII*, c. 3 Prisoners and persones arrested for light suspeccion of felony. *c* **1489** CAXTON *Sonnes of Aymon* vi. 148 Yf ye have ony suspectyon vpon me. **1509** HAWES *Past. Pleas.* XXXV. (Percy Soc.) 180 To cause a lady to have suspection Unto her true lover. **1553** T. WILSON *Rhet.* 50 They make wise men ever after to have them in suspection. **1555** EDEN *Decades* (Arb.) 117 That yowe maye..bee owte of all suspection that yowe shal not bee deceaued. **1588** PARKE tr. *Mendoza's Hist. China* 219 Although they are without suspection of enimies. **1631** CHAPMAN *Caesar & Pompey* II. i. D iv, Suspected? what suspection should feare a friend? **1728** EARL OF AILESBURY *Mem.* (1890) 648 Prosecutions and suspections in relation to great malversations he was charged with.

†**su'spectious**, *a. Obs.* [a. OF. *suspectieux*, f. *suspection*: see prec. and -IOUS.] = SUSPICIOUS.

14.. *Chaucer's Clerk's T.* 540 (Corpus MS.), Suspecious [*other MSS.* Suspecious] was þe defame of þis man. **1422** YONGE tr. *Secr. Secr.* lix. 235 Who-so hath the Paas litill and Swyfte, he is suspeccious, of euyl will. **1477** EARL RIVERS (Caxton) *Dictes* 57 He that trusteth in this worlde is receiued, & he that is suspectious is in grete sorowe. **1521** in Ellis *Orig. Lett.* Ser. II. I. 284 Ye shall shew unto her Grace, the keping that the King her son is in is right susspectious. *a* **1558** in J. R. Boyle *Hedon* (1875) App. 95 That no man harbor within his house anye wavering or suspeccyous persone.

Hence †**su'spectiousness**. *rare*$^{-1}$.

1525 LD. BERNERS *Froiss.* II. clxvii. 187 Se you any suspectiousnes in this mater?

†**su'spectless**, *a. Obs.* [f. SUSPECT *sb.*[1] + -LESS.]

1. Having no suspicion; unsuspecting.

1591 SYLVESTER *Du Bartas* I. ii. 1255 The Wolf and Lamb, Lions and Bucks do row Vpon the Waters, side by side, suspectlesse. **1615** T. ADAMS *White Devil* 6 Judas' traine soone tooke fire in the suspectlesse disciples. **1638** SIR T. HERBERT *Trav.* (ed. 2) 71 Such time poore Abdul Fazel (suspectlesse of any villany) passes by, Radgee falls upon him. *a* **1756** G. WEST *Abuse Trav.* vii, The youthful heart, Exposed suspectless to the traytor's wile.

2. Not liable to suspicion; unsuspected.

1606 SYLVESTER *Du Bartas* II. iv. *Trophies* 505 His son the Prince..warns the Jessean by suspect-lesse signes. **1608** MIDDLETON *Five Gallants* I. ii, It keeps my state suspectless and unknown. **1637** HEYWOOD *Pleas. Dial.* Wks. 1874 VI. 272 This shape may prove suspectlesse, and the fittest To cloud a godhead in.

Hence †**su'spectlessly** *adv.*, unsuspectingly.

1599 LINCHE *Fount. Anc. Fiction* O j, The suspectlesly inchaunted sea-trauellers are infinitely beguiled.

†**su'spectly**, *adv. Obs. rare.* [f. SUSPECT *a.* + -LY[2]. Cf. OF. *suspectement.*] In a way open to

suspicion; suspiciously. So **su'spectness** (*rare*⁻¹), the state of being suspected.

1422 HOCCLEVE *Compl.* 292 Neythar still nor lowde knew they me do suspectly. **1477** *Cov. Leet Bk.* 420 Yf eny persone hereaftur resorte vnto this Cite suspectly. *a* **1577** SIR T. SMITH *Commw. Eng.* II. xxii. (1584) 74 Any that liueth idle and suspectly [*so ed.* **1589**; *ed.* 1609 suspectedly]. **1898** A. F. LEACH *Beverley Act Bk.* (Surtees) I. p. lxxv, J. Binder had been in the usual state of suspectness with the ladies.

suspector (sə'spɛktə(r)). [agent-n. in L. form f. SUSPECT *v.*: see -OR.] One who suspects.

1804 W. TAYLOR in *Ann. Rev.* II. 269 The spy and suspector of his conduct. **1845-6** DE QUINCEY *Gilfillan's Lit. Portraits* Wks. 1859 XII. 293 He was a general disliker and a general suspector.

†**su'spectuous**, *a. Obs. rare*⁻¹. [f. L. *suspectus* (*u*-stem) SUSPECT *sb.*¹ + -OUS. Cf. rare OF. *suspectueux*.] = SUSPICIOUS 2.

1657 *Goodlie Hist. Lucres & Eur.* F vj, I thynke as our Cytezens be suspectuous and full of conjectoures.

suspence, obs. form of SUSPENSE.

suspend (sə'spɛnd), *v.* Also 3 sos-; 5 *pa. t.* and *pple.* suspend(e, *pa. t.* suspent, 5-6 (9 in sense 10 a) *pa. pple.* suspent. [a. OF. *sus-*, *sospendre* or ad. its source L. *suspendĕre* (whence also Pr. *suspendre*, It. *sospendere*, Sp., Pg. *suspender*), f. *sus-*, SUB- ad init. and 25 + *pend-* to hang.]

I. 1. a. *trans.* To debar, usually for a time, from the exercise of a function or enjoyment of a privilege; *esp.* to deprive (temporarily) of one's office. Const. *from*, †*of*.

c **1290** *Beket* 1713 in *S. Eng. Leg.* 155 þe pope him sende lettres..þat he scholde..suspendi þe bischopes þat swuch on-riȝt duden þere. *c* **1380** WYCLIF *Wks.* (1880) 79 þei wolen suspenden pore prestis fro masse & prechynge & alle goddis seruyce. **1387** TREVISA *Higden* (Rolls) VII. 5 þis Odo suspendede kyng Edwynus of Cristendom [HIGDEN *a Christianitate suspendit*], for he was to fervent in leccherie. *c* **1440** *Alphabet of Tales* 460 A bisshopp þat suspent a certan preste in his dioces..þis is þe bisshopp þat tuke fro vs our preste & suspend hym. *c* **1450** *Mirk's Festial* 236 He suspendyt hom of hor pouer þat þay haddyn in Cristys creatures. **1534** tr. *Constit. Otho* in Lyndewode *Constit.* 114 That they be suspended both from offyce and also benefyce. **1586-7** *Reg. Privy Council Scot.* IV. 143 His Hienes and the saidis Lordis hes suspendit..the saidis Maisteris Balcanquell and Williame Watsoun of all..preiching of the Worde. *a* **1628** PRESTON *Saints Daily Exerc.* (1629) 128 They are suspended from receiving the benefit by it. **1687** WOOD *Life* 31 May (O.H.S.) III. 221 The vice-chancellor of Cambridge suspended this month for not admitting father Francis M.A. **1693** *Ibid.* 12 Oct. 432 The society suspended him of his vote. **1699** LUTTRELL *Brief Rel.* (1857) IV. 535 Captain Kirk..is suspended his commission in the earl of Oxfords regiment. **1743-4** in *10th Rep. Hist. MSS. Comm.* App. I. 212, I do hereby suspend you from all further Authority in His Majᵗʸ's Fleet, till His Majᵗʸ's Pleasure shall be known. **1877** FROUDE *Short Stud.* (1883) IV. I. ix. 96 The king had been obliged to suspend the sheriffs in several counties. **1881** GLADSTONE *Sp. in Ho. Comm.* 3 Feb., It becomes my duty to make a Motion for the suspension of the following Members... I have to move that they be severally suspended from the service of the House during the remainder of the day's Sitting.

refl. *c* **1380** WYCLIF *Sel. Wks.* III. 362 ȝif þei wolden suspende hemsilf fro alle þingis but Goddis lawe.

†**b.** To debar temporarily from participation in something, presence in a place, etc. *Obs.*

c **1400** *Rule St. Benet* (verse) 1258 Sche salbe suspend fro þe kirk, Fro mete, & fro al company. *c* **1450** LYDG. & BURGH *Secrees* 2240 Yif he thus offende, Oute of thy presence hym vttirly suspende.

2. a. To put a stop to, usually for a time; *esp.* to bring to a (temporary) stop; to intermit the use or exercise of, put in abeyance. Chiefly in *passive* without implication of a definite agent.

to suspend payment: to cease paying debts or claims on account of financial inability; to become insolvent.

c **1290** *Beket* 856 in *S. Eng. Leg.* 131 þo seide þe bischop of wynchestre: 'sire gilbert, beo stille! We sospendiez swuch conseil, for it nis nouȝt wurth a fille.' *c* **1380** WYCLIF *Sel. Wks.* III. 356 Prove he his power bi þis lese, and suspende assoiling of moneie. **1529** MORE *Suppl. of Soulys* Wks. 326/1 Though he suffer his mercy to be commonly suspended and tempered with the balaunce of his iustice. **1540** *Act 32 Hen. VIII*, c. 48 §1 The same rentis by longe tymes shalbe suspendid and not due to be paid. **1560** DAUS tr. *Sleidane's Comm.* 165 The Emperour doeth suspende all suites and actions in the lawe commenced againste the Protestauntes. **1564** *Reg. Privy Council Scot.* I. 287 The Lordis of Secreit Counsall suspendis the said Robert Lord Sempillis commissioun abonewrittin. **1602** WARNER *Alb. Eng.* Epit. (1612) 355 The Gouernment of the naturall Brittish Kings ..was for many yeeres suspended. **1654** BRAMHALL *Just Vind.* ii. (1661) 16 External actual communion may sometimes be suspended..by the just censures of the Church. **1707** *Curios. Husb. & Gard.* 259 The Course of the nourishing Juice being suspended and turn'd aside. **1751** JOHNSON *Rambler* No. 187 ¶5 By dividing his time between the chace and fishery, [he] suspended the miseries of absence and suspicion. **1761** HUME *Hist. Eng.* I. viii. 178 The king..suspended the payment of Peter's pence. **1777** PRIESTLEY *Matter & Sp.* (1782) I. v. 56 All power of thinking is suspended during a swoon. **1856** SIR B. BRODIE *Psychol. Inq.* I. iv. 138 We may by a powerful effort suspend the action of the respiratory muscles during a limited time. **1860** TYNDALL *Glac.* I. xxvii. 217 A motion which seems not to be suspended even in the depth of winter. **1863** H. COX *Instit.* II. xi. 575 The end of a Prize Court is,—to suspend the property which is the subject of prize, till condemnation. **1883** *Manch. Exam.* 29 Oct. 5/4 The firm had to suspend payment, not from any fault of their own, but from their connection with another firm. **1885** *Law Times* LXXX. 111/1 The right of the railway company to suspend the ordinary service of trains on occasions of..exceptional pressure. **1902** W. W. JACOBS *At Sunwich Port* i. 5 My [master's] certificate has been suspended for six months.

b. To stop or check the action or movement of (something) temporarily; to hold in suspense; †to hold back *from*.

c **1450** *Godstow Reg.* 94 All other every dayes hit shold be lawful to syng j masse with a lowe voyce, and the belle suspended. **1565** *Reg. Privy Council Scot.* I. 413 Thair Hienessis is contentit..to suspend thair handis fra all geving. **1569** UNDERDOWN *Ovid's Invect. Ibis* F iiij, As sone as he sawe his chylde lye before him, he draue on the one syde, and suspended hys plough, and so passed without harme to the chylde. **1643** MILTON *Divorce* vii. Wks. 1851 IV. 36 Nothing more then disturbance of mind suspends us from approaching God. **1710** SHAFTESB. *Charac.* (1737) I. II. ii. 257 The Sublime can no way..bear to be suspended in its impetuous Course. *c* **1750** COLLINS *On Distant View Richmond Ch.* iv, Remembrance oft shall haunt the shore.. And oft suspend the dashing oar To bid his gentle spirit rest! **1753** A. MURPHY *Gray's Inn Jrnl.* No. 33 Both their Sensations being too big for Utterance, their Tongues were suspended. **1836** LANDOR *Pericles & Aspasia* Wks. 1846 II. 373 There is a gloom in deep love as in deep water. There is a silence in it which suspends the foot.

†**c.** *spec.* To put a stop to or interdict the use of (a place of worship), esp. temporarily; hence, to profane. *Obs.*

c **1380** WYCLIF *Wks.* (1880) 69 þei wolen suffre..a chirche or a chirche ȝerde suspendid & no masse seyd þer-inne. *a* **1500** *Bale's Chron.* in *Six Town Chron.* (1911) 120 The first day of July powles church was suspent and the v day folowyng halowed ageyn. **1535** COVERDALE *2 Kings* xxiii. 8 He..suspended yᵉ hye places, where the prestes brent incense. —— *Acts* xxiv. 6 We haue founde this man..a sterer vp of sedicion..& hath taken in hande also to suspende the temple. **1548** UDALL *Erasm. Par. Acts* x. 38 b, Hytherto neuer eate I anye meate that was suspended, or vncleane [orig. *quicquid profanum aut impurum*]. **1560** DAUS tr. *Sleidane's Comm.* 294 His chaplaines before they wold saye any seruice in their churches,..hallowed them againe ..as suspended and polluted with Lutheranisme. **1561** in *Maitl. Club Misc.* III. 270 Ye Lady College Kyrk..is decernit and suspendit ane prophane hows.

†**d.** *gen.* To put a stop to the use of, interdict; to abrogate. *Obs.*

1488 in *Archaeologia* XLV. 115, viij Pillowes of dyvers coloures, besides other that beth suspent & dampned for bad, as appereth in the parcellis of the suspent wares. *c* **1550** ROLLAND *Crt. Venus* III. 369 The law positiue, It did suspend, and haldis as detestine.

e. To cause (a law or the like) to be for the time no longer in force; to abrogate or make inoperative temporarily.

1535-6 *Act 27 Hen. VIII*, c. 10 §8 Provided also that this present acte..be..[not] taken to extincte release discharge or suspende any Statute [etc.]. **1560** DAUS tr. *Sleidane's Comm.* 183 The decree of Auspurge..he suspendeth. **1766** BLACKSTONE *Comm.* II. xviii. 273 The statutes of mortmain were suspended for twenty years by the statute 1 & 2 P. & M. c. 8. **1787** *Constit. U.S.* I. §9 The privilege of the writ of habeas corpus shall not be suspended, unless when..the public safety may require it. **1842** MACAULAY *Ess., Fredk. Gt.* (1877) 700 The authority of laws and magistrates had been suspended. **1879** FROUDE *Cæsar* v. 43 In great danger it was the Senate's business to suspend the constituion.

f. Of an event, condition, etc.: To bring about or entail the temporary cessation of.

1419 *26 Pol. Poems* 71 Encresyng of temperalte Suspende spiritualte. **1684** *Contempl. St. Man* II. iv. (1699) 159 There is no Joy..which can suspend the Grief we suffer from a Finger that is sawing off. **1695** BLACKMORE *Pr. Arth.* III. 587 Wonder almost suspends their Happiness. **1793** BEDDOES *Math. Evid.* p. xiii, Pregnancy suspends consumption. **1805** *Med. Jrnl.* XIV. 142 When the small-pox appeared first, it did not suspend the measles. **1849** MACAULAY *Hist. Eng.* ii. I. 247 The agitation, which had been suspended by the late changes, speedily became more violent than ever. **1901** *Electr. Rev.* 27 Sept. 523/2 A breakdown of a trolley wire.. temporarily suspended the service [of trams].

g. To cease (for a time) from the execution or performance of; to desist or refrain from, esp. temporarily. †Also *absol.* Now *unusual.*

1605 SHAKS. *Lear* I. ii. 86 If it shall please you to suspend your indignation against my Brother, til you can deriue from him better testimony of his intent. **1629** H. BURTON *Babel no Bethel* 69 All saving truthes..must vaile bonnet, and suspend, while Romes Traditions bee serued and obserued. **1715** DE FOE *Fam. Instruct.* (1841) I. I. vii. 125 Suspend your foolish passion about the fellow. **1769** BURKE *Obs. Late St. Nation* Wks. 1842 I. 103 They suspended violence. **1780** COWPER *Nightingale & Glow-worm* 3 A nightingale..Had cheer'd the village with his song, Nor yet at eve his note suspended. **1821** SCOTT *Kenilw.* xvi, Men suspended every, even the slightest, external motion. **1863** GEO. ELIOT *Romola* i, An old woman..for the moment had suspended her wail to listen. **1876** —— *Dan. Der.* lviii, These thoughts, which he wanted to master and suspend.

h. *intr.* for *pass.* To come to a stop for the time, cease temporarily, intermit. *rare.*

1650 FULLER *Pisgah* II. 61 Then Jordan, whose streams hitherto suspended, returned into his channell. **1808** *Med. Jrnl.* XIX. 499 The apoplectic respiration now nearly suspended. **1879** S. C. BARTLETT *Egypt to Pal.* 459 The rain suspended long enough for us to..get fairly under way.

3. a. To put off to a later time or occasion; to defer, postpone. *Obs.* or merged in other senses.

1577 tr. *Bullinger's Decades* (1592) 504 It is..not known what is true, and so the sentence definitiue is suspended. **1581** in Digges *Complete Ambass.* (1655) 388 Her M. suspendeth all resolute answers, till she hear from you. **1646** SIR T. BROWNE *Pseud. Ep.* I. i. 4 So hath he reserved many things unto his owne resolution, whose determinations..we ..must with reverence suspend unto that great day. **1648** GAGE *West Ind.* 202 The old Fryer..thought every day a year that I stayed there, and suspended my Voyage for England. *a* **1700** EVELYN *Diary* 18 June 1683, He would certainly enter judgment against them, which hitherto he had suspended. **1742** WEST *Let.* in *Gray's Poems* (1775) 142 Till that first act is over, every body suspends his vote. **1793** GOUV. MORRIS in Sparks *Life & Writ.* (1832) II. 277 Britain will suspend her blow till she can strike very hard.

Const. *inf.* (or *gerund*). **1566** ABP. PARKER *Corr.* (Parker Soc.) 262 Being informed..that..you suspended to give your furtherance until you had heard our advice. **1581** T. HOWELL *Deuises* (1879) 238 Suspend to deeme the worst,.. And poyse eche poynte before you verdit giue. **1672** EARL ESSEX in *Essex Papers* (Camden) 22 If I shall see that..they doe meritt, I will put it in execution, but if not, I will suspend doeing any thing in it. **1754** EDWARDS *Freed. Will* II. vii. (1762) 71 There is no Medium between suspending to act, and immediately acting.

†**b.** To defer dealing with; to put off consideration of; to pass over for the time; hence *gen.* to disregard. *Obs.*

1581 PETTIE tr. *Guazzo's Civ. Conv.* I. (1586) 6, I would.. a little suspend these seuerall points, and first intreate of this matter in generall. **1632** LITHGOW *Trav.* x. 493 A Regall Commission (which partly being some-where obeyed, and other-where suspended). **1660** R. ELLSWORTH in *Extr. St. Papers rel. Friends* Ser. II. (1911) 121 Their said refuseall, if suspended or conniued att, will cause a general discontent. **1765** T. HUTCHINSON *Hist. Mass.* I. ii. 293 The reason of which..it is better to suspend than too critically to inquire into.

†**c.** Of an event, etc.: To defer or delay the accomplishment of. *Obs.*

1781 GIBBON *Decl. & F.* xxi. (1787) II. 309 The divisions of Christianity suspended the ruin of paganism. **1784** COWPER *Task* II. 197 Will thy discovery of the cause Suspend th' effect, or heal it? **1807** G. CHALMERS *Caledonia* I. II. iii. 253 The bravest efforts of their gallant chiefs could not suspend their destiny.

†**d.** *intr.* To be delayed. *Obs.*

1690 CHILD *Disc. Trade* (1698) 81 Before the use of money falls, which I conclude cannot long suspend.

4. a. *trans.* To keep (one's judgement) undetermined; to refrain from forming (an opinion) or giving (assent) decisively.

†occas. to withhold (assent) *from.*

1553 LATIMER *Serm. Lord's Prayer* i. (1562) 6 b, We should not be to hastye in beleuynge the tale, but rather suspende oure iudgementes till we know the truth. **1620** T. GRANGER *Div. Logike* II. iv, In doubtfull things we suspend our assent, and iudgement. **1667** TEMPLE *Let.* Wks. 1731 II. 27, I suspend my Confidence till the Arrival of my English Letters, which are my Gospel in these Cases. **1742** *Col. Rec. Pennsylv.* IV. 551 He must excuse us if we suspend our belief until we are better satisfied of the Truth of the Facts. **1775** JOHNSON *Tax. no Tyr.* 16 The publick voice suspends its decision. **1791** HAMILTON tr. *Berthollet's Dyeing* I. I. III. ii. 256 On this subject I suspend my opinion. **1885** 'MRS. ALEXANDER' *At Bay* i, He felt strongly disposed to believe that his new acquaintance was thoroughly a lady, though a knowledge of life in most European capitals disposed him to suspend his judgment.

†**b.** *absol.* To suspend one's judgement, to be in doubt; hence *occas.* (with simple obj. or obj. cl.) to doubt; also, to apprehend, suspect. *Obs.*

1585 Q. ELIZ. in *Four C. Eng. Lett.* (1880) 29, I wer out of [my] sences if I shuld not suspend of any hiresay til the answer of your owne action. **1599** B. JONSON *Ev. Man out of Hum.* IV. iv, Pardon me, that's to be suspended, you are too quicke, too apprehensive. **1599** —— *Cynthia's Rev.* IV. ii, These ladies are not of that close, and open behauiour, as happily you may suspend. **1632** LITHGOW *Trav.* VI. 248 [They] sayd, heere Diues the rich Glutton dwelt..: this I suspend. **1646** SIR T. BROWNE *Pseud. Ep.* II. vi. 102 Many things are..believed of other plants, wherein at least we cannot but suspend. **1656** *Burton's Diary* (1828) I. 141 Moses did not suspend that it was to be punished with death. His consultation with God was only about the manner. **1676** MARVELL *Mr. Smirke* Wks. (Grosart) IV. 74 Some divines teach us to believe (though I suspend) that God Himself cannot..compel men to believing. **1749** HARTLEY *Observ. Man* I. Pref., That voluntary Power over our Affections and Actions, by which we deliberate, suspend, and choose.

†**c.** To hold oneself back or refrain *from* doing something. *Obs. rare.*

1598 in Ellis *Orig. Lett.* Ser. I. III. 50 Wisshing us to suspend from embracing any other course in that kinde. **1675** M. CLIFFORD *Hum. Reason* 17 Reason will not presently advise us to a change,..but suspend a while and attempt again. *Ibid.* 89, I must..stand still, that is suspend absolutely from the belief of any Religion.

d. *to suspend disbelief*, to refrain from being sceptical, or from doubting the truth of something. Cf. SUSPENSION 3 b.

1963 *Listener* 28 Feb. 393/2 By the time he arrived at the cliff-hanging conclusion there was nothing for it but to suspend disbelief. **1979** *Amer. N. & Q.* Feb. 97/1 In suspending disbelief, poets could construct a fictitious transitional zone.

5. †**a.** To keep in a state of mental fixity, attention, or contemplation; to rivet the attention of.

1561 T. NORTON *Calvin's Inst.* I. 9 To geue ourselues unto such a searching out of God, as may so holde our witt suspended with admiration [etc.]. **1639** S. DU VERGER tr. *Camus' Admir. Events* a 2, Things which delight and wonderfully suspend the minde. **1667** MILTON *P.L.* II. 555 The harmony..Suspended Hell, and took with ravishment The thronging audience. **1671** WOODHEAD *St. Teresa* II. xi. 91 A Prayer of Quiet in the manner of a Spiritual sleep, which suspends the Soul so, that..we may lose much time. **1744** AKENSIDE *Pleas. Imag.* I. 257 The village-matron, round the blazing hearth, Suspends the infant-audience with her tales. **1804** EUGENIA DE ACTON *Tale without Title* I. 224 She sat suspended, till recollecting the box..she started. **1812** CARY *Dante, Parad.* XXXII. 81 Whatsoever I had yet beheld, Had not so much suspended me with wonder [orig. *Di tanta ammirazion non mi sospese*].

b. To keep in suspense, uncertainty, or indecision. Now *rare*.

1603 B. Jonson *Sejanus* iv. v, Thus he leaues the Senate Diuided, and suspended, all vncertaine. **1653** H. Cogan tr. *Pinto's Trav.* xiii. 39 We were all suspended into divers opinions. **1668** Dryden *Even. Love* Ded., She [*sc.* Victory] seem'd to suspend her self, and to doubt, before she took her Flight. **1719** De Foe *Crusoe* i. (Globe) 247 My Thoughts were a little suspended, when I had a serious Discourse with the Spaniard. **1751** Johnson *Rambler* No. 158 ⁋13 The intent of the introduction is to raise expectation, and suspend it. **1798** Jefferson *Writ.* (1859) IV. 208, I am entirely suspended as to what is to be expected. *c* **1880** *Kirkby* (*Yorks.*) *Dial.*, They were very curious to know the secret but I would not tell them. I suspended them for a whole year. **1962** *Listener* 27 Sept. 483/1 Dostoyevsky harrows and suspends his reader.

6. *Sc. Law.* **a.** *trans.* To defer or stay (execution of a sentence) pending its discussion in the Supreme Court. **b.** *intr.* To present a bill of suspension: see suspension 4, and cf. suspender 3.

1650 *Acts of Sederunt* 16 Jan. (1790) 63 The decreittis, registrate bandis, and uther groundis of the letters and charges craved to be suspendit. **1698** in Sir H. Dalrymple *Decisions* (1792) 1 Sir John C. having charged the Earl.. upon a bond of borrowed money, to pay 1000 l. Sterling, he suspended, and alleged *res judicata*. **1743** Kames *Decis. Crt. Sess. 1730–52* (1799) 65 Begbie occasionally hearing that his decree was suspended, put up his protestation in common form. *Ibid.* 70 W. H., being charged for recourse, suspended upon want of due negociation. **1838** W. Bell *Dict. Law Scot.* s.v. *Suspension*, The party complaining commences proceedings by presenting a bill of suspension..his bill concludes, that the..execution in question ought to be suspended, and therefore he prays for letters of suspension.

7. *Mus.* To prolong (a note of a chord) into the following chord, thus deferring the progression of the part in which it occurs, usually so as to produce a temporary discord.

1853 J. Smith *Treat. Mus.* 35 In Example (97) the diminished and minor seventh are suspended. **1867** Macfarren *Harmony* (1892) 69 Let us suspend every bass note as the inverted 4th of the chord that follows it.

II. 8. a. *trans.* To hang, hang up, by attachment to a support above; = hang *v.* 1. (Often a technical or affected substitute for *hang*.)

c **1440** *Pallad. on Husb.* iii. 832 And after monethes iij do hem suspende. **1593** *Rites of Durham* (Surtees 1842) 34 The iiij[th] bell remaynes ther still and was never rounge synce yt was suspent. **1656** Blount *Glossogr.*, *Suspend*.., to hang up or upon. **1706** Phillips (ed. Kersey), *Suspended*, a Philosophical Word for hanged up. **1719** Quincy *Lex. Physico-Med.* (1722), *Suspended*, or *Appended*, is said of external Remedies, which are wore about the Neck, Wrists, or the like. **1784** Cowper *Task* iv. 774 The most unfurnish'd with the means of life..overhead Suspend their crazy boxes, planted thick, And watered duly. **1796** J. Jordan *Specif. Patent Bridges* (1797) 4 My invention consists in suspending to an arch or arches,..bridges. **1820** W. Irving *Sketch Bk.* II. 52 (*Stage Coach*) Hams, tongues, and flitches of bacon, were suspended from the ceiling. **1836** *Penny Cycl.* VI. 178/2 A collection of pictures..for the present suspended in an apartment at the Pitt press. **1839** Keightley *Hist. Eng.* II. 87 Others [*sc.* rebels] were suspended from the boughs of the oak. **1848** Buckley *Iliad* ii. 293 He suspended from his shoulders his silver-studded sword. **1867** tr. *C'tess Hahn-Hahn's Lives Fathers of Desert* 20 The chandeliers suspended from the roof were of silver.

fig. **1836** J. Gilbert *Chr. Atonem.* ii, Punishments actually denounced, and those punishments suspended over us.

†**b.** *intr.* = hang *v.* 8. *Obs.*

1597 A. M. tr. *Guillemeau's Fr. Chirurg.* 16/2 Because that the wounded partes may suspend & hange in the bellye. **1599** —— tr. *Gabelhouer's Bk. Physicke* 61/2 Let not this little cloth suspend above thre howers therin. *a* **1687** Villiers (Dk. Buckhm.) *Epitaph upon Felton* 1 Here uninter'd suspends..Felton's dead Earth.

c. *trans.* To support (something hanging). *rare*.

1816 Tuckey *Narr. Exped. R. Zaire* iii. (1818) 99 And a silk sash..suspending a ship's cutlass, finished his costume.

d. To attach so as to allow of movement about the point of attachment; = hang *v.* 2.

1827 Faraday *Chem. Manip.* xxiii. (1842) 595 It will, if freely suspended, pass beyond its position of rest to a distance on the left side. **1871** A. Meadows *Man. Midwifery* (ed. 2) 299 An index suspended from a cross-bar.

9. a. *fig.* To cause to depend; *pass.* to depend. Const. *on*, *upon* (rarely *from*). Now *rare*.

1608 Willet *Hexapla Exod.* xxxiv. 820 It seemeth by the Hebrew distinction ouer Iehouah, that this word is suspended from the rest which follow, so that *eel* is one of the epithetes rather..then a proper name of God. **1629** Prynne *Anti-Armin.* 83 If our conuersion, saluation, grace, and glorie, are thus suspended on our most impotent..wills, what man can once be saued? **1653** Milton *Hirelings* Wks. 1851 V. 373 That the Magistrate..should take into his own Power the stipendiary maintenance of Church-ministers,.. would suspend the Church wholly upon the State. **1758** Johnson *Idler* No. 11 ⁋5 The present state of the skies and of the earth, on which plenty and famine are suspended. **1759** —— *Rasselas* xxviii, It is dangerous for a man and woman to suspend their fate upon each other, at a time when opinions are fixed [etc.]. **1829** I. Taylor *Enthus.* x. 278 That the universal prevalence of Christianity..is suspended upon the continuance of missionary zeal. **1844** R. Choate *Addresses* (1878) 334 The peculiarity of this election is that while it involves all the questions of mere policy which are ever suspended on the choice of a president [etc.].

†**b.** To regard as dependent, 'make' (a thing) depend, *upon*. *Obs.*

1638 Chillingw. *Relig. Prot.* i. ii. §69. 79 Your suspending the same [*sc.* salvation of a baptized infant] on the Baptizer's intention. **1797** *Monthly Mag.* III. 262/1 They differed from the above-mentioned theologists and philosophers in this, that the latter suspended every thing from Deity.

10. a. To hold, or cause to be held up, without attachment; = hang *v.* 1 d.

1646 Sir T. Browne *Pseud. Ep.* ii. iii. 72 That in the Temple of Serapis there was an iron chariot suspended by Loadstones in the ayre. **1685** Boyle *Eng. Notion Nat.* ii. 29 That water kept suspended in a sucking Pump, is not in its natural place. **1846** Browning *Luria* ii. 198 The unseen sun above, Which draws and holds suspended all of us, Binds transient mists and vapours into one. **1870** R. R. Coverdale *Poems* 16 A cloud in western skies Suspent, or floating on its way. **1909** C. Keyser in *Hibbert Jrnl.* Jan. 386 The world of things that are finite is strictly an island-world suspent in a sea.

b. To hold, or cause to be held, in suspension; to contain in the form of particles diffused through its substance, as a fluid medium; to cause to be so diffused (*in* the medium).

1737 Bracken *Farriery Impr.* (1757) II. 277 Spirit of Wine singly is not near so efficacious..as when it contains or Suspends some resinous Substance. **1805** W. Saunders *Min. Waters* 162 There is no more carbonic acid, or scarcely more, than is necessary to keep the lime suspended. **1862** Miller *Elem. Chem., Org.* iii. (ed. 2) 244 By suspending the compound of acetylene with subchloride of copper in a solution of ammonia. **1874** Garrod & Baxter *Mat. Med* 115 Fluid Magnesia... Prepare as above, suspend in water and pass pure carbonic acid gas through it. **1880** *Encycl. Brit.* XIII. 81/1 Gold and silver inks are writing fluids in which gold and silver,..are suspended in a state of fine division.

su'spended, *ppl. a.* and *sb.* [f. prec. + -ed[1].]

A. *ppl. adj.* **I. 1.** Temporarily deprived of office, position, or privilege.

1535 in Burnet *Hist. Ref* (1679) I. *Records* 132 Whether any Persons Excommunicate, Suspended or Interdicted, did give Voices in the same Election? **1659** *Clarke Papers* (Camden) IV. 300 The cashiered and suspended officers. **1837** Carlyle *Fr. Rev.* ii. vi. viii, Louis and his sad suspended Household. **1849** Macaulay *Hist. Eng.* ix II. 408 Compton, the suspended Bishop of London. **1901** *Scotsman* 9 Mar. 8/4 One of the suspended members had the first place for an amendment.

2. Undecided, undetermined.

1576 Fleming *Panopl. Epist.* 194 His suspended and doubtfull mynde. **1779–81** Johnson *L.P.*, *Milton* Wks. II. 88 One of his friends who had reproved his suspended and dilatory life. **1881** W. H. White *M. Rutherford's Autobiog.* ii. 20 It is the most difficult thing for us to be satisfied with suspended judgment.

3. Temporarily stopped, intermitted: chiefly in phr. ***suspended animation***, a state of temporary insensibility, esp. that due to asphyxia.

1795 *British Critic* VI. 533 The author having examined the causes of suspended animation in animals that are hanged, drowned, suffocated, or killed by noxious vapours, concludes that it is occasioned solely by the exclusion of vital air from the lungs. **1817** Shelley *Rev. Islam* xi. xi, Why watched those myriads with suspended breath Sleepless a second night? **1820** Good *Nosology* 368 Total suspension of all the mental and corporeal functions..Asphyxy. Suspended animation. **1825** Scott *Betrothed* xiv, In suggesting and applying the usual modes for recalling the suspended sense. **1827** —— *Surg. Dau.* viii, An old servant waited with the means of restoring suspended animation. **1836** I. Taylor *Phys. The. Another Life* xvii. 257 A condition of suspended powers.

4. a. Deferred, or of which the fulfilment or execution is deferred.

1848 Lytton *Harold* viii. vi, Harold parted from his betrothed, without hint of his suspended designs. **1856** Dove *Logic Chr. Faith* v. ii. 325 Inasmuch as perfect justice is not executed in this world, man is in a state of suspended condemnation.

b. ***suspended sentence*** (Law), a sentence which is imposed but remains in suspense provided that the offender commits no further offence within a stipulated period.

The suspended sentence was first introduced in Europe in the late nineteenth cent. Before this the phr. 'to suspend sentence' was used, esp. in the U.S., to denote the remission or commutation of a capital sentence (see quots. 1828, 1860). In Great Britain the suspended sentence became legal only in 1967 (see quot. 1967), and is commonly used in conjunction with the system of probation (see probation 3).

[**1828** De W. Clinton in E. Cowen *N.Y. State Supreme Court Rep.* (1859) IX. 730 If the judiciary be exposed to sudden..attempts on its humanity..to suspend the sentence of the law, what must be the effect on the executive, when it comes before him, backed by judicial authority; a prevalent sentiment against the punishment of death. **1860** N. Howard *Practice Rep. Supreme Court State N.Y.* XX. 119, I have learned by newspapers that the recorder of this city occasionally suspended sentence upon verdicts or pleas of guilty. *Ibid.*, The court does not possess the power to suspend sentence indefinitely. The judge should recommend the prisoner to a pardon and not suspend sentence, in case he thinks no punishment ought to be inflicted.] **1884** *Chicago Legal News* XVI. 392/1 The same ruling might be held to apply as to the enforcement of suspended sentences..if the power of suspension existed. **1912** *Atlantic Reporter* LXXXII. 424/1 The term 'suspended sentence', as used in criminal law, refers to the suspension of the execution of a sentence already imposed, and not correctly to the suspending of a sentence. **1923** *Texas Law Rev.* I. 191 If anyone is to be given a suspended sentence and another chance to 'make good', surely it is the young man who has committed his first misdemeanor. **1947** *Survey* LXXXIII. 219/1 In 1940, 33 percent of our adult offenders were put on probation or granted suspended sentence. **1950** [see box *v.*[2] 2 d]. **1950** *Times* 21 Oct. 3/3 Sir Leo Page had suggested to him that the probation system might be strengthened by the suspended sentence as used in France and other countries. **1957** *Alternatives to Short Terms of Imprisonment* (Home Office) 9 We understand from the Association of Chief Police Officers that there is strong support among the police for the courts being given power to impose a suspended sentence. **1967** *Act Eliz. II* c. 80 §39 A court which passes a sentence of imprisonment for a term of not more than two years for an offence may order that the sentence shall not take effect unless, during a period specified in the order..the offender commits in Great Britain another offence punishable with imprisonment.. and in this Part of this Act 'operational period', in relation to a suspended sentence, means the period so specified. **1971** L. Radzinowicz in M. Ancel *Suspended Sentence* p. vi., The suspended sentence is essentially a continental system. It began its meteoric career over seventy years ago, with the Belgian and French laws of 1888 and 1891... From there it made a *tour du monde*... It eventually reached Israel ..in 1954, before entering the United Kingdom, as a very late immigrant, in 1967. **1972** J. Wilson *Hide & Seek* viii. 151, I got six months suspended sentence last time and fined twenty rotten quid. **1973** F. Rinaldi *Suspended Sentences in Australia* vi. 85 To every suspended sentence there should be added a supervision order. **1979** T. Skyrme *Changing Image Magistracy* x. 125 After the introduction of suspended sentences other forms of penalty, financial as well as custodial, diminished steadily.

c. ***suspended participle*** (Gram.), a participle in an absolute clause or phrase whose subject is omitted, resulting in ambiguity; a dangling participle.

1942 E. Partridge *Usage & Abusage* 93/1 *Confused participles*... Here will be treated what are variously known as disconnected or misrelated or suspended participles... Dr Onions cites the following additional examples:- *Calling upon him last summer*, he kindly offered to give me his copy. (Say: *When I called.*) **1972** R. D. Walshe in G. W. Turner *Good Austral. Eng.* 256 This lapse..has variously been called the..*isolated, suspended*, or *dangling participle* (or *phrase*).

d. ***suspended disbelief***: see suspend *v.* 4 d.

1965 *New Statesman* 20 Aug. 262/1 For a moment you forgot these were actors and participated..in the panic of.. the St Valentine's day massacre... A moment later the curtain came down, the lights went up. The theatre has its own short way with suspended disbelief. **1977** *N.Y. Rev. Bks.* 26 May 13/4 If in the end I remain in a state of suspended disbelief, it is..because I find it hard to believe that there can be a single explanation for so complex a phenomenon.

5. *Mus.* Of a note of a chord: Prolonged into the following chord, usually so as to constitute a temporary discord.

1853 J. Smith *Treat. Mus.* 33 By carrying on some one tone (technically termed a 'suspended note'), from the harmony preceding a dissonant chord. **1867** Macfarren *Harmony* (1892) 66 The suspended discords are the 9th, and the 4th, and also the 5th, from the mediant and leading-note. **1889** Prout *Harmony* xix. 228 The first inversion of the suspended fourth.

II. 6. a. Supported by attachment above; hung; hanging. †***suspended bridge*** = suspension-bridge. ***suspended ceiling***, a ceiling fixed so as to alter the proportions of the room or to give sufficient space above it to accommodate services.

1796 *Monthly Mag.* II. 883 Jordan's Suspended Bridges. **1815** J. Smith *Panorama Sci. & Art* II. 223 The clappers now fly to deposit the electricity they have received upon the central bell. They are then again in a condition to be attracted by the suspended bells. **1861** Stephens & Burn *Bk. Farm-buildings* 368 Suspended or hanging gate for courtyards. **1889** G. Findlay *Eng. Railway* 44 In 1847 Mr. Bridges Adams introduced the suspended joint with fish-plates. **1901** *Black's Illustr. Carp. & Build., Scaffolding* 18 We recognise, by the tell-tale cavities left in the existing stonework, that the scaffolds were suspended ones. **1933** *Archit. Rev.* LXXIV. 54/3 The suspended ceilings are built of steel, wire hangers, steel bars and expanded metal, and plaster. **1955** [see insulation 3 a]. **1978** *Cornish Guardian* 27 Apr. 17/8 (Advt.), The County Council invite offers to submit fixed price tenders for..the provision of a suspended ceiling.

b. *Entom.* (See quots.)

1826 Kirby & Sp. *Entomol.* IV. 300 *Suspended*,..when one part is joined to another by a ligature, without being inserted in it. **1841** Westwood *Brit. Butterflies* 54 The mode in which these caterpillars [of the Peacock Butterfly] change to suspended chrysalides. **1871** E. Newman *Brit. Butterflies* 19 *Suspended*..those in which the chrysalids are attached by the tail only, and hang with the head downwards.

c. *Bot.* Of an ovule (or seed): Attached at or near the summit of the ovary (or fruit) and hanging vertically.

1832 Lindley *Introd. Bot.* 159 When an ovulum..hangs from the summit of the cavity, it is *pendulous*; and when from a little below the summit, it is *suspended*. **1861** Bentley *Man. Bot.* 336 A seed may be erect, inverse or pendulous, suspended, ascending, &c.

7. Held up without attachment; held aloft.

1817 Shelley *Rev. Islam* i. xi, A vapour like the sea's suspended spray Hung gathered.

8. Held in suspension; diffused in a fluid medium, as solid particles.

1832 Babbage *Econ. Manuf.* vii. (ed. 3) 51 The coarsest portion of the suspended matter first subsides. **1851–3** *Tomlinson's Cycl. Arts* (1867) II. 684/1 It..contains suspended impurities coated with albumen. **1877** Huxley *Physiogr.* 141 A part of the suspended sediment falls to the bottom.

B. *sb.* or quasi-*sb. ellipt.* for *suspended sentence*, sense 4 b above. *slang.*

1970 G. F. NEWMAN *Sir, You Bastard* i. 34 The bird'll get a suspended, I don't doubt her old man's had a word somewhere. **1979** M. PAGE *Pilate Plot* ix. 130 If you cooperate, I can probably get you off with a £20 fine and a month's suspended—and no press publicity.

suspendee (sʌspɛn'diː). *nonce-wd.* [f. SUSPEND *v.* + -EE.] One who is suspended.

a **1856** in Olmsted *Slave States* 115, I have heard that the great ordeal, in their [*sc.* negroes'] estimation, a 'seeker' had to pass, was being held over the infernal flames by a thread or a hair. If the thread does not break, the suspendee is 'in the Lord.'

su'spender. [f. SUSPEND *v.* + -ER[1].]

I. One who or that which suspends.

1. One who or that which puts a stop to something, esp. temporarily.

1524 *Extr. Aberd. Reg.* (1844) I. 108 The suspendaris of the said kirk being charply persewit for the said expensis. **1867** *Contemp. Rev.* V. 455 Time itself is the great suspender of controversy.

†**2.** One who suspends his judgement; a doubter, hesitator. *Obs. rare*$^{-1}$.

1625 MOUNTAGU *App. Cæsar* II. v. 146 The cautelousnes of suspenders, and not forward concluders.

3. *Sc. Law.* One who presents a bill of suspension: see SUSPENSION 4, and cf. SUSPEND *v.* 6 b.

1650 *Acts of Sederunt* 16 Jan. (1790) 63 The Lords declairis, That whair the groundis of the chairges are decreittis before inferior judges, the suspender, in that case, is onlie heirby haldin either to produce the decreitt, or ane instrument of refusall theirof. **1698** in Sir H. Dalrymple *Decisions* (1792) 7 The suspender having neglected the legal remedy of suspension. **1774** in A. McKay *Hist. Kilmarnock* (1864) 303 The suspenders have given a very erroneous state of the..manner in which this green was acquired. **1838** W. BELL *Dict. Law Scot.* s.v. *Suspension*, The ordinary course.. is for the suspender to ask the Lord Ordinary to pronounce an order for revising the reasons of suspension and answers. **1868** *Act 31 & 32 Vict.* c. 100 §2 The word 'pursuer' shall include complainer, suspender, petitioner, or appellant.

II. That by which something is suspended.

4. a. One of a pair of straps passing over the shoulders to hold up the trousers: = BRACE *sb.*[2] 9 b: usually in *pl.* Chiefly *U.S.*

1810 *Massachusetts Spy* 23 May 3/2 Part of the buckle of his suspenders and several pieces of his coat..were extracted from the wound. **1830** MARRYAT *King's Own* ii, Loose trousers, tightened at the hips, to preclude the necessity of suspenders. **1841** SYD. SMITH in Lady Holland *Mem.* (1855) II. 442 Correspondences are like small-clothes before the invention of suspenders; it is impossible to keep them up. **1883** 'MARK TWAIN' *Life Mississippi* iv. 45 He wore a leather belt and used no suspenders.

attrib. **1833** [S. SMITH] *Lett. J. Downing* xxii. (1835) 130 And jest then the Gineral got in a way he has of twitchin with his suspender buttons behind.

b. A device attached to the top of a stocking or sock to hold it up in place.

1878 *Queen* 13 July (Advt.), The new stocking suspender (Patent) worn by the leaders of fashion and strongly recommended by the medical profession. **1881** *Queen* 18 June 6/2 (*heading*) The New Stocking Suspender... A handsome pair of..suspenders, in a fancy box. **1895** *Army & Navy Co-op. Soc. Price List* 1082 Ladies' Stocking Suspenders. *Ibid.* 1134 Half Hose Suspenders.

c. suspender belt, an undergarment used for holding up stockings, consisting of a belt and suspenders to which the tops of the stockings are clipped; a garter belt; **suspender clip, end**, the clip on a suspender belt.

1926–7 *Army & Navy Stores Catal.* 667/2 Suspender belts. White only..each 2/6. **1930** A. HUXLEY *Brief Candles* 303 And then that further humiliation of having to ask him to help her look for her suspender belt! **1976** *Vogue* 15 Mar. 79 Blue satin suspender belt, £6.90. **1973** T. PYNCHON *Gravity's Rainbow* (1975) I. 127 Concentrating on gartering her nylons,..suspender-clips glittering silver under or behind her lacquered red fingernails. **1966** *Olney Amsden Price List* 36 *Suspender ends*..Nylon Fitting 6/8 dozen cards.

5. a. An apparatus or a natural structure which supports something suspended.

1839 URE *Dict. Arts* 642 The second improvement described by the patentee, is the construction of 'suspenders', to be substituted instead of the ordinary blocks. **1874** COOKE *Fungi* 168 The suspender of the larger copulative cell. **1895** *Arnold & Sons' Catal. Surg. Instrum.* 704 Suspender (Keetley's), with woollen bag [for scrotal hernia].

b. A tanning-pit in which the hides are suspended.

1882 *Encycl. Brit.* XIV. 384/2 In these pits (also called suspenders) the hides are suspended over poles laid across the pit, and they are moved daily from one to another of a series of four or six.

III. Something that is suspended.

6. A hanging basket, vase, etc., as for flowers.

1878 JEWITT *Ceramic Art* I. 425 Vases, tazzas, brackets, pedestals, suspenders, terminals, flower-vases.

suspendible (sə'spɛndɪb(ə)l), *a. rare*$^{-1}$. [f. SUSPEND *v.* + -IBLE.] Capable of being, or liable to be, suspended. So **suspendi'bility**.

1799 KIRWAN *Geol. Ess.* 407 The solubility or suspendibility, (as some may choose to call it,) in mere water. **1892** *Pall Mall G.* 25 June 1/2 Somebody then would be responsible, and 'suspendible' if legal blunders were found in new laws.

suspending (sə'spɛndɪŋ), *vbl. sb.* [f. SUSPEND *v.* + -ING[1].] The action of the verb SUSPEND.

1. = SUSPENSION 1.

c **1380** WYCLIF *Wks.* (1880) 80 Sumtyme men weren forboden of trewe prestis to vse & do sacramentis in open cursed lif, & þat is trewe suspendynge. *c* **1440** *Jacob's Well* 30 Sentence of cursyng, of suspendyng, of enterdyȝtyng aȝens kyng, lord, baroun. *c* **1585** [R. BROWNE] *Answ. Cartwright* 15 He seemeth to allowe also their suspendings of preachers.

2. = SUSPENSION 2, 4.

1524 *Extr. Aberd. Reg.* (1844) I. 108 The cause of the said kirkis suspending. **1532** MORE *Confut. Tindale* Wks. 595/2 A suspendinge of the vse of yᵉ wyttes. **1673** *Essex Papers* (Camden) I. 49, I long very much for an answer concerning yᵉ Rules. I must needs say that yᵉ Letter for yᵉ suspending of them..has bin of great disadvantage to me. **1696** *Sc. Acts Will. III* (1823) X. 66/1 His Majestie..Ordains that in case of calumnious suspending the Lords of Session Decern a third part more then is Decerned for Expences.

†**3.** = SUSPENSION 7. *Obs.*

1483 CAXTON *Gold. Leg.* 269/1 By the fyrst thre suspendynges that he had ought to be noted he was suspended or taken vp fro the loue of the world and he was suspendyd that is to say ententyf in heuenly loue And he was suspended that is to saye wrappyd in the grace..of God.

su'spending, *ppl. a.* [f. as prec. + -ING[2].] That suspends, in various senses.

1. In non-physical sense: see SUSPEND *v.* 1, 2.

1656 G. COLLIER *Answ. 15 Quest.* Ded. A 2, Mr. Fisher.. hath sent abroad..bitter insinuations against suspending ministers (as he calls them). **1689** TUTCHIN *Heroick Poem* 8 No Poetry must pass, but serv'd the Cause, Or some Suspending Ballad of the Laws. **1824** L. MURRAY *Engl. Gram.* IV. i. §4 (ed. 5) I. 366 It is a general rule, that the suspending pause should be used when the sense is incomplete. **1862** BROUGHAM *Brit. Const.* xvi. 247 James.. assumed the full dispensing and suspending powers. **1910** *Edin. Rev.* Jan. 132 In spite of the Lords' claim to act as a revising and suspending chamber.

2. In physical sense (see SUSPEND *v.* 8), usually applied to the support by which something is suspended (8 c).

1613 in A. F. Steuart *Scots in Poland* (S.H.S.) 69, 16 pairs of suspending eye-glasses. **1796** *Monthly Mag.* II. 883 The patentee..proposes to attach the bridge to these [two parallel elliptic] curves, by means of wrought iron suspending bars. **1797** J. CURR *Coal Viewer* 22 The suspending lug of the corf. **1827** FARADAY *Chem. Manip.* ii. (1842) 51 When the substance is small, the balance delicate, and the suspending line thick. **1846** OWEN in *Rep. Brit. Assoc.* I. 205 The large suspending mastoid to which Muller gives the name of 'temporale'. **1875** KNIGHT *Dict. Mech.* 2462/1 *Suspending-clutch*, a grapple to be fixed to a beam in a barn or warehouse, for the purpose of suspending hoisting-tackle.

†**suspen'sation.** *Obs. rare.* [ad. med.L. *suspensātio*, *-ōnem*, n. of action f. *suspensāre*: see SUSPENSE *v.*] = SUSPENSION.

1571 CAMPION *Hist. Irel.* II. i. (1633) 58 That Mac Murrough..should quietly repossesse the parts of Leinster, which Rodericke with-held by suspensation. *a* **1657** R. LOVEDAY *Lett.* (1663) 267 The malice of the times extends beyond the suspensation of estates, to the separation of friends. ? *a* **1800** MANSFIELD (Worc.), A suspensation of the laws.

suspense (sə'spɛns), *sb.* Also 5–9 suspence, 6–7 -ens. [a. AF., OF. *suspens* m., in phr. *en suspens* (Rolls Parlt., an. 1306) in abeyance, or OF. *suspense* f. deferring, delay, repr. med.L. *suspensum* (in phr. *in suspenso*), **suspensa* (= *suspensio*), neut. and fem. of *suspensus*, pa. pple. of *suspendĕre* to SUSPEND. (The neut. form is represented also in It. *sospeso*, Sp., Pg. *suspenso*.) Cf. the history of DEFENCE and OFFENCE.]

I. †**1. a.** (Chiefly *Law.*) ***in suspense***, not being executed, fulfilled, rendered, paid, or the like; esp. ***to put in suspense***, to defer or intermit the execution, payment, etc. of. *Obs.*

1421 HOCCLEVE *Learn to Die* 138 Whethir not changed may be this sentence; O lord, may it nat put been in suspense? **1492** *Rolls of Parlt.* VI. 445 That by this same Act ..the same Rentes and Services..be not extincted nor put in suspence. **1535** *Act 27 Hen. VIII*, c. 9, The same estatutes ..shalbe in suspence and not to put in execucion duryng the saide tyme. **1544** tr. *Littleton's Tenures* III. x. 124 b, The tenaunt for terme of lyfe hath fe in the seruyces, but seruyces be put in suspence durynge his lyfe. **1576** *Reg. Privy Council Scot.* II. 522 That the saidis landis..remane in the menetyme in suspens un-mellit or intromettit with be ayther of the saidis partiis. **1628** COKE *On Litt.* 313 Albeit during the couerture the seruices shal be put in suspence. **1818** CRUISE *Digest* (ed. 2) IV. 186 It was a springing use, resting in suspence during his life.

†**b.** Hence *gen.* (*a*) Temporary cessation, intermission, abeyance; = SUSPENSION 2. *Obs.*

1584 S. COX in Nicolas *Life Sir C. Hatton* (1847) 396 The long suspense of your favor, hath bred an opinion..that [etc.]. **1588** *Holy Bull & Crusade Rome* 36 Though it were so, that all the same or any of them, did containe any clause contrary to this suspence. **1710** NORRIS *Chr. Prud.* v. 251 In natural Sleep the senses of the Body are bound up, so that there is a suspense of Sensation. **1717** POPE *Eloisa to Abelard* 250 For thee the fates..ordain A cool suspense from pleasure and from pain. **1783** JOHNSON *Let. to Mrs. Thrale* 26 Aug., I hope this little journey will afford me at least some suspense of melancholy. **1818** CRUISE *Digest* (ed. 2) VI. 552 That though, where a number of years directly constituted the term of suspense, property could not be prevented from vesting absolutely during 25 years, [etc.].

†(*b*) Deferment, delay. *Obs.*

c **1590** GREENE *Fr. Bacon* ix. 204 Edward, I accept thee here, Without suspence, as my adopted sonne. **1602** in Moryson *Itin.* (1617) II. 252 These vnreasonable Billes haue been looked into (and so some suspence of paiment made). **1712** STEELE *Spect.* No. 284 ⁋2 Their whole Time is spent in suspense of the present Moment to the next. *a* **1718** PENN *Innocency* Wks. 1726 I. 266 This short Apology,..which had not been thus long retarded, if an Expectation..had not required a Suspense.

2. The state of being suspended or kept undetermined (chiefly ***to hold, keep in suspense***); hence, the action of suspending one's judgement; = SUSPENSION 5.

1560 DAUS tr. *Sleidane's Comm.* 99 b, To geue no credit vnto sclaunders,..but to keepe theyr iudgement in suspence, tyll [etc.]. **1594** HOOKER *Eccl. Pol.* IV. xiv. §6 Suspence of iudgement and exercise of charitie. **1736** BUTLER *Anal.* II. vi. 223 This will afford Matter of Exercise, for religious Suspense and Deliberation. **1794** PALEY *Evid.* III. iv. (1800) II. 314 The miracles did not..so compel assent, as to leave no room for suspense. **1892** WESTCOTT *Gospel of Life* 216 Cases may arise in which it is our duty to hold our judgment in suspense. **1908** *Westm. Gaz.* 16 Jan. 2/2 The plea for a suspense of judgment until the facts are known.

3. a. A state of mental uncertainty, with expectation of or desire for decision, and usually some apprehension or anxiety; the condition of waiting, esp. of being kept waiting, for an expected decision, assurance, or issue; less commonly, a state of uncertainty what to do, indecision: esp. in ***to keep*** (or ***hold***) ***in*** (†***great*** or †***a great***) ***suspense***.

c **1440** CAPGRAVE *Life St. Kath.* IV. 1838 This putte þe puple in conceytes ful suspens. **1526** *Pilgr. Perf.* (W. de W. 1531) 127 Without drede or feare,..suspence & doutfulnes of mynde. **1557** N. T. (Genev.) *Luke* xxiv. 28 *note*, Christe wolde kepe them in suspens til his tyme came to manifest him self vnto him. **1573** G. HARVEY *Letter-bk.* (Camden) 15, I praid him..that he wuld not suffer me to go in as great suspens as I cam. **1621** BURTON *Anat. Mel.* II. ii. VI. i, If he ..be in suspition, suspence, or any way molested, satisfie his mind. **1671** MILTON *Samson* 1569 Suspense in news is torture, speak them out. **1700** C. NESSE *Antid. Armin.* (1827) 58 Men wickedly think that God is such an one as themselves..hanging in pendulous suspences. **1725** DE FOE *Voy. round World* (1840) 82 It was no less than four days before our boat came back, so that the poor men were held in great suspense. **1770** LANGHORNE *Plutarch* (1879) I. 73/1 An incredible silence reigned among the people, anxious for the event, and lost in suspense. **1823** SCOTT *Quentin D.* xxii, All stood in a kind of suspense, waiting the event of the orders which the tyrant had issued. **1849** MACAULAY *Hist. Eng.* ii. I. 170 His opinions oscillated in a state of contented suspense between infidelity and popery. **1871** SPURGEON *Treas. David* Ps. lxxxviii. 18 The ear remains in suspense; until the majestic lxxxixᵗʰ [psalm] shall burst upon it.

†**b.** ***in suspense*** (const. clause, also *of*): undecided, doubtful, uncertain. *Obs.*

1583 STUBBES *Anat. Abus.* II. (1882) 8, I stand in suspence whether hir like were euer borne. **1600** E. BLOUNT tr. *Conestaggio* 92 He stoode in suspence where he should passe. **1629** H. BURTON *Truth's Tri.* 290 To hold their merchants in suspense of making any sauing trade. **1692** DRYDEN *St. Euremont's Ess.* 141 'Tis certain too that Caesar had his Hazards, but..I'm in suspence whether he was ever much Wounded in all his Wars. **1748** *Anson's Voy.* II. ix. 230 They were lying upon their oars in suspence what to do.

c. Objectively, as an attribute of affairs, etc.: Doubtfulness, uncertainty, undecidedness. †***in suspense***: (of a question, etc.) undecided, doubtful.

a **1513** FABYAN *Chron.* v. ciii. (1811) 78 Which innaturall batayll hangynge in suspence to whether of theym the victory shulde turne. *a* **1548** HALL *Chron., Edw. IV*, 246 Meanynge thereby..in the meane season to let that matter be in suspence. **1593** NORDEN *Spec. Brit., M'sex* II. 23 There is a free Schole for the towne, the stipend yet in suspence, the Fishmongers of London contribute twentie pound. **1597** HOOKER *Eccl. Pol.* v. lxxii. §8 Leauing this in suspence as a thing not..certainely knowne. **1623** MASSINGER *Dk. Milan* I. i, It being in suspense on whose fair tent Winged Victory will make her glorious stand. **1741** MIDDLETON *Cicero* I. v. 375 In this suspense of his affairs at Rome. **1815** JANE AUSTEN *Emma* xxxix, Such events are very interesting; but the suspense of them cannot last long. **1874** GREEN *Short Hist.* viii. §2. 461 The first twenty years of Elizabeth's reign were a period of suspense.

†**d.** Doubt as to a person's character or conduct. *Obs.*

1593 SHAKS. *2 Hen. VI*, III. i. 140 'Tis my speciall hope, That you will cleare your selfe from all suspence. **1594** NASHE *Unfort. Trav.* 77 Bring you mee a princoks beardlesse boy..to call my name in suspense?

e. *attrib.* in **suspense account** (*Book-keeping*), an account in which items are temporarily entered until their proper place is determined.

1869 *Bradshaw's Railway Man.* XXI. 383 From this was deducted 31,383 *l.* transferred from suspense account. **1882** BITHELL *Counting-ho. Dict.* (1893) 291. **1905** *Westm. Gaz.* 27 Nov. 11/1 There is the profit of £20,178 transferred to reduction of a suspense account.

4. = SUSPENSION 8. *rare.*

1752 tr. *Rameau's Treat. Mus.* 98 The sounds A keep in Suspence those of B, which naturally ought to have been heard. **1885–94** R. BRIDGES *Eros & Psyche* May xv, Responsive rivalries, that, while they strove, Combined in full harmonious suspense, Entrancing wild desire, then fell at last Lull'd in soft closes.

†**5.** = SUSPENSION 9. *Obs. rare.*

[**1642** FULLER *Holy & Prof. St.* II. xix.* 120* In a defensive warre, when his countrey is hostilely invaded, 'tis pity but his neck should hang in suspence with his conscience that doubts to fight.] **1722** WOLLASTON *Relig. Nat.* v. 99 Must clouds be so precipitated, or kept in suspence, as the case of a particular man or two requires? **1727** SWIFT *Baucis & Philemon* 63 Doom'd ever in suspence to dwell, 'Tis now no kettle, but a bell.

II. Attributive uses and combinations.

6. *attrib.* Of popular literature, etc.: characterized by the capacity to arouse suspense, excitement, or apprehension, as ***suspense novel, story***, etc.

1952 *Spectator* 3 Oct. 452/2 Many of their 'suspense'—as opposed to 'detective'—novels are first-class. **1957** S. BEACH in *This Week's Stories of Mystery & Suspense* 327 In the suspense story the focus..is fixed on the effort of a single individual to overcome danger. **1962** A. LURIE *Love & Friendship* xi. 220 It gave him a dissolute, suspense-movie look which Miranda rather liked. **1963** *Listener* 24 Jan. 158/2 Before compressionism could be taken seriously, suspense drama and the literature of confinement had to be brought together. **1972** J. PHILIPS *Vanishing Senator* III. iii. 150 You said yesterday I should be writing suspense novels. Well, maybe I've read too many of them. **1977** *Amer. N. & Q.* XV. 76/2 Norman Donaldson, an authority on suspense fiction, has written a new introduction for this edition. **1980** D. BLOODWORTH *Trapdoor* xxix. 175 Enemy agents in suspense thrillers who were programmed by post-hypnotic suggestion.

7. *Comb.*, as ***suspense-laden*** adj.

1963 *Times Lit. Suppl.* 24 May 374/4 *Les Gommes*..was conspicuous for..sharp characterization and suspense-laden plotting. **1964** *English Studies* XLV. 375 My chief reason for favoring four beats is therefore that the atmosphere seems more mysterious, suspense-laden, and, as it were, inhuman with four beats than with three.

su'spense, *a.* Now *rare* or *Obs.* Also 5–7 **suspens, suspence**. [a. OF. *suspens-e*, or ad. its source L. *suspensus*, pa. pple. of *suspendĕre* to SUSPEND.]

†**1.** Held in contemplation, attentive. (Cf. SUSPEND *v.* 5 a, SUSPENSION 7.) *Obs.*

c **1450** CAPGRAVE *Life St. Gilbert* vii, In contemplacion [he was] mor suspense þan oþir men. **1556** in W. H. Turner *Select. Rec. Oxford* (1880) 245 In which talk he held men very suspense. **1582** N. T. (Rhem.) *Luke* xix. 48 All the people was suspense [Vulg. *suspensus erat*; ἐξεκρέματο] hearing him.

2. In a state of mental suspense; waiting for the issue; doubtful, uncertain; undecided.

c **1440** CAPGRAVE *Life St. Kath.* v. 881 Thus haue this folkis at Kataryn taken her leue, Walkyng to chaunbre with hertes ful suspens; Keepyng this mater al clos in sylens. *c* **1450** —— *Life St. Aug.* viii, Thus lyued he with suspense mynde, in grete doute. **1546** COVERDALE *Treat. Lord's Supper* A vij, Wt indifferent and suspense mynde. **1596** SPENSER *F.Q.* IV. vi. 34 Whose hart twixt doubtfull feare And feeble hope hung all this while suspence. **1660** MILTON *Free Commw.* Wks. 1851 V. 434 While all Minds are suspense with Expectation of a new Assembly. **1667** —— *P.L.* II. 418 Expectation held His look suspence, awaiting who appeer'd To second, or oppose, or undertake The perilous attempt. **1812** CARY *Dante, Parad.* XXVIII. 37 The guide beloved Saw me in anxious thought suspense [orig. *in cura Forte sospeso*]. **1851** C. L. SMITH tr. *Tasso* VI. xlix, This people and that other stay suspense At [orig. *incerto pende Da*] spectacle so horrible and new.

†**b.** Objectively doubtful or uncertain; undetermined. *Obs.*

1624 BP. MOUNTAGU *Gagg* 64 That leave it so suspence, without distinction. **1657** HAWKE *Killing is M.* Pref., With his Suspence and involved Questions.

†**3.** Refraining from hasty decision or action; cautious, deliberate. *Obs.*

c **1510** BARCLAY *Mirr. Gd. Manners* (1570) B v, To callers importune, of wordes be suspence. **1594** HOOKER *Eccl. Pol.* Pref. ii. §2 The selfe same orders allowed, but yet established in more warie and suspense maner. **1619** HALES *Gold. Rem.* II. (1673) 97 Private meetings in my Lord Bishops Lodging; where upon Wednesday Morning were drawn certain Theses in very suspense and wary terms. **1684** tr. *Bonet's Merc. Compit.* VI. 155 To proceed, to the great Remedies especially, with a suspense pace and slowly.

4. Hung, hung up, hanging; = SUSPENDED 6.

c **1440** *Pallad. on Husb.* I. 500 The pament vnderthirled & suspense. *Ibid.* III. 679 That they suspence aparti so may stonde. **1610** GUILLIM *Heraldry* IV. xv. (1660) 341 These Shields which we call Armes suspence. **1647** H. MORE *Song of Soul* II. iii. III. xlviii, Those higher stars They may as well in water hang suspense As do the Planets. *Ibid.*, *Notes Psychozoia* 349 The imaginative operations of Psyche are more high, more hovering and suspense from immersion into the grosser spirits of this body. **1882** SYMONDS *Animi Figura* 138 Man, The climax of earth's miracle, suspense On the last wave of being.

†**b.** Of a nose: Turned up. *Obs. rare.*

1697 EVELYN *Numism.* ix. 297.

†**5.** Held back, restrained. *Obs. rare.*

1667 MILTON *P.L.* VII. 99 The great Light of Day.. suspens in Heav'n Held by thy voice.

†**su'spense**, *v.* *Obs.* Also 6–7 **-ence**. [f. L. *suspens-*, pa. ppl. stem of *suspendĕre* to SUSPEND, or ad. med.L. *suspensāre* (cf. rare OF. *suspenser*).]

1. *trans.* To keep in abeyance; to defer.

1556 J. HEYWOOD *Spider & F.* xi. 2 This reason dryueth vs now..Streight to your reason, before suspensed. **1626** L. OWEN *Spec. Jesuit.* (1629) 40, I would aduertise the gentle Reader to suspence his beleefe hereof, till hee haue some more credible witnesse.

2. = *dispense with*: DISPENSE *v.* III.

1583 STUBBES *Anat. Abuses* I. (1879) 98 As light and as easie as this punishment is, it may be, and is daiely dispensed [*so ed.* 1595; *ed.* **1585** suspensed] with-all for monie. **1596** R. L[INCHE] *Diella* (1877) 68 With sweete mouth'd Pytho I may not suspence. *a* **1600** DELONEY *Canaans Calam.* Wks. (1912) 450 Perhaps I may take pitty on your case: And graciously withall your faults suspence, And giue you pardon.

So †**su'spensed** *ppl. a.* = SUSPENSE *a.* 1–3; †**su'spensing** *vbl. sb.*, suspension.

1502 ATKYNSON tr. *De Imitatione* III. xxxvi. (1893) 226 About the which [spiritual things] scarsly at any tyme we labour or thynke inwardly with suspensynge of our outwarde sensys. **1526** *Pilgr. Perf.* (W. de W. 1531) 293 Thus they be in herte and wyll eleuate and suspensed from all thynges in heuen and erth. **1591** SAVILE *Tacitus, Hist.* II. iv. 55 Bringing great comfort to the minds of the armies, and prouinces that were suspensed and doubtful. **1594** CAREW *Tasso* II. xxii, Suspenst a while and not so sodaine led To wrath.

suspenseful (sə'spɛnsfʊl), *a.* [f. SUSPENSE *sb.* + -FUL.] Full of suspense; doubtful and apprehensive; uncertain and expectant of the issue.

1637 SANDERSON *Serm.* (1681) II. 72 He that hath a contented mind doth not afflict himself..with suspencefull thoughts, in forecasting both his hopes and fears what he may be. *a* **1731** DK. WHARTON *To Pallas* Poet. Wks. 1735 II. 53, I much rather chose to be at once acquainted with my ill Fortune, than to continue longer in a suspencefull Uncertainty. **1880** *Blackw. Mag.* Feb. 251/2 No other sound is audible but his voice, so suspenseful is the silence.

†**su'spensely**, *adv.* *Obs. rare.* [f. SUSPENSE *a.* – -LY².] Cautiously, deliberately.

1619 HALES *Gold. Rem.* (1673) II. 95 Judges walk suspensly, and are indifferent for either party. **1625** MOUNTAGU *App. Cæsar* I. vii. 59 Our Church, in these deepe and high points, hath in great Wisedome and Prudence, gon on warily and suspensely.

suspensible (sə'spɛnsɪb(ə)l), *a. rare.* [f. L. *suspens-*, *suspendĕre*: see SUSPENSE *v.* and -IBLE. Cf. OF. *suspensible*.] Capable of being suspended. So **suspensi'bility**, capability of being suspended.

1794 KIRWAN *Elem. Min.* (ed. 2) I. 159 Potter's Clay is distinguished, From..Fuller's earth, by..suspensibility in water. **1827** COLERIDGE *Lit. Rem.* (1836) I. 216 The particles themselves must have an interior and gravitative being, and the multeity must be a removable or at least suspensible accident.

suspension (sə'spɛnʃən). Also 6 **-cion, -sioun, -syon**, *Sc.* **-tione**, 6–7 **-tion**. [ad. late L. *suspensio*, *-ōnem*, n. of action f. *suspens-*, *suspendĕre*: see SUSPENSE *v.* Cf. AF. *suspensiun*, mod.F. *suspension*, Pr. *suspensio*, etc.] The action of suspending or condition of being suspended.

I. 1. a. The action of debarring or state of being debarred, esp. for a time, *from* a function or privilege; temporary deprivation of one's office or position.

1528 TINDALE *Obed. Chr. Man* 74 Make them to feare the sentence of the chyrch, suspencions, excommunicacions and curses. *c* **1531** *Pol. Rel. & Love Poems* (1903) 62 Of no maner of man to be vsed,..nor to be red, vnder payne of suspencioun. **1581** MARBECK *Bk. Notes* 1065 Suspention is the censure of the Eldershippe, whereby one is for a time depriued of the Communion of the Sacraments. **1643** *Ord. Lords & Com., Westm. Confess.* (1658) 203 Authoritative suspension from the Lords Table, of a person not yet cast out of the Church, is agreeable to the Scripture. **1682** BURNET *Rights Princes* viii. 267 He..required his Chapter not to receive or instal them, under the pains of suspension. **1726** AYLIFFE *Parergon* 501 Suspension taken in a proper Sense is an Ecclesiastical Censure, whereby a Spiritual Person is either interdicted the Exercise of Ecclesiastical Function, or hindred from receiving the Profits of his Benefice. **1760** *Cautions & Adv. Officers Army* 86 During your Suspension you are a Sort of Prisoner at large and do no Duty. **1870** in J. W. Clark *Ordin. Univ. Camb.* (1904) 306 Members of the University *in statu pupillari*, who are guilty of any of the foregoing practices, render themselves liable to be punished by Suspension, Rustication, Expulsion, or otherwise. **1881** [see SUSPEND *v.* 1].

†**b.** The state of being temporarily kept *from* doing, or deprived *of*, something. *Obs.*

1602 in Moryson *Itin.* II. (1617) 230 Many difficulties at home with himselfe, and actions of others abroad, may make suspension if not diversion from that Spanish invasion. **1637** in *Select. Harl. Misc.* (1793) 316, I was shortly after shut up close prisoner, with suspension of pen, ink, and paper. **1667** *Decay Chr. Piety* Pref. §1 A long indefinite suspension from seeing light.

2. a. The action of stopping or condition of being stopped, esp. for a time; temporary cessation, intermission; temporary abrogation (of a law, rule).

suspension of arms or ***hostilities***, an armistice.

1603 in Rymer *Foedera* (1715) XVI. 494/1 That..you make a Recesse and Suspention of your Negotiation untill you shall have further Warrant..from our said Soveraigne Lord. **1619** in *Eng. & Germ.* (Camden) 51 Their suspension of armes will separate their troupes. **1673** *Essex Papers* (Camden) I. 62 Ye suspencion of ye Rules was mencioned & let fall. **1729** BUTLER *Serm.* Wks. 1874 II. 68 We see men in the tortures of pain..excepting the short suspensions of sleep, for months together. **1748** *Anson's Voy.* II. xi. 253 Occasioned by a casual delay of the galeon..and not by a total suspension of her departure for the whole season. **1835** *Tomlin's Law Dict.* s.v. *Habeas Corpus*, A suspension of the Habeas Corpus Act. **1844** THIRLWALL *Greece* lxi. VIII. 91 He granted a suspension of hostilities. **1874** GREEN *Short Hist.* viii. §2. 477 The suspension of arms lasted through the summer.

b. *Law.* The abeyance of a right, title, etc.

1694 in Cruise *Digest* (ed. 2) III. 221 The suspension in case of coheirs doth not arise from any incapacity either in the blood, or in the persons, of the coheirs. **1728** CHAMBERS *Cycl.*, *Suspension*..is a Temporal Stop of a Man's Right.

c. Stoppage of payment of debts or claims on account of financial inability or failure.

1889 *Standard* 20 Mar. 6/1 It was reported that the creditors of some of the unfortunate brokers who have been caught in the French collapse had offered a composition,.. but no suspension was formally announced. **1893** *Times* 26 April 5/1 The suspension of the London Chartered Bank of Australia was announced to-day.

d. *Palæography.* A form of abbreviation consisting in representing a word by its first letter or letters accompanied by the contraction-mark; also, a word abbreviated in this way.

1896 W. M. LINDSAY *Latin Text. Emend.* Index, Suspension, contractions by. **1912** W. H. STEVENSON in *Eng. Hist. Rev.* Jan. 12 The copyist..appends his mark of suspension to words that he could not fully read. **1915** W. M. LINDSAY *Notae Latinae* 10 By the addition of the final letter the suspension ap was turned into the contraction apd.

3. a. The action of putting off to a later time; deferring, postponement; †respite.

1645 WALLER *Upon Death Lady Rich* 12 With thousand vows and tears we should have sought That sad decree's suspension to have wrought! **1648** BOYLE *Seraph. Love* xiv. (1700) 81 Witness his Suspension of the World's creation, which certainly had had an earlier Date, were not the Deity capable of Want. **1660** R. ELLSWORTH in *Extr. St. Papers rel. Friends* Ser. II. (1911) 120 What reason hath his Maiestie.. to giue any the least suspention vnto those..who haue been ..the Enimies of His Royall person? **1816** DOW *Appeals Ho. Lords* III. 224 This bill was not paid by the acceptors; and a protest was taken, and charge given, to the acceptors and indorsers, for each of whom suspensions were offered. **1912** *Times* 19 Dec. 2/6 In considering what suspension he [*sc.* the judge] ought to impose [as to a bankrupt's discharge].

b. ***(willing) suspension of disbelief***: Coleridge's phrase for the voluntary withholding of scepticism on the part of the reader with regard to incredible characters and events. Now freq. in allusive or extended use.

1817 COLERIDGE *Biog. Lit.* II. xiv. 2 A semblance of truth sufficient to procure for these shadows of imagination that willing suspension of disbelief for the moment, which constitutes poetic faith. **1930** I. A. RICHARDS *Practical Criticism* vii. 277 Coleridge, when he remarked that 'a willing suspension of disbelief' accompanied much poetry, was noting an important fact. **1962** N. COGHILL in Davis & Wrenn *Eng. & Medieval Studies* 210 Here indeed is a call upon us for the suspension of our disbelief. **1962** *Listener* 6 Sept. 366/1 Willing suspension of disbelief doesn't exist for television. **1976** T. SHARPE *Wilt* (1978) ix. 98 Wilt looked desperately round the caravan and met the eyes of the police stenographer. There was a look in them that didn't inspire confidence. Talk about lack of suspension of disbelief.

4. *Sc. Law.* The staying or postponing of the execution of a sentence pending its discussion in the Supreme Court; a judicial order or warrant for such postponement and discussion (in full, ***letters of suspension***). ***bill of suspension***, a petition for suspension formally presented by the party complaining.

1581 *Reg. Privy Council Scot.* III. 435 The suspensioun or supercedere grantit of executioun of letters. **1583** *Leg. Bp. St. Androis* 234 Howliglass..New falsat forged out for to defend him: Ane fair suspentione he hes send him. **1585** *Reg. Privy Council Scot.* III. 748 That all suspensionis aganis letters rasit..salbe deliverit be his Hienes chancellar. **1672** *Justiciary Proceedings* (S.H.S. 1905) II. 76 He had produced a suspension suspending the Warrand. **1765–8** ERSKINE *Inst. Law Scot.* IV. iii. §8 Suspension and reduction are..remedies against the iniquitous..decrees of inferior judges. **1810** Bill of suspension [see INTERDICT *sb.* 2 b]. **1826** G. J. BELL *Comm. Laws Scot.* (ed. 5) I. 385 The bond in a suspension is, that the suspender shall make payment to the charger. **1838** W. BELL *Dict. Law Scot.* 965 A prayer for letters of suspension and interdict in the premises.

5. The action of keeping any mental action in suspense or abeyance: usually in phr., e.g. ***suspension of judgement, opinion***; †also *absol.* hesitation or caution in decision, refraining from decisive action.

1568 in H. Campbell *Love-lett. Mary Q. Scots* (1824) App. 44 They..promised to observe hir Majesty's direction, both in the secresy, and in the suspension of their judgments. **1605** BACON *Adv. Learn.* I. v. §8 An impatience of doubt, and hast to assertion without due and mature suspention of iudgement. **1646** SIR T. BROWNE *Pseud. Ep.* I. viii. 30 In his Indiary relations, wherein are contained.. incredible accounts, he is surely to be read with suspension. *a* **1676** HALE *Prim. Orig. Man.* I. ii. (1677) 58 The Acts of this Faculty [*sc.* the Will] are generally divided into Volition, Nolition, and Suspension. **1680** in Somers *Tracts* (1748) I. 82 Reasons for justifying themselves in the Suspension of their Assent to this. **1694** LOCKE *Hum. Und.* (ed. 2) II. xxi. §47 During this suspension of any desire, before the will be determined to action. **1754** EDWARDS *Freed. Will* II. vii. (1762) 71 The Liberty of the Will in this Act of Suspension, consists in a Power to suspend even this Act, 'till [etc.]. **1862** J. F. STEPHEN *Ess.* 64 An amount of doubt, of suspension of opinion,..and..of aversion to every opinion. **1901** *N. Amer. Rev.* Feb. 296 That state of suspension of judgment which is somewhat inadequately designated agnosticism.

6. The action of keeping or state of being kept in suspense (*spec.* in *Rhet.*); doubt, uncertainty (with expectation of decision or issue); = SUSPENSE *sb.* 3. Now *rare* or *Obs.*

1635 J. HAYWARD tr. *Biondi's Banish'd Virg.* 196 That suspension tormented her not long. **1659** PEARSON *Creed* iv. (1662) 207 The Article immediately preceding leaves us in the same suspension. **1728** CHAMBERS *Cycl.* s.v., In Rhetorick, Suspension is a keeping the Hearer attentive and doubtful. **1798** EDGEWORTH *Pract. Educ.* (1811) I. 123 You may exercise his attention by your manner of telling this story: you may employ with advantage the beautiful figure of speech called *suspension.* **1804** EUGENIA DE ACTON *Tale without Title* I. 79 The face of the father exhibited the appearance of a gathering storm, and after an awful suspension, lightning issued from his eyes.

†**7.** An ecstasy of contemplation. *Obs. rare.*

1671 WOODHEAD *St. Teresa* II. xxvi. 159 Our Lord holding her in a rapt, or suspension.

8. *Mus.* The action of deferring the progression of a part in harmony by prolonging a note of a chord into the following chord, usually producing a temporary discord; an instance of this, a discord so produced.

Sometimes restricted to the case in which the part descends: cf. RETARDATION 3 a.

1801 BUSBY *Dict. Mus.* **1838** G. F. GRAHAM *Mus. Comp.* 28/2 A variety of dissonances termed suspensions, or syncopations. **1853** J. SMITH *Treat. Mus.* 34 A suspension of the leading note, the suspension resolving upwards. **1891** PROUT *Counterpoint* (ed. 2) 17 The suspensions 9 8 and 4 3, with their inversions, are available.

II. 9. a. The action of hanging something up; the condition of being hung, or of hanging from a support; *occas.* hanging as a form of capital punishment; *spec.* in *Med.* the treatment of disease by suspending the patient; see also quot. 1901.

† *bridge of suspension* = SUSPENSION-BRIDGE.

[**1546** BALE *Engl. Votaries* I. (1550) 56 b, Threttenynge the woman suspensyon, ye may call yt hangynge yf ye wyll.] **1656** BLOUNT *Glossogr., Suspension*.., a hanging up. **1657** THORNLEY tr. *Longus' Daphnis & Chloe* 41 They vowed an Anniversary suspension to him of some of the first fruits of the year. **1659** PEARSON *Creed* iv. (1662) 231 True and formal crucifixion is often named by the general word *suspension.* **1713** STEELE *Guard.* No. 131 ⁋2 He hangs 'em over a little Stick, which Suspension inclines them immediately to War upon each other. **1728** CHAMBERS *Cycl.* s.v., Points of Suspension in a Ballance, are those Points in the Axis or Beam wherein the Weights are apply'd; or from which they are suspended. **1819** *Philos. Mag.* LIV. 15 A bridge, upon the principle of suspension. **1821** *Edin. Philos. Jrnl.* V. 237 Description of Bridges of Suspension. **1891** F. TAYLOR *Man. Pract. Med.* (ed. 2) 207 The Method of Suspension [in locomotor ataxy]..was introduced by Professor Charcot. **1901** DORLAND *Med. Dict.* (ed. 2), *Suspension of the uterus*, the operation of suturing the uterus to the abdominal wall. **1909** *Q. Rev.* July 174 A gallows about to be used for the suspension of apprehended robbers.

b. *concr.* Something hanging from a support.

1793 SMEATON *Edystone L.* §143 A strong hawser..being passed under one of the arms of the anchor,..the whole suspension was in that manner purchased.

c. *concr.* A support on which something is hung.

1833 CRABB *Dict. Gen. Knowl.* (ed. 3), *Suspension*, or *Points of Suspension*, those points in the axis..of a balance wherein the weights are applied, or from which they are suspended. **1906** *Daily Chron.* 15 Nov. 3/6 The gear-box will be easily adjustable on its three-point suspension.

d. Attachment such as to allow of movement about the point of attachment; 'hanging', as of a vehicle on springs, straps, etc.

1891 in *Cent. Dict.* **1912** *Sphere* 28 Dec. p. vi/2 Lanchester cars by reason of..their luxurious suspension are well suited for colonial requirements.

10. The action of holding up or state of being held up without attachment.

1646 SIR T. BROWNE *Pseud. Ep.* II. iii. 72 If we conceive ..that bodies suspended in the aire have this suspension from one or many Loadstones placed both above and below it. **1714** R. FIDDES *Pract. Disc.* II. 338 The suspension of the clouds in a medium less gross than themselves.

11. The condition of being suspended, as particles, in a medium. Also *concr.* a collection of suspended particles.

1707 *Curios. Husb. & Gard.* 340 Its Salts..rise upwards, and circulate..around the Glass Vessel. These Salts, being in this suspension,..dispose themselves into Order. **1794** KIRWAN *Elem. Min.* (ed. 2) I. 19 To ascertain the nature of that fluid which was capable of holding in solution or suspension that immense mass of solid substances of which the globe of the earth consists. **1857** MILLER *Elem. Chem., Org.* vii. 505 The gum becoming dissolved, and retaining the resin and oil in suspension. **1863** LYELL *Antiq. Man* iii. 53 Some silt carried down in suspension by the waters of the Forth. **1904** *Brit. Med. Jrnl.* 10 Sept. 564 An arbitrarily chosen bacterial suspension in a test-tube.

12. *attrib.* and *Comb.*, chiefly in sense 9: 'of, pertaining to, or involving suspension', as ***suspension principle***; 'by which something is or may be suspended', as ***suspension apparatus, bolt, joint, -line, -link, -rod***; 'adapted for being suspended', as ***suspension-drill, -scale***; also **suspension-chain**, each of the chains which support a suspension-bridge or similar structure; **suspension dot**, one of a series of dots used to indicate an omission or an interval in a printed text; **suspension-feeder**, a bottom-dwelling aquatic animal which feeds on plankton, etc. found in suspension in the surrounding water; so **suspension-feeding** *ppl. a.* and *vbl. sb.*; **suspension period, point** = *suspension dot* above; **suspension-pier**, a pier supported in the manner of a suspension-bridge, a chain-pier; **suspension polymerization**, polymerization in which the polymer separates out from a dispersion of the monomer in a liquid; **suspension-railway**, a railway in which the wheels run on an elevated rail or pair of rails, the bodies of the carriages being suspended below them; **suspension-tower**, each of the towers to which the chains are attached in a suspension-bridge or the like.

1884 KNIGHT *Dict. Mech.* Suppl. 875 **Suspension Apparatus*..a splint with means of suspension from a frame. **1837** W. B. ADAMS *Carriages* 121 The ends are..curled round a mandril of the size of the *suspension bolt. **1823** SEAWARD in *Philos. Mag.* 31 Dec. 425 Observations on *Suspension Chain Bridges. **1823** in *Daily News* 5 Dec. (1896) 5/7 Over the top of each tower pass the main suspension chains which issue from the body of the cliff. **1949** G. SUMMEY *Amer. Punctuation* viii. 109 *Suspension dots or 'French dots' (*points de suspension*) occur in groups, usually of three, usually spaced but sometimes closed up. They mark preceding material as unfinished, or left dangling an instant for attention. They are used within sentences or as terminal points— sometimes in place of the usual sentence point, sometimes in addition. (Ellipsis dots, in the same form, are discussed in Chapter 9.) **1875** KNIGHT *Dict. Mech.* 2464 **Suspension-drill*,..a vertical drilling-machine having a frame which may be bolted to the ceiling, so as to be out of the way. **1925** O. D. HUNT in *Jrnl. Marine Biol. Assoc.* XIII. 567 Those which feed by selecting from the surrounding water the suspended micro-organisms and detritus,..for want of a better term, may be termed *Suspension-feeders. **1959** A. C. HARDY *Open Sea* II. v. 106 Most animals on rocks or stones will be suspension-feeders, ..because little detritus can remain there. **1975** *Nature* 7 Aug. 521/1 As those samples included some typical 'suspension-feeders' (Porifera, Ectoprocta, Sabellida and so on), a water current able to transport the food items evidently exists and may explain the development of a rich bottom fauna under the Ross Ice Shelf. **1925** *Jrnl. Marine Biol. Assoc.* XIII. 575 The contents of their stomachs resembles closely that of the *suspension-feeding molluscs. **1963** R. P. DALES *Annelids* ii. 53 They [*sc.* sabellids] are not the only ones that have adopted suspension-feeding. **1867** J. HOGG *Microsc.* I. ii. 70 Even after the *suspension joint has become supple by long use. **1884** W. H. GREENWOOD *Steel & Iron* (ed. 2) Index, *Suspension links. **1822** in Picton *L'pool Munic. Rec.* (1886) II. 352 The erection of *suspension piers. **1963** H. SHAW *Punctuate it Right!* xvi. 91 When ellipsis periods come at the end of a statement requiring a period, then four of these 'suspension periods' or '*suspension points'..are occasionally used. **1969** G. SMITH in *Lett. Aldous Huxley* 4 He often used suspension points (...) in place of commas or final stops when typewriting. **1972** *Computers & Humanities* VI. 152 Omit some parenthetic clauses of no importance to the context, and.. replace them by suspension points. **1944** *India Rubber World* CXI. 173/1 More details on *suspension polymerization will be given in another article on this same subject. **1973** *Materials & Technol.* VI. viii. 504 Suspension polymerization is more suited to batch operation and it is difficult to convert it into a continuous process. **1825** *Gentl. Mag.* XCV. I. 628/1 A line of railway..on the *suspension principle having been constructed at Cheshunt. **1835** *Partington's Brit. Cycl. Arts & Sci.* II. 801/2 The bridge over the South Esk at Montrose furnishes a good example of the suspension principle. **1875** KNIGHT *Dict. Mech.* 2464 **Suspension-railway*, a railway in which the carriage is suspended from an elevated track. **1842** *Penny Cycl.* XXIII. 335/1 The *suspension-rods are an inch square, and they support transverse cross-bearers. **1875** KNIGHT *Dict. Mech.* 2464 **Suspension-scale*, one swung by pendent rods from levers above. **1842** *Penny Cycl.* XXIII. 334/2 The roadway, which rises about two feet in the centre between the *suspension-towers.

suspension-bridge.

A bridge in which the roadway is suspended from spans of ropes, chains, or wire cables attached to and extending between supports (in the case of a large bridge, towers of masonry or steel).

Also formerly called *suspended bridge, bridge of suspension, suspension chain bridge* (see SUSPENDED 6, SUSPENSION 9, 12), and CHAIN-BRIDGE.

1821 *Edin. Philos. Jrnl.* V. Index 419 Stevenson, Mr. R... on the history and construction of suspension bridges. **1823** SEAWARD in *Philos. Mag.* 31 Dec. 426 The first suspension bridges that were ever formed, were probably nothing more than two or three ropes or flexible chains stretched across a river from two eminences, upon which boards were placed. **1832** BREWSTER *Nat. Magic* ix. 226 The suspension bridge across the Menai strait in Wales. **1835** *Partington's Brit. Cycl. Arts & Sci.* II. 802/1 The most severe trial to which a suspension bridge can be exposed is that of a body of troops marching over it in regular step. **1876** *Encycl. Brit.* IV. 301/2 A very simple form of suspension bridge has long been used in Peru and Thibet.

suspensive (sə'spɛnsɪv), *a.* [ad. med.L. *suspensīvus* (whence F. *suspensif*, Pr. *suspensiu*, It. *sospensivo*, Sp., Pg. *suspensivo*), f. *suspens-*, pa. ppl. stem of *suspendĕre* to SUSPEND: see -IVE.]

†**1.** Liable to be suspended or temporarily stopped; intermittent. *Obs.*

c **1550** ROLLAND *Crt. Venus* III. 365 (Quod Venus) Quha maid that caus suspensiue: Quha had power sic Actis to decline? **1792** W. ROBERTS *Looker-on* No. 23 (1794) I. 332 The action of bribery being thus suspensive and temporary.

†**2.** Kept undertermined or undecided; subject to doubt. *Obs.*

c **1550** ROLLAND *Crt. Venus* III. 315 This dittay is geuin in sinisterlie: And in the self that point is suspensiue. *Ibid.* 798, I suppone thir wemen ar Include.. For to fulfill the number suspensiue.

†**3.** Liable to be suspended (from office). *Obs.*

1575 *Brieff Disc. Troub. Franckford* (1846) 102 What then shulde haue become off oure church with thies their suspensyve ministers and withe the discipline and all other thinges? **1606** J. CARPENTER *Solomon's Solace* vi. 23 b, Whether his..Maiestie hath holden either of vs or our dealings suspensiue.

4. Having the power or effect of suspending, deferring, or temporarily stopping the operation of something; involving such suspension; *spec.* in *Law*, applied to a condition or obligation of which the operation is suspended until some event takes place.

a **1623** SWINBURNE *Spousals* (1686) 59 That the Verb (*Volo*) doth of its own nature always import a Will, but sometimes a Will suspensive of that which is to come. *a* **1680** BUTLER *Rem.* (1759) I. 346 The Law of Nature (which you say is Legislative, and hath a suspensive Power over all human Laws). **1791** *State Papers* in *Ann. Reg.* 167* The suspensive refusal of the king is thus expressed—*The king will examine.* **1818** COLEBROOKE *Obligations* I. iii. 10 If the agreement bear, that the obligation shall not presently have effect but remain inoperative until the event be certain, the condition is precedent and suspensive; and the conditional obligation is termed a suspensive one. **1821** JEFFERSON *Autobiog.* Writ. 1892 I. 144 Shall the king have a negative on the laws? shall that negative be absolute, or suspensive only? **1822** RANKEN *Hist. France* X. iv. IX. 312 The king.. voluntarily declared his preference of the suspensive veto. **1826** G. J. BELL *Comm. Laws Scot.* (ed. 5) I. 237 Suspensive Conditions are such as suspend the sale and stay the transfer till something be done. **1884** *Spectator* 9 Aug., A suspensive veto in the Lords means the power to compel the House of Commons to pass every great measure twice over. **1902** A. T. CARTER *Law Contract* 70 This is sometimes called a 'suspensive' condition, for it hangs the contract up.

5. Inclined to suspend one's judgement; undecided in mind; of, pertaining to, characterized by, or in a state of suspense. (†rarely predicative.)

1614 JACKSON *Creed* III. xvii §11 The Lord expels not his suspensive rather than diffident admiration with signs and wonders. **1620** RAWLINSON *Conf. St. Aug.* 226 She knew that I was then brought to that suspensive state of mind by his meanes. **1656** *Burton's Diary* (1828) I. 35 You will not longer..be so suspensive what you shall do with him. **1662** HIBBERT *Body Div.* I. 174 In an unconstant man there is.. a doubtful and suspensive life. **1796** MME. D'ARBLAY *Camilla* II. xv, A suspensive discomfort inquieted his mind. **1847** GROTE *Greece* II. xxxvii. IV. 514 That conspicuous characteristic of Grecian philosophy—the antagonist force of suspensive scepticism. **1876** GEO. ELIOT *Dan. Der.* lxvi, The passion for watching chances—the habitual suspensive poise of the mind.

b. Of a word, phrase, etc.: Expressing or indicating suspense; keeping the reader or hearer in suspense.

1711 J. GREENWOOD *Eng. Gram.* I. xxii. 162, I shall therefore divide the Conjunctions into Conjunctions Copulative; into Disjunctive..; into Suspensive, or of doubting; [etc.]. **1836** GLADSTONE in Morley *Life* (1903) I. II. iii. 133 The Duke of Wellington..receives remarks made to him very frequently with no more than 'Ha', a convenient, suspensive expression, which acknowledges the arrival of the observation and no more. **1842** *Blackw. Mag.* LII. 342 We have no long sentences, no careless sentences,..no suspensive sentences.

6. Characterized by physical suspension. *rare.*

1827 FARADAY *Chem. Manip.* xvii. (1842) 477 If a body is to have a suspensive insulation, then silk thread or cord may be advantageously resorted to. **1872** *Daily News* 1 Aug., Any position..perpendicular, horizontal, suspensive, or otherwise.

su'spensively (-ɪvlɪ), *adv.* [f. prec. + -LY[2].] In a suspensive manner. †**a.** = SUSPENSELY. *Obs.* **b.** ***suspensively conditional***, involving a suspensive condition: see prec. 4. **c.** In the way of suspension or hanging; *fig.* in dependence *on.*

1617 COLLINS *Def. Bp. Ely* II. x. 413 The profoundnesse of this mysterie leads vs to wade thus softly and suspensiuely. **1818** COLEBROOKE *Obligations* 212 If either the original or substituted engagement be suspensively conditional. **1872** BUSHNELL *Serm. Living Subj.* 56 We become aerial creatures, resting suspensively on things above the world. *Ibid.* 58 He begins to live suspensively on God.

So **su'spensiveness.**

1816 T. L. PEACOCK *Headlong Hall* xii, An illustrious robber who..was suddenly checked in his career by means of a certain quality inherent in preparations of hemp, which, for the sake of perspicuity, I shall call suspensiveness. **1898** SWEET *New Eng. Gram.* II. 37 The level tone is plaintive.. and suggests the idea of suspensiveness.

suspensoid (sə'spɛnsɔɪd). *Physical Chem.* [a. G. *suspensoid* (P. P. von Weimarn 1908, in *Zeitschr. f. Chem. u. Industr. d. Kolloide* III. 27/2), f. *suspens-ion* SUSPENSION: see -OID.] A lyophobic colloid from which the dispersed phase is readily (and often irreversibly) precipitated by the addition of an electrolyte.

1909, etc. [see EMULSOID]. **1927** [see LYOPHOBE *a.*]. **1936** *Jrnl. Faraday Soc.* XXXII. 1166 The variation of sulphur dioxide and black suspensoids during the fog of 23rd December, 1935, in London, is shown. **1954** [see KERN *sb.*[2] 3]. **1975** *Jrnl. Faculty Fisheries & Animal Husbandry* (Hiroshima Univ.) XIV. 24 Suspensoids were collected from the surface and bottom water samples at stations 3 and 13.

suspensor (sə'spɛnsə(r)). [a. med.L. *suspensor*, agent-n. f. L. *suspens-*, *suspendĕre*: see SUSPENSE and -OR. Cf. F. *suspenseur.*]

†**1.** *Surg.* **a.** A kind of catheter: see quot. *Obs.*

1746 tr. *Le Cat* in *Phil. Trans.* XLIV. 178, I slipt over it the strait Suspensor (a Catheter that opens with a Bow) and dilated the Bladder with the Incision Knife, towards the Pubis, and introduced the lateral Suspensors.

b. A suspensory bandage.

[1803 J. Fox *Med. Dict.*, *Suspensor*, a bandage to suspend the scrotum.] **1896** *Daily News* 14 Dec. 8/2 Electric Belt and Suspensor for Men.

2. *Bot.* The filament by which the embryo is suspended in the seed of phanerogams; also applied to a similar structure in some cryptogams.

1832 LINDLEY *Introd. Bot.* 159 A very delicate thread, the suspensor, descends from the summit of the ovulum into the quintine. **1879** A. W. BENNETT in *Jrnl. Bot.* Mar. 67 The pro-embryo or suspensor (Vorkeim) of Phanerogams.

3. *gen.* That by which something is suspended.

1874 H. H. COLE *Catal. Ind. Art S. Kens. Mus.* 192 Neck Ornament.. Silver-gilt, circular, flower-shaped,..the suspensor formed of twisted..gold thread.

suspensorial (sʌspɛnˈsɔərɪəl), *a.* *Anat.* [f. next + -AL[1].] Pertaining to or of the nature of a suspensorium; suspensory.

1871 HUXLEY *Anat. Vert.* iii. 136 In the *Holocephali* the palato-quadrate and suspensorial cartilages are united with one another and with the skull into a continuous cartilaginous plate. **1873** MIVART *Elem. Anat.* iii. 143 A comparatively minute pair of jaws are suspended at the end of a disproportionately large suspensorial structure.

‖**suspensorium** (sʌspɛnˈsɔərɪəm). [mod.L., neut. sing. of med.L. *suspensōrius SUSPENSORY.]

1. *Surg.* A suspensory bag, bandage, etc.

1758 J. S. *Le Dran's Observ. Surg.* (1771) 239, I advised him to wear a *Suspensorium*.., to favour the spermatick Vessels. **1859** MAYNE *Expos. Lex.*

2. The bone, or series of bones, cartilages, etc., by which the lower jaw is suspended from the skull in vertebrates below mammals.

1869 *Proc. Amer. Philos. Soc.* XI. 577 The suspensorium is slender. **1870** ROLLESTON *Anim. Life* 43 Skeleton of Common Perch... The suspensorium is articulated moveably to the outer and back part of the cranium. **1881** MIVART *Cat* 460 Its mandible directly articulates with the skull, and there is no suspensorium.

suspensory (səˈspɛnsərɪ), *a.* and *sb.* [ad. med.L. *suspensōrius (whence F. *suspensoire* (16th c.), Pr. *suspensori*, It. *sospensorio*, Sp., Pg. *suspensorio*), f. L. *suspens-*, *suspendĕre*: see SUSPENSE and -ORY. As a sb., after F. *suspensoir(e.)*] **A.** *adj.*

I. 1. Having the function of suspending, i.e. supporting something suspended. **a.** *Anat.* Applied to a ligament, muscle, or other structure, by which some part or organ is suspended.

1541 COPLAND *Guydon's Quest. Cyrurg.* I iv b, The synew suspensory and sensyfe that descendeth to the genytalles. **1691** RAY *Creation* II. (1692) 35 To such Beasts as..are forced to hold their Eyes long in a hanging posture,..the seventh or suspensory Muscle is very useful. **1831** YOUATT *Horse* 252 The suspensory ligament is sometimes ruptured by extraordinary exertion. **1839-47** *Todd's Cycl. Anat.* III. 924/1 The true suspensory ligament is calculated by its position and strength to prevent the surgeon from depressing the penis sufficiently to straighten the urethra. **1872** HUXLEY *Physiol.* ix. 227 The crystalline lens..is kept in place by a..membranous frame or suspensory ligament.

b. *Surg.* Applied to a bandage, bag, sling, or the like, in which a diseased or injured part is suspended for support.

1848 DUNGLISON *Med. Lex.* (ed. 7), *Suspensory Bandage* ..is a bandage intended to support the scrotum, in cases of diseases of the testicle or of scrotal hernia. **1884** T. BRYANT *Pract. Surg.* II. 216 If the patient..is unable to keep at rest, the parts must be well supported by a suspensory bandage.

c. In general sense.

1838 *Fraser's Mag.* XVII. 680 A tray hanging forward from a body under the suspensory action of two arms. **1883** *Harper's Mag.* July 930/2 A multitude of suspensory stays of steel wire ropes.

†**2.** Adapted to be hung up. *Obs. rare*[−1].

a **1682** SIR T. BROWNE *Tracts* ii. (1683) 90 The Crowns and Garlands of the Ancients were..Pensile or Suspensory.

II. †**3.** Marked by or indicating mental suspense; doubtful, lacking certainty or assurance.

1611 COTGR., *Suspensoire*,..suspensorie, in suspence. **1682** SIR T. BROWNE *Chr. Mor.* II. iii. (1716) 50 This moves sober Pens unto suspensory and timorous assertions.

4. = SUSPENSIVE 4.

1884 *Truth* 4 Sept. 363/2 The Upper house might be given a suspensory veto on the legislation of the Lower House. **1885** *Law Times' Rep.* LII. 684/2 The Act..gave a short suspensory period during which actions could be brought that would not fall within the limitations of time enacted. **1893** *Times* 17 May 9/4 The Welsh Disestablishment party have themselves recognised the futility of endeavouring to proceed..with the Suspensory Bill.

B. *sb.*

[The following entry in Blount's *Glossogr.* 1656, '*Suspensories*,..certain cords or strings (hanging from the Bedstead) for a sick man to take hold of, and bear himself up with, when he would remove or alter his lying' is a copy of Cotgrave's definition s.v. *Suspensoires*.]

Surg. and *Anat.* A suspensory bandage, ligament, etc. (see A. 1 a, b); a suspensorium.

1699 tr. *De La Vauguion's Chirurg. Oper.* Expl. Figures, Fig. 44. The Suspensory of the Napkin which goes round the Breast. **1706** PHILLIPS (ed. Kersey). **1901** DORLAND *Med. Dict.* (ed. 2).

†**suspensure.** *Obs. rare*[−1]. [ad. L. *suspensūra*, f. *suspens-*, *suspendĕre*: see SUSPENSE and -URE.] A hollow floor 'suspended' or built over a furnace for heating a bath.

c **1440** *Pallad. on Husb.* I. 1085 The cellis suspensuris thus thou dight.

†**suspent,** *ppl. a.* [pa. pple. of SUSPEND *v.*] Interdicted.

1488 [see SUSPEND *v.* 2 d].

†**susper.** *Obs.* App. local abbrev. of SUSPIRAL.

1532-3 *Durham Household Bk.* (Surtees) 267 Operantibus ad le susper, juxta novum pontem, 14d. **1588-9** *Durham Acc. Rolls* (Surtees) 732 For work beyond the Suspers Banke, in Holidays courten. **1594** *Ibid.* 739 At the Susper.

sus. per coll., abbreviation of L. *suspendatur per collum* 'let him be hanged by the neck', in the entry of a capital sentence in the jailer's books; an entry of this against a person's name; hence as *adj.* = hanged.

1560 STAUNFORD *Les Plees del Coron* III. xix. 182 b, Pour chescun felon e le iugement est *quod suspendatur per collum*. Quel in le rolle est enter briefement, s. *sus. per col.*

1827 SOUTHEY *Lett.* (1856) IV. 74 It seems he regards with great pride the *sus-per-coll* in his family tree. **1850** THACKERAY *Pendennis* xiii. Her pedigree with that lamentable note of *sus. per coll.* at the name of the last male of her line. **1875** REYNARDSON *Down the Road* 118 He grew more and more downcast..and one day..he was found 'sus. per col.' in his barn.

Hence **suspercollate** (sʌspəˈkɒleɪt), *v.* (*humorous nonce-wd.*), to hang.

1864 THACKERAY *D. Duval* i. (1869) 1 None of us Duvals have been suspercollated to my knowledge. **1905** *Blackw. Mag.* Aug. 283/2 Suspercollated placards describe the historical development of the pendent machines.

suspescioun, -essyon, -etion, obs. ff. SUSPICION.

suspicable (ˈsʌspɪkəb(ə)l), *a.* Now *rare* or *Obs.* [ad. late L. *suspicābilis* f. *suspicārī* to suspect, f. *su-* SUB- 25 + *spic-*, as in *suspicĕre* to SUSPECT.]

1. That may be suspected or mistrusted; open to suspicion.

1614 BP. HALL *Contempl.*, *O.T.* VI. *Nadab & Abihu*, Suddennesse as it is ever justly suspicable, so then certainly argues anger. **1655-87** H. MORE *App. Antid.* (1712) 192 To proceed from what is plain and unsuspected to what is more obscure and suspicable. **1706** PHILLIPS (ed. Kersey). **1858** J. P. COLLIER *Shaks. Wks.* (ed. 2) I. p. vii, The suspicable (if I may use the word) letter of Jonson to Secretary Cecil.

2. That may be suspected to be so; appearing probable or likely.

1651 H. MORE *Enthus. Tri.* (1712) 31 It is a very suspicable matter that Saturn before the fall was where Mercury, and Mercury where Saturn is. **1653** —— *Conject. Cabbal.* (1713) 183 It is a very suspicable business that he means no more than empty Space by it. **1678** CUDWORTH *Intell. Syst.* I. iv. §15. 269 This makes it still more strongly suspicable, that it was really a Design..of the Devil.

Hence †**suspicaˈbility**, the condition of being open to suspicion.

1660 H. MORE *Myst. Godl.* v. vii. 151 The uncertainty and suspicability of the Story.

†**suspiciency.** *Obs. rare*[−1]. [f. L. *suspicient-*, *-ens*, pr. pple. of *suspicĕre* to SUSPECT: see -ENCY.] = SUSPICION.

a **1690** HOPKINS *Nat. & Necess. Regeneration* (1694) 150 The want of it [*sc.* perfect obedience] should not deject us with a suspiciency of the want of Grace.

suspicion (səˈspɪʃən), *sb.* Forms: α. 3-6 suspecion, 4-5 -ioun, 4-6 -yon, (4-5 susspecyun, -ion, sus(s)pescioun, suspessyon, 6 *Sc.* suspetion, -ione, -ioun). β. 4-5 suspicioun, (5 -ycon, 5-6 -icyon, -ycyon, -ycion, 6 -icioun, sus(s)pissioun), 6-7 suspition, (6 -ioun, -ione, susspitioun), 5- suspicion. [a. AF. *suspecioun* (earlier *suspeziun*), var. OF. *so(u)speçon* (mod.F. *soupçon*) = Pr. *sospeisso*, Pg. *suspeição*:—med.L. *suspectiōnem* SUSPECTION. The orig. form *suspecio(u)n* finally gave way to *suspicion*, which arose in the 14th cent. through the influence of 'learned' OF. *suspicion* or of L. *suspīcio* -*ōnem*, n. of action to *suspicĕre* to SUSPECT.]

1. The action of suspecting; the feeling or state of mind of one who suspects; imagination or conjecture of the existence of something evil or wrong without proof; apprehension of guilt or fault on slight grounds or without clear evidence.

In early use often qualified by *evil*, *wicked*, *false*.

α. **1303** R. BRUNNE *Handl. Synne* 3971 Enuyus man ys so ful of susspecyun þat euyl hym þenketh al, as a felun. **1340** HAMPOLE *Pr. Consc.* 3487 When þou supposes any wykkednes, Thurgh suspecion, þar na es. *c* **1380** WYCLIF *Wks.* (1880) 40 3if..here wyues ben of sich age þat noon euyl suspecion may be reysed of hem. **1489** CAXTON *Faytes of A.* II. xxxvii. 155 Som signe wherby eny suspecion may be had.

β. *c* **1400** *Cato's Morals* in *Cursor M.* App. iv. 311 Qua has ..suspicioun in þo3t þai haue leftese. *c* **1450** *Mirk's Festial* 286 Fals defamacyon fals suspicyon. *a* **1548** HALL *Chron.*, *Edw. IV*, 216 That the duke & all that came with hym, should be taken as hys trew frendes, without fraude or yll suspicion. **1560** DAUS tr. *Sleidane's Comm.* 315 b, Many times woulde they come into the Citie, neither wanted that thinge great suspicion. **1596** SPENSER *State Irel.* Wks. (Globe) 631/2 He may under his mantell goe privilye armed, without suspicion of any. **1611** *Bible* Transl. Pref. ¶ 1 It is welcommed with suspicion in stead of loue. **1662** STILLINGFL. *Orig. Sacræ* I. v. §6. 84 There seems to be very strong ground of suspition that some such thing was designed by Manetho. *a* **1700** EVELYN *Diary* 18 July 1679, [Oates and Bedlow] swearing positively to some particulars, which drew suspicion upon their truth. **1750** JOHNSON *Rambler* No. 79 ¶ 1 Suspicion..has always been considered, when it exceeds the common measures, as a token of depravity. **1828** SCOTT *F.M. Perth* xix, No one may be discovered to whom suspicion attaches. **1889** MARKHAM *Life J. Davis* xiii. (1891) 229 The story is continued by Habakkuk Prickett, whose narrative is open to some suspicion.

personified. **1608** MACHIN *Dumb Knt.* IV. i, Thou curse of greatness, waking-ey'd suspicion. **1609** B. JONSON *Masque Queenes* 56 Wks. (1616) 948 Wild Suspition, Whose eyes doe neuer sleepe. **1613** MARSTON *Insatiate C'tess.* III. Wks. 1856 III. 143 Suspition is a dogge that still doth bite With-out a cause. **1719** D'URFEY *Pills* IV. 47 Suspicion hath double Eyes. **1837** CARLYLE *Fr. Rev.* I. v. iii, There sharpest gazes Suspicion into the pale dim World-Whirlpool.

b. An instance of this.

1382 WYCLIF *1 Tim.* vi. 5 Enuyes, stryues, blasfemyes, yuele suspiciouns. **1398** TREVISA *Barth. De P.R.* XVI. liii. (1495) Liv/2 Iacinctus..dooth away eleyngenes & sorowe, & also vayn suspecyons [*Bodl. MS.* suspessiouns]. **1549** *Compl. Scot.* xiv. 117 He beleuand to keip hym fra ane gritar suspetione. **1577** tr. *Bullinger's Decades* (1592) 131 They of old time did cleere themselues of heinous suspitions by taking of an othe. **1625** BACON *Ess.*, *Suspicion* (Arb.) 528 Svspicions amongst Thoughts, are like Bats amongst Birds, they euer fly by Twilight. **1678** R. L'ESTRANGE *Seneca's Mor.* (1702) 342 Nor is it only by Tales, and Stories, that we are inflam'd, but Suspitions, Countenances [etc.]. **1792** BURKE *Corr.* (1844) III. 370 To lie under those criminal suspicions would be still more grievous to them than the penalties themselves. **1828** SCOTT *F.M. Perth* xii, If you leave me without any better reason but your own nonsensical suspicions. **1873** *Nairne Peerage Evidence* (1874) 129, I have a suspicion that Mrs. Sandeman is suffering from organic disease of the heart.

†**c.** *transf.* A ground of suspicion; a suspicious circumstance. *Obs.*

1592 SHAKS. *Rom. & Jul.* V. iii. 187 3. *Wat.* Here is a Frier. ..We tooke this Mattocke and this Spade from him, As he was comming from this Church-yard side. *Con.* A great suspition. **1687** T. BROWN *Saints in Uproar* Wks. 1730 I. 81, I find you go by different names, a shrewd suspicion of your being cheats.

2. Constructions and phrases.

a. Const. *of* (†*in*, †*to*, †*upon*) the person of whom some evil is suspected.

α. *c* **1290** *St. Sebastian* 29 in *S. Eng. Leg.* 179 Ich habbe to þe suspecion..þat þov a3en me..Itorned hast þi þou3t. *c* **1374** CHAUCER *Troylus* v. 1647 Stod on a day in his malencolye This Troylus and yn suspecion Of here for whom he wende for to dye. *c* **1386** —— *Man of Law's T.* 583 Hem that hadden wronge suspecion Vpon this sely Innocent Custance. *c* **1430** *Syr Gener.* (Roxb.) 89 The king..had no maner suspecion To hem of their fals treason. **1474** CAXTON *Chesse* III. iii. (1883) 102 He vnderstode that the parents and frendes of them had suspecion in hym. **1523** LD. BERNERS *Froiss.* I. xxxii. 46 Desyring hym to haue no suspecyons to hym. *a* **1533** [see d].

β. **1590** SPENSER *Muiop.* 377 Suspition of friend, nor feare of foe..had he at all. **1593** SHAKS. *2 Hen. VI*, I. iii. 210 Let Somerset be Regent o're the French, Because in Yorke this breedes suspition. **1828** SCOTT *F.M. Perth* x, You do wrong even to intimate a suspicion of my Lord of March.

†**b.** Const. *of* the thing of which some evil is suspected. *Obs.*

c **1385** CHAUCER *L.G.W.* 1290 *Dido*, This dido hath suspecioun of this And thoughte wel that it was al a-mys. *c* **1386** —— *Pars. T.* ¶ 380 Whan he hath any wikked suspecion of thyng ther he ne woot of it no soothfastnesse. *c* **1400** *Beryn* 2474 þou3e I suspecioune Have of yeur wordis. **1652** CULPEPPER *Eng. Phys.* (1656) 397 [This] may seem to give some suspition of honesty. **1796** MORSE *Amer. Geog.* I. 312 In order to increase the suspicions already entertained of his generalship.

c. Const. *of* the evil suspected.

a **1350** *St. Andrew* 392 in Horstm. *Altengl. Leg.* (1881) 9 Lat me ett els whore so þou will, For drede of sum suspecion of ill. **1421** *26 Pol. Poems* 82 In towche is susspescioun of mys. **1483-4** *Act 1 Rich. III*, c. 3, Dyvers persones ben.. imprisoned for suspecion of felonie. **1560** DAUS tr. *Sleidane's Comm.* 39 b, Which nation was euer furthest of from all suspecion of Heresye. **1605** SHAKS. *Macb.* II. iv. 27 Malcolme and Donalbaine..Are stolne away and fled, which puts vpon them Suspition of the deed. **1631** JORDAN *Nat. Bathes* Ded. (1669) p. vi, Having removed out of my mind all suspition of misconstruction. **1686** *Col. Rec. Pennsylv.* I. 176 Luke Watson Lay under suspition of being Carnally Concerned with a Woman Servt. **1781** GIBBON *Decl. & F.* xxvii. III. 37 The council of Milan obstinately rejected the suspicion of danger, with a blind confidence. **1806** SURR *Winter in Lond.* III. 53, I..was about to relate my suspicions of the fate of his wife and child. **1866** G. MACDONALD *Ann. Q. Neighb.* i. 5 A minute description of my own person such as would at once clear me from any suspicion of vanity.

d. †*to have*, *take*, occas. *bear suspicion*: to entertain a suspicion. (Now only ***to have a, any, no,*** etc. ***suspicion,*** or ***suspicions.***) †*to give* one *suspicion*: to cause one to suspect.

13.. *K. Alis.* 453 Þeo barouns haddyn suspecioun. *c* **1374** CHAUCER *Troylus* II. 561 As I was comynge Al sodeynly he lefte his compleynynge. Of which I toke somwhat suspecion. *c* **1450** *Mirk's Festial* 10 Nay, syr, not so, lest men wold haue suspessyon of euell. **1471** CAXTON *Recuyell* (Sommer) 90 She..had suspecion that he wold do harme to Iupiter. *c* **1532** DU WES *Introd. Fr.* in *Palsgr.* 1027 Whiche might be occasyon to gyve you suspicion. *a* **1533** LD. BERNERS *Huon* lxv. 222 To thentent that he take in you no suspecyon. **1588** PARKE tr. *Mendoza's Hist. China* 257 More for that none should doo to them any harme, then for any euill suspition they had of them. **1593** SHAKS. *Lucr.* 1321 To cleare her From that suspicion which the world might bear her. **1611** —— *Wint. T.* I. ii. 460 His ill-ta'ne suspition.

a **1700** EVELYN *Diary* 7 May 1685, Under pretence to serve the Church of England, he gave suspicion of gratifying another party.

e. †*of suspicion*: that is (to be) suspected, suspicious. †*without* (or *but*) *suspicion*: without being suspected, unsuspected. †*out of all suspicion*: beyond all doubt. *upon* or *on suspicion* (†*by suspicion*): on the basis of mere supposition (*of* evil or wrongdoing). *above suspicion*: too good or worthy to be suspected of evil.

1340 HAMPOLE *Pr. Consc.* 1652 Or it es a signe of suspecyon þat he es in way of dampnacyon. **1375** BARBOUR *Bruce* x. 555 For I but suspicioun Micht repair till hir preuely. **1514** in Ellis *Orig. Lett.* Ser. I. I. 101 Uppon suspicion he was taken by the Popis commandment and sett in Castill Angill. **1538** STARKEY *England* (1878) 122 Not wythout cause, apon suspycyon only, euery man may frely accuse other of treson. **1560** DAUS tr. *Sleidane's Comm.* 118 Many were apprehended, some by information, and some by suspicion. **1586** A. DAY *Engl. Secretorie* II. (1625) 10 L. thy kinsman..being..brought before a Iustice vpon suspition of his wretched liuing. **1592** SHAKS. *Rom. & Jul.* v. iii. 222 Bring forth the parties of suspition. **1599** — *Much Ado* II. iii. 166 Shee's an excellent sweet Lady, and (out of all suspition,) she is vertuous. **1660** BLOUNT *Boscobel* II. (1680) 8 She procured Him the better Chamber and Accommodation without any suspition. **1683** *Col. Rec. Pennsylv.* I. 84 To aprehend some persons upon suspition of putting away of bad money. **1772** *Jacob's Law Dict.* s.v., A person may be taken up on suspicion, where a felony is done. **1850** MERIVALE *Rom. Emp.* iv. (1865) I. 152 The wife of Caesar must be above suspicion. **1867** *Philatelist* 1 Jan. 18/1 The rare red-brown sixpenny Barbados, unperforated,..is not altogether above suspicion.

†**f.** *in suspicion*: (*a*) suspecting; (*b*) suspected. *to have in suspicion*: to suspect. *to bring in* or *into suspicion*: to cause to be suspected. *to enter into suspicion with*: to become suspicious of. *Obs.*

Cf. quot. *a* 1340 in sense 4.

c **1450** *Merlin* xxvii. 539 Thei wolde not slepe, but were euer in susspecion of the saisnes. **1471** *Arriv. Edw. IV* (Camden) 10 Hymselfe was had in great suspicion. **1484** CAXTON *Fables of Æsop* II. xviii, They..shall euer lyue ryȝte heuyly and in suspycon. *a* **1548** HALL *Chron., Hen. VI*, 181 b, This kyng Iames from his firste rule, began to entre into suspicion with William Erle Douglas. **1555** BRADFORD in Strype *Eccl. Mem.* (1721) III. App. xlv. 131, I declare nothinge to bringe these noblemen into suspition. **1561** T. HOBY tr. *Castiglione's Courtyer* IV. (1577) Y vij b, To commit no vice, nor yet to be had in suspition of any vice. **1568** GRAFTON *Chron.* II. 121 They were had in suspicion to be great Brybers. **1611** SHAKS. *Wint. T.* v. ii. 31 This Newes.. is so like an old Tale, that the veritie of it is in strong suspition. **1635** A. STAFFORD *Fem. Glory* (1869) 80 Hee that ..bringes my Faith to God in suspition. **1665** MANLEY *Grotius' Low C. Wars* 338 He hoped they would not blame the well-known Reputation of the House of Austria, or have him in suspition, now desiring to be the Author of Peace. **1755** MAGENS *Insurances* I. 269 It is not to be presumed that the meadows could be had in Suspicion, for it was never yet to be discovered, that the cause of the Distemper proceeded from the Ground.

3. *gen.* Imagination *of* something (not necessarily evil) as possible or likely; a slight belief or idea of something, or *that* something is the case; a surmise; a faint notion, an inkling. (Chiefly in negative context.)

c **1400** *Beryn* 3831 And ȝit had I nevir suspecioun,..Who did þat cursid dede. **1482** *Monk of Evesham* (Arb.) 59, I neuyr herde before nether hadde any suspycyon hethirto that the kynde of women hadde be deprauyd..by suche a foule synne. *a* **1578** LINDESAY (Pitscottie) *Chron. Scot.* (S.T.S.) I. 86 The Earle of Douglas..was remaining thair.. witht out ony suspetionnis of Schir William Creichtounis gaddering. **1647** CLARENDON *Hist. Reb.* I. §78 There being ..not the least Suspicion or Imagination that the Marriage would not Succeed. **1650** BULWER *Anthropomet.* vii. (1653) 132 A round white..Chin, the Candor whereof seems to introduce into the beholders mind, a certaine suspition of a Rosie colour. *a* **1699** LADY HALKETT *Autobiog.* (Camden) 6 Nott so much as either his sister or mine had the least suspittion of it. **1718** PRIOR *Poems* Ded., The natural Endowments of Your Mind, (which, without suspicion of Flattery) I may tell You, are very Great. **1752** HUME *Ess. & Treat.* (1777) I. 550 This may beget a little suspicion, that even animals depend not on the climate. **1817** JAS. MILL *Brit. India* v. v. II. 524 Tippoo..and M. Lally.. surrounded Colonel Braithwaite before he had received even a suspicion of their march. **1867** AUG. J. E. WILSON *Vashti* xiii, 'Can you conjecture the cause of the present trouble?' 'I have a suspicion.' **1908** *Expositor* July 20 There was no previous suspicion of her future destiny in the Virgin's mind.

†**4.** Surmise of something future; expectation; *esp.* expectation or apprehension of evil. *Obs.* or merged in other senses.

a **1340** HAMPOLE *Psalter* cxviii[i]. 39 Smyte away my reprofe þat i had in suspecion [Vulg. *quod suspicatus sum*]. **1393** LANGL. *P. Pl.* C. XVIII. 315 [They] haueþ suspecion to be saf, boþe sarrasyns and Iewes, Thorwe Moyses and makamede. **1555** EDEN *Decades* (Arb.) 228, I entered into a great suspition of my lyfe. **1576** FLEMING *Panopl. Epist.* 275 The successe of al things..was answerable to our suspicion. **1658** *Tradit. Mem. K. James* 44 So high a suspicion of the immense Treasure. *a* **1700** EVELYN *Diary* 7 Sept. 1666, There was in truth some days before greate suspicion of those two nations joyning. *Ibid.* 18 June 1690, On suspicion that he might..come into the Confederacy of the German Princes.

†**5.** A slight appearance or indication (*of* something). *Obs. rare*⁻¹. (So L. *suspicio*.)

1565 JEWEL *Repl. Harding* (1611) 346 M. Harding, not shewing vs any suspition, or token of inordinate heat in that Reuerend Master of the Church of God.

6. A slight or faint trace, very small amount, 'hint', 'suggestion' (*of* something).

This use app. arose as an englishing of SOUPÇON.

1809 MALKIN *Gil Blas* VIII. iii. ¶3 As for polite literature ..there was not even a suspicion of it in all their talk. **1860** O. W. HOLMES *Elsie V.* v. (1891) 66 Flip,..made with beer and sugar, and a certain suspicion of strong waters. **1871** M. COLLINS *Mrq. & Merch.* III. iv. 107 He was a wall-eyed horse, with a suspicion of spavin.

Hence **su'spicional** *a.*, pertaining to suspicion; †**su'spicionating** *vbl. sb.*, the entertaining of suspicion; **su'spicionful** *a.*, = SUSPICIOUS 2; **su'spicionless** *a.*, devoid of suspicion, unsuspecting.

1890 *Alien. & Neurol.* XI. 347 The same emotional mobility and *suspicional tendencies which characterized her gifted son. *a* **1637** N. FERRAR *110 Consid.* (1638) 311 The *suspicionating, which is as it were a fearing even when it is of the holy spirit. **1911** H. S. HARRISON *Queed* xxiii. (1914) 305 That *suspicionful scrutiny so galling to men of spirit. *c* **1650** *Don Bellianis* 106 Altogether *suspicionlesse of any such treason. **1824** *Blackw. Mag.* XV. 168, I, poor dupe, suspicionless. **1840** GALT *Demon of Destiny* 7 As mourning mortals tell, Suspicionless, to old confiding friends, Disastrous tidings.

su'spicion, *v. dial.* and *colloq.* (orig. *U.S.*). [f. prec.] **a.** *trans.* To suspect. (With simple obj. or obj. cl.)

Quot. *a* 1637 appears to be a fortuitous occurrence unrelated to later uses.

a **1637** N. FERRAR *110 Consid.* (1638) 310 Suspicioning of himselfe, that if he should grow negligent, he might come to loose his magnanimity.

1834 *Kentuckian in New York* I. 64 (Thornton), They began to suspicion, maybe, that they had got the wrong sow by the ear. **1839** MARRYAT *Diary Amer.* Ser. I. II. 212, I suspicion as much. **1853** *Louisville* (Kentucky) *Democrat*, It was considered 'treason' almost to suspicion him of a mean transaction. **1863** ATKINSON *Stanton Grange* (1864) 219 They suspicioned it all wasn't reet. **1876** 'MARK TWAIN' *Tom Sawyer* xxvii, Anybody would suspicion us that saw us. **1902** *Academy* 5 Apr. 359 We suspicion a whiff of democracy in this. **1916** H. L. WILSON *Somewhere in Red Gap* ii. 68 Wilbur says I'm too good, not suspicioning. I'm just being wily, so he says he'll write up and fix it. **1919** J. BUCHAN *Mr. Standfast* xxi. 386 If the Boche once suspicions how little he's got before him the game's up. **1937** C. S. FORESTER *Happy Return* xxii. 259 He is in need of distraction, I suspicion. **1938** S. BECKETT *Murphy* iii. 32 Intense Love nature prominent, rarely suspicioning the Nasty. **1946** S. J. PERELMAN in *New Yorker* 5 Jan. 21/3 Our nineteen-year-old son, which he's home from Yale on his midyears and don't suspicion that his folks are rifting. **1959** *Observer* 22 Mar. 23/6 The major is no fool, and he suspicions as quickly as the audience that the presumed Englishman is a wounded Hungarian on the run. **1961** R. P. HOBSON *Rancher Takes Wife* (1962) viii. 114, I quite often suspicioned this trait of Gloria's but when I found it out for sure it was almost too late. **1973** 'D. SHANNON' *No Holiday for Crime* (1974) vi. 88, I suspicioned what she was, but I didn't have no proof.

b. *absol.* or *intr.*

1905 KIPLING *Actions & Reactions* (1909) 40 An' d'you mean to tell me you never suspicioned? **1946** C. MCCULLERS *Member of Wedding* III. 173 In those bridge games..nobody ever drew a good hand, the cards were all sorry, and no high bids made—until finally Berenice suspicioned, saying: 'Less us get busy and count these old cards.'

†**su'spicionable,** *a. Obs. rare*⁻¹. [f. SUSPICION *sb.* + -ABLE.] Open to suspicion.

1692 BEVERLEY *Disc. Dr. Crisp* 14 It is very suspitionable, the Letting it down lower may have had its Ill, as well as its Good Effects.

†**suspicionous,** *a. Obs.* In 5 suspec-. [a. AF., OF. *suspec-*, *suspicionous*, f. *suspicion* SUSPICION: see -OUS.] = next.

1474 CAXTON *Chesse* III. ii. (1883) 90 We rede that dionyse of zecyll..Was so suspecionous that [etc.]. **1477** EARL RIVERS (Caxton) *Dictes* 119 Of alle other maners & condicions the worst is a man to be suspecionous of his frende. **1481** CAXTON *Godfrey* xli. 80 Themperour.. doubted moche, And had his comyng moche suspecyonous.

suspicious (səˈspɪʃəs), *a.* Forms: α. 4–6 suspecious, (5, -ieuse, 5–6 -yous, 6 -ius), 5 susspecious. β. 4– suspicious, (5 -icyows, -ycyowse, 6 -ycyous, -iciouse, -yciouse, 7 -ycious); 6–7 suspitious, (6 -ius). [a. AF., OF. *suspecious*, *suspicious*, *-eus*, ad. L. *suspīciōsus*, f. *suspīcio* SUSPICION: see -OUS.

For the change of spelling cf. SUSPICION *sb.*]

1. Open to, deserving of, or exciting suspicion; that is or should be an object of suspicion; suspected, or to be suspected; of questionable character.

1340 *Ayenb.* 226 Þe uerste [þing] is him-zelue kepe and priueliche bi ine his house, naȝt uor to uolȝy þe uelaȝredes suspiciouses. *c* **1386** CHAUCER *Clerk's T.* 540 Suspecious was the diffame of this man, Suspect his face, suspect his word also. **1435** *Rolls of Parlt.* IV. 490/1 In crikes, and oyer suspecious places. **1477** *Cov. Leet Bk.* 421 If eny suspect persone..may be founde within this Cite hauyng suspecious langage. **1502** ARNOLDE *Chron.* (1811) 95 Good and honest persones and trewe and not suspecious. **1526** TINDALE *1 Thess.* v. 22 Abstayne from all suspicious thyngs. **1594** NASHE *Terrors Nt.* G iv b, The abrupt falling into his sicknesse was suspitious, proceeding from no apparant surfet or misdiet. **1634** PEACHAM *Compl. Gentl.* xii. 114 All Hebrew Coynes that Antiquaries shew us are suspicious. **1646** SIR T. BROWNE *Pseud. Ep.* I. viii. 34 Authors are also suspicious, nor greedily to be swallowed, who pretend to write of secrets. **1771** *Junius Lett.* xliv. (1788) 247 This sudden alteration of their sentiments..carries with it a suspicious appearance. **1843** R. J. GRAVES *Syst. Clin. Med.* xii. 130 His respiration was interrupted, suspicious, and irregular. **1855** MACAULAY *Hist. Eng.* xxi. IV. 551 Some most suspicious entries had been discovered, under the head of special service. **1889** J. GAIRDNER *Hen. VII*, vii. (1899) 111 This Ludovico had become Duke of Milan himself by the very suspicious death of his nephew.

†**b.** with dependent clause, inf., or *of*. *Obs.*

c **1400** *Rom. Rose* 6110 He wole hym silf suspecious make That he his lyf let couertly..in Ipocrisie. **1527** *Star Chamber Cases* (Selden Soc.) II. 166 All the Barnes..and other suspecyous places..to have hydde corne. **1592** GREENE *Conny Catch.* 18 Citizens..that they finde.. suspitious of the like fault. **1623** MEADE in Ellis *Orig. Lett.* Ser. I. III. 149 The news of the Prince..was suspicious not to be good. **1642** FULLER *Holy & Prof. St.* v. v. 376 'Tis suspicious..that these things might be done by confederacie. **1765** T. HUTCHINSON *Hist. Mass.* I. v. 436 The wife of Richard Cornish was found suspicious of incontinency. **1788** JEFFERSON *Writ.* (1859) II. 552 Symptoms which render it suspicious that the two empires may make their peace with the Turks.

2. Full of, inclined to, or feeling suspicion; disposed to suspect; suspecting; *esp.* disposed to suspect evil, mistrustful.

c **1400** *Cato's Morals* in *Cursor M.* App. iv. 307 Fle to be suspecious, atte þou be noȝt doutous. *c* **1430** LYDG. *Min. Poems* (Percy Soc.) 162 No man of kynde is moore suspecious, Than he that is moost vicious and coupable. **1592** KYD *Sp. Trag.* III. xiv. 160 The world is suspitious, And men may think what we imagine not. **1647** CLARENDON *Hist. Reb.* v. §140 Such Circumstances, as should administer no occasion of Jealousy to the most Suspicious. **1735** POPE *Prol. Sat.* 206 A tim'rous foe, and a suspicious friend. **1842** W. MACGILLIVRAY *Man. Brit. Ornith.* II. 244 This species [of gull]..is vigilant, shy, and suspicious. **1856** KANE *Arctic Expl.* II. xv. 164, I had earned character with these people, at first so suspicious and distrustful.

b. with dependent clause, or *of*.

1474 CAXTON *Chesse* IV. vii. (1883) 180 The aduersaries ben suspecyous that the comyn peple lye In a wayte to Robbe her goodes. **1591** SHAKS. *1 Hen. VI*, IV. i. 153, I see no reason if I weare this Rose, That any one should therefore be suspitious I more incline to Somerset, than Yorke. **1651** HOBBES *Leviath.* IV. xlvi. 379 The best men are the least suspicious of fraudulent purposes. *a* **1721** PRIOR *Dial. Cromwell & Porter* Wks. (1907) 264 You were a Slave to your own Apprehensions, suspicious of every body that came near you. **1783** JOHNSON *Let. to Taylor* 24 July, I was suspicious that you were ill. **1834** J. H. NEWMAN *Par. Serm.* (1837) I. v. 70, I am suspicious of any religion that is a people's religion. **1861** THACKERAY *Four Georges* iii. 134 Like other dull men, the king [*sc.* George III] was all his life suspicious of superior people.

c. *transf.* Expressing, indicating, or characterized by suspicion.

1478 EARL RIVERS *Crystyne's Mor. Prov.* (1859) 3 Woman & man to guider muche Rownyng May often cause suspecieuse slandryng. **1526** *Pilgr. Perf.* (W. de W. 1531) 63 Whose hertes be full of ypocrisy..and suspycyous iudgementes. **1585** T. WASHINGTON tr. *Nicholay's Voy.* IV. xxxv. 158 b, [They] condemned the wise Socrates, for the suspitious opinion they had in him. **1635** QUARLES *Embl.* v. xii. 22 How often hath Thy Hope-reviving Grace Woo'd my suspitious eyes to seek Thy face! **1745** T. RANDALL in *Transl. & Paraphr. Sc. Ch.* XLIX. vi, Love harbours no suspicious thought. **1797** S. & HT. LEE *Canterb. T.* (1799) I. iv. 358 [His conduct] tinctured the mind of his companion with suspicious and black ideas.

†**d.** Showing a suspicion or inkling *of*. *Obs.*

1655 MARQ. WORCESTER *Cent. Inv.* §75 A..Ribbon weaver may set down a whole discourse..without knowing a letter or interweaving anything suspicious of other secret than a new-fashioned Ribbon.

3. *Comb.*, as (in sense 1) *suspicious-looking* adj.; (in sense 2) *suspicious-mindedness*.

1843 *Chambers's Edin. Jrnl.* 46/1 A wiry, crop-eared terrier..; one of those suspicious-looking brutes whom an honest man would shrink from claiming. **1869** TOZER *Highl. Turkey* I. 101 A suspicious-looking mess of fish and vegetables. **1888** DOUGHTY *Arabia Deserta* I. 603 The suspicious-mindedness of the Arabians.

su'spiciously, *adv.* [f. prec. + -LY².] In a suspicious manner.

1. In a way deserving of suspicion; so as to arouse suspicion.

1472 in *Surtees Misc.* (1890) 24 Lawrence of Lawe..lyffez suspeciouslye agayns lawe of this land. **1523** LD. BERNERS *Froiss.* I. xxi. 30 They both dyed suspeciously. **1587** TURBERV. *Epit. & Sonn., To Parker* 192 Their dice are very small,..Not shaking them awhit, they cast suspiciously. **1612** SIR R. NAUNTON in *Buccleuch MSS.* (Hist. MSS. Comm.) I. 118 As if I were too suspiciously inward with Sir F. Gr. **1687** A. LOVELL tr. *Thevenot's Trav.* II. 64 There were Arabs at Mendeli who looked suspiciously. **1823** COOPER *Pioneers* vi, He returned..bringing with him a suspiciously-looking box. **1862** *Morn. Standard* 24 Mar., The sentence above quoted..which looks suspiciously like the Delphic utterance of some South Kensingtonian oracle. **1902** VIOLET JACOB *Sheep Stealers* xiv, 'Oi,' was the reply, which came from suspiciously near the keyhole.

2. In a way showing suspicion; with suspicion; suspectingly.

1549 in Burnet *Hist. Ref.* (1681) II. *Records* 176, I talked in the Matter so suspiciously, as though such an Invasion had been made. **1599** *Life Sir T. More* in Wordsw. *Eccl. Biog.* (1853) II. 70 He would never sinisterlie or suspiciouslie take anie thing written, done, or spoken against him. **1615** G. SANDYS *Trav.* III. 157 The Romanes did keepe a garrison, suspiciously ouer-eying the Temple. **1866** GEO. ELIOT *F. Holt* xxxvi, Is it a pledge you are demanding from me? said Harold, suspiciously. **1868** MISS BRADDON *Run to Earth* xxv, This man looked very suspiciously at the visitor. **1892** 'F. ANSTEY' *Voces Pop.* Ser. II. 24 They watch one another suspiciously.

su'spiciousness. [f. as prec. + -NESS.] The condition or quality of being suspicious.

1. Liability to suspicion; questionable character.

1486 *Year-bk. 2 Henry VII* (1567) 3b, Le felony ou le suspiciousnes. *a* **1716** SOUTH *Serm.* (1717) V. 347 The Reasons, why this inward Voice of the Spirit cannot be the Rule, which Men are to be guided by... Because of its Suspiciousness. **1881** WESTCOTT & HORT *Grk. N.T.* II. 67 Its final conclusions must rest on the intrinsic verisimilitude or suspiciousness of the text itself.

2. Proneness to suspicion; disposition to suspect; mistrustfulness. (In quot. 1525, Suspicion.)

1525 LD. BERNERS *Froiss.* II. xxii. 51 They..went in and out on their maisters busynesse, without any suspeciousness of them. **1526** *Pilgr. Perf.* (W. de W. 1531) 66 Our lorde.. preserue all those that entendeth this holy iourney..from suspycyousnes and wronge iudgementes. **1639** FULLER *Holy War* v. xii. (1647) 251 Suspiciousnesse is as great an enemy to wisdome, as too much credulitie. *a* **1768** SECKER *Serm., Ephes.* v. 11 (1770) II. 351 An immoderate Suspiciousness of innocent Compliances. **1858** FROUDE *Hist. Eng.* IV. xviii. 34 The nation settled back into its old suspiciousness, which it disguised under the name of independence. **1884** R. W. CHURCH *Bacon* ii. 56 Bacon..using every effort and device to appease the Queen's anger and suspiciousness.

†suspiracle. *Obs. rare.* [ad. med.L. *suspīrāculum*: see next.] = next.

1597 A. M. tr. *Guillemeau's Fr. Chirurg.* 50b/1 The suspiracles through the which nature disburseth her selfe of all superfluitys.

†suspiral. *Obs.* Also 5–6 suspyral, -all(e, -irall(e, suspirel, 6 sesperal, susprall, cesperalle. [a. OF. *s(o)uspirail* (mod.F. *soupirail*) = Pr. *sospiralh*, ad. med.L. *suspīrāculum*, f. *suspīrāre* to SUSPIRE + *-culum*, denoting instrument.]

1. A breathing-passage.

c **1400** *Pilgr. Sowle* (Caxton 1483) IV. xxxi. 80 This neck shalle be the suspyralle wherby the brethe shalle be drawen bothe to comforte of the hede and eke of al the body.

2. A vent, esp. for a conduit.

c **1430** in *Lond. & Middlesex Archæol. Trans.* (1870) III. 321 This suspirall seruith for thes ij pipes. *c* **1440** *Promp. Parv.* 485 Suspyral, of a cundyte, *spiraculum*. **1562** in Strype *Stow's Surv.* (1755) II. v. xxi. 411 No man shall..destroy any pipes Sesperals or Wind-vents pertaining to the Conduits.

3. A pipe or passage for water leading to a conduit.

1420 *Cov. Leet Bk.* 21 Ordinatum fuit quod les Suspirales ..deleantur et obstupantur. **1426** *Ibid.* 105 That no welles nor suspiralles, other then ben ordeyned, shuld be had to let the comen Cours of the seid Cundyte. **1543–4** *Act 35 Hen. VIII*, c. 10 To vewe..the said Heddes pipes suspiralles and vaultes, and them to amend repaire translate. [**1656** BLOUNT *Glossogr., Suspiral*,..In the Statute of 35 Hen. 8. Cap. 10. it seems to be taken for a Spring of water, passing under the ground, towards a Conduit or Cestern.]

4. A settling tank; a cesspool.

c **1512** in *Archaeologia* (1902) LVIII. 301 In þe same diche boþe þe suspirel & þe waste pipe awoyde ther water in a gotir of breke. *Ibid.* 302 In the botome of this well undir a stone is a susprall wt a tampioun to clense the home pype. **1583** in N. Bacon *Ann. Ipswiche* (1884) 337 Cesperalle to be made for stopping of filthe by the brooke.

suspiration (sʌspɪ'reɪʃən). Now *rare.* [ad. L. *suspīrātio, -ōnem*, n. of action f. *suspīrāre* to SUSPIRE.]

1. Sighing; a sigh.

c **1485** *Digby Myst., Christ's Burial* 64 O day off suspiratione! Which Iewes shall repent! **1503** HAWES *Examp. Virt.* vii. 115 Peas bytwene the faders hyghenes Of heuen and vs in suspyracyon. *a* **1639** WOTTON *Panegyr. to K. Charles* in *Reliq.* (1651) 136 To have solicited her sister with these panting suspirations. **1641** BROME *Joviall Crew* IV. i. Wks. 1873 III. 420 Ods my life! He sighs again:..Give him more Sack, to drown his Suspirations. **1664** H. MORE *Myst. Iniq.* xii. 40 The devout whispers or suspirations of her affectionate Supplicants. **1786** *Francis the Philanthropist* III. 91 Her lip trembled with suspiration. **1820** SCOTT *Monast.* xvi, I may well heave such a suspiration. **1867** SWINBURNE *Ess. & Stud.* (1875) 128 We have had evidences of religion, aspirations and suspirations of all kinds.

2. (Deep) breathing; breath; a (deep) breath.

1602 SHAKS. *Ham.* I. ii. 79 Nor Customary suites of solemne Blacke, Nor windy suspiration of forc'd breath. **1607** DEKKER *Whore of Babylon* Wks. 1873 II. 193 The nations, Who suspiration draw out of this aire. **1634** S. R. *Noble Soldier* III. i. in Bullen *O. Pl.* (1882) I. 289 We from one climate Drew suspiration. **1892** LD. LYTTON *King Poppy* 121 Its meadowy dales A thousand fragrant suspirations fill'd With incense. **1905** *Westm. Gaz.* 16 Feb. 2/1 The ocean..smooth as glass, without even a suspiration to break the deadly monotony of its surface.

Hence **suspi'ratious, 'suspirative** *adjs.*, sighing.

1824 GALT *Rothelan* II. v. ix. 254 A suspiratious flowing of briny tears. **1872** BROWNING *Fifine* lxi, Not feebly, like our phrase, against the barrier go In suspirative swell the authentic notes I know.

†su'spire, *sb. Obs.* [a. OF. *s(o)uspir* (mod.F. *soupir*) = Pr. *sospir*, It. *sospiro*, Sp., Pg. *suspiro*, or ad. L. *suspīrium*, f. *suspīrāre*: see next.] A sigh.

c **1450** *Envoy to Alison* 25 Suspiris which I effunde in silence! **1549** *Compl. Scot.* vii. 70 The quhilk reproche sche pronuncit vitht mony dolorus suspiris. **1595** *Locrine* V. iv. 2 The circuit of the azure sky Throwes forth sad throbs and grieuous suspirs. **1610** HEYWOOD *Gold. Age* I. i. Wks. 1874 III. 12 Gods are neuer touch't with my suspires, Passions and throbs. **1637** —— *Pleas. Dial.* ii. Wks. 1874 VI. 130 Whence came that deep suspire?

suspire (sə'spaɪə(r)), *v.* Now chiefly *poet.* [ad. L. *suspīrāre* (whence OF. *sospirer*, mod.F. *soupirer*, Pr. *sospirar*, It. *-are*, Sp., Pg. *suspirar*), f. *su-* SUB- 26 + *spīrāre* to breathe.]

1. *intr.* To sigh; *rare* in lit. sense; chiefly *fig.* to sigh or long *for*, yearn *after*.

c **1450** tr. *De Imitatione* III. xxxvii. 107 To be provoked to hyer þinges, &..to suspire þerto by desire. **1532** MORE *Confut. Tindale* Wks. 532/2 Suspyring and sighing after the sight of god. *a* **1542** WYATT *Poet. Wks.*, '*Absens absenting*' vi, To rejoise my wofull herte With sighis suspiring most rufullie. **1610** *Hellish Councell practised by Jesuites* 18 Thy happinesse giues vs leaue to respire, thy absence iustly compels vs to suspire, and the place where we make no doubt thou art, makes vs thither to aspire. **1671** WOODHEAD *St. Teresa* I. Pref. 12 Prayer..consists more in sighing and suspiring after that object, that it is already convinced most to deserve its love. **1855** BROWNING *Serenade at Villa* 12 Earth turned in her sleep with pain, Sultrily suspired for proof. **1887** 'Q' *Dead Man's Rock* 294 Every note breathing pathos or suspiring in tremulous anguish.

2. *trans.* To utter with a sigh, to sigh forth. Also, to breathe out.

1549 *Compl. Scot.* vii. 70 Sche began to suspire lamentabil regrettis. **1865** J. THOMSON *Art* III. ii, Did he ever suspire a tender lay. **1868** BROWNING *Ring & Bk.* x. 997 A bolt from heaven..suspiring flame. **1904** *Blackw. Mag.* Nov. 677 How lustily the bellows did suspire Breath for the flames!

3. *intr.* To breathe.

1595 SHAKS. *John* III. iv. 80 Since the birth of Caine, the first male-childe To him that did but yesterday suspire. **1597** —— *2 Hen. IV*, IV. v. 33 Did hee suspire, that light and weightlesse dowlne Perforce must moue. **1856** MRS. BROWNING *Aur. Leigh* VII. 1061 Fire-flies, that suspire In short soft lapses of transported flame. **1866** SWINBURNE *Poems & Ball., Hermaphroditus* 10 Their breath is fire upon the amorous air, Fire in thine eyes and where thy lips suspire.

Hence **†su'spired** *ppl. a.*, longed for; **†su'spiring** *vbl. sb.*, sighing, a sigh.

1549 *Compl. Scot.* i. 23 The lamentabil suspiring that procedit fra my dolorus hart. *a* **1639** WOTTON *Medit. Christmas Day* in *Reliq.* (1651) 351 The long Suspired Redeemer of the World. **1671** WOODHEAD *St. Teresa* I. Pref. 9 Prayer..by interior frequent suspirings and ejaculations interposed.

suspirious (sə'spɪrɪəs), *a.* [ad. L. *suspīriōsus*, f. *suspīrium* deep breathing, sigh, shortness of breath, SUSPIRE *sb.* Cf. F. *suspirieux.*]

1. Breathing with difficulty or painfully; chiefly *Path.* (see quot. 1896).

1657 TOMLINSON *Renou's Disp.* I. IV. lx. 329 Their [*sc.* hyssop's] faculties..benefit the suspirious and orthopnoical. **1657** *Physical Dict.*, *Suspirious*, broken winded. **1859** MAYNE *Expos. Lex.*, *Suspirious*,..breathing painfully. **1876** BRISTOWE *Theory & Pract. Med.* (1878) 203 Respiration..is then generally slow and suspirious. **1896** *Allbutt's Syst. Med.* I. 565 The respiration..becomes embarrassed and 'suspirious'; marked, that is, by a slow laboured inspiration followed by a quick expiration and a long pause.

2. Full of sighs, sighing.

1751 *Hist. Pompey the Little* 96 When the company had enjoyed enough of this spiritual and suspirious conversation, they proceeded in the last place to singing of psalms. **1809** SYD. SMITH *Methodism* Wks. (1850) 138/1 To estimate what the exertions of the lachrymal and suspirious clergy would be. **1820** H. MATTHEWS *Diary Invalid* (ed. 2) 223 A suspirious, lacrymose, white-handkerchief business.

†suspiry. *Obs. rare.* Also 5 -yry. [ad. L. *suspīrium*: see prec.] A breathing, respiration.

1398 TREVISA *Barth. De P.R.* v. lviii. (Bodl. MS.) lf. 29b/1 By preuey suspiries [*ed.* **1495** suspyries; orig. *respiracula*] and ventinges it [*sc.* the marrow] feleþ þe vertue..of þe mone.

suspition, -ious, obs. ff. SUSPICION, -IOUS.

†suspose, *v.* and *sb. Obs.* Also 5 -owse. Variant of SUPPOSE, influenced by *suspicion.*

a **1325** *Prose Psalter* xlix. 22 [l. 21] Þou wendest wicked-leche, þat y shal be lich to þe; y shal reproue þe of þy susposeing [= supposition]. *c* **1460** *Towneley Myst.* xiii. 514 If ye haue suspowse [= suspicion] to gill or to me.

susprall, var. of SUSPIRAL.

†susprise, *v. Obs. rare.* Also suss-. [f. AF. *suspris-e* = OF. *souspris-e*, pa. pple. of *sou(s)prendre*, by-form of *sourprendre* to SURPRISE.] = SURPRISE *v.* 2, 3, 4.

a **1400–50** *Wars Alex.* 2390 (Dubl. MS.), He wald neuer sussprise [*Ashm. MS.* supprise] no sege vnder heven. *c* **1400** *Anturs of Arth.* (Ireland MS.) xxiv, Thay schalle dee that day,..Sussprisut with a subiecte. **1471** CAXTON *Recuyel* (Sommer) 227 Iupiter felte hym self sore susprised and surmounted of the couetyse of loue.

‖susque deque. *rare.* [L., = lit. both up and down; hence, indifferently.] *pl.* People who are indifferent.

1647 WARD *Simple Cobler* (1843) 50 He hath sounded an alarm to all the *susque deques*, pell-mels, one and alls, now harrasing sundry parts of Christendome.

Susquehannock (sʌskwə'hænək). Now only *Hist.* Forms: 7 **Sasquehanno, Sasquesahanock, -hanough, Sesquesahamock,** 8 **Susquehannah,** 9 **Susquehanno, Susquehanough; Susquehanna,** etc. [a. the name of this people in a neighbouring Algonquian language, lit. 'person (or people) of the Susquehanna River': the river flows from N.Y. State into Chesapeake Bay.] = CONESTOGA 1. Also *attrib.*

1612 J. SMITH *Map of Virginia* 8 To proceed, 60 of those Sasquesahanocks, came to the discouerers with skins, bowes ..and tobacco pipes for presents. *Ibid.*, The description of a Sasquesahanough. *Ibid.* 19 The people differ very much in stature,..some being very great as the *Sesquesahamocks*, others very little, as the Wighcocomocoes. **1676** *Rec. Court of New Castle on Delaware* (1904) 39 If the Sasquehannos should aply to you for anything, you are to use them kindly. **1751** in *New Jersey Archives* (1883) 1st Ser. VII. 598 The Susquahannah Indians only want leave from the Mohawks whom they call their Fathers in order to their accepting of a missionary. **1833** S. KERCHEVAL *Hist. Valley of Virginia* p. xxiv, He ran amongst his men, crying out..these are our friends the Susquehanoughs. **1845** *Encycl. Metrop.* XXV. 937/2 Thus Maryland was inhabited by the Susquehannoes, who were afterwards destroyed by the Iroquois assisted by four nations. **1898** *Contrib. Indian Hist. Lower Susquehanna Valley* (Hist. Soc. Dauphin County, Pa.) 39 Prior to 1600, but how long before is not known, the Susquehannocks were seated upon the river from which they have derived their name. **1910** *Encycl. Brit.* VI. 897/2 *Conestoga*, a tribe of North American Indians of Iroquoian stock... They were sometimes known as Susquehannas... The tribe suffered final extinction in the Indian wars of 1763. **1915** J. BUCHAN *Salute to Adventurers* v. 79, I was with Bacon in '76, in the fray with the Susquehannocks. I speak the Indian tongues. **1940** T. W. CLARKE *Bloody Mohawk* 36 The Iroquois, about 1660, turned their attention to the Andastes, or Susquehannocks of Pennsylvania and southern New York. **1957** *Encycl. Brit.* XII. 683/2 The Iroquoian family occupied three territories, a northern, southern, and southeastern. In the northern area there lived, besides the Iroquois proper, the Conestoga or Susquehanna in Pennsylvania. **1978** *Handbk. N. Amer. Indians* XV. 363/1 The term Sasquesahanough (Susquehannock) was first recited to Capt. John Smith by his Algonquian-speaking interpreter when he was visited by 60 Susquehannocks in 1608. **1978** J. A. MICHENER *Chesapeake* i. 4 The common warriors..felt that for a Susquehannock to pass more than a year in peace would be disgraceful. *Ibid.* 6 He would have to pass two Susquehannock villages to the south.

susreal, var. *surreal*: see SURROYAL.

c **1410** *Master of Game* (MS. Digby 182) ii, Þe first tynde that is next þe heed is ycleped aunteleer, and þe secund reiall, and þe .III. above susreall.

suss (sʌs). *dial.* Also 6 **sose.** [Variant of SOSS *sb.*[1] (sense 3); cf. SOSS-.] A slattern, slut.

15.. *Smyth & his Dame* 251 in Hazl. *E.P.P.* III. 210 He hath amended well thy ble; For yester day,..Thov were a fovle sose [*rimes* thus, Jesus, vs]. **1865** R. HUNT *Pop. Rom. W. Eng.* Ser. I. 97 A great, nasty Suss of a woman.

suss: see SUS, SUSS *sb.*, *v.*

†'sussapine. *Obs.* ? mispr. for GOSSAMPINE.

1594 GREENE & LODGE *Looking Gl.* (1598) D4, Ile deck my Aluida, In Sendall and in costly Sussapine.

sussarara, var. SISERARY.

†sussemy, *a. Obs.* [a. AF. **susseme*, OF. *sousseme*, var. *sourseme*, = med.L. *superseminātus* lit. 'sown over' (see SUPERSEMINATE), applied to measly swine because of their tongues being covered with spots.] Of swine's flesh: Measly.

1421 *Cov. Leet Bk.* 25 Þat no bocher sell..no roten Schep, ne Sussemy flesche, ne non swyn of brym.

Sussex ('sʌsɪks). The name (OE. *Súþseaxe* 'South Saxons') of a maritime county in the south-east of England, used *attrib.* and *absol.* to designate things produced in or peculiar to the county, as breeds of cattle, agricultural implements, etc.

1704 *Dict. Rust.* (1726) s.v. *Plough*, The Sussex single Wheel-Plough. **1818** *Compl. Grazier* (ed. 3) Introd. 3 The Sussex and Hereford breeds [of cows]. **1834** YOUATT *Cattle* 41 The loins of the Sussex ox are wide. **1837** *Brit. Husb.* (Libr. Usef. Knowl.) II. Index, Sussex waggon [described I. 155]. **1846** YOUATT *Pig* (1847) Index, Sussex pigs. **1855** *Poultry Chron.* III. 534/2 My declining to adopt the name of Hamburg for the Bolton Greys and Bays, or that of Dorking for the Sussex fowls. **1875** *Encycl. Brit.* I. 392/2 These sheep are now usually classed as Sussex Downs and Hampshire Downs. **1885** *Ibid.* XIX. 645/2 The Surrey and Sussex fowls are four-toed. **1886** J. MACDONALD *Pringle's Cattle* (ed. 3) vi. 117 The Sussex breed of cattle possesses several of the characteristics of the Devon, but is larger in frame. *Ibid.*, Some fine specimens of Sussex oxen are shown annually. **1919** K. J. J. MACKENZIE *Cattle* x. 144 Today the Sussex is essentially a beef-breed. *Ibid.*, The Sussex inherits some of the faults of the draught-cattle from which he springs. *Ibid.*, The Sussex bullock has to be thoroughly fattened before he is a really good butcher's animal. **1974** *Country Life* 7 Nov. 1396/1 Today the beef animal is supreme—Welsh Black, Sussex, Galloway.

†b. ***Sussex crest***, a name for the cuckold's 'horn'. *Obs.*

1681 T. FLATMAN *Heraclitus Ridens* No. 8 (1713) I. 49 A Cuckold is always to be the last Man that knows he has got a Sussex Crest.

c. Sussex marble, a marble occurring in thin beds in the Wealden clay of Sussex and Kent, formerly much used for pillars in churches; **Sussex spaniel**, a long-coated, stocky, golden-brown spaniel belonging to a breed developed in Sussex and neighbouring counties; also *ellipt.*

1753 *Chambers' Cycl.* Suppl. **1850** ANSTED *Elem. Geol., Min.*, etc. 379 Weald clay, with subordinate limestone (called Sussex marble) and sand. **1856** 'STONEHENGE' *Brit. Rural Sports* 59 A good, useful team of the Sussex spaniels. **1859** [see *Norfolk spaniel* s.v. NORFOLK b]. **1904** H. COMPTON *Twentieth Century Dog* II. 237 The Sussex spaniel is a smaller dog than the Clumber. **1981** C. I. A. RITCHIE *Brit. Dog* vi. 164 In spite of the popularity of land spaniels, such as the beautiful Sussex, the water spaniel was perhaps the favourite.

Hence †**Sussexan**, †**Sussexian** *adjs. rare*, belonging to Sussex.

1612 DRAYTON *Poly-olb.* xvii. 423 Clear Lavant, that doth keep the Southamptonian side (Dividing it well-near from the Sussexian lands). **1614** *Disc. Strange & Monstrous Serpent* B2b, I will conclude this generall discovrse of Serpents, and come to the particular description of our Sussexan Serpent.

sussexite (ˈsʌsɪksaɪt). *Min.* [f. *Sussex*, the name of a county in New Jersey + -ITE¹.] A basic borate of manganese and magnesium, $(Mn,Mg)BO_2OH$, found as white or yellowish orthorhombic crystals, isomorphous with szaibelyite.

1868 G. J. BRUSH in *Amer. Jrnl. Sci.* XCVI. 140 (*heading*) New borate from Mine Hill, Franklin, Sussex Co., New Jersey—sussexite. **1951** C. PALACHE et al. *Dana's Syst. Min.* (ed. 7) II. 375 The names sussexite and szaibelyite are applied to the halves of the series with Mn > Mg and Mg > Mn, respectively. **1954** [see HULSITE]. **1974** *Encycl. Brit. Micropædia* IX. 699/1 Sussexite occurs as hydrothermal fibrous veinlets in the U.S. at Franklin, N.J., and Iron County, Michigan.

†**sussing**, *vbl. sb. Obs. rare.* [Echoic.] The 'spitting' of a cat.

a **1693** *Urquhart's Rabelais* III. xiii. 107 Barking of Currs, bawling of Mastiffs..sussing of Kitnings.

sussingle, obs. from of SURCINGLE.

sussite, var. SUSCITE *v. Obs.*, to resuscitate.

susso (ˈsʌsəʊ). *Austral. slang. Obsolescent.* Also Susso. [f. SUS(TENANCE + -O².] **a.** State government relief paid to the unemployed, *spec.* during the Depression. Also in phr. ***on the susso.***

1941 BAKER *Dict. Austral. Slang* 51 *On the susso*, in receipt of unemployed sustenance. **1942** L. MANN *Go-Getter* 10 Five shillings were five shillings and a handsome help to the sustenance. 'We're on the Susso now.' That was the song they knew and did not sing. **1974** *Times Lit. Suppl.* 15 Feb. 155/4 We're on the Susso now. In the 1930s Melbourne schoolchildren grew up chanting this (to them) cheerful folk song—'Susso' being the state government sustenance available to the unemployed throughout Australia under varying conditions during the Depression.

b. One who draws this relief.

1947 V. PALMER *Cyclone* 8 He thinks it puts hair on his chest knocking about with the sussos. **1963** F. HARDY *Legends from Benson's Valley* 166 The very thought..of the contempt the respectable held for the sussos changed his mood to defiance.

susspecion, -pitioun, etc., obs. ff. SUSPICION.

†**sussy**, *sb. Sc. Obs.* Also 6 sussie, sowcy. [a. OF. *soussy* (mod.F. *souci*), vbl. sb. f. *soussier*: see next.] Care, trouble.

1513 DOUGLAS *Æneis* IV. Prol. 236 Quhat sussy, cuir, and strang ymagyning? *a* **1578** LINDESAY (Pitscottie) *Chron. Scot.* (S.T.S.) I. 307 My lord of Angus tuik lyttill sussie of the samin. **1587** W. FOWLER *Wks.* (S.T.S.) I. 120 He..who hes of his state ones sowcy, cair, and feare. **1591** R. BRUCE *Serm.* iii. G 6, Ane King that hath na kind of cair, nor sussie [*ed.* 1843 soucie] of his subjectis.

†ˈ**sussy**, *v. Sc. Obs.* Also 6 sussie. [a. OF. *soussier*:—L. *sollicitāre* to rouse, excite, SOLICIT.]

1. *intr.* To care, trouble.

c **1550** ROLLAND *Crt. Venus* II. 428 Sussie not, for thow will get reskew. **1570** *Satir. Poems Reform.* xvi. 76 He susseis not thre strais Quha suld be rewlar. *a* **1609** ALEX. HUME *Ep. G. Moncrieff* 318, I sussie not how viuely they be tuitched.

b. With negative and const. inf.: *Not* to refuse *to do* something.

1567 *Gude & Godlie B.* (S.T.S.) 171 Thou susseit nocht to suffer deid. **1570** *Satir. Poems Reform.* xiii. 38 Cain aganis his brother did Rebell, And susseit not to sched his saikles blude. **1580–90** J. STEWART *Poems* (S.T.S.) II. 113 The fengȝeit freind..susseis not to leif his freind in smart.

2. *trans.* To care for, regard.

c **1560** A. SCOTT *Poems* (S.T.S.) xxx. 22 Thay sussy not thair God abufe.

sussy (ˈsʌsɪ), *a. slang.* [Shortened f. SUSPICIOUS *a.* or SUSPECTED *ppl. a.* + -Y¹; cf. SUS, SUSS *sb.*] Suspicious, suspect, suspected.

1965 L. J. CUNLIFFE *Having it Away* xiv. 97 It seemed a bit sussy to me. **1974** G. F. NEWMAN *Price* iii. 97 Sneed's questions were becoming more accusing; there was something sussy about Roger Dawes. **1978** N. MARSH *Grave Mistake* iii. 95 He's done porridge for attempted blackmail and he's sussy for bringing the hard stuff ashore.

sussy, obs. f. SOOSY, E. Indian fabric.

†**sustain**, *sb. Obs. rare.* [f. next.] That which sustains; means of sustenance.

1653 MILTON *Ps. iii*, 14 I lay and slept, I wak'd again, For my sustain Was the Lord.

sustain (səˈsteɪn), *v.* Forms: 3 susteni, -eini, -einy, -eyni, -eyny, sosteine, souste(i)ne, 3–6 susteyne, 3–7 susteine, sustene, 4–5 sustyne, -teene, 4–6 sust(e)igne, susteyn, -tayn, (4 sostene, suste(e)n, -tyene, 5 sousteyne, 6 swstene), 4–7 sustaine, sustayne, 6–7 sustein, 4– sustain. [a. AF., OF. *sustenir*, *so(u)stenir* (mod.F. *soutenir*), pres. stem *sus-*, *so(u)stein-*, *-eign-*, corresp. to Pr., Sp. *sostener*, It. *sostenere*, Pg. *soster*, ad. L. *sustinēre*, f. *sus-* SUB- 26 + *tenēre* to hold, keep.]

1. †**a.** *trans.* To support the efforts, conduct, or cause of; to succour, support, back up. *Obs.*

c **1290** *Beket* 1507 in *S. Eng. Leg.* 149 And bote heo wolden him bi-leue and ne susteyni him non-more. **13..** *Cursor M.* 22102 (Gött.) Bethaida and corozaim, þir tua cites sal susten [*Cott.* foster] him [*sc.* þe anticrist]. *a* **1450** *Knt. de la Tour* lxv, The wiff of the said Amon was not wise..to susteyne hym in his foly. *c* **1500** *Melusine* 111 That..ye..worship with all your power holy chirch, beyng her champyons, the same to susteyne & withstand ayenst alle her euyl wyllers. **1525** LD. BERNERS *Froiss.* II. clxxxvii. 572 That was the duke of Bretaygne, who susteynd the traytour syr Peter of Craon. *a* **1578** LINDESAY (Pitscottie) *Chron. Scot.* (S.T.S.) I. 333 No man sould foster, succour or sustene no Douglasses withtin thair boundis. **1614** RALEIGH *Hist. World* v. i. §6. 349 The Romans resolue to sustaine him, and put themselues in order. **1697** DRYDEN *Æneid* VI. 1122 His Sons, who seek the Tyrant to sustain. **1711** in *10th Rep. Hist. MSS. Comm.* App. I. 143 They brought all the Grenadiers of their army, well sustain'd by a good body of other foot. **1757** W. WILKIE *Epigoniad* I. 16 While Thebes secure our vain attempts withstands, By daily aids sustain'd from distant lands. **1802** JAMES *Milit. Dict.* s.v., To sustain is to aid, succour, or support, any body of men in action, or defence.

†**b.** To uphold, back up, give support to (a person's conduct, a cause, a course of action). Also, to stand by (one's own action or conduct).

1297 R. GLOUC. (Rolls) 7354 þo willam hurde þat he wolde susteini is tricherie. *a* **1300** *Cursor M.* 29275 þam ..þat sustens..Fals trout gain cristen state. *c* **1368** CHAUCER *Compl. Pite* 111 And netheles yit my troth I shall susteen vnto my deth. *c* **1374** —— *Troylus* II. 1686, I wole right fayn with al my myght ben oon. Haue god my trouþe here cause to susteyne. **1483** CAXTON *Gold. Leg.* 154/2 He began to susteyn the feyth to whiche he had ben contrarye. *a* **1575** *Diurn. Occurr.* (Bannatyne Cl.) 281 Johne Knox minister requyrit the lordis to sustene ane book. quhairinto wes contenit that thaj suld ordane..xij superintendentis. **1671** FLAVEL *Fount. Life* vii. Wks. 1701 I. 44/1 His [*sc.* Christ's] Death and Sufferings..must respect others, whose Persons and Cause he sustained in that suffering Capacity. **1752** YOUNG *Brothers* III. i, I'll go; Sustain my part, and echo loud my wrongs.

c. Const. clause or (rarely) acc. and inf.: To support the contention or argument, maintain (that...). Now *rare*.

c **1366** CHAUCER *A.B.C.* 22 As bi riht þei mihten wel susteene. þat j were wurþi my dampnacioun. *c* **1380** WYCLIF *Sel. Wks.* III. 175 þes freres..seyde..þat it is an erroure to susteyne þat dymes ben pure almes. *a* **1450** *Knt. de la Tour* xii, Ther was moche speche whiche he shulde take, mani folke susteninge to take the elder [daughter]. **1456** SIR G. HAYE *Law Arms* (S.T.S.) 209 How it may be sustenyt that the king of Fraunce has na soverane. *c* **1550** R. BIESTON *Bayte Fortune* B ij, With wordes thou wouldest susteine that no good dede is doen without thee. **1609** HUME *Admonit.* in *Wodrow Soc. Misc.* (1844) 570 On the other part, otheris of you..sustene, that, among pastoris, thair sould be imparitie. **1678** G. MACKENZIE *Crim. Laws Scot.* I. xi. §3. (1699) 59 The Justices would not sustain, *minæ per se*, to be a sufficient qualification of self-defence. **1899** *Westm. Gaz.* 8 Sept. 3/1 What patriotic Englishman can for a moment sustain that [etc.]?

2. To uphold the validity or rightfulness of; to support as valid, sound, correct, true, or just.

1415 HOCCLEVE *To Sir J. Oldcastle* 183 Fro Cryst þat right first greew, & if þat we Nat shuln susteene it, we been ful vnwyse. **1425** *Rolls of Parlt.* IV. 271/2 Such possession..ought not to be sustened ne affermed. **1689** *Sc. Acts Will. & Mary* (1875) XII. 47/2 The objectione þerafter putt to the vote and sustained to reject the Commissione be 24 votes. **1754** in *Nairne Peerage Evid.* (1874) 60 [They] sustained and hereby sustain the claim and fand and hereby find that she is a just and lawful creditor. **1756** C. LUCAS *Ess. Waters* II. 67 In the Thesis which I sustained for the degrees in physic at Leyden. **1793** LD. ESKGROVE in Lockhart *Scott* (1837) I. vii. 215 Sustain the Sheriff's judgment, and decern. **1807** LD. ELDON in Vesey *Reports* (1827) XIII. 601 The trustee, having..proved, that he had removed himself from the character of trustee, his purchase may be sustained. **1855** *Poultry Chron.* III. 412 If an objection be made to any entry as being a false one, and such objection be sustained within ten days.

3. To keep (a person or community, the mind, spirit, etc.) from failing or giving way.

13.. *Minor Poems fr. Vernon MS.* xxxii. 984 þat sacrament reconsileþ him ay, Susteyneþ him, þat he ne falle may. *c* **1386** CHAUCER *Man of Law's T.* 62, I prey to god in honour hire susteene. *a* **1400–50** *Wars Alex.* 1749 All þe gracious godis & gudnes..þat..sustaynes þe erth. **1535** COVERDALE *Ps.* iii. 6, I layed me downe and slepte, but I rose vp agayne, for the Lorde susteyned me. **1662** ROWLEY *Birth Merlin* I. ii. 10 That hope alone sustains me. **1742** YOUNG *Nt. Th.* IV. 401 He tunes My voice (if tun'd); the nerve, that writes, sustains. **1837** LOCKHART *Scott* III. x. 334 [He] who, more perhaps than any other master of the pen, had contributed to sustain the spirit of England throughout the struggle. **1843** WORDSW. *Grace Darling* 49 Inwardly sustained by silent prayer.

4. To keep in being; to cause to continue in a certain state; to keep or maintain at the proper level or standard; to preserve the status of.

c **1290** *St. Kath.* 68 in *S. Eng. Leg.* 94 þis Aumperour sende..is sonde þat þe gretteste maistres of clergie to him comen..for to susteinen op heore lawe þoru strencþe of clergie. *c* **1290** *Beket* 1605 *ibid.* 152 He þat sosteinez vuele lawes. **1297** R. GLOUC. (Rolls) 6507 He..muche louede holi chirche & susteinede al so. *Ibid.* 7697 No time nas þet þes bet isusteined þan bi his time was. **1340** *Ayenb.* 57 þo þet þe tauernes sustyeneþ byeþ uelaȝes of alle þe zennen þat byeþ y-do ine hare tauernes. **1377** LANGL. *P. Pl.* B. IX. 108 Trewe wedded libbing folk..mote worche & wynne & þe worlde susteyne. *c* **1386** CHAUCER *Man of Law's T.* 294 The honour of his regne to susteene. *c* **1430** LYDG. *Min. Poems* (Percy Soc.) 210 Trewe juges and sergeauntis of the lawe,..Holde trouthe and sustene rightwisnesse. **1483** CAXTON *Cato* d j, He deyed for to holde and susteyne the lawe and trowthe. **1590** SPENSER *F.Q.* II. ii. 40 That great Queene..That with her soueraigne powre,..All Faery lond does peaceably sustene. **1666** DRYDEN *Ann. Mirab.* xlvii, Two Chiefs..Each able to sustain a Nations fate. **1697** —— *Æneid* I. 400 Remus with Quirinus shall sustain The righteous Laws. **1700** PRIOR *Carm. Sec.* 10 Happy Pow'r sustain'd by wholesom Laws. **1836** J. GILBERT *Chr. Atonem.* vi. (1852) 154 The rule of good, no longer enforced by its proper penalties, requires to be sustained by some equivalent expedient. **1841** MYERS *Cath. Th.* IV. §45. 406 If it [*sc.* Protestantism] has destroyed much it has also created much, and is now sustaining much. **1875** MANNING *Mission Holy Ghost* viii. 211 We are creatures who have come forth from His omnipotence, and are sustained by His almighty power.

5. a. To keep going, keep up (an action or process, †*occas.* a material object); to keep up without intermission; (with mixture of sense 8 or 9), to carry on (a conflict, contest).

c **1330** *Arth. & Merl.* (Kölbing) 9926 Four geauntes,..þat sustend þat bataile. **1405** *Lay Folks Mass Bk.* (1879) 65 Any other anourment whare-wit godes seruys es sustend. *c* **1407** LYDG. *Reason & Sens.* 771 Vertu sensityf..hir quarel doth sustene Ageyns hir ful Rigorously. *c* **1420** ? LYDG. *Assembly of Gods* 1093 Whyle these pety-capteynes susteynyd thus the feelde. *c* **1450** *Godstow Reg.* 602, ij lampes to be susteyned with oyle. **1500–20** DUNBAR *Poems* xlvii. 22 To turne to trew luve his intent, And still the quarrell to sustene. **1544** BETHAM *Precepts War* I. lxxvii. E ij, Men refreshed wyth hote meates, bene hable to susteyne battayle an whole daye. **1553** PAYNELL tr. *Dares' Phryg. Destr. Troy* F ij, Aiax Thelamonius valiantly sustained yᵉ thinge vntill the night departed yᵉ battel. **1697** DRYDEN *Virg. Past.* III. 86 Menalcas shall sustain his under Song. **1760–2** GOLDSM. *Cit. W.* xci, Their perseverance is beyond what any other nation is capable of sustaining. *a* **1774** —— *Hist. Greece* I. 292 At last, the Athenian fleet, after sustaining a long battle, ..was put to flight. **1816** SCOTT *Old Mort.* xxxvi, He felt no sort of desire..to sustain a correspondence which must be perilous. **1817** JAS. MILL *Brit. India* IV. v. II. 205 It was the severest conflict which the English had yet sustained with an Indian army. **1827** FARADAY *Chem. Manip.* iv. (1842) 96 The fire is lighted by a piece of brown paper and a little small coal, and is sustained..with coke and small coal. **1848** DICKENS *Dombey* xxx, The conversation was almost entirely sustained by Mrs. Skewton. **1850** HAWTHORNE *Scarlet L.* iii. (1879) 71 By the Indian's side, and evidently sustaining a companionship with him. **1875** JOWETT *Plato* (ed. 2) III. 46 The arts by which he sustains the reader's interest. **1883** GROVE *Dict. Mus.* III. 638/1 Comical..effects might be got by sustaining such sounds as 'z-z'..'r-r'..or 'ü'. *Ibid.* 639/1 By giving the piano-forte this power of sustaining sound, the special character of the instrument is transformed.

†**b.** To maintain the use, exercise, or occupation of. *Obs.*

1601 B. JONSON *Poetaster* IV. vi, If you thinke gods but fain'd, and vertue painted, Know, we sustaine an actuall residence. **1612** CHAPMAN *Rev. Bussy d'Ambois* III. iv. 5 Since I see You still sustain a jealous eye on me. **1623** *Shakspere's Wks.* Ep. Ded., When we valew the places your H. H. sustaine.

†**6. a.** To support life in; to provide for the life or bodily needs of; to furnish with the necessaries of life; to keep. *Obs.*

c **1290** *St. Edmund* 552 in *S. Eng. Leg.* 447 Swiþe faire under-fongue, And isusteyned in his anuy. **1297** R. GLOUC. (Rolls) 2354 He nadde noȝt inou is kniȝtes to soustene. *Ibid.* 7755 Hom þoȝte in engelond so muche folc neuere nas þat it was wonder ware þoru isousteined it was. **1340–70** *Alex. & Dind.* 797 Alle þe godus þat ȝe geten..Seruen for to sustaine ȝour vnsely wombe. **1377** LANGL. *P. Pl.* B. xv. 275 þorw þe mylke of þat mylde best þe man was susteyned. *c* **1400** MAUNDEV. (Roxb.) xv. 68 Of concubines ilke man takes als many as he may sustene of his gudes. *Ibid.* xxxii. 145 Meet and drink wharwith þe feble body myght be susteynd. **1483** CAXTON *Cato* A iij b, Thou oughtest to loue thy fader and moder nexte after god, and to..susteyne them in theyr necessytees. **1653** HAMMOND *On Matth. iv. 4.* 21 Bread or ordinary means of susteining men. **1667** MILTON *P.L.* v. 415 Whatever was created, needs To be sustaind and fed. *a* **1700** EVELYN *Diary* 26 Oct. 1685, The daughter of a poore labouring man, who had sustain'd her parents..by her labour.

†**b.** Said of the means of support. *Obs.*

1538 STARKEY *England* (1878) 75 Other cuntreys in lyke space or les, dothe susteyn much more pepul then dothe thys ourys. *a* **1578** LINDESAY (Pitscottie) *Chron. Scot.* (S.T.S.) I. 3 Ane hes that micht ane hundreith weill susteine. **1615** G. SANDYS *Trav.* 7 Their territories though large and fruitfull, too narrow to sustaine so populous a State. **1697** DRYDEN *Virg. Georg.* II. 743 Enough remains..His Wife and tender Children to sustain.

†**c.** *refl.* To keep oneself; *occas.* to take food, feed. *Obs.*

a **1300** in *E.E.P.* (1862) 20 Sum þer beþ þat swinkiþ sore winnе catel to hab more ham silf fair to susteni. **1380** in *Eng. Gilds* (1870) 40 He may nought ne haue nouȝthe to susteyne him self. ? *a* **1550** *Freiris Berwik* 226 in *Dunbar's Poems* (1893) 293 That na apperance of feist be heir sene, Bot sobirly our selffis dois sustene. **1640–1** *Kirkcudbr. War-Comm. Min. Bk.* (1855) 157 Thair..families are reducit to extreme miserie..not haveing quhairupon to sustein thame. **1650** W. D. tr. *Comenius' Gate Lat. Unl.* §385 A husbandman that..mainteineth (susteineth) himself with the crop (incom) of his yearly corn.

†**d.** To support (life, nature) with necessaries.

1402 *Pol. Poems* (Rolls) II. 17 Neither they tillen ne sowen,..neither nothing that man should helpe, but only themselves, their lives to susteine. **1483** CAXTON *Cato* h j b, Thou oughtest not to requyre..of god but that whyche is vtyle and prouffytable for to susteyn nature humayn. **1591** SYLVESTER *Du Bartas* I. iii. 694 O sacred simples that our life sustain. **1697** DRYDEN *Virg. Georg.* IV. 82 They..labour Honey to sustain their Lives.

†**e.** To supply (a person's need). *Obs. rare.*

1601 SHAKS. *Twel. N.* IV. ii. 135 Ile be with you againe: In a trice, like to the old vice, Your neede to sustaine.

†**7.** To provide for the upkeep of (an institution, establishment, estate, etc.). *Obs.*

1338 R. BRUNNE *Chron.* (1810) 20 þre þousand marke he gaf..To Petir & Paule of Rome, to susteyn þer light. **1431** *Rec. St. Mary at Hill* (1905) 15 That the same Wardeyns & their Successours fynde & susteyn v tapers of wexe..to brenne vpon my candylstyk. *c* **1450** *Godstow Reg.* 491 And they shold susteyne the seid mese, with ther owne costis, in al so good state or better than they resceived hit. **1544** tr. *Littleton's Tenures* I. viii. 16 Yf a house be let, to holde at wyl, the lessee is nat holden to susteyne or repayre the house. **1592** WEST *1st Pt. Symbol.* §103 C, The saide J. shall well.. sustaine & maintaine the houses & buildings which be.. builded.

8. a. To endure without failing or giving way; to bear up against, withstand.

c **1330** *Arth. & Merl.* (Kölbing) 7152, & he bihinde to ben bi cas, To susten þe paiems ras. **1382** WYCLIF *1 Cor.* xiii. 7 Charite..hopith alle thingis, it susteyneth alle thingis. *a* **1400** CHAUCER *Merciles Beaute* 2 Your yen two wol slee me sodenly, I may the beautè of hem not sustene. **1474** CAXTON *Chesse* I. ii. (1883) 12 The euyll lyf..of the kynge is the lyf of a cruell beste and ought not longe to be susteyned. **1577** GOOGE tr. *Heresbach's Husb.* 125 Asses..able to susteyn blowes, labour, hunger, and thyrst. **1667** MILTON *P.L.* II. 209 This is now Our doom; which if we can sustain and bear, Our Supream Foe in time may much remit His anger. **1817** JAS. MILL *Brit. India* IV. viii. II. 281 He sustained the attack, which, for the space of an hour was vigorously maintained. **1849** MACAULAY *Hist. Eng.* iii. I. 290 Scarce one [of the cities] was now capable of sustaining a siege. **1875** JOWETT *Plato* (ed. 2) V. 263 There is no soul of man..who will be able to sustain the temptation of arbitrary power. **1889** A. R. WALLACE *Darwinism* (1890) 17 Each species [of plant] can sustain a certain amount of heat and cold.

b. †*intr.* (also with *it*) To bear up, hold out (*obs.*). Also occas. *refl.*

1382 WYCLIF *Ps.* cxxix. [cxxx.] 3 If wickidnessis thou shalt al aboute kepe, Lord; Lord, who shal sustene? **1382** —— *Isaiah* lxiv. 3 Whan thou shalt do merueiles, wee shuln not sustene. **1412–20** LYDG. *Chron. Troy* IV. 2029 *heading*, The Troyans and þe Grekes resumede the felde, in þe which the Grekis might not susteyne against þe swerde of Troylus. **1546** LANGLEY tr. *Pol. Verg. De Invent.* I. iii. 5 Other that suppose this worlde had both an originall cause of being, and shall also sustein and ende by putrifaccion. **1573** *Satir. Poems Reform.* xli. 139 In deid that ȝe suld not susteind [= sustain it] He thunderit threitnings to the air. **1598** CHAPMAN *Iliad* II. 287 Sustaine a little then my friendes, that we the trueth may trie: Of reuerend Chalchas prophesy. **1864** TENNYSON *Aylmer's F.* 544 Tho' Averill wrote And bad him with good heart sustain himself.

c. *trans.* To bear, stand the force of (criticism, etc.).

1790 GIBBON *Misc. Wks.* (1814) III. 502 Their opinion will not sustain the rigour of critical enquiry. **1855** MACAULAY *Hist. Eng.* xii. III. 142 The Cathedral..ill qualified to sustain a comparison with the awful temples of the middle ages.

9. a. To undergo, experience, have to submit to (evil, hardship, or damage; now chiefly with *injury*, *loss* as obj., †formerly also *sorrow*, *death*); to have inflicted upon one, suffer the infliction of.

In mod. journalistic use (orig. *U.S.*), to suffer the injury of (a broken limb, or the like).

c **1400** *Destr. Troy* 7179 Why Sustayn ye þat sorow, þat Sewes for euer..? Why proffer ye not pes, or ye payne thole? *c* **1407** LYDG. *Reason & Sens.* 3570 Iason..Fortunyd was for to sustene Al the pereils oon by oon. **1426** in *Surtees Misc.* (1890) 10 After þe grete losses þat I have had and sustened. **1531** ELYOT *Gov.* I. xxvi, The most noble emperour Octauius Augustus,..only for playing at dise and that but seldome, sustaineth a note of reproche. **1542–3** *Act 34 & 35 Hen. VIII*, c. 3, The Offendoures..to susteyne suche further punisshement as shall seme expedient. **1555** EDEN *Decades* (Arb.) 122 The princes are determyned noo longer to susteyne theyr oppressions. **1582** N. LICHEFIELD tr. *Castanheda's Conq. E. Ind.* I. ii. 6 In which time they susteined many and great tempests. **1583** STUBBES *Anat. Abus.* II. (1882) 62 The host of Pharao..who all sustained one kinde of death. **1601** SHAKS. *Twel. N.* I. v. 186 Good Beauties, let mee sustaine no scorne. **1628** DIGBY *Voy. Medit.* (Camden) 3 If either should chance to breake or spring mast or yarde or sustayne any leake or other damage. **1653** R. SANDERS *Physiogn.*, *Moles* 13 She shall sustain thefts, and suffer by fugitive servants. *a* **1700** EVELYN *Diary* 21 Sept. 1674, I went to see the greate losse that Lord Arlington had sustain'd by fire at Goring house. **1771** GOLDSM. *Hist. Eng.* IV. 163 He died of a gangrene, occasioned by the bruises which he had sustained. **1793** SMEATON *Edystone L.* §322 The storms which the building had now sustained, without material damage. **1823** SCOTT *Quentin D.* xvii, He was relating the story of the bastinading which he had sustained. **1825** —— *Betrothed* xiii, Recollecting the loss she had so lately sustained on that luckless spot. **1833** HT. MARTINEAU *Three Ages* ii. 46 His Majesty had sustained a signal defeat abroad. **1865** MORLEY *Mod. Characteristics* 62 A provincial hostess, whose entertainment has gone off flatly, sustains about as much mortification as if her first-born had been attacked by the small-pox. **1880** *Troy* (U.S.) *Daily Times* 28 Aug., [He] fell from a pile of lumber yesterday afternoon and sustained a broken arm.

†*const. inf.* **1559** AYLMER *Harborowe* N iij b, Was it no wronge..that she susteyned..to be first a prysoner..and garded with a sorte of cutthrotes?

†**b.** With neutral obj. *Obs.*

1575 GASCOIGNE *Glasse Govt.* Wks. 1910 II. 9 Having susteyned like adventures. **1577** HARRISON *England* II. ii. (1877) I. 47 Shireburne also susteined the sub-diuision. **1663** *Rec. Meeting of Exercise, Alford* (1897) 9 Mr. John Mair sustained his questionarie tryall, and his tryall in the Languages, and is approven. **1697** DRYDEN *Virg. Georg.* I. 73 That Crop..Which twice the Sun, and twice the Cold sustains. *Ibid.* III. 99 The Bull's Insult at Four she [*sc.* the cow] may sustain.

c. To bear (a burden, charge); †to bear (expense).

1433 *Rolls of Parlt.* IV. 425/1 Ye charges yat he most bere and susteigne. **1530** in W. H. Turner *Select. Rec. Oxford* (1880) 89 The Towne susteyneth nott one peny of the sayd charges. **1533** BELLENDEN *Livy* II. iv. (S.T.S.) I. 142 He was sa fer rvn in age, þat he mycht nocht sustene þe charge of þe consulate. **1601** R. JOHNSON *Kingd. & Commw.* (1603) 196 Neither coulde the King of Spaine sustaine the burden of so many warres. **1651** HOBBES *Leviath.* II. xxiv. 129 That such portion [in the distribution of land] be made sufficient, to susteine the whole expence to the common Peace. **1738** WESLEY *Hymns* LXXIII. iv, The Burthen for me to sustain Too great, on Thee, my Lord, was laid. **1833** HT. MARTINEAU *Manch. Strike* ix. 106 It has enabled us to sustain burdens which would have crushed any other people.

d. To support (a part or character); to play the part of. Also *occas.* to bear (a title).

1560 DAUS tr. *Sleidane's Comm.* 107 Where as they susteyne the persones of intercessours. **1588** KYD *Househ. Philos.* Wks. (1901) 252 [He] ought principally to haue care in choosing of his wife, with whom hee must sustaine the persoune of a Husbande. **1596** DALRYMPLE tr. *Leslie's Hist. Scot.* I. 116 Thay susteine the persone of honest sitizenis. **1643** PRYNNE *Sov. Power Parl.* App. 198 Christ our Saviour who although he were the King of Kings, yet because he then sustained a private person, he payed tribute willingly **1700** WALLIS in *Collect.* (O.H.S.) I. 325 From him that.. sustains that title. **1731** A. HILL (in *Sotheran's Catal.* No. 12. (1899) 26), I am at a loss, how those characters will be sustain'd w[ch] they were to have represented. **1782** COWPER *Parrot* 35 Each character in ev'ry part Sustain'd with so much grace and art. **1884** *Encycl. Brit.* XVII. 88/1 It was in that very opera, *The Siege of Rhodes*, that Mrs. Colman, daughter-in-law of one of the composers, sustained the character of Ianthe. **1939** JOYCE *Finnegans Wake* 49 He may have been the utility man of the troupe capable of sustaining long parts at short notice. **1975** *U.S. News & World Rep.* 3 Mar. 39/2 Students of geopolitics assert that the U.S. has a near-perfect combination to sustain such a role. **1980** M. FONTEYN *Magic of Dance* 312 These ballets seem essential to theatre dance as a whole because they stretch the artist's interpretive powers to the limit in sustaining long roles. **1983** *Financial Times* 16 Feb. 13/4 The solid-voiced baritone Roland Herrmann sustained the killing role of Creon with burly resilience.

†**10.** Const. inf., or acc. and inf., chiefly in negative, conditional, or interrog. use: To reconcile oneself to doing, to bear to do, something; to tolerate or bear that something should be done.

14.. in *Tundale's Vis.* (1843) 113 O who is alas that may sustene To be prowd, consider her mekenes. **1426** LYDG. *De Guil. Pilgr.* 4432, I swepe, I make yt clene, For fylthe noon I may sustene Ther tabyde. **1540–1** ELYOT *Image Gov.* xxvi. 58 b, She coulde not susteyne hyr sonnes wyfe to be called Augusta. **1567** *Gude & Godlie B.* (S.T.S.) 110 We may not sustene To heir thame say, [etc.]. **1700** DRYDEN *Ceyx & Alc.* 19 Can Ceyx then sustain to leave his Wife? *a* **1726** SEWELL *Rich. I* II, He who leads Armies in the Cause of Heaven..Yet can sustain to wrong a King—a Friend.

11. a. To hold up, bear the weight of; to keep from falling by support from below; often simply, to carry, bear. † Also with *up*. Now *rare.*

a **1330** *Roland & V.* 338 Mahoun..dede mani fendes þer in..For to susten þe ymage, & sett him on heiȝe stage. **1390** GOWER *Conf.* III. 108 Whos condicion Is set to be the foundament To sustiene up the firmament. **1470–85** MALORY *Arthur* XVI. ii. 667 Gawayne..lepte vp behynde hym for to sustene hym. **1481** CAXTON *Myrr.* I. xvi. 50 That one [of the four elements] susteyned that other in suche manere, as therthe holdeth hym in the myddle. **1590** SPENSER *F.Q.* II. x. 43 Next whom Morindus did the crowne sustaine. **1592** KYD *Sp. Trag.* II. i. 3 In time the sauuage Bull sustaines the yoake. **1594** —— *Cornelia* II. 339 What e're the massie Earth hath fraight, Or on her nurse-like backe sustaines. **1606** SHAKS. *Ant. & Cl.* III. xi. 45 Well then, sustaine me: Oh. **1697** DRYDEN *Virg. Georg.* III. 256 To harrow Furrows, and sustain the Plough. **1756** E. MOORE *Trial Selim* 27 Her left hand clench'd, her cheek sustain'd **1759** TOPLADY *Poems* (1860) 96 Each a Palm sustain'd In his victorious Hand. **1794** MRS. RADCLIFFE *Myst. Udolpho* xxvi, Here again she looked round for a seat to sustain her. **1831** SCOTT *Cast. Dang.* viii, He found the minstrel seated at a small table, sustaining before him a manuscript. **1832** BREWSTER *Nat. Magic* x. 253 The difficulty..really consists in sustaining the anvil. **1850** MRS. JAMESON *Leg. Monast. Ord.* (1863) 394 Sustained in the arms of two sisters of her Order.

fig. **1390** GOWER *Conf.* III. 136 Pes sustiened up alofte With esy wordes and with softe Wher strengthe scholde lete it falle. **1620** T. GRANGER *Div. Logike* 66 The Adiunct receiued of the Subiect by inherence is infixed, infused, ingrafted, sustained of the subiect.

b. To be the support of, as in a structure or building; to have resting upon it.

c **1386** CHAUCER *Knt.'s T.* 1135 For to make it strong Euery pyler the temple to sustene. *c* **1489** CAXTON *Sonnes of Aymon* xxiv. 505 A forke that susteyned vp their lodges, that was grete and stronge. **1611** CORYAT *Crudities* 325 Two exceeding great Lyons in red marble, that sustaine two goodly pillars. **1697** DRYDEN *Æneid* x. 1189 A Bough his Brazen Helmet did sustain. *a* **1700** EVELYN *Diary* 12 July 1654, The ample Hall and columne that spreads its capital to sustaine the roofe. **1717** PRIOR *Alma* II. 277 The swelling Hoop sustains The rich Brocard. **1784** COWPER *Task* IV. 544 Her head..Indebted to some smart wig-weaver's hand For more than half the tresses it sustains. **1828** SCOTT *F.M. Perth* xxiii, The bier was so placed as to leave the view of the body it sustained open [etc.]. **1856** STANLEY *Sinai & Pal.* x. (1858) 365 The Galilean hills..contain or sustain green basins of table-land just below their topmost ridges.

c. To bear, support, withstand (a weight or pressure). Also in fig. context.

c **1386** CHAUCER *Prioress' T.* 31 My konnyng is so wayk.. That I ne may the weighte nat susteene. **1697** DRYDEN *Virg. Georg.* I. 164 Lest the Stem..Shou'd scarce sustain the Head's unweildy weight. **1774** GOLDSM. *Nat. Hist.* (1776) VI. 91 Though they have but a small weight of body to sustain. **1781** COWPER *Flatting Mill* 9 This process achiev'd, it is doom'd to sustain The thump after thump of a gold-beater's mallet. **1800** VINCE *Hydrost.* ii. (1806) 23 The same pressure must sustain the same weight. **1836** J. GILBERT *Chr. Atonem.* ix. (1852) 268 This external pressure has nothing substantial to sustain it from within. **1860** TYNDALL *Glac.* II. xxx. 404 When the pressure applied becomes too great for the glass to sustain, it flies to pieces.

†**d.** To hold in position, hold erect, etc.; also, to be sufficient to bear the weight of. *Obs.*

1398 TREVISA *Barth. De P.R.* V. xxv. (Bodl. MS.), þe nekke..bereþ and susteyneþ þe heed. **1481** CAXTON *Myrr.* II. xvii. 104 The quyck syluer is of suche nature..that it susteyneth a stone vpon it. **1538** STARKEY *England* (1878) 49 Bycause they [*sc.* the feet] by theyr labour susteyne and support the rest of the body. **1599** ALEX. HUME *Hymns* II. 81 The feit ar swift and members meit, for to susteine the rest. **1668** CULPEPPER & COLE *Barthol. Anat.* IV. vii. 165 If all eight [muscles] act, they hold the Back straight, and do as it were sustain a man.

†**e.** *refl.* and *intr.* To hold oneself upright; also, to be in or maintain a fixed position. *Obs.*

c **1374** CHAUCER *Anel. & Arc.* 177 She ne hath foot on which she may sustene. *c* **1450** *Merlin* 354 He myght no lenger sustene on his feet for the traueile. **1604** SHAKS. *Oth.* V. ii. 260 Behold, I haue a weapon: A better neuer did it selfe sustaine Vpon a Soldiers Thigh. **1728** R. MORRIS *Ess. Anc. Archit.* 35 The Solidity becomes of less Power to sustain in Proportion to its Height.

†**f.** Const. inf. To have sufficient strength to do, be equal to doing, something. *Obs.*

1430–40 LYDG. *Bochas* IX. ii. (MS. Bodl. 263) 408/1 To stonde upriht he myhte nat susteene. **1481** CAXTON *Myrr.* I. xv. 50 No bodyly man may not susteyne for to see hym [*sc.* an angel] in no manere.

12. To be adequate as a ground or basis for. (Cf. SUPPORT *v.* 3 c.)

1828–32 WEBSTER s.v., The testimony or the evidence is not sufficient to sustain the action, the accusation, the charges, or the impeachment. **1866** SEELEY *Ecce Homo* v (ed. 8) 40 We go beyond what the evidence is able to sustain. **1869** J. MARTINEAU *Ess.* II. 361 This passage undoubtedly sustains Mr. Grote's assertion.

¶ **13.** To wait for. (A literalism of translation.)

1382 WYCLIF *Ecclus.* xxxvi. 18 ȝif meede, Lord, to men sustenende thee. **1382** —— *Mark* viii. 2 Now the thridde day thei susteynen [*gloss* or abyden] me.

sustainable (səˈsteɪnəb(ə)l), *a.* [f. prec. + -ABLE. Cf. SUSTENABLE.]

†**1.** Capable of being borne or endured; supportable, bearable. *Obs. rare.*

1611 COTGR., *Soustenable*, sustainable,..abideable.

2. Capable of being upheld or defended; maintainable.

1845–6 DE QUINCEY *Gilfillan's Lit. Portr.* Wks. 1859 XII. 304 From the verdict of a jury,..no candid and temperate man will allow himself to believe any appeal sustainable. **1857** TOULMIN SMITH *Parish* 130 It is the duty of the constable to apprehend offenders taken in the fact, or on sustainable presumption. **1875** *N. Amer. Rev.* CXX. 463 Religion may be morally useful without being intellectually sustainable. **1884** *Law Rep.* 27 *Chanc. Div.* 69 The Defendant has taken several technical objections to the order, none of which..are sustainable.

3. Capable of being maintained at a certain rate or level.

1965 *McGraw-Hill Dict. Mod. Econ.* 501 *Sustainable growth*, a rise in per-capita real income or per capita real gross national product that is capable of continuing for a long time. A condition of sustainable economic growth means that economic stagnation will not set in. **1971** *Nature* 9 July 80/2 The blue whale could have supplied indefinitely a sustainable yield of 6,000 individuals a year. **1976** *Times* 4 Aug. 3/8 The achievement of a sustainable, stationary population.

Hence **sustainaˈbility**.

1972 T. SOWELL *Say's Law* iii. 100 An increase beyond limits of sustainability existing at any given time would lead only to reduced earnings and subsequent contraction of the quantity supplied. **1980** *Jrnl. R. Soc. Arts* July 495/2 Sustainability in the management of both individual wild species and ecosystems..is critical to human welfare.

sustained (səˈsteɪnd), *ppl. a.* [f. SUSTAIN *v.* + -ED[1].]

1. a. Kept up without intermission or flagging; maintained through successive stages or over a long period; kept up or maintained at a uniform (esp. a high) pitch or level.

1796 BURKE *Regic. Peace* i. Wks. 1907 VI. 144 A vehement and sustained spirit of fortitude. **1816** SCOTT *Old Mort.* xxxii, His marksmen, commencing upon the pass a fire as well aimed as it was sustained and regular. **1837** CARLYLE *Fr. Rev.* I. IV. iv, Next day, with sustained pomp, they are.. installed in their *Salle des Menus*. **1853** LYTTON *My Novel* XII. xxxiii, Harley's compassion vanished before this sustained hypocrisy. **1860** *All Year Round* No. 67. 396 Mr. Hyde Clarke is the only man who has attempted a sustained biography of him. **1873** SYMONDS *Grk. Poets* v. 126 The Dorian poets, inspired by a graver and more sustained imagination, composed long and complex odes.

b. *sustained yield* (orig. *Forestry*): the quantity that can be periodically harvested from a crop or population without depleting it in the long term; also *attrib.*

1919 RECKNAGEL & BENTLEY *Forest Management* xii. 124 By sustained yield is understood the yield or cut of timber from a forest which is managed in such a way as to permit the removal of an approximately equal volume of timber, annually or periodically, equal to the increment. **1980** PURDOM & ANDERSON *Environmental Sci.* ix. 219/1 Foresters are finding the sustained yield method, which produces a modest annual timber crop, increasingly more desirable. *Ibid.* x. 245/2 The goal of the fishing industry should be to establish a sustained yield. Closed seasons, catch quotas, nets with larger mesh size, and minimum fish size can help achieve a sustained yield.

c. ***sustained-release*** *a.* (*Pharm.*): applied to a preparation that releases a substance slowly or intermittently into the bloodstream over a period so as to maintain a steady concentration of it, esp. by means of numerous tiny pellets with different coatings contained in and administered orally as a single capsule. Cf. *slow-release* adj. b s.v. SLOW *a.* 16 d, SPANSULE.

1956 *Jrnl. Pharmacy & Pharmacol.* VIII. 975 It was thought that these resins might provide suitable chemical carriers for drugs in sustained release preparations. **1974** SHOTTON & RIDGWAY *Physical Pharmaceutics* xii. 340 Sustained release products can be made by embedding the drug in a hydrophobic matrix from which it is leached out over a period of time. **1979** *Arizona Daily Star* 8 Apr. C10/1 (Advt.), Most products provide short-duration nutritional burst. *Heritage* sustained-release tablets work all day long, up to 12 hours, to release nutrients when you need them.

2. Of a note or tone: **a.** Maintained at the same pitch. *rare.*

1775 T. SHERIDAN *Art Reading* I. 197 That interruption ought to make no change in the proper manner of delivering it, which should be in a sustained note.

b. *Mus.* Maintained (in its full force) through its whole length; see also quot. 1876.

1801 BUSBY *Dict. Mus.* s.v., Notes are said to be *sustained* when their sound is continued through their whole power, or length. **1845** G. DODD *Brit. Manuf.* IV. 156 Unless..it were possible to obtain the sustained tones of the organ. **1876** STAINER & BARRETT *Dict. Mus. T., Sustained note*, a name given to prolonged notes which partake of the character of a pedal-point by their immunity from ordinary harmonic rules, but which cannot with propriety be called pedal-points owing to their occurrence in the middle or upper part.

3. Endured, borne.

1819 BYRON *Mazeppa* ii, This [horse] too sinks after many a league Of well sustain'd but vain fatigue.

4. *Her.* (See quot.)

1882 CUSSANS *Her.* 130 *Sustained*: Usually applied to a Chief or Fess, when a narrow fillet or fimbriation occupies the base of the Charge. This term is seldom used in modern Armory, nor..is it necessary.

Hence **su'stainedly** *adv.*, in a sustained manner.

1842 E. FITZGERALD *Lett.* (1889) I. 219, I think Beethoven is rather spasmodically, than sustainedly, grand. **1857** SPENCER *Ess.* (1858) I. 376 More consistently, more unitedly, and more sustainedly.

sustainer (sə'steɪnə(r)). Forms: 4 **sosteynere**, 5 **suste(y)nour, -tener**, 6- **sustainer**. [Partly a. AF. **sustenour*, OF. *sosteneor, sousteneur*, f. *sostenir* to SUSTAIN; partly directly f. SUSTAIN + -ER[1].] One who or that which sustains.

1. One who or that which upholds, supports, or keeps in being; an upholder, supporter.

a **1400** in *Eng. Gilds* (1870) 349 Principal sosteynere of þe fraunchyse. *c* **1412** HOCCLEVE *De Reg. Princ.* 2856 Honour, long lyfe,..Mot haue oure sustenour, our prince & kyng! **1429** *Rolls of Parlt.* IV. 360/1 Ye seid Inhabitauntz ben susteners and supportours. **1547–64** BAULDWIN *Mor. Philos.* (Palfr.) 126 The sustainers of wrong. *a* **1680** CHARNOCK *Attrib. God* (1682) 709 God is the Lord of all, as he is the sustainer of all by his power. **1726** BUTLER *Serm. Rolls* xiv. 288 When they shall have a Sensation, that He is the Sustainer of their Being, that they exist in him. **1845** *Encycl. Metrop.* II. 861/1 Almighty Creator and Sustainer of all things. **1909** *Q. Rev.* Apr. 657 The aim of our politics can be no other than that the Bohemian people should again become the sustainers of the idea of the State.

†**b.** *pl.* Military supports. *Obs. rare.*

1708 *Lond. Gaz.* No. 4468/2 [They] had for the Attack on the Right 800 Grenadiers,..and for the Left 1600 Grenadiers, with the like number of Sustainers.

c. A thing or circumstance that sustains a condition.

1818 SHELLEY *Rosal. & Helen* 337 The very hope of death's dear rest; Which, since the heart within my breast Of natural life was dispossessed, Its strange sustainer there had been. **1831** LYTTON *Godolphin* ix, It is not always a sustainer of the stage delusion to be enamoured of an actress.

2. †**a.** One who supports or holds a thing. *rare.*

c **1616** CHAPMAN *Homer's Hymn to Vesta & Merc.* 17 Of Heauens golden Rodd The sole Sustainer.

b. A supporting structure or device.

1893 *Westm. Gaz.* 25 Apr. 7/3 The weight of the carriage was 60lb., of the engine 200lb., and of the grating of sustainers 70lb. **1909** *Cent. Dict., Suppl., Sustainer*.., a little disk,..which serves to support in an upright position the wick of a night-light.

†**3.** A sufferer. *Obs. rare.*

c **1611** CHAPMAN *Iliad* XXIII. 524 Thy selfe, hast a sustainer bene Of much affliction in my cause.

4. One who provides another with the necessaries of life. *rare.*

1678 SIR G. MACKENZIE *Crim. Laws Scot.* I. xix. §16. (1699) 106 By sustainers, are meant such as entertain the Thief at bed and board. **1866** J. G. MURPHY *Comm. Exod.* xxii. 22 The decease of the father leaves both the widow and the child without their natural protector and sustainer.

su'staining, *vbl. sb.* [f. SUSTAIN *v.* + -ING[1].] The action of the verb SUSTAIN, in various senses; sustenance, maintenance, support, etc.

c **1383** in *Eng. Hist. Rev.* Oct. (1911) 749 Susteyninge [*sic*] of felowis bi forme of þe gospel þat ben able to performe þe office of þe gospel in good lyuynge. **1398** TREVISA *Barth. De P.R.* XVII. ii. (Bodl. MS.) lf. 188 b/1 For sadnes of þe.. grounde þe herbe hathe grenenes in rote and susteynynge of þe stalke in þee reringe þereof. *c* **1400** *Rom. Rose* 2765 Though he lye in strawe or dust, In Hoope is alle his susteynyng. *c* **1450** *Godstow Reg.* 393 They graunted to hym and to his wyf..a corrodye of one seruant to ther susteynynge. *Ibid.* 438 To the susteynyng of the masse of oure lady seynt marye. **1495** *Naval Acc. Hen. VII* (1896) 159 The Susteynyng & fortyfying of the seid dokke & gates of the same. **1541** COPLAND *Guydon's Quest. Cyrurg.* D ij, Demaunde. Wherfore are the bones made? Answere. Bycause they shulde be the foundacyon of all the body and susteynynge therof. **1593** SHAKS. *Lucr.* 1573 Short time seems long, in sorrowes sharp sustayning. **1607** HIERON *Wks.* I. 170 Without Whose gracious sustaining he should soone returne vnto his first nothing. **1726** LEONI *Alberti's Archit.* I. 76/1 Provisions necessary for the sustaining of a Siege. **1850** McCOSH *Div. Govt.* II. i. (1874) 89 Every one knows how needful the atmosphere is for the sustaining of animal and vegetable life. **1893** *Athenæum* 2 Dec. 767/3 The sustaining of her strong personality..is no easy task.

su'staining, *ppl. a.* [f. SUSTAIN *v.* + -ING[2].]

a. That sustains, in various senses; supporting.

1605 SHAKS. *Lear* IV. iv. 6 Darnell, and all the idle weedes that grow In our sustaining Corne. **1610** —— *Temp.* I. ii. 218 On their sustaining garments not a blemish, But fresher then before. **1817** SHELLEY *Rev. Islam* v. lvi. 6 Melons, and dates, and figs, and many a root Sweet and sustaining. **1820** —— *Prometh. Unb.* III. iii. 91 The many children fair Folded in my sustaining arms. **1828** D'ISRAELI *Chas. I*, I. vi. 163 Mary of Scotland was long the sustaining hope of France, of Spain, and of Rome. **1855** MACAULAY *Hist. Eng.* xv. III. 594 The sustaining power of high religious principle.

b. In technical use.

1839 NOAD *Electricity* iii. 105 The introduction of the 'sustaining' or 'constant' batteries of Messrs. Daniell and Mullins, has..entirely superseded the employment of these simple circles in electro-magnetic investigations. **1842** *Civil Eng. & Arch. Jrnl.* V. 95/1 The meaning of the technical terms of 'retaining' and 'sustaining' walls was—when a wall was used either to support water or earth artificially put together. *a* **1878** SIR G. SCOTT *Lect. Archit.* (1879) I. 281 A narrow vault..which is not necessarily of the same curvature as the sustaining arches.

c. ***sustaining pedal***, (*a*) (see PEDAL *sb.* 1 b); chiefly *U.S.*; (*b*) = *damper-pedal* s.v. DAMPER 8 a.

1889 in *Cent. Dict.* s.v. *Pedal.* **1911** H. E. KREHBIEL *Pianoforte & its Music* iii. 47 On some pianofortes there is a third pedal between the other two, called the Tone Sustaining Pedal, the action of which is to withhold the damper from the string or strings struck just before the depression of the pedal. **1922** A. H. LINDO *Pedalling in Pianoforte Music* I. 14 Students..are frequently told that it [*sc.* the right pedal] should be called, not the 'loud', but the 'sustaining' pedal. **1923** [see ACCENTUATOR]. **1931** G. JACOB *Orchestral Technique* i. 2 In transcribing pianoforte music the effect of the sustaining pedal is often not taken into account. **1976** *Gramophone* Dec. 1016/2 The Gieseking is.. an object-lesson..in how to do without the sustaining-pedal as a prop.

d. ***sustaining programme***, a radio or television programme which is paid for by the broadcasting station. *U.S.*

1931 F. A. ARNOLD *Broadcast Advertising* 31 Sustaining programs are those which are prepared and paid for exclusively by the broadcasting station and in which the advertiser has no participation whatever. **1952** H. L. EWBANK *Broadcasting* viii. 128 A *sustaining* program is neither paid for by a sponsor nor interrupted by spot commercials. **1961** S. P. LAWTON *Mod. Broadcaster* 85 The network contracts themselves,..and the agreements for carrying sustaining programs, all play an important part in the make-up of schedules of affiliate stations. **1973** J. R. GRIMES *Mod. Radio Programming* xii. 173 *Sustaining*, non-sponsored.

Hence **su'stainingly** *adv.*

1640 G. ABBOT *Job Paraphr.* Argt., A little chinke of light whereby he was able to see, and sustainingly to remind himselfe of God's former favours. **1875** *Toxie* I. vi. 101 Holding my soft gloved hand sustainingly to his side.

sustainment (sə'steɪnmənt). Also 5 **sustene-**. [In earliest quot. a. OF. *sus-, sostenement*, f. *sostenir* to SUSTAIN; later f. SUSTAIN *v.* + -MENT.]

1. Means of support; chiefly = SUSTENANCE 1, 2.

c **1450** *Merlin* xxix. 591 Whan Arthur hadde slain Magloras the kinge that was the sustenement of the saisnes. **1588** PARKE tr. *Mendoza's Hist. China* 351 They haue no other sustainment, but only that which this tree yeeldeth. **1670** MILTON *Hist. Eng.* III. Wks. 1851 V. 104 They betook them to the Woods, and liv'd by hunting, which was thir only sustainment.

2. The action of sustaining; *esp.* maintenance in being or activity, in a certain condition or at a certain level; sustentation. (Cf. SUSTENANCE 3.)

1568 HACKET tr. *Thevet's New found World* lxxxii. 135 b, They began to..till the earth, for to receiue the fruits therof for the sustainment of their liues. *a* **1680** CHARNOCK *Attrib. God* (1834) I. 459 God..not..receiving from any place any thing for his preservation or sustainment. **1816** *Q. Rev.* XV. 70 An unnatural and artificial sustainment of the language and imagery. **1833** J. MARTINEAU *Misc.* (1852) 45 In Priestley's case there was not merely a sustainment—but a positive advancement of character in later years. **1857** DICKENS *Lett.* (1880) II. 16 In an impossible attitude for the sustainment of its weight. **1876** LOWELL *Among my Bks.* Ser. II. 50 The Hebrew forerunners, in whose society his soul sought consolation and sustainment.

†**sustantive**, *a. Obs. rare.* In 5 -yf. [? irreg. formed as adj. to SUSTAIN; cf. SUSTENABLE.] Having the function of sustaining physical life.

c **1400** tr. *Secr. Secr., Gov. Lordsh.* 96 Strengthe nutrityf, and infirmatyf, and sustantyf [orig. *nutritiua informatiua & vegetatiua*]. þe wirkynge of þis last, þat þe Auctour clepys vegetatyf, & I here strenght sustantyf, [etc.].

†**sustenable**, *a. Obs.* Also 5 -tin-. [a. OF. *sus-, sostenable*, f. *sostenir* to SUSTAIN.]

1. Capable of being or that is maintained in physical life and growth: in quots. used as synonym for VEGETABLE *a.* 1.

c **1400** tr. *Secr. Secr., Gov. Lordsh.* 90 Some þinges vegetables or sustenables er..by sedys, & with-outen plantyng. *Ibid.* 95 þe composisioun vegitable þat is sustinable is mor noble þan þe originale.

2. Capable of being endured; = SUSTAINABLE *a.* 1.

1471 CAXTON *Recuyell* (Sommer) 320 Hys strookes were not sustenable.

†**sustenal.** *Obs. rare.* [a. OF. *soustenal*, f. *soustenir* to SUSTAIN: see -AL[1].] A support.

c **1400** *Pilgr. Sowle* (Caxton 1483) IV. xxxi. 80 The necke next vnder the hede is set aboue al the body ryght as the sustenal and the piler.

sustenance ('sʌstɪnəns). Forms: 3–4 **sustynance**, 3–6 **-tinaunce**, 4 **sust-**, **sostnaunce**, **sostinonce**, **-tenaunse**, **sustenauns**, 4–5 **-tiena(u)nce**, 4–6 **-ten-**, **-tynaunce**, 5 **-tinens**, **-tenence**, **-tenaunse**, 5–6 **-tinance**, 6 **-tynans**, **-tenans**, **-teynaunce**, **-tainance**, 7–8 **sustinence**, 3– **sustenance**. [a. AF. *sustenaunce*, OF. *sos-, soustenance*, mod.F. *soutenance* (= Pr. *sostenensa*, It. *sostenenza*, OPg. *sustinencia*; cf. late L. *sustinentia*), f. *sostenir* to SUSTAIN: see -ANCE.]

1. Means of living or subsistence; livelihood; †phr. ***to find, win (a) sustenance.***

1297 R. GLOUC. (Rolls) 975 Hii..swonke & tylede hor liflode..Hii founde hom sustenance inou & liuede þus vorþ. **1303** R. BRUNNE *Handl. Synne* 1326 Ȝyf þou þurgh wykked ordynaunce Fordost pore mannys sustynaunce þat aftyrward he may nat lyue. **13..** *Coer de L.* 3757 Kyng Richard gaff castels and touns, To hys eerlys and to barouns, To have therinne her sustynaunce. **13..** *Sir Beues* (A.) 3916 Iosian eueriche a day ȝede aboute þe cite wiþ inne, Here sostenaunse for to winne. *c* **1385** CHAUCER *L.G.W.* 2041 (*Ariadne*), And for myn sustenaunce, yet wil I swynk. *c* **1400** MAUNDEV. (Roxb.) vii. 24 In þis deserte I dwell and gase to gete my sustinaunce. *c* **1460** FORTESCUE *Abs. & Lim. Mon.* xviii. (1885) 154 þe clarkes off is chapell..[shall] be rewarded with pencions..ffor þer rewardes or sustenance. **1568** GRAFTON *Chron.* II. 350 To haue sufficient for their necessarie sustenance. **1687** A. LOVELL tr. *Thevenot's Trav.* I. 243 There is..all that is necessary for the Service of the Church, and the sorry sustenance of the Religious. **1710** PRIDEAUX *Orig. Tithes* i. 30 They reap from them a sustenance in Earthly things. **1836** W. IRVING *Astoria* I. 2 It was the fur trade..which gave early sustenance and vitality to the great Canadian provinces. **1864** TENNYSON *En. Ard.* 258 She..Gain'd for her own a scanty sustenance.

2. Means of sustaining life; food, victuals.

c **1290** *St. Francis* 229 in *S. Eng. Leg.* 60 Miseyse huy hadden þare i-noȝ..For defaute of heore sustinaunce and for defaute of bokes. **13..** *Gaw & Gr. Knt.* 1095 Nauþer of sostnaunce ne of slepe, soþly I knowe. **1377** LANGL. *P. Pl.* B. xx. 7 To clothes and to sustenance. **1390** GOWER *Conf.* II. 83 The cornes and the wynes Ben sustenance to mankinde. **1470–85** MALORY *Arthur* VII. xxvi. 253 Many..merueilled that he desyred his sustenaunce for a twelf monethe. *c* **1491** *Chast. Goddes Chyld.* 13 It is nedeful to take bodily sustenaunce..in resonable manere. **1549** LATIMER *Ploughers* (Arb.) 25 If the ploughemen..were..negligente ..we shoulde not longe lyue for lacke of sustinaunce. **1626** BACON *Sylva* §360 [The Chameleon] feedeth not onely vpon Aire, (though that be his principall Sustenance;) For sometimes hee taketh Flies. **1691** RAY *Creation* I. (1692) 71 Water is one part, and that not the least of our Sustenance. **1760–72** H. BROOKE *Fool of Qual.* (1809) II. 144 Having sold all our moveables..for sustenance. **1808** SCOTT in Lockhart *Life* I. i. 47, I had all the appetite of a growing boy, but was prohibited any sustenance beyond what was absolutely necessary for the support of nature. **1864** TENNYSON *En. Ard.* 550 No want was there of human sustenance, Soft fruitage, mighty nuts, and nourishing roots. **1873** BROWNING *Red Cott. Nt.-cap* II. 1103 Now dying and in want of sustenance!

†**b.** A kind or a quantity of food; *pl.* eatables.

c **1450** *Mirk's Festial* 254 þay..toke no hede what þat þay haden but a sympull sustenaunce. **1528** PAYNEL *Salerne's Regim.* D iij, Nothynge more dangerous than to myngle diuers sustinances to gether. **1615** G. SANDYS *Trav.* 89 Fortie saile of ships..by the trading whereof they bring in that sustenance which the soile affordeth not. **1677** in *Ray's Corr.* (1848) 128, I am apt to believe that water cannot be a competent sustenance for them.

c. *gen.* and *fig.* Nourishment.

c **1489** CAXTON *Sonnes of Aymon* xix. 437 They ete all a lityll therof, whiche gauf theim grete sustenaunse. **1577** GOOGE tr. *Heresbach's Husb.* I. (1586) 18 b, Those [thinges] that require more sustenaunce, are sowen in richer ground. **1671** MILTON *P.R.* I. 429 Lying is thy sustenance, thy food. **1686** W. HOPKINS tr. *Ratramnus* Dissert. v. (1688) 93 This Spiritual virtue [of the Sacrament]..ministering to it the sustenance of Eternal Life. **1742** YOUNG *Nt. Th.* v. 466 Some reject this sustenance divine. **1830** HERSCHEL *Study Nat. Phil.* 65 That dry bones could be a magazine of nutriment,..ready to yield up their sustenance in the form best adapted to the support of life. *a* **1831** A. KNOX *Rem.* (1844) I. 66 The taste once revived, its due sustenance would not be difficult to find. **1849** HELPS *Friends in C.* II. iv. 95 The plants draw most of their sustenance from the air.

3. The action of sustaining life by food; the action of supporting with the means of subsistence; the fact or state of being so sustained.

Tends to merge in sense 2.

c **1386** CHAUCER *Pars. T.* ¶298 Euery tyme that a man eteth or drynketh moore than suffiseth to the sustenaunce of his body. **1389** in *Eng. Gilds* (1870) 46 Ilke broþer and sistir shal ȝeuen..j.d to his sustenauns and releuynge. *c* **1400** *Brut* I. 11 Brut..done mow medes for sustinaunce of hym & of his peple. *a* **1513** FABYAN *Chron.* VI. (1533) 101/2 Other viii. houres he spent in his natural reste, sustinaunce of his body, & the nedes of the realme. **1538** STARKEY *England* (1878) 74 When ther ys of vytayl ouerlytyl for the necessary sustenans and maynteynyng of the same. **1586** B. YOUNG *Guazzo's Civ. Conv.* IV. 224 They take but small refection, a thing most natural for sustainance of life. **1719** DE FOE *Crusoe* I. (Globe) 78 That it was so directed purely for my Sustenance on that wild miserable Place. **1842** COMBE *Digestion* 249 Only two-thirds of the quantity now ascertained to be requisite for human sustenance. **1870** YEATS *Nat. Hist. Comm.* 117 In Europe large spaces are covered with food-grasses and other plants, for the sustenance of the inhabitants. **1913** *Act 3 & 4 Geo. V*, c. 20 §74 Payment..to the bankrupt..of such sum out of the estate as they shall think proper for sustenance.

†4. Endurance. *Obs.*

1390 GOWER *Conf.* II. 131 It is to kinde no plesance That man above his sustienance Unto the gold schal serve and bowe. **1393** LANGL. *P. Pl.* C. IV. 208 Vnsyttynge suffraunce [*v.r.* sustienance]. *a* **1677** BARROW *Serm.* Wks. 1716 I. 350 The willing susception and the cheerful sustenance of the cross.

†5. The action of sustaining, supporting, or upholding. *Obs.*

c **1400** LOVE *Bonavent. Mirr.* xliii. (1908) 238 So hongeth oure lorde onely by thoo two nayles..with outen sustenaunce of the body. *c* **1460** FORTESCUE *Abs. & Lim. Mon.* xiv. (1885) 144 Savynge to hym selff sufficiant ffor the sustenance off his estate. **1836** J. GILBERT *Chr. Atonem.* iv. (1852) 99 Upheld not merely by unreasoning instinct, but by a sustenance of their understandings.

6. Something that sustains, supports, or upholds; a means or source of support.

c **1400** tr. *Secr. Secr., Gov. Lordsh.* 53 þe maners and þe goodis sustinancez of vertues er to guerdon olde trauailles, to reles wrongys, [etc.]. **1526** *Pilgr. Perf.* (W. de W. 1531) 137 b, Whiche two that is grace & the Sacrament..be all our sustenaunce and supportacyon. **1571** GOLDING *Calvin on Ps.* l. 13 Meate and drinke, which are but sustenances of mans infirmitie. *a* **1613** OVERBURY *A Wife*, etc. (1638) 70 The sustenance of his discourse is Newes. **1871** SMILES *Charac.* i. (1876) 6 Simple honesty of purpose..gives him strength and sustenance.

b. Applied to a person.

c **1400** *Beryn* 1176 He toke hir in his armys..And seyd, 'myne ertly Ioy..my lyvis sustenaunce!' *a* **1450** *Knt. de la Tour* xcv, The childe that God gaue me..whiche was alle my ioye and sustenaunce.

7. *attrib.*: **sustenance diet** = *subsistence diet* (SUBSISTENCE 11); **sustenance money** = SUBSISTENCE MONEY 2. (*rare.*)

1886 C. SCOTT *Sheep-farming* 59 The system of carrying on animals to a certain age on merely sustenance diet, before commencing to fatten them. **1905** *Edin. Rev.* Oct. 468 The sustenance-money which was allowed to many *émigrés*.

Hence **'sustenanceless** *a.*, devoid of sustenance or food.

1630 *R. Johnson's Kingd. & Commw.* 87 You have sauce and no sustenance; and so *mich God dich you* with your sustenancelesse sauce.

sustenant ('sʌstɪnənt), *pr. pple.* and *a. rare.* [In A., a. OF. *sustenant*, pr. pple. of *sustenir* to SUSTAIN; in B., f. SUSTENANCE: see -ANT.]

†A. *pr. pple.* Supporting, encouraging. *Obs.*

c **1386** CHAUCER *Pars. T.* ¶366 (MS. Egerton 2726) Sustenaunt [*Ellesm.* sustenynge] the theft of her Ostillers.

B. *adj.* Sustaining. Const. *to*, *of*.

1874 M. COLLINS *Transmigr.* II. vi. 106 The flowers are sustenant and medicinal. **1897** F. THOMPSON *Poems, Anthem of Earth* 147 Mother, I at last Shall sustenant be to thee. **1908** *Edin. Rev.* Oct. 486 So as to make them congruous with it and sustenant of it.

†**sustenate**, *v. Obs. rare*⁻¹. ? Error for SUSTENTATE; but cf. next.

1712 in G. Fox *Hist. Pontefract* (1827) 343 The said lands be granted..for the sustenating an afternoon lecturer.

†**suste'nation.** *Obs. rare.* [f. *sustene*, SUSTAIN *v.* + -ATION, after *sustenance.*] Sustentation; sustenance.

1606 in Davidson *Inverurie* v. (1878) 171 For the upholdin and sustenation of the said scole. *a* **1635** NAUNTON *Fragm. Reg.* (Arb.) 58, 1000 Marks *per annum*, wherewith he lived plentifully in a fine way and garb, and without any great sustenation. **1675** BAXTER *Cath. Theol.* I. I. 25 As he was to dye by Gods withdrawing his Vital influx or sustenation.

sustension, erron. spelling of SUSTENTION.

†**sustent**, *sb. Obs. rare.* [? Shortening of SUSTENTACLE, after OF. *soustien.*] That which sustains or supports.

1664 EVELYN tr. *Freart's Archit.* 125 The Base..imports the sustent, prop or foot of a thing.

†**sustent**, *v. Obs. rare.* [f. L. *sustent-* or ad. L. *sustentāre*: see SUSTENTATE.] *trans.* To sustain.

1512 *Helyas* in Thoms *Prose Rom.* (1828) III. 68 The which..myraclusly there had be nourrisshed and sustented by the divine providence of God. **1591** SYLVESTER *Du Bartas* I. vii. 518 No firmer base her burthen to sustent Then slippery props of softest Element.

†**sustentable**, *a. Obs. rare.* [f. L. *sustentāre* (see SUSTENTATE) + -ABLE.] Capable of being sustained or maintained; maintainable.

a **1623** SWINBURNE *Spousals* (1686) 81 Howsoever the singular Opinion doth seem more probable or more sustentable in the very point of Law.

sustentacle (sə'stɛntək(ə)l). [ad. L. *sustentāculum* (whence OF. *su(b)stentacle*, It. *sostentacolo*, etc.): see SUSTENTACULUM.]

†1. That which sustains or upholds; a support.

1432-50 tr. *Higden* (Rolls) II. 219 Bestes and other creatures, whiche were create to the solace of man, to the sustentacle of recreacion. *c* **1450** CAPGRAVE *Life St Gilbert* vi, Whan he slept his hed hing down with-outen sustentacle and touchid sumtyme his brest. **1545** BALE *Image Both Ch.* I. x. (1550) K vj, Strong sustentacles and sure staves hath God made the vpholders of his true churche. **1642** H. MORE *Song of Soul* II. i. III. xxv, That God's the sustentacle of all Natures. **1653** —— *Conject. Cabbal.* (1713) 189 It will be ἕδρα and ὑποβάθρα,..and, being thus a Sustentacle or Foundation, be fitly represented by the term Earth.

2. = SUSTENTACULUM.

In recent Dicts.

sustentacular (sʌstɛn'tækjʊlə(r)), *a.* [f. next + -AR.] Pertaining to or of the nature of a sustentaculum; supporting.

1890 BILLINGS *Nat. Med. Dict.*, *Sustentacular fibres*, Müller's fibres. **1897** *Allbutt's Syst. Med.* III. 676 The sustentacular ligaments of the peritoneum.

‖**sustentaculum** (sʌstɛn'tækjʊləm). Pl. -a. [L., f. *sustentāre*: see SUSTENTATE and -CULE.]

a. *Anat.* A sustaining or supporting part or organ (only in L. phr., as *sustentaculum lienis, tali*). b. *Zool.*: see quot. 1838.

1838 BLACKWALL in *Trans. Linnean Soc.* (1841) XVIII. 224 *note*, A strong, moveable spine inserted near the termination of the tarsus of each posterior leg, on the under side, in spiders belonging to the genus *Epeira*, which I propose to denominate *sustentaculum*. **1882** *Cassell's Nat. Hist.* VI. 178 In this operation many species are aided by peculiar spines (called *sustentacula*) attached to the last joints of the posterior legs.

'**sustentate**, *v. Obs.* or *arch. rare.* [f. L. *sustentāt-*, pa. ppl. stem of *sustentāre*, f. *sustent-*, pa. ppl. stem of *sustinēre* to SUSTAIN: see -ATE³.] *trans.* To sustain.

a **1564** BECON *Policy War* Pref., Wks. I. 124 Our countrey doeth not onely receaue and ioyfullye sustentate it [*sc.* the body], but also opulently adourne..both that and the minde with most goodly..vertues. **1631** A. B. tr. *Lessius' De Prov. Num.* I. ix. 143 All things being first created by diuyne power, need to be sustentated by the said power. **1861** READE *Cloister & H.* ii, Who have by this divine restorative been sustentated, fortified,..and consoled.

sustentation (sʌstən'teɪʃən). Also 4-5 -acioun, 5-6 -acyon, etc. [a. AF., OF. *sustentacion* = Pr. *sustentacio*, It. *sostentazione*, Sp. *sustentacion*, Pg. *sustentação*, ad. L. *sustentātio*, -*ōnem*, n. of action f. *sustentāre*: see prec.]

†1. a. The action of bearing or enduring; endurance.

In first quot. transl. Vulg. *sustentatio* (= Gr. ἀνοχή).

1382 WYCLIF *Rom.* iii. 26 In the sustentacioun [*gloss* or beringe vp] of God. **1607** J. CARPENTER *Plaine Mans Plough* 134 Patience,..a voluntarie and daily sustentation and tolleration. **1653** BAXTER *Meth. Peace Consc.* 244 Their [*sc.* martyrs'] sufferings and strange sustentations.

†b. The bearing *of* a pecuniary charge. *Obs.*

1553 in Strype *Eccl. Mem.* (1721) III. App. ii. 4 For sustentation of your charges in this behalf.

2. a. The action of keeping up or maintaining an institution, establishment, building, or the like; upkeep, maintenance.

1389 in *Eng. Gilds* (1870) 67 He schal payen, to the sustentacion of this gylde *v.s.* *c* **1450** *Godstow Reg.* 190 Which rent he assigned vnto the sustentacion of the kechyn of the forsaid mynchons. **1486** *Rec. St. Mary at Hill* (1905) 7 The said xx s for the sustentacion of the said v tapers. *Ibid.* 16 Than I bequethe all..to the vse and sustentacion of london Brigge. **1557** in *10th Rep. Hist. MSS. Comm.* App. v. 386 The maynteyninge and sustentacion of the same housse and Colladge. **1627** SIR R. COTTON *Hen. III.* 46 Councellors..are but as accessaries, not principals, in sustentation of the State. **1635** SWAN *Spec. Mundi* (1670) 280 The Stars..stand in need of daily sustentation, like a lamp. **1837** J. D. LANG *New S. Wales* II. 165 The sustentation and maintenance of agriculture and commerce. **1860** HOOK *Lives Abps.* II. ii. 139 The Peter-pence had..been..a charge laid upon the private estates of the king..for the sustentation of the English College at Rome. **1869** RAWLINSON *Anc. Hist.* 49 The taxes, which he imposed on the provinces for the sustentation of his enormous court.

b. The keeping up or preservation *of* a condition or state, esp. human life; also, maintenance of something at a certain level.

1425 *Rolls of Parlt.* IV. 274/1 For ye better sustentation of ye said stile, title, name and worship. *c* **1460** FORTESCUE *Abs. & Lim. Mon.* xiv. (1885) 142 Howe the kyng mey best haue sufficient..livelod ffor the sustentacion off his estate. **1533** CROMWELL in Merriman *Life & Lett.* (1902) I. 356 A certeyn Annuytie of xxvi s. viii d. toward the Sustentacion of his lyvyng for terme of his Naturall life. **1538** STARKEY *England* (1878) 56 Al thyngys necessary and plesaunt for the sustentatyon and quyetnes of mannys lyfe. **1607** J. CARPENTER *Plaine Mans Plough* 68 To till..their fieldes for the better sustentation of mans life. **1785** PALEY *Mor. Philos.* (1818) I. 99 Applied to the sustentation of human life. **1850** W. R. WILLIAMS *Relig. Progr.* iv. (1854) 89 A nation..eager ..for the sustentation and diffusion of freedom. **1856** OLMSTED *Slave States* 279 The improvement, or even the sustentation of the value of his lands became a matter of minor importance. **1878** STUBBS *Const. Hist.* III. xviii. 244 Royal progresses for the sustentation of peace and justice.

3. a. The action of maintaining a person or concrete thing in being or activity, or of keeping it from failing or perishing; esp. in the 17th cent. of divine support. Now *rare.*

1477 EARL RIVERS (Caxton) *Dictes* 11 b, Slepe no more than shall suffyse onely for the Sustentacion of thy body. **1555** WATREMAN *Fardle Facions* App. 325 If menne shal not onely haue regard to their owne priuate profecte, but also to the sustentacion of other. *a* **1617** [see SUAVITY 2 b]. **1624** DARCIE *Birth of Heresies* xxii. 105 The Sunne..by his force and calidity giues sustentation to whatsoeuer liues vpon the earth. **1645** USSHER *Body Div.* (1647) 378 That he would not take his holy Spirit from us in our trialls, but give us sustentation in our temptations. **1675** BROOKS *Gold. Key* Wks. 1867 V. 164 'The preservation and sustentation of all things': Col. i. 17. **1847** GROTE *Greece* II. xxxi. IV. 235 The fruit of the fresh-planted democracy as well as the seed for its sustentation and aggrandisement.

†b. *fig.* A prop, stay, support. *Obs.*

1585 T. WASHINGTON tr. *Nicholay's Voy.* III. xiii. 95 b, They haue some small peeces of money giuen vnto them which is their onely aduantage and sustentation [orig. *soustien*] of their pouerty. **1642** H. MORE *Song of Soul* I. III. xlviii, God..Who is our lifes strong sustentation. *a* **1734** NORTH *Lives* (1826) I. 18 His family was not in a posture to sustain any of the brothers, by estates to be carved out of the main sustentation of the honour.

4. a. The provision *of* a person with a livelihood or means of living; maintenance or support with the means of subsistence; livelihood.

Very common in the 16th century.

1428 *E.E. Wills* (1882) 79, I be-quethe to the sustentacion of that..preest..xx.li. **1530** *Proper Dyaloge* in Roy *Rede me*, etc. (Arb.) 138 Artificers and men of occupacion Quietly wanne their sustentacion. **1547** *Act 1 Edw. VI*, c. 14 §7 Moneye..payed..abowte the fynding, mayntenaunce, or sustentacion of any preistes. **1558** T. WATSON *Seven Sacr.* xxvi. 168 The payment of tythes..for so much as perteineth to..the sustentacion of Gods ministers. **1563** FOXE *A. & M.* 112 The patronages and almoise bestowed by them..for the sustentation of the poore of the realme. **1601** R. JOHNSON *Kingd. & Commw.* (1603) 35 So much [land] was allotted to euery man, as was thought sufficient for the sustentation of his familie. **1609** SKENE *Reg. Maj.* 2 They ordeined to the Justitiar for his sustentation, ilk day of his justice air, fiue pounds. **1677** SCOUGAL *Praise & Thanksgiving* (1770) 14 He that brought it into the World, hath already provided for its Sustentation in it. **1845** STEPHEN *Comm. Laws Eng.* (1874) II. 695 For the proper sustentation and payment of licensed curates, the law has made a variety of provisions. **1852** GLADSTONE *Glean.* (1879) IV. 176 As there is no poor-law under which nations can be rated in proportion to their means, for the sustentation of the impotent.

†b. With *a* and *pl.* A provision or allowance for maintenance; also, one who provides maintenance for others. *obs.*

1461 *Rolls of Parlt.* V. 473/2 Eny Graunte of a Corrodye or Sustentacion made..by th' abbot and Convent. **1568** GRAFTON *Chron.* II. 174 The reuenues..shall be well kept by the handes of the treasurer of Scotlande..sauyng a reasonable sustentation of the lande, Castelles, and ministers of the kingdome. **1622** DONNE *Serm., John xi. 35* (1640) 156 Lazarus, the staffe and sustentation of that family was dead. **1671** J. WEBSTER *Metallogr.* i. 23 To seek for a sustentation by such slavish and drudgery Work.

5. a. The action of sustaining the life of an animate being; the provision of the means of sustenance; feeding, nourishment. Also applied to spiritual nourishment.

c **1440** *Gesta Rom.* xlviii. 218 The water shalle seye..I brynge forþe diuerse kynde of Fishis for thi sustentacioune. *a* **1483** EDW. IV. in Ellis *Orig. Lett.* Ser. II. I. 141 Yeving unto hir for the sustentacion of hir houshold half a beef and ii motons. **1543** *Necessary Doctr.* I iij b, A perpetual fode.. for our spiritual sustentation. **1549** LATIMER *Ploughers* (Arb.) 25 It is necessarie for to haue thys ploughinge for the sustentacion of the bodye. **1605** CAMDEN *Rem.* (1637) 190 All manner of prices of things in this Realme, necessary for sustentation of the people, grew daily excessive. **1658** ROWLAND tr. *Moufet's Theat. Ins.* 903 Unlesse you see that there is not so much Honey left as may serve for the sustentation of the Parents or elder Bees. **1741** WARBURTON *Div. Legat.* IV. v. II. 266 The Country..was rocky and mountainous: which, therefore,..was unfit for the Breed and Sustentation of Horse. **1825** COLERIDGE *Aids Refl.* (1848) I. 193 The part of the plant..suited..to the deposition of its eggs, and the sustentation of the future larva. **1861** HOLLAND *Less. Life* iv. 62 That peculiar element on which the germ must rely for quickening and sustentation.

b. *Physiol.* The action of those vital functions or processes (as digestion, etc.) which sustain the life and normal activity of an organism.

1877 HUXLEY *Anat. Inv. Anim.* Introd. 24 The apparatuses by which certain operations, subsidiary to sustentation and generation, are carried on. **1881** MIVART *Cat* 10 The study of the actions of the system of organs which nourish and support the body: i.e., the study of the function of sustentation.

6. *concr.* That which sustains life; sustenance, food, nourishment. Also applied to spiritual food. (Cf. 5.) Now *rare.*

1537 *Inst. Chr. Man* I v, The sacrament of the Altare..is the very spirituall fode, and the very necessarye sustentation ..of all christen men. **1549** *Compl. Scot.* vi. 38 Beystis.. quhilk past besyde burnis & boggis on grene bankis to seik ther sustentatione. **1552** ABP. HAMILTON *Catech.* (1884) 21 We may lesumlie desyre of God our necessarie sustentatioun. **1630** LENNARD tr. *Charron's Wisd.* I. Pref. 2 To meditate..therein..is the food, sustentation, life, of the spirit. **1646** SIR T. BROWNE *Pseud. Ep.* III. xxi. 163 It is..a very abstemious animall, and such as..will long subsist without a visible sustentation. **1668** WILKINS *Real Char.* II. x. §3. 259 By Sustentation Ordinary..is intended such kind of Food as is usual for ordinary persons, and ordinary times. **1774** T. WEST *Antiq. Furness* (1805) 195 Sustentation and commodities for themselves and their children. **1866** *Reader* 26 May 513 The soil from which they derive their supplies and sustentation.

7. a. The action of holding up or keeping from falling; the condition of being so supported. †Also *concr.*, a support. Now *rare.*

c **1400** *Lanfranc's Cirurg.* 23 It is nessessarie summe lymes to han a sustentacioun. **1482** *Monk of Evesham* (Arb.) 27 And so [he] came to chirche..and without sustentacion or helpe of any thing entrid into the quire. **1555** EDEN *Decades* (Arb.) 349 The most notable pyllers or sustentacions that the earth hath in heauen. **1612** WOODALL *Surg. Mate* Wks. (1653) 93 A convenient Fascia..for the sustentation of the arm. **1650** BULWER *Anthropomet.* 189 Since the Tonique motion of the Muscules is not sufficient for sustentation of the Body. **1669** BOYLE *Contn. New Exper.* I. xxvi. 91 An ordinary School-philosopher would confidently have attributed this sustentation of so heavy a Body to Nature's fear of admitting a Vacuum. **1893** BENT in *Geogr. Jrnl.* II. 140 In difficult places the rocks have been cut [for the old roadways]; walls of sustentation are visible at many points.

b. *Aeronaut.* The action or condition of being aerodynamically supported either by the lift afforded from the motion of an aerofoil or by means of an air-cushion.

1907 [see AEROFOIL]. **1939** *Nature* 18 Feb. 272/1 Most modern air transport is by means of the aeroplane, a body heavier than air, depending upon forward movement for sustentation. **1966** *McGraw-Hill Encycl. Sci. & Technol.* I. 197/2 Another form [of air-cushion vehicle] creates high air pressure beneath its structure for sustentation. **1977** T. K. S. MURTHY in *Proc. 2nd Internat. Waterborne Transportation Conf.* (1978) 308 The sustentation of the vehicle above the water surface is therefore partly due to the pressure of the air in the cushion and partly due to the hydrostatic buoyancy of the submerged hulls.

8. *attrib.*: **sustentation fund**, a fund in the Free Church of Scotland and other bodies for providing adequate support for ministers.

1843 CHALMERS *Consid. Free Ch. Scot.* in Hanna *Mem.* (1852) IV. 564 That the General Fund shall be separated into two parts—a Building and a Sustentation Fund. **1869** *Daily News* 21 Oct., The Free Church of Scotland in 26 years had..raised a sustentation fund of 132,000*l.* per annum, so that every minister should have not less than 150*l.* a year.

sustentative (ˈsʌstənteɪtɪv, səˈstɛntətɪv), *a.* [f. L. *sustentāt-*: see SUSTENTATE and -IVE.]

1. Having the quality of sustaining.

a **1640** JACKSON *Creed* XI. vi. §4 Unless our Being be supported and strengthned by his power sustentative. **1652** URQUHART *Jewel* 278 Dialogismes, displaying their Interrogatory part with communicatively-Pysmatick and Sustentative flourishes.

2. *Physiol.* Pertaining to sustentation.

1877 HUXLEY *Anat. Inv. Anim.* Introd. 24 Each cell..must needs retain its sustentative functions so long as it grows. **1880** J. COOK *Boston Monday Lect.* 203 Sustentative, generative and correlative functions in the lower forms of life are exerted indifferently.

sustentif, v.r. in some MSS. of Langl. *P. Pl.* C. IV. 338, 345, 355, for *su(b)stantif*, SUBSTANTIVE.

sustention (səˈstɛnʃən). Also *erron.* **-sion.** [A modern formation coined, after the analogy of *retain, retention, detain, detention*, to express senses derived immediately from certain spec. senses of SUSTAIN *v.*, and with the purpose of avoiding the general implications of *sustentation.*

Sustencyon in ed. 1542 of Boorde's *Dyetary* vi. (1870) 241 is app. a misprint; edd. 1557 (?) and 1562 read *sustentacion, -tion.*]

1. The action of sustaining or keeping up a condition, feeling, etc.; the holding-on of a musical note.

1868 *Pall Mall Budget* 10 Oct. 66 In the very highest orator, an unlaboured sustention of passion or emotion naturally expresses itself in long and sustained form. **1870** LOWELL *Study Wind.* 277 Pity, a feeling capable of prolonged sustention. **1883** *19th Cent.* May 863 The emission and sustension of sound are subjects of extreme difficulty to singers.

2. The quality of being sustained in argument or style.

1871 MORLEY *Condorcet* in *Crit. Misc.* Ser. I. 98 Condorcet becomes rapturous as he tells in a paragraph of fine sustention [etc.]. **1876** *Macm. Mag.* XXXIV. 94 'Sustained,' in this fashion, Macaulay certainly is not. But in another and a better form of sustension Macaulay is a master.

sustentive (səˈstɛntɪv), *a. rare.* [f. L. *sustent-*, pa. ppl. stem of *sustinēre* to SUSTAIN + -IVE.] Having the quality or property of sustaining.

1662 STANLEY *Hist. Chaldaick Philos.* (1701) 18/2 These Powers the Oracle calls ἀνοχῆας, Sustainers, as sustaining the whole World. The Oracle saith, they are immoveable, implying their setled Power; sustentive, denoting their Guardianship. **1863** DE MORGAN *Pref.* in *Fr. Matter to Spirit* p. xliv, Experiences..of a character not sustentive of the gravity and dignity of the spiritual world.

†**suˈstentment.** *Obs. rare.* [a. OF. *sustentement*, ad. med.L. *sustentāmentum*, f. *sustentāre*: see SUSTENTATE.] Sustentation, support.

c **1400** tr. *Secr. Secr., Gov. Lordsh.* 50 Sustentement of kynges. It most nede be of force þat ilk a kyng haue two helpes to susteyn his kyngdome.

suster, obs. form of SISTER.

ˈsustinent, *a.* and *sb. rare.* [ad. L. *sustinentem, -ens*, pr. pple. of *sustinēre* to SUSTAIN.]

A. *adj.* Sustaining. †**B.** *sb.* Support.

1603 J. DAVIES *Microcosmos* (1878) 70/1 And our right Arme the Weedowe's Sustinent. **1876** DOWDEN *Poems* 13 Gather me close in tender, sustinent arms.

sustren, -yn, sustyr: see SISTER.

‖**susu**[1] (ˈsuːsuː). Also **soosoo, sousou.** [Bengalī.] The Gangetic dolphin, *Platanista gangetica.*

1801 ROXBURGH in *Asiatic Res.* VII. 171 Delphinus Gangeticus... Soosoo is the name it is known by amongst the Bengalese about Calcutta. They are found in great numbers in the Ganges. **1878** J. ANDERSON *Anat. & Zool. Res. Yunnan* I. 422 *Platanista gangetica*... This genus is known by different names along the Ganges, Indus, and Brahmaputra. Along the first-mentioned river, the term generally applied to it is *sus, susu*, or *sunsar*; along the Indus it is called, as a rule, *bulhan.* **1885** *Riverside Nat. Hist.* (1888) V. 191 The Susu (*Platanista gangetica*) inhabits the Brahmapootra as well as the Ganges.

Susu[2] (ˈsuːsuː). Also †**Soosoo, Suzee.** [Native name.] (A member of) a Mande people inhabiting the north-west of Sierra Leone and the southern coastal regions of the Republic of Guinea in West Africa; also, the language of this people. Also *attrib.* or as *adj.*

[**1670** J. OGILBY *Africa* II. 368 The Kingdom of Bena and Sousos, deriving its Name from the inhabitants of its principal Town, which is named Sousos, stands situate about nine days Journey from..the Kingdom of..Serre-Lions.] **1786** J. MATTHEWS *Let.* 20 Feb. in *Voy. River Sierra-Leone* (1791) 13 The river Riopongeos..is..one of the principal rivers for trade... The natives are originally Suzeés. *Ibid.* 20 Nov. 95 The Suzeé language seems to be the root from which the Bagoe..sprung. **1803** T. WINTERBOTTOM *Acct. Native Africans Sierra Leone* I. i. 5 The Bulloms..possessed the whole of the river Kissee, from which they were driven by a nation called Soosoos or Suzees. **1845** *Encycl. Metrop.* XXIV. 579/2 The Súsús were well known to the learned and philosophical Arab historian of Africa. **1846** R. G. LATHAM in *Proc. Philol. Soc.* II. 221 The Susu, of which we have a grammar, is allied to the Mandingo. **1911** [see MALINKE]. **1957** M. BANTON *W. Afr. City* vii. 127 The Susu and Yalunka (or Dyalonke) appear to be two branches of the same people... There are four Susu and three Yalunka chiefdoms. **1977** *Whitaker's Almanack 1978* 758 The southern half of Sierra Leone is inhabited by peoples whose languages fall into the Mende group; the northern half by the Temne, and smaller groups such as the ....Susu.

susuhunan (sʌsuːhuːˈnɑːn). [ad. Javanese *sesuhunan.*] The title of the monarchs of Surakarta (also called Solo) and of Mataram in Java.

1817 T. S. RAFFLES *Hist. Java* II. x. 157 The company and the *susuhúnan* should assist each other. **1831** *Canton Misc.* No. 2. 77 Solo, is the residence of the Susuhunan commonly called the Emperor, and whose ancestors in the 13th and 14th centuries reigned over the greater part of Java. **1915** D. M. CAMPBELL *Java* II. xix. 997 The sultan and susuhunan on state occasions frequently adorn themselves in the Dutch general's uniform. **1973** G. M. D. HOWAT *Dict. World Hist.* 1526/1 The Crown Prince of Mataram, later Susuhunan Amangkurat II (*reg.* 1677–1703).

susumber (səˈsʌmbə(r)). Also **sosuma, soushumber.** [perh. f. Ewe *sũsume* or Twi *nsúsũaa* an edible plant + Twi *mbá* young plants.] A prickly shrub, *Solanum torvum*, of the family Solanaceæ, native to the tropics, esp. America and the West Indies, and bearing clusters of white flowers followed by edible berries; also *attrib.*; = *macaw-bush* s.v. MACAW[2].

1814 J. LUNAN *Hortus Jamaicensis* II. 245 There are two varieties, both very common in Jamaica, the berries about the size of small cherries... They are..known by the names soushumber, cat-nail, Port-Morant tobacco, and macaw bush. **1839** B. M'MAHON *Jamaica Plantership* 27 He then ran after them, flogging, knocking them down, and tumbling them into the susumber bushes, full of thorns. **1913** W. HARRIS *Notes on Fruits & Veg. in Jamaica* 42 The soushumber is used mainly by the natives who..consider it a wholesome vegetable. **1929** M. W. BECKWITH *Black Roadways* 14 Salt cod cooked with..the sosuma berry, is a favourite breakfast dish even upon the tables of the whites. **1953** *Caribbean Q.* III. 1. 10 Susumber berries..grow wild everywhere. **1972** C. D. ADAMS *Flowering Plants Jamaica* 656 *S[olanum] torvum*... Gully Bean, Susumber, Turkey Berry... Shrub 1–4 m high... General in the tropics.

†**susurr**, *v. Obs. rare.* [a. OF. *susurrer*, or its source L. *susurrāre*, f. *susurrus*: see below.] *intr.* To whisper.

1529 W. KNIGHTE *Let. to Wolsey* (MS. Cott. Vit. B. xi. 13) The Cesarians that susurred dayli in the popes ear sumtyme avising, sumtyme thretenyng the pope. **1616** J. LANE *Contn. Sqr.'s T.* x. 400 Tho, to thetherial welkin, he susurrd.

So **susurrant** (s(j)uːˈsʌrənt) *a.*, whispering, softly murmuring; also irreg. **suˈsurrent** *a.*, whence **suˈsurrence** = SUSURRUS; **suˈsurring** *vbl. sb.*, whispering; **suˈsurringly** *adv.*, in a whisper.

1791 E. DARWIN *Bot. Gard.* I. 162 With soft *susurrant voice. **1827** MONTGOMERY *Pelican Isl.* I. 99 Sweet accordance of susurrant sounds. **1891** *Temple Bar Mag.* July 363 A soft susurrant echo. **1909** *Athenæum* 24 Apr. 491/3 The dim *susurrence of cicalas in the trees. **1857** A. DE VERE in *Fraser's Mag.* LVI. 548 The respirations of a southern sea Beat with *susurrent cadence. **1826** *Blackw. Mag.* XX. 9 The silence of the twilight is cheered by a soft *susurring, that whispers innocence and joy. **1830** *Ibid.* XXVII. 267 We answer *susurringly.

susurrate (ˈs(j)uːsʌreɪt, s(j)uːˈsʌreɪt), *v. rare* (chiefly *Lit.*). [f. L. *susurrāt-*, ppl. stem of *susurrāre*, f. *susurrus*: see SUSURRUS, -ATE[3].] *intr.* To whisper.

1623 in COCKERAM. **1957** H. WILLIAMSON *Golden Virgin* III. xxvi. 395 While feet susurrated on the parquet floor made smooth..by scatterings of french chalk. **1968** M. JONES *Day They put Humpty together Again* 45 The lining of her coat susurrated noisily. **1972** *New Yorker* 30 Sept. 6/3 In the Palm Court, violin music susurrates from five to seven.

susurration (s(j)uːsʌˈreɪʃən). Also 5–6 **-acyo(u)n**, 6 *erron.* **sussur-.** [ad. L. *susurrātio, -ōnem*, f. *susurrāre*: see prec. and -ATION.] Whispering; *occas.* a whisper; in early use, malicious whispering, tattle.

a **1400** *Pauline Epistles* 2 Cor. xii. 20 Discencyouns, bacbytyngys, susurracyouns. **1502** *Ord. Crysten Men* (W. de W. 1506) II. ix. 110 Susurration is for to speke cursed langage by malice for to put noyses in some persones. **1503** *Kalender of Sheph.* c vij, The branchys of enwy detraccyon, adulacyon, sussuracyon. **1526** *Pilgr. Perf.* (W. de W. 1531) 90 b, Susurracyon or preuy sclaundre. **1630** I. CRAVEN *Serm.* (1631) 28 The secret susurrations and buzzings of false tongues. **1657** TOMLINSON *Renou's Disp.* 22 Apuleius ....asserts that by a magical susurration..rivers are turned back. **1708** *Brit. Apollo* No. 33. 2/1 To Inlighten their Offuscated Intellects, upon the least Petitionary Susurration. **1825** LAMB *Let. to Manning* in *Final Mem.* vii. 256 Not a susurration of this to anybody! **1855** DE QUINCEY in 'H. A. Page' *Life* (1877) II. xviii. 99 Every syllable and fragment of susurration that might..betray the tendency of our colloquy. **1892** *Harper's Mag.* Aug. 331/1 The crossing of the hands is accompanied by a muttering and susurration of the lips.

b. *transf.* A rustling murmur.

1640 HOWELL *Dodona's Gr.* 2 Those soft susurrations of the Trees. **1867** *Macm. Mag.* Jan. 234/1 There is no sound but the susurration of the taller trees. **1888** *Harper's Mag.* Apr. 736 There is a constant susurration, a blattering and swarming of crustacea.

suˈsurrous, *a. rare.* [f. L. *susurrus* adj. or sb. (see next) + -OUS.] Of the nature of a whisper; characterized by, or full of, whispering.

1859 W. H. RUSSELL *Diary in India* (1860) II. xiii. 247 There were eyes peering through, and a gentle, susurrous whispering. **1886** WEBSTER, *Susurrous*.., whispering;..full of whispering sounds. **1946** M. PEAKE *Titus Groan* lxiv. 388 The long corridors were susurrous with rumour.

‖**susurrus** (s(j)uːˈsʌrəs). [L., = humming, muttering, whispering.] A low soft sound as of whispering or muttering; a whisper; a rustling.

1826 *Blackw. Mag.* XX. 146/2 Through the..range of laughter, from faint susurrus to indomitable guffaw. **1831** SCOTT *Ct. Rob.* Introd. Addr. ¶15 The first thing which alarmed me was a rumour in the village... I was..rather alarmed at this *susurrus.* **1832–4** DE QUINCEY *Cæsars* Wks. 1862 IX. 6 A brief uproar..too feeble..to ascend by so much as an infantine *susurrus* to the ears of the British Neptune. **1847** LONGF. *Ev.* II. iv. 105 The chant of their vespers, Mingling its notes with the soft susurrus and sighs of the branches. **1866** HOWELLS *Venet. Life* xvi. 242 The procession makes a soft susurrus. **1887** BESANT *Kath. Regina* 27 In most assemblies of girls there will be heard a susurrus of universal chatter.

susy, variant of SOOSY.

sutaille, obs. Sc. form of SUBTLE.

sutchong, obs. form of SOUCHONG.

1771 J. R. FORSTER tr. *Osbeck's Voy.* I. 248 Sutchong, or Sootchuen..is the dearest of all the brown teas.

sute, obs. form of SOOT, SUIT.

†**sutel**, *a. Obs.* Forms: 1 **swutol, -el, sutol,** 2–3 **sutel,** 3–4 **sotel.** [OE. (late WS.) *swutol* = Anglian *sweotol*, of obscure origin.] Clear, manifest, evident.

c **897** ÆLFRED *Gregory's Past. C.* xiv. (1871) 83 (Hatton MS.) Ðonne bið hit swutul [*Cott.* sweotol] þæt he bið suiðe ȝȝerisenlice besuapen [etc.]. **971** *Blickl. Hom.* 203 Þa fotlastas wæron swutole and ȝesyne on þæm stane. *c* **1000** *Beowulf* 90 Þþær wæs hearpan sweȝ, swutol sang scopes. *a* **1100** *Gloss Aldhelm* 4538 in Napier *OE. Glosses* 117 *Satis euidens*, ȝenoh sutel. *c* **1200** ORMIN 18862 Azz wass i þiss middellaerd Full sutell & full sene. *c* **1205** LAY. 1519 Ne cume ȝe neauer wið vte scipes bord ær ich ou sende sutel [*c* **1275** sotel] word. *a* **1225** *Leg. Kath.* 1033 In euch þing of þe world beoð sutel....þe weolen of godes wisdom. *a* **1310** in Wright *Lyric P.* iv. 23 Sone is sotel..this shake ich thah hit seme suete.

Hence †**suteliche** *adv.* (1 **swutol(l)ice, swutelice,** 3 **sutel(l)iche**: see -LY[2]), clearly, plainly, evidently.

c **900** tr. *Bæda's Hist.* III. viii. (1890) 174 Moniȝe þara broðra..sæȝdon þæt heo swutolice [*v.rr.* swutollice, sweotolice] engla song ȝehyrdon. *c* **1000** ÆLFRIC *Gen.* xv. 13 Him wæs þa ȝesæd swutelice þurh god, Wite þu [etc.]. *c* **1175** *Lamb. Hom.* 41 We eow wulleð suteliche seggen of þa fredome þe limpeð to þan deie þe is iclepeð su sunedei. *c* **1200** *Trin. Coll. Hom.* 145 Þe holi gost, þe him dide suterliche [*sic*] to understonden þat ure drihten wolde man bicumen. *a* **1225** *Ancr. R.* 112 Þe reisuns hwui beoð her efter suteliche [*v.r.* opinlike] ischeawede. *c* **1230** *Hali Meid.* 23

Feole priuileges scheaweð ful sutelliche hwucche beon þe meidenes.

sutel(e, -ell, obs. forms of SUBTLE.

†**sutele**, *v. Obs.* [OE. *swutelian*, f. *swutol*: see SUTEL *a.*]

1. *trans.* To make clear or manifest.

c **1000** *Ags. Gosp.* Matt. xvi. 21 He ongan swutelian hys leorning-cnihtum þæt he wolde faran to hierusalem. *a* **1225** *Ancr. R.* 154 Hu god hit is forte beon one is boðe iðen olde lawe, & eciðe neowe isuteleð [*sic*] & ischeawed. *a* **1225** *Leg. Kath.* 1036 He schawde, & sutelede inoh, þet he wes soð godd. *Ibid.* 1854 Ure lauerd..schawde him & sutelede him seolf to hire seoluen.

2. *intr.* To become clear or manifest.

a **1000** *Gloria* (Gr.) 32 þine soðan weorc & ðin mycele miht maneȝum swytelað [*v.r.* swutelað]. *a* **1225** *Juliana* 57 Hit schal sone sutelin hu þi wichecreft schal wite þe. *a* **1225** *Leg. Kath.* 1091 þurh þis suteleð soð al þet ich segge.

ˈ**suter**. *Obs.* or *dial.* [Var. of SUITER, SHOOTER.]

1. = SUITER a.

a **1648** DIGBY *Closet Opened* (1677) 219 Set some new whey on the fire, put in your cheese-fat and suter and cloth.

2. A plug used in plug-draining.

1844 H. STEPHENS *Bk. Farm.* I. 601 The next implement used is the *suter* or *plug*, which consists of three or more pieces of wood, 8½ inches in height, 6 inches in length, 4 inches at the top... A single suter of 18 or 24 inches long would answer the same..purpose.

suter, obs. form of SUITOR.

suterkin, variant of SOOTERKIN.

suþ: see SEE *v.*, SITH, SOOTH, SOUTH.

suþdeakne, obs. form of SUBDEACON.

suþe, suthe: see SITH, SOOTH, SOUTH, SWITHE.

suthen, variant of SITHEN *Obs.*

suther (ˈsʊðə(r)), *v. dial.* [Imitative.] *intr.* To sigh, sough. Hence ˈ**suther** *sb.*

1821 CLARE *Vill. Minstr.* II. 105 No noise is heard, save sutherings through the trees, Of brisk wind gushes, or a trembling breeze. **1881** *Leicestershire Words*, *Suther*..the sighing of the wind.

Sutherland (ˈsʌðələnd). The title of Harriet Elizabeth Leveson-Gower, Duchess of *Sutherland* (1806–68), used *attrib.* in ***Sutherland table***, a gate-leg table with rectangular leaves.

1879 *Designs Cabinet Furnit.* (Blyth & Sons) (Index) 2 Sutherland Tables. **1926** R. B. WHIFFEN *Pocket Compend. Furnit.* 99 *Sutherland Table*—A small table with a narrow top (useless when shut) and two large folding leaves, when these are let down it occupies but little space. **1952** F. G. ROE *Victorian Furnit.* xi. 93 The 'Sutherland Table', a Victorian recension of the old flap table with pull-out supports, its name a reminder of that Duchess of Sutherland who had been Queen Victoria's Mistress of the Robes,..and was..Her Majesty's personal friend. **1979** 'J. GASH' *Grail Tree* xvii. 170 Just telling Jimmo here you're wanting a Sutherland table.

sutherly, suthern, suthron, obs. or var. ff. SOUTHERLY, -ERN, -RON.

suthselerere = *southcellarer* (see SOUTH-[2]), subcellarer.

c **1430** *Pilgr. Lyf Manhode* IV. xliv. (1869) 196 Pitaunceere of heere inne, and suthselerere.

suþþe(n, obs. var. SITH, SITHEN.

Suthu, Suto, varr. SOTHO.

sutil(e, -ill, obs. forms of SUBTLE.

sutile (ˈsjuːtɪl, -aɪl), *a. rare.* [ad. L. *sūtilis*, f. *sūt-*, pa. ppl. stem of *suĕre* SEW *v.*[1]] Made or done by stitching or sewing.

a **1682** SIR T. BROWNE *Tracts* ii. (1683) 90 These [crowns and garlands] were made up after all ways of Art, Compactile, Sutile, Plectile. **1758** JOHNSON *Idler* No. 13 ¶8 Half the rooms are adorned with a kind of sutile pictures, which imitate tapestry. **1776** —— *Let. to Mrs. Thrale* 16 May, There was M[rs] Knowles, the Quaker, that works the sutile pictures.

sutle, obs. form of SUBTLE; var. SUTTLE *v.*

sutler (ˈsʌtlə(r)). Also (7 **subtler, suckler, shuttler, sutteler**), 7–9 **suttler**. [a. early mod.Du. *soeteler* (mod.Du. *zoetelaar*) small vendor, petty tradesman, victualler, soldier's servant, drudge, sutler in an army (= MLG. *sut(t)eler, sudeler*), f. *soetelen* to befoul, to perform mean duties, follow a mean or low occupation or trade (cf. LG. *suddeln*, early mod.G. *sudeln* to sully: see SUDDLE).]

One who follows an army or lives in a garrison town and sells provisions to the soldiers.

1590 (Dec. 31) *Ordonances & Instr. Musters*, The Provost Mareschal and Sergeant Maior of euery garrison shal keepe a perfect rolle of all such English victuallers (called in dutch Sutlers) petimarchants,..and other loose persons of the English nation. **1599** NASHE *Lenten Stuffe* C j b, Sutlers booths and tabernacles. **1599** SHAKS. *Hen. V*, II. i. 116, I shal Sutler be vnto the Campe, and profits will accrue. **1611** BEAUM. & FL. *King & No K.* IV, A dry sonnet of my Corporals To an old Suttlers wife. **1627** DRAYTON *Agincourt* ccxc, A few poore Sutlers with the Campe that went. **1645** HARWOOD *Loyal Subj. Retiring-room* 14 Sucklers to your Army. **1649** G. DANIEL *Trinarch., Hen. V*, cclxviii, Hee.. Knocks off the Subtler's tally with a Crowne. **1701** *Lond. Gaz.* No. 3714/4 Mr. Wollaston, Suttler, at the Horse-Guards. **1714** PRIOR *Viceroy* xiii. The suttlers too he did ordain For licences should pay. **1775** R. MONTGOMERY in Sparks *Corr. Amer. Rev.* (1853) I. 498 If they can send down to the army such articles as soldiers choose to lay out their money upon, employing sutlers for that purpose. **1844** *Regul. & Ord. Army* 267 No huts are to be allowed in front of, or between the intervals of the Battalions; their proper situation is in the rear of the line of petty sutlers. **1852** THACKERAY *Esmond* III. v, An honest little Irish lieutenant.. who owed so much money to a camp sutler, that [etc.]. **1877** *Encycl. Brit.* VI. 517/2 Even the licensed sutlers, who follow the autumn manœuvres, are under the Mutiny Act. **1889** *Times* (weekly ed.) 7 June 5/4 Elshe van Aggelin..a sutler with the Dutch at the battle of Waterloo.

fig. **1827** HARE *Guesses* Ser. II. (1873) 302 The sutlers and pioneers..who attend the march of intellect.

†**b.** *gen.* One who furnishes provisions. *Obs.*

1710 *Brit. Apollo* III. No. 43. 3/1 He came to a Sutlers to Dine. *c* **1710** CELIA FIENNES *Diary* (1888) 304 Houses for Suttlers for to provide for the servants. **1793** [EARL DUNDONALD] *Descr. Estate of Culross* 55 Many of the Scots Owners of Collieries acting as Sutlers, and supplying their workmen..with Oatmeal.

†**c.** *slang.* (See quot.) *Obs.*

a **1700** B. E. *Dict. Cant. Crew*, *Sutler*, he that Pockets up, Gloves, Knives, Handkerchiefs, Snuff and Tobacco-boxes, and all the lesser Moveables.

Hence (all *rare*) ˈ**sutlerage** = SUTLERY; ˈ**sutleress**, a female sutler; ˈ**sutlership**, the office or occupation of a sutler.

1854 *Bentley's Misc.* Oct. 323 The slaughterage, the *sutlerage, and the sewerage. **1747** *Gentl. Mag.* Dec. 571/1 To these must be added the *sutleresses. **1871** B. TAYLOR *Faust* II. IV. ii. 308 Speedbooty (sutleress fawning upon him). **1864** WEBSTER, *Sutlership. **1889** *Harper's Mag.* July 178/2 Improper conduct in the disposal of a sutlership or post-tradership in the army.

sutlery (ˈsʌtlərɪ). Also 8 *Sc.* **sutlarie, -y, suttolory**. [f. SUTLER + -Y. Cf. early mod.Du. *soetelrije* 'vile opus, sordidum artificium', etc. (Kilian).]

1. The occupation of a sutler; victualling.

1606 MARSTON *Fawne* IV. i. F iij, Has my sutlery, tapstry, laundrie, made mee be tane vpp at the Court?

2. A sutler's establishment; a victualling establishment or department, esp. for the supplying of soldiers with food and drink.

1636 DAVENANT *Wits* IV. i, A new Plantation..Is made in Covent-Garden, from Sutleries Of German Camps. **1701** *Minute Bk. News Mills Cloth Manuf.* (S.H.S.) 283 Ane order..for roupeing of the breuing looms of the sutlarie &c. *Ibid.* 286 The sutlary accompt. *c* **1730** BURT *Lett. N. Scot.* xiii. (1818) I. 252 The town [of Maryburgh]..was originally designed as a sutlery to the garrison. **1751** *Scott. Forfeited Estates Papers* (S.H.S.) 223 A Brew Seat and Suttolory to be erected at the head quarters of the military. **1777** *Chron.* in *Ann. Reg.* 206/2 A chapel, a keeper's house, taphouse, sutlery, yards [in Newgate jail].

sutor, var. SOUTER, shoemaker; obs. erron. f. SUTURE.

sutorial (s(j)uːˈtɔərɪəl), *a. rare.* [f. L. *sūtōrius*, f. *sūt-*, pa. ppl. stem of *suĕre* SEW *v.*[1]: see -ORY[2] and -AL[1].] Pertaining to sewing, or to the shoemaker's art. So **suˈtorian, suˈtorious** *adjs.*, pertaining or relating to sewing or shoemaking.

1835 KIRBY *Hab. & Inst. Anim.* II. xxiii. 470 In the Indian tailor-birds the object of their *sutorial art is stated above. **1896** *Contemp. Rev.* Apr. 460 The *sutorian art criticism..silenced by his..advice, *ne sutor ultra crepidam.* **1656** BLOUNT *Glossogr.*, *Sutorious, of or belonging to a Shoomaker, or Sewer.

‖**Sutra** (ˈsuːtrə). [Skr. *sūtra* thread, string, (hence) rule, f. *siv* SEW *v.*[1] Cf. F. *soûtra.*] In Sanskrit literature, a short mnemonic rule in grammar, law, or philosophy, requiring expansion by means of a commentary. Also applied to Buddhistic text-books.

1801 COLEBROOKE *Ess., Sanscrit & Prácrit Lang.* (1837) II. 5 Whatever may be the true history of Pánini, to him the *Sútras*, or succinct aphorisms of grammar, are attributed by universal consent. **1876** *Encycl. Brit.* V. 664/1 The Taouist literature, which has its foundation in *The Sûtra of Reason and of Virtue* by Laoutsze, the founder of the sect. **1886** CONDER *Syrian Stone-Lore* ix. (1896) 372 Some of its episodes [i.e. of Sindbad the Sailor] at least are recognised in the Buddhist Sutras.

attrib. **1867** *Chambers' Encycl.* IX. 230 That a habit deeply rooted outlives necessity, is probably also shewn by these Sûtra works. **1881** *Encycl. Brit.* XII. 782/2 Their earliest.. legal writings belong to the Sûtra period, or scholastic development, of the Veda.

suttale, obs. form of SUBTLE.

suttan, variant of SOUTANE, cassock.

1755 *Mem. Capt. P. Drake* II. iii. 145 A Clergyman in his Suttan, or long black Coat.

suttee (sʌˈtiː, ˈsʌtiː). Also 8–9 **sati**, 9 **satti, shuttee**. [a. Skr. (Hindī, Urdū) *satī* faithful or virtuous wife, fem. of *sat* good, wise, honest, lit. being, pr. pple. of *as* to be (see BE *v.*).]

1. A Hindu widow who immolates herself on the funeral pile with her husband's body.

1786 in *Parl. Papers E. India Aff., Hindoo Widows* (1821) 3 We were informed the suttee (for that is the name given to the person who so devotes herself) had passed, and her track was marked by the goolol and betel leaf, which she had scattered as she went along. *Ibid.* 4 As the suttee ascends the pile, she is furnished with a lighted taper. **1787** SIR W. JONES *Let.* in Ld. Teignmouth *Mem.* (1804) 295 My mother.. became a *sati*, and burned herself to expiate sins. **1881** TYLOR *Anthropology* xiv. (1904) 347 There are 'native' districts in India where the *suttee* or 'goodwife' is still burnt on her husband's funeral pile. **1895** MRS. CROKER *Village Tales* (1896) 127 Her relations drove her to the faggots, for the family of a suttee are held in much esteem. **1905** *Westm. Gaz.* 14 Mar. 10/1 The accused Juggernath Missir, beyond saying that his mother died as 'sati' on the same day that his father died, refused to make any statement.

fig. **1849** THACKERAY in *Scribner's Mag.* I. 687/1 You dear Suttees, you get ready and glorify in being martyrized.

2. The immolation of a Hindu widow in this way. Phr. ***to do, perform suttee.***

The custom was abolished by authority in British India in 1829.

1813 in *Parl. Papers E. India Aff., Hindoo Widows* (1821) 33 To require that any express leave..be required, previously to the performance of the act of 'suttee'. **1877** *Encycl. Brit.* VI. 778/2 Suttee in native states..he [*sc.* Lord Dalhousie] kept down with an iron hand. **1885** *Times* (weekly ed.) 2 Oct. 12/2 A ceremony called a 'cold suttee' is described in books on Hindoo customs. When the relatives had a very nice sense of honour, and a widow's proclivities outraged it, they made a feast at which she was the principal guest. She was sumptuously regaled and at the end drugged to death.

fig. **1833** T. HOOK *Love & Pride, Widow* vii, Pratt..gave an account of the proceedings at one of these European suttees. **1859** MEREDITH *R. Feverel* xxxix, He had become resigned to her perpetual lamentation and living Suttee for his defunct rival. **1882** MISS BRADDON *Mt. Royal* I. i. 4 A widower of that kind ought to perform suttee.

attrib. **1823** in *Parl. Papers E. India Aff., Hindoo Widows* (1825) 13 Any general proposition for abolishing the suttee immolation.

Hence **suˈtteeism**, the practice of suttee.

1846 in WORCESTER (citing *Ec. Rev.*). **1867** *Eclectic Rev.* (N.S.) XIII. 94 The Sutteeism of China is by self-strangulation. **1869** *Daily News* 6 Oct., The miserable condition of Hindoo widows after the custom of sutteeism was done away with.

suttel(l, sutteler, obs. ff. SUBTLE, SUTLER.

sutten, dial. pa. pple. of SIT *v.*

sutth(e, -en, variants of SITH *conj. Obs.*

†**suttle** (ˈsʌt(ə)l), *a. Comm. Obs.* [Old variant spelling of SUBTLE *a.* retained in a technical use. Cf. AF. *pois sutil.*] Of weight, after tare, or tret, has been deducted.

In quot. 1695 quasi-sb. by ellipsis.

[**1502–1660**: see SUBTILE *a.* 12, SUBTLE *a.* 12.] **1596** MELLIS *Recorde's Gr. Artes* III. viii. 486 At 16*ll* the 100 suttle, what shall 895*ll* suttle be worth in giuing 4*ll* weight vppone euery 100 for treate? **1622** MALYNES *Anc. Law-Merch.* 33 The diuision of the pound weight for wares, and the correspondence of the hundreth pound, compared to the 100 *ll* Suttle of Antuerp [cf. p. 22 Subtle]. **1695** E. HATTON *Merch. Mag.* 100 In such Commodities wherein Trett is allowed, the Remainer, after the Tare is deducted is called Suttle, out of which Suttle the allowance for Trett is made. **1764** C. HUTTON *Syst. Pract. Arith.* (1766) 72 What remains after the tare is taken from the gross, may be called *tare-suttle*, if there be more deductions... What remains after tret is deducted, may be called *tret-suttle*, if there be any following deduction. **1812** J. SMYTH *Pract. Customs* (1821) 13 Suppose 20 casks of Gentian weigh 120 cwt. 2 qrs. 18 lbs. gross, how many suttle pounds will they contain?

suttle (ˈsʌt(ə)l), *v. Obs.* or *arch.* Also 7–9 **sutle**. [ad. early mod.Du. *soetelen*, or back-formation f. SUTLER, q.v.] *intr.* To carry on the business of a sutler. Chiefly in vbl. sb. ***suttling.***

1648 HEXHAM II, *Zoetelen*, to Suttle [*ed.* **1678** sutle], or to Victuall. **1706** E. WARD *Wooden World Diss.* (1708) 69 He [*sc.* a gunner] can no more abstain from suttling on board, and running Goods a-shore, than he can refrain from talking Bawdy in modest Company. **1757** WASHINGTON *Writ.* (1889) I. 467 To prevent irregular suttling. **1787** NELSON 29 Dec. in Nicolas *Disp.* (1845) I. 263, I have been obliged to punish him for suttling to the Ship's Company and making numbers of them drunk. **1904** *Athenæum* 10 Sept. 339/3 Dismissed for dishonest greed—for suttling, false musters, or turning their ships into merchantmen.

b. in vbl. sb. ***suttling*** used attrib., esp. in **suttling-house**, a house where food and drink are supplied, esp. to soldiers; also ***suttling booth, department, place, shop.***

1691 *Lond. Gaz.* No. 2653/4 Mr. Creggs at the Suttling-House in the Savoy. **1710** STEELE & ADDISON *Tatler* No. 260 ¶3 She came to him in the Disguise of a Suttling Wench, with a Bottle of Brandy under her Arm. **1747** *Gentl. Mag.* Apr. 197/1 The suttling house at the Tilt Yard, Whitehall. **1777** HOWARD *Prisons Eng.* iv. (1780) 110 No sutling place to be kept in this house of correction. **1809** GENERAL J. WILKINSON *Speech in Congress* 19 June (1853) 2439, I shall make such arrangements in the sutling department as entirely to exclude the use of ardent spirits which have been the bane of the service. **1827** HONE *Every-day Bk.* II. 111 Suttling-booths..appeared now on the Thames. **1829** J. T. SMITH *Bk. for Rainy Day* (1905) 282 We entered the parlour of the 'Canteen', that being the sign of the suttling-house of the Palace [Hampton Court]. **1832** SIR J. CAMPBELL *Mem.* I. ii. 35 He..set up a suttling-shop with the money.

suttler, variant of SUTLER.

suttolory, rare obs. form of SUTLERY.

‖**suttoo, suttu** (sʌˈtuː). [Urdū, Hindī *suttū(a).*] (See quots.)

1886 A. H. CHURCH *Food Grains Ind.* 100 The grain [*sc.* barley]..is parched and ground into coarse flour called suttú. **1908** *Animal Managem.* 104 'Suttoo' is a gruel made by stirring finely-ground gram in water.

sut(t)ringee, var. SITRINGEE

sutty, obs. form of SOOTY *a.*

suttyle, -yll, obs. ff. SUBTLE.

sutural ('sju:tjʊərəl), *a.* [a. F. *sutural*, or mod.L. *sūtūrālis*: see SUTURE and -AL[1].] Of, pertaining or relating to, or situated in a suture. **a.** *Bot.* esp. of dehiscence taking place at the suture of a pericarp.

1819 LINDLEY tr. *Richard's Observ. Fruits & Seeds* 21 A seed attached to an axile, parietal, or sutural trophosperm. **1832** —— *Introd. Bot.* 164 If [the dehiscence takes place] along the inner edge of a simple fruit it is called sutural. **1847** W. E. STEELE *Field Bot.* 206 Placentæ sutural, with 1 or 2 seeds. **1870** HOOKER *Stud. Flora* p. x, Ovules sutural or basal. **1872** OLIVER *Elem. Bot.* I. vii. 92 The sutural placentation of apocarpous pistils.

b. *Entom.*, etc. Also *Anat.* pertaining to the sutures of the skull.

1826 KIRBY & SP. *Entomol.* III. xxxv. 600 The sutural and anal angles exist only where the elytra are truncated at the apex. **1836–9** *Todd's Cycl. Anat.* II. 883/2 The common sutural connexion of some of the bones in man. **1854** OWEN in *Orr's Circ. Sci., Org. Nat.* I. 165 They are united together at their thick margins by rough or 'sutural' surfaces. **1876** DUNGLISON *Med. Lex.*, Sutural Ligament.

c. Pertaining to, resulting from, a surgical suture.

1897 *Allbutt's Syst. Med.* III. 595 The sutures were passed through the fibrous structures of the parietes... A little sutural abscess formed about one parietal stitch.

Hence **'suturally** *adv.*, by means of, or in the manner of, a suture or sutures.

1854 OWEN in *Orr's Circ. Sci. Org. Nat.* I. 178 The hæmapophysis is subdivided into two, three, or more pieces, ..suturally interlocked together. **1875** HUXLEY in *Encycl. Brit.* I. 754/2 The short premaxillæ..are united suturally in the middle line.

†**suturate**, *v. Obs. rare.* [f. L. *sūtūra* SUTURE + -ATE[3].] *trans.* To join by a suture.

1666 J. SMITH *Old Age* (1676) 93 Six several bones, which, being most conveniently suturated among themselves, do make up those curious arched chambers.

sutu'ration. *rare.* [f. SUTURE *sb.* + -ATION.] Stitching, sewing.

1891 *Cent. Dict.* **1901** DORLAND *Med. Dict.* (ed. 2).

suture ('sju:tjʊə(r), -tʃə(r)), *sb.* Also 7 *erron.* sutor. [ad. F. *suture* or its source L. *sūtūra*, n. of action f. *sūt-*, pa. ppl. stem of *suĕre* SEW *v.*[1]: see -URE.]

1. a. *Surg.* The joining of the lips of a wound, or of the ends of a severed nerve or tendon, by stitches; also, an instance of this; a stitch used for this purpose.

1541 COPLAND *Galyen's Terap.* 2 G ij, Yf there be daunger of rottennes in the bone, or where sutares [*sic*] behoueth. **1597** A. M. tr. *Guillemeau's Fr. Chirurg.* 15/1 This suture is done with a waxed threde. **1617** MIDDLETON & ROWLEY *Fair Quarrel* v. i, I closed the lips on't [*sc.* the wound] with bandages and sutures. **1651** WITTIE tr. *Primrose's Pop. Err.* I. viii. 30 Simple wounds, for which union alone is sufficient without a suture. **1754–64** SMELLIE *Midwif.* I. 379 The cutis and muscles only should be taken up in the Suture. **1803** *Med. Jrnl.* IX. 165 Two successful operations of the royal suture. **1804** ABERNETHY *Surg. Obs.* I. 36 The edges of the wound were brought together by one suture. **1879** *St. George's Hosp. Rep.* IX. 447 The abdominal wound was closed by silver sutures. **1887** L. OLIPHANT *Episodes* (1888) 204 My right arm was bandaged to my side, so as not to open the sutures.

attrib. **1870** *Daily News* 9 Sept. 6 Plenty of suture needles. **1875** KNIGHT *Dict. Mech.* 2465 Suture-instruments..are.. useful in..operations requiring accurate suture adjustments.

b. *gen.* Sewing, stitching; also, a stitch or seam; †*transf.* adhesion; *fig.* union, now chiefly the union of the parts or sections of a literary composition, or a point at which it is made.

1600 HOLLAND *Livy* XXXVIII. 1001 Three leather thongs hardened and made stiffe with many sutures and seames. **1603** FLORIO *Montaigne* I. xx. (1632) 44 The narrow suture of the spirit and the body. **1656** J. SMITH *Pract. Physick* 358 Suture with glew is convenient. **1791** COWPER *Odyss.* XXII. 214 Till age Had loosed the sutures of its bands. **1883** LD. COLERIDGE in E. H. Coleridge *Life* (1904) II. xi. 335 Here and there..we detect the sutures [in the Æneid], but how seldom! **1887** DOWDEN *Shelley* I. ix. 434 We are whole at that age and have not experienced the manifest sutures of stitches and sutures. **1891** *Nation* (N.Y.) 5 Nov. 360 Page after page, and paragraph after paragraph are extracted from the 'History' to be reset in these 'Sketches',..sometimes with slight modifications of phrase which hardly serve to hide the seams of the literary suture.

2. a. *Anat.* The junction of two bones forming an immovable articulation; the line of such junction; *esp.* any of the serrated articulations of the skull.

1578 BANISTER *Hist. Man* IV. 45 b, The extreme Suture of the iugall bone. **1615** CROOKE *Body of Man* 498 The Sagittall suture or seame. *a* **1631** DONNE *Crosse* 56 As the braine through bony walls doth vent By sutures, which a Crosses forme present. **1650** BULWER *Anthropomet.* Pref., Thy Front towards the Coronal Suture rose. **1696** AUBREY *Misc.* (1857) Introd. p. xi, At eight years old I had an issue (natural) in the coronall sutor of my head. *c* **1720** W. GIBSON *Farrier's Guide* I. vi. (1738) 78 The true Sutures are three in Number, and proper to the Skull only. **1817** COLERIDGE *Zapolya* Prelude i, The unclosed sutures of an infant's skull. **1859** DARWIN *Orig. Spec.* vi. (1873) 158 Sutures occur in the skulls of young birds and reptiles. **1871** —— *Desc. Man* I. iv. 124 In man the frontal bone consists of a single piece, but in the embryo and in children,..it consists of two pieces separated by a distinct suture.

†**b.** (See quots.) *Obs.*

1656 BLOUNT *Glossogr.*, *Suture*,..the line under the yard of a man. **1688** HOLME *Armoury* II. xvii. 381/2 The Suture of the Pallate, is the Seam in the bone in the Roofe of the Mouth. **1725** *Fam. Dict.* s.v. *Lithotomy*, The Suture of the Perinæum.

3. *Zool.* and *Bot.* The junction, or (more freq.) the line of junction, of contiguous parts, e.g. the line of closure of the valves of a shell, the seam where the carpels of a pericarp join, the conflux of the inner margins of elytra, the outline of the septa of the shell of a tetrabranchiate cephalopod.

1677 PLOT *Oxfordsh.* 108 The whole body of the stone [*i.e.* fossil shell]..divided by Sutures,..resembling the leaves of Oak. **1695** WOODWARD *Nat. Hist. Earth* (1723) 24 The same Sutures,..whether within or without the Shell. **1760** J. LEE *Introd. Bot.* I. vi. (1765) 13 The Seeds are fastened along both the Sutures or Joinings of the Valves. **1769** PENNANT *Brit. Zool.* III. 1 Body covered either with a shell or strong hide, divided by sutures. **1785** MARTYN *Lett. Bot.* iii. (1794) 40 The silique opens from the bottom upwards by both sutures. **1826** KIRBY & SP. *Entomol.* IV. xlvii. 368 The straight suture by which the elytra are united. **1851** WOODWARD *Mollusca* I. 101 The line or channel formed by the junction of the whirls is termed the *suture*. **1880** A. GRAY *Struct. Bot.* vi. §6. (ed. 6) 252 For the discharge of the pollen, the cells..open..by a line or chink,..the suture or line of dehiscence.

attrib. **1894** *Geol. Mag.* Oct. 435 The shell is somewhat distorted... Its suture-line cannot be made out.

4. *Geol.* In plate tectonics, the junction or line of junction formed by the collision of two lithospheric plates.

1971 *Nature* 18 June 418/2 Within the present continents these are several linear belts of distinctive oceanic and geosynclinal deposits which apparently mark the boundaries (sutures) between once separated continents. **1977** *Sci. Amer.* Apr. 32/1 Most of the sutures in Eurasia appear to be older than 200 million years.

Hence **'suture** *v. trans.*, (*a*) to secure with a suture, to sew or stitch *up*; (*b*) *Geol.*, to join (lithospheric plates) by means of a suture; often const. *together*; **'sutured** *ppl. a.*, sewn together; **'suturing** *vbl. sb.*

1777 PENNANT *Brit. Zool.* IV. 57 Echinus. Body covered with a sutured crust. **1878** *Masque Poets* 215 From the first skiff of sutured skins or bark To the three-decker with its thundering guns, The thing developed. **1886** *Amer. Jrnl. Philol.* July 233 According to Fick, the present text of the Iliad..is sutured together out of the following pieces. **1890** *Retrospect Med.* CII. 306 By suturing the serous surfaces over the anterior margins of the plates by a few stitches of the continued suture. *Ibid.* 314 The suturing of the mucosa ..is one of the steps of the procedure. **1904** *Brit. Med. Jrnl.* 24 Dec. 1682/2 In suturing up the wound I have again followed Kelly. **1970** *Nature* 14 Nov. 659/1 If..continents are being joined, their suturing prevents further relative motion between the plates on which they ride. **1976** B. E. HOBBS et al. *Outl. Structural Geol.* x. 468 Depositional sites that are subsequently 'sutured' together by convergent plate motion. **1977** *Sci. Amer.* Apr. 32/1 When two continents collide, they suture themselves together to form a larger continent. **1979** *Nature* 6 Dec. 608/2 The act of complete suturing could trap basaltic crust and supracrustals between the two masses.

†**'suty**, *a. Obs.* In 3 suti, swuti, 4 sutty. [Cf. OE. *besútod* defiled, foul.] Foul (*lit.* and *fig.*).

a **1225** *St. Marher.* (1862) 15 þenchen hu swart þing ant hu suti is sunne. *a* **1225** *Leg. Kath.* 452 & ti swuti speche walde of wisdom & of wit beoren þe witnesse. *a* **1225** *Ancr. R.* 228 þe deope dich of sum suti sunne. *a* **1240** *Ureisun* in *O.E. Hom.* I. 185 Mi saule þet is suti ȝet, make hire wurþe to þi swete wunninge. *a* **1400** *Octavian* 885 Clement broght forthe schylde and spere,..Alle sutty, blakk, and unclene.

suuel, obs. var. SOWL *sb.*, relish.

suuen, obs. inf. and pa. pple. of SHOVE *v.*[1]

c **1250** *Gen. & Ex.* 107 Watres ben her ðer-under suuen. *c* **1275** LAY. 17396 Suueþ and hebbeþ mid al ȝoure strengþe.

suum. Imitative of the moaning sound of the wind. (Cf. G. *summ.*)

1605 SHAKS. *Lear* III. iv. 103 Still through the Hauthorne blowes the cold winde: Sayes suum, mun, nonny.

suversed (sju:'vɜ:st), *a. Trig.* Also 8 sup. versed; 9 *erron.* (in Dicts.) subversed. [Orig. *sup.versed*, f. *sup.*, abbrev. of *supplement* + VERSED; cf. CO-VERSED.] ***suversed sine***: the versed sine of the supplement.

1782 HUTTON in *Phil. Trans.* LXXIV. 32 The sum of the radius and cosine will be the sup. versed sine. **1827** AIRY in *Encycl. Metrop.* (1845) I. 674 The versed sine of one is the suversed sine of the other.

suwar, suwarree, var. SOWAR, SOWARRY.

suwarrow, variant of SAGUARO, SAOUARI.

suwe, obs. pa. t. of SAW *v.*; obs. f. SOW *sb.*[1]

suwelsilver, variant of SOWL *silver.*

?**13..** *Cartular. S. Edmundi* lf. 322 (Cowell's *Interpr.* 1701) Ad quemlibet metecorn datur singulis unus denarius ad Suwelsilver.

suwie, var. SUGH *v. Obs.*

suwynge, obs. form of SEWIN.

sux- (sʌks), (before a consonant also **suxa-**), formative element [repr. the sound of *succ-* (sʌks-) in SUCCINYL] in the names of drugs, as in SULFASUXIDINE and SUXAMETHONIUM.

suxamethonium (ˌsʌksəmɪ'θəʊnɪəm). *Pharm.* [f. SUX- + METHONIUM.] = SUCCINYLCHOLINE. Also ***suxamethonium bromide, chloride, iodide.***

1953 J. H. GADDUM *Pharmacology* (ed. 4) xi. 230 Suxamethonium iodide..also causes brief neuromuscular block. **1963** [see DECAMETHONIUM]. **1977** *Lancet* 18 June 1305/2 Prolonged suxamethonium apnœa during a general anæsthetic occurred in a patient with Goodpasture's syndrome who had recently had plasmapheresis.

sux(s)t, obs. 2nd sing. ind. pres. of SEE *v.*

Suycener: see SWISSENER *Obs.*, Swiss.

suyȝen, obs. form of SEE *v.*

suylle, suymme, suyng, suyn(ne, obs. ff. SELL, SWILL, SWIM, SEWING, SUING, SWINE.

suyr(e, suyrte, etc., obs. ff. SURE, SURETY.

suythe, variant of SWITH(E.

suz, suzz (sʌz), *int. U.S.* = Sirs!: see SIR *sb.* 7 b. Also ***my suz!***

1844 'JON. SLICK' *High Life in N.Y.* Gloss. p. xi, Dreadful suz. **1872** S. DE VERE *Americanisms* 639 Law, suzz, what do you mean?

Suze (su:z, ‖syz). [See quot. 1961.] The proprietary name of a yellow, gentian-based aperitif; also, a drink or glassful of this.

1950 D. AMES *Corpse Diplomatique* iii. 22 It..enables one to have another drink... I thought a Suze and a Cinzano? **1961** *Trade Marks Jrnl.* 5 Apr. 483 *Suze*... Aperitif wines having a gentian base. Distellerie de la Suze.., 11, Avenue de Général Leclerc, Maisons-Alfort (Seine), France. **1964** L. DEIGHTON *Funeral in Berlin* xxii. 124, I poured two Suzes into my face. **1974** N. FREELING *Dressing of Diamond* 72 He'd like a big Suze with lots of ice.

suzerain ('s(j)u:zərən), *sb.* (*a.*) (Also -eign.) [ad. F. *suzerain*, older *s(o)userain*, app. f. *sus* above, up (:—L. *sūsum, sursum*, f. *sub* from below, up + *vorsum, versum*, pa. pple. of *vertĕre* to turn), after *souverain* SOVEREIGN.] A feudal overlord. In recent use, with reference to international relations, a sovereign or a state having supremacy over another state which possesses its own ruler or government but cannot act as an independent power.

1807 C. BUTLER *Revol. Germany* III. (1812) 53 The king was called the *Sovereign lord*; his immediate vassal was called the *Suzereign*; and the tenants holding of him were called the *arrière* vassals. **1820** BYRON *Mar. Fal.* IV. ii, A chief in armour is their Suzerain. **1825** SCOTT *Talism.* xi, He answers me ever with cold respects of their relations together as suzerain and vassal. **1853** HALLAM *Mid. Ages* (ed. 10) I. 125 He was constituted..a sort of suzerain, without whose consent the younger brothers could do nothing important. **1855** MILMAN *Lat. Christ.* IX. v. 96 That vague..sovereignty which gave the right of interfering in all the affairs of the realm, as Suzerain as well as Spiritual Father. **1860** GEN. P. THOMPSON *Audi Alt.* III. cxxvi. 81 Two semi-barbarous tribes,..to the great discomfort of the power which professes to be their suzerain, quarrel. **1870** LIDDON *Elem. Relig.* ii. (1881) 56 Egypt was governed by a practically independent Viceroy; the Suzerain's name was mentioned rarely, or only in a formal way.

fig. **1857** LAWRENCE *Guy Liv.* ii, The fact of his father.. having always been suzerain among his women at home.

b. *attrib.* or *adj.*, as ***suzerain lord, power, state.***

1853 M. KELLY tr. *Gosselin's Power Pope Mid. Ages* II. 99 They may hold it in peace, and maintain therein the pure Catholic faith, saving the rights of the suzerain lord. **1868** KIRK *Chas. Bold* III. IV. vii. 120 Sharing the possessions of the house of Burgundy between the two suzerain crowns from which they had been originally derived. **1898** *Daily News* 14 May 6/4 Mr. Kotze had frequently said that there was no Suzerain Power, but the first thing he did after issuing his manifesto was to appeal to England.

Hence **'suzerainship**, suzerainty.

1827 G. S. FABER *Sacr. Calend. Prophecy* (1844) II. 48 The imperial superiority of suzerainship of Charlemagne.

‖**suzeraine** ('s(j)u:zəreɪn, Fr. syzrɛn). [F., fem. of *suzerain* SUZERAIN.] A woman who is in the position of a suzerain.

1880 DISRAELI *Endym.* I. v. 45 The wife of the minister was careful always to acknowledge the Queen of Fashion as her suzeraine. **1881** EARL OF LYTTON in *19th Cent.* Nov. 769 The *Donna* or *Domina* of the Troubadour was the suzeraine of a vassalage which really existed in the social system of his time.

suzerainty ('s(j)u:zərəntɪ). Also 5 suserente. [In sense 1, a. OF. *suserenete*; in sense 2, f. SUZERAIN + -TY, after mod.F. *suzeraineté*.]

†**1.** ? Supremacy. *Obs.*

c **1470** in *Bagford Ballads* (1880) I. 520* Whyche cause gyueth cause to me & myne To serue yᵗ hart of suserente.

2. The position, rank, or power of a suzerain. Appears first in Fr. or semi-Fr. form.

1823 SCOTT *Peveril* xxiii, The family of Peveril, who thereby chose to intimate their ancient suzerainté over the whole country. **1840** *Penny Cycl.* XVIII. 318/1 Albert's successors continued to recognise the suzeraineté of Poland till the treaty of Velau (1657). **1870** *Spectator* 19 Nov. 137 It would be far cheaper to buy from the Sultan the only right which forces us to his side—the suzerainté of Egypt.

1845 S. AUSTIN *Ranke's Hist. Ref.* II. 381 He promised to renounce all his claims..on the suzerainty of Flanders. **1862** HOOK *Lives Abps.* II. ii. 124 He..sought to advance the Pope's claim to a spiritual suzerainty. **1874** GREEN *Short Hist.* iv. §3. 182 The Scotch lords..formally admitted Edward's direct suzerainty. **1874** STUBBS *Const. Hist.* I. i. 4 Its character of nominal suzerainty is exchanged for that of absolute sovereignty. **1881** *Convention of Pretoria* (in *Times* 5 Aug. 3/4) Complete self-government, subject to the suzerainty of Her Majesty,..will be accorded to the inhabitants of the Transvaal territory. **1884** EARL DERBY *Sp. Ho. Lords* 17 Mar., A certain controlling power is retained when the State which exercises this Suzerainty has a right to veto any negotiations into which the dependent State may enter with Foreign Powers.

Suzie-Q, var. SUSIE-Q.

Suzie Wong ('su:zɪ wɒŋ). *slang.* Also **Susie Wong.** The name of the leading character in *The World of Suzie Wong* (1957), a novel by R. L. Mason, applied *transf.* to a woman, esp. a prostitute, in Hong Kong who consorts with visiting servicemen, etc.; also used generically in *sing.*, and *attrib.*

1962 E. SNOW *Other Side of River* xxxvii. 274 What did happen to all these Suzie Wongs? **1965** *Guardian* 24 July 8/5 A teenage English blonde would be far safer in the Suzy Wong quarter of Hongkong than in a side street in Soho. **1971** *Nat. Geographic* Oct. 547/2 Sailors come to sport with Suzie Wong. *Ibid.* 571/2 The fleets of the world have indeed found this superlative anchorage, and the sailors have found Wan Chai, that traditional world of all the Suzie Wongs. **1977** 'J. LE CARRÉ' *Hon. Schoolboy* I. vii. 151 What's happened to Susie Wong since war-weary GIs..have ceased to flock in for rest and recreation? **1978** P. HARCOURT *Agents of Influence* iii. 60 What are you doing here.. enjoying the delights of Suzie Wong land?

‖**suzuribako** (suzuri'ba:ko). [Jap.] In Japan: a box (often, of finely-wrought lacquer-work) in which an inkstone, ink-stick, several brushes, and a small water container are kept; equivalent to an inkstand.

1967 *Times* 7 Mar. 21/6 A suzuribako by Shiomi Masanari. **1974** *Country Life* 6 June p. xii/2 Detail of a suzuribako decorated with a figure of Kajiwara Kagesuye.. Japanese 19th century. **1981** *Jrnl. R. Asiatic Soc.* I. 120 Eight *suzuribako* appear, one (No. 18) with a concealed *waka* poem.

svabite ('svɑ:baɪt). *Min.* [ad. Sw. *svabit* (H. Sjögren 1892, in *Geol. Föreningens i Stockholm Förhandl.* XIII. 789), f. the name of A. *Svab* (1703–68), Swedish mining official: see -ITE[1].] A fluoride and arsenate of calcium found as colourless or light-coloured prismatic crystals of the hexagonal system.

1893 *Jrnl. Chem. Soc.* LXIV. II. 420 Svabite is a new mineral of the apatite group from the Harstig mine. **1966** *Doklady Acad. Sci. USSR: Earth Sci. Sect.* CLXVI. 134/1 Svabite $Ca_5[AsO_4]_3(OH,F,Cl)$, the arsenical counterpart of apatite, is an extremely rare mineral.

Svan (svɑ:n). Also †(pl.) **Ssuanes.** [Russ., cf. L. *Suani* (also used).] (A member of) a southern Caucasian people living in Svanetiya in western Georgia; also, the language of this people. Also **'Svanian, 'Swanian.** Also *attrib.*

1601 P. HOLLAND tr. *Pliny's Nat. Hist.* I. VI. iv. 117 You meet with another river called Charien: upon which bordereth the nation of the Salæ, named in old time Phthirophagi and Suani... The river Cobus,..issueth out of Caucasus, and runneth through the country of the Suani abovesaid. **1814** F. SCHOBERL tr. *von Klaproth's Trav. in Caucasus & Georgia* xxiv. 298 The village of Chulam is inhabited by families of Ssuanes. *Ibid.* xxiv. 292 About six German miles to the south-west of the village of Ckaratschai lies the mountain Dshuman-taw, where commence the settlements of the Ssuanes. **1869** D. W. FRESHFIELD *Trav. in Central Caucasus* x. 292 Suanetia is the general name bestowed..on the upper valley of the Ingur, and is derived from the inhabitants, who from very ancient times have been called the Suani, or Suanetians. **1910** [see SVANETIAN *a.* and *sb.*]. **1939**, **1948** [see LAZ]. **1959** B. GEIGER et al. *Peoples & Lang. Caucasus* iv. 15 Svan... English variants: Svan, Svanetians.... The Svan language is a member of the S. Caucasian..language-family, to which belong.. Mingrelo-Laz and Georgian, the latter languages forming one group as against Svan. **1962** D. M. LANG *Mod. Hist. Georgia* i. 10 The Svans were cut off for centuries from the main stream of Georgian civilization. *Ibid.* 18 Svanian and Mingrelo-Laz..are separate languages.

svanbergite ('svænbɜ:gaɪt). *Min.* [f. the name of Lars F. *Svanberg* (1805–78), Swedish chemist: see -ITE[1].] †**a.** = PLATINIRIDIUM *Obs.* **b.** [ad. Sw. *svanbergit* (L. J. Igelström 1854, in *K. Vetenskaps-Akad. Förhandlingar* XI. 156).] A basic phosphate and sulphate of aluminium and strontium, $SrAl_3PO_4SO_4(OH)_6$, found as translucent rhombohedral crystals.

1857 C. U. SHEPARD *Treat. Mineral.* (ed. 3) 303 *Svanbergite* (S.), Platiniridium, Svanberg.... In small grains and rarely..cubes, with truncated angles. **1866** BRANDE & COX *Dict. Sci., Lit. & Art* II. 532/3 Pissophane. Svanbergite. Amblygonite. **1900** *Mineral. Mag.* XII. 252 Svanbergite is crystallographically very similar both to beudantite and also to hamlinite and florencite. **1979** *Mineral Abstr.* XXX. 422/2 The source of the Sr and P in the svanbergite was probably the basaltic lavas which covered northern Syria in the Quaternary.

Svanetian (svɑ:'ni:ʃən), *a.* and *sb.* Also †**Suanetian.** [f. *Svanet(iya* (see SVAN) + -IAN.] **A.** *adj.* Of or pertaining to the Svans. **B.** *sb.* = SVAN.

[**1788** G. ELLIS *Mem. Map Countries between Black Sea & Caspian* 77 (*heading*) Georgian language. Carduel dialect. Imretian. Suaneti dialect.] **1854** A. VON HAXTHAUSEN *Transcaucasia* v. 159 His wife was the daughter of a Suanetian prince. *Ibid.* 162 The Suanetians have generally blue eyes and blond hair. **1896** D. W. FRESHFIELD *Exploration Caucasus* I. x. 221 The Suanetian language resembles Old Georgian. **1902** *Encycl. Brit.* XXVI. 619/2 The high valleys of the Caucasus are populated by.. Svanetians, Ossets, Pshaves, and Khevzurs in the middle. **1910** *Ibid.* XI. 760/1 The Svanetians, Shvans, or Swanians, on the Upper Ingur. *Ibid.* 761/1 Both the Laz..and the Svanetian present..structural and verbal differences. **1951** W. K. MATTHEWS *Languages U.S.S.R.* v. 87 The rather more divergent Svanetian (Svan). **1959** [see MINGRELIAN *sb.* and *a.*].

‖**svara** ('swara). Also 8 **swara.** [Skr., lit. 'sound, voice'.] In Indian music, a note of a musical scale.

1792 W. JONES in *Asiatick Researches* III. 68 The first of these [notes] is emphatically named *swara*, or *the sound*, from the important office which it bears in the scale. **1891** [see MURCHANA]. **1927** *Grove's Dict. Mus.* (ed. 3) II. 705/2 The second subject..with only two variations, and after these a *Svarā*, or sol-fa'ed passage, by way of a cadenza. **1968** *Indian Mus. Jrnl.* V. 28 He used to play the svara exercises on a single string **1972** P. HOLROYDE *Indian Music* vi. 221 The svaras or notes are still used for vocal gymnastic exercises.

svarabhakti (swara b(h)akti, svara-). *Philol.* [Skr., vowel-separation, f. *svára* vowel + *bhaktí* separation.] The process by which a parasitic vowel is inserted between two consonants. Usu. *attrib.*, esp. as ***svarabhakti vowel.***

1880 A. H. SAYCE *Introd. Sci. of Lang.* I. 317 The insertion..of vowels..goes under the technical name of *Swarabhakti*. This name was imported from the Hindu grammarians by Johannes Schmidt. *Ibid.* 318 Prosthesis, or prothesis..is another illustration of *Swarabhakti*. **1888** [see INDETERMINATE *a.* (*sb.*) 2 e]. **1908** *Indogerm. Forsch.* XXIII. 254 The *-i-* of *pulisa-* and the second *-u-* of *puruṣa* are svarabhakti-vowels. **1942** *Amer. Speech* XVII. 100 A short vowel in E before *r* + a velar is lowered to [ɑ] in the dialect and a svarabhakti [ɪ] develops between the *r* and the velar. **1977** F. COLLINSON in Campbell & Collinson *Hebridean Folksongs* II. 257 The variation of rhythm or melody arising from the presence of a svarabhakti vowel is of constant occurrence in most of the songs.

Hence **svara'bhaktic** *a.*

1894 W. M. LINDSAY *Latin Lang.* 145 The inserted or 'parasitic' vowel (sometimes styled in the terminology of the Sanskrit grammarians 'svarabhaktic' vowel..) is often seen in the older Latin loanwords from Greek. **1965** *English Studies* XLVI. 174 We may here just possibly be..taking.. the *e* to be svarabhaktic.

‖**svarita** ('swarita). Also **Svarita.** [Skr. *svarita.*] A falling glide used in the recitation of Vedic texts (see quots.). Also in extended use.

1916 A. A. MACDONELL *Vedic Gram. for Students* 448 The Svarita is a falling accent representing the descent from the Udātta pitch to tonelessness. **1955** T. BURROW *Sanskrit Lang.* iii. 113 The accent of the syllable immediately following the udātta is termed *svarita-* and it is described by Pāṇini as a combination (*samāhāra-*) of udātta and anudātta. **1957** *New Oxf. Hist. Music* I. iv. 200 The way of chanting the Rigvedic hymns has definite musical importance, as the three accents employed, the *udātta*, the *anudatta*, and the *svarita*, denote a distinct difference in pitch. **1971** *Canadian Jrnl. Linguistics* XVII. 73 The sandhi-organization..is sufficient peculiar origin for Sanskrit svarita. **1973** A. H. SOMMERSTEIN *Sound Pattern Anc. Greek* v. 122 On the vowel following an acute-accented vowel, as also on the latter part of a circumflex-accented vowel, there was a falling glide. [*Note*] Hereinafter often referred to as *svarita*.

svastika, variant of SWASTIKA.

Svedberg ('svɛdbɜ:g). *Biochem.* [The name of Theodor S. *Svedberg* (1884–1971), Swedish chemist.] Also ***Svedberg unit.*** A unit of time equal to 10^{-13} second used in expressing sedimentation coefficients. Symbol S (S 4 d).

1942 *Ann. N.Y. Acad. Sci.* XLIII. 176 The members of the conference..indicated a desire to honor Professor The Svedberg.... It was unanimously decided:..to adopt, as a convenient practical unit for sedimentation constants, the *Svedberg*, to be denoted by the letter *S* and equal to 10^{-13} times the absolute units, which are in seconds. **1944** *Jrnl. Biol. Chem.* CLII. 682 The average sedimentation constant of the iron hydroxide micelle was 150 Svedberg units. **1970** *Nature* 5 Sept. 1068/2 One can comprehend but not condone the biologist's affection for units such as Å, the Svedberg and mmHg. **1976** *Sci. Amer.* Aug. 63/1 It was the expected size (nine Svedberg units).

svelte (svɛlt). Also (*rare*) **svelt.** [F. (= It. *svelto*), :—pop.L. **exvellitu-*, pa. pple. of **exvellĕre*, f. *ex* out + *vellĕre* to pluck.]

a. Slim, slender, willowy.

c **1817** FUSELI in *Lect. Paint.* x. (1848) 594 The Medicean Venus, however 'svelt',..has in length no more than seven heads and a half. **1838** GRANVILLE *Spas Germ.* 246 The tall, *svelte*, pale, and interesting Countess P—k—n. **1887** MISS BRADDON *Like & Unlike* iii, The Matron led the way, lovely, smiling,..*svelte*, and graceful.

b. *transf.* Elegant, smooth, graceful.

1909 E. POUND *Personae* 43 And first the cities of north Italy I did behold, Each as a woman wonder-fair, And svelte Verona first I met at eve. **1967** *Listener* 30 Mar. 434/1 His earlier work, technically less accomplished, rougher, coarser in execution, left a way open—one felt one could break out of the paint. But now his handling is so skilful, svelte, that all other possibilities are closed. **1974** N. MARSH *Black as he's Painted* xi. 78 Is our svelte hired limousine at the door? **1977** *Gramophone* July 202/1 His rhythmic pungency..in the third piece and the svelte charm of the central waltz.. suggest that he might be equally at home with Roussel's symphonic music.

Svengali (svɛŋ'gɑ:lɪ). The name of *Svengali*, musician and hypnotist, a character in the novel *Trilby* (1894) by George Du Maurier, used *transf.* and allusively to designate one who exercises a controlling or mesmeric influence on another, freq. for some sinister purpose. Also *attrib.* and *Comb.*

1914 KIPLING *Divers. Creatures* (1917) 145 I'm glad Zvengali's back where he belongs [referring to a dog with a mesmeric stare]. **1919** C. MACKENZIE *Sylvia & Michael* iv. 92 The juggler..passed into the category of the Svengalis, and became one of a long line of romantic impossibilities. **1934** B. DARWIN *Playing the Like* 121 He believes himself a new Svengali with a second Trilby. **1942** *Amer. Speech* XVII. 90/1 The word 'Svengali' shows the player's ability to keep his opponent so 'hypnotized' that he will not be aware of his trickery. **1962** N. FREELING *Love in Amsterdam* I. 40 He fascinated her. Svengali stuff. **1963** AUDEN *Dyer's Hand* 457 It is impossible to represent Christ on the stage. If he is made dramatically interesting, he ceases to be Christ and turns into a Hercules or a Svengali. **1966** N. MARSH *Black Beech & Honeydew* x. 231 A hideous Svengali-like face. **1972** *Maclean's Mag.* Mar. 41/2 He had a strange hypnotic power—not that he was a Svengali, but when he spoke people listened. **1978** M. DICKENS *Open Book* vi. 59 Charles Pick..already showed the infectious Svengali enthusiasm to which many writers beside me owe the fact that they have had the courage to go on writing.

Sverdrup ('svɜ:drʊp). Also **sverdrup.** [Name of H. U. *Sverdrup* (1888–1957), Norwegian oceanographer and meteorologist.] Also ***Sverdrup unit.*** A unit of flow equal to one million cubic metres per second.

1963 G. L. PICKARD *Descr. Physical Oceanogr.* vii. 117 The most commonly used unit for volume transport is 'one million m^3/sec'..referred to as 'one sverdrup'. **1970** *Sci. Jrnl.* Mar. 58/2 Fifty Sverdrup units of flow approach the east coast of Mindanao in the Philippines and half of this volume turns north into the Kuroshio. **1977** J. D. MACDONALD *Condominium* xxxiv. 341 The..total flow of all the rivers of the world combined..is two sverdrups.

swa, obs. form of SO *adv.* and *conj.*

swab (swɒb), *sb.*[1] (*a.*) Also 8 **swabb.** [f. SWAB *v.*[1] With sense 1 cf. Norw., Sw. *svabb* mop; with sense 2, *svabb*, *svabba* dirty person.]

1. a. A mop made of rope-yarn, etc. used for cleaning and drying the deck, etc. on board ship.

1659 TORRIANO, *Strofinaccio*.., a swab in a ship, a clout-mop in a boat. **1769** FALCONER *Dict. Marine* (1780). **1797** S. JAMES *Narr. Voy. Arabia* 230 We..choaked the pumps up with wringing swabs. **1820** W. SCORESBY *Acc. Arctic Reg.* II. 233 A small broom and a 'swab'. **1893** M. PEMBERTON *Iron Pirate* 182 Others of the crew brought buckets and swabs unbidden, and cleansed the place.

b. Anything used for mopping up; an absorbent mass of rag, cotton-wool, or the like, used for cleansing; any mass or bundle of stuff that takes up moisture, or that, being soaked, is applied to a surface.

Also *Med.* a specimen of a morbid secretion, etc., taken with a swab for bacteriological examination.

1787 M. CUTLER in *Life*, etc. (1888) I. 243 The hostler is at the door, ready to take your horse,..rubs him down, then washes him with a swab and wipes him dry. **1828** *Sporting Mag.* XXII. 354 The swab, which, when well saturated with water, is tied round the outside of the coronets. **1842** MOTLEY *Corr.* (1889) I. iv. 117 The archbishop with a little mop or swab twirling water on all the dignitaries. **1854** *Poultry Chron.* I. 369/1 If they rattle badly in the throat, make a swab by tying a little tow on a small stick, and swab their throats out with the same mixture. **1888** HASLUCK *Model Engin. Handybk.* (1900) 139 The mixture can be applied with a small brush, or a swab tied to the end of a stick. **1903** [see SWAB *v.*[1] 3]. **1907** M. H. GORDON *Abel's Labor. Handbk. Bacteriol.* 165 A plug of sterile wool fixed to a wooden rod or wire (i.e. a 'swab'). **1908** *Animal Managem.* 339 Keep cold swabs over the hoofs.

c. A cylindrical brush or cleaner for cleaning out the bore of a firearm; a soft brush for wetting the mould in founding.

1863 'MARK TWAIN' *Celebr. Jumping Frog* (1867) 73 A sheet was wound around me until I resembled a swab for a Columbiad [cannon]. **1874** tr. *V. Hugo's Ninety-Three* III. I. iii. II. 174 He took the swab and rammer himself, loaded the piece, sighted it, and fired. **1875** KNIGHT *Dict. Mech.* 2465/2 *Swab*..is used..to wet the parting edge before drawing the pattern, and also to moisten parts of the mold requiring repairs.

d. A naval officer's epaulette. *slang.* Also †*transf.*, a naval officer. *Obs.*

1793 C. DIBDIN in *Britannic Mag.* I. 25/2 And there's never a swab but the captain knows the stem from the stern of the ship. **1798** *Sporting Mag.* XII. 35 He makes use of no swabs (gold shoulder knots). **1833** M. SCOTT *Tom Cringle* xv, If half a dozen skippers..were to evaporate during the approaching hot months he may have some small chance of tother Swab. **1834** MARRYAT *P. Simple* xli, I had shipped the swab... I'm lieutenant of the *Rattlesnake*. **1849** CUPPLES

Green Hand i, A fat fellow with red breeches and yaller swabs on his shoulders, like a captain of marines. **1850** H. MELVILLE *White Jacket* II. xliii. 289 Touch your tile whenever a swob (officer) speaks to you.

e. A piece of stuff that hangs loose, trails, etc.

1862 THORNBURY *Turner* II. 322 The swab of a handkerchief hanging from the side-pocket of his tail-coat. **1862** TROLLOPE *N. America* I. 300 At every hundred yards some unhappy man treads upon the silken swab which she trails behind her.

f. *Oil Industry.* A device in the form of a plunger with a valve, used to raise fluid in a well and induce a flow.

1904 *Dialect Notes* II. 391 *Swab*, n., a tool used in drilling... When water comes in faster than it can be got out by the sand-pump, the swab is run down. The fluid passes through it, and by it several hundred feet of fluid can be raised out of the hole at one run. **1916** A. B. THOMPSON *Oil-Field Devel.* x. 482 The early swab consisted of a hollow steel barrel, around which was wrapped sufficient hemp..to tightly fit the well casing when inserted. **1930** W. H. OSGOOD *Increasing Recovery of Petroleum* I. x. 169 Swabbing..may result in the forming of emulsions when the swab is run too low in the fluid and water is present. **1974** P. L. MOORE et al. *Drilling Practices Manual* ix. 241 Swab pressures are associated with fluid flow, caused by pulling equipment out of a liquid filled bore-hole.

2. †**a.** = SWABBER[1] 1. **b.** A term of abuse or (now often mild) contempt: cf. SWABBER[1] 2.

1687 TAUBMAN *London's Tri.* 7 Green-men, Swabs, Satyrs, and Attendants innumerable. **1706** E. WARD *Wooden World Diss.* (1708) 64 Provided always, that the Swab consign him over his Wages for his Labour. **1710** C. SHADWELL *Fair Quaker Deal* I. i. 6 If the Government did but know what a Swabb thou art. **1748** SMOLLETT *Rod. Random* (1812) I. 11 None of your jaw, you swab. **1798** LADY HAMILTON *Let. to Nelson* 8 Sept., I would have been rather an English powder-monkey or a swab in that great victory than an emperor out of it. **1816** SCOTT *Let.* in *Lockhart* (1837) IV. i. 15, I have seen the great swab, who is supple as a glove. **1835** MARRYAT *Jacob Faithful* xx, He said t'other day I was a drunken old swab. **1860** *All Year Round* No. 66. 384 Look there, you swabs! Don't you see that second jib towing overboard? **1887** BESANT *The World Went* xxix, Luke was a grass comber and a land swab. **1899** SOMERVILLE & ROSS *Irish R.M.* 240 The men 'ud rather a lot of swabs, but they know the coast. **1907** QUILLER-COUCH *Poison Island* vii. 60 The Mayor of Falmouth was a well-meaning old swab.

3. *attrib.*: **swab-hitch** *sb.*, *Naut.* (see quot.); hence **swab-hitch** *v.*, to secure with a swab-hitch; **swab-man**, a naval officer wearing epaulettes; **swab-pot** *Founding*, 'an iron vessel containing water and the founder's swab' (Knight *Dict. Mech.* 1875); **swab-rope** *Naut.*, **swab-stick** (see quots.); **swab-washer**, **-wringer** *Naut.*, one who washes or wrings out swabs.

1883 *Man. Seamanship for Boys* 88 A *swab-hitch..is..used for bending a rope's end to swabs when washing them overboard. *Ibid.* 190 Swab-hitch it over the ring and seize the end back. **1836** E. HOWARD *R. Reefer* xl, A little *swab-man..jumped on the..deck. **1867** SMYTH *Sailor's Word-bk.*, **Swab-rope*, a line bent to the eye of a swab for dipping it overboard in washing it. **1839** URE *Dict. Arts* 836 If the ground be very wet, and the hole gets full of mud, it is cleaned out by a stick bent at the end into a fibrous brush, called a *swab-stick. **1890** BILLINGS *Nat. Med. Dict.*, *Swab-stick*, a rod of wood wrapped at one end with cotton, used in making applications to the uterus or vagina. **1836** E. HOWARD *R. Reefer* xxvii, Present that piece of paper..to the head *swabwasher. **1867** SMYTH *Sailor's Word-bk.* s.v., The principal swab-washer, or captain of the head, in large ships. **1821** *Blackw. Mag.* X. 426 A waister, a term which is equally applicable to sweepers, *swab-wringers, ..and drudges of all descriptions.

4. as *adj.* Lubberly.

1914 *Blackw. Mag.* Nov. 648/2 About the swabbest lot that ever left port.

swab (swɒb), *sb.*[2] Now *s.w. dial.* [perh. the same word as prec.] = SWABBER[2].

1681 T. FLATMAN *Heraclitus Ridens* No. 40 (1713) II. 3 He has all the Game in his Hand, all the Trumps and Swabbes. *a* **1840** in C. E. Byles *Life & Lett. R. S. Hawker* vi. (1905) 73 Us was settin' playin' swabs ('all fours') up to 'The Bush'. **1880** *W. Cornwall Gloss.* s.v. *Swabbers*, 'I never cared for whisk since swabs went out of fashion'. Said by an old lady at Penzance about ten years since... Each player before beginning to play puts in the pool a fixed sum for swabs. **1890** *Glouc. Gloss.*, *Swabs* or *Swabbers*, honours at whist.

swab, *sb.*[3] *dial.* [Origin obscure. Cf. SWAD *sb.*[3]] A bean- or pea-shell.

1659 TORRIANO, The swab (or cod, of beanes pease, &c.), *scaffa, guscio* [cf. *Guscio*..swad]. **1706** PHILLIPS (ed. Kersey), *Swab*, a Cod of Beans. **1825–80** JAMIESON, *Swab*, the husk of the pea; *pease swabs.*

Swab (swɒb), *sb.*[4] Also **Suab.** [ad. G. *Schwab*, *Schwabe.*] = SWABIAN.

1663 GERBIER *Counsel* 106 A high German (especially a Swab). **1855** *Poultry Chron.* III. 10/1 The Germans have also what they call a Red Suab, or 'Roth Schwaben'.

swab (swɒb), *v.*[1] Also 9 **swob.** [In branch I, cogn. w. or a. MLG. *swabben* to splash in water or mire, LG. *swabben* to splash, (of soft bodies) to sway, also, to slap, flap. In branch II, back-formation from SWABBER[1].

The root *swab-* denoting backward-and-forward motion, esp. splashing or dabbling in liquid, is repr. in Du. *zwabben* to swab, do dirty work, be tossed about, Norw. *svabba* to spill water, wade, splash, befoul, WFris. *swabje* to swim (of waterfowl), to roam about. See also SWABBLE.]

I. 1. *intr.* To sway about. *dial.*

14.. [see SWABBLE]. *a* **1854** CLARE *MS. Poems*, The billows swab behind. **1854** MISS BAKER *Northampt. Gloss.*, *Swob*, to sway and vibrate with the wind, to wave. **1881** *Leicestersh. Gloss.*, *Swab*, to sway, like boughs in the wind. **1887** *S. Chesh. Gloss.*, *Swob*, to sway beneath the feet; said of marshy ground.

II. †**2.** ? To act like a swab or swabber; to behave in an unmannerly fashion. *Obs. rare.*

1638 FORD *Fancies* II. i, Rudeness! Keep off, or I shall —Sawcy groom, learn manners! Go swab amongst your goblins.

3. To apply a swab to; to cleanse or wipe with or as with a swab; to mop *up*. Also with *down.*

1719 D'URFEY *Pills* (1872) III. 304 All hands up aloft, Swab the Coach fore and aft. **1769** FALCONER *Dict. Marine* (1780), *Fauberter*, to swab a ship's decks, &c. **1834** MARRYAT *P. Simple* vi, The main-deck, which they were swabbing dry. **1836** E. HOWARD *R. Reefer* xliv, 'It melts me,' responded the doctor, swabbing his face with the napkin. **1840** R. H. DANA *Bef. Mast* ii, After we had finished, swabbed down decks, and coiled up the rigging. **1852** DICKENS *Bleak Ho.* xvii, If you only have to swab a plank, you should swab it as if Davy Jones were after you. **1854** [see SWAB *sb.*[1] 1 b]. **1882** BARNETT in *Macm. Mag.* XLVI. 174 The prisoners were 'swabbing' their filthy dens! **1883** F. M. CRAWFORD *Dr. Claudius* ix. 147 A party of red-capped tars were..swabbing the forward deck. **1903** *Lancet* 4 Apr. 946/1 After swabbing out the throat with a swab from the throat of a case of scarlet fever an exudative tonsillitis resulted.

4. To mop *up* (liquid) with or as with a swab.

1745 P. THOMAS *Jrnl. Anson's Voy.* 285 It seems they had ten Men quartered on Purpose to swab up the Blood. **1819** G. BEATTIE *Bark* 128, I swabbed from my cheeks the tears and the spray. **1837** MARRYAT *Snarleyyow* xxxvi, The corporal..swabbed up the blood.

5. To souse as with a mop.

1762 MILLS *Syst. Pract. Husb.* I. 155 Thus we see a smith swab and wet his coals.

6. To draw like a swab over a surface.

1892 *Photogr. Ann.* II. 47 The plate is sloped, and the brush..is swabbed across the required portion.

7. *Oil Industry.* To introduce a swab (SWAB *sb.*[1] (*a.*) 1 f) into (an oil-well) in order to induce a flow.

1916 A. B. THOMPSON *Oil-Field Devel.* x. 482 It was the local custom to swab wells at intervals. **1974** P. L. MOORE et al. *Drilling Practices Manual* ix. 245 This deceleration pressure indicates a well can be swabbed when running pipe into the hole.

†**swab**, *v.*[2] *Obs.* Rare variant of SWAP *v.*

1611 COTGR., *Troquer*, to trucke, chop, swab.

swabber[1] (ˈswɒbə(r)). Also 6 **swaber**, 7–8 **swobber.** [a. early mod.Du. *zwabber*, f. *zwabben*: see SWAB *v.*[1] and -ER[1]. Cf. LG. *swabber* (G. *schwabber*) mop, WFris. *swabber* mop, also roving fellow, vagabond, beggar.]

1. a. One of a ship's crew whose business it was to swab the decks, etc.; a petty officer who had charge of the cleaning of the decks.

1592 WYRLEY *Armorie, Capitall de Buz* 144 Scarce little chip shall lie vpon the hatch, But for the swabber [he] hastely doth call, Cleane and fine ech buisnes to dispatch. **1598** W. PHILLIP tr. *Linschoten* I. xciii. 165/1 The Guardian or quartermaster..hath charge to see the swabers pumpe to make the ship cleane. **1610** SHAKS. *Temp.* II. ii. 48 The Master, the Swabber, the Boate-swaine & I. **1627** CAPT. J. SMITH *Seaman's Gram.* viii. 36 The Swabber is to wash and keepe cleane the ship and maps. **1653** GAUDEN *Hierasp.* 114 By driving the skilful Pilots..from the Helm, and putting in their places every bold Boatswain, and simple Swobber. **1755** *Connoisseur* No. 84. 507 It is beneath the dignity of the British Flag to have an Admiral behave as rudely as a Swabber, or a Commodore as foul-mouthed as a Boatswain. **1769** FALCONER *Dict. Marine* (1780), *Swabber*, ship's sweeper, usually called captain's swabber. **1803** *Royal Proclam.* 7 July, Gunsmiths, Coopers, Swabbers. **1834** *W. Ind. Sk. Bk.* I. 34 A staunch crew too, none of your swabbers and afterguard, able seamen every man on 'em. **1864** E. A. PARKES *Pract. Hygiene* 582 The swabbers, who clean the between-decks, thoroughly ventilate, &c.

b. *transf.* One who uses a mop or cleans up.

1720–1 *Lett. fr. Mist's Jrnl.* (1722) II. 309 Prince Cerberus his Groom of the Stool wants a Swobber. **1931** [see *roach-powder* s.v. ROACH *sb.*[4] 4].

2. One who behaves like a sailor of low rank; a low or unmannerly fellow; a term of contempt. (Cf. SWAB *sb.*[1] 2 b.)

1609 B. JONSON *Sil. Wom.* IV. iv, How these swabbers talke! **1610** —— *Alch.* IV. vii, Doe not beleeue him, sir: He is the lying'st Swabber! **1769** R. CUMBERLAND *Brothers* in *Brit. Theat.* (1808) XVIII. 27 Ridiculous! a poor, beggarly, swabber truly. [**1867** SMYTH *Sailor's Word-bk.*, *Sea-swabber*, a reproachful term for an idle sailor.]

3. A mop or swab; *spec.* a kind of mop for cleaning ovens.

1607 DEKKER *Knt.'s Conjur.* viii. I iij, [Charon loq.] Their ragges serued to make me Swabbers. *a* **1625** FLETCHER *Woman's Prize* III. i, Nothing but brayded haire, and penny riband, Glove, garter, ring, rose, or at best a swabber. **1857** WRIGHT *Dict. Obs. & Prov. Engl.*, *Swabber*,..a kind of broom.

4. *attrib.*: †**swabber-slops**, ? a sailor's wide breeches or garments resembling them.

a **1658** CLEVELAND *Cl. Vind.* Poems (1677) 101 List him a Writer, and you smother Geoffry in Swabber-slops. **1661** K. W. *Conf. Charac., Old Hording Hagg* (1860) 90 Her swetty toes,..the things contained in these swabberslops.

swabber[2] (ˈswɒbə(r)). *Obs.* exc. *Hist.* or *dial.* Also 8–9 **swobber.** [perh. the same word as prec. Cf. SWAB *sb.*[2]] Chiefly *pl.* Certain cards at the game of whist (see first quot.), which entitled the holder to part of the stakes. ***whisk and swabbers***: a form of the game in which these cards were so used.

a **1700** B. E. *Dict. Cant. Crew*, *Swabbers*, the Ace of Hearts, Knave of Clubs, Ace and Duce of Trumps. **1704** T. BAKER *Act at Oxf.* III. ii. 33 We'll sit down to Ombre, Picquet, Wisk, and Swabbers. **1728** SWIFT *Intelligencer* No. 5 ¶7 His Grace said, he had heard that the Clergy-Man used to play at Whisk and Swobbers; that as to playing now and then a sober Game at Whisk for Pastime, it might be pardoned, but he could not digest those wicked Swobbers. **1772** *Test Filial Duty* I. 64 Her thirty thousand pounds would more than discharge all the Knight's play debts, though he should never have a swabber in his hand again. **1812** *Francis Lett.* (1901) II. 670 Last night I had the honour to play at french crowns and swobbers with the following Ladies of quality. **1818** SCOTT *Rob Roy* xiv, The society of half a dozen of clowns to play at whisk and swabbers. **1880**, **1890** [see SWAB *sb.*[2]].

†**ˈswabberly**, *a.* *Obs. rare*[−1]. [f. SWABBER[1] + -LY[1].] Like a swabber or sailor of the lowest rank.

1596 NASHE *Saffron Walden* To Rdr. (ad init.), A base swabberly lowsie sailer.

ˈswabbing, *vbl. sb.* [f. SWAB *v.*[1] + -ING[1].] The action of SWAB *v.*[1]; cleaning with (or as with) a swab or mop; the use of a swab or swabs. Also *concr.* (see quot. 1891).

1840 R. H. DANA *Bef. Mast* xiv, The washing, swabbing, squilgeeing, etc., etc. **1872** O. W. HOLMES *Poet Breakf.-t.* xi, Sparrows..keep up such a swashing and swabbing..round ..the water basins. **1876** BRISTOWE *Theory & Pract. Med.* (1878) 215 The larynx must be treated..by 'swabbing'. **1891** *Labour Commission* Gloss., *Swabbing*, that which is swept up by the swab, a mop used for cleaning the floors in woollen mills. **1921** W. H. JEFFERY *Deep Well Drilling* xii. 338 Swabbing and agitating are sometimes effective in causing wells to resume flowing. **1930** [see SWAB *sb.*[1] 1 f]. **1974** P. L. MOORE et al. *Drilling Practices Manual* xii. 302 When a viscous mud is being used, additional mud weight may be required because of swabbing.

attrib. **1880** BARING-GOULD *Mehalah* vii. (1884) 93 She caught up a swabbing-mop.

swabble (ˈswɒb(ə)l), *v.* *dial.* Also 5 **swable.** [f. SWAB *v.*[1] + -LE.

Cf. LG. *swabbeln* to be agitated, to sway about, reel, make the sound of splashing water, WFlem. *swabbelen, swobbelen* to draw backwards and forwards in water, to make the noise characteristic of this action; so G. *schwappeln* in similar senses; also Sw. *svabel* mop, *svabla* to mop.]

intr. **a.** To sway about. **b.** To make a noise like that of water moved about.

14.. *Promp. Parv.* 481/2 Swablynge, or swaggynge (*A.* swabbyng). **1848** EVANS *Leicester. Words*, *Swabble v.*, to vibrate with a noise, like liquids in a bottle: 'I heard the water swabble in her chest'. **1876** *Whitby Gloss.*, *Swabble*, to reel about.

ˈswabby, *a.* *rare*[−0]. [f. SWAB *sb.*[2] + -Y. Cf. SWADDY *a.*] Having pods or husks.

1659 TORRIANO, Swabbie, *scaffoso.*

Swabian (ˈsweɪbɪən), *a.* and *sb.* Also **Suabian.** [f. *Suabia*, latinized f. G. *Schwaben* + -AN.]

1. a. *adj.* Belonging or pertaining to, or native of Swabia (Schwaben), a former German duchy occupying a region now covered by the state of Baden-Württemberg and part of Bavaria. **b.** *sb.* A native of Swabia.

1785 LATHAM *Gen. Synopsis Birds* V. 60 Swabian B[ittern] ..Inhabits the banks of the Danube. **1831** *For. Q. Rev.* VIII. 348 The Swabian Era [of German literature]. **1840** BROWNING *Sordello* I. 12 They laughed as they enrolled That name at Milan on the page of gold For Godego.., Loria, and every sheep-cote on the Swabian's fief. **1845** S. AUSTIN *Ranke's Hist. Ref.* I. 195 The Swabian league. **1845** *Encycl. Metrop.* XIII. 184/1 The Alemanni or Suabians subdued the portion of Helvetia east of the Reuss. **1905** *Athenæum* 5 Aug. 173/3 A dozen cheery Austrian or Swabian tourists.

c. The dialect of Swabia. Also *Comb.*

1866 J. MACGREGOR *Thousand Miles in Rob Roy Canoe* (ed. 2) v. 76 They were much delighted..and went back prattling their purest Suabian in a highly satisfied frame of mind. **1886** STRONG & MEYER *Outl. Hist. German Lang.* v. 74 Swabian-Alemanic, spoken in Bavaria as far as the Lech, and in Würtemberg. **1937** D. P. INSKIP tr. *E. Tonnelat's Hist. German Lang.* x. 210 It is difficult to draw a boundary between Swabian and Alemanic proper. **1961** R. E. KELLER *German Dialects* 10 Speaking of a certain dialect, e.g. Swabian, implies that such a dialect has an identity which distinguishes it more or less clearly from other dialects. **1981** R. MANNHEIM tr. *G. Grass's Meeting at Telgte* iv. 22 After thirty years of residence in London, the diplomat Weckherlin still spoke an unvarnished Swabian.

2. Name of a variety of pigeon.

1855 *Poultry Chron.* II. 417/1 The beautiful spangled feathering of the Suabian Pigeon. *Ibid.* 516/1 Pens containing Jacobins,..Saxons, Magpies, Owls, Swabians. **1881** LYELL *Pigeons* 99 The ground colour of the Suabian should be of a good metallic black.

ˈswabie. *Sc.* (Shetland). [Shortening of SWARTBACK.] The greater black-backed gull.

1821 SCOTT *Pirate* x, A thousand varying screams, from the deep note of the swabie, or swartback, to the querulous cry of the tirracke. **1837** DUNN *Ornith. Orkney & Shetl.* 110.

swabifi'cation. *humorous nonce-wd.* [f. SWAB *sb.*[1] + -IFICATION.] Mopping.
1833 M. SCOTT *Tom Cringle* xvi, Here a large puff and blow, and a swabification of the white handkerchief, while the congregation blow a flourish of trumpets.

†**swac,** *a. Obs.* [Cognate with or a. MLG. *swac* (LG. *swak*), whence app. early mod.Du. *swack*, Du. *zwak* weak, pliant, MHG., G. *schwach*: cf. SWACK *a.*] Weak, feeble.
c **1250** *Gen. & Ex.* 1528 And helde ȝede on ysaac, Wurðede sighteles and elde swac. [? *Also read* on elde swac *in l.* 1197; *cf. ibid.* 1212 Wintres forðwexen on ysaac And ysmael was him vnswac.]

swach(e, obs. var. SWASH *sb.*[2], SWATCH *sb.*[1]

†**swachele.** *Obs.* Origin and sense unknown.
1600 FORMAN *Diary* (1849) 31, I bought my swachele sword this yer, and did the hangers with silver.

swack (swæk), *sb.* Chiefly *Sc.* Also 4-6, 9 **swak,** 5 **swake,** 9 **swauk.** [Echoic. Cf. *thwack, whack.*] A hard blow; a whack, bang. Also, a violent dash or impetus.
1375 BARBOUR *Bruce* v. 643 The king sic swak him gaiff, That he the hede till harnys claif. *c* **1375** *Sc. Leg. Saints* i. (*Petrus*) 586 He tuk sic a swak, þat harnise, and sched, & body, all fruschit in peciss. *c* **1425** WYNTOUN *Cron.* IX. xii. 1506 Withe a swak þar of his suerde..abuf þe fut He straik þe Lyndissay to þe bane. *c* **1480** HENRYSON *Mor. Fab., Fox, Wolf & Cadger* xx, He hint him be the heillis, And with ane swak he swang him on the creillis. **1513** DOUGLAS *Æneis* I. iii. 22 The jaw of the watter brak, And in ane heip come on thame with ane swak. *Ibid.* v. viii. 10 Now, hand to hand, the dint lichtis with a swak. **1536** BELLENDEN *Cron. Scot.* (1821) II. 511 Sum time rasand this traitour..hie in the aire, and leit him fall doun, with ane swak. **1818** SCOTT *Br. Lamm.* xxiv, The fell auld lord took the whig such a swauk wi' his broadsword that he made twa pieces o' his head. **1819** W. TENNANT *Papistry Storm'd* (1827) 205 There were sic gouffs, and youffs, and swaks. **1886** C. SCOTT *Sheep-Farming* 202 A small dog has less command over the sheep than a large one, which comes round with a heavy swack.

swack (swæk), *a. Sc.* Also 8 **swak.** [app. a. Flem. *zwak* nimble, smart = Du. *zwak* weak, pliant (see SWAC).] Supple; lithe and nimble; smart.
1768 ROSS *Helenore* I. 10 She was swak an' souple like a rae: Swack like an eel an' calour like a trout. *a* **1774** FERGUSON *Poems, Caller Water* viii, Twill mak ye suple, swack and young. **1828** in Buchan *Ball. N. Scotl.* II. 260 The lassie being swack, ran to the door fu' snack. **1868** G. MACDONALD *R. Falconer* I. 272 A good slice of swack cheese. **1871** G. GIBBON *Lack of Gold* xxxix, A swack youth of about eighteen years of age. **1893** F. MACKENZIE *Cruisie Sk.* xviii. (1894) 230 Her tongue was as swack as ever. **1894** J. INGLIS *Oor Ain Folk* vi. 74 He wis a swack man the minister!
Hence **'swacken** *v. intr.*, to become supple.
a **1820** G. BEATTIE *John o' Arnha'* 23 Wi' that her joints began to swacken.

swack (swæk), *v.*[1] *Sc.* Also 4-6, 9 **swak,** 5 **swayk,** 6 **suak, swake.** [Echoic; cf. SWACK *sb.* and obs. Du. *swacken* 'vibrare' (Kilian).]
1. *trans.* To fling, dash; to brandish (a sword).
1375 BARBOUR *Bruce* x. 623 And nocht-for-thi ȝeit ves thar ane Of thame that swakked doun a stane. *Ibid.* XVII. 691 The gynour than gert bend in hy The gyne, and swakked out the stane. [*So ed. Hart 1616*; *v.r.* swappit.] *c* **1375** *Sc. Leg. Saints* xxix. (*Placidas*) 381 To swak sir eustace in þe se. *c* **1425** WYNTOUN *Cron.* IV. iv. 380 That Cyrus suld him tak in yre, And swak him in a birnand fyre. *c* **1480** HENRYSON *Mor. Fab., Fox, Wolf & Cadger* xxi, The hering ane and ane Out of the creillis he swakkit doun gude wane. **1513** DOUGLAS *Æneis* III. ix. 114 The swelland swirl wphesit ws to hevin, Syne wald the wall swak ws doun full evin. *Ibid.* x. x. 78 Bald Lucagus swakkis a burnyst brand. **1560** ROLLAND *Seven Sages* 74 In hir armes culd scho tak Ane mekill stane, and in the well did swak. **18..** *Battle of Otterbourne* in Maidment *Scot. Ballads* (1868) I. 65 They swakked [*v.r.* swapped] their swords, till sair they sweat. **1892** J. LUMSDEN *Sheep-Head & Trotters* 34 Syne swacked they swords in deidly wroth.
absol. *c* **1590** J. STEWART *Poems* (S.T.S.) II. 69/148 Thay suak and poulsis to and fro full fast.
2. *intr.* To strike or dash heavily.
c **1470** HENRY *Wallace* v. 195 At Wallace in the hed he swaket thar. **1819** W. TENNANT *Papistry Storm'd* (1827) 147 Baith totterin' knichts were like to swak Upon the yird thegither.

swack (swæk), *int.* Imitative of the sound of a smart heavy blow.
1673 HICKERINGILL *Greg. F. Greyb.* 141 All stands [*sic*] aloft; swack, swack. **1884** G. H. BOUGHTON in *Harper's Mag.* Dec. 73/1 The swack! swack! of the fagot-cutter's 'bill-hook'.

swacked (swækt), *ppl. a. U.S. slang.* [f. SWACK *v.*[1] in Sc. dial. sense 'to gulp, swill' + -ED[1].] Drunk, intoxicated.
1932 *Amer. Speech* VII. 436 A man drunk is 'limp', 'tight', 'swacked'. **1936** WODEHOUSE *Laughing Gas* ix. 93 My father used to drink till he saw the light, and he prided himself on being able to say anything at any time of the day or night, no matter how swacked he might be, without tripping over a syllable. **1965** H. KANE *Devil to Pay* (1966) iii. 17 I'm slightly swacked on champagne. **1977** J. WAMBAUGH *Black Marble* (1978) vi. 71 They said he was bombed, swacked, bagged. By noon? She wasn't sure if it was booze.

swad, *sb.*[1] *dial.* (eastern). Also **swod.** [Local variant of SWARD *sb.* Cf. SWATH(E[2].] = SWARD *sb.* 1, 2.
c **1460** *Promp. Parv.* (Winch.) 445 Swad, or sward of flesh, *coriana.* **1877** *N.W. Linc. Gloss., Swad, Swod*..(2) The swarth or skin of bacon... *Swarth, Swath, Sward, Swad,* grass-land. **1895** *Gloss. E. Anglia* s.v., Pork swad = brawn.

swad (swɒd), *sb.*[2] Now *dial.* Also 6 **swadde,** 6-7 **swadd.** [? Of Scand. origin: cf. Norw. dial. *svadde* big stout fellow.]
1. A country bumpkin; a clodhopper; a loutish or clownish fellow; a common term of abuse.
c **1570** *Misogonus* II. ii. 6 Dost thou drinke all thy thrift thou swilbold swadd? **1572** GASCOIGNE *Hearbes, Voy. Holland* 70 A Dutche, a Devill, a swadde. **1580** H. GIFFORD *Gilloflowers* (1875) 109 When that this swad long trauailde had, Some seruice to require. **1584** R. WILSON *Three Ladies Lond.* II. A iij b, Thou horson rascall swad auaunt. **1593** G. HARVEY *Pierce's Super.* 151 A hare-braind foole in thy head; a vile swad in thy hart; a fowle lyer in thy throate. **1622** J. TAYLOR (Water P.) *Motto* Wks. II. 46/1 When I see a stagg'ring drunken swad. **1628** R. S. *Counter Scuffle* lxix, Wert not for vs, thou Swad, quoth hee, Where would'st thou fog to get a fee? **1673** S. PARKER *Reproof, Reh. Transp.* 268 Thou dastard craven, thou swad, thou mushroom.
b. *appos.* or as *adj.*
1582 STANYHURST *Æneis* IV. (Arb.) 101 Sister to swad Encelad.
2. A squat fat person. (Cf. SQUAD *a.*, SQUADDY *a.*)
[**1606** HOLLAND *Sueton.* 175 A certeine corpulent and fat swad. **1633** B. JONSON *Tale Tub* II. ii, A blunt squat swad.] **1706** PHILLIPS (ed. Kersey), *Swad,*..a gross fat Woman.

swad (swɒd), *sb.*[3] *dial.* [Origin obscure; perhaps related to SWATHE *sb.*[2], as if = covering, integument.] The pod or husk of peas, beans, etc.
1600 SURFLET *Country Farm* v. xviii. 695 They must bee gathered..presently vpon their being ripe, for else they drie vp and fall out of their swads. **1658** EVELYN *Fr. Gard.* (1675) 197 Gather them when you first perceive their swads below to open and shead. *a* **1693** *Urquhart's Rabelais* III. xviii. 145 The Bean is not seen till..its swad or hull be shaled. **1819** R. ANDERSON *Cumbld. Ball.* 94 They pelt ilk udder wi' swads. **1832** *Scoreby Farm Rep.* 19 in *Libr. Usef. Knowl., Husb.* III, It is the stem and leaf [of beans] that is wanted, more than the swad or grain. **1902** *Speaker* 26 Apr. 100/1 The pods hang down, and only the swad is used for feeding cattle.

swad (swɒd), *sb.*[4] *local.* Also 7 **swadd.** [Origin obscure.] A fish-basket.
1602 in R. G. Marsden *Sel. Pleas. Crt. Admir.* (Selden Soc.) II. Introd. 32, vij oyster swadds. **1847** HALLIWELL, *Swad*..(4) A fish-basket. *Sussex.*

swad (swɒd), *sb.*[5] *dial.* [Perhaps the same word as SWAD *sb.*[2]] A soldier. Also **swad-gill** [GILL *sb.*[7] = fellow], **swadkin.**
1708 *Mem. J[ohn] H[all]* 10 Swad or Swadkin, a Soldier. **1757** W. VERNON *Bardolph & Trulla* i. in *Lond. Chron.* 1-3 Dec. 533/3 Trulla, while I thy love enjoy'd, Nor any of the swads beside, With you might toy and kiss. **1787** W. TAYLOR *Scots Poems* 170 They may..for a swad or sailor sell you In time o' weir. **1796** GROSE *Dict. Vulgar T.* (ed. 3), *Swad,* or *Swadkin,* a soldier. *Cant.* **1812** Swod-gill [see SWADDY *sb.*]. **1853** *Whistle-Binkie* (Sc. Songs) Ser. I. 88 Ilk struttin swad, ilk reelin' sailor. **1867** SMYTH *Sailor's Word-bk., Swad,* or *Swadkin,* a newly raised soldier.

swad (swɒd), *sb.*[6] *Mining. north.* [Possibly a variant of SQUAD *sb.*[2], loose tin or other ore mixed with earth (Cornwall).] A layer of stone or worthless coal at the bottom of a seam.
1860 *Eng. & For. Mining Gloss., Newcastle Terms* (ed. 2) 65. **1865** *Our Coal & Coal-pits* 51 A black substance, called swad, resembling soot caked together.

swad (swɒd), *sb.*[7] *U.S.* Also **swod.** [?] A thick mass, clump, or bunch; hence, a great quantity (also *pl.*).
1828-32 WEBSTER, *Swad*... In New England, a lump, mass or bunch; also, a crowd. (*Vulgar.*) **1833** [SEBA SMITH] *Lett. J. Downing* ii. (1835) 32 Enoch Bissel, as sly as a weasel, slipped in [i.e. into the field-piece] a swad of grass that hit Mr. Van Buren's horse. *Ibid.* iii. 41 There was a swod of fine folks. **1840** HALIBURTON *Clockm.* Ser. III. vi. 83 How is colonist able to pay for all this almighty swad of manufactured plunder? **1844** 'JON. SLICK' *High Life New York* II. 196 The thick swad of hair that hung..all round that harnsome head of her'n. **1855** HALIBURTON *Nat. & Hum. Nat.* II. 124 It ain't good to use such a swad of words.

swa'd, Sc. pa. t. of SWELL *v.*

†**'swadder.** *Cant. Obs.* (See quot.)
1567 HARMAN *Caveat* (1869) 60 A Swadder, or Pedler. These Swadders and Pedlers bee not all evyll. [Cf. *a* **1700** B. E. *Dict. Cant. Crew, Swadlers,* the tenth Order of the Canting Tribe (**1725** *New Cant. Dict. adds* who, not content to rob and plunder, beat and barbarously abuse, and often murder the Passengers).]

†**'swaddish,** *a. Obs. rare.* [f. SWAD *sb.*[2] + -ISH[1].] Clownish, loutish.
1593 G. HARVEY *Pierce's Super.* Wks. (Grosart) II. 273 Bibbing Nash, baggage Nash, swaddish Nash.

swaddle ('swɒd(ə)l), *sb.* Also 6 **swathel(l, swathle, swadel,** 7 **swadle.** [f. next. Cf. MDu. *swadel* and SWEDDLE *sb.*]
1. Swaddling-clothes: also *fig.* Now *U.S.*
1538 ELYOT, *Crepundia*..the fyrst apparayle of chyldren, as swathels, wastcotes, and such lyke. *Ibid., Fascia,* a swathell or swathynge bande. **1605** SYLVESTER *Du Bartas* II. iii. IV. *Captaines* 19 O sacred Place, which wert the Cradle Of th' only Man-God, and his happy Swadle. **1659** TORRIANO, A swadle, or swadling band, or clout, *fascia, benda.* **1881** *Pop. Sci. Monthly* XIX. 146 And under no circumstances any swaddles or baby night-gowns. **1897** *Trans. Amer. Pediatric Soc.* IX. 14 The one reformation of delivering the child from the incarceration of the swaddle.
2. A bandage. *Obs.* or *arch.*
a **1569** KINGESMYLL *Conflict w. Satan* (1578) 22 All full of plasters and bandes and swadels. **1611** COTGR., *Braye*..a trusse, a swathell,..worne by such as are burst [= ruptured]. **1688** HOLME *Armoury* IV. xi. (Roxb.) 444/1 Silk to wipe the Armes of the King after his annoynting and a swadle to bind it on the Armes. **1711** ADDISON *Spect.* No. 90 ¶7 They..ordered me to be..put to Bed in all my Swaddles. **1857** HEAVYSEGE *Saul* (1869) 267 Who will withdraw the swaddles from thine eyes.

swaddle ('swɒd(ə)l), *v.* Forms: *α.* 5 **swaþele,** 6-7 **swathel, swathle.** *β.* 4 **suadil,** 6 **swadel(l, -il, swaddell,** 6-7 **swadle,** 7 **swoddle,** 6- **swaddle.** [f. *swath-* (see SWATHE *sb.*[2]) + -LE, and related to *swethle,* SWEDDLE, as SWATHE to SWETHE; for the phonology (-dl-:—-þl-) cf. *fiddle.* The earliest form in the group to which this verb belongs is *swaðelbond,* SWADDLEBAND.]
1. *trans.* To bind (an infant) in swaddling-clothes.
α. *a* **1425** [see SWADDLING-BAND]. **1577, 1587** [see SWADDLED].
β. **13..** [see SWADDLING-BAND]. **1491** CAXTON *Vitas Patr.* (W. de W. 1495) 94 A lytyll bende to swadle a lytyll chylde beynge in his cradle. **1535** COVERDALE *Luke* ii. 12 Ye shal fynde the babe swadled, and layed in a maunger. **1601** HOLLAND *Pliny* XI. li. I. 353 King Crœsus had a sonne, who lying swaddled [*ed.* **1634** swoddled] in his cradle, spake by that time he was sixe months old. **1633** G. HERBERT *Temple, Mortification* i, Clothes are taken from a chest of sweets To swaddle infants. **1701** C. WOLLEY *Jrnl. New York* (1860) 27 The Children they Swaddle upon a Board. **1789** W. BUCHAN *Dom. Med.* i. (1790) 13, I have known a child seized with convulsion-fits soon after the midwife had done swaddling it. **1873** RICH *Dict. Rom. & Grk. Antiq.* (1884) s.v. *Fascia,* Resembling..the manner in which an Italian peasant woman swaddles her offspring at the present day. **1879** FROUDE *Short Studies* (1883) IV. v. 355 A bambino swaddled round with wrappings.
b. *fig.*, now esp. with reference to the restriction of action of any kind.
1539 *Bible* (Great) Job xxxviii. 9 When I made the cloudes to be a couering for it, and swadled it wyth the darcke. **1613** W. LEIGH *Drumme Devot.* 15 When it pleased him to swaddle us in his mercy. *a* **1631** DONNE *Anat. World* I. 348 When Nature was most busy, the first week Swadling the new-born earth. **1670** EACHARD *Cont. Clergy* 28 The English is the language with which we are swadled and rock'd asleep. **1770** CUMBERLAND *West Indian* III. i, The sun, that..would not wink upon my nakedness, but swaddled me in the broadest, hottest glare of his meridian beams. **1774** GOLDSM. *Nat. Hist.* (1776) VIII. 137 In that state [*sc.* of aurelia] they are not entirely motionless, nor intirely swaddled up without form. **1820** HAZLITT *Lect. Dram. Lit.* 267 [His thoughts] have been cramped and twisted and swaddled into lifelessness and deformity. **1831** LADY GRANVILLE *Lett.* 16 Aug. (1894) II. 107 She looked infinitely handsomer than when in a satin frock, swaddled in jewels. **1882** MISS BRADDON *Mt. Royal* III. iii. 56 You were born and swaddled in the purple of respectability. **1893** *Sketch* 1 Mar. 260/1 The usages and traditions which govern, not to say swaddle, the ordinary theatrical manager.
c. Said of the swaddling-clothes. *rare.*
a **1618** SYLVESTER *Epigr.* Wks. (Grosart) II. 341/2 Clouts swaddle him, whom no Clouds circle can.
2. To wrap round *with* bandages; to envelop with wrappings; to swathe, bandage. Also with *up.*
α. **1597** MORLEY *Canzonets to Foure Voyces* x, Swathele me so that I may runne a gasping. **1615** G. SANDYS *Trav.* III. 133 The corses lie..shrouded in a number of folds of linnen, swathled with bands of the same. [Cf. **1631** WEEVER *Anc. Funeral Mon.* 29.]
β. **1522** MORE *De quat. Noviss.* Wks. 80/1 Twise a day to swaddle and plaster his legge. **1545** ASCHAM *Toxoph.* (Arb.) 121 To swadle a bowe much about wyth bandes. **1581** A. HALL *Iliad* IX.161 To swaddle vp the festred wound. **1589** NASHE in *Greene's Menaphon* Ded. (Arb.) 12 The Scythians, ..if they be at any time distressed with famin, take in their girdles shorter, and swaddle themselues streighter. *a* **1640** DAY *Parl. Bees* v. (1881) 38 To have their temples girt and swadled up With night-caps. **1693** EVELYN *De la Quint. Compl. Gard.* II. 110 Cleft Graffs must be swaddled with fine Earth, and Hay newly prepar'd. **1700** S. L. tr. *Fryke's Voy. E. Ind.* 141 As for our Ship, we were forced to Swaddle it with a four double Cable Rope. **1711** ADDISON *Spect.* No. 90 ¶7 They immediately began to swaddle me up in my Night-Gown with long Pieces of Linnen. **1774** PENNANT *Tour Scotl. in 1772* 284 His ears had never been swaddled down, and they stood out. **1856** KANE *Arctic Expl.* I. xxix. 402 We swaddle our feet in old cloth, and guard our hands with fur mits. **1876** MORRIS *Sigurd* IV. 385 With the golden gear was he swaddled, and he held the red-gold rod. **1897** *Allbutt's Syst. Med.* III. 763 The patient may be kept thus swaddled for six, eight or ten hours.
†**3.** To beat soundly. *colloq. Obs.*
c **1570** *Misogonus* II. i. 62 Thou disardly dronkerd..ile swaddle your skinn. *Ibid.* iv. 32 Gett me dice or I shall yow blesse Yf I haue them not quickly Ile swaddle yow wth a corde. *a* **1575** *Wife Lapped in Morrelles Skin* 846 in Hazl. *E.P.P.* IV. 214 Thy bones will I swaddle. **1607** HARINGTON *Nugæ Ant.* (ed. Park 1804) II. 98 Hercules..swadeled him thriftily with a good cudgell. **1611** BEAUM. & FL. *Knt. Burn. Pestle* II. iv, I know the place where he my loins did swaddle. **1649** DAVENANT *Love & Hon.* I. i. 360 We swadled your duke home; he and the rest Of your bruis'd countrymen have woundrous need Of capons grease. **1694** MOTTEUX

Rabelais v. xxvii. 131 A huge Sandal, with a Pitch fork in his hand, who us'd to.. rib-roast, swaddle, and swindge them. **1822** SCOTT *Nigel* xxviii, If I, with this piece of oak, did not make you such an example.. that it should be a proverb to the end of time how John Christie swaddled his wife's fine leman!

†**'swaddleband**. *Obs.* Forms: α. 2 **swaðel-**, 6 **swathell-**, **swathle-**, 6–7 **swathel-**. β. 5–6 **swadel-**, 6 **-yl-**, **swaddell-**, **swadle-**, 7 **swaddle-**. [f. SWADDLE + BAND *sb.*[1]] = SWADDLING-BAND.

α. *c* **1200** *Vices & Virtues* 49 He lai bewunden on fiteres and mid swaðelbonde ibunden. **1552** HULOET, Swathell, or swathle band for a chyld, *fascia*. **1580** HOLLYBAND *Treas. Fr. Tong, Vne Bande ou Bandelette*,.. a swathel band.

β. **1530** PALSGR. 277/2 Swadylbande, *bande, fasse*. **1530** in *Ancestor* XI. (1904) 179 An egle.. flyeng gryping a child swadeled geules lined ermyns the swadelbond gold. **1578** BANISTER *Hist. Man* IV. 58 The first of these Muscles.. goeth forward fleshy, broad, and thinne like a swadle band. **1639** MASSINGER *Unnat. Combat* IV. ii, Would you have me Transforme.. My corselet to a cradle? or my belt To swaddlebands?

So †**'swaddle-belt**, †**-bind**, †**-binding**.

1467 *Maldon, Essex, Crt. Rolls* (Bundle 43, No. 14), vi. paria caligarum, ii swadel byndes. **1592** *Wills & Inv. N.C.* (Surtees) II. 211 One fine swaddell belt 14[d]. **1653** URQUHART *Rabelais* II. xiv. 99, I swadled him in a scurvie swathel-binding.

†**swaddle-bill**. *Obs. local American*. The shoveller duck.

1709 LAWSON *Voy. Carolina* 151 Swaddle-Bills are a sort of an ash-colour'd Duck, which have an extraordinary broad Bill, and are good Meat. **1785** PENNANT *Arctic Zool.* II. 557.

swaddled ('swɒd(ə)ld), *ppl. a.* [f. SWADDLE *v.* + -ED[1].] Wrapped in swaddling-clothes.

1577 tr. *Bullinger's Decades* (1592) 149 The mothers dugge doth serue the childe, and still attendeth vppon the swathled babe. **1587** A. DAY *Daphnis & Chloe* (1890) 11 The sheepe that whilome sucked the swatheled impe. **1712** W. ROGERS *Voy.* 352 They look like a swadled Child, with its Arms at liberty. **1821** COMBE *Syntax, Wife* v, So careful did the Dame appear To guard from cold her swaddled dear. **1873** MISS BROUGHTON *Nancy* III. 59 The year is no longer a swaddled baby, it is shooting up into a tall stripling. **1911** PETRIE *Rev. Civilis.* iii. 73 The brass of Anne Astley.. with the swaddled twins in her arms.

swaddler ('swɒdlə(r)). [f. SWADDLE *v.* + -ER[1]. For the commonly accepted explanation of this term see quot. 1747. The plausibility of this account is challenged, and another origin is suggested, in *N. & Q.* Ser. IV. I. (1868) 377/1.] orig. A nickname for a Methodist, esp. a Methodist preacher, in Ireland; now, for Protestants in general.

1747 (10 Sept.) C. WESLEY *Jrnl.* (1849) I. 457 We dined with a gentleman, who explained our name to us. It seems we are beholden to Mr. Cennick for it, who abounds in such-like expressions as, 'I curse and blaspheme all the gods in heaven, but the babe that lay in the manger, the babe that lay in Mary's lap, the babe that lay in swaddling clouts', &c. Hence they nicknamed him, 'Swaddler, or Swaddling John'; and the word sticks to us all, not excepting the Clergy. **1771–2** *Ess. fr. Batchelor* (1773) II. 198 Those glorious days, when.. regulators shall disarm troops, and swaddlers superseded [*sic*] the clergy. **1810** J. LAMBERT *Trav. Canada & U.S.* (1816) I. 346 Quakers, Shakers, Swadlers, and Jumpers. **1825** COBBETT *Prot. Ref.* (1847) 105 How the swaddlers would cry out for another 'Reformation'! *a* **1834** in W. J. Fitz-Patrick *Life Doyle* (1880) I. 370 Arrah! hould yer tongue, ye canting Swaddler. **1869** CARD. CULLEN in *Times* 3 Sept. 8/3 Members may be of any religion—Catholics, Presbyterians, Anglicans, Socinians, Arians, Swaddlers. **1894** HALL CAINE *Manxman* 232 To cast ridicule on the 'swaddler' and the 'publican preacher'. **1907** *Catholic Weekly* 29 Nov. 3/3 No priest could enter, and the soupers and swaddlers had all the guidance.. of children and teachers.

swaddling ('swɒdlɪŋ), *vbl. sb.* [f. SWADDLE *v.* + -ING[1].]

1. The action of the vb. SWADDLE; wrapping in swaddling-clothes; swathing, bandaging.

13.., *a* **1425** [see SWADDLING-BAND]. **1522** MORE *De quat. Noviss.* Wks. 80/2 Al our swadlynge and tending with warme clothes. **1611** STAFFORD *Niobe* 161, I would onelie wish, to haue that one ceremonie at my buriall, which I had at my birth; I mean, swadling. *a* **1616** BEAUM. & FL. *Wit without Money* v. i, Hourly troubled, with making broths, and dawbing your decayes with swadling, and with stitching up your ruines. **1826** W. P. DEWEES *Phys. Treatm. Children* 64 The cruel practise of swaddling should be for ever laid aside.

2. *pl.* (rarely *sing.*) Swaddling-clothes; also, a bandage. Also *fig.*

1623 DRUMM. OF HAWTH. *Flowres of Sion* viii, There is hee poorelie swadl'd, in Manger lai'd, To whom too narrow Swadlings are our Spheares. *c* **1645** HOWELL *Lett.* II. lxix. (1892) 495 If you continue to wrap up our young acquaintance.. in such warm choice swadlings, it will quickly grow up to maturity. **1658** A. FOX *Würtz' Surg.* II. xxv. 155 In case the Fracture be next to the Knee from below, then use no swadlings over the Knee. **1661** GLANVILL *Van. Dogm.* 141 Our knowledge, though its Age write thousands, is still in its swadlings. **1882** *Lancs. Gloss.*, *Swaddlins, Swathelins*, wrappers for children. *S. Lancs.* **1899** CROCKETT *Black Douglas* (1900) 330 The head of Gilles de Sillé was still swathed in bandages, when, with an additional swaddling of disguise across his eyes [etc.]. **1905** F. YOUNG *Sands Pleasure* I. v, [A lighthouse] a baby yet, his stone sides hardly out of their swaddling of scaffold!

†**3.** Beating, cudgelling. *Obs.*

1628 R. S. *Counter-Scuffle* cxxx, Behinde the doore he stood to heare, For in he durst not come for feare Of swaddling. **1659** TORRIANO, A swadling, *bastonamento*.

†**4.** [after SWADDLER] Methodism; hence, conduct supposed to be characteristic of Methodists.

1759 *Compl. Lett. Writer* IV. xxx. (1768) 217, I thought if her Sidling and Swaddling, and foolish unalterable Simper, did not provoke the Country Dances to begin, nothing could. **1771–2** *Ess. fr. Batchelor* (1773) I. 49 Swaddling and zeal the female troop enflame.

5. *attrib.* in ***swaddling-robe***, a baby's long-clothes. See also SWADDLING-BAND, -CLOTHES, -CLOUTS.

1845 G. MURRAY *Islaford* 42 To make the swaddling-robe a winding-sheet.

'swaddling, *ppl. a.* [f. SWADDLER: see -ING[2].] Of a Methodist character or practice; Protestant; †canting.

1747 [see SWADDLER]. **1758** WESLEY *Wks.* (1872) II. 449 Swearing he would have none of their swaddling prayers. **1771–2** *Ess. fr. Batchelor* (1773) II. 126 Like the spiritual eye of a Swadling preacher, uplifted to Heaven in a fervour of devotion. **1787** *Minor* 30 The other now resembled a swadling female. **1838** *Blackw. Mag.* May 610/2 You're nothing but a swaddling ould sent ov a saint. **1885** W. J. FITZPATRICK *T. N. Burke* I. 33 No swaddling minister could hold his ground five minutes before them.

'swaddling-band, usually pl. **-bands**. [See SWADDLING *vbl. sb.* and BAND *sb.*[1], BOND *sb.*[1]] = next.

α. *a* **1425** [see β, quot. 13..]. **1609** HOLLAND *Amm. Marcell.* 300 Their king (as yet an infant in his swathling bands).

β. **13..** *Cursor M.* 1343 (Gött.) A new-born child.. bunden wid a suadiling band [*a* **1425** (*Trin. MS.*) swaþeling bonde]. **1560** *Bible* (Genev.) Job xxxviii. 9 When I made the cloudes as a couering thereof, and darkenes as the swadeling bandes thereof. **1590** SPENSER *F.Q.* I. x. 65 As thou slepst in tender swadling band. **1629** MILTON *Christ's Nativ.* 228 Our Babe to shew his Godhead true, Can in his swadling bands controul the damned crew. **1717** PRIOR *Alma* II. 389 One People from their swadling Bands Releas'd their Infants Feet and Hands. **1789** W. BUCHAN *Dom. Med.* i. (1790) 11 Though many of them [*sc.* brute animals] are extremely delicate when they come into the world, yet we never find them grow crooked for want of swaddling bands.

b. *fig.* and *allusively*.

1602 *2nd Pt. Return fr. Parnass.* I. i. (Arb.) 7 Then foule faced Vice was in his swadling bands. **1663** PATRICK *Parab. Pilgr.* xxix. (1687) 347 The Spirit of Man only should.. continue a Child, and never be unloosed from its swadling-bands. **1815** KIRBY & SP. *Entomol.* iii. (1818) I. 69 Having laid aside its mask, and cast off its swaddling bands,.. it is now become a true representative or image of its species. **1837** J. CHANDLER *Hymns* 2 When from the swaddling bands of shade Sprang forth the world so fair. **1845** R. W. HAMILTON *Pop. Educ.* i. (1846) 14 The swaddling-bands of a mistaken kindness.. only cramp its energies. **1875** E. WHITE *Life in Christ* II. ix. (1878) 87 Darkness is necessarily the swaddling-band of mind awakening from nothingness.

'swaddling-clothes, *sb. pl.* [SWADDLING *vbl. sb.*] Clothes consisting of narrow lengths of bandage wrapped round a new-born infant's limbs to prevent free movement. Also *transf.* an infant's long-clothes. Now chiefly *fig.* or *allusively* in reference to the earliest period of the existence of a person or thing, when movement or action is restricted.

α. **1580** HOLLYBAND *Treas. Fr. Tong, Le Berceau d'vn enfant, les langes & petits drapeaux*, a childes cradle, and swatheling clothes. **1596** SHAKS. *1 Hen. IV*, III. ii. 112 (Qo.), This Hotspur Mars in swathling cloaths, This infant warrier. **1612** R. CARPENTER *Soule's Sent.* 84 Some lie in their sinnes as children in their swathling cloathes.

β. **1535** COVERDALE *Luke* ii. 7 She brought forth hir first begotten sonne, & wrapped him in swadlinge clothes, and layed him in a maunger. **1579** W. WILKINSON *Confut. Fam. Love* 48 b, Miracles serued the Church in her swadlyng clothes. **1588** GREENE *Metamorph.* Wks. (Grosart) IX. 52 How did fortune frowne that thou wert not stifled in thy swadling cloathes? **1599** NASHE *Lenten Stuffe* Ep. Ded., This Encomion of the king of fishes was predestinate to thee from thy swadling clothes. **1687** A. LOVELL tr. *Thevenot's Trav.* I. 47 They take care that even their Sucking Children in Swadling Cloaths do not defile themselves. **1712** ARBUTHNOT *John Bull* II. iii, A child in swaddling clothes. **1796** H. HUNTER tr. *St.-Pierre's Study Nat.* (1799) III. 442 He was for many ages in swaddling clothes, begirt by the Druids with the bands of superstition. **1849** JAMES *Woodman* ii, I have never seen him since I was in swaddling-clothes. **1861** MAINE *Anc. Law* (1874) 26 To understand how society would ever have escaped from its swaddling-clothes. **1886** HALL CAINE *Son of Hagar* I. viii, A great child just out of swaddling-clothes. **1897** *Allbutt's Syst. Med.* II. 834 The efficacy of this treatment of snake-poisoning.. seems then undoubted; but it is not yet in a position to put off the swaddling-clothes of the laboratory.

'swaddling-clouts, *sb. pl.* [See SWADDLING *vbl. sb.* and CLOUT *sb.*] = prec.

1530 PALSGR. 819/2 *En maillot*, in their swadlyng cloutes. **1550** HARINGTON tr. *Cicero's Bk. Friendship* (1562) 63 b, That euen as wee came together with them in our swadling cloutes, so we might kepe them compaignie to the windyng sheete. **1592** GREENE *Repentance* Wks. (Grosart) XII. 169, I.. was euen brought vp from my swadling clouts in wickednes, my infancy was sin. **1602** CAREW *Cornwall* 72 b, When mine adverse party was yet scarcely borne, or lay in her swathling clouts. **1655** FULLER *Ch. Hist.* II. ii. §103 A Godfather, which (with Swadling-clouts) they conceive belong to Infants alone. **1658** OSBORN *Q. Eliz.* Ep., Otherwise the most part of New Books.. had still been buried in their Swadling-clouts for want of Transcription. **1678** BUNYAN *Pilgr.* I. Author's Apol. 147 Truth, although the Swadling-clouts.. Informs the Judgment.

swaddy ('swɒdɪ), *sb. slang*. Also **swaddie**, **swoddy**; cf. SWATTY. [f. SWAD *sb.*[5] + -Y.] A soldier. Now generally superseded by SQUADDIE.

1812 J. H. VAUX *Flash Dict.*, *Swoddy* or *Swod-gill*, a soldier. **1828** *Sporting Mag.* XXIII. 176 In one of his journies from Lewes, Tom picked up some swaddies. **1867** SMYTH *Sailor's Word-bk.*, *Swaddie*, a discharged soldier. **1908** A. N. LYONS *Arthur's* II. vii. 165 Up comes a swaddy in a red cap... 'That's a policeman—military policeman. Don't you 'ave no larks with 'im.'

'swaddy, *a. rare*[−0]. [f. SWAD *sb.*[3] + -Y[1].] Bearing 'swads' or pods.

1611 COTGR., *Goussu*.. coddie, hullie, huskie, swaddie.

swade, obs. or dial. f. SUADE *v.*, SWATH(E.

swadeband, obs. form of SWATHE-BAND.

‖**Swadeshi** (swə'deɪʃɪ). *Indian*. [Bengalī, lit. = own-country things, i.e. home industries.] Used chiefly *attrib.* to designate an Indian nationalist movement originating in Bengal, which advocated principally the support of indigenous industries using home-produced materials (esp. cotton), and the boycott of foreign goods. Now (since the partition of 1947) *Hist.* Hence **Swadeshism**.

1905 *Times* 26 Oct. 3/6 They prevent the students from participating in political questions,.. and furthering the Swadeshi movement. **1907** *Missionary Herald* Sept. 261/1 The political aspect of Swadeshism. **1925** S. BANERJEA *Nation in Making* 198 [Jogesh Chunder Chaudhuri] it was who first started an Industrial Exhibition of *Swadeshi* articles as an annexe to the Indian National Congress. That was in 1896. **1936** J. NEHRU *Autobiogr.* xxxv. 266 So far the Congress had thought along purely nationalist lines, and had avoided facing economic issues, except in so far as it encouraged cottage industries and *swadeshi* generally. **1941** L. S. S. O'MALLEY *Mod. India & West* xvi. 762 *Swadeshi* goods.. are goods manufactured in India by Indian labour from Indian raw and basic materials under the guidance of concerns whose capital and management are predominantly Indian, with the proviso that foreign raw or basic materials may be used in cases where India cannot supply them. **1970** 'B. MATHER' *Break in Line* xii. 156 Big coloured Swadeshi towels warming.. by the stove. **1975** E. SHILS in H. M. Patel et al. *Say not the Struggle Nought Availeth* 68 The Indian political movement.. did not cavil at the European substance of higher education. The Swadeshi movement made an issue of it, but it was more concerned with the intentions which were said to underlie it rather than with the substance.

swadge, obs. form of SWAGE *v.*[1]

swad-gill, swadkin: see SWAD *sb.*[5]

swadler: see SWADDER.

swae, obs. Sc. form of SO *adv.* and *conj.*

swæt, var. SWOTE *Obs.*, sweat.

†**swafe.** *Obs.* Also 4–5 **swayf(e**, **sweyf**, **swaffe**, 8 **swave**. [f. ON. *sveif-* in **sveifa* SWAYVE, *sveif* tiller (cf. OHG. *sweib* swinging), related to *svíf-* in *svífa* = OE. *swifan* to SWIVE; the general notion being that of sweeping or swinging.]

1. A swinging stroke or blow; momentum.

13.. *E.E. Allit. P.* B. 1268 Wyth þe swayf of þe sworde þat swolȝed hem alle. *a* **1400–50** *Wars Alex.* 806 (Ashmole MS.) Alexander.. swyngis out his swerde & his swayfe [*Dubl. MS.* swaffe] feches. **14..** *Chaucer's Troylus* II. 1383 (Harl. MS. 3943) þe grete sweyf [*v.rr.* sweyght, sweigh, swey, swough] doþ it þan fal at ones.

2. A kind of sling or ballista; = SWEEP *sb.* 25.

1688 HOLME *Armoury* III. xviii. (Roxb.) 127/2 He beareth Argent a Swafe, or swing stone, sable... These kinds may fitly be termed swafe slings. *Ibid.* 128/2 Some terme this a Slinge tree, but the best name is, a double swafe, or back swafe, to distinguish it from the swafe, or single swafe.

3. A pump-handle; = SWAPE 3, SWEEP *sb.* 24.

1688 HOLME *Armoury* III. 297/1 The Bucket of the Pump, is the like Sucker fastned to an Iron rod, which is moved up and down by the help of the Sweep, or Swafe [**1726** *Dict. Rust.* s.v. *Pump* Swave], or Handle.

†**swaff**[1]. *Obs.* Variant of SWATH[1].

1688 HOLME *Armoury* III. 72/2 A Swaffe, or Sithe Swaffe, as much as the Sithe cuts at one stroak of the Mower. [Also] the Sithe stroaks or marks, which are left in the Grass that the Sithe leaves growing.

swaff[2]. Local variant of SWARF *sb.*[2]; cf. SOIFE.

1846 GREENER *Sci. Gunnery* 141 'Swaff iron forging' is a profitable branch of forging carried on in Birmingham... It is a metal which is composed of iron and steel filings,.. and all other small scraps found in gun-makers' and other work-shops. These are.. sold to the 'swaff-forger'.

swafre, obs. form of SWAVER.

swag (swæg), *sb.* Also 4, 6 **swagge**, 7–9 **swagg**. [In senses 1 and 2 perh. of Scandinavian origin; cf. with sense 2 Norw. dial *svagg* big strong well-grown person. The other senses are mainly direct from SWAG *v.*]

†**1.** A bulgy bag. *Obs.*

1303 R. BRUNNE *Handl. Synne* 502 Þere was a wycche, and made a bagge, A bely of leþyr, a grete swagge.

†**2.** A big blustering fellow. *Obs.*

1588 *Marprel. Epist.* (Arb.) 5 Will you not sweare as commonly you do, like a lewd swag? **1589** NASHE *Martins Months Minde* 42 Kaitiues, lewd swagges, ambicious wretches. **1589** COOPER *Admon.* 62 Hee termeth him a Swag. What hee meaneth by that, I will not diuine: but as all the rest is lewde, so surely herein hee hath a lewde meaning. **1764** *Low Life* (ed. 3) 44 Munster-Cracks, Connaught-Peers, Ulster-Swags, Leinster-Fortune-Hunters, Welch-Gentle Men.

3. A swaying or lurching movement; for spec. dial. uses see quots. 1825–80, 1876.

1660 INGELO *Bentiv. & Ur.* I. (1682) 10 In goes he to the Boat..and the suddenness of the swag, overturn'd the vessel upon the passengers. **1825** J. NICHOLSON *Oper. Mech.* 44 Couplings should be placed near the bearings, as there is there the least swag. **1825** COBBETT *Rur. Rides* (1830) 75 'Oh, yes, Sir,' said he, and with an emphasis and a swag of the head. **1825–80** JAMIESON, *Swag*,..2. Inclination from the perpendicular. **1863** COWDEN CLARKE *Shaks. Char.* x. 251 One would think a 'strong-minded' woman must necessarily have the figure of a horse-guard, the swag of a drayman, and the sensibility of a carcase-butcher. **1876** *Whitby Gloss.*, *Side-swag* or *Side-sway*, a declivity close to the road side, threatening a carriage with an overbalance. **1894** BLACKMORE *Perlycross* 270 The canvas curtain had failed to resist the swag and the bellying of the blast. **1903** KIPLING 5 *Nations* 46, I looked at the swaying shoulders, at the paunch's swag and swing.

†**4.** A pendulum. *Obs.*

So dial. *swagment* (Whitby Gloss. 1876).

1686 MOLYNEUX *Sciothericum Telescop.* x. 45 The Pendulum or swagg is to be lengthned or shortned as is requisite.

5. A heavy fall or drop. *local.*

c **1700** KENNETT *MS. Lansd. 1033* s.v., One that falls down wh some violence and noise is said to come down wh a swag. **1887** *S. Chesh. Gloss.* s.v., One comes down with a swag upon the spring of a bicycle, or upon a hay-stack, or boggy ground, &c. **1912** *Blackw. Mag.* Dec. 805/2 They heard the sound they most desired, the heavy swag as, reassured, he dropped himself down again.

6. a. A wreath or festoon of flowers, foliage, or fruit fastened up at both ends and hanging down in the middle, used as an ornament; also of a natural festoon.

1794 W. FELTON *Carriages* (1801) II. 48 A pair of handsome swags of flowers, painted on the pannels. **1813** *Gentl. Mag.* Mar. 228/2 Swaggs of fruit and flowers. **1846** *Art Union Jrnl.* Jan. 36 A..scroll of foliage..flanked by living birds of a peculiar character (often used by Gibbons in his swags and trophies). **1886** *Law Times* LXXX. 310/1 A deep frieze and cornice, from which depend a series of festoons and swags. **1906** QUILLER-COUCH *Sir J. Constantine* xiv, The creepers which festooned the rock here and there in swags as thick as the *Gauntlet's* hawser.

b. *Theatr.* A festooned stage-curtain or drapery, fastened similarly. Also *transf.* and *attrib.*

1959 RAE & SOUTHERN *Internat. Vocab. Techn. Theatre Terms 58* 74 Swag border. **1961** J. OSBORNE *Entertainer* 11 Different swags can be lowered for various scenes to break up the acting areas. **1982** BARR & YORK *Official Sloane Ranger Handbk.* 136/3 Lots of pretty pelmets and a few swags, variations on the theme of stage curtains—not like those dreadful draped net affairs one sees from the bypass.

7. A sinking, subsidence; *concr.* a depression in the ground which collects water, esp. one caused by mining excavations. *local.*

1848 *Holden's Dollar Mag.* Aug. 475/2 A 'Swag' is often met with in the Western country. It is a concave spot, sunk in below the level by nature. **1856** *Jrnl. R. Agric. Soc.* XVII. II. 518 The wet 'swag' must be relieved by an additional.. channel into the exit-drain. **1883** GRESLEY *Gloss. Coal-mining*, *Swag*, subsidence or weighting of the roof. **1887** *Pall Mall G.* 12 July 8/2 Two brothers..were drowned while bathing in an old colliery swag at Bradley, near Wolverhampton. **1891** *B'ham Weekly Post* 28 July 8/3 The evidence showed that the deceased was bathing in a swag on Saturday.

8. a. *Cant.* A shop. Cf. *swag-shop* (in 12 b).

1676 COLES *Dict.*, *Swag*, a shop. *a* **1700** B. E. *Dict. Cant. Crew.* **1785** GROSE *Dict. Vulgar T.*

b. One who keeps a 'swag-shop'. *slang.*

1851 MAYHEW *Lond. Labour* I. 349 One in Holborn, and the other at Black Tom's (himself formerly a street-seller, now 'a small swag').

9. A thief's plunder or booty; *gen.* a quantity of money or goods unlawfully acquired, gains dishonestly made. *slang.*

1794 *Sessions Papers Central Criminal Court* Jan. 341/1 There are very few gentlemen here on the jury but what know what a *swag* is; the meaning is, a bundle of clothes that are stolen from any place. **1812** J. H. VAUX *Flash Dict.* s.v., *The Swag* is a term used in speaking of any booty you have lately obtained..except money. **1827** SCOTT *Let. to Croker* in Lockhart, I have been stealing from you, and..I send you a sample of the swag. **1838** DICKENS *O. Twist* xix, 'It's all arranged about bringing off the swag, is it?' asked the Jew. **1862** CALVERLEY *Charades* VI. v. in *Verses & Transl.* (ed. 2) 95 While one hope lingers, the cracksman's fingers Drop not his hard-earned 'swag'. **1891** *Newcastle Daily Jrnl.* 18 Mar. 5/3 This genial gentleman went off to America with the swag.

10. *Austral.* and *N.Z.* The bundle of personal belongings carried by a traveller in the bush, a tramp, or a miner. Freq. in colloq. phrases ***to hump the swag***: see HUMP *v.* 2; ***on the swag***: on one's travels.

1853 J. ROCHFORT *Adventurers of Surveyer* vi. 49 Disregarding the state of the roads,..we strapped on our 'swags', consisting of a pair of blankets and a spare pair of trousers, and started for the diggings. **1864** J. ROGERS *New Rush* I. 1 Their ample swags upon a cart are tied. **1881** GRANT *Bush Life Queensl.* I. v. 43 The quart-pots were now put on to boil, swags were opened and food produced. **1889** H. H. ROMILLY *Verandah N. Guinea* 5 Every digger in former days carried in imagination a gigantic nugget in his swag. **1935** J. GUTHRIE *Little Country* xxi. 312 You shouldered your swag and left to seek the foot of another rainbow. **1941** BAKER *N.Z. Slang* v. 41 Such expressions as *to swag it* and *go on the swag* need no elaboration. **1947** D. M. DAVIN *Gorse blooms Pale* 76 Jack went off on the swag for a few years. **1966** J. K. BAXTER *Pig Island Lett.* 16 No books, no bread Are left in my swag. **1971** *N.Z. Listener* 19 Apr. 56/5 He had a compass in his swag but it was pukeroo'd.

11. A great quantity *of* something (now chiefly *Austral.* and *N.Z.*); a large draught of liquor (*dial.*). (Cf. Sc. *swack.*)

1812 J. H. VAUX *Flash Dict.* s.v., A *swag* of any thing signifies emphatically a great deal. **1825–80** JAMIESON, *Swag*, a large draught of any liquid. **1851** MAYHEW *Lond. Labour* I. 373/1 The term *Swag*, or *Swack*, or *Sweg*, is,..a Scotch word, meaning a large collection, a 'lot'. **1863** *Tyneside Songs* 93 An' wishin'..For a swag o' good Newcassel yell. **1929** K. S. PRICHARD *Coonardoo* 49 A boy with a swag of ideals, Hughie was still, Mrs. Bessie realized. **1949** F. SARGESON *I saw in my Dream* ix. 75, I suppose you blokes get told a lot of yarns about a crook missis and a swag of kids. **1963** *Weekly News* (Auckland) 5 June 37/2 There was a big swag of fowls on the station running semiwild. **1973** *New Journalist* (Australia) July–Aug. 4/1 It is cheaper to buy a swag of aged situation comedies..than to produce even the simplest studio-bound program in Australia.

12. *attrib.* and *Comb.* **a. swag lamp, light** *N. Amer.*, an overhead light externally wired so that the flex hangs in a loop across the ceiling towards the power socket; **swag-like** *adv.*, after the fashion of a bushman's 'swag'; **swagman**, (*a*) a man engaged in the 'swag-trade' or who keeps a 'swag-shop' (see b); (*b*) *Austral.* and *N.Z.*, a man who travels with a 'swag'; **swagsman**, †(*a*) = *swagman* (b); (*b*) (see quot. 1890).

1970 *Toronto Daily Star* 24 Sept. 28/6 (Advt.), *Swag lamps; chromed chairs, easy chairs. **1966** M. M. PEGLER *Dict. Interior Design* (1967) 436 **Swag light*, a lamp or light fixture which is hooked into the ceiling with the electric cord ..swagged from the hanging point to the nearest wall, and then down to the floor outlet where it is plugged in. **1890** *Melbourne Argus* 2 Aug. 4/2 He strapped the whole lot together *swag-like. **1851** MAYHEW *Lond. Labour* I. 447/2 The '*swag-men' are often confounded with the lot-sellers'. **1883** KEIGHLEY *Who are You?* 36 (Morris) Then took a drink of tea... Such as the swagmen in our goodly land Have with some Humour named the post-and-rail. **1890** *Melbourne Argus* 7 June 4/2 The regular swagman, carrying his ration bags, which will sometimes contain nearly 20 days' provender in flour and sugar and tea. **1869** in W. M. Hugo *Hist. First Bushmen's Club Austral. Colonies* (1872) 30 A *swagsman, and not ashamed to own it. I have done the 'wallaby' for years past in search of a billet. **1874** A. BATHGATE *Colonial Experiences* xv. 212 One source of annoyance to the squatters is the 'swagsmen'..or men who travel about the country, professedly in search of work, but who do not in reality want it **1879** J. B. STEPHENS *Drought & Doctrine* Wks. 309 (Farmer) A swagsman..with our bottle at his lips. **1880** G. SUTHERLAND *Tales of Goldfields* 89 One of these prospecting swagsmen was journeying towards Maryborough. **1890** BARRÈRE & LELAND *Slang Dict.*, *Swagsman*,..an accomplice who takes charge of the plunder.

b. *slang.* Denoting the trade in certain classes of small, trifling, or trashy articles, those engaged in such trade, etc.

1829 P. EGAN *Boxiana* 2nd Ser. II. 74 It is impossible to describe the applause bestowed upon Delay by the boys of the Blue Anchor, the Cock and Cross, and the Ship and Gun, near the *great swag* shop in the east. **1851** MAYHEW *Lond. Labour* I. 333/2 The slaughterer sells by retail; the swag-shop keeper only by wholesale. *Ibid.* 355/1 Of these swag-barrowmen, there are not less than 150. *Ibid.*, The tinwares of the swag-barrows are nutmeg-graters, bread-graters, beer-warmers, fish-slices, goblets, mugs, save-alls, extinguishers, candle-shades, money-boxes, children's plates, and rattles. *Ibid.* 373/1 The Haberdashery Swag-Shops. By this name the street-sellers have long distinguished the warehouses, or rather shops, where they purchase their goods. *Ibid.* 447/2 The 'penny apiece' or 'swag' trade. **1904** *Daily Chron.* 25 July 6/5 Another showman described himself as 'the cheapest man for all kinds of swag watches, all goers'.

†**swag**, *a.* *Obs. rare.* [attrib. use of SWAG *sb.* 2.] ? Big and blustering.

c **1620** *Trag. Barravelt* II. vii. in Bullen *O. Pl.* (1883) II. 242 Hansom swag fellowes And fitt for fowle play.

swag (swæg), *v.* Now chiefly *dial.* Also 6 swagge, 8–9 swagg. [The existence of this verb is perh. attested for the 15th cent. in *swaggyng* (s.v. SWAGGING *vbl. sb. note*), and in SWAGE *v.*² Its immediate source is uncertain, but it is prob. Scandinavian: cf. Norw. dial. *svagga* and *svaga* to sway (see SWAY *v.* etym.).

The English word might correspond to a Scandinavian form of either type (with *-gg-* or *-g-*), according to dialect; cf., on the one hand, NAG *v.* (Norw., Sw. *nagga*), SAG *v.* (Norw. dial. *sagga*), WAG *v.* (MSw. *wagga*); on the other, DRAG *v.* (ON. *draga*), FLAG *sb.*² (Icel. *flag*, ON. *flaga*), SNAG (Norw. dial. *snag*, *snage*); also Sc. *swaw* = undulating or swinging motion, and FLAW *sb.*¹ (ON. *flaga*).]

1. *intr.* To move unsteadily or heavily from side to side or up and down; to sway without control.

a. of a pendulous part of the body, or of the whole person.

spec. in *Horsemanship*: see quot. 1850.

1530 PALSGR. 744/1, I swagge, as a fatte persons belly swaggeth as he goth, *je assouage.* **1598** R. HAYDOCKE tr. *Lomazzo* II. 13 Mouuing their limmes moderatly, and not permitting them to swag, hang, turne aside and be dilated. **1641** W. HOOKE *New Eng. Teares* 11 Here ride some dead men swagging in their deep saddles. *a* **1712** W. KING *Acc. Horace's Behaviour* Wks. 1776 III. 36 Bless me, Sir, how many craggs You've drunk of potent ale! No wonder if the belly swaggs. **1838** *Fraser's Mag.* XVII. 683 He..swags forward with the gait neither of Christian, Pagan, nor man. **1850** 'H. HIEOVER' (C. Brindley) *Pract. Horsemanship* 11 The idea that tall men are apt to, what is technically termed, 'swag' on the horse. **1859** THACKERAY *Virgin.* ix, The stout chief..sat swagging from one side to the other of the carriage.

b. of a structure or something erected or set in position, a boat, or the like. (Also *occas.* of a rigid body, to get out of line.)

1611 COTGR., *Baccoler*,..to tottar, swag, swing, lift, or heaue often vp and downe. **1633** T. JAMES *Voy.* 79 Which made her [*sc.* a ship] swag and wallow in her Docke. **1641** BROME *Joviall Crew* II. Wks. 1873 III. 393 These pounds are (as I feel them swag) Light at my heart, tho' heavy in the bag. **1664** EVELYN *Sylva* 51 Establish their weak stalks, by siefting some more earth about them; especially the Pines, which being more top-heavy are more apt to swag. *a* **1722** LISLE *Husb.* (1757) 193 Hay will often swag and pitch in the reek after making. **1784** tr. *Beckford's Vathek* 77 These vigilant guards, having remarked certain cages of the ladies swagging somewhat awry. **1793** WASHINGTON *Let.* Writ. 1891 XII. 379 The advantage of this latch is, that let the gate swag as it may, it always catches. **1801** *Encycl. Brit.* Suppl. II. 519/2 The thread, being..unable to bear close packing on the bobin, would swag out by the whirling of the fly. **1812** J. J. HENRY *Camp. agst. Quebec* 58 Though we attempted to steady it, the boat swagged. **1833** LOUDON *Encycl. Archit.* §839 If hurried, the walls will surely be crippled; that is, they will swag, or swerve from the perpendicular. **1867** D. G. MITCHELL *Rural Stud.* 85 The posts are firm and cannot swag.

c. *transf.* and *fig.* To sway; †to vacillate.

1608 MIDDLETON *Mad World* III. i, I'll poise her words i' th' balance of suspect: If she but swag, she's gone. **1649** OWEN *Stedfastness of Promises* (1650) 14 The Promise, that draws the Soul upward, and the weight of its unbelief, that sinks it downward:..the poor Creatures swaggs between both. **1705** J. DUNTON *Life & Errors* 430 If Prerogative swaggs too far on the one side, to step over to Property. **1862** CARLYLE *Fredk. Gt.* XIII. xiii. (1872) V. 130 The Austrian left wing, stormed-in upon in this manner, swags and sways. **1887** G. HOOPER *Camp. Sedan* 128 The front of battle swagged to and fro.

2. To sink down; to hang loosely or heavily; to sag. Also with *down.*

1621 tr. *Drexelius' Angel-Guardian's Clock* 270 His iawes began to drie,..his armes to swagg. *a* **1661** FULLER *Worthies, London* (1662) II. 199 A Swaggerer, so called, because endevouring to make that Side to swag or weigh down, whereon he ingageth. **1713** WARDER *True Amazons* 111 Or else such a Weight will make it swag. **1731** *Phil. Trans.* XXXVII. 31 As the Line swagged down much below the Silk Lines that supported it. **1867** SMYTH *Sailor's Word-bk.*, *Swagg*, to sink down by its own weight; to move heavily or bend. **1876** BLACKMORE *Cripps* xxvi, A timer-dray..with a great trunk swinging and swagging on the road. **1876** *Whitby Gloss.* s.v., 'It swagg'd wi' wet', was depressed with moisture; said of a plant. **1883** M. P. BALE *Saw-Mills* 337 *Swag*, a term applied to driving belts when they are too long or run too loosely.

transf. **1769** *Chron.* in *Ann. Reg.* 154/1 Many dreadful clouds..had been swagging about. **1790** BLACK *Marr. Heaven & Hell* Argt., Hungry clouds swag on the deep.

3. *trans.* To cause to sway uncertainly; to rock about; also, to cause to sink or sag.

c **1530** *Judic. Urines* I. iii. 5 b, Nother that it be not swagged nor borne fro place to place. For shakyng and boystyous ordryng may cause vryne to be trubbled. **1693** EVELYN *De la Quint. Compl. Gard.* Dict. s.v. *Truss*, To Truss up..a Branch of a Wall-Tree..that the Fruit may not ..disfigure the Tree by Swagging it down with its weight. **1708** SEWEL *Eng.-Du. Dict.* s.v., This weight will swag it down. **1777** *Chron.* in *Ann. Reg.* 215/2 He swagged the boat, and in a few minutes filled it and sunk it. **1802** MARIA EDGEWORTH *Rosanna* i, The couplings and purlins of the roof..swagged down by the weight of the thatch.

4. [f. SWAG *sb.* 10.] Chiefly *Austral.* and *N.Z.* **a.** *intr.* *to swag it*: to carry one's 'swag' or bundle of effects. Also in extended use, to travel as a swagman (*up* a region). **b.** *trans.* To pack up (one's effects) in a 'swag'; to carry in a 'swag'; also, to wander about (the land) as a swagman.

1861 T. M'COMBIE *Australian Sk.* 5 The solitary pedestrian, with the whole of his supplies, consisting of a blanket and other necessary articles, strapped across his shoulders—this load is called the 'swag', and the mode of travelling, 'swagging it'. **1861** J. HAAST *Rep. Topographical Exploration Western Districts Nelson Province* i. 16 We again started, on the 11th of February, swagging part of the provisions, &c., down the Buller. **1875** J. JENKINS *Diary Welsh Swagman* (1975) 52 It is better than swagging the country..searching for work. **1883** W. S. GREEN *High Alps N.Z.* 247 We would be obliged..to obtain a sheep and 'swag' it up the glacier again. **1887** W. W. GRAHAM *Climbing the Himalayas* iii. in *From Equator to Pole* 101 We accordingly swagged up our things. **1901** *Bulletin Reciter* (Sydney) 5 And swagging up the long divide that leads to Daybreak Range We came. **1914** A. A. GRACE *Tale of Timber Town* 116 You'll get the tucker..and you'll help swag it. **1939** J. D. PASCOE *Unclimbed N.Z.* 42 We left the hut in auspicious weather to swag up the Mingha riverbed. **1960** 'A. CARSON' *Rose by any Other Name* ix. 50, I was swagging my way up to the Northern Territory.

5. *Criminals' slang.* †**a.** To steal; to make away with (stolen property). *Obs.* **b.** To push (a person) forcefully, to 'shove'; to take or snatch away roughly.

1846 *Swell's Night Guide* 113/2 Bag, to take away, see pinch and swag. **1886** H. BAUMANN *Londinismen* 200/2 *Swag* ..*v.*, plündern, rauben. **1958** F. NORMAN *Bang to Rights* I. 10 So when we got swaged into the meatwagon I asked another geezer the strength of him, and the strength was that he'd got nicked for ponceing. **1978** J. BARNETT *Head of Force* iii. 21 The object is to see if the Commissioner was swagged away by anyone during the demo.

swagait, -gat(is, Sc. var. SOGATE, -GATES.

swag belly, swag-belly. [f. SWAG *v.* + BELLY *sb.*]

1. (as two words) A pendulous abdomen.

[**1604**: implied in SWAG-BELLIED.] **1632** SHERWOOD, A swag bellie, *ventre à poulaine*. *a* **1656** USSHER *Ann.* VI. (1658) 485 He was of an horrid look, short stature, swag belly. **1771** SMOLLETT *Humphry Cl.* 17 May, Great overgrown dignitaries..dragging along great swag bellies. **1820** W. TOOKE tr. *Lucian* I. 469 A multitude of wealthy usurers, all pale with swag-bellies. **1909** *Chambers's Jrnl.* Aug. 541/2 He is rather a decent Christian, with a swag belly and a jolly face.

b. *Path.* = PHYSCONY.

1857 DUNGLISON *Med. Lex.*

2. (with hyphen or as one word) A person having a pendulous abdomen.

1611 COTGR., *Lifrelofre*, a huffesnuffe, swag-bellie, puffe-bag. **1694** MOTTEUX *Rabelais* v. *Pantagr. Progn.* v. 239 So many Swag-bellies and Puff-bags. **1712** —— *2nd Pt. Quix.* xliii. (1749) IV. 64 Confound thee..for an eternal proverb-voiding swag-belly. **1881** *Leic. Gloss.*, *Swag-belly*, i.q. *Sludge-guts*.

Hence **swag-bellied** *a.*, having a 'swag belly' or pendulous paunch.

1604 SHAKS. *Oth.* II. iii. 80 Your Dane, your Germaine, and your swag-belly'd Hollander. **1748** SMOLLETT *Rod. Rand.* ix. (1804) 46 This swag-bellied doctor. **1858** CARLYLE *Fredk. Gt.* x. i. (1872) III. 208 Swag-bellied, short of wind. **1899** F. T. BULLEN *Way Navy* 49 A grimy, swag-bellied drudge of a steam collier.

transf. **1822** W. IRVING *Braceb. Hall* (1845) 334 He saw a swag-bellied cloud rolling over the mountains.

So †**swag-buttocked** *a.*, having large swaying buttocks; †**swag-paunch** = SWAG BELLY.

a **1652** BROME *Damoiselle* v. i, Dat is de gross English douck, fer de *swag-buttock'd wife of de Pesant. **1611** COTGR., *Ventre à la poulaine*, a gulch, big-bellie, gorbellie, *swag-paunch, bundle of guts.

†**swage**, *sb.*[1] [f. SWAGE *v.*[1] Cf. ASSUAGE *sb.*]

1. Alleviation, relief.

a **1300** *Cursor M.* 24350 (Edin.) þat suim was of mi soruing swage [*Cott.* suage].

2. *concr.* The excrement of the otter. *local.* (Cf. SWAGING *vbl. sb.*[1] 3.)

1834 MEDWIN *Angler in Wales* II. 217 Curiosity led me to look if any fresh *swages* of the dourghie [Welsh *dwrfgi* otter] were visible. **1893-4** *Northumbld. Gloss.*, *Swage*, *Spraints*, excrement of the otter.

swage (sweɪdʒ), *sb.*[2] [a. OF. *souage*, *-aige*, later and mod.F. *suage*. See also SWEDGE.]

1. An ornamental grooving, moulding, border, or mount on a candlestick, basin, or other vessel.

1374 *Acc. John de Sleford* (Acc. Exch. K.R. 397/10) m. 2 (Publ. Rec. Off.) Pro duobus paribus legherneys plauntez cum swages de laton' deauratis. **1399** (May 29) *Chancery Warrants* Ser. I. File 601. No. 1891, [Six white silver salt-cellars, gilt on the] swages. **1513** in *Archaeologia* LVI. 333 A bason of syluer all playn the swages gilt. *Ibid.* 335 A litle candelsticke of siluer, swages gilt wt a nose. **1517** *Ibid.* LXI. 86, ij newe chalices with vernacles in the patene the swages of the patens overgilt. **1539** in W. Herbert *Hist. 12 Gt. Livery Comp. Lond.* (1836) II. 196 The said Rob't disceytfully dyd sette swags for feyt to the same pecys [of silver]. **1688** R. HOLME *Armoury* III. xiv. (Roxb.) 4/1 The fillet or swage, is that ring or edge which is on the outside ye brime [of a dish]. **1739** *Act 12 Geo. II* c. 26 §6 Any Sorts of Tippings or Swages on Stone or Ivory Cases.

b. A circular or semicircular depression or groove, as on an anvil (cf. *swage-anvil* in 2 b *attrib.*)

1680 MOXON *Mech. Exerc.* xi. 196 The Point cuts a fine Hollow Circle or Swage in the Flat of the Board. **1688** R. HOLME *Armoury* III. 308/2 In the face of this kinde of Anvil are smal halfe round nicks, which are termed Swages.

2. †**a.** = GAUGE *sb.* II. *Obs.*

1688 HOLME *Armoury* III. 366/2 A..Joyners Gage (of some termed a Swage).

b. A tool for bending cold metal (or moulding potter's clay) to the required shape; also, a die or stamp for shaping metal on an anvil, in a press, etc.

1812 P. NICHOLSON *Mech. Exerc.*, *Smithing* 353 *Swages*, all instruments used to give the form or contour of any moulding, &c. used in the same manner as the rounding tool. **1831** J. HOLLAND *Manuf. Metal* I. ix. 147 The sides of the metal are then bent up with swages in the usual way, so as to bring the two edges as close together as possible. **1832** BABBAGE *Econ. Manuf.* xi. 69 The smith..has small blocks of steel into which are sunk cavities of various shapes; these are called swages, and are generally in pairs. Thus if he wants a round bolt, terminating in a cylindrical head of larger diameter,..he uses a corresponding swaging-tool. **1834-6** *Encycl. Metrop.* VIII. 454/1 (*Pottery*) With..finger and thumb,..or with his fingers only, he gives the first rude form to the vessel, and by a swage, rib, or other utensil,.. smooths the inside. **1839** URE *Dict. Arts* 379 In order to make the bolster of a given size,..it is introduced into a die, and a swage placed upon it. **1883** CRANE *Smithy & Forge* 30 Swages..consist of tools having certain definite shapes, so that the hot iron, being placed in or below them, takes their shape when struck.

attrib. **1843** HOLTZAPFFEL *Turning* I. 225 A swage-tool five feet long worked by machinery. *Ibid.* 231 The holes in the swage block..are used after the manner of heading tools for large objects. *Ibid.* 427 The metal may be gradually reduced by one pair of swage-bits. **1854** MISS BAKER *Northampt. Gloss.*, *Swage*, to work iron in a groove, or into any particular form. The anvil employed for this purpose is called a swage-anvil. **1869** RANKINE *Machine & Hand-tools* Pl. P 9, The swage-hammer.

swage (sweɪdʒ), *v.*[1] *Obs.* exc. *arch.* or *dial.* Also 3-6 **suage**, (4 **squage**, 6 **swadge**, *Sc.* **suaige**). [a. AF. *suag(i)er*, *swag(i)er*, OF. **souagier*, = Pr. *suaujar*, *suauzar*:—pop. L. **suāviāre*, parallel form to **assuāviāre*, whence OF. *asouagier* to ASSUAGE, of which *swage* is partly an aphetic derivative.] = ASSUAGE. **a.** *trans.* To appease, mitigate, pacify, relieve, reduce, abate.

(*a*) emotion, violent action, troubled thoughts, cares, etc.

a **1300** *Cursor M.* 13868 He suaged him wit wordes heind. *c* **1330** R. BRUNNE *Chron. Wace* (Rolls) 4570 Whan sire Cesar..Had pesed & swaged al þer ire. *a* **1450** *Knt. de la Tour* ix, Fastinge is an abstinence of vertu, right couenable to swage the yre of God. *c* **1450** *Guy Warw.* (Cambr. MS.) 5266 Tyll þey be swaged..And chastysed thorow þer owtrage. **1508** FISHER *7 Penit. Ps.* vi. Wks. (1876) 4 The woodnesse of the foresayd wycked spyryte sholde be mytygate and swaged. **1562** PILKINGTON *Expos. Abdyas* Pref. 13 To abate their pride, & swage their malice. **1638-56** COWLEY *Davideis* III. 353 Thus chear'd he Saul, thus did his fury swage. **1667** MILTON *P.L.* I. 556 Nor wanting power to mitigate and swage With solemn touches, troubl'd thoughts. **1671** —— *Samson* 184 Apt words have power to swage The tumors of a troubl'd mind.

(*b*) bodily injury or pain, swelling, etc.

c **1305** *Pilate* 175 in *E.E.P.* (1862) 116 His hurte was al swaged. **1398** TREVISA *Barth. De P.R.* v. xxxiii. (Bodl. MS.), A marie of fatnes..to swage þe coldnes of bones of þe breeste plaate. *c* **1400** *Lanfranc's Cirurg.* 165 ȝeue him metis & drynkis þat mowe swage þe cowȝe. *c* **1480** HENRYSON *Sum Practysis of Medecyne* 33 With þe snowt of ane selch, ane swelling to swage. **1547-64** BAULDWIN *Mor. Philos.* (Palfr.) 163 All doubtfull diseases to swage and to cure. **1582** STANYHURST *Æneis* III. (Arb.) 91 With roots of eeche herb I swadgde my great hunger. **1612** WOODALL *Surg. Mate* Wks. (1653) 32 It swageth the pains and stitches of the breast. **1882** *Lancs. Gloss.*, *Suage*, *swage*..to remove a swelling by fomentation.

(*c*) storm, wind, heat, or other physical force. Also in fig. context (cf. *a*).

a **1340** HAMPOLE *Psalter* lxxxviii. 10 [lxxxix. 9] þou ert lord til þe myght of þe see: þe stirynge..of þe stremys of it þou swagis. **1408** tr. *Vegetius' De Re Milit.* (MS. Digby 233 lf. 225/1) þe hete of þe sonne smotheth and swageth þe scharpe blastes of þe wyndes. *c* **1450** tr. *De Imitatione* III. xxxix. 110 þou..swagist þe mevinges of his flodes. **1513** DOUGLAS *Æneis* I. iii. 84 Thus said he, and with that word hastely The swelland seis hes swagit. **1549-62** STERNHOLD & H. *Ps.* lii. 8 And that my strength may now amend, which thou hast swagde for my trespace. **1582** STANYHURST *Æneis* II. (Arb.) 47 Thee wynds with bloodshed were swagd. *a* **1600** MONTGOMERIE *Misc. P.* xxxi. 43 (Laing MS.) Thy angell withe þame abod þe fyre to suaige. **1635** QUARLES *Embl.* III. iii. 18 Quench, quench my flames, and swage these scorching fires. **1849** FABER *Hymn 'Sweetness in Prayer'* i, What shall I do for thee, poor heart! Thy throbbing heat to swage?

†(*d*) To digest. *Obs.*

1768 ROSS *Helenore* I. 52 Her stammack had nae maughts sick meat to swage.

b. *intr.* (*a*) To be appeased, relieved, or reduced; to decrease, abate.

c **1330** R. BRUNNE *Chron. Wace* (Rolls) 9676 Til he were warysched of his syknesse, Or his penaunce y-swaged lesse. *c* **1375** *Cursor M.* 24350 (Fairf.) Quen þat squyme be-gan to squage. *c* **1412** HOCCLEVE *De Reg. Princ.* 4203 (Roxb.) 151 They felt his expenses swage, And were to hym vnkynde. *a* **1425** tr. *Arderne's Treat. Fistula*, etc. 100 þe pacient was delyuered of akyng and þe arme biganne for to swage. **1525** LD. BERNERS *Froiss.* II. i. 3 Than swaged the loue bitwene him and Sir Barnabo. **1545** RAYNALDE *Byrth Mankynde* II. vii. (1634) 137 If one of the brests swage which before was in good liking, the other remaining sound and safe. *a* **1548** HALL *Chron.*, *Rich. III*, 36 Lest the dukes courage should swage, or hys mynd should agayne alter. **1602** R. CAREW *Cornwall* 106 b, Where salt and fresh the poole renues As Spring and drowth encrease or swage. **1609** *Ev. Woman in Hum.* I. i. in Bullen *O. Pl.* IV, That mooving marish element that swels and swages as it please the Moone. **1702** C. MATHER *Magn. Chr.* VI. ii. (1852) 356 The brains left in the child's head would swell and swage, according to the tides.

†(*b*) *to swage of*: to mitigate, abate. *Obs.*

c **1440** *York Myst.* xxx. 371 Bidde them swage of þer sweying.

†**swage**, *v.*[2] *Obs.* [Of obscure origin; if the root-meaning is 'swing', it is perh. an early form of SWAG *v.*]

1. *intr.* To direct a blow, swing.

c **1400** *Destr. Troy* 7430 þe sun of Theseus..choppit to Ector: With a swyng of his sword swagit on þe prinse.

2. *trans.* To discharge (a gun or ballista).

c **1420** ? LYDG. *Assembly of Gods* 1038 He gan swage gonnes as he had be woode. *c* **1440** *Promp. Parv.* 219 Gunnare, or he þat swagythe a gunne, *petrarius*, *mangonalius*.

swage (sweɪdʒ), *v.*[3] [f. SWAGE *sb.*[2] Cf. SWEDGE *v.*] *trans.* To shape or bend by means of a swage.

1831 J. HOLLAND *Manuf. Metal* I. ix. 141 The article being thus hammered, is next pared with shears to the shape required, after which it is swaged or turned up at the edges. **1832**, **1854** [see SWAGE *sb.*[2] 2 b]. **1838** F. W. SIMMS *Pub. Wks. Gt. Brit.* 48 The bolt to be swaged and made truly cylindrical. **1877** W. JONES *Finger-ring* 266 A ring..found at Fransham, has the hoop swaged or twisted. **1904** *Times* 20 Aug. 7/6 The sectional poles shall be..swaged together when hot so as to make a perfect joint.

†**swaged**, *ppl. a.*[1] *Obs.* [f. SWAGE *v.*[1] + -ED[1].] Reduced, restrained.

a **1603** T. CARTWRIGHT *Confut. Rhem. N.T.* Pref. (1618) 13 They can put no difference betweene a swelling and swaged speech, betweene an honest homely stile, and that which is pricked and pranked vp.

swaged (sweɪdʒd), *ppl. a.*[2] [f. SWAGE *sb.*[2] and *v.*[3] + -ED.]

†**1.** Having a swage or ornamental groove, moulding, etc. *Obs.*

1487 in *Surrey Archæol. Coll.* III. 164, I bequeathe to said Elizabeth my daughter..ii goblettes of silver swaged. **1490** in *Somerset Med. Wills* (1901) 292, 3 bollyd peces swagid. **1535** in Strype *Mem. Cranmer* (1694) App. xvi. 27 Three standing Cups; one plain, and other two swaged with their Covers of silver and gilt. *a* **1548** HALL *Chron.*, *Hen. VIII*, 157 At the nether ende were two broade arches vpon thre antike pillers all of gold, burnished swaged and grauen full of Gargills and Serpentes.

2. Shaped with a swage.

1842 *Civil Eng. & Arch. Jrnl.* V. 286/2 If we only take the trouble to anneal such a swaged axle after it has received the most severe compression. **1859** F. S. COOPER *Ironmongers' Catal.* 169 Candlesticks, Plain Round..Swaged..Plain Oblong. **1894** *Times* 16 Aug. 6/3 Hammered moulds or swaged steel.

†'**swagement.** *Obs. rare.* [f. SWAGE *sb.*[2] + -MENT.] The fluting of a column.

1519 HORMAN *Vulg.* 241 A playted pyller gathereth dust in the swagementis (*in strigilis*).

†'**swager**[1]. *Obs. rare.* [f. SWAGE *v.*[1] + -ER[1].] = ASSUAGER.

1612 WOODALL *Surg. Mate* Wks. (1653) 29 This..plaster is a..good swager of pains.

swager[2] ('sweɪdʒə(r)). Now *rare.* [f. SWAGE *v.*[3] + -ER[1].] One who swages metal.

1881 in *Instructions to Census Clerks* (1885) 91. **1921** *Dict. Occup. Terms* (1927) §190 s.v., Agricultural machine knife swager. **1954** *Times* 9 Apr. 9/4 In my grandfather's lifetime the swager was a familiar figure in the West Country.

swagged (swægd), *ppl. a.* [f. SWAG *v.* + -ED[1].] Sagged, sunken.

1825 C. M. WESTMACOTT *Eng. Spy* II. 83 Cracked walls, swagged floors, bulged fronts, sinking roofs, leaking gutters. **1878** *Cumbld. Gloss.*, *Swag't*, bent downwards in the centre.

swagged, *a.* [f. SWAG *sb.* 6 + -ED[2].] Draped in swags; decorated with swags.

1959 *House & Garden* July 13 For curtains, we suggest.. swagged muslin. **1970** *Daily Tel.* 21 Oct. 15 Two Moroccan woollen belts, about 54in long,..bound and swagged with other bright wools.

swagger ('swægə(r)), *sb.*[1] [f. SWAGGER *v.*]

1. a. The action of swaggering; external conduct or personal behaviour marked by an air of superiority or defiant or insolent disregard of others.

1725 SWIFT *New Song on Wood's Halfpence* viii, The butcher is stout, and he values no swagger. **1809** MALKIN *Gil Blas* IV. v. ¶3 She could put on as brazen-faced a swagger as the most impudent dog in town. **1811** *Sporting Mag.* XXXVII. 86 After much swagger, he asked the constable if he knew who he was? **1871** L. STEPHEN *Playgr. Eur.* (1894) v. 117 Tall, spare,..with a jovial laugh and a not ungraceful swagger. **1877** MRS. FORRESTER *Mignon* I. 21 A man who has outgrown the swagger and affectations of boyhood, and settled down into a..respectable member of society. **1885** RIDER HAGGARD *K. Solomon's Mines* v, He was an impudent fellow, and..his swagger was outrageous.

b. *transf.* Applied to a mental or intellectual attitude marked by the same characteristics.

1819 KEATS *Otho* I. i, No military swagger of my mind, Can smother from myself the wrong I've done him. **1840** DE QUINCEY *Rhet.* Wks. 1859 XI. 33 As to Chrysostom and Basil, with less of pomp and swagger than Gregory, they have not at all more of rhetorical burnish and compression. **1869** LD. COLERIDGE in E. H. Coleridge *Life & Corr.* (1904) II. vi. 165 The mingled swagger and cowardice of the whole transaction. **1908** *Athenæum* 5 Dec. 727/1 He respects the public, contempt for whom is at the root of most artistic display and swagger.

2. Short for *swagger bag*, *cane*, *coat*, etc.: see SWAGGER-. *mod. colloq.*

1929 *Papers Mich. Acad. Sci., Arts & Lett.* X. 327/2 *Swagger* (hospital slang), a tunic for promenade occasions; 'square-push' tunic. **1939** [see *beaver lamb* s.v. BEAVER[1] 6]. **1968** J. IRONSIDE *Fashion Alphabet* 38 *Swagger*, a jacket with a very full back, hanging loose in front. **1979** *Arizona Daily Star* 1 Apr. (Suppl.), In-fashion spring bags... Swaggers, shoulder-straps, double handles.

swagger ('swægə(r)), *sb.*[2] [f. SWAG *v.* or *sb.* + -ER[1].]

I. 1. One who causes a thing to 'swag' or sway.

1653 URQUHART tr. *Rabelais* I. ii. 17 The swagger who th' alarum bell holds out [orig. *Le brimbaleur qui tient le cocquemart*].

II. 2. *Austral.* and *N.Z.* One who carries a swag; a swagman.

1855 *Melbourne Argus* 19 Jan. 6/1 We have observed a great influx of swaggers lately—all seemingly bound for Smith's Creek. **1904** LADY BROOME *Colonial Mem.* 33, I wonder if 'swaggers' have been improved off the face of the country districts of New Zealand? Tramps one would perhaps have called them in England, and yet they were hardly tramps so much as men of a roving disposition, who wandered about asking for work, and they really could and did work if wanted.

swagger (ˈswægə(r)), *a.* *colloq.* or *slang.* [f. next.] Showily or ostentatiously equipped, etc.; smart or fashionable in style, manner, appearance, or behaviour; 'swell'.

1879 *Cambridge Rev.* 26 Nov. 103/2 Is it because the college can't afford to have them [*sc.* railings] painted? Or are they having some swagger new ones made? **1884** *All Yr. Round* 18 Oct. 34/2 She becomes, according to the ideas of her class, quite a 'swagger' personage. **1888** *Echoes fr. Oxford Mag.* (1890) 111 Though Bishops and Dons boss the show, And you think that it's awfully swagger. **1890** F. W. ROBINSON *Very Strange Family* 172 Keeping you company in your swagger chambers. **1896** MARIE CORELLI *Mighty Atom* ii, Sir Charles was a notable figure in 'swagger' society.

swagger (ˈswægə(r)), *v.* [app. f. SWAG *v.* + -ER[5]. Cf. the following:—

1598 CHAPMAN *Achilles Shield* To the Vnderstander B 2, Swaggering is a new worde amongst them, and rounde headed custome giues it priuiledge with much imitation, being created as it were by a naturall *Prosopopeia* without etimologie or deriuation.]

1. *intr.* To behave with an air of superiority, in a blustering, insolent, or defiant manner; now *esp.* to walk or carry oneself as if among inferiors, with an obtrusively superior or insolent air.

1590 SHAKS. *Mids. N.* III. i. 79 What hempen home-spuns haue we swaggering here, So neere the Cradle of the Faierie Queene? **1612** T. TAYLOR *Comm. Titus* i. 6 The cause that now they Swagger, and are masterlesse abroad, is because they were never well mastered at home. *a* **1641** BP. MOUNTAGU *Acts & Mon.* (1642) 323 Antonius..sent away P. Ventidius thither to command in chiefe, whilest himselfe swaggered and revelled (drunken beast as hee was) at Athens. **1726** SWIFT *Gulliver* II. iii, [He] became so insolent ..that he would always affect to swagger and look big as he passed by me. **1765** GOLDSM. *Ess.* x, The bunters who swagger in the streets of London. **1824** W. IRVING *T. Trav.* I. 66 He took complete possession of the house, swaggering all over it. **1853** R. S. SURTEES *Sponge's Sp. Tour* xxii. 113 [He] swaggered about like an aide-de-camp at a review. **1891** E. GOSSE *Gossip in Library* xii. 150 We may think of him as swaggering in scarlet regimentals.

With *it.* **1612** ROWLANDS *Knave of Harts* (Hunter. Cl.) 5 To take a purse, or make a Fray, Tis we that swagger it away. *a* **1656** CAPEL *Rem.* (1658) To Rdr., Alcibiades could swagger it at Athens. *a* **1661** HOLYDAY *Juvenal* (1673) 281 They should..swagger it out bravely in their trappings and chains of gold.

transf. **1613** JACKSON *Creed* II. xvi. §7 To see a grande demure Schoole Diuine,..swaggering it in the metaphoricall cut. **1678** CUDWORTH *Intell. Syst.* 61 It was Atheism openly Swaggering, under the glorious Appearance of Wisdom and Philosophy. **1827** SCOTT *Chron. Canongate* v, A sort of pageant, where trite and obvious maxims are made to swagger in lofty and mystic language.

b. *spec.* To talk blusteringly; to hector; †hence, to quarrel or squabble *with*; also, to grumble. Now only (directly *transf.* from prec. sense), to talk boastfully or braggingly.

1597 SHAKS. *2 Hen. IV*, II. iv. 107 Hee will not swagger with a Barbarie Henne, if her feathers turne backe in any shew of resistance. **1599** —— *Hen. V*, IV. vii. 131 A Rascall that swagger'd with me last night. **1599** NASHE *Lenten Stuffe* 31 Wise men in Greece in the meane while [were trivial] to swagger so aboute a whore [*sc.* Helen]. **1601** ? MARSTON *Pasquil & Kath.* (1878) III. 4 Hee dings the pots about, cracks the glasses, swaggers with his owne shaddow. **1611** CORYAT *Crudities* 236 Some of them beganne very insolently to swagger with me, because I durst reprehend their religion. **1644** TREVOR in T. Carte *Ormond* (1735) III. 267 Sir George Radcliffe and Bathe are very violent, which makes the Irish swagger very severely. **1650** H. MORE *Observ.* in *Enthus. Tri.*, etc. (1656) 127 You swagger and take on..as if..you were of the same fraternity with the highest Theomagicians in the World. **1664** [J. SCUDAMORE] *Homer à la Mode* 1 One Captaine at another swaggers. **1665** GLANVILL *Scepsis Sci.* Address p. iv, The disputes of Men that love to swagger for Opinions. **1670** G. H. *Hist. Cardinals* III. III. 313 The Captains swagger'd [orig. *brontolavano* = grumbled], that they were not obey'd by their Souldiers. **1736** SHERIDAN *Let. to Swift* 31 July, You may think I swagger, but as I hope to be saved it is true. **1854** J. HANNAY *Sat. & Satirists* i. 28 The fellow swaggers and chuckles over every item of his own feast to the men he is entertaining. **1871** L. STEPHEN *Playgr. Eur.* (1894) xiii. 309, I will not say that no mountaineer ever swaggers. **1889** *The County* viii. I. 114 It pays him to have pretty girls about the house and to swagger about his goodness to them.

c. *trans.* To influence, force, or constrain by blustering or hectoring language; to bring *into* or *out of* a state by blustering talk.

1605 SHAKS. *Lear* IV. vi. 240 And 'chud ha' bin zwaggered out of my life. **1606** —— *Tr. & Cr.* v. ii. 136 Will he swagger himselfe out on's owne eyes? **1613** PURCHAS *Pilgrimage* VIII. ix. 655 The Indian iagges himselfe out of humane lineaments the other swaggers himselfe further out of all ciuill and Christian ornaments. **1647** CLARENDON *Hist. Reb.* v. §30 These quick Answers from the King..made it evident to them that he would be no more Swaggered into concessions. **1728** SWIFT *Acc. Crt. & Emp. Japan* ¶12 He would swagger the boldest men into a dread of his power.

2. *intr.* To sway, lurch; *Sc.* to stagger.

1724 RAMSAY *Vision* xix, Staggirrand, and swaggirrand, They stoyter hame to sleip. **1825–80** JAMIESON, To *Swagger*, to stagger, to feel as if intoxicated, *Moray*. **1845** BAILEY *Festus* (ed. 2) 239 The large o'erloaded wealthy-looking wains Quietly swaggering home through leafy lanes.

b. *causatively.*

1851 MAYHEW *Lond. Labour* I. 60, I asked a girl..whether her tray was heavy to carry. 'After eight hours at it,' she answered, 'it swaggers me, like drink.'

swagger-, the verb SWAGGER used in comb.; *swagger-bag*; **swagger-cane, -stick**, an officer's cane or stick; the short cane or stick carried by soldiers when walking out; so *swagger-dress*; **swagger coat**, a three-quarter-length ladies' coat cut with a loose flare from the shoulders (particularly fashionable in the 1930s).

1887 *Times* 11 Apr. 11/5 Their clothes fit them well; they generally carry themselves well; many have swagger-sticks. **1889** *Junior Army & Navy Stores Price List* 669 H, Swagger or Parade Canes. **1890** KIPLING *Soldiers Three* (1891) 24 An' then I meks him [*sc.* a dog] joomp ovver my swagger-cane. **1901** *Westm. Gaz.* 4 Mar. 4/1 The 'swagger', or walking-out, dress of the soldier. **1933** *Bulletin* (Glasgow) 14 Oct. 15/1 A swagger-coat with collarette and gauntlets of black astrakhan. **1938** 'J. BELL' *Port of London Murders* ii. 24 Her hands were pushed into the pockets of an old swagger coat. **1953** 'P. WENTWORTH' *Watersplash* ii. 8 The glove and its fellow had been thrust into the pocket of a blue swagger coat. **1974** *Index-Jrnl.* (Greenwood, S. Carolina) 23 Apr. 3/2 (Advt.), Special selection of baskets, swagger bags, totes, envelopes. **1980** B. BAINBRIDGE *Winter Garden* x. 74 She stood in the gutter in her swagger coat and allowed her teeth to chatter piteously.

swaggerer (ˈswægərə(r)). [f. SWAGGER *v.* + -ER[1].] One who swaggers; †a quarreller.

1592 *Nobody & Someb.* in Simpson *Sch. Shaks.* (1878) I. 292 Your Cavaliers and swaggerers bout the towne That dominere in Taverns, sweare and stare. **1597** SHAKS. *2 Hen. IV*, II. iv. 81 Shut the doore, there comes no Swaggerers heere. **1649** MILTON *Eikon.* ii. Wks. 1851 III. 355 All the passages..be besett with Swords and Pistols cockt and menac'd in the hands of about three hundred Swaggerers and Ruffians. **1779** JOHNSON *L.P.*, *Butler* Wks. II. 186 Hudibras..the hero..compounded of swaggerer and pedant. **1841** DICKENS *Barn. Rudge* x, None of your audacious young swaggerers, who would even penetrate into the bar. **1855** MACAULAY *Hist. Eng.* xvi. III. 641 Some swaggerers, who had..run from the breastwork at Oldbridge without drawing a trigger, now swore that they would lay the town in ashes.

swaggering (ˈswægərɪŋ), *vbl. sb.* [f. SWAGGER *v.* + -ING[1].] The action of the verb SWAGGER; the behaviour of a swaggerer; †quarrelling.

a **1596** *Sir T. More* (Malone Soc.) 865 You think..with your swaggering, you can bear't away. **1611** MIDDLETON & DEKKER *Roaring Girle* D.'s Wks. 1873 III. 170 They keepe a vilde swaggering in coaches now a daies. **1624** CAPT. J. SMITH *Virginia* VI. 223 Much swaggering wee had with them. **1687** T. BROWN *Saints in Uproar* Wks. 1730 I. 72 There is..such swaggering and bouncing..that..I expected every minute it would come to downright kick and cuff between 'em. *a* **1715** BURNET *Own Time* III. (1724) I. 501 (an. 1681) In their cups the old valour and the swaggerings of the Cavaliers seemed to be revived. **1837** W. IRVING *Capt. Bonneville* II. 177 Such is the kind of swaggering and rodomontade in which the 'red men' are apt to indulge in their vainglorious moments.

ˈswaggering, *ppl. a.* [f. SWAGGER *v.* + -ING[2].] That swaggers.

1. Having a blustering or insolent air of superiority; characteristic of a swaggerer.

1596 NASHE *Saffron-Walden* Wks. (Grosart) III. 145 They were two well bumbasted swaggering fat bellies. **1597** SHAKS. *2 Hen. IV*, II. iv. 76 Hang him, swaggering Rascall, let him not come hither. **1600** BRETON *Pasquil's Fooles Cap* lxxxiv, Hee that puts fifteene elles into a Ruffe And seauenteene yards into a swagg'ring slappe. **1612** BEAUM. & FL. *Cupid's Revenge* II. i, He..looks the swaggeringst, and has such glorious cloaths. **1670** EACHARD *Cont. Clergy* 38 The high tossing and swaggering preaching; either mountingly eloquent or profoundly learned. **1727** SWIFT *To Yng. Lady* Wks. 1841 II. 303/1 A tribe of bold, swaggering, rattling ladies. **1790** BURKE *Fr. Rev.* Wks. V. 426 They made a sort of swaggering declaration, something, I rather think, above legislative competence. **1826** COBBETT *Rur. Rides* (1885) II. 105 Great swaggering inns. **1828** LYTTON *Pelham* III. xx, Thornton entered with his usual easy and swaggering air of effrontery. **1838** DICKENS *Nich. Nick.* xxxii, The individual whom he presumed to have been the speaker was coarse and swaggering. **1875** JOWETT *Plato* (ed. 2) I. 171 Our questioner will rejoin with a laugh, if he be one of the swaggering sort, That is too ridiculous [etc.].

2. Lurching, swaying.

1865 A. SMITH *Summer in Skye* I. 301 Through a yellow September moonlight, roll the swaggering wanes.

Hence **ˈswaggeringly** *adv.*, in a swaggering manner, with a swagger.

1611 COTGR., *Guinguois, de guinguois*, huffingly, swaggeringly, aswash. **1685** BUNYAN *Pharisee & Publican* 111 The poor Pharisee..when so swaggeringly he, with his *God I thank thee*, came into the Temple to pray. **1855** *Chamb. Jrnl.* III. 413 He..swaggeringly announced that one Gabriel Derjarvin was below. **1886** MISS BROUGHTON *Dr. Cupid* xi, 'I do not care what she says!' replies Lily swaggeringly.

swaggie (ˈswægɪ). *Austral. colloq.* Also **-y.** [f. *swagman* (see SWAG *sb.* 12) + dim. suffix -IE, -Y.] A swagman.

1892 E. W. HORNUNG *Under Two Skies* 109 Here's a swaggie stopped to camp, with flour for a damper. **1900** H. LAWSON *Over Sliprails* 88 Thefts and annoyances of the above description were credited to the 'swaggies' who infested the roads.

swagging (ˈswægɪŋ), *vbl. sb.* [f. SWAG *v.* + -ING[1].]

Swaggyng in the following quot. may attest the existence of this word for the 15th century, but the true reading is no doubt *swagynge* (i.e. SWAGING, alleviation), as in MS. Rawl. Poet. 32 (cf. v.r. *swagenyng*).

?*a* **1412** LYDG. *Fab. Duorum Merc.* (1897) 511 O weepyng Mirre, now lat thy teerys reyne In to myn ynke so clubbyd in my penne, That rowthe in swaggyng abroode make it renne.

1. a. The action of swaying or rocking to and fro; motion up and down or backwards and forwards; *occas.* wagging (of the head).

1566 STUDLEY tr. *Seneca's Agam.* III, She [*sc.* a ship] with her swaggyng full of sea to bottom lowe doth sinke. **1776** G. SEMPLE *Building in Water* 128 To prevent their wrecking, swagging or dislocating. **1809** MALKIN *Gil Blas* XI. vii. ¶5 A wise swagging to and fro of my head. **1833** LOUDON *Encycl. Archit.* §829 In order to prevent the swagging or sinking of the head or falling style. **1853** SIR H. DOUGLAS *Milit. Bridges* 317 By bracing the beams together, and preventing the bridge from swagging.

fig. **1862** CARLYLE *Fredk. Gt.* XII. xii. (1872) IV. 272 In this manner, Walpole..had balanced the Parliamentary swaggings and clashings.

†**b.** *fig.* Vacillation. *Obs.*

1636 FEATLY *Clavis Myst.* lvii. 778 The people..after much swagging on both sides,..came to fix upon this middle way.

2. Sagging *down*.

1624 WOTTON *Archit.* in *Reliq.* (1651) 224 Because so laid, they [*sc.* brick or squared stones] are more apt in swagging down, to pierce with their points, then in the jacent Posture. **1792** BELKNAP *Hist. New-Hampsh.* III. 75 It is usual for the surveyor to make large measure... Some allow one in thirty, for the swagging of the chain. **1800** *Trans. Soc. Arts* XVIII. 273 A hollow cast-iron roller..in order to bear up the rope, and to prevent it from swagging.

3. *Austral.* and *N.Z.* Travelling as a swagman; carrying one's 'swag', back-packing.

1883 W. S. GREEN *High Alps N.Z.* xvi. 268 Descending to the lower camp..and doing the hard swagging work all over again. **1892** *N.Z. Alpine Jrnl.* I. 100 All our dirty work and heavy swagging will be done for us. **1940** W. S. GILKISON *Peaks, Packs & Mountain Tracks* xiii. 102 Swagging—or, if you prefer it, back-packing—is more or less an essential part of every climbing trip. **1960** 'A. CARSON' *Rose by any Other Name* ix. 50 Swagging is an honourable profession in Australia.

swagging (ˈswægɪŋ), *ppl. a.* [f. SWAG *v.* + -ING[2].]

1. Swaying heavily to and fro; pendulous with weight; hanging loosely.

1593 CHURCHYARD *Challenge* 180 With bellies big, and swagging dugges. **1600** SURFLET *Countrie Farme* II. liv. 369 The brests that are too great & swagging. *a* **1693** *Urquhart's Rabelais* III. xxviii. 230 Swagging cod [orig. *couillon avallé*]. *a* **1722** LISLE *Husb.* (1757) 310 His [*sc.* a ram's] figure should be stately and tall, his belly big, swagging, and woolly. **1727** GAY *Fables* I. xxxvii, Beneath her swagging pannier's load. *a* **1793** G. WHITE *Selborne* etc. (1853) 396 Vast swagging rock-like clouds. **1852** D. JERROLD *Wks.* (1864) II. 497 A purple bloated face and swagging paunch.

b. Of a vehicle: Swaying, lurching, lumbering.

1754 H. WALPOLE *Let. to J. Chute* 21 May, You will dine at Farley in a swagging coach with fat mares of your own. **1827** HONE *Every-day Bk.* II. 1154 The swagging cart.. Reels careless on.

†**2.** ? Big, 'whopping'. *Obs.*

1731 MEDLEY *Kolben's Cape Gd. Hope* I. 203 When the Hottentots louse themselves, they generally pick up the large swagging lice,..and devour them.

swaggy (ˈswægɪ), *a.* *rare*[−1]. [f. SWAG *v.* + -Y.] = SWAGGING *ppl. a.* 1.

1646 SIR T. BROWNE *Pseud. Ep.* III. iv. 112 His swaggy and prominent belly.

†**ˈswaging**, *vbl. sb.*[1] *Obs.* [f. SWAGE *v.*[1] + -ING[1].]

1. Assuagement, alleviation, relief.

1340–70 *Alex. & Dind.* 921 Aftur swaginge of swinc swiþe comeþ ioie. **1382** WYCLIF *Eccl.* xxxvi. 25 If ther is tunge of curing, ther is and of swaging, and of mercy. *c* **1425** WYNTOUN *Cron.* IV. iii. 230 Qwhil þe ost þe huffynge made, And swagyn [*v.r.* swageing] of þe wattyr bayde. **1483** *Cath. Angl.* 373/1 A Swagynge, *mitigacio.* **1531** TINDALE *Expos. 1 John* ii. (1537) 19 The swagynge of woundes. **1543** TRAHERON *Vigo's Chirurg.* v. vi. 170 Yf medicine preuayle not for the swagynge of the toothe ache.

2. Subsidence into a state of quiescence, or the like.

c **1440** *Promp. Parv.* 481/2 Swagynge of blood, *stagnacio.* **1530** PALSGR. 277/2 Swagyng, *refrigeration.*

3. *concr.* An otter's excrement. (Cf. SWAGE *sb.*[1] 2.)

1590 COCKAINE *Treat. Hunting* Dij, Your huntsman.. must goe to the water; and seeke for the new swaging of an Otter.

So †**ˈswaging** *ppl. a.*, alleviating.

1483 *Cath. Angl.* 372/2 Swagynge, *mulcens.*

swaging (ˈsweɪdʒɪŋ), *vbl. sb.*[2] [f. SWAGE *sb.*[2], *v.*[3] + -ING[1].] †**a.** The making of swages or mouldings. **b.** The use of the swage in shaping metal. Also *attrib.*

1688 HOLME *Armoury* III. 259/2 Swaging, is to put edges or Threads to the skirts or any part of a Plate. **1832** [see SWAGE *sb.*[2] 2 b]. **1842** *Civil Eng. & Arch. Jrnl.* V. 285/2 This very cold hammering and swaging, as it is termed. **1880** R. GRIMSHAW (*title*) The History..of Saws of all kinds, with appendices, concerning..Setting, Swaging, Gumming, Filing, etc. **1884** *B'ham Daily Post* 23 Feb. 2/4 Wireing, Swaging and Wheeling Machines.

Swahili (swɑːˈhiːlɪ, swə-). Also **Sowauli, Suhaili, Suaheli, -ele, Swaheli.** [lit. = pertaining to the coasts, f. Arab. *sawāḥil*, pl. of *sāḥil* coast. In Fr. *souayeli*.] **a.** A Bantu people (or one of them) inhabiting Zanzibar and the adjacent coast; also, their language, Kiswahili. **b.** *attrib.* or as *adj.* Hence **Swahiˈlese (Sowhylese), Swaˈhilian** *adjs.*, of or pertaining to (the)

Swahili; **Swahilized** *ppl. a.*, assimilated to the Swahili.

1814 H. SALT *Voy. Abyssinia* etc. App. i. p. iii, Some sailors attached to an Arab boat, who called themselves Sowauli. *Ibid.* p. iv, The Sowauli are sometimes called Sowaiel by their northern neighbours the Somauli. **1833** *W. F. W. Owen's Narr. Voy. Africa*, etc. I. xix. 358 The language of these people differs from that of the Sowhylese. *Ibid.*, Every Arab and Sowhyly carries a sword. *Ibid.* 360 The most wealthy of these Sowhyly states was the Sultany of Patta. **1846** J. R. BROWNE *Etchings Whaling Cruise* xvi. 335 The Sowhelian language is the most generally spoken. **1847** W. W. GREENOUGH in *Jrnl. Amer. Oriental Soc.* I. 263 The Sooahelee has been called a lingua franca. **1850** LATHAM *Nat. Hist. Man* 490 The tribes speaking the Suaheli language. **1893** D. J. RANKIN *Zambesi Basin* xvi. 268 The Swahili and Swahilised natives. **1907** J. H. PATTERSON *Man-Eaters of Tsavo* xviii. 194, I had a long talk with him in broken Swahili.

swaide, swaie: see SWAY *v.*

swaif, obs. Sc. form of SUAVE.

swail, var. SWALE; obs. f. SWEAL.

swaimish, -ous, dial. ff. SQUEAMISH, -OUS.

swain (sweɪn), *sb.* Forms: 2–5 **swein,** 3–5 **sweyn,** 4–5 **swayn,** 4–6 **swayne, squayne,** *Sc.* **swane,** 4–7 **swaine,** (3 **swæin, suein,** 4 **sueyn, suayn, suain,** 5 **sweyne,** 6 **suane),** 3, 7– **swain.** [a. ON. *sveinn* boy, servant, attendant, = OE. *swán* SWON. Occurs as the second element of a compound in *boatswain* (late OE. *bátswegen*), *coxswain*.]

†**1.** A young man attending on a knight; hence, a man of low degree. (Often coupled with *knight*.) *Obs.*

a **1150** *O.E. Chron.* (Laud) an. 1128 Se eorl wearð ȝewunded at an ȝefiht fram anne swein. *c* **1205** LAY. 19156 Næs þer nan swa wracche swein þat he nes a wel god þein. *Ibid.* 28563 Ælc sloh adun riht Weore he swein weore he cniht. *a* **1300** *Cursor M.* 6279 (Cott.) King ne knight, suier ne suain [*Gött.* suayn, *Fairf.* squayne, *Trin.* sweyn]. **13..** *Guy Warw.* (A.) 234 Þai sett hem to mete anon, Erl, baroun, sweyn, & grom. **1375** BARBOUR *Bruce* v. 235 Quhill I liff, and may haf mycht To lede a ȝheman or a swane. *c* **1425** WYNTOUN *Cron.* IX. vii. 904 For ellis alsweil may be slayne A mychty man, as may a swayne. *c* **1430** *Syr Tryam.* 546 Knyghtys, squyers, and swayne. *c* **1572** GASCOIGNE *Posies, Fruites Warre* cx, In regiment.. Where officers.. Shall be abusde by euery page and swayne.

†**2.** A male servant, serving-man; an attendant, follower. *Obs.*

c **1205** LAY. 3505 Forð wende þe king Leir, Nauede he bute enne swein. *c* **1386** CHAUCER *Reeve's T.* 107 Hym boes serue hym selne that has na swayn. *c* **1430** *Hymns Virg.* (1867) 44 Worschipe me here, & bicome my swayn, And y schal ȝeue þee al this. **1568** *Hist. Jacob & Esau* v. ii. F iij, The elder must nowe serue the yonger as his swayne. **1570** LEVINS *Manip.* 200 A squayne, *assecla*. **1579** SPENSER *Sheph. Cal.* Sept. 42 The shepheards swayne you cannot well ken, But it be by his pryde, from other men. **1623** COCKERAM, *Swaine*, a seruant.

†**3.** A man; a youth; a boy. *Obs.*

a **1300** *Cursor M.* 18987 (Gött.) Of mi gast i sal a streme To suayn [*Trin.* mon] and womman giue alsua. [Cf. *Joel* ii. 29.] **13..** *E.E. Allit. P.* B. 1509 Swyfte swaynes ful swyþe swepen þertylle. *c* **1386** CHAUCER *Sir Thopas* 13 Sire Thopas wax a doghty swayn. *c* **1400** *Laud Troy Bk.* 15265 How sche myght venge hir on that swayn That hadde hir two sones sclayn. *c* **1440** *York Myst.* xvii. 207 Nowe shall þei.. tell me of pat litill swayne [*sc.* the child Jesus]. *a* **1508** DUNBAR *Tua Mariit Wemen* 226 Thus beswik I that swane, with my sueit wordis. **1579** SPENSER *Sheph. Cal.* Mar. 79 With that sprong forth a naked swayne [*sc.* Cupid]. **1633** P. FLETCHER *Purple Isl.* XII. lxv, By a mighty swain he [*sc.* the Dragon] soon was led Unto a thousand thousand torturings.

4. A country or farm labourer, *freq.* a shepherd; a countryman, rustic. *arch.*

1579 GOSSON *Apol. Sch. Abuse* (Arb.) 66 Giue them whippes in their handes, and sende them like swaynes to plough and carte. **1590** SPENSER *F.Q.* III. vi. 15 The gentle Shepheard swaynes, which sat Keeping their fleecie flockes. **1594** KYD *Cornelia* III. ii. 39 Lyke morall Esops mysled Country swaine. **1611** SHAKS. *Wint. T.* IV. iv. 9 Your high selfe.. you haue obscur'd With a Swaines wearing. **1663** PATRICK *Parab. Pilgr.* xxix. (1687) 341 Those Swains with their Sheephooks in their hands. **1746** SMOLLETT *Tears Scotl.* 13 Thy swains are famish'd on the rocks, Where once they fed their wanton flocks. **1770** GOLDSM. *Des. Vill.* 2 Where health and plenty cheered the labouring swain. **1809** CAMPBELL *Gert. Wyom.* I. ii, The happy Shepherd Swains had nought to do But feed their flocks. **1840** THACKERAY *Paris Sk.-bk.* (1872) 111 The rural swains. **1892** TENNYSON in Ld. Tennyson *Mem.* (1897) II. xxii. 402, I asked my way ..of a Yorkshire 'swain'.

5. A country gallant or lover; hence *gen.* a lover, wooer, sweetheart, esp. in pastoral poetry.

c **1585** *Fair Em* II. i. 78 In deede my Manuile hath some cause to doubt, When such a Swaine is riuall in his loue! **1591** SHAKS. *Two Gent.* IV. ii. 40 Who is Siluia? what is she? That all our Swaines commend her? **1662** PLAYFORD *Skill Mus.* I. (1674) 67 Will Cloris cast her Sun-bright Eye Upon so mean a Swain as I? **1697** DRYDEN *Virg. Past.* III. 104 To the dear Mistress of my Love-sick Mind, Her Swain a pretty Present has design'd. **1706** ADDISON *Rosamond* II. ii, To be slain By a barbarous swain That laughs at your pain. **1775** SHERIDAN *Duenna* I. v, So! my swain, yonder, has done admiring himself. **1822** W. IRVING *Braceb. Hall* iv. 38 Should any faithless swain persist in his inconstancy. **1864** F. LOCKER *Housemaid* viii, If her Sunday-swain is one Who's fond of strolling. **1881** 'RITA' *My Lady Coquette* iii, She gives such smiles, and looks, and attentions to her devoted swains.

¶**6.** A freeholder within the forest. (A sense invented by Manwood to account for SWANIMOTE.)

1615 MANWOOD *Laws Forest* xxiii. 217 This word *Swaine*, in the Saxons speech is a Bookeland man, which at this day is taken for a Charterar or a freeholder: and so the Swanimote is in English, a Court within the Forest, whereunto all the freeholders doe owe suit and seruice. **1768** BLACKSTONE *Comm.* III. vi. 72 The court of sweinmote is to be holden before the verderors, as judges,.. the sweins or freeholders within the forest composing the jury. **1880** WHITWORTH in *Antiquary* Feb. 94/1 Swanimote, Swaynmote, Swynmote, &c., or meeting of the Forest Swains.

7. *attrib.* and *Comb.* (in sense 4); †**swainloaf** (see 2), bread to be eaten by servants, as opposed to PAIN-DEMAINE, 'panis dominicus' (lord's bread).

1358 *Catal. Anc. Deeds* A. 9847 (1902) IV. 469 [Black loaves called] swaynloves. *a* **1652** BROME *Love sick Court* IV. ii, The chief Swain heads of Thessaly. **1842** *Dumfries Herald* Oct., More swain-like than king-like.

Hence **swain** *v. intr.* (with *it*), to play the lover or wooer; †**'swainess**, a female lover; **'swaining**, love-making, 'spooning'.

a **1652** BROME *Love sick Court* v. iii, That swain-ess was myself. **1840** LADY C. BURY *Hist. of Flirt* xi, He is impatient to swain it with some new face. **1840** MRS. TROLLOPE *M. Armstrong* i, His general manner to ladies had a good deal of what in female slang is called *swaining*.

swaing, obs. form of SWAYING.

swainish ('sweɪnɪʃ), *a.* [f. SWAIN + -ISH[1].] Resembling or characteristic of a swain or rustic; rustic, boorish. Also, of the nature of a rustic lover or rustic love-making. Hence **'swainishness**, boorishness.

1642 MILTON *Apol. Smect.* Wks. 1851 III. 270 [It] argues both a grosse and shallow judgement, and withall an ungentle, and swainish breast. **1645** —— *Colast.* ibid. IV. 362 Ignorant and swainish mindes. **1819** T. CAMPBELL *Spec. Brit. Poets* VI. 99 Some part of the love-story of Palemon is rather swainish. **1840** *Tait's Mag.* VII. 54 Edwin is a sentimental and swainish chap. **1854** EMERSON *Social Aims* Wks. (Bohn) III. 181 Swainish, morose people, who must be kept down and quieted as you would those who are a little tipsy; others, who are not only swainish, but are prompt to take oath that swainishness is the only culture.

†**'swainling.** *Obs.* Also **-lin.** [f. SWAIN *sb.* + -LING.] A poor or young swain or rustic. Also, a rustic female sweetheart.

1615 BRATHWAIT *Strappado* (1878) 135 Ladies & Lordings, Swainelings with their swaines. **1621** —— *Nat. Embassie* etc. 213 Honest Swainling, with his Sweeting. **1638** —— *Barnabees Jrnl.* Ee iij, Bonny blith Swainling [*Vir vere laetus*] intend thy Lamkin. **1651** S. SHEPPARD *Pastorals* 462 They passe us Swainlings all as farr, As doth the Moon the smallest Star. **1672** S. S. *Hist. Dorastus & Fawnia* 18 The swainlings who live neer.

swainmote: see SWANIMOTE.

Swainson ('sweɪnsən). The name of William *Swainson* (1789–1855), English naturalist, used in the possessive to designate birds named in his honour, as **Swainson's †buzzard, hawk,** a dark-coloured buzzard hawk, *Buteo swainsoni*, found in western North America; **Swainson's thrush,** an olive-backed thrush, *Hylocichla ustulata*, found in western North America; **Swainson's warbler,** a brown and white warbler, *Limnothlypis swainsonii*, found in swamp regions of south-eastern North America.

1858 S. F. BAIRD *Birds Pacific Railway Routes* 19 Swainson's Buzzard,.. more nearly related to a generic form of the Old World. *Ibid.* 252 Swainson's Warbler.. South Atlantic States. **1869** *Amer. Naturalist* III. 31 Swainson's Thrush... Common at Cœur d'Alene Mission. **1895** *U.S. Dept. Agric. Yearbk. 1894* 222 The food of Swainson's hawk ..is of much the same character as that of the two preceding species. **1912** C. A. REED *Birds Eastern N. Amer.* 359 Swainson's Warbler is a comparatively rare species found in the Southeastern States. **1939** F. C. LINCOLN *Migration Amer. Birds* 79 Observers in the Great Plains saw large flocks of Red-tailed Hawks, Swainson's Hawks and Rough-legged Hawks wheeling majestically. **1972** *Islander* (Victoria, B.C.) 21 May 6/2 In the evening the sound of the Swainson's thrush. **1976** *National Observer* (U.S.) 31 July 5/2 Southern Swainson's warblers would no doubt agree. **1980** *Country Life* 3 July 46/2, I watched huge flocks of broad-winged hawks.. and a few Swainson's hawks.

†**swaip,** *sb. Obs.* Also 4 **suaip,** 5 **sweype.** [Corresp. in form to ON. *sveipa* (= OE. *swápan* to SWEEP, q.v.) and *sveipr*, but in sense to ON. *svipa* to whip, *svipa* whip. Cf. SWAPE, SWEPE.] A whip, scourge; also, a stroke, blow.

13.. *Cursor M.* 19355 (Edin.) Þan wiþ suaipis [*Cott.* suepes, *Trin.* swappes] þai þaim suang. *c* **1440** *Promp. Parv.* 482/1 Sweype, or swappe (*S.* or strok, *supra*, swype), *alapa*. *Ibid.*, Sweype, for a top, or scoorge, *flagellum*.

So †**swaip** *v. trans.*, to scourge.

13.. *Cursor M.* 24007 (Edin.) Þair swaiping was sa smert. *Ibid.* 24024 Vp reufulli þai gan him raip, Ful snubnerlik him for to swaip.

swaipe, obs. form of SWAPE.

swair, swaird, swairm, swait, obs. ff. SWIRE, SWARD, SWARM, SWOTE.

swaith(e, obs. or dial. forms of SWATH, SWATHE.

swaits, variant of SWATS *Sc.*

swak, obs. form of SWACK.

Swakara ('swækərə). [f. the initials of *S*outh *W*est *A*frica + KARA(KUL.] The coat of a karakul lamb, bred in Namibia, valued as a fur. Chiefly *attrib.*

1966 *Fur Rev.* May 13/1 Selective breeding has improved the.. qualities of S.W.A. Persian Lambskins and brought about a changeover.. to a flat glossy pelt... In order to spread.. the extended range of S.W. African merchandise, a publicity agent has.. [come] up with the clever catchword '*Swakara*'. **1973** *Country Life* 1 Feb. 302/3 Slim little jackets in Swakara broadtail, dyed delectable shades of peach. **1978** *Lancashire Life* Sept. 110/1 Natural grey Swakara Persian lamb has a unique charm.

swal, obs. pa. t. of SWELL *v.*

swale (sweɪl), *sb.*[1] *dial.* Forms: 4 **swayl,** 6 **swaill, swaile, swaule, swawle,** 6–7 **swall(e,** 8–9 **swale,** 9 **swaul.** [Of obscure origin.

If the orig. meaning was a pliant 'swaying' piece of wood, the two types *swail, swall*, may represent an OE. **swæȝ(e)l*, **swaȝol*, f. *swaȝ-*, cogn. with Scand. *svag-* in Norw. *svaga* (see SWAG *v.*); cf. ME. *hail, haul* (OE. *hæȝel, haȝol*), HAIL *sb.*[1]]

Timber in laths, boards, or planks; planking; also, a lath, plank.

For specialized local uses see quots. 1841 and 1903.

1325 *Rolls of Parlt.* I. 434/2 Qu'ele peusse pur swayl & autres busoignes necessaries de la meson, abatre en la dit boys cent rores. **1505–6** *Durham Acc. Rolls* (Surtees) 103 Pro sarracione le swailles pro eisdem [domibus porcorum]. **1531–2** *Durham Househ. Bk.* (Surtees) 80 Pro sarracione ½ rod in swalles 10 d. *Ibid.* 130, 1 lytyll swall and 12 bords. **1557** *Ludlow Churchw. Acc.* (Camden) 80 For swaile for a saunce belle.. ij d. **1574** *Richmond Wills* (Surtees) 249 Foure swawles and foure trists, v[s]. **1582** *Wills & Inv. N.C.* (Surtees 1860) 47, iij swalles for a horse baye. **1597** *Durham Acc. Rolls* (Surtees) 740 For sawinge Sarkyn boordes and Swalles for the churche and the new bridge. **1600** *Knaresb. Wills* (Surtees) I. 222 A swaille of timber lyinge at Beckwithe. **1640** *Gateshead Church Bks.* in *Northumbld. Gloss.* s.v. *Swale*, For 12 swalls for formes for the church. **1648** in *Archaeologia Æliana* (1892) XV. 252 For 20 Swalls to be scaffolds. **1799** *Naval Chron.* I. 176 Stepping down the side of the Yarmouth hulk at Plymouth, he fell against the swale of the vessel. **1841** HARTSHORNE *Salopia Ant.* Gloss. 582 *Swale*, a piece of wood going from an upright shaft in an oatmeal mill to one of the wheels. **1903** *Eng. Dial. Dict.*, *Swauls*, the outside bars in the frame of the bottom of a cart. w. Yks.

swale (sweɪl), *sb.*[2] *dial.*, chiefly *E. Anglian.* Also 7 **swill,** 9 **swail.** [prob. of Scandinavian origin, and related to ON. *svalar* f. pl. (MSw. *svali*, Sw. *svale*, Norw. *sval*) balcony or gallery along the side of a house, ON. *svalr* cool (see SWALE *a.*), ON. (MSw., Sw., Norw.) *svala* to cool.]

Shade; a shady place. Also, the cool, the cold.

c **1440** *Promp. Parv.* 481/2 Swale (*P.* or shadowe), *umbra, umbraculum, estiva*. **1567** GOLDING *Ovid's Met.* v. (1593) 116 Downe she sate among the trees which gaue a plesant swale. **1571** —— *Calvin on Ps.* xxiii. 4 David alludeth to y[e] dark swales or the dens of wyld beastes. **1669** WORLIDGE *Syst. Agric., Dict. Rust.*, *Swill*, used in the Northern parts for shade, or shadow. *c* **1700** KENNETT *MS. Lansd. 1033*, *Swale*, cold or dank air; as, he lies in the swale, i.e. in the open cold air. **1821** CLARE *Vill. Minstr.* I. 139 Granny there was on the bench, Coolly sitting in the swail. **1857** BORROW *Romany Rye* xxv, Turn your horse out to grass.. in the swale of the morn and the evening.

swale (sweɪl), *sb.*[3] *local.* Also 6 *Sc.* **swaill, swayll,** 9 **swail,** *Sc.* **swyle.** [Origin unknown. Prob. conveyed to America from the eastern counties, where it is still in use.] A hollow, low place; *esp. U.S.*, a moist or marshy depression in a tract of land, esp. in the midst of rolling prairie. Also (*U.S.*) a hollow between adjacent sand-ridges.

1584 (Dec. 23) *Reg. Mag. Sig. Scot.* (1888) 239/2 Keipand the stripe quhill it enter in Beildeis swaill, and keipand and ascendand upwith the said swaill quhill it cum to the littill stane calsay. **1615** *Extracts Aberd. Reg.* (1848) II. 324 Hauldand vp the said burne to the roche swaill of Kynmvndie. *Ibid.*, Quhair thair is ane great mother swayll on the south syde of the said Blackburne. *Ibid.* 326 Thairfra doun the said northsyd of the great swayll. **1667** *Dedham Rec.* IV. 135 (Thornton) He may cutt in a place called the Swale, adjoyning to the Ceader Swampe. **1805** T. BIGELOW *Jrnl. Tour Niagra Falls* (1876) 37 (Thornton) A swale or valley affords.. copious springs of water. **1809** KENDALL *Trav.* III. lxxvii. 193 The swales, or rich hollows, lying behind the uplands, by which latter they are separated from the meadows. **1827** J. F. COOPER *Prairie* v, Fire low, boys —level into the swales, for the red skins are settling to the very earth! **1830** GALT *Lawrie T.* III. ii. (1849) 86 Stumps and cradle heaps, mud-holes and miry swails, succeeded one another. **1866** GREGOR *Banffsh. Gloss.*, *Swyle*, a bog. **1874** TRIPPE in Coues *Birds N.W.* 223 An open park-like tract of rolling, grassy prairie, interspersed with groves of pines, low hills, and wet, marshy swales. **1894** *Dialect Notes* I. 334 *Swale*, low land between sand ridges on the coast beaches [of New Jersey]. **1945, 1976** [see *point bar* (*b*) s.v. POINT *sb.*[1] D. 14].

attrib. **1830** GALT *Lawrie T.* VIII. v. (1849) 371 These swale-runnels are often deceptive. **1905** *Blackw. Mag.* Dec. 771/1 That course led him through the swale bottoms. **1911** *Canadian Newspaper*, Their crop is swale hay; in other words swamp grass.

swale (sweɪl), *sb.*[4] *South. dial. local.* [Origin uncertain: cf. SWEAL, SWALE *sb.*, and *swill* sb.[1] 10 in *Eng. Dial. Dict.*] A small broom or brush without a stick for a handle.

1949 K. S. Woods *Rural Crafts of England* III. vii. 123 Some besoms are made without sticks. These are known as swales, an interesting word meaning 'a small bright fire enough to boil a kettle'. Swales are used to brush the flakes from steel-plate. **1968** J. Arnold *Shell Bk. Country Crafts* 100 Like the besom, it has a head of birch..but is without a handle and is called a swale.

swale, *a. north. dial.* [a. ON. *svalr* (MSw., Sw., Norw. *sval*) cool: cf. SWALE *sb.*²] Cool, chill.

1674 Ray *N.C. Words* 47 *Swale*, windy, cold, bleak.

swale, *v.*¹; see SWEAL *v.*

swale (sweɪl), *v.*² [app. of dial. origin (see *swail* in Eng. Dial. Dict.); prob. frequent. f. SWAY *v.* + -LE, but parallels are wanting. Cf. Shropshire dial. *swayl-pole* = *sway-pole*.] *intr.* To move or sway up and down or from side to side. Hence **'swaling** *vbl. sb.* and *ppl. a.*; also **'swalingly** *adv.*, with a swaying motion.

1820 *Blackw. Mag.* VII. 676 Here's a jerked feather that swales in a bonnet. **1822** *Ibid.* XII. 781 With his eternal sidling and sliding about,..and swaling with his coat-tails. *Ibid.* 782 Treading the street with his corn-troubled toes,.. swalingly goes the kind Cockney King. **1824** *Ibid.* XV. 86 He drops a wing..with a swaling and graceful amorousness. **1827** Praed *Red Fisherm.* 221 As the swaling wherry settles down. **1863** Sala *Captain Dangerous* I. iv. 123 The great plumed hat..flapped and swaled over my eyes. **1895** A. Dobson *Poems, Sundial* xi, A soldier gallant.., Swinging a beaver with a swaling plume.

swale, obs. pa. t. of SWELL *v.*

Swaledale ('sweɪldeɪl). The name of a region of North Yorkshire used *absol.* or *attrib.* to designate a long-woolled sheep of the hardy hill breed first developed in the area; also, the breed itself or the long coarse wool produced by a sheep of this kind.

1916 W. J. Malden *Brit. Sheep & Shepherding* vi. 58 Among the remaining breeds of the northern hills may be mentioned the Swaledale, a very hardy breed. **1944** G. Henderson *Farming Ladder* i. 24 The stock consisted of 650 Blackfaced mountain ewes, and thirty pedigree Swaledales. **1961** J. Gunston *Profit from Sheep* ii. 22 Swaledales..do very well in a wide range of hard-grazing and cold districts. **1971** *Farmers Weekly* 19 Mar. 43/3 Certain wool types such as Blackface, Devon and Swaledale have met a better market demand than others. **1980** *Times* 3 Mar. 16/2 A Pennine farmer..was saving 50 bales of hay a day among his Swaledale ewes.

swaler ('sweɪlə(r)). *north-midl. dial.* Also 6 swaller, 8–9 swailer, 9 sweeler. [f. *swale*, SWEAL *v.* + -ER¹.] A dealer in corn: see quots.

1597 *Manch. Crt. Leet Rec.* (1885) II. 130 No swaller that ys a fforrener..shall sell or measure any corne vpon any other daye then vppon the Saturdaye and mundaye. **1743–4** *Alstonfield Par. Const. Acc.* (E.D.D.), Paid for writing warrants for badgers and swalers to take licenses, £00.0.06. **1796** Pegge *Derbicisms* (E.D.S.), *Badger*... He is called also a *swailer*, I suppose from melting or *swealing* the oats; for the *badger* or *swailer* is one that sells oatmeal. **1829** *Glover's Hist. Derby* I. 198 The people who deal in oatmeal are called swalers or mealmen. **1848** Evans *Leicester. Words, Swaler*, a person whose trade it is to prepare oats into grits, meal, &c.: from '*swealing*', or '*swaling*', i.e., wasting or lessening the grain a little. **1887** *Folk-sp. S. Chesh., Sweeler*, a dealer in corn.

swalewe, obs. form of SWALLOW *sb.*¹

†**'swaling**, *vbl. sb. Obs. rare.* [? f. Scandinavian stem *skval-* denoting loud noise.] ? Loud singing (of birds).

c **1400** *Destr. Troy* 1061 Swoghyng of swete ayre, Swalyng of briddes.

†**swall.** *Obs.* Also 4 sual. [a. or corresp. to MLG., LG. *swal(l* whirlpool, swollen mass of water (whence Sw. *svall* surge, swell of the sea), = MHG. *swal* (G. *schwall*); f. *swal-*: *swel-* (see SWELL *v.*).] An agitated mass of water.

a **1340** Hampole *Psalter* xlv[i]. 4 *Fluminis impetus*..þe swall of flode. *Ibid.* lxviii. 3 [lxix. 2] The storme, that is, the sual of malicious men..sloghe me.

swall, var. SWALE *sb.*¹; obs. or dial. f. SWELL.

swallet ('swɒlɪt). *local.* (*s.w.*) [Obscure formation on SWALLOW *v.*, ? after *gullet*.] An underground stream of water such as breaks in upon miners at work. Also (in full, ***swallet hole***), the opening through which a stream disappears underground. Cf. SWALLOW *sb.*² 1 b.

1668 *Phil. Trans.* III. 769 If they find a Swallet, they drive an Adit upon Levell, till 'tis dry. **1761** A. Catcott *Treat. Deluge* III. (1768) 356 The collateral conduits of the swallet-holes, leading down into one great unfathomable cavity in the bowels of the earth. **1778** Pryce *Min. Cornub.* 84 The larger submarine gulphs or swallets. **1856** S. Hughes *Waterworks* 133 Swallet holes and subterranean rivers..in the district of Gower and in the Mendip hills. **1865** *Reader* Jan. 7 This stream is known to commence its subterranean journey about two miles off, where it enters a 'swallet.' **1910** *Spectator* 8 Jan. 47/1 Mendip [has]..underground springs and rivers..faintly indicated by the countless swallets that pit the surface of the hills.

‖**swallo** ('swɒləʊ). Also swala, swalloe, -ow. [a. Malay *suwālā, suwālā*.] = SEA-SLUG 1, TREPANG.

1779 Forrest *Voy. N. Guinea* 373 They see the swallo in clear water, and strike it as it lies on the ground, with an instrument, consisting of four bearded iron prongs. **1792** —— *Voy. Mergui Archip.* 83 They sail in their Paduakans to the northern parts of New Holland..to gather Swallow (*Biche de Mer*). **1802** [see SEA-SWALLOW 3]. **1836** *Penny Cycl.* V. 188/2 The tripang swala, or sea-slug (holothurion), is a valuable article of exportation [from Borneo] to China. **1904** A. H. S. Landor *Gems of East* I. 271 The exports consisting chiefly of Black and White Swallo or Seaslug.

swallow ('swɒləʊ), *sb.*¹ Forms: 1 s(u)ualu(u)ae, swealwe, swalowe, -uwe, -awe, 1, 4 swalewe, swalwe, swolwe, 4 swalugh, swalu, 4–6 swalow(e, 5 swalue, sualowe, 5–7 swallowe, 6– swallow. [Com. Teut. (not recorded for Gothic): OE. *swealwe* wk. fem. = OS. *suala*, MLG. *swalewe, swalue*, MDu. *swâluwe, -ewe* (Du. *zwaluw*), OHG. *swalawa, swalwa* (MHG. *swal(e)we*, G *schwalbe*), ON. *svala* for **svǫlva* (MSw., Sw *svala*, Da. *svale*):—OTeut. **swalwōn-*, the etymological meaning of which is disputed.

Continental Germanic dialects have also forms of other types: without *w* in the final syllable, e.g. MHG. *swal, swale*, MLG. *swale*, WFris. *sweal, swel*; with *m*-suffix, e.g. HG. (local) *schwalm, schwalme*, Flem. *swaelem*; forms with dim. suffix are widespread in LG. and Fris., e.g. MLG. *swalike, swal(e)ke*, LG. *swaalke*, Flem. *swalcke* (Kilian), EFris., NFris. *swâlk*, WFris. *sweaits̆je, sweltsje*.]

1. a. A bird of the genus *Hirundo*, esp. *H. rustica*, a well-known migratory bird with long pointed wings and forked tail, having a swift curving flight and a twittering cry, building mud-nests on buildings, etc., and popularly regarded as a harbinger of summer (cf. c).

a **700** *Epinal Gloss.* 498 *Hirundo*, sualuuae. *c* **950** *Guthlac* x. (1909) 143 þa comon þær sæmninga in twa swalewan fleoȝan, and hi..heora sang upahofon. *c* **1000** *Sax. Leechd.* II. 156 Ȝenim swealwan, ȝebærn..to ahsan. *Ibid.* III. 44 Ȝenim swolwan nest. *c* **1320** *Sir Tristr.* 1566 A swalu ich herd sing. *c* **1374** Chaucer *Troylus* II. 64 The swalwe Proigne, with a sorwful lay,..gan make hir weymentinge. **1398** Trevisa *Barth. De P.R.* XII. xxii. (Bodl. MS.) lf. 122 b/1 In making of nestes þe swalowe is moste sliȝe. *a* **1450** *Knt. de la Tour* lxxx. 102 The dunge of swalues fell into the eyen of this good man Tobie. *a* **1529** Skelton *P. Sparowe* 404 The chattrynge swallow. **1579** Spenser *Sheph. Cal.* Mar. 11 The Swallow peepes out of her nest. **1611** Shaks. *Wint. T.* IV. iv. 119 Daffadils, That come before the Swallow dares. **1750** Gray *Elegy* 18 The swallow twit'ring from the straw-built shed. **1820** Keats *To Autumn* 33 The red-breast whistles from a garden-croft; And gathering swallows twitter in the skies. **1876–82** Newton *Yarrell's Hist. Brit. Birds* II. 345 The migrations of the Swallow are in a direction nearly due north and south.

b. In allusions to the swift flight of the bird.

13.. *K. Alis.* 3775 (Laud MS.), He takes Bulcyphal by þe side, So a swalewe he gynneþ forþ glide. *c* **1380** *Sir Ferumb.* 4232 Þat noble stede, þat al so swyftlyche þanne ȝede So swolwe doþ on flyȝt. *c* **1489** Caxton *Sonnes of Aymon* x. 258 Bayarde went not the lytyll pase, but went lyke a sualowe. **1594** Shaks. *Rich. III*, v. ii. 23 True Hope is swift, and flyes with Swallowes wings.

c. Prov. ***one swallow does not make a summer*** (and allusions to it).

Cf. Gr. μία χελιδὼν ἔαρ οὐ ποιεῖ.

1539 Taverner *Erasm. Prov.* (1552) 25 It is not one swalowe that bryngeth in somer. It is not one good qualitie that maketh a man good. **1546** J. Heywood *Prov.* (1867) 57 One swalowe maketh not sommer (said I) men saie. *a* **1548** Hall *Chron., Hen. IV*, 30 He well remembred that one faire day assureth not a good Sommer, nor one fliyng Swalow prognosticateth not a good yere. **1589** Nashe *Pref. to Greene's Menaphon* Wks. 1905 III. 323, I would preferre diuine Master Spencer..Neither is he the onely swallow of our Summer. **1617** Moryson *Itin.* III. 43 Lest I should seeme by one Swallow to make Summer,..the men of Herefordshire can witnes, that such examples are not rare in England. **1636** Prynne *Rem. agst. Shipmoney* 18 Since in such Taxes commonly, one Swallow makes a kinde of Sommer. **1821** Scott *Kenilw.* xvii, Raleigh..disowning.. that one day's fair reception made a favourite, any more than one swallow a summer.

d. *ellipt.* for *swallow dive* below.

1902 *Encycl. Brit.* XXXIII. 121/2 The 'swallow' is one of the most thrilling dives. **1971** 'D. Halliday' *Dolly & Doctor Bird* xi. 148 Sergeant Trotter himself nipped up the diving-board and executed a swallow and somersault.

e. *transf.* A woman employed by the Soviet intelligence service, who seduces men for the purposes of espionage. *slang.*

1972 D. Bloodworth *Any Number can Play* ix. 69 You have doubtless read about the..'swallows' of the KGB, the young ladies trained..to bed down intelligence targets, so that they can be comfortably and conveniently bugged and photographed in compromising..positions? **1976** 'M. Barak' *Secret List H. Roehm* xii. 130, I need a swallow in America. One..who is sexually skilled and expert in obtaining information. **1979** P. Way *Sunrise* i. 15 Had she been working for the KGB, Joanna would have been.. called a 'swallow'. In the CIA she would have been a 'honeypot'.

2. a. In extended sense, any bird of the swallow kind, or of the family *Hirundinidæ*, e.g. a martin; often misapplied to (and in earlier scientific use including) the swifts, now reckoned as a distinct and unrelated family (*Cypselidæ*).

In OE., *stæpswealwe*, lit. shore-swallow, meant 'sand-martin'. Also, *heoruswealwe*, lit. sword-swallow, occurs in poetry for 'hawk'.

1758 *Phil. Trans.* LI. 464 There are four distinct species of birds, that go under the general name swallow; *viz.* the swift or black martin; 2. the swallow, that builds in chimneys; 3. the martin, that builds against houses; 4. the sand martin, that builds in sand-banks. **1792–5** J. Aikin & Mrs. Barbauld *Evenings at Home* II. 20 The Martins and other swallows. **1867** T. R. Jones *Nat. Hist. Birds* (1872) 51 The extensive race of Swallows and Swifts. **1885** Newton in *Encycl. Brit.* XVIII. 47/2 The *Hirundinidæ* or Swallows.

b. With qualifying words, applied to various species of *Hirundinidæ* or *Cypselidæ*; also to birds of other families resembling swallows: as BANK-*swallow*, BARN-*s.*, CARR-*s.*, CHIMNEY-*s.*, HOUSE-*s.*, SEA-SWALLOW.

cliff swallow, one of several species of the genus *Petrochelidon*, nesting in cliffs. **esculent swallow**, a name for the swifts of the genus *Collocalia*, which construct the 'edible bird's nests' of which soup is made in China. **tree swallow**, (*a*) an Australian swallow of the genus *Hylochelidon*, which lays in holes in trees; (*b*) the N. American white-bellied or white-breasted swallow, *Tachycineta* (*Iridoprocne*) *bicolor*, which nests in trees. †**water swallow**, ? a water-wagtail. **window swallow**, the house-martin, *Chelidon urbica*. **wood swallow**, (*a*) = *swallow-shrike* (see 4); (*b*) = *tree swallow* (b). (Several other species are named in Latham's *Gen. Synopsis Birds*, 1783, and other ornithological works, Morris's *Austral English*, 1898, etc.)

1870 Lowell *Study Wind.* (1886) 18 The *cliff-swallow ..has come and gone. **1783** Latham *Gen. Synopsis Birds* IV. 578 *Esculent Sw[allow]..the nest..is composed of such materials as not only to be edible, but accounted as one of the greatest dainties of the Asiatic epicures. **1813** [see ESCULENT A. 1 ¶]. **1873** Buller *Birds New Zealand* 141 *Hylochelidon nigricans*. (Australian *Tree-swallow.) **1552** Cooper *Elyot's Dict., Cinclos*..the byrde called a *water swallow, not muche bigger than a larke. Eras. saith..that it is a certaine byrd, so weake and feeble, that she can not make hir owne nest, and so laieth hir egges in other byrdes nestes. **1668** Charleton *Onomast.* 108 *Cinclus*..the long-bill'd wagtail, and Half Snipe, aliis Water-Swallow. **1802** Montagu *Ornith. Dict.* I, *Swallow*,..a genus of perchers..of which we have three species natives: the Bank, the Chimney, and the *Window, Swallow. **1817** T. Forster *Observ. Nat. Hist. Swallowtribe* (ed. 6) 6 House Martin, or Window Swallow. **1869** A. R. Wallace *Malay Archip.* I. 338 The curious *wood-swallows (Artami), which closely resemble swallows in their habits and flight..twitter from the tree-tops. **1887** [see *swallow-shrike* in 4]. **1889** Lumholtz *Among Cannibals* 28, I shot a young cuckoo..which was fed by four wood-swallows, (*Artamus sordidus*). **1893** *Scribner's Mag.* June 774/1 The white-breasted or wood-swallow..is called tree-swallow in some regions, because it nests in hollow trees.

3. †**a.** = SEA-SWALLOW 1. **b.** Collector's name for a species of moth: see quot. 1832. **c.** A variety of domestic pigeon: see quot. 1854.

1668 Charleton *Onomast.* 138 *Hirundo*..the Swallow, or Great headed Flying Fish. **1832** J. Rennie *Butterfl. & M.* 34 The Swallow (*Leiocampa dictæa*) appears the beginning of June and August. **1854** Meall *Moubray's Poultry* 288 *Swallow*, distinguished by its 'plunging or sailing in the air, when flying'. **1879** L. Wright *Pigeon Keeper* 205 Swallows are very pretty and very striking birds.

4. *attrib.* and *Comb.*, as ***swallow family***, ***-flight*** (also *fig.*), ***kind***, ***people***, ***tribe***; ***swallow-throated*** adj.; ***swallow-like*** adj. and adv.; also †**swallow-bird** (**-*bridde***), a young swallow; **swallow-chatterer**, the waxwing; **swallow-day**, the day on which the swallows arrive, or are reputed to arrive; **swallow dive**, a forward dive in which the arms are extended sideways, to simulate the outline of a swallow, until just before entry into the water; also *fig.*; so **swallow-diving**; hence **swallow-dive** *v. intr.*; **swallow-fish**, †(*a*) the flying-fish (= SEA-SWALLOW 1); (*b*) the sapphirine gurnard, *Trigla hirundo* (Cent. Dict.); **swallow-fly**, †(*a*) some unidentified swift-flying insect; (*b*) a parasitic fly which infests swallows; **swallow-flycatcher** = *swallow-shrike*; †**swallow-footed** *a.*, swift-footed, running swiftly as a swallow flies; **swallow fork** orig. *Amer.*, a forked cut used in marking cattle or sheep on the ear (see quot. 1966); hence **swallow-fork** *v. trans.*, to cut a swallow fork in (the ear); **swallow-forked** *ppl. a.*, shaped so as to cut a swallow fork; **swallow-hawk**, (*a*) the black-winged kite, *Elanus melanopterus*; (*b*) the swallow-tailed kite, *Elanoides forficatus*; †**swallow('s) herb** = SWALLOWWORT 2; **swallow-kite**, the swallow-tailed kite; **swallow pigeon** = 3 c; **swallow-shrike**, a bird of the genus *Artamus* or family *Artamidæ*, found in India and Australia; **swallow-smolt**, a variety of speckled trout (see SMOLT *sb.*¹ 2); **swallow's nest**, the nest of a swallow; *transf.* applied to a thing lodged at a height; *spec.* a battery of guns or company of shot placed on a height (cf. CROW'S NEST 1); ***swallow's-nest fly***, a fly that infests swallows' nests; also in ***swallow's nest soup***, an oriental dish (see BIRD'S-NEST, BIRD-NEST *sb.* 1); **swallow-stone** (tr. L. *chelidonius lapillus*, Pliny), a stone fabled to be brought from the sea-shore by swallows to give sight to their young; †**swallow-swifter** *comp. adj.* (*nonce-wd.*), swifter than a swallow; **swallow-tick**, a species of tick which infests swallows; **swallow-warbler**, an Australian species of warbler (*Sylvia hirundinacea*), with plumage resembling that of a swallow; **swallow-winged** *a.*, (*a*) swift as the swallow; (*b*) shaped like a swallow's wings; also (of a ship), having sails of such a shape; **swallow-woodpecker**, a woodpecker of the genus *Melanerpes*. See also SWALLOW-TAIL, etc.

a **1325** *Prose Psalter* 180, Y shal alway crye mercy as a *swolwe-bridde. **1688** HOLME *Armoury* III. 291/2 A kind of low footed Stool, or Cricket..with a ledge or border of Board nailed about the top of it, after the manner of a *Swallow Box. **1837** SWAINSON *Nat. Hist. Birds* II. III. vi. 71 Bombycillinæ, or *swallow chatterers. **1808** T. FORSTER *Circle of Seasons* 15 Apr., *Swallow Day. **1898** *Swimming Mag.* Oct. 46/1 To Englishmen the term '*swallow' dive, not 'swan', would best convey the notion of this idealistic manner of reaching the water. **1971** 'D. HALLIDAY' *Dolly & Doctor Bird* xi. 148 Sergeant Trotter, reappearing at the top of the diving-board, swallow-dived efficiently. **1976** 'A. HALL' *Kobra Manifesto* xvi. 215 Sassine had come off his high in a swallow dive. **1897** *Encycl. Sport* II. 425/1 The most graceful is that termed '*swallow-diving', the body being shot out from the board [etc.]. **1858** BAIRD *Cycl. Nat. Sci.*, *Hirundinidæ*, the *Swallow family. **1601** HOLLAND *Pliny* XXXII. xi. II. 452 The sea *Swallow fish. **1661** LOVELL *Hist. Anim. & Min.* 234 Swallow-fish..hath hard flesh and therefore hardly concocted. **1681** GREW *Musæum* I. v. iii. 116 The Swallow-Fish. So called from the length of his Gill-Fins, which reach to the end of his Tail, like a pair of very long Wings. **1850** TENNYSON *In Mem.* xlviii, She.. loosens from the lip Short *swallow-flights of song, that dip Their wings in tears, and skim away. **1883** J. PAYN *Thicker than Water* xxii, After several swallow-flights of talk. **1668** CHARLETON *Onomast.* 43 *Chelidon* (quia volatu post se omnes relinquit) the *Swallow-fly. **1815** KIRBY & SP. *Entomol.* iv. (1818) I. 112 The swallow-fly (*Ornithomyia Hirundinis*..L.)..has been known to make its repast on the human species. **1885** *Encycl. Brit.* XVIII. 38/1 *Swallow-Flycatchers (*Artamus*). **1636** W. DENNY in *Ann. Dubrensia* (1877) 14 The *Swallow-footed Grey-hound. **1636** *Plymouth* (Mass.) *Rec.* (1889) I. 1 Every mans marke of his Cattle... Christopher Waddesworth a *swallow forke. **1869** *Overland Monthly* III. 126 An over-slope and a slit in the right, and a swallow-fork in the left. **1934** *Amer. Ballads & Folk Songs* xvi. 409 They cropped and swallow-forked his ears. **1966** *Publ. Amer. Dial. Soc.* *1964* XLII. 16 *Swallow fork*, two slits run together to form a *W* or an *M*. **1972** P. NEWTON *Sheep Thief* xvi. 134 It was a pair of *swallow-forked ear-markers. **1858** BAIRD *Cycl. Nat. Sci.* s.v. *Milvinæ*, The black winged *swallow-hawk..lives principally upon insects which it catches upon the wing. **1578** LYTE *Dodoens* 32 The great Celandyne is named in Greeke χελιδονιον, that is to say, *Swallow-herbe. **1647** HEXHAM I. (Herbs), Swallowes hearbe, *swaluw-kruydt*. **1687** DRYDEN *Hind & P.* III. 547 Some Swifts, the Gyants of the *Swallow kind. **1773** G. WHITE *Selborne, To Pennant* 9 Nov., All the swallow kind sip their water as they sweep over the face of pools or rivers. **1840** MACGILLIVRAY *Brit. Birds* I. 47 *Nauclerus*. *Swallow-kite. **1582** STANYHURST *Æneis* IV. (Arb.) 101 Furth she quicklye galops, with wingflight *swallolyke hastning. **1606** SYLVESTER *Du Bartas* II. iv. II. *Magnificence* 747 Arm'd with Arrows,..Swift Swallow-like. **1843** *Penny Cycl.* XXV. 272/1 The Swallow-like Campylopterians [humming-birds]. **1896** 'IAN MACLAREN' *Kate Carnegie* 209 Old Sandie Ferguson..whose arrival, swallowlike, heralded the approach of the great occasion. **1730–46** THOMSON *Autumn* 836 Warn'd of approaching Winter, gather'd, play The *swallow-people. **1881** LYELL *Pigeons* 85 The *swallow pigeon..has its name from its resemblance in marking to the tern or sea swallow. **1887** NEWTON in *Encycl. Brit.* XXII. 730/2 The Indian and Australian *Artamus* (the species of which genus are often known as Wood-Swallows, or *Swallow-Shrikes). **1847** STODDART *Angler's Comp.* 36 The *Swallow-Smolt of Tweed. **1604** E. GRIMSTONE *Hist. Siege Ostend* 166 The besieged shot three peeces at the *swalloes nest, and dismounted three of the enemies Canons. **1796** NEMNICH *Polygl.-Lex.*, Swallow's-nest fly, *Hippobosca avicularia*. **1823** SCOTT *Quentin D.* iii, Certain cradles of iron, called 'swallows' nests', from which the sentinels.. could..take deliberate aim. **1849** BALFOUR *Man. Bot.* §1130 The edible swallows'-nests of the East. **1878** MRS. F. D. BRIDGES *Jrnl. Lady's Trav. round World* i. 19 Sept. (1883) 13 We are living with 200 monks in a sort of swallows'-nest monastery, perched half-way up the face of a cliff. **1920** E. & P. SYKES *Through Deserts & Oases Central Asia* iv. 78 Swallows' nest soup is almost unprocurable nowadays. **1976** *Times* 14 Feb. 10/4 A real Thai Chinese restaurant..three colours swallow's nest soup..or even plain shark's fin soup. **1586** BRIGHT *Melanch.* xxxix. 257 The chalydony, or *swallowe stone, found in the mawes of young swallowes. **1668** CHARLETON *Onomast.* 258 *Chelidonius*, Swallow-stone. **1598** SYLVESTER *Du Bartas* II. ii. III. *Colonies* 429 *Swallow-swifter surges. **1879** L. WRIGHT *Pigeon Keeper* 148 If there be white in it or above it under the throat at all, the bird has the fault of being '*swallow-throated'. **1826** SAMOUELLE *Direct. Collect. Insects & Crust.* 55 The Forest Fly, Sheep and *Swallow-tick. **1768** PENNANT *Brit. Zool.* II. 248 Concerning the manner the *swallow tribes dispose of themselves after their disappearance from the countries in which they make their summer residence. **1867** T. R. JONES *Nat. Hist. Birds* (1872) 58 The swallow tribes manifest a decided predilection for the neighbourhood of water. **1801** LATHAM *Gen. Synopsis Birds* Suppl. II. 250 *Swallow Warbler..This is a small species; all above the plumage is black. **1597** *Pilgr. Parnass.* II. 268 Shall not wee..To Parnass hast with *swallow-winged speede? **1629** MASSINGER *Picture* II. i, Ill news, madam, Are swallow-winged. **1865** J. H. INGRAHAM *Pillar of Fire* (1872) 154 A long swallow-winged sail. **1902** *Munsey's Mag.* XXV. 486/1 The swallow-winged Levantine barques. **1837** SWAINSON *Nat. Hist. Birds* II. III. ix. 135 The fifth and last genus (*Melanerpes*) may not unaptly be called *swallow woodpeckers, for they resemble those birds in their migratory habits, their long wings, and their black glossy plumage.

swallow ('swɒləʊ), *sb.*[2] Forms: *α.* 1 **ᵹeswelᵹ, swelh**, 4 **swelw(ȝ)**, *Kent.* **zuelȝ**, 4 **suelhu**, 4–5 **swelowe**, 5 **swelw(h)e, swelgh, sweloghe, sweluh**, 6 *Sc.* **swellie.** *β.* 4 **swolȝ, swolw(ȝ), swolouȝ, -owhe, -ewe**, 4–5 **swolwe, swolow(e**, 5 **swolwh**, 6 *pl.* **swolues**, 7 **swollow.** *γ.* 4–6 **swalowe**, 5 **swalgh, swalo**, (*pl.* **swaloes, sualowe, sqwalowe**), 5–6 **swalow**, (6 *pl.* **swalous**, *Sc.* **swallie**, 9 *north. dial.* **swall(e)y**), 6– **swallow.** [late OE. *ᵹeswelᵹ*, **swelᵹ*, *swelh* gulf, abyss, corresp. to MLG. *swelch* (also *swalch*) throat, whirlpool, gluttony, glutton, OHG. *swelgo* glutton (MHG. *swelhe*, *swelch*, also *swalch* abyss, flood), ON. *svelgr* whirlpool, swallower, devourer; f. *swelg-*: *swalg-* (see SWALLOW *v.*). The phonetic development has followed that of the verb.]

1. A deep hole or opening in the earth; a pit, gulf, abyss. *Obs.* exc. as in b.

α. *a* **1100** in Napier *OE. Glosses* 215/5 *Hiatum, opertionem vel foveam terre*, swelh. **1382** WYCLIF *1 Kings* xi. 27 Salomon beeldide Mello, and euenede the swelwȝ [1388 swolowe] of the citee of Dauid. *c* **1400** MAUNDEV. (Roxb.) viii. 29 Þare er swelghes in þe erthe allway brynnand.

β. **1382** WYCLIF *Prov.* xiii. 15 In the weye of dispiseris a swolwȝ [1388 a swalowe; Vulg. *in itinere contemptorum vorago*]. *c* **1385** CHAUCER *L.G.W.* 1104 (*Dido*) This Eneas is come to Paradys Out of the swolow of helle. **1481** CAXTON *Myrr.* II. xviii. 106 Ther in the myddle of therthe a place whiche is called Abisme or swolowe.

γ. **1388** Swalowe [see 1382 in *β*]. *c* **1530** LD. BERNERS *Arth. Lyt. Bryt.* (1814) 43 The abysme and swalowe of the earth. **1636** R. JAMES tr. *Minucius Felix' Octavius* 22 Into the swallow of a prodigious deepe gulfe. **1665** MANLEY *Grotius' Low C. Wars* 515 They were ignorant, what Swallows and Quagmires lay hid in the deceitful Nature of the Soil. **1694** *Phil. Trans.* XVIII. 6 The Ground..is sunk from the level, ..and ends in a very deep Circular Gulf or Swallow. **1799** KIRWAN *Geol. Ess.* 284 This mountain contains beds of pyrites and vast *swallows*.

b. *spec.* An opening or cavity, such as are common in limestone formations, through which a stream disappears underground: also called *swallow-pit*, SWALLOW-HOLE, and locally SWALLET.

1610 HOLLAND *Camden's Brit.* 297 The [river] Mole [in Surrey]..is swallowed up, and thereof the place is called the Swallow. **1681** BEAUMONT in *Philos. Collect.* No. 2. 3 Certain waters which..were conveyed into the ground by a swallow. *c* **1700** KENNETT *MS. Lansd. 1033*, *Swallow-pit*, where hollow caverns remain in the earth upon mineworks. **1789** E. DARWIN *Bot. Gard.* II. (1791) 96 *note*, The Swallows..or basons on some of the mountains, like Volcanic Craters, where the rain-water sinks into the earth. **1855** J. PHILLIPS *Man. Geol.* 412 Every limestone hill..shows in its swallows and moor pits the erosive power of the atmospheric water. **1895** *Naturalist* 258 A streamlet..runs..eastward, for about fifty yards, and then disappears in a 'swallow', to reappear in another fifty yards and resume its course.

2. A depth or abyss of water; a yawning gulf; a whirlpool. *Obs.* or *arch.*

α. *a* **1100** *Gloss. Aldhelm De Laud. Virg.* (Napier) 119/4620 *Carybdibus .i. uoraginibus*, ᵹeswelᵹum. *c* **1330** R. BRUNNE *Chron. Wace* (Rolls) 1453 So ar þo Nykeres faste aboute.. schipmen..To som swelw [*v.r.* suelhu] to turne or steke, Oþer a-geyn roches to breke. **1382** WYCLIF *Jonah* ii. 4 Alle thi swelowis and wawis passiden on me. **1387** TREVISA *Higden* (Rolls) II. 41 Bytwene þis ilond Mon and Norþ Wales, is a swelowe [*MS. α.* swolwȝ; **1432–50** swalo; CAXTON swolow]. *c* **1400** MAUNDEV. (Roxb.) v. 16 Sum saise þat it es a swelgh [*v.r.* sweloghe] of þe Grauelly See. *c* **1440** *Promp. Parv.* 482/2 Swelwhe, of a water or of a grownde (*K.* swelwe, *S.* swelth, *P.* swelowe), *vorago*.

β. *c* **1380** WYCLIF *Wks.* (1880) 97 Þei may be wel licned to swolwis of þe see. **1387** TREVISA *Higden* (Rolls) I. 65 Þilke tweie swolwes beeþ i-cleped Scylla and Charybdis. *c* **1430** LYDG. *Min. Poems* (1911) 69 Future swolwys of fortunys ffloodys. **1485** CAXTON *Chas. Gt.* III. ii. 205 An abysme or swolowe of water. **1566** STUDLEY tr. *Seneca's Medea* 2649 Amyd the iustlyng swolues of seas that whot with furye frye.

γ. *c* **1400** *Destr. Troy* 13299 Full swift to the swalgh me swinget the flode. **1432–50** tr. *Higden* (Rolls) I. 65 There be other swaloes of the see in the occean. **1470–85** MALORY *Arthur* XVII. ii. 691 There they myght not londe for there was a swalowe of the see. *c* **1510** BARCLAY *Mirr. Gd. Manners* (1570) Cj, Swalous, quicsandes, and fordes perillous. *a* **1533** LD. BERNERS *Gold. Bk. M. Aurel.* (1546) R viij, Wyll ye.. entre agayne into the swalowe of the see, for to engloutte you? **1604** *Meeting of Gallants* 10 And fall into the large swallow of Scylla. **1615** T. ADAMS *Spir. Navig.* Ep. Ded. 2 What Rocks, Gulphs, Swallowes..and other perils that may endanger you are marked out. **1639** HORN & ROB. *Gate Lang. Unl.* vii. §70 A swallow, gulfe or quag-mire. **1887** MORRIS *Odyss.* XII. 350 Better to perish gasping in the swallow of the sea.

†**3.** *fig.* A gulf, abyss, sink (of evil). *Obs.*

c **1380** WYCLIF *Sel. Wks.* III. 390 Also freris ben ressett, and a swolowhe of symonye,..and of thefftis. *c* **1412** HOCCLEVE *De Reg. Princ.* 4479 He is þe swolwe þat is neuere ful: At Auerice now haue here a pul. **1426** LYDG. *De Guil. Pilgr.* 16293 The wofull swolwh off Dysespeyr and Desperacioun. **1563** WINȜET tr. *Vincent. Lirin.* XXX. Wks. (S.T.S.) II. 63 That auld swellie of filthines. **1596** DALRYMPLE tr. *Leslie's Hist. Scot.* I. 118 Mony walde be drawne heidlings into the deip swallie of al abhominable vice. **1621** T. WILLIAMSON tr. *Goulart's Wise Vieillard* 149 To draw vs out of the swallowes and gulfes of intemperance ..and all..excesse. *a* **1624** BP. M. SMITH *Serm.* (1632) 146 Carried head-long by a maine current of disorder, into a bottomlesse swallow of confusion.

4. The passage through which food and drink are swallowed; the throat, pharynx, or gullet, or these collectively; the gorge.

13.. *E.E. Allit. P.* C. 250 A..whal..swyftely swenged hym to swepe & his swolȝ opened. *a* **1400–50** *Wars Alex.* 4507 Bary [*read* Bacy = Bacchus] he was brayne-wode for bebbing of wynes, Forþi þe swire & þe swalow þat swiere he kepis.

1608 TOPSELL *Serpents* 16 Heereby they..make wider their passage or swallow, for then they suddenly goble in the ..meate before them. **1658** A. FOX *Würtz' Surg.* II. x. 86 [If] there is fear that a bloud vein hath been hurt, or that the swallow and throat be cut. **1745** tr. *Egede's Descr. Greenland* 87 All Sorts of Fishes..run into the wide opened Swallow of this hideous Monster. **1873** MIVART *Elem. Anat.* xi. 433 The mouth..which opens behind into the swallow or pharynx. **1884** M. MACKENZIE *Dis. Throat & Nose* II. 157 In most.. cases it is stated that the patient had a 'small swallow' since childhood. **1884** SYMONDS *Shaks. Predec.* iii. 115 Like a shark's open swallow. **1902** *Brit. Med. Jrnl.* 5 Apr., Epit. Lit. 55 Those patients who have stenosis of the swallow.

transf. **1698** FRYER *Acc. E. India & P.* 57 We passed to it through a narrow Bite, which expatiates into a wide Swallow.

b. Considered in relation to its capacity for swallowing; hence *transf.* capacity of swallowing; appetite for food or drink; voracity; also *fig.* appetite, relish, inclination.

1592 NASHE *P. Penilesse* 23 Thou hast a foule swallow, if it come once to carousing of humane bloud. **1596** HARINGTON *Metam. Ajax* Prol. B v, Whose throates haue a better swallow, then their heds haue capacity. **1624** MASSINGER *Parl. Love* IV. v, 'Twill not down, sir! I have no swallow for 't. *a* **1754** FIELDING *Conversation* Wks. 1771 VIII. 126 Methus..measures the honesty and understanding of mankind by a capaciousness of their swallow. **1831** T. L. PEACOCK *Crotchet Castle* i, The Reverend Doctor Folliott, a gentleman endowed with a tolerable stock of learning, an interminable swallow, and an indefatigable pair of lungs. **1871** M. COLLINS *Mrq. & Merch.* III. iii. 78 He..with most voracious swallow Walks into my mutton chops.

5. *fig.* **a.** in reference to consuming or 'devouring' (cf. SWALLOW *v.* 4 a).

1607 *Puritan* III. iv. 58 If I fall into the hungrie swallow of the prison, I am like vtterly to perish. **1628** FELTHAM *Resolves* II. [I.] xlvii. 139 With what a generall swallow, Death still gapes vpon the generall world! **1688** SOUTH *Serm., Prov. xii. 22* (1697) I. 551 His Ungodly swallow, in gorging down the Estates of helpless Widows.

b. in reference to acceptance or belief (cf. SWALLOW *v.* 5).

1624 MIDDLETON *Game at Chess* IV. ii, The swallow of my conscience Hath but a narrow passage. **1662** GURNALL *Chr. in Arm.* verse 17. II. xxvi. §1. (1679) 323/2 One sin will widen thy swallow a little, that thou wilt not so much strein at the next. **1677** W. HUGHES *Man of Sin* II. i. 9 That the Apostles should leave the Care of all the Churches, to take up that of one Particular Church..can never go down with any but a Roman Swallow. **1697** LOCKE *Let. to Molyneux* 10 Apr., Even the largest minds have but narrow swallows. **1757** J. H. GROSE *Voy. E. Indies* 289 Mahomet..knowing as he did the reach and temper of his countrymen, he most probably adapted his religion to their swallow. **1852** THACKERAY *Esmond* II. iii, Of these tales,..Mr. Esmond believed as much as he chose. His kinswoman's greater faith had swallow for them all. **1867** LOWELL *Percival* Pr. Wks. 1890 II. 155 There was no praise too ample for the easy elasticity of his swallow.

†**6.** The function of swallowing; the sense of taste; *transf.* a taste, a small quantity tasted (in quot. *fig.*). *Obs.*

1340 *Ayenb.* 50 Þe mouþ heþ tuo offices huerof þe on belongeþ to þe zuelȝ ase to þe mete an to þe drinke. *Ibid.* 82 Hare wyt is al myswent and corupt ase þe zuelȝ of þe zyke. *Ibid.* 247 Þe ilke greate zuetnesse þet þe herte contemplatif uelþ..ne is bote a litel zuelȝ huerby me smackeþ hou god is zuete.

1826 *Blackw. Mag.* XIX. 659 Patients with callous appetites and hebetated tongues, who have lost the delighted sense of swallow.

7. A single act of swallowing; a gulp.

1822 T. G. WAINEWRIGHT *Ess. & Crit.* (1880) 257, I must drink this glass of sherry exactly at three swallows. **1835** J. WILSON *Noctes Ambr.* Jan., Wks. 1856 IV. 225 The difference between a civilised swallow and a barbarous bolt. **1851** MAYHEW *Lond. Labour* I. 207/2 When she'd had a clean swallow she says [etc.]. **1882** SALA *Amer. Revis.* (1885) 60 He..drank it at one swallow.

b. A quantity (esp. of liquid) swallowed at once; a mouthful swallowed.

1861 DU CHAILLU *Equat. Afr.* vi. 63, I took a swallow of brandy. **1883** *Century Mag.* XXVI. 277/1 To live like an Arab, content with a few dates and a swallow from the gourd. **1904** F. LYNDE *Grafters* ii. 24 The Honorable Jasper ..took a swallow of water from the glass on the desk.

8. a. The space between the sheave and the shell in a pulley-block, through which the rope runs. **b.** In a millstone: see quot. 1880.

c **1860** H. STUART *Seaman's Catech.* 37 Name the parts of a block. The shell, sheave,..swallow, head. **1880** J. LOMAS *Alkali Trade* 217 [In a mill] the 'swallow', or recess cut in the centre of the running stone, must be of ample size.

9. A fish that inflates itself by swallowing air; also called *puffer*, *puff-fish*, or *swell-fish*.

1876 GOODE *Fishes of Bermudas* 22 Chilichthys Spengleri, ..Swallow, Puff-fish.

swallow ('swɒləʊ), *v.* Forms: *α.* 1 **swelᵹan**, (**-sweolᵹan, -swylᵹan**), *3rd sing.* **swilhþ, swilᵹþ, swylᵹþ, -swyleþ, swelhþ, swelᵹþ, swelþ, swelᵹeþ**, 3 **swelȝe(n**, *3rd sing.* **sweleð**, 4 **swelghe, swelugh, -igh, swelwe**, *Kent.* **-zuelȝe**, *3rd sing.* **zuel(ȝ)þ, -zuylþ**, 4–5 **swelewe, -owe**, 5 **-awe, swelle, swelwyn, swellyn**; *Sc.* 4 **swely**, 5–6 **suelly**, 5–6 (9 *dial.*) **swelly**, 6 **swellie**, 9 *dial.* **swill(e)y.** *β.* 2–3 **swoleȝen**, 3 **-uwen, sw(e)olhen, sw(e)olȝe**, *Orm.* **swollȝhenn**, 3–5 **swolewe(n, swolwe**, 4–5 **swolow(e, swolo(n**, 5 **swoolow, sqwolwe**, 6 *Sc.*, 9 *dial.* **swolly**, 6–7 **swollow.** *γ.* 3 **-swalȝe**, 4–6 **swalow(e**, 6 *Sc.* **swallie**, 6–7 **swallowe**, 9 *dial.* **swalley**, 6– **swallow.** *Pa. t. str.* 1 **swealᵹ**, 1–2 **swealh**, 3 **swaluȝ, -sualȝ**, 4 **swalewe**, *Kent.* **-zualȝ**; *wk.* 4 **swelwed, swelowede, suelid, -ud, -yt**, 5

swelwyd, swellyd, swelud; 4 swolȝed, swolewede, swolowyd, squolowde, 5 swolewed, -owed, swolut, sowoluyd; 4 swalud, swalled, 5 swalod, 6- swallowed. *Pa. pple. str.* 1 **-swolȝen, (-swelȝen), 3 iswolwe, isuolȝe, swolȝe(n, 3-5 swolwe, 4 a-swolwe,** *Kent.* **-zuolȝe;** *wk.* **(i)swelewed, -owed, sweliȝhid, swelwid;** *Sc.* and *north.* **5 swelȝed, suelȝit, suelled, 6 suellyit; 4 swolȝed, (i)swolwed, swolewed, -owid, 5 -owet, swolwyd, swolyt, 6** *Sc.* **swolit; 4 swalughid, 5 sualoghed, swaloyd, 6 swalowed, 6- swallowed.** [Com. Teut. orig. str. vb. (not recorded for Gothic): OE. *swelȝan, swealh, swulȝon, swolȝen* = OLFrank. *(far)suelgan*, MDu. *swelgen, swalch, geswolgen* (Du. *zwelgen*), MLG. *swelgen, swelligen*, (LG. *swelgen*), OHG. *swel(a)han, swelgan, swalh, giswolgin* (MHG. *swelhen, swelgen*, G. *schwelgen* wk.), ON. *svelga, svalg, sulgu, solginn*, also wk. (MSw. *svälgha, svalgh, svolgh, sulghen, solghin*, also *swolghet*, Sw. *svälja*, Da. *svælge*); f. base *swelg-: swalg-*, represented also in the forms given s.v. SWALLOW *sb.*²; ulterior relations are undetermined.

As in German and the Scandinavian languages, this verb in English has become weak.

The encroachment of the *o* of the pa. pple. and the *a* of the pa. t. upon the pres. stem is evidenced from the 12th and 13th centuries respectively; it was perhaps furthered by association with SWALLOW *sb.*¹]

1. a. *trans.* To take into the stomach through the throat and gullet, as food or drink. In early use and still *poet.* also more generally = to eat or drink up, devour: cf. FORSWALLOW. Also with *down, in, up* (see 10 a).

α. **c1000** *Sax. Leechd.* II. 230 Laures leaf ceowe and þæt seaw swelȝe. **c1200** *Trin. Coll. Hom.* 43 Ne þaue þu þat storm me duue, ne þat þe deuel me swelȝe. **c1220** *Bestiary* 135 He drageð ðe neddre of ðe ston..and sweleð it. **c1375** *Sc. Leg. Saints* xlvii. (*Effame*) 179 Bestis..þat var of sa gret cruelte, þat þai wald ryf & swely sone Mane or best. **c1380** WYCLIF *Serm.* Sel. Wks. I. 70 Þe more fishes swelewen þe lasse. **c1440** *Promp. Parv.* 482/2 Swelwyn (*K.* swellyn, *P.* swolowyn), *glucio.* **c1480** HENRYSON *Orpheus & Eurydice* 351 Thus Cerberus to swelly sparis nane. **1500–20** DUNBAR *Poems* lviii. 6 Sum swelleis swan, sum swelleis duke. **1536** BELLENDEN *Cron. Scot.* (1821) I. p. xliv, Eftir the..quantite of the dew that thay swellie, thay consave and bredis the perle.

β. [**c1175** *Lamb. Hom.* 123 He..forswoleȝeð þene hoc forð mid þan ese.] **c1200** *Trin. Coll. Hom.* 181 Teð hine grindeð. Tunge hine swoleȝeð. Ðrote turneð hine. **13..** *Sir Beues* (A.) 2764 Ȝenande & gapande on him so, Ase he wolde him swolwe þo. **c1380** WYCLIF *Sel. Wks.* III. 117 þat þou swolow no more þan ys nede. **c1386** CHAUCER *Manciple's Prol.* 36 See how he ganeth lo this dronken wight, As though he wolde swolwe vs anon right. **14..** *Tundale's Vis.* 485 This hogy best..His sette to swolo [*v.rr.* swelowe, swolewe] couetows men. *Ibid.* 491 In tho profecy hit is wryton thus That a best schall swolewo [*v.r.* swelowe] the covetows. **1448–9** METHAM *Amoryus & Cleopes* 1352 Þe serpent a-sundyr þe bak doth byte, And afftyr sqwolwyth yt in.

γ. [**c1205** LAY. 28453 Ævm wurðest þu Winchæstre, þæ eorðe þe scal forswalȝe (**c 1275** for-swolȝe).] **1500–20** DUNBAR *Poems* xi. 27 Syne sall the swallow [*v.r.* swellie] with his mouth The dragone Death. **1534** *Lyndwode's Const. Provinc.* 2 b, Pure wyne onely gyuen to theym to drynke that they maye the more easely & soner swalowe downe the sacramente whyche they haue receyued. **1617** MORYSON *Itin.* I. 245 The Ianizaries..did so swallow our wine, as when it was spent, we were forced to drinke water. **1677** JOHNSON in *Ray's Corr.* (1848) 128 [Salmons] swallow the bait with the hook down into the stomach. **a1700** EVELYN *Diary* 2 Jan. 1684, A fellow who eate live charcoal..champing and swallowing them down **1774** GOLDSM. *Nat. Hist.* (1824) III. 6 There is a power of animal assimilation lodged in the stomach of all creatures..converting substances they swallow into a fluid fitted for their own peculiar support. **1835** T. MITCHELL *Acharn. of Aristoph.* 910 *note*, A prize for the person who..should at a given signal first swallow a certain quantity of wine.

pa. t. str. **c1000** *Eccles. Instit.* in Thorpe *Anc. Laws* (1840) II. 398 He hiȝ swealh, & hiȝ eft aspaw on þa hattestan liȝas. **c1290** *S. Eng. Leg.* I. 19/605 Heo me nam and swaluȝ me in. **c1400** *St. Alexius* (Laud 622) 611 A whal hym swalewe at oo word ffor oo morsel in hast.

pa. t. wk. **a1300** *Cursor M.* 15383 Son it was þat morsel bun,..And Iudas suelid [*Gött.* suelud, *Fairf.* squolowde, *Trin.* swolewed] it onan. **13..** *St. Mergrete* in *Leg. Cath.* (1840) 97 He toke hir in his foule mouthe And swalled hir flesche & bon. **c1330** R. BRUNNE *Chron. Wace* (Rolls) 3785 Man & best he swelwed & et. **c1440** *Alphabet of Tales* 242 Þe devull in liknes of a dragon swalod hym hand & fute. **1481** CAXTON *Reynard* xxvii. (Arb.) 61 The roeke may wel complayne, for I swolowed in dame sharpbeck his wyf. **1821** SCOTT *Kenilw.* xiv, Sussex..swallowed the medicine without farther hesitation.

pa. pple. str. **a1250** *Owl & Night.* 146 Þeos vle..sat toswolle and tobolewe So heo hedde one frogge iswolwe [*v.r.* isuolȝe]. **c1250** *Gen. & Ex.* 1976 Wilde der Hauen min sune swolȝen her. **13..** *Sir Beues* (A.) 786 A..starede on Beues wiþ eien holwe, Also a wolde him haue a-swolwe.

pa. pple. wk. **1387** TREVISA *Higden* (Rolls) IV. 441 Som of hem þat flye,..delyuered hem of ieweles of gold þat þey hadde i-swolwed to fore þat þey flyȝ. **c1450** *St. Cuthbert* (Surtees) 734 Þe seele calfe..þat cuthbert buke had swelyed. **c1450** *Mirk's Festial* 200 A gret horryble dragon..wold haue swolyt her. **1560** ROLLAND *Seven Sages* 61 My self this mater saw..That ane Infant was swellyit with ane sow. **1651** HOBBES *Leviath.* III. xxxii. 195 Pills..swallowed whole, have the vertue to cure. **1779** *Mirror* No. 50 ¶ 11 Having swallowed a short breakfast. **1872** TENNYSON *Gareth & Lynette* 1308 Some hold that he hath swallow'd infant flesh, Monster! **1910** *Encycl. Brit.* II. 28/2 The bait had to be swallowed by the pike before the hook would take hold.

b. In fig. or allusive phr. ***to swallow one's spittle***: (*a*) in renderings of Job vii. 19, where the reference is to the difficulty of swallowing when in distress; † (*b*) to restrain anger or other strong feeling, to repress the rising gorge. ***to swallow a camel, a gudgeon, a spider, a tavern-token***: see CAMEL *sb.* 1 c, GUDGEON *sb.*¹ 2 b, SPIDER *sb.* 1 d, TAVERN *sb.* 4 d. ***to swallow the anchor***, to retire from a sea-faring life; also *transf.* ***to have swallowed the dictionary***: see DICTIONARY 1 c.

c1400 *Pety Job* 40 in 26 *Pol. Poems* 122 Thow woldest suffer neuer more Me to swolowe my salyue? **c1421** 26 *Pol. Poems* 108 How longe sparest þou me noȝt, To swolwe my spotel, bot it me gryue? **1535** COVERDALE *Job* vii. 19 Why goest thou not fro me, ne lettest me alone, so longe till I swalow downe my spetle? [Similarly **1611**.] **1555** EDEN *Decades* (Arb.) 118 Owre men moued with greate hope and hunger of golde, beganne ageine to swalowe downe theyr spettle. **1580** LODGE *Reply Gosson's Sch. Abuse* (Hunter. Cl.) 15 Mithinks while you heare thys I see you swallowe down your owne spittle for reuenge. **a1592** GREENE *Jas. IV* v. iv, None of you both, I see, but are in fault; Thus simple men, as I, do swallow flies. **1631** MASSINGER *Believe as You List* I. ii, Hee durst not stay mee. if hee had, had founde I woulde not swallowe my spettle. **a1714** G. LOCKHART in *L. Papers* (1817) I. 221 [They] were resolved not to swallow a cow and stick at the tail; and as they had begun, carried on, and finished their projects. **1733** SWIFT *On Poetry* 122 And if you find the general vogue Pronounces you a stupid rogue..Sit still, and swallow down your spittle. **1907** J. MASEFIELD *Tarpaulin Muster* xii. 129 An old sailor..had 'swallowed the anchor' in Colon. **1931** A. R. L. GARDNER *Art of Crime* 253 We are glad to be able to quote these..words to..our readers who may entertain..fears lest the crook proper should one day 'swallow the anchor' and retire permanently from the stage. **1977** *Islander* (Victoria, B.C.) 22 May 6/1 But, now he had 'swallowed the anchor', he was a hard-headed business man.

c. *absol.* or *intr.* To take food, drink, etc. into the stomach through the gullet; to perform the act of deglutition, as in an effort to suppress emotion.

a1700 in *Cath. Rec. Soc. Publ.* IX. 345 She not being able to swallow so as to communicate. **1803** *Med. Jrnl.* X. 493 Every time he attempted to speak or swallow, he became more convulsed. **1883** STEVENSON *Treas. Isl.* I. ii, He kept swallowing as if he felt what we used to call a lump in the throat. **1906** CHARL. MANSFIELD *Girl & Gods* xvii, 'I wonder if we hamper Psyche?' 'Don't!' cried Phynides and swallowed quickly.

†2. *trans.* To taste (also *fig.*). *Obs. rare.*

a1340 HAMPOLE *Psalter* xxxiii. [xxxiv.] 8 *Gustate et videte quoniam suauis est dominus*, swelighis and sees for soft is lord. **1340** *Ayenb.* 106 Huanne þe man onderuangþ þise yefþe he zuelȝ[þ] and smackeþ and uelþ þe zuetnesse of God. *Ibid.* 123 Loue of charite nimþ and zikþ and zuelȝþ and halt. **a1400** *Relig. Pieces fr. Thornton MS.* ii. (1914) 48 Þou sese with thyn eghne, heris with thyne eres, Swelawes with thi mouthe, Smelles with þi nese.

3. a. *transf.* To take into itself (physically); to cause to disappear in its interior or depths; to engulf. Also with *down, in, up* (see 10 b).

c1200 ORMIN 10224 Na mannþann helle maȝȝ beon full To swollȝhenn menness sawless. **c1290** *Beket* 2168 in *S. Eng. Leg.* I. 168 Þe eorþe openede under heom for-to swolewen hem a-liue. **a1340** HAMPOLE *Psalter* xiii. 5 A grefe oppynand, þat slas..and swalows þaim in. **13..** *E.E. Allit P.* C. 363 To be swolȝed swyftly wyth þe swart erþe. **c1384** CHAUCER *H. Fame* II. 528 Whan tempest doth the shippes swalowe. **c1400** *Sc. Trojan War* II. 2274 That swelt[h] half of my schippis has Suelled. **c1450** *Mirk's Festial* 4 Helle ȝeonyng, and galpyng..forto swolon hym ynto þe payne þat neuer schall haue ende. **1552** LYNDESAY *Monarche* 5999 The erth sall ryue, And swolly thame, boith man and wyue. **1667** MILTON *P.L.* XII. 196 The Sea Swallows him with his Host. **c1690** tr. *Marana's Lett. Turkish Spy* (1694) I. II. xi. 125 After this Isle was suddenly swallowed down into the Sea. **1855** MOTLEY *Dutch Rep.* VI. i. (1866) 771/2 The lower part of the face was swallowed in a bushy beard. **1905** E. CLODD *Animism* §9. 45 The earthquake that swallowed man and beast.

† b. *refl.* of a river losing itself in another.

1623 tr. *Favine's Theat. Hon.* II. i. 67 Where the Riuer of Lipp..runneth to swallow it selfe [orig. *vient se perdre*] in the Rhine.

4. *fig.* **a.** To make away with, destroy, consume, cause to vanish (as if by devouring or absorption into itself). See also 10 c.

a1340 HAMPOLE *Psalter* cxxiii. 2 [cxxiv. 3] Perauntire þai had swelighid vs lifand. **13..** *E.E. Allit. P.* B. 1268 Wyth þe swayf of þe sworde þat swolȝed hem alle. **c1400** *Destr. Troy* Prol. 12 Sothe stories ben..swolowet into swym by swiftenes of yeres. **c1450** *Cov. Myst.* (Shaks. Soc.) 83 But God in us have habytacion, Peraventure oure enemyes shulde swelle us. **1533** GAU *Richt Vay* 45 As S. Paul sais..Deid is swolit throw wictore. **1610** HOLLAND *Camden's Brit.* (1637) 689 Three Schooles..which the greedy iniquity of these our times hath already swallowed. **1643** in *Verney Mem.* (1907) I. 301, I see my ruine at the very dore ready to swallow mee. **1818** SCOTT *Br. Lamm.* x, The apartment was suddenly illuminated by a flash of lightning, which seemed absolutely to swallow the darkness of the hall. **1837** CARLYLE *Fr. Rev.* II. I. iv, To-day swallowing Yesterday, and then being in its turn swallowed of To-morrow. **1847** TENNYSON *Princess* v. 432 Sloughs That swallow common sense. **1870** MORRIS *Earthly Par.* II. III. 400 All strife was swallowed of festivity.

b. To cause to be 'lost' in something; to 'drown', 'absorb', engross, occupy wholly. (Now only with *up*: see 10 d.)

c1350 *Spec. Gy de Warw.* 642 þe pine of helle hem gan to swolewe. **1434** MISYN *Mending of Life* xi. 125 All my hert..is turnyd in-to heet of lufe, & it is swaloyd In-to a-noþer Ioy and a-nodir form. **1645** G. DANIEL *Wks.* (Grosart) II. To Rdr. 2 In Some I have bene lost and Swallowed from my first intentions, by newer Thoughts. **c1698** LOCKE *Cond. Underst.* §36 The necessary Provison for Life swallows the greatest part of their Time.

c. To take in eagerly, 'devour' (with one's ears or mind).

1387–8 T. USK *Test. Love* Prol. (Skeat) l. 2 Men..that with eeres openly sprad, so moche swalowen the deliciousnesse of jestes and of ryme..that of the goodnesse..of the sentence take they litel hede. **1513** DOUGLAS *Æneis* IV. xii. 35 Now lat ȝone cruell Troiane swelly and see [orig. *hauriat oculis*] This our fyre funerall. **1595** SHAKS. *John* IV. ii. 195, I saw a Smith..With open mouth swallowing a Taylors newes. **c1645** HOWELL *Lett.* (1650) I. 419 A man who weds himself to study, and swallows many books. **1834** MAGINN in *Blackw. Mag.* XXXV. 747 Dosy, who sate in open-mouthed wonder, swallowing them [*sc.* his stories] down as a common-councilman swallows turtle.

d. To take for oneself, or into itself, as a territory or other possession; to absorb, appropriate. (See also 10 e.)

1637 in Foster *Crt. Min. E. Ind. Comp.* (1907) 267 [Without allowing for forfeiture of the bond for private trade, misapplication of the Company's money, or for] swalloweing [Burt's estate]. **a1700** EVELYN *Diary* 18 Nov. 1679, The Duke of Buckingham, much of whose estate he had swallowed. *Ibid.* 23 Sept. 1683, That the French King might the more easily swallow Flanders..whilst we sat unconcern'd. **1888** BRYCE *Amer. Commw.* xci. III. 263 One finds in the United States..many people who declare that Mexico will be swallowed.

e. *Theatr. slang.* To get up (a part) hastily.

1890 BARRÈRE & LELAND *Slang Dict.*, *Swallow the cackle*, (theatrical), to learn a part. **1898** *Tit Bits* 30 July 338/1 The remaining acts [of the play] were in turn 'swallowed' during the successive intervals.

5. a. To accept without opposition or protest; to take (an oath, etc.) without demur or lightly.

a1591 H. SMITH *Wks.* (1867) II. 13 It is very like that these men swallow many sins, for God is never so forgotten as in feasting, and sporting, and bargaining. **1632** MASSINGER *City Madam* I. i, Here's no gross flattery! Will she swallow this? **1646** BP. MAXWELL *Burd. Issach.* in *Phenix* (1708) II. 303, I cannot sufficiently wonder, how the High Court of Parliament of England hath swallow'd and sworn their Covenant. **1762–71** H. WALPOLE *Vertue's Anecd. Paint.* (1786) III. 107 The former laid a wager that there was no flattery so gross but his friend would swallow. **1789** GOUV. MORRIS in Sparks *Life & Writ.* (1832) I. 325 The Representatives of this nation..are ready to swallow this proposition by acclamation. **1810** BENTHAM *Packing* (1821) 191 Give them an oath to swallow. **1822** J. FLINT *Lett. Amer.* 171 In England, affidavits are often managed in a simpler way. *Swallowing* a customhouse oath is there a well known expression. **1853** LYTTON *My Novel* IV. xiv, People take you with all your faults, if you are rich; but they won't swallow your family into the bargain.

b. *esp.* To accept mentally without question or suspicion; to believe unquestioningly. †Also with *down*.

1594 NASHE *Unfort. Trav.* 69 Beleeue nothing,..yet seeme thou as thou swallowedst al, suspectedst none. **1643** *Ord. Lords & Com., Westm. Conf.* Pref. (1658) C 3, So many, especially of the younger sort, do swallow down almost any error that is offered them. **1690** LOCKE *Hum. Und.* I. iv. §24 To make a Man swallow that for an innate Principle, which may serve to his purpose, who teacheth them. **1691** RAY *Creation* II. (1692) 83 He that can swallow the raining of Frogs. **1786** JEFFERSON *Writ.* (1859) I. 516, I find that I could swallow the last opinion, sooner than either of the others. **1791** MME. D'ARBLAY *Diary* 20 Aug., [She] will believe no good of them, and swallows all that is said of evil. **1870** FREEMAN *Norm. Conq.* (ed. 2) II. App. 661 The legend is still swallowed by novelists. **1880** LITTLEDALE *Plain Reas.* lxii. 135 Over-readiness to swallow marvels..is credulity.

6. To put up with, submit to, take patiently or submissively (something injurious or irksome). (Cf. F. *avaler.*)

1611 MIDDLETON & DEKKER *Roaring Girl* D.'s Wks. 1873 III. 185 If I swallow this wrong, let her thanke you. **1613** PURCHAS *Pilgrimage* I. xvii. 80 The mother (not able to swallow her shame and grief) cast her selfe into the lake. **1623** J. CHAMBERLAIN in *Crt. & Times Jas. I* (1848) II. 442 And how many disgraces and indignities he swallowed, to bring his own ends about. **1710** SWIFT *Let. to Abp. King* 10 Oct., They cannot give themselves the little troubles of attendance that other men are content to swallow. **1710** —— *Jrnl. Stella* 2 Nov., I took my four pills last night, and they lay an hour in my throat... I suppose I could swallow four affronts as easily. **1848** THACKERAY *Van. Fair* xvii, He was pompous, but with such a cook what would one not swallow?

7. To refrain from expressing or uttering; to keep down, repress. Also with *down*.

a1642 S. GODOLPHIN *Poems, Ps.* cxxxvii, Deny us freedome of our groans And bid us swallow all our moans. **1719** YOUNG *Busiris* IV. i, They..swallow down their tears to hide them from me. **a1771** GRAY *Dante* 6, I swallow'd down My struggling Sorrow. **1809** MALKIN *Gil Blas* I. v. ¶1 Swallowing my grievances [orig. *dévorant ma douleur*], [I] set myself to wait on my noble masters. **1820** BYRON *Juan* V. xxiv, Swallowing a heart-burning sigh. **1851** D. JERROLD *St. Giles* iv. 31 [She] swallowed her mirth, and..busied herself at the cupboard. **1868** MORRIS *Earthly Par.* (1870) I. I. 325 Then in his throat a swelling passion rose, Which yet he swallowed down. **1878** BOSW. SMITH *Carthage* 296 Hannibal swallowed his resentment.

8. To take back, retract, recant. (Cf. EAT *v.* 2 c.)

1593 SHAKS. *Rich. II*, I. i. 132 As low as to thy heart, Through the false passage of thy throat: thou lyest... Now swallow downe that Lye. **1603** —— *Meas. for M.* III. i. 235 [He] swallowed his vowes whole, pretending in her, discoueries of dishonor. **1703** FARQUHAR *Inconstant* III. i, I have swallow'd my Words already; I have eaten them up. **1848** LOWELL *Biglow P.* Ser. I. iv. 16 A marciful Providence fashioned us holler O' purpose thet we might our principles swaller. **1889** BARRIE *Window in Thrums* xx. 195 If Jamie be living now he has still those words to swallow.

9. To pronounce indistinctly or fail to pronounce; to slur over. (Cf. F. *manger.*)

a **1791** WESLEY *Wks.* (1830) XIII. 479 Some persons mumble, or swallow some words or syllables.

10. swallow up. a. *lit.* To swallow completely or voraciously; to eat up, devour. Also *absol.*

1535 COVERDALE *Obad.* i. 16 Yee dryncke shall they, and swalowe vp, so that ye shall be, as though ye had neuer bene. **1600** J. PORY tr. *Leo's Africa* IX. 346 The crocodile.. swalloweth vp both the baite and the hooke. **1711** ADDISON *Spect.* No. 10 ¶3 Like Moses's Serpent, that immediately swallow'd up and devoured those of the Ægyptians. **1880** STEWART & TAIT *Unseen Univ.* Introd. 15 Just as we cannot conceive of a man swallowing up [*ed.* 1876 devouring] himself, so [etc.].

b. *transf.* To engulf completely; to cause to disappear utterly in its depths. Cf. 3.

1526 TINDALE *Rev.* xii. 16 The erth opened her mought, and swalowed vppe the rever. **1535** COVERDALE *Ps.* cvi. 17 So the earth opened & swalowed vp Dathan. **1560** DAUS tr. *Sleidane's Comm.* 453 The shippes being..swallowed vp of the billowes did perishe. **1596** DALRYMPLE tr. *Leslie's Hist. Scot.* I. 99 Certane difficile myres, quhilkes..sal gaip wyd, and swallie him vp in a maner to the deipth. **1610** HOLLAND *Camden's Brit.* (1637) 587 The first [river] is Hans, which being swallowed up under the ground, breaketh up againe three miles off. **1732** BERKELEY *Alciphr.* IV. §24 Because London was not swallowed up or consumed by fire from heaven. **1803** SCOTT *Let.* in *Lockhart* (1837) I. xi. 392 This district..was swallowed up by the sea. **1823** LAMB *Elia* Ser. II. *Old Margate Hoy*, Sunken ships, and sumless treasures swallowed up in the unrestoring depths. **1832** R. & J. LANDER *Exped. Niger* I. vi. 245 The little legs of the child were swallowed up in his clumsy yellow boots. **1853** JAMES *Agnes Sorel* (1860) II. 103 The Castle gates swallowed them up, and nothing more was seen of them.

c. *fig.* To make away with or destroy completely; to cause to disappear utterly (as if by absorption). Cf. 4 a.

1530 TINDALE *Answ. More* I. xviii. Wks. (1572) 286/2 In yᵉ world to come loue shall swalow vp the other twoo [*sc.* faith and hope]. **1535** COVERDALE *Ps.* lvi[i]. 3 He shal..saue me from the reprofe of him that wolde swalowe me vp. **1626** GOUGE *Serm. Dignity Chivalry* §18 Delight in the things which men do, swalloweth up the pains that is taken about them. **1667** MILTON *P.L.* II. 149 Those thoughts..swallowd up and lost In the wide womb of uncreated night. *c* **1720** DE FOE *Mem. Cavalier* (1840) 121 All people looked upon themselves as ruined and swallowed up. **1758** J. DALRYMPLE *Ess. Feudal Property* (ed. 2) 122 The feudal law carries with it..a system of private rights, which swallow up all others, wherever it comes. **1847** HELPS *Friends in C.* I. vii. 105 Another rule is, not to let familiarity swallow up all courtesy. **1862** STANLEY *Jew. Ch.* (1877) I. v. 96 The man is swallowed up in the cause, the messenger in the message. **1864** BRYCE *Holy Rom. Emp.* v. (1875) 68 Since the powers it gave were autocratic and unlimited, it must swallow up all minor claims and dignities. **1875** JOWETT *Plato* (ed. 2) I. 446 Must not all things at last be swallowed up in death? **1885** *Manch. Exam.* 12 May 5/3 Nearly a month will be swallowed up in the verification of the returns. **1901** *Scotsman* 28 Feb. 7/1 The Irish names in the box swallowed up all the rest.

d. To occupy entirely, engross, 'absorb', 'drown'; = 4 b.

1581 J. BELL *Haddon's Answ. Osor.* 499 b, Blynded with selfe love, drowned in malice, swallowed upp with his owne conceipt. **1738** WESLEY *Ps.* VIII. iii, Wonder dims my aching Eyes, And swallows up my Soul. **1815** J. SMITH *Panorama Sci. & Art* II. 194 The original intention of the experiment was lost sight of, by an unexpected result which swallowed up all their attention. **1857** KEBLE *Let. to Denison* 14 Oct. (in *Maggs's Catal.* Mar. (1897) 54/1) Since I came home [I] have been swallowed up with my little book on Eucharistical Adoration. **1891** KIPLING *Light that Failed* x. 205 He fell to work, whistling softly, and was swallowed up in the clean, clear joy of creation.

e. To take completely into itself, or for oneself; to appropriate, absorb (= 4 d); †in quot. 1544, to take fully upon oneself.

1544 BETHAM *Precepts War* I. lxiii. D iv, A faythfull armye wyll swallowe vp all parylles, before that so lyberall a capytayne shuld haue any shame or reproche. **1654** BRAMHALL *Just Vind.* ii. (1661) 21 The oppressions of the Court of Rome, which would swallow up..all original Jurisdiction. *a* **1700** EVELYN *Diary* 15 July 1683, The French King..having swallow'd up almost all Flanders. **1743** POCOCKE *Descr. East* I. IV. i. 162 In upper Egypt there were formerly twenty-four provinces, but many of them are now swallow'd up by Arab Sheiks. **1884** *Sat. Rev.* 7 June 737/1 Morocco..has escaped being swallowed by France because Spain has guarded it. **1889** GRETTON *Memory's Harkb.* 157 With Exton is joined the hamlet of Horn, now swallowed up in the Park.

†**f.** To take in eagerly: = 4 c. *Obs. rare.*

1593 SHAKS. *Lucr.* 1409 About him were a presse of gaping faces, Which seem'd to swallow vp his sound aduice.

g. To pass over (a distance) rapidly.

(Cf. DEVOUR 8 b.)

1890 'R. BOLDREWOOD' *Col. Reformer* (1891) 188 Three miles had been swallowed up ere the team steadied. [Cf. quot. 1899 s.v. SWALLOWED *ppl. a.*]

swallowable ('swɒləʊəb(ə)l), *a.* [f. SWALLOW *v.* + -ABLE.] Capable of being or fit to be swallowed (*lit.* and *fig.*).

1818 BENTHAM *Ch. Eng.* Introd. 42 This altogether indigestible and scarcely swallowable morsel. **1846–9** S. R. MAITLAND *Ess.*, etc. 315 The reader, who for the first time meets with an anecdote in its hundredth edition, and its most mitigated and swallowable form. **1887** STEVENSON *Let.* 22 Aug., The berths are excellent, the pasture swallowable.

swallowed ('swɒləʊd), *ppl. a.* [f. as prec. + -ED¹.] In senses corresponding to those of the verb (*lit.* and *fig.*).

c **1600** SHAKS. *Sonn.* cxxix, Past reason hated as a swollowed bayt. **1667** *Phil. Trans.* II. 535 The dexterity of disengaging himself from the swallowed hook. **1822–7** GOOD *Study Med.* (1829) I. 120 The swallowed morsel is carried forward into the stomach. **1887** *Pall Mall G.* 23 Nov. 4/2 Why should one more dose of swallowed principles disagree with him? **1899** MEREDITH *Poems, Night-Walk* 42 The posts that named the swallowed mile.

swallower ('swɒləʊə(r)). Also 1 **swelȝere**, 6 *Sc.* **swelliar.** [f. as prec. + -ER¹. In OE. *swelȝere* = OHG. *swelgâri* (MHG. *swelher*, G. *schwelger*) glutton, tippler.] One who or that which swallows.

1. a. *lit.*: see SWALLOW *v.* 1; *esp.* a voracious eater or drinker. Also in Comb., as ***acorn-swallower, sword-swallower.***

a **1000** ÆLFRIC *Colloq.* 16 in Wr.-Wülcker 102 Ic ne eom swa micel swelȝere þæt ic ealle cynn metta on anre ȝereordinge etan mæȝe. **1513** DOUGLAS *Æneis* XIII. vi. 222 Thir akcorne swelliaris, the fat swyne. **1605** *1st Pt. Jeronimo* III. i. 42 Deuourer of apparell, thou huge swallower. **1694** MOTTEUX *Rabelais* IV. xxix. 118 A huge Greedy-Guts, a tall woundy swallower of hot Wardens and Muscles. **1710** FULLER *Tatler* No. 205 ¶2, I..always speak of them with the Distinction of the Eaters, and the Swallowers. **1842** DICKENS *Amer. Notes* vi. (1868) 51 Of all kinds of eaters of fish, or flesh, or fowl, in these latitudes, the swallowers of oysters alone are not gregarious. **1891** HARDY *Tess* xlviii, The enormous numbers that had been gulped down by the insatiable swallower [*viz.* a threshing machine].

b. *spec.* A deep-sea fish, *Chiasmodon niger*, widely distributed in the Atlantic, having an immensely distensible stomach which enables it to swallow fishes larger than itself.

2. *transf.*: see SWALLOW *v.* 3. (In quots. *attrib.*)

1891 MEREDITH *Poems, Eng. bef. Storm* iii, Yon swallower wave with shroud of foam. **1898** —— *Forest History* iv, The forest's heart of fog on mossed morass, On purple pool and silky cotton-grass, Revealed where lured the swallower byway.

3. *fig.* (also with *up*): see SWALLOW *v.* 4, 5, 10 c.

a **1548** HALL *Chron., Hen. VI*, 157 Affirming him to be.. the moste swallower vp and consumer of the kynges treasure. **1810** BENTHAM *Packing* (1821) 191 Give them an oath to swallow, every impure property is, by this consecrated vehicle, carried off. Note that the oath by which the swallower is rendered thus unlikely 'to do wrong,' is the very oath, which..is regularly productive of perjury. **1837** CARLYLE *Fr. Rev.* III. I. vi, Here too is a Swallower of Formulas. **1855** MRS. GASKELL *Let.* Feb. (1966) 332 Meta's atelier is such a swallower-up of time.

'swallow-hole. [f. SWALLOW *v.* or *sb.*² + HOLE *sb.*] = SWALLOW *sb.*² 1 b.

1661 J. CHILDREY *Brit. Baconica* 74 About Badminton also are several holes (called Swallow-holes) where the Waters..fall into the bowels of the earth, and are seen no more. **1829** *Glover's Hist. Derby* I. 11 The channel of the Manifold river is here dry in dry seasons, owing to the vast swallow-holes at Darfa cliff. **1839** *Civil Eng. & Arch. Jrnl.* II. 151/2 These rivulets pour down the hill upon the surface of the tertiary clay, until they arrive at the chalk, where they are entirely absorbed in swallow-holes. **1891** *Leeds Mercury* 5 Nov. 3/6 Shafts being made into it, by which the water absorbed by conites, fissures and 'swallow holes', would be rendered available.

swallowing ('swɒləʊɪŋ), *vbl. sb.* Also 4 **zuelȝinge, swolwyng,** 5 **swelluing, swelwyng(e, swellyng(e.** [f. SWALLOW *v.* + -ING¹.]

I. The action of the verb SWALLOW.

1. Deglutition; †devouring: see SWALLOW *v.* 1.

c **1400** *Apol. Loll.* 55 þe deuowring or swelluing of alle bestis of þe feld. *c* **1440** *Promp. Parv.* 482/2 Swelwyynge of mete (*K.*, *P.* swellynge of mete and drynke), *degluticio.* *c* **1532** DU WES *Introd. Fr.* in *Palsgr.* 903 The swalowyng, *lauailer.* **1725** *Lond. Gaz.* No. 6349/3 His Swallowing is easier. **1780** *Mirror* No. 73 The swallowing of much strong liquor produces a temporary madness. **1803** *Med. Jrnl.* IX. 293 The difficulty of swallowing, known by the name of Dysphagia. **1899** *Allbutt's Syst. Med.* VII. 736 There is rarely any affection of swallowing.

attrib. **1881** CABLE *Mme. Delphine* vi. 27 She..began a faltering speech, with a swallowing motion in the throat.

†**b.** Tasting, sense of taste: see SWALLOW *v.* 2.

1340 *Ayenb.* 91 Be zyȝþe, be hyerþe, be smellinge, be zuelȝynge, and be takynge. *c* **1440** *Jacob's Well* 218 þe iij. gate of þi pytt is tastyng or swelwyng.

2. *fig.* (also with *up*): see SWALLOW *v.* 4, 10 c.

1816 COLERIDGE *Lay Serm.* (Bohn) 318 The oblivion and swallowing-up of self in an object dearer than self. **1830** COBBETT *Rur. Rides* (1853) 604 Which exactions here are swallowed up by the aristocracy and their dependents; but which swallowings are imputed to every one bearing the name of parson.

II. †**3.** A whirlpool: = SWALLOW *sb.*² 2. *Obs.*

Used like OE. pr. pple. *swelȝend* to render L. *vorago.*

1387 TREVISA *Higden* (Rolls) I. 65 þere beeþ many swolwynges and whirlynges of wateres by þe see brynkes. *Ibid.* II. 51 Woodnesse of swolwynge and of whirlynge water.

'swallowing, *ppl. a.* Also 4 **swelwyng.** [f. as prec. + -ING².] That swallows; usually *transf.* or *fig.*: see the verb.

a **1400** *Prymer* (1891) 24 (*Benedicite*) Fier and swelwynghete blesse to the lord. **1548** ELYOT, *Voraginosus*.., full of gulfes or swalowyng pittes. **1555** EDEN *Decades* (Arb.) 193 These blind and swalowyng sandes. *a* **1586** SIDNEY *Ps.* V. iv, Their throate it is an open swallowing grave. **1594** SHAKS. *Rich. III*, III. vii. 128 Almost shoulderd in the swallowing gulph, Of blind forgetfulnesse. **1632** LITHGOW *Trav.* II. 53 Euery swallowing waue threatned our death. **1806** J. BERESFORD *Miseries Hum. Life* I. i. (ed. 3) 13 What is the Country, but a sandy desart at one season or a swallowing quagmire at another? **1852** M. ARNOLD *The Future* 16 Whether he first sees light Where the river..winds through the plain: Whether in sound of the swallowing sea.

swallowling ('swɒləʊlɪŋ). *rare*⁻¹. [f. SWALLOW *sb.*¹ + -LING¹; cf. *duckling.*] A young swallow.

1839 WILLIS *À l'abri* ii. (1840) 9 Her swallowlings..have been hatched a week.

'swallow-pipe. *rare*⁻¹. [f. SWALLOW *v.* or *sb.*² + PIPE *sb.*¹] The gullet.

1786 WOLCOT (P. Pindar) *2nd Ode to R.A.'s* Wks. 1812 I. 134 Not one bit more could pass your swallow-pipe.

swallow-tail, swallowtail ('swɒləʊteɪl). Also in some senses **swallow's tail.** [f. SWALLOW *sb.*¹ + TAIL *sb.*; corresp. to and in certain uses modelled on F. *queue d'aronde*, †*d'arondelle* (senses 5 and 6), G. *schwalbenschwanz* (2 b, 8, etc.), Du. *zwaluwstaart*, MLG. *swalekenstert*, LG. *swalkensteert*, etc.]

1. A tail like that of a swallow; a forked tail.

1703 tr. *Perrault's Abridgm. Vitruvius* I. iv. 30 The Sabliers..joined together by Tenons, in the form of a Swallow-Tail. **1775** DALRYMPLE in *Phil. Trans.* LXVIII. 402 Two birds..with swallow-tails flying above the ship. **1842** G. DARLING in *Proc. Berw. Nat. Club* II. No. 10. 4 Smelts of the Salmon with their silvery sides, dark purply fins, and swallow-tail. **1860** MAYNE REID *Hunters' Feast* iv, The 'passenger' [pigeon]..looks not unlike the kite, wanting the forked or 'swallow' tail.

2. Applied to various animals having a forked tail. †**a.** Some kind of fish: see quot. *Obs.*

1683 POYNTZ *Pres. Prosp. Tobago* 21 The green Swallow-Tail..a Fish not much bigger than a Herring.

b. A swallow-tailed butterfly.

1819 SAMOUELLE *Entomol. Compend.* 416 *Papilio Machaon.* The Swallow-tail. **1868** *Rep. U.S. Commissioner Agric.* (1869) 314 The swallow-tails, belonging to the family *Papilionidæ.* **1880** C. R. MARKHAM *Peruv. Bark* 173 One bright swallow-tail, with blue wings, fringed with crimson.

c. A humming-bird of the genus *Eupetomena.*

1861 GOULD *Monogr. Troch.* II. Plate 42, *Eupetomena Hirundinacea.* Swallow-tail... This species being the most swallow-like member of the entire family of Trochilidæ. **1899** EVANS in *Cambr. Nat. Hist.* IX. 435 *Eupetomena macrura* of Brazil and Guiana, termed the 'Swallow-tail' from its forking rectrices.

d. A swallow-tailed kite.

3. A name for the white willow (*Salix alba*): also ***swallow-tail willow, swallow-tailed willow*** (see next, 2 b).

1626 BACON *Sylva* §475 The Shining Willow, which they call Swallow-Taile. **1766** *Museum Rust.* VI. 81 The bright swallow-tail willow;..next to the Norfolk kind, it is the largest growing sort.

4. A broad or barbed arrow-head; an arrow with such a head.

1545 ASCHAM *Toxoph.* (Arb.) 135 The one..hauyng two ..barbes, lookyng backewarde to the stele and the fethers, which..we call..a brode arrowe head or a swalowe tayle. **1828** SCOTT *F.M. Perth* xxix, The English..sent off their volleys of swallow-tails before we could call on St. Andrew.

†**5.** = DOVETAIL 1 b, 2. *Obs.*

1548 ELYOT, *Securicla*.., a swalowes tayle [**1565** COOPER, swallowe tayle], or a doue tayle in carpenters woorke, whiche is fastnyng of two pieces of timbre..togyther. **1616** BULLOKAR *Eng. Expos.*, *Swallowes tayle*,..a fastening of two peeces of timber so strongly together, that they cannot fall asunder. **1823** P. NICHOLSON *Pract. Builder* 594.

6. *Fortif.* An outwork characterized by two projections with a re-entrant angle between them, suggesting a swallow's tail.

1688 CAPT. J. S. *Fortification* 78 Hornworks..are much more in use than the Tenailes, Swallow Tails, or Priests Bonnets. **1690** D'URFEY *Collin's Walk* I. 11 He..all your Out-works would Assail, With his Eternal Swallows Tail. **1702** *Milit. & Sea Dict.* (1711), *Queue d'yronde*, or *Swallow's-Tail*, a Detach'd or Out-work, whose Sides open towards the Head, or Campaign, and draw closer or narrower towards the Gorge. **1908** MRS. E. WHARTON *Hermit & Wild Woman* 1 A little walled town with Ghibelline swallow-tails.

7. The cleft two-pointed end of a flag or pennon; also, a swallow-tailed flag.

1697 *Lond. Gaz.* No. 3317/3 One with a White Flag, Swallow Tail at Main-top-mast. **1743** BULKELEY & CUMMINS *Voy. S. Seas* 5 The Commander in Chief being distinguish'd by a red broad Pendant with a Swallow's Tail at his Main-top-mast Head. **1753** *Scots Mag.* Aug. 386/2 A yellow jack with a swallow-tail. **1825** SCOTT *Betrothed* xxvii, Methinks, instead of this old swallow's tail, we should muster rarely under a broidered petticoat. **1844** *Regul. & Ord. Army* 10 The Flag of the Guidon of Dragoons to be three feet five inches to the end of the slit of the swallow-tail. **1894** C. N. ROBINSON *Brit. Fleet* 89 The flag..is sometimes square, sometimes a swallow-tail.

b. The cleft tail-end of a vane.

1843 GROVE *Corr. Phys. Forces* (1846) 32 A wind..will instantly arrange these vanes in a definite direction, the arrow-heads or narrow parts pointing one way, the swallow-tails or broad parts another.

8. A swallow-tailed coat. *colloq.*

1835 FRITH *Let.* 2 May, in *Autobiog.* (1888) III. 38, I don't want a dress-coat; besides, I should look a regular guy in a swallow-tail. **1837** DICKENS *Pickw.* ii, The green coat had been a smart dress garment in the days of swallow-tails. **1871** 'M. LEGRAND' *Cambr. Freshm.* 115 Mr. Golightly rose, divested himself of the loose coat he wore in the study, put on his black swallow-tail, and went down to the drawing-room. **1894** WILKINS & VIVIAN *Green Bay Tree* I. 33 The boys..exchanged their tweed coats for the regulation swallow-tails.

b. The tail or skirt of such a coat. *rare.*

1894 LATTO *Tam. Bodkin* vi, I banged roon' my hand, an' lo, there was but ae solitary swallowtail to the fore! **1913** *Play Pictorial* No. 130 The [ladies'] coat..slopes sharply away from the hips, and forms swallow-tails at the back.

9. *attrib.* = SWALLOW-TAILED: as in *swallow-tail butterfly, coat, moth, pennon*; also formerly applied to a cut of the beard with two points. See also *swallow-tail willow* in 3.

1596 NASHE *Walden* Ep. Ded. A iv, Astrologicall Richard ..most studiously compyled a profound Abridgement vpon beards, & therein..frutelessly determined betwixt the swallowes taile cut & the round beard like a rubbing brush. **1602** ROWLANDS *Greene's Ghost* (1872) 9 The vse of the terrible cut, and the Swallow-taile slash. **1745** *Gleditsch's Teutsch-Engl. Lex.*, *Schwalbenschwantz*..a swallow-tail-carving. **1749** WILKES *Engl. Moths & Butterflies* 38 The Swallow-tail Moth..is bred in May and June. *Ibid.* 47 The Swallow-tail Butterfly is produced twice a Year. **1786** *Pogonologia* 27 Those different fashions of wearing the beard called, sharp-pointed, square, round, fan, swallow's-tail, artichoke-leaf, &c. **1816** KIRBY & SP. *Entomol.* xxi. (1818) II. 245 The swallow-tail butterfly (*Papilio Machaon*, L.). **1819** SAMOUELLE *Entomol. Compend.* 253 Our [*apteryx*] *sambucaria* (swallow-tail moth). **1848** LOWELL *Biglow P.* Ser. I. *What Mr. Robinson Thinks*, Parson Wilbur sez he never heerd in his life Thet th' Apostles rigged out in their swaller-tail coats. **1852** BURN *Naval & Milit. Dict.* II. (1863), Swallow tail scarf, *assemblage à queue d'hironde.* **1853** 'C. BEDE' *Verdant Green* I. i, The *toga virilis* of stick-up collars and swallow-tail coats. **1884** E. YATES *Recoll.* I. 45 [The Police, 1836–47] wore swallow-tail blue coats. **1891** DOYLE *White Co.* xiii, The heavy ash spear with swallow-tail pennon.

swallow-tailed ('swɒləʊteɪld), *a.* [f. prec. + -ED².] Having a tail like that of a swallow, or an end or part like a swallow's tail; also, of the form of a swallow's tail.

I. Of natural objects.

1. In names of species or varieties of birds characterized by a long deeply forked tail, as **swallow-tailed duck**, the long-tailed duck, *Harelda glacialis*; **swallow-tailed falcon, hawk** = *s. kite*; **swallow-tailed flycatcher**, the scissor-tail, *Milvulus forficatus* or *M. tyrannus*; **swallow-tailed gull**, a rare American gull, *Creagrus furcatus*; **swallow-tailed kingfisher**, a Surinam species of jacamar, *Galbula paradisea*; **swallow-tailed kite**, a widely distributed American kite, *Elanoides forficatus*; **swallow-tailed sheldrake** = *s. duck.*

1831 SWAINSON & RICHARDSON *Fauna Boreali-Amer.* 460 Swallow-tailed *Ducks. **1781** LATHAM *Gen. Synopsis Birds* I. I. 60 Swallow-tailed *Falcon..is a most elegant species. **1783** *Ibid.* II. I. 356 Swallow-Tailed *Fly catcher..inhabits Mexico. **1872** COUES *Key N. Amer. Birds* 317 Swallow-tailed *Gull..tail white, very much forked. **1771** *Encycl. Brit.* II. 540/2 The [Falco] furcatus, or swallow-tailed *hawk. **1743** EDWARDS *Nat. Hist. Birds* I. 10 The Swallow-tail'd *King-fisher. **1872** COUES *Key N. Amer. Birds* 211 *Nauclerus*, Swallow-tailed *Kite. **1764** EDWARDS *Glean. Nat. Hist.* III. 249 The Swallow-tailed Indian *Roller. *a* **1672** WILLUGHBY *Ornith.* (1678) 364 The Swallow-tail'd *Sheldrake of Mr. Johnson.

2. a. Having a pair of projecting parts suggesting a swallow's tail, as a seed. **b. swallow-tailed willow**: = SWALLOW-TAIL 3.

1712 tr. *Pomet's Hist. Drugs* I. 39 The Seed is Swallow-tail'd and flat. **1764** *Museum Rust.* II. xi. 43, I set twenty willow-sets (the swallow-tail'd willow, or white willow) trunchions. **1884** MILLER *Plant-n.*, *Salix alba*, Common White, Huntingdon, or Swallow-tailed Willow.

3. Having each of the hind wings prolonged into a 'tail', the two together suggesting the forked tail of a swallow, as the **swallow-tailed butterfly** (*Papilio machaon* and other species of *Papilionidæ*) and the **swallow-tailed moth** (*Urapteryx sambucaria*).

1743 G. EDWARDS *Nat. Hist. Birds* I. 34 The dusky and yellow Swallow-tail'd Butter-Fly. **1826** KIRBY & SP. *Entomol.* III. xxx. 148 The beautiful caterpillar of the swallow-tailed butterfly (*Papilio Machaon* L.). **1880** C. R. MARKHAM *Peruv. Bark* 141 Large swallow-tailed butterflies, purple with light-blue spots on the upper wings.

II. Of artificial objects.

4. a. Of a flag or pennon: Having a cleft end with two tapering points.

1697 in *MSS. Ho. Lords* N.S. III. (Hist. MSS. Comm. 1905) 322 Two swallow tailed flags. **1808** SCOTT *Marm.* IV. xxviii, A thousand streamers..Broad, narrow, swallow-tail'd, and square. **1864** BOUTELL *Her. Hist. & Pop.* xvii. (ed. 3) 274 A swallow-tailed pennon.

b. *Naut.* Applied to a kind of topsail.

1794 *Rigging & Seamanship* I. 83 A topsail, called a swallow-tailed topsail.

5. Dovetailed, as a piece of timber or stone; also, having a cleft end, as a part of mechanism, etc.

1726 LEONI *Alberti's Archit.* I. 50 b, Cramps of Brass and Iron are fasten'd in with Lead: But those of Wood are sufficiently secured by their shape, which is made in such manner, that for resemblance, they are call'd Swallow, or Dove-tail'd. **1730** A. GORDON *Maffei's Amphith.* 307 The Key-Stone in the middle is wedged, and, as we say, Swallow-tail'd. **1798** *Hull Advertiser* 11 Aug. 3/1 Mr. Herschell discovered..a new star..it resembles those stars in embroidery called swallow tailed. **1862** *Catal. Internat. Exhib., Brit.* II. No. 4563, The bristles of brushes..are laid upon a principle which prevents their working hollow or wearing swallow-tailed. **1871** tr. *Schellen's Spectr. Anal.* xxvii. 94 The prisms are arranged around this pin, which again is fastened to a swallow-tailed movable bar.

6. Of a coat: Having a pair of pointed or tapering skirts.

1824 J. MORIER *Adventures of Hajji Baba* I. p. xl, I sighed for shaven chins and swallow-tailed coats. **1835** WILLIS *Pencillings* I. xxxiv. 235 He was dressed in an exceedingly well cut swallow-tailed coat. **1882** MISS BRADDON *Mt. Royal* II. x. 212 The atmosphere to-night was as conventional as the men's swallow-tailed coats and white ties. **1889** GUNTER *That Frenchman* viii. 99 A moment after the crowd is swelled by the swallow-tailed gentry, the news having got to the clubs and cafés.

swallowwort ('swɒləʊwɜːt). [f. SWALLOW *sb.*¹ + WORT; in sense 1 rendering early mod.G. *schwalbenwurtz* (cf. obs. Du. *swaelemwortel*) = med.L. *hirundaria*; in sense 2 rendering Du. *zwaluwkruid* = mod.L. *chelīdonium*, Gr. χελιδόνιον (see CELANDINE).]

1. The herb *Vincetoxicum officinale*, formerly called *Asclepias* (or *Cynanchum*) *Vincetoxicum*; from the form of the pods, suggesting a swallow with outspread wings. Hence extended to the genus *Asclepias* generally.

1548 TURNER *Names Herbes* 17 Asclepias..may be called in englishe Swallowurt. **1651** FRENCH *Distill.* ii. 52 Take Swallow-wort. **1785** MARTYN *Lett. Bot.* xvi. (1794) 216 Common Swallow wort, or Tame poison. **1822** GOOD *Study Med.* III. 405 One or two species of asclepias or swallow-wort.

b. An umbelliferous plant, *Elæoselinum* (or *Thapsia*) *Asclepium.*

1866 *Treas. Bot.*

2. The Greater Celandine, *Chelidonium majus.*

1578 LYTE *Dodoens* I. xx. 31 The great Celandyne is called ..in English Celandyne, Swallowurte, and of some Tetter-wurte. **1635** SWAN *Spec. Mundi* (1670) 220 Celandine or Swallow-wort. **1858** IRVINE *Hand-bk. Brit. Plants* Index.

swally, obs. and dial. f. SWALLOW.

†**swalm**, *sb. Obs.* Forms: 3 swalm, 4 sualm, 6 swalme, *Sc.* swame, 7 swawme. [ME. *swalm*, f. *swal-*: *swel-* (see SWELL *v.*); cf. QUALM.]

1. Swelling.

a **1225** *Ancr. R.* 274 Drinc þeonne atterloðe, & drif þene swel [*MS. C.* swalm] aȝeanward urommard þe heorte. **1508** DUNBAR *Tua Mariit Wemen* 167, I sall..me assuage of the swalme, that suellit wes gret. *c* **1583** MONTGOMERIE *Flyting* 336 (Tullibardine MS.), The stane worme, þe ringworme, not slaiking of swame.

2. (An attack of) faintness or sickness. (Cf. SWEAM.)

a **1300** *Cursor M.* 20758 (Cott.), 'Ga to þaa men þat lijs in sualm,' He saic, 'and rine on þam wit it.' **1601** HOLLAND *Pliny* XXIII. Proeme II. 146 Women who being newly conceived and breeding child have many swawms come over their heart. **1609** —— *Amm. Marcell.* XXIV. vi. 255 A cold swawme of feare that quickly came over his heart.

So †**swalm** *v. intr.* and *trans.*, to faint or cause to faint; also in *vbl. sb.*, swooning.

1375 BARBOUR *Bruce* XVII. 648 Sum ded, sum hurt, sum swavnand [*sic*; ? *read* swavmand; *v.r.* swonand]. *c* **1440** *Bone Flor.* 770 Hur fadur nere hande can talme, Soche a sweme hys harte can swalme. *a* **1583** MONTGOMERIE *Flyting* 311 (Tullibardine MS.) With swaming to swelt.

†**swalper**, *v. Obs. rare*⁻¹. [Related to early mod.Du. *swalp* 'fluctus, unda, fluctuatio', Du. *zwalp*, WFlem. *zwalp zwolp* sudden rush of water or other liquid, early mod.Du. *swalpen* 'fluctuare, affluere, iactari fluctibus, undare', Du. *zwalpen*, WFris. *swolpje* to break forth (of water), G. dial. *schwalpen* to flow, sway backwards and forwards, *schwalpig* swaying; prob. of onomatopœic origin.

Similar synonymous roots *skolp-*, *skulp-*, and *skwelp-*, *skwulp-*, are represented by MLG., LG. *schulpen*, *schülpen*, *schülpern*, early mod.Du. *schelpen* (all = Du. *zwalpen*), Da. *skvulpe*, *skulpe* to shake fluid in a vessel, intr. to splash, Icel. *skolp* dish-water.]

intr. To splash or toss about in water.

c **1400** *Destr. Troy* 12526 Fyn-seluyn in the sea sonkyn belyue, Swalprit & swam with swyngyng of armys.

swalt(e, pa. t. of SWELT *v.*

†**swalter**, *v. Obs.* [Cf SWATTER *v.*] *intr.* To wade, splash.

? *a* **1400** *Morte Arth.* 3925 He..Slippes in in the sloppes o-slante to þe girdylle, Swalters upe swyftly with his swerde drawene. *a* **1500** *Colkelbie Sow* I. 228 Than Rany of þe Reidhewch..Licht lap at a lyne He felyeit and he fell in; And Hoge was sa haisty That he swalterit him by.

swalter, obs. variant of SWELTER.

†**swaltish**, *a. Obs. rare*⁻⁰. [f. *swalt*, var. of SWELT + -ISH¹.] Sweltering.

1530 PALSGR. 326/2 Swaltysshe hotte, *fade.*

swalu-, -ugh, swalwe, obs. ff. SWALLOW *sb.*¹

swalud, obs. pa. t. and pple. of SWALLOW *v.*

swaly ('sweɪlɪ), *a. dial.* [f. SWALE *sb.*² + -Y.] Shady.

1820 CLARE *Rural Life* (ed. 3) 70 Shepherds, with their panting sheep, In the swaliest corner creep.

swam, pa. t. and obs. or dial. pa. pple. of SWIM *v.*

swamas, dial. f. SQUEAMOUS.

swame, variant of SWALM, SQUAME *Obs.*, scale.

‖**swami** ('swɑːmiː). Also 8 **swamme, swammy, sawmy,** 9 **swamee, swamy, sammy.** [a. Hindī *swāmī* master, lord, prince, used by Hindus as a term of respectful address, a. Skr. *svāmin* in same senses, also the idol or temple of a god.]

1. A Hindu idol.

1773 E. IVES *Voy. India* 70 Towards the upper end, there is a dark repository, where they keep their Swamme, that is their chief god. **1794** *Indian Observer* 167 (Y.) The gold might for us as well have been worshipped in the shape of a Sawmy at Juggernaut. **1799** WELLINGTON in Gurw. *Desp.* (1837) I. 56 Some brass Swammies which were in the toshekanah were given to the brahmins of different pagodas. **1837** *Lett. fr. Madras* viii. (1843) 64 They admire our dolls so much, that they are almost ready to make Swamies of them. **1884** *Sunday at Home* June 397/1 A fourth [hut], the most pretentious and the best built, was consecrated to the swamie, or god.

2. A title for a Hindu religious teacher.

1901 *Daily News* 2 Dec. 5/1 She was informed that the word Swami meant teacher. **1905** *United Free Ch. Mag.* Feb. 9/2 A distinguished Swami or religious teacher visited Poona lately.

3. *attrib.* **swamy-house**, an idol temple or shrine; **swamy-pagoda**, 'a coin formerly current at Madras; probably so-called from the figure of an idol on it' (Y.).

1778 R. ORME *Hist. Milit. Trans. Indostan* x. II. 443 Until they came in a line with the flank fire of the field-pieces at the swamy house. **1837** *Lett. fr. Madras* (1843) 134 In the middle of the court, round which these galleries of pillars ran, was the Swamy-house, or place in which the idol is enshrined. **1857** H. GREATHED *Lett. Siege of Delhi* (1858) 112 We met Wilby at the advanced post, the 'Sammy House'. **1813** MILBURN *Oriental Comm.* xix. (1825) 233 The old 3 Swamy pagoda, which is about 20⅝ carats fine.

b. Applied to jewellery ornamented with figures of Hindu deities.

1880 BIRDWOOD *Industr. Arts India* I. 152 In the characteristic *swami* work of the Madras Presidency the ornamentation consists of figures of the Puranic gods in high relief. **1882** MRS. B. M. CROKER *Proper Pride* I. iv. 69 My gold swami earrings. **1903** YULE & BURNELL *Hobson-Jobson*, *Swamy Jewelry*, a kind of gold and silver jewelry, made chiefly at Trichinopoly, in European shapes covered with grotesque mythological figures.

swamish, swamous, dial. ff. SQUEAMISH, SQUEAMOUS.

swamp (swɒmp), *sb.* Also 8 **swomp.** [First recorded as a term peculiar to the N. American colony of Virginia, but prob. in local use before in England; cf. quot. 1691 in 1 b, and the app. related SUMP *sb.*

Possibly taken in from LG., where, however, the sense of 'marsh' is not recorded (but cf. LG. *swampen*, used of the quaking of boggy land). The instance of the meaning 'mushroom' (sense 2), which was that of OE. *swamm*, may be due to an occasional borrowing from a foreign source.

Usually referred to the root which is the base of the several Germanic formations **swamp-*, **swamb-*, and **swamm-*, with the meaning 'sponge' or 'fungus', represented by MLG. (LG.) *swamp*, OHG. (MHG.) *swamp*, *swamb-*, ON. *svǫppr* (:—**swampuz*), MSw. *svamper*, Sw., Da. *svamp*, and OE. *swamm*, (M)LG., OHG. *swam* (G. *schwamm*), early mod.Du. *swamme* (Du. *zwam*), Goth. *swamm* acc. sing. The radical notion is perhaps preserved in Gr. σομφός (?:—**swombhós*) spongy, porous.

For other possible relations see SWAMP *a.* and SWANG.]

1. a. A tract of low-lying ground in which water collects; a piece of wet spongy ground; a marsh or bog. Orig. and in early use only in the N. American colonies, where it denoted a tract of rich soil having a growth of trees and other vegetation, but too moist for cultivation (see quots. 1741, 1766, 1875).

1624 CAPT. J. SMITH *Virginia* IV. 163 Some small Marshes and Swamps there are, but more profitable than hurtfull. **1685** PENN *Further Acc. Pennsylv.* 7 Our Swamps or Marshes yeeld us course Hay for the Winter. **1688** CLAYTON *Virginia* in *Phil. Trans.* XVIII. 124 [Musk-rats] build Houses as Beavers do, in the Marshes, and Swamps (as they there call them) by the Water-sides. **1741** TAILFER, etc. *Narr. Georgia* 96 A Swamp is any low watery Place, which is covered with Trees or Canes: They are here of three Sorts, Cypress, River, and Cane Swamps. **1766** STORK *Acc. E. Florida* 26 *note*, The word swamp is peculiar to America; it there signifies a tract of land that is sound and good, but by lying low is covered by water. All the forest trees (pine excepted) thrive best in the swamps, where the soil is always rich. **1875** TEMPLE & SHELDON *Hist. Northfield, Mass.* 21 Swamps.—As used by our fathers in the earliest times, this term did not necessarily denote marshy ground; but flat land which from its peculiar location had escaped the ravages of the annual fires set by the Indians, and was covered with an old growth of wood.

1725 DE FOE *Voy. round World* (1840) 145 Our men..shot a brace of deer, as they were feeding by the side of a swamp or moist ground. **1840** THIRLWALL *Greece* liii. VII. 20 Ground which the rain had turned into a swamp. **1853** J. H. NEWMAN *Hist. Sk.* (1873) II. I. iii. 125 The Pontine Marshes, formerly the abode of thirty nations, are now a pestilential swamp. **1880** HAUGHTON *Phys. Geog.* v. 235 The river Desaguadero..falls into the salt lake and swamps of Aullagas.

fig. **1825** LAMB *Elia* Ser. II. *Convalescent*, In this flat swamp of convalescence, left by the ebb of sickness. **1871**

MORLEY *Carlyle* in *Crit. Misc.* Ser. I. (1878) 173 It has stagnated in the sunless swamps of a theosophy.

b. *local.* See quots., and cf. SUMP *sb.* 1, 2. Also, in *Australia*, a shallow lake or pond.

1691 RAY *S. & E.C. Words* 115 A *Swamp*, a low hollow place in any part of a field. **1881** RAYMOND *Mining Gloss.*, *Swamp*, a depression in a nearly horizontal bed, in which water may collect. **1883** GRESLEY *Gloss. Coal-mining*, *Swamp*, a depression or natural hollow in a seam.

†**2.** A mushroom. *Obs. rare*$^{-1}$.

1631 WIDDOWES *Nat. Philos.* 39 In the body of the [larch] tree groweth Fungus Agaricus, a swamp or mush rome.

3. a. *attrib.* and *Comb.*, as ***swamp-dweller***, ***earth***, ***forest***, ***-jungle***, ***land***, ***-lover*** (see c), ***meadow***, ***muck***, ***mud***, ***peat***, ***region***, ***shell***, ***-side***, ***soil***, ***water***; ***swamp-loving*** adj.; **swamp-angel** (see b); **swamp buggy** *N. Amer.*, a vehicle used in swampy regions; *spec.* a tracked vehicle which can pull a heavily loaded trailer; **swamp-chain**, **-hook** *U.S.*, a long chain, a large hook used in swamping logs; **swamp cooler** *U.S.* (see quot. 1950); **swamp fever**, (*a*) malarial fever prevalent in swampy regions; (*b*) a contagious virus disease of horses, causing anæmia, emaciation, and usually death; **swamp fire** *Canad.*, methane burning in a swampy area; a will-o'-the-wisp (also used in metaphorical comparisons); **swamp-ore** [G. *sumpferz*], bog iron ore; **swamp plough** *N.Z.*, a type of plough with a large mould-board, for use on heavy soils; **swamp rock**, a type of rock music associated with the Southern U.S.; **swamp Yankee** *U.S. dial.* (see quot. 1963).

1941 *Nat. Geogr. Mag.* June 706 Their '*swamp-buggy' is a seagoing amphibious-looking vehicle. Its 10-foot high wheels are equipped with fat, fin-studded oversized tires which act as propellers; when the odd vehicle leaves the land and takes to water, it begins to swim. **1966** *North* July–Aug. 14/2 When the usually dependable swamp buggy breaks down, it's back to the dog team. **1973** *Globe & Mail* (Toronto) 3 Feb. 7/5 While the public sleeps, a Pandora's Box is opening to release a flood of hovercraft, dune buggies, swamp buggies, trail bikes, air sleds and airboats on the long-suffering landscape of crowded Southern Ontario. **1950** *Newsweek* 14 Aug. 51 In dry climates it is possible to rig up a primitive but highly effective cooling system, called a '*swamp cooler'. It consists simply of a fan blowing over an excelsior mat which is drenched with dripping water. **1979** *Tucson* (Arizona) *Citizen* (Weekender Mag.) 28 Apr. 9/1 A swamp cooler has maybe five moving parts; if it quits, you go up on the roof, look to see which part has quit moving, and replace it. **1890** *Swamp-dweller [see PINE LAND]. **1908** RIDER HAGGARD *Ghost Kings* xiv. 193 The Swamp-dwellers, who had their homes upon the banks of the Tugela. **1840** J. BUEL *Farmer's Comp.* 47 To blend with it [*sc.* calcareous soil] quantities of peat or *swamp earth. **1870** KINGSLEY *At Last* xiii, A strong touch of his old *swamp-fever. **1903** *Rep. Min. Agric. Canada 1902* 85 There has been known in the Red River Valley a peculiar and very fatal disease of horses... It is a disease of low lying and swampy country and it is therefore popularly known as swamp fever. **1975** *Daily Colonist* (Victoria, B.C.) 6 July 2/3 Swamp fever..equine infectious anemia—has ravaged almost half of..the little ponies. **1903** S. E. WHITE *Forest* 122 Like *swamp-fire, it lured the imagination always on and on and on through the secret waterways of the uninhabited North. **1954** V. LYSENKO *Yellow Boots* 146 Behind them the swamp fire, like a gigantic Jack o'lantern, bumped and danced and ran around the sky, then finally, as it reached the ground, evaporated into the night air. **1982** H. LIEBERMAN *Night Call* iii. 12 Daughtry's reputation..traveled like swampfire. **1909** GROOM & BALFOUR tr. *Warming's Oecol. Plants* lx. 234 (*heading*) Littoral *swamp-forest. Mangrove. **1955** P. A. BUXTON *Nat. Hist. Tsetse Flies* ix. 269 In places there are 'swamp forests'..the trees growing in a few feet of water at all seasons. **1964** G. B. SCHALLER *Year of Gorilla* (1965) viii. 215 The swamp forest that grows in the low country bordering the South China Sea. **1877** *Lumberman's Gaz.* 22 Dec., *Swamp Hooks, Pevys, Skidding Tongs always on hand. **1902** D. G. HOGARTH *Nearer East* 108 Torrential floods, which..support a dense *swamp-jungle. **1662** in *Connecticut Hist. Soc. Coll.* (1912) XIV. 433 One Parcel of land..being *Swamp land. **1701** *Early Rec. Providence, Rhode Island* (1894) V. 125 A Certaine ffarme or tract of land consisting of upland swampe land & Meadow land. **1791** W. BARTRAM *Carolina* 95 A vast body of rich swamp land, fit for the growth of Rice. **1856** OLMSTED *Slave States* ii. 151 The value of the swamp land varies with the wood upon it. **1826** MISS MITFORD *Village* Ser. II. 173 (*Visit to Lucy*) That *swamp-loving, cold-braving, shade-seeking plant. **1697** *Cambridge* (Mass.) *Proprietors' Rec.* (1896) 344 Four Rods of fence, Lyeing att the head of Samuel Hastings *Swampmeadow. **1880** *Harper's Mag.* June 80 Out in the swamp meadow the tall clumps of boneset show their dull white crests. **1951** R. P. HOBSON *Grass beyond Mountains* 41 We sat around..talking of range cows, and tough trails, slough grass and swamp meadows. **1840** J. BUEL *Farmer's Comp.* 73 Peat earth, or *swamp muck, is vegetable food, in an insoluble state. **1821** *Mass. Spy* 21 Feb. 4/5, I agree that *swamp mud or, as the Scotch and English farmers call it, peat moss..is not manure. **1897** GUNTER *Don Balasco of Key West* xiii. 160 His costume..is covered with swamp mud and coral dust. **1839** URE *Dict. Arts* 834 Bog-ore, *swamp-ore, and meadow-ore. **1863** LYELL *Antiq. Man* ii. 9 The lowest stratum..consists of *swamp-peat composed chiefly of moss or sphagnum. **1930** L. G. D. ACLAND *Early Canterbury Runs* 1st Ser. iii. 42 They..spent a lot of money in cutting the scrub, crushing it down with rollers, and ploughing it in with *swamp ploughs. **1973** *Massey Ferguson Rev.* (N.Z.) Mar.–Apr. 5/1 He..leaves it for two years before getting to work with a 19-inch swamp plough. **1871** NAPHEYS *Prev. & Cure Dis.* I. i. 51 Exposed to *swamp-poison. **1875** tr. *von Ziemssen's Cycl. Med.* II. 564 The warm *swamp-regions of the Australian coast. **1970** *Guardian* 17 Apr. 10/2 Then Creedence. The band['s].. music, like that of Delaney and Bonnie, is called '*swamp rock', and identified with the Southern States of America. **1855** J. PHILLIPS *Man. Geol.* 409 One *swamp shell, viz., Succinea amphibia. **1677** W. HUBBARD *Narrative* (1865) I. 111 They were set upon by many hundreds of the Indians out of the Bushes by the *Swamp-side. **1883** *Science* II. 39/1 Their projection above the level of the roots depending on the depth of the *swamp-waters. **1941** H. KURATH *Linguistic Atlas of New England* II. II. Map 450 The map shows a great variety of terms, largely derogatory and jocular, applied to a person who lives in the country—specifically to an old farmer who seldom visits the village or city. The following terms were recorded in more than one community: rustic, ..*swamp Yankee, hayback, hayseed or hayseeder. **1963** *Amer. Speech* XXXVIII. 121 The term *swamp Yankee* may be defined as 'a rural New England dweller who abides today as a steadfast rustic and who is of Yankee stock that has endured in the New England area since the colonial days.' **1975** G. V. HIGGINS *City on Hill* iv. 104 That back country's full of swamp Yankees, guys..that impregnate their own daughters.

b. In names of animals (mostly birds) inhabiting swamps, as ***swamp adder***, ***bee***, ***bird***, etc.; **swamp-angel** (*U.S.*), a name for the hermit thrush and the wood thrush; also *transf.* or *allusively*; **swamp blackbird** = *marsh blackbird* (see MARSH[1] 4b); **swamp crake**, *Ortygometra tabuensis*, of Australia; **swamp deer**, *Rucervus duvaucelli*, of India; see also BARASINGHA; **swamp hare**, *Lepus aquaticus*, of the southern U.S., also called *water-rabbit*; **swamp hen**, a name for various rails, esp. of the genus *Porphyrio* (cf. *marsh hen*, MARSH[1] 4b); **swamp partridge**, the spruce partridge or Canada grouse; **swamp pheasant**, *Centropus phasianus*, of Australia; **swamp quail**, any species of the genus *Synœcus*, of Australia; **swamp rabbit**, either of two dark brown rabbits of the south-eastern United States, the cane-cutter, *Sylvilagus aquaticus*, or the marsh rabbit, *S. palustris*; cf. *swamp hare*; **swamp robin**, the cheewink or ground-robin, *Pipilo erythrophthalmus*, of N. America; also, = TOWHEE; **swamp sparrow**, (*a*) a species of song-sparrow, *Melospiza palustris*, common in U.S. and Canada; (*b*) *Sphenœacus punctatus* of New Zealand, also called *fern-bird*; **swamp wallaby**, a large wallaby, *Wallabia bicolor*, which has reddish or greyish fur with darker markings; **swamp warbler**, one of several N. American warblers, as *Protonotaria citrea* and *Helmintherus vermivorus*.

1893 CONAN DOYLE *Sherlock Holmes, Speckled Band* 207 It is a *swamp adder!..the deadliest snake in India. **1858** H. C. KIMBALL in *Jrnl. Discourses* V. 31/2 Angels who would thus visit you are *swamp angels,—they are filthy. **1872** SCHELE DE VERE *Americanisms* 117 The Swamp Angel of General Gillmore, as his monster-gun in the swamps was ironically called. **1884** BURROUGHS *Wake-Robin* 38 The wood-thrush..is quite a rare bird,..being found in the Middle and Eastern States,..only in the deepest and most remote forests, usually in damp and swampy localities. On this account the people in the Adirondac region call it the 'Swamp Angel'. **1885** H. C. MCCOOK *Tenants Old Farm* 171, I have heard countrymen call the species of which you speak the *swamp-bee; its scientific name is probably *Bombus separatus*. **1796** NEMNICH *Polygl.-Lex.*, *Swamp bird, the yellow-poll warbler, *Motacilla aestiva*. **1884** SEEBOHM *Brit. Birds* II. 230 Red-throated Pipit. It is very decidedly a swamp-bird. **1891** *Cent. Dict.*, *Swamp-blackbird. **1895** *Outing* (U.S.) XXVII. 75/1 A huge flock of swamp blackbirds covered the ground. **1891** *Cent. Dict.* cites W. L. BULLER for *Swamp-crake. **1874** T. C. JERDON *Mammals of India* 254 The *Swamp Deer... Horns very large and moderately stout. **1891** *Cent. Dict.*, Swamp-deer. **1902** T. W. WEBBER *Forests Upper India* xxi. 312 A very fine specimen of the big swamp deer or barasingha, with 12-tined horns. **1801** LATHAM *Gen. Synopsis Birds* Suppl. II. 206 *Swamp finch. *Fringilla iliaca*. **1891** *Cent. Dict.*, *Swamp-hare. **1897** *Field* 6 Feb. 167/3 The swamp, or northern hare, is a big strong animal. **1898** MORRIS *Austral English*, **Swamp-Hawk*, another name for the New Zealand Harrier. **1848** J. GOULD *Birds Australia* VI. pl. 70 *Porphyrio Bellus*,..*Swamp-Hen, Colonists of Western Australia. **1888** W. L. BULLER *Birds N. Zealand* II. 81 The Swamp-hen is widely distributed over Tasmania, the greater part of the continent of Australia [etc.]. **1874** COUES *Birds N.W.* 394 *Swamp Partridge. **1847** *Swamp-pheasant [see PHEASANT 2]. **1890** LUMHOLTZ *Cannibals* 94 Although it is really a cuckoo, the colonists call it the 'swamp pheasant', because it has a tail like a pheasant. **1895** W. R. OGILVIE-GRANT *Game-Birds* I. 191 The Australian *Swamp-Quail. **1845** C. LYELL *Second Visit U.S.* I. 228, I had heard much of the *swamp-rabbit, which they hunt near the coast in South Carolina and Georgia. **1875** *Fur, Fin & Feather* (ed. 3) 136/1 The 'swamp rabbit' inhabits the heavy timbered woodlands and river bottoms. **1938** M. K. RAWLINGS *Yearling* v. 51 The pair of black swamp rabbits was not new. **1964** W. H. BURT *Field Guide Mammals* (ed. 2) 223 Swamp Rabbit... This is a rich brownish-gray rabbit with coarse hair; feet rusty. **1769** R. SMITH *Jrnl.* 18 May in *Tour of Four Great Rivers* (1906) 41 The lively Note of the *Swamp Robin, the Red Bird and other Birds from the earliest Dawn is entertaining. **1810** WILSON *Amer. Ornith.* II. 36 In Virginia, he [*sc.* the Towhe Bunting] is called the Bulfinch; ..in Pennsylvania, the Chewink, and by others the Swamp Robin. **1955** Swamp robin [see JOREE]. **1811** WILSON *Amer. Ornith.* III. 50 The *Swamp Sparrow is five inches and a half long and seven inches and a half in extent. **1888** W. L. BULLER *Birds N. Zealand* (ed. 2) II. 255 The melancholy cry of the Fern-bird is so general and persistent that its nickname of 'Swamp-Sparrow' is not undeserved. **1896** *Swamp wallaby [see *brush wallaby* s.v. BRUSH *sb.*[1] 4]. **1970** W. D. L. RIDE *Guide Native Mammals Austral.* v. 47 The Swamp Wallaby..is usually placed in a separate genus *Wallabia*. **1859** THOREAU *Jrnl.* 30 Apr. in *Writings* (1906) XVIII. 167 This first *off-coat* warmth just preceding the advent of the *swamp warblers (parti-colored, red-start, etc.) brings them out. **1884** COUES *N. Amer. Birds* 291 *Protonotaria*, Golden Swamp Warblers.

c. Denoting plants or vegetable products (chiefly of North America) growing in swamps, as ***swamp grass***, ***plant***, etc.; ***swamp dock***, ***hellebore***, ***hickory***, ***locust-tree***, ***pine***, ***privet***, ***silk-weed*** (see these words); **swamp-apple** = *honeysuckle-apple* (HONEYSUCKLE 6); **swamp ash**, *Fraxinus sambucifolia*, also called *black*, *ground*, *hoop*, or *water ash*; **swamp azalea** = *swamp honeysuckle*; **swamp blackberry**, a low-growing, semi-evergreen dewberry, *Rubus hispidus*, found near water and marshy ground in parts of Canada and northern and central U.S.A.; **swamp blueberry**, the highbush blueberry, *Vaccinium corymbosum*, or its fruit; **swamp-broom** = SWAMP-OAK 2a (Morris *Austral Engl.*); **swamp-cabbage** = SKUNK-CABBAGE; also, the cabbage palmetto, *Sabal palmetto*; **swamp-cheese** = *swamp-apple*; **swamp-cypress**, the genus *Chamæcyparis*; also, the deciduous cypress, *Taxodium distichum*; **swamp dewberry** = *swamp blackberry* above; **swamp dogwood**, *Cornus alba* and *C. sericea*; also, = *swamp sumach*; **swamp elm**, *Ulmus racemosa*, also called *rock elm*; **swamp gooseberry**, *Ribes lacustre* (Miller *Plant-n.* 1884); **swamp gum**, various species of *Eucalyptus*, of Australia and Tasmania; **swamp hickory**, the water hickory, *Carya aquatica*, or the bitternut hickory, *C. cordiformis*; **swamp honeysuckle**, (*a*) *Rhododendron viscosum* (*Azalea viscosa*); (*b*) a honeysuckle of eastern North America, *Lonicera oblongifolia*, with yellowish flowers and red berries; **swamp laurel**, (*a*) the sweetbay magnolia, *M. virginiana*; (*b*) formerly, also the pale American laurel, *Kalmia polifolia*; **swamp lily**, (*a*) the American Turk's-cap lily, *Lilium superbum*; (*b*) the genus *Zephyranthes*, of Mexico, S. America, and the W. Indies; (*c*) the lizard's-tail, *Saururus cernuus*; (*d*) *Crinum americanum*, which bears white flowers and is native to the south-eastern United States; **swamp loosestrife**, *Decodon verticillatus* or *Nesæa verticillata* (Treas. Bot. 1866); **swamp-lover**, the stud-flower, *Helonias bullata*; **swamp magnolia**, (*a*) = *swamp laurel* (*a*); (*b*) *M. grandiflora*; **swamp mahogany**, a gum tree, *Eucalyptus robusta*, native to coastal regions of eastern Australia; **swamp maple**, the red maple, *Acer rubrum* (Miller); also several other species, as the silver maple, *A. dasycarpum*, the mountain maple, *A. spicatum*, and the allied *Negundo californicum*; **swamp-moss** = *bog-moss* (BOG *sb.*[1] 3); **swamp pea-tree**, sensitive joint-vetch, *Æschynomene hispida*; **swamp-pink** = *swamp honeysuckle*; **swamp rice** = CANADA *rice*; **swamp rose**, *Rosa carolina* (Treas. Bot. 1866); also, another wild N. Amer. rose, *Rosa palustris*; **swamp sassafras** = *swamp laurel* (*a*); **swamp sumach**, the poison sumach, *Rhus vernix*; **swamp tea-tree**, species of *Melaleuca*, of Australia and Tasmania; **swamp-weed**, *Selliera radicans* (Miller); **swamp willow**, the pussy-willow, *Salix discolor*; **swamp-wood**, the N. American leather-wood, *Dirca palustris*. See also SWAMP-OAK.

1846 *Zoologist* IV. 1281 The galls called *swamp-apples. **1847** DARLINGTON *Amer. Weeds*, etc. (1860) 214 The *Azalea nudiflora*, or wild Honeysuckle, has often a singular transformation of its flowers, the parts of the flower becoming enlarged and fleshy,..These succulent excrescences are much sought after by boys who call them 'swamp apples' and 'swamp cheeses'. **1794** W. CLARK *Jrnl.* 15 Sept. in *Mississippi Valley Hist. Rev.* (1914) I. 437 The face [of the land] is nearly covered with a thick groth of Shrubbery, Brush, some Beech, *Swamp Ash. **1842** Z. THOMPSON *Hist. Vermont* I. 211 Black ash. *Fraxinus sambucifolia*..is sometimes called Swamp Ash. **1796** NEMNICH *Polygl.-Lex.*, *Swamp azalea, *Azalea viscosa*. **1958** G. A. PETRIDES *Field Guide to Trees & Shrubs* 365 Swamp Azalea... A medium-sized to tall shrub with leaves glossy above. **1854** THOREAU *Jrnl.* 4 Aug. in *Writings* (1906) XII. 419 The *swamp blackberry on high land, ripe a day or two. **1903** H. L. KEELER *Our Northern Shrubs* 161 Few trailing plants combine a better effect of flower and foliage than our Swamp blackberry. **1975** E. WIGGINTON *Foxfire 3* 285 Swamp blackberry is found in thickets in low, wet places. **1860** THOREAU *Jrnl.* 30 Dec. in *Writings* (1906) XX. 299 Some ten days later comes the high blueberry, or *swamp blueberry, the commonest stout shrub of our swamps. **1917** E. S. BAILEY *Sand Dunes Indiana* 154 There is a chance to study all the sides of a small pond, with the shrub zone of plants in perfect type, such as swamp blueberry, cranberry [etc.]. **1949** *Pacific Spectator* Spring 223 You had to cross the river..to find the low swamp blueberries, lighter blue and sweeter than any other kind. **1793** in *M. Cutler's Life*, etc. (1888) II. 292 Our *Swamp

Cabbage (or Dracontium foetidum). 1880 *Harper's Mag.* June 66 The swamp-cabbage flower..peers above the ground beneath his purple spotted hood. 1938 M. K. RAWLINGS *Yearling* xx. 250 He pulled away layer after layer of the white cores and came at last to the hearts [of palms], crisp and sweet. He said, 'Now I want that fryin' pan, Mr. Penny, please, for my swamp cabbage.' 1942 S. KENNEDY *Palmetto Country* 3 Folks outside the region usually think of the palmetto as the tall palm which is locally called the swamp cabbage or cabbage palm. 1976 *National Observer* (U.S.) 22 May 16-A/1 They were forced to subsist on a diet of unpolished rice, swamp cabbage, and tiny fish. 1847 *Swamp cheeses [see *swamp-apple* above]. 1876 tr. *Heer's Primæval World Switzerland* I. viii. 325 *Taxodium distichum miocenum*, the *swamp-cypress... This species is completely analogous to the swamp-cypress of America (*Taxodium distichum*, Rich., sp.). 1924 C. DEAM *Shrubs Indiana* 109 *Rubus hispidus* Linnæus. *Swamp Dewberry. 1942 L. R. TEHON *Fieldbk. Native Illinois Shrubs* 116 The Swamp Dewberry grows near lakes and marshes, especially at the base of wooded slopes. 1976 *Hortus Third* (L. H. Bailey Hortorium) 985/2 *Swamp dewberry, running blackberry, swamp b.*, slender, hispid, often glandular trailer, laying close to the ground, without prickles. 1817 W. DARBY *Geogr. Descr. Louisiana* 353 *Cornus alba*. *Swamp dogwood. 1847 DARLINGTON *Amer. Weeds*, etc. (1860) 79 Poisonous Rhus. Poison Sumach. Poison Elder. Swamp Dogwood. 1817 W. DARBY *Geogr. Descr. Lousiana* 356 *Ulmus aquatica*. *Swamp elm. 1868 *Rep. U.S. Commissioner Agric.* (1869) 82 Many specimens of *Bryaxis* were beaten off of *swamp grass. 1907 C. HILL-TOUT *Brit. N. Amer., Far West* vi. 119 Various swamp grasses, of which the bulrush is the commonest specimen [used]. 1851 J. MITCHELL in *Pap. & Proc. Roy. Soc. Van Diemen's Land* (1853) II. 132 (Morris) The *Swamp Gum grows to the largest size of any of this family in Van Diemen's Land. 1889 MAIDEN *Usef. Pl. Australia* 27 *Eucalyptus Gunnii*..in South-Eastern Australia..it is known as 'White Gum', 'Swamp Gum', or 'White Swamp Gum'. *Eucalyptus viminalis*,..The 'White Gum', or 'Swamp Gum' of Tasmania. 1762 ELIOT in Mills *System Pract. Husb.* I. 156 Take the roots of *swamp hellebore (known in different places by the several names of skunk cabbage, tickle weed, bear root). 1806 in *Message from President of U.S., communicating Discoveries made in exploring the Missouri by Captains Lewis & Clark* 65 The growth, on the highest [places is] handsome oaks, *swamp hickory, ash, grape vines, &c. 1817 W. DARBY *Geogr. Descr. Louisiana* 354 *Juglans aquatica*. Swamp hickory. 1912 I. S. COBB *Back Home* 306 He was tough as swamp hickory. 1938 C. H. MATSCHAT *Suwannee River* 161 They alus stuck togither tightern the bark on a swamp hickory. 1856 A. GRAY *Man. Bot.* 257 *Azalea viscosa*, Clammy Azalea. White *Swamp-Honeysuckle. 1958 G. A. PETRIDES *Field Guide Trees & Shrubs* 47 Swamp Honeysuckle *Lonicera oblongifolia*... A more or less hairless honeysuckle. 1743 J. CLAYTON *Flora Virginica* 83 *Magnolia Laurifolia*, ..*Swamp-Laurel. 1787 T. JEFFERSON *Notes State Virginia* (1787) 60 Swamp laurel. Magnolia glauca. 1845–50 MRS. LINCOLN *Lect. Bot.* App. 116 *Kalmia glauca* (swamp-laurel). 1869 J. G. FULLER *Uncle John's Flower-Gatherers* 138 The farmers around here call it [sc. *Kalmia*] 'Swamp-Laurel'. 1884 C. S. SARGENT *Rep. Forests N. Amer.* 20 Sweet Bay..Swamp Laurel... A tree 15 to 22 meters in height. 1737 J. BRICKELL *Nat. Hist. N. Carolina* 21 Another Weed, vulgarly called the *Swamp-Lillie..grows in the Marshes and low Grounds, and is something like our Dock in its Leaves. 1814 ROXBURGH *Hort. Bengal.* 23 *Crinum americanum*. Swamp lily. N.S. Wales. 1902 CORNISH *Naturalist Thames* 180 On the green bank of our flower-bordered brook, the American swamp-lily finds its natural place. 1829 LOUDON *Encycl. Plants* 868 *Gleditschia*.. monosperma *Ph.* *Swamp Locust Tree. 1878 MEEHAN *Native Fl. & Ferns U.S.* I. 36 *Swamp-lover. 1872 SCHELE DE VERE *Americanisms* 422 The Sweet Bay is..not to be compared to the *Swamp Magnolia (Magnolia grandiflora). 1884 A. NILSON *Timber Trees New South Wales* 71 *Swamp Mahogany.—A large tree..with a rough furrowed bark. 1886 T. HENEY *Fortunate Days* 50 Swamp-mahogany's floss-flowered arms. 1810 *Swamp maple [see MAPLE TREE]. 1869 MRS. STOWE *Oldtown Folks* xiv. 153 Here and there, a swamp-maple seemed all one crimson flame. 1936 E. B. WHITE *Let.* 3 Sept. (1976) 141 Joe and I have gathered boughs of red swamp maple, to decorate the back porch. 1969 T. H. EVERETT *Living Trees of World* xxii. 221/1 The most important American soft maples are the red or swamp maple..and the silver maple. 1796 NEMNICH *Polygl.-Lex.*, *Swamp pea-tree, *Aeschynomene aquatica*. 1731 MILLER *Gard. Dict.* s.v. *Abies, Pinus*; *Americana, palustris*. The *Swamp Pine. 1743 M. CATESBY *Nat. Hist. Carolina* II. p. xxii, The Swamp Pine grows on barren wet land. 1851 J. S. SPRINGER *Forest Life* 41 This difference is accounted for by ..the tardiness with which the swamp Pine matures. 1958 G. A. PETRIDES *Field Guide Trees & Shrubs* 15 Swamp Pine ..similar to Pitch Pine. 1840 BIGELOW *Plants of Boston* 52 *Azalea viscosa*, Wild honeysuckle, *Swamp pink. 1775 *Nat. Hist.* in *Ann. Reg.* 942 Being a *swamp plant, a north-east aspect will be the properest situation at first to plant it in. 1896 MARY KINGSLEY *W. Africa* 326 From out its dark waters no swamp plant or tree grew. 1861 BENTLEY *Man. Bot.* 697 A serviceable grain known as Canada Rice or *Swamp Rice. 1785 H. MARSHALL *Arbustrum Americanum* 135 *Swamp Pennsylvanian Rose..[rises] to a height of four or five feet. 1814 J. BIGELOW *Florula Bostoniensis* 121 Swamp rose..grows in swamps and wet grounds. 1902 *Outing* June 272/2 The Carolina or swamp rose..is well known to us all. 1796 NEMNICH *Polygl.-Lex.*, *Swamp sassafras, *Magnolia glauca*. 1829 LOUDON *Encycl. Plants* 479 *Magnolia glauca* is deciduous. In America it is known by the names of white laurel, swamp sassafras, and beaver tree. 1887 BENTLEY *Man. Bot.* (ed. 5) 618 *Asclepias incarnata*, *Swamp Silk-weed. 1721 DUDLEY in *Phil. Trans.* XXXI. 145 The Poyson-Wood-Tree..is by some called the *Swamp Sumach. 1814 Swamp sumach [see *poison dogwood* s.v. POISON *sb.* 5 b]. 1945 H. T. DARLINGTON *Higher Plants of Michigan* 25 Red maple and swamp sumac..may add to the brilliant effect. 1862 W. ARCHER in G. Whiting *Products Tasmania* 29 *Swamp Tea-tree (*Melaleuca ericœfolia*). 1765 J. BARTRAM *Jrnl.* 31 July in *Trans. Amer. Philos. Soc.* (1942) XXXIII. 17/1 They have yᵉ upland willow oak with A hoary leafe, & yᵉ *swamp willow with A narrow leafe. 1865 MRS. M. HARRIS *St. Philip's* 23 The pond lay in a sort of basin, with..swamp-willows dipping down into its brink.

swamp (swamp), *a.* *Sc.* and *north. dial.* [Perhaps related to SWAMP *sb.*, the notion of 'depression, subsidence' being the connecting link; there is a remarkable parallel in dial. *swank* sb. = depression in the ground, deep hollow, bog, and *swank* adj. = thin in the belly.] Of a body that may be or is normally distended: That has sunk and become flat; thin from emptiness, as the breasts, the belly, etc.

c 1375 *Sc. Leg. Saints* xxvii. (*Machor*) 1597 Sume [men] throu ydropesy sa gret Swolne þat þai ma ete no mete, Are mad swampe þar. *Ibid.* xl. (*Ninian*) 799. a 1583 POLWART *Flyting w. Montgomerie* 776 (Tullibardine MS.) Swamp sandie, come fra candie, with grandie opprest. 1615 CROOKE *Body of Man* 254 If in a woman with childe the breasts do suddenly fall swampe as we say, then will shee abort or miscarry. 1631 R. H. *Arraignm. Whole Creature* iv. 28 A kind of light Felsie corne, inclosed in certaine eares, which are long and swampe. 1684 MERITON *Yorksh. Dial.* 30 (E.D.S.), Her Ewr's but swampe, Shee's nut for Milk, I trow. a 1708 T. WARD *Eng. Ref.* II. (1710) 105 A useful Sursingle it was,..Which as his Paunch was Full or Swamp, He'd wider make, or straiter cramp. 1885 A. MUNRO *Siren Casket* 90 Their body compress'd and swamp as an eel. 1887 SERVICE *Life Dr. Duguid* t. xxiv. 159 The mortclaith-like goons she puts on gie her a swamp, cauldrife, full-m'unted appearance.

swamp (swɒmp), *v.* [f. SWAMP *sb.*]

1. *pass.* To be entangled or lost in a swamp. *N. Amer.* ? *Obs.*

1688 CLAYTON *Virginia* in *Phil. Trans.* XVII. 986 So that she might turn thereon her weak Cattle, and such as should at any time be swamp'd. 1814 BRACKENRIDGE *Jrnl.* in *Views Louisiana* 210 In spending an hour to relieve a poor ox, which was swamped near the bank.

2. orig. *pass.* To be submerged or inundated with water (or other liquid), as a boat, a piece of ground; hence *actively*, to submerge, inundate, or soak with water, etc.

1772–84 *Cook's Voy.* (1790) IV. 1381 In the morning, the long-boat was found swamped. 1835 LYTTON *Rienzi* v. iii, The ground was swamped with blood. 1835 MARRYAT *Jacob Faithful* xxxvii, The wherry..pitched so heavily, that we were afraid of being swamped. 1865 KINGSLEY *Herew.* vi, At night a sea broke over them, and would have swamped the *Otter*, had she not been the best of sea-boats. 1879 ATCHERLEY *Trip Boërland* 172 The claims were continually being swamped out by the river. 1881 F. WITTI *Diary* 10 June in J. Hatton *New Ceylon* vi. (1881) 166 Towards midnight we awoke in our leaf hut—swamped.

transf. 1858 B. TAYLOR *North. Trav.* xvii. 174 Meat..is rarely properly cooked, and game..is injured by being swamped in sauces. 1883 *Century Mag.* Sept. 643 Sand has beaten in and swamped the vegetation. 1888 *Portfolio* Apr. 68 (Cent. Dict.) Swamped with full washes and blots of colour or strong strokes with the red pen.

3. *intr.* **a.** in passive sense: To be swamped or submerged; to fill with water and sink, as a boat. Also *fig.*

1795 in Nicolas *Disp. Nelson* (1845) VII. p. xxvii, At 11 the yawl astern swamped and was lost with all her furniture. 1821 SCOTT *Pirate* viii, The boats swamped in the current —all were lost. 1858 SEARS *Athan.* iv. 40 A higher step that would have cleared him at once of materialism, and not suffered him to sink back and swamp in it again. 1873 *Forest & Stream* 18 Dec. 290/3, I found him sitting on a log, wet, dirty, and swamping up to his waist.

b. To overflow, cause inundation. *rare.*

1905 *Contemp. Rev.* July 95 Sand, mud, grass and thrift being mingled together, which a spring-tide..was silently swamping over.

4. *fig.* **a.** (*trans.*) To plunge or sink as if in a swamp or in water; to overwhelm with difficulties, or esp. by superior numbers, so as to render inefficient.

1818 TODD, To *Swamp*, to whelm or sink as in a swamp. A modern word. 1833 GREVILLE *Mem.* (1874) II. 380 He said the Tories were indignant at the idea of being compelled to keep quiet, and that if they were to be swamped the sooner it was done the better. 1836 DISRAELI *Lett. Runnymede* 171 The Whigs in 1718 sought to govern the country by 'swamping' the House of Commons; in 1836 it is the House of Lords that is to be 'swamped'. 1846 WELLINGTON in *Croker Papers* (1884) 31 Oct., He.. endeavoured to swamp [the erection of] the statue in Parliament. 1861 HUGHES *Tom Brown at Oxf.* i. (1889) 2 The fast set..swamped, and gave the tone to, the college. 1893 SELOUS *Trav. S.E. Africa* 9, I feel convinced that in South Africa the Dutch element will never become swamped as it has been in America

b. To ruin financially.

1864 MRS. J. H. RIDDELL *Geo. Geith* I. xv. 281 Mortgages enough to have swamped any man. 1879 TOURGEE *Fool's Err.* xviii. 91 If I gave in to them, I..would be swamped by my fertilizer account in the fall.

5. *N. Amer.* To make (a logging-road) in a forest or 'swamp' by felling trees, clearing away undergrowth, etc. Also, to haul (logs) to the skidways. Also with *out.*

1784 M. PATTEN *Diary* 18 Mar. (1903) 480, I swampt out 4 small oak logs the boys saved in cuting wood Ready for hauling out. 1851 J. S. SPRINGER *Forest Life* 84 This is done by an experienced hand, who 'spots' the trees where he wishes the road to be 'swamped'. 1857 THOREAU *Maine W.*, *Allegash & E. Branch* (1912) 289 Making a logging-road in the Maine woods is called 'swamping it'... This was the most perfectly swamped of all the roads I ever saw. 1871 R. L. DASHWOOD *Chiploquorgan* viii. 102 A crew of lumberers have different occupations assigned to them;..the 'swampers', who 'swamp'—cut roads—to the felled trees, to enable the 'teamster' and his assistants to haul them on a 'Bob sled'. 1908 H. DAY *King Spruce* xi. 129 The boys who were swampin' the twitch-roads. 1937 P. K. DEVINE *Devine's Folk Lore of Newfoundland* 50 To swamp a road or path is to build one with a bedding of boughs to be used in hauling slide loads of wood in winter. 1954 C. BRUCE *Channel Shore* 27 [He] had swamped a hauling-road into the middle of the stretch that lay south of the shore road. 1974 D. SEARS *Lark in Clear Air* iii. 40 Where the logs came from and who cut them and the names of the horses that swamped them out.

6. *intr.* To work as a bullock-driver's assistant (also casually, in return for having one's 'swag' carried); to make (*one's way*) by obtaining a lift from a traveller. Cf. SWAMPER 1 c, d. *Austral. slang.*

1926 K. S. PRICHARD *Working Bullocks* 101 Billy Williams the bullocky, and Ern Collins who was swamping for him, turned their team into the yards on the following Monday. 1937 E. HILL *Ports of Sunset* 96 In they came, across the jagged Leopolds, or up from the desert, 'swamping' with a bullocky, staggering behind a pack donkey, or on Shanks' pony. 1944 M. J. O'REILLY *Bowyangs & Boomerangs* 6 My duties were to help to load and unload, bring the horses in the morning, to harness up, help to corduroy bad patches on the track, [etc.]... Fortunately the chap I 'swamped' for was an exceptionally good sort. 1964 T. RONAN *Packhorse & Pearling Boat* 170 If I broke it for a tenner, I'd roll my swag and swamp my way back to Queensland.

Hence **swamped** (swɒmpt) *ppl. a.*, **swamping** *vbl. sb.* and *ppl. a.*

1802 SCOTT *Let.* in *Lockhart* (1837) I. xi. 357 Besides the risks of swamping and breaking our necks. 1828–43 TYTLER *Hist. Scot.* (1864) I. 130 Many..were drowned by the swamping of one of the vessels. 1871 WHITTIER *Sisters* xiii, In peril from swamping sea Or lee shore rocks. 1891 *Law Times* XCII. 74/2 The swamping of the ecclesiastical element in the House of Lords. 1899 *Edin. Rev.* Oct. 302 The swamped area and the rotting vegetation are sufficient cause for the unhealthiness of the tract. 1902 S. E. WHITE *Blazed Trail* vi. 45 Old man Heath was a veteran woodsman who had come to swamping in his old age.

swamper ('swɒmpə(r)). [f. SWAMP *sb.* or *v.* + -ER[1].]

1. *U.S.* **a.** A workman who clears a road for lumberers in a 'swamp' or forest.

1857 THOREAU *Maine W.* i. (1912) 57 The company consists of choppers, swampers,—who make roads,—barker and loader, teamster, and cook. 1880 *Lumberman's Gaz.* 28 Jan., A Wisconsin lumber-camp is divided into 'choppers', 'sawyers' and swampers.

b. A man-of-all-work in a liquor saloon. Also, an assistant to a cook.

1907 in Thornton *American Glossary*. 1907 *Oregonian* (Portland) 13 Oct. 8/1 He was a swamper in a saloon. 1929 *Collier's* 5 Jan. 33/1 As a result it became pay dirt, and in later years the swamper actually had to pay for his job. 1939 P. A. ROLLINS *Gone Haywire* 65 Until the call was given, the average cook permitted nobody to approach the fire except the helper whom he rarely had, and who was known as the flunky, roustabout, swamper, or cook's louse. 1962 E. LUCIA *Klondike Kate* iii. 81 The [theatrical] company had its own bartenders and swampers. 1979 D. ANTHONY *Long Hard Cure* ii. 20 He'd returned promptly to his apartment over the tavern. His Negro swamper bore him out.

c. An assistant to a driver of horses, mules, or bullocks. *slang* (orig. *U.S.*).

1870 *Daily Territorial Enterprise* (Virginia City, Nevada) 21 Apr. 3/1 A 'swamper' is a man who goes with the driver of a 10, 12, or 14-mule team as his assistant—the driver being chief engineer and the swamper first-assistant. 1926 K. S. PRICHARD *Working Bullocks* i. 6 Red Burke shouted to the bullocks... His swamper yelled and danced. 1960 A. DOWNS *Wagon Road North* 43 Many drivers were accompanied by a 'swamper', who was usually a young fellow apprenticed to the teaming business. The swamper looked after the horses, including rounding them up in the morning, usually about four o'clock, and in general assisted the teamster with the over-all duties of freighting.

d. One who travels on foot but has his swag carried on a wagon; hence, one who obtains a lift. Cf. SWAMP *v.* 6. *Austral. slang.*

1901 M. VIVIENNE *Travels in W. Australia* 284 A 'swamper' is a man tramping without his swag, which he entrusts to a teamster to bring on his waggon... While on foot the swamper will generally leave the track, and prospect. 1929 J. RAESIDE *Golden Days* 380 With many a swamper's swag on And many a billy black. 1966 T. RONAN *Once there was Bagman* i. 15 My..fellow swamper tossed his swag off [the mailman's truck] here; he was home.

e. An assistant to the driver of a lorry. *N. Amer. slang.*

1929 *Amer. Speech* IV. 345 *Swamper*, a helper on an auto truck. 1953 C. ARMSTRONG *Catch-as-catch-Can* xiv. 114 The driver of this linen service truck, told his swamper..to stay with it. 1963 *Sun* (Vancouver) 28 Feb. 1/5 A wood truck swamper was charged $25 each for two stolen kisses Wednesday. 1975 E. IGLAUER *Denison's Ice Road* viii. 194 We don't have swampers, a second man on the truck, the way the oil-field men have.

2. An inhabitant of a swampy district. *U.S.*

[1735 J. BELCHER in *New Hampshire Provincial Papers* (1870) IV. 878 The B B's Pr—st is a jolly Fellow. I hear he stood Kick and Cuff upon the Road with some Swampeers.] 1775 *N. Carolina Gaz.* (New Berne) 24 Mar. 3/3 Fellow Dismalites and Swampers, are we not the Men whom God hath appointed to curb the Insolence of Britain. 1857 J. D. LONG *Pictures of Slavery* xvii. 323, I made an appointment to deliver a temperance address to the 'swampers'. 1891 *Boston* (Mass.) *Jrnl.* 9 Apr. 2/3 It has a high reputation among the swampers as a remedy for rheumatism.

3. One who swamps or overwhelms, as by superior numbers. *nonce-use.*

1884 *Sat. Rev.* 12 July 37/2 Mr. Gladstone asks them to swamp themselves without inquiring how they are to be swamped, and to admit their swampers without inquiring how the swampers are to be treated in the way of assigning seats to them.

swampily, swampiness: see after SWAMPY.

swampine ('swɒmpɪn). *U.S.* [ad. mod.L. *swampina* (former specific name), f. SWAMP *sb.*: see -INE[1].] The green killifish, *Fundulus heteroclitus*.

1835 KIRBY *Hab. & Inst. Anim.* I. ii. 122 Another migrating fish was found by thousands in the ponds..of Carolina, by Bosc... They belong to a genus of abdominal fishes [note, *Hydrargyra*] and are called swampines.

swampish ('swɒmpɪʃ), *a.* [f. SWAMP *sb.* + -ISH[1].] = SWAMPY.

1725 *MSS. Dk. Portland* (Hist. MSS. Comm.) VI. 121 The ground is very swampish and damp. **1880** MISS BIRD *Japan* I. 123 Passing over a swampish level.

Hence '**swampishness**.

1879 MISS BIRD *Rocky Mountains* 20 The road at first lay through a valley without a river, but some swampishness nourished some rank swamp-grass.

swamp-oak.

1. In N. America, a name for several species of oak growing in swamps: for distinguishing names of the species see quots. 1817, 1845–50, 1874.

1683 PENN *Let. to Committee* 4 Oak of divers sorts, as Red, White and Black, Spanish Chestnut and Swamp, the most durable of all. **1766** J. BARTRAM *Jrnl.* 4 Jan. in Stork *Acc. E. Florida* 22 The east banks being sandy 8 or 10 foot perpendicular, full of live and swamp-oaks. **1817** W. DARBY *Geogr. Descr. Louisiana* 355 *Quercus lyrata.* Swamp white oak. **1821** T. NUTTALL *Jrnl. Trav. Arkansa Terr.* 71 *Quercus palustris* (the swamp oak). **1845–50** MRS. LINCOLN *Lect. Bot.* App. 152 *Quercus prinus* (swamp chestnut-oak) ..*bicolor* (swamp white-oak). **1854** LOWELL *Indian Summer Reverie* viii, The swamp-oak with his royal purple on, Glares red as blood across the sinking sun. **1874** *Asa Gray's Less. Bot.* 454 *Q. palustris* (Swamp Spanish, or Pin Oak).

2. In Australia: **a.** A leguminous shrub, *Viminaria denudata*, also called *swamp-broom*.

1833 STURT *S. Australia* I. i. 53 Light brushes of swamp-oak, cypress, box, and acacia pendula.

b. Name for various species of *Casuarina*: cf. SHE-OAK.

1837 J. D. LANG *New S. Wales* II. 118 The river Macquarie,..having its banks occasionally ornamented with a handsome though rather melancholy-looking tree, called the swamp-oak. **1882** HARDY in *Proc. Berw. Nat. Club* IX. No. 3. 434 The rough-looking Swamp Oak or Tinian Pine (*Casuarina equisetifolia*), which was first introduced to Britain from the South Sea islands by Admiral Byron in 1766.

swampy ('swɒmpɪ), *a.* [f. SWAMP *sb.* + -Y.] Of the nature of a swamp; abounding in swamps; marshy, boggy.

1697 DAMPIER *Voy.* I. ii. 20 We crossed a deep River.. and marched 7 mile in a low swampy ground. **1716** B. CHURCH *Hist. Philip's War* (1865) I. 102 He..took into the Woods and Swampy thickets. **1791** R. MYLNE *2nd Rep. Thames* 12 The Towing Path is interrupted by a low, swampy Eyot. **1839** DARWIN *Voy. Nat.* x. (1852) 209 The ground is covered by a thick bed of swampy peat. **1874** GREEN *Short Hist.* iii. §4. 128 The town was guarded by the swampy meadows along Cherwell. **1877** HUXLEY *Physiogr.* 145 In many deltas, the alluvial land is swampy.

fig. **1875** MCLAREN *Serm.* Ser. II. vii. 126 The swampy corruption that fills your life.

b. Of or pertaining to a swamp; found in swamps, as ***swampy iron ore*** = bog iron ore (BOG *sb.*[1] 4); proceeding from a swamp.

1796 KIRWAN *Elem. Min.* (ed. 2) II. 183 Swampy Iron ore. *Sumpferz* of Werner. **1798** MALTHUS *Popul.* (1817) I. 214 Swampy exhalations.

Hence '**swampily** *adv.*, '**swampiness**.

1753 RICHARDSON *Grandison* (1766) V. 55 A little swampiness of soil. **1844** H. STEPHENS *Bk. Farm* I. 501 The swampiness of the ground was completely removed. **1890** *Blackw. Mag.* July 57/2 A short cut..has to be circuitously and swampily repented of.

swan (swɒn), *sb.* Forms: 1– **swan**; also 1 **swann, swon, suon,** 1, 4 **suan,** 4–5 **swane,** 4–7 **swanne,** 6 **swonne.** [Com. Teut. (not recorded for Gothic): OE. *swan, swǫn* str. m. = OFris. **swon* (EFris. *swon*, NFris., WFris. *swaan*), OS. *suan*, MLG. *swan, swâne* str. and wk. m., *swôn* str. m., (LG. *swaan*), MDu. *swâne* (Du. *zwaan*), OHG. **swan, swon* str. m., *swana* wk. f. (MHG. *swane, swan* wk. m., G. *schwan* str. m., dial. *schwane, schwone* f.), ON. *svanr* (poet.) str. m. (Norw. *svon* m., *svana* f., Da. *svane* m. f., MSw., Sw. *svan* m.):—OTeut. **swanaz* str. m., **swanon-* wk. m., or **swanôn-* wk. f.

The name was app. applied orig. to the 'musical' swan, having the form of an agent-noun f. Teut. *swan-*:—Idg. *swon-*: *swen-*, represented by Skr. *svánati* (it) sounds, L. *sonit* (it) sounds, (*sonère*, later *sonāre*), Ir. *sennaim* I make music, OE. *ȝeswin* melody, song, *swinsian* to make melody.]

1. a. A large web-footed swimming bird of the genus *Cygnus* or subfamily *Cygninæ* of the family *Anatidæ*, characterized by a long and gracefully curved neck and a majestic motion when swimming; esp. *C. olor, gibbus*, or *mansuetus*, with pure white plumage in the adult, black legs and feet, and a red bill surmounted by a black knob, named specifically the Domestic, Mute, or Tame Swan.

Other important species are **Bewick's swan,** *Cygnus* (*Olor*) *bewicki*; **black swan,** *Chenopsis atratus* of Australia, with plumage almost entirely black; **black-necked swan,** *Cygnus* (*Sthenelides*) *nigricollis* or *melanocoryphus*, with black head and neck, and the rest of the plumage pure white; **trumpeter swan,** *Cygnus* (*Olor*) *buccinator*, of N. America (see TRUMPETER 7); **whistling swan,** (*a*) of Europe, *C.* (*O.*) *musicus* or *ferus*, also called Wild Swan, †Elk, or Whooper; (*b*) of N. America, *C.* (*O.*) *americanus* or *columbianus*.

Swans' quills were used for feathering arrows; hence †*arrows of swan*.

c **700** *Epinal Gloss.* (O.E.T.) 700 *Olor*, suan. *a* **1000** *Phoenix* 137 (Gr.) Ne hornas..ne organan, sweȝleoþres ȝeswin ne swanes feðre. *c* **1050** *Voc.* in Wr.-Wülcker 459/22 *Olor*, swon, ilfetu, swan. *c* **1300** *Havelok* 1726 Biforn hem com þe beste mete þat king or cayser wolde ete; Kranes, swannes, ueneysun. *c* **1340** *Nominale* (Skeat) 838 *Cyne recifle*, swan tissith. *c* **1386** CHAUCER *Prol.* 206 A fat swan loued he best of any roost. **1398** TREVISA *Barth. De P.R.* XII. xi[i]. (Tollem. MS.) Schipmen troweþ, þat it bodeþ good, yf þey meteþ swannes in peryl of schipbreche. *Ibid.* (Bodl. MS.), þe swanne putteþ doune his heed into þe water and secheþ his mete. **1451** *Lincoln Diocese Documents* 57, I wil my nevew Robert constabull haf Al my qwhite Swannes. **1459** *Paston Lett.* I. 482, viij. schefe arrowys of swanne. **1552** HULOET, Swanne, *cygnus*..some take this to be the elke, or wilde swanne. **1552–3** in Feuillerat *Revels Edw. VI* (1914) 138 Pennes of swannes quylles. **1564** *Proclam. Q. Eliz. Conserv. Swans*, It is ordeyned, that no man shal take no gray swannes nor white swannes flying. **1593** in Kempe *Losely MSS.* (1836) 308 All straie swans, all swans unmarked, all wild swans, all tame swans that fly, all swans of felons..are the master of the swans right. **1667** MILTON *P.L.* VII. 438 The Swan with Arched neck Between her white wings mantling proudly, Rowes Her state with Oarie feet. **1674** RAY *Collect. Words* 95 The Elk, Hooper, or wild Swan: *Cygnus ferus*, this bird is specifically distinct from the tame Swan. **1698** WITSEN in *Phil. Trans.* XX. 361 Black Swans, Parrots and many Sea-Cows were found there [*sc.* in Hollandia Nova]. **1717** PRIOR *Alma* I. 379 If You Dine with my Lord May'r, Roast-Beef, and Ven'son is your Fare; Thence You proceed to Swan and Bustard. **1785** PENNANT *Arctic Zool.* II. 542 The Whistling Swan carries its neck quite erect. *Ibid.* 544 The Mute Swan, or that which we call Tame, is found in a wild state in some parts of Russia. **1785** LATHAM *Gen. Synopsis Birds* VI. 438 Black-necked Swan... The plumage the same with the other Swan, except that the neck is of a velvet black. **1789** GOV. PHILLIP *Voy. Botany Bay* xi. 98 A black swan..is here by no means uncommon, being found on most of the lakes. **1814** SCOTT *Ld. of Isles* IV. x, So shoots through the morning sky the lark, Or the swan through the summer sea. **1830** YARRELL in *Trans. Linnean Soc.* XVI. 453 Side view of the sternum and trachea of Bewick's Swan. **1860** TENNYSON *Tithonus* 4 And after many a summer dies the swan.

b. In classical mythology, the swan was sacred to Apollo (hence ***Apollo's swan*** is used allusively) and to Venus (occas., as by Shakespeare, wrongly ascribed to Juno).

1592 *Soliman & Pers.* IV. i. 70 But what two Christian Virgins haue we here?.. I should haue deemd them Iunoes goodly Swannes, Or Venus milke white Doues. **1593** G. HARVEY *New Letter* Wks. (Grosart) I. 277 The brauest man is..A Lion in the field, a Lamme in the towne: A Ioues Eagle in feude, an Apollos Swanne in society. **1600** SHAKS. *A.Y.L.* I. iii. 77 Like Iunos Swans, Still we went coupled and inseperable.

2. *fig.* or *allusively.* **a.** Applied to persons or things, in reference to the pure white plumage of the swan taken as a type of faultlessness or excellence; often in contrast to *crow* or *goose*.

a **1300** *Cursor M.* 17371 (Cott.) His clething als þe suan his suire. *c* **1386** CHAUCER *Sompn. T.* 222 Me thynketh they been lyk Iovinyan Fat as a whale, and walkynge as a swan. —— *Manciple's T.* 29 Whit was this Crowe, as a snow whit swan. **14..** *Sir Beues* (Pynson) 2308 The bysshop crystened Iosian, That was as whyte as any swan. **1457** HARDING *Chron.* in *Eng. Hist. Rev.* Oct. (1912) 745 Iustyse of þese thay bene, as I deme can, As now on days men call the blacke oxe swan. **1589, 1621** [see GOOSE *sb.* 1 d]. **1592** SHAKS. *Rom. & Jul.* I. ii. 92 Compare her face with some that I shall show, And I will make thee thinke thy Swan a Crow. *a* **1617** HIERON *Doctrines Triall* Wks. 1620 II. 16 Though multitudes of good points of Doctrine..fall from vs, as water from a Swannes backe. **1679** PRANCE *Addit. Narr. Pop. Plot* 15 Thus the Accused are all Swans, and the blackness of Guilt is thrown upon the Witnesses for the King. **1858** *Eclectic Rev.* Ser. VI. III. 426 Now it is East, one of the author's white swans..who is guilty of the act of malice we denounce. **1876** LONGF. *Venice* I White swan of cities, slumbering in thy nest. **1884** [see GOOSE *sb.* 1 d]. **1912** FRANCES BALFOUR *Life & Lett. of Jas. MacGregor* xvi. 509 The assistants were to him all 'swans' as soon as they were connected with him or his church.

b. In allusions to the fabulous belief that the swan sings immediately or shortly before its death.

c **1374** CHAUCER *Anel. & Arc.* 346 þe swane..Ageynist his dethe shall synge his penavnse. *c* **1489** CAXTON *Sonnes of Aymon* xxiv. 511 What eileth now that vnhappy folke that make soo grete feest, I byleve that they ben as the swanne is when he shall deye. **1601** SHAKS. *Phœnix & Turtle* 15 Let the priest in surples white, That defunctive musicke can, Be the death-devining swan. **1604** —— *Oth.* v. ii. 247, I will play the Swan, And dye in Musicke. **1621** MIDDLETON *Sun in Aries* Wks. (Bullen) VII. 348 Illustrated by proper emblems..as.. Harmony by a swan. *a* **1718** PRIOR *2nd Hymn Callimachus* 8 And hov'ring Swans, their Throats releas'd From native Silence, Carol Sounds harmonious. **1842** TENNYSON *Morte D'Arthur* 266 Like some full-breasted swan..fluting a wild carol ere her death.

c. Hence used for: A 'singer', bard, poet.

Chiefly in specific designations derived from river-names, cf. ***the Swan of Avon*** (***Avon's Swan***) = Shakespeare. Also, ***the Mantuan Swan*** = Virgil.

Cf. L. *cycnus* (Horace has *Dircæus cycnus* = Pindar), Gr. κύκνος (Anthol. Pal. vii. 19, of Alcman).

1612 C. BROOKE *Elegy Pr. Henry* ix, Yee Isis swannes then, let not Lethe's fowles Prophane his name; but may this prince's glory..Be sung of you in a Mineruall story. **1623** B. JONSON in *Shaks. Wks.* (1st Fol.), Sweet Swan of Auon! what a sight it were To see thee in our waters yet appeare, And make those flights vpon the bankes of Thames. **1691** WOOD *Ath. Oxon.* (1692) II. 292 William D'Avenant.. whom we..may justly stile *the sweet Swan of Isis*. **1728** POPE *Dunc.* III. 20 Taylor,..(Once swan of Thames, tho' now he sings no more). [Cf. *ibid.* III. 155 Each Cygnet sweet, of Bath and Tunbridge race, Whose tuneful whistling makes the waters pass.] **1767** MICKLE *Concub.* xvi, Avons Swan of peerlesse Memorie. **1781** COWPER *Table-T.* 557 Ages elaps'd ere Homer's lamp appear'd, And ages ere the Mantuan swan was heard. **1895** G. B. SHAW *Our Theatres in Nineties* (1932) I. 197 Everyone concerned..is full of earnest belief that the splendor of the Swan will be revealed at last, like the Holy Grail. **1922** JOYCE *Ulysses* 186 Shakespeare..does not stay to feed the pen chivying her game of cygnets towards the rushes. The swan of Avon has other thoughts.

d. ***black swan***: a proverbial phrase (after Juvenal *Sat.* vi. 164) for something extremely rare (or non-existent); a rarity, *rara avis*.

[**1398** TREVISA *Barth. De P.R.* XII. xii. (Bodl. MS.) lf. 120/1 The swanne hatte signus in latine and Olor in grewe, for he is al white in feþeres. for no man findeþ a blacke swanne. **1576** BEDINGFIELD tr. *Cardanus' Comf.* 4 What man is so mad as wil say the swan is black?] **1579** GOSSON *Sch. Abuse* (Arb.) 30 The abuse of such places [*sc.* theatres] was so great, that for any chaste liuer to haunt them was a black swan, and a white crowe. **1606** DAY *Ile of Guls* (1881) 54 The rare..Mopsa, the black swan of beauty & madghowlet of admiration. **1694** N. H. *Ladies Dict.* 192/1 (bis) Husbands without faults (if such black Swans there be). **1764** WESLEY *Jrnl.* 2 Oct., I breakfasted..with Mr. B——, a black swan, an honest lawyer! **1890** W. E. NORRIS *Misadventure* ix, He may not be such a black swan as Aunt Susan makes him out.

e. [f. SWAN *v.*[1] 2.] An apparently aimless journey; an excursion made for reconnaissance or for pleasure. *slang* (orig. *Mil.*).

1946 VISCT. MONTGOMERY *El Alamein* 45 A recurrence of what was then becoming known in the Eighth Army as the 'annual swan' between Egypt and El Agheila. **1958** *Spectator* 23 May 665/2 The General.., yielding to a very natural temptation to go for a 'swan' early in the battle, was away from his headquarters for over thirty-six hours. **1960** C. ACHEBE *No Longer at Ease* xvii. 153 But for an African like you, who has too many privileges as it is, to ask for two weeks to go on a swan, it makes me want to cry. **1968** *Listener* 22 Feb. 238/1 It [*sc.* a festival] has become an accepted 'swan' for the British correspondents. **1974** D. HART-DAVIS *Peter Fleming* iv. 75 The trip as a whole was designed to be what he later called a 'swan'—a general look round. **1979** D. CLARK *Heberden's Seat* vii. 150 'Reed and I may have to go to London for the day.'.. 'It's not just a swan is it?'

3. a. A figure of a swan, as in heraldry.

13.. *E.E. Allit. P.* B. 58 Wyth scheldez of wylde swyn, swanez & cronez. *a* **1400** *Octouian* 1481 Har armes wer gowles and swan, Trappure and scheld. *a* **1490** BOTONER *Itin.* (Nasmith, 1778) 217 Venella apud signum le swan. **1581** PETTIE tr. *Guazzo's Civ. Conv.* II. (1586) 108b, Whereas that hath a flying swan,..this hath besides the shadow of the same swan. **1627** PEACHAM *Compl. Gentl.* xiii. 184 Three Roses Argent betweene as many Swans proper.

b. *Astron.* The northern constellation *Cygnus*.

1551 RECORDE *Cast. Knowl.* (1556) 264 By it [*sc.* Lyra] is the Swanne, named Cygnus. **1606** N. B[AXTER] *Sydney's Ourania* D 4, The siluered Swan that dying sweetly sings, Adorn's with twelue starres her beautifull wings. **1670** *Phil. Trans.* V. 2023 The New Star near the Beak of the Swan. **1868** LOCKYER *Guillemin's Heavens* 328.

†**c.** ***plumed swan***: a colour in alchemy. *Obs.*

1610 B. JONSON *Alch.* II. ii, Your seuerall colours..Of.. the crow, The peacocks taile, the plumed swan.

4. a. *attrib.* and *Comb.*: simple attrib., as ***swan-bevy, comb*** (fig.), ***feast, -feather, -flesh, -flight, -meat, -pie, -plumage***; ***swan-fashion*** adv.; objective, as ***swan-feeder*** (attrib.), ***-hunting, -shooting***; ***swan-delighting, -eating*** adjs.; instrumental, etc. as ***swan-clad, -drawn, -instructed, -poor, -proud*** adjs.; similative and parasynthetic, as ***swan-bosomed, -breasted, -bright, -feathered, -fledged, -plumed, -soft, -sweet, -tuned, -winged*** adjs.

1897 H. N. HOWARD *Footsteps Proserpine* 111 A wench ..*Swan-bosomed. **1930** R. CAMPBELL *Adamastor* 73 The great *swan-breasted seraphs soar and sing. **1923** E. SITWELL *Bucolic Comedies* 35 The *swan-bright fountains. **1646** G. DANIEL *Poems* Wks. (Grosart) I. 27 Swift Arne, the Thuscan Soile, noe more shall beat, Nor *Swan-clad Po run Sweet. **1922** *Swancomb [see *high-reared* s.v. HIGH *adv.* 10 a]. **1936** AUDEN *Look, Stranger!* 41 The *swan-delighting river. **1812** W. TENNANT *Anster F.* I. 3 The *swan-drawn car. **1641** MILTON *Reform.* I. Wks. 1851 III. 18 His canary-sucking and *swan-eating palat. **1849** D. J. BROWNE *Amer. Poultry Yd.* (1855) 242 They would probably please most palates better, if cooked and served *swan fashion. *Ibid.* 250 The '*swan feasts', which sometimes have occurred in England,..have been solemnised in the course of the month of September. *c* **1465** *Chevy Chase* 96 þe *swane fethars þat his arrowe bar with his hart blood þe wear wete. **1953** R. GRAVES *Poems* 17 Past either cheek *Swan-feathered arrows whistle. **1557** GRIMALD in *Tottel's Misc.* (Arb.) 117 *Swan-feeder Temms no furder course can passe. **1862** G. M. HOPKINS *Vision of Mermaids* (1929), And shake From wings *swan-fledged a wheel of watery light. **1557** EDGEWORTH *Serm.* 91 They were forbidden..*swanne flesh. **1959** E. POUND *Thrones* xcviii. 38 The King's job, vast as the *swan-flight. **1708** *Lond. Gaz.* No. 4463/2 The King left Yagersburg on Wednesday last, in order to take the Diversion of *Swan-Hunting. **1870** GILLMORE tr. *Figuier's Reptiles & Birds* 254 Swan-hunting takes place during the season of moulting. **1942** S. SMITH *Magic Morning* in *Coll. Poems* (1975) 206 'Charley, Charley, Charley' cry the *swan-instructed curlews. **1922** JOYCE *Ulysses* 151 Wonder what kind is *swanmeat. **1640** J. D. *Knave in Graine* III. i. Hjb, Wast not an excellent *Swan-pie? **1679** R. MONTAGU in *Buccleuch MSS.* (Hist. MSS. Comm.) I. 331 My wife gives your Lordship her humble thanks for the swan pie. **1953** E. SITWELL *Gardeners & Astronomers* 37 And Cygnus who gave you all his bright *swan-plumage. **1600** TOURNEUR *Transf. Metam.* Epil. 9 *Swan-plum'd Phœbe [= the moon] gards the star-faire night. **1591** SYLVESTER *Du Bartas* I. iv. 364 While tow'rd the Sea, our (then *Swan-poorer) Thames Bare down my Bark upon her ebbing streams. *a* **1618** —— *Sonnets* VII. 9 Sweet Petrarch's Po, and *swan-proud Sein. **1874** J. W. LONG *Amer. Wild-fowl* iii. 71 An excellent decoy for *swan-shooting..is an old white shirt drawn over a bunch of brush. **1596** FITZ-GEFFREY *Sir F. Drake* (1881) 7 Then let thy *swan-sweet voice sing to a Drake. **1604** SCOLOKER *Daiphantus* (1880) 23 Daiphantus hearing such a *Swan-tun'd voyce, Was rauisht. **1798** SOTHEBY tr. *Weiland's Oberon* (1826) II. 215 Through the air the *swan-wing'd chariot flew. **1925** E. SITWELL *Troy Park* 12 In the thick *swan-soft fields.

b. Special Combs.: **swan-animalcule**, an infusorian of either of the families *Trachelocercidæ* and *Tracheliidæ*, esp. *Trachelocerca olor*, having a long flexible and extensible anterior prolongation like a swan's neck; **swan dive** *U.S.*, a swallow dive (see SWALLOW *sb.*[1] 4); hence **swan-dive** *v. intr.*; **swan-down** (see SWAN'S-DOWN); **swan-drop**, (*a*) the knob on a swan's bill; in quot. 1821 *transf.*; (*b*) = *swan-shot*; **swan-egg** = *swan's-egg*; **swan-flower** = *swan-plant* (*a*); **swan-goose**, a large long-necked species of goose from Eastern Asia, *Cygnopsis cygnoides*, also called Chinese or Guinea goose; **swan-mussel**, a common species of freshwater mussel, *Anodonta cygnea*; †**swan-pen** [cf. MDu. *swan(en)penne* swan's quill, *swanenpipe* swan's quill, esp. one used as a drain-pipe] = *swan-quill*; also, a pipe of the width of a swan-quill (cf. PEN *sb.*[2] 3 a) for draining; **swan-plant**, (*a*) an orchid of the S. American genus *Cycnoches*, having flowers with a long curved column like a swan's neck; (*b*) a W. Indian species of birthwort, *Aristolochia grandiflora*, also called Pelican-flower; **swan-post** [ad. F. *poste*; cf. Cotgr., '*Postes*, big haile-shot for Herons, Geese, and other such great fowle'] = *swan shot*; **swanproof** *a. nonce-wd.*, not susceptible to the influence of Shakespeare (cf. sense 2 c); **swan-quill**, a swan's feather, or a pen made of one; **swan's bath** (*pseudo-arch.*), the water, the sea; †**swan's beak, bill**, a kind of surgical forceps (cf. CRANE'S-BILL 2); **swan's egg** (also *swan-egg*), name of a variety of pear; **swan's feather**, collectors' name for a species of moth, *Porrectaria cygnipennella*, with pure white wings (Rennie, 1832); **swan-shot**, a large size of shot, used for shooting swans; also used in angling as a weight; **swan-song** [after G. *schwanen(ge)sang*, *schwanenlied*], a song like that fabled to be sung by a dying swan; the last work of a poet or musician, composed shortly before his death; hence, any final performance, action, or effort; †**swan's tongue**, an old name for hemp-nettle (*Galeopsis Tetrahit*); **Swan Vesta**, the proprietary name of a make of match; cf. VESTA 4. See also SWANHERD, etc.

1865 T. R. JONES in *Intell. Observ.* Mar. 121 A *Swan animalcule (*Trachelocerca olor*). **1898** *Swimming Mag.* Oct. 45/2 The diving..included forward headers,..somersaults and the '*Swan' dive from twenty, thirty, and forty feet. **1912** J. LONDON *Son of Sun* ii. 53, I used to swan-dive a hundred and ten feet in the clear. **1932** E. HEMINGWAY *Death in Afternoon* i. 21 As though a diver could control ..[the] speed..of a swan dive. **1972** B. F. CONNERS *Don't embarrass Bureau* (1973) I. 7 Mrs. Green..executed her swan dive, flopping onto the water with the poise of a stricken bird. **1821** *Blackw. Mag.* IX. 62 Hazlitt I own is not pale, because of his rubicund *swan-drops. **1853** J. PALLISER *Solitary Rambles* ii. 55 My own saddle-bags contained.. powder and shot, and, by great good luck, some swan-drops. **1865** *Pall Mall G.* No. 187. 9/2 Fire-arms..loaded with heavy swan-drops. **1884** MILLER *Plant-n.*, *Swan-flower, of Surinam, *Cycnoches Loddigesii*. **1678** RAY *Willughby's Ornith.* 360 The *Swan-Goose: *Anser cygnoides Hispanicus seu Guineensis*... It is a stately Bird, walking with the Head and Neck decently erected. **1804** BEWICK *Brit. Birds* II. 281 Swan Goose. Chinese, Spanish, Guinea, or Cape Goose. **1777** PENNANT *Brit. Zool.* IV. 96 *Mytilus Cygneus.* *Swan M[ussel] with a thin brittle shell, very broad and convex, marked with concentric striæ. **1864** *Intell. Observ.* Sept. 67 The swan-mussel (*Anodonta*)..is one of the largest of our bivalve molluscs. **1426** *Cov. Leet Bk.* 108 þat ther be no pype [to a conduit] more then a *swan penne. *c* **1480** HENRYSON *Mor. Fab.*, *Lion & Mouse* Prol. vi, Ane roll of paper in his hand he bair; Ane swannis pen [*ed.* **1621** Swane-pen] stikkand vnder his eir. **1841** *Florist's Jrnl.* (1846) II. 135 *Cycnoches Loddigesii.* This is the *swan plant. **1848** SCHOMBURGK *Hist. Barbados* 621 *Aristolochia grandiflora*.. Jamaica, Trinidad. The Swan Plant. **1846** C. ST. JOHN *Wild Sports Highl.* 252 With the double-barrel loaded with *swan-post. **1905** G. B. SHAW in *Shaw on Theatre* (1958) 103 Since Shakespear's words are still the basis of the dialogue, there are moments when the bard enjoys his own again; for all the players are not as completely *swanproof as Mr Tree. **1839** URE *Dict. Arts* 454 Crow quills for draughtsmen, as well as *swan quills, are prepared in the same way. **1900** WEYMAN *Sophia* xxv, She unearthed a pewter ink-pot and an old swan-quill. **1865** KINGSLEY *Herew.* iv, Take to the sea like your forefather, and come over the *swan's bath with me! **1631** H. C[ROOKE] *Expl. Instrum. Chirurg.* 43 Another Instrument called the *Swans beake, the sides whereof are opened by a screw when it is insinuated into the wound. *Ibid.* 41 Those instruments framed to draw out bullets..out of wounds..are almost all called by one generall name Bills or Beakes, as the Crowes Bill, the Cranes Bill, the Drakes Bill, the Parrots Bill, and the *Swans Bill. **1741** *Compl. Fam.-Piece* II. iii. 400 These Pears. [Oct.] Green Sugar, Besidery, *Swan's Egg,..and others. **1767** ABERCROMBIE *Ev. Man his own Gardener* (1803) 672/2 La Marquis, Swan Egg, Virgoleuse, [etc.]. **1843** J. SMITH *Forest Trees* 163 Swan's egg is a small beautifully shaped pear. **1858** GEO. ELIOT *Scenes Cler. Life* 232 Swan-egg pears. **1719** DE FOE *Crusoe* I. (Globe) 235 Large *Swan-Shot, as big as small Pistol Bullets. **1821** SCOTT *Pirate* viii, She will put a hundred swan-shot through a Dutchman's cap at eighty paces. **1856** 'STONEHENGE' *Man. Brit. Rural Sports* 255/2 Swan-shot or lead, in some form, is required to sink the bait. **1882** MISS BRADDON *Mt. Royal* III. iv. 57 He is found with an empty bag, and a charge of swan-shot through his heart. **1971** *Angling Times* 10 June 6/2 Any float will do that a swan shot can't quite take under. **1831** CARLYLE *Sart. Res.* III. vii, The Phoenix soars aloft,..or, as now, she sinks, and with spheral *swan-song immolates herself in flame. **1837** —— *Fr. Rev.* I. II. viii, We will call his Book [Saint-Pierre's 'Paul et Virginie'] the swan-song of old dying France. **1890** *Spectator* 10 May, When Tennyson threw his swan-song ['Crossing the Bar']..before an instantly appreciating world. **1976** *Monitor* (McAllen, Texas) 28 Nov. 11A/4 Rockefeller fairly bubbled with optimism during a recent swan song interview. **1978** G. GREENE *Human Factor* VI. ii. 319 Ivan made his swan song as an interpreter in a building not far from the Lubianka prison. *c* **1450** *Alphita* (Anecd. Oxon.) 80/2 *Herba hircina*, i. tetrahit..anglice *swanestonge. [**1907** *Yesterday's Shopping* (1969) 24/2 Swan White Pine Vestas. (Bryant & May's.).. Doz..0/3½.] **1908** *Trade Marks Jrnl.* 12 Aug. 1340 *Swan Vestas*... Matches. Bryant & May, Limited, Fairfield Works, Bow, London..; match manufacturers. **1958** J. TOWNSEND *Young Devils* vii. 59, I collected..a number of loose Swan Vestas from the class. **1977** 'E. CRISPIN' *Glimpses of Moon* vii. 109 Ling gave his Swan Vesta box an experimental shake.

c. with reference to the keeping of swans and swan-upping, as ***swan-book***, ***-hook***, ***-house***, ***-keeper***, ***laws***, ***-master***, ***-pit***, ***-rights***, ***-warden***, ***-yard***.

1524 in *Archaeologia* (1812) XVI. 156 That there shall no Swannerd keep, or carry any swan book, but the King's Swannerd. *c* **1560** in *Proc. Archæol. Inst., Lincoln* (1850) 305 It is lawful for every owner, swanmaister, or swanheard, to pull up, or cut downe ye birdnet. *Ibid.* 306 If any person.. be found carrijng any swanhooke, and the same person being no swanheard [etc.]. *Ibid.*, They shall pay a land bird to the king, and be obedient to all swan lawes. **1600-1** in Willis & Clark *Cambridge* (1886) III. 594 Pro mending the Swanhouse walles iij[d]. **1733** in *Blackw. Mag.* Dec. (1888) 862/1 [A minute in the books of the Hospital Trust [of St. Helen's, Norwich] says that a new] swan-yard [was constructed in 1793]. **1812** R. SURTEES in J. Raine *Mem. J. Hodgson* (1857) I. 85 Swan-oats are regularly paid by the adjacent properties to the lessee of the old swan-house on the borders of the morass. **1843** YARRELL *Brit. Birds* III. 129 The principal governing officers of the [Vintners'] company for the time being are, a Master and three Wardens, the junior Warden of the year being called the Swan Warden. **1848** BROMEHEAD in *Proc. Archæol. Inst., Lincoln* (1850) 301 *note*, The swanhook, attached to a long pole, by means of which the bird might readily be captured by the neck, is frequently introduced as a symbol amongst the varied devices composing the swanmarks in the MS. **1883** G. C. DAVIES *Norfolk Broads* xxix. 202 The swan-pit, at the back of the Old Man's Hospital, St. Helen's, Norwich. This pit is an oblong pool or tank...with perpendicular sides... Here they [*sc.* cygnets] are fattened for the table, or reared for transmission to their future homes. **1888** *Blackw. Mag.* Dec. 861/2 There are several swan-pits belonging to the various owners of swan-rights on the Norwich rivers. *Ibid.* 862/1 From 80 to 100 cygnets may be seen..undergoing the process of fattening in the swan-pit. **1892** *Pall Mall Gaz.* 2 Aug. 2/1 Fourteen years ago the R.S.P.C.A. prosecuted the swan-masters.

d. with reference to the stories in Aryan mythology of supernatural maidens having the power of transforming themselves into swans by means of a robe of swan's feathers or of a magic ring or chain, as ***swan-bride***, ***-hero***, ***-maid***, ***-maiden*** (after G. *schwanenjungfrau*), ***-wife***, ***-woman***; ***swan-coat***, ***-ring***, ***-shift*** (after G. *schwanenhemd*, *-ring*): also applied to a personage in mediæval story, like Lohengrin, accompanied by a swan, as ***swan-knight*** (= *knight of the swan*, G. *schwanenritter*, F. *chevalier au cygne*).

1859 G. W. DASENT *Pop. Tales from Norse* p. lxi, Brynhildr and the Valkyries..became swan-maidens. **1862** H. MARRYAT *Year in Sweden* lxiv. II. 389 *note*, The smith.. fancied his swan-bride had returned. **1865** TYLOR *Early Hist. Man.* xii. 346 *note*, Three women sit on the shore with their swan-coats beside them, ready to turn into swans and fly away. **1868** BARING-GOULD *Myths Mid. Ages* Ser. II. ix. 298 These swan-maidens are the houris of the Vedic heaven; receiving to their arms the souls of the heroes. *Ibid.* 302 At one time there is but a single swan-woman, at another the sky is dark with their numerous wings. **1880** STALLYBRASS tr. *Grimm's Teut. Mythol.* I. xvi. 427 The swan-hero forsakes his wife the moment she asks the forbidden question. *Ibid.*, Many tales of swan-wives still live among the Norse people. *Ibid.* 428 When they [*sc.* swan-maidens] bathe in the cooling flood, they lay down on the bank the swan-ring, the swan-shift. **1889** R. B. ANDERSON tr. *Rydberg's Teut. Mythol.* 60 Among these swan-maids was Sif. **1911** *Encycl. Brit.* XXI. 133/1 A conclusion, in which the Swan-Knight, Lohengrin is made Parzival's son.

swan, *v.*[1] *nonce-wd.* [f. prec. sb.] **1.** *intr.* (occas. with *it*): To swim like a swan. Also *transf.*

1893 MEREDITH *Ld. Ormont & Aminta* i. I. 9 The forest Goddess of the Crescent, swanning it through a lake. **1938** H. G. WELLS *Apropos of Dolores* vi. 304 He began as an Osteopath but afterwards he became a Mind Healer—with Physical Exercises... He taught them to swan (!?) Swan, you know—like swans. Swanning exercises. Some of them swan now quite beautifully. **1962** *Listener* 13 Sept. 386/2 In his painting Andrea can be seen swanning through the water.

2. To move about freely or in an (apparently) aimless way (formerly, *spec.* of armoured vehicles); hence, to travel idly or for pleasure. Freq. with *about*, *around*, or *off*. *slang* (orig. *Mil.*).

1942 *Daily Tel.* 3 Sept. 6/6 Breaking up his armour into comparatively small groups of..tanks, he began 'swanning about', feeling north, north-west and east for them [*sc.* British tanks]. *a* **1944** K. DOUGLAS *Alamein to Zem Zem* (1946) 24 It seemed crazy to go swanning off into the mist. **1945** *Times* 17 Mar. 4/2 [General Patton's armour]..is 'swanning' more or less unchallenged amid the open moors of the Hunsrück plateau. **1947** C. DAY LEWIS *Poetic Image* 111 A few bold or bomb-happy types still swanning around outside. **1961** G. EGMONT *Art of Egmontese* i. 15 Another excellent way of making contacts is, of course, 'swanning' on the Continent. **1971** *Petticoat* 17 July 28/1 You can't do that if you're swanning around making films all the time. **1980** D. BOGARDE *Gentle Occupation* viii. 200 She swanned about at the party like the Queen Mother.

swan, *v.*[2] *U.S. slang.* [prob. north. Eng. dial. *Is' wan* lit. 'I shall warrant' = I'll be bound; later taken as a mincing substitute for SWEAR *v.* Cf. SWANNY *v.*] ***I swan***, I declare: often in exclamatory asseveration.

I swan to man, a mitigated form of *I swear to God*.

1823 *Missouri Intell.* 20 May (Thornton), I swan it is. **1836** HALIBURTON *Clockm.* (1862) 65 If you hante obsarved it, I have, and a queer one it is, I swan. **1842** MRS. KIRTLAND *Forest Life* I. ii. 20 'Well! I swan!' exclaimed the mamma. **1844** 'JON. SLICK' *High Life N. York* I. 3, I swan if it warn't enough to make a feller dry to see the hogsheads of rum and molasses. **1861** LOWELL *Biglow P.* Ser. II. i. Poems 1890 II. 239 They du preach, I swan to man, it's puf'kly indescrib'le! **1873** CARLETON *Farm Ball.*, '*Betsey & I are out*' ii, 'What is the matter?' say you. I swan it's hard to tell!

swan, variant of SWON *Obs.*, swineherd.

swandown: see SWAN'S-DOWN.

swane, obs. Sc. f. SWAIN; obs. f. SWAN.

Swanee ('swɒnɪ). Also **Swannee**. [Var. of *Suwannee*, the name of a river in Georgia and Florida.] **1.** ***Swanee whistle***, a small woodwind instrument with a slide-plunger to vary the pitch, chiefly used as a toy. Also ***Swanee flute***.

1926 S. T. WARNER *Lolly Willowes* II. 114 She bought a Swanee flute. **1930** R. PAGET *Human Speech* 239 Various forms of mute for converting the whistle sound of a Swannee Whistle into a breathed sound. **1961** A. BAINES *Mus. Instruments through Ages* ix. 235 The Swanee whistle, scored for by Ravel in *Les Enfants et les sortilèges*, is also made by Indian children as a bamboo bird-pipe. **1962** A. NISBETT *Technique of Sound Studio* x. 172 An object (or person) being thrown high into the air might be indicated by the use of a glide up and down on a swannee whistle (this is a whistle which has a slide piston to govern the pitch). **1978** *Times* 15 July 2/4 (*caption*) Pupils..playing a Swanee whistle..and a Melodica, a wind keyboard. **1983** *Daily Tel.* 23 June 18/4 The piece, to be recited by the composer himself, is performed on toy clarinets, saxophones, rattles, swanee whistles, plastic hosepipes and paper-bags.

2. ***to go down the Swanee*** = *to go down the drain* s.v. DRAIN *sb.* 1 e; to become ruined or bankrupt. Cf. RIVER *sb.*[1] 4 c. *slang.*

1977 *Observer* 21 Aug. 1/3 A senior Leyland convener.. called on the Government to give Leyland 'latitude' in settling its pay problems. Without that, he said, the company 'would go down the Swanee'.

swang (swæŋ), *sb.* Chiefly *north. dial.* [Cf. dial. *swank* of the same meaning; both may be derived (with guttural suffix) from the root *swam-*, and so ultimately related to *swamp* (with labial suffix).] A low-lying piece of ground liable to be flooded; a boggy depression, swamp. See also first quot. and cf. SWAMP *sb.* 1 b, quot. 1691.

1691 RAY *N.C. Words* 72 A *Swang*, a fresh piece of green Swarth lying in a bottom among arable or barren Land. A Dool. *Ibid.* 137 A *Swang*, locus paludosus, or part of a Pasture overflow'd with water. **1811** WILLAN *W. Riding Words* in *Archaeologia* XVII. 160 *Swang*, a part of a pasture covered with water. **1891** ATKINSON *Moorland Par.* 70 The swampy, undrained 'swang'.

swang, *v. Obs.* exc. *dial.* [f. root *swang-*: see SWING *v.*] *intr.* To sway or swing to and fro.

13.. *E.E. Allit. P.* A. 111 Swangeande swete þe water con swepe. **1340-70** *Alex. & Dind.* 493 Fihches, þat þere swimmen ful swiþe & swangen aboute.

swang, obs. pa. t. of SWING *v.*

†**swange.** *Obs.* [a. ON. *svangi* (Sw. dial. *svånge*, Norw. *svange*) groin (cf. ON. *svangr* thin, SWONG).] The flank or groin.

13.. *Gaw. & Gr. Knt.* 138 Fro þe swyre to þe swange so sware & so þik. ?*a* **1400** *Morte Arth.* 1129 The kynge.. Swappez in with the swerde þat it þe swange brystedde. *c* **1400** *Anturs of Arth.* xlviii. (Douce MS.), þe swerd swapped one his swange, and one þe mayle slikes.

swangulstoke, obs. variant of SWINGLESTOCK.

swanherd (ˈswɒnhɜːd). Also 6 **swannerd**, *corruptly* **swanyeard, swannyard.** [f. SWAN *sb.* + HERD *sb.*[2]] One who tends swans; an official having charge of swans.

1482 *Rolls of Parlt.* VI. 224/1 Divers Swanherdes, and Kepers of Swannes. **1554** in W. H. Turner *Select. Rec. Oxford* (1880) 220 For ale for the swanyeardys, ij[d]. *Ibid.* 226 Wyne that was geven to swannerds. **1564** *Proclam. Q. Eliz. Conserv. Swans,* Euery swanherde intending to keepe any swannes or signettes. **1602–3** in Willis & Clark *Cambridge* (1888) III. 595 Item y[e] swanherd for vpping swans ij[s]. *a* **1634** COKE *Inst.* IV. (1648) 280 What authority the Kings Swanheard hath, being of ancient time by his Office *Magister deductus Cygnorum,* you may reade Rot. Patentium Anno II H. 4. part. I. m. 14. **1883** in *Standard* 4 Aug. 3/6 The Queen's Swanherd, and the officials of the..Companies, have just concluded their..swan-upping excursion on the Thames.

swanhood (ˈswɒnhʊd). *nonce-wd.* [f. SWAN *sb.* + -HOOD.] The condition of being a (full-grown) swan; in quot. 1857, of being a 'swan' as opposed to a 'goose' (see SWAN *sb.* 2 a).

1857 TROLLOPE *Barchester T.* xx, Clearly showing that Mr. Arabin had not yet proved his qualifications in swanhood to her satisfaction. **1888** *Mag. of Art* Jan. 97 The cygnet is growing up to swanhood alone.

swan-hopper, corruption of SWAN-UPPER.

1641–2 in Willis & Clark *Cambridge* (1886) III. 595 Ricardo Roby le Swanhopper pro le 9 Swans 1[l]. 9[s]. **1827** HONE *Every-day Bk.* II. 914 The..unsuspecting swan-hoppers. **1894** ASTLEY *50 Yrs. Life* I. 12 They [*sc.* the horses] did not half tumble about; neither did the swan-hoppers.

swan-hopping, corruption of SWAN-UPPING.

1598 in W. M. Williams *Ann. Founders' Co.* (1867) 75 Mr. Glover presented a debte of iij s. iiij d. which was laid out for bakeing of Pyes when they went Swan Hopping. **1657** HOWELL *Londinop.* 395 How stately is he attended when he goes to take a view of the River, or a Swan-hopping? **1746** H. WALPOLE *Lett.* (1846) II. 145 Two city companies in their great barges, who had been a swan-hopping. **1833** T. HOOK *Parson's Dau.* III. xi, [Like] my Lord Mayor's barge on the river Thames when his lordship is graciously pleased to go swan hopping. **1854** MEALL *Moubray's Poultry* 29 The Royal Swan Happing (or *upping*, as it was called by the Cockneys). **1884** ALICE CARR in *Harper's Mag.* July 255/2 The City Companies..had been up the river 'swan-hopping'.

swanimote (ˈswɒnɪməʊt), **swainmote** (ˈsweɪnməʊt). *Obs.* exc. *Hist.* Forms: 2–4 **swanimot,** 3 **suanimot, swaynimot, -emot,** 3–4 **swanemot,** 4 **swanymot, swanmot,** *pl.* **swanesmotes,** 5 **swanemoode,** 6 **swanymote, swynemote,** 6–7 **swannimote,** 7 **swanimoote, swannamott, swaynemote, swainemote;** *Hist.* 6–9 **swanimote,** 7 **swainmot,** 7–9 **swainmote,** 8 **swainimote, sweinmote,** 9 **swaynmote, swynmote.** [repr. OE. **swánȝemót* (whence Anglo-L. *suanimotum*), lit. meeting of swineherds, f. *swán* swineherd, SWON + *ȝemót* MOOT *sb.*[1]: the first syllable has been assimilated to SWAIN *sb.*]

A forest assembly held three times a year in accordance with the Forest Charter of 1217, probably orig. 'to enable the forest officers to superintend the depasturing of pigs in the king's woods in the autumn and the clearance of the forest of cattle and sheep while the deer were fawning in the summer'; later, applied vaguely or generically to courts of attachment, inquisitions, etc. (See G. J. Turner, *Select Pleas of the Forest*, 1901.)

The commonly received account of the swanimote is derived from Manwood, who asserted that it was a distinct court of the forest, to which the freeholders (see SWAIN *sb.* 6) were summoned, and having jurisdiction with power to enquire of vert and venison and other trespasses done within the forest.

1189 (Sept. 15) *Carta Abbatis de Burgo* (Cartæ Antiquæ Roll EE 21, P.R.O.) Liberi et quieti ab omni..consuetudine foreste et a swanimot. **1217** *Carta de Foresta* (2 Hen. 3, c. 8) Nullum Suanimotum de cetero teneatur in Regno nostro nisi ter in anno, videlicet in principio quindecim dierum ante festum Sancti Michaelis quando agistatores conveniunt ad agistandum Dominicos boscos nostros & circa festum Sancti Martini, quando agistatores nostri debent recipere Pannagium nostrum;..Et tercium Suanimotum teneatur in inicio quindecim dierum ante festum Sancti Johannis Baptistae, pro feonacione Bestiarum nostrarum. **12..** *Liber Niger Scaccarii* 374 Ipse concessit quod ego, & heredes mei ..quieti sumus de Secta Swanemoti, et de omnibus aliis Sectis illius bosco. **1294** *Yearbks. 22 Edw. I* (Rolls) 627 Nus avum treis swaynemotes par an pur encercher e enquere sy nuly mette plusurs avers ke mettre ne deit. **1311** *Noveles Ordenances* (5 Edw. II), Qe les foresters en qe baillies tieux trespas seront faitz, presentent mesmes les trespas as procheins Swanimotz. **1415–16** in Dugdale *Monast.* (1655) I. 976 Quod omnia bona..sint..quieta..de..Wapentake, & Shewyne & Miskennyng, Swanemoode, et de thesauro ducendo. *c* **1500** in *Essex Rev.* XV. 145 The Clerke of the Swanymote to make relacion to the Kyngs hyghnes of the certente of the deer kyllyd. **1558** *Nottingham Rec.* IV. 118 At the Swynemote at Blydworthe. **1617** ASSHETON *Jrnl.* (Chetham Soc.) 2 Mr. Steward keipping the swainemote. *a* **1634** COKE *Inst.* IV. (1648) 298 There be certain incidents inseparable to every Forest,..Courts of Record, as Courts of Attachments, Swanimote, and Iustice Seats. **1658** *Althorp MS.* in Simpkinson *Washingtons* (1860) App. p. lxxiv, To John Chapman for his chardges at the swannamott held wi[th]in the fforrest of Whitlewood by bill, 00 17 00. **1768** BLACKSTONE *Comm.* III. vi. 72 The court of sweinmote is to be holden before the verderors, as judges, by the steward of the sweinmote thrice in every year. **1837** HOWITT *Rur. Life* v. i. (1840) 355 The Court of Swainmote.

attrib. **1614** SPELMAN *Orig. Four Terms* Eng. Wks. II. (1727) 85 Forasmuch as the Swainmote-Courts are by the ancient Forest-Laws appointed to be kept fifteen Days before Michaelmas. *c* **1645** HOWELL *Lett.* (1655) IV. xvi. 39 A Forest hath her Court of attachments, or Swainmote Court, where matters are as pleadable, and determinable, as at Westminster-Hall. **1670** EVELYN *Sylva* xxxiii. (ed. 2) 209 The great neglect of Swainmote-Courts [should be] reformed. **1809** G. ROSE *Diaries* (1860) II. 368 The business of the Swanimote Court at Lyndhurst.

swank, *sb.*[1] *dial.* [?] (See quots.)

1726 BAILEY (ed. 3), A *swank* (at Bocking in Essex) that Remainder of Liquor at the Bottom of a Tankard, Pot or Cup, which is just sufficient for one Draught; which is not accounted good Manners to divide with the left Hand Man; and according to the Quantity is called either a large or a little Swank. **1813** *Monthly Mag.* XXXVI. 520 [At Braintree, Essex] A pint of beer is divided into three parts or draughts; the first is called Neckum, the second Sinkum, and the third Swank or Swankum.

swank (swæŋk), *sb.*[2] *slang.* [see SWANK *v.*]

1. Ostentatious or pretentious behaviour or talk; swagger; pretence.

1854 MISS BAKER *Northampt. Gloss., Swank,* an ostentatious air, an affectation of stateliness in the walk. 'What a *swank* he cuts!' **1891** *Hartland Gloss., Swank,* s. and v., swagger. **1905** *Daily Chron.* 17 Apr. 6/2 What he said is quite true, barring the whisky—that is all swank. **1909** *Westm. Gaz.* 26 Jan. 4/1 'Swank,' they realised, was the essential qualification for success in the new industry, believing that firms just awaking to its possibilities and the public would take them at their own valuation.

2. = SWANKER[2].

1913 V. SACKVILLE-WEST *Let.* 15 Feb. in V. Glendinning *Vita* (1983) v. 54 [He is] a swank, more swank than you could ever dream of. **1923** 'R. CROMPTON' *William Again* v. 91 He was a pariah, outside the pale, one of the 'swanks' who lived in big houses and talked soft. **1949** W. C. WILLIAMS *Autobiogr.* xxxii. 190 We were not concerned with the moving-picture colony or the swanks.

swank, *a.*[1] *Sc.* [app. a. MLG. *swank*, MDu. *swanc* flexible, supple, slender, = MHG. *swanc* (G. *schwank*); f. *swank-*, appearing also, with suffix, in OE. *swancor* pliant, supple, agile, MHG. *swankel* supple, and parallel to *swang-*, appearing in ON. *svangr* thin, lean, SWONG, *svangi* SWANGE, early mod.G. *schwang* (= *schwank*).

For other derivatives of the widespread *swink-*: *swank-* and *swing-*: *swang-*, see SWINK, SWENCH, SWING, SWINGE, SWENGE.]

Agile, active, nimble.

1786 BURNS *To Auld Mare* iii, A filly buirdly, steeve, an' swank. **1901** 'IAN MACLAREN' *Yng. Barbarians* iv. (ed. 3) 68 Ye're to tak' thirty swank fellows that can run. **1912** *Blackw. Mag.* Apr. 487/2 To ride among the swank, well-fed lads in the Bewcastle chase.

swank (swæŋk), *a.*[2] *colloq.* (chiefly *U.S.*). [f. SWANK *sb.*[2] or *v.*] Stylish; 'posh', 'classy'. (Freq. applied to shops, hotels, or apartments.)

1913 [see SWANK *sb.*[2] 2]. **1919** W. DEEPING *Second Youth* xvii. 145 Look here, come for a ride. Had this new swank machine just a week. **1928** *Publishers' Weekly* 30 June 2578 From honor and riches to poverty and shame—from the swankest hunting set of England to a garret in the Latin Quarter of Paris. **1947** D. RIESMAN in *University Observer* Winter 20/1 John..refuses to angle for the mastership of..one of the swank Harvard Houses. **1957** L. STERN *Midas Touch* I. xii. 98 These were the women..who patronized the swank Michigan Avenue specialty shops. **1972** 'E. LATHEN' *Murder without Icing* (1973) xx. 179 He was thrilled at having a swank apartment. **1981** R. BARNARD *Mother's Boys* i. 12 Have you got a big box of chocks? Something real swank?

swank (swæŋk), *v. slang.* [A midl. and s.w. dial. word taken into general slang use at the beginning of the 20th cent.

The etymological meaning is uncertain, but perh. the orig. notion is that of swinging the body, and the word is ultimately related to OHG., MHG. *swanc* swinging motion, MHG. *swanken* (G. *schwanken*) to sway, totter, etc. (cf. SWANK *a.*[1]).

The immediate source of sense 2 (= SWINK *v.*) is prob. different, but ultimate identity of origin may be presumed.]

1. a. *intr.* To behave ostentatiously, to swagger; also, to pretend by one's behaviour to be something superior to what one is; *gen.* to make pretence.

1809 BATCHELOR *Anal. Eng. Lang.* 144 (Bedfordshire dialect) *Swangk,* to strut. **1848** EVANS *Leic. Words & Phrases* s.v., I met him swanking along the road, ever so genteel. **1903** A. MCNEILL *Egregious Englishm.* x, To see your wife in the Peeresses' Gallery on great occasions, and your sons swanking about town with Hon. before their names.

b. To boast.

1874 HOTTEN *Slang Dict.* 316 *Swank,* to boast or 'gas' unduly. **1914** G. B. SHAW *Fanny's First Play* III. 211, I used to boast about what a good boy Bobby was. Now I swank about what a dog he is; and it pleases people just as well. **1950** *Sport* 7–13 Apr. 9/2 Lest I may appear to be swanking, let me hasten to add that all of the credit went to someone else. **1960** J. RAE *Custard Boys* I. vii. 80 'You think that I am swanking too much, John?' With his accent the slang word sounded very strange. **1980** *London Rev. Bks.* 17 Apr. 6/2 Anonymity..is no guarantee against a tendency on the part of informants to swank about their supposed religious experiences.

2. To work hard, to 'swot'.

1890 BARRÈRE & LELAND *Slang Dict., Swank* (public and military schools), to work hard. **1911** A. G. C. *Through College Keyhole* (Cambr.) 11 E'en have I dreamed of a minute Swanking to claim a degree.

ˈswanker[1]. *dial.* [f. SWANK *a.*[1] or SWANKING *a.*] = SWANKY *sb.*[1]

1811 WILLAN in *Archaeologia* XVII. 160 (W. Riding Words) *Swanker,* or *Swankie, s.* a strapping young man.

swanker[2] (ˈswæŋkə(r)). *dial.* or *slang.* [f. SWANK *a.*[1] or SWANK *v.* + -ER[1].] One who swanks.

a **1846** M. H. BARKER *Nights at Sea* (1858) 35 There used to be a lot of outrageous tarnation swankers meet there for a night's spree. **1890** BARRÈRE & LELAND *Slang Dict., Swanker* (public and military schools), one who works hard. **1909** *Westm. Gaz.* 31 Aug. 8/3 When Smith cried out that he was stabbed, she replied, 'Go on, you are a good old swanker.' She thought he was joking until she saw he was bleeding.

swankily (ˈswæŋkɪlɪ), *adv. slang.* [f. SWANKY *a.*[2] + -LY[2].] In a swanking or ostentatious manner; boastfully.

1924 D. MOORE *Fen's First Term* viii. 87 Angela did it first, and did it swankily. **1940** E. F. BENSON *Final Edition* xiii. 284, I swankily told my friend..that I had decided not to go to the Coronation but to give my place to someone else. **1951** *Sport* 6–12 Apr. 11/1 You are unfortunate in not..being able to play swankily to the gallery, not having the peculiar knack some players have of catching the eye.

swankiness (ˈswæŋkɪnɪs). *slang.* [f. SWANKY *a.*[2] + -NESS.] The quality of being swanky; swagger.

1920 *Christian World* 2 Sept. 4/2 The average American is free from swankiness. **1965** *Listener* 22 July 125/1 The 'swankiness' inside the school was matched in the streets outside. 'Grammar grubs', the secondary schoolboys shouted at us, and we passed by, noses lifted... We thought them the bottom.

†**swanking**, *sb. Sc. Obs. rare*[−1]. [Cf. SWANK *a.*[1], SWANKY *sb.*[1]] A fine strapping fellow.

1500–20 DUNBAR *Poems* lxxv. 26 My sweit swanking [1568 *Bannatyne MS.* swanky], saif ȝow allane, Na leid I luiffit all this owk.

ˈswanking, *a. Sc.* [Cf. SWANKY, SWANKIE *sb.*[1] (*a.*[1]).] Strong and active, stout, strapping.

a **1704** T. BROWN *Lett. fr. Dead* II. (1707) 84 There goes a tall Ensign, there's a swanking Fellow for you. **1818** SCOTT *Br. Lamm.* xxiv, I lived on his land when I was a swanking young chield. **1877** BLACK *Green Past.* xliv, Tall, swanking fellows with big riding-boots and loose jackets.

ˈswanking, *vbl. sb. slang.* [f. SWANK *v.* + -ING[1].] = SWANK *sb.*[2]

1900 *Manch. Guardian* 5 Dec. 3/8 (E.D.D.) Smith picked up a piece of paper, and attempted to light it, but did not do so. The deceased said, 'None of your swanking, Smith, you can light it well enough'. **1916** *Captain* June 231/1 (*heading*) The perils of swanking. **1918** *Daily Express* 2 Oct. 2/2 History will declare that by swanking the Hohenzollerns fell.

ˈswanking, *ppl. a. slang.* [f. SWANK *v.* + -ING[2].] That swanks; boastful, ostentatious, pretentious.

1918 *Daily Express* 2 Oct. 2/2 The swanking dustman is a nuisance. So is the swanking duke.

swankpot (ˈswæŋkpɒt). *slang.* [f. SWANK *sb.*[2] + POT *sb.*[1]] An ostentatious or boastful person; one who is full of swank.

1914 *Picture Fun* 26 Dec. 1/6 Brimstone..and Billy kept the old swankpot nicely on the trot. **1927** H. WALPOLE *Jeremy at Crale* xii. 212 He's an awful swankpot. **1936** J. B. PRIESTLEY *They walk in City* v. 115 Silly swank-pot! **1959** I. & P. OPIE *Lore & Lang. Schoolch.* xiii. 302 If a boy is under the necessity of coming to school in a new suit his fellows greet him with,..'Swank pot', 'Posh guy'.

ˈswanky, swankie, *sb.*[1] (*a.*[1]). *Sc.* and *north. dial.* [Related to SWANK *a.*[1], SWANKING *sb.* and *a.*]

A smart, active, strapping young fellow.

1508 DUNBAR *Flyting* 130 Sueir swappit swanky, swyne-keper ay for swaittis. **1513** DOUGLAS *Æneis* VIII. Prol. 68 Swingeouris and scurrevagis, swankeis and swanis. **1715** RAMSAY *Christ's Kirk Gr.* II. vii, The young swankies on the green Took round a merry tirle. *c* **1756** JANE ELLIOT *Flowers of Forest* 9 In Har'st at the shearing, nae swankies are jeering. **1820** SCOTT *Monast.* xvi, There is a young swankie here who shoots venison well.

b. *adj.* = SWANK *a.*[1], SWANKING *a.*

1838 JAS. STRUTHERS *Poetic Tales* 78 Aye try to please My swankie joker. **1898** N. MUNRO *John Splendid* xix. 188 Airlie's troopers, swanky blaspheming persons.

ˈswanky, swankey, *sb.*[2] *dial.* [Perhaps a use of *swanky* adj. (see prec.) with the connotation 'thin, poor'.] Small beer, or other poor or weak liquor. Also *attrib.*

1841 HARTSHORNE *Salopia Antiqua* Gloss. 583. **1863** *Tyneside Songs* 25 We've Tom-an'-Jerry an' swanky shops, An' places where yor claes they pops. *a* **1872** *Newfoundland Fisheries* 110 (Schele de Vere) Each man..took his turn at the swankey pail. **1893** J. A. BARRY *Steve Brown's Bunyip* 295 The captain certainly had sent them a couple of dozen of porter. But, as one explained.—What's the good of sich rubbishin' swankey? **1908** W. M. J. WILLIAMS *King's Revenue* xi. 80 The 'Swankey shops', which were houses where beer at $1\frac{1}{2}d.$ the quart was sold without a licence.

swanky *a.*[1]: see SWANKY *sb.*[1]

'swanky, *a.*[2] *slang.* [f. SWANK *sb.*[2] or *v.* + -Y.] Swaggering; 'swagger', pretentiously grand. Also, boastful. Of things: imposing, stylish, 'posh'.

1842 AKERMAN *Wiltshire Gloss.*, *Swankey*, swaggering, strutting. **1883** in *Hampsh. Gloss.* **1912** *World* 6 Aug. 243/2 Some girls have such awfully swanky ideas, haven't they? **1929** 'R. CROMPTON' *William* i. 9 'I read that too,' interrupted Ginger, 'so you needn't be so swanky.' **1940** C. DAY LEWIS tr. *Virgil's Georgics* II. 49 No mansion tall with a swanky gate. **1959** *Spectator* 25 Sept. 406/3 An English producer and a London critic..in the swanky bar of the Excelsior. **1974** *Sunday Tel.* 8 Dec. 8/6 Swanky Christmas presents, beautifully wrapped in red and gold.

'swan-like, *a.* (*adv.*) [f. SWAN *sb.* + -LIKE.] Like a swan, or like that of a swan.

1591 SYLVESTER *Du Bartas* I. v. 727 White (Swan-like) wings. **1607** *Barley-Breake* (1877) 12 Her Swan-like brest, her Alabaster hands. **1697** DRYDEN *Virg. Past.* IX. 48, I.. gabble like a Goose, amidst the Swan-like Quire. **1726** POPE *Odyss.* XIX. 649 Fast by the limpid lake my swan-like train I found. **1812** CARY *Dante, Purg.* XIX. 45 With swan-like wings dispred. **1838** LYTTON *Alice* II. i, Love swelled the swanlike neck, and moulded the rounded limb.

b. *esp.* in reference to the fabled singing of the swan just before its death: cf. SWAN *sb.* 2 b.

1592 GREENE *Groat's W. Wit* To Gentl. Rdrs., Greene.. sends you his Swanne-like song, for that he feares he shal neuer againe carroll to you woonted loue layes. **1596** SHAKS. *Merch. V.* III. ii. 44 If he loose he makes a Swan-like end, Fading in musique. **1600** BRETON *Melancholike Hum.* Wks. (Grosart) I. 9 My poore swanlike soule, (alas) hath no such power to sing. **1629** PRYNNE *Anti-Armin.* (1630) 261 His last Swan like Sermon. **1678** *Yng. Man's Call.* 10 The swan-like song of the dying martyr, 'None but Christ! None but Christ!' **1837** HALLAM *Lit. Eur.* (1847) I. i. §2. 2 The swanlike tones of dying eloquence.

c. *adv.* Like or in the manner of a swan.

1635 A. STAFFORD *Fem. Glory* 166 This holy man..in a divine Rapture Swanne-like (his death being then at hand) sung this his sweetest Ditty. **1844** A. B. WELBY *Poems* (1867) 49 Who would not, Swan-like, waste his sweetest breath To ..die so sweet a death?

'swan-mark. [MARK *sb.*[1]] An official mark of ownership cut on the beak of a swan, on the occasion of SWAN-UPPING.

c **1560** in *Proc. Archæol. Inst., Lincoln* (1850) 309 If any person..by sale, or exchaunge have obteined any swan-marke, and hath any game of the same. **1586** *Will of Buckworth* (Somerset Ho.), I geue to my son my swannemarke of the hokys in fee symple. **1602–3** in Willis & Clark *Cambr.* (1886) III. 595 Bond for going to S[t] Iues about our swanmarke xij[d]. **1662–3** *Ibid.*, For the Alienacion of the Swanne marke, oo. 07. 08. **1842** [see below]. **1883** G. C. DAVIES *Norfolk Broads* xxix. (1884) 225 This privilege of swan-mark was a heritable property. **1886** WILLIS & CLARK *Cambridge* I. 438 One of the doors..has the College swan-mark engraved upon it.

So **'swan-ˌmarker**, an official who marks swans, a swan-upper; **'swan-ˌmarking**, the operation of marking swans.

1842 *Penny Cycl.* XXIII. 372/1 In creating this privilege the crown grants a swan-mark (cygninota), for a *game* of swans... The swan-markers of the crown and the two Companies [*sc.* Dyers and Vintners] of the city of London go *up* the river [Thames] for the purpose of..marking the young birds. **1900** *Daily News* 27 Sept. 5/1 This year's swan-marking.

†'swannage. *Obs.* Also 4 swanadge. [f. SWAN *sb.* + -AGE.] Payment for the right to keep swans.

1398 *Cockersand Chartul.* (Chetham) 1083 Quite of amerciament..of the helpes of worke of any Castells, houses,..dyches, swanadge, warpenye, tethingepeny. **1610** FOLKINGHAM *Art of Survey* III. iv. 70 Wrecks, Swannage, Warrenage, Commonage, Piscage.

'swan-neck. Also swan's neck. [Cf. G. *schwanenhals*, Sw. *svanhals*; in MHG. *swanhals* = narrow sickle.]

1. A neck like that of a swan; a long slender (white) neck.

Quots. 1823 and 1867 refer to the cognomen *Swanneshals* (see HALSE *sb.*) = 'swan's neck' of a certain Eadgyth (Edith), a mistress of Harold, king of the English (*De Inv. Sanctæ Crucis Walthamensis* xxi, 12th c.).

[**1823** LINGARD *Hist. Eng.* (1855) I. vi. 190 *note* 3 They sent for Harold's mistress, Editha, surnamed 'The Fair', and the 'Swan's Neck.'] **1837** CARLYLE *Fr. Rev.* III. I. i, The fair swan-bevies of *Citoyennes* that have alighted in Churches, and sit there with swan-neck. **1867** FREEMAN *Norm. Conq.* III. v. §5. 514 Eadgyth of the Swan's Neck.

2. Name for various structural parts or contrivances having a curved cylindrical form like a swan's neck.

1686 PLOT *Staffordsh.* 376 The Head..that makes the body of the Spurr..with swan-necks. **1823** P. NICHOLSON *Pract. Builder* 201 A Swan-neck, in dog-legged and open-newelled stair cases, is a portion of the rail, consisting of two parts, the lower being concave and the upper convex. **1923** G. STURT *Wheelwright's Shop* 223 *Swan-necks*, curved hooks fastened to the shafts of a dung-cart, for attaching the shafts to the body. **1935** *Discovery* Jan. 9/1 The adjustment of these beams was generally effected by bending the swan-necks in or out so as to alter the arm lengths. **1967** *Gloss. Sanitation Terms* (*B.S.I.*) 51 *Swan-neck*, a short bent delivery pipe attached to the outlet of a tap.

3. = *swan-plant* (*a*): see SWAN *sb.* 4 b.

1866 *Treas. Bot.*, Swan-neck, or Swanwort, *Cycnoches*.

4. *attrib.* Of a curved form like a swan's neck.

1844 H. STEPHENS *Bk. Farm* II. 208 The steam-pipe.. takes a swan-neck bend downwards to within 12 inches of the floor. *Ibid.* 680 The tines are always in this machine made of the swan-neck or self-cleaning form. **1884** KNIGHT *Dict. Mech.* Suppl., *Swan-neck Needle Forceps* (Surgical), an instrument for use through curved passages difficult to reach. **1891** KIPLING *Light that Failed* xiv. 305 A pair of swan-neck spurs.

'swan-necked (-nɛkt), *a.* [Cf. prec.]

1. Having a long slender neck.

1703 *Lond. Gaz.* No. 3938/4 A black Gelding..Swan Neck'd. **1869** FREEMAN *Norm. Conq.* III. App. NN. 764 The swan-necked lady [*sc.* Eadgyth] of the Waltham story. **1908** *Animal Management* (Vet. Departm., War Office) 24 A 'Cock-throttled' or 'swan-necked' horse is one which has a neck like a fowl.

2. Having (or having some part of) a curved cylindrical form like a swan's neck.

1745 W. ELLIS *Mod. Husbandman* Aug. vii. 62 Their five-toothed, long, Swan-neck'd, wooden..Rake. **1825** J. NICHOLSON *Oper. Mech.* 604 Hand-railing, whether ramped, swan-necked, level, circular, or wreathed. **1901** *Scotsman* 5 Nov. 8/1 The swan-necked putter [at golf].

swanner ('swɒnə(r)). Also 6 swaner. [Partly reduced form of *swannerd*, SWANHERD, partly a MDu. *swanier* swan-warden, with assimilation to sbs. in -ER[1].] = SWANHERD.

1524 in *Archaeologia* (1812) XVI. 155 The King's Swannerd, or his Deputy, shall give warning unto the rest of the Swanners, when that he..will go a rowing,..for to go a merkinge..of any other swans. **1555–6** in W. H. Turner *Select. Rec. Oxf.* (1880) 260 Payed to swanners for there fee ijs. vjd. **1594–5** in Willis & Clark *Cambridge* (1886) III. 596 [Five shillings] to a Swaner for bringing a swane mark. **1842** *Gentl. Mag.* Jan. 45/2 The swan with two nicks, the way in which the swanner still marks his birds.

swannerd, obs. form of SWANHERD.

swannery ('swɒnəri). Also 8 swanery. [f. as SWANNER: see -ERY. Cf. MDu. *zwaenerie* right to keep swans.] **†a.** The keeping of swans (?). **b.** A place where swans are kept and reared.

1570 in *Archaeologia* (1812) XVI. 159 The true Copy of an old Paper, touching the Swannery found among my Father's Books, and intituled a Copy of the Ordinances for Swans, &c. **1754** POCOCKE *Trav.* (Camden) 95 At the swanery..the walls are built of a stone full of shells. **1774** HUTCHINS *Hist. Dorset* I. 538/1 A little W. of the town [*sc.* Abbotsbury] is a noble swannery, much visited by strangers. **1888** *Blackw. Mag.* Dec. 857/2 How many years previous to that time the abbots..had 'enjoyed' the privilege of maintaining a swannery is not recorded.

†'swannet. *Obs. rare.* [f. SWAN *sb.* + -ET[1].] A young swan, cygnet; chiefly applied *fig.* to a poet (cf. SWAN *sb.* 2 c).

The reading in the first quot. is doubtful.

c **1560** in *Proc. Archæol. Inst., Lincoln* (1850) 308 It is ordeined, that no person shall take any gray swannet or cignettes. **1605** DANIEL *Philotas* Epistle 53 Though you haue a Swannet of your owne, Within the bankes of Douen meditates Sweet notes to you. **1612** C. BROOKE *Elegy Pr. Henry* viii, In Tagus then some swannet dip his pen, And of this eaglet-issue, sing the fame.

swanning ('swɒnɪŋ), *vbl. sb. slang* (orig. *Mil.*). [f. SWAN *v.*[1] + -ING[1].] The action of the verb (sense 2).

1951 E. LINKLATER *Campaign in Italy* v. 257 Some..were indulging in a favourite pastime of the army, known as swanning. The swan..has the habit of taking short flights that create appreciable commotion but have no serious purpose. Officers who spent their spare time in swanning had in a like manner no graver reason than a desire to watch some particular fragment of a battle, or to visit friends. **1960** *Times Lit. Suppl.* 16 Sept. 587/2 The 22nd Armoured Brigade was continually exercised in a swanning role, of the kind which had so often led to defeat in the past. **1975** *Bookseller* 12 Apr. 2095/1 Harold Latham, the Macmillan editor,..was on a casual swanning tour round Georgia.

swannish ('swɒnɪʃ), *a. rare.* [f. SWAN *sb.* + -ISH[1].] Swan-like.

a **1586** SIDNEY *Arcadia* II. (1622) 216 Long since, alas, my deadly swannish musick Hath made itself a cryer of the morning. **1591** W. R. *Murther John Ld. Bourgh* B, A swannish tune becomes my morning song. **1630** DRAYTON *Muses' Elysium* Nymphal i. 77 My swannish Breast brancht all with blew. **1631** [MABBE] *Celestina* XVIII. 187 This hoarse swannish voyce of mine.

swanny ('swɒni), *a.* [f. SWAN *sb.* + -Y.]

1. Full of or abounding in swans.

1567 GOLDING *Ovid's Met.* VII. (1593) 163 The swannie Temp [orig. *Cycneia Tempe*] and Hyries poole he viewed from above. **1640** J. GOWER *Ovid's Festiv.* IV. 87 Next Camarine with Swanny Tempe [orig. *Heloria Tempe*] fair. **1859** in Campbell *Tales W. Highlands* xvii. c. (1860) I. 291 From the loved swanny glen.

2. Of or pertaining to, or resembling that of, a swan.

1598 F. ROUS *Thule* T 3 b, But O my pen transforme thy swanny face, And in eternall streames my inck shall weepe. **1602** tr. *Guarini's Pastor Fido* I. i. B 1 b, More purely white then swanny downe. **1604** PRICKET *Honors Fame* (1881) 29 A Swanny whitenes. **1748** RICHARDSON *Clarissa* (1811) IV. v. 22 The swanny glossiness of a neck late so stately. **1829** W. TAYLOR *Hist. Surv. Germ. Poetry* II. 114 Girt in the swanny arms of fair Glycera. **1871** G. M. HOPKINS *Jrnls & Papers* (1959) 207 Clouds..in burly-shouldered ridges swanny and lustrous.

swanny, *v. U.S. slang.* [prob. north. Eng. dial. *Is' wan ye* lit. 'I shall warrant you'.] = SWAN *v.*[2]

1839 *Salem Advertiser* 18 Sept. 3/2 (Thornton) 'Capt. Center, didn't I tell you Van Buren was not the man?' 'Yes you did, I swanney.' **1844** 'JON. SLICK' *High Life N. York* II. 132, I swanny, it eenamost made me boo-hoo right out.

swan-pan, var. SUAN-PAN.

Swan River. The name of a river in Western Australia, used *attrib.* in **Swan River daisy**, an annual herb of the genus *Brachycome*, esp. *B. iberidifolia*, belonging to the family Compositæ, native to Western and South Australia, and bearing pinnate leaves and blue, violet, or white flowers resembling daisies.

[**1841** J. LINDLEY in *Edward's Bot. Reg.* XXVII. 9 Mr. Lowe, of Clapton, has also raised the Large Swan Daisy.] **1873** W. B. HEMSLEY *Handbk. Hardy Trees, Shrubs, & Herbacious Plants* 235 Swan River Daisy.—An erect glabrous annual about a foot high. **1915** W. STEVENS *Let.* 25 July (1967) 184 Another new thing was what is called swan-river daisies from Australia. **1957** J. S. DAKERS *Annuals* xiii. 92 Swan River Daisy..one of the most beautiful of all our annuals. **1962** R. PAGE *Educ. Gardener* xi. 302 The cypresses are underplanted with sheets of..the blue Swan River daisy.

Swanscombe ('swɒnzkəm). The name of a village in north-west Kent, used *attrib.* to designate a Middle Pleistocene fossil hominid, an early type of *Homo sapiens*, known from parts of a skull found in a gravel pit near Swanscombe in 1935 and subsequent years. Also ***Swanscombe skull.***

1938 W. LEG. CLARK in *Jrnl. R. Anthropol. Inst.* LXVIII. 58 (*title*) General features of the Swanscombe skull bones. **1940** *Nature* 13 July 51/2 Swanscombe man appears..in gravels heralding the third glacial stage. **1946** F. E. ZEUNER *Dating Past* viii. 279 The view..is beginning to be held generally, and especially on the strength of the Swanscombe skull, that *H[omo] sapiens* evolved during the Penultimate Interglacial. *Ibid.* ix. 298 Swanscombe Man..is a member of the *sapiens* group. **1962** *Listener* 22 Nov. 878/2 For those who think Pleistocene is a substance, Mary Cathcart Boxer's *Mankind in the Making*..will prove a model of clarity that.. sorts the jumble of prehistory in a manner that even those as thick of skull as Swanscombe Woman can grasp. **1973** B. J. WILLIAMS *Evolution & Human Origins* x. 169/2 The bone of the Swanscombe skull is thinner than that of Peking Man but thicker than in modern man's. **1975** J. G. EVANS *Environment Early Man Brit. Isles* i. 1 Many dramatic environmental changes separate Swanscombe Man by more than 150,000 years from the development and eventual spread into Britain of farming communities.

swan's-down, swansdown ('swɒnzdaʊn). Also swandown. [Cf. G. *schwanendaune*, Sw. *svandun*, Da. *svanedun.*]

1. The down or soft under-plumage of the swan, used for dress-trimmings, powder-puffs, etc.

1606 SHAKS. *Ant. & Cl.* III. ii. 48 The Swannes downe feather That stands vpon the Swell at the full of Tide: And neither way inclines. **1807–26** S. COOPER *First Lines Surg.* (ed. 5) 208 To keep the swelling covered with a piece of swan's-down, or rabbit's skin. **1835** *Court Mag.* VI. p. xiv/2 Others have, in addition to the knots, a row of swansdown on each side of the front. **1855** LONGF. *Hiaw.* xvi. 193 With his plumes and tufts of swan's-down. **1891** DOYLE *White Company* xxiii, Swathed in swan's-down and in ermine.

2. a. A soft thick close woollen cloth. **b.** A thick cotton cloth with a nap on one side, also called *Canton* or *cotton flannel.*

1801 *Sporting Mag.* XVII. 177 The blankets of the finest swansdown. **1824** SCOTT *St. Ronan's* xv, If a gold-laced waistcoat has an empty pouch, the plain swan's-down will be the brawer of the twa. **1877** J. W. HAYES *Draper & Haberdasher* (ed. 4) 97 Swansdown is a loose thick make of white and unbleached calico, with a raised surface, like blankets. **1883** SIMMONDS *Dict. Trade* Suppl., *Swandown*, a kind of twilled fustian, like moleskin.

3. *attrib.* (in sense 1 or 2).

1798 *Hull Advertiser* 13 Oct. 2/2 Swansdown stocks. **1803** *Censor* 1 Apr. 46 A common swandown waistcoat. **1858** SIMMONDS *Dict. Trade* s.v. *Swan*, Their skins enter into commerce for swans'-down trimmings. **1867** URE *Dict. Arts* etc. III. 858, 500,000 puffs, made annually from about 7000 swans' down skins, imported into Britain. **1877** MAR. M. GRANT *Sun-maid* vii, He wrapped her in her swansdown mantle. **1885** *Encycl. Brit.* XVIII. 829/2 It is filtered through chamois leather or swansdown calico.

fig. **1880** MRS. LYNN LINTON *Rebel of Family* ii. (1901) 21 Her soft swan's-down kind of nature soothed him.

Swansea ('swɒnzi). The name of a city in South Wales, used *attrib.* and *absol.* to designate pottery and porcelain made at the Cambrian Pottery there from 1764 to 1870.

1863 W. CHAFFERS *Marks & Monograms on Pott. & Porc.* 131 *Swansea.* This china was introduced about 1800, and was remarkable for the beautiful delineation of birds, butterflies, and shells. **1879** M. E. BRADDON *Vixen* II. ii. 19 Old Worcester teacups..or flowered Swansea. *Ibid.* vii. 107 The Swansea tea-set. **1895** *Wales* Aug. 372/2 The best Swansea china is exquisitely beautiful. **1904** [see DUCK'S EGG d]. **1957** MANKOWITZ & HAGGAR *Encycl. Eng. Pott. & Porc.* 216/2 These [fakes], however, are mostly distinguishable from true Swansea as the style of decoration and often the forms and shapes are quite dissimilar. **1967** W. H. BOORE *Cry on Wind* x. 95 An old, long-settled place..has its own surprising treasures..a bardic chair..some priceless Swansea porcelain [etc.]. **1976** *Western Mail* (Cardiff) 27 Nov. 16/3 (Advt.), Collector wishes to purchase Swansea Pottery and Porcelain.

swan's feather: (*a*) see SWAN *sb.* 4b; (*b*) a corruption of *swine's feather* (see SWINE *sb.*).

swanskin ('swɒnskɪn). Also **swan's-skin.** [Cf. Sw. *svanskinn.*]

1. The skin of a swan (with the feathers on); *transf.* a soft or delicate skin.

1610 [see 3]. **1842** *Penny Cycl.* XXIII. 375/2 *Cygnus Buccinator*,..to which the bulk of the swan-skins imported by the Hudson's Bay Company belong. **1846** J. E. TAYLOR *Fairy Ring, Six Swans* 66 The swans flew to her,..their swans' skins fell off, and her brothers stood before her in their natural form.

2. A fine thick kind of flannel; also, a woollen blanketing used by printers and engravers as an elastic impression-surface.

1694 MOTTEUX *Rabelais* v. *Pantagr. Prognost.* x. 246 Furr'd Gowns, Swans-Skins, and other warm Cloths. **1706** PHILLIPS (ed. Kersey), *Swans-skin*, a sort of fine Flannel, so call'd on account of its extraordinary Whiteness. **1844** *Ladies' Hand-bk. Haberdashery* 31 Swanskin is..especially employed by the laundress, as a covering for her tables. **1863** *Alpine Jrnl.* Mar. 27 Very stout and dense scarlet blanketing (of the description known to the trade as swan-skin).

3. a. *attrib.* Made or consisting of swanskin. *swanskin flannel* = sense 2.

1610 B. JONSON *Alch.* III. iii, I' the swan-skin couerlid, and cambrick sheets. **1740** RICHARDSON *Pamela* (1824) I. xx. 32, I brought two flannel undercoats; not so good as my swanskin and fine linen ones. *c* **1790** IMISON *Sch. Arts* II. 49 Directions for laying the Mezzotinto Ground... Laying your plate with a piece of swanskin-flannel under it, upon your table. **1903** W. CHURCHILL *Crossing* I. vi, He wore jauntily a swanskin three-cornered hat.

b. *fig.* Soft and delicate, smooth like swanskin. (Only found in the work of E. Sitwell.)

1925 E. SITWELL *Troy Park* 38 Once, plumaged like the sea, his swanskin head Had wintry white quills. **1936** —— *Victoria of England* xvi. 197 Wild violets beneath their swan-skin leaves.

SWANU ('swɑːnuː). [Acronym f. the initial letters of *S*outh *W*est *A*frica(n) *N*ational *U*nion.] An African nationalist organization in Namibia. Cf. SWAPO.

1962 *Rep. U.N. Spec. Comm. S.W. Afr.* 14 Sept. 3 Mr. Kozonguizi explained that he represented the South West Africa Union (SWANU)... The aims of SWANU were to achieve independence for South West Africa. **1963** R. FIRST *South West Afr.* v. iv. 200 The following month the South West African National Union, known as the 'First S.W.A.N.U.', was established. **1970** J. WORONOFF *Organizing African Unity* iii. 265 Several nationalist groups were formed as of 1959. First was the South West African National Union (SWANU). **1973** *Black World* Oct. 35/2 Free the land FROLIZI. Swing in there SWANU.

'swan-ˌupping. Also corruptly SWAN-HOPPING, q.v. [See UPPING *vbl. sb.*] The action or practice of 'upping' or taking up swans and marking them with nicks on the beak in token of being owned by the crown or some corporation.

[**1570** in *Archaeologia* (1847) XXXII. 428 The Maister of the Swannes is to haue for euery white Swanne and gray vpping a penny.] **1810** J. T. SMITH *Bk. Rainy Day* (1861) 194 Swan-upping..has been changed..into Swan-hopping. **1885** *Pall Mall G.* 2 Feb. 1/2 The 'swan-uppings' on the Thames of the Vintners and Dyers.

So **'swan-ˌupper**, an official who takes up and marks swans.

1557–8 in W. H. Turner *Select. Rec. Oxford* (1880) 272 The charges goynge wᵗ the swane uppers iij dayes vj *s.* iiij *d.* **1913** *Standard* 25 July 13 The little company of swan-uppers which annually leaves Southwark.

'swan-white, *a. poet.* [Cf. MLG. *swanewit*, G. *schwanenweiss*, ON. *svanhvítr* (as a proper name).] As white as a swan; snow-white.

1393 LANGL. *P. Pl.* C. XXI. 215 Yf alle þe worlde were whit oþer swan-whit alle þynges. **1508** DUNBAR *Tua Mariit Wemen* 243 Swan-quhit of hewis. *a* **1618** SYLVESTER *Mem. Mortalitie* II. xlix, To note An old Sir Tame-ass..swan-white to dote On Venus' Dovelings. **1794** BURNS *O Mally's Meek* iii, Her yellow hair..Comes trinkling down her swan-white neck. **1823** JOANNA BAILLIE *Poems, Ship's Return* i, Thy swan-white sails exulting spread. *a* **1900** T. W. ROLLESTON *The Dead at Clonmacnois* v, Many a blue eye of Clan Colman the turf covers, Many a swan-white breast.

swanwort ('swɒnwɜːt). [f. SWAN *sb.* + WORT *sb.*] †**a.** (Only OE.) Some unidentified (? aquatic) plant. **b.** A book-name for the genus *Cycnoches*: = *swan-flower, swan-plant* (*a*): see SWAN *sb.* 4b, SWAN-NECK 3.

c **1000** *Sax. Leechd.* II. 74 Wiþ deadum swile, ȝenim swane wyrt. **1866** [see SWAN-NECK 3].

swanyeard, obs. form of SWANHERD.

swap, swop (swɒp), *sb.* Also 4–7 **swappe,** 5 **swape, (sqwappe, squappe),** 8 *s.w. dial.* **zwap, zwop,** 9 **swapp.** [f. next. The spelling *swap* for both is recommended.]

I. 1. An act of 'swapping' or striking; a stroke, blow; †*occas.* a kiss. *Obs.* exc. *dial.*

α. **13..** *E.E. Allit. P.* B. 222 Fendez ful blake Weued at þe fyrst swap as þe snaw þikke. *c* **1384** CHAUCER *H. Fame* II. 35 (Fairf.) With hys grym pawes stronge,..Me fleynge in a swappe [*Bodl. MS.* yn a swape, CAXTON at a swap] he hente. *c* **1400** *Anturs of Arth.* xlii. (Douce MS.) Withe a swap [*v.r.* sqwappe] of a swerde þat swaþel him swykes. *c* **1440** CAPGRAVE *Life St. Kath.* III. 313 The gate shal open lightly at a swap. *c* **1440** *York Myst.* xxxiii. 362 Swete may þis swayne for sweght of our swappes! **1530** PALSGR. 842/2 Swappe for Swappe, *coup pour coup.* **1545** ASCHAM *Toxoph.* (Arb.) 48 Halfe oure tyme..is at one swappe quite taken awaye. *a* **1553** UDALL *Royster D.* IV. iv. (Arb.) 66, I with my newe broome will sweepe hym one swappe. *a* **1566** R. EDWARDS *Damon & Pithias* (1571) Fiij b, If ich could not steale one swap at their lippes. *a* **1625** FLETCHER *Nice Valour* III. i, There's no new-fashioned swappe that ere came up yet But I've the first on 'em. **1654** GAYTON *Pleas. Notes* I. viii. 30 The Usher gives him a shrewd swap on the very end of the elbow. **1818** HOGG *Brownie of Bodsbeck* I. viii. 135 Whan a thing comes on ye that gate, that's a dadd... Then a paik, that's a swapp or a skelp like. **1822** —— *Perils of Man* xix. II. 243 Pell-mell, swap for swap, was a' that they countit on.

β. **1746** *Exmoor Scolding* (E.D.S.) 100 Gi' me a Zwop?—Ad! chell gi' tha a Wherret, or a Zlat in the Chups. **1863** BARNES *Dorset Gloss.*, *Swop*, a strong whop.

II. 2. a. An act, or the action, of 'swapping' or exchanging; (an) exchange. *slang* or *colloq.*

α. **1625** PURCHAS *Pilgrimes* I. IV. iv. §2. 418 They..will either beg them, or make a swap with you in priuate. **1711** N. BLUNDELL *Diary* (1895) 90, I proposed a Swap with Samw. Edw. between my Button and his Gray Galloway. **1785** BURNS *1st Ep. J. Lapraik* xviii, We'se..hae a swap o' rhymin-ware Wi' ane anither. **1798** T. MORTON *Speed the Plough* I. i. (1800) 7 Drabbit it, only to think of the zwaps and changes of this world! **1805** JAMES *Milit. Dict.* (ed. 2) s.v., A writership or a military appointment given for a seat in parliament may be called a swap. **1822** COBBETT *Rur. Rides* (1830) 117 *Lord Castlereagh..was accused of making a swap, as the horse-jockeys call it, of a writer-ship against a seat. **1888** 'R. BOLDREWOOD' *Robbery under Arms* viii, A big, brown, resolute, well-bred horse he had got in a swap because the man that had him was afraid of him.

β. **1682** T. FLATMAN *Heraclitus Ridens* No. 72. (1713) II. 191 They'd almost threaten to flee the Land, and put themselves under the Protection of the French King... And a fair swop, cry I. **1702** BAYNARD *Cold Baths* II. (1706) 172 It cur'd her Ague, but made a worse swop; for she was..seiz'd with Epileptick Fits. **1714** ADDISON *Spect.* No. 559 ¶6 These [two gentlemen] had made a foolish Swop between a Couple of thick bandy Legs, and two long Trapsticks that had no Calfs to them. **1851** MAYHEW *Lond. Labour* I. 370/1 The glass wares are so very rarely sold..'Swop, sir,' I was told repeatedly, 'they all goes in swop.' **1882** SALA *Amer. Revis.* (1885) 365 [Railway] tickets are..the object of..barter, 'swop' and 'trade' generally. **1884** *Manch. Exam.* 6 Dec. 5/5 It is probable that Mr. Master will find little to complain of in the swop he has effected.

†**b.** ? An allowance made in exchanging. *Obs.*

1595 *Compt Bk. D. Wedderburne* (S.H.S.) 31 Item xs. for the swap to be allowit in the Witsonday termes meill nixt.

c. *slang.* ***to get*** (or ***have***) ***the swap***: to be dismissed from employment. (Cf. SWAP *v.* 9a.)

1890 BARRÈRE & LELAND *Slang Dict.* s.v. *Swop.* **1905** WELLS *Kipps* I. v. §3 Every time I've had the swap I've never believed I should get another Crib.

3. *Finance.* In foreign exchange operations: an exchange of an amount of money at different rates (i.e. a 'spot' sale for a 'forward' purchase). More generally, an arrangement between the central banks of two countries for stand-by credit to facilitate the exchange of each other's currency. Chiefly *attrib.*

1963 *Economist* 14 Dec. 70/1 A permanent system of automatic swap-lines as opposed to the existing three-monthly swaps is favoured together with easier facilities for medium term credit. **1968** *Times* 9 Sept. 1/2 *Swap arrangements.* The 12 members of the Basle central bankers' club have made reciprocal arrangements to make short-term loans to each other in the event of any currency coming under severe pressure. **1970** SLOAN & ZURCHER *Dict. Econ.* (ed. 5) 425 Swap credits are used especially in periods of emergency when a particular country's currency..comes under pressure because speculators are selling it on the world markets. **1975** *Financial Times* 29 Oct. 7/1 A classic swap is a transaction in which a spot purchase of a given currency, is covered by a forward sale of the same amount. **1979** *Bank of England Q. Bull.* June 131 The Federal Reserve and the US Treasury again repaid some swap debt to other central banks.

4. Special combinations. **swap fund** *U.S. Stock Exchange*, a fund which investors enter by exchanging securities directly for shares in the fund, obtaining a diversified portfolio without selling stock, and thereby avoiding liability for capital gains tax on the sale of these securities; **swap meet** chiefly *U.S.*, a gathering at which enthusiasts discuss, exchange, or trade items of common interest; **swap shop**, an agency for putting people with articles to exchange or trade in touch with one another; also *fig.*

1966 *Economist* 23 July 380/1 The Revenue Service..will no longer permit investors to defer capital gains tax on the appreciation of stocks exchanged for shares of the special swap funds. **1973** *Daily Tel.* 25 Aug. 16/1 A market has been established in them [*sc.* bottles] and regular 'swop-meets' are arranged so that enthusiasts can buy and sell among themselves. **1976** *Billings* (Montana) *Gaz.* 11 July 3-B/1 The swap meet has become an annual event that attracts visitors from Canada and other states to exchange information about antique cars and parts, he said. **1976** *Milton Keynes Express* 18 June 27/6 (Advt.), Dishot Swop Shop. **1976** *Sunday Post* (Glasgow) 26 Dec., Just before half-time some fans not involved in the beer can 'swop-shop' took refuge on the park. **1977** *Skateboard Special* Sept. 2/1 If you want to take up our super Swap-Shop offer now's your chance. **1979** *Guardian* 5 July 4/4 Instead of handing down golden tablets..the Schools Council will become more of a swap shop for ideas.

swap, swop (swɒp), *v.* Forms: α. 4– **swap,** 4–7 **swappe,** (5 **squappe, swape**), 6–7 **swapp;** *pa. t.* 3–6 **swapte,** 4 **swappede,** (5 **sqwapputte**); *pa. t.* and *pple.* 4– **swapped, swapt;** *Sc.* and *north.* 4–5 **swappyt,** 4–6 **swappit,** 6 **swapit,** (**suapit**). β. 5–6 **swope,** 7– **swop;** *pa. t.* and *pple.* 7– **swopped, swopt.** [prob. of echoic origin, signifying a smart resounding blow (cf. SWAP *adv.*). So G. dial. *schwappe* resounding box on the ear, *schwappen* to make a clapping or splashing noise, to strike with a resounding blow.

The development of the sense of concluding a bargain from that of striking is paralleled in various uses of *strike*; cf. also L. *fœdus ferire.*]

I. † **1. a.** *trans.* To strike, hit, smite (*occas.* used of kissing). Also *fig. Obs.*

a **1400** *Leg. Rood* (1871) 142 A swerd swapped hire þorw þe brest. *c* **1400** *Destr. Troy* 1271 With a swinge of his sworde [he] swappit hym in þe fase. *c* **1400** *Anturs of Arth.* xl. (Douce MS.) He swapped [*v.r.* sqwapputte] him yne at þe swyre, with a swerde kene. *c* **1440** *York Myst.* xxx. 286 A sweuene þat swiftely hir swapped, Of one Jesu þe juste man. **1534** MORE *Comf. agst. Trib.* III. xxiv. Wks. 1256/2 They that lye in a plewrosy, thinke that euery time they cough, they fele a sharp sweorde swap them to the heart. **1557** PHAER *Æneid* VI. Rj b, Anon the giltie soules..Tisiphonee doth take, and scourging them she swappes with whippes. **1577–82** BRETON *Flourish upon Fancie* (Grosart) 6/2 To..swap ech slut vpon the lippes, that in the darke he meetes.

b. To strike or smite *off*, *in two*, etc.; to cut or chop off or asunder at one blow; to drive *out*, etc. by striking. *Obs.* exc. *arch.* Also †*to swap to* (*the*) *death*, *of live*, to kill at a blow.

c **1350** *Will. Palerne* 3609 To haue with his swerd swapped of his hed. **1375** BARBOUR *Bruce* XVII. 691 The gynour than gert bend in hy The gyne, and swappit out the stane. *c* **1386** CHAUCER *Sec. Nun's T.* 247 Who so wol nat sacrifise Swape [*v.rr.* swap, swappe] of his heed. *a* **1400–50** *Wars Alex.* 957 (Ashm. MS.) He swyngis out with a swerd & swappis him to dethe. *c* **1400** *Destr. Troy* 6699 With a swyng of his sword [he] swappit hym of lyue. *c* **1400** *Anturs of Arth.* xl. (Ireland MS.) Syxti maylis and moe, The squrd squappes [*Douce MS.* swapt] in toe. ? *a* **1500** *Chester Pl.* xiv. 389 The Devill Swapp [*MS. W.* **1592** swope] of my Swyre, if I do it without hyre. **1581** A. HALL *Iliad* x. 186 The king for thirtenth Diomede out life to death doth swap. **1582** STANYHURST *Æneis* III. (Arb.) 92 Feare thear vs enforced..Too swap of our cables. **1600** FAIRFAX *Tasso* XX. xxxiii, And then Alarcos head she swapt off cleene.

1888 DOUGHTY *Trav. Arabia Deserta* II. 17 Drawing his sword, he..swapt off at once the miserable man's head.

c. To cut or reap (corn or other crops) close to the ground with a 'swap-hook' (see 6). *dial.*

1853 W. D. COOPER *Sussex Gloss.* (ed. 2) *Swap*,..to cut wheat in a peculiar way, more like chopping than reaping. S. **1861** *Jrnl. R. Agric. Soc.* XXII. II. 378 Both crops were 'swapped', or cut close to the ground. **1903** *Sat. Rev.* 8 Aug. 168/2 It is time..to go swapping the laid piece down by Kixes Wood.

2. *intr.* To strike, smite, deal a blow or blows. Now *rare* or *Obs.*

? *a* **1400** *Morte Arth.* 1129 He..Swappez in with the swerde þat it þe swange brystedde. *Ibid.* 1795 He spede hym fulle ȝerne, Swappede owtte with a swerde. *c* **1400** *Destr. Troy* 5936 He swappit at hym swithe with a swerd felle. *c* **1400** *Song Roland* 747 He drawithe out his swerd, and swappithe hym about. *c* **1465** *Chevy Chase* xxxi. in Child *Ballads* (1889) III. 309/1 The swapte togethar tylle the both swat, With swordes that wear of fyn myllan. **1535** STEWART *Cron. Scot.* (Rolls) I. 206 Tha swapit ouir quhill all the swyir did swydder. **1819** W. TENNANT *Papistry Storm'd* (1827) 63 Wi' angry bill, and will theretill, They wapp't and swapp't, and flapp't and slapp't.

3. *trans.* To move (something) quickly or briskly, esp. so as to impinge upon something else; to fling, cast, throw (*down*, etc.) forcibly; to bang (a door) *to*; *refl.* to sit *down* with force, plump oneself *down*. *Obs.* exc. *dial.*

13.. *Sir Beues* (A.) 1899 Beues is swerd anon vp swapte. *c* **1374** CHAUCER *Troylus* IV. 245 His hed to þe wal, his body to þe grounde Ful ofte he swapte. **1375** BARBOUR *Bruce* x. 623 Ȝeit ves thar ane Of thame that swappit doun a stane. *c* **1425** WYNTOUN *Cron.* VIII. xiii. 2022 (Wemyss MS.) He swappit egirly þe blude Rycht in till William Wallace face. *c* **1440** *Gesta Rom.* i. 3 (Harl. MS.) He swapte his hed vndir þe watir. *c* **1590** GREENE *Fr. Bacon* i. 111 Sheele swap thee into hir plackerd. **1592** BABINGTON *Comf. Notes Gen.* xviii. 71 b, We swap vs downe in our places most vnreuerently. **1596** NASHE *Saffron Walden* P iv, He runs and swapps the doore too. **1642** *Life Hen. II* in *Harl. Misc.* (Malh.) V. 235 Because the legate was not to remove, and the archbishop would not remove, therefore he most unmannerly swopped him down on the Archbishop of Canterbury's lap. **1794** WOLCOT (P. Pindar) *Frogs & Jupiter* Wks. 1812 III. 259 Down he swopp'd A monstrous Piece of Wood. **1825** MACKENZIE *Hist. Northumbld.* I. 149 *note*, To *swap the door*..is as much as to say, shut it violently. **1846** W. E. FORSTER in Reid *Life* (1888) I. vi. 186 Only think of poor self swapped down in the midst of forty Quakeresses.

4. a. *intr.* To move with haste or violence, esp. so as to strike or impinge upon something; to fall *down* suddenly or with a 'flop'; to sink *into* a swoon; to come hastily or forcibly, fling oneself *into* a place, etc. Now *rare* or *Obs.*

The instance of *swapte* in the later text of Layamon 26775 (Beofs to him swapte [*earlier text* him biarnde] and mid harmes hine biclupte) is prob. an error for *swipte* (see SWIP), a frequent form in Layamon.

1375 BARBOUR *Bruce* XVII. 683 The stane smertly swappit out. *c* **1386** CHAUCER *Clerk's T.* 1099 Al sodeynly she swapte [*v.r.* swapped] adoun to grounde. *a* **1400** *Minor Poems Vernon MS.* (1901) 621 Heo swapte on swownyng. *c* **1470** HENRY *Wallace* VII. 349 As bestly folk [thai] tuk off thaim selff no keip..Through full gluttre in swarff swappyt lik swyn. **1530** LYNDESAY *Test. Papyngo* 184 Scho..flatlyngis fell, and swappit in to swoun. **1592** WYRLEY *Armorie*,

Capitall de Buz 113 With chilling fear, the Ladies swapped downe, In deadly sownd. **1600** SURFLET *Country Farm* I. xv. 93 The kite,.. which sometimes will not let to swap into the very broode-house to.. carrie away the chickens. *c* **1700** KENNETT *MS. Lansd. 1033, To swapp or swoop at*, catch hastily as a kite is said to swapp at chickens. **1728** VANBR. & CIB. *Prov. Husb.* v. iii, So in swops me, with my Hoop stuff'd up to my Forehead! **1770** FOOTE *Lame Lover* II. Wks. 1799 II. 79 There he swops with both his knees on the ground.

b. To flap or beat up and down: also with *it*.

c **1520** SKELTON *Magnyf.* 775 Thy slyppers they swap it, yet thou fotys it lyke a swanne. **1535** STEWART *Cron. Scot.* (Rolls) III. 561 Vpoun ane suey ay swappand vp and doun. **1884** 'MARK TWAIN' *Huck. Finn* viii, There was freckled places on the ground where the light sifted down through the leaves, and the freckled places swapped about a little, showing there was a little breeze up there.

c. *trans.* To pounce upon, seize.

a **1712** W. KING *Eagle & Robin* 137 They'll swop our chicken from the door. **1821** [see SWAPPING *ppl. a.* 1].

†**5.** *trans.* To drink *off* quickly, toss off; to eat *up*, devour. *Obs.*

1508 DUNBAR *Tua Mariit Wemen* 243 Thai swapit of the sueit wyne. **1582** STANYHURST *Æneis* I. (Arb.) 41 At a blow hee lustelye swapping, Thee wyne.. swild vp to the bottom. **1592** NASHE *Four Lett. Confut.* Ep. Ded., Wks. 1904 I. 258 That thou mightst swappe off a hartie draught to the success of this voiage. **1593** G. HARVEY *Pierce's Super.* Wks. (Grosart) II. 231 Thou hast swapped-downe a pounde of Butter at a peece of a Breakefast. **1609** HEALEY *Discov. New World* I. 1 Where that huge.. Birde called Rvc, snatcheth vp.. a whole Elephant at a stoope, and swappes him vp at a bit.

6. *Comb.*: **swap-hook** *dial.*, a kind of reaping-hook for cutting crops close to the ground (see 1 c); †**swap-tail** *a.*, that strikes with its tail.

1863 *Standard* 10 Sept. (Sussex provincialism), *Swap-hook. **1875** PARISH *Dict. Sussex Dial.*, *Swap*, to reap corn and beans. *Swap-hook*, the implement used for swapping. **1883** JEFFERIES *Life of Fields* (1884) 84 [In Sussex] They call their reaphooks swaphooks or swophooks. **1681** GREW *Musæum* I. II. iii. 46 The *Swaptail Lizard. *Uromastix vel Caudiverbera*.

II. †**7. a.** *absol.* or *intr.* app. To 'strike hands' in token of an agreement or bargain. *Obs. rare*⁻¹.

13.. *Gaw. & Gr. Knt.* 1108 Swete, swap we so, sware with trawþe.

†**b.** *trans.* To strike (a bargain). Also with *up*.

1590 LODGE *Rosalind* (1592) F ij, Aliena.. swapt a bargaine with his Landslord. **1592** GREENE *Black Bookes Messenger* Wks. (Grosart) XI. 17 Wee like two good Horse-corsers, made a choppe and change, and swapt vp a Rogish bargaine, and so he married my wife and I his. **1650** J. REYNOLDS *Flower of Fidelity* 147 They forth with swapt a bargain. **1692** [A. PITCAIRN] *Assembly* IV. i. (1766) 46, I must know what you can do, ere I swap a Bargain.

8. a. To give or dispose of in exchange *for* something else; to exchange (a thing) *with* another person. Also, to give (something) to (a person) by way of exchange; ***to swap horses in midstream***: see HORSE *sb.* 18. Chiefly, now only, *slang* or *colloq.*

Probably orig. a horsedealer's term: cf. 1592 in 7b.

α. **1594** LYLY *Mother Bombie* v. iii, Ile not swap my father for all this. **1600** —— *Love's Metam.* I. ii, Inconstancie is a vice, which I will not swap for all the vertues. **1646** J. HALL *Poems, To Mr. Hall on his.. Detractors*, Thy works purchase thee more Then they can swappe there Heritages for. **1679** *Lond. Gaz.* No. 1423/4 He swapt a sorrel Stonehorse near Ripon about 14 or 15 hands high. **1708** N. BLUNDELL *Diary* (1895) 61 He was about swaping his Running Hors with my Lord Mountg[arret]. **1798** ROOT *Amer. Law Rep.* I. 66 One Rose and Charles Knot.. proposed to swap shoe buckles. **1823** MOORE *Mem.* (1853) IV. 149 Find that the man with whom I wished to swap ponies requires five pounds with mine. **1825** J. NEAL *Bro. Jonathan* I. 154 He will 'swap' anything with you. **1830–2** CARLETON *Traits* (1843) I. 263, I offer up a *pater* and *ave* for you, and you again for me. This is called swapping or exchanging prayers. **1861** THACKERAY *Four Georges* i. (1876) 7 [He] swapped a battalion against a dancing-girl's diamond necklace. **1864** ABRAHAM LINCOLN in E. R. Jones *Lincoln*, etc. (1876) 59, I am reminded.. of a story of an old Dutch farmer, who remarked.. 'that it was not best to swap horses when crossing a stream.' **1888** EGGLESTON *Graysons* x. 109 Farmers frequented the town, to meet old friends and get the better of them in swapping horses. **1891** *Boston* (Mass.) *Jrnl.* 12 Sept. 5/1 As they sat in the tavern, swapping stories. **1934** D. HAMMETT *Thin Man* iii. 14 Right now I'd swap you all the interviews with Mayor-elect O'Brien ever printed.. for a slug of whis——. **1940** W. FAULKNER *Hamlet* I. ii. 38 The team Stamper had swapped him stopped now with their heads down. **1948** —— *Intruder in Dust* (1949) ix. 192, I swapped Crawford Gowrie a German pistol.

β. **1624** QUARLES *Job* i, There dwelt a man brought from his linniage That for his belly swopt his heritage. *a* **1658** CLEVELAND *Poems, To T.C.* 45 For to make Mummie of her Grease, Or swop her to the Paper Mill. **1660** *Okie's Lament.* 38 My Horses swopt for light Nags. **1764** H. WALPOLE *Let. to Mann* 27 July, I believe my Lady Temple would.. be heartily glad to swop situations with you. **1800** MAR. EDGEWORTH *Castle Rackrent* Gloss. p. xxxviii, He makes me an offer to swop his mare that he couldn't sell at the fair of Gurtishannon. **1824** SCOTT *St. Ronan's* xviii, The new-fashioned finery which she swopt her character for. **1860** O. W. HOLMES *Elsie V.* vii. (1891) 96, I wish our little man and him would swop pulpits. **1882** MISS BRADDON *Mt. Royal* II. iv. 66 He bought and sold and swopped horses. **1890** YOUNGHUSBAND *Polo in India* iii. 42 Jones's Rs. 500 pony had been swopped for a worthless mare.

b. with advs. *away*, *off*.

1589 R. HARVEY *Pl. Perc.* 1 He.. swapt away his siluer for Copper retaile. **1683** TRYON *Way to Health* 500 They swap us away for a little Money to the Butcher. **1708** *Lond. Gaz.* No. 4404/3 He rode a stout black Mare the Day before taken, which he swop'd away. **1841** J. T. HEWLETT *Parish Clerk* I. 204 Two cover-hacks.. were exchanged, or rather, in stable phrase, swapped away. **1862** LOWELL *Biglow P.* Ser. II. iii. 140 Swappin' silver off for lead ain't the sure way to win. **1866** WHITTIER *Summer with Dr. Singletary* vi, I've noticed that your college chaps swop away their common sense for their larning. **1907** KATE D. WIGGIN *New Chron. Rebecca* viii. 230 He breaks all the young colts and trains them, and swaps off the poor ones.

c. *absol.* To exchange, make an exchange. Also with indirect obj., to make an exchange of some specified item with (someone). *colloq.*

1778 MISS BURNEY *Evelina* lxxxiii, Doff your coat and waistcoat, and swop with Monsieur Grinagain here. **1809** KENDALL *Trav.* III. lxix 37 To buy, to sell, to exchange, or, as they term it, to swap, are the pursuits in which they wish to be constantly engaged. **1857** HUGHES *Tom Brown* I. ix, I know something of him at home, and should like to excuse him—will you swop? **1885** J. K. JEROME *On the Stage* 153 If any gentleman has more friends of that kind than he wants, and would care to have a few of the opposite stamp, I am quite ready to swop with him. **1976** *Evening Chron.* (Newcastle) 26 Nov., As Coun. Collins says this council work will suit a pensioner, if he will answer this letter and tell me how many council meetings he has in a week, I will swap him.

9. *transf.* in various slang uses. **a.** To dismiss or be dismissed from employment. **b.** To cheat, take in. **c.** To change one's clothes.

1862 *Macm. Mag.* Nov. 34 The assistant [in a linen-draper's].. 'swops' or is 'swopped', or gets or gives 'the sack'. **1880** J. C. HARRIS *Uncle Remus* iv, Den Brer Fox know dat he bin swop off mighty bad. **1904** SLADEN *Playing the Game* II. xiv, My man can bring my dress things later, if you'll give me a room to swop in. **1905** WELLS *Kipps* I. v. *heading*, 'Swapped!' [= dismissed].

swap, swop, *adv.* (*int.*) Now *dial.* (see Eng. Dial. Dict.) [The stem of SWAP *v.* Cf. G. *schwapp(s)*, LG. *swaps* int.] At a blow; with sudden violence; suddenly and forcibly.

1672 VILLIERS (Dk. Buckhm.) *Rehearsal* II. iii. (Arb.) 57 His spirits exhale with the heat of his passion, and all that, and swop falls asleep. **1687** MONTAGUE & PRIOR *Hind & P. Transv.* 20 She's in the right on't; but mind now, she comes upon her swop! **1702** *Mouse grown a Rat* 4, I came upon him swop with Abundance of Confidence. **1728** VANBR. & CIB. *Prov. Husb.* I. ii, And straight upo' that, swop comes somewhat across my forehead. *a* **1818** M. G. LEWIS *Jrnl. W. Ind.* (1834) 297 The waves.. hovering for a while over the ship, and then coming down upon us swop.

swape (sweɪp). *dial.* Also 5 swaype, 6 swaipe, 7 swap (?). [orig. f. ON *sveip-*, denoting sweeping or circle-wise motion, repr. by *sveipa* to sweep, wrap, swaddle, swoop (see SWOPE *v.*), *sveipr* fold of garment, in comb. *ǫldusveipr* 'wave-sweeper', oar. In later usage influenced by, or varying locally with, SWEEP *sb.*]

I. †**1.** Applied to various contrivances of the form of a lever: see quots. *Obs.*

1492–3 *Rec. St. Mary at Hill* 186 The swaype of þe cherch dore. **1666** in *Archæol. Æliana* XVII. 133 For swapes for yᵉ bells 1s. **1793** SMEATON *Edystone L.* §333 *note*, A Swape (a north country term for a Lever, when fixed upon a centre, and acted upon by the hand).

2. A large oar, esp. one used for steering a barge: = SWEEP *sb.* 28.

1592 *Wills & Inv. N.C.* (Surtees 1860) 252 Half a kurvell lighter, with hir furnytter, that is, j ore and a swaipe [etc.]. **1789** BRAND *Hist. Newcastle* I. 261 *note*, [The keelmen] call the great oar, used as a kind of rudder at the stern of this vessel, the swape. **1864** SMILES *G. & R. Stephenson* II. i. (1868) 67 The vessel being guided by the aid of the 'swape,' or great oar.

3. A long pole supported on a fulcrum and carrying a bucket for raising water; also, a pump-handle: = SWEEP *sb.* 24. Also in comb., as ***swape-well*** (for other combs. see Eng. Dial. Dict.).

1773 *Phil. Trans.* LXIII. 229 A pump.. whose handle (or swape, as it is called hereabout [*sc.* Ripley, Yorks.]) is all of iron, very thick and long. **1890** *N. & Q.* 7th Ser. X. 240/1 Dwellers in the Eastern Counties may be credited with knowing what a swape-well is.. A swape-well is a well from which the water is raised by a loaded lever. **1908** [MISS FOWLER] *Betw. Trent & Ancholme* 369, I remember the two Roxby 'Swape-wells'.. the woman pulling down the swape by the chain.

4. A sconce for a light.

1867 SMYTH *Sailor's Word-bk.* **1875** KNIGHT *Dict. Mech.*

5. (See quot.)

1881 RAYMOND *Mining Gloss.*, *Swape*, an implement for shaping the edge of a boring-bit.

II. †**6.** The crop of hay taken up from a meadow: = SWEEP *sb.* 13.

1613 MARKHAM *Eng. Husbandman* II. II. vii. (1635) 85 The swap, and first crop is all the maine profit you can challenge your owne. **1622** tr. *Indenture an. 1456* in *Gentl. Mag.* May (1863) 629 It is agreed the Prior of malton and Co'uent.. shall haue swape of Certen medowes.

SWAPO ('swɑːpəʊ). Also **Swapo**. [Acronym f. the initial letters of *South West Africa(n) People's Organization*.] An African nationalist organization in Namibia. Cf. SWANU.

1962 A. K. LOWENSTEIN *Brutal Mandate* vi. 117 SWAPO grew out of the Ovamboland People's Organization. **1970** C. P. POTHOLM *Four African Pol. Systems* iv. 100 In South West Africa, the South West Africa People's Organization (SWAPO) likewise undertook a modest policy of selective sabotage. **1973** *Times* 25 Aug. 5/1 The Swapo youth wing's statement.. says that its protests at 'Boer' injustices in Namibia have been met with imprisonment, torture, brutality and other forms of oppression. **1976** *Plain Truth* Dec. 6/2 The South West Africa People's Organization (SWAPO), despite its terrorist activities and opposition to the conference, has been invited to be the proposed new government's political opposition.

swapper, swopper ('swɒpə(r)). [f. SWAP *v.* + -ER¹.]

1. Something very big; a 'whopper'; *spec.* a 'thumping' lie. *slang* or *dial.*

c **1700** KENNETT *MS. Lansd. 1033*, *Swapper*, a great lie is called a swapper. **1715** M. DAVIES *Athen. Brit.* I. Pref. 36 After they have confess'd their swappers to the Jesuits or some of the Regulars. **1818** MAGINN in *Blackw. Mag.* IV. 321 I'm a swapper, as every one knows, In my pumps six feet three inches high.

2. One who 'swaps', exchanges, or barters. *slang* or *colloq.*

1680 *Reflect. on Late Libel* 28 The Author had.. been Lecturer there at this day, (for he is no Starter, nor Shifter, nor Swapper of Livings). ? *a* **1700** in S. de Vere *Americanisms* (1872) 308 The headlong fool who wants to be a swopper Of gold and silver coin for English copper. **1893** *Columbus* (Ohio) *Dispatch* 14 Nov., In this case a man casting other than a straight ticket may be called a 'trader' or 'swapper.'

†**swappes.** *Obs. rare*⁻¹. [Cf. SWAB *sb.*¹ 2 b.] A term of reproach or contempt.

1626 BRETON *Pasquil's Madcappe* xix, This swappes, that neuer bloodied sword.

swapping, swopping ('swɒpɪŋ), *vbl. sb.* [f. SWAP *v.* + -ING¹.] The action of the verb SWAP.

†**1.** Striking, smiting; smiting or cutting off. *Obs.*

c **1400** *Destr. Troy* 1889 With swappyng of swerdys. *Ibid.* 5785 Swordis, with swapping, swaruyt on helmes. **1515** *Scottish Field* 465 in *Chetham Soc. Misc.* (1856) II, There were swinging out of swordes, and swapping of heddes.

2. Exchanging of one thing for another; exchange, barter. *slang* or *colloq.*

1695 J. EDWARDS *Author. O. & N. Test.* III. 231 Swapping or bartering of one thing for another. **1695** *Whether Parlt. be not dissolved by Death of Princess of Orange* 21 The Blessings.. which we had gotten.. by swopping of Kings. *a* **1739** JARVIS *Quix.* III. vii. (1742) I. 110 The laws of chivalry.. do not extend to the swapping of one ass for another. **1825** J. NEAL *Bro. Jonathan* I. 23 After having grown old in the ways of the world.. hypocrisy, 'swapping', trading, and evil speaking. **1861** GEO. ELIOT *Silas M.* iii, Dunsey Cass, whose taste for swopping and betting might turn out to be a sowing of something worse than wild oats. **1900** W. R MOODY *Life D. L. Moody* ii. 31 'Swapping' is a Yankee weakness.

3. *Finance.* The action or process of making a swap (sense 3).

1957 *Times* 19 Dec. 15/1 There was rather more outright buying of Dominion and Colonial stocks.., as well as a fair amount of swapping among Crown Colony loans. **1971** *Guardian* 8 Sept. 1/8 Of this inflow, £500 millions was used, indirectly, to support the dollar by 'swapping forward'—Britain actually claimed only a small proportion of the foreign currency due to her, and took the rest in foreign IOUs.

'swapping, swopping, *ppl. a.* Also 5 schwoppinge. [f. as prec. + -ING².]

1. †Striking; †flapping; *dial.* swooping, pouncing.

c **1450** *Cov. Myst., Innoc.* (Shaks. Soc.) 182 With swappynge swerde now is he shorn The heed ryght fro the nekke! **1575** CHURCHYARD *Chippes* (1578) C iij, With swapping Besome in her hand. **1642** H. MORE *Song of Soul* II. i. I. xi, Fowls flie by, and with their swapping wings Beat the inconstant aire. **1821** CLARE *Vill. Minstr.* I. 18 Chick, and duck, and gosling gone astray; All falling prizes to the swopping kite.

2. Very big, 'thumping', 'whopping'. *slang* or *colloq.*

c **1440** WALSINGHAM in Hone *Year Bk.* (1832) 90 In delvinge he myghte.. find a schwoppinge mallarde imprisoned in the sinke or sewere. **1589** NASHE *Countercuffe* Wks. 1904 I. 61 Pasquill met him.. with.. a swapping Ale-dagger at his back. **1624** MIDDLETON *Game at Chess* IV. ii, Ay, marry, sir, here's swapping sins indeed! *c* **1662** in Wood *Life* (O.H.S.) III. 513 Hee was a swapping swapping mallard. *a* **1843** SOUTHEY *Comm.-pl. Bk.* IV. 425/1 A swopping mallard found which used to come and feed there. **1886** *Pall Mall G.* 28 Oct. 6/1 We have seven professors of the jargon called law, and all with swopping salaries.

†**swappit,** *a.* *Sc. Obs.* [Cf. SWAPPER 1, SWAPPING *ppl. adj.* 2.] ? Very big.

1508 DUNBAR *Flyting* 130 Sueir swappit swanky.

†**swap thak.** *Sc. Obs.* [f. SWAP *v.* in the Sc. sense of 'to gird' + THACK *sb.*] 'Thin boards of wood firmly fastened over a thatched roof, as a girding for the thatch' (Jam.).

1496 *Acc. Ld. High Treas. Scot.* I. 310 Item, to the sawaris, for swap thak sawing to the samyn hous,.. xxx s.

†**swar.** *Sc. Obs.* [Origin unknown. Cf. SWARL.] A snare.

c **1470** HENRY *Wallace* II. 169 He caucht is in the swar [*ed.* 1570 snair]. *Ibid.* VII. 211 Be he entrit, hys hed was in the swar [*ed.* 1570 snair].

swar, variant of SWARE *sb. Obs.*

Swaraj (swə'rɑːdʒ, swɑː-). *Indian Hist.* Also **swaraj**. [ad. Skr. *svarāj* self-ruling (*svarājya* own dominion), f. *sva* one's own + *rāj* to reign, rule.] Self-government (for India); the agitation in favour of this.

[**1845** *Encycl. Metrop.* XXI. 679/2 The Swa-ráj, or 'Own Sovereignty', secured to him all the territory possessed by Sivá-ji.] **1907** *Westm. Gaz.* 18 Dec. 1/3 The movement known as Swaraj. **1908** *Times* 27 Oct. 8/3 There is a good deal of talk going on in these days about 'swaraj', or the making of India a self-governing country. **1920** M. K. GANDHI *Non-Co-operation* 12 Aug. (1921) 2 Mr. Tilak lived for his country. The inspiration of his life was freedom for his country which he called Swaraj. **1945** R. HARGREAVES *Enemy at Gate* 182 It was a deadlock..which forced the sponsors of *Swaraj* to try and 'save face' by endeavouring to shift the whole matter on to a basis of pacifism and 'appeasement'. **1965** J. K. MITTAL in *University of Allahabad Studies: Law Section* 39 In 1927, the Swaraj Constitution, based on a declaration of rights, was framed to give momentum to the fight for *Swaraj* (i.e. Self-Government). **1977** C. ALLEN *Raj* x. 129/2 All Anglo-India knew that one day *swaraj* (home rule) must inevitably come.

Hence **Swa'rajist**, one who advocated self-rule for India; also *attrib.*

1908 *Westm. Gaz.* 24 June 5/1 The family lawyer.. introduced him to two men..who were ardent Swarajists. **1923** *Glasgow Herald* 12 Dec. 8 Failing unconditional assent, the Swarajist intention is to obstruct every official measure coming before the Assembly. **1953** EARL WINTERTON *Orders of Day* x. 133 The Swarajists were very active..in India.

swarbout: see SWORBOTE.

sward (swɔːd), *sb.* Forms: 1, 7–8 **sweard**, 4 **suerd**, 5 **swerde, swarde**, 5–6 **sworde**, 5–9 (now *dial.*) **swerd**, 6 **suard, swart**, 6–7 **swarde**, 6–8 *Sc.* **swaird**, 7 **swort**, 7–9 **sword**, 5– **sward**. See also SWAD *sb.*[1] *β.* 6 **soord**, 6–7 **soard**, 7 **sourd**, 7–9 (now *dial.*) **sord**. [OE. *sweard* ? m., corresp. to OFris. *swarde* f., skin of the head (NFris. *swârd, sûrd*, EFris. *swôed, swode*, WFris. *swaerd* rind of pork, surface of fenland), MLG. *swarde* f., thick hairy skin, esp. scalp of man, skin of pig, (LG. *swaarde*, also *grönswaarde* greensward), MDu. *swarde* f. (Du. †*swaerd*, †*zwaard*, mod. *zwoord* n., infl. by Fris. forms), MHG. *swarte* f., hairy skin, scalp, bacon rind, (G. *schwarte*), ON. *svörðr*, gen. *svarðar*, skin, esp. of the head, walrus hide, *svarð-* in comb., greensward, walrus hide, (Icel. *grassvörðr* greensward, MSw. *grönsvärdher* greensward, Sw. dial. *svärd*, Norw. *svord, svor* skin, greensward, also *grassvord, -svoor*, Da. *svær*, also *fleskesvær* bacon rind, *grønsvær*); f. Teut. stem *sward-, swarð-*: *swarþ-* (see SWARTH *sb.*[1]), the ultimate origin of which is unknown. The OE. word, if indeed it survived, was reinforced in ME. by the Scandinavian forms, and possibly from LG.]

1. The skin of the body; *esp.* (now *dial.*) the rind of pork or bacon. † ***head sward***: the scalp.

c **725** *Corpus Gloss.* (Hessels) V 222 *Vistula*, suᵹesweard. *c* **1050** *Voc.* in Wr.-Wülcker 265/9 *Cutis*, sweard. **13..** *K. Alis.* 5950 Caluȝ was his heuede swerd. *c* **1375** *Sc. Leg. Saints* xlv. (*Christina*) 227 þat luge..gert tak hyr in teyne, & schawe hir heid to þe suerd. *c* **1430** *Two Cookery-bks.* 6 Sethe..porke þer-ynne, an pulle of þe swerde, an pyke owt þe bonys. *c* **1440** *Promp. Parv.* 482/1 Swarde, or sworde of flesche, *coriana*. **1607** *Lingua* II. i. Civ, If they would.. brandish no swords but swerds of Bacon. **1610** MARKHAM *Masterp.* II. cii. 385 Annoynt the cronet of the hoofe with the fat swarde of bacon. **1663** COWLEY *Ess. Verse & Pr., Country Mouse* 19 And for a *Haut goust* there was mixt with these The swerd of Bacon, and the coat of Cheese. **1747–96** MRS. GLASSE *Cookery* v. 85 To dress a ham à la braise,..take off the swerd. **1829** *Glover's Hist. Derby* I. 133 *note*, She [*sc.* a sow] proved when fat, good bacon, juicy and tender; the rind or sword was remarkably thin.

β. **1598** BP. HALL *Sat.* IV. ii. 36 Reez'd bacon soords shall feast his familie. **1598** FLORIO, *Cotenna*..the soard [*ed.* **1611** sord] of bakon.

2. † **a.** Usually with defining phr. *of the earth*, etc.: The surface or upper layer of ground usually covered with herbage. *Obs.*

c **1440** *Pallad. on Husb.* I. 58 Se not the swerd al nakid, white, vnclene. *c* **1440** *Promp. Parv.* 506 Turfe of flagge, swarde of þe erþe (*S.* turfe, flag, or sward of erþ), *cespes, terricidium*. **1473** *Rental Bk. Cupar-Angus* (1879) I. 171 They sal neuer cast [= dig] bot onder a fourhed, leuand a pair of the mos in the ground and fylland behynd tham with the sward of the mos. *a* **1552** LELAND *Itin.* (1712) VIII. 119 Ovar growen in the Swart with fine Grase. **1577** HARRISON *England* II. xvi. in *Holinshed* I. 91 b/2 Great plentye of water ..betweene the new loose swart and the olde hard earth,.. being drawne awaie. **1601** HOLLAND *Pliny* XVI. xxxi. I. 477 The roots of the Apple-tree, Olive, and Cypresse, lie very ebbe, and creepe hard under the sourd of the ground. **1626** A. SPEED *Adam out of E.* xvi. (1659) 138 Some will burn to Ashes, Roots, and Stubble, the sword and swarth of the Ground.

b. Qualified by *green, grassy, grass, of grass*, etc.: The surface of soil covered with grass or other herbage; turf, GREENSWARD.

1513 DOUGLAS *Æneis* VI. iii. 65 A pair of dowis..on the greyn sward thair place tuke law. **1610** HOLLAND *Camden's Brit.* (1637) 336 A pretty hillocke to be seene apparelled in a fresh suit of green sord. **1667** MILTON *P.L.* XI. 433 Ith' midst an Altar as the Land-mark stood Rustic, of grassie sord. **1725** RAMSAY *Gentle Sheph.* IV. ii. Prol., The green swaird grows damp with falling dew. **1741** *Compl. Fam.-Piece* III. 417 If the Turf hath a good Sward of Grass upon it. **1846** MCCULLOCH *Acc. Brit. Empire* (1854) I. 9 The western mountains..are mostly covered with a fine green sward. **1866** LIVINGSTONE *Last Jrnls.* (1873) I. xii. 326 The grassy sward. **1881** 'RITA' *My Lady Coquette* iv, The grass sward..slopes invitingly before her.

c. (*a*) Without qualification: = b.

1508 DUNBAR *Tua Mariit Wemen* 520 The sueit sawour of the sward, and singing of foulis. **1512** *Reg. Mag. Sig. Scot.* 797/2 Una cum acra de le suard vel medow pro pastura animalium. **1530** PALSGR. 284/1 Turfe flagge sworde, *tourbe*. **1649** BLITHE *Eng. Improv.* 34 So cut the Turfe, that the Soard may have all the Winters frost to wroxe, and moulder it. **1660** SHARROCK *Vegetables* 90 Plant them thereupon with the Soard downward. **1747** E. POSTON *Pratler* I. 85 The Sord which I pared off the Earth, commonly called Turf. **1785** BURNS *Addr. Deil* xv, The fragrant, flow'ry swaird. **1794** VANCOUVER *Agric. Cambridge* 177 The toughness of the fen swerd. **1832** TENNYSON *Œnone* 3 There is a dale in Ida,..beautiful With emerald slopes of sunny sward. **1834** *Brit. Husb.* I. 80 The grass of lawns, mown solely to keep the sward in order. **1837** LYTTON *E. Maltrav.* I. ix, The moon-light slept soft upon the sward. **1879** JEFFERIES *Wild Life in S. Co.* 36 It has become the fashion..to break up the sward of the downs.

(*b*) A growth of grass; a stretch of greensward.

1733 TULL *Horse-hoeing Husb.* xx. 289 The Grass from the Edges will spread and form a new Turf (or Swerd) on the other Side. **1816** J. SMITH *Panorama Sci. & Art* II. 619 To make a close thick sward. **1843** LYTTON *Last Bar.* I. i, A considerable plot toward the centre presented a level sward. **1881** DARWIN *Veg. Mould* 10 Wherever a path crosses a heath its surface becomes covered with a fine short sward.

† **3.** *transf.* The surface (of water). *nonce-use.*

1606 S. GARDINER *Bk. Angling* 22 Such as plodde wholy in the mudde and myre of the worlde, will neuer rise vp to the sword of the water.

4. *attrib.* and *Comb.*, (in sense 2), as ***sward ground, land***; ***sward-crested, -like*** adjs.; **sward-cut** *v.*, *trans.* to cut (land) with a sward-cutter; **sward-cutter**, an implement for cutting a tough sward in preparation for ploughing; **sward-earth**, † (*a*) *Sc.* grass-land; (*b*) turf.

1854 H. MILLER *Sch. & Schm.* xxv. (1858) 558 The *sward-crested trap-rock. **1797** *Encycl. Brit.* (ed. 3) I. 276/1 The land may lie several months in winter after being *sward-cut. **1786** R. SANDILANDS (*title*) A description of the patent instrument called a *sward-cutter. **1797** *Encycl. Brit.* (ed. 3) I. 276/1 One sward-cutter will cut as much in one day as six ploughs will plough. **1858** SIMMONDS *Dict. Trade, Sward-cutter*, a machine for bringing old grass-lands into tillage. **1799** *View Agric. Lincoln.* 71 A *sward-dresser has been found very useful upon the meadows and pastures of Brothertoft. **1541** *Reg. Mag. Sig. Scot.* 565/1 Marresiam de Farneis et lie *swarde-yird ejusdem. **1634** *Ibid.* 19/2 Cum eorum terris tam arabilibus quam non arabilibus lie sward-eardis. **1852** WIGGINS *Embanking* 237 A tile drain on a sole filled part of the way, say 1 foot, over, with any loose material, and the sward earth over that. **1608** WILLET *Hexapla Exod.* 241 The greene grasse and *sword ground. **1744** W. ELLIS *Mod. Husbandman* Jan. i. 12 (*heading*) The Gloucestershire way of preparing and sowing *sward-Land with corn. **1805** R. W. DICKSON *Pract. Agric.* II. 604 That potatoes may be grown in a very beneficial manner on sward lands. **1905** *Westm. Gaz.* 31 July 4/1 Old sward land.

sward (swɔːd), *v.* Also 7 **sword, soard(e.** [f. SWARD *sb.*]

1. *intr.* To form a sward; to become covered with grassy turf.

1610 FOLKINGHAM *Feudigr.* I. xi. 35 A loose and light Sand swords slow. **1644** G. PLATTES in *Hartlib's Legacy* (1655) 236 [Ground] that..will not sward again, or gather a good head of grass, for the first, 3, 4, 5, 6, or 7 years, when laid down after Ploughing. **1649** BLITHE *Eng. Improv.* xv. 84 It hath one halfe yeare more to Soard in. *a* **1735** EARL HADDINGTON *Forest Trees* (1765) 45 The ground, immediately after corn, is many years before it swards.

2. *trans.* To cover with a sward; chiefly *pass.* to be covered with grass or herbage.

1610 FOLKINGHAM *Feudigr.* IV. Concl. 87 The Soile is a sandy Clay of 18 Inches Crust close sworded. **1649** BLITHE *Eng. Improv.* 32 How to level Land, and the suddainest way to Soarde it. **1760** WASHINGTON *Diary* 7 Mar., Writ. 1834 II. 513 The ground being well swarded over, and very heavy ploughing. **1786** tr. *Beckford's Vathek* 23 A high mountain, whose sides were swarded with wild thyme and basil. **1841** *Penny Cycl.* XX. 33/1 Hedge-banks may be improved..by being swarded. **1888** STEVENSON *Black Arrow* 75 It was a pillared grove..open and smoothly swarded. *a* **1904** A. ADAMS *Log Cowboy* v. 56 The prairies were swarded with grass and flowers.

swarded ('swɔːdɪd), *ppl. a.* [f. SWARD *sb.* or *v.* + -ED.] Covered with a sward or grassy turf; turfed.

1513 DOUGLAS *Æneis* XII. Prol. 65 The swardit soyll enbrovd wyth selcouth hewis. **1669** WORLIDGE *Syst. Agric.* (1681) 231 To pare off the Turf of soarded-Land. **1788** HURDIS *Village Curate* (1797) 48 A green swarded wain-way. **1800** —— *Fav. Village* 131 The mellow ground Along the swarded vale. **1868** *Rep. U.S. Commissioner Agric.* (1869) 351 The..escape of rain-fall from the surface of cleared and swarded land. **1879** STEVENSON *Trav. Donkey* 173 Many.. chestnuts stood together, making an aisle upon a swarded terrace.

swarding ('swɔːdɪŋ), *vbl. sb.* Also 6 **swayrdynge**, 7 **swoording, soarding**, 8 **swerding, swording.** [f. SWARD *sb.* or *v.* + -ING[1].]

† **1.** ? The squaring of timber preparatory to sawing. *Obs.*

Cf. LG. *swaarde*, the first and last piece of a tree trunk sawn lengthwise (*Brem. Wbch.*).

c **1480** *Durham Acc. Rolls* (Surtees) 157 Carpentariis operantibus per iiij dies in lez Swardyng meremii apud Shynkley bankez. **1532–3** *Durham Househ. Bk.* (Surtees) 231 For fellyng of 19 treys, 6s. 4d. For toppynge and swayrdynge off te sayme, 19s.

2. The action of forming a sward; the process of covering, or becoming covered, with grassy turf.

1610 FOLKINGHAM *Feudigr.* II. i. 48 The soile is so apte to fast-matting and swoording. **1649** BLITHE *Eng. Improv.* vi. 35 The thinner is thy Corne,..the more Grasse will grow among, which will help thee more in the Soarding of it. **1707** MORTIMER *Husb.* (1721) I. 33 The Clays that are long in swerding. *a* **1722** LISLE *Husb.* (1757) 247 The broad-clover would, when it decayed, prevent the ground from swording to natural grass.

swardy ('swɔːdɪ), *a.* [f. SWARD *sb.* + -Y.] Covered with sward, swarded, turfy.

1639 T. DE GREY *Compl. Horsem.* 244 Soft moyst swardy ground. **1733** TULL *Horse-hoeing Husb.* xx. 292 Must we have Recourse to the Spade for breaking up our rich, strong, swerdy Land? **1857** G. H. KINGSLEY *Sport & Trav.* (1900) 448 Her swardy, heathery, broom-birch-and-gorse-fringed banks. **1899** J. MACTAGGART *Mackinnon & Bards* I. vi. 7 Late primroses and bright bluebells Bloom'd by them in the swardy dells.

† **sware**, *sb.* *Obs.* Also 4 **suar, suare, swar.** [Partly OE. **swaru*, in *andswaru* ANSWER *sb.*, *mánswaru* perjury (cf. MANSWEAR); partly a. ON. *svar* answer: f. root *swar-* (see SWEAR *v.*). Cf. next.]

1. Swearing; an oath.

c **1200** *Trin. Coll. Hom.* 163 Curs, and leasinges, and sware, and alle swikele speches. *c* **1250** *Hymn to God* 35 in *Trin. Coll. Hom.* App. 259 Mid wicke speche & false sware. *c* **1275** LAY. 10893 þo was wo Coel..þat he sahtnesse mid sware [*c* 1205 treoðe] hadde ifastned. *a* **1327** *Pol. Songs* (Camden) 247 Y charge ou by oure sware, That ȝe to Engelonde be trewe. *a* **1400** *Pauline Epistles* Gal. iii. 17 þis ..testament confermyd of god þurgh sware. *c* **1430** *Free-masonry* 257 Ny no fals sware sofre hem to make.

2. Answer, reply.

c **1200** ORMIN 2422 Whi ȝaff ȝho swillc anndswere onnȝæn?.. Nu wile I shæwenn ȝuw forrwhi ȝho ȝaff swillc sware onnȝæness. *a* **1400–50** *Wars Alex.* 1184 þe bischop.. Gase him doun..Swiftly to þe swiars & þam his sware ȝeldis.

3. Saying, speech, word.

a **1300** *Cursor M.* 17819 (Cott.) þai hailsed þaim wit suetli suar. *c* **1325** *Metr. Hom.* 17 Scho wiped his feet wit her hare, And kissed thaim wit suetli suare. *c* **1400** *Destr. Troy* 1200 Sum swalt in a swym with-outen sware more.

† **sware**, *v.* *Obs.* [a. ON. *svara*, f. root *swar-* (see SWEAR *v.*). Cf. prec.] *intr.* and *trans.* To answer.

c **1200** ORMIN 8938 Off þatt he wass full ȝæp & wis To swarenn & to fraȝȝnenn. **13..** *E.E. Allit. P.* B. 1415 Symbales & sonetez sware þe noyse. **13..** *Gaw. & Gr. Knt.* 2011 He called to his chamberlayn, þat cofly hym swared. *a* **1400–50** *Wars Alex.* 2069 And þai swiftly him sward & swyth þus him tellis.

sware, arch. pa. t. of SWEAR.

sware, obs. f. SQUARE, SWEER; var. SWIRE *Obs.*

swared: see SWARVE *v.*[1]

swarf (swarf), *sb.*[1] *Sc.* Forms: 5, 8 **swarff**, 6 **swerfe, suerf**, 6–9 **swerf**, 7 **swarfe**, 7– **swarf.** [Related to SWARF *v.*] A swoon, a fainting-fit; a state of faintness or insensibility.

c **1470** HENRY *Wallace* VII. 349 The Sotheron..Throuch full gluttre in swarff swappyt lik swyn. **1508** DUNBAR *Tua Mariit Wemen* 225 With that I seme for to swoune, thoghht I na swerf tak. *c* **1590** J. STEWART *Poems* (S.T.S.) II. 43/14 The scorching sychs,..Quhilk vith suerfs oursets his hardie hart. **1606** BIRNIE *Kirk-Buriall* (1833) 13 As if such superciliosity could sweeten the bitter swarfes of their sowre death. **1676** ROW *Contn. Blair's Autobiogr.* ix. (1848) 143 Mr. Blair did fall into a fit of fainting or a kind of swarf. **1742** J. MILL *Diary* (S.H.S.) 3, I..fell down suddenly by a swerf or stoppage of blood. **1871** W. ALEXANDER *Johnny Gibb* xlix, Aw heard that he was feerious far gane in a swarf the tither day. **1894** CROCKETT *Raiders* 208 She wad gang aff again in a swarf.

swarf (swɔːf, swɑːf), *sb.*[2] Also 6 **swarfe**, 9 **swarff**; see also SWAFF[2], SWARTH *sb.*[3], SOIFE. [repr. OE. *ᵹeswearf, ᵹesweorf, ᵹeswyrf* filings, or a. ON. *svarf* file-dust, related to *sverfa* to file: see SWERVE.] **a.** The wet or greasy grit abraded from a grindstone or axle; the filings or shavings of iron or steel. Hence, any fine waste produced by a machining operation, esp. when in the form of strips or ribbons.

1566 *Act 8 Eliz.* c. 11. §3 No person..shall die..black, any Cappe wth Barke or Swarfe, but only wth Copperas and Gall or wth Wood [*v.r.* Woade] and Madder. **1583** MASCALL tr. *Profitable Bk.* D ij, Put..halfe so muche of swarfe of the grindstone. **1640** in Entick *London* (1766) II. 174 Fileings of iron, called swarf. **1706** PHILLIPS (ed. Kersey), *Axungia*, the Grease or Swarf in the Axle-tree of a Wheel. **1858** SIMMONDS *Dict. Trade, Swarf*, iron filings. **1884** H. J. PALMER in *Eng. Illustr. Mag.* Aug. 666/1 The knife-grinder ..is saturated with the wet 'swarff' (powdered stone) which dyes him a deep saffron colour from head to toe. **1917** *Yorkshire Post* 3 Jan. 4/6 Rough copper, copper ore, and copper scrap and swarf in the possession of or due under existing contract to a manufacturer. **1953** *Times* 23 Oct. 5/3 There's swarf—chips of wood, metal, etc.—grinding around in your expensive machinery and shortening its life. **1970** P. DICKINSON *Seals* ii. 41 Down the inside rim of the second key-hole there was..a thin curl of swarf still attached to the main brass. **1973** J. G. TWEEDDALE *Materials Technol.* II. vi. 142 In more ductile materials chips may remain partially bonded to each other to form continuous severely-work-hardened ribbons sometimes called swarf.

Comb. **1909** *Spectator* 25 Dec. 1094/2 A swarf-stained son of 'the wheel'.

b. *spec.* The material cut out of a gramophone record as the groove is made.

1935 H. C. BRYSON *Gramophone Record* x. 275 When metal is recorded upon..it is often necessary to arrange for the removal of the swarf either by blowing..or by means of a small brush. **1947** *Jrnl. Inst. Electr. Engineers* XCIV. III. 288/2 By using a suction system to remove swarf continuously while recording, these troubles are avoided. **1977** *Times* 18 Apr. (Gramophone Suppl.) p. iv/7 For a long-playing record, this swarf, a strip narrower than a human hair, might be half a mile long.

Hence (*rarely*) as *v. trans.* with *up*, to make dirty with swarf; **swarfed** *ppl. a.*, dirtied with swarf, mucky. *colloq.*

1914 D. H. LAWRENCE *Widowing of Mrs. Holroyd* I. i. 4 A man in blue overalls, swarfed and greased. *Ibid.* 5 *Mrs. Holroyd*: ..Here, take hold, and help me fold it. *Blackmore*: I shall swarf it up.

†**swarf**, *sb.*³ *Obs.* Also 7 swarfe, swarff. [Variant of SWARTH *sb.*¹: see TH (6).]

1. = SWARD *sb.* 2.

1599 *Reg. Mag. Sig. Scot.* 284/1 Lie Elie-law et totum lie swarf ei adjacentem. **1603** *Ibid.* 524/2 Lie swarff, wrak et wair eisdem adjacentibus. **1664** O. HEYWOOD *Diaries* etc. (1883) III. 84 The whole field hath a little swarfe with grasse at the top.

2. *fig.* Surface. *nonce-use.*

a **1599** ROLLOCK *Lect. Passion* etc. xli. (1616) 408 His joye is light, and proceedes onely from the swarfe of the soule.

†**swarf**, *a. Obs.* Variant of SWARTH *a.* (Cf. prec.)

1619 HEATH *House of Correction* B 2 b, Because I'me black and swarfe. **1621** QUARLES *Argalus & P.* (1678) 96 Her face did shrowd A swarff Complexion. **1622** MABBE tr. *Aleman's Guzman d'Alf.* II. 200 A dainty fine shee-slaue, not swarfe and tawney..but faire and well-favour'd.

So †**swarfish** *a.* = SWARTHISH; †**swarfy (-fie, -ffie, -vy)** *a.* = SWARTHY *a.*¹

1602 *Salmasis & Hermaphroditus* D 2 b, While the black night with her pitchie hand Tooke just possession of the swarfie land. **1643** BAKER *Chron., Rich. III.* 137 His face little and round, his complexion swarfie. **1671** BLAGRAVE *Astrol. Physic* 77 Complexion muddy or swarfish. **1688** HOLME *Armoury* I. 13/2 Swart, Swarvy or Tawny-moor colour.

swarf (swarf), *v. Sc.* and *north. dial.* Also 6 swarth, 7 swerf, 7, 9 swarve, 9 swerve, swairf, swaif, etc. (see *Eng. Dial. Dict.*). [? a. ON. *svarfa* to upset (Norw. *svarva* to agitate or be agitated, *lit.* and *fig.*), with specialized development of meaning. See SWERVE *v.*]

1. *intr.* To faint, swoon.

1513 DOUGLAS *Æneis* XI. xv. 116 All paill and bludles swarthis [*v.r.* swarfis] scho rycht thair. *c* **1614** MURE *Dido & Æneas* II. 760 He..stood vnmov'd, whill I for greiff did swarve. **1637–50** ROW *Hist. Kirk* (Wodrow Soc.) 324 No sooner did he heare a ham spoken of but he swarfed. **1660** A. HAY *Diary* (S.H.S.) 234 After sermons my wiffe swerfed in the kirk. **1790** BURNS *Battle of Sheriffmuir* iv, Mony a huntit, poor red-coat, For fear amaist did swarf. **1816** SCOTT *Antiq.* xxvii, He was like a man awa frae himsell..and I thought he wad hae swarv't a' thegither. *a* **1837** R. NICOLL *Poems* (1843) 143 The bairnies crowd round him his stories to hear Whill maistly the wee things are swarfin' in fear. **1892** LUMSDEN *Sheep-head & Trotters* 32 Old Magge..drew near And swarf'd outright wi' gladsome fright.

2. *trans.* To cause to faint; to stupefy.

1813 PICKEN *Poems* I. 120 A sight had nearhaun swarf'd the callan. **1824** MACTAGGART *Gallovid. Encycl.* s.v. *Luscan*, The scene..swarf'd him so, that he could not utter a word.

swarf: see SWERVE.

swarfish, swarfy: see SWARF *a.*

†**swarf-money, -penny.** *Obs. local.* [perh. a corruption of **warth-money*, *-penny* = **ward-money*, WARD-PENNY; cf. WROTH SILVER.] A due paid in commutation of the service of CASTLE-GUARD, -WARD.

? **16..** in Manley *Cowell's Interpr.* (1672) s.v., The Swarff-money is one peny half-peny, it must be paid before the rising of the Sun [etc.]. **1730** THOMAS *Dugdale's Warwickshire* I. 4/2 A certain rent due unto the Lord of this hundred [*sc.* Knightlow], called *Wroth* money, or *Warth* money' or *Swarff* peny, probably the same with *Ward* penny.

†**swarl**, *v. Obs. rare*⁻⁰. [Origin unknown. Cf. SNARL *v.*¹ and SWAR.] *trans.* To ensnare.

c **1460** *Promp. Parv.* (Winch.), Marlyn, or swarlyn, *illaqueo. Ibid.*, Ruffelone, or swarlyn, *illaqueo.*

swarm (swɔːm), *sb.* Forms: 1 suearm, swearm, swerm, 4–7 swarme, 6 swerm, 4– swarm. [OE. *swearm*, = Fris., MLG. *swarm*, OHG. *suar(a)m* (MHG. *swarem, swarm*, G. *schwarm*) swarm of bees or insects, ON. *svarmr* tumult (Norw. dial. *svarm*):—OTeut. **swarmaz*.

The root is usually identified with that of Skr. *svárati* sounds, resounds, *svará, svára* sound, voice, and connected further with *sur-* in L. *susurrus* hum, MLG. *surren* to hum, MHG. *surm* humming, Lith. *surmà* pipe, etc. But the etymological meaning may be that of agitated, confused, or deflected movement, in which case SWARM and SWERVE might arise from parallel formations on the same base; cf. the parallelism of SWARM *v.*² and SWARVE *v.*²; Norw. dial. *svarma* to be giddy, stagger, dream, and *svarva* to turn, go in a circle, stagger, be agitated (see SWARF *v.*); Icel. *svarfla* and *svarmla* 'praecipitanter contrectare, huc illuc raptare'; also the meanings of G. *schwärmen* to swarm, rove, riot, fall into reverie, rave.

The existence of a mutated form in OE. (early WS. **swierm*) cannot be inferred with certainty from the late instance of *swerm* (Napier *OE. Glosses* 156/21), but such a form is found on the Continent in WFris. *swerm*, MLG., MDu. *swerm* (Du. *zwerm*), Da. *sværm*, Sw. *svärm*; cf. the vb.]

1. a. A body of bees which at a particular season leave the hive or main stock, gather in a compact mass or cluster, and fly off together in search of a new dwelling-place, under the guidance of a queen (or are transferred at once to a new hive).

c **725** *Corpus Gloss.* (Hessels) E 506 *Examen*, sueᵃrm. *a* **1100** *Aldhelm Gloss.* I. 3521 (Napier 101/2) *Examen, .i. multitudo apium*, swearm *ad aluearium*, to hyfen. **13..** *Cursor M.* 7113 (Gött.) A swarm [*Cott.* bike] of bes þar-in war bred. **13..** *E.E. Allit. P.* B. 223 Þikke þowsandez..Fellen fro þe fyrmament,..Hurled in-to helle-hole as þe hyue swarmez. *c* **1374** CHAUCER *Troylus* II. 193 For neuere yet so þikke a swarm of been Ne fleygh as Grekes gonne fro hym flen. *c* **1412** HOCCLEVE *De Reg. Princ.* 3380 Do no cruelte vnto þe swarm, But mekely hem gouerne. *c* **1440** *Pallad. on Husb.* I. 1039 His hyuys hauynge redy forto take His swarmys yonge. **1523** FITZHERB. *Husb.* § 122 If a swarme be caste late in the yere. **1603** DEKKER *Wonderfull Yeare* Wks. (Grosart) I. 143 He strucke so sweetely on the bottome of his Copper instrument, that he would emptie whole Hiues, and leade the swarmes after him only by the sound. **1677** PLOT *Oxfordsh.* 182 They can take swarms out of any stock that is able, and neglects to swarm, without any prejudice to the stock. **1774** GOLDSM. *Nat. Hist.* (1824) III. 281 When a hive sends out several swarms in the year, the first is always the best and the most numerous. **1817** KIRBY & SP. *Entomol.* xix. (1818) II. 166 A swarm seldom..takes place except when the sun shines and the air is calm. **1864** in *N. & Q.* 3rd. Ser. VI. 492/2 A swarm of bees in May Is worth a load of hay. A swarm of bees in June Is worth a silver spoon. A swarm of bees in July Is not worth a butterfly. **1870** YEATS *Nat. Hist. Comm.* 341 Each swarm contains not only the recently-hatched young bees, but also a portion of the old inhabitants.

b. *allusively* of persons who leave the original body and go forth to found a new colony or community.

1659 in *Burton's Diary* (1828) IV. 352 They are rather inferior than superior: but a swarm from you. You are the mother-hive. They are but a rib from your side. **1761** HUME *Hist. Eng. to Hen. VII* (1762) I. ii. 55 A new swarm of Danes came over this year [875]. **1827** G. HIGGINS *Celtic Druids* 78 It is very probable that a great swarm from the hive bearing the name of Scythians may have arrived in Germany. **1900** G. C. BRODRICK *Mem. & Impr.* 213 The learned theory of Mr. H. Rashdall, that as Oxford was (or must have been) a swarm from Paris, so Cambridge was (or must have been) a swarm from Oxford.

2. A very large or dense body or collection; a crowd, throng, multitude. (Often *contemptuous.*)

(*a*) of persons.

1423 JAS. I *Kingis Q.* clxv, And euer I sawe a new[e] swarm [of folk] abound. **1542** UDALL *Erasm. Apoph.* 291 There shall..come leapyng footh whole swarmes, of bothe horsemen and footemen. **1549** HOOPER *Funerall Oratyon* B vij, As black is contrarye vnto whyte: and the catholycke churche of Christ, to the smerm [*read* swerm] and multytude of Antichriste. **1553** BECON *Reliques of Rome* (1563) 87 b, A swarme of Bishops to the number..of CCCL. **1605** *1st Pt. Jeronimo* I. iii. 22 Farmers that crack barns With stuffing corne, yet starue the needy swarmes. *a* **1661** FULLER *Worthies* (1662) II. *Worc.* 183/1 England in swarms did into Holland throng. **1685** BAXTER *Paraphr. N.T.* 2 Cor. xi. 13 It's no wonder then if there be swarms of false Ministers, pretending to be the true Ministers of Christ. *a* **1715** BURNET *Own Time* III. (1724) I. 257 We saw what swarms of sects did rise up on our revolt from Rome. **1852** TENNYSON *Ode Wellington* 110 Beating from the wasted vines Back to France her banded swarms. **1878** BOSW. SMITH *Carthage* 310 The onset of a second son of the same dreaded chieftain, who would sweep down with new swarms of Gauls and Spaniards from the north.

(*b*) of insects or other small creatures, esp. flying or moving about; †rarely of large animals.

1560 *Bible* (Genev.) Exod. viii. 21, I wil send swarmes of flies bothe vpon thee, & vpon thy seruants. *a* **1569** KINGESMYLL *Man's Est.* xi. (1580) 73 There was fleshe enough to satisfie that swarme of adders, the Pharisees. **1600** J. PORY tr. *Leo's Africa* I. 39 Great swarmes of tigres, which are very hurtfull both to man and beast. *Ibid.* 51 Swarmes of a kinde of fowles of the bignes of duckes. **1684** *Contempl. St. Man* I. x. (1699) 116 Locusts..in great swarms shall disperse themselves over the Face of the whole Earth. **1780** COWPER *Progr. Err.* 431 The wriggling fry soon fill the creeks around, Pois'ning the waters where their swarms abound. **1842** TENNYSON *Locksley Hall* 10 Many a night I saw the Pleiads..Glitter like a swarm of fire-flies tangled in a silver braid. **1914** *Brit. Mus. Return* 197 A swarm of cockroaches..in a house at Chislehurst.

(*c*) of inanimate objects or abstract things. *spec.* (i) of asteroids or meteors (cf. *meteor-swarm* s.v. METEOR 6 d); (ii) of earthquakes; cf. also *dike-swarm* s.v. DIKE, DYKE *sb.*¹ 10.

1582 BENTLEY *Mon. Matrones* ii. 1 My sinnes..are so manie, that the infinit swarme of them [etc.]. **1596** SHAKS. *1 Hen. IV.* v. i. 55 This swarme of faire aduantages. **1684** BUNYAN *Pilgr.* II. 6 Upon this, came into her mind by swarms, all her unkind, unnatural, and ungodly Carriages to her dear Friend. **1698** FRYER *Acc. E. India & P.* 2 Such a swarm of Vessels of greater bulk. **1785** BURKE *Sp. Nabob of Arcot's Debts* Wks. 1842 I. 340 He is overpowered with a swarm of their demands. **1866** WHITTIER *Snow-bound* 33 A night made hoary with the swarm And whirl-dance of the blinding storm. **1890** *Nature* 20 Mar. 473/2 There are swarms of dust travelling thro' space. **1929** J. JEANS *Universe around Us* iv. 242 The asteroids occur as a single swarm. **1958** C. F. RICHTER *Elem. Seismol.* I. vi. 71 Certain localities are..visited by earthquake swarms, long series of large and small shocks with no one outstanding principal event. Such swarms are common in volcanic regions. **1959** *Listener* 30 July 172/2 The Trojans, whose mean distances from the Sun are the same as that of Jupiter, so that they lie far beyond the main swarm [of asteroids]. **1962** F. I. ORDWAY et al. *Basic Astronautics* iii. 105 Many swarms of meteors orbit the Sun and some periodically intersect the orbit of the Earth causing meteor showers. **1979** *Nature* 25 Oct. 661/1 Earthquake swarms, consisting of many earthquakes of nearly equal magnitude within a small area, often occur in areas of recent or current volcanic or tectonic activity. **1981** I. RIDPATH *Young Astronomer's Handbk.* 197/1 At various times of the year, the Earth crosses the orbits of certain comets, encountering whole swarms of meteors.

(*d*) *Biol.* A cluster of free-swimming cells or unicellular organisms moving in company.

1900 B. D. JACKSON *Gloss. Bot. Terms.*

(*e*) *Ecol.* = *hybrid swarm* s.v. HYBRID *a.* 3.

1926 *Nature* 30 Oct. 624/1 Where a specific name has been given to a smaller group within the swarm..we may adopt this name for the minor group. **1963** DAVIS & HEYWOOD *Princ. Angiosperm Taxon.* xiv. 483 Hybrids..may even become established and form large swarms many miles from either parent.

3. *attrib.* and *Comb.*: *swarm-formation*; **swarm-cell** *Biol.* = *swarm-spore* (*a*); **swarm-movement** *Biol.*, the movement of swarm-spores in 'swarming' (SWARM *v.*¹ 1 c); **swarm-spore** *Biol.* (cf. SWARM *v.*¹ 1 c), (*a*) a motile spore in certain Algæ, Fungi, and Protozoa, a zoospore; (*b*) the free-swimming embryo or gemmule of freshwater sponges.

1882 VINES tr. *Sachs's Bot.* 38 Much quicker movements ..occur in cells either before their growth, as in *swarm-cells, or when it is nearly completed. **1946** *Nature* 21 Sept. 423/1 The most important biological attribute of an outbreak centre is to provide conditions for survival and multiplication of locusts at those times when their range of dispersal is at a minimum, and also to provide conditions necessary for an increase in that range of dispersal (by *swarm-formation). **1953** J. S. HUXLEY *Evolution in Action* iii. 72 At least six species [of malaria-carrying mosquitoes] must be distinguished..some mating without swarm-formation, others requiring the stimulus of swarming. **1898** PORTER tr. *Strasburger's Bot.* I. i. 50 The swarm-spores of the Myxomycetes soon lose this characteristic *swarm-movement. **1859** J. R. GREENE *Man. Anim. Kingd., Protozoa* 42 Ciliated *swarm spores, similar to those which are found in Spongilla. **1874** A. W. BENNETT in *Pop. Sci. Rev.* XIII. 29 The production of spontaneously motile zoospores, or 'swarm-spores'. **1880** BESSEY *Botany* 36 The swarm-spores..are naked masses of freely moving protoplasm.

swarm (swɔːm), *v.*¹ Also 4–7 swarme, (5 swerme), 6 *Sc.* suarm, 7 *Sc.* swairme. [f. SWARM *sb.*: cf. MLG., MHG. *swarmen*; also, with mutation, OE. **swierman*, *swirman*, MLG., MDu. *swermen* (Du. *zwermen*), MHG. *swärmen* (G. *schwärmen*), Sw. *svärma*, Da. *sværme*.]

1. *intr.* Of bees: To gather in a compact cluster and leave the hive in a body to found a new colony: see SWARM *sb.* 1. Also with *off.*

c **1386** CHAUCER *Sompn. Prol.* 29 Right so as bees out swarmen [*Corpus & Camb. MSS.* swermen] from an hyue. **1573** TUSSER *Husb.* (1878) 114 Take heede to thy bees, that are readie to swarme. **1609** C. BUTLER *Fem. Mon.* v. (1623) I 3, Those that swarme before the blowing of knap-weed come in very good time. **1697** DRYDEN *Virg. Georg.* IV. 28 The youthful Prince, with loud allarm, Calls out the vent'rous Colony to swarm. **1818** SCOTT *Rob Roy* xvii, Ye see this is the second swarm, and whiles they will swarm off in the afternoon. The first swarm set off sune in the morning. **1875** *Encycl. Brit.* III. 502/1 It often happens that bees give every indication of an intention to swarm, and cluster idly outside the hive..for..weeks before they really emigrate.

b. *allusively*: cf. SWARM *sb.* 1 b.

1609 *Bible* (Douay) 2 Macc. i. 12 He made them swarme out of Persis. **1745** *Season. Adv. Protest.* 17 Protestants, who from a common Ancestor..have swarmed into many Stocks. **1821–30** LD. COCKBURN *Mem.* vii. (1874) 401 Jealousies and dissensions..induced the artists to swarm off, and begin the Academy. **1909** J. T. FOWLER in *Yorks. Archæol. Jrnl.* XX. 1 The number of monks increased so rapidly that they were soon obliged to swarm off, like bees, into new monasteries of the same Order.

c. *Biol.* Of certain spores or reproductive bodies: To escape from the parent organism in a swarm, with characteristic movement; to move or swim about in a swarm, as zoospores ('swarm-spores') do in the cell just before escaping, and in the water after escaping.

1864, 1867, 1875, 1882 [see SWARMING *ppl. a.* 4, *vbl. sb.* 2]. **1875** BENNETT & DYER tr. *Sachs's Bot.* 674 In Algæ of simple structure..the swarmspores are also formed in the night, but swarm only with access of daylight.

d. *trans.* in causative sense.

1827 J. F. COOPER *Prairie* iv, 'Swarm your own hive', returned the discontented bee-hunter.

2. *intr.* To come together in a swarm or dense crowd; to collect, assemble, or congregate thickly and confusedly; to crowd, throng; also, to go or move along in a crowd.

c **1386** CHAUCER *Sqr.'s T.* 181 Greet was the prees þat swarmeth to and fro To gauren on this hors that stondeth so. **1513** DOUGLAS *Æneis* VI. v. 23 Thiddir to the bray swarmit all the rout Of deid gaistis. **1515** BARCLAY *Egloges* II. (1570) Biv/2 If the dishe be pleasaunt,.. Ten handes at once swarme in the dishe. **1526** TINDALE *Acts* xxi. 30 All the cite was moved, and all the people swarmed togedder. **1551** ROBINSON tr. *More's Utopia* II. (1895) 179 All the people were swarmed furth into the stretes. **1604** DEKKER *Honest Wh.* Wks. 1873 II. 96 They swarme like Crickets to the creuice of a Brew-house. **1764** BURN *Poor Laws* 205 The religious houses sent abroad their friers mendicant, who swarmed about the kingdom. **1847** TENNYSON *Princess* Concl. 37 The crowd were swarming now, To take their leave, about the garden rails. **1867** LADY HERBERT *Cradle L.* iv. 126 The English were swarming out of this inn. **1875** JOWETT *Plato* IV. 233 The ideas swarming in men's minds.

3. To occur or exist in swarms or multitudes; to be densely crowded or congregated; to be very numerous, abound excessively. (Often in reproach or contempt, esp. when said of persons.)

1399 LANGL. *Rich. Redeles* II. 21 Signes þat swarmed so thikke þoru-oute his lond.. þat [etc.]. *a* **1548** HALL *Chron., Hen. V*, 54 Their bodies whiche swarmed euery day about thenglishe shippes. **1570** GOOGE *Pop. Kingd.* IV. (1880) 47 b, Puddings every wheare Do swarme. **1594** GREENE & LODGE *Looking Gl.* III. ii, When falshood swarmeth both in old and youth. **1634** BRERETON *Trav.* (Chetham Soc.) 13 Arminians, Brownists, and Anabaptists, and Manists, do lurk here and also swarm. *a* **1700** EVELYN *Diary* 19 Aug. 1641, The Sectaries that swarm'd in this Citty. **1721** BAILEY, To *Swarm*.. to abound, spoken of Vermin. **1742** YOUNG *Nt. Th.* IX. 765 Bright legions swarm unseen, and sing.. the glorious Architect. **1849** MACAULAY *Hist. Eng.* vii. II. 239 Roman Catholics already swarmed in every department of the public service. **1883** GILMOUR *Mongols* xv. 167 Native doctors swarm in Mongolia.

4. ***to swarm with***: to be crowded or thronged with; to contain swarms or great numbers of; to abound greatly in. Now only in material sense.

a **1548** HALL *Chron., Hen. V*, 46 The countree swarmed with men of warre. **1548** UDALL, etc. *Erasm. Par. Matt.* vii. 49 They that swarme with much greater vices. *a* **1592** GREENE *Jas. IV*, v. ii, Oh, what are subtile meanes to clime on high, When euery fall swarmes with exceeding shame? **1593** SHAKS. *Rich. II*, III. iv. 47 Her wholesome Herbes, Swarming with Caterpillers. **1667** MILTON *P.L.* VII. 400 Each Creek & Bay With Frie innumerable swarme. **1732** BERKELEY *Alciphr.* II. §13 All kinds of animals, with which the creation swarms. **1849** MACAULAY *Hist. Eng.* ix. II. 484 A market-place swarming with buyers and sellers. **1893** FORBES-MITCHELL *Remin. Gt. Mutiny* 269 The river swarmed with alligators.

†**b.** Similarly, ***to swarm full of***, ***to swarm in***.

1482 *Monk of Evesham* (Arb.) 40 The lenthe of that valey.. was so full of fowyls, as hyues swarmyn ful of bees. **1560** DAUS tr. *Sleidane's Comm.* 36 They shall not onely not take awaye theyr sectes, but increase and swarme in the same. **1561** T. NORTON *Calvin's Inst.* II. iii. (1634) 127 The soule.. while it swarmeth full of such diseases of vices. **1694** ATTERBURY *Serm., Prov. xiv. 6* (1726) I. 198 The Great Lords of the Earth, who swarm in all the Delights of Sense.

5. *trans.* To fill or beset as, or with, a swarm; to crowd densely, throng. Chiefly *pass.*

1555 EDEN *Decades* III. (Arb.) 188 The barbarians.. came swarmyng the bankes on bothe sydes the ryuer, to the number of syxe thousande men. **1559** *Mirr. Mag., Induct.* lxxv, The rout Gan all in heapes to swarme vs round about. *a* **1586** SIDNEY *Ps.* XXXII. vii, Who on God his trust invokes With mercies shall be swarmed. **1647** FANSHAWE *Æneid* IV. Poems 287 How did thy sences quayle Seeing the shoares so swarm'd. **1810** *Sporting Mag.* XXXV. 8 Your house is so swarmed with rats. **1823** MOORE *Mem.* (1853) IV. 121 Poor wretches, who marry upon the strength of this pied-à-terre, and swarm the little spot they occupy with children. **1847** *Zoologist* V. 1899 Brighton was swarmed with lady-birds on Saturday and Sunday. **1886** R. L. DE BEAUFORT *Lett. Geo. Sand* I. 130 You will also see the towers of Notre Dame; they are swarmed with swallows.

6. To breed or produce a swarm of. *rare*[−1].

1842 TENNYSON *Will Waterproof* xxv, Ere days, that deal in ana, swarm'd His [*sc.* the Poet's] literary leeches.

swarm (swɔːm), *v.*[2] [Of unascertained origin. Perh. orig. a sailor's word borrowed from the Continent, but no trace of the meaning has been discovered for phonetically corresponding words. Cf. the synonymous SWARVE *v.*[2] and etymol. remarks s.v. SWARM *sb.*

Connexion with *squirm* is out of the question, on historical and phonological grounds.]

1. *intr.* To climb *up* (†*upon*) a pole, tree, or the like, by clasping it with the arms and legs alternately.

15.. *Sir A. Barton* in *Surtees Misc.* (1890) 72 Then he swarmd up the maine mast tree [cf. SWARVE *v.*[2], quot. *a* 1650]. *c* **1550** [see SWARVE *v.*[2]]. **1607** DEKKER *Knt.'s Conjur.* B j b, The waues.. boylde vp to such heigth, as if they meant that all men should swarm in heauen, and shippes to sayle in the Skie. **1653** H. MORE *Antid. Ath.* III. iv. §3 Swarming upon Trees as nimbly as Cats. **1701** C. WOLLEY *Jrnl. New York* (1860) 41 We follow'd a Bear from Tree to Tree, upon which he could swarm like a Cat. **1804** *Naval Chron.* XI. 103 He swarms up to his seat. **1872** CALVERLEY *Fly Leaves, Changed* v, They fright me, when the beech is green, By swarming up its stem for eggs. **1893** SELOUS *Trav. S.E. Africa* 433, I.. could have swarmed up the branchless stem of the sapling.

b. *transf.* To climb a steep ascent or the like by clinging with the hands and knees, or in some way compared to this.

1681 COTTON *Wond. Peak* (ed. 4) 17 Having swarm'd sevenscore paces up,.. you find a kind of Floor. **1848** DICKENS *Dombey* ii, The smallest boy but one divining her intent, immediately began swarming upstairs after her—if that word of doubtful etymology be admissible—on his arms and legs. **1851** HELPS *Comp. Solit.* vi. (1874) 98 People who are swarming up a difficult ascent. **1890** W. CLARK RUSSELL *Ocean Trag.* II. xviii. 107 Onward she held her course, swarming steadily forward in long gliding curtseyings over each frothing surge.

2. *trans.* with the pole, etc. as obj.

1668 H. MORE *Div. Dial.* I. II. vi. 207 Endowing them with such.. Nimbleness in swarming of trees, as Apes.. have now. *a* **1769** JOHNSON in Boswell *Life* (1831) IV. 451 Why, I can swarm it now, [replied Dr Johnson,.. on which he ran to the tree, clung round the trunk, and ascended to the branches]. **1787** 'G. GAMBADO' *Acad. Horsemen* (1809) 23 Like swarming the bannisters of a stair-case. **1859** F. E. PAGET *Curate of Cumberworth* 72 She rushed towards a clean-stemmed beech, apparently with the intention of swarming it.

swarmed ('swɔːmɪd, swɔːmd), *ppl. a. poet. rare.* [f. SWARM *v.*[1] + -ED[1].] Of a place: crowded, thronged. Of people: assembled in a crowd, congregated, massed.

1885 G. M. HOPKINS *Poems* (1967) 98 How then should Gregory, a father, have gleanèd else from swarm-èd Rome? **1951** R. GRAVES *Poems & Satires* 37 Tormented by his progress he displays An open flank to the swarmed enemy.

swarmer[1] ('swɔːmə(r)). [f. SWARM *v.*[1] + -ER[1].]

1. One of a number that swarm; one of a swarm (as of insects); in *Biol.* a swarm-spore; in *Bacteriol.*, a swarmer cell.

1844 DICKENS *Mart. Chuz.* lii, 'Oh, vermin!' said Mr. Pecksniff. 'Oh, bloodsuckers!.. vermin and swarmers.' **1872** J. G. MURPHY *Comm. Lev.* xi. 20 Winged creepers or swarmers are so called from their minuteness and their multitude. **1898** H. M. WARD in *Ann. Bot.* XII. 301 The obvious suspicion arose that an intruding swarmer had got into my hanging-drop. **1900** *Nature* 21 June 191/1 The beetles are late swarmers, appearing chiefly in July. **1964** *Bacteriol. Rev.* XXVIII. 242/2 If the swarmer is to become a recognizable caulobacter cell, it must develop a stalk after cell division.

2. A bee-hive adapted for swarming, or from which a swarm is sent forth.

1855 *Poultry Chron.* III. 300/1, I have found hives in which the combs ranged in the way most common, from front to back, indifferently swarmers or non-swarmers. **1883** in *Standard* 15 Feb. 5/2 'Artificial swarmers'.. have displaced the old fashioned 'skep'.

3. swarmer cell *Bacteriol.*, a flagellated motile cell produced by the stalked cell of certain species of stalked bacteria.

1950 *Biochimica & Biophysica Acta* V. 41 A study was made of the flagellation of swarmer cells of *Proteus vulgaris.* **1976** *Jrnl. Bacteriol.* CXXVIII. 456/1 The stalked cell [of *Caulobacter crescentus*] divides repeatedly to produce new swarmer cells, whereas the swarmer cell, which cannot divide, loses motility and develops into a stalked cell.

†'**swarmer**[2]. *Pyrotechny. Obs.* [ad. G. *schwärmer* or Du. *zwermer*, f. *schwärmen*, *zwermen* to rove, stray.] A cracker or serpent.

1765 R. JONES *Fireworks* iv. 149 Rockets which go under the denomination of swarmers, are those from two ounces downwards. **1799** G. SMITH *Laboratory* I. 7 Cases for Swarmers, or Rockets.

swarming ('swɔːmɪŋ), *vbl. sb.* [f. SWARM *v.*[1] + -ING[1].] The action of SWARM *v.*[1]

1. The action of assembling in a swarm or dense crowd; *spec.* the gathering and departure from the hive of a swarm of bees; also *transf.* of persons (usually with *off*).

1550 BALE *Engl. Votaries* II. 77 b, A myddle swarmynge of Antichristes sectes in England. **1573** TUSSER *Husb.* (1878) 110 Watch bees in May, for swarming away. **1661** CHILDREY *Brit. Baconica* 26 The chief time of the swarming (as one would say) of Pilchards about the shores of Cornwall, is from July to November. **1675** GEDDE *New Discov. Bee-houses* 16 When Bees are at the Swarming. **1707** MORTIMER *Husb.* (1721) I. 271 Observe what you can of the usual Signs that precede their Swarming. **1817** KIRBY & SP. *Entomol.* xix. (1818) II. 167 Sometimes, when every thing seems to prognosticate swarming, a cloud passing over the sun calms the agitation. **1911** J. H. ROSE *W. Pitt* vii. 168 The divisions, by the process of swarming-off, rapidly extended the organisation.

2. *Biol.* The movement characteristic of swarm-spores; reproduction by swarm-spores.

1867 *Chambers's Encycl.* IX. 234/2. **1875** BENNETT & DYER tr. *Sachs's Bot.* 673 The swarming of zoospores. **1882** VINES tr. *Sachs's Bot.* 4 *note*, The term 'swarming' is applied to any apparently spontaneous motion imparted to a naked protoplasmic body by vibratile cilia.

3. *attrib.*, as ***swarming-place***, ***season***, ***time***.

Used spec. in names of apparatus for transferring a swarm of bees to a new hive, as ***swarming-bag***, ***-basket***, ***-box***, ***-hook*** (in recent Dicts.).

1707 MORTIMER *Husb.* (1721) I. 270 In Swarming time the Hives that you are minded to use, rub with sweet Herbs. **1855** *Poultry Chron.* III. 206/2 Watching and hiving for several weeks in the swarming season. **1892** ZANGWILL *Childr. Ghetto* I. 3 At last it [*sc.* the Ghetto] becomes only a swarming-place for the poor and the ignorant.

'**swarming**, *ppl. a.* [f. SWARM *v.*[1] + -ING[2].]

1. Assembling or moving in a swarm; forming a swarm or dense crowd; thronging; very numerous.

1590 SPENSER *F.Q.* II. x. 63 Those spoilefull Picts, and swarming Easterlings. **1725** POLE *Odyss.* XIII. 179 The swarming people hail their ship to land. **1784** COWPER *Task* III. 555 Moisture and drought, mice, worms, and swarming flies. **1817** SHELLEY *Rev. Islam* V. xxxviii, To see Earth from her general womb Pour forth her swarming sons to a fraternal doom. **1856** FROUDE *Hist. Eng.* I. i. 40 Barges pursuing their now difficult way among the swarming steamers.

2. *spec.* of bees; also *transf.* of persons: see SWARM *v.*[1] 1, 1 b.

1553 GRIMALDE *Cicero's Offices* I. (1558) 69 Being swarming [orig. *congregabilia*] by kinde they work their combes. **1697** DRYDEN *Virg. Past.* VII. 18 See.. How black the Clouds of swarming Bees arise. **1713** YOUNG *Last Day* II. 51 Swarming bees,.. Charm'd with the brazen sound. **1869** FREEMAN *Norm. Conq.* III. xii. 147 Whence Ambigatus had sent forth his swarming colonists.

3. Filled with a swarm or multitude; densely crowded; thronged; very populous.

1810 MONTGOMERY *West Indies* II. 117 That stock he found on Afric's swarming plains. **1842** TENNYSON *Talking Oak* 213 The swarming sound of life. **1858** HAWTHORNE *Fr. & It. Note-bks.* (1872) I. 16 A swarming city.

4. *Biol.* Emerging as swarm-spores, or moving in the way characteristic of them: see SWARM *v.*[1] 1 c.

1864 *Reader* 30 Apr. 548/3 The swarming-spores of certain Algæ. **1882** VINES tr. *Sachs's Bot.* 232 In many of the more highly developed Thallophytes this power of motility is however limited to the male 'swarming' fertilising elements.

swarmy ('swɔːmɪ), *a. rare*[−1]. [f. SWARM *sb.* + -Y.] Swarming, thronged.

1858 HAWTHORNE *Fr. & It. Note-bks.* (1872) II. 192 This market is the noisiest and swarmiest centre of noisy and swarming Florence.

swarne, obs. pa. pple. of SWEAR *v.*

swarry ('swɒrɪ). Also **-ee**, **-ey**. Humorous spelling of SOIRÉE (repr. a vulgar or careless Eng. pronunciation).

1837 DICKENS *Pickw.* xxxvii, A friendly swarry, consisting of a boiled leg of mutton with the usual trimmings. **1848** THACKERAY *Van. Fair* xlii, At one of her *swarreys* I saw one of 'em speak to a dam fiddler. **1884** *Illustr. Lond. News* 15 Nov. 467/2 The complaint of the 'English Hostess' that ladies and gentlemen invited to dinner have become so.. unpunctual that, as the lady calls it: 'There will be no dinners in London and we shall be reduced to cold swarries.'

swart (swɔːt), *a.* (*sb.*) Now only *rhet.* or *poet.* (or *dial.*) Forms: 1 **sweart**, 2 **sward**, 3 **swært**, **sweort**, **swerd**, **suart**, 5 **swertt**, 5–6 **swarte**, 5, 7 **swert**, 1– **swart**. [Com. Teut.: OE. *sweart*, = OS., OFris. *swart* (NFris. *sûart*, EFris. *suurt*, WFris. *swart*), MLG., LG. *swart*, MDu. *swart* (Du. *zwart*), OHG., MHG. *swarz* (G. *schwarz*), ON. *svartr* (Sw. *svart*, Da. *sort*), Goth. *swarts*; f. root *swart-* 'dark', of which another grade is found in ON. *sorta* black dye, *sorti* black cloud, *sortna* to grow black, *Surtr* (see SURTURBRAND).

While surviving as the regular colour-word in the Continental languages, it has been superseded in ordinary use in English by *black*.]

1. Dark in colour; black or blackish; dusky, swarthy. **a.** *gen.*

Beowulf 167 (Gr.) Heorot eardode, sincfaȝe sel sweartum nihtum. *Ibid.* 3145 Wudurec astah sweart. *c* **1000** *Sax. Leechd.* I. 310 Đeos wyrt.. ys þyrnihton stelan.. & bradran leafon þonne leac & sweartran. **1122** *O.E. Chron.* (Laud), þa wearð swiðe mycel wind fram þa undern dæies to þa swarte nihte. *a* **1200** *Moral Ode* 278 in *O.E. Hom.* I. 177 Nis þer neure oþer liht þanne þe swarte leie. *c* **1205** LAY. 11974 Swurken vnder sunnen sweorte weolcnen. **1297** R. GLOUC. (Rolls) 10049 Vor he vel of is palefrey & brec is fot.. So suart so eni crowe amorwe is fot was. **13..** *E.E. Allit. P.* C. 363 To be swolȝed swyftly wyth þe swart erþe. *c* **1430** *Hymns Virg.* etc. (1895) 119 Hitt shalle be swarte as any pyche. **1578** LYTE *Dodoens* 38 It is smaller, smother, and of a swarter colour. **1601** HOLLAND *Pliny* XXIII. i. II. 149 Foule and unseemly swert skars, it reduceth to the fresh and naturall colour. **1602** MARSTON *Antonio's Rev.* I. i. Wks. 1856 I. 73 You horrid scouts That centinell swart night. **1682** SIR T. BROWNE *Chr. Mor.* III. §6 Nor deepen those swart Tinctures, which Temper, Infirmity, or ill habits have set upon thee. **1794** COLERIDGE *Koskiusko* 4 Through the swart air.. on the chill and midnight gale Rises.. The dirge of murder'd Hope! **1811** SCOTT *Don Roderick* I. liii, Swart as the smoke from raging furnace. **1890** 'R. BOLDREWOOD' *Col. Reformer* (1891) 283 The trees upon the swart hillsides were visible.. as at midday.

b. *spec.* Of the skin or complexion, or of persons in respect of these.

a **1395** HYLTON *Scala Perf.* (W. de W. 1494) II. xii, Beholde me not that I am swart [*ed.* 1533 blacke] for the sonne hath defaded me. *a* **1400–50** *Wars Alex.* 3970 þa swart men of ynde. *c* **1407** LYDG. *Reason & Sens.* 3791 Vulcanus.. For his smotry, swarte face He stood clene out of hir grace. **1568** GRAFTON *Chron.* II. 192 This king was of stature talle, somewhat swarte or black of colour. **1590** SHAKS. *Com. Err.* III. ii. 104 *Anti.* What complexion is she of? *Dro.* Swart like my shoo, but her face nothing like so cleane kept. **1614** SYLVESTER *Bethulia's Rescue* III. 36 The swelting coasts of swartest Abyssine. **1613–16** W. BROWNE *Brit. Past.* I. iv, The swart ploughman for his breakfast staid. **1634** MILTON *Comus* 436 No goblin, or swart faëry of the mine. **1810** SHELLEY *Solitary* ii, The swart Pariah in some Indian grove. **1825** SCOTT *Talism.* xxvii, Their countenance swart with the sunbeams. **1901** E. L. ARNOLD *Lepidus* 154 This swart adventurer made love to the girl that was all in all to me.

†**c.** Livid through suffering or emotion. *Obs.*

a **1400** *Sir Beues* (S.) 1912 For teene he wexe al swert. *c* **1485** *Digby Myst., Mary Magdalene* 780, I wax alle swertt! **1567** GOLDING *Ovid's Met.* XII. (1593) 288 Al his body waxt starke cold and died swart. **1581** in Farr *S.P. Eliz.* (1845) II. 395 Who alwaies thinkes of death Shall neuer looke with cheerefull face, But swarte, and wan. **1590** BARROUGH *Meth.*

Phisic I. iii. (1639) 5 Their face is..full and pale, and their eyes are swolne and swart.

d. quasi-*adv.* qualifying an adj. of colour.

In first quot. *swarte* is a disyllable, as if repr. OE. *swearte* adv.

c **1384** CHAUCER *H. Fame* III. 557 Blak blo grenyssh swarte Red. *c* **1530** *Judic. Urines* II. xiv. 45 b, Lyke as we see whan a thyng that is swart grene. **1578** LYTE *Dodoens* 82 Small round beries of a swarte redde colour. **1841** BROWNING *Pippa Passes* II. 51 An Almaign Kaiser,..Swart-green and gold, with truncheon based on hip.

2. *transf.* Producing swarthiness of complexion.

Applied by Milton to some heavenly body, perhaps the dog-star (cf. Hor. *Od.* III. xxiii. 9), in reference to the heat of summer; hence in echoes of Milton, sometimes in sense 'malignant' (cf. 3 b).

1637 MILTON *Lycidas* 138 Ye valleys low..On whose fresh lap the swart Star sparely looks. **1759** MASON *Caractacus, Ode* II. iii, From the sultry south alone The swart star flings his pestilential fire. **1818** KEATS *Endym.* II. 15 Swart planet in the universe of deeds! **1862** TRENCH *Poems* 254 (*Sonnet*) The swart sun's blaze Down beating with unmitigated rays. **1892** HENLEY *Song of Sword* etc. 15 From swart August to the green lap of May.

b. Dressed in black.

Cf. MLG. *swartbroder*, ON. *svartmunkr*, etc., a Dominican, black friar.

1688 MRS. BEHN *Fair Jilt* Plays etc. 1871 V. 206 Canonesses, Begines, Quests, Swart-Sisters, and Jesuitesses. **1856** AYTOUN *Bothwell* II. ix, There he stood,..Swart in the Congregation's garb.

3. *fig.* **a.** 'Black', wicked, iniquitous. **b.** Baleful, malignant.

a **900** CYNEWULF *Juliana* 313 (Gr.) Wraþra fela..bealwa..sweartra synna. *c* **1000** ÆLFRIC *Hom.* (Th.) I. 54 Swa lange swa he hylt ðone sweartan nið on his heortan. *a* **1225** *Ancr. R.* 304 A domesdei schulen ure swarte sunnen bicleopen us stroncliche of ure soule murðre. **1594** CAREW *Tasso* IV. xx. (1881) 78 Whereto booted this, if they ne mote Of these vncertaine broyles the issue cleere?.. Nor hels swart cunning could to truth direct? **1852** ROCK *Ch. Fathers* III. ix. 222 Whenever any swart evil had betided this land. **1867** EMERSON *Poems, The Past* 8 Nor haughty hope, nor swart chagrin, Nor murdering hate.

4. *Comb.*, as ***swart-coloured***, ***-complexioned***, ***-faced***, ***-featured***, ***-visaged*** adjs. (Cf. OE. *swearthǽwen*.)

1620 T. GRANGER *Div. Logike* 67 Vnder the North pole they are browne, and *swart coloured. *c* **1600** SHAKS. *Sonn.* xxviii, The *swart complexiond night. **1821** SCOTT *Kenilw.* xi, A..*swart-faced knave of that noble mystery. **1905** TUCKWELL *Remin. Radical Parson* xii. 181 A great gathering of swart-faced enthusiasts in the Black Country. **1837** CARLYLE *Fr. Rev.* II. IV. iv, So many *swart-featured haggard faces. **1858** O. W. HOLMES '*This is it*' 57 in *Aut. Breakf.-t.* ii, Bare-armed, *swart-visaged, gaunt, and shaggy-browed.

†**B.** *sb.* A person of swarthy complexion; in quot. *c* 1425 *fig.* as a term of reproach. *Obs. rare.*

c **1425** *Cast. Persev.* 2211 in *Macro Plays* 143 Charyte, þat sowre swart, with fayre rosys myn hed gan breke. **1867** SMYTH *Sailor's Word-bk.*, *Swarts*, a name formerly applied by voyagers to Indians and negroes.

† **swart**, *v. Obs.* [f. SWART *a.* In OE. *sweartian*, corresp. to MLG. *swarten*, also *swerten*, OHG. *suarzên*, MHG. *swarzen*, also OHG. *suarz(i)an*, *suerzen*, MHG. *swerzen* (G. *schwärzen*); cf. ON. *svartaðr* dyed black.]

1. *intr.* To become swart, dark, or dusky.

c **1000** ÆLFRIC *Saints' Lives* xviii. 151 Efne ða aras se wind and ða wolcnu sweartodon. *c* **1000** *Sax. Leechd.* III. 104 þanne sweartigeð hy [*sc.* the teeth] & fealleð.

1581 A. HALL *Iliad* v. 86 Hir colour gay So bright that was, beginnes to swarte.

2. *trans.* To make swart; to darken (esp. the skin or complexion).

1577 GRANGE *Golden Aphrod.* Nj, Vulcane beyng..swarted with the..smoke of his forge. **1614** GORGES *Lucan* VI. 217 The skinne it scorching swarts. **1628** *Brittain's Ida* in *Spenser's Wks.* (1862) 502/2 Jove upon him downe his thunder darted, Blasting his splendent face, and all his beauty swarted. **1646** SIR T. BROWNE *Pseud. Ep.* VI. x. 326 The heate of the Sun, whose fervor may swarte a living part, and even black a dead or dissolving flesh.

swart, obs. form of SWARD.

swartback, **swarthback**. *local.* Also 5 **suerthbak**, 7 **swarth bag**. [ad. Icel. *svartbakur* (whence Norw. *svartbak*, Da. *svartbagmaage*): see SWART *a.*, SWARTH *a.* + BACK *sb.*[1] Cf. SWABIE.] The great black-backed gull, *Larus marinus*.

c **1450** HOLLAND *Howlat* 180 The Goule was a gryntar, The Suerthbak a sellerar. **1676** STERPIN *Descr. Fœroe* 141 The Swarth bag is a great Bird like a Kite, it is white all over, but the back. **1678** RAY *Willughby's Ornith.* 344 In the Feroe Islands it is called, The Swarth-back. **1805** BARRY *Orkney* III. i. 304 The Great Black and White Gull..our black-backed maw, or as it is sometimes called swartback, is the largest of the gull kind in our seas. **1821** SCOTT *Pirate* x, Thy foot had been on the Maiden-skerrie of Northmaven, known before but to the webbed sole of the swartback. *Ibid.* [see SWABIE].

‖**swart gevaar** (swart xə'fa:r). *S. Afr.* [Afrikaans, lit. 'black peril', f. Du. *zwart* SWART, black + *gevaar* danger, peril.] The name given in South Africa to the threat to the Western way of life and white supremacy believed to be posed by the black races. Cf. *yellow peril* s.v. YELLOW *a.* 1 d.

[**1939** R. F. S. HOERNLÉ *S. Afr. Native Policy* 1 To protect White South Africa against 'the Native Danger'—*die donker gevaar* or *die swart gevaar*—is..the simple pole towards which the needle of Native Policy steadily points.] **1948** *Hansard S. Afr.* 20 Jan. 111 In a pathetic attempt to get into power they have dropped Republicanism and adopted the Swart Gevaar. **1970** *Cape Times* 28 Oct. 9/2 They introduce *swart gevaar* where it suits them. **1979** *Economist* 8 Sept. 59/1 Afrikaner Nationalists, brought up for more than half a century on the politics of *swart gevaar* (black danger).

swarth (swɔ:θ), *sb.*[1] Now only *dial.* Also 7 **sworth**, 8 **swarthe**. [OE. *swearþ*: see SWARD *sb.* and cf. SWARF *sb.*[3]]

1. Skin, rind; *fig.* the surface, outside.

c **725** *Corpus Gloss.* C 198 *Cater*, suearth. *c* **1050** *Ags. Voc.* in Wr.-Wülcker 363/9 *Catrum*, swearð. *c* **1450** *St. Cuthbert* (Surtees) 2280 For oft knelyng his knees boun, A grete swarth was on þaim groune. **1807** STAGG *Poems* 49 Lest for the swarth I past retrievan, The substance torfeit. **1869** *Lonsdale Gloss.*, *Swarth*,..any outward covering, as the rind of bacon. **1878** *Cumbld. Gloss.*, *Swarth*, the skin of hams and bacon.

2. Green turf, grass land, greensward.

?*a* **1400** *Morte Arth.* 1126 One the erthe [he] hitez A swerde lenghe with-in þe swarthe. *Ibid.* 1466 Swyftly with swerdes, they swappene there-aftyre,..That alle swellttez one swarthe. *a* **1552** LELAND *Itin.* (1906) VI. 79 In Cairarvonshire..is Llin edwarchen, wher [is] the Swymming Island, and ther of it hath the name as of a suimming swarth of yerth. **1594** PLAT *Jewell-ho.* I. 19 Cloddes of earth..such as are full of swarth. **1616** SURFL. & MARKH. *Country Farm* v vi. 533 New broken swarthes. **1664** EVELYN *Sylva* 18 The swarth par'd first away, and the earth stirred a foot deep or more. **1770–4** A. HUNTER *Georg. Ess.* (1803) I. 141 Two acres of rich sand land, which the year before had been ploughed out of swarth. **1794** VANCOUVER *Agric. Cambridge* 93 The old swarth produces a very indifferent herbage, but may be much improved, by breaking up, [etc.]. **1798** *Trans. Soc. Arts* XVI. 242 He has it in contemplation to leave the rest to swarth without sowing seeds on it.

b. qualified by *green* (or *grassy*).

1616 SURFL. & MARKH. *Country Farm* III. i. 335 As soone as you see these bankes firme, and beginning to grow to haue a greene swarth vpon them. **1637** B. JONSON *Sad Shepherd* I. v, On every greene swarth, and in every path. **1751** R. PALTOCK *P. Wilkins* xi. (1883) 34/1, I walked over the green swarth to the wood. **1784** COWPER *Task* I. 110 Through lanes, Of grassy swarth close cropt by nibbling sheep.

†**c.** *transf.* Applied to the top layers of soil. *Obs.*

1649 BLITHE *Eng. Improv.* vii. 38 This..cold hungry water is found, beneath the first and second swarth of thy Lands.

d. *attrib.*

1598 *Fitzherbert's Husb.* viii. (1882) 132 If you sowe Winter-corne..vpon swarth ground. **1607** MARKHAM *Caval.* VI. ii. 5 Some plaine leuell Meddowe or such like greene swarth ground. **1794** *Act for inclosing South Kelsey* 26 Any old Green Swarth Ground. **1876** *Mid-Yorks. Gloss.* s.v., 'Swarth-balks', the end portions of a field, left unploughed, for a cart-way.

swarth (swɔ:θ), *sb.*[2] Now *dial.* [Obscure altered form of SWATH[1].]

1. = SWATH[1] 3.

1552 HULOET, Swarth of grasse newe mowen. **1688** HOLME *Armoury* III. 72/2 The Swarth..are the rows of the cut Grass as the Sithe leaves it. **1706** *Phil. Trans.* XXV. 2237 The Waves came rolling down, like long Swarths of Grass, one upon another. **1713** *Ibid.* XXVIII. 91 When it is cut, it must in most Years lie 5 or 6 Days in swarth. *a* **1722** LISLE *Husb.* (1757) 277, I could have no prospect of mowing a good swarth in the French-grass. **1763** *Museum Rust.* (ed. 2) I. 236 In Buckinghamshire they cannot use a cradle, their crops being in general so heavy, that the workmen could not carry over the swarth. **1817–18** COBBETT *Resid. U.S.* (1822) 181 They mow four acres of oats, wheat, rye, or barley in a day, and, with a cradle, lay it so smooth in the swarths, that it is tied up in sheaths with the greatest neatness and ease. **1861** HUGHES *Tom Brown at Oxf.* xxiii. (1889) 221 There were groups of children in many parts of the field, and women to look after them, mostly sitting on the fresh swarth.

attrib. **1813** VANCOUVER *Agric. Devon* 171 The barley is gathered from the swarth into sheaves,..and, after the swarth-corn is secured, the fields are carefully raked.

b. *to mow in swarth*: see quots.

1763 *Museum Rust.* (ed. 2) I. 235 Horse-beans..they usually mow with a bare scythe, in swarth, as they term it; that is, they mow the beans towards the beans. **1764** *Ibid.* III. lxxvi. 336 As to mowing wheat in swarth, I think it will litter about very much, for beans do so.

c. Applied to growing grain: cf. SWATH[1] 3 b.

1880 SIR J. B. PHEAR *Aryan Village* i. 4 These open spaces..are..covered..by green waving swarths of rice.

2. *transf.* and *fig.* = SWATH[1] 4 a, b.

†*at full swarth*: (app.) 'in full swing' (Davies), like a scythe making swaths.

1601 SHAKS. *Twel. N.* II. iii. 162 An affection'd Asse, that cons State without booke, and vtters it by great swarths. **1713** *Gentl. Instructed* III. iii. (ed. 5) 403 Tho' his Design miscarried, his Malice was at full swarth. **1847** LE FANU *T. O'Brien* 257 Old time sweeps in his swarth. **1854** J. S. C. ABBOTT *Napoleon* (1855) II. ix. 139 He sees the course of his heroes by the black swarth of dead men.

swarth (swɔ:θ), *sb.*[3] Variant of SWARF *sb.*[2]

With quot. 1596 cf. quot. 1566 s.v. SWARF *sb.*[2]

1596 *Wills & Inv. N.C.* (Surtees 1860) 259 In dieng stuffe..In brasell, half a hundreth and xj pounds, 46s. 8d. In galles, viij poundes, 6s. In swarthe, iiij pounds, 3d. **1783–4** *London Sessions Papers* 472 He told me that there was some swarth, that is iron file dust. **1892** RIGBY in *Min. Proc. Inst. Civ. Engin.* CXI. 140 A capillary brass tube [in a drilling-machine], supplying soap-and-oil emulsion at a pressure of 80 lbs. on the inch. This washes out the 'swarth' and cools the cutting-edge.

swarth, *sb.*[4] *dial.* [perh. subst. use of SWARTH *a.* But cf. Sc. *warth*, var. *wraith*.] The apparition of a dying person; a wraith.

1674 RAY *N.C. Words* 47 A *Swarth*, Cumb., the Ghost of a dying man. **1790** GROSE *Provinc. Gloss.*, *Pop. Superstitions* 13 These apparitions are called Fetches, or Wraiths, and in Cumberland, Swarths.

swarth, *a.* (*sb.*[5]) [Obscure variant of SWART *a.*; cf. SWARTHY *a.*[1], and SWARF *a.*, SWARFISH, SWARFY.] Dusky, swarthy, black.

c **1530** [implied in *swarthness*]. **1569** C. T[YE] *Nastagio & Traversari* A vj b, A knight, of colour swarthe. **1600** SURFLET *Country Farm* VI. xxii. 787 Such women as..are subiect to pale and swarth colours. **1600** E. BOLTON *Palinode* in *Eng. Helicon* B iv b, Swarth clowdes. **1613** FLETCHER, etc. *Captain* II. ii, He looks Of a more rusty swarth Complexion Than an old arming Doublet. **1784** COWPER *Task* IV. 749 A swarth Indian with his belt of beads. **1814** SCOTT *Ld. of Isles* I. vii, Where thwarting tides, with mingled roar, Part thy swarth hills from Morven's shore. **1851** MAYNE REID *Scalp Hunters* vii. 55 The complexion, from tan and exposure, was brown and swarth.

fig. **1621** FLETCHER *Isl. Princess* v. i, Foule swarthe ingratitude.

b. *sb.* Swarthiness; dusky complexion or colour. *rare.*

a **1661** HOLYDAY *Juvenal* (1673) 258 The skies Face and black swarth of cloud threaten no ill: 'Tis summer-thunder. **1872** BROWNING *Fifine* xv, First Let me..pourtray you..The gypsy's foreign self, no swarth our sun could bake.

Hence **'swarthish** *a.*, somewhat swarthy; **'swarthness**, swarthiness, duskiness.

c **1530** *Judic. Urines* II. ii. 11 b, A swarthnes, a derknes & dymnes in the vryne, most to blaknesse warde. **1653** RAMESEY *Astrol. Restored* 86 A..long visage, and a swarthish complexion.

swarth, *v.*[1] Now *dial.* [f. SWARTH *sb.*[1]] *trans.* and *intr.* = SWARD *v.* 1, 2.

1610 FOLKINGHAM *Feudigr.* I. vi. 13 With what Herbage the Crust or Sword is matted, mantled and swarthed. **1765** *Museum Rust.* IV. xxi. 95 If, through..some mischance in the hay-seeds, it should not swarth well. **1858** *Jrnl. R. Agric. Soc.* XIX. I. 256 Where land is of a rich loamy character, there is no difficulty in getting it to swarth over with grass of good quality.

swarth (swɔ:ð, -θ), *v.*[2] *rare.* [f. SWARTH *a.*] *trans.* To make swarthy, to darken.

1846 G. WARBURTON *Hochelaga* II. 161 Complexion fresh and ruddy but swarthed over by sun and wind. *a* **1889** G. M. HOPKINS *Poems* (1967) 180 His cheeks the forth-and-flaunting sun Had swarthed about with lion-brown.

swarth, obs. var. SWARF *v.*, to faint.

swarthback: see SWARTBACK.

swarthily ('swɔ:ðılı, -θ-), *adv.* [f. SWARTHY *a.*[1] + -LY[2].] With a swarthy colour.

1755 JOHNSON, *Swarthily*, blackly; duskily; tawnily. [Hence in later Dicts.] **1955** J. THOMAS *No Banners* v. 40 De Laurière was a tall man, swarthily handsome. **1981** *Times Lit. Suppl.* 20 Feb. 198/4 A swarthily soulful young boy sitting all alone on a chair in a predominantly bare room.

swarthiness ('swɔ:ðınıs, -θ-). [f. as prec. + -NESS.] The quality of being swarthy; duskiness; darkness of colour or complexion.

1577 B. GOOGE *Heresbach's Husb.* II. (1586) 67 b, The ripenesse whereof is deemed by the swarthinesse and the softnesse of the berrie. **1628** FELTHAM *Resolves* II. [I.] xxxvi. 111 It thickens the complexion, and dyes it into an vnpleasing swarthinesse. **1668** WILKINS *Real Char.* II. viii. 224 Yellowness and Swarthiness of colour, accompanied with faintness. **1758** *Descr. Thames* 179 The Fat is thought excellent against Redness, or Swarthiness. **1823** SCOTT *Quentin D.* v, The complexion of the face..in its ordinary state of weather-beaten and sunburnt swarthiness. **1884** JEFFERIES in *Pall Mall Gaz.* 8 Aug. 4/2 A clear swarthiness—a translucent swarthiness—clear as the most delicate white.

swarthish, swarthness: see after SWARTH *a.*

swarthy ('swɔ:ðı, 'swɔ:θı), *a.*[1] [Obscure variant of SWARTY: cf. SWARTH *a.*, SWARF *a.*, SWARFISH, SWARFY.] Of a dark hue; black or blackish; dusky.

a. *gen.* = SWART *a.* 1 a.

1577 [implied in SWARTHINESS]. **1596** GOSSON *Quippes Upstart Gentlewom.* 99 in Hazl. *E.P.P.* IV. 254 The swarthie-blacke, the grassie-greene, The pudding-red, the dapple graie. **1602** MARSTON *Ant. & Mel.* I. Wks. 1856 I. 16 Swarthy darknesse popt out Phoebus eye. **1697** DRYDEN *Virg. Georg.* III. 596 Search his Mouth; and if a swarthy Tongue Is underneath his humid Palate hung [etc.]. **1786** tr. *Beckford's Vathek* (1868) 35 From a swarthy crimson to a bright rose colour. **1827** HEBER *Europe* 270 The swarthy vintage. **1842** TENNYSON *Morte d'Arthur* 269 Like some full-breasted swan That..takes the flood With swarthy webs.

b. of or in reference to the complexion: = SWART *a.* 1 b.

1591 SHAKS. *Two Gent.* II. vi. 26 Siluia..Shewes Iulia but a swarthy Ethiope. **1601** B. JONSON *Poetaster* v. i, Let our Roman eagles flie On swarthy Ægypt. **1634** SIR T. HERBERT *Trav.* 14 The people are of a swarthy darke colour. **1638–56** COWLEY *Davideis* III. 178 Your Name..That to rich Ophirs rising Morn is knowne, And stretcht out far to the burnt swarthy Zone. **1744** MITCHELL in *Phil. Trans.* XLIII. 122 If we proceed from the swarthiest white Person to the palest

Egyptian, from thence to the fairest Mustee, Molatto, Moor, &c. to the darkest Indian. **1833** TENNYSON *Dream Fair Wom.* xxxii, A queen, with swarthy cheeks and bold black eyes. **1879** S. C. BARTLETT *Egypt to Pal.* xxv. 493 Six swarthy Arabs pulled our oars as we headed north.

c. *fig.* 'Black', 'dark', malignant, dismal: cf. SWART *a.* 3.

1651 J. S. *Prince of Priggs Revels* III. 9 You (Parson).. Black best becomes your swarthy function Whose Doctrine ..damns more souls Then Lucifer by all his stratagems. **1756** AMORY *Buncle* (1825) I. 2 My lot has been a swarthy one in this first state.

d. *Comb.*

1587 TURBERV. *Trag. Tales* (1837) 31 A hydeous knight, to seeming swarthie hewde. **1689** *Lond. Gaz.* No. 2433/4 A swarthy Complexioned Boy. **1891** DOYLE *White Company* xxiv, A raw-boned, swarthy-cheeked man.

Hence †**swarthy** *v. trans.*, to make swarthy.

1663 COWLEY *Cutter Colman St.* IV. vi, Now will I and my Man John swarthy our Faces over as if that Country's Heat had made 'em so.

†**swarthy**, *a.*[2] *Obs. rare*[−1]. [f. SWARTH *sb.*[1] + -Y.] = SWARDY.

1613 [STANDISH] *New Direct. Planting* 8 The best way to inclose, is (if it be in swarthy grounds) to set [etc.].

swartish ('swɔːtɪʃ), *a.* Also 6 swerttysshe. [f. SWART *a.* + -ISH[1].] Somewhat swart, dusky, or dark-coloured. Also *advb.*

1483 *Chaucer's H. Fame* III. 557 Black, blo, grenyssh, swartysh [*MSS.* swart(e) rede. *c* **1530** *Judic. Urines* I. iii. 8 The womans vryne is more swartyshe..than is mannes vryne. *Ibid.* III. v. 50 A vapourus superfluyte, swerttysshe and dymmysshe. **1545** RAYNALDE *Byrth Mankynde* 43 The couloure swartisshe blacke. **1630** *R. Johnson's Kingd. & Commw.* 59 The Tartars are swartish, illfavoured, with a great thick lip. **1647** LILLY *Chr. Astrol.* viii. 58 His complexion pale, swartish or muddy.

'**swartly**, *adv. rare.* [f. as prec. + -LY[2].] So as to be or become swart; swarthily.

1582 STANYHURST *Æneis* IV. (Arb.) 111 When she the gift sacrifice with the incense burned on altars..thee moysture swartlye was altred. **1607** *Puritan* IV. ii. 16 How do's hee looke..? very swartlie, I warrant, with black beard, scorcht cheekes, and smokie eyebrowes.

swartness ('swɔːtnɪs). [f. as prec. + -NESS.] The quality of being swart; swarthiness, duskiness.

a **1100** *Aldhelm Gloss.* I. 4681 (Napier 121/1) *Nigredine*, sweartnysse. *a* **1395** HYLTON *Scala Perf.* (W. de W. 1494) II. xii, The swartnesse [1533 blackenes] that I haue is all wythoute. **1530** PALSGR. 278/1 Swartnesse, *estalleure*. **1584** B. R. tr. *Herodotus* II. 75 The blacknesse and swartnesse of the people. **1590** BARROUGH *Meth. Phisick* III. xix. (1639) 133 It chanceth sometime the face to be made very red..but this colour turneth againe into swartnesse. **1823** SCOTT *Peveril* xxvi, She..denounced the plague of swartness to the linen, of leanness to the poultry, of dearth and dishonour to the housekeeping.

'**swart,rutter.** *Obs.* exc. *Hist.* Also 6 swartroter, swart(e) rutter, swartrytter, swarthrutter. [a. early mod.Du. *swartrutter* (in Kilian *swerte ruyters* pl.): see SWART *a.* and RUTTER[1].] One of a class of irregular troopers, with black dress and armour and blackened faces, who infested the Netherlands in the 16th and 17th centuries.

1557 in *Cecil Papers* (Hist. MSS. Comm.) I. 144 A number of our Swartroters took Scheney. **1558** in Feuillerat *Revels Q. Eliz.* (1908) 94 The performaunce of A Maske of swart-rutters. **1572** BUCHANAN *Detection Mary Q. Scots* D iij b, Put on ane lose cloke, sic as the Swartrytters weare. **1598** E. GUILPIN *Skial.* (1878) 36 Like a Swartrutters hose his puffe thoughts swell, With yeastie ambition. **1634** W. TIRWHYT tr. *Balzac's Lett.* I. 128 The novelty of these barbarous faces, and of those great lubberly Swa[r]t-rutters, might easily have affrighted us. **1657** REEVE *God's Plea* 81 Fitter for Swartrutters and Ruffians, then for true Penitents. [**1706** PHILLIPS (ed. Kersey), *Swart-Reyter*, (Dutch) a Horseman with black Armour.] **1900** F. W. MAITLAND in Fisher *Biog.* (1910) 122 The English government's one idea of carrying on a big war..was that of hiring German 'swart-rutters'.

Hence †**swartrutting** *a. nonce-wd.*, behaving like a swartrutter.

1592 GREENE *Upst. Courtier* D 4, Making no brawles to haue wounds, as swartrutting veluet breeches dooth.

‖**swartwitpens** (svart'vɪtpɛns). *S. Afr.* Also **swart witpenz, zwart wit pens.** [Afrikaans, f. *swart* black + *wit* white + *pens* belly.] = *sable antelope* s.v. SABLE *sb.*[2] 5.

1869 T. BAINES *Diary* 31 Aug. (1946) I. 137 We saw a fine troop of *Zwart-wit-pens*..or Harris bucks. **1880** E. F. SANDEMAN *Eight Months in Ox Waggon* 254 We rode along ..hoping to find..a swartwitpense [*sic*] feeding on the luxuriant grass. **1889** H. A. BRYDEN *Kloof & Karroo* xvi. 284 The Sable antelope, 'zwart wit pens'—i.e. black with white belly. **1939** S. CLOETE *Watch for Dawn* xx. 265 Game was abundant: eland, giraffe, wildebeeste, zebra, swart witpenz,..and innumerable rhinoceros. **1951** *Cape Argus* 8 Dec. 4/3 He and Conroy spotted a fine buck—a swartwitpens.

swarty ('swɔːtɪ), *a.* Now *rare* or *Obs.* [f. SWART *a.* + -Y[1].] = SWARTHY *a.*[1]

1572 J. JONES *Bathes Buckstone* 1 b, It should not onely bee of another collour marly yellow, or swarty greene. **1582** STANYHURST *Æneis* III. (Arb.) 72 With black weede the altar is hanged, With tree swartye Cipers. **1600** SHAKS. *Tit. A.* II. iii. 72 (Qo.) Your swartie [*Folios* swarth] Cymerion. **1609** HEALEY *Discov. New World* I. xii. 55 A stonie, swartie, barren, Grass-lesse, sandie soyle. **1613–16** W. BROWNE *Brit. Past.* I. v, The swarty Smith spits in his Buckhorne fist. **1656** HEYLIN *Surv. France* 205 A beard..black and swarty. **1888** DOUGHTY *Trav. Arabia Deserta* II. 69 Before us appeared that great craggy blackness—the Harra, and thereupon certain swarty hills and crests.

Comb. **1635** R. N. tr. *Camden's Hist. Eliz.* II. 189 Frobisher..under the Latitude of 63 degrees..found men ..swarty coloured.

swarve (swɔːv), *v.*[1] *local* (Kent and Sussex). Also 5–6 *pa. pple.* **swared.** [Cf. the synonymous QUAR *v.*[1]] Chiefly *pass.*, to be choked *up* with sediment, to be silted *up*. Hence '**swarving** *vbl. sb.*

1485 *Rolls of Parlt.* VI. 331/1 The said Ryver, at the said place called Sarre..is so swared, growen, and hyghed with wose,..that nowe no Fery..may be there. **1548** *Act 2 & 3 Edw. VI*, c. 30 The Channell there is so choked swared and fylled uppe, that there cannot lye in the same Harborowe [of Camber, near Rye] above thirtie or fowrtie saylle of Shippes. **1562** in *W. Holloway's Hist. Romney Marsh* (1849) 141 A creek or waterway swawed [*sic*] or dried up. **1587** FLEMING *Contn. Holinshed* III. 1545/2 The hauens mouth would.. haue soone beene swarued vp. **1603** KNOLLES *Hist. Turks* (1621) 544 A narrow way almost swarved up with rubbidge. **1665** in *W. Holloway's Hist. Romney Marsh* (1849) 165 When the ditches and bounds be swarved up. **1701** WALLIS in *Phil. Trans.* XXII. 978 At Hythe in Kent (which is one of the Cinq-Ports) there was..a Convenient Harbour for small Vessels; which is now swarved up. **1904** MAUD S. RAWSON *Apprentice* 17 The swarving of river channels with sand and shingle. **1906** KIPLING *Puck of Pook's Hill* 250 Next floods the brook'll swarve up.

†**swarve**, *v.*[2] *Obs.* [Of doubtful origin; see the synonymous SWARM *v.*[2] (North. dialects have *swarble* beside *swarmle* in the same sense.)] = SWARM *v.*[2] (*intr.* and *trans.*).

15.. *Isumbras* 351 (Douce MS. 261, lf. 7) He swarued [*ed. Copland* (*c* 1550) swarmed] vp in to a tree Whyle ether of them myght other see. *a* **1613** OVERBURY *A Wife*, etc. (1638) 107 He swarves up to his seat as to a saile-yard. *a* **1650** *Sir A. Barton* liii. in Child *Ballads* (1889) III. 341/2 With that hee swarued the maine-mast tree [*another version, ibid.* 345/1 Then up the mast-tree swarved he]. **1844** *M. A. Richardson's Historian's Table-bk., Leg. Div.* II. 393 Now leaping, now swarving the slipp'ry steep.

swarve: see SWARF *v.*, SWERVE.

swash (swɒʃ), *int.* or *adv.* and *sb.*[1] Also **swosh.** [Imitative of the sound of splashing or agitated water, or of a resounding blow. Cf. *swish*.]

A. *int.* or *adv.* Expressive of the fall of a heavy body or blow: With a crash.

1538 BALE *Thre Lawes* 393 Haue in than at a dash, With swash myry annet swash. **1582** STANYHURST *Æneis* II. (Arb.) 58 Pat fals thee turret, thee Greeks with crash swash yt heapeth. **1863** MRS. GASKELL *Sylvia* xv. II. 7 If a hadn't been too quick for her, it would have a' gone swash down i' t' litter. **1927** J. MASEFIELD *Midnight Folk* 92 He swung Blackmalkin [*sc.* a cat] round his head and pitched him swosh into the mud.

B. *sb.*

I. 1. a. Pig-wash; also, wet refuse or filth.

1528 TINDALE *Parable Wicked Mammon* Wks. (1573) 65/1 His stomacke abhorreth longyng after slibbersause and swashe, at which a whole stomacke is readye to cast hys gorge. **1634** MERES *Wits Commonw.* II. 50 Swine..refuse partriges and delicats, and doe greedily hunt after Acornes and other swash. **1847** HALLIWELL, *Swash*..(4) Refuse; hog-wash. **1878** *Cumbld. Gloss.*, *Swash*, wet stuff. **1893** *Times* (weekly ed.) 10 Feb. 114 The well-filled troughs of swash and potatoes round which I have seen pigs crowd.

†**b.** *transf.* Nonsense; worthless stuff. Cf. HOG-WASH b. *slang. obs.*

1895 W. C. GORE in *Inlander* Nov. 65 *Swosh*,..nonsense; inferior work. **1924** GALSWORTHY *White Monkey* II. v. 162 Anyway sentiment was swosh! Cut it out!

2. A body of water moving forcibly or dashing against something.

An alleged sense 'stream, puddle of water', entered in Phillips's *World of Words*, ed. Kersey, 1706, is not otherwise authenticated.

1671 SKINNER *Etymol.*, Swash, a great Swash of water, *magnus & cum magno impetu ruens aquarum Torrens*. **1844** W. H. MAXWELL *Wanderings in Highlands* xviii. II. 5 Some 'swash' in the Goodwins. **1852** HAWTHORNE *Blithedale Rom.* xxvii, Up came a white swash to the surface of the river. It was the flow of a woman's garments. **1860** *Wilts. Archæol. Mag.* VI. 380 *note*, A man in answer to my question of how the rain seemed to fall, said 'It came down in swashes'.

3. Chiefly *U.S.* = SWATCH *sb.*[3]

1670–1 NARBOROUGH *Jrnl.* in *Acc. Sev. Late Voy.* I. (1694) 46 It drains into salt Water-swashes. *Ibid.* 52, I sent the Boat for Water to a Swash on the East-side. **1775** ROMANS *Florida* App. 78 As the bank is bound with a reef here, you must pick your way through that, which you may, as there are several swashes, which though they are narrow, have no less than 11 or 12 feet thro'. **1788** JEFFERSON *Writ.* (1859) II. 453 Having got themselves near the swash, at the mouth of the Boristhenes. **1869** *New Orleans Bee* in Schele de Vere *Americanisms* (1872) 556 It is said they took refuge in the swash behind the house.

4. A heavy blow, esp. of, or upon, some yielding substance; the sound of this.

1789 DAVIDSON *Seasons, Spring* 32 Forthwith amain he [*sc.* the salmon] plunges on his prey, Wi' eager swash. **1853** KANE *Grinnel Exp.* xxvi. (1856) 211 The voices of the ice and the heavy swash of the overturned hummock-tables. **1865** G. MACDONALD *Alec Forbes* 29 The cruel serpent of leather went at him, coiling round his legs with a sudden, hissing swash. **1866** GREGOR *Banffsh. Gloss.*, *Swash*, (1) a severe blow. (2) A severe dash. **1898** J. PATON *Castlebraes* ii. 49, I laid ma Heezel Rung, a second swash, athwart the safter pairts.

5. a. The action of water dashing or washing against the side of a cliff, ship, etc. or of waves against each other; the sound accompanying this.

1847–54 WEBSTER, *Swash*..2. Impulse of water flowing with violence. **1849** CUPPLES *Green Hand* ix, The lazy swash of the water round our fore-chains. **1849** W. S. MAYO *Kaloolah* ii. (1850) 21 The captain fancied that he heard the swash of the water against the sides of a ship. **1863** HAWTHORNE *Our Old Home* (1879) 279 The swash and swell of the passing steamers. **1883** G. H. BOUGHTON in *Harper's Mag.* Feb. 393/1 We were steaming along splendidly now, sending up a fine wash and swash along the banks. **1892** H. HUTCHINSON *Fairway Island* 25 The swash of the sea at the cliff foot.

b. *Physical Geogr.* The rush of sea water up the beach after the breaking of a wave.

1919 D. W. JOHNSON *Shore Processes & Shoreline Development* x. 514 Since there are a variety of marks left on the sand by wave action, and the present feature is peculiarly a product of the swash, I have given it the name of 'swash mark'. **1934** *Geogr. Jrnl.* LXXXIII. 485 When the swash dies out the backwash of the wave returns directly down the steepest slope to the sea. **1976** P. D. KOMAR *Beach Processes & Sedimentation* ii. 14 The return flow of the swash collides with the incoming surf bores.

6. A watery condition of land; ground under water.

1864 CARLYLE *Fredk. Gt.* XVI. xiv. IV. 478 Waters all out, ground in a swash with December rains. **1891** *The Auk* Jan. 65 Here [*sc.* Andros in the Bahamas] the ground is soft, and in wet weather almost entirely under water; hence the peculiar appropriateness of the local term *swash*.

II. 7. A swaggerer; a swashbuckler; now *Sc.* an ostentatious person (cf. SWASH *a.*[1], SWASHING *ppl. a.* 1).

1549 CHALONER *Erasm. on Folly* D iij b, Commenly thei that bringe any valiant feate to passe, are good blouddes, venturers, compaignions, swasshes. **1579** GOSSON *Sch. Abuse* (Arb.) 46 Every Duns will be a Carper, every Dick Swash a common Cutter. **1584** R. WILSON *Three Ladies Lond.* (1592) A 3, I will flaunt it and brave it after the lusty swash. **1593** G. HARVEY *Pierce's Super.* 117 The noddy Nash, whom euery seruing Swash With pot-iestes dash, and euery whipdog lash. **1637** I. JONES & DAVENANT *Brit. Triumphans* 17 With Courtly Knights, not roaring country swashes, Hath beene her breeding still. **1659** T. PECKE *Parnassi Puerp.* 16 Two Swashes did the fair Camilla court. **1693** SOUTHERNE *Maid's last Prayer* II. ii, I remember your Dammee-boys, your Swashes, your Tuquoques. **1824** MISS FERRIER *Inher.* xviii, A great gormandizing swash. **1866** GREGOR *Banffsh. Gloss.*, *Swash*..(4) A vapouring dandy.

8. Swagger; swashbuckling.

1593 G. HARVEY *Pierce's Super.* ***j, If nothing can the booted Souldiour tame..But Swash will still his trompery aduaunce. **1605** A. WARREN *Poor Man's Pass.* E 3, I would elect, Flaunt, Cut, and Swash for mates, For choise Companions, pleasure, mirth, delight. **1822** MAGINN in *Blackw. Mag.* XI. 370* The stamping, ramping, swaggering, staggering, leathering swash of an Irishman. **1854** MISS BAKER *Northampt. Gloss.* s.v., What a swash he cuts! **1866** GREGOR *Banffsh. Gloss.*, *Swash*..(3) The act of walking with a haughty, silly air.

III. 9. *attrib.*: (sense 5 b) *swash mark, -slope, -zone*; **swash bank** (see quot.); **swash channel, swash-way**, 'a channel across a bank, or among shoals, as the noted instance between the Goodwin Sands' (Smyth *Sailor's Word-bk.*, 1867); **swash-plate** *Engin.*, a disc mounted obliquely on the end of a revolving shaft, which can impart to a rod in contact with the edge of the disc a reciprocating motion parallel to the axis of the shaft.

1852 WIGGINS *Embanking* 25 The *swash bank, which, having only to sustain the broken tops of the waves, is but 2½ feet high and 2½ feet wide at top. **1885** *Century Mag.* XXIX. 742 The *Minnesota*, taking the middle or *swash channel. **1919** *Swash mark [see sense 5 b above]. **1982** *Sci. Amer.* Aug. 130/2 Seaward of a swash mark on some beaches one is likely to find smaller diamond-shaped markings left by the backwash. *a* **1877** KNIGHT *Dict. Mech.* III. 2467/2 *Swash-plate. **1913** W. E. DOMMETT *Motor Car Mech.* 158 The plungers are driven by a swash-plate mechanism. **1977** *Design Engin.* July 92/1 (Advt.), To obtain precise control in many fields, e.g. valves, or engine throttle position, or a pump swashplate, you need a remote position actuator. **1931** *Geogr. Jrnl.* LXXVIII. 134 They [*sc.* waves]..on nearing high-water mark were busily pushing forward shingle to the top of their *swash slope. **1839** *Civil Engin. & Arch. Jrnl.* II. 221/1 Forming track-paths across *swash-ways in Loch Dochfour. **1883** *Chambers's Jrnl.* 18 Aug. 525/2 Certain narrow fareways which seam the sands at low tide,..are called on the south side of the Roach 'swatch'-ways, but beyond the Crouch 'swash'-ways. **1976** P. D. KOMAR *Beach Processes & Sedimentation* ii. 14 Schiffman..defines a transition zone between the surf and *swash zones.

swash, *sb.*[2], **swesh.** *Sc. Obs.* exc. *Hist.* Forms: 6 swasche, (suasche, squasche, swach(e, swass, sc(h)osche?), 6, 9 swash; 6 swesch(e, swech(e, (suech, suis, suishe, swische), 6, 9 swesch, swesh, 7 swy(s)che. [Perh. orig. in full *swasche, swesche*, or *swische ta(l)burne* (see TABORN *sb.*), but the orig. meaning and source of *swasche*, etc. are unknown.] A kind of drum. Also *attrib.* **swash-head**, a drum-head; **swash-man** = SWASHER[1].

1533 *Acc. Ld. High Treas. Scot.* VI. 159 For ane swasche talburne to the futmen xxs. **1541** *Ibid.* VII. 478 The twa Toddeis that playis vpoun the Swische taburn. **1543–4** *Ibid.* VIII. 250 Thre playarris upon the swesche. **1560** ROLLAND *Seven Sages* 20 With trumpet, schalme, drum, squasche & clarioun. **1562** *Extr. Aberd. Reg.* (1844) I. 343 Passing throw the toun with ane swech. **1571** *Extr. Burgh Rec. Lanark*

(Burgh Rec. Soc.) 55 That thei nychtly wache with the balleis fra the strak of the secund strak of the suishe. **1574-5** *Burgh Rec. Glasgow* (1876) I. 455 Item, to Thomas Downy for inputting of the schoscheheid vs. Item, for ane perchement skyn to Robert Muir to cover the scosche iij s. vj d. **1576** in *Maitl. Club Misc.* (1840) II. 343 For ane swasche to our moustiris iiij^l. **1593** *Extr. Aberd. Regr.* (1848) II. 81 Andro Inglis, sweschman, commoun servand to the toun. **1598** in Pitcairn *Crim. Trials* II. 30 'Stryke þe swasch' and 'Ryng þe commoun bell'! **1625-6** *Charters* etc. *Peebles* (1872) 414 Item, gewine John Robeine for striking of the swyche, xij s. **1672** *Burgh Rec. Peebles* (1872) 336 At the stryking of the swysche.

¶ Misused for: A trumpet. Also *swash-trump*.

This is the only meaning given by Jamieson, 1808, on the authority of quot. 1609; cf. also the following, where the Latin original would seem to warrant such a meaning:—

1533 BELLENDEN *Livy* II. lxiv. (S.T.S.) 238 Horsmen with swasche and taberne [orig. *cornicines tubicinesque in equis impositos*].

1609 SKENE *Reg. Maj., Stat. Gild* 143 After they heare the striak of the swesch (or the sound of the trumpet). **1819** TENNANT *Papistry Storm'd* (1827) 47 Wi' swesch-trump in his hand. **1871** WADDELL *Ps. in Scottis* xlvii. 5 God has gane up wi' a sugh; the Lord wi' the tout o' a swesch.

†**swash** (swɒʃ), *sb.*³ *Obs.* [Derived from or forming the radical of ASWASH *adv.* = aslant. Cf. SWASH *a.*²] **a.** *Turning*, etc., A figure or ornament the lines or mouldings of which lie obliquely to the axis of the work. **b.** *Printing.* The flourished extension characteristic of swash letters (see SWASH *a.*² 2).

1680 MOXON *Mech. Exerc.* xiv. 241 You set it to that Slope you intend the Swash on your Work shall have. *Ibid.* Explan. Terms LL 2 b, *Swash.* A *Swash* is a Figure whose Circumference is not Round, but Oval; and whose Moldings lye not at Right Angles, but Oblique to the Axis of the Work. **1683** *Ibid., Printing* xiii. ¶4 *2*, whose Swashes come below the Foot-Line.., ought to have the.. Sholder of that Swash Sculped down straight.

swash, *a.*¹ [f. SWASH *sb.*¹]

†**1.** = SWASHING *ppl. a.* 2. *Obs.*

1599 MINSHEU *Sp. Dict., Dial.* (1623) 30 This wound hurts me not much, for it is giuen with the hand vpward, but beware of the swash blow [Spanish *el rebés*], for I will draw it with the hand downwards.

2. †**a.** ? Swashbuckling, swaggering: = SWASHING *ppl. a.* 1. *Obs.* **b.** 'Swell', 'swagger', showy. *dial.*

c **1600** DAY *Begg. Bednall Gr.* II. ii. (1881) 39 Old Simsons son.. that wears his great gall gaskins o' the Swash-fashion, with 8 or 10 gold laces of a side. **1635** J. GOWER *Pyrgomachia* A 3 b, Some others.. Are of the rash-swash-fellowes band. **1713** S. SEWALL *Diary* 5 Nov., I first see Col. Tho. Noyes in a swash Flaxen Wigg. **1866** GREGOR *Banffsh. Gloss., Swash*, (1) gaudy; showy... (2) Of ostentatious manners. **1877** *Holderness Gloss., Swash*, showy; gaudy.

swash (swɒʃ), *a.*² [app. SWASH *sb.*³ used attrib.]

1. *Turning*, etc. Inclined obliquely to the axis of the work.

swash-work, work in which the cuttings or mouldings traced round a cylinder are inclined to the axis; also called ***pumped work***. ***swash-engine***, an apparatus for turning swash-work. ***swash-board***, ***swash-plate***, 'a rotating, circular plate, inclined to the plane of its revolution so as to give a vertical reciprocation to the rod, whose foot rests thereupon, and which moves between lateral guides' (Knight *Dict. Mech.*, 1875); also called *pumping-plate*.

1680 MOXON *Mech. Exerc.* xiv. 241 To the Turning of Swash-Work you must have two such Puppets as the Fore-puppet described in §22. *Ibid.*, Upon both the Flat sides of this Swash Board in a Diametrical Line is fastned up-right an Arch of a Quadrant made of a Steel Plate... The convex edges of these Quadrants are cut into Notches,.. that according as you may have occasion to set the Swash-Board more or less a-slope, you may be accommodated with a Notch or Tooth to set it at. *Ibid.* 242 These Oval-Engines, Swash-Engines, and all other Engines. **1688** HOLME *Armoury* III. 360/1 The Turning Engine [is] for the turning of Oval Work, Rose Work, and Swash Work. **1703** *Lond. Gaz.* No. 3887/4 A Gold Watch in a Grav'd Case..; with a Moco Stone Swash. **1812** P. NICHOLSON *Mech. Exerc.* 356 Turning is also of different kinds, as Circular Turning, Elliptic Turning, and Swash Turning.

2. *Printing.* Applied to old-style capital letters having flourished strokes designed to fill up unsightly gaps between adjacent letters.

1683 MOXON *Mech. Exerc., Printing* xiii. ¶4 Swash-Letters, especially *2*. **1867** BRANDE & COX *Dict. Sci.*, etc., *Swash Letters*.. have been revived of late years with the reintroduced old-fashioned types. **1899** DE VINNE *Pract. Typogr.* (1902) 271 *note*, An excellent form of old-style italic of bold face, with the swash letters and other features of quaintness.

swash, *a.*³ *dial.* [Cf. SWASHY.] Soft; also, fuddled.

1711 RAMSAY *On Maggy Johnstoun* vi, We did baith.. pish and spew, and yesk and maunt, Right swash I true. **1728** *Ramsay's Poems* II. Gloss., *Swash*, squat, fuddled. *a* **1800** PEGGE *Suppl. Grose, Swash*, and *Swashy*, soft, like fruit too ripe. Derb. **1888** *Sheffield Gloss.*

swash (swɒʃ), *v.* [Echoic. Cf. SWASH *sb.*¹]

1. *trans.* To dash or cast violently.

1577 HOLINSHED *Chron.* II. 444/2 The Archbyshop of Yorke.. swasht him down, meaning to thrust himselfe in betwixt the Legate, and the Archb. of Canterbury. **1582** STANYHURST *Æneis* I. (Arb.) 19 This Queene wyld lightninges from clowds of Iuppiter hurling Downe swasht theyre nauy. **1710** RUDDIMAN *Douglas' Æneis* Gloss. s.v. *Squat*, Scot. *swash*, Ang. *squat* is to cast against the ground. **1866** GREGOR *Banffsh. Gloss.*

2. *intr.* To dash or move violently *about*; also occas. *refl.*

1583 GOLDING *Calvin on Deut.* cxxxi. 807/1 As a swyne when he hath once winded his meat, runnes on to swash himself in it [orig. *se fourrer là*]. **1609** HOLLAND *Amm. Marcell.* XXXI. vii. 413 On all sides swords swashed and darts flew as thicke as haile.

1831 CARLYLE *Sart. Res.* II. ii, If.. your House fell, have I not seen five neighbourly Helpers appear next day; and swashing to and fro,.. complete it again before nightfall? **1837** —— *Fr. Rev.* II. IV. vi, Your dusty Mill of Valmy.. may furl its canvas, and cease swashing and circling. **1879** STEVENSON *Trav. Donkey* 139 A jolting trot that set the oats swashing in the pocket of my coat. **1889** 'MARK TWAIN' *Yankee at Crt. K. Arthur* vii, The gusts of wind were flaring the torches and making the shadows swash about.

3. To make a noise as of swords clashing or of a sword beating on a shield (cf. SWASHBUCKLER); to fence with swords; to bluster with or as with weapons; to lash *out*; hence, to swagger.

1556 [see SWASHING *vbl. sb.* 1 and *ppl. a.* 1]. **1565** COOPER *Thesaurus* s.v. *Concrepo*, *Concrepare gladiis ad scuta*, to swashe, or make a noyse with swoordes agaynst tergattes. **1593** LODGE *Will. Longbeard* C 3 b, He over-maistered [them] by his attendants swashing out in the open streets uppon everie light occasion. **1593** *Bacchus Bountie* in *Harl. Misc.* (Mahl.) II. 265, I giue them right to sweare it out with wordes, I giue them might to swash it out with swordes. **1600** BRETON *Pasquil's Fooles Cap* xl, Shee that.. Ruffin-like, will sweare, and swash it out. **1611** FLORIO, *Cortellare*, to fence, to swash with swords, to swagger. **1629** Z. BOYD *Last Battell* 673 [They], in hight of stomacke, ruffling & swashing, did tread vpon God's turtles.

a **1825** FORBY *Voc. E. Anglia, Swash*, to affect valour; to vapour or swagger. **1837** CARLYLE *Fr. Rev.* I. VII. ii, Captains of horse and foot go swashing with 'enormous white cockades'. **1850** —— *Two-hundred & Fifty Y. Ago* Ess. 1857 IV. 321 Bucklers went out.. 'about the twentieth of Queen Elizabeth'; men do not now swash with them, or fight in that way. **1890** *Pall Mall G.* 1 July 2/2 When Mr. Caine joined Lord Randolph in swashing at the Government. **1893** BARING-GOULD *Cheap Jack Zita* xxxv. III. 111 He will swash about with his toasting-fork as if 'twere a cutlass.

4. *trans.* To dash or splash (water) about; to dash water upon, souse with water or liquid (of water) to beat with a splash against.

1589 FLEMING *Virg. Georg.* IV. 64 *note*, Gargarise, or swash in and about the mouth. **1656** [? J. SERGEANT] *tr. T. White's Peripat. Inst.* 67 As it happens in liquids when they are swash'd up and down. **1721** BAILEY, To *Swash*, to make fly about, as Water. **1828** MOIR *Mansie Wauch* xix. 281 Having a bucket.. I swashed down such showers on the top of the flames. **1836** W. IRVING *Astoria* v. (1849) 61 For three hours and a half did they tug.. at the oar, swashed occasionally by the surging waves of the open sea. **1862** G. H. KINGSLEY *Sport & Trav.* (1900) 375 Men swishing and swashing and brooming about. **1863** W. W. STORY *Roba di R.* II. i. 1 The boards on which the meats are laid are swashed constantly with water. **1876** R. BRIDGES *Growth of Love* xxvii, What grisly beast of scaly chine That champ'd the ocean-wrack and swashed the brine. **1887** *Pall Mall G.* 28 Sept. 8/1 He added that the excursion boats also swashed the *Thistle*, damaging her to a certain extent.

5. *intr.* Of water or of an object in water: To dash with a splashing sound; to splash *about*.

1836 W. IRVING *Astoria* lviii. (1849) 477 The next wave threw their bodies back upon the deck, where they remained swashing backward and forward. **1843** CARLYLE *Misc., Dr. Francia* (1857) IV. 269 You have all got linen bathing-garments, and can swash about with some decency. **1847** H. MELVILLE *Omoo* x, The water fairly poured down in sheets.. swashing about. **1876** HOLLAND *Sev. Oaks* v. 65 Flocks of ducks.. swashed down with a fluttering ricochet into the water. **1892** H. HUTCHINSON *Fairway Island* 25 The sea at the cliff foot—swashing ever louder and louder.

†**swa'shado.** *nonce-wd.* [f. SWASH *v.* + -ADO.] A swashbuckler.

1663 *Proposal to use No Conscience* 4 A company of Swashado's beat the Watch.

swashbuckler ('swɒʃ,bʌklə(r)). [f. SWASH *v.* + BUCKLER *sb.*²; hence *lit.* one who makes a noise by striking his own or his opponent's shield with his sword.] **a.** A swaggering bravo or ruffian; a noisy braggadocio.

1560 PILKINGTON *Expos. Aggeus* ii. 8–9 (1562) 266 Too be a dronkarde,.. a gamner, a swashe-buckeler, he hath not alowed thee one mite. **1593** NASHE *Christ's T.* Wks. 1904 II. 148 No Smithfield ruffianly Swashbuckler will come of with such harshe hell-raking othes as they. **1648** JENKYN *Blind Guide* i. 14 He speaking.. more like a swash-buckler than a Bishop. *a* **1680** BUTLER *Charact., Hermetic Philos.*, Make those spiritual Swash-Bucklers deliver up their Weapons, and keep the Peace. *a* **1721** PRIOR *Dial. Dead, Charles & Clenard* Wks. 1907 II. 218 When ever You have Thought and Conquered with your Ruyters & Swashbucklers. **1809** W. IRVING *Knickerb.* VI. i. (1861) 184 He had a garrison after his own heart.. guzzling, deep-drinking swashbucklers. **1828** SCOTT *F.M. Perth* iv, Neither did his frank and manly deportment.. bear the least resemblance to that of the bravoes or swash-bucklers of the day. **1899** E. GOSSE *Life J. Donne* I. 32 He shows himself.. a daring.. young swash-buckler of poetry.

attrib. **1620** MELTON *Astrolog.* 13 What a quarrelling Swash-buckler Mars. **1672** MARVELL *Reh. Transp.* I. 260 Men.. do.. cut and slash about vestments.. rather in a swash-buckler and Hectoring way, than.. like.. Christians. **1816** SINGER *Hist. Cards* 258 *note*, The swash-buckler manners of the youth of fashion in the reign of Elizabeth. **1896** GEN. H. PORTER in *Century Mag.* Nov. 25 The most approved swashbuckler style of melodrama.

b. A book, film, or other work portraying swashbuckling characters.

1975 *Daily Colonist* (Victoria, B C.) 27 July 20/3 Clavell's most ambitious novel—an oldfashioned swash-buckler complete with all the popular ingredients. **1977** *Time* 30 May 42/2 *Star Wars* is a combination of *Flash Gordon, The Wizard of Oz*, the Errol Flynn swashbucklers of the '30s and '40s and almost every western ever screened.

Hence (*nonce-wds.*) **'swash,bucklerdom, -ism, -,bucklery**, the conduct of a swash-buckler; also **'swash,bucklering** = SWASH-BUCKLING *a.*

1862 MRS. SPEID *Last Years Ind.* 91 A sort of paralytic attempt at *swashbucklerdom and swagger. **1884** *19th Cent.* Dec. 1023 The *swash-bucklering and speculative fashion which the Republican supporters.. extolled. **1914** G. K. CHESTERTON *Flying Inn* 180 Such swashbucklering comedy. **1892** *Review of Rev.* 14 Apr. 360/1 Mr. Gladstone has.. been so sedulous an opponent of *swashbucklerism. **1889** D. HANNAY *Life F. Marryat* 21 He would have condemned.. such a piece of frantic *swashbucklery as the last fight of the *Revenge*.

'swash,buckling, *a.* [f. SWASHBUCKLER (apprehended as an agent-n. in -ER¹) + -ING².] Acting like, or characteristic of the conduct of, a swashbuckler; noisily swaggering, blustering. So **'swash,buckling** *sb.*

a **1693** *Urquhart's Rabelais* III. xlii. 349 The huff, snuff,.. swash-buckling High Germans. **1863** SALA in *Temple Bar* IX. 65 The Hungarian are stout wines, of a swash-buckling flavour. **1865** KINGSLEY *Herew.* xxxii, A swash-buckling ruffian. **1888** *Boston* (Mass.) *Transcript* 7 July 4/4 Swashbucklers are generally satisfied with swashbuckling. **1889** T. B. REED in *Boy's Own Paper* 3 Aug. 696/1 A score of more of swashbuckling 'prentices were on board the ship. **1894** *Athenæum* 27 Oct. 565/3 The one occasionally degenerates into artifice, and the other into literary swashbuckling.

Hence (back-formation) **'swash,buckle** *v.*, to swagger noisily, act like a blustering bravo.

1897 *Westm. Gaz.* 6 Jan. 3/1 He strikes one as a bravo, he swashbuckles and swaggers. **1939** W. FORTESCUE *There's Rosemary, There's Rue* vi. 41 One proud day I was promoted to study the part of Rosalind in 'As You Like It', and I swashbuckled round that flat in imaginary doublet and hose. **1979** R. BLYTHE *View in Winter* ix. 312, I knew a remittance man in Kenya.. swashbuckling about with a revolver in his belt.

swasher¹, **swesher.** *Sc. Obs.* exc. *Hist.* In 6 **swasche(a)r, swacher, suescher, swescher, -eour.** [f. SWASH *sb.*², SWESH + -ER¹.] A drummer.

15.. *Aberd. Reg.* (Jam.) Commoun tabernar and swescher. **1576** in *Maitl. Club Misc.* (1840) II. 340 Gevin Carsane the swaschear that day we moustirit xxx s. **1600** in Pitcairn *Crim. Trials* II. 245 To the townes twa swascheris.

swasher² ('swɒʃə(r)). [f. SWASH *v.* + -ER¹.] A swashbuckler; a blustering braggart or ruffian; *Sc.* a swaggerer, showy fellow. See also quot. 1866.

1589 [? NASHE] *Almond for Parrat* Ded. 3 Neither must you thinke his worship is to pure to be such a swasher. **1599** SHAKS. *Hen. V*, III. ii. 28 As young as I am, I haue obseru'd these three Swashers. **1619** A. NEWMAN *Pleas. Vis.* 30, I no blaspheming Roarer was, No Swasher, no Repent-too-late. **1621** BURTON *Anat. Mel.* I. ii. III. xv. 170 They cannot.. make congies, which euery common swasher can doe. **1821** SCOTT *Kenilw.* iii, Known for a swasher and a desperate Dick. **1866** GREGOR *Banffsh. Gloss.*, *Swasher*, (1) a person of tall stature, and somewhat ostentatious manners. (2) Anything whatever large and attracting attention. **1889** T. STODDART *Angling Songs* 300 Sic a swasher I ween Is rare to be seen.

swashing ('swɒʃɪŋ), *vbl. sb.* [f. SWASH *v.* + -ING¹.]

1. Ostentatious behaviour; swaggering.

(Cf. SWASH *sb.*¹ 7, 8, SWASH *a.*¹ 2, SWASH *v.* 3, SWASHER², SWASHING *ppl. a.* 1.)

1556 OLDE *Antichrist* 138 b, The ruffling and ioyly swashing of a princes courte. **1587** GREENE *Carde of Fancie* Wks. (Grosart) IV. 14 To see my sonne,.. consume his time.. in swearing and swashing.

2. Violent or noisy striking.

a **1661** FULLER *Worthies, London* II. (1662) 199 Swash-Buckler [so called] from swashing, or making a noise on Bucklers.

3. Dashing or splashing of water.

1819 C'TESS SPENCER *Let.* 3 Nov. in *Corr. Lady Lyttelton* viii. (1912) 215 Only that we still keep up that rare and useless custom of washing and swashing, we should pig it as comfortably as they wallow in Italy. **1864** CARLYLE *Fredk. Gt.* XVII. v. IV. 558 The primordial diluviums and world-old torrents,.. with such storming, gurgling, and swashing. **1870** J. SHARPE in *Eng. Mech.* 4 Mar. 608/3 'Rushing' and 'swashing' in millstones is caused by not driving the stone from its centre. **1872** O. W. HOLMES *Poet Breakf.-t.* xi. (1885) 287 Sparrows.. keep up such a swashing and swabbing and spattering round.. the water basins.

swashing ('swɒʃɪŋ), *ppl. a.* Also 7 **swassing.** [f. SWASH *v.* + -ING².]

1. Characterized by ostentation, or by showy or blustering behaviour; swaggering; swash-buckling; dashing. (Cf. prec. 1.)

1556 OLDE *Antichrist* 147, I speake not now of mytred bishoppes, and swashing abbottes. **1600** SHAKS. *A.Y.L.* I. iii 122 Weele haue a swashing and a marshall outside. *c* **1600** DAY *Begg. Bednall Gr.* IV. i. (1881) 77 The name and habit of some swashing Italian or French Noble-man. **1665** G. HAVERS *P. della Valle's Trav. E. India* 181 By profession Souldiers, sufficiently swashing and brave. **1684** OTWAY *Atheist* IV. i, A blustering, roaring, swashing Shark. **1809** MALKIN *Gil Blas* IV. iii. ¶4 With the swashing outside of a gay spark. **1821** SCOTT *Kenilw.* iv, Lay aside your swashing look. **1885** STEVENSON *Prince Otto* I. iv, The song went to a rough, swashing, popular air.

2. Applied to a particular stroke in fencing, perh. the 'stramazon'; also of a weapon: Slashing with great force. In mod. use only in reminiscences of Shakspere. (Cf. SWASH *a.*[1] 1, WASHING.)

1611 BEAUM. & FL. *Philaster* v. iv, With this swashing blow,..I could hulk your Grace, and hang you up cross-leg'd. *c* **1615** *Shaks.'s Rom. & Jul.* I. i. 70 (Qo. 4) Gregorie, remember thy swashing [*Qo.* 2 & 3, *Fo.* washing] blowe. **1670** MILTON *Hist. Eng.* II. Wks. 1851 V. 70 The Britans had a certain skill with their broad swashing Swords and short Bucklers. **1862** G. A. LAWRENCE *Barren Honour* I. x. 210 Even 'Lanky Jem' recovered after a while from Somers' swashing blow. **1876** TREVELYAN *Life & Lett. Macaulay* II. xii. 253 *note*, He soon showed that he had not forgotten his swashing blow. **1905** *Times* 17 June 4/6 [He] is a swashing foe of all accepted or debated theories but his own.

3. Of water, etc.: Dashing and splashing.

1620 J. TAYLOR (Water P.) *Praise Hemp-seed* (1623) 31 Drencht with the swassing waues, and stewd in sweat. **1853** KANE *Grinnell Exp.* xiv. (1856) 101 Rendered dangerous.. by the swashing ice and a growing fog.

Hence **'swashingly** *adv.*, swaggeringly; in a swashbuckling style.

1664 COTTON *Scarron.* IV. (1741) 79 He wore a Hat Instead of Sattin lac'd with Fat, Which being limber grown we find Most swashingly pinned up behind. **1891** *Sat. Rev.* 15 Aug. 179/2 Mr. Balfour spoke..swashingly about Sir William Harcourt.

†**'swashly**, *adv. Obs.* [f. SWASH *int.* or *a.*[1] + -LY[2].] With a sound of dashing or splashing.

1582 STANYHURST *Æneis* II. (Arb.) 50 Their tayls with croompled knot twisting swashlye they wrigled.

swash-man: see SWASH *sb.*[2]

swash-pen. [f. SWASH *v.* + PEN *sb.*[1], after *swashbuckler.*] A literary braggadocio.

1593 G. HARVEY *Pierce's Super.* 155 Meridarpax..neuer made such a hauocke of the miserable frogges: as this Swash-pen would make of all English writers.

†**swashruter.** *Obs.* If not a misprint, ? a combination of SWASHBUCKLER and SWART-RUTTER.

1582 STANYHURST *Æneis* I. 15 Then sootherne swashruter [orig. *procacibus Austris*]..Flundge vs on high shelueflats.

swash-work: see SWASH *a.*[2]

swashy ('swɒʃɪ), *a.* [f. SWASH *sb.*[1] or *v.* + -Y.] Sloppy, watery. Also *fig.* 'watery', 'washy'.

1796 J. OWEN *Trav. Europe* I. 70 Some part of the track.. was piled into heaps of swashy clay. **1803** J. BUNTING *Let.* 23 Sept., in *Life* (1859) I. x. 182 When I hear such preaching as Mr Jay's, I..wonder that the people should ever like to listen to my poor swashy sermons. **1876** *Whitby Gloss.*, *Swashy*, wet ground. 'Swashy stuff', poor beverage. **1890** *Temple Bar* Sept. 127 The pavement was swashy with three inches of half-melted snow.

swasion, -ive, obs. ff. SUASION, SUASIVE.

†**swa'sivious**, *a. Obs. rare*[−1]. [f. It. *suasivo* SUASIVE + -IOUS.] Agreeably persuasive.

1592 R. D. *Hypnerotomachia* 39b, With pleasurable actions, maydenly iestures, swasiuious behauiours.

swass, swassing, var. SWASH *sb.*[2], SWASHING *ppl. a.*

swastika ('swɒstɪkə, formerly 'swæstɪkə). Also svast-, -ica. [Skr. *svastika*, f. *svastí* well-being, fortune, luck, f. *sú* good + *astí* being (f. *as* to be).] **1.** A primitive symbol or ornament of the form of a cross with equal arms with a limb of the same length projecting at right angles from the end of each arm, all in the same direction and (usually) clockwise; also called GAMMADION and FYLFOT. Also *attrib.*

1871 ALABASTER *Wheel of Law* 249 On the great toe is the Trisul. On each side of the others a Swastika. **1882** E. C. ROBERTSON in *Proc. Berw. Nat. Club* IX. No. 3. 516 In Japan ..the cross-like symbol of the sun, the Swastica, is put on coffins. **1895** *Reliquary* Oct. 252 The use of the Swastica cross in mediaeval times. **1904** *Times* 27 Aug. 10/3 [In Tibet] a few white, straitened hovels in tiers... On the door of each is a kicking swastika in white, and over it a rude daub of ball and crescent.

2. a. This symbol (with clockwise projecting limbs) used as the emblem of the German (and other) Nazi parties; = HAKENKREUZ, HAKENKREUZ. Also, a flag bearing this emblem.

1932 'NORDICUS' *Hitlerism* ii. 17 Thousands flocked to his standard—the 'Hakenkreuz'—(swastika), the ancient anti-semitic cross in a color scheme of red-white-black in memory of the colors of the old army. **1933** [see ARYAN *a.* 2]. **1941** G. ZIEMER *Educ. for Death* i. 4 A squad of Nazi youngsters in..brown shirts decorated with swastikas. *Ibid.* ii. 30 A luxury hotel managed by a Jew... The swastika over it fluttered gaily. **1951** L. HAGEN *Follow my Leader* i. 6 Most of the men in my Sturm wore at least part of a uniform, and all I could do was wear a swastika armlet. *Ibid.* vii. 266 Our compatriots..clung to their German ways and..flew the swastika on our national holidays. **1967** T. GUNN *Touch* 15 A silk tent of swastikas. **1977** E. HEATH *Travels* iv. 113 Along this street had stretched the Nazi columns... Gone, now, were the crowds and the bright-red banners flaunting their swastikas over the streets. **1979** J. BURMEISTER *Glory Hunters* i. 5 In addition to her national flag she [*sc.* a ship] also flew the Swastika.

b. *attrib.* and *Comb.*

1934 *Ann. Reg. 1933* I. 179 Minor acts of defiance towards the Austrian Government..such as..the lighting of Swastika fires and the daring hoisting of forbidden Swastika banners under the eyes of the police..and the hoisting of Swastika flags. **1940** H. G. WELLS *All Aboard for Ararat* iv. 101 As regards the olive branch incident, it is to be noted that the leaves were blood-stained and tied with a swastika ribbon. **1946** J. FLANNER in *New Yorker* 5 Jan. 46/1 Ten years ago, he [*sc.* Goering] was baying 'Heil' as he strutted the swastika-hung streets. **1957** T. GUNN *Sense of Movement* 36 The swastika-draped bed. **1960** *Jewish Chronicle* 8 Apr. 14/3 The recent swastika-daubings in this country.

Hence **'swastika'd** *a.*, decorated with or wearing a swastika, esp. as a badge of Nazism.

1965 *New Statesman* 15 Oct. 552/3 Buckley has.. described the American Nazi Party as 'two dozen swastika-ed cretins who go about plying their pathology in the fever-swamps of the crazy-Right'. **1969** *Listener* 14 Aug. 225/3 Where do those swastika'd Hell's Angels types fit in?

swat (swɒt), *sb.*[1] *north. dial.* and *U.S.* Also swot. [f. SWAT *v.*[1] Cf. SQUAT *sb.*[1]] A smart or violent blow. Also, a heavy fall.

a **1800** PEGGE *Suppl. Grose* (MS.), *Swat*, a Blow. **1847** HALLIWELL, *Swat*..(4) A knock, or blow; a fall. *North.* **1894** *Outing* (U.S.) XXIV. 417/2 One 'swat' from his [*sc.* a bear's] mighty fore-paw. **1909** JACK LONDON in *Contemp. Rev.* June 704, I..ducked a swat from a club.

swat, *sb.*[2], a hard worker: see SWOT *sb.*

Swat (swɒt), *sb.*[3] [The name of a district in the Malakand Division of North-west Frontier Province, Pakistan.] = (and superseded by) SWATI. Also *attrib.* or as *adj.*

1897 *Westm. Gaz.* 8 Sept. 2/2 The Afridi rising..was all a matter of wire-pulling on the part of..the Swat Fakirs. **1911** G. P. GOOCH *Hist. our Times* vii. 170 A rising began in 1897 among the Swats, Mohmands, and Afridis.

swat, *a.*, obs. and dial. var. SQUAT *a.*

1656 S. HOLLAND *Zara* II. v. (1719) 79 Thy breeding no better then that the Boars of Belgia afford their swat-bodied Bantlings.

swat (swɒt), *v.*[1] Also 7 **swatt**, 9 **swot**. [north. dial. and U.S. variant of SQUAT *v.*]

1. *intr.* To sit down, squat. *north.*

1615 BRATHWAIT *Strappado* (1878) 129 Swatt on thy tayle man, heeres a blythy place, And ile ensure thee how I gat this grace. **1804** R. ANDERSON *Cumbld. Ball.* (*c* 1850) 49 They swattet tem down. *Ibid.* 83 Come swat thy ways down on the sattle.

2. *trans.* To hit with a smart slap or a violent blow; also, to dash. Now esp. to crush (a fly, etc.) with a blow.

a **1796** PEGGE *Derbicisms* (E.D.S.), *Swat* a thing on the ground; to swat a person's brains out. *a* **1800** PEGGE *Suppl. Grose* (1814), *Swat*, to throw down forcibly. North. **1848** in Bartlett *Dict. Amer.* s.v., Tell me that again, and I'll swot you over the mug. **1905** D. WALLACE *Lure of Labrador Wild* vi. 83 George effectually disposed of the wounded goose by swatting him over the head with the paddle. **1911** *Daily Record & Mail* 15 July 3 A big army for the destruction of the house fly with 'Swat the Fly' as its battle-cry. **1916** A. HUXLEY *Let.* 29 Sept. (1969) 114 A poem..which..is destined to become a cause of rupture in the world, dividing it up into..Monts and Caps, Mouldiwarpians and Swat-that-Moleites. **1942** *R.A.F. Jrnl.* 18 Apr. 9 The familiar white butterflies should be 'swatted' wholesale. **1958** R. K. NARAYAN *Guide* vii. 139 He repelled me with a back-stroke of his left hand as if swatting a fly. **1962** K. KESEY *One Flew over Cuckoo's Nest* (1973) 9 One swats the backs of my legs with a broom handle to hurry me past. **1976** *Times Lit. Suppl.* 12 Nov. 1414/2 Identical communities to Tolmers Square have been swatted from the urban map.

swat, *v.*[2], to study hard: see SWOT *v.*

swat: see SWEAT *v.*, SWOTE *Obs.*, sweat.

Swatantra (swɑː'tɑːntrə). [Hindi, (one who is) self-determined or self-motivated.] In full, ***Swatantra party***. A liberal conservative political party (the Freedom Party) in the Republic of India from 1959 to 1972. Also *attrib.*

1959 *Hindu* 8 June 1/5 Addressing a..public meeting in Royapettah last evening, Mr. C. Rajagopalachari explained the aims and policies that would be pursued by the new Opposition party, which he said, would be called the Swatantra Party. **1963** H. TINKER *Democratic Ideal in Asia* 23 C. R. Rajagopalachari, the veteran Swatantra statesman. **1966** *Economist* 24 Dec. 1319/3 The rajahs who joined Swatantra in droves were angry with Congress for having reduced them to commoners. **1979** V. L. PANDIT *Scope of Happiness* ii. 13 A merger of Congress (O), Swatantra party, Jan Sangh, and Bharatiya Lok Dal.

swatch (swɒtʃ), *sb.*[1] orig. *Sc.* and *north.* Also 6–7 **swache**, 7 **suache**, **swatche**. [Origin unknown.]

1. †The 'foil' or 'counterstock' of a tally (*obs.*); in Yorkshire, a tally 'affixed to a piece of cloth before it is put with others into the dye-kettle' (Robinson *Whitby Gloss.* 1876).

1512 *Northumbld. Househ. Bk.* (1770) 60 That the said Clerkis of the Brevements entre all the Taills of the Furniunturs in the Jornall Booke in the Countynghous every day furthwith after the Brede be delyveret to the Pantre and then the Stoke of the Taill to be delyveret to the Baker and the Swache to the Pantler. **1691** RAY *N.C. Words*, *A Swache*, a Tally: that which is fixt to Cloth sent to Dye, of which the Owner keeps the other part. *a* **1800** PEGGE *Suppl. Grose* (1814), *Swatch*, a pattern, or tally, a term among dyers in Yorkshire, &c.

2. A sample piece of cloth. Hence, of other materials (see also *S.N.D.*). Also, a collection of samples bound together, a swatch-book.

1647 in *Sc. Jrnl. Topog.* (1847) I. 95/1, I..tryid for ye neirest swachis of clothe I could find conforme to ye orders reseuid. **1690** *Records New Mills Cloth Manuf.* (S.H.S.) 219 That swatches of the most fashionable collours be sent to David Maxwell that he may dye them. **1830** GALT *Lawrie T.* VII. xi. (1849) 352, He had come with his swatches, in consequence of hearing I was likely to require a coloured coat. **1874** CROOKES *Dyeing & Calico-Printing* 658 Few colours..do not show a distinction if a swatch be cut in halves and preserved, the one in darkness and the other in the light. **1953** *Times* 23 July 1/4 (Advt.), Duffle jackets and duffle coats... Swatches sent on request. **1973** *Sci. Amer.* June 119/2 Continue..until a piece of filter paper or swatch of cotton held close to the exit by means of long metal forceps begins to burn. **1982** *Daily Tel.* 2 Aug. 9/2 He wears swatches of the hats he is currently working on, hat-pinned to his tie for inspiration.

transf. *a* **1708** T. WARD *Eng. Ref.* I. (1710) 14 Those little swatches, Us'd by the Fair sex, called Patches. **1928** P. GREY *Making of King* 6 Ye'll mind an' bring a swatch o' yer wallpaper wi' ye. **1957** *Brit. Commonwealth Forest Terminol.* II. 192 *Swatch*, a sample sheet of veneer, usually 3 ft. long and the full width of the flitch. **1965** G. MCINNES *Road to Gundagai* iii. 38 One's wants were provided for by a swatch of neatly cut squares from the Hobart *Mercury* struck on a nail in the wall. **1973** *Sci. Amer.* Apr. 41/1 A swatch of inks as rendered by Kodak color slide films that maximize consumer satisfaction with the greenness of grass, the blueness of sky, and the healthy glow of complexions. **1981** N. GORDIMER *July's People* 54 She knew it was impossible that he could have made free of the still-thick swatch of notes, lying swollen as the leaves of a book that has got wet and dried again.

3. *fig.* A sample, specimen. Also extendedly (esp. without the notion of a sample), a portion, a clump.

1697 J. SAGE *Fundamental Charter of Presbytery* Pref. (ed. 2) C vj b, Such a sample of him; such a swatch (pardon the word, if it is not English) of both his Historical and his Argumentative Skill. **1708** *Caldwell Papers* (Maitl. Cl.) I. 216 My Lord Macclesfield and his retinue they took for a swatch of the nation. **1719** RAMSAY *To Arbuckle* 95 Ye's get a short swatch of my creed. **1785** BURNS *Holy Fair* x, On this hand sits a chosen swatch, Wi' screw'd up grace-proud faces. **1823** GALT *R. Gilhaize* xiv, Truly..thou's no an ill swatch o' the Reformers. *a* **1841** R. W. HAMILTON *Nugæ Lit.* 355 [On Yorks. Dial.] A *Swatch*, or *smatch*, is an attack, not very serious, of any evil. 'A swatch of the fever.' **1930** *Aberdeen Press & Jrnl.* 19 May 5/2 Swatches from Shakespeare... The miscellany consisted of excerpts from 'Henry IV',..the ghost scene in 'Hamlet', [etc.]. **1950** A. LOMAX *Mister Jelly Roll* 30 The hollows of his cheeks and temples showing dark against silvery skin, and up towards the ceiling a swatch of silvery hair. **1961** J. STEINBECK *Winter of our Discontent* 358 A swatch from Lincoln's Second Inaugural. **1963** *Punch* 31 July 165/1, I..consumed unbelievable swatches of it [*sc.* electricity]. **1972** J. MOSEDALE *Football* ii. 23 A swatch of astroturf in the Hall leads to the present. **1975** *Times Lit. Suppl.* 24 Oct. 1254/1 Mr Boston gives a fair selection: the life and death of the Admirable Crichtoun from *The Jewel*, a reasonable swatch of *Logopandecteision*.

4. Comb. **swatch-book**, a book of samples.

1956 *Archit. Rev.* CXIX. 286/1 One of the first firms to pin their colours to this mast is T. & W. Farmiloe Ltd., the manufacturers of Nine Elms Paints, who present the full range in the form of a truly magnificent swatch-book. **1978** *Times* 26 Jan. 13/5 Some of the collections were just dull... Why not just send for the swatch-book?

swatch, *sb.*[2] *Obs.* exc. *dial.* [app. an irreg. variant of SWATH[1]. Cf. dial. *swatch* = SWATHE *v.*] A row (of corn or grass) cut.

1573 TUSSER *Husb.* (1878) 131 One spreadeth those bands, so in order to ly, As barlie (in swatches) may fill it thereby. **1901** (Lancashire) in *Eng. Dial. Dict.*

swatch (swɒtʃ), *sb.*[3] *local.* [In local English use chiefly in eastern counties. Its relation to SWASH *sb.*[1] 3 is not clear.] A passage or channel of water lying between sandbanks or between a sandbank and the shore.

1626 in Foster *Eng. Factories India* (1909) III. 117 [Anchored] without the swatch of Swally. **1726** G. ROBERTS *Four Yrs. Voy.* 336 From a Mile distance off, to the Shore, are several Swatches and Channels to go through, having Water enough for any Ship. **1775** ROMANS *Florida* App. 86 There are two swatches thro' the east breaker. **1830** LYELL *Princ. Geol.* I. 243 A nearly circular space called the 'swatch of no ground' [in the middle of the Bay of Bengal]. **1889** A. T. PASK *Eyes Thames* 66 The famous 'Swatch' caused by the meeting of the Thames and Medway tides. **1912** HANNAY in *Blackw. Mag.* Mar. 369/1 The access to the roadstead was through 'swatches'.

b. *Comb.* **'swatchway** = *swash way* (SWASH *sb.*[1] 9).

1798 *Hull Advertiser* 29 Dec. 2/1 Anchors and cables, lost and left in the Humber..in the open of Patrington Swatch Way. **1851** TAYLOR *Improvem. Tyne* 85 Such is an origin of swatchways in tidal rivers. **1890** *Nature* 10 Apr. 539/2 The Duke of Edinburgh Channel, the deepest swatchway of the estuary. **1903** CHILDERS *Riddle of Sands* xii. 154 We traversed the Steil Sand again, but by a different swatchway.

†**swatche**, *v. Obs. rare.* Variant of SQUATCH *v.*

a **1300** *E.E. Psalter* cv. 29 [cvi. 30] The scatthinge [*v.rr.* sqwattinge, swacching; L. *quassatio*] lefte ilkadele. *Ibid.* cix. 7 [cx. 6] Sqwat [*v.rr.* swatche, squatche; L. *conquassabit*] sal he heuedes, blode and bane.

swatchel ('swɒtʃəl). *slang.* Also 9 **schwassle**. [Perh. f. G. *schwätzeln*, frequentative form of *schwatzen* to chatter, tattle.] An older form of

SWAZZLE; also interpreted as the name for Mr. Punch in a Punch and Judy show. Freq. *attrib.*, as ***swatchel box, cove*** (see quots.).

1854 *Househ. Words* 24 Sept. 76/1 A Punch's show [is] a schwassle-box. **1864** HOTTEN *Slang Dict.*, *Swatchel-cove*, the master of a Punch-and-Judy exhibition who..does the necessary squeak for the amusement of the bystanders. **1887** W. E. HENLEY *Villon's Good-Night* in J. S. Farmer *Musa Pedestris* (1896) 174 You swatchel-coves that pitch and slam. **1900** *Sat. Rev.* 19 May 613/1 Students of Romany..will find some interest in a list furnished to a friend who handed it on to me by a 'swatchel-cove' or peregrinating Punch-exhibitor. **1921** *Glasgow Herald* 24 June 7 'Swatchel' is Mr Punch, hence 'Swatchel-box' the show, and 'Swatchel cove' the patterer. *c* **1938** A. HAMBLING *Punch & Judy* 3 Wet the swatchel, and having fixed the thread, put it on the tongue crosswise. **1983** *Listener* 22 Sept. 14/3 The word 'swatchel' is Punch and Judy showmen's slang for the figure of Punch.

swatching ('swɒtʃɪŋ), *vbl. sb.* [Origin unknown.] A method of taking seals: see quot. 1901.

1883 *Fisheries Exhib. Catal.* (ed. 4) 175 Swatching and Trolling Old Hoods. **1901** W. T. GRENFELL in *Blackw. Mag.* Nov. 692/1 Many seals are taken by the process known as 'swatching'... On finding a clear piece of water, called a 'pond', we built a shelter of ice, called a 'gaze'. Here one sits and waits till a seal puts up his head.

swath[1] (swɔːθ, swɒθ), **swathe** (sweɪð). Forms: 1 **swæþ, swaþu**, 3 **swaðe**, (4 **swethe** ?, 6 **swade, suath**, 7 **swaithe, sweath**, 7–9 **swaith**), 4– **swath, swathe.** [OE. *swæþ* str. n., *swaþu* str. fem. trace, track, corresp. to MLG. *swat, swâde* furrow, swath, measure of land (LG. *swad, swatt*), MDu. *swat* (*-d-*), **swâde* (Du. *zwad, zwade*) swath, MG. *swade* wk. m. swath, piece of flesh torn off longways (G. *schwad* str. m. and n., *schwade* wk. m. and f. swath, space covered by the scythe in a swing); Fris., (M)LG., early mod.Du. *swade* have also the meaning 'scythe'. The ulterior relations and original meaning of the underlying Teut. root *swaþ-* are uncertain.

Evidence is not available for determining the date of the appearance of the form with a long vowel typically represented by the spelling *swathe*, since in the early periods *swathe, swathes*, are phonetically ambiguous; in modern local use, *swathe* is characteristic of the northern counties; its use in literature has prob. been furthered by association with SWATHE *sb.*[2]]

†**1.** Track, trace. *lit.* and *fig. Obs.*

Chiefly or ? only OE.; quot. *c* 1250 is dubious.

Beowulf 2098 (Gr.), Hwæþre him sio swiðre swaðe weardade hand on Hiorte. *c* **888** ÆLFRED *Boeth.* xxxix. §1 He ..ne forlæt nan swæð ær he ȝefehð þæt þæt he æftersþyreð. *a* **900** *O.E. Martyrol.* 5 May 74 On Oliuetes dune syndon nu ȝyt þa swæðe dryhtnes fotlasta..ne mihte seo his swaðu.. beon þæm oðrum florum ȝeonlicod. *c* **900** tr. *Bæda's Hist.* IV. iii. (1899) 350 þa swaðe awuniað reȝollices lifes [*orig. regularis vitæ vestigia permanent*]. *c* **1250** *Gen. & Ex.* 3786 Gret fier..for-brende hem..Oc aaron al hol and fer, Cam him no fieres swaðe ner.

2. a. The space covered by a sweep of the mower's scythe; the width of grass or corn so cut.

c **1475** *Cath. Angl.* 373/2 (Addit. MS.), Swathe, *orbita falcatoris est.* **1523** FITZHERB. *Husb.* §23 Take hede that thy mower..mowe his swathe cleane thorowe to that that was laste mowen before. **1664** SPELMAN *Gloss.* s.v. *Dolæ*, Illud terræ spacium quod uno falcis ictu messor radit. Angl. swath. *c* **1830** *Glouc. Farm Rep.* 27 in *Libr. Usef. Knowl., Husb.* III, The mowing should be so performed, that neither the strokes of the scythe nor the junction of the swaths can be discerned. **1849** THOREAU *Week Concord Riv.* Sat. 41 The great mower Time, who cuts so broad a swathe. **1879** J. D. LONG *Æneid* IX. 415 While I cut right and left, And mow thee in advance a good wide swath.

b. As a measure of grass land: A longitudinal division of a field, ? orig. reckoned by the breadth of one sweep of the scythe. *local.*

c **1325** in Kennett *Par. Ant.* (1818) I. 573 Duæ Swathes dicti prati jacent ut sequitur. *Ibid.*, Dimidia roda et dimidia Swathe apud Shortedolemede. **1526** *Lincoln Wills* (Linc. Rec. Soc.) V. 166, I bequeth vj swades off medow grounde lyeng att byllesby croffte end for to kepe an obbyt for my soule. **1625** *Deed* in *Sheffield Gloss.* (1888) s.v., All those foure swathes of land lying and being in Crigleston. **1664** *N. Riding Rec. Soc.* (1886) IV. 162 All those sixteene swaithes of meadowe-ground lyeing etc. within the lord-shippe of Cropton. **1787** *Survey* in *N.W. Linc. Gloss.* (1877) s.v., All the grass lands in the Ings are laid out in Gads or swaths. **1839** STONEHOUSE *Axholme* 158 Two swathes [of land] in the Ings Meadow.

†**c.** The extent of sweep of a scythe. *Obs. rare.*

Misunderstood by R. Holme *Armoury* III. 332/2 as 'the long crooked Staff or Pole' of a scythe.

1577 B. GOOGE *Heresbach's Husb.* I. (1586) 41 b, In other places they vse a greater Sythe with a long Suath.

d. A stroke of the scythe in reaping. *rare.*

a **1643** W. CARTWRIGHT *Poems, On Birth Dk. of York* 38 A strangled snake, Kill'd before known, perhaps 'mongst Heathen hath Been thought the deed and valour of the Swath. **1874** HARDY *Far fr. Madding Crowd* II. iii. 30 The hiss of tressy oat-ears rubbing together as their perpendicular stalks of amber-yellow fell heavily to each swath.

3. a. A row or line of grass, corn, or other crop, as it falls or lies when mown or reaped; also *collectively*, a crop mown and lying on the ground; phr. ***in*** (***the***) ***swath*** (cf. LG. *in't swatt*), lying in this condition.

Sometimes, 'the quantity falling at one sweep of the scythe' (Robinson *Whitby Gloss.* 1876 s.v. *Sweeathe*).

c **1325** *Gloss. W. de Bibbesw.* in Wright *Voc.* 154 *Une andeyne de prée*, a swathe [*v.r.* a swethe of mede]. *c* **1340** *Nominale* (Skeat) 112 M[an] mawith of mede a swath. ? *a* **1400** *Morte Arth.* 2508 A mede..Mawene and vne-made, ..In swathes sweppene downe, fulle of swete floures. **1573** TUSSER *Husb.* (1878) 122 Grasse latelie in swathes is hay for an ox. **1606** SHAKS. *Tr. & Cr.* V. v. 25 The straying Greekes ripe for his edge, Fall downe before him, like the mowers swath. **1614** SYLVESTER *Bethulia's Rescue* V. 499 Long Swathes of their degraded Grasse, Well show the way their sweeping Scithes did pass. **1616** SURFL. & MARKH. *Country Farm* IV. vi. 499 If there be plentie of grasse, and that you see it lye thicke in the swathes. **1622** DRAYTON *Poly-olb.* xxii. 678 Swaths of new-shorn grass. **1766** GOLDSM. *Vicar W.* vi, We turned the swath to the wind. **1766** *Compl. Farmer*, *Grips*, the swaiths, or small heaps of corn, lying in the field, as it is cut down with the scythe. **1813** T. DAVIS *Agric. Wilts* Gloss. s.v., Hay [is] in swath when just mowed. **1831** *Sutherland Farm Rep.* 74 in *Libr. Usef. Knowl., Husb.* III, That it may come early to the swaith, it is never permitted to eat it down in autumn. **1834** *Brit. Husb.* I. 73 As clover.. is rarely tedded, it should be sufficient to leave every tenth swathe for the tithe. **1840** *Florist's Jrnl.* (1846) I. 70 Though the swathe from some grounds is not heavy, the quality will everywhere be very superior. **1857** G. MUSGRAVE *Pilgr. Dauphiné* I. xi. 243 The grass had been cut, and left in swaths. **1883** SYMONDS *Ital. Byways* i. 1 Men..were mowing the frozen grass..and as the swathes fell, they gave a crisp..sound.

b. *transf.* Applied to growing grass or corn ready for mowing or reaping.

1577 B. GOOGE *Heresbach's Husb.* I. (1586) 45 b, To the ende the after swath may be mowed in Autume. **1612** DRAYTON *Poly-olb.* xiv. 100 Whose burden'd pasture bears The most abundant swathe. **1819** KEATS *To Autumn* 18 While thy hook Spares the next swath and all its twined flowers. **1846** J. BAXTER *Libr. Pract. Agric.* (ed. 4) I. 366 In June there was a heavy swath, which was mown for seed. **1868** MORRIS *Earthly Par.* (1870) I. II. 592 Within the flowery swathe he heard The sweeping of the scythe.

c. ***to cut a swath*** (U.S. slang): to make a pompous display, swagger, 'cut a dash'. Now freq. ***to cut a wide swath.***

1848 BARTLETT *Dict. Amer.* s.v. *Cut.* **1855** *Knickerb. Mag.* Dec. 617 [He] might better have cut just as big a swath somewhere else. **1902** H. L. WILSON *Spenders* 348 You folks been cuttin' a pretty wide swath here in New York. **1929** *Amer. Speech* V. 119 [Maine] Someone conceited..'feels his oats', 'cuts a wide swath', 'is one of the big bugs'. **1960** I. WALLACH *Absence of Cello* (1961) 241 He was determined to cut a wide swath with the girls—no easy trick in Philadelphia.

4. *transf.* and *fig.* **a.** A broad track, belt, strip, or longitudinal extent of something.

? **1605** DRAYTON *Poems Lyr. & Past.* Ode vii. B8 b, Yet many riuers cleere Here glide in siluer swathes, And what of all most deare Buckstons delicious bathes. **1681** GREW *Musæum* IV. ii. 367 The Notch fortify'd with a Swath of split Quill. **1715** tr. *Gregory's Astron.* (1726) I. 256 The.. Ecliptic, or rather Zodiac, (for like a Belt or Swath, it is 20 deg. broad). **1818** HOGG *Brownie of Bodsbeck* I. iii. 41, I began to look o'er my shouther, but there was naething there but the swathes o' mist. **1849** CUPPLES *Green Hand* xiii, Where you saw the water winding about the horizon in long swathes, as it were. **1859** MAURY *Phys. Geog.* vi. §339. 105 A breadth or *swath* of winds in the north-east trades. **1867** SMYTH *Sailor's Word-bk.*, *Swathe*, the entire length of a sea-wave. **1909** R. F. ANDERSON *Logie 100 Years Ago* 9 An auld wifie laying out a swath of unbleached cotton.

b. Something compared to grass or corn falling before the scythe or sickle; *esp.* used of troops 'mown down' in battle.

1852 M. ARNOLD *Human Life* 19 As the foaming swath Of torn-up water, on the main, Falls heavily away with long-drawn roar. **1856** RUSKIN *Mod. Paint.* IV. v. vi. §9. 89 The sound of every drooping swathe of rain. **1873** LONGF. *Wayside Inn* III. *Scanderbeg* 19 The rearguard as it fled, Mown down in the bloody swath Of the battle's aftermath. **1895** A. I. SHAND *Life Gen. Sir E. B. Hamley* I. iv. 92 We see the dead lying in swathes as they had fallen.

5. *attrib.* and *Comb.*, as ***swath-width***; **swath-board**, a slanting board attached to the cutter-bar of a mowing machine, designed to force the cut grass, etc., into a narrower swath; **swath(e)-balk**, a ridge of grass left unmown between the swaths, or between the sweeps of the scythe; hence **swath(e)-balked** *a.*; **swath(e)-rake**, 'a wooden rake the breadth of the swath, used to collect the scattered hay or corn' (E.D.D.); **swath-turner**, a machine used for turning over swaths of hay.

1691 RAY *N.C. Words*, A **Swathe bauk*, a Swarth of new mowen Grass or Corn. **1811** WILLAN in *Archaeologia* XVII. 160 (*W. Riding Words*), *Swath-Bauks*, the edges of grass between the semicircular cuttings of the scythe. *a* **1800** PEGGE *Suppl. Grose*, **Swath-bawk'd*, grass that has escaped the scythe. Lanc. **1952** J. W. DAY *New Yeomen of England* vii. 87 After mowing, the lucerne is tedded to remove the wad, left by the *swathe board, and is then swept to the tripods and cocked. **1963** *Listener* 28 Mar. 552/1 The swathe-board..of a grass-mower. **1652** *Inv.* in *N.W. Linc. Gloss.* (1877) s.v., Two yron *swath rakes. **1658** R. HUBBERTHORN *Rec. Sufferings for Tythes* (MS.) Sweath-rake. **1764** *Museum Rust.* II. 31 The swathe-rake; a rake about two yards long, with iron teeth, and a beam in the middle, to which a man fixes himself with a belt. **1766** *Compl. Farmer*, *Swath-rake*...much used in Essex for gathering barley after mowing. **1922** JOYCE *Ulysses* 699 Grindstone, clodcrusher, *swatheturner, carriagesack. **1958** *Times* 27 Oct. 15/4 A swath-turner was used to invert the swath and move it onto dry ground. **1778** [W. MARSHALL] *Minutes Agric., Observ.* 24 In the middles of some of the *swath-widths. **1970** G. F. BURNETT in H. W. Mulligan *African Trypanosomiases* xxiv. 506 When treating an area of woodland, the aircraft must pass over it on parallel runs at regularly spaced intervals, each of which is referred to as a 'swath width'.

swath[2], **swathe**, local variant of SWARTH *sb.*[1] (Cf. SWAD *sb.*[1])

1776 in *Trans. Soc. Arts* (1784) II. 68 Holes, which will hold water, and quite spoil the Turf or new Swath. **1826** SCOTT *Woodst.* xxxiii, I have made him plough in my furrow, when he thought he was turning up his own swathe. **1873** *Swaledale Gloss.*, *Swath*, the skin of bacon. **1877** *N.W. Linc. Gloss.*, *Swarth, Swath, Sward, Swad*, grass-land.

swath, obs. form of SWATHE.

†**swath-band, swathe-band.** *Obs.* Forms: 4 **suaþebend**, 6 **swadeband, sweathband**, 6–7 **swathe-band**, (9 *Hist.*) **swath-band**; 7 **swathe-bond.** [f. stem of SWATHE *v.* + BAND *sb.*[1] (BEND *sb.*[1], BOND *sb.*[1]). Cf. SWATHING-BANDS.]

1. *pl.* Swaddling-bands, swaddling-clothes.

c **1315** SHOREHAM III. 127 In suaþebendes hy hyne dyȝte, Ase hyt hys þe chyldes ryȝte. **1563** *Mirr. Mag.*, *Hastings* xcii, Euen in thy Swathebands out commission goeth To loose thy breath, that yet but yongly bloweth. **1596** SPENSER *F.Q.* VI. iv. 23 Euery part, that vnder sweathbands lay. **1632** B. JONSON *Magn. Lady* III. iv, Could they teach each other how to win I' their swath bands. **1641** J. TRAPPE *Theol. Theol.* i. 6 The Babe of Bethlehem (lapt up in the swath-bands of the holy History). **1652** SPARKE *Prim. Devot.* (1663) 534 Did not princes Christ in swath-bands greet? **1656** J. SMITH *Pract. Physick* 208 After four Months the Hands and Arms may be let loose from swath-bands.

2. A bandage, binder.

1556 J. HEYWOOD *Spider & F.* lxxx. 32 One leg, and his waste, in swadeband rold to be, And crutches by his side. **1615** SYLVESTER *Job Triumph.* IV. 408 Whenas I made the Cloud a clowt for it, And blackest Darkness as a swath-band fit. **1672** *Ovid de Arte Amandi* 76 About a faint and slender body wear A flannel swathband or warm stomacher. **1688** HOLME *Armoury* III. 434/2 A Swathe Band..Of some called a Rowller, or a Linnen Rowller.

3. *transf.* An enveloping membrane. *rare.*

1668 CULPEPPER & COLE *Barthol. Anat.* I. xvii. 45 Another external [membrane] from the Peritonæum, which adhæres but loosely, whence they term it the Swath-band of the Kidneys [i.e. *fascia renum*].

†**swath-clouts**, *sb. pl. Obs.* Also 4 clut; 6 **swathe.** [f. stem of SWATHE *v.* + pl. of CLOUT *sb.* Cf. SWATHING-CLOUTS.] Swaddling-clothes.

c **1325** *Gloss. W. de Bibbesw.* in Wright *Voc.* 143 (Camb. MS.) Lors deyt estre maylolez [*gloss* swath-clut]. **1579** LYLY *Euphues* (Arb.) 60 When children are in their swathe cloutes. **1580** *Ibid.* Ep. Ded. 214 The other (right Honourable) being but yet in his swathe cloutes, I commit..to your Lordships protection. **1583** MELBANCKE *Philotimus* H iv b, Was it not better for the two twinnes Romulus and Remus, to be caste oute in their swath clowtes? **1592** LYLY *Gallathea* III. i, Beeing yet scarce out of his swath-clowtes.

swathe, *sb.*[1]: see SWATH[1].

swathe (sweɪð), *sb.*[2] Also 7–8 **swaith, swath.** [OE. **swæþ* (?), *swaþ-*, only in dat. pl. *swaþum*; for related forms see SWATHE *v.*, SWETHE, SWADDLE, SWEDDLE.]

1. A band of linen, woollen, or other material in which something is enveloped; a wrapping; sometimes, a single fold or winding of such; also *collect. sing.* **a.** *gen.*

c **1050** *Voc.* in Wr.-Wülcker 484/17 *Institis*, in swaþum. [Gloss on John xi. 44.] **1598** FLORIO, *Banda*..a skarfe or a swathe. **1666** WOOD *Life* (O.H.S.) II. 88, 3 crevetts, 4 swaiths, 2 handkerchiefs. **1681** GREW *Musæum* IV. iii. 373 The Handle, adorned with fine Straws laid along the sides, and lap'd round about it, in several distinct Swaths. **1711** ADDISON *Spect.* No. 90 ¶7 Long Pieces of Linen, which they folded about me till they had wrapt me in above an hundred Yards of Swathe. **1737** WHISTON *Josephus, Antiq.* III. vii. §3 A cap,..made of thick swaths. **1818** KEATS *Prophecy* 21 Though the linen that will be Its swathe, is on the cotton tree. **1911** 'GEO. A. BIRMINGHAM' *Lighter Side Irish Life* vii. 159 Young men masked and disguised with swathes of straw tied over their clothes.

†**b.** *sing.* & *pl.* An infant's swaddling-bands. *Obs.*

1565 COOPER *Thesaurus*, *Crepundia*..the first apparayle of children, as, swathes,..and such lyke. **1580** *Fermor Acc.* in *Archæol. Jrnl.* (1851) VIII. 186 Yᵉ other daughter to be pictured [on the side of the Tomb] as dieinge in yᵉ cradle or swathes. **1607** SHAKS. *Timon* IV. iii. 252 Had'st thou like vs from our first swath proceeded. **1646** LLUELYN *Men-Miracles*, etc. 98 Thou that in Conquests didst thy Non-age bathe, And like Alcides combate in thy Swathe. **1742** BLAIR *Grave* 138 Like new-born Infant wound up in his Swathes. **1786** *Misc. Ess.* in *Ann. Reg.* 125/1 [The infant] is not there swaddled and filleted up in a swathe.

c. A surgical bandage.

1615 CROOKE *Body of Man* Pref. 1 Engines, Swathes, Ties, Bands and Ligatures, described by Hippocrates. **1656** J. SMITH *Pract. Physick* 162 Swaths, which are either of leather..or of woollen. **1722** DOUGLAS in *Phil. Trans.* XXXII. 85, I turn'd a swath a little broader than the Patient's Hand once round him. **1806** J. BERESFORD *Miseries Hum. Life* III. (ed. 3) 43 My limping gait, and this bewitching swathe about my head. **1897** *Allbutt's Syst. Med.* II. 376 Strips of lint..may be laid along the..swelling ..and covered with the flannel swathe as before.

2. *transf.* **a.** A natural formation constituting a wrapping; †a covering membrane, integument; an object that enwraps something, as a cloud.

1615 CROOKE *Body of Man* 191 The outward coate inuesting the kidneyes which is commonly called *fascia* or the swath. **1733** CHEYNE *Engl. Malady* I. x. §4. 98 These Swaiths and Membranes burst and break naturally. **1871** *Daily News* 19 Aug., Grey swathes of cloud still hung about the hills. **1880** BROWNING *Pan & Luna* 49 The downy swathes [of cloud about the moon] combine. **1891** MEREDITH *Poems, Eng. bef. Storm* iv, When..high in swathe of smoke the mast Its fighting rag outrolled.

†**b.** = LIST *sb.*³ 6 b, LISTEL. *Obs.*

1673 MOXON tr. Barozzio's *Vignola* 22 The nether Band or Swathe of the Column. *Ibid.* 58 The upper Torus, or Swathe.

c. *fig.* Something that restricts or confines like a swaddling-band.

1864 *Spectator* 31 Dec. 1500 Tied up helplessly in tight swathes of ignorance. **1906** *Ibid.* 3 Feb. 176/1 Within the swathes and fetters of civilisation.

3. *Comb.*: †**swathe-fish**, the ribbon-fish.

1668 CHARLETON *Onomast.* 126 *Tænia*..the Swath-fish. **1901** CLIVE HOLLAND *Mousmé* 89 With a graceful bending of her knees beneath her swathelike kimono.

swathe (sweɪð), *v.* Also 6-7 **swath**. [late OE. *swaþian*, f. *swaþ*: see SWATHE *sb.*²]

1. *trans.* To envelop in a swathe or swathes; to wrap up, swaddle, bandage.

11.. *MS. Cott. Vesp. D. 14* in Kluge *Angelsächs. Lesebuch* 73 Heo hine baðede..and frefrede and swaðede and roccode. **13..** *Bonaventura's Medit.* 974 Marye, with a swote cloute, Swaþed here sones hede all aboute. *c* **1425** *Cursor M.* 11236 (Laud) Suche clothis as she had to hond With suche she swathid [*Cott.* suedeld, *Gött.* swetheled] hym & bond. *c* **1440** *Pallad. on Husb.* IV. 78 Swathe [*v.r.* swethe] a tender vyne in bondes softe. **1538** ELYOT, *Fascior* .., to swathe a chylde. **1611** COTGR., *Bander*..to bind, swaddle, swath, tye with bands. **1697** DAMPIER *Voy.* I. xv. 408 From their Infancy their Feet are kept swathed up with bands. **1742** RICHARDSON *Pamela* IV. 319, I have seen poor Babies roll'd and swath'd, ten or a dozen times round, then Blanket upon Blanket, Mantle upon that. **1819** SCOTT *Ivanhoe* xlii, I found my arms swathed down, my feet tied. **1824** —— *Redgauntlet* let. xi, His legs stretched out before him, and swathed up with flannel. **1863** TYNDALL *Heat* i. 6 Two glasses are swathed thickly round with listing, to prevent the warmth of the hands from reaching the mercury. **1892** K. TYNAN in *Speaker* 3 Sept. 290/1 In the winter [the roses] were swathed in cocoanut fibre and sacking.

b. Said of the swathe or wrapping.

1856 MISS MULOCK *John Halifax* xxii, The showiest of cambric kerchiefs swathing him up to the very chin. **1909** *Daily Graphic* 4 Oct. 13/2 This scarf-like trimming also swathes the high toques of pleated velvet.

c. To wrap round something, as or like a swathe or bandage.

1656 J. SMITH *Pract. Physick* 163 The second band laid on they swathe with fewer rollings. **1824** W. IRVING *T. Trav.* IV. 279 He..had a red belt or sash swathed round his body. **1833** M. SCOTT *Tom Cringle* xv. (1859) 369, I can swathe a bandage too, although no surgeon. **1909** *Daily Graphic* 4 Oct. 13/1 [To] wear their hair swathed round their heads à la Récamier.

2. *transf.* and *fig.* To envelop or surround as with a wrapping; to enwrap, enfold; †to encircle so as to confine or restrain.

1624 QUARLES *Job* Sect. xviii. N 4 b, Who is't that tames the raging of the Seas, And swathes them vp in mists, when-e're he please? **1692** BP. HOPKINS *Disc. Providence* in *Expos. Lord's Prayer*, etc. 276 Who hath swathed in the great and proud Ocean, with a Girdle of Sand. **1781** COWPER *Retirem.* 527 [God] swathes about the swelling of the deep, That shines and rests, as infants smile and sleep. **1809** DE QUINCEY in 'H. A. Page' *Life* (1877) I. vii. 145 My cottage ..being swathed about by a little orchard. **1860** FROUDE *Hist. Eng.* xxxv. VI. 528 In that brief time she had swathed her name in the horrid epithet which will cling to it for ever. **1860** TYNDALL *Glac.* I. xxi. 145 The Riffelberg was swathed in a dense fog. **1860** FARRAR *Orig. Lang.* vi. 141 The mists that swathed the primeval chaos. **1866** G. MACDONALD *Ann. Q. Neighb.* xv. (1878) 308 The water swathed their stems with coolness and freshness. **1884** W. C. SMITH *Kildrostan* 43 Dim-lettered texts from the Holy Word; But all in the damp moss swathed and bound.

¶**3.** To make into sheaves. *Obs. rare*$^{-0}$.

1611 COTGR., *Javelé*, swathed, or made into sheaues. *Ibid.*, *Javeler*, to swathe, or gauel corn; to make it into sheaues, or gauells.

swathe-band: see SWATH-BAND.

swathed (sweɪðd, *poet.* 'sweɪðɪd), *ppl. a.* [f. SWATHE *v.* + -ED¹.]

†**1.** Wrapped in swaddling-clothes, swaddled. *Obs.*

1608 HEYWOOD *Lucrece* Wks. 1874 V. 167 He..first deposd My father in my swathed infancy. **1627** DRAYTON *Agincourt* lxxi, An eagle..A swathed Infant holding in her foote.

2. Enveloped in a wrapping or bandage or in clothes draped round the figure; in recent dressmaking, arranged in or characterized by folds resembling those of a bandage.

1815 KIRBY & SP. *Entomol.* iii. (1818) I. 66 The swathed appearance of most insects in this state [*sc.* the pupa state]. **1821** JOANNA BAILLIE *Metr. Leg., Malcolm's Heir* iii, The Swathed Knight walks his rounds. **1852** THACKERAY *Esmond* I. xiii, With a laugh and a look at his swathed [gouty] limb. **1896** *Daily News* 1 Dec. 5/6 The swathed bodice was ornamented with straps of embroidery. **1899** MARG. BENSON & GOURLAY *Temple of Mut* i. 11 An Arab girl with solemn eyes and swathed form.

swathel, obs. form of SWADDLE.

swather¹ ('sweɪðə(r)). *rare.* [f. SWATHE *v.* + -ER¹.]

¶**1.** (See quot. and SWATHE *v.* 3.) *Obs. rare*$^{-0}$.

1611 COTGR., *Iaveleur*, a swather, or binder vp of corne into gavells.

2. One who swathes.

1833 J. DAVIDSON *Embalming* 6 It [*sc.* the body] was then washed, and by the χολχιται, or swathers, closely wrapped in cloth.

swather² ('swɔːθə(r), 'swɒθə(r)). [f. SWATH¹ + -ER¹.] (See quot.)

1875 KNIGHT *Dict. Mech.*, *Swather*, a device attached to the front of a mowing-machine for the purpose of raising the uncut fallen grain and marking the line of separation between the cut and the uncut grain. **1929** *Kansas City* (Missouri) *Times* 26 June, The swather, or windrowing machine, is proving almost as popular as the older combine, which it complements. **1958** *Times* 24 Nov. 15/4 There is still a great deal of room for improvement in the design of combine harvesters and swathers. **1976** *Billings* (Montana) *Gaz.* 17 June 6-F/2 (Advt.), Swather, with conditioner. 14' auger head, industrial gas engine.

swathing ('sweɪðɪŋ), *vbl. sb.* [f. SWATHE *v.* + -ING¹.]

1. The action of the verb SWATHE; wrapping or binding up; swaddling.

1375, etc. [implied in SWATHING-BAND, -CLOTHES, -CLOUTS]. *c* **1440** *Promp. Parv.* 482/1 Swathynge of chyldyr. **1650** BULWER *Anthropomet.* 185 The Pergamites..had a great affectation..in streight swathing of their children. **1684** tr. *Bonet's Merc. Compit.* VIII. 272 Swathing egregiously stops Bleeding. **1698** FRYER *Acc. E. India & P.* 198 They use no swathing to their Babes. **1796** MORSE *Amer. Geog.* II. 489 The smallness of their feet is reckoned a principal part of their beauty, and no swathing is omitted ..to give them that accomplishment.

2. *concr.* That with which something is swathed; a wrapping; a bandage; a swaddling-band; also *fig.* (Most commonly in *pl.*)

1652 COTTERELL tr. *Calprenède's Cassandra* II. 132 Putting his hands where he found his hurts paine him, he met with the plaisters and swathings which had bin applyed to them. *a* **1711** KEN *Sion* Poet. Wks. 1721 IV. 33 To..heal each Wound, Which there is with soft Swathing bound. **1822-7** GOOD *Study Med.* (1829) II. 630 Flannel swathing around the body. **1860** TYNDALL *Glac.* II. iii. 246 Were the earth unfurnished with this atmospheric swathing. **1884** J. COLBORNE *Hicks Pasha* 58 The women in a blue calico swathing. **1904** BUDGE *3rd & 4th Egypt. Rooms Brit. Mus.* 117 The linen swathings of mummified bodies.

'swathing, *ppl. a.* [f. SWATHE *v.* + -ING².] That swathes; enveloping, enwrapping.

1844 MRS. BROWNING *Drama of Exile* 1943 The slow procession of the swathing seas. **1890** R. BRIDGES *Shorter Poems* v. xv. 15 No bud had burst its swathing hood.

'swathing-band.

1. = SWADDLING-BAND. Usually *pl.*

c **1435** *Torr. Portugal* 2017 Vp they toke the child ying, .. And vndid the swathing band. **1632** J. HAYWARD tr. *Biondi's Eromena* 192 They scorned to serve a babe in his swathing bands. *a* **1668** LASSELS *Voy. Italy* (1698) II. 211 An angel of silver..presenting to our Lady a child of gold in swathing-bands. **1702** N. TATE *Hymn*, '*While shepherds*' iv, The heavenly Babe..All meanly wrapt in swathing bands. **1875** *Encycl. Brit.* III. 189/1 Among neither people, however, did art altogether escape from the swathing-bands of its nursery.

†**2.** A bandage, a band of stuff for winding round a body. Also *transf. Obs.*

1615 CROOKE *Body of Man* 143 *Fascia renum*, that is, the Kidneyes swathing band. **1625** K. LONG tr. *Barclay's Argenis* v. i. 328 Hee takes off the swathing-band from the most dangerous wound. **1683** LORRAIN *Muret's Rites Funeral* 3 Afterwards they anointed it [*sc.* the corpse] outwardly all over with a certain gum; wrapt it in swathing-bands of very fine linnen. **1684** T. BURNET *Th. Earth* I. 268 As so many girdles or swathing-bands about the body of the earth.

†**'swathing-clothes,** *sb. pl. Obs.* = SWADDLING-CLOTHES.

1382 WYCLIF *Wisd.* vii. 4, I was nurshid in swathing clothis. **1551** ROBINSON tr. *More's Utopia* II. (1895) 162 They maye laye downe the yong infauntes..take them out of their swathynge clothes and holde them to the fyere, and refreshe them with playe. **1596** SHAKS. *1 Hen. IV*, III. ii. 112 Thrice hath the Hotspur Mars, in swathing Clothes, This Infant Warrior..Discomfited great Dowglas. **1611** COTGR. s.v. *Aube, En mes aubes*, in my infancie, or swathing clothes; when I was in my cradle.

†**'swathing-clouts,** *sb. pl. Obs.* = SWADDLING-CLOUTS.

1375 *Creation* 763 in Horstm. *Altengl. Leg.* (1878) 133 A ȝong child..In þe swaþyng cloutis wounde. **1585** GREENE *Planetom.* Wks. (Grosart) V. 69 A disease rooted in women from their swathing cloutes. **1594** GREENE & LODGE *Looking Gl.* (1598) I 4 b, Wrapt in the foldes and swathing cloutes of shame. **1602** SHAKS. *Ham.* II. ii. 401 That great Baby you see there, is not yet out of his swathing clouts [*1st Qo.* swadling clowts]. **1675** COTTON *Scoffer Scoft* 68 What a Filou in swathing Clowts?

swathy ('swɔːθɪ, 'sweɪðɪ), *a. rare.* Also 8 **swathey**. [f. SWATH¹ + -Y.] Of, pertaining to, or consisting of swaths.

a **1627** MIDDLETON *Witch* I. ii, I'll mar their syllabubs and swathy feastings Under cows' bellies with the parish youths. *a* **1790** JOANNA BAILLIE *Summer's Day* 75 Forth hies the mower..And lays the grass in many a swathey line.

Swati ('swɒtɪ). Also †**Swa(u)tee, Swathi.** [f. SWAT *sb.*³ + -I.] A member of a people inhabiting the district of Swat in Pakistan. Also *attrib.* or as *adj.*

1815 M. ELPHINSTONE *Acct. Kingdom of Caubul* II. xii. 319 The Swautees..appear to be of Indian origin... Swaut and Boonair, their last seats, were reduced by the Eusofzyes in the end of the fifteenth century. **1866** T. SEATON *From Cadet to Colonel* II. 202 Afreedees and Swatees, Affghans and Maguls. **1897** W. S. CHURCHILL in *Daily Tel.* 7 Oct. 11/1 The Swatis, Bonerwals, Mohmands and other frontier tribes with whom the Malakand Field Force is at present engaged are brave and warlike. **1927** *Rep. Admin. Border N.W.F.P. 1925–26* (Calcutta) 7 Extensive smuggling of *charas* into Peshawar which was known to be carried on by Swathi traders. **1955** *Times* 25 June 7/7 Swati politics are quite straight-forward. **1977** D. MURPHY *Where Indus is Young* 10 That battered bus, full of Swatis on their way home.

Swatow ('swɑːtaʊ, 'swɒ-). The name of a port (now Shantou) in the province of Guandong, China, used to designate a type of porcelain produced in the Ming dynasty (A.D. 1368–1644) (see quots.).

1925 R. L. HOBSON *Later Ceramic Wares China* xii. 111 A type of coarse porcelain, distinguished by an iron-red biscuit and accretions of..grit in the base..known among Chinese dealers as Swatow ware. **1945** W. B. HONEY *Ceramic Art China* i. 21 The red-and-green and green-and-blue wares made for export in Southern China (the 'Swatow wares' of the English collector). *Ibid.* ii. 127 Plates and dishes of the Swatow class. **1953** S. JENYNS *Ming Pottery & Porcelain* 147 The so-called 'Swatow' plates, which we now believe..to have been made at, or near, Shih-ma in Fukien. **1970** *Oxf. Compan. Art* 235/1 The still unidentified makers of 'Swatow' porcelains, which are chiefly large dishes coarsely but attractively painted in red and green.

swats (swɒts), *sb. pl. Sc.* Also 6 **swaits, swaittis,** 9 **swatts.** [repr. OE. *swatan* 'cervisia', beer.] New small beer or ale; also see quot. 1888.

1508 DUNBAR *Flyting* 130 Sueir swappit swanky, swyne-keper ay for swaittis. **1572** *Satir. Poems Reform.* xxxiii. 261 Now drink thay Mylk and Swaits in steid of Aill. *a* **1682** SEMPILL *Blythesome Wedding* 69 There will be..swats, and scraped paunches. **1717** RAMSAY *Elegy on Lucky Wood* vi, She ne'er..kept dow'd tip within her waws, But reaming swats. **1791** BURNS *Tam o' Shanter* 40 Reaming swats, that drank divinely. **1871** C. GIBBON *Lack of Gold* xxx, However, he took a draught of swats (small ale). **1888** EDMONSTON & SAXBY *Home Naturalist* 209 Swatts is the water that covers sowens, and is used to thin the sowens, or as a drink.

swatt, swatte: see SWEAT *v.*, SWOTE *Obs.*

swatter ('swætə(r)), *v. Sc.* and *north. dial.* [Echoic. Cf. SQUATTER; also early mod.Du. *swadderen* to slaver (of serpents), to splash in water (Kilian), dial. *zwadderen* in the latter sense, WFlem. *zwadderen* to speak slaveringly, G. dial. *schwadern* to disturb (water), splash, be agitated (of liquids), to tipple, also to prattle, babble; f. root *swad-* (: *swat-*) + frequent. suffix -ER⁵.]

1. *intr.* To flutter and splash in water like ducks or geese; to splash water about or splash about in water; †*fig.* to wallow.

1501 DOUGLAS *Pal. Hon.* I. xxv, In that desert..Quhair dragouns, lessertis, askis, edders, swatterit, With mouthis gapand. *a* **1599** ROLLOCK *Lect. Passion* etc. xxxviii. (1616) 371 Hee swatters and swimmes,..hee drownes not altogether. **1606** BIRNIE *Kirk-Buriall* (1833) 20 Tymes wherein the world lay..swattering in all sorte of superstition. **1637** RUTHERFORD *Let. to Lady Culross* 15 June, Oh, to be swattering, & swimming over head & ears in Christ's love! ? *a* **1800** *Twa Sisters* xi. in Child *Ballads* (1882) I. 135 Aye she swattered [*other vers.* swittert] and aye she swam, Until she came to the mouth of the dam. **1816** SCOTT *Bl. Dwarf* xvii, Before he lap the window into the castle moat, and swattered through it like a wild duck. **1821** —— *Pirate* xxx, I swattered hard for my life, wi' the help of ane of the oars. **1871** G. LAWRENCE *Anteros* xx. (1872) 177 'Pray, gently, on the right'—cries the mild Master, in the act of swattering through a miry pool.

†**b.** *transf.* To 'flutter'. *Obs. rare.*

1676 ROW *Contn. Blair's Autobiog.* iii. (1848) 122 Out of the dreary vale of tears My soul hath swattered out. **1843** *Whistle-binkie* (1890) II. 43 The blude a swatert through my hert.

2. To fritter *away* (as time, money).

1690 C. NESSE *Hist. & Myst. O. & N. Test.* I. 78 Such as swatter away all their youth-time..in ways of both vanity and villany. **1790** GROSE *Provinc. Gloss.* (ed. 2), *Swatter*, to scatter or waste. He swattered away all his money. North. **1905** *19th Cent.* Sept. 404 Proof that..it [*sc.* the poor rate] does not go to the poor, but is just 'swattered away'.

swatter ('swɒtə(r)), *sb.* [f. SWAT *v.*¹ + -ER¹.] An instrument for swatting flies. Also occasionally, one who swats flies (with a swatter).

1917 [see *fly-swatter* s.v. FLY *sb.*¹ 11]. **1923** *Dundee Tel.* 21 July 3/3 We have tried fly-papers, swatters, formaline solution, and nets. **1926** *Glasgow Herald* 4 Oct. 8 Poultry food is made from the Mexican bluebottle, professional 'swatters' making a good living by catching them. **1947** J. STEINBECK *Wayward Bus* i. 8 The death of a fly by swatter, or slowly smothered in the goo of fly paper. **1967** O. WYND *Walk Softly, Men Praying* iii. 35 The Principal turned back to pick up a swatter on his desk, then lashed out.

swattle ('swæt(ə)l), *v. north. dial.* [f. the same root as SWATTER *v.* + frequent. suffix -LE. Cf. G. dial. *schwatteln* to splash, etc.]

1. *intr.* To make a splashing or spluttering noise in or with water. (Cf. SWATTER *v.* 1.)

1671 *Depos. Cast. York* (Surtees) 186 That she carryed him downe and threw him in the becke, and that he swattled after he came in the becke. *c* **1700** KENNETT *MS. Lansd.* *1033*, *Swattle*, to drink as ducks doe water.

b. *intr.* and *refl.* To tipple or guzzle drink.

1785 *Bran New Wark* (E.D.S.) 460 He can be naa nebbour at dow, that tipples and swattles, and idles fra morning to neet. *c* **1826** Hogg in *J. Wilson's Wks.* (1855) I. 224 Some wouldna gie misery a dram Though they swattle themselves till they spew.

2. = swatter *v.* 2.

1681 H. More *Expos. Dan.* Pref. 93 By making them swattle away their love and zeal upon false objects. **1691** Ray *N.C. Words*, To *Swattle* away, to waste. **1876** *Mid-Yorks. Gloss.* s.v., Till thou'd swattled it clean away, bit by bit.

swatty ('swɒtɪ). *U.S. slang.* = swaddy *sb.*

1901 H. W. Phillips *Red Saunders* 4 A flat-faced swatty at Fort Johnson halted me. **1901** *Munsey's Mag.* XXIV. 481/2 A stray 'swatty' or two going back and forth between the post and Stringtown.

swauk, Sc. form of swack *sb.*

swaule, obs. variant of swale *sb.*[1]

swave, obs. form of suave; variant of swayve.

S wave: see S 6.

swaver ('sweɪvə(r)), *v. north. dial.* Also 4 swafre. [? f. Scand. stem *sveif-*: see swayve and -er[5]. Cf. ON. *sveifla* to swing (Norw. dial. *sveivla* to fan, waft), and Eng. dial. *swavel* to reel, stagger, sway about.] *intr.* To stagger, totter. Also *fig.* to decline *away from*.

?*a* **1400** *Morte Arth.* 3970 Than swetes the swete kynge and in swoune fallis, Swafres vp swiftely, and swetly hym kysses. *c* **1485** *Digby Myst.*, *Conversion of St. Paul* 447 Thowȝe on do swauer away from our lore. **1768** Ross *Helenore* I. 20 She wins to foot, an' swavering makes to gang. **1866** Gregor *Banffsh. Gloss.* s.v., He swavert o' the edge o' the rock, an' syne fell our. **1866** Buchanan *Lond. Poems* 230 His heart fail'd, he swaver'd forth again. **1874** —— *Scaith o' Bartle* Poet. Wks. I. 199 Swavering down the path, he took my arm.

swaviloquent, obs. form of suaviloquent.

swawle, obs. variant of swale *sb.*[1]

sway (sweɪ), *sb.* Forms: 4–5 **sweighe**, 4–5, 8 **sweigh**, 4–6 (9 *dial.*) **swey**, 5 **swegh**, **sweyh**, **sweyȝ**, **swyȝe**, 5–6 **sweygh**, 6 **swaie**, **swaye**, **swaigh(e**, **swea**, **suey**, **suai**, 8–9 *dial.* **swee**, **swye**, 6– **sway**. [In branch I f. sway *v.*; with sense 1 cf. EFris. *swei* movement in a curve. In branch II partly of different origin; for sense 12 cf. ON. *sveigr* (Sw. *sveg*, Norw. *sveig*) switch, twig.]

I. The action of the verb sway.

†**1.** The motion of a rotating or revolving body.

c **1374** Chaucer *Boeth.* I. met. v. 13 (Camb. MS.) O Thow..which..tornest the heuene with a Rauessyng sweyh [*v.r.* sweighe]. *Ibid.* II. pr. i. 22 The swyftnesse and the sweyȝ [*v.r.* sweyes] of hir [*sc.* Fortune's] turnynge wheel. *c* **1386** —— *Man of Law's T.* 198 O firste moeuyng crueel firmament, With thy diurnal sweigh that crowdest ay And hurlest al from Est til Occident. **1412–20** Lydg. *Chron. Troy* II. 2024 As Fortune..List on hir whele make a man ascende,..And with a swyȝe þrow hym to meschaunce. **1426** —— *De Guil. Pilgr.* 12234, iiij spookys..Set vp-on an Extre large, Of the sweygh to bere the charge. **1598** Sylvester *Du Bartas* II. i. iv. *Handie-crafts* 578 To know Heav'n's course, and how their constant swaies Divide the year in months, the months in dayes. **1601** Shaks. *Jul. C.* I. iii. 3 Are not you mou'd, when all the sway of Earth Shakes, like a thing vnfirme? **1610** *Histrio-m.* I. 227 Turne a huge wheele: contrary to the sway Place me a flye uppon't.

2. a. The sweeping or swinging motion of a heavy body, a storm, etc.; the impetus or momentum of a body, etc. in motion. *Obs.* or *dial.*

c **1374** Chaucer *Troylus* II. 1383 Whan þat þe sturdy ok.. Receyued hath þe happy fallyng strok The grete sweigh doth it to come al at onys. *c* **1540** tr. *Pol. Verg. Eng. Hist.* (Camden No. 29) 16 The bridge..being broken with the swey of people that thronged over the same. **1568** V. Skinner tr. *Montanus' Inquisition* 24 b, That he may fall downe with a sway. **1577** B. Googe *Heresbach's Husb.* IV. (1586) 188 Great Maules and Beetels, which the more angerly the Beare shoueth aside, with the greater sway they come vppon his head agaıne. **1590** Spenser *F.Q.* II. x. 15 Untill a nation straunge,..with their importune sway, This land invaded with like violence. **1645** Ussher *Body Div.* (1647) 74 In a field there are many battels,..yet all turn head with one sway at once. **1667** Milton *P.L.* VI. 251 With huge two-handed sway Brandisht aloft the horrid edge came down. **1700** Dryden *Ceyx & Alc.* 167 The hero tenth advanc'd before the rest Sweeps all before him with impetuous sway. **1757** Gray *Bard* 75 Regardless of the sweeping whirlwind's sway. **1802** James *Milit. Dict.*, *Sway*, the swing or sweep of a weapon. **1815** Shelley *Alastor* 387 Seized by the sway of the ascending stream. **1825** Scott *Talism.* xxvii, The glittering broadsword..descended with the sway of some terrific engine.

fig. **1553** Grimalde *Cicero's Offices* I. (1558) 47 They feele nothing but pleasure and therunto be caried with their holle sweygh [orig. *omni impetu*]. **1579** Fenton *Guicciard.* 831 So that the whole swaigh or burden of the Warre lay upon the Swizzers.

†**b.** A swinging stroke or blow. *Sc. Obs.*

1535 Stewart *Cron. Scot.* (Rolls) II. 383 This schiphird carle he gaif him sic ane swey [etc.].

c. A turn, veer. *Sc.*

1818 Hogg *Brownie of Bodsbeck* viii. I. 139 Ye ken the wind very often taks a swee away round to the east i' the night time. **1875** W. McIlwraith *Guide Wigtownsh.* 126 The [flat-bottomed] boats were liable to give a sudden swee.

†**3.** Force or pressure bearing or inclining its object in one direction or another. *Obs.*

1565 Peend *Hermaphroditus* B v b, Such be the..fits which in the blinded brayne Of wanton women often times with swinging swey doth reigne. **1597** Hooker *Eccl. Pol.* v. xlix. §6 As long as the sway of euill custome ouerbeareth them. **1601** Dent *Pathw. Heaven* 305 The sway of the world doth weigh downe all things that can be spoken out of the word of God. **1667** Milton *P.L.* VI. 234 Expert When to advance, or stand, or turn the sway Of Battel. **1757** W. Wilkie *Epigon.* III. 52 Push'd and yielding to superior sway, ..the Spartan ranks gave way. **1791** J. Learmont *Poems* 32 Sic is Britain's present state. A sweigh will coup her ony gate.

†**4.** Inclination or bias in a certain direction; *occas.* deviation *from* a course of action. *Obs.* (in later use *Sc.*).

a **1586** Sidney *Arcadia* III. xxiii. (1912) 490 [He] suffred.. his imaginations to be raised even by the sway, which hearing or seing, might give unto them. **1595** Shaks. *John* II. i. 578 This aduantage, this vile drawing byas, This sway of motion. **1596** Bacon *Max. Com. Law* iii. (1636) 10 This rule doth give them a sway to take the law more certainly one way. *a* **1601** ? Marston *Pasquil & Kath.* (1878) I. 188 Their verie wish..had some sway from dutie. **1645** Milton *Tetrach.* 29 Such a peculiar sway of liking, or disliking in the affairs of matrimony. **1730** T. Boston in Morrison *Mem.* x. (1899) 316 A plain sway to the other side appearing in that committee. **1820** Hogg *Winter Even. T.* I. 253 (Jam.) Its your mind that I'm sad for they'll gie't a wrang swee.

5. Prevailing, overpowering, or controlling influence.

a **1510** Douglas *King Hart* II. 216 No dar I nocht be no way mak travale, Bot quhair I se my maister get a swey. **1575** Gascoigne *Kenelworth* Wks. 1910 II. 103 You fishes all, and each thing else, that here have any sway. **1586** A. Day *Engl. Secretary* I. (1625) 26 My Lord the Duke is here of great sway. **1671** Milton *Samson* 791 The jealousie of Love, powerful of sway In human hearts. **1705** Addison *Italy* 31 This renders it very suspicious, that the Interests of Particular..Religious Orders..have too great a Sway in their Canonizations. **1762–71** H. Walpole *Vertue's Anecd. Paint.* (1786) II. 57 His Countess, who had great sway with him, being notoriously corrupt. **1849** Macaulay *Hist. Eng.* vii. II. 188 The sovereign of this country, acting in harmony with the legislature, must always have a great sway in the affairs of Christendom. **1879** Dixon *Windsor* II. ii. 16 The girl had fallen under the sway of nuns and priests.

6. a. Power of rule or command; sovereign power or authority; dominion, rule.

1586 A. Day *Engl. Secretary* I. (1625) 33 In causes of sway and government. **1616** B. Jonson *Epigr.* xxxv. 2 A prince that rules by example, more than sway. **1681** Dryden *Abs. & Achit.* 780 For who can be secure of private Right, If Sovereign Sway may be dissolv'd by Might? **1683** Temple *Mem.* Wks. 1720 I. 458 There were two ruling Burgomasters of Amsterdam..who had the whole Sway of that Town. **1706** Prior *Ode to Queen* xxv, France on universal Sway intent. **1836** Thirlwall *Greece* xvi. II. 372 Her sway was exclusively acknowledged by her Peloponnesian allies. **1872** Yeats *Growth Comm* 181 Western India from Ormuz to Ceylon owned the sway of Portugal. **1875** Fortnum *Maiolica* ii. 14 There were two periods of Mahommedan sway in Spain.

b. *transf.* and *fig.*

1597 Shaks. *Lover's Compl.* 108 That horse his mettell from his rider takes Proud of subiection, noble by the swaie. **1644** Milton *Educ.* 1 Either by the definite will of God so ruling, or the peculiar sway of nature. **1692** Prior *Ode Imit. Hor.* iv, The Sun absent, with full sway the Moon Governs the Isles. **1714** R. Fiddes *Pract. Disc.* II. 220 The soul.. originally govern'd the body with an absolute sway. **1805–6** Cary *Dante, Inf.* VIII. 16 A small bark..under the sole sway Of one that ferried it. **1871** Palgrave *Lyr. Poems* 136 In the hearts of men is thy sway.

c. *contextually.* (*a*) Means of government. (*b*) Position of authority or power.

c **1645** Howell *Lett.* (1655) IV. xlvii. 111 The Sword is the surest sway over all people who ought to be cudgel'd rather then cajoll'd to obedience. **1765** Goldsm. *Double Transform.* 101 No more presuming on her sway, She learns good-nature every day. **1805–6** Cary *Dante, Inf.* VII. 84 One nation rises into sway, Another languishes. **1825** Scott *Talism.* xi, He had been raised to the ducal sway in the German empire.

7. Phr. *to bear* (†*a* or *the*) *sway*, etc. (also †*to carry sway*): to rule, govern; to hold the (highest) position in authority or power; to exercise influence, carry weight. Also, † *to carry the sway of.*

1550 Crowley *Last Trumpet* 1309 Let them two [*sc.* knowledge and fear of the Lord] bear all the swea In thy doinges. **1555** Watreman *Fardle Facions* II. vi. 151 Nexte vnto the kinges maiestie, the communaltie bare the swaye. **1567** Fenton *Trag. Disc.* 8 Suche as in many ages before had borne the grettest swaighe in that publike weale. **1570** Walsingham in D. Digges *Compleat Ambass.* (1655) 8 Montmorencie..now carrieth the whole sway of the Court. **1573** G. Harvey *Letter-bk.* (Camden) 3 Wilfulnes wil beare a suai, if it be not bridelid. **1581** Mulcaster *Positions* xxxvii. (1887) 150 One prince beareth the sway. **1636** Massinger *Gt. Dk. Florence* II. ii, This is the man that carries The swey, and swinge of the Court. **1651** Hobbes *Leviath.* I. v. 19 As it comes to bear sway in them. **1715** Pope *Iliad* I. 285 Let revenge no longer bear the sway. **1759** Robertson *Hist. Scot.* vi. Wks. 1813 I. 459 Huntly and Bothwell, who bore the chief sway in the kingdom. **1779** *Mirror* No. 66. ⁋5 He knows..that, in Lady Anne, vanity bears absolute sway. **1845** M. Pattison *Ess.* (1889) I. 9 The ages when the Church bore sway over every action of life.

8. Manner of carrying oneself; carriage, deportment. ?*Obs.*

1753 Hogarth *Anal. Beauty* iii. 20 The Antinous's easy sway must submit to the stiff and straight figure of the dancing master. **1796** W. H. Marshall *Planting* II. 40 The Evergreen Bignonia..will form at a distance a grand figure from the sway they bear. **1845** J. Keegan *Leg. & Poems* (1907) 263 From time out of mind, this parish has been famous for its dances, and our boys and girls always.. brought the sway, both for step and figure, and carriage, too.

9. a. The action of moving backward and forward or from side to side.

1846 Holtzapffel *Turning* II. 917 The sway of the blades of jointed shears is prevented, by allowing the moving arm to pass through a loop or guide which may retain it in position. **1865** A. L. Gordon *Vis. Smoke* viii. Poems (1912) 85 A sway in the crowd—a murmuring hum! **1912** J. Masefield in *Eng. Rev.* Oct. 338 The poise [of a ship] At the roll's end, the checking in the sway.

b. *Naut.* A rhythmic linear motion of a vessel from side to side (as distinguished from the rotatory motion of a roll).

1957 *Trans. Inst. Naval Architects* XCIX. 121/1 Sway accelerations were actually measured to a good approximation in the form of the displacement of the apparent vertical. **1968** Rawson & Tupper *Basic Ship Theory* xii. 427 Disturbances in the yaw, surge and sway modes will not lead to such an oscillatory motion..when the ship is in a seaway. **1977** *Offshore Engineer* May 44/3 During these tests, the data acquisition system recorded waves,.. sway and yaw of the lay barge, pull and length of mooring cables, and anchor positions.

II. Concrete senses.

†**10.** ? The pole of a cart. *Sc. Obs.*

1535 Stewart *Cron. Scot.* (Rolls) III. 561 Fast festnit on ane tre, Out throw the toun tha gart him drawin be, Vpoun ane suey ay swappand vp and doun.

11. A lever, crowbar. *dial.*

1545 *Acc. Ld. High Treas. Scot.* VIII. 423 Sweyis, oxin bollis, and other necessaries pertening to the said monitioun. **1547** *Ibid.* IX. 88 Thair ten cairttis laidint with ..extreis, sweyes, sowmes, ȝokes, oxin bowes and other necessarres for the said artalȝere. **1566** *Inventories R. Wardr.* (1815) 170 Item fyve sweis of tymmer Item certane hand spakkis. **1793** *Young's Ann. Agric.* XXI. 621 A gentlewoman in the vicinity of Edinburgh..has always been used to Churn..in a plunge Churn, with a swee (a lever applied to the end of the Churn-staff). **1808** Jamieson, *Swey*, a long crow for raising stones. **1823** Moor *Suffolk Words*. **1876** Atkinson *Cleveland Gloss.*, *Sway*, a wooden lever.

12. A small pliable twig or rod, esp. one used in thatching (see quot. 1949); a switch. *dial.*

1630 *Churchw. Acc. St. Peter Mancroft, Norwich* in *Norf. Antiq. Misc.* (1883) II. 341 Item paid Thomas Seamer for swaies or wandes..iij. d. **1787** W. H. Marshall *Rural Econ. Norfolk* Gloss. (E.D.S.). **1847** Halliwell, *Sway*..a switch used by thatchers to bind their work... *East.* **1949** K. S. Woods *Rural Crafts of Eng.* IV. xiii. 203 The light timbers that support the thatch are 'flues' laid upward from eaves to ridge like rather thin rafters; 'sways' or long laths are laid horizontally across them at frequent intervals. **1966** *Punch* 10 Aug. (Advt. following p. 216), Hazel rods or 'sways' are used in conjunction with iron hooks to fasten the thatch to the roof timbers.

13. A flat iron rod suspended in the chimney, on which pots and kettles are hung. *Sc.* and *north.*

1825 Jamieson. **1870** J. K. Hunter *Life Stud. Charac.* xli. 257 Willie's lum was one of an old-fashioned wideness, with a rungiltree instead of a swee.

sway (sweɪ), *v.* Forms: 4 **sweȝe**, 4–5 **swye**, 4–6 **sweye**, 4–7 (8–9 *dial.*) **swey**, (6 **sweie**, **swaye**, 7–9 **sweigh**, 8–9 *Sc.* **swee**), 6– **sway**; *3rd sing.* 6 **swayth**, **swaieth**, **sweath**; *pr. pple.* 6 *Sc.* **sweand**; *pa. t.* (*str.*) 4 **sweȝe**, **swey**, **swe**; *pa. t.* and *pple.* 4 **sweȝed**, **sweyed**, 4–5 **swyed**, 5 **sweyd**, **sweyt**, 6–7 **swaid(e**, **swayd**, **swaied**, 7 **swai'd**, **sued** (?), 7– **swayed**. [Properly two distinct words. (1) ME. *sweȝe* (14th c.), conjugated strong and weak, also *swye*, to go, move (cf. ME. *forsueie* to go astray), may have been a native word orig. of the OE. type **sweȝan*, (3 pres. ind. **swiȝeþ*), pa. t. **swæȝ*, parallel to OE. *weȝan* to move, carry, weigh, (*wiȝeþ*), *wæȝ*, ME. *weȝe*, occas. *wye*, pa. t. *weȝe*, *wei(ȝ)*, *wei(e)de*. (Cf. also the parallelism of *swag* and *wag*, *sweight* and *weight*.) Formally, *sweȝe* might also be ad. ON. *sveigja* to bend (a bow), swing (a distaff), etc., give way, yield (cf. *sveigr* switch, twig), causative vb. f. *svig-*, in *svig* bend, curve, *svigi* switch, *svigna* to give way; but the ME. and ON. verbs do not agree in sense. (2) The modern *sway* dates only from *c* 1500, and agrees in form and sense with, and appears to be ad., LG. *swâjen* to be moved hither and thither by the wind (whence Sw. *svaja* to swing, Da. *svaie* to move to and fro, G. *schwaien*, *schweien*), Du. *zwaaien* to swing, wave, walk totteringly, slant, bevel.]

I. † **1.** *intr.* To go, move. *Obs.*

13.. *E.E. Allit. P.* B. 87 Swyerez þat swyftly swyed on blonkez. *Ibid.* C. 72 Now sweȝe me þider swyftly & say me þis arende. *Ibid.* 151 þe sayl sweyed on þe see. **13..** *Gaw. & Gr. Knt.* 1429 Al in a semblé sweyed to-geder. ?*a* **1400** *Morte Arth.* 57 [He] Sweys in-to Swaldye wiþ his snelle houndes.

†**b.** Often with *down*: To go down, fall (*lit.* and *fig.*); *spec.* to fall or sink *into* a swoon. *Obs.*

13.. *Gaw. & Gr. Knt.* 1796 Sykande ho sweȝe doun, & semly hym kyssed. **13..** *E.E. Allit. P.* B. 956 þe rayn rueled adoun..Of felle flaunkes of fyr..Swe aboute sodamas. *Ibid.* C. 429 þe soun of oure souerayn þen swey in his ere. ?*a* **1400** *Morte Arth.* 1467 So many sweys in swoghe swounande att ones! *Ibid.* 3676 With þe swynge of þe swerde sweys þe mastys. *c* **1400** *Destr. Troy* 9454 Parys..Sweyt into swym, as he swelt wold. *a* **1400–50** *Wars Alex.* 2057 (Dublin), þe power owt of perse..Sweyd sleghtly downe slayn of þair blonkes. *c* **1415** *Crowned King* 29 Swythe y swyed in a sweem þat y swet after. **1513** Douglas *Æneis* II. x. 86 Quhar thir towris thou seis doun fall and sweye, And stane fra stane doun bet. **1533** BELLENDEN *Livy* IV. xv. (S.T.S.) II. 103 Þe hewmondis of romanis semyt as þai war sweyand doun.

†**c.** *causative.* To cause to go or move; to drive. *Obs. rare.*

13.. *E.E. Allit. P.* C. 236 Styffe stremes.. þat drof hem dryȝlych adoun þe depe to serue, Tyl a swetter ful swyþe hem sweȝed to bonk.

II. 2. *intr.* To move or swing first to one side and then to the other, as a flexible or pivoted object: often amplified by phr., e.g. *backwards and forwards*, *to and fro*, *from side to side.*

Not common before the 19th century.

c **1500** *Bk. Mayd Emlyn* 334 in Hazl. *E.P.P.* IV. 94 An halfepeny halter made hym fast, And therin he swayes. **1555** EDEN *Decades* (Arb.) 120 Yet are they [*sc.* the branches of the trees] tossed therewith, and swaye sumwhat from syde to syde. **1797** S. & HT. LEE *Canterb. T.* (1799) I. 375 The lamp swayed with the blast. **1859** TENNYSON *Marr. Geraint* 171 A purple scarf, at either end whereof There swung an apple of the purest gold, Sway'd round about him as he gallop'd up. **1863** MRS. OLIPHANT *Salem Chapel* x, That stick over which his tall person swayed with fashionable languor. **1874** L. STEPHEN *Hours in Libr.* (1892) II. ii. 51 The dreary estuary, where the slow tide sways backwards and forwards.

b. *fig.* To vacillate. *rare.*

1563 WINȜET tr. *Vincent. Lirin.* xv. Wks. (S.T.S.) II. 35 Thai, sweand and swounand betuix thame twa, determinatis nocht quhat wes specialie erast to be chosin be thame. **1825** JAMIESON, *Swee*,.. to be irresolute. **1871** B. TAYLOR *Faust* (1875) II. I. i. 5 When the crowd sways, unbelieving.

3. *trans.* To cause to move backward and forward or from side to side (cf. 2). (See also 13.)

Not common before the 19th century.

1555 EDEN *Decades* (Arb.) 152 Swayinge her bodye twyse or thryse too and fro. **1667** MILTON *P.L.* IV. 983 As when a field Of Ceres ripe for harvest waving bends Her bearded Grove of ears, which way the wind Swayes them. **1717** PRIOR *Alma* II. 215 Have you not seen a Baker's Maid Between two equal Panniers sway'd? **1784** COWPER *Task* VI. 73 The roof,.. moveable through all its length As the wind sways it. **1819** SHELLEY *Julian* 276 The ooze and wind Rushed through an open casement, and did sway His hair. **1865** TROLLOPE *Belton Est.* xii. 137 He swayed himself backwards and forwards in his chair, bewailing his own condition. **1902** R. BAGOT *Donna Diana* xv. 178 When the cool breeze sweeps up from the sea, gently swaying the tops of the cypress-trees.

b. *fig.*

a **1586** SIDNEY *Arcadia* II. xxix. (1912) 330 He was swayed withall.. as everie winde of passions puffed him. **1592** WYRLEY *Armorie, Ld. Chandos* 29 Some turning fate, Which like wild whirlwind all our dooings sweath. **1596** SHAKS. *Merch. V.* IV. i. 51 Affection, Maisters [? = Mistress] of passion, swayes it to the moode Of what it likes or loaths. *a* **1650** MAY *Old Couple* II. i. (1658) C 2, He has got A great hand over her, and swayes her conscience Which way he list. **1866** G. MACDONALD *Ann. Q. Neighb.* xv. (1878) 307, I was swayed to and fro by the motions of a spiritual power. **1870** *Edin. Rev.* Oct. 388 Dr. Newman.. tells us.. with the utmost frankness, the persons who.. swayed his beliefs hither and thither.

4. *intr.* To bend or move to one side, or downwards, as by excess of weight or pressure; to incline, lean, swerve.

In mod. quots. only a contextual use of 2.

1577 HOLINSHED *Chron.* II. 1624/1 The left side of the enimies.. was.. compelled to sway a good way backe, and giue grounde largely. **1593** SHAKS. *3 Hen. VI*, II. v. 5. **1610** BOYS *Wks.* (1622) 223 The tree falleth as it groweth.. Learne then in growing to sway right. **1624** BACON *Consid. War w. Spain* Wks. 1879 I. 542/1 In these personal respects, the balance sways on our part. **1631** GOUGE *God's Arrows* III. §48. 273 Aaron and Hur.. kept his hands that they could not sway aside one way or other. **1670–1** NARBOROUGH *Jrnl.* in *Acc. Sev. Late Voy.* I. (1694) 166 Could not get the Ship off, for the Water did Ebb, and the Ship Sued above 3 Foot. **1860** TYNDALL *Glac.* I. xxvii. 196 The carriage swayed towards the precipitous road side. **1881** 'RITA' *My Lady Coquette* xv, She sways towards him like a reed.

†**b.** *transf.* To have a certain direction in movement; to move. *Obs.*

1597 SHAKS. *2 Hen. IV*, IV. i. 24 Let vs sway-on, and face them in the field. **1601** —— *Twel. N.* II. iv. 32 So swayes she leuell in her husbands heart. **1605** —— *Macb.* V. iii. 9 The minde I sway by, and the heart I beare, Shall neuer sagge with doubt, nor shake with feare. **1650** W. D. tr. *Comenius' Gate Lat. Unl.* §233 Man's estate swaieth (is going downwards) [L. *vergit*] towards a declining age.

c. To move *against* in a hostile manner. *rare.*

1590 SPENSER *F.Q.* II. viii. 46 How euer may Thy cursed hand so cruelly haue swayd Against that knight. *Ibid.* x. 49 Yet oft the Briton kings against them [*sc.* the Romans] strongly swayd. **1603** KNOLLES *Hist. Turks* (1621) 195 A man would have thought two rough seas had met together swaying one against the other. **1871** DIXON *Tower* III. xxvi. 284 The Duke had grown too great to live. All passions swayed against him.

5. *trans.* To cause to incline or hang down on one side, as from excess of weight; *dial.* to weigh or press down; also, to cause to swerve.

1570 BUCHANAN *Chamæleon* Wks. (S.T.S.) 45 The said Chamæleon.. changeing hew as the quene sweyit ye ballance of hir mynd. **1625** BACON *Ess., Simulation* (Arb.) 509 To keepe an indifferent carriage, betweene both, and to be Secret, without Swaying the Ballance, on either side. **1663** CHARLETON *Chor. Gigant.* 27 As that no force of wind or tempest.. by diminishing the gravity on one side, might incline or sway them to sink down on the other. **1664** POWER *Exp. Philos.* II. 145 The greater weight of water in the pendent Leg [of the Syphon].. sways down that in the shorter, as in a pair of Skales. **1678** BUTLER *Hud.* III. II. 1368 As Bowls run true, by being made Of purpose false, and to be sway'd. **1797** HOLCROFT tr. *Stolberg's Trav.* (ed. 2) II. xliii. 81 The.. tower of Pisa.. is swayed fifteen feet from the centre. **1846** HOLTZAPFFEL *Turning* II. 848 They have learned to avoid swaying down the file at either extreme. **1856** KANE *Arctic Expl.* II. xiv. 143 These swayed the dogs from their course. **1857** WHITTIER *Poems, Funeral Tree Sokokis* Argt., The surviving Indians 'swayed' or bent down a young tree until its roots were upturned.

absol. **1624** BEDELL *Lett.* v. 84 A little weight is able to sway much, where the beame it self is false.

†**b.** To strain (the back of a horse): see SWAY-BACKED, SWAYED 1. *Obs. rare.*

1611 COTGR., *Esflanquer*, to sway in the backe. **1639** T. DE GREY *Compl. Horsem.* 42 He might wrinch any member, or sway his back.

6. a. To turn aside, divert (thoughts, feelings, etc.); to cause to swerve *from* a course of action.

1596 SHAKS. *1 Hen. IV*, III. ii. 130 Heauen forgiue them, that so much haue sway'd Your Majesties good thoughts away from me. **1616** *Marlowe's Faustus* IV. ii. (1631) F j, Let vs sway [*ed.* 1624 stay] thy thoughts, From this attempt. **1673** CAVE *Prim. Chr.* II. vi. 135 No dangers could then sway good men from doing of their duty. **1679** J. GOODMAN *Penit. Pard.* I. iii. (1713) 69 An huge advantage may sway him a little aside. **1822** B. W. PROCTOR *Ludovico Sforza* ii, No ill has happened.. to sway Your promise from me? **1874** GREEN *Short Hist.* vi. §6. 335 No touch either of love or hate swayed him from his course.

†**b.** To influence in a specified direction; to induce *to do* something. *Obs.*

1625 *Impeachm. Dk. Buckhm.* (Camden) 292 To sweigh the people to accept the King's offers. **1634** SIR T. HERBERT *Trav.* 63 He answered, his businesse swayed him to another end. **1667** MILTON *P.L.* VIII. 635 Least Passion sway Thy Judgement to do aught, which else free Will Would not admit. **1712** ADDISON *Spect.* No. 357 ¶14 The Part of Eve .. is no less.. apt to sway the Reader in her Favour. *a* **1720** SEWEL *Hist. Quakers* (1795) II. VII. 83 He so swayed the master that at last he agreed. **1807** WORDSW. *White Doe* VI. 48 Even that thought, Exciting self-suspicion strong, Swayed the brave man to his wrong.

†**c.** To give a bias to. *Obs.*

1593 BACON *Let. to Burghley* Apr., I spake simply and only to satisfy my conscience, and not with any advantage, or policy to sway the cause.

†**7.** *intr.* To incline or be diverted in judgement or opinion; to swerve *from* a path or line of conduct; to lean (towards a side or party). *Obs.*

1556 J. HEYWOOD *Spider & F.* xxv. 94 We sweie From the streight lyne of iustice. **1581** LAMBARDE *Eiren.* II. iv. (1588) 166 The common opinion swayeth to the other side. **1594** R. CAREW *Huarte's Exam. Wits* iii. (1596) 24 With which of these opinions the truth swaieth, time serueth not now to discusse. **1599** SHAKS. *Hen. V*, I. i. 73 He seemes indifferent: Or rather swaying more vpon our part, Then cherishing th' exhibiters against vs. **1659** W. GUTHRIE *Chr. Gt. Interest* (1724) 80 This imports a Sort of Impropriation: For the Heart, pleasing that Device, in so far swayeth towards it. *Ibid.*, *Explic. Sc. Words*, To *sway* or *swey* towards a Thing, is to bend towards it.

8. *trans.* To wield as an emblem of sovereignty or authority; esp. in phr. ***to sway the sceptre***, †***the sword*** (also, by extension, †***the diadem***, †***the rule***), to bear rule.

Cf. Du. *den schepter zwaaien.*

1575 GASCOIGNE *Weedes, In Praise of Gentlewoman* 5 Golden Marcus he, that swaide the Romaine sword. **1576** —— *Steele Gl.* (Arb.) 61 You should not trust, lieftenaunts in your rome, And let them sway, the scepter of your charge. **1590** SPENSER *F.Q.* II. x. 20 Madan was young, vnmeet the rule to sway. **1590** GREENE *Orl. Fur.* Wks. (Rtldg.) 99/1 It fits me not to sway the diadem. **1593** SHAKS. *3 Hen. VI*, III. iii. 76 Though Vsurpers sway the rule a while. **1671** MILTON *P.R.* III. 405 If I mean to raign David's true heir, and his full Scepter sway. **1750** GRAY *Elegy* 47 Hands, that the rod of empire might have sway'd. *a* **1828** H. NEELE *Lit. Rem.* (1829) 26 Had Charles I. continued to sway the English sceptre.

b. *transf.* To wield (an implement or instrument). *poet.*

c **1600** SHAKS. *Sonn.* cxxviii, When thou gently sway'st, The wiry concord that mine eare confounds. **1810** SCOTT *Lady of L.* II. vii, This harp, which erst Saint Modan swayed. **1867** MORRIS *Jason* VI. 239 Erginous now, Great Neptune's so the brass-bound tiller swayed.

9. To rule, govern, as a sovereign. Chiefly *poet.*

1595 SHAKS. *John* I. i. 13 To lay aside the sword Which swaies vsurpingly these seuerall titles. *Ibid.* II. i. 344 By this hand I sweare That swayes the earth this Climate ouerlookes. **1613** PURCHAS *Pilgrimage* VI. viii. 502 The Great Turke swayeth with his Ottoman Scepter.. this Kingdome of Tunis, and all Africa, from Bellis de Gomera to the Redde Sea. **1634** MILTON *Comus* 825 A gentle Nymph.. That with moist curb sways the smooth Severn stream. **1709** WATTS *Hymn, 'The Lord! how fearful is his Name'* vi, Now let the Lord for ever reign, And sway us as he will. **1812** BYRON *Ch. Har.* II. xlvii, With a bloody hand He sways a nation, turbulent and bold. **1896** A. AUSTIN *Eng. Darling* I. i, Buhred hath fled the land By him for two-and-twenty winters swayed.

b. *transf.* To have the command or control of; to control, direct.

1587 GOLDING *De Mornay* xxiv. (1592) 366 There must be some pretie speech of Fortune, which swayth the battels. As for God.. not one word. **1590** SHAKS. *Mids. N.* I. i. 193 Teach me.. with what art You sway the motion of Demetrius hart. *Ibid.* II. ii. 115 The will of man is by his reason sway'd. **1665** BOYLE *Occas. Refl.* VI. iii. (1848) 352 Custom has much a larger Empire than men seem to be aware of, since whole Nations are wholly swai'd by it. **1791** BURKE *Corr.* (1844) III. 268, I have been long persuaded, that those in power here, instead of governing their ministers at foreign courts, are entirely swayed by them. **1874** GEO. ELIOT *Coll. Breakf.-P.* 412 A sword.. With edge so constant-threatening as to sway All greed and lust by terror.

10. *intr.* (occas. ***to sway it.***) To rule; to hold sway. Also *fig.*

1565 J. PHILLIP *Patient Grissell* Pref. (Malone Soc.) 17 Let Grissills Pacience swaye in you. **1586** A. DAY *Engl. Secretary* I. (1625) 16 Yours while life swaieth within me. **1591** SHAKS. *1 Hen. VI*, III. ii. 135 A gentler Heart did neuer sway in Court. **1615** ROWLANDS *Melanch. Knight* 23 For shee's a Gentlewoman (though I say it) That doth deserue to domineere and sway it. **1633** BP. HALL *Hard Texts* 1 Cor. vi. 3 Those evill and apostate spirits, which doe now sway so much in the world. **1667** MILTON *P.L.* x. 376 There let him still Victor sway, As Battel hath adjudg'd. **1711** in *10th Rep. Hist. MSS. Comm.* App. v. 114 A tyrant is he.. who swayes for his own onely pleasure. **1725** POPE *Odyss.* III. 401 Lawless feasters in thy palace sway. **1853** J. HUNT *Spir. Songs, 'Let all the world rejoice'* ii, He rules by sea and land, O'er boundless realms he sways. **1886** A. T. PIERSON *Crisis of Missions* 117 Turkey.. still sways over one million square miles.

†**11.** To have a preponderating weight or influence, prevail. *Obs.*

This use combines senses 4 and 10.

1586 A. DAY *Engl. Secretary* I. (1625) 126 His counsell.. swaieth not.. in our mindes, so much as it might haue done with many others. **1610** HOLLAND *Camden's Brit.* (1637) 586 Wee may understand.. that gold swaied much yea in Church matters, and among Church-men. **1647** N. BACON *Disc. Govt. Eng.* I. lxx. (1739) 187 Nor did the King's Proclamation sway much this or that way. **1710** LADY M. W. MONTAGU *Let. to Mr. W. Montagu* 14 Nov., If my opinion could sway, nothing should displease you. **1768** TUCKER *Lt. Nat.* I. I. v. §7. 96 To distinguish what motive actually swayed with him upon every particular occasion.

12. *trans.* To cause (a person, his actions, conduct, or thoughts) to be directed one way or another; to have weight or influence with (a person) in his decisions, etc.

1593 G. HARVEY *Pierce's Super.* Wks. (Grosart) II. 46 Had not affection otherwhiles swinged their reason, where reason should haue swayed their affection. **1605** B. JONSON *Volpone* IV. vi, *Lady P.* You shall sway me. *a* **1674** CLARENDON *Surv. Leviath.* (1676) 108 Inclinations which sway them as much as other men. **1681** DRYDEN *Abs. & Achit.* I. 939 Thus long have I by Native Mercy sway'd, My Wrongs dissembl'd. **1743** BULKELEY & CUMMINS *Voy. S. Seas* 31 Believing we can sway most of the Seamen on Shore. **1760–2** GOLDSM. *Cit. W.* lvii, Swayed in their opinions by men who.. are incompetent judges. **1818** SCOTT *Br. Lamm.* xxxiii, The honour of an ancient family, the urgent advice of my best friends, have been in vain used to sway my resolution. **1852** MISS YONGE *Cameos* I. xii. 76 Bribery and every atrocious influence swayed the elections. **1870** MAX MÜLLER *Sci. Relig.* (1873) 292 The authority of their names continues to sway the public at large. **1892** *Speaker* 3 Sept. 279/1 The jury.. was swayed by the customary ethical code in these matters.

13. To swing (a weapon or implement) about; *dial.* to swing (something) to and fro, or from one place to another. Also *intr.* to swing.

1590 SPENSER *F.Q.* I. xi. 42 When heauie hammers on the wedge are swaid. *Ibid.* III. i. 66 She.. Here, there, and every where, about her swayd Her wrathfull steele. **1815** SCOTT *Guy M.* xlvi, Meg.. lifted him into the vault 'as easily,' said he, 'as I could sway a Kitchen's Atlas'. **1818** MISS FERRIER *Marriage* xxxii. (1881) I. 320 Do I look like as if I was capable of hindering boys from sweein' gates? **1822** HOGG *Perils of Man* iv. I. 60 Bairns, swee that bouking o' claes aff the fire. **1823** SCOTT *Quentin D.* xxi, He.. caught hold of one of the chains.. and.. swayed himself out of the water. **1894** P. H. HUNTER *James Inwick* xiv. 170 Ye've been sweein on the yett for a gey while.

14. *Naut.* (usually with *up*). To hoist, raise (esp. a yard or topmast).

1743 BULKELEY & CUMMINS *Voy. S. Seas* 15 He immediately gave Orders to sway the Fore-yard up. **1768** J. BYRON *Narr. Patagonia* (ed. 2) 15 He was going forward to get the fore-yard swayed up. **1835** MARRYAT *Jacob Faithful* xi, Forward there, Jacob, and sway up the mast. **1883** *Man. Seamanship for Boys* 61 A spanker is fitted with an outhaul and brails, the gaff being kept always swayed up in place.

b. *absol.*

1836 MARRYAT *Midsh. Easy* xii, How long will it be, sir, before you are ready to sway away? **1840** R. H. DANA *Bef. Mast* xvii, We got a whip on the main-yard, and, hooking it to a strap round her body, swayed away. **1867** SMYTH *Sailor's Word-bk.*, *Sway*, or *Sway away*, to hoist simultaneously; particularly applied to the lower yards and top-masts, and topgallant-masts and yards. *To sway away on all top-ropes*, to go great lengths (colloquially).

†**c.** To weigh (anchor). *Obs.*

1772–84 *Cook's Voy.* (1790) IV. 1405 The gale having subsided they swayed the anchor.

sway, obs. Sc. form of SO *adv.* and *conj.*

sway-, the vb.-stem or sb. used in comb: **sway-bar**, (*a*) a circular piece of timber on the hinder end of the fore-hounds of a carriage, resting on the coupling-poles and sliding on them when the carriage turns; (*b*) chiefly *N. Amer.*, a bar joining the suspension assemblies of corresponding wheels at either side of a motor vehicle so as to reduce rolling when cornering; an anti-roll bar; **sway-beam**, an early name for the side-lever in a steam-engine; = BEAM *sb.*[1] 11; **sway-bracing**, diagonal bracing of a bridge designed to prevent swaying; so **sway-brace** *sb.*; **sway-brace** *v.*, to strengthen with a sway-brace; **sway plate**, the plate covering the sway-bar; †**sway tree**, ? a crane.

1801 W. FELTON *Carriages* II. Suppl. 18 For the purpose of putting in new futchels, a *sway bar, [etc.]. **1812** *Chron.* in *Ann. Reg.* 148/1 The shock.. broke a sway-bar, and threw the state coachman off the box. **1890** *Lincoln Gaz.* 6 Sept. 6/5 To.. unship pole and sway-bars. **1973** *Hot Rod* Oct. 108/1 Also known as stabilizer bars, antiroll bars, or just plain sway bars, these little goodies.. can make so much difference you wouldn't believe it. **1979** *Tucson* (Arizona) *Citizen* 3 Oct. c. 14/5 (Advt.), 69 MGB... High performance sway bars, Monza exhaust system. **1839** R. S. ROBINSON *Naut. Steam Eng.* 69 The *sway beams or side levers, two of which are attached to each engine. **1909** *Century Dict., Suppl.*, **Sway-brace*, a diagonal bracing used to resist side- or swaying-strains. **1894** W. H. WARREN *Engin. Construction* xix. 304 High trestle piers of timber present great varieties in design. They should be thoroughly *sway-braced. **1903** *Sci. Amer.* 19 Sept. 202/3 The two legs of the tower will be heavily sway-braced. **1864** WEBSTER, **Sway-bracing* (Engin.), the horizontal bracing of a bridge, which prevents its swaying. **1852** BURN *Naval & Milit. Dict.* (1863), *Sway plate, *coiffe de grande sassoire*. *c* **1632** in Brand *Newcastle* (1789) I. 370 *note*, One *swea tree with two rolles for taking and laying down lair-stones.

'swayable, *a.* [f. SWAY *v.* + -ABLE.] Capable of being swayed or influenced.

1642 *Fuller Answ. to Dr. Ferne* 16 The Members..are lesse swayable, as not easily reducible to one head of private interest. **1978** C. TOMLINSON *Shaft* 42 A wind is having its way with all swayable things, Combing through flag and steam, streaming-out hair. **1982** *Washington Post* 4 May C5/4 As hostess, you should generally give the impression of someone who has rules but is swayable.

‖**swayamvara** (ˌswajam'vaːra). *India.* Also **swayambara, swayamvar.** [Skr., lit. 'self-choice'.] A Hindu ceremony in which a woman chooses her husband from amongst several contenders; a symbolic representation of this, preceding an arranged marriage.

1831 H. H. MILMAN in *Q. Rev.* XLV. 17 A solemn assemblage, called the *Swayambara*, or self-election, where the princess is to designate the favoured suitor by throwing a wreathe of flowers round his neck. **1863** M. WILLIAMS *Indian Epic Poetry* 100 Draupadi was about to hold her swayamvara. **1932** J. NEHRU *Let.* 23 June in *Glimpses of World Hist.* (1939) 210 There is a long poem about one of these Chalukyan kings, and in this it is stated that he was chosen by his wife at a public swayamvara. **1970** *Times* 28 Feb. 6/1 The wedding began on Monday with the Swayamvara ceremony, in which the Hindu girl accepts her parents' choice of husband by garlanding him.

swayback, *sb.* and *a.*

A. *sb.* **1. a.** Sway-backed condition. Also, an instance of this.

a **1913** in DORLAND *Med. Dict.* **1939** J. CARY *Mister Johnson* 156 She is a huge, lumbering woman... She has a sway back..and long heels like a hen. **1946** *Richmond* (Va.) *News-Leader* 14 Nov. 30 (*heading*) Swayback is figure fault. Exercises quickly correct.

b. A sway-backed horse or lamb. Also *transf.*, of a person.

1874 *Rep. Vermont Board Agric.* II. 402 The buckskin McClellan was a regular hollow or sway back. **1921** S. KAYE-SMITH *Joanna Godden* I. 35 'He'd three sway-backed lambs at Rye market on Thursday.' 'Sway-backs!' 'Three. 'Twas a shame.' **1934** S. BECKETT *More Pricks than Kicks* 68 A woman..is either: a short-below-the-waist, a big-hip, a sway-back, a big-abdomen or an average. **1974** M. LAURENCE *Diviners* iv. 80 Make pemmican out of the swayback which dropped dead of exhaustion on the Back Forty.

2. A copper deficiency disease affecting the nervous system of young lambs, causing paralysis. Cf. RENGUERRA.

1938 *Nature* 5 Mar. 400/1 Swayback..accounts from time to time for many lambs. **1947** *Sci. News* V. 100 Research has been going on into a disease of newborn lambs called swayback. **1960** *Farmer & Stockbreeder* 1 Mar. 105/3 Injection of a copper preparation..into a ewe during pregnancy can prevent swayback in its lambs. **1970** 'J. HERRIOT' *If only they could Talk* xxv. 149 The diseases which beset the lambs themselves—swayback, pulpy kidney, dysentery. **1980** *Daily Tel.* 16 Feb. 12/6 Thousands of lambs may die from a nervous disorder called swayback.

B. *adj.* Sway-backed.

1887 T. N. PAGE *Ole Virginia* (1893) 118 A man riding a sway-back sorrel horse.

'sway-backed, *a.* [Of Scandinavian origin: cf. obs. Da. *sveibaget*, also Da. *sveirygget*, †*svegrygget*, Sw. dial. *svegryggad*, in the same sense.] Of an animal, esp. a horse: Having a downward curvature of the spinal column; strained in the back, as by overwork. Also *transf.*

1680 *Lond. Gaz.* No. 1561/4 An old White Nag.., sway Back'd. **1876** LANIER *Poems, Clover* 25 Dick..upbraids The sway-back'd roan. **1880** 'MARK TWAIN' *Tramp Abroad* I. 257 These rambling, swaybacked tunnels. **1884** *Bath Chron.* 12 June 6/6 In Kent there is a large proportion of sway-backed lambs among the flocks. **1919** T. K. HOLMES *Man from Tall Timber* ix. 101 'Does seem a pretty springtime, after all,' Aunt Tabby ruminated, as she rocked in a swaybacked chair. **1950** *Audio Engin.* Sept. 30/2 If the *lows* and *lower highs* are both present to excess, the system is *sway-backed*. **1965** J. A. MICHENER *Source* (1966) 730 Shmuel Hacohen, a sway-backed Jew from Russia, sought an opposing judgment. **1976** H. MACINNES *Agent in Place* xviii. 197 It was a steep pull, the stone steps made sway-backed by centuries of..feet. **1977** D. HARSENT *Dreams of Dead* 49 On knees and palms, swaybacked like a stricken runner..she begged, 'Pleasure me, pleasure me.'

swayed (sweɪd), *ppl. a.* [pa. pple. of SWAY *v.*]

†**1.** Of a horse: Having a depression in the spinal column, caused by strain. Also *back-swayed*, SWAY-BACKED. *Obs.*

In Shaks. *Tam. Shr.* III. ii. 56 *swayed* is a conjecture of Hanmer's for the reading *Waid* of the folios and quarto. **1577** B. GOOGE *Heresbach's Husb.* III. (1586) 134 b, Which will make him draw his legges after him, and goe as if he were swaide in the chine. **1600** SURFLET *Country Farm* I. xxviii. 189 For a horse sweide in the backe,..apply vnto the reines of his backe an emplaster. **1685** *Lond. Gaz.* No. 2089/4 A Great Spread black Cart-Gelding,..having a rowling gate, formerly Sway'd in the back. *a* **1722** LISLE *Husb.* (1757) 225 A strait flat back, or a little swayed. **1852** BURN *Naval & Milit. Dict.* (1863), Back swayed, *élancé, efflanqué*.

2. *gen.* Bent.

1688 HOLME *Armoury* III. xv. (Roxb.) 25/2 An old Leger booke, with turned vp leaues and a swayed or bent back.

swayer ('sweɪə(r)). [f. SWAY *v.* + -ER[1].] One who or that which sways, wields, or rules.

1598 FLORIO, *Dominatore*, a ruler, a gouernor, a lord, a swayer. **1679** J. BROWN *Life of Faith* (1824) II. xvii. 325 He is the happiest swayer of a sceptre that ever was. **1691** WOOD *Ath. Oxon.* II. 178 Pym, Hamden, and Strode were esteemed Parliament-drivers, or Swayers of all the Parliaments wherein they sat. **1832** *Examiner* 773/2 Eloquence and truth united are greater swayers of opinion than either wealth, wigs, or woolsacks. **1853** KINGSLEY *Misc.* (1860) I. 300 To talk loud about the poet's divine mission, as the prophet of mankind, the swayer of the universe, and so forth.

swayf(e, variants of SWAFE.

'swayful, *a. rare.* [f. SWAY *sb.* + -FUL.] Able to exercise sway, powerful.

1767 FAWKES *Theocritus* Idyll. xxviii. 7 Cytherea's swayful power.

swaying ('sweɪɪŋ), *vbl. sb.* [f. SWAY *v.* + -ING[1].]

1. The action of the verb SWAY; movement to and fro; vacillation; influencing, controlling, etc.

a **1665** J. GOODWIN *Being filled with the Spirit* (1867) 240 For the swaying and ordering of our judgments in the question in hand. **1837** CARLYLE *Fr. Rev.* III. II. ii, Bread not to be had except by Ticket from the Mayor,..after long swaying, with firm grip, on the chain of the Queue. **1849** KINGSLEY *Misc.* (1860) II. 275 The swaying of the fir boughs in the gale. **1850** HT. MARTINEAU *Hist. Peace* IV. xiv. II. 200 His life had been a swaying between contemplation and action. **1867** LADY HERBERT *Cradle L.* iv. 132 The low murmur and swaying to and fro of the dense crowd.

2. *swaying of* or *in the back*: the condition of being swayed in the back (SWAY *v.* 5 b) or SWAY-BACKED. Also *back-swaying*.

1598 FLORIO, *Feruto*, a disease in a horse called the swaying of the neck [*sic*]. **1704** *Dict. Rust.* (1726) s.v. *Sway'd, Swaying in the Back*, a Distemper in Horses that comes many ways. *c* **1720** W. GIBSON *Farrier's Guide* II. lxviii. (1738) 225 By a Swaying of the Back is properly to be understood a stretching and relaxation of the Muscles and Ligaments. **1852** BURN *Naval & Milit. Dict.* (1863) s.v., Back swaying, *effort des reins*.

swaying ('sweɪɪŋ), *ppl. a.* [f. SWAY *v.* + -ING[2].]

I. †**1.** Moving. *Obs. rare.*

13.. *E.E. Allit. P.* B. 420 [The ark] Drof vpon þe depe dam..With-outen..any sweande sayl to seche after hauen.

II. 2. Exercising power, influence, or control; influential, controlling. *Obs.* exc. as the second element of compounds, e.g. *all-swaying*.

1625 in Foster *Eng. Factories India* (1909) III. 106 [All matters of moment are to be determined by the three captains..; Weddell to have] a double or swaying voyce. **1647** CLARENDON *Hist. Reb.* VII. §319 A Member of the House of Commons, and of a swaying Interest there. **1684** O. HEYWOOD *Diaries*, etc. (1885) IV. 111 A sweying man.. to moderate the bench. **1711** in *10th Rep. Hist. MSS. Comm.* App. v. 171 A directing and swayeing head.

3. Vacillating.

1688 HOLME *Armoury* III. 74/2 The Laws of Coursing.. often alter according to some Mens swaying Fancies.

4. In horses, 'a hollow sinking down of the Back-bone' (Bailey, 1726).

5. Moving to and fro.

1847 THACKERAY *Lords & Liv.* iii, The mad swaying rush of the horses was reduced to a..steady gallop. **1875** MCLAREN *Serm.* Ser. II. vii. 121 The swaying branches creak and groan. **1899** E. J. CHAPMAN *Drama of Two Lives, Snake-Witch* 53 The flood-swept land and the swaying sea.

Hence **'swayingly** *adv.*, with a swaying motion.

c **1854** in *Circ. Sc.* (*c* 1865) I. 294/2 On the tall poplar tree Perch'd swayingly. **1882** PROCTOR in *Contemp. Rev.* Mar 476 Carried, not bodily, but still swayingly, against the direction of rotation.

swayless ('sweɪlɪs), *a. poet. rare.* [f. SWAY *sb.* + -LESS.] Not swayed or swaying; unmoved, immovable.

1856 *Tait's Mag.* XXIII. 548/1 A gnarled tree, which.. free and swayless in the fresh air grew. **1897** F. THOMPSON *New Poems* 12 And with her magic singing kept she..That garden of enchanting In visionary May; Swayless for my spirit's haunting.

swayme, swaymish, -ous, var. SWEAM, SQUEAMISH, SQUEAMOUS.

swayn(e, swayth(e, obs. ff. SWAIN, SWATHE.

swayve, *v. dial.* Also 4 sweyue, 9 swave. [ad. ON. **sveifa* (cf. Norw. dial. *sveiva* to swing, *sveiv* whirl, vortex), related to *svífa* to rove, drift (see SWIVE).] *intr.* To move to and fro; to flow.

13.. *E.E. Allit. P.* C. 253 Þenne he [*sc.* the whale] swengez & swayues to þe se boþem. **1377** LANGL. *P. Pl.* B. Prol. 10 As I lay and lened and loked in þe wateres, I slombred in a slepyng it sweyued [*v.r.* sweyed, *A-text* sownede, *v.rr.* swiȝede, swyed] so merye. **1847** HALLIWELL, *Swave*, to pass backward and forward. *Cumb.* **1878** *Cumbld. Gloss.*, *Swayve*.

Swazi ('swɑːzɪ), *sb.* and *a.* [ad. Nguni *Mswati*, the name of a former king of the Swazi.]

A. *sb.* **a.** A (member of a) people of mixed stock, predominantly Nguni, inhabiting the kingdom of Swaziland (independent since 1968) and parts of eastern Transvaal in the Republic of South Africa. **b.** A dialect of Nguni spoken by the Swazi. **B.** *adj.* Of, pertaining to, or characteristic of this people.

[*a* **1857** J. SHOOTER *Kafirs of Natal & Zulu Country* 391 The Amaswazi partially shave their head [*sic*].] **1872** C. A. PAYTON *Diamond Diggings of S. Afr.* 142 A book of very great interest on new African sport and travel, entitled, I believe, 'Swazi Kafirs and Swazi Game'. **1878** A. AYLWARD *Transvaal of To-day* 182 The Swazis transferred the fidelity and love they bore him. **1884** K. JOHNSTON *Africa* xxvi. 461 The most..numerous..are the Bechuanas..cut off from the Zulus and Swazi by the Quathlamba range on the east. **1902** *Encycl. Brit.* XXXIII. 111/2 The Swazies are a branch of the Bantu family... Swazieland was first constituted a petty native state in 1843, when the Barabuza people under their chief, Swaze, rose against their Zulu oppressors, and according to custom took their name from the founder of their chieftaincy. **1910** J. BUCHAN *Prester John* xi. 193 There were tall Zulus and Swazis with *ringkops* and feather head-dresses. **1919** H. H. JOHNSTON *Compar. Study of Bantu & Semi-Bantu Languages* 298 The Zulu-Kafir Languages.. Swazi..Tekele. **1937** N. J. VAN WARMELO in I. Schapera *Bantu-Speaking Tribes* iii. 51 Commencing with the increasing power of the Ngwane Chief Sobhuza (*ca* 1820), the 'Swazi' people gradually began to come into being. **1947** J. STEVENSON-HAMILTON *Wild Life S. Afr.* xxiii. 188 The man (a Swazi) entered, and almost immediately was attacked by the leopard. **1956** H. BLOOM *Episode* v. 72 She wagged her head and huffed her shoulders and muttered in Swazi. **1961** W. VAUGHAN-THOMAS *Anzio* ix. 197 The cheerful Swazi Pioneer..dashed around the football field in an enormous beret. **1973** 'S. HARVESTER' *Corner of Playground* III. ii. 181 A Swazi king in eighteen-fiftyfour raided the Tsonga to find boys and girls to sell to the Boers. **1982** *Times* 1 June 8/1 We [*sc.* the Zulus] are their countrymen, and yet they are prepared to sell us out to the Swazis in a clandestine deal.

swazzle ('swɒz(ə)l). Also swozzle. [Var. SWATCHEL.] In a Punch and Judy show: an instrument consisting of two convex metal pieces bound together with a length of tape stretched from side to side between them, which is held in the mouth of the puppeteer and is used to produce the characteristic squeaking voice of Mr. Punch.

Mayhew's *call* (CALL *sb.* 6 e), described in *London Labour* (1861) III. 45/2.

1942 S. DE HEMPSEY *How to do Punch & Judy* 86 Amongst the professional Punch and Judy performers the gadget for the Punch voice is popularly known as a 'Swazzle'. **1951** G. SPEAIGHT in *Oxf. Compan. Theatre* 644/2 [Punch] spoke in a high squeak, formed by inserting a 'swazzle' or squeaker into the mouth of the speaker. **1959** *Times* 13 Aug. 10/6 My friend, removing his top and bottom dentures, put my swazzle in his mouth and gave an expert demonstration of the Punch voice. **1962** *Guardian* 31 Mar. 6/5 The swozzle—the hand-made reeded 'call' which the operator keeps in his mouth to reproduce the Punch squawk. **1973** G. SIMS *Hunters Point* ii. 13 Mr. Punch's high-pitched buzzing voice was..achieved by using a 'swozzle', a piece of linen stretched between two flat pieces of silver, bound together with more linen, and placed at the back of Mr. Jackman's throat. **1983** *Daily Tel.* 11 Apr. 12/4 The swazzle, the flat metal instrument bound with black thread which the Punchinello keeps in his mouth (at some risk of swallowing) to make Mr Punch's nasal squeak.

swch(e, swdan, obs. ff. SUCH, SUDDEN.

swe, obs. form of SUE.

†**sweak**, *v. Obs. rare*[−1]. [Cf. SWEEK.] *trans.* app. To swing.

1567 GOLDING *Ovid's Met.* VIII. 108 As he sweakt his axe asyde to fetch his blow.

sweak(e, obs. and dial. form of SQUEAK; var. SWEEK.

sweal, swale (swiːl, sweɪl), *sb. dial.* Also swaile, sweel. [f. next.] A blaze, flame; the guttering of a candle.

1781 J. HUTTON *Tour to Caves* (ed. 2) Gloss. (E.D.S.) *Swaile, Sweal*, a flame. **1878** *Cumbld. Gloss.*, *Sweel*..the melting of a lighted candle in a draught. **1882** *Lanc. Gloss.*, *Sweel*, a great blaze.

sweal, swale (swiːl, sweɪl), *v.* Now *dial.* Forms: 1 swælan, 3 swælen, *pa. t.* swelde, 3–4 swale, 4 swayle, (also 9) swele, 4, 7–9 swaile, 5 sweile, sweyle, 6–7 sweale, 7–9 swail, 8–9 sweel, (9 squail, zwele, zweel, etc.), 6– sweal, 7– swale. [OE. *swǽlan* wk. trans. to burn, related to OE. *swelan* str. intr. to burn (which may be in part also the source of this word) = (M)LG. *swelen* to singe, wither (of grass), make hay, etc. (whence G. *schwelen, schwälen* to burn slowly without flame, NFris. *swîal* to singe, EFris. *swêl* to glow), ON. *svæla* to smoke out, *svæla* thick mist or smoke, f. Teut. root *swel-* to be subjected to heat or slow burning (cf. OHG. *suilizôn* to burn slowly).

Other grades of the root are represented by OE. *swol*, *swolig* (cf. SOOLY), *swoloþ* burning, heat, LG. *swôl*, *swûl*, *swôlig*, *swûlig* oppressively hot, sultry (whence G. *schwül*, earlier †*schwul*), Du. *zwoel* sultry.

Cognates outside Teut. are recognized in Lith. *svilti* to scorch, *svilus* glowing, *svilmis* smell of burning, Lett. *swelt* to scorch.]

1. *trans.* To consume with fire, burn; to set fire to (e.g. gorse, etc., soot in a chimney); to singe, scorch; *locally*, to singe (a hog), (in Ireland) to roast (a sheep) whole in its skin.

[*Beowulf* 3041 (Gr.) Gledum beswæled.] *c* **1000** *Lambeth Ps.* xxv[i]. 2 Onæl..*vel* swæl *vel* bærn lendenu..mine. *c* **1205** LAY. 1647 Berneð heore halles..& swaleð heore bures. *c* **1275** *Ibid.* 25594 þo com þar..a bernen[d]e drake, borwes he swelde. **1387** TREVISA *Higden* (Rolls) III. 325 He ..sweled of his berd heer with a firy cole. *Ibid.* VIII. 143 He ..schewed hym his heed þat was i-sweled and i-scalded. *c* **1400** *Beryn* 2349 For to swele his vlyes He stert in-to the bern & aftir stre he hies. *c* **1410** *Lanterne of Liȝt* ix. 78 þat lust of þe fleische mai be sweilid from coueiting of yuel [orig. *ut conbusta caro non concupiscat malum*]. **1573** TWYNE *Æneid* XII. Ll 4, His huge beard brent a light, And swealed caused a stinke. **1591** SYLVESTER *Du Bartas* I. iv. 253 Summers-guide, the Crab comes..To bring us yearly in his starry shell, Many long dayes the shaggie Earth to swele. **1609** C. BUTLER *Fem. Mon.* (1634) 36 If you must use many [hives]; then, having wet the skirts with a cloth, singe or sweal the inside. **1669** WORLIDGE *Syst. Agric.* (1681) 322 To *Sweal* a Hog, to singe a Hog. **1795** *Trans. Soc. Arts* XIII. 183 The gorse..is used for sweeling ships [*i.e.* applying a torch to the greased and tarred bottom that the fat, etc. may penetrate]. **1800** HURDIS *Fav. Village* 52 To see the thunder-bolt with fiery arm Arrest the mountain top and sweal his brow. **1846** J. BAXTER *Libr. Pract. Agric.* (ed. 4) II. 310 In order to have good bacon the hair should be sweeled off—not scalded. **1883** *Almondbury & Huddersfield Gloss.*, *Sweal*, to burn the soot out of the chimney. **1883** *Standard* 12 Sept. 2/2 'Sweel' is an odd Sussex word, meaning to singe linen. **1911** *Daily News* 22 Dec. 12/1 Strong overgrown heather which.. would have to be torched or 'swaled' before young plants.. could take possession of that area.

b. To cause (grass, etc.) to dry or wither.

1796 PEGGE *Derbicisms* (E.D.S.) s.v., The wind sweals the grass; not only checks its growth, but cuts off and consumes its blade. **1881** *Leicester. Gloss.* s.v., 'It'—the hay—'is swaled enow, an' way'll hack it in'.

2. *intr.* To burn with fire, or as a fire; to be consumed with fire; to be scorched; to be burning hot.

[*Beowulf* 2713 (Gr.) Sio wund ongon..swelan and swellan. *a* **900** CYNEWULF *Crist* 987 (Gr.) On fyrbaðe swelað sæfiscas.] *c* **1205** LAY. 16219 þe castel gon to bernen, bures þer swælden [*MS.* slælden]. **1382** WYCLIF *Matt.* xiii. 6 Sothely the sunne sprung vp, thei swaliden [*gloss* or brenden for hete]. —— *Rev.* xvi. 9 Men swayleden [**1388** swaliden; Vulg. *æstuaverunt*] with greet heete. **1388** —— *Jer.* xx. 9 The word of the Lord was maad, as fier swalynge [1382 gretly hetende] in myn herte. **1811** WILLAN in *Archaeologia* XVII. 160 (*W. Riding Words*), *Sweal*, to blaze, to burn away rapidly. **1861** E. BROWN *Seaman's Narr.* xxii. 251 The flesh swealed with the heat of the irons, and a blue steamy smoke arose. **1882** *Lanc. Gloss.* s.v., A fire or anything else is said to sweel when it burns fiercely.

3. Of a candle: To melt *away*; to gutter. Also said of the tallow or wax. Hence *fig.* to waste away.

1653 H. MORE *Conject. Cabbal.* (1713) 80 That they can burn thus with their heads downwards, and not presently sweal out and be extinguished, as our ordinary Candles are. **1671** SKINNER *Etymol.*, To Sweal away, *eliquescere instar candelæ*, vox agro Linc. usitatissima. **1816** SCOTT *Old Mort.* v, Mind ye dinna let the candle sweal as ye gang alang the wainscot parlour. **1827** T. WILSON *Pitman's Pay* II. iii, The unsnuff'd lights are now burnt low, And dimly in their sockets sweeling. **1858** FABER *Bartoli & Maffei's Life Xavier* 396 The wax which had swealed from it [*sc.* a candle]. **1870** KINGSLEY *At Last* viii, The soil is half pitch, half brown earth, among which the pitch sweals in and out, as tallow sweals from a candle. **1881** *Pall Mall G.* 9 Mar. 10 The candles they have to light them to their rooms are swaling. **1893** *Wiltshire Gloss.*, *Squail*..(4) Of a candle, to gutter.

4. *trans.* To cause to waste away like a guttering candle. Chiefly *fig.*

1655 GURNALL *Chr. in Arm.* I. 298 Lest this sin of pride (as a thief in the candle) should swail out thy joy. **1662** HIBBERT *Body Div.* I. 144 An intemperate man is one that, like some candles, sweals away his life. **1673** *True Worship of God* 65 The wasting and swealing out the Lights of the Church. *a* **1679** T. GOODWIN *Unregenerate Man* XIII. ix, Immoderate sorrows swale our life. **1697** CONGREVE *Mourning Bride* III. vi, Our Hymeneal Torch..dashed with Rain from Eyes, and swail'd with Sighs. **1702** C. MATHER *Magn. Chr.* III. I. i. (1852) 275 Reckoning..the time not spent in study, for the most part sweeled away. **1862** [C. C. ROBINSON] *Dial. Leeds* s.v., Mind an' doan't sweal t'cannel.

sweal, dial. form of SQUEAL.

swealed (swi:ld), *ppl. a.* Also 8 **swilled**. See also SWOLED. [f. SWEAL *v.* + -ED[1].] Scorched, singed; (of a sheep) roasted whole in the skin.

c **1000** ÆLFRIC *Voc.* in Wr.-Wülcker 149/30 *Fomes*, ȝeswælud spoon, *uel* tynder.

1674 RAY *S. & E.C. Words* s.v. *Sweale*, A sweal'd pig, a singed pig. **1732** MRS. DELANY *Life & Corr.* (1861) I. 365 A 'swilled mouton,' that is a sheep roasted whole in its skin, scorched like a hog. **1863** W. BARNES *Dorset Gloss.* s.v. *Zweal*, He is lik' a swealed cat; better than he do look vor.

'swealer. *dial.* Also **sweeler**; see also SWALER. [f. SWEAL *v.* + -ER[1].] (See quot. 1877.)

1877 *N.W. Linc. Gloss.*, *Swealer*, a speck of foreign matter in the grease of a candle which causes it to sweal. **1896** N. MUNRO *Lost Pibroch*, etc. 121 Had it been shrouds instead of sweelers.

'swealing, 'swaling, *vbl. sb.* [f. SWEAL *v.* + -ING[1].] Burning; singeing: for special uses see quots. and SWEAL *v.*

c **1410** *Lanterne of Liȝt* iii. 6 Euery proud soule..schal be in to sweyling [orig. *erit in combustionem*]. **1549** *Compl. Scot.* ii. 24, I sal visee ȝou vitht dreddour, vitht fyir, ande vitht suellieg [*sic*]. **1694** J. HOUGHTON *Collect. Improv. Husb.* No. 95 ⁋2 Swealing of Sheep in Ireland. **1759** R. FORSTER in J. Nichols *Collect. Hist. Berks* (1783) 56 The singeing of a pig they call sweeling. **1805** R. W. DICKSON *Pract. Agric.* II. 1201 When cured as bacon, it is the practice in Kent to singe off the hairs, by making a straw fire round the hog, an operation which is termed swaling. **1892** *Pall Mall G.* 16 Apr. 7/2 The wanton practice of 'swaling' [*sc.* 'firing the heather' on Dartmoor]. **1899** J. M. FALKNER *Moonfleet* vii, There is a swealing of the parchment under the hot wax. **1902** E. PHILLPOTTS *River* 251 These spring fires, or 'swaleings', had been deliberately lighted that furze and heather might perish, and the grasses, thus relieved, prosper for flocks and herds.

'swealing, 'swaling, *ppl. a.* [f. SWEAL *v.* + -ING[2].] Burning, blazing; (of a candle) guttering.

a **1023** WULFSTAN *Hom.* xliii. (1883) 213 He ða sende of heofonum beornend ren and swælende leȝ. *c* **1420** *Prymer* (1895) 10 (*Benedicite*) Fier & swellynge heete [*ignis et æstus*]. **1807** J. STAGG *Poems* 24 Swift the sweelin hether flies. **1812** COLMAN *Br. Grins, Lady of Wreck* II. xxviii, A swaling candle.

swealtie, obs. form of SWELTY.

†**sweam**, *sb. Obs.* Forms: 3 **swem**, 5 **swayme, sweme, sweem, sqweme**, 6 **sweame**, 7 **swaim, sweam.** [f. SWEAM *v.* (Cf. SWIME.)

Sense 2 may have been borrowed from ON. *svimi*, *svimr* giddiness, swooning, or the ON. word itself may have been actually taken over, *ī* becoming *ē* as in native words.]

1. Grief, affliction. ***to think sweam*** (impers. with dat.): to be grievous to. ***to be sweam***: to be a pity. So ***for sweam!***

c **1250** *Gen. & Ex.* 391 Of paradis hem ðinkeð swem, Of iwel and dead hem stondeð greim. *Ibid.* 1961 He missed Ioseph and ðhogte swem. *c* **1430** LYDG. *Min. Poems* (Percy Soc.) 38 His hert began to melt, For veray sweme of this swemeful tale. *c* **1440** *Promp. Parv.* 482/2 Sweem, of mornynge, *tristicia*, *molestia*, *meror*. *c* **1450** *Cov. Myst.* xi. 127 That mannys sowle it xulde perysche it wore sweme. *c* **1460** METHAM *Wks.* (1916) 43 Ful grete sqweme for yowre absens I schal haue. *Ibid.* 62 Alas, for sqweme! *c* **1491** *Chast. Goddes Chyld.* 92 The olde enmye the deuyl hath fered me by swemes. ? *a* **1500** *Chester Pl.* (E.E.T.S.) xi. 8 And nowe that fitt may I not flee, thinke me never so swem.

2. A sudden fit of sickness or fainting; a swoon.

c **1400** *Destr. Troy* 3895 He swat neuer for þat swynke, ne in swayme felle. *c* **1415** *Crowned King* 29 Swythe y swyed in a sweem, þat y swet after. *a* **1440** *Sir Degrev.* 1211 (Camb. MS.) Loke at þ[u] come at þ[t] tyme Oþer swowne shal I sweme þe lady shall I se [*Thornton MS.* And ane of us salle ly in swyme]. **1587** *Mirr. Mag.*, *King Jago* Lenuoy i, A warning this may be, Against the slothfull sweames of sluggardye. *Ibid.*, *Vitellius* ii, By blindnesse blunt, a sottishe sweame hee feeles: With ioyes bereft, when death is hard at heeles. **1677** HOLYOKE *Dict.*, A sweam or swaim, *subita ægrotatio.*

Hence †**'sweamful** (5 **swem-, sqwem-, swymful**) *a.*, grievous, distressing; †**'sweamfully** *adv.*; †**'sweamly (swemly)** *a.*, distressful.

a **1400** *Leg. Rood* (1871) 135 [He] sweltep heerin a swemly swouh. *c* **1420** ? LYDG. *Assembly of Gods* 1223 Then seyde Frewyll & swemfully spake. *c* **1430** [see SWEAM *sb.* 1]. *c* **1460** METHAM *Wks.* (1916) 43 At her sqwemfful departyng. *c* **1460** *Play Sacram.* 807 Now alle my pepulle wt me ye dresse ffor to goe see that swymfulle syght. **1469** *Paston Lett.* Suppl. 128 It is gret pety to here the swemefull and petowse compleyntis of the pore tenauntis.

†**sweam**, *v. Obs.* Forms: 3 **sweamen**, 3–6 **sweme.** [OE. **swǣman*, found only in the compound *áswǣman* to be grieved or afflicted. Cf. prec.]

1. *trans.* To afflict, grieve. Hence **'swemand** *ppl. a.*, afflicting, grievous.

c **1205** LAY. 16099 He scal alle þa swiken swemen [*printed* swenien] mid eiȝe. *a* **1225** *Ancr. R.* 312 Beo we sorie þet we euer schulden wreððen swuch feder, & sweamen [*v.r.* sweme] swuchne wardein. *Ibid.* 398 Non vuel ne schal hermien þe, no þing ne schal sweamen þe. *c* **1230** *Hali Meid.* 17 Hwa þat sehe þenne hu þe engles beo isweamed þat seoð hare suster swa fohrfulliche afallet. **13..** *E.E. Allit. P.* B. 563 þe swemande sorȝe soȝt to his hert. *c* **1450** *Mankind* 868 in *Macro Plays* 33 Yt swemyth my hert, to thynk how onwysely I hawe wroght.

2. *intr.* To grieve, mourn. Also in *vbl. sb.*

c **1450** *Cov. Myst.* (Shaks. Soc.) 81 Your swemynge smytyht to myn herte depe. **14..** *Promp. Parv.* 482/2 Swemyn, *molestor*, *mereo*..Swemynge, or mornynge.

3. *pass.* and *intr.* To be overcome with faintness.

c **1440** *York Myst.* xl. 40 þane on his bakke bare he þame by, A crosse vnto Caluery, þat swettyng was swemyed for swetyng. **1501** DOUGLAS *Pal. Hon.* III. xc, I..langit sair for to haue swemit agane.

sweamish, dial. form of SQUEAMISH.

sweande, obs. pr. pple. of SWAY *v.*

sweap, variant of SWAPE; obs. f. SWEEP.

sweaple, variant of SWIPPLE.

swear (swɛə(r)), *sb.* Now *colloq.* [f. SWEAR *v.*] An act of swearing; an oath.

1. A formal or solemn oath.

a **1643** W. CARTWRIGHT *Ordinary* IV. iv, Gull'd by my swear, by my swear gull'd. **1691** *Pol. Ballads* (1860) II. 31 You must either take the swear, or starve. *a* **1704** T. BROWN *Dial. Dead, Reas. Oaths* Wks. 1711 IV. 79 [He has] faced about to the Right, and taken the Swear. **1899** E. PHILLPOTTS *Human Boy* ii. 38 We swore by a tremendous swear, to obey Trelawny. *Ibid.* iv. 108 She kept her swear all right.

2. A profane oath, a swear-word; also, a fit or bout of swearing.

1871 C. GIBBON *Lack of Gold* v, A good swear is a cure for the bile, so swear away. **1873** CARLETON *Gone with a Handsomer Man* i. in *Farm Ball.* 27 I've choked a dozen swears. **1894** BESANT *Equal Woman* 127 He swore a swear. **1915** D. L. R. LORIMER *Pashtu* I. 194 Khlākah. Damn me. (An Afridi swear, said to be properly *Khudākē*.)

b. A harsh noise made by an angry cat, bird, etc.

1895 J. G. MILLAIS *Breath fr. Veldt* (1899) 98 Its cry of alarm (a jarring swear) is almost exactly like that of the common starling.

swear (swɛə(r)), *v.* Pa. t. swore (swɔə(r)); pa. pple. sworn (swɔ:n). Forms: 1–2 **swerian**, (1 **swer(i)ȝan, suerian**, 2 **sweriȝen**), 2–4 **swerie(n, sweren**, (3 **swærie, suerie**, 4 **swery(e**, *Ayenb.* **zuerie**), 3–5 **swer**, 4–5 **suer**, 4–6 **suere**, 4–7 **swere**, (4 **squere**, 5 **sqwere, sweire, sweyre, suerne**, 6 **shwere**), 5–9 *Sc.* **sweir**, (6 *Sc.* **sueir**), 6–7 **sweare**, 6–8 **sware**, 6– **swear.** *Pa. t.* α. 1–5 **swor**, 2–4 **suor**, 3 **sweor**, 4 **suore**, *Ayenb.* **zuor**, 4–5 *Sc.* **swour, swoir**, 4–5 (8–9 *Sc.*) **swoor**, 6 *Sc.* **swoyr**, 7 **swoare**, 3– **swore.** β. 3–4 **swar**, 4 **suar(e, square**, 4–7, 9 *arch.* **sware.** γ. 4 **swer, suer**, 4–5 **swere, squere.** δ. 1 **swerede**, 6 **swered**, 7 (9 *dial.*) **sweared**; 5 **swarid, sward.** *Pa. pple.* α. 1–6, 8 **sworen**, 3 **sweoren**, 4 **suorn**, 4–5 **squorn(e**, 5 **suoren**, 5–7 **sworne, suorne**, (6 **swarne, soren, sorne, shorne**, *Sc.* **suoryne**), 4– **sworn**; 2 **ȝesworen**, 3–4 **i-, ysworen**, 4–5 **ysworn(e.** β. 3–5 **suore**, 3–5, 7–9 (now *dial.* or *vulgar*) **swore**; 3 **ysuore**, 3–5 **iswore**, 4–5 **yswore**, 5 **iswoor, (i-swere).** γ. 4 **yswered.** [Com. Teut. str. vb. (sporadically wk.) with *j*-present stem: OE. *swęrian*, *swór*, rarely *swerede*, *-swaren*, usually *-sworen*, = OFris. *swaria*, *swera*, also *swara*, *swora*, OS. *swerian*, *-swôr*, *-sworen*, (M)LG. *sweren*, *swôr*, *swâren*, *swôren*, MDu. *sweren*, (Du. *zweren*), OHG. *suuerian*, *suuerran*, *suôr*, *giswaran* (for **giswaran*), MHG. *swern*, *swûr*, *swuor*, dial. *swerete*, *gesworn*, *geswarn* (G. *schwören*, *schwur*, †*schwor*, *geschworen*), ON. *sverja*, *sór*, *svór*, *svarinn*, also wk. *svarði*, *svarðr* (Sw. *svärja*, Da. *sværge*):—OTeut. **swarjan* (not in Goth., which has a new formation *swaran*), f. *swar-*, whence also ON. *svar* answer, *svara* to answer, SWARE, and OE. *and-swaru* ANSWER. The ulterior relations of the root are uncertain.

The conjugation of this verb has been influenced from early times by that of BEAR *v.* (OE. *beran*). The regular pa. t. *swore* (OE. *swór*) has never ceased to be extensively current, but from the 15th to the 17th cent. *sware*, formed on the analogy of *bare* (OE. *bær*, *bǣron*), was widespread; *swar* occurs as early as the first text of Layamon; *suar(e* is the prevailing form in the Cotton MS. of *Cursor Mundi*; *sware* and *swore* are both used in Malory's *Morte Darthur*; *sware* is the only form in the Bible of 1611 (exc. in the Apocrypha), but is rare in the 1st Folio of Shakspere. In the 14th and 15th a by-form *swere* occurs, after *bere*.]

I. 1. *intr.* To make a solemn declaration or statement with an appeal to God or a superhuman being, or to some sacred object, in confirmation of what is said; to take an oath.

Const. *by*, *on*, or *upon* that to which appeal is made (see 13, 16), in OE. *on*, *þurh*, *under*.

a **900** *Laws of K. Ælfred* Introd. c. 48 Ne swerȝen ȝe næfre under hæðne godas. *c* **950** *Lindisf. Gosp.* Matt. v. 34 *Ego autem dico uobis non iurare omnino*, ic uutetlice cueðo iuh to ne suerige æfre [*Rushw.* þæt ȝe ne sellaþ hað *vel* swerȝe allunga, *Ags. Gosp.* þæt ȝe eallunga ne swerion, *Hatton* sweriȝan]. *a* **1225** *Ancr. R.* 70 ȝe ne schulen uor none þinge ne warien, ne swerien, bute ȝif ȝe siggen witterliche, oðer sikerliche. **1340** *Ayenb.* 6 Ine non oþre manyere ne is no riȝt to zuerie. *c* **1410** *Lanterne of Liȝt* xii. 89 ȝit enemyes purswen aȝen þis comaundement, & seyn þat Crist him silf swore, and hise seintis boþe. *a* **1425** *Cursor M.* 6848 (Trin.) Trowe on no goddes fals, Swereþ not I bidde ȝou als. **1660** in *Extr. St. Papers rel. Friends* Ser. II. (1911) 122 Wee dare not sware least we sin against our God. **1716** HEARNE *Collect.* (O.H.S.) V. 382 Charlett himself told me I should be forced to quit, if I did not swear (as I was resolved not to do). **1798** COLERIDGE *Fears in Solitude* 73 The Book of Life is made A superstitious instrument, on which We gabble o'er the oaths we mean to break; For all must swear. **1815** SCOTT *Guy M.* xxxii, 'As a magistrate,..if you refuse to answer my questions, I must put you upon your oath.' 'Troth, sir, I am no free to swear.'

2. To promise or undertake something by an oath; to take an oath by way of a solemn promise or undertaking. (Const. as in 1; also const. dat. or *to* the person to whom the promise is made.)

a. *intr.* (See also 17 a.)

c **825** *Vesp. Psalter* xiv. [xv.] 4 *Qui jurat proximo suo et non decepit eum*, se swereð ðæm nestan his & ne beswac hine. *c* **1205** LAY. 22865–7 Ærst sweor Arður..seoððen sworen eorles. *c* **1250** *Gen. & Ex.* 2433 Iosep swor him al-so he bad. *a* **1300** *Cursor M.* 18362 (Cott.) Þou has þam drund and don forfare, Als þou til ur for-eildres suare. *c* **1385** CHAUCER *L.G.W.* 1321 *Dido*, And so ȝe wele me now to wiue take As ȝe han sworne. *c* **1400** *Destr. Troy* 11837 Priam on his part, & his prise knightes, Sweryn all swiftly, & no swyke thoghtyn. **1562** A. SCOTT *Poems* (S.T.S.) i. 134 Credence is past off promeis, tho' thai sweir. **1634** MILTON *Comus* 1011 From her fair unspotted side Two blissful twins are to be born, Youth and Joy; so Jove hath sworn. **1662** STILLINGFL. *Orig. Sacræ* II. vi. §6 God is said to swear when he binds himself absolutely to performance. **1837** DICKENS *Pickw.* ii, 'Can I rely upon your secrecy?'..'You can'..'Hear me swear——'. 'No, no..don't swear, it's quite unnecessary.' **1902** VIOLET JACOB *Sheep-Stealers* viii, 'Swear, I tell ye.' 'I swear it, so help me God.'

fig. **1610** SHAKS. *Temp.* I. i. 62 Hee'l be hang'd yet, Though euery drop of water sweare against it, And gape at widst to glut him.

b. with inf.

1154 *O.E. Chron.* (Laud MS.) an. 1140 Alle diden him manred, & suoren þe pais to halden. *c* **1290** *Beket* 1007 in *S. Eng. Leg.* 135 He suor to holde þe eorþelich honur and hath i-broke is oth. *c* **1330** *Arth. & Merl.* 3405, xi kinges & doukes on Han ysworn, Arthour to slon. *c* **1400** *Destr. Troy* 13643 Fayne were þo freikes..And swiftly þai sware..To be lell to þe lord all his lyf tyme. **1441** *Extr. Aberd. Reg.* (1844) I. 7 He sall swere to keep this statute. *a* **1548** HALL *Chron., Hen. V*, 71 All maner persones of holy Churche..that shal swere to kepe this presente accord. **1667** MILTON *P.L.* I. 322 Or in this abject posture have ye sworn To adore the Conquerour? **1797** MRS. RADCLIFFE *Italian* xvii, I have sworn to speak the truth only. **1832** W. IRVING *Alhambra* II. 274 [He] swore not to raise his camp until he had gained possession of the place. **1867** HOWELLS *Ital. Journ.* 105 At last we leave the gates, and swear each other to come again many times while in Naples.

ellipt. **1600** SHAKS. *A.Y.L.* v. iv. 107 They shooke hands, and swore brothers.

c. with clause (occas. with quoted words).

c **1000** ÆLFRIC *Josh.* ii. 12 Sweriað me nu þurh drihten, þæt ȝe don eft wið me swilce mildheortnisse, swa ic macode wið eow. *c* **1200** *Trin. Coll. Hom.* 213 Þe sullere..swereð þat he hit nele lasse selle, þe beggere..swereð þat he nele more geuen. *c* **1205** LAY. 29078 Heo..sworen þat heo wolden Heore forward halden. *c* **1275** *Ibid.* 5866 We ȝou wolleþ swerie Vppen houre swerdes þat we wolleþ ȝou bi-fore Libbe oþer ligge. *a* **1300** *Cursor M.* 3225 (Cott.) Apon his kne he did him suere [*Fairf.* squere] þat he suld be lel errand berer. **1387** TREVISA *Higden* (Rolls) VI. 445 He hadde byhote and i-swore þat he schulde ȝelde Normandye to Richard. *c* **1420** *Sir Amadace* (Camden) xxii, Thenne he squere, 'Be Ihesu, Mare sun, That body schalle neuyr in the erthe come, My siluyr tille that I haue.' *c* **1470** HENRY *Wallace* v. 864 He..swour he suld be wengit on that deid. *a* **1529** SKELTON *E. Rummyng* 164 Elynour swered, Nay, Ye shall not beare away My ale for nought, By hym that me bought! **1592** *Soliman & Pers.* v. ii. 63 He lept for ioy, swearing and promising That our reward should be redoubled. **1689** in *Acts Parl. Scot.* (1875) XII. 51/1, I faithfully promitt in presence of the almighty god and swear þat I shall demean my self faithfully. **1813** SCOTT *Rokeby* IV. xiv, Rokeby sware, No rebel's son should wed his heir.

d. *trans.* With pron. as obj.

[*a* **1000** *Elene* 686 (Gr.) Ic þæt ȝeswerȝe þurh sunu meotodes..þæt ðu hungre scealt..cwylmed weorðan.] *c* **1205** LAY. 22507 Ælche ȝere ȝiuen [ich] þe wulle æhte..þis ich wullen þe swerien. *a* **1225** *Ancr. R.* 96 Ich heuede isworen hit, luuien ich mot te. *c* **1300** *Havelok* 398 Godard stirt up, an swor al þat þe king him bad. *c* **1369** CHAUCER *Dethe Blaunche* 1231 As I best koude I swore hir this. *c* **1412** HOCCLEVE *De Reg. Princ.* 2331 He rathir chees be disobedient..Than be forsworn of þat he swoor so depe. **1567** *Gude & Godlie Ball.* (S.T.S.) 91 Quhateuer he sweir to ony man,..His promeis he will keip. **1667** MILTON *P.L.* IV. 96 How soon Would highth recal high thoughts, how soon unsay What feign'd submission swore. **1869** FREEMAN *Norm. Conq.* III. xii. 246 Harold then..swore, but what he swore is as uncertain as it is when and where he swore it.

3. *trans.* With certain sbs.: To promise or undertake on oath to observe or perform (something).

a. fidelity, allegiance, etc.

a **1154** *O.E. Chron.* an. 1123 (Laud) Se ærceb[iscop] swor him underþeodnysse of ealle ða þing [etc.]. *c* **1290** *Beket* 1017 in *S. Eng. Leg.* 135 Þou suore þe kynge eorþelich honour and nelt don him non. **13..** *K. Alis.* 7427 (Laud MS.), Hij duden hym alle feute And sworen to hym also leute. **1387** TREVISA *Higden* (Rolls) V. 331 Arthur..ȝaf hym Hampschire and Somersete..and fey was i-swore to hym. *c* **1440** *Partonope* (1862) 2723 The king of Fraunce tolde homage And ther-to suer hostage, That they shulde him bere fayth and trouth. **1591** SHAKS. *1 Hen. VI*, v. iv. 169 Then sweare Allegeance to his Maiesty. **1595** —— *John* v. iv. 19 That Altar, where we swore to you Deere Amity, and euerlasting loue. **1600** E. BLOUNT tr. *Conestaggio* 76 That the Noblemen and Commons shoulde presently sweare obedience vnto them. **1675** CROWNE *Andromache* IV, Go, swear to her, the faith thou swor'st to me. **1848** THACKERAY *Van. Fair* xviii, While the French nation and army were swearing fidelity round the eagles in the Champ de Mars.

absol. *a* **1400–50** *Wars Alex.* 2104 Þar sere citis of þa sidis to him-selfe sweren. **1605** SHAKS. *Macb.* IV. ii. 47 *Son.* What is a Traitor? *Wife.* Why one that sweares, and lyes.

b. an action that is to be accomplished.

a **1300** *Cursor M.* 3994 (Cott.) Lauerd, þou send me now þi rede, Gains esau has suorn [*Fairf.* squorne] mi dede. **15..** *Christ's Kirk* 25 in *Bann. MS.* (Hunter. Cl.) 283 Thocht all hir kin had sworn hir deid. *a* **1533** LD. BERNERS *Huon* lxxxvii. 277 Thus duke Raoull sware the deth of Huon. *a* **1575** *Diurn. Occurr.* (Bannatyne Cl.) 308 Be the tennour heirof sueris and promeissis ane cessatioun and abstinence from hostilitie. **1592** *Arden of Feversham* II. ii. 131 The villaine hath sworne the slaughter of his maister. *a* **1774** GOLDSM. *Hist. Greece* II. 150 Whose destruction they had more than once swore. **1859** FITZGERALD *Omar* lxx, Repentance oft before I swore.

c. conditions, an agreement.

a **1154** *O.E. Chron.* an. 1094 (Laud) Þær seo forewarde ær wæs ȝewroht and eac ȝesworen. **1387** TREVISA *Higden* (Rolls) VIII. 51 Þe articules þat he hadde i-swore in his crownynge. **1601** SHAKS. *Jul. C.* II. i. 113 *Cas.* And let vs sweare our Resolution. *Brut.* No, not an Oath. *a* **1649** DRUMM. OF HAWTH. *Poems* Wks. (1711) 49 Thou ne're swore our covenant. *a* **1715** BURNET *Own Time* an. 1675 (1724) I. 381 When the long Parliament engaged into the league with Scotland, he would not swear the Covenant. **1757** W. WILKIE *Epigon.* VI. 167 A truce we swore; Jove witnessed the deed.

4. To affirm, assert, or declare something by an oath; to make oath to the truth of a statement. (Const. as in 1.) **a.** (*a*) *intr.*: *spec.* to give evidence on oath (*against* a person). Now *rare*.

c **825** *Vesp. Psalter* ci. 9 [cii. 8] *Adversum me jurabant*, [hi] wið me sworun. *c* **1385** CHAUCER *L.G.W.* Prol. 58 Al swere I nat, of this I wol nat lye. *c* **1420** *Sir Amadace* (Camden) xxiii, Quen Sir Amadace herd that he hade squorne. *c* **1450** CAPGRAVE *Life St. Gilbert* xxi, He was reqwyred to come be-fore þe iuges & make þer a bodely oth wheythir he was gilty in þis mater or nowt. But þis refused he, for he saide he had leuer be exiled þan swere. **1580** LYLY *Euphues* (Arb.) 242 That which followeth I saw, where-of who so doubteth, I will sweare. **1596** SHAKS. *Merch. V.* III. ii. 206 Swearing till my very rough [= roof] was dry With oathes of loue. **1613** —— *Hen. VIII*, v. i. 133 At what ease Might corrupt mindes procure, Knaues as corrupt To sweare against you. **1681** DRYDEN *Abs. & Achit.* I. 1012 Against themselves their Witnesses will Swear. **1810** CRABBE *Borough* xxii. 274 Why ask my father?—that old man will swear Against my life; besides, he wasn't there.

(*b*) With *home* or hyperbolical expressions, as *through a two-inch board*; also, ***to swear one's way through***...: denoting hard swearing.

1678 RAY *Prov.* (ed. 2) 271 He'll swear through an inch board, dagger out of sheath, the devil out of hell, 'till he's black in the face. **1680** in *Hickeringill's Wks.* (1716) II. 202 He swore home, or (as we say, through an Inch-board) against Records. **1722** [see HOME *adv.* 5]. **1728** EARL OF AILESBURY *Mem.* (1890) 372 Then he went through thick and thin, and, according to an old English phrase, swore through a two-inch board. **1865** DICKENS *Mut. Fr.* I. xv, That severe exertion which is known in legal circles as swearing your way through a stone wall.

b. with clause (or equivalent obj. and compl. or acc. and inf.): often also, to affirm emphatically or confidently (without an oath).

688–95 (*c* **950**) *Laws of Ine* (Liebermann) c. 56 Oððe swerie þæt he him nan facn on nyste. *c* **1000** *Ags. Gosp.* Matt. xxvi 74 Ða ætsoc he & swerede þæt he næfre þone man ne cuþe. **1038** *Charter of Harold Harefot* in Kemble *Cod. Dipl.* IV. 57 Se king..swor..under god ælmihtine & under ealle halȝan þarto þæt hit næfre næs na his ræd na his dæd. *c* **1250** *Gen. & Ex.* 1964 Til him he sweren ðat he liued. *a* **1300** *Cursor M.* 17493 Der yee suer, for godds blis, þat yee herd and sagh al þis? *c* **1374** CHAUCER *Anel. & Arc.* 122 He wolde preyen her to swere What was that worde. **1377** LANGL. *P. Pl.* B. XIV. 34 Haukyn..ligtly gan swerye, 'Who so leueth ȝow, by owre lorde I leue nouȝte he be blissed.' *c* **1385** CHAUCER *L.G.W.* 1378 *Hypsipyle*, O oftyn sworist thow that thow woldist deye. *c* **1386** —— *Prol.* 454, I dorste swere they weyeden ten pound. **1484** CAXTON *Fables of Alfonce* iii, [He] swore vpon the holy euangely that he toke none of the ryche mans oylle. *a* **1548** HALL *Chron., Edw. IV*, 232 b, Sweryng by sainct George that the kyng of Englande was not extracted of no noble house. *c* **1600** SHAKS. *Sonn.* cxlvii, I haue sworne thee faire, and thought thee bright. **1621** LADY M. WROTH *Urania* 468 She swore I loued her not, began to lament her selfe, wept, and cryd; O vnconstant men. **1674** C. F. *Wit at a Venture* 60 Our Town..Can't shew the like I'le sware. **1711** in *10th Rep. Hist. MSS. Comm.* App. v. 116 To refuse sweareing the said Queen to be head..of the English church, was a premunire. **1717** LADY M. W. MONTAGU *Let. to C'tess of Bristol* 1 Apr., I dare swear..that..'tis a very comfortable reflection to you. **1726** SWIFT *Gulliver* II. viii, His men came back in a fright, swearing they had seen a swimming house. **1848** THACKERAY *Van. Fair* xxxix, He swore it was as good as a play to see her in the character of a fine dame. **1865** TROLLOPE *Belton Est.* iv. 39 He swore to himself that he did love her.

c. *trans.* with pron. as obj.

c **1200** *Vices & Virtues* 9 Al þat we more sweriȝeð, swo it is euel and senne. *c* **1275** *Sinners Beware* 19 in *O.E. Misc.* 72 Ah ich hit segge and swerie. *c* **1300** *Havelok* 647 Soth it is, þat men seyt and suereth. *c* **1400** *Rom. Rose* 7638 But trustith wel, I swere it yow. That it is clene out of his thought. **1638** in *Verney Mem.* (1907) I. 124 By my soule I dare swear itt. **1649** C. WALKER *Hist. Independ.* II. 105 Should they Vote..Oliver's Nose a Ruby, they would expect we should sweare it, and fight for it. **1818** SCOTT *Hrt. Midl.* xxi, Her father..tormented himself with imagining what the one sister might say or swear.

5. *trans.* With certain sbs.: **a.** To take an oath as to the fact or truth of; to confirm (a statement) by oath. Also † ***to swear sooth, truth.***

1377 LANGL. *P. Pl.* B. XX. 160 Her syre was a sysour þat neure swore treuthe. **1382** WYCLIF *Eccl.* ix. 2 As a for-sworn, so and he that soth swerth [orig. *ut perjurus, ita et ille qui verum dejerat*]. **1565** *Reg. Privy Council Scot.* I. 404 Havand diverse of thair servandis fylit in the billis of Elname Newtoun..quhilkis billis ar sworne. *a* **1715** BURNET *Own Time* III. (1823) II. 300 Depositions were prepared for them: and they promised to swear them. **1755** JOHNSON s.v., He swore treason against his friend. **1818** CRUISE *Digest* (ed. 2) V. 387 Every such affidavit..shall be sworn before a person duly authorized to take affidavits in this court. **1847** LADY BLESSINGTON *Marmaduke Herbert* lxii, Two men..against whom Mr. Herbert had sworn information for a conspiracy to extort money from him.

b. To proclaim or declare with an oath or solemn affirmation.

to swear the peace against: see PEACE *sb.* 9 b.

13.. *Gaw. & Gr. Knt.* 1825 He..swere swyftely his sothe; þat he hit sese nolde. **1390** GOWER *Conf.* II. 300 Whan he hath his trouthe suore. **1599** SHAKS. *Much Ado* II. i. 175, I heard him sweare his affection. **1667** MILTON *P.L.* v. 814 The just Decree of God, pronounc't and sworn. **1709** STRYPE *Ann. Ref.* I. li. 513 That they should swear his supremacy, and obedience to him before some priest. **1871** MORLEY *Carlyle* in *Crit. Misc.* Ser. I. (1878) 168 A man of genius is at liberty to..swear all his conclusions.

c. To value on oath *at* so much.

1854 SURTEES *Handley Cr.* lxv. (1901) II. 199 She died. —Her wealth was great..and the Captain..soon discovered he might swear the property under twelve thousand pounds, without defrauding himself. **1873** *Chambers's Jrnl.* 10 May 304/2 James Wood, of Gloucester, who died in 1836, possessed of property sworn under £900,000. **1896** *Law Times* C. 508/1 The gross personal estate is sworn at £37,405. 16. 10.

6. To take or utter (an oath), either solemnly or profanely (cf. 8). Also const. as in 1, 2, 4.

Beowulf 472 (Gr.) He me aþas swor. *c* **1050** *O.E. Chron.* an. 1049 (MS. C) [He] cwæð þæt he him aþas sweriȝan wolde & him hold beon. *a* **1123** *Ibid.* an. 1109 Ðær wurdon..þa aðas ȝesworene his dohter þam Casere to ȝifene. *c* **1205** LAY. 653 Þe king wes swiðe wrað & swar muchelne oað. *a* **1225** *Ancr. R.* 198 Þisses hweolpes [*sc.* Blasphemy] nurice is þe þet swereð greate oðes. *a* **1300** *Cursor M.* 4650 Al þat barunage, ..To þis ioseph an ath þai suare. *c* **1380** *Sir Ferumb.* 82 By Mahomet ys oþ þanne a swer. *Ibid.* 1045 Y til him am trewe ypliȝt & haue myn oþ yswered. *a* **1450** *Knt. de la Tour* Prol. 2 Grete fals othes that the fals men vsen to swere to the women. **1470–85** MALORY *Arthur* VIII. ii. 275 He..sware a grete othe that he shold slee her but yf she told hym trouthe. *a* **1548** HALL *Chron., Hen. VII*, 17 b, Thys othe he sware in the great Church of Bruges. *c* **1643** LD. HERBERT *Autobiog.* (1824) 74 [Queen Elizabeth] swearing her usual oath demanded, who is this? **1784** COWPER *Task* IV. 629 He.. mumbling, swears A bible-oath to be whate'er they please. **1823** SCOTT *Quentin D.* xxxiii, Never was false oath sworn on this most sacred relique but it was avenged within the year. **1852** THACKERAY *Esmond* I. ix, My lord swore one of his large oaths that he did not know in the least what she meant.

transf. **1592** SHAKS. *Rom. & Jul.* I. iv. 87 Being thus frighted, [he] sweares a prayer or two & sleepes againe. **1823** BYRON *Juan* XIV. xxxiv, Sires, The Nestors of the sporting generation, Swore praises, and recall'd their former fires.

†**7.** To use (a sacred name) in an oath; to invoke or appeal to (a deity, etc.) by an oath: = 13 a.

c **1250** *Gen. & Ex.* 3498 Tac ðu nogt in idel min namen, Ne swer it les to fele in gamen. **1303** R. BRUNNE *Handl. Synne* 608 Swere nat hys name yn ydulnys. *c* **1380** WYCLIF *Wks.* (1880) 60 Many..men sweryngе herte & bonys & nailis & oþere membris of crist. *c* **1400** *Rom. Rose* 5965 Yit wolde I swere, for sikirnesse, The pole of helle to my witnesse. **1430–40** LYDG. *Bochas* VIII. xiv. (MS. Bodl. 263) 384/1 Nat afferd to suere goddis bonys With horrible othes of bodi flessh & blood. **1509** BARCLAY *Shyp of Folys* (1570) 174 But nowe eche sweareth the Eucharist commonly. **1605** SHAKS. *Lear* I. i. 163 *Lear.* Now by Apollo. *Kent.* Now by Apollo, King, Thou swear'st thy Gods in vaine.

8. a. *intr.* To utter a form of oath lightly or irreverently, as a mere intensive, or an expression of anger, vexation, or other strong feeling; to use the Divine or other sacred name, or some phrase implying it, profanely in affirmation or imprecation; to utter a profane oath, or use profane language habitually; more widely, to use bad language. (See also 12.) † ***to swear and stare***: see STARE *v.* 3 a.

c **1430** *How Good Wife taught Dau.* 62 in *Babees Bk.* (1868) 39 To swere be þou not leefe. **1531** ELYOT *Gov.* I. xxvi, They wyll say he that swereth depe, swereth like a lorde. **1577** B. GOOGE *Heresbach's Husb.* I. (1586) 15 b, Let him..in no wyse suffer them [*sc.* servants] to sweare or to blaspheme. **1583** STUBBES *Anat. Abus.* I. (1877) 72 Then fell shee to sweare and teare.., to cursse and banne. **1593** SHAKS. *2 Hen. VI*, I. i. 188 Oft haue I seene the haughty Cardinall..Sweare like a Ruffian. **1706** E. WARD *Hud. Rediv.* III. 17 Your Folly makes me stare; Such talk would make a Parson swear. **1706** —— *Wooden World Diss.* (1708) 45 He never swears but in his Cups. **1841** THACKERAY *Gt. Hoggarty Diam.* ix, O, sir, it would have frightened you to hear a Christian babe like him swear as he did. **1902** G. K. MENZIES *Prov. Sk.* 17 Where a golfer, club in hand, Freely swears As he hacks with all his might.

b. To utter a harsh guttural sound, as an angry cat or other animal. *colloq.*

c **1700** KENNETT *MS. Lansd. 1033* s.v., The dog swears when he grumbles and snarles. **1753** MISS COLLIER *Art Torment.* Concl. 232 [The cat] swears, she growls, and shews all the salvage motions of her heart. **1896** F. GALTON in *Spectator* 11 Apr. 515 When Phyllis was a kitten she had wild fits, tearing round the room and 'swearing' horribly. **1902** *Strand Mag.* Jan. 72/2 Away to the east an angry [locomotive] engine was swearing.

9. *trans.* **a.** To bring or get into some specified condition or position by swearing. (See also IV.)

1588 SHAKS. *L.L.L.* v. ii. 275 Berowne did sweare him-selfe out of all suite. **1616** S. S. *Honest Lawyer* IV. G 4 b, I would sweare them to the Gallous, as well as they swore me out of my money. **1728** [DE FOE] *Street-Robberies* 6 She might have swore her Eyes out of her Head, for the unbelieving Wretches did not mind what she said or swore. **1818** SCOTT *Rob Roy* vii, The miller swore himself as black as night that he stopt them at twelve o'clock. **1846** D. JERROLD *Mrs. Caudle* x, Because once in your lifetime your shirt wanted a button, you must almost swear the roof off the house.

b. To put *upon* or ascribe *to* a person in a sworn statement.

1754 GOODALL *Exam. Lett. Mary Q. Scots* I. Introd. 12 To the end that they might convict Murray and his party, both of murdering the King, and of forging papers, and then swearing them upon her. **1785** TRUSLER *Mod. Times* II. 142 To..lay them [*sc.* their bastards] at the doors of some gentlemen's houses, or swear them to persons that had been their common disturbers. **1900** WEYMAN *Sophia* iii, A silver tankard and twenty-seven guineas she took with her, and I'll swear them to you.

II. 10. a. Orig. *pass.* To be bound by oath (see also *sworn brother*, etc. s.v. SWORN); hence *actively*, to cause to take an oath; to bind by an oath; to put (a person) upon his oath; to administer an oath to. Also const. *on* as in 1.

c **1050** *Voc.* in Wr.-Wülcker 375/21 *Conspirati*, onan ȝeswonene. *a* **1400** *Minor Poems fr. Vernon MS.* xlix. 148 Good schame, holynesse, & curtesye As breþuren ben sworen. **1431** *E.E. Wills* 88 [I bequeath] To Maude Wilbe, xx li, so am y sworne. *a* **1450** *Knt. de la Tour* xvii, Thereof y am suore. **1483-7** *Star Chamber Proc.* (Som. Rec. Soc. 1911) 43 The same abbot wold not be sworne vppon eny answer. **1514** *Extr. Aberd. Reg.* (1844) I. 90 To be suorn the gret bodelie aitht. **1545** in Leadam *Sel. Cases Crt. Requests* (Selden Soc.) 80 William Warwyck..sworen vpon his othe sayth. **1596** SHAKS. *Merch. V.* v. i. 301 The first intergatory That my Nerrissa shall be sworne on. **1681** *Trial S. Colledge* 35 *Mr. Att[orney] Gen[eral].* Swear Stevens. (*Which was done.*) **1776** *Trial of Nundocomar* 52/1 You have sworn me upon the waters of the Ganges: how can I tell more than I remember? **1802-12** BENTHAM *Ration. Judic. Evid.* (1827) I. 418 Tender the oath: if he accepts it, swear him. **1827** HALLAM *Const. Hist.* i. (1854) I. 19 Commissioners were appointed throughout the Kingdom to swear every man to the value of his possessions. **1912** *Times* 19 Dec. 12/6 A member of a French Roman Catholic Sisterhood objected to be sworn on the Testament.

with compl. *a* **1548** HALL *Chron., Hen. VI*, 137 He..hanged the Frenchmen, because thei wer once sworne English, and after, brake their othe. **1610** SHAKS. *Temp.* II. ii. 156 Ile sweare my selfe thy Subiect. **1682** DRYDEN *Mac-Fl.* 113 Hannibal did to the Altars come, Swore by his Syre a mortal Foe to Rome.

†**b.** *to have, make, take* (a person) ***sworn***: to administer an oath to. *Obs.*

c **1400** *Anturs of Arth.* liv, þay made hyme sworne to Sir Gawane. **15..** *Sir A. Barton* in *Surtees Misc.* (1890) 69 And ther he tooke me sworne. **1556** *Chron. Grey Friars* (Camden) 46 The erle of Angwyche..whome the kynge..had hym with the other lordes of Scotlonde shorne and resevyd the sacrament that [etc.]. ? *a* **1600** *Lord of Learne* 289 in Furniv. *Percy Folio* I. 192, I am tane sworne vpon a booke, & forsworne I will not bee.

c. Const. *to* a person (i.e. in allegiance or service), a rule, a course of action, a declaration, etc. Similarly const. *against*.

Now chiefly in ***to swear to secrecy***.

1297 R. GLOUC. (Rolls) 5520 Sire..ich was ysuore to him ar to þe. *a* **1325** *MS. Rawl. B.* 520 lf. 32b, Eche man..i suuore ant assised to armes..þat is to wite to viftene pond worth of londe. **1338** R. BRUNNE *Chron.* (1725) 168 Now is Cipres lorn fro Isaac & hise, & to R. suorn for his valiantise. c **1386** CHAUCER *Sqr.'s T.* 10 As of the secte of which þat he was born He kepte his lay, to which þat he was sworn. *a* **1400** *St. Matthew* 270 in Horstm. *Altengl. Leg.* (1881) 135 To chastite þan was scho sworn. c **1430** *Freemasonry* (1840) 436 And alle these poyntes hyr before, To hem thou most nede be y-swore. **1509** in Leadam *Sel. Cases Star Chamber* (Selden Soc.) 277 Eche of them had offendid the sayd statute of the Cyte whervnto they ware swarne. **1549** LATIMER *7th Serm. bef. Edw. VI* (Arb.) 185, I woulde not haue men to be sworne to them, and so adicte as to take hand ouer hed whatsoeuer they say. **1684** *Pennsylv. Archives* I. 87 That the Lord Balltemoare had sworne all the Inhabitants..with faith and Alleigense to him. **1690** DRYDEN *Don Sebastian* v. (1692) 108 Let me swear you all to secresy. **1700** TYRRELL *Hist. Eng.* II. 779 The King had sent Commissioners to Swear Men to the Observation of the Charters. **1745** R. LEVESON GOWER in Jesse *Selwyn & Contemp.* (1843) I. 75 We have all been swore to our depositions. **1814** SCOTT *Ld. of Isles* III. xxiv, Sworn to vigil and to fast. **1852** THACKERAY *Esmond* I. vii, He swore Harry to secrecy too, which vow the lad religiously kept. **1859** [MISS PIDDINGTON] *Last of Cavaliers* xlii. III. 138 Oh, was that Heaven itself sworn against me, that this was always hidden from me, to crush me so at last!

d. with inf.

c **1325** *Poem Times Edw. II* (Percy) x, The erchedeknes that beth sworn To visite holy cherche. c **1374** CHAUCER *Troylus* III. 312, I am sworn to holden it secree. **1470-85** MALORY *Arthur* Table Contents 9 He was sworne vpon a book to telle the trouthe of his queste. *a* **1530** DK. NORFOLK in Ellis *Orig. Lett.* Ser. III. I. 378, I have soren all the Commissioners not to disclose any parte thereof to any other creature. **1531** in J. Bulloch *Pynouris* (1887) 62 Five of the best pynouris..sorne the grit aytht to be leill and trew to the merchandis. *a* **1548** HALL *Chron., Hen. VIII*, 50b, [The] crowner..assembled a quest..and hath sworne theim truely to enquire of the death of one Rychard Hun. **1594** SHAKS. *Rich. III*, I. iv. 213 Thy Sou'raignes Sonne, Whom thou was't sworne to cherish and defend. **1686** GOAD *Celest. Bodies* I. ix. 29 They do not swear us to believe All they deliver. **1773** BLACKSTONE *Comm.* I. ii. (ed. 5) 180 A select committee of fifteen members, who are sworn well and truly to try the same. **1805** COLEBROOKE *Védas* Misc. Ess. 1837 I. 43 The priest swears the soldier by a most solemn oath, not to injure him. **1827** HALLAM *Const. Hist.* ix. (1854) II. 96 The..keeper of the great seal was to be sworn to issue writs for a new parliament.

e. with clause. ? *Obs.*

a **1450** *Knt. de la Tour* xix, They were suoren that none shulde late his wiff haue weting of her wager. **1570** in *Archaeologia* XL. 392 This examynate dyd swere hym upon a booke that he shuld not practys the same. *a* **1593** MARLOWE *Edw. II*, I. i. 83 [We] were sworne to your father at his death, That he should nere returne into the realme. **1679** *Establ. Test* 21 His Father swore him before the Altars..that he should be *perpetuus Romani nominis Osor*.

f. Phr. ***I dare be sworn, I'll be sworn***, expressing strong affirmation, properly implying readiness to take an oath upon the fact. *arch.*

1596 SHAKS. *Merch. V.* v. i. 172, I dare be sworne for him, he would not leaue it. **1598** —— *Merry W.* I. iv. 156 Ile be sworne on a booke shee loues you. **1610** —— *Temp.* III. iii. 26 Ile be sworne 'tis true. **1693** *Humours Town* 4 I'll be sworn, it has seem'd an Age to me. **1835** LYTTON *Rienzi* I. ix, I dare be sworn the good man spent the whole night in painting it himself.

11. *spec.* **a.** To admit to an office or function by administering a formal oath. (See also 21.)

a **1049** *O.E. Chron.* an. 1041 (MS. C) He..wæs to cinge ȝesworen. *a* **1400** *Old Usages Winchester* in *Eng. Gilds* 350 þer sholde be twey baylyues y-swore in þe Citee. **1560** DAUS tr. *Sleidane's Comm.* 86b, He appointeth and sweareth others in theyr steade. **1568** GRAFTON *Chron.* II. 130 Men empaneled and sworne for to enquire of the aforesayd articles. **1623-4** *Act 21 Jas. I*, c. 31 §1 To..choose and sweare one Master two Wardens sixe Searchers and foure and twentie Assistantes. **1681** *Trial S. Colledge* 21 Mr. Sheriff, there are a great many of the Jury that are not Sworn, they are discharged. **1712** PRIDEAUX *Direct. Ch.-wardens* (ed. 4) 46 If any Arch-Deacon..shall refuse to Swear a Church-warden into his Office. **1837** CARLYLE *Fr. Rev.* I. VII. xi, Lafayette..swears the remaining Bodyguards, down in the Marble-Court. **1857** TOULMIN SMITH *Parish* 91 A Churchwarden may execute his office before he is sworn. **1880** MISS BRADDON *Just as I am* viii, The jury were sworn.

b. with compl., usually expressing the office or function to which the person is appointed.

c **1205** LAY. 30128 Kinges heo weoren ihouene & kinges iswerene. **1556** *Chron. Grey Friars* (Camden) 73 The xx[ti] day of December [1551] was sorne the byshoppe of Ely lorde [chancellor of Engla]nd. **1598** SHAKS. *Merry W.* II. iii. 55, I am come to fetch you home: I am sworn of the peace. **1608** in *Capt. J. Smith's Wks.* (Arb.) p. xc, Master Archers quarrell to me was..because I would not sware him of the Councell for Virginia. **1626** EARL OF WINTOUN in *10th Rep. Hist. MSS. Comm.* App. I. 45 Sum ladys ar suorne of the Quenis bed chalmer. **1628** *Ibid., Var. Coll.* IV. 238 A certificate..that he..be fitt to be sworne a free citizen. **1665** in *Verney Mem.* (1907) II. 244, I am told Sir John Dynham's Lady and fine Mrs. Middleton are sworne the Queen's Dressers. **1727** POPE, etc. *Art of Sinking* 125 This may be obviated by swearing those six persons of his majesty's privy council. **1855** MACAULAY *Hist. Eng.* xii. III. 151 Richard..had been sworn of the Irish Privy Council.

III. 12. swear at ——. **a.** To imprecate evil upon by an oath; to address with profane imprecation; *gen.* to utter maledictions against; to curse.

1680 H. MORE *Apocal. Apoc.* 357 The Wits of this age that are ready to swear and flear at any such profession. **1779** WARNER in Jesse *Selwyn & Contemp.* (1844) IV. 13 In a fury, swearing like an Emperor at all the world. **1845** DISRAELI *Sybil* III. iii, Master Joseph Diggs did nothing but blaspheme and swear at his customers. **1863** SUSAN WARNER *Old Helmet* xxiii, He swore at them [*sc.* drives in the park] for the stupidest entertainment man ever pleased himself with. **1891** 'J. S. WINTER' *Lumley* iv, This important man, who was probably swearing at fate that he must pass the next two hours [etc.].

b. *fig.* Of colours, etc.: To be violently incongruous or inharmonious with. *colloq.* (Cf. F. *jurer*.)

1884 *Daily News* 10 Nov. 3/1 Two tints that swear at each other. **1889** *Harper's Mag.* Jan. 258/2 What is new in it in the way of art, furniture, or bric-à-brac..may 'swear' at the old furniture and the delightful old portraits.

13. swear by ——. **a.** To appeal to, or use a formula of appeal to (a divine being or sacred object, or something affectedly or trivially substituted therefor) in swearing; to say 'by...' as a form of oath: cf. BY *prep., adv.* (*a., sb.*[1]) 2.

to swear by no beggars, by no bugs: see BEGGAR *sb.* 1 c, BUG *sb.*[1] 1.

c **1220** *Bestiary* 597 He sweren bi ðe rode, bi ðe sunne & bi ðe mone. *a* **1300** *Cursor M.* 6847 (Cott.) Bi fals godds suer yee nan. *a* **1300** *Pol. Songs* (Camden) 70 Sire Simond de Mountfort hath swore bi ys chyn [etc.]. *Ibid.*, Sire Simond de Montfort hath suore bi ys cop [etc.]. **1340** *Ayenb.* 45 A knyȝt wes þet zuor be godes eȝen. c **1386** CHAUCER *Miller's Prol.* 17 In Pilates voys he gan to crie And swoor by Armes, and by blood, and bones. **14..** *R. Gloucester's Chron.* (Rolls) App. K. 3 (MS. β) þer of we schul awreke beo, I swere be my heued. c **1470** *Gol. & Gaw.* 1045, I swere be suthfast God, that settis all on sevin! **1599** SHAKS. *Much Ado* IV. i. 278 *Bene.* By my sword Beatrice thou lou'st me. *Beat.* Doe not sweare by it and eat it. *a* **1631** DONNE *Sat.* i. 13 First sweare by thy best love in earnest..Thou wilt not leave mee in the middle street, Though some more spruce companion thou dost meet. **1721** WODROW *Hist. Suff. Ch. Scot.* (1838) I. I. iv. 333/2 That to swear by faith, conscience, and the like, were innocent ways of speaking. **1781** GIBBON *Decl. & F.* xxxi. III. 229 They had sworn, by the sacred head of the emperor himself. **1842** TENNYSON *Godiva* 24 He laugh'd, and swore by Peter and by Paul. **1877** —— *Harold* v. i. 67 The strange Saints By whom thou swarest.

b. To swear to or be sure of the existence of (cf. 17 b): in phr. ***enough to swear by***, expressing a very slight amount. *colloq.* or *slang*.

1756 C. LUCAS *Ess. Waters* III. 138 They prescribe them ..in some quantity, though it be but enough to swear by. **1884** 'H. COLLINGWOOD' *Under Meteor Flag* 40 The two ships touched with a shock which was barely perceptible, just enough in fact to 'swear by,' as the gunner remarked.

c. To accept as an infallible authority; to have absolute confidence in. *colloq.*

c **1815** JANE AUSTEN *Persuas.* vi, I have no very good opinion of Mrs. Charles's nursery-maid... Mrs. Charles quite swears by her. **1864** YATES *Broken to Harness* x. I. 173 He is always..changing his medical system; now vaunting the virtues of blue-pill, now swearing by homœopathy. **1890** HENTY *With Lee in Virginia* 91 We have a first-rate fellow in command of the cavalry..His fellows swear by him.

14. swear for ——. To answer for under oath, or with assurance. ? *Obs.*

1579 GOSSON *Sch. Abuse* (Arb.) 60 It is hard to say that all offend, yet I promise you, I wil sweare for none. **1611** SHAKS. *Wint. T.* IV. iv. 155 Ile sweare for 'em.

15. swear off ——. To abjure, forswear, renounce. (Cf. 22 c.) *colloq.* or *slang*.

1898 A. F. LEACH *Beverley Act Bk.* (Surtees) I. 315 Ingelram keeps a concubine... Confesses and swears off her.

16. swear on (or **upon**) ——. To take an oath, symbolically touching or placing the hand on (a sacred object); †formerly also, to swear by (a deity, etc.) = 13 a: cf. ON *prep.* 1 f.

c **950** *Lindisf. Gosp.* Matt. xxiii. 18 *Quicumque iurauerit in altari*, seðe suerias on wiȝ-bed. c **1205** LAY. 22860 Bringeð þene halidom, And ich wulle swerien þer on. c **1300** *Havelok* 1077 The king aþelwald me dide swere Vpon al þe messegere þat [etc.] *Ibid.* 1082 þat gart he me sweren on þe bok. **1362** LANGL. *P. Pl.* A. I. 97 Dauid..Dubbede knihtes, Dude hem swere on hear swerd to serue treuþe euere. c **1400** *Destr. Troy* 11381 All sweire þai, full swiftly, vpon swete haloues. **1553** *Respublica* 1131 For my parte, I will sware the gosspell booke vppon. **1610** SHAKS. *Temp.* II. ii. 130 I'le sweare vpon that Bottle, to be thy true subiect. **1821** JOANNA BAILLIE *Metr. Leg., Lord John* xiv, Were I on my father's sword to swear.

17. swear to ——. **a.** To promise or undertake with a solemn oath (an act or course of action): cf. 2. Now *rare*.

[**1028-60** *Laws Northumbrian Priests* §57 (Liebermann 384/1) þæt hi hit ȝegaderian and eft aȝifan, swa hi durran to swerian.] **1588** SHAKS. *L.L.L.* I. i. 53 *Longa.* You swore to that Berowne, and to the rest. **1671** H. M. tr. *Erasm. Colloq.* 401 Even when he had deeply sworn to it. **1710** PRIDEAUX *Orig. Tithes* v. 275 The English..made all, that reigned over them, to sware to the keeping of them. **1818** SCOTT *Br. Lamm.* xx, I have sacrificed to you projects of vengeance long nursed, and sworn to with ceremonies little better than heathen.

b. To affirm with an oath; to express assurance of the truth of (a statement), or the identity of (a person or thing), by swearing.

1601 SHAKS. *All's Well* v. iii. 291 He knowes I am no Maid, and hee'l sweare too 't. *a* **1718** PRIOR *Better Answer to Chloe Jealous* iii, Od's Life! must One swear to the Truth of a Song? **1757** HUME *Hist. Gt. Brit.* II. iii. 120 The greatest interest could not engage him [*sc.* a quaker], in any court of judicature, to swear even to the truth. **1802** MARIA EDGEWORTH *Moral T., Forester* xix, Mr. W—— held the book to him, and demanded whether he would swear to the person from whom he received the note. **1841** THACKERAY *Gt. Hoggarty Diam.* xii, Mr. Abednego and the two gentlemen from Houndsditch were present to swear to their debts. **1848** G. WYATT *Revelat. an Orderly* (1849) 82 They came and swore to having served the dustucks. **1859** H. KINGSLEY *G. Hamlyn* v. I. 42 There was something about his *toute ensemble*..that would have made an Australian policeman swear to him as a convict without the least hesitation. **1908** R. BAGOT *A. Cuthbert* xxiv. 315 You could swear to its authenticity, or the reverse, if necessary?

18. swear with ——. = sense 12 b. *rare*.

1789 H. WALPOLE *Let.* 2 July (1961) XXXI. 306, I do not propose putting your name.., as I think it would swear with the air of ancientry you have adopted in the signature and notes. **1976** C. OMAN *Oxf. Childhood* 101 It was decreed that she must wear a rose-pink robe which swore most horribly with her greatest asset.

IV. 19. swear away. To take away by swearing; to give evidence on oath so as to destroy or cause the loss of.

a **1763** W. KING *Lit. & Polit. Anecd.* (1819) 191 Who for a small bribe would swear away any man's life. **1873** EDITH THOMPSON *Hist. Eng.* xxxv. 172 By him and by others who made a profit of perjury, the lives of many innocent Romanists were sworn away. **1879** TOURGEE *Fool's Err.* xi. 50 What! allow a nigger to testify! allow him to swear away your rights and mine!

20. swear down. a. To put down or put to silence by swearing. **b.** To bring or call down by swearing.

[c **1386** CHAUCER *Miller's T.* 659 With othes grete he was so sworn adoun That he was holde wood.] **1590** SHAKS. *Com. Err.* v. i. 227 There did this perjur'd Goldsmith sweare me downe. **1603** —— *Meas. for M.* v. i. 243 Though they would swear downe each particular Saint.

21. swear in. To admit or induct into an office by administering a prescribed oath.

a **1700** EVELYN *Diary* 15 Oct. 1673, To Council, and swore in Mr. Locke, secretary. **1768** GRAY in *Corr. w. Nicholls* (1843) 80 As soon as I have been sworn in, and subscribed. **1828** ELLENBOROUGH *Diary* (1881) I. 8 Went to the Cottage to be sworn in as a Privy Councillor and Lord Privy Seal. **1857** G. A. LAWRENCE *Guy Liv.* iv, The municipal authorities..swore in no end of specials as a reserve. **1891** *Times* (weekly ed.) 16 Aug. 641/3 The process of swearing-in the members of the Lower-House began.

22. swear off. †**a.** To resign one's office. *Obs.* **b.** To get rid of or pass off on somebody with an oath or asseveration. **c.** To abjure something, esp. intoxicating drink (cf. 15). More recently, with obj. expressed. Chiefly *U.S.*

1698 LUTTRELL *Brief Rel.* (1857) IV. 414 This day Mr. Howard, wine cowper, was chose sherif of London, in room of Mr. Moor that swore off. **1737** BRACKEN *Farriery Impr.* (1757) II. 14 They..make nothing of turning any common Cart-Horse to the Road,..and swear him off to their best Friend for an excellent Hunter. **1839** *Spirit of Times* 16 Nov. 434/1 Like swearing off from liquor and going into a grog-shop. **1853** MRS. STOWE *Key to Uncle Tom's Cabin* 91/2 Well, after all, I suppose, Mr. Legree, you wouldn't have any objections to swarin' off? **1896** *Spectator* 15 Feb. 235 Just as a man who has 'sworn off,' for a long time, loses the desire for drink. **1922** 'MARK TWAIN' in *Harper's Mag.* Mar. 457/1, I..swore off my taxes like the most conscienceless of the lot. **1960** R. ST. JOHN *Foreign Correspondent* v. 88 He became a newspaper reporter and swore off personal involvement in politics, at least for the time.

23. swear out. †**a.** To utter a solemn charge or challenge in regard to. Also *absol.* *Obs.*

a **1440** *Sir Eglam.* 1249 Harowdes of armes swore owt than, 'Yf ther be ony gentylman, To make hys body gode.' **1575** GASCOIGNE *Glasse Govt.* I. v, If any gentleman offer you the least parte of injury, Dicke must be sent for to sweare out the matter.

†**b.** To forswear, abjure. *Obs.*
1588 Shaks. *L.L.L.* ii. i. 104, I heare your grace hath sworne out Housekeeping.
c. To turn out or expel by an oath.
c **1665** Mrs. Hutchinson *Mem. Col. Hutch.* (1846) 393 The colonel, thinking it a ridiculous thing to *swear out* a man ..when they had no power to defend themselves against him.
d. To obtain the issue of (a warrant for arrest) by making a charge upon oath. *U.S.*
1898 Hamblen *Gen. Manager's Story* xv. 236 The president [of the railroad]..swore out warrants for the arrest of all the members of the committee. **1912** *Times* 19 Oct. 5/6 The warrant was 'sworn out' by the girl's mother at Minneapolis.

swear, sweard: see sweer *a.*, sward *sb.*

swearer ('swɛərə(r)). Forms: 4 sweryar, sueryar, swerier; 4 suerere, 4–5 swerere, 4–6 swerer, 5 swerare, 5–6 swerar, 6 *Sc.* sweirar, 6– swearer. [f. swear *v.* + -er¹.] One who swears.
1. One who takes an oath; *spec.* one who takes or has taken an oath of allegiance; = juror 4; †also, a juryman; = juror 1. ***false swearer***, one who swears falsely, or who breaks his oath; a perjurer. See also non-swearer.
c **1380** Wyclif *Wks.* (1880) 242 A meyntenour of wrongis at louedaies, a fals suerere, a manquellere. *c* **1390–1400** *R. Gloucester's Chron.* (Rolls) 8833 (MS. B.) He hem out drou, And false sueryars [*v.r.* sweryars, swerier s] of assyses, & dude hem ssame ynou. *c* **1440** *Promp. Parv.* 482/2 Swerare, *jurator, juratrix*. *Ibid.* 483/1 Swerare, þat ofte ys forswore, *labro*. **1441** in *10th Rep. Hist. MSS. Comm.* App. v. 297 The swerere, if he be pleyntif, shal losse his action. **15..** *Adam Bel* 275 in Hazl. *E.P.P.* II. 149 The justice with a quest of swerers That had juged Cloudesle there hanged to be. **1598** Shaks. *Merry W.* ii. ii. 41 *Fal.* Good maid, then. *Qui.* Ile be sworne, as my mother was the first houre I was borne. *Fal.* I doe beleeue the swearer. **1635** Jackson *Creed* viii. xviii. § 5 It must consist of swearing men, or of swearers; a new title given by some Roman regular Catholiques,..unto such Seculars of their owne profession, as will take the oath of allegiance. **1720** Swift (*title*) The Swearer's-Bank: or, Parliamentary Security for Establishing a New Bank in Ireland. **1837** Carlyle *Fr. Rev.* ii. i. vi, Consider..how Bailly, the great Tennis-Court swearer, again swears. **1855** Macaulay *Hist. Eng.* xiv. III. 447 The swearers..avoided coming to close quarters with the nonjurors on this point. **1859** Dickens *T. Two Cities* ii. iii, The watchful eyes of those forgers and false swearers.
2. One who uses profane oaths; a person addicted to profane language. Also with objective *of*.
c **1386** Chaucer *Pars. T.* ¶ 518 Euery greet swerere, nat compelled lawefully to swere. *c* **1450** *Mirk's Festial* 229 Scho..ys a claterer, a ianguler, a flyter, a curser, a swerer, and a skold. **1509** Barclay *Shyp of Folys* (1570) 172 *heading*, Blasphemers and swearers of the name of God, and of his Saintes. **1564** *Reg. Privy Council Scot.* I. 298 Anent the sweraris of abhominabill aithis. **1597** in *Maitl. Club Misc.* I. 89 The sweiraris and banneris. **1633** G. Herbert *Temple, Ch. Porch* x, Take not his name, who made thy mouth, in vain;..the cheap swearer through his open sluce Lets his soul runne for nought. **1659** D. Pell *Impr. Sea* 103 Hee was a most damnable Swearer, and inventer of new Oaths. **1711** Steele *Spect.* No. 8. ¶ 3, I know the Lanes and Allies that are inhabited by common Swearers. **1800** Gilpin *Serm.* II. xxvii. (R.) The swearer continues to swear: tell him of his wickedness he allows it is great, but he continues to swear on.
3. One who administers an oath to another (const. *of*). Also ***swearer-in*** (see swear *v.* 21).
1597 E. S. *Discov. Knts. Poste* B 2 b, I graunt he is a broker,..but he was first a bailer and a swearer. **1676** Marvell *Mr. Smirke* K 2 b, Provided they could be the Swearers of the Prince to do all due Allegiance to the Church. **1678** Sir G. Mackenzie *Crim. Laws Scot.* ii. xxiii. §2. (1699) 246 An Act is to be extracted upon their said absence, and is to be delivered to the Swearer, or his Clerk. **1827** in Hone *Every-day Bk.* II. 86, I was obliged to hire a man as a 'swearer-in'. **1865** Dickens *Mut. Fr.* i. xii, I am not a swearer in of people, man.

swearing ('swɛərɪŋ), *vbl. sb.* [f. swear *v.* + -ing¹.] The action of the verb swear.
1. The action of taking an oath. ***false swearing***, perjury. ***hard swearing***: see hard *a.* 19 b.
c **1200** *Vices & Virtues* 9 Of oðe(s) sueriingge. **1303** R. Brunne *Handl. Synne* 2724 By þis tale ȝe mowe se alle þat fals sweryng wyl euyl befalle. *c* **1425** J. Hill in *Illustr. Anc. State & Chivalry* (Roxb.) 9 Whanne he is called to his first ooth, thanne sitteth it to alle his forsaide Counsaille to goo with hym..for to here..how he swereth, and what countenaunce he haueth in his sweryng. **1526** *Pilgr. Perf.* (W. de W. 1531) 94 Swerynge whan it is with deliberacyon for ony thynge yᵗ is false or vayne, it perteyneth to periury. **1561** T. Hoby tr. *Castiglione's Courtyer* ii. (1577) M iij, I beleeue withoute swearing that you haue no faith also in Christe. **1601** Shaks. *Twel. N.* v. i. 277 And all those sayings, will I ouer sweare, And all those swearings keepe as true in soule. **1651** Hobbes *Govt. & Soc.* ii. §20. 32 Swearing is a speech joyned to a promise, whereby the promiser declares his renouncing of Gods mercy, unlesse he perform his word. *a* **1704** T. Brown *Dial. Dead, Reas. Oaths* Wks. 1711 IV. 81 The Doctor considered the taking of the Oaths to be only an indifferent thing..for otherwise it had been his Duty to dissuade all Persons..from Swearing. **1837** Carlyle *Fr. Rev.* ii. i. viii, The February swearing has set them all agog. **1887** [see hard *a.* 19 b].
2. The uttering of a profane oath; the use of profane language.
1340 *Ayenb.* 63 Hi ne conne noþing zygge wyþ-oute zueriynge. *c* **1380** Wyclif *Wks.* (1880) 120 Ydel sweryinge of herte & bonys of crist. **1500–20** Dunbar *Poems* ix. 106, I knaw me vicious, Lord,..In aithis sweiring, leising, and blaspheming. **1542** Boorde *Dyetary* vii. (1870) 243 In all the worlde there is not suche odyble swearyng as is vsed in Englande. **1623–4** *Act 21 James I,* c. 20 For as much as all prophane Swearing and Cursing is forbidden by the Word of God, Be it therefore enacted..That no person or persons shall from henceforth prophanely sweare or curse. **1657** in *Trans. Cumbld. & Westmorld. Antiq. Soc.* (N.S.) XIV. 189 Convict..for the swearinge of 5 profane oaths upon the same day (viz.) 3 of them by god, one by his troth and one by his soule. **1663** Dryden *Wild Gallant* i. ii, He has been a great fanatic formerly, and now has got a habit of swearing, that he may be thought a cavalier. **1764** Gray *Jemmy Twitcher* 16 All the town rings of his swearing and roaring. **1867** Smyth *Sailor's Word-bk.* s.v., Habitual swearing was usually typical of a bad officer.
3. The action of administering an oath, *spec.* of admitting a person into office with an oath. Also ***swearing-in***: see swear *v.* 21.
a **1400** *Old Usages Winchester* in *Eng. Gilds* (1870) 362 So þᵗ, byfore answere, ne legge non oþer delay, but ȝif hit be for swerynge of mo parteneres of play of londe by ryȝt. **1722** Prideaux *Direct. Ch.-wardens* (ed. 4) 47 There is a Writ at Common-Law issuable out of the King's-Bench to command the Swearing of him. **1863** H. Cox *Instit.* i. vi. 42 As there is no election of a Speaker, and no general swearing of members. **1900** *Westm. Gaz.* 4 Jan. 7/3 The swearing-in of the Volunteers at the Guildhall.
4. *attrib.*
1569 J. Sanford tr. *Agrippa's Van. Artes* liv. 72 b, Who is that whiche seethe a man goo with a cocke pase, with a swearinge gesture, with a fierce countenaunce,..with an vnpleasaunt speache, with wild manners,..that doth not iudge him to be a Germane? **1705** tr. *Bosman's Guinea* 149 Every Person entring into any Obligation is obliged to drink this Swearing Liquor. *a* **1718** T. Ward *Eng. Ref.* iv. (1710) 102 Cowper, who kept the Swearing Office, Instructed wisely ev'ry Novice, In what concern'd the Swearing Art **1721** Amherst *Terræ Fil.* No. 41. (1754) 218 [I] swore engag'd my soul, And paid the swearing-broker whole Ten shilling. **1842** D. G. Rossetti *Let.* 1 Sept. (1965) I. 7 Uncle Henry's Swearing-book combines both Bible and Prayer-Book. **1899** Swearing-habit [see *drinking-habit* s.v. drinking *vbl. sb.* 4 c]. **1939** Joyce *Finnegans Wake* 524 Mr. Cockshott, as he had his assignation with, present holder by deedpoll and indenture of the swearing belt.

'swearing, *ppl. a.* [-ing².] That swears.
1. That takes or has taken an oath, esp. an oath of allegiance.
1727 P. Walker *Vind. Cameron's Name* in *Biog. Presbyt.* (1827) I. 248 We have the Parallel Case in Scotland this Day, putting the Swearing Ministers in Place of the Actually-indulged. **1837** Carlyle *Fr. Rev.* ii. i. vi, Saw the Sun ever such a swearing people? **1855** Macaulay *Hist. Eng.* xiv. III. 447 The swearing clergy, as they were called, were not a little perplexed by this reasoning.
2. That utters a profane oath; given to profane language.
1796 J. Woodforde *Diary* 10 Oct. (1929) IV. 312 My Boy, John Brand, left my Service to day, as he had proper Notice so to do, being the most saucy swearing Lad that ever we had. **1862** Borrow *Wales* lxviii, Night came quickly upon me after I had passed the swearing lad. **1887** F. Francis Jun. *Saddle & Mocassin* 5, I guess they [*sc.* the Mormons] smokes more, and stands for the swearingest people as there is anywhere.
Hence **'swearingly** *adv.*
a **1617** Hieron *Wks.* (1620) II. 340 Now it curseth man, talkes viciously, speaks swearingly; suddenly it is framing some words of holinesse and deuotion.

'swear-word. *colloq.* (orig. *U.S.*) [f. swear *v.* + word *sb.* Cf. *cuss-word* s.v. cuss *sb.* 3.] A word used in profane swearing, a profane word.
1883 A. M. Gow *Primer Politeness* 58 A youth who mixed his conversation with many swear-words. **1893** Dunmore *Pamirs* I. 344 A string of naughty swear words. **1904** H. Jenner *Cornish Lang.* xiii. 154 Cornish is a disappointing language in respect of swear-words.

sweat (swɛt), *sb.* Forms: 4 suet, 4, (8 *Sc.*) sweet, 4–6 swete, suete, swett(e, 4–7 swet, (5 suett, squete), 5–7 *Sc.* sweit, (6 sweth, *Sc.* sueit), 6–7 sweate, 6– sweat. [ME. *swet, swete*, alteration of *swot(e* (see swote) after *swete*, sweat *v.* First exemplified from northern texts, in which close and open *e* rimed together as early as the fourteenth century; hence, on the one hand, *swet*: *feit* (OE. *fét*) and *bete* (OE. *bétan*), on the other, *swet*: *gret* (OE. *grǽt*).]
I. †**1.** The life-blood: in phr. ***to tine, leave, lose the sweat***: to lose one's life-blood, die. *Obs.*
The existence of this use is difficult to account for, since the sense of 'blood' which belonged to OE. *swát* (e.g. *swát forlǽtan*) did not survive in ME. swote.
c **1320** *Sir Tristr.* 2904 His frende schip wil y fle; Our on schal tine swete [*rime* to bete]. **13..** *E.E. Allit. P.* C. 364 And alle þat lyuyes here-inne [to] lose þe swete. **1375** Barbour *Bruce* xiii. 32 Sum held on loft, sum tynt the suet [*rime* feit]. ? *a* **1400** *Morte Arth.* 2145 By that swyftely one swarthe þe swett es by-leuede. *Ibid.* 3360 Many swayne wiþ þe swynge has the swette leuede. *c* **1470** Henry *Wallace* iii. 194 The Scottis on fute gert mony loiss the suete [*rime* feit]. **1513** Douglas *Æneis* i. iii. 10 Quhar that the vailȝeand Hector lowsit the sweit [*rime* spreit] On Achillis speir. *Ibid.* vii. ix. 130 About hym fell down deid, and lost the sueit [*rime* spreit] Mony of the hyrd men.
II. 2. a. Moisture excreted in the form of drops through the pores of the skin, usually as a result of excessive heat or exertion, also of certain emotions, or of the operation of sudorific medicines; sensible perspiration.
c **1375** *Sc. Leg. Saints* xviii. (*Egipciane*) 305 For rednes tuk hyme sic abaysinge, þat þe swet til his fete ran. *a* **1400–50** *Wars Alex.* 3790 All ware þai swollen of þe swete & sweltid on þe son. **1485** Caxton *St. Wenefr.* 4 Wypyng her visage and clensynge it fro the duste and swette. **1508** Dunbar *Flyting* 202 Ane caprowsy barkit all with sweit. **1533** Bellenden *Livy* iii. ix. (S.T.S.) I. 282 Als sone as his govne was dicht fra suete and duste of pow[d]er. **1667** Milton *P.L.* viii. 255 Soft on the flourie herb I found me laid In Balmie Sweat, which with his Beames the Sun Soon dri'd. **1693** Dryden *Juvenal* i. 253 A cold Sweat stands in drops on ev'ry part. **1798** Coleridge *Anc. Mar.* iv. viii, The cold sweat melted from their limbs. **1822–7** Good *Study Med.* (1829) V. 549 The matter of sweat and that of insensible perspiration are nearly the same. **1857** Hughes *Tom Brown* i. vii, His face, all spattered with dirt and lined with sweat. **1899** *Allbutt's Syst. Med.* VIII. 725 The sweat does not appear on the foot of which the nerve is cut.
b. In phr. ***the sweat of*** (one's) ***brow*** (†***brows***), ***face***, etc., expressing toil (cf. 9): after Gen. iii. 19.
c **1380** Wyclif *Wks.* (1880) 51 þei ben tauȝt to lyue in swet of here body bi comaundement of god. **1535** Coverdale *Gen.* iii. 19 In the sweate of thy face shalt thou eate thy bred. **1553** T. Wilson *Rhet.* Pref. (1580) A vij b, Who would trauaile and toile with the sweate of his browes? **1621** Brathwait *Nat. Embassie* (1877) 136 Liue on the sweat of others browes. **1643** Trapp *Comm. Gen.* ii. 15 It was after his fall laid upon him as a punishment, Gen. iii. 19. to eat his bread in the sweat of his nose. [**1718** Prior *Solomon* iii. 362 E'er yet He earns his Bread, a-down his Brow, Inclin'd to Earth, his lab'ring Sweat must flow.] **1779** Earl Carlisle in Jesse *Selwyn & Contemp.* (1844) IV. 257 You are entitled to some happiness, for you have earned it with the sweat of your brow. **1816** Southey *Ess.* (1832) I. 179 When he receives his daily wages for the sweat of his brow. **1886** 'Sarah Tytler' *Buried Diamonds* xxvi, A day laborer, who could..earn enough by the sweat of his brow to keep his wife and sick daughter from starving.
c. ***bloody sweat***: (*a*) that of Jesus in the Garden of Gethsemane: see Luke xxii. 44.
1526 *Pilgr. Perf.* (W. de W. 1531) 249 b, That moost paynfull agony of his blody swet. **1548–9** (Mar.) *Bk. Com. Prayer, Litany*, By thyne agony and bloudy sweate..Good lorde deliuer us. [**1701** Stanhope *Pious Breathings* vii. vii. (1704) 329 The Sweats of blood, which streamed from thy holy body.] **1819** Shelley *Cenci* i. i. 113 Tears bitterer than the bloody sweat of Christ.
transf. **1594** Kyd *Cornelia* i. 183 Warre..Which yet, to sack vs, toyles in bloody sweat T'enlarge the bounds of conquering Thessalie.
(*b*) *Path.*: see hæmatidrosis.
1848 Dunglison *Med. Lex.* **1876** [see hæmatidrosis].
3. a. A condition or fit of sweating as a result of heat, exertion, or emotion; diaphoresis.
†***breathing sweat***: see breathing *ppl. a.* d. ***cold sweat***, sweating accompanied by a feeling of cold, esp. as induced by fear or the like; freq. in phr. ***in a cold sweat*** (also *fig.*). Cf. sense 10.
c **1400** *Pilgr. Sowle* (Caxton) i. xxii. (1859) 25 Yf thou myghtest dayes two or thre Haue such a swete, it wold auayle the. *c* **1420** *Avow. Arth.* xlii, That heuy horse on him lay, He squonet in that squete. *c* **1420** ? Lydg. *Assembly of Gods* 2044 My body all in swet began for to shake. *a* **1548** Hall *Chron., Hen. VII*, 3 b, Sodenly a deadly and burnyng sweate inuaded their bodyes. **1581** Mulcaster *Positions* xxxv. (1887) 132 The rule is, change apparell after sweat. **1617** Moryson *Itin.* iii. 84 In Summer time this kind of lodging is vnpleasant, keeping a man in a continuall sweat from head to foote. **1706** E. Ward *Wooden World Diss.* (1708) 25 They hear him cuff about the Bed and Bedpolls, and crying out in a cold Sweat. **1719** De Foe *Crusoe* i. (Globe) 87 An Ague very violent; the Fit held me seven Hours, cold Fit, and hot, with faint Sweats after it. **1791** Mrs. Radcliffe *Rom. Forest* iv, I turned all of a cold sweat in a minute. **1840** Lytton *Money* (ed. 2) iii. vi. 94 'Poor fellow! He'll be ruined in a month.'..'I'm in a cold sweat.' **1853** Kingsley *Hypatia* xiii. 164 His knees knocked together; a faint sweat seemed to melt every limb. **1864** Mrs. Carlyle *Lett.* (1883) III. 211 A heap of blankets that kept me in a sweat. **1905** *Brit. Med. Jrnl.* 25 Feb. 406 He had a shaking chill followed by a sweat. **1941** C. Mackenzie *Red Tapeworm* xii. 153 He would..have broken out in a cold sweat at the thought of what might have happened. **1966** C. Aird *Relig. Body* xvii. 158 Cousin Harold must have been in a cold sweat in case his father died before he got to Cullingoak.
†**b.** = sweating-sickness. *Obs.*
a **1517** in G. P. Scrope *Castle Combe* (1852) 294 The wyche freer dyyd of the swet in my howse. **1551** Edw. VI *Lit. Rem.* (Roxb.) II. 329 At this time cam the sweat into London, wich was more vehement then the old sweat. **1576** Newton *Lemnie's Complex.* (1633) 164 The English Sweat, the accident of which disease is sowning and grievous paine at the heart, joyned with a byting at the Stomacke. **1596** Dalrymple tr. *Leslie's Hist. Scot.* I. 5 That sair seiknes, named the sueit of Britannie. *a* **1614** D. Dyke *Myst. Self-deceiving* (ed. 8) 26 Thus it was in that great Sweat in the time of King Edward. **1661** J. Childrey *Brit. Baconica* 123 There was a fourth sweat between the years 1517 and 1551.
4. A fit of sweating caused for a specific purpose.
a. as a form of medicinal treatment or to reduce one's weight. (In quot. 1779 used jocularly.)
1632 B. Jonson *Magn. Lady* iii. iv, To clense his body, all the three high wayes; That is, by Sweat, Purge, and Phlebotomy. **1779** G. Keate *Sketches fr. Nat.* (1790) II. 60 Paying my half-crown, I took a sweat, on one of the snug superannuated benches [in a hot ballroom]. **1780** Cowper *Progr. Err.* 221 He..Prepares for meals as jockies take a sweat. **1807** P. Gass *Jrnl.* 219 Yesterday we gave him an Indian sweat, and he is some better to-day. **1856** 'Stonehenge' *Brit. Sports* ii. v. 418/2 To hunt three days a-week, and shoot the other three, by way of a moderate sweat.
b. A run given to a horse (often in a coat) as part of his training for a race.
1705 *Lond. Gaz.* No. 4149/4 A 12 Stone Plate..will be run for..by Hunters..that..have [not] been kept in Sweats above 12 weeks before the day of Running. **1737** [see sweat

v. 4 b]. **1828** *Sporting Mag.* XXIII. 106 The management of a Flighty Horse in his exercise or sweat. **1856** 'STONEHENGE' *Brit. Sports* II. I. vi. §6. 335/1 The conclusion of the second preparation should be a severe sweat.

c. A long training run for schoolboys. *Public Schools' slang.*

1916 E. F. BENSON *David Blaize* xiv. 274 You brutes have been having an innocent happy sweat along the road. **1924** KIPLING *Debits & Credits* (1926) 93 For the juniors, a shortish course.. while Packman lunged Big Side across the inland and upland ploughs, for proper sweats. **1983** W. BLUNT *Married to Single Life* iv. 62 Long melancholy 'sweats' (runs) over the downs [at Marlborough].

5. *transf.* Something resembling sweat; drops of moisture exuded from or deposited on the surface of a body; an exudation.

1387 TREVISA *Higden* (Rolls) I. 269 The snowe þat lieþ vppon Alpes þat brekeþ out on sweet. **1555** EDEN *Decades* (Arb.) 294 The swette of heauen, or as it were a certeyne spettyl of the starres. **1616** W. BROWNE *Brit. Past.* II. ii. 2 The Mvses friend (gray-eyde Aurora) yet Held all the Meadowes in a cooling sweat. *a* **1631** DONNE *Elegies* viii. 1 The sweet sweat of Roses in a Still. **1646** SIR T. BROWNE *Pseud. Ep.* I. vii. (1686) 19 The sea was but the sweat of the Earth. **1712** BLACKMORE *Creation* II. 66 The fragrant Trees .. Owe all their Spices to the Summer's Heat, Their gummy Tears, and odoriferous Sweat. **1788** M. CUTLER in *Life*, etc. (1888) I. 428 A serious sweat over the mountain. **1847** L. HUNT *Jar Honey* ix. (1848) 116 The pleasant meadows sadly lay In chill and cooling sweats.

6. A process of sweating or being sweated; exudation, evaporation, or deposit of moisture, fermentation, partial fusion, etc., as practised in various industries.

1573 TUSSER *Husb.* (1878) 125 Let shock take sweate, least gofe take heate. **1707** MORTIMER *Husb.* 115 Those [beans] that are to be kept are not to be thrashed till March, that they have had a thorough sweat in the Mow. **1765** *Museum Rust.* III. 225 The same barley.. will not malt alike well at all times:.. take it as soon as it is housed, it comes well, but whilst it is in its sweat, by no means. **1813** VANCOUVER *Agric. Devon* 240 After undergoing the first sweat, [they] should be ground, pressed, fermented, and casked a-part from each other. **1843** *Florist's Jrnl.* (1846) IV. 220 There will be found to have commenced a process of fermentation, technically called a 'sweat'. **1876** SCHULTZ *Leather Manuf.* 23 The American process is called cold sweat.

†**7.** A medicine for inducing sweat; a sudorific, diaphoretic. *Obs.*

1655 CULPEPPER, etc. *Riverius* I. i. 3 The custom of taking Purges, Sweats, Diureticks, or provokers of Urine. **1681** ASHMOLE *Diary* 6 Apr. in *Mem.* (1717) 64, I took my usual Sweat, which made me well. *Ibid.* 2 Oct. 65, I took my Sweat for Prevention of the Gout. *a* **1776** R. JAMES *Diss. Fevers* (1778) 75 Thus much cannot be said with respect to any other vomit, any other purge, or any other sweat.

8. *U.S.* Name for a gambling game played with three dice. (Cf. *sweat-cloth* in 11.)

1894 MASKELYNE *Sharps & Flats* 253.

III. 9. *fig.* **a.** Hard work; violent or strenuous exertion; labour, toil; pains, trouble. *arch.*

a **1300** *Cursor M.* 921 (Cott.) Of erth þou sal, wit suete and suinc, Win þat þou sal ete and drinc. *c* **1375** *Sc. Leg. Saints* xxvii. (*Machor*) 1241 With swink & swet Hiddir þai come & trawall gret. *c* **1380** WYCLIF *Serm.* Sel. Wks. I. 259 þer ben sum men þat lyven here in swete and bisynesse. **1533** GAU *Richt Vay* 93 Lat wsz notht liff of the sweyt and blwid of the pwir. **1590** SHAKS. *Mids. N.* II. i. 94 The Oxe hath therefore stretch'd his yoake in vaine, The Ploughman lost his sweat. **1610** —— *Temp.* II. i. 160 All things in common Nature should produce Without sweat or endeuour. **1642** ROGERS *Naaman* 100 All well affected Christians would be loth to lose their labour and sweat, till they haue enjoyed the promise. **1751** CHAMBERS *Cycl.* s.v. *Approach*, The curve of equable Approach.. has caused some sweat among analysts. **1821** BYRON *Cain* I. i, Who bids The Earth yield nothing to us without sweat. **1879** J. D. LONG *Æneid* IX. 598 They recognize the spoils the Volscians bring,.. and, regained At such a sweat, their own insignia.

b. *old sweat*: see OLD *a.* E. 4.

10. a. A state of impatience, irritation, anxiety, or the like, such as induces sweat; a flurry, hurry, fume. Chiefly *Sc.* and *U.S.*

1715 PENNECUIK *Descr. Tweeddale*, etc. 139 This put our Conjurer in a deep Sweet, who now had only one Shift left him, which was this, [etc.]. **1753** MISS COLLIER *Art Torment., Gen. Rules* 216 You may talk in such a manner of the pleasure you enjoyed in their absence, as will put your husband in a sweat for you. **1884** 'MARK TWAIN' *Huck. Finn* xx. 200 He was in a sweat to get to the Indian Ocean right off. **1895** H. WATSON in *Chap Book* III. 502, I passed the half-hour that ensued in a sweat of conjecture, as to what was to fall out.

b. *no sweat*: see NO *a.* 5 d.

IV. 11. *attrib.* and *Comb.*, as ***sweat-drop***, ***labour***, ***-scraper***, ***-secretion***, ***-stain***; *spec.* = 'exciting or relating to the secretion of sweat', as ***sweat-absorber***, ***apparatus***, ***canal***, ***centre***, ***coil***, ***fibre***, ***nerve***; ***sweat-dried***, ***-marked***, ***-shining***, ***-soaked***, ***-stained***, ***-wet*** adjs.; also **sweat-band**, (*a*) a band of leather or other substance forming a lining of a hat or cap for protection against the sweat of the head; (*b*) in *Sport*, a strip of material worn around the (fore)head or wrist to absorb perspiration; **sweat-bath**, a steam-bath or hot-air bath, esp. among N. American Indians; cf. SWEAT-HOUSE 1; **sweat-bee**, a name for the small bees of the family *Andrenidæ*; **sweat-box**, (*a*) a narrow cell in which a prisoner is confined (*slang*); also *U.S.*, a room in which a prisoner undergoes intensive questioning (see quot. 1931); (*b*) a box in which hides are sweated; (*c*) a large box in which figs are placed to undergo a 'sweat'; (*d*) *transf.* and *fig.*, *spec.* a heated compartment in which perspiration is induced, to encourage weight loss, etc.; **sweat-cloth**, a cloth or handkerchief used for wiping off sweat; a sudary; see also quot. 1872; **sweat cooling** *Engin.*, a form of cooling in which the coolant is passed through a porous wall and evenly distributed over the surface, which is cooled by its evaporation; hence **sweat-cooled** *ppl. a.*; **sweat-cyst** *Path.*, a cyst resulting from some disorder of the sweat-glands; **sweat-duct** *Anat.*, the duct of a sweat-gland, by which the sweat is conveyed to the surface of the skin; **sweat equity** *U.S.*, an interest in a property earned by a tenant who contributes his labour to its upkeep or renovation; **sweat flap**, a leather flap in harness, for protecting the rider's leg from the sweat of the horse; **sweat-gland** *Anat.*, each of the numerous minute coiled tubular glands just beneath the skin which secrete sweat; **sweat heat** *Gardening*, the heat at which fermentation takes place; **sweat-hog** *U.S. slang*, a difficult student singled out in school or college for special instruction; †**sweat-hole**, = *sweat-pore*; **sweat-leather**, (*a*) a leather sweat-band in a hat or cap; also **sweat lining**; (*b*) = *sweat-flap*; **sweat-lodge**, = SWEAT-HOUSE 1; **sweat-orifice** = *sweat-pore*; **sweat pants** chiefly *U.S.*, trousers of thick cotton cloth worn by athletes, esp. before or after strenuous exercise; tracksuit trousers; **sweat-pit**, †(*a*) the arm-pit exuding sweat (*obs. nonce-use*); (*b*) in *Tanning*, a pit in which hides are sweated, a sweating-pit; **sweat-pore** *Anat.*, each of the pores of the skin formed by the openings of the sweat-ducts; **sweat-rag** (*slang*), any cloth used for wiping off sweat, or worn round the head to keep sweat out of the eyes; **sweat-rash** *Path.*, an eruption caused by obstruction of the sweat-pores; **sweat-room**, a room in which tobacco is sweated; **sweat root**, *Polemonium reptans* (Dunglison *Med. Lex.* 1857); **sweat rug** a rug put on a horse after exercise; **sweat-shirt** orig. *U.S.*, a loose shirt; *spec.* a long-sleeved, high-necked pullover shirt of thick cotton cloth (usu. with a fleecy lining), worn by athletes to avoid taking cold before or after exercise (cf. SWEATER 7 b); hence **sweat-shirted** *a.*; **sweat-shop** orig. *U.S.*, a workshop in a dwelling-house, in which work is done under the sweating system (or, by extension, under any system of sub-contract); also *fig.* and *attrib.*; **sweat-stock** *Tanning*, a collective term for hides which are being or have been sweated (see SWEAT *v.* 13); **sweat-suit** orig. *U.S.*, an athlete's suit consisting of a sweat-shirt and sweat-pants; †**sweat-sweet** *a. nonce-wd.*, having a sweet exudation; **sweat vesicle** *Path.*, = *sweat-cyst*; **sweat-vessel** *Anat.*, = *sweat-duct*; **sweat-weed**, marsh mallow, *Althæa officinalis* (Billings *Med. Dict.* 1890). See also SWEAT-HOUSE.

1956 S. BECKETT *Malone Dies* 93 A *sweat-absorber for the armpit. **1883** F. T. ROBERTS *Handbk. Med.* (ed. 5) 960 Affections of the *sweat-apparatus. **1891** *Pall Mall G.* 28 Sept. 2/3 An American chemist.. threatens us with lead-poisoning from the '*sweat-band'. **1956** R. H. APPLEWHAITE *Lawn Tennis* i. 12 Sweatbands.. are worn round the wrist to prevent perspiration running down the arms into the hands. **1977** J. F. FIXX *Compl. Bk. Running* xii. 134 When I started running, I saw a lot of runners wearing sweatbands, so after sweat had dripped into my eyes a few times I went out and bought one. **1877** S. POWERS *Tribes of California* xxvi. 244 [The Shasta Indians] have no assembly chamber..; nothing but a kind of oven large enough that one person may stretch himself therein and enjoy a *sweat-bath. **1921** J. HASTINGS *Encycl. Relig. & Ethics* XII. 128/2 When we turn to the Old World, we find a striking resemblance to the American customs in Herodotus's description of the use of the sweat-bath among the Scythians as a means of purification, after mourning. **1963** E. WAUGH *Let.* Sept. in C. Sykes *Evelyn Waugh* (1975) xxvi. 439, I have sat in a 'sweat-bath' and been severely massaged. **1965** S. G. LAWRENCE *40 Yrs. on Yukon Telegraph* xiv. 75 They [*sc.* some Indians] stayed over a day and all the old men took sweat baths. **1894** *U.S. Dept. Agric., Div. Veg. Physiol. & Path.* Bulletin v. 79 (Cent. Dict., Suppl.) The *sweat bees of the genus Halictus and Andrena. **1870** *U.S. Navy Gen. Orders & Circulars* (1887) 97 He was.. gagged and confined in a *sweat-box of such dimensions that it was impossible to sit down. **1888** CHURCHWARD *Blackbirding in S. Pacific* 28 This sweat-box is a sort of cell in the lowest part of the ship, pitch dark, and hot as hell. **1890** BARRÈRE & LELAND *Slang Dict.*, *Sweat-box*, the cell where prisoners are confined on arrest previous to being brought up for examination before the magistrate. **1895** *Pop. Sci. Monthly* XLVI. 345 When sympathetic visitors crowded around his sweatbox. **1897** *Chicago Tribune* 10 July 1/4 The upper gallery commonly known as the 'sweat box' in regular theaters. **1900** *Yearbk. U.S. Dept. Agric.* 94 After the figs were dried they were placed in sweat boxes holding about 200 pounds each, where they were allowed to remain for two weeks, to pass through a sweat. **1901** 'J. FLYNT' *World of Graft* 102 He was copped out on suspicion. They put him in the sweat-box, made him cough, an' you know the rest. **1931** Z. CHAFEE et al. in *Rep. Nat. Comm. Law Observance & Enforcement* (U.S.) ii. 38 The original 'sweat box' used during the period following the Civil War.. was a cell in close proximity to a stove, in which a scorching fire was built and fed with old bones, pieces of rubber shoes, etc., all to make great heat and offensive smells, until the sickened and perspiring inmate of the cell confessed in order to get released. **1973** 'H. HOWARD' *Highway to Murder* ii. 28, I ought to stick you in the sweat box until you told me the name of your client. **1974** J. ENGELHARD *Horsemen* vi. 38, I never go in a sweatbox... I lose all the weight I want playing tennis. **1890** BILLINGS *Med. Dict.*, **Sweat canal*, excretory duct of a sweat-gland. *Ibid.*, *Sweat centre. **1898** *Allbutt's Syst. Med.* V. 200 The effect of this [accumulation of carbonic acid in the blood] being to stimulate the sweat centres. **1872** SCHELE DE VERE *Americanisms* 329 The *sweat-cloth, a cloth marked with figures, and used by gamblers with dice. **1894** *Athenæum* 24 Feb. 239/3 The appearance of the sweat-cloth is a very characteristic mark. **1899** *Allbutt's Syst. Med.* VIII. 741 An uninterrupted series of changes in the *sweat-coils was observed from the beginning up to the end of the disease. **1948** *Technical Publ. Amer. Inst. Mining & Metall. Engineers* No. 2343. Class E. 1 In designing a *sweat cooled part it is imperative to assure a given rate of flow of coolant. *Ibid.*, A less orthodox method consists of making the part to be cooled of a porous material, so that the cooling fluid can be forced through the pores... This method, referred to as '*sweat cooling', was proposed at the Jet Propulsion Laboratory in September 1944. **1969** E. C. ROBERTSON *Now Bks. Rocket Motors* iv. 29 Many devices have been tried to keep the walls of the chamber cool and techniques have ranged from sweat cooling.. to the one that is most common today. **1898** HUTCHINSON *Archives Surgery* IX. 160 My patient had been liable to unilateral sweating of the face... The vesicles or little cysts.. varied in size from pins' heads to peas... There could be little doubt that these were *sweat-cysts. **1885** B. HARTE *Maruja* iii, As he groomed the *sweat-dried skin of the mustang. **1776** MICKLE tr. *Camoens' Lusiad* 304 Fell the hot *sweat-drops as he champt the rein. **1817** BYRON *Mazeppa* xi, And my cold sweat-drops fell like rain Upon the courser's bristling mane. **1881** HUXLEY *Elem. Physiol.* v. (new ed.) 114 Cells lining the *sweat duct. **1973** *Time* 16 July 43 A group of poor, racially mixed tenants took over a nearby city-owned tenement, stripped the shabby interiors and are building modern apartments to replace the narrow, cold-water flats... In return for their '*sweat equity', the builder-residents will make payments as low as $80 per month and ultimately own the building as a cooperative. **1980** B. VILA *This Old House* v. 83/1 The calculations you make in a sweat equity job are different from those in a project in which you are employing professionals. **1908** *Animal Managem.* 182 The *sweat flap of the girth. **1845** TODD & BOWMAN *Phys. Anat.* I. 423 The *sweat-glands exist under almost every part of the cutaneous surface. **1843** *Florist's Jrnl.* (1846) IV. 225 A '*sweat heat' of from 85° to 95° temperature. **1976** *Senior Scholastic* 4 May 41 John Travolta.. [is] back in the classroom.. as the leader of the *sweathogs in ABC's *Welcome Back, Kotter*. **1979** BROOKS & MARSH *Compl. Directory Prime Time Network TV Shows, 1946–Present* 673/1 Gabe's 'sweathogs' were the outcasts of the academic system, streetwise but unable or unwilling to make it in normal classes. **14..** *Nom.* in Wr.-Wülcker 679/16 *Hic porus*, a *swetholle. **1527** ANDREW *Brunswyke's Distyll. Waters* F j b, [Veronica water] is good to be dronke for the flyenge sore, for it openeth the swete holes. **1612** WOODALL *Surg. Mate* Wks. (1653) 368 Nature striveth to thrust out her venemous enemy.. by the sweatholes. *a* **1674** TRAHERNE *Chr. Ethics* (1675) 261 All the *sweat labour of the martyrs, all the persecutions and endeavours of the apostles. **1970** *Islander* (Victoria, B.C.) 22 Nov. 5/1 Little by little they cleared each acre with axe and cross-cut saw. It was slow, sweat-labor. **1884** KNIGHT *Dict. Mech.* Suppl. s.v. *Sweat Rolling Machine*, The *sweat-leather lining of hats. *Ibid.*, *Sweat Sewing Machine*, a machine for sewing the *sweat lining in hats. **1887** *Amer. Soc. Psych. Research* Dec. 141 When persons are taking a bath in the *sweat-lodge. **1973** *New Society* 19 July 137/2 A 'sweat lodge', or hut fashioned from rocks, branches and a sacred blanket. The sauna-like action of a fire inside the hut helps purify his soul along with his body. **1977** *Rolling Stone* 7 Apr. 55/3 She learned of the sweat lodge and the sacred pipe ceremony and the Sun Dance while researching her Indian history book, and then began to understand them as part of the present. **1914** D. H. LAWRENCE *Prussian Officer* 20 His *sweat-marked horse swishing its tail. **1897** *Allbutt's Syst. Med.* III. 308 The *sweat-nerves leave the spinal cord by the anterior roots. **1957** H. ROOSENBERG *Walls came tumbling Down* v. 127 They had noticed that Nell's green skirt was badly worn—would she try on these *sweat pants and see if they fitted? **1978** R. B. PARKER *Judas Goat* vi. 33 My blue sweat pants worn stylishly with the ankle zippers open. **1708** T. WARD *Terræ-filius* v. 27 The Effluvia that arises from her *Sweat-Pits. **1852** MORFIT *Tanning & Currying* (1853) 323 Eight stone sweat-pits, with pointed arches and flues. **1899** *Allbutt's Syst. Med.* VIII. 742 The obstruction at the orifice of the *sweat-pore. **1843** 'R. CARLTON' *New Purchase* I. xi. 73 This luxury.. was used only as a '*sweat rag', and not 'as a nose-cloth'. **1902** H. LAWSON *Children of Bush* 9 He wiped his face, neck, and forehead with a big speckled 'sweat-rag'. **1930** *Aberdeen Press & Jrnl.* 28 Mar. 7/5 Making a swab with a sweat-rag, he attempted to stop the flow of blood. **1953** X. FIELDING *Stronghold* 256 The dirty old sweat-rag which he had worn round his head for the last three months. **1974** D. STUART *Prince of My Country* v. 32 Father puts down his knife and wipes his face with the sweatrag at his neck. **1899** *Allbutt's Syst. Med.* VIII. 586 'Red gum', 'teething rash', usually regarded as a *sweat-rash. **1971** M. BRANDER *Horseman's Vade Mecum* 439 **Sweat-rug*, a string rug put on under a reversed top rug when a horse has been sweating. **1978** 'F. PARRISH' *Sting of Honeybee* i. 11 She had taken off his saddle and put on a sweat-rug. **1908** *Animal Managem.* 60 *Sweat scrapers are long flexible blades of smooth metal. **1899** *Allbutt's Syst. Med.* VIII. 666 Over markedly ichthyotic parts, *sweat-secretion is usually diminished. **1923** D. H. LAWRENCE *Birds, Beasts & Flowers* 172 And dance, and dance, forever dance, with breath half sobbing in dark, *sweat-shining breasts. **1929** *Sears, Roebuck Catal.* Spring/Summer 394 Every Man and Boy Wants A *Sweat Shirt. **1938** E. HEMINGWAY *Fifth Column* (1939) 291 He'd pull on a rubber shirt over a couple of jerseys and a big sweat shirt over that. **1948** *Daily Express* 4 Sept. 2/5 (*caption*) The fluffy blonde in pale lemon sweat shirt. **1958** J. & W. Hawkins *Death Watch* (1959) i. 16 She was wearing jeans, moccasins and a white sweat shirt. **1978** L. Heren *Growing up on The Times* ix. 307 Another [young lad] exchanged his jeans and sweatshirt for a white dinner jacket and plum-coloured trousers. **1977** R. Barnard *Blood Brotherhood* i. 14 The be-jeaned and *sweat-shirted figure. **1892** *Charities Rev.* Jan. 115 What relaxation or excitement can a car-driver or a *sweat-shop tailor get except by drinking? **1895** *Westm. Gaz.* 2 Nov. 2/3 All but fifteen of the 385 wholesale clothing manufacturers in New York have their goods made in '*sweat shops'. **1900** F. H. Stoddard *Evol. Eng. Novel* 172 The contract system—the familiar sweat-shop system of more modern days. **1903** *Bond of Brotherhood* (Calgary, Alberta) 12 June 4/1 Healthy niggers sound in wind and limb well broke to handcuffs, two pair of genuine sweat shop overalls given with each piece of ebony. **1906** Olive C. Malvery *Soul Market* xi. 185 Under the 'Sweat-shop' Law of the State of New York, the manufacture of articles of wearing apparel is now specifically forbidden in any tenement house without a license. **1938** *Times Lit. Suppl.* 3 Dec. 767/2 The story of two Jews who, in youth, work in the same tailoring sweat-shop. **1959** *Daily Tel.* 17 Apr. 13/8, I cannot really think that he should want my job. Whitehall, and certainly Downing Street, is nothing but a sweatshop. **1972** *Bookseller* 4 Mar. 1476/1 If 28 jobs were costing only £6,000 a year..then the N.B.L. were running a sweat shop. **1944** K. Levis in Murdoch & Drake-Brockman *Austral. Short Stories* (1951) 429 Our shirts *sweat-soaked under the midday sun. **1973** 'R. MacLeod' *Burial in Portugal* i. 29 His sweat-soaked shirt was sticking to his back. **1973** R. Busby *Pattern of Violence* vi. 96 There was a dark *sweat stain down the back of his shirt. **1932** W. Faulkner *Light in August* ii. 28 Byron watched him standing there and looking at the men in *sweat-stained overalls. **1975** H. R. F. Keating *Remarkable Case* i. 3 His jacket and trousers were..worn and sweat-stained. **1882** Paton in *Encycl. Brit.* XIV. 384/1 Among non-acid tanners the plumping of *sweat stock in which there is no lime is secured in the weak acid liquors of the colouring and handling pits. **1930** L. W. Olds *Track Athletics & Cross Country* i. 4 *Sweat suits should be fleece-lined, washable and worn for warmth rather than a flashy appearance. **1951** I. Shaw *Troubled Air* x. 158 Archer lay on the mat in a sweatsuit. **1979** J. P. R. Williams *JPR* iv. 91 An Adidas sweat-suit keeping out the elements. **1591** Sylvester *Du Bartas* i. vi. 148 The *sweat-sweet Civit. **1901** Osler *Princ. & Pract. Med.* i. (ed. 4) 17 Cases that have not been carefully sponged may shew *sweat vesicles. **1682** T. Gibson *Anat.* (1697) 12 These *Sweat-vessels arise from the glands that the skin is every where beset with. *a* **1963** S. Plath *Crossing Water* (1971) 58 Tangled in the *sweat-wet sheets I remember the bloodied chicks.

sweat (swɛt), *v.* Forms: 1 swǣtan, 3 swæten, sweten, 3 *sing. pres. ind.* swet, 3–6 swete, (4 squete), 4–5 suete, sweete, (5 sweet, swett), 5–6 *Sc.* sweit, (6 swheate), 6–7 sweate, swet, 6– sweat; 8 *Sc.*, 9 *dial.* swat. *Pa. t.* 1 swætte, 3–5 swatte, 3, 7 swate, (4 squat), 4–6, 8 *Sc.*, 9 *Sc.* and *dial.* swat, 5 suatte; 3–7 swette, 4 suet(t, (squette), 4–7 swet, 6 swett, 6–9 sweat, 7 sweatt, sweate; 4 sweted, 7– sweated. *Pa. pple.* 3 -swæt (see besweat), 3–6 swat, 4–7 swet, 5 swette, 5–7 swett, 6–8 sweat; 5 sweted, 7– sweated; (7 *in rime*, 9 *pseudo-arch.* sweaten). [OE. *swǣtan*, f. *swāt* swote. Cf. Fris. *swêt*, *swette*, *switte*, MLG. *swêten* (LG. also *swetten*), MDu. *swêten* (Du. *zweeten*), OHG. *sweizzan* (MHG. *sweizen*, G. *schweissen* in technical use), ON. *sveita* (Sw. *svetta*, Da. *svede*).

Avoided in refined speech in the ordinary physical senses; cf. quot. 1791 s.v. perspire *v.* 3.]

I. 1. *intr.* To emit or excrete sweat through the pores of the skin; to perspire (sensibly).

c **900** tr. *Bæda's Hist.* iii. xiv. [xix.] (1890) 216 He swa swiðe swætte swa in swole middes sumeres. *c* **1000** *Sax. Leechd.* II. 290 ða him þonne to his neste & bewreo hine wearme & licge swa oþ he wel swæte. *c* **1205** Lay. 19797 Of þan watere he dronc & sone he gon sweten. *a* **1225** *Ancr. R.* 360 Hwon þet heaued swet wel, þet lim þet ne swet nout, nis hit vuel tokne? *c* **1290** *St. Mary* 174 in *S. Eng. Leg.* 266 Þe Monek swatte for drede. *c* **1386** Chaucer *Can. Yeom. Prol. & T.* 7 His hakeney which þat was al pomely grys So swatte [*v.rr.* swette, swete], that it wonder was to see. *a* **1400** *Minor Poems fr. Vernon MS.* xxiii. 903 Whon he sweted In his gret Agonye. *c* **1400** *Beryn* 2007 Beryn..for angir swet. *a* **1450** *Knt. de la Tour* xciv, They saide vnto hym that he shulde be all hole in hasti tyme after that he had slepte and swette. **1533** More *Apol.* 204 Fryth labored so sore that he swette agayne, in..wrytyng agaynst the blessed sacrament. *a* **1547** Surrey in *Tottel's Misc.* (Arb.) 217 Such was my heate, When others frese then did I swete. *a* **1585** Montgomerie *Cherrie & Slae* 577 Wald thou nocht sweit for schame? **1590** *Tarlton's News Purgat.* (1844) 54 At this sodaine sight [I] fell into a great feare, in somuch that I sweat in my sleep. **1657** Reeve *God's Plea* 192 Andreas Maro Brixianus made verses, till his brows sweatt. **1667** N. Fairfax in *Phil. Trans.* II. 547 She affirm'd, she never swet in her life. **1681** *Lond. Gaz.* No. 1599/4 Saturday was allotted them to sweat and wash in the Royal Bagnio. **1705** Addison *Italy, Pesaro* 165 We were sometimes Shivering on the Top of a bleak Mountain, and a little while after Sweating in a warm Valley. **1725** Ramsay *Gentle Sheph.* ii. iii, Mungo's mare stood still and swat wi' fright. **1737** Bracken *Farriery Impr.* (1757) II. 148 If he sweat out well..it betokens him in good Wind. **1741–2** Gray *Agrippina* 97 Have his limbs Sweat under iron harness? **1821** Byron *Cain* iii. i. 109, I have toil'd, and till'd, and sweaten in the sun. **1829** E. Everett *Orat. & Sp.* (1850) II. 34 He sweat plentifully during the night, and the fever left him.

2. a. *trans.* To emit or exude through the pores of the skin, as or like sweat. Also with *out*.

Freq. *to sweat blood* in reference to the bloody sweat of Jesus (see sweat *sb.* 2 c).

[In OE., what is exuded is expressed by a dative or instrumental (cf. 10), repr. occas. in ME. by *of*; e.g.:—

a **1000** in Cockayne *Narratiunculæ* (1861) 35 Hi..fleoð and blode hi swætað. *c* **1275** *Passion our Lord* 378 in *O.E. Misc.* 48 Pilates..hyne heyghte bete, þat al his swete likame of blode gon to swete.

a **1225** *Ancr. R.* 110 He..deiȝede ȝeond al his bodi, ase he ear ȝeond al his bodi deaðes swot swette. *a* **1310** in Wright *Lyric P.* xxv. 70 Love the made blod to sueten. *c* **1386** Chaucer *Sec. Nun's T.* 522 She sat al coold and feeled no wo, It made hire nat a drope for to sweete. *c* **1400** *Pilgr. Sowle* (Caxton) i. xxii. (1859) 25 Thou hast not swette out of thyn eye a tere. *a* **1536** Tindale *Brief Declar. Sacram.* Bj, He sweat water and bloud of a very agonye conceyued of his passyon so nye at hande. **1590** Lodge *Rosalind* (1592) Mij, What the Oxe sweates out at the plough, he fatneth at the cribbe. **1602** Marston *Ant. & Mel.* iii. Wks. 1856 I. 42 Ile sweate my blood out, till I have him safe. **1687** A. Lovell tr. *Thevenot's Trav.* i. 245 It is sweated out as fast as one drinks it. **1700** Dryden *Cock & Fox* 27 With Exercise she sweat ill Humors out. **1713** Young *Last Day* i. 184 Thou, who..hast..sweat blood. **1854** S. Dobell *Balder* xix. 80 These..or crouched in dark and foul Discovery, or swat a cancerous pool Of poison, and lay hid. **1860** Emerson *Cond. Life, Fate* Wks. (Bohn) II. 325 The slug sweats out its slimy house on the pear-leaf.

b. *fig.* To give forth or get rid of as by sweating; *slang*, to spend, lay out (money). Also with *away*, *out*. In slang phrases: ***to sweat one's guts out*** (see quot. 1890); ***to sweat blood***, (*a*) to exert oneself to the utmost; (*b*) to be terrified.

1592 Greene *Disput.* 1 Hath your smooth lookes linckt in some Nouice to sweate for a fauour all the byte in his Bounge? *c* **1620** *Women Saints* 140, I could not sweate out from my hart that bitternes of sorrow. [**1667** Dryden & Dk. Newcastle *Sir M. Mar-all* v. ii, If my shoulders had not paid for thi fault, my purse must have sweat blood for't.] **1727** De Foe *Hist. Appar.* iv. (1840) 28 A set of human bodies..that could live always in a hot bath, and neither sweat out their souls, or melt their bodies. **1791** Beckford *Pop. Tales Germans* II. 80 His intractable pupil had entirely sweated away his Creed during the night! **1890** Barrère & Leland *Slang Dict.*, *Sweat one's guts out*, a vulgar expression, meaning to work very hard. **1911** G. S. Porter *Harvester* xvii. 405 He just sweat blood to pacify her, but he couldn't make it. **1924** D. H. Lawrence in M. Magnus *Mem. Foreign Legion* 53, I sweat blood every time anybody comes through the door. **1937** 'G. Orwell' *Road to Wigan Pier* xii. 228 It makes one sick to see half a dozen men sweating their guts out to dig a trench.., when some easily devised machine would scoop the earth out in a couple of minutes. **1950** 'J. Tey' *To Love & be Wise* xiii. 163, I expect he sweats blood over his writing. He has no imagination. **1961** R. Jeffries *Evidence of Accused* v. 45 You sweated your guts out for months and finished your book, then the public looked the other way. **1973** W. M. Duncan *Big Timer* xxi. 138, I was sitting there sweating blood when those damned cops arrived.

†**c.** *intr.* (*fig.*) To suffer waste or loss. *Obs.*

1533 More *Debell. Salem* Wks. 1002/1 Hys soule is safe ynoughe, though hys purse may happe to sweate, if he bounde himself to prouide the thinge at his own perill.

d. With *off*. To (cause to) lose (weight, etc.) through strenuous exercise; *spec.* in *Boxing* (see quot. 1955).

1895 Kipling *Day's Work* (1898) 347, I sweated the beef off 'em, and then I sweated some muscle on to 'em. **1899** — *Stalky & Co.* 129 We've sweated a stone and a half off him since we began. **1955** F. C. Avis *Boxing Dict.* 110 *Sweat off*, to lose weight through perspiration caused by vapour baths, etc., in an effort to bring the body to the poundage required for a given championship grade. **1976** *Southern Even. Echo* (Southampton) 12 Nov. 27/5 The..finalist outboxed his opponent, who was weakened after sweating off six pounds during the week.

†**3.** To sweat upon; to wet, soak, or stain with sweat. Also with *out*. *Obs.*

1599 B. Jonson *Cynthia's Rev.* ii. i, He dares tell 'hem, how many shirts he has sweat at tennis that weeke. **1607** Dekker & Webster *Northw. Hoe* iv. iii, I..lend Gentlemen holland shirts, and they sweat 'em out at tennis. **1807** J. Barlow *Columb.* i. 42 Who now..indungeon'd lies, Sweats the chill sod and breathes inclement skies.

4. a. To cause to sweat; to put into a sweat.

With quots. 1748, 1764 cf. sweating *vbl. sb.* 5.

1621 T. Williamson tr. *Goulart's Wise Vieillard* 26 We commonly see the most part of men sweated to death with hote burning feauers. **1712** Arbuthnot *John Bull* iv. i, He should be purged, sweated, vomited, and starved, till he came to a sizeable bulk. **1726** Leoni *Alberti's Archit.* I. 6/2 They will sweat themselves for some Days, and so recover their Health. **1748** Smollett *Rod. Random* xlvi, We should scour the hundreds, sweat the constable..and then reel soberly to bed. **1764** Churchill *Duellist* iii. 378 To knock a tott'ring watchman down, To sweat a woman of the Town. *a* **1776** R. James *Diss. Fevers* (1778) 56 Sir Thomas continued the use of the Powder in smaller doses, which had the good effect of sweating him gently. **1808** *Compl. Grazier* (ed. 3) 69 The tendency of animals to become fat is materially promoted by sweating them. **1841** Catlin *N. Amer. Ind.* lviii. II. 225 The labouring man, who is using his limbs the greater part of his life in lifting heavy weights.. sweats them with the weight of clothes which he has on him.

b. To give (a horse) a run for exercise.

1589 [see sweating *vbl. sb.* 1]. **1737** Bracken *Farriery Impr.* (1757) II. 148 Those Horses which are sweat without Covering, or with a very thin one, should run a long Sweat.

c. *slang.* To subject (a prisoner, etc.) to close interrogation †or torture; to give the 'third degree' to (someone). Cf. *sweat-box* s.v. sweat *sb.* 11.

1764 *Select Trials* I. 285, I..had heard him say, that Capt. Clark was a very great Rascal; and at Admiral Knowles's Trial, he would sweat Capt. Clark if he was examined, and if he could not sweat him there, he would sweat him another way. **1892** 'Mark Twain' *Amer. Claim.* xix. 194 It seems a piteous thing to sweat this poor ancient devil for a burglary he hadn't the least hand in. **1926** J. Black *You can't Win* xviii. 260, I wasn't taken out of my cell and 'sweated' or third-degreed, or beaten up. **1979** 'J. le Carré' *Smiley's People* (1980) xix. 237 Probably Mikhel intercepted and read it... We could sweat him, but I doubt if it would help.

II. 5. a. *intr.* To exert oneself strongly, make great efforts; to work hard, toil, labour, drudge. Often with inf.

In early use freq. in collocation with *swink*.

c **897** Ælfred *Gregory's Past. C.* xxxix. 285 Ðæm ðe nu on godum weorcum ne swæt and suiðe ne suinceð. *a* **1300** *Cursor M.* 1047 (Cott.) Adam..suanc and suet. **13..** *E.E. Allit. P.* A. 585 Oþer..þat swange & swat for long ȝore. **1362** Langl. *P. Pl.* A. vii. 121 We mowe nouþur swynke ne swete, such seknes vs eileþ. **1382** Wyclif *Eccl.* ii. 11 The trauailes in whiche in veyn I hadde swat. *a* **1425** tr. *Arderne's Treat. Fistula*, etc. 3, I haue swette and trauailed ful bisily and pertinacely. **1535** Coverdale *Eccl.* ii. 20 To leaue his labours vnto another, yᵗ neuer swett for them. **1632** Milton *L'Allegro* 105 He..Tells how the drudging Goblin swet, To ern his Cream-bowle duly set. **1684** *Contempl. St. Man* ii. iii. (1699) 154 Sweating and toiling for a small part of the Goods of this World. **1786** Burns *To Jas. Smith* xvii, Some, lucky, find a flow'ry spot, For which they never toil'd nor swat. **1821** Byron *Sardanap.* i. i. 24 He sweats in palling pleasures. **1861** Reade *Cloister & H.* xlvi, Lovers of money must sweat or steal.

b. To toil *after*, *along*, etc. in pursuit or the like; *transf.* (with *up*) to rise steeply.

1815 Scott *Guy M.* xxxix, Some of them are always changing their ale-houses, so that they have twenty cadies sweating after them. **1856** Kane *Arctic Expl.* I. xvi. 187 In about ten minutes, we were sweating along at eight miles an hour. **1904** R. J. Farrer *Garden Asia* 139 The track sweats up through the woodland on to the open ground of the mountain.

c. *spec.* Formerly, in the tailoring trade, To work at home overtime.

1851 Mayhew *Lond. Labour* I. 62/1 One couple..who were 'sweating' for a gorgeous clothes' emporium. **1889** in *Pall Mall G.* 7 May 1/2 The school-boy working out of school hours, the tailor working out of shop hours was said to be 'sweating'.

d. *Cards.* (*U.S.*) 'To win a game by careful and watchful play, avoiding risks' (*Standard Dict.*).

1907 *Hoyle's Games* 411 *Sweating out.* Refusing to bid when nearly out, so as to get out by picking up a few points at a time.

6. *trans.* **a.** To exact hard work from.

1821 Byron *Sardanap.* i. ii. 231, I have not..sweated them to build up pyramids.

b. *spec.* To employ in hard or excessive work at very low wages, esp. under a system of subcontract. See also sweated *ppl. a.* 2, sweating *vbl. sb.* 2 b, 6 (*sweating system*).

1879 Sims *Social Kaleidoscope* Ser. i. ix. 58 One master man employs a number of men and women at a weekly wage, and 'sweats' them to show his profit. **1887** *19th Cent.* Oct. 489 They declared that they were being 'sweated'—that the hunger for work induced men to accept starvation rates.

7. a. *trans.* To work *out*; to work hard at; to get, make, or produce by severe labour. *rare.*

1589 [? Lyly] *Pappe w. Hatchet* D ij, Let them but chafe my penne, & it shal sweat out a whole realme of paper. **1643** Trapp *Comm. Gen.* iii. 19 This is a law laid upon all sorts to sweat out a poor living. **1649** Milton *Tenure of Kings* 3 Then comes the task to those Worthies which are the soule of that Enterprize, to bee swett and labour'd out amidst the throng and noises of vulgar and irrationall men. **1760** H. Walpole *Let. to Earl Strafford* 7 June, Doddington stood before her [*sc.* the Spanish ambassadress]..sweating Spanish at her. **1817** Byron *Beppo* lxxiv, Translating tongues he knows not even by letter, And sweating plays so middling, bad were better. **1822** — *Let. to Moore* 27 Aug., Leigh Hunt is sweating articles for his new Journal.

b. *Naut.* To set or hoist (a sail, etc.) taut, so as to increase speed (also *intr.*); also with the ship as obj.

1890 W. Clark Russell *Ocean Trag.* I. iv. 73 You will still go on sweating—pray pardon this word in its sea sense..—your craft as though the one business of the expedition was to make the swiftest possible passage. **1895** *Outing* (U.S.) XXVI. 46/2 Hoist up on the halyards and sweat up with the purchase. **1899** W. Clark Russell *Ship's Adventure* iv, Smedley..never sweated his yards fore and aft.

8. *intr.* To undergo severe affliction or punishment; to suffer severely. Often ***to sweat for it***, to suffer the penalty, 'get it hot'. Now *rare* or *Obs.*

[*c* **1386** Chaucer *Miller's T.* 516 Wel litel thynken ye vp on my wo That for youre loue I swete ther I go No wonder is thogh that I swelte and swete. **1605** Shaks. *Macb.* ii. iii. 7 Haue Napkins enow about you, here you'le sweat for 't.] **1612** Beaum. & Fl. *Coxcomb* v. i, Thou hadst wrongs, & if I live some of the best shall sweat fort. **1671** Flavel *Fount. Life* ii. 4 He [*sc.* our Lord before the Incarnation] was never sensible of pains and tortures..tho' afterwards he groaned and sweat under them. **1755** Smollett *Quix.* (1803) I. 77 It is odds but they..have us apprehended; and verily, if they do, before we get out of prison, we may chance to sweat for it.

fig. **1647** Trapp *Marrow Gd. Authors* in *Comm. Ep.* 603 The variety of meats, wherewith great mens tables usually sweat.

9. a. To suffer perturbation of mind; to be vexed; to fume, rage. Now *rare* or *Obs.*

a **1400–50** *Wars Alex.* 5325 'I swete', quod þe swete kyng, 'þat I na swerd haue'. **1662** Dryden *Wild Gallant* i. i, I sweat to think of that Garret. **1735** Pope *Prol. Sat.* 227, I ne'er with wits or witlings pass'd my days..Nor at Rehearsals sweat, and mouth'd, and cry'd. **1741** Warburton *Div. Legat.* II. Pref. 10 The Press sweat with Controversy. **1846** Landor *Imag. Conv.* Wks. II. 54/1

Germans had no objection to the bill of fare, but stamped and sweated to see the price of the dishes.

b. *trans.* With *out*, to await or endure anxiously or with unease. Esp. in phr. ***to sweat it out***. *colloq.*

1876 'Mark Twain' *Tom Sawyer* xx. 200 Well, it's a kind of a tight place for Becky Thatcher... Just..let her sweat it out! **1942** E. Colby *Army Talk* 229 *Sweat*..is a synonym for wait. You sweat a man out when you are waiting for him. You 'sweat out' a chow line while waiting for your turn for the sergeant to put your food in the mess kit. **1945** 'L. Lewis' *Birthday Murder* (1951) xiii. 191, I haven't much time..but I'll sweat it out awhile. **1960** *News Chron.* 29 Sept. 1 Mr. Khruschev is just sweating it out in New York for an announcement of a manned flight in orbit. **1976** 'D. Fletcher' *Don't whistle 'Macbeth'* 148, I had no intention of telling Hugo... Let him sweat that one out.

c. *intr.* With *on*, to await anxiously (an event or person); *spec.* in the game of lotto. Also *transf.*, to be close to attaining, as in phr. ***to sweat on the top-line***. *slang* (chiefly *Austral.*) orig. *Mil.*

1917 A. G. Empey *From Fire Step* xix. 127 Sometimes you have fourteen numbers on your card covered and you are waiting for the fifteenth to be called. In an imploring voice you call out, 'Come on, Watkins, chum, I'm sweating on "Kelly's Eye".' *Ibid.* 252 *Sweating on leave.* Impatiently waiting for your name to appear in orders for leave. **1919** *Athenæum* 1 Aug. 695/2 'Sweating on the top line' is to be within an ace of obtaining what you want. **1959** S. J. Baker *Drum* 150 *Sweat on*, to wait, usually to wait anxiously (for something to happen). **1968** S. L. Elliott *Rusty Bugles* in E. Hanger *3 Austral. Plays* I. iv. 62 Wimpy sweats on me see ..waits his chance..puts on a hut raid the other night and finds me mosquito net's not down and I lose my stripes.

d. *intr.* To experience discomfort through anxiety or unease (*colloq.*). In phr. ***don't sweat it*** (U.S. slang), don't worry.

1963 *Amer. Speech* XXXVIII. 271 *Don't sweat it* means 'don't worry about it'. **1973** R. Hayes *Hungarian Game* xxxix. 234 'Hold off for a moment. I want to watch him sweat.' 'The guy's about to faint from pain.' **1976** N. Thornburg *Cutter & Bone* x. 238 Cutter reached over and covered her hand with his own, patted it. 'Don't sweat it, kid,' he said. 'It's nothing.' **1978** D. Devine *Sunk without Trace* ix. 92 No point in being early. Let him sweat.

III. 10. a. *intr.* To exude, or to gather, moisture so that it appears in drops on the surface.

In OE. the matter exuded is expressed by a dative or instrumental: cf. 2.

c **893** Ælfred *Oros.* iv. viii. 188 Mon ȝeseah tweȝen sceldas blode swætan. *c* **1000** Ælfric *Hom.* (Th.) II. 162 Ða ȝebroðra ða eodon..to ðam mercelse, and ȝemetton ðone clud ða iu swætende. [*c* **1290** *Michael* 596 in *S. Eng. Leg.* 316 Þe sonne..makez þe wateres breþi upriȝt as þei scholden swete.] *c* **1400** Maundev. (Roxb.) xvii. 80 If venym or puyson be broȝt in place whare þe dyamaund es, alsone it waxez moyst and begynnez to swete [orig. Fr. *suer*]. **1483** Caxton *Gold. Leg.* 147/2 They wente and fonde the montaygne all swetyng. **1598** *Epulario* L j b, Put them [*sc.* eggs] into the white embers..and when they sweat, they are rosted. **1657** R. Ligon *Barbadoes* (1673) 42 The air being moist, the stones often sweat. **1731** Miller *Gard. Dict.* s.v. *Winter*, If Stone or Wainscot that has been used to sweat, (as it is call'd) be more dry in the Beginning of Winter. **1847** Smeaton *Builder's Man.* 59 Plaster or mortar made with salt water, will always sweat with a moist atmosphere. **1870** *Eng. Mech.* 11 Feb. 525/2 His object glass may have had a deposit formed between its component lenses, or in vulgar parlance 'sweated'.

b. Said *spec.* of products to be stored, or substances in preparation, which are first set aside to exude their moisture.

c **1440** *Pallad. on Husb.* i. 486 The coriaunder leuis, lest hit [*sc.* the wheat] swete, Is put theryn. *Ibid.* ii. 424 So lette hem [*sc.* laurel berries] sething longe tyme swete. **1523** Fitzherb. *Husb.* §25 Make it in greatter hey-cockes, and to stande so one nyghte or more, that it maye vngiue and sweate. **1577** B. Googe tr. *Heresbach's Husb.* i. (1586) 45 b, Good husbandes doo not lay it [*sc.* grass] vp in their Loftes, till suche time as it hath sweat in the Feelde. **1615** W. Lawson *Country Housew. Garden* (1626) 51 Lay..the longest keeping Apples ..on dry straw,..that they may sweat. **1725** *Fam. Dict.* s.v. *Oats*, Oats newly housed and thrashed, before they have sweat in the Mow. **1766** *Compl. Farmer* s.v. *Threshing*, Beans and peas always thresh best after they have sweated in the mow. **1838** *Trans. Provinc. Med. & Surg. Assoc.* ii. VI. 200 The apples [for Devonshire cider] are collected into heaps and allowed to sweat or pass into a state of fermentation. **1843** *Penny Cycl.* XXV. 16/2 [The cut tobacco plants] are left to sweat for three or four days. **1852** Morfit *Tanning & Currying* (1853) 327 Salted hides.. require..rather longer to sweat.

†**c.** To undergo fusion, as metal: cf. 17. *Obs.*

1709 T. Robinson *Nat. Hist. Westmoreld.* xi. 65 We put it [*sc.* the ore] into the great Furnace, where we let it lie sweating in a soft and slow Fire..until the taste and smell of Sulphur be quite gone off.

d. To exude nitroglycerine, as dynamite.

1900 *Westm. Gaz.* 16 July 8/2 Sometimes the cordite 'sweats,'..we put it in a warm place for a time, when the sweated substance is absorbed.

11. *trans.* To emit (moisture, etc.) in drops or small particles like sweat; to exude, distil. Also with *out*.

1398 Trevisa *Barth. De P.R.* xvii. clx[i]v. (Bodl. MS.) lf. 231 b/1 Terebintus..is a tre þat sweteþ rosine. *c* **1440** Capgrave *Life St. Kath.* v. 1959 It longeth to flowres swhiche lycoure for to swete. *c* **1450** *Mirk's Festial* 166 Hard ston and þorne summe tyme swetyþe watyr. **1577** B. Googe *Heresbach's Husb.* ii. (1586) 111 The Cedar sweateth out Rozen and Pitche. **1605** Shaks. *Macb.* iv. i. 65 Greaze, that's sweaten [*rime* eaten] From the Murderers Gibbet, throw Into the Flame. **1607** —— *Cor.* v. iii. 196 It is no little thing to make Mine eyes to sweat compassion. **1638–56** Cowley *Davideis* i. 236 The silver Moon with terrour paler grew, And neighb'ring Hermon sweated flowry dew. **1712** Addison *Spect.* No. 415 ¶3 The Earth..sweated out a Bitumen or natural kind of Mortar. **1884** Roe *Nat. Ser. Story* viii, The clover was piled up.., to sweat out its moisture. **1891** W. A. Jamieson *Dis. Skin* ii. (ed. 3) 19 Alkaline soaps, which improve when kept, because they sweat-out the excess of soda.

12. *intr.* To ooze *out* like sweat; to exude.

a **1425** tr. *Arderne's Treat. Fistula*, etc. 39 Superflue watrenes swette out fro þe place þat was wonte for to file many lynnen cloþes putte atwix. **1555** Eden *Decades* (Arb.) 174 They gather pytche whiche sweateth owte of the rockes. **1668** Culpepper & Cole *Barthol. Anat.* ii. vi. 99 But some particles thereof sweat through the Parenchyma into the Ventricles. **1744** Berkeley *Siris* §38 This balsam, weeping or sweating through the bark. **1839** Ure *Dict. Arts* 30 This alloy is next exposed to a heat just sufficient to melt the lead, which then sweats out..from the pores of the copper. **1884** C. G. W. Lock *Workshop Receipts* Ser. iii. 3/1 By applying heat too suddenly, the metals which fuse at lower degrees of heat, sweat out. **1884** *Marshall's Tennis Cuts* 63 Blue stone dust being again spread over it to absorb the surplus tar, which is sure to 'sweat out' from time to time.

13. a. *trans.* To cause to exude moisture, force the moisture out of; *spec.* to subject to a process of sweating (see 10 b).

1686 W. Harris tr. *Lemery's Chem.* ii. ix. (ed. 3) 404 Make a strong decoction of other Balm, and pour of it into the pot enough to swet it sufficiently. **1733** W. Ellis *Chiltern & Vale Farm.* 98 Extracting the Sap out of Planks for Ship-building, by sweating them in hot Sand. **1754** *Phil. Trans.* XLVIII. 827 Some white marble lime; which was what they call sweated, that is wrapp'd in dung. **1826** *Art Brewing* (ed. 2) 93 Taking the barley from the kiln, for the purpose of sweating it. **1836** in *Chambers' Edin. Jrnl.* 31 Dec. 389 After the fish has been dried to that degree, or rather more, which we shall call thoroughly dried,..it is put up into one large pile, and left to stand for ten or twelve days, which is called sweating it. **1881** Greener *Gun* 314 The stoving sweats the powder, and drives off any remaining moisture. **1882** Paton in *Encycl. Brit.* XIV. 383/2 [Hides] are still sometimes, especially on the Continent, sweated, that is, they are laid in heaps and kept wet and warm.

b. *Cookery.* To heat (meat or vegetables, etc.) in a pan with fat or water, in order to extract the juices.

1877 E. S. Dallas *Kettner's Bk. of Table* 452 *Sweat, to*, is not a pretty phrase, but it expresses clearly..the act of making meat yield its juices by being heated in a pan with little or no water... The heat applied must be low and slow. **1942** [implied at sweating *vbl. sb.* 3 c]. **1953** N. Heaton *Cassell's Cooking Dict.* 171 *Sweat*, to heat gently to extract flavour. **1972** *Guardian* 18 Aug. 11/3 Finely chop one large onion and two cloves garlic. Sweat these in a little oil in a thick saucepan.

14. *slang.* To deprive of or cause to give up something; to rob, 'fleece', 'bleed'. Also *transf.* to rob (a vessel) of some of its contents.

1847 W. *Sk. Irel. 60 Yrs. Ago* i. 14 On the 29th of July, 1784..They determined to amuse themselves by 'sweating' him, *i.e.*, making him give up all his fire-arms. **1860** *Slang Dict.*, *Sweat*, to extract money from a person, to 'bleed', to squander riches. *Bulwer.* **1867** Smyth *Sailor's Word-bk.*, *Sweating the Purser*, wasting his stores. Burning his candles, &c. **1869** Conington tr. *Horace's Sat.*, etc. (1874) 167 Kind to his wife, indulgent to his slave, He'd find a bottle sweated [Ep. ii. ii. 134 *signo læso..lagœnæ*] and not rave.

15. To lighten (a gold coin) by wearing away its substance by friction or attrition.

1785 [see sweating *vbl. sb.* 4]. **1796** Wolcot (P. Pindar) *Bozzy & Piozzi* ii. 204 Wks. 1816 I. 278 His each vile sixpence that the world hath cheated, And his, the art that ev'ry guinea sweated. **1865** Dickens *Mut. Fr.* iii. i, I suppose..you haven't been lightening any of these... *You* understand what sweating a pound means; don't you?

16. *slang.* To pawn.

c **1800** *Irish Song, Nt. bef. Larry was Stretched* 4 They sweated their duds till they riz it.

17. To subject (metal) to partial fusion; to fasten or join by applying heat so as to produce partial fusion; in *Metallurgy*, to heat so as to melt and extract an easily fusible constituent. (After G. *schweissen*.)

The 9th c. form *gisuetit*, glossing 'ferruminatus' (in Goetz *Glossæ Latinogr.* (1888) 579/58), is not certainly OE., and the instance 1575–6 s.v. sweating *vbl. sb.* 3 may be only a casual borrowing from the Continent.

1884 W. H. Wahl *Galvanoplastic Manip.* 112 (Cent. Dict.) The junction of the coil wires with the segments of the commutator is made through large copper plugs, which are sweated in to secure perfect contact. **1890** *Times* 6 Dec. 12/4 It is admitted that 'a few' screws did work loose... It [*sc.* the defect] was remedied by sweating in the screws.

Hence **'sweatable** *a. rare*, capable of becoming sweated labour or a sweated labourer.

1922 G. B. Shaw in S. & B. Webb *Eng. Prisons* p. xlvi, The supply of sweatable labor. **1928** —— *Intelligent Woman's Guide* xli. 158 Our capitalist traders..were the enemies of every country, including their own, where there was a sweatable laborer to make dividends for them.

sweated ('swɛtɪd), *ppl. a.* [f. prec. vb. + -ed[1].] In senses corresp. to various trans. senses of the verb.

1. a. Saturated or covered with sweat. **b.** Exuded as or like sweat.

1654 Gayton *Pleas. Notes* iii. iii. 81 Sancho should have rode him about the grounds,..and then tied him (well cloath'd) to the Racks, and some three or foure houres after, refreshed his sweated body with a mesh. *a* **1711** Ken *Psyche* Poet. Wks. 1721 IV. 181 Bath'd in a Purple Flood Of sweated Blood. **1900** [see sweat *v.* 10 d].

2. Employed in very hard or excessive work at very low wages; oppressively overworked and underpaid; also said of the labour so imposed or exacted.

1883 *Nonconf. & Indep.* 28 Dec. 1177/1 [In the outfitting trade] the sweaters themselves are only just one remove above the sweated. **1889** S. Webb in *Contemp. Rev.* Dec. 880 A low type of 'sweated' and overworked labour is employed at starvation wages. **1894** *Westm. Gaz.* 2 May 2/3 The state of things described by Kingsley still remains in the lower strata of these sweated industries.

3. Of gold coins: Lightened by friction or attrition.

1869 *Latest News* 29 Aug. 8 To get rid of more than 2,000 'sweated' sovereigns per week without exciting an inconvenient amount of attention.

sweatee (swɛ'tiː). [f. as prec. + -ee.] A sweated worker or employee: see prec. 2.

1889 *Charity Organis. Rev.* Jan. 12 The subordinate workers—the 'sweatees'—who are employed by the sub-contractors. **1890** *Times* 8 Apr. 10/1 A competent 'sweatee' can earn about 26*s.* in a busy week.

sweater ('swɛtə(r)). [f. as prec. + -er[1].]

1. a. *lit.* One who sweats or perspires; *spec.* one who takes a 'sweating bath'.

1562 Bulleyn *Bulwark, Bk. Sick Men* (1579) 21 b, Take heede to sutch sweaters, and idle eaters. **1579** Twyne *Phisicke agst. Fort.* i. xviii. 23 Compare with these, those sweaters, and belchers. **1611** Cotgr., *Racletorets*, such as rub sweaters in hot bathes.

b. with *out*: One who gives forth or exudes something in the manner of sweat; in quot. *fig.*

1612 Chapman *Rev. Bussy d'Ambois* i. i. 350 Every innovating Puritan, And ignorant sweater-out of zealous envy.

†**c.** Name for a variety of pear. *Obs.*

1629 Parkinson *Parad.* (1904) 593 The Sweater is somewhat like the Windsor [pear] for colour and bignesse.

2. a. One who works hard, a toiler; *spec.* a tailor who worked for an employer overtime at home (now disused: see sweat *v.* 5 c). Also *transf.* (see quot. 1887).

a **1529** Skelton *El. Rummyng* 105 To trauellars, to tynkers, To sweters, to suynkers, And all good ale drynkers. **1628** tr. *Mathieu's Powerfull Favorite* 145 Of the blood of sweaters, and of the teares of the people. **1851** Mayhew *Lond. Labour* II. 304/1 Amongst the 'sweaters' of the tailoring trade Sunday labour..is almost universal. **1887** Atkin *House Scraps* 13 *Sweater*,..a broker who works for such small commissions as to prevent other brokers getting the business, whilst hardly being profitable to himself. **1889** in *Pall Mall G.* 7 May 1/2 Originally the tailoring was carried on in work-rooms belonging to the tailors' shops, and the name of 'sweater' was first given as a term of reproach to the tailor who worked at home. **1895** Meredith *Amazing Marriage* ix, The dirty sweaters are nearer the angels for cleanliness than my Lord and Lady Sybarite out of a bath, in chemical scents.

b. A servant. *Winchester College slang.*

1900 J. S. Farmer *Public School Word-Bk.* 198 *Sweater* ..(Winchester), a servant. **1973** *Country Life* 19 July 147/1 This is a souvenir plaque..showing the famous painting of the 'Trusty Servant' at Winchester College..or 'Sweater' as he is sometimes called.

3. A medicine that induces sweat; a sudorific, diaphoretic.

1684 W. Russell *Phys. Treatise* 13 Seeing it is evident, that Vomiting and Purging Medicines never become Sweaters or Binders. **1856** 'Stonehenge' *Brit. Sports* ii. vii. ii. §2. 451/2 This is no doubt a strong sweater, but it upsets the stomach.

4. One of a set of street ruffians in the 18th century, who threatened or attacked people so as to make them sweat. *Obs.* exc. *Hist.*

1712 Steele *Spect.* No. 332 ¶2 These Sweaters..seem to have at present but a rude Kind of Discipline amongst them. **1878** Lecky *Eng. in 18th Cent.* I. iii. 482 The 'sweaters' who formed a circle round their prisoner and pricked him with their swords till he sank exhausted to the ground.

5. One who exacts hard work at very low wages; an employer or middleman who overworks and underpays those working under him: see sweat *v.* 6 b, and cf. 2 above.

1846 *Manch. Guardian* 21 Mar. 7/4 A sort of middlemen, called 'sweaters', who get it [*sc.* tailoring work] by men and women at starvation prices. **1850** Kingsley *Alton Locke* x, Were not the army clothes, the post-office clothes, the policemen's clothes, furnished by contractors and sweaters, who hired the work at low prices, and let it out again to journeymen at still lower ones? **1869–70** Latham *Dict.*, *Sweater*..Middlemen between slopsellers and working tailors. *Colloquial.* **1879** Sims *Social Kaleidoscope* Ser. i. ix. 58 The half-starved women and men, who put the things together in top garrets in back slums, or are nigger-driven by a 'sweater' in an East-end workroom. **1890** Earl Dunraven *Draft Rep. Sweating Syst.* §7 The sweater may employ only two or three persons, or he may have two or three score in his service; but the great bulk of the sweated class work for small masters and in rooms or shops where from two or three to a dozen or twenty are employed.

6. One who 'sweats' gold coins: see sweat *v.* 15.

1845 *Currency Theory Reviewed* 69 It being obvious that the coinage, in the very nature of things, must be for ever, unit by unit, falling under depreciation by the mere action of ordinary and unavoidable abrasion—(to say nothing of the inducement which every restoration of the coinage holds out to the whole legion of 'pluggers' and 'sweaters'). **1868** Seyd *Bullion* (1880) 550 To the sweater it really can make no difference whether the mint takes his lightened sovereigns. **1875** Jevons *Money* x. 115 No one now actually refuses any gold money in retail business; so that the sweater..has all the opportunities he can desire.

7. †**a.** *pl.* Clothes in which a horse or a man in training is exercised, to produce profuse sweating.

1828 *Sporting Mag.* XXIII. 104 A craving, strong horse, going along in his sweat, loaded with sweaters. **1856** 'STONEHENGE' *Brit. Sports* II. v. 420/1 Let him put on his sweaters, including a flannel pair of drawers, two pair of trowsers, a flannel jersey [etc.].

b. A woollen vest or jersey worn in rowing or other athletic exercise, orig. (cf. a) in order to reduce one's weight; now commonly put on also before or after exercise to prevent taking cold. Hence, a similar garment for general informal wear; a jumper or pullover.

1882 FLOYER *Unexpl. Baluchistan* 74 Barja is resplendent in my rowing 'sweater', covered by a scarlet blanket, worn as a coat. **1886** *Referee* 12 Dec. (Cassell's) Want of food..and exercise in sweaters. **1890** R. C. LEHMANN *Harry Fludyer* 97 As for Pilling [the cox], the little ruffian actually weighs over 8 stone; but we're going to make him run a mile every day, with four sweaters, and three pairs of flannel trousers on. **1895** *Century Mag.* May 25/2 His brawny, muscular chest, which was covered only by a dark, close-fitting 'sweater', was that of an athlete. **1912** J. SANDILANDS *Western Canad. Dict. & Phrase-Bk.*, *Sweater*, a woollen jacket, much worn in Canada during the winter both indoors and outdoors, and sometimes a somewhat gaudy article of wear. **1957** *Times Lit. Suppl.* 25 Oct. 640/1 A tall, bespectacled young man in turtle-necked sweater. **1981** G. SWIFT *Shuttlecock* i. 13 Martin has a red polo-neck sweater and Peter a brown one and they both wear identical child's blue jeans.

8. An occupation, etc. that makes one sweat or exert oneself. *colloq.*

1851 MAYHEW *Lond. Labour* I. 126/2 The business is a sweater, sir; it's heavy work. **1856** MRS. STOWE *Dred* xlii, You ought to read Fletcher's book; that book, sir, is a sweater, I can tell you. I sweat over it, I know.

9. *attrib.* and *Comb.*, as (sense 7 b) ***sweater blouse, coat, dress, -suit***; **sweater girl** *U.S.*, a girl, esp. a model or actress, who wears tight-fitting sweaters; orig. a name applied to the American actress Lana Turner (b. 1921) who wore such a sweater in the film *They won't Forget* (1937), and in subsequent publicity photographs; **sweater-shirt**, (*a*) *U.S.*, a knitted garment that may be worn as a sweater or a shirt; (*b*) = *sweat-shirt* s.v. SWEAT *sb.* 11.

1925 *Vogue* Early Mar. 60 (*caption*) This straight-line *sweater blouse from Molyneux..is fashioned of fine dark-blue tricot covered with an all-over woven pattern in gold thread. **1954** *New Yorker* 27 Nov. 141/1 A wool jersey sweaterblouse, lavender or white, has cap sleeves and a scoop neck ornamented with gold thread and tiny pink felt buds. **1911** *Sweater coat [see LOVAT]. **1963** *Vogue* Dec. 190 Sweater-coat hand-knitted in Italy. **1965** *Harper's Bazaar* May 6 (Advt.), An enchanting cashmere *sweater-dress. **1940** *Movie Mirror* June 9/1 (*caption*) Sweet and sophisticated sixteen: Lana Turner, at the time her face hit a thousand papers as the '*Sweater Girl'. **1941** *Life* 14 Apr. 33/2 Mr. Breen's letter left movie-makers wondering..what to do with their up-and-coming sweater girls. **1956** S. ERTZ *Charmed Circle* 71 Among all the 'sweater girls' she looked, in her unrevealing black dress, as if she had strayed in by mistake. **1971** D. MACKENZIE *Sleep is for Rich* iii. 66 Crying Eddie was getting plenty of attention from the sweater girls. **1964** *New Yorker* 12 Oct. 15 *Sweater-shirt of pink cashmere. **1977** *Private Eye* 4 Mar. 20/2 (Advt.), American styled printed sweatershirts and T-shirts. **1929** M. LIEF *Hangover* 232 'You're looking fine,' said Whippet, admiring her..slim figure in a neat-fitting *sweater-suit. **1964** *Glamour* Sept. 160 Town sweater-suits [are] booted for the summer.

Hence **'sweatered** *a.*, wearing a sweater; clothed in a sweater.

1901 S. E. WHITE *Claim Jumpers* i. 11 Two sweatered and white-ducked individuals. **1936** R. CHANDLER in *Trouble is my Business* (1954) 205 The sweatered man snatched the gun up. **1971** C. MCCULLERS *Mortgaged Heart* (1977) 74 His blue sweatered shoulders were shaking.

sweatful ('swɛtfʊl), *a.* Chiefly *poet.* [f. SWEAT *sb.* + -FUL.] Full of or abounding in sweat; inducing or accompanied by sweat; toilsome, laborious; distressing, oppressive.

1615 SYLVESTER *Job Triumph.* I. 361 Man, for Sin, must toile him servily, In Sweatfull Labour. **1623** B. HONE in Cockeram *Eng. Dict.* A vij b, If things farre fetch'd are dearest, most esteem'd, which by times sweatful houres haue been redeem'd. **1876** BLACKIE *Songs Relig. & Life* 53 Lift up thy head, O Man,..To sway with sweatful plan The stubborn-breasted earth. **1885** LOWE *Bismarck* xiv. II. 403 The bloated armaments under which all Europe is bending to the earth with sweatful groans.

sweath, obs. form of SWATH[1], SWEDE *sb.*

'sweat-house.

1. A hut or other structure in which hot-air or vapour baths are taken, among the N. American Indians and other peoples.

1750 C. GIST *Jrnls.* (1893) 33, I..sweated myself according to the Indian Custom in a Sweat-house. **1877** G. GIBBS *Tribes Washington* 208 Their sweat-houses are partially excavated in the ground, just large enough to contain the body of one person. **1898** J. HERON *Celtic Church Irel.* I. ii. 39 Perhaps the most singular of primitive Irish structures is the *Teach-an-alais*, or 'sweat-house'.

2. *Tanning.* A building in which hides are sweated: see SWEAT *v.* 13.

3. (See quot.) Cf. *sweat-box* (*c*) s.v. SWEAT *sb.* 11. *rare.*

1882 *Harper's Mag.* Nov. 872/2 The grapes for raisin-making..are removed to an airy building known as a 'sweat-house', where they remain possibly a month, till the last vestiges of moisture are extracted.

sweatily, sweatiness: see after SWEATY.

sweating ('swɛtɪŋ) *vbl. sb.* [f. SWEAT *v.* + -ING[1].] The action of the verb SWEAT.

1. a. Emission of sweat from the pores of the skin; the process of inducing this, esp. in preparing a person for athletic contests or a horse for a race.

c **1205** LAY. 17763 Wreoð nu wel þene king þæt he ligge a swæting. *c* **1400** tr. *Secr. Secr., Gov. Lordsh.* 73 Vse of bathynge and swetynge. *c* **1440** *York Myst.* xl. 40 þat swettyng was swemyed for swetyng. **1563** T. GALE *Antidot.* II. 23 The patyente maye not goe abroade after hys swettynge. **1589** R. HARVEY *Pl. Perc.* (1590) 21, I would we had an Ostler to giue them a turne or two till their sweating were done. **1617** MORYSON *Itin.* III. 60 If he..can find..by the swetting of the horse, that hee hath ridden an extraordinary pace. **1639** MAYNE *City Match* v. iii, You were better match a ruin'd Bawd; One ten times cured by sweating, and the Tub. **1732** ARBUTHNOT *Rules of Diet* in *Aliments*, etc. 272 Sweating often thickens the Blood. **1848** DUNGLISON *Med. Lex.* (ed. 7), Sweating of blood. **1856** 'STONEHENGE' *Brit. Sports* II. I. ix. § 3. 351/1 Sweating will seldom be necessary until the spring. *a* **1883** FAGGE *Princ. Med.* (1886) II. 531 One of the most striking symptoms of acute rheumatism..is sweating.

†**b.** = SWEATING-SICKNESS. *Obs.*

a **1585** MONTGOMERIE *Flyting* 317 The powlings, the palsay, with pockes like pees, The swerfe and the sweiting.

2. a. Toiling, labouring, severe exertion.

c **1430** *Pilgr. Lyf Manhode* III. xix. (1869) 145, j gripe.. that that oothere hauen laboured and conquered with here swetinge. **1551** ROBINSON tr. *More's Utopia* II. (1895) 281 Hollye set vpon the dessire of the lyffe to come; by watchynge and sweatynge hoping shortely to obtaine it. **1596** DALRYMPLE tr. *Leslie's Hist. Scot.* II. 146 Sik heit, in sueiting, trauel, and fechteing. **1633** P. FLETCHER *Purple Isl.* I. xxxviii, You search farre distant worlds with needlesse sweating. **1764** FOOTE *Mayor of G.* II. Wks. 1799 I. 186 After all his..sweatings, his swimmings; must his dear blood be spilt by a broker!

b. *spec.* (*a*) The practice of doing piece-work overtime; (*b*) the practice of exacting hard work from employees for low wages, esp. under a middleman by sub-contract. (See SWEAT *v.* 5 c, 6 b.)

1843 *Mech. Mag.* XXXIX. 443 All owing to their buying ready-made large shoes, and not having patience to let a good working tradesman make them (leaving out the Moses and Son principle of sweating). **1850** KINGSLEY *Alton Locke* x, When this piece-work and sweating first came in. **1888** *Times* 20 Sept. 7/3 Mr. Booth calls sweating the advantage that may be taken of unskilled and unorganised labour under the contract system.

3. a. The action or process of exuding moisture, or of condensing it in drops on the surface (also *concr.*); also, any one of various processes likened to emission of sweat, as of evaporation, fermentation, partial fusion, etc., or the action of exposing something to such process. Also with *out.* (See SWEAT *v.* 10 b, c, 12, 13, 17.)

1545 ELYOT, *Aspergines parietum*, sweatynge of stone walles. **1575-6** *Reg. Privy Council Scot.* II. 512 Gold and silver that salbe recoverit be sweting, melting, affynning or utherwayis. **1699** L. MEAGER *Art of Gardening* 74 Well line the Bottom or Sides of the [Fruit-] Sieves with Fern..to keep them from brusing, and likewise to prevent their sweating. **1707** MORTIMER *Husb.* x. 205 The Bees will hover about the Doors in cold Evenings, and Mornings, there will be a moisture or sweating upon the Stool. **1764** *Museum Rust.* III. li. 225 Yet after it [*sc.* barley] has done sweating, it comes well again. **1808** HOLLAND *Agric. Cheshire* xiii. 283 If the fermentation, or sweating, has been imperfect..the cheese will be liable to become *hove*. **1826** *Art Brewing* (ed. 2) 78 After it [*sc.* malt] is getting out of its first sweating, they take it from the kiln. **1834** *Brit. Husb.* I. 497 A moderate degree of fermentation, or sweating of hay in the stack. **1834** *Penny Cycl.* II. 191/2 The best mode [of preserving apples] is to allow the fruits..to lie till their superfluous moisture has evaporated, which is what is technically called sweating. **1845** DODD *Brit. Manuf.* Ser. v. 133 (*Tobacco*) Sweating..is in its nature a slight degree of fermentation. **1876** BRISTOWE *The. & Pract. Med.* (1878) 825 The sweating of this fluid through the walls of the smaller arteries. **1882** PATON in *Encycl. Brit.* XIV. 383/2 In America the sweating is performed cold; the hides are hung up wet in a damp underground cellar. **1969** BENNISON & WRIGHT *Geol. Hist. Brit. Isles* iii. 43 The last major effect of the metamorphism was the 'sweating out' of synorogenic pegmatites which cross-cut some of the Inverian structures. **1971** I. G. GASS et al. *Understanding Earth* iii. 46/2 The present oceans and atmosphere of the Earth are secondary features due to the subsequent dewatering or 'sweating out' of the Earth's interior.

b. (See quot.)

1909 *Hawkins' Mech. Dict.*, *Sweating On*, the soldering of metallic surfaces without the aid of a copper bit... Sweating on is often employed for the temporary holding together of work which has to be turned or shaped, and which could not be so conveniently held by other methods.

c. *Cookery.* The action or process of SWEAT *v.* 13 b.

1942 C. SPRY *Come into Garden, Cook* xi. 137 Cook the sliced vegetables first in a little fat... This preliminary sweating of the vegetables draws out the flavour.

4. The practice of lightening gold coins by friction.

1785 GROSE *Dict. Vulgar T.*, *Sweating*, a mode of diminishing the gold coin, practised chiefly by the Jews, who corrode it with aqua regia. **1878** F. A. WALKER *Money* x. 195 Whether the loss of the precious metal in the coin results from an external abrasion..or through the clipping or sweating of the coin.

5. a. The practices of the ruffians called 'sweaters' in the 18th century.

1785 GROSE *Dict. Vulgar T.*, *Sweating*,..a diversion practised by the bloods of the last century who stiled themselves Mohocks.

b. Extortion of a confession (from a prisoner, etc.) by close interrogation †or torture. Cf. SWEAT *v.* 4 c.

1824 J. DODDRIDGE *Notes Settlement Indian Wars* II. xii. 122 The torture of sweating..that is of suspension by the arms pinioned behind the backs, brought a confession. **1904** *Cincinnati* (Ohio) *Enquirer* 21 Oct. 4 He confessed, under sweating, that he broke into several offices. **1949** *Amer. Speech* XXIV. 262 The device of *sweating* consisted of suspending the offender from the limb of a tree by his arms, and laying lashes on him.

6. *attrib.*, as ***sweating process***; in sense 1, = used to induce sweating or profuse perspiration, as ***sweating-bath, -bench, -closet, -coop, -draught, oil, -tub*** (cf. TUB *sb.* 1 b); = characterized by sweating, as ***sweating stage*** (in ague or other febrile disease); in sense 2 b, as ***sweating den, shop, system***; in sense 3 b, as ***sweating socket***; **sweating-bag**, a bag used by thieves for sweating gold coins; **sweating-band** = *sweat-band* (see SWEAT *sb.* 11); †**sweating-cloth** = *sweat-cloth* (see SWEAT *sb.* 11); **sweating club**, a club of the ruffians called 'sweaters' in the 18th century; **sweating-fever** = SWEATING-SICKNESS; **sweating-furnace** (see quot.); **sweating-iron** = *sweat-scraper* (see SWEAT *sb.* 11); **sweating pen** *Austral.*, a pen in which sheep are kept (formerly, to sweat so as to soften the wool) before shearing; = *holding pen* s.v. HOLDING *vbl. sb.* 6 b; **sweating-pit**, in *Tanning*, a pit in which hides are sweated; **sweating-place**, (*a*) a building or chamber in which sweating-baths are taken; (*b*) an establishment in which work-people are sweated (see sense 2 b); **sweating plant**, *Eupatorium perfoliatum* (Dunglison *Med. Lex.* 1848); **sweating-room**, (*a*) a room in which persons are sweated, as in a Turkish bath; (*b*) a room in which cheeses are 'sweated' or deprived of superfluous moisture; **sweating-stock**, in *Tanning* = *sweat-stock* (see SWEAT *sb.* 11). See also SWEATING-HOUSE, -SICKNESS.

1617 MORYSON *Itin.* I. 117 Leander thinkes this place to haue been a *sweating bath. **1799** TOOKE *View Russian Emp.* III. iii. II. 262 The russian baths are..sweating-baths. *Ibid.* 261 After remaining awhile they come down from the *sweating-bench, and wash their body with warm or cold water. **1648** HERRICK *Hesper.*, *Panegerik* 121 To build A *Sweating-Closset, or to anoint the silke-soft-skin, or bath in Asses' milke. **1585** HIGINS *Junius' Nomencl.* 172/2 *Sudarium*..a *sweating-cloth: a towell. **1825** R. CHAMBERS *Tradit. Edinb.* II. 260 The *Sweating Club flourished [in Edinburgh] about the middle of the last century. **1751** J. BARTRAM *Observ. Trav. Pennsylv.*, etc. 33, I have seen many of these places in my travels. They differ from their *sweating coops, in that they are often far from water, and have a stake by the cage. **1894** DOLLING in C. E. Osborne *Father Dolling* (1903) xiii, The *sweating dens of financiers. **1822-7** GOOD *Study Med.* (1829) II. 116 *Ephemera Sudatoria.* *Sweating Fever. **1875** KNIGHT *Dict. Mech.*, **Sweating-furnace* (Metallurgy), a liquation furnace of peculiar construction, in which a *matte* of copper and argentiferous lead is heated to deprive the copper of the metals combined therewith. **1753** CHAMBERS *Cycl. Supp.*, **Sweating-iron*, in the manege, is a piece of a scythe about a foot long... When a horse is very hot, and the grooms have a mind to lessen the sweat,..they take this knife or iron.. and gently run the cutting edge along the horse's skin..with intent to scrape off the sweat. **1831** YOUATT *Horse* xxii. 387 An infusion of two ounces of flies..when sufficiently lowered with common oil,..is called a *sweating oil. **1882** ARMSTRONG & CAMPBELL *Austral. Sheep Husbandry* xv. 176 On each side of the board are built the sheep pens, which are filled from a race on each side..which is in its turn filled from the *sweating pen. *c* **1929** H. B. SMITH *Sheep & Wool Industry in Austral. & N.Z.* (ed. 3) x. 73 After drafting, the sheep to be shorn are run up a ramp into the sweating pens of the shed. **1965** J. S. GUNN *Terminol. Shearing Industry* II. 29 *Sweating pen*, sometimes used in the same sense as 'holding pen', although there is no longer any suggestion of deliberately 'sweating' the sheep. **1591** PERCIVALL *Sp. Dict.*, *Sudadero*, a *sweating place. **1850** KINGSLEY *Cheap Clothes* 11 In some sweating places, there is an old coat kept called a 'reliever,' and this is borrowed by such men as have none of their own to go out in. **1849** CLARIDGE *Cold Water Cure* 7 The wet sheet..has gradually superseded the *sweating process. **1852** MORFIT *Tanning & Currying* (1853) 171 All methods of fermentation [for the depilation of hides] are termed sweating processes. **1741** *Phil. Trans.* XLI. II. 855 A Roman Hypocaustum or *Sweating-Room. **1808** HOLLAND *Agric. Cheshire* xiii. 284 Every dairy should be furnished with a regular sweating-room. **1855** MAYNE *Expos. Lex.*, *Laconicum*,..old term for a sweating-room or stove; a vapour-bath. **1880** SIMS *Social Kaleidoscope* Ser. II. xii. 83 The women and children from..the '*sweating' shops in the neighbourhood. **1908** *Installation News* II. 70/1 The grips are provided with a *sweating socket to receive the earth conductor. **1803** *Med. Jrnl.* X. 86 The *sweating stage ..does not appear with any regularity at the second or third return of the paroxysm. *a* **1851** in Mayhew *Lond. Labour* II. 328/2 The *sweating system increases the number of hands to an almost incredible extent. **1879** SIMS *Social Kaleidoscope* Ser. I. ix. 58 The bulk of the work..is done on the 'sweating' system. **1883** *Nonconf. & Indep.* 28 Dec. 1176/3 The sweating system of the outfitting trade. **1660**

MILTON *Free Commw.* Wks. 1851 V. 445 These Tigers of Bacchus, these new Fanatics of not the preaching but the *sweating-tub, inspir'd with nothing holier than the Venereal Pox.

'sweating, *ppl. a.* [f. as prec. + -ING².] That sweats, in various senses.

1. Exuding sweat, perspiring.

1393 LANGL. *P. Pl.* C. IX. 241 With swynke and with swot, and swetynge face. **1592** SHAKS. *Ven. & Ad.* 25 With this she ceazeth on his sweating palme. **1612** WOODALL *Surg. Mate* Wks. (1653) 349 Gently provoke him to be in a sweating manner. **1697** DRYDEN *Virg. Past.* II. 96 The sweating Steers unharness'd from the Yoke. **1791** COWPER *Iliad* VIII. 629 Each his sweating steeds released. **1899** *Allbutt's Syst. Med.* VIII. 728 Warm sweating hands are best treated with weak alkaline baths.

2. Exuding or condensing moisture, etc.: see SWEAT *v.* 10.

1578 LYTE *Dodoens* 411 It..sticketh fast..upon moyst or sweating rockes. **1593** G. HARVEY *Pierce's Super.* 15 A sweating Impe of the euer-greene Laurell. **1718** LADY M. W. MONTAGU *Let. to C'tess of Bristol* (1887) I. 236 [He] gravely asserts, that he saw in Sancta Sophia a sweating pillar. **1976** K. BONFIGLIOLI in *Winter's Crimes 8* 44 The sweating heel of some nameless cheese. **1981** J. B. HILTON *Surrender Value* vi. 47 A sweating expresso machine.

3. Toiling; toilsome, laborious.

1586 A. DAY *Eng. Secretary* II. (1625) 58 The long sweating paines, wherein your good selfe..haue lately trauelled. **1633** P. FLETCHER *Purple Isl.* I. xlix, None felt hard labour, or the sweating plough. **1674** BUNYAN *Light in Darkness* II. Wks. (ed. Offor) I. 435 Believing is now sweating work; for Satan will hold as long as possible, and only steadfast faith can make him fly.

4. *spec.* **a.** Working overtime. **b.** Exacting hard work for very low wages. (See SWEAT *v.* 5 c, 6 b.)

1850 CARLYLE *Latter-d. Pamph.* v. (1872) 133 Poor sweating tailors. **1886** *Echo* 1 Dec. (Cassell's) Recently a trade journal published a list of sweating firms in the clothing trade.

Hence **'sweatingly** *adv.*, in or as in a sweat.

1578 BANISTER *Hist. Man* v. 65 The intercourse of Veynes and Arteries..in those partes sweatyngly poure forth bloud.

sweating-house.

1. A house or building in which persons are sweated, esp. by way of curative treatment; *spec.* among the N. American Indians = SWEAT-HOUSE 1.

1664 PEPYS *Diary* 16 Sept., The general cure for all diseases there [*sc.* Russia] is their sweating houses. **1791** J. LONG *Voy. Indian Interpr.* 47 When the pipe has gone round, a sweating-house is prepared with six long poles fixed in the ground [etc.]. **1837** W. IRVING *Capt. Bonneville* I. 276 Making a rude sweating-house on the banks of the river.

2. In Spain, a hut into which sheep are crowded together so as to sweat, in order to soften the wool for shearing.

1832 *Encycl. Amer.* XI. 353 A narrow, long, low hut, called the sweating-house, where the sheep, being much crowded, perspire freely.

sweating-sickness. [Cf. early Du. *sweetende siechte* (Kilian), after Eng.; also mod.Du. *zweetziekte*, G. *schweisssucht*, Sw. *svettsjuka*.] A febrile disease characterized by profuse sweating, of which highly and rapidly fatal epidemics occurred in England in the 15th and 16th centuries. Now chiefly *Hist.* in reference to these.

1502 ARNOLDE *Chron.* A vij, This yere [*sc.* 1485] was a grete deth and hasty callyd th swetynge syknes. **1542** BOORDE *Dyetary* xxvii. (1870) 289 Whan the Plages of the Pestylence or the swetynge syckenes is in a towne,..the people doth fle. **1560** DAUS tr. *Sleidane's Comm.* 83 This yeare [*sc.* 1529] also was Germany sore afflicted with a newe kynde of disease called the Sweathing sicknes. **1661** J. CHILDREY *Brit. Baconica* 122 The first time of this sweating sickness was in the year 1485. **1758** JORTIN *Erasm.* I. 36 The sweating sickness..began at first in 1483, in Henry the Seventh's army, upon his landing at Milford haven. **1839** KEIGHTLEY *Hist. Eng.* I. 423 The sweating sickness was a rapid fever, carrying people off in 24 hours.

fig. or *allusively*. **1594** NASHE *Unfort. Trav.* Wks. 1904 II. 228 Let mee..tell a little of the sweating sicknes, that made me in a cold sweate take my heeles and runne out of England. **1639** MASSINGER *Unnat. Combat* IV. ii, [We will] ease you Of your golden burthen: the heavy carriage may Bring you to a sweating sickness.

sweatless ('swɛtlɪs), *a. rare.* [f. SWEAT *sb.* + -LESS.] Without sweat; *fig.* without toil or labour, indolent, idle.

1605 SYLVESTER *Du Bartas* II. iii. III. *Law* 839 Thou.. That sweat-lesse eat'st, and without sowing reap'st. **1642** VICARS *God in Mount* 45 A sweatlesse swarm of droanish Deans. **1893** *19th Cent.* Dec. 900 Whose example keeps alive among the masses a craving for something not entirely tame and sweatless.

swea tree: see SWAY-.

sweaty ('swɛtɪ), *a.* Forms: 4–5 **swety,** 6 **swettie,** 6–7 **sweatie,** 7 **sweatty, swetty,** 7– **sweaty.** [f. SWEAT *sb.* + -Y.]

1. Causing sweat: **a.** Heating, excessively hot. **b.** Toilsome, laborious.

c **1374** CHAUCER *Former Age* 28 The tyme..þat men fyrst dede hir swety bysynesse To grobbe vp metal. **1599** B. JONSON *Ev. Man out of Hum.* v. iv, Spare no sulphurous jest that may come out of that sweatie forge of thine. **1600** CORNWALLIS *Ess.* I. ii. C iij, The life of Industries first fruite is somewhat sweatie, and painful. **1602** SHAKS. *Ham.* I. i. 77 What might be toward, that this sweaty hast Doth make the Night ioyn-Labourer with the day. **1641** *Protestation Protested* 10 Witnesse Dr. Hals sweatty discourses. **1673** [R. LEIGH] *Transp. Reh.* 21 Captain Zuinglius, and John Calvin, converted more with Swords and Guns, then with their sweaty Preaching. **1709** PRIOR *First Hymn of Callimachus* 85 Those who labor The sweaty Forge. **1776** MICKLE *Camoens' Lusiad* IX. 370 And measured echoing shouts their sweaty toils attend. **1821** *Blackw. Mag.* IX. 60 The sugar..which the hands of the sooterkin negro Reared..in the island of sweaty Jamaica. **1823** BYRON *Juan* XIII. xlviii, 'Tis..a pity.. To lose those best months in a sweaty city. **1908** *Blackw. Mag.* Dec. 770/1 Thank Heaven he's let us alone this sweaty afternoon.

c. Severe, demanding. *colloq.*

1919 A. LUNN *Loose Ends* iii. 27 'It's a sweaty house for new men.' Cluff shook his head sadly. 'Yes, it's a hard life for new men.' *Ibid.* xiii. 118 These Blues are sometimes rather sweaty. They think it lip if you cut your work for a man who's been a Blue. **1973** M. AMIS *Rachel Papers* 85 I'm not trying to be sweaty or anything, but, um—just out of interest—how long have you known De Forest?

2. a. Covered with sweat; wet, moist, or stained with sweat.

1590 SPENSER *F.Q.* I. vii. 3 Hee..bayes His sweatie forehead in the breathing wind. **1591** —— *Daphn.* iv, When the wearie Sun After his dayes long labour drew to rest, And sweatie steeds now hauing ouer run The compast skie, gan water in the west. **1601** SHAKS. *Jul. C.* I. ii. 247 The rabblement..threw vppe their sweatie Nightcappes. **1664** COTTON *Scarron.* Wks. (1725) 126 His sweaty Pumps are in my Nose still. **1759** B. STILLINGFLEET tr. *Hasselgran's Swedish Pan* in *Misc. Tracts* (1762) 345 The plants ought not to be handled by sweaty hands. **1831** TRELAWNY *Adv. Younger Son* lix, The groans of the slaves,..their sweaty brows, wan eyes, and galled backs.

b. Of persons: Laborious, toiling.

1603 DEKKER *Wonderfull Yeare* Wks. (Grosart) I. 108 The swetty hinde (that digs the rent he paies thee out of the entrailes of the earth) he is sent for. **1659** W. CHAMBERLAYNE *Pharonnida* II. 150 These glittering Jems had been By sweaty Labourers dig'd. **1667** MILTON *P.L.* XI. 434 Thither ..A sweatie Reaper from his Tillage brought First Fruits.

c. *transf.* Full of or exuding moisture like sweat.

1600 SURFLET *Country Farm* III. xxviii. 484 The apple tree ..loueth to haue the inward part of his wood moist and swettie. **1623** LISLE *Ælfric on O. & N. Test.* Ded. xx, Then selfe-sown Wheat shall grow and ripen afield, And sweatie vent of oke pure honie yeild.

3. Consisting of sweat.

1731 SWIFT *Poems, Strephon & Chloe* 12 No noisome whiffs, or sweaty streams.

Hence **'sweatily** *adv.*; also *fig.*, anxiously, feverishly; **'sweatiness.**

1688 HOLME *Armoury* III. 128/1 Terms of Art used in Barbing... Rub the Hair with a Napkin, is to dry it from its swettiness. **1727** BAILEY vol. II, *Sweatiness.* **1818** TODD, *Sweatily*, so as to be moist with sweat; in a sweaty state. **1975** *Times* 4 Sept. 12/8 Men talking sweatily about the upcoming upcurve in house prices. **1978** W. F. BUCKLEY *Stained Glass* iii. 21 On the occasions when they found themselves trapped in his company at a dinner party, they would sweatily engage other members of the party..in concentrated, often nonsensical, discussions.

sweaven, variant of SWEVEN, dream.

sweb (swɛb), *v.* Now *north. dial.* [repr. OE. *swebban* to put to sleep (see SWEVE).] *intr.* To faint, swoon. Hence **'swebbing** *vbl. sb.*

1599 *Warn. Faire Wom.* II. 567 Looke in my purse for a peece of ginger; I shall sweb, I shall swound. **1667** DRYDEN & DK. NEWCASTLE *Sir M. Mar-all* III. ii, Pray your Lordship keep her from swebbing. **1674** RAY *N.C. Words* 47 To *Sweb*, to swoon. **1888** *Sheffield Gloss.*

sweche, obs. form of SUCH.

swecht, Sc. form of SWEIGHT.

sweddle ('swɛd(ə)l), *sb. Obs.* exc. *dial.* Forms: α. 1 **suaeðil, suoeðel, sweþil, -el,** 4–5 **swethel, sueþel,** (4 **squeþel**); β. 5 **swedyll,** 9 *dial.* **sweddle.** [OE. **sweþel*:—**swaþil-*, f. *swaþ-* in *swaþian* to SWATHE + instrumental suffix (-LE). Cf. SWADDLE and SWETHE.] = SWADDLE *sb.* 1.

c **725** *Corpus Gloss.* (Hessels) F 26 *Fasciarum*, suaeðila. *c* **950** *Lindisf. Gosp.* John xi. 44 *Ligatus pedes et manus institis*, ȝebundeno foet & hond suuoeðles. *c* **1050** *Voc.* in Wr.-Wülcker 400/41 *Fasciarum*, sweþelum, wræda. *Ibid.* 403/4 *Fascia*, sweþil, wræd. *c* **1450** *Mirk's Festial* 231 When he was bowndyn hondys and fote wyth his sweþeles. **1877** *Holderness Gloss.*, *Sweddle*, a swathing-band for infants. **1887** *South Chesh. Gloss.*, *Sweddles*, a child's swaddling-band.

b. *attrib.*, as **†sweddle- (swethel-) band** = SWADDLE-BAND; **†sweddle-clout** = SWADDLING-CLOUTS.

a **1300** *Cursor M.* 1343 (Cott.) A new born barn... Bondon wit a sueþelband [*v.rr.* squeþel bande, suadiling band, swaþeling bonde]. *c* **1325** *Metr. Hom.* 91 A womman ..That bar a child in hir arm, In swethel cloutes liand warm. *c* **1460** *Towneley Myst.* xvi. 310 On lyfe lyefe none of tho that lygys in swedyll clowte.

'sweddle, *v. Obs.* exc. *dial.* Forms: α. 4 **swethel, -il;** β. 4 **suedel,** 5 **swedyll,** 6–7 **sweddell, swedle.** See also SWEEL *v.* [f. prec.] = SWADDLE *v.* 1, 2.

a **1300** *Cursor M.* 11236 (Cott.) Sli clathes als sco had to hand Wit suilk sco suedeld [*Gött.* swetheled] him and band. *Ibid.* 11271 þe child þat suedeld [*Gött.* swethild] was, Lai in crib tuix ox and ass. **13..** *Gaw. & Gr. Knt.* 2034 þenn dressed he his drurye double hym aboute; Swyþe sweþled vmbe his swange swetely. *c* **1460** *Towneley Myst.* xiii. 433, I shall swedyll hym right In my credyll. **1535** COVERDALE *Job* xxxviii. 9 When I made the cloudes to be a coueringe for it, and swedled it with yᵉ darcke. —— *Ezek.* xvi. 4 Thou wast nether rubbed with salt, ner swedled in cloutes. **1615** BRATHWAIT *Strappado* (1878) 129 Thou hardly had a lapp to swedle thee.

Hence **'sweddling** *ppl. a.* (in quot., ? wrapped in swaddling-clothes).

? *a* **1500** *Chester Pl.* (E.E.T.S.) viii. 392 That ilke swedling swayne I shall swap of his head.

Swede (swiːd), *sb.* Also 7 **Sweath, Swead, Suede, Sweed.** [a. MLG., MDu. *Swede* (mod. *Zweed*), = HG. *Schwede* native of SWEDEN, q.v.

The OE. name was *Swéon* (pl.), in ON. *Svíar* (Sw. *Svear*), whence L. *Suiones* (see SUIOGOTHIC), med.L. *Swei*; also OE. *Swéoþéod* (*Swǽþéod* in the Peterborough Chron. an. 1025), ON. *Svíþjóð* (= lit. Swede-people), whence, it has been conjectured, arose the forms from which *Swede* and *Sweden* are derived.

The med.L. forms for the name of the country are *Suecia* (whence It. *Svezia*, Sp., Pg. *Svecia*), *Suedia*, and *Sueonia*; for the adj. of nationality *Suecus* (whence Sp., Pg. *Sueco*), *Suecicus*, and *Suedus*.]

I. 1. A native of Sweden.

In quot. 1614 incorrectly tr. L. *Suevi* Swabians; May's version (1627) has *Sueuians*.

1614 GORGES *Lucan* II. 45 Let red-haird Sweaths powre showrs of darts. **1644** (*title*) Good news for England; or a relation of more victories obtained by the Sweads against the king of Denmarke. *c* **1655** MILTON *1st Sonn. to C. Skinner* 8 And what the Swede intend, and what the French. **1663** WOOD *Life* (O.H.S.) I. 486 Mr. Thomas Baltzar, the Sweed, and great violinest. **1698** G. THOMAS *Pensilvania* 51 The way of Worship the Sweeds use in this Countrey, is the Lutheran. *a* **1700** EVELYN *Diary* 1 Oct. 1661, At the reception of the Sweeds Ambassador. **1734** POPE *Ess. Man* IV. 220 Heroes are much the same,..From Macedonia's mad-man to the Swede. **1831** SIR J. SINCLAIR *Corr.* II. 209 Both the Danes and Swedes endeavour to follow the example of their wealthier neighbours, in keeping up a splendid court. **1876** BANCROFT *Hist. U.S.* II. xxiv. 124 The Swedes and Finns and Dutch were invested with the liberties of English-men.

2. A Swedish ship. *rare*⁻¹.

1799 R. SMELT in B. Ward *Dawn Cath. Revival* (1909) II. 219 Mr. Wyndham with other ministers chartered a large Swede of 600 tons.

II. (Now with lower-case initial.) **3.** (= earlier *Swedish turnip*.) A large variety of turnip with yellow flesh, *Brassica campestris*, var. *Rutabaga*, first introduced into Scotland from Sweden in 1781–2.

1812 SIR J. SINCLAIR *Syst. Husb. Scot.* I. 112 With turnips, particularly the Swedes, there is no occasion to give any corn to oxen. **1844** H. STEPHENS *Bk. Farm* II. 17 If weight of crop, nutritious property, and durability of texture are valuable properties in a turnip, none can exceed the Swedes. **1882** HARDY in *Proc. Berw. Nat. Club* IX. No. 3. 550 Wood-pigeons..stripped the leaves off most of the Swedes.

4. *attrib.* and *Comb.* in sense 3, as ***swede-field, -hacking, -trimming, turnip***; **swede-basher** *slang*, a farm worker; hence, a rustic (cf. BASHING *vbl. sb.* 3); so **swede-bashing** *a.*; **swede greens, swede tops,** the tops of swedes eaten as greens.

1851 'CECIL' *Stud Farm* vi. 98 Swede turnips or parsnips are far superior [to carrots]. **1887** JEFFERIES *Amaryllis* iii, If you can get fresh swede tops you don't want a doctor within twenty miles. *Ibid.*, Swede greens be the top of all physic. **1891** HARDY *Tess* xliii, The swede-field in which she and her companion were set hacking. *Ibid.*, When it was not swede-hacking it was swede-trimming. **1936** J. CURTIS *Gilt Kid* iv. 40, I know you're not a swede-bashing judy. **1943** HUNT & PRINGLE *Service Slang* 63 *Swede-basher*, agricultural worker; country bumpkin. **1948** A. BARON *From City, from Plough* 84 There's a lot o' these swedebashers go down the farms every night. **1966** *New Statesman* 18 Mar. 363/1 Sir Gerald Nabarro is said to have remarked on TV that the fate of the nation depended on a few swede-bashers. **1976** J. GRENFELL *Joyce Grenfell requests Pleasure* (1977) xiii. 190, I tried to sing a song appropriate for the swede-bashers from Lincolnshire, the Cockneys, Scots.., and so on.

Swede (swiːd), *a.* Chiefly *Canad.* [f. the sb.] = SWEDISH *a.*; *spec.* in ***Swede saw***, a type of saw having a bow-like tubular frame and a sharp blade with many cutting teeth.

1934 G. BETTANY *Valley of Lost Gold* 29 I've been to the Swede settlement west of the hills. **1950** J. HAMBLETON *Abitibi Adventure* 120 It looked just like any other 'Swede saw', with its tubular metal frame, painted blue, and a thin, keen blade which was kept taut by a clamp. **1971** D. C. BROWN *Yukon Trophy Trails* ii. 39 Louis packed the axe and the Swede saw, and I carried the gun and lunch. **1981** *Nordic Skiing* Jan. 30/2 Lee saws firewood with the Swede saw and I get the honor of splitting it into burning size.

Sweden ('swiːd(ə)n). Also 6 *Sc.* **Suethin, Suadene,** 7 **Swethen,** *Sc.* **Swaden.** [a. MLG., MDu. *Sweden* (Du. *Zweden*), in HG. *Schweden*, prob. dat. pl. of the national name *Swede* SWEDE *sb.*, q.v. In F. *Suède*.

In OE. the country was named *Swéoland* and *Swéo-*, *Swioríce* (= ON. *Svíaríki*, Sw. *Sverige*); these names did not survive.

In AF. of the 12th and 13th c. (e.g. Gaimar) the form is *Suane*, *Swane* (with adj. *Suaneis*). In Sc. *Swane*, *Swaine*, occurs in the 16th c. (e.g. 1559 Burgh Rec. Peebles, 1872, 262); cf. Gaelic *Suain*.

Forms with *th* appear in English in the 14th c., e.g. *Sweþerlond* (? for *Sweþelond*) in Trevisa's Higden, *Swetherwyke* in Morte Arthure, an error for *Swetheryk*, with which *Swethrik*, occurs in Wyntoun's Chron.; *Swadrik* of the Bannatyne MS. belongs to the same series. The simple *Swethe* is used in Mirrour of Our Ladye (15th c.). From the 16th to the 18th c. typical forms are *Swethland*, *Swed(e)land*, *Sweedland*.

Forms approximating to the present form appear in Sc. in the 16th c., as *Suethin*, *Suadene*, *Swadne*. These forms seem to have been felt appropriate for adjectival uses, and in early 17th c. English usage *Sweden* appears as the name of the people, *Swedeland* being the name of the country.]

1. The name of one of the Scandinavian countries; †used attrib., *spec.* in ***Sweden boards*** (Sc.).

1503 *Acc. Ld. High Treas. Scot.* II. 273 For ij[e] fiue score viij Suethin burdis, ilk pece xij d. **1543** *Aberd. Reg.* XVIII. (Jam.) Tymmer skowis, Suadene buirdis, guird stringis and boddumis. **1612** *Bk. Rates* in *Halyburton's Ledger* (1867) 290 Swaden boordes of the great sort the hundreth . . xxiiii li. *Ibid.* 316 Spanish Spruce and Swadens Irne the stane weght thairof . . xiii *s.* iiii *d.* **1665** BRATHWAIT *Comm. Two Tales* 164 This Mother-Midnight, shap'd like a Sweden Hag.

†**2.** = SWEDE *sb.* 1.

1600 W. WATSON *Decacordon* (1602) 276 The Spaniard, the Polonian, the Sweden. **1612** in *Eng. Hist. Rev.* Apr. (1914) 249 Another part [of their country is] usurped . . by the Swedens. *Ibid.* 255 The Swethen hath likewise abused them.

Swedenborgian (swiːd(ə)n'bɔːdʒɪən), *a.* and *sb.* [f. the name of Emanuel *Swedenborg* or Svedberg (see below) + -IAN.] **a.** *adj.* Of or pertaining to Emanuel Swedenborg, a Swedish scientific and religious writer (1688–1772), or the body of followers of his religious teachings, organized in 1788 and styled by themselves 'The New Church'. **b.** *sb.* A follower of Swedenborg. Hence **Sweden'borgianism**, also *rarely* **'Swedenborgism**.

1791 J. LACKINGTON *Mem.* xxv. 195 The *Swedenborgians*, or *New Jerusalemists*, are gaining ground very fast. **1802** M. CUTLER in *Life* etc. (1888) II. 114 In the evening the Swedenborgian preached in the Hall. **1807** SOUTHEY *Lett. from Eng.* III. lxii. 144 (*heading*) Account of Swedenborgianism. *Ibid.*, The New Jerusalem, or Swedenborgian chapel. **1810** CRABBE *Borough* iv. 168 Some Swedenborgians in our streets are found, Those wandering walkers on enchanted ground. **1825** SYD. SMITH *Sp.* Wks. 1859 II. 199/1 They never can mean that our government is essentially Presbyterian, essentially Swedenborgian, essentially Ranting, or essentially Methodist. **1842** C. FOX *Jrnl.* 6 June in *Memories of Old Friends* (1882) viii. 160 Thomas Carlyle came in . . and we presently got, I know not how, to Swedenborgianism. **1854** EMERSON *Lett. & Soc. Aims*, *Immortality* (1883) 242 Some neat and plausible system, as Calvinism, Romanism, or Swedenborgism, for household use. **1856** *Spiritual Herald* June 147 The Lord may be better represented by an animated and intelligent orb . . than by a Whewellite or Swedenborgian star. **1863** E. H. PLUMPTRE in *Smith's Dict. Bible* III. s.v. *Science*, A spurious theosophy—of which Swedenborgianism is, perhaps, the nearest modern analogue. **1914** C. MACKENZIE *Sinister Street* II. III. ix. 682, I should love to be a sort of Swedenborgian with all sorts of fanciful private beliefs. **1920** M. BEER *Hist. Brit. Socialism* II. III. i. 12 William Hill, a Swedenborgian preacher and a grammarian. **1976** *Gramophone* June 32/1 Pitcairn wished to sponsor the promotion and recording of his fellow Swedenborgian's music.

swedge (swɛdʒ), *sb.* [Variant of SWAGE *sb.*[2]] = SWAGE *sb.*[2] 2 b. Also *attrib.*

1825–80 JAMIESON, *Swedge*, an iron chisel with a bevelled edge, used for making the groove round the shoe of a horse, Roxb. To *Swedge*, to make a groove in a horse-shoe for receiving the nails, Roxb. This is done by such a chisel as that above described. **1881** GREENER *Gun* 181 This shell is found to be rather uncertain in exploding, therefore Forsyth brought out the swedge shell as an improvement. *Ibid.*, The base of the bullet is . . passed through a screw swedge, which . . makes the bullet appear as one piece. **1908** *Animal Managem.* 234 The 'swedge,' 'crease,' or 'concave tool,' . . is a mould through which the hot bar is pulled by the smith, whilst it is hammered by the striker.

swedge (swɛdʒ), *v.* [f. prec. sb.] *trans.* = SWAGE *v.*[3] (also *transf.* to double back or round an object). Also (*U.S. Naut. slang. rare*) *intr.*, to go *off* or depart without paying.

1844 H. STEPHENS *Bk. Farm* III. 1079 A blade of rolled cast-steel swedged into a form. *Ibid.*, The swedged or moulded back. **1881** GREENER *Gun* 181 Two pairs of moulds and one swedging machine. **1884** J. H. WALSH *Sportsman's Gun & Rifle* II. 314 Conical [bullets] . . may be 'swedged' or driven into a suitably constructed die by blows upon a punch applied to the base of the bullet. **1897** KIPLING *Capt. Cour.* v. 124 'Seems kinder unneighbourly to let 'em swedge off like this,' Salters suggested, feeling in his pockets. **1901** —— *Kim* xiv, He bound them into a neat packet, swedging down the stiff, sticky oil-cloth at the corners.

†**'Swedian.** *Obs. rare.* [f. SWEDEN + -IAN.] A Swede.

1573 L. LLOYD *Marrow of Hist.* (1653) 139 The Swedian a light talkative person.

Swedish ('swiːdɪʃ), *a.* and *sb.* Also 7 **Swethish**, 8 **Sweedish.** [f. SWEDEN or SWEDE *sb.* + -ISH[1], after G. *schwedisch*, MDu. *swedesch*, *sweets(ch)*, Du. *zweedsch.*]

A. *adj.* Of or belonging to Sweden or the Swedes; native to or living in Sweden, or of Swedish descent.

Swedish clover: = ALSIKE. ***Swedish coffee***: see COFFEE *sb.* 4 b. ***Swedish drill***, ***gymnastics***, ***movements***, a system of muscular exercises as a form of hygienic or curative treatment. ***Swedish exercises*** = *Swedish drill*; also *fig.* ***Swedish feather***: see FEATHER *sb.* 14. ***Swedish glove***: see SUEDE. ***Swedish massage***, a system of massage combined with manipulation of the joints and muscles, first devised in Sweden; hence ***Swedish masseur***, (fem.) ***-euse***, one trained in the practice of Swedish massage. ***Swedish modern*** = *Danish modern* s.v. DANISH *a.* (cf. SCANDINAVIAN *a.* 2). ***Swedish nightingale***, the thrush nightingale, *Daulias philomela*; also misapplied to the redwing. ***Swedish turnip*** = SWEDE *sb.* 3. ***Swedish work***, a kind of hand-weaving: see quot. 1882. Also in reference to iron obtained, or processes of iron manufacture introduced, from Sweden.

1632 (*title*) The Swedish Discipline, Religiovs, Civile, and Military. **1652** [see FEATHER *sb.* 14]. **1656** *Act Commw.* c. 20 Rates (1658) 469 Iron Amys, Spanish, Spruce, and Swethish, the Tun 16 00 00. **1738** *Gentl. Mag.* Nov. 594/1 Lord and Master of the Swedish Nation. **1756** F. HOME *Exper. Bleaching* 164 There would appear . . a greater difference than this, betwixt the Swedish ashes, if that is the true process. **1786** GROSE *Milit. Antiq.* I. 165 Rests thus armed [with spikes, etc.], were called swines or Sweedish feathers, and were contrivances preceding the use of the bayonet. *c* **1791** *Encycl. Brit.* VIII. 761/1 The ruta baga, or Swedish turnip, is a plant from which great expectations have been formed. **1799** MALTHUS *Diary* 27 July (1966) 191 The son-in-law told us that a Norway lap must not go into Sweden, nor a Swedish lap come into Norway. **1819** SCOTT *Leg. Montrose* ii, I was often obliged to run my head against my old acquaintances, the Swedish feathers, whilk your honour must conceive to be double-pointed stakes, shod with iron at each end, and planted before the squad of pikes to prevent an onfall of the cavalry. *Ibid.* xi, The Captain . . whistled a Swedish retreat. **1852** BURN *Naval & Milit. Dict.* (1863), Swedish ship, *crayer.* **1879** E. P. WRIGHT *Anim. Life* 235 The Swedish Nightingale (*Daulias philomela*) does not occur in Great Britain. **1882** CAULFEILD & SAWARD *Dict. Needlework* 466 *Swedish Work*, a kind of weaving much practised in Sweden. . . It is worked in a small frame, shaped like a comb, and with two sets of threads to form the woof, while the warp is made by a thread wound upon a very thin shuttle. **1884** [see NIGHTINGALE[1] 1 b]. **1884** W. H. GREENWOOD *Steel & Iron* 130 It is not unusual to find Swedish pigs whose fracture presents a skin of . . chilled iron. *Ibid.* 233 The Lancashire Hearth or Swedish Finery. **1885** 'MRS. ALEXANDER' *Valerie's Fate* i, A many-buttoned tawny Swedish glove. **1890** BILLINGS *Med. Dict.*, *Swedish bitters*, compound tincture of aloes. *Swedish gymnastics*, a system of exercises . . in which active and passive movements are combined with massage. **1896** *Times* (weekly ed.) 16 Feb. 126/4 A poniard . . a 'knuckle-duster,' and a so-called Swedish knife. **1899** tr. *Wide's Handbk. Med. Gymnastics* Pref. p. v, The whole civilized world . . honours not only the master but also the land to which he [*sc.* P. H. Ling] belonged by its general adoption of the term 'Swedish Gymnastics'. **1899** *Allbutt's Syst. Med.* VI 605 Galvanism, shampooing and Swedish movements. **1908** *Animal Managem.* 109 Alsike, . . sometimes called Swedish clover, is often grown instead of the red varieties. **1911** *Daily Colonist* (Victoria, B.C.) 8 Apr. 5/2 (Advt.), Swedish Massage, Medical Sick-Gymnastic, Electric Vibrations. . . Above treatments highly recommended by leading physicians. **1911** Swedish masseur [see OPSONIST]. **1912** 'SAKI' *Unbearable Bassington* vii. 124 A sporting cat . . watching the Swedish exercises of a well-spent . . mouse. **1916** J. LEWIS *Swedish Drill Illustr.* 3 A Swedish Drill lesson. **1923** WODEHOUSE *Inimit. Jeeves* xi. 123 If she had knocked off starchy foods and done Swedish exercises for a bit, she might have been quite tolerable. **1948** A. H. RUTT *Home Furnishing* (ed. 2) xiii. 217 Swedish Modern is a favorite style which successfully combines native, Classical, Empire, and Modern ideas. **1958** 'S. MARLOWE' *Second Longest Night* iii. 26 The living-room was Swedish modern . . with black lacquered pieces and high-grained white ash. **1959** A. GLYN *I can take it All* ii. 30 'But you live in—' I was going to say Helsinki, but I remembered . . that she was a Swedish Finn '—in Helsingfors?' **1966** J. MITFORD in *McCall's* Mar. 190/2 A splendid Swedish masseuse . . rubs you all over with cream. **1970** D. BAGLEY *Running Blind* vii. 156 The room was decorated in that generalized style known as Swedish Modern. **1975** C. YOUNG *Massage* ii. 16 In the beginning of the nineteenth century a Swedish fencing master, Peter Henrik Ling, introduced a system of movement that consisted of massage and exercises. . . This method . . became the basis for . . Swedish massage. **1979** J. TATE tr. *Martenson's Death calls on Witches* v. 33 Her parents were Swedish-Americans.

B. *sb.* The language of Sweden.

1605 VERSTEGAN *Dec. Intell.* Ep. to Nation, High, Low, and Eastlandish Teutonic, together with respect vnto the dependant Danish and Swedish. **1605**, **1797**, **1841** [see NORWEGIAN B. 2].

swedle, obs. variant of SWEDDLE *v.*

†**swedyr,** *v. Obs. rare*[−1] (Meaning uncertain.)

c **1400** *Song of Roland* 337 Hou wondirly on they set with dentis felle; speris to-brast and in pecis flowen, . . swerdis swedyrd out and laid hem doun.

swee (swiː). [Echoic.] A South African species of waxbill (*Estrilda dufresnii*), so called from its note. So **swee-swee** *v. intr.* to utter a note like the syllable 'swee' repeated; to chirp shrilly.

1839 MOIR *Mansie Wauch* xxii, The grand carved roofs, where the swallows swee-sweed as they darted through the open windows. **1908** HAAGNER & IVY *Sk. S. Afr. Bird-Life* iv. 68 The Swee Waxbill (*E[strilda] dufresnii*) is the best known species in the South-eastern Province of Cape Colony. **1913** PETTMAN *Africanderisms*, Swee, . . *Estrilda dufresnii.* It owes its popular name to its cry of 'swee-swee'.

swee, dial. form of SWAY.

sweeal, dial. form of SQUEAL.

Sweed, obs. form of SWEDE *sb.*

†**sweedle** ('swiːd(ə)l), *v. Obs. slang.* [Blend of SWINDLE *v.*[2] and WHEEDLE *v.*] *trans.* To swindle by wheedling. Hence **'sweedling** *vbl. sb.* and *ppl. a.*

1908 H. A. JONES *Dolly reforming Herself* IV. 94 I'm not going to be sweedled!—*Matt.* What is sweedled? *Harry.* Sweedling is sweedling! It's part swindling and part wheedling! **1908** *Westm. Gaz.* 4 Nov. 5/2 Dolly is a 'sweedling' extravagant little vixen. **1909** *Daily Chron.* 19 Jan. 4/4 He circumvented Isengrim the Wolf and 'sweedled' King Noble the Lion. **1914** *Angl. Forsch.* XLII. 20 The mind, hesitating between *swindle* and *wheedle*, compromises on *sweedle*. When the result pleases the coiners, it sometimes continues in family use, as *sweedle* in the case of a Nebraska family.

†**sweek.** *Obs.* Also 6 **sweake**, 7 **sweeke.** [If the primary sense be 'swing', this word is related to SWEAK *v.* and to the dial. *sweak* swing-bar in a fireplace for kettles, etc., *swake* pump-handle.] Part of a trap for catching birds.

1594 BARNFIELD *Affect. Sheph.* (Arb.) 13 If thou wilt Make pit-falls for the Larke and Pheldifare, Thy prop and sweake shall be both ouer-guilt. **1623** C. BUTLER *Fem. Mon.* vii. (1634) 120 The three sides or parts of the Prop (the Poste, the Sweeke, and the Brace,) are three Stiks: all, almost half an inch broad, and half a quarter of an inch thik. *Ibid.* 121 First bait the Sweek with a thin piece of good Cheese, or Bacon, or Suet.

sweel (swiːl), *v. Sc.* Forms: 6 **sweil**, 7 **swill**, 7–8 **swyle**, 8 **swayl**, 9 **sweal**, **sweel.** [Contracted f. SWEDDLE *v.*] *trans.* To swaddle, swathe. Hence **'sweeling** *vbl. sb.*, attrib. in † ***sweilling clais***, swaddling-clothes.

1567 *Gude & Godlie Ball.* (S.T.S.) 50 The Sylk and Sandell the to eis, Ar hay, and sempill sweilling clais. *a* **1583** MONTGOMERIE *Flyting w. Polwart* 286 [292] (Tullib. MS.) Swir sweillit [*Harl. MS.* sweddelled; *ed.* **1629** swyld; *ed.* **1688** swill'd] in ane swyneskin. **1768** ROSS *Helenore* III. 110, I hae a ribbon twa ell lang, . . Gin it hae monie marrows I'm beguil'd, 'Twas never out o' fauld syn she was swyl'd. **1858** M. PORTEOUS *Souter Johnny*, *To Shade of Burns*, In blanket sweel'd. **1890** SERVICE *Notandums* xiv. 101 Them that were hurt they sweeled in a barrie o' dirty linen.

sweel, dial. f. SQUEAL; obs. f. SWEAL; dial. f. SWILL, SWIVEL.

sweem, Sc. f. SWIM.

sweemish, north. dial. f. SQUEAMISH.

sween, obs. var. SWEVEN, dream.

Sweeney ('swiːnɪ). *slang.* Also **sweeney**, **Sweeny.** [f. the name of *Sweeney* Todd, a barber who murdered his customers, the central character of a play by George Dibdin Pitt (1799–1855), and of later plays.] **1.** In full ***Sweeney Todd.*** Rhyming slang for 'Flying Squad'. So, a member of the Flying Squad.

1936 J. CURTIS *Gilt Kid* xxii. 223 The slops had been turning up at the block of flats just as he was making his getaway. Yes, and coming along in a jam jar too. That made them look like Sweenies. **1938** F. D. SHARPE *Sharpe of Flying Squad* 333 *The Sweeney Todd*, the Flying Squad. **1956** J. D. CARR *Patrick Butler for Defence* xiii. 140 The Flying-Squad people are called sweenies, from Sweeny Todd. **1967** N. LUCAS *C.I.D.* xiii. 195 By the way, don't bother to call the Sweeny (Sweeny Todd—Flying Squad). **1971** R. BUSBY *Deadlock* I. v. 56, I was with the sweeney before this firm. . . The Sweeney Todd—crime squad. . . If you're an old sweeney man too, we'll get along all right. **1977** *Guardian Weekly* 17 July 10/1 Was designed—as they say in The Sweeney—to put the frighteners on Labour knockers.

2. A (nickname for a) barber.

1966 'L. LANE' *ABZ of Scouse* 104 I'm goin' ter Sweeny ter 'ave me hur cut. **1980** *Globe & Laurel* July/Aug. 217/2 It has been noted that a significant number of the ship's company now have a 'Sweeney' Barber special.

sweenge, Sc. f. SWINGE.

sweenied ('swiːnɪd), *a. U.S.* Also **sweeneyed**, **swinneyed**, **swyneyed.** [f. SWEENY + -ED[2].] Suffering from sweeny. Hence ***sweenied-looking*** adj.

1861 *Harper's Mag.* Aug. 421/2 The people have been fed on buncombe, while a lot of spavined, ring-boned, . . swyneyed, split-headed . . polleviled politicians have had their noses in the public crib. **1872** *Rep. Indian Affairs 1871* (U.S.) 554 The three mules were thin, and one of them lame in the right shoulder, 'sweenied'. **1872** *Borderer* (Las Cruces, New Mexico) 5 Oct. 2/4 God Almighty only knows the age of 'em!—three footed, one-eyed, sweeneyed, spavined, broken-down ex-livery stable stock, 'political hacks', and sway-backed horses. **1960** V. WILLIAMS *Walk Egypt* 188 Mule and tree had grown old and swinneyed together. *Ibid.* 240 He picked up a mule. . . It was a swinneyed-looking thing.

sweens, var. SOWENS.

sweeny ('swiːnɪ). *U.S.* Also **swinn(e)y.** [prob. f. G. dial. *schweine* emaciation, atrophy, *schweinen* to become emaciated.] Atrophy of the shoulder-muscles in the horse. Also *fig.* of the 'stiffness' of pride or self-conceit.

1813 E. GERRY *Diary* 23 June (1927) 131, I answered he [*sc.* a horse] was foundered, but was informed that it was another complaint called the sweeney. **1832** J. P. KENNEDY *Swallow Barn* II. i. 22 He professed to cure the colt's distemper, sweeny, and other maladies. **1855** H. C. KIMBALL in *Jrnl. Discourses* II. 158/1 Too many have got the sweeny, and the skins are growing tight on their flesh. **1887** *Sci. Amer.* 30 July 72/3 The shrinkage of the muscles of the shoulder, and which is commonly called 'sweeny', is due to some lameness of the foot or limb.

sweep (swiːp), *sb.* Forms: 6 **swiepe**, 6–7 **sweepe**, **sweape**, 7 **swepe**, 7–8 **sweap**, 7– **sweep.** [Mainly

f. SWEEP *v.* In senses 26, 28, app. a local variant of SWAPE, q.v.]

I. The action of sweeping.

1. a. An act of sweeping or clearing up or (usually) away; a clearance: freq. ***a general***, (now) ***a clean sweep***.

1552 in *Vicary's Anat.* (1888) App. xvi. 293 Thynkyng.. this Hospital should haue made a generall swiepe of all poore and afflicted. **1712** SWIFT *Jrnl. to Stella* 1 July, Here has been a great sweep of employments, and we expect still more removals. **1720** —— *Run on Bankers* Wks. 1755 IV. I. 22 The bold encroachers on the deep Gain by degrees huge tracts of land, Till Neptune with one gen'ral sweep Turns all again to barren strand. **1801** JEFFERSON *Writ.* (ed. Ford) VIII. 64 In Connecticut alone a general sweep seems to be called for. **1848** CLOUGH *Amours de Voy.* I. 24 Would to Heaven the old Goths had made a cleaner sweep of it! **1868** MILMAN *St. Paul's* 229 To make the last remorseless sweep of these riches. **1869** TOZER *Highl. Turkey* II. 144 A clean sweep had been made of all the beasts of burden in the neighbouring districts. **1889** JESSOPP *Coming of Friars* v. 236 There had been a clean sweep of the old incumbents from all the parishes for miles round.

b. An act of passing over an area in order to capture or destroy the occupants of it. Also *spec.* with reference to aircraft patrols, usu. offensive, but occas. also for reconnaissance purposes.

1837 W. IRVING *Capt. Bonneville* I. 186 [They] had taken the lead, and hoped to have the first sweep of the hunting ground. **1889** *19th Cent.* Nov. 758 The hopes that the few remaining hundreds of the aborigines might be captured in one sweep. **1916** *Edin. Rev.* July 172 The Grand Fleet had been engaged in carrying out one of those frequent 'sweeps' of the North Sea on which it has been employed for months in order to find the enemy. **1940** *Sun* (Baltimore) 21 Feb. 1/6 In a daylight sweep over the Channel.. British fighters set another Nazi E-boat afire. **1942** *Ann. Reg. 1941* 52 About the middle of June the Royal Air Force began to make what were called 'offensive sweeps'.. seeking for enemy machines. **1959** R. COLLIER *City that wouldn't Die* x. 167 Some fifty day-fighters and thirty night-fighters had taken part in this spectacular sweep. **1973** 'R. LEWIS' *Blood Money* viii. 106 The helicopter seemed to have completed its sweeps... The shadows.. had made spotting difficult.

c. ***at one*** or ***a sweep***: with a single blow or stroke.

1834 L. RITCHIE *Wand. Seine* 96 Seventeen persons were drowned by the bar at one sweep. **1870** BURTON *Hist. Scot.* (1873) VI. lxxii. 256 The Tables resolved to take them at one sweep out of the hands of the Government. **1877** *Daily News* 25 Oct. 5/4 If the best mines are liable to explosion, killing hundreds of men at a sweep.

d. *Sport.* Victory in all the games in a contest, tournament, etc., by one team or one competitor, or the winning of all the places in an event or competition. orig. and chiefly *U.S.*

1960 WENTWORTH & FLEXNER *Dict. Amer. Slang* 531/1 *Sweep n.*, the act or an instance of one athlete or team winning a tournament without losing an individual game or contest. **1974** *State* (Columbia, S. Carolina) 31 Mar. 5-D/4 The Gamecocks claimed all three places for a sweep of the 880 as John Brown rolled home with a time of 1:56.6 to best teammates Mike Sheley and Don Brown. **1977** *Hongkong Standard* 12 Apr. 12/7 John Mayberry also drove in two runs to help Royals complete a season-opening sweep of the three-game series against the Tigers. **1979** *Arizona Daily Star* 1 Apr. C1/1 James Frazier led an Arizona sweep in the high jump with a winning leap of 7-3¾, followed by Roger Curtis' 7-1¾.

2. The action of a person or animal moving along with a continuous motion, esp. with a magnificent or impressive air. Also with advs., as ***sweep-by, sweep-past***.

1607 SHAKS. *Timon* I. ii. 137 What a sweepe of vanitie comes this way. **1775** MME. D'ARBLAY *Let.* in *Early Diary* Nov., Nothing could be more noble than her entrance. She took a sweep from the full length of the stage. **1827** HONE *Every-day Bk.* II. 57 Private carriages.. draw up to the box door with a vigorous sweep. **1856** MRS. MARSH *Ev. Marston* xviii. II. 93 The stillness being only broken by.. the noiseless sweep by of the large white owl. **1895** SNAITH *Mistr. D. Marvin* vi, She cantered him [*sc.* a horse] gently to the far end of the yard to give him a good sweep for the spring.

3. a. The rapid or forcible and continuous movement of a body of water, wind, etc.

1708 J. PHILIPS *Cyder* II. 83 A Torrent swell'd With wintry Tempests, that disdains all Mounds,.. and involves Within its Sweep, Trees, Houses, Men. **1754** GRAY *Pleasure* 59 With resistless sweep They perish in the boundless deep. **1801** SOUTHEY *Thalaba* VIII. viii, The wind Swept through the moonless sky,.. And in the pauses of its sweep They heard the heavy rain Beat on the monument above. **1821** CLARE *Vill. Minstr.* I. 76 The river pours Its guggling sounds in whirling sweep. **1837** CARLYLE *Fr. Rev.* III. I. vi, Brawny Danton is in the breach.. amid the sweep of Tenth-of-August cannon. **1898** *Jrnl. Sch. Geog.* (U.S.) Oct. 298 To anchor at some distance off-shore, exposed to the full sweep of the long rollers.

b. semi-*concr.* of a forcibly moving body of water.

1815 SHELLEY *Alastor* 362 Suspended on the sweep of the smooth wave, The little boat was driven. **1864** TENNYSON *En. Ard.* 55 He thrice had pluck'd a life From the dread sweep of the down-streaming seas. **1867** AUGUSTA WILSON *Vashti* xxvii, He might as well have attempted to catch.. in the hollow of his hand the steady sweep of Niagara.

4. An action, or a process in expression, thought, etc., figured as movement of this kind.

1662 GRAUNT *Bills of Mortality* ii. 16 In Countries subject to great Epidemical sweeps man may live very long. **1817** COLERIDGE *Biog. Lit.* (Bohn) 272 It was easy to excuse some inaccuracy in the final sounds if the general sweep of the verse was superior. **1840** DE QUINCEY *Style* I. Wks. (1860) 164 Whatever sweep is impressed by chance upon the motion of a period. **1842** TENNYSON *Epic* 14, I heard The parson taking wide and wider sweeps. **1858** CARLYLE *Fredk. Gt.* VII. ix. (1872) II. 340 The first sweep of royal fury being past. **1872** MORLEY *Voltaire* i. (1886) 1 As if the work had been wholly done.. by the sweep of deep-lying, collective forces.

5. a. The action of driving or wielding a tool or weapon, swinging an arm, etc., so as to describe a circle or an arc.

1725 POPE *Odyss.* VII. 419 Justly tim'd with equal sweep they row. **1831** SCOTT *Cast. Dang.* iii, The sweep of a brown bill. **1849** JAMES *Woodman* iii, The woodman had pulled his axe from his belt, and with a full sweep of his arm struck a blow. **1850** TENNYSON *In Mem.* lxxxix, The sweep of scythe in morning dew. **1861** HUGHES *Tom Brown at Oxf.* vi, The long steady sweep of the so-called paddle tried him. **1890** R. BRIDGES *Windmill* ii, Its hurtling sails a mighty sweep Cut thro' the air.

b. *Cricket.* An attacking stroke made on the front foot, in which the batsman brings the bat across his body to hit the ball square or backward of square on the leg side.

1888 R. H. LYTTELTON in Steel & Lyttelton *Cricket* ii. 65 George Parr's leg hit.. was the sweep to long leg off a shortish ball. **1920** D. J. KNIGHT in P. F. Warner *Cricket* 35 The sweep to leg is a very paying and useful stroke, although not elegant. It is effected by sinking almost down on the right knee and sweeping the ball right round in the direction of long leg. **1955** *Times* 9 May 15/1 He had played some good drives and sweeps. **1970** *Times* 19 Aug. 6/5 Most of the Yorkshire batsmen were obsessed by that ugly and risky stroke, the sweep.

6. a. The action of moving in a continuous curve or a more or less circular path or track: said, e.g., of the movements of an army or a fleet, the turn of a river's course; †formerly also of the rotation or revolution of a body; *occas.* a single revolution.

1679 MOXON *Mech. Exerc.* ix. 166 A Door is said to Drag when.. the bottom edge of the Door rides (in its sweep) upon the Floor. **1680** *Ibid.* xiii. 220 (Turning Hard Wood) They lay their Tool flat and steddy upon the Rest; which being hard held in this position, does by the coming about of the Work, cut or tear off all the Extuberances the Tool touches in the sweep of the Work... For should it in one sweep of the Work be thrust nearer the Axis in any place, it would there take off more than it should. **1780** J. ADAMS in *Fam. Lett.* (1876) 386 The French and Spanish fleets have made a sweep of sixty upon the English East India and West India fleets. **1798** S. & HT. LEE *Canterb. T.* II. 441 Taking suddenly a bold sweep, the stream smoothed.. ere it discharged itself into the sea. **1821** CRAIG *Lect. Drawing*, etc. v. 284 The species of sweep, curve, or twist, which the branches take in diverging from the trunk. **1869** RANKINE *Machine & Hand-tools* Pl. D 5, The top of the jib, and consequently the forked hanger suspended from it.. make a sweep from side to side in front of the furnace. *a* **1900** S. CRANE *Gt. Battles* (1901) 15 The sweep of the Allies under Graham around the French right. **1914** *Times* 12 Sept. 8/3 When the enemy's sweep to the south-east of Paris was checked on the Grand Morin.

†**b.** The course (of a river). *Obs. rare.*

1596 LAMBARDE *Peramb. Kent* (ed. 2) 259 Neither of them standeth in the full sweepe, or right course, of those Riuers, but in a diuerticle, or by way.

c. *Gunnery.* The lateral movement of a gun in distributing fire over a given front.

1907 BETHELL *Mod. Guns & Gunnery* 172 If we multiply the front of the target in degrees by 10, this will give the outward deflection and sweep required in minutes.

d. *Electronics.* A steady movement across the screen of a cathode-ray tube of the spot produced by the electron beam; the moving spot itself, or the line it generates.

1924 *Wireless World* 5 Mar. 705/2 The approximate form of transient phenomena may also be indicated, if the frequency is low enough to enable a single sweep of the ray across the screen to be seen. **1946** *Radar: Summary Rep. & Harp Project* (U.S. Nat. Defense Res. Comm., Div. 14) 144/1 By making this motion rapid and continuous, the point of light becomes a line of light, and is called a sweep. **1958** *New Scientist* 10 Apr. 17/2 A ray of greenish-blue light —the sweep—pivots on the centre of the tube like the spokes of a wheel. **1966** M. WOODHOUSE *Tree Frog* xxi. 154 The bright scanning sweep swung around the orange tube face of the monitor like the seconds' hand of a stop-watch. **1975** G. J. KING *Audio Handbk.* v. 114 The oscilloscope's time-base is switched off and the horizontal sweep provided by high-level signal from the audio oscillator.

e. *Electronics.* A steady, usu. repeated, change in the magnitude or frequency of a voltage or other quantity between definite limits.

1930 *Proc. IRE* XVIII. 590 A single sweep, exposing each tone about 1/150th of a second was found sufficient to give a useful record. **1966** *McGraw-Hill Encycl. Sci. & Technol.* XIII. 336/1 Hyperbolic sweeps may be generated as a modification of the type of circuitry used in the generation of saw-tooth sweep waveforms. **1975** D. G. FINK *Electronics Engineers' Handbk.* XVI. 29 Circuits delivering a linear voltage sweep fall into two categories, the Miller time base and bootstrap time base.

7. *Astr.* A term used by Sir William Herschel to denote a method of surveying the heavens in sections (see quots. and cf. SWEEP *v.* 21); also, one of such sections of observation. Rarely *gen.* the survey of an extensive region.

1784 SIR W. HERSCHEL *Sci. Papers* (1912) I. 165 It occurred to me that the intermediate spaces between the sweeps might also contain nebulæ. **1786** *Ibid.* 261 The instrument was.. either lowered or raised about 8 or 10 minutes, and another oscillation was then performed like the first. Thus I continued generally for about 10, 20, or 30 oscillations,.. and the whole of it was then called a Sweep. **1841** MYERS *Cath. Th.* III. §45. 172 A rich apparatus fitted alike for the wide sweep of celestial scenery, and the strictest scrutiny of a terrestrial atom. **1867** G. F. CHAMBERS *Astron.* (1876) 920 *Sweep, sweeping*, terms introduced by Sir W. Herschel to describe his practice of surveying the heavens by clamping his telescope in successive parallels of declination, and allowing during a series of equal intervals of time, portions of the sky to pass under view by diurnal motion.

8. a. An act of sweeping with a broom.

Also with advs.: e.g. ***to give a room a good sweep, sweep-out***, or ***sweep-up***.

1818 SCOTT *Br. Lamm.* xv, When his [*sc.* a spider's] whole web.. is destroyed by the chance sweep of a broom. **1908** *Contemp. Rev.* Feb. 155, I have known outdoor paupers who.. would let their rooms go for the month without ever a single 'sweep-up'.

b. *fig.* A comprehensive search, esp. in relation to crime investigation; *spec.* a search for electronic listening devices. *colloq.* (orig. *U.S.*).

1966 *Wall St. Jrnl.* 17 Feb. 1/4 In Burns' 'sweeps'.. specialists check furniture, light switches, air vents, drapes, rugs, telephones, pictures and walls with.. detection gear. **1973** *Times* 18 June 2/7 One of the largest British-based international companies recently employed a security firm to conduct 30 anti-bugging 'sweeps' on its premises every month. **1974** *Union* (S. Carolina) *Daily Times* 20 Apr. 1/7 Police mounted a room-by-room sweep of hotels.. in search of Dantzler. **1978** J. GARDNER *Dancing Dodo* xiii. 93 '*Overshoot?*' Dobson queried reflectively... 'Will you do a sweep of the files?'

9. The action of a garment, etc. brushing, or of the hand or an instrument passing in continuous movement, along or over a surface.

1820 SHELLEY *Sensit. Pl.* II. 27 Wherever her aëry footstep trod, Her trailing hair from the grassy sod Erased its light vestige, with shadowy sweep. **1855** BROWNING *Fra Lippo* 52 A sweep of lute-strings. **1856** MISS WARNER *Hills Shatemuc* xl, The old man's brush made long sweeps back and forward over the shining gunwale. **1863** GEO. ELIOT *Romola* xliii, The tramp of footsteps, and the faint sweep of woollen garments. **1893** J. A. HODGES *Elem. Photogr.* (1907) 59 The developer is now poured, with a gentle sweep, over the plate.

10. *Cards.* **a.** In the game of casino, a pairing or combining all the cards on the board, resulting in the removal of all of them. **b.** In whist, the winning of all the tricks in a hand; a slam.

1814 *Hoyle's Games Improved* 161 (*Cassino*) Do not neglect sweeping the board when opportunity offers; always prefer taking up the card laid down by the opponent, also as many as possible with one; endeavouring likewise to win the last cards or final sweep. **1879** in WEBSTER Suppl.

11. *Physics.* A process of settling, or tending to settle, into thermal equilibrium.

1903 W. S. FRANKLIN in *Science* 20 Nov. 647/2 The settling of a closed system to thermal equilibrium is called a *simple sweep*.

II. Range, extent.

12. Compass, reach, or range of movement, esp. in a circular or curving course.

1679 MOXON *Mech. Exerc.* ix. 159 If the Boards of the Floor chance to swell within the sweep of the Door. **1680** *Ibid.* x. 184 The Sweep of the Treddle being so small. **1748** *Anson's Voy.* II. xi. 251 The whole sweep of our squadron, within which nothing could pass undiscovered, was at least twenty-four leagues in extent. **1779** J. MOORE *View Soc. Fr.* (1789) I. xix. 154 All within one sweep of the eye. **1853** KANE *Grinnell Exp.* v. (1856) 38 In our wake, and just outside the sweep of our oars. **1861** CRAIK *Hist. Eng. Lit.* II. 158 From the minutest disclosures of the microscope to beyond the farthest sweep of the telescope. **1878** CONDER *Tentwork Pal.* I. viii. 242 Huge camels, loaded with fire-wood, come rolling by, and oblige you to crouch against the wall to avoid the sweep of the load. **1886** *Field* 20 Mar. 353/1 The fishermen waiting till they see a salmon show within the sweep of the net.

13. a. Extent of ground, water, etc.; an extent, stretch, or expanse, such as can be taken in at one survey or is included in a wide-spreading curve.

1767 JAGO *Edge-hill* II. 92 The Lawns, With spacious Sweep, and wild Declivity. **1791** W. GILPIN *Forest Scenery* II. 49 It's woody scenes, it's extended lawns, and vast sweeps of wild country. **1842** TENNYSON *Audley Crt.* 12 By many a sweep Of meadow smooth from aftermath. **1856** STANLEY *Sinai & Pal.* ii. 128 The whole sweep of mountains which enclose the western plains of Asia. **1871** L. STEPHEN *Playgr. Eur.* (1894) v. 131 So noble and varied a sweep of glacier is visible nowhere else in the Alps. **1885** RIDER HAGGARD *K. Solomon's Mines* (1889) 35 A lovely coast.. with its red sand-hills and wide sweeps of vivid green. **1906** SIR F. TREVES *Highways Dorset* xii. 192 A long sickle-shaped sweep of fawn-coloured sand.

b. A series (of buildings); †a suite (of rooms).

1751 SMOLLETT *Per. Pickle* cv, The rooms were every way suitable,.. and our hero imagined they had made a tour through the whole sweep, [etc.]. **1772** T. NUGENT tr. *Grosley's Tour Lond.* I. 348 The apartment of the first story, consisting of a sweep of seven chambers. **1858** HAWTHORNE *Fr. & It. Note-bks.* (1872) I. 42 A sweep of shops.. and all manner of open-air dealers.

14. Extent or range of thought, observation, experience, influence, power, etc.

1781 COWPER *Table-T.* 474 Tyranny sends the chain, that must abridge The noble sweep of all their privilege. **1839** HALLAM *Lit. Eur.* III. vi. §87 He wanted that large sweep of reflection and experience which is required for the greater diversity of the other sex. **1855** *Edin. Rev.* July 296 The extensive sweep of these four great principles did not escape the penetration of Russia. **1874** GREEN *Short Hist.* viii. §5. 501 London.. was brought within the sweep of Royal extortion. **1877** C. GEIKIE *Christ* i. I. 5 [Christ] threw down the wall of separation, and consecrated the whole sweep of existence.

15. *Aeronaut.* = *sweepback* s.v. SWEEP- 3.

1914 *Aeroplane* 26 Mar. 358/2 (*caption*) Plan view of the Grahame-White biplane, showing sweep of wings. **1947** *Aircraft Engin.* June 180/2 As can be seen .. the sweep is 38° .. for the main plane and rather less for the tail plane. **1976** *Farnborough Internat. Exhibition* (Official Programme) 41 Studies indicate that, by adjusting the angle of sweep, fuel consumption .. can be materially reduced.

III. A curve or curved object, etc.

16. a. A curved line or form; a curve; also, curvature.

1715 DESAGULIERS *Fires Impr.* 85 The Model, by means of which the Workman may give Chimneys that Sweep or Curvature which they ought to have. **1731** W. HALFPENNY *Perspective* 27 Take OC, strike a sweep towards B; from B, draw a Line to I. **1739** S. SHARP *Treat. Surgery* x. 51 Having made one Incision .. a little circularly, begin a second in the same Point as the first, bringing it with an opposite Sweep to meet the other. **1804** C. B. BROWN tr. *Volney's View Soil U.S.* 91 An extensive meadow, through which the St. Laurence flows, in three sweeps or bends. **1825** J. NICHOLSON *Oper. Mech.* 637 Glass can be bent to circular sweeps. **1855** *Orr's Circ. Sci., Inorg. Nat.* 150 A soft rock .. has been scooped out into sweeps and rounded surfaces. **1881** YOUNG *Ev. Man his own Mechanic* §38 It admits of being bent almost double without snapping and on that account it is well adapted to be used for curved work if the sweep be not too small.

b. The continuously curved part of an arch.

1685 DRYDEN *Albion & Albanus* Frontispiece c j, On the sweep of the Arch lies one of the Muses. **1721** BAILEY, *Key-Stone* .. is the middle Stone of an Arch, to bind the Sweeps of the Arch together. **1835** J. GREENWOOD *Tour Thornton Abbey* 36 A pointed window of three lights, with perpendicular tracery in the sweep.

†**c.** *Shipbuilding.* An arc or curved line used in a plan to indicate the shape of the timbers; the curve of a ship's timbers. *Obs.*

1627 CAPT. J. SMITH *Sea. Gram.* ii. 3 Those ground timbers doe giue the floore of the ship, being straight, sauing at the ends they begin to compasse, and there they are called the Rungheads, and doth direct the Sweepe or Mould of the Foot-hookes and Nauell timbers. *a* **1647** PETTE in *Archaeologia* XII. 248 The great platform, .. where all the lines of the midship bend were drawn .. with their centres, perpendiculars, and sweeps. **1664** BUSHNELL *Compl. Ship-Wright* 14 Here in this Draught I draw a Sweepe, or a piece of a Circle from the point G. *Ibid.* 15 Then make the Moulds by their Sweepes. **1704** J. HARRIS *Lex. Techn.* I. s.v., The Seamen call the Mold of a Ship when she begins to compass in at the Rungheads, the Sweep of her; or the Sweep of the Futtocks. **1797** *Encycl. Brit.* (ed. 3) XVII. 378/2 (*Shipbuilding*) A frame of timbers is commonly formed by arches of circles called sweeps. There are generally five sweeps, .. the floor sweep .. the lower breadth sweep .. the reconciling sweep .. the upper breadth sweep .. the top timber sweep.

d. A flowing line (of drapery, hair, the contour of a limb, etc.); also semi-*concr.*

1784 COWPER *Task* I. 352 Well-roll'd walks, With curvature of slow and easy sweep. **1818** SCOTT *Hrt. Midl.* x, That graceful and easy sweep of outline which at once indicates health and beautiful proportion of parts. **1823** —— *Quentin D.* xiii, The dark and downward sweep of his long-descending beard. **1858** KINGSLEY *Misc., My Winter-Garden* (1859) I. 153 See the depth of chest, the sweep of loin. **1868** HELPS *Realmah* viii. (1876) 214 She trails after her in the muddy streets an ample sweep of flowing drapery. **1890** *Atlantic Monthly* Mar. 353/2 Deep, wistful gray eyes, under a sweep of brown hair that fell across his forehead. **1894** CROCKETT *Raiders* v, Narrow tongues of fire and great sweeps of smoke drove to leeward.

e. A projecting contour or face of a wall, column, etc.

1726 LEONI *Alberti's Archit.* II. 20 The Sweeps are two, one at the top and the other at the bottom of the Column, and are called Sweeps upon account of their running out a little beyond the rest of the Shaft. **1731** *Gentl. Mag.* Nov. 488/1 The Descent formerly craggy .. is now firm, .. by 17 Traverses, the Sweeps and Angles wall'd with Stones. **1816** J. SMITH *Panorama Sci. & Art* I. 146 The shafts do not in this style generally stand free, but are parts of the sweep of mouldings.

f. *Forestry.* The natural curve of a tree or log of wood.

1932 CHAPMAN & DEMERITT *Elem. Forest Mensuration* xi. 179 The extent of the actual loss of boards by reason of crook or sweep depends on the minimum length of a merchantable board. **1946** *Q. Jrnl. Forestry* XL. 52 Many of the trees had a severe 'sweep' which resulted in the very poor output of suitable telegraph pole material. **1957** *Brit. Commonw. Forest Terminol.* II. 192 *Sweep*, the natural bend of a log, generally applied to long gentle bends.

17. Concrete uses.

a. A curved mass of building or masonry.

1766 ENTICK *London* IV. 414 The pillars are terminated to the east by a sweep, .. in a kind of semicircle. **1825** J. NICHOLSON *Oper. Mech.* 87 A curved wall or sweep of masonry, which is made concentric with the wheel. **1859** DICKENS *Tale Two Cities* II. ix, Two stone sweeps of staircase meeting in a stone terrace before the principal door.

b. 'A semicircular plank fixed up under the beams near the fore-end of the tiller, which it supports' (*Rudim. Navig.* c 1850); a similar support on which a gun travels.

1756 *Gentl. Mag.* Jan. 15/1 The tiller .. having born so hard upon the sweep as almost to have worn it through. **1837** *Civil Engin. & Arch. Jrnl.* I. 28/1 Her armament .. consists of 14 long 32-pounders, and two 84-pounders on circular sweeps.

c. A curved carriage drive leading to a house.

1797 JANE AUSTEN *Sense & Sens.* III. xiv. (1811) 326 They could superintend the progress of the parsonage .. could choose papers, project shrubberies, and invent a sweep. **1838** LYTTON *Alice* I. ix, The narrow sweep that conducted from the lodge to the house. **1897** STEVENSON *St. Ives* xii, The lane twisted .. and showed me a gate and the beginning of a gravel sweep.

d. In pattern-making, a short segment of a circle used in making a ring, being shifted round on its centre several times in succession until the ring is completed.

1885 [HORNER] *Pattern Making* 82 The sweep, with its bosses and prints, is rammed up in sand level with its top face, and withdrawn. It is then carried round exactly one-sixth of its circumference and its right-hand print and boss is dropping into the impression just made by its left-hand print and boss. There the sweep is again rammed up, to be again withdrawn and removed, until the ring, with its six bosses and six prints is completed.

IV. That which is swept up.

†**18.** The crop of hay raised from a meadow. *Obs. local.*

1672 MANLEY *Cowell's Interpr., Swepage*, is the Crop of Hay got in a Meadow, called also *The swepe* in some parts of England [referring to Coke *On Litt.* fol. 4: see SWEEPAGE 2.]

19. *coll. sing.* or *pl.* The sweepings of gold and silver dust from the workshops of goldsmiths, silversmiths, etc.

a **1771** H. PEMBERTON *Course Chem.* 282 Our refiners have an operation something similar to this, which they call melting their sweep. **1778** PRYCE *Min. Cornub.* 246 The inhabitants of Africa .. dress their Gold-dust in small bowls, after the manner that Gold-smiths wash their sweeps. **1852** *Househ. Words* V. 275/2 A lot of 'good handy sweeps'! **1884** in *Standard* 4 Jan. 2/5 They were blockers, and had to remove the gold waste from the books .. that were being gilt. That was called 'sweep'.

20. = SWEEPSTAKE 3.

1849 *Bentley's Misc.* XXVI. 573 The public-house wherein the 'sweep' is got up so philanthropically. **1888** KIPLING *Departm. Ditties, Maxims of Hafiz* xii, The gold that we spend On a Derby Sweep.

21. That which is swept up, in, along, etc.

1838 JAMES *Robber* vi, He thought it would be a good sweep for us all, if we could get the bags. **1873** TRISTRAM *Moab* xi. 196 The sweep of sediment which comes down with the floods. **1893** *Daily News* 25 Dec. 2/1 This gathering is not a mere sweep in from the streets.

22. = ALMOND-FURNACE.

After G. *gekrätzofen*, lit. sweepings-furnace.

1706 PHILLIPS (ed. Kersey). **1728** CHAMBERS *Cycl.*, The *Almond-Furnace*, called also the Sweep, is usually six Foot high, four wide, and two thick.

V. Apparatus that sweeps or has a sweeping motion.

†**23.** A broom or mop: in *oven-swepe*. *Obs.*

c **1475** *Promp. Parv.* (Phillipps MS.) 323/2 Ouen swepe, *dossorium, tersorium.*

24. An apparatus for drawing water from a well, consisting of a long pole attached to an upright which serves as a fulcrum; hence, a pump-handle.

1548 ELYOT, *Telo*, .. a great poste and high is set faste, then ouer it cometh a longe beame, whiche renneth on a pynne, so that the one ende hauyng more poyse then the other, causeth the lighter ende to rise; with suche beere brewers in London dooe drawe vp water, thei call it a sweepe. **1598** FLORIO, *Toleone, Tolleone*, an engine to draw vp water, called a sweepe. **1660** R. D'ACRES *Water-drawing* II. i. 11 Those that are moved to and fro, men cannot so well command with that free and full strength, as they may the perpendicular sweaps which move up and down. **1747** HOOSON *Miner's Dict.* Q ij, Those common Pumps used in the Mines, such as Raggs, Churns, Sweaps, Forces. **1825** J. NICHOLSON *Oper. Mech.* 105 Mr. Smeaton always used such sweeps, .. it is certainly preferable to any intricate work in the form of the buckets. **1896** HOWELLS *Impressions & Exp.* 257 The boatmen smoked on the gunwales or indolently plied the long sweeps of their pumps. **1913** *Blackw. Mag.* Sept. 324/1 Wells with the old-fashioned 'sweep'.

†**25.** A ballista. *Obs.* (exc. *Her.*).

1598 FLORIO, *Telone*, an instrument of warre like that which brewers vse with a crosse beame to drawe water, it is called a sweepe. **1661** MORGAN *Sph. Gentry* II. viii. 104 Argent a Sweep azure, charged with a Stone Or, [borne] by the name of Magnall. [**1892** WOODWARD & BURNETT *Her.* 365.]

26. Applied to various kinds of levers, or to a long bar which is swept round so as to turn a shaft.

1657 R. LIGON *Barbadoes* (1673) 89 The Horses and Cattle being put to their tackle, they go about, and by their force turne (by the sweeps) the middle roller. **1688** HOLME *Armoury* III. xxi. (Roxb.) 267/1 The Sweep and String, is the moveing beame .. which hanging by the middle .. so that drawing the end down, by the tackle; the other end riseth, and with it string draws vp the Leaded Hammer. **1763** *Museum Rust.* I. lxi. 259 F, is the sweep, whereby the cutter plays up and down when in use. **1799** A. YOUNG *Agric. Linc.* 152 Two sweeps annexed to the wheels, and going the circle with them. **1875** KNIGHT *Dict. Mech., Sweep* .. the lever of a horse-power or pug-mill. **1884** C. T. DAVIS *Manuf. Bricks*, etc. v. (1889) 144 Broad, curved pieces of iron, called sweeps, pressers, or pushers, .. their use is to force the tempered clay through an opening near the bottom, in the side of the cylinder or box inclosing the pug-mill.

27. A sail of a windmill. Also *occas.* a paddle of a water-wheel.

1702 W. J. *Bruyn's Voy. Levant* xxxii. 124 Several Wind-Mills .. The Sweeps whereof are more Numerous than ours are. **1731** *Gentl. Mag.* I. 221/2 As Mr. Richards .. was viewing a Windmill by Bow the Sweeps turning of a sudden dash'd out his Brains. **1741** J. TAYLOR *Patent Specif.* No. 576 Every one of these sweeps is a thin board or plate of such wedth and depth as fit the wedth and depth of the box exactly. **1836** *Boston* etc. *Herald* 12 Apr. 2/5 Miss P. incautiously ventured out on the platform or gallery, and received two violent blows from the sweeps of the mill. **1923** H. BELLOC *Sonnets & Verse* III. 119 The sweeps have fallen from Ha'nacker Mill. **1968** J. ARNOLD *Shell Bk. Country Crafts* 170 The original form of sweep consisted of a light framework mounted on each stock, or sail-arm, over which a canvas sail was set or furled according to the wind.

28. A long oar used to propel a ship, barge, etc. when becalmed, or to assist the work of steering.

1800 *Asiat. Ann. Reg., Misc. Tr.* 223/1 These vessels should .. be so constructed as to be rowed by sweeps (or large oars) in calm weather. **1833** M. SCOTT *Tom Cringle* xv. (1842) 377 The wind died away altogether—and 'out sweeps' was the word. **1890** HOSIE *Three Yrs. W. China* 68 Our craft, guided by stern and bow sweeps, dashed four and five feet at a bound. **1892** W. PIKE *North. Canada* 6 The boats are steered with a huge sweep passed through a ring in the stern post. **1894** C. N. ROBINSON *Brit. Fleet* 204 Sweeps, or long pulling oars .. were also furnished to every vessel.

29. A plate, frame, or the like for sweeping off, up (etc.), grain, soil, etc.

1825 J. NICHOLSON *Oper. Mech.* 449 The sweep, making part of the inner rake, occasionally let down for sweeping off all the seed.

30. A length of cable used for sweeping the bottom of the sea, in mine-laying, mine-sweeping, etc.

1775 FALCK *Day's Diving Vessel* 49 When a cable .. is used in its full length, without making it into any particular form, it is generally called in this operation a sweep. **1904** *Daily Chron.* 30 Nov. 8/1 The 'sweep,' which consists of a surface line 20 fathoms, or 120 feet long, carrying under-water charges of guncotton. **1915** *Chambers's Jrnl.* June 387/2 Those six small gray ships will return with .. a fearsome tale of many mines caught in their sweeps and destroyed. **1923** *Man. Seamanship* (Admiralty) II. 172 The vessel .. puts the end of the sweep on a slip somewhere on her quarter-deck. **1943** *His Majesty's Minesweepers* (Min. of Information) 8/1 The thud of the explosion as a mine, caught in a sweep, detonated under a trawler's counter.

31. An instrument used for drawing curves at a large radius, a beam-compass. Also, a profile tool for cutting mouldings in wood or metal in a lathe.

1680 MOXON *Mech. Exerc.* xiii. 226, I placed the Center-point of the Sweep in a Center-hole made in a square Stud of Mettal... I provided a strong Iron Bar for the Beam of a Sweep. **1711** W. SUTHERLAND *Shipbuild. Assist.* 77 The instruments which we term Sweeps, to mark out the Curves that compose the Body. **1847** HALLIWELL, *Sweep*... (3) An instrument used by turners for making mouldings in wood or metal.

32. *Founding.* A movable templet used in loam-moulding, a striking-board.

1864 in WEBSTER.

VI. One who sweeps (and derived senses).

33. a. A chimney-sweeper.

Prob. taken from the chimney-sweeper's street cry 'Sweep!' as CHIMNEY-SWEEP (1614 Chapman in Chris. Brooke's *Poems*, ed. Grosart, 50) was from the earlier cry 'Chimney sweep!' See also *sweep-chimney* (s.v. SWEEP- 2) and SWEEPY *sb.*

1812 H. & J. SMITH *Rej. Addr., Archit. Atoms*, A mingled noise of dustmen, milk, and sweeps. **1827** HOOD *Bianca's Dream* 108 In skin as sooty as a sweep. **1861** E. T. HOLLAND in *Peaks, Passes, & Glaciers* Ser. II. I. 91 The small black particles filled our eyes, .. and our faces soon became almost as black as sweeps.

Phr. **1842** LOVER *Handy Andy* i. 8 That peculiar pace which is elegantly called a sweep's trot. **1878** WALSHAM *Surg. Pathol.* xiii. 369 From the great frequency with which it occurs in chimney-sweepers, cancer of the scrotum is generally designated the soot- or sweep's-cancer.

b. *the Sweeps*: a nickname for the Rifle Brigade.

1879 *All Year Round* 5 Apr. 371/2 The Sweeps and the Jollies—the active and intrepid lads of the Rifle Brigade and the Marine Light Infantry. **1888** *Nicknames in Army* 112 Rifle Brigade.—'The Sweeps,' from its dark coloured uniform and facings.

c. A disreputable person; a scamp, blackguard. *slang* and *dial.*

1853 *Househ. Words* VIII. 75/2 A low person is a snob, a sweep, and a scurf. **1888** W. E. NORRIS *Chris* vi, Fancy making up to a drunken sweep like that just because he has a few thousands a year! **1903** FARMER & HENLEY *Slang, Sweep* .. A term of contempt: *e.g.* 'What a sweep the man is'; 'You dirty sweep'.

d. Name for two Australasian marine fishes, *Scorpis æquipennis* and *Incisidens simplex*.

1840 F. D. BENNETT *Whaling Voy.* I. 23 They were chiefly of the kinds known as 'rock-cod', 'snappers', or gilt-heads, 'sweeps', and 'rudder-fish', or scad. **1883** E. P. RAMSAY *Food Fishes N.S. Wales* 12 (Fish. Exhib. Publ.) The 'sweep,' *Scorpus æquipinnis*, is the only fish of this family that is used with us as an article of food.

34. a. A crossing-sweeper. **b.** *U.S.* A servant who looks after university students' rooms. Chiefly at Yale University. ? *Obs.*

1858 SIMMONDS *Dict. Trade, Sweep*, a crossing-sweeper. **1900** *Dialect Notes* II. 65 *Sweep, n.*, a care-taker of college rooms at Yale, where negro boys are employed. **1950** *Harvard Alumni Bull.* 22 Apr. 590/3 In early times, sweeper was in use instead of goody, and even now at Yale College the word sweep is retained.

VII. 35. *attrib.* and *Comb.*, as (sense 6 d, e) ***sweep amplifier***, ***generator***, ***oscillator***, ***voltage***; (in sense 17 c) ***sweep-gate***; (in sense 19) ***sweep-smelter***, ***-washer***, ***-washings***; (sense 20) ***sweep-ticket***; (in sense 34) ***sweep-boy***; **sweep-head**, the upper end or handle of a large oar (sense 28); **sweep-swinger** *U.S.*, an oarsman in a racing boat. (See also SWEEP-.)

1947 R. LEE *Electronic Transformers & Circuits* i. 4 Make efficient transformers for the non-sinusoidal wave shapes such as are encountered in pulse, video, and *sweep amplifiers. **1818** MAGINN in *Blackw. Mag.* III. 53 I'd rather see a *sweep-boy suck a penny roll, Than listen to a criticising woman. **1798** JANE AUSTEN *Northang. Abb.* xxix, To have it [*sc.* a post-chaise] stop at the *sweep-gate was a sight to brighten every eye. **1847** MRS. GORE *Castles in Air* xxv. II. 305 On approaching the sweep-gates of the villa. **1946** *Radar: Summary Rep. & Harp Project* (U.S. Nat. Defense Res. Comm., Div. 14) 144/1 **Sweep circuit* or *generator*, a circuit which produces at regular intervals an approximately linear or circular, or other form of movement (sweep) of the beam of the cathode-ray tube. **1975** D. G. FINK *Electronics Engineers' Handbk.* XVI. 29 Sweep generators may also be looked upon as integrators with a constant-amplitude input signal. **1881** KIPLING *Departm. Ditties, Galley-Slave* ii, We gripped the kicking *sweep-head and we made that galley go. **1939** H. J. REICH *Theory & Application Electron Tubes* xv. 596 Practical *sweep oscillators do not furnish a voltage that satisfies the requirements for a perfect sweep voltage. **1967** *Electronics* 6 Mar. 2 (Advt.), All solid-state Hewlett-Packard 3211A sweep oscillators..meet virtually all of your swept frequency testing requirements. **1949** *N.Y. Times* 12 June 48/4 Hundreds of *sweepswingers are sweating it out..on Connecticut's Thames River. **1971** L. KOPPETT *N.Y. Times Guide Spectator Sports* xviii. 234 A crewman is a 'sweepswinger'. **1930** *Daily Express* 23 May 3/4 Who sent out the Mayfair Luncheon Club's £20,000 *sweep tickets? **1934** J. H. REYNER *Television* vii. 78 The spot can be shifted horizontally or vertically, as required, irrespective of the *sweep or work voltages. **1962** SIMPSON & RICHARDS *Physical Princ. Junction Transistors* xvii. 443 The simplest sweep voltage is obtained by suddenly applying a d.c. voltage *V* to a resistor *R* and a capacitor *C* in series and taking the voltage across the capacitor as the output. **1815** J. T. SMITH *Anc. Topog. Lond.* 20 The *Sweepwasher is a person who buys the sweepings of the floors of the working gold and silver smith and also the water in which the workmen wash their hands. **1833** in R. Ellis *Customs* (1840) IV. 154 Sweep-washer's dirt may be landed and delivered without entry, on due examination. **1839** URE *Dict. Arts* 1225 *Sweep-washer*, is the person who extracts from the sweepings, potsherds, etc., of refineries of silver and gold, the small residuum of precious metal. **1875** KNIGHT *Dict. Mech.*, **Sweep-washings*, the refuse of shops in which gold and silver are worked.

sweep (swiːp), *v.* Forms: 4–6 **swepe**, 4–7 **sweepe**, 5 **swep**, 6 **sweppe**, **swyp(e**, *Sc.* **sweip**, 6–7, 9 *dial.* **swip(e**, 6– **sweep**. *Pa. t.* 4 **swepid**, **sueped**, **swepte**, 5 **sweppit**, 7 **sweeped**, 6– **swept**. *Pa. pple.* 4 **sweped**, **sueped**, **-et**, **iswepid**, **squepid**, 5 **swyped**, 6–8 **sweeped**, 7 **sweept**, 7–8 **sweep'd**; 5 **yswepped**, 5–6 **swepte**, 6– **swept** (9 *dial.* **swep'**, *Sc.* **sweepit**); *str.* 5 **yswepe**, **sweppene**. [ME. *swepe* (taking the place of the original SWOPE, OE. *swápan*, *swéop*, *swápen*), first recorded from northern texts; of uncertain origin. Two suggestions of source have been made, both of which involve phonological difficulties. (1) The mutated stem *swǽp-* (cf. *ȝeswǽpa* beside *-ȝeswáp* sweepings, *ymbswǽpe* 'ambages'). This would normally have produced a mod.Eng. **sweap*, but in its transference from the northern to the southern area, *swepe* may have been assimilated to words like *slepe* (OE. Anglian *slépan*) to SLEEP, or *crepe* (OE. *créopan*) to CREEP, the process being perhaps assisted by the pa. t. *swep-e* (OE. *swéop*) of the original strong verb. (2) ON. *svipa* to move swiftly and suddenly. This etymology involves the assumption that ON. *ĭ* became ME. *ē*, which is not otherwise clearly authenticated, and that the intransitive sense (22) is the original.

The shortening of the stem-vowel in pa. t. and pa. pple. is shown in spellings *c* 1400.

The order of sense-development presents difficulties, it being uncertain whether the transitive or intransitive meanings are the primary ones. The present arrangement of the word is adopted as convenient from the modern point of view, since the whole word is now coloured by the meaning 'cleanse or remove with a broom'.]

I. Senses with that which is removed or moved along as the object, and derived uses.

1. a. *trans.* To remove, clear *away*, *off* (etc.) with a broom or brush, or in a similar way by friction upon a surface; to brush away or off.

a **1300** *Cursor M.* 26672 (Cott.), I haue mi hert soght ilk a delle, And sueped [*Fairf.* squepid out] wel þat was þar-in. [After *Psalm* lxxvii. 6; cf. quot. *a* 1300 in sense 13.] **1382** WYCLIF *Isa.* xiv. 23, I shal destroȝe Babyloynes name..I shal sweepen it in a besme. **1552** HULOET, Swepe away, *euerro*. **1560** DAUS tr. *Sleidane's Comm.* 158 Certen Cardinalles standing about him, whiche with foxes tayles tied to staues lyke besomes, sweepe all thinges vpsyde downe. **1579** in *Archaeologia* LXIV. 357 For swipping and bearing rubbitch out of the hous. **1590** SHAKS. *Mids. N.* v. i. 397, I am sent with broome before, To sweep the dust behinde the doore. **1650** W. D. tr. *Comenius' Gate Lat. Unl.* §582 Sweepings and scraps are swept away with besoms. **1746** FRANCIS tr. *Hor., Sat.* II. viii. 15 Another sweeps the fragments of the feast. **1866** GEO. ELIOT *F. Holt* i, The old lodge-keeper..was wanted at the Court to sweep away the leaves. **1902** R. BAGOT *Donna Diana* xiii. 139 Leaving his housekeeper to clear away the empty plates and dishes and sweep the breadcrumbs off the wine-stained table cloth.

b. *Curling.* = SOOP *v.*[3] Also *absol.*

1811 *Acc. Game Curling* 44 A player may sweep his own stone the whole length of the rink; his party not to sweep until it has passed the hog-score at the farther end. **1910** *Encycl. Brit.* VII. 647 (*Curling*), No party except when sweeping according to rule, shall go upon the middle of the rink, or cross it.

2. a. To cut *down* or *off* with a vigorous swinging stroke. Now *rare* or *Obs.*

? *a* **1400** *Morte Arth.* 2508 Now ferkes to þe fyrthe thees fresche mene of armes..In the myste mornynge one a mede falles,..In swathes sweppene downe, fulle of swete floures. *c* **1440** CAPGRAVE *Life St. Kath.* v. 1572 Thi owen wyues heed of þou dede sweepe. **1823** SCOTT *Quentin D.* vi, I would rather you swept my head off with your long sword; it would better become my birth, than to die by the hands of such a foul churl. **1840** THACKERAY *Catherine* viii, The reapers sweeping down the brown corn.

b. *Cricket.* To hit (the ball) with a sweep (sense 5 b). Also *absol.* or *intr.*, to play a sweep.

1920 [see SWEEP *sb.* 5 b]. **1958** D. BRADMAN *Art of Cricket* 80 An inviting half-volley comes along... The greater scoring medium would be to sweep it fine. **1963** *Times* 19 Feb. 4/2 He is a fine cutter and an enthusiastic sweeper. Today he swept only twice, lest the shot should get him into trouble, as it sometimes does. **1965** D. SILK *Attacking Cricket* iv. 60 The batsman must always try to sweep the ball along the ground. **1976** *Star* (Sheffield) 30 Nov., Fletcher eventually fell lbw sweeping at Eknath Solkar.

3. To remove with a forcible continuous action; to brush *off*, *away*, *aside*.

1577 B. GOOGE *Heresbach's Husb.* IV. (1586) 188 b, The mothes, if they appeare, must bee sweeped away. **1590** SHAKS. *Mids. N.* IV. i. 126 My hounds..their heads are hung With eares that sweepe away the morning dew. **1632** LITHGOW *Trav.* x. 469 The Gouernour caused Areta..to gather and swipe the Vermine vpon me. **1829** *Chapters Phys. Sci.* 449 The same diluvial agency..appears also to have swept off the superior strata from extensive tracts. **1857** MILLER *Elem. Chem., Org.* (1862) 17 The gases are to be swept out of the apparatus in the manner already described. **1865** KINGSLEY *Herew.* xxvii, Sweep the chessmen off the board. **1867** W. W. SMYTH *Coal & Coal-mining* 64 The upper part of the series..has been swept away by denudation. **1867** AUGUSTA WILSON *Vashti* xxviii, Leaning against the railing, she impatiently swept off the snowy lemon leaves. **1908** S. E. WHITE *Riverman* ix, Miss Bishop turned to the piano, sweeping aside her white draperies as she sat. *Ibid.* xvii, She swept aside the portières.

4. *transf.* chiefly with adv. or advb. phr.: To clear out, drive away, or carry off *from* a place or region, (as if) forcibly or by violence. Also *fig.*

1593 SHAKS. *3 Hen. VI*, v. vii. 13 Thus haue we swept Suspition from our Seate, And made our Footstoole of Security. **1605** —— *Macb.* III. i. 119 Though I could With bare-fac'd power sweepe him from my sight. **1613** —— *Hen. VIII*, v. iv. 13 Vnlesse we sweepe 'em from the dore with Cannons. **1645** GATAKER *God's Eye on Israel* 29 Who draw up whatsoever cometh to hand, with the hooke, and sweep all away hand over head, with their net. **1700** S. L. tr. *Fryke's Voy. E. Ind.* 67 Those that were still coming up..we swept down like a swarm of Bees, with our..Fire-arms. **1771** SMOLLETT *Humphry Cl.* 29 May, The tide of luxury has swept all the inhabitants from the open country. **1779** *Mirror* No. 36 ¶2 When Xerxes..saw all his troops ranged in order before him, he burst into tears at the thought, that ..they would be sweeped from the face of the earth. **1831** D. E. WILLIAMS *Life & Corr. Sir T. Lawrence* II. 257 A..storm..In its fury it had just swept away the pier at Ryde. **1835** LYTTON *Rienzi* II. i, Let us sweep, then, our past conference from our recollection. **1842** LOVER *Handy Andy* i. 13 Divil sweep you! **1855** PRESCOTT *Philip II*, I. vi. (1857) 106 The Moslems..butchered the inhabitants, or swept them off into hopeless slavery. **1906** ALICE WERNER *Natives Brit. Centr. Afr.* xii. 284 When the invaders retired, they..cultivated their gardens in the plains, but only to have their crops swept off by fresh raids.

5. Chiefly with *away*: To remove forcibly or as at one blow from its position or status, or out of existence; to do away with, destroy utterly.

1560 *Bible* (Genev.) Isa. xxviii. 17 The haile shal swepe away the vaine confidence. **1611** —— Jer. xlvi. 15 Why are thy valiant men swept away? **1632** SANDERSON *Serm.* 316 When He..sweepeth away religious Princes, wise Senatours, zealous Magistrates. **1643** HOWELL *Twelve Treat.* (1661) 238 The ragingst Plague that ever was in Spain ..happen'd of late years, which sweep'd away such a world of people. *a* **1720** SEWEL *Hist. Quakers* (1795) I. Pref. p. xvi, These God will leave to be trodden down and swept away by the Gentiles. **1726** POPE *Odyss.* XXIV. 134 Did the rage of stormy Neptune sweep Your lives at once, and whelm beneath the deep? **1833** LANDOR *Imag. Conv., P. Scipio Æmilianus*, etc. Wks. 1846 II. 246/2 In one Olympiad the three greatest men that ever appeared together were swept off. **1847** L. HUNT *Men, Women, & Bks.* II. viii. 158 The heart of man is constantly sweeping away the errors he gets into his brain. **1878** BOSW. SMITH *Carthage* 31 Long after Carthage and the Carthaginians had been swept away. **1878** DALE *Lect. Preach.* iii. 83 In the early part of the third chapter the last hopes of the Jews are swept away.

6. a. To carry or drive along with force; to carry *away* or *off* by driving before it, as a wind, tide, stream, etc.

1743 FRANCIS tr. *Hor., Odes* I. vii. 24 The south wind often ..Sweeps off the clouds. **1783** CRABBE *Village* I. 128 Till some fierce tide..Sweeps the low hut and all it holds away. **1813** BYRON *Giaour* 18 If at times a transient breeze..sweep one blossom from the trees. **1840** MARRYAT *Poor Jack* ix, The tide was sweeping us past. **1853** KINGSLEY *Hypatia* v, He was swept, along with the mob in which he had been fast wedged, through a dark low passage. **1879** FARRAR *St. Paul* v. xx. I. 360 They might find the bridges shattered and swept away by the sudden spates of rushing streams.

fig. **1867** PARKMAN *Jesuits N. Amer.* xx. (1875) 303 The fury of the minority swept all before it.

b. *to sweep off*: to drink off, swallow down quickly. *Obs.* or *dial.*

1706 E. WARD *Wooden World Diss.* (1708) 83 He sweeps off the lusheous Stuff [*sc.* lobscouse] as cleverly as a Dairy-Maid does her Butter. **1863** MRS. TOOGOOD *Yorksh. Dial.* (MS.) Take the pint and sweep it off.

c. *to sweep* (a person) *off his feet*: to affect with overwhelming enthusiasm, to infatuate. Also *transf.* Cf. *to carry* (a person) *off his feet* s.v. FOOT *sb.* 27.

1913 F. L. BARCLAY *Broken Halo* xiv. 151, I remember being swept completely off my feet when I first met Jim. **1937** W. R. INGE *Rustic Moralist* I. ii. 46, I do not approve of concentration camps, or of Jew-baiting, or of sabre-rattling. I only want to understand a movement which has swept a great nation off its feet. **1977** *Daily Mirror* 16 Mar. 13/5 Mr. Lipscombe's daughter Gillian was swept off her feet by De Roth.

7. a. To drive together or into a place by or as by sweeping; to gather or take *up*, esp. so as to allocate or consign to a place, object, or purpose.

1340 HAMPOLE *Pr. Consc.* 4947 Þan sal alle þe fire be sweped doune In-til helle. *c* **1386** CHAUCER *Can. Yeom. Prol. & T.* 385 The Mullok on an heepe sweped [*v.rr.* yswoped, iswepid, yswepped] was. **1538** ELYOT Addit., *Conuerro*,..to swepe to gether into one place. **1560** DAUS tr. *Sleidane's Comm.* 394 b, Oure aduersaries..destroyinge the wealthe of the Empire, swepe all into theyr owne coffers. **1570** FOXE *A. & M.* (ed. 2) II. 926/2 The Dominicke Friers..so had sweapt all the fatte to their own beardes, from the order of the Franciscanes, that all the almes came to theyr boxe. **1652** EARL MONM. tr. *Bentivoglio's Hist. Relat.* 63 The fire thereof was rather sweep'd up then quench'd by the twelve years Truce. *a* **1700** EVELYN *Diary* an. 1646 (1879) I. 279 As if Nature had here swept up the rubbish of the earth in the Alpes to forme and cleere the plaines of Lombardy. **1706** E. WARD *Wooden World Diss.* (1708) 68 He is sure to sweep fifty Pounds at least into his Pocket. **1861** READE *Cloister & H.* lxv, Her glorious eyes fringed with long thick silken eyelashes, that seemed made to sweep up sensitive hearts by the half dozen. **1871** FREEMAN *Norm. Conq.* IV. xvii. §2. 38 The heritage of many such being swept in a mass into the hands of some insatiable stranger. **1885** 'MRS. ALEXANDER' *Valerie's Fate* iii, Sybil swept her much-enduring instructress up to her room. **1900** *Times* 25 July 4/5 Any mass of weed or *débris* that comes down with the stream will be swept into the angle of one of these *sudd* traps. **1911** E. RUTHERFORD in *Encycl. Brit.* XXII. 794/1 If a sufficiently strong field is used, the ions are all swept to the electrodes before appreciable loss of their number can occur by recombination.

b. *fig.* To include in its scope; to extend to.

1692 R. L'ESTRANGE *Fables* lxxiii. 73 The Letter of the Law Sweeps All in such a Case, without Distinction of Persons. **1886** SIR J. PEARSON in *Law Rep. 32 Chanc. Div.* 47 The words of this clause sweep in, as far as I can see, every possible liability of the company.

8. a. To gather in or up, collect wholesale or at one stroke; esp. in phr. ***to sweep the stakes*** (cf. SWEEPSTAKE).

1635 SHIRLEY *Traitor* v. i, Death's a devouring gamester, And sweepes up all. **1672** DRYDEN *Conq. Granada, Heroique Plays* ad fin., I have already swept the stakes; and with the common good fortune of prosperous Gamesters, can be content to sit quietly. **1693** —— *Persius* III. 94 My Study was ..To shun Ames-Ace, that swept my Stakes away. **1705** tr. *Bosman's Guinea* 90 A Portuguese or Interloper..by selling cheap, sweeps a great part, if not all their Gold. **1732** POPE *Ep. Bathurst* 71 If the stakes he sweep. **1907** *Daily Chron.* 7 June 6/6 Sweepstakes are always swept by the man who does not want the money.

b. *U.S.* To win every event in (a series of sporting events, etc.), or to take each of the main places in (a contest or event).

[**1942** BERREY & VAN DEN BARK *Amer. Thes. Slang* §650/7 *Phlanx, sweep the event*, to win all of the main events in all three first places in a meet.] **1960** WENTWORTH & FLEXNER *Dict. Amer. Slang* 531/1 *Sweep ...v.t.*, to win a tournament without losing a game or contest. **1974** *Greenville* (S. Carolina) *News* 22 Apr. 15/1, I didn't think either team would sweep this series. **1979** *Tucson* (Arizona) *Citizen* 20 Sept. 8D/3 Montreal swept a double-header from New York, 3–1 and 4–1.

9. To carry or trail along in a stately manner, as a flowing garment.

1591 SHAKS. *1 Hen. VI*, III. iii. 6 Let frantike Talbot triumph for a while, And like a Peacock sweepe along his tayle. **1798** S. & HT. LEE *Canterb. T.* II. 90 The self-named heiress..swept her long mourning robes through the whole train of sycophants, to an upper seat in the room.

10. To move or draw (something) over and in contact with a surface.

1825 SCOTT *Talism.* xxvi, Again sweeping his fingers over the strings. **1894** BARING-GOULD *Kitty Alone* II. 141 He swept the brush vigorously about, so as to disperse over the floor any particles.

11. To move (something) *round* with force and rapidity, or over a wide extent; to take *off* (one's hat) with a sweep of the arm.

1845 J. COULTER *Adv. in Pacific* xiv. 217 He..ended the matter by sweeping round quickly our canoe, and capsized the other. **1867** THOMSON & TAIT *Nat. Phil.* I. I. §106 It is the case of a common spinning-top..sweeping its axis round in a cone whose axis is vertical. **1868** WHITMAN *Amer. Feuillage* Poems 92 The scout..ascends a knoll and sweeps his eye around. **1885** 'MRS. ALEXANDER' *At Bay* i, He swept off his hat in continental style.

12. *intr.* and *trans.* [f. SWEEP *sb.* 28.] To row, or to propel (a vessel), with sweeps or large oars. Also *intr.* of the vessel. ? *Obs.*

1799 H. DIGBY in *Naval Chron.* II. 342 The enemy.. preserved his distance by towing and sweeping to the Westward. **1804** W. CARR *ibid.* XII. 71 Obliged..to tow and sweep her out in a dead calm. **1839** MARRYAT *Phant. Ship* xxiii, They discovered a proa,..sweeping after them.

II. Senses with that over which something moves or is moved as the object.

13. a. *trans.* To pass a broom or brush over the surface of (something) so as to clear it of any small loose or adhering particles; to cleanse with a broom or brush (as a floor, room, or house of dust and small refuse, a path or street crossing of dirt, etc., or a chimney of soot). Also with *down*, *out*, *up*; and with *clean* as compl. Also (rarely, but cf. b) said of the broom.

a **1300** *E.E. Psalter* lxxvi. 7 [lxxvii. 6], I swepid mi gaste [orig. *scopebam spiritum meum*]. *c* **1325** *Gloss. W. de Bibbesw.* in Wright *Voc.* 157 Si le festes nette baler [*gloss* suepet klene]. *c* **1386** CHAUCER *Can. Yeom. Prol. & T.* 383 As vsage is, lat sweepe [*v.rr.* swepe, swope, swoope] the floor as swithe. *c* **1440** *R. Gloucester's Chron.* (Rolls) 6945 (MS. δ) On þe bar erþe yswepe [*v.rr.* yswope, iswope, clene swope]. *a* **1450** *Knt. de la Tour* viii. 11 To suepe and to kepe clene the chirche. **1483** CAXTON *G. de la Tour* cxxi. 169 Theyr chambres were..dayly made swyped clene. **1495** *Trevisa's Barth. De P.R.* XVII. clix. (W. de W.) T viij b/1 Therwyth houses ben swepte [*Bodl. MS.* iswope] & clensyd. **1534–5** *MS. Rawl. D.* 777 lf. 78 Sweppyng and makyng Clene the said walk. **1535** COVERDALE *Luke* xv. 8 She..swepeth the house, and seketh diligently, tyll she fynde it. **1573** TUSSER *Husb.* (1878) 123 Where chamber is sweeped, and wormwood is strowne. **1592** in *Essex Rev.* (1907) XVI. 162 He hadd seene a broome in his house swype the house without any hands. **1593** SHAKS. *2 Hen. VI*, IV. vii. 34, I am the Beesome that must sweepe the Court cleane of such filth as thou art. **1633** G. HERBERT *Temple, Elixer* v, Who sweeps a room, as for thy laws, Makes that and th' action fine. **1683** WILDING in *Collect.* (O.H.S.) I. 258 For sweeping my Chimney..00 00 04. *a* **1756** ELIZA HAYWOOD *New Present* (1771) 255 The steps ought to be swept down every day. **1775** *Lett. John Murray* (1901) 225 Be carefull to have the used Chimneys sweep'd once a month. **1841** THACKERAY *Gt. Hoggarty Diam.* xiii, The black man who swept the crossing. **1853** KINGSLEY *Hypatia* x, The attendants..came in to sweep out the lecture-rooms. *a* **1859** MACAULAY *Hist. Eng.* xxiii. (1861) V. 45 Charles Duncombe, who was born to carry parcels and to sweep down a countinghouse. **1885** 'MRS. ALEXANDER' *Valerie's Fate* ii, She..noticed..that her fire was bright, her hearth swept up, her lamp lighted.

b. *absol.* or *intr.*; also often said of the broom, esp. in prov. ***new brooms sweep clean***.

c **1340** *Nominale* (Skeat) 186 W[oman] with besome sweputh. *c* **1386** CHAUCER *Clerk's T.* 922 She gan the hous to dighte..Preyynge the chambreres..To hasten hem, and faste swepe and shake. **1495** *Coventry Leet Bk.* 565 That all persones þat haue shopes..shall swep & make clene wekely before theire shopes. **1562** [see SWEEPER 1]. **1579** W. WILKINSON *Confut. Fam. Love* 16b, The besome.. wherewith the woman swept. **1656** in *Nicholas Papers* (Camden) III. 261 There is reason to sweepe cleane where the venom sticks soe close. **1789** MRS. PIOZZI *Journ. France* II. 376 Nasty, ill-looked fellows come in one's room to sweep. **1809** MALKIN *Gil Blas* XI. ii. (Rtldg.) 395 New brooms, they say, sweep clean! **1865** H. KINGSLEY *Hillyars & Burtons* xxix, There was another forge established at the bottom of Church Street, and our business grew a little slack (for new brooms sweep clean). **1886** W. J. TUCKER *E. Europe* 353, I never allow my maid to go to that part of the room, but sweep and dust myself there.

c. *trans.* To do the chimney-sweeping for. *colloq.* or *vulgar*.

1848 THACKERAY *Van. Fair* lx, Mr. Chummy, the chimney-purifier, who had swep' the last three families.

d. *fig.* To examine (premises, telephone lines, etc.) for electronic listening or recording devices. *colloq.* (orig. *U.S.*).

1966 *Wall Street Jrnl.* 17 Feb. 1/4 The companies also are having their offices regularly 'swept'—checked by professional sleuths to find any hidden transmitters. **1968** [see SWEEPER 5 b]. **1970** K. BENTON *Sole Agent* xx. 210 This room's all right. It was 'swept' only a few weeks ago. **1979** J. BARNETT *Backfire is Hostile!* iii. 37 'How safely can we speak on this line?'..'The line is swept every fifteen minutes and it is very clean.'

14. a. To pass over the surface of (something) in the manner of a broom or brush; to move over and in contact with; to brush, rub like (or as with) a brush.

1500–20 DUNBAR *Poems* xiv. 73 Sic fowill tailis, to sweip the calsay clene. **1538** ELYOT Addit., *Atta*, is he that gothe so on the soles of his fete, that he swepeth the grounde, rather than walketh. **1582** STANYHURST *Æneis* I. (Arb.) 33 His neck and locks fal a sweeping Thee ground. **1638** JUNIUS *Paint. Ancients* 285 That garment is decently put on, Which doth not sweep the dust. **1697** DRYDEN *Virg. Georg.* III. 98 With her length of Tail she [*sc.* a cow] sweeps the Ground. **1770** GOLDSM. *Des. Vill.* 152 The long-remember'd beggar was his guest, Whose beard descending swept his aged breast. **1823** SCOTT *Quentin D.* xxxiii, The plume of feathers which he wore was so high, as if intended to sweep the roof of the hall.

b. *Ent.* To drag a net over the surface of (herbage, etc.) in order to catch insects. Cf. SWEEP-NET 2.

1826 KIRBY & SPENCE *Introd. Entomol.* IV. l. 517 For this last operation—sweeping the grass, &c.— ..you will find a net invented by Mr. Paul..a very useful implement. **1926** A. H. HAMM in J. J. Walker *Nat. Hist. Oxf. District* 263 *Hemerodromia precatoria* Fln. and *H. raptoria* Mg. have been captured by sweeping water plants in 'Mesopotamia'. **1977** RICHARDS & DAVIES *Imms's Gen. Textbk. Entomol.* (ed. 10) II. III. 1205 The adults are most often obtained by sweeping or shaking the vegetation.

†**15.** To wipe; *spec.* in *Falconry* of a hawk, to wipe (the beak), = SEW *v.*[3] *Obs.*

c **1532** DU WES *Introd. Fr.* in *Palsgr.* 950 To swepe the nose, *moucer*. *Ibid.* 956 To swepe, *torcher*. **1625** B. JONSON *Staple of N.* II. iii. 19 *stage direct.*, He sweepes his face. **1658** PHILLIPS s.v., A Hawk after she hath fed, is said to sweep, not wipe her beake.

16. *transf.* and *fig.* To clear *of* something by vigorous action compared to that of a broom; *spec.* to clear (a place) *of* enemies or a mob by firing amongst them.

to sweep the board (or †*table*): see BOARD *sb.* 5 c. ***to sweep the deck*** or (usu.) ***decks***: to clear the deck of a ship (as by artillery, or as a wave breaking over); also *fig.*

1627 DRAYTON *Agincourt* xlvi, First seauen Ships from Rochester are sent, The narrow Seas, of all the French to sweepe. **1678** MARVELL *Growth Popery* 54 The false Dice must at the long run Carry it, unless discovered; and when it comes once to a great Stake, will Infallibly Sweep the Table. **1748** *Anson's Voy.* III. viii. 379 The Commodore's grape-shot swept their decks so effectually,..that they began to fall into great disorder. **1817** SCOTT *Harold* IV. i, To sweep out And cleanse our chancel from the rags of Rome. **1832** GEN. P. THOMPSON *Exerc.* (1842) II. 63 A scheme..so feeble, and so swept of everything like manly wisdom,..as this. **1836** THIRLWALL *Greece* xxvi. III. 423 The country was completely swept of every thing valuable. **1856** MRS. STOWE *Dred* II. viii. 91 In one day houses are swept of a whole family. **1878** JEFFERIES *Gamekeeper at H.* vii, These fellows..will completely sweep a lane of all the birds whose song makes them valuable. **1880** *Times* 17 Dec. 5/6 The Casco..is reported..to have arrived at Philadelphia with decks swept, boats carried away..and with loss of sails.

17. To draw something, as a net or the bight of a rope, over the bottom of (a body of water) in search of something submerged; to drag. Also *intr.* to search *for* in this way. Also *trans.* to catch (something submerged) in this way.

1637 B. JONSON *Sad Sheph.* I. ii, Earine was drown'd!.. Have you swept the river, say you, and not found her? **1748** *Anson's Voy.* II. ii. 133 We were much concerned for the loss of our anchor, and swept frequently for it. **1769** *De Foe's Tour Gt. Brit.* (ed. 7) IV. 297 Divers went to Work, and swept for her. **1805** *Naval Chron.* XVI. 328 The Pilots.. swept for and weighed the..anchors. **1820** SCORESBY *Acc. Arctic Reg.* II. 293 When they [*sc.* whales] hang perpendicular, or when they cannot be seen, they are discovered by a process called 'sweeping a fish'. **1836** *Uncle Philip's Convers. Whale Fishery* 82 While they are.. sweeping for these lines, some of the men..jump upon the whale and lash the fins together. **1882** NARES *Seamanship* (ed. 6) 167 Sweep the upper fluke with the bight of a hawser. **1901** *Daily Chron.* 12 Oct. 3/5 He then swept an area of half a mile from the wreck buoy to the north-westward.

18. a. To move swiftly and evenly or with continuous force over or along the surface of; in weakened sense, to pass over or across. Also *fig.*

1590 SHAKS. *Mids. N.* III. ii. 23 As..russed-pated choughes,..(Rising and cawing at the guns report) Seuer themselues, and madly sweepe the skye. **1697** DRYDEN *Virg. Georg.* I. 432 All the warring Winds that sweep the Skies. **1725** POPE *Odyss.* XIII. 186 Swift as a swallow sweeps the liquid way. **1749** SMOLLETT *Regic.* II. iv, More swift than gales that sweep the plain. **1808** SCOTT *Marm.* I. Introd. 11 An angry brook, it sweeps the glade. **1813** BYRON *Giaour* 73 Before Decay's effacing fingers Have swept the lines where beauty lingers. **1879** S. C. BARTLETT *Egypt to Pal.* xi. 238 The bed of the valley was swept along some parts of its width by winter torrents. **1913** *Daily Graphic* 26 Mar. 8/4 The storm which swept the Central States on Sunday. **1957** W. S. CHURCHILL *Hist. English-Speaking Peoples* III. vii. 272 Although his generals and Ministers were reluctant and apprehensive a kind of delirium swept the martial classes of the Empire. **1958** P. H. GIBBS *Curtains of Yesterday* xix. 156 That was a gruesome sight! The whole country is swept by typhus. I guess some of us may be unlucky. It may be difficult to dodge.

b. To achieve widespread popularity throughout (a town, country, etc.). Also *spec.* in Politics, to gain control of by an overwhelming margin.

1892 *Times* 9 July 11/1 Mr Gladstone is not likely to 'sweep' the counties any more than he has 'swept' the boroughs. **1931** W. HOLTBY *Poor Caroline* vii. 278 Tell her that that C.C.C. is going to *sweep England*. **1950** *Times* 27 Apr. 4/3 Any party which, at the next election, pledged itself to forming a coalition Government no matter how big a majority it obtained would sweep the country. **1960** *Sunday Express* 14 Aug. 12/3 The short cut is sweeping the town. **1970** *Morning Star* 29 May 1 Ceylon's Left wing United Front led by Mrs Sirimavo Bandaranaike swept the polls here today. **1974** *News & Courier* (Charleston, S. Carolina) 10 Mar. 9-A/2 Sweep the Negro vote..and pick up enough whites to come out of the primary with something more than 50 per cent of the ballots.

19. a. To range over (a region of sea or land), esp. to destroy, ravage, or capture; to scour. Also *spec.* with an aircraft as subject.

1788 GIBBON *Decl. & F.* lxviii. VI. 489 Their artillery swept the waters. **1809** MALKIN *Gil Blas* v. i. ⁋68 To fit out a vessel, for the purpose of sweeping the sea and committing acts of piracy. **1825** SCOTT *Betrothed* xxix, The Welsh.. sweep the villages, and leave nothing behind them but blood and ashes. **1864** BURTON *Scot Abr.* I. iii. 115 The Earls.. swept the country as far as Edinburgh with more than the usual ferocity of a Border raid. **1884** *Times* (weekly ed.) 7 Mar. 3/1 The force advanced—the scouts sweeping a large area on both flanks. **1897** J. F. INGRAM *Natalia* i. 11 With his magnificently organised armies he pitilessly swept the country. **1941** E. SHEPHERD *Mil. Aeroplane* 26 These aeroplanes have to sweep the seas and watch enemy harbours. **1959** R. COLLIER *City that wouldn't Die* iv. 56 At 9.35 p.m. the usual dusk patrol, a few day and night fighters, sweeping the raiders' normal routes. **1976** A. WHITE *Long Silence* vii. 53 We had picked up our fighter escort... Every so often, one or the other would peel off and sweep an observation circuit.

b. Of artillery: To have within range, to command (an extent of territory).

1748 *Anson's Voy.* II. xiv. 287 The cannon of the men of war would have swept all the coast to above a mile's distance from the water's edge. **1829** SCOTT *Anne of G.* xxxvi, The cannon, judiciously placed to sweep the pass. **1855** MACAULAY *Hist. Eng.* xii. III. 244 Macarthy placed his cannon in such a manner as to sweep this causeway.

20. a. To pass the fingers over the strings of a musical instrument so as to cause it to sound. (With the strings, or the instrument, as obj.) Chiefly *poet.*

1637 MILTON *Lycidas* 17 Begin, and somwhat loudly sweep the string. **1708** POPE *Ode St. Cecilia* 4 Wake into voice each silent string, And sweep the sounding lyre! **1805** SCOTT *Last Minstr.* I. Introd. 92 He swept the sounding chords along. **1831** JAMES *Phil. Augustus* I. vii, He took his harp from a page, and sweeping it with a careless but a confident hand [etc.].

b. *transf.* To produce or elicit (music) by such action. *poet.*

1815 SHELLEY *Alastor* 166 Her fair hands..sweeping from some strange harp Strange symphony. **1850** TENNYSON *In Mem.* ciii, The wind began to sweep A music out of sheet and shroud.

21. To direct the eyes, or an optical instrument, to every part of (a region) in succession; to take a wide survey of, to survey or view in its whole extent, esp. with a glass or telescope. Also *absol.* or *intr.*; in *Astron.* to make systematic observations of a region of the heavens (cf. SWEEP *sb.* 7).

1727–46 THOMSON *Summer* 435 O'er heaven and earth, far as the ranging eye Can sweep. *Ibid.* 1408 Here let us sweep The boundless landscape. **1786** SIR W. HERSCHEL in *Phil. Trans.* LXXVI. 460, I..began now to sweep with a vertical motion. **1793** SMEATON *Edystone L.* §322, I swept with my telescope..the line of the horizon. **1830** *Edin. Rev.* LI. 94 The heavens were..swept for double stars. **1883** PEARD *Contrad.* xviii, Before they reach the door, Dorothy has swept the garden with her eye. **1890** W. J. GORDON *Foundry* 26 The gun would remain in sight only long enough to fire. The enemy at sea would sweep the chalk hill in vain for a sign of its presence other than the smoke.

III. Intransitive senses denoting movement (esp. in a curve), and derived uses.

22. *intr.* To move with a strong or swift even motion; to move along over a surface or region, usu. rapidly, or with violence or destructive effect; sometimes, to come with a sudden attack, to swoop.

a. of a person, an animal, a ship (or the like).

13.. *E.E. Allit. P.* B. 1509 Swyfte swaynes ful swyþe swepen þer-tylle. *a* **1547** SURREY *Æneid* IV. 779 With ships the seas ar spred, Cutting the fome, by the blew seas they swepe. **1599** SHAKS. *Hen. V*, III. v. 48 Harry.., that sweepes through our Land With Penons painted in the blood of Harflew. **1602** —— *Ham.* I. v. 31 That I, with wings as swift As meditation, or the thoughts of Loue, May sweepe to my Reuenge. **1697** DRYDEN *Æneid* II. 271 Two Serpents.. smoothly sweep along the swelling Tide. **1715** POPE *Iliad* II. 947 Now, like a Deluge, cov'ring all around, The shining Armies swept along the Ground. **1735** SOMERVILLE *Chase* III. 94 Down we sweep, as stoops the Falcon bold To pounce his Prey. **1810** SCOTT *Lady of L.* IV. xii, When the deer sweeps by, and the hounds are in cry. **1864** G. A. LAWRENCE *Maurice Dering* II. 215 As she swept down The Row at a slinging canter. **1888** STEVENSON *Black Arrow* 76 A whole company of men-at-arms came driving round the corner,.. swept before the lads, and were gone again upon the instant.

b. of water, wind, flame, etc.

13.. *E.E. Allit. P.* A. 111 Swangeande swete þe water con swepe. *c* **1400** *Destr. Troy* 342 There was wellit to wale water full nobill,..With a swoughe and a swetnes sweppit on þe grounde. **1617** MORYSON *Itin.* III. 107 When the South East wind blowes, and sweepes vpon the plaine. **1794** MRS. RADCLIFFE *Myst. Udolpho* xxxi, Their deep silence, except when the wind swept among their branches. **1835** MARRYAT *Jacob Faithful* xxxix, The breeze swept along the water and caught the sails of the privateer. **1845** J. COULTER *Adv. in Pacific* xiv. 219 There were light breezes sweeping up. **1865** KINGSLEY *Herew.* xxxi, On came the flame... The archers.. fell, scorched corpses, as it swept on. **1877** HUXLEY *Physiogr.* 73 South and south-west winds sweeping across that ocean.

c. of non-physical things.

1832 LONGF. *Coplas de Manrique* xxx, Our theme shall be of yesterday, Which to oblivion sweeps away, Like days of old. **1876** TREVELYAN *Macaulay* vii. II. 16 All its associations and traditions swept at once across his memory. **1889** JESSOPP *Coming of Friars* iv. 170 The plague swept over Europe.

d. To move a limb forcibly from side to side; *spec.* of a wounded whale swinging the flukes from side to side.

1839 CAPT. WILSON in *Mag. Nat. Hist.* Oct. 519 On endeavouring to raise the [saw-]fish it became most desperate, sweeping with its saw from side to side.

23. To move or walk in a stately manner, as with trailing garments; to move along majestically; 'to pass with pomp' (J.). Also with *it*.

1590 GREENE *Never too late* (1600) 35 Her pace was like to Iunoes pompous straines, When as she sweeps through heauens brasse-paued way. **1593** SHAKS. *2 Hen. VI*, I. iii. 80 She sweepes it through the Court with troups of Ladies. **1600** —— *A.Y.L.* II. i. 55 Sweepe on you fat and greazie Citizens. **1632** MILTON *Penseroso* 98 Som time let Gorgeous Tragedy In Scepter'd Pall com sweeping by. **1814** SCOTT *Ld. of Isles* I. xvi, Let them sweep on with heedless eyes! **1847** C. BRONTË *Jane Eyre* ii, I heard her sweeping away. **1854** STANLEY *Mem. Canterb.* ii. (1857) 74 The indignant silence with which Becket had swept by. **1869** TROLLOPE *He knew*, etc. vi, Having so spoken, she swept out of the room. **1913** *Standard* 20 June 7/7 As the long line of carriages swept along the broad, green pathway.

fig. **1822** LAMB *Eliana, J. Kemble & Godwin's 'Antonio'*, The first act swept by, solemn and silent.

24. To move along a surface or in the track of something like a trailing robe; to trail *after*; to brush *along*. Also *fig.*

1642 MILTON *Apol. Smect.* Wks. 1851 III. 317 Those things which are yours take them all with you, and they shall sweepe after you. **1670** EACHARD *Cont. Clergy* 117 The Land, that goes sweeping away with the Eldest Son. **1839** LONGF. *Hymn to Night* i, I heard the trailing garments of the Night Sweep through her marble halls!

25. To move continuously in a long stretch or over a wide extent, esp. *round* or in a curve; †to take a curve.

1725 W. HALFPENNY *Sound Building* 35 How to form the Arch or Mold of the Hand-Rail of a Pair of Stairs that sweeps two Steps quicker than in the foregoing Examples. **1826** SCOTT *Jrnl.* 6 Oct., The first flight of the hawks, when they sweep so beautifully round the company. **1830** HERSCHEL *Study Nat. Phil.* 280 Magnificent bodies united in pairs,..sweeping over their enormous orbits, in periods comprehending many centuries. **1831** JAMES *Phil. Augustus* I. iii. Her eyes were long,..and the black lashes that fringed them..swept downward and lay upon her cheek. **1867** AUGUSTA WILSON *Vashti* xv, As she passed him,..her muslin dress swept within reach of his spur. **1875** DARWIN *Insectiv. Pl.* i. 10 The tentacles in the act of inflection sweep through a wide space. **1907** BETHELL *Mod. Guns & Gunnery* 171 The line of fire of the left gun should sweep from point 7½ to point 42½.

26. a. To extend continously through a long stretch, or widely around; to present a surface of wide extent.

1789 W. GILPIN *River Wye* 52 Grand woody hills sweeping, and intersecting each other. **1794** MRS. RADCLIFFE *Myst. Udolpho* l, The forests of pine and chestnut that swept down the lower region of the mountains. **1798** SOUTHEY *Engl. Ecl., Old Mansion-House* 36 A carriage road That sweeps conveniently from gate to gate. **1808** SCOTT *Marm.* I. i, The flanking walls that round it sweep. **1821** CLARE *Vill. Minstr.* I. 72 A road swept gently round the hill. **1871** L. STEPHEN *Playgr. Eur.* (1894) iii. 71 The.. glacier, sweeping in one majestic curve from the crest of the ridge. **1879** S. C. BARTLETT *Egypt to Pal.* ii. 23 The Plain El Murka sweeps north, unbroken and entirely level.

b. *trans.* with cognate obj. To perform or execute (such a movement); to make (a curtsey), deal (a blow), with a sweeping motion.

[*a* **1553** UDALL *Royster D.* IV. iv. (Arb.) 66, I with my newe broome will sweepe hym one swappe.] **1848** THACKERAY *Van. Fair* li, Becky..swept the prettiest little curtsey ever seen. **1896** 'H. S. MERRIMAN' *Sowers* iv, She..swept him a deep curtsey. **1900** H. SUTCLIFFE *Shameless Wayne* xii. (1905) 158 He sweeps two blows [of his sword] in for every one of ours.

27. *trans.* To describe, trace, mark out (a line, esp. a wide curve, or an area); *spec.* in *Shipbuilding*: see quots., and cf. SWEEP *sb.* 16 c.

1664 E. BUSHNELL *Compl. Ship-wright* iv. 9 Shewing, how to sweepe out the Bend of Moulds upon a Flat. *Ibid.* vii. 23 To finde the Sweepe..that will round any Beame, or other piece of Timber that is to be Sweept. **1669** STURMY *Mariner's Mag.* II. ii. 53 You must have..a pair of Beam-Compasses, for to sweep the Arches. **1725** W. HALFPENNY *Sound Building* 1 Open your Compasses.., and setting one Foot in the Point A, with the other sweep the Arch *e e.* **1805** *Shipwright's Vade-M.* 171 The centre for sweeping the stem ..must be set off thus. **1837** WHEWELL *Hist. Induct. Sci.* (1857) I. 324 The areas described or swept, by lines drawn from the sun to the planet. **1843** RUSKIN *Mod. Paint.* I. II. III. iii. §8 They..found it much easier to sweep circles than to design beauties. *c* **1850** *Rudim. Navig.* (Weale) 124 In those lines are found the centres for sweeping the lower and upper breadth sweeps. **1909** *Westm. Gaz.* 9 Sept. 4/2 The erection of the main framing from the platform and bottom sides, which is, in coachmakers parlance, also swept to shape.

28. *Founding.* To form (a mould) with a sweep (SWEEP *sb.* 31).

1885 [HORNER] *Pattern-making* ii. 13 Lay one edge of each sweeped piece on its respective pitch-line. **1909** *Hawkins' Mech. Dict., Sweep*..In founding, to work a loam mould up to the proper outline, by means of profile boards moved over it under mechanical guidance. **1910** J. G. HORNER in *Encycl. Brit.* X. 744/1 That group of work in which the sand or loam is 'swept' to the form required for the moulds and cores by means of striking boards, loam boards, core boards or strickles. *Ibid.*, These joints also are swept by the boards. *Ibid.*, Its mould also is swept on bricks.

sweep, *adv.* and *int.* [The stem of the vb. SWEEP; cf. *bang, crash, dash,* etc.] With a sweeping movement or a swoop.

1670 EACHARD *Cont. Clergy* 86 Sweep comes the Kite, and carries away the fattest and hopefullest of all the Brood. **1694** ECHARD *Plautus, Epidicus* II. iii, Sweep says my Worship with as much Mony as he pleases. **1756** MRS. CALDERWOOD in *Coltness Collect.* (Maitl. Cl.) 225 Whenever a street makes a turn, sweep go about the houses built upon it, as if it had been turned after they were all set. **1849** CUPPLES *Green Hand* v, You felt her shoving the long seas aside..then sweep they came after her.

sweep-, the verb-stem in combination.

1. In attrib. relation to the second element. (In some of these the first element may be SWEEP *sb.*) **sweep-bar** = *sway-bar* (see SWAY-); **sweep-board** (see quot.); **sweep-brush,** a brush used by paperhangers for smoothing paper as it is laid on; **sweep hand** = *sweep second(s hand*; **sweep-head** *a.*, applied to a miner's pick with a curved head; **sweep-panelled** *a.*, ? having curved panels; **sweep-piece** *Shipbuilding*, **sweep-plate** (see quots.); **sweep-rake,** (*a*) see quot. 1884; (*b*) a wheeled frame with long teeth for sweeping up crops lying in swath; **sweep-rod,** a long rod operating as a lever; **sweep-rope** = SWEEP *sb.* 30; **sweep-saw,** a saw adapted for cutting sweeps or curves; a bow-saw, turning-saw; **sweep second(s (hand)** orig. *U.S.* = *centre-second(s* s.v. CENTRE, CENTER *sb.* and *a.* 19; hence ***sweep-seconds watch***; **sweep-seine,** = SWEEP-NET 1; hence **sweep-seining,** the use of a sweep-seine; **sweep-slide** = *sweep-piece*; **sweep-table** [= F. *table à balais*], = *sweeping-table* (SWEEPING *vbl. sb.* 3); † **sweep tail,** a long sweeping tail; **sweep wire,** a wire used in sweeping for something under water; **sweep-work,** curved work. See also SWEEP-NET.

1802 JAMES *Milit. Dict.*, **Sweep-bar*, of a waggon, is that which is fixed on the hind part of the fore guide, and passes under the hind pole, which slides upon it. **1876** VOYLE & STEVENSON *Milit. Dict.*, *Sweep Bar*, the rear bar of a siege howitzer limber (O.P.), which connects the futchels. **1911** WEBSTER s.v. *Strickle*, The strickle is drawn laterally along a guideway, or rotated with a vertical spindle. In the latter case it is more commonly called *sweepboard or striking board. **1901** *J. Black's Carp. & Build., Home Handicr.* 77 The *sweep brush or smoothing roller is taken from the apron pocket and smooths the paper on to the ceiling progressively. **1948** *Wrist Watches, Pocket Watches & Clocks* iii. 185 Watch stops... This may be caused by ..*sweep hand rubbing on dial. **1967** R. MEYERS *Dolphin Rider* (1968) i. 22 Henries..listened while he watched the sweep hand of his watch. **1977** *Times Lit. Suppl.* 24 June 779/1 The sweep hand of my watch is there in order to make seconds easier to read. **1883** GRESLEY *Gloss. Coal-mining*, **Sweep-head Pick*, a pick the form of the head of which is made curved instead of elbowed or anchored, as other kinds are termed. **1843** C. J. C. DAVIDSON *Trav. Upper India* ix. II. 209 Buggies, full, half, or *sweep-panelled. **1867** SMYTH *Sailor's Word-bk.*, **Sweep-piece*, a block at the bottom of the port-sill for receiving the chock of the gun-carriage, and to aid in training the gun. **1851** GREENWELL *Coal-trade Terms Northumb. & Durh.* 54 **Sweep-plates*, curved plates for laying barrow-way round a turn. **1884** KNIGHT *Dict. Mech.* Suppl., **Sweep Rake*, the rake that clears the table of a self rake reaper. **1910** *Encycl. Brit.* XIII. 108/1 An American invention known as the sweep rake was introduced..into England in 1894. **1867** W. W. SMYTH *Coal & Coal-mining* 184 When pumps are to be worked, it is usually by *sweep-rods passing from the crank on the main shaft to quadrants or bell-cranks at the shaft mouth. **1848** JAL *Gloss. Naut.*, **Sweep-rope*, corde employée à draguer les objets restés au fond de la mer. **1846** HOLTZAPFFEL *Turning* II. 728 The turning-saw, or *sweep-saw..also called the frame-saw, or bow-saw. **1948** *Wrist Watches, Pocket Watches & Clocks* ii. 154 Remove *sweep seconds hand. **1953** W. J. GAZELEY *Watch & Clock Making* iii. 48 Nowadays..we have what are termed sweep-seconds watches. At one time these were referred to as centre-seconds. **1962** E. BRUTON *Dict. Clocks & Watches* 170 *Sweep seconds*, American name for centre seconds. **1962** J. D. MACDONALD *Girl, Gold Watch, & Everything* viii. 101 Uncle Omar's gold watch..had an hour hand, a minute hand and a sweep second hand. **1969** *Guardian* 20 Aug. 7/1 All the clocks..have a sweep second hand. **1979** *Sci. Amer.* May 145/1 A sweep second hand on a wristwatch will also serve. **1856** OLMSTED *Slave States* 351 The shad and herring fisheries upon the sounds and inlets of the North Carolina coast..The largest *sweep seines in the world are used. **1838** *Civil Eng. & Arch. Jrnl.* I. 353/1 She mounts two 84 pounders bow and stern, on *sweep slides. **1839** URE *Dict. Arts* 816 At the upper part of these five *sweep tables, the materials which are to undergo washing are agitated in two boxes..by small paddle-wheels. **1686** *Lond. Gaz.* No. 2190/4 A Bay Nag with a *Sweep Tail. **1909** *Westm. Gaz.* 15 July 7/1 The torpedo boat No. 99 has been anchored to her by *sweep wires. **1847** SMEATON *Builder's Man.* 93 In bending and glueing-up stuff for *sweep-work.

2. With the second element in objective relation: **sweep-all** *nonce-wd.*, one who 'sweeps up' or appropriates all, = SWEEPSTAKE 1; **sweep-chimney** *Obs.* or *dial.*, a chimney-sweeper; † **sweep-gallery, -house,** a person employed to sweep a gallery or a house, a menial servant; † **sweep-street,** (*a*) ? one whose long garments sweep the street; (*b*) a street-sweeper.

1695 J. EDWARDS *Author. O. & N. Test.* III. 583 The avaritious and extorting Pretor of Sicily is by Tully call'd Verrens, *Sweep-all. **1657** BAXTER *Min. agst. Malign.* §12. 6, I would be a Plow-man,..if not a *sweep-Chimney, rather then a Minister. **1716** M. DAVIES *Athen. Brit.* III. 87 It [*sc.* a conduit of stone for water] serves only for Sweep-Chimneys to stand by,..and therefore vulgarly call'd Sweep-Chimneys-Hall. **1826** *Times* 5 Jan. 3/4 He was a sweep-chimney by profession. **1858** HUGHES *Scour. White Horse* v. 94 Amongst 'em a sweep chimley and a millurd. **1705** in *Ushaw Mag.* (1903) Dec. 299 Bernard ye *sweepgallery. **1621** SIR S. D'EWES in *College Life t. Jas. I*, iii. (1851) 50 Two base *sweep-houses belonging to him, who were recusants. **1553** BALE *Vocacyon* 43 They are but pilde peltinge prestes,..though they be sir *Swepestretes, maistre doctours, and lorde bishoppes. **1612** tr. *Benvenuto's Passenger* II. i. 423 Shoomakers, Woodmongers, Sweepe-streetes [orig. *Spaza camini*], Faulkners.

3. With advbs.: **sweepback** *Aeronaut.*, the form of an aircraft wing that is angled backwards, so that the part farther from the fuselage is aft of the nearer part; the angle made by such a wing with a line at right angles to the fuselage; **sweep-forward** *Aeronaut.*, the form of an aircraft wing that is angled forwards, so that the part further from the fuselage is forward of the nearer part; **sweep-out,** an act of sweeping out; (*U.S. colloq.*) a clearance or purge.

1914 *Aeroplane* 19 Mar. 308/1 Owing to the *sweep back on the wings the side area of these struts may be regarded as taking the place of tail fins. **1918** H. J. STEPHENS *Gloss. Aeronaut. Words* (ed. 2) 36 *Sweepback*, the angle at which the planes slope backwards each side of the fuselage. **1939** *Aircraft Engin.* Apr. 159/3 The basic characteristic of sweepback on a rectangular wing would appear to be an early stalling of the tips which may or may not produce greater lateral stability. **1968** MILLER & SAWERS *Technical Devel. Mod. Aviation* vi. 204 The slightly greater sweep-back of the 707's wing means that it takes off at a greater angle of attack. **1977** *Jrnl. R. Soc. Arts* CXXV. 349/2 We can use the improved methods..to reduce wing sweepback (thus improving take-off and landing). **1932** *Technical Rep. Aeronaut. Res. Committee 1930–1* I. 39 *Sweep-forward increases the maximum lift and considerably delays the stall. **1953** M. RAUSCHER *Introd. Aeronaut. Dynamics* ix. 378 A wing without pronounced sweep-back or sweep-forward. **1975** L. J. CLANCY *Aerodynamics* xvi. 532 Sweep forward would have a de-stabilizing effect. **1947** *Sun* (Baltimore) 16 Aug. 12/8 Governor Lane has ordered a *sweep-out at the Board of Supervisors of Elections... About 30 places on the pay roll..are slated to be pulled out from under employés who are on the wrong side of the Democratic factional fence. **1978** *Detroit Free Press* 6 Apr. E 5/3 A total of 47 rookies won jobs this season, reflecting a lot of dead wood on the rosters. 'Next year', predicts our source, 'will see an even bigger sweep-out.'

sweepage (ˈswiːpɪdʒ). Also 7 swepage. [f. SWEEP *v.* + -AGE.]

1. = SWEEPING *vbl. sb.* 2, 2 b.

1606 S. GARDINER *Bk. Angling* 149 The veriest mennow among men, the salt and sweepage of the court, dare.. contriue the death of the Prince of the court.

2. a. *spec.* 'The Crop of Hay got in a Meadow' (Cowell *Interpr.*, 1672, s.v. *Swepage*): cf. SWEEP *sb.* 18; *gen.* what is mown. **b.** *dial.* (See quot. 1895.)

1628 COKE *On Litt.* I. i. §1. 4 b, He shall haue the vesture of the land, (that is) the corne, grasse, vnderwood, swepage, and the like. **1857** WRIGHT *Dict. Obs. & Prov. Engl.*, *Swepage*, the rough grass in a meadow which cattle will not eat, and which has to be mown or swept off. **1895** *E. Anglian Gloss.*, *Sweepage*, the right of cutting faggots, grass, &c., on a several or common allotment. **1910** *Encycl. Brit.* VI. 782/1 Sweepage (i.e. everything which falls to the sweep of the scythe).

sweepdom (ˈswiːpdəm). *nonce-wd.* [f. SWEEP *sb.* 33 + -DOM.] Sweeps collectively.

1855 A. C. COXE *Impress. Eng.* (1856) 70 Jack-in-the-Green, on a May-day in London..this beneficial anniversary of sweepdom.

sweeper (ˈswiːpə(r)). Also 5 swepare, 6 -er, -ar, 7 sweaper. [f. SWEEP *v.* + -ER¹.]

1. a. *gen.* One who or that which sweeps (something): usually with objective *of.*

1530 PALSGR. 278/1 Swepar of chymneys. **1552** HULOET, Sweper of houses, *scoparius*..Sweper of the ground wyth hys fete, *atta.* **1562** J. HEYWOOD *Prov. & Epigr.* (1867) 137 New broome swepeth cleane, in the cleane swepers hande. **1706** E. WARD *Hud. Rediv.* I. I. 18 The Sweeper of a Chimney. **1769** FALCONER *Dict. Marine* (1780), *Sweeper* of the sky.. a name given by sailors to the N.W. winds of America. **1812** COBBETT in *Examiner* 19 Oct. 671/1 Noble Ladies, who..condescended to become housekeepers and sweepers of malls.

†**b.** A broom for sweeping out an oven. *Obs.*

c **1440** *Promp. Parv.* 323/2 Malkyne, mappyl, or ouen swepare, *dossorium, tersorium.* **1580** [see *oven-sweeper*, OVEN *sb.* 4].

c. One who or a vessel which sweeps for something under water. Now usu. short for *mine-sweeper*.

1775 FALCK *Day's Diving Vessel* 46 The boat should advance but very slowly, and the sweepers should hold the line in their hands all the while. **1915** S. H. CARDEN in M. Gilbert *Winston S. Churchill* (1972) III. Compan. I. 405 Battleships preceded by sweepers making way up towards Narrows. **1941** S. O'CASEY *Let.* 28 Apr. (1975) I. 886 Delighted to hear John [Allen]'s allright on a sweeper. **1979** D. GURR *Troika* i. 5 Losses of submariners trying to run the Baltic minefields without benefit of sweepers were appalling.

d. *Cricket.* A batsman who sweeps (sense 2 b).

1961 *Times* 21 Aug. 3/3 There can be few more effective sweepers. **1963** [see SWEEP *v.* 2 b]. **1965** D. SILK *Attacking Cricket* iv. 60 The best sweepers bring the bat down on the ball from above as well as across.

e. *Assoc. Football.* One who plays as the last line of defence except the goalkeeper, across the width of the field (i.e. as opposed to a right or left back, etc., in other systems).

1964 *Times* 13 Apr. 4/1 Moore..played a giant part in his role as 'sweeper' of the rear. **1971** *Times* 15 Feb. 9/2 Of the other younger England [hockey] players Perry had a solid game as sweeper. **1973** *Daily Pennsylvanian* 9 Oct. 6 We knew they were using a sweeper, so we had to run to the corners to draw him out. **1976** *Denbighshire Free Press* 8 Dec. 24/2 Even with Bernie Welsh operating as sweeper behind a defensive line of four, Courtaulds were far from impressive at the back when the ball was in the air.

2. a. A person employed in sweeping a room, chimney, house, ship, etc.; *spec.* in India, a person of the lowest caste. Also in comb., as CHIMNEY-SWEEPER, CROSSING-*sweeper*. Also *attrib.* as ***sweeper caste***.

1657 J. WATTS *Scribe, Pharisee*, etc. I. 267 Those chimney houses, so foul, and black, and sooty, that they need the sweeper to come to them quickly. **1670** G. H. *Hist. Cardinals* I. III. 76 The four private Sweepers [in the papal household]. **1675** J. SMITH *Chr. Relig. Appeal* III. i. §6. 12 Hybreas the Oratour, in lineaments of Face and whole Body was so peer'd by the sweeper of his School, as [etc.]. **1714** PARKYNS *Inn-Play* 13 A Sweeper and Pump-Dresser to a Fencing School. **1715** HEARNE *Collect.* (O.H.S.) V. 47 A Woman and a Girl..not sworn or admitted to be Sweepers. **1769** FALCONER *Dict. Marine* (1780), *Swabber*..ship's sweeper, usually called captain's swabber. **1790** *Laws of Harvard Coll.* 58 The Steward shall also engage proper sweepers for the Colleges. **1815** W. H. IRELAND *Scribbleomania* 82 Whose rhymes are so bad, he was never yet able To serve as last sweeper in Pegasus' stable. **1844** W. H. SLEEMAN *Rambles & Recollections Indian Official* I. viii. 64 The right of sweeping within a certain range is recognised by the caste to belong to a certain member... If any house-keeper..happens to offend the sweeper..none of his filth will be removed. **1859** LANG *Wand. India* 259 Two sweepers —men of the lowest caste of Hindoos. **1861** *Macm. Mag.* Feb. 268/2 The rooms [in an American College] were supposed to be taken care of by three or four men called 'sweepers', whose duty extended only to making the beds daily, and sweeping the rooms occasionally.

attrib. **1837** *Lett. fr. Madras* x. (1843) 89 He kept no sweeper-woman, and, as may be supposed, the dirt crunched under our feet as we walked. *a* **1851** MRS. SHERWOOD *Poor Burruff* 11 Marten, who sent the sweeper-man immediately to the poor dog, to remove the arrow. **1859** MRS. R. M. COOPLAND *Lady's Escape from Gwalior* iii. 58 Matrané, a woman of the sweeper caste. **1909** J. HASTINGS *Encycl. Relig. & Ethics* II. 551/2 The sweeper or scavenger caste of Hindustan.

b. One who sweeps the ice at curling.

1789 DAVIDSON *Seasons* 165 Allan of Airds, a sweeper good.

†**3.** A pliant rod forming part of a snare for catching birds. *Obs.*

1621 MARKHAM *Hunger's Prevent.* vi. 42 The sweaper or maine plant, which as it is prescribed of Hazell, Elme, or Witchen, so in this case it may be of Willow. **1681** WORLIDGE *Syst. Agric.* 245 The main Plant, or Sweeper must be also proportionable to the strength of the Fowl.

4. A telescope used for 'sweeping' the sky: cf. SWEEP *sb.* 7, *v.* 21. ? *Obs.*

1786 SIR W. HERSCHEL *Sci. Papers* (1912) I. 294 This nebula was discovered.. with an excellent small Newtonian Sweeper of 27 inches focal length, and a power of 30. **1792** —— in *Phil. Trans.* LXXXII. 24.

5. a. A mechanical apparatus for sweeping a floor, road, etc.; a sweeping-machine.

1862 *Catal. Internat. Exhib., Brit.* II. No. 6139, The dust, lint, and even hairs, pins, needles, &c. are taken up directly into the box and there retained as the sweeper moves along. **1892** A. E. LEE *Hist. Columbus* (Ohio) II. 528 [In 1886] N. B. Abbott began running a fourhorse sweeper on High Street six nights per week.

b. *colloq.* An electronic device for detecting listening or recording apparatus. Also, a person operating such a device.

1968 *Observer* 16 June 7/2 To help in the job of debugging, Mr. Johnson is having electronic 'sweepers' manufactured... Small ones can be operated by firms' security officers to keep a boardroom 'clean' after it has been 'swept'. It was with one of these 'sweepers' that an attempt to smuggle a bug into a boardroom in the bottom of a coffee pot was recently foiled. **1972** K. BENTON *Spy in Chancery* xi. 116 They sent a 'sweeper' team.. and they went through the rooms in Chancery. **1979** F. FORSYTH *Devil's Alternative* x. 232 A secure room regularly checked by the 'sweepers' who are.. looking for.. listening devices.

6. A tree growing close to the margin of a stream and overhanging it. Also, a partially fallen or drifting tree. *N. Amer.*

1888 S. M. ST. MAUR *Jrnl.* 19 July in *Impressions of Tenderfoot* (1890) vii. 95 We glided through the water at about ten miles an hour, sometimes rushing.. within a few inches of a sweeper, as they call the trees which hang across the river. **1929** L. JOHNSTON *Beyond Rockies* 191 'Where are them sweepers, Charlie?' (sweepers being the river term for drifting trees, which may in a moment upset the craft of an unwary skipper). **1977** *New Yorker* 9 May 120/2 Over the cut bank a sweeper had recently fallen, a spruce whose trunk reached into the river... Sweepers tend to trap boats.

7. *Electronics.* A sweep generator or oscillator. *colloq.*

1967 *Electronics* 6 Mar. 2 (Advt.), The main frame of the 3211A contains everything you could hope to find in a sweeper. **1976** *Physics Bull.* Sept. 411/1 The hired equipment included spectrum analysers, signal generators, sweepers, oscilloscopes, [etc.].

Hence **'sweeperess** *nonce-wd.*, a female (crossing-) sweeper.

1848 THACKERAY *Van. Fair* xlii, The sweeperess at the crossing.

sweeping ('swiːpɪŋ), *vbl. sb.* [f. SWEEP *v.* + -ING[1].] **1.** The action of the verb SWEEP.

a. Cleansing, or removing, with or as with a broom or brush: also *fig.*

c **1480** HENRYSON *Mor. Fab., Cok & Jasp.* i, Scraipand amang the ass.. He fand ane Ioly Iasp,.. Was castin furth be sweping of the houss. **1519** in *Archaeologia* XXV. 423 Pd to John ye Scott of Ryngstede, for swepyng of ye Kechyn Chymnye. ijd. **1558** *Nottingham Rec.* IV. 119 The sweppyng and dressyng of the Counsell' Housse. **1591** *Shuttleworths' Acc.* (Chetham Soc.) 70 Dressinge of privies and swypinge of chimnes for onne holl yere xvjd. **1639** *Crabtree Lect.* 25 Thou biddest them everie night looke to the sweeping of thy shop. **1770** LANGHORNE *Plutarch* II. 460 Fine gardens and walks that require much watering and sweeping. **1825** COBBETT *Rur. Rides* (1853) 337 It is impossible for any just man to regret the sweeping away of this base race of Squires. **1863** KINGSLEY *Water-Bab.* i, The chimneys wanted sweeping. **1867** W. W. SMYTH *Coal & Coal-mining* 205 We must provide for the sweeping away of the products of breathing and combustion. **1884** H. P. SPOFFORD in *Harper's Mag.* Nov. 889/2 She tied up her mouth when sweeping was in progress. **1900** *Daily Tel.* 2 Oct. (Ware) Though the time has come when Volunteers, Yeomen, and Guards should be sent home, there is still a good deal of sweeping up to be done in the Transvaal.

b. Dragging for something under water: see SWEEP *v.* 17. Also in ***mine-sweeping***.

1704 J. HARRIS *Lex. Techn.* I, *Sweeping*, at Sea, signifies dregging along the Ground.. with a Three-fluked Grapnel, to find some Hawsar or Cable, which is slipped from an Anchor. **1775** FALCK *Day's Diving Vessel* 50 Out of the various methods of sweeping,.. I pursued.. the most eligible. **1896** *Daily News* 14 Nov. 6/7 Her whereabouts were discovered by 'sweeping'.

c. *Astron.*: see SWEEP *v.* 21.

1786 SIR W. HERSCHEL *Sci. Papers* (1912) I. 260 My apparatus.. being from time to time adapted to the different views I had in sweeping. **1881** J. W. WEBB in *Nature* 10 Nov. 36/2 It [*sc.* a star-cluster] may be found without circles, by patient sweeping.

d. Movement over a surface, or in an extended curve: see SWEEP *v.* 22, 26.

1830 TENNYSON *A Character* 16 He spake of virtue.. And with a sweeping of the arm,.. Devolved his rounded periods. **1837** CARLYLE *Fr. Rev.* II. I. xii, There is wheeling and sweeping, to slow, to quick and double-quick time. **1853** M. ARNOLD *Church of Brou* iii. 43 In the sweeping of the wind your ear The passage of the Angels' wings will hear.

e. Rowing with sweeps: see SWEEP *v.* 12.

1831 TRELAWNY *Adv. Younger Son* xxxii, The sweeps were got out under the hot sun... With what little air there was, and with sweeping, we continued to drop the frigate.

f. *Gunnery.* (See quot.)

1907 BETHELL *Mod. Guns & Gunnery* 172 In a wider sense sweeping means distributing fire laterally over a given front.

g. The formation of a mould with a sweep.

1902 *Lockwood's Dict. Terms.*

2. a. That which is swept up; matter, esp. dust or refuse, that is swept together or away.

†*sing.* **1480** *Cov. Leet Bk.* 461 þat þe people of the Citie car on their Donge, Ramell, & swepyng of their houses. **1541** in W. H. Turner *Select. Rec. Oxford* (1880) 162 To cary all swepyng of mens howses, and the dyrte that commythe of the sweppyng of the strettes. **1665** in De Foe *Plague* (Rtldg.) 63 That the Sweeping and Filth of Houses be daily carry'd away by the Rakers.

pl. **1489** CAXTON *Faytes of A.* II. xiii. 114 The fylthes and swepynges of the hous. **1555** EDEN *Decades* (Arb.) 157 As a beasome gathereth the swepynges of a house. *c* **1604** *Acc. Bk. W. Wray* in *Antiquary* XXXII. 180 The markyt corne and markitte swepings was firste geven to this wakeman, 153-. **1630** B. JONSON *New Inn, Ode* iii, There, sweepings do as well As the best order'd meale. **1665** BOYLE *Occas. Refl.* I. xxxii. (1848) 92 Gold-smiths and Refiners are wont.. carefully to save the very sweepings of their Shops. **1742** *Lond. & Country Brew.* III (ed. 4) 230 At every Brewing after he had strained the Sweepings of his Coolers through a Flannel-bag. **1868** *Rep. U.S. Commissioner Agric.* (1869) 286 Sweepings of threads, formerly thrown away because the workmen could not unravel them. **1884** *Standard* 4 Jan. 2/5 Gold leaf, known in the trade as sweepings.

b. *fig.* (*pl.*) of persons or things, in depreciative sense: Rubbish, riff-raff.

1641 MILTON *Prel. Episc.* Wks. 1851 III. 92 Confronting .. the sacred verity of Saint Paul with the offalls, and sweepings of antiquity. **1795** J. ROBERTSON *Agric. Perth* 59 The deformed spawn and jail sweepings of great towns. **1832** MARRYAT *N. Forster* xl, I wish I had fifty more of the same sort, instead of the sweepings of the gaols. **1878** STUBBS *Study Med. & Mod. Hist.* viii. (1900) 182 The population [of Armenia] was composed largely of the sweepings of Asia Minor, Christian tribes which had taken refuge in the mountains.

3. *attrib.*, as ***sweeping-brush, -day, -gear, -machine***; **sweeping-bar** = *sweep-bar* (SWEEP- 1); **sweeping-net** = SWEEP-NET; **sweeping-table** (cf. *sweep-table*, SWEEP- 1), a sloping table on which ore is washed by a current of water.

1859 F. A. GRIFFITHS *Artil. Man.* (1862) 63 Limbers have the Futchells, Splinter, or *Sweeping-bar, of ash. *a* **1828** D. WORDSWORTH *Jrnl.* (1941) II. 329 Presently a Man enters with a *sweeping brush, to '*arrange*'. **1922** JOYCE *Ulysses* 327 Gob, he'd adorn a sweepingbrush,.. if he only had a nurse's apron on him. **1889** MARY H. FOOTE *Last Assembly Ball* III. iv, Friday.. was general *sweeping-day at Mrs. Dansken's. **1909** *Daily Chron.* 28 Aug. 3/4 Boats.. have been sweeping for dummy mines in the Thames estuary. The boats operate in couples, dragging their *sweeping gear between them. [**1858** SIMMONDS *Dict. Trade*, *Street-sweeping Machine*, a cart fitted with revolving brooms, or a rotatory brush and scraper, for cleansing public thoroughfares.] **1899** *Daily News* 5 Dec. 9/2 It is a *sweeping-machine, and not a cart. **1809** SCOTT *Poacher* 77 The fish-spear barb'd, the *sweeping net are there. **1913** *Proc. Ashmolean Nat. Hist. Soc.* (1914) 39 Insects were somewhat disappointingly scarce, the sweeping-net only producing the large brown *Dascillus cervinus*, *Mantura matthewsi* and *Meligethes solidus*. **1896** NICHOLS & FRANKLIN *Elem. Physics* I. xii. 200 A homogeneous substance not in a state of thermal equilibrium undergoes a *sweeping process as the substance settles down to a state of thermal equilibrium. Such a process is absolutely irreversible. **1839** URE *Dict. Arts* 819 In certain mines of the Hartz.. tables called *à balais*, or *sweeping tables, are employed.

'sweeping, *ppl. a.* [f. as prec. + -ING[2].]

1. That sweeps with a broom: also said of the broom. *rare.*

1611 COTGR., *Balayeuse*, a drudge, or sweeping wench. **1671** M. BRUCE *Gd. News in Evil Times* (1708) 14 When his Anger comes with the sweeping Besom of Destruction.

2. a. Moving forcibly over a surface, etc. so as to clear it; rushing violently; carrying all before it.

1611 *Bible* Prov. xxviii. 3 A poore man that oppresseth the poore, is like a sweeping raine which leaueth no food. **1642** H. MORE *Song of Soul* I. II. cxxix, A sweeping torrent that beats down the corn. **1757** GRAY *Bard* 75 Regardless of the sweeping Whirlwind's sway. **1787** BURNS *Death Sir J. H. Blair* xi, She said—and vanish'd with the sweeping blast. **1822** BYRON *Heaven & Earth* i, The stillness of The untrodden forest, only broken by The sweeping tempest through its groaning boughs. **1830** COBBETT *Hist. George IV* iii. §142 The French were carrying on a sweeping and successful war upon the continent.

b. Moving continuously over a surface or through a wide extent; trailing, passing with stately movement.

1610 FOLKINGHAM *Feudigr.* I. v. 10 All sweeping or floating Waters, which flit and fleete to and fro with wind-catches. **1697** DRYDEN *Virg. Georg.* I. 504 Seeming Stars.. shooting through the Darkness, gild the Night With sweeping Glories, and long Trails of Light. —— *Æneid* I. 560 In length of Train descends her sweeping Gown. *Ibid.* III. 375 The Seamen ply Their sweeping Oars: the smokeing Billows fly. **1712–14** POPE *Rape Lock* I. 84 Peers, and Dukes, and all their sweeping train. **1821** CLARE *Vill. Minstr.* (1823) I. 85 As the sweeping swallows stop Their flights along the green. **1859** *Habits of Gd. Society* iv. (new ed.) 179 For state dinners it [*sc.* the dress] should be long, and fresh, and sweeping.

c. *transf.* of movement or action.

1760–72 H. BROOKE *Fool of Qual.* (1809) I. 63 Away the coach drove at a sweeping gallop. **1812** *Sporting Mag.* XXXIX. 26 Richardson was thrown by a half jirk of the hip, followed by a sweeping cross-buttock. **1814** SOUTHEY *Roderick* III. 419 Looking round with sweeping eyes. **1818** SCOTT *Br. Lamm.* xi, With a sweeping blow, he threw down from a shelf some articles of pewter and earthenware. **1825** HONE *Every-day Bk.* I. 880 The mower begins to make his sweeping cuts. **1864** *Even. Standard* 26 May, The sweeping action of the Derby horse exciting general admiration. **1879** MORLEY *Burke* i. 14 The very boldness and sweeping rapidity of Bolingbroke's prose. **1883** J. PAYN *Thicker than Water* xxxix, Mary made him a sweeping curtsey.

3. Extending through a long stretch or wide space, esp. in a curve; having a long curving outline or contour.

1772 MASON *Eng. Garden* I. 11 Where'er she [*sc.* Nature] takes Her horizontal march, pursue her step With sweeping train of forest. **1794** MRS. RADCLIFFE *Myst. Udolpho* xxxii, Emily.. winding round the rock saw, within the sweeping bay beyond,.. two groups of peasants. **1821** SCOTT *Kenilw.* xxv, Its stately towers, rising from within a long sweeping line of outward walls. **1837** CARLYLE *Fr. Rev.* III. VII. ii, Her sweeping tresses snooded by glittering antique fillet. **1855** *Orr's Circ. Sci., Inorg. Nat.* 185 The sweeping form given to snow by winds. **1888** MORRIS *Dream J. Ball* i, The narrow stretch of bright green water-meadows that wind between the sweeping Wiltshire Downs.

4. *fig.* Having a wide scope; extensive, comprehensive, all-inclusive; wholesale, indiscriminate.

1771 BURKE *Corr.* (1844) I. 276 A general sweeping censure of my whole conduct. **1802** JAMES *Milit. Dict.*, *Sweeping*, a word which is peculiarly attached to one of the sections or clauses in the Articles of War, namely, the 24th. Hence *Sweeping Clause.* **1822** HAZLITT *Table-t.* Ser. II. iii. (1869) 56 A sweeping, unqualified assertion ends all controversy. **1833** T. HOOK *Parson's Dau.* I. v, A sweeping suspicion of female virtue, and a splendid contempt for female intellect. **1858** KINGSLEY *Misc.* (1859) I. ii. 125 A sweeping measure of sanitary reform. **1910** *Encycl. Brit.* III. 38/2 The general election.. resulted in a sweeping victory for the Social Democrats.

sweepingly ('swiːpɪŋlɪ), *adv.* [f. prec. + -LY[2].] In a sweeping manner (*lit.* or *fig.*).

1. With a sweeping movement; so as to sweep over a surface.

1830 *Blackw. Mag.* XXVII. 509 Those tragedies which go sweepingly over the bloody stage. **1854** *Chamb. Jrnl.* II. 120 Their outer integuments have a tendency.. to trail sweepingly at the heels.

2. So as to have a wide scope; comprehensively; indiscriminately.

1822 *Examiner* 802/1 Is it to be tolerated that men.. should be thus sweepingly branded with the ignominy of guilt? **1881** MISS BRADDON *Asph.* II. 137 All wild and rugged coasts she denounced sweepingly, as dangerous to life and limb.

So **'sweepingness**.

1831 *Examiner* 306/1 The.. Tories have themselves alone to blame for the sweepingness which they ascribe to the Reform Bill. **1881** W. CLARK RUSSELL *Ocean Free-Lance* II. ii. 111 A sublime curtsey, the overwhelming sweepingness of which was no doubt meant to cover me with confusion.

sweeple, variant of SWIPPLE.

sweep-net. [SWEEP- 1.]

1. A large net used in fishing, enclosing a wide space; a kind of seine. Also *fig.*

1605 CAMDEN *Rem., Anagrams* 154 She [*sc.* Q. Eliz.] was as a Sweepnet for the Spanish ships, which.. happily fell into her net. **1611** COTGR., *Esparvier*,.. a great Sweepe-net for fishing. **1721** in Bailey. **1834** JARDINE in *Proc. Berw. Nat. Club* I. No. 2. 51 In the rivers they [*sc.* herling] are caught with the common sweep-nets. **1866** *Daily Tel.* 5 Jan. 5/1 The sweep-net and circle and shrimp nets, which certainly do entrap immense quantities of immature fry. **1894** A. ROBERTSON *Nuggets*, etc. 130 She guessed her guess, and made a cast with her sweep-net of questions and caught him in the meshes.

2. A net used for catching insects by sweeping it over herbage, etc.

1872 *Routledge's Ev. Boy's Ann.* Sept. 634/1 The larva of this insect may be found plentiful, especially if the sweep-net be used.

sweepstake ('swiːpsteɪk), **sweepstakes** (-steɪks). Also 5–6 **swepe-**, 6 **sweepestake**, 6 **swepstacke**. [f. SWEEP *v.* 8 (SWEEP- 2) + STAKE *sb.*[2] Cf. SWOOPSTAKE.]

†**1.** One who 'sweeps', or takes the whole of, the stakes in a game, etc.; usually *fig.* one who takes or appropriates everything; from the 15th to the 17th cent. commonly used as a ship's name.

a. **1495** *Naval Acc. Hen. VII* (1896) 159 The Kinges Bark called the Swepestake. **1520** in *Lett. & Papers Hen. VIII*, III. II. 1541 To John Hopton, wages of the Swepestake row-barge, and for rigging other ships, 100 l. **1527** *Will of J. Piper* (Somerset Ho.), My shipp called the Mary Swepestake. **1540** PALSGR. *Acolastus* b iv, Pantolabus signifieth *omnia capiens*, one that is a swepestake and all is fysshe that commeth to the nette with hym. **1545** in *12th*

Rep. Hist. MSS. Comm. App. VII. 8 The second rancke of the vaunt-ward:—The greate gallye. The Swepstacke. **1593** G. HARVEY *Pierce's Super.* Wks. (Grosart) II. 111 He that will exploit wonderments, and karrie all before him, like a sweepe-stake. **1593** in J. Morris *Troubles Cath. Forefathers* (1877) 163 The gleaners, as sweepstakes, who raked up without scruple all that whereof the other made some conscience. **1595** *Roxb. Ball.* (1889) VI. 409 The George-Aloe and the Sweep-stake too. **1632** BROME *Novella* II. ii, Shee will runne on the faster... She will prove the only Sweep-stake In all the city. **1687** MIEGE *Gt. Fr. Dict.*, Sweep-stake, He that gets all the Stakes, *Celui (ou Celle) qui tire l'Enjeu*.

β. *c* **1650** (*title of ballad*) The Seaman's only Delight: Shewing the brave Fight between the George-Aloe, the Sweepstakes and certain French Men at Sea. **1669** NARBOROUGH *Jrnl.* 15 May in *Acc. Sev. Late Voy.* (1711) I, I received..my Commission to Command his Majesty's Ship the Sweepstakes. **1673** R. HEAD *Canting Acad.* 18 Thy Sweep-stakes still shall bare the Bell, No Fire-ship yet aboard it fell.

†**2.** The act of sweeping everything away; a clean sweep; total removal or clearance. Only in form *sweepstake*: usually in phr. ***to make sweepstake, to play (at) sweepstake.*** *Obs.*

1542 UDALL *Erasm. Apoph.* 323 Verres wheresoeuer he came plaied swepestake [orig. *quod omnia uerreret*]. *c* **1555** [COVERDALE] *Exhort. carienge of Chrystes crosse* xii. 133 If the pope and his prelates were charitable, they woulde, I trowe, make swepe stake at once wyth purgatorye. **1557** R. EDGEWORTH *Serm.* 314 And this boke made swepestake of the blessed sacrament, declaring there to be nothing els but bare bread and wine. **1581** J. BELL *Haddon's Answ. Osor.* III. 403 b, Leo the 10...devising..to make sweepe-stake for money [orig. *de emungenda pecunia*]. **1589** NASHE *Martins Months Mind* To Rdr., For the moste parte..they maie in the end with a tripsie Tray, carrie all awaie smoothe; and come once to the sweepestake. **1613** J. TAYLOR (Water P.) *Heav. Blessing* Wks. 1630 III. 123/2 Death..whose auaritious greedy mood, Doth play at sweepe-stake with all liuing things. **1648** in Rushw. *Hist. Coll.* IV. (1659) II. 1227 The Scots play Sweep-stake, take nothing but all Moveables. *a* **1650** ABP. WILLIAMS in Hacket *Life* II. (1693) 172, I cannot conceive from what ground this general Sweepstake of Archbishops, Bishops, Parsons, Vicars,.. should proceed. **1653** *Vind. Christmas* Title-p., The lamentable game called Sweepstake, acted by Gen. Plunder and Maj. Gen. Tax.

3. orig. A prize won in a race or contest in which the whole of the stakes contributed by the competitors are taken by the winner or by a certain limited number of them; hence (now usually), the race or contest itself. (Cf. STAKE *sb.*[2] 3.)

1773 MME. D'ARBLAY *Early Diary* (1889) I. 234 The great Sweep Stakes of the asses were half-a-guinea; the second prize a crown, and the third half-a-crown. **1785** W. PICK (*title*) Authentic Historical Racing Calendar of all the Plates, Sweep-stakes, Matches, &c., run for at York, 1709–1785. **1835** H. HAREWOOD *Dict. Sports* s.v. *Woodpecker*, At Newmarket Spring Meeting, 1777, Woodpecker won a sweepstakes of 1500 gs. **1854** *Poultry Chron.* I. 616/1 A Sweepstake for Dahlias, of 2s. 6d. each (open to the County).

b. A betting or gambling transaction in which each person contributes a stake, and the whole of the stakes are taken by one or divided among several under certain conditions.

1862 SALA *Seven Sins* III. v. 121 A lucky draw in a sweep-stakes on one of the minor races. **1901** HALL & OSBORNE *Sunshine & Surf* ii. 18 We had nothing so modern or up to date as sweepstakes on the day's run [of the ship].

4. *attrib.*

1599 MINSHEU *Sp. Dict., Pleas. Dial.* (1623) 25 It is not, but that you will not haue any game of vertue but sweepe stake play. **1779** *Sylph* I. 238 My former winnings are in the sweep-stake-pool at the commerce-table. **1896** *Peterson Mag.* Jan. 89/2 Four miles the old mule took at sweepstake pace. **1897** *Westm. Gaz.* 29 May 10/1 The amount spent on sweepstake tickets during the autumn race meeting totalled up to the respectable sum of £107,164.

Hence **'sweep,staking**, gambling in the way of sweepstakes.

1882 S. G. THOMAS in Burnie *Mem. & Lett.* xv. (1891) 179 There is a good [deal] of card-playing on board, and some 'sweepstaking'.

sweepy ('swi:pɪ), *sb. dial.* Also 8 *s.w. dial.* **zweepy.** [? f. *sweep-chimney* (SWEEP- 2) + -Y dim. suffix. (Slightly earlier than SWEEP *sb.* 33; cf. SWEETIE.)] A chimney-sweep or his boy.

1798 T. MORTON *Speed the Plough* I. ii. (1800) 10 Little zweepy do tell I he can zee a bit out from the top of the chimbley. **1825–80** JAMIESON, *Sweepie*, a chimney sweeper, Aberd.

sweepy ('swi:pɪ), *a.* Chiefly *poet.* [f. SWEEP *sb.* or *v.* + -Y.] Characterized by sweeping movement or form; sweeping.

1697 DRYDEN *Virg. Georg.* I. 651 The King of Floods.. rowling onward, with a sweepy Sway, Bore Houses, Herds, and lab'ring Hinds away. **1700** —— *Ovid's Met., Acis, Pol. & Galatea* 127 The sweepy weight Of Ews that sink beneath the Milky fraight. **1722** W. HAMILTON *Wallace* 116 Bars, Bolts, and brazen Hinges..tumbl'd down before the sweepy Stroke. **1725** POPE *Odyss.* IV. 644 The Nile, who from the secret source Of Jove's high seat descends with sweepy force. **1790** A. WILSON *Thunderstorm* Poet. Wks. (1846) 33 Hail furious flew and sweepy light'ning shone. **1821** JOANNA BAILLIE *Metr. Leg., Columbus* xvi, Groves, where each dome of sweepy leaves In air of morning gently heaves. **1821** T. G. WAINEWRIGHT *Ess. & Crit.* (1880) 184 His lines are flowing and sweepy. **1850** BROWNING *Christmas Eve* viii. 9, I saw the back of Him—no more:..No face only the sight Of a sweepy garment, vast and white.

sweer (swɪə(r), swir), *a. Sc.* and *north. dial.* Forms: 1 **swær (suuer, swer), swære,** 3 *Ormin* **sware,** 3–7 **swere,** 4 **suer,** 4–5 **suere,** 4–6 **swer,** 6 **sweyr,** 6–7 **sueir,** 6–9 **sweir,** 7 **sweare,** 7, 9 **swear,** 8– **sweer.** [Com. Teut. adj. (= heavy, grievous, grave):—OE. *swǽr, swǽre*, also *swár*, = OFris. *swêre* (WFris. *swier*, E. and NFris. *swâr*, only fig.), OS. *swâr*, MLG. *swêr* and *swâr*, MDu. *swær* and *swâre* (Du. *zwaar*), OHG. *suâri* and *suâr* (MHG. *swære*, *swære*, and *swâr*, G. *schwer*), ON. *svárr* (Sw. *svår*; Da. *svær* from LG.), Goth. *swêrs* only in sense 'honoured, worthy' :—OTeut. **swǣrja-* and **swǣra-* (cf. Lith. *sveriù* to lift, weigh, *svarùs* heavy).

Ormin's form *sware* is from ON. The physical meaning 'heavy' did not survive the OE. period.]

†**1.** Grievous, oppressive. *Obs.*

a **900** CYNEWULF *Crist* 1412 (Gr.) Þær þu þolades siþþan.. sar & swar ȝewin & sweartne deað. *a* **1000** *Cædmon's Gen.* 472 (Gr.) Swa him æfter þy yldo ne derede ne suht sware. *c* **1200** ORMIN 16280 Forr hefiȝ & forr sware unngripþ þatt hæþenn follc þær wrohhte. *a* **1225** *Juliana* 46 Ne set me neuer naþing swa luðere ne swa swere.

†**2.** Oppressed in mind, grieved, sad. *Obs.*

c **1000** *Ags. Ps.* (Th.) ci. 4 [cii. 5] Forðon me is swære stefne, hefiȝ, gnorniende. *c* **1375** *Sc. Leg. Saints* vi. (*Thomas*) 480 Þat lichtis þe hart & makis It clere, þat Ignorance before mad swere.

3. Disinclined for effort, inactive; indolent, slothful.

c **725** *Corpus Gloss.* (Hessels) D 26 *Desis*, suuer. *c* **950** *Lindisf. Gosp.* Matt. xxv. 26 *Serue male et piger*, ðeȝn ðe yfle & swer. *c* **1375** *Sc. Leg. Saints* vii. (*Jacobus Min.*) 12, I tak na tym to tel It here, For I ame ald & sumdele swere. *a* **1500** *Wisd. Solomon* 549 in *Ratis Raving*, etc. 17 He sais, þat the full suere man plettis his handis one his brest. **1500–20** DUNBAR *Poems* xxvi. 70 Mony sweir bumbard belly huddroun. **1513** DOUGLAS *Æneis* III. viii. 15 Nocht sweir, bot in his deidis diligent. **1596** DALRYMPLE tr. *Leslie's Hist. Scot.* I. 286 Ydle, sueir, and sleuthfull. **1609** SKENE *Reg. Maj., Stat. Alex. II*, 14 The swere and slowfull man will not plowe. **1668** R. B. *Adagia Scot.* 3 An oleit [= active] Mother makes a sweir Daughter. **1865** G. MACDONALD *A. Forbes* iv, It's a sweer (*lazy*) thochtless way to gang to the Almichty wi' ilka fash.

4. Loth, reluctant, unwilling, disinclined (*to do* something).

a **1300** *Cursor M.* 28284 Ic ha ben bath reckeles and suere To helpe nedy in þair mistere. *c* **1375** *Sc. Leg. Saints* vi. (*Thomas*) 685 Þocht to treu he wes swere, Quhen he can goddis wordis here. *a* **1510** DOUGLAS *K. Hart* II. 24 In fayth ȝe cum nocht heir; Rin on thy way, or thow sall beir ane route: And say, the portar he is wonder sweir. **1560** in *Maitl. Club Misc.* III. 217 We haif our lang abstractit ourselfis and beyne sweir in adjwning ws to Christes Congregatioun. **1724** RAMSAY *Tea-t. Misc.* (1733) I. 26 But O I'm wae And unko sweer to die. **1816** SCOTT *Antiq.* xv, 'Very right, my little man,' said Ochiltree, turning the reluctant pony's head towards Monkbarns, 'but we'll guide him atween us, if he's no a' the sweerer.' **1896** BARRIE *Marg. Ogilvy* vi. (1897) 107 I'm sweer to waken him—I doubt he was working late.

†**'sweerdom.** *Sc. Obs. rare*[−1]. In 4 **suer-.** [f. prec. + -DOM.] = SWEERNESS 1.

c **1375** *Sc. Leg. Saints* xl. (*Ninian*) 233 Suerdome & Idilnes forto fle.

sweere, obs. form of SWIRE.

†**sweering.** *Obs. rare*[−1]. In 4 **sueryng.** [irreg. f. SWEER *a.* + -ING[1].] Sloth, negligence.

a **1300** *Cursor M.* 28329 Ic ha þere ben in present þar man wit-vten testament, Wit-vten scrift and preist rede, Thoru mi sueryng mai fall was dede.

'sweerness. *Sc.* and *north. dial.* [OE. *swǽrnes* = MLG. *swêr-*, *swârnisse*: see SWEER *a.* and -NESS.]

1. Indolence, laziness, sloth.

c **888** ÆLFRED *Boeth.* xxxv. § 1 Þeah sio swærnes ðæs lichoman & þa unþeawas oft abiseȝien þæt mod mid oferȝiotulnesse. *a* **1300** *Cursor M.* 28370 My suernes me has don for-gette. *c* **1400** *Apol. Loll.* (Camden) 107 Superfluite, glotany, and lust, and swernes. **1456** SIR G. HAY *Bk. Knighthood* Wks. (S.T.S.) II. 59 Suerenes is a vice quhilk makis a man to hate all gudelynes and to lufe all viciousnes. **1533** GAU *Richt Vay* 20 Sweirnes is aganis the thrid command. **1595** DUNCAN *App. Etym.* (E.D.S.), *Segnities*,.. sweirnes; *desidia*. **1676** ROW *Contn. Blair's Autobiogr.* ix. (1848) 129 Checking himself for swearness, laziness, and loving of his bed too well.

2. Unwillingness, disinclination (*to do* something).

1533 BELLENDEN *Livy* V. xxiv. (S.T.S.) II. 231 For swernes þat ȝe haue to big, ȝe ar reddy to suffer all þir schamefull..dammaigis. **1659** *Melrose Regality Records* (S.H.S. 1914) I. 218 [He] burstit [a mare]..puting and binding three harrowes togither for hes sueirnes to lift the ane at the land end.

sweert (swirt), *a. Sc.* Also **sweered, sweerd, sweired, sweirt, swear't.** [? f. SWEER *a.* + -ED (-*t*). Cf. *swippert* (see SWIPPER).] = SWEER 3, 4.

1817 *Lintoun Green* Errata etc. 167 Sweered, yet willing. **1824** MISS FERRIER *Inher.* iv. (1825) I. 39 He maun tak what the doctor sends him..but 'tweel he's very sweered to tak them whiles, tho' I'm sure muckle money they cost. **1870** RAMSAY *Remin.* (ed. 18) p. xv, A man sae sure o' Heaven and sae sweert to be going taet. **1885** BLACK *White Heather* xx, I was sweirt to trouble his lordship with my small affairs.

sweesh, Sc. form of SWISH.

sweet (swi:t), *sb.* Forms: see next. [SWEET *a.* used subst.]

1. a. That which is sweet to the taste; something having a sweet taste. Chiefly *poet.*

a **1300** *Cursor M.* 7126 Of þe etand þe mete vt sprang, And þe suete vte o þe strang. *Ibid.* 23979 He dranc þe sure and i þe suete. **1390** GOWER *Conf.* I. 82 Fulofte and thus the swete soureth, Whan it is knowe to the tast. **1590** SPENSER *F.Q.* I. iii. 30 A dram of sweet is worth a pound of sowre. **1607** SHAKS. *Cor.* III. i. 157 Let them not licke The sweet which is their poyson. **1611** *Bible* 1 Esdras ix. 51 Goe then and eate the fat, and drinke the sweet. **1781** COWPER *Conversat.* 440 The mind..Visiting ev'ry flow'r with labour meet, And gathering all her treasures sweet by sweet.

b. A sweet food or drink.

c **1400** *Destr. Troy* 13683 Fortune..Lurkis in lightly with lustis in hert, Gers hym swolow a swete, þat swellis hym after. **1660** F. BROOKE tr. *Le Blanc's Trav.* 22 The Nobility of the Country affect much to eat Ambar, Musk, and other sweets. **1697** DRYDEN *Virg. Georg.* IV. 300 Such Rage of Honey in their Bosom beats: And such a Zeal they have for flow'ry Sweets. **1743** FRANCIS tr. *Hor., Odes* IV. xii. 22 Bring the glad merchandise, with sweets replete. **1802** *Eng. Encycl.* V. 610/2 The purer sweets, as sugar... The unctuous and mucilaginous sweets, as the impure sugars, liquorice, &c. **1861** FLOR. NIGHTINGALE *Nursing* (ed. 2) 51, I have never known a person take to sweets when he was ill who disliked them when he was well. **1887** JEFFERIES *Amaryllis* iii, If there were two courses, then bread between to prepare the palate, and to prevent the sweets from quarrelling with the acids.

c. *pl.* Syrup added to wine or other liquor to sweeten and improve its flavour; hence, wine or other liquor thus sweetened; applied *spec.* to British wines and cordials.

a **1679** SIR J. MOORE *Eng. Interest* (1703) 33 The best way to Order your Sugar before you put it into your Cyder, is to make it into a kind of Syrup or Sweets. **1696** *Act 7 & 8 Will. III*, c. 30 § 6 Mixed Liquors commonly called and known by the Name of Sweets, made from foreign or English Materials. *a* **1700** B. E. *Dict. Cant. Crew, Sweets*, the Dreggs of Sugar used by Vintners, to allay the undue fermenting or fretting of their Wine. **1765** BLACKSTONE *Comm.* I. viii. 320 All artificial wines, commonly called sweets. **1842** *Penny Mag.* 29 Oct. 431/1 Mark Beaufoy..entered his name at the Excise as a 'maker of sweets' about a century ago. **1845** DODD *Brit. Manuf.* 98 At first the name of 'sweets' was confined principally to the varieties of raisin-wine. **1889** *Act 52 & 53 Vict.* c. 42 § 28 The expression 'sweets or made wines' shall mean any liquor which is made from fruit and sugar..and which has undergone a process of fermentation.

d. *spec.* A sweet dish (a pudding, tart, cooked fruit, etc.), or one of several such, forming a separate course at a meal. Usu. *pl.* in early use.

1832 F. TROLLOPE *Domestic Manners Americans* II. xxviii. 131 They are 'extravagantly fond'..of puddings, pies, and all kinds of 'sweets'. **1834** DICKENS *Sk. Boz, Steam Excurs.*, The sweets [on the table] shook and trembled till it was quite impossible to help them. **1852** THACKERAY *Esmond* II. xv, By the time the soup came he fancied they must have been hours at table; and as for the sweets and jellies, he thought they never would be done. *a* **1864** HAWTHORNE *Grimshawe* xix. (1891) 246 And *entremets*, and 'sweets', as the English call them. **1890** R. C. LEHMANN *H. Fludyer* 41 There was a delicious sweet for luncheon... It was like a sort of bird's-nest in spun barley-sugar with whipped cream eggs inside. **1954** J. BETJEMAN *Few Late Chrysanthemums* 95, I know what I wanted to ask you—Is trifle sufficient for sweet? **1968** [see PUDDING *sb.* 6 a]. **1979** J. COOPER *Class* xii. 202 Everything from lemon water ice to jam roly-poly pudding, Caroline would call 'pudding'. She would never say 'sweet' or 'dessert'.

e. A sweetmeat, esp. in lozenge or 'drop' form.

SWEETIE is earlier in this sense.

1851 MAYHEW *Lond. Labour* I. 203/2 Rose acid, which is a 'transparent' sweet. **1865** DICKENS *Mut. Fr.* I. v, The basket supplied the few small lots of fruit and sweets that he offered for sale. **1877** R. J. MORE *Under the Balkans* xv. 216 Sweets, jelly, and water were then handed round by the bridesmaids to the assembled guests.

f. *pl.* Drugs, *esp.* amphetamines. *U.S. slang.*

1961 [see HOLD *v.* 15 f]. **1979** S. SMITH *Survivor* xxi. 221 A whole load of minor drugs, mostly amphetamines—known as 'sweets', 'blues' and 'black bombers'.

2. Sweetness of taste; sweet taste. *rare.*

c **1381** CHAUCER *Parl. Foules* 161 For thu of loue hast lost thi tast, y gesse As seek man hath of swete & bitternesse. **1705** BEVERLEY *Virginia* II. iv. § 13. (1722) 113 Their [*sc.* mulberries'] Taste..being of a faintish Sweet, without any Tartness. **1887** LADD *Physiol. Psychol.* II. iii. § 13. 313 It seems tolerably well established that sweet and sour are tasted chiefly with the tip of the tongue.

3. a. That which is pleasant to the mind or feelings; something that affords enjoyment or gratifies desire; (a) pleasure, (a) delight; the pleasant part *of* something. In later use chiefly in *pl.*, the pleasures or delights *of* something.

Often in contrast with *bitter*, *sour*, and in expressions retaining literal phraseology, e.g. *to taste* or *suck the sweet(s) of.*

sing. **1377** LANGL. *P. Pl.* B. XI. 250 Al though it be soure to suffre þere cometh swete [C. XIII. 143 a swete] after. **1423** JAS. I *Kingis Q.* clxxxii, Euery wicht his awin suete or sore Has maist In mynde. *c* **1440** *Jacob's Well* 106 He had leuere lesyn thre massys þan to forgo oo slepe or o sweet in þe morwenyng. **1553** T. WILSON *Rhet.* (1580) 31 Where the sweete hath his sower ioyned with hym. **1560** ROLLAND *Seven Sages* 70 He..had slokinnit of bedsolace the sweit. **1589** COOPER *Admon.* 178 Princes..which suck the sweete from the people of God. **1611** SHAKS. *Wint. T.* IV. iii. 3 When Daffadils begin to peere,..Why, then comes in the sweet o' the yeere. **1637** HEYWOOD *Pleas. Dial.* Wks. 1874 VI. 302 Who can know the sweet of ease, That never was in paine? **1697** DAMPIER *Voy. round World* (1699) 64 Our Jamaica-men Trade thither indeed, and find the sweet of it. **1725** POPE *Odyss.* V. 152 Love, the only sweet of life. **1878** BROWNING *La Saisiaz* 310 Must..Every sweet warn "Ware my bitter!"

pl. **1583** MELBANCKE *Philotimus* C iij, Alwayes shun such bitter sweets. **1590** LODGE *Rosalind* (1592) G iij, Of all soft sweets, I like my mistris brest. **1596** SHAKS. *Tam. Shr.* I. i. 28 To sucke the sweets of sweete Philosophie. **1607** TOURNEUR *Rev. Trag.* IV. i. G j, An incredible Act.. Twixt my Step-mother and the Bastard, oh, Incestuous sweetes betweene 'em. **1694** tr. *Milton's Lett. State* Wks. 1738 II. 175 Your Lordships.. who.. enjoy the sweets of Peace both at home and abroad. **1697** DRYDEN *Æneid* XI. 417 The Gods have envy'd me the sweets of Life. **1749** FIELDING *Tom Jones* III. vi, Surfeited with the sweets of marriage, or disgusted by its bitters. **1826** F. REYNOLDS *Life & Times* II. 436 Being now compelled daily, to taste more and more of the sweets of management. **1858** R. S. SURTEES *Ask Mamma* xlv. 200 Mr. Bankhead, knowing the sweets of office, again aspired to high places. **1861** HUGHES *Tom Brown at Oxf.* x, The run.. up to town to.. taste some of the sweets of the season.

b. Contrasted with *sweat*.

1588 KYD *Househ. Philos.* Index, Wks. (1901) 236 Gaine purchased with sweat or sweete. **1607** HIERON *Wks.* I. 397 We haue heard hitherto of the sweat, now let vs heare the sweet of religion. **1610** MASON *Turke* V. i, Ere we had relisht the sweete of her sweete [*sic*], that is the fruit of her labors. **1667** FLAVEL *Saint Indeed* (1754) 129 He that will not have the sweat, must not expect the sweet of religion. **1670** RAY *Prov.* 146 No sweet without some sweat.

4. A beloved person, darling, sweetheart. (Cf. SWEET *a.* 8 c.)

In ME. verse *that swete* is freq. used conventionally.

13.. *Guy Warw.* (A.) 4578 No y no loued non bot þat swete. *c* **1369** CHAUCER *Dethe Blaunche* 832 Hyt was my swete ryght al hir selve. *c* **1400** *Destr. Troy* 10567 Myche sorow hade his Syre the sun to behold, And oft swonyt that swete, & in swyme felle. *c* **1480** HENRYSON *Mor. Fab., Cock & Fox* vii, At his end I did my besie curis To hald his heid .. Syne at the last, the sweit swelt in my arme. **1592** SHAKS. *Rom. & Jul.* III. iii. 162 Bid my Sweete prepare to chide. **1640** tr. *Verdere's Rom. of Rom.* III. 66 Among the which [gentle-women] perceiving my Claristea (so is this inexorable sweet named) to be one. **1664** BUTLER *Hud.* II. I. 394 This made the beauteous Queen of Crete To take a Town-Bull for her Sweet. **1703** *Rules of Civility* 25 As, for a Governor, speaking of his Wife, to say,.. My Sweet is the most prudent. **1855** TENNYSON *Maud* I. XXII. xi, She is coming, my own, my sweet. **1868** MORRIS *Earthly Par.* (1870) I. I. 289 What feat do ye This eve in honour of my sweet and me?

5. a. A sweet sound. *poet.* *rare*$^{-1}$.

1590 SPENSER *F.Q.* I. xii. 39 Yet wist no creature, whence that heauenly sweet Proceeded.

b. *pl.* A woman's breasts. *poet.*

1817 KEATS *Poems* 49 Ah! who can e'er forget so fair a being? Who can forget her half retiring sweets? **1870** D. G. ROSSETTI *Poems* (ed. 2) 111 Your silk ungirdled and unlac'd And warm sweets open to the waist.

6. Sweetness of smell, fragrance; *pl.* sweet odours, scents, or perfumes. *poet.*

1594 DRAYTON *Sonn., Amour* xxv, Some muz'd to see the earth enuy the ayre, Which from her lyps exhald refined sweet. *c* **1600** SHAKS. *Sonn.* xcix, More flowers I noted, yet I none could see, But sweet, or culler it had stolne from thee. **1612** WEBSTER *White Devil* II. i. 165 The naturall sweetes Of the Spring-violet. *a* **1718** PRIOR *2nd Hymn Callimachus* 50 Perfumes distill their Sweets. **1784** COWPER *Task* I. 444 He .. riots in the sweets of ev'ry breeze. **1820** SHELLEY *Skylark* 55 The scent it gives Makes faint with too much sweet those heavy-wingèd thieves. **1821** CLARE *Vill. Minstr.* II. 81 Perfuming evening with a luscious sweet.

7. *pl.* Substances having a sweet smell; fragrant flowers or herbs; †scents, perfumes. Now *rare*.

1602 SHAKS. *Ham.* V. i. 266 Sweets, to the sweet. **1639–40** in Swayne *Churchw. Acc. Sarum* (1896) 320 Sweetes to burne in the Church at Chrismass. **1667** MILTON *P.L.* V. 294 Through Groves of Myrrhe, And flowring Odours... A Wilderness of Sweets. **1691** *Lond. Gaz.* No. 2641/4 The Bottle of Sweets [*viz.* perfume]. **1784** COWPER *Task* II. 257 Strew the deck With lavender, and sprinkle liquid sweets. **1837** HT. MARTINEAU *Soc. Amer.* II. 63 The rich carnations and other sweets that bloomed in the garden.

8. *attrib.* and *Comb.* (chiefly in sense 1 e), as ***sweet-box***, ***coupon***, ***-maker***, ***-making***, ***paper***, ***ration***, ***rationing***, ***-shop***, ***-stall***, ***-standing***; (sense 1 d) ***sweet course***; **sweet trolley**, a dining trolley from which a choice of cold sweet dishes may be offered in a restaurant.

1943 N. LAST *Diary* 25 Dec. in *Nella Last's War* (1983) 270 Not a flower, a card—or a sweet, although you had the *sweet coupons in your pocket. **1974** G. MARKSTEIN *Cooler* xlvi. 164 Grace spent all the sweet coupons he had left on buying a bar of chocolate. **1892** *Girl's Own Paper* 23 Apr. 476/2 The *sweet course can also be arranged for by having some stewed fruit.. with a mould of rice or cornflour. **1981** P. VAN GREENAWAY *'Cassandra' Bell* vii. 83 The evening meal.. lasted ten minutes... Cherry stabbed a fork at his once or twice, derided the sweet course, and went. **1896** *Westm. Gaz.* 18 Mar. 8/2 A Hoxton sugar-boiler and *sweet-maker. **1731–3** P. SHAW *Chem. Lect.* xi. (1755) 203 The Art of *Sweet-Making might receive a high Degree of Improvement, by using pure Sugar as one general wholesome Sweet, instead of those infinite Mixtures of Honey, Raisins, Syrups, Treacle, Stum, Cyder, &c. wherewith the Sweet-Makers supply the Wine-Coopers. **1964** *Guardian* 1 Feb. 8/3 An occasional *sweetpaper flutters striped among the bushes. **1979** M. INGATE *Tomb of Flowers* xxi. 153 A few sweet papers, and one or two bottles. **1944** *Sweet ration [see RATION 3 c]. **1978** E. MALPASS *Wind brings up Rain* i. 11 She tried to take back the toffee—she *needed* her sweet ration. **1942** *Times* 24 July 2/6 As a prelude to the introduction of chocolate and *sweet rationing.. there is heavy selling at some retail shops. **1879** MISS E. K. BATES *Egypt. Bonds* II. vi. 166 The *sweet-shops, with their sugary wares. **1882** *East. Daily Press* 17 July 3 All day long the *sweet stalls.. were besieged by battalions of the common honey bee. **1902** 'Q' *White Wolf* 91 He had bought a packet off one of the *sweet-standings. **1963** *P.M.L.A.* Dec. p. vii/2 [U.K.] *sweet trolley: [U.S.] dessert cart. **1964** L. DEIGHTON *Funeral in Berlin* xv. 93 The steak was O.K. and I was strong-willed enough not to hit the sweet-trolley too hard. **1981** *Radio Times* 19–25 Sept. 21/1 It's irritating being pointed at in a restaurant, like a sweet trolley.

sweet (swiːt), *a.* and *adv.* Forms: 1 **swoete**, *Northumb.* **suoet**, **suet**, 1–6 **swete**, 2–6 **swet**, 3–6 **suete**, 4–5 **suet**, *Sc.* **sweyt**, 4–8 *Sc.* **sweit**, 5–7 **sweete**, (2 **sweote**, 3 **swiete**, 4 **suette**, **swett**, **squete**, **sweyte**, *Kent.* **zuete**, 5 **swette**, **sqwete**, **swyte**, 6 *Sc.* **sweitt**, **sueit**, 7 **suiet**, 8 *Sc.* **suit**), 6– **sweet**. *Comp.* 1 **swet(t)ra**, 3–5 **swettere**, (1 **swoetra**, 3 **swettre**, **swetture**, 4 **-ore**, **-our**, 5 **-ir**, **-ur**; 4 **squetter**, **suetter**), 4–5 **swetter**; 4 **swetere**, *Sc.* **-are**, 6 *Sc.* **-ar**, **suetar**, 5– **sweeter**. *Sup.* 1–5 **swetest**, 2–5 **-este**, 5 **-ist**, 5– **sweetest**; also 3–5 **swetteste**, 4–5 **-est**, 5 **-ist**. [Com. Teut.: OE. *swéte*, = OFris. *swêt*, OS. *swôti*, MLG. *sote*, *sute*, (LG. *söte*, *söt*), MDu. *soete*, *suete* (Du. *zoet*), OHG. *suozi*, *swuozi* (MHG. *sueze*, G. *süss*), ON. *sœtr* (Sw. *söt*, Da. *sød*):—OTeut. **swōtja-*, **swōti-*, f. *swōt-* (whence OE. *swóte* SOOT *adv.*):—Indo-Eur. *swād-* (with variant *swăd-*), in Skr. *svādús* sweet, *svádati* to be sweet, Gr. ἡδύς sweet, ἥδεσθαι to rejoice, ἡδονή pleasure, ἁνδάνειν (ἕαδον, ἕαδε) to please, L. *suāvis* (:—**swādwis*) sweet, *suādēre* to advise (properly, to make something pleasant to). Gothic shows another grade of the root in *sūts*.]

A. *adj.*

1. a. Pleasing to the sense of taste; having a pleasant taste or flavour; *spec.* having the characteristic flavour (ordinarily pleasant when not in excess) of sugar, honey, and many ripe fruits, which corresponds to one of the primary sensations of taste. Also said of the taste or flavour. Often opposed to *bitter* or *sour* (so also in *fig.* senses).

See also special collocations in C. 1.

c **888** ÆLFRED *Boeth.* xxxix. §9 þæt is forhwi se gooda læce selle þam halum men seftne drenc & swetne. *a* **1000** *Phœnix* 193 (Gr.) þa swetestan somnað & gædrað wyrta wynsume & wudubleda. *c* **1250** *Death* 106 in *O.E. Misc.*, Hwer beoð þine dihsches Midd þine swete sonde? **1303** R. BRUNNE *Handl. Synne* 1398 Delytable, & swete of sauoure. **1377** LANGL. *P. Pl.* B. XII. 264 þe larke.. is.. swifter þan þe pecok, And of flesch... fatter and swetter. **1393** *Ibid.* C. XIX. 60 Somme [apples] ar swettere þan some and sonnere wollen rotye. *c* **1449** PECOCK *Repr.* I. xiii. 67 Hony is swettist to him of alle othere metis. **1523** FITZHERB. *Husb.* §23 The yonger and the grener that the grasse is, the softer and sweter it wyll be, whan it is hey. **1574** NEWTON *Health Mag.* I j b, The fleash that is about the bones is sweeter and better to digest then other. **1594** MARLOWE & NASHE *Dido* II. i, Ile giue thee Sugar-almonds, sweete Conserues. **1596** *Edward III*, II. i. 406 A sugred, sweet and most delitious tast. **1667** MILTON *P.L.* V. 68 O Fruit Divine, Sweet of thy self, but much more sweet thus cropt. **1765** *Museum Rust.* IV. 398 Fine-flavoured, mellow, sweet beef from beasts fed with oil-cakes. **1818** SCOTT *Br. Lamm.* xi A tart—a flam—and some nonsense sweet things, and comfits. **1827** FARADAY *Chem. Manip.* xxiv. (1842) 629 The liquid will communicate a very aromatic sweet taste to it. **1883** *Cassell's Dict. Cookery* 772/1 Rose Sauce for Sweet Puddings. **1887** BENTLEY *Man. Bot.* (ed. 5) 824 Secondary products of metastasis, some of which, as sweet secretions, &c., are necessary for the perpetuation of the species.

b. In similative and other proverbial phr.

c **825** *Vesp. Ps.* xviii. 11 [xix. 10] *Dulciora super mel & favum*, swoetran ofer hunig & biobræd. *c* **1386** CHAUCER *Miller's T.* 20 He hym self as sweete as is the roote Of lycorys. *a* **1400–50** *Wars Alex.* 3855 Was neuir na hony in na hyue vndire heuen swettir. *c* **1403** LYDG. *Temple of Glas* 1251 Swete is swettir eftir bitternes. **14..** *Lat. & Eng. Prov.* (MS. Douce 52) lf. 16 b, Hungur makyth harde bonys swete. **1546** J. HEYWOOD *Prov.* (1867) 16 Sweete meate will haue sowre sawce. *a* **1553** UDALL *Royster D.* I. iii. (Arb.) 20 Soft fire maketh sweete malte, good Madge. **1600** SHAKS. *A.Y.L.* III. ii. 115 Sweetest nut, hath sowrest rinde. **1607** [see SAUCE *sb.* 1 b]. **1671** T. HUNT *Abeced. Scholast.* 79 The sweetest flesh is next the bone. **1697** DRYDEN *Virg. Past.* vii. 53 Fair Galathea, with thy silver Feet, O, whiter than the Swan, and more than Hybla sweet. **1721** BAILEY s.v., After sweet Meat comes sowr Sauce. **1898** W. W. JACOBS *Sea Urchins, Choice Spirits* (1906) 90 'The meat's awful.' 'It's as sweet as nuts,' said the skipper.

2. a. Pleasing to the sense of smell; having a pleasant smell or odour; fragrant. Also said of the smell or odour.

900 tr. *Bæda's Hist.* III. viii. (1890) 174 Hordærn.. balsami & þara deorwyrðestena wyrta & þara swetestena þara þe in middangearde wæron. **971** *Blickl. Hom.* 59 þa swetan stencas gestincað þara wuduwyrta. *c* **1175** *Lamb. Hom.* 53 þe sweote smel of þe chese. *c* **1220** *Bestiary* 508 Vt of his ðrote is smit an onde, Ðe swetteste ðing ðat is o londe. *a* **1272** *Luue Ron* 151 in *O.E. Misc.* 97 þu art swetture þane eny flur. *a* **1300** *Cursor M.* 1381 Cipres, be þe suete sauur, Bitakens ur suete [*Fairf.* squete] sauueur. *c* **1386** CHAUCER *Prol.* 5 Zephirus.. with his swete breeth. *c* **1425** *Cast. Persev.* 801 in *Macro Plays* 101 Parkys, poundys, & many pens, þei semyn to zou swetter þanne sens. **1542** BOORDE *Dyetary* xx. (1870) 281 Parsley.. doth cause a man to haue a swete breth. **1590** SHAKS. *Mids. N.* II. i. 252, I know a banke .. Quite ouer-cannoped.. With sweet muske roses, and with Eglantine. **1596** —— *Tam. Shr.* Induct. i. 49 Burne sweet Wood to make the Lodging sweete. **1650** FULLER *Pisgah* III. ii. §5 Pillasters.. of.. Almuggin trees.. which, if odoriferous,.. made that passage as sweet to the smell, as specious to the sight. **1781** COWPER *Hope* 290 Sweet scent, or lovely form, or both combined. **1850** TENNYSON *In Mem.* lxxxvi, Sweet after showers, ambrosial air.

†**b.** *spec.* Perfumed, scented. See also *sweet-bag*, *-ball*, *-powder* (in C. 1 a), SWEET-WATER. *Obs.*

1573–4 in Feuillerat *Revels Q. Eliz.* (1908) 208 Sweete lightes of white wex for the same vii^{s}. **1592** *Acc.-Bk. W. Wray* in *Antiquary* XXXII. 79 A barrell swet sop, xxix *s.* **1611** SHAKS. *Wint. T.* IV. iv. 253 You promis'd me a tawdry-lace, and a paire of Sweet Gloues. **1656** EARL MONM. tr. *Boccalini's Pol. Touchstone* 407 The Monopoly of making sweet Gloves to that Nation whose hand did stink insufferably.

3. a. Free from offensive or disagreeable taste or smell; not corrupt, putrid, sour, or stale; free from taint or noxious matter; in a sound and wholesome condition.

c **1250** *Gen. & Ex.* 3302 A funden trew ðor-inne dede Moyses, and it wurð swet on ðe stede. *a* **1300** *Cursor M.* 6352–4 þe water was al suete alson, þe water þat sua fuli stanc, Suetter neuer þai siþen drank. **1501** *Reg. Privy Seal Scotl.* I. 100/1 [3½] lastis of salmond, ful, rede, and swete. **1596** HARINGTON *Metam. Ajax* E iv b, Because hee had not seene better to the keeping sweet of the streets. **1607** DEKKER *Westw. Hoe* I. Wks. 1873 II. 291 He hath an excellent trick to keepe Lobsters and Crabs sweet in summer. **1655** MARQ. WORCESTER *Cent. Inv.* § 100 [They] furnish Cities with Water.. as well as keep them Sweet, running through several Streets. **1681** LANGFORD *Plain Instr. Fruit-trees* 139 Cyder Fruit.. laid upon a sweet and dry floor, in a heap. **1685** *Compl. Servant Maid* 144 You must wash your own Linen, keeping your self sweet and clean. **1754** *Compl. Cyder-man* 114 A sufficient Number of sweet Casks to put it into. **1791** *Trans. Soc. Arts* IX. p. xvii, Preserving Fresh Water sweet, for the use of Seamen during long voyages. **1859** JEPHSON *Brittany* v. 55, I question whether the beds would be so clean and sweet. **1861** MRS. BEETON *Bk. Househ. Managem.* (1880) 385 In choosing a ham, ascertain that it is perfectly sweet. **1883** GRESLEY *Gloss. Coal-mining*, *Sweet*, free from fire-damp or other gases, or from fire-stink.

b. *spec.* Of water: Fresh, not salt. Also of butter: Fresh, not salted. (Cf. G. *süsswasser*, F. *eau douce*, etc.) See also SWEET WATER.

c **1000** *Sax. Leechd.* II. 134 Drince wegbrædan seaw on swetum wætre. *c* **1220** *Bestiary* 320 He lepeð ðanne wið mikel list, Of swet water he haueð ðrist. *a* **1425** *Cursor M.* 6349 (Trin.) þei fond.. Watir bittur as any bryne. As bryne hit was & no swettur. **1480** CAXTON *Myrr.* xx. 109 Alle watres come of the see; as wel the swete as the salt. **1553** EDEN *Treat. Newe Ind.* (Arb.) 26 In this deserte are.. founde bytter waters: but more often fresshe and sweete waters. **1591** A. W. *Bk. Cookrye* 8 b, In the seething pot put in a peece of sweet Butter. **1661** LOVELL *Hist. Anim. & Min.* Introd., Living in rivers and other sweet waters. **1709** T. ROBINSON *Nat. Hist. Westmoreld.* iv. 23 The subterrene Waters are those sweet Mineral Feeders, which do implete the Body of the Earth. **1796** MORSE *Amer. Geog.* I. 84 Animals which.. live alternately on land or in sweet water. **1925** *N.Y. Produce Rev.* 27 May 95 (Advt.), Specializing in sweet butter. **1952** M. SMALL *Special Diet Cook Bk.* 201 Grocers.. catering to the Jewish trade usually carry sweet butter. **1971** S. WALKER *Highland Cookbook* 8 Scones are delicious with sweet butter, in Scotland called fresh butter.

†**c.** Of bread (in 16th c. versions of and allusions to Scripture): Unleavened. (Opposed to *sour* as in SOUR-DOUGH.) *Obs.*

1526 TINDALE *Mark* xiv. 12 The first daye of swete breed. **1535** COVERDALE *Exod.* xxxiv. 18 The feast of swete bred shalt thou kepe. **1593** NASHE *Christ's T.* Wks. 1904 II. 48 The feast of Tabernacles, the feast of sweet Bread, and the feast of Weekes.

d. Of milk: Fresh, not sour: see *sweet milk* in C. 1 a.

1812 SIR J. SINCLAIR *Syst. Husb. Scot.* I. 105 The milk can be sold sweet, as taken from the cow.

e. *Old Chem.* and *Metallurgy*. Free from corrosive salt, sulphur, acid, etc. In mod. use also in the *Oil Industry*, of petroleum or natural gas: free from sulphur compounds, *esp.* hydrogen sulphide or alkyl mercaptans.

1666 BOYLE *Orig. Formes & Qual.* II. iv. 315 Chymists.. terme the Calces of Metals and other Bodies dulcifi'd, if they be freed from all corrosive salts and sharpness of Tast, sweet, though they have nothing at all of positive sweetness. **1863** *Edin. Rev.* Apr. 411 The 'sweetest' kinds of coal (the freest from sulphur) are reserved for the smelting furnace. **1881** RAYMOND *Mining Gloss.*, *Sweet-roasting*. **1911** *Rep. Brit. Assoc. Adv. Sci. 1910* 612 The Coal Measures include 'sweet', *i.e.*, non-sulphurous, coals at several horizons. **1919** E. W. DEAN *Motor Gasoline Properties* (U.S. Bur. Mines Techn. Paper No. 214) 25 If the liquid remains unchanged in color and if the sulphur film is bright yellow or only slightly discolored.., the test shall be reported negative and the gasoline considered 'sweet'. **1950** [see HYDRODESULPHURIZATION]. **1975** *Offshore Engineer* Sept. 44/3 The sweet gas is extracted through wells drilled by a Saipem rig. **1980** *Blair & Ketchum's Country Jrnl.* Oct. 6/3 Light, so-called 'sweet', crude yields a high percentage of automotive gasoline.

4. a. Pleasing to the ear; having or giving a pleasant sound; musical, melodious, harmonious: said of a sound, a voice, an instrument, a singer or performer on an instrument.

c **900** tr. *Bæda's Hist.* IV. iii. (1890) 264 þa geherde he.. þa swetestan stefne & þa fægrestan singendra. *a* **1300** *Cursor M.* 1030 þar sune es soft and suet sang. ? *a* **1366** CHAUCER *Rom. Rose* 768 In loreyn her notes bee Fulle swetter than in this contre. *c* **1460** *Towneley Myst.* xv. 13 A! myghtfull god, what euer this ment, so swete of toyn. *c* **1500** *Melusine* i. 7 He stood styl.. to here her swette & playsaunt voyce. **1530** PALSGR. 278/1 Swetetunyng, *modulation*. *a* **1548** HALL *Chron., Hen. VIII*, 214 b, iiii. Muses plaiyng on seueral swete instrumentes. **1560** *Bible* (Geneva) 2 Sam. xxiii. 1 Dauid.. the swete singer of Israel. **1599** SHAKS., etc. *Pass. Pilgr.* 282 Cleare wels spring not, sweete birds sing not.

1602 —— *Ham.* III. i. 166 Like sweet Bels iangled, out of tune, and harsh. **1604** E. G[RIMSTONE] *D'Acosta's Hist. Indies* VII. iii. 500 Their tongue and pronountiation is very sweete and pleasant. **1617** MORYSON *Itin.* I. 152 A paire of Organs doth make sweet musicke. **1697** DRYDEN *Virg. Georg.* IV. 680 Th' Infernal Troops..list'ning, crowd the sweet Musician's side. **1780** COWPER *Doves* 37 Thus sang the sweet sequester'd bird, Soft as the passing wind. **1836** DUBOURG *Violin* i. (1878) 11 The viol instruments were decidedly sweet, but comparatively dull. **1859** TENNYSON *Marr. Geraint* 329 The sweet voice of a bird.

b. Hence, applied to music, esp. jazz, played at a steady tempo without improvisation, or to this style of playing and its exponents. Cf. HOT *a.* 8 g. Orig. and chiefly *U.S.*

1924 [see HOT *a.* 8 g]. **1927** *Melody Maker* May 477/1 A really good saxophonist..must be able to render a sweet melody correctly phrased and as though his soul were in it, without a trend to exaggerate sloppy sentiment. **1933** *Fortune* Aug. 47/1 He is decidedly not a *sweet* trombonist—he doesn't play sentimentally with lots of *vibrato*. **1934** S. R. NELSON *All about Jazz* iii. 66 If it is of the melody type, and without much syncopation, the number is treated in the 'sweet' manner. **1956** A. HODEIR *Jazz: its Evolution & Essence* viii. 129 Both 'straight' jazz and 'sweet' music..make use of a sonority and a melodic and harmonic language that are exaggeratedly sugar-coated. **1981** *Oxford Times* 6 Feb. 13/1 The Dorseys' orchestra at this time was sweet rather than swinging, which will disappoint those like myself who prefer the jazzier side of Jimmy and Tommy Dorsey.

5. Pleasing (in general); yielding pleasure or enjoyment; agreeable, delightful, charming. (Only literary in unemotional use: cf. e.)

a. to the mind or feelings.

c **888** ÆLFRED *Boeth.* xxxv. §4 Hi..meahton eaðe seggan soðspell, ʒif him þa leasunga næren swetran. *c* **900** tr. *Bæda's Hist.* v. xxiii. (1890) 482 Me symble swete & wynsum wæs, ðæt ic oþþe leornode oþþe lærde oððe write. *c* **1200** *Trin. Coll. Hom.* 33 Ac swo þe wowe þinkeð biter, þe hwile þe he lesteð, swo þincð wele þe swettere þan hit cumeð þarafter. *a* **1225** *Ancr. R.* 294 Drauh, ase he dude, þet swete likunge into smeortunge. *c* **1250** *Gen. & Ex.* 210 Paradis, An erd al ful of swete blis. *c* **1320** *Sir Tristr.* 631 Þe ring was fair to se, Þe ʒift was wel swete. **1362** LANGL. *P. Pl.* A. Prol. 83 Persones and parisch prestes..askeþ leue..To singe þer for Simonye, for seluer is swete. **1377** *Ibid.* B. xv. 179 Þough he bere hem no bred, he bereth hem swetter lyflode. **1393** *Ibid.* C. XXI. 219 He hadde nat wist wyterly wheþer deþ wer soure oþer sweyte. *c* **1449** PECOCK *Repr.* I. xiii. 66 In the historial parties of the Oold Testament and of the Newe, is miche delectable and sweete. **1560** DAUS tr. *Sleidane's Comm.* 337 b, How swete is yᵉ name of peace, and how comfortable a thing it is. **1567** MAPLET *Gr. Forest* 4 b, [It] is otherwise effectuous to bring a man in sweete sleepe. **1575** GASCOIGNE *Glasse Govt.* IV. vi, Although it seeme unto some men a sweete thing to commaunde. **1600** SHAKS. *A.Y.L.* II. i. 12 Sweet are the vses of aduersitie. **1604** —— *Ham.* III. iv. 209 (Qo. 2) O tis most sweete When in one line two crafts directly meete. **1609** [see REVENGE *sb.* I]. **1638** JUNIUS *Paint. Ancients* 119 Art, abounding with many sweet vices, drew still the eyes..of unadvised spectators. **1643** TRAPP *Comm. Gen.* xl. 3 A sweet providence; that these obnoxious officers should be sent to Joseph's prison. **1738** WESLEY *Hymn*, '*Let us go forth*' ii, When He vouchsafes our Hands to use, It makes the Labour sweet. **1784** COWPER *Task* I. 94 Sweet sleep enjoys the curate in his desk. *Ibid.* II. 482 Oh, popular applause, what heart of man Is proof against thy sweet seducing charms? **1801** WORDSW. *Sparrow's Nest* 19 A heart, the fountain of sweet tears. **1876** MISS BRADDON *J. Haggard's Dau.* x, It was sweeter to you to help others than to be happy yourself. **1882** SERJT. BALLANTINE *Exper.* iv. 41, I received half a guinea, the sweetest that ever found its way into my pocket.

b. to the senses; esp. to the sight = Lovely, of charming appearance.

? *a* **1366** CHAUCER *Rom. Rose* 622 And thus he walketh to solace Hym and his folk for sweeter place To pleyn ynne he may not fynde. **1375** BARBOUR *Bruce* XVI. 66 Quhen byrdis syngis on the spray,..For softnes of that sweit sesoune. *c* **1430** *Chev. Assigne* 44 A seluer cheyne Eche on of hem hadde, a-bowte his swete swyre. **1590** SPENSER *F.Q.* II. x. 47 Warlike Cæsar, tempted with the name Of this sweet Island. **1617** MORYSON *Itin.* I. 99 The place where the Marchants meete, called *la Loggia*, lying vpon the sea, is as sweete an open roome, as euer I saw. **1632** LITHGOW *Trav.* IV. 137 The sweetest face, the youngest age, and whitest skin was in greatest value and request. **1645** SYMONDS *Diary* (Camden) 175 His Majestie lay at Mr. Crompton's howse, a sweet place in a fyne parke. *a* **1700** EVELYN *Diary* 23 Apr. an. 1646, This sweete Towne [*sc.* Vincenza] has more well-built Palaces than any of its dimensions in all Italy. **1812** BYRON *Ch. Har.* I. lxxix, On high The corse [of the bull killed in the bull-fight] is piled—sweet sight for vulgar eyes. **1837** CAMPBELL *Cora Linn* ii, It was as sweet an Autumn day As ever shone on Clyde. **1842** BORROW *Bible in Spain* xxvi. 282 It is a sweet spot, and the prospect which opens from it is extensive.

¶ The phr. *sweet in* (*the, one's*) *bed* has been used with various implications.

a **1300** *Havelok* 2927 [He] dide him þere sone wedde Hire þat was ful swete in bedde. **1721** KELLY *Sc. Prov.* 290 Sweet in the Bed, and sweir up in the Morning, was never a good Housewife. *a* **1800** in Laing *Sel. Anc. Pop. P. Scotl.* (1822) xxiii. Introd., A Clown is a Clown both at home and abroad; When a Rake he is comely, and sweet in his bed.

c. Of song or discourse, and hence *transf.* of a poet, orator, etc., with mixture of sense 4: Pleasing to the ear and mind; pleasant to hear or listen to; sometimes implying 'persuasive, winning', †or in bad sense, 'alluring, enticing'.

c **1386** CHAUCER *Prol.* 265 Somwhat he lipsed for his wantownesse To make his englissh sweete vp on his tonge. **1423** JAS. I *Kingis Q.* ix, His metir suete..full of moralitee. *c* **1480** HENRYSON *Mor. Fab.* Prol. i, Thair polite termes of sweit Rhetorie. **1526** TINDALE *Rom.* xvi. 18 By swete preachynges and flatterynge wordes [they] deceave the hertes of the innocentes. *a* **1533** LD. BERNERS *Gold. Bk. M. Aurel.* (1546) Ej, He was so swete in his wordes, that many tymes he was harde more than thre houres togyther. **1612** BRINSLEY *Lud. Lit.* xiii. (1627) 175 Such a one [*sc.* book] as is most easie, both for the sweetest Latine and choisest matter. **1632** MILTON *L'Allegro* 133 Sweetest Shakespear fancies childe. **1746** FRANCIS tr. *Horace, Art of Poetry* 113 Whose rapid Numbers, suited to the Stage,..With sweet Variety were found to please.

d. *ironically*: cf. FINE *a.* 12 c.

1656 G. COLLIER *Answ. 15 Quest.* 18 Here's another sweet inference. **1677** MIEGE *Eng.-Fr. Dict.* s.v., I should have made a sweet business on't for my self. **1725** T. THOMAS in *MSS. Dk. Portland* (Hist. MSS. Comm.) VI. 133 We had a specimen of the sweet road we were to clamber through,..a pretty sharp ascent..full of loose, ragged stones. **1850** SMEDLEY *F. Fairlegh* xl, Oh! they made a sweet row, I can tell you.

e. In colloq. use, an emotional epithet expressive of the speaker's personal feelings as to the attractiveness of the object.

1779 *Mirror* No. 41 ⁋7 Miss Betsy had taken down some sweet copies of verses, as she called them, in her memorandum book. **1782** MISS BURNEY *Cecilia* I. iv, 'I assure you', she continued, 'she has all Paris in her disposal; the sweetest caps! the most beautiful trimmings! and her ribbons are quite divine!' **1840** THACKERAY *Barber Cox* June, Honourable Tom Fitz-Warter, cousin of Lord Byron's; smokes all day; and has written the sweetest poems you can imagine. **1884** *Boston* (Mass.) *Jrnl.* 22 Nov. 2/5 A new fashion in false hair is quite sweet. **1887** JESSOPP *Arcady* viii. 240 She falls in love with some sweet thing in hats or handkerchiefs.

f. Used as an intensifier in certain slang phrases (often of a coarse nature) meaning 'nothing at all'. See also *F.A.* s.v. F III. 3, FANNY ADAMS 2, *S.F.A.* s.v. S 4 a. Also ***sweet nothing***.

1958 F. NORMAN *Bang to Rights* I. 28 You can do sweet B.A. about it. **1959** I. & P. OPIE *Lore & Lang. Schoolch.* xvii. 365 They stand on the field and they rave and they shout On subjects they know sweet nothing about. **1973** B. BROADFOOT *Ten Lost Years* ix. 95 The government provided sweet bugger all. Absolutely sweet bugger all. **1973** B. TURNER *Hot-Foot* vi. 43 What had I gained for my trouble? Sweet nothing, that's what.

6. In extended use: Having an agreeable or benign quality, influence, operation, or effect. Chiefly technical: see quots.

a. Favourable, genial.

13.. *E.E. Allit. P.* C. 236 Styffe stremes & streʒt hem strayned a whyle..Tyl a swetter ful swyþe hem sweʒed to bonk. **1594** PLAT *Jewell-ho.* I. 50 Some further & sweeter helps for her barren groundes. **1824** LOUDON *Encycl. Gard.* §3295 After the bed has come to a sweet heat, shut down close at night.

b. Of land, products, or the like: Free from bitter or similar deleterious qualities.

1577 GOOGE tr. *Heresbach's Husb.* 24 The land..is..called..pleasaunt ground, sweete, blacke, rotten, and mellowed, which are the signes of good ground. **1578** LYTE *Dodoens* VI. xxiv. 688 Bay..groweth plentifully..by the sea syde in saltishe groundes..and dieth not in the winter season, as it doth in sweete groundes. **1649** BLITHE *Eng. Improv.* xxiii. 140 Which sorts of Land if Rich, and Sweet, will lose Advance by Ploughing. **1765** *Museum Rust.* III. 239 The land most suitable for this plant [*sc.* teazel] is that of a thin sweet surface, and marly bottom. **1839** MURCHISON *Silur. Syst.* I. x. 135 From its sulphureous properties, it is also preferred to coal of the sweetest and best quality. **1840** *Civil Eng. & Arch. Jrnl.* III. 296/2 Iron of an excellent quality, which they term sweet-iron.

c. Easily managed, handled, or dealt with; working or moving easily or smoothly.

1673 R. HEAD *Canting Acad.* 192 The fourteenth a Gamester, if he sees the Hic sweet, He presently drops down a Cog in the street. **1725** *New Cant. Dict.*, *Sweet*, easy to be taken in: Also expert, dexterous, clever: As, *Sweet's your Hand*, said of one who has the Knack of stealing by Sleight of Hand. **1801** STRUTT *Sports & Past.* I. i. 16 Beasts of sweet flight,..the buck, the doe, the bear, the rein deer, the elk, and the spytard. **1883** STEVENSON *Treas. Isl.* II. vii, You never imagined a sweeter schooner—a child might sail her. **1915** *Blackw. Mag.* Sept. 316/1 She was a sweet ship in a seaway if one knew her idiosyncrasies. **1937** *Times* 11 Dec. 4/7 The engine is, in my opinion, more responsive and sweet than its predecessor. **1955** *Times* 10 May 7/6 The clutch is exceptionally sweet in operation, a point which helps to make the car easily manoeuvrable. **1975** *Washington Post* 25 Jan. A19/1 As J. Robert Oppenheimer said of the hydrogen bomb: 'It was so technically sweet, we had to do it.'

†**d.** *Art.* Delicate, soft. *Obs.* (Cf. SWEETEN 8 b.)

1662 EVELYN *Chalcogr.* 66 So sweet, even and bold was his work. **1662** FAITHORNE *Graving & Etching* xvii. 21 It is at the first operation, that you are to cover all the faintest and sweetest places.

7. *transf.* (chiefly in phr.) Fond of or inclined for sweet things, esp. in *sweet tooth* (see C. 1 a).

1591 SHAKS. *Two Gent.* III. i. 330 She hath a sweet mouth.

8. a. Dearly loved or prized, precious; beloved, dear.

a **900** CYNEWULF *Juliana* 94 (Gr.) Ðu eart dohtor min seo dyreste & seo sweteste. *c* **1275** *Passion our Lord* 64 in *O.E. Misc.* 39 Vor vuele he dude god, þer-vore hi at þen ende schedden his swete blod. *a* **1300** *Cursor M.* 14401 God luued þe Iuus lang beforn þat his suet [*Fairf.* squete, *Gött.* suete, *Trin.* swete] sun was born. *c* **1375** *Lay Folks Mass Bk.* (MS. B.) 449 Swete ihesu make me saue. *c* **1385** CHAUCER *L.G.W.* 1042 *Dido*, Whom schulde he louyn but this lady swete? *c* **1386** —— *Prol. Melibeus* ⁋18 By goddes swete pyne. *c* **1400** *Destr. Troy* 11381 All sweire þai, full swiftly, vpon swete haloues. *c* **1425** *Seven Sag.* (P.) 2080 Thou wylt by schent, by swyte Jhesus. *a* **1533** LD. BERNERS *Huon* ii. 3, I..render grace..to god my swet creatore. **1579** LYLY *Euphues* (Arb.) 74 He will be..readie to offer himselfe a Sacrifice for your sweete sake. **1583** EARL NORTHAMPTON *Def. agst. Prophecies* Pp iv b, Policarpus, the sweete Martir of our Lorde. **1591** SHAKS. *Two Gent.* II. vi. 30 Ayming at Siluia as a sweeter friend. **1591** —— *1 Hen. VI*, IV. vi. 55 Thy Life to me is sweet. **1780** MME. D'ARBLAY *Diary* (1842) I. 359 Ah, how different and how superior our sweet father.

b. In forms of address, freq. affectionate, but formerly also (now *arch.*) respectful or complimentary.

a **1225** *Leg. Kath.* 1536 Mi swete lif, se swoteliche he smecheð me..þet al me þuncheð..þet he sent me. *c* **1330** *Spec. Gy de Warw.* 555 Swete lord, forʒiue þu me. *c* **1350** *Will. Palerne* 4579 Swete sire,..Wharfore was al þis fare formest bi-gunne? **1593** SHAKS. *3 Hen. VI*, II. v. 137 Nay take me with thee, good sweet Exeter. **1605** —— *Lear* I. v. 50 O let me not be mad, not mad, sweet Heauen. **1617** R. FENTON *Treat. Ch. Rome* 145 Sweet Jesus, had it not beene for these and these, we had neuer beene enabled to preach thy Gospell. **1693** *Humours Town* 31 Ah sweet Mr. Jovial, you mistake me quite. **1782** COWPER *Parrot* iii, 'Sweet Poll!' his doting mistress cries, 'Sweet Poll!' the mimic bird replies. **1807–8** SYD. SMITH *Plymley's Lett.* i. (ed. Cassell) 10 In the first place, my sweet Abraham, the Pope is not yet landed. **1833** TENNYSON *Miller's Dau.* iii, Give me one kiss: My own sweet Alice, we must die. **1849** FABER *Hymn*, Sweet Saviour, bless us ere we go. **1875** JOWETT *Plato* (ed. 2) I. 25 Be cheerful, sweet sir, and give your opinion.

c. *absol.* in affectionate address: Beloved, dear one; also in *superlative*. (Cf. SWEET *sb.* 4.)

c **1300** *K. Horn* 465 (Harl. MS.) Help me þat ych were Ydobbed to be knyhte, Suete, bi al þi myhte. **13..** *Sir Beues* (A.) 279 'Haue', a seide, 'ber þis sonde Me leue swet!' *c* **1386** CHAUCER *Frankl. T.* 250 Haue mercy sweete or ye wol do me deye. *a* **1400–50** *Wars Alex.* 2826 Here send I þe, my swete, salutis & ioy. **1588** SHAKS. *L.L.L.* v. ii. 373 Gentle sweete, Your wits makes wise things foolish. **1590** —— *Mids. N.* III. ii. 247 Sweete, do not scorne her so. *a* **1658** LOVELACE *To Lucasta, going to the Wars* i, Tell me not, sweet, I am unkind. **1814** SHELLEY *To M. W. Godwin* v, We are not happy, sweet! **1818** —— *Rosal. & Helen* 73 Thou lead, my sweet, And I will follow. **1885** 'MRS. ALEXANDER' *At Bay* x, I would give my life to buy peace for you, sweetest.

d. Dear to the person himself; usually *sarcastically*, 'pet', 'precious': chiefly qualifying *self* or *will*. *at one's own sweet will*: just as one likes. Also in phrs. ***to bet one's sweet life***, ***to take one's own sweet time***, ***to go one's own sweet way***, and varr.

1621 *Chas. I's Answ. to Petit. Comm.* in Rushw. *Hist. Coll.* (1659) I. 49 Let us not so far wrong the Jesuites, as to rob them of their sweet Positions and practice in that very point. **1746** FRANCIS tr. *Hor., Sat.* II. v. 61 Bid him go home, of his sweet self take care. *a* **1774** TUCKER *Lt. Nat.* (1834) II. 401 Nor yet need he be too secure against all damage to his own sweet person. **1802** WORDSW. *Sonn., Westm. Bridge* 12 The river glideth at his own sweet will. **1846** TENNYSON *Lit. Squabbles* iii, The petty fools of rhyme..Who..strain to make an inch of room For their sweet selves. **1862** WHITTIER *Amy Wentworth* 151 Love has never known a law Beyond its own sweet will. **1873** SYMONDS *Grk. Poets* xi. 344 The monk Planudes..remodelled the Greek Anthology of Cephalas at his own sweet will. **1889** KIPLING *From Sea to Sea* II. xxxii. 110 The younger ones [*sc.* Mormons]..*will* mix with the Gentile..and you bet your sweet life there's a holy influence working toward conversion in the kiss of an average Gentile. **1942** BERREY & VAN DEN BARK *Amer. Thes. Slang* §54/3 Not hurry..take one's (own) sweet time. **1945** A. KOBER *Parm Me* 85 You betcha sweet life I'll give you a buzz. **1946** *Civil & Mil. Gaz.* (Lahore) 19 July 6/4 The station authorities..took their own sweet time in handing the driver the token for him to proceed on his journey. **1968** M. ALLINGHAM *Cargo of Eagles* iv. 52, I let him pass, making sure he'd turn off, but not on your sweet life. He was right with me all the way. **1970** 'D. HALLIDAY' *Dolly & Cookie Bird* vii. 105 You go your own sweet way, or so the evidence tells me. **1975** D. DELMAN *One Man's Murder* ii. 49 So you're finally here... You took your own sweet time about it. **1976** H. MACINNES *Agent in Place* xi. 120 Katie has complicated everything in her own sweet way. **1978** 'G. VAUGHAN' *Belgrade Drop* v. 33 If one single person's seen you get on this lorry..you can bet your sweet life they'll turn it inside out.

9. Having pleasant disposition and manners; amiable, kindly; gracious, benignant. **a.** Of persons, etc.

c **825** *Vesp. Ps.* xxiv. 8 *Dulcis et rectus Dominus*, swoete & reht dryten. *c* **1200** ORMIN 1258 Cullfre iss milde, & meoc, & swet. *c* **1275** *Moral Ode* 381 in *O.E. Misc.* 71 God is so swete & so muchel in his godnesse. **1297** R. GLOUC. (Rolls) 4088 Ou iesu þat þulke day worþ me suete & god. **1375** BARBOUR *Bruce* I. 390 Quhen he wes blyth, he wes lufly, And meyk and sweyt in cumpany. **1382** WYCLIF *Ps.* xcix. [c.] 5 Preise ʒee his name, for swete is the Lord. **1553** *Respublica* I. i. 108, I doubte not a shewete Ladye I shall fynde hir. *c* **1610** *Women Saints* 176 She was a verie courteous and sweete woman. **1693** J. EDWARDS *Author. O. & N. Test.* 350 Very good-natur'd, sweet, and benign persons. **1799** WORDSW. *Lucy Gray* ii, The sweetest thing that ever grew Beside a human door! **1859** TENNYSON *Marr. Geraint* 393 Seeing her [*sc.* Enid] so sweet and serviceable. **1905** ELINOR GLYN *Viciss. Evangeline* 157 At luncheon she was sweet to me at once.

ironical. **1608** ARMIN *Nest Ninn.* D ij, His report..making no bones of the sweet youth gaue his doings thus. **1644** PRYNNE & WALKER *Fiennes's Trial* 26 *note*, Was not this a sweet Governour, that professeth he had no more charge of his chiefest Fort, then of any house in the Towne?

b. Of personal actions or attributes.

a **1300** *Cursor M.* 20086 He þat nam of hir his flexs, Als his suet will al wess. *c* **1330** *Spec. Guy de Warw.* 998 Þo seide anon þe profete To þe widewe wordes swete. *c* **1400** *Laud Troy Bk.* 18657 God..graunte vs of his swete grace Ther-In to haue a swete place! **1473** *Rental Bk. Cupar-Angus* (1879) I. 177 The ourman quhilk the Abbot assignis for kepyn of gud and suet nichtburhed. **1546** J. HEYWOOD *Prov.* (1867) 44 To see his sweete lookes, and here his sweete wurdes. **1590** SHAKS. *Com. Err.* II. ii. 112, I, I, Antipholus, looke strange and frowne, Some other Mistresse hath thy sweet aspects. **1647** HERRICK *Noble Numb.*, *Almes* I, Give, if thou canst, an Almes; if not, afford, Instead of that, a sweet and gentle word. *a* **1661** FULLER *Worthies, Westmoreld.* (1662) II. 140 One of a sweet nature, comely presence, courteous carriage. **1705** STANHOPE *Paraphr.* II. 265 His Temper and Conversation is sweet and obliging. **1849** MACAULAY *Hist. Eng.* viii. II. 321 His person was pleasing, his temper singularly sweet. **1886** 'OUIDA' *House Party* v. (1887) 92 How are your children? Do they still care for me? That is very sweet of them.

†**c.** Gentle, easy. *Obs.*

1607 MARKHAM *Caval.* (1617) II. iv. 50 A smooth Cannon ..is of all bytts the sweetest. *Ibid.* IV. viii. 39 You shall.. carrie an euen and sweet hand vpon him. **1622** T. SCOTT *Belg. Pismire* 37 To know the natures of all people, and to be able to carry a sweet hand, wherewith to manage them easily. **1655** FULLER *Ch. Hist.* IX. vii. §24 That he was made a Cardinall of purpose to be sent then into England for the sweet managing of those Affairs.

d. *to keep* (someone) *sweet*: to keep (someone) well-disposed towards oneself, *esp.* by complaisance or bribery.

1939 C. DAY LEWIS *Child of Misfortune* II. vi. 241 It was necessary to keep the wealthier parishioners sweet. **1944** 'N. SHUTE' *Pastoral* viii. 202 Mine won't worry, but I'd like to keep them sweet. **1965** N. GULBENKIAN *Pantaraxia* xi. 228 Mr. Sheets..had what he described as 'a wonderful idea' to keep the Russians sweet politically. **1972** G. BROMLEY *In Absence of Body* vi. 69 Joe Retford..helps to keep him sweet —wines him and dines him and all that. **1978** N. FREELING *Night Lords* iii. 17 The cops were capable of leaking the most dreadful nonsense if one didn't take pains to keep them sweet.

10. *to be sweet on* (*upon*): †**a.** To behave affectionately or gallantly towards, treat caressingly.

1694 ECHARD *Plautus* Pref. a 7 This Stripling began to be sweet upon her, and waggish upon me too. *a* **1700** B. E. *Dict. Cant. Crew, To be Sweet upon*, to coakse, wheedle, entice or allure. **1716** ADDISON *Freeholder* No. 44 ⁋5 What still gave him greater offence, was a drunken bishop, who reeled from one side of the court to the other, and was very sweet upon an Indian queen. **1754** *Connoisseur* No. 7 ⁋11, I would recommend it to all married people, but especially to the ladies, not to be so sweet upon their dears before company.

b. To have a particular fondness or affection for (one of the opposite sex); to be enamoured of or smitten with. Also *transf.*

1740 tr. *De Mouhy's Fort. Country-Maid* (1741) I. 42 He ..is very sweet upon her; but I shall watch him so narrowly, that he'll not find an Opportunity of speaking to her, but when I am by. **1844** DICKENS *Mart. Chuz.* xi, I think he is sweet upon your daughter. **1853** 'C. BEDE' *Verdant Green* I. xii, The bar was presided over by a young lady, 'on whom' he said 'he was desperately sweet'. **1862** WHYTE MELVILLE *Inside Bar* iii. (ed. 12) 256 If he should see any gentleman rather sweet upon the nag.

11. *Austral. slang.* Fine, in order, ready.

1898 *Bulletin* (Sydney) 17 Dec. (Red Page), *Sweet, roujig* and *not too stinkin'* are good. **1939** K. TENNANT *Foveaux* 312, 'I brassed a mug yesterday,' he told her, 'and everything's sweet again.' He flashed a roll of notes. **1949** L. GLASSOP *Lucky Palmer* 242 'Everything jake?' he asked. 'She's sweet,' said Max. **1962** S. GORE *Down Golden Mile* 120 Might as well be in it. We'll be sweet for getting back. **1975** X. HERBERT *Poor Fellow my Country* 353 Mossie came in..to say cheerfully, 'She's sweet.'

B. *adv.* Sweetly; so as to be sweet (*lit.* or *fig.*).

1. = SWEETLY *adv.* 1. (Chiefly with vb. *smell.*)

c **1250** *Gen. & Ex.* 2443 Iosep dede hise lich..riche-like smeren, And spice-like swete smaken. **1362** LANGL. *P. Pl.* A. VII. 206 þei schule soupe þe swettore whon þei han hit deseruet. *a* **1425** *Cursor M.* 1014 (Trin.) Floures þat ful swete smelles. **1592** SHAKS. *Rom. & Jul.* II. ii. 44 (Qo. 1) Whats in a name? That which we call a Rose, By any other name would smell as sweet. *c* **1640** SHIRLEY *Cont. Ajax & Ulysses* (1659) 128 Onely the actions of the just Smell sweet, and blossom in their dust. **1667** FLAVEL *Saint Indeed* (1754) 21 When the salt of heavenly-mindedness is again cast into the spring, the streams will run clearer and sweeter. **1746** FRANCIS tr. *Hor., Ep.* I. xix. 6 Soon the tuneful Nine At Morning breath'd, and not too sweet, of Wine.

2. = SWEETLY *adv.* 2.

15.. *Christ's Kirk* 39 in *Bann. MS.* (Hunter. Cl.) 283 He playit so schill and sang so sweit. **1592** SHAKS. *Rom. & Jul.* II. ii. 166 How siluer sweet, sound Louers tongues by night. *a* **1708** T. WARD *Eng. Ref.* I. (1710) 96 She Psalms wou'd often sing in Meeter Like Hopkins, but a great deal Sweeter. **1851** TENNYSON *E. Morris* 113 Then low and sweet I whistled thrice. **1891** FARRAR *Darkn. & Dawn* xxii, 'I think', said Nero, savagely, 'that swans sing sweetest before they die.'

3. a. = SWEETLY *adv.* 4.

a **1300** *Cursor M.* 15186 þe lauerd..ansuard þam ful suete. **1338** R. BRUNNE *Chron.* (1810) 275 Doun Sir Richard went, & spak to þam lufly, Many of þam he knewe, so fair spak & so suete. *c* **1386** CHAUCER *Miller's T.* 119 He kist hire sweete. *c* **1520** SKELTON *Magnyf.* III. xxvii. 1802 So I wolde clepe her! so I wolde kys her swete! **1535** STEWART *Cron. Scotl.* (Rolls) I. 517 Beseikand thame richt sweit to cum him to. **1592** SHAKS. *Rom. & Jul.* II. iii. 32 Good morrow, Father. *Fri.* Benedicite. What early tongue so sweet saluteth me?

b. = SWEETLY *adv.* 4 d.

1846 HOLTZAPFFEL *Turning* II. 689 The generality of other saw-files are single or float-cut, that kind of file tooth being considered to 'cut sweeter'. **1862** PYCROFT *Cricket Tutor* 26 There is one way..to make the ball fly away like a shot, going so clean off the bat that you scarcely feel it; and this is the test of clean hitting—of the ball going off 'sweet'.

4. = SWEETLY *adv.* 3.

1592 SHAKS. *Rom. & Jul.* II. ii. 188 Sleepe dwell vpon thine eyes, peace in thy brest. Would I were sleepe and peace, so sweet to rest. **1596** —— *Merch. V.* v. i. 54 How sweet the moone-light sleepes vpon this banke. **1757** GRAY *Bard* 118 Her lyon-port, her awe-commanding face, Attemper'd sweet to virgin-grace. **1813** SHELLEY *Q. Mab* VI. 73 The stars, Which on thy cradle beamed so brightly sweet.

C. Combinations and special collocations.

1. of the adj. **a.** With sbs.: **sweetback** *U.S. slang*, a woman's lover, a ladies' man; a pimp; also *sweetback man* (cf. *sweet man* below); † **sweet-bag**, a small bag or sachet filled with a scented or aromatic substance, used for perfuming the air, clothes, etc.; occas. *transf.* of the honey-bag of a bee; † **sweet-ball**, a ball of scented or aromatic substance; **sweet band** orig. and chiefly *U.S.*, a band which plays sweet music; **sweet biscuit**, a biscuit flavoured with sugar; † **sweet-blanch**, a dish made with the flesh of chickens and almond milk; **sweet-bone(s** *dial.*, 'a griskin of pork' (Miss Baker *Northampt. Gloss.* 1854); **sweet-cake**, a kind of cake made with a specially large proportion of sugar; † **sweet-cheese** (see quot.); **sweet dreams** *int.*, a farewell to someone going to bed; **sweet Jesus** *int.*, used as an oath or exclamation (cf. JESUS 1 b); **sweet life** = DOLCE VITA; hence **sweet-lifer**, one who leads the sweet life; † **sweet-love**, a term of affection for a beloved person; **sweet mama** *U.S. slang* (see quots.); **sweet man** *U.S. slang* = *sweetback* above; **sweet-mart**, a name for the pine-marten, as distinguished from the *foulmart*, FOUMART, or polecat (see MART *sb.*[1]); **sweet milk**, fresh milk having its natural sweet flavour, as distinct from skimmed milk, or from 'sour milk', i.e. buttermilk; also *attrib.*, as *sweet-milk cheese*, cheese made from unskimmed milk; **sweetmouth** *v. trans. slang*, to flatter; **sweet music**, light instrumental music of a popular or conventional character (cf. SWEET *a.* 4 b); also *fig.*, esp. in allusion to love-making; **sweet nothings** *colloq.*, sentimental trivia, endearments; **sweet oil**, any oil of pleasant or mild taste, *spec.* olive oil; **sweet papa** *U.S. slang* (see quot. 1970); † **sweet-powder**, perfumed powder used as a cosmetic; **sweet-spittle** *Path.*, an increased secretion of saliva having a sweetish taste; **sweet spot**, the point on a bat, club, racket, etc., at which it makes most effective contact with the ball; cf. MEAT *sb.* 3 f; **sweet-stuff**, sweetmeats, sweets, confectionery; also *attrib.* and *Comb.*; now freq. in *pl.*; †also *euphem.*, gin (*obs.*); **sweet tooth** (TOOTH *sb.* 2 a), a taste or liking for sweet things; also *transf.* and *fig.*; **sweet wine**, wine having a sweet taste (as distinguished from *dry* wine); wine in the manufacture of which 'sweets' or syrup is added. See also SWEETMEAT, SWEET SINGER, SWEET WATER.

1929 in P. Oliver *Screening Blues* (1968) vi. 206 Had a man, good old *sweetback **1935** A. J. POLLOCK *Underworld Speaks* 117/2 *Sweet back*, a pimp. **1950** BLESH & JANIS *They all played Ragtime* ii. 39 The dapper, foppish 'macks' or 'sweet-back men'..got their gambling stakes from the girls. **1974** Sweetback [see SUPERFLY *sb.*]. **1615** in Foster *Lett. E. India Co.* (1897) III. 16 Some pillow *sweetbag or other like thing of the rockwork used lately in England. **1626** BACON *Sylva* §385 When Bodies are Moved or Stirred, though not Broken, they Smell more; As a Sweet-Bagge waved. **1648** HERRICK *Hesper.*, *The Bag of the Bee* 1 About the sweet bag of a Bee, Two Cupids fell at odds. **1707** CIBBER *Double Gallant* I, Her Sweet-bags, instead of..Musk and Amber, breathe nothing but..Hartshorn, Rue and Assafœtida. **1821** SCOTT *Kenilw.* xx, Hast thou no perfumes and sweet bags, or any handsome casting bottles, of the newest mode? **1617** *Janua Ling.* 76 The Queene with her courtiers that weare feathers..smell of *sweete-balls. **1637** HEYWOOD *Pleas. Dial.* ii. Wks. 1874 VI. 130 This sweet-Ball, Take it to cheare your heart. **1650** W. D. tr. *Comenius Gate Lat. Unl.* §587 Sweet-powders, sweet balls, and besprinklings out of sweet-glass bottles. **1935** *Vanity Fair* (N.Y.) Nov. 71/2 Hot musicians look down on *sweet bands, which faithfully follow the composer's arrangements. **1938** *Sat. Even. Post* 7 May 23/1 Art Hickman and the first wave of big sweet bands [were] calling the country's dance tunes. **1974** *Listener* 24 Oct 532/1 Would Albert McCarthy..say that Glenn Miller's was the best dance/swing/'sweet' band? [**1926–7** *Army & Navy Stores Catal.* 6/2 Assorted biscuits. A choice selection of Plain, Sweet, and Fancy kinds.] **1929** W. FAULKNER *Sartoris* 165 Negroes lounged, skinning bananas or small florid cartons of *sweet biscuits. **1941** *Ration Craft* 9 The present shortage of sweet biscuits is well known. **1977** *Lancashire Life* Feb. 19/1 Sweet biscuits were unknown until about sixty years ago. Before that the only biscuits made were ship's biscuits. *c* **1430** *Two Cookery-bks.* 112 *Sweteblanche.—Nym chikons or hennes, skald hem ..& seth hem with good beofe. **1826** HAN. MORE in W. Roberts *Mem.* (1835) IV. 304 The spare-rib, *sweet-bone, ears, and snout [of a pig]. **1969** C. DRUMMOND *Odds on Death* vii. 130 Sister has some Wiltshire sweetbones done under crisp suet crust. **1726** SWIFT *Gulliver* II. iii, I..sat down..to eat a piece of *sweet-cake for my breakfast. **1825** T. HOOK *Sayings* Ser. II. *Man of Many Fr.* (Colburn) 112 The fruits, sugars, wines, creams, and sweet-cakes [after dinner]. *a* **1881** M. CLARKE in *Mem.* (1884) 143 He..got a big piece of sweet-cake, and put it in the pocket of his little jumper. **1688** HOLME *Armoury* II. 173/1 **Sweet-Cheese*, Fleeting strained through a fine Cloth and Sugared. **1908** *Sears Roebuck & Co. Catal.* 138/1 Tenor Solos..Good Bye, *Sweet Dreams, Good Bye. **1970** *New Yorker* 28 Feb. 70/2 Good night, sleep tight, sweet dreams. **1981** P. NIESEWAND *Word of Gentleman* xvii. 109 I need some sleep.'.. 'Sweet dreams, then.' **1932** W. FAULKNER *Light in August* viii. 182 'Come on out,' the blonde woman said. 'For *sweet Jesus,' Max said. **1955** F. O'CONNOR *Wise Blood* v. 95 Oh sweet Jesus, come on! **1973** 'D. JORDAN' *Nile Green* xxxiii. 157 Her voice so still, so soft, and I believed her, sweet Jesus, I believed her. **1962** *Sunday Express* 18 Feb. 13/5 Klaus was tired of being respectable and hungered for 'the *sweet life'. **1974** M. CECIL *Heroines in Love* ix. 218 The sweet life was turning sour on heroines in the late 1960s. **1967** D. SKIRROW *I was following this Girl* iii. 16 I've been tailing that toffee-nosed *sweet-lifer. *a* **1560** PHAER *Æneid* VIII. Y iv, O husbande *sweetloue most disierd. **1950** A. LOMAX *Mister Jelly Roll* 19 Now these boys used to all have a *sweet mama ..they was what I would call, maybe a fifth-class whore. **1970** C. MAJOR *Dict. Afro-Amer. Slang* 111 *Sweet mama*, black female lover. **1942** BERREY & VAN DEN BARK *Amer. Thes. Slang* §443/5 *Beau*,..*sweet man. *Ibid.* §508/3 *Pimp* ..sweetman. **1952** S. SELVON *Brighter Sun* ii. 21 Look how Ah take up meself and leave sweetman life in town. **1959** [see *saga boy* s.v. SAGA[1] 3]. **1972** J. MARYLAND in T. Kochman *Rappin' & Stylin' Out* 211 Damn, Rev., that's some real cruel shit, suggesting a sweet man [pimp] be iced. **1788** W. MARSHALL *Rural Econ. Yorks.* (E.D.S.), **Sweet-mart*, the marten. **1847** HALLIWELL, *Sweet-mart*, the badger. *Yorksh.* **1905** *Athenæum* 26 Aug. 262/1 Cumberland had its almost distinctive sports, such as foulmart hunting and sweetmart hunting. *c* **1420** *Liber Cocorum* (1862) 17 Take *swete mylke and put in panne. **1787** BURNS *Holy Fair* vii, Wi sweet-milk cheese, in mony a whang. **1820** HOGG *Tales & Sk.* (1836) II. *Welldean Hall* 224 That whining sweet-milk boy. **1844** H. STEPHENS *Bk. Farm* II. 713 Hard-boiled picks of porridge, with a little sweet-milk in the dish. **1877** *Encycl. Brit.* VII. 649/2 Edam..gives its name to a well-known description of 'sweetmilk' cheese. **1895** *Oracle Encycl.* I. 556/1 Butter-Milk, the liquid which remains after the churning of cream or sweet-milk for the preparation of butter. **1948** *Publ. Amer. Dial. Soc.* IX. 81 Employment [by the Gullahs] of groups of words for..verbs..or other parts of speech (such as..*to *sweet mouth* 'to flatter'). **1950** *Language* XXVI. 330 Not recorded in the Atlas but commonly considered to be of Negro origin are such metaphors as sweet-mouth 'to flatter' and bad-mouth 'to curse'. **1973** J. JONES *Touch of Danger* xli. 238 He went on sweetmouthing me, with his slippery mean eyes. **1967** *Guardian* 28 Sept. 4/5 If pop music should be a fad that passes he sees Radio One as becoming a '*sweet music' station. **1970** *Ibid.* 10 Mar. 1/3 A..choice between.. pop music on Radio 1 and 'sweet' music on Radio 2. **1971** R. GADNEY *Somewhere in England* xxi. 180 A small black girl.. offered him 'some sweet music'. **1977** J. WAINWRIGHT *Day of Peppercorn Kill* 99 [They] should be making sweet music, every night of the week. **1981** H. R. F. KEATING *Go West, Inspector Ghote* iii. 29 Rock music, country music, sweet music, pop music—all or any of these..at the touch of a button. **1900** FAZL-I-HUSAIN *Diary* 20 May in A. Husain *Fazl-i-Husain* (1946) ii. 35 The *sweet nothings so often talked of in the romantic descriptions. **1934** C. LAMBERT *Music Ho!* III. 212 The blues have a certain austerity that places them far above the sweet nothings of George Gershwin. **1973** M. AMIS *Rachel Papers* 119 Half the guests, including DeForest (after a minute of sweet-nuthins with Rachel), had wisely got the hell out as soon as dinner was over. *a* **1585** in *Eng. Hist. Rev.* (1914) XXIX. 519 All our wolle oyles and *swete oyles. **1757** BROMFEILD *Eng. Nightshades* 74 The red oil, produced by distillation from bitter almonds, after the sweet oil had been expressed. **1776** PIGOU in *Gentl. Mag.* (1792) Jan. 14/2 We found relief by rubbing the parts with sweet oil. **1857** MILLER *Elem. Chem., Org.* iii. 158 If this liquid [*sc.* sulphethylic acid] be boiled, sweet oil of wine mingled with sulphurous acid passes over. **1867** BLOXAM *Chem.* 580 Salad oil, or sweet oil.., is obtained by crushing olives. *c* **1923** in *W. C. Handy's Coll. Blues* (? 1925) 28 Ashes in my *sweet pa-pa's bed So that he can't slip out. **1941** W. C. HANDY *Father of Blues* x. 141 The sweet papa who happened to be shining around the absentee prisoner's gal at the moment. **1970** C. MAJOR *Dict. Afro-Amer. Slang* 111 *Sweet papa*, a sugar-daddy and sweet man. **1573–4** in Feuillerat *Revels Q. Eliz.* (1908) 208 *Sweete powder made of Musk & Amber. **1709** STEELE *Tatler* No. 52 ⁋1 The Expence of Sweet Powder and Jessamine are considerably abated. **1710** C. SHADWELL *Fair Quaker Deal* II. 25 He's for turning the Gun powder into Sweet-Powder, and the Iron Balls into Wash-Balls. **1820** GOOD *Nosology* 13 Apocenosis, ptyalismus, mellitus..*Sweet-spittle. **1976** *National Observer* (U.S.) 1 May 10/4 The *sweet spot—the precise point of contact on the racket face where all the force of a swing goes into the ball without jarring the arm—was considerably farther from the center than anyone had ever suspected. **1976** *Golf International* 13–29 May 21/1 Because we use investment casting, the head weight is distributed over a wider area, increasing the sweet spot. We call this Perimeter Weighting. **1980** *Esquire* Mar. 78 Tennis players, of course, are accustomed to a long racquet, but they're also accustomed to a nice fluffy projectile and the luxury of a forgiving 'sweet spot'. **1835** DICKENS in *Even. Chron.* 7 Feb. 3/3 Wretched houses with..'*sweet-stuff' manufacturers in the cellars. **1851** MAYHEW *Lond. Labour* I. 204/1 The sweet-stuff maker (I never heard them called confectioners). **1862** SALA *Accepted Addr.* 96 The back parlour of the little sweetstuff shop. **1908** *Chambers's Jrnl.* Feb. 204/1 The scent for sweetstuffs is very strongly developed in the Customs officer, and he has found sugar in such an unlikely article as blacking. **1911** J. H. HART *Cacao* ii. 18 The bean may be used in the same way as almonds, and boiled to sweetstuff with sugar. **1963** *Times* 18 May 9/4 We teach our students the harmful effects of the consumption of sweetstuffs between meals. **1390** GOWER *Conf.* I. 14 Delicacie his *swete toth Hath fostred. **1580** LYLY *Euphues* (Arb.) 308, I am glad that my Adonis hath a sweete tooth in his head. **1625** B. JONSON *Staple of N.* II. Interm., I haue a sweet tooth yet. **1710** ADDISON *Tatler* No. 255 ⁋2 A liquorish Palate, or a sweet Tooth (as they call it). **1899** J. LONDON *Let.* 29 July (1966) 45 If you're a sweet tooth you will not receive accommodation here except in the fruit line and the candy stores. **1904** P. FOUNTAIN *Gt. North-West* x. 96 Americans have the sweet-tooth highly developed. **1946** DYLAN THOMAS *Deaths & Entrances* 14 Till the sweet tooth of my love bit dry. **1960** *Times* 5 July 16/5 A symphony for sweet-tooths. *c* **1386** CHAUCER *Wife of Bath's Prol.* 459 When I had dronke a draughte of *swete wyn. **1430–1** *Rolls of Parlt.* IV. 369/1 Every Tonne of swete Wyn..commyng in to this saide Roialme, be weye of Merchandise. **1542** BOORDE *Dyetary* xxiv. (1870) 296 Swete wynes be good for them the whiche be in consumpcion. **1797** *Encycl. Brit.* (ed. 3) XII. 202/1 The white of an egg, milk, and sweet-wine. **1857** MILLER *Elem. Chem., Org.* II. 118 The liquid..acquires a ropy consistence as is sometimes observed when sweet wines are kept for a time.

b. *spec.* in distinctive names of sweet-scented or sweet-flavoured species or varieties of plants, fruits, etc., as ***sweet almond***, †***ballocks***, ***basil***, ***bent***, ***birch***, ***calabash***, ***calamus***, ***cassava***, ***cicely***, ***clover***, ***coltsfoot***, ***gum (-tree)***, ***horse-mint***, ***locust***, ***marjoram***, ***maudlin***, ***navew***, ***oleander***, ***orange***, ***pepper-bush***, ***pine-sap***, ***pishamin***, ***sorghum***, †***stones***, ***sultan tea***, ***trefoil***, ***violet***, ***virgin's bower***, ***woodruff*** (see also these words); **sweet Alice**, sweet alyssum, *Lobularia maritima* (cf. ALYSSUM 2) or *Arabis alpina*, another small cruciferous herb with white flowers; **sweet-apple**, a name for the SWEET-SOP, also called *sugar-apple*; **sweet bay**, (*a*) the bay laurel, *Laurus nobilis*; (*b*) in N. America applied to *Magnolia virginiana*, also called white bay; also attrib. and in comb., as **sweet bay laurel** = (*a*); **sweet-bay (-leaved) willow**, *Salix pentandra*; **sweet-bough** *U.S.*, an early variety of apple or the tree that bears it; **sweet broom**, (*a*) ? some species of broom (*Cytisus* or *Genista*); (*b*) a name for *Scoparia dulcis* (N.O. *Scrophulariaceæ*), also called **sweet broom-weed**; **sweet buckeye**, a yellow-flowered horse chestnut, *Aesculus octandra*, found in eastern North America; **sweet cane**: = *sweet flag*; **sweet chestnut**, the common or Spanish chestnut, *Castanea sativa*, as distinguished from the bitter inedible HORSE-CHESTNUT; also, the fruit or timber of this tree; **sweet corn** *U.S.*, a sweet-flavoured variety of maize; **sweet fern**, a name for two plants with fern-like leaves and aromatic scent: (*a*) locally in England, the sweet cicely, *Myrrhis odorata* (N.O. *Umbelliferæ*); (*b*) in N. America, the shrub *Comptonia asplenifolia* (N.O. *Myricaceæ*); **sweet flag**, a rush-like plant, *Acorus Calamus* (N.O. *Araceæ* or *Orontiaceæ*), widely distributed in the North Temperate zone, growing in water and wet places, with an aromatic odour, and having a thick creeping rootstock of a pungent aromatic flavour; **sweet gum(-tree)** = LIQUID-AMBAR 2; **sweet melon** = SPANSPEK; **sweet milk-vetch**, *Astragalus glycyphyllus*, with sweet-flavoured leaves; **sweet olive**, an evergreen shrub, *Osmanthus fragrans*, of the family Oleaceæ, native to eastern Asia and bearing clusters of small fragrant white flowers; **sweet pepper**, (*a*) = PEPPER *sb.* 2 b; (*b*) = *sweet pepper-bush*; **sweet plum**, (*a*) see quot. 1796; (*b*) the Queensland plum, *Owenia cerasifera*; (*c*) a species of hog-plum, *Spondias pleigyna*; **sweet potato**, the edible tuber of a perennial vine, *Ipomœa batatas*, native to South America and widely cultivated elsewhere; **sweet scabious**, *Scabiosa atropurpurea*; also applied to the N. American *Erigeron annuus* (N.O. *Compositæ*); also *E. philadelphicus*; **sweet sedge** = *sweet flag*; **sweet vernal grass**, *Anthoxanthum odoratum* (see VERNAL 3 c); **sweet willow**, (*a*) = *sweet-bay willow* (see WILLOW); (*b*) = SWEET-GALE. See also SWEET-BRIER, SWEET-GALE, SWEET-PEA, SWEET-WILLIAM, etc.

1886 BRITTEN & HOLLAND *Dict. Eng. Plant-Names* 459 *Sweet Alice. *Arabis alpina*, L... A corruption of Sweet Alison, which name belongs more properly to *Alyssum maritimum*, L. **1927** V. WOOLF *To Lighthouse* I. iv. 38 She was picking Sweet Alice on the bank. **1719** QUINCY *Compl. Disp.* 114 *Sweet Almonds.—These are of a soft, sweet, grateful Taste. **1760** J. LEE *Introd. Bot.* App. 305 *Apple, Sweet, *Annona*. **1597** GERARDE *Herbal* I. cii. 169 *Testiculus odoratus*... Ladies traces:..of some *sweete Ballocks, sweete Cods, sweete Cullions. **1647** HEXHAM I. (*Herbs*), *Sweete Basill, *Wilde Christus oogen, ofte Gennettekens*. **1820** KEATS *Isabella* lii, She..o'er it set Sweet Basil, which her tears kept ever wet. **1716** *Petiveriana* I. 246 Barbadoes *Sweet-Bay. **1766** J. BARTRAM *Jrnl.* 9 Jan. in Stork *Acc. E. Florida* 29 On it grew great magnolia, sweet-bay, live-oak, palms. **1850, 1903** Sweet bay [see *laurel magnolia* s.v. LAUREL *sb.*[1] 6]. **1858** BAIRD *Cycl. Nat. Sci.* s.v. *Lauraceæ*, The common, or sweetbay laurel, *Laurus nobilis*. **1938** M. K. RAWLINGS *Yearling* xviii. 217 The sweet bay was still in bloom, filling the sink-hole with its fragrance. **1958** G. A. PETRIDES *Field Guide to Trees & Shrubs* 303 Sweet-bay Magnolia... A large shrub or small tree with thick, rather leathery, elliptic leaves that are evergreen. **1857** MISS PRATT *Flower. Pl.* V. 78 *S[alix] pentandra* (*Sweet Bay-leaved Willow). **1796** NEMNICH *Polygl.-Lex.*, *Sweet birch, *Betula nigra*. **1861** BENTLEY *Man. Bot.* 652 The bark of *B[etula] lenta*, known in the United States as Sweet Birch or Cherry Birch. **1850** *Rep. Comm. Patents: Agric. 1849* (U.S.) 281 Of summer apples, the best..are the early-harvest and early *sweet-bough. **1906** *Harper's Mag.* Apr. 667 He halted under the sweet-bough and gave one branch a shake. **1736** BAILEY *Househ. Dict.* 554 *Sweet-Broom. **1884** MILLER *Plant-n.*, *Scoparia dulcis*, Sweet Broom. **1890** *Cent. Dict.* s.v. *Scoparia*, *S[coparia] dulcis* is used as a stomachic in the West Indies, and is called *sweet broomweed and licorice-weed. **1815** D. DRAKE *Cincinnati* ii. 77 *Sweet buckeye. **1943** R. PEATTIE *Great Smokies* 155 The sweet buckeye or horse chestnut is found here up to 125 feet in height. **1969** T. H. EVERETT *Living Trees of World* xxii. 224/2 The largest of the Americans is the sweet or yellow buckeye. **1796** NEMNICH *Polygl.-Lex.*, *Sweet calabash, *Passiflora laurifolia*. **1611** *Sweet cane [see CANE *sb.*[1] 2]. **1718** J. QUINCY *Compleat Eng. Dispensatory* II. i. 85 Sweet-Cane.. is a spicy bitterish Root. **1822** J. CAMPBELL *Trav. S. Afr.: 2nd Journey* I. xx. 226 A constant succession of fresh visitants arrived, several of whom brought us presents of sweet cane. **1818** SCOTT *Hrt. Midl.* xxxii, Large *sweet-chesnut trees and beeches. **1838** J. C. LOUDON *Arboretum & Fruticetum Britannicum* III. 1983 The term Sweet Chestnut is applied with reference to the fruit. **1909** ELWES & HENRY *Trees Gt. Brit. & Ireland* IV. 844 The Sweet or Spanish Chestnut..is..one of the largest trees in England. **1956** *Handbk. Hardwoods* (Forest Prod. Res. Lab.) 72 Sweet chestnut bears a close resemblance to oak but is more easily worked. **1977** *New Yorker* 4 July 22/2 If he could, he would supplement local bounty only with sweet chestnuts and Korean pears. **1981** G. KEYNES *Gates of Memory* xxix. 351 Nearer to us were glorious stands of trees, ..sweet chestnuts hundreds of years old with twisted trunks. **1874** A. GRAY *Man. Bot.* (ed. 5) 128 *Melilotus*,.. Melilot. *Sweet Clover. *Ibid.* 227 *Nardosmia*, *Sweet Coltsfoot. **1646** E. HOPKINS *Let.* 20 Mar. in *Coll. Mass. Hist. Soc.* (1863) 4th Ser. VI. 334 Wequash Cooks brother tooke from him..2 bushell of *sweet corne. **1810** T. JEFFERSON *Garden Bk.* (1944) 424 [Sowed]..Sweet or shriveled corn in the N.W. corner. *a* **1817** T. DWIGHT *Trav. New Eng.*, etc. (1821) I. 49 At New-Haven the sweet corn may be had in full perfection for the table by successive plantings from the middle of July to the middle of November. **1909** 'O. HENRY' *Roads of Destiny* 364 Cigarettes rolled with sweet corn husk were as honey to Buck's palate. **1917** WILL & HYDE *Corn among Indians* 118 The Upper Missouri tribes prepared this 'sweet corn' for winter use in two ways: by boiling it in kettles, and by roasting it in fires. **1974** A. PRICE *Other Paths to Glory* II. iii. 139 To the north..of the house there had been..a single tiny field of sweet corn. **1787–9** WITHERING *Brit. Plants* (1796) II. 306 *Scandix odorata*..Sweet Cicely ..*Sweet Fern. **1849** BALFOUR *Man. Bot.* §1037 The leaves of *Comptonia asplenifolia*, Sweet Fern, are found..to contain peculiar glands. [**1640** J. PARKINSON *Theatrum Botanicum* xlviii. 139 This sweet smelling Flagge hath many flaggy long and narrow fresh greene leaves. **1728** R. BRADLEY *Dictionarium Botanicum* I. s.v., Calamus aromaticus Off. is also call'd Acorus, and in English, The sweet smelling Flag.] **1790** L. CASTIGLIONI *Viaggio regli Stati Uniti* II. 185 Acorus verus..*Sweet-flagg. **1796** WITHERING *Brit. Plants* (ed. 3) III. 917 Sweet Flag. **1858** SIMMONDS *Dict. Trade*, *Sweet-flag*..is..employed to scent aromatic baths, perfumery, and hair-powder. **1700** *Baltimore Rent Rolls* in *Maryland Hist. Mag.* (1924) XIX. 367, 127 acre Sur[veyed]..begun at a bounded *sweet gum. **1709** J. LAWSON *New Voy. Carolina* 95 The sweet Gum-Tree, so call'd, because of the fragrant Gum it yields in the Spring-time, upon Incision of the Bark, or Wood. **1717** *Petiveriana* III. 195 Sweet-gum. Because in the Spring it yeilds a fragrant Gum, upon cutting its Bark or Wood, of great use in Tetters, Scurfs, Inflammations, etc. **1856** A. GRAY *Man. Bot.* (1860) 148 *Liquidambar*, Sweet-Gum Tree. **1867** AUGUSTA WILSON *Vashti* iii, The trunk of a decayed and fallen sweet-gum. **1884** [see COPALM]. **1981** A. MITCHELL *Gardener's Bk. Trees* 101/1 For summer foliage and autumn colours the Sweet gum has few equals. **1819** *Sweet locust [see *honey-locust* s.v. HONEY *sb.* (*a.*) 7 b]. **1863** *Chambers's Encycl.*, *Honey Locust Tree*..also known as the Sweet Locust and Black Locust. **1565** COOPER *Thesaurus*, *Amaracus*..*sweete [1545–52 ELYOT, soote] maioram. **1601** SHAKS. *All's Well* IV. v. 17 Indeed sir she was the sweete Margerom of the sallet, or rather the hearbe of grace. **1883** J. ROTH *Man. S. Afr. Gardening* 78 The Water Melons must not be ripped or cut, as required by *Sweet Melons. **1970** *Rand Daily Mail* 28 Feb. 7/4 South Africans also speak of ..'sweet melons'. **1860** *Chambers's Encycl.* I. 504/1 The *Sweet Milk-vetch, or Wild Liquorice. **1886** YULE & BURNELL *Hobson Jobson*, **Sweet Oleander*,..the common oleander, *Nerium odorum*. [**1789** W. AITON *Hortus Kewensis* I. 14 Sweet-scented Olive. Nat[ive] of Cochinchina, China, and Japan.] **1861** S. K. HOLMES *Jrnl.* 15 Oct. in *Brokenburn* (1955) 61 Mrs. Carson gave Mamma plants of *sweet olive ..and purple magnolia. **1899** [see CITRONELLE]. **1958** S. A. GRAU *Hard Blue Sky* iii. 122 There was..the winey odor of the sweet olive. **1785** J. WOODFORDE *Diary* 19 Apr. (1926) II. 185 To a Dozen of *sweet Oranges to carry home p^d o. I. 6. **1796** NEMNICH *Polygl.-Lex.*, Sweet orange, *Citrus aurantium sinense*. **1861** BENTLEY *Man. Bot.* 495 The rind of the Sweet Orange is an aromatic stimulant and tonic. **1923** *Sweet pepper [see PEPPER *sb.* 2 b]. **1944** E. A. HOLTON *Yankees were like This* 84 The perfume of bush honeysuckle and sweet pepper from the swamps. **1969** *Oxf. Bk. Food Plants* 128/1 The larger-fruited kinds [of *Capsicum annuum*] are quite mild in taste and are known as 'sweet peppers'. **1972** *Country Life* 16 Mar. 625/3 Every garden that can provide lime-free soil ought to contain a bush of the Sweet Pepper, *Clethra alnifolia*. **1814** O. O. RICH *Synopsis Genera N. Amer. Plants* 50 Clethra. *Sweet Pepper-Bush. **1846–50** A. WOOD *Class Bk. Bot.* 373 *Clethra alnifolia*. Sweet-pepper Bush. **1901** C. T. MOHR *Plant Life Alabama* 652 Sweet Pepper Bush... Common in the coast plain on swampy banks of pine-barren streams. **1976** *Hortus Third* (L. H. Bailey Hortorium) 286/2 Sweet pepperbush... Summer to autumn. **1874** A. GRAY *Man. Bot.* (ed. 5) 304 *Schweinitzia*, *Sweet Pine-sap. **1829** LOUDON *Encycl. Plants* 1286 *Carpodinus*, *Sweet Pishamin..produces green flowers. **1796** NEMNICH *Polygl.-Lex.*, *Sweet plumb, *Prunus americana*. **1874** *Treas. Bot.* Suppl. 1324/2 *Owenia cerasifera* is called the Sweet Plum or Rancooran. **1889** MAIDEN *Usef. Pl. Australia* 599 *Spondias pleiogyna*,..'Sweet Plum', or 'Burdekin Plum'. **1750** J. BIRKET *Some Cursory Remarks* 9 They have..abundance of..the *Sweet Potatoe. **1775**, etc. [see POTATO 3 a]. **1832** [see BATATA]. **1972** Y. LOVELOCK *Veg. Bk.* I. 233 Sweet potato is now grown throughout the tropics. **1976** M. H. KINGSTON *Woman Warrior* (1977) 79 My mother liked to look at the ducks and plan how she would dig a pond for them near the sweet potato field. **1789** W. AITON *Hortus Kewensis* I. 137 *Sweet Scabious. Nat[ive]. **1796** NEMNICH *Polygl.-Lex.*, Sweet scabious, *Scabiosa atropurpurea*. **1828** C. RAFINESQUE *Med. Flora* I. 162 *Erigeron Philadelphicum*... Vulgar Names—Skevish, Scabish, Sweet Scabious [etc.]. **1856** A. GRAY *Man. Bot.* (1860) 198 *Erigeron annuum*..(Daisy Fleabane. Sweet Scabious). **1937** *Range Plant Handbk.* (U.S. Dept. Agric. Forest Service) W67 Annual wild-daisy (*E. annuus*) and Philadelphia wild-daisy, misnamed sweet scabious..are other wild-daisies with similar properties. **1976** *Hortus Third* (L. H. Bailey Hortorium) 1014/1 Sweet scabious.. naturalized in California. **1857** MISS PRATT *Flower. Pl.* V. 323 *Acorus* (*Sweet Sedge). **1697** RAY in *Phil. Trans.* XIX. 635 They tasted somewhat like the Root of Seleri, or *Sweet Smallage. **1597** GERARDE *Herbal* I. cii. 167 The first kind of *Sweete stones is a small, base, and lowe plant. **1706** J. GARDINER tr. *Rapin's Gardens* I. 34 *Sweet-Sultans nam'd from the Byzantine King. **1859** MAYNE *Expos. Lex.*, **Sweet Trefoil*, common name for the *Trifolium cæruleum*. **1845** LINDLEY *Sch. Bot.* 143 *Anthoxanthum odoratum* (*Sweet Vernal Grass). **1597** GERARDE *Herbal* III. lxviii. 1228 *Myrtus Brabantica, siue Elæagnus Cordi*, Gaule, *sweete Willow, or Dutch Myrtle tree. **1731** Sweet willow [see WILLOW *sb.* 2 a]. **1776** W. WITHERING *Bot. Arrangement Veg. Gt. Brit.* 610 Gale..Sweet Willow. Dutch Myrtle. In marshy barren ground. **1839** J. J. AUDUBON *Ornith. Biogr.* V. 288 A heavy growth of cotton-wood, ash, and sweet-willow. **1855** A. PRATT *Flowering Plants & Ferns Gt. Brit.* V. 56 Sweet Gale, or Dutch Myrtle..is called Sweet Willow. **1800** J. E. SMITH *Eng. Bot.* XI. 755 *Asperula odorata*. *Sweet Woodruff or Woodroof.

c. Parasynthetic, as ***sweet-beamed***, ***-blooded***, ***-breathed*** (-breθt), †***-conditioned***, ***-dispositioned***, ***-eyed***, ***-faced***, ***-flavoured***, ***-fleshed***, ***-flowered***, ***-leafed***, ***-mannered***, ***-minded***, ***-natured***, †***-numbered*** (NUMBER *sb.* 18 b), ***-savoured*** (cf. ME. *swote sauoured*), ***-shaped***, †***-smelled*** (= SWEET-SMELLING), ***-souled***, †***-sounded*** (= sweet-sounding), ***-tasted***, ***-tempered***, ***-toned***, ***-tuned***, ***-voiced*** adjs.; see also **sweet-breasted**, etc. in 3 below. Also SWEET-SCENTED.

1730–46 THOMSON *Autumn* 29 Attempered suns arise, *Sweet-beamed. **1859** GEO. ELIOT *Adam Bede* I. v, Those large-hearted, *sweet-blooded natures that never know a narrow or a grudging thought. **1617** DRUMM. OF HAWTH. *Forth Feasting* 34 *Sweet-breath'd Zephyres. **1623** WEBSTER *Devil's Law-Case* I. ii, O sweet-breath'd monkeys, how they grow together! **1814** WORDSW. *Excurs.* VII. 731 The sweet-breathed violet of the shade. **1881** O. WILDE *Poems* 209 Most bounteous Spring! That cans't give increase to the sweet-breath'd kine. **1949** M. MEAD *Male & Female* xiv. 283 Life is a race that boys and girls must run clear-eyed, sweet-breathed, well bathed. **1624** MASSINGER *Renegado* V. ii, Our *sweet-conditioned princess, fair Donusa. **1646** W. BRIDGE *Saints Hiding-Place* (1647) 30 We have a meek and *sweet disposition'd Saviour. **1812** W. TENNANT *Anster F.* I. xxxi, *Sweet-eyed lass. **1590** SHAKS. *Mids. N.* I. ii. 88 Piramus is a *sweet-fac'd man. **1612** BEAUM. & FL. *Coxcomb* III. i, Good sweet fact serving-man! **1885** 'H. CONWAY' *Slings & Arrows* 168 A pale, sweet-faced woman,..who was dressed as a Sister of Charity. **1981** M. WARNER *Joan of Arc* xiii. 267 The young Joan of Arc, the sweet-faced child of hagiography. **1952** A. G. L. HELLYER *Sanders' Encycl. Gardening* (ed. 22) 9 [*Actinidia*] *purpurea*, *sweet-flavoured purple berries. **1923** D. H. LAWRENCE *Birds, Beasts & Flowers* 41 A rock-living, *sweet-fleshed sea-anemone. **1611** COTGR., *Sequinant*, the *sweet-flowred Rush tearmed Squinant. *a* **1586** SIDNEY *Arcadia* II. (1912) 225 Whom yet with a *sweete-graced bitternes they blamed. **1749** SHENSTONE *Ode after Sickness* 30 The *sweet-leaft eglantine. **1887** G. M. HOPKINS *Let.* 25 Dec. (1956) 183 The youngest boy Leo is a remarkably winning *sweetmannered young fellow. *a* **1586** SIDNEY *Arcadia* II. (1912) 169 The *sweete minded Philoclea. **1650** STAPLYTON *Strada's Low C. Wars* VI. 23 A plaine and *sweete-natured man. **1876** GEO. ELIOT *Dan. Der.* lviii, The sweet-natured, strong Rex. **1598** SYLVESTER *Du Bartas* II. ii. II. *Babylon* 590 *Sweet-numbred Homer. **1530** PALSGR. 326/2 *Swete savoured, *aromaticq*. **1590** SHAKS. *Com. Err.* II. ii. 119 That neuer words were musicke to thine eare,..That neuer meat sweet-sauour'd in thy taste. **1632** RUTHERFORD *Lett.* (1862) I. 82 The *sweetest-smelled flowers. **1747** SHENSTONE *Lett.* xlv. (1777) 120 That *sweet-souled bard Mr. James Thomson. **1790** WOLCOT (P. Pindar) *Ep. to Sylv. Urban* Wks. 1812 II. 262 Each sweet-soul'd Stanza. **1932** D. H. LAWRENCE *Etruscan Places* i. 12 Those pure, clean-living, sweet-souled Romans, who smashed nation after nation. **1659** O. WALKER *Oratory* 25 Words, smooth and *sweeter-sounded ..are easie to be read. **1807** T. THOMSON *Chem.* (ed. 3) II. 74 A *sweet-tasted salt, called muriate of glucina. **1913** J. MASEFIELD *Daffodil Fields* 31 Cropping sweet-tasted pasture. **1632** MASSINGER & FIELD *Fatal Dowry* III. i, *Sweet-tempered lord, adieu! **1749** FIELDING *Tom Jones* XI. ii, She's a sweet-tempered, good-humoured lady. **1845** DICKENS *Chimes* iv. 145 The sweetest-looking, sweetest-tempered girl, eyes ever saw. **1870** BRYANT *Iliad* I. IX. 274 A *sweet-toned harp. **1598** SYLVESTER *Du Bartas* II. i. I. *Eden* 129 The Nightingal's *sweet-tuned voice. **1760–72** H. BROOKE *Fool of Qual.* (1809) IV. 119 A well-known and sweet-tuned voice. ?**1807–8** WORDSW. *Somnambulist* 17 A Bird of plumage bright, *Sweet-voiced. **1919** J. MASEFIELD *Reynard the Fox* 11 John Pym..Gross and blunt-headed like a shrike. Yet sweet-voiced as a piping flute.

d. with sbs., forming adjs. having the sense of parasynthetic combinations, as ***sweet-breath*** (= sweet-breathed); **sweet-lip**, any of several marine fishes with prominent mouths, esp. an Australian food fish, *Lethrinus chrysostomus*, or a brightly coloured tropical fish of the family Plectorhynchidæ; also †**sweet-lips**, a delicate eater, epicure; **sweet-throat**, sweet-voiced.

1648 HERRICK *Hesper.*, *Meddow Verse* 8 While *sweet-breath Nimphs, attend on you this Day. **1934** T. WOOD *Cobbers* xvii. 223 *Sweet-lip, and barracouta, a slim silver sword. **1951** T. C. ROUGHLEY *Fish & Fisheries Austral.* (rev. ed.) 75 The best-known of the emperor breams is the sweet-lip or red-mouthed emperor. **1974** J. M. THOMSON *Fish of Ocean & Shore* xiii. 142 The sweetlip emperor, or simply sweetlip..is highly regarded for the table. **1580** HOLLYBAND *Treas. Fr. Tong*, *Vn friand, friolet*, a licorous felow, a *sweete lips. **1870** MORRIS *Earthly Par.* IV. 74 The bright-billed *sweet-throat bird.

2. Combinations of the adv. (or in which *sweet* is in adverbial relation to the second element). **a.** with pples. and ppl. adjs., as ***sweet-bleeding***,

-breathing, *-complaining*, *-flowering*, *-flowing*, *-looking*, *-murmuring*, † *savouring*, *-set*, *-singing*, *-smiling*, *-sounding*, *-spun*, *-suggesting*, *-touched*, *-whispered*: see also **sweet-recording**, **sweet-spoken** in 3 below, and SWEET-SMELLING. **b.** with adjs. (chiefly poetic, denoting a combination of sweetness with some other quality), as *sweet-bitter*, *-bright*, *-chaste*, *-familiar*, *-sad*.

Combs. of this class were much favoured by Sylvester, who has *sweet-charming*, *-piercing*, *-rapting*, *-sacred*, *-sweating*, *-warbling*.

1591 SYLVESTER *Du Bartas* I. vi. 133 He doth discharge On other's shoulders his *sweet-bitter charge. **1690** DRYDEN *Amphitryon* III. i, The stern goddess of sweet-bitter cares. **1590** SPENSER *F.Q.* I. i. 9 The Mirrhe *sweete bleeding in the bitter wound. *a* **1586** SIDNEY *Arcadia* II. (1912) 176 It might seeme that Love..was there to refreshe himselfe betweene their *sweete-breathing lippes. **1819** SHELLEY *Cyclops* 524 Pied flowers, sweet-breathing. **1856** VAUGHAN *Mystics* (1860) I. 23 The sweet-breathing air. **1598** BARNFIELD *Remembr. Eng. Poets* ii, Daniell, praised for thy *sweet-chast Verse. **1591** SHAKS. *Two Gent.* III. ii. 86 The nights dead silence Will well become such *sweet complaining grieuance. **1865** G. M. HOPKINS *Poems* (1967) 21 New-dated from the terms that reappear, More *sweet-familiar grows my love to thee. **1596** *Edw. III*, III. ii. 47 *Sweete flowring peace. **1721** RAMSAY *Petition to Whin-bush Club* i, *Sweet-flowing Clyde. **1784** COWPER *Poplar Field* 12 The scene where his melody charm'd me before, Resounds with his sweet-flowing ditty no more. **1845** DICKENS *Chimes* iv. 145 The *sweetest-looking, sweetest-tempered girl, eyes ever saw. **1742** BLAIR *Grave* 100 In grateful Errors thro' the Under-wood *Sweet-murmuring. **1946** A. HUTCHINGS in A. L. Bacharach *Brit. Music* xvi. 200 Parts were Arthur Blissy, and none the worse for that; parts were *sweet-sad and Englysshe. **1962** R. PRAWER JHABVALA *Get Ready for Battle* ii. 97 There was music blaring out of various radios, sweet-sad music played at top volume. **1382** WYCLIF *Ezek.* xxvii. 19 *Swete sauerynge spice. **1596** DALRYMPLE tr. *Leslie's Hist. Scot.* I. 44 Sueit sairing flouris. **1592** *Arden of Feversham* III. v. 146 How you women can insinuate, And cleare a trespasse with your *sweete set tongue! **1593** MARLOWE *Hero & Leander* II. 162 *Sweet singing Mere-maids, sported with their loues. **1740** MRS. DELANY in *Life & Corr.* (1861) II. 131 Do you ever hear from sweet-singing Birch? **1625** MILTON *Death Fair Infant* 53 Wert thou that *sweet smiling Youth? **1595** *Locrine* I. i. 239 Plaidst thou as sweet, on the *sweet sounding lute. **1743** FRANCIS tr. *Hor., Odes* IV. iii. 17 Goddess of the sweet-sounding lute. **1910** W. DE LA MARE *Three Mulla-Mulgars* v. 71 When you hear my sweet-sounding..song. **1649** G. DANIEL *Trinarch., Hen. V*, cccixxx, Nor lov'd Court-Sweets, nor *Sweet Spun Dialects. **1591** SHAKS. *Two Gent.* II. vi. 7 O *sweet-suggesting Loue. *a* **1593** MARLOWE *Ovid's Elegies* III. xi. 40 *Sweet toucht harpe that to moue stones was able. **1843** JAMES *Forest Days* (1847) 209 Many a *sweet-whispered word.

3. Miscellaneous Special Combinations: **sweet-and-twenty**, a Shakespearian phrase (see TWENTY A. 2), misunderstood by later writers to mean 'a sweet girl of twenty years old'; † **sweet-breasted** *a.* [see BREAST *sb.* 6], sweet-voiced; **sweet-lipped**, **-lipt** *a.*, having sweet lips; usually, speaking sweetly; **sweet-mouthed** (-maʊðd) *a.*, †(*a*) fond of sweet-flavoured things, dainty; (*b*) speaking sweetly (usually ironically); † **sweet-recording** *a.* [RECORD *v.* 3], singing sweetly, tuneful; **sweet-seasoned** *a.*, 'seasoned' or imbued with sweetness; **sweet seventeen**: see SEVENTEEN *a.* 2; now more usually, **sweet sixteen** (cf. SIXTEEN *sb.* 4); **sweet-spoken** *a.*, speaking sweetly, using pleasant language (cf. *plain-spoken*); **sweet-throated**, sweet-voiced; **sweet-tongued** (-tʌŋd) *a.*, having a sweet tongue or utterance, sweet-voiced, sweet-spoken; **sweet-toothed** (-tuːθt) *a.*, having a 'sweet tooth', fond of sweet things or delicacies.

1601 SHAKS. *Twel. N.* II. iii. 52 Then come kisse me *sweet and twentie. **1887** J. ASHBY STERRY *Lazy Minstrel* (1892) 76, I love the eyes of peerless blue, And nameless grace of Sweet-and-Twenty! **1901** G. K. MENZIES *Prov. Sk.* (1902) 48 When one's special sweet-and-twenty Is enshrined in one's Canader on the Cher. *a* **1623** FLETCHER *Love's Cure* III. i, A proper man,..*Sweet breasted, as the Nightingale, or Thrush. *a* **1644** QUARLES *Sol. Recant.* Sol. viii. 81 And Candle-light devotion, trim'd and straw'd With *sweet-lipt Roses. **1783** W. GORDON *Livy* III. lxviii, The embellishments of a sweet-lipped tribune. *a* **1845** HOOD *Lamia* v. 1 Nay, sweet-lipped Silence, 'Tis now your turn to talk. **1542** UDALL *Erasm. Apoph.* 45 For that he was so *sweete mouthed, and drouned in the voluptuousnesse of high fare. **1611** COTGR., *Leschard*, a lickorous, or sweet-mouthed slapsawce. **1623** MIDDLETON & ROWLEY *Sp. Gipsy* II. (1653) D 1, This cherry-lip'd, sweet-mouth'd villaine. *a* **1722** LISLE *Husb.* (1757) 409 Nuts, being so sweet, would make them so sweet-mouthed, that [etc.]. **1886** J. F. MAURICE in *Lett. fr. Donegal* Pref. p. vi, The class which Mr. Parnell never speaks of except as the 'felon' landlords, just as his sweet-mouthed friends speak of *The Times*. **1598-9** E. FORDE *Parismus* I. (1661) 10 They heard the sound of most *sweet recording musick which made Dionysius wonder. **1601** CHESTER *Love's Mart.*, etc. (1878) 123 The sweete recording Swanne Apolloes ioy. *c* **1600** SHAKS. *Sonn.* lxxv, So are you to my thoughts as food to life, Or as *sweet season'd shewers are to the ground. **1632** LITHGOW *Trav.* I. 9 A bitter pleasant tast, of a sweete-seasoned sowre. **1826** *Blackw. Edin. Mag.* XX. 138/1 A bright-eyed, round-limbed virgin of *sweet sixteen. **1898** J. THORNTON (*song-title*) When you were sweet sixteen. **1977** *Grimsby Even. Tel.* 5 May 12/3 Unfortunately everybody can't be sweet 16 and there are many shops catering for the older woman. **1716** ADDISON *Drummer* IV. i, You are such a *sweet-spoken man, it does one's heart good to receive your orders. **1887** J. R. LOWELL *Credidimus* in *Atlantic Monthly* Feb. 251 Who knows but from our loins may spring (Long hence) some winged *sweet-throated thing. **1928** W. B. YEATS tr. *Sophocles' King Oedipus* 5 What message of disaster from that sweet-throated Zeus? **1598** MARSTON *Pygmal.*, *Sat.* v, *Sweet tongu'd Orpheus. *a* **1758** RAMSAY in *Evergreen* Contents vii, Sweit tungd Scot, quha sings the welcum hame. **1837** CARLYLE *Fr. Rev.* II. v. viii, Beautiful sweet-tongued Female Citizens. **1615** MARKHAM *Eng. Housew.* II. ii. (1668) 51 She must not be butter-fingred, *sweet-toothed, nor faint-hearted. **1682** WHELER *Journ. Greece* II. 203 The Turks are very sweet-tooth'd and love all Kind of sweet Meats. **1808** JAMIESON s.v. *Slaik*, Our use of the word seems indeed to have been borrowed from the nasty habits of sweet-toothed cooks. **1975** *Times* 31 May 7/2 The puddings, often a weakness in French restaurants from a sweet-toothed British customer's point of view.

sweet, *v.*[1] Now *rare*. [f. SWEET *a.*; in OE. *swétan* = OHG. *suozen* (MHG. *suezen*).]

1. *trans.* To make sweet, sweeten. **a.** *lit.* (to the taste, smell, etc.).

c **1000** *Sax. Leechd.* III. 58 Nim þonne huniȝ be dæle & swet þone drænc. *c* **1200** ORMIN 1649 þe sallt þatt ure mete swetep. *c* **1440** CAPGRAVE *Life St. Kath.* v. 1959 It longeth to flowres swhiche lycoure for to swete. **1542** UDALL *Erasm. Apoph.* 3 b, Hounger is the best sauce..Because the same bothe sweeteth all thynges, and also is a thyng of no coste ne charge. **1545** RAYNOLD *Byrth Mankynde* 131 With fayre water fyrste soden and sweted with sugre. **1580** NEWTON *Approved Med.* 24 The Nutmegge..stayeth vomittes, & sweeteth the Breathe. **1604** DRAYTON *Owle* 69 Sweeting her Nest, and purging it of Doung. **1622** WITHER *Philarete* D v b, The mornings dewie roses: That..Cast perfumes that sweet the Aire. **1765** *Proc. Gen. Court Martial on Lieut. Gov. P. Thicknesse*, etc. 49 It is the Lieutenant-Governor's Orders that the soldiers in Garrison sweet and clean the parade..twice a week. **1896** *Godey's Mag.* Feb. 173 When..pine-woods sweet the air.

b. *fig.* (to the mind, feelings, etc.).

a **900** CYNEWULF *Juliana* 525 (Gr.) He [*sc.* the devil] mec feran het..þæt ic þe sceolde synne swetan. **1542** UDALL *Erasm. Apoph.* E.'s Pref., What thyng better sweetteth yᵉ endityng of Marcus Tullius? **1597** BRETON *Auspicante Jehova* Wks. (Grosart) II. 11/2 Beeing clensed from my sinne..and sweeted in my soule, by the oile of Thy grace. **1600** —— *Daffodils & Primroses* ibid. I. 14/2 Queene of suche powre As sweeteth euery sowre. *a* **1601** ? MARSTON *Pasquil & Kath.* (1878) II. 37, I haue a thankefull heart, Tho not a glorious speech to sweet my thankes. **1609** *Bible* (Douay) Ecclus. xxvii. 26 In the sight of thyne eyes he will sweete his mouth.

2. To affect in a sweet or pleasant way; to give pleasure to, delight, gratify.

c **1555** HARPSFIELD *Divorce Hen. VIII* (Camden) 292 To sweet the people's ears with pleasant words [he] told them [etc.]. *a* **1600** in Ashmole *Theat. Chem. Brit.* (1652) 196 In thyne owne howse thow mast well gett A good Morsell of meat thy mouth to sweet. **1602** MARSTON *Antonio's Rev.* III. iii, Heavens tones Strike not such musick to immortall soules As your accordance sweetes my breast withall. **1879** *Blackw. Mag.* Jan. 58 [West Indian Negro] You will hear of something that will sweet you greatly.

† **sweet**, *v.*[2] *Obs. rare.* [Echoic: cf. SWEET-SWEET.] *intr.* To pipe, chirp, or twitter, as a bird.

1677 N. COX *Gentl. Recreat.* III. 57 When you have so tamed them [*sc.* captured nightingales] that they begin to Cur and Sweet with chearfulness. *Ibid.*, Those Birds that are long a feeding, and make no Curring nor Sweeting.

sweet, obs. form of SWEAT.

Sweet Adeline (swiːt 'ædɪlaɪn). *U.S.* A name in a popular close-harmony song (see quot. 1903), used in *pl.* to denote a group or organization of female barber-shop singers (cf. BARBER-SHOP 2 b). Also *attrib.* in *sing.*

[**1903** ARMSTRONG & GERARD *You're the Flower of my Heart, Sweet Adeline* (song) 5 Sweet Adeline. For you I pine.] **1947** *Harmonizer* Nov. 37/1 The Sweet Adelines, women's quartet organization, held their first convention and contest in Tulsa in October. **1958** *Music Jrnl* Nov.-Dec. 67/2 A Sweet Adeline Chapter..is a chorus and usually meets once a week. **1969** *Pitch Pipe* Summer 7/1 We as Sweet Adelines have a..responsibility to present ourselves as an 'in' group..capable of presenting..choruses and performances. **1972** *Music Educators Jrnl.* Dec. 71/1 'The Sweet Adelines', an organization for women, have been largely responsible for keeping alive this style of singing. **1979** *Tucson* (Arizona) *Citizen* 20 Sept. (Old Pueblo Suppl.) 2/4 On the bill for the 5 p.m. show are the Arizona Opera Puppets..the Old Pueblo Sweet Adelines.

So as *v. intr.*, to sing in barber-shop style; hence **Sweet 'Adelin(e)ing** *vbl. sb.*

1949 *Educational Music Mag* Nov.-Dec. 38/3 So—get four boys 'Sweet Adelining' around the place if you want to start a real male section to your choir. **1961** *Pitch Pipe* Aug. 13/2 I've just completed one of the most fabulous weekends in my career of 'Sweet Adelining'. **1966** *Ibid.* Spring 6/1 Sweet Adeline-ing is almost as habit-forming as a drug!

sweet and sour, **sweet-sour**, *adj. phr.* [f. the adjs.] **1.** = SOUR-SWEET *a.* Also, alternatively sweet and sour.

1594 DANIEL *Cleopatra* IV. Wks. (1717) 286 To have eat the sweet-sower Bread of Poverty. **1707** MORTIMER *Husb.* (1721) II. 352 It will taste a little Sweet-sour, from the Sugar and from the Currant. *c* **1879** G. M. HOPKINS *Poems* (1967) 179 When the air was sweet-and-sour of the flown fineflour of Those gold-nails and their gaylinks that hang along a lime. **1909** E. B. TITCHENER *Text-Bk. Psychol.* I. xxxvii. 141 The mixed sweet-sour stimulus affects only the sour-sensitive bulbs. **1959** *Vogue* Dec. 120 This sweet-and-sour glimpse of the cultured Sahib chez soi continually excites by its freshness. **1967** P. D. JAMES *Unnatural Causes* III. iv. 211 Dalgliesh could smell his breath, the sweet-sour trace of too much drinking. **1975** *Chem. in Brit.* XI. 18/3 If it [*sc.* the chemical industry] is subjected to short term sweet-and-sour treatments of restraints, constraints, stimuli, and instant statute, it could very easily be damaged beyond repair.

2. *Cookery.* Cooked in or flavoured with sugar and vinegar or lemon. Now esp. of Chinese food. Also *absol.* as *sb.*

1723 J. NOTT *Cook's & Confectioner's Dict.* sig. L l 2, To make a sweet-sour-tart. Boil..Sugar in..Verjuice, or Lemon Juice. **1932** L. GOLDING *Magnolia Street* v. 103 Mrs. Emmanuel brought in some fish cooked in sweet-and-sour sauce. **1951** *Good Housek. Home Encycl.* 360/2 The soup should have a pleasant 'sweet-sour' taste. **1959** E. MANNIN *Blue-Eyed Boy* I. xi. 129 'A little more sweet-and-sour?' 'A lot,' said Len. He added, 'It's tasty, I must say.' **1961** [see CHOW MEIN]. **1977** *Times* 7 May 9 The usual chow meins and sweet-and-sours can be had. **1978** *Texas Highways* Feb. 16/2 Hong Kong chicken in a sweet-sour sauce. **1982** C. THOMAS *Jade Tiger* 5 The German Chancellor's top adviser..struck down by sweet and sour pork.

sweetbread ('swiːtbrɛd). (Also formerly as two words.) [app. f. SWEET *a.* + BREAD *sb.*, but the reason for the name is not obvious.]

1. The pancreas, or the thymus gland, of an animal, esp. as used for food (distinguished respectively as ***heart***, ***stomach***, or ***belly sweetbread*** and ***throat***, ***gullet***, or ***neck sweetbread***): esteemed a delicacy.

1565 COOPER *Thesaurus*, *Animellæ*, the sweete breade in a hogge. **1578** BANISTER *Hist. Man* VII. 90 A certaine Glandulous part, called Thimus, which in Calues..is most pleasaunt to be eaten. I suppose we call it the sweete bread. **1598** CHAPMAN *Iliad* I. 458 [They] Cut off their thighes dubd with the fatte,..And pricke the sweetebreads thereupon. *a* **1613** OVERBURY *A Wife*, etc. (1630) L i j b, For an inward bruise, Lambstones and sweet-breads are his onely *Sperma Ceti*. **1653** H. COGAN tr. *Pinto's Trav.* xxx. (1663) 121 Some sell their pigs, and some again sell nothing but the chitterlings, the sweet-breads, the blood, and the haslets. **1791** BOSWELL *Johnson* 9 May an. 1778, He gave her her choice of a chicken, [or] a sweetbread. **1797-8** LAMB *Ros. Gray* xi. Wks. 1903 I. 26, I ordered my dinner—green peas and a sweetbread. **1824** in *Spirit Pub. Jrnls.* (1825) 281 We've gullet-sweetbreads, veined with red. **1846** SOYER *Gastron. Regen.* 681 If I cannot meet with heart sweetbreads, I in general satisfy myself with the throats. **1884** G. ALLEN *Philistia* III. 156 Oysters, game, sweetbreads, red mullet, any little delicacy of that sort.

† **2.** A bribe, *douceur*. *Obs. slang* or *colloq.*

a **1670** HACKET *Abp. Williams* II. (1693) 163, I obtain'd that of the fellow,..with a few Sweetbreads that I gave him out of my Purse.

'sweet-,brier, **-,briar**. (Also as two words.) Forms: see SWEET *a.* and BRIER *sb.*[1] A species of rose, the Eglantine, *Rosa rubiginosa* (and some other species, as *R. micracantha*), having strong hooked prickles, pink single flowers, and small aromatic leaves; freq. cultivated in gardens.

1538 TURNER *Libellus*, *Cynorrhodos*..swete brere aut Eglentyne. **1548** —— *Names Herbes* 33 Cynorrhodus named of the latines Rosa canina, is called in englishe a swete brere or an Eglentyne. **1625** BACON *Ess.*, *Gardens* (Arb.) 562 Some Thickets, made onely of Sweet-Briar, and Honny-suckle, and some Wilde Vine amongst. *a* **1631** DONNE *Epicedes*, *Elegie on the L.C.* 9 If a sweet briar, climbe up by a tree. **1774** G. WHITE *Selborne*, *To Pennant* 2 Sept., The fly-catcher..builds in a vine, or a sweet-brier. **1796** WITHERING *Brit. Plants* (ed. 3) II. 467 In the Garden Sweet-briar the leaves [are] beset above with very short hairs, oval-eggshaped. **1802** BLOOMFIELD *Rur. Tales*, *Dolly* 45 The sweet-brier op'd its pink-ey'd rose, And gave its fragrance to the gale.

allusively. **1599** MASSINGER, etc. *Old Law* II. ii, *2 Court.* O sweet precious bud of beauty! Troth, she smells over all the house, methinks. *1 Court.* The sweetbriar's but a counterfeit to her—It does exceed you only in the prickle.., lady. **1638** FORD *Fancies* II. ii, Bill, pigeon, do; thou'st be my cat-a-mountain, and I thy sweet-briar, honey.

attrib. **1796** WITHERING *Brit. Plants* (ed. 3) II. 467 Rosa..eglanteria... Sweet-briar Rose. **1857** G. *Bird's Urin. Deposits* (ed. 5) 236 The sweet-briar odour was frequently present. **1884** MILLER *Plant-n.*, *Bedeguar*, or *Sweet Briar Sponge*, a gall found on the Sweet Briar and other Roses. **1900** H. SUTCLIFFE *Shameless Wayne* xiii. (1905) 179 The sweetbriar hedges.

Hence **sweet-briery** *a.*, full of sweet-brier.

1828 MOORE '*We may roam through this world*' ii, The wild sweet-briery fence.

sweetch (swiːtʃ), *int.* or *adv. nonce-wd.* An imitative word expressing the sound of a whip.

1859 MEREDITH *R. Feverel* ii, Sweetch went the mighty whip, well swayed.

sweeten ('swiːt(ə)n), *v.* [f. SWEET *a.* + -EN[5].]

1. *trans.* **a.** To make sweet to the taste; *esp.* to add sugar or other sweet substance to (food or drink) so as to impart a sweet flavour; also *absol.*

1552 HULOET, Sweten or make swete, *dulco*. **1597** SHAKS. *Lover's Compl.* 272 Loues armes are peace,..And sweetens in the suffring pangues it beares, The Alloes of all forces. **1665** BOYLE *Occas. Refl.* I. IV. iv. (1848) 68 The Fruit..being neither sweetned nor concocted by Maturity. **1711** ADDISON *Spect.* No. 69 ¶ 4 The Infusion of a China Plant sweetned with the Pith of an Indian Cane. **1747-96** MRS. GLASSE *Cookery* xiv. 210 Add half a pint of white wine, and sweeten to your palate. *a* **1777** in *Jrnl. Friends' Hist. Soc.* Oct. (1914) 188 Sweeten it to your taste and put in a Quarter of a pound of plimpd Currants. **1833** HT. MARTINEAU *Briery Creek* iii. 60 To get something to sweeten my husband's toddy with. **1883** *Cassell's Dict. Cookery* 771/2 Rose Custard. Boil a pint of good milk,..sweeten to taste, adding some essence of rose.

b. To make sweet to the smell; to fill or imbue with fragrance.

a **1586** SIDNEY *Arcadia* II. (1912) 229 The world the garden is, she is the flower That sweetens all the place. **1611** SHAKS. *Cymb.* IV. ii. 220 With fayrest Flowers..I'le sweeten thy sad graue. *c* **1645** HOWELL *Lett.* (1655) II. 34 This perfume..hath ascended to my brain, and sweetned all the cells thereof. **1867** O. W. HOLMES *Pages fr. Old Vol. Life* v. (1891) 153 The azalea, wild honeysuckle, is sweetening the roadsides.

2. To free from offensive taste or smell; to render fresh; to free from taint, purify, bring into a wholesome condition.

1599 B. JONSON *Cynthia's Rev.* Induct., I would thou hadst some sugar candied to sweeten thy mouth. **1605** SHAKS. *Macb.* v. i. 57 Heere's the smell of the blood still: all the perfumes of Arabia will not sweeten this little hand. **1611** —— *Wint. T.* II. i. 156 There's not a graine of it, the face to sweeten Of the whole dungy-earth. **1675** SOUTH *Serm., Judg. viii. 34–5* (1697) I. 514 The Sea swallows them [*sc.* rivers of fresh water] all, but is not at all changed, or sweetned, by them. **1711** ADDISON *Spect.* No. 16 ¶2 The one might be employ'd in healing those Blotches and Tumours which break out in the Body, while the other is sweetning the Blood and rectifying the Constitution. **1722** DE FOE *Plague* (Rtldg.) 307 Measures for airing and sweetning their Houses. **1794** R. J. SULIVAN *View Nat.* I. 287 Fixed air most assuredly has the power of sweetening the putrid effluvium.

3. To make sweet to the ear; to impart a pleasant sound to.

1578 H. WOTTON *Courtlie Controv.* 90 Mine aduersary (who as the crafty fowler sweeteneth his voice to deceiue). *c* **1618** MORYSON *Itin.* IV. IV. iii. (1903) 377 The language of the Netherlanders is a Dialect of the German toung, but sweetned with the leuity of the French toung. **1794** MRS. RADCLIFFE *Myst. Udolpho* xxxvi, The horns, placed in a distant part of the woods where an echo sweetened and prolonged their melancholy tones, broke softly on the stillness of the scene.

4. To make pleasant or agreeable; sometimes, to make more pleasant, add to the sweetness of.

a **1586** SIDNEY *Arcadia* II. (1912) 214 One was the Prince Plangus (whose name was sweetened by your breath, peerlesse Ladie, when the last daie it pleased you to mention him unto me). **1597** HOOKER *Eccl. Pol.* v. lxxxi. §2 That comfort which sweetneth life to them that spend it in these trauayles vpon their owne. *a* **1601** ? MARSTON *Pasquil & Kath.* (1878) Introd. 19 His industrie should sweat To sweeten your delights. **1641** J. JACKSON *True Evang. T.* I. 5 The whole sentence is sweetned with a continued allegory. **1712** ADDISON *Spect.* No. 471 ¶11 The Influence of Hope in general sweetens Life. **1742** GRAY *Eton* 34 Graver hours that bring constraint To sweeten liberty. **1857** RUSKIN *Pol. Econ. Art* I. xiv. 21 All acts and services were..to be sweetened by brotherly concord. **1888** MISS BRADDON *Fatal Three* I. iv, The home ties and tender associations which sweeten other lives were unknown to her.

with advs. **1594** MARLOWE & NASHE *Dido* I. i, Venus Swannes shall shed their siluer downe, To sweeten out the slumbers of thy bed. **1611** B. JONSON *Catiline* II. i, I would have my love Angry sometimes, to sweeten off the rest Of her behaviour. *a* **1644** QUARLES *Sol. Recant.* Sol. ix. 75 Goe, sweeten up thy labours and thy life With fresh delights. *Ibid.* x. 26 She will..direct thy ways In sacred Ethicks, sweetning out thy days With season'd Knowledge.

5. a. To make less unpleasant or painful; to alleviate, lighten, mitigate.

a **1586** SIDNEY *Arcadia* II. (1912) 155 She the sweetnesse of my harte, even sweetning the death, which her sweetnesse drew upon me. **1598** SYLVESTER *Du Bartas* II. ii. I. *Ark* 338 Thus Noah sweetens his Captivity, Beguiles the time, and charms his misery. **1622** PEACHAM *Compl. Gentl.* x. 78 To sweeten your seuerer studies, by this time vouchsafe Poetry your respect. **1682** MRS. BEHN *Round-heads* IV. ii, This mighty pleasure comes A propos To sweaten all the heavy toyls of empire. **1706** *Art of Painting* (1744) 75 He us'd to sing to himself to sweeten his labour. **1844** KINGLAKE *Eothen* xviii, The [burial] ground..has nothing to sweeten melancholy. **1870** J. H. NEWMAN *Gram. Assent* II. x. 396 Hope of future good, as we know, sweetens all suffering.

b. To make less harsh, offensive, or objectionable; to soften, palliate, extenuate. Now *rare* or *Obs.*

1635 in Foster *Crt. Min. E. Ind. Comp.* (1907) 115 Wherein hee shall find any harsh or bitter language, to sweeten the same in a more mild and gentle phrase. **1665** J. WEBB *Stone-Heng* (1725) 10 Learned Men have usually extenuated and sweetned the Failures and Mistakes of others. **1700** RYCAUT *Hist. Turks* III. 333 He endeavoured to sweeten the matter, and render the case as plausible as might be.

6. With personal object (a person, or his mind, temper, etc.):

a. To produce a pleasant disposition in; to make gracious, mild, or kind; to refine.

1561 T. HOBY tr. *Castiglione's Courtyer* II. (1577) Hiij, Those sightes sweeten the mindes of the hearers. *a* **1628** PRESTON *Saints Daily Exerc.* (1629) 138 It sweetens his spirit, it makes him more gracious. **1662** STILLINGFL. *Orig. Sacræ* II. iv. §7 Rather to transport men beyond the power of their reason, then to compose and sweeten it. **1706** STANHOPE *Paraphr.* III. 31 Though it be the very End of this Religion to correct and sweeten the Tempers of Men. **1867** TROLLOPE *Chron. Barset* II. lvi. 123 [Her] temper..was not sweetened by her husband's very uncivil reference to her sex. **1883** H. DRUMMOND *Nat. Law in Spir. W.* (1884) 192 He whose spirit is purified and sweetened becomes proof against these germs of sin.

b. To make things pleasant for, relieve, comfort, soothe, gratify. Now *rare* or *Obs.*

1647 MAY *Hist. Parl.* I. vii. 76 [They] would still take all harsh, distastefull things, upon themselves, to cleare, to sweeten their Master. **1652** HEYLIN *Cosmogr.* IV. 112 A Crown being sent him by King Iames with many other rich presents, the better to sweeten and oblige him. **1666** BUNYAN *Grace Abound.* §202 Something..which, with this Text, did sweeten my heart. **1833** TENNYSON *Dream Fair Wom.* lix, The kiss he gave me, ere I fell, Sweetens the spirit still.

c. To free from bitter or angry feeling; to mollify, appease. Now *rare* or *Obs.*

1657 SPARROW *Bk. Com. Prayer* (1661) Pref., He will perhaps be so sweetned as..to pardon those who [etc.]. **1691** tr. *d'Emiliane's Frauds Rom. Monks* 392 The Abbot having heard what they had to say, endeavour'd what he could to sweeten them,..but all this did but incense them the more. **1693** *Mem. Cnt. Teckely* II. 124 The Emperor to sweeten the People, restor'd the Confiscated Goods. **1714** BUDGELL tr. *Theophrastus* i. 6 He redoubles his Professions of Friendship, and sweetens him out of his Resentments.

7. To persuade by flattery or gifts; to cajole; to decoy, take in; to bribe. Also with *up*. (Cf. SWEETENER 3.) Now only *slang* or *dial.*

1594 R. CAREW *Huarte's Exam. Wits* xiii. (1596) 202 With his lips he sweetneth, and in his heart he betraieth thee. **1623** in *Impeachm. Dk. Buckhm.* (Camden) 72 What somme wilbe fitt..to sweeten him for their future occasions. **1664** PEPYS *Diary* 16 June, The talke..is..that the Holland Embassador here do endeavour to sweeten us with fair words. **1678** [? WINSTANLEY] *Four for a Penny* 8 Which Species of Wheedling in Terms of their [*sc.* the Bum-bailiffs'] Art is called Sweeten and Pinch. *a* **1700** B. E. *Dict. Cant. Crew, To Sweeten*, to decoy, draw in. **1821** *Life D. Haggart* (ed. 2) 61 We went to jail to see the boy, and sweetened the toping cove [= hangman] with plenty of budge [= drink]. **1872** J. HARTLEY *Yorks. Ditties* Ser. II. 96 All seekin' for orders an' jobs An' sweetenin th' sarvents wi' tips. **1875** 'MARK TWAIN' in *Atlantic Monthly* Aug. 195/1 Stephen sweetened him up and put him off a week. **1971** 'E. LATHEN' *Ashes to Ashes* x. 99, I know Unger is just trying to sweeten us up... Maybe we should be trying to sweeten him up.

8. In various technical uses: To bring to the desired quality or condition. **a.** To make pliable; to cause to work smoothly or easily.

1607 MARKHAM *Caval.* II. iv. (1617) 51 This [smooth] Cannon ordreth and sweetneth the Horses mouth. **1898** KIPLING *Day's Work* 74 Every inch of her [*sc.* a ship]..has to be livened up and made to work wi' its neighbour—sweetenin' her, we call it, technically.

b. *Painting* and *Drawing*. To free from harshness, soften (a tint, line, etc.).

1688 HOLME *Armoury* III. 152/2 *Sweeten your Shaddow*, is to breath on the Glass, and strike it lightly over with the Washer Brush. **1695** DRYDEN tr. *Dufresnoy's Art Paint.* lxx. §530 Correggio has made his Memory immortal..by sweetning his Lights and Shadows, and melting them into each other so happily, that they are even imperceptible. *c* **1790** IMISON *Sch. Arts* II. 62 Sweeten that part with the finger as little as possible. **1873** E. SPON *Workshop Receipts* Ser. I. 100/2 The chief use of the badger tool is to soften or sweeten broad tints.

c. To render (soil) mellow and fertile.

1733 W. ELLIS *Chiltern & Vale Farm.* 36 This sort of Ploughing sweetens the Ground better than bouting. **1842** *Penny Cycl.* XXIII. 313/2 The system of fallowing to clean the land, and to 'sweeten' it, as old farmers say. **1851** *B'ham & Midl. Gardeners' Mag.* Apr. 30 Many of the little growers in the North..were compelled to cleanse and sweeten their soils for Carnations by baking them in small ovens.

d. To neutralize (an acid) by means of an alkali.

[**1681**, etc., implied in SWEETENER 1 b]. **1885** HUMMEL *Dyeing Textile Fabrics* v. 83 Another plan to avoid tendering, is to let the goods steep in a weak soda-ash solution for a short time... This is termed 'sweetening' the goods.

e. *Oil Industry*. To free (petroleum products) from sulphur or sulphur compounds.

1924 *Industr. & Engin. Chem.* Nov. 1113 Although naphthas and kerosenes have been sweetened by the sodium plumbite method for many years, the process is entirely empirical. **1975** W. G. ROBERTS *Quest for Oil* (rev. ed.) ix. 92 The lighter distillates, liquid petroleum gas, gasolenes and kerosenes, can be sweetened by simple chemical treatments which either remove the sulphur compounds or turn them into harmless and non-smelly forms.

9. *slang*. **a.** *Cards*. To increase the stakes; *esp.* at poker, to increase the stakes in a pot that has not been opened. **b.** To bid at an auction merely in order to raise the price. **c.** *Finance*. To increase the collateral of a loan by adding further securities.

1896 [see SWEETENING *vbl. sb.* 1 d]. **1903** FARMER & HENLEY *Slang, Sweeten*,..To contribute to the pool. Hence *Sweetening* = money paid into the pool or kitty. **1904** [see SWEETENER 3 b]. **1910** *Encycl. Brit.* XXI. 901/1 *Sweeten*, chipping to a jack-pot after a failure to open.

10. *intr.* To become sweet (in various senses).

1626 BACON *Sylva* §325 Where a waspe..hath bitten, in a Grape, or any Fruit, it will sweeten hastily. **1765** *Museum Rust.* IV. 178 Those lands which have that bitterness are several years a sweetening. **1794** MCPHAIL *Treat. Cucumber* 73 When frames are new painted, they should be suffered to lie and sweeten for some time. **1840** *P. Parley's Ann.* I. 173 The various articles of wearing apparel, hung out to dry and sweeten. **1851** T. T. LYNCH *Unaddr. Lett.* iv. in *Lett. to Scattered* (1872) 184 Papa..laughed, and said, George was coming on; he would sweeten by and by. **1858** GLENNY *Gard. Every-day Bk.* 163/1 The soil laid in a heap to sweeten.

sweetened ('swiːt(ə)nd), *ppl. a.* [f. prec. + -ED[1].] Made sweet, in any sense: see prec. and SWEET *a.*

1567 DRANT *Horace, Ep. Arte Poet.* Bj, Plautus rymes and tothesume sweetned vayne. **1616** W. BROWNE *Brit. Past.* II. ii. 475 Where Philomela and such sweetned throates, Are for the mastry tuning various notes. **1682** N. O. *Boileau's Lutrin* I. 174 The Sweetned Prelate rises from the Table. *a* **1708** BEVERIDGE *Thes. Theol.* (1711) III. 250 If he casts darts infected with pleasure, faith shews they are sweetened poisons. **1797** MRS. BERKELEY in *G. M. Berkeley's Poems* Pref. p. cccx, Sweetened sand, called sugar. **1890** *Retrospect Med.* CII. 39 Bromoform is conveniently administered suspended in sweetened water. **1924** *Industr. & Engin. Chem.* Nov. 1113 The reactions involved..have furnished explanations of the various complications which appear in sweetening, including..the sourness developed in rerunning a sweetened oil.

sweetener ('swiːt(ə)nə(r)). [f. as prec. + -ER[1].]

1. a. That which makes something sweet to the taste or other sense; something that imparts a sweet flavour.

1719 QUINCY *Compl. Disp.* 96/1 All those which usually pass for Sweetners. **1884** DOWELL *Taxation* v. ii. I. 132 Sugar..began to displace honey as a sweetener for food.

b. An alkali or similar substance used to neutralize acidity; something which renders soil rich and mellow.

1681 tr. *Belon's Myst. Physick* Introd. 34 Alcalies and other Sweetners should be employed. *a* **1699** TEMPLE *Misc.* III. *Health & Long Life* Wks. 1720 I. 286 Powder of Crabs-Eyes and Claws, and burnt Egg-Shells are often prescribed as Sweetners of any sharp Humours. **1712** STEELE *Spect.* No. 547 ¶10, I..having a Constitution which naturally abounds with Acids..have found it a most excellent Sweetner of the Blood. **1765** *Museum Rust.* IV. xl. 178 During that year, one may sow either oats, corn, peas or beans, or any sweetener. **1794** VANCOUVER *Agric. Cambridge* 201 The plough is..used with great propriety, as a sweetener of the soil.

c. *Painting*. A brush used for 'sweetening': see SWEETEN 8 b.

1859 GULLICK & TIMBS *Painting* 198 Most artists also use a brush made of badger's hair. It bears the significant names of 'softener' and 'sweetener', and is used to blend the colours and remove 'edginess', by being swept to and fro over them while freshly laid.

2. a. A person or (more usually) a thing that renders something pleasant or agreeable (or mitigates its unpleasantness).

a **1649** DRUMM. OF HAWTH. *Madrigals, A Kiss*, This Sweetner of Annoyes, This Nectare of the Gods. **1670** BROOKS *Wks.* (1867) VI. 368 The communion with God, that is the life of your graces, the sweetener of all ordinances. **1710** NORRIS *Chr. Prud.* viii. 350 Wisdom..the great Up-holder and Sweetner of all Society. **1742** BLAIR *Grave* 89 Friendship!.. Sweetner of Life! and Solder of Society! **1865** MRS. GASKELL *Wives & Dau.* l, Molly stood by,..and only kept where she was by the hope of coming in as sweetener or peacemaker. **1871** SMILES *Charac.* ix. (1876) 260 Grace is a sweetener and embellisher of life.

†**b.** One who softens, palliates, or extenuates; a flatterer, cajoler. *Obs.*

1724 SWIFT *Drapier's Lett.* vii. Wks. 1755 V. II. 150 Those softners, sweetners, compounders, and expedient-mongers. **1728** *Capt. G. Carleton's Mem.* 202 When any Officers had asserted the Falsity of those Inventions (as they all did, except a military Sweetner or two). **1729** SWIFT *Poems, Libel on Delany* 154 You, who till your fortune's made Must be a sweetener by your trade, Should swear he never meant us ill.

c. Something that produces (or restores) pleasant feeling; something pleasing, gratifying, or comforting; also, a means of persuasion, an inducement (cf. next sense); a bribe; a concession or appeasement (esp. in politics, business, etc.). Cf. DOUCEUR 3.

1741 MIDDLETON *Cicero* (1742) II. viii. 235 A sweetner for my Cato. **1754** E. FARNEWORTH tr. *Life Sextus V*, IV. (1766) 190 This was what the gamesters call a Sweetner, to draw them on, and made them labour more earnestly. **1782** S. CRISP *Let. to Mme. D'Arblay* 5 Apr., And now, Fanny, after this severe lecturing, I shall give you a sweetener to make it up with you. **1829** P. EGAN *Boxiana* 2nd Ser. II. 415 As a reward, or sweetener for his numerous defeats,..the above unexpected victory has put Sampson once more into good humour with himself. **1847** A. HARRIS *Settlers & Convicts* vi. 89 The handsome 'sweeteners' (bribes) which old D——'s profits enabled him to give the constables. **1903** G. H. LORIMER *Lett. Self-made Merch.* xiii. 186, I met him coming in from his route looking glum; so I handed him fifty dollars as a little sweetener. **1955** *Times* 24 May 16/2, I suggest that what you got from Carroll Levis was a sweetener or a bribe. **1959** *Economist* 28 Mar. 1176/1 The main attraction of the Kennedy Bill is its 'sweeteners' in the form of amendments, made to the order of the labour leaders, to the basic Taft-Hartley Act regulating trade union activities. **1960** *Wall St. Jrnl.* 26 Sept. 11 The State Department responded..by permitting the imports but removing the sweetener—the premium that other sugar suppliers enjoy in their sales to the U.S. **1975** *Times* 10 Apr. 8/2 Mr Nixon used the threat of renewed bombing as a sweetener to get the reluctant President Thieu to sign the agreements. **1979** G. HAMMOND *Dead Game* x. 138 Everybody gives 'sweeteners' of some kind or another, even if it's only a bottle at Christmas.

3. *slang*. **a.** A decoy, cheat, sharper. ? *Obs.*

a **1700** B. E. *Dict. Cant. Crew, Cog*,..the Money..the Sweetners drop to draw in the Bubbles. *Ibid., Sweetners*, Guinea-Droppers, Cheats, Sharpers. **1707** LUTTRELL *Brief Rel.* (1857) VI. 223 Being one of the gang, and a sweetner, he goeing to the innocent persons to perswade them to make up the same by giving money. **1714** *Lond. Gaz.* No. 5272/9 Whereas divers Persons, commonly called Sweetners, have cheated many People of considerable Sums of Mony, by plausible Pretences.

b. One who bids at an auction merely in order to raise the price.

1823 in *Spirit of Public Jrnls.* (1825) 508 Here the music of bidding grows loud and more loud—Here the sweetener is conning his hints for the day. **1865** *Slang Dict.* **1904** *Daily Chron.* 23 Sept. 6/4 'Safe bidding' or 'sweetening' at an auction sale was a fraud on the public. Most men bidding at an auction trusted the other bidders. A 'sweetener' was a man who was not 'playing the game'.

sweetening ('swiːt(ə)nɪŋ), *vbl. sb.* [f. as prec. + -ING[1].]

1. The action of the verb SWEETEN. **a.** The imparting of a sweet taste or smell; †perfuming; the freeing from taint, staleness, or impurity.

1591 Wotton *Lett.* (1907) I. 270 There is a certain English northern man in this town..lives now by sweetening of gloves. **1599** B. Jonson *Ev. Man out of Hum.* III. i, Which sute (for the more sweetning) now lies in lavender. **1617** J. Taylor (Water P.) *Trav. to Hamburgh* B j, As if her selfe..had layen seauen yeares in Lauender on sweetning in long Lane. *a* **1774** Tucker *Lt. Nat.* (1834) II. 380 Some to be hung in the winds for sweetening, some plunged into rapid waters to wash away their filth. **1876** B. Martin *Messiah's Kingd.* I. iii. 31 The sweetening of the waters at Marah.

fig. **1740** Cheyne *Regimen* 339 To..pass over every Impulse, Sweetning, or Glance of Light. **1883** H. Drummond *Nat. Law in Spir. W.* (1884) 192 The acrid humours that are breaking out all over the surface of his life are only to be subdued by a gradual sweetening of the inward spirit.

b. *Painting* and *Drawing*. (See SWEETEN 8 b.)

1688 Holme *Armoury* III. 149/2 *Sweetning*, is the working one colour into another with a soft Pencil: that they will look as one colour, though they be diverse. *c* **1790** Imison *Sch. Arts* II. 63 To use his crayon in sweetening as much, and his finger as little, as possible.

c. The action of rendering pleasant, alleviating, palliating, making gracious, etc.

1592 Nashe *P. Penilesse* F j b, If I were to paint Sloth (as I am not seene in the sweetening)..I would draw it like a Stationer that I know, with his thumb vnder his girdle. **1597** Hooker *Eccl. Pol.* v. xxxviii. §2 For the raysing vp of mens hearts, and the sweetning of their affections towards God. **1829** Newman in Liddon, etc. *Life Pusey* (1893) I. viii. 167 You will be doing as much to the sweetening of your book.. as by your humanities towards Mr. R.

d. *slang*. (See SWEETEN 9.)

1896 Lillard *Poker Stories* viii. 191 Then along came a big jack pot that had been enlarged by repeated sweetenings. **1903** [see SWEETEN 9]. **1904** [see SWEETENER 3 b].

e. *Oil Industry*. The process of freeing petroleum products of sulphur or sulphur compounds.

1924 *Industr. & Engin. Chem.* Nov. 1113 Sweetening consists in the removal of hydrogen sulfide and of alkyl mercaptans which are the only compounds responsible for sourness. **1959** H. M. Noel *Petroleum Refinery Man.* v. 153/1 Kerosene stocks which are too low in smoke point to be finished by simple sweetening. **1970** C. L. Thomas *Catalytic Processes & Proven Catalysts* xix. 199 Mercaptans in gasoline have an objectionable odor ('sour' gasoline). By converting them to disulfides which have less odor, a 'sweet' gasoline is produced; hence the term 'sweetening'.

2. That which sweetens; something that imparts a sweet flavour.

long sweetening*, *short sweetening: see LONG *a.* 18.

1819 Moore *Rhymes on Road* xv. 18 Him Whose bitter death-cup from above Had yet this sweetening [*later altered to* cordial] round the rim. **1872** Schele de Vere *Americanisms* 206 The backwoodsman finds at home, besides honey, the long and short sweetening, peculiar to the West. **1884** Roe *Nat. Ser. Story* ix, Berries, to which the sun had been adding sweetening. **1890** *Boston* (Mass.) *Jrnl.* 20 May 2/2, I..made a year's sweetening from maple sirup.

'sweetening, *ppl. a.* [f. as prec. + -ING[2].] That sweetens.

1. Imparting a sweet taste, smell, etc.; freeing from taint, purifying.

1707 Mortimer *Husb.* (1721) I. 351 Sweetning Vapours of the Air. **1804** Bewick *Brit. Birds* (1847) II. 204 When they have undergone a certain sweetening process before cooking. **1830** M. Donovan *Dom. Econ.* I. 269 The sugar of the grape..differs from common sugar..in having less sweetening power. **1867** Smyth *Sailor's Word-bk.*, *Sweetening cock*, a wholesome contrivance for preventing fetid effluvia in ships' holds.

2. Rendering something pleasant or delightful; producing pleasant feeling or gracious disposition; †soothing.

1644 Bulwer *Chirol.* 78 Drawing our Hand with a sweetning motion over the head. **1648** Owen *Right. Zeal Encouraged* Wks. 1851 VIII. 152 A close labouring in all his ways without the least sweetening endearments. **1810** Southey *Kehama* VIII. xi, No sweetening vengeance roused a brave despair. **1886** Dickie *Words Faith*, etc. (1892) 135 He adds His sweetening blessing to it.

sweet-field: see SWEET-VELD.

'sweetful, *a.* Now *dial.* [f. SWEET *a.* + -FUL 1; cf. *grateful*, *sadful*, *strangeful*.] Full of sweetness.

1589 Lodge *Scillaes Met.* (1819) 4 And from a brier a sweetfull branch did plucke. *a* **1825** Forby *Voc. E. Anglia*, *Sweetful*, delightful; charming; full of sweets.

'sweet-gale. Also 7 -gaule. [See SWEET *a.* and GALE *sb.*[1]] The bog myrtle, *Myrica Gale*.

1640 Parkinson *Theat. Bot.* 1451 *Rhus sylvestris sive Myrtus Brabantica aut Anglica.* Sweete Gaule. **1838** Mary Howitt *Birds & Fl., Pheasant* iii, The spicy sweet-gale. **1845** Lindley *Sch. Bot.* (1862) 128 The Sweet Gale..has amentaceous achlamydeous flowers. **1851** Tennyson *E. Morris* 110, I..heard..The Sweet-Gale rustle round the shelving keel.

'sweet-grass. [See SWEET *a.* and GRASS *sb.*]

a. Any kind of grass (or herb called 'grass') of a sweet taste serving as fodder; *spec.* a book-name for the genus *Glyceria*; also locally, the woodruff, *Asperula odorata*, and the grass-wrack, *Zostera marina* (Britten & Holland). Also applied to a species of *Heracleum*: see quot. 1784.

1577 Googe *Heresbach's Husb.* I. 45 The best hearbe for Pasture or Meddowe, is the Trefoyle or Clauer: the next is sweete Grasse. **1709** T. Robinson *Nat. Hist. Westmoreld.* iii. 20 Bituminous Peat Earth..when burnt, limed, and manured..will produce a new Set of sweet Grass, as Clover, both white and red. **1784** King *Cook's Voy. Pacific* III. 336 The other plant alluded to is called the sweet grass; the botanical description is *Heracleum Sibericum foliis pinnatis* [etc.]..In May..it was..covered with a white down, or dust,..it tasted as sweet as sugar; but was hot and pungent. **1908** *Animal Managem.* 109 The 'Reed Sweet grass,' 'Floating sweet grass'.

b. *S. Afr.* = SWEET-VELD.

1812 A. Plumptre tr. *Lichtenstein's Trav. S. Afr.* I. II. xv. 204 On the high hills, sweet grass grows in tolerable plenty. **1838** W. B. Boyce *Notes S. Afr. Affairs* 186 Men should be sent from..the sweet-grass and karoo farms. **1897** [see NUM-NUM]. **1913** Pettman *Africanderisms*, *Sweet grass*, the food plants growing on rich alluvial soil.

c. *N. Amer.* One of several scented grasses, esp. *Hierochloë odorata*, used in basket-making.

1926 *Daily Colonist* (Victoria, B.C.) 24 Jan. 20/1 From making sweet-grass baskets on the shores of the lake of Bays to singing before royalty in the Albert Hall is a far cry. **1968** E. Buckler *Ox Bells & Fireflies* xv. 227 Her contentment grows as the sweet-grass basket fills. **1973** A. H. Whiteford *North Amer. Indian Arts* 43 Sweet grass is widely used in coils.

sweetheart ('swiːthɑːt), *sb.* Forms: see SWEET *a.* and HEART *sb.*

1. a. (Properly two words: see HEART *sb.* 14.) A term of endearment = darling: used chiefly in the vocative. Also used ironically or contemptuously.

c **1290** *St. Kenelm* 140 in *S. Eng. Leg.* 349 Alas..þat ich scholde.. a-bide þat mi child, mi swete heorte, swych cas schal bi-tide. *c* **1325** *Orfeo* 100 Swete hert, he sayde, how may this be? *c* **1374** Chaucer *Troylus* III. 1183 For-yeue it me myn owene swete herte. [Cf. 1820 Troylus..Is with Criseyde his owne herte swete.] **1509** Hawes *Past. Pleas.* xvi. (Percy Soc.) 65 Alas! fayre lady, and myne owne swete herte. **1588** Shaks. *L.L.L.* v. ii. 221 Curtsie sweet hearts, and so the Measure ends. **1596** Nashe *Saffron Walden* Wks. 1905 III. 108 So hath he his Barnabe and Anthony for his minions and sweet-harts. **1601** Shaks. *All's Well* II. iii. 285 *Ros.* Vndone, and forfeited to cares for euer. *Par.* What's the matter sweet-heart? **1613** Middleton *Triumphs Truth* Wks. (Bullen) VII. 241 O welcome, my triumphant lord, My glory's sweetheart! **1648–9** in *Eikon Bas.* (1649) App. 274 The King taking the Duke of Glocester upon His Knee, said, Sweet-heart now they will cut off thy Fathers Head. **1679** *Tryals Robt. Green*, etc. 65 My Husband..called to me, prithee, sweetheart, what hast thou got for my Supper? **1727** Mrs. Delany in *Life & Corr.* (1861) I. 136 What interest I have, I shall be very willing to make use of for my sweetheart's service, but nothing can be done till he is sent to school to Westminster. **1845** James *Arrah Neil* i, A gay cavalier..pulled up..and seeing the girl he exclaimed, ..'Which is the way to Bishop's Merton, sweet-heart?' **1859** Tennyson *Grandmother* xiii, Sweetheart, I love you so well that your good name is mine. **1890** Hall Caine *Bondman* III. vi, 'Ot's the name of your 'ickle boy?' 'Ah, I've got none, sweetheart.' **1941** B. Schulberg *What makes Sammy Run?* iv. 51 (*addressing a man*) 'Hiya, sweetheart,' he said. **1977** F. Parrish *Fire in Barley* viii. 82 Try harder, sweetheart, or I'll plug you in the guts.

b. *N. Amer.* Anything especially good of its kind. Cf. HONEY *sb.* (*a.*) 5 b.

1942 *Amer. Speech* XVII. 105/1 *Sweetheart*, piece of equipment which performs well. **1970** *Globe & Mail* (Toronto) 28 Sept. 27/7 (Advt.), 68 Renault R10, deluxe, radio, a little sweetheart. **1978** *Detroit Free Press* 2 Apr. 15F/4 (Advt.), Lovely 3 bedrm brick ranch, $1\frac{1}{2}$ baths, re rm, a sweetheart for $45,900.

†2. One who is loved illicitly; a paramour. *Obs.*

1589 [? Lyly] *Pappe w. Hatchet* Wks. 1902 III. 399 Ye like not a Bishops rochet, when all your fathers hankerchers were made of his sweete harts smocke. **1610** Holland *Camden's Brit.* (1637) 379 Edith his wife, who..had been one of King Henrie the First his sweet hearts and lig-bies. **1696** Aubrey *Misc., Appar.* (1784) 107 A gentlewoman, a handsome woman, but common, who was Mr. Mohun's sweet heart. **1796** *Grose's Dict. Vulgar T.* (ed. 3), *Sweet Heart*,..a girl's lover, or a man's mistress.

3. A person with whom one is in love.

1576 Fleming *Panopl. Epist.* 309 One hanges himselfe under his sweetehartes windowe with a twyned haulter. *c* **1597** Breton *Figure of Foure* II. §89 Foure creatures goe willingly to their businesse: a Bride to Church, a boy to breckfast, an heire to his land, and a sweet-heart to his loue. **1600** Holland *Livy* XXVI. 623 Your sweet-heart and best beloved [orig. *sponsa*] I have entertained, as well,..as she should have bene with your father and mother in law. **1711** Budgell *Spect.* No. 161 ¶3 Her Sweet-heart, a Person of small Stature. **1782** *Jrnl. Yng. Lady of Virginia* (1871) 38 Miss Nancy's sweetheart came to-day. **1802** in *Nairne Peerage Evidence* (1874) 165, I shall be well pleased to hear from M. Serre the sweet heart of Sussanne all that concerns them. **1855** Dickens *Dorrit* II. xxiii, Your old sweetheart an't far off, and she's a blabber. **1863** Reade *Hard Cash* li, The prejudiced statements of friends and sweethearts, who always swear from the heart rather than from the head and the conscience.

4. *colloq.* and *dial.* in various transf. senses.

a. A sugar cake in the shape of a heart; a jam tart. **b.** Applied to the burs or thorny seeds or sprays which attach themselves to a person's clothes; also, a plant bearing these, as species of *Desmodium*. **c.** A tame rabbit.

1732 Swift *Exam. Abuses Dublin* Wks. 1735 IV. 321 There is another Cry.., and it is that of *Sweet-hearts* [*Note*, A Sort of Sugar-Cakes in the Shape of Hearts]. **1750** G. Hughes *Barbados* 213 Sweet-Heart. The pod is intirely incrusted with small *setæ* or hooked bristles, by which means they tenaciously stick to the cloaths of those who walk among them. **1840** Blaine *Encycl. Rur. Sports* §2683 Four kinds of rabbits are acknowledged among dealers and fanciers,—warreners, parkers, hedgehogs, and sweethearts. .. Sweethearts are the tame varieties. **1877** *N.W. Linc. Gloss.*, *Sweetheart*, a piece of thorn or briar which becomes attached to a woman's dress and drags along after her. **1888** *Sheffield Gloss.*, *Sweetheart*, a thin tart made by spreading a layer of jam between thin slices of paste. **1913** Pettman *Africanderisms*, *Sweethearts*, the hooked seeds of *Bidens pilosa*.

5. A variety of *Rosa wichuraiana* developed by M. H. Walsh about 1903 which bears clusters of small pink flowers; also = *sweetheart rose*, sense 6 b below.

1905 *Country Life Amer.* VII. 625 Sweetheart..delicate blush. **1920** R. Pyle *How to grow Roses* 106 Some roses have acquired new names... Sweetheart P. Mlle Cecile Brunner. **1955** H. van P. Wilson *Climbing Roses* v. 75 Sweetheart (1901)... Rose-pink buds open to very double, $2\frac{1}{2}$-inch, white flowers that are richly fragrant.

6. *attrib.* or as *adj.* **a.** Designating a contract, agreement, etc., arranged privately (i.e. without genuine collective bargaining) by trade unions and employers which is beneficial to themselves but prejudicial to the interests of the workers; hence applied to persons, etc., prone to such collaboration. Also *transf. colloq.* (orig. and chiefly *U.S.*).

1959 *Washington Post* 5 Feb. A2/2 The Administration's ban..would stop an honest union from picketing a shop that had made a substandard 'sweetheart' deal, recognizing a racket union. **1962** N. S. Falcone *Labor Law* xi. 321 Some employers engaged in collusion with unions and paid union officials to get 'sweetheart' contracts. **1965** *Wall St. Jrnl.* (Eastern ed.) 23 Sept. 1/6 The mine manager is a 'sweetheart' operator... In the classic 'sweetheart' situation, corrupt union leaders accept or extort payoffs from employers in exchange for assuring labour peace or winking at contract violations. **1967** G. Tyler *Labor Revolution* xi. 243 The contract is a 'sweetheart agreement' to give the union heads an income, to give the employer relief from a real union, and to give the workers nothing. **1974** *Australian* 12 Nov. 3 Miss Martin said Mr Jones' description of the..award as a sweetheart agreement was farcical. The award had been decided by arbitration, not by negotiation between Qantas and the unions. **1975** *Publishers Weekly* 14 July 54/2 She takes us to three factors, one unorganized, a second with a sweetheart union, the third with an excellent local. *Ibid.* 24 Nov. 53/1 Caffery, a 35-year-old hockey star... Keeping his medical problem secret Caffery negotiates a sweetheart contract to jump league to Texas. **1977** *Time* 1 Aug. 32/2 William Safire.. raised the question of whether the $3.4 million loan that was granted on Jan. 7, after Lance had accepted the sensitive OMB job, was a 'sweetheart loan'. **1979** *Times* 21 Nov. 20/3 What are known as 'sweetheart' transactions (when [supermarket] checkout operators reduce the bill for those they know). **1981** *Times* 30 Nov. 15/1 Mobil has accused US Steel of an illegal 'sweetheart deal' with Marathon board members at the expense of the shareholders.

b. Special Comb.: **sweetheart neck(line)**, a heart-shaped neckline on a dress, blouse, etc. (see quot. 1968); **sweetheart plant**, either of two species of *Philodendron*, *P. cordatum* or *P. scandens*, epiphytic herbs of tropical America which have large heart-shaped leaves; **sweatheart rose** *U.S.*, one of several roses having small pink, white, or yellow flowers, particularly attractive as buds, esp. the climbing polyantha Cécile Brunner; see also sense 5 d above.

1965 *Housewife* Jan. 16/1 She has a great feeling for a return to the late forties. 'Wide shoulders, *sweetheart necks.' **1980** B. Bainbridge *Winter Garden* xvi. 129 Enid.. sauntered through the cool reception hall in her pink summer dress with the sweet-heart neck and emerged into the evening sunshine. **1968** J. Ironside *Fashion Alphabet* 54 **Sweetheart neckline*, a neckline cut in front in two almost semicircular curves, like a heart. **1974** *Country Life* 17 Jan. 106 Sweater with a sweetheart neckline. **1981** *Daily Tel.* 21 May 17/2 The bride, of course, was a stunner—all demure in white broderie anglaise with a sweetheart neckline. **1963** *Reader's Digest Compl. Libr. of Garden* II. 658/1 *P[hilodendron] scandens* (*sweetheart plant) origin: Puerto Rico, Panama. A popular and attractive climbing plant. **1981** *Times* 28 Mar. 11/4 A $6\frac{1}{2}$ ft sweetheart plant..cost £29. **1936** J. H. Nicolas *Year in Rose Garden* xv. 72 Cécile Brunner (*Sweetheart Rose): Light pink tea-like flowers. **1976** *Columbus* (Montana) *News* 27 May 6/4 She carried a bouquet of yellow sweetheart roses.

Hence **'sweetheartdom**, **'sweetheartship** (*nonce-wds.*): see -DOM, -SHIP.

1887 Augusta Wilson *At Mercy of Tiberius* xiv, In the magical days of sweetheartdom, a silvery glorifying glamour wraps the world. **1898** *Tit-Bits* 30 Apr. 85/1 The premature sweetheartship that existed between them.

'sweetheart, *v.* [f. prec.]

1. *trans.* To make a sweetheart of; to court, make love to.

1804 R. Anderson *Cumbld. Ball.* 79, I yence sweethearted Madge o' th' Mill. **1861** Mayhew *Lond. Labour* III. 390 One of his mates sweethearted the servant. **1893** Baring-Gould *Cheap Jack Z.* II. 87 Mark Runham running after two girls, sweethearting both.

2. *intr.* To be, or act the part of, a sweetheart; to court a sweetheart, make love.

1798 T. Morton *Speed the Plough* v. i. (1800) 70 Remember how I used to let thee zit up all night a sweethearting. **1824** Mactaggart *Gallovid. Encycl.* 444

Teevo, .. one who learns the rules of affectation, who *sweethearts* with warmness seemingly. **1873** G. C. DAVIES *Mount. & Mere* xvi. 135 He had gone in the country for his Sunday outing, sweethearting. **1883** *Harper's Mag.* July 165/1 The lanes in which he has sweethearted. **1898** R. KEARTON *Wild Life at Home* 53, I watched a pair of red-backed shrikes or butcher-birds, sweethearting.

Hence **'sweethearting** *vbl. sb.* and *ppl. a.*; also **'sweethearter**.

1812 COLERIDGE in *Lit. Rem.* (1839) IV. 68 Then her Spanish sweet-hearting, doubtless in the true Oroondates style. **1851** MAYHEW *Lond. Labour* I. 379/2 It's that I go for, love and sweet-hearting. **1854** R. S. SURTEES *Handley Cross* lxxix. (1901) II. 276 Venting her spleen on Doleful and all dilatory sweethearters. **1861** HUGHES *Tom Brown at Oxf.* xxiii, There was this sweethearting after old Simon's daughter. **1866** *Morn. Star* 18 Apr. 4/5 The sweet-hearting portion of the audience. **1874** LISLE CARR *Jud. Gwynne* I. iv. 104 She remembered .. how she and William had carried on in those happy sweethearting days. **1886** HALL CAINE *Son of Hagar* I. vii, You Colebank chaps are famous sweethearters, I hear.

sweet-hearted, *a.* [f. SWEET *a.* + HEART *sb.* + -ED[2].] Of sweet disposition. Hence **sweet-heartedness**.

1850 TENNYSON *In Mem.* xcvi, You say, but with no touch of scorn, Sweet-hearted, you, .. You tell me, doubt is Devil-born. **1865** SWINBURNE *Chastelard* IV. i. 163 Soft hearts would weep and weep and let men die For very mercy and sweet-heartedness.

sweetie ('swiːtɪ); usually in pl. **sweeties**. orig. *Sc.* Also **sweety**. [f. SWEET *a.* + -IE. Earlier than SWEET *sb.* 1 e (cf. SWEEPY *sb.* and SWEEP *sb.* 33).]

1. a. A sweetmeat, lollipop. Also, sweet cake or the like.

1721 RAMSAY *Conclusion* 22 To wrap Up snuff, or sweeties, in a shap. **1824** W. HAVERGAL *Let.* in *Life* (1882) 55 Baby .. was satisfied with a bit of sweetie. **1860** THACKERAY *Round. Papers, Christmas Tree*, Instead of finding bonbons or sweeties in the packets which we pluck off the boughs. **1874** CHRISTINA ROSSETTI *Speaking Likenesses* 73 Burnt almonds, chocolate, and 'sweeties' of every flavour. **1899** CROCKETT *Kit Kennedy* 25 She gied me a' the sweeties she had.

b. *attrib.*

1790 D. MORISON *Poems* 18 Rob tak's them to a sweety bench Where a' thing's fit for eatin'. **1808** JAMIESON s.v. *Yule*, What the vulgar call a sweetie-skon, or a loaf enriched with raisins, currants, and spiceries. **1813** G. ROBERTSON *Agric. Surv. Kincard.* 406 The sweety-men, or confectioners. **1821** *Blackw. Mag.* VIII. 423 The Sweety-wife .. Spreads out her sweeties, and adjusts her scale. **1837** LOCKHART *Scott* I. vii. 224 A 'sweetie wife' (that is, an itinerant vender of gingerbread, &c.). **1893** BARING-GOULD *Cheap Jack Z.* I. 51 Money .. for sweetie stuff. **1895** CROCKETT *Bog-Myrtle & Peat* IV. ii. (1899) 332 The row of sweetie-bottles. **1928** J. BUCHAN *Runagates Club* ii. 85 Some biscuits which I bought at a sweetie shop. **1980** *Times* 11 Dec. 11/2 Cheery old Mrs Mutterance has a Battersea sweetie shop.

2. *colloq.* (orig. *U.S.*). **a.** A sweetheart, a lover; a lovable person. Also as a term of endearing address.

1778 [see YANKEE 1 a]. **1925** F. SCOTT FITZGERALD *Great Gatsby* ii. 42 Tom's the first sweetie she ever had. **1932** WODEHOUSE *Hot Water* xv. 248 'I'll drop down off the balcony with the stuff.' .. 'You won't hurt yourself, sweetie?' **1949** A. CHRISTIE *Crooked House* vi. 34 The poor old Sweetie... He .. was just on ninety. **1958** *Listener* 3 July 31/1 His *fiancée*, Julia, who is a sweetie. **1964** G. MCDONALD *Running Scared* i. 14 'Where is Dad?' 'He's in Washington, I think, Sweetie.' **1975** *Times* 19 Sept. 9/3 Karen Black as the steely sweetie on the way up. **1977** N. MARSH *Last Ditch* ii. 40 'Sweetie,' Julia cried extravagantly, 'you *are* such heaven!'

b. *Comb.*, as ***sweetie-pie***.

1928 WODEHOUSE *Money for Nothing* iv. 76 'Hello, sweetie-pie,' said Miss Molloy. **1937** D. B. WYNDHAM LEWIS in L. Russell *Press Gang!* 239 Follies show-girl Gladileen ('Sweetie-Pie') Kisse. **1955** LD. WINTERTON *Fifty Tumultuous Years* 28 She is not his daughter; as I tell you, she his girl; how you say, his 'sweetie-pie'. **1957** E. HYAMS *Into Dream* I. 77 'I think they're all perfect sweetie-pies,' Barbara said. **1977** 'L. EGAN' *Blind Search* v. 83 He's .. the kind of man who calls anything female 'honeybunch' and 'sweetie-pie'.

'sweetikin(s. By-form of SWEETKIN.

1596 NASHE *Saffron Walden* Wks. 1905 III. 129 She is such a hony sweetikin. **1974** I. MURDOCH *Sacred & Profane Love Machine* 81 Oh my sweetikin, how can such a love as ours stop? **1978** C. MACLEOD *Rest you Merry* (1979) vi. 56 Next time you drop one of your time bombs into the punch bowl, sweetiekins, you clean the bathrooms.

sweeting[1] ('swiːtɪŋ). Also 4–6 **sweting**, (4 **suetyng**, 5 **swettyng**). [f. SWEET *a.* + -ING[3].]

1. A 'sweet' or beloved person; dear one, darling, sweetheart. Chiefly as an endearing term of address. *arch.*

a **1300** *K. Horn* 230 (Laud MS.) Hom rod him aylmer king, And wit horn þe sweting. **13..** *K. Alis.* 914 (Laud MS.), Cler & fair is day springyng And makeþ many departyng Bituene kniȝth & his suetyng. *c* **1440** *York Myst.* xl. 40 Þat swettyng was swemyed for swetyng. *a* **1530** J. HEYWOOD *Wether* Plays (1905) 97 A special good lover and she his own sweeting. **1600** BRETON *Daffodils & Primroses* Wks. (Grosart) I. 19/1 Litle birdes wowld cary tales Twixte Susen and her Sweetinge. **1740** RICHARDSON *Pamela* (1741) I. xxii. 57 A Blessing attend my little Sweeting, .. wher-ever you go! **1812** COLMAN *Br. Grins, Vagaries Vind.* xxxvii, A curate who .. can boast .. a sweeting, soured by care, to patch his gown. **1857** THORNBURY *Songs Cavaliers & Roundh.* 272 How her little heart was beating, As I clasped her round—the sweeting. **1895** A. AUSTIN in *Blackw. Mag.* Apr. 519 The swain and his sweeting met and kissed.

c **1350** *Will. Palerne* 916 'Nai sertes, sweting', he seide, 'þat schal I neuer.' *c* **1400** *Beryn* 327 Nowe mercy, dere sweting! I wol do so no more. *c* **1460** *Towneley Myst.* xii. 476 Haylle, maker of man, haylle, swetyng! **1596** SHAKS. *Tam. Shr.* IV. iii. 36 How fares my Kate, what sweeting all a-mort? **1638** FORD *Fancies* II. ii, Attend within, sweeting. **1721** CIBBER *Rival Fools* II, Why, how now, Sweeting—What, a whole half-hour from me? **1863** HOLME LEE *A. Warleigh* III. 117, I will be patient as Job, pretty sweeting! go on. **1890** CONAN DOYLE *White Company* vii, I am a lonely man, my sweeting.

2. Name for a sweet-flavoured variety of apple.

1530 PALSGR. 278/1 Swetyng an apple, *pomme doulce*. *a* **1568** ASCHAM *Scholem.* I. (Arb.) 36 A childe will chose a sweeting, because it is presentlie faire and pleasant, and refuse a Runnet, because it is than grene, hard, and sowre. **1592** SHAKS. *Rom. & Jul.* II. iv. 83 Thy wit is a very Bitter-sweeting, It is a most sharpe sawce. **1656** BEALE *Heref. Orchards* (1657) 18 The Gennet moyle, the Kydoddin, the Sweeting, and the French Cornell. **1878** T. L. CUYLER *Pointed Papers* 130 In God's orchards there are .. rich, juicy 'sweetings' like Rutherford and Baxter. **1908** [MISS FOWLER] *Betw. Trent & Ancholme* 379 Some remaining Pear and 'Sweeting' trees.

† **'sweeting**[2]. *Obs.* [f. SWEET *a.* + -ING[1].] Sweet flavouring; sweetness.

1600 BRETON *Daffodils & Primroses* Wks. (Grosart) I. 17/1 Reasons sence and learninges sweetinge. *a* **1672** BAXTER in *Lauderdale Papers* (Camden) III. App. ii. 238 That all this glory will quickly set in the shadows of death, & that all this sweeting will turn soure!

sweetish ('swiːtɪʃ), *a.* [f. SWEET *a.* + -ISH[1].] Somewhat or slightly sweet.

1580 HOLLYBAND *Treas. Fr. Tong, Douceastre*, sweetish. **1601** HOLLAND *Pliny* XIV. vi. I. 414 Sweetish they be, and yet otherwhiles they have an unripe and harsh rellish of the wood. **1681** GREW *Musæum* IV. I. 354 It becomes sweetish, and makes no Effervescence upon the injection of the Chalk. **1778** PRYCE *Min. Cornub.* 56 If the acid becomes a little sweetish, Lead is certainly mixed with the Mercury. **1803** SOUTHEY in *Ann. Rev.* I. 69 A lake of sweetish water, much frequented by water fowl. **1871** NAPHEYS *Prev. & Cure Dis.* III. ii. 626 When the odor [of the breath] is sickly sweetish, we may conclude the lungs are out of order. **1880** 'VERNON LEE' *Italy* iii. 151 A grandiloquent poem, stately and sweetish, full of gods, goddesses, and little chubby Cupids.

advb. **1864** GARROD *Mat. Med.* (ed. 2) 256 Of a sweetish-bitter taste. **1895** KIPLING *2nd Jungle Bk.* 186 A sweetish-sourish smell.

Hence **'sweetishness**.

1752 BERKELEY *Th. Tar-water* Wks. 1784 II. 645 A fade sweetishness, offensive to the palate. **1831** J. WILSON in *Blackw. Mag.* XXIX. 8 A peculiar sort o' wersh fuzionless nonsense that's gotten a sweaty sweetishness aboot it.

sweet John. A name for the narrower-leaved varieties of a species of pink, *Dianthus barbatus*, as distinguished from those called SWEET-WILLIAM.

1573 TUSSER *Husb.* (1878) 96 Herbes .. for windowes and pots... Sweete Johns. **1597** GERARDE *Herbal* II. clxxiv. 478 Sweete Iohns hath round iointed stalkes, as haue the Gilloflowers. **1629** PARKINSON *Parad.* 319 The sweete Iohn hath his leaues broader, shorter and greener then any of the former Gilloflowers, but narrower than sweete Williams. **1721** MORTIMER *Husb.* (ed. 5) II. 238 Sweet Williams, or Sweet Johns, are of several sorts, but the double and the Velvet are chiefly worth your propagating. **1911** C. MACKENZIE *Passionate Elopement* xxix. 257 The very heart of high June and hot July dwelt in that fragrant enclosure. Sweet Johns and Sweet Williams with Dragon flowers and crimson Peaseblossom.

† **sweetkin.** *Obs. rare*$^{-1}$. [f. SWEET + -KIN; cf. Du. *soetken* (Kilian).] A term of endearment: in quot. *attrib.* = darling.

1599 NASHE *Lenten Stuffe* Wks. 1905 III. 187 Flocking to hansell him and strike him good luck as the Sweetkin Madams did about valiant S. Walter Manny.

sweetleaf ('swiːtliːf). A tree or shrub, *Symplocos tinctoria*, of the southern U.S., having sweet-flavoured leaves eaten by horses and cattle.

1829 LOUDON *Encycl. Plants* 1076 The leaves .. of Symplocos tinctoria are used in America under the name of Sweet-leaf, for dying yellow.

sweetling ('swiːtlɪŋ). *rare.* [f. SWEET *a.* + -LING[1].]

1. A term of endearment for a beloved person: = SWEETING[1] 1.

1648 HERRICK *Hesper., Connubii Flores* 40 And (Sweetling) marke you, what a Web will come Into your Chests. **1789** CONWAY *False Appearances* Epil. 74 Wedded sweetlings, mutually sincere, Who mean, 'My devil!' when they lisp, 'My dear'. **1872** MORRIS *Love is Enough* (1873) 23 Mother and sister, and the sweetling that scorned me .. All are departed. **1903** *Speaker* 25 Apr. 76/2 'Sweetling, show me thy face,' cried he.

2. A small sweet thing.

1840 BROWNING *Sordello* II. 693 John's cloud-girt angel .. with, open in his hand, A bitter-sweetling of a book. [See *Rev.* x. 9, 10.] **1874** R. BUCHANAN *London Lyrics* iv. 12 Little barefoot maiden, Selling violets blue, Hast thou ever pictured Where the sweetlings grew?

† **'sweetly**, *a. Obs.* Also 4 **suetli**, **-ly**, 6 **swe(e)tely**. [f. SWEET *a.* + -LY[1]. Cf. MDu. *soetelijc* (Du. *zoetelijk*), MHG. *suezlich* (G. *süsslich*); also OE. *swótlic*.] Sweet.

a **1300** *Cursor M.* 17819 Þai hailsed þaim with suetli suar. *a* **1310** in Wright *Lyric P.* xvi. 52 A suetly suyre heo hath to holde. ? *a* **1500** *Chester Pl.* (Shaks. Soc.) II. 2 Fayne maye thy frendes be in fere, To see thy sweetlye [*v.r.* frely] face. **1530** PALSGR. 842/2 Swetely of savoure, *souef*. **1592** WYRLEY *Armorie, Capitall de Buz* 156 By sweetely Lord, that straied sinners sought. **1601** HOLLAND *Pliny* XXXVI. v. II. 565 Agoracritus of Paros, whome hee loved also for his sweetly youth.

sweetly ('swiːtlɪ), *adv.* Forms: see SWEET *a.* and -LY[2]. [Cf. MLG. *sôt(e)lîken*, MDu. *soetelîke*, MHG. *suezlîche*; also ME. *swoteliche*, SOOTLY.] In a sweet manner; with sweetness.

1. With a sweet taste or smell.

[*c* **900**: see 3.] **1530** PALSGR. 842/2 Swetely of taste, *doucement*. *a* **1547** SURREY *Eccles.* v. 13 Humble vowes fullfilld by grace right swetly smoke. *c* **1565** SPARKE *Hawkins' 2nd Voy.* in Hakluyt *Voy.* (1600) III. 515 They [*sc.* turtle's eggs] did eat very sweetly. **1611** *Bible* Song Sol. vii. 9 Like the best wine .. that goeth downe sweetely. **1850** NEALE *Med. Hymns* (1867) 121 Now the myrrh of Cyprus groweth, Widelier spreadeth, sweetlier bloweth.

2. With a sweet sound or voice.

1340 *Ayenb.* 61 Nykeren þet .. zuo zuetelich zingeþ þet hi makeþ slepe þe ssipman. **1398** TREVISA *Barth. De P.R.* v. xxiii. (Bodl. MS.) lf. 13/2 Þe pipe singeþ swetelich while þe fouler disseyueþ þe bridde. **1500–20** DUNBAR *Poems* lxxvii. 45 Madinis ȝing .. Playand on timberallis, and syngand rycht sweitlie. **1598** SYLVESTER *Du Bartas* II. i. III. *Furies* 56 An Instrument .. Whose symphony resounded sweetly-shrill The Almightie's praise. **1629–30** MILTON *Circumcision* 4 Ye flaming Powers .., That erst with Musick, .. So sweetly sung your Joy. **1781** COWPER *Retirem.* 568 Streams tinkle sweetly in poetic chime. *a* **1839** PRAED *Lidian's Love* xx, She .. sang as sweetly as a caged canary.

3. So as to be pleasing to the mind or the feelings; pleasurably; comfortably.

c **900** tr. *Bæda's Hist.* v. xxiii. Concl. (1890) 486 Swetlice drincan þa word þines wisdomes. *c* **1350** *Will. Palerne* 1329 Nobul leches .. þat seide he schuld be sauf & sweteliche heled. **1435** MISYN *Fire of Love* II. xii. 103 Þis meruellus heet, þe qwhilk þe mynd swetelyest gladyns. **1533** FRITH *Answ. More* (1548) H viij, Yf a man be faythfull, the Spiryte of God worketh in hys heart very swetelye at hys communion. **1535** COVERDALE *Prov.* iii. 24 Thou shalt not be afrayed, but shalt take thy rest & slepe swetely. **1599** SHAKS. *Much Ado* IV. i. 226 Th' Idea of her life shal sweetly creepe Into his study of imagination. **1606** SYLVESTER *Du Bartas* II. iv. II. *Magnificence* 1215 Sweetly-rapt in sacred Extasie. **1640** QUARLES *Enchirid.* II. xxvii, If thou labour in a painefull calling .. thou shalt be .. sweetlier satisfied at the time of death. **1784** COWPER *Task* I. 89 The nurse sleeps sweetly, hir'd to watch the sick, Whom snoring she disturbs. **1803** VISCT. STRANGFORD *Camoens, Sonn.* vii. (1810) 93 The sweetly sad remembrances of yore! **1847** C. BRONTË *Jane Eyre* viii, Nor was that problem solved to my satisfaction ere I fell sweetly asleep.

b. ironically, esp. with *pay*, *cost*.

1579 TOMSON *Calvin's Serm. Tim.* 243/2 It is sure, that this his high place will cost him sweetely. **1585** FETHERSTONE tr. *Calvin on Acts* xxii. 28 How can it be that thou beeing some base fellowe of the countrie of the Cilicians, shouldest obtayne this honour, for which I paid sweetly? *a* **1617** HIERON *Wks.* II. 311 It cost Dauid sweetly for passing ouer the murder of Amnon, done by his sonne Absolom. **1855** *Poultry Chron.* III. 514/1 Having, as may be supposed, paid *sweetly* for them, and having fitted up house, nests and roosts, with the greatest care. **1882** STEVENSON *New Arab. Nts.* (1884) 112 Everything in this world has to be paid for, and some things sweetly.

4. So as to be pleasing to the sight or the æsthetic sense; delightfully, charmingly.

1576 FLEMING *Panopl. Epist.* 55 Sithence you haue written thereof in a certaine treatise very sweetly and pleasantly. **1617** MORYSON *Itin.* I. 45 One market-place sweetly shaded with trees. **1650** BULWER *Anthropomet.* 88 The Eye-brows ought to be .. sweetly arched. *a* **1700** EVELYN *Diary* 8 May 1666, Went to visite my Co. Hales at a sweetly-water'd place at Chilston. **1766** GOLDSM. *Vicar W.* viii, The two lovers so sweetly described by Mr. Gay, who were struck dead in each other's arms. **1837** CARLYLE *Fr. Rev.* III. III. iv, Vergniaud denounces and deplores; in sweetly turned periods. **1879** S. C. BARTLETT *Egypt to Pal.* xxiv. 490 The lights and shadows lie sweetly on the hillsides at night and morning.

b. as a technical term of *Art*.

1662 EVELYN *Chalcogr.* 69 Had he perform'd his heightnings with more tendernesse, and come sweetly off with the extremities of his hatchings. **1709** POPE *Ess. Crit.* 489 When the ripe colours soften and unite, And sweetly melt into just shade and light.

c. with emotional or sentimental colouring.

1840 THACKERAY *Barber Cox* Aug., 'How sweetly the dear Baron rides,' said my wife, who was ogling at him. **1907** PHYLLIS DARE *From School to Stage* ii. 21 That sweetly pretty play, 'Ib and Little Christina.'

d. In vaguer sense: In a desirable or satisfactory way; favourably; †delicately; now *esp.* in reference to the working of machinery: Smoothly, easily.

1594 PLAT *Jewell-ho.* I. 6 A Christall stone .. hauing a good foyle sweetlie conueyed within the concaue superficies thereof. **1651** FRENCH *Distill.* VI. 178 In these colder countreys they .. never yeeld any fruit, .. but if at any time nature be wittily and sweetly helped, then Art can perfect what nature could not. **1825** *Edin. Rev.* XLIII. 14 Like .. the jerks of a machine not working sweetly. **1876** W. CUDWORTH *Round abt. Bradford* 120 The engines .. although thirty years old .. do their work 'sweetly'.

5. With graciousness of action or treatment; with kindly disposition or intent; graciously.

a **1225** *Ancr. R.* 430 Lihtliche & sweteliche uorȝiueð ham hore gultes. *a* **1300** *Cursor M.* 14884 (Cott.) Suetli he wald þam drau him to. *c* **1386** CHAUCER *Prol.* 221 Ful swetely herde he confession, And plesaunt was his absolucion. **1471** CAXTON *Recuyell* (Sommer) 51 Whan he had herd her answers and had seen how swetly she had taken hit. **1502** *Ord. Crysten Men* (W. de W.) I. iii, That it wolde please yᵉ swetely to beholde hym or her thy seruaunt. **1589** R. HARVEY *Pl. Perc.* (title-p.), Sweetly indevvring with his blunt persuasions to botch vp a Reconciliation. **1621** ELSING *Debates Ho. Lords* (Camden) 48 The sentence in the Star Chamber, the which he confesseth justly imposed and swetely. **1673** S. C. *Art of Complaisance* 15 We must represent things which appear difficult and greivous by insinuating them sweetly into the spirit of those to whom we speak. **1794** MRS. RADCLIFFE *Myst. Udolpho* xli, She used to try so sweetly to oblige him.

6. With pleasantness of manner or address; in sweet terms; hence, affectionately, lovingly.

a **1225** *Ancr. R.* 264 In eueriche time hwon ȝe neode habbeð, scheaweð so sweteliche to his swete earen. *a* **1300** *K. Horn* 404 (Camb.) On knes he him sette, And sweteliche hure grette. **13..** *Cursor M.* 15651 (Gött.) Ful suetli to þaim he spack, 'breþer, quat nu do ȝe?' *c* **1440** *Jacob's Well* 267 Be fayr of speche, answere swetely! *a* **1533** LD. BERNERS *Huon* lxxxv. 267 He..toke leue of hym, & swetely kyssyd hym. **1592** SHAKS. *Rom. & Jul.* I. v. 111 O trespasse sweetly vrg'd. **1602** tr. *Guarini's Pastor Fido* II. i. E j b, Let's kisse and striue Who can kisse sweetliest among our selues. **1743** FRANCIS tr. *Hor., Odes* I. xxii. 24 The nymph, who sweetly speaks, and sweetly smiles. **1852** MRS. STOWE *Uncle Tom's C.* xx, The child looked perplexed and sorrowful, but said sweetly—'Poor Topsy, why need you steal?' **1867** TROLLOPE *Chron. Barset* II. xlv. 14 He was disappointed..although she had spoken to him so sweetly.

7. Qualifying pples. used adj., often hyphened (in any of the preceding senses), as ***sweetly-breathing, -budding, -fenced, -smelling, -swelling, -written***; occas. with adjs., as ***sweetly-pensive, -wise***; also less correctly used for 'sweet' in parasynthetic combination, as ***sweetly-scented, -tasted, -toned.***

a **1586** SIDNEY *Arcadia* II. (1912) 219 Of pretious pearle the double rowe, The second sweetly-fenced warde, Her heav'nly-dewed tongue to garde. *Ibid.* III. 447 Her roundy sweetly swelling lippes. **1641** in *Verney Mem.* (1907) I. 229 A most noble and sweetly disposed lady. **1743** FRANCIS tr. *Hor., Sec. Poem* 100 Sweetly-shining queen of night. **1760–72** H. BROOKE *Fool of Qual.* (1809) IV. 37 In a sweetly-breathing accent..scarcely audible. *a* **1774** TUCKER *Lt. Nat.* (1834) II. 475 Hymns, meditations, and sweetly-written books. **1844** KINGLAKE *Eothen* xviii, Spices or sweetly-burning woods. **1846** H. G. ROBINSON *Odes of Horace* II. xii, Thy mistress Lycimnia's sweetly-ton'd voice. **1871** B. TAYLOR *Faust* (1875) II. II. iii. 120 She thanked with sweetly-wise and conscious tongue. **1875** W. MCILWRAITH *Guide Wigtownshire* 18 The sweetly-scented birch.

sweetmeat ('swi:tmi:t), *sb.* Now chiefly *arch.* [See SWEET *a.* and MEAT *sb.* Cf. OE. *swétmettas, swótmettas* delicacies.]

1. *collect. pl.* (and †*sing.*) †Sweet food, as sugared cakes or pastry, confectionary (*obs.*); preserved or candied fruits, sugared nuts, etc.; also, globules, lozenges, 'drops,' or 'sticks' made of sugar with fruit or other flavouring or filling; *sing.* one of these.

c **1480** HENRYSON *Test. Cress.* 420 The sweit Meitis, seruit in plaittis clene, With Saipheron sals of ane gud sessoun. ?*a* **1500** *Chester Pl.* (Shaks. Soc.) I. 143, I knowe that in thy childehoode Thou wylte for sweete meate loke. **1584** LYLY *Sappho* v. ii. 9 Giue him some sweete meates. **1592** SHAKS. *Rom. & Jul.* I. iv. 76 Their breath with Sweet meats tainted are. **1626** BACON *Sylva* §756 Teeth are much hurt by Sweet-meats. **1640** A. RIGBY in Rushw. *Hist. Coll.* (1721) IV. 129 Or, like little Children, when we have been whipt and beaten, be pleased again with Sweetmeats. **1683** TRYON *Way to Health* 489 Nor [is it] lawful for any of us to eat Sweet-Meats or delicious Tarts, after we have eaten sufficiently of other simple & natural Food. *a* **1700** EVELYN *Diary* 10 Sept. 1677, To the Towne-house, where they presented us a collation of dried sweet meates and wine. **1750** JOHNSON *Rambler* No. 51 ¶6 She should be ashamed to set before company..sweetmeats of so dark a colour as she had often seen at Mistress Sprightly's. **1812** SHELLEY *Devil's Walk* xiv. Tired, [he] gives his sweetmeat, and again Cries for it, like a humoured boy. **1825** J. NEAL *Bro. Jonathan* I. 76 Here were 'sweetmeats', i.e. preserved plums. **1858** SIMMONDS *Dict. Trade, Sweetmeats*, a general name for succades; fruits preserved in sugar, and confectionery articles made of sugar. **1880** 'OUIDA' *Moths* i, You eat heaps of sweetmeats. You take too much tea, too much ice, too much soup, too much wine!

fig. **1690** C. NESSE *Hist. & Myst. O. & N. Test.* I. 49 This is Satan's sweet-meat to make Sinners like filthy dogs. **1854** THACKERAY *Newcomes* I. 168 Gandish was always handing him sweetmeats of compliments.

2. A varnish, consisting principally of linseed oil, used in the preparation of patent leather.

1875 KNIGHT *Dict. Mech.* s.v. *Patent Leather.*

3. *attrib.* and *Comb.*, as ***sweetmeat glass, pan, pot, shop, spoon; sweetmeat-seller.***

1669 R. MONTAGU in *Buccleuch MSS.* (Hist. MSS. Comm.) I. 448 One sweetmeat pan, with a skimmer. **1705** *Lond. Gaz.* No. 4104/4, 2 Sweet-meat Spoons forked. **1769** MRS. RAFFALD *Eng. Housekpr.* (1778) 225 Put it into flat sweet-meat pots, and tie it down with brandy paper. **1857** DICKENS & COLLINS in *Househ. Words* 10 Oct. 338/1, I see a sweetmeat shop. **1895** KIPLING *2nd Jungle Bk.* 92 It was the wife of the sweetmeat-seller. **1897** A. HARTSHORNE *Old English Glasses* xviii. 299 The bowls of the cut sweetmeat glasses have the edges engrailed, vandycked, or faceted. **1971** *Country Life* 9 Sept. 639/2 Exquisite sweetmeat glasses with elaborately cut bowls and sturdy facet-cut stems were made between 1740 and the 1780s.

Hence **sweetmeat** *v.* (*nonce-wd.*) *trans.*, to furnish with sweetmeats.

1764 H. WALPOLE *Let. to Earl Hertford* 24 Feb., The fairies had so improved upon it, had so be-garlanded, so sweetmeated, and so desserted it [*sc.* a supper-room], that it looked like a vision.

sweet Nancy. *local.* The pheasant-eyed narcissus, *Narcissus poeticus*, esp. the double variety.

1848 MRS. GASKELL *M. Barton* viii, In his button-hole he stuck a narcissus (a sweet Nancy is its pretty Lancashire name). **1873** MISS BROUGHTON *Nancy* I. 94 The hyacinth bells, and the sweet Nancies..blowing all together.

sweetness ('swi:tnɪs). Forms: see SWEET *a.* [OE. *swétnes* (*suoet-*): see -NESS. Cf. MDu. *soetenisse*; also SOOTNESS (OE. *swótnes*).] The quality of being sweet, *concr.* something sweet.

1. a. Of taste or flavour.

c **897** ÆLFRED *Gregory's Past. C.* xvii. 125, & eac sceal bion on ðæm breostum ðæs monnan swetnes. **1340** *Ayenb.* 55 Þe zuetnesse of þe mete. *a* **1425** tr. *Arderne's Treat. Fistula*, etc. 89 One [oil] for þe rednes and swetnez is called sanguis veneris. **1477** EARL RIVERS (Caxton) *Dictes* 68 The bittrenesse of the aloe tre distroyeth the swettenesse of the hony. **1555** EDEN *Decades* (Arb.) 110 These apples..haue a certeyne sweetnes myxte with a gentell sharpnes. **1588** KYD *Househ. Philos.* Wks. (1901) 247 The Malmesey and Greeke and Roman Wines..haue some kind of sweetnes. **1704** SWIFT *Batt. Bks.* Wks. 1841 I. 128/2 Instead of dirt and poison, we have rather chosen to fill our hives with honey and wax, thus furnishing mankind with the two noblest of things, which are sweetness and light. **1781** COWPER *Charity* 190 Has God then giv'n its sweetness to the cane..in vain? **1855** BAIN *Senses & Int.* II. ii. §9 The sweetness of every kind of fruit [etc.] is known to arise from sugar.

¶ Phr. ***sweetness and light***, taken from Swift (see quot. 1704 above) and used with æsthetic or moral reference; now usu. in trivial (freq. ironic) use, under influence of senses 6, 7: pleasantness, good will.

1869 M. ARNOLD *Cult. & An.* 28 Their ideal of beauty and sweetness and light, and a human nature complete on all its sides. **1879** FARRAR *St. Paul* (1883) 410 Gallio..was pre-eminently endowed with that light and sweetness which are signs of the utmost refinement. **1927** WODEHOUSE *Meet Mr Mulliner* vi. 186 He had been all sweetness and light and had not done a thing to them. **1949** N. BALCHIN *Sort of Traitors* xi. 191 You know how it is when you've got to poke about round somebody else's work—it's not all sweetness and light as a rule. **1953** P. WENTWORTH *Anna, where are You?* vii. 45 A desire to spread sweetness and light. **1968** G. JONES *Hist. Vikings* II. iii. 106 Anskar, the monk of Corbey,..whose sweetness and light were probably much lightened and sweetened by his biographer Rimbert. **1974** *Times* 16 Jan. 16/5 When this Act was introduced it was done..to create sweetness and light between management and unions. **1982** *Sunday Tel.* 12 Dec. 14/5 Hell hath no fury like a peace-woman scorned, by comparison with whom even a Cruise missile becomes a soft symbol of sweetness and light.

b. *concr.* Something sweet to the taste; a sweet substance. *spec.* molasses. (*Canad.*)

c **725** *Corpus Gloss.* (Hessels) A 524 *Ambrosea*, suoetnis. **1382** WYCLIF *Joel* ii. 18 And it shal be, in that day mounteyns shuln droppe swetnes. **1398** TREVISA *Barth. De P.R.* XIX. xliii. (W. de W.), Swetnesse layed to the tonge openyth moderatly and hetyth moderatly. **1553** EDEN *Treat. Newe Ind.* (Arb.) 42 Who hath not of sowrenes felte the bitter tast, Is not worthy of swetenes to take his repast. **1655** G. S. in Hartlib *Ref. Commw. Bees* 27 There is worthily a great difference to be acknowledged between Honey and other inspissated sweetnesses. **1890** *Opelousas* (Louisiana) *Democrat* 20 Dec. 2/1 Sweetness by the barrel, bon-bons, sugar plums [etc.]. **1912** N. DUNCAN *Best of Bad Job* xxi. 143 T' beg a barrel o' flour an' a gallon o' sweetness. **1920** W. T. GRENFELL *Labrador Doctor* viii. 164 The fact that we were without butter, and that 'sweetness' (molasses) was low, was scarcely even noticed.

2. Of smell or odour: Fragrance.

c **900** tr. *Bæda's Hist.* IV. x. (1890) 292 Micel swetnes wundorlices stences. *c* **1175** *Lamb. Hom.* 145 Þer scal beon..smellinge mid swetnesse. *c* **1220** *Bestiary* 750 Ut of his ðrote cumeð a smel..ðat ouer-cumeð haliweie wið swetnesse. *c* **1380** WYCLIF *Wks.* (1880) 216 Whanne men schullen..smelle..þe swettenesse & good odour of herbis. *c* **1385** CHAUCER *L.G.W.* Prol. 120 Floures..Of swich swetnesse and swich odour ouer al. **1626** BACON *Sylva* §489, I thinke Rosemary will leese in Sweetnesse, if it be set with Lauender. **1750** GRAY *Elegy* 56 Full many a flower is born to blush unseen, And waste its sweetness on the desert air. **1870** SPURGEON *Treas. Dav.* Ps. xlv. 8 All his dress is fragrant with all sweetness.

3. a. Of sound: Melodiousness, musical quality.

1398 TREVISA *Barth. De P.R.* v. xxiii. (Bodl. MS.), Orpheus..plesid treen wodes hulles and stones with swetnes of his voice. **1448–9** METHAM *Amoryus & Cleopes* 410 Syngyng in ther lay With mornyng joy in sqwetnes off songe. **1553** T. WILSON *Rhet.* (1580) 30 The swetenesse of the tongue, the wholsomnesse of the aire in other countries. **1590** SPENSER *F.Q.* III. xii. 6 The rare sweetnesse of the melody. **1681** DRYDEN *Abs. & Achit.* To Rdr., There's a sweetness in good Verse, which Tickles even while it Hurts. **1797** MRS. RADCLIFFE *Italian* i, The sweetness and fine expression of her voice. **1836** DUBOURG *Violin* ix. (1878) 273 His violoncellos..are..not so strong..as old Forster's, but in sweetness and purity, excelling them. **1849** MACAULAY *Hist. Eng.* i. I. 30 Rude societies have versification, and often versification of great power and sweetness.

b. A sweet sound or tone. *rare.*

c **1400** *Destr. Troy* 342 There was wellit to wale water full nobill,..with plentius stremes, With a swoughe and a swetnes sweppit on þe grounde. **1632** MILTON *L'Allegro* 140 With many a winding bout Of lincked sweetnes long drawn out. **1651** JER. TAYLOR *Serm. for Year, Summer* xix. 238 It is not the eye that sees the beauties of the heaven, nor the ear that hears the sweetnesses of musick. **1895** F. THOMPSON *New Poems* 107 The wailful sweetness of the violin Floats down the hushed waters of the wind.

4. In specific uses, denoting various desirable physical qualities, *e.g.* freshness (as opp. to saltness, putridity, etc.), mellowness (of soil), etc.

c **1400** MAUNDEV. (1839) i. 7 The Watre of the See is fressche and holdethe his swetnesse 20 Myle within the See. **1607** MARKHAM *Caval.* II. (1617) 52 It giueth libertie to the tongue,..and keepeth the mouth in tendernesse and sweetnesse. *a* **1700** EVELYN *Diary* 25 Jan. 1645, These [beds] are in a very long rome having an inner passage..with as much care, sweetenesse, and conveniency as can be imagin'd. **1733** W. ELLIS *Chiltern & Vale Farm.* 46 The Remedy of this is, to give it constantly its due Course of Fallowings, whereby it may enjoy a thorough Sweetness. **1815** J. SMITH *Panorama Sci. & Art* II. 355 This powder will also restore the sweetness of flesh-meat but slightly tainted with putridity. **1844** H. STEPHENS *Bk. Farm* III. 1046 Oil-cake..is an excellent medicine for live-stock,..giving to the hide a sweetness of coat unattainable by other means. **1894** WALROND *Archery* xvii. 297 No bow can come up to a good self for sweetness, softness, and steadiness in the hand when it is loosed.

5. a. Pleasantness to the senses generally, esp. the sight; pleasantness of aspect, artistic effect, etc.

a **1568** ASCHAM *Scholem.* II. (Arb.) 138 The right forme..fit and dew, to the dignitie of a man, to the bewtie of a woman, to the sweetnes of a yong babe. **1617** MORYSON *Itin.* I. 118 Baie, an ancient Citie, and for the sweetnesse preferred to Rome by Horace. *a* **1661** FULLER *Worthies* (1840) I. 224 It is confessed that Oxford far exceeds it [*sc.* Cambridge] for sweetness of situation. **1707** MORTIMER *Husb.* (1721) I. 285 The use that is made of it [*sc.* wax] for Lights, the clearness and sweetness of which makes it preferr'd before all other Sorts. *a* **1822** SHELLEY *Pr. Wks.* (1888) I. 407 The curved lines of her fine limbs flow into each other with a never-ending sinuosity of sweetness. **1888** MISS BRADDON *Fatal Three* I. v, The house and gardens had all the sweetness and freshness of a scene to which one is restored after absence.

b. as a technical term of *Art.*

1695 DRYDEN tr. *Dufresnoy's Art Paint.*, etc. 220 He painted with great Strength, great Heightning, great Sweetness, and liveliness of Colours. **1706** *Art of Painting* (1744) 68 His colouring had not the vigour and sweetness of Giacomo Bassano's. **1816** SIR J. REYNOLDS *Life Raffaello*, etc. 156 The gliding motion of his [*sc.* Correggio's] outline, and the sweetness with which it melts into the ground. **1816** J. SMITH *Panorama Sci. & Art* II. 770 The pen should have a diamond point, which..imparts an admirable degree of regularity and sweetness to the work.

6. a. Pleasantness to the mind or feelings; delightfulness.

c **900** tr. *Bæda's Hist.* IV. xxiv. (1890) 346 Bi swetnesse þæs heofonlecan rices he moniȝ leoð ȝeworhte. **971** *Blickl. Hom.* 37 Swa we sceolon eac ure heortan ȝefyllan mid þære swetnesse godcundra beboda. *a* **1310** in Wright *Lyric P.* xxv. 68 Iesu, suete is the love of the, Al that may with eȝen se, Haveth no suetnesse aȝeynes the. **1340** *Ayenb.* 92 Þe more þet lykeþ þe zuetnesse of þe worlde þe lesse me wylneþ þe zuetnesse of god. **1390** GOWER *Conf.* II. 57 Thei..resten as hem liketh best In all the swetnesse of delices. *c* **1440** *York Myst.* xlvii. 137 All kynnys swetnesse is þer-in. **1528** TINDALE *Obed. Chr. Man* 15 b, To translate it welfaveredly, so that it have the same grace and swetnesse..in the latyne, as it hath in the hebrue. **1585–7** T. ROGERS *39 Art.* xi. (1625) 55 Neither shall they bee partakers of the sweetnesse of this truth which say, that [etc.]. **1699** T. BAKER *Refl. Learn.* iv. 38 He..to whom he gives the Force of Demosthenes, the Sweetness of Isocrates, and the Copia of Plato. **1748** J. GEDDES *Comp. Antients* 7 The two things then, which every good writer either in prose or verse is to aim at, are sweetness and dignity. **1840** J. H. NEWMAN *Par. Serm.* (1842) V. xxii. 365 Even sorrow must have a sweetness, if love be in it.

b. Pleasant feeling, delight, pleasure; also, a source of delight or pleasure. Now *rare* or merged in other senses.

a **1225** *Ancr. R.* 102 Þes cos..is a swetnesse & a delit of heorte, so unimete swote & swete. *c* **1230** *Hali Meid.* 7 Swuch swetnesse þu schalt ifinden in his luue & in his seruise..þet [etc.]. *a* **1240** *Ureisun* in *O.E. Hom.* I. 183 Ihesu min hali loue min sikere swetnesse [*printed* spetnesse]. *c* **1386** CHAUCER *Melib.* ¶192 Salomon seith That ..'the conseil of trewe freendes yeveth swetenesse to the soule.' *a* **1400** *Prymer* (1891) 51 Heyl queene moder of mercy, oure lyf and oure swetnesse. *c* **1440** *Jacob's Well* 280 Whan þin herte is harde as a stone, & hath no deuocyoun to god, ne loue, ne dreed, ne swetnesse. *c* **1485** *Digby Myst., Mary Magdalene* 794 O lord Iesu, ower mellefluess swettnesse. **1526** *Pilgr. Perf.* (W. de W. 1531) 159 b, To..use yᵉ maner of prayer..in yᵉ whiche he fyndeth moost swetnes. *Ibid.* 287 Swetenesses of grace. **1612** BRINSLEY *Lud. Lit.* 9 They feele such a sweetnesse in play and idlenesse, as they can hardly bee framed to leaue it. **1863** PUSEY *Serm. Matt.* v. 4. 6 Rather it is an abiding sorrow, sweeter than all life's sweetnesses. **1870** BRYANT *Iliad* I. III. 102 Such glow of love Possesses me and sweetness of desire. **1886** *Pall Mall G.* 14 Sept. 5/2 She was one of those brave souls who have fought the good fight with little help of spiritual sweetnesses.

7. Of disposition, manner, or conduct: Graciousness, gentleness, kindliness, mildness.

c **1000** *Ags. Ps.* (Th.) xxx. 21 [xxxi. 19] Hu micel..is seo mycelnes þinre swetnesse. *a* **1225** *Ancr. R.* 254 Jesu Cristes deorewurðe wordes & werkes, þet weren alle ine luue & ine swetnesse. *a* **1300** *Cursor M.* 9803 Mikel it was his suetnes þan, Mikel reuth he had þat sith o man **1340** *Ayenb.* 145 Mansuetudo oþer beningnitas þet is zuyetnesse of herte. *c* **1366** CHAUCER *A.B.C.* 51 Glorious mayde and moder..ful of swetnesse and mercy euer. *c* **1450** *Mirk's Festial* 220 Aȝeynes passyon he schowyd louyng swetenes. **1598** B. JONSON *Ev. Man in Hum.* II. i, So full of man, and sweetnesse in his carriage. **1641** J. JACKSON *True Evang. T.* II. 102 Grace of Regeneration..introduceth gracious habits of sweetnesse, peace and love. **1680** OTWAY *Orphan* I. i, They're both of Nature mild, and full of sweetness. **1784** COWPER *Task* II. 708 In his speech was heard Paternal sweetness, dignity, and love. **1848** THACKERAY *Van. Fair* xxxiv, She repaid Miss Crawley's engouement by artless sweetness and friendship. **1891** FARRAR *Darkness & Dawn* x, In his eyes and mouth there was an expression of honesty and sweetness which endeared him to the heart of the lonely prince.

†8. Addiction to sweet things; self-indulgence. *Obs. rare.*

c **1440** *Gesta Rom.* xxx. 110 (Harl. MS.), He yaf him so muche to this swettnes, that he wolde not thens, but yete hony, and made him murye. **1603** SHAKS. *Meas. for M.* II. iv. 45 To remit Their sawcie sweetnes, that do coyne heauens Image In stamps that are forbid.

'sweet 'pea. a. The common name of *Lathyrus odoratus*, a climbing annual leguminous plant, indigenous to Sicily, cultivated in numerous varieties for its showy variously-coloured sweet-scented flowers; formerly called *sweet-scented pea* (see SWEET-SCENTED b).

1732 R. FURBER *Flower Gard. Displ.* 57 Purple Sweet Pea. This is what we call the Sweet-scented Pea. **1816** KEATS '*I stood tip-toe upon a little hill*' 57 Here are sweet peas, on tip-toe for a flight.

b. The scent of the sweet pea, esp. as used in cosmetics, etc.

1890–1 *T. Eaton & Co. Catal.* Fall & Winter 42/2 Colgate's perfumes—white rose, sweet pea, Cashmere bouquet. *c* **1938** *Fortnum & Mason Catal.* 54/1 Soaps.. sandal wood.. sweet pea.. verbena. **1972** [see LILAC 2 c].

'sweet rush.

1. The lemon-grass or camel's hay, *Andropogon Schœnanthus*; also the allied species *A. laniger*.

1598, 1601 [see SQUINANT]. **1874** *Treas. Bot.* Suppl.

2. The sweet flag, *Acorus Calamus*.

1607 TOPSELL *Four-f. Beasts* 116 Roes.. loue the lakes and strong streames, breaking the floods to come by fresh pasture, as sweet rushes and Bul-rushes. **1760** J. LEE *Introd. Bot.* App. 325. **1785** MARTYN *Lett. Bot.* xviii. (1794) 251 Calamus Aromaticus or Sweet Rush.

sweet-scented (stress variable), *a.* Having a sweet-scent; sweet-smelling, fragrant.

1591 COKAINE *Treat. Hunting* B 3 b, Sweet sented Roe. **1606** N. BAXTER *Sydney's Ourania* L iv b, The fragrant smell, Of sweetest sented flowers. **1730** BAILEY (fol.), *Aromatical*, having a Spicey Smell, sweet scented. **1837** CARLYLE *Fr. Rev.* II. IV. vii, Thus go they plunging; champ the sweet-scented forest-herb. **1843** PRESCOTT *Mexico* (1850) I. 62 He was arrayed in a splendid dress, regaled with incense, and with a profusion of sweet-scented flowers.

b. *spec.* in names of species or varieties of plants having sweet-smelling flowers, leaves, etc.

sweet-scented pea, an early name for the SWEET PEA.

1666 R. PRESTON *Let.* in *Essex Rev.* (1908) XVII. 133 One hogshead of Sweet-sented tobacco. **1688** CLAYTON in *Phil. Trans.* XVII. 943 There is not only the two distinct sorts of a Sweet-scented, and Aranoko Tobacco, but of each of these be several sorts much different. **1728** BRADLEY *Dict. Bot.* II, *Lathyrus*, in English Cicheling, is a kind of Pulse, which has many varieties.. of these is our fine sweet scented Pea. **1753** *Chambers' Cycl.* Suppl. s.v. *Rubus*, The sweet scented rubus. **1796** WITHERING *Brit. Plants* (ed. 3) II. 59 Sweet-scented Vernal-grass. **1846–50** A. WOOD *Class-bk. Bot.* 258 *Calycanthus floridus*, Carolina Allspice. Sweet-scented Shrub.

sweet singer. *Hist.* 1. The phr. *sweet singer* (see SWEET *a.* 4), more fully ***sweet singer of Israel*** (app. with reminiscence of 2 Sam. xxiii. 1, where David is called 'the sweet psalmist of Israel'), designating a sect or sects which flourished in the latter years of the 17th cent.: see quots.

1680 H. MORE *Let.* in R. Ward *Life* (1710) 356, I partly have some Knowledge of the Sweet Singers of Israel. But to say or sing sweetly is little to the Purpose, while there is a False Principle at the Heart... What a Discord in Your Sweet Singer was the Admiration of that roaring Wretch you described, that lately hanged himself! **1681** *Act of Counc.* in Wodrow *Hist. Suff. Ch. Scot.* (1722) II. 221 Edinburgh, August 2, 1681. His Royal Highness and Lords of Privy Council, having considered the Condition of these Prisoners, called the sweet Singers, David Jamison, John Gib,.. and some Women, give Order to the Magistrates to liberate them. **1687** MIÈGE *Gt. Fr. Dict., Eng.-Fr.* s.v., Tis a late blasphemous Sect, which call themselves the Sweet Singers of Israel. Whereof one John Taylor was Head, who had a Congregation of them at Guildford in Surrey. **1692** *Life of John Bunyan* 22 A Sect of loose prophane Wretches, afterward called Ranters and sweet Singers. **1704** SWIFT *Mech. Operat. Spir.* in *T. Tub*, etc. 319. **1711** *Mem. Visct. Dundee* p. ix, At this Time, about thirty of these deluded People left their Families and Business, and went to the Hills, where they lived in Rocks and Caves for some Weeks. .. They called themselves The Sweet Singers of Israel, eat nothing that there was Salt in, or paid Tax to the King, blotted the Name of King out of their Bibles, and cohabited all together. **1732** P. WALKER *Life of Cargill* in *Biogr. Presbyt.* (1827) II. 16 These People.. were commonly called Sweet-singers, from their frequently meeting together, and singing these tearful Psalms over the mournful Case of the Church, Psal. 74, 79, 80, 83, 137.

2. a. A religious poet.

1560, etc. [see SINGER[1] 2]. **1892** J. JULIAN *Dict. Hymnol.* 1284/2 William Williams, of Pantycelyn, was the Sweet Singer of Wales. **1933** *Sign* July 92/2 The sweet singer, Christina Rossetti.

b. A popular, esp. sentimental, writer or singer.

[**1878** J. A. MOORE (*title*) Sweet singer of Michigan.] **1936** *New Statesman* 25 Jan. 113/2 Kipling.. was a sweet singer to the last. He could bring home the colours and savours of many distant places... But he was not a faultless writer. **1958** *Listener* 4 Dec. 913/1 The latest hit of one of the sweet singers of Hong Kong, Li Li Hua or Yao Lee.

sweet-smelling (stress variable), *a.* Smelling sweet; sweet-scented.

1388 WYCLIF *Ezek.* xxvii. 22 Alle the beste swete smellynge spices. *c* **1400** *26 Pol. Poems* xxvi. 4 A place.. Y-set aboute with floures so swete smellyng. **1535** COVERDALE *Jer.* vi. 20 Swete smellinge Calamus from farre countrees. **1585** T. WASHINGTON tr. *Nicholay's Voy.* III. xxii. 112 A vyoll full of sweet smelling water. **1667** MILTON *P.L.* IV. 709 Flowers, Garlands, and sweet-smelling Herbs. **1731** MILLER *Gard. Dict.* s.v. *Agrimonia*, The Sweet-smelling Agrimony is by some preferr'd to the common sort for medicinal Uses. **1855** TENNYSON *Brook* 122 He led me thro' the short sweet-smelling lanes. **1890** *Science-Gossip* XXVI. 146/1 The innocent-looking, sweet-smelling mint (*Melissa officinalis*).

sweetsome ('swiːtsəm), *a. dial.* [f. SWEET *a.* + -SOME[1].] Sweet, pleasant. Also *advb.*

1799 S. J. PRATT *Glean. Eng.* IV. 377 The yard is a kind of grove. I remember it sweetsome to behold. **18..** R. H. GROOME *Aftermath, Only Darter* (Cent. Dict. Suppl.), I nivver h'ard her sing so sweetsome as she did then.

'sweet-sop. [SOP *sb.*[1]] The sweet fruit of a tree or shrub, *Anona squamosa*, allied to the SOUR-SOP, extensively cultivated in tropical countries. Also the tree or shrub itself. (Cf. *sugar-apple* in SUGAR *sb.* 5 c.)

1696 SLOANE *Catal. Plantarum in Jamaica* 205 Anona, foliis odoratis minoribus, fructu conoide squamoso parvo dulci... *Sweet-sop.* In pratis & agris campestribus ubique spontanea reperitur. **1756** P. BROWNE *Jamaica* 256 The Sweet-sop or Sugar Apple Tree. **1834** *Penny Cycl.* II. 54/1 The sweet-sop.. is often only a small bush,.. it bears a greenish fruit covered with scales, and having the appearance of a young pine cone. **1871** KINGSLEY *At Last* ii, The sweet sop—a passable fruit, or rather congeries of fruits, looking like a green and purple strawberry, of the bigness of an orange.

sweet-sour: see SWEET AND SOUR, SWEET-SOUR *adj. phr.*

sweet-sweet. An imitation of the musical chirp of a bird (with suggestion of SWEET *a.*): cf. SWEET *v.*[2] Often addressed to pet cage-birds.

1605 SYLVESTER *Du Bartas* II. iii. I. *Vocation* 1019 A Sparrow's head he shall (even flying) split: And in the ayre shall make the Swallow cease His sweet-sweet note, and slicing nimbleness.

sweet-talk ('swiːt tɔːk), *v. colloq.* (orig. and chiefly *U.S.*). [f. (as) next.] a. *trans.* To cajole, flatter, persuade. Cf. SMOOTH-TALK *v.*

1936 M. MITCHELL *Gone with Wind* xlvii. 836 Don't try to sweet talk me. **1955** T. WILLIAMS *Orpheus Descending* II. iv. 80 I'd say a peculiar slew-footer that sweet talks you while he's got his hand in the cashbox. **1965** *Listener* 27 May 791/1 There she worked her life away on the edge of poverty, sweet-talking her customers as she lathered them. **1970** J. H. GRAY *Boy from Winnipeg* 199 The 'puller' would come out and sweet-talk them into the store. **1981** *Observer* 17 May 19/6 Many have tried over the years to sweet-talk Walsh into selling, but he remained strongly independent until the last.

b. *intr.* To talk persuasively or flatteringly.

1956 H. GOLD *Man who was not with It* (1965) iv. 33, I would just have to sweet-talk a little. **1968** L. DEIGHTON *Only when I Larf* viii. 102 He'll switch on the charm and sweet-talk so hard that I am throwing my arms around him.

Hence **'sweet-talker; 'sweet-talking** *ppl. a.* and *vbl. sb.*

1946 MEZZROW & WOLFE *Really Blues* p. vi, To the sweettalkers, the gumbeaters, the highjivers. **1956** R. ELLISON in *New World Writing* IX. 230 Now he ain't like that ole clarinet; clarinet so sweet-talking he just *eases* you in the dozens. **1966** J. B. PRIESTLEY *Salt is Leaving* vi. 81, I still say, my sweet-talking friend, that.. you'd have.. forgotten me. **1979** *Arizona Daily Star* 1 Apr. H 1/1 Why did he let himself be wheedled out of a lifetime job? Some sweet-talker, that Lyndon Johnson. **1981** P. NIESEWAND *Word of Gentleman* xxxii. 221 We tried diplomacy and sweet talking.

'sweet talk, *sb. colloq.* (orig. *U.S.*). [SWEET *a.*] Endearment, blandishment, flattery.

1945 L. SHELLY *Jive Talk Dict.* 35/1 *Sweet talk*, endearing terms. **1968** S. ELLIN *Valentine Estate* III. viii. 163 'And stop calling me baby!' she said with sudden heat. 'It's not Tinpan Alley sweet talk, the way you say it... It sounds full of contempt.' **1979** J. W. WAINWRIGHT *Tension* xlv. 142 A touch of sweet-talk and a winning smile.

sweet-veld. Also † -feldt, † -field. [ad. Cape Du. *zoetveld*, lit. sweet field.] In South Africa, an area of land providing good nutritious grazing; also, the vegetation of an area of this kind.

1785 G. FORSTER tr. *Sparrman's Voy. Cape G. Hope* (1786) I. 250 By the Sweet-fields (*Zoete-velden*) are meant such places as do not correspond to the descriptions given above of the *Zuure* and *Carrow veld.* **1850** R. G. CUMMING *Hunter's Life S. Afr.* (1902) 10/2 Those from about the frontiers of the colony, or anywhere beyond the Orange River, are termed 'Sweet-feldt' oxen. **1852** M. B. HUDSON *S. Afr. Frontier Life* I. 137 The sheep from the sweet veld fall sick on karroo. [**1876**: see VELDT 1.] **1896** R. WALLACE *Farming Industries Cape Colony* 82 Animals brought from sweet veld suffer from what is termed veld sickness. **1905** *Sci. S. Afr.* 383–4 (Pettman) Wherever it [*sc.* lime] does occur marked fertility and sweet-veld results. **1937** *Handbk. Farmers S. Afr.* 381 The types of grass found in the sweet veld maintain their feed value after maturity. **1948** H. V. MORTON *In Search of S. Afr.* 86 There is sweet veld and sour veld, high veld and low veld. **1972** *Even. Post* (Port Elizabeth) 19 Feb. (Weekend Mag.) 2 Somerset East was, with its wonderful water supply and sweet veld, a choice place for men and beasts to rest.

sweet water, sweet-water.

1. (as two words) Fresh water (see SWEET *a.* 3 b); *attrib.* (usually with hyphen or as one word), living in or consisting of fresh water.

1608 TOPSELL *Serpents* 287 There was a magicall.. vse of these Sweete-water-Tortoyces agaynst Hayle. **1861** *Chambers' Encycl.* II. 668/2 [Catabrosa] is sometimes called Whorl Grass, and sometimes Sweet Water Grass. **1872** RAYMOND *Statist. Mines & Mining* 11 Sweet-water springs. **1895** P. HEMINGWAY *Out of Egypt* II. 149 A party of women washing linen in some sweetwater canal.

†2. (as two words, or with hyphen) A sweet-smelling liquid preparation; a liquid perfume or scent. *Obs.*

1544 PHAER *Regim. Lyfe* (1560) M viij b, As concernynge sweete waters to sprinkle upon your clothes. **1588** SHAKS. *Tit. A.* II. iv. 6 Call for sweet water, wash thy hands. **1688** HOLME *Armoury* III. 398/1 A small Chafer (which they [*sc.* barbers] use to carry about with them..) to carry their sweet water.. in. **1769** LADY MARY COKE *Jrnl.* 27 Nov., All sorts of sweet waters & fine pomatums. **1859** *Habits of Gd. Society* ii. (new ed.) 125 Banish.. every essence, cosmetic, or sweet-water from your toilet.

b. Technically applied to sweet liquids obtained as by-products in certain manufactures.

1885 W. L. CARPENTER *Soap, Candles*, etc. xiii. 295 (*Glycerin*) The whole is then blown out into a tank, and the 'sweet-water' is run off. **1910** *Encycl. Brit.* V. 178/2 (*Candles*) On standing the product separates into two layers —'sweet water' containing glycerin below, and the fatty acids with a certain amount of lime soap above.

3. (with hyphen, or as one word) A variety of white grape, of specially sweet flavour.

1786 ABERCROMBIE *Arrangem.* in *Gard. Assist.* 15 Grapes. .. White sweet-water. Black sweet-water. **1848** LOWELL *Biglow P.* Ser. I. Introd., He affirmed that.. he had never seen a sweet-water on a trellis growing so fairly.. as a fox-grape over a scrub-oak in a swamp. **1865** SALA *Diary in Amer.* II. v. 159 The black Hambros, or the juicy sweet-waters, or the fragrant muscatels.

sweetweed ('swiːtwiːd). Name for two scrophulariaceous plants of the West Indies and tropical America, *Capraria biflora*, also called goatweed or West Indian tea, and *Scoparia dulcis*, also called sweet broomweed or liquorice-weed.

1760 J. LEE *Introd. Bot.* App. 329. **1771** J. R. FORSTER *Flora Amer. Septentr.* 28.

sweet-william (swiːt 'wɪljəm). (Also as two words, with or without capitals, or rarely as one word without hyphen.)

1. A species of pink, *Dianthus barbatus*, cultivated in numerous varieties, bearing closely-clustered flowers of various shades of white and red, usually variegated or parti-coloured.

1573 TUSSER *Husb.* (1878) 96 Herbes, branches and flowers, for windowes and pots... Sweete Williams. **1578** LYTE *Dodoens* II. vii. 154 The third [sort of gillofer] is that which we cal in Englishe Sweete Williams and colmeniers. **1616** W. BROWNE *Brit. Past.* II. iii. 62 They did.. intwine The white, the blewe, the flesh-like Columbine With Pinckes, Sweet-williams. **1786** J. ABERCROMBIE *Arrangem.* in *Gard. Assist.* 68/1 Double mule, or sweet-william pink. **1796** C. MARSHALL *Garden.* xix. (1813) 355 Sweet William (or bearded pink) is distinguished into broad and narrow leaved sorts. **1866** M. ARNOLD *Thyrsis* vii, Sweet-William with his homely cottage-smell. **1879** DOWDEN *Southey* 4 A house rich in old English comfort, with its diamond-tiled garden-way,.. its sweet-williams and stocks and syringas.

b. Applied to other species of pink, also to plants of other genera:

Childing Pink, *Dianthus prolifer* (Childing Sweet-william); the Deptford Pink, *D. Armeria* (also called Sweet-william Catchfly); †the Wallflower, *Cheiranthus Cheiri* (obs.); Lobel's Catchfly, *Silene Armeria* (Treas. Bot.); the Scarlet Lychnis, *L. chalcedonica* (U.S.); *Phlox maculata* (Wild Sweet-william), of N. America; and *Ipomœa Quamoclit*, of Barbados.

1562 BULLEIN *Bulwarke, Bk. Simples* (1579) 46 The whyte and yellow Gilloflower, called sweete William, or hearts ease. **1633** JOHNSON *Gerarde's Herbal* II. clxxxiv. 599 *Armeria prolifera, Lob.* Childing sweet Williams. **1760** J. LEE *Introd. Bot.* App. 329 Sweet William of Barbadoes, *Ipomœa.* **1856** A. GRAY *Man. Bot.* (1860) 330 *Phlox maculata*.. (Wild Sweet-William).

2. †a. Applied to the tope or dog-fish. b. A local name for the goldfinch.

1730 DALE *Hist. Harwich* 420 Cartilagineous Fishes. I. The Dog-kind, or such are as long... The Sweet-William. **1848** *Zoologist* VI. 2258 The goldfinch is called a 'red-cap', a 'sweet-William', a 'proud tailor'.

sweetwood ('swiːtwʊd). A name for various trees and shrubs, chiefly lauraceous, of the West Indies and tropical America, some of which furnish valuable timber; also the tree itself.

black sweetwood, *Strychnodaphne* (*Ocotea*) *floribunda*. **loblolly s.**, *Oreodaphne* (*Ocotea*) *Leucoxylon*; also *Sciadophyllum Jacquini* (N.O. *Araliaceæ*). **lowland, pepper**, or **yellow s.**, *Nectandra sanguinea*. **mountain s.**, *Acrodiclidium jamaicense*. **Rio Grande s.**, *Oreodaphne Leucoxylon*. **shrubby s.**, the genus *Amyris* (N.O. *Rutaceæ* or *Amyridaceæ*). **timber s.**, *Oreodaphne* (*Nectandra*) *exaltata*, *N. leucantha*, and *Acrodiclidium jamaicense*. **white s.**, *Nectandra leucantha* and *N. sanguinea*. The name is also given to *Croton eleuteria* of the W. Indies and Bahamas, which yields cascarilla bark. (See *Treas. Bot.* and Miller *Plant-n.*)

1607 in *3rd Rep. Hist. MSS. Comm.* 53/2 The soil.. covered with good oak, ash, walnut tree, poplar, pine, sweet woods. **1624** CAPT. J. SMITH *Virginia* 197 Many huge bone-fires of sweet-wood. *c* **1711** PETIVER *Gazophyl.* viii. 71 Mexican sweet Wood... This is a pale coloured Wood with brownish Clouds, it has a very fragrant Smell especially if chewed. **1721** *Act 8 Geo. I*, c. 12 §2. **1811** TITFORD *Sk. Hortus Bot. Amer.* Expl. Plate vii, p. ii, White Sweet- wood (*laurus leucoxylon*). **1858** HOGG *Veg. Kingd.* 623 The wood of *O[reodaphne] exaltata* is yellow, very hard and durable, and is called *Sweetwood*, in Jamaica. **1866** *Chambers' Encycl.* VIII. 491/1 The compound decoction, formerly known as the Decoction of Sweet Woods.

b. *attrib.*, as *sweetwood tree*; **sweetwood bark**, a name for cascarilla bark.

1750 G. HUGHES *Barbados* 157 The Sweet Wood-tree. **1846** JUDGE LEES in Lindley *Veg. Kingd.* 279 The plant is scarcely known here [Bahamas] by the name of Cascarilla, but is commonly called Sweet Wood Bark.

sweet-wort (ˈswiːtwɜːt). [WORT *sb.*[2]] A sweet-flavoured wort; *esp.* the infusion of malt, before the hops are added in the manufacture of beer. Also *attrib.*

1567 *Richmond Wills* (Surtees) 203 In the bachousse and brewhouse.. a swete worte toube. **1567** *Wills & Inv. N.C.* (Surtees 1835) 267 A lead, a maskfatt and a swett wort fatt. **1707** MORTIMER *Husb.* (1721) I. 279 Of all Food [for bees], Honey is the best.. if it is mixed well with a moderate Proportion of good Sweet-wort. **1793** BEDDOES *Sea Scurvy* 91 Sweet wort, or the extract of malt. **1851–4** TOMLINSON *Cycl. Arts* (1867) II. 667/1 This vitreous mass was formerly obtained by rapidly boiling down a concentrated solution of sugar in barley-water or sweet-wort, and hence the name of barley-sugar applied to sticks of it. **1876** HARLEY *Mat. Med.* (ed. 6) 322 Alcohol is obtained by the distillation of any saccharine fluid which has been subjected to fermentation. Sweet worts are formed for this purpose by the action of diastase on the starch of the cereals or the potato.

¶ Webster's (1847–54) definition 'Any plant of a sweet taste', copied by later Dicts., cannot be authenticated.

sweety: see SWEETIE.

sweevil, Sc. f. SWIVEL.

swefel, sweft, swefne, obs. ff. SWIVEL, SWIFT, SWEVEN.

swegh, sweigh: see SWAY.

†**sweight.** *north. dial.* and *Sc. Obs.* In 5 **sweght, sweyght,** 6 (9) *Sc.* **swecht.** [app. f. *sweȝ-* (repr. by the early forms of SWAY *v.*) + -T *suffix*[3] a.] 'The force of a body in motion' (Jam.); impetus.

14.. *Chaucer's Troylus* II. 1383 (MS. St. John's Camb.) Whan that the sturdy ook.. Receyued hath the happy fallynge strooke The grete sweyght [*also Harl. 1239*; *v.rr.* sweigh, swey, sweyf, swough] makith it come al at ones. *c* **1440** *York Myst.* xxxiii. 362 Swete may þis swayne for sweght of our swappes! **1513** DOUGLAS *Æneis* IX. ix. 36 Tho wyth thar swechtis, as thai reyll and leipe, The byrnand towyr doun rollis with a rusche. *Ibid.* XII. xi. 159 Like as the gret roch crag.. Is maid to fall and tumble with all his swecht. [**1819** W. TENNANT *Papistry Storm'd* (1827) 173 Round him they rush't, and push't, and pecht To overturn him wi' their swecht.]

b. *fig.* (See quot.)

a **1800** PEGGE *Suppl. Grose* (1814), *Sweight*, the greatest part of any thing. North.

sweile, sweill, obs. ff. SWEAL, SWEEL.

swein, sweingeor, sweinmote, obs. ff. SWAIN, SWINGER[1], SWANIMOTE.

sweir, Sc. f. SWEAR *v.*, SWEER.

sweit, obs. Sc. f. SWEAT, SWEET.

swelawe, obs. f. SWALLOW *v.*

swelchie (ˈswɛlxɪ). *Sc.* ? *Obs.* Also 7 **swelchee.** [ad. ON. *svelgr*: see SWALLOW *sb.*[2]] A whirlpool; also, the local name for the race in Pentland Firth.

a **1688** J. WALLACE *Descr. Orkney* i. (1693) 5 On the North side of this Isle, is a part of the Firth called the Swelchee of Stroma.. very dangerous. **1805** BARRY *Orkney* I. ii. 44 Did we credit the tales of former times, wells and swelchies, gulphs and whirlpools, are constantly surrounding this island [*sc.* Swanay], like so many gaping monsters. **1821** SCOTT *Pirate* xxix, Through all the waws, wells, and swelchies of the Pentland Firth.

swele, obs. f. SQUEAL, SWEAL, SWELL *sb.*, SWILL.

swelewe, swel(i)gh, obs. ff. SWALLOW.

swelk, such: see SWILK.

swell (swɛl), *sb.* Also 3 **swel,** 4 **swele.** [In sense 1 prob. repr. OE. *ȝeswel* (:—**gaswaljo-*), corresp. to MLG. *geswel(le, swel, swele*, MDu. *geswel, swel, sweel(e* (Du. *gezwel*); in the other senses f. SWELL *v.*, q.v.]

†**1.** A morbid swelling. *Obs.*

a **1225** *Ancr. R.* 274 Auh drinc þeonne atterloðe, & drif þene swel [*v.r.* swalm] aȝeanward urommard þe heorte, þet is to siggen, þenc oðe attrie pinen þet God suffrede oðe rode & þe swell schal setten. **13..** *Seuyn Sag.* (W.) 1566 He.. usede sinne sodomighte. So long he pleiede with yong man, A swele in his membres cam than.

2. a. The condition of being swollen, distended, or increased in bulk; swelling or protuberant form, bulge; *concr.* a protuberant part, protuberance.

In technical use *spec.*, e.g. the enlargement near the muzzle of a gun, the enlarged and thickened part of a gunstock, the entasis of a column.

1683 J. REID *Scots Gard'ner* (1907) 39 Grass, or brick-walkes may have, for thirty foot broad, six inches of swell. **1726** LEONI *Alberti's Archit.* II. 20 The swell or belly of the shaft. **1733** W. ELLIS *Chiltern & Vale Farm.* 45 Not being able to make their growing Progress, for want of Room in the Earth, for the Swell and Multiplicity of their several Stalks. **1741** *Compl. Fam.-Piece* III. 512 The [pigeons called] Crappers are valuable for their Swell. **1758** REID tr. *Macquer's Chym.* I. 374 During the calcination of the Tin,.. you perceive in several places a small swell of a certain matter which bursts. **1768** *Woman of Honor* II. 201, I think I see the hardly suppressed swell of face of one of those immortal geniuses. **1802** C. JAMES *Milit. Dict.* s.v. *Secure arms!*, Quit the butt with the left hand, and seize the firelock with it at the swell. **1822–7** GOOD *Study Med.* (1829) V. 94 When pregnancy takes place, and the uterus enlarges, the breasts exhibit a correspondent increase of swell. **1831** J. HOLLAND *Manuf. Metal* I. 73 The irregular swells and hollows on the surface of a casting. *Ibid.* 195 This bore is a piece of strong iron, ten or twelve inches in length: near to each end there is a knob or swell of steel. **1833** *Ibid.* II. 204 The shanks consist of tubes of brass covering iron rods, and screwed together at the swells. **1846** MRS. A. MARSH *Father Darcy* II. xix 327 There was a slight swell in his chest—the *hysterica passio* of poor Lear rose.. in his throat. **1848** THACKERAY *Van. Fair* xlv, Pitt looked down.. at his legs, which had not.. much more symmetry or swell than the lean Court sword which dangled by his side. **1849** FREEMAN *Archit.* v. 88 Ornamental balusters with a single swell are found. **1876** *Encycl. Brit.* IV. 490/1 If a column be intended to have a swell in the middle.

b. *fig.* Increase in amount. *rare.* ? *Obs.*

1768 *Woman of Honor* III. 227 His plan of concealing the enormous swell of his fortune. **1842** ALISON *Hist. Europe* lxxviii. X. 1009 The augmentation of wealth, the swell of pauperism.

3. a. The rising or heaving of the sea or other body of water in a succession of long rolling waves, as after a storm; *concr.* such a wave, or, more usually, such waves collectively. (See also GROUND-SWELL.) Also *spec.* in *Meteorol.* and *Oceanogr.*, wave movement persisting after the wind causing it has dropped, or due to disturbance at a distance. Contrasted with SEA *sb.* 5 d.

1606 SHAKS. *Ant. & Cl.* III. ii. 49 The Swannes downe feather That stands vpon the Swell at the full of Tide, And neither way inclines. **1725** DE FOE *Voy. round World* (1840) 326 Fenced nowhere from the least surge or swell of the water. **1727** A. HAMILTON *New Acc. E. Ind.* II. xlii. 114 There being nothing to keep the great Swell of rolling Seas off them. **1748** *Anson's Voy.* II. iii. 139 A most excellent harbour.. for its security against all winds and swells. **1805** H. K. WHITE *Lett.* Poems (1837) 266 Some tremendous swells which we weathered admirably. **1808** PIKE *Sources Mississ.* (1810) 21 My boat ploughed the swells, sometimes almost bow under. **1833** HT. MARTINEAU *Cinnamon & Pearls* i. 13 Old Gomgode's flat-bottomed fishing-boat.. was pitching in the rising swell. **1865** PARKMAN *Huguenots in Florida* ii, Their water-casks.. rocking on the long swells of subsiding gales. **1930** *Meteorol. Gloss.* (Meteorol. Office) (ed. 2) 188 Swell is wave motion in the ocean persisting after the originating cause of the wave motion has ceased or passed away. **1957** *Encycl. Brit.* XXIII. 442A/1 When wind-raised waves travel out of a storm area they advance as 'swell', and after having travelled large distances become a series of long, low and fairly regular undulations. **1977** [see SEA *sb.* 5 d].

fig. **1798** LANDOR *Gebir* IV. 33 Such ebbs of doubt, and swells of jealousy. **1871** MORLEY *Carlyle* in *Crit. Misc.* Ser. I. (1878) 175 The full swell and tide and energy of genius.

b. The rising of a river above its ordinary level. ? *Obs.*

1758 *Ann. Reg., Hist. War* 46/2 The swell of the river had rendered all relief impossible. **1760** *Ibid.* 38/2 Notwithstanding.. the great swell of the waters.. he passed the Rhine. **1769** *Ibid.* 25/2 A sudden and extraordinary swell of the.. Niester.. totally destroyed the bridge. **1796** MORSE *Amer. Geog.* I. 176 Rapids; which.. with a swell of two or three feet, become very passable for boats. **1812** BRACKENRIDGE *Views Louisiana* (1814) 48 The annual swell, which is early in the spring of the year, raises the water fifty or sixty feet.

4. a. A piece of land rising gradually and evenly above the general level; a hill, eminence, or upland with a smooth rounded outline and broad in proportion to its height; a rising ground. Also, a similar feature on the sea bed; a relatively elevated part of a lithospheric plate.

Orig. with qualifying phr., e.g. *swell of ground*, which is still usually felt to be necessary by English writers; the absol. use is specially American.

1764 DODSLEY *Leasowes* in *Shenstone's Wks.* (1777) II. 308 A swell of waste furzy land, diversified with a cottage, and a road. **1792** YOUNG *Trav. France* (1889) 20 The swells margined with wood. **1808** PIKE *Sources Mississ.* II. (1810) 135 The prairie rising and falling in regular swells, as far as the sight can extend. **1818** SCOTT *Rob Roy* xxvii, An uninterrupted swell of moorland. **1825** LONGF. *Burial Minnisink* 1 On sunny slope and beechen swell. **1869** PARKMAN *Disc. Gt. West* xxv. 337 The grassy swells were spangled with the bright flowers for which Texas is renowned. **1908** RIDER HAGGARD *Ghost Kings* v. 55 Following a game-path through the dew-drenched grass which grew upon the swells and valleys of the veld. **1963** G. L. PICKARD *Descriptive Physical Oceanogr.* ii. 10 The characteristic features [of the deep-sea bottom] are.. either basically long and narrow.. or of roughly equal lateral extent (swells and basins). **1971** *Nature* 30 Apr. 555/1 Many areas such as Kenya mark igneous provinces of characteristic per-alkaline magma.. which are up-swollen portions ('swells') of the African plate some 1,000 km across.

b. *Coal-mining.* (See quots.)

1855 J. PHILLIPS *Man. Geol.* 193 [The seam] is.. cut into 'swills' [*sic*] or 'horse backs', which rise up from the floor. **1882** GEIKIE *Text-Bk. Geol.* (1885) 467 The stratification of the later accumulation will end off abruptly against the flanks of the older ridge, which will appear to rise up through the overlying bed. Appearances of this kind are not uncommon in coal-fields, where they are known to the miners as 'rolls', 'swells', or 'horses' backs'. **1883** GRESLEY *Gloss. Coal-mining*, *Swell*, a kind of fault. See *Horses*. *Ibid.*, *Horses* or *Horsebacks*, natural channels cut, or washed away by water, in a coal seam, and filled up with shale and sandstone.

5. a. Of sound, esp. musical sound: Gradual increase in loudness or force; hence, a sound or succession of sounds gradually increasing in volume, or coming upon the ear more and more clearly.

1803 SCOTT *Gray Brother* xxiii, The heavy knell, the choir's faint swell, Came slowly down the wind. **1822** *Q. Mus. Mag.* IV. 35 The swell, or gradual increase of sound, is produced by opening the door of the box in which this part of the organ is inclosed. **1833** TENNYSON *May Queen* III. viii, And up the valley came a swell of music on the wind. **1839** MOORE *Alciphron* iii. 121 There came A swell of harmony as grand As e'er was born of voice and hand. **1848–9** [see FLAM *sb.*[2]]. **1894** HALL CAINE *Manxman* VI. xii, As Philip lay alone the soar and swell of the psalm filled the room.

b. *spec.* in *Mus.* A gradual increase of force (*crescendo*) followed by a gradual decrease (*diminuendo*), in singing or playing; hence, a character composed of the *crescendo* and *diminuendo* marks together, denoting this: < >.

1757 FOOTE *Author* Epil., Divine Mingotti! what a swell has she! **1833** J. RUSH *Philos. Hum. Voice* (ed. 2) 259 A gradual strengthening and subsequent reduction of the voice, similar to what is called a swell in the language of musical expression. **1848** RIMBAULT *First Bk. Piano.* 65.

6. A contrivance for gradually varying the force of the tone in an organ or harmonium (also in the harpsichord and some early pianos), consisting of a shutter, a lid, or (now usually) a series of slats like those of a Venetian blind, which can be opened or shut at pleasure by means of a pedal or (in the harmonium) a knee-lever. Also short for *swell-box, swell keyboard*, or *swell organ* (see below).

Used attrib. in names of apparatus connected with or actuating the swell, as *swell-coupler, keyboard, manual, pedal*; *swell-box*, the box or chamber, containing a set of pipes or reeds, which is opened and closed by the swell in an organ or harmonium; *swell organ*, the set of pipes enclosed in this, forming one of the partial organs which make up a large organ.

1773 BARRINGTON in *Phil. Trans.* LXIII. 271 The insipidity of the upper part of the flute stop of an organ, which hath not the modern improvement of a swell. **1774** GILLESPY in *Abridgm. Specif. Patents, Mus.* (1871) 10 My new constructed principle of putting on the quills to strike the strings of a harpsichord with a peddle and swell. **1801** BUSBY *Dict. Mus.* s.v., A certain quantity of pipes inclosed in a large wooden case called the Swell Box. **1822** *Q. Mus. Mag.* IV. 35 Three.. distinct sound-boards; the great organ, the choir organ, and the swell. **1865** *Chambers' Encycl.* VII. 111/1 Above the choir-organ is the swell-organ, whose pipes are enclosed in a wooden box with a front of louvre-boards like venetian blinds. **1869** *Eng. Mech.* 31 Dec. 386/1 The swell box.. covers the top of the reed chest or 'pan'. **1875** STAINER & BARRETT *Dict. Mus. Terms* s.v. *Organ Construction* §17 In 1712, Abraham Jordan invented the 'Nag's-head swell', as it was afterwards termed. It consisted of an echo organ, having, instead of a fixed front, a moveable shutter working up and down in a window sash. **1881** W. E. DICKSON *Organ-Build.* xii. 151 To give promptness to the return of the swell-pedal.. by attaching a strong spiral spring to the pedal. *Ibid.* 155 The simplest form of swell-coupler. **1883** A. J. HIPKINS in Grove *Dict. Mus.* III. 489 The Potsdam harpsichords were made with Shudi's Venetian Swell. **1889** STAINER *ibid.* IV. 8 The early swell-organs were of very limited compass... For many years the compass did not extend below tenor C..; but in all instruments with any pretension to completeness the Swell manual is made to CC, coextensive with the Great and Choir.

7. A lever in a loom (see quot.).

1894 T. W. FOX *Mech. Weaving* xiii. 318 All looms are provided with curved levers called swells, which.. serve the twofold purpose of protecting warp from being broken when a shuttle is in the shed, and also of stopping a shuttle from rebounding after entering a box.

8. The action or condition of swelling, in fig. senses. **a.** Of a feeling, emotion, etc. (cf. SWELL *v.* 7). Now *rare* or *Obs.*

1702 STEELE *Funeral* IV. i. 51 It Moderates the Swell of Joy that I am in, to think of your Difficulties. **1781** COWPER *Charity* 246 The swell of pity, not to be confin'd Within the scanty limits of the mind. **1822** LAMB *Elia* Ser. I. *Old Actors*, Of all the actors who flourished in my time.. Bensley had most of the swell of soul, was greatest in the delivery of heroic conceptions, the emotions consequent upon the presentment of a great idea to the fancy.

b. Proud or arrogant, or (in later use) pompous or pretentious air or behaviour; (a piece of) swagger. *to cut a swell*, to 'cut a dash', swagger. (Cf. SWELL *v.* 9, 10.) ? *Obs.*

1724 *Briton* No. 28. 123 There is such a Swell and Insolence in most of those who can maintain any Degree of Mastery. **1751** JOHNSON *Rambler* No. 179 ¶4 The softness of foppery, the swell of insolence, the liveliness of levity. **1800** in *Spirit Pub. Jrnls.* IV. 61 To see our young lords and our young gentlemen 'cutting a swell', as the fashionable phrase is. **1823** *Ibid.* 232 The trio, having been to the play, agreed to call in at Smith's, by way of a swell, to get sixpennyworth of oysters each. **1847** BUSHNELL *Chr. Nurt.*

II. i. (1861) 235 They practice it [*sc.* the child] in shows and swells and all the petty airs of foppery and brave assumption.

†**c.** Turgid or inflated style of language. *Obs.*

1742 YOUNG *Nt. Th.* VII. 595 Pride, like the Delphic priestess, with a swell, Rav'd nonsense, destin'd to be future sense. **1783** BLAIR *Rhet.* xiii. I. 264 Sentences constructed with the Ciceronian fulness and swell. **1843** *Blackw. Mag.* LIV. 62 The air of pretence, the craving after effect, the swell.

9. *colloq.*, orig. *slang.* A fashionably or stylishly dressed person; hence, a person of good social position, a highly distinguished person.

1786 *Sessions Papers* 13 Dec. 92/2 Here is a *swell* a coming. What is the meaning of that?—I do not know what meaning they give to it, without it is a gentleman. [**1804** *Times* 25 Feb., A number of young gentlemen, on the King's establishment, have lately been dismissed on account of their having formed an expensive club, under the title of the Swell!] **1811** *Lexicon Balatronicum, Cadge the swells*, beg of the gentlemen. **1812** J. H. VAUX *Flash Dict.*, *Swell*, a gentleman; but any well-dressed person is emphatically termed a swell, or a rank swell. **1819** *Blackw. Mag.* IV. 566 The third was one than whom no heavier swell Thy groaning pavement, Street of Princes, vext. **1836** MARRYAT *Midsh. Easy* xviii, I never was a gentleman—only a swell. **1838** J. BLACKWOOD in Mrs. G. Porter *Ann. Publishing Ho.* (1898) III. 11 The Baron is a most capital fellow, and a very big swell; he is chamberlain to the King of Prussia. **1861** HUGHES *Tom Brown at Oxf.* i, Pictures of old swells, bishops and lords chiefly. **1885** 'MRS. ALEXANDER' *Valerie's Fate* i, The girls were no end of swells, such lovely sable trimmings to their jackets! **1892** *Law Times* XCIII. 459/2 The plaintiff stated that the defendant was one of the greatest swells in the City..and had often readily paid £20 or £30.

b. *transf.* One who is distinguished or eminent in achievement; one who is very clever or good *at* something.

1816 MOORE *Epist. fr. Tom Crib to Big Ben* 23 Having floor'd, by good luck, the first swell of the age, Having conquer'd the prime one, that mill'd us all round. **1846** DE QUINCEY *Syst. Heavens* Wks. 1862 III. 171 To insinuate the possibility of an error against so great a swell as Immanuel Kant. **1879** E. K. BATES *Egypt. Bonds* I. viii. 180, I know you are a swell at that sort of thing. **1886** 'OUIDA' *House Party* v. (1887) 82 Russians are tremendous swells at palaver,.. gammon you no end.

swell, *a.* *colloq.* Now chiefly *U.S.* [attrib. use of SWELL *sb.* in sense 9.] That is, or has the character or style of, a 'swell'; befitting a 'swell'.

a. Of persons: Stylishly or handsomely dressed or equipped; of good (social) position; of distinguished appearance or status. More recently, in weakened use as a general expression of approval.

1810 in *Spirit Pub. Jrnls.* XV. 29 My great swell pris'ner and his pal are flown! **1823** BYRON *Juan* XI. xix, So prime, so swell [*note* gentlemanly], so nutty, and so knowing. **1826** *Sporting Mag.* XVIII. 279 The two very swell coachmen who drove them out of London. **1845** DISRAELI *Sybil* VI. viii, Why are we not to interfere with politics as much as the swell ladies in London? *a* **1876** M. COLLINS *Pen Sk. by Vanished Hand* (1879) I. 113 How 'swell' they are! how carefully-gloved and glossily-hatted. **1890** 'R. BOLDREWOOD' *Col. Reformer* xiv. (1891) 147 A decent sort of fellow belonging to swell people. **1926** MAINES & GRANT *Wise-Crack Dict.* 13/1 *Swell dish*, very beautiful girl. **1951** M. MCLUHAN *Mech. Bride* (1967) 60/2 He was a swell kid. **1977** I. SHAW *Beggerman, Thief* II. iii. 141 That's great. She's swell, a real lady. What a difference between her and some of the dames we had to put up with on the boat.

b. Of things: Distinguished in style; stylish; first-rate, tip-top. Also similarly weakened: 'great', 'fine', etc.

1812 J. H. VAUX *Flash Dict.* s.v., Any thing remarkable for its beauty or elegance, is called a swell article; so, a swell crib, is a genteel house. **1831** *Lincoln Herald* 21 Oct. p. iv/5 We had some slap-up and swell lingo against the church. **1849** THACKERAY *Pendennis* iii, A youth..appeared..in one of those costumes to which the public consent..has awarded the title of 'Swell'. **1876** C. D. WARNER *Wint. Nile* xii. 159 It is getting to be considered that cigars are more 'swell' than pipes. **1897** S. CRANE *Third Violet* vii. 44 You don't look as if you had such a swell time. **1930** E. H. LAVINE *Third Degree* xi. 128 The swell time he had with the swell broads in the swell musical comedy company. **1947** A. MILLER *All my Sons* II. 62 We're eating at the lake; we could have a swell time. **1952** S. KAUFFMANN *Tightrope* viii. 142 A play like this, with a swell part for her..all that may not come along again for five years. **1968** *Amer. Speech* XLIII. 223 It was a swell date. **1978** J. KRANTZ *Scruples* iii. 77 All in all, a swell arrangement, and Spider learned a great deal during the year he was Levy's assistant.

c. swell mob, a class of pickpockets who assumed the dress and manners of respectable people in order to escape detection. Hence **swell-mobsman**, a man belonging to the swell mob. *slang.* Now *Obs.* or *Hist.*

1836 MARRYAT *Midsh. Easy* xii, A man who has belonged to the swell mob is not easily repulsed. **1843** *Sessions Papers* 6 Jan. 38, I have heard..that the prisoner is a swell mob's man. **1851** MAYHEW *Lond. Labour* (1861) II. 369/1 Swell mobsmen, and thieves, and housebreakers. **1886** J. K. JEROME *Idle Thoughts* i. 7 He enters..giving himself really the air of a member of the swell mob. **1886** D. C. MURRAY *Cynic Fort.* x, When he had worn something of the air of a dandy—or, at the worst, of a successful swell-mobsman.

d. *predic.* Most pleasant or kind; very effective; 'splendid'. *U.S.*

1926 *Scribner's Mag.* Aug. 198/2 He also knew that the yeggs were not trained fur-thieves... 'They were swell on safes, but a bum would have showed better judgment on furs.' **1931** H. CRANE *Let.* 2 June (1965) 370 Moisés has been swell to me. **1942** WODEHOUSE *Money in Bank* (1946) ii. 16 You eat vegetables and breathe deep and dance around in circles. It's supposed to be swell for the soul. **1965** A. LURIE *Nowhere City* IV. xxi. 237 Yeah; that'd be really swell, if you would.

e. *int.* As an expression of satisfaction.

1930 D. HAMMETT *Maltese Falcon* xvii. 201 'She's full of gas and ready to go.' 'Swell.' **1935** WODEHOUSE *Luck of Bodkins* xxii. 289 'Swell,' said Mabel, placing the document in her vanity-bag. **1976** *Daily Record* (Glasgow) 22 Nov. 10/3 My fellow Scot agreed that you could call it that. 'Swell,' said the reporter.

swell (swɛl), *v.* Pa. t. **swelled** (swɛld); pa. pple. **swollen** ('swəʊl(ə)n), **swelled.** Forms: 1 **swellan**, (2 *3rd sing.* **swelð**), 3–6 **swelle**, 6–7 **swel**, (5 **suell**, 6 *Sc.* **swoll**, 9 *Sc.* **swall, swaul**), 5– **swell.** *Pa. t.* α. 1 **sweall**, *pl.* **swullon**, 3–5 **swal**, 5 **swalle**, *pl.* **swollen**, 6–7, 9 *dial.* **swole**, 7–9 (*arch.*) **swoll.** β. 5 **swelde**, (*Sc.* 6 **swellit, swollit, swa'd**), 6– **swelled.** *Pa. pple.* α. 1 **-swollen, (suollaen)**, 4–7 **swolne**, (4 *Sc.* **swolline**, 5 **swollyn**, 6 **swolen, swollne, solne, swone**), 6–9 **swoln**, 4– **swollen**; 4 **(i-)swolle**, 5 **y-swolle, suoll(e, swalle**, 9 *dial.* **swole.** β. 5 **i-sweld**, 6 **swelde**, 6–7 **sweld, swel'd**, 5– **swelled.** [Com. Teut. str. vb.: OE. *swellan*, pa. t. *sweall*, *swullon*, pa. pple. *-swollen* = OFris. **swella* (in 3rd sing. *swilith*), OS. **swellan* (in 3rd pl. *suellad*), MLG., MDu. (also wk.) *swellen, swillen* (LG. *swillen*, pa. t. *swull*, pa. pple. *swullen*, Du. *zwellen*), OHG. *swellan*, pa. t. *swall*, *s(w)ullum*, pa. pple. *gis(w)ollan* (MHG. *swellen*, G. *schwellen*, pa. t. *schwoll*, earlier *schwall*, pa. pple. *geschwollen*), ON. *svella*, pa. t. *sval*, *sullu*, pa. pple. *sollinn* (Sw. *svälla*, Norw. *svelle*):—OTeut. **swellan*. A causative (wk.) vb. **swalljan* is represented by MLG., MDu. *swellen, swillen*, OHG. *-swellan*, (MHG. *swellen*, G. *schwellen*), ON. *svella*; cf. Goth. *ufswalleins* state of being puffed up, φυσίωσις.

The following forms belong to various grades of the same root: (M)LG. *swal* (G. *schwall*) swollen mass of water, SWALL, OE. *ȝeswell*, SWELL *sb.*, MLG. *(ge)swel*, Du. *gezwel*, MLG. *swul, swuls(t)*, OHG. *giswulst* (MHG. *ge-swulst*, G. *geschwulst, schwulst*), swelling, ON. *sullr* boil, OE. *swile, swyle*, (M)LG., Fris. *swil*, Du. dial. *zwil*, OHG. *swilo, (ga)suil* (MHG. *swil, geswil*, G. *schwiele*) callosity.]

1. a. *intr.* To become larger in bulk, increase in size (by pressure from within, as by absorption of moisture, or of material in the process of growth, by inflation with air or gas, etc.); to become distended or filled out; *esp.* to undergo abnormal or morbid increase of size, be affected with tumour as the result of infection or injury. Also with *out, up.*

Beowulf 2713 (Gr.) Ða sio wund ongon..swelan ond swellan. *c* **1000** *Sax. Leechd.* III. 86 Wið wunda ðe swellaþ. *c* **1205** LAY. 19800 His wombe gon to swellen. *a* **1225** *Ancr. R.* 274 So louh wunde ne dred tu nout to sore, bute ȝif hit to swuð swelle. *c* **1275** *Sinners Beware* 297 in *O.E. Misc.* 82 For hunger ich swal þar-vte. **1377** LANGL. *P. Pl.* B. XIX. 278 Shulde neuere mete ne mochel drynke Make hym to swelle. *c* **1386** CHAUCER *Pard. Prol.* 26 If Cow or Calf or Sheepe or Oxe swelle That any worm hath ete or wyrm ystonge. *c* **1400** *Laud Troy Bk.* 4534 For tene his herte began to bollen, And bothe his chekes gret swollen. **1470–85** MALORY *Arthur* IV. xviii. 729 Whanne he had eten hit, he swalle soo tyl he brast. **1526** TINDALE *Acts* xxviii. 6 They wayted when he shulde have swolne or fallen doune deed sodently. *a* **1578** LINDESAY (Pitscottie) *Chron. Scot.* (S.T.S.) II. 246 This serwand persaving the eird evir to ryve and to swoll quhair he stuid. **1614** PURCHAS *Pilgrimage* I. ii. (ed. 2) 11 Thus doth this Globe [*sc.* the earth] swell out to our vse, for which it enlargeth it selfe. **1799** KIRWAN *Geol. Ess.* 284 Most probably then the pyrites swoll, uplifted the whole [etc.]. **1833** N. ARNOTT *Physics* (ed. 5) II. 86 When the liquid swells out into an air or gas. **1837** P. KEITH *Bot. Lex.* 37 The vessels become convoluted and swell up into a bunch. **1853** SOYER *Pantroph.* 304 They placed barley in water, and left it there until it swelled. **1860** TYNDALL *Glac.* I. xxii. 159 His knee swelled, and he walked with great difficulty. **1877** BLACKIE *Wise Men* 121 The solid ground did rock, and swoll and sobbed. **1898** R. BRIDGES *Hymn Nat.* iii, Every flower-bud swelleth.

b. Of a body of water: To rise above the ordinary level, as a river, or the tide; to rise in waves, as the sea in or after a storm; to rise to the brim, well up, as a spring (also said of tears).

1382 WYCLIF *Isa.* li. 15, I..am the Lord thi God, that disturbe the se, and swellen his flodis. *c* **1435** *Torr. Portugal* 147 He swellyd ase dothe the see. *a* **1513** FABYAN *Chron.* VI. ccvi. (1811) 219 He went vnto yᵉ Thamys syde, and beheld howe the water swelled or flowed. **1555** EDEN *Decades* (Arb.) 140 That south sea doth soo in maner boyle and swelle, that when it is at the hyghest it doth couer many greate rockes, which at the faule therof, are seene farre aboue the water. **1588** SHAKS. *L.L.L.* IV. iii. 37 Do but behold the teares that swell in me. **1610** HOLLAND *Camden's Brit.* (1637) 286 Thus farre swelleth the Tamis with the accesse of the flowing tide. **1634** MILTON *Comus* 732 The Sea o'erfraught would swell. **1742** SHENSTONE *Schoolmistress* 179 Her sad grief that swells in either eye. **1758** *Ann. Reg., Hist. War* 70/1 A prodigious surf swelled all along the shore. **1812** BYRON *Ch. Har.* II. xxviii, As breezes rise and fall and billows swell. **1813** HOGG *Queen's Wake, Kilmeny* iv, Where the river swa'd a living stream. **1817** COLERIDGE *Biog. Lit.* 268 My eyes felt as if a tear were swelling into them. **1830** W. TAYLOR *Hist. Surv. Germ. Poetry* III. 337 The waters rush'd, the waters swoll. **1849** CUPPLES *Green Hand* vi. (1856) 62 Now and then a bigger wave than ordinary would go swelling up. **1883** TYLOR in *Encycl. Brit.* XV. 199/2 They can bring rain and make the rivers swell.

c. Expressing form (not movement or action): To be distended or protuberant; to be larger, higher, or thicker at a certain part; to rise gradually and smoothly above the general level, as a hill.

1679 MOXON *Mech. Exerc.* ix. 157 If the edge swell in any place, then plain off that swelling till it comply as aforesaid. **1791** W. GILPIN *Forest Scenery* I. 183 A varied surface—where the ground swells, and falls. *a* **1817** T. DWIGHT *Trav. New Eng.*, etc. (1821) II. 253 The surface here began to swell, and to be covered with oak, walnut, and chestnut. **1849** KINGSLEY *Misc.* (1860) II. 240 One long grey hill after another swelled up browner and browner before them. **1859** MURCHISON *Siluria* v. (ed. 3) 101 This zone of..rock varies much in dimensions..it so swells out in the parishes of Church Preen and Kenley, that [etc.]. **1869** BOUTELL *Arms & Armour* iii. (1874) 44 Swelling with graceful curves in the middle of the blade.

2. a. *trans.* (see also 3): To make larger in bulk, increase the size of, cause to expand; to enlarge morbidly, affect with tumour. Also with *out, up.*

c **1400** *Destr. Troy* 13683 Fortune..Gers hym swolow a swete, þat swellis hym after. *a* **1400–50** *Wars Alex.* 4276 Haue we no cures of courte ne na cointe sewes Swanes ne na swete thing to swell oure wames. **1484** CAXTON *Fables of Æsop* II. xx, Men sayn comynly Swelle not thy self to thende that thow breste not. **1535** COVERDALE *Isa.* xliv. 14 The Fyrre trees which he planted himself, and soch as the rayne hath swelled. **1592** KYD *Midas* III. ii, I am one of those whose tongues are swelde with silence. **1597** DONNE *Poems, The Storme* 21 Sweet, As to a stomack sterv'd, whose insides meete, Meate comes, it came; and swole our sailes. **1598** SHAKS. *Merry W.* III. v. 16 The water swelles a man; and what a thing should I haue beene, when I had beene swel'd? **1735** JOHNSON *Lobo's Abyssinia, Descr.* xv. 137 It..swell'd up my Arm, afflicting me with the most horrid Torture. *c* **1790** *Encycl. Brit.* (ed. 3) V. 490/2 By swelling out its cheeks and gill covers to a large size. **1812** J. WILSON *Isle of Palms* III. 121 Till the land-breeze her canvas wings shall swell. **1818** *Art Bk.-binding* 3 Swell, to make the back thicker by opening the foldings with the fingers. **1848** DICKENS *Dombey* x, The Major, straining with vindictiveness, and swelling every already swollen vein in his head. **1856** KANE *Arctic Expl.* II. xxv. 247 They were to be calked and swelled and launched and stowed, before we could venture to embark in them.

b. To cause (the sea, a river, etc.) to rise in waves, as the wind, or (more usually) above the ordinary level, as rain.

1605 SHAKS. *Lear* III. i. 6 [He] Bids the winde blow the Earth into the Sea, Or swell the curled Waters 'boue the Maine. **1662** STILLINGFL. *Orig. Sacræ* III. iv. §6 The rain-water..doth..swell the Rivers which thereby run with greater force. **1697** DRYDEN *Æneid* XI. 607 What heaps of Trojans by this Hand were slain, And how the bloody Tyber swell'd the Main. **1709** T. ROBINSON *Nat. Hist. Westmoreld.* i. 10 These slow running Rivers do gradually swell up the Sea into such a gibbosity, as contributes to that annual Flux, or overflowing of Nilus. **1813** SCOTT *Trierm.* III. v, The upland showers had swoln the rills.

3. a. In pa. pple. *swollen*, less usually *swelled*, without implication of subject (in some cases possibly belonging to the *intr.* sense): Increased in bulk, dilated, distended; affected with morbid enlargement or tumour.

c **700** *Epinal Gloss.* 1018 *Tuber, tumor*, suollaen. *c* **1375** *Sc. Leg. Saints* xxvii. (*Machor*) 1596 Sume [men] throu ydropesy sa gret Swolne þat þai ma ete no mete. **1387** TREVISA *Higden* (Rolls) I. 299 Men [with] bocches vnder þe chyn i-swolle and i-bolled as þey he were double chynned. **1422** YONGE tr. *Secreta Secret.* lviii. 227 Tho that haue ribbis bocchynge owtwardes like as they weryn y-swolle, bene yanglours. **1530** PALSGR. 582/1 Me thynke you have the tothe ake, for your cheke is swollen. **1538** STARKEY *England* (1878) 79 In a dropcy the body..solne wyth yl humorys, lyth idul. **1605** SHAKS. *Macb.* IV. iii. 151 Strangely visited people All swolne and Vlcerous. **1637** MILTON *Lycidas* 126 The hungry Sheep..swoln with wind. **1697** DRYDEN *Virg. Georg.* I. 425 While yet the Head is green, or lightly swell'd With Milky-moisture. **1715** LADY M. W. MONTAGU *Let. to Lady Rich* 17 June, The next morning..my face was swelled to a very extraordinary Size. **1791** MRS. RADCLIFFE *Rom. Forest* vii, With eyes swollen with weeping. **1829** *Chapters Phys. Sci.* 173 The stomach..by being swoln out or contracted [etc.]. **1831** SCOTT *Cast. Dang.* ii, His features were still swollen with displeasure. **1857** MILLER *Elem. Chem., Org.* 98 It furnishes a coke which is much swollen, caked together, and possessed of a high lustre.

b. Of a body of water, esp. a river: see 1 b, 2 b.

1588 KYD *Househ. Philos.* Wks. (1901) 240 The Ryuer.. was swoln so high as it farre surpast the wonted limmits. **1636** E. DACRES tr. *Machiavel's Disc. Livy* I. 72 The Albanlake being miraculously sweld. **1770** LANGHORNE *Plutarch* (1879) II. 673/1 A torrent swelled with sudden rains. **1810** WELLINGTON in Gurw. *Desp.* (1837) VII. 2 The rivulets were so much swelled yesterday that we could see nothing on their right. **1869** PHILLIPS *Vesuv.* ii. 30 A mere brook occasionally swollen to a torrent.

c. Of a distended form, protuberant, bulging: see 1 c.

1708 J. CHAMBERLAYNE *St. Gt. Brit.* II. I. ii. (1710) 327 The Countrey is generally swell'd with Hills. **1796** WITHERING *Brit. Plants* (ed. 3) IV. 48 Plant pendent, cracked and swollen. **1875** *Encycl. Brit.* II. 441/2 Friezes, instead of being sculptured, are swollen. **1877** F. E. HULME *Wild Fl.* p. vi, Stems forking, swollen at the nodes, about three feet high.

4. a. *intr.* To become greater in amount, volume, degree, intensity, or force: now only in immaterial sense (see also 6).

c **1450** *St. Cuthbert* (Surtees) 4176 His sekenes began to suell. **1598** BASTARD *Chrestol.* V. iv. 107 Gæta from wooll and weauing first beganne, Swelling and swelling to a gentleman... At last..He swole to be a Lord: and then he burst. **1611** SHAKS. *Cymb.* III. i. 50 Cæsars Ambition, Which swell'd so much, that it did almost stretch The sides o' th'

World. *c* **1645** HOWELL *Lett.* (1650) II. xxxix. 50 Divers reports for peace have swoln high for the time, but they suddenly fell low, and flat again. **1662** *Bk. Com. Prayer* Pref., To make the number swell. **1776** GIBBON *Decl. & F.* vi. (1782) I. 173 The murmurs of the army swelled with impunity into seditious clamours. **1854** R. S. SURTEES *Handley Cross* iv, The names which had first amounted to fifty had swelled into a hundred and thirteen. **1862** LATHAM *Channel Isl.* III. xvi. (ed. 2) 379 The number, however, soon swoll. **1895** *Times* 10 Jan. 5/1 The ranks of the unemployed are..daily swelling.

b. Of a receptacle: To be filled to overflowing. *poet*, *rare*.

1616 R. C. *Times' Whistle* (1871) 94 The husbandman, if that his crops proove well, Hath his heart fild with joy 'cause his barnes swell. **1908** [see SWELLING *ppl. a.* 4b].

5. a. *trans.* To make greater in amount, degree, or intensity; to increase, add to. Also with *out*, *up*. (See also 6b.)

1599 MARSTON *Antonio's Rev.* III. iii, And now swarte night, to swell thy hower out, Behold I spurt warme bloode in thy blacke eyes. **1653** W. RAMESEY *Astrol. Restored* 173 It is not for me to insist on every particular in every house, for that would swell this Volume to a bulk as large again as it is. **1754** GRAY *Pleasure* 50 The simplest note that swells the gale. **1781** GIBBON *Decl. & F.* xxi. (1787) II. 261 The presence of the monarch swelled the importance of the debate. **1849** MACAULAY *Hist. Eng.* x. II. 558 The prince's party was now swollen by many adherents who had previously stood aloof from it. **1867** AUGUSTA WILSON *Vashti* xxvii, The property left me by Mr. Evelyn swelled my estate to very unusual proportions. **1868** FREEMAN *Norm. Conq.* II. App. A. 518 The Winchester Annals swell out the story into a long romance. **1874** GREEN *Short Hist.* iv. § 2. 169 The long peace and prosperity of the realm [etc.] ..were swelling the ranks and incomes of the country gentry.

b. To fill (a receptacle) to overflowing. *poet. rare*.

1601 B. JONSON *Poetaster* III. i, Swell me a bowle with lustie wine. **1697** DRYDEN *Virg. Georg.* III. 484 The still distended Udders never fail; But when they seem exhausted swell the Pail.

c. *pa. pple.* (sense 4 or 5: cf. 3): Increased in amount or extent.

1641 J. JACKSON *True Evang. T.* III. 230 A..great Commentatour upon holy Scripture; whose volumes are swelled to that proportion that they take up halfe a *Classis* in our publique Libraries. **1675** G. HARVEY *Dis. Lond.* 296 This Treatise being swelled beyond my Intention. **1725** *Wodrow Corr.* (1843) III. 169, I have formed my first draught of Mr. Robert Bruce's Life, which is swelled very much.

d. To magnify; to exalt. Now *rare* or *Obs.*

1600 MARSTON, etc. *Jack Drums Entert.* I. (1601) A4b, After your decease your issue might swell out your name with pompe. [**1601** SHAKS. *All's Well* II. iii. 134 Where great additions swell's [= swell us], and vertue none, It is a dropsied honour.] **1796** MORSE *Amer. Geog.* II. 474 The emperor's titles are swelled with all the pomp of eastern magnificence. **1827** LYTTON *Pelham* lxvii, Those which we receive as trifles, swell themselves into a consequence we little dreamt of.

6. a. *intr.* Of sound, esp. music: To increase in volume, become gradually louder or fuller; to come upon the ear with increasing clearness, or with alternate increase and diminution of force. Also of a musical instrument: To give forth a swelling sound or note.

1749 SMOLLETT *Regic.* III. ii, The trumpet swells! **1769** GRAY *Installation Dk. Grafton* 24 Choral warblings round him swell. **1794** MRS. RADCLIFFE *Myst. Udolpho* xv, A chorus of voices and instruments now swelled on the air. **1842** TENNYSON *Sir Galahad* vii, Thro' the mountain-walls A rolling organ-harmony Swells up. **1891** FARRAR *Darkn. & Dawn* xxiv, Then the strain swelled louder.

b. *trans.* To utter with increase of force, or with increasing volume of sound. *rare*.

1775 J. STEELE *Ess. Melody Speech* 47 That speech.. which I..have noted in the stile of a ranting actor, swelled with *forte* and softened with *piano*. **1824** W. IRVING *T. Trav.* I. 326 The choir swelling an anthem in that solemn building. **1833** J. RUSH *Philos. Hum. Voice* (ed. 2) 203 But if the voice is swelled to a greater stress as it descends, the grave severity and dignified conviction of the speaker becomes at once conspicuous.

7. *fig. intr.* **a.** Of a feeling or emotion: To arise and grow in the mind with a sense as of distension or expansion.

c **1386** CHAUCER *Wife's T.* 111 Hir thoughte it swal so soore aboute hir herte, That nedely som word hire moste asterte. **1421–2** HOCCLEVE *Min. Poems* 96/29 The grefe abowte my harte so sore swal..That nedes oute I muste there-with-all. **1593** SHAKS. *Rich. II*, IV. i. 298 The vnseene Griefe That swells with silence in the tortur'd Soule. **1770** GOLDSM. *Des. Vill.* 82 Remembrance.. Swells at my breast, and turns the past to pain. **1848** DICKENS *Dombey* liv, Her purpose swelling in her breast. **1849** MACAULAY *Hist. Eng.* viii. II. 304 The spirit of Englishmen..swelled up high and strong against injustice. **1902** VIOLET JACOB *Sheep-Stealers* ix, Something swelled up in his heart.

b. Of a person, the heart, etc.: To be affected with such an emotion; to have a mental sensation as of enlargement or expansion; to be puffed up, become elated or arrogant. Const. *with* (esp. pride, indignation, etc.).

c **1386** CHAUCER *Knt.'s T.* 1885 Swelleth the brest of arcite and the soore Encreesseth at his herte. **14..** *Gower's Conf.* I. 54 Sche for anger þerof swal. **1576** GASCOIGNE *Philomene* xcv, Malice made Hir venging hart to swell. **1627** MAY *Lucan* VIII. (1631) 335 He swell'd to see Varus a suppliant growne. **1711** ADDISON *Spect.* No. 93 ¶5 His Heart burns with Devotion, swells with Hope. **1797** MRS. RADCLIFFE *Italian* i, Vivaldi's heart swelled at the mention of a rival. **1848** THACKERAY *Van. Fair* li, Little Becky's soul swelled with pride and delight at these honours. **1849** MACAULAY *Hist. Eng.* iii. I. 323 His stout English heart swelled with indignation at the thought. **1868** FREEMAN *Norm. Conq.* (1877) II. ix. 331 Events which may well make every English heart swell with pride.

8. *trans.* To affect with such an emotion; to cause a sense of enlargement in; to puff up, inflate. Often in pa. pple. (which may sometimes belong to the *intr.* sense, 7b); const. *with*. (Also said of the emotion.)

c **1200** *Vices & Virtues* 65 *Scientia inflat, karitas edificat.* He seið þat ðis scarpe iwitt swelð ðane mann, ðe hes haueð wiðuten charite. **14..** *Langland's P. Pl.* C. VII. 154 (MS. F.) 3it I spak no speche it swal so my breste, þat I chewed it as a cowe. *a* **1450** *Knt. de la Tour* cx, There be mani women that haue thayre hertys suolle fulle of pride. **1594** KYD *Cornelia* III. iii. 211 Caesar, swolne with honors heate, Sits signiorizing in her seate. **1597** SHAKS. *2 Hen. IV*, IV. v. 171 If it did..swell my Thoughts, to any straine of Pride. **1599** MARSTON *Antonio's Rev.* v. i, The States of Venice are so swolne in hate Against the Duke. **1649** MILTON *Eikon.* xi. 112 What other notions..could swell up Caligula to think himself a God? *c* **1685** POMFRET *Cruelty & Lust* 129 Swell'd with success, and blubber'd up with pride. **1741** WATTS *Improv. Mind* I. iii. §4 You value, exalt, and swell yourself as though you were a man of learning already. **1752** HUME *Ess. & Treat.* (1777) I. 231 Their heart, swoln with the tenderest sympathy and compassion. **1830** GREVILLE *Mem.* (1874) II. 65 Intoxicated with his Yorkshire honours, swollen with his own importance. **1891** HARDY *Tess* xl, Inwardly swollen with a renewal of sentiments that he had not quite reckoned with.

9. a. *intr.* To show proud or angry feeling in one's action or speech; to behave proudly, arrogantly, or overbearingly; to be 'puffed up'; to look or talk big. *Obs.* or *arch.* (partly merged in sense 10).

a **1250** *Owl & Night.* 7 Eyþer ayeyn oþer swal [*v.r.* svall], And let þat vuele mod vt al. **1526** TINDALE *1 Cor.* iv. 6 That one swell not agaynst another. *Ibid.* 18 Some swell as though I wolde come no more at you. **1553** T. WILSON *Rhet.* (1580) 130 When we heare one saie, sutche a man swelled, seyng a thyng against his minde, we gather that he was then more then halfe angrie. **1583** STUBBES *Anat. Abus.* II. (1882) 3 Herod and Nabuchadnezer swelling in sinne, and rising vp against the maiestie of God. **1593** NASHE *Christ's T.* Wks. 1904 II. 83 The rich Cittizen swells against the pryde of the prodigall Courtier; the prodigal Courtier swels against the welth of the Cittizen. **1599** MARSTON *Antonio's Rev.* II. ii. 109, I will not swell, like a tragedian, In forced passion of affected strains. **1648** MILTON *Ps. lxxxiii.* 5 Thy furious foes now swell And storm outrageously. *a* **1704** T. BROWN *Praise Poverty* Wks. 1720 I. 104 Men..being obliged to discard imaginary Merit, would seek the real, wou'd swell no more on the borrow'd Greatness of Ancestors. **1706** E. WARD *Wooden World Diss.* (1708) 79 Vex him then, and he shall swell and sputter like a roasted Apple.

b. Used in reference to turgid or inflated style of language.

1712 ADDISON *Spect.* No. 285 ¶6 He must not swell into a false Sublime, by endeavouring to avoid the other Extream.

10. To behave pompously or pretentiously, swagger; to play the 'swell'. Also with *it*.

1795 WOLCOT (P. Pindar) *Pindariana* Wks. 1812 IV. 183 Tis laughable to see a Frenchman swell. **1841** *Punch* 23 Oct. 178/2 Father Thames..has been 'swelling it'..through some of the streets of the metropolis. As if to inculcate temperance, he walked himself down into public-house cellars, filling all the empty casks with water. **1863** *Tyneside Songs* 22 Two sots wi' eyes a' bleary, Doon Sangyet street did swell. **1884** HOWELLS *Silas Lapham* (1891) I. 106, I couldn't have father swelling on so, without saying something. **1888** 'R. BOLDREWOOD' *Robbery under Arms* xii, While he was swelling it in the town among the big bugs.

swell-, the verb-stem in combination (in some cases also referable to the sb.): **swell-fish**, a fish that inflates itself by swallowing air, also called *puffer* or *puff-fish* (see PUFF *sb.* 9b); **swell-front** *U.S.*, a bow-front of a house, i.e. one segmentally curved on plan (see BOW *sb.*[1] 12 e); *transf.* a house having such a front; **swell-head** *colloq.* = *swelled head* (see SWELLED b); also, a person affected with 'swelled head'; **swell-headed** *a. colloq.*, affected with 'swelled head'; **swell-rule** *Printing* (RULE *sb.* 22), a 'rule' or dash of swelling (usually diamond) form in the middle (Jacobi *Printers' Voc.* 1888); **swell-shark**, (*a*) a small shark, *Scyllium ventricosum*, of the Pacific coast of America; (*b*) a Californian shark, *Catulus uter*, which when caught inflates itself by swallowing air; **swell-work**, work characterized by enlargement or protuberance in certain parts designed for ornament.

1839 STORER in *Boston Jrnl. Nat. Hist.* II. 513 *Tetraodon turgidus*, Mitchell. The *Swell Fish. Puffer. **1860** O. W. HOLMES *Elsie V.* xxxii. (1891) 484, I was walking with a young friend along by the *swell-fronts and south-exposures. **1872** HOWELLS *Wedd. Journ.* (1892) 67 A humble three-story swell-front up at the South End. **1845** J. J. HOOPER *Some Adventures Simon Suggs* iv. 46 As for the present directory, they're all a pack of d——d *swell-heads. **1867** G. W. HARRIS *Sut Lovingood* 61 Wif an onintemitant attack of swell-head. **1884** *St. James's Gaz.* 10 May 5/1 'Mugwump'..is 'synonymous with the New York term "big bug," or the Washington expression "swellhead".' **1901** G. DOUGLAS *House w. Green Shutters* 214 Lord, but young Gourlay was the fine fellow! Symptoms of swell-head set in with alarming rapidity. **1817** COBBETT *Wks.* XXXII. 43 The upstart, big-bellied, *swell-headed farmer can bluster and bully..about Sinecures. **1906** *Daily Chron.* 11 May 7/3 Gangs of swell-headed agents in plain clothes.. persecuting inoffensive citizens. **1891** *Cent. Dict.* s.v. *Scyllium*, *S. ventricosum* is the *swell-shark, a small voracious species found on the Pacific coast from California to Chili. **1833** J. HOLLAND *Manuf. Metal* II. 198 The various descriptions of reeded and other *swell-work, exhibited by some superb brass fenders.

swelldom ('swɛldəm). *colloq.* [f. SWELL *sb.* 9 + -DOM.] The realm or world of 'swells'; people of rank and fashion, or of distinction of any kind.

1855 THACKERAY *Newcomes* xliii, When all Swelldom is at her feet. **1864** J. R. GREEN *Lett.* II. (1901) 152, I..discover what a false pretence antiquarian swelldom is. **1885** *Graphic* 21 Feb. 174/2 In the railway train, we sit either in exclusive 'swelldom' in the first, or herd with 'the vulgar' in the third class.

swelle, obs. form of SWALLOW *v.*, SWELL.

swelled (swɛld), *ppl. a.* [Weak pa. pple. of SWELL *v.*: see -ED[1]. Less frequent as an adj. in most senses than the strong pa. pple. SWOLLEN.]

a. In senses of SWELL *v.*, *lit.* and *fig.*; *esp.* in sense 'morbidly enlarged, affected with tumour'.

1611 SHAKS. *Cymb.* v. v. 162 Hearing vs praise our Loues of Italy For Beauty, that made barren the swell'd boast Of him that best could speake. **1670** DRYDEN *1st Pt. Conq. Granada* II. i, The swell'd Ambition of his Mind. **1726** *Dict. Rust.*, *Swelled pizzle*, a kind of hardness that proceeds from a Horse's being bruised by Riding. **1733** in *10th Rep. Hist. MSS. Comm.* App. I. 251 He has so bad a cold, and swelled face. **1753** J. BARTLET *Gentl. Farriery* 296 *margin*, How swelled heels should be treated. **1842** *Civil Eng. & Arch. Jrnl.* V. 81/2 Swelled Friezes.—This invention bears a close resemblance to an article of dress said to have been used by our great grandmothers, called a bustle. **1869** TANNER *Clin. Med.* (ed. 2) 312 The symptoms..are..fœtid breath, swelled belly, emaciated extremities. **1913** DORLAND *Med. Dict.*, *Roup*, an infectious respiratory disease of poultry.. sometimes called avian diphtheria and swelled head.

b. *swelled head* (fig.): inordinate self-conceit, excessive pride or vanity (humorously regarded as a morbid affection); also, a person affected with 'swelled head'. *colloq.* Hence *swelled-headedness*.

Cf. the earlier *swell-head(ed* s.v. SWELL-.

1862 *Harper's Mag.* June 33/1 He was set down as a born aristocrat and 'swelled head'. **1891** KIPLING *Light that Failed* iv. 69 Dick, it is of common report that you are suffering from swelled head. **1900** *Times* 7 July 10/1 The Queen's-hall was filled with swelled heads, and, judging from your correspondent's note, the swelled heads elected one of their own body. **1907** E. REICH (*title*) Germany's Swelled Head. *Ibid.* 1 The Germans are afflicted with the severest attack of swelled-headedness known to modern history.

sweller ('swɛlə(r)). *rare.* [f. SWELL *v.* + -ER[1].] One who or that which swells.

c **1374** CHAUCER *Boeth.* III. pr. vi. (1868) 77 O glorie glorie, ..þou nart no þing ellys to þousandes of folkes but a gret sweller of eres [orig. *auribus inflatio magna*].

swellie, obs. Sc. form of SWALLOW *sb.*[2] and *v.*

swelling ('swɛlɪŋ), *vbl. sb.* [f. SWELL *v.* + -ING[1]. In OE. *swelling* (once); cf. MLG. *swillinge*, MDu., MHG. *swellinge*.]

1. The process of becoming, or condition of having become, larger in bulk, as by internal pressure; distension, dilatation, expansion.

1577 B. GOOGE *Heresbach's Husb.* I. (1586) 39 The waxing yellowe, and swelling of the knoppes that holde the seede. **1593** NASHE *Christ's T.* (1613) 145 They shew the swellings of their mind, in the swellings and plumpings out of their apparrayle. **1688** HOLME *Armoury* III. 259/2 *Swelling*, is to give it [*sc.* the metal] its shape, and make it proportionable. **1780** SIR J. REYNOLDS *Disc.* x. (1876) 10 There is given to Hercules an extraordinary swelling and strength of muscles. **1842** LOUDON *Suburban Hort.* 32 The swelling of the buds, and the expansion of the leaves. **1875** BENNETT & DYER tr. *Sachs' Bot.* III. iv. 697 These organised bodies are..all capable of swelling; *i.e.* they have the power of absorbing water or aqueous solutions between their solid particles with such force that the particles are forced apart.

b. *concr.* A swollen, distended, or protuberant part of something; a protuberance, prominence; †a swell of ground.

In OE. applied to a bellying sail.

a **900** CYNEWULF *Elene* 245 (Gr.) þær meahte ʒesion, se ðone sið beheold, brecan ofer bæðweʒ, brimwudu snyrʒan under swellingum. **1615** CROOKE *Body of Man* 732 The fleshy swellings which the Chyromanticks call hyllockes or Monticles do make the brawne or pulpe of the hand. **1630** *R. Johnson's Kingd. & Commw.* 43 Mountaines be naturall swellings of the earth, above the usuall levell or surface of it. *a* **1634** CHAPMAN & SHIRLEY *Chabot* II. iii. 139 He..cannot ..stand at all parts So truly circular, so sound, and solid, But have his swellings-out, his cracks and crannies. **1679** [see SWELL *v.* 1c]. *a* **1700** EVELYN *Diary* 10 Sept. 1677, Euston.. is seated in a bottome between two gracefull swellings. **1789** J. WILLIAMS *Min. Kingd.* II. 368 Some of the bellies, pipes, or swellings of the veins. **1834–5** J. PHILLIPS *Geol.* in *Encycl. Metrop.* VI. 702/2 The little pillars [*sc.* of the bridge over the Wear] are worked with various swellings and mouldings. **1847** W. C. L. MARTIN *Ox* 15/1 The convexity and bold swellings of the forehead. **1883** M. P. BALE *Saw-Mills* 337 *Swelling*, an excrescence upon the exterior of a tree. **1885** C. G. W. LOCK *Workshop Receipts* Ser. IV. 232/2 Too thick a thread will make the 'swelling' (the rising caused in the back by the thread) too much.

2. *spec.* Abnormal or morbid distension or enlargement of some bodily part or member.

Also in *Path.* with defining words, as *cloudy swelling*, a form of albuminous degeneration of various tissues

(Billings); ***glassy swelling***, amyloid degeneration (Dorland); ***white swelling***, a form of swelling without redness, *spec.* (*a*) a tuberculous arthritis; strumous synovitis of a joint; (*b*) *phlegmasia alba dolens* (see PHLEGMASIA), milk-leg, white-leg.

1377 LANGL. *P. Pl.* B. v. 122 May no sugre ne swete þynge asswage my swellynge. **1382** WYCLIF *Acts* xxviii. 6 Thei gessiden him to be turned into swellinge, and sudenly to fallinge, and for to deie. **1398** TREVISA *Barth. De P.R.* v. xxviii. (Bodl. MS.), Fulnes blaynes and bladdres swellinges. **14..** *Langland's P. Pl.* A. VII. 204 (MS. U.) For swellynge of heore wombes. **1573** TUSSER *Husb.* (1878) 52 If ratling or swelling get once to the throte, Thou loosest thy porkling. **1592** KYD *Murther I. Brewen* Wks. (1901) 289 A strong deadly poyson whose working was to make speedy haste to the heart, without any swelling of the body, or other signe of outward confection. *a* **1604** HANMER *Chron. Irel.* (1809) 156 Her shinne, her knee, and her thigh,..and some parts above, tooke swelling. **1702** J. PURCELL *Cholick* (1714) 15 There is no Swelling, neither does any Pain follow from thence. **1704** *Dict. Rust.* (1726), *Swelling*, a disease which Goats are apt to be troubled with, after they have brought forth their Young. **1803** *Med. Jrnl.* IX. 374 The remedies for white swelling. **1872** T. BRYANT *Pract. Surg.* (1884) I. 69 When a visible part is inflamed, there are four notable phenomena to be observed, namely:—redness, heat, pain, and swelling.

b. *concr.* An abnormal or morbid enlargement in or upon any part or member; a tumour.

1542–3 *Act 34 & 35 Hen. VIII*, c. 8 §3 Any..outwarde swelling or disease. **1577** B. GOOGE *Heresbach's Husb.* III. (1586) 143 The swelling betwixt the two Clewes must be cut. **1650** W. D. tr. *Comenius' Gate Lat. Unl.* §307 A swelling riseth (swelleth up) and falleth again. **1704** *Dict. Rust.* (1726) s.v. *Swelled*, Swellings or Tumours in Horses, come by Heats, by hard Riding or by sore Labour. *c* **1720** DE FOE *Mem. Cavalier* I. 28 The Swelling broke. **1789** W. BUCHAN *Dom. Med.* (1790) 399 The white swellings of the joints. **1808** SCOTT in Lockhart *Life* (1839) I. i. 13 The slightest cold occasioned swellings in her face. **1835** *Cycl. Pract. Med.* II. 738/1 The swelling may be fixed or moveable.

3. The rising of water above its ordinary level (as of a river in flood); the swell (of the sea); the rise (of the tide); the welling up (of a spring). *Obs.* or *arch.*

1557 *Tottel's Misc.* (Arb.) 190 Hie springes may cease from swellyng styll, but neuer dry away. **1560** *Bible* (Genev.) Jer. xii. 5 What wilt thou do in the swelling of Iorden? **1601** HOLLAND *Pliny* III. v. I. 58 He [*sc.* the Tiber] hath many and those suddaine swellings. **1754** FIELDING *Voy. Lisbon* Wks. 1882 VII. 112 My whole comfort was to find, by the captain's relation, that the swelling was sometimes much worse. **1764** J. FERGUSON *Lect.* ii. 27 The swelling of the tide..occasioned by the influence of the moon.

b. *concr.* A swelling wave, tide, or flood. *Obs.* or *arch.*

1387 TREVISA *Higden* (Rolls) VIII. 231 Þe swellynge of þe see as mylk we schal souke. **1560** *Bible* (Genev.) Jer. xlix. 19 He shal come vp like a lyon from the swelling of Iorden. **1676** OTWAY *Don Carlos* III. i, Rock'd on the Swellings of the floating Tide. **1697** DRYDEN *Æneid* VIII. 120 He rowld his River back; and pois'd he stood; A gentle Swelling, and a peaceful Flood. **1781** COWPER *Retirem.* 527 He swathes about the swelling of the deep. **1905** J. B. BURY *Life St. Patrick* vii. 134 He first crossed over a river-swelling, and then found a second swelling in front of him.

4. Of sound: see SWELL *v.* 6; cf. SWELL *sb.* 5.

1818 KEATS *Endym.* I. 117 A faint breath of music.. Within a little space again it gave Its airy swellings, with a gentle wave.

5. *fig.* Inflation by pride, vanity, etc.; proud, haughty, or indignant feeling; also, proud or arrogant behaviour or talk, swagger. *Obs.* or *arch.*

c **1386** CHAUCER *Pars. T.* ¶ 324 Swellynge of herte is whan a man reioyseth hym of harm that he hath doon. *c* **1410** *Lanterne of Liȝt* iii. 6 Euery proud soule þat risiþ in swelling aȝens his God. *c* **1425** *Cursor M.* 12083 (Trin.) Þourȝe swellyng of his herte To Ioseph spake he wordis smerte. **1535** COVERDALE *2 Cor.* xii. 20, I feare..lest there be among you, debates, envyenges, wrathes, stryuynges, bacbytinges, whysperinges, swellinges, vproures. **1593** NASHE *Christ's T.* Wks. 1904 II. 83 From the rich to the poore (in euery street in London) there is ambition, or swelling aboue theyr states. **1625** BACON *Ess., Truth* (Arb.) 501 So alwaies, that this prospect, be with Pitty, and not with Swelling, or Pride. *a* **1639** WOTTON *Portraict. Chas. I* in *Reliq.* (1685) 156 In your aspect no swelling, nothing boysterous. **1711** ADDISON *Spect.* No. 40 ¶5 Their Swelling and Blustring upon the Stage very much recommends them to the fair Part of their Audience. **1756** BURKE *Subl. & Beaut.* I. xvii, A sort of swelling and triumph, that is extemely grateful to the human mind. **1825** SCOTT *Talism.* xxv, Thus the proud swelling of his heart further suggested.

6. The rising *of* emotion.

1709 *Tatler* No. 114 ¶1 My heart was torn in pieces to see the Husband..suppressing and keeping down the swellings of his grief. **1750** JOHNSON *Rambler* No. 29 ¶9 To repress the swellings of vain hope.

'swelling, *ppl. a.* [f. as prec. + -ING².] That swells, in various senses.

1. Increasing in bulk, as by absorption or inflation; becoming distended or filled out; bellying, as a sail; undergoing morbid enlargement, breaking out as a tumour.

c **1000** ÆLFRIC *Exod.* ix. 9 Swellende blæddran. *c* **1000** *Sax. Leechd.* II. 6 Wiþ ælcre yfelre swellendre wætan. **1382** WYCLIF *Exod.* ix. 10 Woundes of the swellynge bleynes. *a* **1591** H. SMITH *Wks.* (1867) II. 397 Botches and swelling sores. *c* **1591** ROYDON *Elegy for Astrophel* i, No swelling clouds accloyed the air. **1697** DRYDEN *Virg. Past.* III. 129 The Show'rs are grateful to the swelling Grain. —— *Georg.* I. 269 The hissing Serpent, and the swelling Toad. —— *Æneid* III. 692 Breath on our swelling Sails a prosp'rous Wind. *a* **1721** PRIOR *Past. Dial.* 5 Young tender Plants and swelling buds appear. **1859** *Habits Gd. Society* ii. (new ed.) 121 Swelling glands are prevented. **1877** RAYMOND *Statist. Mines & Mining* 156 The swelling ground crushes in the timbers.

b. *causatively.* Producing distension. *rare.*

1398 TREVISA *Barth. De P.R.* VII. viii. (Bodl. MS.) lf. 50/2 He schalle spare swelling metes and greete [orig. *ab inflatiuis cibis*].

2. Having the form of something distended; protuberant, bulging; rising evenly and smoothly above the general surface, as a hill or piece of ground.

1544 *N. Country Wills* (Surtees 1908) 194 An olde gowne with a swelling welte faced with blacke budge. *a* **1586** SIDNEY *Arcadia* III. xvi. (1912) 447 Her roundy sweetly swelling lippes a little trembling. **1667** MILTON *P.L.* IV. 495 Half her swelling Breast Naked met his. **1697** DRYDEN *Æneid* v. 15 A swelling Cloud hung hov'ring o're their Head. **1728** R. MORRIS *Ess. Anc. Archit.* 43 There is less Substance in the streight Column..than there is in that which is swelling. **1794** COLERIDGE *Fears in Solit.* 4 The hills are heathy, save that swelling slope. **1839** MURCHISON *Silur. Syst.* I. xxvi. 331 The hard volcanic grit wraps round the swelling concretionary masses of this trap. **1872** JENKINSON *Engl. Lake Distr.* (1879) 287 The great swelling masses of Whiteside and Grasmoor are directly opposite.

3. Rising in waves, or as a wave; rising in level, becoming fuller, as a river or the tide. Chiefly *poet.*

1549 *Compl. Scot.* vi. 39 Throcht virkyng of the suelland vallis of the brym seye. **1582** STANYHURST *Æneis* I. (Arb.) 19 This Queene..Doune swasht theyre nauy, thee swelling surges vp-haling. **1585** JAS. I *Ess. Poesie* (Arb.) 72 Ilk saile Of dyuers ships vpon the swolling wawes. **1610** HOLLAND *Camden's Brit.* (1637) 241 Rivers, swelling Brookes, and rils of ever-living fountaines. **1633** P. FLETCHER *Pisc. Ecl.* VII. xix, The earth her robe, the sea her swelling tide. **1745** P. THOMAS *Jrnl. Anson's Voy.* 53 We had a great swelling Sea. **1746** COLLINS *Ode to Evening* ix, Be mine the hut That from the mountain's side Views wilds and swelling floods.

b. *transf.* Becoming full to overflowing, as the eyes with tears; said also of the tears.

1593 SHAKS. *Lucr.* 1228 The maid with swelling drops gan wet Her circled eien. **1596** —— *1 Hen. IV*, III. i. 202 That pretty Welsh Which thou powr'st down from these swelling Heauens. **1760–72** H. BROOKE *Fool of Qual.* (1809) III. 103 Taking out her handkerchief, she wiped away a swelling tear. *Ibid.* 141 With..trembling lips, and swelling eyes.

4. Becoming greater in amount, increasing, growing; *loosely*, great in amount, full, abundant. *rare.*

1628 FELTHAM *Resolves* II. [I.] i. 1 Hee carelesly waues himselfe in the swelling plenty. **1829** SCOTT *Anne of G.* xxvii, To supply the public wants from their own swelling hoards! **1854** *Poultry Chron.* I. 61/2 Witness our weekly swelling list of promised exhibitions.

b. Of a receptacle: see SWELL *v.* 4 b. *poet.*

1908 *Blackw. Mag.* Oct. 538 There easier toil Brings to the swelling bin a more abundant spoil.

5. Of sound: Gradually increasing in force or volume; becoming louder and fuller.

1753 HOGARTH *Anal. Beauty* xii. 97 As the gradating shade pleases the eye, so the increasing, or swelling note, delights the ear. **1797** MRS. RADCLIFFE *Italian* xxii, Hearing at intervals swelling though feeble groans. **1810** SCOTT *Lady of Lake* I. x, The dingle's hollow throat Prolong'd the swelling bugle-note.

†**b.** ***swelling organ***, an earlier name for the swell organ (see SWELL *sb.* 6). *Obs.*

1712 in Grove *Dict. Mus.* (1889) IV. 8 [The first attempt at a] swelling organ [was made by Jordan in 1712]. **1837** *Stranger's Guide York* (ed. 6) 77 There are..9 [stops] to the choir organ, 12 to the swelling organ.

6. *fig.* Of a feeling or emotion (usually pleasurable): Arising and growing in the mind with expansive force; causing the heart to 'swell' with emotion.

1593 SHAKS. *3 Hen. VI*, IV. viii. 42 My mildnesse hath allay'd their swelling griefes. **1697** COLLIER *Ess. Mor. Subj.* II. (1703) 64 A swelling discontent is apt to suffocate and strangle, without passage. **1700** PRIOR *Carmen Seculare* iii, They scarce Their swelling Thirst of Fame could hide. **1749** FIELDING *Tom Jones* XII. x, The warm, solid content, the swelling satisfaction, the thrilling transports. **1760–72** H. BROOKE *Fool of Qual.* (1809) IV. 82 He..hid the tears of his swelling delight.

7. Inflated, or showing inflation, with pride or the like; proud, haughty; arrogant, puffed up. **a.** Of the heart, mind, etc.; †rarely of the person.

a **1586** SIDNEY *Ps.* XVII. viii, Cruell wordes their swelling tongues do chatt. **1604** SHAKS. *Oth.* II. iii. 57 Three else of Cyprus, Noble swelling Spirites... Haue I to night fluster'd with flowing cups. **1630** tr. *Camden's Hist. Eliz.* I. 91 She, to restraine the young Kings swelling minde,..had begun to set her husbands name after her owne in the publicke Acts. **1702** ROWE *Tamerl.* I. ii. 684 While th' avenging hand of Heav'n is on thee And presses to the Dust thy swelling Soul. **1735** JOHNSON *Lobo's Abyssinia, Descr.* x. 106 The ridiculous Speculations of those swelling Philosophers, whose Arrogance would prescribe Laws to Nature. **1846** MRS. A. MARSH *Father Darcy* II. xi. 201 'Insulting!' said the proudly swelling heart.

b. Of the feeling or mental state; †also of speech (*obs.*).

1579 W. WILKINSON *Confut. Fam. Love* 6 b, His swellyng wordes of vanitie. **1590** NASHE *Pasquil's Apol.* I. Wks. 1904 I. 114 Thys swelling and sawcie humour..against her Maiesties right honourable priuie Counsell. **1610** HOLLAND *Camden's Brit.* (1637) 108 Possessed they were with swelling pride. **1680** ROSCOMMON *Horace's Art of Poetry* Poet. Wks. (1749) 155 Peleus and Telephus, exil'd and poor, Forget their swelling and gigantic words. **1817** CHALMERS *Astron. Disc.* iv. (1852) 92 What an impressive rebuke does it bring on the swelling vanity of science. **1843** BORROW *Bible in Spain* xxxvi, Insignificant are the results of man's labours compared with the swelling ideas of his presumption.

8. Of style or language: Grand, magnificent, stately, majestic; usually in bad sense, Inflated, bombastic, turgid, pretentiously pompous.

1596 SHAKS. *Merch. V.* I. i. 124 A more swelling port Then my faint meanes would grant continuance. **1597** MORLEY *Introd. Mus.* 183 To decke a lowlie matter with loftie and swelling speech. **1599** SHAKS. *Hen. V*, I. Prol. 4 O for..A Kingdome for a Stage, Princes to Act, And Monarchs to behold the swelling Scene. **1617** PURCHAS *Pilgrimage* v. xi. §2 (ed. 3) 634 The swelling stile of this King of Bisnagar. *a* **1661** FULLER *Worthies* (1662) II. 127 His stile, conceived by some to be swelling, is allowed for lofty and full by others. **1680** MORDEN *Geog. Rect., Spain* (1685) 171 The Vulgar Spanish or Castilian..is said to be a brave lofty swelling Speech. **1712** ADDISON *Spect.* No. 279 ¶5 Those swelling Sentiments which are so frequent in Statius. **1812** H. & J. SMITH *Rej. Addr.* x. (1873) 92 A swelling opening is too often succeeded by an insignificant Conclusion. **1846** KEIGHTLEY *Notes Virg., Bucol.* v. 36 Perhaps this [sc. *mandavimus*] is too swelling a term for bucolic simplicity. *a* **1859** MACAULAY *Hist. Eng.* xxiii. (1861) V. 6 Those swelling sentiments of liberty which abound in the Latin poets and orators. **1895** M. R. JAMES *Abbey St. Edmund at Bury* 125, I will render Leland's swelling Latin into literal English.

swellingly ('swɛlɪŋlɪ), *adv.* [f. prec. + -LY².] In a swelling manner; with swelling form or outline; also, with swelling sound; *fig.* grandiloquently, †bombastically.

a **1652** BROME *City Wit* IV. i, As for Corantoes, &c.—I speak it not swellingly, but I subscribe to no man. **1833** L. RITCHIE *Wand. Loire* 180 Meadows and cultivated fields sweep swellingly away from the water's edge. **1839** *Fraser's Mag.* XIX. 215 No longer Pyrrhias, Dromio, Tibias, But Megabyzus, Megacles, Protarchus Swellingly styled. **1879** MEREDITH *Egoist* vii, He was of a sensitiveness terribly tender. A single stroke on it reverberated swellingly within the man. **1894** *Cornh. Mag.* Jan. 91 As burly a billow of cloud as ever sailed swellingly over the broad Atlantic.

swellish ('swɛlɪʃ), *a. colloq.* [f. SWELL *sb.* 9 + -ISH¹.] Characteristic of or befitting a 'swell'; stylish, dandified. Hence **'swellishness**.

1820 *Sporting Mag.* VII. 144 The look of Williams was swellish in the extreme. **1856** in *Brasenose Ale* 133 Which ornament [*sc.* the moustache] (swellish, yet somewhat *outré*), Can be only assumed with the hood of B.A. **1863** W. H. KNIGHT *Diary of Pedestrian in Cashmere & Thibet* v. 186 One..group of Mahomedan exquisites..had, in addition to their heavy swellishness, an air of Eastern listlessness. **1890** JEAN MIDDLEMASS *Two False Moves* II. xiii. 198 The bigger the swell, the more money he expects to get for his swellishness and his title.

swellism ('swɛlɪz(ə)m). *colloq.* [f. SWELL *sb.* 9 + -ISM.] The character, style, or practice of a 'swell'.

1840 *Tait's Mag.* VII. 796/2 The only point of swellism which the Lord Advocate usually lacks, is white kids. **1870** MISS BRIDGMAN *R. Lynne* II. ix. 188 Selwyn would be.. contemptuous of Blake's swellism.

swell mob, -mobsman: see SWELL *a.* c.

swellness ('swɛlnɪs). *rare.* In 6 swellenes. [f. SWELL *sb.* or *v.* + -NESS.]

†**1.** Protuberance. *Obs.*

a **1583** in Halliwell *Rara Mathem.* (1841) 38 You shall see youre owne face..to bee in swellenes accordinge to the forme of the hylling or bossing outwardes.

2. The condition of a 'swell' or person of distinction. *colloq.*

1894 HUXLEY in *Life* (1900) II. xxii. 373 My swellness is an awful burden.

swelluing, obs. f. SWALLOWING.

swelly ('swɛlɪ), *sb. Coal-mining.* (*north. dial.*) Also **swally, swolly.** [? Local variant of SWALLOW *sb.*² Cf. SWILLY *sb.*] A depression in coal strata; a local thickening in a seam of coal.

1849 GREENWELL *Coal-trade Terms Northumb. & Durh.* (1851) 54 *Swelly*, or *Swally*, a gradual depression or dish in the strata. **1863** WARRINGTON SMITH *Addr. Brit. Assoc.*, Swellies, or narrow depressions in the Low Main coal. **1883** GRESLEY *Gloss. Coal-mining*, *Swelly*, also *Swally*, also *Swilly*.

'swelly, *a. rare*⁻¹. [f. SWELL *sb.* + -Y.] Characterized by swells.

1722 W. HAMILTON *Wallace* 123 So Triton when at Neptun's high Command He heaves the swelly Surge above the Land.

swelly, obs. Sc. form of SWALLOW *v.*

swellynge, obs. f. SWALLOWING, SWELLING.

†**swelme.** *Obs.* [f. *swel-*, root of SWEAL *v.* + *-m* suffix. Cf. early mod.G. *schwelm* 'fomes'.] The heat (of anger or the like).

13.. *E.E. Allit. P.* C. 3 When heuy herttes ben hurt wyth heþyng oþer elles, Suffraunce may aswagen hem & þe swelme leþe. *a* **1400–50** *Wars Alex.* 750 Alexander..Lete a-swage or he sware þe swelme of his angirs.

sweloghe, -owe, obs. ff. SWALLOW *sb.*² and *v.*

swelp, perversion of *so help*, in the oath 'so help me God': see SO *adv.* and *conj.* 19, and cf. S'ELP, S'HELP.

1894 [see DICKEN, DICKIN *int.*]. **1899** WHITEING *No. 5 John St.* vi. 54 Swelp me lucky I ain't tellin' yer no lie! **1901** H.

FURNISS *Confess. Caricaturist* I. vii. 283 Your hasting steed pull up, I say! S'welp me, draw your rein! **1937** N. MARSH *Vintage Murder* x. 112 It's true... S'welp me. **1981** J. BARNETT *Firing Squad* vii. 74 'Think again—harder.' 'Swelp me, Mr Smiff—.'

swelt (swɛlt), *v.* Now *dial.* Forms: 1 **sweltan**, 2–4 **swelten**, (*Ormin* **swelltenn**), 4–6 **swelte**, (4 **suelt, squelt, swellte**, 5, 8 **swalt**), 4– **swelt**. *Pa. t.* 1 **swealt**, *pl.* **swulton**, *Northumb. wk.* **-suelte**, 3 *Ormin* **swallt**, *pl.* **swulltenn**, 4–5 **swalt, swelte**, 4–6 **suelt, swelt**, 4– **swelted**, (9 **sweltit, swilted**). *Pa. pple.* 1 **ȝeswolten**, 4, 7 **swelt**, 5 **sweltid**, 6 **swolt**, 6– **swelted**. [Com. Teut. str. vb.: OE. *sweltan*, pa. t. *swealt*, *swulton*, pa. pple. *ȝeswolten* = OS. *sweltan*, pa. t. *swalt* to die, MDu. *swelten* to faint, die, OHG. *swelzan* (MHG. *swelzen*) to burn away, languish, ON. *svelta*, pa. t. *svalt*, *svultu*, pa. pple. *soltinn* to die, starve, (Sw. *svälta*, *svalt*, *sultin* to die of hunger, Da. *sulte* to hunger, starve, back-formation f. pa. pple. *sulten* hungry, dial. *svelta*, pa. t. *svalt*, *svolt*, pa. pple. *svolten*, *svulten*, *svoltet*), Goth. *swiltan*, pa. t. *swalt*, *swultum*, pa. pple. *swultans* to die.

The Teut. root *swelt-*: *swalt-*: *swult-* appears also in ON. *svelta* (causative) to put to death, starve, Crim-Gothic *swalth* death, Goth. *swultawairþja* near to death, ON. *sultr* hunger (MSw. *sulter*, Da. *sult*, dial. *svolt*, *svult*), OE. *swylt* (:—**swultiz*) death, *swyltan* to die, and prob. SULTER. It is perhaps a secondary formation on the root *swel-* to burn slowly (see SWEAL *v.*). As in other Germanic languages, the word has in ME. the sense of 'faint, languish', which is not, however, recorded for OE.]

I. *intr.* **1.** To die, perish.

Beowulf 892 (Gr.) Draca morðre swealt. *c* **888** ÆLFRED *Boeth.* x. §1 Mænegum men is leofre þæt he ær self swelte ær he gesio his wif & his bearn sweltende. *c* **1000** ÆLFRIC *Saints' Lives* iii. 592 þu scealt sweltan synna and criste lybban. *c* **1000** —— *Exod.* xxi. 12 Se þe mann þe wundað and wyle hine ofslean swelte he deaðe. *c* **1200** *Trin. Coll. Hom.* 181 Gief þu etest of þe forbodene trewe, þu shalt adeðe swelte. *c* **1200** ORMIN 5321 Þe Laferrd Cristess posstles, þatt ..forr to reȝȝsenn Crisstenndom, Full bliþelike swulltenn. **13..** *E.E. Allit. P.* A. 816 For vus he swalt in Ierusalem. *c* **1375** *Sc. Leg. Saints* xvii. (*Martha*) 197 Vith þat scho swelt, & gawe þe gest. *a* **1400** *Minor Poems fr. Vernon MS.* 615/111 For to winne al þis werld þat swelte vndur þe deueles swerd. *c* **1400** *Destr. Troy* 10905 With swappis of hor swordes swelt mony knightes. *c* **1460** *Towneley Myst.* xxi. 280 My hart is fulle cold nerehand that I swelt. **1513** DOUGLAS *Æneis* VIII. Prol. 5 Swownand as he suelt wald. **1535** STEWART *Cron. Scot.* (Rolls) I. 144 Mony ane swolt and mony fell in swoun. *Ibid.* II. 661 He slew him self thair suddantlie and suelt. **1794** W. HUTCHINSON *Hist. Cumbld.* I. 220 *note*, Provincial words: *swelting* for expiring. **1897** in *Eng. Dial. Dict.*

2. To be ready to perish with the force of strong emotion, or a fit of sickness; to be overcome, faint, swoon.

In the 16th c. the notion of fainting from the *heat* of emotion prevailed: cf. 3.

c **1320** *Sir Tristr.* 242 Sorwe it was to se, þat leuedi swelted swiþe. *c* **1350** *Will. Palerne* 4268 Sche swelt for sorwe & swoned rit þere. *c* **1374** CHAUCER *Troylus* III. 347 His olde wo þat made his herte to swelte. *c* **1400** *Destr. Troy* 8319 With Swym vnder swerd swalton full mony. *c* **1430** LYDG. *Min. Poems* (Percy Soc.) 38 Aboute his hert he thoughte he gan to swelt. *a* **1450** *Knt. de la Tour* xxxiv, God..sent the ladi suche a sodein sikenesse that she swalt there she stode, and that no man wost whedir she shulde leue or deye. *c* **1480** HENRYSON *Mor. Fab., Fox, Wolf & Cadger* xxxiii, He..hit him with sic will vpoun the heid, Quhill neir he swonit and swalt [*v.r.* swelt]. **1565** GOLDING *Ovid's Met.* III. (1593) 70, I do both set on fire, And am the same that swelteth too through impotent desire. **1575** GASCOIGNE *Dan Bartholomew* Wks. 1907 I. 109 When absent Troylus did in sorowes swelt. **1596** SPENSER *F.Q.* IV. vii. 9 Her deare hart nigh swelt, And eft gan into tender teares to melt. *a* **1643** W. CARTWRIGHT *Ordinary* III. i, I swelt here as I go; Brenning in fire of little Cupido. **1691** NICHOLSON in Ray *N.C. Words* 149 To Swelt, *deficere*, to Sownd. **1703** ELIZ. WEST in *Mem.* (1865) 216, I was in such an extreme trouble that..vent it must have, or then I must swelt. **1836** M. MACKINTOSH *Cottager's Daughter* 99 When she heard that she sweltit at their feet. **1850** *Tales Kirkbeck* Ser. II. 197, I felt sae sick and unsattled, an' then a' at ance I clean swilted awa.

3. To be overpowered or faint with heat; to suffer oppressive heat, swelter, 'melt'. †Also *refl.*

c **1386** CHAUCER *Miller's T.* 516 Wel litel thynken ye.. That for youre loue I swete ther I go, No wonder is thogh that I swelte and swete. *c* **1400** *Laud Troy Bk.* 9278 Many on swalt In his owne gres. *a* **1500** *Flower & Leaf* (Skeat) 360 The ladies eek to-brent..The Knightes swelt, for lak of shade ny shent. **1583** MELBANCKE *Philotimus* E e j, Here did Philotimus that swet and swelted almost, sette himselfe to refreshe his weakned limmes. **1591** SYLVESTER *Du Bartas* I. v. 271 In a cold sweat, shaking, and swelt almost. **1600** MORLEY *Madrigals to foure Voices* xvi, Soft a while, not away so fast, they melt them. Piper! Piper! Piper! Be hang'd a while knaue, looke, the dauncers swelt them. **1614** GORGES *Lucan* I. 39 The Fire would then the Earth haue melt, And with thy flames the heau'ns haue swelt. **1768** ROSS *Helenore* II. 82 Wi' faut an' heat I just was like to swelt, An' in a very blob o' sweat to melt. **1820** KEATS *Isabella* xiv, And for them many a weary hand did swelt In torched mines and noisy factories.

†**b.** To burn or rage as with fever. *Obs.*

1590 SPENSER *F.Q.* I. vii. 6 Till..chearefull bloud in faintnesse chill did melt, Which like a feuer fit through all his body swelt. *Ibid.* III. xi. 27 With huge impatience he inly swelt.

†**4.** To exude with heat. *Obs.*

c **1530** *Judic. Urines* I. ii. 2 All the Iuce and all the humydyte sweteth and swelteth oute of hym to the lyuer. Ryght as mylke swelteth & sweteth oute of the koowes body in to the vdder. **1614** GORGES *Lucan* x. 445 Each where the pitch and tarre that melts Amongst the timbers burning swelts.

†**b.** To be oppressive with heat, swelter. *Obs.*

1630 J. TAYLOR (Water P.) *Anagrams & Sonn.* Wks. II. 256 The dogged dog daies now with heat doe swelt.

†**5.** ? To welter, wallow (*fig.*). *Obs.*

1575 GASCOIGNE *Dan Bartholomew* Wks. 1907 I. 105 When he thought his hap to be most hye,..And that he swelt in all prosperitie.

II. *trans.* †**6.** To cause to perish. *Obs.*

Perhaps partly ad. ON. *svelta*, causative of *svelta*; but cf. FORSWELT 2.

13.. *K. Alis.* 7559 (Linc. Inn MS.) To brenne brout and to beo swelt. **13..** *E.E. Allit. P.* B. 332 Þis meyny of aȝte I schal saue of monnez saulez, and swelt þose oþer.

7. To overheat, broil, scorch; to oppress or overwhelm with heat; also in fig. phr. *to swelt one's heart*, to exert oneself to the utmost. Now *dial.*

a **1400–50** *Wars Alex.* 3790 Alle ware þai swollen of þe swete & sweltid on þe son. **1555** WATREMAN *Fardle Facions* I. vi. 98 When thei see the Locustes come..thei set al on fire, and so swelte theim in the passyng ouer, that thei..fall to the grounde. **1584** R. WILSON *Three Ladies Lond.* I. Cj, He shall neuer haue better eating fellowes if hee woulde swelte his hart. **1599** NASHE *Lenten Stuffe* Wks. 1905 III. 221 Let the cunningest lickespiggot swelt his heart out, the beere shal neuer foame or froath in the cupp. **1608** SYLVESTER *Du Bartas* II. iv. III. *Schism* 413 Not a breath is felt, But hectick Auster's, which doth all things swelt. **1651** Bp. HALL *Soliloquies* lxxiv, Is the Sun to be blamed that the Travellers cloak swelts him with heat? **1684** MERITON *Yorks. Dial.* 525 (E.D.S.) If we sud swelt our hearts, it will nut deau. **1811** WILLAN in *Archaeologia* XVII. 160 (*W. Riding Words*), *Swelted*, overcome with heat and perspiration. **1886** *S.W. Linc. Gloss.* s.v., It's so hot it's fit to swelt you.

'swelted, *ppl. a. dial.* [f. prec. + -ED[1].] Overpowered with heat; scorched; 'broiled', 'melted'.

a **1640** DAY *Peregr. Schol.* (1881) 54 The beauteous flowers..were nothing else but swelted weeds and fruitless mosse. *a* **1800** PEGGE *Suppl. Grose* (1814), *Swelted* and *Swelter'd*, overpowered with heat. Derb. **1848** A. B. EVANS *Leicestersh. Words* s.v., It's so warm! and Maria's very swelted.

'swelter, *sb.* [f. next.] A sweltering condition. Also in phr. (slang) *to do a swelter*, to perspire.

1851 *Illustr. Lond. News* 23 Aug. 234/3 Perspiring multitudes who stand the swelter with a pluck which would do honour to niggers. **1884** *Punch* 11 Oct. 180/1 So I let them as liked do a swelter.

¶ Equivalent to *sweltered venom* (see SWELTERED 1), or confused with WELTER = slough.

1894 CROCKETT *Mad Sir Uchtred* 156 He skimmed the green swelter of the bottomless shaking bogs. **1914** J. K. GRAHAM *Anno Domini* 138 Knowledge of falsehood dug out of the swelter of the pit.

swelter ('swɛltə(r)), *v.* Also 5 **sweltre**, 6 **squelter**; 5 **swalt(e)ryn, sqwalt-, squalt(e)ryn**. [f. root of SWELT *v.* + -ER[5]. Cf. SULTER.

Promp. Parv. has a variant derived from the grade *swalt-*; cf. *swaltyng* s.v. SWELTING *vbl. sb.*, and SWALTISH.]

1. *intr.* To be oppressed with heat; to sweat profusely, languish, or faint with excessive heat.

c **1403** LYDG. *Temple of Glas* 358 Þuruȝ myn axcesse..I sweltre and swete. *c* **1440** *Promp. Parv.* 471/1 Sqwalteryn, for hete or oþer cawsys (*P.* squaltryn or swaltryn), *sincopo, exalo. Ibid.* 481/2 Swalteryn for hete, or febylnesse, or other cawsys (*P.* or swownyn), *exalo, sincopizo.* **1575** GASCOIGNE *Dan Bartholomew* Wks. 1907 I. 123 My seale is sorrowes sythe, within a fielde of flame, Which cuts in twaine a carefull heart, yt sweltreth in the same. **1624** QUARLES *Sion's Elegies* viii. 9 Oh, let me swelter in those sacred beams. **1624** —— *Sion's Sonn.* i. 5, I was enforc'd to swelter in the Sunne. **1662** TRENCHFIELD *Chr. Chym.* 3 Like Physitians who willing to appeare richly clad, swelter in Plush in hot summer. **1714** MANDEVILLE *Fab. Bees* (1729) II. 24 The venerable Counsellor,..that at his great Age continues sweltering at the Bar to plead the doubtful Cause. **1825** SCOTT *Let. to Morritt* 3 Aug., in *Lockhart*, Your kind letter ..finds me sweltering under the hottest weather I ever experienced. **1880** L. OLIPHANT *Land of Gilead* xi. 313 A fat offical sweltering in his uniform under the burning sun.

fig. **1582** STANYHURST *Æneis* I. (Arb.) 31 Thee labor hoat sweltreth [L. *Fervet opus*]. **1716** M. DAVIES *Athen. Brit.* III. 10 Were they treated by Church-Zealots with a more Charitable Indifferency or Pity,..they would soon swelter away..to the Church Communion.

b. Said of natural objects.

1635 QUARLES *Embl.* III. xiv. 17, I behold..the battlements of heav'n Sweltring in Flames. **1833** I. TAYLOR *Fanat.* vi. 197 The very bowels of the world swelter and are molten. **1840** DICKENS *Old C. Shop* xlv, Stagnant pools, which here and there lay idly sweltering by the black roadside. **1865** PARKMAN *Champlain* i. in *Pioneers France N. World* (1876) 201 It was late in August, and the leafy landscape sweltered in the sun.

c. *fig.* with reference to the heat of burning desire, or the oppressiveness of a burden.

1571 JEWEL *Def. Apol.* etc. viii. II. 219 Better it is to Marrie, then to swelter inwardely with filthy affections. **1620** *Swetnam Arrayned* (1880) 43 As if they meant to dye for loue, When they but swelter in the reeke of Lust. **1675** BROOKS *Gold. Key* Wks. 1867 V. 212 Shall he lie sweltering under his Father's wrath? **1715** M. DAVIES *Athen. Brit.* I. 136 He chose rather to swelter under the Weight of the learned Mr. Selden's Authority.

d. To move slowly or painfully (as if) oppressed with heat.

1834 M. SCOTT *Cruise Midge* (1863) 162 The labouring ship sweltered about on the boiling sea. **1884** *Manch. Exam.* 15 Nov. 5/1 In the height of summer English troops were to swelter through the desert.

2. *trans.* To oppress with heat; to cause to sweat, languish, or faint with oppressive heat. Chiefly *pass.*

1601 W. CORNWALLIS *Ess.* II. xlvi. (1631) 263 As painfull, as a body sweltred in a crowde. **1609** HOLLAND *Amm. Marcell.* 262 Sweltered with the flaming heat of the Sun. **1650** FULLER *Pisgah* IV. iv. 70 Say not that the High-priest was sweltred, being built so many stories high in his garments. **1763** *Brit. Mag.* IV. 405 We were sweltered in the sun, or blown through with a north-east wind. **1825** J. NEAL *Bro. Jonathan* I. 368, I was half sweltered to death, under a great pile o' blankets. **1890** J. PULSFORD *Loyalty to Christ* I. 140 The heat that swelters a bear is the delight of a lark.

b. *fig.* with reference to the heat of strong emotion or desire.

1582 STANYHURST *Æneis* IV. (Arb.) 115 Shee stormeth sweltred in anger. **1765** FALCONER *Demagogue* 279 He.., swelter'd with revenge. **1835** BECKFORD *Recoll.* 158 The.. stranger, who felt..sufficiently annoyed and sweltered.

†**3.** *intr.* and *pass.* To be bathed *in* liquid; hence, to welter, wallow (*lit.* and *fig.*). *Obs.*

1595 *Locrine* III. iv, I long to see The trecherous Scithians squeltering in their gore. **1596** LODGE *Marg. Amer.* 136 A soule sweltered in sinnes. **1610** G. FLETCHER *Christ's Tri.* II. xx, Acquieting the soules, that newe before Their way to heav'n through their owne blood did skore, But now.. Swelter in quiet waves of immortalitie. *a* **1640** DAY *Parl. Bees* (1881) 75 The mossie weeds, halfe swelter'd, serv'd As beds for vermin hunger-sterv'd. **1647** C. HARVEY *Schola Cordis* xxxviii. (1778) 119 Swelter'd and swill'd in sweat. **1654–66** EARL ORRERY *Parthen.* (1676) 324 He fell on the ground, sweltering in a Sea of Bloud. **1865** BUSHNELL *Vicar. Sacr.* III. v. (1866) 271 The transgressor could as easily regather his money sown upon the Gulf Stream, as gather himself back out of the penal causations in which he is sweltering.

4. *trans.* with allusion, more or less precise, to Shakspere's *sweltered venom* (see next, 1): To exude (venom); also *absol.*, and *intr.* for *pass.*

1834 LYTTON *Pompeii* III. x, Burn flame—simmer herb —swelter toad. **1837** DICKENS *Pickw.* li, A reptile contemporary has recently sweltered forth his black venom in the..attempt [etc.]. **1842** F. E. PAGET *Milford Malvoisin* 165 The concentrated venom which was sweltering in her countenance. **1847** L. HUNT *Men, Women, & Bks.* I. xiv. 234 The fat seemed sweltering and full of poison.

sweltered ('swɛltəd), *ppl. a.* [f. prec. + -ED[1].]

1. Exuded like sweat (as if) by heat. Only in *sweltered venom* in and after Shaks.; cf. prec. 4.

1605 SHAKS. *Macb.* IV. i. 8 Toad, that vnder cold stone.. ha's..Sweltred Venom sleeping got. **1814** MOORE *Anacreontic, To Plumassier* 33 Books, that, far from every eye, In 'swelter'd venom sleeping' lie! **1856** F. E. PAGET *Owlet of Owlst.* 57 They produce their most sweltered venom.

2. Bathed in, or oppressed with, great heat.

1798 COLERIDGE *Fire, Famine, & Slaughter* 53 It was so rare a piece of fun To see the sweltered cattle run. **1821** CLARE *Vill. Minstr.* I. 108 The rose reviving blows Upon the swelter'd bower.

sweltering ('swɛltərɪŋ), *vbl. sb.* [f. SWELTER *v.* + -ING[1].] **a.** Fainting, swooning. **b.** A condition of suffering from oppressive heat.

c **1440** *Promp. Parv.* 481/2 Swalterynge, or swownynge, *sincopa. Ibid.* 482/2 Sweltrynge, or swalterynge.., *sincopa.* *a* **1586** SIDNEY *Arcadia* III. (1598) 341 To asswage the sweltring of my hellish longing. **1657** R. LIGON *Barbadoes* 102 Neither themselves, nor any other, can remaine in them [*sc.* their houses] without sweltring. **1846** JAS. HAMILTON *Mount of Olives* viii. 191 When the fret and worry and sweltering of their jaded day is done.

'sweltering, *ppl. a.* [f. SWELTER *v.* + -ING[2].]

†**1.** Exuding with heat. *Obs. rare.*

1575 GASCOIGNE *Dan Bartholomew* Wks. 1907 I. 112 The droppes of sweltring sweate, Which trickle downe my face.

2. Of heat, weather, a season, etc.: Oppressive or overpowering with great heat; causing or accompanied by profuse sweating or suffocation through extreme heat.

1591 SYLVESTER *Du Bartas* I. iii. 182 The sweltring heat, and shiv'ring cold. *c* **1620** Z. BOYD *Zion's Flowers* (1855) 40, I here doe lye, Without a shed scorch'd with a swelt'ring skye. **1650** W. D. tr. *Comenius' Gate Lat. Unl.* §275 The sweltring heat of the heart is cooled by the lungs (lights) lying next to it. **1661** HICKERINGILL *Jamaica* 7 The sweltering and sultry Climes within the Tropicks. **1706** BAYNARD in Sir J. Floyer *Hot & Cold Bath.* II. 384 He was wrapt..in Flannels,..but..threw off all his Sweltering Harness. **1798** SOUTHEY *Cross Roads* vii, In such a sweltering day as this A knapsack is the devil. **1863** DICEY *Federal St.* II. 49 That dull still closeness which foretels a day of sweltering heat. **1899** SOMERVILLE & ROSS *Exper. Irish R.M.* xii, The dances lasted a sweltering half-hour.

b. *fig.* of the heat of feeling. Now *rare* or *Obs.*

In quot. 1820 with reminiscence of Shakspere's *sweltered venom*: see SWELTERED 1.

1586 A. DAY *Engl. Secretorie* I. (1625) 112 Shunning to be tainted with the least touch of sweltring griefe. **1587** —— *Daphnis & Chloe* IV. (1890) 14 With a maner of sweltring kind of disdaine. **1602** MARSTON *Antonio's Rev.* I. i, I burnt in inward sweltring hate. **1820** BYRON *Mar. Fal.* II. i. 427 The blighting venom of his sweltering heart.

3. a. Of persons: Suffering from or overpowered by oppressive heat.

1652 BENLOWES *Theoph.* IV. xlvi, How in Love's torrid zone thy swelt'ring martyr stews. **1825** HONE *Every-day Bk.* I. 1199, I forced myself through the sweltering press. **1883** *Harper's Mag.* Oct. 804/2, I was starved and sweltering.

b. Of localities, etc.: Excessively hot or sultry.

1845 HIRST *Com. Mammoth*, etc. 93 As he strode Along the sweltering glade. **1886** *Athenæum* 20 Feb. 259/2

Whether in the sweltering cities of the south or in dirt-begrimed Peking. **1888** G. ALLEN in *Longm. Mag.* July 306 All the parts of the camel's body which touch the sweltering sand in his ordinary patient kneeling position are provided with callosities of thickened hide. **1890** R. BRIDGES *Shorter Poems* II. v. 9 Swift from the sweltering pasturage he flows.

Hence **'swelteringly** *adv.*

c **1890** A. MURDOCH *Yoshiwara Episode* 13 It was August, and consequently swelteringly hot.

sweltery, variant of SWELTRY.

† **swelth**¹. Chiefly *Sc. Obs.* Also 4 **suelth, swelt,** 6 **sweltht, swelf,** 7 **suald.** [Representing or related to OE. *ȝeswelȝ, swelh* or ON. *svelgr* SWALLOW *sb.*²]

1. A whirlpool.

c **1375** *Sc. Leg. Saints* xxxiv. (*Pelagia*) 181 Men but nombre als haf I Gert synk in-to þe suelth of syne. *c* **1400** *Sc. Trojan War* (Horstm.) II. 2273 That swelt half of my schippis has Suellede ande all þat in þaime was. *c* **1460** *Promp. Parv.* (Winch.) 445 Swelth of a water or grownd, *vorago.* *c* **1500** *Lancelot* 1317 Thi schip, that goth apone the stormy vall, Ney of thi careldis in the swelf it fall. **1513** DOUGLAS *Æneis* I. iii. 42 Thryise thair the fluide quhirlit about round, The sowcand sweltht. *Ibid.* iv. 73 The ragis of Silla that huge swelth in the se 3e haue eschapit. **1601** *Reg. Mag. Sig. Scot.* 391/2 Passand..be the eist syid of ane arne or aller bus in the lin or suald of Schirestoun.

2. Foul or troubled water.

Prob. due to misapprehension of a passage in G. Douglas.

1563 *Mirr. Mag., Induct.* xxxi, A deadly gulfe where nought but rubbishe growes, With fowle blacke swelth in thickned lumpes yᵗ lyes. *Ibid.* lxix, Rude Acheron,..That boyles and bubs vp swelth as blacke as hell.

swelth² (swɛlθ). Now *dial.* (see Eng. Dial. Dict.). [f. SWELL *v.* + -TH¹.] (A) swelling (*lit.* and *fig.*).

1631 BYFIELD *Doctr. Sabb.* 101 His wound and bruise could be seene no where but on his head, necke and face in swelth and blacknesse. **1647** TRAPP *Comm. Matt.* xix. 23 The greatest wealth is ordinarily tumoured up with the greatest swelth of rebellion against God. **1671** GREW *Anat. Plants* vi. §2 The continuance and ampliation or, (as I may call it) the swelth and superbience of the Inner Part thereof. **1681** —— *Musæum* II. I. i. 183 Neither is it only the swelth of the Barque, but the Wood it self is augmented.

† **'swelting,** *vbl. sb. Obs.* [f. SWELT *v.* + -ING¹.]

a. A fainting or being overcome with heat. **b.** Sweltering heat.

c **1460** *Promp. Parv.* (Winch.), Swaltyng, or swownyng, *Sincopa uel Extasis.* **1571** GOLDING *Calvin on Ps.* lviii. 5 Some kyndes of poyson kill with theire coldenesse and other-some consume the partes of lyfe with sweltinge and burninge. **1607** MARKHAM *Caval.* I. iv. (1617) 30 Either for casting their Foales, swelting or other violent euill proceeding from wildnesse.

† **'swelting,** *ppl. a. Obs.* [f. as prec. + -ING².]

1. Dying.

?*a* **1400** *Morte Arth.* 1465 They..Swappez doune ffulle sweperlye swelltande knyghtez. *Ibid.* 2146 Swerdez swangene in two, sweltand knyghtez Lyes wyde opyne.

2. = SWELTERING *ppl. a.*

a **1542** WYATT in *Tottel's Misc.* (Arb.) 59 Regard at length..The sweltyng paynes of my desire. **1568** T. HOWELL *Arb. Amitie* (1879) 49 Nor swelting heat, whose flames yᵉ pastures fry. **1605** SYLVESTER *Du Bartas* II. iii. III. *Law* 963 The first drops [of rain] to cool their swelting heat.

sweltry ('swɛltrɪ), *a.* Now *arch.* and *dial.* Also 6–7 **sweltrie,** 7–8 **swealtry, sweltery.** [f. SWELTER *v.* + -Y. Cf. SULTRY.]

1. Of heat, weather, etc.: Oppressively hot, sweltering, sultry.

1576 TURBERV. *Venerie* 118 The vehement sweltrie heate thereof [*sc.* the sun]. **1661** EVELYN *Fumifugium* Misc. Writ. (1805) I. 216 The drier aer is generally the more salutary and healthy, so it be not too sweltery. **1775** ADAIR *Amer. Ind.* 7 When they are waddling, whooping, and prancing it away, in their sweltery town-houses,..around the reputed holy fire. **1843** *Blackw. Mag.* LIII. 499 The fierce heat of the sun had rendered the atmosphere sweltry and oppressive.

b. *transf.* of feeling or action.

1748 THOMSON *Cast. Indol.* I. xi, The wretched thrall Of bitter dropping sweat, of swealtry pain. **1819** [H. BUSK] *Vestriad* IV. 801 Labouring thro' the sweltry dance.

2. Oppressed or languishing with heat.

1635 J. HAYWARD tr. *Biondi's Banish'd Virg.* 121 Phebus now hastened to bathe his swealtry Steeds in the foaming Ocean. **1796** COLERIDGE *Destiny of Nations* 150 Along the rough-hewn bench The sweltry man had stretched him.

'swelty, *a.* Now *dial.* Also 6 **swealtie,** 7 **sweltie.** [f. SWELT *v.* + -Y.] Sweltering, sultry.

1586 WARNER *Alb. Eng.* I. iv. (1592) 11 The swealtie Sun..So vehementlie did shine vpon the oosie plashes myerd. **1623** tr. *Favine's Theat. Hon.* III. iii. 355 The Raynie sweltie heates. **1886** *S.W. Linc. Gloss., Swelty,* close, hot and smothering.

swelugh, swelw(e, swely, obs. ff. SWALLOW *sb.*² and *v.*

swem(me, swemyle, swen: see SWIM, SWIMBLE *v.*, SUE *v.*

† **swench.** *Obs.* Forms: 1 **suoenc, suenc,** (**ȝe**)**swenc,** 1–3 **swench,** 3–4 **suench, swunch.** [OE. *swenc* (also *ȝe-*):—**swaŋki-*, f. *swaŋk-*: cf. next and SWINCH. For the variant *swunch* cf. STENCH *sb.*] In OE., affliction, trial; in ME., labour, toil.

c **950** *Lindisf. Gosp.* Luke xxii. 28 *In temtationibus meis,* in suoenccum [*Rushw.* swencum] minum. *Ibid.* xxiv. 20 *In damnationem mortis,* in niðrung *vel* in suoenc deaðes [*Rushw.* in swenche *vel* costunge deoðes]. *c* **1000** in Cockayne *Narrat. Angl.* (1861) 40 Hu se eadeȝa margareta ȝeþrowade ..& þurh þæt ȝeswenc to ece reste becom. *c* **1200** *Trin. Coll. Hom.* 179 On sore eche we hider cumen. On swunche we here wunien. In wowe we henne witeð. *c* **1290** *St. Brendan* 623 in *S. Eng. Leg.* 237 A Monek liuez muche bi swunche [*v.rr.* swench, swinche] of mannes honde. **1297** R. GLOUC. (Rolls) 962 To ȝiue hom to libbe by bi suench [*v.rr.* swinch, swynke] of hor honde. *Ibid.* 4810 Alle leuede bi hor suench.

† **swenche,** *v. Obs.* Forms: 1 (**ȝe**)**swencan, swencean,** (**suoenca**), 2–3 (**i**)**swenche(n,** *Ormin* **swennchenn;** *pa. t.* 1–2 **swencte;** *pa. pple.* 1 **ȝeswenced, -swenct,** 2 **-swenched, i-swenced;** see also SWEYNT. [OE. *swencan* (also *ȝe-*) :—**swaŋkwjan,* causative of **swiŋkwan* to SWINK, q.v.] *trans.* To trouble, harass, afflict.

Beowulf 1510 (Gr.) Ac hine wundra þæs fela swencte on sunde. *c* **888** ÆLFRED *Boeth.* xxiv. §1 Ælc deaðlic man swencð hine selfne mid mistlicum & mæniȝfealdum ymbhoȝum. *c* **1000** *Ags. Gosp.* Luke iv. 38 Ða wæs simones sweȝer ȝeswenced [*Hatton* ȝeswenched] on mycelum feferum. **1154** *O.E. Chron.* (Laud MS.) an. 1090 Se cyng wæs smæȝende hu he mihte wrecon his broðer Rodbeard, swiðost swencean, & Normandiȝe of him ȝewinnan. *c* **1175** *Lamb. Hom.* 13 Euwer feond eou ne scal derien ne swenchen. *Ibid.* 101 Sume men festen swa þet hi swencten swiðe heom seolfe. *c* **1200** ORMIN 12216 To swennchenn Cristess þeowwess. *c* **1205** LAY. 15787 Monine mon on sweuene ofte heo swencheð. *c* **1230** *Hali Meid.* 35 Hwil þu swenchest te ter wið iþi deaðes dute.

b. To mortify.

971 *Blickl. Hom.* 81 þa lareowas sceolan heora aȝenne lichoman swencean on forhæfdnesse. *c* **1200** ORMIN 15764 ȝiff þatt we don itt all þwerrt ut..forr to swennchenn ure life To betenn ure sinness. *a* **1225** *Ancr. R.* 134 So wisliche heo schal þauh swenchen þet flesch.

swene, obs. variant of SWEVEN.

† **sweng.** *Obs.* [OE. *swęng* (cf. OFris. *sweng*):—**swaŋgwiz,* f. *swaŋgw-* (see SWING *v.*¹).] A stroke, blow; also applied widely to various kinds of violent action, e.g. a fall at wrestling, a swing, a military assault.

Beowulf 1520 (Gr.) Mæȝenræs forȝeaf hildebille, hond swenge ne ofteah. *a* **1000** *Elene* 239 (Gr.) Bord oft onfeng.. yða swengas. *a* **1225** *Ancr. R.* 80, & ine uondunges to wrastlen stalewardliche aȝein þes deofles swenges. *a* **1225** *St. Marher.* (1866) 14 ȝef ha et stonden wulleð mine unwreste wrenches ant mine swikele swenges, wrestlin ha moten ant wiðerin wið ham seoluen. *a* **1250** *Owl & Night.* 797–9 ȝif tveie men goþ to wraslinge,..An þe on can swenges suþe fele,..An þe oþer ne can sweng but anne. *Ibid.* 1286 Go so hit go at eche fenge, þu fallest mid þine ahene swenge. *c* **1290** *S. Michael* 173 in *S. Eng. Leg.* 304 Fram þe hexte stude þat is with one swenge he cam To þe loweste stude. *Ibid.* 179 A wonder sweng, me þinchez, he made! *c* **1400** *Sege Jerus.* (E.E.T.S.) 317 Many swykel at þe sweng to þe swerd ȝede. *Ibid.* 1172 Eleuen hundred þousand Jewes in þe mene whyle Swalten, while þe sweng last by swerd & by hunger.

b. Toil, labour; = SWING *sb.*¹

13.. *E.E. Allit. P.* A. 575 þaȝ þay com late & lyttel wore, & þaȝ her sweng wyth lyttel at-slykez.

† **swenge,** *v. Obs.* (Also *pa. t.* 3 **sweinde,** 3–5 **swende.**) [OE. *swęngan*:—**swaŋgwjan* (as in Goth. *afswaggwjan*): cf. prec. and see SWING. This vb. reappears later as SWINGE *v.*¹, q.v.]

1. *trans.* To shake, shatter.

a **1000** *Voc.* in Wr.-Wülcker 224/14 *Discutiens, i. iudicans, querens, uel* swengende. *c* **1050** *Ibid.* 396/10 *Excussit,* fram swengde. *c* **1440** *Promp. Parv.* 482/2 Swengyn, or schakyn, as menne done clothys. *Ibid.*, Swengynge, *excussio.*

2. To smite; to dash, fling; = SWING *v.*¹ 2.

c **1205** LAY. 6424 þat Morpidus..Seouen hundred of-sloh and swenden mið wepuen. *Ibid.* 22839 [He] nimeð al his nexte cun..and swengeð of þa hafden mid breoden euwer sweorden. *a* **1225** *St. Marher.* 10 þe drake rahte ut his tunge and swende hire in ant forswalh. *a* **1225** *Ancr. R.* 280 He.. sweinde ham þuruh prude adun into helle grunde. **13..** *E.E. Allit. P.* C. 108 He swenges me þys swete schip swefte fro þe hauen. **14..** *Sir Beues* 248 þre hondred heuedes of a slende [*v.rr.* swengde, swende] Wiþ is brond.

b. To beat up (eggs); = SWING *v.*¹ 1 c.

c **1430** *Two Cookery-bks.* 25 ȝolkys of eyroun y-swengyd, & a-lyid. *Ibid.* 40 Take Eyroun with alle þe whyte, & swenge hem.

3. *intr.* To make a dash, move violently; to dash, fling (*at*); = SWING *v.*¹ 3.

c **1000** *Ags. Hom.* (Assmann) xviii. 207 þa swengde sio lio sona forð and forswealh uncerne hlaford biforan unc. *c* **1205** LAY. 8183 Æft he him to sweinde. *a* **1225** *Ancr. R.* 290, & breid up þene rode stef, & sweng [*MS. T.* swench] him aȝean a uour halue. *c* **1275** LAY. 27787 Sweord aȝein sweorde sweynde wel ilome. **13..** *E.E. Allit. P.* C. 253 þenne he swengez & swayues to þe se boþem. *c* **1350** *Will. Palerne* 3444 þe swerd swiftili swenged þurth þe bode euen. *a* **1375** *Joseph Arim.* 529 þei come swiftly vppon and swengeden to-gedere.

† **swenk,** *v. Obs.* Occasional variant in Ormin of SWENCHE, prob. due to pa. t. *swencte,* pa. pple. *ȝeswenct,* or 2 and 3 pres. ind. *swencst, swencþ*: cf. *cwennkenn,* QUENCH.

c **1200** ORMIN 8942 Whi didesst tu, lef sune, þuss Wiþþ uss, forr uss to swennkenn?

† **Swenk'feldian.** *Obs.* Also 6 **Swinke-,** 7 **Suenc(k)-, Swenckfeldian, Swinkfieldian,** 8 **Swinfeildian.** = SCHWENKFELDIAN.

1564 DORMAN *Proofe Cert. Articles Relig.* 133 Be they Swenckfeldians, be they if yow list Dauid georgians. **1579** FULKE *Heskins' Parl.* 232 The Swinkefeldians, Anabaptistes, Libertines, Henrinicolaites. **1637** GILLESPIE *Engl. Pop. Cerem.* III. viii. 143 Anabaptisticall or Swenckfeldian-like enthysiasmes. **1677** GILPIN *Dæmonol.* (1867) 166 The Swinkfieldians assumed the title of 'the Confessors of the Glory of Christ'. **1796** MORSE *Amer. Geog.* I. 289 A few of the German inhabitants..styled Swinseildians [*sic*].

swenkt, *ppl. a.* Error for *swinkt*: see SWINKED.

1837 CARLYLE *Fr. Rev.* II. IV. vi, The swenkt grinders in this Treadmill of an Earth have ground out another Day.

sweoke, sweor: see SWIKE, SWIRE.

sweot, variant of SWOTE *Obs.*, sweat.

† **swepe,** *sb.*¹ *Obs.* Forms: 1 **swipu, swipe** (**suib-, swiop-, suiop-, sweop-, suyppu, swypu**), 2–4 **swepe,** (2 **swupe,** 4 **suepe,** 5 **swip**). [OE. *swipu* str. fem., *swipe* wk. fem., corresp. to ON. *svipa* str. fem., whip, f. weak grade of Teut. *swaip-*: *sweip-*: *swip-*: see SWOPE *v.*¹ and cf. SWAIP, SWAPE.] A scourge, whip.

a **700** *Epinal Gloss.* 641 *Mastigia,* suipan [*Erfurt* suibae]. *c* **975** *Rushw. Gosp.* John ii. 15 *Cum fecisset quasi flagellum de funiculis,* miððy ȝiworhte swelce swiopa [*Ags. Gosp.* swipe] of rapun. *a* **1000** *Sal. & Sat.* 121 (Gr.) Swiðmode sweopan. *a* **1175** *Cott. Hom.* 231 Mid gode repples and stiarne swepen. *Ibid.* 239 þe weregede gastes þe hine uniredlice underfangeð min stiarne swupen. *c* **1200** ORMIN 15565 Crist himm wrohhte an swepe þær..& draf hemm alle samenn ut. *a* **1300** *Cursor M.* 19355 For þan wit suepes þai þam suang, And scurged sare, þai let þam gang. *c* **1460** *Towneley Myst.* xxiii. 470 Blo and blody thus am I bett, Swongen with swepys and alle to-swett.

† **swepe,** *sb.*² *Obs.* [Obscure; possibly an early instance of SWEEP *sb.* in fig. sense.] ? Scope, significance (of a dream).

c **1250** *Gen. & Ex.* 2086 'Me wore leuere', quad Ioseph, 'Of eddi dremes rechen swep.' *Ibid.* 2112. *a* **1400–50** *Wars Alex.* 248 For þai can swyth of a sweuyn all þe swepe telle.

† **swepe,** *v. Obs.* Also 8 *Sc.* **sweap.** [? f. SWEPE *sb.*¹ or ad. ON. *svipa* to whip. Cf. SWIP *v.*] *trans.* To scourge. Also † **sweping** *vbl. sb.*

a **1300** *E.E. Psalter* xxxiv. [xxxv.] 15 Samened on me swepinges [L. *flagella*]. *Ibid.* xxxvii[i]. 18 [17] In swepinges am I dight. **1710** RUDDIMAN *Gloss. Douglas' Æneis* s.v. *Swipper, Sweap, Scot.*,..signifying *to scourge.*

sweper, -ir, etc., obs. ff. SWIPPER.

swept (swɛpt), *ppl. a.* [pa. pple. of SWEEP *v.*]

1. In senses of the verb. Also with advs., as ***swept-out***; ***swept-up***: *spec.* of hair, brushed up towards the top of the head. Freq. as the second element of compounds, as ***air-***, ***breeze-***, ***bullet-***, ***wind-swept***.

1552 HULOET, Swept howse, *tersa domus.* **1707** MORTIMER *Husb.* (1721) I. 346 Then he fills up the said swept place with Malt cast into a round from the sides. **1852** DICKENS *Bleak Ho.* v, Groping among the swept-out rubbish for pins and other refuse. **1893** G. D. LESLIE *Lett. Marco* i. 6 Piles of swept-up leaves. **1895** M. HEWLETT *Earthwork Tuscany* 12 Gas-lamps in swept streets flickered dirty yellow in the garish light. **1903** *Daily Chron.* 28 May 7/3 A sword with a 'swept' hilt of large proportions. **1948** 'J. TEY' *Franchise Affair* xviii. 217 With her hair swept up and some make-up on, she would look quite different. **1959** *News Chron.* 18 Aug. 6/7 Swept-up hair styles which straggle down the neck. **1973** M. WOODHOUSE *Blue Bone* vi. 58 She was about five feet six, with butterfly glasses and swept-up hair.

2. *Electronics.* Of (the frequency of) a signal: increased (or decreased) through a range of values, usu. rapidly and repeatedly.

1965 *Wireless World* Aug. 384/1 A random vibration testing technique which was similar to a swept sinewave frequency test except that the single frequency was replaced by a narrow band of noise. **1980** *IEEE Trans. Microwave Theory & Techniques* XXVIII. 792/1 An automated swept-frequency absorption spectrometer.

3. Special collocations: **swept-back** *a. Aeronaut.*, (of a wing) having its leading edge angled backwards (cf. *sweepback* s.v. SWEEP- 3 and *delta wing* s.v. DELTA 4); also *transf.*; **swept valley** *Building* [VALLEY *sb.* 4] (see quot. 1964); **swept volume** *Mech.*, the volume through which a piston or plunger moves as it makes a stroke; **swept wing** *Aeronaut.*, a swept-back wing; freq. *attrib.*; also as *sb.*, a swept-wing aircraft.

1914 *Aeroplane* 26 Feb. 213/2 *Swept-back wings with negative tips must always have their centre of side pressure farther back relatively to their centre of lift than normal wings. **1951** *Engineering* 20 Apr. 474/3 The third type of British swept-back 'delta'-wing experimental aircraft. **1959** *Ibid.* 16 Jan. 95/1 At each side of the column just below the engine are 'swept back' service ducts extending to the cell walls. **1976** B. JACKSON *Flameout* x. 169 Fast aircraft with swept-back wings are susceptible to dutch rolls. **1926** G. ALLEN *Smaller House of Today* vi. 96 *Swept valleys are very suitable for slated and stone roofs. **1951** N. WYMER *Village Life* iii. 64 A particularly unusual feature of the Cotswold roof is the 'swept valley'. **1964** J. S. SCOTT *Dict. Building* 326 *Swept valley,* a valley formed of shingles, slates, or tiles cut or made to a taper so as to eliminate the need for a flexible-metal valley. A tile-and-a-half tile is used and cut to shape so that its tail is narrower than its head. **1918** W. E. DOMMETT *Dict. Aircraft* 45 **Swept Volume.* The volume swept by the piston equals area of piston multiplied by the stroke. **1930** *Flight* 24 Jan. 144/2 The engine is of the five-cylinder radial type of 150 cub. ins. swept volume. **1971** B. SCHARF *Engin. & its Lang.* xiii. 193 Volumetric efficiency. This is the ratio of the actual volume discharged [from a pump] (capacity) to the displacement or swept volume of the cylinder(s). **1947** *Jrnl. R. Aeronaut. Soc.* LI. 15/2 Whether or not the delta wing is a better compromise than the *swept wing..must await the verdict of appropriate researches. **1955** *Times* 25 June 6/2 The R.A.F.'s latest type of Hawker Hunter swept-wing fighter, the Mark IV, is being used for the first time. **1978** A. WELCH *Bk. Airsports* i. 9/2 In between are swallow-tails, swept-wings without tails and even the occasional biplane.

swepyll, swepyr: see SWIPPLE, SWIPPER.

swer, obs. form of SURE, SWEAR.

swer(e: see SWEAR, SWEER, SWIRE.

swerd, obs. form of SWARD, SWART, SWORD.

swerel, obs. form of SQUIRREL.

a **1430** *Sev. Sages* (Cott. Galba) 3104 He gert it dub.. With swerel tailes ful blak also.

swerf, -fe, -ff, obs. forms of SWARF *sb.*[1] and *v.*

swerill, north. dial. form of SQUIRREL.

†**swerk**, *v. Obs.* In 1 sweorcan (see etym.), 3 **swærken**, *pa. t. pl.* **swurken**. [OE. *sweorcan*, pa. t. *swearc*, **swurcon*, pa. pple. -*sworcen* = OS. *swerkan* to become sad, pa. pple. *gisworkan* clouded, darkened (lit. and fig.), LG. in pa. pple. *sworken* and *besworken*, *-ed* clouded, OHG. *swercan* to become dark or gloomy (lit. and fig.), f. Teut. root *swerk-* (:*swark-*, *swurk-*), whence also OE. *ȝesweorc* cloud, *swearcian* to be darkened, OS. *giswerk* darkness, (M)LG. *swerk*, *swark* dark clouds, sorrow, grief, MDu. *gheswerc*, *swerc* (Du. *zwerk*) clouds, cloudy sky, OHG. *giswerc*, *kiswerc* dark clouds, and OE. *áswarcan*, 'tabescere', *ásweorcan* 'elanguere', *áswarcod* 'reveritus'; ulterior connexions undetermined.] *intr.* To be or become dark; in OE. often, to become gloomy, troubled, or sad.

Beowulf 1737 (Gr.) Ne him inwitsorh on sefan sweorceð. *a* **1000** *Andreas* 372 (Gr.) Wedercandel swearc, windas weoxon. *a* **1000** *Boeth. Metr.* iii. 2, & hu grundleasum seaðe swinceð þæt sweorcende mod. *c* **1205** LAY. 11973 Swurken vnder sunnen sweorte weolcnen. *Ibid.* 22030 þenne swelleð þe mære, þenne swærkeð þa vðen.

swerle, obs. form of SWIRL.

†'**swermer**. *Obs.* [ad. early mod.G. *schwermer* (mod. *schwärmer*), a favourite word of Luther's, esp. for the Anabaptists, f. *schwermen*, *schwärmen* to swarm, rove, riot, rave (see SWARM *sb.*).] A sectarian, fanatic. Hence † **swer'merian** in the same sense.

1585-7 T. ROGERS *39 Art.* xxiii. (1625) 137 The Anabaptisticall Swermers. *Ibid.* xxvii. 169 Some vtterly deny that Infants..are to be baptized; so..doe the Swermerians (a sect among the said Anabaptists).

swert, obs. form of SWART.

swerte, obs. form of SURETY.

swerve (swɜːv), *sb.* Also 8 swarve. [f. next.] An act of swerving, turning aside, or deviating from a course; in *Cricket* and *Baseball*: see SWERVE *v.* 7 b. Also *attrib.*, as ***swerve-bowler***, ***-bowling***.

1741 *Compl. Fam.-Piece* II. i. 310 If there be no such Swarve,..then that Dog that is nearest the Deer when he swarves..wins the Match. **1840** E. E. NAPIER *Scenes & Sports For. Lands* I. i. 13, I missed him with my first barrel, but from the swerve he gave after my second attempt..I was aware he was hit. **1857** DICKENS *Dorrit* II. xix, Every swerve of the carriage and every cry of the postilion. **1865** A. L. GORDON *Poems, Vis. Smoke* iv, On! on! to the cannon's mouth they stride, With never a swerve nor a shy. **1900** A. W. PULLIN *Talks with Old Eng. Cricketers* 125 One hears occasionally of swerving balls, but the swerve depends very much on the air. **1901** *Westm. Gaz.* 16 Aug. 8/2 Hirst..has a peculiar 'knack'..of making the ball swerve in the air... Yesterday the 'swerve' showed itself. **1930** C. V. GRIMMETT *Getting Wickets* iii. 67 In swerve bowling, like other branches of the art, it must be the bowler's object so to regulate his swerve that the ball will hit the wicket. **1944** E. BLUNDEN *Cricket Country* iii. 37 A large wrathful swerve-bowler using the wind..to the immediate..destruction of all.

fig. **1871** DORA GREENWELL *Colloquia Crucis* iii. 63 A warp and swerve in nature that seems to demand a mighty work of restoration.

swerve (swɜːv), *v.* Forms: α. 3-4 *pa. t.* **swarf**, 4- **swerve**, (6 *Sc.* **suirve**, **suerwe**, *pa. pple.* **swarven**); β. 5- (now *dial.*) **swarve** (6 **swarfe**, *Sc.* **suarve**, 7 **swarv**). [Com. Teut. (orig.) str. vb. with a variety of meanings: ME. *swerve*, pa. t. *swarf* to turn aside, repr. OE. *sweorfan*, pa. t. *swearf*, pa. pple. *sworfen* to file, scour, = OFris. *swerva* to creep, (WFris. *swerv(j)e*, pa. t. *swurf*, pa. pple. *swurven* to wander, hurry away, NFris. *swarwi*), OS. **swerban* to wipe, only in pa. t. *swarf*, MDu. *swerven* (Du. *zwerven*) to rove, stray, LG. *swarven* to swerve, stray, riot, OHG. *swerban* (MHG. *swerben*) to wipe, to move quickly backwards and forwards, whirl or twirl round (mod.G. has a derivative form *schwirbeln*), ON. *sverfa*, pa. t. *svarf*, *svurfum*, pa. pple. *sorfinn* to file, (Norw. *swerva* to whirl, swirl), Goth. *-swairban* in *afswairban*, *biswairban* to wipe (away).

The original sense of the radical may be that of agitated, irregular, or deflected movement: cf. SWARM *sb.*, etym. The sense of fling did not survive the OE. period, but is preserved in the derivative sb. SWARF *sb.*[2] The sudden emergence of the sense of 'turn aside' in ME. is remarkable; the presumption is that it existed in OE., since there is no known foreign source to account for it.]

†**1.** *intr.* To depart; to make off. *Obs. rare.*

a **1225** *Leg. Kath.* 2132 Heo swarf to Criste upon þe þreo & twentuðe dei of Nouembres moneð. *c* **1400** *Destr. Troy* 2358, I..swaruyt out swiftly, might no swayne folo.

2. a. To turn aside, deviate in movement from the straight or direct course.

In early use, of a glancing blow or weapon.

α. *c* **1330** *Arth. & Merl.* 9359 (Kölbing) þe dint swarf & flei for bi. *c* **1380** *Sir Ferumb.* 743 þat swerd on ys syde swarf. **1390** GOWER *Conf.* III. 7 As a drunke man I swerve. *Ibid.* III. 92 Riht so was This erthe set..That it may swerve to no side. **1541** COPLAND *Guydon's Quest. Cyrurg.* L iij, Ye ought to haue a quyll w[t] a hole in the syde wher with the other syde of the lyppe shal be steyed, bycause it shall nat swerue. **1642** FULLER *Holy & Prof. St.* v. xix. 436 As if Nature on set purpose mistook her mark, and made her hand to swerve. **1784** COWPER *Task* I. 161 His lab'ring team, that swerv'd not from the track. **1816** SCOTT *Old Mort.* iii, The animal swerved at the moment his master fired. **1854** R. S. SURTEES *Handley Cr.* xxxii, Nothing looks so pusillanimous as to see a chap ride bang at a fence as though he would eat it, and then swerve off for a gate or a gap. **1864** G. A. LAWRENCE *Maurice Dering* II. 19 The bullet did not swerve from its mark one hair's-breadth. **1901** [see SWERVE *sb.*].

β. *c* **1400** *Destr. Troy* 5785 Swordis, with swapping, swaruyt on helmes. *c* **1450** *Merlin* xx. 341 Yef the swerde hadde not swarued, maymed hadde he ben for euer. **1526** *Pilgr. Perf.* (W. de W. 1531) 166 Yf it [*sc.* the ball] be cast vp crokedly, it swarueth & falleth on that one syde or on y[t] other. **1553** BRENDE *Q. Curtius* B v, With hys sword drawen [he] ran at hys sonne, who by swaruing with hys body, avoyded the stroke. **1557** EDGEWORTH *Serm.* Repert. A iij, In Croked thinges the midle swarueth from the extremities. **1590** SPENSER *F.Q.* I. x. 14 Vp to heauen..Her stedfast eyes were bent, ne swarued other way. **1598** BARCKLEY *Felic. Man* 173 The beasts that drew Darius wagon hauing no man to gouerne them, were swarued out of the high way. **1607** MARKHAM *Caval.* II. xxiii. (1617) 248 The very center of the ring, from which your eye in running must not swarue. **1625** N. CARPENTER *Geogr. Delin.* I. x. (1635) 220 The Sunne neuer swaruing from his Eclipticke, hath his course equally diuided by the Horizon. **1741** [see SWERVE *sb.*]. **1818** SCOTT *Br. Lamm.* xxiv, The horse swarved round.

b. To turn in a specified direction; to be deflected (statically).

c **1600** SHAKS. *Sonn.* lxxxvii, And so my pattent back againe is sweruing. **1607** MARKHAM *Caval.* VII. xlii. 60 Waights of such sufficient poise as may either drawe the Crest vp straight, or els mak it leane to that side from whence it swerueth. **1820** L. HUNT *Indicator* No. 40 (1822) I. 316 While the leaves issue from it, and swerve upwards with their elegant points. **1863** COWDEN CLARKE *Shaks. Char.* vi. 157 In those secluded villages where the high post and railroads swerve in the distance. **1883** *Mag. Art* Aug. 398/1 The road swerves to the left.

†**c.** *trans.* To deviate from (a path). *Obs. rare.*

a **1513** FABYAN *Chron.* VII. 627 When the duke had wyttynge of the Kynges great power, he swaruyd the way from the Kynges hoost and toke the way towarde London. **1587** TURBERV. *Trag. Tales* (1837) 140 It [*sc.* sin] makes him passe beyond the boundes of kynde, And swerve the trade where truth and vertues lay.

3. a. *intr.* To turn away or be deflected from a (right) course of action, a line of conduct, an opinion, etc.; †to waver, vacillate.

a **1400** ? CHAUCER *Compl. to Mortal Foe* 29, I preye, as he that wol nat swerve, That I may fare the better for my trouthe. *a* **1547** SURREY *Æneid* II. 714 Neoptolem is swarved out of kinde. **1557** *Tottel's Misc.* (Arb.) 176 Since so vnconstantly thou wilt Not loue, but still be swaruing. **1599** SHAKS. *Hen. V*, II. ii. 133 Are they..Constant in spirit, not sweruing with the blood? **1667** MILTON *P.L.* IX. 359 Firm we subsist, yet possible to swerve. **1810** WORDSW. *Sonn.*, '*Avaunt all specious pliancy of mind*' 7 Honour that knows the path and will not swerve. **1847** EMERSON *Repr. Men, Swedenborg* Wks. (Bohn) I. 334 With a tenacity that never swerved..he adheres to this brave choice. **1873** DIXON *Two Queens* XII. ii. II. 293 She argued with him, but he would not swerve a jot. **1884** L. J. JENNINGS *Croker Papers* I. x. 278 Mr. Croker..never swerved in his support of every well-directed measure for Catholic relief.

b. (*a*) Const. *from.*

α. **1390** GOWER *Conf.* I. 240 So that I mihte..Fro suche that mi ladi serve Hire herte make forto swerve. *Ibid.* II. 42 And yit therfro mai noman swerve, That he ne mot his lawe obeie. **1535** JOYE *Apol. Tindale* (Arb.) 30 He wold..neuer haue had so farre swaruen from his principal, as [etc.]. [*Cf.* boden *and* stoken *in the preceding context.*] **1554** *Act 1 & 2 Phil. & Mary* c. 8 §1 As well the Spiritualtie as the Temporaltie..have swerved from the Obedience of the See Apostolike. **1606** SHAKS. *Tr. & Cr.* III. ii. 191 If I be false, or swerue a haire from truth. **1626** MIDDLETON *Women Beware Women* v. i. 163 This swerves a little from the argument. **1664** H. MORE *Myst. Iniq.* II. i. i. §3. 206 The..converting of Christendom to that ancient and Apostolick purity..from which they have so long time swerved. **1756** C. LUCAS *Ess. Waters* I. Pref., It will to some appear most..impudent to attempt to swerve from the spelling received and established. **1822** LAMB *Elia* Ser. II. *Conf. Drunkard*, What hinders in your instance that you do not return to those habits from which you would induce others never to swerve? **1868** E. EDWARDS *Ralegh* I. xxvii. 683 From the resolute vindication of the Guiana enterprise itself Sir Walter never really swerved. **1874** GREEN *Short Hist.* ix. §10. 710 The wealth around him never made Walpole swerve from a rigid economy.

β. *a* **1513** FABYAN *Chron.* VII. 510 If he or ye kynge of Nauerne wolde swarue from any poynt or artycle of the sayd former agrement. **1521** in *Bradshaw's St. Werburge* (1887) 202 Thys soule..from vertue neuer swarued [*rime* preserued]. **1535** COVERDALE *Ps.* cxviii[i]. 110 Yet swarue not I from thy commaundementes. **1582** STANYHURST *Æneis* To Rdr. (Arb.) 11 As what shal seeme too swarue from theyre maximes, they wyl not stick too skore vp for errours. **1611** *Bible* 1 Tim. i. 6 From which [*sc.* charity] some hauing swarued, haue turned aside vnto vaine iangling. *a* **1632** T. TAYLOR *God's Judgem.* I. II. vii. (1642) 177 Astyages..so much swarved from humanity, that he gave in strict charge that..his own daughter's sonne..should be made away. **1642** CHAS. I *Answ. Declar. Lds. & Comm.* 19 May 6 We have not at all swarved or departed from Our Resolution. **1684** BUNYAN *Pilgr.* II. 20 Let him never suffer me To swarve or turn aside From his free grace.

†(*b*) To forsake, desert, be disloyal to (a person); also, to differ from, be discrepant from.

a **1400** ? CHAUCER *Compl. to Lode-sterre* 40 My herte and body, shal I never swerve From you. ? **1566** R. W[ITC] *To the vnconstant E.T.* xxvi, Frequent not Womens company but see thou from them swarue. **1579** LYLY *Euphues* (Arb.) 191 That thy nature should not swerue from thy name. **1584** B. R. tr. *Herodotus* I. 55 b, From whom the Caryans themselues doe greatly dissent and swarue in opinion. **1590** SPENSER *F.Q.* II. x. 55 The Captaines on her side, Corrupted by Paulinus, from her sweru'd. **1607** TOPSELL *Four-f. Beasts* Ep. Ded. A vj, In the names of the Beasts and the Physicke I have not swarued from him at all. *a* **1656** USSHER *Power Princes* I. (1683) 3 Neither doth St. Peter any whit swerve from his beloved brother Paul.

c. Const. *to*, *towards*, †occas. *on.*

c **1550** R. BIESTON *Bayte Fortune* B ij b, By arrogance oultrageous thy tounge on vaunting swerueth. **1570** T. NORTON *Nowel's Catech.* 9 Our soules are sayd to be defiled with adulterie, when they swarue [*orig. deflectunt*] from God to idolatrie and superstition. *a* **1586** SIDNEY *Ps.* XXXVII. xviii, Who be swarved To ill, both they and theirs shall wrack. **1850** TENNYSON *In Mem.* lxxxv, My passion hath not swerved To works of weakness. **1882** J. H. BLUNT *Ref. Ch. Eng.* II. 485 Charles..was never in danger of swerving toward either Romanism on the one hand, or Puritanism on the other. **1885-94** R. BRIDGES *Eros & Psyche* March x, And to the Cretan maid her worship swerved.

†**d.** Without constr.: To deviate from the right; to err; to go astray, esp. morally; to transgress.

1576 W. RAWELY in Gascoigne *Steele Gl.* Wks. 1910 II. 139 The life likewise, were pure that never swerved. **1576** FLEMING *Panopl. Epist.* 163 Saying, that at no time our deedes haue so swerued, that they might be amended. **1602** WARNER *Alb. Eng.* XIII. lxxvii. (1612) 318 How all these Deities than Men more brutishly did swerue. **1611** SHAKS. *Cymb.* v. iv. 129 But (alas) I swerue.

†**e.** To go back on what one has said. *Obs.*

1527 *St. Papers Hen. VIII*, VI. 593 He many tymes swarfethe in wordes. **1529** *Ibid.* VII. 160 As thEmperouris folkis first sayd, but nowe swarfe.

†**4.** To give way; to sway, totter; *fig.* to shrink from action. *Obs.*

1573 *Satir. Poems Reform.* xxxix. 158 The Suddartis swarfit, and said thay wald not sar. *a* **1586** SIDNEY *Arcadia* III. xxv. (1912) 502 My Muse hath swarved, From such deepe plaint as should such woes descrie. **1590** SPENSER *F.Q.* II. iii. 42 With that she swaruing backe, her Iauelin bright Against him bent. **1596** DRAYTON *Legends* iv. 276 With faintness shee began to reele, Shewing her selfe a little as shee swarv'd. **1611** SPEED *Hist. Gt. Brit.* IX. xx. §68 This so round and quicke dealing with the Earles complices.., startled his shallow..inuentions, and made their whole bulke to swarue and splinter. **1649** MILTON *Tenure of Kings* 4 Another sort..begin to swerve and almost shiver at the majesty..of som noble deed, as if they were newly enter'd into a great sin. **1650** W. D. tr. *Comenius' Gate Lat. Unl.* §538 Beginning to totter and reel (swerve and lean to a side) it [*sc.* a house] must needs be shored up with some arch. **1667** MILTON *P.L.* VI. 386 The battel swerv'd, With many an inrode gor'd. **1818** SHELLEY *Euganean Hills* 41 Every little living nerve That from bitter words did swerve Round the tortured lips and brow.

5. To rove, stray. Also *fig.* to digress.

1543 BECON *New Year's Gift* Wks. 1564 I. 175 b, Al are swarued and clene gone out of the way. **1648** HERRICK *Hesper., Cheat of Cupid* 10, I [*sc.* Cupid] a Boy am, who By Moonlesse nights have swerved. **1655** in Hartlib *Ref. Commonw. Bees* 9 In case that upon the neglect any be swarved forth, and settled unto some tree. **1658** A. FOX *Würtz' Surg.* II. vi. 61 Now it is time to come to the Wound itself,..hitherto I swarved round about. **1698** A. BRAND *Emb. Muscovy to China* 111 He had swarved about the Desart for three days. **1745** *Gleditsch's Teutsch-Engl. Lex.* s.v. *Schwärmen*, He swerves about by night.

†**6.** = SWARM *v.*[2], SWARVE *v.*[2] *Obs.*

1606 DRAYTON *Odes* (1619) *Skeltoniad* 29 Parnassus is not clome By euery such Mome; Vp whose steep side who swerues, It behoues t' haue strong Nerues. **1692** DRYDEN *Amaryllis* 24 Nimbly up, from bough to bough I swerv'd. **1697** —— *Æneid* II. 606 Some mount the scaling Ladders; some more bold, Swerve upwards, and by Posts and Pillars hold.

7. a. *trans.* To cause to turn aside or deviate (*lit.* and *fig.*).

1390 GOWER *Conf.* I. 54 Bot he his yhe awey ne swerveth Fro hire. *Ibid.* III. 25. *a* **1552** LELAND *Itin.* (1769) V. 73 He hath suarvid his Course a good But Shotte of. *c* **1590** J. STEWART *Poems* (S.T.S.) II. 204/6 That schrink of sorrow nether suerwe nor smart The Interpryse of thy magnanime hart. **1615** BRATHWAIT *Strappado* (1878) 10 How manie haue wee in this error swerud Who in themselues haue iustly wel deserud. **1617** SWETNAM *Sch. Sci. Defence* 142 The defence of this guard..is to swerue his vper-hand, this way, or that way. **1629** SIR W. MURE *Sonn.* ix. 2 A constant course

..each creature keeps, Not swarving from thine ordinance their ends. **1659** Gauden *Tears Ch.* iv. xi. 460 Those Scotish motions and pretentions..swerved them..from the former good constitution of the Church of England. **1723** Dk. Wharton *True Briton* No. 9. I. 77 To swerve them from that Allegiance. **1801** Eliz. Helme *St. Marg. Cave* II. 263 Your son has received my decided opinion, and from which nothing shall swerve me. **1816** Scott *Antiq.* viii, Swerve the yard a bit—Now—there! there she sits safe on dry land. **1878** Proctor *Pleas. Ways Sci.* iii. (1879) 69 We determine Jupiter's mass..by noting how he swerves his moons at their respective (estimated) distances. **1897** Flora A. Steel *On Face of Waters* i. vi. 74 Swerving his bullock to give them room.

b. *Cricket* and *Baseball.* To cause a ball to deflect by imparting a spinning motion to it as it leaves the bowler or pitcher. Chiefly *intr.* Of a delivery: to deviate in the air. Of a bowler: to bowl with a swerve.

1894 *Cricket Field* 437 Lockwood was bowled by a ball that swerved considerably in the air. **1903** C. B. Fry *Let.* Sept. in P. F. Warner *How we recovered Ashes* (1905) ii. 15 Much will depend on how you work your bowlers. I wonder which of your 'swervers' will swerve best in Australia? **1906** *N. & Q.* 10th Ser. V. 426/1 The word 'swerve' has been used in cricket for the last two seasons, as applied to the bowling of B. J. T. Bosanquet... He intentionally imparts a direction to the ball in its flight through the air before it touches ground. **1911** P. F. Warner *Cricket* 29 Such a [bowler] as Hirst, who swerves from the off at a fast pace. [Cf. swerve *sb.*, quot. 1901.]

swerve, variant of swarve *v.*[1]

1764 *Museum Rust.* II. xxxi. 103 (Sussex) The tides brought up the mud with them, and swerved to the depth, at some places, of six or eight feet. **1790** E. Hasted *Hist. Kent* III. 442 The river Limene's course hither by that means swerved up, and directed wholly into another channel.

swerve, dial. var. swarf *v.*, to swoon.

swerveless ('swɜːvlɪs), *a.* [f. swerve *v.* + -less.] Unswerving; also, that may not be swerved from.

1863 P. S. Worsley *Poems & Transl.* 5 He..spake, appealing to that swerveless oath. **1869** Mrs. Whitney *Hitherto* xxxiv, His..spirit looked forth at me from pure, swerveless eyes. **1882** Ella W. Wilcox *Poems, 'Let me lean hard'* iii, That swerveless force Which speeds the solar systems on their course.

swerver ('swɜːvə(r)). Also 6–7 **swarver.** [f. swerve *v.* + -er[1].] †**a.** One who swerves from the right path, a transgressor. **b.** A person or animal that swerves; in *Cricket* and *Baseball*, a player or a ball that swerves.

1598 Florio, *Preuaricatore*,..a swaruer from truth. *Ibid.*, *Trasgressore*, an offender..a trespasser, a swaruer. **1611** Shaks. *Wint. T.* ii. i. 93 Shee's A Bed-swaruer. **1892** *Field* 20 Feb. 244/1 A well-known mare swerved at a fence... The rider of the swerver got a shaking fall. **1902** *Sat. Rev.* 5 July 12/2 One good ball, a 'swerver' that comes in a lot from the off. **1903** [see swerve *v.* 7 b]. **1911** P. F. Warner *Cricket* 55 It is impossible to go in first and not meet with a 'swerver'; for every county team possesses one.

swerving ('swɜːvɪŋ), *vbl. sb.* [f. swerve *v.* + -ing[1].] The action of the vb. swerve; deviation; departure *from* a norm, a prescribed or right course, etc.; †error, transgression.

1513 More *Rich. III* (1641) 246 The smalest swarving that is possible (if the thing bee misconstrued) may bee the cause of the destruction of many giltlesse persons. **1545** Bale *Myst. Iniq.* 29 Bynde vp her head for sweruynge, lappe vp her bodye warme for surfetynge. **1561** Norton & Sackv. *Gorboduc* i. ii. 20 Their vnworthy life,..their lawlesse swaruynge out of kinde. **1561** Daus tr. *Bullinger on Apoc.* (1573) 125 b, Corrupt doctrine and swaruyng from the fayth. **1594** Hooker *Eccl. Pol.* i. iii. §1 That which Angels doe cleerly behold, and without any swaruing obserue, is a Law celestiall and heauenly. **1607** Hieron *Wks.* I. 151 The swaruing and straying from the will of God. **1607** Markham *Caval.* ii. (1617) 199 Making a horse doe them iust and strongly without either reeling or swaruing. *a* **1656** Hales *Gold. Rem.* (1673) 53 Our Sermons, in which the swarvings of that Church are necessarily to be taxt by us. *a* **1661** Fuller *Worthies* (1662) ii. 120 The Swervings and Aberrations of men. **1842** Manning *Serm.* (1848) I. 55 The holiest will..is clogged and checked by the swerving and burden of the flesh. **1859** Tennyson *Geraint & Enid* 1355 At a sudden swerving of the road. **1883** *Sat. Rev.* 27 Oct. 537/2 It seems that Bendigo, after swerving, had dashed up close to the rails and won by a neck.

'swerving, *ppl. a.* [f. swerve *v.* + -ing[2].] That swerves; deviating; making a swerve; diverted from the straight or right path; †erroneous.

1534 Whitinton *Tullyes Offices* ii. (1540) 86 The more swaruyng [orig. *versutior*] and craftyer that a man is. *a* **1547** Surrey *Æneid* ii. 283 The swarving axe when he [*sc.* a bull] shakes from his neck. **1549** Latimer *Ploughers* (Arb.) 19 Not to a swaruinge fayeth, but to a fayeth that embraceth Christe. *a* **1638** Mede *Wks.* (1672) 581, I dare not be confident that this Order and Series..is in no part thereof faulty and swerving. **1665** Bunyan *Holy Citie* (1669) 50 All swerving and unsound opinions. **1697** Dryden *Virg. Georg.* ii. 453 The swerving Vines on the tall Elms prevail. **1815** Scott *Dance of Death* iii, Where held the cloak'd patrol their course, And spurr'd 'gainst storm the swerving horse. **1867** W. W. Smyth *Coal & Coal-mining* 77 In consequence of the swerving direction of a great east and west dislocation. **1898** *Westm. Gaz.* 21 Oct. 4/3 The swerving gallop of the polo-ponies. **1900** [see swerve *sb.*]. **1903** *Westm. Gaz.* 18 Aug. 3/1 Hirst proceeded to bowl us out, or, rather, get us caught.. from that swerving ball of his. **1911** P. F. Warner *Cricket* 62, I have selected..Hirst as the fast 'swerving' left-hander.

swesh, swesher: see swash *sb.*[2], swasher.

swet(e, obs. ff. suet, suit, sweat, sweet.

†**sweth.** *Obs.* Misprint for *siueth*, var. of civet *sb.*[2], chive.

1562 Turner *Herbal* ii. 9 b, Syues or sweth..hath the same propertie that vnyons hath. **1597** Gerarde *Herbal* i. lxxxvii. §2. 140. **1611** Cotgr. s.v. *Brelles.*

†**swethe**, *v. Obs.* Also 5 **sweethe.** [OE. **sweþian* (in *besweþian*), related to *swaþian* to swathe (q.v.).] *trans.* To swathe.

c **1440** *Pallad. on Husb.* iv. 78 And swethe a tender vyne in bondes softe. *Ibid.* vi. 19 And swethed [*v.r.* sweethed] hem to geder se, Lest wyndes rude hem breke & ouerthrowe.

swethe, obs. form of swath.

swethel, var. sweddle.

swett(e, obs. ff. suet, sweat, sweet.

†**swetter**, *v. Sc. Obs.* [Variant of swatter.] *intr.* To wallow.

1536 Lyndesay *Answ. to Kingis Flyting* 58 Wald God the Lady..Had sene ȝow thair ly swetterand lyke twa swyne.

†**swetterly**, *adv. Obs.* [f. *swetter*, comp. of sweet *a.* + -ly[2]. Cf. *swifterly*.] More sweetly.

a **1340** Hampole *Psalter* xi. 7 Imange all metalles nan is þat swetterly chymes þan syluere.

†**sweve**, *v. Obs.* (Also 3 *pa. pple.* **iswaued.**) [Three OE. verbs coalesced under this form: (1) *swefan* (pa. t. *swæf*, *swǽfon*) str. intr. to sleep; (2) (*ʒe*)*swebban* (pa. t. *-swefede*, pa. pple. *swefed*) wk. trans. to put to sleep or to death (cf. sweb), corresponding to OS. *an-swebian*, OHG. *int-swebben* (MHG. *ent-sweben*), ON. *svefja* :—**swafjan*; (3) *ʒeswefian* (pa. t. *ʒeswefode*, pa. pple. *ʒeswefod*) to put to sleep; f. *swef-*: *swaf-*: *swuf-* (cf. ON. *sofa*, *svaf*, *svofinn* to sleep and *søfa* to put to death): see sweven.]

I. 1. *intr.* To sleep, sink to rest, become quiet.

Beowulf 119 (Gr.) Fand þa ðær inne æþelinga ʒedriht swefan æfter symble. *a* **1000** *Cædmon's Exod.* 36 (Gr.) Swæfon seledreamas. *c* **1205** Lay. 25548 Wederen alre selest, and þa sæ sweuede.

II. 2. *trans.* To put to sleep (or to death), lull to rest; also, to stupefy.

Beowulf 679 (Gr.) Ic hine sweorde swebban nelle. *c* **725** *Corpus Gloss.* (Hessels) S 399 *Sopio*, suebbo. *a* **950** *Guthlac* vi. (1909) 136 Þa wæs he sæmninga mid leohte slæpe swefed. *c* **1000** Ælfric *Hom.* II. 474 Se apostol Matheus þa dracan ʒeswefode. *a* **1175** *Cott. Hom.* 233 He blisseð hus mid dʒeies [*sic*] licht, he sweueð hus mid þiestre nicht. *c* **1205** Lay. 3073 Mid þære wræððe he wes isweued [*later text* igremid] þat he feol iswowen. *Ibid.* 15706 Þenne ich wæs on bedde iswaued.

†**swevel(l.** *Obs.* [For **swervel*, ad. WFris. (? Flem.) *swervel*, f. *swervje* to rove (see swerve). Cf. swarmer[2].] (See quots.)

1634 J. B[ate] *Myst. Nat.* 76 Swevels are nothing else but Rockets, having instead of a rod (to ballast them) a little cane bound fast unto them. **1688** R. Holme *Armoury* iii. xvi. (Roxb.) 91/2 A Swevell or Rockett.

swevell, obs. form of swivel.

sweven ('swɛv(ə)n), *sb. Obs.* exc. *arch.* Forms: 1 **swefen (suoefn, soefn, swæfn)**, 1, 3 **swefn**, (3 **suefen, sweoven**), 4–5 **swefene, sueven(e, swevene**, (4 **squeven, -yn, -in**, 4–5 **swevon**, 5 **swevn, swyven, swene, sween, sweine, sweyne**), 5–6 **swevin**, (5 **swevyn**, 6 *Sc.* **swewyn, sweving, -yng**), 6–8 **sweaven**, (7 **sweeven**), 3– **sweven.** [OE. *swef(e)n* str. neut., sleep, dream = OS. *sweban* str. m., ON. *svefn* str. m.:—OTeut. **swefno-*:—Indo-eur. **swepno-*, f. *swep-*.

The parallel formations **swepno-*, *swopno-*, *supno-* are represented outside Teutonic by Skr. *svápnas*, Gr. ὕπνος, L. *somnus*, Arm. *khun*, OIr. *suan*, W. *hun*, OSl. *sŭnŭ*, Lith. *sãpnas*; and, with secondary suffix, Skr. *svápn(i)yam*, Gr. ἐνύπνιον, L. *somnium*, OSl. *sŭnije*. From Indo-eur. *swep-*: *swop-*: *swup-* are derived also Skr. *svápiti* to sleep, L. *sopor* sleep, OE. *swefan* (see sweve), OSl. *sŭpati* to sleep.]

1. A dream, vision.

c **897** Ælfred *Gregory's Past. C.* xvi. 101 For ðære ʒesihðe ðe he on ðæm swefne ʒeseah. *c* **950** *Lindisf. Gosp.* Matt. i. 20 *In somnis*, in suoefnum *vel* in slepe. *a* **1000** *Cædmon's Dan.* 496 (Gr.) Him wearð on slæpe swefen ætywed. *c* **1205** Lay. 25552 Alse þe king slepte, A sweuen him imette, Feorlic wes þat sweouen. *a* **1225** *Ancr. R.* 268 Hit bringeð to nout alle þes deofles wieles..as lease swefnes, & false scheauwinges. *c* **1250** *Gen. & Ex.* 224 God dede ðat he on sweuene cam, And in ðat sweuene he let him sen Mikel ðat after sulde ben. *c* **1305** *St. Kenelm* 147 in *E.E.P.* (1862) 51 Þis sueuene bicom soþ ynouȝ. *c* **1386** Chaucer *Nun's Pr. T.* 101 Allas and konne ye been agast of sweuenys No thyng god woot, but vanitee in sweuene is. *c* **1420** *Chron. Vilod.* 1668 A merueylle swene he dude þo mete. **1422** Yonge tr. *Secreta Secret.* 199 Manasses..beleuyd swenys and sorsrie. *a* **1450** *Le Morte Arth.* 3226 In stronge sweyneys I haue bene stad. **1470–85** Malory *Arthur* i. xiii. 53 Alle that herd of the sweuen said it was a token of grete batayll. ? *a* **1500** *Chester Pl., Balaam* 382 Then shold our childre prophesie, ould men meet swevens [*v.r.* sweens] wytterly. **1513** Douglas *Æneis* ii. xii. 64 The figour fled as lycht wynd, or son beyme, Or mast liklie a waverand sweving [*v.r.* sweuin] or dreyme. *c* **1570** *Pride & Lowl.* (1841) 65, I looked all my chamber round about, And called to remembraunce all my sweven. **1594** *Zepheria* iii, I as out of sweauen, My selfe gan rowse, like one from sleepe awaked. *a* **1643** W. Cartwright *Ordinary* ii. ii. (1651) 26 Dan Cupido Sure sent thylke sweven to mine head. *a* **1650** *St. Aldringa* 77 in Hales & Furniv. *Percy Folio* I. 169, I had thought sweuens had neuer been true. *a* **1650** *Robin Hood & Guy of Gisborne* iv, Sweauens are swift, master..As the wind that blowes ore a hill. *a* **1832** Motherwell *Poems, Sabbath Summer Noon* xx, Fast fade the cares of life's dull sweven. **1840** Kingsley *Weird Lady* Poems (1892) 211 Mary Mother she stooped from heaven; She wakened Earl Harold out of his sweven.

†**2.** Sleep. *Obs. rare.*

a **1000** *Cædmon's Gen.* 720 (Gr.) Hit wæs deaðes swefn.. menniscra morð.

c **1645** *Enquiry*, &c. in *Harl. Misc.* (Malh.) V. 503 If they [*sc.* swallows] should have no occasion for breath, while they lie in their sweeven, or winter-sleep. [Cf. swevet, quot. 1623.]

†**sweven**, *v. Obs.* [OE. *swefnian* trans. to appear to in a dream, intr. to dream, f. *swefn*: see prec.] *intr.* To dream.

c **1000** *Sax. Leechd.* III. 212 Ʒif ðu swefnast ðe tweʒe monan ʒeseon. **1382** Wyclif *Isa.* xxix. 8 As sweueneth the hungrende, and eteth, whan forsothe he were wakid, voide is his soule. **14..** *Langl. P. Pl.* Prol. 10 (MS. Univ. Coll. e. 45), I slombride on a slepynge & sweuenyd so myrie, þan gan y to mete a merueylous sweuene. **1532** *Chaucer's Wks.*, *Troylus* iii. 1190 If ye be wyse Sweueneth [*MSS.* swouneth, etc.] not nowe, leste more folke aryse.

Hence †'**swevener** (also 6 *Sc.* **suengour, swevyngeour**), a dreamer.

1382 Wyclif *Jer.* xxvii. 9 Ȝoure profetus, and deuynoures, and sweueneres. **1513** Douglas *Æneis* viii. Prol. 171 Suengouris [*v.r.* swevyngeouris] that slummeris nocht weil.

†**swevening**, *vbl. sb. Obs.* Forms: 3–4 **swevening**, (4 **suev-**, 4–5 **-yng**), 4–5 **swefnyng(e.** [f. sweven *v.* + -ing[1].] Dreaming; a dream.

c **1275** Lay. 19701 He..com to þan kinge þar he lay a sweuekinge [*read* sweueninge]. *a* **1300** *Cursor M.* 4513 (Cott.) Pharaon þe king Sagh in slepe suilk a sueuening. *a* **1300** *St. Kenelm* 116 in *E.E.P.* (1862) 50 A sweueninge þat þe child mette. ? *a* **1366** Chaucer *Rom. Rose* 1 Many men sayn þat in sweueninges Ther nys but fables & lesynges. ? *a* **1400** *Morte Arth.* 759 With þe swoghe of þe see in swefnynge he felle. *c* **1400** Maundev. (Roxb.) vii. 27 Þe seuen deed qwhete eres, whilk kyng Pharao sawe in swefnyng. **1423** Jas. I *Kingis Q.* clxxiv, Though that my spirit vexit was tofore In sueuenyng, alssone as euer I woke, By twenty fold It was In trouble more.

So †'**swevening** (6 *Sc.* **sweyning**) *ppl. a.*, dreaming.

1570 *Satir. Poems Reform* x. 12 Dame Dreming, all clad in blak Sabill, With Sweyning Nymphis in cullouris variabill.

†**swevet.** *Obs.* Forms: 1 **swefet, sweofot**, 3 **swevet, sweovet**, 7 **swivet.** [OE. *swefet*, *sweofot*, f. *swef-* (see sweven).] Sleep, slumber.

Beowulf 1581 (Gr.) He Hroðgares heorðʒeneatas sloh on sweofote. *c* **1200** *Trin. Coll. Hom.* 77 Þat we don alse þing doð þe haueð lein on swe[ue]te, forquichieth þan here time cumeð. *c* **1205** Lay. 17773 Þe king læi on sweuete. *a* **1225** *Leg. Kath.* 1427 Ha slepten swoteliche a sweouete.

1623 C. Butler *Fem. Mon.* iii. (ed. 2) G iij, If there happen a milde and warme houre, they [*sc.* bees] presently perceiuing it, awake out of their swiuet. [Cf. sweven *sb.* 2, quot. *c* 1645.]

†**Swevian**, *a.* and *sb. Obs.* [f. med.L. *Suēvus*, used erron. for *Suecus* or *Suedus* Swede *sb.* + -ian.] **a.** *adj.* Swedish. **b.** *sb.* A Swede.

1601 R. Johnson *Kingd. & Commonw.* (1603) 129 The Sweuian horsemen are deuided into thirteene companies: Sweueland and Gothland mainetaine eleuen, and Finland two. *Ibid.* 130 In warring with the Muscouite the Sweuian hath the most aduantage.

†'**Swevical**, *a. Obs.* [f. mod.L. *Suēvicus*, f. *Suēvia* Swabia or *Suēvus* Swabian: see -ic and -al[1].] = Swabian *a.*

1560 Daus tr. *Sleidane's Comm.* 322 b, The Emperoure Maximilian, by the aid of the Sweuical league,..made warre with the Swisses.

swevil(l, -vyl(l, -wyl, obs. or dial. ff. swivel.

swewyt, obs. Sc. pa. t. of swive.

†**swey**, *v. Obs.* [OE. *swéʒan* to make a noise, sound, move with a noise:—**swōgjan* (cf. Goth. *gaswōgian*, *ufswōgjan* to sigh), cogn. w. *swéʒ*, earlier *swoeʒ* sound, noise = ON. *sœgr* :—**swōgiz*, f. *swōg-*, root of OE. *swóʒan*: see sough *v.*[1] The form *swey* in quot. 13.. is either an abnormal str. pa. t. or repr. OE. *swéoʒ*, pa. t. of *swóʒan*.] *intr.* To sound, make a sound, resound. Hence †'**sweying** *vbl. sb.*, noise; *ppl. a.*, resounding.

c **1000** Ælfric in *Ags. Hom.* (Assmann) 56 Swa þæt heora bodunge sweʒ sweʒde ʒeond eall. *c* **1000** —— *Hom.* (Th.) I. 104 Þæs Fæder stemn of heofenum hlude sweʒde, ðus cweðende. *a* **1240** *Ureisun* in *O.E. Hom.* I. 193 Murie dreameð engles biuoren þin onsene, Pleieð, & sweieð, & singeð bitweonen. **13..** *E.E. Allit. P.* C. 429 Þe soun of oure sourerayn þen swey in his ere. **14..** *Langl. P. Pl.* Prol. (ed. Wright) 10 As I lay and lenede, And loked on the watres, I slombred into a slepyng, It sweyed [*v.rr.* swiȝede, swyed, sownede, sweyued] so merrily. *a* **1400–50** *Wars Alex.* 5019 With a sweȝand swoȝe þis sware scho him ȝeldis. *c* **1440** *York Myst.* xxx. 371 Crye pece in this prese,..Bidde them swage of þer sweying.

swey: see sway *sb.* and *v.*

sweymows, obs. form of squeamous.

sweyn, sweyne, obs. ff. SWAIN, SWINE.

†**sweynt**, *ppl. a. Obs.* [pa. pple. of SWENCHE *v.*] Wearied, tired, inactive.
c 1384 CHAUCER *H. Fame* III. 693 Ye be like the sweynte [*Fairf.* swynt, *late versions* slepy] Catte That wolde haue fyssh; but, woste what? He wolde no thinge wete his clowys.

sweype, sweyr, sweyre, sweyt(e, sweythyli, swferane, swhyve: see SWAIP *Obs.*, SWEER *a.*, SWEAR, SWEET, SWITHLY, SOVEREIGN, SWIVE.

†**swibber-swill.** *Obs. rare.* (The first element is a var. of or error for *slibber* in SLIBBER-SAUCE.)
1546 BALE *1st Exam. Anne Askewe* 37 God was not wyse ynough in settynge the order therof [*sc.* of the Scriptures], but they must adde therunto their swybber swylle.

swible, obs. form of SWIVEL.
1647-60 HEXHAM, A Swible of yron which turneth round about. 1714 *Lond. Gaz.* No. 5218/3 A Gold Chain.., with 4 Steel Swibles. [Cf. *sweaple*, SWIPPLE 2.]

swic, obs. var. SWIKE.

swice, obs. f. SWISS.

swich, var. SWASH *sb.*² drum; obs. f. SUCH, SWITCH.

swick, mod. dial. f. SWIKE *v.*

†**swickle**, *sb. Obs.* [f. SWIKE *sb.*² + -LE.] A loop or noose in a trap. Hence †**swickle** *v., trans.* to noose.
1621 MARKHAM *Hunger's Prevent.* vi. 39 At the top you shall fasten a very strong loope or swickell of aboue an hundred Horse haires. *Ibid.* 41 They shall no sooner touch the Springe..but they shall presently be taken, and that member swickled which first toucheth the Springe.

swidden ('swɪdən). *Agric.* [f. *swidden*, var. SWITHEN *v.* (see *Eng. Dial. Dict.*: also, as a place-name element in Yorks.); in mod. use, a conscious readoption of the dialect word (see sense 2, quot. 1951).] **1. a.** An area of land that has been cleared for cultivation by slashing and burning the vegetation cover. Formerly only *north. dial.* (see quot. 1868).
1868 J. C. ATKINSON *Gloss. Cleveland Dial.* 514 *Swidden*, any place on the moor from which the Ling and other herbage has been burnt away, and which still shows signs of burning. 1957 *Proc. 9th Pacific Sci. Congress* (1958) XX. 127/1 They maintain permanent villages.., constructing temporary simple houses in their swidden, where at least part of the family lives during those times of the year when the swidden requires a great deal of care. 1961 *Current Anthropol.* II. 27/2 The specific form that a system of swidden agriculture may exhibit..depends on..the dispersal of swiddens... Swiddens may or may not be fenced. 1972 *Nature* 3 Mar. 41/1 In one case a specific tree is found growing in the new swidden.
b. *ellipt.* for *swidden cultivation.*
1955 *Proc. Prehistoric Soc.* XXI. 45 Even if *swidden* (clearance of woodland by burning) was not widely practised before Neolithic times, [etc.]. 1971 D. J. ROBINSON in Blakemore & Smith *Latin Amer.: Geogr. Perspectives* v. 191 Swidden appears to have formed the basis of the subsistence agriculture of..a part of the tropical zone. 1977 J. J. FOX *Harvest of Palm* i. 38 The Timorese have been forced..to rely even more heavily on swidden.
2. *attrib.* = SLASH-AND-BURN *attrib. phr.* (The principal use.)
1951 K. G. IZIKOWITZ *Lamet Hill Peasants in French Indo-China* 7 This is a book about the Lamet, swidden cultivators in the northern part of Laos. [*Note*] The primitive system of farming which involves clearing and burning the forest... In English it is sometimes called 'shifting cultivation' or 'slash and burn'. There is no single word in ordinary English which covers the meaning, since the method is no longer used in England... In searching for an English word I have taken..a dialect word, *swidden.* 1957 *Proc. 9th Pacific Sci. Congress* (1958) XX. 127/1 We have swidden cultivators who are sedentary in Southeast Asia and other parts of the humid tropics. 1965 G. A. COLLIER *Fields in Tzotzil* iii. 60 Virtually all are subsistence corn farmers who utilize the slash-and-burn or 'swidden' system of agriculture. 1971 *Sci. Amer.* Sept. 101/2 There is a structural similarity between a swidden garden and a tropical rain forest. 1978 KUNSTADTER & CHAPMAN in P. Kunstadter et al. *Farmers in Forest* i. 3/2 Swidden fields are usually located at some distance from markets, generally on land that is considered marginal... Swiddening is often carried out primarily as a subsistence operation..rather than as a source of cash crops.
Hence (as a back-formation) *v. trans.*, to cultivate by the swidden method; '**swiddener**, '**swiddening** *vbl. sb.*
1971 *Sci. Amer.* Sept. 119/1 Between one month and four months after clearing begins..the felled litter on the site is burned. This is a step of considerable importance in the swiddening regime. 1975 J. NANCE *Gentle Tasaday* xvi. 282 Swiddeners did not uproot the growth, but burned it over and planted within it. 1978 KUNSTADTER & CHAPMAN in P. Kunstadter et al. *Farmers in Forest* i. 7/2 The land that is swiddened may or may not be claimed by a village unit as a whole.

swidder, var. SWITHER.

Swiderian (swɪ'dɪərɪən), *a. Archæol.* [ad. F. *swidérien*, G. *swiderien*, f. *Swidry*, the name of an archæol. site near Warsaw (see quot. 1936): cf. -AN.] Of, pertaining to, or characteristic of a (principally) mesolithic culture in Poland and neighbouring countries, or its artefacts. Also *absol.* as *sb.*
[1922 *Wiadomosci Archeologiczne* VII. 96 Dans la formation III on trouve des documents archéologiques se rapportant aux industries magdalénienne moyenne, swidérienne, azilienne.] 1936 J. G. D. CLARK *Mesolithic Settlement N. Europe* ii. 62 Two alternative names have been put forward..to label a culture..centering on the valleys of the Vistula and the Bug-Swiderian, after the site at Swidry..and Chlebowician... Numerous Swiderian sites are known from Poland. 1939 V. G. CHILDE *Dawn Europ. Civilization* (ed. 3) i. 4 The *Swiderian* culture, represented by assemblages of small flint tools collected from sand-dunes in Russia and Poland, sometimes under fossil turf-lines of Atlantic age, is characterized by small asymmetrically tanged-points..used presumably as arrow-heads. 1948 A. KROEBER *Anthropol.* (ed. 2) xvi. 270 *Swiderian*, Poland, Rumania; smallish, tanged blades; early Mesolithic—in fact apparently late Palaeolithic also. 1951 [see LYNGBY]. 1960 C. WINICK *Dict. Anthropol.* 518/2 *Swiderian*, a culture found in Poland, with the tranchet as a typical tool. Its remains, mostly kitchen middens, resemble the Campignian culture, which is found further south.

†**swie**, *v. Obs.* Also 3 swiȝe, swihe. [OE. *swīȝan* and *swīȝian*, corresp. to OFris. *swīgia*, OS. *swīgôn*, MLG., MDu. *swīgen* (Du. *zwijgen*), OHG., MHG. *swīgên* (G. *schweigen*); ultimately related to Gr. σιγή silence, σιγᾶν to be silent.] *intr.* To be silent. Also in *ppl. a.* (**swihende**), silent.
Beowulf 1699 (Gr.) Ða se wisa spræc sunu Healfdenes (swiȝedon ealle). c 900 *Bæda's Hist.* II. ix. (1890) 124 He..oft longe ana sæt swiȝende muðe. c 1205 LAY. 16820 Alle heo weoren stille & swiȝeden mid stæuen. c 1200 *Trin. Coll. Hom.* 101 Bitwenen his þrowenge & his ariste he lai on his sepulcre & swiede. a 1225 Swihende wike [see below].
Hence †**swidaȝ**, any of the last three days of Holy Week; †**swimesse** [MASS *sb.*¹], the canon of the mass, which is said in a low voice (cf. early mod.G. *stillmesse*, now = low mass); †**swiwike** [WEEK *sb.*], Holy Week (cf. G. *stillwoche*).
c 1000 ÆLFRIC *Hom.* (Th.) I. 218 Circlice þeawas forbeodaþ to secgenne ænig spel on þam þrym swig-dagum. c 1000 in Napier *Contrib. OE. Lexicogr.* (1906) 60 Se prest stod on þære swimæsse. *Ibid.* He wæs on þere swigmesse & ȝeornlice bæd for þon cincge. c 1200 *Trin. Coll. Hom.* 101 þe þre daȝe biforen estre cleped swidaȝes. *Ibid.* 97 þe holi word þe ure helende..seide..and efter him prest hem seð atte swimesse. a 1225 *Ancr. R.* 70 Al þe swiðwike [? swiȝwike; *v.rr.* swihende wike, swiwike] uort non of Ester euen.

swier, obs. f. SQUIRE = ESQUIRE.
a 1400-50 [see SWIMBLE *v.*]. 1450 in *Catal. Anc. Deeds* IV. 327 Comeng..to excuse hym opon a boke be for John Hudelston swier.

swier, swiete, swife, swiff: see SWEER, SWEET, SWIVE.

†**swift**, *sb.*¹ *Obs. Naut.* App. = SWIFTER.
Knight *Dict. Mech.* gives this form with the definitions of SWIFTER a, b, but they seem to be wrongly inferred from the entry *swift* in Smyth's *Sailor's Word-bk.*
1336-7 *Acc. Exch. K.R.* 19/31 m. 5 (P.R.O.) In D. Swiftes emptis in Grosso apud lenne de Iohanne de Kynge-stone. *Ibid.*. In ij. petris cord. de canabo..pro swifftes et robond inde faciendis.

swift (swɪft), *sb.*² [subst. use of SWIFT *a.*]
I. 1. The common newt or eft. Now only *dial.* **b.** A name for several swift-running small lizards, as the N. American fence-lizard, *Sceloporus undulatus.*
1530 PALSGR. 278/2 Swyfte, worme, *lesarde.* 1559 W. CUNNINGHAM *Cosmogr. Glasse* 173 Venomous beastes, and Wormes, as Ranny, Tode, Eddy, Snack, swift. 1606 N. B[AXTER] *Sydney's Ourania* G 3, The Neught, the Swift, lurking in the Roade. 1650 W. D. tr. *Comenius' Gate Lat. Unl.* §215 The lizzard, the evet, the swift..walk on their feet. 1668 CHARLETON *Onomast.* 26 *Lacerta Stellio*..the Swift. 1848 *Zoologist* VI. 2186 If you were to ask here [*sc.* in Norfolk] whether there were any swifts about, you would be told 'Yes, plenty in the clay-pits': the only creature known by that name is the water-eft. 1889 [see *fence-lizard* s.v. FENCE *sb.* 11].
2. A bird of the family *Cypselidæ*, comprising numerous and widely distributed species, outwardly resembling swallows (cf. SWALLOW *sb.*¹ 2), and noted for their swiftness of flight; *esp.* the common swift, *Cypselus apus*, a summer visitant to the British Isles and Europe generally.
1668 CHARLETON *Onomast.* 90 *Hirundo Apos Major*..the Horse-Marten, or Swift. a 1672 WILLUGHBY *Ornith.* (1678) 214 The black Martin or Swift. *Hirundo apus.* 1687 DRYDEN *Hind & P.* III. 547 Some Swifts, the Gyants of the Swallow kind. 1769 G. WHITE *Selborne, To Pennant* 8 Dec., The invariable early retreat of the *Hirundo apus*, or swift, so many weeks before its congeners. 1866 DARWIN *Orig. Spec.* vii. (ed. 4) 281 One of the swifts of North America makes its nest..of sticks agglutinated with saliva. 1870 NICHOLSON *Man. Zool.* (1875) 508 In the Swifts..all four toes are present, but they are all turned forwards.
b. Name for a breed of domestic pigeons having some resemblance to swifts. Also *swift pigeon.*
1879 L. WRIGHT *Pigeon Keeper* 197 Swifts are named from the great resemblance of their long flights and tails to the Martin and Swallow tribe of birds. 1881 LYELL *Pigeons* 113 The Swift pigeon..is of Eastern origin.
†**3.** A proper name for a swift-running hound.
1602 *2nd Pt. Return fr. Parnass.* II. v. 904 The Buck broke gallantly: my great Swift being disaduantaged in his slip was at the first behinde. 1677 COLES, *Argus*..swift, a dogs name, Ulysses's dogs name.
4. Collectors' name for moths of the genus *Hepialus* or family *Hepialidæ*, distinguished by their rapid flight. Also *swift moth.*
1819 SAMOUELLE *Entomol. Compend.* 245 Hepialus Humuli (ghost swift). Hep. Mappa (map-winged swift). Hep. Hectus (golden swift). 1870 *Eng. Mech.* 21 Jan. 449/3 The subterranean Caterpillars of the Swift Moths.
II. 5. A light kind of reel, usually of adjustable diameter, upon which a skein of silk, yarn, etc. is placed in order to be wound off. See also quot. 1878.
1564 *Inv.* in Noake *Worcestershire Relics* (1877) 13 In the weaving shoppe..ij pare of shuttels a swiste [*sic*] and a knave to the quiltourne. 1795 W. HUTTON *Hist. Derby* 208 The machine continually turns a round bobbin, or small block of wood, which draws the thread from the slip, while expanded upon a swift, suspended on a centre. The moment the thread breaks, the swift stops. 1805 GODWIN *Fleetwood* xi, The reels, or, as the English manufacturers call them, swifts, which received the silk, as it was devolved from certain bobbins [*sic*]. 1825 J. NICHOLSON *Oper. Mech.* 395 Each of the skeins is extended upon a slight reel called a swift..composed of four small rods, fixed into an axis, and small bands of string are stretched between the arms to receive the skein,..the bands admit of sliding to a greater or less distance from the centre, so as to increase the effective diameter of the reel, according to the size of the skein. 1876 PREECE & SIVEWRIGHT *Telegraphy* 176 The galvanized iron wire is placed on a simple loose wheel, or 'swift'. 1878 *Cumbld. Gloss.*, *Garn winnels, Swifts*, a wooden cross from which yarn is wound off. 1884 W. S. B. MCLAREN *Spinning* (ed. 2) 182 The only objection to this machine is the danger to the workers, for the swift is not stopped with each change of wool.
b. A cylinder in a carding-machine.
1853 URE *Dict. Arts* I. 765 The cards employed for tow are machines of considerable weight and importance, the main cylinder, or, as it is sometimes called, 'swift', being from 4 to 5 feet diameter. 1888 *Encycl. Brit.* XXIV. 659/1 The angle stripper passes the wool from the doffer to the next cylinder, which is called a 'swift'.
†**6.** A rapid current; a rapid. *Obs. rare.*
1661 WALTON *Angler* xiv. 198 He [*sc.* the Barbel] is able to live in the strongest swifts of the Water. 1712 *Lond. Gaz.* No. 5026/6 Another we sunk, who in the swift of the Sea turn'd bottom up.
7. The sail of a windmill. *dial.*
1763 MILLS *Pract. Husb.* III. 125 By working the bellows with swifts like those of a mill. 1796 *Lond. Chron.* 21 Jan. 72 As a boy was at play near the windmill belonging to Rye,..the swifts struck him on the head.
8. *Printers' slang.* A quick or expeditious typesetter.
1841 SAVAGE *Dict. Print.* 229 Compositors who are expeditious workmen are styled Fire Eaters, and also Swifts. 1896 *Indianapolis Typogr. Jrnl.* 16 Nov. 405 Owing to the linotype machines, several 'swifts' were thrown out of employment.
III. 9. *attrib.* and *Comb.*, as *swift-like* adj. or adv.; **swift moth**, = 4; **swift pigeon**, = 2 b; **swift reel**, = 5; **swift-shrike**, a bird of the genus *Ocypterus.*
1839 BAILEY *Festus* 144, I was at home in Heaven: *Swift-like I lived above. 1868 *Rep. U.S. Commiss. Agric.* (1869) 288 The skeins are slipped upon octagonal, wicker '*swift' reels. 1841 *Penny Cycl.* XXI. 416/1 The *swift shrikes (*Ocypterus*, Cuv.), so named from their very long wings.

swift, *a.* (*adv.*) Also 1, 4-6 swyft, 1, 3-4 (6 *Sc.*) suift, 4-6 **swifte**, 5-6 **swyfte**, (4 **sweft, sweyft, squift**, *Ayenb.* **zuift, zuyft**, 4-5 **squyft(e**, 5 **suyfte, sqwyft(e, swyfht**, 6 **swiyft**), *Sc.* **swuft, swofte, suofte**, (7 **suifte**, *Anglo-Ir.* **shwift**(e). [OE. *swift*:—prehistoric ***swipt-**, repr. Indo-eur. root (*swoib-*) *sweib-, swib-*: (*swoip-*), *sweip-, swip-* to move in a sweeping manner (see SWOPE *v.* and SWIVE *v.*) with ppl. suffix *-to-*. The relations of the following phonologically equivalent forms to each other and to this word are not determinable: WFris. *swift* adj. restless, disturbed, stormy, *swift* sb. worthless fellow, swindler, LG. *swift* small lean person, Sw. dial. *svift* speedy, swift (cf. *sviftande* instantaneous movement).]
A. *adj.* **1. a.** 'Moving far in a short time' (J.); moving, or capable of moving, with great speed or velocity; going quickly or at a great rate; rapid, fleet.
Beowulf 2264 (Gr.) Se swifta mearh. c 888 ÆLFRED *Boeth.* xxxvi. §3 Ic hæbbe swiðe swifte feþera, þæt ic mæȝ fliogan ofer þone hean hrof þæs heofones. c 1205 LAY. 5902 þa oðere weoren swifte [c 1275 swihte], heore wepnen weoren lihte. *Ibid.* 26068 Ardur wes swiftre and of-toc þene eotend. a 1300 *Cursor M.* 17288 + 186 (Cott.) Peter & Iohne to-geder ran..But Iohne was þe swifter. ? a 1366 CHAUCER *Rom. Rose* 949 The swiftest of these Arowis fyue. c 1375 *Cursor M.* 3730 (Fairf.) Goddote Am I noȝt so squyft on fote. 1390 GOWER *Conf.* I. 119 The grete hert.. Whiche swifte feet sette upon grounde. *Ibid.* II. 328 A Swalwe swift of winge. c 1450 HOLLAND *Howlat* 138 The Swallowe so swyft. 1533 GAU *Richt Vay* 66 Our bodis sal be na mair hewy or sweir bot swuft. 1596 DALRYMPLE tr. *Leslie's Hist. Scot.* I. 91 Swiftnes of fute, in quhilke thay walde ouirrin the swoftest horse. 1628 MILTON *Vac. Exerc.* 96 Severn swift, guilty of Maidens death. 1667 —— *P.L.* I. 326 His swift pursuers. 1696 PHILLIPS (ed. 5) s.v., A Planet is said to be swift in Motion, when by its own proper Diurnal Motion, he moves farther than his mean Diurnal Motion. a 1700 EVELYN *Diary* 7 Mar. 1690, A vessell..built with low decks,..and..so light and swift of sailing, that [etc.]. 1784

COWPER *Task* III. 325 Delights which who would leave.. For all the savage din of the swift pack, And clamours of the field? **1843** JAMES *Forest Days* iii, They watched the swift fish darting along the stream. **1852** MRS. STOWE *Uncle Tom's C.* xvii. 161, I will.. engage him to come behind on his swift nag.

in similative and proverbial phrases.

a **1225** *Ancr. R.* 196 Vre widerwines beoð swifture þen þe earnes. *c* **1386** CHAUCER *Prol.* 190 Grehoundes he hadde, as swift as fowel in flight. *c* **1400** *Rom. Rose* 5024 Present tyme abidith nought, It is more swift than any thought. **1560** *Bible* (Geneva) Eccl. ix. 11 The race is not to the swift, nor the battel to the strong. *a* **1593** MARLOWE tr. *Lucan* I. 231 Swifter then bullets throwne from Spanish slinges. **1599** PORTER *Angry Wom. Abingt.* (Percy Soc.) 41 A swift horse will tier, but he that trottes easilie will indure. **1692** PRIOR *Ode Imit. Hor.* vi, Fate has swifter Wings than Fear.

b. Of movement, or action regarded as movement: Taking place or executed at high speed; rapid, quick.

a **1050** *Wærferth's Gregory's Dial.* II. vii. 115 He.. mid swiftum [*earlier version* færlicum] ryne eft ȝecyrde. **1398** TREVISA *Barth. De P.R.* III. xvii. (1495) d iv/2 An oore yᵗ semyth broken in yᵉ water for swyft meuinge of yᵉ water. *a* **1542** WYATT *Song of Iopas* 15 With great swift sway, the first [= *primum mobile*].. Carieth it self. **1606** SHAKS. *Tr. & Cr.* I. i. 119 *Troy*. But to the sport abroad, are you bound thither? *Æne.* In all swift hast. **1634** MILTON *Comus* 114 The Starry Quire, Who.. Lead in swift round the Months and Years. **1662** PLAYFORD *Skill Mus.* I. x. (1674) 33 This Mood.. is of two Motions, the one slow, the other more swift. **1784** COWPER *Task* I. 139 That play of lungs.. Respiring freely the fresh air, that makes Swift pace or steep ascent no toil to me. **1851** CARLYLE *Sterling* I. iv, A swift but not very legible or handsome penmanship. **1860** TYNDALL *Glac.* II. x. 279 The non-coincidence of the point of swiftest motion with the centre of the glacier. **1867** AUGUSTA WILSON *Vashti* xii, The swift clicking of her knitting-needles.

2. a. Coming on, happening, or performed without delay; prompt, speedy.

c **1000** ÆLFRIC *Hom.* I. 618 Se miccla Godes dæȝ is swiðe ȝehende and ðearle swyft. **1377** LANGL. *P. Pl.* B. XI. 370 Suffraunce is a souereyne vertue, And a swyfte veniaunce. **1603** SHAKS. *Meas. for M.* IV. iii. 107 Make a swift returne, For I would commone with you of such things, That want no eare but yours. **1667** MILTON *P.L.* V. 907 Those proud Towrs to swift destruction doom'd. **1697** DRYDEN *Æneid* VIII. 230 And, when to Morrow's Sun reveals the Light, With swift Supplies you shall be sent away. **1755** WESLEY *Prim. Physick* p. xxi. (Postscr.), It was a great Surprize to the Editor of the following Collection, that there was so swift and large a Demand for it. **1870** DICKENS *E. Drood* iii, She looks up at him with a swift bright look. **1904** R. C. JEBB *Bacchylides* (Proc. Brit. Acad.) 15 This art of swift transition ..was one which Pindar seems to have regarded as peculiarly his own.

b. Acting, or disposed to act, without delay; prompt, ready. Usually const. *to* with inf. or sb.

1340 *Ayenb.* 141 Efterward þe milde is wel zuift and wel ingnel. **1340** HAMPOLE *Pr. Consc.* 792 He es swyft to spek on his manere. **1382** WYCLIF *Jas.* i. 19 Be ech man swift for to here, forsothe slowe for to speke. *c* **1477** CAXTON *Jason* 47 b, Ye ben hasty & moche swift in your werkes. *c* **1586** C'TESS PEMBROKE *Ps.* LXXXVI. v, Thou, Jehova, swift to grace. **1667** MILTON *P.L.* IX. 633 He.. To mischief swift. **1681** DRYDEN *Abs. & Achit.* 191 Swift of Dispatch and easie of Access. **1784** COWPER *Task* II. 251 All were swift to follow whom all lov'd. **1827** SCOTT *Surg. Dau.* ii, Richard is not swift,.. but then he is sure. **1847** HELPS *Friends in C.* I. 11 Let us not be swift to imagine that lies are never of any service. **1855** KINGSLEY *Westw. Ho!* xxxiii, Crafty of counsel, and swift of execution.

3. Done or finished within a short time; passing quickly, of short continuance, that is soon over, brief. Chiefly *poet.*

a **1225** *Leg. Kath.* 2156 Þis swifte pine, þet aswikeð se sone. **1590** SHAKS. *Mids. N.* I. i. 144 Swift, as a shadowe; short, as any dreame. **1608** —— *Per.* III. i. 13 Lucina,.. make swift the pangues Of my Queenes trauayles! **1611** *Bible* Job vii. 6 My dayes are swifter then a weauers shuttle. **1820** SHELLEY *Sensit. Pl.* III. 22 Swift Summer into the Autumn flowed. **1821** —— *Epithal.* 7 Hence, swift hour! and thy loved flight Oft renew. **1848** A. B. EVANS *Leicestersh. Words, Swift*, fast consuming: 'The Snibston coal is very *swift*.'

B. *adv.* (Now chiefly *poet.*)

1. = SWIFTLY 1.

13.. *E.E. Allit. P.* C. 108 He swenges me þys swete schip swefte fro þe hauen. *c* **1400** *Destr. Troy* 13299 Full swift to the swalgh me swinget the flode. *c* **1430** *Chev. Assigne* 113 Thenne an hynde kome fro þe woode rennynge fulle swyfte. **1596** in *Spalding Club Misc.* I. 85 Thow.. rann.. alss swoft, as apperit to him, as ane arrow culd be schot furth of ane bow. **1606** SHAKS. *Tr. & Cr.* II. iii. 277 Light Botes may saile swift, though greater bulkes draw deepe. **1667** MILTON *P.L.* III. 714 Swift to thir several Quarters hasted then The cumbrous Elements. **1729** SWIFT *Lett. Irish Coal* 23 Oct., The latter [*sc.* Irish coal] consumed away very swift in a blaze. *a* **1774** GOLDSM. *Surv. Exp. Philos.* (1776) II. 224 Wood rubbed very swift with a circular motion takes fire. **1781** COWPER *Retirem.* 435 Then swift descending with a seaman's haste. **1852** THACKERAY *Esmond* I. xiii, A light chaise.. running as swift.. as a Lap-lander's sledge.

2. = SWIFTLY 2, 3.

† *soft swift*: 'not so fast'; 'don't be too hasty'.

c **1375** *Cursor M.* 341 (Fairf.) Al his comandement was done Squyfter [*Cott.* suiftliker] þan any eye may wynke. **1596** SHAKS. *Merch. V.* III. ii. 199 My eyes my Lord can looke as swift as yours. **1597** MORLEY *Introd. Mus.* 123 Soft swift, you who are so ready to find faultes, I pray you let vs see howe you can mend them. **1667** MILTON *P.L.* VI. 190 A noble stroke.. Which hung not, but so swift with tempest fell On the proud Crest of Satan, that [etc.]. **1808** SCOTT *Marm.* VI. xxii, Himself he swift on horseback threw.

¶ Hyphened to pres. pple. and occas. to a finite part of a verb, on the analogy of combs. in C. 3.

1727 THOMSON *Summer* 490 [588] Swift-shrinking back, I stand aghast. **1729** SAVAGE *Wanderer* II. 371 The Roof swift-kindles from the beaming Ground. **1735** SOMERVILLE *Chase* I. 109 To rein the Steed Swift-stretching o'er the Plain. **1820** KEATS *Lamia* I. 116 She.. Blush'd a live damask, and swift-lisping said [etc.]. **1887** MORRIS *Odyssey* XI. 5 Pouring the tear-drops swift-following each on each.

C. Combinations, etc.

1. Special collocations of the adj.: **swift cut** = *speedy cut* (SPEEDY 7); also in names of species of animals distinguished by swift running or flight, as ***swift lizard, snake, swallow, tern.***

1725 *Bradley's Fam. Dict.* II. 5 Y 4 b/2 If Scabs be under his Knee on the inside, it is the *Swift-Cut, and he will illy endure galloping. **1802** SHAW *Gen. Zool.* III. I. 251 *Swift Lizard. *Lacerta Velox. Ibid.* II. 510 *Swift Snake. *Coluber Cursor.* **1601** HOLLAND *Pliny* XI. xlvii. I. 351 That Martinets have feet: like as also the *swift Swallow called Oce. **1817** STEPHENS in *Shaw's Gen. Zool.* X. I. 97 Swift Swallow (*Hirundo Velox*). **1889** H. SAUNDERS *Man. Brit. Birds* 640 The *Swift Tern. *S[terna] bergii* of Lichtenstein (*S. velox* of Rüppell).

2. Combs. of the adj.: parasynthetic, as ***swift-fated, -handed, -heeled*** (= SWIFT-FOOTED), ***-hoofed*** (†***-hoved***), ***-paced, -streamed, -tongued***; also † **swift-flight** *a.*, flying swiftly; with other adjs., expressing a combination of two qualities, as ***swift-frightful, -slow.*** Also † **swift horse running**, horse-racing.

1723 BLACKMORE *Alfred* III. 559 The *swift-finn'd Racers of the Flood. **1592** *Soliman & Pers.* I. iii. 42 To change a bullet with our *swift flight shot. **1837** CARLYLE *Fr. Rev.* III. v. vi, A thing so incalculable, *swift-frightful. **1840** —— *Heroes* ii, A *swift-handed, deep-hearted race of men. **1634** HABINGTON *Castara* I. (Arb.) 43 No suppliant breath Stayes the speed of *swift-heel'd death. **1702** CONGREVE *Ode to Ld. Godolphin* viii, Varying anon her Theme, she takes Delight The swift-heel'd Horse to praise. **1615** CHAPMAN *Odyss.* VI. 149 In the wilde Bores chace; Or *swift-hou'd Hart. **1500–20** DUNBAR *Poems* xxxix. 9 Halking, hunting and *swift horss rynning. **1598** BP. HALL *Sat.* IV. iii. 52 Say'st thou this Colt shall proue a *swift-pac'd steed Only because a Iennet did him breed? **1716** *Loyal Mourner* 69 From swift-paced Time's destructive Power free. **1870** BRYANT *Iliad* II. XIV. 59 For much he feared to offend the swift-paced Night. **1598** SYLVESTER *Du Bartas* II. I. *Eden* 226 Painfull griefes, whose *swift-slow posting pase.. our dying life doth chase. **1594** *Selimus* 2407 Leaving the banks of *swift-stream'd Thermodon. **1746** FRANCIS tr. *Hor., Sat.* I. vii. 10 The *swift-tongued Barrus.

3. Combs. of the adv. with pples., as ***swift-advancing, -burning, -darkening, -declining, -eddying, -falling, -flashing, -flowing, -flying, -gliding, -moving, -posting, -pursuing, -recurring, -revenging, -running, -rushing, -sliding, -sprung, -starting, -stealing, -striding, -swimming.***

1859 GEO. ELIOT *A. Bede* xxxv, Not knowing where to turn for refuge from *swift-advancing shame. **1834–5** J. PHILLIPS *Geol.* in *Encycl. Metrop.* (1845) VI. 592/2 *Swift-burning thick coals. **1933** W. DE LA MARE *Fleeting* 33 Even the wise.. Have smiled with *swift-darkening eyes. **1590** GREENE *Orl. Fur.* I. i, To Tanuis, whose *swift declining flouds [etc.]. **1923** H. BELLOC *Sonnets & Verse* 13 Anchor hold against *swift-eddying time. **1791** BLAKE *French Rev.* in *Compl. Writings* (1972) 141 Aumont, whose chaos-born soul Eternally wand'ring a Comet and *swift-falling fire, pale enter'd the chamber. **1951** W. DE LA MARE *Winged Chariot* 38 Swift-falling flower, slowly fretting stone Clock on unheeded those who lie alone. **1855** W. WHITMAN *Leaves of Grass* 62 The great gay-pennanted.. steamboat.., with her.. delicate *swift-flashing paddles. **1930** BLUNDEN *Summer's Fancy* 44 With swift-flashing hope. **1848** BUCKLEY *Iliad* 97 A *swift-flowing river. **1605** SYLVESTER *Du Bartas* II. iii. III. *Law* 62 A *swift-flying Fame, Which (lately but) from stately Memphis came. **1871** LONGF. *Div. Trag.* I. ix. 70 The swift-flying vapours hid themselves In caverns. **1715** POPE *Iliad* III. 17 *Swift-gliding mists the dusky fields invade. **1872** W. WHITMAN *As Strong Bird on Pinions Free* 4 Thee as another equally needed sun, America-radiant, ablaze, *swift-moving, fructifying all. **1955** J. R. R. TOLKIEN *Return of King* v. i. 19 He wondered if he was.. still in the swift-moving dream in which he had been wrapped. **1610** DRAYTON *Leg. Robt. Normandie* xliii, Times *swift posting hours [*edd.* 1605, 1608 times ne'r-turning howres]. **1785** T. DWIGHT *Conquest of Canäan* VIII. 188 Once hast thou fled the *swift-pursuing spear, But fled'st in vain. **1948** R. GRAVES *Coll. Poems 1914–47* 231 The swift-pursuing reed. **1841** BROWNING *Pippa Passes* I. 278 At *swift-recurring intervals. **1590** GREENE *Orl. Fur.* v. i, And neuer sheath thy *swift reuenging swoorde Till.. The highest mountaines swimme in streames of bloud. **1538** ELYOT, *Alipedes*, *swyfte runnynge horses. **1833** J. RENNIE *Alph. Angling* 59 The fish more peculiar to swift-running waters. **1625** MILTON *Death Fair Inf.* 67 To turn *Swift-rushing black perdition hence. *a* **1618** SYLVESTER *Spectacles* v, Yon silver Brooks,.. Whose smooth *swift-sliding pase Still, still roules down apace. **1935** KIPLING *King & Sea* in *Times* 17 July 19/4, I opened him all the guile of the seas—Their sullen, *swift-sprung treacheries. **1596** *Edw. III*, IV. vii. 2 *Swift starting feare Hath buzd a cold dismaie through all our armie. **1669** STURMY *Mariner's Mag.* I. ii. 16, I hope to ..hear, That the English Mariner will make better use of *swift-stealing Time. **1929** KIPLING *Poems 1886–1929* III. 341 One silent, swart, *swift-striding camel, oceanward wending. **1888** GOODE *Amer. Fishes* 78 It is a *swift-swimming fish.

swift, *v.*¹ *Naut.* [Owing to the scantiness and the chronological discrepancy of the early evidence, the mutual relation and immediate source of this word, SWIFT *sb.*¹, and SWIFTER, cannot be clearly ascertained. They are presumably of Scand. or LG. origin: cf. ON. *svipta* ('svɪfta) to reef, *sviptingar, -ingr, -ungr* reefing-ropes, Du. *zwichten* to take in (sails), roll up (ropes), *zwichtings, zwichtlijnen* cat-harpings, WFris. *swicht* partly or completely furled sail, G. *schwigten* to snake two ropes together, *schwigting, schwigtleine* snake-line, Da. *svigte* to take in (sail): prob. allied ultimately to SWIFT *a.*] *trans.* To tighten or make fast by means of a rope or ropes drawn taut; e.g. the rigging or masts, the capstan-bars, or a boat or ship by passing a rope round the gunwale, or round the bottom and upperworks, to prevent strain. Cf. SWIFTER *sb.*

1485 *Naval Acc. Hen. VII* (1896) 47 Swyftyng takles.. xj. **1487** *Ibid.* 62 Swiftyng takles.. viij. **1495** *Ibid.* 275 The pollankers and Swifting takles of the foremaste. *a* **1625** *Nomenclator Navalis* (Harl. MS. 2301) *Swifteing*. When wee bring Shipps agrounde, or Careene them, wee vse to Swift the Masts, to ease them and strengthen [them], wᶜʰ is done in this manner: they Lash fast all the Pendants of the Swifters, and Tackles, wᵗʰ a Roape, close to the Mast, as neare their Blocks as they cann. **1704** J. HARRIS *Lex. Techn.* I, *Swifting* the Capstan-Bars, is straining a Rope all round the outer ends of the Capstan-Bars, in order to strengthen them, and make them bear all alike, and together, when the Men heave or work there. **1799** *Hull Advertiser* 19 Oct. 2/1 One ship's main-mast, one fore-mast, and one mizen-mast, all swifted together, which were towing at the stern of the brig. **1840** R. H. DANA *Bef. Mast* xxxv, We were obliged to go aloft upon the ropes and shearpoles with which the rigging was swifted in. **1867** SMYTH *Sailor's Word-bk.* s.v., The rigging is.. swifted down preparatory to replacing the ratlines truly horizontal after setting up. **1883** *Man. Seamanship for Boys* 200 *Q.* What do you mean by rigging the capstan? *A.* The bars being shipped, pinned, and swifted in place.

swift, *v.*² *rare.* [f. SWIFT *a.*] *intr.* To move swiftly; to hasten. Now only as *nonce-usage.*

a **1618** SYLVESTER *Mem. Mortalitie* II. iv, Time flits as Winde, and as a Torrent swifteth. **1722** RAMSAY *Three Bonnets* IV. 169 Between your houghs gae clap your gelding, Swift hame and feast upon a speldìng. **1935** R. MACAULAY *Personal Pleasures* 195 There goes the Atalanta among cars; see how it swifts along, passing all others.

swiften ('swɪft(ə)n), *v. rare.* [f. SWIFT *a.* + -EN⁵.]

1. *trans.* To make swift or swifter, hasten.

1638 SIR T. HERBERT *Trav.* (ed. 2) 202 Our Ambassador to swiften his dispatch, visited.. the grand Favorite Mahomet Ally-beg. **1647** BOYLE in Birch *Life* B.'s Wks. 1772 I. p. xxxix, The dictionary, whose edition, had my wishes the power to swiften it, should be very sudden.

2. *intr.* To become swift or swifter; *loosely*, to move swiftly, hasten, hurry. Hence **swiftening** *ppl. a.*

1839 BAILEY *Festus* ii. 8 The thought comes swiftening over us Like a small bird winging the still blue air. **1848** LYTTON *K. Arthur* II. lxxviii, Still, while he sped, the swifter wings that lead Seem'd to rebuke for sloth the swiftening steed. **1889** *Scribner's Mag.* May 603 High places where on quiet afternoon A shadow swiftens by.

swifter ('swɪftə(r)), *sb.* [See SWIFT *v.*¹]

1. *Naut.* A rope used for swifting (see SWIFT *v.*¹). **a.** One of a pair of shrouds, fixed above the other shrouds, for swifting or stiffening a mast. **b.** A rope passed through holes or notches in the outer ends of the capstan-bars and drawn taut. **c.** A rope passed around a boat or ship as a protection against strain or collision.

a **1625** *Nomenclator Navalis* (Harl. MS. 2301) *Swifters*.. Doe belong to the Maine and fore-mast, and are to succor the Shrowdes, and keepe stiff the Mast, they haue Pendants, wᶜʰ are made faste vnder the Shrowdes, at the head of the Mast, with a double Block, through wᶜʰ is reeued the Swifter, wᶜʰ at the Standing parte hath a single Block with a hooke, which is hitched in a Ring by the Chaine Wale, and soo the fall being hal'd doth helpe to strengthen the Mast. **1627** CAPT. J. SMITH *Sea. Gram.* v. 19 Ouer the heads of those Masts are pendants, for Tackels and Swifters vnder them. **1769** FALCONER *Dict. Marine* (1789) L 2 b. **1836** MARRYAT *Midsh. Easy* xl, 'Down, my lads, in a moment by the swifters,' cried Jack. **1847** A. C. KEY *Narr. Recov. H.M.S. Gorgon* 18 A swifter consisting of three turns of twelve-inch hemp cable, was passed round the ship. **1883** *Man. Seamanship for Boys* 200 In each end of the bars [of the capstan] there is a notch; a piece of rope called the swifter is passed round in each notch, and swab-hitched to the end of each bar.

2. *N. Amer. Logging.* A cable or spar used to secure a raft of logs.

1870 *Overland Monthly* 5 July 58/1 In a 'square' raft, long, slender spars, called 'swifters', are placed. **1975** H. WHITE *Raincoast Chron.* (1976) 150/1 They were using a hand winch to pull the swifters across that locked the logs in place.

Hence **'swifter** *v. trans.* to fasten a swifter to, or tighten with a swifter: = SWIFT *v.*¹

1794 *Rigging & Seamanship* I. 198 The shrouds are then swiftered together. **1881** W. CLARK RUSSELL *Ocean Free-Lance* II. iv. 170, I had the lower rigging swiftered.

† **'swifterly,** *adv. Obs.* [f. compar. of SWIFT *a.* + -LY². Cf. SWETTERLY.] More swiftly.

c **1425** *Found. St. Bartholomew's* (E.E.T.S.) 45 That his way begonne, the swyfterly he myght parforme.

'swift-foot, *a.* and *sb.*

A. *adj.* = SWIFT-FOOTED.

1594 KYD *Cornelia* III. ii. 4 The Scithian swift-foote feareles Porters. **1598** SYLVESTER *Du Bartas* II. ii. III. *Colonies* 792 The swift-foot Tiger or fierce Lionesse. *c* **1611** CHAPMAN *Iliad* XXIV. 151 Go, swift foot Iris. **1635** QUARLES *Embl.* IV. iii. 25 The streames of swift-foot Rhene. **1875**

MORRIS *Æneid* IV. 180 Swift are her wings to cleave the air, swift-foot she treads the earth.

B. *sb.* A swift-footed person or animal, a fast runner; *spec.* = COURSER[3].

1825 SELBY *Illustr. Brit. Ornith.* I. 334 Cream-coloured Swiftfoot. *Cursorius Isabellinus.* **1869** RUSKIN *Q. of Air* i. §20 The two Harpies, 'Stormswift' and 'Swiftfoot', are the sisters of the rainbow. **1887** MORRIS *Odyss.* XII. 539 The spirit of the Swiftfoot, the glorious Æacus' seed.

swift-footed (stress variable), *a.* Having swift feet; running or going swiftly.

c **1600** SHAKS. *Sonn.* xix, Do what ere thou wilt swift-footed time To the wide world. **1617** DRUMM. OF HAWTH. *Forth Feasting* 47 Some swiftest-footted get her hence. **1631** MASSINGER *Emperor East* IV. ii, Swift-footed Atalanta. *c* **1714** ARBUTHNOT, etc. *Mem. M. Scribl.* xiii, Man-tiger.. made a circle round the Chamber, and..the swift-footed Martin pursued him. **1870** BRYANT *Iliad* I. 1. 5 Achilles the swift-footed, answered thus.

† **swifthede.** *Obs. rare*[−1]. In 4 (*Ayenb.*) zuyft-. [f. SWIFT *a.* + *-hede*, -HEAD.] Swiftness.

1340 *Ayenb.* 78 Uayrhede of bodye, prouesse, strengþe, zuyfthede.

Swiftian ('swɪftɪən), *a.* [f. the name of the satirist Jonathan *Swift* (1667–1745) + -IAN.] Pertaining to or characteristic of Swift or his works. Hence '**Swiftianism**, a piece of writing or an expression characteristic of Swift.

1762 BP. FORBES *Jrnl.* (1886) 181 Struan was greatly of the Swiftian Taste. **1826** SCOTT *Jrnl.* 21 March, Joseph Hume, indeed!—I say Joseph Hum—and could add a Swiftian rhyme, but forbear. **1826** —— *Diary* 15 April, So hey for a Swiftianism. **1895** SIR J. SKELTON *Table Talk of Shirley* 122 This..sardonic Timon held aloof from his fellows, and regarded them with tacit or even Swiftian disapprobation.

swiftie ('swɪftɪ). Also **swifty.** [f. SWIFT *a.* + -Y[6], -IE.] **1.** A fast-moving person: a rapid runner, a quick thinker. Also *ironically. colloq.*

1945 *Sun* (Baltimore) 24 Feb. 9/1 Dan Ferris..says that the Swedish swiftie's provisional entry still is among the 36 hopefuls in the 3-mile run. **1946** J. IRVING *Royal Navalese* 170 *Swifty*, a derisive nickname for any particularly lugubrious and slow-moving man. **1969** N. FREELING *Tsing-Boum* xvii. 126 Make no mistake about those feminine nails: a swifty.

2. An act of deception, a trick or sleight; = ROUGHIE 3. Also in phr. *to pull a swiftie* (cf. *to pull a fast one* s.v. FAST *a.* 11, and PULL *v.* 20 d). *Austral. slang.*

1945 BAKER *Austral. Lang.* xv. 265 *Swiftie*..will..be heard in male conversation to describe a joke or trick that is either agreeable or disagreeable. **1953** 'CADDIE' *Sydney Barmaid* 224 'You didn't work a swiftie on them, did you?' I asked suspiciously. For I was already aware that Bill was collecting three doles for himself. **1962** R. TULLIPAN *March into Morning* 43 If these mugs hadn't pulled a swifty they wouldn't have been working for me at all. **1969** *Sunday Truth* (Brisbane) 23 Mar. 28/4 Police..arrested him for his Sydney swiftie. **1976** *Sydney Morning Herald* 9 Apr. 6 The Queensland Premier..is now worried that the Federal Treasury may be trying to pull a swiftie.

swifting tackle: see SWIFT *v.*[1]

swiftlet ('swɪftlɪt). [f. SWIFT *sb.*[2] + -LET.] A little or young swift; a small species of swift, as those of the genus *Collocalia*, which construct the edible birds' nest of China.

1892 *Cornh. Mag.* May 535 Would the swift have to go nestless, to the inconvenience, if not fatal prejudice, of generations of swiftlets unborn? **1898** *Sven Hedin's Through Asia* xix. 245 The edible nests of the swallow, or, more correctly swiftlet.

swiftly ('swɪftlɪ), *adv.* Forms: see SWIFT *a.* and -LY[2]; also 4 **swiflich**, *sup.* **swifliest**, 5 **swyfliche.** [f. SWIFT *a.* + -LY[2].] In a swift manner; with swift movement or action.

1. With great speed or velocity; at a great rate; = QUICKLY 2 a.

c **1000** ÆLFRIC *Hom.* I. 580 Zacheus ða swyftlice of ðam treowe alihte. *c* **1000** *Lambeth Ps.* vi. 11 *Uelociter*, hredlice *vel* swiftlice. *a* **1023** WULFSTAN *Hom.* xlii. (1883) 200 Heora fyðera swegað swa swa wæteres dyne..hi fleoð swiftlice. *a* **1325** *Prose Psalter* xliv. 2 [xlv. 1] My tunge is penne of þe scriuayn swiflich wrytand. *c* **1350** *Will. Palerne* 3454 Wel was him in þe world þat swifliest miȝt hiȝe. *c* **1385** CHAUCER *L.G.W.* Prol. 200 Home to myn house ful swiftly I me sped. **1447** BOKENHAM *Seyntys* (Roxb.) 20 They rent hyr flesh.. So dispetously that than a ryver Hyr blood to grounde swyftlyere dede glyde. **1593** SHAKS. *3 Hen. VI*, II. i. 109 Tydings, as swiftly as the Postes could runne, Were brought me of your Losse. **1647** H. MORE *Poems* Notes 399 Ethereall matter floweth swiftlier in those places. **1735** BERKELEY *Querist* §22 Whether..less money, swiftly circulating, be not, in effect, equivalent to more money slowly circulating? **1798** COLERIDGE *Anc. Mar.* VI. xiii, Swiftly, swiftly flew the ship. **1877** LADY BRASSEY *Voy. Sunbeam* xv. (1878) 255 The currents run very swiftly between these islands. **1907** J. H. PATTERSON *Man-Eaters of Tsavo* i. 17 A swiftly-flowing stream.

b. *transf.* Steeply.

1893 STEVENSON *Catriona* i. 4 The narrow paved way descended swiftly.

† **c.** *swiftly horsed, mounted*, mounted on a swift horse. *Obs. rare.*

c **1611** CHAPMAN *Iliad* IV. 246 His swiftly mounted Greekes. **1654–66** EARL ORRERY *Parthen.* (1676) 37, I should commit you to the charge of some Gentleman, swiftly Hors'd.

2. Within a short space of time; = QUICKLY 2 b. *Obs.* or merged in sense 1.

a **1300** *Cursor M.* 341 (Cott.) All his comament was don, Suiftliker þen hee may wink. *c* **1430** *How Good Wife taught Dau.* 89 Þouȝ ony man speke to þee, Swiftli þou him grete. *c* **1440** *York Myst.* xxix. 244 Swiftely he swapped of my nere. **1817** SHELLEY *Rev. Islam* VI. xi. 4 Those slaves were swiftly overthrown. **1837** CARLYLE *Fr. Rev.* III. VII. v, A swiftly-appointed, swift Military Tribunal.

3. Without delay; after a very short, or no, interval of time; = QUICKLY 2 c.

c **1000** ÆLFRIC *Hom.* I. 452 Þa ferde his gast swyftlice. *a* **1225** *Leg. Kath.* 690 Wittie wordes, þe schulen þe flit of þine fan swiftliche afellen. **1340** *Ayenb.* 140 Þe ournemens of boȝamnesse byeþ zeuen. Þet ys, þet me bouȝe prestliche, gledliche, simpleliche, klenliche, generalliche, zuyftliche, and wiluolliche. *a* **1400–50** *Wars Alex.* 2069 (Dubl. MS.), Þai swyftly hym sware & sothly hym tald. *c* **1475** *Rauf Coilȝear* 949 Thay swoir on thair swordis swyftlie all thre. *a* **1593** MARLOWE *Hero & Leander* I. 292 Hate me not, nor from me flie To follow swiftly blasting infamie. **1596** SHAKS. *Tam. Shr.* V. i. 1 Softly and swiftly sir, for the Priest is ready. *a* **1729** CONGREVE *Ovid's Art of Love* 672 Swiftly seize the Joy that swiftly flies. **1907** *Verney Mem.* II. 450 Her life came gently but swiftly to a close.

swiftness ('swɪftnɪs). [f. SWIFT *a.* + -NESS.]

1. The quality of being swift; rapidity.

a. of something moving, or of movement or physical action; in early use sometimes nearly = 'rapid movement'.

c **888** ÆLFRED *Boeth.* xxxix. §3 Hwa unlæredra ne wundrað þæs roderes færeldes & his swiftnesse? *c* **1000** *Ags. Ps.* (Th.) xxxii. 15 [xxxiii. 17] Þi byð dysiȝ, se þe ȝetruwað on his horses swiftnesse. *a* **1300** *Cursor M.* 23381 (Cott.) In suiftenes þou sal be sa suift, Þat als suith som þou mai lift Þine eie up þe lift to se, Als suith þar þan sal þou be. **1340** HAMPOLE *Pr. Consc.* 7933 Þe secunde blys after es swyftnes, Þat ilk body sal be have þat ryghtwise es. **1484** CAXTON *Fables of Æsop* V. x, For the swyftnesse of the water he must nedes passe vnder the whele of the mylle. **1559** W. CUNNINGHAM *Cosmogr. Glasse* 12 To cary the heauens of the Planetes, by his swiftnes about th' earth with him. **1596** DALRYMPLE tr. *Leslie's Hist. Scot.* I. 20 The secund kynde of hunting dog is ..a beist of a meruellous audacitie and suiftnes. **1613** SHAKS. *Hen. VIII*, I. i. 142 We may out-runne By violent swiftnesse that which we run at; And lose by ouer-running. *a* **1700** EVELYN *Diary* 2 June 1662, The rich gondola..was not comparable for swiftnesse to our common wherries. **1781** COWPER *Anti-Thelyphth.* 194 The barb sprang forward, and his lord, whose force Was equal to the swiftness of his horse, Rushed with a whirlwind's fury on the foe. **1811** MISS MITFORD in L'Estrange *Life* (1870) I. v. 120 The creature [*sc.* a snake] got away with incredible swiftness. **1816** J. SMITH *Panorama Sci. & Art* I. 560 The swiftness of Saturn's motion on his axis produces an oblate figure. **1841** BORROW *Zincali* I. IV. II. 301 With the swiftness of lightning.

b. of something figured as moving or as movement (e.g. thought, time, etc.).

a **1340** HAMPOLE *Psalter* ciii 4 [civ. 3] Þou passis all swyftnes of our thouȝtis. *c* **1400** *Destr. Troy* 12 Sothe stories ben..swolowet into swym by swiftenes of yeres. **1605** BACON *Adv. Learn.* I. To the King §2, I have been.. possessed with an extreme woonder at..the swiftnesse of your Apprehension. **1662** DRYDEN *To Ld. Chancellor* 109 Such is the mighty Swiftness of your Mind That, like the Earth's, it leaves our Sense behind. **1891** MEREDITH *One of our Conq.* x, If you would like a further definition of Genius, think of it as a form of swiftness.

2. The fact of happening, or acting, without delay; promptitude; †haste, rashness.

a **1400–50** *Wars Alex.* 1017 My couatyng is elder þe sadnes of slike men, þan swyftnes of childir. **1535** COVERDALE *2 Esdras* viii. 18, I haue herde the swiftnes of the iudge, which is to come. **1599** SHAKS. *Hen. V*, I. ii. 306 Let ..all things [be] thought vpon, That may with reasonable swiftnesse adde More Feathers to our Wings. **1607** —— *Cor.* III. i. 313 This Tiger-footed-rage, when it shall find The harme of vnskan'd swiftnesse, will (too late) Tye Leaden pounds too 's heeles. **1706** PRIOR *Ode to Queen* xx, He wept the Swiftness of the Champion's Fall. **1820** SHELLEY *Prometh. Unb.* IV. 379 With earthquake shock and swiftness making shiver Thought's stagnant chaos.

† **swiftship.** *Obs. rare*[−1]. In 3 **-schipe.** [f. SWIFT *a.* + -SHIP 1.] Swiftness.

a **1225** *Ancr. R.* 398 Asaeles swiftschipe, þet strof wið heortes ouervrn.

'**swift-winged**, *a.* Having swift wings, flying swiftly, rapid in flight (*lit.* and *fig.*).

1591 SHAKS. *1 Hen. VI*, II. v. 15 Yet are these Feete.. Swift-winged with desire to get a Graue. **1592** *Soliman & Pers.* II. ii. 33 Thou great commander of the swift wingd winds. **1619** A. NEWMAN *Pleas. Vis.* B ij, When youthfull Spleene Had ne're the wiles..of Pleasure seene, Nor dreampt, how pretious is swift-winged Time. **1725** POPE *Odyss.* XV 566 The hawk, Apollo's swift-wing'd messenger. **1785** BURNS *Cotter's Sat. Nt.* v, The social hours, swift-wing'd, unnotic'd fleet. **1874** WOOD *Nat. Hist.* 696 The first family of the Moths is the Sphingidæ, a group which contains a great number of swift-winged insects.

swifty ('swɪftɪ), *a. rare* (chiefly *poet.*). [f. SWIFT *a.* + -Y.] Swift. Hence †'**swiftiness.**

c **1380** WYCLIF *Sel. Wks.* II. 407 Crist is swiftier in hise werkes þan oure tungis ben in her speche. **1460** CAPGRAVE *Chron.* (Rolls) 36 Al manere games that longyn to power or switnesse [*v.r.* swiftinesse]. **1563** B. GOOGE *Eglogs*, etc. (Arb.) 71 His Spurres with heeles he strykes, And forewarde ronnes with swiftye race. **1567** DRANT *Horace, Ep.* II. ii. H vj, As gliding waues in swiftye streames are quickly cumd, and gone. **1596** COLSE *Penelope* (1880) 170 To swifty Dolon take good heede. *a* **1890** R. F. BURTON tr. *Catullus' Carmina* lv. 26 Rhesus borne in swifty car snow-white.

swig (swɪg), *sb.*[1] *slang* or *colloq.* Also 6 **swyg**, 7 **swigge.** [Origin unknown.]

1. Drink, liquor. ? *Obs.*

1548 UDALL *Erasm. Par. Luke* vi. 74 Hauing been long accustomed to the olde soure swyg of Moses lawe they could not awaie with the muste of euangelical charitie. **1635** J. TAYLOR (Water P.) *Old Parr* C 2 b, And for his daily swig, Milk, Butter-milk, and Water, Whay, and Whig.

b. Applied locally to special drinks: see quots.

1827 R. COOK *Oxford Night Caps* 30 The Wassail Bowl, or Swig, as it is termed at Jesus College in this University. *Ibid. note*, Swig was formerly almost exclusively confined to Jesus College; it is now, however, a great favourite through-out the University. **1841** HARTSHORNE *Salopia Ant.* 584 *Swig*, I. Toast and ale.

2. An act of 'swigging'; a deep or copious draught of a beverage, esp. of intoxicating liquor; a 'pull'.

1621–3 MIDDLETON & ROWLEY *Changeling* IV. ii, But one swig more, sweet madam. **1622** MABBE tr. *Aleman's Guzman d' Alf.* II. 208 He takes the flagon of wine in his hands, and giues it a good swigge. **1687** *Renowned Hist. Sir. J. Hawkwood* ix. 17 After they had taken several lusty swigs, so that their spirits came (as it were) again. **1726–31** WALDRON *Descr. Isle of Man* (1865) 70 After a good hearty swig out of one of the bottles of ale. **1842** LOVER *Handy Andy* xxxvi, 'Hand us that whisky'—he put the bottle to his mouth and took a swig. **1849** THACKERAY *Pendennis* xxviii, And now for another swig at the beer. **1899** R. WHITEING *No. 5 John St.* xi, I buy a ha'porth of bread, take a swig at a fountain, and tramp the East End parks to kill time.

b. Drinking; *to play at swig*, to indulge in drinking. ? *Obs.*

1688 W. SCOT *Hist. Fam. Scot* (1776) 32 A vitious, odious King [*sc.* Donald V], he play'd at swig, Whilst he lost Scotland all to Striviling-bridge.

3. *Comb.*, as *swig-bowl, -day* (see quots.).

1832 HONE *Year Bk.* 265 Swig Day, at Cambridge [*sic*]. **1870** MISS JACKSON *Shropsh. Word-bk.*, *Swig*, spiced ale and toast... *Swig-bowl*, the large bowl—like a punch-bowl—in which swig is served.

† **swig**, *sb.*[2] *Cards. Obs.* [Cf. SWIG *v.*[1] It is not certain that the quots. refer to the same game. Quot. *c* 1700 suggests derivation from a form related to OE. *swiȝian*, SWIE, to be silent.] (See quots.)

1598 FLORIO, *Trinca*, a game at cards called swig or new cut. *c* **1700** KENNETT in *MS. Lansd. 1033* lf. 398 (Hall.) A sort of play at cards in the North, in which all the gamesters are to be silent, is calld swig.

swig, *sb.*[3] *Naut.* Also **swigg.** [Cf. SWIG *v.*[3]]

1. A tackle the falls of which are not parallel.

1807 T. YOUNG *Lect. Nat. Philos.* II. 197/2 A pulley with ropes not parallel is called by seamen a swigg. **1852** BURN *Naval & Milit. Dict.* (1863), Swig, *palan.*

2. The act of 'swigging' at a rope: see SWIG *v.*[3] 3. (In quots., a punning use of SWIG *sb.*[1])

1849 H. MELVILLE *Redburn* I. ix. 94 Every once in a while, the men went into one corner, where the chief mate could not see them, to take a 'swig at the halyards', as they called it;..'to taper off'. **1904** *Westm. Gaz.* 9 July 12/2 Take a swig on those halliards.

† **swig**, *v.*[1] *Cards. Obs.* [Cf. SWIG *sb.*[2]]

1591 FLORIO *2nd Fruites* 69 *S.* Will you put it to me? *A.* You bid me to losse. *S.* Will you swigg? *A.* Tis the least part of my thought. **1598** FLORIO, *Amonte*, to swig or deale againe at cards. *Ibid.*, *Metter a' monte*, to heape vp, to swigge the cardes. **1605** VERSTEGAN *Dec. Intell.* (1634) 232 *Swyca.* A beguiler, wee aske at Cards if one will swig, that is, whether hee will beguile or bee beguiled.

swig, *v.*[2] *slang* or *colloq.* Also 8 **swigg.** [app. f. SWIG *sb.*[1]] To drink (esp. intoxicating liquor) in deep draughts; to drink eagerly or copiously. **a.** *trans.* (with the vessel, or the drink, as obj.).

1682 *Wit & Drollery, Tom-a-Bedlam* iv. 151 When short I have shorn my Sows face, And swigg'd my Horned Barrel. *c* **1688** *Roxb. Ball., Jolly Welsh Woman* v. (1893) VII. 724 Now while hur had gotten the jugg at her snout,..Hur gave it a tug, 'till hur swigg'd it half out. **1762** BRIDGES *Burlesque Trans. Homer* (1772) 246 (Farmer) When my landlord.. fairly fills it full, I just can swigg it at one-pull. **1837** MARRYAT *Snarleyyow* ix, You sailors will ever be swigging your can.

1780 R. TOMLINSON *Slang Pastoral* 3 With such a companion,..To swig porter all day. **1819** MOORE *Tom Crib* App. i. 39 The Hero, that sits there, Swigging Blue Ruin, in that chair. **1838** JAS. GRANT *Sk. Lond.* 62 The oceans of 'Entire' which they are everlastingly swigging. **1841** DICKENS *Barn. Rudge* xxxi, Beer; of which he swigged such copious draughts that most of his faculties were utterly drowned and washed away. **1854** THACKERAY *Newcomes* xxxvi, He swigged off a great bumper as he was making the remark. **1871** RUSKIN in Collingwood *Life* (1893) II. 127 'I am..drinking as much tea,'—taking his second cup—'as I can swig.'

b. *absol.* or *intr.*

c **1654** L. PRICE *Dead & Alive* II. v. in *Roxb. Ball.* (1891) VII. 389 The second time that he set [up] the bottle to his snout, He never left off swigging, till he had suckt all out. *a* **1734** NORTH *Autobiog.* xi. §184 in *Lives* (1890) III. 143, I went to a dairy-house and swigged of the milk and water. **1792** J. BUDWORTH *Fortn. Ramble* i. 4 He pulled a bottle of chamomile tea out of his pocket, and swigged heartily. **1837** DICKENS *Pickw.* xli, Them down-hearted fellers as can't svig avay at the beer. **1838** BARHAM *Ingol. Leg.* Ser. I. *St. Nicholas* lix, Swigging as though he would empty the Rhine.

Hence '**swigging** *vbl. sb.* and *ppl. a.*

1702 YALDEN *Æsop at Court, Fox & Flies* iv, I'll brush those Swigging Dogs away, That on thy Blood remorseless Prey. **1723** VANBRUGH *Let.* in *Athenæum* 6 Sept. (1890) 322/3, I have been drinking waters at Scarborough three or four days, and am to return thither.. for a weeks swigging more. **1826** W. E. ANDREWS *Crit. Rev. Fox's Bk. Mart.* III. 288 They had a swigging bout in prison. **1865** E. BURRITT *Walk to Land's End* 268 This would be called in America pretty large swigging for one family.

swig, *v.*[3] [The general sense may be 'to cause to sway about, pull about, pull', and relation to SWAG is probable; but it is not clear that all the senses below belong to the same word.]

1. *trans.* To castrate (a ram) by tying the scrotum tightly with a string.

1663 BOYLE *Usef. Exp. Nat. Philos.* II. v. xii. 234 A Servant of mine that deals much in Cattle, and had lately divers Sheep swigg'd (as they call it) after this manner. *a* **1722** LISLE *Husb.* (1757) 315 Swigging, which is girding them hard round the cods, and cutting the cod away close to the string.

2. ? To pull about.

1684 CREECH *Virg. Ecl.* iii, The Lambkins swigg the Teat, But find no moisture. **1697** DRYDEN *Æneid* IX. 73 The bleating Lambs Securely swig the Dug, beneath the Dams.

3. *Naut.* To pull at the bight of a rope which is fast at one end to a fixed object and at the other to a movable one; to pull (a sail, etc.) *up* in this manner. Also *intr.*, to pull *on* a rope (see quot. 1961).

1794 *Rigging & Seamanship* I. 176 *Swigging off*, pulling upon the middle of a tight rope that is made fast at both ends. **1827** *Examiner* 154/1 Taking about a calendar month to swig up her mainsail. **1882** NARES *Seamanship* (ed. 6) 57 *Swinging or swigging off*, that is, pulling at right angles to a taut rope. **1917** A. T. QUILLER-COUCH *Mortallone & Aunt Trinidad* ix. 77 He had now to hoist sail; which he did very leisurably.. swigging on the uphaul till he had it chock-a-block. **1939** A. RANSOME *Secret Water* xxi. 250 'It's just the wind we want,' panted Daisy swigging on her halyard. **1961** F. H. BURGESS *Dict. Sailing* 203 *Swig*, to swig on a rope is to take half a turn with one hand, whilst heaving and taking up the slack with the other.

4. *intr.* To sway about, waver; to move with a swaying motion.

1833 M. SCOTT *Tom Cringle* xv, Her long slender wands of masts which used to swig about. **1896** KIPLING *Seven Seas, Rhyme Three Sealers* 8 The landward breeze Brings up the harbour noise, And ebb of Yokohama Bay Swigs chattering through the buoys.

swiggle ('swɪg(ə)l), *v. rare.* Also 7 swigle. [app. frequent. of SWIG *v.*[3]; cf. SQUIGGLE *v.*]

†**1.** *trans.* To sprinkle. *Obs. rare*$^{-1}$.

1683 PETTUS *Fleta Min.* I. (1686) 73 Put ground Bone-Ashes in it, and swigle or strew it over the test.

2. *intr.* (or *trans.* with cogn. obj.) To wriggle.

1837 HALIBURTON *Clockm.* Ser. I. xxii. 230 When he was in full rig a swigglin away at the top of his gait. **1840** *Ibid.* Ser. III. xi. (1848) 86 With that he swiggled his way thro' the crowd, to the counter. **1907** J. M. SYNGE *Playboy* II. 39 To think of you swaying and swiggling at the butt of a rope.

3. *trans.* To shake about (liquid in a vessel, or something in a liquid). Also with vessel (spec. a beer glass) as obj. *dial.*

1943 *Pub & People* (Mass Observation) vi. 185 Some people have a habit of what may be called 'swiggling' their glasses, which consists in moving them round and round in circles, either on the bar counter or table top, or up in the air.

Hence '**swiggling** *vbl. sb.*

1948 L. A. G. STRONG *Trevannion* xiii. 229 There was a wild splashing; Trevannion, craning forward, saw the gleam of a silver belly, and heard a madly energised swiggling and slithering. **1971** *Weekly Guardian* 2 Jan. 19/3 Such categories of pub behaviour as 'Swiggling'—the habit of moving a beer glass round and round between sips.

†**swigman.** *Obs. Cant.* Also 6 swygman. [?] (See quots.)

1561 AWDELAY *Frat. Vacab.* (1869) 5 A Swygman goeth with a Pedlers pack. **1673** R. HEAD *Canting Acad.* 82 These Irish Toyls, or Swig-men, being much alike, I joyn.. together, who carry pins, points and laces, and such like wares about. *a* **1700** B. E. *Dict. Cant. Crew, Swig-men*, the 13th Rank of the Canting Crew.

swike, *sb.*[1] *Obs.* (exc. *dial.*). Forms: 1–2 **swica**, 2 **swice**, 2–4 **swike**, **suike**, 3 **sweoke**, **swoke**, (**swiche**), 3–4 **suyke**, 5 **sweke**. [OE. *swica*: see SWIKE *v.* In Sc. and north. dial. *swaik, swyke, swick* = deceitful person, worthless fellow.] A deceiver; a traitor.

c **1000** *Ags. Gosp.* Matt. xxvii. 63 We ȝemunon þæt se swica sæde þa he on life wæs æfter þrym daȝon ic arise. *a* **1100** *O.E. Chron.* an. 1055 Utlaȝode mann Ælfar eorl forðon him man wearp on þæt he wæs þes cynges swica. **1154** *Ibid.* an. 1135 þa ricemen þe wæron swikes. *a* **1200** *Moral Ode* 103 in *O.E. Hom.* I. 165 þa swicen [*Egerton MS.* swikele, *later copy* swikene] and ta forsworene. *a* **1225** *Ancr. R.* 98 Ueond þet þuncheð freond is swike ouer alle swike. *c* **1230** *Hali Meid.* 45 Ne geineð þe nawt, sweoke. *c* **1300** *Havelok* 1158 þat wicke þral, þat foule swike. *c* **1400** *R. Gloucester's Chron.* 6399 (MS. β) Alle traitours & luþer swikes [*v.rr.* suiken, sweken, swykes] god late hom so spede.

swike, *sb.*[2] *Obs.* (exc. *dial.*). Forms: 1 **swic**, ? **swica**, **swice**, 3–4 **swike**, 3–5 **swik**, (**swiche**), 4 **suike**, **suik**, (**suiche**), **squike**, **squyke**, 4–5 **swyke**, 5 **swyk**, **swyck**. [OE. *swic* ? n., chiefly in compounds, *swice* str. m., escape, outcome, issue, deceit, treachery, stumbling-block, *swice* wk. f., or *swica* wk. m., trap: cf. MHG. *swîch, swîche* deceit, and see SWIKE *v.*]

1. Deceit, deception, treachery; an act of deception, a trick.

In ME., *withouten* or *but swike* was used as a metrical tag. In mod.Sc. and north. dial. in the forms *swike, swyke, swick*, with the sense 'cheat, deception'; also in Sc. phr. *the swick of*, the responsibility for (something blameworthy).

c **893** ÆLFRED *Oros.* III. vii. 114 He.. ealle þa cyningas mid biswice [*Cott. MS.* mid his swice] ofsloȝ. *c* **1220** *Bestiary* 445 Ðe deuel is tus ðe fox ilik mið iuele breides & wið swik. *c* **1250** *Hymn to God* 19 in *Trin. Coll. Hom.* App. 258 He vs bouchte wið his blod of þe feondes swiche. *a* **1300** *Cursor M.* 818 (Cott.) þe find.. þat wit his suik bi-suak adam. *Ibid.* 2097 Asie es, wit-outen suike, Sua mikel als europ and affrike. *Ibid.* 6514 'þi folk,' he said, 'has don a suik.' *c* **1425** WYNTOUN *Cron.* VII. viii. 1616 (Wemyss MS.) He gat nocht þat bischoprik Nocht wiþ lawte, bot with swik. *a* **1500** *Ratis Raving* I. 1031 Bot always serf hyme elyk, Quhill þow haf tan thi leif but swik.

†**2.** A snare, trap. *Obs.*

This use is perh. continued under the form SWEEK, q.v. (where, however, another explanation has been suggested). Cf. SWICKLE.

a **1100** *Gloss Aldhelm* I. 4982 (Napier 127/2) *Decipulam*, swican. **13..** *Coer de L.* 4081 Under the brygge ther is a swyke, Corven clos, joynand queyntlike. *c* **1400** *Ywaine & Gaw.* 677 Under that than was a swyke, That made Syr Ywain to myslike; His horse fote toched thareon, Than fel the port-culis onone. **14..** *Guy Warw.* (Camb. MS.) 7580 He ys black as any pyck, And also felle as a lyon in his swyck. *c* **1475** *Nom.* in Wr.-Wülcker 703/7 *Hec discipula* [= *decipula*], a swyke.

†**swike**, *a. Obs.* [OE. *swice* (Genesis 1996, where the meaning is doubtful): see next.] Deceitful; treacherous; traitorous.

c **1175** *Lamb. Hom.* 53 þenne þe mon wule tilden his musestoch he bindeð uppon þa swike chese. *c* **1205** LAY. 14865 He.. minne fader biswak þurh swike his craftes [*later version* mid his luþer craftes]. *c* **1250** *Gen. & Ex.* 2845 He ledden feren swike, Ðe sulden him deren witterlike.

swike, *v. Obs.* exc. *Sc. dial.* Forms: α. 1 **swican**, 2–5 **swike**, 4 **suike**, **squike**, **squyke**, *Ayenb.* **zuyke**, 4–5 (9 *dial.*) **swyke**; β. 1 **swician**, 2 **swikian**, 3 **swic**, 4 **suick**, **squeke**, 6 **swik**, **swyk**, 9 *dial.* **swick**. *Pa. t.* α. 1–3 **swac**, (*pl.* 1 **swicon**, 2 **suyken**), 2–3 **-swak**, 3–5 **-swok(e**, 4 **suak(e**, **squake**; β. 1 **swicode**, (**-ade**, **-ede**), 4–5 **swykede**, **swykkede**, 6 *Sc.* **swikit**. *Pa. pple.* α. 1–3 **-swicen**, 2–5 **swiken**, 4 **squikin**, 5 **suiken**; β. 9 *Sc.* **swicket**. [OE. *swícan* str. vb., pa. t. *swác, swicon*, pa. pple. *swicen*, and *swician* wk. vb., to wander, depart, cease, fail in loyalty, deceive, 'scandalizare', also in compounds *á-, be-, ȝeswícan, á-, beswician* (see ASWIKE, BESWIKE, ISWIKE). The str. vb., repr. a Com. Teut. vb. *sweikan with a variety of meanings, corresponds to OFris. *swîka* to keep far from, OS. *swîkan*, pa. t. *swêk* to leave in the lurch, to languish, be disloyal, MLG. *swîken* to give way, MDu. *zwîken* to escape, desert, depart, (also *bezwîken* to faint, to leave in the lurch, Du. *bezwijken* to give way, sink), OHG. *swîhhan, swîchan*, MHG. *swîchen* to faint, desert, allow to perish, also OHG. *swîchôn* to wander, stray (G. dial. *schweichen* to wander round, to deceive), ON. *svíkva, svíkja*, pa. t. *sveik, sviku*, pa. pple. *svikinn* to betray (MSw. *swika*, Sw. *svika*, Da. *svige*). The wk. vb. is from the weak grade of the root, whence also OE. *swica, swice, swic* SWIKE *sb.*[1] and [2], *swice* SWIKE *a.*, MLG. *swik*, OHG. *biswih* deceit, treachery, ON. *svik* (MSw. *swik, swek*, Sw. *svek*, Da. *svig*) treachery, *-sviki* traitor, and OE. *swicol* SWICKLE.]

I. †**1.** *intr.* To leave off, cease. *Obs.*

In OE. const. gen. or *from*; in ME. the gen. sing. can be apprehended as pl., which then appears to be a direct object.

c **897** ÆLFRED *Gregory's Past. C.* xxviii. 195 Ærest mon hnappað; ȝif he ðonne ðære hnappunge ne swicð, ðonne hnappað he oð he wierð on fæstum slæpe. *a* **900** CYNEWULF *Juliana* 373 (Gr.) Ic hine þæs synnum onæle þæt he byrnende from ȝebede swiceð. *c* **1175** *Lamb. Hom.* 15 þas reueres & þas þeues þet nulleð nu nefre swike heore ueeles. *c* **1220** *Bestiary* 193 No mod ðu ne cune,.. oc swic of sineginge. *a* **1225** *Leg. Kath.* 1937 Swa þet Katerine.. swike hire sotschipes, & ure wil wurche. *c* **1240** *Cuckoo Song*, Cuccu! cuccu! Wel singes þu cuccu; ne swik þu nauer nu. *a* **1310** in Wright *Lyric P.* xv. 48 Nou y swyke, y mei nout so, Hit [*sc.* gout] siweth me so faste. **1340** *Ayenb.* 157 Vor hy ne zuyke þ neure ni3t ne day ac alneway bieþ in waytinge uor ous.

†**2.** *intr.* To act deceitfully, practise deceit. *Obs.*

c **1000** ÆLFRIC *Hom.* I. 316 Hwi woldest ðu swician on ðinum aȝenum? *c* **1000** —— in *Ags. Hom.* (Assmann) i. 121 Ure wiðerwinna is witodlice se deofol, þe embe us swicað mid his searacræftum. *c* **1205** LAY. 2349 Ah ne dude he nawiht swo for swiken [*c* **1275** swike] he þohte. *a* **1300** *Cursor M.* 19093 (Cott.) Yee suak and nitt be-for pilate, And demed als ye-seluen wate. *c* **1300** *K. Horn* 711 (Laud) Ne shal ich neuere swike, Ne do þat þe mislike.

II. 3. *trans.* To deceive, cheat, ensnare.

In OE. const. dative.

c **950** *Lindisf. Gosp.* Matt. xxiv. 11 *Multi pseudo-prophetae surgent et seducent multos*, moniȝo lease witȝo arisað & swicað moniȝo. *c* **1000** ÆLFRIC *Exod.* xxxiv. 15 Ne nim þu nane sibbe wið þæs landes menn, þe læs þe hira æniȝ þe swice. *a* **1023** WULFSTAN *Hom.* xxxiii. (1883) 160 Mæst ælc swicode and oðrum derede wordes and dæde. *c* **1050** *O.E. Chron.* an. 1049 (Cott. MS.) Ða wende Beorn for þære sibbe þæt he him swican nolde. *c* **1205** LAY. 3948 Poreus hauede þe heorte swa luþer.. þat swiken he him wolde a sumes kinnes wisen. *c* **1220** *Bestiary* 601 He ðe swiken ðer imong, ðin a3te wið swiking, ði soule wið lesing. *a* **1300** *Cursor M.* 819 (Cott.) God wist wel þe find him suak. *Ibid.* 14840 Quer he haf suiken [*Fairf.* squikin] wit his art, Ani lauerding apon vr part. *Ibid.* 26572 If þou will noght þi saul suick [*Fairf.* squike] þou sceu þi sin all openlike. *a* **1340** HAMPOLE *Psalter* xxxvi. 34 For þe rightwismannys life is vnlike til his, he thynkis him to swyke. *c* **1375** *Cursor M.* 26456 (Fairf.) Qua wraþþis his lorde he dos him squeke, Quen he of merci has funden him meke. **1513** DOUGLAS *Æneis* IV. ii. 72 Sum tyme wald scho Ascanius, the page.. in hir bosum brace, gif scho tharby The luif vntellable mycht swyk or satisfy. **1514** in *Rec. Earldom of Orkney* (S.H.S.) 88 It is weill knawin and fund that he swekit and defraudit his bruthir.

†**b.** Of a thing: To prove false to, disappoint the expectation of, fail (a person). *Obs.*

In OE. also, 'to be a traitor, desert'.

Beowulf 1460 (Gr.) Næfre hit [*sc.* the sword] æt hilde ne swac manna ængum. ? *a* **1400** *Morte Arth.* 1795 Whene his spere was sprongene, he spede hym fulle ȝerne, Swappede owtte wiþ a swerde, that swykede hym neuer. *Ibid.* 3361 For whilles thow swanke with the swerde, it swykkede þe neuer. *a* **1400–50** *Wars Alex.* 4999 And þou may swythe haue a sware, at swike sall þe neuire.

†**c.** To surprise, take unawares. *Obs. rare*$^{-1}$.

c **1400** *Anturs of Arth.* xlii. (Douce MS.) Withe a swap of a swerde þat swaþel him swykes.

d. To get dishonestly, 'sneak'. *Sc. dial.*

1889 EDWARDS *Strathearn Lyrics* 33 My heaviest care was the loss o' a bool, When 'twas stown or 'swicket' at Auld Jenny's Schule.

Hence †**swiking** (OE. **swicung**) *vbl. sb.*, deceit, fraud; †**swiking** *ppl. a.*, whence †**swikingly** (**swicandliche**) *adv.*, treacherously.

c **1000** *Sax. Leechd.* III. 198 Swicunge ceapes. *c* **1000** in *Anglia* (1889) XI. 117/29 *Inlusione diabolica*, mid swicunge deoflicre. *c* **1175** *Lamb. Hom.* 25 þenne cumeð her under þe deofel swicandliche. *c* **1220** *Bestiary* 602 [see 3 above].

†**swikebert.** *Obs. rare*$^{-1}$. An alleged name for the hare.

c **1300** *Names of Hare* in *Rel. Ant.* I. 133.

†**swikedom.** *Obs.* Forms: see SWIKE *sb.*[2] and -DOM. [OE. *swicdóm*, f. *swik-*: see SWIKE *v.* and -DOM.] Deceit, fraud; treachery, treason.

c **893** ÆLFRED *Oros.* II. iv. 76 Se ȝionga cyning swiðor micle wenende wæs þæt hie þonon fleonde wæren þonne hie æniȝne swicdom cyþan dorstan. *Ibid.* IV. v. 168 þa tuȝon hie hiene þære burge witan þæt he heora swicdomes wið Alexander fremmende wære. *c* **1100** *O.E. Chron.* an. 1087 Ða þe cyng underȝeat.. hwilcne swicdom hi dydon to weard his. *c* **1175** *Pater Noster* 10 in *Lamb. Hom.* 55 þurh beelzebubes swikedom. *c* **1205** LAY. 5520 Belin & his broðer beien weoren warre of þon swikedome þe heom com of Rome. *a* **1250** *Owl & Night.* 167 Svikedom haueþ schome and hete If hit is ope and vnderyete. **1297** R. GLOUC. (Rolls) 2294 Vor to do a suikedom no conseil ne ssolde faile. *c* **1325** *Chron. Eng.* 838 in Ritson *Metr. Rom.* II. 305 Knout.. made hem telle here suykedom Ant for that tresoun that hy dude Hy were to-drawen. *c* **1400** *R. Gloucester's Chron.* (Rolls) App. X. 3 Vor after þat seint kenelm þoru swikedom ded lay Fourti ȝer after.

'**swikeful**, *a. Obs.* exc. *Sc. dial.* Forms: see SWIKE *sb.*[2] and -FUL. [OE. *swicfull* = ON. *svikfullr* (Sw. *svekfull*, Da. *svigefuldt*), f. *swik-*: see SWIKE *sb.*[2] and -FUL.] Deceitful, treacherous.

c **1100** *Aldhelm Gloss* I. 732 (Napier 21/1) *Strofose*, swicfulles. *c* **1205** LAY. 10535 þis iherde Cyrian speken þene swikeful mon. *a* **1300** *Cursor M.* 4412 (Cott.) Ioseph.. þat suikeful fals, þat fole lichour. *c* **1425** WYNTOUN *Cron.* VII. vii. 1373 (Wemyss MS.) His ministeris.. Prevely put in þe chalice Wenamous poisoun.. Be sic swikfull seruice þan Hastely deit þis haly man.

Hence †**swikefully** *adv.*

c **1425** WYNTOUN *Cron.* VI. xv. 1581 (Wemyss MS.) A fals tratour callit Gudwyne.. murtherist him swikfully. *Ibid.* VIII. iii. 384 (Cott. MS.) Fals was his relacion, And informyt richt falsly, And set the case all swykfully.

†**swikehede.** *Obs.* [f. SWIKE *sb.*[1] or *a.* + *-hede*, -HEAD.] = SWIKEDOM.

a **1250** [see SWIKELHEDE].

†**swikel**, *a. Obs.* Forms: 1 **swicol**, 2–4 **swikel**, 3 **suykel**, 3–4 **suikel**, 4 **swikil(l**, **-yll**, **swykile**, (**sikil**), 4–5 **swykel**. [OE. *swicol*, corresp. to OHG. *pi-swichal* 'subdolus', ON. *svikall* (MSw. *swikul*), f. *swik-*: see SWIKE *v.* and -LE.] Deceitful, treacherous, crafty.

c **1000** ÆLFRIC *Hom.* I. 82 Se swicola Herodes. *c* **1000** *Sax. Leechd.* III. 428 Næs heo swicol nanum þæra þe hyre to ðohte. *c* **1175** *Lamb. Hom.* 43 Heo wes.. liȝere & swikel. *a* **1225** *Ancr. R.* 180 Inre vondunges.. swikele þouhtes, þet þuncheð þauh gode. *a* **1250** *Prov. Ælfred* 356 in *O.E. Misc.* 124 Mony mon haueþ swikelne muþ. *c* **1300** *Havelok* 1108 Ioie he made hire swiþe mikel, But neþeles he was ful swikel. *a* **1340** HAMPOLE *Psalter* xlii. 1 Wickid is he þat does ill apertly, sikil, þat priuely synnes. *a* **1400** *Prymer* (1891) 34 A swykel tunge. *a* **1400** *Siege Jerusalem* (E.E.T.S.) 18/317 Many swykel at þe sweng to þe swerd ȝede.

Hence †'**swikeldom**, †'**swikelhede**, †'**swikelness**, deceitfulness, treachery; †'**swikelly** *adv.*, deceitfully, treacherously.

a **1250** *Owl & Night.* 162 (Cott.) Schamie þe for þin unrede, Vnwroȝen is þi *svikel-hede; Schild þine *swikeldom vram þe liȝte [*Jesus MS.* swikehede.. swikedom]. **1297** R. GLOUC. (Rolls) 7332 þo willam bastard hurde telle of haraldes suikelhede. *a* **1023** WULFSTAN *Hom.* vii. (1883) 55 Hy.. leatað þæt to wærscype, þæt hy oðre maȝan swa *swicollice þæcan. *a* **1340** HAMPOLE *Psalter* v. 11 [9] With þair tonges swikilly þai wroght. *a* **1023** WULFSTAN *Hom.* vii. (1883) 55 Antecrist lærð unsoðfæstnysse and *swicolnesse. *c* **1275** in *O.E. Misc.* 143/88 þer wurþ ioye & mury song, Wiþ-vte swikelnesse.

swile (swaɪl). *Newfoundland.* Also swoil(e. Irregular var. of SEAL *sb.*[1] Cf. SOILE.

1802 J. MURPHY *Old Sealing Days* (1916) 2 [J]ars, Doaters and Gunswoils and many others brew upon the rocks. *c* **1845** in *Dict. Newfoundland Eng.* (1982) 450/2 When we got into the jam the swoiles were very thick. **1878** in C. HALLOCK *Hallock's Amer. Club List & Sportsman's Gloss.* p. xi/2 Swile. **1907** J. G. MILLAIS *Newfoundland* ii. 39 Swoiles (seals) was much to us in the spring, for it meant 'bout what we lived on. **1924** F. BAIRD *Parson John of Labrador* iii. 64 It's t' good Lard as does it,.. as made t' harbours for we, an' sends t' fish, an' t' swiles. **1969** H. HORWOOD *Newfoundland* xii. 83 Seals on the north-east coast are called swiles, and the guns used for hunting them are swilin' guns. **1974** F. MOWAT *Boat who wouldn't Float* vi. 58 A number of swile guns—longbarrelled, smooth-bore guns intended for killing seals.

Hence as *v. intr.* = SEAL *v.*[3]; **swiling** *vbl. sb.*

c **1894** in *Dict. Newfoundland Eng.* (1982) 455/2 Ma shall have a new silk dress, When Da comes home from swoiling. **1897** B. WILLSON *Tenth Island* 110, I was no good for 'swilin'' any more. **1905** N. DUNCAN *Dr Grenfell's Parish* 40, I been swilin'.. in these seas every spring for fifty-seven years. **1906** J. LUMSDEN *Skipper Parson on Bays & Barrens of Newfoundland* 90 If the Canadians come down here to take our country I'll get down my 'swiling gun', and we'll go out and meet 'em. **1969** [see the sb. above].

swiler ('swaɪlə(r)). *Newfoundland.* [f. SWILE *v.* + -ER[1].] **1.** = SEALER *sb.*[2] 2.

1883 HATTON & HARVEY *Newfoundland* 88 The roads.. begin to be enlivened by the appearance of the sealers, or, as they are called in the vernacular, 'silers', their enterprise being designated 'swile huntin''. **1927** in *Dict. Newfoundland Eng.* (1982) 455/1 We are swoilers fearless, bold. **1958** M. HARRINGTON *Sea Stories from Newfoundland* 118 She sailed.. with Skipper Ned Dower in command, and a crew of able 'swoilers'. **1976** *Globe & Mail* (Toronto) 27 Nov. 35/3 It's the swoilers of Newfoundland and the pea-soupers of Quebec, symbols of cultures that in their turn have been despised for different reasons.

2. = SEALER *sb.*[2] 1.

1897 B. WILLSON *Tenth Island* 110 When the 'swiler' came to start I give my place to another man. **1900** in Oliver & Burke *People's Songster* 46 The interest of all the people was centred on the 'swoilers'. **1959** in Ryan & Small *Haulin' Rope & Gaff* 70 You'll need no Daylight Bill When a 'swiler' first is sighted From the tower upon the 'Hill'.

†**swilk**, *dem. adj.* and *pron.* (and *adv.*). *Obs.* Forms: α. 3–4 swilc, (3 *Orm.* swillc, swillk-; swiulc, suwilk, squilk, 4 squylk), 3–5 swilk, suilk, 4–5 swilke, swylk(e, suylk; 5 swelk, suelc. β. 3 selk(e, 3–4 sulk(e, 4–5 silk(e, sylk(e, (4 schilke). γ. 4–5 swyk. [Northern unpalatalized form corresp. to *swilč*, *swilch*, *swelč*, *sulch*, *swich*: see SUCH and cf. SIC.]

1. As *dem. adj.* in ordinary attributive, predicative, or complemental use: = SUCH I.

α. *c* **1200** ORMIN 201 Witt sinndenn off swillc elde nu þatt witt ne muȝhenn tæmenn. *Ibid.* 15811 Whatt læn þeȝȝ shollden unnderrfon Att Godd forr swillke dedess. *c* **1220** *Bestiary* 440, & deuel geld swilk billing wið same & wið sending. *c* **1250** *Gen. & Ex.* 3726 Leateð ben swilc wurdes ref. *a* **1300** *Cursor M.* 4133 (Cott.) If yee do suilk an outrake. *Ibid.* 6258 And yee sal cum al hal to land, Swilk es þe vertu of þis wand. **1375** BARBOUR *Bruce* VII. 364 He suld nouthir haff hert no will Swilk inperdy till vndirta. *c* **1400** tr. *Secr. Secr., Gov. Lordsh.* 89 Two precious stoones.. þat n en fynden yn rynnand waters, of whom þe wyrkynges er swylk. *c* **1440** *York Myst.* iii. 53 To swilke a lorde in alle degree Be euer-more lastand louynge.

β. *a* **1300** *Siriz* 101 That I shal don selk falsete. *Ibid.* 264, I shal kenne hire sulke a lore. *c* **1330** R. BRUNNE *Chron. Wace* (Rolls) 1513 How dar ȝe do sylk a þyng? **13..** *Cursor M.* 23153 (Edinb.) Al þat are schilke. *Ibid.* 24548 Of bale and bot sulk was mi soru. *c* **1400** *Apol. Loll.* 7 þat.. silk indulgencis rennun not forþ aȝen þe ordinaunce of God.

γ. *a* **1500** *Ratis Raving* Prol. 11 And gyf swyk causs sall fal in the, Trow weill at þow sal punyst be.

2. With correlative or dependent clause: = SUCH II.

α. *c* **1200** ORMIN 5413 þa shall Godess kinedom All all swillc beon onn eorþe, Alls itt iss upp inn heoffness ærd. **12..** *Will of Ælfgar* (anno 958) in Birch *Cartul.* III. 215 In to squilke haleȝen stowe squilk hire red likes. *c* **1250** *Gen. & Ex.* 1937 Swilc nið & hate ros hem on, He redden alle him for to slon. *a* **1300** *Body & Soul* in *Map's Poems* (Camden) 339 The fendes kasten suwilk a ȝel, the erthe it openede anon. *a* **1300** *Cursor M.* 2848 (Cott.) Suilk als þai brued now ha þai dronken. *c* **1300** *Havelok* 2123 So stod ut of his mouthe a glem, Rith al swilk so þe sunne-bem. **1340** HAMPOLE *Pr. Consc.* I. 658 Swilk als þe tre es with bowes, Swilk es þe fruyt þat on it growes. **1375** BARBOUR *Bruce* II. 337 Wyrk yhe then apon swylk wyss, That ȝour honour be sawyt ay. **1444** *Test. Ebor.* (Surtees) II. 105 Swilk composicion and avise as sall be made betwen ye said Maire.. and Hugh Cliderhowe. **1451** *Lincoln Diocese Documents* 52 With suylke stufe of vetell as was purwad for my howsald.

β. *c* **1400** *Apol. Loll.* 59 Oþer sacramentis are ȝeuen to ilk man for himsilf, and silk þey are to ilk man as þei are tane wiþ hart and concience. **1457** *Test. Ebor.* (Surtees) II. 207 Silke as the custom of the kirk of the cite of York requires.

γ. *c* **1400** tr. *Secr. Secr., Gov. Lordsh.* 101 Yn pryue conseils er swyk þinges shewed to oon, þat byfore many or mo shold noght be shewyd.

3. *swilk and swilk*: see SUCH *a.* 16 b. (Cf. 4.)

c **1200** ORMIN 1006 All þeȝȝre lac wass swillc & swillc. *a* **1300** *Cursor M.* 4413 (Cott.) Al suilk and suilk, sir, was þe scam þat he can seke on mi licam.

4. *absol.* or as *pron.* = SUCH IV.

[*c* **888** ÆLFRED *Boeth.* xxxviii. §1 Be swilcum & be swylcum þu miht ongitan þæt se cræft þæs lichoman bið on þa mode.] *c* **1200** ORMIN 9381 All swillc & swillc comm Sannt Johan To shæwenn & to kiþenn. *Ibid.* 13935 Wel he wisste himm sellf forr whatt He nollde swillke chesenn. *c* **1300** *Havelok* 644 Al with suilk Shole we sone þe wel fede. *a* **1340** HAMPOLE *Psalter* xxxix. 21 Swilk ere fikil louers and fals. *c* **1400** tr. *Secr. Secr., Gov. Lordsh.* 50 To swilk.. þat souereyn god iugys vnworthi & enemys. *c* **1460** *Towneley Myst.* xxviii. 333 Whils I am werere of swylke, the longere mercy may I call.

5. With *one*, *none*, *another*: = SUCH 26–28.

α. *c* **1200** ORMIN 11595 þatt swillc an sholde muȝhenn beon Shippennd off alle shaffte. *a* **1300** *Cursor M.* 77 (Cott.) Suilk in herth es fundun nan. *Ibid.* 1942 For nakin schaunce Sal i ta suilk a noiþer wengance. *Ibid.* 18142 For þar mai be nanoþer suilk. *c* **1400** tr. *Secr. Secr., Gov. Lordsh.* 107 If þou fynde non swylke. **1483** *Cath. Angl.* 374/2 Swilkone,.. *talio*.

β. *a* **1300** *Siriz* 245 For none selke werkes. *c* **1400** *Laud Troy Bk.* 15508 In al this world is non silke [*rime* mylke].

6. With numeral, expressing multiplication: = SUCH 32.

13.. *Evang. Nicod.* 386 in Herrig *Archiv* LIII. 398 [It] es more syn þan swilk seuen. *c* **1400** *Ywaine & Gaw.* 1886 Sum he losed of hys men, Bot the evil lost swilk ten. *c* **1425** *Seven Sag.* (P.) 1196 Swylke seven clerkys hadde hee Undir hym as have ȝe.

B. *adv.* So, likewise; as. Cf. SUCH *adv.*

12.. [see 2 above]. *c* **1250** *Gen. & Ex.* 143 Ðe mone is more bi mannes tale, Ðan al ðis erðe in werldes dale; And egest swilc ðe sunnes brigt, Is more ðanne ðe mones ligt.

C. *Comb.*: **swilk-like** = SUCH-LIKE.

c **1400** tr. *Secr. Secr., Gov. Lordsh.* 97 Chaterynge of bryddes, and swylk lyk souns. *Ibid.*, A rappyngge togedre of stones, hewynge of wode, and swylk lyk. **1439** *Charters &c. of Edinb.* (1871) 64 Payand yerly.. swylk like annuales as thai dede to.. Schir Robert.

swilk, *v. dial.* [Echoic.] *intr.* To splash or dash about, as liquid. So '**swilker** *v. dial.*

1674 RAY *N.C. Words*, To *Swilker* ore: to dash over. **1853** ANNA M. HOWITT *Art Student in Munich* 198 The water dashed over the little raft, swilkering between the mighty stems. **1865** WAUGH *Lanc. Songs* 46 Th' owd lad he's fairly made 'em swilk. **1867** SMYTH *Sailor's Word-bk.*, *To Swilker*, a provincialism for splashing about.

†**swilkin(s**, *a. Obs.* [f. SWILK + KIN *sb.*[1] 6 b. Cf. SICCAN.] = SUCHKIN.

a **1300** *Cursor M.* 857 (Cott.) Leue we now o suilkin spel Of our stori forth to tell. *Ibid.* 18064 He þat suilkins mightes moght.

swill (swɪl), *sb.*[1] *north.* and *E. Anglian.* Also 4 sqwill(e, 4–7 swille. [Origin unknown.]

1. A large shallow basket, made roughly with strips of oak, unpeeled willows, or the like.

1395 *Cartular. Abb. de Whiteby* (Surtees) II. 604 Fro ij cannis et j sqwill, subulcc, vj. d. **1569** *Richmond Wills* (Surtees) 218, vj sand pokes with iij great swilles. **1650** in *Trans. Cumb. & Westm. Antiq. Soc.* (N.S.) IX. 291 The Miller.. shall not lette any moulter stay in swilles.. above half a peck. **1701** in W. O. Blunt *Ch. Chester-le-Street* (1884) 103 Paid for a swill for yᵉ cuishon 00 00 03. **1811** WILLAN in *Archaeologia* XVII. 160 (*W. Riding Words*) *Swill*, a wicker basket, used by washer-women. **1829** BROCKETT *N.C. Gloss.*, *Swill*, a round basket of wicker work; generally carried on the head. **1894** H. D. RAWNSLEY *Lit. Assoc. Engl. Lakes* I. 123 Here he worked at his baskets and swills for five and a half years.

b. *spec.* A basket in which fish, esp. herrings, are landed or carried to market; hence as a measure, containing from 500 to 660 herrings. †Formerly also for oysters.

1352 *Excheq. Acc. Q.R.* Bundle 20. No. 27 (P.R.O.) De id. ob. solutis pro uno sqwille empto. **1398** *York Memo. Bk.* (Surtees) I. 164 Ceaux qe vendount oistres desormes facent vendre par swilles. **1657** in Sir C. Sharp *Chron. Mirab.* (1841) 33 (*Wolsingham*) George Greeinewell, the swill maker. **1853** *Househ. Words* VI. 425/2 At Yarmouth.. the fish are landed in certain convenient and quaintly-shaped baskets, called 'swills'. **1856** *Illustr. Lond. News* 12 Apr. 374/1 (*Yarmouth*) A number of baskets called 'swells', somewhat [similar] in shape to a baker's basket, but considerably longer, with a broad flat handle in the centre, at top. **1894** R. LEIGHTON *Wreck Golden Fleece* 14 Many's the time I've risked my life for a swill o' mackerel or a line of haddocks.

†**2.** A washing-tub. *Obs.*

1624 in *Archaeologia* XLVIII. 147 (*Yorks.*) In the Wash-house. Tubbs 3. Swills 3. Soaes 3. 2 cloth baskettes. **1674** RAY *N.C. Words*, *A Swill*, a keeler to wash in, standing on three feet.

swill (swɪl), *sb.*[2] Also 6 swyl, swyll, 6–7 swil. [f. SWILL *v.*]

1. a. Liquid, or partly liquid, food, chiefly kitchen refuse, given to swine; hog-wash, pig-wash.

a **1570** *Black-Letter Ball. & Broadsides* (1867) 131, I serue your swyne with draffe and swyl. **1570** FOXE *A. & M.* (ed 2) I. 138/1 Swyl and draffe, wont to be giuen to their hogs. **1626** BRETON *Fantastickes* Wks. (Grosart) II. 13/2 The Hogges cry till they haue their swill. **1666** J. ALLEINE *Let.* xxvi. in *Life* (1672) 93 Every Swine will have his swill. **1707** MORTIMER *Husb.* (1721) I. 249 'Tis good to give them [*sc.* pigs] such swill as you have every Morning and Evening to make them come home to their Coats. **1817–18** COBBETT *Resid. U.S.* (1822) 174 The milk and fat pot-liquor and meal are, when put together, called, in Long Island, *swill*. **1864** H. JONES *Holiday Papers* 45 Many a time have I watched the yardman baling out swill for the pigs with a ladle. **1913** G. G. COULTON in *Rep. 7th Ann. Meeting Hist. Assoc.* 13 The pig bred for pork, to which everything is given indiscriminately and simultaneously, in the form of swill or slop.

b. *fig.*

1553 M. WOOD tr. *Gardiner's True Obed.* To Rdr. B iv, He.. geueth vs leaue, according to our demerites, to be fed with the swil and draffe, of masing masses. **1554–5** HOOPER in Foxe *A. & M.* (1563) 1061/1, I am swill and sincke of sin. **1613** PURCHAS *Pilgrimage* VII. ii. 555 And yet our country-man Harding, leauing the cleare waters of truth, hath swallowed the same swill, as the Iewell of our Church hath taught him. *a* **1653** G. DANIEL *Idyll.* v. 107 Throw yᵉ Course Branne, with the Swill of Humors, a Mash made For Sickly Tirants. **1901** WINSTON CHURCHILL *Crisis* I. x, You will not think of us as foreign swill, but as patriots.

c. *transf.* A liquid or partly liquid mess, a slop.

1665 NEDHAM *Med. Medicinæ* 47 It contemns all those large Pectoral Swils, long Syrups, and Electuaries. **1897** *Allbutt's Syst. Med.* III. 499 If the state of the ingesta is usually rather that of a sour fermented 'swill'. **1903** CUTCLIFFE HYNE *McTodd* iv. 87 The place was full of steam, too, from the swill slopping against the boiler fires.

2. a. Copious or heavy drinking; liquor, esp. when drunk to excess; †a draught or swig (of liquor).

1602 BRETON *Mother's Blessing* xlv, Weare not a feather in a showre of raine, Nor swagger with a Swiser for his swill. **1641** H. L'ESTRANGE *God's Sabbath* 132 To spend the hole day in swinish swill, lascivious wantonnesse,.. and in the true service of Satan. **1654** R. CODRINGTON tr. *Iustine* XXIV. 339 The Gauls falling to their swill of Wine as to their prey. **1726–31** WALDRON *Descr. Isle of Man* (1865) 56 As soon as he had recruited himself with a hearty swill of brandy. **1730–46** THOMSON *Autumn* 538 As they swim in mutual swill. **1846** LD. STANLEY in *Croker Papers* (1884) III. 87 A pail of ale, with a bottle of gin in it, from which every man takes a swill. **1864** CARLYLE *Fredk. Gt.* XV. i. IV. 7 Eminent swill of drinking, with the loud coarse talk supposable, on the part of Mentzel and consorts did go on.

b. *six o'clock swill*, the customary bout of hasty drinking in public houses at the end of the working day, occasioned by the former six-o'clock-closing regulations. *Austral.* and *N.Z. colloq.*

[**1951** A. W. UPFIELD *New Shoe* 93 It wanted ten minutes to the fatal hour of six, and the enforced National Swill was in full flood.] **1955** A. ROSS *Australia 55* 81 This evening ritual, known amongst Australians as the 'six o'clock swill'. **1961** F. HARDY *Hard Way* 73 The [prison] yard was filling steadily, mostly with drunks, and a few victims of the six o'clock swill. **1970** D. HORNE *Next Australia* 160 The 'six o'clock swill' before the lavatory-tiled bars closed was one of the continuing tests of masculinity.

3. *Comb.*, as ***swill-barrel***, ***-bucket***, ***-cistern***, ***-house***, ***-pail***; ***swill-engrossing*** adj.; †**swill-milk** *U.S.*, inferior milk produced by cows fed entirely on swill (*obs.*).

(See also SWILL *v.* 5; also SWILL-TUB.)

1869 MRS. STOWE *Oldtown Folks* xxxvi. 469 The wasteful excesses she had seen in the minister's *swill-barrel. **1932** KIPLING *Limits & Renewals* 311 Enoch sat helpless on a *swill-bucket. **1975** *Country Life* 13 Mar. 666/1 Those happy-go-lucky swill-bucket days. **1833** LOUDON *Encycl. Archit.* §866 *Swill-cisterns and tanks for holding liquid food. **1631** FULLER *David's Heinous Sin* (1867) 212 *Swill-engrossing swine, with greedy throats. **1833** LOUDON *Encycl. Archit.* §866 Gloss., **Swill house*, place for preparing pigs' food. **1853** *Hunt's Merch. Mag.* XXVIII. 684 The whole business [is] in the hands of the *swill milk manufacturers. **1894** P. L. FORD *Hon. Peter Stirling* 72 The press began, too, a crusade against the swill-milk dealers. **1741** *Boston News-Let.* 12 Feb. 2/1 Taken up by John Morey, Esq... a *swill-Pale, otherwise called a Hog-Pale. **1889** FERNALD in *Voice* (N.Y.) 3 Oct., Buy green apples at the highest market price, and throw them into the swill-pail.

swill (swɪl), *v.* Forms: 1 swillan (suillan), swilian (swylian), 3–4 swyle, 4 swile, 6 swyll, swil, *Sc.* sweill, 7 swille, 6– swill. [OE. *swillan*, *swilian*, of which no certain cognates are known.]

1. *trans.* To wash or rinse *out* (a vessel or cavity), or, now usually, to cause water to flow freely upon (a surface, floor, etc.) in order to cleanse it; †formerly also in wider use, to wash, bathe, drench, soak.

c **725** *Corpus Gloss.* (Hessels) G 3 *Gargarizet*, gagul suille. *c* **1000** *Lambeth Ps.* vi. 7 [6] *Lauabo.. lectum meum lacrimis meis*, ic ðwea *vel* ic swilige.. min bed mid minum tearum. *c* **1000** *Sax. Leechd.* II. 24 Seoh þurh linenne clað & swile mið þæt geagl. *a* **1300** *Body & Soul* in Böddeker *Altengl. Dichtungen* (1878) 239 þe þridde day shal flowe a flod þat al þis world shal hyle; boþe heye & lowe, þe flume shal hit swyle. *c* **1300** *Havelok* 919 Ful wel kan ich dishes swilen. **1303** R. BRUNNE *Handl. Synne* 5826 He meked hym self ouer skyle, Pottes and dysshes for to swele [*v.r.* swyle]. **1530** PALSGR. 745/2, I swyll, I rynce or clense any maner vessell, *je raince.* **1582** STANYHURST *Æneis* I. (Arb.) 24 With wyne theire venison was swyld. **1599** SHAKS. *Hen. V*, III. i. 14 A galled Rocke.. Swill'd with the wild and wastfull Ocean. **1619** DRAYTON *Bar. Wars* II. xiv, The Siluer Trent.. Which, with the store of liberall Brookes supplyde, Th' insatiate Meads continually doth swill. **1638** RIDER *Horace, Odes* iii. 12 He in Tiber's streams hath swill'd His oyly shoulders. **1647** C. HARVEY *Schola Cordis* (1778) 119 Swelter'd and swill'd in sweat. **1801** tr. *Gabrielli's Myst. Husb.* III. 77 There, slip these on,.. and I will swill out your other stockings in the morning. **1802** BEDDOES *Hygeia* VIII. 19 The patient had carefully swilled out her stomach with water. **1842** T. MARTIN in *Fraser's Mag.* Dec. 652/2 Ducking and diving into the basin-stand, and swilling his face and neck with oceans of water. **1879** JEFFERIES *Wild Life in S. Co.* 69 The dairy, which has to be constantly 'swilled' out and mopped clean.

absol. **1860** GEO. ELIOT *Mill on Floss* III. vi, Kezia, the good-hearted, bad-tempered housemaid,.. had begun to scrub and swill.

b. To stir (something) about in a vessel of liquid; to shake or stir (liquid) in a vessel by moving the vessel about.

1580 FRAMPTON *Joyful News, Two Med. agst. Venome* 138 It is good to have a peece of a right Unicornes horne in a smal cheyne of golde, that it may bee swilled continually in the water that shall bee dronke. **1600** SURFLET *Country Farm* I. xii. 59 They swill the vrine round about the basen. *c* **1650** *K. Arthur & K. Cornwall* 278 in Hales & Furniv. *Percy Folio* I. 73 Then Sir Tristeram tooke powder forth of that box, & blent it with warme sweet milke; & there put it vnto that horne, & swilled it about in that ilke.

c. To carry by a current of water, to wash down, against something, etc. Also, to pour or carry (liquid) freely down.

1598 SYLVESTER *Du Bartas* II. i. III. *Furies* 307 Bloud, tears, bowrs, towrs; she spils, swils, burns, and razes. **1633** P. FLETCHER *Purple Isl.* III. xx, The worst..distilling To divers pipes, the pale cold humour swilling, Runs down to th' Urine-lake. **1850** *Jrnl. R. Agric. Soc.* XI. I. 155 The first rains..swill the soil into the rock beneath. **1902** *Daily Chron.* 15 Sept. 6/4 He clutched at everything he could feel. He was 'swilled' against a post.

2. *intr.* To move or dash about, as liquid shaken in a vessel; to flow freely or forcibly; to flow or spread over a surface.

1642 H. MORE *Song of Soul, Notes Psychath.* Wks. (Grosart) 152/1 The acceleration or retardation of the motion of the Earth will make the sea fluctuate or swill, like water in a shaken vessel. **1659** —— *Immort. Soul* III. xiii. §6. 465 The Spirit of Nature in some regards leaves the motion of Matter to the pure laws of Mechanicks, but within other bounds checks it, whence it is that the Water does not swill out of the Moon. **1884** R. PATON *Scott. Church* vii. 62 Than if their heads were channels for any rubbish to swill through that happened to be in the way. **1895** G. PARKER *Adventurer of North* 183 The river went swishing, swilling past. **1896** KIPLING *Seven Seas, Rhyme of 3 Sealers* 119 O rainbow-gay the red pools lay that swilled and spilled and spread.

3. To drink freely, greedily, or to excess, like hogs devouring 'swill' or 'wash'. **a.** *trans.* (Occas. with *down*, formerly also *in.*)

1561 AWDELAY *Frat. Vacab.* (1869) 13 A licoryce knaue that will swill his Maisters drink. **1563** *Homilies* II. *Agst. Gluttony* Eee ij b, He left not his banqueting, but in one night swilled in so much wyne, that he fell into a feuer. **1617** MORYSON *Itin.* III. 91 Their women swill Wine and Beere daily, and in great excesse. **1674** tr. *Martiniere's Voy. North. Countries* 32 They drank of our beer.., but not with the gust and delight they swill down their own. **1712** STEELE *Spect.* No. 474 ¶6, I would be brisk in swilling Bumpers. **1732** ARBUTHNOT *Rules of Diet* in *Aliments*, etc. 391 Swilling down great Quantities of cold watery Liquors. **1808** SCOTT *Marm.* I. xxii, Let Friar John..Roast hissing crabs, or flagons swill. **1821** —— *Kenilw.* ii, These empty stoups,.. which my nephew and his drunken comrades have swilled off. **1850** DICKENS *Dav. Copp.* xxvi, I sat swilling tea. **1853** HAWTHORNE *Tanglewood T., Circe's Palace* (1879) 138 How they swilled down the liquor.

transf. and *fig.* **1566** STUDLEY tr. *Seneca's Agamemnon* 2273 The sacred tombes and alter stones our blood haue dronke and swyld. **1591** SYLVESTER *Du Bartas* I. i. 438 Those that the Sea hath swill'd. **1690** C. NESSE *Hist. & Myst. O. & N. Test.* I. 97 That bitter cup which..they should have been swilling and swallowing down for ever. **1744** ARMSTRONG *Preserv. Health* IV. 168 In the tempting bowl Of poison'd nectar sweet oblivion swill. **1818** SHELLEY *Lines Euganean Hills* 223 That the brutal Celt may swill Drunken sleep with savage will.

b. *intr.* (*esp.* to tipple, booze).

c **1530** [see SWILLING *vbl. sb.* 2]. *a* **1583** MONTGOMERIE *Flyting* 494 (Tullibard. MS.) Vnto þe cocatrice in ane creill they send it [*sc.* the crocodile]; quhair, sevin ȝeiris, it sowkit, sweillit, singit and sarie. *c* **1590** MARLOWE *Faustus* xiii, He would not banquet, and carowse, and swill Amongst the Students. *a* **1625** FLETCHER *Bloody Brother* II. ii, Then let us swill boyes for our health, Who drinks well, loves the commonwealth. **1678** R. L'ESTRANGE *Seneca's Mor.* (1702) 252 When he had Swill'd..to a Beastly Excess he was carry'd away..to bed. **1775** SHERIDAN *Duenna* III. v, Ye eat, and swill, and sleep, and gourmandise. **1780** COWPER *Progr. Err.* 266 To swill and swallow at a trough. **1845** DICKENS *Chimes* ii. 60 Not that you should swill, and guzzle, and associate your enjoyments, brutally, with food. **1887** JEFFERIES *Amaryllis* vii, They went along..en route to swill and smoke and puff and guffaw somewhere else.

4. *trans.* To cause to drink freely; to supply with abundance or excess of liquor; to fill with drink; *refl.* to drink one's fill. Const. *with*, †*in*.

1548 ELYOT, *Appotus*, well wette with drynke, welle wasshed or swilled with drynke, almost drunke. **1583** STUBBES *Anat. Abus.* I. (1879) 104 Wee must not swill and ingurgitate our stomacks so ful. **1648** CRASHAW *Delights Muses, Muses Duel* 76 Sweet-lipp'd Angell-Imps, that swill their throats In creame of Morning Helicon. **1710** ADDISON *Tatler* No. 154 ¶13 Several Souls, who..flock about the Banks of the River Lethe, and swill themselves with the Waters of Oblivion. **1728** VANBR. & CIB. *Prov. Husb.* I. ii, I wonder..you will encourage that lad to swill his guts thus with such beastly lubberly liquor. **1772** NUGENT tr. *Grosley's Tour Lond.* I. 81 Tied in a file to posts at the extremity of the grass-plat, they [*sc.* cows] swill passengers with their milk, which.. is served..in little mugs. **1866** GEO. ELIOT *F. Holt* xi, Till they can show there's something they love better than swilling themselves with ale.

b. To supply or feed (a hog) with swill.

a **1722** LISLE *Husb.* (1757) 411 Hogs should be well swilled with wash before they are put up for fatting.

5. *Comb.* **a.** with adv., as †**swill-down** *a.*, that swills down liquor, addicted to excessive drinking. **b.** with sb. in objective relation, as †**swill-belly**, a great drinker; so **swill-bellied** *a.*; SWILL-BOWL, **swill-flagon, swill-pot**, one who swills a bowl (flagon, pot), an excessive drinker, a toper.

1699 R. L'ESTRANGE *Erasm. Colloq.* (1725) 124 Their brawny, *swill-bellied monks. *a* **1700** B. E. *Dict. Cant. Crew*, **Swill-belly*, a great Drinker. *a* **1693** *Urquhart's Rabelais* III. xxxi. 256 Such a *Swill-down Bouser. **1829** SCOTT *Anne of G.* xxiii, Out, thou eternal *swill-flagon! **1653** URQUHART *Rabelais* I. xxxiii, That unworthy *Swill-pot Grangousier.

Hence **swilled** (swɪld) *ppl. a.*, filled with liquor, inebriated, drunken.

1634 MILTON *Comus* 178, I should be loath To meet the rudenesse, and swill'd insolence Of such late Wassailers.

swill (also 6 **swyll**), dial. var. SWEAL *v.*

1543 *St. Papers Hen. VIII*, III. 444 To storke [? scorke] or swyll the eares of wheate, and eate the same. **1841** J. T. HEWLETT *Parish Clerk* II. 88 The smell and the crackling noise..occasioned by 'swilling', or scorching it [*sc.* a pig].

'Swill, euphemistic shortening of *God's will*, used as an asseveration.

1601 MARSTON *Ant. & Mel.* v. i. 45 *Alb*... How shall I purchase love of Rossaline? *Feli.* 'Swill, flatter her soundly.

swill-bowl ('swɪlbəʊl). *Obs.* or *arch.* Forms: see SWILL *v.* and BOWL *sb.*[1]; also 6 **swielbolle, swylbowle,** 6–7 **swilbol.** [f. SWILL *v.* + BOWL *sb.*[1]] One who habitually 'swills the bowl' or drinks to excess; a toper, drunkard.

1542 UDALL *Erasm. Apoph.* 330 b, The greatest swielbolle of wyne in the world. **1583** STUBBES *Anat. Abus.* I. (1879) 86 The Drunkards & swilbowles, vppon their ale benches. **1601** HOLLAND *Pliny* XXIII. viii. II. 171 Lustie tosse-pots and swill-bolls. **1616** DEACON *Tobacco Tortured* 57 Alas poore Tobacco, my pretie Tobacco; thou that hast bene hitherto accompted the Ale-knights armes, the Beere brewers badge,..the Swil bols swine-troffe, the Tinkers trull. **1655** R. YOUNGE *Agst. Drunkards* (1863) 5 Though these swinish swill-bouls make their gullet their god. *a* **1845** MRS. BRAY *Warleigh* xviii. (1884) 149, I will allow nothing to make you the companions of swillbowls and ranters.

swiller[1] ('swɪlə(r)). [f. SWILL *v.* + -ER[1].] One who swills.

†**1.** One who swills dishes; a scullion. *Obs.*

c **1475** *Pict. Voc.* in Wr.-Wülcker 769/24 *Hic lixa*, a swyllere.

2. One who drinks greedily or to excess.

1598 FLORIO, *Sorbibruodo*, a greasie, slouenly feeder, a sipper of broth, a swiller. *c* **1618** MORYSON *Itin.* IV. (1903) 224 These Judges were..great swillers of Spanish sacke. **1694** MOTTEUX *Rabelais* v. Prol. A 6 b, What Swillers, what Twisters will there be! **1845** FORD *Handbk. Spain* I. 71 The genuine Goths, as happens everywhere to this day, were great swillers of ale and beer.

swiller[2]. *north. dial.* [f. SWILL *sb.*[1] + -ER[1].] One who makes swills or baskets.

1859 W. DICKINSON *Gloss. Words & Phrases Cumberland* 116 *Swiller*,..a swill-maker. **1901** C. W. BARDSLEY *Dict. Eng. & Welsh Surnames* 522/2 In Ulverston registers to this day a maker of *swills* (i.e. baskets) is set down as a *swiller*. **1949** K. S. WOODS *Rural Crafts of Eng.* III. viii. 142 In Furness the baskets are known as swills, and the craftsmen as swillers. Whether the word is a form of scull or scuttle, or whether it means swaler, is not known. **1972** *Daily Tel.* 5 Aug. 9/4 The Lancashire mountains near Ulverston, home of the 'swillers', or basket-makers. *Ibid.*, With a short and very sharp knife the swiller slices his oak into ribs which he fixes across a hazel rim.

swilley: see SWILLY *sb.*

swilling ('swɪlɪŋ), *vbl. sb.* Forms: see SWILL *v.*; also 1 **swiling,** 5 **swelyng,** 6 **swellyng;** 6 **swildyng, swyldyng;** 7 *Sc.* (*pl.*) **swillons.** [f. SWILL *v.* + -ING[1].] The action of the verb SWILL; also *concr.*

1. Washing, etc. (see SWILL *v.* 1).

c **1000** *Sax. Leechd.* II. 2 Clæsnunga & swiling wið hrum & ȝillistrum to heafdes hælo. *c* **1430** *Syr Gener.* (Roxb.) 2375 With swilling thries and oones wrong, Therabout stoode she not long, She gate awey the spottes in hast. **1888** *Times* 31 Dec. 7/4 The recent swilling of the floor of Barrett's stable.

2. Heavy or excessive drinking, tippling.

c **1530** *Jyl of Brentford's Test.* (1871) 7 Come you nere, & take parte of our swyllyng. **1576** FLEMING *Panopl. Epist.* 382 Who is giuen to excessiue swilling so much as hee? **1638** 'R. JUNIUS' *Drunkard's Char.* 45 What so much as swilling blowes up the cheekes with wind, fills the nose and eyes with fier, loads the hands and legs with water? **1714** MANDEVILLE *Fab. Bees* (1725) I. 117 The cramming and swilling of ordinary Tradesmen at a City Feast. **1843** R. J. GRAVES *Syst. Clin. Med.* v. 68 The continued swilling of even the most innocent fluids will bring on heaviness of stomach. **1858** LYTTON *What will He do?* IV. iv, All is noise and bustle, and eating and swilling.

3. *concr.* (usually *pl.*) = SWILL *sb.*[2] 1. ? *Obs.*

a **1529** [implied in *swyllynge tubbe*: see 5]. **1537** COVERDALE *Expos. Ps. xxii.* B vij b, These worldlye goodes are hys draff and swellynges, wherwith he fylleth the hogges belyes. **1583** MELBANCKE *Philotimus* D iij, A swete swillings, I would the swine had her. **1614** MARKHAM *Cheap Husb.* (1623) 123 Filling their troughes with Draffe and Swilling, let them fill their bellies. **1707** MORTIMER *Husb.* (1721) I. 337 The Chaff and the Dust..are very good Swine's-meat, mixt either with Whey or Swillings.

b. The feeding (of a hog) with swill.

a **1722** LISLE *Husb.* (1757) 413, I bought a hog, and when it was swilled, the farmer commended very much the swilling of it.

4. Dirty liquid such as that produced by the washing out of casks or other vessels; also, poor liquor.

1545 BALE *Myst. Iniq.* 40 And nothynge do ye at all but vomete fylthye swyllynges. *a* **1603** T. CARTWRIGHT *Confut. Rhem. N.T.* (1618) 587 The same stroake..should much more wipe away your traditions as swaddes and swillings of mens brewing. **1637** J. TAYLOR (Water P.) *Drinke & Welcome* A 4, A heartlesse liquor much of the nature of Swillons in Scotland, or small Beere in England. **1891** *Daily News* 26 Dec. 3/5 The swillings from these barrels. **1899** H. COBBE *Luton Ch.* 495 The coarse swillings of bad fermented liquor.

5. *attrib.* and *Comb.*, as †*swilling-pan*, †*-pot*, †*-tub* (= SWILL-TUB).

1459–60 *Durham Acc. Rolls* (Surtees) 89, j patella vocata Stokton vel le Swelyngpan. **1485–6** *Ibid.* 98 Swyllyngpan. *a* **1529** SKELTON *El. Rummyng* 173 Stryke the hogges with a clubbe, They haue dronke vp my swyllynge tubbe! *a* **1539** *Cartular. Abb. de Rievalle* (Surtees) 342 A swyldyng pott of brass. **1601** *Strange Rep. Sixe Notorious Witches* A iiij, He thrust his head into a swilling Tubbe full of Swines meate. **1897** *Jrnl. Iron & Steel Inst.* LII. 32 After the plates are removed from the swilling tanks. *Ibid.*, The wet plates from the swilling-troughs of the white pickling machine.

'swilling, *ppl. a.* [f. as prec. + -ING[2].] That swills or drinks greedily; addicted to excessive drinking. Also of a draught of liquor, Abundant, 'deep'.

1633 P. FLETCHER *Purple Isl.* VII. lxxv, Among the bows did swilling Bacchus ride. **1687** DRYDEN *Hind & P.* III. 124 When at the fountains head..you take a swilling draught. *a* **1716** SOUTH *Serm.* (1727) VI. 347 Of so peculiar a Force is Temperance against the fiercest Assaults of the Devil, and so unfit a Match is a soaking, swilling Swine to encounter this roaring Lion. **1802** COLMAN *Br. Grins, Elder Bro.* xx, But there are swilling Wights, in London town, Term'd—Jolly dogs,—Choice Spirits. **1826** DISRAELI *Viv. Grey* VI. i, A boisterous..party of swilling varlets.

swilling: see SULING.

†**swill-pough, -pow.** *Obs.* = DILLING; also *attrib.* (*transf.*).

1611 COTGR., *Besot*, a dilling, or swill-pough. *a* **1693** *Urquhart's Rabelais* III. xxvi. 217 Swillpow cock.

swill-tub ('swɪltʌb). [f. SWILL *sb.*[2] 1 + TUB *sb.*] A tub for swill or hog-wash. Occas. *attrib.* Also *fig.* with allusion to heavy drinking.

1575 *Gammer Gurton* IV. ii, Art thou sure diccon, the swil tub standes not here aboute? **1633** P. FLETCHER *Purple Isl.* VII. lxxvii, Soure swil-tub sinne, of all the rest the sink. **1725** BAILEY *Erasm. Colloq.* (1878) 387 The Husband..has been call'd Blockhead, Toss-Pot, Swill-Tub. **1736** F. DRAKE *Eboracum* I. iii. 84 The inhabitants..have a custom..to make Pyes in the Form of a Swill, or Swine-Tub. **1756** *Poor Robin* June B j b, Who makes a swill tub of his womb, Is but a speaking, prattling tomb. **1899** 'OUIDA' in *Fortn. Rev.* Nov. 813 Hogs do not rend the man who carries the swill-tub.

swilly ('swɪlɪ), *sb. dial.* Also **swilley.** [app. var. of SWELLY *sb.*]

1. A detached portion of a coal-seam; also, a local thickening of a coal-seam: = SWELLY *sb.*

1836 T. THOMSON *Min. Geol.*, etc. ii. 162 These little basins are provincially called swilleys. They seldom exceed a mile or a mile and a half in length, and none of them has been worked.

2. An eddy or whirlpool; also in comb. *swilly-hole* (see quot.).

1890 W. A. WALLACE *Only a Sister* 95 I'd sooner lig like an eel in a swilly hole all my days. *Note*, A swilly hole = a pool at the bend of a stream.

3. 'A hollow place;..a gutter washed out of the soil' (E.D.D.).

1899 *Evesham Jrnl.* Mar. 25 (E.D.D.) The drainage was what was locally known as discharging into 'swilleys'.

'swilly, *a. rare*[−1]. [f. SWILL *sb.*[2] 2 or *v.* 3 + -Y.] Addicted to swilling or heavy drinking.

1824 in *Spirit Pub. Jrnls.* (1825) 199 Father Crackenthorpe jovial, and stuffy, and swilly.

swim (swɪm), *sb.* Also 6 **swym(me,** 7 **swimme,** 8 *Sc.* **soom.** [f. SWIM *v.*]

†**1.** The clear part of a liquid which floats above the sediment: = SUBLATION 1, SUBLIMATION 3.

1547 RECORDE *Judic. Ur.* 16 b, The sedyment or grounde, the sublacion or swymme, and the cloude. **1625** HART *Anat. Ur.* I. iii. 34 The urine in this disease was..variable and inconstant in the swimme and sublimation. **1676** JAS. COOKE *Marrow Chirurg., Inst.* III. iii. 39 The Sediment possesses the bottom; the Swim the middle, the Cloud at top.

2. A smooth gliding movement of the body. Also *fig.*

1599 B. JONSON *Cynthia's Rev.* II. iv, *Mer.* A happy commendation, to dance out of measure. *Mor.* Save only you wanted the swim i' the turne. **1654** WHITLOCK *Zootomia* 505 An even unruffled swimme of Affaires, and Fortunes. **1681** OTWAY *Soldier's Fort.* II. i, The modish swim of your body. **1703** STEELE *Tender Husb.* III. i, Your Arms do but hang on, and you move perfectly upon Joints. Not with a Swim of the whole Person—. **1760–72** H. BROOKE *Fool of Qual.* (1809) IV. 27 That easy swim of movement..which.. distinguishes the ladies of this country.

†**3.** The swimming-bladder or sound of a fish.

a **1649** WINTHROP *New Eng.* (1825) I. 272 Distinct bodies in the form of a globe, not much unlike the swims of some fish. **1684** R. WALLER *Nat. Exper.* 67 The greater part of the Air in the bladder, by forcing, or taring the Swim, gets out through some invisible Passages. **1787** BEST *Angling* (ed. 2) 1 An air bladder, or swim, to enable them to rise or sink to any height or depth of water, at pleasure. **1833** *Penny Cycl.* I. 242/1 The..functions of the air-bladder, or, as they [*sc.* fishermen] most commonly call it, the *swim*.

4. a. An act of swimming.

1764 J. WESLEY *Jrnl.* 16 Jan. (1914) V. 44 My mare lost both her fore feet, but she gave a spring, and recovered the causeway; otherwise we must have taken a swim, for the water on either side was ten or twelve feet deep. **1805** HAYLEY *Ballads* I. xv, 'Twas Edward's pleasure, after toil, To take a fearless swim. **1828** WHEWELL in *Life* (1881) 126 A piece of water..where, I believe,..I should find water-fowl of various kinds, tame and wild, taking their morning swim. **1890** 'R. BOLDREWOOD' *Col. Reformer* xvii. (1891) 199 Parklands..had..a swim with Brandon and Mr. Neuchamp in the river. **1895** MEREDITH *Amazing Marr.* i, The tale of her swim across the Shannon river and back.

b. A piece of water to be crossed by swimming. *local.*

1880 Miss Bird *Japan* II. 130 The Aino guide took to the water without giving us any notice that its broad eddying flood was a swim, and not a ford. **1895** *Queenslander* 7 Dec. 1061 The Diamantina River is a swim at Elderslie.

5. A swimming motion; *colloq.* or *dial.* a swimming or dizzy sensation. (Cf. SWIME.)

1817 Keats *'I stood tip-toe'* 114 The moon lifting her silver rim Above a cloud, and with a gradual swim Coming into the blue with all her light. **1818** —— *Endym.* I. 571 Visions.. The which became more strange, and strange, and dim, And then were gulph'd in a tumultuous swim. And then I fell asleep. **1829** E. Elliott *Village Patriarch* III. iv, The laws allow His [*sc.* the coach-horse's] ever-batter'd hoof, and anguish'd limb, Till death-struck, flash his brain with dizzy swim. **1886** Elworthy *W. Somerset Word-bk.*, *Swim.. sb.* State of giddiness or faintness. My 'ead's all of a swim.

6. a. A part of a river or other piece of water much frequented by fish, or in which an angler fishes.

1828 *Sporting Mag.* XXII. 25 It is an excellent part of the stream, and has many good swims and deep holes. **1840** Blaine *Encycl. Rur. Sports* VIII. ix. §3427 It is a method [of catching barbel] principally applied to the more quiet swims. **1864** Hibberd in *Intell. Observer* V. 17 Angling for grayling beside a poor swim on the banks of the Wye, the Dove, or the Ribble. **1867** F. Francis *Bk. Angling* i. (1880) 38 Roach and dace for the most part bite in the same swims.

b. fig. phr. ***in the swim with***: in the same company with, in league with.

1885 *Graphic* 3 Jan. 11/2 A combination of leading jockeys and others 'in the swim' with them. **1889** R. Bridges *Growth of Love* lxiii, And since I see Myself in swim with such good company.

7. *fig.* The current of affairs or events, *esp.* the popular current in business, fashion, or opinion; chiefly in phr. ***in (out of) the swim***.

1869 *Macm. Mag.* Nov. 70/2 A man is said to be 'in the swim' when any piece of good fortune has happened, or seems likely to happen, to him.. The metaphor is piscatorial. **1874** *Siliad* II. 30 'He's in the swim', another swift replies; 'Hot wather, thin, he loiks', Obroian cries. **1879** McCarthy *Own Times* xxvi. II. 264 Palmerston is to all appearance what would be vulgarly called 'out of the swim'. **1884** *Graphic* 29 Nov. 562/3 The second category of companies is usually so managed that the originators do pretty well out of it whether those of the shareholders who are not 'in the swim' gain a profit or lose their Capital.

b. with qualifying words.

1884 H. P. Spofford in *Harper's Mag.* Nov. 891/1 She is in the swim of the world, turning night into day. **1888** Gunter *Mr. Potter* xiv. 167 Who knows nearly everybody in the swim of European society. **1891** Mrs. L. B. Walford *Mischief of Monica* xxix, They have got into the Schofield swim, and in the Schofield swim they must remain.

8. An enterprise, scheme, 'game'. *colloq.* or *slang.*

1860 Sala *Baddington Peerage* I. vii. 138 Perhaps, though, I'd better work with Jack; I don't like being alone in a swim. **1869** 'Wat Bradwood' *The O.V.H.* (1870) 211, I suppose your master aint the sort to stand in for a swim is he? **1876** 'Annie Thomas' *Blotted Out* xvi. 147 You should have taken Claire into your confidence respecting this swim we're in about getting the money from your father.

9. (See quot. 1867.)

1867 Smyth *Sailor's Word-bk.*, *Swims*, the flat extremities of east-country barges. **1883** *Pall Mall G.* 8 Dec. 4/1 When .. the steersman has taken his place in the front swim, and the horse has been attached by a long rope, the vessel is ready to start.

10. a. Simple attrib. 'Worn while swimming', as ***swim-cap***, ***-pants***, ***-shorts***, ***-trunks***, ***-wear***. Cf. SWIMMING *vbl. sb.* 6.

1964 *Harper's Bazaar* Nov. 102 Black and white felt, close as a swimcap. **1942** N. Last *Diary* 5 June in *Nella Last's War* (1983) 207 Arthur stripped off to a pair of swim-pants, to get sun-browned. **1977** J. D. MacDonald *Condominium* xxxiv. 328 He wore brief turquoise swim pants and large, very dark sunglasses. **1973** G. Beare *Snake on Grave* iv. 22 All he wore was swim-shorts and leather sandals. **1959** *Spectator* 21 Aug. 223/1 Several were wading about in the water. Two were braving it out in swim-trunks. **1979** G. Mitchell *Mudflats of Dead* iii. 35 He.. put on his swim-trunks, and slung a towel around his shoulders. **1935** A. P. Herbert *What a Word!* iv. 115, I have been implored by many to attack 'neck-wear', 'foot-wear', 'sleep-wear', and 'swim-wear'. **1962** *Punch* 23 May p. xiii/1 Harvey Nichols have a new range of Californian swimwear. **1976** J. Archer *Not Penny more, not Penny Less* x. 104 I'll never get into the swimwear I'm.. modelling next week.

b. Special combinations. **swim-feeder**, in coarse fishing: a short length of perforated plastic tube about an inch in diameter, used to contain maggots, which escape gradually once it is sunk in the water; **swimgloat**, Logan Pearsall Smith's term for the enjoyment of brief social success without becoming corrupted by it; **swim-hole** = *swimming hole* s.v. SWIMMING *vbl. sb.* 6; **swim-pool** = *swimming-pool* s.v. SWIMMING *vbl. sb.* 6; **swimsuit**, a (woman's) bathing costume; hence **swim-suited** *a.*

1958 F. Oates *Coarse Fishing Baits* ix. 68 Another method of ground baiting is by the use of a new gadget called a 'swim-feeder'. **1981** B. Walsh *Live Bait* v. 33, I used a paternoster rig, with a swimfeeder and a coffin leger to hold the bottom. **1943** J. Lees-Milne *Jrnl.* 5 Sept. in *Ancestral Voices* (1975) 236 He [*sc.* Logan Pearsall Smith] calls Stuart's social success a 'swimgloat'. **1974** *Times Lit. Suppl.* 11 Oct. 1112/3 Logan Pearsall Smith coined a word for the buoyant negotiation of the vanities and temptations of society..: 'swimgloat'. It is a term which suggests the eternal resilience of the picaresque hero. **1924** Kipling *Debits & Credits* (1926) 321 There was a wet ditch at the bottom that I had wanted.. to dam up to make a swim-hole for Mrs. Bevin's ducks. **1958** J. Kerouac *On Road* I. i. 10 My boyhood in those dye-dumps and swim-holes. **1964** C. Barber *Ling. Change Present-Day Eng.* ii. 21 Recently I have seen.. *swim-pool* in a high-class newspaper. **1970** *New Yorker* 10 Oct. 80/1 (Advt.), Two swim pools. **1977** *Lancashire Life* Mar. 115/1 Britain has some of the finest swim pool engineers in the world. **1934** *Times* 18 July 17/6 The one-piece swimsuits with attached skirt are still the most popular. **1948** J. Betjeman *Coll. Poems* (1958) 148 Don't hang swimsuits out on sills (A line has been provided at the back). **1980** B. Castle *Castle Diaries* 151 To the disapproval of the department I insisted on taking an hour off on my way to the office to try to buy a swimsuit for my holiday. **1955** *New Statesman* 16 July 66/2 Brutally honest was the Visual Arts float: the Visual Arts.. were.. represented by a number of swim-suited young women. **1979** 'J. Ross' *Rattling of Old Bones* iii. 32 She was all fresh and rosy and swimsuited.

swim (swɪm), *v.* Pa. t. **swam** (swæm); pa. pple. **swum** (swʌm). Forms: 1 **swimman, (swymman)**, 2–7 **swimme**, 3–7 **swymme**, 4–5 **sweme**, 4–6 **swime**, 5–6 **swym(e**, 7–9 *Sc.* **sweem**, (3 **swemme**, 4 **suemme, suim, suiymme, squim**, 5 **swymb**, 6 **swymm**), 6– **swim**; *Sc.* 4–6 **swome**, 6 **soume, sowme, swoume**, 8 **sume**, 8–9 **soum, sowm, s(w)oom**. *Pa. t. str.* 1 **swamm**, 3–4 **suam**, (4 **squam**), 4–6 **swame**, 5–7 **swamme**, 1– **swam**; *pl.* 1 **swummon**, 2 **swummen**, 3 **svommen**, 3–5 **swomme**, 4 **swumme**; 1, 4–7 (9 *dial.*) **swom**, 4–7 **swomme**, 6–7 **swumme, swome**, (6 **swoome, swume, swomm**), 6–9 **swum**; *wk.* 3 **swymde**, 5 **swymyd**, 6 **swymmed**, *Sc.* **swoumit**, 6–8 (9 *dial.*) **swimmed**, 7 **swimed**, 9 *Sc.* **soomed**. *Pa. pple. str.* 1 **(ȝe)swummen**, 4, 7 **swommen**, 6–7 **swom(m)e**, (7 **swoome, swumme, swom, swimme**), 6– **swum**; 7– (now *incorrect*) **swam**; *wk.* 6 **swymmed**, *Sc.* **swymmit**, 6–7 (9 *dial.*) **swimmed**, 9 *Sc.* **soomed, sweemed**. [Com. Teut. str. vb. (not recorded for Gothic): OE. *swimman*, pa. t. *swamm*, also *swam*, *swom*, pl. *swummon*, pa. pple. *swummen*, = OFris. *swimma* (WFris. *swimme*, *swom* or *swimde*, *swommen*), MLG. *swemmen*, MDu. *swemmen*, *swimmen*, *swam*, *swommen* (Du. *zwemmen*, *zwom*, *gezwommen*), OHG. *swimman*, *swam*, *swummun*, (MHG. *swimmen*, G. *schwimmen*, *schwamm*, *geschwommen*), ON. *svimma*, *svamm*, *summu*, *sommet*, (MSw. *symma*, **svamm*, *summo*, *summith*, Sw. *simma*, *sam*, *summit*, ODa. *svemme*, *svømme*, *svam*, *svemde*, *svemmet*, *sømmet*, Norw., Da. *svømme*).

The Scand. langs. show the following secondary forms, in mod. dial, often with wk. conjugation: ON. *svima* and *symja*, *svam*, *svámu*, *svimit*, MSw. *sima*, *sam*, *samo*, *sumit*, Norw. *svemja*, *svømja*, and *symja*, *svam*, *svom*, and *svamde*, *sumde*, *svomet*, *s(v)oomt*, *swamt*.

Related forms in Germanic containing other vowel-grades are: NFris. *swum*, *swomme*, EFris. *swom* (:—**swomma*), MLG. *swommen*, *swummen* wk. to swim, OHG. *geswumft*, *swummôth* swimming, Goth. *swumfsl* pool, OE. *sund* SOUND *sb.*[1]; MHG. *swamen* to swim, ON. *svamla* to swim with much noise (cf. Norw. dial. *sumla*). A causative form **swam(m)jan* is represented by OE. *beswemman*, MHG. *swemmen* (G. *schwemmen*).

The Indo-eur. root *swem-* with the wider meaning of 'to be in motion' is found in W. *chwyf* motion, OIr. *do-sennaim* I hunt, Lith. *sùndyti* to chase.]

I. Intransitive senses.

1. a. To move along in or on water by movements of the limbs or other natural means of progression.

Beowulf 1624 (Gr.) Com þa to lande lidmanna helm swiðmod swymman. *a* **1000** *Riddles* LXXIII. 4 (Gr.) Ic.. fleah mid fuȝlum & on flode swom. *c* **1000** Ælfric *Hom.* II. 516 Ða ȝeseah he swymman scealfran on flode. *c* **1050** *Voc.* in Wr.-Wülcker 454/30 *Nat*, swam, swimð. *c* **1175** *Lamb. Hom.* 51 Heo bi-gon to swimmen forðward mid þe streme and swam hire þer aȝen. *Ibid.* 129 Alle þe fiscas þe swummen in þere se. *c* **1205** Lay. 1342 Þa mereminnen heom to svommen. *c* **1275** *Ibid.* 28078 Com þar a fisc swemme. *c* **1290** *St. Patrick's Purgat.* 350 in *S. Eng. Leg.* 210 In þat water, ..þis gostes swymden op and doun. *a* **1330** *Otuel* 1617 Summe swumme & summe sunke. *c* **1375** *Sc. Leg. Saints* xvii. (*Martha*) 108 He enterit in riuere faste, & swemand ay, til and mycht leste. **1375** Barbour *Bruce* III. 431 Sum off thaim couth swome full weill. **1382** Wyclif *Acts* xxvii. 42 Lest ony schulde scape, whanne he hadde swymmed [**1526** Tindale, **1535** Coverdale, **1560** *Geneva* swome] out. *c* **1386** Chaucer *Miller's T.* 389 Thanne shal I swymme [*v.r.* sweme] as myrie,.. As dooth the white doke after hire drake. *c* **1470** Henry *Wallace* v. 515 Quhen he is strest, than can he swym [*v.r.* swoome] at will. **1535** Coverdale *Ezek.* xlvii. 5 The water was so depe, that it was nedefull to haue swymmed. *a* **1593** Marlowe *Hero & Leander* II. 250 Vouchsafe these armes some little roome, Who hoping to imbrace thee, cherely swome. **1597** Beard *Theatre God's Judgem.* (1612) 273 They swum through the waters amaine. **1606** Sylvester *Du Bartas* II. iv. III. *Schism* 431 The Crystall Wave, Over the which so often swom they have. **1635** R. N. tr. *Camden's Hist. Eliz.* I. 66 Being shipwrack't ..he had swumme till his strength and his armes failed him. **1638** Mayne *Lucian* (1664) 174 In the sight of all he swumme over to the enemies. **1653** Walton *Angler* vi. 135 Some.. young Salmons, which have been taken in Weires, as they swimm'd towards the salt water. **1670** Milton *Hist. Eng.* II. Wks. 1851 V. 57 His Foot so pass'd over, his Horse waded or swom. *a* **1676** Hale *Prim. Orig. Man.* II. vii. (1677) 202 Though it hath been observed that Bears have swimmed into Islands many Leagues from the Continent. **1676** Shadwell *Virtuoso* II, Admirably well struck! rarely swom! **1701** J. Brand *New Descr. Orkney*, etc. (1703) 110 Betaking themselves to Sea, they endeavour to sweem to the next Isle. **1750** Johnson *Rambler* No. 24 ¶9 Who, being shipwrecked, had swam naked to land. **1776** Mickle tr. *Camoens' Lusiad* Introd. 112 His poems, which he held in one hand, while he swimmed with the other [etc.]. **1827** Carlyle *Germ. Rom.* I. 161 The messengers.. had swam across the Elbe and the Moldau. **1853** Kingsley *Hypatia* iii, Luckily Philammon.. was a bather, and swam like a water-fowl. **1890** 'R. Boldrewood' *Col. Reformer* xiv. (1891) 156 Maories and Kanakas can swim, repeated the old man... White men like you and me can only paddle.

b. *fig.* or in fig. context or phrase.

to swim between two waters (occas. erron. ***streams***), tr. F. prov. *nager entre deux eaux*: to steer between two extremes.

c **1400** *Rom. Rose* 7007 Al amydde I bilde and mak My hous and swimme [*MS.* swmme] and pley therynne Bet than a fish doth with his fynne. *c* **1400** *Pety Job* 83 in *26 Pol. Poems* 123 For Mary loue, that mayde so fre, In whos blode thy son swamme. *c* **1480** Henryson *Mor. Fab., Paddock & Mouse* xxiii, Mannis bodie, swymand air and lait In to this warld,.. quhilis plungit vp, quhilis doun. **1561** tr. *Calvin's 4 Serm. Idol.* i. A vj b, Thei that swim (as the common saying) betwixt two waters allege [etc.]. **1567** *Satir. Poems Reform.* iii. 53 He swoumit in the fluidis of Poetrie. **1595** Spenser *Col. Clout* 782 Vnlesse he swim in loue vp to the eares. **1598** Chapman *Marlowe's Hero & Leander* III. 100 When on his breasts warme sea she sideling swims. **1642** H. More *Song of Soul*, *Oracle* Wks. (Grosart) 134 Well hast thou swommen out, and left that stage Of wicked Actours. **1649** Howell *Pre-em. Parl.* 17 My whole life (since I was left to my self to swim, as they say without bladders). **1738** Wesley *Hymn*, *'Of Him who did Salvation bring'*, He suffer'd; All our Guilt's forgiven; And on his Blood we swim to Heaven. **1888** *Times* (weekly ed.) 3 Feb. 9/2 These documents went swimming to and fro in the Admiralty. **1889** J. M. Duncan *Clin. Lect. Dis. Wom.* xxviii. (ed. 4) 229 A woman who for a long time swam for her life, having had an attack of pyæmia in the course of her recovery from a perimetric abscess. **1890** Barrère & Leland *Slang Dict.* s.v., To make a man *swim* for it, is to cheat him out of his share. **1893** Stevenson *Catriona* xi. 120, I could lay all these troubles by..; swim clear of the Appin murder, [etc.].

c. phr. ***to swim with*** or ***down the stream*** or ***the tide***, to act in conformity with prevailing opinion or tendency (see STREAM *sb.* 2 f); so, in opposite sense, ***to swim against the stream*** or ***the tide***.

a **1592** T. Watson *Tears of Fancy* xliii, Long haue I swome against the wished waue. **1592** [see STREAM *sb.* 2 f]. **1597** Shaks. *2 Hen. IV*, v. ii. 34 You must now speake Sir Iohn Falstaffe faire, Which swimmes against your streame of Quality. **1602** Fulbecke *2nd Pt. Parall.* Introd. 3 Because I would not swim against the streame, nor be vnlike vnto my neighbours. **1631** R. Bolton *Comf. Affl. Consc.* 227 A notorious wretch which hath swumme downe the current of the times, and wallowed in worldly pleasures. **1697** Collier *Ess. Mor. Subj.* II. (1703) 74 A popular man always swims down the stream. **1705** Ld. Fermanagh *Let.* 18 Nov. in M. M. Verney *Verney Lett.* (1930) I. xiii. 229, I fancy Mr. Gape may lose it... Its hard Swimming against the Tyde. **1712** Steele *Spect.* No. 492 ¶4 There is no help for it, we must swim with the Tide. **1760–72** H. Brooke *Fool of Qual.* (1809) IV. 21 Our young Englishman swam willingly down the stream of pleasure. **1855** Motley *Dutch Rep.* III. vi. (1866) 452/1 The President stoutly told him that he was endeavouring to swim against the stream, that the tax was offensive to the people. *Ibid.* v. iv. 727/1 They.. had sought to swim on the popular tide when it was rising. **1971** *Nature* 22 Oct. 515/3 The Sira Institute seems to be swimming against the economic tide.

2. a. To float on the surface of any liquid; to be supported on water or other fluid; not to sink; to form the upper part of a mass of liquid. Sometimes, To rise and float on the surface.

c **1000** *Sax. Leechd.* II. 88 Wiþ circul adle ȝenim doccan þa þe swimman wille. **1382** Wyclif *2 Kings* vi. 6 Felle the yren of the axe in to the watir.. Thanne he hewede of a tree, and putte thider; and the yren swam. **1558** Warde tr. *Alexis' Secr.* 44 b, Take vp with a.. spone,.. all the oyle that shall swim aboue. **1560** Rolland *Seven Sages* 23 Thay gar sweit licour swym aboue, and gall is at the ground. **1607** *God's Warning* in *Harl. Misc.* (Malh.) III. 66 Sheepe swimming upon the waters dead. **1650** W. D. tr. *Comenius' Gate Lat. Unl.* §71 If one plunge or drown anie thing under it [*sc.* water], it will swim out again. **1665** Hooke *Microgr.* vi. 12 Several distinct Liquors, which swimming one upon another, will not presently mix. **1775** Johnson *Diary* 23 Oct. in *Boswell*, The cannon ball swam in the quicksilver. **1798** in Nicolas *Disp. Nelson* (1845) III. 51 A boat, the only one that could swim. **1807** T. Thomson *Chem.* (ed. 3) II. 407 On standing, the mixture separated into two portions; the alcohol holding the salt in solution sunk to the bottom; the ether swam on the surface. **1884** *Chr. Commonw.* 23 Oct. 20/3 Men are skimming the milk before much of the cream has had time to swim.

b. To be supported in a fluid medium.

1547 Recorde *Judic. Ur.* 17 If it [*sc.* the sediment in urine] be so lyght, that it swym in the myddle region of the urine, then it is called the sublation or swym. *a* **1661** Boyle *Cert. Physiol. Ess.* iv. (1660) 131 Amongst whose little Crystals nevertheless there appear'd to swim very little grains. **1817** Shelley *Rev. Islam* v. iv, Methought, his voice did swim As if it drowned in remembrance were Of thoughts. **1895** Crockett *Men of Moss-Hags* xli. 296 When my minnie gaed to him with the guid kail broo and the braxy sooming amang it.

c. *fig.* and in fig. context.

1547–64 Bauldwin *Mor. Philos.* (Palfr.) 144 A very fruitlesse and dead faith,.. which swimmeth like a fume in the outward parts of mens thoughts. **1563** Becon *Demands Script.* Pref. (1577) A iij, This holy woord of God among you, swimmeth not in your lippes only, but it also shineth in your lyfe and conuersation. **1587** Fleming *Contn. Holinshed* III. 1353/1 Why we let them [*sc.* God's laws] swim in our lips, and slip from our liues, as the vaine Iewes did. **1788** Sir J. Reynolds *Disc.* vi. 219 The principles on which the work is wrought.. do not swim on the superficies, and consequently are not open to superficial observers. **1850** Tennyson *In Mem.* cviii, On the depths of death there swims The reflex of a human face.

d. Phr. in which *swim* is opposed to *sink*; esp. ***sink or swim*** (occas. ***swim or drown***), used *spec.* in reference to the ordeal of suspected witches (cf. 14 b), hence *fig.* = 'whatever may happen'.

c 1410 Lanterne of Liȝt 106 þei charge not wheþir þei [*sc.* souls] synk or swyme, so þei moun regne as lordis. 1538 Starkey England (1878) 85 For the rest they care not (as hyt ys commynly sayd) whether they synke or swyme. a 1553 Udall Royster D. i. iii. (Arb.) 22, I care not to let all alone, choose it swimme or sinke. 1611 Cotgr. s.v. Nager, A fauourite of the time, or of authoritie, may boldly swimme where another would sinke. 1786 Burns Earnest Cry & Prayer v, Let posts an' pensions sink or swoom. 1825 [see sink *v.* 1 *Phr.*]. 1860 Whyte Melville Holmby House xviii. I. 274 Well, it's 'over shoes over boots now', and sink or swim, I won't give in for the fear of a ducking! 1887 Stevenson Thrawn Janet in Merry Men, etc. (1905) 132 The guidwives..pu'd her doun the clachan to the water o' Dule, to see if she were a witch or no, soum or drown.

3. a. To move or float along on the surface of the water, as a ship. Now *poet.*

c 1000 Wanderer 53 (Gr.) Secga ȝeseldan swimmað eft onweȝ. a 1300 K. Horn 203 (Camb. MS.) Wiþute sail & roþer Vre schip bigan to swymme [*v.r.* swemme] To þis londes brymme. 1513 Douglas Æneis ix. iii. 95 O ȝe my schippys,..Go furth and swome as Goddessis of the see. 1617 Moryson Itin. ii. 84 The carkasse of a broken ship swimming by vs. 1624 Bacon Consid. Warre w. Spaine Misc. (1629) 41 The greatest Nauy that euer swam vpon the Sea. 1664 Pepys Diary 22 Dec., To Redriffe..and saw the new vessel..launched... It swims and looks finely. 1669 Sturmy Mariner's Mag. v. xii. 81 The Ship was free, and swimmed. 1765 R. Rogers Acc. N. Amer. 18 Having good anchoring ground, and water sufficient for any ship that swims. 1817 Shelley To one Singing 1 My spirit like a charmed bark doth swim Upon the liquid waves of thy sweet singing.

b. To be conveyed by a body floating on the water. Also *fig.* as in phr. 'to be in the same boat with' (boat *sb.* 1 d).

c 1386 Chaucer Miller's T. 364 A knedyng trogh or ellis a kymelyn,..In whiche we mowe swymme [*v.r.* sweme] as in a barge. 1571 Satir. Poems Reform. xxxi. 100 Yai wald haif wist hir swoumand Intil a bait vpon Lochlowmond. 1600 Shaks. A.Y.L. iv. i. 38, I will scarce thinke you haue swam in a Gundello. 1650 Fuller Pisgah 410 The gold of Ophir swimming unto him in the ships of Tarshish. 1869 'Wat Bradwood' The O.V.H. (1870) 215 Half the world will think we have scratched to swim in the same boat with Fisherman.

4. To move as water or other liquid, esp. over a surface; to flow.

c 1400 Song Roland 70 It [*sc.* the wine] swymyd in ther hedis and mad hem to nap. c 1572 Gascoigne Posies, Fruites Warre ccii, As long as any Sunne May shine on earth, or water swimme in Seas. 1582 Stanyhurst Æneis iii. (Arb.) 90 Thee goare blood spouteth..And swyms in the thrashold. 1683 J. Reid Scots Gard'ner (1907) 82 Husbandmen's watering is, by running plough-furrowes and trenches where needful,..so as the water may gently sweem over the whole. 1725 Fam. Dict. s.v. Pears, Comfit your Fruit as readily as you can, to the end, that the liquid Part may continually swim over the Fruit. 1831 Society I. 2 The..occasional tears which swam in the light blue eyes of her Hebe-looking companion.

5. a. To glide with a smooth or waving motion.

a 1553 Udall Royster D. ii. iii. (Arb.) 36 Ye shall see hir glide and swimme, Not lumperdee clumperdee like our spaniell Rig. c 1563 Jack Juggler Bj, She minceth, she brideleth, she swimmeth to and fro. a 1591 H. Smith Serm. (1637) 175 Noblemen, when they..look upon their train swimming after them. 1623 Drumm. of Hawth. Flowres of Sion viii, Thus singing through the Aire the Angels swame. 1728–46 Thomson Spring 784 The peacock spreads His every-coloured glory to the sun, And swims in radiant majesty along. 1760–72 H. Brooke Fool of Qual. (1792) II. 71 Turning away, she swam and disappeared in an instant. 1773 Goldsm. Stoops to Conq. Epil. 28 [She] Doats upon dancing, and in all her pride, Swims round the room, the Heinel of Cheapside. 1830 Macaulay in Trevelyan Life & Lett. (1876) I. iv. 164 Showy women swimming smoothly over the uneasy stones. 1888 Stevenson Black Arrow 209 She..swam across the floor as though she scorned the drudgery of walking.

b. Of a plough (in full, ***to swim fair***): To go steadily (see quots.).

1797 Encycl. Brit. (ed. 3) XV. 75/1 When the plough goes on steadily, without any effort of the ploughman, it is said to be in trim, and to swim fair. 1842 Jrnl. R. Agric. Soc. III. ii. 357 The action of the plough was in no way deranged by that of the slicers; it 'swam fair' on the furrow bottom. 1844 H. Stephens Bk. Farm I. 435 This plough, with its sole upon the surface of two years' old lea, and the coulter alone in the soil, the bridle having been adjusted to make it swim without any undue tendency.

6. a. To move, or appear to move, as if gliding or floating on water; *esp.* to move, glide, or be suspended in the air or ether, occas. by mechanical means.

1661 Boyle Certain Physiol. Ess. (1669) 191 Those little moats that from a shady place we see swimming up and down in the Sun-beams. 1669 Sturmy Mariner's Mag. i. ii. 3 The Compass swings in the Boxes,..the Chard swimming well on the Pin perpendicular in the middle of the Box. 1676 Wood Jrnl. in Acc. Sev. Late Voy. i. (1694) 149 The Sun..having no Depression towards the Horizon, but always swimming about at the same hight. 1708 Brit. Apollo No. 22. 2/1, I observ'd a Kite in the Air to swim several times round in a Circle. 1732 Arbuthnot Rules of Diet in Aliments, etc. 414 This Disease may be easily communicated by the Contagion or steams of an infected Person swimming in the Air. 1780 Cowper Progr. Error 333 The Muse, eagle-pinioned,..Down, down the wind, she swims, and sails away. 1833 Tennyson Two Voices 262 High up the vapours fold and swim; About him broods the twilight dim. 1872 Black Adv. Phaeton xxi. 303 The moon had swum further up into the heavens. 1895 R. W. Chambers King in Yellow, Street of Our Lady of Fields iv. (1909) 253 The dome of the Pantheon swam aglow above the northern terrace, a fiery Valhalla in the sky.

b. Said of the apparent motion of objects before the eyes of a person whose sight is troubled or blurred.

1678 Dryden All for Love iii. ad fin., My sight grows dim, and every object dances, And swims before me, in the maze of death. 1697 —— Æneid x. 1050 A hov'ring Mist came swimming o're his sight. 1709 E. Smith Phædra & Hippolytus i. 7 Priests, Altars, Victims swam before my Sight! 1818 Shelley Rosalind 194 Then all the scene was wont to swim Through the mist of a burning tear. 1818 Byron Ch. Har. iv. cxl, The arena swims around him—he is gone. 1857 Dufferin Lett. High Lat. (1867) 62 The room swam round before me. 1888 'R. Boldrewood' Robbery under Arms xviii, There was a sound like rushing waters in my ears, and the courthouse and the people all swam before my eyes.

†c. To 'float' in the mind. *Obs.*

1627 Lisander & Cal. x. 215 The admirable attractions of her surmounting beauty swome in her minde. 1639 S. Du Verger tr. Camus' Admir. Events 87 Seeking to feed his eyes with the sight of this faire image, which swimmed in his fantasie.

7. a. Of the head or brain: To be affected with dizziness; to have a giddy sensation. Also, of the head, ***to swim round*** = to be in a whirl.

1702 Steele Funeral i. (1734) 19 My Head swims, as it did when I fell into my Fit, at the Thought of it. 1782 Cowper Jackdaw 10 Look up—your brains begin to swim. 1829 Lytton Devereux i. iii, My head swam round. 1851 D. Jerrold St. Giles xi. 108 His brain swam with the thought, and he almost fell to the earth. 1871 C. Gibbon Lack of Gold xx, My head's bizzing, and sooming, and burning. 1886 Stevenson Kidnapped xvii, My own sides so ached, my head so swam,..that I lay beside him like one dead.

b. Of the eyes: To be troubled or blurred: with mixture of sense 10.

1817 Shelley Rev. Islam vi. xxxvi, When the faint eyes swim Through tears of a wide mist boundless and dim. 1820 W. Irving Sketch Bk., Rip Van Winkle (1821) I. 63 At length his senses were overpowered, his eyes swam in his head. 1847 Tennyson Princ. vi. 193 Who turn'd half-round to Psyche as she sprang To meet it, with an eye that swum in thanks. 1860 Tyndall Glac. i. xxii. 155 On suddenly raising it [*sc.* my head] my eyes swam as they rested on the unbroken slope of snow.

†8. *transf.* To abound *with* swimming animals.

c 1381 Chaucer Parl. Foules 188 (Harl. MS.) Colde welle stremes,..þat swommyn ful of smale fysshes lyht. a 1578 Lindesay (Pitscottie) Chron. Scot. (S.T.S.) I. 337 The stankis..was sowmond full of all delecat fisches. 1596 Dalrymple tr. Leslie's Hist. Scot. I. 23 A pleasand Loch swomeng full of fyne perchis.

9. a. To float, be immersed or steeped, *in* a fluid; also in fig. context (cf. b).

c 1450 Mirk's Festial 14 þay vndedyn hit [*sc.* a tomb], and fonden his bones swymmyng yn oyle. a 1586 Sidney Ps. xvii. viii, Their eies doe swimme, their face doth shine in fatt. 1605 B. Jonson Volpone i. i, When you do come to swim in golden lard, Up to the arms in honey. 1655 Culpepper, etc. Riverius ii. vi. 337 The Water corrupted in the Abdomen, doth also corrupt the Bowels that swim therein. 1663 Unfort. Usurper i. ii. 5, I expected to see him almost drown'd with sorrow, But find him swiming, and almost drown'd in's Liquor. 1698 Fryer Acc. E. India & P. 188 Rice thrives best in Watery Places, it swimming always therein till Harvest. 1719 Ozell tr. Misson's Mem. Trav. Eng. 314 Five or six Heaps of Cabbage..or some other Herbs..., well pepper'd and salted, and swimming in Butter. 1719 Ramsay To Hamilton (Herrings) i, Your herrings..In healsome brine a' soumin. 1775 R. Chandler Trav. Asia M. viii. (1825) I. 29 A cotton-wick swimming in oil.

b. *fig.* To be immersed or sunk *in* pleasure, grief, etc.; †to abound *in.*

c 1412 Hoccleve De Reg. Princ. 1254 They þat swymmen in richesse Continuelly, and han prosperitee. 1526 Tindale 2 Thess. i. 3 Every one of you swymmeth in love towarde another betwene youre selves. 1575 Gascoigne Flowers Wks. 1907 I. 94, I seeme to swime in such a sugred joye, As did (parcase) entise them to delight. 1590 Spenser F.Q. ii. iii. 39 There thou maist loue, and dearely loued bee, And swim in pleasure. 1637 Gillespie Engl. Pop. Cerem. iv. vi. 30 They slept upon beds of yvorie, and swimmed in excessive pleasures upon their couches. a 1644 Quarles Sol. Recant. Sol. iii. 38 At noon we swim in wine; at night, in tears. 1652 Crashaw Carmen Deo Nostro, Sancta Maria iv, She sees her son..swimme In woes that were not made for Him. 1667 Milton P.L. ix. 1009 As with new Wine intoxicated both [*sc.* Adam and Eve] They swim in mirth. 1760–72 H. Brooke Fool of Qual. (1809) IV. 27 My soul swims in delight.

10. a. To be covered or filled with fluid; to be drenched, overflowed, or flooded. Const. *with, in.*

a 1542 Wyatt Of Mean & Sure Estate 7 When the furrowes swimmed with the rayne. 1560 Bible (Genev.) Ps. vi. 6, I cause my bed every night to swimme. 1560 Daus tr. Sleidane's Comm. 251 While they seke howe to make slaughter in Germanye, and that all thynge maye swymme full of theyr blud, that professe Chryst. 1595 Locrine ii. v. 66 The currents swift swimme violently with blood. a 1658 Cleveland Inund. Trent 86 Some say the Meadows swim, some say they'r drown'd. 1697 Dryden Æneid iii. 822 With spouting Blood the Purple Pavement swims. 1709 Steele Tatler No. 104 ¶1 To see her Eyes swimming in Tears of Affection. 1711 Addison Spect. No. 83 ¶1 When the Heavens are filled with Clouds, when the Earth swims in Rain. 1735 Johnson Lobo's Abyssinia, Descr. iii. 54 Every thing they eat smells strong and swims with Butter. 1827 Lytton Pelham liv, Ellen, whose eyes swam in tears, as they gazed upon her brother. 1884 Gilmour Mongols 169 Great parts of the causeway swim with deep black mud. 1891 Farrar Darkn. & Dawn lxvi, The marble floors of the Temple of Jerusalem swam in blood.

b. *fig.* To be full to overflowing *with.*

1548 Udall, etc. Erasm. Par. Luke v. 67 Whereas themselfes swimmed as full as theyr skinnes might holde of many great vices. a 1614 D. Dyke Myst. Selfe-Deceiuing (1630) 56 The wickeds Table, though swimming neuer so much with dainties. 1676 Bunyan Strait Gate Wks. (1692) 636/2 Beware..of the Man whose Head swims with Notions, but his Life is among the unclean. 1762–71 H. Walpole Vertue's Anecd. Paint. (1786) IV. 297 The eyes swimming with youth and tenderness. 1845 G. Oliver Coll. Biog. Soc. Jesus 76 He tells Dorothy in a letter, that his heart is now swimming with joy. 1895 Meredith Amazing Marr. iv, The upper sky swam with violet. 1902 R. W. Chambers Maids of Paradise vi. 93 The room in the turret was now [*sc.* after the battle] swimming in smoke and lime dust.

II. Transitive senses.

11. a. To traverse or cover (a certain distance) by swimming. Also, to perform (a stroke or evolution) by swimming.

c 1000 Epist. Alex. ad Arist. in Cockayne Narrat. Angl. (1861) 10 þa hie ða hæfdon feorðan dæl þære ea ȝeswummen. c 1290 St. Brendan 169 in S. Eng. Leg. 224 He swam more þan tuei myle. a 1586 Sidney Arcadia ii. xxiv. (1912) 306, I had swomme a very little way. 1590 Shaks. Mids. N. ii. i. 174 Be thou heere againe, Ere the Leuiathan can swim a league. 1610 —— Temp. iii. ii. 16, I swam, ere I could recouer the shore, fiue and thirtie Leagues. 1848 Blackw. Mag. Dec. 723/1 Gazing at the gold-fish that swam their monotonous circle in the basin. 1893 F. M. Crawford Children of King I. iv. 114 He could not swim a stroke.

b. To glide smoothly through. *rare.*

1725 Pope Odyss. vi. 188 Stately in the dance you swim th' harmonious maze.

12. a. To pass or cross by swimming; to move in, on, or over by swimming; to swim across.

1591 Shaks. Two Gent. i. i. 26 You are ouer-bootes in loue, And yet you neuer swom the Hellespont. 1667 Milton P.L. i. 202 That Sea-beast Leviathan, which God of all his works Created hugest that swim th' Ocean stream. 1697 Dryden Æneid iv. 764 Parti-colour'd Fowl, Which haunt the Woods, or swim the weedy Pool. 1746 Hervey Medit. (1769) I. 203 All that wing the Firmament, or tread the Soil, or swim the Wave. 1813 Scott Rokeby vi. ii, The otter.., prowling by the moon-beam cool, Watches the stream or swims the pool. 1841 Elphinstone Hist. India I. 617 They swam the river to the spot where the king's tent was pitched.

b. To float on the surface of (water). *rare.*

1855 Singleton Virgil I. 137 Nor less, too, swims the seething surge The buoyant alder, wafted on the Po.

13. a. To cause (an animal) to swim, esp. across a river, etc.

1639 T. de Grey Compl. Horsem. 306 After swim him, and apply bathes. 1714 tr. Joutel's Jrnl. Voy. Mexico (1719) 133 Handing over our Goods from one to another, and swimming over our Horses. 1722 Acts Assembly Pennsylv. (1762) I. 96 For every Cow or other neat Cattle, boated or swam, Three Half-pence. 1818 Scott Rob Roy xxxiii, Sometimes swimming their horses, sometimes losing them and struggling for their own lives. 1890 Stevenson Let. to H. James (1899) II. 213 The place is awkward to reach on horseback. I had to swim my horse the last time I went to dinner. 1903 Morley Gladstone I. ii. 47 How he..swam the Newfoundland dog in the pond.

b. To convey by swimming. *rare.*

1613 Heywood Brazen Age i. B4b, I'le vndertake to swimme her Vnto the furthest strond, vpon my shoulders. 1939 A. Ransome Secret Water xxvi. 315 You'll just have to lie on your back and keep still, and I'm going to swim you ashore. 1953 Sun Mag. (Baltimore) 25 Oct. 29/1 The gun fires and the bay dog is over with a splash. Exultantly he swims the dead game back to his master.

c. To cause (something) to pass over the surface of water; to float.

1743 Bulkeley & Cummins Voy. S. Seas 160 The People swam off three Casks of Water. 1800 Moore Anacreon lii. 5 Teach me this, and let me swim My soul upon the goblet's brim. 1836 T. Hook G. Gurney I. 38 Two of the boys proceeded to a pond, for the purpose of swimming a gallipot.

d. Of a rushing force of water: To carry or sweep away in its course.

1858 Carlyle Fredk. Gt. ix. x. (1872) III. 171 Two villages, Fuhrenheim and Sandhausen, it swam away, every stick of them. 1865 Ibid. xx. vii. IX. 129 Reach the bridge before it be swum away.

14. a. To cause to float; to buoy up.

1669 Sturmy Mariner's Mag. v. xii. 81, 5 Tun of Cask will swim a Canon of 8 or 9000 weight. 1779 Phil. Trans. LXX. 107 This deck..was laid at five feet five inches above the bottom of the keel,..and swam the ship at twelve feet five inches water. 1800 S. Standige in Naval Chron. III. 474 Cann Buoys to swim the buoy-rope,..are the most buoyant. 1820 W. Scoresby Acc. Arctic Reg. II. 478 We had not before ascertained how far the contrivance of swimming the ship by the ceiling could be depended on. 1842 Jrnl. R. Agric. Soc. III. ii. 303 Steep the seed in brine that will swim an egg. 1854 Bowlker's Art of Angling 58 Put on a cork float sufficiently large to swim a Gudgeon, or large Minnow, at mid-water.

b. To put (a person suspected of witchcraft) to the ordeal of being immersed in water, the proof of innocence being that the person did not sink.

1718 F. Hutchinson Hist. Ess. Witchcraft 65 Hopkins [the Witch-finder] went on searching and swimming the poor Creatures. 1748 in Gentl. Mag. Mar. (1867) 320 Alice, the wife of Thomas Green, labourer, was swam, malicious..people having raised an ill report of her for being a witch. 1818 Scott Hrt. Midl. xl, The folk are speaking o' swimming her i' the Eden. 1825 Ann. Reg., Chron. 98/1 A man was swam for a wizard at Wickham-Keith..in the presence of some hundreds of people!

c. To furnish sufficient depth of water for (something) to swim or float in.

1794 M. Parry Jrnl. 23 May in Kentucky Hist. Soc. Register (1936) XXXIV. 380 Forded Buffaloe Creek, at the mouth, which did not quite swim them [*sc.* the horses]. 1815

SCOTT *Guy M.* ix, We'll drink the young Laird's health in a bowl that would swim the collector's yawl. **1817** M. BIRKBECK *Notes Journ. Amer.* (1818) 82, I guess it [*sc.* the creek] will swim your horse. **1887** I. R. *Lady's Ranche Life Montana* 25 Wide rivers, very rapid and almost deep enough to swim a horse.

d. (See quot.)

1864 WEBSTER, *Swim, v.t.*...2. To immerse in water that the lighter parts may swim; as, to *swim* wheat for seed.

†**15.** To carry (a publication) to success. *Obs.*

1870 'MARK TWAIN' *Lett. to Publishers* (1967) 45 Launch a book right on our big tidal wave and swim it into a *success.* **1890** G. MEREDITH *Let.* 19 Nov. (1970) II. 1012 If clogged with the letter-press, I should have my doubts of success, even with his name to swim the book.

swimathon ('swɪməθɒn). Also **swim-a-thon.** [f. SWIM *v.* + -ATHON.] A long-distance swimming race; a marathon (often sponsored) swimming event.

1968 *Telegraph* (Brisbane) 20 Dec. 2/2 Six Gold Coast girls will take part in a swimathon at Southport's Olympic Pool. **1976** *Estevan* (Saskatchewan) *Mercury* 23 June 16/3 A swim-a-thon will be held at Woodlawn Swimming Pool June 27... Proceeds will go toward the aquatic club.

'swim-ˌbladder. [f. SWIM *v.* Cf. G. *schwimmblase.*] A fish's swimming-bladder (see SWIMMING *vbl. sb.* 6).

1837 P. KEITH *Bot. Lex.* 375 Ascending or descending chiefly by means of the compression or dilatation of the swim-bladder, an organ with which most fishes are furnished. **1883** *Knowledge* 30 Mar. 191/1 Isinglass..is.. the swim-bladder of the sturgeon and similar fishes cut into shreds. **1896** tr. *Boas' Text Bk. Zool.* 344 In most Fish..the lung..simply possesses the power of diminishing the specific gravity of the animal, and is termed the swim-bladder.

†**swimble,** *sb. Obs. rare.* In 5 **swymbul.** [Related to next.] A swaying motion.

c **1386** CHAUCER *Knt.'s T.* 1121 (Harl. MS.) A foreste,.. With knotty knarry bareyn trees olde Of stubbes sharpe and hidous..to biholde; In which ther ran a swymbul and a swough, As though a storm sholde bresten every bough.

†**swimble,** *v. Obs. rare.* In 5 **swemyle.** [a. west Scand. *svimla* (Norw. dial. *svimla*, Da. *svimle*) to be giddy, stagger, f. *swim-* (see next) + frequent. suffix. Cf. (M)LG. *swîmel* staggering, swooning, *swimel(e)n* to swoon, MHG. *swimmel, swim(m)eln*, early mod.Du. *swijmel, swijmelen*, G. dial. *schweimel, swîmel.*] *intr.* To feel dizzy.

a **1400–50** *Wars Alex.* 156 Swiers swemyle, swouned ladys.

†**swime,** *sb. Obs.* Forms: 1 **swima,** 3–4 **suim(e, suijm,** 4 **suuime,** 4 **squyme,** 4–5 **swym(e.** [OE. *swíma* = MLG. *swîm, swîme*, Du. *zwijm*, G. dial. *schweim* giddiness, swooning, related immed. to (M)LG., MDu. *swîmen* to become faint (Du. *zwijmen*), MHG. *swîmen*, pa. t. *sweem* (G. dial. *schweimen*), and, with variety of vowel-grade, to OE. *-swǽman* (:—**swaimjan*) SWEAM, OFris. *swima* swoon, *swima* to swoon, (M)LG. *sweimen, swimen, swêmen* to stagger, faint, swoon, ON. *svimi* giddiness; f. Teut. root *swaim-*: *swĭm-*, whence also the forms s.v. SWIMBLE.] Dizziness, giddiness, or a fit of this; swooning, a swoon.

a **900** CYNEWULF *Crist* 1300 (Gr.) þær hi ascamode, scondum ȝedreahte, Swiciað on swiman. *a* **1000** *Judith* 106 (Gr.) He on swiman læȝ, druncen & dolhwund. *c* **1000** *Sax. Leechd.* III. 48 Wið ðone swiman nim rudan [etc.]. *a* **1300** *Cursor M.* 5072 (Cott.) þai fell in suijm and cried 'merci!' *Ibid.* 24350 þat suime was o mi soruing suage. ? *a* **1400** *Morte Arth.* 4246 He swounnes one þe swarthe, and one swym fallis. *c* **1460** *Towneley Myst.* ii. 27 Ye stand as ye were fallen in swyme.

fig. *c* **1400** *Destr. Troy* Prol. 12 Sothe stories ben stoken vp, & straught out of mynd, And swolowet into swym by swiftenes of yeres.

†**swime,** *a. Obs.* In 4 **swym.** [f. prec.] Used vaguely (like the sb.) in *Destr. Troy* = giddy, dazed, and (actively) stunning.

c **1400** *Destr. Troy* 3604 With þi swerde is to swinke & not with swym thoghtes. *Ibid.* 9561 Alto swappon vs with swerdes & with swym strokes.

swim-in ('swɪmɪn). [f. SWIM *v.* + -IN[3].] A form of protest or recreation at which a number of people swim together. Cf. SIT-IN *sb.* 1.

1960 *Daily Progress* (Charlottesville, Va.) 2/3 Other white bathers cleared out of the immediate vicinity of the swim-in. **1977** *Navy News* Sept. 25/2 Other events on the social programme have included a barbecue and a 'swim-in' at the local pool.

swimmable ('swɪməb(ə)l), *a.* [f. SWIM *v.* + -ABLE.] Capable of being swum; (also ***swimmable-in***) suitable for swimming in.

1852 M. W. SAVAGE *R. Medlicott* IV. iv, I rode everything rideable,..swam everything swimmable. **1866** *Reader* 10 Feb. 145/1 Within swimmable distance of the shore. **1963** P. MCCUTCHAN *Man from Moscow* ix. 91 The sea's swimmable-in, if you're a Spartan. **1966** *Telegraph* (Brisbane) 3 Feb. 18 (*caption*) Bare midriff camisole tops are the latest on the patio this summer. Worn with snug hip-hugger jams in nylon knit. Both are completely swimable. **1976** *National Observer* (U.S.) 13 Mar. 7/2 Congress poured money into it to help cities do their part in achieving 'swimmable, fishable' waters.

swimmer ('swɪmə(r)). [f. SWIM *v.* + -ER[1]. Cf. MLG. *swemmer*, also *swommer*, MHG. *swimmer* (G. *schwimmer*), Du. *zwemmer.*]

1. A person (or animal) that swims in the water.

1377 LANGL. *P. Pl.* B. XII. 167 þe swymmere þat is sauf bi so hym-self lyke. **1398** TREVISA *Barth. De P.R.* XIII. xvii. (Bodl. MS.), Swymmers beþ ofte yperissched in swalowes. **1578** H. WOTTON *Courtlie Controv.* 135 Ye swimmer Leander. **1593** SHAKS. *Lucr.* 1098 The other wild, Like an vnpractiz'd swimmer plunging still, With too much labour drowns for want of skill. **1663** DRYDEN *Rival Ladies* Ep. Ded., Ess. (1900) I. 4 Like an ill swimmer, I have willingly staid long in my own depth. **1810** SCOTT *Lady of L.* II. xxxvii, The swimmer plied each active limb. **1908** *Animal Managem.* 140 The horse is a powerful natural swimmer.

2. a. An animal that (habitually) swims, or whose structure is adapted for swimming; *spec.* a bird of the order *Natatores*, a swimming bird.

1399 LANGL. *Rich. Redeles* III. 86 Thanne sighed þe swymmers ffor the swan ffailed. **1599** T. M[OUFET] *Silkwormes* 44 The whitest Swimmer nature e're begate, Suspition blacke and iealousie defiles. **1630** DRUMM. OF HAWTH. *Flowres of Sion, Shadow of Judgem.* 246 The Woods wilde Forragers doe howle and roare, The humid Swimmers dye along the shoare. **1646** SIR T. BROWNE *Pseud. Ep.* V. i. 234 In latirostrous or flat bild birdes, which being generally swimmers, the organ is wisely contriv'd unto the action, and they are framed with fins or oares upon their feet. **1718** ROWE tr. *Lucan* IX. 1214 The Swimmer there the crystal stream pollutes. **1835–6** *Todd's Cycl. Anat.* I. 269/2 The Swimmers [*sc.* Natatores]..are..recognizable by the structure and position of their oar-like feet. **1872** COUES *N. Amer. Birds* 14 Among swimmers, the body is always more or less depressed, or flattened horizontally.

b. *Entom.* (*a*) One of a tribe of spiders (*Araneidæ natantes*) which live in water; a swimming spider, water-spider. (*b*) A swimming beetle of the group *Hydradephaga* or *Hydrocanthari.*

1815 KIRBY & SP. *Entomol.* xiii. (1818) I. 427 Walckenaer's Swimmers the last of his grand tribes of spiders.

3. a. The swimming-bladder of a fish. Now *dial.*

1579 T. STEVENS in Hakluyt *Voy.* (1599) II. II. 99 Which combe standeth vpon a thing almost like the swimmer of a fish in colour and bignesse. **1886** ELWORTHY *W. Somerset Word-bk.*, *Swimmer*, the air-bladder of a fish. (Always.) In bloaters this silvery-looking purse is very conspicuous.

†**b.** *Farriery.* A protuberance on the leg of a horse. *Obs.*

? **1726** *Farrier's Dict.* (Johnson), The swimmer is situated in the fore legs of a horse, above the knees, and upon the inside..; this part is without hair, and resembles a piece of hard dry horn.

c. A swimming organ of an animal; *esp.* an anal appendage in certain aquatic insect larvæ. (Cf. SWIMMERET.)

1816 KIRBY & SP. *Entomol.* xxii. (1818) II. 295 There are two descriptions of larvæ of *Hydrophili*, one furnished with swimmers or anal appendages, by means of which they are enabled to swim. **1828** J. FLEMING *Hist. Brit. Animals* 29 In this animal [*sc.* the sea-cow], the fore-swimmers (fins or paws) are furnished with the rudiments of nails.

d. An appliance for buoying up or supporting something in the water.

1799 G. SMITH *Laboratory* I. 21 How to make Water-rockets, Water-brands, Water-cats, Water-ducks, &c., that turn themselves in the Water... Having fixed a wooden swimmer below the neck, it [*sc.* the water-brand] is dipped in wax and pitch, and is ready for use.

4. a. A thing which floats upon the surface of a liquid; *spec.* an angler's float; see also quot. 1854.

a **1609** DENNIS *Secrets Angling* I. xiii. (1613) Biij, Then take good Corke, as much as shall suffice, For every Line to make his swimmer fit. **1664** EVELYN *Sylva* vii. 24 Let the Nuts be first spread to sweat;..a Moneth being past, plunge them in Water, reject the Swimmers. **1837** CARLYLE *Fr. Rev.* II. I. iii, Shall we say, the Revolution-element works itself rarer and rarer; so that only lighter and lighter bodies will float in it; till at last the mere blown-bladder is your only swimmer? **1854** MISS BAKER *Northampt. Gloss.*, *Swimmer*, a wooden trencher, or two short pieces of flat wood nailed across floating upon a bucket of water to prevent its washing over as it is carried along.

b. *Brewing.* A vessel containing ice or iced water floating on the wort in a fermenting-tun. (Cf. G. *schwimmer.*)

1881 WERSHOVEN *Techn. Voc. Eng.-Fr.* 263 The fermenting tun, the gyle-tun, *la cuve guilloire*, the swimmer, *le flotteur.*

†**5.** A cup or goblet 'swimming' or brimming over; a 'bumper'. *Obs.*

1682 N. O. *Boileau's Lutrin* I. 180 [He] takes himself a lusty Beer-bowl brimmer Of Racy Claret, and Commends a Swimmer To the good Company. **1706** BARNES in Hearne *Collect.* 18 July (O.H.S.) I. 273 Some Brimmer And Swimmer, Wth Nectar shall flow.

†**6.** *slang.* (See quots.) *Obs.*

a **1700** B. E. *Dict. Cant. Crew*, *Swimmer*, a Counterfeit (old) Coyn. **1812** J. H. VAUX *Flash Dict.*, *Swimmer*, a guard-ship, or tender; a thief who escapes prosecution, when before a magistrate, on condition of being sent on board the receiving-ship, to serve His Majesty, is said by his palls to be swimmered.

7. *slang.* A swimming costume. Now (*Austral.*) *pl.* const. *sing.* Cf. BATHER 3.

1929 *Daily Tel.* 3 June 7/1 Two coloured swimmer with brassiere attached. **1967** *Sunday Truth* (Brisbane) 23 July 1/1 Bikini girls at Parliament House..when a parade of new season's swimmers..will be on show. **1978** *Courier-Mail* (Brisbane) 22 Feb. 1/9, I am not an exhibitionist and if I go swimming on the main beach, I would wear swimmers.

8. Special combination. **swimmer's itch** *Med.*, a painful dermatitis caused by the cercaria of certain species of blood flukes, notably *Schistosoma mansoni*, which penetrate human skin (or mucous membrane) during swimming.

1928 *Minnesota Med.* XI. 573/1 There has been reported from several lake regions in Minnesota a peculiar type of skin eruption locally called 'swimmer's' itch. **1969** *Trans. R. Soc. Trop. Med. & Hygiene* LXIII. 557 Visitors to that camp suffered severe swimmer's itch when bathing in one of the rock pools.., and subsequently developed schistosomiasis.

Hence †**swimmer** *v.* (see quot. 1812 in sense 6 above).

swimmeret ('swɪmərət). [f. SWIMMER + -ET[1].] An abdominal limb or appendage of a crustacean, adapted for swimming; a swimming-foot, pleopod.

1840 *Cuvier's Anim. Kingd.* 416 The second family of Decapoda,—Decapoda Macrura..,—is distinguished by having at the extremity of the tail, on each side, appendages, ordinarily forming a swimmeret [orig. F. *nageoire*]. **1874** A. WILSON *Stud. Guide Zool.* 96 All the varied segments and appendages of the lobster—eyes, feelers, jaws, legs, and swimmerets—are merely modifications of a common structural plan. **1880** HUXLEY *Crayfish* i. 20 Attached to the sternal side of every ring of the abdomen of the female there is a pair of limbs, called swimmerets.

†**swimmering,** *vbl. sb. Obs. rare.* [Cf. ON. *svimra* to be giddy.] Giddiness; = SWIMMING *vbl. sb.* 4. Also *ppl. a.*, giddy = SWIMMING *ppl. a.* 5.

1650 W. D. tr. *Comenius' Gate Lat. Unl.* §297 Head-ache and the megrim causseth either giddiness (dizziness, swimmering), or dotage. **1650** H. MORE *Observ.* in *Enthus. Tri.*, etc. (1656) 118 This is but idle treading of the air, and onely a symptome of a light swimmering fancy.

swimming ('swɪmɪŋ), *vbl. sb.* [f. SWIM *v.* + -ING[1].] The action of the verb SWIM.

1. The action of moving along in the water by natural means of progression.

1377 LANGL. *P. Pl.* B. XII. 166 He þat neuere ne dyued ne nouȝt can of swymmynge. **1398** TREVISA *Barth. De P.R.* XVIII. xxix. [xxx.] (Bodl. MS.) lf. 263 b/1 In swymmynge þe strenger [harts] swymmeþ bifore. *a* **1513** FABYAN *Chron.* VII. ccxxxviii. (1811) 277 Swymynge of fysshes, & fleynge of fowlys. **1533** BELLENDEN *Livy* IV. xiv. (S.T.S.) II. 99 Vthiris þat war crafty in swomyng war sa sare woundit..þat þai drownit in þe streme. **1638** RAWLEY tr. *Bacon's Life & Death* (1650) 40 Exercise within cold water, as swimming, is very good. **1683** J. REID *Scots Gard'ner* (1907) 90 The larger your pondes or rivers be,..and the more moved by horse, geese and ducks, in their sweeming, the sweeter it will be. **1771** SMOLLETT *Humphry Cl., Let. to Sir W. Phillips* 1 July, I love swimming as an exercise, and can enjoy it at all times of the tide. **1835** *Partington's Brit. Cycl. Arts & Sci.* II. 803/2 In ordinary easy swimming, the hands are not used to propel, but merely to assist in keeping on the surface.

2. a. The action of moving or floating on the surface of the water, as a ship.

1719 DE FOE *Crusoe* II. (Globe) 405 The Fire so burn'd the upper Part, that it soon made them unfit for swimming in the Sea as Boats. **1827** FARADAY *Chem. Manip.* ii. (1842) 62 When surrounded by the fluid, its density was in some degree judged of by the sinking or swimming of the included bulb.

b. *concr.* A thing which floats upon the surface.

1833 LOUDON *Encycl. Archit.* §1262 The swimmings, or light grains that are skimmed off in the cistern.

†**3.** A watered pattern in a fabric. *Obs. rare.*

1611 FLORIO, *Nuóta*, a waue, a swimming as in damaske or chamblet.

4. A state of dizziness or giddiness; vertigo. Usually ***swimming of the head*** or ***brain.***

1530 PALSGR. 278/2 Swymyng in the hed, *bestournement.* **1556** WITHALS *Dict.* (1568) 72 b/1 Swimming in the heade, *vertigo.* **1581** MULCASTER *Positions* xxi. (1887) 90 It is commended for a remedie against the swiming of the head. **1601** HOLLAND *Pliny* XXI. xxx. II. 111 It is good for the swimming and dizzinesse of the braine. **1684** W. RUSSELL *Phys. Treatise* 135 A Man of middle Age having..a Swimming in his Head. **1770** FOOTE *Lame Lover* II, A faintness, a kind of swimming. **1871** L. STEPHEN *Playgr. Eur.* (1894) xiii. 305, I could not look over a precipice without a swimming in the head.

fig. **1649** MILTON *Eikon.* xxviii. 240 Upon a sudden qualm and swimming of thir conscience.

5. An appearance as of something floating or wavering before the eyes.

1760–72 H. BROOKE *Fool of Qual.* (1809) II. 95 My knees trembled..; a swimming came before my eyes. **1771** SMOLLETT *Humphry Cl., Let. to Lewis* 8 May, The continual swimming of those phantoms before my eyes, gave me a swimming of the head. **1833** L. RITCHIE *Wand. Loire* 234 He was affected by a reeling of the brain and a swimming of the eyes.

6. *attrib.* and *Comb.*, as ***swimming-apparatus, -belt, costume, -fin, -foot, -girdle, -leg, -organ, -paddle, -paw, -plate, suit, trunks, -web; swimming-bath, -place, -pond, -school;*** **swimming-bell,** a bell-shaped part or organ, as a nectocalyx, by which an animal propels itself through the water; **swimming-bladder,** (*a*) the air-bladder of a fish, which enables it to keep its balance in swimming; (*b*) an inflated bladder to assist a person in swimming; **swimming hole** chiefly *U.S.*, *Austral.*, and *N.Z.*, a bathing place in a stream or river; **swimming pool**, an artificial pool designed for swimming in; **swimming-tub** *Calico-printing* etc., a tub of colours, with a floating layer of fabric, on which a block is laid to colour its surface.

1875 Knight *Dict. Mech.*, **Swimming-apparatus*.., a float or dress to sustain a person in the water. **1900** B. D. Jackson *Gloss. Bot. Terms*, *Swimming-apparatus*, in Azolla, three apical episporic spongy masses of tissue, surrounding a central conical body with an array of fine filaments (Campbell). **1742** *Daily Advertiser* 28 May (*N. & Q.* 10th Ser. X. 89), The Pleasure or *Swimming Bath, which is more than forty-three Feet in length. **1868** A. J. Symonds *Let.* 29 July (1967) I. 828, I went..to the Victoria Swimming Baths, as I occasionally do, to smoke my cigar & to learn the secrets of Form. **1892** H. Lane *Differ. Rheum. Dis.* (ed. 2) 103 The ladies' swimming bath at the New Royal Baths. **1982** *Financial Times* 9 Dec. 9/1 Proposals are being investigated for private sector school meals and cleaning, the running of swimming baths, [etc.]. **1861** J. R. Greene *Man. Anim. Kingd., Cœlent.* 27 The 'nectocalyces', or '*swimming bells', with which the hydrosoma may be provided. **1856** 'Stonehenge' *Brit. Sports* 512/1 Various kinds of Apparatus have been recommended for sustaining the body, as cork-jackets, *swimming-belts, bladders, &c. **1713** Derham *Phys. Theol.* 10 *note*, If the *Swimming-Bladder of any Fish be pricked or broken, such a Fish sinks presently to the bottom. **1843** Holtzapffel *Turning* I. 155 Isinglass..is prepared from the sound or swimming-bladder of the sturgeon. **1858** O. W. Holmes *Aut. Breakf.-t.* ii. (1883) 32 Don't puncture their swimming-bladders; don't break the ends of their brittle and unstable reputations. **1904** R. Thomas *Swimming* 112 It is very difficult to get photographs of amateur ladies in *swimming costume. **1962** F. C. Avis *Swimming Dict.* 95 *Swimsuit*, a superior or elegant swimming costume, with particular reference to the female bather. **1977** N. Slater *Crossfire* iii. 58 A twenty-nine-year-old married woman..who wore a bathing cap and a one-piece swimming costume. **1861** P. P. Carpenter in *Rep. Smithsonian Inst.* 1860, 240 The animal has a broad *swimming fin, armed with an operculum. *Ibid.* 234 *Aclesia* is like *Aplysia*, without shell or *swimming flaps. **1816** Kirby & Sp. *Entomol.* xxii. (1818) II. 303 The envelope of the intermediate tarsi..is fringed on one side with hairs, to enable the insects to use them as *swimming feet. **1626** Bacon *New Atl.* 42 Wee haue Shipps and Boates for Going under Water, and Brooking of Seas; Also *Swimming-Girdles and Supporters. **1700** T. Brown *Amusem. Ser. & Com.* 111 Under that Bulk was a Projector clicking off his Swimming Girdles, to keep up Merchants Credits from sinking. **1835** *Partington's Brit. Cycl. Arts & Sci.* II. 803/2 The swimming girdle, about five inches wide, is placed round the pupil's breast. **1867** G. W. Harris *Sut Lovingood* 25 He wer aimin fur the *swimin hole in the krick. **1912** J. H. Moore *Ethics & Educ.* 128 The boy's love for the water, his affection for the old swimming-hole. **1928** [see bogy[2], bogey[2]]. **1975** D. Bagley *Snow Tiger* ii. 33 The bluff ..projected into the river..and that was where they had their swimming hole. **1871** Darwin *Desc. Man* II. ix. I. 328 The males..alone are furnished with perfect *swimming-legs. **1861** J. R. Greene *Man. Anim. Kingd., Cœlent.* 115 The endodermal lining of the polypite passes into the central cavity of the *swimming-organ. **1895** *Oracle Encycl.* I. 567/2 The forelimbs, represented by *swimming-paddles, are of small size. **1808** J. Fleming in *Mem. Wernerian Nat. Hist. Soc.* (1811) I. 134 There were two *swimming-paws (if I may be allowed the expression), corresponding to the pectoral fins in fishes, situated in the forepart of the body [of the narwal] towards the under-side. **1591** Percivall *Sp. Dict.*, *Nadadero*, a *swimming place, **1840** *Cuvier's Anim. Kingd.* 417 The lateral swimming-pieces at the extremity of the tail..are thrown back at its sides... The six or four following legs terminate in a *swimming-plate. **1833** Loudon *Encycl. Archit.* §1443 A garden containing a bowling-green, quoit-ground, cricket-ground, *swimming-pond, and baths. **1899** *Scribner's Mag. Advertiser* Jan. 26/2 You can enjoy..a plunge into the great marble *swimming pool, where the water is tempered according to season. **1921** A. Huxley *Crome Yellow* iii. 19 The stone-brimmed swimming-pool. **1972** *Punch* 1 Mar. 266/3 Our goals are increasingly the same—a bigger car, an expense account, and a swimming-pool in every back garden. **1835** *Partington's Brit. Cycl. Arts & Sci.* II. 803/2 Every *swimming school ought to have a leaping tower. **1742** *Daily Advertiser* 18 May (*N. & Q.* 10th Ser. X. 89), *Swimming-Stays are made by the above Exchange-Keeper to the utmost Perfection. **1926** E. Hemingway *Sun also Rises* II. xix. 245, I found my *swimming suit, wrapped it with a comb in a towel. **1971** 'D. Halliday' *Dolly & Doctor Bird* vi. 83 My swimming-suit, helmet and towel. **1943** *New Yorker* 22 May 26/1 He was big, stalwart, and dressed only in *swimming trunks. **1978** I. Murdoch *Sea* 70 Shall I come and bring my swimming trunks? **1839** Ure *Dict. Arts* 240 The *swimming or colour-tub is usually double, and serves for two tables. **1871** Darwin *Desc. Man.* II. xii. II. 24 The hind-feet are provided with a *swimming web.

swimming ('swɪmɪŋ), *ppl. a.* [f. swim *v.* + -ing[2].] That swims, in various senses.

1. Moving along in the water by natural means of progression; that habitually swims, as some birds and insects.

c **1000** Ælfric *Gen.* i. 20 Teon nu þa wæteru forð swimmende cynn cucu on life. *c* **1050** *Byrhtferth's Handboc* in *Anglia* (1885) VIII. 310 He ȝescop eall wyrmcynn & creopende & fleoȝende & swymmende. *c* **1460** *Towneley Myst.* i. 55 The water to norish the fysh swymand. **1605** Shaks. *Lear* III. iv. 134 Poor Tom, that eates the swimming Frog. **1804** Shaw *Gen. Zool.* V. 463 Swimming Pegasus... Native of the Indian seas. **1859** *Todd's Cycl. Anat.* Index, *Swimming birds* (Natatores). **1862** Ansted *Channel Isl.* II. ix. (ed. 2) 232 The spider crab, and swimming or velvet crab, are also eaten.

b. *fig.* Characterized by easy smooth motion or progress, as of a person swimming; free from obstruction or difficulty.

1760–72 H. Brooke *Fool of Qual.* (1809) II. 88 During a swimming period of six years, I scarce remember to have experienced the smallest discontent. **1830** in Cobbett *Rur. Rides* (1885) II. 320 Emigration is going on at a swimming rate. **1854** H. Miller *Sch. & Schm.* xxii. (1857) 496, I.. carried my election by a swimming majority.

c. *Stock Exchange.* (See quot.)

1870 Medbery *Men & Myst. Wall Str.* 138 Swimming market—the opposite of a sick market. Everything is buoyant.

2. Floating in the water; *spec.* in *Bot.* (see quot. 1859).

c **1000** Ælfric *Hom.* II. 60 Se swymmenda arc [= Noah's ark]. **1548** Turner *Names Herbes* 65 Potamogeton..maye be named in englishe Pondplantayne, or swymmynge plantayne. **1597** Gerarde *Herbal* II. cclxxxvii. 680 (*heading*) Of Duckes meate, and other swimming herbes. **1706** E. Ward *Wooden World Diss.* (1708) 1 A Ship of War... It's the most admirable swimming Contrivance, that ever mortal Thought brought forth. **1793** Martyn *Lang. Bot.*, *Swimming* or Floating leaf. **1859** Henslow *Dict. Bot. Terms*, *Swimming*, used vaguely for aquatics, which either float on the surface, or have their leaves floating. More restrictedly applied to aquatics which are wholly immersed, and also free from attachment to the bottom. **1870** tr. *Pouchet's Universe* (1871) 42 The swimming fucus or sea-weed. **1879** Tyndall *Fragm. Sci.* (ed. 6) I. xiii. 374 When the pole of an ordinary magnet is brought to act upon the swimming needle [*i.e.* floating upon a liquid].

b. *swimming stone*: a kind of stone so light as to float upon water; = float-stone 2.

1758 Borlase *Nat. Hist. Cornw.* 111 In a copper-mine.. near Redruth, they have a stone which they call the Swimming-stone. **1841** *Penny Cycl.* XIX. 199/2 Cavernous quartz is termed Spongiform quartz or Swimming stone.

†**c.** *fig.* Wavering, unsteady. *Obs. rare.*

1596 Nashe *Saffron Walden* 71 Certaine strange dreames ..which wel she hoped were but idle swimming fancies of no consequence. **1603** Bacon *Valerius Terminus* i. Wks. 1857 III. 239 As far as a swimming anticipation could take hold.

†**d.** *fig.* Superficial, on the surface. *Obs. rare.*

a **1679** T. Goodwin *Work of Holy Spirit* v. vi. Wks. 1703 V. I. 205 An abundance..of swimming knowledg, common enlightning.

†**3.** Of the carriage of the body: Characterized by a smooth waving motion. *Obs.*

1590 Shaks. *Mids. N.* II. i. 130 Which she with pretty and with swimming gate Following..Would imitate, and saile vpon the Land. **1694** N. H. *Ladies Dict.* 169/2 A Swimming Gate, or an affected Pace, as if you were..measuring the ground by the Foot as you pass along. *Ibid.* 495/2 He.. admires her swiming Carriage. **1709** Steele *Tatler* No. 52 ¶2 That swimming Air of your Body. **1731** Lady M. W. Montagu *Poems, Farew. to Bath* vi, Somerville, of courteous mien,..With swimming Haws, and Brownlow blithe.

4. Overflowing (in quot. *transf.*).

c **1586** C'tess Pembroke *Ps.* xcviii. iii, You streamy rivers clapp your swymming hands.

b. Of the eyes: Suffused with tears; watery.

a **1729** Congreve *Tears of Amaryllis* 126 From her swimming eyes began to pour Of softly falling rain a silver show'r. **1864** Tennyson *En. Ard.* 322 She rose, and fixt her swimming eyes upon him.

c. *advb.*

1887 *Suppl. Jamieson's Sc. Dict., Addenda, Swimming*.. also used as an *adv.*, as in the phrase *swimming full*, i.e. abundantly, copiously full or filled, well stocked.

5. Affected with, or characterized by, dizziness or giddiness.

1607 Topsell *Four-f. Beasts* 555 For the..curing of the swimming dizzines or giddines in the head. **1688** *King's Declar.* 21/2 Yet you..are in no Danger at all of Falling Down, from any other Cause, but the Swimming Conceipt of your Own Head. **1760–72** H. Brooke *Fool of Qual.* (1809) II. 59 A swimming kind of stupor would fall..upon my soul. **1818** Byron *Mazeppa* xviii, The cold, dull, swimming, dense Sensation of recurring sense. **1842** Mrs. Carlyle *Lett.* (1883) I. 178 My head got into a swimming condition. **1885–94** R. Bridges *Eros & Psyche* April xxix, She yielded, and was borne with swimming brain And airy joy, along the mountain side.

b. Of the eyes or sight (cf. L. *oculi natantes, lumina natantia*).

1697 Dryden *Virg. Georg.* IV. 717 An Iron Slumber shuts my swimming Eyes. **1697** —— *Æneid* v. 1113 The Pilot.. Soon clos'd his swimming Eyes, and lay supine. **1819** Keats *Eve of St. Mark* 55 With aching neck and swimming eyes, And dazed with saintly imag'ries. **1819** Byron *Juan* II. cxii, And slowly by his swimming eyes was seen A lovely female face. **1827** Lytton *Pelham* lxxv, No trembling of the hand, no error of the swimming sight.

swimmingly ('swɪmɪŋlɪ), *adv.* [f. prec. + -ly[2].] In a swimming manner.

1. With easy smooth progress; smoothly and without impediment; with uninterrupted success or prosperity. †In early use, esp. with *bear, carry*: With conspicuous success, with *éclat*.

1622 Fletcher & Mass. *Prophetess* I. iii, *Max.* Can such a Rascal as thou art, hope for honour?.. *Geta.* Yes, and bear it too, And bear it swimmingly. **1654** *Nicholas Papers* (Camden) II. 51 Lord Percey carried himselfe swimmingly and said more for then against the Chancelor. **1668** Etheredge *She Would if She Could* I. i, Prithee let us dine together to-day, and be swimmingly merry. **1678** Otway *Friendship in F.* I. i, He never dreams how swimmingly his own Affairs are manag'd at home. **1696** Vanbrugh *Relapse* IV. i, So, matters go swimmingly. **1754** Warburton in *W. & Hurd's Lett.* (1809) 186 Only this last year or two I was going swimmingly on. I have now struck upon a rock. **1824** Lady Granville *Lett.* 14 Mar. (1894) I. 266 The interview went off very swimmingly. **1844** Macaulay in Trevelyan *Life & Lett.* (1876) II. x. 152 The article on Chatham goes on swimmingly. **1893** Forbes-Mitchell *Remin. Gt. Mutiny* 155 Everything went swimmingly with the prosecution.

2. With a smooth gliding movement.

1745 *Gentl. Mag.* July 384/2 Like fluttering angels they swimmingly move. **1816** J. Scott *Vis. Paris* (ed. 5) 37 Perhaps the reality did not appear quite so swimmingly elegant..as the fancy of the thing [*sc.* a rustic dance] had been. **1842** Browning *Waring* I. iv, E'en so, swimmingly appears, Through one's after-supper musings, Some lost Lady of old years.

swimmingness ('swɪmɪŋnɪs). *rare.* [f. swimming *ppl. a.* + -ness.] **a.** A misty or moist appearance (of the eyes). **b.** Smooth gliding movement.

1700 Congreve *Way of World* III. v, You see that picture has a sort of a—Ha, Foible! a Swimmingness in the eyes. **1746** H. Walpole *Let. to Conway* 24 Oct., His eyes..had.. a certain melancholy swimmingness, that described hopeless love rather than a natural amorous languish. **1835** T. Hook *G. Gurney* I. vii. 283 There was a swan-like swimmingness about her air and gait.

swimmist ('swɪmɪst). [f. swim *v.* + -ist.] A habitual or professional swimmer.

1881 *Cuckoo* 22 June, Champion swimmists like Webb and Beckwith. **1885** *Graphic* 3 Jan. 11/3 The Serpentine Christmas Day Morning Handicap, to the decision of which so many swimmists look forward.

swimmy ('swɪmɪ), *a.* [f. swim *v.* + -y.]

a. Inclined to dizziness or giddiness. Also in *Comb.*

1836 F. S[ykes] *Scraps fr. Jrnl.* 123 To look down was quite enough to cause one's head to be unpleasantly swimmy. **1881** C. Whitehead *Hops* 42 The operators must not be swimmy-headed. **1892** Stevenson *Vailima Lett.* xvii. (1895) 153 My head rather swimmy.

†**b.** Graceful, elegant. *Obs. nonce-use.*

1827 Coleridge *Let.* 2 June (1971) VI. 687 A fine, tall, slim, swimmy, glidy lass.

c. Of the eyes: watery, tearful. Also, of tears.

1936 J. B. Priestley *They walk in City* vii. 178 She had a round moist face, with swimmy eyes. **1978** J. Irving *World according to Garp* xvii. 358 The woman's..face, dissolving before him in his own swimmy tears.

Hence '**swimminess**, dizziness.

1894 Conan Doyle *Parasite* 96, I had a dizziness and swimminess which rapidly passed away.

Swinburnian (swɪn'bɜːnɪən), *a.* [f. the name of the English poet Algernon Charles *Swinburne* (1837–1909) + -ian.] Of, pertaining to, imitative or characteristic of Swinburne or his poetry. Hence **Swin'burnianism**, **'Swinburnism**.

1867 E. B. Lytton *Let.* 25 Jan. in *Lett. R. Lytton* (1906) I. 207 The 'Gyges and Candaules' have some dangerous supersensual lines which I advise you to reconsider. It will not do for you to be 'Swinburnian'. **1868** A. J. Symonds *Let.* 24 Apr. (1967) I. 803 Courthope..is full of the gall of bitterness against the Apostles of Swinburnism. **1892** W. B. Scott *Autobiogr. Notes* I. xxii. 300 When the Swinburnian passion for French things..had infected nearly all our young writers. **1920** *Glasgow Herald* 30 Dec. 4 The 'Various' verses show now and then a Swinburnian touch. **1931** G. K. Chesterton *All is Grist* xxxviii. 212 Something that is connected not only with Swinburne but with Swinburnianism. **1949** A. Huxley *Let.* 6 Apr. (1969) 595 Any equivalent in English becomes automatically Swinburnian, that is to say rich without the weight..which Latin imposes. **1960** J. Betjeman *Summoned by Bells* vii. 75, I was released Into Swinburnian stanzas with the wind. **1974** E. Hardwick *Seduction & Betrayal* 109 A Swinburnian mood of spankings and teasing degradation. **1976** *Times Lit. Suppl.* 26 Nov. 1495/2 [Gilbert Murray's] translations of Greek tragedies are still to be found on the shelves of college bookstores today, in spite of all the rude things that have been said about their Swinburnianism.

†**swinch.** *Obs.* Forms: 3 **swinche, suinch,** 4 **swinch, swynche,** *Ayenb.* **zuynch.** [Aphetic f. i-swinch. Cf. swench.] Toil, labour.

12.. *Moral Ode* 369 in *O.E. Hom.* I. 181 þer is wele abute grame and reste abuten swinche. **1297** [see swench]. **1340** *Ayenb.* 83 Alle þise þinges makeþ zuete zuynch zorȝes tyeares and wepinges.

†**swind**, *v. Obs.* Also 4 **swynde.** [OE. *swindan*, pa. t. *swand, swundon*, pa. pple. *-swunden* = OHG. *suuintan, suindan*, pa. t. *suant*, (MHG. *swinden*, occas. *swinten*, G. *schwinden, schwand, geschwunden*, whence Da. *svinde*), a formation with *-nd-* on the Teut. root *swĭ-* (cf. Icel. *svía* to abate), parallel to a formation with *-n-*, repr. by OHG. *swînan* (MHG. *swînen*, G. *schweinen*) of the same meaning, MLG. *swînen* to be slow, ON. *svina* to subside, and to a formation with *-m-*, repr. by swime and the related forms.] *intr.* To waste away, languish; to dwindle, decrease; to vanish, disappear. Hence †**swinden** *ppl. a.*, enfeebled, enervated (cf. aswind 2, for-swounden).

c **900** tr. *Bæda's Hist.* IV. xxv. (1899) 500 Ealle..oððe hefiȝe slæpe swundon, oððe to synnum wacedon. *c* **1000** *Ags. Ps.* (Spelman) xxxviii. 15 [xxxix. 11] Swindan ðu dydest.. sawle his. *a* **1200** *Moral Ode* 57 in *O.E. Hom.* I. 163 Vre swinc and ure tilþe is ofte iwoned to swinden. *c* **1275** Lay. 23670 þanne mai me singe Of one swindene kinge þat his beot haueþ imaked And his cniht-sipe forsake. **13..** *St. Erkenwolde* 342 in Horstm. *Altengl. Leg.* (1881) 274 Sodenly his swete chere swyndid & faylide. *a* **1327** *Pol. Songs* (Camden) 150 Thus me pileth the pore that is of lute pris: Nede in swot and in swynk swynde mot swo. *a* **1380** *Minor Poems fr. Vernon MS.* xxviii. 56 Heil lenere and louere of largenesse, Swete and swettest þat neuer may swynde.

swindge, swindgel, var. SWINGE, SWINGLE.

swindle, *sb.*[1] Local variant of SWINGLE *sb.*[1] Also in *Comb.* **swyndilland** = SWINGLE-HAND.

14.. *Nom.* in Wr.-Wülcker 696/7–8 *Hoc exculidium*, a swyndylstoc. *Hoc excudium*, a swyndilland. 1857 Borrow *Rom. Rye* xxx, I drank with the harvesters, who sang me songs about rural life, such as—'Sitting in the swale; and listening to the swindle of the flail, as it sounds dub-a-dub on the corn, from the neighbouring barn.'

† **swindle**, *sb.*[2] *Obs.* [ad. early mod.Du. *swindel* (Du. *zwendel*) = MHG. *swindel, swintel* (G. *schwindel*), f. Teut. *swind-*: see SWIND *v.* and -LE. Cf. SWINDLING *vbl. sb.*[1]] Giddiness, vertigo.

1559 Morwyng *Evonym.* 137 This lyquor is good for the headache, fallinge sicknesse, frensye, swindle or turnsicknes.

swindle (ˈswɪnd(ə)l), *sb.*[3] [f. SWINDLE *v.*[2]]

1. a. An act of swindling; a fraudulent transaction or scheme; a cheat, fraud, imposition.

1833 in A. Bunn *Stage* (1840) I. 134 There was a universal cry of 'off-off'—'swindle-swindle'. 1852 C. W. Day *Five Yrs'. Resid. W. Indies* II. 185 The West India Islands are full of the swindles of European tradesmen. Wine and spirits are shockingly adulterated, [etc.]. 1881 *Jrnl. Inst. Bankers* Nov. 573 The trustees under liquidation never have their bills taxed; they charge what they like and do what they like; it is a perfect swindle with them.

b. *spec.* (slang or local): see quots.

1870 *Law Reports, Davey* v. *Walmsley* (Farmer), Lotteries are announced and commonly known as swindles. 1872 Schele de Vere *Americanisms* 576 When he [*sc.* a Western man] wishes to know what he has to pay, he asks, What's the damage? or, not so charitably, What's the swindle? 1890 Barrère & Leland *Slang Dict.* s.v., When a proposition is made to toss for a drink by spinning a coin, the phrase is generally 'let's have a swindle'.

2. Something that is not what it appears or is pretended to be; a 'fraud'. *colloq.*

1866 Howells *Venet. Life* i. 4 Let us take, for example, that pathetic swindle, the Bridge of Sighs. 1882 T. G. Bowles *Flotsam & Jetsam* 395 As a sea the Mediterranean is a mere swindle. It is, indeed, not a sea at all, but a miserable puddle.

3. Special combination. **swindle sheet** *slang* (chiefly *U.S.*), an expense account; also (*joc.*) in extended use, of other documents which conceal (or reveal) fraudulence and other 'swindles', as a log-book or time sheet.

1923 *N.Y. Times* 9 Sept. VII. 2/3 *Swindle sheet*, the advance agent's expense account. 1934 J. O'Hara *Appointment in Samarra* ii. 42 The Apollo [hotel] got a big play from salesmen who had their swindle sheets to think of. 1936 *Times Lit. Suppl.* 15 Feb. 125/3 The 'swindle-sheet' for the average motor-car shows that 40 per cent of the fuel energy goes into the cooling water. 1960 H. L. Lawrence *Children of Light* v. 77 The fare's ten bob... Put it on the swindle sheet. 1971 M. Tak *Truck Talk* 161 *Swindle sheet*, the daily log book, mandatory for all drivers.

† **swindle**, *v.*[1] *Obs.*: see SWINDLING *vbl. sb.*[1]

ˈ**swindle**, *v.*[2] [Back-formation f. SWINDLER.]

1. *intr.* To act the swindler; to practise fraud, imposition, or mean artifice, esp. for the purpose of obtaining money.

1782 Bailey, *Swindle*, to get Money on false Pretences. 1802 James *Milit. Dict.*, *Swindle*, .. a cant word signifying to cheat. 1820 Shelley *Hymn Merc.* xlix, Those Who swindle, house-break, sheep-steal, and shop-lift. 1848 Thackeray *Van. Fair* xxxvi, Hardy English adventurers who have.. swindled in all the capitals of Europe.

2. *trans.* To cheat, defraud (a person) *out of* money or property.

1803 Syd. Smith *Delphine* Wks. 1859 I. 46/1 Though she swindles Delphine out of her estate. 1858 J. Martineau *Stud. Christ.* 243 Having been intrusted with the management of a bank in the *Piscina publica*, he swindled and ruined the depositors. 1908 R. Bagot *A. Cuthbert* xiv. 162 It appears that del Monte has swindled his wife—his widow—out of every sixpence she possessed.

b. To bring into some specified condition by swindling.

1810 in *Life Adam Clarke* viii. (1834) 192, I might swindle away this poor Sarah Boswell from your chapels to ours. 1839 Thackeray *Fatal Boots* Oct., When I had paid the debt into which I had been swindled by her.

3. To get or gain by swindling. ? *Obs.*

1804 *Revol. Plutarch* II. 306 The convention of Alexandria, which Buonaparte swindled from the trembling Melas. 1837 Carlyle *Fr. Rev.* III. I. v, Lamotte.. had.. swindled a sum of three-hundred livres from one of them.

swindleable (ˈswɪndləb(ə)l), *a.* *nonce-wd.* [f. SWINDLE *v.*[2] + -ABLE.] Capable of being or liable to be swindled.

1874 M. Collins *Th. in Garden* (1880) I. vii. 283, I have had to pay many of their bills, chiefly I think because I look easily swindleable (to coin a word).

swindledom (ˈswɪnd(ə)ldəm). *nonce-wd.* [f. SWINDLE *sb.*[3] + -DOM.] The realm or domain of swindles.

1893 *Scott. Leader* 10 June 10 (*heading*) The latest from swindledom.

swindler (ˈswɪndlə(r)). [ad. G. *schwindler* giddy-minded person, extravagant projector, esp. in money matters, cheat, f. *schwindeln* to be giddy, act thoughtlessly or extravagantly, swindle, going back to MHG. *swindeln*, OHG. *suintilôn* (cf. MHG. *swindel, swintel*, OHG. *suuintilôd* dizziness), frequent. f. *suintan* to waste away, languish, lose consciousness, etc.: see SWIND *v.* and -LE. Cf. Du. *zwendelaar*.

Orig. a cant word, said to have been introduced into London by German Jews about 1762, and to have been first used in literature by Lord Mansfield. See Bailey's Dict. ed. 1782, and *Slang Dict.* (1873) 317.]

One who practises fraud, imposition, or mean artifice for purposes of gain; one who systematically defrauds or cheats others; a cheat.

1774 W. Hawke (*title*) The life, trial, &c. of William Hawke... To which is added a full description of the impositions and deceptions practiced by the swindlers, sharps, gamblers.. in and about London. 1775 *Ann. Reg.*, *Chron.* 175/2 Dupes to the designing arts of the wretches distinguished by the name of Swindlers. 1797 (*title*) Adventures of the Extravagant Wit; or the English Swindler, shewing the various Frauds and Tricks he committed in London and the most distant parts of the Globe. 1819 Shelley *Peter Bell 3rd* II. i., A swindler, living as he can. 1889 Jessopp *Coming of Friars* iii. 159 The swindler always thinks his victim a fool

Hence (all *nonce-wds.*) ˈ**swindlerdom**, the realm of swindlers, swindlers collectively; ˈ**swindlership**, the condition of a swindler; ˈ**swindlery**, the practice of a swindler, swindling.

1865 *Pall Mall G.* 16 Aug. 9/1 The enterprise of London *Swindlerdom seems to be illimitable. 1862 Carlyle *Fredk. Gt.* XII. xi. III. 341 What is truth, falsity, human Kingship, human *Swindlership? 1833 —— *Misc. Ess., Cagliostro* (1872) V. 93 Had there been no sumptuary or adultery or *swindlery Law-acts. 1837 —— *Fr. Rev.* I. II. vi, Swindlery and Blackguardism have stretched hands across the Channel, and saluted mutually. 1869 Dickens in *All Year Round* 2 Jan. 109/2 Swindlery in doubtful boots, on the sharp look-out for any likely young gentleman.

† ˈ**swindling**, *vbl. sb.*[1] *Obs. rare.* In 6 swyndelynge. [ad. G. *schwindelung* (OHG. *suintilunga*, MHG. *swindelunge*), f. *schwindel* SWINDLE *sb.*[2], *schwindeln* vb., formations on Teut. *swind-* (see SWIND *v.*).] Swimming in the head, dizziness, giddiness.

1527 Andrew *Brunswyke's Distyll. Waters* K iv b, [It] is good agaynste the swyndelynge in the hede.

swindling (ˈswɪndlɪŋ), *vbl. sb.*[2] [f. SWINDLE *v.*[2] + -ING[1].] The action of SWINDLE *v.*[2]; the practice of a swindler; fraud or imposition for purposes of gain; systematic cheating.

1788 *Gentl. Mag.* LVIII. 1154/2 As *swindling* is a word that occurs not in our dictionaries, and yet we often meet with it in modern writers.., we should be obliged to any gentleman among your correspondents.., to define it; or.. inform us what.. distinguishes it from other modes of fraud and imposition. 1792 H. Walpole *Let. to W. Beloe* 24 Sept., A deep laid plan of political swindling. 1855 Macaulay *Hist. Eng.* xviii. IV. 177 He seems not to have taken up the trade of a false witness till he could no longer support himself by begging or swindling. 1869 *Adam Smith's W.N.* I. II. ii. 326 *note*, Free trade in banking, it has been wisely and wittily said, is free trade in swindling.

ˈ**swindling**, *ppl. a.* [f. SWINDLE *v.*[2] + -ING[2]. Cf. prec.]

1. That swindles; acting or dealing fraudulently.

1795 Kirwan *Elem. Min.* (ed. 2) I. Pref. p. xv, Ignorant or swindling dealers at Naples. 1809 J. Adams *Wks.* (1854) IX. 610 Our medium is depreciated by the multitude of swindling banks. 1877 Black *Green Past.* xiv, The swindling old heathen.

2. Of acts, etc.: Involving a swindle, fraudulent.

1809 Malkin *Gil Blas* VII. xii. ¶11 He declared his.. abhorrence of becoming a party.. in a mere swindling trick. 1879 Geo. Eliot *Theo. Such* xvi. 283 Since his name for virtue served as an effective part of a swindling apparatus.

Hence ˈ**swindlingly** *adv.*

1887 Mrs. Daly *Digging & Squatting* xvi. 171 The break-up of many of the more swindlingly formed enterprises naturally ensued.

swine (swaɪn). Pl. swine. Forms: *Singular* and *Plural.* 1–4 **swin**, 1–6 **swyn**, 4–5 **suyn**, 4–7 **swyne**, (4 **suine, swiyn, squine**, *Ayenb.* **zuyn**, 4–5 **squyne**, 5 **swyyn, swyyne, sweyne, sqwyne**, 6 **suyne, swyin, swyen**, 7 **sweyn, shwine**), 5– **swine**. *Plural* in *-s*. 5 **swynes**, 6, 8–9 **swines**. [Common Teutonic: OE. *swín* str. n. = OFris., OS., MLG. *swîn*, MDu. *swijn*, (NFris. *swinn*, EFris. *swin*, WFris. *swyn*, LG. *swien*, Du. *zwijn*), OHG., MHG. *swîn*, (G. *schwein*), ON. *svín*, (Sw. Da. *svin*), Goth. *swein*:—OTeut. **swīnom*, neut. of adj. formation with suffix *-īno-* (cf. L. *suīnus*, OSl. *svinŭ* swinish, and see -INE *suffix*[1]) on the root of L. *sūs*, Gr. ὗς, and SOW *sb.*[1]

The orig. use may have been either generic or restricted to the young of the swine; for the latter cf. Goth. *gaitein*, OHG. *geizzîn* young goat, kid, cogn. w. OE. *gǣten* of goats, L. *hædīnus* of kids:—Indo-eur. **ghaidīno-*, f. *ghaid-* GOAT.]

1. a. An animal of the genus *Sus* or family *Suidæ*, comprising bristle-bearing non-ruminant hoofed mammals, of which the full-grown male is called a *boar*, the full-grown female a *sow*; esp. the common species *Sus scrofa*, domesticated from early times by Gentile nations for its flesh, and regarded as a type of greediness and uncleanness. (Now only literary, dialectal, or as a generic term in zoology, etc., being superseded in common use by *pig* or *hog*: see these words.)

(*a*) *sing.* c725 *Corpus Gloss.* (Hessels) S 700 *Suis*, swin. a1000 *Riddles* xli. [xl.] 105 (Gr.) Mara ic eom & fættra, þonne amæsted swin. a1122 *O.E. Chron.* (Laud MS.) an. 1085, Ne an cu ne an swin næs belyfon. a1200 *Moral Ode* 143 in *O.E. Hom.* I. 169 Swines brede is swiðe swete, swa is of wilde dore. c1205 Lay. 468 Al swa þat wilde swin þ wroteð ȝeond þan grouen. a1225 *Ancr. R.* 128 Ase swin ipund ine sti uorte uetten. a1300 *Cursor M.* 26751 (Cott.) þai sal yow vp on balkes lift Als suine [*Fairf.* squine] þat ar to salting tift. c1330 R. Brunne *Chron. Wace* (Rolls) 12342 By a mykel fir he sat, Rostyng a swyn gret & fat. a1440 *Sir Degrev.* 1398 Sche brouȝt fram the kychene A scheld of a wylde swynne. 1535 Coverdale *1 Macc.* i. 47 To offre vp swynes flesh and other vnclene beastes. 1596 Shaks. *Tam. Shr.* Induct. i. 34 Oh monstrous beast, how like a swine he lyes. 1634 Milton *Comus* 53 Circe.. Whose charmed Cup Whoever tasted, lost his upright shape, And downward fell into a groveling Swine. 1682 Shadwell *Lanc. Witches* II, Coursing had gotten me a woundy stomach, and I eat like a Swine. 1780 Cowper *Love of World Reproved* 3 There is a part in ev'ry swine No friend or follower of mine May taste. 1799 S. Freeman *Town Off.* 58 He found a swine going at large in the town.

(*b*) *pl.* c888 Ælfred *Boeth.* xxxvii. §4 He bið anlicost fettum swinun þe syle willað licgan on fulum solum. c1200 *Trin. Coll. Hom.* 37 Ðet oref þe þis dear waneð beð shep & reðeren & get & swin. a1300 *Cursor M.* 4711 [þai] soght þam rotes, als þe suine. c1375 *Sc. Leg. Saints* xxix. (*Placidas*) 319 He.. al his bestiale sleu in hy,.. assis, mulis, schepe & swyne. 1421 *Cov. Leet Bk.* 27 We commaund þat no man haue no Swyne goyng in the hyȝe streit. c1452 *Termes of Venery* in J. Hodgkin *Proper Terms* 56/2 Sundyr of wylde Swyne, Dryfte of Tame Swyne. 1528 Roy *Rede me* (Arb.) 113 There is grountynge of pigges and swyne With lowynge of oxen and kye. 1562 Leigh *Surv.* (1577) F iv b, Neither maie Geese or Swine haue common, but by the lordes sufferaunce. 1671 Milton *P.R.* IV. 630 Thee and thy Legions, yelling they shall flye, And beg to hide them in a herd of Swine. 1796 W. H. Marshall *Rural Econ. W. Eng.* II. 222 Of Swine, Somersetshire appears still to persevere in the old white breed. 1846 Youatt *Pig* 24 Swine are the most prolific of all domesticated animals. 1870 Morris *Earthly Par.* IV. 296 The rooting swine Beneath the hedge-row oak-trees grunt and whine.

β. 1483 Caxton *G. de la Tour* G j, His Swyneherd, he that kept his swynes. 1551 in Strype *Eccl. Mem.* (1721) II. II. v. 285 Beeves, muttons, veals, swines. 1738 [G. Smith] *Cur. Relat.* II. 421 When Swines continue longer than ordinary in the Mire. 1759 Brown *Compl. Farmer* 41 Young shoots, which are swines of about three quarters of a year old. 1850 H. Melville *White Jacket* I. xv. 93 Some of you chaps haven't no more manners than so many swines!

b. In proverbial and allusive expressions, and in fig. context.

c1000 *Ags. Gosp.* Matt. vii. 6 Ne ȝe ne wurpen eowre meregrotu toforan eo wrum swynon. c1175 *Lamb. Hom.* 135 Ne sculen ȝe nawiht ȝimstones leggen swinen to mete. 13.. *Guy Warw.* (A.) 3680 þou sest Mahoun ne Apolin Be nouȝt worþ þe brestel of a swin. c1386 Chaucer *Man of Law's T.* 647 And stolen were hise lettres pryuely Out of his box whil he sleep as a swyn. 1390 Gower *Conf.* II. 360 The servantz lich to drunke Swyn Begunne forto route faste. 1542 Udall *Erasm. Apoph.* 342 b, A swyne to teache Minerua, was a prouerbe [etc.]. 1560 in *Maitl. Club Misc.* III. 210 That lecherous Swyne the Byschop of Rome (quhai hais rutet wp the Lordis wyneyard sa far as in him wes). 1588 Shaks. *L.L.L.* IV. ii. 91 Fire enough for a Flint, Pearle enough for a Swine. 1590 Greenwood *Collect. Sclaund. Art.* G j, We sayd you shall finde it.. a pyg of that Swyne. 1598 Shaks. *Merry W.* IV. ii. 109 'Tis old, but true, Still Swine eats all the draugh. a1600 Montgomerie *Misc. P.* xxx. 42 (Laing MS.) Lat me nocht sleip in sleuth, In stinkand sty with sathanis sinfull suyne. 1608 Willet *Hexapla Exod.* 683 A certaine Sorbonist, then a popish bishop.. a swine out of the same stie. 1761 *Brit. Mag.* II. 440 The tricks of old Circe deter us from Wine, Tho' we honour a Boar, we won't make ourselves Swine. 1821 Scott *Kenilw.* xix, He that does me not reason is a swine of Sussex, and I'll make him kneel to the pledge, if I should cut his hams, and smoke them for bacon.

2. *fig.* Applied opprobriously to a sensual, degraded, or coarse person; also (in mod. use) as a mere term of contempt or abuse.

c1380 Wyclif *Serm.* Sel. Wks. I. 263 Mannis lawis hav distemperid kynde of men, and turned hem into swyn. c1384 Chaucer *H. Fame* III. 687 Ye maisty Swyne ye ydel wrechhes. 1430–40 Lydg. *Bochas* I. xi. (MS. Bodl. 263) 51/2 How that this swyn.. This Thiestes, afftir Europa Lay bi his douhter callid Pellopia. 1531 Tindale *Expos. 1 John* ii. 13–17 (1537) 42 Lechery.. maketh a man altogether a swyne. 1594 Shaks. *Rich. III*, V. ii. 10 This foule Swine Is now euen in the Centry of this Isle. 1842 Browning *Soliloquy Span. Cloister* ix, Gr-r-r—you swine! 1891 Farrar *Darkness & Dawn* xxxviii, I shall be butchered to amuse these swine. 1907 H. Wyndham *Flare of Footlights* xxxv, The swine might have had the decency to have made up his alleged mind a bit sooner.

b. Of a thing: = PIG *sb.*[1] 1 c. *slang.*

1933 Dylan Thomas *Let.* Oct. (1966) 31 This method of letter writing.. is very satisfying, but it's a swine in some ways. 1938 N. Marsh *Artists in Crime* iii. 38 'It's a swine of a pose, Miss Troy.' 'Well, stick it a bit longer.' 1967 K. Giles *Death in Diamonds* ii. 41 The Inspector groaned. 'Could be heroin. That's a swine.' 1976 H. MacInnes *Death Reel* iii. 19 This car's.. a swine to drive at slow speeds.

3. = *swine-fish*: see 5.

1844 W. H. MAXWELL *Sports & Adv. Scot.* xv. (1855) 143 The 'wolf-fish', here 'swine', (*anarhichas lupus* of Linnæus).

4. Obvious Combinations: attrib., as ***swine-bristle, -fat, -flesh, †-greun*** [GROIN *sb.*², snout], ***-leather*** [cf. G. *schwein(s)leder*], ***-market, †-pork, -trough***, etc.; adj. = SWINISH, as in ***swine enjoyment, security***; objective, etc., as ***swine-buyer, -catcher, -dealer, -eater, -keeper, -keeping; swine-eating*** adj.; ***swine-like*** adj. and adv.; parasynthetic (similative), as ***swine-faced, -headed, -mouthed, -snouted*** adjs.; occas. with *swine's*, as ***† swine's-faced***.

c **1440** *Alphabet of Tales* 396 Þe harys on his browis war lyke *swyne-brustyls. **1831** CARLYLE *Sart. Res.* III. i, Working on tanned hides, amid pincers, paste-horns, rosin, swine-bristles, and a nameless flood of rubbish. **1707** *Lond. Gaz.* No. 4318/4 Richard Wells, of Ingoldsby in Lincolnshire, *Swinebuyer. **1835** *App. Munic. Corpor. Rep.* IV. 2652 (Congleton) The *swine-catcher, levying 1*s.* upon each vagrant pig. *c* **1592** MARLOWE *Jew of Malta* II. i, These *swine-eating Christians. **1742** YOUNG *Nt. Th.* v. 14 Wit.. lifts our *swine-enjoyments from the mire. **1595** *Enq. Tripe-wife* (1881) 150 The pudding house, Where *swine facde beautie onely sate in pride. **1596** NASHE *Saffron Walden* Wks. 1905 III. 134 Two or three sturdie Plow-men (such as his swines fac't bluecoate was). **1597** *1st Pt. Return fr. Parnass.* I. i. 281 What an unmanerlie microcosme was this swine-faced clowne. **1922** JOYCE *Ulysses* 468 Her odalisk lips ..smeared with salve of *swinefat. **1398** TREVISA *Barth. De P.R.* XVIII. i. (Bodl. MS.), *Swyne flesche and schepe flesche is better rosted þan sode. *c* **1400** MAUNDEV. (Roxb.) ix. 36 Þe Sarzenes also bringes furth na grysez, ne þai ete swyne flessch. **1884** J. TAIT *Mind in Matter* 189 The Jews.. prohibited from using swine-flesh. **1691** RAY *N.C. Words* 138 **Swine-greun*, a Swines snout. **1710** SIBBALD *Hist. Fife* 53 *Swine-headed and mouth'd and backed. **1922** Swineheaded [see DOG *sb.*¹ 19 c]. **1508** DUNBAR *Flyting* 130 Sueir swappit swanky, *swynekeper ay for swaittis. **1596** SHAKS. *1 Hen. IV*, IV. ii. 38 A hundred and fiftie totter'd Prodigalls, lately come from *Swine-keeping. **1409** in *Beverley MSS.* (Hist. MSS. Comm. 1900) 100 Calf-lethyr, *swyn-lether. **1575–85** ABP. SANDYS *Serm.* 156 Let vs not *swinelike returne to wallowe in that slime againe. **1604** JAS. I *Counterbl. to Tobacco* (Arb.) 106 Olde drunkards thinke they prolong their dayes, by their swinelike diet. **1624** QUARLES *Job* xix, In Pleasure's sincke, he takes a swinelike Pleasure. **1888** *Pall Mall G.* 26 May 11/1 Creatures more swine-like than human. **1467–8** *Rolls of Parlt.* V. 603/2 A Strete called *Swynemarket. **1610** HOLLAND *Camden's Brit.* (1637) 441 Rumford, the glory whereof dependeth on a swine mercat. **1456** SIR G. HAY *Gov. Princes* Wks. (S.T.S.) II. 157 Sum man luxurious as a *swyne pork, and sum chaste as a turtur dowe. **1633** FORD *Broken H.* III. ii, To one that franks his lust In *swine-security of bestial incest. **1887** MORRIS *Odyssey* x. 239 And *swine-shape they had, and the voice..of the boar. **1840** LONGF. *Sp. Student* I. iv, I tell you this is nothing but Vino Tinto of La Mancha, with a tang of the *swine-skin. **1592** NASHE *P. Penilesse* Wks. 1904 I. 169 Hee will..sonnet a whole quire of paper in praise of Lady *Swin-snout, his yeolow-fac'd Mistres. **1900** W. ARCHER tr. *Ibsen's When we dead Awaken* I. 14 Lop-eared, low-browed dog-skulls, and fatted swine-snouts. **1602** BRETON *Wonders worth Hearing* Wks. (Grosart) II. 8/1 Squinte eyed, *Swine snouted, wry bodyed, and splay footed. **1579** FULKE *Heskins' Parl.* 124 Let him resorte to M. Heskins' *swyne-trough. **1616** DEACON *Tobacco Tortured* 57 The Swil bols swine-troffe. **1619** in Ferguson & Nanson *Munic. Rec. Carlisle* (1887) 278 Keping of swine troughes in the hye streyt. **1827** SCOTT *Chron. Canongate* ii, They come, with the prodigal son, to the husks and the swine-trough. **1559** *Richmond Wills* (Surtees) 135 One *swyne tubbe.

5. a. Special Combinations (also with *swine's*): **swine-back**, (*a*) a convex or arched back like that of a swine (= HOGBACK 1); (*b*) in *Coal-mining* = HOGBACK 2 b, HORSE-BACK 4; **swine-backed** (-bækt) *a.*, having a back like that of a swine; *spec.* in *Archery*, having a convexly curved outline (opp. to *saddle-backed*); **swine-badger** = *hog-badger* (HOG *sb.*¹ 13 c); **swine-chopped** *a.*, of a hound: having the lower jaw projecting forward of the upper one; so **swine-chop**, a malformation of this kind; **swine-crew (crue), -cruive** *dial.* [CREW *sb.*, CRUIVE], a pigsty; **† swine-drunk** *a.* [cf. ON. *svíndrukkinn*], excessively drunk, beastly drunk; so **† swine drunkenness**; **swine erysipelas**, an infectious, sometimes fatal, disease of pigs, caused by the bacterium *Erysipelothrix rhusiopathiæ*, and characterized by fever, reddish spots on the skin, and general debility; **swine-eyes**, eyes like those of a swine, which cannot be directed upwards; **swine fever**, a name for two infectious diseases of swine (produced by different bacteria), distinctively called *hog-cholera*, chiefly affecting the intestines, and *swine-plague*, chiefly affecting the lungs (see below); **swine-fish**, the wolf-fish, *Anarrhichas lupus*, so called from the movement of its snout; **swine flu** = *swine influenza* below; **† swine-garth**, an enclosure for swine, a pigsty; **swine-girl**, a girl who tends swine; **swine-grease** (see *swine's grease* below); **swine-hound** *slang rare*, tr. G. *schweinehund* SCHWEIN(E)HUND (quot. in Mil. context); **swine influenza**, an infectious virus disease of pigs, esp. young ones, characterized by fever, coughing, and difficulty in breathing; also, influenza in man caused by the same (or a closely related) virus; **swine('s)-head**, a swinish or self-indulgent person; **† swine-hog** = HOG *sb.*¹ 1; **† swine-house** [cf. ON. *svínahús*], a building in which swine are kept; hence **† swine-housegarth**, an enclosed piece of ground containing such a building; **swine-hulk, -hull** *dial.* [HULK *sb.*¹, HULL *sb.*¹ 4 b], a pigsty; **† swine-louse**, a woodlouse, hog-louse, or sow-bug; **swine-meat** *dial.*, food for swine, hog-wash; **swine-oat** *local* (see quot.); **swine('s)-penny** *local* (see quots.); **swine-plague**, an infectious disease of swine, resembling but distinct from hog-cholera (see *swine fever* above); **swine's back**, local name for a narrow hill-ridge (cf. HOGBACK 2 a); **† swine-seam**, = *swine's-grease*; **† swine's evil**, = SCROFULA; **swine's grease** (occas. ***swine-grease***), now *dial.*, the fat of a swine, lard; **swine-shott, † -shoute** *dial.* [SHOAT²], a young pig; **swine-skeel** *dial.*, a tub for hog-wash; **† swine-sought**, = SWINE-POX 2; **† swine's-pike** *Mil.*, = SWINE'S FEATHER; **† swine's pudding** = HOG'S PUDDING; **† swine's-stead**, a building in which swine are kept; **swine vesicular disease**, an infectious virus disease of pigs (similar to foot-and-mouth disease) characterized by mild fever and blisters round the mouth and feet; **† swine-wroting**, a place in which swine root. (See also SWINE'S FEATHER.)

1675 *Lond. Gaz.* No. 976/4 A..bay Nag, with a Blaze down his Face, a *Swine-back. **1883** GRESLEY *Gloss. Coal-mining*, *Swine-back* (S.W.). See *Horses*. *Ibid.*, *Horses* or *Horsebacks*, natural channels cut, or washed away by water, in a coal seam, and filled up with shale and sandstone. Sometimes a bank or ridge of foreign matter in a coal seam. **1545** ASCHAM *Toxoph.* (Arb.) 133 The *swyne backed fashion, maketh the shaft deader. **1710** [see *swine-headed* in 4]. **1890** DOYLE *White Company* xxxiv, It has been my wont to choose a saddle-backed feather for a dead shaft, and a swine-backed for a smooth flier. **1768** PENNANT *Brit. Zool.* I. 66 Naturalists once distinguished the badger, by the names of the *swine-badger, and the dog-badger; from the supposed resemblance of their heads to those animals. **1962** *Times* 9 June 11/4, I have seen..puppy show prizes awarded to young hounds with *swine-chop. **1930** KIPLING *Thy Servant a Dog* 20 Moore-man lifted Ravager's head and opened his mouth... 'Look, m'lord. He's *swine-chopped.' **1965** D. MOORE *Bk. Foxhound* ii. 29 The forehead and nose merge invisibly, giving always a rather stupid expression, and sometimes accompanying a swine-chopped mouth. **1669–81** *Swine-crue [see CREW *sb.* 1]. **1501** *Extr. Aberd. Regr.* (1844) I. 70 That al the tovn be devoyen of *swn croffis. *c* **1575** [see CRUIVE 2]. **1616** *Reg. Privy Council Scotl.* X. 559 Hiddin in swyne crooves and middingis. **1592** NASHE *P. Penilesse* Wks. 1904 I. 207 The third [stage] is *Swine drunke, heauy, lumpish, and sleepie, and cries for a little more drinke. **1601** SHAKS. *All's Well* IV. iii. 286 Drunkennesse is his best vertue, for he will be swine-drunke. **1547–64** BAULDWIN *Mor. Philos.* (Palfr.) 124 Of all other most odious is *swine drunkennesse, wherewith both the body & soule is deformed. **1898** M. M. HAYES tr. *Friedberger & Fröhner's Vet. Pathol.* 72 *Swine erysipelas (or swine measles)..is a specific septicæmia produced by a minute bacillus. **1922** A. T. KINSLEY *Swine Practice* xii. 338 Swine erysipelas is an infective disease of swine characterized by a high temperature, cerebral disturbances and discoloration of the skin. **1970** W. H. PARKER *Health & Dis. in Farm Animals* x. 141 A disease which can easily be confused with swine fever is swine erysipelas. **1872** JEFFERIES *Toilers of the Field* (1892) 323 Curses on our insular *swine-eyes that could not see it. **1898** *Daily News* 15 Sept. 3/2 Provided..that the swine are not in a *swine-fever infected place. **1863** WOOD *Illustr. Nat. Hist.* III. 289 The Sea Wolf, Sea Cat, or *Swine-fish. **1921** *Wallace's Farmer* 25 Feb. 371/1 So-called '*swine flu', a name which, while it became quite popular thru its association with the human disease, is nevertheless a misnomer, is primarily a bronchitis. **1976** *National Observer* (U.S.) 21 Aug. 2/2 The swine-flu insurance bill was signed by President Ford, clearing the way for mass inoculations in about six weeks. **1981** *Sci. Amer.* Oct. 46/2 Epidemiologists determined.. that recipients of the swine-flu vaccine were developing Guillain-Barré syndrome at a rate several times the usual one. **1459–60** *Durham Acc. Rolls* (Surtees) 88 Pro mundacione de le *Swynegarth. **1886** C'TESS E. MARTINENGO-CESARESCO *Ess. Study Folk-Songs* 199 The *swine girl went up to the mountain top and sang and sang. *c* **1386** CHAUCER *Reeve's T.* 341 He seyde, thou Iohn, thou *swynesheed awak. **1819** KEATS *On C. A. Brown* ii, He 'sdeigned the swine-head at the wassail-bowl. **1548** *Durham Wills* (Surtees) I. 12, ij *swyn houggs xs. **1601** in W. Jackson *Cumbld. & Westmoreld. Papers* (1892) I. 155 Item a swyne hogge xii s. **1916** 'BOYD CABLE' *Action Front* 245 'Sulky, eh, my *swine-hound!' said the officer. 'But I think we can improve those manners.' **1576** E. WORSELY *Surv. Mannor Felsted, Essex* 150 (MS.) To repaire and maintaine ..the lord's hoggs-cote or *swinehouse. **1675** HOBBES *Odyssey* (1677) 168 As many swine-houses replete with swine. **1466–7** *Durham Acc. Rolls* (Surtees) 91 Pro operacione et emendacione pavimenti..in le *swynhousgarth. **14..** *Metr. Voc.* in Wr. Wülcker 626/1 *Ara*, stye, or a *swyne holke. **1566** in Leader *Rec. Burgery Sheffield* (1897) 15 Hughe Storey for a smythye and a *swyne hoowle iij s. **1674** RAY *N.C. Words* 47 A *Swinhull* or *Swine-crue*, a Hogs-stye. **1807** R. ANDERSON *Cumberld. Ball.* 145 To the sweyne-hull hie an' swat thee. **1922** *Jrnl. Amer. Vet. Med. Assoc.* LXI. 178 We must be able to differentiate between hog cholera, necrotic enteritis,..broncho-pneumonia or *swine influenza, and many others. **1935** *Lancet* 11 May 1123/2 It seems to me..exceedingly probable that the virus of swine influenza is really the virus of the great [influenza] pandemic of 1918 adapted to the pig and persisting in that species ever since. **1969** C. W. SCHWABE *Vet. Med. & Human Health* (ed. 2) vii. 216/2 Swine influenza was not known before the human influenza pandemic of 1918. **1976** *Globe & Mail* (Toronto) 26 Mar. 1/1 Ontario residents probably will be vaccinated against a deadly swine influenza virus, Alan Backley, Ontario's deputy health minister, said yesterday. **1585** LUPTON *Thous. Notable Th.* (1675) 50 Little worms with many feet (of some called *Swine-lice). **1583** *Durham Wills* (Surtees) II. 78, j other tubbe, for *swine meat 12 d. **1819** REES *Cycl.* XXXIV, **Swine-Oat*,..a particular kind of oat, which is cultivated for the use of pigs..in some parts of Cornwall..the naked oat, or *avena nuda*. **1610** HOLLAND *Camden's Brit.* 550 The Roman Emperours coine: which because swine many times rooting into the ground turne up with their snouts, the country people [at Littleborough] call *Swines-penies. **1723** W. STUKELEY in *Mem.* (Surtees) III. 149 Many coyns found in one field towards that bridg [at Littleborough]. They call 'em Swine-pennys. **1891** BILLINGS *Med. Dict.* **Swine plague* .., an acute, epidemic, contagious, and usually fatal disease of swine, with..rapid and labored respiration, and sometimes diarrhœa. **1826** W. A. MILES *Deverel Barrow* 15 On its ridge [*sc.* a range of chalk], or to use a more common term, on the **swine's back*, is a cluster of tumuli. **1562–3** *Acc. Ld. High Treas. Scot.* XI. 248 Item, for *swyne same..iij li. iiij s. **1528** PAYNELL *Salernes Regim.* R j, By *swynes yuell is vnderstande inflasion vnder the chynne about the throte. **1584** COGAN *Haven Health* cx. (1636) 111 A plaster made of figges..are good for the swines evill. *a* **1425** tr. *Arderne's Treat. Fistula*, etc. 11 Ane emplastre of maluez & *swynes grese. **1463–4** *Compota Domest.* (Abbotsf. 1836) 45, xij petrarum de Swynegrece. **1530** PALSGR. 278/2 Swynes grease, *sayn de pourceau*; *gresse de porc*. **1600** SURFLET *Country Farm* II. xlviii. 307 This roote roasted and stamped with olde swines grease, and applyed to the cornes of the feet. **1581** *Durham Wills* (Surtees) II. 35, v *swyne shoates. **1901** TROTTER *Galloway Gossip* 332 (E.D.D.) Stots, an hoggs, an swine-shotts. **1559** *Richmond Wills* (Surtees) 135 One *swyne skele. **1483** *Cath. Angl.* 375/1 Þe *Swynsoghte, *porrigo*. **1638** WARD *Animadv. War* I. cclxxxi. 393 (*heading*) The Description of an Instrument, invented by King Henry the fifth, at the Battell of Agincourt, and since used by the King of Sweden, and by him called a *Swines-Pike. **1639** *Ibid.* II. 90 These Shot ought to have each man his Swines-Pike at his girdle, to stick down against the Horse. **1647** TRAPP *Comm. Mark* vii. 3 Sometimes they wear a sausage or a *swines-pudding in place of a silver or gold chain. **1596** SPENSER *State Irel.* Wks. (Globe) 645/1 A delighte to keepe his sayde howse neate and cleanlye, which nowe being.. rather *swynes-steades then howses, is the chiefest cause of his soe beastly manner of life. **1972** *Guardian* 16 Dec. 1/8 The outbreaks of suspected foot-and-mouth disease in the Midlands have turned out to be a rare virus which affects only pigs. Its new name, invented by the Ministry of Agriculture yesterday, is *swine vesicular disease. **1981** *Vet. Rec.* 30 May 468/3 The relative decline in the number of cases of swine vesicular disease this year suggests that the campaign against the disease is achieving worthwhile results. *c* **1475** *Pict. Voc.* in Wr.-Wülcker 798/30 *Hic scrobs*, a *swynwrotyng.

b. In names of plants, usually with *swine's* (cf. HOG *sb.*¹ 13 d, PIG *sb.*¹ 14 b, SOW *sb.*¹ 8 b): **swine-arnot** *Sc.*, the marsh betony, *Stachys palustris*; **swine-arnuts** *Sc.*, tall oat-grass, *Avena elatior*; **swine('s) fennel, finkle**, *Peucedanum officinale*, also called HOG'S FENNEL and *sow-fennel* (SOW *sb.*¹ 8 b); **swine's snout** (see quot. 1863); **swine's succory** (see SUCCORY 2); **swine('s) thistle** *dial.* = SOW-THISTLE 1. (See also SWINE'S CRESS, SWINE'S GRASS.)

1812 SOUTER *Agric. Surv. Banffs.* App. 38 If it [*sc.* the land] be pestered with quicken, *swine-arnot or other such spreading roots. **1777** LIGHTFOOT *Flora Scot.* (1789) I. 105 *Avena elatior*..Tall Oat-Grass. *Anglis*. *Swines Ar-Nuts, or Earth-Nuts. *Scotis*. *c* **1400** *MS. Laud* 553 lf. 11 Feniculus porcinus is an herbe þ*t* me clepitth *swynesfenel or wormeseed. **1529** *Grete Herball* cccxxx. S v b/1 Peucedane is an herbe or wode called dogfenell or swynefenel. **1842** BROWNING *Solil. Sp. Cloister* ii, What's the Latin name for 'parsley'? What's the Greek name for *Swine's Snout? **1863** PRIOR *Pop. Names Brit. Plants* 222 Swine's snout, L. *rostrum porcinum*, from the form of the receptacle, the dandelion. *a* **1500** *Gl. Harl. 3388* in *Sax. Leechd.* III. 346/2 *Swines thistell, *sonchus oleraceus*. **1796** NEMNICH *Polygl.-Lex.*, *Swine thistle*, the sow-thistle. **1824** MACTAGGART *Gallovid. Encycl.* 104 s.v. *Burr-thristles*, There are five kinds of thistles common in Scotland—the burr or horse thristle; the corn thristle; the moss thristle; the swine thristle; and the Scotch thristle.

swine-bread ('swaɪnbrɛd). Also 6–7 **swines-bread.** [Cf. G. *schwein(s)brot*, mod.L. *panis porcinus*.]

† 1. The plant Cyclamen; = SOWBREAD. *Obs.*

1591 SYLVESTER *Du Bartas* I. iii. 704 Swines-bread, so used, doth not onely speed A tardy Labour; but (without great heed) If over it a Child-great Woman stride, Instant abortion often doth betide. **1648** HEXHAM I. *Herbs*, Sow bread, or Swyne bread.

† 2. Truffles. *Obs.*

1677 MIÉGE *Fr. Dict.*, *Trufe*, Sow-bread, or swine bread (a most dainty kind of round and russet root). **1696** tr. *Du Mont's Voy. Levant* vi. 68 Tis not so hard a Task to know the delicious Earth-Apples or Swine-bread [orig. *Trufes*]. **1755** JOHNSON, *Swinebread*, a kind of plant; truffles.

3. Locally applied to the earth-nut or pig-nut, *Bunium flexuosum*.

1888 *Sheffield Gloss.*, *Pig-nut*, sb. the earth nut. *Bunium flexuosum*. Called *Swine-bread* in Inverness-shire.

swine-cote. Now only *Hist.* or *dial.* Forms: see SWINE and COTE *sb.*¹; also 6 **swynne-coote**, 7 **swincoate, -coote**; 5 **swynce cote**, 6 **swynsecote**; 5 **swynnen cote.** [f. SWINE + COTE *sb.*¹] A pigsty.

c **1380** WYCLIF *Sel. Wks.* III. 277 Now þei [*sc.* abbeys] ben fallen doun, or maad swyn-kotis, stablis, or bark-houses. *c* **1440** *Promp. Parv.* 449/2 Schudde, hovel, or swyne kote. *Ibid.* 475/1 Sty, swynce cote (*K.* swynys howus, *S.* swyn cote, *A.* styy, swynnen cote). **1447** BOKENHAM *Seyntys* (Roxb.) 291 In a taverners hous in a swyncote lay she Tyl mydnyht. **1546** *Supplic. Poore Commons* (E.E.T.S.) 78 Would ye commyt them to the kepyng & fedyng of such swynherdes as did not know theyr swynsecotes when thei sawe theym? **1557** *Scotter Manor Rec.* in *N.W. Linc. Gloss.*, That euery man shall haue a sufficient swynne-coote. **1604** *Manch. Court Leet Rec.* (1885) II. 199 Iohn Chester hath a swinecoate at the backsyde of his house verie pestiferous. **1659** in Picton *L'pool Munic. Rec.* (1883) I. 192 The swynecoate joyneing unto the Church wall be puled downe. **1730** P. WALKDEN *Diary* (1866) 117 Spent the day at home in repairing our swine cote side, and painting it. **1830** tr. *Aristoph., Wasps* 147 *Philocleon.* What is this? *Bdelycleon.* A swine-cote of Vesta. **1869** *Lonsdale Gloss.*, *Swine-cote, Swine-hull, Swine-sty*, a pig-sty.

swineherd (ˈswaɪnhɜːd). Not in colloq. use. Forms: see SWINE and HERD *sb.*[2]; also 5–6 **swynnard(e**, 5–6 **swynard**, 6–7 **swinheard**, 7 **swinherd, swiniard**, (also 9 *dial.*) **swin(e)yard**; 5 **swynshyrd.** [late OE. *swýnhyrde*: see SWINE and HERD *sb.*[2] Cf. MLG. *swînherde*, OHG. *swînhirti* (MHG. *-hirte*, G. *schwein(e)hirt*), ON. *svínahirðir* (Sw. *svinherde*, Da. *svinehyrde*).

The normal form of the word would be represented by the pronunciation (ˈswɪnəd); cf. the old spellings *swynnard*, *swinherd*, and GOZZARD, SHEPHERD (ˈʃɛpəd). The word has been refashioned in modern times on its etymological elements. For the variants *swin(e)yard*, etc., cf. *swanyeard*, etc., SWANHERD. See also SWINWARD.]

1. A man who tends swine, esp. for hire.

a **1100** in *Zeitschr. für deutsches Altertum* XXXIII. 239 *Subulcus*, swynhyrde. **1338** R. BRUNNE *Chron.* (1810) I. 9 A suynhird smote he to dede vnder a thorn busk. *c* **1440** *Promp. Parv.* 483/2 Swyyne herd (*K.* swynshyrd). *a* **1450** *Knt. de la Tour* lxxii, Ye shall sitte downe and ete here with the swyne-herthe. **1451** *Lincoln Diocese Documents* 51, I will my scheperd hafe vj. wedyr hogges; & my Swynnard iiij. Swynne. **1526** TINDALE *Mark* v. 14 The swyne heerdes fleed and tolde it. **1547–64** BAULDWIN *Mor. Philos.* (Palfr.) 19 This man [*sc.* Justinus] in his youth was but a swin-heard. **1590** T. WATSON *Eglogue Death Walsingham* Poems (Arb.) 157 When eurie swynard shall exceede his borne. *c* **1622** ROWLEY, etc. *Birth of Merlin* III. iv. 5 A swinherds wife, keeping hogs by the Forestside. **1640** *J. Dyke's Sel. Serm.* Ep. Ded. A iij b, The cooke, and the swineyard, the weaver, and kember. **1687** BISHOP *Marrow of Astrol.* I. 36 Herdsmen, or swinyards. **1691** WOOD *Ath. Oxon.* II. 504 Mr. Corbet.. had his head cut off by two Swiniards in the time of the Rebellion in Ireland, an. 1641. **1726** POPE *Odyss.* XVII. 254 Where goes the swine-herd, with that ill-look'd guest? **1819** SCOTT *Ivanhoe* xxv, I, Gurth, the son of Beowulph, the swineherd. **1846** YOUATT *Pig* ii. 14 The swineherds [in Egypt] formed an isolated race, outcasts from society. **1872** TENNYSON *Last Tourn.* 626 When had Lancelot utter'd aught so gross Ev'n to the swineherd's malkin in the mast?

†**2.** 'A term for a boar, he being the head or master of the herd' (Nares). *Obs.*

1607 *Christmas Prince* (1816) 24 Then sett downe y[e] Swineyard, The foe to y[e] Vineyard... Lett this Boares-head and mustard Stand for Pigg, Goose and Custard.

Hence ˈ**swine,herding**, the tending of swine; ˈ**swine,herdship**, the position of swineherd.

1586 WARNER *Alb. Eng.* IV. xxi. (1589) 88 An Vnder-Swineheard ship did serue, he sought not to be chiefe. **1872** YEATS *Nat. Hist. Comm.* 113 Cattle-breeding and swine-herding. **1899** *Q. Rev.* Apr. 443 (tr. *Heine*), I have returned to God like the prodigal son after my long swineherdship among the Hegelians.

swinehood (ˈswaɪnhʊd). [f. SWINE + -HOOD.] The condition of a swine; also *fig.*

1822 LAMB *Elia* Ser. I. *Diss. upon Roast Pig*, The grossness and indocility which too often accompany maturer swinehood. **1886** MARG. BURT *Browning's Women* (1887) 164 Elvire.. sees only the swinehood that hath no remedy.

swinely (ˈswaɪnlɪ), *a. rare.* [f. as prec. + -LY[1].] Pertaining to or characteristic of swine; swinish. Also *adv.*, swinishly.

1434 MISYN *Mending Life* 116 Is not glotony & lichery swynely filth? **1880** W. S. BLUNT *Love Sonn. Proteus* cviii, Than their ain swine begotten swinelier.

swinepipe (ˈswaɪnpaɪp). [A book-name, still retained; of undetermined origin.] The redwing.

1668 WILKINS *Real Char.* II. viii. §4. 149 Redwing, Swinepipe. *Turdus iliacus.* **1676** WILLUGHBY *Ornith.* 139 *Turdus Iliacus sive Illas aut Tylas*, the Redwing, Swine-pipe, or Wind-Thrush.

swine-pox. ? *Obs.* Also 7 **swine's-pox.**

1. A name for chicken-pox.

Retained as a synonym in 19th cent. medical works.

1530 PALSGR. 278/2 Swyne pockes, *farcin.* *c* **1550** LLOYD *Treas. Health* R j, The great swyne pokes. **1624** MASSINGER *Renegado* I. iii, The Swine's-pox overtake you! There's a curse For a Turk, that eats no hog's flesh. **1659–60** PEPYS *Diary* 13 Jan., Thence I went to Mrs. Jem, and found her up and merry, and that it did not prove the small-pox, but only the swine-pox. **1676** JAS. COOKE *Marrow Chirurg.* IV. II. ix. 739 These they call Cristals, but Country-people call them Swine-Pox, Hen-Pox, &c.

2. An eruptive disease in swine.

1704 *Dict. Rust.* (1726), *Swine-pox*, an ill sore in Hogs which spreads abroad, and is a very grievous Scab. **1898** *Syd. Soc. Lex.*, *Swine-pox*, a disease in which tubercles come out on the legs and thighs of swine. Around and under each tubercle is highly inflamed tissue.

swinery (ˈswaɪnərɪ). [f. SWINE *sb.* + -ERY; cf. *piggery*.]

1. A place where swine are kept; a piggery. Also *fig.*

1778 [W. MARSHALL] *Minutes Agric., Digest* 22 The Swinery.. is very commodious. **1792** WOLCOT (P. Pindar) *More Money* Ode ii. 12 Thus are parterres of Richmond and of Kew Dug up for bull and cow, and ram and ewe, And Windsor Park so glorious, made a swinery. **1895** MEREDITH *Amazing Marr.* I. viii. 89 There is to be an extra bedroom secured at her hotel. That swinery of a place she insists on visiting is usually crammed. **1895** *Arena* (Boston) Aug. 434 His neighbor keeps a swinery in his garden.

2. A swinish condition; swine collectively.

1849 CARLYLE *Irish Journey* 28 July (1882) 201 Human swinery has here reached its acme, happily. **1888** LEES & CLUTTERBUCK *B.C. 1887* xxxiv. (1892) 376 A squealing, grunting, parti-coloured streak of swinery went scuttering past.

swine's cress. Also 5 **swynescars**, 6 **swineskerce, swine carse.** [Cf. G. *schwein(s)kresse.* Through the phonetic similarity of such forms as *swinescres*, *-kers*, *-kars*, and *swinesgres*, *-gers*, *-gars*, this word and SWINE'S GRASS were formerly synonymous.]

†**a.** = SWINE'S GRASS, knotgrass. **b.** The cruciferous plant *Senebiera Coronopus*; called also *buckshorn* and *wart-cress.* **c.** Fool's watercress, *Helosciadium nodiflorum. local.* **d.** Ragwort, *Senecio Jacobæa. local.* **e.** Nipplewort, *Lapsana communis.*

c **1440** *MS. Laud 553* lf. 8 b, Centinodium is an herbe þat me cleputh centinodie or sparitonge or swynescars that herbe groweth welney ouer alle & hath mony knottes in on stalk. **1541** *Bk. Properties Herbs* D viij, Lingua hi[r]cina. This is called Buckeshorne or Swineskerce. **1578** LYTE *Dodoens* I. lxiv. 95 In some places of England they call it [*sc.* Coronopus Ruellii] Swynescressis. **1597** GERARDE *Herbal* App., *Swine Carse* is knotgrasse. **1700** WALLACE *Acct. Orkney* ii. 17 *Ambrosia campestris repens*, Swines cresses. **1803** SIR J. E. SMITH *Sowerby's Eng. Bot.* XVI. 1130 *Senecio Jacobæa.* Common Ragwort... In Yorkshire this plant is sometimes called Swine's Cresses. **1850** MISS PRATT *Comm. Things Sea-side* i. 87 The common swine-cress, or wart-cress of our inland waste places. **1857** —— *Flower. Pl.* III. 218 *L[apsana] communis* (common Nipplewort).. is sometimes called Swine's-cress.

swine's feather. *Mil.* (now only *Hist.*) Also **swine-feather; sweynes-feather, swan's-feather.** [ad. G. *schweinsfeder* (1) boar-spear (= early mod.Du. *swijnspriet*, *-spiesse*, *-staf*, *-stock*), (2) rifleman's lance used as a rest for the rifle and, in numbers, as chevaux-de-frise.] A pointed stake or pike, used as a weapon of defence against cavalry, being either fixed in the ground as a palisade (PALISADE *sb.* 2) or carried in a musket-rest like a bayonet. Also called *Swedish feather* (FEATHER *sb.* 14) and *swine's-pike* (SWINE 5).

1635 BARRIFFE *Milit. Discipl.* xcv. (1643) 307 Those parts which lye most open to the fury of the enemies Horse, ought to bee impaled with pallisadoe (or swines-feathers). **1639** SIR A. JOHNSTON (Ld. Wariston) *Diary* (S.H.S.) 50 We have receaved no spades, nor howes, no swyne feathers wherby we may intrinch ourselves. **1646** DK. ALBEMARLE *Obs. Milit. & Polit. Aff.* viii. (1671) 26 So many Musqueteers as you have more than Pikemen in your Army ought to have Swine-feathers with heads of rests fastned to them. **1786** GROSE *Milit. Antiq.* I. 165. **1824** MEYRICK *Ant. Armour* III. 78. **1834** *Penny Cycl.* II. 376/1 The sweynes-feather was invented in the reign of James I. During the civil wars, its name was sometimes corrupted into swan's-feather.

swine's grass. Also 3 **swines gres**, 5 **swynegrece, swynesgarce**, 6 **swyne gyrs**; 7 **swine-grasse.** [Cf. local G. *schweingras.*] Knotgrass, *Polygonum aviculare*; also, locally, ragwort, *Senecio Jacobæa.* (Cf. SWINE'S CRESS.)

12.. *Herbarium* in *MS. Bodl. 130* lf. 42 b, Swines gres [*in another hand* blod[w]ert .i. suines gres]. *c* **1450** *Alphita* (Anecd. Oxon.) 38/1 *Centinodium*, populus uel poplius, longam habet hastam et gracilem et folia longa. angl. swynegrece uel cattesgres. *Ibid.* 104/1 *Lingua passeris*, poligonia, proserpinata, centinodium idem. angl. swynesgarce. **1538** TURNER *Libellus, Poligonon...* Hanc uulgus appellat swyne gyrs, & knotgyrs. **1597** GERARDE *Herbal* II. clxi. 452 Knot grasse.. is giuen vnto swine.. when they are sicke.. whereupon the countrie people do call it Swines grasse, and Swines skir [? swineskirs = swine's cress]. *a* **1697** *Aubrey's MS.* (Royal Soc.) 12 (Britten & Holl.) Raggewort (Jacobæa) vulgò Swine-grasse growes.. plentifully in good ground from Notts to the Bishopricke of Durham. *a* **1722** LISLE *Husb.* (1757) 331 Poligona, knot-grass, swine's-grass, or blood-wort.. is very pernicious to sheep.

swinestone (ˈswaɪnstəʊn). [ad. G. *schweinstein* (see SWINE and STONE *sb.*), = mod.L. *lapis suillus.*] An early name for ANTHRACONITE, a variety of limestone containing bituminous matter, which emits a fetid odour when struck or rubbed; also called *stinkstone.*

1794 W. HUTCHINSON *Hist. Cumbld.* I. App. 44/1 Swine Stone. *Lapis Suillus.*—Almost black, of fine scaly texture. **1819** BRANDE *Chem.* 210. **1876** PAGE *Adv. Text-bk. Geol.* xiv. 244.

swine-sty (ˈswaɪnstaɪ). Now chiefly *dial.* Forms: see SWINE and STY; also 5 **swinysty, swynysty**, 6 **swines-stie.** [f. SWINE + STY *sb.* Cf. MDu. *swijnstie*, ON. *svínstí.*] A pigsty.

1340 HAMPOLE *Pr. Consc.* 9002 Als mykelle difference.. suld be Bitwene heven and swilk a cete, Als es bitwene a kynges palays And a swynsty. **1423** *Cov. Leet Bk.* 59 þai orden þat.. all þe pryves & swynesties þeron be done away. *c* **1440** *Promp. Parv.* 483/2 Swyyne kote, howse for swyyn (*K.* swinysty, or sty). **1587** HOLINSHED *Chron.* III. 83/2 To reuoke the king.. from the swines-stie of vice to the statelie throne of vertue. **1647** TRAPP *Comm. Heb.* xii. 16 Many such Edomites.. now-adaies that prefer earth before heaven, a swine-sty before a sanctuary. **1756** C. LUCAS *Ess. Waters* II. 13 There are waters.. smelling as offensively as a swine-stie. **1857** DUFFERIN *Lett. High Lat.* xii. (ed. 3) 370 She.. conceals the Jarl and his companion in a hole dug for this purpose, in the swine-stye, and covered over with wood and litter. **1887** MORRIS *Odyssey* x. 389 She opened the swine-stye door And drave them out.

swineyard, obs. var. SWINEHERD.

†**swing**, *sb.*[1] *Obs.* [OE. *ȝeswing*, in form and origin identical with *ȝeswing* SWING *sb.*[2] (sense 1), f. Teut. *swiŋgw-* (see SWING *v.*[1]) used in the same sense as the parallel form *swiŋkw-* (see SWINK *v.*, to toil).] Labour, toil.

c **1000** *Ags. Ps.* (Spelman) lxxxix. 11 [xc. 10] *Eorum labor et dolor*, heora ȝeswing & sar. *c* **1175** *Lamb. Hom.* 145 þer scal beon.. hele wið-uten unhele, reste wið-uten swinge. *c* **1250** *Gen. & Ex.* 566 Ðor buten noe long swing he dreȝ.

swing (swɪŋ), *sb.*[2] Also 4–5 **swyng(e**, 6–7 **swinge.** [In sense 1 app. representing OE. *ȝeswing* (see also prec. sb.) in comp. *hand-*, *sweordȝeswing* stroke with a weapon in fight (otherwise only in phr. *ýða ȝeswing* impetus of waves; cf. sense 6), f. Teut. *swiŋgw-* (see SWING *v.*[1]), whence also OE. *swinge* wk. f., stroke with a rod or scourge, corresp. to OFris. *swing* (also *swang*, *sweng*) blow, sprinkling, *swinge* swingletree, OHG. *swingâ* swinglestaff, wing, MHG. *swinge*, G. *schwinge* winnowing-fan, pl. wings. (Cf. SWENG.) For sense 2, see note there. The other senses are directly from SWING *v.*[1]]

I. Abstract senses.

†**1. a.** A stroke with a weapon. *Obs.*

1375 BARBOUR *Bruce* XV. 188 The Mawndwell by his armyng He knew, and roucht him sic a swyng That he till erd ȝeid hastely. ? *a* **1400** *Morte Arth.* 3360 Many swayne with þe swynge has the swette leuede. *c* **1400** *Destr. Troy* 1271 With a swinge of his sworde [he] swappit hym in þe fase. *c* **1400** *Laud Troy Bk.* 9018 Odemoun.. Toke Menelaus In that swyng And him bare ouer his hors tayl. *a* **1400–50** *Wars Alex.* 1232 With a swyng of a swerd [he] swappis of hes hede.

b. *in a swing*: suddenly. (Cf. F. *tout d'un coup.*) *Obs.*

1375 BARBOUR *Bruce* XVII. 574 Sic abasing Tuk thame, but mar, in-to a swyng, Thai gaf the bak all, and to-ga.

†**2.** *to bear the swing*: to have full sway or control. Also (*to have*) *swing and sway*. *Obs.*

In this use *swing* app. arose as a substitute or variant of *swinge*: see SWINGE *sb.*[1] 1.

1552 LATIMER *Cert. Godly Serm.* (1562) 132 b, At the tyme when the Cardinall was aloft, and beare the swynge [*ed.* **1584** swyng]. **1565** *Reg. Privy Council Scot.* I. 370 Sa lang as sum of thame buir the haill swynge with us thame selffis. *a* **1568** ASCHAM *Scholem.* (1570) 15 b, Whan honest Parmenos shall not be hard, but beare small swing [*ed.* **1571** swinge] with their masters. **1570** *Satir. Poems Reform.* xi. 49 Throw the all Tratoures blythlie sing... Throw the murther wald beir the swing. **1622** MASSINGER & DEKKER *Virgin Martyr* II. i. D ij b, Shee tooke vs, tis true, from the gallowes, yet I hope she will not barre yeomen sprats to haue their swinge. **1631** MASSINGER *Emperor East* IV. i. (1632) H 2, That shee might still continue Her absolute sway, and swing ore the whole state. **1633** G. HERBERT *Temple, The Glance* ii, Had the malicious and ill-meaning harm His swing and sway.

3. The course of a career, practice, period of time, etc., esp. as marked by vigorous action of some kind. Now chiefly in phr. *in full swing*, *in the full swing of...*

1570 FOXE *A. & M.* I. 1/2 The time of Antichrist, or desolation of the Churche, whose full swinge conteineth the space of 400 yeares. *a* **1618** W. BRADSHAW *Medit. Mans Mortal.* (1621) 19 Sleepe is but short... And as it is but short of it selfe, though it should last the full swinge of nature: so the soundest sleepe, is easily broken. **1680** C. NESSE *Church-Hist.* 220 Thinking to take a long swing in sin. **1689** T. R. *View Govt. Europe* 31 Puft up and wanton with their new acquisitions and swing of fortune. **1702** FARQUHAR *Twin Rivals* IV. i, To disturb me thus, just in the swing and stretch of my full Fortune! **1850** GROTE *Greece* II. lvii. (1862) V. 119 She [*sc.* Athens] was in the full swing of hope. **1861** MEREDITH *Evan Harrington* xlv, A barrister in full swing of practice. **1861** HUGHES *Tom Brown at Oxf.* iv, He had had his full swing of success for two years. **1864** HUXLEY in *Life* (1900) I. xviii. 253 My lectures tire me, from want of practice... I shall soon get into swing. **1894** HALL CAINE *Manxman* V. iii, It was still early in the herring season, but the fishing was in full swing.

†**4.** Impulse; inclination, tendency: = SWINGE *sb.*[1] 3. *Obs.*

1538 *St. Papers Hen. VIII*, III. 39 The saide Lorde Deputie refused to accepte the same, whiche afterwarde, of his awne swynge.. he receyved. **1549** LATIMER *5th Serm. bef. Edw. VI* (Arb.) 150 They would haue a Kynge of theyr owne swinge and of theyr owne election. *a* **1568** ASCHAM *Scholem.* (1570) 14 b, Where the swing goeth, there to follow, fawne, flatter. *a* **1607** BRIGHTMAN *Bright. Rediv.* iii. (1647) 50 Christ did not of his own Swing and Counsell leap into the Office of Reconciliation. **1614** D. DYKE *Myst. Selfe-Deceiuing* 335 If wee can follow the swing and sway of our owne proud, and vaineglorious affections. *a* **1704** LOCKE in Ld. King *Life* (1830) II. 220 From their cradles some.. have been.. given up to the conduct and swing of their inconsiderate desires. *a* **1716** SOUTH *Serm.*, *1 Kings* xiii. *33–4* (1727) I. 137 Were it not for these, Civil Government were not able to stand before the prevailing Swing of corrupt Nature.

5. Freedom of action, free scope: = SWINGE *sb.*[1] 2; esp. in phr. *to take, have one's (full) swing*, to allow oneself every freedom, indulge oneself to the full, have one's fling. (See note under sense 8.)

1584 LYLY *Campaspe* III. ii. 34 *Psyllus.* How canst thou thus diuine, deuide, define, dispute, and all on the suddaine? *Manes.* Wit wil haue his swing. **1587** HARRISON *England* II. xvi. in *Holinshed* I. 199/2 Wherby it appeereth that some sort of youth will oft haue his swinge, although it be in a halter. **1697** DRYDEN *Virg. Georg.* Ded., He had, (according to our homely Saying) his full swing at this Poem, beginning it about the Age of Thirty Five; and scarce concluding it before he arriv'd at Forty. **1698** FARQUHAR *Love & Bottle* II. iii, The fellow will have his swing, tho he hang for't. **1712** STEELE *Spect.* No. 503 ⁋2 This Creature came among us only to give herself Airs, and enjoy her full Swing in being admir'd. **1731** FIELDING *Letter-Writers* I. ii, I resolved to take one swing in the charming plains of iniquity. **1808** SCOTT *Marm.* I. xvii, Let the wild falcon soar her swing. **1860** MISS YONGE *Hopes & Fears* I. 244 Trust me that things will adjust themselves all the better for letting them have their swing. **1873** M. ARNOLD *Lit. & Dogma* (1876) 16 The giving free swing to one's temper and instincts. **1908** S. E. WHITE *Riverman* ix, She was a kindly girl, whose parents gave her free swing.

6. a. Forcible motion of a body swung or flung. (Also *fig.*) *arch.*

1595 *Locrine* V. iv. 189 That..she might haue died a death Worse then the swing of old Ixions wheele. **1606** SHAKS. *Tr. & Cr.* I. iii. 207 The Ramme that batters downe the wall, For the great swing and rudenesse of his poize [etc.]. **1697** DRYDEN *Æneid* XI. 933 Swelling Surges..Bound o're the Rocks, incroach upon the Land;..Then backward with a Swing, they take their Way. *Ibid.* XII. 1335 And rising as he threw, With its full swing the fatal Weapon flew. **1895** MORRIS *Beowulf* xiv. 30 The dread swing of the waves [*orig.* atol yða ȝeswing] was washing all mingled With hot blood.

b. Continuous vigorous movement or progress.

1856 H. H. DIXON *Post & Paddock* i. 24 He [*sc.* a horse] would insist on walking through the brook instead of taking it in his swing. **1861** HUGHES *Tom Brown at Oxf.* xi, The..casual voyager..might have beheld the..eight-oar coming with a steady swing up the last reach. **1865** *Morn. Star* 5 July, When the train was getting on the 'swing' (attaining a high speed).

c. ***full swing*** (advb. phr.): at full speed; with the utmost vigour or energy.

1848 H. MILLER *First Impr. Eng.* vii. (1857) 110 He returned full swing to the gratification of the grosser propensities of his nature. **1854** R. S. SURTEES *Handley Cr.* li, Round they go, full swing, every hound throwing his tongue. **1887** JESSOPP *Arcady* viii. 236 While the northern mail was coming along full swing through the parish.

d. A swift tour or journey (*through* a place) involving a number of stops or visits. Now *spec.* a political campaign tour; also, ***swing around the circle***, a campaigning tour of a constituency or larger area. Cf. SWING *v.*[1] 11 c. *U.S.*

1860 H. J. HAWLEY *Jrnl.* 22 Apr. in *Wisconsin Mag. Hist.* (1936) XIX. 330 Had a fine time a nice swing..saw sights and returned. **1905** *Springfield* (Mass.) *Weekly Republican* 6 Oct. 1 Will the appropriated money be available for campaigning swings around the circle? **1929** *Sun* (Baltimore) 23 Oct. 2/7 Mr. Hoover has undergone much strain on this swing and he showed it as he waved a weary adieu to the hospitable Ohioans. **1949** *Manch. Guardian Weekly* 1 Sept. 2 Before his recent swing around the Marshall countries. **1967** *Boston Globe* 5 Apr. 51/1 Dizzy Dean's wife once traveled with him on an Eastern swing by the Cardinals. **1972** *Even. Telegram* (St. John's, Newfoundland) 27 June 5/3 Senior citizens can call a number and a van will come by to pick them up on swings through the city. **1978** L. HEREN *Growing up on The Times* iii. 92, I..was sharing a room..with Colin Reid of the *Daily Telegraph*, who was on a swing from Beirut.

e. A worker's rest period between duties; a shift system which incorporates such breaks. Also, time off work as leave, furlough. Cf. *swing-shift* s.v. SWING- 2 a. *U.S. slang.*

1917 D. C. ROPER *U.S. Post Office* 353 *Swing*, period of time within the day's tour or 'trick' when an employee is temporarily off duty. **1918** *Outlook* (N.Y.) 17 July 443/2 [On a street railway] The 'swings', or free time between runs, are for the most part so arranged as to be inconvenient for going home. **1945** *Transit News* (Capital Transit Co., Washington, D.C.) 15 June, A 'Swing' works during the morning rush hour, and the operator is then off until time to start the evening rush hour. **1972** J. MILLS *Report to Commissioner* 129, I went on my swing after that.

f. In colloq. phr. ***to go with a swing***: said of a lively, successful party or other entertainment or undertaking.

1976 *Bridgwater Mercury* 21 Dec. 9/3 Families may soon be enjoying a tipple at the bar to make their parties held in the community centre go with a swing.

7. a. The act of swinging or waving about a weapon or other body; a movement describing a curve, such as that made in flourishing a weapon, raising the arm or hand to give a blow, etc.

1635 QUARLES *Embl.* III. xii. 30 The farther off we go, The swing of Iustice deales the mightier blow. **1771** LONNERGAN *Fencer's Guide* 87 By the swing you give, you may find way still for a thrust to enter upon me, if you do not disarm me; but if your wrist is swung too far from the Line, you must spring back to avoid a thrust that may come at you. **1839** URE *Dict. Arts* 582 He now heats the bulb in the fire,..and by a dexterous swing or two he lengthens it. **1853** R. S. SURTEES *Sponge's Sp. Tour* iii. 10 [He] brought his right arm round with a sort of military swing to his forehead. **1876** TENNYSON *Harold* V. i, Swaying his two-handed sword about him, Two deaths at every swing. **1887** *Field* 19 Feb. 242/2 By 'swing' I understand keeping the gun moving with the object for a short time before firing. **1891** H. HERMAN *His Angel* ii. 31 The woodwork of the car was flying in splinters under the rapid swing of an axe. **1892** GREENER *Breech Loader* 205 Those who shoot with the gun on the swing. **1899** HUTCHINSON, etc. *Bk. Golf* ii. 42 Instantaneous photographs of first-class players taken when at the top of the swing. **1908** T. BURNS *Scientific Boxing* ii. 33 The quickest punches are necessarily the straight arm ones. They will always get there quicker than any round arm swing.

b. *Boxing.* A punch delivered with a sweep of the arm; a swinging blow. Also in gen. colloq. use, esp. in phr. ***to take a swing at*** (someone).

1910 [see HOOK *sb.*[1] 13 b]. **1962** *Times* 28 Apr. 3/5 Barlow came rushing in attempting to land with right swings to the head. **1983** W. WINWARD *Last & Greatest Art* 211 If I stand here much longer I'm going to be tempted to take a swing at you.

8. a. The act of swinging or oscillating, as a suspended body, or a body turning (to and fro, or in either direction) upon a fixed centre or axis, e.g. upon a hinge; an oscillating or swaying movement, oscillation; also, the amount of oscillation, the arc or curve traced or moved through in this way. Also with adv., as ***swing-to***, the act of swinging to.

In quot. 1589 with reference to hanging and play on sense 5, where cf. quots. 1587, 1698.

1589 NASHE *Martins Months Minde* To Rdr., Wks. (Grosart) I. 160 If these men may haue their swaie (but wee hope first they shall haue their swing). **1630** J. TAYLOR (Water P.) *Necessitie of Hanging* Wks. II. 133/1 One hanging is a necessary thing, Which is a pretty gamball, cald a Swing. [*note*] A swing or stretch for exercise and health. **1677** MIEGE *Fr. Dict.*, To give one a great swing, *donner à quêcun une grande secousse.* **1729** BOYER *Royal Dict.* s.v., He may have a Swing, (or be hang'd) for't. **1775** J. STEELE *Ess. Melody Speech* 68 The rhythmical pulsation is regularly periodical and constant as the swings of a pendulum. **1777** COOK *Voy. Pacific* III. ix. (1784) II. 167 They say, that a goddess, having a lump or mass of earth suspended in a cord, gave it a swing, and scattered about pieces of land. **1827** FARADAY *Chem. Manip.* ii. (1842) 56 A swing of a foot or two in extent should then be given to it, so as to produce centrifugal force. **1853** DALE tr. *Baldeschi's Ceremonial* 35 He..incenses the Celebrant with three double swings. **1854** R. S. SURTEES *Handley Cr.* xxvii, Charley was speedily at a white gate, whose sound and easy swing denoted an entrance of some pretension. **1867** MORRIS *Jason* IX. 288 Argo, leaping forward to the swing Of measured oars. **1869** *Routledge's Ev. Boy's Ann.* 443 At first the time is bad, there is not sufficient 'swing' or 'catching at the beginning'. **1883** GRESLEY *Gloss. Coalmining*, *Swing*, the arc or curve described by the point of a pick or maundril when being used by a holer or in cutting coal; called the swing of the pick. **1901** G. DOUGLAS *House w. Green Shutters* 289 The sharp swing-to of the door. *a* **1903** 'H. S. MERRIMAN' *Last Hope* ii, The swing of her tapering masts spoke of the heaving seas she had left behind.

fig. **1877** R. GIFFEN *Stock Exch. Securities* 153 There is an upward and downward swing, as of a pendulum, in the prices of securities. **1891** SIR R. BALL *Ice Age* 167 At the other end of the swing the summer in the Northern hemisphere will be seven days shorter than the winter in the same hemisphere.

b. ***on the swing***: swinging from side to side, oscillating.

1854 R. S. SURTEES *Handley Cr.* xxxviii, His dressing-table was covered with blacks—his looking-glass was on the swing—his soap was reduced to a wafer. **1882** SALA *Amer. Revis.* (1885) 166 The..doors were..on the swing. **1890** 'R. BOLDREWOOD' *Col. Reformer* xiii. (1891) 128 The pace was frightful by this time, the coach on the swing.

c. A form of penance performed by Hindus: see SWING *v.*[1] 6 (*b*).

1852 [MRS. F. L. MORTIMER] *Far Off, Hindostan* 103 There is another way of torture quite as painful—it is the swing. Those [Hindoos] who determine to swing, allow the blacksmith to drive hooks into the flesh upon their backs, and hanging by these hooks they swing in the air.

d. The distance which determines the diameter of the work that can be admitted by a lathe.

1875 in KNIGHT *Dict. Mech.*

e. A sweeping movement.

1897 *Badminton Mag.* IV. 386 Presently the hounds took a swing to the left and over the edge of the hill again.

f. The leaning outward from the vehicle of the upper part of a wheel.

1875 in KNIGHT *Dict. Mech.*

g. *Cricket.* A curving deviation of a ball from a straight line of flight on delivery, occasioned by a combination of the angle of its seam and the relative smoothness of the leather each side of this.

1906 *Cricket* 29 Nov. 450/1 He and Raynor..were two of the best boy bowlers I have seen, and the latter had more break—not swing—in the air than anyone else I ever saw. **1920** LYTTELTON & WILSON in P. F. Warner *Cricket* (ed. 2) 270 Baker did not swing too much..and he combined swing with length. **1976** J. SNOW *Cricket Rebel* 101 It is not often in Australia that the atmospheric conditions encourage swing.

h. An observable movement in general opinion away from one position towards another. Hence *spec.* in *Pol.*, a change in the relative distribution of popular support for political parties, often measured in terms of percentage gains or losses by each party at a poll. Formerly also † ***swing of the pendulum***.

1899 *Pall Mall Mag.* Jan. 42 Affairs took a swing under me and took me off my balance. **1912** *Contemp. Rev.* Dec. 835 It is evident that a swing of public opinion has occurred. **1933** D. W. BROGAN *Amer. Polit. System* x. iv. 368 The strength of American parties is, as a rule, too sectional, too much divorced from any current national controversies, for there to be anything like our 'swing of the pendulum'. **1940** *Economist* 5 Oct. 421/2 The swing in American public opinion has been such that the Nazis may well despair of keeping the United States out of a long war. **1945** *Times* 27 July 4/1 When the votes were counted..it was revealed that the Government formed by Mr Churchill on the break-up of the Coalition had been decisively beaten by a surging swing of opinion to the Left. **1955** *Times* 26 May 10/1 The absence of any pronounced 'swing' towards the Government. **1960** *Where?* III. 17 '*Swing*', *the*, jargon for the relatively recent tendency among sixth form pupils to specialize in science rather than arts subjects. *a* **1974** R. CROSSMAN *Diaries* (1975) I. 493 It was only a 3·1 swing, and by God a 3·1 swing can become a 4·0 counter-swing very quickly indeed. **1976** H. WILSON *Governance of Britain* ii. 38 We had bad county council results in April, including Lancashire though with a favourable swing in Greater London.

i. *Electr.* An increase or decrease in the magnitude of a current or voltage, the difference between its greatest and smallest values.

1908 *Rep. Brit. Assoc. Adv. Sci.* 1907 622 These [oscillations]..are transferred..into a closed air-condenser circuit, which, when its swings reach a maximum, overflows into the coherer. **1957** *Practical Wireless* XXXIII. 562/2 It is possible to increase the anode voltage swing and the anode peak current. **1978** *Sci. Amer.* Dec. 54/1 Load-following generators are started daily and run most of the time to cope with daily swings in the load; they may be shut down at night.

j. *Psychol.*: see *mood swing* s.v. MOOD *sb.*[1] 3 f.

k. *Bridge.* The difference between the total scores of two teams of two pairs playing the same deal at two tables, each team having north-south positions at one table and east-west at the other.

1945 S. J. SIMON *Why You lose at Bridge* 24 In Room 1, North-South bid six Spades and made five. In Room 2, North-South stopped in 4 spades and declarer, playing for safety, made three. No swing! **1949** *Contract Bridge Jrnl.* Feb. 5/2 On the very next hand the Scots repaid the compliment; at this stage they were going great guns, and on Board 54 came the biggest swing to-date. **1961** *Listener* 10 Aug. 222/3 The swing on the board was 2,080, or 11 match points.

9. Movement of the body or limbs in a manner suggesting the action of swinging.

1730 SWIFT *Tom & Dick* Wks. 1755 IV. I. 261 Tom had the genteeler swing, His hat could nicely put on. *a* **1739** JARVIS *2nd Pt. Quix.* II. xiii. (1742) II. 157 Don Quixote, who was not used to alight without having his stirrop held, ..threw his body off with a swing. **1752** JOHNSON *Rambler* No. 194 ⁋6 One was detected by his gait, and another by the swing of his arms. **1807–8** W. IRVING *Salmag.* (1824) 388 An easy swing in my walk. **1901** *Daily News* 1 Apr. 5/7 [In rowing] Their recovery was lively, their swing-forward remarkably steady and well-balanced.

10. a. A steady vigorous rhythm or movement characterizing a verse or musical composition.

1829 CUNNINGHAM *Brit. Paint.* I. 171 Distinguished by a vigorous swing of versification. **1879** CHURCH *Spenser* 46 In the Shepherd's Calender we have for the first time in the century, the swing, the command, the varied resources of the true poet. **1884** *Congregationalist* Feb. 109 The 'swing' and 'go'..of these popular religious ballads.

b. *Mus.* A quality of jazz, dance music, etc., that has a flowing but strongly compelling rhythm; since the mid-thirties (esp. for a decade), applied to a variety of big dance-band music played in this style. Cf. SWING- 2 d.

(*a*) **1899** H. H. MINCER (*song-title*) Virginia. Two-step & hot rag swing. **1917** *Sun* (N.Y.) 5 Aug. 3/7 Jazz is based on the savage musician's wonderful gift for progressive retarding and acceleration guided by his sense of swing. **1924** (*music-title*) Lou'siana swing [performed by Piron's New Orleans Orchestra]. **1932** 'DUKE' ELLINGTON (*song-title*) It don't mean a thing (If it ain't got that swing). **1939** —— in *Melody Maker* 15 July 8/3 No notes represent swing. You can't write swing because swing is the emotional element in the audience and there is no swing until you hear the note. **1954** *Grove's Dict. Music* (ed. 5) IV. 600/1 'Swing' ..can only be said to designate the regular but subtle rhythmic pulsation which animates 4-4 time and must be present in every good jazz performance. Swing is essentially the performer's concern: it cannot be indicated in musical notation except implicitly.

(*b*) **1936** *Delineator* CXXIX. 10/1 This swing, it's nothing more or less than jazz, is it? **1937** L. ARMSTRONG *Swing that Music* xiv. 117 Even now, thirty years after Swing was born, this book is the first history of swing music, and of the men who made it, to be published in the English language. **1943** D. WELCH *Maiden Voyage* xiv. 110 'What kind of records have you got?' 'There's plenty of swing.' **1957** R. HOGGART *Uses of Literacy* v. 129 The emotional patterns bodied out by 'swing' are quite close to those of the older, waltz-derived, styles: in fact, 'swing' has been adapted and assimilated; a modern 'swing' song and an old-fashioned waltz tune live together with ease. **1973** J. WAINWRIGHT *Pride of Pigs* 61 It wasn't jazz. Not *real* jazz... Swing..that's what they'd called it, when [Artie] Shaw had introduced it in the 1930's.

II. Concrete senses.

11. a. A contrivance used for recreation, consisting of a seat which is suspended from above on ropes or rods and on which a person may sit and swing to and fro; also = *swing-boat* (SWING- 2).

1687 A. LOVELL tr. *Thevenot's Trav.* I. 45 In the Morning the Streets are full of Swings, adorned with Festoons. **1799** S. & HT. LEE *Canterb. T.* III. 325 There once hung my infantine swing between two limes. **1813** *Sporting Mag.* XLII. 20 There were the usual swings, ups-and-downs, and roundabouts. **1886** RUSKIN *Præterita* xii. §258. I. 428 A post to tie a swing to.

b. Colloq. phr. ***to gain on the swings and lose on the roundabouts*** and varr., according to which one's losses in one quarter balance one's gains in another. Also *allusively*.

1912 P. R. CHALMERS *Green Days & Blue Days* 20 For 'up an' down an' round,' said 'e, goes all appointed things, An' losses on the roundabouts means profits on the swings! **1927** *Times* 24 Mar. 15/5 By screwing more money out of taxpayers he diminishes their savings, and the market for trustee securities loses on the swings what it gains on the roundabouts. **1944** G. B. SHAW *Everybody's Political What's What* xv. 121, I was taxed at a higher rate than my fellow capitalists who had smaller incomes. But then I had to pay at a lower rate than others who had bigger incomes. Whether I lost on the swings what I gained on the roundabouts I do not know. **1964** *English Studies* XLV. (Suppl.). 98 The more a word loses in meaning, the more it gains in functional, as distinct from semantic, importance. What we lose on the swings we win on the roundabouts. **1976** *Listener* 18 Nov. 641/1 There is a certain rough justice in charging for the possibility of using the [broadcasting] service... Swings and round-abouts.

12. †**a.** A pendulum. *Obs.*

1696 DERHAM *Artif. Clock-m.* ii. 14.

†**b.** A noose for hanging, halter. *Obs.*

1697 ABELL in Potter *Antiq. Greece* I. xxv. I. 126 That he might there make swings above the floor For all his nasty Queans, who'd play'd the Whore.

c. A hawser for making fast a boat.

1834 H. MILLER *Scenes & Leg.* xii. (1850) 177 The small hawser attached to the stem, known technically as the *swing*, which he wound securely round a jutting crag.

d. The rope or chain attached to the tongue of a wagon, along which the draught animals between the leaders and the wheelers are attached, they being said to be ***in the swing***; hence, the animals occupying that position (more fully, ***swing-pair, -steer, -team***).

1869 [see LEAD *sb.*[2] 11 b]. **1891** in *Cent. Dict.* **1907** *Morn. Post* 21 May 9/3 The splendid sextet, Jim and Henry in the wheel, Billy and Phil in the swing, and Mace and Dude in the lead. **1909** *Westm. Gaz.* 28 May 9/3 The two wheelers of the team.. The swing pair,..and the two leaders. **1909** *Cent. Dict., Suppl., Swing-team*, in a logging-team of six, the pair between the leaders and the butt team.

e. The outriders who keep a moving herd of cattle in order. Also ***swing-men, -riders***. *U.S.*

1903 A. ADAMS *Log Cowboy* iii. 28. *Ibid.* x. 137 He rode up from his position of third man in the swing.

f. 'A kind of suspensory cradle or sling for a broken leg' (Dorland *Med. Dict.* 1901).

g. *Photogr.* = *swing-back* (SWING- 2).

1878 ABNEY *Photogr.* (1881) 244 On one side of the picture a near object may have to be represented; by using the horizontal swing, it may often be brought into focus.

Swing, *sb.*[3] Now *Hist.* Used, chiefly *attrib.*, to designate a system of intimidation practised in agricultural districts of the South of England in 1830–1, consisting in sending to farmers and landowners threatening letters over the signature of a fictitious Captain Swing, followed by the incendiary destruction of their ricks and other property.

Three pretended lives of Swing appeared: *The Life and History of Swing, the Kent Rick-burner, written by himself*, 1830, *A Short Account of the Life and Death of Swing, the Rick-burner, written by one well acquainted with him*, by H. N. Coleridge, and *The Genuine Life of Mr. Francis Swing*, 1831. A review of the first of these, by Gen. P. Thompson, entitled 'On Machine-breaking', in the Westminster Review, Jan. 1831, was republished in pamphlet form, 'In answer to "Swing".'

1830 *Poor Man's Guardian* 31 Dec. 8/1 There is no doubt that the fire was caused by an incendiary, as Mr. Ley had previously received a 'Swing' letter, threatening that his place should be fired before the 10th of January. [**1832** *Let. to J. Keate* (Headmaster of Eton) in *N. & Q.* 7th Ser. VII. 268/1 If you do not lay aside your Thrishing machine you will hear further from..SWING.] **1836–7** DICKENS *Sk. Boz, Tales* viii, 'But this letter..is anonymous.' 'I see—bit o' Sving, eh?' [**1842** BARHAM *Ingol. Leg.* Ser. II. *Babes in Wood* xvii, And Captain Swing came in the night, And burnt all his beans and his barley.] **1845** W. WING *Antiq. Steeple Aston* 58 The riots in the agricultural districts in 1830–1, called the 'Swing-riots'. **1859** *Times* 21 Nov., Excesses of the Luddites and Swing. [**1861** HUGHES *Tom Brown at Oxf.* xxxix, And while Swing and his myrmidons were abroad in the counties.] **1888** *World* 2 May 5 He quoted the example of the Swing Fires as an example of an evil which may have averted greater evils.

swing (swɪŋ), *v.*[1] Pa. t. swung (swʌŋ), *rarely* swang (swæŋ); pa. pple. swung. Forms: 1 swingan, (suinga), 2 swingen, (4 suing(e, squynge), 4–5 swynge, 4–6 swinge, swyng, 5– swing. *Pa. t. str.* 1, 3, 5– swang (1 *pl.* swungon, 3 *pl.* swonge(n), 4 suang, squang(e, 4–5 swange, swonge, 4–7 swong, 8– swung; *wk.* 4 swyngede, 5 swynget, swinget, 6 swynged, 7 swinged. *Pa. pple. str.* 1 swungen, (1, 4 suungen), 3 iswonge, 4 yswonnge, yswongen, iswungen, suongen, swngen, squongin, 4–5 swongen, swonge, (5 swongyn, -on), 8– swung; *wk.* 6 swynged, 6–8 swinged. [OE. *swingan*, pa. t. *swang*, *swungon*, pa. pple. *ȝeswungen* to scourge, chastise, beat up, intr. to move violently or impetuously, related to OFris. *swinga* (also *swenga, swanga*) to fling, besprinkle, MLG. *swingen* str., to fling, hurl, swingle flax, intr. to fling oneself, fly, *swengen* wk., intr. and refl. to throw oneself in any direction, rotate, wheel round, LG. *swingen* to swingle, OHG. *swingan* to hurl, fling, beat, intr. to move rapidly, fly, (MHG. *swingen*, G. *schwingen* to brandish, flourish, shake, winnow, swingle, intr. or refl. to swing, oscillate, swing oneself up, etc., bound, soar, rise, whence Sw. *svinga*, Da. *svinge*), Goth. *afswaggwjan* in pass. rendering ἐξαπορηθῆναι to be in doubt or anxiety; f. Teut. *swiŋgw-*, older *sweŋgw-*: *swaŋgw-* (*swaŋgwj-*), to be or to put in violent (circular or rotatory) motion; whence also the forms recorded s.v. SWANG *v.*, SWING *sb.*[1] and [2], SWING *v.*[2], SWENG, SWENGE, SWINGE, and prob. SWANGE, SWONG.]

†**1.** *trans.* To scourge, whip, flog, beat (a person); also, to strike with a weapon or the hand.

*c*725 *Corpus Gloss.* (Hessels) E 477 *Exalaparetur*, suungen. **971** *Blickl. Hom.* 15 Hie hine bindað & swingaþ & spætliað on his onsyne. *Ibid.* 23 Hie hine swungon, & bundon. *Ibid.* 243 Swingaþ hine on his muð. *c* **1000** ÆLFRIC *Saints' Lives* xxxvii. 158 And hine man þa swang & mid saglum beot. *c* **1175** *Lamb. Hom.* 149 [He] ofte for his sunne swingeð him mið smele twige. *a* **1300** *Cursor M.* 26019 Efter he was wit skurges suungen [*Fairf.* squongin]. *c* **1330** *Assump. Virg.* (B.M. MS.) 443 With oute gult þei me swongen, And to a piler þei me bounden. *c* **1330** R. BRUNNE *Chron. Wace* (Rolls) 13054 Ilk oþer wroþ, ilk oþer swong. *a* **1400** *Octavian* (Sarrazin) 2 Jesu, þat was..for vs hard and sore yswonnge. *c* **1450** *Mirour Saluacioun* (Roxb.) 5 How xrist was with scourgis swongyn. *c* **1460** *Towneley Myst.* xxiii. 470 Blo and blody thus am I bett, Swongen with swepys.

b. To beat (the flesh) *from*, (the blood) *out of*.

a **1300** *Cursor M.* 9102 (Cott.) Vte of his bak þe blode þai suang. *a* **1400** *Leg. Rood* (1871) 142 þe flesch was from þe bones swonge.

c. *Cookery.* To beat up, 'whip' (milk, eggs, etc.). *Obs.*

c **1000** *Sax. Leechd.* III. 24 ȝif þoc sy on eaȝan nim arsapan & hinde meoluc mæng to somne & swyng. ? *c* **1390** *Form of Cury* in Warner *Antiq. Culin.* (1791) 10 Breke ayrenn and do thereto; and swyng it wel togydr. *c* **1420** *Liber Cocorum* (1862) 11 Swyng eyryn, and do þer to. *a* **1500** *Recipes* in *Babees Bk.* (1868) 53 Recipe brede gratyd, & eggis; & swyng þam to-gydere.

d. *intr.* To strike a blow *with* a sword; to come *together* with blows; to deliver a blow *at*.

c **1350** *Will. Palerne* 3856 Swiftli seþþe with swerdes swonge þei to-gider. *a* **1375** *Joseph Arim.* 576 þe white kniht wiþ his swerd swyngede to hem sone. *a* **1400–50** *Wars Alex.* 957 He swyngis out with a swerd & swappis him to dethe. *c* **1400** *Destr. Troy* 13590 Pirrus swappit out his sword, swange at þe kyng. *c* **1470** HENRY *Wallace* IV. 314 Wallace thar with swyth with a suerd out swang.

†**2.** *trans.* To throw with force, fling, hurl.

a **1300** *Cursor M.* 7527 (Cott.) His arms fra him did he suing [*Fairf.* squynge]. *c* **1480** HENRYSON *Mor. Fab., Fox, Wolf & Cadger* xviii, He hint him be the heillis, And with ane swak he swang him on the creillis. **1495** *Trevisa's Barth. De P.R.* xv. cii. (W. de W.), He swange [*Bodl. MS.* swenged] the adder in to the fire.

†**3.** *intr.* To move or go impetuously; to rush; to fling oneself. *Obs.*

Beowulf 2264 (Gr.) Nis hearpan wyn,..ne god hafoc ȝeond sæl swingeð, ne se swifta mearh burhstede beateð. *a* **1300** *Cursor M.* 7582 Wit þat stan he laid in sling, Sua stalworthli he lete it suing þat in his frunt þat stan he fest. **13..** *E.E. Allit. P.* A. 1059 þat foysoun flode..Swyþe hit swange þurȝ vch a strete. **13..** *Gaw. & Gr. Knt.* 1562 þe lorde..Swez his vncely swyn, þat swyngez bi þe bonkkez. **14..** *Sir Beues* 497 (Pynson) Al at onys on hym they swonge And gaue hym woundes wyde and longe. *a* **1553** UDALL *Royster D.* II. iii. (Arb.) 35 *Tib. Talk.* Well Trupenie neuer but flinging. *An. Alyface.* And frisking? *Trupenie.* Well Tibet and Annot, still swingyng and whiskyng? **1582** STANYHURST *Æneis* II. (Arb.) 50 Two serpents..Plasht the water sucking to the shoare moste hastelye swinging.

b. *trans.* To carry or drive forcibly. *Obs.*

c **1400** *Destr. Troy* 13299 Full swift to the swalgh me swinget the flode. **1582** STANYHURST *Æneis* I. (Arb.) 33 With steeds he is swinged, downe picht in his hudge wagon emptye.

4. *trans.* †To draw *out* (a sword) with a vigorous movement (*obs.*); to flourish, brandish, wave *about*; in later use with mixture of sense 7 or 12: to wield (a weapon or implement), or move (a body held or grasped) with an oscillating or rotatory movement; also (*Austral. slang.*), ***to swing Kelly*** (or ***Douglas***), to wield an axe, to do axework.

a **1400–50** *Wars Alex.* 806 Alexander..Swythe swyngis out his swerde. *c* **1400** *Destr. Troy* 7275 He..swynget out a sword, swappit at þat other. *Ibid.* 10390 þen he swange out a sword swicly with þat. **1513** DOUGLAS *Æneis* IX. vii. 161 He ..thame stoutly assalit,..And euer his schynand swerd about him swang. **1581** A. GILBY *Test. 12 Patriarchs* 27 b, I tooke hym by the Hornes, and swinged hym aboute, and finally killed hym. **1592** SHAKS. *Rom. & Jul.* I. i. 118 The fiery Tibalt, with his sword prepar'd, Which..He swong about his head. *c* **1611** CHAPMAN *Iliad* III. 393 An emptie helme, That then he swong about his head, and cast among his friends. **1626** BACON *Sylva* §310 Take Bottles, and Swing them. **1646** CRASHAW *Sospetto d'Herode* xl, Swinging a huge scythe, stands impartial Death. **1666** DRYDEN *Ann. Mirab.* xcvii, If some one approach to dare his Force, He swings his Tail. **1671** MILTON *Samson* 1240 Go baffl'd coward, lest I..swing thee in the Air. **1725** *Fam. Dict.* s.v. *Sallet*, Lettice, Cresses, Radish, &c. must..be..swing'd and shaken gently. **1815** SCOTT *Guy M.* xx, He..swung his arms like the sails of a wind-mill. **1860** TENNYSON *Sea Dreams* 24 For sideways up he swung his arms. **1873** B. HARTE *Fiddletown*, etc. 107 Each swung a lasso. **1909** STACPOOLE *Pools of Silence* xxx, Adams had swung the man aloft and dashed him against the wall. **1945** BAKER *Austral. Lang.* i v. 78 *Kelly* and *douglas*, an axe (from the names of makers), with their derivatives *to swing kelly* or *douglas*, to do axework. **1966** 'J. HACKSTON' *Father clears Out* 98 The scholars..could have passed with honours in such subjects as milking, swinging Douglas, panning off.

†**5.** To whirl (a wheel) round. *Obs.*

a **1225** *Juliana* 58 [He] dude..fore of his cnihtes forte turnen þat hweol..ant het swingen hit swiftliche abuten ant tidliche turnen.

6. *intr.* To move freely backwards and forwards, as a body suspended from a support above; to oscillate below a point of support, as a pendulum or the like. For spec. use in Hindu asceticism, see (*b*).

Occas. the intr. sense corresp. to 7 d.

1545 ASCHAM *Toxoph.* I. (Arb.) 47 Moche lyke the pastyme that boyes vse in the churche when their master is awaye, to swinge and totter in a belrope. **1660** BOYLE *New Exp. Phys. Mech.* xxvi. 202 We thought it not amiss to try if a Pendulum would swing faster, or continue swinging longer in our Receiver. **1710** STEELE *Tatler* No. 96 ¶5 His Arms naturally swang at an unreasonable Distance from his Sides. **1782** COWPER *Gilpin* 107 A bottle swinging at each side. **1816** J. SMITH *Panorama Sci. & Art* II. 133 A great beam, suspended on gudgeons at the middle, and swinging like the beam of a balance. **1839** FR. A. KEMBLE *Resid. Georgia* (1863) 19 The mocking birds are swinging and singing even now. **1842** TENNYSON *Sir Galahad* iii, The shrill bell rings, the censer swings. **1844** A. B. WELBY *Poems* (1867) 44 Her cottage bonnet filled with flowers, Hung swinging from her arm. **1864** TENNYSON *Aylmer's F.* 19 Sir Aylmer Aylmer,..Whose blazing wyvern weathercock'd the spire,..And swang besides on many a windy sign. *a* **1900** KIPLING *A Dedication* vi, One stone the more swings to her place In that dread Temple of Thy worth. **1912** H. BELLOC *Four Men* 25 His arms dangled rather than swang.

(*b*) **1773** ED. IVES *Voy. to India* I. ii. 27 On the 9th of April, annually, at Bengal the natives undergo a very uncommon kind of penance:..In a large plain about a mile from Calcutta, there are erected about thirty Bamboos, at least twenty feet high; on the top of these they contrive to fix a swivel, and another bamboo of thirty feet or more crosses it, at both ends of which hangs a rope. One end of this rope, the people pull down, and the devotee placing himself under it, the Brahmin pinches up a large piece of skin under both the shoulder blades,..and thrusts a strong iron-hook through each... When this is done, the people haul down the other end of the bamboo, by which means the devotee is immediately lifted up..from the ground, and then run round as fast as their legs will carry them. This throws the devotee out to the full length of the rope, where as he swings, he plays a thousand antic tricks. **1793** *Medical Spectator* II. No. 39. 246 All the information that I could get from our Banyan relative to this strange custom was, that they swing for a good conscience.

b. Of a person: To move backwards and forwards through the air upon a suspended rope or a swing (SWING *sb.*[2] 11), as a sport; to ride in a swing.

[**1545**: see 6.] **1662** J. DAVIES tr. *Olearius' Voy. Ambass.* 93 They have also ropes to swing in. **1665** SIR T. HERBERT *Trav.* (1677) 130, I saw ropes or cords stretched from tree to tree in several gardens, Boys and Girls..swinging upon them. **1714** GAY *Sheph. Week* Monday 104 On two near elms the slacken'd cord I hung, Now high, now low my Blouzelinda swung.

c. Of a (suspended) bell: To give forth a sound by swinging; to sound, ring *out*.

1632 MILTON *Penseroso* 76 Oft..I hear the far-off Curfeu sound, Over som wide-water'd shoar, Swinging slow with sullen roar. **1812** COLMAN *Br. Grins, Lady of Wreck* II. xii, A sound swung down the glen..From Bunamargy Friary bell. **1874** GREEN *Short Hist.* ii. §6. 90 The burgesses gathered in town-mote when the bell swung out from St. Paul's.

d. *fig.* To waver, vacillate; to change from one condition or position to the opposite (esp. in fig. phrases with *pendulum* as subj.: see PENDULUM *sb.* 2).

1833 CHALMERS *Power of God* II. x. 106 We swing as it were between two assumptions. **1836** [see PENDULUM *sb.* 2]. **1877** R. GIFFEN *Stock Exch. Securities* 152 He should endeavour..not to invest when the pendulum has swung upwards. **1890** *Retrospect Med.* CII. 378, I am by no means sure that the pendulum may not have swung too far in the opposite direction.

e. *trans.* To mark or indicate by swinging; ***to swing seconds***, to oscillate once in every second.

1736 DERHAM in *Phil. Trans.* XXXIX. 202 The next Experiments I shall mention, I made..by the Help of a good Month-Piece that swings Seconds. **1764** MASKELYNE *ibid.* LIV. 373 A little clock..having a pendulum swinging seconds.

7. *trans.* To cause to oscillate, as a body suspended from a support above; to move or sway (something) to and fro in this or a similar manner.

Phr. ***to swing a cat*** (i.e. holding it by the tail); in ***no room to swing a cat in*** and similar expressions, said of a confined or narrow space. ***to swing the lead***: see LEAD *sb.*[1] 6 b.

1560 DAUS tr. *Sleidane's Comm.* 295 They hange out the dead body by a chaine ouer the walle, and after they had swynged it a whyle to and fro, they let it fall into the ditche. **1665** *Medela Pestil.* 57 They had not space enough (according to the vulgar saying) to swing a Cat in. **1706** E. WARD *Wooden World Diss.* (1708) 5 When they walk, they swing their Corps like a Pendulum. **1771** SMOLLETT *Humphry Cl.* 8 June, I am pent up in frowzy lodgings, where there is not room enough to swing a cat. **1827** FARADAY *Chem. Manip.* xx. (1842) 543 The flasks should be well rinsed, and..swung in the hand to shake out adhering drops. **1844** DICKENS *Mart. Chuz.* xvi, The colonel..took his seat upon the table, and swung his legs. **1849** CLOUGH *Poems, Natura Naturans* viii, Big bees their burly bodies swung. **1850** DICKENS *Dav. Copp.* xxxv, Mrs. Crupp had indignantly assured him that there wasn't room to swing a cat there; but, as Mr. Dick just observed to me,..'You know, Trotwood, I don't want to swing a cat. I never do swing a cat.' **1906** Raven *Bells* 41 Arrangements for hanging bells in turrets and swinging them.

b. To cause (a person) to oscillate as in a swing; to give (one) a ride in a swing.

1615 G. Sandys *Trav.* 56 By two ioyning ropes that are fastned aboue, they will swing themselues as high as the transome. **1712** Steele *Spect.* No. 492 ¶3 They get on Ropes, as you must have seen the Children, and are swung by their Men Visitants. **1783** Justamond tr. *Raynal's Hist. Indies* V. 40 Their slaves had no other employment but to swing them in their hammocks. **1838** Lytton *Alice* III. vii, Come to-morrow, and swing Sophy—no nice swinging since you've been gone.

c. Of a bell: To send *forth* a peal of sound.

1818 Scott *Rob Roy* xxi, The hour of twelve o'clock swung its summons over the city from the belfry. **1852** Rock *Ch. of Fathers* III. ix. 294 The bells in every church steeple swung forth their peals of gladsomeness.

d. To lift and transport (something suspended), as with a crane; *transf.* to convey or transport from point to point.

1856 Emerson *Eng. Traits, Stonehenge* Wks. (Bohn) II. 126 Men..swinging a block of granite..with an ordinary derrick. **1862** H. Kingsley *Ravenshoe* li, Who could tire,.. at the strange dim vista of swinging horses between decks? **18..** *Jrnl. Mil. Service Inst. U.S.* X. 588 (Cent. Dict.) By means of the railroad, troops can be swung across from bay to bay as the exigencies of the war may require.

e. *refl.* To hoist oneself up or transport oneself from point to point by grasping a support above. Also *intr.*

1899 Crockett *Black Douglas* i, The young man..swung lightly off his charger. *Ibid.* ii, The Douglas swung himself into the saddle. **1902** Violet Jacob *Sheep-Stealers* xi, Putting his foot on the axle and swinging himself up. **1907** J. H. Patterson *Man-Eaters of Tsavo* xii. 133 All kinds of monkeys chatter..overhead as they swing themselves from branch to branch.

8. *intr.* To be suspended from a support above (without necessarily implying oscillation).

a. *spec.* To be hanged; to suffer death by hanging. *slang* or *colloq.*

1542 Udall *Erasm. Apoph.* 122 Diogenes..had a great zele..to see theim euery one swyngyng & tottreyng in halters. **1592** Nashe *P. Penilesse* (ed. 2) 10 What pennance can be greater for Pride, than to let it swinge in hys owne halter? **1725** *New Cant. Dict., To Swing*, to hang. **1728** [De Foe] *Street-Robberies* 8 They all lovingly swung together at Execution-Dock. **1841** Dickens *Barn. Rudge* lxii, It is..a choice between his life and death. If you refuse, he swings. **1884** 'Edna Lyall' *We Two* xl, I don't wish any man to swing for me—I have always disapproved of the death-penalty.

b. *gen.* To be suspended, to hang; *transf.* to appear as if suspended (= hang *v.* 12). Also *fig.* (*swing from*, to depend or 'hinge' on).

1641 Tatham *Distracted State* v. i, *Agath.* And now you see the Pinacle from which You must be tumbled down, away with him... *Fellow.* If you please to walk that way you may see Oleander swinging for his life. **1781** Cowper *Charity* 615 His Budget, often filled, yet always poor, Might swing at ease behind his study door. **1829** Scott *Anne of G.* xxiii, 'Yonder swings the Flying Stag', said Ital, pointing to an immense sign. **1859** Tennyson *Marr. Geraint* 170 A purple scarf at either end whereof There swung an apple of the purest gold. **1867** Augusta Wilson *Vashti* xix, In the west, where a waning moon swung on the edge of the distant misty hills. **1888** G. A. Smith *Isaiah* xiii. (1891) 229 As this one [word] is obscure in its English guise, and the passage really swings from it, we may devote a paragraph to its meaning. **1898** Rider Haggard *Dr. Therne* i. 14 A lantern swung from the roof of the coach.

9. *trans.* To hang, suspend; *rarely*, to hang (a person), put to death by hanging (*slang* or *colloq.*).

1528 More *Dyaloge* III. xi. (1529) 82b, In the tother [wallet] he layeth vp all hys owne and swyngeth yt at hys backe. **1811** *Regul. & Orders Army* 249 The Men's Hammocks must be swung regularly by Companies. **1816** 'Quiz' *Grand Master* VII. 202 Had he the pow'r he'd change the case, And swing some col'nels in their place. **1848** Lytton *K. Arthur* I. xliii, A slender draw-bridge, swung from brink to brink. **1860** *All Year Round* No. 73. 550 The heavy vehicle so ill swung,..as springless as an artillery tumbril. **1911** Max Beerbohm *Zuleika Dobson* v. 61 You would be driven to Court in my state-coach. It is swung so high that the streetsters can hardly see its occupant.

b. To strain (the back of a horse): = sway *v.* 5 b.

1844 H. Stephens *Bk. Farm* III. 1258 If she [*sc.* a mare] ..has met with an accident, such as having swung her back.

10. *intr.* To oscillate (without suspension); to move to and fro, or from side to side; to sway; to hover; *spec.* to sway the body backward and forward in rowing.

1607 Chapman *Bussy d'Ambois* v. I j, Not so the surges of the euxine Sea..Swell being enrag'd,..As Fortune swings about the restlesse state Of vertue. **1712** Arbuthnot *John Bull* II. iv. 17 If the Coach swung but the least to one side, she used to shriek so loud, that all the Street concluded she was overturn'd. **1828** Wordsw. *Power of Sound* x, While Fauns and Satyrs beat the ground In cadence,—and Silenus swang This way and that, with wild-flowers crowned. **1860** Tyndall *Glac.* I. xv. 101 A single hawk swung in the atmosphere above us. **1879** *Oxf. & Camb. Undergrad. Jrnl.* 13 Mar. 292/2 Prest is getting more and more used to the boat, but he still swings short and stiffly.

11. To turn in alternate directions, or in either direction (usually horizontally), around a fixed axis or point of support; *spec. Naut.* said of a vessel riding at a single anchor or moored by the head, and turning with the wind or tide. Also with *to*, *open*, *wide*, etc.

1769 Falconer *Dict. Marine* (1780), *To Swing*, to turn round the anchors, or moorings, at the change of the wind, or tide. **1812** J. Wilson *Isle of Palms* III. 929 While safely she at anchor swings. **1819** Shelley *Cenci* IV. ii. 41 It is the iron gate, Which ye left open, swinging to the wind. **1860** A. Cumming in *Merc. Marine Mag.* VII. 102 Let them..swing to one anchor. **1863** Reade *Hard Cash* xx, But in the middle of the joyous whirl, Julia's quick ear on the watch all the time, heard the gate swing to. **1892** Greener *Breech Loader* 215 The shot will..fly in that direction in which the gun was swinging when the charge of shot left the muzzle. **1892** Gunter *Miss Dividends* (1893) 33 He swings around suddenly and quickly to see who interrupts him.

b. To go along or round in a curve or with a sweeping motion; to wheel, sweep.

1810 Scott *Lady of L.* I. xx, So forth the startled swan would swing. **1853** Kingsley *Hypatia* xxii, A choir of nymphs swung round him hand in hand. **1856** Miss Warner *Hills Shatemuc* xxxv, With wind and headway the sloop gently swang up to her appointed place. **1865** Kingsley *Herew.* xv, In marched Hereward and all his men, and swung round through the gateway into the court. **1914** *Times* 8 Sept. 9/1 The battle line proceeds due east to Sézanne and Vitry-le-François, and then swings north-east round the plain of Châlons to the fortress of Verdun.

c. *to swing around the circle*, to make a political tour of a constituency or larger area. *U.S.*

1866 E. McPherson *Polit. Man.* v. 58 We swing around the circle of the Union with a fixed and unalterable determination to stand by it. **1871** G. W. Peck *Adventures Terence McGrant* iv. 27 Until me Cousin Ulissis gets through swinging around the circle. **1887** *Chicago Tribune* 2 Oct., President Andrew Johnson originated the phrase 'swinging round the circle' on the occasion of his famous tour to Chicago..in September, 1866. **1910** *N.Y. Evening Post* 29 Oct. 2 To stem the rising tide against him, Col. Roosevelt is to swing around the circle in Brooklyn to-night.

d. *Cricket.* Of a bowler: to impart swing to the ball on delivery. Also with the ball as subj. Cf. swing *sb.*[2] 8 g.

1900 P. F. Warner *Cricket in Many Climes* 84 Morton.. has a beautiful natural action, and swings in the air with his arm. *Ibid.* 179 Rowe..has, too, a very good fast 'yorker' which swings in the air. **1952** *M.C.C. Cricket Coaching Bk.* ii. 37 The farther up the ball is pitched, the more 'room' it has in which to swing. **1977** *World of Cricket Monthly* June 30/1 Bowling medium-pace, he got the ball to swing in the heavy atmosphere.

e. Of a spacecraft: to pass *by* a planet using its gravitational field to change course.

1967 [implied in *swing-by* s.v. swing- 2 a]. **1970** *Nature* 1 Aug. 434/2 The spacecraft will be launched in the autumn of 1973, swinging by Venus at a distance of 3,000 miles. **1976** *Sci. Amer.* May 116/2 These two spacecraft are scheduled to be launched in 1977 and to swing by Jupiter in 1979.

12. *trans.* To cause to turn in alternate directions, or in either direction, on or as on an axis or pivot; to turn or cause to face in another direction.

1768 Tucker *Lt. Nat.* I. xxii. 114 The boy who wished to be a king that he might have an officer appointed to swing him all day long upon a gate. **1783** Cowper *Epit. Hare* 24 To skip and gambol like a hare And swing his rump around. **1784** —— *Ep. Jos. Hill* 21 Swinging the parlour-door upon its hinge. **1818** Scott *Br. Lamm.* x, Ae leaf of the muckle gate has been swung to wi' yestreen's wind. **1883** *Harper's Mag.* Jan. 284/1 What maddening whirls when he called, 'Swing partners!' **1887** *Field* 19 Feb. 223/2 A good practical exponent of 'the art of shooting flying' states..that he never met with a first-rate shot who 'swings' his gun—*i.e.* keeps it moving in the direction of the bird's flight. **1890** 'R. Boldrewood' *Miner's Right* vi. I. 139 The base line is altered or 'swung', *i.e.* freshly marked on another imaginary course. **1892** E. Gosse *Secr. Narcisse* iii. 80 As he was about to turn towards the window, Rosalie swang herself violently back.

b. *Naut.* To turn (a ship) to all points in succession, in order to ascertain the deviation of her magnetic compass.

1859 in *Merc. Marine Mag.* (1860) VII. 49 The necessity of having all iron steamships..swung, in order to ascertain the deviation of their compasses. **1877** Spry *Cruise H.M.S. Challenger* x. (1878) 176 Some hours were spent swinging for magnetical purposes.

c. To drive or cause to move in a curve; also, to make or execute by moving in a curve (in phr. *to swing a cast*, in hunting: see cast *sb.* 41).

1819 J. G. Lockhart *Peter's Letters* (ed. 2) III. lxix. 203 The balls..being swung to and fro in a terrific manner, by means of long queues with elastic shafts. **1854** R. S. Surtees *Handley Cr.* li, The hounds dash towards the fence beyond, and swing their cast without a whimper. **1889** Gunter *That Frenchman* v. 46 He swings his team into the Avenue de l'Impératrice. **1897** *Outing* (U.S.) XXX. 127/1 The dogs have changed direction by the left flank... We swing them, make a short cut through a bit of brush.

d. In fig. phr. *to swing it on* or *across* (someone) = *to put it across* s.v. put *v.*[1] 36 a (*b*).

1923 *Daily Mail* 16 June 11 Too experienced to let even a thundering smart girl swing it on him as easily as that. **1943** N. Marsh *Colour Scheme* iv. 64 You saw Questing swing it across me. **1950** T. E. Lawrence *Mint* 39 'Swinging it on the..rookies, they are, the old sweats' grumbled Tug.

e. *to swing the gate* (see quot. 1933). Cf. drag *v.* 9 b and *swing-gate* s.v. swing- 2 a. *Austral.* and *N.Z. slang.*

1933 L. G. D. Acland in *Press* (Christchurch, N.Z.) 16 Dec. 21/8 *Swing the gate*, to be the fastest shearer in the shed. **1941** [see drag *v.* 9 b]. **1965** J. S. Gunn *Terminol. Shearing Industry* II. 12 A ringer is..said to 'swing the gate', presumably because he keeps the catching-pen gate swinging.

f. To turn a starting-handle in order to start (a motor vehicle, its engine). Also with *over*. *colloq.*

1927 R. Lehmann *Dusty Answer* III. 164 It took ten minutes to get the car started, with Martin and Roddy madly swinging her by turns. *a* **1938** in T. E. Lawrence *Lett.* (1938) 495 S[haw] was asked to swing the car for the old boy. **1957** L. F. R. Williams *State of Israel* iv. 42 Two men break off for a moment from swinging the engine of a tractor. **1977** *Daily Tel.* 12 Jan. 10/2 Attempting to 'swing over' modern high-compression engines would tax the strength of all but the most muscular.

g. *Cricket.* Of a bowler: to bowl (the ball) with swing. Cf. swing *sb.*[2] 8 g.

1948 [see *seam bowler* s.v. seam *sb.*[1] 10].

13. *intr.* To go along with undulating or swaying movement, or in a vigorous manner; to walk with swinging step. (See also swinging *ppl. a.* 3.)

1854 R. S. Surtees *Handley Cr.* lxii, Pulling up at the door of the Turtle Doves Hotel, he threw himself carelessly off the half cover-hack..and..swung into the hall with a noisy flourish. **1884** W. Black in *Harper's Mag.* Dec. 30/2 The coach swings along pleasantly. **1894** J. A. Steuart *In Day of Battle* xviii, The camels, swinging at a steady trot.

14. *trans. fig.* To direct or control the movement or action of; to sway; to wield. *U.S.*

1889 *Voice* (N.Y.) 2 May, The rum wing purposes swinging the party. The temperance innocents will have to submit or step out. **1890** 'Mark Twain' in *Pall Mall G.* 10 Sept. 3/2 His great charm to me is the way he swings nervous English! **1908** U. Sinclair *Money-Changers* ii. 35 He can swing the market so as to break a man.

b. To bring (something uncertain) about; to contrive or manage; to 'wangle'. Freq. with *it*. *colloq.*

1934 E. Pound *Let.* 7 Jan. (1971) 250 A guy named Collis. .. Wants me to edit a mag again. I have replied that..I wd. edit an annual... If he swings it, I shd. want to see a batch of yr. mss. in say about 6 months' time. **1937** Wodehouse *Summer Moonshine* (1938) i. 14 'The idea is to get him to trim the thing a little.' 'How do you expect to swing that?' **1941** B. Schulberg *What makes Sammy Run?* vi. 104 And Julian actually has a real job?.. How the hell did you swing it? **1955** 'J. Christopher' *Year of Comet* ii. 77 I'm not promising anything, but there's a chance I may be able to swing something useful there. **1962** 'K. Orvis' *Damned & Destroyed* x. 71 Phil had gotten himself a white nest-egg. Now how..could a half-broke addict-musician have swung that? **1975** M. Bradbury *History Man* viii. 138 You can't con me, but you might swing it with someone else.

15. a. To fix (the work) on the centre or centres in a lathe. **b.** Of a lathe: To have a 'swing' or capacity of (so much): see swing *sb.*[2] 8 d.

1884 F. J. Britten *Watch & Clockm.* 201 The work is 'swung' or arranged so as to yield an unequal pressure in polishing. **1888** Hasluck *Model Engin. Handybk.* (1900) 22 Three inch centres—that is, a lathe which swings six inches.

16. a. *Mus. intr.* To play jazz music with swing (see swing *sb.*[2] 10 b). Also, *to swing it*.

[**1918** (*music-title*) Swinging along. **1928** (*music-title*) Swing on the gait.] **1931** (*music-title*) Swing it. **1933** [see get *v.* 70 l]. **1934** *Esquire* Feb. 96/2 This still leaves a comfortable margin of popular acclaim for the boys who couldn't read it, but who, in the parlance of *hot*, knew how to *swing* it. **1935** *Swing Music* Nov.–Dec. 248/2 In the Duke's band the brass section may swing while the rhythm-section and reed-section provide a harmonic..background. **1937** L. Armstrong *Swing that Music* xiii. 114 A lot of Americans in Paris came to hear me swing. **1955** in Shapiro & Hentoff *Hear Me Talkin' to Ya* xviii. 289 Don't let Benny scare you, you're a *piano player*, Johnny—and you *swing*. **1966** T. Pynchon *Crying of Lot 49* iii. 48 The early crowd tends to dig your Radio Cologne sound. Later on we really swing. **1977** J. Wainwright *Do Nothin' till you hear from Me* viii. 125 He sometimes plays pure 'Palm Court'.., and without that extra lift which can make a band swing.

b. *Mus. trans.* To play (a tune) with swing.

1936 (*music-title*) Swingin' them Jingle Bells. **1938** *Times Herald* (Dallas) 1 Apr. III. 11 The Detroit station pull[ed] .. Tommy off the air for 'swinging' Loch Lomond. **1947** *Penguin Music Mag. II* May 28 His instructions in the introduction to the score are that these are to be slightly 'swung', and he admits the influence upon his music of all Negro spirituals. **1954** *Grove's Dict. Music* (ed. 5) 600/2 A score can at most be more or less susceptible to being 'swung'. One band may swing an arrangement while another may play the same arrangement without a touch of swing. **1968** *Blues Unlimited* Nov. 23 The waltz, swung so gently and delicately by the cajuns, is in constant demand.

c. *intr.* To enjoy oneself, have fun, esp. in pursuit of what is considered fashionable or in a manner free of conventional constraints; to be up to date. Also of a place, to provide lively enjoyment.

1957 N. Mailer in *Dissent* Summer 288 Still I am just one cat in a world of cool cats, and everything interesting is crazy, or at least so the Squares who do not know how to swing would say. **1966** *Reporter* 24 Mar. 22/1 Surprising nightlife. Amsterdam *swings*. **1967** *Wall St. Jrnl.* 24 Jan. 30 He has to really swing: Motor-cycle racing, free-fall parachuting, [etc.]. **1975** D. Lodge *Changing Places* ii. 59 Jane Austen and the Theory of Fiction. Professor Morris J. Zapp... 'He makes Austen swing,' was one comment. **1983** *Times* 25 Oct. 10/1 The fashion collections..are supposed to have proved..that 'London swings again'.

d. To engage in (promiscuous) sexual intercourse; *spec.* to advocate or engage in group sex or swapping sexual partners. Also, *to swing both ways*, to enjoy both heterosexual and homosexual relations. *slang.*

1964 W. & J. Breedlove *Swap Clubs* iii. 73 Almost everyone in the group knows one or more couples with which they swing who were not accepted by the recruitment committee. **1970** E. M. BRECHER *Sex Researchers* ix. 251 If only one-tenth of one percent of married couples (one couple in a thousand) swing, however, the total still adds up to some 45,000 swinging American couples. **1972** J. G. VERMANDEL *Last seen in Samarra* xxii. 153 As for the mystery that still surrounded Robin Aseltine's death, the police had picked up and questioned several former girl and boy friends, Robin having been found to swing both ways.

e. Of a party: to go with a swing (see SWING *sb.*[2] 6f). *colloq.*

[**1963** *Amer. Speech* XXXVIII. 171 [Kansas University slang.] A particularly rough and noisy party..*swinger*.] **1975** D. LODGE *Changing Places* ii. 87 The party's beginning to swing. **1978** J. ANDERSON *Angel of Death* xii. 128 They were trying hard to make the party swing, but..there seemed a forced air about the revelry.

†**swing**, *v.*[2] *Obs.* Pa. t. 3 **swang**, 4 **swange**, **swong**. [OE. *swingan*, corresp. in form and meaning to SWING *sb.*[1], and so ultimately identical with SWING *v.*[1]] *intr.* To labour, toil; = SWINK *v.* 1.

c **1000** ÆLFRIC *Exod.* xviii. 14 Hwæt dest þu on þis folce? hwi swingst þu ana? *c* **1000** *Ags. Ps.* (Spelman) cxxvi[i]. 1 Buton drihten timbriende hus on ydel swingað ða ðe timbriað hi. *c* **1275** LAY. 7488 He swang [*c* 1205 swonc] in þan fihte, þat he leþerede a swote. **13..** *E.E. Allit. P.* A. 586 þat swange & swat for long ȝore. **13..** *Guy Warw.* (A.) 3589 Herhaud þat day so sore swong, þat þurch his mouþe þe fom it sprong. *c* **1480** HENRYSON *Mor. Fab., Wolf & Lamb* xx, His seruand nor his self may not be spaird To swing and sweit, withouttin Meit or wage.

†**swing**, *adv. Obs. rare*[−1]. In 5 **swingge**. [Stem of SWING *v.*[1]] With a sudden blow or impact; 'slap'.

c **1400** *St. Alexius* (Laud 108) 443 As man þat hadde deþes wounde He fel swingge doun to grounde.

swing- in combination.

1. In general attrib. or adj. use (mostly without hyphen, as a separate word). **a.** Applied to a piece of mechanism, apparatus, or utensil suspended, hinged, or pivoted so as to be capable of oscillating or turning to and fro: = SWINGING *ppl. a.* 1, 2. (See also 2.)

1791 *Rep. Comm. Thames-Isis Navig.* 15 At the lower End of this Channel there is a Pen formed by a Swing Stride and Flood Gates. **1828** P. CUNNINGHAM *N.S. Wales* (ed. 3) II. 213 Swing stoves and charcoal put on board, to carry about into the damp corners. **1833** LOUDON *Encycl. Archit.* §1112 Centre point, or swing hinges, appear to be of two kinds. **1843** HOLTZAPFFEL *Turning* I. 257 The whole load is quickly immersed by a swing crane into a tank of water about five feet deep. **1855** LEIFCHILD *Cornwall* 257 The miners worked in a swing stage, which they dropped against such parts of the side as they intended to take away. **1858** SIMMONDS *Dict. Trade*, *Swing Tea-kettle*, a kettle on a stand for table use, moving on pivots. **1869** RANKINE *Machine & Hand-tools* Pl. 02, The shaft, v, which is supported by fixed bearings, K, and the swing or movable bearings. **1885** LADY BRASSEY *The Trades* 379 The perpetual rolling and tossing of the vessel had warned us that in all probability the maximum clinometrical angle of the swing-table would ere long be reached. **1888** *Lockwood's Dict. Terms Mech. Engin.* 363 *Swing Table*, the table of a drilling machine which is made to swing or swivel around the central pillar..in order to bring any desired portion of the work underneath the drill. **1909** 'Q' *True Tilda* xix, A swing-lamp shone down upon a white-covered table.

b. = SWINGING *ppl. a.* 3. *rare.*

1809 W. IRVING *Knickerb.* III. ix. (1861) 112 He proceeded on a long swing trot through the muddy lanes of the metropolis. **1863** TREVELYAN *Compet. Wallah* (1866) 95 Going the whole way at a swing trot.

c. With advbs. forming attrib. phrases in sense 'that swings in the direction specified', as (hyphened) ***swing-away***, ***-down***, ***-out***. See also sense 2a below.

1965 *Wireless World* July 3 (Advt.), Swing-away, lift-off mounting (optional). **1949** *Archit. Rev.* CV. 241 A slightly less conventional example is the swing-down metal wash-basin with which the Viking is equipped. **1977** *Times* 29 Apr. 13/4 There are 156 A class cabins each with two sofa beds, swing-down bunks, lavatory and shower. **1967** K. M. SMITH *Insect Virol.* v. 103 In this gradient a discrete band was obtained after 60 minutes centrifugation in a swing-out (Spinco SW25) head at 24,000 rpm.

2. a. Special Combinations: **swing-back**, (*a*) the back of a photographic camera, carrying the sensitized plate, arranged so as to be 'swung' or turned on a hinge or pivot into any required position; (*b*) the backward swing of a body, weapon, etc.; back-swing; (*c*) a movement of reaction to(wards) a previous state; (*d*) applied *attrib.* to a style of coat or jacket cut to swing as the wearer moves; **swingball**, a game of table-skittles in which a suspended ball is thrown to hit the skittles on the return pass; also (*U.S.*), a larger-scale version of the game played in a doorway; see also quot. 1980; **swing-bar**, a bar arranged to turn on a pivot; *spec.* a swingletree; **swing-beam**, a beam arranged to turn, or to enable something to turn, on a pivot or the like (see quots.); **swing-bed**, a movable stool-bed in a gun-carriage; also attrib., as ***swing-bed-plate***; **swing-boat**, a boat-shaped swing used for amusement at fairs, etc.; **swing bowler** *Cricket*, a bowler who makes the ball swing; also **swing bowling**; **swing-bridge**, a form of drawbridge which turns horizontally on a pivot (either at one end or in the centre); **swing-by**, a change of course made by a spacecraft by using a planet's gravitational field (see also quot. 1967); **swing-cart**, a cart 'swung' or suspended on springs, a spring-cart; **swing-chair**, a rocking-chair; **swing-coat**, a fashionable coat cut to give a swinging motion when the wearer moves (cf. *swing-back* (*d*) above); **swing-door**, a door constructed to swing to or shut of itself; *pl.* a door made in two leaves, which are hung separately and furnished with springs that bring them back to meet in the middle when pushed open in any direction; **swing-front**, in a photographic camera (cf. *swing-back*); **swing-gate**, a gate constructed to swing to or shut of itself; *spec.* a form of this used in Australia for drafting sheep; **swing-glass**, a looking-glass suspended on pivots; **swing hand** *Bridge*, a hand which proves to be decisive for a team in the overall result of a rubber or match; **swing-handle**, a handle turning on pivots, esp. such an arched handle of a basket, pail, etc.; **swing-jack** (JACK *sb.*[1] 10), see quot.; **swing-jointed** *a.*, jointed so as to turn to and fro on a pivot; **swing label** = *swing ticket* below; **swing man**, (*a*) *U.S.* = SWING *sb.*[2] 12e; (*b*) *Mus.*, a jazz musician who plays swing music (see also sense 2d below); (*c*) *U.S. Sports slang*, a versatile player who can play effectively in different positions; (*d*) *slang*, a drug pedlar; **swing mirror** = *swing-glass*; **swing needle**, a sewing-machine needle which can move sideways to the direction of work to accomodate another needle or to form zigzag or patterned stitches; freq. *attrib.*; **swing-over**, a change to a contrastive state or opinion; **swing pass** *U.S. Football*, a short pass to a back running to the outside; **swing-plough** (cf. G. *schwingpflug*), a plough without wheels; **swing room** *U.S.*, a room in which employees may relax while (temporarily) off duty; **swing-round**, a striking change or reversal of direction (in quots., *fig.*); **swing set**, a set of children's play equipment, including one or more swings, supported by a rigid frame; **swing-shift** *U.S.*, a work shift between the standard day and night shifts, esp. from the afternoon to late evening; applied to other irregular shift arrangements; **swing-stoppered** *a.*, applied to a bottle whose stopper is clamped in place by a wire mechanism about the bottle-neck; **swing-tail**, †(*a*) a long tail that swings about; also *attrib.* having a sweeping tail or train; (*b*) *Aeronaut.*, a hinged rear section of a fuselage which can be swung to one side to facilitate the loading of large items of cargo; freq. *attrib.*; **swing-tailed** *a.*, having a long swinging tail; **swing-tap**, a tap constructed to turn horizontally on the supply-pipe and thus open or close the valve as required; **swing-ticket**, a tag or label which carries a guarantee or other information, and hangs loosely from the article to which it is attached; **swing-tool** (see quot. 1875); **swing vote(r)** *U.S.*, the independent vote(r) that often decisively influences the result of a poll; also, a casting voter; **swing-wheel**, the escape-wheel of a clock, which drives the pendulum; also, the balance-wheel of a watch; also *attrib.*; **swing wing**, an aircraft wing whose sweep can be increased at high speeds to delay the development of shock waves and decreased at low speeds to provide more lift; freq. *attrib.* (with hyphen); cf. *variable sweep*. See also SWING-ROPE, etc.

1862 *Catal. Internat. Exhib., Brit.* II. No. 3064, Portrait Camera, and lens with *swing back. **1878** ABNEY *Photogr.* xxxiii. 269 A fair general focus can..be obtained by using with the camera a vertically-pivoted swing-back. **1890** H. G. HUTCHINSON et al. *Golf* iv. 98 It is an effect of stretching after an artificially long swing back. **1924** *Public Opinion* 4 July 16/2 The swing-back to biblicism appears as an accomplished fact. **1945** *N.Y. Times* 12 Aug. IV. 6/2 Legislation will be necessary to tide over those men who are unemployed while the gigantic swing-back to peacetime industry is being accomplished. **1952** W. CUNNINGTON *Eng. Women's Clothes in Present Cent.* viii. 280 Coats were swing-back, flared or tiered [in 1945]. **1972** *Daily Tel.* 1 Mar. 5/1 The firm has charted a remarkable swing-back among its African personnel from rejection to timid acceptance. **1973** *Country Life* 15 Mar. 723/1 Swing-back jacket in showerproof Terylene/cotton twill. **1935** *Popular Mechanics* Dec. 925 (*heading*) '*Swing Ball' table top action game of skill. **1955** D. A. HINDMAN *Handbk. Indoor Games & Stunts* xii. 188 *Swingball bowling...* The player takes the ball and carries it any desired distance away from the doorway. **1977** *Sci. Amer.* Dec. 39/2 They range from simple board games [to]..indoor versions of miniature golf, swingball bowling (the ball is tethered to the top of a doorframe). **1980** *Trade Marks Jrnl.* 23 July 1316/2 Swingball... Games (other than ordinary playing cards) and playthings incorporating the use of balls. Dunlop Holdings Limited,..London, SW1Y 6PX; a holding company. **1844** H. STEPHENS *Bk. Farm* II. 293 These studs are inserted into a *swing-bar that can be bolted to the horizontal rails of the framing, in such position as will bring the intermediate wheels into proper pitch with the principals. **1852** BURN *Naval & Milit. Dict.* (1863), Swing bar or *beam of a rocket frame. **1857** P. COLQUHOUN *Comp. 'Oarsman's Guide'* 32 The swing beams are the long beams running along the [lock-]gates, by which they are pushed open. **1875** KNIGHT *Dict. Mech.*, *Swing-beam.* 1. (*Railway Engineering.*) A cross-piece suspended from the truck, and sustaining the car-body, so that it may have independent lateral motion. 2. (*Carpentry.*) A cross-beam supporting an over-head mow in a barn. **1852** BURN *Naval & Milit. Dict.* (1863), *Swing bed of a field gun. **1861** MAYHEW *Lond. Labour* III. 107/2 All the caravans and *swing-boats, and what not, used to assemble there. **1958** *Times* 11 Nov. 15/2 He made an uppish defensive shot against medium-paced *swing bowler, Strauss. **1953** *Times* 27 Aug. 3/7 Wind tunnel experiments at this university have shown that spin plays only a secondary part in *swing bowling. **1963** A. ROSS *Australia* 63 iii. 87 This was swing bowling of the kind Statham does not often manage. **1791** *Estimate Works Thames-Isis Navig.* 3 At Duxford Wear, a *Swing-Bridge for Towing-Horses, and Fence-Gates. **1898** W. W. JACOBS *Sea Urchins, Grey Parrot* (1906) 213 The gangway was shipped, and..the *Curlew* drifted slowly away from the quay and headed for the swing bridge slowly opening in front of her. **1967** *Britannica Bk. of Year 1966* 804/3 **Swing-by*, an interplanetary mission in which a space vehicle utilizes the gravitational field of a planet near which it passes for changing course (a *swing-by* through the gravitational field of Venus on the way to Mars). **1970** *Nature* 1 Aug. 434/2 The next opportunity to make a similar swing-by flight to Mercury will not occur until 1982. **1796** H. HUNTER *London* (1811) II. 107 Raspberries, which are raised chiefly for the use of the distillers, and conveyed to London in *swing carts. **1833** LOUDON *Encycl. Archit.* §697 A *swing chair, formed out of ten pieces of elder tree. **1900** ELINOR GLYN *Visits Elizabeth* (1906) 18 She was lying in a swing chair, showing lots of petticoat and ankle. **1935** *Times* 4 Nov. 7/1 There is a new flat *swing-coat in shower-proof Llamavel curl. **1939** *Country Life* 11 Feb. p. xxxvii/2 (Advt.), The three-quarter 'swing' coat of dyed baby sealskin obtainable in black, brown, or cafe. **1833** LOUDON *Encycl. Archit.* §765 The use of the *swing door..is to prevent the door from ever being left open in severe weather. **1863** MISS BRADDON *J. Marchmont* I. i. 23 He was gone, and the swing-door slammed in Edward Arundel's face. **1895** P. HEMINGWAY *Out of Egypt* I. i. 3 As the waiters pushed aside the swing-doors of the buffet. **1892** *Photogr. Ann.* II. 884 The wide angle lens is attached to the *swing front ready for work. **1774** *Garton Inclos. Act* 5 No *swing-gates or other gates shall at any time be suffered. **1805** R. W. DICKSON *Pract. Agric.* I. 143 In the construction of the swing-gate, the bars are so long, that too much weight is often thrown upon the hinges. **1878** E. S. ELWELL *Boy Colonists* 214 This was something like a 'race' for drafting sheep, with a swing gate. **1890** 'R. BOLDREWOOD' *Squatter's Dream* ix. 91 Mr. Stangrove..has no more idea of a swing-gate than a shearing-machine. **1809** R. LANGFORD *Introd. Trade* 81 A Dressing Table, and a *Swing Glass..£2 10s. **1847** DISRAELI *Tancred* II. vii, She threw a glance at her swing-glass. **1960** T. REESE *Play Bridge with Reese* x. 41 Playing in a team-of-four match against strong opponents, I pick up this *swing hand. **1891** *Cent. Dict.*, *Swing-handle. **1896** *Jrnl. R. Horticult. Soc.* Nov. 202 All fruit should be carefully placed in the basket (which is preferable lined or padded, and if with a swing-handle all the better). **1875** KNIGHT *Dict. Mech.*, **Swing-jack*, a jack for replacing cars on the track; the bottom of the standard is a cylindrical segment, and has a toe working in a slot in the base of the jack. A pair are used, and the car being lifted while the standards are vertical, the latter are canted to or swung over, bringing the wheels of the car in line with the rails. **1844** H. STEPHENS *Bk. Farm* II. 595 The marker *mn* is another appendage to the [drill sowing-]machine... It consists of the bar *mm*, and the marking-rod *mn*. The latter is *swing-jointed on a stud fixed in the ends of the marker-bar *mm*. **1968** J. IRONSIDE *Fashion Alphabet* 100 **Swing label*, the cardboard label hanging from a garment giving name of manufacturer, size, price, etc. **1903** A. ADAMS *Log of Cowboy* iii. 20 The herd trailed along behind the leaders..guarded by outriders, known as *swing men. **1936** *Delineator* CXXIX. 10/3 There have been many other great *swingmen* whose names have become tradition. **1957** D. HAGUE in S. Traill *Concerning Jazz* 123 Many years ago the best alto player among the swingmen was Johnny Hodges—and to-day he is still tops! **1969** *Daily Progress* (Charlottesville, Va.) 6 Aug. A6/1 As the swingman last year the former Lane High All-Stater was used as a replacement for either of the Browns' starting offensive guards. **1972** T. A. BULMAN *Kamloops Cattlemen* xii. 72 Another rider, called the swing man, cut in about the middle of the bunch. **1972** *Sunday Sun* (Brisbane) 2 July 14/2 Now he [drug supplier] is called the connection, the bagman, the swing man, the dealer. **1973** J. WAINWRIGHT *High-Class Kill* 157 Tell us about all the dope he pushed... He was taking from *his* swingman. **1930** *Heal & Son Catal.: Matter of Taste in Furnit.* (1972) 11 Toilet Table with two drawers and oval *swing mirror. **1978** *Cornish Guardian* 27 Apr. 10/4 (Advt.), Mahogany swing mirror. **1954** M. B. PICKEN *Singer Sewing Bk.* (ed. 2) 246/1 The twin needles provided for the *Swing Needle Machine allow you to do beautiful double stitching, using two different-colour threads. **1959** R. P. GILES *Needlework* i. 6 The more recently introduced swing needle machines..are able to stitch automatically many embroidery stitches. **1961** *Observer* 28 May 33/1 Swing-needle (zigzag) machines.. range from £50 upwards. **1927** *Daily Tel.* 1 Nov. 13/5 Harden was twitted with the violence of his *swing-over. **1977** G. CLARK *World Prehistory* (ed. 3) II. 56 The most striking change in respect of animals was a swing-over from heavy emphasis on gazelle to sheep and goat. **1960** *Washington Post* 3 Jan. C4/2 They prattle knowingly of splits and gaps,..of flare passes and *swing passes. **1979** *Tucson* (Arizona) *Citizen* 20 Sept. 1D/1 The hardest thing on a linebacker is the swing pass. **1733** W. ELLIS *Chiltern & Vale Farm.* 309 The Foot Plough, the Kentish Broad-board Plough, the Creeper, and the *Swing Plough. **1807** A. YOUNG *Agric. Essex* (1813) I. 127 In favour of the swing-plough it is contended that it is better calculated for fallowing, as the soil can be broken up to a greater depth. **1846** MCCULLOCH *Acc. Brit. Empire* (1854) I. 147 The Scotch, or swing-plough, drawn by 2 horses driven by the ploughman. **1917** D. C. ROPER *U.S. Post Office* xxv. 291 The modern '*swing' rooms of many large post offices.. have been made ideal club rooms. **1973** 'E. MCBAIN' *Hail to Chief* iv. 56 Patrolman Gomez.. was watching television in the swing room on the ground floor. **1940** W. EMPSON *Gathering Storm* 71 The *swing-round of the Trade Unions to rearmament. **1959** *Times* 16 Jan. 14/6 (*heading*) Swing-round in Paris markets. **1951** *Sears, Roebuck & Co. Catal.* Spring and Summer 958/2, 3-Stunt *Swing Set. Non-tilt enameled wood swing seat.. wood trapeze bar.. metal trapeze rings, wood grips. **1978** J. IRVING *World according to Garp* xii. 230, I can travel across lawns, over porches, through swing sets. **1943** *Sun* (Baltimore) 26 Mar. 1/5 (*heading*) *Swing-shift workers cross border for 15-cent highballs after California bars close. **1974** *Spartanburg* (S. Carolina) *Herald-Jrnl.* 20 Apr. B5/1 (Advt.), Baby sitter.. needed for swing shift in Pacolet area. [**1957** *Encycl. Brit.* I. 225/1 Swing lever stoppered bottles.] **1972** E. FLETCHER *Bottle Collecting* iii. 51 In 1894, *swing-stoppered bottles were introduced for sterilized milk. **1683** *Lond. Gaz.* No. 1861/8 One Bay Gelding.. Aged about four years, with a *Swi[n]g Tail lately cut off. **1865** HUNT *Pop. Rom. W. Eng.* I. 274 The squire.. saw the old woman beating her step-daughter.. about the head with the skirt of her swing-tail gown. **1959** *Wall St. Jrnl.* (Eastern ed.) 20 Feb. 12/2 Feature of the cargo planes is a 'swing tail', which permits the whole aft section of the fuselage to swing aside. *Ibid.*, Although there are other aircraft with rear-loading doors, the flight characteristics of the new swing-tail planes would be considerably better. **1963** *Economist* 21 Sept. 1013/2 The swing-tail version of the Bristol Britannia. **1980** *Jane's Encycl. Aviation* II. 370/1 Commercial Forty-Fours.. were built with swing-tails for straight-in loading as CL-44D4s. **1609** BLUNDEVIL *Art of Riding* I. xiii. Div, Ouermuch spurringe wil make him *swing tailed, and speciallye if he be a Gennet, or Turkye horse, whose tayles be alwayes lose and at libertye. **1892** *Photogr. Ann.* II. 466 A galvanised iron cistern.. fitted with nickel-plated *swing tap. **1962** *B.S.I. News* July 10/1 Many of the chromium-plated goods on show carried the now familiar *swing ticket indicating that the chrome conformed to British Standard. **1972** *Times* 27 June 11/4 Size and price can both go on swing tickets. **1846** HOLTZAPFFEL *Turning* II. 849 Various kinds of *swing tools, used by watchmakers in filing and polishing small flat works. **1875** KNIGHT *Dict. Mech.*, *Swing-tool*, a holder which swings on horizontal centers, so as to yield to unequal pressure and keep the plate flat against the face of the file. **1970** *New Yorker* 12 Dec. 63/3 Sellers told him that Fong was one of the *swing votes. **1978** H. KEMELMAN *Thursday Rabbi walked Out* (1979) iii. 21 Blair and Mitchener will vote for it... So that leaves Cunningham. He's the swing vote. **1966** *Economist* 5 Mar. 898/2 He is expected to join Mr Daane as a '*swing voter', leaving Mr Martin with only one conservative colleague. **1696** DERHAM *Artif. Clockm.* i. 4 The Crown-Wheel in Small pieces, and *Swing-Wheel in Royal Pendulums, is that Wheel which drives the Ballance, or Pendulum. **1826** T. REID *Clock & Watch Making* xii. 275 A spring, acting on the pin, brought the nib in a contrary direction, to act on the third wheel teeth, by which it gave motion to the swing-wheel during the time of winding. **1846** HOLTZAPFFEL *Turning* II. 826 Balance-wheel or swing-wheel files, the convex side cut, the angular sides safe. **1965** *New Scientist* 22 Apr. 217/1 One new project in view is the development.. of a *swing-wing aeroplane. **1976** *Farnborough Internat. Exhibition* (Official Programme) 8/1 Swing wings.. permit Tornado to achieve its best performance in all sections of its flight. **1978** G. VIDAL *Kalki* i. 5, I persuaded Boeing to drop the variable-geometry (or swing-wing) aircraft in favor of the fixed delta-shaped wing and tail plane.

b. In designations of the swingle and swingle-tree used in dressing flax.

(Cf. MHG. *swinge-blok*, swingletree, G. *schwingstock*, *schwingbrett*, *schwingmesser*.)

1825 JAMIESON, *Cogster*, the person who, in the act of swingling flax, first breaks it with a swing-bat, and then throws it to another. **1839** URE *Dict. Arts* 486 Two distinct pieces of apparatus belong to it [*sc.* winnowing of flax], namely, the swing-stock and the swing-knife.

c. *Dynamics.* In terms used by Clifford for various geometrical figures or lines having relation to the oscillation of a body, as ***swing-conic, -ellipse, -ellipsoid, -quadric, -radius.***

1887 W. K. CLIFFORD *Elem. Dynamic* I. IV. 17 The second moment of an area in regard to any line, divided by the area itself, is the square of a length which is called the swing-radius of the area in regard to the line, or of the line in regard to the area. *Ibid.* 24, 34.

d. *Mus.* The jazz sense of 'swing' (SWING *sb.*[2] 10 b) used *attrib.* and in *Comb.*, as ***swing band, craze, music,*** etc.; ***swing-minded*** adj.

1933 *Fortune* Aug. 90/3 The best white ensembles usually compromise by playing both *sweet* and *hot* music. This is true of Ben Pollack's excellent *swing* band of Chicago (with Trombonist Teagarden and other crack soloists). **1935** (*title*) Swing music. **1937** L. ARMSTRONG *Swing that Music* xiv. 117 People were beginning now to understand more clearly the difference between a swing orchestra and an ordinary popular orchestra. **1938** *Sat. Even. Post* 7 May 112/2 If any one musician brought about the Swing Age, it is Benny Goodman. **1939** A. HUXLEY *After Many a Summer* I. xiii. 178 Real romance, like in the pictures, with moonlight, and swing music. **1941** *Melody Maker* 12 July 4/2 Which would you say is the most swing-minded provincial town in the British Isles? **1945** KOESTLER *Twilight Bar* 11 The swing-band at the Ritz is also on strike, so they play for them. **1947** R. DE TOLEDANO *Frontiers of Jazz* v. 68 A combination of events set off the 'swing' craze. **1949** L. FEATHER *Inside Be-Bop* i. 3 The swing era brought jazz to the attention of the public in the 1930's. **1952** A. LOMAX *Mister Jelly Roll* 292 Jelly Roll tried to compete with the swing bands. **1956** M. STEARNS *Story of Jazz* (1957) xvi. 189 It was this style, made famous by Benny Goodman and brought to a peak by the Count Basie Band, that characterized the Swing Era. **1968** *Blues Unlimited* Nov. 23 It features a superb vocal with encouragement from someone in the band in the true hot western swing tradition of Bob Wills. **1976** A. MURRAY *Stomping Blues* vii. 107 (*caption*) The Savoy, the most famous ballroom in Harlem during the so-called Swing Era.

3. In *attrib.* or semi-adjectival use.

a. The electoral sense of 'swing' (SWING *sb.*[2] 8 h) applied to a marginal constituency, state, etc.

1964 *Economist* 4 July 44/2 That interesting phenomenon, a 'swing' state. **1974** *Times* 2 Mar. 4/5 The two major parties have very efficient organizations, as would be expected in a swing constituency. **1980** *Washington Post* 19 Oct. A5/5 An effort to improve his chances of carrying the 26 electoral votes of that swing state.

b. Designating a nation that has the capacity to adjust oil production according to demand; also applied to the oil itself.

1973 *Synagogue Light* Sept. 76/2 U.S. Treasury Deputy Secretary William H. Simon has identified Saudi Arabia as the 'swing nation', capable of a huge increase in its oil production. **1975** *Offshore Engineer* Sept. 24/1 Acting as a 'swing producer', Saudi Arabia has absorbed the biggest drop in oil income. **1980** *Times* 5 Feb. 18/2 Oil is the present 'swing' or 'balancing' fuel. Its flexibility of marketing and supply allows it to be easily taken up or cut back according to demand.

swinge (swɪndʒ), *sb.*[1] *Obs.* exc. *dial.* Also 6 swynge, 6–7 swindge. [Related to SWINGE *v.*[1]]

†**1.** Sway, power, rule, authority, influence: esp. ***to have*** or ***bear swinge, the*** (***full, whole, chief***) or ***all the swinge***, etc. *Obs.*

1531 TINDALE *Expos. 1 John* v. 21 (1538) 83 Yf in .x. paryshes rounde ther be not one learned and discrete to helpe the other, then the deuell hath a greate swynge amonge vs, that the byshops officers that dwel so farre of, must abuse vs as they do. **1536** *Rem. Sedition* 16 The euyl be mo in nombre, they bere the swynge. *a* **1548** HALL *Chron., Hen. VI*, 151 She bare the whole swynge, as the strong oxe doth, when he is yoked in the plough with a pore silly asse. **1581** MULCASTER *Positions* xxxvii. (1887) 150 An oligarchie: where some few beare all the swinge. **1585** FETHERSTONE tr. *Calvin on Acts* iv. 33 The Sadduces.. did then beare the chiefe swindge. **1601** J. WHEELER *Treat. Comm.* 37 The Antwerpians.. in all the Marts, & Faires in Dutchland, bare the chiefest swindge. **1612** CHAPMAN *Rev. Bussy d'Ambois* I. i, When Glory, Flatterie, and smooth applauses of things ill Vphold th' inordinate swindge of downe-right power. **1629** MASSINGER *Picture* II. ii. (1630) E 2 b, What wise man.. But must confesse that fortunes swinge is more Ore that profession, then all kinds else Of life pursu'd by man? **1636** —— *Gt. Dk. Florence* II. ii, This is the man that carries The sway, and swinge of the Court.

†**2.** Freedom of action, free scope, licence; liberty to follow one's inclinations: = SWING *sb.*[2] 5. Phr. ***to have*** or ***take one's swinge, to give*** (a person or thing, oneself) ***swinge***. *Obs.*

1542 BOORDE *Dyetary* xvi. (1870) 273 Sensuall appetyde muste haue a swynge, all these thinges notwithstandynge. **1545** ASCHAM *Toxoph.* I. (Arb.) 52 Shooting hath two Tutours.. the one called Daye light, ye other Open place, whyche .ii. keepe shooting from euyl companye, and suffers it not to haue to much swinge. **1575–85** SANDYS *Serm.* viii. §10 Youth they say must haue his swinge. **1597** BEARD *Theatre God's Judgem.* (1612) 272 They giue the full swindge to their bold and violent affections. **1598** CHAPMAN *Iliad* v. [IX.] 617 For whose sake I will lose the raynes, and giue mine anger swindge. **1615** —— *Odyss.* XXII. 597 That then-streight bed Is sowre to that swindge, in which she was bred. **1622** FLETCHER *Span. Cur.* v. ii, I'le have my swindge upon thee. **1631** CHAPMAN *Cæsar & Pompey* II. i. 12, I had able means, And spent all in the swinge of lewd affections. **1668** H. MORE *Div. Dial.* III. xxiii. (1713) 233 By preferring the full swindge of the Animal life before the orderly Pleasures.. of the Divine. **1675** CROWNE *Country Wit* I. i, I am perswaded the bounds of his land have been the utmost extent of his travel; except since his Parents death he has given himself a swinge to some race or fair. **1687** tr. *Sallust* (1692) 8 A savage sort of People, living at their full swinge of Liberty and Licence.

†**b.** ***of, at one's own swinge***: said of a person being entirely his own master. *Obs.*

1536 *St. Papers Hen. VIII*, II. 322 That he shulde rule of his owne swynge, so as noon of us durste advise him to the contrary. **1576** FLEMING *Panopl. Epist.* 290 In his lustie yeares, he is at his own swinge. [**1663** HEATH *Flagellum* 4 His Father dying soon after and leaving him to his swinge.]

†**3.** Impetus, impulse, driving power (of something non-physical, as passion, will, etc.); inclination; drift, tendency. ***of one's own swinge***: of one's own free choice, of one's own accord, spontaneously. *Obs.*

a **1548** HALL *Chron., Hen. VII*, 36 They of their awne swynge pacefied them selfes, and beganne to turne to their .. naturall liege lorde. **1548** UDALL, etc. *Erasmus Par. Matt.* iii. 28 He rushed not furth of his owne swinge to preache. **1552** R. HUTCHINSON *Declar. Christes Supper* iii. (1560) K j b, As long as they folowe the wyld swynge of their youth. *a* **1618** SYLVESTER *Christian's Conflict* 87 The swinge of custome (whirl-wind-like) Rapting my Passion. **1621** HAKEWILL *David's Vow* 105 He goes on with an high hand and a stiffe neck, and is carried with a swinge, as a ship under full saile. **1651** CULPEPPER *Astrol. Judgem. Dis.* (1658) 80 He follows the swinge of the times. *a* **1677** BARROW *Serm.* (1687) I. xi. 144 Ascribing them to the mere conduct and agency of visible causes, hurried by a necessary swindge. **1686** tr. *Chardin's Coronat. Solyman* 86 The great ones following his example give themselves the liberty to follow the swinge of their own Arbitrary Wills. **1804** JEBB in *Knox & Jebb's Corr.* (1834) I. 95 What greater punishment.. can there be, than to be given up, by God, to the swinge of a man's own lusts?

†**4.** Impetus (of motion); impetuous or forcible sweeping or whirling movement. *Obs.*

1583 H. HOWARD *Defensative* L iij b, As we see that barges which are forced by the strength of oares, haue a kinde of gate or swinge when the stroke of dooth cease. **1599** NASHE *Lenten Stuffe* Wks. 1905 III. 164 In the swindge of his trident he constituted two Lord admirals ouer the whole nauy of England. *a* **1600** DELONEY *Canaans Calamitie* 915 The Romaines full of hot reuenge.. Troopt to the Temple, with a mighty swinge. *c* **1600** *Distracted Emp.* IV. i. in Bullen *O. Pl.* (1884) III. 235 A thynks me fallinge & avoyds my Swindge. **1646** SIR T. BROWNE *Pseud. Ep.* To Rdr. a iij b, Whirled on by the swindge and rapt of the one [wheel]. *a* **1661** HOLYDAY *Juvenal* (1673) 247 The swindge or circling motion of the arm in shaking the sistrum. **1696** ALSOP *God in Mount* 9 They have been heaving with all their strength to roll it away, and when they have hoped they were just turning it over,.. it has come upon them with the greater swinge.

†**5.** The lashing (of a tail). *Obs. rare.*

1627 MAY *Lucan* I. 225 When his Tailes swindge has made him hot,.. He [*sc.* a lion] roares from his wide throat. *c* **1640** WALLER *Battle of Summer Isl.* III. 22 The shallow water doth her force infringe, And renders vain her tail's impetuous swinge.

b. *gen.* A stroke, blow. *dial.*

1823 MOOR *Suffolk Words.*

6. A leash for hounds. *Obs.* exc. *dial.*

a **1661** FULLER *Worthies*, *Yorks.* III. (1662) 221 A Gentleman of this County, being to let slip a brace of Grey-hounds, to run for a great wager, so held them in the Swinge, that they were more likely to strangle themselves then kill the Hare. **1895** *E. Angl. Gloss.*, *Swinge*, a leash or couple by which hounds are led.

swinge, *sb.*[2] [f. SWINGE *v.*[2]] A singe.

App. inferred in Dicts. erron. from the foll. passage, where the word is SWING *sb.*[2] 8.

a **1619** FLETCHER, etc. *Q. Corinth* I. i, If to feed Vultures here, after the halter Has done his part, or if there be a Hell, To take a swinge or two there [etc.].

swinge (swɪndʒ), *v.*[1] Also 6 swynge, 6–8 swindge; *pres. pple.* and *ger.* 6–8 swindging, 7 swindgeing, 6– swinging, 7– swingeing. [Later form of ME. SWENGE.]

1. *trans.* To beat, flog, whip, thrash. †Also with *off. arch.* or *dial.*

a **1553** UDALL *Royster D.* II. iv. (Arb.) 38, I will rather haue my cote twentie times swinged, Than on the naughtie wag not to be auenged. **1595** SHAKS. *John* II. i. 288 Saint George that swindg'd the Dragon. **1596** —— *Tam. Shr.* v. ii. 104 If they denie to come, Swinge me them soundly forth vnto their husbands. **1606** HOLLAND *Sueton.* 222 Hee was roiotous, wild and wanton: in so much as his father swindged him well and soundly for it. **1660** H. MORE *Myst. Godl.* III. xiii. 85 These sad Ceremonies they also used in Peru, where they swinged themselves with stinging Nettles, and struck themselves over the shoulders with hard stones. *a* **1700** B. E. *Dict. Cant. Crew*, *I Swing'd him off*, I lay'd on and beat him well-favoredly. **1764** FOOTE *Mayor of G.* I, I would so swinge and leather my lambkin. **1786** BURNS *The Ordination* xi, See, see auld Orthodoxy's faes She's swingein thro' the city. **1828** SCOTT *F.M. Perth* xi, We have swinged them as far as the Abbey-Gate. **1888** DOUGHTY *Trav. Arabia Deserta* II. 232, I swinged him soundly in a moment and made all his back smart.

†**b.** *fig.* To chastise, castigate; to pay out, serve out. *Obs.*

1560 T. WILSON *Rhet.* Prol., Hauyng been thus swinged, and restrained of libertie. **1636** WENTWORTH in Carte *Ormonde* (1735) III. 5 The proof was once clear,.. and he a spirit that will deserve well to be swinged into the knowledge of himself and the duty he owes the state. **1690** DRYDEN *Amphitryon* I. ii, Jupiter can swinge you off, if you swear by him, and are forsworn. **1693** J. DRYDEN in *Dryden's Juvenal* XIV. (1697) 349 This very Rev'rend Leacher.. swinges his own Vices in his Son. **1710** *Dublin Examiner* 26 Dec., The Printer.. brought along with him a Bundle of those Papers, which in the Phrase of Whig Coffee-houses have Swinged off the Examiner. **1711** SWIFT *Jrnl. to Stella* 16 Oct., One Boyer, a French dog, has abused me..: the Secretary promises me to swinge him.

†**c.** ? To pillory (*fig.*). *Obs. rare*[−1].

1546 *Supplic. Poore Commons* (E.E.T.S.) 69 When thei katch any thyng that soundeth to the contrary, it shall not escape so, we warrant you. It shalbe swynged in euery pulpyt wyth, this is the Kynges gratious wyll.

†**d.** To bear heavily upon. *Obs. rare.*

1681 PRIDEAUX *Lett.* (Camden) 96 The innkeeper.. swinged them in their reckoneing most abominably, makeing them pay five times the price for every thing they had.

†**e.** *slang.* = SWIVE. See also quot. *a* 1700.

1622 FLETCHER *Beggar's Bush* III. i, Give her cold jelly To take up her belly, And once a day swinge her again. **1688** MIÈGE *Gt. Fr. Dict.*, To Swinge off,.. *il se dit aussi dans un Sens Venerien*. *a* **1700** B. E. *Dict. Cant. Crew*, *He is Swing'd off*, damnably Clapt.

†**2.** To drink *up* or *off*, 'toss *off*'. *Obs. slang.*

a **1529** SKELTON *E. Rummyng* 568 She swynged vp a quarte At ones. **1570** B. GOOGE *Pop. Kingd.* IV. 48 And cleane they swinge of euery cup. **1649** J. TAYLOR (Water P.) *Wand. West* 7 Mine Host swing'd off halfe a pot to me.

3. To cut down with a scythe. *dial.*

1573 TUSSER *Husb.* (1878) 117 Swinge brembles & brakes. **1854** MISS BAKER *Northampt. Gloss.*, *Swinge*, 2. To cut the nettles, &c. from hedges to make them neat.

†**4.** To brandish, flourish; to lash (the tail, or something with the tail). Also *transf. Obs.*

1591 SYLVESTER *Du Bartas* I. vi. 410 The Lion.. often swindging, with his sinnewy train, Somtimes his sides, somtimes the dusty plain. *Ibid.* vii. 507 Th' Air corrupteth soon, except With sundry winds it oft be swing'd and swept. **1607** [B. BARNES] *Devil's Charter* v. iv. L j b, When I was a Scholler in Padua, faith then I could haue swingd a sword and a buckler. **1629** MILTON *Nativity* xviii, Th' old Dragon under ground.. Swindges the scaly Horrour of his foulded tail.

†**5.** To bear sway over. (After SWINGE *sb.*[1] 1.)

1593 G. HARVEY *Pierce's Super.* 12 Had not affection otherwhiles swinged their reason, where reason should haue swayed their affection.

†**6.** To whirl round (e.g. a wheel). *Obs.*

1548 ELYOT, *Roto*,.. to tourne a thyng lyke a whiele, to swynge about. **1561** T. HOBY tr. *Castiglione's Courtyer* III.

Ffiij, Like a whiele that longe swynged about with violence [etc.]. **1612** SHELTON *Quix.* I. viii. 50 Their Sayles [*sc.* of windmills], that are swinged about by the Winde. **1677** MIÈGE *Dict. Eng. Fr.*, Swinged, or turned about, *roué, tourné en roué*.

†**7.** *intr.* To have free scope or course, to indulge one's inclination. (After SWINGE *sb.*[1] 2.)

1613 CHAPMAN *Rev. Bussy d'Ambois* I. Bj, To what will this declining Kingdome turne, Swindging in euery license [etc.]?

†**8.** In combination with a noun in obj. relation, as **swinge-bow** (see I e); **swinge-buckler** = SWASHBUCKLER. *Obs.*

1579 NORTHBROOKE *Dicing* 25 b, If these and such like lawes were executed iustlie.. there would not be manie.. Blasphemers, & Swinge Bucklers. **1597** SHAKS. *2 Hen. IV*, III. ii. 24 You had not foure such Swindge-bucklers in all the Innes of Court againe. **1675** COTTON *Burlesque upon B.* 83 Is the old Letcher A Swinge-bow of so high renown, A Wench can't sooner take him down?

swinge (swɪndʒ), *v.*[2] Now *dial.* and *U.S.* [? Alteration of SINGE, perh. influenced by SWEAL.] *trans.* To singe, scorch.

1590 SPENSER *F.Q.* I. xi. 26 The scorching flame sore swinged all his face. **1600** SURFLET *Country Farm* I. xxiv. 150 To haue his haire swinged off with straw. **1790** GROSE *Provinc. Gloss.* (ed. 2), *Swinge*, to singe. North. **1844** *Maj. Jones's Courtship* 185 (Bartlett), I don't think I ever did see things jest sprawled out and swinged up so with the sun before. [In various dial. glossaries, northern, west-midland, and south-western.]

† **swingebreech.** *Obs. nonce-wd.* [? f. *swinge*, SWING *v.*[1] + BREECH *sb.* 4.] ? One who struts or flaunts about.

1581 [A. GILBY] *Pleas. Dial. Soldier & Chapl.* M 3. Their [*sc.* the bishops'] pompous trayne of proud idle swinge-breeches, in the steede of Preachers & Schollers.

swingeing, swinging ('swɪndʒɪŋ), *vbl. sb.* [f. SWINGE *v.*[1] + -ING[1].] The action of SWINGE *v.*[1]; scourging, flogging, beating, dealing of blows.

1603 HOLLAND *Plutarch's Mor.* 10 This course of swinging and beating seemeth meete for bondslaves. **1664** BUTLER *Hud.* II. II. 56 Whether it be direct infringing An Oath, if I should wave this swinging. **1844** *Maj. Jones's Courtship* 180 (Bartlett) Go it, old fellow; give the goats a swinging every time you come across them. **1869** BLACKMORE *Lorna D.* ii, To these we paid no heed.., being in the thick of swinging.

swingeing ('swɪndʒɪŋ), *ppl. a.* (*adv.*) Also 6–9 **swinging**, 7–9 **swindging**. [f. SWINGE *v.*[1]]

1. That swinges; scourging, flogging. *rare.*

1614 D. DYKE *Myst. Selfe-Deceiuing* xvii. 229 He tels him of the seuere schoole-master, of the swindging roddes, of the hard feruler. **1618** —— *Two Treat., School of Affliction* 339 The first Schoolemaster is Affliction. A sharp, and seuere and swinging Schoolemaster indeed.

2. Very forcible, great, or large; huge, immense. Chiefly, now only, *colloq.* or *slang*; mostly *arch.* or *dial.* (Cf. *thumping*, *whopping*.)

c **1590** GREENE *Fr. Bacon* xv. 34 May not a man haue a lustie fier there, a pot of good ale, a paire of cardes, a swinging peece of chalke, and a browne toast? **1597** TOFTE *Laura* xiii, Thicke swinging showers. *a* **1600** *Flodden F.* viii. (1664) 80 And swindging swaps made many swelt. **1677** W. HUGHES *Man of Sin* II. vii. 111 Many other of those foolish and childish Penances may be seen in the Author quoted... There is one swinging one, I can't pass over. **1678** DRYDEN *Limberham* V. i, I dream'd.. that a great swinging Thief came in, and whipt 'em out. **1691** MRS. D'ANVERS *Academia* 30, I had a swinging mind to go, And hear the Organs. **1694** MOTTEUX *Rabelais* IV. xii, My Gentleman must pay him such swindging damages, that his acres may bleed for't. **1706** HEARNE *Collect.* 17 Feb. (O.H.S.) I. 187 That Swinging Orthodox G. Burnett Bp. of Sarum. **1711** SWIFT *Jrnl. to Stella* 13 Nov., I.. now have got a swingeing cold. **1748** RICHARDSON *Clarissa* VII. 19 Lady Sarah Sadleir and Lady Betty Lawrance, will also die, and leave me swindging legacies. **1749** FIELDING *Tom Jones* VIII. iii, He hath devoured two swinging butter-toasts this morning for breakfast. **1771** GOLDSM. *Haunch of Venison* 82 At the top a fried liver and bacon were seen; At the bottom was tripe, in a swinging tureen. **1844** DICKENS *Mart. Chuz.* xxviii, To make a swingeing profit. **1857** BORROW *Rom. Rye* xliii, The horse fetched a good swinging price. **1876** R. BRIDGES *Growth of Love* xxvii, Old Leviathan.. Had never rib nor bray nor swindging fan Like his iron swimmer of the Clyde or Tyne. **1904** *Times* (Lit. Supp.) 15 July 218/3 The jury gave swinging damages.

b. as *adv.* Hugely, immensely.

1690 DRYDEN *Amphitryon* I. i, He has sent me to will and require you to make a swinging long night for him. **1706** HEARNE *Collect.* 16 Sept. (O.H.S.) I. 288 A swinging fat Wife. **1711** SWIFT *Jrnl. to Stella* 7 June, At dinner there fell the swingingest long shower. **1810** SCOTT *Lady of L.* VI. v, Our vicar still preaches that Peter and Poule Laid a swinging long curse on the bonny brown bowl. **1836** HALIBURTON *Clockm.* (1862) 20 A swingeing big Pig. **1872** C. D. WARNER *Backlog Studies* 246 Christmas Eve was.. a placid, calm, swingeing cold night.

†**3.** (After SWINGE *sb.*[1] I.) Powerful, authoritative. *Obs.*

1567 TURBERV. tr. *Mantuan's Ecl.* iii. 18, I wote not who doth rule the winds and beares the swinging swaye.

Hence **'swing(e)ingly** *adv.* (*colloq.* or *slang*), very greatly or forcibly, hugely, immensely.

1672 DRYDEN *Assignation* III. iii, I have sin'd swingingly, against my Vow. **1691** SHADWELL *Scowrers* I. i, We drunk swingingly last night. **1703** DE FOE *Misc., Freeholder's Plea* 172 Only we find we are swingingly tax'd; and they tell us 'tis done by the Parliament. **1720** SWIFT *Poems, Excellent New Song* 31 This wicked rogue Waters.. if swearing can do't, shall be swingingly mawl'd. **1778** FOOTE *Trip Calais* I. Wks. 1799 II. 341, I reckon, your lordships were swingingly sous'd on the road. **1903** KIPLING *Five Nations, The Lesson* 6 This was not bestowed us under the trees, nor yet in the shade of a tent, But swingingly, over eleven degrees of a bare brown continent.

swingel ('swɪndʒəl), var. SWINGLE.

swinger[1] ('swɪndʒə(r)). *Sc.* ? *Obs.* Also 6 **swenȝour, sweyngeour, swingeour, -or, swyngeour, -or, swenger, sweingeor,** 7 *Sc.* **swyngour, swynger, swounger.** [Of uncertain origin; prob. a cant term and perh. a derivative of early Flem. *swentsen* 'vagari' (Kilian), orig. with the sense of 'vagabond'; cf. early mod.G. *schwänzer* 'otiosus, ambulator', *schwänzen* to go about aimlessly, in thieves' cant, to ride, travel.] A rogue, rascal, scoundrel.

1500–20 DUNBAR *Poems* lxxxii. 44 Ȝour burgh of beggeris is ane nest, To schout thai swenȝouris will nocht rest. **1513** DOUGLAS *Æneis* VIII. Prol. 68 Swingeouris and scurrevagis, swankeis and swanis. **1528** LYNDESAY *Dreme* 962 Tha sweir swyngeoris thay tuke of me non heid. **1567** *Satir. Poems Reform.* viii. 31 Sweingeor, cum, sweir þe saikles sone, Deny þe evill þat þow hes done. **1613** *Reg. Privy Council Scot.* X. 3 Quhat wer it to tak the buttoun or blason af his breist, and to lay ane lumder uponn sic a swounger as throw [*read* thow] art. **1618** *Extr. Aberd. Reg.* (1848) II. 356 Mr. Henrie wes convict.. for iniuring the said Willeame Gray.. in calling him febill swynger. **1640** ROTHES in Napier *Mem. Montrose* xiii. (1856) I. 231 That swinger, the Treasurer, has so calumniated the whole estates to his Majesty. **1739** A. NICOL *Poems, Nat. without Art* (1766) 19 If some auld swinger snap to speak Of pink-ey'd queans, he gives a Squeek.

attrib. **1542** *Records of Elgin* (New Spald. Cl. 1903) I. 68 Iohne Innes wrangit in the calling of Nicoll Moressone swenger carle and birsyn carle. *a* **1550** LYNDESAY *Descr. Peder Coffeis* 17 Ane swyngeour coife, amangis the wyvis.

swinger[2] ('swɪndʒə(r)). [f. SWINGE *v.*[1] + -ER[1].]

†**1.** One who acts vigorously or forcibly; a vigorous performer; a powerful fellow. *Obs.*

1583 MELBANCKE *Philotimus* L iij, The three Sisters Litæ .. were left a loofe behind her far out of sight, not able to keepe pace with such a swinger. **1679** DRYDEN *Limberham* I. i, Before George, a proper fellow! and a Swinger he shou'd be, by his make! **1679** —— *Troil. & Cress.* I. ii, Is't not a brave Man that? he's a Swinger, many a Grecian he has laid with his Face upward. **1684** SOUTHERNE *Disappointm.* II. i, I' gad I was a Swinger in those days; let me see,—I cou'd have done—I don't know what I could have done.

2. Something forcible or effective; *esp.* something very big; a 'whopper'. *colloq.* or *slang*; now *rare* or *local*. Cf. SWINGEING *ppl. a.* 2.

1599 *Warn. Faire Wom.* II. 1524, I am sure there is a gallowes big enough to hold them both.. 'tis a swinger yfayth. **1648** HERRICK *Hesper., Twelfe Nt.* 24 And thus ye must doe To make the wassaile a swinger [*rime* ginger]. **1677** *2nd Pacquet Advices* 42 They are likely to give us nothing New but a New Parliament, and that shall be a Swinger, as the Dissolver hath promised us. **1712–13** SWIFT *Jrnl. to Stella* 25 Jan., I saw a hundred tiles fallen down; and one swinger fell about forty yards before me, that would have killed a horse. *a* **1734** NORTH *Lives* (1826) II. 70 This motion at that time was indeed a swinger; for, in consequence, the execution of it by such a pardon of all convictions had lost the King irrecoverably. *a* **1734** —— *Exam.* II. iv. §10 (1740) 236 We had.. diverse [plots] of most desperate Reach; witness that of Fitzharris, which was a Swinger. **1853** C. B. MANSFIELD *Paraguay*, etc. (1856) 425, I started off.. with a tremendous toothache, one of my old swingers. **1872** SCHELE DE VERE *Americanisms* 557 In Virginia.. boys have for more than two centuries called a large snake or other formidable creature a swindger.

†**b.** *spec.* A great or bold lie, a 'bang'. *Obs.*

1671 EACHARD *Observ. Answ. Cont. Clergy* 153 How will his puling Conscience be put to it, to rap out presently half a dozen swingers to get off cleaverly? **1727** SWIFT *Art Polit. Lying* Wks. 1755 III. I. 122 The Whig-party do wisely to try the credulity of the people sometimes by swingers. **1781** M. MADAN *Thelyphthora* III. 148 Is it possible that, when St. Bernard told this swinger, he could believe it, himself?

c. A forcible blow or stroke.

1836 E. HOWARD *R. Reefer* xxv, He applied across my shoulders one of the most hearty.. swingers that ever left a wale behind it. **1841** J. T. HEWLETT *P. Priggins* II. xi. 169 Another pleasant occupation was having to jump two or three feet from the ground, and then to be knocked down by his master, who stood on a form for the purpose. This was called 'tipping a neat swinger'. **1890** BARRÈRE & LELAND *Slang Dict., Swinger* (Charterhouse), a box on the ears.

3. A tool with a raised point, used for levering timbers, etc.

swinger[3] ('swɪŋə(r)).

I. [f. SWING *v.*[1] + -ER[1] 2.] One who or that which swings.

1. One who flourishes something about, or causes it to oscillate.

1543 BALE *Yet a Course* 88 Holy water swyngers, and euen songe clatterers. **1897** *Daily News* 27 May 2/5 Club Swinging... The well-known swinger of Indian clubs, brought his attempt to swing a pair of two pound clubs for thirty consecutive hours to a successful conclusion.

2. a. (*a*) A person who swings.

1712 STEELE *Spect.* No. 492 ⁋3 These [familiar romps], Mr. Spectator, are the Swingers... They get on Ropes, as you must have seen the children, and are swung by their Men Visitants. **1877** G. H. KINGSLEY *Sport & Trav.* (1900) 331 The strong man becomes a swinger in hammocks, a sucker of oranges, a smoker of pipes.

(*b*) A Hindu who performs the penance of swinging: see SWING *v.*[1] 6 (*b*).

1793 *Medical Spectator* II. No. 39. 242 Every thing being ready for the swinger, he kneels upon the ground, when a very dexterous operator fixes two strong iron hooks into the common integuments betwixt his shoulders. **1893** *Times* 11 July 3/6 The writer afterwards interviewed a swinger. He was rather the worse for opium, but none the worse for his swing.

b. A thing that swings to and fro; †a swing for recreation; a kind of lever; a coat with swinging tails or skirt. See also JIM-SWINGER.

three legs and a swinger: said of an animal which has only three sound legs, the fourth hanging or dragging limp through injury; hence of a dilapidated chair, etc.

1662 J. DAVIES tr. *Olearius' Voy. Ambass.* 93, I have seen publick Swinging-places, They.. giving two or three pence to little Boies who keep Swingers ready. **1825** J. NICHOLSON *Oper. Mech.* 426, 19 and 20 act as swingers or levers from the joints 21 and 22. **1863** B. BRIERLEY *Chron. Waverlow* 147 The latter people did not care for misfits at all, and would don a broad-lapped 'swinger' or a swallow-tailed coat with equal indifference. **1893** *Westm. Gaz.* 12 May 1/3 Royal Hampton had no pretensions to winning although he took the City and Suburban on 'three legs and a swinger' in the following spring. **1916** C'TESS BARCYNSKA *Honey-Pot* ii, Be careful of the chair! It's a real antique, only three legs and a swinger!

c. *Cricket.* A ball that swings in the air on delivery; an inswinger or outswinger.

1920 LYTTELTON & WILSON in P. F. Warner *Cricket* (ed. 2) 266 He bowled a swinger, an off break, and a fast ball, which went with his arm. **1948** *Sporting Mirror* 21 May 2/3 Heath bowls medium fast swingers and opens the bowling. **1966** [see CUTTER *sb.*[1] 5 b]. **1977** *Listener* 11 Aug. 182/4 Waving at a late swinger outside the off stump.

d. A gramophone record with an eccentric spindle-hole.

1935 H. C. BRYSON *Gramophone Record* vi. 147 The central hole has to be made perfectly true, for were it the least eccentric with the grooves, the records produced from it would be swingers. **1961** E. N. BRADLEY *Records & Gramophone Equipment* i. 22 The most likely cause of wow is a swinger—a record whose spindle hole is not exactly central and so turns eccentrically as a result. **1981** *Hi-Fi Answers* Apr. 74/2 If you press the grooves off-centre relative to the centre hole it sounds terrible. A swinger that would just be okay at 33 will not do at 45.

3. a. *Mus.* A musician who plays jazz with swing.

1934 in B. Rust *Jazz Records 1897–1942* (1969) 1516 (recording artists) The Six Swingers. **1958** K. GOODWIN in P. Gammond *Decca Bk. of Jazz* xiii. 151 There are some *real* swingers on the coast, among them a young coloured pianist —Hampton Hawes. **1962** *Sunday Times* (Colour Suppl.) 10 June 3 Unexcelled as a technician and swinger, Baker is said by some to lack a musical heart and personality of his own.

b. A lively person who keeps up with what is considered fashionable; one who is 'with it'.

1965 P. KAEL *I lost it at Movies* 19, I think in treating indiscriminateness as a *value*, she has become a real swinger. **1966** *Economist* 11 June 1240/3 No attempt has been made to attract the wilder London 'swingers' of *Time*-fame. **1967** H. KEMELMAN *Nine Mile Walk* (1968) 149 In the parlance of the undergraduate.. Professor John Baxter Bowman.. was a swinger, with a taste and interest in clothes not usually associated with the professoriat. **1972** J. GORES *Dead Skip* (1973) xiv. 96 The Dukum Inn.. looked.. like an aging swinger getting up in the morning with his teeth still in the water glass. **1977** M. FRENCH *Women's Room* (1978) i. 14 I'd meet some middle-aged swinger with a deep tan and sideburns.

c. A person who is sexually promiscuous; *spec.* one who advocates or engages in group sex or the swapping of sexual partners. Also, a homosexual. *slang.*

1964 W. & J. BREEDLOVE *Swap Clubs* i. 37 We will on occasion utilize 'swinger' and 'swinging' to describe the advocate of sexual partner exchange and the exercising of that practice. **1966** T. PYNCHON *Crying of Lot 49* vi. 147, I had a date last night with an eight-year-old, And she's a swinger just like me. **1972** G. BAXT *Burning Sappho* iii. 47 Flo pondered the invitation... 'You sure you ain't no swinger?' 'I assure you my dear,' said Lady Molly.. 'I am *not* a womaniser.' **1977** *Time* 4 July 38/2 Some operators have converted nudist colonies into 'swinger camps', the new rural retreats for the randy.

†**4.** ? A large sword. (Cf. early Flem. *swinghe*.)

1673 HICKERINGILL *Greg. F. Greyb.* 42 The old Bishops.. that ne'r.. so much as knew how to set the Periwig and Galloshoes, much less the true timing and accenting of a Rapper, and double swinger.

II. [f. SWING *sb.*[2] 12 d + -ER[1] I.] **5.** Each of the middle pair of horses in a team of six.

a **1872** *Trip to the West* 137 (S. de Vere) Each wagon is usually drawn by three span of mules, of which the lighter and forward, are leaders, the next pair swingers, and the rear, or heaviest pair, wheelers.

Swingfelter, aberrant f. SCHWENKFELDER.

1792 MORSE *Amer. Geog.* 313.

swinging ('swɪŋɪŋ), *vbl. sb.* [f. SWING *v.*[1] + -ING[1].] The action of SWING *v.*[1]

†**1.** Beating, scourging. *Obs.*

c **1200** *Trin. Coll. Hom.* 57 We shulen leden al þis leinten on festing.. on smerte swinginge & on oðre swiche gode dedes. *a* **1340** HAMPOLE *Psalter* xxxi. 13 Eftere þe bridel comes þe swyngynge for to teme him þat is wilde.

2. Flourishing, waving about.

c **1400** *Destr. Troy* 12526 Hym-seluyn in the sea sonkyn belyue, Swalprit & swam with swyngyng of armys. **1897** [see SWINGER[3] I].

3. a. (*a*) Movement to and fro, as of a suspended body; oscillation, swaying, etc.: see the verb.

1669 STURMY *Mariner's Mag.* VII. xxxiii. 48 It will strike what Hour of the Day or Night it is, and then leave off striking, and swinging also. **1771** SMOLLETT *Humphry Cl.* 26 June, I have suffered more from jolting and swinging than ever I felt in the whole course of my life, although the carriage is remarkably..well hung. **1771** LUCKOMBE *Hist. Print.* 331 A low man cannot pull the handle of the Bar at so great a force..as a tall man; but will require the swinging of his whole body backwards to add force to the Pull. **1816** SHELLEY *Mont Blanc* ii, Thy giant brood of pines..in whose devotion The chainless winds still come..their mighty swinging To hear. **1849** JAMES *Woodman* ix, No sound was heard, except the swinging of the great bell. **1867** AUGUSTA WILSON *Vashti* xxxiii, The peculiar, free, childish swinging of the left arm.

(*b*) See SWING *v.*[1] 6 (*b*).

1793 *Medical Spectator* II. No. 39. 242 A few days after this, came on the annual custom of swinging. *Ibid.* 246 Some who have got marks of the wounds made on their backs by the swinging-hooks. **1857** LADY CANNING in Hare *Story Two Noble Lives* (1893) II. 284 Dr. Duff says the swinging festival went off very mildly this year.

b. The sport of riding in a swing. Also *attrib.*

1610 HEALEY *St. Aug. Citie of God* 698 These swinging-games had origin all from hence [*sc.* Italy]. **1662** J. DAVIES tr. *Olearius' Voy. Ambass.* 93 Their husbands are very glad to give them this kind of sport, and sometimes help them in their swinging. **1838** [see SWING *v.*[1] 7 b].

4. *slang* or *colloq.* Hanging. Also *attrib.*

1591 PERCIVALL *Sp. Dict.*, *Columpio*, swinging in a halter. **1879** BROWNING *Ned Bratts* 95, I think he pulled a face, next Sessions' swinging-time! **1883** STEVENSON *Treas. Isl.* II. xi, They [*sc.* gentlemen of fortune] risk swinging.

5. Indulgence in sexual promiscuity; *spec.* engaging in group sex or the exchanging of sexual partners. *slang.*

1964 [see SWINGER[3] 3 c]. **1967** W. & J. BREEDLOVE *Swinging Set* v. 65 The act of prostitution is separate from 'swinging'. **1970** E. M. BRECHER *Sex Researchers* ix. 250 What happened during the 1960's was that group sex in public—swinging—emerged from the brothels and became an established though minor feature of American urban and suburban life. **1973** *New Society* 24 May 437/1 'Swinging' is extra-marital sex by both spouses, at the same time and usually in the same place.

'swinging, *ppl. a.* [f. as prec. + -ING[2].] That swings.

1. a. Moving to and fro as or like a suspended body; oscillating; swaying.

a **1560** PHAER *Æneid* x. (1562) Dd iv b, He swam with swinging sides. **1716** GAY *Trivia* I. 157 But when the swinging signs your ears offend With creaking noise, then rainy floods impend. **1803** SCOTT *Cadyow Castle* xi, The drawbridge falls—..Clatters each plank and swinging chain. **1815** SHELLEY *Alastor* 563 A pine..stretched athwart the vacancy Its swinging boughs. **1833** LOUDON *Encycl. Archit.* § 662 Swinging cribs and cradles are now justly exploded. **1848** LYTTON *K. Arthur* x. xcix, With lifted cross and swinging censer. **1900** CONAN DOYLE *Green Flag*, etc. 127 He punched the swinging ball and worked with the dumb-bells.

fig. **1915** J. KELMAN *Salted with Fire* xii. 180 The devious and swinging balance of power with which diplomacy has hitherto concerned itself.

b. Of a blow: Characterized or accompanied by a swing of the arm, etc.

1850 HOLTZAPFFEL *Turning* III. 1190 The toothed saws for stone are used with a swinging stroke. **1898** 'H. S. MERRIMAN' *Roden's Corner* xxx. 320 Von Holzen ran at him with his arm outstretched for a swinging stab. **1902** S. E. WHITE *Blazed Trail* I. vi, He saw his opening and let out with a swinging pivot blow.

2. Turning or adapted to turn freely in either direction upon a fixed axis or centre, as a gate or door, a hinged piece of mechanism, etc.; in technical use = SWING- (see also 4).

1730 *Inv. D. Bond's Goods* (1732) 34 A square Walnut-tree Table and Swinging Glass. **1868** *Rep. to Govt. U.S. Munitions War* 51 Mr. Joslyn's rifle, calibre 0·500, has a swinging breech-piece of a peculiar pattern. **1885** MABEL COLLINS *Prettiest Woman* x, He opened the swinging door for her. **1879** *Man. Artill. Exerc.* 71 The butt of the swinging derrick is made fast to the upright spar. **1904** *Windsor Mag.* Jan. 300/2 The girl turned about on the swinging stool where she sat.

3. a. Applied to a steady vigorous rhythmical onward movement (pace, step, etc.) accompanied, or such as is commonly accompanied, by a swaying from side to side; hence used of a rhythm in verse or music suggesting such a movement.

1818 SCOTT *Br. Lamm.* xxii, Onward they came at a long swinging trot. **1881** FENN *Off to Wilds* viii, The boy pressed his horse's sides, and went off at a swinging canter. **1884** J. G. ROGERS in *Congregationalist* Feb. 104 These swinging congregational melodies. **1887** *Westm. Rev.* June 380 A long swinging dactylic measure in rhyming couplets. **1902** J. BUCHAN *Watcher by Threshold* 76, I heard a long swinging step outside.

b. *Mus.* Applied to a musician who plays jazz with swing; also, to the music itself. Cf. SWING *sb.*[2] 10 b.

1955 in A. J. McCarthy *Jazzbook 1955* 31 It has been satisfying to witness the renewed success within the past two years of Count Basie's orchestra, as the swinging spearhead of coloured jazz. **1956** B. HOLIDAY *Lady sings Blues* (1973) xxiii. 189 They were the swingingest cats I ever heard. **1958** K. GOODWIN in P. Gammond *Decca Bk. of Jazz* xiii. 153 Mel Lewis—..easily the most swinging drummer ever to work with the Kenton band.

c. Uninhibited, ignoring conventions; lively and up to date: applied to persons, places (*swinging London*), etc., and *spec.* to the 1960s (*swinging Sixties*). Also, as a general term of approval: fine, splendid, 'great' (temporarily contrasted with *dodgy*). *colloq.*

1958 *Publ. Amer. Dial. Soc.* xxx. 47 *Swingin'*, the highest term of approval. May be applied to anything a jazzman likes, or any person. **1959** *Manch. Guardian* 25 June 8/7 [She] informed him that she wants a large place 'in a swinging part of town'..so he is looking around in Chelsea and Knightsbridge. **1962** J. BALDWIN *Another Country* (1963) II. iii. 299 'You feeling all right?'.. 'He's going to feel just swinging.' **1964** N. VAUGHAN in *T.V. World* 24 Sept. 48 When people ask me how I feel about the months ahead, I tell them: 'Sometimes it's a bit dodgy, but most of the time it's swinging!' **1965** *Weekend Telegraph* 16 Apr. 12/2 Diana Vreeland..editor of *Vogue*..has said simply 'London is the most swinging city in the world at the moment'. **1966** *Time* 15 Apr. 11/3, I know this world, this swinging London... But I wouldn't describe myself as a swinger. **1967** *Listener* 19 Jan. 107/1 He does not fit into the *Zeitgeist* of the swinging 'sixties. **1967** F. MULLALLY *Prizewinner* iii. 41 The swinging London Percy had read so much about. **1971** H. WILSON *Labour Govt.* xxxvii. 766 The press publicized what they called the new swinging style of the Downing Street receptions. **1976** P. CAVE *High Flying Birds* iii. 25 Young people from all over the world—draft-evading Americans, poker-faced Germans, swinging Swedes and the comic-clown Dutch. **1980** M. SELLERS *Leonardo & Others* x. 56 Zuleika lived life to the full. She was a product of the swinging sixties. **1982** S. BRETT *Murder Unprompted* v. 51 The British film industry..was committed to making zany films about Swinging London.

d. Of or pertaining to one who engages in promiscuous sexual activity (esp. group sex or the swapping of sexual partners). *slang.*

1964 W. & J. BREEDLOVE *Swap Clubs* ii. 43 A 'swinging couple'. **1978** *Bulletin* (Sydney) 11 Apr. 6/2 'Swinging couples' are no longer addicted to square dancing but to the less innocuous pastime of wife-swapping.

4. Special collocations or combinations: **swinging-bar** = *swing-bar* (SWING- 2); **swinging-boom** *Naut.*, a boom swung or suspended over the ship's side, used to stretch the foot of a lower studding-sail, and (when at anchor) for a boat to ride by; **swinging-bridge**, (*a*) see quot. 1892; (*b*) = *swing-bridge* (SWING- 2); **swinging-tree** *dial.* = SWINGLETREE.

1859 JEPHSON *Brittany* xi. 188 To the end of the pole is attached a *swinging-bar and a pair of traces for a leader. **1840** R. H. DANA *Bef. Mast* xi, Bracing the yards forward so that the *swinging-boom nearly touched the sprit-sail yard. **1708** in *Rec. Early Hist. Boston* (Boston Registry Dept.) (1883) VIII. 52 The way leading from Madam Butlers Corner..to the *Swinging Bridg. **1892** PHILIPS *Fortification* 244 Flying or Swinging Bridges.—A flying bridge is one in which the action of the current is made to move a boat, or raft of two piers, across a stream, by acting obliquely against its side. **1908** *Westm. Gaz.* 23 Nov. 5/3 The city of Cleveland, Ohio,..desired to convert the viaduct-bridge over the Cuyahoga River into a swinging-bridge.

Hence **'swingingly** *adv.*, with swinging movement.

1882 'ANNIE THOMAS' *Allerton Towers* II. vi. 105 A long, lithe, lean-headed mare,..with action so swingingly easy..that her rider never swerves by a hair's-breadth in the saddle. **1891** *Murray's Mag.* X. 662 To strut swingingly up the Cathedral to the Dean's pew.

swinging, -ly, var. SWINGEING, -LY.

swingism ('swɪŋɪz(ə)m). *rare.* See SWING *sb.*[3] and -ISM.

1841 LYTTON *Nt. & Morn.* III. viii, At one time we have burking—at another, swingism—now, suicide is in vogue.

swingle ('swɪŋg(ə)l), *sb.*[1] Also 5 **swengyl, swyngel, -il, -yl(l, swangul-, sungylle-,** 5–6 **swyngell,** 6 **swyngle,** 7 **swingow,** 6–9 **swingell,** 9 *local* **swindgel(l, swingel, -jel** ('swɪndʒ(ə)l). [a. MDu. *swinghel* swingle for flax, corresp. in form to OE. *swingell, -el(l)e, swingle* stroke or stripe with a rod, etc., whipping, scourging, chastisement, affliction, scourge, whip, also once, swingle or distaff (transl. *colus*), f. SWING *v.*[1] + -LE 1; or partly a. (M)LG. *swengel* bell-clapper, pump-handle, swipe, MDu. *swenghel* swipe, Du. *zwengel* swingle, MHG. *swengel* (G. *schwengel* swipe, bell-clapper, swingletree, etc.):—**swaŋgwil-*, f. *swaŋgw-* (see SWING *v.*[1]). Some forms (*swengyl, swangull, sungylle*) show divergent stem-vowels the immediate source of which is not clear.]

1. A wooden instrument resembling a sword, used for beating and scraping flax or hemp so as to cleanse it of woody or coarse particles; also called *swingle-hand*, *-staff*, or *-wand*, *swingling-bat*, *-knife*, or *-staff*.

c **1325** *Gloss. W. de Bibbesw.* in Wright *Voc.* 156 *Le pesselin*, the swingle. *c* **1440** *Promp. Parv.* 482/2 Swengyl, for flax or hempe, *excudium*. *c* **1462** *Wright's Chaste Wife* 216, I haue both hempe and lyne..And a swyngyll good and grete. *Ibid.* 387 Sche brought a swyngyll att þe last. **1847** *Jrnl. R. Agric. Soc.* VIII. II. 446 The swingle or scutching tool. **1850** J. WARNES *Flax v. Cotton* 13 The first blow of the swingle is the commencement of wages.

2. The striking part or swipple of a flail. *local.*

c **1440** *Promp. Parv.* 482/2 Swengyl, of a fleyle or oþer lyke, *feritorium*. **1547** SALESBURY *Welsh Dict.*, *Fustwial*, a swyngell. **1570** FOXE *A. & M.* (ed. 2) III. 2233/2 A blow with the swingell of a flayle. **1821** CLARE *Vill. Minstr.* (1823) I. 90 While distant thresher's swingle drops With sharp and hollow-twanking raps. *a* **1825** FORBY *Voc. E. Anglia.* **1889** F. LUCAS *Sk. Rural Life, The Tasker* xvi, Then let our floors send up the sound Of the swinjel's measured stroke.

b. A weapon resembling a flail; a kind of cudgel.

1818 W. CHAFIN *Cranbourn Chase* 35 They [*sc.* deer-stealers] came in the night..armed with deadly offensive weapons called swindgels, resembling flails to thresh corn. **1904** *Daily News* 7 Nov. 9 The keeper drew a 'swingle' round his legs, bringing him to the ground. **1905** J. C. COX *Royal Forests Eng.* 84 Helmets and swindgel of the deer hunters of Cranbourn Chase.

†**3.** The clapper of a bell. *Obs. rare*$^{-0}$.

14.. *Voc.* in Wr.-Wülcker 567/39 *Batillus*, a belle clapere *vel* a swyngell.

4. a. A spoke or lever for turning the barrel in wire-drawing or the roller of a plate-press. **b.** A crank.

1674 RAY *Coll. Words, Wire working* 133 Underneath is fastened to the barrel a spoke of wood, which they call a Swingle which is drawn back a good way by the calms or cogs in the Axis of the wheel, and draws back the barrel which falls to again by it's own weight. **1787** MARSHALL *Rural Econ. Norfolk* (1795) II. Gloss. (E.D.S.) *Swingle, sb.* a crank. **1875** KNIGHT *Dict. Mech.*

swingle ('swɪŋg(ə)l), *sb.*[2] *N. Amer. slang.* [Blend of SWINGING *ppl. a.* 3 c, d and SINGLE *sb.* 5 c.] A 'swinging' single or unaccompanied person; *spec.* one in search of a sexual partner.

1967 *Glamour* June 82 Hilton Swingles Week. We created a week for people like you: Swinging Singles. **1973** *Newsweek* 16 July 53 The sheer number of singles, meshed with the media's seductive imagery (singles who swing are jauntily dubbed 'swingles'), is gradually revising society's view of its unwed members. **1978** *Chatelaine* (Canada) Dec. 106/3 When she went out with her women friends for an evening, their husbands felt she was luring their wives into swingles bars and white slavery.

'swingle, *v.*[1] Forms: see SWINGLE *sb.*[1]; also 5 **swyngill, (squyngyl),** 8 *dial.* **sungle.** [a. MDu. *swinghelen*, f. *swinghel* SWINGLE *sb.*[1]]

1. *trans.* To beat and scrape (flax or hemp) with a swingle, in order to cleanse it of the coarser particles; to scutch. Also *absol.*

c **1325** *Gloss. W. de Bibbesw.* in Wright *Voc.* 156 *Estonger vostre leyn*, to swingle the flax. **14..** *Lat.-Eng. Voc.* in Wr.-Wülcker 581 *Excudio*, to squyngyl. *c* **1462** *Wright's Chaste Wife* 389 'Good syres', sche seyd, 'swyngylle on fast; For no þing that ye blynne'. *Ibid.* 401 Þe stuard þat was so stowde, Was fayne to swyngelle þe scales owte. *c* **1480** HENRYSON *Mor. Fab., Swallow*, etc. xxx, The carle pullit the lyne,.. swyngillit it weill, and hekkillit in þe flet. **1590** *Shuttleworths' Acc.* (Chetham Soc.) 61 Foure womene wch did brake hempe and swynglye. **1615** [see SWINGLETREE 1]. **1711** S. SEWALL *Diary* 15 Jan., It came by a man's blowing out his pipe, who was swingling Flax. **1776** *Pennsylvania Even. Post* 24 Sept. 478/2 Choice swingled Flax. **1794** *Piper of Peebles* 6 (E.D.D.) Lint was beaten wi'a mell An' ilk ane sungled to themsell. **1844** G. DODD *Textile Manuf.* v. 150 Weeding, steeping, grassing, and swingling or cleaning the flax. **1883** *Harper's Mag.* Aug. 390/1, I found a group of bare-armed women under the trees swingling flax.

2. To cut off the tops of (weeds) without uprooting. *local.* (Cf. SWINGE *v.*[1] 3.)

a **1825** FORBY *Voc. E. Anglia.*

'swingle, *v.*[2] [frequent. of SWING *v.*[1]]

†**1.** *trans.* To swing or flourish about. *Obs.*

c **1450** [see SWINGLING *vbl. sb.*[2]].

2. *intr.* To swing; to hang, be suspended. *dial.*

1755 JOHNSON, *To Swingle*, v.n. 1. To dangle; to wave hanging. 2. To swing in pleasure. **1830** HOGG *Greek Pastoral* 15 Where clouds and mountains seem'd to swingle, And Ossa with Olympus mingle.

swingle- in comb.: **swingle-bar** = SWINGLETREE 2; † **swingle-foot,** = SWINGLE *sb.*[1] 1; also *attrib.*; † **swingle foot hards** (see quot.); † **swingle-head** (?), **-staff** = SWINGLE *sb.*[1] 1; **swingle-stick, -stock** = *swing-stock* (SWING- 2 b); **swingle-tail,** name for a species of shark, = THRASHER[1] 2; **swingle-wand** = SWINGLE *sb.*[1] 1.

1849 DE QUINCEY *Eng. Mail-Coach* II. Wks. 1854 IV. 343 Either with the *swingle-bar, or with the haunch of our near leader, we had struck the off-wheel of the little gig. **1907** 'Q' (Quiller-Couch) *Poison Isl.* i. 8 The Royal Mail pulled up before Minden Cottage with a merry clash of bits and swingle-bars. **1500** *Ortus Vocab.*, *Excussorium*, a *swyngelfote. **1611** COTGR., *Farasse*..the coursest of Hempe, Swingle foot herds, course towe. **1688** R. HOLME *Armoury* III. iii. 106/1 A Swingle Foot. A Swingle Hand, corruptly a Swingow Hond: a thing like a Wooden Fauchion with a square hole or handle. **1677** COLES, *Excudia* and *-ium*, a *swingel-head. **1664** GOULDMAN *Lat. Eng. Dict.*, A *swingle-staff or bat to beat flax, *scutula*. **1883** *Harper's Mag.* Aug. 390/1 The women stood about the fire, each beside her swingle-staff. This instrument is like a wooden pocket-knife, about two feet long, with legs supporting it at the height of a table. *c* **1325** *Gloss. W. de Bibbesw.* in Wright *Voc.* 156 *Vostre pessel*, a *swinglestyk. *c* **1340** *Nominale* (Skeat) 545 *Swangulstoke riplingcombe swyngilwande. **14..** *Voc.* in Wr.-Wülcker 581/29 *Excudia*, a swyngylstok. *c* **1475** *Pict. Voc.* in Wr.-Wülcker 795/11 *Hec excudia*, a sungyllestok. **1483** *Cath. Angl.* 374/2 A Swyngilstoke, *excudia, excudium*. **1839** STORER in *Boston Jrnl. Nat. Hist.* II. 529 *Carcharias vulpes*. Lin... This species..is called by the fishermen 'Thresher', and '*Swingle tail'. *c* **1340** *Swyngilwande [see *swingle-stock*]. **1808** JAMIESON, *Swingle-wand*, the instrument with which flax is swingled.

swingle-hand. Also 5 swyngilland, 7 *Sc.* svinglent, 9 *Sc.* swinglind. [See prec. and HAND *sb.* 24 (?).] = SWINGLE *sb.*[1] 1.

c **1475** *Pict. Voc.* in Wr.-Wülcker 795/12 *Hec excudiatorium*, a sungyllehand. **1483** *Cath. Angl.* 375/1 A Swyngylhande (*A.* Swyngilland). **1500** *Ortus Vocab.*, *Excudia die*, a swyngelhand vel excussorium. **1689** A. HAIG in Russell *Haigs* (1881) 479 Half ane stane of heckis, rokis, spindillis, svinglinstokis, svinglentis, vinddillis. **1806** J. HOGG *Poems* 72 (Jam.) They laid sae fast upo' the boards, The swinglinds gaed lik horsemen's swords. **1825** J. NICHOLSON *Oper. Mech.* 420 A long flat straight piece of wood, usually termed a swingle-hand or scotcher.

swingletree ('swɪŋg(ə)ltriː). Forms: see SWINGLE and TREE. [f. SWINGLE *sb.*[1] + TREE *sb.*]

1. A board used in dressing flax or hemp: = *swing-stock*, *swingle-stock* (see SWING- 2 b, SWINGLE-). Also called ***swingletree block***. ***swingletree dagger*** = *swing-knife* (SWING- 2 b), SWINGLE *sb.*[1] 1. *Obs.* or *dial.*

c **1462** *Wright's Chaste Wife* 528 One of hem knockyd lyne, A-nothyr swyngelyd good and fyne By-fore the swyngyll tre. **1615** MARKHAM *Eng. Housew.* II. v. (1668) 133 After your Hemp and flax is brak't, you shall then swingle it, which is upon a swingle tree blocke made of an half inch boord about four foot aboue ground, and set upon a strong foot or stock. *Ibid.* 134 A piece of Wood called the Swingle-tree dagger. **1825** JAMIESON, *Swingle-tree*, the stock over which flax is scutched, Dumfr.; synon. *Swingling-stock*.

2. In a plough, narrow, carriage, etc., a crossbar, pivoted at the middle, to which the traces are fastened, giving freedom of movement to the shoulders of the horse or other draught-animal.

An altered form SINGLE-TREE, due to association with *double-tree* (= the crosspiece to which the swingletree is attached), is common in U.S.

1483 *Cath. Angl.* 375/1 A Swyngilstre (*A.* Swyngyltre) of a harowe, *protectorium*. **1523** FITZHERB. *Husb.* §15 The horses..must haue..a swyngletre to holde the tresses abrode, and a togewith to be bytwene the swyngletre and the harowe. **1620** MARKHAM *Farew. Husb.* II. xiii. (1668) 61 To the big end of this harrow, you shall fix a strong rope with a swingle-tree. **1688** R. HOLME *Armoury* III. viii. 336/1 The Swingle Tree of a Coach Pole..fastned by..pinns to the Coach Pole, to the which Horses are fastned by their Harnish when there is more then two to draw the Coach. **1765** A. DICKSON *Treat. Agric.* (ed. 2) II. v. 200 It [*sc.* the bridle or muzzle of the plough] has notches by which the cleek of the swingle-tree may be fixed. *a* **1817** W. MUIR *Poems* (1818) 8 The very pettle, riest an' seath,..The swingle-trees an' a' the graith. **1844** H. STEPHENS *Bk. Farm* I. 417 To the shackle is appended the swivel-hook, to which is attached the main draught-bar, or swingle-tree of the yoke. **1859** F. A. GRIFFITHS *Artil. Man.* (1862) 104 One swingle-tree between the footboard and the splinter bar. **1889** GRETTON *Memory's Harkb.* 115 His leaders.. wrenched the swingletrees off the pole, and the uncoupled reins out of the coachman's hands.

attrib. **1819** T. RADCLIFF *Agric. E. & W. Flanders* x. §2. 115 The extremity of the handle..strikes against, and rests upon the swingle-tree bar. **1852** BURN *Naval & Milit. Dict.* (1863), Swingle-tree clasp, cramp, clip or socket.

3. = SWINGLE *sb.*[1] 2. *dial.*

1858 SIMMONDS *Dict. Trade*, *Swingle-tree*,..in Scotland the striking end of a flail. **1907** T. M. ALLISON in *Country-Side* 16 Nov. 27/1 The handle [of the flail]..was held in the hands, and the beater, or 'swingle-tree' was swung round behind the head.

Swinglian, obs. f. ZWINGLIAN.

swinglind, Sc. f. SWINGLE-HAND.

†**swingling** ('swɪŋglɪŋ), *vbl. sb.*[1] *Obs.* In 1 swinglung, (swinclung), 5 swyngyllyng. [Cf. Icel. *svingla* to rove, Da. *svingla* to reel, stagger, *svingling* reeling, giddiness. The form in the northern *Alph. Tales* may be from Scandinavian.] Giddiness, dizziness, vertigo.

c **1000** ÆLFRIC *Gloss.* in Wr.-Wülcker 112/18 *Scotomic*, swinglung. *c* **1000** *Sax. Leechd.* I. 344 Ðam mannum þe swinclunge [*v.r.* swinglunge] þrowiað. *c* **1440** *Alphabet of Tales* 19 And þer fell a swyngyllyng in his hede þat he wex fonde with.

†**swingling**, *vbl. sb.*[2] See SWINGLE *v.*[2] 1.

c **1450** in Aungier *Syon* (1840) 300 Goynge..withe oute swyngylynge of armes or of handes.

swingling ('swɪŋglɪŋ), *vbl. sb.*[3] [f. SWINGLE *v.*[1] + -ING[1].] The process of dressing flax or hemp with a swingle; scutching.

c **1462**, etc. [see b]. **1688** R. HOLME *Armoury* III. iii. 106/2 *Swingowing*, is the beating off the brused inward Stalk of the Hemp or Flax, from the outward pill. **1765** *Museum Rust.* IV. cvi. 456 When the flax grows crooked, it is more liable to be hurt in the rippling and swingling. **1847** NICHOLLS in *Jrnl. Roy. Agric. Soc.* VIII. II. 457 Scutching or Swingling ..is the act of clearing the fibre [of flax] from the woody part of the stalk after it has been bruised and loosened by the break.

b. *attrib.*, as ***swingling machine***, ***operation***; **swingling-bat**, **-knife**, **-staff** = SWINGLE *sb.*[1] 1; **swingling-board**, **-post**, **-stock** = *swingle-stock*, *swing-stock* (see SWING- 2); **swingling-hand** = SWINGLE-HAND; **swingling-tow**, the coarse part of flax, separated by swingling.

c **1462** *Wright's Chaste Wife* 386 The wyfe þrew hym a swyngelyng stocke. **1552** HULOET, Swynglyngbatte, or staffe to beate flaxe, *scutula*. **1583** *Wills & Inv. N.C.* (Surtees 1860) 78 Two swinglinge stockes withe theire swynglinges. **1689** [see SWINGLE-HAND]. **1819** *Mass. Spy* 3 Nov. 2/2 My wife threw a swinglin; board at the man who had me by the hand. **1825** JAMIESON, *Swingling-hand*, a wooden lath or sword for dressing flax. **1827** CARLYLE *Germ. Rom.* I. 39 Spinning-wheel and reel, swingling-stake [*sic*] and hatchel. **1828–32** WEBSTER, *Swingling-tow*, the coarse part of flax, separated from the finer by swingling and hatcheling. **1839** URE *Dict. Arts* 493 The scutching or swingling machine. **1851** A. MARSHALL in Schroeder *Ann. Yorks.* I. 419 Making less dust in the swingling operation. **1902** A. THOMSON *Lauder & Lauderd.* xxii. 259 A swingling post, sloping slightly, was firmly fixed in the floor of the barn.

swingometer (swɪŋ'ɒmɪtə(r)). [f. SWING *sb.*[2] 8 h + -OMETER, after *barometer*, etc.] A device consisting of a dial with a movable pointer, used to demonstrate (esp. on television) how a likely or observable 'swing' should influence the outcome of an election. Also *transf.* and *fig.*

1965 *B.B.C. Handbk.* 36 (*caption*) Robert McKenzie demonstrating the Swingometer. **1969** D. WIDGERY in Cockburn & Blackburn *Student Power* 128 Eventually the 'swingometer' which the UCL NUS Committee had installed in their Gower Street office moved slowly in favour of the ISC and the Executive. **1974** *Daily Tel.* 22 Oct. 18 After five or six results, Robert McKenzie's famous swingometer accurately showed what was to be in the event a majority of 40 or so for Labour over Conservative. **1978** *Sunday Times* 19 Mar. (Weekly Rev.) 37 Guardians of the social swingometer..have been drawing attention to punk rock. **1979** H. WILSON *Final Term* v. 84 This figure headed the election night screens, until the 'swingometer' working on the first declarations rapidly moved into a much more moderate posture.

'**swing-rope.** [f. SWING- + ROPE *sb.*]

1. *Naut.* †**a.** ? = SHEET *sb.*[2] 1. *Obs.* **b.** A small rope by which a boat 'swings' (SWING *v.*[1] 11).

1336 *Roll 'W.N.'* 579 in Nicolas *Hist. Royal Navy* (1847) II. 471 [For skin ('pelle') bought of divers persons to make two] swengeropes [therewith, 2 s.]. **1844** in W. H. Maxwell *Sports & Adv. Scot.* (1855) 323 The tie of the last net is.. fixed to the swing-rope, a small hawser attached to the stern, and the boat rides to her drift as if at anchor. **1879** *Encycl. Brit.* IX. 252/2 If there is a great deal of wind more swing-rope is allowed, so that the nets may not be dragged through the water.

2. A rope for a swing (SWING *sb.*[2] 11).

1815 *Sporting Mag.* XLV. 153 Good swing ropes and jump cords.

swingster ('swɪŋstə(r)). *slang.* [f. SWING *sb.*[2] 10 b + -STER.] = SWINGER[3] 3 a.

1937 *Nebraska State Jrnl.* (Lincoln, Nebraska) 22 Aug. CD-9/4 Swingsters got the best touch of feet-itch of the season. **1946** *Jazz Writings* 19/2 Holmes' jazz is 'grown-up' jazz—as opposed to the 'adolescent' jazz of the swingsters. **1952** B. ULANOV *Hist. Jazz in Amer.* xxii. 307 It was an old war in jazz; it had not been declared by the swingsters or the boppers.

swing-swang ('swɪŋˌswæŋ). Also **swing swong**. [Reduplicated f. SWING *v.*[1] with change of vowel.] A swinging to and fro; a (double or complete) oscillation; a reciprocating movement, *occas.* see-saw. Also *fig.* and *attrib.*

c **1683** HOOKE *Posth. Wks.* (1705) 472 Not that I pretend to discover any new Thing,..'tis, as trivial as the pendulous vibrating Motion, which, in Contempt, hath been call'd Swing Swangs. **1773** C. DIBDIN *Deserter* I. ii. (1775) 10 The parish-bell may toll, Gra'mercy on my soul! Ding dong! Swing swong! **1829** R. L. SHEIL in *New Monthly Mag.* Aug. 98 In a beautiful walk of trees, which ran down from the rear of the building through the play-ground, I saw several French boys playing at swing-swang. **1829** [H. BEST] *Pers. & Lit. Mem.* 174 A friend of mine at Oxford called it the swing-swang style. **1887** MAX MÜLLER in *Fortn. Rev.* May 704 Is, then, our knowledge nothing but a perpetual swing-swang? **1910** G. CHRYSTAL *Seiches*, etc. *Lake Surfaces* i. 29 The swing-swang of a clock-pendulum.

swing-tree ('swɪŋtriː). = SWINGLETREE 2.

1396–7 *Durham Acc. Rolls* (Surtees) 214, iiij harpice cum iij Swyngtreys ferreis. **1802** JAMES *Milit. Dict.*, *Swing-tree* of a waggon. **1812** SIR J. SINCLAIR *Syst. Husb. Scot.* II. App. 46 The..swing-trees, to which the horses are attached when ploughing. **1883** JEFFERIES *Nature near Lond.* 86 The traces are taut, the swing-tree like a yard braced square.

swingy ('swɪŋɪ), *a. colloq.* [f. SWING *sb.*[2] + -Y[1].] That swings; characterized by swing. In various senses. **1.** Of music: see SWING *sb.*[2] 10 b.

1933 *Melody Maker* 25 Nov. 3/1 (*song-title*) Swingy little thingy. **1956** E. DELANEY in S. Traill *Play that Music* 54 Do you remember the Gerry Mulligan sounds?—easy, swingy and very *quiet*. **1968** *Melody Maker* 30 Nov. 22/2 The arrangements are tight and swingy. **1973** J. WAINWRIGHT *Pride of Pigs* 46 The trombonist..improvised a tidy, swingy, four-bar lead-in.

2. Of garments, esp. skirts.

1937 *Evening News* 1 Feb. 1/3 Skirts will be shorter and swingier.., in keeping with swing music. **1960** *She* Dec. 8 It's the swingiest thing! Lister 'Crimplene' in party casuals. **1981** *Times* 28 Apr. 10/6 Chic tweed suits with swingy skirts.

3. Of movement, gait, etc.

1943 J. STEINBECK *Once There was a War* (1959) 22 A band of pipers marches out in kilts, with bagpipes and drums and the swingy march of pipers. **1944** D. BURLEY *Handbk. Jive* 85 You bend your knees halfway and rock back and forth on your heels and toes with a swingy sway.

Swinhoe ('swɪnhəʊ). The name of Robert *Swinhoe* (fl. 1862–3), British consul in Taiwan, used in the possessive, as **Swinhoe's pheasant** (occas. **kaleege** [KALEEGE, KALIJ]), to designate *Lophura swinhoei*, a brightly coloured pheasant native to Taiwan, where he first collected it in 1862. Also *ellipt.* as **Swinhoe's.**

1863 *Proc. Zool. Soc.* 119 (*heading*) Swinhoe's pheasant. **1921** W. BEEBE *Monogr. Pheasants* II. 78 We have no definite information as to the distribution of Swinhoe's kaleege, except that it is not found near the coast of Formosa, but only in the..interior. *Ibid.* 80 The price for the first pair of Swinhoes was between four and five thousand francs. **1951** J. DELACOUR *Pheasants of World* 162 Swinhoe's Pheasant has developed an interesting mutation in captivity. **1965** P. WAYRE *Wind in Reeds* xv. 212 The male Swinhoe's is.. magnificent.., his neck, underparts, rump and outer tail feathers being a dark metallic blue; a white crest tops his head and there is a white patch on his back; his scapulars are bright maroon. **1973** *Sci. Amer.* June 40/1 The birds are Swinhoe's pheasant, the mikado pheasant, [etc.].

swiniard, obs. var. SWINEHERD.

swinish ('swaɪnɪʃ), *a.* [f. SWINE *sb.* + -ISH[1].]

1. Having the character or disposition of a swine; hoggish, piggish; sensual, gluttonous; coarse, gross, or degraded in nature.

c **1200** *Trin. Coll. Hom.* 37 [They] ben icleped swinisse men & on hem wuneð þe deuel. **1588** *Marprel. Epist.* (Arb.) 24 The Lorde B. and your Antichristian swinish rable. **1592** NASHE *P. Penilesse* Wks. (Grosart) II. 43, I loue the quicke-witted Italians..because they mortally detest this surley swinish Generation. **1606** S. GARDINER *Bk. Angling* 22 Drunkards, swinish Epicures, heretiques. **1685** BAXTER *Paraphr. N.T.* Luke viii. 32 Swinish sinners. **1790** BURKE *Fr. Rev.* 117 Learning will be cast into the mire, and trodden down under the hoofs of a swinish multitude. **1829** LYTTON *Disowned* lxxxiii, The reeking, gaping, swinish crowd. **1829** SCOTT *Anne of G.* xxiii, 'The swinish mutineers!' said Schreckenwald. **1857** H. S. BROWN *Manliness* 2 Far be it from me to say that *the* multitude is swinish, but certainly there is a swinish multitude.

b. Of actions, etc.: Characteristic of or befitting a swine; coarse, degraded, beastly.

1426 LYDG. *De Guil. Pilgr.* 3718 He, in hys swynys lawe, Off hys rudnesse bestyal, Ne kan no ferther se at al Toward the hevene. ? **1563** VERON (*title*) A Frvtefvl treatise of predestination,..with an apology of the same, against the swynyshe gruntinge of the Epicures and Atheystes of oure time. **1604** SHAKS. *Ham.* I. iv. 19 (Qo. 2) They clip vs drunkards, and with Swinish phrase Soyle our addition. **1605** —— *Macb.* I. vii. 67 When in Swinish sleepe, Their drenched Natures lyes. **1613** PURCHAS *Pilgrimage* IX. viii. 717 In this swinish education he had not so much as learned to reade. **1694** F. BRAGGE *Disc. Parables* xi. 381 Drunkenness, that swinish vice. **1817** BENTHAM *Parl. Reform* Wks. 1843 III. 469 Swinish the character, of the vast majority of that vast multitude. **1865** DICKENS *Mut. Fr.* III. x, In his worse than swinish state..he was a pretty object for any eyes.

2. Pertaining to or fit for swine.

1592 BRETON *C'tess Pembroke's Love* Wks. (Grosart) I. 22/2 The sweetest wine, is but as swinish wash, Vnto the water, of the well of life.

3. Having the nature of swine; that is a swine; consisting of swine.

1612 ROWLANDS *Knaue of Harts* (Hunter. Cl.) 27 Directly like the swinish Hogge he liues, That feeds on fruit which from the tree doth fall. **1799** S. TURNER *Anglo-Sax.* II. vii. 316 Ina..was amazed to find..a swinish litter on the couch of his repose. **1830** CARLYLE in *For. Rev. & Cont. Misc.* V. 10 All sorts of bovine, swinish, and feathered cattle. **1891** FARRAR *Darkn. & Dawn* lxvi, To have its site defiled with swinish offerings and Pagan shrines.

b. Resembling a swine or that of a swine, in aspect or other physical quality.

1805 [S. WESTON] *Werneria* 13 The swinish smell Most fetid [of swine-stone]. **1815** *Ann. Reg., Chron.* 17/2 There is hardly a company in which this swinish female [having features like a pig] is not talked of. **1889** W. CLARK RUSSELL *Marooned* xiv, The swinish outline of the porpoise.

Hence '**swinishly** *adv.*; '**swinishness**.

1545 BALE *Image Both Ch.* I. 39 b, For so muche as thou haste not..bene thankfull vnto God for such an heauenly gift, but rather swynishly troden it vnder thy feete. **1591** PERCIVALL *Sp. Dict.*, *Porqueria*, swinishnes. **1655** GURNALL *Chr. in Arm.* I. iii. (1669) 26/2 The Drunkard has nothing to say for himself, when you ask him why he lives so swinishly. *a* **1775** J. RUTTY in Boswell *Johnson* (1848) 551/2 [Johnson laughed heartily..at his mentioning, with such a serious regret, occasional instances of] swinishness in eating. *a* **1868** in Farrar *Seekers* (1875) 333 It stands out in noble contrast to the swinishness of the Campanian villas.

swink (swɪŋk), *sb. arch.* Forms: 1, 3–4 swinc, 2–3 swink-, 3 swinck-, swunk, *Orm.* swinnc, 3–5 swynk, swynke, 3, 6–7 swinke, 4 suink(e, suinc(k, suynk, (squink, squynk(e, 5 suenk), 6 swinck(e, 3–7 (9 *arch.*) swink. [OE. *swinc* str. n. (1) trouble, chastisement, (2) labour, toil (cf. *swincfull* SWINKFUL, *swincléas* SWINKLESS, *swinclíc* laborious), also *ȝeswinc* I-SWINCH, I-SWINK, nouns of action to *swincan* to SWINK, q.v.; cf. SWINCH and SWING *sb.*[1]]

†**1.** Trouble, affliction. *Obs. rare.*

c **1000** *Sax. Leechd.* III. 198 Erian se þe hine ȝesihð swincu mæste him onȝean cumað. **1154** *O.E. Chron.* (Laud MS.) an. 1137 On al þis yuele time heold Martin abbot his abbotrice..mid micel suinc. *c* **1430** *Erthe upon Erthe* x. 35 Whanne þat erþe upon erþe is brouȝt withinne þe brink, þan schal erþe of þe erþe haue a rewful swynk.

2. Labour, toil.

c **1175** *Lamb. Hom.* 155 Ach hwider wenden heo?..fram hele in vnhele, from reste in to swinke [*Trin. Coll. Hom.* 147 swinche]. *c* **1200** ORMIN 6103 Swa þatt tin swinnc be clene swinnc & att rihht time swunnkenn. *c* **1205** LAY. 2281 Moni swinc moni swæt Monine seorhfulne pleiȝe. *a* **1225** *Leg. Kath.* 805 Lure ow is to leosen Ower swinkes lan. *a* **1300** *Cursor M.* 921 Of erth þou sal, wit suete and suinc, Win þat þou sal ete and drinc. *c* **1386** CHAUCER *Prol.* 540 Hise tithes payde he ful faire and wel Bothe of his propre swynk and his catel. *c* **1400** *Rom. Rose* 5687 But right anoon aftir his swynke He goth to tauerne forto drynke. *c* **1450** *Mirk's Festial* 2 He most trauayl his body yn good werkes, and gete his lyfe wyth swynke. **1575** *Gammer Gurton* II. i. B ij, Chad a goodly dynner for all my sweate and swyncke. **1579** SPENSER *Sheph. Cal.* May 36 How great sport they gaynen with little swinck. **1624** SANDERSON *Serm., Ad Pop.* v. (1657) 306 So into these spiritual Sacrifices of Thanksgiving.. we infuse a quantity of our own swinke and sweat. **1638** W. LISLE *Heliodorus* x. 186 This [translation] have I wrought with day-and-nightly swinke. **1819** W. TENNANT *Papistry Storm'd* (1827) 112 The plew-man frae his day-lang swink Lay restin' on the kitchen-bink. **1896** A. AUSTIN *England's Darling* II. i, Who recks of summer sweat and swink, Or winter's icy pang?

attrib. *c* **1250** *Gen. & Ex.* 3172 Was hem noȝt werned ðat he crauen, For here swinc-hire he nu hauen.

†**3.** Heavy drinking: cf. next, 3. *Obs. rare*$^{-1}$.

1611 COTGR. s.v. *Dodo, Apres bu dodo*, Prov. After swink sleepe. [Cf. s.v. *Bu*, After liquor lazinesse.]

swink (swɪŋk), *v. arch.* and *dial.* Forms: 1 swincan, 3 swinken, (*Orm.* swinnkenn, 3–4 suink(e, 4 suinc, suynk, squink, squynke, *Ayenb.* zuynke), 3–6 swynke, 4–6 swynk, 4–7 swinke, (6 swincke), 4– swink. *Pa. t.* α. 1–3 swanc, (1 *pl.* swuncon), 3–4 swonke, swank, 3 swunke, swonc, (4 suanc, squank, 5 swanke). β. 4 swinkid, 8 swinked. *Pa. pple.* 3 i-swunke(n, swunnkenn, 4 (i-)swonke, 6 -swonck, 7 swonk, 9 swunk. β. 6, 9 swinked, 7–8 swinkt. [OE. *swincan*, pa. t. *swanc*, *swuncon*, pa. pple. **swuncen*, parallel formation to *swingan*, SWING *v.*[1]]

1. *intr.* To labour, toil, work hard; to exert oneself, take trouble.

Often alliterating with *sweat*.

Beowulf 517 (Gr.) ðit on wæteres æht seofon niht swuncon. *c* **1000** ÆLFRIC *Hom.* (Th.) II. 441 Martha swanc, and Maria sæt æmtiȝ. *a* **1200** *Moral Ode* 254 in *O.E. Hom.* I. 175 [Hie] luueden..hordom & drunken & a doules werche bliþeliche swunken. *c* **1200** *Trin. Coll. Hom.* 179 Ðe underlinges þenchen oðe dai hu hie muȝen mest swinken and spenen here flesh & here blod. *c* **1205** LAY. 7488 He swonc i þon fehte þat al he laude asweote. *Ibid.* 17408 Heo swunken [*c* **1275** swonke] ful swiðe. *a* **1225** *Ancr. R.* 404 Ase þauh a mon þet heuede longe i-swunken and failede efter his sore swinke. *c* **1250** *Gen. & Ex.* 2877 Ic..swanc and michil sorwe dreȝ. *a* **1300** *Cursor M.* 1047 Adam..suanc and suet and eue his wif, Of þe erth to win þar lijf. *c* **1300** *Havelok* 798 Swinken ich wolde for mi mete. It is no shame forto swinken. **13..** *Sir Beues* (A.) 3107 Þow hauest so swonke on hire to niȝt [etc.]. *c* **1384** CHAUCER *H. Fame* III. 85 Hit.. maketh alle my wyt to swynke On this castel to be-thynke. ? *a* **1400** *Morte Arth.* 2961 He..Sweltes ewynne swiftly, and swanke he no more! **1426** AUDELAY *Poems* 57 Let me never in slouth stynke, Bot grawnt me grace for to swynke. **1560** BECON *New Catech.* Pref., Wks. 1564 I. 289 Their pelfe, for the which they haue so swincked and sweate. **1591** SPENSER *M. Hubberd* 163 For they doo swinke and sweate to feed the other. **1622** FLETCHER *Span. Cur.* III. ii, We'll labour and swinck. **1642** H. MORE *Song of Soul* II. I. II. xii, Long have I swonk with anxious assay To finden out what this hid soul may be. **1714** CROXALL *Anoth. Canto Spenser* xxxiv, Many to up-climb it vainly strove, Swinking and sweating with their utmost Might. **1748** THOMSON *Cast. Indol.* II. ii, And they are sure of bread who swink and moil. **1820** SHELLEY *Let. to Mar. Gisborne* 59 That dew which the gnomes drink When at their subterranean toil they swink. **1872** O. W. HOLMES *Poet Breakf.-t.* i. 10 We poor wives must swink for our masters. **1885** STEVENSON *Pr. Otto* II. i. 68 The fellow swinking in a byre, whom fools point out for the exception.

†**b.** To journey toilsomely, travel. *Obs. rare*$^{-1}$.

c **1250** *Gen. & Ex.* 1656 Laban faȝnede him in frendes wune, Feren swunken ysaaces sunen. Iacob tolde him for quat he swanc So fer.

2. *trans.* †**a.** with cognate obj.; also, to gain by labour. *Obs.*

c **1200** [see SWINK *sb.* 2]. *c* **1200** *Moral Ode* 321 in *Trin. Coll. Hom.* 229 Swunke [*Egerton MS.* sswunche] we for godes luue half þat we doð for eihte Nare we naht swo ofte bicherd ne swo euele bikeihte. *a* **1225** *Ancr. R.* 110 Al his swinc foreloren þet he swonc on eorðe. **1340–70** *Alex. & Dind.* 855 Whan ȝe mow take..No swiche werkus to swinke as oþur swainus vsen. *c* **1386** CHAUCER *Sec. Nun's Prol.* 21 And to deuouren al that othere swynke.

†**b.** To cause to toil; to set to hard work, to overwork; *refl.* = sense 1. *Obs.*

c **1250** *Gen. & Ex.* 4018 He..wende wended godes ðoȝt, Oc al he swinked him for noȝt. *a* **1300** *Cursor M.* 23051 Þai ..suonken þam bath dai and night, For to beserue vr lauerd dright. *c* **1384** CHAUCER *H. Fame* I. 16 Ne neuer thinke To besely my Wytte to swinke To knowe of hir signifiaunce.

†**3.** *trans.* and *intr.* To drink deeply, tipple. (Cf. SWINGE *v.*[1] 2, SWINK *sb.* 3.) *Obs.*

c **1550** BALE *K. Johan* (Camden) 78, I am sure then thu wylt geve it hym in a drynke. Marry that I wyll & the one half with hym swynke, To encourage hym to drynke the botome off. **1581** J. BELL *Haddon's Answ. Osor.* 319 Swill and swincke soundly, make meery mightely. **1590** GREENE *Mourn. Garm.* (1616) 15 That one Darius, a great king, being dry was glad to swink his fill of a Shepheards bottle. **1590** *Cobler Canterb.* 68 Yet to drinke he would neare lin: But swincked with all his might.

swinked, swinkt (swɪŋkt, also 'swɪŋkɪd), *ppl. a. arch.* (after Milton). [f. SWINK *v.* + -ED[1].] Wearied with toil; overworked.

1634 MILTON *Comus* 293 That time the laboured Oxe In his loose traces from the furrow came, And the swink't hedger at his Supper sate. **1788** HURDIS *Village Curate* (1797) 77 The swinkt mower sleeps. **1845** AIRD *Old Bachelor* xv. 115 The swinkt labourers of the sweltering day. **1881** E. ARNOLD *Indian Poetry* 127 The sacristan, Leading his swinkèd ringers down the stairs. **1886** *Ch. Q. Rev.* XXII. 296 The care-worn mothers, the swinked toilers.

Swink(e)f(i)eldian: see SWENKFELDIAN.

swinker ('swɪŋkə(r)). *arch.* [f. SWINK *v.* + -ER[1].] One who swinks; a toiler, labourer.

1340 *Ayenb.* 90 Yef he deþ workes bodylyche as doþ þise zuynkeres and þise gememen. *c* **1386** CHAUCER *Prol.* 531 With hym ther was a Plowman,..A trewe swynkere and a good was he. **1393** LANGL. *P. Pl.* C. xx. 173 A fayre lye, That serueþ þese swynkeres to seo by a nyghtes. *a* **1450** *Tourn. Tottenham* 14 Theder com al the men of the contray,..And all the swete swynkers. *a* **1529** SKELTON *El. Rummyng* 105 She maketh therof port sale..To sweters, to swynkers, And all good ale drynkers. **1582** STANYHURST *Æneis* I. (Arb.) 17 Thee sulcking swincker. **1623** COCKERAM, *Swynker*, labourer [*mispr.* tabourer]. **1886** J. W. GRAHAM *Neaera* (1887) I. vi. 74 What do these rough swinkers know of these things? **1893** K. GRAHAME *Pagan Papers* 105 With most of us who are labourers in the vineyard, toilers and swinkers, the morning pipe is smoked in hurry and fear.

†**'swinkful,** *a. Obs.* [OE. *ȝeswincfull*, later *swincfull*: see SWINK *sb.* and -FUL.]

1. Full of toil or trouble; disastrous; troublesome, irksome; painful, distressing.

c **888** ÆLFRED *Boeth.* XIV. § 1 ðif hi yfele sint & lytiȝe þonne sint hi þe pliolicran & ȝeswincfulran hæfd ðonne næfd. *a* **1100** *O.E. Chron.* (Laud MS.) an. 1085, & þæs ilcan ȝeares wæs swiðe hefelic ȝear & swiðe swincfull. *c* **1175** *Lamb. Hom.* 7 Þeos world is..swiðe lewe & swincful. *a* **1225** *Ancr. R.* 292 Þu schalt ȝiuen me, Louerd, heorte-scheld aȝean þe ueonde; þet beoð þine swincfule pinen.

2. Hard-working, industrious, diligent.

c **1200** ORMIN 2621 Ȝho wass swinncfull..Inn alle gode dedess.

Hence †**'swinkfulness,** diligence.

c **1200** ORMIN 2526 Ȝho wass..Alt full..Off rihhtwis swinncfullnesse.

†**swinkhede.** *Obs. rare*$^{-1}$. In 4 swinched. [f. SWINK + *-hede*, -HEAD. For the formation cf. OE. (*ȝe*)*swincnis* 'tribulatio'.] A state of labour or toil.

c **1315** SHOREHAM vii. 737 In swinched þou schalt þy lyf leade, And ete ine swote.

'swinking, *vbl. sb. arch.* [f. SWINK *v.* + -ING[1].]

1. The action of the verb SWINK; toiling, toil, labour.

c **1175** *Lamb. Hom.* 69 Þurh trowþe & þurh swincunge. **1375** in Horstm. *Altengl. Leg.* (1878) 130/1 He tauȝte hem.. How þeȝ myȝte hem frutes gete Wiþ swet & swynkynge sore. *c* **1400** *Rom. Rose* 6703 Whanne her swynkyng is agone, They rede and synge in chirche anone. *a* **1500** *Erthe upon Erthe* xiii. 104 That erthe schuld labour the erthe In trowthe and sore swynkynge. **1906** CONAN DOYLE *Sir Nigel* xiii, Peter the Plowman grows weary of swinking in the fields.

†**2.** Deep drinking. *Obs.*

1590 *Cobler Canterb.* 60 But with swinking at hir will Shee lookt red about the gill.

'swinking, *ppl. a. arch.* [f. SWINK *v.* + -ING[2].] **a.** That swinks; labouring, toiling. **b.** Involving toil, laborious, toilsome.

a **1225** *Ancr. R.* 260 Two maner men habbeð neode uorte eten wel,..swinkinde men, & blod-letene. *a* **1693** *Urquhart's Rabelais* III. xv, Desist from all your swinking painful Labours. *a* **1849** J. C. MANGAN *Poems, Message to Iron Foundry* (1859) 51 Here, late and early, swinking hands, Fed volumed flames and blazing brands. **1860** SIR T. MARTIN *Horace* 10 While swinking Vulcan strikes the sparkles fierce and red. **1865** S. FERGUSON *Poems, Forging of Anchor* ii, And thick and loud the swinking crowd at every stroke pant 'ho!'

†**'swinkless,** *a. Obs.* In 1 swincleas, 4 suincless, 4–5 swynk(e)les. [f. SWINK *sb.* + -LESS.] Free from toil or trouble; painless.

c **1000** ÆLFRIC *Hom.* (Th.) II. 364 We sceolon on andwerdum life hine herian, ðæt we moton becuman to ðære swincleasan herunge. *a* **1300** *Cursor M.* 9421 Sa suincless [*v. rr.* swynkles, suynkles, swynkeles] and sua fair and bright, Als þat time was the sun o light.

swinney, swinny, var. SWEENY.

†**'swinward.** *Obs. rare*$^{-1}$. Alteration of *swinnard*, obs. var. of SWINEHERD, by assimilation to WARD *sb.*, keeper, guardian.

1613 W. BROWNE *Sheph. Pipe* ii. (1614) Dj, Neere to the May-pole on the way This sluggish Swinward met me.

swinyard, obs. var. of SWINEHERD.

†**swip,** *sb.*[1] *Obs.* Also swipe, *pl.* swippes. [f. SWIP *v.*]

1. A stroke, blow; = SWAP *sb.* 1.

c **1205** LAY. 7648 Nas næuere þe ilke bern þe auere iboren weoren þat of þen ilke sweorde enne swipe [*c* **1275** swip] hefde..þat he nes sone dæd. *Ibid.* 16498 þa swipen weoren grimme. *c* **1275** *Ibid.* 28551 Drowen sweorde longe and smiten on þe healmes..þe swippes were bitere.

2. Forcible movement; a rush.

c **1205** LAY. 31925 Þa fusden touward sæ fifti þusende baldere beornen..Mid þan formeste swipen [*c* **1275** swipe] her comen þreo hundred scipen.

†**swip,** *sb.*[2] *Obs.* [App. shortened f. SWEEP *sb.*] = SWAPE 3, SWEEP *sb.* 24, SWIPE *sb.*[1]

1639 HORN & ROB. *Gate Lang. Unl.* liii. § 583 A man may draw with a swip, and a scoop or a bucket. **1657** C. BECK *Univ. Char.* L 5, A swip to draw water.

†**swip,** *v. Obs.* Forms: 3–4 swippe, 4–5 swyppe, (5 squyppe), 7 swip; *pa. t.* 3 swipte, suipte, 4 swypped, swypte, 7 swipte; *pa. pple.* 3 i-swipt. [ME. *swippen*, pa. t. *swipte*, pointing to OE. **swippan*, by the side of **swipian* (recorded only in 3rd pers. ind. *sweopaþ*, and doubtfully in pa. t. *swipode*); f. *swip-*, represented also by OE. *swipu*, *swipe* scourge, ON. *svipa* whip (see SWEPE), *svipr* sudden sweeping movement, glimpse, fleeting appearance, *svipa* to swoop, flash, refl. to glance after or at, OHG. *swipfen* to move quickly in a curve, MG. *-swif* (gen. *-swiffes*) quick turning, in *nider-*, *ummeswif*; related to *swaip-* (see SWOPE *v.*[1]).]

1. *trans.* To strike, hit, smite. (Cf. SWAP *v.* 1, 1 b.)

c **1205** LAY. 878 Ich wulle mid swerde his heued of swippen. *Ibid.* 16518 [He] mid muchelere strengðe hine adun swipte. *a* **1225** *Leg. Kath.* 2452 He..hef þet hatele sweord up, & swipte hire of þet heaued.

b. To wield (a weapon) forcibly, esp. in a downward direction.

c **1205** LAY. 23978 Arður..his sweord Caliburne swipte mid maine. *c* **1275** *Ibid.* 16510 [He] heȝe hefde his sweorde and hit adun swipte.

c. *intr.* To deal a blow *at*. *rare.*

c **1380** WYCLIF *Serm.* Sel. Wks. I. 201 Cristis disciplis.. liȝten on þe corner stoon..and þanne fendis of helle dreden hem to swippen at hem.

2. *intr.* To move with haste or violence; to make a dash; to slip away, escape. (Cf. SWAP *v.* 4.)

c **1205** LAY. 28956 Þer weoren twenti and æhte of eorlene streone Suipten from londe seouen hundred scipene. *a* **1225** *Ancr. R.* 252 Ine swifte wateres..þe þet is isundred, he is sone iswipt forð. *c* **1275** LAY. 27627 Ridwalþan his sweord droh and swipte to þan kinge. **13..** *S.E. Leg.* (MS. Bodl. 779) in Herrig's *Archiv* LXXXII. 309/148 Moyses hadde a ȝerd, & to þe ground it cast: anon it worþ an addre & gan to swype fast. **13..** *E.E. Allit. P.* B. 1253 Alle þat swypped vnswolȝed of þe sworde kene. **1340** HAMPOLE *Pr. Consc.* 2196 When þe saul fra þe body swippes.

fig. *a* **1500** *Bernardus de cura rei fam.*, etc. (E.E.T.S.) iii. 214 Þow swerys wonder Swyftly, & Swyppe may it euer.

Hence †**'swipping** *vbl. sb.*, striking; *ppl. a.*, moving quickly.

c **1420** *Anturs of Arth.* 55 (Ireland MS.) The squyppand watur, that squytherly [*read* squyperly] squoes. *a* **1450** [see SWIPPLE 2].

swipe (swaɪp), *sb.*[1] Also 7 swype. [app. local variant of SWAPE *sb.* or SWEEP *sb.*] A contrivance of the form of a lever for raising a weight, *esp.* for raising water; = SWEEP *sb.* 23, 24, 26. (Cf. SWAFE *sb.* 3, SWAPE *sb.* 3, SWIP *sb.*[2])

1600 HOLLAND *Livy* XXIV. xxxiv. 533 He devised a crane or swipe to be planted aloft upon the wals, having at the one end, which hung over the sea, a drag or grappling hooke of yron like an hand,..which tooke hold upon the proo of a gallie, [etc.]. **1611** COTGR., *Bascule*, a swipe, scoope, or putgally to draw vp water withall. **1661** BLOUNT *Glossogr.* (ed. 2), *Swepe* or *Swipe* [*ed.* 1656 Sweep], was an instrument of war; like that which Brewers use with cross beams to draw water. **1699** POTTER *Antiq. Greece* III. xvi. 143 Ἀντλίον, ἄντλον, in Latin, *haustrum, tolleno*, or *tollena*, &c. a Swipe, or Engine to draw up Water. **1706** PHILLIPS (ed. Kersey), *Swipe*, an Engine to draw up Water; also another sort to throw Granadoes. *a* **1825** FORBY *Voc. E. Anglia*, *Swipe*, the lever or handle of a pump. **1852** BURN *Naval & Milit. Dict.* (1863) s.v., Swipe or bar of a sluice-gate with a counter-poise. **1905** *Sat. Rev.* 15 July 82/2 The 'swipe' of British brickfields.

b. *attrib.*: **swipe-beam,** the counterpoise lever of a drawbridge.

swipe (swaɪp), *sb.*[2] Also 9 swype. [? local variant of SWEEP *sb.* and therefore partly identical with prec.]

I. †**1.** An instrument used in cutting peas: see quot. *dial. Obs.*

1750 W. ELLIS *Mod. Husb.* IV. v. 41 [They cut pease] with their two instruments, called, in the hither part of this country, next London, swipe and pix: with the pix, or picks, a man hawls a parcel to him with his left hand, and cuts them with the swipe in the other hand.

2. a. A heavy blow; *spec.* a driving stroke made with the full swing of the arms, in cricket or golf; *transf.* one who makes such a stroke. *colloq.*

a **1807** J. SKINNER *Amusem. Leis. Hours* (1809) 42 Francie Winsy steppit in,..Ran forrat wi' a furious din, And drew a swinging swype. **1825** C. M. WESTMACOTT *Eng. Spy* I. 32 With the cricketers he was accounted a hard *swipe*, an active *field*, and a stout bowler. **1862** PYCROFT *Cricket Tutor* 44 The favourite swipe is sure to be risked. **1886** *Field* 4 Sept. 377/1 In driving for Tel-el-Kebir [a golf-hole], Kirk had a long swipe off the tee. **1893** FURNIVALL *Three Kings Sons* I. Forewords p. v, In all the battles, no one is split in two; no one has his head clean cut off at one swipe.

b. (*a*) A row or line of corn as it falls when mown; = SWATH[1] 3. (*b*) A streak or stripe produced as if by swiping.

1869 BLACKMORE *Lorna D.* xxix, Three good swipes he cut of corn, and laid them right end onwards. **1890** *Advance* (Chicago) 24 Apr., A long swipe of dirt across her dimpled cheek.

3. A copious draught. *dial.*

1866 GREGOR *Banffs. Gloss.* Addit.

II. [Miscellaneous senses of uncertain affiliation.] **4.** A groom or stableboy. *U.S. slang.*

1929 S. ANDERSON in *Mercury Story Bk.* 221, I had taken a job as swipe with one of the two horses Harry was campaigning. **1954** W. FAULKNER *Fable* 178 He hasn't got any money... What little there might have been, that cockney swipe threw away long ago on whores and whisky.

5. An objectionable person; also, such persons considered *collect. slang*.

1929 D. H. LAWRENCE *Pansies* 138 And do you think it's my business to be handing out money to a lot of inferior swipe? **1944** J. DEVANNY *By Tropic Sea & Jungle* xviii. 163 Some swipe has lost the fishing lines. **1951** R. PARK *Witch's Thorn* xiv. 177 His tormentors leapt off him... 'Bloody little swipes!' said Mr Mate Solivich.

6. The penis. *slang* (*U.S. Blacks*).

1967 'I. SLIM' in T. Kochman *Rappin' & Stylin' Out* (1972) 389 Slim, pimping ain't no game of love, so prat 'em and keep your swipe outta 'em.

swipe (swaɪp), *v.* [? partly local variant of SWEEP *v.*, partly f. SWIPE *sb.*[2]]

1. *trans.* and *intr.* To drink hastily and copiously; to drink at one gulp. (Cf. *sweep off*, SWEEP *v.* 6 b.) *slang* or *colloq.*

1829 BROCKETT *N.C. Words* (ed. 2), *Swipe*, to drink off to the very bottom. **1876** *Whitby Gloss.*, *Swipe*, *v.* to drink the whole at one draught. 'Swipe it off.' **1890** 'R. BOLDREWOOD' *Col. Reformer* (1891) 134 At the public, he talks a deal more than he swipes.

2. *intr.* **a.** (See quot. 1825.) *Sc.* **b.** To strike *at* with the full swing of the arms; chiefly in cricket (see SWIPE *sb.*[2] 2).

1825 JAMIESON, *To Swipe*, *v.n.* 1. To move circularly, Lanarks. 2. To give a stroke in a semicircular or elliptical form, as when one uses a scythe in cutting down grass, S. **1857** *Chambers' Inform.* II. 690/2 Always treat them [*sc.* 'shooting-balls'] entirely on the defensive in preference to 'swipeing away' at them blindly. **1857** HUGHES *Tom Brown* II. viii, The first ball of the over Jack steps out and meets, swiping with all his force. **1869** *Routledge's Ev. Boy's Ann.* 638 Wilson was now as bold as a lion, swiping at every ball.

c. *trans.* To deal a swinging blow or hit at (esp. in cricket).

1851 W. CLARKE in W. Bolland *Cricket Notes* vii. 148 Some would shut their eyes at a fast one, but might perchance swipe away a slow one for four. **1881** *Leicestershire Gloss.*, *Swipe*, *v.a.*, to hit anything a heavy blow, as a cricket-ball, &c. **1886** *Trans. Amer. Philol. Assoc.* XVII. 45 A vulgar but strong expression in the South for a severe beating is, 'He swiped up the very earth with him', or 'He swiped the whole thing out'—in these cases meaning about the same as sweep. **1888** *Sheffield Gloss.* s.v., The bat is swung round horizontally, and not in the usual way. A cricketer would say 'he fairly swiped it off his wicket'.

3. *intr.* and *trans.* = SWEEP *v.* 17.

1881 *Times* 22 Dec. 3/6 The men went out for the purpose of swiping for anchors. **1883** G. C. DAVIES *Norfolk Broads* xl. (1884) 314 Rusty anchors which have been 'swiped' up out of the deep. **1893** COZENS-HARDY *Broad Norfolk* 77 *Swiping*, raising old anchors for an Admiralty reward.

4. *trans.* To steal, 'appropriate'; to loot. *slang* (orig. *U.S.*)

1889 *Seattle Post-Intelligencer* 5 Dec. 8/1 'By adopting this method,' said the merchant, 'we can stand back and laugh at their vain attempts to 'swipe' our goods.' **1890** BARRÈRE & LELAND *Slang Dict.*, *Swipe* (American), to appropriate. Frequently said of actors or exhibitors who take the stage jokes of others, and pass them off for their own. **1896** *Boston* (Mass.) *Jrnl.* 5 Nov. 10/1 There must have been something of interest in the newspaper,..for I notice that somebody has swiped ours. **1900** KIPLING in *Daily Mail* 23 Apr. 4/5 He was in luck. Had helped 'swipe' a Boer wagon overturned by our shell fire. **1936** WODEHOUSE *Laughing Gas* xxii. 238 You expect me, do you, not only to act as a stooge for you in front of the camera, but to sit smiling in the background while you horn in and swipe my interview. **1946** 'S. RUSSELL' *To Bed with Grand Music* ii. 27 Is there another drink going before you swipe the lot? **1970** T. ROETHKE *Let.* (1970) 10 June 263 That beautiful Greek anthology you sent me some student swiped. **1982** *Verbatim* Autumn 3/1 The hero gallantly sets out to recover the item, which he does after much derring-do—climbing walls, crawling through windows, swiping addresses out of locked desk drawers.

Hence **'swiping** *vbl. sb.*

1833 in G. W. Ormerod *Ann. Teignbridge Cricket Club* (1889) 14 And when he's in the swiping mood, My stars! how Johnny works 'em! **1860** JAS. THOMSON in H.S. Salt *Life* (1889) ii. 39 O it's then we're on the loose, and the swiping grows profuse, And we drink rivers, lakes, and seas. **1862** PYCROFT *Cricket Tutor* 47 As to the Drive, (1) avoid 'Swiping', or hitting the ball in the air. **1883** G. C. DAVIES *Norfolk Broads* clxi. (1884) 314 The process of raising the anchors is called 'swiping'.

swiper ('swaɪpə(r)). [f. prec. vb. + -ER[1].]

1. A copious drinker. *slang* or *colloq.*

1836 F. MAHONY *Rel. Father Prout* (1859) 179 'Consule scholas Jesuitarum', exclaims the Lord Chancellor Bacon, who was neither a quack nor a swiper, but 'spoke the words of sobriety and truth'. **1878** *Cumberld. Gloss.*, *Swiper*, a hard drinker.

2. One who deals a swipe or driving stroke; also, a swipe.

1853 F. GALE *Public School Matches* 59 Swiper has the ball; now, if there is one ball which Swiper hits harder than any other, it is an on[-side] long hop rather wide to the leg. **1857** HUGHES *Tom Brown* II. viii, Jack Raggles the long-stop, toughest and burliest of boys, commonly called 'Swiper Jack'. **1860** LD. W. LENNOX *Pict. Sporting Life* I. 281 A 'swiper' (we adopt the phraseology of an old Westminster) might..smash the pane of a travelling-carriage.

swiper, obs. form of SWIPPER *a.*

swipes (swaɪps). *slang* or *colloq.* Also **swypes**. [? f. SWIPE *v.* (sense 1).] Poor weak beer; small beer; hence, beer in general.

1796 *Grose's Dict. Vulgar T.* (ed. 3), *Swipes*, purser's swipes; small beer; so termed on board the king's ships, where it is furnished by the purser. **1812** *Murphy Delany's Feast* 8 The Rattle-belly vengeance flew about, Swipes, 'tis call'd in common. **1821** SCOTT *Fam. Lett.* 6 Apr., I am bringing down with me a tankard for swipes. **1838** DICKENS *O. Twist* xxxix, It's been as dull as swipes. *a* **1845** HOOD *Sniffing a Birthday* x, To me it seems this is a day For bread and cheese and swipes. **1895** MEREDITH *Amazing Marriage* xv, You may get as royally intoxicated on swipes as on choice wine.

swipey ('swaɪpɪ), *a. rare.* [f. prec. + *-ey*, -Y.] Somewhat intoxicated; tipsy.

1821 P. EGAN *Life in London* II. ii. 181 If the latter are caught in any ways inclined to roosting from being swipy, the young buzzmen will make them pay dearly for the few winks they may enjoy. **1844** DICKENS *Mart. Chuz.* xxviii, 'He ain't ill. He's only a little swipey you know.' Mr. Bailey reeled in his boots, to express intoxication. **1865** —— *Mut. Fr.* III. x, A muddling and a swipey old child.

swiple, variant of SWIPPLE.

swipper ('swɪpə(r)), *a.* Now *dial.* Forms: 4-5 swiper(e, swyper, 4-6 *Sc.* swepyr, 5 swypir, -yr, swepir, -er, 6 swip(p)ir, swypper, shwyper, 6- swipper. [repr. (with change of meaning) OE. *swipor*, *ʒeswipor* crafty, cunning, corresp. to OHG. *swephar*, *sweffar*, *swepfar*, also *swef(f)ari*, *sweffri*, in the same sense; f. *swip-* to move quickly, root of SWIP *v.* Cf. LG. *swipp(e* clever, ON. *svipull* fickle.

In ME. texts the *þ* has been sometimes misread as *þ*, and this again changed to *th*. The Sc. variant *swippert* is found from the 18th c.; for the form cf. SWEERT = SWEER.]

Quick, nimble, active.

c **1375** *Sc. Leg. Saints* vii. (*Jacobus Minor*) 514 þane Iosaphus, as a wicht man & swepyr alswa, a swerd gat. **1387** TREVISA *Higden* (Rolls) III. 361 Aristotle..was sweper [*some MSS.* sweper, swyþer; *ed.* **1527** shwyper] and swift, and cleer of witte. **1398** —— *Barth. De P.R.* XII. xxi (Tollem. MS.), þe swalowe is..swiper and most swyfte of flyȝte. *c* **1412** HOCCLEVE *De. Reg. Princ.* 5221 Swypir [*v.r.* swepir] feendly hand with strook vengeable. *c* **1440** *Promp. Parv.* 484/1 Swypyr, or delyvyr, *agilis*. **1513** DOUGLAS *Æneis* VI. v. 20 Als fery and als swipper as a page. **1674** RAY *N.C. Words* 47 *Swipper*, nimble, quick. **1867** WAUGH *Old Cronies* viii, They were a lot o' th swipper'st stark'est, lads in Christendom, wur th' Lancashire Volunteers.

Hence †**'swipperly** *adv.*, quickly, nimbly.

? *a* **1400** *Morte Arth.* 1128 Bot ȝit the kynge sweperly fulle swythe he by-swenkez. *Ibid.* 1465 They..Swappez doune ffulle sweperlye swelltande knyghtez. *c* **1420** *Anturs of Arth.* 55 (Irel. Ms.) The squyppand watur, that squyperly [*printed* squytherly; *cf.* squeturly l. 540 *infra*] squoes. **1513** DOUGLAS *Æneis* IX. ii. 34 Furth fleand swepyrly.

swipple ('swɪp(ə)l). Also 5 **swepelles, swepyl, swipylle**, 7 **sweaple**, 7-9 **swiple**, 9 *Sc.* **swoople, swupple**. See also SUPPLE *sb.*[1] [prob. orig. f. *swēp-*, SWEEP *v.* or *swip-*, SWIP *v.* + instrumental suffix -ELS. Cf. LG. *swepelbessen* broom with which chaff is swept up.]

†**1.** A besom, mop. *Obs.*

14.. *Voc.* in Wr.-Wülcker 616/12 *Tersorium*, a swepelles (a malkyn).

2. The part of a flail that strikes the grain in thrashing.

a **1450** *Tourn. Tottenham* 167 Of sum were the hedys brokyn..Wyth swyppyng of swepyls [*v.r.* swipylles]. **1609** *Shuttleworths' Acc.* (Chetham Soc.) 184 For hollyn swipples, vijd. **1619** *Ibid.* 239 Twelve swipples. **1688** HOLME *Armoury* III. 333/1 The Swiple [of a Flail or Threshal is] that part as striketh out the Corn. **1824** MACTAGGART *Gallovid. Encycl.* s.v. *Barnman's-jig*, The swoople on the end of the hand-staff. **1902** A. THOMSON *Lauder & Lauderdale* xxiii. 261 An early working model of the threshing mill consisted of a series of flails or swiples..dangerous to approach. **1907** M. C. F. MORRIS *Nunburnholme* 249 The sound of the swipple on the barn floor was heard every working day all through the winter.

†**3.** app. A swivel. *Obs.*

1691 *Lond. Gaz.* No. 2632/4 A Gold Japanned Watch, with a Gold Chain, and 3 Sweaples.

swipy ('swaɪpɪ), *a.* [f. SWIPE *sb.*[2] + -Y.] Characterized by swipes or swinging strokes.

1852 in Bettesworth *Walkers of Southgate* (1900) 252 When, in the course of a swipy lucky innings straight balls are pulled to the leg.

swire (swaɪə(r)). Forms: α. 1 **sweora**, 2 **sweor**, 2-3 **swore**, 2-4 **sweore**; 3-4 **suere**, 3-5 **swere**, (4 **zuere**), 4-6 **sweere**. β. 1 **swiora, swyra, swira, suira, swura**, 3 **swiere**, 3-4 **swure**, (4 **suire, suyre, swyer**), 4-6 **swyr**, (5 **squyre**, 6 **swyir**, 7 **suir**), 4-9 **swyre**, 3- **swire**. γ. Chiefly *Sc.* 5-6 **swar**, 5-6, 9 **sware**, 6, 8-9 **swair**, (9 **squair**). [OE. *sweora*, *swiora*, Northumb. and late WS. *swira*, late WS. *swýra*, *swúra* wk. m.:—OTeut. *swerhan-, related to ON. *sviri* neck, beak of a ship, local name of a neck-shaped ridge in Iceland :—*swerhjan-; ulterior relations uncertain.

It is not certain whether the forms *swar(e*, *swair*, which are chiefly Sc., have arisen from false analogy (cf., e.g., *quair*, *quere*, QUIRE, and *sware*, *swere*, *swire*), or through exigency of rime.]

†**1.** The neck. *Obs.*

α. and β. *c* **888** ÆLFRED *Boeth.* xix. § 1 þæt ȝe underlutan mid eowrum swiran þet deaðlice ȝeoc. *a* **900** *Lorica Gloss.* 21 in *O.E. Texts* 172 *Cladam*, swiran [*altered to* swioran *later*]. **971** *Blickl. Hom.* 223 þa he þa Sanctus Martinus þæt ȝeseah, þa dyde he sona þæt hræȝl of his sweoran. *Ibid.* 241 ðif eow swa liciȝe uton sendon rap on his swyran. *c* **1000** ÆLFRIC *Gloss.* in Wr.-Wülcker 157/38 *Collum*, sweora *uel* swura. *c* **1175** *Lamb. Hom.* 49 þenne ualleð he þer inne þet him brekeð þe sweore. *c* **1200** *Moral Ode* 146 in *Trin. Coll. Hom.* 224 Swines brade is wel swete swo is of wilde diere Ac al to dire he hit abuið þe ȝieft þar-fore his swiere [*earlier version* dore, swore]. *c* **1205** LAY. 4012 Heo cærf him þene swure [*c* **1275** swere] atwa. *a* **1225** *Leg. Kath.* 2233 Streche forð þine swire scharp sweord to underfonne. **1303** R. BRUNNE *Handl. Synne* 5028 Ely..fyl bakward of hys chayre, And brak on two hys swyer. **13..** *K. Alis.* 1938 (Laud MS.) Vp he dresseþ heued & swire And gynneþ speke on þis maner. *c* **1380** *Sir Ferumb.* 3643 Ys scheld þan heng he aboute ys swyre, And forþ he prykede with gret yre. **1390** GOWER *Conf.* II. 30 Sche aboute hire whyte swere It dede, and hyng hirselven there. *a* **1400** *Leg. Rood* (1871) 134 Mi mouþ I pulte, my sweore I streiȝt To cusse his feet. *c* **1400** *Melayne* 36 Ladyes swete of Swyre. *c* **1430** *Syr Gener.* (Roxb.) 1175 She leid hir arme about his swere, She kyssed him with hertie chere. *c* **1470** HENRY *Wallace* IV. 316 Vpon the hede he straik with so gret ire, Throu bayne and brayn in sondyr schar the swyr. **1501** DOUGLAS *Pal. Hon.* I. xvii, Vp be the swire Myself I hangit. ? *a* **1600** *Marr. Sir Gawain* II. 58 in *Percy's Reliques* (1857) 388 Sir Kay beheld that lady's face And looked upon her sweere.

γ. *c* **1440** *Bone Flor.* 441 But yf he to hym hys doghtur geve, That ys so swete of sware [*rimes* fare, thare, mare]. *c* **1450** HOLLAND *Howlat* 171 Swannis suowchand full swyth, swetest of swar [*rimes* blythar, war, ar]. *c* **1470** *Gol. & Gaw.* 1053 Mony sweit thing of sware swownit full oft. **1501** DOUGLAS *Pal. Hon.* I. x, A Quene, as lyllie sweit of swair. **1513** DOUGLAS *Æneis* I. ii. 37 That lillie quhite of [*ed.* 1553 *erron.* as] swair.

2. A hollow near the summit of a mountain or hill; a gentle depression between two hills. *local* (occurs in several place-names in Scotland and the north of England).

OE. *ȝesweoru* translates Latin *colles* in *Ags. Ps.* (ed. Thorpe). OE. *sweoru* is used also = neck of water or strait, L. *fretum*.

c **1050** *Voc.* in Wr.-Wülcker 427/13 *Iuga*, duna swioran. *c* **1216** *Newminster Cartul.* (1878) 77 Ad crucem positam super le Swire de Fastside. **1375** BARBOUR *Bruce* XVII. 13 Fra Redis swyr till Orkynnay. *a* **1508** DUNBAR *Tua Mariit Wemen* 519 The soft souch of the swyr, and sovne of the stremys. **1513** DOUGLAS *Æneis* IV. iv. 50 Lo! ther the rais, rynning swyft as fyre, Drevin from the hychtis brekkis out at the swyre. **1573** *Satir. Poems Reform.* xxxix. 350 He raid throw montanes mony, mose, and myre..Then wes he worsland our ane wondie swyre. *a* **1598** D. FERGUSON *Prov.* (1641) § 608 Little kens the wife that sits by the fire, how the wind blaws on hurly-burly swire. **1790** A. TAIT in *Contemp. Burns* (1844) 144 Then from Dewar's Swair I tripped on my shanks. **1820** W. CHAMBERS *Life Bl. Dwarf* (1885) 1 A gentle rising hill to the south-west, called Manor Swire. **1893** *Northumbld. Gloss.*

3. *attrib.* and *Comb.* †**swire-bone** = NECKBONE; †**swireforth** *adv.*, neck forward, headlong.

c **825** *Vesp. Hymns* vi. 28 in *O.E.T.* 408 *Usque ad cervices*, oð swirban. *c* **1230** *Hali Meid.* 23 Leste hwase leope..& driue adun swireuorð, wiðuten ikepunge, deope into helle. ? *a* **1400** *Morte Arth.* 2959 The swyers swyre-bane he swappes in sondyre!

swire, dial. form of SQUIRE *sb.*

†**swirk**, *v. Sc. Obs.* [? f. root of next + *-k*. Cf. *twirk* and *twirl*.] *intr.* To spring *forth*.

1503 DUNBAR *Thistle & Rose* 8 Full craftely conjurit scho the Yarrow, Quhilk did furth swirk als swift as ony arrow.

swirl (swɜːl), *sb.* Also 5 **swyrl(l)e**, 6 **swirle**, *Sc.* **sworle, sworll**. [orig. Sc.: of uncertain source; if not of independent onomatopœic formation, prob. related to the similar Norw. dial. *svirla*, Du. *zwirrelen* to whirl, G. dial. *schwirrlen* to totter, which have the form of frequentatives of the stem contained in Da. *svirre*, Norw. dial. *sverra*, *svirra*, Sw. dial. *svirra* to whirl, G. *schwirren* to whiz, whir, chirp.]

1. a. An eddy, a whirlpool; an eddying or whirling body of water, in later use also of cloud, dust, etc.

c **1425** WYNTOUN *Cron.* IV. iii. 261 Than gert he draw þat ryvere all In foure hundreth and sexty small Narow swyrlis. **1513** DOUGLAS *Æneis* III. viii. 113 The swelland swirl wphesit ws to hevin. *Ibid.* IX. iii. 66 Be that ilk pyky laik, wyth brais blak And laithly sworlis [*ed.* **1553** swirlis]. *Ibid.* XII. xi. 125 A sworll of fyre blesis vpthraw!

1834 M. SCOTT *Cruise Midge* vi. (1836) I. 182 A white sheet of buzzing water,..in the small yeasty swirls of which the moon and stars sparkled diamond-like. **1840** CARLYLE *Heroes* i. (1904) 19 The Nottingham bargemen, when the River is in a certain flooded state (a kind of backwater, or eddying swirl it has, very dangerous to them), call it *Eager*. **1853** RUSKIN *Stones Venice* II. vi. § 8. 156 Seen through clefts in grey swirls of rain-cloud. **1861** J. R. GREEN *Lett.* (1901) 84 Fresh swirls of flame..leapt ever onward to some new prey. **1894** CROCKETT *Lilac Sunbonnet* 53 The keen, acrid swirls of wood-smoke blew into his eyes.

b. A fairground roundabout with freely-pivoted cars drawn by a spider frame. *slang.*

1962 *Sunday Express* 4 Feb. 1/4 She had four rides on the merry-go-round, two trips on the ghost train, and rides on the 'swirl' and the dodgems. **1968** D. BRAITHWAITE *Fairground Architecture* vi. 107 In the 1920's Savages of King's Lynn produced a ride known as the 'Womp'. This was a variant of the 'Whip'... Re-named the 'Swirl' by showmen, this ride was considerably refined by Thurston, Thurston and Lakin's Patents of 1929 and became one of the fastest rides on the fairground.

2. a. A whirling or eddying motion; a whirl, gyration.

1818 SCOTT *Br. Lamm.* xxxiv, The leaves are withering fast on the trees, but she'll never see the Martinmas wind gar them dance in swirls like the fairy rings. **1818** KEATS *Endym.* III. 630 Headlong I darted; at one eager swirl Gain'd its bright portal. **1871** H. MACMILLAN *True Vine* v. (1872) 201 The slender, fragile, branched corals, yield to the swirl of the surging sea. **1902** S. E. WHITE *Blazed Trail* xviii, He stepped.. out on the flat rock to which his guide brought the canoe with a swirl of the paddle.

fig. **1791** LEARMONT *Poems* 51 The tricks o' ilka ill gi'en churle He brawlie tells, An' a' their deeds winds to a swirl Wi' logic spells. **1880** T. A. SPALDING *Eliz. Demonol.* 133 The very rush and swirl of town life.

b. *Engin.* A circular motion imparted to the mixture entering the cylinder of an internal-combustion engine. Freq. *attrib.*

1926 *Engineering* 27 Aug. 279/1 It is possible with sleeve valve operation to provide a high degree of swirl in the cylinder, which.. serves to bring the air to the fuel. **1940** C. B. DICKSEE *High-Speed Compression-Ignition Engine* vii. 170 The swirl ratio, i.e. the ratio between the rate of air swirl and the rotational speed of the engine, varies in different designs. *Ibid.* The effect of the squish is.. to increase the swirl already present. **1979** P. J. BOWYER *Boat Engines* ii. 48 The mixing of air and fuel is all important so that the design of the inlet and exhaust ports, as well as the combustion area, is arranged to cause phenomena such as 'squish' or swirl.

3. a. A twist or convolution; a curl of hair; a knot in the grain of wood.

1786 BURNS *Twa Dogs* 36 His gawsie tail, wi' upward curl, Hung owre his hurdies wi' a swirl. **1825** JAMIESON, *Swirl*,.. a twist or contortion in the grain of wood. S. **1844** H. STEPHENS *Bk. Farm* II. 217 The hair.. which, notwithstanding its different swirls, all tends from the upper to the lower part of the body.

b. A tress of hair or strip of material round the head or hat. (Cf. SWIRL *v.* 1 b.) Also *attrib.*

1909 *Daily Mail* 3 Aug., A swirl of tulle.. draped to suggest the irregular surface of fur. **1909** *Daily Graphic* 4 Oct. 13/1, The adjustment of the new hats.. demands the new swirl coiffure. **1909** *Punch* 10 Nov. 326/1 Put off, put off your alien 'swirls', Resume.. Those little inexpensive curls.

4. Special Comb.: **swirl chamber** *Engin.*, a chamber in an internal-combustion engine fashioned so as to impart a whirling motion to the mixture passing through it into the cylinder; **swirl skirt**, a skirt cut circular or with many gores, so as to swirl when the wearer walks.

1934 *Proc. Inst. Mech. Engineers* CXXVIII. 169 In some types of engine a very distinct improvement had been effected by making an additional passage from the cylinder head into the swirl chamber, so that the 'squish' was allowed to interfere.. with the swirl. **1976** *Daily Tel.* 3 Nov. 12/3 The swirl chamber in the 2068cc Rekord engine is specially designed for the best mixture and combustion of the fuel. **1962** *Harper's Bazaar* Aug. 32 Dashing young suit with a swirl skirt. **1976** *Morecambe Guardian* 7 Dec., Wearing a Russian-style fur hat, boots and a warm-coloured burgundy coat with swirl skirt, the Princess was escorted.. to the private dining room at Cartmel College.

swirl (swɜːl), *v.* Also 6 Sc. **sworl.** [orig. Sc.: see prec.]

1. *trans.* To give a whirling or eddying motion to; to bring into some position by a whirling motion; to whirl, brandish.

1513 DOUGLAS *Æneis* VIII. ii. 64 The lang stremis and wallis[= waves] round sworling.

1790 A. WILSON *Poems, The Pack* 61 Fearfu' winds loud gurl'd, An' mony a lum dang down, an' stack, Heigh i' the air up swirl'd. **1818** MISS FERRIER *Marriage* xxvi, Some withered leaves were swirled round and round, as if by the wind. **1844** *Ayrshire Wreath* 192 He swirled his brand wi' a' his mycht. **1879** SEGUIN *Black For.* ii. 72 The immense mass of floating timber, swirled and carried along by the raging waters. **1898** WATTS-DUNTON *Aylwin* III. iv, Great isles and continents of cloud were rolled and swirled from peak to peak.

b. To give a twisted or convolute form to; to wind round (hair, trimming) in a 'swirl'; also, to wrap round *with* something.

1902 *Westm. Gaz.* 31 July 3/2 The trimming,.. just a nice ribbon swirled round the crown. **1908** *Ibid.* 6 June 13/2 A black or dark straw hat swirled with tulle. **1909** *Daily Mail* 30 Sept. 5/3 Women.. with their tresses dressed in the new manner swirled compactly about the head.

2. *intr.* **a.** Of water or of objects borne on water: To move in or upon eddies or little whirlpools.

1755 R. FORBES *Ajax's Sp.* in *Poems in Buchan Dial.* (1785) 3 Wha.. in a tight Thessalian bark To Colchos' harbour swirl'd. **1785** BURNS *Winter Night* ii, While burns, wi' snawy wreeths up-choked, Wild-eddying swirl. **1816** L. HUNT *Story Rimini* I. 24 The far ships.. chase the whistling brine, and swirl into the bay. **1858** KINGSLEY *Misc., Chalk-stream Stud.* (1859) I. 167 The low bar over which the stream comes swirling and dimpling. **1902** S. E. WHITE *Blazed Trail* xlvii, The drivers were enabled to prevent the timbers from swirling in the eddies.

b. Of other objects: To move rapidly in eddies or in a whirling or circular course.

1858 KINGSLEY *Misc., Chalk-stream Stud.* (1859) I. 175 Great tails and back-fins are showing above the surface, and swirling suddenly among the tufts of grass. **1863** —— *Water Bab.* iii, While the fish are swirling at your fly as an oar-blade swirls in a boatrace. **1877** KINGLAKE *Crimea* VI. xii. 247 Pouring through its two embrasures, or swirling round by its flanks, the bulk of the Grenadier Guards [etc.]. **1882** B. HARTE *Flip* i, The stage-coach swirled past the branches of a fir. **1885** M. ARNOLD *Poor Matthias* 144 Swallows trooping in the sedge, Starlings swirling from the hedge. **1896** CROCKETT *Cleg Kelly* (ed. 2) 21 The wind swirled about the old many gabled closes of Edinburgh.

3. Of the head, etc.: To swim, to be giddy or dizzy.

1818 HOGG *Brownie of Bodsbeck* I. xiii. 288 We'll never mair.. swirl at the gelloch o' the ern. **1891** DOYLE *White Company* xvi, Even as he spoke,.. his head swirled round.

Hence **swirled** *ppl. a.*, **'swirling** *vbl. sb.*

1825 JAMIESON, *Swirling*, giddiness, vertigo. **1882** *Daily Tel.* 12 Sept. 2/2 A furious swirling of foam. **1899** *Westm. Gaz.* 6 Apr. 3/2 These swirlings of tulle. **1909** *Daily Mail* 9 Oct. 11/4 The softly swirled folds of velvet.

swirl, north. dial. f. SQUIRREL.

swirling ('swɜːlɪŋ), *ppl. a.* [f. SWIRL *v.* + -ING².] That swirls.

1. Characterized by twists or convolutions; curling; twisted.

1807 TANNAHILL *Poet. Wks.* (1846) 21 Auld, swirlon, slaethorn, camsheugh, crooked Wight. **1831** *Sutherland Farm Rep.* 83 in *Libr. Usef. Knowl., Husb.* III, Covered with short, white, flat-growing, swirling hair. **1883** G. H. BOUGHTON in *Harper's Mag.* Apr. 685/1 The rapid increase of swirling ornament as a feature of domestic.. architecture.

2. Moving in eddies or whirlpools, or with a circular motion or course; whirling.

1849 KINGSLEY *Misc., N. Devon* (1859) II. 246 A deep dark pool of swirling orange-brown. **1853** RUSKIN *Stones Ven.* II. iv. § 10. 63 The great mouldering wall.. worn by the rain and swirling winds into yet unseemlier shape. **1887** T. A. TROLLOPE *What I remember* II. ii. 32 The white gulls.. started from their roosting-places.. or returned to them from their swirling flights. **1898** H. DAY *K. Spruce* xx. 242 Blinking the big flakes out of his eyes as he breasted the swirling storm.

swirly ('swɜːlɪ), *a.* [f. SWIRL *sb.* + -Y.]

1. Twisted; knotty, gnarled (cf. SWIRL *sb.* 3).

1785 BURNS *Halloween* xxiii, A swirlie, auld moss-oak. **1825** JAMIESON, *Swirlie*.., entangled; applied to grass that lies in various positions, so that it cannot be easily cut by the scythe. **1828** P. CUNNINGHAM *N.S. Wales* (ed. 3) II. 165 The swirly bark always denoting a swirly fibre in the wood.

2. = SWIRLING *ppl. a.* 2. Also *fig.*

1912 W. R. TITTERTON *From Theatre to Music Hall* II. i. 117 Viennese operetta, luscious and swirly. **1939** A. RANSOME *Secret Water* xxvii. 317 The water would be a good deal higher.., and already felt swirly and strong. **1979** R. JAFFE *Class Reunion* (1980) I. ii. 38 Her favorite black taffeta dress with the swirly pleated skirt.

swirrel, north. dial. f. SQUIRREL.

swirt, north. dial. f. SQUIRT.

swirtie, obs. Sc. form of SURETY.

swis, obs. 3 sing. pres. ind. of SUE *v.*

1435 MISYN *Fire of Love* II. vi. 84 Alle þinge he suld caste downe þat emnyly lufars swis.

swish (swɪʃ), *int.* or *adv.* and *sb.*¹ [Imitative.]

A. *int.* or *adv.* Expressive of the sound made by the kind of movement defined in B. 1; with a swish. Also reduplicated ***swish, swish.***

1837 HOOD *Agric. Distress* 35 When swish! in bolts our bacon-hog Atwixt the legs o' Master Blogg. **1890** *Scribner's Mag.* Nov. 565/2 Swish went the whip. **1899** CROCKETT *Kit Kennedy* 181 Swish-swish went Kit's feet through the dew-drenched grass. *a* **1911** in 'G. A. Birmingham' *Lighter Side Irish Life* (1912) iv. 72 So the executioner swung his sword and swish went poor John's [the Baptist's] head.

B. *sb.*

1. a. A hissing sound like that produced by a switch or similar slender object moved rapidly through the air or an object moving swiftly in contact with water; movement accompanied by such sound.

1820 CLARE *Rural Life* (ed. 3) 60 I'd just streak'd down, and with a swish Whang'd off my hat soak'd like a fish. **1862** KINGSLEY in *Macm. Mag.* Oct. 443 The salmon.. went on.. with a swish or two of his tail which made the stream boil again. **1862** TYNDALL *Mountaineer.* vi. 45 The swish of many a minor streamlet mingled with the muffled roar of the large one. **1878** STEVENSON *Inland Voy.* 200 The rhythmical swish of boat and paddle in the water. **1886** J. R. REES *Divers. Bookworm* iii. 95 The swish of the angler's rod. **1887** KNOX LITTLE *Broken Vow* vi. 86, I drew the curtains away with a good swish behind the dressing-table. **1895** MEREDITH *Amazing Marriage* ix, The willowy swish of silken dresses. **1896** 'IAN MACLAREN' *Kate Carnegie* 289 In my study I hear the swish of the scythe.

b. Reduplicated ***swish, swish*** or ***swish-swish.***

1833 M. SCOTT *Tom Cringle* viii, I heard the frequent swish-swish of the water, as they threw bucketsful on the sails to thicken them. **1894** A. ROBERTSON *Nuggets*, etc. 61 The swish-swish of wild cats and the cries of opossums were heard. **1900** M. H. GRANT *Words by Eyewitness* vii. (1902) 145 The incessant swish, swish of bullets.

c. A rough hiss heard at each revolution of a faulty gramophone record.

1949 G. A. BRIGGS *Sound Reproduction* xxi. 130 A background noise of even volume.. is much more tolerable than a sudden or changing sound such as the click of a damaged surface or the swish of a warped record. **1978** *Gramophone* Jan. 1307/1 Background noise can be at remarkably low levels on disc—though admittedly in only the best examples, and with an ever-present risk of warps, swishes and other annoyances.

2. A 'dash' of water upon a surface.

1851 G. H. KINGSLEY *Sport & Trav.* (1900) 524 So up we went.. getting a shivering 'swish' of ice-cold water in our faces. **1867** SMYTH *Sailor's Word-bk.*, *Swish*, an old term for the light driving spray of the sea. **1879** BLACK *White Wings* xvii, The brave *White Dove* goes driving through those heavy seas,.. followed by a swish of water that rushes along the lee scuppers.

3. Short for *swish-broom*, *-tail* (see SWISH-).

1844 H. STEPHENS *Bk. Farm* II. 697 A neat swish is all that is requisite [for a draught-horse] at any time. **1873** E. SPON *Workshop Receipts* Ser. I. 62/1 A small broom, termed a swish, made from the waste cuttings of cane. **1901** ALLDRIDGE *Sherbro* xxiii. 246 A Madeira mosquito swish, which was simply a horse's tail fastened to the end of a short stick.

4. A cane or birch for flogging; also, a stroke with this.

1860 *Sat. Rev.* 12 May 600/2 If he flogs, it is according.. to a fixed tariff of 'swishes'. **1885** MEREDITH *Diana* xxvi, A man who has not blessedly become acquainted with the swish in boyhood.

5. A male homosexual; an effeminate man. *U.S. slang.*

1941 B. SCHULBERG *What makes Sammy Run?* iv. 71 If.. that fat swish lets the producer know he did all the writing, you're dead. **1967** L. FORRESTER *Girl called Fathom* xiv. 178 'I think he's a swish.' 'A—what?' 'Faggot. Queer.' **1975** J. F. BURKE *Death Trick* (1976) iv. 62 [He] dresses mod, and he talks like some kind of a swish.

6. *Cricket.* A rapid or careless attacking stroke. *colloq.*

1963 *Times* 25 Feb. 4/1 He resorted at last to the swish, an invitation to the disaster which presently befell him. **1977** *Daily Mirror* 15 Mar. 31/3 The striking sequence that whistled young Hookes from 36 to 56 was as follows: An enormous one-bounce slog over mid-off; a swish to long leg [etc.].

swish (swɪʃ), *sb.*² [? Native name.] A native mortar of West Africa. Also *attrib.*

1863 R. F. BURTON *W. Africa* II. 240 The town is filled with deep holes, from which the sand mixed with swish for walls has been dug. **1879** —— *El-Medinah* xiii. (ed. 3) 174 He sees a plain like swish-work [*ed.* 1855 tamp-work], where knobs of granite act daisies. **1881** *Standard* 12 Nov. 5/1 The 'swish' used in ordinary houses is simply red earth worked up with water until it thus acquires a certain degree of tenacity. **1897** MARY KINGSLEY *W. Africa* 113 The swish huts of the Effiks.

swish (swɪʃ), *v.* [Imitative. Cf. SWISH *int.* or *adv.* and *sb.*¹]

1. *intr.* To move with a swish (see SWISH *sb.*¹ 1); to make the sound expressed by 'swish'.

1756 [E. PERRONET] *Mitre* I. liii, Next see two huge Academies:.. With these conjoin a thousand more, Of vaulted roof, or humble floor;.. Where swish the rods or whirl the toys. **1860** G. H. K. in *Vac. Tour.* (1864) 116 The rain pattering against the window-panes, and the birches outside swishing and rasping against the walls. **1860** O. W. HOLMES *Elsie V.* x. (1891) 139 The rustic who was.. swishing through the grass with his scythe. **1877** BLACK *Green Past.* xviii. 147 The wheels swished through the pools. **1885** *Chamb. Jrnl.* 15 Aug. 515/2 The water swishing amongst the pebbles at the far end of the cove. **1898** G. W. STEEVENS *With Kitchener to Khartum* 146 The bullets were swishing and lashing now like rain on a pond.

2. *trans.* To cause to move with a swish; *esp.* to whisk (the tail) about.

1799 COLERIDGE *Devil's Thoughts* ii, And backward and forward he swish'd his long tail As a Gentleman swishes his cane. **1862** WHYTE-MELVILLE *Inside Bar!* 347, I confess I have no great confidence in a thorough-bred mare, that swishes her tail a good deal in harness. **1880** JEFFERIES *Greene Ferne Farm* 263 Swishing the briar, which bent easily.

b. *intr.* (const. *with*).

1854 P. B. ST. JOHN *Amy Moss* 106 As he advanced swishing before him with a stick he had picked up. **1866** BLACKMORE *Cradock Nowell* xix, He swished away very hard with the broom the moment he saw such a visitor.

c. *trans.* To move or remove with (or as with) a swishing movement.

1894 *Daily News* 25 Sept. 5/6, 80,000 men equipped as a modern army cannot be swished about in the sort of way that is assumed in these discussions. **1904** A. ST. H. GIBBONS *Africa* I. v. 59 We were again swished downstream at the rate of some ten miles an hour.

3. *intr.* To jump a high hedge, brushing through the twigs at the top and making them bend. Also ***to swish a rasper*** (see Eng. Dial. Dict.).

1825 ALKEN *Nat. Sports Gt. Brit.* (1903) Plate 15 Swishing at a Rasper. **1864** G. A. LAWRENCE *M. Dering* II. 22 Breaking through the irregular line [of the enemy].. as they would have 'swished' through a bulfinch in the Shires.

4. *trans.* To flog, esp. at school.

1856 THACKERAY *Misc., Fashionable Authoress* II. 470 Doctor Wordsworth and assistants would swish that error out of him in a way that need not here be mentioned. **1872** *Routledge's Ev. Boy's Ann.* 614/2 As he wouldn't tell he must be swished. **1875** REYNARDSON *Down the Road* 18 How he [*sc.* Dr. Keate] used to 'swish' a fellow if he caught him up at barracks! **1896** E. A. KING *Ital. Highways* 339 One small boy is being horsed on the back of another and soundly swished.

5. To brush with a swishing sound.

1889 *The County* xxx, The long grass moistly swishes my petticoats.

Hence **swished**, **'swishing** *ppl. adjs.*; also **'swisher**, a flogger.

1860 THACKERAY *Round. Papers, Hundred Y. Hence* (1861) 137 Here are the scourges. Choose me a nice long, swishing, buddy one. **1869** GIBBON *R. Gray* vii, The brig was cutting through the water with a swishing sound. **1884** E. YATES *Recoll.* I. ii, A desperate swisher the doctor. **1891** ZANGWILL *Bachelor's Club* 181 Large banks of clouds.. melted into swishing showers. **1898** WOLLOCOMBE *Morn till*

Eve vii. 83 The leading crew, with a long swishing stroke, pass the barges.

swish (swɪʃ), *a. colloq.* [Perh. f. as prec.] Smart, elegant, fashionable.

1879 *N. & Q.* 5th. Ser. XI. 116 Provincialisms..in the neighbourhood of Lydford... *Bain't you swish?* = How smart you are. **1922** E. RAYMOND *Tell England* II. xi. 269 Really, under these conditions, the Peninsula, we felt, would be quite 'swish'. *Ibid.* xii. 273 'If I'm killed you can put those lines over me.'.. 'They are rather swish,' I murmured. **1933** AUDEN *Witnesses* in *Listener* 12 July (Suppl.) p. ii/1 He was born in a palace, his people were swish. **1960** *Guardian* 14 July 7/7 A party at a swish place with the best people. **1972** *Daily Tel.* (Colour Suppl.) 7 Jan. 7/1 He..is a lover of the sea, food, lilies, the Old Vic, and swish cars: he is contemplating the purchase of a £5,380 Mercedes 350SL Coupé. **1974** P. DICKINSON *Poison Oracle* ii. 60 The architects..had made their name running up swish hotels in Beirut.

swish-, the vb.-stem used attrib. or advb.: **swish-broom**, a short-handled broom, usually made of twigs, for swishing water, etc.; **swish-cane**, a light slender cane such as can be swished; so **swish-whip**; **swish cut** *sb.* (see quot. 1725); *a.* (see quot. 1831); **swish-tail**, †(*a*) *slang*, a pheasant; (*b*) a long flowing tail which can be swished about (earlier SWITCH *tail*); also *attrib.*

1891 N. GOULD *Double Event* 151 A light *swish cane he twirled about. **1725** *Fam. Dict.* II. 5 Y 4/2 [A horse] that.. neither cuts under his Knee, which is call'd the **Swish Cut*, nor crosses, nor claps one Foot on another. **1831** *Lincoln Herald* 11 Feb. 1 The tail of the coat swish cut (cut off towards a point). **1796** *Grose's Dict. Vulgar T.* (ed. 3), **Swish Tail*, a pheasant; so called by the persons who sell game for the poachers. **1826** *Sporting Mag.* XVIII. 431 [He] had four swishtail greys, but not of the right cut. **1844** J. T. HEWLETT *Parsons & W.* iii, His swish tail ain't long enough. **1845** J. T. SMITH *Bk. for Rainy Day* 93 He..carried a *swish-whip when he walked.

'swishing, *vbl. sb.* [f. SWISH *v.* + -ING[1].]

1. The action of moving with a swishing sound; a swishing movement or sound.

1860 THACKERAY *Round. Papers, On being found out* (1861) 126 What a butchery,..what an endless swishing of the rod! **1891** in Mrs. A. P. Martin *Cooee* 277 The swishing of the ducks' wings. **1897** S. CRANE *Third Violet* xxvi. 177 Hawker heard a step and the soft swishing of a woman's dress.

2. A flogging; esp. so called at Eton. Also *attrib.*

1859 J. PAYN *Foster Brothers* ix. 134 The Times controversy upon the great 'swishing' case at Winton. **1863** KINGSLEY *Water-Bab.* i, The birches birched him as soundly as if he had been a nobleman at Eton, and over the face too (which is not fair swishing, as all brave boys will agree). **1890** R. C. LEHMANN *H. Fludyer* 47 Don't let the Mater know about this; but nobody..thinks anything of a swishing. **1901** *Athenæum* 27 July 121/1 Had not our young friend enjoyed better luck than he deserved, his visits to the 'swishing-room' would have been even more frequent.

swish-swash ('swɪʃ,swɒʃ), *sb.* (*adv.*). Also 6 **swyshe swashe**. [Reduplicated f. SWISH with alternating vowel.]

1. An inferior or wishy-washy drink. Also *attrib.*

1547 BOORDE *Introd. Knowl.* ii. (1870) 126 Swyshe swashe metheglyn I take for my fees. **1577** HARRISON *England* III. i. 96/2 in *Holinshed*, There is a kind of swish swash made also in Essex,..wyth Hony and water, which the countrey wiues putting some pepper & a little other spyce among, call meade. **1881** J. SARGISSON *Joe Scoap's Jurneh* 49 It was sad swish-swash stuff, an nut hoaf boilt. **1884** DOWELL *Taxation England* IV. 55 The small sour swish-swash of the poorer vintages of France.

†**2.** A violent or swaggering person. Also *attrib.* Cf. SWASHBUCKLER. *Obs.*

1582 STANYHURST *Æneis* III. (Arb.) 92 Vp to the sky reatching, thee breetherne swish swash of Ætna. **1593** G. HARVEY *Pierce's Super.* Ffiv b, Quiet thy rage, Imperious Swish-swash.

B. *adv.* expressing alternation or repetition of a swishing movement.

1865 G. MACDONALD *Alec Forbes* 29 And still the instrument of torture went swish-swash round his little thin legs. **1913** M. ROBERTS *Salt of Sea* xix. 461 The sea had a motion in it, up and down, swish-swash.

swish-swish: see SWISH *sb.*[1] 1 b.

swishy ('swɪʃɪ), *a.* [f. SWISH *sb.* or *v.* + -Y.]

1. Characterized by swishing.

1828 C. J. MATHEWS in Dickens *Life* (1879) I. x. 308 A young foal ambling after her aged mother, and now and then seizing her by her swishy tail. **1875** MISS COBBE *False Beasts* 71 Two little fishy, swishy arms. **1890** JESSOPP *Trials Country Parson* ii. 68 Our brooms are so new, so swishy.

2. *slang.* Characteristic of a male homosexual; effeminate. Also as *sb.*

1941 G. W. HENRY *Sex Variants* II. 1177 *Swishy.* The reference is to the peculiarly effeminate walk of many male homosexuals. **1954** C. ISHERWOOD *World in Evening* II. 125 You thought it meant a swishy little boy with peroxided hair, dressed in a picture hat and a feather boa, pretending to be Marlene Dietrich? Yes, in queer circles, they call *that* camping. **1959** J. OSBORNE *World of Paul Slickey* I. v. 48 He's a cad... He's contrary, he's a swishy. **1968** *Globe & Mail Mag.* (Toronto) 13 Jan. 6/3 Though they ordinarily despise swishy gestures, even masculine homosexuals will sometimes camp (exhibit feminine mannerisms).

Swiss (swɪs), *sb.* and *a.* Forms: 6 **Swyce**, *pl.* **Swices, Swesses**, 6–7 **Swisse**, 7 **Swizz**, 7–8 **Suisse**, 7– **Swiss**. [ad. F. *Suisse*, ad. MHG. *Swiz* (cf. MDa. *Svids, Suitz*).]

A. *sb.* **1.** (Pl. *the Swiss*; †formerly *the Swisses.*) A native or an inhabitant of Switzerland.

pl. (*a*) **1515** PACE in *St. Papers Hen. VIII*, VI. 39, I be this day butt forti milis fromme the Swisses. **1522** J. CLERK in Ellis *Orig. Lett.* Ser. III. (1846) I. 312 He shewed me also that the Bastard of Savoy was with the Swices. **1535** *Lincoln Diocese Documents* 251 After them came the swesses euery man with his Javelinge in his hande. **1577–8** W. DAVISON in Nicolas *Mem. Sir C. Hatton* (1847) 45 He..solicited the succour and assistance of..the Swisses. **1608** CHAPMAN *Byron's Trag.* I. i. 8 At fourteene yeares of age he was made Colonell To all the Suisses seruing then in Flanders. **1687** DRYDEN *Hind & P.* III. 177 Those Swisses fight on any side for pay. **1735** BERKELEY *Querist* §324 What sea-ports or foreign trade have the Swisses? **1796** [see BASTARD *a.* 4]. **1801** tr. *Gabrielli's Myst. Husb.* IV. 265 The Swisses excepted.

pl. (*b*) **1678** BUTLER *Hud.* III. iii. 458 Lawyers..make their best Advantages, Of other quarrels, like the Swiss. *a* **1700** EVELYN *Diary* Apr. 1646, I..pass'd the guard of Swisse. **1799** *Med. Jrnl.* II. 494 The Swiss are indebted, it is thought, to the vigorous tone of their digestive organs, for the long preservation of their lives. **1831** SIR J. SINCLAIR *Corr.* II. 404 The Scots and the Swiss have always felt a strong predilection for each other.

sing. **1632** MASSINGER & FIELD *Fatal Dowry* I. ii, And thou thyself slave to some needy Swiss. **1770** LD. HUNTINGDON in *3rd Rep. Hist. MSS. Comm.* 430/2 The imputation..of being an accommodating man, that voted like a Swiss with every administration. **1771** FLETCHER *Checks* Wks. 1795 II. 357 Like a true Suisse I love blunt honesty. **1829** SCOTT *Anne of G.* xxviii, 'I set at all', said the daring young Swiss.

2. The Swiss dialect of German or other language spoken by the Swiss. *rare.*

1846 WORCESTER. *Swiss*, a native, or the language, of Switzerland. **1949** J. C. HEROLD *Swiss without Halos* i. 15 There are several popular misconceptions concerning the language situation in Switzerland. Some believe that the Swiss speak a language called Swiss. **1972** L. P. JOHNSON in M. Pasley *Germany* i. 19 Alsatian, Swabian and Swiss are forms of Alemannic.

3. Short for *Swiss muslin*. Freq. *dotted Swiss*.

1895 *Montgomery Ward Catal.* Spring & Summer 19/1 Imported Curtain Swiss, white with woven coin spots. **1897** *Sears, Roebuck Catal.* 214/1 *Shirt*..With wide pleated puff bosom of snow white dotted Swiss. **1909** *Public Ledger* (Philadelphia) 24 June 5/7, 50c. for 75c. to $1. Dressing Sacques: Lawns and Swisses. **1924** C. E. MULFORD *Rustlers' Valley* vi. 68 He thought he could make out an oval face drawing back from the dotted Swiss. **1948** E. B. WHITE *Let.* June (1976) 294 Mrs. Dow has just entered this room bearing fresh dotted Swiss curtains. **1978** J. UPDIKE *Coup* (1979) iv. 157 An overheated room with..dotted Swiss curtains.

4. A tournament, usu. of bridge or chess, played in accordance with the Swiss system (see sense 1 b of the adj. below).

1953 *British Chess Federation Year Bk. 1951–52* 150 Do not expect the Swiss to do more than it is capable of doing. **1965** *Listener* 29 Apr. 651/2 It is usual, for publicity purposes, to pair the favourite with one of the local hopes in the first round of a Swiss. **1975** *Games & Puzzles* June 4/2 A 5-round Swiss would make an excellent final.

B. *adj.*

1. a. Of, belonging to, or characteristic of the Swiss or Switzerland; native to, or coming from, Switzerland. Also *Swiss-French*, *-German* adjs. and sbs., (designating) the dialect of French or German spoken in Switzerland, or a speaker of this. Cf. *French-Swiss, German-Swiss* at first element.

1530 PALSGR. 278/1 Swyce or swycers pype, *fleuste dalemant.* **1613** CHAPMAN *Maske Inns Court*, A strange person..half French, halfe Swizz. **1706–7** FARQUHAR *Beaux Strat.* v. v, My Valour is downright Swiss; I'm a Soldier of Fortune, and must be paid. **1843** *Penny Cycl.* XXVI. 32/1 A dialect of the Swiss-German is the language of the country. **1846** LINDLEY *Veg. Kingd.* 707 Arnica montana, a Swiss herb, called in our gardens Mountain Tobacco. **1857** *Ch. Times* 20 Aug. 186/1, I never yet saw a Swiss breakfast without a bowl of honey on the table. **1941** M. F. K. FISHER in *As they Were* (1983) 58 She..stood close against the stone, saying, 'Oh, you are adorable, adorable'..in..Swiss-French. **1961** L. F. BROSNAHAN *Sounds of Lang.* vii. 166 [pf, ts] and [kx] are still almost exclusively characteristic of High German, the former two in the standard language, the last confined to a few of the Swiss-German dialects. **1964** M. A. K. HALLIDAY et al. *Linguistic Sciences* 83 Germanic speakers in Switzerland regard themselves..as speaking a distinct 'Swiss-German'. **1969** R. PETRIE *Despatch of Dove* I. i. 19 Her French was fluent, without the savoyard singsong you could so often detect in Swiss-French. **1970** *Guardian* 2 June 15/4 Mr Schwarzenbach is a Swiss-German. **1979** T. BARLING *Olympic Sleeper* i. 17 Her accent could have been Swiss-French.

b. Designating a system of organizing tournaments, usu. of bridge or chess, under which each player or team is matched, in each round except the first, against an opponent with a similar score, but no two opponents may meet more than once.

1953 *Brit. Chess Federation Year Bk. 1951–52* 150 The Swiss system in the last few years..has become increasingly popular. **1964** FREY & TRUSCOTT *Official Encycl. Bridge* 599/1 *Swiss system* (for multi-session team-of-four events), a method which has been used successfully for many years in major chess tournaments. When insufficient time is available for a complete round robin, a partial round robin is played. **1965** *Listener* 29 Apr. 651/1 The most popular method of deciding a large tournament is now the Swiss system, a hybrid of the conventional all-play-all event and a knock-out. **1973** *Jewish Chron.* 19 Jan. 43/2 This is the first time the English Bridge Union have held a 'Swiss' teams event.

2. In names of things, animals, etc. actually or reputedly coming from Switzerland: e.g. ***Swiss cambric, chalet, clock, copper, darning, deal, embroidery, flute, franc, lace, milk, muslin, patchwork, pigeon, pine, shell, watch*** (see quots.); **Swiss bank**, a bank in Switzerland, often chosen by international clients, whose anonymity and security are preserved by a system of numbered accounts (see NUMBERED *ppl. a.* 2); also **Swiss banker, banking**; **Swiss chard** = *silver beet* s.v. SILVER *sb.* and *a.* 21 e; **Swiss cottage**, a chalet; hence, a type of tent; **Swiss cream**, a type of trifle; **Swiss drill**, a cylindrical drill with the cutting point shaped into two pyramidal planes; **Swiss file** (see quot. 1964); **Swiss guards**, mercenary soldiers from Switzerland used as a special bodyguard by former sovereigns of France and other monarchs: still employed at the Vatican; **Swiss Itch** *U.S. slang* (see quot. 1967); **Swiss melilot**, a plant, *Trigonella cœrulea*; **Swiss plover** or **sandpiper**, a large plover (*Squatarola helvetica*) having four toes like a sandpiper; **Swiss roll**, a 'sweet' consisting of sponge cake rolled up with a layer of jam; **Swiss steak** *U.S.*, a steak (usu. round) cooked by dipping in flour, pounding and braising, and served with vegetables; hence, a steak (usu. a less tender cut) suitable for cooking in this way; **Swiss stone-pine**: see STONE-PINE; **Swiss sword**, a basket-hilted sword used in the 16th c. by Swiss foot-soldiers; **Swiss tapeworm**, the broad tapeworm, *Bothriocephalus latus*; **Swiss tea**, an infusion of several herbs of the genus *Achillea*, common in the Swiss Alps.

1949 M. CRANSTON *Introd. Switzerland* v. 54 To have one's money in a Swiss bank is to have it somewhere secure against wars and revolutions. *Ibid.* Capital flowed into Switzerland during the two decades between the wars, and Swiss bankers were able to take advantage of this. **1962** SAYERS & LINDER in R. S. Sayers *Banking in Western Europe* 188 The Swiss banker does not regard bonds as a really attractive use of resources. **1981** P. O'DONNELL *Xanadu Talisman* ix. 187 Your Swiss banker telephones confirmation of receipt. **1982** D. WILTSE *Wedding Guest* xvi. 215 The reputation of the entire Swiss banking community, depends on reliability in following procedures the client stipulates. **1882** CAULFEILD & SAWARD *Dict. Needlework* s.v. *Swiss Cambric*, This is a cotton material, manufactured at Zurich and St. Gall for a long period before muslins..were produced in England. **1879** I. L. BIRD *Lady's Life in Rocky Mts.* v. 58 A small house, which bore a delightful resemblance to a Swiss châlet. **1970** 'D. HALLIDAY' *Dolly & Cookie Bird* iii. 33 The story..about Diana doing her Swiss chalet housekeeping last winter. [**1731** P. MILLER *Gardeners Dict.* s.v. *Beet*, The Swiss or Chard Beet.] **1832** Swiss chard [see CHARD[2]]. **1900** L. H. BAILEY *Cycl. Amer. Hort.* I. 289/1 This vegetable is also known as Sea-kale Beet and Swiss Chard. **1950** *N.Z. Jrnl. Agric.* Jan. 10/1 Silver beet also called Swiss chard and sea kale beet is grown for its foliage. **1980** *Times* 23 June 16/5 The Swiss chard, a spinach-like green, was developing brown dry spots on the leaves. **1897** M. H. KINGSLEY *Trav. W. Africa* i. 16 Manchester cottons and shawls, Swiss clocks, and..vividly coloured china. **1982** R. LUDLUM *Parsifal Mosaic* xix. 306 'Pretty punctual, huh?' 'Like a Swiss clock.' **1881** DALPAYRAT *Limoges Enamels* 8 Of the kind called virgin or Swiss Copper. **1820** M. WILMOT *Let.* 1 Aug. (1935) 75 A beautiful Swiss Cottage, built in the most correct manner. **1884** T. H. LEWIN *Fly on Wheel* iv. 117 The 'Swiss cottage' tent, on which I decided [in 1862], as it had the advantage of being divisible into two compartments, with, in addition, a small bathing-room, and large outer flaps which served as shelter for my servants. **1968** *Sat. Rev.* (U.S.) 27 July 40/1 Take the omnibus..to the Swiss Cottage—the play-chalet which Prince Albert designed for his children. **1971** A. D. GORWALA *Queen of Beauty* 70 In the snug well-lighted Swiss Cottage tent that was his itinerant home and office for weeks on end while on tour. *Ibid.* 77 There were quite a number of places at which the old Swiss Cottage proved useful. **1845** E. ACTON *Mod. Cookery* xx. 527 (*heading*) Swiss cream, or trifle. (Very good.) **1861** MRS. BEETON *Bk. Househ. Managem.* 748 *Swiss cream*..¼lb. of macaroons or 6 small sponge-cakes, sherry, 1 pint of cream, 5 oz. of lump sugar, 2 large tablespoonfuls of arrowroot, the rind of 1 lemon, the juice of ½ lemon, 3 tablespoonfuls of milk. **1903** JOYCE *Let.* 26 Feb. (1966) II. 31 Today for dejeuner I had some cold ham, bread and butter, Swiss cream with sugar. **1882** CAULFEILD & SAWARD *Dict. Needlework* s.v. *Swiss Darning*, The method of reproducing Stocking-web by means of a darning needle and a thread of yarn worked double. **1843** HOLTZAPFFEL *Turning* I. 107 The sounding boards of..most.. instruments, are made of the Swiss deal. **1846** HOLTZAPFFEL *Turning* II. 547 It is sometimes called the Swiss drill, and was employed..for making the numerous small holes, in the delicate punching machinery for manufacturing perforated sheets of metal and pasteboard. **1882** CAULFEILD & SAWARD *Dict. Needlework* s.v. *Swiss Embroidery*, This Embroidery is the same as is known as Broderie Anglaise, Irish Work, and Madeira Work. **1960** E. L. DELMAR-MORGAN *Cruising Yacht Equipment & Navigation* xiv. 163 The Swiss files are most useful for repair jobs. **1964** S. CRAWFORD *Basic Engin. Processes* i. 8 Needle files or Swiss files, small fine-cut files of various cross-sections, used for instrument work and in the match-making industry. **1852** SEIDEL *Organ* 105 Swiss flute is an open flue-register. **1934** WEBSTER, Swiss franc. **1938** M. MUGGERIDGE *In Valley* ix. 62, I wrote a cheque for twenty Swiss francs. **1973** 'G. BLACK' *Bitter Tea* i. 11 She had just made quite a killing..and had invested her take in

Swiss francs. *a* **1700** Evelyn *Diary* 22 Oct. 1644, In this Palace the Duke ordinarily resides, living with his Swiss guards. **1823** Scott *Quentin D.* Introd., With his usual attendants of two files of Swiss guards preceding, and the same number following him. **1959** *Life* 7 Dec. 51/1 The technique..was..old stuff to mature Americans who in Prohibition days had used it, complete with salt, as the safe way to take bathtub gin, then called 'Swiss Itch'. **1967** *Amer. N. & Q.* June 152/1 '*Swiss Hitch*'.., I believe the correct form is Swiss Itch, and I suspect that there is more than one recipe, but I have always heard the term applied to the process by which one places a pinch of salt on the back of the hand, then licks it off, and takes immediately a jigger of tequila, and follows *that* by immediately biting into a segment or a slice of lime. **1865** *Reading Industr. Exhib. Catal.* in *Reading Mercury* (1968) 17 Aug. 11 Swiss lace, tambour muslin, leno and every description of curtain materials. **1882** Caulfeild & Saward *Dict. Needlework* s.v. *Swiss Lace*, Lace was manufactured in Switzerland during the sixteenth century. **1889** *Girl's Own Paper* Summer No. 13/1 A small tin, which everyone supposed was Swiss milk, but which proved to be a shilling tin of cream. **1898** *Jrnl. Sch. Geog.* (U.S.) Oct. 296 He had brought up a family of thirteen children entirely on Swiss milk and American flour. **1832** T. S. Fay *Dreams & Reveries* I. 155 If I had any-thing to say about bobbinet or Swiss muslin collars, I should at least wait till he had reached some passage not particularly remarkable for beauty. **1882** Caulfeild & Saward *Dict. Needlework* s.v. *Swiss Muslin*, Muslin was manufactured at St. Gall and Zurich long prior to the production of the textile in England. It is a coarse description of buke or book muslin, much used for curtains, made with raised loose work in various patterns, and also plain. **1882** Caulfeild & Saward *Dict. Needlework* s.v. *Patchwork, Raised [Patchwork]*. This is also known as Swiss Patchwork, and is made by stuffing the patches out with wadding so that they are well puffed up. **1855** *Poultry Chron.* III. 140/1 (*Pigeons*) Gulls or Swallows, Shields, Swiss. **1881** Lyell *Pigeons* 101 The Swiss pigeon..also goes by the name of moon, crescent, and badge of honour pigeon. **1879** *Man. Artill. Exerc.* 71 Swiss pile drivers. **1896** A. J. Hipkins *Pianoforte* 122 *Swiss Pine*, a name applied by pianoforte makers to the finer qualities in growth and grain of *Abies Excelsa*, the Spruce Fir. **1874** Coues *Birds N.W.* 449 Black-bellied, Gray and Swiss Plover. **1897** *Econ. Confect. Bk.* 13 Swiss Roll. Ingredients. ½ lb. of Flour. ½ lb. of Castor Sugar. 9 eggs. A pinch of Volatile Salts. 6 drops Essence of Lemon. **1753** Chambers *Cycl., Supp.* s.v. *Trumpet-Shell*, The rough *buccinum*, called the Swiss-shell. **1932** E. Craig *Cooking with Elizabeth Craig* 175 Swiss Steak... Take a..2 pound slice of steak. Sprinkle thickly with flour. Pound... Brown steak on both sides. **1947** L. P. De Gouy *Gold Cookery Bk.* vi. 345 Swiss Steak. The original name of this recipe was 'Schmor Braten.' It is three centuries old. **1973** *Black Panther* 12 May 10/1 Safeway was charged with.. mislabeling swiss steaks as round steak for an extra profit of ten cents per pound. **1860** Hewitt *Anc. Armour* III. 617 The basket-hilted sword does not appear till the middle of the [sixteenth] century. It is often called by old writers the 'Swiss sword'. **1860** *Chambers' Encycl.* I. 29/1 The inhabitants of the Alps..use them [*sc.* leaves of Achillæa] for making what is called Swiss Tea. **1885** C. M. Yonge *Two Sides of Shield* I. iii. 28 Her mother's little Swiss watch. **1977** H. Kaplan *Damascus Cover* (1978) xvi. 174 The Colonel had honed the movements of the two Israeli agents with the precision of a Swiss watch.

Swiss cheese. 1. Cheese from Switzerland.

1822 Lamb *Let. to Coleridge* 9 Mar., Your potted char, Swiss cheeses, French pies.

2. *fig.*, with reference to the pitted or honeycombed structure of some varieties of Swiss cheese. Freq. *attrib.*

1924 Novak & Martzloff in *Amer. Jrnl. Obstetrics & Gynecol.* VIII. 387 We are accustomed to speak of the endometrium as presenting a 'swiss cheese' pattern in these cases. *Ibid.* 409 The glands are of the 'swiss cheese' pattern, large dilated glands being found side by side with glands which are small and narrow. **1929** Hall & Niles *One Man's War* i. 5 Passing out of the up-rush, I dropped into what was then known as a Swiss cheese section of air. **1949** *Bull. Geol. Soc. Amer.* LX. 1290/1 Collapsed pumice fragments, usually less resistant than the matrix, weather to give the rock a Swiss-cheese appearance. **1968** *Nature* 10 Feb. 513/2 Such a universe can be simulated by a 'swiss cheese' model in which spherical perturbations..are distributed through space. **1970** J. R. Lincke *Jenny was no Lady* vi. 81 The planes ran into 'Swiss-cheese' air, downdrafts..and violent gusts. **1974** A. Lurie *War between Tates* i. 13 Their friendship now is full of Swiss-cheese holes in which sit things which cannot be discussed.

3. Special combination: **Swiss cheese plant**, an evergreen climbing plant, *Monstera deliciosa*, of the family Araceæ, native to central America and often cultivated as a house plant for the sake of its large ovate perforated leaves.

1946 M. Free *All about House Plants* xviii. 267 One of the most interesting [aroids] is the..Swiss Cheese Plant, because of the holes naturally formed in the much-divided leaves. **1955** W. E. Shewell-Cooper *Pot Plants* i. 15 *Monstera deliciosa*..is usually called the Swiss Cheese plant. **1970** *Sunday Tel.* 3 May 19/2 A variation of the 'Swiss cheese plant' has golden marking besides the familiar 'holes' in the leaves. **1981** 'J. Ross' *Dark Blue & Dangerous* xxiii. 130 An immense Swiss Cheese plant climbed a cement pillar.

†**'Swissener.** *Obs. rare.* In 6 Suycener. [f. MHG. *Swicen(lant)* or MDu. *Switsen(lant)* Switzerland + -er[1]. (Cf. next.)] A Swiss.

1542 Udall *Erasm. Apoph.* 276 The Suyceners are yᵉ whole nacion of Suycerlande.

†**'Swisser.** *Obs.* Forms: 6 Swycer, Swycher, Suisser, Swizer, 6–7 Swizzer, 6–8 Swisser, 7 Swizar, Swiser. See also Switzer. [ad. MHG. *Swycer, Schwyczer*, var. *Sweitzer* Switzer, or f. F. *Suisse* Swiss + -er[1].] A Swiss.

1530 Palsgr. 278/1 Swyce or swycers pype, *fleuste dalemant*. **1549** Thomas *Hist. Italie* 38 Out of the bisshops palaice came his garde of Suizzers all in white harneis. **1593** Nashe *Christ's T.* Wks. 1904 II. 99 Law, Logique, and the Swizers, may be hir'd to fight for any body. **1596** —— *Saffron Walden* Wks. 1905 III. 35 A payre of Swissers omnipotent galeaze breeches. **1600** Marston, etc. *Jack Drum's Entert.* i. (1601) Bj, Nor do I enuy Poliphemian puffes, Swizars slopt greatnes. **1602** Shaks. *Ham.* iv. v. 97 Where are my Switzers [*Quartos* Swissers]? **1602** Breton *Mother's Blessing* xlv, Nor swagger with a Swiser for his swill. **1611** Cotgr. s.v. *Papier, Vin papier*, white wine; (called so by some Swizzers). **1671** tr. *Palafox's Conq. China* xxix. 524 Two handed like the Swissers Swords. **1734** Ozell tr. *Brantome's Sp. Rhodom.* (1744) 210 They left only some Swissers in the Rear.

'Swissess. *rare.* [f. Swiss + -ess.] A female Swiss; a Swiss woman or girl.

1793 A. C. Bower *Diaries & Corr.* (1903) 144 She is a Swissess and speaks pretty broken English. **1818** Shelley *Let.* Pr. Wks. 1888 II. 241 A Mr. and Mrs. Hoppner, the gentleman an Englishman, and the lady a Swissesse.

swissing ('swɪsɪŋ), *vbl. sb.* Also **swizzing**. [Origin unascertained.] The calendering of bleached cloth by passing it between pairs of rollers after damping.

1888 Sansone *Dyeing* 223 Three bowl swizzing calender. **1910** *Encycl. Brit.* X. 379/1 The pieces are simply passed through for 'swissing', i.e. for the production of an ordinary plain finish.

swit, obs. Sc. form of soot *sb.*[1]

a **1583** Polwart *Flyting w. Montgomerie* 685 (Tullibardine MS.) Thy sentences of swit richt sweitlie smellis, Thow sat neir the chymlay niuk þat maid þame.

switch (swɪtʃ), *sb.* Also 7 **swits, swytche, swich.** [In branch I.: early forms *swits, switz* (see next); prob. ad. Flem. or LG. word represented by Hanoverian *swutsche*, variant of LG. *zwukse* long thin stick, switch (cf. *zwuksen* to bend up and down, also, to make a swishing noise like a lash). In branch II., f. switch *v.*]

I. 1. a. A slender tapering riding whip.

Phr. ***switch and spurs, upon the switch and spur*** = at full speed, in hot haste: see spur *sb.*[1] 2 a, quots. 1592–1708.

1592 Shaks. *Rom. & Jul.* ii. iv. 73 Swits and spurs, Swits and spurs, or Ile crie a match. ? *c* **1600** *Distracted Emp.* iii. ii. in Bullen *O. Pl.* (1884) III. 220, I must tyre, Theres not a swytche or prycke to quycken me. **1609** B. Jonson *Masque of Queens* Wks. (1616) 956 A Cloud of pitch, a spurre, and a switch, To haste him away, and a whirlewind play. **1655** Bp. Hall *Serm. Higham* 1 July, Rem. Wks. (1660) 209 The dog fears the whip, & the horse the switch. **1791** Boswell *Johnson* 16 Oct. 1773, He preferred riding with a switch. *c* **1815** Jane Austen *Persuas.* x, To cut off the heads of some nettles..with his switch. **1894** Weyman *Under Red Robe* ii. (1897) 31 Thundering on the door with my riding switch.

†**b.** *fig.* Stimulus, incentive. *Obs. rare.*

1630 J. Taylor (Water P.) *Gt. Eater Kent* 12 Any sawcy spurre or switch of sowre veriuce or acute vineger.

2. a. A thin flexible shoot cut from a tree.

1610 Beaum. & Fl. *Scornf. Lady* v. iii, One that vpon the next anger of your brother, must raise a sconce by the high way, and sel switches. **1613** Shaks. *Hen. VIII*, v. iv. 9 Fetch me a dozen Crab-tree staues, and strong ones: these are but switches to 'em. **1693** Evelyn *De la Quint. Compl. Gard.* II. 114 Some fix spikes from space to space into the Wall, sticking out about two Inches, to fasten Laths, Poles, Perches, or Switches upon them. **1711** Addison *Spect.* No. 117. ⁋5 There was not a Switch about her House which her Neighbours did not believe had carried her several hundreds of Miles. **1801** J. Thomson *Poems Sc. Dial.* 133 A switch o' rowan-tree. **1845** S. Hislop in G. Smith *Life* ii. (1888) 57 The cotton is a low growing shrub, consisting of little more than two switches branching from each other.

b. A massage instrument made of twigs.

1887 D. Maguire *Art Massage* iv. (ed. 4) 114 Percussions with the closed hand, the palette, switch, or any other instrument of percussion.

3. Name for various mechanical devices for altering the direction of something, making a connexion or disconnexion, or other purposes.

a. On a railway: A movable rail or pair of rails pivoted at one end, forming part of the track at a junction with a branch line, siding, etc., and used to deflect or 'shunt' a train, car, etc. from one line to another; often made tapering, and in that case distinctively called ***split switches, point-switches***, or *points* (point *sb.*[1] 3 f). Also, by extension, the whole apparatus of which this is the essential part.

1797 Curr *Coal Viewer* 27 The part (*h*) being a stop to prevent the switch (*g*) from flying out too far. **1837** *Civil Eng. & Arch. Jrnl.* I. 71/2 The switches so arranged, that an engine can never run off the line. **1845** *Ann. Reg.* 89 A 'switch' which, when turned in one direction allows the train to pass direct on. **1898** Hamblen *Gen. Manager's Story* iv. 40, I ran ahead.., opened and closed switches, cut off and coupled on the engine [etc.].

b. In an electric telegraph, telephone, signalling-, lighting-, or other apparatus: A lever, plug, or other device for making or breaking contact, or altering the connexions of a circuit, e.g. for connecting a trunk line with one or other of various other lines. Also *loosely* = switchboard.

1865 W. H. Preece *Railway Electric Signalling* 16 The instrument which is employed to raise and lower the signal is called a 'Switch'. **1866** R. M. Ferguson *Electr.* 240 The clerk..thereupon turns the switch and sets the clock-work in motion. **1889** Preece & Maier *Telephone* xxx. 461 This switch consisted of a board provided with as many spring plates as there were transmitters, and which allowed the switching on or off the batteries working the microphones. **1899** J. L. Williams *Stolen Story*, etc. 42 Mr. Stone pulled down the switch and shut off the circuit of the Day's outer office. **1909** Le Queux *House of Whispers* xviii. (1913) 128 She touched the switch, and the place became flooded by a soft, mellow light from lamps..concealed behind the bookcases against the wall.

c. 'A key on a gas-burner to regulate the amount of gas passing, and, consequently, the light' (Knight *Dict. Mech.* 1875).

d. *fig.* or in fig. contexts, esp. with reference to railway or electrical switches; ***asleep at the switch***, etc. (*U.S. colloq.*), negligent of or oblivious to one's responsibility, off guard.

1898 G. B. Shaw *Let.* 16 Mar. (1972) II. 16, I am very cross and incommoded..by having to adapt myself [to a new secretary]... For three sentences, I feel resentful..and quite put out. At the fourth the switch operates and I am on to the new line as if I had never dictated to anybody else. **1906** H. Green *At Actors' Boarding House* 368 Snow.. awoke the startled Williams, asleep at the switch. **1932** W. Faulkner *Light in August* viii. 161 Mind and body as if on the same switch, believing that he had seen a movement among the shadows. **1958** *Observer* 19 Oct. 18/4 The television play], though a bit slow off the switch, scored well over half-marks for sincerity and realism. **1966** C. Achebe *Man of People* iv. 51 We must not let up. We just must not be caught sleeping on the switch again.

e. *Computers.* A program instruction that selects one or other of a number of possible paths according to the way it is set.

1951 M. V. Wilkes et al. *Preparation of Programs for Electronic Digital Computer* 167 Numbers at one end of a permitted range can be detected by adding a constant and testing the sign, and then the result of the discrimination may be used to operate a multiway switch. **1962** R. S. Ledley *Programming & utilizing Digital Computers* vi. 227 The switch designator is of the form name[n] where name is the name of the switch corresponding to the switch declaration and n is an integer telling which label of the switch declaration to use. **1970** O. Dopping *Computers & Data Processing* v. 89 A switch can consist of a branch instruction, the address part of which can be altered by the program.

4. A long bunch or coil of hair, esp. of false hair worn by women to supplement the natural growth of hair.

1870 L. M. Alcott *Old-Fashioned Girl* xi. 223 So much hair of her own, that she never patronized either rats, mice, waterfalls, switches, or puff combs. **1878** B. Harte *Man on Beach* 87 'If I couldn't afford any other clothes, I might wear a switch, too!' hissed the Amazonian queen. **1882** J. E. Sandeman in *Proc. R. Geog. Soc.* N.S. IV. 264 One Kachin *swaba*..had two switches of hair of the thickness of one's thumb, and four cubits long. **1888** *Pall Mall G.* 4 Aug. 5/1 The list of switches, such as the Jeunesse, the Frou Frou, the Basket Plait, and the Queen Anne.

5. A stag having switch-horns.

1912 *Blackw. Mag.* Dec. 805/2 'He's nobbut a "switch",' he whispered into Lord Donald's ear.

II. 6. An act of switching; a blow with a switch; also in *Angling* (cf. next, 3).

1809 T. Donaldson *Poems* 199 I'll gie ye still anither switch, Or a' be done. **1839** Mrs. Kirkland *New Home* xxvi. 166 Henry gave Job such a switch across the knuckles as effectually cleared the bridle. **1867** F. Francis *Angling* v. 130 The running line goes before the casting line, and it requires a sharp switch or cut to get the casting line fairly forward. **1883** Mrs. E. Kennard *Right Sort* xxi, [She] raised her whip-hand and gave the mare a smart switch.

7. Gunnery. ***angle of switch*** = switching angle (switching *vbl. sb.* 5).

8. a. A change from one state or course to another; an alteration of position, policy, etc.

1920 Ade *Hand-Made Fables* 27 A switch had to be made. The Wholesaler..wished him on to the Banker. **1941** *News Rev.* 14 Aug. 4/2 The Soviet's entry into the war against Nazi Germany meant a switch in the Communist Party's home policy as well as its foreign outlook. **1951** M. McLuhan *Mech. Bride* (1967) 151/2 In the space of six months it recently shifted a large section of its enterprises from murder to love comics. The combined attacks of Dr. Frederic Wertham, Mr. G. Legman, and others suggested the advisability of a partial switch from Death to Love. **1960** *Economist* 15 Oct. 260/2 Large-scale cultivation of wheat in the new areas would make possible a switch to industrial crops in the older agricultural parts. **1977** 'E. Crispin' *Glimpses of Moon* viii. 151 If you're thinking I could have done some sort of a switch at some stage, you can put the idea out of your mind straight away. **1981** F. Hoyle *Ice* x. 158 It is satisfactory that both of the switches, to and from an ice-age condition, can arise from the same kind of cosmogonic event.

b. *Bridge.* A change of suit either in bidding or play. Cf. sense 7 b of the vb.

1921 A. M. Foster *Auction Bridge* 70 The take-out or switch. **1923** [see assist *sb.* a]. **1939** N. De V. Hart *Bridge Players' Bedside Bk.* iv. 38 It was a clever switch, and at once turned the hand into a difficult problem. **1952** I. Macleod *Bridge is Easy Game* xii. 141 Here you dare not concede the opening trick for a Heart switch will surely defeat you. **1980** R. Markus *Bridge-Table Tales* vi. 19 Declarer was forced to win East's king for fear of a spade switch.

c. An exchange; *spec.* a substitution which involves criminal deception. *colloq.* and *slang*.

1935 Wodehouse *Luck of Bodkins* xiv. 144, I plunged into ..your state-room..and gave the sleeping figure..a hearty wallop..and it was Gertrude... 'What's the idea? Why the switch?' **1938** F. Chester *Shot Full* xxv. 302 Another of

Lewis's rackets was to pose as a buyer of loose diamonds, and then substitute glass for the stones... This form of robbery is known as 'the switch'. **1955** W. GADDIS *Recognitions* II. ii. 369 Somebody pulled the old twenty-dollar-bill switch on her, Ellery said looking up from his magazine.

III. 9. *attrib.* and *Comb.*, as ***switch-cord, -box, -gear, -handle, -lever, -plug, -stick, -whip***; **switch-bar**, a bar connected with a switch (on a railway or electrical apparatus); **switch base** (see quot. 1940); **switch-blade,** (*a*) the 'blade' or hinged strip of metal of a 'knife-switch' in an electrical apparatus, which is inserted between the jaws to complete the circuit; (*b*) a pocket knife with a blade released by pressing a button or similar device on the handle (cf. *flick-knife* s.v. FLICK *sb.*[1] 4); in full, ***switch-blade knife***; **switch cane**, a large bamboo, *Arundinaria gigantea* subsp. *tecta*, native to southern N. America; **switch-clerk**, a telephone clerk or operator; **switch dealing** *Econ.*, purchase and resale, or sale and repurchase, of a commodity in order to profit by differential values of currency; repurchase or resale through a third party; hence **switch deal, dealer; switch dollar** *Econ.* (see quots.); **switch-engine** = *switching-engine* (SWITCHING *vbl. sb.* 5); so **switch-engineer**, the driver of a switch-engine; **switch gear**, the assembly of switching devices and associated equipment used in the generation and transmission of electric power; **switch gene** *Genetics*, a gene whose presence or absence determines whether a group of other genes is expressed; **switch-girl** *Austral.* = *switchboard girl* s.v. SWITCHBOARD b; **switch-grass**, the couch-grass or squitch, *Triticum repens*; **switch-hitter** *U.S. Baseball*, an ambidextrous batter; also *transf.* (colloq.) in sporting and gen. contexts; *slang*, a bisexual; also **switch-hitting** *ppl. a.* and *vbl. sb.*; **switch hook** *Teleph.*, the hook or support in a telephone set which operates the circuit switch when the receiver is placed upon or removed from it; **switch-horn**, a stag's horn without branches; also, a stag having such horns; **switch-knife** = *switch-blade* (*b*) above; **switch-lamp, -lantern**, a lamp or lantern fixed on a railway switch to indicate which track is open; **switch-light** *U.S.* = *switch-lamp, -lantern*; also *transf.* (see quot. 1960); **switch mechanism** *Genetics*, the mechanism by which a switch gene operates; **switch-plant** *Bot.*, a plant having green switch-like branches, nearly or quite leafless, which perform the function of leaves; **switch-rail** = sense 3 a; **switch-reference** *Linguistics* (see quot. 1972); **switch-room**, a room containing the switches of an electrical system (telegraph, telephone, etc.); **switch selling**, a sales technique whereby cheap goods are displayed in order to lead the consumer to buy similar but more expensive items; also *transf.*; hence **switch-selling** *ppl. a.* and (as a back-formation) **switch-sell** *v. intr.*; **switch-signal**, a signal indicating the position of a railway switch; **switch-snake** = WHIP-SNAKE; **switch-sorrel**, name in Jamaica for the shrub *Dodonæa viscosa*, from the sour taste of its leaves; **switch-stand**, a stand or support for the levers and other apparatus connected with a set of railway switches; **switch-table**, a form of switchboard shaped like an ordinary table; **switch tail** = *swish-tail* (see SWISH-); also *attrib.* having such a tail; **switch-tender**, a man who attends to a set of switches on a railway, a switchman, pointsman; **switch-tower** *U.S.*, a building containing the levers or other appliances for working a set of switches on a railway, etc.; a signal-box, -cabin, or -tower; **switch trading** *Econ.*, international trading in commodities conducted through media other than currency (cf. *switch deal* above); **switchyard** *U.S.*, (*a*) an area of a railway taken up by points, and in which trains are made up; also *transf.*; (*b*) an enclosed area of a power system which contains the switchgear. See also SWITCHBOARD, SWITCHMAN.

1837 *Civil Eng. & Arch. Jrnl.* I. 52/2 The *switch bars corresponding with the straight line. **1940** *Chambers's Techn. Dict.* 826/1 **Switch-base*, the insulating base on which a switch is mounted. **1967** M. CHANDLER *Ceramics in Mod. World* iv. 114 For telegraph or telephone insulation, as for domestic switch-bases, fuse-holders, bulb-sockets, and so on, almost any kind of insulating material will work. **1909** *Installation News* III. 119/2 The *switch blades are fitted with sparking contacts. **1932** L. HUGHES *Negro Mother* 13 'Cause I carries a switch-blade And I swing it a-hummin', And if I don't get you goin', I'll cut you down comin'. **1950** PATTERSON & CONRAD *Scottsboro Boy* II. ii. 96 He put the shears in his pocket and went to his cell. I had a switch-blade knife. I went looking for him. **1957** *New Yorker* 5 Oct. 64/1 A fist fight between two champions, but there are emotional complications, and the switch-blade knives are put to work. **1975** P. THEROUX *Great Railway Bazaar* xxx. 342, I would have plotted myself into danger; Sadik would have had a switchblade and gold teeth. **1940** *Chambers's Techn. Dict.* 826/1 **Switch-box*, an enclosure housing one or more switches operated by means of an external handle **1978** W. F. BUCKLEY *Stained Glass* xxii. 217 Blackford walked to the switch box. **1845** W. T. PORTER *Big Bear Arkansas* 132 They circled about among the *switch-cane and priscimmon bushes a long time. **1954** W. FAULKNER in *Holiday* XV. 36/3 The Natchez doctor was clearing the land fast now, plowing under the..switch cane of the creek and river bottoms. **1889** PREECE & MAIER *Telephone* xiv. 230 No *switch-clerk is permitted to have charge of more than fifty renters. *Ibid.*, The testing of the *switch-cords is a matter that must not be overlooked. **1973** 'D. JORDAN' *Nile Green* xxi. 85 KK hovered in his office, too, doing a quick *switch deal in forward dollars. **1967** *Economist* 14 Jan. 143/1 When the Russians don't wish to take up a consignment of Moroccan oranges to which they are committed under a bilateral trade agreement, they go to a specialist known as a *switch dealer in one of Europe's financial centres and he arranges a resale to someone else, at a discount. That, in a nutshell, is the mysterious art of switch trading. **1957** *Ibid.* 21 Dec. 1082/1 Commodity shunting in general virtually stops when the margin between transferable sterling and official sterling is a little less than three per cent. But '*switch' dealings in platinum are possible at a narrower margin. **1964** *Times Rev. Industry* Sept. 17/1 All purchases of foreign exchange for investment in non-Sterling Areas are subject to control... Direct investment projects..may be financed..either by borrowing abroad or by using the non-sterling currency proceeds of the sale of foreign securities..; i.e., so-called '*switch dollars'. **1978** J. PAXTON *Dict. European Econ. Community* (rev. ed.) 236 *Switch dollar market*. Investment in foreign securities by United Kingdom residents is not normally allowed.., but existing holdings may be realised and the proceeds switched into (*i.e.* used to buy) other securities, or sold..to other United Kingdom residents who wish to purchase foreign securities. For convenience, such funds, whatever the currency, are expressed in terms of United States dollars called Switch, security or investment dollars. **1896** *Nebraska St. Jrnl.* 15 Feb. 8/4 He was struck by the footboard of an approaching *switch engine. **1906** *Westm. Gaz.* 24 Dec. 8/1 To regulate the seniority list of the *switch engineers. **1901** *Ibid.* 31 Oct. 8/1, 6,000 horse-power in boilers, engines, dynamos, and *switch gear. **1930** *Times* 29 Mar. 19/4 Out metal is now being adopted as a substitute for non-magnetic iron in many instances, such as in the large casings for metal-clad switchgear. **1958** *Optima* Sept. 130/2 The electrical industry uses platinum for switchgear contacts in such equipment as traffic lights, telephone exchanges, radio stations and generating stations. **1978** *Jrnl. R. Soc. Arts* CXXVI. 609/2 Continued improvements in control circuitry and microprocessors are likely to..further increase the utilization of transformers, switchgear and circuits. [**1941** MATHER & DE WINTON in *Ann. Bot.* V. 310 The more rigorous the selection of illegitimacy to outbreeding conditions the more efficient it is as an in-breeding mechanism when the switching genes are changed.] **1942** *Nature* 14 Nov. 564/1 Mather and de Winton have recently spoken of such genes as '*switch genes'. **1968** R. D. MARTIN tr. *Wickler's Mimicry in Plants & Animals* vii. 82 Polymorphisms is sometimes controlled by single genes, sometimes by groups of genes, and..switch genes (as explained for *Papilio dardanus*) may also play a part. **1943** K. TENNANT *Ride on Stranger* xi. 120 Some of them would be asking for letters at the *switch-girl's desk. **1969** *Southerly* XXIX. 93 The tea-lady panders to the biological necessities of life, the switchgirl makes communication easier. **1840** J. BUEL *Farmer's Comp.* 232 The quack, *switch, or witch grass, a variety of the fiorin. **1876** PREECE & SIVEWRIGHT *Telegraphy* 107 The *switch-handle itself is in connection with the back contact of the key K. **1948** L. DUROCHER *Dodgers & Me* vii. 49 Cullenbine, a *switch hitter, and Steve Rachunok..were two athletes we had picked up..from Detroit. **1956** H. KURNITZ *Invasion of Privacy* iii. 25 A free-swinging round-house slap..landed high on his cheek... 'What do you know!' he said softly. 'A southpaw!' 'Wrong,' said the girl. 'A switch-hitter.' **1960** WENTWORTH & FLEXNER *Dict. Amer. Slang* 534/1 *Switch-hitter*, a bisexual person. **1972** *Pussycat* XXXIII. LIX. 8/1 The buddy would shove cock to me. I can still remember the first switch-hitter. **1938** *Philadelphia Rec.* 5 Feb. 15/6 A signed contract has been received from Emmett Mueller, *switch-hitting rookie whom the Phils rescued from the Cardinal chain gang this winter. **1952** *Sun* (Baltimore) 25 Feb. (B ed.) 14/6 He also picked up a switch-hitting style from baseball. Gordie is the only player..who has mastered the art of switching hands on his stick, so that he can shoot from either his right or left side without warning. **1970** *N.Y. Times* 16 Aug. II. 1/1 Chock full of scenes of what people apparently *want* to see today..lesbianism, switch-hitting, group gropes. **1922** *Telegr. & Teleph. Jrnl.* VIII. 82/2 If a subscriber leaves his receiver off the *switchhook..the switching equipment is automatically released after a certain interval. **1975** D. G. FINK *Electronics Engineers' Handbk.* XXII. 4 In the *common-battery* [telephone] *set*..a circuit closure, activated by the switch hook, serves to alert the central office. **1880** H. C. ST. JOHN *Wild Coasts Nipon* 276 A stag with *switch horns. **1907** *Spectator* 5 Jan. 11/1 The 'hummel' stag—that ungainly beast with no horns at all—is a better fighter than the 'switch-horn'. **1955** *Time* 6 June 27/3 They manufacture pistols, carry *switchknives and use them. **1957** WODEHOUSE *Over Seventy* xv. 144 At Eightieth Street he produced a switch-knife... 'This is a stick-up', he announced. **1898** HAMBLEN *Gen. Manager's Story* ii. 12 An old man..who was trimming *switch lamps. **1875** KNIGHT *Dict. Mech.*, **Switch-lantern*, a lantern on the lever of a railway-switch, to indicate the condition of the switch either by its position or by the display of a colored light. *Ibid.*, **Switch-lever*, the handle and bar by which the switch is moved. **1892** *Harper's Mag.* Dec. 80 He saw the station agent running down the tracks with the red *switch-light. **1929** W. FAULKNER *Sartoris* IV. 350 Along the tracks green switch-lights were steady in the dusk. **1960** *Listener* 18 Aug. 250/2 When a hungry young boomer came in and demanded..'a couple of switch lights in the fog'..what he really wanted was..two fried eggs with the grease poured over them. **1941** *Ann. Bot.* V. 308 The *switch mechanism at the S,s locus offers the possibility of a very different adjustment to changed breeding conditions. **1953** J. S. HUXLEY *Evolution in Action* I. 29 Some genetic differences act as a switch mechanism, turning on a whole battery of further processes. **1894** OLIVER tr. *Kerner's Nat. Hist. Plants* (1902) I. 330 Another group of plants known by the name of '*switch' plants..are characterized by their rod-shaped stems and branches... The *Spartium* belongs to those switch-plants which are not entirely leafless. **1901** *Brit. Med. Jrnl.* 9 Mar. 573/2 A workman had fixed a brass socket (to hold the *switch plug). **1797** CURR *Coal Viewer* 26 The mode of turning out to the right hand, and passing, which is done..without a *switch rail, as is required in common waggon ways. **1967** W. JACOBSEN in Hymes & Bittle *Stud. in Southwestern Ethnolinguistics* 238 This paper discusses a device for pronominal references, denominated '*switch-reference', which is found, with considerable differences of detail, in three languages of the Hokan-Coahuiltecan group. **1972** D. HYMES in M. E. Smith *Stud. in Linguistics in Honor of G. L. Trager* 105 The use of separate forms of third person to keep track of discourse is best treated under the general heading of 'switch reference'... It may be preferable to abandon use of the term 'fourth person' altogether, speaking simply of 'inclusive', 'obviative'.., and 'switch reference'. **1978** *Language* LIV. 220 The presence of switch-reference morphemes..also appears to be an areal feature in parts of California. **1885** *List of Subscribers, Classified* (United Telephone Co.) (ed. 6) 8 Each subscriber is furnished with a set of instruments..which is connected with a wire communicating with the Exchange or *Switch Room nearest his address. **1901** *Westm. Gaz.* 7 Dec. 7/3 The switch-room system is making its *debut* in London. This is known as the central battery system. [**1930** *Amer. Speech* VI. 128 To switch a customer is to quote to him a low price on an article to inspire him, and then to direct his interest to another article.] **1960** *Guardian* 30 Nov. 2/7 The practice of *switch selling of sewing and other machines..from misleading advertisements. **1965** E. GUNDREY *Foot in Door* ii. 20 The fast-talking, switch-selling, hard-pressing salesman. *Ibid.* xxxviii. 219 It should..be made illegal to 'switch-sell'. **1971** H. WILSON *Labour Govt.* xix. 361 Mr Kosygin..was escorted throughout the day by..the Secretary of State, who had been told about the American exercise in switch-selling the night before and had been asked to watch out for any signs of reaction. **1838** *Civil Eng. & Arch. Jrnl.* I. 358 Railway *Switch Signal. **1791** W. BARTRAM *Carolina* 196 [The tail] not small and slender as in the *switch snake. **1864** *Switch Sorrel [see SORREL *sb.*[1] 4]. **1875** KNIGHT *Dict. Mech.*, **Switch-stand* (Railway) a fulcrum and locking-device for the levers whereby switch-rails are moved. **1858** LYTTON *What will He do?* III. xvi, In his hand he carried a supple *switch-stick. **1884** KNIGHT *Dict. Mech.* Suppl., The '*switch' tables, of which there are twelve in the Cincinnati [telephone] Exchange. **1689** *Lond. Gaz.* No. 2473/4 A sand grey Mare,..with a *switch Tail. **1776** *Pennsylv. Even. Post* 4 June 280/2 A bright bay horse, ..three white feet, a switch tail, shod all round. **1853** SURTEES *Sponge's Sp. Tour* iii. 11 He had a famous switch tail, reaching nearly to his hocks. **1871** *Routledge's Ev. Boy's Ann.* May 280 A bare-backed, switch-tail horse. **1853** *Putnam's Mag.* July 34/2 We went roaring, rushing, screaming, up the valley of the Susquehanna, occasionally passing a *switch-tender with his white lights. **1870** E. E. HALE *Ten Times One* i. (Cent. Dict.), Her husband, who is now switch-tender, lost his arm in the great smash-up. **1897** KIPLING in *Scribner's Mag.* Aug. 146/1 They were at the far north end of the yard, now, under a *switch-tower, and looking down on the four-track way of the main traffic. **1901** *Munsey's Mag.* XXV. 699/1 The locomotive..stopping only once to allow McCann to drop another set of running orders at a switch tower on the next division. **1967** *Switch trading [see *switch dealer* above]. **1974** *Harper's Mag.* Dec. 54 What Intertel does is.. advise on geopolitical 'switch-trading opportunities'. **1815** SCOTT *Guy M.* xxxviii, Slapping his boots with his *switch-whip. **1888** *Austin* (Texas) *Statesman* 1 Nov. 6/6 In the *switch yards of the Chicago & Alton.. nearly all the men reported for duty this morning. **1943** J. S. HUXLEY *TVA* 85 The transformers and switchyard..are not applied to a predetermined structure, they are part of it. **1956** H. GOLD *Man who was not with It* (1965) x. 70, I was at the switch-yards, still running, and then I was clambering in the coupling of a moving freight. **1969** *Daily Colonist* (Victoria, B.C.) 16 Oct. 40/7 Work is to begin immediately on placing the..generators at the underground powerhouse ..and the switchyard and central control building on the surface. **1971** *Sci. Amer.* June 60 Near the end of its trip the electron beam passes through a 'beam switchyard' before reaching the target areas.

switch, *v.* Also 7 switz, swich. [f. prec.]

1. a. *trans.* To strike, hit, beat, flog, or whip with or as with a switch.

c **1611** CHAPMAN *Iliad* XXIII. 315 Thy right horse, then switching; all thy throate (Spent in encouragements) giue him. *a* **1625** FLETCHER *Nice Valour* I. i, Has been thrice switz't from seven a clock till nine. **1656** EARL MONM. tr. *Boccalini's Advts. fr. Parnass.* I. xxxi. (1674) 36 [He] did so seasonably switch and put on his Horses. **1688** HOLME *Armoury* III. xix. (Roxb.) 179/2 Any gentleman of noble extraction..that had married for couetousnesse or with a woman of meane condition, was to be switched with wands. **1832** HT. MARTINEAU *Demerara* i. 11 She switched her brother with the cane she snatched from his hand. **1845** S. JUDD *Margaret* II. viii, You must truss-up a cow's tail if you don't want to be switched when you're milking. **1866** R. M. BALLANTYNE *Shifting Winds* ix. (1881) 88 We heard him switching his boots as he passed along the street.

b. *intr.* or *absol.* To strike, deal a blow or blows, with or as with a switch.

1612 DRAYTON *Poly-olb.* xviii. 390 With his revengeful sword [he] swich'd after them that fled. **1676** HOBBES *Iliad* (1677) 149 Ulysses with his bow still switching on. **1678** R. L'ESTRANGE *Seneca's Mor.* III. 130 To be perpetually switching, and spurring, makes him [*sc.* a horse] Vitious, and Jadish. **1691** SHADWELL *Scowrers* I. ii, You women are for the young stripling, that switch, and spur a short race.

c. ***I'll be switched***, a mild indication of exasperation, denial, or surprise. *N. Amer. colloq.*

1838 *U.S. Mag.* I. 427, I'll be switched if I do. **1841** J. B. Jones *Wild Western Scenes* xiv. 178 I'll be switched if many folks lives in *higher* houses than I does. **1901** *Daily Colonist* (Victoria, B.C.) 4 Oct. 3/7 'Well, I'll be switched!' ejaculated the chatterer. **1941** L. I. Wilder *Little Town on Prairie* ix. 99 'Well, I'll be switched!' said Pa... It takes you to think up a chicken pie, a year before there's chickens to make it with.

2. a. *trans.* With adverbial extension: To drive with or as with a switch.

a **1616** Beaum. & Fl. *Wit without M.* II. iv, Go switch me up a Covey of young Scholars. **1625** Massinger *New Way* I. i, I shall switch your brains out! **1824** Scott *St. Ronan's* iii, Honest Nelly switched her little fish-cart downwards to St. Ronan's Well. **1890** 'R. Boldrewood' *Col. Reformer* xviii. (1891) 218 He..observed his master switch beast after beast into the..receptacles for cattle.

†**b.** *fig.* To urge on, impel, incite. *Obs.*

1648 Winyard *Midsummer-Moon* 2 He comes forth like mad Orestes switched on by furies. **1659** in *Burton's Diary* (1828) IV. 297 To retrench the time is very acceptable; but why we should go to it so switched and spurred, I know not. **1672** *Mede's Wks.* Life p. xlv, How this, I say, would switch and spur on their Industries.

3. a. To flourish like a switch, to whisk, lash; to move (something) with a sudden jerk; *spec.* in *Angling* (see quot. 1867).

1842 J. Wilson *Chr. North* I. v. 205 Not a bird can open his wing, nor a rat switch his tail, without scattering the straw like chaff. **1856** Miss Mulock *John Halifax* xiv, He ..stood switching his riding-whip after the old habit. **1867** F. Francis *Angling* v. 138 In very windy weather, or in difficult places,..the angler..will have to switch his line. Raising the point of the rod high in the air,..he must make a sharp forward and downward cut. **1870** Rock *Textile Fabr.* I. 51 The..animal has switched its tail into the last link of the chain.

b. *intr.* To bend as a switch or flexible twig.

1854 Ruskin *Lect. Archit.* ii. §37 A branch of wild rose, which switches round at the angle, embracing the minute figure of the bishop.

4. *trans.* To cut off the switches or projecting twigs from; to trim (a tree, hedge, etc.).

1811 W. Nicol *Planter's Kal.* (1812) 460 Switch and clip thorn and other deciduous hedges. **1812** [see switching *vbl. sb.* 3]. **1826** Scott *Jrnl.* 29 Oct., Elms cruelly cropped, pollarded, and switched. **1843** A. Hepburn in *Zoologist* I. 297 [Hedges] are commonly pruned or *switched* every year.

5. ***to switch a rasper***: see swish *v.* 3.

1836 T. Hook *G. Gurney* I. 225 He was killed, switching a rasper.

6. a. To turn (a railway train, car, etc.) on to another line by means of a switch; to shunt; also *intr.* for *pass.* **b.** *intr.* Of a railway line: To branch or turn *off* at a switch. *U.S.*

1853 'Mark Twain' *Let.* in *Iowa Jrnl. Hist.* (1929) XXVII. 413 Our train ran back half a mile and switched off another track, and stopped. **1875** L. F. Tasistro tr. *Comte de Paris's Civ. War Amer.* I. 230 Two branches of the Alexandria and Lynchburg line switch off to enter the Valley of Virginia. **1891** C. Roberts *Adrift Amer.* 60 The car that I was in was switched out of the train and left in the yard there. **1901** *Munsey's Mag.* XXV. 698/2, I knew they changed engines here, but they switched the train, and I lost it. **1904** *Daily News* 15 July 7/1 The freight train was switching, and thus occupied both tracks.

7. *fig.* To turn *off*, divert. Chiefly *U.S.*

1860 O. W. Holmes *Elsie V.* xvii. (1861) 209 That curious state which is so common in good ministers,..in which they contrive to switch off their logical faculties on the narrow side-track of their technical dogmas. **1897** *Globe* 18 Feb. 1/4 Mr. Julian Hawthorne has explained to an interviewer that his recent infertility as a novelist is due to the fact that he has 'somehow been switched off into journalism'. **1897** Conan Doyle *Trag. Korosko* vi, The Colonel..switched the conversation off to the chances of the morrow.

b. *intr.* To change or transfer from one thing to another; to alter to another state or activity. Also with preps. and advbs. *spec.* in *Bridge*, to change to another suit in bidding or in play (see sense 8 b of the sb.).

1906 *Westm. Gaz.* 20 Oct. 14/1 It is possible that the king will be held up, in which case, after making the ten, knave in dummy, he will switch to diamonds. **1921** A. M. Foster *Auction Bridge* 32 Your partner..can support your call or switch into another bid. **1932** *Daily Tel.* 8 Oct. 15/5 At Contract he has the..duty of raising the opener's bid..and, if he switches, of deciding whether to make a pre-emptive bid or not. **1952** I. Macleod *Bridge is Easy Game* xiv. 189 Switching to Diamonds declarer made her contract. **1980** R. Markus *Bridge-Table Tales* iv. 16 West won and switched to a spade.

1923 H. Crane *Let.* 20 Jan. (1965) 117, I..urged him not to 'waste his time' on any magazine project. But after his visit here last summer I quickly switched about. **1930** H. Zink *City Bosses in U.S.* x. 207 He bolted the regulars and switched to reform groups. **1954** J. Steinbeck *Sweet Thursday* v. 34 He knows when high-school boys have switched from gin to marijuana. **1962** *Rep. Comm. Broadc. 1960* 239 in *Parl. Papers 1961–2* (Cmnd. 1753) IX. 259 Viewers who did not switch would find themselves exposed at some time of the evening to informational material. **1978** M. Amis *Success* ix. 173 Some dead-end toiler asked to switch from one equally meaningless chore to another.

c. *trans.* To exchange (items), esp. with intent to deceive.

1897 *Columbus* (Ohio) *Dispatch* 18 June 5/2 An opportunity presented itself to 'switch' the bottles. **1917** *Dialect Notes* IV. 330 *Switch, v.t.*, to exchange, esp. surreptitiously. 'I thought I was getting title to this land, but they switched deeds on me in the office.' Neb. **1948** C. L. B. Hubbard *Dogs in Britain* III. xv. 130 A business in which dogs have been 'switched' (and doped) and the results manipulated is questionable. **1978** F. Weldon *Praxis* x. 75 Praxis managed to switch envelopes so that an empty one was dispatched instead.

d. To change or alter (*from* one thing *to* another); to transfer. Also, with items involved in the change as plural obj.

1919 Wodehouse *My Man Jeeves* 157 It struck me that I'd no right to butt in on his secret sermons, so I switched the conversation. **1931** W. G. McAdoo *Crowded Years* x. 157 Sullivan switched the fifty-eight votes of Illinois from Clark to Wilson. **1957** A. C. Clarke *Deep Range* xxi. 188 The very idea of switching our entire herds to milking instead of slaughtering is just crazy. **1959** *Daily Tel.* 15 Oct. 12 Among those who have switched offices, Mr. Watkinson's is perhaps the most surprising translation. **1963** *Listener* 28 Feb. 363/2 The government was forced to switch the full campaign towards the less flexible statutory committees. **1975** D. Lodge *Changing Places* vi. 229 Philip switches channels until he hits the transmission of the Plotinus March.

8. a. *trans.* In electrical apparatus: To direct (a current) by means of a switch; to put *on* or *off*, i.e. connect or disconnect with a battery, or with a particular line or circuit, e.g. on a telephone; to turn (an electric light, radio, television, etc.) *on* or *off*; to turn *out* (an electric light). Also, to change the state of (a two-state device).

1881 *Daily News* 14 Nov. 5/3 Subscribers have become accustomed to be 'switched on' to each other. **1884** C. G. W. Lock *Workshop Receipts* Ser. III. 72/1 The current will be 'switched' into the signalling apparatus. **1891** *Times* 28 Sept. 13/5 By automatically switching in or out of circuit a larger or smaller number of accumulator cells. **1907** H. Wyndham *Flare of Footlights* ii, She..switched on a single electric light. **1935** *Radio Times* 13 Sept. 4/3 If you were to switch on your set..you would have no difficulty in distinguishing..who was speaking or singing. **1954** I. Murdoch *Under Net* iii. 53, I didn't switch out the light, but covered the lamp up again with gauzy stuffs until it gave only a faint glow. **1960** Haley & Scott *Analogue & Digital Computers* vii. 188 The core is switched from the 1 to the 0 state. **1964** F. L. Westwater *Electronic Computers* iv. 79 This is..got round by first switching a wound core..and then allowing the read current in this core to be used to write in the appropriate row and column. **1983** J. Fuller *Convergence* xix. 210 It is no sweat. Easy as switching on the old FM.

(ii) ***to switch in***: to bring into a circuit by the operation of a switch; similarly ***to switch out***.

Cf. quot. 1891, sense 8.

1957 *Practical Wireless* XXXIII. 734/1 A resistor could be switched in initially to limit the maximum possible current flowing to 10 mA. **1970** J. Earl *Tuners & Amplifiers* iii. 67 The loudness control filter..can be switched out allowing the volume control to work in the ordinary, uncompensated manner. **1978** *SLR Camera* Aug. 90/1 To switch in the automatic exposure control system all he need do is turn the shutter speed setting dial to the position marked 'Auto'.

(iii) *intr.* Of a two-state device: to pass to the other state. Of its state: to change.

1964 F. L. Westwater *Electronic Computers* iv. 77 The resulting change of flux as the core switches will cause an electromotive force in the read wire. **1981** J. D. Lenk *Handbk. Digital Electronics* ii. 41 Inputs cause the state of the circuit to switch, reversing the output.

b. *intr.* or *absol.* To turn *on* (or *off*) a radio or television set, or other device. Cf. turn *v.* 74 h, 75 a.

1932 *Even. Standard* 21 Jan. 3/3 The best plan is to tell listeners what is going to happen and let them decide whether they switch off or not. **1951** 'J. Wyndham' *Day of Triffids* xi. 206, I could not hear above the noise of the engines. We both switched off. **1958** *Listener* 20 Nov. 849/3 Many viewers may have missed it by switching off in fatigue. **1975** *Ibid.* 9 Jan. 38/2 They do it because someone's just switched on. **1977** *Rep. Comm. Future of Broadcasting* (Cmnd. 6753) iii. 19 Viewers and listeners cannot..express ..disapproval, except by switching off.

c. *intr.* To change *over* to another state by means of a switch; *spec.* to alter the receiving channel of a radio or television set.

1937 *Discovery* Nov. 348/2 By switching over from white light to black an entire scene can be changed instantaneously. **1940** N. Mitford *Pigeon Pie* v. 85 It would be difficult to do better, for an account of the Wig Inquest than to switch over, as they say on the wireless, to the columns of the *Evening Runner*. **1958** *Sunday Times* 26 Jan. 6/5, 200 pages of mumbo-jumbo which would make anyone switch over to another programme. **1961** S. Price *Just for Record* i. 13 The phone hasn't rung all day because I've switched over to the answering service.

d. *trans.* To turn *off* (a television or radio programme, or its content).

1947 G. B. Shaw *How to become Musical Critic* (1960) 321 [The B.B.C.'s] worst concessions to popular bad taste..are very horrible. I switch them off so promptly that I am hardly qualified to condemn them. **1962** *Listener* 18 Oct. 633/3 The archness of the dialogue had to be heard to be switched off.

e. To direct (a telephone link) *through* to a subsidiary receiver by means of a switch.

1971 'S. Smith' *Grave Affair* xii. 181 The telephone had not been switched through to my study deliberately. **1976** J. Tate tr. *A. Bodelsen's Operation Cobra* xvii. 83 They switched the telephone through and went on up.

9. *transf.* and *fig.* **a.** To turn *on* or *off*, as if by means of a switch.

1929 W. J. Locke *Ancestor Jorico* viii. 111 Without great discourtesy one couldn't switch off Binkie. **1934** *Discovery* Sept. 259/2 In this way she succeeded in switching off any unpleasant dream. **1966** *Listener* 24 Mar. 426/1, I have always found it very easy to 'switch on' emotion. **1967** B. Patten *Little Johnny's Confession* 54 Those couples who Having been switched off permanently, Are so very still. **1980** *Nature* 27 Mar. 379/2 The prose style is guaranteed to switch off all but the most ardent student.

b. *intr.* for *refl.* With *off*. Of persons: to cease listening, to lose concentration; to become bored or inattentive.

1921 G. B. Shaw *Back to Methuselah* III. 94 Dont switch off. Listen. This American has invented a method of breathing under water. **1928** [see easy *adv.* 4 b]. **1955** *Times* 22 June 11/5 Does he seriously maintain that in a class of 24 boys, where 23 are working keenly and well, it is invariably the master who is to blame because No. 24 always 'switches off'? **1976** J. I. M. Stewart *Memorial Service* vii. 108 He was heavy alike with his years and his whisky and wine, and he may simply have switched off. **1980** D. Bloodworth *Trapdoor* xx. 121 For some reason he could not fathom she had switched off. Her love had died.

switchable (ˈswɪtʃəb(ə)l), *a.* [f. switch *v.* + -able.] Capable of being switched between different positions or modes of operation. Freq. in *techn.* contexts.

1961 [see *dual-standard* s.v. dual *a.* (*sb.*) 3]. **1970** J. Earl *Tuners & Amplifiers* vi. 142 Signal in the i.f. channel also operates the tuning meter, switchable to a.m. by the f.m./a.m. changeover switch. **1977** *Nature* 6 Jan. 92/1 The range is −0·05 to 1·999A with a switchable decimal point and double over-range indication. **1982** *Sunday Times* 31 Oct. 57/1 Switchable pension... Switching is allowed among six funds (corresponding text).

switchback (ˈswɪtʃbæk), *a.* and *sb.* [f. switch *v.* 6 + back *adv.*]

A. *adj.* **a.** Applied to a form of railway used on steep slopes, consisting of a zigzag series of lines connected by switches, at each of which the train or car is 'switched back' or reversed in direction. Also *fig.* and in extended *transf.* uses. **b.** Applied to a railway consisting of a series of steep alternate ascents and descents, on which the train or car runs partly or wholly by the force of gravity, the momentum of each descent carrying it up the succeeding ascent; *esp.* to such a railway constructed for amusement at a pleasure-resort. Hence *transf.* of a road having steep alternate ascents and descents.

1887 R. Fry *Let.* 21 Nov. (1972) I. 117 Some of us went on a switchback railway (the sensation of which I thought very pleasant). **1888** Lees & Clutterbuck *B.C. 1887* xxxiv. (1892) 373 We began the ascent of the range, which..is accomplished by what is called a 'switchback' railway. This contrivance is a series of zigzags, and has no similarity to the ..sport lately introduced into England under the same name. **1896** *Gentl. Mag.* CCLXXX. 126 The effect on the infamous road we travelled was a combination of the switchback railway and 'razzle-dazzle'. **1899** *Daily News* 8 May 5/5 The switchback road of Earlswood-common. **1908** F. W. Lanchester *Aerodonetics* 30 A magnificent flight, remarkable 'switch-back' flight path, distance, relative to the wind, probably over 600 yards. **1912** G. Mackenzie *Carnival* ix. 90 Jenny thought what horrible places they were, these sweeping moorland wastes..with switchback stone walls. **1961** *Daily Tel.* 5 Sept. 12/2 Where Mr Hill made much more sense was in criticising what he called the Government's 'switchback economies'. **1965** *Daily Mail* 28 Oct. 5/3 A dangerous 'switchback' course can build up as the plane descends. **1978** S. Wilson *Dealer's Move* vii. 116, I got hung up behind a couple of lorries... It was switch-back country and there was no way you could see what was coming.

B. *sb.* A switchback railway (in either sense); also *transf.* and *fig.*; applied in N. Amer. to a tight bend on an ascending road or trail.

1863 *Harper's Mag.* Sept. 465/1 We descend from our high elevation by gravity, changing our direction at various points by means of what is called a Switch-back. **1887** A. A. Hayes *Jesuit's Ring* 162 A temporary expedient in the way of a switch-back. **1888** *Pall Mall G.* 8 Sept. 4/1 The popularity of the switchback is due to the exhilaration and excitement of a jerky rush through the air at a speed over varying angles suggestive of danger. **1895** J. G. Millais *Breath fr. Veldt* (1899) 129 Fortunately the switchback of human sensations brings us back again and again to the pinnacle of hope. **1897** Mrs. A. Tweedie *Through Finland* vii. 139 The Finlanders put up a *Kälkbacke* or *Skrinnbacke*, in imitation of their Russian friends... They are really switchbacks made of ice and snow. **1933** *Nat. Geogr. Mag.* Feb. 196 (*caption*) An excellent highway climbs by turns and switchbacks through natural timber to the top of the towering dome. **1934** [see *giant racer* s.v. giant *sb.* 6]. **1965** *Daily Mail* 28 Oct. 5/3 If the Vanguard..was on the down-slope of a switchback when the talk-down was ended,..probably no further cause for the crash need be sought. **1969** *Islander* (Victoria, B.C.) 9 Nov. 7/1 Steep grades are not the only challenge on this road. Several of the switchbacks are so tight that much manoeuvring is required to get around them. **1976** J. Snow *Cricket Rebel* 61 Each time I was to find the county side at a lower ebb, with the team on a down slide of the switchback we rode in the 1960s.

Hence **ˈswitchback** *v. intr.*, to take a zigzag course like a switchback railway (A. a); **ˈswitch-backed** *ppl. a.*, **ˈswitchbacking** *vbl. sb.* and *ppl. a.*

1903 *Blackw. Mag.* Apr. 499/2 The railway cork-screwed and switch-backed up a rise of a couple of thousand feet in seventeen miles. **1913** *Outing* Jan. 498/1 Switch-backing or zigzagging up a hill is simply striking off to the right, for instance, at an angle and then turning off to the left. **1930** J. Collier *His Monkey Wife* vi. 72 Electric light cables.. switch-backed along the undulating coast. **1963** *Times* 16 Feb. 11/1 Another short drop leads to the edge of the lake with its bathing station and a surrealist structure built for high diving and switchbacking into the water. **1972** *Daily Tel.* (Colour Suppl.) 13 Oct. 86/2 A switchbacking lane over the heath to Studland. **1976** B. Bova *Multiple Man* (1977) vi. 65 My rented car climbed the switch-backed driveway.

switchboard ('swɪtʃbɔəd). [f. SWITCH *sb.* 3 b + BOARD *sb.*] **a.** A board or frame bearing a set of switches for connecting and disconnecting the various circuits of an electrical system, as of a telegraph, telephone, etc.

1873 *Harper's Mag.* Aug. 349/2 The switch-board..is the central ganglion of the whole [telegraphic] system. **1879** *Nature* 11 Sept. 461/2 The switch-board at the central office. **1884** *Pall Mall G.* 8 July 2/1 The necessary batteries and switchboards. **1889** PREECE & MAIER *Telephone* xiv. 216 The switchboard is an apparatus which enables each subscriber of the telephonic network to call the exchange and to enter into communication with it, and which further enables the operator at the exchange to effect the connection of any two subscribers in the shortest and safest manner.

b. *attrib.*, esp. as ***switchboard girl, operator.***

1903 *P.O. Telephone Service* 77 The current from the 'busy-back' and 'don't answer' commutators is not led directly to the switchboard terminals. **1925** F. G. C. BALDWIN *Hist. Telephone in U.K.* xi. 301 Switchboard cable containing 42 wires was employed between the test board and the first switch section. **1952** *Traffic* Apr. 34 (Advt.), Suppliers to the World for all Telecommunication products ..Automatic telephone equipments for main and satellite exchanges..Telephone instruments and accessories. Switchboard lamps (Hivac Ltd.). **1961** M. KELLY *Spoilt Kill* II. 105 He just wouldn't have anything to do with her. A girl from the works, the switchboard girl! **1967** N. FREELING *Strike out where not Applicable* 111 'All right,' said the switchboard girl indifferently. **1974** A. MORICE *Killing with Kindness* ii. 18 The call came through a switchboard operator.

switched (swɪtʃt), *a.* and *ppl. a.* [f. SWITCH *sb.* and *v.* + -ED.]

†**1.** *adj.* Of a horse: Having a switch tail (see SWITCH *sb.* 9). *Obs.*

1769 *Stratford Jubilee* I. i. 8 The full tailed blacks, and the switched roans.

2. *ppl. a.* Of cream: Whipped. Also, of an egg. *rare.*

1909 *Brown & Polson's Corn-Flour Recipe Bk.* 26 When cold, turn out and serve with switched cream. **1931** A. J. CRONIN *Hatter's Castle* III. ix. 602 I'm to have a switched egg.

3. a. Of a mechanism: turned *on* or *off* by a switch. Also *fig.*

1962 *Listener* 28 June 1131/1 His characters were understandably so permanently switched on that their moments of crisis were brought about by the small talk of others. **1968** P. MARLOWE *Hire me a Hearse* vii. 101 He hung up the picture with the switched-off mike. **1968** *Listener* 25 July 127/2 The screen of a switched-on television. **1974** J. WAINWRIGHT *Evidence I shall Give* i. 9 The switched-on light would emphasise the possible importance of..the one room..with the light still burning. **1977** *Times* 15 Aug. 2/1 Switched-off heating in every unoccupied room.

b. ***switched-on***: aware of all that is considered fashionable and up to date. Cf. *turned on* s.v. TURNED *ppl. a.* 8. Less frequently, in contrast, ***switched-off***. *slang.*

1964 *House & Garden* Nov. 78/2, I..want..to open a department store which caters for switched-on people. **1966** *Punch* 29 June 946/1 But nowhere have I come across a word of guidance for the 'out' crowd—the vast, non-swinging, switched off, palateless, utterly without-it lot who dominate the community. **1967** N. FITZGERALD *Affairs of Death* viii. 141 They must be more switched on than I gave them credit for being. **1970** D. DEVINE *Illegal Tender* ii. 25 Her mother wasn't switched on, she knew nothing of modern fashion. **1972** D. WESTON *Poor, Poor Ophelia* xxv. 153 The fine beautiful free life. The switched-on scene. **1979** 'A. HAILEY' *Overload* IV. iii. 302 She had delivered the tapes to that switched-on black woman who worked for a newspaper. **1982** *London Rev. Bks.* IV. XXIV. 7/2 What Amis's *sprezzatura* is saying is that most of his readers are out of touch, old fogies, Prufrock retreads, switched-off.

4. *adj.* and *ppl. a. Electr.* Having a switch; obtained by switching; subjected to switching.

1961 *IBM Jrnl. Res. & Devel.* V. 93 A phase reversal data transmission system is described, capable of operating at 2000 bauds over private telephone lines and at 1200 bauds over switched networks. **1971** *Gloss. Electrotechnical, Power Terms (B.S.I.)* III. vi. 12 Switched beam direction finder. **1971** *Physics Bull.* Oct. 612/3 The instrument can be used for checking all types of digital logic... Three switched frequency ranges are standard (0–50 kHz, 0–500 kHz, 0–5 MHz). **1974** HARVEY & BOHLMAN *Stereo F.M. Radio Handbk.* v. 106 (*caption*) Mullard switched decoder.

switchel ('swɪtʃəl). *N. Amer.* Also -ell. [Origin unknown. Cf. SWIZZLE.] **a.** A drink made of molasses and water, sometimes with vinegar, ginger, or rum added; also applied to various strong drinks sweetened and flavoured.

1790 P. FRENEAU in *Daily Advertiser* (N.Y.) 22 Mar. 3/1 Not wretched switchel and vile hogo drams. **1800** WEEMS *Washington* ix. (1877) 81 The dauntless Yankees still drank their Switchel. **1840** HALIBURTON *Clockm.* Ser. III. xi. (1848) 85 What will you have? cocktail, sling, julip, sherry cobbler, purl talabogus, clear sheer or switchell? **1843** *Family Herald* 29 July 183/1 The drinks ain't good here;.. no white noses..switchel-flip..or nothin', but that heavy, stupid, black, fat porter. *a* **1848** in Bartlett *Dict. Amer.* s.v. *Liquor*, Switchel-flip. **1925** *Dialect Notes* V. 344 [Newfoundland] *Switchel*, a drink of water and molasses. **1959** W. R. BIRD *These are Maritimes* vii. 190 She kept the jug in the cellar and boy when you came in and had a mug of that switchel it was worth while. **1977** *New Hampshire Times* 27 July VII. 20/3 Switchel was a concoction of cold water, sugar, ginger and vinegar, and..it was more or less thirst-quenching.

b. *Newfoundland.* (A drink of) tea, esp. amongst fishermen and sealers (see quots.).

1897 *Jrnl. Amer. Folklore* X. 211 *Switchel*, a mug of weak tea given to the sailors between meals when at the seal fishing. **1924** G. A. ENGLAND *Vikings of Ice* 50 Some were devouring beans and salt meat; others, gulping tea that steamed. 'Switchel', this tea was; that is, boiled-over tea whereto new and again fresh leaves are added. **1963** *Amer. Speech* XXXVIII. 300 *Switchel*, cold tea. **1974** *National Geographic* Jan. 114/2 [We] snugged down in the cabin for a 'cup o' switchel', as they call strong tea.

switcher ('swɪtʃə(r)). [f. SWITCH *v.* + -ER[1].] One who or that which switches, in any sense: *spec.* **a.** A switch or slender rod used as a whip; also, a person who wields a switch. **b.** A switching-engine. **c.** An angler who 'switches': see SWITCH *v.* 3.

1847 HALLIWELL, *Switcher*, a small switch. *North.* **1852** BURN *Naval & Milit. Dict.* (1863), Switcher, *aiguilleur.* **1882** *Sun* 14 May 6/6 The switcher [*sc.* engine] came with a rush. **1893** J. GRANT in *Westm. Gaz.* 25 Feb. 8/1 One of the best old Spey fishers was my father,..who had the reputation of being a crack switcher.

d. One who changes or transfers something to another position; a person who exchanges items, or substitutes one for the other. *slang* and *colloq.* (orig. *U.S.*).

1914 [see FLOPPER 2]. **1958** *Wall St. Jrnl.* 3 Nov. 1/1 Almost a third of the voters who plan to vote mostly for Republican candidates tomorrow are recent 'switchers', who until a few days ago either had planned to vote Democratic or were still undecided. **1978** *Economist* 1 Apr. 26/1 Singapore, South Korea and the Philippines as well as eastern European countries are said to be among the more determined switchers out of dollars.

switcheroo (swɪtʃə'ru:). *colloq.* (chiefly *U.S.*). [f. SWITCH *sb.* + -EROO.] = SWITCH *sb.* 8 a, c; a change of position or an exchange, esp. one intended to surprise or deceive; a reversal or turn-about; *spec.* an unexpected change or 'twist' in a story. Also *attrib.*, reversible, reversed.

1933 *Forum* Dec. 372/2 We'll pull a switcheroo. We'll use olives instead [of cherries]. **1941** B. SCHULBERG *What makes Sammy Run?* iv. 81 All you gotta do to that story is to give it the switcheroo. Instead of the minister you got a young dame missionary, see. **1949** *Sun* (Baltimore) 22 Sept. 7 (Advt.), Girls' 'switcheroo' jacket. One side's red or green corduroy and..the other side's a gay..wool plaid. **1953** C. M. KORNBLUTH *Syndic* v. 52 Two strapping girls..began to tear *his* clothes off, laughing at their switcheroo on the year's big gag. **1961** *N.Y. Times Bk. Rev.* 21 May 6/3 In Chapter X, then, with a neat whodunit switcheroo, Radin puts the finger on that most obvious suspect who, it appears, was cleared in too much haste. **1970** 'A. GILBERT' *Death wears Mask* vi. 102, I ought to have suggested it was a switcheroo. You know—criminal makes the discovery and informs the police. **1980** *Fortune* (Chicago) 7 Apr. 44/3 The arbitrator.. turned out to be Daniel Collins,..who had upheld Equity in the 1976 row... Collins this time came down on the side of management. It was one of those great switcheroo endings.

switchfoot ('swɪtʃfʊt). *Surfing.* Pl. -foots. [f. SWITCH *v.* 7 + FOOT *sb.*] (See quot. 1970.) Also **switch-footer**.

1970 *Studies in English* (Univ. of Cape Town) I. 30 The few surfers who are able to ride with equal skill with either right or left foot forward, are known as switchfoots. **1971** *Ibid.* II. 26 Finally, surfers differentiate among themselves between naturals,..goofies..and switchfooters, who can switch stance. **1978** G. WRIGHT *Illustr. Handbk. Sporting Terms* 147/4 *Switchfoot*, a surfer who can ride with either his left foot or right foot forward.

switching ('swɪtʃɪŋ), *vbl. sb.* [f. SWITCH *v.* + -ING[1].]

1. A beating with a switch; a flogging; the striking of an object with a switch.

a **1625** FLETCHER *Fair Maid Inn* I. iii, The switching him duld him [*sc.* a horse]. **1658** OSBORN *Jas. I*, Index, Wks. (1673) 23 A Character of Philip Earl of Mongomery; How patiently he took his Switching by Ramsey at Croydon. **1866** *Morn. Star* 20 Aug. 5/2 If he chooses to profit by the switching which he has received he will make for himself a deservedly great reputation. **1888** BURGON *Lives 12 Gd. Men* II. xii. 377 The signal..being the switching of his bedroom window-pane with a long wand. **1904** S. E. WHITE *Forest* xiv, You stumble, you break through the bush, you shut your eyes to avoid sharp switchings.

2. *Angling.* (See SWITCH *v.* 3.)

1867 F. FRANCIS *Angling* ix. 285 Switching..is a species of cast that is made when there are high banks or rocks at the angler's back, so that he cannot send his line behind him. **1893** J. GRANT in *Westm. Gaz.* 25 Feb. 8/1, I can cast a long line overhead, yet by switching I can cast farther.

3. The trimming of a hedge, etc. by cutting off projecting branches or twigs.

1812 SIR J. SINCLAIR *Syst Husb. Scot.* I. 44 Hedges.. ought to be cut into the shape of what is called a hog-main, i.e. brought to a point along the top, and preserved in that form by yearly switching. **1844** H. STEPHENS *Bk. Farm* II. 563 Switching consists of lopping off straggling branches that grow more prominently from a hedge than the rest.

4. a. Shunting of railway trains, etc.; connexion or disconnexion (***switching on*** or ***off***) of electric circuits; also *fig.*: see SWITCH *v.* 6–8.

1889 [see SWITCH *sb.* 3 b]. **1897** *Allbutt's Syst. Med.* IV. 146 This switching off of the skin from its connection with the respiratory and placing it in relation with the portal system. **1898** HAMBLEN *Gen. Manager's Story* xii. 175 When I got there, I found four hours' switching..to get my train together.

b. Changing or transferring from one position to another; exchanging.

1904 'No. 1500' *Life in Sing Sing* 253/1 *Switching*, transferring; passing to another. **1957** *Publ. Amer. Dial. Soc.* 1956 XXVI. 40 Precision would thus require us to distinguish three stages in diffusion: (1) *switching*, the alternate use of two languages, [etc.].

c. *Stock Exchange.* The purchase (or sale) of one stock, and the sale (or purchase) of another stock, at a stipulated price difference.

1932 *Literary Digest* 30 Jan. 49/1 (*title*) 'Switching' in a bear market. **1936** *Economist* 1 Feb. 248/2 The available evidence suggests that 'switching' has not greatly affected the past year's results. Some trusts..have increased their American holdings. **1960** *Ibid.* 15 Oct. 288/3 Buying in the gilt edged market increased..and demand from both home and continental buyers, including some switching and investment buying, remained high. **1981** *Times* 18 Aug. 18 The shares managed a 16p rise..with heavy switching from the ordinary into the NV.

5. *attrib.* and *Comb.*: *spec.* (*a*) used in switching hedges, etc., as ***switching-bill, -knife***; (*b*) used in or for shunting on a railway, as ***switching-engine*** or ***-locomotive, -eye*** (see quot. 1884), ***-ground***; **switching yard** = *switchyard* a, s.v. SWITCH *sb.* 9; (*c*) used for connecting electric circuits, as ***switching-plug***; pertaining to the switching of electrical apparatus or electronic devices, as ***switching centre, circuit, speed, station, theory, time.*** Also **switching angle** *Gunnery*, the angle between the lines of fire of the directing gun when the latter is brought to bear on the left of the new target.

1844 H. STEPHENS *Bk. Farm* I. 224 He handles the small cutting-axe and switching-knife with the force and neatness with which a dragoon wields his sabre. *Ibid.* II. 563 This operation is performed with the switching-bill. **1871** DARWIN *Desc. Man* II. xiii. 64 The *Scolopax Wilsonii* of the United States makes a switching noise whilst descending rapidly to the earth. **1875** KNIGHT *Dict. Mech.*, *Switching-engine*, a yard-engine, or donkey-engine, used about a station or depot for making up trains or moving engines which have not steam up. **1882** *Sun* 14 May 6/6 A large freight-engine with tender..had been at switching work. **1884** KNIGHT *Dict. Mech.* Suppl., *Switching Eye* (Railway), a cast-iron socket on the corner of a freight-car, to which a chain or push-bar may be applied by an engine on an adjoining track. *Switching-in Plug* (Electricity), a plug having its two brass sides insulated from each other by a strip of hard rubber [etc.]. **1894** *Daily Ardmoreite* (Ardmore, Okla.) 28 Mar. 1/8 There came very near being a disastrous collision..in the upper switching yards of the Santa Fe. **1897** KIPLING *Capt. Cour.* viii. 179 The familiar noise of a switching-engine coughing to herself in a freight-yard. **1907** BETHELL *Mod. Guns & Gunnery* 173 For large angles..the switching angle must be calculated or measured ..with the field plotter. **1939** H. J. REICH *Theory & Applic. Electron Tubes* xii. 459 Two high-vacuum amplifier tubes.. are alternately overbiased by the voltage drop through the anode resistors of the switching circuit. **1959** J. M. PETTIT *Electronic Switching, Timing, & Pulse Circuits* iii. 73 The switching speed of a triode in ordinary circuits is impaired by capacitances rather than by transit time of electrons in the tube. **1960** *McGraw-Hill Encycl. Sci. & Technol.* XIII. 357/1 The bulk of switching theory is concerned with circuits made of binary (two-valued) devices, since these are most common. **1960** R. S. LEDLEY *Digital Computer & Control Engin.* xxi. 697 The value of *Rc* can be estimated by means of considerations concerning the switching time of the core, the time τ required to switch or flip a core. **1962** *B.B.C. Handbk.* 113 The EBU is responsible for the coordination of the programme, legal, and technical aspects of Eurovision, and operates the switching centre in Brussels. **1968** Switching station [see FEEDER 10 a]. **1969** *Jane's Freight Containers 1968–69* 116/3 Progress has been made in reducing the time cars spend in switching yards. **1973** *Times* 30 Oct. 1/2 Engineers who man power stations and switching centres will refuse to turn out if a breakdown or other difficulty arises while they are off duty. **1977** *Sci. Amer.* Sept. 212/3 Switching theory, which was developed to help design the relay-operated switching networks of automatic telephone systems, provided guides that enabled a designer to formulate a network with the minimum number of relays for accomplishing some given logical operation. **1978** *Ibid.* Mar. 61/2 (*caption*) Supervisory and switching circuits in the central office connect the two sets for the conversation and disconnect them when the call is over.

'switching, *ppl. a.* [f. as prec. + -ING[2].] That switches; striking as or as with a switch.

switching neck (U.S.): a name for the Louisiana heron. **18..** MEDWIN *Suggestions during Hot Weather* i. (in *Sotheran's Catal.* Apr. (1907) 58) Armed with a switching, cutting Rod. **1891** *Auk* Jan. 77 (Cassell's Suppl.) *Ardea tricolor ruficollis* (Gosse). Louisiana Heron. 'Switching Neck.'

switchman ('swɪtʃmən). [f. SWITCH *sb.* 3 a + MAN *sb.*[1]] A man who works a switch or set of switches on a railway; a pointsman.

1843 *Civil Eng. & Arch. Jrnl.* VI. 23/1 General regulations for police, superintendent, inspectors, constables, switchmen and gatekeepers. **1898** HAMBLEN *Gen. Manager's Story* x. 137 When an accident occurs, conductors, brakemen, and switchmen all unite to swear the blame on the unfortunate engineer.

'switch-off. [f. vbl. phr. *to switch off*: see SWITCH *v.* 8.] The turning off of an (electrical) power supply, television set, etc., by means of a switch. Also *attrib.* and *transf.*

1947 *Times* 11 Feb. 2/3 Liverpool electricity undertaking ..reduced its load by about 55 per cent, during both the morning and afternoon switch-off periods. **1966** *Listener* 7 July 9/2 Television is continually at the mercy either of switch-off or switch-over. **1974** *Times* 15 Jan. 14/3 A mass switch-off of electrical appliances. **1978** *Nature* 5 Jan. 10/3

This suggests that the switch-off of interferon production is due to cessation of mRNA synthesis as well as to its inactivation. **1980** *Daily Tel.* 10 Mar. 13/2 The home viewer who cannot cope with BBC2 or the switch-off button is going to feel swamped by the Olympics.

'switch-on. [f. vbl. phr. *to switch on*: see SWITCH *v.* 8.] The switching on of an (electrical) power supply, light, etc. Also *transf.*

1950 *Sun* (Baltimore) 4 Mar. 2/7 A new electric 'pick-proof' motor car lock which..permits switchon, and starts with a single key, is being manufactured in Stockholm, Sweden. **1976** *Sunday Mail* (Glasgow) 28 Nov. 11/6 Councillor Brian Meek..will attend the district council's tree switch-on. **1978** *Nature* 5 Jan. 10/3 Thus the switch-on of interferon synthesis requires new transcription.

'switch-over. [f. vbl. phr. *to switch over*: see SWITCH *v.* 8c.] A switch or change from one state or course to another; a change-over.

1928 *Daily Express* 12 Nov. 10/2 The opening left by America's switch-over to the 'talkies' can be brilliantly exploited. **1937** *Essays & Stud.* XXII. 148 The cross-currents, switch-overs, throw-backs, and quasi-automatic tags of *The Waste Land.* **1941** 'R. WEST' *Black Lamb & Grey Falcon* I. 159 He believes that any moment the whole process of life may make a slight switch-over and that every thing will be agreeable for ever. **1952** S. KAUFFMANN *Philanderer* (1953) iv. 66 So six months after we start, we've got the name of the book banged into the public's head, and maybe..we've held on to a lot of the confession readers in the switch-over. **1962** *Rep. Comm. Broadc. 1960* 210 in *Parl. Papers 1961–2* (Cmnd. 1753) IX. 259 *The method of changing the line standard...* It considered the possibility of 'a simultaneous change-over throughout the country'—that is, a 'switchover'. **1979** *Financial Rev.* (Sydney) 6 July 46/4 Each of the..pulse generators across Australia required manual switchover in the event of failure.

switchy ('swɪtʃɪ), *a. rare.* [f. SWITCH *sb.* + -Y.] Of the nature of or resembling a switch or slender rod; moving or bending like a switch.

1812 COMBE *Picturesque* xx. 227 And now, perhaps, her switchy tail Hangs on a barn-door from a nail! **1856** RUSKIN *Mod. Paint.* IV. v. i. §10 They have the exact switchy sway of the sail that is always straining against the wind. **1879** ELIZ. S. PHELPS *Sealed Orders* (1880) 157 It's a slender, switchy stock, Mr. Graven; may bend, may break.

swith (swɪθ), *adv. arch.* or *dial.* (in later use chiefly *Sc.*) Forms: α. 1–3 **swiðe**, 1–4 **swyðe**, 1–5 **swiþe**, 2–3 **swuðe**, 2–4 **suithe, suythe**, (2 **swuþe**, 3 **swðe**), 3–4 **suyþe**, 4 (*Ayenb.*) **zuyþe**, 4–5 **swyþe, suiþe**, (**swyde** ?), (4 **squiþe, squyþe**, 4–5 **squythe**, 5 **squithe, sqwithe**), 4–6 **swythe**, 3–5, 9 *arch.* and *rare* **swithe**. β. 3 **swuð** ?, 4 **suiþ**, (**suit, squyþ**, *comp.* **swyþþer**), 4, 6 *Sc.* **suith, suyth**, 4–5, 6 *Sc.* **swyth**, 5 **swiþ**, (*Sc.* **swycht**), 5–6 *Sc.* **swyith**, (6 *Sc.* **switht**), 4–6, 8 *Sc.*, 9 *arch.* and *Sc.* **swith**. [OE. *swiðe* = OS. *swîðo* (MLG. *swide, swît*), OFris. *swîthe, swîde*, OHG., MHG. *swinde* (later *swint, schwind(t)*, mod.G. *geschwind*, dial. *schwind-e*), adv. of Com. Teut. adj. represented by OE. *swiþ* strong (surviving in ME. only in the compar. SWITHER) = OS. *swîði, swîð* strong, powerful, sudden (MLG. *swîde, swît*), OHG., MHG. *swinde* strong, rapid (as the second element in many personal names, as *Wolfswind, Amalswind*), early mod.G. *schwind-e*, ON. *svinnr* swift, quick, wise, Goth. *swinþs* strong; of doubtful origin.

The normal modern representative of OE. *swiðe* would have been (swaɪð). The reduction of ME. *swīthĕ* to one syllable (swiːð) took place first in the north (*Cursor Mundi*). Evidence of normal shortening of the stem-vowel in the compar. *swyþþer* appears late in the 14th cent.; there is no clear evidence of shortening in the positive till late in the 16th cent.]

†**1.** Qualifying a finite verb or a participle: Strongly, forcibly; very greatly, very much, extremely, excessively; in *sup.* most, most especially.

Beowulf 997 (Gr.) Wæs þæt beorhte bold tobrocen swiðe. **971** *Blickl. Hom.* 223 Þæs he wæs ðonne ealles swiþost to hergenne. *a* **1122** *O.E. Chron.* (Laud MS.) an. 959 He wearð wide, ʒeond þeodland, swiðe ʒeweorðad. *c* **1175** *Lamb. Hom.* 119 We sculen hine efre mid alle ure heorte..herian and swiþest on þissere halie tide. *a* **1225** *Ancr. R.* 178 3if eni ancre is þet ne veleð none uondunges, swuð drede hire iðet point, þet heo beo ouer muchel & ouer swuðe ivonded. *c* **1230** *Hali Meid.* 39 Hit ah meiden to eggi þe swiðre þer framward. *c* **1320** *Cast. Love* 1039 Þe fend wondrede swiþe, and seide 'What artou?' **13..** *E.E. Allit. P.* B. 987 Wyth lyʒt louez vplyfte þay loued hym swyþe. **1387** TREVISA *Higden* (Rolls) III. 479, I wil not greve þe to swiþe [CAXTON swyth]. **1398** —— *Barth. De P.R.* IV. xi. (Tollem. MS.) Hete worcheþ ful swyþe [orig. *nimis*] in þe substaunce of flewme and brenneþ it.

†**2.** Qualifying an adj. or adv.: Excessively, extremely, very. *Obs.*

971 *Blickl. Hom.* 27 He hine lædde upon swiþe hea dune. *c* **1000** *Ags. Gosp.* Matt. vii. 13 Se weʒ is swyþe rum þe to forspillednesse ʒelæt. **1154** *O.E. Chron.* (Laud MS.) an. 1140 Hit ward sone suythe god pais. *c* **1250** *Hymn Virgin* 2 in *Trin. Coll. Hom.* App. 257 Moder milde flur of alle þu ert leuedi swuþe treowe. **1297** R. GLOUC. (Rolls) 5616 þe king ..auised hym suiþe wel, wat man it were. *c* **1375** *Cursor M.* 14335 (Fairf.) Vn-til his fader he made a bone & he hit herde squiþe sone. **1387** TREVISA *Higden* (Rolls) I. 293 Þe water of þat welle is swiþe good for men and nouʒt for wommen. *c* **1425** *Seven Sag.* (P.) 2 In Rome was an emperour, A man of swyth mikil honur. *c* **1450** *Hymns Virgin*, etc. (1867) 119 The iiij^te day ys swythe longe, With wepynge & wyth sorow amonge.

3. At a rapid rate, very quickly, swiftly, rapidly. Now *arch.* or *dial.*

α. *c* **1205** LAY. 28469 Ut of Eouerwike..heo iwende, & touward Karliun tuhte, Swa swithe swa heo mahte. **13..** *K. Alis.* 5540 (Laud MS.) To his folk he com ful swiþe, And of his comyng hij weren bliþe. **13..** *Gaw. & Gr. Knt.* 1424 Þe howndez..hastid þider swyþe. *c* **1400** MAUNDEV. (Roxb.) xxxiii. 150 It es ane of þe swythest rynnand waters of þe werld. *c* **1412** HOCCLEVE *De Reg. Princ.* 744 Þe day passiþ swiþe. *c* **1430** *Two Cookery-bks.* 39 Late hem nowt sethe to swythe, & þan lat hem kele.

β. *a* **1352** MINOT *Poems* v. 67 Þe schipmen of Ingland sailed ful swith þat none of þe Normandes fro þam might skrith. *c* **1380** *Sir Ferumb.* 816 Olyuer sone y-seʒ þat cas, & swyþþer bi-gan to haste. *c* **1400** *Destr. Troy* 13156 Whan I hade leingit qwile me list, I launchit on swith. *c* **1400** *Beryn* 583 The Pardoner ran so swith, þe panne fil hym fro. *c* **1450** HOLLAND *Howlat* 171 Swannis suowchand full swyth, swetest of swar. **1892** J. LUMSDEN *Sheep-Head & Trotters* 40 But daffin jigs, an' sangs, an' tales, Sped far too swith the hours on.

4. Quickly, without delay, forthwith, instantly, immediately, directly, at once. Also as *int.* = Quick! hence! away! Now *arch.* or *dial.*

α. *c* **1175** *Lamb. Hom.* 13 Stala and steorfa swiðe eow scal hene. *c* **1205** LAY. 25794 We þe scullen fusen to, swa we hit swiðest maʒen don [*c* **1275** so swiþe so we mawe do]. *a* **1225** *Ancr. R.* 236 Go & slep swiðe. *c* **1250** *Gen. & Ex.* 1086 Ðis angeles..Bid him, or day, redi ben And swiðe ut ðis burʒes flen. *c* **1300** *Havelok* 140 He sende writes sone on-on..That he shulden comen swiþe Til him, that was ful vnbliþe. **1340–70** *Alex. & Dind.* 921 Aftur swaginge of swinc swiþe comeþ ioie. **1388** WYCLIF *John* xiii. 27 That thing that thou doist, do thou swithe. *c* **1420** *Avow. Arth.* xxv, He stroke him sadde and sore, Squithe sqounut he thore. *c* **1435** *Torr. Portugal* 1116 'Swith', he seith, 'that this be done.' **1575** *Gammer Gurton* I. iv, That chal gammer swythe and tyte, and sone be here agayn. **1907** J. DAVIDSON *Triumph Mammon* v. ii, Wherefore upon rebellion swithe I loosed With my own hand the reservoir of death.

β. *a* **1300** *Cursor M.* 1902 Sco went forth and com ful suith [*rime* eftsith]. **1375** BARBOUR *Bruce* II. 316 Till armys swyth, and makys ʒow ʒar! *c* **1420** *Avow. Arth.* xxx, Sethun thay busket hom ʒare, Sqwith with owtun any mare. *c* **1475** *Rauf Coilʒear* 625 Let him swyith in. **1513** DOUGLAS *Æneis* I. ii. 61 Swiht the cluddis, hevin, sone, and days licht Hid. **1528** LYNDESAY *Dreme* 971 Swyith, harlote, hy the hence. **1570** *Pride & Lowl.* (1841) 58 Then called I the Shoemaker and Smyth, The Tanner, Graisier, and the Vintener; Who ready were at hand and came full swith. **1615** BRATHWAIT *Strappado* (1878) 129 Pray thee (good Billy) tell me swith and soone, Iockie may doe what Billy late has done. **1725** RAMSAY *Gentle Sheph.* IV. i, Swith tak him deel, he's our lang out of hell! **1788** BURNS '*Louis, what reck I by thee*' ii, Kings and nations—swith, awa! **1805** SCOTT *Last Minstr.* IV. xxii, My Ladye reads you swith return. **1838** J. STRUTHERS *Poetic Tales* 20 Swith he left his pipe and plaid. **1900** C. MURRAY *Hamewith, Winter* viii, Swith to the fleer ilk eager chiel Bangs wi' his lass to start the reel.

†**b.** *as* (*als, also*) *swithe as* (*als swither*), as soon as. *Obs.*

a **1300** *Cursor M.* 8167 (Cott.) Alsuith sum [*Gött.* also suith as] he þat king had knaun, He said, 'sir welcum to þin aun.' *c* **1400** *Gamelyn* 541 (Harl. MS.) As swithe as thei haddyn wroken hem on her foon. *c* **1420** *Avow. Arth.* xliv, Als squithur thay ar ʒare, To masse ar thay wente.

†**c.** *ellipt.*: see ALSWITHE 2, ASWITHE = as soon as possible, at once, immediately. *Obs.*

swithe, *v. Obs.* exc. *dial.* (swid). Forms: 3 **swiðe, -sweðen**, 4 **swiþe**, *pa. t.* **swath**, 4 **swyþe**, 5 *pa. pple.* **-swythyn**, 6 *pa. pple.* **swithen**. [a. ON. *sviða*, pa. t. *sveið*, pa. pple. *sviðinn* to singe, to smart (MSw. *swidha, swe(e)dh, swidhin* to singe (trans. and intr.), to smart, Sw. *svida* to smart, Norw. *svida*, Da. *svide, svie*), related to ON. *svið* singed sheep's heads, *sviða* roasting, burning, singeing, *sviði* (MSw. *swidhi*) smart from burning: see also SWITHEN, SWITHER *v.*[2] The verb occurs compounded in pr. pple. *forswiðande* (Ancr. R., Titus MS.) and inf. *forsweðen* (Gen. & Ex.): see FOR- *pref.*[1] 5.]

1. *trans.* To burn, scorch, singe.

c **1220** *Bestiary* 70 Ðe sunne swiðeð [*MS.* swideð] al his [*sc.* the eagle's] fliʒt. *a* **1300** *E.E. Psalter* cv[i]. 18 Þe lowe it swath sinful dounright. **13..** *E.E. Allit. P.* C. 478 Þe warme wynde of þe weste wertes he swyþez. [*c* **1440** *Alphabet of Tales* 497 A dynt of þe throndre smate þaim bathe down, so at þe clerk lay vnder-nethe þe preste,..and all þe preste membrys war all to-swythyn.] **1590** R. BERNARD tr. *Terence, Adelphos* v. iii, I will make her as swithen and blacke as a coale.

2. *intr.* To smart. *north. dial.*

1876 *Whitby Gloss.*, *Swid, Swidge*, or *Swither*..'My hand swidded'.

'swithen, *v. Obs.* exc. *dial.* (swidden, swizzen). [a. ON. *sviðna* to be singed (cf. ON. *sviðningr* clearing of land made by burning, Da. *svidning* burning, singeing): see prec.] *trans.* = prec. 1. Also *intr.* to be singed.

1600 SURFLET *Country Farm* III. xx. 471 The northeast winde..is sharpe and swithning, verie hurtfull for all sortes of plants. **1690** O. HEYWOOD *Diaries*, etc. (1885) IV. 138 The ground being very chapt and grasse exceedingly swithened. **1691** RAY *N.C. Words* 72 To *Swizzen*, to Singe. **1788** W. H. MARSHALL *Rural Econ. E. Yorksh.* Gloss. (E.D.S.), *Swidden*, to singe, or burn off, as heath, &c. **1811** WILLAN *W. Riding Words* (E.D.S.), **1876** *Whitby Gloss.*, *Swidden, Swizzen*, or *Sizzen*, to singe, as flannel too near the fire. *Swiddening*, scorching. **1892** M. C. F. MORRIS *Yorkshire Folk-Talk* 112 And a shirt that is scorched at the fire; [they say,] 'Diz tha see? Lawks a massy! it swizzens!'

swither ('swɪðə(r)), *sb. Sc.* and *dial.* Also 8–9 **swidder** (see *Eng. Dial. Dict.*). [f. SWITHER *v.*[1]]

1. A state of agitation or excitement; a flurry, fluster.

a **1768** *Gude Wallace* xvii. in Child *Ballads* VI. 268 The gude wife ran but, the gude man ran ben, They pat the house all in a swither. **1785** BURNS *Death & Dr. Hornbook* vi, I there wi' Something does forgather, That pat me in an eerie swither. **1816** SCOTT *Antiq.* xxxvi, She's been in a swither about the jocolate this morning, and was like to hae toomed it a' out into the slap-basin. **1893** STEVENSON *Catriona* xix. 226 She told me..in what a swither she was in about her papa.

2. A state of perplexity, indecision, or hesitation; doubt, uncertainty.

1719 RAMSAY *Epist. to Arbuckle* 3 [He] stands some time in jumbled swither, To ride in this road, or that ither. **1788** E. PICKEN *Poems* 93 Doun in the yird thou e'en maun lie, Without a swither. **1838** J. STRUTHERS *Poetic Tales* 47 Nae swither checked his onward step. **1895** CROCKETT *Men of Moss-Hags* xxxv. 253 'Mean!' said he, 'mean ——' speaking vaguely as one in a swither.

†**swither**, *a. Obs.* [OE. *swiþra*, comp. of *swiþ* strong: see SWITH *adv.*] The right (hand, side, etc.).

c **950** *Lindisf. Gosp.* Matt. v. 29 *Oculus tuus dexter*, eʒo ðin suiðre. *c* **1000** *Sax. Leechd.* I. 384 Nim eorþan, oferweorp mid þinre swiþran handa under þinum swiþran fet. *a* **1175** *Cott. Hom.* 229 Drihten..astah to heofene..& sit an þar swiðeran halfe his faðer. *c* **1205** LAY. 1548 Breid he mid swiðeren hond a sweord muchel & swide [*v.r.* swiðe] strong.

swither ('swɪðə(r)), *v.*[1] *Sc.* and *dial.* Also 6 **swider, sueidder, swydder**, 6–9 **swidder**. [Of uncertain origin.

Continuity or connexion with the foll. OE. words cannot be assumed with certainty: (*ʒe*)*-sweðrian, -swiðrian* to abate, subside, dwindle, fail; *ʒesweð(e)rian, ʒeswiðrian* to cause to fail or disappear, weaken, destroy; *swaðrian, swæðorian* to subside; *ʒeswæðrung* failure (of mind).]

intr. To be or become uncertain; to falter; to be perplexed or undecided; to hesitate.

1501 DOUGLAS *Pal. Hon.* III. lv, Than on the wall ane garitour I consider, Proclamand loud that did thair hartis swidder. **1535** STEWART *Cron. Scot.* (Rolls) II. 56 Quhilk causit mony for to sueit and swidder. **1570** *Satir. Poems Reform.* xx. 56 Lat na mans feid..Ʒour hartis mak to swidder. **1730** RAMSAY *Fables* xx. viii, Our passions gods, that gar us swither. **17..** *Johnnie Faa* 56 in Child *Ballads* (1857) IV. 285 But the virtue o' a leal woman I trow wad never swither O. **1768** ROSS *Helenore* II. 88 There's nae time to swidder 'bout the thing. **1830** GALT *Lawrie T.* VIII. v. (1849) 371 A child would not have swithered to step over it. **1881** *Fraser's Mag.* Jan. 136 Sir William Harcourt was supposed to be swithering under the dictation of certain federated societies which are powerful at Derby. **1889** STEVENSON *Master of B.* iv. 101, I might have stood there swithering all night, had not the stranger turned.

Hence **'swithering** *vbl. sb.* and *ppl. a.*[1]

a **1585** MONTGOMERIE *Cherrie & Slae* 1007 Considering the swidering [*v.r.* sueiddring] Ʒe fand me first into. **1834** *Tait's Mag.* I. 429/1 I have a swithering, and a leaning, and a hankering and relenting. **1902** N. MUNRO *Children of Tempest* iii, Without a moment's swithering he gave it [*sc.* the money] all to the Jesuits. **1917** KIPLING '*Holy War*' in *Land & Water* Christmas No., The Pope, the swithering Neutrals, The Kaiser and his Gott—..He knew and drew the lot.

'swither, *v.*[2] *dial.* [a. ON. *sviðra* to burn, singe: see SWITHE *v.* and -ER[5]. Cf. SWITHEN.]

1. *trans.* = SWITHE *v.* 1; also *intr.* to burn. Hence **'swithering** *ppl. a.*[2], scorching, parching.

1865 B. BRIERLEY *Irkdale* xv. I. 239 Let it swither away like matchwood. **1886** *S.W. Linc. Gloss.*, *Swither*, to parch, wither up. It's such a swithering day. The plants are quite swithered up. **1886** *Rochdale Gloss.*, *Swuther*, to burst into a flame, as fire which has been smouldering. **1895** CROCKETT *Men of Moss-Hags* xxvi. 196 On that day of swithering heat.

2. *intr.* = SWITHE *v.* 2.

1876 *Whitby Gloss.*, *Swither*, to tingle... 'A sair swithering an warking', a sore tingling and aching.

†**'swithly**, *adv. Obs.* Forms: 1 **swiþ-, swið-, suiðlice**, 2–3 **swiþe-, swiðelic(c)he**, 4 **swyþely**, 4–5 **swythly**, 6 **sweythyli**, *Sc.* **swy(i)thlie**. [OE. *swiþlíce*, f. *swiþ* strong, etc.: see SWITH and -LY[2].]

1. = SWITH *adv.* 1, 2.

c **888** ÆLFRED *Boeth.* xxxvi. §4 Me ðincð nu þæt þin ʒecynd & ðin ʒewuna flite swiðe swiðlice wið ðæm dysiʒe. *c* **1000** *Ags. Gosp.* Matt. xxvii. 14 Se dema wundrode swiþlice. *c* **1175** *Lamb. Hom.* 45 We aʒen þene sunne dei swiþeliche wel to wurþien. *c* **1205** LAY. 4421 And þe king him answerede swiðeliche fæire.

2. = SWITH *adv.* 3, 4.

13.. *Gaw. & Gr. Knt.* 1479 Sir Wawen Settez hir sof[t]ly by his syde, & swyþely ho laʒez. ? **1370** *Robt. Cicyle* (Harl. MS. 525) in Warton *Hist. Eng. Poetry* (1840) I. 185 The sexteyne of the cherche att last Swythly to hym he ganne goo fast. *a* **1400–50** *Wars Alex.* (Dublin MS.) 1184 Þe Bishop.. Gase hym downe..Swythly to þe swyers & þaim þe sware ʒeldez. **1560** ROLLAND *Seven Sages* 99 And the trew treuth swyithlie I sall him schaw. **15..** *King & Barker* 104 in Hazl. *E.P.P.* (1864) I. 9 The hors sped him sweythyli, he sped him wonderley fast.

†**'swithness.** *Sc. Obs. rare*[−1]. = SWIFTNESS.

1536 BELLENDEN *Cron. Scot.* XII. viii. (1541) 178/1 Herald namit for his gret swithnes, hairfut.

swiðwike: see under SWIE.

'switter, *v. dial.* [Imitative.] *intr.* = SWATTER *v.* 1. So **switter-swatter** *adv.* (imitative of the sound made by ducks splashing in water).

1694 *Urquhart's Rabelais* I. xxi. 78 The total Welfare of our humidity doth not depend upon drinking, switter, swatter [*ed.* 1653 in a rible rable; orig. *à tas, à tas*] like Ducks. ? *a* **1800** *Bonnie Milldams of Binnorie* xi. in Child *Ballads* (1882) I. 129/2 Aye she switterit, and aye she swam, Till she cam to yon bonnie mill-dam. [Cf. quot. ? *a* 1800 s.v. SWATTER *v.* 1.]

Switzer ('swɪtsə(r)). *arch.* Also 6 **Switser, Zuitzer,** 7 **Swytzer, Switzard, Zwitzer, -ar.** See also SWISSER. [ad. MHG. *Switzer, Schwytzer*, etc. (early mod.G. *Schweytzer*, now *Schweizer*), or MDu. *Switser, Swytzer* (Du. *Zwitser*); cf. MDa. *Svidser, Suitzer*, Fris. *Sweitser*, etc.; f. *Switz(en)*, etc., Switzerland: see SWISS.]

1. = SWISS *sb.* 1.

1577 tr. *Bullinger's Decades* II. viii. 193/1 Wee Switzers saye: *Vrteilen oder erteilen oder richten.* **1597** SKENE *De Verb. Sign.* s.v. *Menetum*, I haue seene the like in the Cuntrie of Helvetia..amangst the Zuitzers. **1624** CAPT. J. SMITH *Virginia* III. xi. 88 One William Volday, a Zwitzar by birth. **1664** BUTLER *Hud.* II. iii. 1134 A Monster with huge Whiskers, More formidable than a Switzers. **1754** FIELDING *Voy. Lisbon* Wks. 1882 VII. 92 The honesty and freedom of the Switzer. **1810** SCOTT *Lady of L.* VI. iii, The mountain-loving Switzer. **1883** *American* VII. 186 Born, reared and educated a Switzer.

2. *pl.* = *Swiss guards* (SWISS *a.* 2): rarely *sing.* Also *fig.*

1591 *Garrard's Art Warre* 348 But against the Switzers and Launce Knights, the Launce auaileth litle. **1602** SHAKS. *Ham.* IV. v. 97 *King.* Where are my Switzers? Let them guard the doore. **1638** BAKER tr. *Balzac's Lett.* (vol. II) 81 He will never suffer..that a Swytzer shall keep them from entring his base court. **1724** J. MACKY *Journ. thro' Eng.* I. ii. 29 A Guard-Hall, where the Switzers, or the Yeomen of the Guards, as they are called here [*sc.* Windsor Castle], do Duty. **1892** LOUNSBURY *Stud. Chaucer* III. vii. 193 That literary proletariat of the last century whose members.. threatened at one time to develop into an organized band of scribbling Switzers.

3. *attrib.* or *adj.* = SWISS *a.*

1598 BARRET *Theor. Warres* V. ii. 172 A seruant..(who spake the Switzer tong perfectly well). **1818** SCOTT *Battle Sempach* vii, The Switzer priest has ta'en the field. **1829** —— *Anne of G.* x, Now thou hast seen us more closely, what thinkest thou of the Switzer youth?

Hence **'Switzeress**, a female Switzer, a Swiss woman or girl. (The allusion in quot. 1719 is doubtful.)

1719 *Freethinker* No. 132 ¶7 It was impossible he should ever love such a Switzeress as the Queen. **1895** *Punch* 28 Sept. 147/3 Simple Switzeresses outside toybooths..all in national costume.

switzerite ('swɪtsəraɪt). *Min.* [f. the name *Switzer* (see quot. 1967) + -ITE[1].] A hydrated phosphate of manganese and iron, (Mn, Fe)$_3$(PO$_4$)$_2$.4H$_2$O, found as pink to brown monoclinic crystals.

1967 LEAVENS & WHITE in *Amer. Mineralogist* LII. 1595 The name switzerite is proposed for the mineral in honor of George Switzer, Chairman, Department of Mineral Sciences, Museum of Natural History, Smithsonian Institution. **1978** *Rocks & Minerals* LIII. 160 A number of new minerals..from the Quarry include switzerite, eakerite and brannockite.

swive (swaɪv), *v. Obs.* or *arch.* Also 4-5 **swyve,** 5-6 **swyfe,** 6 **swiff, swhyve;** 5 (*Sc.*) *pa. pple.* **swyffit, swywit,** 6 (*Sc.*) *pa. t.* **swiffit, swewyt.** [app. representing, with change of conjugation, and a specialized meaning not found in the cognate words, the OE. str. vb. *swífan*, pa. t. *swáf*, pa. pple. *-swifen* to move in a course, sweep.

OE. *swifan* corresponds to OFris. *swiva* to be uncertain, ON. *svifa* to rove, ramble, drift:—**swīban*, f. Teut. *swīb-*: *swaib-*: *swib-* (cf. OHG. *sweib* swinging, *sweibôn*, MHG. *schweiben* to sway, hover, OFris. *swif* (?) sudden movement, vibration, ON. *svif* turn, veering of a ship, OHG. *swebên*, MHG. *sweben*, G. *schweben* to hover; see also SWAFE, SWAYVE).]

1. *trans.* To have sexual connexion with, copulate with (a female).

c **1386** CHAUCER *Miller's T.* 664 Thus swyued was this Carpenteris wyf For al his kepyng and his Ialousye. *c* **1425** WYNTOUN *Cron.* VIII. xiii. 2008 (Wemyss MS.) Thy dame wes swyffit [*v.r.* swywit] or þou wes borne. **1539** *Extr. Aberd. Reg.* (1844) I. 159, I sell leid the to the place for the freir swewyt the. **1596** SIR J. DAVIES *Epigrams* ix, He sweares he hath foure onely swiude, A maide, a wife, a widow and a whoore. **1598** FLORIO s.v. *Fottere.* *a* **1722** PENNECUIK *Scots Poems* (1756) 100 And why was all this mighty pother, But for to swive some jade or other? **1884** J. PAYNE *Tales fr. Arabic* I. 230 So he ate and drank and lay with her and swived her.

2. *intr.* To copulate.

c **1440** in *Rel. Ant.* (1843) II. 281 If he may wele swyfe. **1500-20** DUNBAR *Poems* xxxiv. 67 The Feind me ryfe, Gif I do ocht bot drynk and swyfe. **1646** H. MILL *Night's Search* II. 130 She scorn'd to swive Under a Crown, with any man alive. **1694** WOOD *Life* 26 May (O.H.S.) III. 453 Mason, minister of Water Stratford in Bucks: he and his disciples.. live in common... Eat, drink, and sleep, dance, swive. **1898** *Secreta Secret.* (E.E.T.S.) 76 *marg.*, Don't bathe on a full stomach: nor swive.

Hence **swived** *ppl. a.*, **swiving** *vbl. sb.*; also † **swive** *sb.*, an act of swiving; **'swiver**, one who swives; one given to sexual indulgence.

a **1300** *Pol. Songs* (Camden) 69 Richard of Alemaigne, whil that he wes kyng, He spende al is tresour opon swyvyng. *c* **1440** in *Rel. Ant.* (1843) II. 282 Mete and drynke thay hafe ynoghe, bot swyvyng thame wanntis. *Ibid.*, And now are sary swywers brokyne owte of bande. *c* **1500** *Blowbol's Test.* 231 in Hazl. *E.P.P.* I. 102 Alle feeble swyvers. *c* **1560** A. SCOTT *Poems* (S.T.S.) iv. 36 Wedow men þat wantis To steil. a pair of swyvis. **1611** COTGR., *Chevaucherie*, a riding; a swiuing. *a* **1680** BUTLER *Characters*, etc. (1908) App. 457 In the Scotch translation Genesis is rendered the Buke of Swiving. **1707** MARKLAND in Hearne *Collect.* 30 Sept. (O.H.S.) II. 56 Drunkards and Swivers Are never long livers. *a* **1722** PENNECUIK *Scots Poems* (1756) 101 The goddess, who lou'd swiving. **1869** FURNIVALL in *Wright's Chaste Wife* Pref. p. vii *note*, The swived wife and broken arm that he [*sc.* Chaucer] gives his befooled Oxford tradesman in the Milleres Tale.

swivel ('swɪv(ə)l), *sb.* Forms: 4 **swyuel, swewyl, suawel(le,** 5-6 **swevill(e, -yll, -ell,** (5 **swefel, sewevelle),** 5-7 **swivell,** 6 **swyuell, swyvle, (swyffvyll),** 7 **swyvile,** 7-8 **swivle,** 8 **swyvil, swivil,** (9 *Sc.* **sweevil),** 7- **swivel.** *β.* 6 *Sc.* **swele,** 7 **sweell.** *γ.* 6 *Sc.* **sowl, swoll, swoul,** 9 **soul, sooal,** etc. [f. weak grade *swif-* of OE. *swifan* (see SWIVE) + *-el* (see -LE).]

1. a. A simple fastening or coupling device made so that the object fastened to it can turn freely upon it, or so that each half of the swivel itself can turn independently; *e.g.* a ring or staple turning on a pin or the like.

1307-8 *Acc. Exch. K.R.* Bd. 14. No. 14 (P.R.O.), In quodam haunser empto..pro dicta masta tractanda, iiij.s. viij.d...in vno swyuel de ferro empto..pro dicta Masta, .x.d. **1330** *Chancellor's Roll 123* m 20 *dorso*, In..uno swyvel de ferro..pro dicta bargia. **1353** in *Pipe Roll 32 Edw. III*, m. 36 Pro factura de .iij. Swyuels pro towagio ij. mast[orum] de hortepole et .j. masti de scharburghe. *Ibid.* 36/1 *dorso* De .j. ancre cum vno suawel sine anulo in capite. **1411** *Nottingham Rec.* II. 86, iij. swefels, ijd. **1424-5** *Foreign Accounts* 59 m. 26, De j ferro vocato swevill de novo facto ad towandum quoddam malum grossum. **1426-7** *Rec. St. Mary at Hill* 65 For a key & a swevyll to þe chirche dore vij d. **1482-4** *Acc. Exch. K.R.* Bd. 496. No. 28 (P.R.O.) Cymenting barres Swevilles Steybarres pro fenestris. **1502-3** in C. Kerry *Hist. St. Lawrence, Reading* (1883) 53 A bolte and a swevyll to the trendyll. **1525** *MS. Acc. St. John's Hosp., Canterb.*, Payd for ij swevyllys for calues ij d. **1535** *MS. Rawl. D.* 777 lf. 84 b A new swyffvyll ffor the buket of the said well. **1575** TURBERV. *Faulconrie* 173 Take a small corde of the bignesse of a bowstring or little more, put it through a ring and binde it about the stone, in such sorte that the ring or swyvle may go rounde about the stone, without any stoppe or lette. **1598** FLORIO, *Accialino*,..the swiuell of a chaine. **1651** T. BARKER *Art of Angling* (1653) 4 Two hairs twisted for the bottom.. with a Swivel nigh the middle of your line. **1672** T. VENN *Milit. Discipl.* 8 He is to have a good Harquebuz, hanging on a Belt, with a swivel. **1682** *Lond. Gaz.* No. 1710/4 A Ger Faulkon of the King's,..having one of the King's Varvels upon one Leg, and a Brass Swivel upon the other. **1695** *Ibid.* No. 3070/4 Lost.., a Steel Chain and Swivles of the same, belonging to a Watch, having the Key and two Seals upon the Swivles. **1791** SMEATON *Edystone L.* §126 Two 40 fathom chains were to be joined together by one of the loops of the large swivel,..one of the anchors..being laid to the westward..from the swivel. **1802** JAMES *Milit. Dict.*, *Swivels*,..commonly called Loop and Swivel, and Guard and Swivel,—Two iron rings attached to a musquet, through which the sling passes. **1887** HARDY *Woodlanders* I. iii. 44 He carried a horn lantern which hung upon a swivel, and, wheeling as it dangled, [etc.].

β. **1502** Swele [see 4]. **1688** HOLME *Armoury* III. xviii. (Roxb.) 134/2 A carbine..is hung by the mans side in a belt ouer his left shoulder, and vnder his right Arme: with a sweell or sweeth vpon it, which by the help of a spring in it, taks hold of a ring, on a side bar..screwd on the stock.

γ. **15..** *Lichtoun's Dream* 64 in *Bann. MS.* lf. 101 b, Thair tedderis wer maid weill grit to graip, With silkin schakillis and sowlis [*Maitland MS.* swollis] of quhyte saip. *c* **1536** LYNDESAY *Compl. Bagsche* 202 Thocht ȝe be cuplit all to gidder With silk, and swoulis of syluer fyne. **1878** *Cumbld. Gloss.*, *Sooals*, a swivel joint in a chain, commonly termed a pair of sooals.

fig. **1775** SHERIDAN *Rivals* IV. iii, T'other [eye] turned on a swivel, and secured its retreat with a frown! **1836** I. TAYLOR *Phys. Theory* xvi. 208 That the sun is the mere lamp and hearth of the planetary system or only the swivel of its revolutions.

b. *spec.* A pivoted rest for a gun, esp. on the gunwale of a boat, enabling it to turn horizontally in any required direction.

1697 DAMPIER *Voy. round World* (1699) 30 She had 4 Patereroes, and some long Guns plac'd in the Swivel on the Gunnel. **1745** P. THOMAS *Jrnl. Anson's Voy.* 288 She had.. twenty-eight Brass Patareroes..mounted on Swivels on the Gun-walls. **1878** A. H. MARKHAM *Gt. Frozen Sea* i. 4 They were both provided with harpoon guns fixed on swivels in the bows.

2. Short for *swivel-gun*: see 4 b.

1748 *Anson's Voy.* II. iv. 169 Four four pounders, and two swivels. **1761** *Ann. Reg., Chron.* 97/2 The Vainqueur of 10 guns, 16 swivels, and 90 men. **1816** TUCKEY *Narr. Exped. R. Zaire* iii. (1818) 109 On his landing I saluted him with four swivels. **1876** BANCROFT *Hist. U.S.* IV. xxxv. 573 At daybreak it was boarded by the provincials, who carried off four four-pounders and twelve swivels.

3. A kind of small shuttle used in ribbon-weaving, etc. (Cf. *swivel-loom* in 4 b.)

1894 T. W. FOX *Mech. Weaving* XII. 313 If the two systems are compared as to beauty of effect, variety of detail, and general excellence of workmanship, swivels are vastly superior to lappets. *Ibid.* 314 Swivels have been made in power-looms for upwards of twenty years, but they are still, to a large extent, produced on hand-looms.

4. *attrib.* and *Comb.*: in names of various parts of machinery, etc. = forming or connected with a swivel, so as to turn on some other part or allow it to turn, as ***swivel-bar, -bearing, -bed, -belt, -coupling, -hanger, -head, -joint, -link, -pipe, -plate, -ring, rocker, -seat, -table***, etc.; also ***swivel-like*** adj. and adv.

1502 *Acc. Ld. High Treas. Scot.* II. 46 For ane elne gray damas to be ane swele belt for hir credill, xxijs. **1725** *Fam. Dict.* s.v. *Windmill*, That the Handle or Rod of the Bucket, be so made, that it may, swivel-like, turn any way. **1769** FALCONER *Dict. Marine* (1780) s.v. *Moorings*, To this swivel-link are attached the bridles, which are short pieces of cable. **1792** BELKNAP *Hist. New Hampsh.* III. 105 The invention of the swivel-chain. **1825** J. NICHOLSON *Operat. Mech.* 56 The gives..should not be immovably fixed to the arms, but hung by a swivel joint. **1838** *Civil Eng. & Arch. Jrnl.* I. 263/1 One of these guns will be placed forward, and the other aft,..on sliding swivel beds. **1844** H. STEPHENS *Bk. Farm* II. 534 A carriage of a nearly triangular form is very generally adopted, the apex being in front over the swivel-bar. *Ibid.* III. 1103 The end..is furnished with ferule and swivel-ring. **1856** 'STONEHENGE' *Brit. Rural Sports* 255 The Single Swivel-Trace consists of about 12 inches of gut or gimp, with a hook-swivel at one end. **1869** RANKINE *Machine & Hand-tools* Pl. P 4, A swivel bearing fixed in the arms of the quadrants. *Ibid.* P 11, Connected to the mains by elastic pipes or swivel couplings. **1875** KNIGHT *Dict. Mech.*, *Swivel-joint*, a section in a chain or a joint on a rod, which allows the parts to twist without kinking or distortion. **1908** *Westm. Gaz.* 17 Oct. 12/2 The eyes of the chameleon.. appear to be mounted on ball-sockets, that act in a swivel-like manner. **1916** *Blackw. Mag.* Oct. 475/1 He walked unsteadily across the room and sat down on a swivel-seat. **1975** Swivel rocker [see *saddle brown* s.v. SADDLE *sb.* 12].

b. Special Combs.: **swivel-bridge**, a swing-bridge; **swivel-chair**, a chair the seat of which turns horizontally on a pivot; † **swivel-engine** = *swivel-loom*; **swivel eye** *colloq.* or *slang*, a squinting eye (cf. 1775 in 1 *fig.*); an eye that rolls in its socket; hence **swivel-eyed** *a.*, squint-eyed, squinting; **swivel-gun**, a gun or cannon, usually a small one, mounted on a swivel (sense 1 b) so as to turn horizontally in any required direction; **swivel hips** *Trampolining*, an exercise consisting of a seat drop followed by a half-twist into another seat drop (constr. *sing.*); also *transf.*; **swivel-hook**, a hook fastened to something, *e.g.* a pulley-block, by means of a swivel; hence **swivel-hooked** *a.*; **swivel-loom**, ? a loom having swivels (sense 3) on the batten, used in ribbon-weaving; **swivel-plough**, a turn-wrest plough; **swivel-shuttle**, = sense 3; **swivel-weaving**, weaving with a swivel-shuttle; so **swivel-weft**.

1754 POCOCKE *Trav.* (Camden) II. 66 The Wye [= Wey], over which there is a long *swivil bridge which turns with one hand. **1848** DICKENS *Dombey* ix, A little canal near the India Docks, where there was a swivel bridge which opened now and then to let some wandering monster of a ship come roaming up the street like a stranded leviathan. **1858** *Merc. Marine Mag.* V. 124 The Swivel Bridge across the New Cut at Swansea Harbour. **1884** HOWELLS *Silas Lapham* (1891) I. 22 Lapham..lifted his bulk up out of his *swivel-chair. **1795** J. AIKIN *Manchester* 163 Ingenious mechanics [were] invited over to construct *swivel engines. **1765** S. CIBBER *Let.* 3 Oct. in *Private Corresp. David Garrick* (1831) I. 201, I hope you remember that I have lost poor little *swivel-eye, that was blind, and also that you promised me a dog that could see. **1865** DICKENS *Mut. Fr.* II. xii, She found herself possessed of what is colloquially termed a swivel eye... She was not otherwise positively ill-looking. **1896** A. D. COLERIDGE *Eton in Forties* (1898) 174 He glared with his swivel eye at the congregation. **1781** C. JOHNSTON *Hist. J. Juniper* I. 21 Some witch or fairy..must have stolen away her own child..and left this *swivel-eyed elf in his place. **1889** CONAN DOYLE *Micah Clarke* 244 Your blue-coated, gold-braided, swivel-eyed, quarter-deckers. **1712** E. COOKE *Voy. S. Sea* 125, I went away in our Pinnace, with..a *Swivel-Gun in the Boat. **1748** *Anson's Voy.* II. v. 179 The Commodore ordered..a swivel gun-stock to be fixed in the bow. **1769** COOK *Voy. round World* I. x. (1773) 102, I mounted six swivel guns upon the fort, which I was sorry to see struck the natives with dread. **1846** GREENER *Sci. Gunnery* 283 The longest duck or swivel guns. **1943** L. GRISWOLD *Trampoline Tumbling* 49 As the legs are swung through the vertical position, the twist is made to right or left and the hips are flexed to assume the sitting position for landing. The movement performed by the hips is called '*swivel hips'. **1948** *Ibid.* (ed. 2) vi. 46 This exercise—popularly called 'swivel hips'—consists of a seat-drop take-off, a half twist, and a seat-drop landing. **1964** *Trampolining* ('Know the Game' Series) 22/1 The first one [*sc.* bounce] to practise is the seat bounce with half twist known as the swivel hips. **1966** ROTE & WINTER *Lang. Pro Football* III. 141/1 *Swivel hips*, elusive ball carrier who fakes potential tacklers by shifting hips from side to side. **1980** *Sci. Amer.* Mar. 118/2 An astronaut in space could easily reorient himself in any direction with swivel hips and tuck drops. **1788** JEFFERSON *Writ.* (1859) II. 379 Hook the instrument by its *swivel hook. **1844** H. STEPHENS *Bk. Farm* I. 425 The draught swivel-hook is attached to the shackle. **1883** *Man. Seamanship for Boys* 136 Fall Blocks, for Top-Tackle Pendants, Are iron-bound, *swivel-hooked blocks. **1795** J. AIKIN *Manchester* 175 Some attempts have been made to work a number of looms together by machinery. The first was upon the introduction of *swivel-looms, about thirty years since. **1875** KNIGHT *Dict. Mech.*, *Swivel-loom*, a kind of loom (formerly) used for the weaving of tapes and narrow goods. *Ibid.*, **Swivel-plow*... Known in England as a *turn-wrest* plow; in the United States as a Side-hill Plow. **1894** T. W. FOX *Mech. Weaving* XII. 314 In power-looms, *swivel shuttles are fitted in a movable carrying frame attached to the front of a slay. *Ibid.*, *Swivel-weaving consists in adding ribbon shuttles to an ordinary loom in such a manner that they can be held out of the way, dropped upon the race board, and moved under lifted warp at pleasure. *Ibid.* VI. 162 This machine makes imperfect cloth, because ground weft floats under the figure in precisely the same manner as *swivel weft.

'swivel, *v.*^{1} [f. prec. sb.]

1. *trans.* To turn (something) on or as on a swivel.

1794 *Sporting Mag.* III. 162/2 Our hobs can swivel noses at single stick who fight. **1832** *Prop. Regul. Instr. Cavalry* II. 41 The..men..swivel their carbines. **1876** C. D. WARNER *Wint. Nile* xxv. 311 He simply swivels his eye around and brings it to bear on the object. **1879** *Cassell's Techn. Educ.* IV. 343/1 It swivels or adjusts itself so as to prevent irregular cutting. **1914** J. G. HORNER *Gear Cutting* 89 The tooth flank is swivelled about the apex of the cone of the gear.

2. *intr.* To turn or rotate as, or as on, a swivel.

1846 HOLTZAPFFEL *Turning* II. 854 If the jaws are closed upon a taper object,..the two parts of the vice swivel horizontally on a joint. **1869** RANKINE *Machine & Hand-tools* Pl. L 4, Each of the lower speed cones, F, is so mounted as to be capable of swivelling about the shaft, E. **1884** KNIGHT *Dict. Mech., Suppl.* 754/2 A street car mounted on its running gear so as to swivel thereon and turn end for end, dispensing with a turn-table.

3. *trans.* To furnish with a swivel; to fasten *to* something by means of a swivel.

1870 *Eng. Mech.* 14 Jan. 429/3 Arms swivelled to a revolving disc. **1891** *Pall Mall G.* 10 Dec. 2/2 The electric current not only rings the alarm bell but also swivels up the harness of the horses that draw the fire-engine. **1901** *Daily News* 9 Jan. 3/3 The weapons are also fitted with a short sling attached to the ring swivelled on to the fore band of the piece.

Hence **swivelled** ('swɪv(ə)ld) *ppl. a.*, furnished with a swivel; **'swivelling** *vbl. sb.* and *ppl. a.*

1869 RANKINE *Machine & Hand-tools* Pl. O 4, A suitable swivelling joint being provided to enable the crane to make complete revolutions. **1871** *Routledge's Ev. Boy's Ann.* Oct. 594 Joined together by a swivelling-pin over the driving-wheel. **1884** F. J. BRITTEN *Watch & Clockm.* 138 The upper slide is swivelled. **1894** T. W. FOX *Mech. Weaving* XII. 316 A rack is usually governed by the Jacquard through a cam, a series of links, and an upright shaft, and means are provided for putting the rack out of action whenever it becomes necessary to stop swivelling. **1911** *Encycl. Brit.* XXVII. 164/1 Modern car bodies are mounted either on a single four-wheeled truck, with a fixed or rigid wheel-base, or on two four-wheeled bogies or swivelling trucks. **1914** J. G. HORNER *Gear Cutting* 168 The swivelling movement of the cutter head.

swivel ('swɪv(ə)l), *v.*^{2} [Alt. f. SHRIVEL *v.*; for an equivalent change of initial *shr-* to *sw-*, compare U.S. dial. *swimp* shrimp.] *intr.* To shrivel. Also const. *up. U.S. dial.*

1898 'R. SANDERS' *Sk. Country Life* xxv. 155 Sometimes I think to myself if Christmas didn't come reglar onest a year ..this old world would soon swivel and swink up and die out with the dry rots. **1957** W. FAULKNER *Town* (1958) vii. 103 Old hermits setting on rocks out in the hot sun..watching their blood dry up and their legs swivelling.

Hence **'swivelled** *ppl. a.*

1898 'R. SANDERS' *Sk. Country Life* viii. 53, I..filled my pockets full of scalybarks and peanuts and some swivelled up apples of my own raisin. **1938** M. K. RAWLINGS *Yearling* xvii. 204 The one we cain't spare was the one was takened. ..And him a swivveled, no-account thing, too. **1975** E. WIGGINTON *Foxfire 3* 258 It'll be a little bitty old swivelled up thing.

swivet ('swɪvɪt). *dial.* (chiefly *U.S.*). Also **swivvet, swi(v)vit.** [Origin unknown.] A state of agitation; a fluster or panic. Also, a hurry. Freq. in phr. ***in a swivet.***

1892 *Dialect Notes* I. 232 *Swivet* (swivit),..'Don't be in such a swivet.' *a* **1904** in *Eng. Dial. Dict.* (1904) V. 893/2 What a swivit ee's in. **1913** H. KEPHART *Our Southern Highlanders* xiii. 294 When a man is..in a hurry, he is in a swivvet. **1917** *Dialect Notes* IV. 418 [N. Carolina] *Swivvit*, n., hurry. 'He's always in a swivvit.' Also La. **1933** I. S. COBB *Murder Day by Day* xvi. 209 And Hilda, so Verity said, was in quite a swivit over the prospect of being interviewed again. **1955** *N.Y. Sunday News* 27 Mar. 100/1 She does not get in 'swivets' or 'tizzies', either, and she does not often sulk. **1962** M. CARLETON *Dread Sunset* (1963) v. 81 'Don't get into a swivet,' Ellen soothed. **1978** C. MACLEOD *Rest You Merry* xxiv. 168 Jemina was always in a swivet about something.

swivet, var. SWEVET *Obs.*

Swizar, -er, Swizzer, var. SWISSER *Obs.*

swizz (swɪz). *slang.* Also **swiz.** [Shortened f. SWIZZLE *sb.*^{2}] A disappointment or 'swindle.' Freq. in the exclamation 'What a swizz!'

1915 W. OWEN *Let.* 19 Mar. (1967) 328 What a swizz about Harold! **1921** V. BRITTAIN *Let.* Nov. in *Testament of Youth* (1933) x. 513 What a swiz for all the people who swore that there was nothing in it between Ramage and Cathleen Nesbitt. **1932** G. CLARK *Mistress* II. v. 186 They want us to go lunch. Just round the corner here... Bit of a swiz, isn't it? I did my best to get out of it. **1937** S. SMITH *Good Time was had by All* 38 The people say that spiritism is a joke and a swizz. **1959** R. FULLER *Ruined Boys* II. ix. 144 He's given him not out. What a sodding swiz. *a* **1974** R. CROSSMAN *Diaries* (1976) II. 208 We were drinking cheerfully when up came that phrase Quintin Hogg is always using: 'Really, it's only a swizz.'

Hence as *v. trans.*, to trick by swindling, to subject to disappointment (in quot., *pass.*).

1961 H. & M. WILLIAMS *Irregular Verb to Love* in J. C. Trewin *Plays of Year* XXIII. 84, I..felt I'd been swizzed —not just of sex though that was part of it.

swizzing: see SWISSING.

swizzle ('swɪz(ə)l), *sb.*^{1} *slang* or *colloq.* [Origin unknown. Cf. SWITCHEL.] A name for various compounded intoxicating drinks; sometimes vaguely used for intoxicating drink in general.

1813 COL. HAWKER *Diary* (1893) I. 68 The boys..finished the evening with some prime grub, swizzle, and singing. **1843** LE FEVRE *Life Trav. Phys.* III. III. i. 86 A glass of swizzle, the most salubrious beverage in hot weather. **1848** ALB. SMITH *Chr. Tadpole* xlv. 304 'What sort of swizzle do you keep here?' 'Swizzle, sir?—yes, sir,' answered the waiter, not exactly knowing what to reply. 'Drink, I mean,' the other continued; 'lush!—will that do?' **1879** BODDAM-WHETHAM *Roraima*, etc. 129 A certain institution of Demerara known as 'swizzles'... The exact receipt for a swizzle I cannot give. **1899** C. H. ROBINSON in *World Wide Mag.* July, After partaking of the inevitable brandy cocktail or 'swizzle' as it is called in the West Indies.

swizzle ('swɪz(ə)l), *sb.*^{2} *slang* (chiefly *Schoolchildren's*). [Prob. altered f. SWINDLE *sb.*^{3}] = SWIZZ.

1913 A. H. DAWSON *Dict. Eng. Slang & Colloquialisms* 139 *Swizzle.* (1) Any sort of drink. (2) A swindle, fraud. Also a verb in both senses. **1931** C. MACKENZIE *Buttercups & Daisies* v. 59 'What a swizzle you can't eat rats,' Roger sighed. *Ibid.* xviii. 229 What a swizzle it's so late. **1950** A. BUCKERIDGE *Jennings goes to School* i. 12 It was a rotten swizzle, sir, because we flew through low cloud and we couldn't see a thing. *a* **1976** A. CHRISTIE *Autobiogr.* (1977) IX. v. 476 This place is awful, Mother... As for those bathrooms,..it's an absolute swizzle! They're never used.

'swizzle, *v. slang* or *colloq.* and *dial.* [f. SWIZZLE *sb.*^{1}]

1. *intr.* To drink to excess, swig, tipple. Hence **'swizzled** *ppl. a.*, drunk, 'sozzled'; influenced or induced by heavy drinking.

1843 *Knickerbocker* XXII. 366 We were never 'groggy', ..'swizzled' or 'tight', but once. **1847** HALLIWELL, *Swizzle* ..to drink, or swill. **1888** *Texas Siftings* 14 Jan. 8/2 Old Shep, with a swizzled intuition, would darkly imagine that the singers were alluding to his calcium nose. **1903** MCNEILL *Egregious English* 155 There he gorges and swizzles till the warning bell advises him of the departure of his train. **1918** G. FRANKAU *One of Them* ix. 65 Some quaff th'embittered cocktail, or the rum Whose swizzled headaches heavy on to-morrow weigh. **1934** *Amer. Spectator* July 2/3 The editors of *The American Spectator* got somewhat swizzled one night last week and didn't feel so good the next day.

2. *trans.* To stir with a swizzle-stick.

1859 TROLLOPE *West Indies* iii. (1860) 46 A long bitter duly swizzled is your true West Indian syren. **1885** LADY BRASSEY *The Trades* 151 The whole is mixed with powdered ice, and stirred or 'swizzled' until it froths well.

'swizzler. *dial.* and *slang.* Now *rare.* [f. SWIZZLE *v.* + -ER^{1}.] **a.** A drunkard. **b.** A swindler.

1876 F. K. ROBINSON *Gloss. Whitby* 192/1 *Swizzler*, a drunkard. **1936** 'N. BELL' *Crocus* ix. 235 Oh, he didn't diddle me... I knew him for a swizzler from the word go. **1938** J. W. DAY *Dog in Sport* xvii. 233 Lights gleamed in a building ashore. The Cockney swizzlers were still at it.

'swizzle-stick. [f. SWIZZLE *sb.*^{1} + STICK *sb.*^{1}]

1. A stick used for stirring drink into a froth. Also, a rod used to stir a mixed drink, or to flatten the effervescence of a cocktail, etc.

1879 J. W. BODDAM-WHETHAM *Roraima & Brit. Guiana* xii. 129 The revolutions of a peculiar instrument called the swizzle-stick. **1885** LADY BRASSEY *The Trades* 152, I mean.. to take home some 'swizzle-sticks'. They are cut from some kind of creeper, close to a joint, where four or five shoots branch out at right angles, so as to produce a star-like circle. **1899** C. J. C. HYNE *Further Adventures Capt. Kettle* v. 135 Shout for your boy to bring the cocktail... Where's the swizzle-stick? **1951** *N.Y. Herald-Tribune* 9 Mar. 18/3 Under Otto Preminger's direction it is all as frothy and inevitable as the action of a swizzle stick in a champagne glass. **1964** WODEHOUSE *Frozen Assets* ii. 36 The way the mere sound of her voice got inside one and stirred one up as with a swizzle-stick. **1976** J. I. M. STEWART *Young Pattullo* iii. 69, I was being officiously counselled not to commit the solecism of using a swizzle-stick too soon.

2. *transf.*

1962 J. GLENN in *Into Orbit* 44 A simple little rod... It is ten inches long, has a hook on the end of it for pulling at levers and a stub for pushing at buttons. You grasp it in your glove if you know you are not going to be able to reach something with your fingers... We call it, naturally, a 'swizzle stick'. **1977** *Lancet* 16 Apr. 836/2 The swizzlestick consists of a handle fastened to a small stainless steel circular platform to which is also fastened a stainless steel displacement probe having a diameter slightly less than the bore of a capillary tube and a volume equal to the volume of blood required for the assay.

3. *Comb.*, as **swizzle-stick tree**, a small aromatic evergreen tree, *Quararibea turbinata*, of the family Bombacaceæ, found in the W. Indies and tropical South America.

1943 RECORD & HESS *Timbers New World* 98/1 All specimens of *Quararibea* without distinct heartwood... Common names: Garrocho, swizzle-stick tree. **1951** E. MITTELHOLZER *Shadows move among Them* I. xvi. 153 Wild cacao and swizzle-stick trees and ferns..grew out of reddish sand.

swk, obs. Sc. form of SUCK *v.*

swld(e, obs. ff. *should*, pa. t. of SHALL.

swm(e, obs. Sc. ff. SOME.

swmmer, obs. form of SUMMER *sb.*^{2}

swmyr, obs. Sc. f. SUMMER *sb.*^{1}

swn, swne, obs. forms of SUN.

swndre, obs. Sc. f. SUNDER *v.*

swne, obs. Sc. f. SOON *adv.*, SWOON.

swnye, var. SONYIE *v. Obs.*

swoap, obs. dial. f. SOPE.

swob, swobber, var. SWAB, SWABBER.

swoch, Sc. var. SOUGH *v.*^{1}, SWOW *sb.*; obs. form of SUCH.

swod, variant of SWAD *sb.*^{1}, ^{7}.

swoddle, obs. form of SWADDLE *v.*

swoddy, variant of SWADDY *sb.*

†**swoft.** *Obs. rare.* [app. f. ME. SWOP-E + -T.] Sweepings.

c **1250** *Death* 152 in *O.E. Misc.* 176 Me wule swopen þin hus & ut mid þe swoft.

swofte, obs. Sc. var. SWIFT.

†**swog,** *v. Obs. rare.* [? A mixture of SWAY or SWING and JOG.] *intr.* ? To make one's way heavily.

1637 WHITING *Albino & Bellama* 105 He..with all speed was swogging to the hall.

swogh(e, swoȝ(e: see SOUGH, SWOW *sb.*

swohinge, variant of SWOWING *vbl. sb.*

swoir, obs. Sc. pa. t. of SWEAR *v.*

swolde, rare obs. pa. pple. of SELL *v.*

†**'swolder,** *v. Obs. rare.* [? Miswritten for **swolter*, possibly a variant of SWALTER.] *intr.* To wallow, welter.

c **1200** *Trin. Coll. Hom.* 7 Longe we habben lein on ure fule synnes & swoldred þaron alse slou man doð on swete slape.

swole, obs. pa. t. of SWELL *v.*

swoled, dial. variant of SWEALED *ppl. a.*

1709 W. KING *Art of Cookery* 35 Others, to shew the largeness of their Soul, Prepare you Muttons swol'd, and Oxen whole. *Ibid., Let.* 21 A swol'd Mutton, which is a Sheep roasted in its Wool.

†**swole-hot,** *a. Obs.* = *swoly hot*: see SWOLY.

1721 BAILEY, *Swole-hot*, sultry, hot. *O.* [= Old Word].

swolewe, obs. form of SWALLOW.

swoling, obs. form of SULING.

swolks, app. a meaningless perversion of SWOUNDS.

1731-8 SWIFT *Pol. Conversat.* ii. 173 Swolks, I must be going, by'r Lady.

swollen ('swəʊl(ə)n), *ppl. a.* Forms: see SWELL *v.* [Strong pa. pple. of SWELL *v.*]

1. a. Increased in bulk, as by internal pressure; distended, filled out; *esp.* morbidly enlarged, affected with tumour; also, of a distended form, bulging, protuberant.

c **1325** *Song of Merci* 162 in *E.E.P.* (1862) 123 We loue so slouþe, and harlotrie, We slepe a[s] swolle swyn in lake. **1538** ELYOT, *Tumidus*,..swollen. **1558** WARDE tr. *Alexis' Secr.* 23 b, To heale swollen knees or legges. **1590** SPENSER *F.Q.* II. i. 13 Her swollen eyes were much disfigured. **1598** BP. HALL *Sat.* IV. i. 69 His pouting cheeks puff vp aboue his brow Like a swolne Toad toucht with the Spiders blow. **1683** PRIOR *Pastoral* 14 Nor let those sighs from your swoln bosom rise. **1688** HOLME *Armoury* II. 4/2 Æolus..an ancient Man with swolne Blub Cheeks. **1742** COLLINS *Oriental Eclogues* ii. 63 The silent asp shall creep..Or some swoln serpent twist his scales around. **1816** BYRON *Prisoner of Chillon* viii, I've seen it on the breaking ocean Strive with a swoln convulsive motion. **1838** DICKENS *Nich. Nick.* xix, The swollen veins stood out like sinews on Ralph's forehead. **1839** FR. A. KEMBLE *Resid. Georgia* (1863) 61 Upon this great tray are piled the swollen..cotton bags. **1884** BOWER & SCOTT *De Bary's Phaner.* 519 Plants which, in their wild form, have thin roots, but in many cultivated varieties are provided with fleshy swollen roots. **1890** *Retrospect Med.* CII. 326 The swollen, vascular state of the tongue.

b. Of a body of water: cf. SWELL *v.* 1 b, 2 b, 3 b.

1652 MAYNE tr. *Donne's Epigrams* lvi. 9 Here the swoln sea views the inferiour ground. **1794** MRS. RADCLIFFE *Myst. Udolpho* l, The swollen torrents that descend from the heights. **1856** RUSKIN *Mod. Paint.* v. xvi. §20 Cliffs..of which every thunder-shower dissolves tons in the swoln blackness of torrents. **1913** G. M. TREVELYAN *J. Bright* Introd. 1 His oncoming was as the surge of the full swollen tide, not of the sea in storm.

c. Increased in amount or degree.

a **1631** DONNE *Elegies* xi[i]. 110 At thy lives last moment, May thy swolne sinnes themselves to thee present. **1871** R. H. HUTTON *Ess.* (1877) I. 61 The inroads of unjust and swollen powers. **1911** G. ELLIOT SMITH *Anc. Egyptians* ii. 15 The writings that..fill the swollen shelves of our libraries.

2. *fig.* **a.** Said of a feeling or mental state such as causes a sense of distension or expansion, or of a person affected with such a feeling, etc.; *esp.* inflated with pride, puffed up.

c **1386** CHAUCER *Clerk's T.* 894 With humble herte and glad visage, Nat with no swollen thoght in hire corage. **1412-20** LYDG. *Chron. Troy* IV. 4889 Eneas Of Ire & rancour so [a]meved was Ageyn þe kyng, with a swollen herte. **1592** *Soliman & Pers.* III. ii. 15 And here my swolne harts greef doth stay my tongue. **1625** J. ROBINSON *Observations* xxii. 130 Of them I have known some so swoln in the mouth, as they have thought, that if they gave their Servant a better name, then *Sirra*, or *Boy*, they lost of their authoritie. **1697** DRYDEN *Æneid* VI. 251 Swoln with Applause. **1838** DICKENS *Nich. Nick.* xii, His swollen heart almost bursting.

b. Of language: Turgid, inflated, bombastic.

1605 *1st Pt. Jeronimo* I. i. 56 Let him.. Stretch his mouth wider with big swolne phrases. **1783** BLAIR *Lect.* xviii. (1812) II. 27 The swoln imagery. *a* **1834** COLERIDGE *Shaks. Notes* (1849) 49 Swoln panegyrics.

c. *swollen head*: excessive pride, or a person suffering from it; also, a hangover. *colloq.* Cf. SWELLED *ppl. a.* b.

1899 N. GOULD *Landed at Last* vi. 59 You have got a swollen head this morning... Had too much to drink last night. **1922** F. HAMILTON *P.J., Secret Service Boy* vi. 242 You don't strike me, somehow, as being liable to swollen head. **1928** *Daily Express* 23 July 9 British film-producers.. are.. annoyed with me for saying that their swollen-headed outlook was the root-trouble... I feel certain that the swollen heads will bring about many crashes in British film-production.

3. *Comb.*, as *swollen-cheeked*, *-eyed*, *-faced*, *-headed*, etc., adjs.

1591 PERCIVALL *Sp. Dict.*, *Carrillado*, *swolen cheeked. **1837** CARLYLE *Fr. Rev.* III. I. vii, A man bodily and mentally swoln-cheeked. **1930** E. POUND *XXX Cantos* xv. 67 Ἡέλιον τ' Ἡέλιον blind with the sunlight, *Swollen-eyed, rested. **1977** N. SAHGAL *Situation in New Delhi* xvi. 153 The girl raised her head, swollen-eyed. *a* **1618** SYLVESTER tr. *Dicher's Lat. Verses* Wks. (Grosart) II. 337/2 The boy'strous billows Of *swolne fac't Auster. **1647** H. MORE *Min. Poems, Exorcismus* iv, Those Eastern spatterd lights.. And that *swoln-glowing ball. **1928** *Swollen-headed [see sense 2 c above]. **1983** D. FRANCIS *Danger* i. 13 Chasing personal glory. Stupid, swollen-headed, lethal human failing.

b. Special combination. **swollen shoot**, a virus disease of cocoa trees, spread by mealy bugs and distinguished by swelling of the young shoots, leading to the death of infected trees.

1936 W. F. STEVEN in *Gold Coast Farmer* V. 144/1 A new disease of cocoa.. has provisionally been named 'Swollen Shoot and Die-back'. **1950** *Times* 2 Feb. 9/2 We shall test our proposed method for the prevention of swollen shoot disease of cocoa in the Gold Coast, using systemic insecticides. **1972** P. F. ENTWISTLE *Pests of Cocoa* x. 170 At the time of discovery of swollen shoot disease planting in the Eastern Region was still expanding.

swollenness ('swəʊl(ə)nnɪs). [f. prec. + -NESS.] The state or appearance of being swollen.

1902 E. SELOUS *Thought Transference in Birds* (1931) 14 In a very little while.. this swollenness subsides and there is the same average appearance of the birds.

swolling, obs. form of SULING.

swolly, swolo(w), swolwe, etc., obs. ff. SWALLOW.

swoln: see SWELL *v.*, SWOLLEN *ppl. a.*

swolten ('swəʊlt(ə)n), *ppl. a. rare*[-1]. [str. pa. pple. of SWELT.] Oppressed with heat, sultry.

1876 C. J. WELLS *Joseph & Brethren* II. i, Dreamy Egyptians in the outer field Scatter the grain in swolten idleness.

†**swoltery**, *a. Obs. rare.* [f. **swolter*, *swalter*, var. of SWELTER (cf. SWALTISH) + -Y.] Sultry.

1603 SHAKS. *Ham.* v. ii. 101 (Qo. 1) Very swoltery [*1st Fo.* soultry] hot.

swolues, obs. pl. of SWALLOW *sb.*[2]

†**'swoly**, *a. Obs.* Also 6 swooly, sooly(e. [Represents OE. *swoliȝ*, f. *swol-*: *swel-* (see SWEAL *v.*).] Oppressively hot, sultry. Also *advb.*

1496 *Bk. St. Albans, Fishing* 22 A swoly hote weder. **1556** WITHALS *Dict.* (1568) 3 a/2 Feruent heate, or swoly hotte. **1570** FOXE *A. & M.* (ed. 2) II. 1071/2 The soolye [*later edd.* sooly] heat of y[e] prison.

swom, obs. pa. t. of SWIM *v.*

swomp, obs. form of SWAMP.

†**swon.** *Obs.* Forms: 1 swan, 4 suan, 5 swan, swon. [OE. *swán* swineherd = MLG. *swên*, *swein* herd, esp. swineherd, young man, LG. *sween*, *swên*, OHG. *swein* (G. dial. *schwein*), ON. *sveinn* boy, servant, whence SWAIN (Sw. *sven*, Da. *svend* boy, lad):—OTeut. **swainaz*, referred by some to root *swa-*, *swe-* oneself, and taken to mean orig. 'a person belonging to oneself, adherent, attendant'.] A swineherd.

a **700** *Epinal Gloss.* 961 in *O.E. Texts* 92 *Sabulcus*.. suan. **900-30** *O.E. Chron.* an. 755 (Parker MS.) He þær wunade oþ þæt hiene an swan ofstang æt Pryfetes flodan. **1395** *Cartular. Abb. de Whiteby* (Surtees) 614 Item j suan per xxiiij dies minanti plaustra .iiij.s. **1421** *Coventry Leet Bk.* 27 We commaund.. that the Swan of this Cite drive the Swyne of this Cite to wastes and marreys a-bout this cite. *c* **1440** *Pallad. on Husb.* III. 1086 Thi swon may se their noumber & up saue Thoppressed pigge.

swon, swonne, obs. ff. SWAN, SWOON.

swonds, variant of SWOUNDS.

swone, obs. form of SWOON.

swones, variant of SWOUNDS.

†**swong**, *a. Obs.* [ad. ON. *svangr*, related to *svangi* SWANGE groin, f. *swaŋgw-*, perh. identical with *swaŋgw-*, grade-variant of *swiŋgw-* to SWING, q.v.; cf. the parallel formations s.v. SWANK *a.*[1]] Thin, lean, as from hunger.

a **1300** *Estorie del Evangelie* 284 (Vernon MS.) in *Engl. Stud.* VIII. 258 Þe hungri in god he made stronge, And þe riche he lette al swonge. *c* **1440** *Promp. Parv.* 484/2 Swonge, smal and long (or gawnte, *supra*), *gracilis*.

swong(e, obs. pa. t. and pple. of SWING *v.*

swoo, obs. form of SOE, SOUGH *v.*[1]

swoof, swuff, *v. Sc.* ? *Obs.* Also 6 suoufe. Variants of SOUGH *v.*[1], SOWFF. So **swoof** *sb.* = SOUGH *sb.*[1]

1595-6 BUREL *Pilgr.* in Watson *Coll. Sc. Poems* (1709) II. 34 Than softlie did I sucufe and sleep. **1822** HOGG *Perils of Man* II. vii. 256, I was.. keeping a good look out a' round about, and Will he was swuffing and sleeping. **1825** JAMIESON, *Swuff, Swoof, s.*, the act of whizzing. **1834** J. YOUNGER *Poems, Thoughts as they Rise*, I love the *swuff* of every out-field feather. *a* **1835** HOGG *Good Man of Alloa* vii, With a holy psalm sung ower mine head, And swoofit with my last breath. **1835** JOS. GRANT *Dreams of Absence* ii, The cauld winds did swoof through the rifted roof.

swooly, variant of SWOLY *a. Obs.*

swoom, Sc. and north f. SWIM *v.*

swoon (swu:n), *sb.* Forms: 4 *north.* suun, squowen, -in, 4-5 swon-e, swoun-e, swown-e, (5 swon, swonne ?, suoun), 5-6 swoone, swown 5-7 swoun(e, swowne, (6 *Sc.* swne, 7 swoone), 7- swoon. [Orig. in phr. *in swoune*, etc. (sense 1), alteration of *a swoun*, ASWOON, q.v.; otherwise f. SWOON *v.* Cf. the parallel SWOW and ASWOUGH, ASWOW(E.

In the following quot. the spelling *swoon* is used where the rime requires *swound*,

1682 N. O. *Boileau's Lutrin* II. 16 Thus spoke our Lover whining, plain and round, And clos'd her speech with an half-dying swoon.]

1. The action of swooning or the condition of one who has swooned; syncope.

a. Without article, in phr. *to fall, lie in* (occas. *on, of*) *swoon. arch.*

13.. *Guy Warw.* (A.) 557 Adoun he fel a-swounie; & when he gan to dawei [etc.]. *c* **1386** CHAUCER *Doctor's T.* 245 And with that word she fil aswowne [*v.rr.* on swoune on swoun, a swoun, in swoune] anon. **1390** GOWER *Conf.* III. 310 For sorwe a swoune [*v.r.* aswoune] he overthrew, That noman wiste in him no lif. [For later examples see ASWOON.]

a **1300** *Cursor M.* 11722 Þai fell in suun al þat þar war. **13..** *E.E. Allit. P.* A. 1180 A longeyng heuy me strok in swone [*rimes* regioun, etc.]. **1340** HAMPOLE *Pr. Consc.* 7289 Þai salle.. deghe ever-mare lyfand with-alle, Als men dose þat we se in swowne falle. **1390** GOWER *Conf.* II. 249 And with that word sche gan doun falle On [*v.rr.* Of, Inne] swoune. *a* **1400-50** *Wars Alex.* 734 (Dublin MS.) [She] drowpys doun in swone. *c* **1440** *Generydes* 4095 Clarionas.. fylle down in swoune [*rime* doon = down]. *c* **1480** HENRYSON *Mor. Fab., Swallow*, etc. XXXVII, That bludie bowcheour beit thay birdis doun.. Sum with ane staf he straik to eirth on swoun. *c* **1489** CAXTON *Blanchardyn* iv. 19 They were bothe fal in swone. **1535** STEWART *Cron. Scot.* (Rolls) I. 408 Helmes wer hewin to the schulderis doun, Rycht mony suelt and mony fell in swoun. *a* **1578** LINDESAY (Pitscottie) *Chron. Scot.* (S.T.S.) I. 208 The king.. was sa brucklit in his harnis witht the fall that he fell in deidlie swne. **1856** MRS. BROWNING *Aur. Leigh* I. 570 As one in swoon, To whom life creeps back in the form of death.

b. In particularized use: A fainting-fit.

1390 GOWER *Conf.* III. 371, I was out of mi swoure affraied. **14..** *Sir Beues* 2753 + 77 (MSS. S. & N.) Of his swon sir B. awooke. *c* **1440** *Generydes* 2359 He bledde so fast that he felle in A swonne [*rime* sone]. *c* **1489** CAXTON *Blanchardyn* iv. 20 After that they had layen in a swoune a goode while. *a* **1533** LD. BERNERS *Huon* xvii. 231 They came to Esclaramonde, who lay on y[e] erth in a swone. **1613** PURCHAS *Pilgrimage* I. xviii. 82 And falling in a dead swowne, sinketh downe with horror. **1653** R. LOVELL in *Nicholas Papers* (Camden) II. 36 M[r] D[ean] Cosens, as hee was readeing evening prayer, fell down in a swoone. **1662** H. MORE *Apology* 503 No heart could escape from being struck into a swoun at the sight of so overcoming a Beauty and Majesty. **1719** DE FOE *Crusoe* I. 12, I was so surprized, that I fell down in a Swoon. **1833** TENNYSON *Eleanore* 134 Then, as in a swoon, With dinning sound my ears are rife. **1865** KINGSLEY *Herew.* vii, The knight, awakening from his swoon, struggled violently.. to escape.

fig. **1613** PURCHAS *Pilgrimage* VI. viii. 498 A swoune meane-while did Rome sustaine. **1643** SIR T. BROWNE *Relig. Med.* 66, I wonder.. in what swoun their Reasons lay, to content themselves.. with such a.. ridiculous reason as Plutarch alleadgeth for it. *a* **1677** BARROW *Serm.* Wks. 1716 I. 269 Anger (that swoon of reason). **1817** SHELLEY *Rev. Islam* II. xiv. 4 Like a sulphurous hill, Which on a sudden from its snows has shaken The swoon of ages.

†**2.** A (deep or sound) sleep. *Obs. rare.*

1590 SPENSER *F.Q.* I. i. 41 A trickling streame.. Mixt with a murmuring winde, much like the sowne Of swarming Bees, did cast him in a swowne. *Ibid.* III vi. 7 Her selfe she layd To sleepe, the whiles a gentle slombring swowne Vpon her fell.

swoon (swu:n), *v.* Forms: α. [3 suowene], 4 swowene, swoȝene, -y, swouȝne. β. 4-6 swoune, swowne, (4 suoun, squoen ?, swoune, 5 sqwowne), 7 swoun, 7, 9 swown. γ. 4-5 swone, (5 suone, swoyne), 5-7 swoone, 7- swoon. [ME. *swoȝene*, *swoȝeny*, *swowene*, possibly a back-formation from *swoȝning*, *swowening*, SWOONING, q.v. Three types were developed: (1) *swoune*, *swowne*, which would have given mod. *swown* (swaʊn); (2) *swōne*, arising from loss of *ȝ* or *w*, whence the mod. *swoon*; cf. ME. *woe* for *woȝe* (OE. *wóȝian*), and *wooe* by the side of *wowe* in Spenser; (3) *sounye*, *soune*, whence SOUND *v.*[2]]

1. *intr.* **a.** To fall into a fainting-fit; to faint.

α. [*c* **1290**: see SWOONING *vbl. sb.* 1.] **13..** *K. Alis.* 5841 (Laud MS.), Þe kyng swoȝened for þt wounde. *c* **1330** R. BRUNNE *Chron. Wace* (Rolls) 1841 Þe geaunt.. in his armes so hym wente þat Gogmagog gan to swowene. *a* **1375** *Joseph Arim.* 513 Mony swouȝninge lay þorw schindringe of scharpe. *c* **1400** *St. Alexius* 222 (Trin. MS.) To swoȝeny he be-gan.

β. **13..** *Guy Warw.* (A.) 468 Adoun he fel and swoune bigan. **1377** LANGL. *P. Pl.* B. xx. 104 Many a louely lady.. Swouned and swelted for sorwe of dethes dyntes. *c* **1385** CHAUCER *L.G.W.* 872 *Thisbe*, And how sche lyth & swounnyth [*v.rr.* swowneth, souneth, suowneth, swouneth, swonyth, sowneth] on the grounde. **1426** LYDG. *De Guil. Pilgr.* 4816 Wych shal.. Maken hyre in Terys drowne, And offte sythes for to swowne. **1448-9** METHAM *Amoryus & Cleopes* 399 As offtyn sqwowny[n]g, as I remembyr her bryght face. *a* **1508** DUNBAR *Tua Mariit Wemen* 225 With that I seme for to swoune, thought I na swerf tak. **1598** B. JONSON *Ev. Man in Hum.* v. ii, Take my armour of quickly, 'twill make him swoune, I feare. **1601** —— *Poetaster* II. ii. 192 Sometimes froward, and then frowning, Sometimes sickish, and then swowning. **1633** P. FLETCHER *Pisc. Ecl.* III. xx, So down he swowning sinks. *a* **1656** BP. HALL *Mourner in Sion* Rem. Wks. (1660) 164 Those faint hearts that are ready to swoun away for the scratch of a finger. **1865** DICKENS *Mut. Fr.* I. xvi, You pray that your Granny may have strength enough left her at the last.. to get up from her bed and run and hide herself, and swown to death in a hole, sooner than [etc.].

γ. **13..** *Cursor M.* 14287 (Gött.) Till hir broþer graue scho gas, þar forto suoun [*Fairf.* squoen, *Trin.* swowne]. *c* **1374** CHAUCER *Anel. & Arc.* 169 (Shirley MS.) Sheo weopeþe waylepe swooneþe [*v.rr.* swoneth, swouneth, swowneth] pytously. **1375** BARBOUR *Bruce* XVII. 648 (Edin. MS.) Sum ded, sum hurt, and sum swonand. *c* **1400** *Destr. Troy* 8046 [Bresaid] ay swonit in swyme, as ho swelt wold. *c* **1480** HENRYSON *Mor. Fab., Fox, Wolf & Cadger* xxxiii, He.. hit him with sic will vpoun the heid, Quhill neir he swonit and swalt in to that steid. *c* **1489** CAXTON *Sonnes of Aymon* xxi. 466 Reynawde.. was swoninge for sorowe. **1595** R. JOHNSON *7 Champions* (1608) 60 His joy so exceeded that he swooned in his daughters bosome. **1600** SHAKS. *A.Y.L.* IV. iii. 159 Many will swoon when they do look on bloud. **1697** DRYDEN *Æneid* VIII. 774 He said, and, swooning, sunk upon the ground. **1748** *Anson's Voy.* I. x. 101 This lassitude at last degenerates into a proneness to swoon. **1859** DICKENS *T. Two Cities* II. v, If a girl.. swoons within a yard or two of a man's nose, he can see it without a perspective-glass. **1865** TENNYSON *Princess* v. 533 Home they brought her warrior dead; She nor swoon'd, nor utter'd cry.

b. *fig.* said of natural phenomena.

1818 KEATS *Endym.* I. 286 Strange ministrant of undescribed sounds, That come a swooning over hollow grounds. **1833** TENNYSON *Lotos-eaters* 5 All round the coast the languid air did swoon. **1875** LONGF. *Birds of Passage* IV. *Amalfi* 80 All the landscape seems to swoon In the happy afternoon. **1876** B. HARTE *Gabriel Conroy* III. viii, A sudden sense of some strange, subtle perfume.. came swooning over him.

c. To sink *to* or *into* a less active condition or a state of rest.

1821 CLARE *Vill. Minstr.* II. 75 Till morn's long streaking shadows lose their tails, And cooling winds swoon into faultering gales. **1871** ROSSETTI *Poems, Card-dealer* i, Though its splendour swoon Into the silence languidly As a tune into a tune. **1887** HALL CAINE *Deemster* xxxix, The light was gone and another day had swooned to another night.

2. *pass.* To fall into a swoon; chiefly *pa. pple.* or *ppl. a.*: In a swoon.

c **1450** *Mirk's Festial* 206 Scho nys not dede, but swownyd [*v.r.* sownyd] for drede. **1795** *Jemima* II. 175 Rosina.. was swooned away in Levet's arms. **1820** KEATS *Lamia* I. 132 He.., lighting on the printless verdure, turn'd To the swoon'd serpent. **1837** CARLYLE *Fr. Rev.* I. v. vi, She lies swooned on a paillasse.

swoond, obs. or dial. form of SWOUND.

swooner ('swu:nə(r)). [f. SWOON *v.* + -ER[1].]

1. One who swoons or faints, or pretends to do so.

1911 K. D. WIGGIN *Mother Carey* xxx. 263 Nancy had secretly trained Peter so that he was the best swooner of the family. **1951** M. MCLUHAN *Mech. Bride* (1967) 28/2 There's no need to reassure the swooner that Lana is human flesh and blood. **1966** *New Statesman* 19 Aug. 269/3 Olga Ferri accepted the chance to appear more of a queen, less of a lyrical swooner.

2. *U.S.* One who sings in a manner which resembles crooning. Also (nonce-wd.) *swooner-crooner*.

1944 *Amer. Speech* XIX. 102/1 *Swooner-crooner* is a characterizing term in current use among journalists and humorists for the singer Frank Sinatra. It made its advent in late 1943. **1952** B. ULANOV *Hist. Jazz in Amer.* xxi. 268 His voice.. never falls into the whispering faint that makes listening to the swooners and crooners so disturbing.

swoones, variant of SWOUNDS.

swooning ('swu:nɪŋ), *vbl. sb.* Forms: see SWOON *v.* [ME. *suoweningue*, *swoȝning*, app. f. *i-swowen*, *i-swoȝen* SWOW(N *pa. pple.* + -ING[1].]

1. Fainting, syncope.

a. c **1290** *Mary Magd.* 375 in *S. Eng. Leg.* 473 ȝif is moder mouwe ȝuyt of hire suoweningue awake. *a* **1300** *K. Horn* 474 Rymenhild.. Wakede of hire swoȝning [*v.r.* swowneynge.]. **13..** *St. Alexius* 142 (Trin. MS.) þo hy of swoȝenynge a-ros [*Laud MS. 463* þo she of swounynge ros].

β. a **1375** *Joseph Arim.* 543 He was in swounynge and fel to þe grounde. *c* **1386** CHAUCER *Clerk's T.* 1024 O which a pitous thyng it was to se Hir swownyng. **14..** *Sir Beues* (E.) 4313 + 88 Iosyan.. Fyl on swownyng on þat grounde. *c* **1440** *Generydes* 6569 With that he fell in swounyng for very payn. **1544** PHAER *Regim. Lyfe* (1553) E iij, Swouning is a takinge awaie of the feeling and mouing of the bodi by weaknes of the hert. **1590** BARROUGH *Meth. Phisick* III. iv. (1639) 105 When.. venimous and gnawing humours be kept in the stomach.. they cause swowning.

γ. a **1300** *Cursor M.* 4202 He morn mare þan .i. can tell, Al-mast in suoning þar he fell. *a* **1400** *Isumbras* 656 And als sone als scho saw it with syghte, In swonyng than felle that swete wyghte. *c* **1420** *Sir Amadace* (Camden) lxvi, Doune on squonyng ther con thay falle. *a* **1500** *Lancelot* 2716 In swonyng thore he fell one to the ground. **1530** PALSGR. 278/2 Swonyng a disease, *espaumure*. **1650** W. D. tr. *Comenius' Gate Lat. Unl.* §302 Faintings, qualms, and swooning, are relieved by vinegar. **1656** J. SMITH *Pract. Physick* 16 It differs from swooning, because in swooning the colour of the face is changed. **1822-7** GOOD *Study Med.* (1829) IV. 543 Vertigo.. occasionally terminates in swooning; and.. swooning is not unfrequently succeeded by vertigo.

2. A swoon; a fainting-fit.

13.. *Guy Warw.* (A.) 518, & seþþe me comeþ swouninges þre. *c* **1490** *Plumpton Corr.* (Camden) 83 Such sicknes my wyfe hath,.. puts her in joperty of hir life with a swonnyng. **1622** MABBE tr. *Aleman's Guzman d'Alf.* II. 158 In these his swounings, I did comfort my selfe, that if he should chance to dye [etc.]. **1671** MILTON *Samson* 631 Thence faintings, swounings of despair. **1725** DE FOE *Voy. round World* (1840) 178 Swoonings and faint sweats. **1789** W. BUCHAN *Dom. Med.* liv. (1790) 621 Even disagreeable smells will sometimes occasion swoonings. **1815** KIRBY & SP. *Entomol.* x. (1818) I. 329 The Chinese, when about to speak in public.. eat an ounce of it [*sc.* wax] to prevent swoonings.

3. *attrib.*, as **swooning bed, fit, passion, state**; †**swooning-ripe** *a.*, ready to swoon; †**swooning-water**, a 'water' used as a remedy for fainting.

1574 in *MSS. Ld. Middleton* (Hist. MSS. Comm. 1911) 447 To Mrs. Banyster for a swoninge water for my Mrs... vs. **1598** SYLVESTER *Du Bartas* II. i. III. *Furies* 567 The Falling-sickness, and pale Swouning-passion. **1630-1** MILTON *On University Carrier* II. 17 On his swooning bed outstretch'd. **1652** C. B. STAPYLTON *Herodian* I. 6 But swooning ripe he backward fell in bed. **1694** SALMON *Bate's Dispens.* 180/2 *Essentia Regia*.. a most odoriferous Essence.. takes away Fainting, and Swooning Fits. **1880** BROWNING *Dram. Idylls* Ser. II. *Pan & Luna* 90 First moon-eclipse.., first swooning-fit which puzzled sore The early sages.

swooning ('swu:nɪŋ), *ppl. a.* [f. SWOON *v.* + -ING².] That swoons or faints; characterized by swooning.

1646 N. LOCKYER (*title*) England faithfully watcht with in her wounds, or Christ as a father sitting up with his children in their swooning state. **1820** KEATS *Lamia* I. 219 She.. fell into a swooning love of him. **1831** SCOTT *Ct. Rob.* xxxi, The father's attention was instantly called to support his swooning child. **1886** SYMONDS *Renaiss. It., Cath. React.* (1898) VII. xii. 201 A tone of swooning piety blent with sensuous luxuriousness. **1904** M. HEWLETT *Queen's Quair* III. ii. 366 She drowsed into a swooning sleep.

Hence **'swooningly** *adv.*

[*c* **1475** *Partenay* 3566 Zownyngly she fil wofully to grounde.] **1864** in WEBSTER.

swoons, obs. form of SOWENS.

1739 A. NICOL *Nat. without Art* 99 Swoons and Pottage.

swoony ('swu:nɪ), *a.* [f. SWOON + -Y.]

1. Inclined to swoon.

a **1919** In recent Dicts. **1978** M. DICKENS *Open Book* (1980) ii. 26 For one of her heroes, in the style she originated as a swoony girl in Dulwich, Fanny wrote: [etc.].

2. Inducing a swoon; hence, distractingly attractive, delightful. *colloq.*

1934 in WEBSTER. **1960** WENTWORTH & FLEXNER *Dict. Amer. Slang* 534/2 *Swoony*,.. *adj.*, attractive. Teenage use, *c*1940. More often in movies and stories about teenagers than used by teenagers. **1973** T. PYNCHON *Gravity's Rainbow* I. 57 Those eyes she could never quite see into were so swoony. **1974** 'R. TATE' *Birds of Bloodied Feather* ii. 26 Champers and strawberries and Ronald and swoony lanes on the way back. **1976** P. FLOWER *Crisscross* i. 11 Their kiss was long and deep and swoony.

Hence **'swooniness**, a quality suggestive of a swoon.

1909 R. BRIDGES in R. W. Dixon *Poems* p. xxx, The faintness and swooniness is in some sort akin to the remoteness and misty atmosphere of antiquity.

swoop (swu:p), *sb.* Forms: 6 soope, 6-7 swoope, 7 swope, swoup, 7- swoop. [f. next; but the source of sense 1 is not clear.]

†**1.** A blow, stroke; also *fig.*; in *Fencing*, see quot. 1711. *Obs.*

1544-5 PAGET in Waters *Chesters of Chicheley* (1878) I. iv. 33 Some in dede shall wynne by it, who owe more than they have here, but.. dyvers others a greate nombre are like to have a great swoope by it [*sc.* the embargo on English goods] having much here and owing nothing or little. **1589** *Hay any Work* 11, I come vpon you.. with 4. or 5. such drie soopes, as Iohn of London with his two hand sword neuer gaue the like. **1711** WYLDE *Eng. Master Defence* 26 A Blow I call the Swoop, is made when you lie upon an outside thus, Let your Point drop Hanging-wise, and bring it round the Point of your Opponent's Sword, and Pitch it home to his Face.

†**2.** An act of sweeping or clearing away; a clearance. Cf. SWEEP *sb.* 1. *Obs. rare.*

1612-39 BRETON *Wits Private Wealth* Wks. (Grosart) II. 8/2 Death where he commeth, makes a swoope with all persons.

3. The act of swooping down; *esp.* the sudden pouncing of a bird of prey from a height upon its quarry.

1605 [see b]. **1698** FRYER *Acc. E. India & P.* 292 Some of them [*sc.* hawks] in their Swoops are so couragious, as to seize the Heads of Deer or Antelopes. **1795** COLERIDGE *To Author of Poems* 14 The vapour-poison'd Birds, that fly too low, Fall with dead swoop, and to the bottom go. **1841** S. BAMFORD *Life of Radical* (1844) 116 Darkness came down like a swoop. **1847** LONGF. *Ev.* I. i. 115 Swift as the swoop of the eagle. **1852** R. F. BURTON *Falconry Valley Indus* v. 62 The kite.. wriggled out of the way of their swoop.

b. *at one (fell, etc.) swoop*, at one sudden descent, as of a bird of prey; hence, at a single blow or stroke.

1605 SHAKS. *Macb.* IV. iii. 219 Oh Hell-Kite! All? What, All my pretty Chickens, and their Damme At one fell swoope? **1612** WEBSTER *White Devil* I. i. 6 If she [*sc.* Fortune] give ought, she deales it in smal percels, That she may take away all at one swope. **1692** R. L'ESTRANGE *Fables* lxxii. I. 70 The Eagle.. fell into his [*sc.* the fox's] Quarters and carry'd away a Whole Litter of Cubbs at a Swoop. **1825** T. HOOK *Sayings* Ser. II. *Sutherl.* (Colburn) 30 That the whole of this detail would probably reach Mr. Lazenby's ears, and destroy, at one fell swoop, all his hopes and expectations. **1847** DISRAELI *Tancred* II. v, The Church Temporalities' Bill in 1833, which at one swoop had suppressed the Irish episcopates. **1865** DICKENS *Mut. Fr.* I. iv, The huffing of Miss Bella, and the loss of three of her men at a swoop.

c. A sudden descent, as by a body of troops, esp. *upon* something which it is intended to seize.

1824 W. IRVING *T. Trav.* II. iv. (1848) 108 He made one fell swoop upon purse, watch, and all. **1837** —— *Capt. Bonneville* I. xii. 211 A swoop was made through the neighbouring pastures by the Blackfeet, and eighty-six of the finest horses carried off. **1871** L. STEPHEN *Playgr. Eur.* (1894) xi. 262 Any one.. who has trembled at the deadly swoop of the gale. **1885** RUNCIMAN *Skippers & Sh.* 59 As the ship gave her long swoops down the sides of the seas. **1894** J. A. STEUART *In Day of Battle* xv, It was the pipes that won Waterloo, that saved Lucknow, that broke the Russian swoop at Balaclava. **1895** HUXLEY in *Life* (1900) II. xxiii. 400 Influenza came down upon me with a swoop.

swoop (swu:p), *v.* Forms: 6 swoupe, 6-7 swoope, 7 swoup, 7- swoop; also 6 sooup, 6-7 soup, 7 soupe, soop(e. [app. a dialectal development of OE. *swápan*, SWOPE *v.*¹, prob. influenced by Sc. and north. dial. SOOP *v.* (a. ON. *sópa*).]

†**1.** *intr.* To move or walk in a stately manner, as with trailing garments; to sweep along. Also with *it*. *Obs.*

1566 DRANT *Horace, Sat.* I. ii. B j b, He swings and swoupes from streete to streete, with gowne that sweepes the grounde. **1597** BP. HALL *Sat.* I. iii. 23 Soouping in side robes of Royalty. **1598** MARSTON *Sat.* III. viii, O now me thinks I heare swart Martins cry, Souping along in warres fain'd maskerie. **1602** *2nd Pt. Return fr. Parnass.* v. i. 1965 England affordes those glorious vagabonds,.. Coursers to ride on.. Sooping it in their glaring Satten Sutes. **1617** BP. HALL *Quo Vadis?* xii, The persecutors of S. Thomas of Canterbury, whose posteritie (if we believe.. Degrassalius) are borne with long and hairie tails souping after them. **1622** DRAYTON *Poly-olb.* xxviii. 229 And in her winding Banks along my bosome led, As shee goes swooping by.

†**2.** *trans.* To sweep *up, away, off*, etc.; to remove forcibly from its position or out of existence.

1600 HOLLAND *Livy* v. xiii. 189 The forraiers.. encountred the residue.. of this battaile.. and swoopt them up cleane. **1609** —— *Amm. Marcell.* XVI. iv. 61 A rich patrimonie.. he swoopt away. **1611** BEAUM. & FL. *Philaster* v. iii, Like a wild overflow, that soops before him A golden Stack, and with it shakes down Bridges. **1615** T. ADAMS *White Devil* 26 A starre placed high in the orbe of the Church, thogh swooped downe with the Dragons taile because not fixed. **1623** T. GODWIN *Rom. Antiq.* II. III. xiii. (1658) 117 Look who threw an Ace and Sice together, for every Dye he staked and laid to stake a Denere; which he took up and swooped all clean. **1625** LISLE *Du Bartas, Noe* 24 Make haste and soop the wat'r away That hides the land from Heav'n. **1634** FORD *Perkin Warbeck* I. ii. B iij b, So Pasture fields Neighbouring too neere the Ocean, are soopd vp And knowne no more. *c* **1685** *Lintoun Green* (1817) 165 They Donald gar'd their victuals dress, Knives clean,.. And swoop dirt pulverized Ilk morning gray. **1791** LEARMONT *Poems* 180 Doctors, wi' hocus-pocus faith Gie poison, an swoop aff your waith. **1819** W. TENNANT *Papistry Storm'd* I. (1827) 6 The whirlwind's blast, That.. swoops the hay-cocks aff the lea. **1888** CHILD *Ballads* III. 103/1 Robin swoops off Red Roger's head.

†**b.** To utter forcibly. *Obs. rare.*

1605 CAMDEN *Rem., Languages* 23 The Northerne Nations of the world, who are noted to soupe their words out of the throat with fat and full spirits.

†**c.** To drink off or swallow down quickly the contents of; = SWEEP *v.* 6 b. *Obs.*

1648 G. DANIEL *Eclog* iii. 138 With bended knee, Swoope of a vessel bigger then all three. **1654** GAYTON *Pleas. Notes* III. vi. 103 A thorough.. draining, and swooping the whole vessell.

†**3.** To pounce upon, as a bird of prey; to seize, catch up with a sweeping movement. Also *fig.*

1638 WILKINS *New World* I. xiv. (1640) 238 If there bee such a great Ruck in Madagascar.. which can soope up a horse and his rider, or an elephant, as our kites doe a mouse. **1649** G. DANIEL *Trinarch., Hen. V*, lxviii, As ore a Hill, Where lanke-wing'd Puttocks hope to catch their Prey They hover, till it Stirre, and Swoop't away. *a* **1653** —— *Idyll.* iv. 32 Though Tyranny, (big-Swolne, in all formes, Vulture or Moll) doe Swoop, or hunt out wormes. **1661** GLANVILL *Van. Dogm.* 247 The Physitian looks with another Eye on the Medicinal hearb, then the grazing Oxe, which swoops it in with the common grass. **1670** DRYDEN *1st Pt. Conq. Granada* I. i, Till now at last you came to swoop it all. **1672** MARVELL *Reh. Transp.* I. 35 He [*sc.* the pope] would have swoop'd up the Patriarchate of Lambeth to his Mornings-draught, like an egg in Muscadine. **1678** OTWAY *Friendship in F.* v, Thou shalt every morning swoop the Exchange in triumph to see what gaudy bauble thou canst first grow fond of. **1688** BUNYAN *Jerus. Sinner Saved* (1886) 78 Why the text swoops you all... It has a particular message to the biggest sinner. I say, it swoops you all. **1818** MILMAN *Samor* IV. 681 To grapple with these vultures, whose broad vans.. would swoop us. **1822** BYRON *Werner* III. i. 157 'Tis but a snare he winds about us both, To swoop the sire and son at once.

4. *intr.* To make a rapid sweeping descent through the air *upon* its prey, as a bird.

1837 W. IRVING *Capt. Bonneville* I. xiii. 222 Like a hawk in a cage, who hears his late companions swooping and screaming in wild liberty above him. **1852** R. F. BURTON *Falconry Valley Indus* vi. 68 Jerking the prey out of her reach as she swoops at it. **1873** BLACK *Pr. Thule* xxvii. 454 Sea-gulls were swooping down and around the tall masts. **1894** WEYMAN *Under Red Robe* vii. (1897) 178 The frogs croaked in the pool and a bat swooped round us in circles.

5. To come down *upon* suddenly with a sweeping movement, esp. with the intention of seizing, as a body of troops.

1797 MRS. RADCLIFFE *Italian* xiii, Those Carmelites may swoop upon us all of a sudden, before we can help ourselves. **1859** MASSON *Brit. Novelists* i. 71 Turning over the leaves of the large folio, and swooping down on the text here and there. **1860** TYNDALL *Glac.* I. iii. 30 At other times a breeze would swoop down upon us. **1873** DIXON *Two Queens* I. VIII. vii. 95 Descending from Pamplona, he could swoop on either Zaragoza or Valladolid. **1874** BURNAND *My Time* xv. 130 She swooped down before the fire. **1884** MAHAFFY in *Contemp. Rev.* July 89 The wild mountaineers, who used to swoop down on the rich trading cities of the coast.

Hence **'swooper**, a person or thing that swoops.

a **1849** J. C. MANGAN *Poems, The Diver*, What in Charybdis's caverns dwells No chronicle.. tells;.. the shattered masts and the drifting keel Alone tell the tale of the swooper's prey. **1880** *Libr. Univ. Knowl.* (N.Y.) X. 496 Classification [of birds] based on Cuvier [etc.]... I. Robbers. *a.* Swoopers. Eagles, hawks, vultures. *b.* Stealers.

swooping ('swu:pɪŋ), *ppl. a.* [f. SWOOP *v.* + -ING².]

†**1.** Sweeping along the ground; trailing. *Obs.*

1581 A. GILBY *Pleas. Dial.* B ij, In this swouping blacke gowne, and this sarcenet flaunting tippet. **1602** *2nd Pt. Return fr. Parnass.* I. ii. 262 Thy plainer verse.. Is grac'd with a faire end and sooping traine.

2. a. Descending with a rapid sweeping movement.

1846 PROWETT *Prometh. Bound* 18 The swooping thunder-bolt with flaming breath. **1857** J. HAMILTON *Less. fr. Great Biog.* 188 The Sea of Galilee.. its waters.. splashed up for a moment by the swooping pelican.

b. Of a surface: sloping sharply or steeply.

1956 G. DURRELL *My Family & Other Animals* viii. 103 One of the first to arrive was Zatopec, an Armenian poet, a short, stocky individual with a swooping eagle nose. **1979** *Jrnl. R. Soc. Arts* Nov. 744/1 The gently upturned, swooping roofs.

swoople, Sc. form of SWIPPLE.

†**'swoopstake**, *sb.* and *adv. Obs.* [Alteration of SWEEPSTAKE after SWOOP *v.*] **a.** *sb.* = SWEEPSTAKE 2. **b.** *adv.* By sweeping all the stakes at once; hence, indiscriminately.

1600 HEYWOOD *2nd Pt. Edw. IV*, I. vi. (1613) O iij, Heres vying of villianie who shall haue all,.. I would the diuell were there to crie swoope stake. **1602** SHAKS. *Ham.* IV. v. 142 That soop-stake you will draw both Friend and Foe, Winner and Looser.

†**swoor**, obs. or Sc. pa. t. of SWEAR *v.*

swoord, obs. form of SWARD, SWORD.

swoose (swu:s). [Blend of SWAN *sb.* and GOOSE *sb.*] A bird that is the offspring of a swan and a goose. Also *transf.*

1920 *Daily Mail* 13 July 7/5 A bird prodigy of evil and hybrid character is the despair of a Norfolk farmer. It rejoices in the name of the 'swoose', a portmanteau word indicating its origin, for its father was a swan and its mother a goose. This ill-assorted pair had three children—three 'sweese'. **1927** *Daily Express* 12 July 8/4 The swoose is a cross between the goose and the swan. **1954** *Sun* (Baltimore) 27 Apr. 1/7 A Democratic swan.. who fell in love with a common farmyard goose today became the father of a 'swoose'. **1964** *Sunday Mail* (Brisbane) 24 May 29/2 By salvaging parts from the damaged planes, airmen resurrected a few bombers like the Swoose. The name Swoose, for part-swan, part-goose, reflects the plane's patchwork rebirth. **1976** *Sydney Sun* 20 Aug. 16/2 Like the 'swoose' (a cross between a swan and a goose) the 'churkey' is a mythical bird.

swoosh (swu:ʃ), *v.* [Imitative.] *intr.* To make a noise expressed by the syllable 'swoosh'. So **swoosh** *sb.*, such a noise, or movement accompanied by such a noise.

1867 F. FRANCIS *Bk. Angling* ix. (1880) 323 When I hear an angler's rod 'swooshing' through the air. **1885** *Chamb. Jrnl.* 12 Sept. 578/2 Great foam-crested billows.. passing harmlessly under her stern with a swoosh. **1906** *Daily Chron.* 20 Aug. 4/4 The sea swooshed along the groynes and revetments. **1916** BOYD CABLE *Action Front* 252 The next instant a dark object fell with a swoosh and a thump in the bottom of the trench.

swoot(e, variants of SOOT a. and sb.², SWOTE.

swop (swɒp), informal contraction of 'so help': see S'ELP, SWELP.

1890 P. H. EMERSON Wild Life 46 Swop my bob. 1912 W. DEEPING Sincerity xxviii. 214 Swop me bob, somebody else will be callin' for the police.

swop: see SWAP.

†**swope**, v.¹ Obs. Forms: 1 swapan, 3–5 swope, 4 Ayenb. zuope, 5 swoope, 6 suope. Pa. t. 1 sweop, 4 swepe, 9 dial. swap(e. Pa. pple. 1 swapen, 3–4 swopen, 4 isuope, iswope, swope, swpen, 4–5 yswope(n, 9 dial. swapen; weak 5 yswoped, iswoped, 5 swoped, -it. [OE. swápan, pa. t. swéop, pa. pple. swápen to sweep with a broom, brandish (a sword), intr. to rush, dash, = OS. *swêpan, only in pa. t. farswêp swept away, OFris. swêpa to sweep, OHG. sweifan to set in circular motion, wind, (MHG. sweifen, pa. t. swief, G. schweifen intr. to rove, ramble, trans. to sweep in a curve, etc., winnow), ON. sveipa, pa. t. sveip, usually wk. sveipaða, pa. pple. sveipinn, f. Teut. root swaip- (whence also the causative vbs. MHG. sweifen, G. schweifen to swing, ON. sveipa, sveipta to throw, sling, wrap; see also SWAIP, SWAPE). For representatives of the weak grade of the root see SWEPE, SWIFT, SWIP, SWIPPER.] To sweep.

1. trans. = SWEEP v. 1, 7, 13.

c1000 Ags. Ps. (Lambeth) lxxvi[i]. 6 Ic sweop minne gast [scobebam spiritum meum]. c1000 ÆLFRIC Gram. xxviii. (Z.) 169 Uerro, ic swape. c1200 Trin. Coll. Hom. 87 He..cumeð þerto & fint hit emti & mid beseme clene swopen. a1225 Ancr. R. 314 3if hit dusteð swuðe, heo vlaskeð water þeron, & swopeð hit ut awei efter al þet oðer. 1297 R. GLOUC. (Rolls) 6945 Me broȝte vorþ þis fury [= fiery] ssares and leide is al arewe In þe bar erþe isuope. c1320 Sir Tristr. 2193 Þe flore was swopen clene. 1362 LANGL. P. Pl. A. v. 102 3if schrift schulde hit þenne swopen out. 1408–17 in Rec. St. Mary at Hill Introd. p. xcvi, The church and the chauncell flore most be..fayre swoped with a Besom. 14.. Chaucer's Can. Yeom. Prol. & T. 385 The mullok on an heep yswoped [v.rr. iswoped, yswopen, sweped, iswepid, yswepped] was. c1480 HENRYSON Mor. Fab., Cok & Jasp. ii, Iowellis ar tint ..Vpon the flure, and swopit furth anone. a1800 PEGGE Suppl. Grose (1814), Swoop, the Preterit of Sweep. North. 1862 [C. C. ROBINSON] Dial. Leeds, Swap, p.t. of sweep. 'Swap it off wi' his arm.' 1876 Holderness Gloss., Swape, p.t. of to sweep. Swapen, p.p. of to sweep.

2. intr. = SWEEP v. 22, 23.

a1000 Boeth. Metr. vii. 20 Hus on munte..on swift wind swapeð. a1000 Cædmon's Exod. 480 (Gr.) Brim..wide wæðde, wælfæðmum sweop. 13.. E.E. Allit. P. C. 341 Þenne he swepe to þe sonde in sluchched cloþes. a1552 LELAND Itin. (1768) VII. 83 Kenet towchithe the Towne withe his lifte Ripe suopinge in a low Botom.

Hence †'swopen ppl. a., swept.

13.. S.E. Leg. (MS. Bodl. 779) in Herrig's Archiv LXXXII. 318/451 Vppon þe swpen grounde eche nyȝt he lay.

†**swope**, sb. and v.² Also 7 swoup. Obs. or dial. form of SUP sb.¹ and v.¹

[1617 MORYSON Itin. III. 81 The Germans..serue to the Table sower Cabbages, which they call Crawt, and beere (or wine for a dainty) boyled with bread, which they call Swoope.] Ibid. 86 They will spend an Age in swoping and sipping. 1639 R. JUNIUS Sinne Stigmatizd 316 Pledge me quickly, and carouse it off every swoup. 1807 R. ANDERSON Cumbld. Ball. 116, I wish I'd but seav'd a swope geuseberry wine.

swope, obs. f. SOAP, SOPE, SWAP, SWOOP.

swor, obs. f. SURE a.; obs. pa. t. of SWEAR v.

†**sworbote**. Obs. Also 6 swarbout. In God sworbote, corruption of God's forbote: see FORBODE sb. b, c.

1581 W. STAFFORD Exam. Compl. i. 39 God sworbote [version c 1550 God forbid], that euer wee shoulde haue any such Tyrauntes come among vs. 1598 R. BERNARD tr. Terence, Phormio v. ix, Marrie God Swarbout.

sword (sɔːd, sɔəd), sb. Forms: 1–4 sweord, (1 sueord, swurd), 1, 4 (6 Sc.) suord, 1, 6 swyrd, 3–5 (6 Sc.) suerd, 3–6 swerd, (3 swærd, swuerd), 4–6 swerde, sworde, (4 surd, squorde, Ayenb. zuord, 4–5 swerid, swert, 5 sward, swirde, swhirde, squrd, sqwerd, 6 sweard(e, swyrde, swurde, shorde, showrde, swourd, swoord(e, Sc. swrd, sourd), 1, 5– sword. [OE. sweord str. n. = OS., OFris. swerd, MLG. swert, MDu. swaert (Du. zwaard), OHG., MHG. swert (G. schwert), ON. sverð (Sw. svärd, Da. sværd):—OTeut. *swerdom.]

1. a. A weapon adapted for cutting and thrusting, consisting of a handle or hilt with a cross-guard, and a straight or curved blade with either one or two sharp edges and a sharp point (or sometimes with blunt edges, and used only for thrusting).

Swords are of various shapes and sizes, some with distinctive names, as BROADSWORD, CLAYMORE, RAPIER, SABRE, SCIMITAR, etc.; but, without qualification, the word is commonly understood to mean a large weapon such as those used in warfare.

Beowulf 2638 (Gr.) Helmas and heard sweord. 971 Blickl. Hom. 11 Anra gehwylc hæfde sweord ofer his hype. a1000 Fight at Finnsburg 17 (Gr.) Sigeferð and Eaha hyra sword getugon. c1000 Ags. Gosp. Matt. xxvi. 47 Mid swurdum & sahlum. c1205 LAY. 8908 Þi mon he sæl bi-cumen..& þat ich þe wullen swerien Uppen mine sweorden. c1250 Gen. & Ex. 1307 Ysaac..bar ðe wude..And abraham ðe fier and ðe swerd bar. c1275 Passion of Our Lord 200 in O.E. Misc. 43 Þo iseyh ihesu crist þat peter so dude, Put in, he seyde, þi sweord. 1297 R. GLOUC. (Rolls) 386 Corineus suerd sone brac, so strong he smote & vaste. a1300 Cursor M. 15721 (Cott.) Sper and suerd [Gött. surd] and mace þai bring. Ibid. 21710 (Edin.) Mocht na kingis suorde [Fairf. squorde] do mare. 1340 Ayenb. 48 Mid oȝene zuorde man may himzelue sle. c1386 CHAUCER Prol. 112 And by his syde a swerd and a bokeler. c1400 Destr. Troy 5741 Mony Troiens..Thurgh swap of his sword sweltyn belyue! 1451 Lincoln Diocese Documents 50 A hole harnor of plate & my Swirde. 1534 in W. Kelly Notices Illustr. Drama (1865) 191, I borrowyd a shorde and a bokelar, wch showrde and bokelar he allmust bothe loste. 1539 Bible (Great) Matt. xxvi. 52 One of them which were wyth Iesus, stretched out his hande, and drue his swearde... Then sayd Iesus vnto hym: put vp thy swearde into hys sheath. 1546 J. HEYWOOD Prov. (1867) 53 The prouerbe saith, he that striketh with the swoorde, Shalbe strikyn with the scaberde. 1600 BRETON Pasquil's Fooles-cappe xliii, Hee that..by his side can finely weare his swearde. 1601 SHAKS. Twel. N. v. i. 191 You drew your sword vpon me without cause. 1782 COWPER Royal George 21 His sword was in the sheath. 1847 TENNYSON Princess v. 528 A moment hand to hand, And sword to sword, and horse to horse we hung. 1851 D. WILSON Preh. Ann. (1863) II. IV. x. 511 A fine specimen of the old Scottish two handed sword.

b. As used on ceremonial occasions as a symbol of honour or authority (**sword of honour, of state**, etc.).

1429 Pol. Poems (Rolls) II. 146 The toon was a swerde of mercy, the oothir of astate. 1483 Coron. Rich. III in L. G. W. Legg Eng. Coron. Rec. (1901) 195 Therle of Northumberland..with the Pointless Sword naked in his hand, which signifyed Mercie... Therle of Kent bare ye second sword..with a Point which signifyed Justice to the Temporallitee, The Lord Lovell bare ye third Sword..with a Point which signifyed Justice to the Cleargie... Therle of Surrey bare ye fourth Sword..with a rich scabbard, being called the Sword of Estate. 1556 Chron. Grey Friars (Camden) 81 And he delyveryd hare the swerde, and she toke it to the erle of Arnedelle, and he bare it before hare. 1578 MOYSIE Mem. (Bannatyne Cl.) 11 The erles of Angus quho buir the croune, the erle of Lennox the septer, and the erle of Mar the suord of honour. 1831 GREVILLE Mem. (1874) II. 137 The tall, grim figure of Lord Grey close beside him with the sword of state in his hand. 1891 A. H. CRAUFURD Gen. Craufurd 271 To subscribe in order to present this General with a sword of honour.

c. phr. (a) Fencing (see quot. a 1700). (b) **sword-in-hand**, armed with a sword; fig. militant.

a1700 B. E. Dict. Cant. Crew, Within the Sword, from the Sword to the Right Hand. Without the Sword, all the Man's Body above the Sword. 1838 J. MITCHELL Thoughts on Tactics 37 The Russians never ventured, unless when covered by chevaux-de-frise, to await the sword-in-hand onsets of the Turks. 1906 Daily Chron. 23 Aug. 4/6 A typical South American sword-in-hand politician.

d. A wooden imitation of a sword, used in fencing exercise, etc.; also, the blade of a foil.

c1643 LD. HERBERT Autobiog. (1824) 64 The Fort or strong [of a foil], which extends from the part of the hilt next the Sword about a third part of the whole length thereof. 1697 J. LEWIS Mem. Dk. Glocester (1789) 9 Accoutred with paper caps, and wooden swords. 1746 FRANCIS tr. Horace, Epist. I. i. 2 note, The Gladiators, in learning their Exercises, played with wooden Swords, called rudes.

e. pl. One of the four suits in packs of playing-cards used in Italy and in Spanish-speaking countries, and in tarot packs. Cf. SPADE sb.²

1816 G. W. SINGER Researches into Hist. Playing Cards I. 17 The four suits, Spade, (swords,) Coppe, (cups,) Denari, (money,) and Bastone, (clubs,) adopted both by the Italians and Spaniards, were probably the suits of the Eastern game. 1848 W. A. CHATTO Facts & Speculations on Origin & Hist. Playing Cards iv. 191 The earliest writers who mention Tarocchi as a kind of cards, always speak of them as consisting of four suits,—Swords, Cups, Batons, and Money. Ibid. 227 The cards most commonly used in Italy in the latter part of the fifteenth century, were those which had ..Swords, Cups, Batons, and Money,—as the marks of the suits. 1892 'PAPUS' Tarot of Bohemians v. 44 When we consider the four colours of the Tarot, new deductions will be called forth... The Sword represents the union of the two by its crucial form. 1911 A. E. WAITE Pictorial Key to Tarot I. iv. 36 We must forbear from saying, for example, that the Conditions of Life correspond to the Trumps Major ..and the conditions of life to Swords. 1934 J. D. CARR (title) The eight of swords. 1952 V. WILKINS King Reluctant III. iii. 230 He..produced two [tarot] cards... 'The King of Swords and the King of Cups!' he said. 1978 Jrnl. Playing-Card Soc. Feb. 90 It comprises 52 cards, with suits of Swords, Batons, Cups and Pomegranates.

2. fig. **a.** Something that wounds or kills, a cause of death or destruction, a destroying agency; also, something figured as a weapon of attack in spiritual warfare.

c1000 ÆLFRIC Hom. II. 218 [Eph. vi. 17] Nymað þæs geleafan scyld, and ðæs hihtes helm, and þæs Halgan Gastes swurd, þæt is, Godes word. c1200 Vices & Virtues 91 Nim ðin sweord, ðat is, godes word. c1200 Trin. Coll. Hom. 61 Bute we turnen to gode anradliche, he wile his swerd draȝen, þat is his wrake. 13.. Cursor M. 11371 (Gött.) þe suord of soru thoru hir hert stod. c1385 CHAUCER L.G.W. Prol. 127 Wyntyr that..with his swerd of cold so sore hadde greuyd. 1426 LYDG. De Guil. Pilgr. 7985 The Swerd, I mene, of Ryghtwysnesse. 1513 BRADSHAW St. Werburge I. 3467 The sharpe swerde of deth..Spared no creature. 1514 Extr. Aberd. Reg. (1844) I. 90 This violent and contageous suord of pestilence. c1530 Hickscorner 104 They saye they be smyten with the swerde of poverty. 1539 Bible (Great) Ps. lvii. 4 Whose tethe are speares and arowes, and their tonge a sharpe swerd. 1605 SHAKS. Macb. IV. iii. 87 This Auarice ..hath bin The Sword of our slaine Kings. a1628 PRESTON Effectual Faith (1631) 47 Though the Law bee a sword, yet unlesse God take that sword into his hand [etc.]. 1655 VAUGHAN Silex Scint., Rules & Lessons xii, If thou giv'st words, Dash not with them thy friend, nor Heav'n;..some Syllables are Swords. 1825 SCOTT Talism. xxiv, You are the leader of our expedition, the sword and buckler of Christendom. 1895 S. WHEELER Ameer Abdur Rahman 66 Sharpening the sword of intention, to speak Asiatically, but not knowing when it might be used.

b. at the sword's point: under pressure of a threat or an urgent demand; **at swords' points**: in a state of open hostility. Cf. DAGGER sb. 2.

1895 A. BEARDSLEY Let. Nov. (1970) 104 The dreadful thing was a blaze up with Lane-cum-Mathews, and a drawing to be produced at the sword's point. 1909 WEBSTER, At swords' points. 1963 M. MCCARTHY Group x. 214 Mrs Hartshorn and her dead husband had had a running battle over Wilson and the League, and now Priss and Sloan were at swords' points over Roosevelt and socialized medicine.

3. transf. The use of the sword in warfare, massacre, etc.; hence, slaughter; warfare; military force or power; also, the military profession or class, the army.

c1000 Ags. Gosp. Matt. x. 34 Ne wene ge þæt ic come sybbe on eorþan to sendanne, ne com ic sybbe to sendanne ac swurd [Lindisf. suord]. 1382 WYCLIF Rom. viii. 35 Who therfore schal departe vs from the charite of God? tribulacioun, or angwisch, or hungur, or nakidnesse, or persecucioun, or perel, or swerd? c1410 Lanterne of Liȝt viii. 45 Excesse of mete & drink sleeþ many moo þan doiþ þe swerid. c1520 SKELTON Magnyf. 1522 Alerycus, that rulyd the Gothyaunce by swerd. 1549 Compl. Scot. xv. 123 Thai recompens me vitht hungyr, and vitht the sourd. 1559 Mirr. Mag., Dk. Glocester viii, Wasting the Countrey with swurde and with fyer. 1590 MARLOWE 2nd Pt. Tamburl. IV. i, See now ye slaues, my children stoops your pride And leads your glories sheep-like to the sword. 1598 SHAKS. Merry W. I. i. 41 If I were yong againe, the sword should end it. 1649 MILTON Eikon. x. 96 It hath bin oft anough told him, that he hath no more autority over the sword then over the law. 1682 DRYDEN Medal 306 The Cut-throat Sword and clamorous Gown shall jar. 1724 RAMSAY Vision xxiii, I still support my precedens Abune them all for sword and sens. 1766 GRAY Kingsgate 21 Purg'd by the sword, and purified by fire. 1823 SCOTT Quentin D. i, These hireling combatants sold their swords for a time to the best bidder. 1832 AUSTIN Jurispr. (1879) I. vi. 245 This influential portion [sc. the sovereign's counsellors] was formed by the nobility of the sword, the..clergy, and the members of the parliaments. 1839 LYTTON Richelieu II. ii, The pen is mightier than the sword. 1849 MACAULAY Hist. Eng. i. I. 141 Anomalies and abuses, which were in strict conformity with the law, and which had been destroyed by the sword. Ibid. vi. II. 16 Some of the exiles offered their swords to William of Orange.

b. to put (†do) to the sword, to kill or slaughter with the sword.

1338 R. BRUNNE Chron. (1725) 47 Agode Erle of Warwik was don to þe suerd. 1600 SHAKS. A.Y.L. v. iv. 164 To take His brother..and put him to the sword. 1603 KNOLLES Hist. Turks (1621) 35 The Turkes..put to sword all that came in their way. 1759 HUME Hist. Eng. Ho. Tudor, Edw. VI, ii. I. 323 De Thermes..took the fortress of Broughty, and put the garrison to the sword. 1891 HALL CAINE Scapegoat xvii, A warrant to put every man, woman, and child to the sword.

c. Contrasted with ploughshare (in allusion to Isaiah ii. 4 and Micah iv. 3), as types respectively of war and peace: see PLOUGHSHARE 1. Esp. in phr. **to beat swords into ploughshares**.

1924 L. P. SMITH S.P.E. Tract XVII. 38 We must take them [sc. words] as they come to our hands; if they are ploughshares which have been beaten into swords, tools which have been made into battle-axes, they are tools nevertheless for which we have no substitutes. 1976 N. THORNBURG Cutter & Bone x. 242 You know the old phrase about beating swords into plowshares—well I think you've beaten your grief into a sword.

4. As the instrument or symbol of penal justice; hence, the authority of a ruler or magistrate to punish offenders; more generally, power of government, executive power, authority, jurisdiction; also, the office of an executive governor or magistrate.

1382 WYCLIF Rom. xiii. 4 Sothli if thou doist yuel thing, drede thou; for not withoute cause he berith the swerd. 1549 COVERDALE, etc. Erasm. Par. Rom. Prol., In the .xiij. he teacheth to honour the worldly and temporall swearde. 1549 LATIMER 1st Serm. bef. Edw. VI (Arb.) 23 Let ye preacher teach, improue, amende, an[d] instructe in rightwesnes, wyth the spyrytuall swearde. 1592 NASHE P. Penilesse Wks. 1904 I. 179 Burgomasters and Gentlemen beare all the swaye of both swords, spirituall and temporall. a1628 DABORNE Poor-man's Comf. v. (1655) H2, You have felloniously usurpt The sword of Government. 1633 T. STAFFORD Pac. Hib. I. i. (1821) 4 Upon the taking of our Sword, and chiefe charge of that our Realme of Ireland, as our Deputie. 1634 E. REYNOLDS Shieldes of Earth (1636) 19 Jurisdiction coercitive, or the power of the Sword. 1650 HOBBES De Corp. Pol. 66 This Power Coercive, or (as men use to call it) the Sword of Justice. 1651 —— Leviath. II. xvii. 85 Covenants, without the Sword, are but Words. 1673 Essex Papers (Camden) I. 60 A very great part of this ground ..has ever..belong'd to ye Sword. 1677 Ibid. II. 124, I should with some regret have parted with ye sword into ye hands of my Lord Conway. 1676 DRYDEN Aurengz. II. 29 Justice to merit does weak aid afford; She trusts her Ballance, and neglects her Sword. 1769 BLACKSTONE Comm. IV. i. 8 The magistrate..who bears the sword of justice by the consent of the whole community. 1915 Eng. Hist. Rev.

Apr. 219 Richemont..had been offered the sword of constable of France.

5. A material object resembling a sword.

a. One of various mechanical devices in the form of a flat wooden blade, bar, or rod.

1530 PALSGR. 278/2 Sworde for a flaxe wyfe, *guinche.* **1667** in Pettus *Fodinæ Reg.* (1670) 35 Five Pair of large Smelting Bellows with Beams, Frames, Swords. **1766** *Compl. Farmer* s.v. *Flax*, The sword, or upright timber-rod between the treadle and the treadle crank. **1797** *Encycl. Brit.* (ed. 3) XVIII. 835/2 The workman closes it [*sc.* the woof] by one or two strokes of the lay or batten, of which WB, WB are called the swords. *c* **1860** H. STUART *Seaman's Catech.* 32 Every other part is..forced close home to the bolt with a wooden sword. **1863** J. WATSON *Art of Weaving* 149 Swords are these parts of the loom that the lay is fixed to. **1883** *Man. Seamanship for Boys* 182 A piece of wood made in the shape of a knife, called a sword, is..inserted between the alternate parts of the warp. **1886** J. BARROWMAN *Sc. Mining Terms* 66 *Sword*, a rod connecting a pump bucket with the foot rod. *a* **1919** *Advt.*, A strong useful Cart, fitted with Wing Boards and Tipping Sword. **1942** R. DAVEY *Measurement of Trees* ii. 28 When a tree lies on the ground, there may be some difficulty in passing the tape beneath it. A flat piece of metal with a hook at one end, called a 'timber sword' may be used for this purpose. **1953** H. L. EDLIN *Forester's Handbk.* xiv. 213 Find the mid-point of the log, and pass a girthing tape around it; with large logs, the device called the timber-measurer's sword will be of assistance.

b. The sharp projecting jaw-bone of the swordfish.

1641 SYMONDS *Serm. bef. Ho. Comm.* D iv, They say there is a fish that hath a sword but no heart. **1681** GREW *Musæum* I. v. i. 87 The Sword grows in a level, not from the upper but the under Jaw. **1860** WRAXALL *Life in Sea* v. 108 The keel of an East Indiaman was once bored by a twenty-foot Xyphias so violently, that the sword went in up to the roots.

c. A sword-like ray or flash of light.

1866 B. TAYLOR *Poems, Hymn to Air*, The Sun's uplifted sword of flame. **1890** W. J. GORDON *Foundry* 93 While swords of vivid light are brandished to and fro on to the hurrying clouds.

6. *attrib.* and *Comb.* **a.** Simple attrib., as ***sword-blow, -clash, -edge, -exercise, -fight, -flash, -frog*** [FROG[3] I], ***-game, -handle, -hanger*** [HANGER *sb.*[2] 4 b], ***-hate, -hilt, -point, -rust, -scabbard, -sheath, -stroke, -sweep, -thrust, -tip, -wound***, etc. **b.** Instrumental, as ***sword-armed, -girded, -girt*** adjs.; ***sword-hunter.*** **c.** Objective, as ***sword-maker, -making, -setter; sword-rusting*** adj.; similative, etc., as ***sword-keen, -like, -shaped*** adjs.

1640 J. GOWER *Ovid's Festiv.* IV. 84 But e're the evening doth the sights conclude, *Sword-arm'd Orion in the waves is stew'd. **1898** ROSSETTI in *Ruskin*, etc. (1899) 28 The sword-armed angels. **1816** SCOTT *Old Mort.* xxxiii, Firearms were discharged and *sword-blows given for upwards of five minutes. **1946** R. CAMPBELL *Talking Bronco* 45 Amidst the *sword-clash of the reeds. **1969** G. M. BROWN *Orkney Tapestry* 74 It was a long stern battle, hurling of missiles and sword-clash. **1809** ROLAND (*title*) The Amateur of Fencing; or a Treatise on the Art of *Sword-Defence. **1852** BAILEY *Festus* (ed. 5) 291 The third one simply smote by the *sword-edge All who dared doubt his darkly chequered tale. **1796** (*title*) Rules and Regulations for the *Sword Exercise of the Cavalry. **1627** HAKEWILL *Apol.* IV. iv. §8. 316 Some they set to fight with beasts, some to fight one with another. These they called *Gladiatores* swordplayers, & this spectacle, *munus gladiatorium*, a *sword-fight. **1635** J. HAYWARD tr. *Biondi's Banish'd Virg.* 150 Where with single sword-fight they ended their quarrell, by dying both. *a* **1661** HOLYDAY *Juvenal* (1673) 96 Shee's past a blush..That has renounc'd her sex, and, sleighting fears, Admires the sword-fights so. **1647** HEXHAM, A *sword-fighter, *een swaerdt-vechter.* **1874** R. BUCHANAN *Poet. Wks.* III. 228 Feeble as a maid who hides her face In terror at a *sword-flash. **1868** *Regul. & Ord. Army* ¶615 The waist-belt with the *Sword-frog supplied with the tools, is to be worn over the belt from which the tools are suspended. **1618** BOLTON *Florus* III. xx. (1636) 239 To fight..about the funerall fire, as if it would cleere all passed disgrace, if of a sword player, hee become a giver of *sword-games. **1889** R. B. ANDERSON tr. *Rydberg's Teut. Mythol.* 216 The souls of warriors who had fallen in battle, and now imitated the sword-games they had played on earth. **1338** R. BRUNNE *Chron.* (1725) 44 An armed knyght ..*Suerd girded & lance in hand. *Ibid.* 159 Armed and *suerd girte. *a* **1593** MARLOWE *Lucan* I. 664 Sword-girt Orions side glisters too bright. **1855** BAILEY *Mystic*, etc. 131 Some crowned and sword-girt conqueror. **1799** HERSCHEL in *Phil. Trans.* XC. 63 In clear nights..we may see a whitish patch in the *sword-handle of Perseus. **1851** NICHOL *Archit. Heav.* 14 The spot in the Sword-handle of Perseus. **1591** PERCIVALL *Sp. Dict.*, *Talabarte*, *sword hangers. **1912** E. POUND *Ripostes* 29 Disease or oldness or *sword-hate Beats out the breath from doom-gripped body. **1455** in Meyrick *Ant. Armour* (1824) II. 144 A Scottysh *swerde hylte and pomell covered with sylver. **1601** SHAKS. *Jul. C.* v. v. 28 Hold thou my Sword Hilts, whilest I runne on it. **1706** *Lond. Gaz.* No. 4257/4 A Sword Hilt Maker. **1781** COWPER *Charity* 50 The hand, that slew till it could slay no more, Was glued to the sword-hilt with Indian gore. **1833** J. HOLLAND *Manuf. Metal* II. 72 It was..not uncommon for the expiring knight to fix his eyes upon his sword hilt as a lively symbol of his faith. **1865** KINGSLEY *Herew.* xxxvi, Hereward swore awfully, and laid his hand on his sword-hilt. **1867** BAKER (*title*) The Nile Tributaries of Abyssinia, and the *Sword Hunters of the Hamran Arabs. **1901** KIPLING *Kim* viii. 209 He caught Mahbub's *sword-keen glance. **1578** J. JONES *Preserv. Bodie & Soule* I. xl. 87 Launcelike, *swordlike. **1655** VAUGHAN *Silex Scint.*, *Stars* iv, A swordlike gleame Kept man for sin First Out. *a* **1711** KEN *Hymns Evang.* Poet. Wks. 1721 I. 184 Maternal Pity pierc'd her through and through, Up to the hilt her Sword-like Sorrow flew. **1852** BAILEY *Festus* (ed. 5) 495 A stranger star, Swordlike in shape. **1592** *Arden of Feversham* v. i. 69 He lyke a foole beares his *sword point halfe a yarde out of danger. **1610** HOLLAND *Camden's Brit.* (1637) 519 Rather to try the Title by the sword point than by point of Law. **1657** J. BENTHAM *Two Treat.* 27 They stand at sword point against sin and transgressions. **1821** SCOTT *Kenilw.* xxxix, His sword-point turned to the ground. **1923** D. H. LAWRENCE *Birds, Beasts & Flowers* 54 Think of it, from the iron fastness Suddenly to dare to come out naked, in perfection of blossom, beyond the *sword-rust. **1930** T. S. ELIOT tr. *St.-J. Perse's Anabasis* 47 In the mirror of our dreams, the *sword-rusting sea. **1758** J. S. *Le Dran's Observ. Surg.* (1771) 340 Such Wood as they make Bandboxes or *Sword-Scabbards with. **1575–6** in Wodderspoon *Mem. Ipswich* (1850) 174 Prynters, fyshemongers, *swordsetters. **1776** J. LEE *Introd. Bot.* Explan. Terms 386 *Ensiforme*, *sword-shaped, double-edged, gradually lessening from the Base to the Point. **1832** LINDLEY *Introd. Bot.* 382 *Sword-shaped*.., lorate, quite straight, with the point acute. **1858** SIMMONDS *Dict. Trade*, **Sword-sheath*, the scabbard or case for a sword. **1891** CONAN DOYLE *White Company* xx, In vain were sword-sheaths, apple branches, and belts linked together, thrown out to him by his companions. **1829** SCOTT *Anne of G.* vi, [He] stood firm within *sword-stroke of his adversary. **1880** SWINBURNE *Stud. Shaks.* 79 Swift alike of speech and sword-stroke. **1808** SCOTT *Marm.* VI. xxv, With *sword-sway, and with lance's thrust. **1828** —— *F.M. Perth* xxxiv, To get within the *sword-sweep of those opposed to them. **1857** G. A. LAWRENCE *Guy Liv.* xxv. 243 Guy fairly staggered, as if he had received a *sword-thrust. **1852** THACKERAY *Esmond* I. vi, 'I have found..only the weapons with which beauty is authorized to kill,' says he, pointing to a wig with his *sword-tip. **1902** F. E. HULME *Proverb-Lore* 114 *Sword-wounds may be healed, word-wounds are beyond healing.

d. Special Combs.: **sword-and-buckler** *a.*, armed with or using a sword and buckler; pertaining to or performed with sword and buckler; †*fig.* bragging, blustering (*obs.*); so **sword-and-dagger** *a.*; **sword-arm**, the arm with which the sword is wielded, the right arm; also rhetorically = military power or action, and *fig.*; **sword-bayonet**, a form of bayonet which may be used as a sword; **sword-belt**, a belt by which the sword in its scabbard is suspended; **sword-bill**, a South American humming-bird, *Docimastes ensiferus*, with a very long bill; **sword-breaker**, a device, as a dagger or buckler with a notch or hook, for breaking the blade of an adversary's sword; **sword-cane**, a hollow cane or walking-stick containing a steel blade which may be drawn or shot out and used as a sword; **sword-case**, a case to hold a sword; in mod. use, a receptacle at the back of a carriage for swords, sticks, or other articles; **sword-craft**, the art of using, or skill in the use of, the sword; military power; **sword-cut**, (*a*) a cutting stroke or blow dealt with the edge of a sword; (*b*) a wound or scar produced by such a stroke; **sword-cutler**, a cutler who makes sword-blades or swords; so **sword-cutlery**; † **sword dagger**, ?a heavy dagger; **sword-dance** [cf. MLG. *swertdans*, G. *schwertertanz*, etc.], a dance in which the performers go through some evolutions with swords, or in which a person dances among naked swords laid on the ground; also *fig.*; so **sword-dancer, -dancing**; **sword dollar**, name for a Scottish silver coin of James VI, of the value of 30 shillings Scotch (= 2*s.* 6*d.* English), with the figure of a sword on the reverse; † **sword-fencer**, a gladiator; **sword-flighted** *a.*, said of a bird having some of the wing-feathers contrasted in colour with the rest, suggesting a sword carried at the side; † **sword-girdle** = *sword-belt*; **sword-hand**, the hand with which the sword is wielded, the right hand; **sword-knot**, a ribbon or tassel tied to the hilt of a sword (originating from the thong or lace with which the hilt was fastened to the wrist, but later used chiefly as a mere ornament or badge); **sword-law**, government by the power of the sword, or by military force; martial law; **sword-leaved** *a.*, having sword-shaped or ensiform leaves; **sword-mat** *Naut.*, a piece of matting used to protect parts of the rigging, etc., so called from the wooden 'sword' with which the fabric is beaten close in weaving; so **sword-matting**; † **sword-minded** *a.*, of cruel or sanguinary disposition, bloody-minded; **sword-proof** *a.*, proof against the sword; capable of resisting the stroke of a sword; **sword-rattling** *a. fig.*, that threatens military action; aggressive, pugnacious; also as *sb.* = *sabre-rattling* vbl. sb. s.v. SABRE *sb.* 4 a; **sword-salve**, salve applied to a sword, and supposed to cure the wound inflicted by it (cf. *weapon-salve*); **sword-service**, military service rendered as a due to the overlord; **sword-side** [cf. OFris. *swerdsîda*, MLG. *swerdhalve, -side*, G. *schwertseite*, etc.], the male line in descent (= *spear-side*, SPEAR *sb.*[1] 10); **sword-smith**, a smith who makes swords, a sword-cutler; **sword-stand** = *sword-case*; **sword-star**, poetic name for a comet supposed to resemble a sword; **sword-stick** = *sword-cane*; **sword-swallower**, one who entertains for money by swallowing or pretending to swallow swords; so **sword-swallowing**; **sword-tail**, an animal of the group *Xiphosura*, comprising only the genus *Limulus*; a king-crab; so **sword-tailed** *a.*, having a sword-like tail; **sword-taker**, one who 'takes the sword' (Matt. xxvi. 52) without authority or right, a lawless killer; **sword-tash**, used by Carlyle for *sabre-tash*, SABRETACHE; **sword-whale**, the grampus, also called SWORDFISH; **sword-work** = SWORD-PLAY 1; also *fig.*; † **sword-wrack**, destruction by the sword. See also SWORD-BEARER, -BLADE, etc.

1596 SHAKS. *1 Hen. IV*, I. iii. 230 That same *Sword and Buckler Prince of Wales. **1599** PORTER *Angry Wom. Abingt.* (Percy Soc.) 61, I see by this dearth of good swords that dearth of swoord and buckler fight begins to grow out:..a man, a tall man, and a good sword and buckler man, will be spitted like a cat or a conney. *Ibid.* 98, I..put on my fellow Dickes sword and buckler voyce and his swounds and sbloud words. *a* **1635** NAUNTON *Fragm. Reg.* (Arb.) 47 As he lived in a ruffling time, so he loved sword and buckler men. **1646** G. DANIEL *Essay* 23 Wks. (Grosart) I. 80 Nor would I ..engage My selfe in Controversie to the Age, With Sword and Buckler Langvage. **1818** SCOTT *Rob Roy* xxviii, Our two sword-and-buckler men gave up their contest with as much indifference as they had entered into it. **1860** FAIRHOLT *Costume* (ed. 2) 228 Sword-and-buckler play formed the usual relaxation of the London apprentices on ordinary occasions [*temp.* Hen. VIII]. **1821** SCOTT *Kenilw.* xii, Any of these *sword-and-dagger men. **1692** SIR W. HOPE *Fencing-Master* (ed. 2) 159 Stand not to an Ordinary Guard, for then he would Disable your *sword Arm. **1760–72** H. BROOKE *Fool of Qual.* (1809) IV. 95, I feel a little smart in my sword-arm. **1833** *Regul. & Instr. Cavalry* I. 133 The 'Guard' is continued by moving the sword-arm..to the right. **1838** LYTTON *Leila* II. i, Methinks our best wisdom lies in the sword-arm. **1895** SIR E. WOOD *Cavalry in Waterloo Campaign* iv. 107 His sword-arm being so hacked by sabres as to be practically severed. **1916** BUCKLE *Life Disraeli* IV. xiii. 480 Gathorne Hardy, who succeeded to Cairns's place as his 'sword-arm' when the fight was fierce in the House of Commons. **1844** *Regul. & Ord. Army* 94 Rifle, Rammer, and *Sword Bayonet. **1521** *Extr. Burgh Rec. Stirling* (1887) 13 Item, ane swourd, buklar and *swourd belt, vj s. **1534** *Acc. Ld. High Treas. Scot.* VI. 184 Ane swerd belt of fresit ledder. **1777** ROBERTSON *Hist. Amer.* (1783) III. 88 Hunger compelled them..to gnaw the leather of their saddles and sword-belts. **1824** SCOTT *Redgauntlet* ch. xiii, He wore a smart hanger and a pair of pistols in a sullied sword-belt. **1861** W. F. COLLIER *Hist. Eng. Lit.* 177 His broad sword-belt, supporting a Spanish rapier. **1861** GOULD *Monogr. Trochilidæ* IV. Pl. 233 *Sword-bill. **1830** MEYRICK & SKELTON *Illustr. Ant. Arms* II. Plate 100 A *sword breaker. .. The teeth give way in order to receive a blade struck against them, and close over it so that by a slight motion of the wrist it can be broken. **1837** CARLYLE *Fr. Rev.* II. III. v, Snatch your..*sword-canes, secret arms, and tickets of entry. **1576–7** *Registers S. Mary Woolnoth* (1886) p. xxiv, To the joyner for mendyng the *sworde case for the Lorde Maior to sett up in the church against the pewe. **1699** in *10th Rep. Hist. MSS. Comm.* App. v. 511 A sword case to hould the King's sword. **1794** W. FELTON *Carriages* (1801) I. 15 The sword-case, so called from its length and convenience for carrying swords or sticks,..is sometimes called a boodge. **1852** OSBORNE in *Times* 3 Nov., A neat London-built brougham, with his lordship and the chaplain inside, the episcopal mace in the sword case. **1855** MOTLEY *Dutch Rep.* Introd. vi. (1866) 17 They learn to tremble as little at priest-craft as at *sword-craft. **1897** 'H. S. MERRIMAN' *Kedar's Tents* xxv. (*heading*) Sword-craft. **1818** SCOTT *Rob Roy* xxxv, To have as many *sword-cuts made, and pistols flashed at me, as [etc.]. **1859** TENNYSON *Elaine* 258 Seam'd with an ancient swordcut on the cheek. **1678** *Lond. Gaz.* No. 1363/4 Mr. Job Jeffs, *Sword Cutler under the Greyhound Tavern in the Strand. **1714** MANDEVILLE *Fab. Bees* (1725) I. 80 Without being themselves guilty of, or accessary to them, any otherwise than by way of Trade, as a Druggist may be to Poysoning, or a Sword-Cutler to Blood-shed. **1833** J. HOLLAND *Manuf. Metal* II. 74 In France a sword-cutler is still called *fourbisseur.* **1837** CARLYLE *Fr. Rev.* III. v. vi, Do not..iron stanchions [transmute themselves] into the white-weapon.., by *sword-cutlery? **1567** in Picton *L'pool Munic. Rec.* (1883) I. 109 A very good yew bow and..a *sword dagger. **1604** MARSTON *Malcontent* I. iii. B 2 b, Heres a Knight..shall..Doe the *sword daunce with any Morris-dauncer in Christendome. **1712** N. BLUNDELL *Diary* (1895) 103, I made a Sword Dance against my Marlpit is flower'd. **1814** SCOTT *Diary* 7 Aug., in *Lockhart*, The sword-dance, now almost lost, but still practised in the Island of Papa. **1868** Q. VICTORIA *Life Highl.* 14 The piper played, and one of the highlanders danced the Sword dance. **1884** WHITTIER in *Harper's Mag.* Jan. 179/1 The midnight sword-dance of the northern sky. **1648** HEXHAM II, *Een sweerat-dansser*, a *Sword-dauncer. **1777** BRAND *Pop. Antiq.* 175 The Fool Plough goes about, a Pageant that consists of a Number of Sword Dancers, dragging a Plough, with Music. **1811** *Gentl. Mag.* LXXXI. I. 423/2 In the North Riding of Yorkshire... On the feast of St. Stephen..6 youths (called sword-dancers, from their dancing with swords)..begin to travel from village to village, performing a rude dance, called the sword dance. **1897** *Q. Rev.* Oct. 489 The sword-dancers from Papa. **1648** HEXHAM II, *Een sweerdt-dans*, a *Sword-dauncing with the point upon the palme of ones hands, or teeth. **1712** N. BLUNDELL *Diary* (1895) 105 We.. had Sword Dansing and a Merry-Night in yᵉ Hall and in yᵉ Barne. **1847** HALLIWELL s.v., There is a very singular custom, called *sword-dancing*, prevalent in many parts of Northumberland, and in the county of Durham, during the Christmas holidays. **1825** JAMIESON, *James Ryall*, the name of the silver coin of James VI. of Scotland, vulgarly called the **Sword Dollar.* **1600** HOLLAND *Livy* XVI. Argt. 390 Combates of *swordfensors at the sharpe to the utterance. **1615** CROOKE *Body of Man* 355 In the single Combats of Sword-Fencers (called *Gladiatores*). **1868** DARWIN *Anim. & Pl.* xxvi. II. 349 Pouters properly have white primary wing-feathers, but not rarely a '*sword-flighted' bird, that is, one with the few first primaries dark-coloured, appears. *c* **1325** *Gloss. W. de Bibbesw.* in Wright *Voc.* 165 *Ta renge*, thi *swerd-girdel. **1523** in W. H. Turner *Select. Rec. Oxford* (1880) 43 It' for ij swerde gyrduls. **1574** tr. *Marlorat's Apoc.* 22 A swoordgirdle decked with golde [Rev. i. 13] is a souldiorlyke furniture. **1601** Holland *Pliny* xxxiii. xii. II. 483 Their sword girdles..gingle againe with thin plates of silver. **1647** Hexham i, A sword-girdle, *een swaerdt-riem.* **1531** *Acc. Ld. High Treas. Scotl.* (1905) VI. 21 To be scalbartis and to bynd *swerd handis to the King, ane alne and half quartar veluett. **1632** J. Hayward tr. *Biondi's Eromena* 145 Wounding him with a main blow on the elbow of the sword hand. **1705** Collier *Ess. Mor. Subj.* iii. *Pain* 26 'Tis like a Wound in the Sword Hand; the Man is disabled in that which should defend him. **1881** Tennyson *Charge Heavy Brigade* iv, They rode, or they stood at bay—Struck with the sword-hand and slew. **1694** N. H. *Ladies Dict.* 407/1 (bis) Your Spruce Crevat-strings, *Swords-knots, and the rest of your Finical Dress. **1712–14** Pope *Rape Lock* i. 101 Where wigs with wigs, with sword-knots sword-knots strive, Beaux banish beaux, and coaches coaches drive. **1802** James *Milit. Dict.* s.v., All officers belonging to the British army are directed to wear sword-knots of a peculiar colour and make. **1881** Kipling *Departm. Ditties*, etc. (1899) 68 One sword-knot stolen from the camp. **1667** Milton *P.L.* xi. 672 So violence Proceeded, and Oppression, and *Sword-Law. **1805** James *Milit. Dict.* (ed. 2), *Sword-law*, When a thing is enforced, without a due regard being paid to established rules and regulations, it is said to be carried by sword-law, or by the will of the strongest. **1837** Browning *Strafford* iv. i, Who bade him break the Parliament, Find some pretext for setting up sword-law! **1807** J. E. Smith *Phys. Bot.* 368 Mr. Gawler's elucidations of the *Ensatæ*, *Sword-leaved plants. **1851** H. Melville *Moby Dick* II. v. 31 Queequeg and I were mildly employed weaving what is called a *sword-mat, for an additional lashing to our boat. *c* **1860** H. Stuart *Seaman's Catech.* 32 What is the use of a sword mat? To keep the chafes off the lanyards of lower rigging, backstays, &c... Sword mats are usually made with nettle stuff. **1882** Nares *Seamanship* (ed. 6) 126 The furling gaskets..are made of *sword matting. **1603** Florio *Montaigne* ii. xvi. (1632) 356 Those men *sword-minded can death entertaine. *a* **1593** Marlowe *Edw. II*, i. ii, Vnlesse his brest be *sword proofe he shall die. ? *a* **1625** Webster *Appius & Virginia* v. iii, My skin is not sword-proof. **1821** Praed *Gog* i. Poems 1865 I. 96 Sword-proof thenceforth from top to toe. **1914** *Bulwark* June 84/2 No doubt the Germans will know how to make their Prince acquainted with the unpopularity of his *sword-rattling swagger. **1955** *Times* 12 May 1 (*heading*) Afghan 'sword rattling'. *Ibid.*, I would like to ask my Afghan friends whether they really think such a sword-rattling and offensive attitude is going to help them. **1978** *Guardian Weekly* 29 Jan. 6/3 There are 1,500 British troops in Belize.., as the result of Guatemala's sword-rattling last July. **1647** Trapp *Comm. 1 Pet.* ii. 24 We can hardly believe the power of *sword-salve. **1630** *R. Johnson's Kingd. & Commw.* 182 The [French] King hath nothing of his Noblesse, but *Sword-service. **1892** Cochran-Patrick *Mediæval Scot.* i. 6 Strangers in blood to the tribe often joined a sept, and received a portion from the chief, giving in return their sword-service and customary dues. **1854** R. G. Latham *Native Races Russian Emp.* 189 Sarmatian (as a Scandinavian would say) on the *sword-side. *a* **1861** Sir F. Palgrave *Norm. & Eng.* ii. iii. (1864) III. 173 He argued, that he and Duke Robert were of equal rank, by reason of their consanguinity, Sword-side and Spindle-side counter-changed. **1872** Cutts *Scenes & Char. Mid. Ages* 320 Some *swordsmiths chanted magical verses as they welded them. **1894** *Archaeologia* LIV. 45 Of the churches in the City to-day, thirty have one *sword-stand each. **1852** Bailey *Festus* (ed. 5) 520 Once more the blazing *swordstar shewed in Heaven. **1858** Simmonds *Dict. Trade*, **Sword-stick*, a walking-cane concealing a sharp, rapier-like weapon. **1906** C. N. & A. M. Williamson *Car of Destiny* xxxviii, The old man had come out of the house with a Toledo sword-stick. **1827** Hone *Every-day Bk.* II. 1196 He was assisted by a wretched looking female, who was a *sword-swallower. **1901** W. R. H. Trowbridge *Lett. her Mother to Eliz.* xxxi. 153 The sword-swallower did some amazing things, and smacked his lips, as if the swords tasted nice. **1873** *Routledge's Yng. Gentl. Mag.* Feb. 137/2 What he told me about his *sword swallowing was even more curious. **1858** Baird *Cycl. Nat. Sci.*, *Xiphosura*, ..*Sword-tails. **1660** *Swordtaker [see SWORD-BEARER d]. **1858** Carlyle *Fredk. Gt.* viii. ii. (1872) III. 9 He wears his sword, but has no *sword-tash (*porte-epee*). **1860** Wraxall *Life in Sea* i. 16 The Grampus, or *Sword-whale..attains a length of twenty-five feet. **1913** *Nation* 28 June 484/2 Not only has he [*sc.* Sir John Simon] shown his greatest skill in this *sword-work [etc.]. **1977** P. Scupham *Hinterland* 58 Boughs come adrift Over the splayed sword-work of spring flowers. **1646** G. H. Hils tr. *Casimire's Odes* 21 Forbeare cruell men to multiply With fire, *sword-wrack, your single destiny.

e. In names of plants having sword-shaped leaves or other parts, as **sword aloe** (see quot.); **sword-bean**, the genus *Entada*, and *Canavalia gladiata*, from their large flat pods; **sword-fern**, name for several ferns with long narrow fronds, as the genus *Xiphopteris*, *Polystichum munitum*, native to western North America, *Nephrolepis exaltata* and other species, and *Grammitis australis*; **sword-flag**, the yellow water-flag, *Iris Pseudacorus*; **sword-flax**, a name for the New Zealand flax, *Phormium tenax*; **sword-lily** [cf. Du. *zwaardlelie*, G. *schwertlilie*, etc.], the genus *Gladiolus*; in quot. 1845 applied to some water plant; **sword-rush**, **-sedge**, an Australian sedge, *Lepidosperma gladiatum*; **sword-weed**, a name for *Cassia occidentalis*, from its sword-shaped pods. See also SWORD-GRASS.

1731 Miller *Gard. Dict.* s.v. *Aloe, Africana caulescens, foliis minus glaucis caulem amplectentibus, floribus rubris.* The *Sword Aloe. **1875** *Encycl. Brit.* III. 460/2 Beans or pulse, of no small importance as articles of diet, such as the ..*sword bean of India. **1829** Loudon *Encycl. Plants*, *Xiphopteris.* *Sword-Fern. **1899** E. Cotes *Path of Star* i. 4 The bunch of sword-ferns..grew beside the door. **1932** J. Steinbeck *Pastures of Heaven* vi. 126 Swordferns grew rankly under the alders. **1976** *Islander* (Victoria, B.C.) 4 Jan. 5/1 Most of the park is forest, the damp coastal rain forest of huge sword-ferns and gigantic cedar trees. **1884** Jefferies *Life of Fields* 56 You must push through the reed grass to find the *sword-flags. **1871** R. H. Hutton *Ess.* I. 61 The little clover competes successfully even with the *phormium tenax*, the *sword-flax. **1786** Abercrombie *Arr.* in *Gard. Assist.* 73 *Gladiolus*, *sword-lily, or corn-flag. **1845** Browning *Flight of Duchess* xiii, Where the bold sword-lily cuts the clear waters. **1875** *Melbourne Spectator* 21 Aug. 190/1 The wrapping-paper, manufactured from the *Sword-rush growing at Portland. **1877** Von Mueller *Bot. Teach.* 124 (Morris) *Lepidosperma gladiatum*, the great *Sword-sedge of our coasts.

sword, *v. rare.* [f. prec. sb.]

1. *trans.* To equip or arm with a sword. (See also SWORDED.)

In quot. used satirically in reference to the previous speaker's words, and in double sense: see 2.

a **1616** Beaum. & Fl. *Little Fr. Lawyer* iv. i, *Sam.* My kingdom for a sword! *Cham.* I'le sword you presently, I'le claw your skin coat too.

2. To strike, slash, or kill with a sword. Also *absol.* or *intr.*

1863 Sala *Captain Dangerous* III. iv. 142 That confounded Officer that I sworded. **1871** Tennyson *Last Tourn.* 473 Swording right and left Men, women, on their sodden faces. **1882** Jefferies *Bevis* I. i. 14 The burdocks and the rest were not high enough yet, the Paynim scoundrels had not grown tall enough..to be slain with any pleasure, and a sense that you were valiantly swording.

3. *trans.* (*fig.*) To thrust or put forth like a sword. *nonce-use.*

1827 Clare *Sheph. Cal.* 53 And mint and flagleaf, swording high Their blooms to the unheeding eye.

sword(**e**, obs. forms of SWARD.

'sword-bearer. [Cf. ON. *sverðberari.*] A person who bears a sword. **a.** *spec.* A municipal official who carries a sword of state before a magistrate on ceremonial occasions.

1431 *Rec. St. Mary at Hill* (1905) 15 The Mayres Swerd berer for the tyme beyng. *a* **1471** *Rolls of Parlt.* V. 396/1 Kerver and Swordberer to the saic moste heynous Traytour. **1518** *Star Chamber Cases* (Selden Soc.) II. 143 Officers of the same Towne, as Recorder, Towne Clerke, Swordberer, attorney and other. *a* **1674** Clarendon *Hist. Reb.* xvi. §118 The City of London sent a Letter to him by their Sword-Bearer. **1708** *Lond. Gaz.* No. 4464/5 His Lordship..carried the Sword bareheaded before Her Majesty..to the Church, where the City Sword-bearer receiv'd it from his Lordship. *a* **1734** North *Lives* (1826) I. 251 There was one Row in office of swordbearer; which in that town [*sc.* Bristol] is pronounced sorberer. I thought it sounded like Cerberus. **1835** *App. Munic. Corpor. Rep.* i. 60 The Sword-bearer [of Gloucester] is elected for life by the corporation... His only duties are to attend upon the mayor, and to carry the sword.

b. An attendant on a military man of rank, or on a chief, who carries his master's sword when not worn.

1660 in *Verney Mem.* (1904) II. 151 What the Sword-bearer brought of Monke's coming up, may bee falsly rendered by him.

c. *gen.* One who carries or wears a sword.

1530 Palsgr. 278/1 Swerdeberer, *porteur despee.* **1538** Elyot, *Macherophorus*, a sworde bearer. **1570** Jewel *View Bull Pius V* (1582) 4 [Saint] Paule the Swordebearer. **1802** James *Milit. Dict.*, *Sword-bearer*, one who wears a sword.

d. A ruler or magistrate having authority to punish offenders (with allusion to Rom. xiii. 4).

1660 R. Coke *Justice Vind.* 32 Though he makes no difference between Swordbearers and Swordtakers, between Gods Ministers, and Theeves and Robbers; yet the Holy Ghost does, for Gods Minister is a Swordbearer. **1691** Baxter *Nat. Ch.* xi. 49 Supposing such Bishops qualified.., and usurping none of the Sword-bearers power.

e. One of an order of knights in Poland, founded in 1204: see PORT-GLAIVE.

1656 [see PORT-GLAIVE]. **1693** *d' Emiliane's Hist. Monast. Orders* 287 Of the Order of Teutonick Knights, Marrianes, or Sword-bearers. **1728** Chambers *Cycl.* s.v. *Teutonic*, In 1204, Duke Albert had founded the Order of Sword-bearers, *Port-Glaives.* **1784** H. Clark *Hist. Knighthood* II. 88 Albert then Bishop of Livonia..prescribed to these Knights the Cistercian rule and habit, *viz.* a long white mantle and black hood; on the breast two swords in saltire, whence they had the title of Brethren Sword-Bearers. **1841** *Penny Cycl.* XX. 248/1 Most of these [German] families settled there [*sc.* in the Baltic provinces] when the Order of the Knights Sword-bearers was the acknowledged sovereign of these countries (from 1300 to 1530).

Hence **'sword,bearership**, the office of a sword-bearer (sense a).

1535 Cranmer *Let. to Crumwell* in *Misc. Writ.* (Parker Soc.) II. 307 His preferment unto the room of the sword-bearership of London.

'sword-,bearing, *a.* Bearing a sword; that is a sword-bearer.

a **1000** *Cædmon's Gen.* 1060 (Gr.) þe æðelingas sweord-berende settan heton. **1601** Weever *Mirr. Mart.* (Roxb.) 217 The king..As Gods sword-bearing minister appointed. **1890** *Cent. Dict.* s.v. *Docimastes*, Sword-bearing Humming-bird (*Docimastes ensiferus*).

'sword-blade. The blade of a sword.

1409 *Durham Acc. Roll* in *Eng. Hist. Rev.* (1899) XIV. 521 Et soluta Johanni Felanceby pro ii swerdblad pro les belowes [of the forge], ii *d.* **1545** *Rates of Custome Ho.* b vj b, Knyues called swerdblades the dossen vi.s. viii.d. **1620** in Foster *Eng. Factories Ind.* (1906) 215 There is scarce a kniffe or a swordblade in the fleete. *a* **1700** Evelyn *Diary* 30 Sept. 1644, The Mills where they hammer and polish the sword-blades. **1784** Cowper *Task* ii. 318 It [*sc.* satire] may correct a foible, may chastise The freaks of fashion, regulate the dress, Retrench a sword-blade, or displace a patch. **1842** Borrow *Bible in Spain* xxxvi, In old times..the sword-blades of Toledo were held in great estimation. **1852** Thackeray *Esmond* iii. xiii, She..turned pale at the sight of her brother and kinsman, drawn swords, broken sword-blades, and papers yet smouldering in the brazier.

b. *attrib.* ***Sword-blade bond, note***, one of the securities issued by the *Sword-blade Company*, a speculative company in London incorporated 15 Sept. 1691 for the manufacture of hollow sword-blades in the North of England, which failed and was taken over by London merchants who speculated in forfeited lands in Ireland.

[**1703** *Jrnls. Ho. Commons Ireland* 9 Oct. 331/1 The Governor and Company for hollow Sword-Blades in England.] **1707** Luttrell *Brief Rel.* (1857) VI. 192 It's said a quo warranto will be brought against the sword blade company. **1708** *Lond. Gaz.* No. 4422/8 Lost.., between the Mine-Adventure-Office on Snow-hill, and the Sword-Blade-Office in Birchin-lane, a..Pocket-Case, in which were the following Notes:..Three Sword-Blade-Notes,.. No. 41. for 12l. 10s., No. 19. for 23l. 10s., No. —— for 30l. **1725** in J. Collyer *Rep. Cases Crt. Chancery* (1847) II. 363 *note*, A. B., being ill of the sickness whereof he died..said, 'Now, my dear Ann, take these (viz. a bank note and a sword-blade bond), they are yours.'

†**sword-brother.** *Obs.* [f. SWORD *sb.* + BROTHER *sb.* Cf. MLG. *swertbroder*, MHG. *swertbruoder* (G. *schwertbruder* Hist.), MDa. *sværdbroder* = SWORD-BEARER e.] A comrade in arms.

c **1205** Lay. 4144 Ich wulle mine rihte faren to stal fehte to-gene þene swerd broþeren þe beiene beoh for-sworne. *Ibid.* 30523 He bigon þene swikedom uppen his sweord broþeren.

sworded ('sɔːdɪd, 'sɔədɪd), *a.* [f. SWORD *sb.* + -ED[2].] Equipped or armed with a sword.

c **1000** Ælfric *Gram.* xliii. (Z.) 257 *Gladius* swurd, *gladiatus* ȝeswurdod. *c* **1000** *Vercelli MS.* lf. 78 b (in Napier *Contrib. OE. Lexicogr.*) þa cwomon þær semninga tweȝen englas to him ȝescildode & ȝesweordode [*Blickl. Hom.* 221 ȝesceldode & ȝesperode]. *c* **1400** Maundev. (1839) xii. 137 Thei knowen not how to ben clothed; now long, now schort, ..now swerded, now daggered. **1470–85** Malory *Arthur* viii. xxxix. 333 Whan sir Tristram was armed as hym lyked best and wel shelded and swerded. **1629** Milton *Hymn Nativ.* xi, The helmed Cherubim And sworded Seraphim. **1634** W. Wood *New Eng. Prosp.* ii. vii, Being double pistold, and well sworded. **1711** E. Ward *Vulgus Brit.* viii. 87 Such a brave surprizing Train Of sworded Boys, and armed Men. **1798** W. Taylor in *Monthly Mag.* V. 367 Nor James, nor sworded Paul, Watch in the cross-shap'd hall; Nor the first martyr of a madding crowd. **1805** Coleridge *Separation* i A sworded man whose trade is blood. **1854** Whittier *The Rendition* ii, I thought of Liberty Marched hand-cuffed down that sworded street. **1880** L. Wallace *Ben-Hur* 507 A Caesar helmed and sworded.

b. *transf.* Having some part resembling a sword.

1681 Grew *Musæum* i. v. i. 87 Whether this Fish be Viviperous, is uncertain; yet being of the Sworded-kind, I have ventur'd here to describe the Head. **1852** Bailey *Festus* (ed. 5) 495 A marvel mightier than the sworded star. **1897** F. Thompson *Ode Setting Sun* New Poems 116 Where is the Naiad 'mid her sworded sedge?

sworder ('sɔːdə(r), 'sɔədə(r)). [f. SWORD *sb.* + -ER[1], after L. *gladiātor* GLADIATOR.]

1. One who kills another with a sword, an assassin, cut-throat; one who habitually fights with a sword; a gladiator.

1593 Shaks. *2 Hen. VI.* iv. i. 135 A Romane Sworder, and Bandetto slaue Murder'd sweet Tully. **1606** —— *Ant. & Cl.* iii. xiii. 31 Cæsar will.. be Stag'd to th' shew Against a Sworder. **1828** Scott *F.M. Perth* vi, I am honest, and so forth, you would say, but a hot-brained brawler, and common sworder or stabber. **1837–42** Hawthorne *Twice-told T.* (1851) II. ii. 35 These mercenary sworders and musketeers. **1895** *Athenæum* 15 June 778/2 A naked babe.. turns his smiling face to the truculent sworder who is about to execute the behest of the weak Herod.

b. = SWORD-BEARER e.

1537 [Coverdale] *Orig. & Sprynge of Sectes* 33 The Swearders. This order weareth whyt also, & .ii. reede sweardes crosse waye vpon a whyte cole [? cote], which signify theyr bloudy knight hode.

2. One skilled in the use of the sword; a swordsman.

1814 Scott *Ld. of Isles* ii. xviii, With blade advanced, each Chieftain bold Show'd like the Sworder's form of old. **1820** Byron *Juan* iv. xlix, The third, a wary, cool old sworder, took The blows upon his cutlass. **1876** Earl Albemarle *Fifty Years Life* I. 106 A splendid horseman, a dexterous sworder.

'swordfish. [f. SWORD *sb.* + FISH *sb.*[1] Cf. MLG. *swertvisch*, G. *schwertfisch*, etc.]

1. The common name of *Xiphias gladius*, a large fish of the Atlantic, Mediterranean, and Pacific, having the upper jaw prolonged into a sword-like weapon; the flesh is used for food. Also extended to other species of the genus *Xiphias* and related genera.

Also applied locally to several fishes of slender elongated form, as the garfish or garpike (*Belone vulgaris*), the butter-fish or spotted gunnel (*Centronotus* or *Murænoides gunnellus*), also called SWORDICK, and the cutlass-fish or silvery hair-tail (*Trichiurus lepturus*). Also, the grampus or killer (*Orca gladiator*), a ferocious toothed cetacean.

c **1400** *Brut* cclvii. 523 This yere were taken iiij gret ffisshes bitwen Greth & London: one was called mors marine, þe secund, A swerd fyssh, & þe other tweyn wer whalles. *c* **1460** J. Russell *Bk. Nurture* 836 Salt swyrd-fysche savery & fyne. *a* **1586** SIDNEY *Arcadia* III. (1912) 517 The sword-fish, against the whale; the Rhinoceros against the elephant. **1613** *Descr. Bermudas* in Force *Tracts* (1844) III. III. 22 The Sword-fish swimmes vnder the Whale, and pricketh him vpward. **1646** SIR T. BROWNE *Pseud. Ep.* III. xxiii. 168 The horne of the Pristis or Sword-fish. **1658** GURNALL *Chr. in Arm.* verse 14. II. iv. 47 The sword-fish, which Plutarch saith, hath..a sword in the head, but no heart to use it. **1706** PHILLIPS (ed. Kersey), *Sword-Fish*, a Sea-fish which has at the end of the upper Jaw, a Weapon like a Sword..; It also has Vents near the Eyes, to spout forth Water, with seven Fins. **1769** PENNANT *Brit. Zool.* III. 128 The sword fish is said to be very voracious. **1820** SHELLEY *Arethusa* 68 The shadowy waves Are as green as the forest's night:—Outspeeding the shark, And the sword-fish dark. **1839** T. BEALE *Nat. Hist. Sperm Whale* 49 It is said by whalers, that the 'thresher' and the sword-fish attack the whale in conjunction.

b. *attrib.*

1888 GOODE *Amer. Fishes* 249 Upon the end of the 'shank' fits the head of the harpoon, known by the names of Sword-fish iron, lily-iron, and Indian-dart. **1891** *Cent. Dict.* s.v., *Swordfish sucker*, a remora, *Echeneis brachyptera*, which often fastens on swordfishes. **1897** KIPLING *Capt. Cour.* viii. 190 A Gloucester sword-fish boat.

2. The southern constellation *Dorado* or *Xiphias*.

1771 *Encycl. Brit.* I. 487 The new Southern Constellations [include]..Dorado, *Xiphias*, The Sword Fish.

Hence **'sword,fisherman**, a vessel employed in fishing for swordfish; **'sword,fishery**, **'sword,fishing**, fishing for swordfish.

1879 *The Congregationalist* 20 Aug. (Cent. Dict.) Swordfishing is the most popular way of spending the day [at Block Island]. **1885** C. F. HOLDER *Marvels Anim. Life* 61 The Thumbscrew was a sword-fisherman, long, low and rakish.

'sword-grass. A name for several different plants with sword-shaped leaves, as the sword-lily (*Gladiolus*), *Arenaria* (*Spergularia*) *segetalis*, *Melilotus segetalis* or *sulcata*, and various grasses and sedges, as the reed canary-grass *Phalaris arundinacea*, *Arundo conspicua* of New Zealand, and *Cladium psittacorum* of Australia.

1598 FLORIO, *Gladolo*, an herbe called great Galangall or swordgrasse. **1647** HEXHAM I. (*Herbs*), Sedge, or Sword-grasse, *Water-lisch.* **1728** CHAMBERS *Cycl.* s.v. *Acorus*, The false Acorus is the common Sword-grass. **1749** [see b]. **1823** *Blackw. Mag.* XIV 190 A sort of long sword-grass that grows about marshes and the sides of lakes. **1833** TENNYSON *May Queen* II. vii, When..the summer airs blow cool On the oat-grass and the sword-grass, and the bulrush in the pool. **1859** MAYNE *Expos. Lex.*, Sword-grass, common name for the *Phasganium*. **1872** A. DOMETT *Ranolf* x. ii. 172 The great plumes far and wide of the sword-grass aspire.

b. *attrib.* in collectors' names for moths of the genus *Calocampa*.

1749 B. WILKES *Eng. Moths & Butterflies* 8 The Sword-grass moth. Mr. Rosel informs us, That the Caterpillar of this Fly feeds on the Orache;..I once took one of these Caterpillars, full grown, feeding on the Sword-grass in the Marshes at Rotherhith. **1832** J. RENNIE *Butterfl. & M.* 65 The Sword Grass (*C*[*alocampa*] *exoleta*..) appears in April or May, and the middle of October.

swordick ('sɔːdɪk). [Obscure.] A local name of the butter-fish (cf. SWORDFISH 1).

1805 BARRY *Orkney* 292 The Spotted Blenny (*blennius gunnellus*, Lin. Syst.) which, from the form of its body, has here got the name of swordick. **1863** [see GUNNEL].

'swording, *vbl. sb.* [f. SWORD *v.* + -ING[1].] Striking with a sword; exercise with the sword, fencing (in quot. 1899 *attrib.*).

1891 *Cent. Dict.*, *Swording*, slashing with a sword. **1899** CROCKETT *Black Douglas* (1900) 94, I also won the swording prize at the last wappenshaw.

'swording, *ppl. a. Obs.* or *arch.* [f. SWORDER: see -ING[2].] Martial, warlike, military.

1611 SPEED *Hist. Gt. Brit.* IX. xvi. §68 The Duke brought with him foure hundreth men, the Earle of Salisbury fiue hundreth, the Earle of Warwicke sixe hundreth: The Dukes of Excester and Sommerset eight hundreth, the Earle of Northumberland, the Lords Egremont and Clifford fifteene hundreth. This was the fashion of that swording age. *a* **1659** BP. BROWNRIG *Serm.* (1674) II. ii. 20 Our Fore-fathers.. lived in those Swording times, when all was in an uprore. **1860** SWINBURNE *Queen-Mother* I. iii, These swording-men are holier things than we.

swordless ('sɔːdlɪs, 'sɔədlɪs), *a.* [f. SWORD *sb.* + -LESS.] Destitute of a sword; not having, carrying, or using a sword.

c **1440** *Partonope* 4334 Hys swerde he smotte a-geyne the gysharne Be the hylt hit brake,.. The danys were gladde.. For swerdeles was Partonope. **1470–85** MALORY *Arthur* I. v. 41 And so I thought my broder syr kay shold not be swerdles. *a* **1814** *Spaniards* III. i. in *New Brit. Theatre* III. 224 My hand..Instinctive rushes to my swordless side. **1815** BYRON *Parisina* ix, With swordless belt, and fetter'd hand. **1883** WHITTIER *Our Country* xviii, The swordless commonwealth of Penn. **1889** CORBETT *Monk* xiii. 187 In their midst rode Lambert with swordless scabbard.

swordlet ('sɔədlɪt). *nonce-wd.* [f. SWORD *sb.* + -LET.] A small sword.

1884 R. F. BURTON *Bk. Sword* 169 A specimen of the Manquema Swordlet drawn to scale.

†swordling. *Obs. rare*[−1]. In 6 swerdlynge. [ad. early mod.G. *swertlinch*, f. *swert* SWORD *sb.* + *-linch*, *-ling*, -LING[1] 2; a rendering of L. *gladiolus*.] In quot. app. denoting the yellow iris or water-flag (*Iris Pseudacorus*).

1562 TURNER *Herbal* II. 23 Iris..hath leaues like vnto the herbe called Gladiolus, that is to saye, the gladdon or swerdlynge.

'swordman. Now *rare* or *Obs.* (replaced by SWORDSMAN). Pl. **-men.** [f. SWORD *sb.* + MAN *sb.*[1]]

1. A man who uses or fights with a sword; a gladiator; one skilled in, or addicted to, using a sword; *spec.* one skilled in fencing: = SWORDSMAN 1.

1387 TREVISA *Higden* (Rolls) V. 23 Þat swerdman was i. slawe. *c* **1440** *Promp. Parv.* 483/1 Swerde man, or he þat vsythe a swerde, *gladiator*. **14..** *Gest of Robyn Hode* clxix. in Child *Ballads* (1888) III. 64/2 Thou art one of the best sworde-men That euer yit sawe I. **1500** *Ortus Vocab.*, *Gladiator*, a swerd mane. **1649** JER. TAYLOR *Gt. Exemp.* II. Ad Sect. xii. 58 Peter was the boldest of the twelve, and a good Sword-man. **1652** *Nicholas Papers* (Camden) 290 It is here said your favourite Dr. Froissard is become of late a quarrelsome sword-man. **1670** MILTON *Hist. Eng.* IV. Wks. 1851 V. 148 Cuichelm..sent privily Eumerus a hir'd Sword-man to assassin him. **1692** SIR W. HOPE *Fencing-Master* (ed 2.) 164, I have given you the Directions to make you a Sword-Man. **1728** D. MCBANE (*title*) The Expert Sword-Man's Companion: or the True Art of Self-Defence.

b. A soldier who fights with a sword; one of a body of troops armed with swords; hence, an armed follower.

c **1400** *Laud Troy Bk.* 16673 The speremen ride, the bowemen schote,..The swordmen smyte & strokes ȝeue. **1422** YONGE tr. *Secr. Secr.* 215 In the ryght hande of thyne enemys, the Swerde mene; In the lyfte hande, the Iusters wyth Speris. **1610** *Cal. St. Papers Irel.* (1874) 416 It is to be wished that the swordmen, not only of Ulster but of Connaught, were transmitted upon this occasion to Swethen or Virginia. **1612** SIR J. DAVIES *Why Ireland*, etc. (1787) 35 They and all their sword-men should clearly relinquish..unto the King..all their lands..which they held in Leinster. **1617** MORYSON *Itin.* II. 100 Two things remained to settle the Kingdome. First the ridding Ireland of the Swordmen. **1632** *Star Chamber Cases* (Camden) 113 There were manie accusacions against Hugh Erswicke and his sword-man. **1669–70** R. MONTAGU in *Buccleuch MSS.* (Hist. MSS. Comm.) I. 468 The sword men are discontented to hear they are not likely to be employed for a year at least.

2. A man 'of the sword'; a warrior, military man, fighter, soldier. Also *fig.*

1601 SHAKS. *All's Well* II. i. 62 Worthy fellowes, and like to prooue most sinewie sword-men [*printed* -man]. **1621–31** LAUD *Serm.* (1847) 13 David was a swordman with a witness:—one of the greatest warriors that ever was. **1647** CLARENDON *Hist. Reb.* II. §26 The Earl of Essex..the most Popular man of the Kingdom, and the Darling of the Sword-men. **1651** HOWELL *Venice* 188 How much it did misbecom Bishops..who make profession of a life differing from Sword-men, to change the Crosier into Musket rests. **1668** R. L'ESTRANGE *Vis. Quev.* (1708) 73 Sword-Men; As Generals of Armies, Captains, Lieutenants, Common Soldiers. **1679** C. NESSE *Antichrist* 39 His sworn swordmen the jesuits. **1708** J. CHAMBERLAYNE *St. Gt. Brit.* I. III. iv. (1710) 190 This..Degree [of Knight Batchelor]..was.. bestowed upon Gown-Men, contrary to the nature of the thing (as Degrees in the Universities are sometimes bestowed on Sword-men). [**1900** MORLEY *Cromwell* v. iv. 413 Such an innovation should be a warning not to vote for swordmen nor for the Protector's friends.]

Hence **swordmanship** = SWORDSMANSHIP.

1781 COWPER *Charity* 509 No skill in swordmanship, however just, Can be secure against a madman's thrust.

sword-pink: see PINK *sb.*[1] (Cf. G. *schwertboot.*)

1614 T. GENTLEMAN *Eng. Way to Wealth* 14 These are Vessels of diuers fashions, and not like vnto the Busses,.. and they bee called some of them, Sword-pinks, Flat-bottomes, Holland-toads. **1616** CAPT. J. SMITH *Descr. New Eng.* 12, 2 or 3000 Busses, Flat bottomes, Sword pinks.

'sword-play. [OE. *sweordplega*, f. SWORD *sb.* + PLAY *sb.*]

1. †**a.** Fight, battle. *OE.* **b.** The action of plying or wielding a sword briskly, as in fencing; the art or practice of fencing.

a **1000** *Waldere* 13 (Gr.) Ðy ic ðe ȝesawe æt ðam sweord-pleȝan..wiȝ forbuȝan. **1627** HAKEWILL *Apol.* IV. iv. §9. 319 Truly I thinke there is at no time a greater concourse of the people then at the sword-playes. **1647** STAPYLTON *Juvenal* 48 When there was any sword-play, or fighting on the stage. **1889** CONAN DOYLE *Micah Clarke* 205, I studied sword-play under Signor Cantarini. **1904** *Windsor Mag.* Jan. 298/2 His sword-play was like flashes of lightning. **1910** EGERTON CASTLE in *Encycl. Brit.* X. 250/2 The new [17th century] French sword-play was..very neat,..and..even more deadly than the old fence.

c. *fig.* Spirited or skilful controversy or debate.

1847 BUNSEN *Church of Future* Pref. p. xxvii, I have not the slightest intention..of involving myself in any literary sword-play. **1902** L. STEPHEN *Stud. Biogr.* III. vi. 189 To enjoy the spectacle of intellectual swordplay.

2. A kind of sword-dance. *rare.*

1882 ELTON *Origins Eng. Hist.* v. 123 If no duel occurred during the meal, the guests were entertained with a sword-play.

'sword-,player. Now *rare* or *Obs.* One skilled in sword-play; chiefly, a gladiator; also, a fencer.

14.. *Nom.* in Wr.-Wülcker 696/37 *Hic gladiator*, a swerd-plaer. **1538** ELYOT Addit., *Bustuarij*, sworde players, whiche went before the ded corpsis whan they were borne to be burned. **1555** EDEN *Decades* (Arb.) 115 Settinge them in order of battell after his swoordeplayers fasshion. **1586** J. HOOKER *Hist. Irel.* in *Holinshed* II. 27/1 The plaie or game of swordplaiers or maisters of defense. **1608** WILLET *Hexapla Exod.* 640 A Romane Emperour is said to haue seene in his smaragd the sword players as they did fight. **1627** [see *sword-fight*, SWORD *sb.* 6 a]. **1671** MILTON *Samson* 1323 Have they not Sword-players, and ev'ry sort Of Gymnic Artists? **1693** DRYDEN *Juvenal* iv. (1697) 71 In a Prize of Sword-Players, when one of the Fencers had the other at his Mercy, the Vanquish'd Party implor'd the Clemency of the Spectators. **1823** SCOTT *Quentin D.* xxxv, 'Nay!' said the Countess,..'Would you hold me out as a prize to the best sword-player?'

So †**sword-playing** = SWORD-PLAY 1 b.

14.. *Lat.-Eng. Voc.* in Wr.-Wülcker 586/35 *Gladiatura*, a swerdpleyynge, or bokeler pleyynge. **1587** GOLDING *De Mornay* xx. (1592) 315 Justs,..Swordplayings, Wrestlings, buffetings.

†**sword-sliper.** *Sc.* and *north. dial. Obs.* Also 6 -slippar, -slypper, -slyper, 6–8 -slipper, 7–8 -sleiper. [Of Scand. origin (cf. MSw. *swerdslipare*): see SLIPE *v.*[1]] A sword-sharpener.

1478–9 in R. Davies *Extr. Munic. Rec. York* (1843) 64 Solut. Robson Swerdsliper pro j vagina de novo fact. magno gladio majoris. **1541** *Acc. Ld. High Treas. Scot.* VII. 480 To Thomas Softlaw, suerd slipper, for his fe in making of the Kingis grace skalbertis..xx li. **1584** *Rec. Elgin* (New Spald. Club 1903) I. 175 Johne Wmfray swordslypper in Elgin. **1601** in Pitcairn *Crim. Trials* (Bannatyne Cl.) II. II. 357 Hector Dauidsoune, sword-slipper in Edinburgh. **1661** BLOUNT *Glossogr.* (ed. 2), *Sword-sleiper*,..a dresser or maker of Swords. So used in the North of England; And a Cutler with them deals onely in knives. **1678** SIR G. MACKENZIE *Crim. Laws Scot.* I. xxviii. §2. (1699) 145 In Anno 1634, James Clerk was pursued, because a Sword being sent by Cuthbertson to Moubray a Sword-slipper [etc.]. **1688** *Par. Reg. Hexham* in *Chron. Mirab.* (1841) 156 William, son of William Hutchinson, Sword Sliper. **1714** *Extracts Burgh Rec. Stirling* (1889) 133 John Allan, sword slipper in Doune.

swordsman ('sɔːdz-, 'sɔədzmən). Pl. **-men.** [f. gen. of SWORD *sb.* + MAN *sb.*[1]]

1. A man who uses, or is skilled in the use of, a sword; *spec.* one skilled in fencing.

a **1680** BUTLER *Rem.* (1759) I. 219 As Swordsmen use to fence With blunted Foyles. **1802** C. JAMES *Milit. Dict.*, *Swordsman*,..at present it generally means a person versed in the art of fencing. **1825** LYTTON *Zicci* I. i, The Sicilian was a renowned swordsman; nevertheless, in the third pass he was run through the body. **1828** SCOTT *F.M. Perth* xv, Had a common swordsman struck this fatal blow, he had harmed the bone and damaged the muscles. **1868** E. EDWARDS *Ralegh* I. xv. 306 His animosities were held in check by only one curb—he was no swordsman.

b. = SWORDMAN 1 b.

1865 J. H. INGRAHAM *Pillar of Fire* (1872) 188 The Egyptian army consists of swordsmen, macemen, slingers, and other corps.

2. = SWORDMAN 2.

1701 J. PRINCE (*title*) Danmonii [*sic*] Orientales Illustres: ..wherein the Lives..of the Most famous Divines, Statesmen, Swordsmen, Physicians [etc.], Natives of that most noble Province [*sc.* Devon]..are memoriz'd. **1851** MRS. BROWNING *Casa Guidi Wind.* I. 693 The swords-man's pass.

So **'swordswoman.**

1883 *Pall Mall G.* 24 Dec. (Cassell's) A company of twelve Viennese swordswomen will shortly arrive in Paris to give a series of entertainments.

'swordsmanship. [f. prec. + -SHIP.] The quality or art of a swordsman; skill in the use of the sword.

1851–2 RUSKIN *Stones Venice* I. App. xiv. 382 The mere swordsmanship and marksmanship of the troops are of small importance in comparison with their disposition. **1891** *Times* 20 Feb. 7/6 Mr. Egerton Castle discoursed on the 'Story of Swordsmanship, especially considered in its connexion with the rise and decline of duelling.' **1899** *Daily Tel.* 10 Nov. 10/1 The latter bear terrible evidence of the swordsmanship of our cavalry.

b. *fig.* Skill in controversy or debate.

[**1879** MCCARTHY *Own Times* I. 43 Lord John Russell's swordsmanship was the swordsmanship of Saladin, and not that of stout King Richard.] **1886** BLACKIE *What does Hist. Teach* 86 The spiritual swordsmanship of St. Paul.

'swordster. *nonce-wd.* [f. SWORD *sb.* + -STER.] One addicted to the use of the sword.

1881 HENTY *Cornet of Horse* vii. (1888) 64, I would not on any account that any one thought I was a quarrelsome swordster.

swore, pa. t. and obs. pa. pple. of SWEAR *v.*; obs. f. SWIRE.

sworl, Sc. and north. dial. f. SWIRL.

sworn (swɔːn), *ppl. a.* [Pa. pple. of SWEAR *v.*]

1. That has taken or is bound by an oath.

sworn brother: either of two companions in arms who took an oath according to the rules of chivalry to share each other's good and bad fortunes; hence, either of two comrades or friends who are absolutely faithful or devoted to each other; a close or intimate friend or companion. So ***sworn friend***. ***sworn enemy***, ***foe***: one who has vowed perpetual enmity against another; hence, a determined or irreconcilable enemy.

c **1250** *Gen. & Ex.* 824 He woren breðere of kinde boren, And abram woren he breðre sworen. *c* **1384** CHAUCER *H. Fame* III. 1010, I wol ensuren the..That I shal neuer fro the go But be thyn ovne sworen brother. *c* **1440** *Generydes* 4834 His sworn broder he was in sothfastnes. *c* **1460** *Oseney Reg.* 5 Robert Doyly and Roger of Iuory, sworne brethren and i-confederyd..euerich to other by feythe and sacrament, come to the conquest of Inglonde with Kyng William bastarde. **1576** FLEMING *Panopl. Epist.* 21 Although I had beene your sworne and professed foe. **1593** SHAKS. *Rich. II*, v. i. 23, I am sworne Brother (Sweet) To grim Necessitie;

and hee and I Will keepe a League till Death. **1599** —— *Much Ado* I. i. 73 Who is his companion now? He hath euery month a new sworne brother. **1603** KNOLLES *Hist. Turks* (1621) 1152 Those sworne enemies of the Christian Religion. **1611** SHAKS. *Wint. T.* I. ii. 167 Now my sworne Friend, and then mine Enemy. *a* **1661** FULLER *Worthies* (1840) II. 538 Private profit is (though a secret) a sworn enemy to the general good. **1780** COWPER *On Burning Ld. Mansfield's Library* 2 The Vandals of our isle, Sworn foes to sense and law. **1848** DICKENS *Dombey* x, That boy's father and myself, Sir, were sworn friends. **1870** FREEMAN *Norm. Conq.* (ed. 2) I. App. 690 Cnut..proposes that they [*sc.* he and Eadmund] shall..divide the Kingdom and become sworn brothers ('fratres adoptivi').

b. With other sbs. (esp. agent-nouns): Thoroughly devoted or addicted to some course of action; resolute, out-and-out, inveterate.

1607 SHAKS. *Timon* III. v. 68 He's a sworne Riotor. **1808** SCOTT *Marm.* VI. xvi, Thou sworn horse-courser, hold thy peace. **1837** CARLYLE *Fr. Rev.* II. I. ii, The Soldiers at Jalès ..were in heart sworn Sansculottes. **1856** MERIVALE *Rom. Emp.* xl. (1871) V. 10 Every theory had its special teacher, every paradox its sworn defender.

2. Appointed or admitted with a formal or prescribed oath to some office or function.

sworn broker: see quots. 1855, 1901.

1433 *Rolls of Parlt.* IV. 432/1 Certain bokes and recordes of youre Eschequier, made by youre sworn Officers. **1445** *Extr. Aberd. Reg.* (1844) I. 14 They sal sell na flesche quhill it be prisit be the sworne prisaris. **1499** in J. Bulloch *Pynours* (1887) 57 It was deliuerit be ane suorne assiss Alexander Chamer forspekar that the pynouris sal pay [etc.]. **1603** SHAKS. *Meas. for M.* II. i. 20 The Iury..May in the sworne-twelue haue a thiefe, or two Guiltier then him they try. **1605** —— *Lear* III. iv. 84 Sweare not, commit not with mans sworne Spouse. **1702** *Post Man* 1–3 Jan. 2/2 Advt., At the Office of Mr. Temple, Sworn Broker of London. **1707** E. SMITH (*title*) Phædra and Hippolitus. A Tragedy as it is Acted at the Queen's Theatre..by Her Majesty's Sworn Servants. **1793–4** *Matthews's Bristol Directory* 30 Dunn, John, Sworn-measurer, Glocester-lane. **1818** SHELLEY *Rosal. & Helen* 289 To be His sworn bride eternally. **1823** SCOTT *Quentin D.* xxx, The Duke of Burgundy, the sworn vassal of France. **1842** *Act 5 & 6 Vict.* c. 103. §1 The Offices of Comptrollers of the Hanaper, Six Clerks, Sworn Clerks, and Waiting Clerks..are hereby abolished. **1848** DICKENS *Dombey* ix, One Brogley, sworn broker and appraiser, who kept a shop where every description of second-hand furniture was exhibited. **1855** F. PLAYFORD *Pract. Hints Investing Money* 21 Sworn-brokers, who, not content with having gained private confidence, have complied in addition with certain City regulations; as becoming citizens of London, and being sworn in before the Lord Mayor. **1901** *Westm. Gaz.* 15 Aug. 7/1 There are some firms who to this day have the words 'Sworn brokers' printed upon their business cards... All who aspired to carry on business as brokers had to attend the Court of Aldermen and be formally sworn.

b. *sworn man* (formerly written in one word): *gen.* a man bound by oath to the performance of a duty or office; hence, a man bound to strict service, a 'vassal', 'henchman'; †*spec.* a 16th century name for the church officers appointed to assist the churchwardens, later called *side(s)men*.

1571 GRINDAL *Injunctions* §22. C iij, That the Churchwardens and sworne men of euerie Parishe shall halfe-yearely..present to the Ordinarie the names of all such persons of their Parishe, as be..blasphemers of the name of God [etc.]. **1582** FETHERSTONE *Dial. agst. Dancing* C 5, By this you seeme to burthen Churchwardens and sworne men with periurie. **1593** R. HARVEY *Philad.* 4 Brute and his fellowes swornemen were worth all the rest. **1611** *Bible* Transl. Pref. ¶9 They will not trust the people with it [*sc.* the Scripture], no not as it is set foorth by their owne sworne men. **1617** MORYSON *Itin.* III. 204 Being found guilty by a Iurie of twelue sworne men. **1800** *Med. Jrnl.* IV. 88 To remove all doubt, six sworn men were appointed from different places in the neighbourhood to watch her day and night. **1821** SCOTT *Kenilw.* vii, Richard Varney is my sworn man, and a close brother of my secret council. **1890** ELIZ. LAMOND tr. *Walter of Henley's Husb.* 7 Survey your lands and tenements by true and sworn men.

3. Affirmed or promised by an oath; confirmed by swearing; to which one is sworn.

1818 SCOTT *Br. Lamm.* xxxiii, Are you willing to barter sworn faith..to this wretched hypocritical sophistry? **1830** JAMES *Darnley* I. v. 107 If it had been to-morrow, I'd not have gone upon the thing, for to-day my sworn service is out. **1909** tr. *Hopf's Hum. Species* 7 The Koran requires no such sworn evidence.

b. with prep. or adv.: cf. SWEAR *v.* III, IV.

1869 *Adam Smith's W.N.* I. v. I. 45 *note*, Bullion..not the produce of English coin..being called technically *sworn-off* gold. **1898** *Westm. Gaz.* 1 July 4/2 Their statistics and almost sworn-to facts could not hold water.

swosh, variant of SWASH.

swot, swat (swɒt), *sb. slang.* [Dialectal variant of SWEAT *sb.*

According to a contributor to *N. & Q.* 1st Ser. I. 369/2, the term originated at the Royal Military College, Sandhurst, in the use on one occasion of the expression 'It mades one swot' (= sweat) by the Scotch professor of mathematics, William Wallace.]

1. Work or study at school or college; in early use *spec.* mathematics. Hence *gen.* labour, toil.

1850 *N. & Q.* 1st Ser. I. 352/2, I have often heard military men talk of *swot*, meaning thereby mathematics; and persons eminent in that science are termed 'good swots'. **1899** CROCKETT *Kit Kennedy* 307 Mary is a good girl, but I own it is no end of a swot to have to see her home from night-school. **1905** H. A. VACHELL *The Hill* iii. 51 Our object is..to get through the 'swat' with as little squandering of valuable time as possible.

2. One who studies hard.

1850 [see sense 1]. **1866** *Routledge's Every Boy's Ann.* 220 'Oh, you swat!' met us at every turn..and yet the real truth was, that neither Jack nor myself did 'swat'. **1899** 'MARTELLO TOWER' [CAPT. NORMAN] *At School & Sea* 40 Sometimes a knot of us..would persuade a good-natured swot to construe the forthcoming lesson to us.

swot, swat (swɒt), *v. slang.* [f. prec.] *intr.* To work hard at one's studies; to 'bone *up*'. Also *trans.*, to 'get *up*', 'mug *up*' (a subject); more rarely, without *up*.

1860 *Slang Dict.* (ed. 2), *Swot*,..to work hard for an examination, to be diligent in one's studies.—*Army*. **1866** [see prec. 2]. **1899** E. PHILLPOTTS *Human Boy* 120 He was swatting like anything in play-hours for a special Old Testament history prize. **1901** *Chambers's Jrnl.* July 445/2 Dick was 'swotting' blue china for all he was worth, at the British Museum and elsewhere. **1908** *Athenæum* 25 July 93/2 It is the case that boys deliberately set themselves to 'slack' or 'swot' for longer or shorter periods. **1913** *Wireless World* I. 37/2 There will be a chance for fellows like me, who have been swatting up Fleming's books. **1931** R. CAMPBELL *Georgiad* i. 18 All who..of despair have baulked the yawning precipice By swotting up his melancholy recipes For 'happiness'. **1955** *Times* 26 May 13/2 Mr. Forester must have 'swotted up' the subject of wartime Atlantic convoys just as he 'swotted up' the subject of the Navy in Nelson's time. **1967** K. GILES *Death in Diamonds* vi. 114 Been swatting the maps, I see. **1977** *N.Y. Rev. Bks.* 23 June 3/2 Our culture hound..swots up in the Encyclopedia before distinguished guests arrive.

swot(e: see SOOT *sb.*[1], *a.* and *sb.*[2], *adv.*

†**swote.** *Obs.* Forms: 1, 3–5 swat, 3 (*Lay.*) swæt, sweot, 1, 3–5 swot, 4 (*Ayenb.*) zuot, 4–5 swote, swoot, soot, sot, 5 sote. *β. north.* 4–6, 8 swat, 6 swatt, *Sc.* swait. [Com. Teut. (wanting in Gothic): OE. *swát* str. n. = OS., OFris., LG. *swêt*, (M)Du. *zweet*, OHG., MHG. *sweiz* str. m. (G. *schweiss*), ON. *sveiti* wk. m. (MSw. *svet(t)e*, Sw. *svett*, Da. *sved*):—OTeut. **swait-*:—Indo-eur. **swoid-*, whence also Skr. *svēdas*, L. *sūdor* (:—**swoidos*). From the weak grade of the same root are Skr. *svidyate* to sweat, Arm. *khirtn* sweat, Gr. ἱδρώς, OHG. *suizzan* (MHG. *swizen*, G. *schwitzen*) to sweat, W. *chwŷs* sweat, Lett. *swidri* (pl.). In several of the Germanic languages the word has the twofold signification of sweat and blood; the second survives in G. hunting parlance.]

1. = SWEAT *sb.* 2.

c **897** ÆLFRED *Gregory's Past. C.* xxxvii. 268 Ðær wæs swiðe swiðlic ʒeswinc, & ðær wæs micel swat agoten. *c* **1000** ÆLFRIC *Gen.* iii. 19 (Gr.) On swate þines and wlitan þu bricst þines hlafes. *c* **1000** *Ags. Gosp.* Luke xxii. 44 His swat wæs swylce blodes dropan on eorðan yrnende. *c* **1205** LAY. 7489 He swonc i þon fehte þat al he lauede asweote [*c* **1275** a swote]. *a* **1225** *Ancr. R.* 112 þet ilke blodi swot of his blisfule bodie. *c* **1250** *Gen. & Ex.* 364 In swinc ðu salt tilen ði meten, Ðin bred wid swotes teres eten. *c* **1300** *Havelok* 2662 [þei] fouhten so þei woren wode, þat þe swot ran fro þe crune. *c* **1380** *Sir Ferumb.* 719 þay smyte to gadre þo so feste ..þat þe soot fram hem gan breste. *c* **1386** CHAUCER *Can. Yeom. Prol. & T.* 25 A Clote leef he hadde vnder his hood For swoot. *c* **1400** *Lanfranc's Cirurg.* 197 Also her breeþ wole stynke & her sotes. *c* **1430** LYDG. *Venus-Mass* in *Lay Folks Mass Bk.* App. v. 394 To wypen away the soot of myn inportable labour. **1483** CAXTON *Gold. Leg.* 313/2 Goo to fraunceys and saye to hym that he selle to the a penyworthe of his swote.

β. **1375** BARBOUR *Bruce* XI. 613 That all thair flesche of swat wes wete. *c* **1425** WYNTOUN *Cron.* III. i. 90 He wes all for rynnyng hat, And oure drawkit all with swat. **1513** DOUGLAS *Æneis* VII. viii. 115 Our all his body bristing furth did creip The warm swait.

2. = SWEAT *sb.* 3.

c **1205** LAY. 17803 þene king..laï on sweouete & on muchele swate. *a* **1250** *Prov. Ælfred* 292 in *O.E. Misc.* 120 If heo ofte a swote for-swunke were. **1340** *Ayenb.* 31 Hi hedden leuere lyese vour messen þanne ane zuot oþer ane slep. *c* **1400** *Beryn* 493 He cauʒt a cardiakill & a cold sct. *c* **1425** *Cast. Persev.* 1227 in *Macro Plays* 114 Men lofe wel now to lyë stylle, In bedde to take a þorowe swot.

b. = SWEAT *sb.* 3 b.

1481 CAXTON *Godfrey* lxvii. 111 The heete, and also the swote destroyed them. **1551** in *Archaeologia* (1860) XXXVIII. 107, June, 1551. The Swatt called new acquyrtance alles Stoupe knave and know thy Master began the xxiiij[th] of this monethe.

3. *fig.* = SWEAT *sb.* 9.

Usually in collocation with *swink* (= labour); orig. denoting the actual sweating accompanying labour, with special reference to Gen. iii. 19.

971 *Blickl. Hom.* 59 On hungre, & on þurste, and on cyle he bið afeded, on ʒewinne & on swate he leofaþ. *c* **1275** LAY. 2281 Moni swinc mani swot [*c* **1205** swæt]..þolede ich in velde. *c* **1320** *Cast. Love* 200 In swynk and swot in world to liue. **1398** TREVISA *Barth. De P.R.* XIV. xlix. (Tollem. MS.) þe felde is a place of besinesse, of trauayle, and of swot. *c* **1450** *Mirk's Festial* 66 þer þay schulden..gete hor mete wyth labour and swot.

'**swother**, *v. Obs.* exc. *dial.* Forms: 1 swodrian, 3 swoudri(e, suoddre, 8–9 *dial.* swather, swother. [OE. *swodrian*, of unascertained origin.] *intr.* To sleep, slumber; also, to swoon. Hence '**swother** *sb.* (**swather, zwodder**), slumber, drowsiness; '**swodder** *a.*, drowsy.

c **1000** *Ags. Ps.* (Spelman) iii. 5 *Ego dormivi, et soporatus sum*, ic hnæppode and ic swodrode. *c* **1290** *St. Edmond* 268 in *S. Eng. Leg.* 439 Alutel he bigan to swoudri as a slep him nome. þo þoʒte him in his swoudringe þat a whit coluere com Fram heuene. **1297** R. GLOUC. (Rolls) 5340 A day as he weri was & a suoddringe him nom. *c* **1730** J. HAYNES *Voc. Dorset* in *N. & Q.* 6th Ser. VIII. 45 A *swather*, slumber. **1825** JENNINGS *Observ. Dial. W. Eng.*, *Zwodder*, a drowsy and stupid state of body or mind. **1847** HALLIWELL, *Zwodder*, drowsy and dull. *West.* **1854** G. WILLIAMS *Gloss.* in *N. & Q.* 1st Ser. X. 400 *Swothered*, stifled. **1873** WILLIAMS & JONES *Somerset. Gloss.*, *Swather*, or *Swother v.*, to faint.

†**swotred**, *pa. pple.* or *a. Obs.* (?)

a **1400** *Octouian* 1022 Clement ofsent hys armes blyue, Swot reed hyt was and euell to thys schyue. *Ibid.* 1045 The launce was swot red and croked.

swotter ('swɒtə(r)). *slang.* [f. SWOT *v.* + -ER[1].] = SWOT *sb.* 2. Also *swotter-up*.

1919 in *Cassell's New Eng. Dict.* **1925** *Times Lit. Suppl.* 26 Mar. 219/1 If we allow contempt to confuse thought, the 'swotter', for all his dullness, will have us on the hip. **1931** R. CAMPBELL *Georgiad* iii. 62 Swotters-up of philosophic blisses.

swotting ('swɒtɪŋ), *vbl. sb. slang.* [f. SWOT *v.* + -ING[1].] = SWOT *sb.* 1; hard work at one's studies.

1873 *Punch* 11 Jan. 19/2 For downright hard 'swotting' there's no place like School. **1959** I. & P. OPIE *Lore & Lang. Schoolch.* x. 179 'Swotting' or 'mugging up' is only considered good form if a person is on the point of taking an exam. **1974** 'J. HERRIOT' *Vet in Harness* v. 37 He had been blessed with the kind of brain which made swotting irrelevant.

†'**swoty**, *a. Obs.* Also 3 swoti, swati. [OE. *swátiʒ* sweaty, bloody = MLG. *swêtich*, early Flem. *sweetigh*, MHG. *sweizec* (G. *schweissig*), ON. *sveitugr*: see SWOTE and -Y[1].] = SWEATY 2.

c **893** ÆLFRED *Oros.* III. ix. 124 þa ongan he hine baðian þæron swa swatiʒne. *a* **1225** *Ancr. R.* 104 Swoti [*v.r.* swati] hateren. *a* **1275** *Prov. Ælfred* 292 in *O.E. Misc.* 121 Gif he for-swunken swoti wuere. *c* **1400** *Destr. Troy* 2366 My horse, þat hote was of Rennyng, All swoty for..his swift course.

swouch, obs. f. SOUGH *sb.*[1], *v.*[1]

swoue, variant of SWOW *Obs.*

†**swough.** *Obs.* Forms: 4 suowe, 4–5 swough(e, 5 swowe. [Representing an original **swog(h)-*, prob. related to **sweg(h)-*, base of ME. *sweʒe* (see SWAY *sb.*, SWAY *v.*, branch I).] A forcible movement; impetus.

1338 R. BRUNNE *Chron.* (1725) 170 Bot he com with a suowe, þat þe schip to rof. *c* **1386** CHAUCER *Man of Law's T.* 198 (Harl. 7334) O firste meuyng cruel firmament With þi diurnal swough [*other MSS.* sweigh] þat crowdest ay. ? *a* **1400** *Morte Arth.* 1127 Nere swounes þe kynge for swoughe of his dynttez! *c* **1435** *Torr. Portugal* 548 To the chyld he toke a flyght With an howge swowe. *a* **1440** *Sir Eglam.* 391 He come to hym wyth a swowe, Hys gode stede undur hym he slowe. **1470–85** MALORY *Arthur* V. iv, The dragon..come doune with suche a swough and smote the bore.

swough(e, obs. ff. SOUGH *sb.*[1], [2], var. SWOW.

swoun(e, obs. forms of SWOON.

swound (swaʊnd), *sb.* Now *arch.* and *dial.* Forms: 5 **swownyd**, 5–7 **swounde**, 6–7 **swownd**, 7–8 **swond**, 7 (9 *dial.*) **swoond**, 6– **swound**. [Later form of *swoune*, SWOON, with excrescent *d*.] A fainting-fit; = SWOON *sb.* 1 b.

c **1440** *Alphabet of Tales* 460 He was so flayed he was like hafe dyed, & fell in a swownyd [*sic MS.*]. **1470–85** MALORY *Arthur* XX. xxii. 838 Syr Gauwayn synked doun vpon hys one syde in a swounde. **1596** SPENSER *F.Q.* IV. vii. 9 When she lookt about, and nothing found But darknesse and dread horrour,..She almost fell againe into a swound. **1615** HIERON *Wks.* I. 597 As when one is in a swond or a sleepe. *c* **1645** HOWELL *Lett.* v. 38 My Lord of Sunderland..got a bruise..which put him in a swound. **1700** DRYDEN *Pal. & Arc.* I. 537 His Spirits are so low, his Voice is drown'd, He hears as from afar, or in a Swound. **1709** in *Law's Mem.* (1818) 245 *note*, She immediately fell into a swond for a considerable time. **1798** COLERIDGE *Anc. Mar.* v. xxii, It flung the blood into my head, And I fell down in a swound. **1856** AYTOUN *Bothwell* II. vi, I wakened in the Hermitage Up from my heavy swound [*rime* wound]. **1863** LONGF. *Wayside Inn* I. *Finale* 7 The Landlord stirred, As one awakening from a swound. **1897** STEVENSON *St. Ives* (1898) 165, I believe I nearly went off into a swound.

fig. **1595** MARKHAM *Sir R. Grinvile* (Arb.) 73 The bellowing shotte which wakened dead mens swounds. **1600** BRETON *Pasquil's Fooles-Cap* Wks. (Grosart) I. 25/1 While healthfull spirits fall into a swound. **1602** DEKKER *Satirom.* K j, I Wish..that..Time, Were in a swound; and all his little Houres, Could neuer lift him vp with their poore powers. **1624** QUARLES *Sion's Sonn.* Poems (1717) 346 My Faith fell in a swound. **1639** FULLER *Holy War* v. vii. (1647) 241 They feared if Abbeys were only left in a swound, the Pope would soon get hot water to recover them. **1691** E. TAYLOR *Behmen's Theos. Philos.* viii. 9 As the life lies in a swound in vegetables till revived by the return of the spring. **1817** SHELLEY *Rev. Islam* IX. xi, A visioned swound, A pause of hope and awe the City bound.

b. without article: = SWOON *sb.* 1 a. *rare.*

1880 W. WATSON *Prince's Quest* (1892) 61 Long time the Prince was held in swound.

swound (swaʊnd), *v.* Now *arch.* and *dial.* Also 6–7 **swounde, swond,** 7 (9 *dial.*) **swoond.** [See prec.] *intr.* To swoon, faint.

1530 PALSGR. 745/2, I swounde, *je me espaume.* **1570** FOXE *A. & M.* (ed. 2) II. 1031/1 In the tyme of his tormentyng he swonded [*ed.* 1576 swounded]. **1590** BARROUGH *Meth. Phisick* I. xv. (1639) 23 Take heed you let him not bleed until he swond. **1653** H. COGAN tr. *Pinto's Trav.* xl. 159, I and my fellows were ready to swoond for very astonishment. **1685** R. Burton *Eng. Emp. Amer.* ii. 35 They instantly swounded away for want of Air. **1821** W. Gifford in Smiles *Mem. J. Murray* (1891) II. xxi. 55, I thought..that both the damsels would have swounded. **1873** J. Spilling *Molly Miggs*, etc. (1903) 22, I wor that terrified that I fell down..and swounded right off.

fig. **1603** Dekker *Wonderful Year* Cjb, (Our fruitfull souereigne) Iames, at whose dread name Rebellion swounded.

Hence '**swounding** *vbl. sb.* (also *attrib.*) and *ppl. a.*

1570 Foxe *A. & M.* (ed. 2) I. 307 The swondyng of the Prior before the kyng. **1597** Breton *Auspicante Jehoua* Wks. (Grosart) II. 6/1 Ouercome with the comfort of Thy vnspeakable kindenes, in the swounding traunce of the treasure of Thy loue. **1615** —— *Characters vpon Ess., Loue*, In the swounding delight of his sacred Inspiration. **1615** Crooke *Body of Man* 253 Light faintings, desperate swoondings. **1650** Earl Monm. tr. *Senault's Man bec. Guilty* 337 Those who feared that the Suns swounding did foretoken the world's end. **1654–66** Earl Orrery *Parthen.* (1676) 17 She fell into divers fits of swounding. **1671** Salmon *Syn. Med.* III. xxii. 394 Motherwort, it is good in swounding fits [etc.]. **1843** Landor *Imag. Conv., O. Cromwell* Wks. 1846 II. 228/1 With a sad sinking of spirit, to the pitch well-nigh of swounding. **1854** Mrs. Gaskell *North & S.* xix, I'm all in a swounding daze to-day. **1901** N. Munro *Doom Castle* xxxi, His temporary sense of swounding helplessness.

†**swounds**, *int. Obs.* Forms: 6 **swown(e)s, swouns, swonds, sowns, 'sowns,** 6–7 **swoundes, swones,** 7 **swoones, 'swounds, swounds.** A euphemistic abbreviation of *God's wounds* (see GOD *sb.* 14 a) used in oaths and asseverations. Cf. ZOUNDS.

1589 [? Nashe] *Almond for Parrat* Ded. Aijb, Some rufling Courtier, that sweares swoundes and blood. *c* **1590** Marlowe *Faustus* iv, How, boy? swowns, boy. **1599** Hayward *1st Pt. Life Hen. IV*, 19 Sir Hugh swore, swownes, and snayles, let vs set vpon them. **1599** Porter *Angry Wom. Abingt.* 335 Sowns, go to, put up your bodkin. **1604** [? Chettle] *Wit of Woman* E 3, Foh, swoundes Sir, tis a Sir reuerence. **1620** I. C. *Two Merry Milk-maids* IV. i. Ljb, O Swoones he has stabd me.

swoup(e, obs. forms of SWOOP.

swour, obs. Sc. pa. t. of SWEAR *v.*

†**swow, swough**, *sb. Obs.* Forms: 3 **swoȝ**, 4 **swouȝ, swoue, swouh, sogh,** 4–5 **swough(e, swogh(e, swow(e,** 5 **swowgh, swowȝe, sowe,** 6 *Sc.* **swoch.** [app. arising from the analysis of ASWOUGH, ASWOW as = *a swough, a swow*: cf. SWOW *pa. pple.* and *v.*[1]]

1. A swoon.

c **1250** *Gen. & Ex.* 484 Til he fel dun on dedes swoȝ. **13..** *Sir Beues* (A.) 1563 Whan he awakede of þat swouȝ, þe tronsoun eft to him a drouȝ. *c* **1369** Chaucer *Dethe Blaunche* 215 What she said more in þat swow I mai nat telle ȝow as now. *a* **1400** *Leg. Rood* (1871) 135 His flesch is smite wiþ deþes þarmes, And swelteþ heer in a swemly swouh [*c* **1425** swow]. *c* **1400** *Destr. Troy* 3551 He..felle to þe ground In a swyme & a swogh, as he swelt wold. **1447** Bokenham *Seyntys* (Roxb.) 14 Whan of his swow As a man amasyd he sodeynly dede abreyde. *c* **1460** *Towneley Myst.* xv. 68 As I lay in a swogh.

b. phr. ***to fall on, in swough***: to swoon. (Cf. next.)

13.. *Sir Beues* (A.) 1309 Terri fel þer doun and [?= an] swouȝ. *c* **1350** *Will. Palerne* 87 Reuliche gan he rore..& fel doun on swowe. *c* **1400** *Laud Troy Bk.* 4376 And thei of Troye bakward drowe; And many fel ded In sowe. *c* **1440** Capgrave *Life St. Kath.* III. 1214 Wyth þese swete wordes sche fel in swow. *a* **1450** *Le Morte Arth.* 1634 Than was the quene glad I-noghe Whan she saw launcelot du lake, That nyghe for Ioy she felle in swoughe.

2. A state of sleep or trance.

c **1403** Clanvowe *Cuckow & Night.* 87, I fel in suche a slomber and a swow, Not al a-slepe, ne fully wakinge. *c* **1440** Capgrave *Life St. Kath.* III. 649 Whan þat same Adam slepte in a swow, Oure lord oute of his syde þan made Eue. **1513** Douglas *Æneis* VIII. i. 62 The profund swoch of sleip had thaim ourtayne.

†**swow, swown**, *pa. pple. Obs.* Forms: α. 1 **ȝeswoȝen,** 3 **iswoȝe(n,** 3–4 **iswowe(n, ysown, swoune,** 5 **suoun.** β. 3 **isuowe, isuoȝe,** 3–4 **yswowe, yswoȝe,** 4 **isowe, ysow(e, ysowȝ, swowe, swoghe.** [OE. *ȝeswoȝen.* Cf. ASWOON, ASWOUGH, ASWOW(E.] Fainting, in a swoon: orig. and chiefly in predicative use with *fall*.

c **1000** Ælfric *Saints' Lives* xii. 63 [He] began to etenne; he feoll þa æt ðære forman snæde underbecc ȝeswoȝen. *c* **1000** —— *Hom.* II. 356 Se læȝ..ȝeswoȝen betwux ðam ofsleȝenum. *c* **1000** *Sax. Leechd.* II. 196 Þæt hie syn sona ȝeswoȝene ȝif hie þone mete næbben. *c* **1205** Lay. 3074 Mid þære wræðe he wes isweued þat he feol iswowen [*c* 1275 hiswoȝe]. *Ibid.* 4516 Stille he wes iswoȝen [*c* **1275** iswoȝe] on his kine-stole. *c* **1290** *St. Clement* 173 in *S. Eng. Leg.* 327 Þis womman feol a-don i-swowe. **13..** *Sir Beues* (A.) 446 Þat emperur fel swowe adoun [*MS. C.* yn swowne downe]. **1362** Langl. *P.Pl.* A. v. 222 Sleuþe for serwe fel doun I-swowene. *a* **1375** *Joseph Arim.* 583 Whon Eualac þat sauȝ, he fel to þe grounde, And Seraphe also, and boþe lye swoune. *c* **1380** *Sir Ferumb.* 2497 For hungre þai fulle y-sowe. **1387** Trevisa *Higden* (Rolls) VI. 477 Þe kyng was astonyed, and fil doun to þe grounde as þeyȝ he were i-sowe [*MS. β.* a swowe; *MS. γ.* y-swowe]. **1390** Gower *Conf.* III. 357 Mi dedly face pale and fade Becam, and swoune I fell to grounde. **1423** Jas. I *Kingis Q.* lxxiii, I..lent, amaisit verily, Half sleping and half suoun.

b. as *ppl. a.* ? 'Dead' (silence).

13.. *Gaw. & Gr. Knt.* 243 Al stouned at his steuen..In a swoghe sylence..As al were slypped vpon slepe.

†**swow**, *v.*[1] *Obs.* [f. prec.] *intr.* To swoon, faint.

a **1225** *Ancr. R.* 288 Þe heorte..ȝeieð creaunt, creaunt, ase swowinde. **13..** *E.E. Allit. P.* C. 442 Þer he swowed & slept sadly al nyȝt. **1377** Langl. *P.Pl.* B. v. 154 Hir were leuere swowe or swelte þan suffre any peyne.

swow (swaʊ), *v.*[2] *U.S. colloq.* [*I swow* app. = *Is' vow* (I shall vow); cf. SWAN *v.*[2]] *I swow*, I declare; = SWAN *v.*[2]

[**1790** *Mass. Spy* 30 Dec. 1/1 In one village you will hear the phrase 'I snore,'—in another, 'I swowgar,'—and in another, 'I van you, I wunt do it.'] **1844** 'Jonathan Slick' *High Life N. York* I. 104, I swow, Miss Miles, you look as harnsome as a full blown rose this morning. **1872** Schele de Vere *Americanisms* 595, I swan, I swad, I swow, I swamp, and I vum, for I swear, and I vow.

swow(e, swowȝ(e, swowgh(e, swowh: see SOUGH, SWOUGH.

†'**swowing**, *vbl. sb. Obs.* Forms: 1 **ȝeswowung, ȝeswoȝung,** 3 **swouing,** 4 **swohing,** 6 **swowyng.** [OE. *ȝeswoȝung*, noun of action corresp. to *ȝeswoȝen* SWOW *pa. pple.*: see -ING[1].] Swooning.

c **1000** *Sax. Leechd.* II. 160 Hu se hata omihta maȝa unȝemet þurst & swol þrowað..& ȝeswoȝunga. *Ibid.* 206 Se mon ȝeswoȝunga þrowað & modes ȝeswæþrunga. *a* **1290** *St. Eustace* 163 in Horstm. *Altengl. Leg.* (1881) 214 Þe kniȝt wes ney I-swowe..þo he hof swouing [*printed* swoning] aros [etc.]. *c* **1300** *K. Horn* 474 (Laud MS.) Þo reymyl þe ȝenge Com of hire swohinge [*other MSS.* swoȝning, swowenynge]. **1525** tr. *Brunswyke's Handywork Surg.* xv. Dj, Spasmus whiche is yᵉ crampe or Cincopis that is the swowyng.

swown(e, obs. forms of SWOON.

swown(e)s, variants of SWOUNDS.

swoyr, obs. Sc. pa. t. of SWEAR *v.*

swozzle, var. SWAZZLE.

swre, swth, swt(t)e, obs. ff. SURE, SOOTH, SUIT *sb.*

swuc, swuc(c)h, swuer, swuff, swuft, swuling: see SUCH, SURE, SWOOF, SWIFT, SULING.

swum, pa. t. and pple. of SWIM *v.*

swung (swʌŋ), *ppl. a.* Also 5 **swonge(n.** [Pa. pple. of SWING *v.*[1]]

†**1.** *Cookery.* Beaten up. *Obs.*

c **1420** *Liber Cocorum* (1862) 36 Take swongen eyrene and floure þer to. *c* **1467** *Noble Bk. Cookry* (1882) 120 Grind raw pork and temper them with swonge egges.

2. Caused to oscillate; suspended; wielded with rotatory movement, etc.: see the verb.

1812 Sir T. Lawrence in Williams *Life & Corr.* (1831) I. 318 A wee modest cart, with an old higgler in it, sitting on a swung seat. **1908** Binyon *Lond. Visions* 14 Out of its slumber roused, intense, To the swung axe a demon calls.

3. ***swung dash***, a curved dash ~, used in dictionaries to stand for the headword of an entry or for a specified part of it.

In Oxford dictionaries first used in the first edition of *The Little Oxford Dictionary* (1930) but there called a tilde.

1951 *Conc. Oxf. Dict.* p. iii, In this edition..the swung dash has been freely employed. **1975** *Amer. N. & Q.* XIV. 60/1 *ER*, like most dictionaries, uses a swung dash to denote the entry word.

swunk (swʌŋk), *ppl. a. pseudo-arch.* [pa. pple. of SWINK *v.*] Wearied with toil; = SWINKED *ppl. a.*

1858 Hogg *Life Shelley* II. x. 353 His lively fancy had transmuted him into the swunk freedman.

swupple, swuttie: see SWIPPLE, SOOTY *a.*

swy (swaɪ). *Austral. slang.* Also **swi.** [ad. G. *zwei* two.] **1.** Two; *spec.* a two-shilling coin or a two-year prison sentence.

1924 *Truth* (Sydney) 27 Apr. 6 *Swy*, two. **1941** Baker *Dict. Austral. Slang* 75 *Swy*, the game of two-up. (2) A sentence of two years' gaol. (3) A florin. **1983** *Age* (Melbourne) 15 Dec. 13 (*caption*) Exhibition of used coin of the realm: bank notes, collector's items, swys, deaners, zacs, treys, brass razoos.

2. The game of two-up (see also quot. 1950). Also ***swy-up***.

1940 *Bulletin* (Sydney) 17 Jan. 34/3 The crown-and-anchor seminary he avoids; When swi-up's on, a different direction He takes. **1941** [see sense 1 above]. **1950** K. S. Prichard *Winged Seeds* 63 What set the whole town agog, though, was their attempt to visit the 'swy': the famous two-up ring on a sand hill near the old Rising Sun Inn. **1953** R. Braddon in I. Bevan *Sunburnt Country* 127 Swy is a game of chance, requiring the tossing of two or three pennies into the air and the betting of those who watch their rise and fall on whether they come down heads or tails. **1969** *Courier-Mail* (Brisbane) 24 Sept. 1/1 He said two-up (or swy) was Australia's national game. **1976** *Sunday Mail* (Brisbane) 24 Oct. 16/4 The police know they will never stop goldfielders playing swy.

3. *Comb.*, as **swy game**, a game of two-up; **swy school**, a group of persons who have gathered to play two-up.

1950 *Austral. Police Jrnl.* Apr. 118 *Swi*, 2s., but a swi-game is a two-up game. **1953** K. Tennant *Joyful Condemned* xxix. 284 There's all these little crims in the swi-game and the S.P. betting. **1969** *Telegraph* (Brisbane) 14 May 8/4 Otherwise they blow it at the pub, or at the swy game. **1921** *Aussie* 15 Mar. 54 Just done me last dollar up at the swi school. **1956** S. Hope *Diggers' Paradise* 59 Neither shalt thou play two-up for lucre in the street, nor attend such swy schools in any private or public premises.

swy, obs. form of SUE *v.*

Swyce, Swycer: see SWISS, SWISSER.

swych(e, Swycher, swycht, swye, swyer, swyfe, swyffit: see SUCH, SWISSER, SWITHE *adv.*, SWAY *v.*, SQUARE, SQUIRE, SWIVE.

swyȝe, swyith, swyk, swylk: see SWAY *sb.*, SWITHE *adv.*, SWILK.

swyle, swyll: see SWALE *sb.*[3], SWEAL *v.*, SWEEL *v.*, SWILL.

swyl(l)ing, obs. forms of SULING.

swynacy(e, -asy, -aysy, -esye, obs. ff. SQUINACY, quinsy.

swyneyed, var. SWEENIED *a.*

swyng, swynge, obs. ff. SUING, SWING, SWINGE.

swyper, -ir, etc., obs. ff. SWIPPER.

swyr(e, obs. ff. SQUIRE, SURE, SWIRE.

swyte, obs. form of SWEET.

swythare, variant of SIQUARE.

c **1375** *Sc. Leg. Saints* xxxiii. (*George*) 56 He..sla but bad quham-euir he fande In þat swythare hym nere-hande.

swyther, error for *swyper*, SWIPPER.

sy: see SAY *v.*[1], SEE *v.*, SIȜE *Obs.*

-sy, hypocoristic dim. suffix added to (i) proper names, as *Betsy, Patsy, Topsy*, also in the form *-cy*, as *Nancy*, (ii) common nouns, as *babsy, ducksy*, MOPSY, *petsy*, POPSY (*popsy-wopsy*). In adjectival formations expressing a degree of mocking contempt, as *artsy-and-craftsy, artsy-fartsy, backwoodsy, bitsy, booksy, folksy, itsy-bitsy, teensy*, etc., the suffix may be considered to represent a nursery form (cf. -Y[6]), or the *pl.* (or even a singular ending) in *-s* + -Y[1].

‖**syagush** ('sjɑːguːʃ). Also [7 **siyah-ghush**], 8 **siagush, shoegoose, shah goest, shargoss,** 9 **syah-gush.** [Urdū = Pers. *siyāh gosh* black ear. (Friar Jordanus, 14th cent., has the form *siagois*.)] The caracal, a feline animal.

[**1677** Charleton *Exercit. de Diff. et Nom. Anim.* 21 Inter alia nomina, Persice dicitur *Siyah-Ghush*, i.e. *Nigris auribus* prædita, Black-ear.] **1727** A. Hamilton *New Acc. E. Ind.* I. xi. 124 They hunt with Dogs, Leopards, and a small fierce Creature, called by them a Shoegoose. **1759** *Ann. Reg., Chron.* 119/2 A very beautiful and uncommon animal, lately arrived from the East Indies,..is lodged in the Tower. It is called, in the Indostan language, a Shah Goest. **1774** Goldsm. *Nat. Hist.* II. 322 All animals of this kind pursue in a pack... The jackall, the syagush, the wolf, and the dog, are of this kind. *a* **1793** J. Hunter *Ess. & Observ. Nat. Hist.* etc. (1861) II. 50 Of the Shargoss. This animal is about the size of a common fox. It is of the genus of the cats. **1813** J. Forbes *Oriental Mem.* I. x. 277 The Moguls train another beast for antelope-hunting, called the syah-gush.

syar, obs. f. SIRE *sb.*

syaticke, obs. f. SCIATIC.

syb, obs. form of SIB.

sybarite ('sɪbəraɪt), *sb.* and *a.* Also 7 **Siberite, -arite, -aryte,** and with capital initial. [ad. L. *Sybarīta*, ad. Gr. Συβαρίτης, f. Σύβαρις Sybaris (see below). Cf. F. *Sybarite*.]

A. *sb.* **1.** (With capital initial.) A native or citizen of Sybaris, an ancient Greek city of southern Italy, traditionally noted for its effeminacy and luxury.

1598 Bp. Hall *Sat.* v. ii. 58 All dumb and silent, like the dead of night, Or dwelling of some sleepy Sybarite. **1599** Nashe *Lenten Stuffe* Wks. 1905 III. 189 *margin*, The Sybarites neuer woulde make any banquet vnder a twelue-moneths warning. **1601** R. Johnson *Kingd. & Commw.* (1603) 64 The pleasure of Tarent and the soile of the Siberites were inchantments sufficient to make men effeminate. **1660** Stanley *Hist. Philos.* IX. *Pythagoras* xi. (1687) 499/2 The Crotonians joyning with the Sybarites and the Metapontines, determined to expel the rest of the Grecians out of Italy. **1787** Beckford *Lett. Italy* xxix. (1805) I. 291, I have some noisy tradesmen near me, that the Sybarites would not have permitted in their city. **1834** K. H. Digby *Mores Cath.* v. vi. 182 The Sybarites of old would not allow a cock to be in their city, lest it should disturb their matutinal slumbers.

2. A person devoted to luxury or pleasure; an effeminate voluptuary or sensualist.

1623 Drumm. of Hawth. *Flowres of Sion, Hymne True Happinesse* 44 Fraile Beautie to abuse, And (wanton Sybarites) On past or present touch of sense to muse. **1628** Le Grys tr. *Barclay's Argenis* 41 Not to haue their stables full, (as in an Army of Sibarytes) of capreoling Horses. **1809** Mrs. Jane West *The Mother* (1810) 35 Some feeble Sybarite, Pain'd by a crumpled rose-leaf. **1820** Byron *Mar. Fal.* III. ii. 160 The Lords of Lacedæmon were true soldiers, But ours are Sybarites. **1863** Miss Braddon *J. Marchmont* III. i. 7 It was a handsome room, certainly—the very room for an artist and a sybarite. **1880** DISRAELI *Endym.* xxxvii, The dinner was refined, for Mr. Bertie Tremaine combined the Sybarite with the Utilitarian sage.

transf. **1852** H. ROGERS *Ecl. Faith* (1853) 30 'This,' said I, 'is the plea of intellectual Sybarites.'

B. *adj.* = SYBARITIC.

1599 NASHE *Lenten Stuffe* Wks. 1905 III. 189 Hydra herring will haue euery thing Sybarite dainty, where he lays knife aboord. **1608** TOPSELL *Serpents* 227 So great is the poyson of the Sibarite Scorpion, that the dung thereof being trode vppon breedeth vlcers. **1660** STANLEY *Hist. Philos.* IX. *Pythagoras* xvii. (1687) 504/1 These Sybarite-Ambassadors. **1831** YOUATT *Horse* iv. 43 The Sybarite horses began to dance. **1838** PRESCOTT *Ferd. & Is.* (1846) I. xi. 454 This Sybarite indulgence.. does not seem to have impaired the martial spirit of the nobles. **1897** GUNTER *Ballyho Bey* xv. 178 Irene Vannos, even as she fans her sybarite mistress, falls fainting on the deck.

So **'sybarism**, sybaritism; **'sybarist**, a sybarite; **'sybarital** *a.*, sybaritic; † **sybaritan** [L. *Sybarītānus*] *a.* and *sb.* = SYBARITE; **'sybaritish** *a.* (also 7 *erron.* **sabar-**), sybaritic; **'sybaritism**, sybaritic habits or practices, effeminate voluptuousness.

1889 B. WHITBY *Awakening Mary Fenwick* II. vii. 169, I am ashamed of your selfish *sybarism! **1652** N. CULVERWEL *Lt. Nature* I. xvii. (1661) 153 The soft *Sybarist.. complain'd in the morning of his weariness. **1839** J. E. READE *Deluge*, etc. 149 Soft abandonment to ease, reclining In *Sybarital luxury. **1607** TOPSELL *Four-f. Beasts* 310 Where-upon the *Sibaritan horsses came running & dancing among their aduersaries. **1608** D. T[UVILL] *Ess. Pol. & Mor.* 118 That speech of the Sibaritans, concerning the Lacedæmonians austerer kind of living. **1631** R. H. *Arraignm. Whole Creature* v. 32 That abound in all Asian luxuries, and more than *Sabaritish delights. *a* **1656** HALES *Gold. Rem.* I. (1673) 67 All this is but out of a Sybaritish ridiculous daintiness. **1821** *Examiner* 253/1 Sybaritish enjoyment. **1883** W. E. NORRIS *No New Thing* II. xiii. 4 We sit.. hugging ourselves in a sybaritish contentment. **1840** G. DARLEY *Wks. Beaum. & Fl.* Introd. (Rtldg.) p. xxiii, It is quite a mistake to imagine *Sybaritism did not commence in England till the reign of Charles the Second, when it was rather at its climax. **1870** *Echo* 9 Nov., Modern Republics like ancient Carthage swim in gold and sybaritism.

sybaritic (sɪbə'rɪtɪk), *a.* Also 7 *erron.* **Sabariticke**, and with capital initial. [ad. L. *Sybarīticus*, ad. Gr. *Συβαρῖτικός*, f. *Συβαρίτης* SYBARITE.]

1. (With capital initial.) Of or pertaining to Sybaris or its inhabitants.

Sybaritic fables (Gr. *λόγοι Συβαριτικοί, ἱστορίαι Συβαριτικαί*), a class of fables or stories which appear to have been concerned only or mainly with human beings and to have involved humorous or ridiculous situations or conversations.

1786 POLWHELE tr. *Theocritus, Idyl.* v. (1792) II. Notes 100 Long after the destruction of the old Sybaritic republic. **1840** tr. *C. O. Müller's Hist. Lit. Greece* xi. §15. 145 The Sybaritic fables mentioned by Aristophanes [*Wasps*]. *Ibid.*, Doubtless, therefore, the Sicilian poet Epicharmus means, by Sybaritic apophthegms, what others call Sybaritic fables. **1889** J. JACOBS *Æsop* I. 203 It is possible that the collections on which we are commenting have a connection.. with the 'Sybaritic Jests'.

2. Characterized by or devoted to excessive luxury; effeminately luxurious.

1619 H. HUTTON *Follie's Anat.* B iv b, His belly is a Cesterne of receit,.. A Sabariticke Sea, a depthlesse Gulfe. **1759** WARBURTON *Let. to Hurd* 30 Jan., On the 4th, I shall get to town, when I hope you will dine with me on a single dish, to atone to Philosophy for the Sybaritic dinners of Prior-Park. **1835** MARRYAT *Olla Podr.* III. 252 The Sybaritic sheet of finest texture. **1849** THACKERAY *Lett.* (1887) 56 It was a Sybaritic repast, in a magnificent apartment, and we were all of us young voluptuaries of fashion. **1876** *World* V. No. 117. 12 They do what they please,.. and inhale an atmosphere of sybaritic enjoyment.

sybaritical (sɪbə'rɪtɪkəl), *a.* Now *rare.* [f. L. *Sybarīticus*: see prec. and -ICAL.] = prec.

a **1617** HIERON *Aarons Bells* (1623) 14 Their Sybaritical feasts and banquets consecrated to Flora. **1621** BURTON *Anat. Mel.* I. ii. III. xiii, Those prodigious prodigals, & mad Sybaritical spendthrifts. **1651** H. MORE *Second Lash* in *Enthus. Tri.*, etc. (1656) 214 Clothed with transparent lawns or sybaritical tiffanies. **1725** BAILEY *Erasm. Colloq.* (1878) I. 112 *Ch.* If you will have me, I'll make a Sybaritical Appointment... *Pe.* What Appointment is that? *Ch.* The Sybarites invited their Guests against the next Year, that they might both have Time to be prepar'd. **1898** L. STEPHEN *Stud. Biogr.* II. iv. 145 They.. became soured, or mildly.. sybaritical.

Hence **syba'ritically** *adv.*, voluptuously.

1846 *Blackw. Mag.* LX. 84 We battened sybaritically. **1897** *Daily News* 7 Oct. 6/5 Our quarters here are nothing less than sybaritically luxurious.

So † **sybaritican** *a.*

1623 COCKERAM, *Sybaritican-meale*, a rich costly meale. **1671** H. M. tr. *Erasm. Colloq.* 103, I see an Epicurean dinner, that I say not a Sybaritican.

Sybil, etc.: see SIBYL, etc.

sybotic (saɪ'bɒtɪk), *a. rare* (*affected*). [ad. Gr. *συβωτικός*, f. *συβώτης* swineherd.] Pertaining to a swineherd or his occupation. So **sybotism** ('sɪbətɪz(ə)m), the tending of swine.

1876 *Daily Tel.* 4 Dec. (Cassell's). He was twitted with his sybotic tendencies,.. and was asked what a scholar and a gentleman could possibly see in a fat hog. *Ibid.*, Sybotism.

sybow ('saɪbəʊ). *Sc.* Forms: 6 **sebowe**, *pl.* **sybees, sybbow**, 7 *pl.* **sybeis**, 8 *pl.* **sybouse**, 8– **sybo**, 9 **seybo(w, se(i)bow, sibow, syboe, sibba, saybee, seybie**, 7– **sybow**. [Sc. variant of CIBOL, CIBOULE, q.v.] Orig. = CHIBOL 1; now, a young or spring onion with the green stalk attached = CHIBOL 2.

1574 in Row *Hist. Kirk* (Wodrow Soc.) 50 That teind sybbows, leeks, kaill, and onyons, be discharged. **1580** *Min.* in D. D. Black *Hist. Brechin* iii. (1867) 44, 40*s.* resting of £8 due James Watt for Sybees that grew in his yard. **1653** *Culross Session Minutes*, Cited for pulling sybows on the Lords Day. **1659** *Melrose Regality Rec.* (S.H.S. 1914) 218 [The agreed-on price of] certane sybeis [bought from him]. *a* **1682** SEMPILL *Blythsome Wedding* 55 With sybows and rifarts and carlings. **1727** P. WALKER *Semple* Biog. Presbyt. (1827) I. 162, I have beheaded your Duke like a Sybow. **1818** SCOTT *Old Mort.* xxxii, The head's ta'en aff them, as clean as I wad bite it aff a sybo. **1819** W. TENNANT *Papistry Storm'd* (1827) 39 Sebows and leeks.

attrib. **1752** *Records of Elgin* (New Spald. Cl. 1903) I. 462 Ilk firkin of onions or sybowheads 9^{d}. **1786** BURNS *Ep. to M'Adam* v, A lee dyke-side, a sybow-tail, And barley-scone, shall cheer me.

sybrade, -brede, etc., obs. ff. SIBRED.

syc, obs. form of SIC, SIKH.

sycamine ('sɪkəmɪn, -aɪn). *arch.* [ad. Gr. *συκάμῖνον* mulberry, *-ος* mulberry tree (late L. *sycamīnus*), ad. Heb. *shiqmah* (Aram. pl. *shiqmīn*), with assimilation to *σῦκον* fig.] The common black mulberry, *Morus nigra.*

1526 TINDALE *Luke* xvii. 6 Yf ye.. shulde saye vnto thys sycamyne tree [so **1611**] plucke thy silfe vppe by the rotes and plant thy silfe in the see. [**1849** BALFOUR *Man. Bot.* §1023 The Mulberry is the *συκαμινος*, or Sycamine-tree of the New Testament.]

sycamore, sycomore ('sɪkəmɔə(r)). Forms: 4–7 **sicamour**, (4 **sika-, sicomour, sicomore, syca-, sykamoure**, 5 **sycomour, -owre, secomoure, sichomure, cicomour, cycomyr, sygamour(e)**, 6–7 **siccamore, sycamour**, (6 **segamore**, 7 **sicamor(e, cycamore**), 4– **sycomore**, 7– **sycamore**. [a. OF. *sic(h)amor*, *-more*, later *sicomore*, mod.F. *sycomore*, = It., Sp., Pg. *sicomoro*, ad. late L. *si-*, *sycomorus*, ad. Gr. *σῡκόμορος*, f. *σῦκον* fig + *μόρον* mulberry. The spelling *sycamore* is the more usual, but *sycomore* is retained in mod. edd. of the Bible, and is used by some writers in sense 1 for the sake of distinction.]

1. A species of fig-tree, *Ficus Sycomorus*, common in Egypt, Syria, and other countries, and having leaves somewhat resembling those of the mulberry.

13.. *Propr. Sanct.* (Vernon MS.) in Herrig's *Archiv* LXXXI. 319/14 In to a treo he wente þerfore, A Sikamour, to seon him þore. **1388** WYCLIF *Isaiah* ix. 10 Thei han kit doun sicomoris. *a* **1400–50** *Wars Alex.* 4973 Oleues out of lebany.. With sichomures & sipresses. *c* **1440** *York Myst.* xxv. 427 A nobill tree þou secomoure. **1530** PALSGR. 269/2 Sicomer, frute. Sicomour, tree. **1601** HOLLAND *Pliny* XIII. vii. I. 389 The Sycomore.. is called the Ægyptian Figtree. The tree for leafe, bignesse, and barke, is like unto the Mulberie tree. **1633** G. HERBERT *Temple, World* iii, That Sycomore, Whose leaves first sheltred man from drought and dew. **1720** POPE *Iliad* XXI. 44 As from a sycamore, his sounding steel Lopp'd the green arms to spoke a chariot-wheel. **1867** BAKER *Nile Tribut.* i. (1872) 3 We climbed the steep sandy bank and sat down beneath a solitary sycamore. **1910** MRS. H. M. TIRARD *Bk. of Dead* iii. 73 In Egypt sycomores often grow on the edge of the desert.

2. A large species of maple, *Acer Pseudo-platanus*, introduced into Britain from the Continent, and grown as a shady ornamental tree and for its wood.

Also with distinguishing adj., ***bastard, false, vulgar sycamore***.

1588 SHAKS. *L.L.L.* v. ii. 89 Vnder the coole shade of a Siccamore, I thought to close mine eyes some halfe an houre. **1653** WALTON *Angler* iv. 121 We.. sate as quietly.. under this Sycamore, as Virgils Tityrus and his Melibœus did under their broad beech tree. **1657** S. PURCHAS *Pol. Flying-Ins.* I. xv. 94 Sycomore, or great Maple. **1728** BRADLEY *Dict. Bot.*, *Sycamore vulgar*, i.e. Acer majus. **1760** J. LEE *Introd. Bot.* App. 329 Sycamore, False, *Acer.* **1765** GRAY *Lett., to Wharton* (1912) III. 84 The enclosures, that surround the house, are border'd with 3 or 4 ranks of sycomores, ashes, & white poplars of the noblest height. **1777** LIGHTFOOT *Flora Scot.* (1789) 639 The Great Maple, or Bastard Sycomore. **1850** TENNYSON *In Mem.* lxxxix, Thou, with all thy breadth and height Of foliage, towering sycamore. **1889** A. C. BENSON *Altar Fire* (1907) 89 There were many ancient elms and sycamores forming a small park.

3. a. In N. America, a plane or tree of the genus *Platanus*, esp. the buttonwood, *P. occidentalis.*

1814 PURSH *Flora Amer. Septentrionalis* 635 *Platanus occidentalis*... On the banks of rivers: Canada to Florida, and in Louisiana... This tree is known by the name of Button-wood, Water Beech, Sycamore and Plane Tree; in Canada Cotton Tree. **1872** SCHELE DE VERE *Americanisms* 413 Buttonwood.. The tree is known also as Sycamore and Plane-Tree.

b. In Australia and elsewhere applied (with or without epithet) to various trees: see quots.

1866 *Treas. Bot.* s.v. *Melia*, *M[elia] Azedarach*, vulgarly known as the Pride of India, False Sycamore, Holy-tree. *Ibid.*, Sycamore.. New South Wales. *Brachychiton luridum.* **1889** MAIDEN *Usef. Pl. Australia* 368 *Achras laurifolia*.. Called 'Sycamore' in Southern New South Wales. *Ibid.* 410 *Cryptocarya obovata*.. 'Sycamore', 'White Sycamore', 'Bastard Sycamore'. **1898** MORRIS *Austral Eng.* s.v. *Laurel*, Native L[aurel].. *Panax elegans*.. also called Light or White Sycamore.

4. The wood or timber of the sycamore (usually in sense 2).

c **1384** CHAUCER *H. Fame* III. 188 Ther saugh I Colle tregetour Vpon a table of Sygamour Pley an vncouthe thynge to telle. *a* **1500** *Eger & Grine* 971 in Furniv. & Hales *Percy Folio* I. 384 His sadle with sekamoure [*printed* selc-] was sett. **1506** *Paston Lett.* III. 408 A payre of beddes of segamore. **1842** GWILT *Archit.* §1724 Old houses.. floored with sycamore and wainscotted with poplar.

5. Short for *sycamore-moth* (see 6).

1843 WESTWOOD *Brit. Moths* I. 193 *Apatela aceris* (the sycamore). **1869** NEWMAN *Brit. Moths* 251/2 The Sycamore (*Acronycta Aceris*)... This caterpillar feeds on the sycamore (*Acer pseudoplatanus*).

6. *attrib.* and *Comb.*, as ***sycamore fruit, key*** (KEY *sb.*[1] 14), ***leaf***; **sycamore-fig**, the fig-tree *Ficus Sycomorus*, or its fruit; † **sycamore-locust** (see quot.); **sycamore maple** = sense 2; **sycamore(-tussock)-moth**, a noctuid moth, *Acronycta (Apatela) aceris*, the larva of which feeds on the sycamore (sense 2).

1615 G. SANDYS *Trav.* 121 Variety of excellent fruites; as orenges, lemons, pomegranats,.. *Sicamor figs. **1861** BENTLEY *Man. Bot.* 639 The Sycamore Fig is said to have yielded the wood from which mummy-cases were made. **1899** MARG. BENSON & GOURLAY *Temple of Mut* i. 3 Groves of palm mingled with the thicker foliage of the sycamore-fig and tamarisk. **1611** *Bible* Amos vii. 14, I was an heardman, and a gatherer of *Sycomore fruit. **1657** AUSTEN *Fruit Trees* I. 138 Setting.. Ash-keyes, *Cycamore-keyes. **1664** POWER *Exp. Philos.* I. 32 The Sycomore-Locust.. is a pretty little yellow Insect, which is bred, and feeds on the *Sycomore-leaves, which at first hath no wings, but six leggs and two horns. **1712** tr. *Pomet's Hist. Drugs* I. 154 The Leaves are a little less than the Sicamore Leaves. **1887** W. PHILLIPS *Brit. Discomycetes* 198 Wherever decaying sycamore-leaves are found. **1664** *Sycamore locust [see *sycamore leaf* above]. **1796** WITHERING *Brit. Plants* (ed. 3) II. 369 Sycamore Tree. *Sycamore Maple. **1833** *Penny Cycl.* I. 76/2 *Acer striatum*, the striped-bark maple.. frequently grows to thrice its native size, in consequence of being grafted upon the sycamore maple. **1753** CHAMBERS *Cycl. Suppl.*, **Sycamore-moth*,.. a peculiarly large and beautiful moth,.. so called, from its caterpillar feeding on the leaves of the sycamore. **1861** MORRIS *Brit. Moths* II. 73 *Acronycta Aceris.* Sycamore Moth... It feeds on the sycamore and the horse-chesnut. **1749** B. WILKES *Eng. Moths & Butterflies* 32 The *Sycamore Tussock-Moth. You may find the Caterpillars on Sycamore Trees. **1832** J. RENNIE *Butterfl. & M.* 78 The Sycamore Tussock (*Apatela Aceris*, Stephens) appears the end of June. **1854** RONALDS & RICHARDSON *Chem. Technol.* (ed. 2) I. 195 *Sycamore wood.

'sycamore-tree. = prec. (in various senses).

13.. *Propr. Sanct.* (Vernon MS. fol. ccxxvii.) þis ilke Sicomours [*sic*] tre In wȝuche clomb vp Zachee. **1382** WYCLIF *Luke* xix. 4 He rennynge bifore, stiȝede in to a sycamoure [**1388** sicomoure] tree. **14..** *Nom.* in Wr.-Wülcker 715/43 *Hic cicomorus*, a cycomyrtre. **1597** GERARDE *Herbal* III. cxii. 1300 The great Maple, not rightly called the Sycomore tree.. is a stranger in England. *a* **1600** in Chappell *Pop. Music* (1855) I. 207 The poor soul sat sighing by a sicamore tree. **1611** *Bible* Ps. lxxviii. 47 He destroyed their vines with haile: and their Sycomore trees with frost. **1872** SCHELE DE VERE *Americanisms* 413 Buttonwood is the popular name of the so-called Sycamore-tree (*Platanus occidentalis*). **1898** MORRIS *Austral Eng.*, *Sycamore Tree*... In New South Wales, the name is given to *Brachyc[h]iton luridus.* **1908** R. M. WATSON in *Athenæum* 4 Apr. 418/3 The west shone pale through the boughs of the sycamore tree As the rooks sailed home to their haunt in the dusky park.

syce, sais (saɪs). Forms: 7 **seis**, 7–8 **seise**, 7– **sais**, 8 **scise**, 9 **sayse, sâees, saice, sice, syce**, 20 **saïs**. [ad. Arab. *sā'is*, f. *sūs* to tend a horse; in the 18th and 19th centuries, adopted from Hindustani into Anglo-Indian use.] In parts of Africa and Asia, and esp. in India, a servant who attends to horses, a groom; also, an attendant who follows on foot a mounted horseman or a carriage.

1653 GREAVES *Seraglio* 141 The.. Master of the horse hath the charge.. of all his other horses, mules, camels, and all his cattle.. having.. many ordinary grooms which are to look to them, and see that the Seises keep them in good case. **1675** COVEL in *Early Voy. Levant* (Hakluyt Soc.) 172, I had my servant, and a seis or groom, to look after my horse. **1779** in H. E. Busteed *Echoes Old Calcutta* (1882) 230 The bearer and scise.. came to the place where I was. **1815** MRS. SHERWOOD in *Life* xxvi. (1847) 437 The Sais, or horse-attendant,.. took charge of my horse. **1825** T. HOOK *Sayings* Ser. II. *Passion & Princ.* iii, The gallant aide-de-camp mounted his little Arabian, and followed by his sice at full speed, galloped away to head-quarters. **1832** MARRYAT *N. Forster* xxxviii, Syces were fanning the horses with their chowries. **1854** THACKERAY *Newcomes* lxvi, The Course is at Calcutta.. he calls his grooms *saices!* **1887** KIPLING *Plain Tales from Hills* (1888) 28 He.. deserved a V.C., if it were only for putting on a *sais*'s blanket. **1896** 'H. S. MERRIMAN' *Flotsam* xxii. 254 The carriages rolled up to the cathedral doors, and the syces.. cried frantically to the throng to make room. **1924** L. ECKENSTEIN *Tutankh-aten* ii. 24 The *saïses* running on either side of the chariots as only outrunners in Egypt can run. **1927** R. J. H. SIDNEY *In Brit. Malaya Today* 143 The Malay *saises* will all be playing cards. **1936** W. H. S. SMITH *Let.* 26 June in *Young Man's Country* (1977) ii. 11, I said good-bye to Peter and his sais yesterday morning. **1953** J. MASTERS *Lotus & Wind* viii. 113 I'll walk back to your bungalow with you. My sais can bring Beauty along. **1975** T. DINESEN *My Sister, Isak Dinesen* v. 56 The sais (horse-keeper) was to bring the horses up after us.

syce, obs. form of SICE, SIZE *sb.*[1], [3].

sycee (saɪ'siː). Also 8 **sisee, seze**. [Chinese *sí* (pronounced in Canton *sai, sei*) *sz'* fine silk: 'so called because, if pure, it may be drawn out into fine threads' (Giles in Yule and Burnell *Hobson-Jobson*).] Fine uncoined silver in the form of lumps of various sizes, usually having a banker's or assayer's seal stamped on them, formerly used by the Chinese as a medium of exchange. Also *sycee silver*.

1711 LOCKYER *Acc. Trade India* v. 135 Formerly they used to sell for Sisee, or Silver full fine;.. 10 Tale of Gold 93 fine, sold for 94 Tale weight of Sisee Silver is 7 above Touch. **1834** *Jrnl. Asiatic Soc. Bengal* App. 29 Sycee silver.. is the only approach to a silver currency among the Chinese. **1865** RENNIE *Peking & Pekingese* II. 116 The purchase money consisting of sixty-two shoe-shaped ingots of Sycee silver. **1882** *'Fan Kwae' at Canton* 58 Shroffs were also 'changers'—providing when required either Sycee, chopped dollars, or gold—as well as bankers.
attrib. **1875** JEVONS *Money* xii. 148 Either rupees as in India, sycee bars as in China, or silver dollars.

sycers, obs. f. SCISSORS.

sych(e, obs. ff. SIGH, SUCH.

sychare, variant of SIQUARE *Obs.*
c **1375** *Sc. Leg. Saints* vi. (*Thomas*) 382 þane al þe sek men, þat come þare, Parfyt heyle gat in þat sychare.

sycher, obs. form of SICKER *a.*

sychnocarpous (sɪknəʊˈkɑːpəs), *a. Bot.* [f. Gr. συχνός many + καρπός fruit + -OUS.] Bearing fruit many times, as a perennial plant; polycarpous.
1832 LINDLEY *Introd. Bot.* 401 *Polycarpous* (better *sychnocarpous*); having the power of bearing fruit many times without perishing.

sychon = *such a one*: see SUCH *dem. adj.* 28.

†**sycht**. *Sc. Obs. pl.* 'The front parts of a gown, coat, etc.' (Jam.).
Cf. *foirsycht, foirbreist* in Jam.
1542 *Inv. R. Wardr.* (1815) 101 Item ane schort gown of sad cramasy velvott lynit with quhyt taffateis the sychtis with quhyt letuis. **1543** *Acc. Ld. High Treas. Scot.* VIII. 187 Item, deliverit to lyne the sychtis thairof, v quarteris blak teffites of Janis. **1548** *Ibid.* IX. 222 Item, vj quarteris taffateis [of] foure thredis to lyne the sychtis of hir goun, xxiiijs.

sycht, obs. Sc. form of SIGHT.

syck(e, obs. ff. SICK, SIKE.

syclatoun, -owne, sycle, var. CICLATOUN, SICLE *Obs.*

sycoceric (sɪkəʊˈsɛrɪk, -ˈsɪərɪk), *a. Chem.* [f. Gr. σῦκον fig + κηρός wax + -IC.] Of, pertaining to, or derived from the waxy resin of an Australian species of fig, *Ficus rubiginosa*; as in ***sycoceric acid***, a crystalline compound, $C_{18}H_{28}O_2$; so ***sycoceric alcohol, aldehyde***. So **sycoˈceryl**, the hypothetical radical of the sycoceric compounds (also *attrib.*); hence **sycoceˈrylic** *a.* = sycoceric.
1860 DE LA RUE & MÜLLER in *Phil. Trans.* CL. 47 *Acetate of Sycoceryl.* We assign this name.. to the crystallizable substance.. obtained when the residue, left after the treatment of the original resin with cold alcohol, is dissolved in boiling alcohol, and the solution allowed to cool. *Ibid.* 50 The new alcohol which we propose to call Sycocerylic Alcohol. **1873** WATTS *Fownes' Chem.* (ed. 11) 791 Sycoceryl Alcohol is produced by the action of alcoholic soda on sycoceryl acetate.

†**ˈsycomancy.** *Obs.* Also 7 **-manty, sico-**. [f. Gr. σῦκον fig + μαντεία divination: see -MANCY.] Divination by means of figs or fig-leaves.
1652 GAULE *Magastrom.* xix. 166 Sycomancy, [divining] by Figgs. *a* **1693** *Urquhart's Rabelais* III. xxv. 209 By Sicomancy; O Divine Art in Fig-tree Leaves! [**1895** ELWORTHY *Evil Eye* 445 Conjuring with fig leaves was called sycomancy.]

sycomore: see SYCAMORE.

sycon (ˈsaɪkɒn). *Bot.* [a. Gr. σῦκον fig.]
†**1.** = SYCONIUM. *Obs.*
1845 *Encycl. Metrop.* VII. 51/1 A sycon is a fleshy, concave receptacle surrounding the fruits.., which are numerous, small, and distinct. **1900** B. D. JACKSON *Gloss. Bot. Terms* 262/1 Sycon.. a multiple hollow fruit, as that of the fig.
2. [Adopted as a generic name by A. Risso, *Hist. Nat. Europe Méridionale* (1826) V. 368.] A calcareous sponge of the genus of this name; also, a stage in the development of sponges in which flagellated chambers are developed and lined with choanocytes.
1882 W. J. SOLLAS in P. M. Duncan *Cassell's Nat. Hist.* VI. 326 A transitional series of species can be shown to exist between a simple Ascon and a Sycon in which radiate buds have all united.. to form a complex tubulated wall. **1912** *Phil. Trans. R. Soc.* B. CCII. 170 The normal young Sycon has a beautiful double ascular crown of long monaxons. **1932** BORRADAILE & POTTS *Invertebrata* iii. 113 The three grades of sponge structure.. are known as the 'Ascon', 'Sycon', and 'Leucon' grades.

‖**syconium** (saɪˈkəʊnɪəm). *Bot.* [mod.L., f. Gr. σῦκον fig: see also SYCON.] A multiple fruit developed from numerous flowers imbedded in a fleshy receptacle, as in the fig.
1856 HENSLOW *Dict. Bot. Terms, Syconium, Syconus.* **1880** GRAY *Struct. Bot.* vii. §2 (ed. 6) 303 The Syconium.. results from a multitude of flowers concealed in a hollow flower-stalk,.. which becomes pulpy and edible when ripe.

‖**syconus** (saɪˈkəʊnəs). *Bot.* [mod.L., f. Gr. σῦκον fig.] = SYCONIUM.
1832 LINDLEY *Introd. Bot.* 180 *Syconus*.. a fleshy rachis, having the form of a flattened disk, or of a hollow receptacle, with distinct flowers and dry pericarpia. **1861** BENTLEY *Man. Bot.* 327 The *Dorstenia*.. is another example of the syconus, although it differs a good deal from the Fig in its general appearance.

sycophancy (ˈsɪkəfənsɪ, -fænsɪ). [ad. L. *sycophantia*, a. Gr. συκοφαντία, f. συκοφάντης SYCOPHANT.] The practice or quality of a sycophant.
1. The trade or occupation of an informer; calumnious accusation, tale-bearing. Now only in *Gr. Hist.*: see next, 1.
1622 BP. HALL *Contempl., N.T.* III. iv, It was hard to hold that seat [*sc.* the publican's] without oppression, without exaction: One that best knew it, branded it with poling, and sycophancy. **1721** BAILEY, *Sycophancy*.. false Dealing, false Accusation, Tale-bearing. **1808** MITFORD *Hist. Greece* xxi. §1. III. 18 That evil which, with the name of Sycophancy, so peculiarly infested Athens. **1850** GROTE *Greece* II. lxv. (1862) V. 562 Men (says Xenophon) whom every one knew to live by making calumnious accusations (called Sycophancy).
2. Mean or servile flattery; the character of a mean or servile flatterer.
1657 TRAPP *Comm. Esther* iii. 1 Whether it was also by flattery or sycophancy.. that Haman had insinuated himself into the Kings favour. **1742** RICHARDSON *Pamela* (1824) I. xcv. 472 The child will reject with sullenness all the little sycophancies that are made to it. **1821** SYD. SMITH *Wks.* (1867) I. 338 Abject political baseness and sycophancy. **1860** MILL *Repr. Govt.* (1865) 67/1 The people, like the despot, is pursued with adulation and sycophancy. **1873** DIXON *Two Queens* IV. XXII. ix. 225 Neither of these critics had the sycophancy to approve his lines.

sycophant (ˈsɪkəfənt, -fænt), *sb.* (*a.*) Also 6 (sicophanta), sichophant, 6–7 scico-, sico-, 7 sicco-, scyco-, 7–8 sycho- (9 syko-). [ad. L. *sycophanta*, ad. Gr. συκοφάντης, f. σῦκον fig + φαν-, root of φαίνειν to show. (Cf. F. *sycophante* (16th c.), †*sichophant*, It., Sp. *sicofanta*, Pg. *sycophanta*.)
The origin of the Gr. word, lit. = 'fig-shower', has not been satisfactorily accounted for. The explanation, long current, that it orig. meant an informer against the unlawful exportation of figs cannot be substantiated. It is possible that the term referred orig. to the gesture of 'making a fig' or had an obscene implication: cf. FIG *sb.*[2] (See Boisacq *Dict. Étym. de la langue grecque*.)]
1. *Gr. Hist.* One of a class of informers in ancient Athens: see quots. and etymology above.
1579–80 NORTH *Plutarch* (1595) 101 (*Solon*) Wee may not altogetehr discredite those which say, they did forbid in the olde time that men should carie figges out of the countrie of Attica, and that from thence it came that these picke thankes, which bewray and accuse them that transported figges, were called *Sycophantes.* **1656** STANLEY *Hist. Philos.* v. (1701) 171/1 Crobulus the Sycophant met him, accompanying Chabrias to the Tower, and said unto him, Do you come to help others, you know not that the poyson of Socrates is reserved for you? **1748** HUME *Ess., Inq. Hum. Underst.* xi, If Epicurus had been accused before the people by any of the sycophants or informers of those days. **1838** THIRLWALL *Greece* xxxi. IV. 181 A class of men who were universally odious,.. the informers, or sycophants as they were called at Athens, who had perverted the laws [etc.].
†**2.** *transf.* and *fig.* An informer, tale-bearer, malicious accuser; a calumniator, traducer, slanderer. *Obs.*
[**1537** CROMWELL in Merriman *Life & Lett.* (1902) II. 84 Whereas Michael Throgmerton.. hathe.. taken vppon him .. to become bothe a Sicophanta in Writing and a most vnkynde deuiser.. of thinges most.. traytorous against hys sayd Souereigne lorde.] *a* **1548** HALL *Chron., Hen. IV* 2 b, He.. was very glad (as tell tales and scicophantes bee..) to declare to the kyng what he had heard. **1561** B. GOOGE *Palingenius' Zodiac of Life* To Rdr., Who can scape the poisened lips of slandrous sicophants? **1612** T. TAYLOR *Comm. Titus* iii. 2. (1619) 568 As sycophants who make the scapes of men farre greater then they are. **1697** POTTER *Antiq. Greece* I. xxi. (1715) 122.
3. A mean, servile, cringing, or abject flatterer; a parasite, toady, lickspittle.
1575 GASCOIGNE *Glasse Govt.* Prol. 18 What subtile snares these Sycophants can use. *a* **1633** AUSTIN *Medit.* (1635) 224 Such is his [*sc.* the Pope's] power, attributed to him by his Sycophants that there can bee no Saints but of his making! **1702** ROWE *Tamerl.* I. i, A noble Freedom.. unknown to fawning Sycophants. **1736** BOLINGBROKE *Patriot.* (1749) 139 Crowds of spies, parasites and sycophants, will surround the throne under the patronage of such ministers. **1843** PRESCOTT *Mexico* II. i. (1850) I. 183 The young monarch was accompanied by a swarm of courtly sycophants. **1877** MRS. OLIPHANT *Makers Flor.* x. 252 The real sentiments of this great prince.. were very different from those of his sycophants.
†**4.** Vaguely used for: Impostor, deceiver. *Obs.*
1589 [? NASHE] *Almond for Parrat* 16 Am not I old *Ille ego qui quondam* at yᵉ besleeuing of a sichophant? **1606** CHAPMAN *Gentl. Usher* v. I 4 b, Presumptuous Sicophant, I will have thy life. **1651** WITTIE tr. *Primrose's Pop. Err.* 163 The good man Daniel Sennertus,.. being deceived by a Germane sycophant. **1653** GATAKER *Vind. Annot. Jer.* 13 It is not any spurious or seditious doctrine in their Teachers, by this foul-mouthed Sycophant, so falsely fathered upon Calvin. **1728** CHAMBERS *Cycl., Sycophant*,.. the term became used.. at last, for a Lyer, Imposter, &c.
5. *Comb.*, as ***sycophant-like*** adj.
1601 B. JONSON *Poetaster* v. iii. 112 An honest sycophant-like slaue. **1627** [R. NICCOLS] *Beggers Ape* B 3, With Sycophantlike trickes, hee tooke delight, With euery Iacke to play the Parasite.
B. *attrib.* or *adj.* Sycophantic.
1692 E. WALKER tr. *Epictetus' Mor., In praise Epictetus*, The bended knee Of Sycophant Servility. *a* **1700** EVELYN *Diary* 25 Mar. 1657, The Protector,.. now affecting Kingship, is petition'd to take the Title on him by all his new-made sycophant Lords. **1747** RICHARDSON *Clarissa* (1811) II. xxvi. 169 A sycophant creature. **1763** WILKES *Corr.* (1805) I. 236 This sycophant court language. **1847** C. BRONTË *Jane Eyre* Pref. to ed. 2, Ahab did not like Micaiah, because he never prophesied good concerning him..: probably he liked the sycophant son of Chenaannah better.

†**sycophant**, *v. Obs.* [f. prec.] *trans.* To act the sycophant towards. **a.** To slander, calumniate, traduce. **b.** To flatter meanly; also *intr.* to play the sycophant (= SYCOPHANTIZE 2). Hence †**sycophanting** *ppl. a.*
1637 HEYWOOD *Pleas. Dial.* xiv. Wks. 1874 VI. 230 Nor sycophant they us, such things to attaine By us. **1642** MILTON *Apol. Smect.* Wks. 1851 III. 261 By sycophanting and misnaming the worke of his adversary. **1674** *Govt. Tongue* viii. 150 His Sycophanting arts being detected. **1704** J. MACMILLAN in H. M. B. Reid *Cameronian Apostle* (1896) App. i. 223 A sycophanting age.

sycophantic (sɪkəˈfæntɪk), *a.* [ad. Gr. συκοφαντικός, f. συκοφάντης SYCOPHANT.]
a. Having the character of, or characteristic of, a sycophant; meanly flattering; basely obsequious. **b.** Calumnious, slanderous.
1676 ROW *Contn. Blair's Autobiogr.* xii. (1848) 547 The base sycophantic fools magnify and extol Sharp. **1782** V. KNOX *Ess.* lvii. (1819) II. 3 Mean, unprincipled, selfish, and sycophantic deceivers. **1801** MASON *Suppl. to Johnson, Sycophantick*, adj., tale bearing; maliciously officious. **1828** D'ISRAELI *Chas. I*, I. ix. 274 That sycophantic blasphemy, which the Court-bishops.. carried to an incredible excess. **1854** J. S. C. ABBOTT *Napoleon* (1855) II. i. 24 Upon sycophantic knees they bowed before the conqueror. **1870** BINNIE *Psalms* II. x. 348 Sycophantic divines have often made of it [*sc.* divine right] a flattering unction for the ears of princes.

†**sycoˈphantical**, *a. Obs.* [See prec. and -ICAL.]
1. Calumnious, slanderous.
a **1566** R. EDWARDS *Damon & Pithias* (1571) E iij b, Either you talke of that is done, or by your Sicophanticall enuye, You pricke forth Dionisius the sooner, that Damon may die. **1587** M. GROVE *Pelops & Hipp.* (1878) 6 A railing rout of Sycophanticall brablers. **1644** PRYNNE & WALKER *Fiennes's Trial* 11 Colonell Fiennes.. in a sycophanticall way alleadged, that we suspected the integrity of that Court.
2. Meanly flattering; basely obsequious.
1632 LITHGOW *Trav.* v. 217 Herod.. eaten of wormes, after the Sycophanticall people called his.. oration, the voyce of God. *a* **1716** SOUTH *Serm.* (1744) VIII. 192 They have.. suffered themselves to be cheated and ruined by a sycophantical parasite.

sycophantically (sɪkəˈfæntɪkəlɪ), *adv.* [See prec. and -ICALLY.] In a sycophantic manner; like a sycophant; in the way of mean flattery.
1643 *Necess. Christ. Subjection* 6 The States of England, as some of their Preachers.. have sycophantically phrased them. **1728** MORGAN *Algiers* I. iv. 90 Scurrilously railing against the triumphant Belisarius, yet most sycophantically adulating the half-desponding Gilimen. **1857** BORROW *Romany Rye* App. x, In these days, when it is dangerous to say anything about him but what is sycophantically laudatory.

sycophantish (ˈsɪkəfəntɪʃ, -fæntɪʃ), *a.* [f. SYCOPHANT *sb.* + -ISH[1].] Basely obsequious. Hence **ˈsycophantishly** *adv.*
1821 R. LEE *Diary* 20 Oct. (1897) 26 Mr. L. said that although he admired Sir W. Scott's talents, still there was something about him which he did not like—a sneaking, flattering, sycophantish manner. **1840** DE QUINCEY *Essenes* II. Wks. 1897 VII. 133 Vespasian was shrewd enough from the first to suspect him for the sycophantish knave that he was. **1847** —— *Sp. Mil. Nun* xxv, Neither proud.. nor sycophantishly and falsely humble. **1873** 'ANNIE THOMAS' *Two Widows* I. iii. 79 [He] vibrated between melodramatic reserve and sycophantish smiling.

ˈsycophantism. [f. as prec. + -ISM.] = SYCOPHANCY 2.
1821 V. KNOX *Spirit of Despotism* ix. (ed. 2) 22/2 Panic fears, servile sycophantism, and artful bigotry. **1831** *Fraser's Mag.* III. 204 Mr. Bulwer's sycophantism of the Editor.

ˈsycophantize, *v. rare.* [f. as prec. + -IZE.]
†**1.** *intr.* To utter malicious accusations; to slander, calumniate. *Obs.*
1634 BP. REYNOLDS *Shieldes of Earth* (1636) 32 The Accuser.. doth not informe, but sycophantize and calumniate.
2. To deal in mean or servile flattery. Hence **ˈsycophantizing** *vbl. sb.* and *ppl. a.*
1605 G. POWEL *Refut. Epist. Puritan Papist* To Rdr. *2 b, Thus they sycophantize; *Puissant Prince and orient Monarch.* **1631** R. H. *Arraignm. Whole Creature* xviii. 321 By Sycophantizing and observance, he might have beene a Favorite to Alexander. **1640** BASTWICK *Lord Bps.* App. L 3, His flattering and Sycophantising Prelates. **1709**

SACHEVERELL *Serm.* 15 *Aug.* 8 Scycophantizing Flattery. **1830** *Fraser's Mag.* I. 158 Dr Bowring should not sycophantise.

†'**sycophantly**, *a. Obs. rare*−1. [f. as prec. + -LY1.] = SYCOPHANTIC.

a **1680** in R. L'Estrange *Answ. Litter of Libels* 9 Sycophantly Knave.

'**sycophantly**, *adv. rare.* [f. SYCOPHANT *a.* + -LY2.] In the manner of a sycophant; sycophantically.

1672 PENN *Spir. Truth Vind.* 94 We deny not the use of *Master, Father, Son, Servant,* &c., when they are significantly, and not improperly and Sycophantly used. **1871** *Member for Paris* II. 13 Self-styled Democrats, who refuse homage to a king, but fawn sycophantly upon the mob.

†'**sycophantry.** *Obs.* [f. SYCOPHANT *sb.* + -RY.] = SYCOPHANCY.

1670 OWEN *Refl. Libel* Wks. 1853 XVI. 272 He seems to design himself an example in the art of sycophantry. *a* **1677** BARROW *Serm. Matt. vii. 1* Wks. 1687 I. 280 Rather backbiting, whispering, supplanting, or sycophantry, than fair and lawfull judging. **1705** HICKERINGILL *Priest-cr.* II. iii. 33 Princes..cajol'd..by Flattery and Sycophantry. **1728** MORGAN *Algiers* I. Pref. p. ii, This is no Sycophantry, no Adulation.

sycoretin (sɪkəʊ'riːtɪn). *Chem.* [f. Gr. σῦκον fig + ῥητίνη resin.] An amorphous white neutral substance obtained from the resin of an Australian species of fig (*Ficus rubiginosa*).

1860 DE LA RUE & MÜLLER in *Phil. Trans.* CL. 44. **1873** WATTS *Fownes' Chem.* (ed. 11) 791.

sycorie, -y, obs. forms of CHICORY.

c **1450** *M.E. Med. Bk.* (Heinrich) 146 Betoyne, hertestonge, sycory, violet, welcressen. **1565** COOPER *Thesaurus, Ambubeia,* the common sycorie [1538–52 ELYOT cykory(e] with the longe leafe and blew flower.

‖**sycosis** (saɪ'kəʊsɪs). *Path.* [mod.L., a. Gr. σύκωσις, f. σῦκον fig.]

1. Applied to various kinds of ulcer or morbid growth on the skin, resembling a fig. ? *Obs.*

1580 NEWTON *Approved Med.* 77 A certaine disease of the eye Lyddes which is called Sycosis. **1693** tr. *Blancard's Phys. Dict., Sycosis,* an Excrescence of the Flesh about the Fundament. 'Tis also an Ulcer so called from the resemblance of a Fig. **1820** GOOD *Nosology* 155 *Sycosis,* tumour excrescent; fleshy; fig-shaped.

2. An eruptive disease characterized by inflammation of the hair-follicles, esp. of the beard.

1822–7 GOOD *Study Med.* (1829) II. 352 Sycosis..is seated sometimes on the beard, and sometimes in the hair of the head. **1883–4** *Medical Annual* 23/1 Eczema of the chin and cheeks of adults..the non-parasitic sycosis of many writers.

sycur, obs. form of SICKER *a.*

syd, sydar, obs. ff. SIDE, CIDER.

Sydama, var. SIDAMO.

syddir, obs. f. CEDAR, CIDER.

syde, obs. f. SIDE *sb.*1, *adv.*1, *v.*1; var. SIDE *a.*

Sydenham ('sɪdənəm). *Path.* [The name of Thomas *Sydenham* (1624–89), English physician, who described the chorea in *Schedula Monitoria de Novæ Febris Ingressu* (1686).] *Sydenham's chorea*: a self-limited disorder of childhood or pregnancy that is a neurological manifestation of rheumatic fever, affecting the motor activities of the nervous system and characterized by involuntary movements.

1892 *Med. Record* (N.Y.) XLI. 285/2 There are many cases of Sydenham's chorea in which voluntary effort arrests the movements. **1954** *Handbk. for Mental Nurses* (ed. 8) vi. 162 Sydenham's Chorea. This, also known as St. Vitus's Dance, is..much commoner in girls than in boys. **1976** SMYTHIES & CORBETT *Psychiatry* vii. 128 Sydenham's chorea occurs in younger people, there is no family history, no dementia and the course is not progressive.

syder, -ir, obs. ff. CIDER.

syderal, -ation, -eal, -ite, obs. ff. SIDERAL, etc.

sydlop, sydlyng(s, obs. ff. SEEDLIP, SIDELING(S.

Sydnæan, var. SIDNEIAN *a.*

Sydney ('sɪdnɪ). [The name of the capital city of New South Wales.] **1.** In *Austral.* colloq. phr. ***Sydney or the bush***, all or nothing. Cf. BUSH *sb.*1 9.

1924 *Truth* (Sydney) 27 Apr. 6 *Sydney or the bush,* all or nothing. **1930** E. SHANN *Econ. Hist. Austral.* 365 'Sydney or the bush!' cries the Australian when he gambles against odds. **1970** R. BEILBY *No Medals for Aphrodite* 34 'Here we go,' Turk murmured grimly, climbing in behind the wheel. 'It's Sydney or the bush! Keep your fingers crossed.'

2. Special combinations. **a. Sydney-side** [SIDE *sb.*1 15 b], Sydney and the surrounding area; also as *adj.*; **Sydneysider**, a resident or native of Sydney or of New South Wales.

[**1872** W. M. HUGO *Hist. First Bushmen's Club in Austral. Colonies* 108 Very frequently, however, they are not allowed to proceed so far as the city, but get 'bailed up', as they call it on the Sydney side, before they reach their destination.] **1888** 'R. BOLDREWOOD' *Robbery under Arms* I. i. 1 My name's Dick Marston, Sydney-side native. **1928** 'BRENT OF BIN BIN' *Up Country* v. 67 She was..supposed to be..a descendant..of the famous Sydney-side sire 'Clifton'. **1941** BAKER *Dict. Austral. Slang* 75 *Sydneyside,* originally the area which is now N.S.W. Later, especially the area of Sydney. **1865** H. KINGSLEY *Hillyars & Burtons* III. xiii. 144 The Sydney-siders' loss is considered by him to have been far greater. **1931** *Times Lit. Suppl.* 1 Oct. 738/1 A fear of its [*sc.* Melbourne's] writers..echoed the nationalist emotion, but in abstract terms that lacked the appeal of the Sydneysiders. **1980** N. MARSH *Photo-Finish* vii. 199 He was a self-made man, a Sydneysider.

b. *Nat. Hist.* In the names of plants or animals associated with the region, as **Sydney blue gum**, a flooded gum, *Eucalyptus saligna*; **Sydney golden wattle**, a shrub or small tree, *Acacia longifolia*; **Sydney silky** (also **silkie**), a small stocky terrier of the breed so called, with long, silky, grey-blue fur and tan markings.

1932 R. H. ANDERSON *Trees N.S.W.* v. 101 Sydney Blue Gum... A tall-growing, shaft-like species. **1933, 1965** Sydney blue gum [see FLOODED *ppl. a.*]. **1909** A. E. MACK *Bush Calendar* 20 Flowers blooming [in September]. *Acacia longifolia.* Sydney golden wattle. **1976** *Hortus Third* (L. H. Bailey Hortorium) 6/1 Sydney golden wattle..flower heads in loose spikes. **1945** Sydney silky [see AUSTRALIAN *sb.* 3]. **1965** *Austral. Encycl.* III. 265/2 The Sydney silky, classed as a toy dog,..has a coat of steel-blue, silky hair up to 6 inches long, with a tan face, legs and points. **1977** *N.Z. Herald* 8 Jan. 4-9/7 (Advt.), Sydney silkie dog pups, 6 wks. old.

Sydnian, var. SIDNEIAN *a.*

sydre, sydur, obs. ff. CIDER.

sydyr, obs. f. CEDAR, CIDER.

†**sye, sie,** *sb.*1 *Obs.* or *dial.* Also 5 scye. [Of Scand. origin; cf. Norw. *si* (also *baatsi*) cowhair (and wool) or rope-fibre used for caulking.] Tow or oakum used for caulking; see also quot. 1866.

1295 *Acc. Exch. K.R.* 518 m. 2 (P.R.O.) Et vj. d. ob. in Sy. empto et filo inde faciendo pro dicta Galea obstupenda. **1495** *Naval Acc. Hen. VII* (1896) 153 For Sye and spynnyng of the same..vs. **1497** *Ibid.* 294 For here & Scye occupyed & layed in the Semys of the seid Ship. [**1866** EDMONDSTON *Shetland & Orkney Gloss., Sie,* a narrow strip of cloth which, after having been soaked in tar, is placed between the overlaps of a clinker-built boat.]

sye (saɪ), *sb.*2 *Obs.* exc. *dial.* Forms: 5 syhe, 6 syghe, 6, 9 sye, 7–9 seigh, sigh, 9 sey, si', sie. [f. SYE *v.*2, or a. ON. *sía* or MDu. *sye, sie* (Du. dial. *zië,* Flem. *zie, ziig,* †*sijghe*), corresp. to MLG. *sie, sihe, sige,* OHG. *sîha* (MHG. *sîhe,* G. *seihe* strainer, colander, filter, dregs):—OTeut. **sīχwōn*. OE. had *seohhe* sieve:—OTeut. **seχwōn*.]

1. A sieve, strainer (esp. for milk).

1468 *Medulla Gram.* in *Promp. Parv.* 79 *note, Colum,* a mylke syhe, or a clansynge syfe. **1688** HOLME *Armoury* III. 335/1 A kind of Wooden Dish with a large round hole in the bottom..by Milk Women called a Seigh; and having a Cloth tied about the hole, Milk runs through it, which takes away all hairs from the Milk; this in our Country is termed Seighing of Milk. **1846** J. BAXTER *Libr. Pract. Agric.* (ed. 4) I. 209 The whole mass..with the cream and new milk is run through the searce into the milk-sye.

b. *Comb.* (partly from SYE *v.*2) as *sye-bowl, -clout, -dish.*

1878 *N. & Q.* 5th Ser. X. 39/1 In Worcestershire a '*sigh-bowl' is the name of the implement used for straining milk. *a* **1650** *Bell My Wiffe* 30 in Furniv. & Hales *Percy Folio* II. 323 My cloake..is now but a *sigh clout, as you may see; It will neither hold out winde nor raine. **1562** *Lanc. Wills* (Chetham Soc.) II. 33 One skymmer ijd..one *syghe dyshe iijd. **1844** H. STEPHENS *Bk. Farm* III. 835 The milk..is passed through the milk-sieve, or sey-dish, as it is named.

2. A drop; also, a spot or stain made by a drop of liquid (cf. SYE *v.*2 2).

1781 J. HUTTON *Tour to Caves* (ed. 2) Gloss. (E.D.S.) *Sye, Sie,* a drop. **1838** HOLLOWAY *Prov. Dict., Sigh,* a drop. **1855** ROBINSON *Whitby Gloss.,* A *Sie,* a slightly soiled appearance on linen or paper.

sye, *v.*1 *Obs.* exc. *dial.* Forms: 1 sigan, 3 siȝe, sihe, sie, 3–5 seȝe, 4–5 sye, (4 seige ?, 5 syeȝe, cy(e, cygh, *3rd sing.* seis, 9 *dial.* sigh). *Pa. t.* α. 1–3 sah, (1 saag, sagh, *pl.* siȝon), 2–3 sæh, 3 seh, soh, 4–5 sey; β. 5 seit, seyt, seyit. *Pa. pple.* 1 siȝen, 3 isiȝe(n, isihen, 4 seȝen. [OE. *sīȝan,* pa. t. *sāh* (older *saag*), *siȝon,* pa. pple. *siȝen,* = MLG., MDu. *sîgen,* pa. t. *seeg, seech, seghen,* pa. pple. *gesehen* to sink (Du. *zijgen* intr. to sink down, droop), OHG. *sîgan,* pa. t. *sêg, sigen,* pa. pple. *sigen* to fall, fall in drops (MHG. *sîgen,* G. *seigen* to strain), ON. *síga* to sink gently down, glide, move slowly, pa. t. *seig, sé, sigum,* pa. pple. *siginn* (MDa. *sighe, sige* wk.).

The orig. meaning was prob. 'to fall in drops'; cf. the related forms L. *siat* makes water (= **sijat*:—**sigat*), OHG. *seihhen* to make water, ON. *sík, síki* ditch, trench, and Skr. *siñcáti, sécate* pours out, OSl. *sîcati* to make water, and SYE *v.*2, the forms of which in Engl. and the cognate langs. are often indistinguishable from those of this verb.]

1. *intr.* To sink, fall, descend (*lit.* and *fig.*); to collapse.

Beowulf 1251 (Gr.) Siȝon þa to slæpe. *c* **888** ÆLFRED *Boeth.* xxxiii. §5 Ne nanwuht eorðlices hi ne healt þæt hio ne siȝe. *c* **897** —— *Gregory's Past. C.* xix. 142 Ða men þe sigað on ðisses middanȝeardes lufan. *c* **960** *O.E. Chron.* (Parker MS.) an. 937, Siðþan sunne up on morgen tid..oð sio æþele ȝesceaft sah to setle. *c* **1200** *Trin. Coll. Hom.* 109 þe sunne..arist anes â daí and eft sigeð. *c* **1205** LAY. 10255 þa þe king sah to grunde. *Ibid.* 27635 His fule saule sæh in to helle. *a* **1330** *Otuel* 1393 He sey doun of his stede. *c* **1374** CHAUCER *Troylus* v. 182 For whan she gan here fader fer aspye, Wel neigh doun on here hors she gan to sye. *c* **1375** *Sc. Leg. Saints* xliii. (*Cecile*) 535 A bose, of wynd þat fillit ware, & with a prene Mocht out be latine..& seige [?], and to-giddire fal. *a* **1400–50** *Wars Alex.* 980 (Ashmole MS.) He seis [*Dubl. MS.* sittes] doune in þe sete with septer in hande. *c* **1400** *Destr. Troy* 6644 He gird to þat greke..þat he seyt to þe soile, & soght out of lyue. **1896** *Warwicksh. Gloss., Sigh,* to fade, decrease. 'This pimple's beginning to sigh.'

2. To go, proceed; *fig.* to proceed or come from a source, be derived.

Beowulf 307 (Gr.) Guman onetton, siȝon ætsomne. *c* **1052** *O.E. Chron.* (MS. C.) an. 1052, Godwine sah him æfre to werd Lundenes. *c* **1205** LAY. 23811 Seoððen þer gunnen ut siȝen sixti þusende Bruttes. *a* **1225** *Leg. Kath.* 2055 þet heaðene folc þet alle weren isihen hider. *c* **1230** *Hali Meid.* 47 Wið þene seli brudgume þet siheð alle selhðe of. *c* **1400** *Destr. Troy* 2512 Then he..Seyit furth with sory chere. *Ibid.* 7129 After settyng of þe Sun þai Seyn to þe ȝates. *a* **1400–50** *Wars Alex.* (Ashmole MS.) 2182 He seȝis to þe Synagog.

b. To come, arrive (*fig.* of a condition, time, etc.); *occas.* to befall, happen.

c **1205** LAY. 2918, & seoððen þer seh [*c* **1275** soh] toward swiðe muchel seorwe. *Ibid.* 4023 þa wes þe muchele speche ..of þare seoreȝe þe isiȝe wes to lond. *Ibid.* 4566 He þoðte heo to habben to his awere bihoue, & oðer weis hit sæht [? *read* sæh]. *Ibid.* 24043 þe dæi sæh to burhȝe þe Arður iset hafde. **13..** *Gaw. & Gr. Knt.* 1958 Til þe sesoun was seȝen, þat þay seuer moste. *c* **1400** *Destr. Troy* 3398 When yt seyit to Sopertyme.

c. *to sye hethen* (= hence) or *of life,* to depart this life, die.

13.. *Gaw. & Gr. Knt.* 1879 He..prayed hym..þat he wolde..lern hym..How his sawle schulde be saued, when he schuld seye heþen. *a* **1400–50** *Wars Alex.* 716 (Ashmole MS.) Wele semys slike a sacchell to syeȝe þus of lyfe! *Ibid.* 4333 Ne seȝes na segge of oure sede sodanly of lyue.

Hence **sying** *vbl. sb.*1, sinking, etc.

c **1400** *Promp. Parv.* 77/1 Cyynge downe, or swownynge (*P.* cyghinge or swonynge downe), *sincopacio.* *Ibid.* 455/2 Syynge downe, or swonynge, *sincopacio.*

sye, sie, *v.*2 *Obs.* exc. *dial.* Forms: 1 sion, seon, (*3rd pers. sing.* siid), 2 *pa. t.* seh, 4–5 (9 *dial.*) sie, 4–6 (9 *dial.*) sye, (5 syee, cy(e, sigh, 6 sighe), 7 seigh, 9 *Sc.* sey. [OE. *síon, séon* (:—**sīhan*), pa. t. *sáh,* pa. pple. *siȝen, siwen,* later *seowen, séon,* = MLG. *sîgen, sihen, sîen,* MDu. *sighen, sijghen, siën, ziën* (pa. t. *seech,* pa. pple. *gesegen, gesiet,* Du. *zijgen*), OHG. *sîhan,* pa. t. *sêh, siwan,* pa. pple. *gisigan* (MHG. *sîhen, sîgen,* pa. t. *seic, sigen,* pa. pple. *gesigen,* G. *seihen*), ON. *sía*:—OTeut. **sīχwan*. Cf. prec.]

1. *trans.* To strain, pass through a strainer; also, to strain out. †Also with *up.*

c **725** *Corpus Gloss.* (Hessels) E 461 *Excolat,* siid. *c* **1000** *Saxon Leechd.* III. 14 Seoh ðurh clað. *c* **1380** WYCLIF *Sel. Wks.* II. 383 Blynde leders, syynge þe gnatte and swolowe þe camel. *c* **1420** *Liber Cocorum* (1862) 17 Take swete mylk.. And sethe and sye hit thorowghe a cloth. **1523** FITZHERB. *Husb.* §146 Milke thy kye, socle thy calues, sye vp thy mylke. **1530** PALSGR. 717/2, I sye mylke, or clense, *je coulle du laict.* This terme is to moche northerne. **1559** MORWYNG *Evonym.* 392 Aromaticall wynes..the spyces beaten together, sighed and streined a few tymes through a streiner or Hippocras bag of wull. **1847** HALLIWELL, *Sie*..(4) to strain milk... It is still used in Derbyshire. **1895** PINNOCK *Black Country Ann.* (E.D.D.) To sye it thru a jelly bag.

2. *intr.* To drop as a liquid, drip, drain, ooze.

c **893** ÆLFRED *Oros.* I. vii. 38 þa wæron swiðe hreowlice berstende, & þa worms utsionde. *c* **1000** ÆLFRIC *Saints' Lives* xx. 64 Hi cwædon þa sume þæt se læce sceolde asceotan þæt geswell..and þær sah ut wyrms. *c* **1175** *Lamb. Hom.* 121 Mid þornene crune his heaued wes icruned swa þet þet rede blod seh ut. *c* **1440** *Pallad. on Husb.* XI. 326 And into a wyn barel doun let hem sie. **1450–1530** *Myrr. our Ladye* 108 That there shulde no thorrocke that myghte syee or droppe in therto. **1868** [see b].

b. *trans.* To mark or stain by dropping.

1855 ROBINSON *Whitby Gloss.* s.v. *Sie,* Not stained, but sied all over. **1868** ATKINSON *Cleveland Gloss., Sie, v.n.,* to drop, to mark by dropping.

Hence **sying** *vbl. sb.*2 and *ppl. a.*, straining; oozing, etc.

c **1000** *Saxon Leechd.* II. 314 Wiþ seondum geallan ete rædic. *c* **1440** *Promp. Parv.* 455/2 Syynge, or clensynge (*S.* syftynge, *P.* siffinge), *colacio, colatura.* **1450–1530** *Myrr. our Ladye* 109 A place in the bottome of a shyppe wherein ys gatheryd all the fylthe that cometh in to the shyppe, other by lekynge or by syinge in to yt by the bourdes. **1688** [see SYE *sb.*2 1].

sye, obs. pa. t. and pple. of SEE *v.*; obs. f. SIGH.

syecle, Syed, syege, syell(e: see SIECLE, SAYYID, SIEGE, SILE *sb.*1 and 2.

syen: see SCION, SEE *v.*, SYNE.

syence, -ens(e, obs. ff. SCIENCE.

syenite ('saɪənaɪt). *Min.* Also sienite. [ad. F. *syénite,* G. *syenit,* ad. L. *Syēnītēs* (*lapis*), (stone) of Syene, f. *Syēnē,* Gr. Συήνη, a town of upper Egypt, the modern Assouan.] A crystalline rock allied to granite, mainly composed of hornblende and feldspar, with or without quartz.

1796 KIRWAN *Elem. Min.* (ed. 2) I. 341 Sienite. An aggregate of quartz, hornblende, and felspar. **1813** BAKEWELL *Introd. Geol.* (1815) 116 The transitions by which granite passes into sienite, and the latter into porphyry, trap, and basalt. **1842** SEDGWICK in *Hudson's Guide Lakes* (1843) 230 The red syenite of Ennerdale and Buttermere. **1854** HOOKER *Himal. Jrnls.* II. xxix. 297 Enormous rounded blocks of syenite.

b. *attrib.* and *Comb.*

1832 DE LA BECHE *Geol. Man.* (ed. 2) 267 Granite and sienite mountains. **1835** R. GRIFFITH in *Trans. Geol. Soc.* (1840) Ser. II. V. 180 Syenite veins passing through mica slate. **1876** ELLEN E. FREWER tr. *Verne's Adv. 3 Eng. & 3 Russ. S. Afr.* viii. 66 Its [*sc.* the baobab's] syenite-coloured bark gave it a peculiar appearance.

syenitic (saɪə'nɪtɪk), *a.* Also si-. [f. prec. + -IC. So F. *syénitique*.] Of, pertaining to, composed of, allied to, or having the character of syenite.

1799 KIRWAN *Geol. Ess.* 343 The porphyritic and sienitic hills. **1835** R. GRIFFITH in *Trans. Geol. Soc.* (1840) Ser. II. V. 180 Two..veins of syenite, which pass into syenitic greenstone. **1868** WATTS *Dict. Chem.* V. 647 The occurrence of hornblende in granite renders it more or less syenitic.

Syenna, obs. var. SIENA.

syenodiorite (saɪənəʊ'daɪəraɪt). *Petrogr.* [f. *syeno-*, comb. form of SYENITE + DIORITE.] A plutonic rock of a kind intermediate between syenite and diorite, containing both alkali feldspar and plagioclase.

1917 A. JOHANNSEN in *Jrnl. Geol.* XXV. 89 Syenodiorite, syenogabbro, and granogabbro are introduced as new terms. **1940** *Bull. Geol. Soc. Amer.* LI. 1592 The laccolith near the abandoned wax factory on Fresno Creek..is composed of a striking augite syenodiorite. **1977** A. HALLAM *Planet Earth* 162/1 Color index rises to about 50 in the gabbros and is between 20 and 50 in the diorites and syenodiorites.

syepoorite ('saɪpʊəraɪt). *Min.* [f. *Syepoor* or *Saipūr*, in N.W. India, where found: see -ITE[1].] A native sulphide of cobalt, of a steel-grey colour inclining to yellow.

1849 J. NICOL *Min.* 458 *Syepoorite.* This name may be given to a sulphuret of cobalt,..found in primary rocks with pyrite and chalcopyrite at Syepoore near Rajpootanah.

syeppaling, syer, syeth, syeue: see SIPLING, SIRE, SYVER, SCYTHE, SIEVE *v.*

Syeud, variant of SAYYID.

syfe, syff(e, syfle, syfte, obs. ff. SIEVE, SIFFLE, SIFT.

syg, obs. pa. t. of SEE *v.*

sygalder, -drye, var. SIGALDER, -DRY *Obs.*

sygale, -alle, obs. ff. *cigale*: see CIGALA.

1484 CAXTON *Æsop* IV. xvii. 123 (*heading*) The xvij fable is of the Ant and of the sygale. *Ibid.*, This present fable, Of the sygalle, whiche in the wynter tyme..demaunded of the ant somme of her Corne for to ete.

sygge, obs. f. SAY *v.*

sygh(e, obs. pa. t. of SEE *v.*; obs. f. SIGH.

syght, syghth, sygle, sygn, obs. ff. SIGHT, SITH, SICKLE, SIGN.

sygneoury, sygnory, obs. ff. SIGNORY.

sygnet, -ett(e, obs. ff. CYGNET, SIGNET.

syh(e, obs. pa. t. of SEE *v.*; obs. f. SIGH.

syhedrite (saɪ'hiːdraɪt). *Min.* [Improperly for **syhadrite*, f. the Syhadree Mountains in Bombay, where found: see -ITE[1].] A mineral of uncertain composition, supposed to be related to stilbite.

1865 SHEPARD in *Amer. Jrnl. Sci.* Ser. II. XL. 110 Syhedrite. I have thus named, from its locality... The mineral occurs in trap at Thore-Ghat, in the Syhedree Mountains, Bombay.

syht, syhþ, obs. 3 sing. pres. of SEE *v.*

syhte, obs. f. SIGHT.

syide, syik, syike, obs. ff. SIDE, SIC, SICK, SIKE *sb.*[1]

syis, obs. f. SICE; Sc. pl. of SITHE *sb.*[1] *Obs.*; obs. Sc. f. SIZE *sb.*[1]

syister, obs. f. SISTER.

syith, obs. f. SCYTHE; Sc. var. SITHE *sb.*[1] *Obs.*

syk, obs. f. SIC, SICK, SIKE.

syke, obs. f. SEEK, SIC, SICK, SIKH; var. SIKE.

sykel(le, -ol, -yl(l, obs. ff. SICKLE.

syker(e, etc., **sykkyr**, obs. ff. SICKER.

Sykes (saɪks). The name of William Henry *Sykes* (1790–1872), English soldier and naturalist, used in the possessive in **Sykes'(s) monkey**, to designate *Cercopithecus albogularis*, a blue-grey guenon native to East Africa.

[**1831** *Proc. Zool. Soc.* 105 Major Sykes subsequently called the attention of the Committee to a Monkey presented by him to the Society.] **1864** *Ibid.* 709 Sykes's Monkey. **1905** [see MONKEY *sb.* 1 b]. **1914** R. C. F. MAUGHAM *Wild Game in Zambezia* xi. 252 Sykes' Monkey is a comparative rarity. **1932** S. ZUCKERMAN *Soc. Life Monkeys & Apes* xi. 185 Loveridge found that Sykes' monkeys were plentiful at Morogoro in East Africa. **1963** A. SMITH *Throw out Two Hands* xiii. 132 We had initially been concentrating on a group of Sykes's monkeys.

syklatown, var. CICLATOUN *Obs.*

sykþ, obs. 3 sing. pres. of SEE *v.*

syl-, assimilated form of SYM- before *l.*

sylde, sylden, -on, syler, sylf, sylibewk, sylie, syll(e: see SELD, SELDOM, SILOUR, SELF, SILLIBOUK, SILLY, SELL, SILL.

'syllab, 'syllabe. *Obs.* exc. *dial.* Forms: 5 *north.* silapp(e, sylypp, 6 sillab(e, syllape, 6–7 syllabe, 7–8 syllab, 9 *Sc.* syllup. [a. OF. *sillabe* (mod. *syllabe*): see SYLLABLE *sb.*] = SYLLABLE *sb.*

c **1440** *Alphabet of Tales* 104 Silappis & wurdis þat er ouerhippid, & also versis of þe salter & wurdis er mombled. *c* **1440** *York Myst.* x. 26 Abram first named was I, And sythen he sette a sylypp ma. **1509** BARCLAY *Shyp of Folys* (1874) I. 144 Homo est Asinus is cause of moche stryfe Thus passe forth these folys the dayes of theyr lyfe In two syllabis. **1529** LYNDESAY *Compl.* 91 The first sillabis that thow did mute Was 'pa, Da Lyn, vpon the lute'. *a* **1533** FRITH *Answ. More* (1548) C vj b, I neuer altered one syllabe of Gods worde. *a* **1568** ASCHAM *Scholem.* II. (Arb.) 148 Their feete be ..not distinct by trew quantitie of sillabes. **1625** B. JONSON *Staple of N.* v. ii. 37, I will not change a syllab, with thee, more. **1636** —— *Eng. Gram.* i. §2 A Word..consisteth of one or more Syllabes. **1762** BRIDGES *Homer Travest.* (1797) I. 102 With staring looks and open jaws They catch each syllab as it flows. **1785** in Shirrefs *Poems* (1790) 318 Sic verses.. And no ae syllab' o' them wrang. **1889** BARRIE *Window in Thrums* xix. 181 There hasna been a syllup aboot it.

‖**syllabarium** (sɪlə'bɛərɪəm). Pl. -ia. [mod.L., neut. of med.L. *syllabārius*, f. *syllaba* SYLLABLE.] = next.

1850 DONALDSON *New Cratylus* §109 (ed. 2) 166, [a] is.. the fundamental vowel with which every consonant in the old syllabarium was articulated. **1858** BIRCH *Anc. Pottery* II. 207 Two of these vases..had a Greek alphabet and syllabarium scratched on them. **1873** EARLE *Philol. Engl. Tongue* (ed. 2) §90 A syllabarium, which is a set of phonetic characters, not of vowels and consonants but of syllables.

syllabary ('sɪləbərɪ). Also 6 -ery. [ad. mod. L. *syllabārium*: see prec. Cf. F. *syllabaire*, Sp. *silabario* spelling-book.] A collection, set, system, list, or table of syllables. Also *attrib.*

1586 FERNE *Blaz. Gentrie* To Gentl. Inner Temple A v, If any neuer so meere a Syllabery, or Christ crosse losell, haue clumperd vp (with the helpe of some rude and grosse Minerua) any worke, straightwaies it is meete for all to reade. **1654** BROOKSBANK *Rules Syllabication* (title-p.), With Directions for the use of the English Syllabary, and the English Monosyllabary. **1839** *Proc. Amer. Philos. Soc.* I. 121 The Japanese syllabary. **1873** EARLE *Philol. Engl. Tongue* (ed. 2) §91 The Chinese writing has led to syllabaries among the Japanese, and to an alphabet among the Coreans. **1879** JEFFERIES *Wild Life in S. Co.* 149 The starling has a whole syllabary of his own, every note of which evidently has its meaning. **1883** SAYCE *Fresh Light fr. Anc. Mon.* Introd. 12 The Persian cuneiform system must have consisted of an alphabet, and not of a syllabary.

‖**syllabatim** (sɪlə'beɪtɪm), *adv. rare.* [L. *syllabātim* (Cicero), f. *syllaba* SYLLABLE, after *gradātim*.] By syllables; syllable by syllable.

1628 J. MEAD in *Crt. & Times Chas. I* (1848) I. 344 He.. examined every one *syllabatim* by the records. **1668** H. MORE *Div. Dial.* II. 337 To tell you *syllabatim* in the words of any Language what they naturally signifie. **1791–1823** D'ISRAELI *Cur. Lit.* (1866) 550/2 Mr. Littleton said, that he had examined every one *syllabatim*.

syllabation (sɪlə'beɪʃən). *rare.* [f. L. *syllaba* SYLLABLE *sb.* + -ATION. Cf. F. *syllabation* and med.L. *syllabāre*.] = SYLLABIFICATION.

1856 CALDWELL *Compar. Gram. Dravidian* 138 The chief peculiarity of Drâvidian syllabation is its extreme simplicity and dislike of compound or concurrent consonants. **1871** *Public Sch. Lat. Gram.* §11. 5 The following rules are observed in Latin Syllabation.

syllabi, plural of SYLLABUS.

syllabic (sɪ'læbɪk), *a.* and *sb.* [ad. mod.L. *syllabicus* (Priscian), ad. Gr. συλλαβικός, f. συλλαβή SYLLABLE *sb.* Cf. F. *syllabique* (1704 in Hatz.-Darm.), It. *sillabico*, Sp. *silábico*.]

A. *adj.*

1. a. Of, pertaining or relating to, a syllable or syllables.

1755 JOHNSON, *Syllabick*, relating to syllables. **1782** V. KNOX *Ess.* xxiii. (1819) I. 132 There are many passages.. which, if you attend to the accentual and not to the syllabic quantity, may be scanned like hexameter verses. **1795** MASON *Ch. Mus.* ii. 95 In the responses.., which are noted for various voices, this syllabic distinction is sufficiently attended to. **1852** *Proc. Philol. Soc.* V. 156 In English pronunciation syllabic quantity is..imperfectly marked. **1860** ADLER *Prov. Poet.* i. 6 Versification founded on a combination of the rhyme with the syllabic accent. **1892** LOUNSBURY *Stud. Chaucer* I. iii. 286 In his endeavors to impart to the line syllabic regularity.

b. Forming or constituting a syllable. ***syllabic augment***: see AUGMENT *sb.* 2.

1728 CHAMBERS *Cycl.* s.v., The first [augment] call'd Syllabic, which is when the Word is increas'd by a Syllable. **1837** G. PHILLIPS *Syriac Gram.* 25 Whenever the noun in its primitive form receives a syllabic augment. **1888** SWEET *Engl. Sounds* §21 A sound which can form a syllable by itself is called *syllabic*... The distinction between syllabic and non-syllabic is generally parallel to that between vowel and consonant. But..'vowellike' or 'liquid' voiced consonants ..are often also syllabic... Even voiceless consonants can be syllabic, as in *pst*, where the *s* is syllabically equivalent to a vowel. **1908** —— *Sounds of English* § 149 In such a word as *little* litl the second l is so much more syllabic than the preceding voiceless stop that it assumes syllabic function.

c. Denoting a syllable; consisting of signs denoting syllables.

1804 J. BARROW *Trav. in China* vi. 270 [The Manchu writing-system] is alphabetic, or, more properly speaking, syllabic. **1838** P. DU PONCEAU *Chinese System of Writing* p. xii, Syllabic alphabets, besides, have considerable advantages over those that we make use of. **1865** TYLOR *Early Hist. Man.* v. 104 Writing his language in syllabic signs. **1875** RENOUF *Egypt. Gram.* 1 All other Egyptian phonetic signs have syllabic values. **1884** W. WRIGHT *Empire Hittites* 70 A syllabic writing evidently of immense antiquity.

d. Of verse or metre: based upon or determined by the number of syllables in a line, etc.

1923 L. ABERCROMBIE in *Times Lit. Suppl.* 12 Apr. 247/1 English metre, according to many theorists, is neither syllabic nor quantitative, but simply accentual. **1965** A. F. SCOTT *Current Lit. Terms* 282 The determining feature of syllabic verse is the number of syllables in the line, not the stress nor the quantity. **1970** G. S. FRASER *Metre, Rhyme & Free Verse* iv. 50 Purely syllabic metrics seems..not suitable to the prosody of English as a natural language.

2. a. Applied to singing, or a tune, in which each syllable is sung to one note (i.e. with no slurs or runs).

1789 BURNEY *Hist. Mus.* III. 389 Nothing now but syllabic and unisonous psalmody was authorised in the Church. **1834** K. H. DIGBY *Mores Cath.* v. iii. 75 That syllabic composition of song in Pindar's style.

b. Pronounced syllable by syllable; uttered with distinct separation of syllables.

1890 SARAH J. DUNCAN *Social Departure* xiii. 122 His English was careful, select, syllabic. **1899** *Allbutt's Syst. Med.* VII. 64 'Scanning', 'staccato', or 'syllabic' speech is one of the symptoms of [disseminate sclerosis].

3. Consisting of mere syllables or words; verbal. *rare*$^{-1}$.

1850 P. CROOK *War of Hats* 35 The mere syllabic air Of words in formal orisons bestowed.

B. *sb.* (elliptical use of the adj.)

1. A syllabic sign; a character denoting a syllable.

1880 *Encycl. Brit.* XI. 800/2 A determinative [attached to an ideographic sign] often indicates to the reader..this radical change in the use of the sign. In this case the sign is said to be employed as a syllabic. **1885** *Athenæum* 4 Apr. 436/3 Eight syllabic signs..are verified by their close accordance of form with Cypriote syllabics.

2. A syllabic sound; a vocal sound capable by itself of forming a syllable, or constituting the essential element of a syllable.

1890 SWEET *Primer of Phonetics* §150 Hence the ear learns to divide a breath-group into groups of vowels (or vowel-equivalents), each flanked by consonants (or consonant-equivalents)—or, in other words, into syllable-formers or syllabics, and non-syllabics, each of these groups constituting a syllable. **1908** —— *Sounds of English* §149 The more sonorous a sound is, the more easily it assumes the function of a syllabic.

3. A syllabic utterance; a word or phrase pronounced syllable by syllable. *nonce-use.*

1893 T. B. FOREMAN *Trip to Spain* 30 A welcome relief to the hard syllabics, 'Splendid!' 'Beautiful!'

4. *pl.* Syllabic verse.

1964 *Times Lit. Suppl.* 16 Jan. 53/4 Syllabics are as legitimate a metrical device as any other. *Ibid.*, Syllabics accommodate speech rhythms... MacBeth and..B.S. Johnson, independently discovered this quality of syllabic metre a few years ago. **1977** *Ibid.* 8 Apr. 428/2 The line in Bridges's use of neo-Miltonic syllabics is fundamentally of twelve syllables.

sy'llabical, *a.* Now *rare* or *Obs.* Also 6–7 sill-. [f. mod.L. *syllabicus*: see -ICAL.]

1. = prec. A. 1 b.

1530 PALSGR. 83 Verbes actives parsonals have..addynge of sillabicall adjections. **1602** [J. WILLIS] *Art Stenogr.* D 5, Syllabicall adiections vsed in the Latine tongue. **1671** PHILLIPS (ed. 3), *Syllabical Augment*, is an augmentation which is made in Greek verbs, by prefixing ἐ (and thereby adding one syllable).

2. = prec. A. 3.

1606 S. GARDINER *Bk. Angling* 117 Orators, and Poets.., the quintessence of whose wittes, are nothing else but waues of wast words, a streame of sillabical slight inuention.

3. = prec. A. 1.

1620 W. COLSON *Fr. Gram.* 15 Contraction or distraction litterall or syllabicall. **1641** 'SMECTYMNUUS' *Vind. Answ.* §1. 4 If we were called to give an account of this Syllabicall Errour before a Deske of Grammarians. **1774** J. BURNET (Ld. Monboddo) *Orig. & Progr. Lang.* II. 299 We have.. accents in English, and syllabical accents too: but they are of a quite different kind from the antient accents. **1775** TYRWHITT *Cant. Tales Chaucer* IV. *Essay* 88 In order..to form any judgement of the Versification of Chaucer, it is necessary that we should know the syllabical value (if I may use the expression) of his words, and the accentual value of his syllables.

†4. Considered in relation to every syllable or detail: cf. next, 2. *Obs.*

1647 N. BACON *Disc. Govt. Eng.* I. iii. (1739) 6, I must allow it to pass for current for the substance, not justifying the syllabical writing thereof.

5. = prec. A. 2 b.

1708 CALAMY *Life* vi. (1829) II. 98 The speech was syllabical, and there was a distinct heave and breathe between each syllable.

syllabically (sɪˈlæbɪkəlɪ), *adv.* [f. prec. + -LY^{2}; see -ICALLY.] In a syllabic or syllabical manner.

1. †In syllables, in audible words, articulately (*obs.*); syllable by syllable, with distinct utterance of the syllables; as a separate syllable.

1610 HEALEY *St. Aug. Citie of God* x. xv. 381 Wherein [*sc.* in the mouths of Angels] Gods person would appeare, and speake syllabically in a mans voyce, unto us. *a* **1660** HAMMOND *Serm. Rom. i. 26* Wks. 1684 I. 657 The first voice of nature..which it uttered..when it was an infant in the World, and therefore perhaps..not so plainly, and syllabically, and distinctly, as could have been wished. **1811** SOUTHEY in *Q. Rev.* Oct. 278 They first read the words syllabically. **1837** HALLAM *Lit. Eur.* I. I. viii. §26. 433 It is necessary to presume that many terminations, now mute, were syllabically pronounced. **1862** SALA *Seven Sons* II. xi. 286 Tottenham — he pronounced the word very syllabically.

†**2.** Syllable for syllable; word for word;

1654 WARREN *Unbelievers* 55 The Scripture doth syllabically repeat these words. **1661** GAUDEN *Consid. Liturgy* 25 These and many like places,..though they do not literally and syllabically agree with the quotation,..may sufficiently justifie that place..to be..a Divine Scriptural Truth. **1698** [R. FERGUSON] *View Eccles.* 7 Scrupling, at certain Words and Phrases, which were not ῥητῶς, or Literally, and Syllabically Canonical. *a* **1778** TOPLADY *Wks.* (1828) III. 446 It is called St. Athanasius's Creed; not because it was syllabically composed by him, but [etc.].

3. In relation to a syllable or syllables; by syllabic characters.

1795 MASON *Ch. Mus.* ii. 95 Those parts or versicles which..are syllabically distinguished by notes of different musical duration. **1888** [see SYLLABIC A. 1 b]. **1908** *Westm. Gaz.* 9 Dec. 10/3 Showing how Chinese sounds could be reproduced alphabetically or syllabically.

sy'llabicate, *v.* [Back-formation f. next.] *trans.* To form into syllables. Also *intr.*, to form or construct syllables; to divide a word or passage into syllables.

1654 J. BROOKSBANK *Plain, Brief, Rules of Syllabication Eng. Words* 27 To Syllabicate, which is to find out a word by its syllables. **1775** in ASH *Suppl.* **1831** J. BOADEN *Life of Mrs. Jordan* II. xx. 178 He did not syllabicate, his notion of a word was often caught from vulgar speakers. **1902** H. BRADLEY *Let.* 9 Jan. in *Corresp. Bridges & Bradley* (1940) 9 If the Greeks syllabicated like this..a syllable ending in *one* or more consonants is long. **1971** *Language* XLVII. 138 *Perpetual* is syllabicated as *per. pety. u. al.*

syllabication (sɪˌlæbɪˈkeɪʃən). [ad. med.L. *sill-, syllabicātio, -ōnem*, n. of action f. *syllabicāre*, f. *syllaba* SYLLABLE.] **a.** = SYLLABIFICATION.

Tending to give way to *syllabification*.—R.W.B.

1631 [MABBE] *Celestina* xviii. 180, I sweare unto thee by the crisse-crosse row, by the whole Alphabet, and Sillabication of the letters. **1654** BROOKSBANK (*title*) Plain, brief, and pertinent Rules for the..Syllabication of all English Words. **1754** GOODALL *Exam. Lett. Mary Q. Scots* I. v. 110 The syllabication of the Scottish word *nouther*.. had been changed, after the English orthography, into *neither*. **1791** BURNS *Let.* Wks. (Globe) 496 Thou faithful recorder of barbarous idiom: thou persecutor of syllabication. **1863** NUTTALL *Standard Dict.* Pref., Orthography..comprehends the correct spelling and syllabication of words. **1933** L. BLOOMFIELD *Language* vii. 121 The ups and downs of *syllabication* play an important part in the phonetic structure of all languages. **1971** *Language* XLVII. 138 The rule for the devoicing of liquids follows syllabication.

b. The action of making syllabic; pronunciation as a distinct syllable.

1857 CRAIK *English of Shaks., Jul. C.* I. i. (1869) 73 The distinct syllabication of the final *ed*.

syllabicity (sɪləˈbɪsɪtɪ). [f. SYLLABIC *a.* + -ITY.] = SYLLABICNESS.

1933 L. BLOOMFIELD *Language* viii. 130 Syllabicity determined also by manner of articulation. **1944** L. M. HARTMAN in *Language* XX. 33 One of these [morphophonemic changes] is the loss of syllabicity either by this or by the preceding syllable. **1952** A. COHEN *Phonemes of Eng.* iii. 62 There does not seem to be any need for assuming a special phoneme of syllabicity. **1968** F. G. LOUNSBURY in J. A. Fishman *Readings Sociol. of Lang.* 53 What we have accomplished is to suppress from our transcription the representation of features of the acoustic stimulus (voicing, syllabicity, laryngeal order, and position of the accent) which do not serve as cues for differential responses on the part of the native subjects. **1977** *Archivum Linguisticum* VIII. 87 There is no experimental evidence for, and some experimental evidence against, the necessary presence of such pulses as physiological correlates of syllabicity.

sy'llabicness. [f. SYLLABIC *a.* + -NESS.] The quality of being syllabic.

1888 SWEET *Hist. Engl. Sounds* §21 Syllabicness implies an appreciable duration and force. *Ibid.* §22 A vowel..can lose its syllabicness, especially in combination with another vowel, with which it then forms a diphthong.

syllabification (sɪˌlæbɪfɪˈkeɪʃən). [n. of action f. med.L. *syllabificāre*, f. *syllaba* SYLLABLE: see -FICATION.] Formation or construction of syllables; the action or method of dividing words into syllables.

1838 GUEST *Engl. Rhythms* I. 23 The early systems of syllabification. **1843** POE *Premature Burial* Wks. 1864 I. 330 What he said was unintelligible; but..the syllabification was distinct. **1862** J. ANGUS *Hand-bk. Engl. Tongue* 495 Rules of syllabification. **1972** *Webster's New World Dict.* (Delux Color ed.) p. x, The syllabifications used in this dictionary are in the main those in general use by printers since the 18th century. **1977** *Archivum Linguisticum* VIII. 87 Such questions, he states, are now 'reduced to practical matters of articulatory adjustment in particular languages'..—which would seem to imply that syllabification rules are part of particular phonologies. **1979** *Collins Eng. Dict.* p. x, Syllabification breaks are shown for all headwords. **1980** *Verbatim* Spring 19/1 Lexicography is not simply adding one good point to another to make an ideal dictionary, but balancing the saving of space against fullness of information, the amount of information against cost, a more exact pronunciation guide against added difficulty for some users, the addition of extra information (pronunciation or syllabification) in the headword at the expense of its clean appearance.

sy'llabify, *v.* [Back-formation f. prec. But cf. OF. *sillabifier* (15th c.).] *trans.* 'To form or divide into syllables' (Webster, 1864). Also *intr.*

1926 [see SYLLABIZATION]. **1954** F. G. CASSIDY *Robertson's Devel. Mod. Eng.* (ed. 2) xii. 381 Though the American may syllabify more fully where the Englishman elides, he also slurs more. **1972** *Language* XLVIII. 357 If one assumes that ø is the alternative to syllabifying *-s*, then one can establish a graded gamut of markedness among the three alternants.

syllabism (ˈsɪləbɪz(ə)m). [f. L. *syllaba*, Gr. συλλαβή SYLLABLE + -ISM, after *syllabize*. Cf. F. *syllabisme*.] **a.** The use of syllabic characters. **b.** Division into syllables. **c.** Theory concerning syllables (*Cent. Dict.*, 1891).

1883 I. TAYLOR *Alphabet* I. i. §6. 33 Syllabism..finds its best illustration in the development of the Japanese writing out of the Chinese. **1892** H. D. DAREISHIRE in *Classical Rev.* Feb. 57/1 The accentuation is matér-,..the syllabism is māt-ér-.

syllabist (ˈsɪləbɪst). *rare*$^{-1}$. [Formed as prec. + -IST.] One versed in the division of words into syllables.

1846 WORCESTER cites *Fo. Qu. Rev.*

syllabi'zation. [f. SYLLABIZE *v.* + -ATION.] = SYLLABIFICATION.

1926 H. W. FOWLER *Mod. Eng. Usage* 590/2 A verb & a noun are clearly sometimes needed for the notion of dividing words into syllables. The possible pairs seem to be.. syllabify..syllabification [etc.]... The best thing would be to accept the most recognized verb *syllabize*, give it the now non-existent noun *syllabization*, [etc.]. **1929** *S.P.E. Tract* XXXIII. 436 Under *syllabize etc.* he [*sc.* Fowler] exposes a want in our vocabulary, which perhaps indicates a general lack of interest in *syllabization*. **1976** *Archivum Linguisticum* VII. 181 In Adrados's explanation, these forms without colouring of the vowel occur in a different syllabization.

syllabize (ˈsɪləbaɪz), *v.* [ad. med.L. *syllabizāre*, ad. Gr. συλλαβίζειν, f. συλλαβή SYLLABLE *sb.*: see -IZE. Cf. F. *syllabiser*.]

1. *trans.* To form or divide into syllables; to utter or articulate with distinct separation of syllables.

1656 BLOUNT *Glossogr.*, *Syllabize*, to divide by syllables. **1660** HOWELL *Parly of Beasts* Pref. Verses b ij, 'Tis Mankind alone Can Language frame, and syllabize the Tone. **1831** *Examiner* 694/1 Every word is syllabized, and every syllable protracted to three times its due quantity.

2. *intr.* To sing notes to syllables, as in solmization. *nonce-use.*

1782 BURNEY *Hist. Mus.* II. ii. 105 It may be said, that to *syllabize* in quick passages is little more than to speak, but to *vocalize* is to sing.

Hence **'syllabized** *ppl. a.*; **'syllabizing** *vbl. sb.* and *ppl. a.*

1831 *Examiner* 259/2 A drawling tone and syllabizing pronunciation. *Ibid.* 822/1 The syllabizing of the dialogue, and the roulading of the music, are equally out of place. **1885** *Athenæum* 13 June 762/3 Irish metric, like that of the Slavonic peoples, has passed from an original purely syllabizing system to an accentuating one. **1957** A. ORAS in N. Frye *Sound & Poetry* 112 Milton's growing dislike of syllabized *-ed* endings. **1969** *Computers & Humanities* III. 257 The latter is based upon successive scanning of the syllabized text in groups of four, three, two and one characters.

syllable (ˈsɪləb(ə)l), *sb.* Forms: 4–7 **sillable**, (4 **silable**, 5 **sillabil, -byl, sylable, -bul, syllabylle, cyllable,** 7 **sillabell**), 6– **syllable.** *β. dial.* 5, 9 **sinnable,** 9 **synnable.** [a. AF. *sillable* = OF. *sillabe* (12th c.), mod.F. *syllabe*, ad. L. *syllaba*, a. Gr. συλλαβή, f. συλλαμβάνειν to take, put, or bring together, f. σύν SYN-^{1} + λαμβάνειν (stem λαβ-) to take.]

1. a. A vocal sound or set of sounds uttered with a single effort of articulation and forming a word or an element of a word; each of the elements of spoken language comprising a sound of greater sonority (vowel or vowel-equivalent) with or without one or more sounds of less sonority (consonants or consonant-equivalents); also, a character or set of characters forming a corresponding element of written language.

c **1384** CHAUCER *H. Fame* III. 8 Though somme vers fayle in A sillable. *c* **1386** —— *Sqr.'s T.* 93 After the forme vsed in his langage With outen vice of silable or of lettre. **1387** TREVISA *Higden* (Rolls) II. 437 Ascanius was i-cleped Iulus ..a name of tweie silables. *c* **1430** *Stans Puer* (Lamb. MS.) 98 in *Babees Bk.* (1868) 33 In þis writynge..Yf ouȝt be mys, in worde, sillable, or dede, I submitte me to correccioun withoute ony debate. *a* **1491** J. ROWS *Roll* vii. (1859) B 3 b, The furst sinnable of hys naavm [*sc.* Arth-gallus] that ys to seey Arth or Narthe is asmuch to sey in Walsh as a bere. **1526** *Pilgr. Perf.* (W. de W. 1531) 158 Not clipping the syllables, nor skyppyng ony worde. **1555** WATREMAN *Fardle Facions* I. iv. 40 Yeat ware not their Letters facioned to ioyne together in sillables like ours. *a* **1568** ASCHAM *Scholem.* II. (Arb.) 145 Our English tong, hauing in vse chiefly, wordes of one syllable. **1612** BRINSLEY *Posing Parts* (1669) 90 When is a Noun said to increase? *A.* When it hath more syllables in the Genitive case, than in the Nominative. *a* **1711** KEN *Psyche* Poet. Wks. 1721 IV. 281 Return, Re—— in this Syllable she fail'd. **1762–71** H. WALPOLE *Vertue's Anecd. Paint.* (1786) I. 277 On the back ground the front of a castle with columns; on the bases of which are the syllables Es—sex. **1880** W. S. ROCKSTRO in Grove *Dict. Mus.* I. 734/1 The sounds [of each hexachord] are sung..to the syllables *ut, re, mi, fa, sol, la*, the semitone always falling between the syllables *mi* and *fa*. **1890** [see SYLLABIC B. 2]. **1899** R. J. LLOYD *Northern English* §105 Speech is a succession of sounds continually rising and falling in sonority. Each single short wave of sonority, one rise and one fall, is a syllable. *Ibid.* §107 The most sonorous phone of a syllable is its vowel: the rest are its consonants. **1908** SWEET *Sounds of English* §150 The beginning of a syllable corresponds to the beginning of the stress with which it is uttered. Thus in *atone* the strong stress and the second syllable begin on the *t*, and in *bookcase* bukːkeis on the second *k*.

b. Used pregnantly of a word of one syllable, or in reference to a part of a word, considered in relation to its significance.

1390 GOWER *Conf.* III. 343 That o sillable [*sc.* nay] hath overthrowe A thousend wordes. **1577** VAUTROUILLIER *Luther on Ep. Gal.* 21 Learne this definition diligently, and especially so exercise this pronoune *our*, that this one sillable being beleeued, may swallow vp all thy sinnes. **1577** HARRISON *England* II. v. (1877) I. 115 This syllable Sir, which is the title whereby we call our knights. **1603** OWEN *Pembrokeshire* (1892) 267 [The Fox and Marton] are desired onelye for the two last sillables of theire Carcases [*i.e.* 'cases' = skins]. **1781** COWPER *Hope* 690 Those awful syllables, hell, death, and sin. **1796** BURKE *Corr.* (1844) IV. 397 What can make us in love with oppression because the syllables 'Jacobin' are not put before the 'ism'?

c. Colloq. phr. *in words of one syllable*, in simple language.

1922 F. H. BURNETT *Head of House of Combe* xvii. 206 The French Revolution..—the cataclysms of agony—need not have been, but they *were*. To put it in words of one syllable. **1941** V. WOOLF *Between Acts* 218 Let's talk in words of one syllable, without larding, stuffing or cant. **1966** 'E. LATHEN' *Murder makes Wheels go Round* xxi. 166 'John,' he said breathlessly, 'would you please explain in words of one syllable.' **1970** *Guardian* 9 Mar. 24/1 Why don't they tell us precisely, in words of one syllable, how they would behave if they were in our place?

2. a. The least portion or detail of speech or writing (or of something expressed or expressible in speech or writing); the least mention, hint, or trace *of* something: esp. in negative context.

1434 MISYN *Mending Life* 118 All our prayer with desire and effect sal be, so þat we ouer-rynne not þe wordis, bot nerehand all sillabyls with grete cry & desire we sal offyr to owr lorde. **1533** MORE *Apol.* 8 b, Of all theyr owne wordes I leue not one syllable out. **1583** MELBANCKE *Philotimus* Cc iv, One sillable of thine shall more perswade mee, then the sage sentences of anye other. **1604** SHAKS. *Oth.* IV. ii. 5, I heard, Each syllable that breath made vp betweene them. **1605** —— *Macb.* v. v. 21 To the last Syllable of Recorded time. **1687** ATTERBURY *Answ. Consid. Spirit Luther* 47 To this there's not a syllable of proof offer'd. **1768** GOLDSM. *Goodn. Man* II. i, I know every syllable of the matter. **1771** SMOLLETT *Humphry Cl., Let. to Lewis* 2 Apr., Don't say a syllable of the matter to any living soul. **1801** COLMAN *Poor Gentl.* III. i. 34 There isn't a syllable of sense in all you have been saying. **1876** GREEN *Stray Stud.* 189 The name of Dante is mentioned but once, and then without a syllable of comment. **1885** D. C. MURRAY *Rainbow Gold* II. iii, I ain't a-going to breathe a synnable.

†**b.** *pl.* Minute details of language or statement; exact or precise words. *Obs.*

1597 HOOKER *Eccl. Pol.* v. lxviii §2 Our imitation of him consisteth not in tying scrupulously our selues vnto his sillables. **1614** SELDEN *Titles Hon.* II. i. 173 Whose syllables I the rather cite, because..he iustifies himself out of the Instrument of that Donation, which, by his assertion, he made vse of.

†**3.** With reference to the etymological sense: A composite thing, a compound. *Obs. nonce-use.*

1678 CUDWORTH *Intell. Syst.* I. v. 849 Life and Understanding..are no Syllables or Complexions,..nor can either the Qualities of Heat and Cold, Moist and Dry; or else Magnitudes, Figures, Sites, and Motions, however Combined together, as Letters Spell them out, and make them up.

4. *attrib.* and *Comb.*, as *syllable-count, -division, stress*, etc.; *syllable-counting, -final, -initial* adjs.; **syllable-monger** (*nonce-wd.*), one who makes verses (regarded merely as an orderly arrangement of syllables); **syllable-timed** *a.*, of or having a rhythm in which syllables occur at roughly equivalent time intervals; opp. *stress-timed* adj. s.v. STRESS *sb.* 11; hence **syllable-timing**.

1969 *Language* XLV. 250 The text itself is composed in syllable-count verse forms. **1983** *Listener* 6 Jan. 21/3 Pop lyrics writers throw in an 'oh yeah' or a 'baby' wherever the syllable-count needs padding out. **1959** *PMLA* LXXIV. 588/2 This has been done on strictly accentual (plus syllable-counting) principles. **1978** *Early Music* Oct. 587/3 He describes in detail three kinds of relationship.. between words and music in the period—the metrical.. the accentual ..the syllable-counting (the characteristic mode of Christian and much courtly poetry). **1888** Sweet *Hist. Engl. Sounds* §19 It is possible to alter the syllable division by shifting the stress from one element to another. **1964** B. Malmberg in D. Abercrombie et al. *Daniel Jones* 116 Many languages have an opposition between explosive (syllable-initial) and implosive (syllable-final) consonant. **1978** *Language* LIV. 23 Durand.. points out that the [t] in *petit orage* 'little storm' is syllable-initial, while the [t] in *petite orange* 'little orange' appears to be syllable-final for most speakers. **1890** Sweet *Primer Phonetics* §150 Syllable-formers [see syllabic B. 2]. **1964, 1978** Syllable-initial [see syllable-final *adj.* above]. **1784** Cowper *Let. to W. Unwin* 5 Apr., As my two syllablemongers, Beattie and Blair, both agree that language was originally inspired [etc.]. **1924** H. E. Palmer *Gram. Spoken Eng.* I. 6 *Word-stress* (in the opinion of the author the term *syllable-stress* would be more appropriate). This term is used with reference to a syllable. **1964** W. S. Allen in D. Abercrombie et al. *Daniel Jones* 14 These remarks on English verse are intended only to apply to the 'syllable-stress' metres. **1890** Billings *Med. Dict.*, *Syllable-stumbling*, a form of paralytic dysphasia in which there is difficulty in speaking a word as a whole, although each letter and syllable can be distinctly sounded. **1947** K. L. Pike *Phonemics* I. ii. 13/1 In English one tends to hear stress-timed rhythm in contra-distinction to a syllable-timed rhythm. In the syllable-timed type the syllables themselves tend to be more or less equally spaced... As a result of the syllable timing the vowels are likely to be clear cut. **1980** *English World-Wide* I. 1. 108 This, as well as the syllable-timed rhythm, gives rise to the staccato impression often noticed by outsiders. **1964** M. A. K. Halliday et al. *Linguistic Sci.* 72 The English type of rhythm is known as 'stress-timing', by contrast with the 'syllable timing' of French.

'syllable, *v.* [f. prec. sb.]

1. *trans.* ? To arrange in syllables. *rare*$^{-1}$.

c **1475** *Partenay* 6581 Als the frensh staffes silabled be More breueloker and shorter also Then is the english lines vnto see.

2. To utter or express in (or as in) syllables or articulate speech; to pronounce syllable by syllable; to utter articulately or distinctly; to articulate. Also *fig.*

1633 P. Fletcher *Poet. Misc.*, tr. *Asclepiads* 3 Unwritten Word, which never eye could see, Yet syllabled in flesh-spell'd character. **1634** Milton *Comus* 208 Airy tongues, that syllable mens names On Sands, and Shoars, and desert Wildernesses. **1751** Ld. Stormont *On Death Frederic Pr. Wales* 6 in *Epicedia Oxon.* C 2, To syllable new sounds in accent strange. **1820** Byron *Mar. Fal.* III. i. 58, I cannot shape my tongue To syllable black deeds into smooth names. **1852** Whittier *First-Day Thoughts* 7 There syllabled by silence, let me hear The still small voice which reached the prophet's ear. **1886** Miss Braddon *One Thing Needful* v, The first prayer those lips had ever syllabled.

b. To read (something) syllable by syllable; to read in detail or with close attention; to spell out. *rare.*

1728 P. Walker *Peden* in *Biog. Presbyt.* (1827) I. p. xxxi, This bruitish, carnal Age knows not what it is to syllable the Scriptures, or feed upon them. **1831** Carlyle *Sart. Res.* II. ii, These things were the Alphabet, whereby in after-time he was to syllable and partly read the grand Volume of the World.

c. To represent by syllables. *rare.*

1887 Newton in *Encycl. Brit.* XXII. 200/2 Loud notes [of a snipe] that have been syllabled *tinker, tinker, tinker*.

3. *intr.* To utter syllables, to speak. *nonce-use.*

1829 Keats *Lamia* I. 244 Turn'd—syllabling thus, 'Ah, Lycius bright'.

Hence **'syllabled** (-b(ə)ld) *ppl. a.*; **'syllabling** *vbl. sb.*

1819 *Metropolis* I. 215 The three words drawn to the utmost extent of syllabling. **1843** Carlyle *Past & Pr.* II. xvii, Men had not a hammer to begin with, not a syllabled articulation. **1865** Mrs. Whitney *Gayworthys* xxvii. (1879) 269 The tree-whispers sounded like a syllabled sympathy. **1876** Ruskin *Fors Clav.* lxxi. §2. 360 The painted syllabling of it. **1885** J. H. Dell *Dawning Grey, Songs Surges* 98 The songs of the surges I shaped to a syllabled sound.

syllablize ('sɪləb(ə)laɪz), *v. rare*$^{-1}$. [f. syllable *sb.* + -ize.] *trans.* = syllabize 1.

1877 May Laffan *Hon. Miss Ferrard* I. vii. 207 Those marks indicate the syllablising of the word and its pronunciation.

syllabub: see sillabub.

syllabus ('sɪləbəs). Pl. **syllabi** ('sɪləbaɪ) or **syllabuses** ('sɪləbəsɪz). [mod.L. *syllabus*, usually referred to an alleged Gr. σύλλαβος. *Syllabus* appears to be founded on a corrupt reading *syllabos* in some early printed editions—the Medicean MS. has *sillabos*—of Cicero Epp. ad Atticum IV. iv, where the reading indicated as correct by comparison with the MS. readings in IV. v. and viii. is *sittybas* or Gr. σιττύβας, acc. pl. of *sittyba*, σιττύβα parchment label or title-slip on a book. (Cf. Tyrrell and Purser *Correspondence of Cicero* nos. 107, 108, 112, Comm. and Adnot. Crit.) *Syllabos* was græcized by later editors as συλλάβους, from which a spurious σύλλαβος was deduced and treated as a derivative of συλλαμβάνειν to put together, collect (cf. syllable).

In the passage from S. Augustine's *Confessions* XIII. xv. ('ibi legunt [*sc.* angeli] sine syllabis temporum quid velit aeterna voluntas tua') commonly adduced as further evidence of L. *syllabus*, the word is clearly *syllaba* syllable.]

1. a. A concise statement or table of the heads of a discourse, the contents of a treatise, the subjects of a series of lectures, etc.; a compendium, abstract, summary, epitome.

1656 Blount *Glossogr.*, *Syllabus*, a Table or Index in a Book, to shew places or matter by Letters or Figures. **1667** Jer. Taylor *Gt. Exemp.* (ed. 4) I. vi. §22. 160 The Apostle expresses it still by Synonyma's, *Tasting of the heavenly gift, and made partakers of the holy Ghost*..; all which also are a syllabus or collection of the several effects of the graces bestowed in Baptism. **1775** T. Sheridan *Art Reading* 11 The first article in the syllabus, entitled, A scheme of the vowels. **1796** Morse *Amer. Geog.* I. 526 Presenting to the students a compend or syllabus of their lectures. **1818** Scott *Hrt. Midl.* i, Syllabus of lectures. **1822-7** Good *Study Med.* (1829) I. 123 He preached with as much fluency as ever.., with nothing more than a syllabus of his discourse before him. **1881** *Southern Law Rev.* (St. Louis, Missouri) VII. 298 Among these duties [of the official reporter of a Court] is the preparation of syllabi of all decisions. **1886** *Athenæum* 2 Oct. 431/1 The 'Retrospections' should have been furnished.. with a copious syllabus or list of contents.

b. *spec.* a statement of the subjects covered by a course of instruction or by an examination, in a school, college, etc.; a programme of study.

1889 *Rep. Higher Educ. in London* p. ix, in *Parl. Papers* (C. 5709) XXXIX. 323 The colleges having no *locus standi* to make representations to the authorities of the university either as to the settlement or alteration of the 'syllabus' by which the course of the examinations is regulated. **1955** E. Blishen *Roaring Boys* III. 117 The history syllabus for the school had been drawn up by Mr Benson. **1972** *Daily Tel.* (Colour Suppl.) 1 Dec. 15 Schools should allow pupils to determine syllabi.

c. *fig.*

1938 Auden *Commentary* in *Journey to War* (1939) 290 And the young emerging from the closed parental circle, to whose uncertainty the certain years present their syllabus of limitless anxiety and labour.

2. (With capital initial.) *R.C. Ch.* A summary statement of points decided and errors condemned by ecclesiastical authority; *spec.* that annexed to the encyclical *Quanta cura* of Pope Pius IX, 8 Dec. 1864.

1876 B. Martin *Messiah's Kingdom* v. i. 229 The right of the Pope to depose princes.. is reaffirmed in the *Syllabus*. **1907** *Edin. Rev.* Oct. 416 The Syllabus is a voice speaking in a dead language from a dead world.

‖**syllepsis** (sɪ'lɛpsɪs). Pl. **syllepses** (-iːz). Also 6 sill-. [a. late L. *syllēpsis*, a. Gr. σύλληψις, f. σύν syn-[1] + λῆψις taking (f. ληβ-, Attic f. λᾱβ-, lengthened f. λαβ-, stem of λαμβάνειν to take).]

1. *Gram.* and *Rhet.* A figure by which a word, or a particular form or inflexion of a word, is made to refer to two or more other words in the same sentence, while properly applying to or agreeing with only one of them (e.g. a masc. adj. qualifying two sbs., masc. and fem.; a sing. verb serving as predicate to two subjects, sing. and pl.), or applying to them in different senses (e.g. literal and metaphorical). Cf. zeugma.

1577 Peacham *Gard. Eloquence* F j. **1586** A. Day *Engl. Secretorie* II. (1625) 82 *Syllepsis*, when one verbe supplyeth two clauses, one person two roomes, or one word serueth to many senses, as, thus, Hee runnes for pleasure, I for feare. **1589** Puttenham *Engl. Poesie* III. xii. (Arb.) 176 But if such want be in sundrie clauses, and of seuerall congruities or sence, and the supply be made to serue them all, it is by the figure *Sillepsis*, whom for that respect we call the double supplie... as in these verses,.. Here my sweete sonnes and daughters all my blisse, Yonder mine owne deere husband buried is. Where ye see one verbe singular supplyeth the plurall and singular. **1616** S. Ward *Balm fr. Gilead* (1628) 55 He that hath them not.. may well conclude, Wee are assured [etc.]... He speakes it in the plurall number by way of Syllepsis, changing the number, because hee would haue it the word of euery Christian. **1813** Jefferson in H. S. Randall *Life* (1858) III. ix. 391 Fill up all the ellipses and syllepses of Tacitus, Sallust, Livy, etc., and the elegance and force of their sententious brevity are extinguished. **1882** Farrar *Early Chr.* II. 560 By the figure of speech called zeugma, or rather syllepsis, the same word.. is.. made to serve two purposes in the same sentence. A verb is often used with two clauses which is only appropriate to one of them, as in Pope's line—'See Pan with flocks, with fruits Pomona crowned.'

2. In etymological sense: A taking together; a summary. *nonce-use.*

a **1834** Coleridge in *Lit. Rem.* (1839) IV. 191 A Creed is ..a *syllepsis* of those primary fundamental truths.. from which the Christian must commence his progression.

sylleptic (sɪ'lɛptɪk), *a.* [ad. Gr. συλληπτικός, f. σύλληψις syllepsis. Cf. F. *sylleptique.*] Pertaining to, of the nature of, or involving syllepsis. Also **sy'lleptical** *a.* Hence **sy'lleptically** *adv.*

1802 A. Crombie *Etym. & Syntax Eng. Lang.* II. (1830) 260 'He addressed you and me, and desired *us* to follow him', where *us* sylleptically represents the two persons. **1846** Worcester, *Sylleptical*, relating to, or implying, syllepsis. *Crombie.* **1860** Farrar *Orig. Lang.* viii. 174 That sylleptical tendency which seems to have marked the earliest stage of language. **1865** —— *Chapt. Lang.* vi. 77 It [*sc.* gesture] is.. obscure because it is sylleptic, i.e. it expresses but the most general facts of the situation.

syller, obs. Sc. form of silver.

syllibub, obs. form of sillabub.

syllid ('sɪlɪd), *sb.* and *a.* [ad. mod.L. family name *Syllidæ*, f. generic name *Syllis* (J. B. P. A. de M. de Lamarck *Hist. Nat. Animaux sans Vertèbres* (1818) V. 317) + -id[3].] **A.** *sb.* A small errant polychæte worm of the family Syllidæ, distinguished by three tentacles on its head and found on rocky shores. **B.** *adj.* Of or pertaining to an animal of this kind. Also † **sy'llidian** *sb.*

1888 Rolleston & Jackson *Forms Animal Life* (ed. 2) 607 The parent-form in these Syllidians remains non-sexual. **1910** *Encycl. Brit.* V. 793/1 There are even dimorphic forms among the Syllids. **1928** Russell & Yonge *Seas* ii. 52 The little syllid worms break up.. into fragments of a few segments, each of which.. develops into a full-sized worm. **1930** *Q. Jrnl. Microsc. Sci.* LXXIII. 651 (*heading*) On a new Hermaphrodite Syllid. **1963** R. P. Dales *Annelids* i. 30 The nephridiostome remains as a recognisable notch or pocket in the larger coelomostome, as it does.. in some syllids. **1971** *Oxf. Bk. Invertebrates* 96 Syllids usually cling to sea-vegetation or nestle in empty shells and crevices. *Ibid.* 96/2 *Syllis* shows well the typical syllid processes arising from the sides of the body.

syllit, obs. f. *ceiled*, pa. pple. of ceil *v.*

a **1578** Lindesay (Pitscottie) *Chron. Scot.* (S.T.S.) I. 336 This palice withtin was weill syllit and hung witht fyne tapistrie.

‖**sylloge** ('sɪlədʒiː). *rare.* [a. Gr. συλλογή, f. συλλέγειν to collect.] A collection; a summary.

1686 Goad *Celest. Bodies* III. i. 364, I do not intend to tie my self to any one Individual Aspect, but of the whole Sylloge. **1697** Evelyn *Numism.* vii. 244 Luckius.. who set forth his Sylloge of many Illustrious Persons of the last Century. **1787** Pegge (*title*) A Sylloge of the remaining Authentic Inscriptions relative to the erection of our English Churches. **1880** *Encycl. Brit.* XIII. 131/1 Of the documents belonging to the later period a very comprehensive though not quite complete *sylloge* is given.

syllogism ('sɪlədʒɪz(ə)m). Forms: 4 **silogime,** 4–6 **silogisme,** 5–6 **sylogysme,** 5–7 **sillogisme,** 6 **silogysme, sellogisme,** 6–7 **syllogisme, sylogisme,** 7 **sillogism,** 7– **syllogism.** Also 6 in Lat. form **syllogismus** (sill-, sil-). [a. OF. *silogime*, later *sil(l)ogisme*, F. *syllogisme* (= It. *sillo-*, *silogismo*, Sp. *silogismo*, Pg. *syllogismo*), or ad. L. *syllogismus*, a. Gr. συλλογισμός, f. συλλογίζεσθαι to syllogize.]

1. *Logic.* An argument expressed or claimed to be expressible in the form of two propositions called the premisses, containing a common or middle term, with a third proposition called the conclusion, resulting necessarily from the other two. Example: *Omne animal est substantia, omnis homo est animal*, ergo *omnis homo est substantia.*

The kind of syllogism illustrated by the above example is called *simple* or *categorical*. In valid categorical syllogisms, the premisses have the major and minor terms so disposed in respect of the position of the middle (see figure *sb.* 23) and the quality and quantity of the premisses (see mood *sb.*[2] 1) that the conclusion affirms or denies the major term of the minor.

For *hypothetical* (also called *complex*), *conjunctive*, *connexive*, *disjunctive syllogism*, see these words. ***demonstrative syllogism***: one in which the premisses are true and necessary. † *horned syllogism* (see horned 1 b): the dilemma.

1398 Trevisa *Barth. De P.R.* XIX. cxxvi. (1495) mm b/2 Without nombre is not.. Subiectum knowe fro the Predicatum: nother the conclusyon in Silogismes [*orig.* in sillogisticis] is distyngued fro the premysses. *c* **1430** *Pilgr. Lyf Manhode* I. xix. (1869) 14 If ye wol eyther make jugementes, silogismes, other argumentes with oute me, shule ye neuere haue conclusioun. *c* **1480** Henryson *Mor. Fab.* Prol. vii, Ane sillogisme propone and eik conclude. **1528** More *Dyaloge* I. Wks. 125/2 Well quod I and yet he commeth to hys perswasion by a sylogysme & reasonninge, almost as formall as is the argument, by whiche ye proue the kinde of man reasonable, wherof what other colleccion haue you that brought you first to perceiue it than that this man is resonable, and this man, & this man, and this man, and so forth all whom ye se. **1530** Tindale *Answ. More* I. xxvii. Wks. (1572) 288/1, I would fayne know in what figure that silogismus is made. **1532** More *Confut. Tindale* Wks. 504/1 This sillogisme is mine. And thys sillogisme yf Tindall would fayne wit in what figure it is made: he shal finde it in the first figure, and the third mode, sauing that yͤ mynor carieth his proofe wᵗ him, which woulde elles in the same figure and the same mode haue made another sillogisme. **1542** Udall *Erasm. Apoph.* 90 b, *marg.*, A syllogisme, is a perfecte argumente of logike, in whiche, two thynges or moo, first putte, & the same graunted, the conclusion dooeth ineuitably foloe of necessitee. *c* **1590** Marlowe *Faustus* 140, I that haue with Consis sylogismes Graueld the Pastors of the Germane Church. **1633** G. Herbert *Temple, Ch. Mil.* 55 Prayers chas'd syllogismes into their den, And *Ergo* was transform'd into *Amen.* **1646** Sir T. Browne *Pseud. Ep.* VI. i. 275 Men do speak.. in simple tearms and words, expressing the open notions of things, which the second act of reason compoundeth into propositions, and the last into syllogisms and forms of ratiocination. **1649** Evelyn *Liberty & Servitude* ii, Certaine it is, that our understanding cannot always impedite itselfe, that it should not acquiesce at the Conclusion of a demonstrative syllogisme, having before comprehended the first and second propositions. **1691** Norris *Pract. Disc.* 143 The Sum of the whole may be reduced to this practical Syllogism. That which will bring a man peace at the last, is to be chiefly minded: But a Life of Piety and Vertue will bring a man Peace at the last. Therefore a Life of Piety and Vertue is to be chiefly minded.

1748 W. DUNCAN *Elem. Logic* III. i. (1752) 194 As every Act of Reasoning implies three several Judgments, so every Syllogism must include three distinct Propositions. **1781** COWPER *Conversat.* 93 Though syllogisms hang not on my tongue, I am not surely always in the wrong! **1827** HUYSHE *Logic* 85 A syllogism is an argument in which the terms are so placed with respect to each other, that the conclusion results necessarily from the premises, from the mere force of the expression, and without any consideration of the meaning of the terms themselves. **1830** SCOTT *Demonology* ix. 306 The pedantic sovereign considered the execution of every witch who was burnt as a necessary conclusion of his own royal syllogisms. **1833** SIR W. HAMILTON in *Edin. Rev.* LVII. 220 Hypothetical syllogisms, in the present acceptation, were first expounded, and the name first applied to them by Theophrastus and Eudemus. **1840** MACAULAY *Ess., Clive* (1843) III. 201 Here the House stopped. They had voted the major and minor of Burgoyne's syllogism; but they shrank from drawing the logical conclusion. **1850** KINGSLEY *Alton Locke* xxxviii, The unconscious logic of association is often deeper and truer than any syllogism. **1892** J. TAIT *Mind in Matter* (ed. 3) 312 The 'fool' who said in his heart that 'there was no God' no doubt thought he had wiped Him out by a syllogism.

b. *transf.* and *allusively.* An argument or something ironically or humorously regarded as such, *esp.* a specious or subtle argument or piece of reasoning; †in early use, a subtle or tricky speech; a poser; more widely, an artifice, trick.

1387 TREVISA *Higden* (Rolls) VII. 371 He coude what hym nedede for to konne, outake fables and poetes, and wily and sly silogismes, þat he wolde nouȝt on caas vouchesauf forto lerne. **1390** GOWER *Conf.* III. 366, I syh there Aristotle also, Whom that the queene of Grece so Hath bridled, that in thilke time Sche made him such a Silogime, That he foryat al his logique. *c* **1400** *Rom. Rose* 4457 Whanne she wole make A fulle good silogisme, I dreede That aftirward ther shal in deede Folwe an evelle conclusioun. **1402** *Pol. Poems* (Rolls) II. 63 Go grees a shoep undir the taile, that semeth the beter than with sotil sillogismes to parbrake thi witt. **1484** CAXTON *Fables of Æsop* V. xiv, Thow hast not yet wel studyed, and knowest not yet the Sylogysmes. **1591** GREENE *Farew. Folly* Wks. (Grosart) IX. 251 Measure not the length of an other mans foot by your owne shoe, but ioine the souldier and scholler in one sillogisme, and then the premises equall, conclude how you list. **1860** MOTLEY *Netherl.* I. viii. 501 An absolute sovereign, even without resorting to Philip's syllogisms of axe and faggot, was apt in the sixteenth century to have the best of an argument with private individuals. **1879** FARRAR *St. Paul* I. 225 They took refuge in what St. Chrysostom calls 'the syllogism of violence'.

2. In generalized sense: The form of such arguments, or argumentation in that form; the form or instrument of reasoning from generals to particulars. Also, as a mental act: mediate inference or deduction (as distinguished from immediate inference and induction).

1588 FRAUNCE *Lawiers Logike* I. ii. 7 Questions.. to be concluded by syllogisme, the onely iudge of all coherence or consequence. **1603** HOLLAND *Plutarch's Mor.* 1356 Of the present dependeth all Syllogisme and reasoning, and that by the vertue & efficacie of a conjunction: for that if this thing be, such a thing went before: and *conversim*, if this be; that shall be. **1605** BACON *Adv. Learn.* II. xiii. §4. 50 b, Certaine it is, that Middle Propositions, cannot be diduced from them [*sc.* some axioms] in Subiect of Nature by Syllogisme, that is, by Touch and Reduction of them to Principles in a Middle Terme. *Ibid.* II. xiv §12. 57 b, There being but foure kindes of demonstrations, that is by the immediate consent of the Minde or Sence; by Induction; by Syllogisme; and by Congruitie. **1690** LOCKE *Hum. Und.* IV. xvii. §4 We reason best and clearest, when we only observe the connexion of the Proofs, without reducing it to any Rule of Syllogism. *Ibid.* §6 A Man knows first, and then he is able to prove syllogistically. So that Syllogism comes after Knowledge, and then a Man has little or no need of it. **1704** NORRIS *Ideal World* II. Pref. 8 What is syllogism but only a more recollected and express way of reasoning, the putting together of all the parts of an argument, and nothing but those parts, and that in their due form and order? **1774** REID *Aristotle's Log.* Wks. (1846) 712/1 In reasoning by syllogism from general principles, we descend to a conclusion virtually contained in them. The process of induction is more arduous, being an ascent from particular premises to a general conclusion. **1821** *Aldrich's Artis Logicæ Rudim.* (ed. 2) 110 The office of syllogism is not the discovery, but the application of truth; it consists in the practical use of knowledge, rather than the primary acquisition of it. **1843** MILL *Logic* II. i. I. 223 Reasoning, in the extended sense in which I use the term, and in which it is synonymous with Inference, is popularly said to be of two kinds: reasoning from particulars to generals, and reasoning from generals to particulars; the former being called Induction, the latter Ratiocination or Syllogism. **1867** FOWLER *Deduct. Logic* III. iii. 80 (*heading*) On Mediate Inference or Syllogism. **1870** JEVONS *Elem. Logic* xv. 127 Syllogism may thus be defined as the act of thought by which from two given propositions we proceed to a third proposition. **1877** E. CAIRD *Philos. Kant* I. 134 Syllogism is just the activity of thought whereby a judgment is made complete, as judgment is the activity of thought whereby a conception is made distinct.

syllogist (ˈsɪlədʒɪst). [f. SYLLOGISM or SYLLOGIZE: see -IST.] One who reasons by syllogisms; one versed in syllogism.

1799 J. SCOTT *Bahar-Danush* I ii. 13 As the syllogists of deep judgment, [he was] skilled in eloquence. **1806** W. TAYLOR in *Ann. Rev.* IV. 219 They come again a posteriori to the usage which an a priori syllogist had exploded. **1836** LANDOR *Pericles & Asp.* cxcvi. Wks. 1846 II. 436/2 It is only since the departure of the sedate unostentatious Anaxagoras, that syllogists have snapped their fingers at experiment.

syllogistic (sɪləˈdʒɪstɪk), *a.* (*sb.*) [ad. L. *syllogisticus* (Quintilian) or Gr. συλλογιστικός, f. συλλογίζεσθαι to SYLLOGIZE: see -IC and -ISTIC. Cf. F. *syllogistique*, Ital. *sillo-*, *silogistico*, etc.] Of, pertaining to, of the nature of, or consisting of a syllogism or syllogisms.

1669 GALE *Crt. Gentiles* I. I. ii. §14 The more simple mode of philosophizing by Dialogues,.. which was the main Logic used in al the Grecian.. Scholes, before Aristotle brought in the syllogistic forme of Mode and Figure. **1678** CUDWORTH *Intell. Syst.* I. v. 770 To put the Argument into a more Approveable Syllogistick Form, Whatsoever is Extended, is Body, or Corporeal; But Whatsoever Is, is Extended. Therefore Whatsoever Is, is Body, or Corporeal. And by Consequence there can be no Incorporeal Deity. **1697** tr. *Burgersdicius' Logick* II. vi. 22 The Syllogistick Form is only an apt Disposition of the three Propositions for the necessary Collection of a Conclusion from the Premises. **1751** JOHNSON *Rambler* No. 152 ¶10 If a disputed position is to be established, or a remote principle to be investigated, he may detail his reasonings with all the nicety of syllogistic method. **1821** *Aldrich's Artis Logicæ Rudim.* (ed. 2) 110 The harshness and apparent tautology of the formal syllogism has been one occasion of prejudice against the syllogistic system. **1855** SPENCER *Princ. Psychol.* II. VI. vii. 73 So-called syllogistic reasoning passes into what is commonly known as reasoning by analogy. **1867** FOWLER *Deduct. Logic* III. iii. 90 We shall first enumerate and explain certain syllogistic rules (derived from the definition of a syllogism) which will exclude illegitimate moods.

B. *sb.* Reasoning by syllogisms; that department of logic which deals with syllogisms. Also *pl.* (see -ICS). *rare.*

1833 SIR W. HAMILTON *Discuss.* (1853) 135 Dr. Whately makes the process of reasoning not merely its [*sc.* logic's] principal, but even its adequate object;.. In this view Logic is made convertible with Syllogistic. **1837** CARLYLE *Fr. Rev.* III. II. v, The rest.. welter amid Law of Nations, Social Contract, Juristics, Syllogistics. **1847** SIR W. HAMILTON *Let. to De Morgan* 3 The principle of Syllogistic, afforded by the quantification—the expressed quantity—of the predicate.

syllo'gistical, *a.* Now *rare.* [f. as prec. – -AL[1]: see -ICAL.] = prec. adj.

a **1529** SKELTON *Replyc.* 97 In your dialecticall And principles silogisticall, If ye to remembraunce call Howe [etc.]. **1563** [see DEMONSTRATION 3]. **1570** DEE *Math Pref.* b iij b, Hard enough to frame to the Conclusion Syllogisticall. **1592** in J. Morris *Troubles Cath. Forefathers* (1877) 22 The poor man unlearned, having by chance read *Seaton's Logic*, to the interrogatories of the bishop and his chaplain made such syllogistical answers that they thought him a great clerk. **1600** W. WATSON *Decacordon* Pref. (1602) A v b, Arguments sillogisticall, enthimematicall and inductiue. **1653** GATAKER *Vind. Annot. Jer.* 131 Let your Argument be drawn into a syllogistical form. **1674** HICKMAN *Quinquart. Hist.* Ep. (ed. 2) a 3 b, They had strange Schools, in which a man could never hear a Syllogistical Disputation. **1697** tr. *Burgersdicius' Logic* II. ix. 41 In that [*sc.* the first figure] there appears the Necessity of the Syllogistical Sequel, and the Dictum of All and None. **1698** STILLINGFL. *Answ. Locke's 2nd Let.* 120 Here we have no general principles; no Criterion, no Antecedents and Consequents; no Syllogistical Methods of Demonstration.

b. Addicted to reasoning by syllogisms; dealing in syllogisms.

1599 NASHE *Lenten Stuffe* Wks. 1905 III. 185 A colony of critical Zenos, should they sinnow their sillogisticall cluster-fistes in one bundle to confute and disproue mouing. **1674** HICKMAN *Quinquart. Hist.* (ed. 2) 16 He is no Syllogistical man, and therefore I will not tie him to the strict rules of argumentation. **1837** *Fraser's Mag.* XV. 393 A peripatetic logician, as disputatious and as syllogistical as any of the *Magistri nostri.*

†c. Corresponding or agreeing like the propositions in a syllogism; consistent. *Obs. nonce-use.*

1672 MARVELL *Reh. Transp.* (1673) II. 68 That it should remain upon Record how Syllogistical a life his hath been to the Stile and Principles that he has manag'd and prosecuted.

syllogistically (sɪləˈdʒɪstɪkəlɪ), *adv.* [f. prec. + -LY[2]; see -ICALLY.] In a syllogistic manner; by means of a syllogism or syllogisms; by the method of syllogisms. Also *gen.* with logical formality or precision, by the rules of logic.

1584 FENNER *Def. Ministers* (1587) 25, I meane not to inferre all absurdities on his sayings, which might Sillogisticallie bee deducted out of his wordes. **1588** FRAUNCE *Lawiers Logike* I. ii 9 In placing them axiomatically, syllogistically, or methodically, wee argue some other thing either by explication or confirmation. **1619** SIR J. SEMPIL *Sacrilege Handled* App. 10 What more reason is there heere to separate Tithing from the Patriarch and the Promises, then to separate Blessing, seeing all three are so syllogistically wouen and interlaced? **1630** RANDOLPH *Aristippus* 12 If you discourse but a little while with a Courtier, you presently betray your learned Ignorance, answering him he concludes not Syllogistically, and asking in what Mood and figure he speakes in. **1690** [see SYLLOGISM 2]. **1782** ELIZ. BLOWER *Geo. Bateman* II. 46 Consider the matter syllogistically. It is the voice of the public that confers infamy, but the public will never know of this transaction; therefore the public cannot confer infamy on you. **1837** LYTTON *E. Maltrav.* I. xvi, No man can mathematically or syllogistically contend, that the world, which a God made, and a Saviour visited, was designed to be damned! **1864** BOWEN *Logic* xi. 351 We must reason syllogistically whenever we use language with any perception of its meaning. **1871** SPENCER *Princ. Psychol.* §305 (1872) II. 99 In the fore-going section.. we saw that there are many inferences of a kind so certain as to be called axiomatic, which do not admit of having their terms arranged syllogistically.

†syllogistry. *Obs. nonce-wd.* [f. SYLLOGISTICAL, after *sophistry.*] Sophistical syllogistic reasoning.

1592 NASHE *Strange Newes* C ij b, I would foorthwith haue writ in praise of Ropemakers, & prou'd it by sound sillogistry to be one of the 7 liberal sciences. **1593** G. HARVEY *Pierce's Super.* Wks. (Grosart) II. 276.

syllogization (ˌsɪlədʒaɪˈzeɪʃən). *rare.* [f. next + -ATION: in med.L. *syllogizatio.*] The action of syllogizing; syllogistic reasoning.

1660 FISHER *Rusticks Alarm* Wks. (1679) 597 From *may be* to *must be* is such a silly sort of Sillogization, as is not owned in *foro Academico.* **1744** HARRIS *Three Treat.* Notes (1765) 265 From mathematical Bodies.. they passed to.. Intuition and Syllogization.

syllogize (ˈsɪlədʒaɪz), *v.* Forms: 5 sylogyse, sillogise, 7 sillogize, 6– syllogize, 7– syllogise. [a. OF. *sil(l)ogiser*, or ad. med.L. *syllogizāre* (Boethius, Thomas Aquinas), ad. Gr. συλλογίζεσθαι, f. σύν SYN-[1] + λογίζεσθαι to reckon, calculate, compute, conclude, infer, f. λόγος discourse, reason, consideration, account.

Syllogize has often been explained as meaning literally 'to collect', L. *colligere* being regarded as the etymological equivalent of Gr. συλλογίζεσθαι (perh. by association with συλλογή collection, συλλέγειν to collect); cf. Milton's *Logic* II. ix, eam ratiocinantis quasi collectionem vox ipsa syllogismi significat. It has otherwise been interpreted as 'to add up, make a sum of', as if συλλογίζεσθαι were an intensive of λογιζέσθαι in the sense of 'to calculate, compute']

1. *intr.* To argue by syllogisms; to reason syllogistically; also *gen.* (Also with *it.*)

c **1420** ? LYDG. *Assembly of Gods* 19 Me nought auaylyd ayene hym to sylogyse. **1509** HAWES *Past. Pleas.* ix. (1555) E ij b, But rude people, opprest with blyndnes Agaynst your fables, wyll often solisgyse [*sic*]. **1594** NASHE *Terrors of Night* Wks. (Grosart) III. 250 All receipts and authors you can name he syllogizeth of. **1616** R. C. *Times' Whistle* etc. (1871) 146 Though they can sillogize with arguments Of al things. **1631** [see ELENCHIZE]. **1632** J. HAYWARD tr. *Biondi's Eromena* 93 This constant concealing himselfe put her in doubt, causing her to syllogize; That who so loveth, the same obeyeth the thing or subject beloved, but he obeyed not (because he told her not who hee was) and therefore he loved her not. **1663** COWLEY *Cutter Colman St.* IV. iv, I have heard him syllogize it with Mr. Soaker in Mood and Figure. **1697** tr. *Burgersdicius' Logic* II. vi. 20 To Syllogise is to collect, that is, conclude, or from some certain Propositions to draw up the Summ of an Argument or Proof. **1759** STERNE *Tr. Shandy* I. xvi, And then he would do nothing but syllogize within himself for a stage or two together, How far the cause [etc.]. **1788** T. TAYLOR *Proclus* I. 54 *note*, Thus we may syllogize in the first figure, Everything white, is an animal: Every bird is white: Therefore, Every bird is an animal. **1875** W. JACKSON *Doctr. Retribution* i. 54 They [*sc.* first-truths] cannot be proved deductively, because, being first, there is nothing *prior* from which to syllogize. **1907** F. HARRISON *Creed of a Layman* 168 He does not syllogize about the origin of things, but he goes straight to the practical work of religion.

b. *trans.* To argue (a person) *out of* a condition, etc.

1718 *Free-thinker* No. 14 ¶6 A Scholastick Jugler, who plays his Legerdemain Tricks to Syllogize the Ignorant out of their Understanding and their Senses. **1809** SOUTHEY in *Q. Rev.* II. 51 That [he] should of a sudden fall in metaphysics, and, by a few miserable sophisms syllogize himself out of all hopes of an hereafter.

c. To deduce by syllogism.

Only in transl. and echoes of Dante *Paradiso* x. 138 sillogizzò invidiosi veri = 'drew true conclusions which brought odium upon him' (Tozer).

1867 LONGF. tr. *Dante, Paradise* x. 138 Sigier, Who, reading lectures in the Street of Straw, Did syllogize invidious verities. **1870** LOWELL *Among my Bks.* Ser. I. (1873) 337 The men who attack abuses are not so much to be dreaded by the reigning house of Superstition as those who, as Dante says, syllogize hateful truths. **1884** —— *Democracy* (1887) 15 It is then only that they syllogize unwelcome truths.

2. *intr.* (*nonce-use*, after *sympathize.*) To agree in ways of thinking.

1800 MACKINTOSH *Let. to Moore* 27 Sept., in *Mem.* (1835) I. 141 There is no body to whom I speak with such unreserved agreeable liberty, because we so much sympathise and (to borrow Parr's new coined word) syllogise.

Hence **'syllogizer**, a syllogistic reasoner; **'syllogizing** *vbl. sb.*, reasoning by syllogisms.

1588 J. HARVEY *Disc. Probl.* 96 These cunning *Syllogizers, or any like Sophisticall concluders. **1606** J. DOVE *Def. Church Govt.* 72 It is not a noueltie of 60. yeares old, as this syllogiser hath obiected. **1642** SIR E. DERING *Sp. on Relig.* xvi. 86 Every Syllogizor is not presently a match to cope with Bellarmine. *c* **1449** PECOCK *Repr.* I. xiv. (Rolls) 76 For that thei trusten and trowen the premisse be trewe, eer that thei seen the premisses sufficientli proued bi *sillogizing. **1569** J. SANFORD tr. *Agrippa's Van. Artes* xcvii. 169 They hauing recourse to interpreting, to expounding, to glossinge, and to sillogisinge, do rather geue it some other sence, then the proper meaninge of the letter. **1654** J. WEBSTER *Acad. Examen* 38 The vain glory of Syllogizing Sophistry. **1656** tr. *Hobbes's Elem. Philos.* (1839) 57 Errors which happen in reasoning, that is, in syllogizing, consist either in the falsity of the premises, or of the inference. **1666** BP. S. PARKER *Free & Impart. Censure* (1667) 36 Plato's manner of arguing is more succinct than the tedious way of Syllogising. **1699** T. BAKER *Refl. Learn.* v. 58 The way of Syllogizing seem'd to him very fallacious and too dependent upon words, to be much rely'd on. **1806** W. TAYLOR in *Ann. Rev.* IV. 722 The reasoning power he [*sc.* Newton] displayed in the mathematical forms of syllogizing. **1877** E. CAIRD *Philos. Kant* I. 134 There is no ground for saying that reason, the faculty of syllogising, is different and distinct from understanding, the faculty of judging.

syllour, -ure, sylor, -our, var. CELURE, SILOUR, *Obs.*

syllup: see SYLLAB.

†**sylly-jestical,** *a. Obs. nonce-wd.* Perversion of SYLLOGISTICAL intended to suggest *silly jest*.

1601 BP. W. BARLOW *Defence* 69 Faine would this disputer with his sylly-iesticall method conclude vs all to be infidels.

Sylow ('siːlɒf). *Math.* The name of P. L. *Sylow* (1832–1918), Norwegian mathematician, used *attrib.* and in the possessive to designate concepts in group theory propounded by him (*Math. Annalen* (1872) V. 584), as **Sylow (p-)subgroup**, a subgroup whose order is the largest power of the prime *p* which divides the order of the group; **Sylow's theorem** (see quots. 1897, 1975).

1893 *Proc. Lond. Math. Soc.* XXV. 14 It is then shown that Sylow's theorem leads to relations between the numbers of operations of different orders which it is impossible to satisfy. **1897** W. BURNSIDE *Theory of Groups of Finite Order* vi. 91 We shall divide the proof of Sylow's theorem into two parts. First we show that, if p^a is the highest power of a prime *p* which divides the order of a group, the group must have a sub-group of order p^a; and secondly that the sub-groups of order p^a form a single conjugate set and that their number is congruent to unity, mod. *p*. **1905** *Messenger Math.* XXXV. 48 A group..all of whose Sylow subgroups are cyclical. **1975** I. STEWART *Concepts Mod. Math.* vii. 104 The best that can be said in general is Sylow's theorem; if *h* is a power of a prime and divides the order of a group *G*, then *G* has a subgroup of order *h*. **1976** *Nature* 20 May p. vii (Advt.), The classification of nonsoluble groups with abelian sylow 2-subgroups.

sylph (sɪlf). [ad. mod.L. (pl.) *sylphes*, G. *sylphen* (Paracelsus *De Nymphis*, etc.), mod.L. *sylphi* (Ibid., Wks. 1658 II. 391). Cf. F. *sylphe*, Sp. *silfo*, Pg. *sylpho*, etc.

Littré conjectures a Gaulish origin, citing *sulfis* dat. pl. from *Inscr. Helvet.* no. 117 of Orelli, who connects the form with *suleviæ* female tutelary spirits venerated in Gaul (see Holder *Altcelt. Sprachschatz* s.v.). But Paracelsus's word may be an arbitrary coinage, perh. a blending of *sylvestris* SYLVESTER *sb.*[1] 1 and *nympha* NYMPH *sb.*]

1. a. One of a race of beings or spirits supposed to inhabit the air (orig. in the system of Paracelsus).

1657 H. PINNELL *Philos. Reformed* I. i. 26 (from Paracelsus) To the Earth doe belong Gnoms, Lemurs, Sylphs. **1680** A. L[OVELL] tr. *Montfaucon de Villars' Cnt. of Gabalis* 29 The Sylphs are composed of the purest atomes of air. **1699** DRYDEN *Let. to Mrs. Eliz. Thomas* 12 Nov., Wks. 1800 I. II. 97 Whether Sylph or Nymph, I know not: those fine creatures..have a mind to be christen'd. **1712** [see SALAMANDER *sb.* 2b]. **1714** POPE *Rape Lock* I. 65 The light Coquettes in Sylphs aloft repair, And sport and flutter in the fields of Air. **1812** SIR H. DAVY *Chem Philos.* 17 The Rosicrucian philosophy, in which gnomes, sylphs, salamanders, and nymphs were the spiritual agents, supposed capable of being governed or enslaved by man. **1830** SCOTT *Demonol.* x. 347 They affirmed that they could bind to their service and imprison in a ring, a mirror, or a stone, some fairy, sylph or salamander. **1856** MISS MULOCK *John Halifax* x, Though this lady did not look like a sylph or a wood-nymph—being neither very small nor very slight.

b. Applied to a graceful woman or girl; usually with implication of slender figure and light airy movement. (Cf. NYMPH *sb.* 2.)

1838 DICKENS *Nich. Nick*, xxv, She's the only sylph I ever saw, who could stand upon one leg, and play the tambourine on her other knee, like a sylph. **1847** DISRAELI *Tancred* IV. xi, The mother..seemed a sylph or a sultana.

2. Gould's name for various humming-birds with long forked tails.

1861 GOULD *Monogr. Trochilidæ* III. Pl. 172 *Cynanthus cyanurus.* Blue-Tailed Sylph. *Ibid.* 173 *Cynanthus smaragdicaudus.* Green-Tailed Sylph.

3. *Comb.*, as ***sylph-like*** adj. and adv., ***sylph-looking*** adj.

1801 C. WILMOT *Let.* 13 Dec. in T. U. Sadleir *Irish Peer* (1920) 15 Madame, their Mother, was too much en bon point to have such a sylphlike appearance as her daughters. **1818** SCOTT *Br. Lamm.* xviii, The sylph-like form, disencumbered of her heavy riding-skirt and mantled in azure silk. **1825** T. HOOK *Sayings* Ser. II. *Passion & Princ.* vii. III. 82 A sylph-like gracefulness in their figures and actions. **1833** —— *Parson's Dau.* III. ix, Lady Catherine.. gliding sylph-like across the room, seated herself by his side. **1834** H. MILLER *Scenes & Leg.* xx. (1857) 289 There tripped lightly along a sylph-looking creature.

Hence **'sylphic, 'sylphish, 'sylphy** *adjs.*, pertaining to, resembling, of the nature of, or characteristic of a sylph; sylph-like; **'sylphize** *v.*, *trans.* to give a sylphish character to.

1821 *New Monthly Mag.* II. 361 This..cannot but be considered as an improvement even by the most prejudiced of the *sylphic race. **1825** C. M. WESTMACOTT *Engl. Spy* I. 227 The sylphic daughters of Terpsichore. **1754** *Adventurer* No. 93. II. 136 The images, customs, and employments of his [*sc.* Pope's] sylphs are exactly adapted to their natures..; are all, if I may be allowed the expression, *Sylphish. **1834** MEDWIN *Angler in Wales* II. 233 She was of a slender, delicate, and sylphish form. **1802** ANNA SEWARD *Lett.* (1811) VI. 27 The Gothic mythology, demonized by the elder bards of Caledonia, *sylphized by Shakespeare, and the British poets. **1836** T. HOOK *G. Gurney* I. vii. 283 There was a swan-like swimmingness about her air and gait—a sort of *sylphy something that rivetted the attention. **1842** *United Service Mag.* I. 383 Her chaplet of bright flowers and expanded sylphy wing.

sylphid ('sɪlfɪd), *sb.* (*a.*) Also -ide. [ad. F. *sylphide* (1671 in Littré), f. *sylphe*: see prec. and -ID[2].] A little or young sylph.

1680 A. L[OVELL] tr. *Montfaucon de Villars' Cnt. of Gabalis* 67 As to marriage, I would advise you to take a sylphide. **1714** POPE *Rape Lock* II. 73 Ye Sylphs and Sylphids, to your chief give ear! **1803** H. K. WHITE *Clifton Grove* 48 in *Rem.* (1807) II. 12 Hosts of Sylphids on the moon-beam sail. *a* **1814** *Gonzanga* v. i. in *New Brit. Theatre* III. 145 Let me catch my runaway sylphid by the leg, what a delightful scene of raillery I'll have with him. **1837** LYTTON *E. Maltrav.* III. ii, Worse than the Rosicrucians, it is to make a sacrifice of all human beauty for the smile of a sylphid, that never visits us but in visions. **1849** THACKERAY *Pendennis* xxxviii, Our little sylphide, who scarcely ate at dinner more than the six grains of rice of Amina. **1897** GUNTER *Susan Turnbull* xxi. 276 She bounds with the grace of a sylphide.

b. *attrib.* or as *adj.* = SYLPHIC, SYLPHISH.

1779 *Sylph* I. 195 My connexion with the Sylphiad [*sic*] tribe. **1803** JANE PORTER *Thaddeus* xxii, He ventured to look once only at her Sylphid figure. **1808** SCOTT *Marm.* II. Introd. 90 If to Sylphid Queen 'twere given, To show our earth the charms of Heaven, She could not glide along the air, With form more light. **1853** MISS E. S. SHEPPARD *Ch. Auchester* II. 204 If he were small and sylphid seated by his majestic mother, how tiny was that delicate satellite of his.

Hence **'sylphidine** *a.* (*nonce-wd.*), like a sylphid.

1885 MEREDITH *Diana* xiii, She swam above them in a cocoon of her spinning, sylphidine, unseizable.

Sylphon ('sɪlfɒn). Also **sylphon**. [Invented word.] A proprietary name (see quots. 1906, 1916, 1933) used esp. to designate concertina-like metal bellows and devices employing them.

1906 *Official Gaz.* (U.S. Patent Office) 3 Apr. 1643/1 Heat-regulators for use on boilers, furnaces, and stoves... *Sylphon.* **1916** *ibid.* 25 July 1432/1 *Sylphon*... A hollow expansible and contractible corrugated tubular metal device. **1933** *Trade Marks Jrnl.* 2 Aug. 925/2 *Sylphon*... Valves, hot and cold water mixers and dampers all being parts of steam boilers... The Fulton Sylphon Company.., Knoxville, Tennessee. **1937** *Jrnl. Psychol.* IV. 281 The essential unit is a small capacity sylphon or thin-gauge metal bellows enclosed in an airtight metal housing. **1938** *Jrnl. R. Aeronaut. Soc.* XLII. 1072 The valves of these tanks may be operated by a sylphon bellows. **1945** H. D. SMYTH *Gen. Acct. Devel. Atomic Energy Mil. Purposes* x. 110 The pumps used were sylphon-sealed reciprocating pumps.

sylring, var. of CELURING *Obs.*

1628 in *Maitland Club Misc.* III. 372 The law galerie without to have ane fair border round about from the sylring to the heid of the windowis.

sylue, obs. form of SELF.

1426 LYDG. *De Guil. Pilgr.* 3396 Ryht in the sylue wyse.

syluer, -ir, -ur, -yr(e, obs. ff. SILVER.

sylueren, obs. f. SILVERN.

sylure, var. CELURE, SILOUR, *Obs.*; obs. f. SILVER.

‖**sylva, silva** ('sɪlvə). [L. *silva* a wood, forest, woodland: commonly misspelt *sylva* in imitation of the synonymous Gr. ὕλη (see HYLE).]

1. a. A title for a treatise on forest trees, or a descriptive list or catalogue of trees. (Cf. FLORA 2.)

1664 EVELYN (*title*) Sylva, Or a Discourse of Forest-Trees. **1859** W. S. COLEMAN *Woodlands* (1866) 63 Its [*sc.* the walnut's] importance as a timber and fruit tree is so great that we must introduce it as a member of our Sylva.

b. The trees of a particular region or period collectively. (Cf. FLORA 3.)

1846–8 LOWELL *Biglow P.* Ser. I. *2nd Let. fr. B. Sawin* Postscr., In the *sylva* of our own Southern States, the females of my family have called my attention to the china-tree. **1882** 'OUIDA' *Maremma* I. 148 The rich sylva and flora which the central part of the Maremma possesses.

†**2.** A title for a collection of pieces, esp. of poems; also, a thesaurus of words or phrases.

After the title (*Silvæ*) of Statius's collection of occasional poems.

[**1626** BACON (*title*) Sylva Sylvarvm: or A Naturall Historie. In ten Centvries.] **1636** A. C[OWLEY] (*title*) Sylva, or Divers Copies of Verses Made upon sundry occasions. **1675** ALSOP *Anti-sozzo* iii. §2. 259 What ever other Synonima his Sylva will furnish him with. **1728** CHAMBERS *Cycl.*, *Sylva*, in Poetry, a poetical Piece, composed, as it were, at a Start; in a kind of Rapture or Transport,..its chief Use, in our Language is, metaphorically, to express certain Collections of poetical Pieces, of various Kinds, and on various Subjects. **1787** (*title*) Sylva; or, the Wood: being a Collection of Anecdotes, Dissertations, Characters, Apophthegms, Original Letters, Bons Mots, and other little things... By a Society of the Learned.

sylvage ('sɪlvɪdʒ). *rare*[−1]. [f. L. *sylva, silva* a wood (see prec.) + -AGE.] Woody growth, boscage.

1773 GOLDSM. *Ess.* xxi. Wks. (Globe) 345/1 The brook assumed a natural sylvage; and the rocks were covered with moss.

sylvan, silvan ('sɪlvən), *sb.* and *a.* Also 6 -ein, 6–7 -ane, (9 -ain). [ad. F. *sylvain* (only sb.; in Marot, 1539, *silvans, sylvans* pl.) or ad. L. *silvānus, sylvānus* (in early use only sb. fem. pl. *silvānæ* goddesses of the woods), f. *silva, sylva*: see prec. and -AN.

The Latin masc. adj. *Silvanus* was used as the proper name of a divinity of the fields and forests, identified with Pan, etc.; it has been occas. anglicized as *Silvan*, e.g. Milton *Comus* 268, *Il Pens.* 134.]

A. *sb.* One who (or something that) inhabits a wood or forest; a being of the woods.

a. *Mythol.* An imaginary being supposed to haunt woods or groves; a deity or spirit of the woods.

1565 GOLDING *Ovid's Met.* I. 222 Satyres, Faunes, and sundry Nymphes, with Silvanes eke beside. **1586** L. BRYSKETT in *Spenser's Astrophel, Aeglogue Sir P. Sidney* 116 Ye Siluans, Fawnes, and Satyres, that emong These thickets oft haue daunst after his pipe. **1616** DRUMMOND OF HAWTH. *Poems* (S.T.S.) I. 39 Goate-feete Syluans. **1675** SHADWELL *Psyche* I, Then an Entry danc'd by four Sylvans, and four Dryads, to rustick Musick. *a* **1758** RAMSAY *Yellow haird Laddie* ii, Silvans and Fairies unseen danc'd around. **1831** SCOTT *Ct. Rob.* xvi, The ancient belief in the god Pan, with his sylvans and satyrs. **1845** DISRAELI *Sybil* II. i, Ionic columns of black oak, with a profusion of fruits and flowers, and heads of stags and sylvans.

b. A person dwelling in a wood, or in a woodland region; a forester; a rustic.

1589 PUTTENHAM *Engl. Poesie* I. xv. (Arb.) 49 The Satyre was pronounced by rusticall and naked Syluanes speaking out of a bush. **1698** FRYER *Acc. E. India & P.* 146 Daily disturbance from these Sylvans and Mountaineers. **1703** POPE *Vertumnus* 20 Her private orchards, wall'd on ev'ry side, To lawless sylvans all access deny'd. **1824** SCOTT *St. Ronan's* xxv, They [*sc.* two girls] were encountered by a country fellow..up came cousin Francis.., and soon put the silvan to flight.

c. An animal, esp. a bird, living in or frequenting the woods.

1612 DRAYTON *Poly-olb.* xiii. 44 Hunts-up to the Morn the feath'red Sylvans sing. **1613–16** W. BROWNE *Brit. Past.* II. iii. 891 A little grove..Where every morne a quire of Silvans sung. **1831** J. WILSON in *Blackw. Mag.* XXIX. 291 Shyest of the winged silvans, the cushat. **1831** SCOTT *Ct. Rob.* xvi, The sylvan [an orang-outang] looked fixedly upon Count Robert, almost as if he understood the language used to him.

d. ? A forest tree, shrub, etc. *rare.*

1632 LITHGOW *Trav.* x. 498 Clydes fragrant fields,.. Bedeckt with Siluans. **1787** *Generous Attachment* II. 97 The verdant sylvans.

B. *adj.* **1.** Belonging, pertaining, or relating to, situated or performed in, associated with, or characteristic of, a wood or woods. (In earliest use of deities or nymphs: see A.)

1580–3 GREENE *Mamillia* II. Wks. (Grosart) II. 283 The Syluein Nimph Oenone. *a* **1586** SIDNEY *Arcadia* II. iv. (1912) 172 A goodly white marble stone, that should seeme had bene dedicated in ancient time to the Silvan gods. **1638** COWLEY *Love's Riddle* I. i, May all the Sylvan Deityes Bee still propitious to you. **1697** DRYDEN *Æneid* IX. 549 If e're my Pious Father, for my sake, Did grateful Off'rings on thy Altars make; Or I increas'd them with my Silvan toils. **1741** SHENSTONE *Judgem. Hercules* 57 The silvan choir, whose numbers sweetly flow'd. **1750** JOHNSON *Rambler* No. 66 ¶9, I once knew a man..who..found himself irresistibly determined to sylvan honors;..he..spent whole days in the woods, pursuing game. **1810** SCOTT *Lady of L.* II. ii, Good hawk and hound for sylvan sport. **1821** —— *Kenilw.* xxxiv, Elizabeth's silvan dress..was of a pale blue silk. **1831** —— *Ct. Rob.* xxvii, A sylvan man, or native of the woods [an orang-outang]. **1847** L. HUNT *Jar Honey* viii. (1848) 104 The Italians identify the pastoral with the sylvan drama. **1885** R. BUCHANAN *Annan Water* viii, Deep sylvan silence.

b. Of woods as a subject of cultivation or observation. *rare.*

1830 J. G. STRUTT *Sylva Brit.* 42 These would form a volume in themselves, a Sylvan Chronicle of times past. **1834** *Tait's Mag.* I. 665/1 The new system of silvan-culture introduced by Violaines, for the regeneration of the Royal forests.

2. Consisting of or formed by woods or trees.

1594 NASHE *Unfort. Trav.* Wks. (Grosart) V. 120 As many sortes of shrill breasted birdes as the Summer hath allowed for singing men in hir siluane chappels. **1615** CHAPMAN *Odyssey* XIX. 599 Steepe Parnassus, on whose forehead grow All syluan off-springs round. **1667** MILTON *P.L.* V. 377 So to the Silvan Lodge, They came. **1697** DRYDEN *Virg. Past.* VI. 15 And all the Silvan reign shall sing of thee. **1784** COWPER *Task* I. 588 The houseless rovers of the sylvan world. *a* **1822** SHELLEY *Fragm. Unfinished Drama* 225 The pillared stems Of the dark sylvan temple. **1857** LIVINGSTONE *Trav.* xii. 212 The islands at a little distance seem great rounded masses of sylvan vegetation.

3. Furnished with, abounding in, or having as its chief feature, woods or trees; wooded, woody.

1667 MILTON *P.L.* IV. 140 Cedar, and Pine, and Firr, and branching Palm A Silvan Scene. **1697** DRYDEN *Æneid* XI. 874 To share with me The Silvan Shades. **1794** MRS. RADCLIFFE *Myst. Udolpho* xxxiv, All the charms of sylvan and pastoral landscape. **1798** WORDSW. *Tintern Abbey* 56 How oft, in spirit, have I turned to thee, O sylvan Wye! thou wanderer thro' the woods! **1814** SCOTT *Wav.* xxii, The glen widened into a silvan amphitheatre. **1870** EDGAR *Runnymede* 23 The towns assumed a sylvan aspect, and the churches were converted into leafy tabernacles. **1880** LD. BEACONSFIELD in *Daily News* 27 Mar. 6/5 Sylvan scenery never palls. **1883** STEVENSON *Silverado Sq.* 60 The whole neighbourhood..now so quiet and sylvan, was once alive with mining camps.

Hence **syl'vanity** (sɪl-), sylvan quality or character; **'sylvanize** *v. trans.*, to render sylvan; **'sylvanly** *adv.*, in a sylvan manner or style; **'sylvanry**, sylvan scenery.

1832 J. WILSON in *Blackw. Mag.* XXXII. 852 Manners.. full of rurality, or *silvanity, or urbanity. **1907** *Times* 1 July

7/4 Mr. Knight's 'Sylvanus Urban'..combined the urbanity of a true man of letters with the sylvanity (if it may be called so) of a Yorkshireman. **1835** *Blackw. Mag.* XXXVII. 606 The winds..would..have called from their sleep of years the satyrs to *sylvanize the spot again. **1800** COLERIDGE in Robberds *Mem. W. Taylor* (1843) I. 318 Something very *sylvanly romantic. **1844** MRS. BROWNING *Lost Bower* xxiv, The wild hop..And the large-leaved columbine, Arch of door and window-mullion, did right sylvanly entwine. **1821** *New Monthly Mag.* II 46 Perch'd upon a green and sunny hill, Gazing upon the *sylvanry below. **1901** *Pall Mall G.* 29 May 1/3 You shall find..quite unsuspected sylvanry in..Kensington Gardens.

Sylvaner (sɪl'vɑːnə(r)). Also **sylvaner**. [a. G. *silvaner, sylvaner*: cf. SYLVAN, SILVAN *sb.* and *a.*]

1. A variety of vine first developed in German-speaking districts, the dominant form bearing white grapes; a vine or grape of this variety. Also *attrib.*

1928 P. M. SHAND *Bk. French Wines* vi. 201 The Gutedel ..Ortlieber, Burger, Sylvaner, and Klevner are grown besides [in Alsace]. **1963** *Times* 17 Jan. 4/6 It has the typical flavour of a wine made from Sylvaner grapes. **1965, 1976** [see PINOT]. **1981** T. MCLEAN *Medieval Eng. Gardens* ix. 256 The Müller-Thurgau vine..is a cross between a Riesling and a Sylvaner.

2. The white wine made from the Sylvaner grape.

1958 A. L. SIMON *Dict. Wines, Spirits & Liqueurs* 152/2 *Sylvaner*, a free-bearing white-wine grape grown extensively in Germany and in Alsace. Much Alsatian wine (white) made from Sylvaner grapes is marketed under the name of *Sylvaner*. **1961** *Spectator* 24 Nov. 756 [The wines] are labelled according to the grapes used, as in Alsace... The commonest names are Riesling..Sauvignon, Sylvaner, [etc.].

sylvanite ('sɪlvənaɪt). *Min.* [f. (*Tran*)*sylvania*, where found: see -ITE[1]. Cf. *sylvanium* (G. *sylvan*, Werner), an old name for tellurium.]

a. Native tellurium, with slight admixture of gold, iron, etc. ? *Obs.* **b.** A telluride of gold and silver (sometimes also containing lead), occurring in crystals or masses of a steel-grey, silver-white, or yellow colour with metallic lustre.

1796 KIRWAN *Elem. Min.* (ed. 2) II. 324, I call it [*sc.* the new semi-metal] Sylvanite, from its being found in Transylvania. **1811** PINKERTON *Petral.* II. 239 Bornite,.. with sylvanite, from Nagyag in Transilvania. **1868** DANA *Min.* (ed. 5) 81 Sylvanite... Comp... Tellurium 55·8, gold 28·5, silver 15·7. Antimony sometimes replaces part of the tellurium, and lead part of the other metals.

Hence **sylva'nitic** *a.*, containing sylvanite.

1796 KIRWAN *Elem. Min.* (ed. 2) II. 101 The Sylvanitic Ore..is..of a whitish colour.

sylvar, obs. form of SILVER.

sylvate, silvate ('sɪlveɪt). *Chem.* [f. SYLVIC + -ATE[1] c.] A salt of sylvic acid.

1836 BRANDE *Chem.* (ed. 4) 978 The silvates of potassa, soda, and ammonia, are soluble in water;..the silvate of magnesia..is soluble in alcohol.

sylvatic, silvatic (sɪl'vætɪk), *a.* Also 8 **selvatick** (after It. *selvatico*). [ad. L. *silvāticus*, f. *silva*: see SYLVA and -ATIC. Cf. F. *sylvatique*.]

1. Belonging to or found in woods; of the nature of a wood or woodland; sylvan; † *transf.* rustic, boorish (*obs.*). *rare.*

1661 LOVELL *Hist. Anim. & Min.* Isagoge a v b, Insectivorous,..and..not melodious, as the..swallow, wild and riparie;..titmouse, great fennish, sylvatick, black, ceruleous. **1668** H. MORE *Div. Dial.* III. xxxiv. (1713) 271 Fauns and Satyrs and other Sylvatick Genii. *Ibid.* v. xxi. 474 How rough and unpolish'd, how rude and sylvatick the spirit of Elias will appear. **1755** T. H. CROKER *Orl. Fur.* XXIV. xci, Concealed in the selvatick brake. **1814** T. HAYNES *Treat. Strawberry*, etc. (ed. 2) 5 *note*, Others assert the large Carolinian [strawberry] to be an inhabitant of sylvatic situations.

2. *Med.* Also (*rare*) **selvatic**. Applied to certain diseases (as rabies, yellow fever, plague, and Chagas's disease) when contracted by wild rather than domesticated animals, and to the pathogens causing them. [ad. F. *selvatique* (R. Jorge *Les Rongeurs & leurs Puces dans la Propagation de la Peste* (1928) ii. 36); cf. L. *silvāticus* wild.]

1931 C. O. STALLYBRASS *Princ. Epidemiol.* ix. 310 In this way arise two types of epizoötic [plague]... One.. among wild rodents, spreading slowly from colony to colony, independent of man's lines of communication..; to this type of epizoötic Jorge (1928) has given the title selvatic plague. **1935** *Jrnl. Amer. Med. Assoc.* 17 Aug. 535/2 The invasion of sylvatic plague among the ground squirrels of the foothills of the Sierras and Cascade Mountains creates a widening menace in the United States. **1936** WU LIEN-TEH in Wu Lien-Teh et al. *Plague* vi. 195 Jorge..distinguished between the pandemic plague introduced..by..'domestic' rodents, and selvatic plague, dangerous to man only when he invades the remote endemic areas populated by wild rodents. **1970** *Sci. Jrnl.* Apr. 35/1 There has been a steady and alarming increase in rabies in wild animals—so-called sylvatic rabies. **1978** *Nature* 27 Apr. 820/1 We have identified distinct sylvatic and domestic strain-groups of *T*[*rypanosoma*] *cruzi*, apparently circulating independently and transmitted by different vector species.

So † **syl'vatical** *a.* (*obs. rare*[−0]).

1656 BLOUNT *Glossogr.*, *Sylvatical.*

† **sylve.** *Obs.* Pedantic *nonce-use.* [ad. L. *sylva, silva* a wood.]

1694 MOTTEUX *Rabelais* v. 251 Incluse with Sylves behind, and Lakes before us, Our outward man wants something that's calorous.

† **sylvester**, *sb.*[1] *Obs.* Also silv-. [In sense 1, ad. L. *syl-, silvestris*; in sense 2, ad. L. *silvestre* (sc. *grānum* seed), neut. of *silvestris*: see SYLVESTER *a.*]

1. In the system of Paracelsus, a spirit of the woods.

1657 H. PINNELL *Philos. Reformed* I. i. 27 In the Aire or our airy world there are Umbratils, Silvesters, Satyrs, whose Monsters are the Gyants. *Ibid.* II. 15 *marg.*, Gnomes, Sylvesters and Lemures.

2. Name for an inferior kind of cochineal (supposed, like the true cochineal, to be the seed of a plant).

1697 DAMPIER *Voy.* I. v. 124 The Friers get plentiful incomes..in other places where they plant Cochoneel Trees, or Silvester Trees. *Ibid.* viii. 229 The Silvester is a red grain growing in a Fruit much resembling the Cochineel-fruit. **1703** *Lond. Gaz.* No. 3895/3 Goods out of the Mary Man of War from Vigo, consisting of Sugars,.. Campuchina, or Silvester. [**1791** HAMILTON tr. *Berthollet's Art of Dyeing* II. II. III. iii. 170 The sylvestris is a sort of cochineal.]

Sylvester ('sɪlvɪstə(r), sɪl'vɛstə(r)), *sb.*[2] [Proper name.] St. Sylvester's day, Dec. 31. ***Sylvester-eve, -night*** [G. *Sylvesterabend*], the evening or night of Dec. 31, New Year's Eve.

1838 S. JACKSON tr. *Strauss' Remin. Early Life Lutheran Clergyman* I. 50, I have never been able to feel joyful on Sylvester-eve, when I have spent it wholly in company. **1852** THACKERAY *Esmond* II. vii, And so the sylvester night passed away. **1866** ENGEL *Nat. Mus.* viii. 276 In the villages of Northern Germany, it is not unusual for the cow-herd,.. at midnight of Sylvester, to..sing a sacred hymn.

† **sylvester, sil-**, *a. Obs. rare.* [ad. L. *sil-, sylvester, -tris*, f. *silva*, SYLVA.] = SYLVESTRIAN *a.*[1] So **syl'vestral** *a. Bot.*, growing in woods or woodland places; of a type found in woods; † **syl'vestrial**, † **syl'vestric**, † **syl'vestrious**, † **syl'vestrous** *adjs.* = SYLVESTRIAN *a.*[1]

1578 T. N. tr. *Conq. W. India* (1596) 378 They did maintaine themselves with rootes, hearbes, and *silvester frutes. **1720–1** *Lett. fr. Mist's Jrnl.* (1722) II. 169 One Time a mighty Plague did pester All Beasts Domestick and Sylvester. **1858** IRVINE *Hand-bk. Brit. Plants* 80 *Sylvestral plants..grow chiefly in woods; but some..also in hedges, and more in bushy places. **1863** J. G. BAKER *N. Yorksh.* 181 Aboriginal species characteristically paludal, uliginal, ericetal, and sylvestral. **1607** TOPSELL *Four-f. Beasts* 630 All wilde *siluestriall beastes are dryer then the tame, modern, and domesticall. **1620** VENNER *Via Recta* iii. 64 It [*sc.* the pheasant] may of all syluestriall Fowle, well challenge the first place at tables. **1623** COCKERAM I, *Sylvestrick, wilde, rusticall. **1656** BLOUNT *Glossogr.*, *Sylvestrick*, *Sylvestrious ..of Wood or Forest, full of Trees or Wood, woody. **1653** R. MASON in Bulwer *Anthropomet.* Lett. to Author **4, The ruder crouds and *sylvestrous heards of mankinde.

sylvestrene (sɪl'vɛstriːn). *Chem.* [ad. G. *sylvestren* (A. Atterberg 1877, in *Ber. Deut. Chem. Ges.* X. 1203), f. L. *sylvestr-is* found in woods (f. *silva*: see SYLVA, SILVA), specific epithet of the Scots pine, *Pinus sylvestris*: see -ENE.] A liquid monocyclic terpene, $C_{10}H_{16}$, known in two optically active forms and formerly believed to be a natural constituent of pine oil, but now recognized as a product of the extraction process.

1877 *Chem. News* 6 July 7/1 A. Atterberg has examined the crude '*Wood-Spirit from Norwegian Pines*', and found in the higher boiling portions..a new turpentine, to which he assigns the name *sylvestrine*. **1931** [see ISOPRENE b]. **1952** TURNER & HARRIS *Org. Chem.* xix. 317 Simonsen..showed that the precursor of sylvestrene is the naturally occurring (+)-Δ^3-carene.

sylvestrian, sil- (sɪl'vɛstrɪən), *a.*[1] [f. L. *silvestris* (see SYLVESTER *a.*) + -AN.] Belonging to or found in woods; sylvan, rustic.

1657 TOMLINSON *Renou's Disp.* 229 Mallows..is either Hortensian..or Sylvestrian. **1716** M. DAVIES *Athen. Brit.* III. *Diss. Physick* 37 There's nothing now remaining of those Sylvestrian Herbalists. *a* **1732** GAY *Wine* 131 Sylvestrian gods! **1866** J. B. ROSE tr. *Ovid's Fasti* II. 289 Silvestrian deities. **1867** —— tr. *Virg. Æneid* 62 The Nymphs sylvestrian.

Syl'vestrian, *a.*[2] and *sb. Ch. Hist.* [f. *Sylvester* (see below) + -IAN.] Belonging to, or a member of, an order of Benedictines founded by Sylvester Gozzolini in 1231. Also † **Sylvestrin(e** [F. *Sylvestrin* sb.] *a.* and *sb.*

1693 tr. *d'Emilianne's Hist. Monast. Orders* xii. 100 Of the Sylvestrin Order. The Congregation of Sylvestrins began to be established in the year 1269..by Sylvester Gozolini. **1753** CHALLONER *Cath. Chr. Instructed* 182 Other Religions, professing the Rule of St. Benedict, as the Silvestrines. **1882–3** *Schaff's Encycl. Relig. Knowl.* III. 2275 Sylvestrians. **1905** *United Free Ch. Mag.* Apr. 13/2 The convent of San Marco..was originally a foundation of Sylvestrian monks.

sylviad ('sɪlvɪæd), *sb.* (*a.*) *Ornith.* [f. mod.L. *Sylviadæ*, variant form for *Sylviidæ*, f. *Sylvia*, name of the typical genus: see -ID[3], and cf. -AD 1 b.] A bird of the family *Sylviadæ* (*Sylviidæ*); a warbler. Also *attrib.* or as *adj.*

1867 *Ibis* Jan. 73 If we cast our eye down the catalogue, we find sixty-one species of the Sylviads enumerated. *Ibid.* 74 There are two very distinct tides of Sylviad immigration in Palestine.

† **sylvian**, *a.*[1] *Obs. rare*[−1]. Incorrectly for SYLVAN.

1698 FRYER *Acc. E. India & P.* 64 Those slender Fences only designed to oppose the Sylvian Herd, are thrown down to erect others of a more War-like Force.

Sylvian ('sɪlvɪən), *a.*[2] *Anat.* [ad. F. *sylvien*, f. the name of François de la Boë *Sylvius*, a Flemish anatomist (1614–1672); often erroneously referred to that of Jacques Dubois, latinized Jacobus *Sylvius*, an earlier French anatomist (1478–1555).] Described by or named after the anatomist Sylvius: applied to certain structures in the brain, viz.:

Sylvian aqueduct (***aqueduct of Sylvius***), the passage between the third and fourth ventricles of the brain. ***Sylvian artery***, the middle cerebral artery. ***Sylvian fissure*** (***fissure of Sylvius***), the fissure between the anterior and middle lobes of the cerebrum. ***Sylvian fossa***, a depression of the cerebral hemispheres in the middle of the Sylvian fissure, containing the island of Reil. ***Sylvian ventricle***, the fifth ventricle of the brain.

1828 J. QUAIN *Elem. Anat.* ix. 613 The angular part of the anterior lobe..is included between the internal termination of the fissure of Sylvius, the longitudinal fissure, and the commissure of the optic nerves. **1839–47** [see ROLANDO a]. **1849** S. G. MORTON *Illustr. Syst. Human Anat.* 547 The insula [of Reil] consists of five or six small convolutions grouped and concealed within the Sylvian fissure. **1871** HUXLEY in Darwin *Descent of Man* vii. (1874) 204 In the human foetus, the sylvian fissure is formed in the course of the third month of uterogestation. **1888** [see REIL]. **1890** BILLINGS *Med. Dict.*, Sylvian fossa..Sylvian ventricle. **1899** *Allbutt's Syst. Med.* VI. 773 Lesions in or about the nuclei in the gray matter of the Sylvian Aqueduct. *Ibid.* VII. 608 The middle cerebral, or Silvian artery, is practically the direct continuation of the internal carotid. **1939** [see REIL]. **1980** A. SILVERSTEIN *Human Anat. & Physiol.* xiii. 278/2 Viewed from the side, the cerebrum looks something like a large mitten, with the wrist at the back and the fingers at the front of the head. The 'thumb' of the mitten is separated from the remainder by another prominent groove, the lateral fissure or fissure of Sylvius.

sylvian, *a.*[3] (*sb.*) *Ornith.* [f. mod.L. *Sylvia* (Scopoli, 1769), f. L. *silva* a wood: see SYLVA and -AN.] Belonging to the genus *Sylvia* or family *Sylviidæ* of oscine passerine birds (the warblers). **b.** *sb.* A bird of this genus or family.

In mod. Dicts.

sylvic, silvic ('sɪlvɪk), *a. Chem.* [ad. F. *sylvique* (*a* 1836), f. L. *sylva, silva* a wood: see -IC 1 b.] ***sylvic acid***: a colourless crystalline substance, isomeric with pinic acid, and, like it, forming a constituent of colophony or turpentine-resin.

1836 BRANDE *Chem.* (ed. 4) 978 Silvic Acid..is insoluble in water, fusible at about 212°, soluble in alcohol and ether, and in sulphuric acid. **1838** T. THOMSON *Chem. Org. Bodies* 506 That portion of the resin which remains undissolved when the turpentine freed from its oil is digested in cold alcohol of 0·867, has been called *silvic acid* by Unverdorben, and *resin beta* by Berzelius. **1844** FOWNES *Chem.* 500 Pure sylvic acid crystallizes in small, colourless, rhombic prisms.

sylvicoline (sɪl'vɪkəlaɪn), *a.* and *sb. Ornith.* [ad. mod.L. *Sylvicolīnæ* pl., f. *Sylvicola*, a former generic name, = L. *silvicola* inhabiting woods: see -INE[1].] **a.** *adj.* Belonging to the *Sylvicolinæ*, a former division of the family then called *Sylvicolidæ* (now *Mniotiltidæ*), comprising the typical American warblers. **b.** *sb.* A bird of this division.

1872 COUES *Key N. Amer. Birds* 91 The student will be able to assure himself that his specimen is a sylvicoline. **1878** —— *Birds Colorado Valley* 484 The genus *Icteria*..seems decidedly Tanagroid or Sylvicoline.

sylviculture, silvi- ('sɪlvɪkʌltjʊə(r), -tʃə(r)). [ad. F. *sylvi-, silviculture*, f. L. *sylva, silva* a wood + F. *culture* cultivation.] The cultivation of woods or forests; the growing and tending of trees as a department of forestry.

1880 *Nature* 5 Feb. 330/1 A recent instructive experiment in sylviculture. **1893** M. G. WATKINS in *Academy* 15 July 55/2 Sylviculture..means the culture of timber for profit, as opposed to arboriculture, or the growing of beautiful specimen trees in park and garden.

Hence **sylvi'cultural** *a.*, belonging or relating to sylviculture (whence **sylvi'culturally** *adv.*); **sylvi'culturist**, a person engaged or skilled in sylviculture.

1889 *Nature* 12 Dec. 122/2 *Sylvicultural systems—that is different methods under which the creation, regeneration, tending, and utilization of woods are effected. **1893** NISBET (*title*) British Forest Trees and their Sylvicultural Characteristics and Treatment. **1903** *Board Agric. Leaflet* No. 91. 4 It is to the action of the beetle that the chief silvicultural damage is due. **1903** *Forestry Quart.* Nov. 36 (Cent. Dict., Suppl.) *Silviculturally of interest is the note that in a spruce stand undergrown with beech no beetles were found, although a neighboring stand was greatly damaged. **1887** *Pop. Sci. Monthly* Sept. 636 A French *sylviculturist has devised a method of clothing the stripped oak-trees.

sylviine ('sɪlvɪaɪn), *a. Ornith.* [ad. mod.L. *Sylviinæ* pl., f. *Sylvia*: see SYLVIAD and -INE[1].] Belonging to the *Sylviinæ*, either as a synonym of *Sylviidæ* reckoned as a subfamily of a larger family, or as a subfamily of *Sylviidæ* comprising the warblers of the Old World.

1884 COUES *Key N. Amer. Birds* (ed. 2) 260 *Polioptila* has been sometimes associated with the *Paridæ*, but differs decidedly and is apparently Sylviine.

sylvine ('sɪlvɪn). *Min.* [a. F. *sylvine* (Beudant, 1832), from the old name of the salt, *sal digestivus Sylvii* 'digestive salt of Sylvius': see -INE[5].] Native potassium chloride, occurring in some salt-mines and on Mount Vesuvius. Also called **sylvite** ('sɪlvaɪt).

1850 ANSTED *Elem. Geol., Min.* etc. §370 *Sylvine*, Chloride of potash. **1868** DANA *Min.* (ed. 5) 111 Sylvite. **1913** *Illustr. Lond. News* 22 Feb. 238/3 Sylvine happens to be one of the minerals which, in one of its forms, emits electricity on compression.

sylvinite ('sɪlvɪnaɪt). *Min.* [ad. G. *sylvinit*, f. G. *sylvin* SYLVINE: see -ITE[1].] A commercial name for a mixture of sylvite and halite (the form in which sylvite commonly occurs).

1896 A. H. CHESTER *Dict. Names Minerals* 263 *Sylvinite*, the commercial name for sylvite. **1962** *Economist* 31 Mar. 1274/3 The D'Arcy Exploration Company..found..potash-bearing brine and sylvinite (a mixture of potassium chloride and salt) in a boring near Whitby. **1980** H. BLATT et al. *Origin Sedimentary Rocks* (ed. 2) xv. 558 Sylvinite is composed of sylvite (KCl) and halite (NaCl).

sylvre, -vryn, -vyrn, obs. ff. SILVER, SILVERN.

sylwes, obs. f. *shelves*, pl. of SHELF *sb.*[1]

sylypp, obs. form of SYLLAB, syllable.

sym- (sɪm), *prefix*, repr. Gr. συμ-, assimilated form of συν-, SYN-[1], before labials (β, μ, π, φ, ψ), hence in words of Greek derivation in Latin and modern languages before *b*, *m*, *p*. **symmorphic** (sɪ'mɔːfɪk), *a. nonce-wd.* [f. Gr. σύμμορφος (μορφή form) + -IC], having the same or a like form; conformed; so **sy'mmorphism**, likeness of form, condition of being conformed. **sympalmograph** (sɪm'pælməʊgrɑːf, -æ-) [Gr. παλμός vibration: see -GRAPH], an apparatus for exhibiting the combination of vibrations, consisting of a double pendulum the two parts of which can be caused to vibrate in different directions and at varying rates, with a style attached so as to trace the resulting curves on a prepared surface. **sympatetic** (sɪmpə'tɛtɪk), *nonce-wd.* [after PERIPATETIC], a fellow-walker, a companion in a walk. **sympelmous** (sɪm'pɛlməs), *a. Ornith.* (also *erron.* **syn-**) [Gr. πέλμα sole of the foot: see -OUS], having the tendons of the deep flexors of the toes united before separating to each of the four digits. **symperitoneal** (sɪm,pɛrɪtəʊ'niːəl), *a.* (see quot.). **sympetalous** (sɪm'pɛtələs), *a. Bot.* (also *erron.* **syn-**), having the petals united; gamopetalous. **sympha'langism** *Anat.* [L. *phalang-*: see PHALANX], a condition in which the middle phalanx of a finger or toe is properly developed in length but its proximal (or distal) joint is imperfect or absent. **'symphile** *Ent.*, an insect that lives with ants or other social insects as a guest in a relationship of symphilism; hence **sym'philic** *a.*, pertaining to or being a symphile; also *fig.* **symphilism** ('sɪmfɪlɪz(ə)m), *Biol.* [ad. G. *symphilie* (M. E. Wasmann 1896, in *3me Congr. Internat. Zool.* 412), f. Gr. συμφιλεῖν to love mutually + -ISM], term for a kind of friendly symbiosis or commensalism existing between ants or termites and certain other insects which they feed and tend as guests, and which in some cases yield a sweet substance as food for them; also **symphily** ('sɪmfɪlɪ) [ad. Gr. συμφιλία]. Hence **symphilous** ('sɪmfɪləs) *a.*, characterized by symphily. **symphonesis** (sɪmfə'niːsɪs), *Philol.* [Gr. φώνησις PHONESIS; cf. Gr. συμφώνησις agreement] (see quot. and DING-DONG C. 1). **symphonetic** (sɪmfə'nɛtɪk), *a.* [Gr. φωνητικός PHONETIC], (*a*) *Mus.* consisting of parts in harmony; polyphonic; (*b*) *Philol.* exhibiting symphonesis. **symphrase** ('sɪmfreɪz), *Gram.*, a word consisting of a phrase or number of words run into one. **symphrattic** (sɪm'frætɪk), *a. Geol.* [irreg. f. Gr. συμφράττειν to press together + -IC], produced by pressure, as regionally metamorphosed rocks; so **sym'phrattism**, metamorphism caused by pressure. **symphronistic** (sɪmfrə'nɪstɪk), *a. nonce-wd.* [f. Gr. συμφρονεῖν to be of one mind; after *synchronistic*], involving coincidence or identity of thought; embodying the same ideas. **'symphylan, 'symphylid** *adjs.* and *sbs. Ent.* [mod.L. *Symphyla*, name of a class of arthropods (J. A. Ryder 1880, in *Amer. Naturalist* XIV. 376), f. Gr. φυλή tribe: so called from their combining characteristics of several other classes] (of or pertaining to) an arthropod of the class Symphyla, the members of which resemble centipedes, having soft bodies and many legs. **symphyllous** (sɪm'fɪləs), *a. Bot.* [Gr. φύλλον leaf: see -OUS], having the perianth-leaves united; gamophyllous. ‖**sympneuma** (sɪm'pnjuːmə), pl. **-ata** [Gr. πνεῦμα spirit], a supposed companion spirit, or spiritual bride or bridegroom; hence **sympneu'matic** *a.*, of or pertaining to a 'sympneuma'; so **sym'pneumatism**, the theory of 'sympneumata'; also, agreement in 'spirit', disposition, or mental attitude. **sympolar** (sɪm'pəʊlə(r)), *a. Geom.*, reciprocally polar: said of a pair of polyhedra so related that every face of each corresponds to a summit of the other. **sympolity** (sɪm'pɒlɪtɪ) [Gr. συμπολίτης fellow-citizen, after POLITY], mutual relation of, or a body of, fellow-citizens. **'symport** *Biochem.* [after TRANSPORT *sb.*], flow of two substances through a membrane in the same direction in which the rate is increased by a cooperative effect. †**sympresbyter** *obs.* (also *erron.* **syn-**) [ad. Gr. συμπρεσβύτερος (1 Pet. v. 1)], a fellow-presbyter, fellow-elder. **sympsychograph** (sɪm'psaɪkəʊgrɑːf, -græf), *nonce-wd.* [PSYCHOGRAPH], an imaginary composite portrait produced by superposition of images of the same object as conceived by different minds; so **sympsy'chographer, -graphy**.

1851 G. S. FABER *Many Mansions* 103 Our spiritualised human bodies..thus conformed or (as the Greek has it [Philipp. iii. 21])..made *symmorphic to his spiritualised Body. *Ibid.*, They would neither have this declared *symmorphism, nor..be fitted for a perpetual abode..with the Lord their glorious pattern. **1895** C. E. BENHAM in *Engineering* 26 July 127 (*title*) The *Sympalmograph. **1832** MAGINN in *Blackw. Mag.* XXXII. 413 Without..interrupting..the dialogue of the two venerable *sympatetics. **1890** SEEBOHM in *Ibis* Jan. 31 In *synpelmous birds the plantars do not cross each other at the back of the tarsus.., but coalesce at the point where they usually cross. **1885** *Stand. Nat. Hist.* (1888) IV. 369 An arrangement to be called synpelmous, since the two tendons are completely blended... The synpelmous distribution of the deep plantar tendons obtains especially in the swifts, humming birds..and their allies. **1898** *Syd. Soc. Lex.*, Sympelmous. **1903** DORLAND *Med. Dict.* (ed. 3), **Symperitoneal*..uniting two or more parts of the peritoneum artificially. **1870** A. W. BENNETT in *Jrnl. Bot.* June 192, I would propose..terms similar to those applied to the pistil, where we use 'apocarpous', and 'syncarpous'... The terms 'aposepalous', 'synsepalous', 'apopetalous', and '*synpetalous', would at once convey their meanings. **1877** A. W. BENNETT tr. *Thomé's Bot.* 129 The corolla is gamopetalous or *sympetalous (less correctly 'monopetalous'), when the petals are more or less coherent. **1916** H. CUSHING in *Genetics* I. 91 This paper will present a much more complete family record of an inherited trait... The malformation will be designated *symphalangism. **1943** *Jrnl. Heredity* XXXI. 344/1 Similar reports of abnormalities of hands and feet including symphalangism, syndactylism, and polydactyly..seem to agree that many anatomical anomalies may be inherited as single dominant traits. **1965** *Arch. Internal Med.* CXV. 580/1 Symphalangism (congenital fusion of the phalanges) is occasionally associated with brachydactyly. **1910** *Symphile [see *synœkete* s.v. SYN-]. **1960** H. OLDROYD tr. *Jeannel's Introd. Entomol.* viii. 212 The greater number of symphiles are beetles, cherished by the ants, and carried with them wherever the nest is moved, but nevertheless terrible enemies of the colony because of the great damage they do to it. **1971** E. O. WILSON *Insect Societies* xx. 403/1 Many of the better-integrated symphiles dispense attractive substances to their hosts from epidermal glands. **1919** W. OSLER *Old Humanities & New Sci.* ii. 12 This attention is what our *symphilic community—to use a biological term—bestows on you. **1927** H. ST. J. K. DONISTHORPE *Guests of Brit. Ants* p. xvi, They mostly possess characteristic or 'symphilic' colours and texture—a yellow-red, with an oily looking surface. **1971** E. O. WILSON *Insect Societies* xx. 403/2 A large percentage of the symphilic beetles..possess peculiar tufts of red or golden hairs. **1903** *Nature* 12 Feb. 351/1 The phenomenon of '*symphilism', that is to say, the harbouring of insects, &c., of various foreign species in the nests of ants and termites. It is stated that the number of *symphilous arthropods exceeds a hundred. **1899** D. SHARP in *Cambridge Nat. Hist.* VI. 183 The relations between ants and their guests..Wasmann..arranges..in four categories: 1, '*Symphily' for the true guests, which are fed and tended by the ants, the guests often affording some substance the ants delight in. **1872** A. J. ELLIS *Presid. Addr. to Philol. Soc.* 13 The Dingdong! theory..; let us call it **symphonesis*. **1721** A. MALCOLM *Treat. Mus.* xi. §2. 332 A compound Song is where Two or more Voices go together,..so that the Melody each of them makes, is a distinct and different simple Song..; ..all such Compositions are very properly called *symphonetick Musick, or Musick in Parts. **1872** A. J. ELLIS *Presid. Addr. to Philol. Soc.* 15 Is it [*sc.* the word 'scrumptious'] interjectional, imitational, or symphonetic? **1893** *Smithsonian Rep.* 41 He was able to ascertain and formulate the principles..governing the number, kind, and position of notional stems in *symphrases, or word-sentences. **1904** A. W. GRABAU in *Amer. Geol.* Apr. 236 *note*, Rocks of this type may be called *symphrattic rocks. *Ibid.* 236 Whether the metamorphism be due..to mountain making processes (regional or dynamo-metamorphism, or *symphrattism). **1828** CARLYLE *Germ. Rom.* IV. 145 Another series of..occurrences, not so much of a synchronistic, as of a *symphronistic kind. **1898** A. S. PACKARD *Text-bk. Entomol.* 21 He..believed that the Symphyla are the forerunners of the myriapods, and not of the insects, his genealogical tree representing the *symphylan and thysanuran phyla as originating from the same point. **1964** U. LANHAM *Insects* i. 19 Two of these classes [of many-legged arthropods]— the pauropods and the symphylans—are small, obscure creatures... The other two—centipedes and millipedes—are larger, more conspicuous. **1979** W. D. RUSSELL-HUNTER *Life of Invertebrates* xvi. 301 In some structural features, symphylans resemble the centipedes and in others the apterygote insects. **1936** *Trans. Soc. Brit. Entomol.* III. 14 The contention that the opisthogoneate condition in insects has been derived from *Symphylid stock. *Ibid.* 16 The heart, haemocoel, fat-body and anal glands have all been inherited from the Symphylids. **1973** *Nature* 16 Nov. 128/1 It is of interest that certain of the symphilids carry styli on the base of the second and third pairs of legs. **1974** *Encycl. Brit. Macropædia* XII. 771/1 Symphilid species are small, fragile, and lacking pigmentation. **1877** A. W. BENNETT tr. *Thomé's Bot.* 134 The perianth..may be gamophyllous or *symphyllous..on the one hand; or [etc.]. **1885** L. OLIPHANT *Sympneumata* v. 81 United with a '*Sympneuma' free from the gross external covering of outer body. *Ibid.* xii. 179 The electric *sympneumatic life. *Ibid.* xiii. 201 The conscious notes echoed from the unconscious sympneumatic depths. **1891** *Pall Mall G.* 9 July 2/2 The *sympneumatism between the *Times* and the 'Tories' Last Hope'. **1892** *Daily News* 16 July 5/2 The young lord who is bitten by 'Sympneumatism', or the theories of Mr. Laurence Oliphant. **1873** B. GREGORY *Holy Cath. Ch.* xv. 146 There does arise a new *sympolity, a fellow-citizenship of the saints. **1963** P. MITCHELL in *Biochem. Soc. Symp.* XXII. 148 Over a certain range of concentration, the asymmetry of distribution of the molecules of one substrate across the membrane gives rise to an increased flow of the second substrate in the same direction. We will call this type of coupled movement *symport. **1978** *Nature* 2 Mar. 97/1 There are discussions of algal ion transport and of Na^+/organic solute cotransport (symport). **1671** BAXTER *Power Mag. & Ch. Pastors* ii. §44. 35 The Major Vote of his *Syn-Presbyters are against it. *a* **1677** BARROW *Serm. Heb.* xiii. 17, Wks. 1686 III. 280 The same titles, which the Apostles assumed to themselves, they ascribe to their Sympresbyters. **1896** D. S. JORDAN in *Pop. Sci. Monthly* Sept. 601 We are enabled to present a copy of the resultant *sympsychograph. *Ibid.* 602 One suggestion was that this was the blind spot on the retina in each of the *sympsychographers. *Ibid.* 601 From seven ideals, sympathetically combined, the true cat would be developed. This combination is the essence of *sympsychography.

syma, obs. form of CYMA.

syman, obs. form of CEMENT.

a **1583** in Halliwell *Rara Math.* (1841) 40 The Glasse..ys made fast with syman vppon a smalle block.

symar, var. CYMAR, SIMAR.

symbal(e, -all, obs. forms of CYMBAL.

symbilyne, ? obs. Sc. form of CYMBALLING.

1500–20 DUNBAR *Poems* lxxxvi. 15 Quhar cherubyne syngis sweit Osanna, With organe, tympane, harpe, and symbilyne.

Symbionese (,sɪmbɪə'niːz), *a.* [f. SYMBIO(SIS + -*n*- + -ESE, after group and people names in -*nese* (*Chinese*, *Lebanese*, etc.): see quot. 1974.] *Symbionese Liberation Army*, the name adopted by a socialist revolutionary group active in the United States in the mid-1970s.

1973 *N.Y. Times* 10 Nov. 1/4 Two days ago, a group calling itself the Symbionese Liberation Army took the responsibility for the killing. **1974** *Black Panther* 23 Feb. 11/2 The Symbionese Liberation Army is made up of the aged, youth and women and men of all races and people. The name Symbionese is taken from the word symbiosis and we define its meaning as a body of dissimilar bodies and organisms living in deep and loving harmony and partnership in the best interest of all within the body. **1975** *Times* 20 Nov. 1/3 Miss Patricia Hearst, the runaway heiress..was arrested..[in] a routine check on the movements of people associated with the Symbionese Liberation Army (the SLA). **1976** M. J. LASKY *Utopia & Revolution* (1977) 603 Six leading American members..of the so-called Symbionese Liberation Army were killed in Los Angeles in a gun fight [in 1974] with the local police.

symbiont ('sɪmbɪɒnt, -baɪ-). *Biol.* Also (in Dicts.) **symbion.** [irreg. f. Gr. συμβιῶν, pr. pple. of συμβιοῦν: see SYMBIOSIS.] Either of two organisms living in symbiosis; a commensal.

1887 GARNSEY & BALFOUR tr. *De Bary's Fungi* 360 The results of the reciprocal action of the two symbionts. **1902** H. M. COULTER *Plant Studies* 162 In symbiosis one of the symbionts may be an animal.

symbiose ('sɪmbaɪəʊz), *v.* [Back-formation from next.] *intr.* To live as a symbiont.

1960 *McGraw-Hill Encycl. Sci. & Technol.* XI. 546/2 Strains of each species show marked host specificities in their abilities to symbiose with the plants within each group. **1971** M. ALEXANDER *Microbial Ecol.* xi. 266 A single fungus can apparently symbiose with dissimilar species of algae.

‖**symbiosis** (sɪmbɪ'əʊsɪs, -baɪ-). Pl. **symbioses.** [mod.L., ad. Gr. συμβίωσις a living together, companionship, f. συμβιοῦν, συμβιόειν to live together, f. σύμβιος adj. living together, sb. companion, partner, f. σύν SYM- + βίος life.]

1. Living together, social life.

1622 MISSELDEN *Free Trade* 60 To study and inuent things profitable for the publique Symbiosis. **1910** *Spectator* 30 July 173/2 The savage with his..sense of 'participation', of 'symbiosis'. **1920** *Q. Rev.* July 164 So long as the people concerned can talk freely together, they form one spiritual symbiosis, and their culture will be the same.

2. a. *Biol.* Association of two different organisms (usually two plants, or an animal and a plant) which live attached to each other, or one as a tenant of the other, and contribute to each other's support. Also more widely, any intimate association of two or more different organisms, whether mutually beneficial or not.

Also called *commensalism* or *consortism*; distinguished from *parasitism*, in which one organism preys upon the other. Rarely in extended use, including parasitism; or including mutually beneficial association without bodily attachment

1877 BENNETT tr. *Thomé's Bot.* (ed. 6) 267 In the Lichens we have the most remarkable instance in the vegetable kingdom of..symbiosis or commensalism. **1882** H. N. MOSELEY in *Times* 30 Aug. 7/4 Certain animals have imbedded in their tissues numbers of unicellular algæ, which are not to be regarded as parasites, but which thrive in the waste products of the animal, while the animal feeds upon the compounds elaborated by the algæ. This combined condition of existence has been named by Dr. Brandt symbiosis. **1909** tr. *Warming's Oecol. Plants* xxv. 84 Parasitism is a form of symbiosis. **1941** H. KIRBY in Calkins & Summers *Protozoa in Biol. Res.* xix. 891 De Bary..used symbiosis as a collective term, the subdivisions of which include parasitism and mutualism; he recognized two main categories, antagonistic and mutualistic symbiosis. **1953** [see SYMBIOTE]. **1953**, etc. [see MUTUALISM 2]. **1973** R. G. KRUEGER et al. *Introd. Microbiol.* xxxi. 748/1 Three or more different kinds of organisms are involved in some symbioses. **1977** R. L. SMITH *Elem. Ecol. & Field Biol.* x. 268/1 Mutualism is often termed symbiosis. Actually symbiosis.. includes mutualism, commensalism, and parasitism.

b. *transf.* and *fig.*

1921 G. B. SHAW *Back to Methuselah* II. 79 Let the Creator say, if you like, 'I will establish an antipathetic symbiosis between thee and the female.' **1955** *Bull. Atomic Sci.* Apr. 143/2 Two world wars predetermined the henceforth inevitable symbiosis of scientific activity and political decision. **1963** *Listener* 28 Feb. 386/1 The agreement between Castro and the Communist Party early in 1958..began the process of symbiosis which worried many of the more thoughtful *fidelistas*. **1967** M. J. RUGGLES in D. H. Perman *Bibliogr. & Historian* (1968) II. 22 A symbiosis between scholar and librarian is necessary. **1976** *New Yorker* 17 May 127/1 In the symbiosis that will link the candidates and the press throughout this election year, many representatives of each are out in Iowa. **1982** *Listener* 23 & 30 Dec. 29/2 The politician and the journalist exist in a state of uneasy symbiosis.

Hence **symbiote** ('sɪmbɪəʊt, -baɪ-) [for ending cf. *zygote*], (*a*) a combination of two symbiotic organisms; (*b*) = SYMBIONT; also *fig.*; **symbiotic** (sɪmbɪ'ɒtɪk, -baɪ-), *a. Biol.* associated or living in symbiosis; relating to or involving symbiosis; also *transf.* and *fig.*; **symbi'otically** *adv.*, in a symbiotic manner, in the way of symbiosis; **'symbiotism** (*rare*), symbiosis.

1897 *Nature* 2 Dec. 119/1 It may be a *symbiote involving some gigantic rhizopod..and a bacterial organism. **1923** *Anat. Rec.* XXV. 2 Portier believes that the 'symbiotes' are especial microorganisms found in great abundance in nature. They are constantly entering and leaving the host organism. **1925** *Jrnl. Infectious Dis.* XXXVI. 94 The intracellular bacteria have been designated as 'symbiotes'. **1953** R. P. HALL *Protozoology* x. 528 Endoparasites which participate in symbiosis, an association involving mutual benefits to host and parasite, are known as symbiotes. **1953** [see MUTUALISM 2]. **1970** *Times Lit. Suppl.* 14 Aug. 899/5 His suggestion of a future man as a bio-mechanical symbiote. **1882** *Academy* 4 Feb. 86/2 Prof. Moseley..expresses the view that the chlorophyllaceous corpuscles.., long known as constituents of the living substance of large Foraminifera, are *symbiotic algae. **1894** OLIVER tr. *Kerner's Nat. Hist. Plants* I. 254 Animals and Plants considered as a great symbiotic community. **1900** J. HUTCHINSON in *Archives Surg.* XI. 224 The tubercle bacillus is probably present in symbiotic and often latent union with the tissues. **1951** R. FIRTH *Elem. Social Organization* i. 10 It is most evident in the case of an African tribe having its members living intermingled with those of other tribes and in symbiotic relationship with them. **1956** *Psychiatric Research Rep.* No. 3. 8 A therapeutic move of considerable importance in such a situation is for the physician to function as the other half of the patient's 'symbiotic' system. **1962** *Lancet* 19 May 1033/2 The human infant in its first year is more precariously placed than has hitherto been appreciated since mother and child form a symbiotic union. **1970** *Nature* 6 June 905/1 Throughout its auspicious history the Botanical Society of Edinburgh has had a symbiotic relationship with the Royal Botanic Garden. **1979** W. STYRON *Sophie's Choice* vi. 150 Höss eventually developed what might be called a fruitful—or at least symbiotic—relationship with the man who was to remain his immediate superior. **1888** VINES in *Encycl. Brit.* XXIV. 128/2 A Lichen is a compound organism consisting of a Fungus and an Alga living *symbiotically. **1895** OLIVER tr. *Kerner's Nat. Hist. Plants* II. 233 Several plants..live symbiotically with certain.. ants. The plants afford the ants lodging..and give them nourishment..; the ants in return defend the foliage against the attacks of leaf-eating animals. **1902** *Encycl. Brit.* XXV. 272/2 The remarkable *symbiotism between Algæ and Fungi.

symbiotrophic (ˌsɪmbaɪəʊ'trəʊfɪk, -'trɒfɪk), *a. Ecol.* [f. SYMBIO(SIS + -TROPHIC.] Obtaining nourishment through symbiosis.

1905 B. D. JACKSON *Gloss. Bot. Terms* (ed. 2) 358/1. **1974** D. H. LEWIS in Carlile & Skehel *Evolution in Microbial World* 386 Chemoheterotrophs, including animals, may derive nutrients in the free-living state (saprotrophic) or following intimate contact with other organisms (symbiotrophic). **1978** *Proc. Indian Acad. Sci.* B. LXXXVII. x. 243 Despite high salinity and acidity an acid sulfate soil harboured N_2-fixing symbiotrophic organisms with appreciable efficiency.

‖**symblepharon** (sɪm'blɛfərɒn). *Path.* [mod.L., f. Gr. σύν SYM- + βλέφαρον eyelid.] Adhesion of the eyelid to the eyeball.

1819 S. COOPER *First Lines Surg.* (ed. 4) I. 438 Concretions of the eyelids... One, termed *symblepharon*, in which the inner lining of one or both eyelids has become adherent to the eyeball. **1875** H. WALTON *Dis. Eye* 468 Where the palpebral and ocular conjunctiva are cut through, these are apt to unite and produce symblepharon.

symbly, var. SEMBLE *a. Obs.*, like, similar.

a **1500** *Ratis Raving* I. 1355 As arestotyll and ypocras Has vyting in syk symbly cas.

symbol ('sɪmbəl), *sb.*[1] Also 6 simbole, 6–7 symbole, -boll, 7 simbol; also in L. form. [ad. late L. *symbolum* (partly through F. *symbole*, 16th c. = It., Sp. *sim-*, Pg. *symbolo*), a. Gr. σύμβολον mark, token, ticket, 'tessera', f. σύν SYM- + root of βολή, βόλος a throw (cf. συμβάλλειν to put together, f. σύν SYM- + βάλλειν to throw).]

1. a. A formal authoritative statement or summary of the religious belief of the Christian church, or of a particular church or sect; a creed or confession of faith, *spec.* the Apostles' Creed.

This use is traceable to Cyprian, Bishop of Carthage (*c* 250), who applies L. *symbolum* to the baptismal creed, this creed being the 'mark' or 'sign' of a Christian as distinguished from a heathen. The notion, long current, that the creed was so called because it was 'put together' by the Apostles is without foundation in fact.

1450–1530 *Myrr. our Ladye* III. 312 Thys crede ys called *Simbolum*, that ys to say a gatherynge of morselles. for eche of the .xii. apostels put therto a morsel. **1490** CAXTON *How to Dye* 4 The credo and symbole of the fayth. **1536** HEN. VIII in Burnet *Hist. Ref.* (1679) I. *Collect. Rec.* 306 All..things..which be comprehended in the whole body and Canon of the Bible, and..in the three Creeds or Symbols. **1539** HILSEY *Man. Prayers* C iij b, The Symbole or Crede of the greate doctour Athanasius. **1585** T. WASHINGTON tr. *Nicholay's Voy.* IV. xiii. 126 b, He sayde.. the Lordes Prayer, the salutation of the Aungell, and the Symbole of the Apostles. **1602** PARSONS *Warn-word* I. xiv. 100 b, The Symbolum or Creed of the Apostles. *a* **1638** in Chillingw. *Relig. Prot.* I. iv. §27. 205 The Symbole is a briefe yet entire Methodicall summe of Christian Doctrine. **1699** T. BAKER *Refl. Learn.* xiv. 175 Enquiring into the number of Symbols, he adds a fourth to the other three. **1887** *Ch. Q. Rev.* Apr. 20 The symbolum *Quicunque vult*, whether regarded as an actual Creed..or as a hymn on the Creed.. has an intense value of its own. **1887** CAROLINE HAZARD *Mem. J. L. Diman* vii. 150 The Nicene Creed, the great symbol in which the divinity of Christ is asserted and defined. **1912** *Ch. Q. Rev.* July 349 Salnar, in 1581, gathered the ten chief Symbols of the Reformed Churches in his *Harmonia Confessionum Fidei*.

†**b.** *transf.* A brief or sententious statement; a formula, motto, maxim; *occas.* a summary, synopsis. *Obs.*

1594 NASHE *Unfort. Trav.* 50 The simbole thereto [*sc.* to the helmet] annexed was this, *Ex lachrimis lachrimæ*. **1644** BULWER *Chirol.* 94 The Cynique in his symbole advising men to adde benignity to their courtship. **1656** BLOUNT *Glossogr.* [from Cotgrave], *Symbole*..a short and intricate riddle or sentence. **1662** OWEN *Disc. Liturgies* iii. 16 That they might have [in the Lord's Prayer] a summary Symbole of all the most excellent things they were to ask of God. **1751** JOHNSON *Rambler* No. 117 ¶3 The celebrated symbol of Pythagoras, ἀνεμῶν πνεόντων τὴν ἠχὼ προσκύνει; 'when the wind blows, worship its echo.'

2. a. Something that stands for, represents, or denotes something else (not by exact resemblance, but by vague suggestion, or by some accidental or conventional relation); *esp.* a material object representing or taken to represent something immaterial or abstract, as a being, idea, quality, or condition; a representative or typical figure, sign, or token; †*occas.* a type (of some quality). Const. *of.*

1590 SPENSER *F.Q.* II. ii. 10 That, as a sacred Symbole, it [*sc.* a blood-stain] may dwell In her sonnes flesh. **1604** SHAKS. *Oth.* II. iii. 350 To renownce his Baptisme, All Seales, and Simbols of redeemed sin. **1612** DEKKER *London Triumphing* Wks. 1873 III. 245 Euery one carrying..a Symbole, or Badge of that Learning which she professeth. **1615** G. SANDYS *Trav.* II. 139 They [*sc.* ostriches] are the simplest of fowles, and symbolls of folly. **1641** J. JACKSON *True Evang. T.* III. 170 They play and sport together. A thing so true a symbole of deerenesse. **1646** SIR T. BROWNE *Pseud. Ep.* V. xxi. 265 Salt as incorruptible, was the Simbole of friendship. **1686** SOUTH *Serm., Isa. v. 20* (1727) II. 333 Words are the Signs and Symbols of Things; and, as in accounts, Cyphers and Figures pass for real Sums; so.. Words and Names pass for Things themselves. **1688** HOLME *Armoury* III. 127/1 In Arms..Changes [are] the simbol of Dissimulation. **1765–8** ERSKINE *Inst. Law Scot.* III. iii. §5 Another symbol was anciently used in proof that a sale was perfected, which continues to this day in bargains of lesser importance among the lower rank of people, the parties licking and joining of thumbs. **1769** ROBERTSON *Chas. V*, III. x. 238 There was engraved on it a cap, the ancient symbol of freedom. **1816** SCOTT *Old Mort.* xix, 'I deliver to you, by this symbol,' (here she gave into his hand the venerable gold-headed staff of the deceased Earl of Torwood)—'the keeping and government and seneschalship of my Tower of Tillietudlem'. **1833** TENNYSON *Miller's Dau.* 233 The kiss, The woven arms, seem but to be Weak symbols of the settled bliss, The comfort, I have found in thee. **1849** RUSKIN *Seven Lamps* iv. §2. 95 The fluting of the column, which I doubt not was the Greek symbol of the bark of the tree. **1862** H. SPENCER *First Princ.* I. iv. §22. (1875) 68 Ultimate religious ideas and ultimate scientific ideas, alike turn out to be merely symbols of the actual, not cognitions of it. **1865** R. W. DALE *Jew. Temp.* xvi. (1877) 180 The offering of incense is a natural symbol of adoration. **1909** RIDER HAGGARD *Yellow God* 108 The symbols of the good and evil genii on a Mohammedan tomb.

b. An object representing something sacred; *spec.* (*absol.*) either of the elements in the eucharist, as representing the body and blood of Christ.

1671 EVELYN *Let. to Father Patrick* 27 Sept., After the prayer..the symbols become changed into the body and blood of Christ, after a sacramental, spiritual, and real manner. **1704** NELSON *Fest. & Fasts* ix. II. (1739) 579 Bread and Wine..by Consecration being made Symbols of the Body and Blood of Christ. **1781** J. MORISON in *Transl. & Paraphr. Sc. Ch.* XXXV. ii, That symbol of his flesh he broke. **1845** FORD *Handbk. Spain* I. III. 364 The injuries began the very day after the conquest, when..the white-washings and removals of Moslem symbols commenced. **1845** S. AUSTIN *Ranke's Hist. Ref.* III. 385 Whether the body [of Christ] was really in the symbols. **1870** M. D. CONWAY *Earthw. Pilgr.* ix. 119 We read of many..religions,..all of them surrounded with fables and symbols... Of all the symbols, the most universal was the Cross. **1877** E. PETERS tr. *Pfleiderer's Paulinism* vi. I. 240 This mystical element [lies] at the very root of the ancient idea of worship; the symbol is here never mere symbol, but..medium of a real connection with the actual..object of worship. **1899** W. R. INGE *Chr. Mysticism* vii. 258 We should..train ourselves..to consider them [*sc.* the sacraments] as divinely-ordered symbols, by which the Church,..and we as members of it, realise the highest and deepest of our spiritual privileges.

c. *Numism.* A small device on a coin, additional to and usually independent of the main device or 'type'.

1883 P. GARDNER *Types Grk. Coins* ii. 53 The symbol..is a copy or replica of the signet of the magistrate who is responsible for the coin. **1886** B. V. HEAD in *L. Jewitt's Eng. Coins & Tokens* 102 Small objects represented either in the field or the exergue as adjuncts to the main type are called *symbols*.

d. Symbols collectively; symbolism. *rare.*

1856 EMERSON *Eng. Traits, Aristocr.* Wks. (Bohn) II. 77 Proud..of the language and symbol of chivalry. **1875** E. WHITE *Life in Christ* IV. xxv. (1878) 410 Other portions of [the Apocalypse], and those the least loaded with prophetic symbol.

3. A written character or mark used to represent something; a letter, figure, or sign conventionally standing for some object, process, etc.

e.g. the figures denoting the planets, signs of the zodiac, etc. in astronomy; the letters and other characters denoting elements, etc. in chemistry, quantities, operations, etc. in mathematics, the faces of a crystal in crystallography.

c **1620** A. HUME *Brit. Tongue* (1865) 7 The symbol..I cal the written letter, quhilk representes to the eie the sound that the mouth sould utter. **1700** MOXON *Math. Dict.*, *Symboles*, are Letters used for Numbers in Algebra. **1805–17** R. JAMESON *Char. Min.* (ed. 3) 184 The different letters which compose the symbol. **1827** WHATELY *Logic* I. §4 (ed. 2) 36 The advantage of substituting for the terms, in a regular syllogism, arbitrary unmeaning symbols, such as letters of the alphabet, is much the same as in mathematics. **1844** FOWNES *Chem.* 180 Table of symbols of the elementary bodies. **1849** BALFOUR *Man. Bot.* §713 It is usual in descriptive works to give a list of the authors, and the symbols for their names. **1882** MINCHIN *Unipl. Kinemat.* 186 Suppose $x = f(a, b, t)$, $y = g(a, b, t)$, where f and g are symbols of functionality.

4. *attrib.* and *Comb.*, as ***symbol-essence, -figure, -flower, -god, -maker, -making, -object, -printing, -system, -user***; ***symbol-making, -minded, -using*** adjs.

1818 KEATS *Endym.* III. 700 If he explores all forms and substances..to their symbol-essences. **1895** ELWORTHY *Evil Eye* 249 The typical symbol-figures representing the four Evangelists. **1821** SHELLEY *Hellas* 1095 Not gold, not blood, their altar dowers, But votive tears and symbol flowers. **1866** LYTTON *Lost Tales Miletus, Secret Way* 4 Egypt's vast symbol gods. **1981** F. INGLIS *Promise of Happiness* iii. 85 The nineteenth-century novelists were the symbol-makers for a new order. **1953** R. LEHMANN *Echoing Grove* 28 Its one round turret, its weather-cock and flag-pole all supernaturally designed in the last sun's last symbol-making glow. **1962** W. NOWOTTNY *Lang. Poets Use* viii. 180 A kind of linguistic ambiguity..seems frequently to occur in poems bent on symbol-making. **1936** O. NASH *Primrose Path* 55 Still, I think, a pig's a pig—Ah, there, symbol-minded Sig! **1977** *N.Y. Times* 20 Jan. 4/3 Ever since he walked home from his inauguration, Mr. Carter has presented the country with a symbol-minded Presidency. **1913** L. BLOOMFIELD in C. F. Hockett *Leonard Bloomfield Anthol.* (1970) 43 This symbol-object is..the word: without it no concept of action, quality, or relation can exist. **1964** E. BECKER in I. L. Horowitz *New Sociol.* 119 Man..possesses both thing-objects, like all other animals; and, uniquely, symbol-objects. **1875** KNIGHT *Dict. Mech.*, *Symbol-printing* (Telegraphy), a system of printing in dots and marks.., or other cipher, as distinct from printing in the usual Roman letter. **1946** F. P. CHISHOLM in W. S. Knickerbocker *Twentieth Cent. Eng.* II. 183 The communication process involves both speakers and listeners, writers and readers, using a socially-constructed symbol-system, in whose structure 'reality' must be represented. **1964** R. H. ROBINS *Gen. Linguistics* 13 Among symbol systems language occupies a special place. **1946** F. P. CHISHOLM in W. S. Knickerbocker *Twentieth Cent. Eng.* II. 172 Our distinguishing human characteristic is that we are symbol-users. **1951** J. HOLLOWAY *Lang. & Intelligence* vi. 95 Intelligence displayed in a symbol-using planning sequence sometimes enables us to reduce the sequence of actions to a sequence of routines. **1977** R. HOLLAND *Self & Social Context* i. 18 Ethnomethodology..embraces a phenomenological concern for the experiencing, symbol-using self.

†**symbol**, *sb.*[2] *Obs.* (Also in L. form.) [ad. L. *symbola*, a. Gr. συμβολή, f. συμβάλλειν (see SYMBOL

sb.[1]). Cf. obs. F. *symbole* 'a shot, a collation' (Cotgr.).] A contribution (properly to a feast or picnic); a share, portion.

Quot. 1627 echoes the L. phr. *symbolarum collatores* (Plautus), those who contribute their shot to a feast.

1627 B. JONSON in Drayton *Battle Agincourt*, etc. Pref. Verses a j, This reck'ning I will pay, Without conferring symboles. **1653** JER. TAYLOR *Serm. for Year, Winter* i. 3 The persons who are to be judged..shall all appear to receive ther Symbol. *Ibid.* xx. 271 He refused to pay his Symbol, which himself and all the company had agreed should be given. *a* **1661** FULLER *Worthies, Chester* (1662) I. 291 Let me contribute my Symbole on this Subject. **1667** OLDENBURG in *Phil. Trans.* II. 414 That they would be pleased..to joyn their Symbola's, and to send in their Proposals. **1683** A. HILL *Life Barrow* B.'s Wks. 1687 I. c 2, I wish they [*sc.* his friends] would..bring in their Symbols toward the History of his Life. **1767** A. CAMPBELL *Lexiph.* (1774) 57 Misocapelus instigated by the ramifications of private friendship disbursed the symbol. **1822** LAMB *Elia* Ser. I. *Compl. Decay Beggars*, To have sat down at the cripples' feast, and to have thrown in his benediction, ay, and his mite too, for a companionable symbol.

'symbol, *v.* [f. SYMBOL *sb.*[1]]

1. *trans.* = SYMBOLIZE 3.

1832 *Examiner* 595/1 English Justice, being, as she is symboled, hoodwinked. **1861** MEREDITH *Evan Harrington* xi, Bread and cheese symbolled his condition. **1864** TENNYSON *Aylmer's F.* 535 [She] read, and tore, As if the living passion symbol'd there Were living nerves to feel the rent. **1874** SYMONDS *Sk. Italy & Greece* (1898) I. xi. 213 Angels..with fluttering skirts..and mouths that symbol singing.

2. *intr.* To make signs, to signal. *nonce-use.*

1864 CARLYLE *Fredk. Gt.* XVI. i. IV. 248 They say and symbol to me, 'Tell us of him!'

symbolæography (ˌsɪmbəliːˈɒgrəfɪ). *rare.* Also 7 sim-, -le- (*erron.* -li-), 6–7 -ie. [ad. Gr. συμβολαιογραφία, f. συμβολαιογράφος notary, f. συμβόλαιον mark, sign, contract, etc. + -γράφος writing (see -GRAPHER).] The art of writing out or drawing up legal instruments.

1590 WEST (*title*) Συμβολαιογραφία. Symbolæographia. Which may be termed The Art, Description, or Image of Instruments, Couenants, Contracts, &c. Or The Notarie or Scriuener... The Contents of the Bookes of Symbolæographie. **1610** FOLKINGHAM *Feudigr.* I. i. 2 The Legall part..comprehends the Symboliographie or Clarkeship, and penning of the Suruey.

symbolatry (sɪmˈbɒlətrɪ), shortened form of SYMBOLOLATRY (cf. *idolatry*). So **sym'bolater**, **sym'bolatrous** *a.*

1871 BARING-GOULD *Orig. & Developm. Relig. Beliefs* I. ix. 186 The Arabian monotheist cannot be excepted, for all his artistic advance was due to friction against symbolatrous peoples. *Ibid.*, Of the immense debt of gratitude we owe to symbolatry it is impossible to speak too highly. **1916** *Daily News* 27 Mar. 4 Blind Symbolaters.

symboled: see SYMBOLLED *a.*

symbolic (sɪmˈbɒlɪk), *a.* (*sb.*) [ad. late L. *symbolicus*, a. Gr. συμβολικός, f. σύμβολον SYMBOL *sb.*[1]: see -IC. Cf. F. *symbolique* (from 16th c.), It., Sp. *sim-*, Pg. *symbolico.*]

A. *adj.* **1. a.** Having the character of a symbol or representative sign or mark; constituting or serving as a symbol (*of* something).

1680 PLEYDELL *Serm. Funeral Glanvill* (1681) 2 It may be well doubted whether their symbolick divinity were not design'd rather to conceal their own ignorance. **1704** NELSON *Fest. & Fasts* vi. (1739) 78 The Apostles..laid their Hands upon them; an ancient Symbolic Rite of Investiture and Consecration. **1841** MYERS *Cath. Th.* III. §11. 41 The Old Testament..is Prophetic and Symbolic of the Revelations of the New. **1864** PUSEY *Lect. Daniel* (1876) 411 The symbolic animal. **1871** R. W. DALE *Commandm.* ii. 58 Jewish priests who offered a mere symbolic sacrifice might properly wear symbolic robes. **1899** W. R. INGE *Chr. Mysticism* vii. 254 All voluntary external acts are symbolic of (that is, vitally connected with) internal states.

b. *Gram.* (See quot., and cf. PRESENTIVE.)

1871 EARLE *Philol. Eng. Tongue* 195 The Symbolic words are those which by themselves present no meaning to the mind, and which depend for their intelligibility on a relation to some presentive word or words.

2. a. Consisting of, denoted by, or involving the use of written symbols or significant characters.

1656 HOBBES *Six Lessons* Wks. 1845 VII. 264 You demonstrate nothing to anybody but those who understand your symbolic tongue. **1669** GALE *Crt. Gentiles* I. I. xi. 64 The Egyptian Language..was twofold, Symbolic and Hieroglyphic, or Simple. **1741** WARBURTON *Div. Legat.* IV. iv. 144 Symbolic Writing, the more it receded from the Proper Hieroglyphic, the more it became obscure. **1805–17** R. JAMESON *Char. Min.* (ed. 3) 184 All this description may be exhibited in symbolic language. **1839** DE MORGAN in *Trans. Camb. Phil. Soc.* VII. 173 The method of giving meaning to the primary symbols, and of interpreting all subsequent symbolic results. **1901** F. S. DELLENBAUGH *N.-Americans of Yesterday* 69 In Symbolic Writing, a single characteristic part or trait serves to represent the whole object; thus the track of an animal will stand for the animal itself.

b. *Math.* Denoted by, relating to, or involving some special set or system of symbols, esp. simple or brief symbols used instead of fuller or more lengthy expressions, or symbols of operation treated as themselves subject to operation like symbols of quantity.

1846 SIR W. R. HAMILTON in *Camb. & Dubl. Math. Jrnl.* I. 49 Calling this act of connection of symbols, the operation of *addition*; the added symbols, *summands*; and the resulting symbol, a *sum*; we may..say..that this symbolic sum of lines represents the total (or final) effect of all those successive rectilinear motions..which are represented by the several summands. **1886** J. C. FIELDS in *Amer. Jrnl. Math.* VIII. 367 (*heading*) Symbolic Finite Solutions and Solutions by Definite Integrals of the Equation $\frac{d^ny}{dx^n} = x^my$. **1888** W. W. JOHNSON *ibid.* X. 94 (*heading*) Symbolic Treatment of Exact Linear Differential Equations.

c. ***symbolic logic***, logic that employs a special technical notation of symbols; formal or mathematical logic (see MATHEMATICAL *a.* 1 e). Hence ***symbolic logician.***

1856 A. DE MORGAN in *Trans. Cambr. Philos. Soc.* IX. 83, I think it reasonably probable that the advance of symbolic logic will lead to a calculus of opposite relations, for mere inference, as general as that of + and − in algebra. **1881** VENN (*title*) Symbolic Logic. **1903** B. RUSSELL *Princ. Math.* ii. 10 Symbolic or Formal Logic—I shall use these terms as synonyms—is the study of the various general types of deduction. The word *symbolic* designates the subject by an accidental characteristic, for the employment of mathematical symbols, here as elsewhere, is merely a theoretically irrelevant convenience. *Ibid.* vi. 74 By symbolic logicians..this will be felt as a reactionary view. **1933** C. A. MACE *Princ. Logic* iv. 64 The fact that symbolic logicians have not generally recognized this form compels us to introduce a symbol that is not in common use. **1941** [see *mathematical logic* s.v. MATHEMATICAL *a.* 1 e]. **1958** *Times Lit. Suppl.* 19 Dec. 729/3 Professor Sparshott quotes the dying symbolic logician—'complete rigour at last!' **1968** *Brit. Med. Bull.* XXIV. 239/2 The final study to be reviewed concerns diagnosis by the computer using a combination of symbolic logic..and similarity coefficients. **1973** *Sci. Amer.* Apr. 101/3 First Frege, then Peano and finally Russell turned to symbolic logic as a potential source of the fundamental notions necessary for a theory of natural number.

d. ***symbolic address*** (Computers), an address consisting of a symbol chosen by the programmer for its convenience; so ***symbolic addressing.***

1953 *Trans. IRE Professional Group on Electronic Computers* Mar. 10/1 Programs for automatic calculators can be written with symbolic addresses instead of actual addresses. **1970** O. DOPPING *Computers & Data Processing* xix. 308 In automatic coding..each data item receives a name, or symbolic address. **1977** *Gloss. Terms Data Processing* (*B.S.I.*) VII. 13/1 Symbolic addressing. **1981** M. E. WALSH *Understanding Computers* iii. 48 This process of using mnemonic instructions..and symbolic addressing and having them translated into machine language is called assembling a program.

3. a. Expressed, denoted, or conveyed by means of a symbol or set of symbols; concerning, involving, or depending upon representation by symbols; also, dealing with or using symbols.

symbolic delivery: see SYMBOLICAL 3 b.

1684 SIR G. MACKENZIE *Inst. Law Scot.* II. i. (1694) 56 The..most ordinary way of acquiring of Property is by Tradition,..and this translation is made either by the real delivery of the thing it self, as of a Horse, a Cup &c. or by a Symbolick delivery. **1831** CARLYLE *Sart. Res.* III. iii, In Death too, in the Death of the Just, as the last perfection of a Work of Art, may we not discern symbolic meaning? **1846** TRENCH *Mirac.* xxxiii. (1862) 460 An allegorical, or more truly a symbolic, meaning underlying the literal. **1850** MᶜCOSH *Div. Govt.* III. i. (1874) 264 The Symbolic power, which enables us to represent objects by signs. **1861** TRENCH *Comm. Ep. Churches Asia* 26 What we may call the mystical or symbolic interest..predominates over the actual. **1899** W. R. INGE *Chr. Mysticism* vii. 257 There are two views of this sacrament which the 'plain man' has always found much easier to understand than the symbolic view which is that of our Church. **1908** R. H. STRACHAN in *Expositor* Feb. 114 Apart from the much larger question of the symbolism of the Gospel, he [*sc.* John] displays what might be called the 'symbolic' mind, a mind that is especially open to any suggestion of spiritual truth conveyed by the actual facts.

b. *Art* and *Literature.* Having the characteristics of symbolism (see SYMBOLISM 1 d).

1910 B. W. WELLS *Modern Fr. Lit.* xiii. 485 Here [*sc.* in 'La petite paroisse'] first Daudet adopted the symbolic method that Zola and Ibsen also use with such effect.

c. ***symbolic interaction*** (Social Psychol. and Sociol.), the sharing and use of common symbols in human communication; freq. *attrib.*; also ***symbolic interactionist***, an adherent of the theory that the child is formed into a social being through learning the common meaning attached to symbols by his or her group; also *attrib.* or as *adj.*; hence ***symbolic interactionism.***

1937 H. BLUMER in E. P. Schmidt *Man & Society* 153 The group of social psychologists who may be conveniently labelled 'symbolic interactionists'. *Ibid.* 174 It is clearly an instance of the symbolic interaction. *Ibid.* 191 The stimulus-response approach is interested in *reaction*; the symbolic interaction view in *action*. **1961** D. MARTINDALE *Nature & Types Sociol. Theory* xiv. 339 The symbolic interaction school took shape in America, primarily under the influence of pragmatism. **1967** *Sociol. Q.* VIII. 149 (*title*) On the edge of rapprochement: was Durkheim moving toward the perspective of symbolic interaction? **1969** H. BLUMER (*title*) Symbolic interactionism. *Ibid.* i. 1 George Herbert Mead who, above all others, laid the foundations of the symbolic interactionist approach. **1972** S. MENNELL in Cox & Dyson *20th-Cent. Mind* III. v. 160 Another kind of social action theory has also been influential, especially in the last decade. It is usually known as 'symbolic interactionism', and has deep roots in American sociology. **1977** J. A. KOTARBA in Douglas & Johnson *Existential Sociol.* ix. 272 The concept of illness as deviant behavior..is built upon the labeling theory of the symbolic interactionist perspective. **1979** *Human Relations* Sept. 803 Symbolic interaction stresses the personal definition of the situation, while frame analysis seeks to uncover the background assumptions within which interaction takes place. **1982** *Jrnl. Learning Disabilities* XV. 347 Using a symbolic interaction perspective, the study focused on the extent of agreement..in referring children..to a university clinic for psycho-educational assessment.

4. Pertaining to or of the nature of a formal creed or confession of faith (SYMBOL *sb.*[1] 1).

1867 *Chambers's Encycl.*, *Symbolic Books*, in the language of the church, is a phrase that signifies the same as Creeds and Confessions. **1887** *Ch. Q. Rev.* Apr. 18 It is implied in the Augsburg Confession,..the *Confessio Gallicana*, and..several cognate symbolic documents.

B. *sb.* [after G. *symbolik.*] **a.** = SYMBOLICS 2. *rare*⁻⁰. **b.** A symbolic word (see 1 b above). *rare*⁻¹.

1864 WEBSTER, *Symbolic, n.*.. That branch of historic theology which treats of creeds; symbolism. **1871** EARLE *Philol. Eng. Tongue* 210 Symbolics.

symbolical (sɪmˈbɒlɪkəl), *a.* [f. late L. *symbolicus*: see prec. and -ICAL.]

1. = prec. 1.

1620 T. GRANGER *Div. Logike* 176 The Primarie [distribution], is when the totall proper[ly] so called is distinguished into true, and symbolicall parts [*margin*, symbols or notes of the causes or effects]. **1646** SIR T. BROWNE *Pseud. Ep.* I. iv. 16 By this incroachment Idolatry first crept in, men converting the symbolicall use of Idols into their proper worship. **1657–83** EVELYN *Hist. Relig.* (1850) I. 20 Some..made it [*sc.* an egg] symbolical of the world. **1681** B. KEACH *Tropologia* (1779) 230 By which typical and symbolical Image the four universal Kingdoms ..are..shadowed. **1681–6** J. SCOTT *Chr. Life* II. vii. §5 (1718) 401 His laying his Hand upon the Head of his Sacrifice, was a Symbolical Action. **1793** HORSLEY *Serm.*, *Luke iv. 18–19* (1816) I. 215 Our Lord's miracles, which, for the most part, were actions distinctly symbolical of one or other of the spiritual benefits of the redemption. **1848** LYTTON *Harold* I. i, A small circular table..supported by symbolical monsters quaintly carved. **1862** BURTON *Bk. Hunter* (1863) 64 The hand pouring oil into a lamp.. symbolical of the nutriment supplied to the intellectual flame. **1874** MICKLETHWAITE *Mod. Par. Churches* 6 Ceremonial was sometimes symbolical.

2. = prec. 2.

1654 J. WEBSTER *Acad. Examen* 24 The Hieroglyphical, Emblematical, Symbolical and Cryptographical learning. **1656** tr. *Hobbes' Elem. Philos.* (1839) 316 This doth not properly belong to Algebra, or the analytics specious, symbolical, or cossick; which are, as I may say the brachygraphy of the analytics. **1660** BARROW *Euclid* Pref. (1714) 3 Those who are delighted more with symbolical than verbal Demonstrations. **1805–17** R. JAMESON *Char. Min.* (ed. 3) 184 In order to prevent beginners from finding any thing ambiguous in the symbolical mode of writing. **1841** J. R. YOUNG *Math. Dissert.* Introd. 3 Some of the symbolical expressions most familiar to the algebraical student.

b. *Math.* = prec. 2 b.

1830 G. PEACOCK *Treat. Algebra* xi. (1845) II. 2 The operations..of Arithmetical and Symbolical Algebra. *Ibid.*, The rules of operation in Symbolical Addition and Subtraction. **1846** SIR W. R. HAMILTON in *Camb. & Dubl. Math. Jrnl.* I. 45 The present paper is an attempt towards constructing a symbolical geometry. **1852** SYLVESTER *Ibid.* VII. 83 Take the symbolical product of the first line.

3. = prec. 3.

1607 BP. ANDREWES *Serm.*, *Resurrection* ii. (1629) 399 Symbolicall Divinitie is good: but, might we see it in the rationall, too? **1650** BULWER *Anthropomet.* 124 They had a respect to a Symbolical intent. **1656** BLOUNT *Glossogr.*, *Symbolical Philosophy*, is that kinde of Learning and Wisdom, which..teach us how to make or expound those mystical and artificial bodies called Symboles. **1664** H. MORE *Myst. Iniq.* vi. 16 Whether it be referred to God himself, or to his Symbolical presence in the Ark of the Covenant, it is manifest that the worship was intended to God. *a* **1682** SIR T. BROWNE *Tracts* 75 The mystery and symbolical sense is chiefly to be looked upon. **1816** J. SMITH *Panorama Sci. & Art* II. 524 Bergman has adopted a symbolical mode of representing affinities. **1856** MAX MÜLLER *Chips* (1867) II. xvi. 104 *note*, People who wished to find a symbolical significance in every act of their traditional ritual. **1899** W. R. INGE *Chr. Mysticism* vii. 261 The objective or symbolical type of Mysticism.

b. Sc. Law. ***symbolical delivery***, ***possession***: see quot. 1838. *Hist.*

1681 STAIR *Inst. Law Scot.* xiii. §17. 239 The delivery of Symbolical Possession, by the Superiour or his Bailzie, to the Vassal or his Acturney, by delivery of Earth and Stone, and other Symbols. *a* **1688** G. DALLAS *Stiles* 45 Symbolical forms of giving sasine in Scotland. **1838** W. BELL *Dict. Law Scot.* s.v. *Delivery*, Actual delivery of heritage is impracticable; but the law of Scotland has recognised a symbolical delivery, which is indispensable in the transference of such property. *Ibid.* s.v. *Symbols*, Heritable property is transferred by the delivery of symbols:.. wherever sasine is requisite, the longest possession is insufficient without symbolical possession... In giving sasine of lands, the symbols are earth and stone of the lands; ..of fishings, net and cobble;..of patronage teinds, a sheaf of corn.

4. = prec. 4.

symbolical books, (spec.) the authentic documents (the Confession of Augsburg, etc.) constituting the Lutheran confession of faith.

1745 *Gleditsch's Teutsch-Engl. Lex.* **1764** MACLAINE tr. *Mosheim's Eccl. Hist.* Cent. XVII. II. II. i. §22. (1768) IV. 449 What the members of our communion call their Symbolical Books,..which..all candidates for the ministry would be obliged to subscribe, as containing the true and genuine doctrine of the Lutheran church. **1889** C. A. BRIGGS *Whither?* 19 Most Christian Churches have such symbolical books, which constitute the standard of orthodoxy for their own church organizations. **1912** *Ch. Q. Rev.* July 351 A maintenance of Symbolical doctrines.

†**5.** = SYMBOLIZING *ppl. a.* 1 a. *Obs. rare*⁻¹.

1667 O. HEYWOOD *Heart-Treasure* xiv. 170 Transmutation is easie in Symbolical Elements, such as agree in some prime qualities.

symbolically (sɪmˈbɒlɪkəlɪ), *adv.* [f. prec. + -LY².] In a symbolical way.

1. In the manner of a symbol or emblem; by means of a symbol or symbols; emblematically.

1603 HOLLAND *Plutarch's Mor.* 1307 Neither describeth he them symbolically.., but in proper and plaine termes. **1607** TOPSELL *Four-f. Beasts* 484 The lyon when he sleepeth hath his eies open,..and therefore the ancients did symbolically picture a lyon vpon the doors of their temples. **1646** SIR T. BROWNE *Pseud. Ep* I. ix. 36 Others symbolically intended are literally received. *a* **1677** MANTON *Exp. Lord's Pr.* Matt. vi. 9 Wks. 1870 I. 58 In the temple..God was present symbolically, because there were the signs and tokens of his presence. **1681** STAIR *Inst. Law Scot.* xii. §15. 197 Possession is attained Symbolically, where there is not use of the whole or a part, but only of a Symbol or Token. **1744** BERKELEY *Siris* §269 The Egyptians did symbolically represent the supreme Divinity sitting on a lotus. **1856** R. A. VAUGHAN *Mystics* (1860) I. 54 The heaven those vain builders sought to reach, signifies symbolically the mind. **1899** W. R. INGE *Chr. Mysticism* vii. 252 Light and darkness are..only symbolically connected with life and death.

2. By, or in relation to, written symbols or significant characters; *spec.* in *Math.* (see SYMBOLIC 2 b).

1846 SIR W. R. HAMILTON in *Camb. & Dubl. Math. Jrnl.* I. 48 We shall interpret an equation such as $DC = BA$..as denoting that the two lines, of which the symbols are equated, have equal lengths and similar directions;..if we call such lines symbolically equal, it will be allowed [etc.]. **1851** RANKINE *Misc. Sci. Papers* (1881) 50 To illustrate this symbolically, let V represent the volume occupied by unity of weight of the substance, [etc.]. **1876** PREECE & SIVEWRIGHT *Telegraphy* 24 The binoxide of manganese is reduced to a lower oxide... What actually takes place may be symbolically represented as follows.

So **symˈbolicalness**, the quality of being symbolical.

1633 D. R[OGERS] *Treat. Sacraments* I. 66 The Sacramentalnesse and Symbolicalnesse of the things of God. **1827** HARE *Guesses* Ser. I. (1847) 93 Nor is it without a prophetic symbolicalness that the sea fills so important a part in both the Homeric poems.

†**symˈbolicly**, *adv. Obs. rare*⁻¹. [f. SYMBOLIC *a.* + -LY².] Symbolically.

1669 GALE *Crt. Gentiles* I. III. vii. 75 The Poets..make Pyrrha the wife of Deucalion: whereby they symbolicly signifie [etc.].

symbolics (sɪmˈbɒlɪks). [pl. of SYMBOLIC used subst. (see *-ics*, -IC 2), chiefly after G. *symbolik* or F. *symbolique*.]

†**1.** The use of written symbols, as in mathematics. *Obs.*

1657 HOBBES *Absurd Geom.* Wks. 1845 VII. 379 The best masters of symbolics.

2. The study of creeds and confessions of faith, as a branch of theology.

1847 WEBSTER, *Symbolics*, the science of creeds. **1885** SCHAFF *Christ & Chr.* 5 The new name of Symbolics, which includes Irenics as well as Polemics. Symbolics is the science of symbols or creeds. It is comparative dogmatics. **1907** C. G. MCCRIE *Confessions Ch. Scot.* v. 209 Professor Philip Schaff..the greatest Protestant authority on Symbolics, set forth the uses of creeds in four particulars.

3. The study of symbols, or of symbolic rites and ceremonies, as a branch of anthropology.

1850 OGILVIE, *Symbolics*, the name given by the Germans to the study of the symbols and mysterious rites of antiquity.

symboling: see SYMBOLLING *vbl. sb.*

symbolism (ˈsɪmbəlɪz(ə)m). [f. SYMBOL *sb.*¹ + -ISM, partly after F. *symbolisme*, G. (mod.L.) *symbolismus*.]

I. 1. The practice of representing things by symbols, or of giving a symbolic character to objects or acts; the systematic use of symbols; hence, symbols collectively or generally.

1654 J. WEBSTER *Acad. Exam.* 24 Who can be ignorant of the..compendious use of all sorts of Symbolismes, that have but any insight into Algebraick Arithmetick? **1840** CARLYLE *Heroes* iv. (1841) 198 'You do not believe,' said Coleridge; 'you only believe that you believe.' It is the final scene in all kinds of Worship and Symbolism. **1850** BLACKIE *Æschylus* I. 327 These volcanic movements in the religious symbolism of early Greece became giants. **1870** ROCK *Text. Fabr.* Introd. vii. p. cxxxvii, Heraldry grew out of symbolism. **1874** MICKLETHWAITE *Mod. Par. Churches* 6 Durandus himself, the prophet of symbolism, often gives alternative interpretations. **1882** FARRAR *Early Chr.* II. 273 Every item of the symbolism..is borrowed from ancient prophecy.

b. A symbolic meaning attributed to natural objects or facts.

1835 J. B. ROBERTSON tr. *von Schlegel's Philos. Hist.* Life p. xiv, All the divine symbolism in nature and in man. **1871** FRASER *Life Berkeley* iii. 63 The theory of sense symbolism, which connected Berkeley with the Baconian movement.

c. *pl.* Symbolical figures. *rare.*

1876 'OUIDA' *Winter City* xiv. 388 To embroider..the loveliest Bacchic symbolisms.

d. The use of symbols in literature or art; *spec.* the principles or practice of the Symbolists (see next, 2 c).

1866 *Contemp. Rev.* May 60 By Symbolism in art, poetic or pictorial, we understand the attempt to suggest higher, wider, purer, or deeper ideas by the use of simpler, humbler, or more familiar thoughts or objects. **1898** R. N. BAIN in *Literature* 12 Nov. 453/1 Symbolism is the name given by French critics to that revolt against the dryness and photographic exactness of naturalism, which..is characterized, at its best, by a..somewhat dreamy poetry, and half-naïve, half-mystical attempt to interpret the moods of nature through the medium of human sensations.

2. The use, or a set or system, of written symbols.

1864 RUSKIN in *Reader* IV. 678/1, I had..invented a short-hand symbolism for crystalline forms. **1868** *Chambers's Encycl.* X. 289/1 There are two principles employed in [writing],..Ideographism and Phonetism. An ideograph is either a picture of the object..or..some symbol which stands..for the object, in which case it is called Symbolism.

3. = SYMBOLICS 2.

1846 WORCESTER, *Symbolism*, an exposition or comparison of symbols or creeds. *Robertson.* **1907** C. G. MCCRIE *Confessions Ch. Scot.* i. 1 Symbolism is that branch of theology which stands between the Biblical..and the Dogmatic or Systematic.

†**II. 4.** See quots. and cf. SYMBOLIZATION 1 a. *Obs. rare*⁻⁰.

1722 QUINCY *Lex. Physico-Med.* (ed. 2), *Symbole*, and *Symbolism*, is said either of the Fitness of Parts with one another, or of the Consent between them by the Intermediation of Nerves, and the like. **1753** CHAMBERS *Cycl. Supp. Symbolism*, a word used by some of the chemical writers to express a consent of parts.

symbolist (ˈsɪmbəlɪst). [f. SYMBOL *sb.*¹ + -IST; cf. prec. In sense 2 c after F. *symboliste*.]

1. *Ch. Hist.* One who holds that the elements in the Eucharist are mere symbols of the body and blood of Christ. *Obs. exc. Hist.*

1585–7 T. ROGERS 39 *Art.* xxviii. (1625) 176 The Symbolists, Figurists, and Significatists, who are of opinion that the faithfull at the Lords Supper, doe receiue nothing but naked, and bare signes. **1839** MILMAN *Life Gibbon* v. 144 *note*, An amicable compromise between the Symbolists and Anti-Symbolists of Germany.

2. a. One who uses symbols, or practises symbolism.

1812 SOUTHEY *Omniana* I. 48 The whim of some violent symbolist. **1865** C. STANFORD *Symb. Christ* vii. 183 'My dark and cloudy words, they do but hold The truth, as cabinets enclose the gold.' So did the Puritan symbolist speak.

b. One who uses written symbols.

1881 VENN *Symbolic Logic* Introd. p. xxxiii, Examples which however simple they may seem to a modern symbolist represent a very great advance beyond the syllogism.

c. One who uses symbolism in art or literature: (*a*) A painter who aims at symbolizing ideas rather than representing the form or aspect of actual objects; *spec.* applied to a late nineteenth-century school of painters who used representations of objects and schemes of colour to suggest ideas or states of mind. (*b*) One of a late nineteenth-century school of French poets who aimed at representing ideas and emotions by indirect suggestion rather than by direct expression, and attached a symbolic meaning to particular objects, words, sounds, etc. (Cf. quots. s.v. SYMBOLISM 1 d.) Also *attrib.*

1888 G. MOORE *Confessions of Young Man* vi. 147 Like a white flag fluttering faintly, Symbolists and Decadents appeared. **1892** *Spectator* 30 Jan. 168/1 (*heading*) Art. At the Old Masters. II. [Dialogue between] A Symbolist [and] an Impressionist. **1894** *Tablet* 27 Jan. 122 Verlaine, and the other French 'Symbolists' as they are called, in poetry. **1899** A. SYMONS (*title*) The Symbolist Movement in Literature. **1902** *Encycl. Brit.* XXVIII. 497/1 The Symbolist school.. aimed at greater freedom, a less strict prosody, and a more musical poetry. **1905** *Westm. Gaz.* 25 Feb. 16/3 'Well, do as you like,' the symbolist [*sc.* Boecklin] said, 'but without a vermilion cow you'll never make a picture of that thing.' **1907** *Dublin Rev.* Oct. 407 The great Symbolist, Joris Karl Huysmans.

3. One versed in the study or interpretation of symbols or symbolism.

1839 T. MITCHELL *Frogs of Aristoph.* Introd. p. lxxxiii, The authorities on which the learned symbolist relies. **1907** *Westm. Gaz.* 20 Feb. 4/3 Blake's 'Jerusalem'..is not easy reading even to a symbolist confident of his key.

Hence **symboˈlistic, -ical** *adjs.*, pertaining to or characteristic of a symbolist (esp. in sense 2 c); belonging to or characterized by symbolism; **symboˈlistically** *adv.*, in the manner of a symbolist; in the way of symbolism.

1864 WEBSTER, *Symbolistic, Symbolistical*, characterized by the use of symbols; as, symbolistic poetry. **1903** F. B. SMITH *How Paris Amuses Itself* ii. 42 The pensive, long-haired devotees of the symbolistic school. **1912** *English Rev.* Dec. 86 The scenes..reverting, symbolistically..to the scene started from, where the 'stranger' is seen sitting on a bench, scratching the sand with a stick.

‖**symboliste** (sɛ̃bɔlist). Also with capital initial. [Fr.: cf. SYMBOLIST.] = SYMBOLIST 2 c (*b*). Chiefly *attrib.*

1925 [see CROCEAN *a.*²]. **1957** J. HOLLANDER in N. Frye *Sound & Poetry* 67 Professor Knight has elevated his rather *symboliste* construction of the word 'music' to the heights proclaimed in Verlaine's manifesto. **1966** *Listener* 17 Mar. 378/1 T. S. Eliot..found the clues he needed..in the French *Symbolistes* like Laforgue. **1980** A. ALPERS *Life K. Mansfield* vii. 135 A little *symboliste* prose-poem.

†**symbolizant**, *a. Obs. rare*⁻¹. [ad. F. *symbolisant*, †*-izant*, pr. pple. of *symboliser*, †*-izer*, or mod.L. *symbolizans*, pr. pple. of *symbolizāre* to SYMBOLIZE.] = SYMBOLIZING *ppl. a.* 1 a.

1685 J. CHAMBERLAYNE *Coffee, Tea & Choc.* 61 Two predominant qualities..which agree very well together and for that reason are called symbolizant.

symbolization (ˌsɪmbəlaɪˈzeɪʃən). [ad. F. *symbolisation*, †*-ization* (Rabelais), n. of action f. *symboliser* to SYMBOLIZE.]

1. †**a.** The fact of 'symbolizing' in nature or quality; agreement or participation in qualities.

1607 B. BARNES *Divils Charter* (ed. McKerrow) 3144 Through operation, conuersation, and simbolisation, With matter in the subiect properly, With th'elements in body quadrifarie, With growing plants in vertue vegitatiue, In sence with beasts. **1622** MALYNES *Anc. Law-Merch.* 64 The elements are ioined by Symbolization, the aire to the fire by warmenesse, the water to the aire by moysture, the earth to the water by coldnesse. **1658** J. ROBINSON *Endoxa* 81 That common Salt..doth, by symbolization, easily turn into nitre. *a* **1693** *Urquhart's Rabelais* III. iii. 40 There would.. be..no manner of Symbolization..amongst the Elements.

b. The action of 'symbolizing' in tenets or practice; conformity (*with*). Now *rare* or *Obs.*

1633 PRYNNE *Histrio-m.* 48 A degenerous, and Vnchristian symbolization with his present World. **1884** *Chr. Commonw.* 14 Feb. 415/2 They enfeeble [their principles] by symbolisation or adulteration with some Sub-Apostolic, or Patristic,..or other spurious form of ceremonies, of doctrine, or of ordinances.

2. The action of symbolizing; representation by a symbol or symbols; *transf.* something in which this is exemplified; a symbol or symbolism.

In 1st quot., the action of making or accounting symbolic.

1603 HOLLAND *Plutarch's Mor.* 1316 The utility and symbolization heereof [*i.e.* of certain animals]:..as touching the goat, the sheepe and the Ichneumon,..they honor them for the use and profit they receive by them... The serpent *Aspis*..the wezill and the flie called the bettill, they reverence, because they observe in them I wot not what little slender images..of the divine power. **1646** SIR T. BROWNE *Pseud. Ep.* v. xxi. 264 The Hieroglyphicall symboles of Scripture..are oft times wrackt beyond their symbolizations, and inlarg'd into constructions disparaging their true intentions. **1669** GALE *Crt. Gentiles* I. II. viii. 114 The ancient Persian Magi..received their first..Rites from the Zabii, which is sufficiently evident by their Symbolisation. **1827** G. S. FABER *Sacr. Cal. Prophecy* (1844) I. p. xiv, Political convulsions typified (on the well-ascertained laws of symbolisation) by signs in the heavenly bodies. **1858** SEARS *Athan.* xvii. 146 To them the grand and beautiful in the external world are not the symbolization of spiritual qualities. **1861** J. Y. SIMPSON *Archæology* 62 [He] placed..on the altar..a piece of fresh turf in symbolization of his royal land-gift.

b. Representation by written symbols; *transf.* a set of written symbols or characters.

1842 G. S. FABER *Prov. Lett.* (1844) I. 122 The Systematic Employment of miniature in Hieroglyphical Symbolisation. **1864** ELLIS in *Reader* 3 Sept. 304/1 To appreciate and symbolize the sounds is far more difficult than to utter them from the symbolization.

symbolize (ˈsɪmbəlaɪz), *v.*¹ Also 6–7 sim-. [ad. F. *symboliser*, †*-izer*, ad. mod.L. *symbolizāre*, f. *symbolum* SYMBOL *sb.*¹: see -IZE. Cf. It. *simboleggiare* to concur, *simbolizzare* to symbolize, Sp. *simbolizar*, Pg. *symbolizar*.]

I. †**1.** *intr.* To agree or harmonize in qualities or nature (or in some quality): *symbolize with*, to partake of the qualities or nature of; hence often = to be like, resemble. (A technical term of early physics, said of elements or other substances having qualities in common; hence in general use.) *Obs.*

1591 SYLVESTER *Du Bartas* I. ii. 265 But Aire turne Water, Earth may Fierize, Because in one part they do symbolize. **1598** *Ibid.* II. ii. IV. *Columnes* 377 Such Shape and Name.. As with their Natures neerly symbolize. **1613** JACKSON *Creed* II. xxxi. §15 Thrice happie is that Land..where ciuill pollicie and spiritual wisedome..doe rightly symbolize. **1642** HOWELL *For. Trav.* (Arb.) 50 The Brittaines in Wales, with whom..the Biscayner doth much symbolize in many things. **1687** H. MORE *Answ. Psychop.* (1689) 134 It is as much Spiritual as before, and does not herein symbolize with Matter, but approves itself contrary thereto. *a* **1711** KEN *Sion* Poet. Wks. 1721 IV. 387 You..Would tune your Harp to symbolize with me. **1816** T. TAYLOR *Ess.* VIII. 457 Our intellect, in a descending state, must aptly symbolize with the divinity of Ceres.

†**b.** To enter into union, combine, unite, as elements having qualities in common; to form a harmonious union or combination. *Obs.*

In quot. 1601 app. including the idea of transmutation of elements: cf. quots. 1591 in sense 1, and 1660 s.v. SYMBOLIZING *ppl. a.* 1 a.

1601 WEEVER *Mirr. Mart.* F j, The fyre, red-blushing of his fact ashamed, Clad him in Smoke, the smoke to Aire he turned, That aire to water, water earth receiued, Earth like the fyre to melt to water burned: Earth, Water, Aire, Fyre, symboliz'd in one, To quench, or coole, Oldcastl's Martyrdome. *a* **1628** F. GREVIL *Sidney* iv. (1652) 51 Affirming that to associate by an uniform bond of conscience, for the protection..of Religion and Liberty, would prove a more solid union, and symbolize far better against their Tyrannies, than any Factious combination in policy.

†**c.** *trans.* To mix, combine, unite (elements or substances, esp. those of similar qualities). *Obs.*

1590 MARLOWE *2nd Pt. Tamburl.* I. iv, Water and ayre being simbolisde in one Argue their want of courage and of wit. **1595** B. BARNES *Spir. Sonn.* lxxx, A blast of winde, a momentarie breath, A watrie bubble simbolizde with ayre. **1607** TOPSELL *Four-f. Beasts* 351 The disease..proceedeth of too great aboundance of fleme and choler, simboliz'd together. **1610** MARKHAM *Masterp.* I. iv. 12 These humours are simbolized or mixt through euery part of the body.

†**d.** To liken or compare, as having similar qualities or attributes. *Obs. rare*⁻¹.

1652 *Hermeticall Banquet* B 2, I strike againe at this little World Man:..and the Head I Symbolize with the Elementary upper Regions, Fire and Aer.

2. *intr.* To agree in belief or practice (esp. religious); to hold the same opinions or principles; to comply, conform. Frequent in 17th c., esp. in controversial use; now *rare* or *Obs.*

1605 *Answ. Supposed Discov. Romish Doctr.* 12 We haue not now an other Queene Marie..to be ioyned in mariadge with a potent Prince..; simbolizing with husband, conformitie in countrie discipline is neuer like to breed you scruples in this behalfe. *c* **1645** HOWELL *Lett.* (1650) I. 338 With the Jew they symbolize..in circumcision, in refraining from swine's flesh, in detestation of images. **1656** *Artif. Handsom.* 154 [They] oft symbolize, and comply with the vulgar humor. **1732** NEAL *Hist. Purit.* I. 69 To continue the use of those Garments, was in his [*sc.* Hooper's] opinion, to symbolize with Antichrist. **1845** MIALL in *Nonconf.* V. 73 In early life Dr. Arnold appears to have been a republican, ..of late years he symbolised principally with the whigs. **1869** A. W. HADDAN *Apost. Succession* ii. (1879) 30 Those who profess to be Churchmen, but in this particular symbolize with..Nonconformists.

II. 3. *trans.* **a.** To represent by a symbol or symbols. Also *absol.*

1606 HOLLAND *Sueton.* 70 Under obscure and doubtfull titles symbolizing somewhat else. *c* **1620** A. HUME *Brit. Tongue* (1865) 7 The thing symbolized I cal the sound quhilk the mouth utteres quhen the eie sees the symbol. *Ibid.* 16 To symboliz right, the sound of the voual is first to be observed. **1829** I. TAYLOR *Enthus.* iii. (1867) 59 A change of moral dispositions so entire as to be properly symbolized by calling it a new birth. **1838** DE MORGAN *Ess. Probab.* 47 Twelve halfpence..are thrown up, required the probability of all the cases which can happen, and which we shall symbolise thus: (H_3T_9) means that there are three heads and nine tails. **1840** CARLYLE *Heroes* i. (1841) 55 They would go on singing, poetically symbolizing, as our modern Painters paint, when it was no longer from the innermost heart. **1864** [see SYMBOLIZATION 2 b].

b. To be a symbol of; to represent or stand for, as a symbol; to typify.

1603 HOLLAND *Plutarch's Mor.* 1316 Many..say, that the male wezill engendreth with the female by her eare, and that she bringeth forth her yoong at the mouth: which symbolizeth..the making and generation of speech. *Ibid.* Gloss., To *Symbolize*, that is, by certeine outward signes, to signifie some hidden things: Thus an eie symbolizeth vigilancy. **1840** CARLYLE *Heroes* i. (1841) 9 But consider whether Bunyan's Allegory could have preceded the Faith it symbolizes! The Faith had to be already there,..of which the Allegory could then become a shadow. **1874** SPURGEON *Treas. Dav.* Ps. lxxxiv. 6 As the valley of weeping symbolizes dejection, so a 'well' symbolizes ever-flowing salvation and comfort. **1879** H. PHILLIPS *Addit. Notes Coins* 1 The owl, which is the crest, symbolizes wisdom and learning.

4. To make into or treat as a symbol; to regard as symbolic or emblematic. *rare.*

1646 SIR T. BROWNE *Pseud. Ep.* VII. iv. 347 Some pious and Christian pens have onely symboliz'd the same [*sc.* the rainbow] from the mystery of its colours. **1658** *Ibid.* VII. i. (ed. 4) 421 We read in Pierius, that an Apple was the Hieroglyphick of love..; and there want not some who have symbolized the Apple of Paradise unto such constructions. **1903** [implied in SYMBOLIZER 3].

III. 5. To formulate or express in a creed or confession of faith: cf. SYMBOL *sb.*¹ 1.

1895 *Funk's Stand. Dict., Symbolize*..4. To formulate into a creed or confession of faith; as, the Council of Nicea symbolized the orthodox faith. **1912** [see SYMBOLIZED 2].

†**symbolize,** *v.*² *Obs. rare*⁻⁰. [f. SYMBOL *sb.*² + -IZE.] (See quot.)

1656 BLOUNT *Glossogr.*, To *Symbolize*..to joyn purses, or pay rateably towards any charge, to club.

symbolized (ˈsɪmbəlaɪzd), *ppl. a.* [f. SYMBOLIZE *v.*¹ + -ED¹.]

1. Represented by a symbol.

1844 W. H. MILL *Serm. Tempt. Christ* iii. 62 The doom on the symbolized tempter. **1874** SAYCE *Compar. Philol.* vii. 263 To mistake the symbol for the symbolised.

2. Expressed in a formulated creed.

1912 W. W. PEYTON in *Contemp. Rev.* Jan. 101 Chalmers ..had his doubts about the symbolised metaphysics.

symbolizer (ˈsɪmbəlaɪzə(r)). *rare.* [f. as prec. + -ER¹.] One who or that which symbolizes.

†**1.** A person or thing that agrees, harmonizes, or conforms with another. *Obs.*

But in 1st quot. perh. = That which represents something symbolically.

1607 *Schol. Disc. agst. Antichr.* I. ii. §31. 107 The Emperour of Æthiopia when he goeth foorth, hath a Crosse carried before him, and an earthen pitcher full of earth: the one signifying his profession, the other his mortalitie... It is ..by the adiunct or effect of mortalitie that he Symbolizeth with the same, and a Metonimicall Symbolizer, the Crosse is as well as he. **1659** GAUDEN *Tears Ch.* IV. xxi. 591 The discontented Presbyters of Scotland, and their ambitious Symbolizers in England.

2. = SYMBOLIST 2.

1854 EMERSON *Lett. & Soc. Aims* i. (1875) 61 The poet is representative,..symbolizer, emancipator.

3. = SYMBOLIST 1.

1903 J. C. LAMBERT *Sacraments in N.T.* ix. 370 They themselves no more think of taking ἐστι literally..than the barest symboliser does.

symbolizing (ˈsɪmbəlaɪzɪŋ), *vbl. sb.* [f. as prec. + -ING¹.] The action of the verb SYMBOLIZE.

1. †Agreement in nature or qualities, resemblance, congruity, analogy (*obs.*); agreement in tenets or practices, conformity, compliance (now *rare* or *obs.*).

1605 [see SYMBOLIZE *v.* 2]. **1607** (*title*) A Scholasticall Discovrse against Symbolizing with Antichrist in Ceremonies: especially in the Signe of the Crosse. **1641** *Answ. Vind. Smectymnuus* 58 Could you instance, This prayer is Superstitious, that Idolatrous,..you might have just reason to except at any touch of our symbolizing with them. *a* **1661** FULLER *Worthies, Kent* (1662) I. 62 There is a great Symbolizing betwixt them in many concurrences. **1759** HUME *Hist. Eng.* II. iii. 506 Every compliance, they said, was a symbolizing with Antichrist. **1822** R. HALL *Notes Serm.* v. Wks. 1832 V. 35 Though unitarians repel..the charge of symbolizing with deists.

2. The action of using symbols, or of representing something by a symbol.

1887 BROWNING *Parleyings, B. de Mandeville* viii, What need of symbolizing? Fitlier men Would take on tongue mere facts. **1908** *Expositor* Mar. 251 Shortening and symbolizing of imitative curses and prayers is an often observed phenomenon.

ˈsymbolizing, *ppl. a.* [f. as prec. + -ING².] That symbolizes.

1. †**a.** Agreeing in nature or qualities; congruous, concordant, similar. *Obs.*

1611 COTGR., *Symbolizant*, symbolizing, sympathizing. *a* **1652** J. SMITH *Sel. Disc.* VI. iv. (1821) 210 A discerning of that sympathizing and symbolizing complexion of their own bodies with some other bodies without them. *Ibid.* ix. 272 Any admirable discourses, in which there is a cheerful and free flowing forth of a rich fancy.., are apt to beget a symbolizing quality of mind in a by-stander. **1660** BOYLE *New Exp. Phys. Mech.* xxii. 179 We might easily subjoyn the Authority of Aristotle, and..the Schools who are known to have taught, that Air and Water being Symbolizing Elements (in the quality of moisture) are easily transmutable into one another. **1661** —— *Scept. Chym.* v. (1680) 325 These Symbolizing Bodies, Aire and Fire.

b. Agreeing, or showing agreement, in tenets or practices; conforming. ? *Obs.*

1732 NEAL *Hist. Purit.* (1754) I. ii. 46 Hooper was as much for the clergy's wearing a decent and distinct habit from the laity, as Ridley, but prayed to be excused from the old symbolizing popish garments.

2. Using, or representing things by, symbols.

1909 *Spectator* 10 Apr. 570/2 It was not until comparatively late that the symbolising instinct of a simple age felt that the ideal purity of the Lord's Mother was best expressed in the purity of white lilies.

symbolled (ˈsɪmbəld), *a.* Also **symboled.** [f. SYMBOL *v.*¹ or *sb.*¹ + -ED.]

1. Represented or expressed by a symbol; symbolized.

1829 E. ELLIOTT *Village Patriarch* II. viii, When History's page no symbol'd thought retains. **1852** TUPPER *Proverb. Philos., Of Writing* 164 As a fossil in the rock,..So the symbolled thoughts tell of a departed soul.

2. Furnished or adorned with symbols or symbolical figures.

1895 E. MASON *Flamma Vestalis* 7 The Vestal Virgin passes down the street,..With half-told beads, and symbolled raiment. **1935** DYLAN THOMAS in *New Verse* Aug.–Sept. 3 The invalid rivals, Voyaging clockwise off the symboled harbour.

symbolling (ˈsɪmbəlɪŋ), *vbl. sb. U.S.* usu. **symboling.** [f. SYMBOL *v.*¹ + -ING¹.] **a.** The action of symbolizing; *transf.* something that symbolizes, symbolism. **b.** The use of symbols in communication.

1842 TUPPER *Proverb. Philos.* Ser. II. 229 Animal creation, with sciences, and things..Contributed their symbollings.. wherewith to title men. **1910** MEREDITH *Celt & Saxon* xv. 216 After she and the captain had spelt the symbolling in turns. **1974** H. G. BURGER in *Gen. Systems* XIX. 64/1 What appears to be non-language..is probably a precisely coded symboling of a non-standard dialect. **1977** —— in B. Bernardi *Concept & Dynamics of Culture* 419 Between the gross human ability of symboling, so well known, and the peculiarly human institutions, also well known, lie special symboling processes. **1977** *Dædalus* Summer 62 Process theory is no longer linked, as in its earlier heyday, with Gumplowicz's notion that 'man's material need is the prime motive of his conduct'; it now recognizes the critical importance of meaning and symboling.

symbolling, var. SEMBLING.

symbolo-, combining form of Gr. σύμβολον SYMBOL *sb.*¹, as in **symbolo-fideism** (ˌsɪmbələʊˈfaɪdiːɪz(ə)m) [F. *symbolo-fidéisme*], the theory that symbols are of the essence of religious dogma, and that the attitude of faith has priority over intellectual belief (see quot. 1921); hence ˌ**symbolo-ˈfideist,** one who holds this theory; ˌ**symboloˈmania** *nonce-wd.*, excessive use of symbols.

[**1897** A. SABATIER *Esquisse d'une Philosophie de la Réligion* III. vii. 406 En combinant les vues de M. Ménégoz et les miennes qui se complètent en effet réciproquement, on a pu baptiser la conception nouvelle de *symbolo-fidéisme.*] **1903** *Hibbert Jrnl.* I. 555 In these two principles,—the symbolic, pictorial character of all the concepts and terms of religion, and the distinction just mentioned between faith and belief, —we have the germs of Symbolo-fideism. The name appears to have been given to the school by an anonymous writer in 1894. **1921** *Encycl. Relig. & Ethics* XII. 151 Symbolofideism is the name given to the theology taught in the second half of the 19th cent. at the Protestant Faculty of Paris by Professors Auguste Sabatier and Eugène Ménégoz. **1949** E. L. MASCALL *Existence & Analogy* v. 93 Modern Roman Catholic theologians..under the stress of their controversy with symbolo-fideists and modernists of various kinds, have discussed the doctrine of analogy at great length. **1970** *Nature* 4 Apr. 47/2 Such a hornet's nest of symbols, wiggly lines,..and the like, that the reader, despairing of ever reaching the goodies obscured by the fog of symbolomania, may come to think that this new approach to mathematics is not worth while.

symbolography (sɪmbəˈlɒgrəfɪ). [f. Gr. σύμβολον SYMBOL *sb.*¹ + -γραφία -GRAPHY.]

1. Description of symbols. *rare*⁻⁰.

1656 BLOUNT *Glossogr.*, *Symbolography*..a description of Symboles, a writing or expression of things by signs and tokens.

2. The writing or tracing of symbolic characters or figures, or such characters or figures collectively; symbolic writing.

1865 *Athenæum* 14 Oct. 495/1 The cross, the comb and mirror, the interlaced serpents, the chase, and other indicia of Christian symbolography. **1887** SIR S. FERGUSON *Ogham Inscript.* 150 The type must be looked for in Byzantine symbolography.

symbology (sɪmˈbɒlədʒɪ). [ad. mod.L. *symbologia*, shortened form for **symbolologia*, f. Gr. σύμβολον SYMBOL *sb.*¹: see -LOGY.] The science or study of symbols; *loosely*, the use of symbols, or symbols collectively; symbolism.

1840 DE QUINCEY *Essenes* Wks. 1862 IX. 271 *note*, In the symbology of the Jewish ritual. **1853** J. MILLS (*title*) Sacred Symbology: or, An Inquiry into the Principles of Interpretation of the Prophetic Symbols. **1883** SINNETT *Esoteric Buddhism* Pref. (1884) p. xv, Ideas..in more or less embarrassing disguise of mystic symbology. **1896** E. P. EVANS *Anim. Symbolism* v. 246 Whimseys of Ecclesiology and Symbology.

So **symboˈlogical** *a.*, pertaining to symbology; **symˈbologist**, one versed in symbology (*rare*).

1864 WEBSTER, Symbological. *Ibid.*, Symbologist. **1924** *Glasgow Herald* 4 Apr. 13 Professor Stern returns to the attack upon this theory-mongering, always recalling the symbologists and complex-jargonists to a consideration of practical realities as a test of their deductions. **1976** *N.Y. Rev. Bks.* 15 Apr. 29/2 He considered the Papal Bull of 1950 declaring the Assumption of the Virgin an article of faith to be the most important symbological event since the Reformation.

symbololatry (sɪmbəˈlɒlətrɪ). [f. Gr. σύμβολον SYMBOL *sb.*¹ + λατρεία worship: see -LATRY.] Worship of or excessive veneration for symbols (in any sense). Also SYMBOLATRY, q.v.

1828 PUSEY *Hist. Enq.* I. 82 Confusion and symbololatry alone could arise from terming them [*sc.* books] 'inspired'. **1888** SCHAFF *Hist. Chr. Ch., Mod. Chr.* i. §9. 40 This Protestant bibliolatry and symbololatry.

syme, syment, symeter, -itare, obs. ff. SEEM *v.*², CEMENT, SCIMITAR.

symitriall: see SYMMETRIAL.

symly, obs. form of SEEMLY.

c **1470** HENRY *Wallace* XI. 758 Byschop Synclar..Com out off Bute with symly men to sycht.

symmachy (ˈsɪməkɪ). *rare.* [ad. Gr. συμμαχία alliance in war, f. σύμμαχος adj. fighting together or in alliance, sb. an ally, f. σύν with + μάχη fight.]

1623 COCKERAM, *Symmachie*, aide in warre. **1658** PHILLIPS, *Symmachy*, a joyning in war against a common enemy. **1911** C. PHILLIPSON *Internat. Law & Custom Ancient Greece & Rome* I. ix. 222 The relationship existing between those cities which constituted the military symmachy in Italy.

symmedian (sɪˈmiːdɪən), *sb.* and *a. Geom.* [f. Gr. σύν SYM- + MEDIAN *a.*¹ and *sb.*¹]

symmedian, or ***symmedian line***, each of three lines drawn from the angles of a triangle at inclinations to the angle-bisectors equal to those of the medians (i.e. the lines from the angles to the middle points of the opposite sides). ***symmedian point***, the point at which the symmedians meet.

1885 J. CASEY *Analyt. Geom.* 45 The three lines which make with the bisectors of a triangle, on the opposite sides, angles equal to those which the medians make, are called the symmedians of the triangle, and their point of intersection its symmedian point. *Ibid.* 247 If figures directly similar be described on the sides of the triangle *ABC*, the symmedian lines of the triangle (*abc*) formed by any three corresponding lines pass respectively through the vertices of Brocard's second triangle.

‖**symmelia** (sɪˈmiːlɪə). *Path.* [mod.L., f. Gr. σύν SYM- + μέλος limb: see -IA¹.] A malformation in which a pair of limbs, esp. the hinder limbs, are fused into one. Hence **syˈmmelian** *a.*, characterized by symmelia; *sb.* an animal so characterized.

1894 BATESON *Study of Variation* I. xviii. 458 In vertebrates such union is especially well known.. producing the cyclopic, synotic and symmelian conditions respectively. *Ibid.* 459 The body of the symmelian ends posteriorly in an elongated lobe made up of parts of the posterior limbs compounded together by homologous parts. *Ibid. note*, To the determination of the morphology of the hind limb the structure of the symmelian monster is of unique importance. **1901** DORLAND *Med. Dict.* (ed. 2), *Symmelia*.. fusion of the feet and legs.

symmer, obs. Sc. form of SUMMER.

symmetallism (sɪmˈmɛtəlɪz(ə)m). *Econ.* Also **Symmetallism.** [f. SYM- + BI)METALLISM.] A proposed monetary system based on the use of an amalgam of gold and silver as a standard (see quot. 1979). Hence **symmeˈtallic** *a.*; **symˈmetallist** *sb.* an advocate of symmetallism (also *attrib.* or as *adj.*).

1895 F. Y. EDGEWORTH in *Econ. Jrnl.* V. 443 The arrangement that there should be a *joint demand* for gold and silver money might, perhaps, be called *symmetallism*, to distinguish it from the arrangement that there should be a *composite supply* which is called bimetallism. *Ibid.* 444 Suppose England with India adopts one symmetallic ratio. **1897** *Daily News* 30 Nov. 4/6 [A man] may be a Symmetallist, and believe that standard coins should be made from a mixture of silver with gold. *Ibid.*, Whether a symmetallist coinage be possible or not, it is certain that we have a symmetallist Administration. **1923** A. MARSHALL *Money, Credit & Commerce* 64 Although coinage of gold and silver at a fixed ratio causes movements of prices to be governed chiefly by the production of gold and silver alternately, a plan can be devised which would make the two metals work together: it may be called Symmetallism. **1934** *Sun* (Baltimore) 24 May 10/2 It [*sc.* the President's proposal] does not involve either bimetallism or symmetalism [*sic*]. **1979** *Econ. Jrnl.* LXXXIX. 29 Consider now Marshall's.. proposal for a 'stable bimetallism', which is usually called symmetallism. Under this system the central bank does not attempt to stabilise the price of either gold or silver separately, but rather pegs the price of a reserve unit that corresponds to a specified combination of the two metals. **1980** *Internat. Econ. Rev.* XXI. 675 Under a symmetallic standard.. the monetary authority does not set prices for individual commodities.

symmetral (ˈsɪmɪtrəl), *a.* [f. Gr.-L. *symmetros* (Vitruvius), Gr. *σύμμετρος* commensurate, proportionable, symmetrical (f. *σύν* SYM- + *μέτρον* measure) + -AL[1].]

†**1.** Agreeing in measurement, proportionable, commensurate. *Obs. rare*[−1].

1660 H. MORE *Myst. Godl.* v. xvi. 185 The Temple and Altar of God that are Symmetral or commensurable to the Angels measure [Rev. xi. 1].

†**2.** *fig.* Commensurate with the Divine idea or pattern; agreeing with the Word of God (cf. quot. 1680 s.v. ASYMMETRAL, and 1683 below): applied to the early church, or its times, etc. *Obs.*

1660 H. MORE *Myst. Godl.* v. xvii. §3. 204 It was both the Doctrine of the Apostles, and Practice of the Church, while it was Symmetral, to obey the Magistrate. **1664** —— *Myst. Iniq.* 472 The Church was Symmetral for about four hundred years after Christ. **1681** —— *Expos. Dan.* App. ii. 270 The end of the Symmetral Ages of the Church and the beginning of the Asymmetral or of the Apostasy. **1683** G. HICKES *Case Inf. Bapt.* 82 The purity of the Apostolical Ages, when the Church was.. represented as Symmetral by the Spirit of God, under the Symbol of Measuring the Temple of God and the Altar. **1685** H. MORE *Reflect. on Baxter* 29 An Authentick Church, reformed to the Pattern of the Symmetral or Primitive Ages.

3. *Math.* †**a.** *Arith.* and *Alg.* Having a common measure, commensurable. *Obs.*

1674 JEAKE *Arith.* (1696) 295 Commensurable, called also Symmetral, is when the given Numbers have a Common Divisor. *Ibid.*, Symmetral Surdes.

b. *Geom.* Related to or determining symmetry; about which a figure is symmetrical; as in ***symmetral axis, plane*** = axis or plane of symmetry.

1878 GURNEY *Crystallogr.* 27 The two halves on either side of this symmetral plane are in all respects similar. *Ibid.* 37 An axis of symmetry or a symmetral axis.

†**symmetrial,** *a. Obs. rare*[−1]. In 7 symitriall. [f. L. *symmetria* SYMMETRY + -AL[1].] = SYMMETRICAL 1.

1612 tr. *Benvenuto's Passenger* II. i. 429 Degenerating, swaruing and digressing from this qualitie, symitriall and iust proportion, there ensues a distempered temperature.

†**syˈmmetrian.** *Obs. rare.* [f. as prec. + -AN.] = SYMMETRIST.

a **1586** SIDNEY *Arcadia* I. xvi. (1912) 102 Her face was a thought longer then the exacte Symmetrians perhaps would allow. **1613** PURCHAS *Pilgrimage* v. xvii. 459 Statues.. fiue or sixe fathomes high, which these Symmetrians proportioned to the stature of Adam. **1623** COCKERAM I, *Simmetrian*, a painter or grauer, one that considereth the due proportion of a thing. **1656** [see SYMMETRIST].

†**syˈmmetriated**, *ppl. a. Obs. rare*[−1]. [ad. It. †*symmetriato* (= obs. F. *symmetrié*), ad. mod.L. **symmetriātus*: see -ATE[3].] Symmetrical.

1592 R. D. *Hypnerotomachia* 45 b, A.. Pallaice of a noble simmetriated [orig. It. *symmetriata*] architecturie.

symmetric (sɪˈmɛtrɪk), *a.* [f. SYMMETRY + -IC, after *geometric*. Cf. F. *symétrique*, †*symmetrique* (1529).] **1. a.** = SYMMETRICAL.

1796 BURNEY *Mem. Metastasio* II. 332 The air should be phrased and symmetric. **1816** TUCKEY *Narr. Exped. R. Zaire* iii. (1818) 108 The faces of many of the women were by no means unprepossessing, and their forms extremely symmetric. **1853** SYLVESTER in *Phil. Trans.* CXLIII. 434 Calculating the symmetric functions as a function only of *x* [etc.]. **1854** CAYLEY *Math. Papers* II. 233 The covariant may in the former case be called a symmetric covariant, and in the latter case a skew covariant. **1860** TYNDALL *Glac.* II. xxix. 403 The ripples from the two sides form a pair of symmetric curves. **1871** BROWNING *Balaust.* 1656 While still one's heart, in time and tune, Paced after that symmetric step of Death. **1885** BURTON *Arab. Nts.* (1887) III. 12 Perfect in beauty and loveliness and stature and symmetric grace.

b. Math. and Logic. ***symmetric difference*** (see quot. 1936); ***symmetric group***, the group of all the permutations of a set of unlike entities.

1936 *Trans. Amer. Math. Soc.* XL. 38 The Union (modulo 2), or symmetric difference, of two classes is the class of objects belonging to one or the other, but not to both, of those classes. **1971** J. H. CONWAY in Powell & Higman *Finite Simple Groups* vii. 225 If some non-empty $\mathscr{C}$-set has fewer than five elements, every set of the same cardinal would be a $\mathscr{C}$-set,.. and by taking symmetric differences we should obtain every two-element set.. as a $\mathscr{C}$-set, which cannot be. **1897** W. BURNSIDE *Theory of Groups of Finite Order* viii. 139 The group of order *n*! which consists of all the substitutions that can be performed on *n* symbols is called the symmetric group of degree *n*. **1955** L. MIRSKY *Introd. Linear Algebra* ix. 257 In addition to the symmetric group.. there are other groups of permutations, all of them naturally subgroups of the symmetric group.

c. *Physics.* = SYMMETRICAL *a.* 2 b.

1935 CONDON & SHORTLEY *Theory of Atomic Spectra* iii. 165 If the atom is at a certain moment in a symmetric state it will always remain in a symmetric state. **1965** H. MUIRHEAD *Physics Elem. Particles* ix. 369 It is apparent from this equation that parallel spin states.. are symmetric. **1979** *Nature* 29 Mar. 404/2 Certain baryons.. contain three identical quarks with parallel spins in a state which is symmetric (the wave function does not change sign) to the interchange of a pair of quarks.

2. *Logic.* Of a binary relation: such that when two terms for which it is true are interchanged, it remains true.

1933 *Mind* XLII. 34 Not even God himself can make men into women by shifting words, or make what we call 'implies' symmetric by changing names. **1968** *New Scientist* 16 May 339/1 Equality is symmetric as well as being reflexive. **1979** K. J. DEVLIN *Fund. Contemp. Set Theory* i. 14 A binary relation on a set is an equivalence relation just in case it is reflective, symmetric, and transitive.

symmetrical (sɪˈmɛtrɪkəl), *a.* [f. SYMMETRY + -ICAL, after *geometrical*. Cf. prec. and next.] Characterized by or exhibiting symmetry.

1. Having the parts or elements regularly and harmoniously arranged; regular in form; well-proportioned; balanced. (Said of natural or artificial bodies or structures, or of abstract or immaterial things; cf. SYMMETRY 2.)

1751 JOHNSON *Rambler* No. 94 ¶4 Some of the lines of this description are.. defective in harmony, and therefore by no means correspondent with that symmetrical elegance.. which they are intended to exhibit. **1833** LYELL *Princ. Geol.* III. 319 The oldest lavas of Etna were poured out many thousand.. years before the newest, and yet they have produced a symmetrical mountain. **1841** DICKENS *Barn. Rudge* viii, That I had but eyes!.. to behold my captain's symmetrical proportions. **1870** ROLLESTON *Anim. Life* p. xxiii, An increase in our knowledge.. may.. overthrow the most perfectly symmetrical of systems. **1886** RUSKIN *Præterita* I. 272 The symmetrical clauses of Pope's logical metre.

2. a. *Geom.*, etc. Said of a figure or body whose points or parts are equably distributed about a dividing line, plane, or point, i.e. arranged in pairs or sets so that those of each pair or set are at equal distances on opposite sides of such line, plane, or point; consisting of, or capable of being divided into, two or more exactly similar and equal parts. Also said of the form of such a figure or object, of its parts or their arrangement, or of any part in relation to the corresponding part.

1794 R. J. SULIVAN *View Nature* xxix. I. 423 In the passing of a substance from a fluid into a solid state, it almost universally appears.. to have its parts arranged in a symmetrical order. **1805–17** R. JAMESON *Char. Min.* (ed. 3) 146 When the nucleus has not what is called a symmetrical form, as when it is a parallelopiped, whose faces differ in the respective inclinations of their faces, or in the measure of their angles. **1850** GROVE *Corr. Phys. Forces* (ed. 2) 88 Those crystals which have one axis of figure, or a line around which the figure is symmetrical. **1885** LEUDESDORF *Cremona's Proj. Geom.* 267 The point *M* (and the symmetrical point in which the parabolas intersect again) can then be constructed. **1889** COCKSHOTT & WALTERS *Geometr. Conics* 40 The ellipse is symmetrical with respect to the minor axis. **1894** C. SMITH *Geometr. Conics* 4 When.. corresponding to any point of the curve there is another point such that the chord joining the two points is bisected perpendicularly by [a] straight line, then the curve is said to be symmetrical about the straight line, and the straight line is called an axis of the curve.

b. *Alg.* and *Higher Math.* Applied to an expression, function, or equation whose value is never altered by interchanging the values of any two of the variables or unknown quantities. In *Physics* also applied to a state represented by such a wave function. Also in *Logic*, = SYMMETRIC *a.* 2.

symmetrical or ***symmetric determinant***: a determinant in which the constituents in each row are the same respectively, and in the same order, as those in the corresponding column, and which is therefore symmetrical about its principal diagonal.

1816 tr. *Lacroix' Diff. & Int. Calc.* 536 On the supposition that $f(\alpha, \beta, \gamma, \&c.)$ is symmetrical with respect to all the roots, except α. **1854** *Orr's Circ. Sci., Math.* 217 Thus $x + y = a$; $x^2 + 3xy + y^2 = b$;.. are.. symmetrical equations; because for every *x* you may put *y*, and for every *y*, *x*, without altering either of the equations. **1863** FROST & WOLSTENHOLME *Solid Geom.* 29 To find the symmetrical equations of a straight line. **1878** W. K. CLIFFORD *Math. Papers* (1882) 317 If *n* is odd,.. the determinant is skew symmetrical, and being of odd order it necessarily vanishes. **1903, 1937** [see REFLEXIVE *a.* 7]. **1930** P. A. M. DIRAC *Princ. Quantum Mech.* xi. 201 It is quite possible for only symmetrical or antisymmetrical states to occur in nature... One assumes the symmetrical states for photons. **1954** I. M. COPI *Symbolic Logic* v. 141 Various symmetrical relations are designated by the phrases: 'is next to', 'is married to', and 'has the same weight as'. A symmetrical relation is one such that if one individual has that relation to a second individual, then the second individual must have that relation to the first. **1963** R. P. FEYNMAN et al. *Feynman Lect. Physics* I. xi. 2 The laws of physics are symmetrical for translational displacements,.. in the sense that the laws do not change when we make a translation of our coordinates. **1973** B. H. BRANSDEN et al. *Fundamental Particles* iv. 79 The triplet spin state is symmetrical. **1979** GEORGACARAKOS & SMITH *Elementary Formal Logic* ix. 329 When a relational expression has this property, we say that it is symmetrical.

c. *Photogr.* Applied to a lens of symmetrical form; also *ellipt.* as *sb.* = symmetrical lens.

1890 *Anthony's Photogr. Bull.* III. 326 Rapid, and portable symmetrical lenses, and a whole plate rapid symmetrical for long distance work. **1892** *Photogr. Ann.* II. 355 The lens is a rapid symmetrical with revolving diaphragms.

d. Math. and Logic. ***symmetrical difference*** = *symmetric difference* s.v. SYMMETRIC *a.* 1 b.

1978 C. H. GREENSTEIN *Dict. Logical Terms & Symbols* 172 Symmetrical difference. **1979** KANDEL & LEE *Fuzzy Switching & Automata* ii. 53 The symmetrical difference (or Boolean sum) of two fuzzy sets.

3. a. *Bot.* Of a flower: Having the same number of parts in each whorl: = ISOMEROUS 1.

1849 BALFOUR *Man. Bot.* §644 In speaking of flowers, it is usual to call them symmetrical when the sepals, petals, and stamens follow the law mentioned, even although the pistil may be abnormal. Thus, many Solanaceæ are pentamerous, and have a dimerous ovary, yet they are called symmetrical. .. In Papilionaceous flowers, the parts are usually symmetrical, there being five divisions of the calyx, five petals, and ten stamens in two rows.

b. (*a*) *Anat.* and *Zool.* Having similar or corresponding parts or organs on opposite sides of a dividing plane, or regularly arranged around an axis or centre; consisting of two or more similar or corresponding divisions. Also said of the parts. (*b*) *Path.* Of a disease: Affecting such corresponding parts or organs simultaneously. (Cf. SYMMETRY 3 c.)

1851 RICHARDSON *Geol.* viii. (1855) 230 Some have internal symmetrical bones, as the Sepia and Loligo. **1851** WOODWARD *Mollusca* I. (1856) 62 Unlike most of the mollusca, they are symmetrical animals, having their right and left sides equally developed. *a* **1883** FAGGE *Princ. Pract. Med.* (1886) II. 669 Remarkable cases of symmetrical gangrene of the extremities. **1892** H. LANE *Differ. Rheum. Dis.* (ed. 2) 46 Rheumatoid Arthritis.. affection of joints often symmetrical.

Hence **symmetriˈcality** = SYMMETRICALNESS.

1893 *Chamb. Jrnl.* 21 Jan. 44/2 With regard to symmetricality, Nature, when she has a purpose to serve, is nowise loth to depart from it.

symmetrically (sɪˈmɛtrɪkəlɪ), *adv.* Also 6–7 simm-. [f. SYMMETRY + -ICALLY, after *geometrically*. Cf. F. *symétriquement*, †*symmetriquement* (1529).] In a symmetrical manner; so as to be symmetrical; with symmetry.

1575 LANEHAM *Let.* 67 A square pilaster.. Simmetrically pierced throogh from a foot beneath, untill a too foot of the top. **1638** SIR T. HERBERT *Trav.* (ed. 2) 338 They write neither to the right hand nor to the left,.. but right downe and simmetrically. **1831** BREWSTER *Optics* xli. §197. 338 The pencils [of light] from every part of the object will fall symmetrically upon the lens, and be symmetrically refracted. **1838** DICKENS *Nich. Nick.* xxi, Mr. Mantalini was disclosed to view, with his shirt collar symmetrically thrown back. **1859** PARKINSON *Optics* (1866) 13 Since *u*, *v* are symmetrically involved in the equation $\frac{1}{v} + \frac{1}{u} = \frac{2}{r}$. **1878** GURNEY *Crystallogr.* 27 Every diameter of a circle divides it symmetrically. **1896** H. WOODWARD *Guide Fossil Reptiles Brit. Mus.* 114 This sub-order.. comprises the symmetrically-formed Cod-fishes.

So **syˈmmetricalness,** †(*a*) the quality of being SYMMETRAL (sense 2), (*b*) the quality of being symmetrical; symmetry.

1684 H. MORE *Answer* Pref. b j, The Symmetricalness of the Primitive Ages. **1858** W. BAGEHOT in *National Rev.* Oct. 460 The mode in which those opinions are expressed, and.. the mode in which they are framed, affect us.. with a sensation of symmetricalness. **1874** *Contemp. Rev.* Nov. 931 There is.. a symmetricalness and consistency about these peasants.

†**symmetrician.** *Obs. rare*⁻¹. Also 6 **simmetricien.** [f. SYMMETRY, after *geometrician.*] = SYMMETRIAN, SYMMETRIST.

1577 HARRISON *England* I. iv. in *Holinshed* I. 4 b/1 Sith yᵉ longest rib is commonly about yᵉ fourth part of a man, as some Simmetriciens [*ed.* **1587** symmetricians] affirme.

†**sy'mmetrious,** *a. Obs. rare.* [f. SYMMETRY + -OUS.] Symmetrical; corresponding. Hence †**sy'mmetriously** *adv.*, symmetrically.

1656 W. COLES *Art of Simpling* 148 A Body so symmetriously composed. **1667** WATERHOUSE *Narr. Fire in London* 85 Its Franchises being all Emblematical of, and Symmetrious with the Greater Ones of the Nation.

symmetrist ('sɪmɪtrɪst). *rare*⁻¹. [f. SYMMETRY + -IST.] An advocate of, or one studious of, symmetry.

1624 WOTTON *Archit.* in *Reliq.* (1672) 56 Some exact Symmetrists have been blamed for being too true. **1656** BLOUNT *Glossogr.*, *Symmetrist* or *Symmetrian*..one that considers the due proportion of a thing, and how well the parts agree with the whole; one skilled in proportions.

symmetrize ('sɪmɪtraɪz), *v.* [ad. F. *symétriser* (in sense 1 below), or f. SYMMETRY + -IZE.]

1. *intr.* To be symmetrical; to correspond symmetrically. *rare.*

1749 J. CLELAND *Mem. Woman of Pleasure* II. 233 An air of becoming manliness..that symetriz'd [*sic*] nobly with that air of distinction..with which nature has stamped it [*sc.* his face]. **1786** H. WALPOLE *Let. to C'tess Ossory* 28 Sept., With a mound of vermilion on the left side of his forehead to symmetrise with a wen on the right.

2. *trans.* To make symmetrical; to reduce to symmetry. Also *absol.*

1796 BURKE *Let. Noble Ld.* Wks. VIII. 46 He would soon have supplied every deficiency, and symmetrized every disproportion. **1853** *Blackw. Mag.* LXXIV. 735 A picturesque scene, however seemingly unsymmetrical, will be found..to be symmetrised at least aerially, by the influence of light, shade and colour. **1874** *Contemp. Rev.* Aug. 439 Charm of incident, grace of narrative,..majesty of eloquence,—all perfectly symmetrized with incomparable artistic skill. **1973** *Sci. Amer.* Jan. 111/2 This leaves one column and one row, with the poison piece at the vertex... From now on the first player 'symmetrizes'. Whatever his opponent takes from either line, he takes equally from the other.

Hence **'symmetrized, 'symmetrizing** *ppl. adjs.*; also ˌ**symmetri'zation**, the action or process of symmetrizing.

1854 *Fraser's Mag.* XLIX. 149 The philosophic classes have never admitted that a moral change can be effected by political change, that a realized idea needs symmetrization in statute. **1862** R. H. PATTERSON *Ess. Hist. & Art* 60 When the several parts of an object..present a resistance to its [*sc.* the mind's] synthetical or symmetrising power,—it imputes to such objects a character of force and energy, which purely symmetrical compositions do not suggest. **1890** *Q. Jrnl. Microsc. Sci.* Aug. 448 The larva emerges..as a symmetrical animal, but the details of the process of 'symmetrisation'—the strongly marked character of which justifies the use of an otherwise undesirable term—are still rather obscure. **1966** *Math. Rev.* XXXI. 36/1 (*heading*) Matrix applications of a quadratic identity for decomposable symmetrized tensors. **1979** *Nature* 29 Feb. 597/2 It is the interference between the two parts of the symmetrised wave-functions..that leads to the intensity interference.

symmetrodont (sɪ'mɛtrəʊdɒnt), *sb.* and *a.* [f. mod.L. order name *Symmetrodonta* (G. G. Simpson 1925, in *Amer. Jrnl. Sci.* CCX. 560), f. SYMMETR(Y + Gr. ὀδούς, ὀδοντ- tooth, in allusion to the form of the teeth (see quot. 1979²).]

A. *sb.* A fossil mammal of the order Symmetrodonta, known from remains found in North America and Europe. **B.** *adj.* Of or pertaining to an animal of this kind or the order including it.

1933 A. S. ROMER *Vertebr. Paleont.* xii. 260 The symmetrodonts seem to have been somewhat off the main evolutionary line. **1950** *Nature* 21 Oct. 696/2 The specimen can easily be described as a lower symmetrodont cheek tooth. **1977** A. HALLAM *Planet Earth* 223 Triconodont and symmetrodont mammals died out during the Cretaceous. **1979** R. C. FOX in Fairbridge & Jablonski *Encycl. Paleont.* 429/2 Symmetrodonts were small shrew-sized mammals, probably having insectivorous food habits. *Ibid.*, Symmetrodont molars are highly characteristic; both upper and lower crowns formed simple occlusal triangles... The lower molar triangles are reversed in respect to the uppers and occlusion was alternate in the sense that each molar occluded within the embrasure between two successive molars on the opposite jaw.

symmetroid ('sɪmɪtrɔɪd). *Geom.* [irreg. f. SYMMETRY + -OID.] Cayley's name for a certain surface of the fourth order: see quot.

1870 CAYLEY *Math. Papers* VII. 134 The surface which I call a symmetroid; viz., the surface represented by an equation $\Delta = 0$, where Δ is a symmetrical determinant of the 4th order the several terms whereof are linear functions of the coordinates (x, y, z, w).

symmetrophobia (ˌsɪmɪtrəʊ'fəʊbɪə). Also **symmetriphobia.** [irreg. f. SYMMETRY + -*o* + -PHOBIA.] Dread or avoidance of symmetry, as shown or supposed to be shown in Egyptian temples, Japanese art, etc.

1809 W. R. HAMILTON *Remarks Turkey* I. 131 Another instance of the *Symmetrophobia* of the architects of antient Egypt is visible in the difference of the spaces between the sphinxes and crio-sphinxes. **1865** J. FERGUSSON *Hist. Archit.* I. iv. I. 103 The buildings..are..generally affected with a symmetriphobia that it is difficult to understand. **1881** R. S. POOLE in *Contemp. Rev.* Sept. 373 Symmetrophobia, shown in the placing columns of different orders opposite one another, and a colonnade on one side only of a court. **1894** LOCKYER *Dawn Astron.* viii. 75 At Karnak..we can see how closely the walls reflect the orientation of the included temples, even when they seem most liable to the suggestion of symmetrophobia.

symmetry ('sɪmɪtrɪ). Also 6 **symmetrye, simetrie, 6–7 simetry, sym(m)etrie, 7 simmetry, -ie, symetry.** [a. F. †*symmetrie* (1529), mod. *symétrie* (= It. *simm-*, Sp. *sim-*, Pg. *symetria*), or ad. late L. *symmetria*, a. Gr. συμμετρία, f. σύμμετρος, f. σύν SYM- + μέτρον measure (see METRE).]

†**1.** Mutual relation of the parts of something in respect of magnitude and position; relative measurement and arrangement of parts; proportion.

With qualifying adj. such as *just*, *right*, *true*, coinciding with sense 2.

1563 SHUTE *Archit.* A iij b, Concerning yᵉ proportion and simetry to vse the accustomed terme of the arte of the fornamed columbes. *Ibid.* B j b, They not knowing any measure of pillours considered howe to make a iust Symetrie,..after that they deuised to make a temple to the goddesse Diana, wherein they dyd deuise an other Symetrie, for that temple. **1570** DEE *Math. Pref.* a iv, The exhibiting to our eye,..the plat of a Citie,..or Pallace, in true Symmetry. *Ibid.* c iij b, Now, may you, of any Gunne,..make an other, with the same Symmetrie..as great, and as little, as you will. **1624** WOTTON *Archit.* in *Reliq.* (1672) 23 Man..is..as it were the Prototype of all exact Symmetrie. **1650** BULWER *Anthropomet.* 241 True and native beauty consists in the just composure and symetrie of the parts of the body. **1730** A. GORDON *Maffei's Amphith.* 313 He marks out a Stair..which agrees not with the Symmetry of the Building.

2. Due or just proportion; harmony of parts with each other and the whole; fitting, regular, or balanced arrangement and relation of parts or elements; the condition or quality of being well-proportioned or well-balanced. In stricter use (approaching or passing into 3 b): Exact correspondence in size and position of opposite parts; equable distribution of parts about a dividing line or centre. (As an attribute either of the whole, or of the parts composing it.)

a. of natural objects or structures, esp. the human or animal body: often (esp. in early use) = regularity and beauty of form, fair or fine appearance, comeliness.

1599 B. JONSON *Cynthia's Rev.* I. iii, If I had thought a creature of her symmetry, could have dar'd so improportionable, and abrupt a digression. **1633** G. HERBERT *Temple, Ch. Porch* lxx, Who marks in church-time others symmetrie, Makes all their beautie his deformitie. **1635** A. STAFFORD *Fem. Glory* (1869) 5 Whether her Beauty chiefly consisted in colour, in symmetry of parts, or both. **1778** HAN. MORE *Bleeding Rock* 224 Hers every charm of symmetry and grace. **1820** W. IRVING *Sketch Bk.* I. 185 The small Italian hound of exquisite symmetry. **1853** C. BRONTE *Villette* xxiv, Her pale, small features, her fairy symmetry, her varying expression. **1858** O. W. HOLMES *Aut. Breakf.-t.* xii. 113 One of the finest trees in symmetry and beauty I had ever seen.

†(*b*) in semi-*concr.* sense: (Well-proportioned) figure or form (of a person or animal). *Obs.*

1602 MARSTON *Ant. & Mel.* II. Wks. 1856 I. 25 Ladie, erect your gratious simmetry. **1633** FORD *Love's Sacr.* II. E j, She cannot..more really, behold her owne Symmetry in her glasse. **1794** W. BLAKE *Songs Exper., Tiger* 4 What immortal hand or eye Could frame thy fearful symmetry?

b. of artificial things or structures, esp. buildings.

1601 HOLLAND *Pliny* XXXIV. viii. II. 499 The Symmetrie, which..he observed most precisely in all his workes, is a tearme that cannot properly be expressed by a Latine word. *Ibid.* XXXV. x. 543 Asclepiodorus, whome for his singular skill in observing symetries and just proportions, Apelles himselfe was woont to admire. **1702** W. J. *Bruyn's Voy. Levant* ix. 31 There is no regularity of Architecture nor any Symmetry observ'd in it. **1723** CHAMBERS tr. *Le Clerc's Archit.* I. 97 This Column..must have a Pilaster by its side, to make a Symmetry with that on the other side the Window. **1820** LAMB *Elia* Ser. I. *Two Races of Men*, Spoilers of the symmetry of shelves. **1849** LONGF. *Building Ship* 179 Till, framed with perfect symmetry, A skeleton ship rose up to view! **1907** *Verney Mem.* I. 15 The utter disregard of symmetry evinced by our ancestors which is one secret of the picturesqueness of their groups of buildings.

c. (*a*) in general sense, or of immaterial or abstract things, as action, thought, discourse, literary composition, etc.

1603 HOLLAND *Plutarch's Mor.* 60 Beautie and fauour is composed..of many numbers meeting and concurring in one..and that by a certaine symmetrie, consonance and harmonie. **1609** BP. ANDREWES *Serm.*, *Resurrection* iv. (1631) 420 The way, to peace, is the mid way: neither..too much; nor..too little. In a word; all analogie, symmetrie, harmony, in the world, goeth by it. **1643** SIR T. BROWNE *Relig. Med.* II. §9 Whatsoever is harmonically composed, delights in harmony; which makes me much distrust the symmetry of those heads which declaime against all Church musicke. **1711** SHAFTESB. *Charac.* IV. ii. (1737) I. 139 The ordering of Walks, Plantations, Avenues; and a thousand other Symmetrys, will succeed in the room of that happier and higher Symmetry and Order of a Mind. **1742** WEST *Let.* in *Gray's Poems* (1775) 142 The connection and symmetry of such little parts with one another must naturally escape me, as not having the plan of the whole in my head. **1860** PUSEY *Min. Proph.* 291 This book, Micah, has remarkable symmetry. Each of its three divisions is a whole, beginning with upbraiding for sin, threatening Gods judgments, and ending with promises of future mercy. *a* **1862** BUCKLE *Civiliz.* (1864) II. vi. 445 Into that dense and disorderly mass, did Adam Smith introduce symmetry, method, and law. **1904** HUGH BLACK *Practice of Self-Culture* v. 132 Culture..aims at symmetry of life.

(*b*) Agreement, consistency, consonance, congruity, keeping (*with* something). *rare* or *Obs.*

1654 H. L'ESTRANGE *Chas. I* (1655) 9 You furnished my Father with..supply's, but they held no symmetry or proportion with the charge of so great an enterprise. **1659** EVELYN *Let. to R. Boyle* 3 Sept., I will..shew what symmetry it [*sc.* the building] holds with this description. **1878** STUBBS *Lect. Med. & Mod. Hist.* viii. (1900) 192 It is in exact symmetry with Western usage, that this great compilation was not received as a code until the year 1369.

3. Various specific and technical uses.

†**a.** *Physiol.* Harmonious working of the bodily functions, producing a healthy temperament or condition. *Obs. rare.*

1541 COPLAND *Galyen's Terap.* 2 E j b, In Symmetrye, that is to say..in competent [? competence] and commoderacyon of smal conduites lyeth and consisteth the helth. And in Ametrie, that is to saye, in vncompetence and immoderacyon in them the dysease.

b. (*a*) *Sci.* Exact correspondence in position of the several points or parts of a figure or body with reference to a dividing line, plane, or point (or a number of lines or planes); arrangement of all the points of a figure or system in pairs (or sets) so that those of each pair (or set) are at equal distances on opposite sides of such line, plane, or point. More widely, a property by virtue of which something is effectively unchanged by a particular operation; an operation or set of operations that leaves something effectively unchanged; in *Physics*, a property that is conserved (cf. *symmetry operation*, sense 4 below).

Symmetry, e.g. in crystals, may be of various grades, according to the number of radiating or non-parallel lines or planes about which the figure or body is symmetrical.

axis of symmetry, centre of s., plane of s., the line, point, or plane about which a figure or body is symmetrical, i.e. which bisects every straight line joining a pair of corresponding points of such figure or body.

1823 H. J. BROOKE *Introd. Crystallogr.* 13 From the perfect symmetry of its form, the cube has a similar axis in four directions. **1837** BREWSTER *Magnet* 39 A horse-shoe magnet..was made to revolve..about its axis of symmetry. **1850** McCOSH *Div. Govt.* II. i. (1874) 119 The oblong, or two-and-two-membered symmetry, may be traced..among crystals and flowers, as may also the three-membered symmetry. **1877** HUXLEY *Physiogr.* (1878) 56 The best example of this hexagonal symmetry..is furnished by crystals of snow. **1878** GURNEY *Crystallogr.* 29 A plane..through the centre of a model of a crystal will be a plane of symmetry, if the perpendiculars drawn to it from every point of the model, on being produced to equal distances on the other side..will terminate in points of the model similar to those from which they are drawn. **1908** H. HILTON *Theory of Groups of Finite Order* iv. 42 If a movement (other than identity) brings every point of a figure F into the position previously occupied either by itself or by some other point of F, F is said to possess symmetry. **1941** BIRKHOFF & MACLANE *Survey Mod. Algebra* vi. 122 The algebra of symmetries has its genesis in the fact that we can multiply two motions by performing them in succession. **1965** R. P. FEYNMAN et al. *Feynman Lect. Physics* III. xvii. 8 Symmetry with respect to displacements in time implies the conservation of energy; symmetry with respect to position in x, y, or z implies the conservation of momentum. **1967** *Physical Rev. Lett.* XIX. 1264/2 As far as we know, two of these symmetries are entirely unbroken: the charge Q..and the electron number N. **1968** M. S. LIVINGSTON *Particle Physics* xii. 201 One consequence of the translational symmetry of space is the invariance of physical laws under translation from one location to another. **1974** FRAUENFELDER & HENLEY *Subatomic Physics* vi. 154 Some of the symmetries are perfect even under closest scrutiny, and no breakdown in the corresponding conservation law has ever been found. Rotational symmetry and conservation of angular momentum are one example.

(*b*) *Alg.*, *Higher Math.* and *Logic.* The fact of being symmetrical, as an expression or function: see SYMMETRICAL *a.* 2 b.

1888 *Amer. Jrnl. Math.* X. 173 Notes on Geometric Inferences from Algebraic Symmetry. **1950** [see REFLEXIVITY]. **1967** S. C. KLEENE *Math. Logic* iii. 158 Sometimes 'equality' is used in a different sense, so that it possesses only the first three properties (reflexivity, symmetry and transitivity).

c. (*a*) *Anat.* and *Zool.* Arrangement of parts or organs in pairs or sets on opposite sides of a dividing plane, or around an axis or centre; repetition of similar corresponding parts in the two halves, or other number of divisions, of the body. (Nearly coinciding with 3 b or the stricter use in 2, except that corresponding parts are not necessarily equal, nor do all the parts necessarily correspond.) (*b*) *Path.* Affection of such corresponding parts simultaneously by the same disease.

1849–52 *Todd's Cycl. Anat.* IV. 845 Symmetry is a word used to express..the fact, that one half of an animal is usually an exact reversed copy of the other... To this there are numerous exceptions. *a* **1883** FAGGE *Princ. Pract. Med.* (1886) II. 619 Symmetrical distribution means that exactly the corresponding parts on the right and left side are simultaneously affected... This is bilateral symmetry, but we also see examples of serial symmetry in pathology where the same condition is seen on the elbow and the knee, the wrist and the ankle.

d. *Bot.* Equality of the number of parts in the several whorls of the flower: see SYMMETRICAL 3 a.

1845–50 MRS. LINCOLN *Lect. Bot.* 138 The symmetry of structure observable in [Enchanter's Night-shade] is seen in many flowers. **1849** BALFOUR *Man. Bot.* §643 When the number of parts is two, the flower is dimerous.. and the symmetry two-membered. When the number of parts is three, the flower is trimerous, and when the parts are arranged in an alternating manner, the symmetry is trigonal or triangular [etc.]. **1908** HENSLOW *How to Study Wild Fl.* 113 The flowers [of *Lythrum Salicaria*] vary in symmetry; for sometimes the central flower will differ from the lateral ones in the number of parts.

4. *attrib.* and *Comb.*, as ***symmetry principle, property***; **symmetry-breaking** *ppl. a.* and *vbl. sb. Physics*, (causing) the absence of manifest symmetry in a situation despite its presence in the laws of nature underlying it; **symmetry group**, a group (GROUP *sb.* 5 a) whose elements are all the symmetry operations of a particular entity; **symmetry operation** *Physics*, an operation or transformation that leaves something effectively unchanged.

1961 M. GELL-MANN in Gell-Mann & Ne'eman *Eightfold Way* (1964) We attempt.. to treat the eight known baryons as a supermultiplet, degenerate in the limit of a certain symmetry but split into isotopic spin multiplets by a symmetry-breaking term. **1977** *Dædalus* Summer 29 As a result of this symmetry-breaking, the quanta of the weak interactions are predicted to acquire a mass approximately forty or more times heavier than that of a proton. **1981** *Nature* 10 Dec. 522/1 The usual analogy used for spontaneous symmetry breaking is ferromagnetism. Maxwell's equations are rotationally invariant; however, below the Curie temperature the rotational invariance of a ferromagnet is spontaneously broken when the magnetization chooses a specific direction. **1956** *Ibid.* 10 Mar. 458/1 To-day the instinctive reaction of every theoretical physicist, confronted with an unexplained regularity in the behaviour of elementary particles, is to postulate an underlying symmetry-group. **1975** I. STEWART *Concepts Mod. Math.* vii. 97 Every shape has a symmetry group. **1981** *Sci. Amer.* Apr. 50/2 The $SU(2) \times U(1)$ theory is only a partial unification because it still includes two distinct forces, each with its own symmetry group and its own coupling constant. **1952** H. WEYL *Symmetry* 27 For forms fixed to the bottom of the ocean the direction of gravity is an important factor, narrowing the set of symmetry operations from all rotations around the center P to all rotations about an axis. **1973** B. H. BRANSDEN et al. *Fundamental Particles* iv. 56 The symmetry operations with which we are concerned are transformations of the dynamical variable that leave the Hamiltonian operator unaltered. **1968** M. S. LIVINGSTON *Particle Physics* xii. 201 It is possible that the number of such symmetry principles is limited and that they are interrelated. *Ibid.*, One of the most basic symmetry principles is that of the homogeneity of space and the associated symmetry of time. **1977** *Dædalus* Fall 31 Some theorists turned to the study of symmetry principles and conservation laws, which can be applied to physical phenomena without detailed dynamical calculations. **1935** PAULING & WILSON *Introd. Quantum Mech.* xiv. 388 The symmetry properties of molecular wave functions. **1968** M. S. LIVINGSTON *Particle Physics* iii. 58 The type of quantum statistics which applies to a system of particles (all of one kind) is related to the symmetry properties of the wave function describing this system of particles.

symmography (sɪ'mɒgrəfɪ). [f. SYMM(ETRY + -OGRAPHY.] = *string art* s.v. STRING *sb.* 32. Also **'symmograph**, a pattern or picture made by symmography; **symmo'graphic** *a.*

1971 L. KREISCHER *Symmography* 4 Symmography is an art form using yarn, wood, and nails as the media. *Ibid.* 5 The materials you need to begin a symmograph are basically quite simple. *Ibid.*, The nails I use for my symmographic creations are.. bright steel wire. **1975** *String Art Encycl.* 9 Whereas originally string-craft creations were often symmographs—art works in which string was wound attractively and symmetrically around nails in a board—this book deals with string in other artistic forms as well.

symmorphic, -morphism: see SYM-.

symmory ('sɪmərɪ). *Anc. Gr. Hist.* [ad. Gr. συμμορία, f. σύμμορος adj. sharing (*sc.* the burden of taxation), f. σύν SYM- + μορ- (: μέρος portion, share).] Each of the companies or fellowships, graded according to wealth, into which the citizens of Athens and other cities were divided for purposes of taxation.

[**1835** T. MITCHELL *Acharn. of Aristoph.* 453 *note*, Property-taxes are often mentioned in connexion with the resident aliens. This class of settlers composed distinct symmoriæ (μετοικικαί συμμορίαι), which had treasurers of their own; and a fixed contribution was settled for each one.] **1847** GROTE *Greece* II. xiii. III. 247 The territory of the town was distributed amongst a certain number of towers, to each of which corresponded a symmory or section of the citizens having its common altar and sacred rites. **1891** *Athenæum* 25 July 128/1 The proposition of Demosthenes was that 2,000 citizens should be placed in the symmories.

†**symmyst, symmist.** *Obs.* Also 7 symist. [ad. late L. *symmysta* (Jerome), med.L. *symmista*, *symmystēs* (Apuleius), colleague in the priesthood, ad. Gr. συμμύστης fellow-initiate, f. σύν SYM- + μύστης one initiated into mysteries: cf. MYST. The unetymological but more frequent spelling with *i*, already found in med.L., is due to association with words in -IST.] **a.** An associate in a 'mystery', i.e. a secret belief or practice; a fellow-initiate. **b.** A colleague in a sacred office.

1607 TOPSELL *Four-f. Beasts* 474 All the Easterne wise men beleeued the transmigration of spirites.. and insinuated so much to their symmists and disciples. **1635** PAGITT *Christianogr.* 180 The sacred Symists of his Religion, are especially to be honoured: Some examples of this also I mean to produce, that their follies may.. appear, who would detract due honour from the sacred Ministers of Almighty God. *a* **1680** GLANVILL *Sadducismus* I. (1726) 63 One of the.. most religious Symmysts of that stupendious secret of Nullibism. *a* **1693** *Urquhart's Rabelais* III. xlviii. 391 The other Mole catching Symmists [orig. *les Symmystes taulpetiers*].

symon ('saɪmən) *local.* [var. SIMMON *sb.*[1]] Name for a kind of red shale; also *attrib.* **symon fault**, an interruption of a seam of coal by shale or other material (see quots.).

1834–6 PRESTWICH in *Trans. Geol. Soc.* Ser. II. (1840) V. 432 'Symon fault'.. is occasioned by the gradual.. substitution of the coal by clay, shale, or sandstone,.. the proportion of which rapidly increases, until it entirely replaces the coal. **1839** MURCHISON *Silur. Syst.* I. vii. 101 Even the coal.. tapers away and disappears amid the shales and sandstones, constituting what are locally termed 'Symonfaults'. **1881** MISS JACKSON *Shropsh. Word-bk.*, *Symon*, a sort of red shale, same as Calaminca, q.v.—Colliery; M[iners'] T[erm].

symond(e, -ont: see SIMMON *sb.*[1], SIMONT.

Symondite ('sɪməndaɪt). Now *Hist.* [f. the name of Rear-Admiral Sir William *Symonds* (1782–1856): see -ITE[1].] A small warship designed by Sir William Symonds in his capacity as surveyor to the Royal Navy.

1927 B. M. CHAMBERS *Salt Junk* iv. 27 The *Eurydice* was what was known as a Symonite [*sic*] or Jackass frigate, i.e., something between a sloop and a frigate. **1932** A. H. LONG *Round the Bill* 9 She was a good little boat, about seven feet beam, drew three feet six inches, and had a regular Symondite bottom, like the *America*. **1935** H. I. CHAPELLE *Hist. Amer. Sailing Ships* 156 As a class, the Symondites were very unsteady gun-platforms. **1957** *Mariner's Mirror* XLIII. 337 For rolling, pitching and lee-lurches the Symondites beat the lot.

sympalmograph, -patetic: see SYM-.

†**sympatheal**, *a. Obs. rare*[−1]. [f. Gr. συμπάθεια SYMPATHY + -AL[1].] Sympathetic.

1600 W. WATSON *Decacordon* (1602) Pref. A iv b, So sweet a sympatheall harmonie in English hearts.

sympathectomy (sɪmpə'θɛktəmɪ). *Surg.* Also **sympathetectomy**. [f. SYMPATH(ETIC + Gr. ἐκτομή excision.] Excision of a sympathetic ganglion or other part of the sympathetic nerve.

1900 *The Physician & Surg.* I. No. 7. 314 European Oculists and Surgeons have performed sympathectomy for glaucoma and exophthalmic goiter. **1903** *Med. Record* LXIII. 875/2 So far as the question of choice of operation between hemisection and sympathectomy went, he believed that the Jennesco operation gave better results. **1936** *Q. Jrnl. Med.* XXIX. 438 Of all the 'sympathectomies' which have been proposed and tried, 'ganglionectomy' is the only one really worth doing. **1955** *Sci. News Let.* 22 Oct. 262/1 The nerve-cutting operation, called sympathectomy, is to dilate arteries that have been stopped. **1968** G. MAXWELL *Raven seek thy Brother* ii. 29 There was no alternative, he said, to lumbar sympathectomy. **1979** *Molecular Pharmacol.* XV. 35 Microsomal preparations derived from several peripheral organs of cats or rabbits following chemical sympathectomy.

Hence **sympa'thectomized** *a.*, that has undergone sympathectomy.

1928 *Amer. Jrnl. Physiol.* LXXXV. 493 Table 3 shows the changes produced in the relative mononuclear count in sympathectomized animals. **1970** H. SHANDS *Semiotic Approaches to Psychiatry* xxiii. 396 He [*sc.* the schizophrenic] thrives (relatively speaking) when, like Cannon's sympathectomized cats, he is never exposed to normally expectable variation.

sympathetic (sɪmpə'θɛtɪk), *a.* (*sb.*) [ad. mod.L. *sympathēticus*, a. Gr. συμπαθητικός, f. συμπαθεῖν, after παθητικός PATHETIC.]

A. *adj.* **1. a.** Pertaining to, involving, depending on, acting or effected by 'sympathy', or a (real or supposed) affinity, correspondence, or occult influence; esp. in ***sympathetic powder*** = 'powder of sympathy': see SYMPATHY I. Now chiefly *Hist.*

1644 DIGBY (*title*) Discourse concerning the Cure of Wounds, by the Sympathetic Powder. **1664** BUTLER *Hud.* II. III. 296 He would.. Cure Warts and Corns, with application Of Med'cines to th' Imagination... And fire a Mine in China, here, With Sympathetick Gunpowder. *a* **1665** DIGBY *Receipts in Physick*, etc. (1668) 45 A Sympathetick cure for the Tooth-ach.—With an Iron-nail raise and cut the Gum from about the Teeth, till it bleed, and that some of the blood stick upon the nail; then drive it into a wooden beam up to the head: After this is done, you never shall have the tooth-ach in all your life. **1665** GLANVILL *Scepsis Sci.* xxi. 134 To conferr at the distance of the Indies by Sympathetick conveyances, may be as usual to future times, as to us in a litterary correspondence. **1713** ADDISON *Guard.* No. 119 ¶5 The Friend.. saw his own Sympathetick Needle moving of it self to every Letter which that of his Correspondent pointed at. **1768** TUCKER *Lt. Nat.* I. II. xix. 32 Those sympathetic cures spoken of by Sir Kenelm Digby, who tells you that wounds have been healed by applying salves and plaisters to the instrument that made them. **1804** MRS. BARBAULD *Life Richardson* I. 12 In those times talismans and wounds cured by sympathetic powder.. were seriously credited. **1905** CLODD *Animism* §13. 66 The numerous practices which come under the head of 'sympathetic magic', or the imitation of a cause to produce a desired effect.

b. ***sympathetic ink***: a name for various colourless liquid compositions used as ink, the writing with which remains invisible until the colour is developed by the application of heat or some chemical reagent. Also *fig.*

1721 BAILEY, *Sympathetick Inks*, are such as can be made to appear or disappear, by the Application of something that seems to work by Sympathy. **1796** *Phil. Trans.* LXXXVI. 333 The phænomena which heat produces on the solution of cobalt in muriatic or nitro-muriatic acid, called sympathetic ink. **1822** IMISON *Sci. & Art* II. 309 Make a drawing representing a Winter scene in which the trees appear void of leaves, and.. put the leaves on with this sympathetic ink. **1848** RICHTER *Levana* xiii, Like sympathetic ink, it becomes as quickly invisible as visible. **1866** CARLYLE *Remin.* (1881) I. 158 All written in us already.. in sympathetic ink. **1907** *Verney Mem.* I. 297 He writes topsy-turvy in sympathetic ink, between the lines of a letter ostensibly full of public news.

c. *Physiol.* and *Path.* Produced by 'sympathy' (see SYMPATHY 1 b): applied to a condition, action, or disorder induced in a person, or in an organ or part of the body, by a similar or corresponding one in another.

1728 CHAMBERS *Cycl.*, *Sympathetic*, is particularly applied to all Diseases which have two Causes; the one remote, the other near. In which Sense, the Word is opposed to *Idiopathetic.* **1774** GOLDSM. *Nat. Hist.* (1824) I. 211 He had only to gape, or yawn, and the professor instantly caught the sympathetic affection. **1804** ABERNETHY *Surg. Obs.* I. 22 Perhaps these vessels undergo a kind of sympathetic enlargement. **1849** NOAD *Electricity* (ed. 3) 486 The action of Electricity on the muscles and nerves produces two distinct kinds of contractions; the first, which he [*sc.* Marianini] calls *idiopathic*, are the result of the immediate action of the current on the muscles; and the second, which he calls *sympathetic*, arise from the action of Electricity on the nerves which preside over the motions of the muscles. **1872** T. BRYANT *Pract. Surg.* (1884) I. 385 Sympathetic ophthalmia is.. a peculiar form of inflammation.. in one eye in consequence of morbid changes.. in the other.

d. *Anat.* Designating one of the two great nerve-systems in vertebrates (the other being the *cerebro-spinal*), consisting of a double chain of ganglia, with connecting fibres, along the vertebral column, giving off branches and plexuses which supply the viscera and blood-vessels and maintain relations between their various activities; belonging to or forming part of this system. Also applied to a similar set of nerves supplying the viscera in some invertebrates.

1769 JOHNSTONE in *Phil. Trans.* LX. 35 The intercostal, or as they are otherwise called, the great sympathetic nerves. **1830** R. KNOX *Béclard's Anat.* 337 The particular action of the heart.. is directly under the influence of the sympathetic nerve;.. digestion, under the combined influence of the par vagum and sympathetic nerve. **1873** MIVART *Elem. Anat.* ix. 403 The sympathetic system is made up of.. small nerves and ganglia closely connected with the arteries and the viscera. **1880** BASTIAN *Brain* 46 The 'sympathetic' or visceral ganglia of the Frog. **1888** ROLLESTON & JACKSON *Anim. Life* 149 The respiratory sympathetic system [in the Sphinx-larva].

transf. **1878** KINGZETT *Anim. Chem.* 52 Sympathetic saliva is furnished on irritation of the sympathetic nerve.

e. *Physics.* Used in reference to sounds produced by responsive vibrations induced in one body by transmission of vibrations from another. Also *spec.* in Mus., ***sympathetic strings***: (see quot. 1960).

1832 BREWSTER *Nat. Magic* viii. 182 The subdivision of the string, and consequently the production of harmonic sounds, may be effected.. by means of a sympathetic action conveyed by the air. **1836** MRS. SOMERVILLE *Connex. Phys. Sci.* Introd. (ed. 3) 2 Oscillations, which correspond in their periods with the cause producing them, like sympathetic notes in music. **1884** F. NIECKS *Dict. Mus. Terms* s.v. *Viola d'amore*, a bow stringed instrument a little longer than the viola, with seven (sometimes fewer) catgut strings about the fingerboard, and seven sympathetic wire strings below it. **1888** HIPKINS & GIBB *Mus. Instruments* 53 In the beautifully carved and inlaid instrument here drawn, a perfect viola d'amore in form.., the sympathetic strings are absent. **1898** STAINER & BARRETT *Dict. Mus. Terms* s.v. *Pianoforte*, The player controls all this wealth of sympathetic vibration with the damper pedal. **1908** L. J. DE BEKKER *Stokes' Encycl. Mus. & Musicians* 706/2 The sympathetic strings give a beautiful effect. **1928** E. BLOM *Romance of Piano* x. 178 In the treble, the sympathetic strings of the Blüthnor piano are tuned in unison with the ordinary strings. **1940** C. SACHS *Hist. Musical Instruments* xvi. 365 Sympathetic strings had come to England from the Near East, apparently in the sixteenth century. Praetorius related that the English used sympathetic viol strings. **1960** H. HAYWARD *Antique Coll.* 297/2 *Viola d'amore*, a musical instrument.. notable for its system of 'sympathetic' strings... Although out of reach of the bow and fingers these strings vibrate freely in sympathy with the notes played and produce a peculiarly ethereal effect. **1966** *Melody Maker* 7 May 10 The sympathetic strings [in a sitar] vibrate when the main strings are played, giving an answering drone. **1976** *Early Music* July 303 This viol still bore twelve wrestpins in the end block which would have originally carried sympathetic strings added in the 18th century. *Ibid.* 305 A viola bastarde.. with six sympathetic strings beneath the six bowed strings.

2. a. †Agreeing, harmonious, befitting, consonant, accordant (*obs.*); according with one's feelings or inclinations, congenial. (Now only as coloured by or *transf.* from 3.)

1673 S. PARKER *Reproof Reh. Transp.* 471 Thou thyself instead of coarse drugget shalt wear sympathetick silk. **1789** WORDSW. *Even. Walk* 316 Now o'er the soothed accordant heart we feel A sympathetic twilight slowly steal. **1875** H. JAMES *Trans. Sketches* 291 My imagination..refused to project into the dark old town and upon the yellow hills that sympathetic glow which forms half the substance of our genial impressions. **1910** HIRTH in *Encycl. Brit.* VI. 191/2 That natural philosophy of the 'male and female principles', according to which all good things and qualities were held to be male, while their less sympathetic opposites were female.

b. Tending to elicit sympathy (senses 3 b, d) or to induce a feeling of rapport; also *loosely*, pleasant, likeable. Cf. SYMPATHIQUE *a.*

1900 M. BEERBOHM in *Sat. Rev.* 10 Mar. 295/2 The true Don Juan..is..not a 'sympathetic' part. **1926** FOWLER *Mod. Eng. Usage* 590/2 Macbeth..is not made sympathetic, however adequately his crime may be explained & palliated, by being the victim of a hallucination. **1965** *Listener* 23 Dec. 1045/1 Being a lover of the south, I personally found it [*sc.* a novel] more sympathetic. **1976** A. EDEN *Another World* iv. 54 It was not a sympathetic house and the furnishing and pictures were ugly.

3. a. Feeling or susceptible of sympathy; sharing or affected by the feelings of another or others; having a fellow-feeling; sympathizing, compassionate. (With various shades of meaning: cf. SYMPATHY 3 a–d.)

a **1718** PRIOR *Epil. Lucius* 29 Your Sympathetic Hearts She hopes to move. **1764** GOLDSM. *Trav.* 43 He, whose sympathetic mind Exults in all the good of all mankind. **1837** CARLYLE *Fr. Rev.* I. II. v, Beyond the Atlantic.. Democracy..is struggling for life and victory. A sympathetic France rejoices over the Rights of Man. **1856** MRS. BROWNING *Aur. Leigh* II. 185 Your quick-breathed hearts, So sympathetic to the personal pang. **1867** DICKENS *Lett.* (1880) II. 281 An unusually tender and sympathetic audience. **1875** J. P. HOPPS *Princ. Relig.* xvi. (1878) 50 You have faith in a friend..when you know he is unselfish, and truthful, and sympathetic.

b. Pertaining to, of the nature of, characterized by, arising from, or expressive of sympathy or fellow-feeling. (With various shades of meaning as in a.) ***sympathetic strike***, a strike by workers in support of the action of strikers in another union, industry, etc.

a **1684** ROSCOMMON *Ess. Transl. Verse* 97 United by this sympathetic bond, You grow familiar, intimate, and fond. **1754** GRAY *Progr. Poesy* 94 Thine too these golden keys,.. This can unlock the gates of Joy;..that..ope the sacred source of sympathetic Tears. **1782** MISS BURNEY *Cecilia* v. i, A look of sympathetic concern from Cecilia. **1813** SCOTT *Rokeby* v. xi, For cold reserve had lost its power In sorrow's sympathetic hour. **1853** C. BRONTE *Villette* xviii, The sympathetic faculty was not prominent in him; to feel, and to seize quickly another's feelings, are separate properties. **1853** J. MARTINEAU *Stud. Christ.* (1858) 230 Thought, conscience, admiration in the human mind were..the sympathetic response of our common intellect, standing in front of Nature, to the kindred life of the Divine intellect behind Nature. **1901** *Daily Chron.* 7 Aug. 6/2 The head of the Coal Miners' Union is opposed to sympathetic strikes. **1906** *Lit. World* 15 Nov. 520/1 Professor Dowden's article on Henrik Ibsen..is sympathetic, but critical as well. **1913** in J. O'Connor *Hist. Ireland 1798–1924* (1925) II. xvii. 192 They followed by a somewhat lame conclusion that the 'sympathetic strike was being met with the sympathetic lock-out.' **1958** *Times Rev. Industry* Aug. 7/2 The merest murmur of the words 'sympathetic strike' will command the dockers' attention.

B. *sb.*

1. *Anat.* Short for *sympathetic nerve* or *system*: see A. 1 d above.

1808 BARCLAY *Muscular Motions* 254 These branches, proceeding from the trunks of the eighth pair, *par vagum*, or middle sympathetic, enter the thorax. **1826** KIRBY & SP. *Entomol.* IV. xxxvii. 20 The ganglions of the great sympathetics. **1871** ALLBUTT in *Brit. & For. Med.-Chirurg. Rev.* XLVIII. 51 We all know that a galvanized sympathetic causes contractions of blood-vessels. **1872** HUXLEY *Physiol.* vi. 145 The combined blushing and sweating which takes place when the sympathetic in the neck is divided.

2. a. A person affected by 'sympathy' (SYMPATHY 1 b); one who is susceptible or sensitive to hypnotic or similar influence. **b.** A sympathetic person, sympathizer. *rare.*

1888 C. L. NORTON in *N. Amer. Rev.* June 705 Favorable conditions may make any one hypnotic to some extent... Naturally enough a company of sympathetics may be similarly influenced. **1906** *Westm. Gaz.* 22 Sept. 6/2 The unburdenings to a sympathetic of the griefs which he too has felt and can understand.

Hence **sympa'theticism** (-sɪz(ə)m), sympathetic tendency, susceptibility to sympathy (used disparagingly); **ˌsympathe'ticity** (-'tɪsɪtɪ), **sympa'theticness**, the quality of being sympathetic.

1884 HOWELLS *Silas Lapham* II. 289 Penelope..received her visitors with a piteous distraction, which could not fail of touching Bromfield Corey's Italianised sympatheticism. **1891** *Murray's Mag.* Mar. 316 The deep vein of tenderness, of womanly sympatheticness. **1893** *Graphic* 25 Mar. 318/1 A good cook cannot teach you how to make the pasty..by word of mouth. She may show you something, but the secret lies in your handling, in a sort of sympatheticity.

†sympa'thetical, *a. Obs.* Also 7 sim-. [f. mod.L. *sympathēticus*: see prec. and -ICAL.]

1. = SYMPATHETIC *a.* 1, 1 b, 1 c.

1639 WOODALL *Treat. Plague* Wks. 360 There is a farre greater sympatheticall danger [of infection] betwixt Children, then betwixt Men and Women. **1646** SIR T. BROWNE *Pseud. Ep.* I. iv. 16 The grosse mistakes, in the cure of many diseases, not only from..sympatheticall receits, but amulets, charms, and all incantatory applications. **1651** WITTIE tr. *Primrose's Pop. Err.* IV. xlviii. 400 The weapon-salve, otherwise called the sympatheticall, magneticall, and starry oyntment. **1662** R. MATHEW *Unl. Alch.* §113. 184 The powder of Sympathy, or the Sympathetical Powder, made of Roman Vitriol. **1669** W. SIMPSON *Hydrol. Chym.* 275 There is a sympathetical combination betwixt the matrix and the stomach. **1672** SIR T. BROWNE *Let. Friend* §2 To wonder that you had not some secret..intimation [of his death] by dreams..or sympathetical insinuations. **1677** W. HARRIS tr. *Lemery's Course Chym.* I. xi. 143 Inks called Sympathetical. **1678** CUDWORTH *Intell. Syst.* I. i. §27. 29 The Sensible Idea's of Hot and Cold, Red and green..may be easily apprehended as Modes of Cogitation, that is, of Sensation, or Sympathetical Perception in us. **1696** TRYON *Misc.* Pref. 5 One Body works upon another, by a certain natural attraction and simpathetical Inclination. **1743** tr. *Heister's Surg.* 189 This sort of Cure seems to be sympathetical and superstitious.

2. = SYMPATHETIC *a.* 2.

1848 *Blackw. Mag.* LXIII. 576 Their varnished boots even have a dull lustreless look that is..sympathetical with the general gloom.

3. = SYMPATHETIC *a.* 3.

1650 H. BROOKE *Conserv. Health* 237 A sympathetical spirit..towards one another. **1753** MISS COLLIER *Art Torment* II. iii. 136 Where good-fellowship, good wine, and a certain sympathetical idleness, draw people together.

sympathetically (sɪmpə'θɛtɪkəlɪ), *adv.* [f. prec. + -LY².: see -ICALLY.] In a sympathetic manner; by, with, or in the way of sympathy (in various senses).

1. (See SYMPATHETIC *a.* 1, 1 c, 1 e, SYMPATHY 1, 1 b, 1 c.)

1621 BURTON *Anat. Mel.* I. i. III. iv. 53 The first [kind of melancholy] proceeds from the sole fault of the Braine..: the second sympathetically proceedes from the whole Body, when the whole temperature is Melancholy. **1669** WORLIDGE *Syst. Agric.* (1681) 192 Take a live Coal, and hold it as near..to the place as you can..endure it, which will Sympathetically attract the fiery venom that by the sting was left in the wound. **1678** CUDWORTH *Intell. Syst.* I. iii. 161 The Plastick Nature acting neither by Knowledge nor by Animal Fancy..must be concluded to act Fatally, Magically and Sympathetically. **1785** WARTON *Note Milton's Ode Passion* 43 He seems..to have catched sympathetically Sandys's sudden impulse to break forth into a devout song. **1851** H. MAYO *Pop. Superst.* (ed. 2) 42 The..directly or sympathetically disordered brain. **1860** W. COLLINS *Wom. White* I. ix. 47 No serious alteration could take place in any one of us which did not sympathetically affect the others. *Mod.* When one string of a piano is struck with the pedal held down, other strings vibrate sympathetically.

2. (See SYMPATHETIC *a.* 3, SYMPATHY 3.)

1825 SCOTT *Betrothed* xxix, A faithful domestic sympathetically agitated by the bad news with which he was about to afflict his master. **1870** SPURGEON *Treas. Dav.* Ps. li. 13 He will speak sympathetically, as one who has felt what he declares. **1885** *Manch. Exam.* 4 Nov. 3/3 A.. sympathetically written criticism.

sympatheticism, -ity, -ness: see after SYMPATHETIC.

sympatheticotonia, -ic: see SYMPATHICOTONIA.

sympathic (sɪm'pæθɪk), *a.* Now *rare* or *Obs.* Also 7 sim-. [ad. F. *sympathique* (= It., Sp. *simpatico*, Pg. *sympathico*), ad. mod.L. **sympathicus* (whence also G. *sympathisch*), f. *sympathia* SYMPATHY: see -IC. Cf. *idiopathic.*]

†1. = SYMPATHETIC *a.* 1, 1 c, 2. *Obs.*

1659 TATHAM *London's Tri.* 7 As th' Magnetique Courts, the Adamant With her Simphatick faculty,..So we from most parts of the Universe Are sought, rather petitioned for Commerce. **1663** GERBIER *Counsel* 11 The fit mixture of Materials, Morter, Brick and Stone, being Simpathike stuff. **1684** tr. *Bonet's Merc. Compit.* VI. 199 Whether the Cataphora be sympathick from the full and fuming Præcordia, or Idiopathick.

2. *Anat.* = SYMPATHETIC *a.* 1 d.

1836 SHUCKARD tr. *Burmeister's Man. Entom.* 286 The sympathic system is peculiar to all insects, but in the several orders it takes a different form. **1880** GÜNTHER *Fishes* 108 The sympathic trunks run along each side of the aorta and the back of the abdomen.

So **†sym'pathical** *a.* (also erron. **-pati-**); whence **†sym'pathically** *adv.*

1570 DEE *Math. Pref.* A j, A certaine Sympathicall forewarnyng. **1652** *Hermeticall Banquet* 6 Let Appetite satisfie it self with some one Dish most Sympaticall to your Stomack. *Ibid.* 68 Sympaticall Physick. **1684** tr. *Bonet's Merc. Compit.* XVI. 580 Vapors, that Sympathically annoy the Brain.

sympathico-: see SYMPATHO-.

symˌpathico'tonia. *Physiol.* Also anglicized as **symˌpathico'tony.** [f. SYMPATHICO- + -TONIA.] The state or condition in which there is increased influence of the sympathetic nervous system and heightened sensitivity to adrenalin. Also **sympaˌthetico'tonia, -'tonus**, in the same sense.

1916 J. P. STEWART *Diagnosis of Nervous Dis.* (ed. 4) xx. 356 Vago-tonus and sympathetico-tonus.—Individuals may be classified into two great vegetative types, according as their autonomic sensitiveness prevails over their sympathetic, or *vice versa.* **1923** *Handbk. for Mental Nurses* (Medico-Psychol. Assoc.) (ed. 7) ix. 375 The condition is then known as sympathetico-tonus or vagotonus, as the case may be. **1930** J. E. NICOLE *Psychopathology* ix. 77 The characteristics of vagotonia might be due to the thymus and pituitary glands, while the adrenals and thyroid would account for sympatheticotonia. **1948** A. BRODAL *Neurol. Anat.* xi. 371 Frequently persons are also met with in whom only one organ reveals a clear-cut parasympathetic or sympathetic dominance (local vagotonia or sympathicotonia). **1977** *Lancet* 12 Nov. 1027/2 During sympathicotony the organism is already making use of Nature's reserve supply of lachrymal fluid.

Hence **sympaˌthetico'tonic, symˌpathico'tonic** *adjs.*, displaying or promoting sympathicotonia; also as *sbs.*, a sympathicotonic person.

1916 J. P. STEWART *Diagnosis of Nervous Dis.* (ed. 4) xx. 357 Sympathetico-tonic individuals are specially sensitive to adrenalin which exaggerates all their characteristics. **1930** J. E. NICOLE *Psychopathology* viii. 70 The sympatheticotonics ..have dry skins, prominent eyes, dilated pupils, and are possessed of great energy, both mental and physical. **1944** L. J. BENDIT *Paranormal Cognition* iii. 47 She was of the sympathicotonic type, given to attacks of vomiting when emotionally upset. **1954** S. DUKE-ELDER *Parsons' Dis. Eye* (ed. 12) xxi. 235 It is seen particularly in those who are highly strung, anxious in disposition and sympatheticotonic in type. **1975** *Year Bk. Ear, Nose & Throat* 273 Sympathicotonic influences might cause hypertonicity of the cricopharyngeus muscle.

symˌpathico'tropic (-'trəʊpɪk, -'trɒpɪk), *a.* *Pharm.* [f. SYMPATHICO- + -TROPIC.] Possessing an affinity for the sympathetic nervous system. Also **ˌsympatho'tropic** *a.*, in the same sense.

1914 *Jrnl. Amer. Med. Assoc.* 22 Aug. 619/2 Epinephrin.. affects especially the sympathetic... It is therefore spoken of as a sympathicotropic drug. **1964** *Internat. Jrnl. Neuropharmacol.* III. 217 When evaluating the effect of indirectly acting sympathotropic substances one must first ascertain whether the tissue stores endogenous catecholamines. **1975** *Acta Biol. Med. Germanica* XXXIV. 661 (*heading*) The action of sympathicotropic substances upon liver microsomes in vivo and in vitro.

sympathin ('sɪmpəθɪn). *Physiol.* [f. SYMPATH(O- + -IN¹.] A hormone which acts as a mediator of nerve impulses at sympathetic nerve synapses; now effectively a disused synonym of NORADRENALINE.

1931 CANNON & BACQ. in *Amer. Jrnl. Physiol.* XCVI. 411 Because the substance is derived from structures under sympathetic control, when they are influenced by sympathetic impulses, we suggest that it be called sympathin. **1938** *Nature* 12 Feb. 266/2 The authors reject Bacq's rather factious criticisms of their theory of sympathins *E* and *I*. **1946** *Ibid.* 20 July 88/1 In Cannon's remaining active years he was largely concerned with evidence as to the nature of the sympathetic transmitter 'sympathin', which he believed to be not identical with adrenaline. **1971** *Ibid.* 2 Apr. 340/2 In an attempt to demonstrate this increase the transmitter 'sympathin' liberated from sympathetic nerve to the spleen was examined.

‖**sympathique** (sɛ̃patik), *a.* [Fr.: see SYMPATHIC *a.*] Of a thing, place, etc.: agreeable, to one's taste, suitable. Of a person: likeable, *en rapport* with one, congenial. Cf. SYMPATHETIC *a.* 2 b.

1859 QUEEN VICTORIA *Let.* 27 Apr. in R. Fulford *Dearest Child* (1964) 187 The sight of a professor or learned man alarms me, and is not sympathique to me. **1865** —— *Let.* 30 Dec. in *Ibid.* 52 Oh if only Antoinette was in Ali's place! She is so much more *sympathique* and *grande dame.* **1869** W. JAMES *Let.* 1 Nov. in R. B. Perry *Thought & Char. W. James* (1935) I. 308 England is evidently *sympathique* to you. **1897** A. BEARDSLEY *Let.* Apr. (1970) 305 The Baronne Dufour came to see us today... How sweet and sympathique she is. **1930** E. WAUGH *Vile Bodies* vii. 116, I do think, when you get to my age, dear, there is something *sympathique* about a wig, don't you? **1960** *Harper's Bazaar* July 25 A warm and *sympathique* personality. **1975** D. GRAY *Ride on Tiger* ii. 14, I find you *sympathique.*

‖**sympathisch** (zʏm'pa:tɪʃ), *a.* Also *erron.* **sympatisch.** [Ger.: see SYMPATHIC *a.*] = SYMPATHIQUE *a.*

1911 R. BROOKE *Let.* 13 Dec. (1968) 325, I find that Creative Artists are so particularly *sympathisch.* **1922** D. H. LAWRENCE *Let.* 25 Oct. (1932) 559 But it [*sc.* New Mexico] isn't *sympatisch* like Australia. **1937** AUDEN in Auden & MacNeice *Lett. from Iceland* viii. 100 You I find sympatisch, a good townee. **1976** P. HENISSART *Winter Quarry* I. vii. 72 Another lie? It's what makes you so *sympatisch*, isn't it? **1982** *N.Y. Times Mag.* 17 Oct. 100/5 The personality of the singer himself—warm, intelligent, *sympathisch*, recognizable.

sympathist ('sɪmpəθɪst). *rare.* [f. SYMPATHY + -IST.] One who sympathizes, a sympathizer.

c **1819** COLERIDGE *Lit. Rem.* (1836) II. 220 The.. consciousness..of human auditors—of flesh and blood sympathists—acts as a support and a stimulation. **1897** *Chicago Advance* 4 Feb. 154/1 Nature..is a natural sympathist.

†sympathizant. *Obs. rare*⁻¹. In 7 -isant. [a. F. *sympathisant*, pr. pple. of *sympathiser* (see next).] A thing that has affinity with another: cf. next, 2, and SYMPATHY 1, 2.

1620 J. PYPER tr. *Hist. Astrea* I. v. 146 All things corporall or spirituall haue euery one their contraries, and their sympathisants.

sympathize (ˈsɪmpəθaɪz), *v.* Also 6–7 sim-. [a. F. *sympathiser* (from 16th c.), f. *sympathie* SYMPATHY: see -IZE. Cf. It. *simpatizzare*, etc.]

1. *intr.* To suffer with or like another; to be affected in consequence of the affection of some one or something else; to be similarly or correspondingly affected; to respond sympathetically to some influence; *spec.* in *Path.*, to be or become disordered in consequence of the disorder of some other part: cf. SYMPATHY 1, 1 b. Const. *with*.

In mod. use often coloured by, or taken as *fig.* from, sense 4.

1597 A. M. tr. *Guillemeau's Fr. Chirurg.* 48/2 As soone as the actione of one parte is hindered, al the other partes of the body doe therwithe conspire and sympathise. **1621** BURTON *Anat. Mel.* I. i. III. ii. 48 The Heart, and other inferiour parts, which sympathize and are much troubled. **1632** [see SYMPATHIZING *vbl. sb.*]. **1674** W. BATES *Harmony Div. Attrib.* ix. (1688) 176 The Earth trembled and the Rocks rent; the most insensible Creatures sympathiz'd with him. **1797** M. BAILLIE *Morb. Anat.* (1807) 288 The stomach sympathizes with this state of the kidneys, for it is affected with sickness and vomiting. *a* **1812** BUCKMINSTER *Serm.* (1827) I. 49 The mind will sympathize so much with the anguish and debility of the body, that it will be..too distracted to fix itself in meditation. **1876** LOWELL *Among my Bks.* Ser. II. 250 In the great poets there is an exquisite sensibility both of soul and sense that sympathizes like gossamer sea-moss with every movement of the element in which it floats. **1879** ROOD *Chromatics* xlv. 61 The landscape ..sympathizes with the sky, and near the sun..assumes an orange..hue.

†**b.** *trans.* in causal sense: To make 'sympathetic', cause to be similarly affected. *Obs. rare.*

1661 GLANVILL *Van. Dogm.* 205 That some have conferr'd at distance by sympathized hands,..the hands of two friends being sympathized by a transferring of flesh from one into the other..; the least prick in the hand of one, the other will be sensible of,..in the same part of his own.

†**2.** *intr.* **a.** To have an affinity; to agree in nature, disposition, qualities, or fortunes; to be alike; with *with*, to be like, resemble. Cf. SYMPATHY 2. *Obs.*

1591 SYLVESTER *Du Bartas* I. iv. 101 So, did he make.. The Heav'ns and Stars, of one same substance bright; To th' end these Lamps dispersed in the Skies, Might, with their Orb, it with them sympathize. **1599** SHAKS. *Hen. V*, III. vii. 158 The men doe sympathize with the Mastiffes, in robustious and rough comming on. *a* **1643** W. CARTWRIGHT *Siege* v. viii, Your Majesty And I do sympathize most strangely in Our Fortunes, that we should both of 's be married Just at one very instant. **1668** *The Rivals* 6 My thoughts are of the same complexion too, Our fears do Sympathize, just like our Loves.

†**b.** To agree, be in harmony, accord, harmonize. Const. *with*. *Obs.*

1600 MARSTON, etc. *Jack Drums Entert.* II. (1601) C iv b, Let me liue lou'd in my husbands eies, Whose thoughts with mine, may sweetly simpathize. **1610** FOLKINGHAM *Feudigr.* I. xi. 37 Strong and long rootes neuer Sympathize with firme hard and solid soyles. **1629** MILTON *Hymn Nativ.* i, Nature in aw to him Had doff't her gawdy trim, With her great Master so to sympathize. **1632** LITHGOW *Trav.* B j, So doth it also best simpathize with reason. **1683** SALMON *Doron Med.* I. 133 Make choice of a Purgative simpathizing with those parts. **1695** DRYDEN tr. *Dufresnoy's Art Paint.* (1716) 183 Blue and Yellow are two Colours which sympathize. **1711** [see SYMPATHIZING *vbl. sb.*].

†**3.** *trans.* To agree with, answer or correspond to, match. *Obs.*

1593 SHAKS. *Rich. II*, v. i. 46 The sencelesse Brands will sympathize The heauie accent of thy mouing Tongue, And in compassion, weepe the fire out. **1593** —— *Lucr.* 1113 True sorrow then is feelinglie suffiz'd, When with like semblance it is simpathiz'd. **1596** SPENSER *Hymn Beauty* 192 In your choice of Loues..That likest to your selues ye them select, The which your forms first sourse may sympathize. **1606** WARNER *Alb. Eng.* XIV. To Rdr. 333 Seeke Loues that ours shall sympathize.

†**b.** To represent or express by something corresponding or fitting; to apprehend mentally by the analogy of something else. *Obs.*

c **1600** SHAKS. *Sonn.* lxxxii, Thou truly faire, wert truly simpathizde, In true plaine words, by thy true telling friend. **1600** S. NICHOLSON *Acolastus' After-witte* D j b, Who right conceiues the miseries of Iob,..Can fittest deeme their griefes true qualitie, And sympathize poore Souldiers miserie. **1638** SIR T. HERBERT *Trav.* (ed. 2) 12 Some Boobyes, weary of flight, made our Ship their pearch, an animall so simple as suffers any to take her without feare,.. which to sympathize I have as simply for your sport depicted. **1645** R. BEAKE *Let. fr. Sommer Isl.* in Prynne *Discov. Blazing Stars* App. 10 Able to sympathize another mans case by his owne.

†**c.** To make up or compound of corresponding parts or elements; to form or contrive harmoniously or consistently. *Obs.*

1588 SHAKS. *L.L.L.* III. i. 52 A message well sympathis'd, a Horse to be embassadour for an Asse. **1590** [see SYMPATHIZED]. **1606** SYLVESTER *Du Bartas* II. iv. II. *Magnificence* 1343 Of this great Frame, the parts so due-devis'd, This Bodie, tun'd so, measur'd, sympathiz'd.

4. *intr.* To feel sympathy; to have a fellow-feeling; to share the feelings of another or others; to be affected by the condition or experience of another with a feeling similar or corresponding to that of the other; *spec.* to be affected with pity for the suffering or sorrow of another, to feel compassion. (Cf. SYMPATHY 3 a–c.) Const. *with* a person (or, in extended or *fig.* use, a thing), *in*, *with* (rarely †*at*) a feeling, experience, etc.

1605 B. JONSON *Volpone* III. iv, There was but one sole man..With whom I ere could sympathize. **1644** CROMWELL in Ellis *Orig. Lett.* Ser. I. III. 300 It's our duty to sympathize in all mercyes; that wee praise the Lord together, in chastisements or tryalls, that soe wee may sorrowe together. **1685** O. HEYWOOD *Diaries*, etc. (1885) IV. 114 Friends and foes pittyed my case, sympathized with me. **1749** FRANCIS tr. *Horace, Art of Poetry* 146 With them, who laugh, our social Joy appears; With them, who mourn, we sympathise in Tears. **1762** GOLDSM. *Cit. W.* xxi, A heart that sympathises at human happiness. **1784** COWPER *Task* IV. 340 We may with patience bear our mod'rate ills, And sympathise with others, suff'ring more. **1838** LYTTON *Alice* I. i, The elder of the two seemed the most to sympathize with her mirth. **1850** A. L. WARING *Hymn*, '*Father, I know*' ii, A heart at leisure from itself, To soothe and sympathize. *a* **1862** BUCKLE *Misc. Wks.* (1872) I. 166 Commerce first made nations sympathise with each other. **1874** GREEN *Short Hist.* ii. §8. 101 He was..without the imagination and reverence which enable men to sympathise with any past at all. **1888** *Poor Nellie* II. ix. 152, I do sympathise in the anxiety you will feel about George!

b. *transf.* To express sympathy, esp. for another's sorrow or suffering; to condole (*with* a person).

1748 [see SYMPATHIZING *vbl. sb.*]. **1841** LD. COCKBURN *Jrnl.* (1874) I. 295 A public meeting held..for the purpose of 'sympathising' with the seven ministers. **1908** [MISS FOWLER] *Betw. Trent & Ancholme* 311 A clergyman and his wife went to sympathise with a neighbour.

c. In weakened sense: To agree or be disposed to agree in some opinion or way of thinking, to be of (about) the same mind *with* a person or party; also, with *in* or (now usually) *with*, to approve or incline to approve, to regard with favour (a scheme, cause, etc.). Cf. SYMPATHY 3 d.

1828 D'ISRAELI *Chas. I*, I. Pref. 16 In his terror of Papistry he sympathized with the Puritans. *a* **1842** ARNOLD *Fragm. on Church* (1845) 220 There will be much in it in which you will heartily sympathize. **1864** NEWMAN *Apol.* i. (1904) 8/1 As far as I know, on this point alone, he and Hurrell Froude intimately sympathized. **1880** L. STEPHEN *Pope* vii. 160 Pope..sympathized with his schemes.

†**sympathized**, *ppl. a.* *Obs. rare.* [f. prec. + -ED[1].] **a.** ? Compounded of corresponding parts or elements, complicated: cf. SYMPATHIZE 3 c.

1590 SHAKS. *Com. Err.* v. i. 397 All..That by this simpathized one daies error Haue suffer'd wrong.

b. Rendered 'sympathetic': see SYMPATHIZE 1 b.

1661 [see SYMPATHIZE 1 b].

sympathizer (ˈsɪmpəθaɪzə(r)). [f. as prec + -ER[1].] One who or that which sympathizes; *esp.* one disposed to agree with or approve a party, cause, etc.; a backer-up.

1815 JANE AUSTEN *Emma* III. vi, His patient listener and sympathizer. **1838** GEN. P. THOMPSON *Exerc.* (1842) IV. 336 A new name is invented for the sufferers [*sc.* U.S. citizens taken in the Canadian insurrection]—Sympathisers. **1865** J. S. MILL in *Evening Star* 10 July, Lovers of England, ..sympathisers with the English people. **1888** BURGON *Lives 12 Gd. Men* II. v. 46 There never was a more enthusiastic sympathizer with his Clergy. **1901** DORLAND *Med. Dict.* (ed. 2), *Sympathizer*..an eye which becomes inflamed through sympathy with disease of its fellow. **1918** *Times, Lit. Supp.* 14 Mar. 123/1 Our Balkan allies and sympathizers.

sympathizing (ˈsɪmpəθaɪzɪŋ), *vbl. sb.* [f. as prec. + -ING[1].] The action of the verb SYMPATHIZE, q.v., in various senses.

1632 J. HAYWARD tr. *Biondi's Eromena* 81 Among the hidden secrets of nature, that of sympathizing is one of the truest. **1654–66** EARL ORRERY *Parthen.* (1676) 145 If I am in any trouble, it only proceeds from sympathizing in these disasters you were fallen into. **1711** SHAFTESB. *Charac.* (1737) II. 362 A universal union, coherence, or sympathizing of things. **1748** SMOLLETT *Rod Random* xxii, An old gentlewoman, under pretence of sympathizing, visited me.

ˈ**sympathizing**, *ppl. a.* [f. as prec. + -ING[2].] That sympathizes, in various senses.

†**1.** Being similarly affected, or having an affinity, *with* something else: see SYMPATHIZE 1, 2. *Obs.*

a **1628** SIR J. BEAUMONT *To Prince Charles* 52 And feele their strokes with sympathyzing brests. **1635** SWAN *Spec. Mundi* vi. (1643) 290 The sympathizing Turcois true doth tell, By looking pale the wearer is not well. *a* **1652** J. SMITH *Sel. Disc.* vi. (1821) 210 That sympathizing and symbolizing complexion of their own bodies with some other bodies without them.

2. Feeling sympathy; sympathetic: see SYMPATHIZE 4.

1683 NORRIS *Passion of Saviour* 162 So long the sympathising sun his light withdrew, And wonder'd how the stars their dying Lord could view. **1737** *Gentl. Mag.* Sept. 567/1 Fain would my sympathizing breast extend A world of comfort to an unknown friend. **1746** HERVEY *Medit.* (1767) I. 21 Feeling some Touches of sympathizing Concern. **1755** DODDRIDGE *Hymn*, '*Father of mercies, send thy grace*' ii, O may our sympathizing breasts That generous pleasure know, Promptly to share in others' joy, And weep for others' woe. **1849** MACAULAY *Hist. Eng.* ii. I. 177 To New England, where he was likely to find sympathising friends. **1865** LIVINGSTONE *Zambesi* xx. 417 With sympathizing hearts the little band..assisted the bereaved husband in burying his dead.

Hence ˈ**sympathizingly** *adv.*, in a sympathizing way, sympathetically.

1840 MILL *Diss. & Disc.* (1859) I. 288 To enter sympathizingly into the peculiar feelings which pervade them [*sc.* De Vigny's writings]. **1876** *Fam. Herald* 2 Dec. 66/2 'You do look seedy', said Algy, sympathisingly.

sympatho- (ˈsɪmpəθəʊ), combining form of SYMPATHETIC *a.* (*sb.*), used to form terms relating to the sympathetic nervous system; also **symˈpathico-**; ˌ**sympathoˈgonia** (-ˈgəʊnɪə) *sb. pl.* *Med.* [ad. G. *sympathogonien* (H. Poll 1906, in O. Hertwig *Handb. d. vergleichenden und exper. Entwickelungslehre d. Wirbeltiere* V. III. i. 460), f. Gr. γόνος offspring, begetting], undifferentiated embryonic cells of the sympathetic nervous system which give rise to sympathoblasts; also used as *sing.*; ˌ**sympathogoniˈoma**, **symˌpathicogoniˈoma** [-OMA], a malignant tumour composed chiefly of sympathogonia.

1934 *Jrnl. Path. & Bacteriol.* XXXIX. 28 The sympathogonia from which the medulla of the suprarenal takes origin, as first described by Wiesel (1902), began to invade the anlage of the adrenal cortex. **1966** *Pharmacol. Rev.* XVIII. 659 The common progenitor, called sympathogonia, is a small lymphocyte-like cell with a dense, chromatin-rich, spherical or pyriform nucleus and a scanty rim of clear, poorly-staining cytoplasm. **1934** *Jrnl. Path. & Bacteriol.* XXXIX. 28 Those formed of sympathogonia have been classified as sympathogoniomas. **1966** *Pharmacol. Rev.* XVIII. 659 Each of these three types of sympathetic cell may give rise to a tumor: the sympathogonia to a sympathogonioma; the sympathoblast to a sympathoblastoma; and the ganglion cell to a ganglioneuroma. **1974** *Oncology* XXIX. 521 Tumour biopsies of a..sympathicogonioma..were obtained when the tumours were removed surgically.

ˌ**sympatho-adˈrenal**, *a.* *Physiol.* [f. SYMPATHO- + ADRENAL *a.*] Pertaining to or involving the sympathetic nervous system and the medulla of the adrenal gland, and their activity. Also **symˌpathico-adˈrenal** *a.*, in the same sense.

1928 *Amer. Jrnl. Physiol.* LXXXIV. 560 Previous investigations..have emphasized the emergency functions of the sympathico-adrenal mechanism. **1949** KOESTLER *Insight & Outlook* v. 59 The whole complex of sympathico-adrenal excitation which characterizes laughter is not only absent in crying, but is replaced..by parasympathetic excitation, or..by types of reaction, for example, fatigue, which are the direct opposites of sympathetic excitation. **1965** *Jrnl. Physiol.* CLXXIX. 290 Three drugs which are known to have various actions on the sympatho-adrenal system were tested. **1974** *Jrnl. Appl. Physiol.* XXXVI. 183/1 Sympathicoadrenal medullary secretion of catecholamines is increased during acute cold exposures. **1979** *Med. Hypotheses* V. 317 Some disorders in which excessive sweating..is a symptom are also characterized by increased sympatho-adrenal activity.

sympathoblast (ˈsɪmpəθəʊblæst). *Med.* [f. SYMPATHO- + -BLAST.] A small, relatively undifferentiated cell formed in the early development of nerve tissue which develops into a sympathetic neurone. Also **symˈpathicoblast**, in the same sense.

1927 *Amer. Jrnl. Path.* III. 212 These lesions represent a tumor of a more primitive type of cell (sympathicoblast) than the sympathetic neuroblast. **1934** *Jrnl. Path. & Bacteriol.* XXXIX. 28 Different stages in development may be present in the same tumour *e.g.* sympathogonia, sympathoblasts and ganglion cells. **1966** *Experientia* XXII. 297 In the developing CNS [*sc.* central nervous system] and the spinal ganglia, only the sympathoblasts of the primary and secondary trunk of chick embryos contain a varying amount of catechol amine-containing granules.

Hence **symˌpathicoblaˈstoma**, (less commonly ˌ**sympathoblaˈstoma**) [-OMA], a malignant tumour composed chiefly of sympathoblasts.

1927 *Amer. Jrnl. Path.* III. 213 The sympathicoblastomas have often been described as consisting of two types of tissue. **1934** *Jrnl. Path. & Bacteriol.* XXXIX. 29 Sympathicoblastomata are the commonest sympathetic tumours found. **1960** *Hirosaki Med. Jrnl.* XII. 92 (*heading*) A case of sympathoblastoma, suspected to be Ewing's tumor. **1974** *Oncology* XXIX. 521 Tumour biopsies of a sympathicoblastoma..were obtained when the tumours were removed surgically.

ˌ**sympatholytic** (-ˈlɪtɪk), *a.* *Med.* [f. SYMPATHO- + -LYTIC.] Annulling or opposing the transmission of nerve impulses in the sympathetic system. Also **symˌpathicoˈlytic** *a.*, in the same sense.

1947, **1948** Sympathicolytic [see ADRENO-]. **1951** Sympatholytic [see DIOXAN]. **1952** *Acta Endocrinol.* IX. 116 The alarm reaction caused by adrenaline..can be counteracted by using a sympathicolytic agent. **1954** *Brit. Jrnl. Pharmacol.* IX. 236 The assay of sympatholytic (anti-adrenaline) drugs. **1961** *Lancet* 26 Aug. 475/1 Failures of wholly different origin are those due to administration of sympatholytic or ganglion-blocking drugs. **1977** *Ibid.* 19 Mar. 650/2 The medical treatment of essential hypertension is currently based almost exclusively on sympatholytic drugs of one kind or another on the assumption that the disease is caused by over-activity of the sympathetic nervous system.

ˌ**sympathomiˈmetic**, *a.* (and *sb.*) *Pharm.* [f. SYMPATHO- + MIMETIC *a.* (and *sb.*).] Producing physiological effects characteristic of the sympathetic nervous system (as raised blood pressure and rate and depth of breathing, decreased secretion and tone of smooth muscle) by promoting stimulation of sympathetic nerves. Also as *sb.*, a substance which does this. Also **sym,pathicomi'metic** *a.* (and *sb.*), in the same sense.

1910 BARGER & DALE in *Jrnl. Physiol.* XLI. 21 A term at once wider and more descriptive than 'adrenine-like' seems needed to indicate the type of action common to these bases. We propose to call it 'sympathomimetic', a term which indicates the relation of the action to innervation by the sympathetic system. **1949** KOESTLER *Insight & Outlook* xx. 281 In contrast to the sympathomimetic hormones, the vagus substance is rapidly destroyed. **1956** *Nature* 7 Jan. 44/2 The presence of sympathomimetic activity in adrenergic nerve tissue has been demonstrated. **1958** *Dis. of Chest* XXXIII. 18 (*heading*) Depressed response to intravenous sympathicomimetic agents in humans during acidosis. **1964** W. G. SMITH *Allergy & Tissue Metabolism* ix. 91 Sympathomimetic amines and theophylline are believed to work by a bronchodilator action. **1966** *Acta Physiol. Scand.* LXVII. 482 Peripherally they are generally classified as indirectly acting sympathomimetics, i.e. they depend on an intact sympathetic nervous system for their activity. **1970** PASSMORE & ROBSON *Compan. Med. Stud.* II. ix. 6/1 Many of the substances most useful in asthma, e.g. sympathomimetic drugs.., act not as specific agents but by producing an opposing, and often overriding, effect on the bronchi. **1973** *Brit. Jrnl. Hosp. Med.* IX. 21/1 Inhalation challenge using agents producing a type I skin response often induce immediate airways obstruction with asthma, reversible by sympathomimetics. **1983** *Amer. Rev. Respiratory Dis.* CXXVII. 413 Airway resistance..and lung volume were assessed before and after inhalation of a β2-sympathicomimetic.

sympathy ('sɪmpəθɪ), *sb.* Also 6–7 sim-, -ie. [ad. late L. *sympathia*, a. Gr. συμπάθεια, f. συμπαθής having a fellow feeling, f. σύν SYM- + παθ-, root of πάθος suffering, feeling, πάσχειν to suffer. Cf. F. *sympathie* (from 15th c.), It., Sp. *simpatia*, Pg. *sympathia*.]

1. a. A (real or supposed) affinity between certain things, by virtue of which they are similarly or correspondingly affected by the same influence, affect or influence one another (esp. in some occult way), or attract or tend towards each other. *Obs.* exc. *Hist.* or as merged in other senses.

powder of sympathy (*sympathy-powder*), a powder supposed to heal wounds by 'sympathy' on being applied to a handkerchief or garment stained with blood from the wound, or to the weapon with which the wound was inflicted: also called *sympathetic powder* (see SYMPATHETIC *a.* 1).

[**1579** J. JONES *Preserv. Bodie & Soule* Ep. Ded. p. vi, Plato also testifieth suche a *Sympathia* to be betweene the bodye and the soule, that if either exceede the meane, the one suffereth with the other.] *a* **1586** SIDNEY *Arcadia* III. xvii. (1912) 455 His Impresa was a Catoblepta, which so long lies dead, as the Moone (whereto it hath so naturall a sympathie) wants her light. **1601** HOLLAND *Pliny* II. Explan. A vj b, *Sympathie*, i. a fellow-feeling, used in Plinie for the agreement or amitie naturall in divers senselesse things, as betweene yron and the loadstone. *Ibid.* XXIV. i. II. 175 In every..corner of the world there may be observed both sympathies and antipathies (I meane those naturall combinations and contrarieties in these creatures). **1613** PURCHAS *Pilgrimage* v. xii. 431 Crabbes heere with vs haue a sympathy with the Moone, and are fullest with her fulnes. **1658** R. WHITE (*title*) A late Discourse Made..in France, By Sr. Kenelme Digby..Touching the Cure of Wounds by the Powder of Sympathy. **1668** SEDLEY *Mulberry Gard.* III. ii. 43, I have Sympathy-powder about me, if you will give me your handkercher while the blood is warm, will cure it immediately. **1711** STEELE *Spect.* No. 53 ¶3 Those Applications which are said to convey their virtues by Sympathy. **1815** J. SMITH *Panorama Sci. & Art* II. 181 The cures said to have been performed by magnetic sympathy. **1883** W. G. BLACK *Folk-Medicine* iii. 50 That doctrine of sympathy which accompanies all remedies by association.

b. *Physiol.* and *Path.* A relation between two bodily organs or parts (or between two persons) such that disorder, or any condition, of the one induces a corresponding condition in the other.

1603 HOLLAND *Plutarch* Explan. Words, *Sympathie*, that is to say, A fellow feeling, as is between the head and stomacke. **1655** CULPEPPER, etc. *Riverius* VII. i. 146 Breathing is hindered by sympathy or consent from other parts. **1668** —— & COLE *Barthol. Anat.* I. xvii. 47 The Sympathy between the Kidneys and the Stomach, as when persons diseased in their Kidneys, are troubled with Stomach-sickness and vomiting. **1836** A. COMBE *Physiol. Digestion* II. iv. (ed. 2) 161 The sympathy between them [*sc.* the skin and the mucous coat of the alimentary canal] is.. very rapid and intimate. Eruptions on the skin, for example, are almost always owing to disorder of the digestive organs; and bowel-complaint, on the other hand, is often produced by a sudden chill on the surface. **1871** A. MEADOWS *Man. Midwifery* (ed. 2) 167 The child should be put to the breast ..as this.., through the sympathy between the breast and uterus, is sure to excite uterine action.

c. *Comm.* in phr. ***in sympathy with***, used in market reports in reference to a rise or fall in the price of a commodity induced by a rise or fall in that of another, or by some event or circumstance.

1897 *Daily News* 7 May 7/2 Corn opened easy, with July ⅛c. down.., but recovered in sympathy with wheat. **1912** *Times* 19 Dec. 20/4 Lard... American refined in pails is easier in sympathy with advices from the other side.

2. Agreement, accord, harmony, consonance, concord; agreement in qualities, likeness, conformity, correspondence. *Obs.* or merged in 3 a.

[**1567** FENTON *Trag. Disc.* ii. (1898) I. 90 If he had bene aunswerd with a *sympathia*, or equalitie of frendshipp. *Ibid.* xiii. II. 247 Whereof [*sc.* of the passion or fever of love] there seamed alredie a *sympathia*, or equalitie, betwene the two younglinges. **1574** J. JONES *Nat. Beginning Grow. Things* 29 Of the good effectes, *Simpathia*, vnity, agreements of the spirites, humors and members, health is..preserued.] **1579** LYLY *Euphues* (Arb.) 48 Doth not the simpathy of manners make the coniunction of mindes? **1588** SHAKS. *Tit. And.* III. i. 148 O what a simpathy of woe is this! **1589** PUTTENHAM *Engl. Poesie* II. x. [xi.] (Arb.) 98 If it please the eare well, the same represented by delineation to the view pleaseth the eye well..: and this is by a naturall simpathie, betweene the eare and the eye, and betweene tunes and colours, even as there is the like betweene the other sences and their obiects. **1590** GREENE *Mourn. Garment* Wks. (Grosart) IX. 179 Iubal exercised Musike, and spent his time in practising the simpathy of sundry sounds. **1592** SHAKS. *Rom. & Jul.* III. iii. 85 O he is euen in my Mistresse case..O wofull simpathy. **1598** —— *Merry W.* II. i. 7, 9, 10. **1604** —— *Oth.* II. i. 232 There should be..simpathy in yeares, Manners, and Beauties: all which the Moore is defectiue in. **1684** BUNYAN *Pilgr. P.* II. (1900) 234, I think there was a kind of a Sympathy betwixt that Valley and him. **1777** WATSON *Philip II* (1793) II. XI. 8 He was strongly attached by sympathy of manners to the Princes. **1847** L. HUNT *Jar Honey* xii. (1848) 159 One of those sympathies of colour which are often finer than contrast.

3. a. Conformity of feelings, inclinations, or temperament, which makes persons agreeable to each other; community of feeling; harmony of disposition.

1596 SPENSER *Hymn Beauty* 199 Loue is a celestiall harmonie, Of likely harts..Which ioyne together in sweete sympathie, To worke ech others ioy and true content. **1633** HEYWOOD *Eng. Trav.* I. i, So sweet a simpathie, As crownes a noble marriage. **1775** HARRIS *Philos. Arrangem.* Wks. (1841) 291 There is..a social sympathy in the soul of man, which prompts..individuals..to congregate, and form themselves into tribes. **1822–7** GOOD *Study Med.* (1829) IV. 61 The sympathies and antipathies, the whims and prejudices that..haunt us. **1833** HT. MARTINEAU *Briery Creek* ii. 26 It was impossible that there could be much sympathy between two men so unlike. **1876** MOZLEY *Univ. Serm.* x. (1877) 206 They enjoy the sympathy of kindred souls.

b. The quality or state of being affected by the condition of another with a feeling similar or corresponding to that of the other; the fact or capacity of entering into or sharing the feelings of another or others; fellow-feeling. Also, a feeling or frame of mind evoked by and responsive to some external influence. Const. *with* (a person, etc., or a feeling).

1662 R. MATHEW *Unl. Alch.* p. x, Out of faithful and true simpathy and fellow-feeling with you. **1667** MILTON *P.L.* IV. 465 With answering looks Of sympathie and love. *Ibid.* x. 540 Horror on them fell, And horrid sympathie. **1756** BURKE *Subl. & Beaut.* I. xiii, Sympathy must be considered as a sort of Substitution, by which we are put in the place of another man, and affected in many respects as he is affected. **1784** COWPER *Task* VI. 1 There is in souls a sympathy with sounds..Some chord in unison with what we hear Is touched within us, and the heart replies. **1833** COLERIDGE *Table-t.* 30 Aug., For compassion a human heart suffices: but for full and adequate sympathy with joy, an angel's only. **1856** FROUDE *Hist. Eng.* I. v. 447 Our sympathies are naturally on the side of the weak and the unsuccessful. **1859** HAWTHORNE *Fr. & It. Journals* II. 277 Such depth and breadth of sympathy with Nature. **1862** SIR B. BRODIE *Psychol. Inq.* II. iii. 99 A cheerful disposition..leads to sympathy with others in all the smaller concerns of life. **1880** DISRAELI *Endym.* xvi, The sympathy of sorrow is stronger than the sympathy of prosperity. **1907** *Verney Mem.* I. 76 A favourite daughter, to whom he turned on all occasions for sympathy and affection.

c. *spec.* The quality or state of being thus affected by the suffering or sorrow of another; a feeling of compassion or commiseration. Const. *for*, *with* (a person), *for*, *in*, *with*, †rarely *of* (an event, experience, etc.).

1600 S. NICHOLSON *Acolastus' After-witte* D 2, The showres which daily from mine eyes are raining, Draw the dum creatures to a sympathie. *a* **1701** MAUNDRELL *Journ. Jerus.* (1732) 34 A kind of Sympathy in the River, for the Death of Adonis. **1777** S. J. PRATT *Emma Corbett* (ed. 4) II. 107, I wanted to express my sympathy of your present misfortune. **1783** BURKE *Sp. Fox's E. India Bill* Wks. 1808 IV. 20 To awaken something of sympathy for the unfortunate natives. **1796** —— *Corr.* (1844) IV. 360 Your sympathy makes our ill-health a great deal more tolerable. **1807** SOUTHEY *Espriella's Lett.* (1808) II. 323 They have.. little sympathy for distresses which they have never felt. **1829** LANDOR *Imag. Conv., Penn & Peterborough* II. 269 Joining in the amusements of others is..the next thing to sympathy in their distresses. **1850** TENNYSON *In Mem.* lxxxv. 88 Canst thou feel for me Some painless sympathy with pain? **1872** KINGSLEY *Lett.* (1878) II. 381 Every expression of human sympathy brings some little comfort. **1893** *Academy* 30 Dec. 581/1 Sympathy with the bereaved parents and for the bride was..deeply felt.

d. In weakened sense: A favourable attitude of mind towards a party, cause, etc.; disposition to agree or approve. Const. *with*, rarely *for*, *in*.

1823 SOUTHEY *Hist. Penins. War* I. 526 Their sympathy in the instinct and principle by which it was carried on. **1838** SIR F. B. HEAD *Narrative* 9 Feb. xi. (1839) 384 American 'sympathy' for our absconded [Canadian] traitors was unbridled and unchecked. **1852** HAWTHORNE *Blithedale Rom.* ix, Priscilla's silent sympathy with his purposes, so unalloyed with criticism. **1864** NEWMAN *Apol.* i. (1904) 8/2 In his [*sc.* Whately's] special theological tenets I had no sympathy. **1893** FORBES-MITCHELL *Remin. Gt. Mutiny* 293 He had no sympathy with the anti-opium party.

4. *Comb.* **sympathy card**, a printed card expressing condolence on a bereavement; **sympathy strike** = *sympathetic strike* s.v. SYMPATHETIC *a.* 3 b; hence **sympathy striker**.

1967 'T. WELLS' *Dead by Light of Moon* (1968) x. 102 'Sympathy cards? Oh yes.' I remembered now. She wrote greeting card verses. **1976** *Billings* (Montana) *Gaz.* 27 June 3-D/4, I left it in a phone booth while I was writing a sympathy card to be mailed. **1937** *Sun* (Baltimore) 19 Mar. 2/3, 200 women in the South Unit sewing department.. struck because of a wage dispute. Some 280 other women seamstresses in the North Unit staged a one-hour 'sympathy strike'. **1981** *Sunday Tel.* 22 Mar. 6/6 The first sympathy strike by students of an American university has been organised in support of demands made by students on strike at a brother-campus in Britain. **1973** *Morning Star* 28 Aug. 3 (*heading*) Chrysler hit by sympathy strikers.

†'sympathy, *v. Obs. rare.* [f. prec. sb.] *intr.* To have 'sympathy' or affinity; to agree in nature or qualities (*with* something).

1615 BRETON *Charac.* 19 It [*sc.* love] simpathies with life, and participates with light, when the eye of the minde sees the ioy of the heart. *a* **1634** RANDOLPH *Muse's Looking Glass* II. iii, Pleasures, that are not mans, as man is man, But as his nature sympathies with beasts.

sympatisch, erron. var. SYMPATHISCH *a.*

sympatric (sɪm'pætrɪk), *a. Biol.* [f. SYM- + Gr. πάτρα fatherland: see -IC.] Occurring in the same geographical region, or in overlapping regions. Opp. ALLOPATRIC *a.*

1904 E. B. POULTON in *Trans. Entomol. Soc.* V. p. xc, Forms found together in certain geographical areas and not in other areas. Such groups may be called *Sympatric*. **1942** E. MAYR *Systematics & Origin of Species* vii. 149 The gaps between sympatric species are absolute, otherwise they would not be good species; the gaps between allopatric species are often gradual and relative. **1953, 1958** [see ALLOPATRIC *a.*]. **1974** *Nature* 16 Aug. 540/1 The two species are sympatric throughout much of their range. **1978** *Ibid.* 21 Sept. 256/1 White makes a good argument for sympatric speciation on small oceanic islands with many species and also for allochronic speciation.

Hence **sym'patrically** *adv.*; **'sympatry**, the occurrence of sympatric species or forms.

1904 E. B. POULTON in *Trans. Entomol. Soc.* V. p. xc, The occurrence of forms together may be termed Sympatry, and the discontinuous distribution of similar forms Asympatry. **1968** *Amer. Mus. Novitates* No. 2349. 6 The grasslands of this region are generally similar to those of the area of sympatry west of Bahía Blanca. **1970** *S. Afr. Jrnl. Sci.* LXVI. 392/1 The two species have been found to occur sympatrically over a depth range of 14 to 33 metres. **1973** *Nature* 9 Feb. 406/2 The planting of dense agricultural stands of larval foodplants..[is] believed to have affected the species' geographical ranges and abundances, causing extensive sympatry over much of the eastern United States. **1975** *Jrnl. Zool.* CLXXVII. 330 True polymorphism is thus restricted to multiple forms of a species which regularly occur sympatrically (and synchronically) within a population.

sympelmous to **symphalangism**: see SYM-¹.

†symphan, *sb. Obs.* Also 4 symphayne, -fan, 5 synphane, -fan, sinfon, simphan(n)e, 6 cymphan. [a. OF. *simphaine, semphaine, var. of *simphoine*, earlier *cinfonie*, *cifonie*, *siphonie*, ad. L. *symphōnia* SYMPHONY; the majority of the Eng. forms show assimilation in the final syllable to TYMPAN.] = SYMPHONY 1.

1303 R. BRUNNE *Handl. Synne* 4769 As Dauyd seyþ yn þe sautere, 'Yn harpe, yn thabour, and symphan gle, Wurschepe God.' *c* **1330** —— *Chron. Wace* (Rolls) 11387 Harpes, pypes, & tabours,..Belles, chymbes, & symfan. **1435** MISYN *Fire of Love* II. ii. 72 His prayars he sall synge with a gostly synphane. **1509** HAWES *Past. Pleas.* XVI. xi. (Percy Soc.) 61 There sat dame Musyke, with all her mynstrasy; As tabours, trumpettes,..Sakbuttes, organs,.. Harpes, lutes,..Cymphans, doussemers.

Hence **†symphan** *v. intr.*, to play on a 'symphan'.

1483 *Cath. Angl.* 340/1 To Synfan, *simphonizare*.

symphile, symphilic, etc.: see SYM-.

†symphioun. *Obs. rare*⁻¹. Altered form of SYMPHAN: cf. SUMPHION.

1560 ROLLAND *Seven Sages* 20 Harp, Lut, Organe, Symbal and Symphioun.

†'symphona. *Obs. rare.* [L., neut. pl. of **symphōnus* (SYMPHONOUS) used as sing. like *antiphōna* ANTIPHON.] ? A harmonized or concerted piece of music.

1691 WOOD *Ath. Oxon.* I. 680 [Joh. Gwyneth] had published..certain Symphona's, Antiphona's, and divers Songs for the use of the Church.

Similarly **†symphonask** [of obscure formation].

1621 RAVENSCROFT *Whole Bk. Ps.* Pref., The fiue lines are vsed for Symphonaskes or Parts Compounded of 2. 3. 4. 5. 6. voices, &c.

†symphone. *Obs. rare*⁻¹. [? Back-formation f. SYMPHONY.] (See quot.)

1572 BOSSEWELL *Armorie* II. 64 b, The Delphine..wil harken and delight to heare the tune of the Simphoni: and therfore he is called a Symphone, because he hath great liking in harmonie.

†symphoner. *Obs. rare.* In 5 sim-. [a. AF. **symphoner* = OF. *symphonier*, *-ieur*, f. *symphonie* SYMPHONY.] A player on the 'symphony' (SYMPHONY 1).

14.. *Nom.* in Wr.-Wülcker 697/2 *Hic simphonista*, a simphoner.

symphonesis, symphonetic: see SYM-.

symphonette (sɪmfəˈnɛt). *rare.* [f. SYMPHON(Y + -ETTE.] A popular musical composition in classical symphonic form (cf. *symphonic jazz* (*a*) s.v. SYMPHONIC *a.* (*sb.*) 3); a short symphony.

1947 A. EINSTEIN *Mus. Romantic Era* xi. 131 *Overture, Scherzo, and Finale*.., a work that Schumann in all seriousness wanted to bring out as his Second Symphony, or at least as a 'Symphonette'. **1955** L. FEATHER *Encycl. Jazz* 201/1 Completed mambo symphonette in three movements, March 1955.

‖**symphonia**¹ (sɪmˈfəʊnɪə). Also 6 sum-. [L. *symphōnia*, a. Gr. συμφωνία SYMPHONY.]

1. = SYMPHONY 2, 3.

1579 LODGE *Def. Plays* (Shaks. Soc.) 21 [Music] drawing his original from the motion of the stars, from the agreement of the planets..and from al those celestial circles where there is ethir perfit agreement or ony *Sumphonia*.

2. = SYMPHONY 1. (After Vulgate, Dan. iii. 5.)

1864 PUSEY *Lect. Daniel* i. 29 There is no evidence of any actual instrument called 'symphonia', until times when it would be altogether a new instrument.

3. = SYMPHONY 5.

1724 *Short Explic. For. Wds. in Mus. Bks.*, *Symphonia*, or *Simphonia*, a Symphony; by which is to be understood Airs in Two, Three, or Four Parts, for Instruments of any Kind; or the Instrumental Parts of Songs [etc.].

‖**symphonia**². *Obs.* [med.L., reduced f. med.L. *symphoniaca*, a. Gr. συμφωνιακή. Cf. OF. *simphonie*.] **a.** The plant henbane, or a drug made from it. **b.** A species of amaranth.

In mod. *Bot.*, a genus of the N.O. *Guttiferæ*.

1579 LANGHAM *Gard. Health* (1633) 308 Poysoned, drinke one dramme of Symphonia. **1728** BRADLEY *Dict. Bot.*, *Symphonia*, i.e. Amaranthus tricolor.

†symˈphoniac, *a.* *Obs.* *rare*⁻¹. [ad. L. *symphōniacus* or Gr. συμφωνιακός, f. συμφωνία SYMPHONY: see -AC.] Characterized by 'symphony' or harmony; in quot., sung by the whole choir together, as opp. to *antiphonal*. So ††**symphoˈniacal** *a.*, harmonious; consonant, accordant; whence †**symphoˈniacally** *adv.*, in a consonant manner.

1635 BRATHWAIT *Five Senses* II. v. 136 Yet may wee collect Symphoniacally, though not analogically nor proportionably, by the Excellence of the Creature, the infinite goodnesse of the Creator. **1650** CHARLETON *Paradoxes* Ep. Ded. 10 That the Latin is the most symphoniacall and Concordant Language. **1665** E. MAYNWARING *Treat. Scurvy* 56 A pitch of energy, symphoniacal with vital principles. **1776** HAWKINS *Hist. Mus.* I. III. iv. 289 *note*, This distinction between symphoniac and antiphonal psalmody.

†symˈphonial, *a.* *Obs.* *rare*⁻¹. [f. L. *symphōnia* SYMPHONY + -AL¹.] Harmonious.

1773 J. ROSS *Fratricide* II. 123 (MS.) Let this our best symphonial song Each day at noon be chanted up to Heav'n.

symphonic (sɪmˈfɒnɪk), *a.* (*sb.*) [f. SYMPHONY + -IC, after *harmonic*.]

1. a. *Welsh Prosody.* Involving similarity of sound: cf. SYMPHONIZE 1 b, SYMPHONY 2, quot. 1856. **b.** Having the same sound, pronounced alike; = HOMOPHONOUS 2. **c.** Applied to a shorthand sign denoting more than one sound; also as *sb.*

1856 J. WILLIAMS *Gram. Edeyrn* §1785 There are three kinds of resumption; namely, resumption of letters.., resumption symphonic.., and sense-producing.. resumption. **1880** J. A. H. MURRAY in *Trans. Philol. Soc.* 33 Special facilities of comparing whole classes of symphonic words with each other and their earlier forms. **1904** W. E. THOMSON tr. *Javal's Blind Man's World* 154 Phonography with Symphonics. A symphonic sign is one which expresses more than one speech-sound.

2. Harmonious. *rare.*

1864 WEBSTER. **1872** C. KING *Mountaineering Sierra Nev.* viii. 175 As we marched down the road, unconsciously keeping step, the sound of our boots had quite a symphonic effect; they were all full of water, and with soft, melodious slushing acted as a calmer upon our spirits.

3. *Mus.* Of, pertaining to, or having the form or character of a symphony. Also *transf.* (in reference to poetry), and *fig.*

symphonic ballet, a ballet choreographed to the music of a symphony, with an emphasis on pattern rather than plot. ***symphonic jazz***, (*a*) jazz influenced by the form and instrumentation of classical music; (*b*) classical music scored and performed in jazz style. ***symphonic poem*** (tr. G. *symphonische dichtung*, Liszt), a descriptive orchestral composition of the character and dimensions of a symphony, but freer in form, founded on some special poetic theme or idea.

1864 WEBSTER. **1873** *N. Amer. Rev.* CXVI. 241 Liszt, in his Symphonic Poems, has also tried to express poetical thoughts by music alone. **1881** *Athenæum* 26 Mar. 438/1 Smetana's symphonic poem 'Vltava' had been produced at the Crystal Palace concert. **1881** *Cornh. Mag.* Mar. 312 Alone in this elemental overture to tempest I..felt through self-abandonment to the symphonic influence how [etc.]. **1883** *Harper's Mag.* Mar. 541/1 The full growth from small beginnings of both symphonic and dramatic forms in music. **1886** A. L. ALGER tr. *Reissman's Life & Works R. Schumann* iii. 57 Schumann took an important step forward in the path of his progress... Thus arose: 'The Carnival'.., the 'Symphonic Studies' (Op. 13, 1834) [etc.]. **1889** C. H. H. PARRY in Grove *Dict. Mus.* IV. 33/1 Mendelssohn's only other symphonic work was the Lobgesang. *Ibid.* 34/2 The manner [of Schumann's 1st Symphony] is thoroughly symphonic, impressive and broad. **1913** *Times* 3 Oct. 8/5 The two new works—Sir Edward Elgar's symphonic study for orchestra, *Falstaff*, and Mr. Hamilton Harty's setting.. of..'The Mystic Trumpeter'. **1926** WHITEMAN & MCBRIDE *Jazz* iii. 58 Symphonic jazz had proved so successful that the Alexandria's cover receipts had risen from $300 to $1200 a day. **1929** *Metronome* Jan. 32/1 Whiteman put jazz in its Sunday dress and made it respectable. He applied the jazz treatment to the classics and established symphonic jazz which could be scored on paper. **1934** S. R. NELSON *All about Jazz* v. 101 Grofé has added 'Grand Canyon Suite'.. to his personal contribution to the field of symphonic Jazz. **1936** *Times* 24 June 14/3 'Les Presages'. M. Massine's first symphonic ballet..was revived at Covent Garden last night. **1947** W. MELLERS *Stud. Contemp. Mus.* xi. 176 The string quartet Variations, and even Rawsthorne's biggest and most important work, the Symphonic Studies, are more freely based on the same notion of the variation of form. **1958** G. LASCELLES in P. Gammond *Decca Bk. Jazz* viii. 104 Paul Whiteman absorbed the nucleus of the Goldkette Orchestra into his own symphonic jazz group. **1964** RAFFÉ & PURDON *Dict. Dance* 487/1 Most choreographers who have attempted symphonic ballet have..used the music as a basis for vague generalisations by way of theme, while avoiding the technical aridity of 'abstract ballet'. **1976** *New Yorker* 26 Jan. 96/3 The big symphonic ballet in the Allegretto is a space-filling geometrical composition.

†symˈphonical, *a.* *Obs. rare.* [f. as prec.: see -ICAL.] Harmonious: = prec. 2.

1589 PUTTENHAM *Engl. Poesie* II. vii. (Arb.) 93 Your verses answering eche other by couples, or at larger distances in good cadence is it that maketh your meeter symphonicall. **1650** *Anthroposophia Theomagica* 92 Such chiming and clinching of words, Antithetall Librations, and Symphonicall rappings

symphonically (sɪmˈfɒnɪkəlɪ), *adv.* [f. SYMPHONIC *a.*: see -ICALLY.] In a symphonic manner; as or like a symphony. Also *transf.*

1854 H. F. CHORLEY *Mod. German Mus.* v. 274 We may arrive at some canons of dramatic orchestral effect, not easy to reconcile with the practice of those writers who have treated Opera symphonically. **1923** G. SAINTSBURY in *Times Lit. Suppl.* 4 Jan. 2/1 There undoubtedly is room for ametric and unrhymed but symphonically rhythmed verse. **1927** R. VAUGHAN WILLIAMS in *Radio Times* 3 June 440/3 The words as well as the music are treated symphonically. **1929** *Sunday Dispatch* 13 Jan. 16 Paul Whiteman records have a wonderful following—chiefly because he can treat jazz symphonically. **1972** *Human World* Feb. 3 Hence the aptness of the symphonically deployed arch-motif in the imagery [of Racine's *Phèdre*]—the repeated reference to monsters. **1977** *Gramophone* Mar. 1457/1, I like both symphonies very much indeed even though I am not sure that they work symphonically.

symphonious (sɪmˈfəʊnɪəs), *a.* Only in literary use. [f. L. *symphōnia* SYMPHONY + -OUS, after *harmonious*.]

1. Full of or characterized by 'symphony' or harmony of sounds (SYMPHONY 2); sounding pleasantly together or *with* something else; concordant; harmonious: = HARMONIOUS 2.

1652 BENLOWES *Theoph.* VI. lxix, All, what symphonious breaths inspire, all, what Quick fingers touch. **1667** MILTON *P.L.* VII. 559 The sound Symphonious of ten thousand Harpes, that tun'd Angelic harmonies. **1757** GRAY *Bard* 119 What strings symphonious tremble in the air! **1784** COWPER *Task* IV. 162 The sprightly lyre..And the clear voice symphonious, yet distinct. **1818** SHELLEY *Q. Mab* VI. 41 Of purest spirits, a pure dwelling-place, Symphonious with the planetary spheres. **1858** CARLYLE *Fredk. Gt.* VII. v. (1872) II. 295 Their life was not quite symphonious. **1878** STEVENSON *Inland Voy.* 53 The shadows, the rich lights and the silence, made a symphonious accompaniment about our walk. **1835** W. HAY in *Blackw. Mag.* XXXVIII. 401 Whom the Muse taught to steal..Tones from the lyre symphonious with her own! **1841** HOR. SMITH *Moneyed Man* I. viii. 226 Listening entranced to the symphonious music of the spheres. **1865** TRENCH *Poems, Prize of Song* v, At that melody symphonious Joy to Nature's heart was sent.

b. *fig.* or *gen.* Marked by 'symphony' or agreement (SYMPHONY 3); agreeing, accordant: = HARMONIOUS 1. Const. *to*, *with*. (Often with direct allusion to prec. sense.)

1742 YOUNG *Nt. Th.* IV. 617 Future life symphonious to my strain, (That noblest hymn to heav'n). **1770** LANGHORNE *Plutarch* (1879) II. 793/2 The word *menoikes*..signifies what is symphonious to the mind, what soothes its weakness. **1813** SHELLEY *Q. Mab* VI. 41 Of purest spirits, a pure dwelling-place, Symphonious with the planetary spheres. **1858** CARLYLE *Fredk. Gt.* VII. v. (1872) II. 295 Their life was not quite symphonious. **1878** STEVENSON *Inland Voy.* 53 The shadows, the rich lights and the silence, made a symphonious accompaniment about our walk.

2. Sounding together or in concert.

1816 T. L. PEACOCK *Headlong Hall* xi, In conjunction with the symphonious scraping of fiddles. **1862** SYMONDS in H. F. Brown *Life* (1895) I. v. 255 Strange inexplicable chords and combinations of symphonious instruments.

3. Sounded alike: = SYMPHONIC 1 b. *rare*⁻¹.

1786 PINKERTON *Anc. Sc. Poems* I. p. cxliii, Synorthographic and Symphonious Words.

Hence **symˈphoniously** *adv.*, harmoniously.

1764 [see MELLIFLUENT]. **1804** J. GRAHAME *Sabbath* 78 A thousand notes symphoniously ascend. **1842** G. S. FABER *Prov. Lett.* (1844) II. 223 [The Church] symphoniously declares..these things, as having only one mouth.

symphonism (ˈsɪmfənɪz(ə)m). [f. SYMPHON(Y + -ISM.] Music of a symphonic kind; symphonies collectively.

1965 *Listener* 27 May 805/2 Operatic music, which has to encompass drama and accommodate it as a further musical element, needs a more flexible technique than the pure music of symphonism. **1973** *Radio Times* 15 Nov. 60 A series of 13 concerts. 7: 'Cyclic' Symphonism.

symphonist (ˈsɪmfənɪst). [f. SYMPHONIZE *v.* or SYMPHONY + -IST. Cf. F. *symphoniste* (18th c. in Hatz.-Darm.).]

†**1.** (See quot., and cf. next, 1.) *Obs. rare*⁻⁰.

1656 BLOUNT *Glossogr.*, *Symphonist*..a Chorister, one that sings with true tune and time.

2. †An orchestral performer who plays in a symphony (SYMPHONY 5 a) (*obs.*); a player in a symphony orchestra (*rare*).

1767 *Ann. Reg.*, *Ess.* 196/2 The singers and the symphonists in the orchestra. **1790** *Bystander* 178 These symphonists were first placed between the wings of the stage. **1964** M. MCLUHAN *Understanding Media* (1967) II. xxiii. 378 The satisfactions are just as few for the.. symphonists, since a player in a big orchestra can hear nothing of the music that reaches the audience.

3. A composer of symphonies (SYMPHONY 5 b).

1789 BURNEY *Hist. Mus.* IV. x. 595 John Christian Bach, the late celebrated opera composer and symphonist. **1820** *Q. Mus. Mag.* II. 63 The ponderous and heavy style of the early symphonists. **1845** E. HOLMES *Mozart* 166 The great career of Mozart as symphonist and dramatic musician. **1884** *Encycl. Brit.* XVII. 96/2 Next in chronology [to Haydn] as a symphonist stands Mozart.

symphonize (ˈsɪmfənaɪz), *v.* [ad. med.L. *symphōnizāre* (f. *symphōnia*), or directly f. SYMPHONY: see -IZE.]

1. a. *intr.* To sing or sound together, in concert, or in harmony. Now *rare* or *Obs.*

1491 CAXTON *Vitas Patr.* (W. de W. 1495) I. xlviii. 92 b/1 Melodyouse songes and armonyous, as of Infenyte nombre of people; Symphonysynge more swetter thanne ony other Instrumentes. *a* **1618** SYLVESTER *Miracle of Peace* xxxv, When many tunes do gently symphonize. **1787** *Gentl. Mag.* Dec. 1073/2 On the Coryphæus it depended..that the chorus altogether should symphonize. *a* **1859** DE QUINCEY *Posth. Wks.* (1893) II. 134 His first little wolfish howl..may have symphonized with the ear-shattering trumpet.

b. *Welsh Prosody.* To have the same or a similar sound, to sound alike. Now *rare* or *Obs.*

1856 J. WILLIAMS *Gram. Edeyrn* §1804 When the syllable next to the main rhyme symphonises or co-rhymes with one of the preceding pauses.

†**2.** To agree, be in accordance, harmonize (*with* something). *Obs.*

1661 BOYLE *Style of Script.* 71 They decline the commonest Acceptions, but to make the Texts.. Symphonize with their Tenents. *Ibid.* 253 The Law and Prophets Symphonizing with the Gospel. **1712** SIR G. WHELER *Liturgy after Model of Ancients* 145 That we might symphonize with the Universal Church.

3. a. To play a symphony (SYMPHONY 5 a). Now *rare* or *Obs.*

1833 *New Monthly Mag.* July 292 To enable the orchestra to symphonize, and the singer to warble.

b. *trans.* To accompany musically. Now *rare* or *Obs.*

1801 C. WILMOT *Let.* 29 Nov. in T. U. Sadleir *Irish Peer* (1920) 4 During the dinner..we were symphoniz'd by republican tunes, play'd outside the window. **1802** —— *Let.* 19 Oct. in *Ibid.* 103 A Gothic Castle..symphonis'd by the music of the waters.

4. To give the character or style of a symphony to (a piece of music), to render symphonic.

1932 *Amer. Speech* Apr. 241 Jazz is meant for the mass, it isn't meant to be symphonized, and all attempts at symphonization have been no more than negligible.

Hence **symphoniˈzation;** **ˈsymphonized** *ppl. a.*, composed in the manner of a symphony.

1932 Symphonization [see sense 4 of the vb. above]. **1946** R. BLESH *Shining Trumpets* i. 14 A spate of symphonized jazz and pseudo-jazz master-works.

symphonous (ˈsɪmfənəs), *a. rare.* ? *Obs.* [f. Gr. σύμφωνος (see next) + -OUS.] = SYMPHONIOUS 1. (In first quot. *ironical*.)

1814 *Q. Rev.* Apr. 97 The symphonous expression 'mully-grubs'. **1831** J. WILSON in *Blackw. Mag.* XXX. 403 Hear! hear! bursts in symphonous cadence from the manly bass of Grahame.

symphony (ˈsɪmfənɪ). Forms: 3–5 **symphanye**, 4 **symfonye**, 4–5 **symphonye**, 4–7 **symphonie** (4 syn-), 5–6 **simphony(e**, 5–7 **simphonie**, 6 **simphoni**, 5– **symphony.** [a. OF. *simphonie* (from 12th c.), mod.F. *symphonie* = It., Sp. *sinfonia*, Pg. *senfoni*, ad. L. *symphōnia* sound of instruments, instrumental harmony, voices in concert, musical instrument (*Dan.* iii. 5, *Luke* xv. 25), a. Gr. συμφωνία agreement or concord of sound, concert of vocal or instrumental music, ? musical instrument, f. σύμφωνος harmonious, f. σύν SYM- + φωνή sound.]

†**1.** Used vaguely, after late L. *symphōnia*, as a name for different musical instruments. (See also SYMPHAN.) *Obs.*

c **1290** *St. Thomas* 80 in *S. Eng. Leg.* I. 379 Tabours and fiþele and symphanye. *c* **1380** WYCLIF *Serm.* Sel. Wks. II. 73 Symphonye and croude weren herd whanne apostlis knewen alle wittis. **1382** —— *Dan.* iii. 7 Anoon as alle peplis harden the sown of trumpe, pype, and harpe, sambuke, and sautrie, synphonie, and al kynde of musikis. [So COVERDALE, *Douay*, and **1611** (margin).] *c* **1386** CHAUCER *Sir Thopas* 104 With harpe and pype and symphonye. **1398** TREVISA *Barth. De P.R.* XIX. cxxxvi. (1495) 00 j b/2 The Symphonye is an Instrument of Musyk: and is made of an holowe tree closyd in lether in eyther syde And Mynstralles betyth it wyth styckes. **1426** LYDG. *De Guil. Pilgr.* 11620 To pleye on sondry Instrumentys, On harpe, lut, & on gyterne,.. On rebube and on symphonye. **1567** MAPLET *Gr. Forest* 42 Hereof [*sc.* elder] are made certain kinds of instruments and especially a kinde of Symphonie whiche the common sort call a Pipe: the learned and more ciuil kinde of men name it a Dulcimer. **1602** MARSTON *Antonio's Rev.* IV. v, The strings of natures symphony Are crackt. **1898** STAINER & BARRETT *Dict. Mus. Terms* s.v., (4) In the seventeenth century the virginal was sometimes spoken of as a symphony. (5) A bagpipe has also been called a symphony, perhaps a corruption of the word *sampogna*.

2. Harmony of sound, esp. of musical sounds; concord, consonance. Also occas. of speech-sounds, as in verse. Now *rare* or *Obs.*

c **1440** CAPGRAVE *Life St. Kath.* I. 385 Armonye is in voyse, in smytyng or wynde, Symphonye & euphonye arn of hys kynde. *c* **1480** HENRYSON *Orpheus & Eurydice* 114 Fyve hevynly symphonyis.. First dyatesseron,.. And dyapason, symple and duplycate, And dyapente, componyt with a dys. **1589** PUTTENHAM *Engl. Poesie* I. ii. (Arb.) 22 By reason of our rime and tunable concords or simphonie. *Ibid.* III. xvi. 185 A rime of good simphonie should not conclude his concords with one and the same terminant sillable,.. but with diuers and like terminants. **1603** HOLLAND *Plutarch's Mor.* 228 The harmonie of musicke.. hath symphony by antiphony (that is to say) the accord ariseth from discord. **1660** WATERHOUSE *Arms & Arm.* 25 As in Consorts notes answer each other to a Symphony, so in Armory there must be regularity. **1797** MRS. RADCLIFFE *Italian* i, She touched her lute in sweet symphony. **1837** DISRAELI *Venetia* IV. ii, Stanzas glittering with refined images, and resonant with subtle symphony. **1856** J. WILLIAMS *Gram. Edeyrn* §1787 The resumption of letters and symphony takes place when the verses harmonise together at the beginning; as.. *Pum heryr.. Pum haerwy*.

3. Harmony (in general), agreement, accord, concord, congruity. Now *rare* or *Obs.*

1598 STOW *Surv.* 462 To conclude therefore the estate of London for gouernment is so agreeable a Symphony with the rest, that there is no feare of dangerous discord to ensue thereby. **1647** JER. TAYLOR *Lib. Proph.* iii. 61 The Jewes pretend that the Christians have corrupted many places, on purpose to make symphony between both the Testaments. **1691** NORRIS *Pract. Disc.* 327 To disturb the moral Harmony of the Universe, to hinder the symphony and agreement of the Two Worlds. **1752** HUME *Ess. & Treat.* (1777) II. 324 He must move some universal principle.. and touch a string, to which all mankind have an accord and symphony. **1858** CARLYLE *Fredk. Gt.* x. ii. (1872) III. 224 Their domestic symphony was liable to furious flaws.

4. a. (transf. from 2.) Music in parts, sung or played by a number of performers with pleasing effect; concerted or harmonious music; a performance or strain of such music. Chiefly *poet.* or *rhet.*

1599 T. STORER *Life & Death Wolsey* K 3, Sweete songs of many parts, Angells the quire, whose Symphonie to heare, Is able to prouoke conceiuing harts, To misconceiue of al inticing Arts. **1629** MILTON *Hymn Nativ.* xiii, Ring out ye Crystall sphears,.. And with your ninefold harmony Make up full consort to th' Angelike symphony. **1667** —— *P.L.* v. 162 Ye Sons of light, Angels,.. with songs And choral symphonies, Day without Night, Circle his Throne rejoycing. **1700** DRYDEN *Flower & Leaf* 210 From afar I heard a suddain Symphony of War. **1797** MRS. RADCLIFFE *Italian* vi, Her sorrow did not allow her to join in the choral symphonies of the nuns. **1814** SCOTT *Ld. of Isles* I. i, Ne'er to symphony more sweet Gave mountain echoes answer meet. **1845** DISRAELI *Sybil* IV. vi, Suddenly the organ burst forth, a celestial symphony floated in the lofty roof.

b. *fig.* A collection of utterances, or sounds of any kind, likened to concerted music; a 'chorus' (of praise, etc.).

1654 WHITLOCK *Zootomia* 456, I have seldome heard in any Discourse of but foure, or five Parts.. a Symphony of Commendations of an absent man,.. without some one.. striking a *F Fa ut—But* of Diminution. **1713** *Guardian* No. 29. ¶6 We now and then discharge our selves in a Symphony of Laughter. **1728–46** THOMSON *Spring* 579 While I deduce, From the first note the hollow cuckoo sings, The symphony of Spring. **1849** LONGF. *Seaside & Fireside* Ded. x, The grand, majestic symphonies of ocean. **1862** GOULBURN *Pers. Relig.* II. x. (1873) 139 Praying and giving thanks.. will constitute.. a beautiful symphony in the ears of the Most High.

c. Applied to a collection or composition of various colours which harmonize, with pleasing or brilliant effect.

1874 R. TYRWHITT *Sketch. Club* 257 Symphonies of colour, like Whistler's. **1885** *Harper's Mag.* Mar. 524/1 The mantel is exquisite, a symphony in white and gold. **1895** R. W. CHAMBERS *King Yellow, Str. Lady of Fields* iv, Neat girls.. bearing milliners' boxes, students with black portfolios and high hats,.. quick-stepping officers, symphonies in turquoise and silver.

5. *Mus.* **a.** A passage for instruments alone (or, by extension, for a single instrument) occurring in a vocal composition as an introduction, interlude, or close to an accompaniment (partly = RITORNELLO); also, a short instrumental movement occurring between vocal movements, as the 'Pastoral Symphony' in Handel's 'Messiah'; also formerly applied to a more extended instrumental piece, often in several movements, forming the overture to an opera or other vocal work of large dimensions (cf. next sense).

1661 PEPYS *Diary* 19 May, Captaine Cooke, Mr. Gibbons, and others of the King's musicians were come to present my Lord with some songs and symphonys, which were performed very finely. **1662** *Ibid.* 14 Sept., Having vialls and other instruments to play a symphony between every verse of the anthem. **1667** MILTON *P.L.* III. 368 Thir gold'n Harps they took,.. and with Præamble sweet Of charming symphonie they introduce Thir sacred Song. **1763** J. BROWN *Poetry & Mus.* xii. 207 Whoever is inclined to hear a Succession of Symphonies and Songs, set off with.. all the Refinement of Execution that can Inchant the Ear, let him attend the Opera. **1778** MISS BURNEY *Evelina* xxi. (1784) 159 During the symphony of a song.. young Mr. Braughton said, 'Its my belief that that fellow is going to sing another song.' **1810** SCOTT *Lady of L.* I. xxx, She sung, and still a harp unseen Fill'd up the symphony between. **1836** DICKENS *Sk. Boz, Streets-Night*, Smuggins, after a considerable quantity of coughing by way of symphony,.. sings a comic song.

b. An elaborate orchestral composition in three or more movements, originally developed from the operative overture (see prec. sense), similar in form to a sonata, but usually of grander dimensions and broader style.

1789 BURNEY *Hist. Mus.* IV. vi. 482 His [*sc.* J. C. Bach's] symphonies, quartets, and concertos for almost every species of instrument. **1830** *Examiner* 148/2 Beethoven's symphony led off. **1866** ENGEL *Nat. Mus.* v. 179 A composition for a number of different instruments in combination,—as, for instance, a Symphony or any other orchestral work. **1880** GROVE *Dict. Mus.* I. 352 *Choral Symphony*, the ordinary English title for Beethoven's 9th Symphony,.. the Finale of which is a chain of variations for solos and chorus. *Ibid.* II. 671 *Pastoral Symphony, The.* 'Sinfonia Pastorale, No. 6', is the title of the published score of Beethoven's 6th Symphony. **1889** C. H. H. PARRY *ibid.* IV. 15 Emmanuel Bach.. began writing symphonies in 1741, when Haydn was only nine years old. *Ibid.* 799 *Toy Symphony* (Ger. *Kindersinfonie*..), the English name by which a certain work of Haydn's is known... The toy instruments employed are a 'cuckoo'.., a trumpet and drum.., a whistle, a triangle, and a 'quail'... Andreas Romberg wrote a symphony for much the same instruments... Mr. Franklin Taylor has written one for piano and toys.

†**c.** Singing by the whole of a choir or congregation together. *Obs.*

1776 HAWKINS *Hist. Mus.* I. III. iv. 289 The second and third [methods of singing psalms] were.. distinguished by the names of symphony and antiphony.

d. *ellipt.* for 'symphony orchestra'.

1926 WHITEMAN & MCBRIDE *Jazz* xiv. 287 The unknown composer has to pay to get his compositions played by a good symphony. **1934** S. R. NELSON *All about Jazz* v. 87 Symphony work, although of the highest *ton*, is not very lucrative, and most players have additional sources of income. **1968** *Globe & Mail* (Toronto) 17 Feb. 23/4 The former manager of the Vancouver Symphony. **1977** *Times* 23 Apr. 11/3 The seven arias skimpily supported by the Barcelona Symphony.

6. *attrib.* and *Comb.*, as (sense 5 b) ***symphony concert, form, orchestra.***

1863 *Dwight's Jrnl. Mus.* XXIII. 110/3 Our concern now is with the concerts... To begin with the most important, those of the Orchestra, the so-called 'Philharmonic', or Symphony concerts. **1919** *Daily Mail Year Bk.* 200/1 Conductor of the Promenade Concerts since 1895, the Queen's Hall Symphony Concerts. **1956** A. H. COMPTON *Atomic Quest* ii. 68 On one occasion, Mrs. Edward Ryerson saw me as I was seeking a little relaxation at a symphony concert. **1911** *Contemp. Rev.* May 615 The idea that the symphonic poem is a further development of the symphony form. **1881** in Grove *Dict. Mus.* (1884) IV. 43/1 Orchestra to be permanent, and to be called The Boston Symphony Orchestra. **1932** *Daily Tel.* 8 Oct. 1/6 London Symphony Orchestra. **1978** *Ann. Reg. 1977* 404 Their success went a good way towards discounting the much-publicized theory that the conventional symphony orchestra now exists only for the purpose of playing music from the past.

symphrase to **symphyllous**: see SYM-.

symphyo- (ˈsɪmfɪəʊ), before a vowel **symphy-**, used as combining form of Gr. συμφυής growing or grown together, in some modern scientific terms, chiefly of Botany. **symphyˈantherous** *a.*, having the anthers united, synantherous, syngenesious (Treas. Bot. 1866). **symphyˈcarpous** *a.* [irreg. for **symphyocarpous*, f. Gr. καρπός fruit], having confluent fruits. **ˈsymphynote** *a.* [irreg. for **symphyonote*, f. Gr. νῶτον back], having the valves of the shell soldered together at the back or hinge, as certain molluscs of the family *Unionidæ*. ‖**symphyocephalus** (-ˈsɛfələs) [mod.L., f. Gr. κεφαλή head], a double monster with a single head (Dorland *Med. Dict.* 1901). ‖**symphyogenesis** (-ˈdʒɛnɪsɪs) [mod.L.: see -GENESIS], formation of some structure by union of previously separate parts; so **symphyogeˈnetic** *a.*, formed in this way. **symphyoˈstemonous** *a.* [Gr. στήμων, taken as = stamen], having the stamens united by their filaments, as a monadelphous flower.

1870 I. LEA *Synopsis Unionidæ* p. xv, I.. presumed.. that the first division of the family would be *symphynote and non-symphynote Unionidæ. **1887** GARNSEY & BALFOUR tr. *De Bary's Fungi* Gloss. 500 **Symphyogenetic*, formed by union of previously separate elements.

symphysial (sɪmˈfɪzɪəl), *a.* Also **-eal.** [f. SYMPHYSIS + -AL[1].] Of or pertaining to, situated at, or forming a symphysis. ***symphysial angle***: see quot. 1890.

1835–6 *Todd's Cycl. Anat.* I. 277/1 The anterior symphyseal or dental portion of each ramus first unites with its fellow at the symphysis. *a* **1856** H. MILLER *Footpr. Creat. Notes Suite Fossils* (1861) 322 The two bones of the under jaw, with their symphysial teeth. **1875** HUXLEY in *Encycl. Brit.* I. 755/1 A short curved rod of bone, which unites with its fellow in the symphysis, and is, in fact, the ossified symphysial end of Meckel's cartilage. **1890** BILLINGS *Med. Dict.*, *Symphyseal angle*.., that between line drawn from lower incisor teeth to point of chin and the plane of lower border of inferior maxillary bone.

So **symphysian** (sɪmˈfɪzɪən), *a.* [ad. F. *symphysien*], in same sense.

symphysian angle, in *Craniometry*, the angle between the profile of the symphysis and the plane of the inferior border of the lower jaw.

In recent Dicts.

symphysio-, also **-eo-** (after Fr. *-éo-*, from stem συμφυσε- of Gr. σύμφυσις), combining form of next, in the foll. surgical terms. **symphysiorrhaphy** (ˌsɪmfɪzɪˈɒrəfɪ), suture of a divided symphysis (Dorland *Med. Dict.* 1901). **symphysiotome** (-ˈfɪzɪəʊtəʊm) [Gr. -τομος cutting], a knife used in symphysiotomy (Knight *Dict. Mech.* 1875). **symphysiˈotomist**, an advocate of symphysiotomy. **symphysiotomy** (ˌsɪmfɪzɪˈɒtəmɪ) [Gr. -τομία cutting], the operation of cutting through the symphysis pubis to facilitate delivery.

1846 BRITTAN tr. *Malgaigne's Man. Oper. Surg.* 574 Symphysiotomy. There are two proceedings; one by ordinary, and the other by subcutaneous, incision. **1888** *Buck's Handbk. Med. Sci.* VI. 700/2 The medical profession became divided into Symphysiotomists and Cæsareanists, each advocating the one plan of delivery to the disparaging of the other. **1893** *Brit. Med. Jrnl.* 29 Apr. 915/2 The zeal with which several former advocates of Cæsarean section.. have taken up symphysiotomy.

‖**symphysis** (ˈsɪmfɪsɪs). [mod.L., a. Gr. σύμφυσις a growing together, esp. of the bones, f. σύν SYM- + φύσις growth.]

1. *Anat.* and *Zool.* The union of two bones or skeletal elements originally separate, either by fusion of the bony substance (*synostosis*) or by intervening cartilage (*synchondrosis*); the part, or line of junction, where this takes or has taken place: used esp. of such union of two similar bones on opposite sides of the body in the median line, as that of the pubic bones (*symphysis pubis*) or of the two halves of the lower jaw-bone (*s. mandibulæ* or *menti*).

1578 BANISTER *Hist. Man* I. 4 That kynde of coniunction of bones, that is called *Symphysis*: as when they are so vnited together that they haue motion neither manifest, nor obscure. **1634** T. JOHNSON *Parey's Chirurg.* VI. xlii. (1678) 165 The bones are composed after two sorts, that is, by Arthrosis.. and by Symphysis. **1779** *Monthly Rev.* LX. 61 The room gained by slitting the Symphysis of the Pubis will not, in many cases, allow the child's head to pass. **1800** *Phil. Trans.* XC. 433 The two portions of the lower jaw, instead of terminating at the symphisis [*sic*], where they join, become two thin plates, and are continued forwards. *a* **1856** H. MILLER *Footpr. Creat., Notes Suite Fossils* (1861) 317 The fourth tooth of the under jaw, reckoning from the symphysis. **1870** GILLMORE tr. *Figuier's Reptiles & Birds* ii. 44 The two halves of the lower jaw in Ophidians.. are not united by a bony symphysis, but by an elastic ligament. **1870** ROLLESTON *Anim. Life* Introd. 51 Except in *Rhea*, the ischia [in birds] never form any symphysis; nor do the pubic bones, except in *Struthio Camelus*.

b. Occasionally applied to a union or fusion, or a point or line of junction, of other parts either originally or normally separate.

1891 *Cent. Dict.* s.v., The symphysis of the optic nerves, .. the symphysis of teeth with the jaw. **1913** DORLAND *Med. Dict.* s.v., *Cardiac s[ymphysis]*, adhesion of the parietal and visceral layers of the pericardium.

†**c.** *Surg.* (See quots.) *Obs.*

1767 GOOCH *Treat. Wounds* I. 160 We see what wounds are curable by Symphysis, and what by Syssarcosis. **1828–32** WEBSTER, *Symphysis*... In *surgery*, a coalescence of a natural passage; also, the first intention of cure in a wound.

2. *Bot.* Coalescence or fusion of parts of a plant normally distinct.

1866 *Treas. Bot.*, *Symphysis*, a growing together.

†**symphysy.** *Obs. rare.* [irreg. ad. mod.L. *symphysis*: see prec.] Union or fusion of two bodies or parts of a body.

1655–87 H. MORE *App. Antid. Ath.* (1712) 233 The Dæmon.. rather seems by temporaneous constriction to keep the parts together, than to join them by any permanent Symphysy. *Ibid.* 234 This.. would be so, if the Devil, by a true Symphysy, could co-unite the parts; but if he only holds them together,.. the parts of the body are no more coherent than a handful of sand.

symphytic (sɪmˈfɪtɪk), *a. rare.* [ad. Gr. συμφυτικός, f. συμφύειν to make to grow together, f. σύν SYM- + φύειν to grow.] Formed by or involving coalescence or fusion of two parts or elements. Hence **symˈphytically** *adv.*, in the way of such coalescence or fusion; so **ˈsymphytism**, (tendency to) such coalescence or fusion; **ˈsymphytize** *v.*, *intr.* to become fused, to coalesce.

1871 EARLE *Philol. Engl. Tongue* v. 220 Symbolic words are marked by a.. tendency to attach themselves to other words;.. this tendency.. we will.. call.. *symphytism*. *Ibid.* 223 The tendency to a symphytic coalition. *Ibid.* viii. 408 A tendency to symphytize again once more with the word which they have already absorbed. *Ibid.* 417 The.. adverb at one time attached itself closely to the verb, indeed almost symphytically. *Ibid.* ix. 445 Conjunctions formed by the symphytism of a preposition with a noun, as in..*belike.* **1900** B. D. JACKSON *Gloss. Bot. Terms, Symphytic,* formed by fusion of several nuclei, as a gameto-nucleus.

sympiesometer (ˌsɪmpɪɪ'sɒmɪtə(r)). Also **-piez-**. [irreg. (for **sympiesiometer*) f. Gr. συμπίεσις compression (f. συμπιέζειν to compress, f. σύν SYM- + πιέζειν to press) + -OMETER. In Fr. *sympiézomètre.*]

1. A form of barometer in which the column of liquid in the tube has above it a body of confined air or other gas (instead of a vacuum as in the mercurial barometer), so that the pressure of the atmosphere acts against the weight of the liquid and the elastic pressure of the gas; a thermometer is attached for correction of the readings according to the expansion or contraction of the gas with changes of temperature.

1817 *Blackw. Mag.* I. 418 Mr. Adie has given it the name of sympiesometer (or measure of compression). **1843** *Mech. Mag.* XXXVIII. 117 The sympiesometer, from its delicacy and susceptibility to changes in the atmospheric pressure.. seems peculiarly fitted for the purpose of an indicator of danger in the mine. **1851** H. STEPHENS *Bk. Farm* (ed. 2) II. 301/2 One mercurial barometer, two sympiesometers with oil in the tube, and two more with a mineral solution in the tube. **1869** A. R. WALLACE *Malay Archip.* I. 49 The height, as measured by a sympiesometer, was about 2,800 feet.

2. An instrument for measuring the pressure or velocity of a current of water or other liquid, by the difference of level of the liquid in two bent tubes with open submerged ends pointing in opposite directions, against and with the current.

In Dicts.

sympil(e, -ill, -le, obs. ff. SIMPLE.

symplasm ('sɪmplæz(ə)m). *Biol.* [f. SYM- + PLASM.] **a.** *Bacteriol.* A group of bacterial cells that have coalesced into one amorphous mass. ? *Obs.*

1916 LÖHNIS & SMITH in *Jrnl. Agric. Res.* VI. 680 Type D is in most cases the dissolution product either of the large forms [of *Bacillus azotobacter*]..or of the small cells... As it is made up by a thorough mixing or melting of a frequently large number of cells, spores, or gonidia, the term *symplasm* or *symplastic stage* seems to be a correct and convenient name. **1923** *Anat. Rec.* XXVI. 69 The bacteria coalesce and resolve into a sort of plasmodium. This plasmodium is the symplasm. Later, in the completion of the life-cycle, bacteria are again formed by the breaking up of the symplasm. **1934** A. T. HENRICI *Biol. Bacteria* ix. 153 Such symplasms are found in old cultures and they probably represent masses of gum secreted by the bacteria, or more likely, masses of débris formed from dead and dissolved bacterial cells.

b. *Bot.* The cytoplasm of a symplast (sense b); an interconnected mass of cytoplasm.

1948 *Recueil d. Travaux botaniques Néerlandais* XLI. 5 Up until now, only a few publications have dealt with estimations as to what extent the symplasm is permeable for solutes. **1954** *Nature* 31 July 223/2 The transport in the cytoplasm from cell to cell..without loss to the outer solution indicates that plasma connexions between the cells must exist. The cells behave like a 'symplasm'. **1973** *Planta* CXII. 293 Stelar tissues only accumulate ions when these are supplied through the root symplasm.

Hence **sym'plasmic** *a.*, of or pertaining to (a) symplasm.

1923 *Anat. Rec.* XXVI. 70 The symplasmic stage in the life-cycles of bacteria appear[s] to be universal. **1971** *Protoplasma* LXXII. 315 The concept of symplasmic transport between plant cells must take account of the possible role of plasmodesmata.

symplasma (sɪm'plæzmə). *Med.* Pl. **-plasmata.** [mod.L., coined in Ger. (R. Bonnet 1903, in *Monatsschr. f. Geburtshülfe u. Gynaekol.* XVIII. 8): see SYM- and PLASMA.] A mass of cell nuclei and cytoplasm regarded as formed by the breaking down of the cell walls of the outer layer of the placenta.

1908 *Q. Jrnl. Microsc. Sci.* LIII. 134 The maternal tissue ..is universally recognised to undergo catalytic changes, and to pass into a symplasma, towards the composition of which superficial epithelium, proliferated epithelium of crypts and glands, subepithelial connective tissue, leucocytes, and blood have all largely contributed. **1910** F. H. A. MARSHALL *Physiol. of Reproduction* x. 414 After the destruction of the epithelium, the villi penetrate into the deeper tissues of the mucosa by gradually absorbing the symplasmata, and branch to form secondary and tertiary villi. **1923** *Q. Jrnl. Microsc. Sci.* LXVII. 146 A degenerating syncytium is called a symplasma.., a term which can be correctly applied only to maternal structures of a degenerate nature contained in the plasmodium. **1973** BOVING & LARSEN in Hafez & Evans *Human Reproduction* vii. 149/1 By this stage, the rabbit uterine epithelium has become converted into a 'symplasma' or multinucleated syncytium through the disappearance of the cell membranes between the epithelial cells.

symplasmatic (sɪmplæz'mætɪk), *a.* [f. prec. after *plasma, plasmatic.*] **a.** *Med.* Of or pertaining to a symplasma. **b.** *Bot.* = SYMPLASMIC *a.*

1923 *Q. Jrnl. Microsc. Sci.* LXVII. 156 In the symplasmatic zone of the diploplasma are to be found remains of maternal nuclei, maternal blood corpuscles and various granules. **1974** *Planta* CXIX. 47 Transients are observed in mutated cells when the illuminated green leaf sample also comprises normally green cells and there is a symplasmatic connection between the 2 types of cells.

symplast ('sɪmplɑːst, -æ-). *Bot.* [f. SYM- + -PLAST.] †**a.** [ad. G. *symplast* (J. von Hanstein 1880, in *Bot. Abh.* IV. II. 9).] A multinucleate cell created either by the fusion of cells into one cytoplasmic mass, or by the division of the nucleus of a single energid. *Obs.*

1894 *Jrnl. R. Microsc. Soc.* 376 Klemm objects to the term 'unicellular' as applied to *Caulerpa prolifera* and similar organisms. They should be regarded rather as 'symplasts', composed of a number of energids. **1900** *Ibid.* 475 When the polyplasts are so completely fused together that their cytoplasms form a single mass in which a number of nuclei are imbedded, Hanstein's term 'symplasts' may be applied. **1912** L. A. BORRADAILE *Man. Elem. Zool.* vi. 116 Groups of similar, unseparated energids are known as syncytia. They may be plasmodia, formed by the union of free energids, or symplasts, formed by the division of the nucleus of a single energid.

b. [ad. G. *symplast* (E. Münch *Die Stoffbewegungen in der Pflanze* (1930) 73).] A continuous network of interconnected plant cell protoplasts.

1938 *Amer. Jrnl. Bot.* XXV. 529/2 Studies on the occurrence of plasmodesmata in living tissues show that where pits occur the protoplasts are commonly connected by these strands. Consequently the 'symplast'..of the root must constitute an interconnected protoplasmic unit. **1976** B. E. S. GUNNING in Gunning & Robards *Intercellular Communication in Plants: Studies on Plasmodesmata* I. 2 Following the evolution of plasmodesmata, the plant body is ..composed of two major compartments, for which the terms apoplast and symplast are convenient (Münch, 1930). .. The term symplast refers to the interconnected protoplasts, all bounded by a continuous plasmalemma.

Hence **sym'plastic** *a.*, of or pertaining to a symplast or symplasm; ***symplastic growth***, the expansion of a common wall between adjacent plant cells during cell enlargement.

1916 [see SYMPLASM a]. **1930** J. H. PRIESTLEY in *New Phytologist* XXIX. 132 It is proposed to call this alternative method of growth now described symplastic growth. **1981** J. R. BARNETT *Xylem Cell Devel.* ii. 63 This symplastic growth hypothesis..could not explain satisfactorily the type of growth in which an enlarging cell, such as a fibre, increases the number of cells with which it is in contact as it grows.

symplectic (sɪm'plɛktɪk), *a.* and *sb.* [ad. Gr. συμπλεκτικός twining or plaiting together, copulative, f. σύν SYM- + πλέκειν to twine, plait, weave: see -IC.] **A.** *adj.* **1.** *Anat.* and *Zool.* Epithet of a bone of the suspensorium in the skull of fishes, between the hyomandibular and the quadrate bones.

1839–47 *Todd's Cycl. Anat.* III. 833/1 The symplectic bones seem to be peculiar to Fishes.

2. *Petrol.* Of a rock or its texture: exhibiting an intimate intergrowth of two different minerals, esp. one where one mineral has a vermicular habit within the other as a result of secondary action. [ad. G. *symplektisch* (C. F. Naumann *Lehrb. der Geognosie* (1850) I. 667.]

1916 J. J. SEDERHOLM in *Bull. de la Comm. Géol. de Finlande* No. 48. 46, I..take the liberty of proposing that the term symplektic, or symplektitic should be used preferably as a designation of secondary intergrowths of two different minerals. **1949** F. H. HATCH et al. *Petrol. Igneous Rocks* (ed. 10) iv. 281 A characteristic feature of certain noritic rocks is the development of symplectic intergrowths along intercrystal boundaries. **1971** *Nature* 3 Dec. 251/3 The decomposition of a fayalitic olivine (Fe_2SiO_4) to symplectic metallic iron and cristobalite provides confirmation of a very low oxygen fugacity.

B. *sb. Anat.* and *Zool.* The symplectic bone.

1870 ROLLESTON *Anim. Life* 44 The synchondrosis between the hyomandibular and the symplectic. **1880** GÜNTHER *Fishes* 55 The mesotympanic or symplectic appears as a styliform prolongation of the lower part of the hyomandibular.

Hence **sym'plectite**, an intergrowth of this kind; **symplec'titic** *a.*

1916 J. J. SEDERHOLM in *Bull. de la Comm. Géol. de Finlande* No. 48 46, I..propose to use for these intergrowths of two minerals plaited together, and generally of second origin, the common designation symplektites (or symplectites). **1949** F. H. HATCH et al. *Petrol. Igneous Rocks* (ed. 10) iv. 282 (*caption*) Myrmekite-like symplectites of orthopyroxene and plagioclase are lobed into the labradorite. **1976** *Nature* 22 Apr. 673/2 Rare symplectites of spinel and pyroxene may result from the dehydration of amphibole. **1979** *Ibid.* 5 Apr. 512/2 Symplectitic diopside is not different from coarser, recrystallised diopside.

symplesite ('sɪmpləzaɪt). *Min.* [ad. G. *symplesit* (A. Breithaupt 1837, in *Jrnl. f. prakt. Chem.* X. 501), f. Gr. πλησιάζειν to bring together (in allusion to its relations to other minerals): see SYM- and -ITE¹.] A hydrated ferrous arsenate, $Fe_3(AsO_4)_2.8H_2O$, found as green triclinic crystals (altering to blue), usu. in aggregates having a coarsely fibrous radial structure.

1844 J. D. DANA *Syst. Min.* (ed. 2) VI. 532 Symplesite... Occurs at Lobenstein in Voigtland, with cobaltic pyrites and dolomite. **1968** I. KOSTOV *Mineralogy* 453 Symplesite is found in spherical aggregates, light green to indigo-blue when oxidized.

‖**symploce** ('sɪmpləsiː). *Rhet.* Also 6 **-che; symploke** (-əkiː). [Late L. *symplocē*, a. Gr. συμπλοκή an interweaving, f. σύν SYM- + πλέκειν (see SYMPLECTIC). Cf. F. *symploque, symploce.*] A figure consisting in the repetition of one word or phrase at the beginning, and of another at the end, of successive clauses or sentences; a combination of *anaphora* and *epistrophe.*

1577 PEACHAM *Gard. Eloquence* I j b, *Symploce*,.. comprysing..both *Epanaphora* and also *Epiphora.* **1589** PUTTENHAM *Engl. Poesie* III. xix. (Arb.) 209 Take me the two former figures and put them into one, and it is that which the Greekes call *symploche*, the Latines *complexio*, or *conduplicatio*, and is a maner of repetition, when one and the selfe word doth begin and end many verses in sute. *a* **1679** HOBBES *Rhet.* IV. v. (1681) 150 When both of these [*sc.* anaphora and epistrophe] are joyned together, it is called a coupling or Symploce [*mispr.* symplote]. **1952** J. D. DENNISTON *Gr. Prose Style* v. 90 Occasionally repetition occurs both at beginning and at end of clause, anaphora being combined with antistrophe. This is the figure known as symploke.

sympneuma, etc.: see SYM-.

sympode ('sɪmpəʊd). *Bot.* Anglicized form of SYMPODIUM. (Cf. F. *sympode.*)

1880 GRAY *Struct. Bot.* v. (ed 6) 154 The inflorescence.. is a sympode, i.e. consists of a series of seemingly superposed internodes which belong to successive generations of axes. **1888** *Encycl. Brit.* XXIV. 237/2 The most generally accepted explanation is the 'sympodial' one. According to this, the shoot of the vine is a 'sympode', consisting of a number of 'podia' placed one over the other in longitudinal series.

‖**sympodia** (sɪm'pəʊdɪə). *Anat.* [mod.L., f. Gr. συμποδ-, σύμπους adj. with the feet together + -IA.] A malformation in which the legs or lower extremities are united.

1848 DUNGLISON *Med. Lex.* (ed. 7). **1849–52** *Todd's Cycl. Anat.* IV. 964 Sympodia or Siren-like form is the fourth species of defective formation of the trunk. **1912** KEITH *Human Body* viii. 124.

sympodia, plural of SYMPODIUM.

sympodial (sɪm'pəʊdɪəl), *a.* [In sense 1, f. SYMPODIUM; in sense 2, f. SYMPODIA: see -AL¹.]

1. *Bot.* Pertaining or relating to, of the nature of, or producing a sympodium.

1875 BENNETT & DYER tr. *Sachs' Bot.* 157 The Development of Dichotomous Systems may take place either in a forked or a sympodial manner. **1880** BESSEY *Botany* 140 Sympodial dichotomy, in which one of the branches of each bifurcation develops more than the other. **1888** [see SYMPODE].

2. *Anat.* Affected with sympodia; having the lower extremities united.

1902 *Brit. Med. Jrnl.* 15 Mar. 671 His identification of the Siren with the sympodial fetus.

Hence **sym'podially** *adv. Bot.*, in the manner of, or so as to produce, a sympodium.

1875 BENNETT & DYER tr. *Sachs' Bot.* 157 The dichotomous system is developed sympodially when at each bifurcation one branch developes more strongly than the other. **1884** BOWER & SCOTT *De Bary's Phaner.* 279 A cauline bundle, the corners of which are composed of the sympodially united leaf-traces of a single bundle.

‖**sympodium** (sɪm'pəʊdɪəm). *Bot.* Pl. **-ia.** [mod.L., f. Gr. σύν SYM- + ποδ-, πούς foot.] An apparent axis or stem in a dichotomously branched plant, made up of the bases of successive branches so arranged as to resemble a simple or monopodial axis; a pseudaxis (see PSEUDO- 2).

1862 F. CURREY tr. *Hofmeister's Higher Cryptogamia* 224 Those plants whose sympodium (which has the appearance of a principal axis) bears no fronds. *Ibid.* 225, I have met with sympodia four feet long devoid of fronds. **1875** BENNETT & DYER tr. *Sachs' Bot.* 157 The apparent primary shoot, which in fact consists of the bases of consecutive bifurcations, may..be termed a Pseud-axis or Sympodium.

sympolar, -polity: see SYM-.

†**sympose.** *Obs. rare*⁻¹. Anglicization of SYMPOSIUM (in quot., in sense 1 b).

1621 T. WILLIAMSON tr. *Goulart's Wise Vieillard* 95 A manner of speech..among the Grecians, as Plato mentioneth in his Sympose.

symposia, plural of SYMPOSIUM.

symposiac (sɪm'pəʊzɪæk), *sb.* and *a.* Also 6 **-ake,** 7 **-ach, -acke, -aque,** 7–8 **-ack.** [ad. late L. *symposiacus* adj. (Gellius), in neut. pl. *symposiaca* also as sb. applied to certain writings of Plutarch (see A. 2 below), or Gr. συμποσιακός adj., f. συμπόσιον SYMPOSIUM: see -AC.]

A. *sb.* †**1.** = SYMPOSIAST 1. *Obs. rare*⁻¹.

1581 MULCASTER *Positions* xxxv. (1887) 129 Dipnosophistes, symposiakes, antiquaries.

2. A symposiac meeting or conversation, or an account of one; a symposium. Now *rare* or *Obs.*

1603 HOLLAND *Plutarch's Mor.* 641 (*heading*) The Symposiaqves or Table-questions. **1646** SIR T. BROWNE *Pseud. Ep.* II. iv. 81 Plutarch speakes positively in his Symposiacks, that amber attracteth all bodies. **1651** JER. TAYLOR *Serm. for Year, Summer* xiv. 179 That which was fine in discourse at a Symposiack, or an Academical dinner. **1683** DRYDEN *Life Plutarch* in *P.'s Lives* (1758) p. xvi, A man ..of whom Plutarch has made frequent mention in his Symposiaques or Table Conversations. **1748** J. GEDDES

Comp. Antients 110 In the Symposiac, or banquet [of Plato], where a variety of characters are brought in. **1792** W. Roberts *Looker-on* No. 30 (1794) I. 432 Taciturnity was.. the best recommendation to the symposiacs of sages, and the lectures of philosophers. **1828** *Blackw. Mag.* XXIV. 252 At a Symposiac, near London. **1842** *Tait's Mag.* IX. 683 Politics and symposiacs go ill together.

B. *adj.* Of, pertaining to, or suitable for a symposium; of the nature of a symposium; convivial.

1642 Cudworth *Union Christ & Ch.* 21 He [*sc.* Plato] therefore in that excellent Symposiack dialogue concerning the nature of Love, brings in Aristophanes discoursing in this manner. **1646** Sir T. Browne *Pseud. Ep.* v. xxi. 266 The ancient custome in Symposiacke meetings, to weare chapletts of Roses about their heads. **1731** Arbuthnot *Aliments* Pref. (1735) A ij, In some of those symposiac Disputations amongst my Acquaintance. **1840** G. C. Lewis tr. *C. O. Müller's Hist. Lit. Greece* x. §16. 124 These elegies, like those of Archilochus, Solon, Theognis, &c. were symposiac. **1850** Mure *Lit. Greece* III. 100 The next.. order of symposiac performance.. resembles our.. custom of laying each guest under an obligation to sing his song. **1898** Stainer & Barrett *Dict. Mus. Terms, Symposiac,* a term applied to cheerful and convivial compositions for voices, as glees, catches, rounds, &c.

So **symposiacal** (sɪmpəʊˈzaɪəkəl) *a. rare*$^{-1}$.

1826 *New Monthly Mag.* Jan. 17 Symposiacal forth-pourings of gratitude.

symposial (sɪmˈpəʊzɪəl), *a.* [f. symposium + -al[1].] = symposiac *a.*

1775 Sir E. Barry *Observ. Wines Ancients* 276 The different symposial topics of conversation. **1880** J. Cairns *Unbelief in 18th Cent.* iii. (1881) 72 An account of a pantheistic club.. with a description of their.. symposial usages.

symposiarch (sɪmˈpəʊzɪɑːk). [ad. Gr. συμποσίαρχος, f. συμπόσιον symposium + ἀρχός ruler, chief.] The master, director, or president of a symposium; the leader of a convivial gathering.

1603 Holland *Plutarch's Mor.* 641 What maner of person the Symposiarch or master of the feast ought to be. **1660** Stanley *Hist. Philos.* ix. (1701) 431/1 He staid for the chief Magistrate. As soon as he came, he was made Symposiarch, Master of the Feast. *a* **1704** T. Brown *Declam. in Def. Gaming* Wks. 1709 III. 139 Under the.. direction of some certain prudent and sober Symposiarchs, or Masters of the Feasts. **1787** Hawkins *Life of Johnson* 258 So was Johnson [born] for the office of a symposiarch, to preside in all conversations. **1878** F. Ferguson *Pop. Life Christ* i. xii. 133 We shall be ready to exclaim with Cana's surprised symposiarch, 'Thou hast kept the good wine until now.' **1882** *Athenæum* 14 Jan. 54/1 The criticisms of Shakspeare's plays that went on at the Mermaid under symposiarch Ben Jonson. **1895** Burness in Anna M. Stoddart *Blackie* II. xxi. 245 Fixing his eye on the symposiarch, he rose to propose the health of that gentleman.

symposiast (sɪmˈpəʊzɪæst). [ad. Gr. type *συμποσιαστής, f. συμποσιάζειν to drink together, f. συμπόσιον symposium.] One who takes part in a symposium.

1. A member of a drinking-party; a banqueter.

In first quot. confused with symposiarch; the definition is taken from Cotgr. s.v. *Symposiarque.*

1656 Blount *Glossogr., Symposiast,* the master or overseer of a Feast, a Feast-maker.

1830 Gen. P. Thompson *Exerc.* (1842) I. 199 The symposiasts of Whitby. **1835** T. Mitchell *Acharn. of Aristoph.* 129 *note,* That the Spartans had distinguished themselves by their agreeable manners, but that the Athenians had carried away the palm, as symposiasts at the entertainment. **1900** W. Tuckwell *Remin. Oxford* 13 The delightful symposiasts.. are gone to.. the Mansion of Hades.

2. One who contributes to a 'symposium' on some topic (symposium 2).

1878 R. Wallace in Smith & Wallace *Life & Last Leaves* (1903) 244 The view of Mr. Gladstone and the symposiasts. **1930** *Time & Tide* 16 May 638 This new sally is directed against the Religious Symposiasts of the popular press, against the well-known writers who take part in those series called 'Is Prayer Answered?' [etc.]. **1978** *Social Sci. & Med.* XII. 185 The symposiasts insist that their analyses are stimulated by the cultural science, yet cannot specify just how.

symposiˈastic, *a.* [ad. med.Gr. συμποσιαστικός, f. *συμποσιαστής: see prec. and -ic.] = symposiac *a.*

1669 Gale *Crt. Gentiles* i. iii. iv. 54 Plato, in his Symposiastic Dialogue.. mentions [etc.]. **1866** Blackmore *Cradock Nowell* xl, He thought about Socrates, and his symposiastic drolleries.

symposium (sɪmˈpəʊzɪəm). Also 7–9 **-ion**. Pl. **-ia** (rarely **-iums**). [a. L. *symposium,* ad. Gr. συμπόσιον, f. συμπότης fellow-drinker (cf. συμπίνειν to drink together), f. σύν sym- + πότης drinker (cf. πότιμος drinkable, ποτόν drink).]

1. a. A drinking-party; a convivial meeting for drinking, conversation, and intellectual entertainment: properly among the ancient Greeks, hence generally.

1711 Addison *Spect.* No. 9. ¶11 The rules of a Symposium in an ancient Greek author. **1748** Chesterf. *Let. to Son* 29 Oct., I take it for granted, that.. your Symposion [is] intended more to promote conversation than drinking. **1781** Warton *Hist. Eng. Poetry* xliv. IV. 18 It appears that the company dined so very late [in 1609], as at half an hour after eleven in the morning; and that it was the fashion to ride to this polite symposium on a Spanish jennet. **1787** Hawkins *Life of Johnson* 360 Our symposium at the King's head broke up. **1816** Scott *Antiq.* vi, You are welcome to my symposion. **1828** D'Israeli *Chas. I,* I. viii. 270 His symposia attracted a closer observation from the freedom of his conversation. **1866** Felton *Greece Anc. & Mod.* I. ii. iv. 336 If he [*sc.* Socrates] went to a symposium, he was likely to stay all night.

b. An account of such a meeting or the conversation at it; *spec.* the title of one of Plato's dialogues.

a **1586** Sidney *Apol. Poetry* (Arb.) 57 One.. that should bid one read Phædrus, or Symposium in Plato. **1603** Holland *Plutarch's Mor.* 689 Epicurus.. in his Symposium or banquet, hath discussed the question. **1776** Mickle tr. *Camoens' Lusiad* Introd. p. cxxxv. *note,* The passage stands in the Symposion of that author [*sc.* Plato] as follows.

2. *transf.* **a.** A meeting or conference for discussion of some subject; hence, a collection of opinions delivered, or a series of articles contributed, by a number of persons on some special topic.

1784 (*title*) Symposia; or, Table Talk in the month of September, 1784, being a rhapsodical hodge-podge. **1869** Ticknor in Hillard *Life,* etc. (1876) I. i. 12 Alexander and Edward Everett, Edward T. Channing, Nathan Hale, William Powell Mason, and Jacob Bigelow constituted this *symposium.* **1877** Shields *Final Philos.* 57 Foulke Greville seems to have held a symposium for the liberal discussion of the Copernican system. **1882** *Glasgow News* No. 2607. 2/3 A symposium is commenced in the Clerical World this week on the question 'Within what limits are "Schools of Thought" desirable in a religious community?'

b. A book consisting of essays on various aspects of a subject contributed by a number of different authors.

1946 *Nature* 19 Oct. 534/1 Advances in biological sciences in the U.S.S.R. within the recent 25 years, 1917–1942. Symposium. Editor-in-chief: L. A. Orbeli. (In Russian.) Pp. 356. **1969** *Listener* 15 May 696/1 A symposium on 20th-century music, published in 1960, contained a fulsome and over-extended reference to a then almost unknown French composer. **1972** *Daily Tel.* 30 Mar. 6 This generously illustrated symposium, by contributors of different denominations, covers a world-wide range of Christian art and architecture. **1979** *Nature* 1 Mar. 102/1 Symposia are at present, perhaps, an over-popular form of publication: in many of them the thread of supposed common interest which binds the essays together is far too tenuous, and indeed, in the case of some complimentary volumes such as this, completely non-existent.

3. *Comb.*

1856 R. A. Vaughan *Mystics* (1860) II. 115 Such symposium-loving scholars.

sympotic (sɪmˈpɒtɪk), *a.* [f. as next.] = sympotical *a.*

1972 P. M. Fraser *Ptolemaic Alexandria* I. x. 565 In other fields Asclepiades shows himself an innovator in his adaptation of existing poetical genres to the epigram. This is clearly shown in his sympotic epigrams, which form a main category of his work. **1981** *Times Lit. Suppl.* 6 Nov. 1307/5 The archaic age was the great age of sympotic pottery: potters and painters became rich and famous, producing shapes and painting designs which echoed the sympotic preoccupations of their aristocratic patrons.

sympotical (sɪmˈpɒtɪkəl), *a. rare.* [f. late L. *sympoticus* (Gellius) or Gr. συμποτικός (f. συμπότης fellow-drinker, boon-companion) + -al[1].] = symposiac *a.*

1825 *Blackw. Mag.* XVII. 679 The light sympotical mode with which he [*sc.* Socrates] treats the most difficult points of philosophy. **1981** *Times* 5 Aug. 12/6 The sympotical form is still quite distinctive of British culture from pubs to clubs.

sympresbyter to **sympsychography**: see sym-.

symptom (ˈsɪmptəm), *sb.* Forms: 4–5 **synthoma**, *pl.* **syn-**, **sinthomata**, 6 **symptoma**, 7 **syntoma**; 6–7 **symptome** (6 **sinthom**, **syntone**), 7 **symtom(e**, **simptome**, (**syntome**, **sintum**), 7– **symptom**. [In early use, in med.L. form *synthoma, sinthoma,* corrupt ff. late L. *symptōma,* a. Gr. σύμπτωμα chance, accident, mischance, disease, f. συμπίπτειν to fall together, fall upon, happen to (cf. πτῶμα fall, misfortune), f. σύν sym- + πίπτειν to fall. In mod. use, ad. F. *symptome,* †*sinthome,* or directly ad. L. *symptōma.* Cf. It. *sintomo,* Sp. *síntoma,* Pg. *symptoma.*]

1. a. *Path.* A (bodily or mental) phenomenon, circumstance, or change of condition arising from and accompanying a disease or affection, and constituting an indication or evidence of it; a characteristic sign *of* some particular disease. Esp., in mod. use, a subjective indication, perceptible to the patient, as opposed to an objective one or sign (sign *sb.* 7f).

1398 Trevisa *Barth. De P.R.* v. ii. (1495) g j b/1 Yf the heed be corrupte & dystemperate wyth Synthoma of corrupcion of heed ache. *Ibid.* v. iii. g iij/2 Yf dryenesse [of brain] encreasyth wyth heete there.. comyth worse Synthomata, euylles & syknesses. *a* **1425** tr. *Arderne's Treat. Fistula,* etc. 57 Oþer sinthomata i.[e.] perilez as scharp akyng and prikkyng, brynnyng, ychyng, smertyng. **1602** *2nd Pt. Return fr. Parnass.* ii. i. (Arb.) 21, I haue considered of the crasis, and syntoma of your disease. **1605** Daniel *Queen's Arcadia* i. iv, We shall soone preuent this growing plague, Of pride, and folly, now that she discry The true symptoma of this maladie. **1541** Copland *Galyen's Terap.* 2 A iij b, Those thynges are as symptomes and accydentes of the sayde vlceres, which yf they be present may hynder and let the curacion. **1562** Bullein *Bulwarke, Dial. Sorenes & Chir.* 26 Alienacion of minde, with other sinthoms whiche in this case, are.. signes of colde death. **1594** Carew *Huarte's Exam. Wits* (1616) 180 Counting the damages which the feauer produceth, with those of the Syntones of the euill. **1601** Holland *Pliny* xxi. xiii. II. 94 The symptomes or accidents that ensue upon the eating of this honey, are these. *Ibid.* xxix. v. 362 That symtome of beeing afraid of water; which is incident unto such as be so bitten. **1603** —— *Plutarch's Mor.* 123 Swelling is a symptome or accident following upon a great wound or hurt in the flesh. **1621** Burton *Anat. Mel.* i. iii. viii. 429 Feare, sorrow, suspition, bashfulness and those other dread Symptomes of body and mind, must needs aggravate this misery. **1643** Baker *Chron., Edw. III* 170 If he had not fallen into Symptomes of a Dropsie. **1660** R. Coke *Justice Vind.* 10 As when a Physitian from the symptoms of his indisposed Patient, endeavors to find out the causes of his distemper. **1692** *Lond. Gaz.* No. 2801/3 The Small-Pox being come out with all the good simptomes that could be wish'd. *a* **1700** in *Cath. Rec. Soc. Publ.* IX. 345 She perceived in herself yᵉ sintums of her neer aproching death. **1798** Ferriar *Illustr. Sterne* iii. 81 Symptoms of fever appearing, he was removed. **1804** Abernethy *Surg. Obs.* 175 His skin was hot, and his pulse strong. These symptoms could be attributed to.. inflammation of the brain. **1842**, etc. [see sign *sb.* 7e]. **1846** Trench *Mirac.* xxvii. (1862) 367 All the symptoms.. exactly agree with those of epilepsy. **1869** S. Fenwick *Med. Diagnosis* i. 2 Diseases are distinguished from each other either by such alterations in the organs themselves, or their secretions, as can be ascertained by the senses of the observer (physical signs); or by changes in the functions of the parts affected (symptoms). **1922** *Amer. Jrnl. Med. Sci.* CLXIV. 684 The first sign noticed was cyanosis and the first symptom shortness of breath on exertion.

b. *attrib.* and *Comb.*: as ***symptom-free*** adj.; **symptom-complex**, **-group**, a set of symptoms occurring together and characterizing or constituting a particular disease or affection.

1897 *Allbutt's Syst. Med.* II. 865 Delirium tremens seems to have been first recognised as a symptom group, and separated from acute mania by Dr. Thomas Sutton.. in 1813. *Ibid.* III. 70 The symptom-complex here presented is.. unlike that of any other disease. **1962** *Lancet* 27 Jan. 212/2 Most remain symptom-free, apart from aching calves, thighs and backs. **1980** *Recent Advances in Surgery* X. 396 Only about 45 per cent of patients achieve a perfect, symptom-free, Visick grade I result.

2. a. *gen.* A phenomenon or circumstance accompanying some condition, process, feeling, etc., and serving as evidence of it (orig. and properly of something evil); a sign or indication *of* something.

1611 B. Jonson in *Coryat's Crudities* Charact. Auth. bj b, He free from all other Symptomes of aspiring, will easily outcary that. **1626** Prynne *Perpet. Regen. Man's Est.* Ep. Ded., It is a sure syntome, that iniquitie doth abound among vs. **1638** Sir T. Herbert *Trav.* (ed. 2) 42 Furnisht with language, and many symptomes of education. **1641** Sir E. Nicholas in *N. Papers* (Camden) I. 55 Jalousies and private devisions ware never good simptomes in a State. **1647** H. More *Song of Soul* i. ii. cx, Ill symtomes men descry In this thy Glaucis, though the nimble wench So dexterously can pray and prophecy. **1673** (*title*) The Character of a Coffee-House, with the Symptomes of a Town-Wit. **1698** Fryer *Acc. E. India & P.* 13 The Morn appears, but with the Symptoms of a blowing Day. **1769** Robertson *Chas. V,* iv. Wks. 1813 V. 373 They observed many symptoms of a boundless ambition in that young prince. **1776** Adam Smith *W.N.* ii. v. I. 455 The carrying trade is the natural effect and symptom of great national wealth. **1831** Scott *Ct. Rob.* xvi, Nor was it long ere symptoms of his approach began to be heard. **1852** R. B. Mansfield *Log Water Lily* 12 The river.. showed symptoms of rising. **1855** Macaulay *Hist. Eng.* xviii. IV. 120 Symptoms of discontent began to appear. **1871** R. W. Dale *Commandm.* vii. 189 There are some symptoms in the general habits.. of society which seem to me somewhat ominous.

b. With negative expressed or implied: A slight, or the least, sign *of* something; a trace, vestige.

1722 Wollaston *Relig. Nat.* ix. 186 We perceive not the least symptom of cogitation or sense in our tables, chairs, &c. *a* **1797** H. Walpole *Mem. Geo. III* (1845) I. xi. 171 Europe could scarce amass the symptom of a fleet. **1821** Scott *Kenilw.* xxviii, He.. attempted to pass him.. without any symptom of recognition. **1873** Tristram *Moab* vii. 27 Scarce a symptom of spring could as yet be seen.

¶ Misused for or confused with *symbol.* (Cf. symptomatic ¶.)

a **1687** Cotton *Poems, On Lord Derby* 32 Those Judges.. Who, in the symptomes of thy ruin drest, Pronounc't thy Sentence.

Hence ˈ**symptom** *v. trans. rare*$^{-1}$, to indicate as by a symptom; *loosely,* to symbolize.

1648 Earl of Westmorland *Otia Sacra* (1879) 65 To dwell with Dust and Clay, Which Symptome may Mans Low condition.

†**symptomates**, *sb. pl. Obs. rare.* [ad. F. *symptomates* (Rabelais) or ad. L. *symptōmata,* pl. of *symptōma* symptom.] Symptoms.

1590 Barrough *Meth. Phisick* v. ii. (1639) 255 The symptomates or accidents which are commonly incident to these tumors.

symptomatic (sɪmptəˈmætɪk), *a.* (*sb.*) [ad. F. *symptomatique* or late L. *symptōmaticus* (cf. Gr. συμπτωματικός exposed to chance), f. *symptōmat-, symptōma* symptom: see -ic.]

1. *Path.* Of the nature of, or constituting, a symptom of disease; *spec.* applied to a secondary disease or morbid state arising from and accompanying a primary one (opp. to *idiopathic*).

1698 FLOYER *Asthma* iii. (1717) 110, I shall next describe those Symptomatic Asthma's, which succeed Cephalic Diseases. **1710** T. FULLER *Pharm. Extemp.* 64 Fevers.. accompanied with a Symptomatic Flux of the Belly. **1742** FIELDING *J. Andrews* I. xiii, If his fever should prove more than symptomatic, it would be impossible to save him. **1802** GOUV. MORRIS in Sparks *Life & Writ.* (1832) III. 166 This will give what doctors call a symptomatic indication. **1822-7** GOOD *Study Med.* (1829) IV. 245 This..is..sometimes denominated symptomatic amaurosis, being the mere effect of another disease, which is the primary one. **1834** J. FORBES *Laennec's Dis. Chest* (ed. 4) 451 The symptomatic dropsy may accompany almost every disease. **1877** F. T. ROBERTS *Handbk. Med.* (ed. 3) I. 296 Symptomatic Parotitis differs from the idiopathic form in its great tendency to end in suppuration.

b. Const. *of*.

1814 L. HUNT *Feast Poets* Notes (1815) 100 Symptomatic of a weak state of stomach. **1831** SCOTT *Cast. Dang.* x, A species of dotage of the mind, which is sometimes found concomitant with and symptomatic of this disorder. **1874** CARPENTER *Mental Phys.* I. iv. (1879) 156 The flashes of light which are symptomatic of disease of the Retina or of the Optic nerve.

2. Relating to or concerned with symptoms.

1767 S. PATERSON *Another Trav.* I. 321 The symptomatic art..the learned faculty of medicine have an undoubted right to. **1843** R. J. GRAVES *Syst. Clin. Med.* ix. 101 The mere symptomatic practitioner would be unable to acquire anything more than a loose and undefined notion. *Ibid.* 758 [Epilepsy] received from our ancestors the apt symptomatic name of the 'falling-evil' or 'falling-sickness'.

3. *gen.* That is a symptom of something; accompanying and indicating some condition, quality, etc.; characteristic and indicative *of*.

1751 SMOLLETT *Per. Pickle* (1779) IV. xc. 84 The friendship..had of late suffered several symptomatic shocks. **1803** *Edin. Rev.* Jan. 497 Symptomatic of rather a rancourous spirit of controversy. **1837** HALLAM *Lit. Eur.* I. I. i. §80 He shows..a regard to profane literature, unusual in the darker ages, and symptomatic of a more liberal taste. **1847** J. MARTINEAU *Chr. Life* (1867) 326 The symptomatic smoke has puffed up from the social volcano. **1878** C. J. VAUGHAN *Earnest Words* 120 All that remains is symptomatic—this is essential.

¶ Misused for or confused with *symbolic* or *emblematic*. (Cf. SYMPTOM ¶.)

1852 DICKENS *Bleak Ho.* xlviii, With ashes (or hair-powder) on their heads, symptomatic of their great humility. **1881** *Manch. Guard.* 27 Jan., [He] referred to the right hon. gentleman's red stockings as being 'symptomatic of the seas of gore' through which the Government meant to wade in Ireland.

B. *sb.* in *pl.* **symptomatics** (sɪmptə'mætɪks) = SYMPTOMATOLOGY.

1748 SMOLLETT *Rod. Random* xvi. (1804) 315 Wagtail.. harangued upon prognostics, diagnostics, symptomatics. **1830-2** CARLETON *Traits* (1842) I. 135 The differential symptomatics between a Party Fight..and one between two Roman Catholic Factions.

symptomatical (sɪmptə'mætɪkəl), *a.* Now *rare* or *Obs.* [Formed as prec.: see -ICAL.]

1. *Path.* = prec. 1.

1586 BRIGHT *Melanch.* xvi. 89 In simptomaticall euents in sicknes. **1625** HART *Anat. Ur.* I. iii. 33 Whether the feaver be primarie, or a principall guest, or symptomaticall, accompanying the disease as the shadow doth the bodie. **1663** BOYLE *Usef. Exp. Nat. Philos.* II. v. xx. 295 In (not, Symptomatical, but) Essential Feavers. **1702** C. MATHER *Magn. Chr.* III. II. v. (1852) 386 He fell into a quinsie, with a symptomatical fever. **1748** R. JAMES *Fevers* (1749) 5 Sweats, which are not spontaneous, but extorted, generally prove symptomatical and noxious, instead of being critical and salutary. *a* **1776** *Ibid.* (1778) 65 Other evacuations.., as they only arise from the symptoms, or from the agonies of nature, unequal to the task of surmounting the difficulties she is oppressed with..are called symptomatical.

2. *gen.* = prec. 3.

1628 JACKSON *Creed* VI. I. i. §2 The more right resemblances we make to ourselves of any thing, the greater will be the symptomatical impression of the latent truth. **1742** RICHARDSON *Pamela* (1785) III. xl. 387, I dare say, your Thoughtfulness is but symptomatical, and will go off, in proper Time. **1816** SCOTT *Antiq.* xiv, Visions..very symptomatical of poetic fury.

symptomatically (sɪmptə'mætɪkəlɪ), *adv.* [f. prec. + -LY²; see -ICALLY.] In a symptomatic manner; in the way of, or as, a symptom (formerly often opp. to *critically*); in relation to symptoms.

1615 CROOKE *Body of Man* 416 It is one thing for a thing to be done critically, and another thing to be done symptomatically; one thing to be done by force & contention of Nature, another by the force and contumacy of the malady. **1655** CULPEPPER, etc. *Riverius* VI. iv. 135 Somtimes abundance of Blood flows from the Gums, either Critically, or Symptomatically. **1713** SPREGNELL in *Phil. Trans.* XXVIII. 130 If the Hæmorrhages had happened critically, and not symptomatically. **1742** RICHARDSON *Pamela* (1785) III. xli. 391 A Train of Thinking which sometimes I get into ..; I hope, only symptomatically, as you say. **1822-7** GOOD *Study Med.* (1829) I. 410 The disease [*sc.* jaundice] is also found symptomatically in pregnancy, colic, and fevers of various kinds. **1876** BARTHOLOW *Mat. Med.* (1879) 492 When a poisonous dose has been taken the stomach should be emptied, and the systemic efforts should be treated symptomatically. **1898** P. MANSON *Trop. Diseases* xviii. 291 Gangrenous dysentery is symptomatically but an aggravated form of acute ulcerative dysentery.

So **sympto'maticalness** *rare*⁻⁰.

1727 BAILEY vol. II, *Symptomaticalness*..being attended with Symptoms.

symptomatize ('sɪmptəmətaɪz), *v.* [f. Gr. συμπτωματ-, σύμπτωμα SYMPTOM + -IZE.] *trans.* To be a symptom of; to characterize or indicate as a symptom.

1794 COLERIDGE *Lett., to Southey* (1895) 81, I think of her ..with unspeakable tenderness, with that inward melting away of soul that symptomatizes it. **1817** —— *Biog. Lit.* x. (1907) I. 131 The exhaustion had produced a cold fit of the ague which was symptomatized by indifference among the many, and a tendency to infidelity or scepticism in the educated classes. **1875** *Encycl. Brit.* II. 171/1 Amnesic aphasia is symptomatised very variously. **1880** *Ibid.* XIII. 109/1 Senile insanity is symptomatized by dementia with frequent intercurrent attacks of mania.

symptomatography (ˌsɪmptəmə'tɒgrəfɪ). *rare*⁻⁰. [ad. mod.L. *symptōmatographia*, f. *symptōmat-*, *symptōma* SYMPTOM + *-graphia* -GRAPHY.] The, or a, description of symptoms.

1736 BAILEY (folio) Pref., *Symptomatography*..a Discourse or Treatise of the various Accidents common to animal Bodies. **1859** MAYNE *Expos. Lex.*, *Symptomatographia*..term for a description of the signs or symptoms of disease: symptomatography.

symptomatology (ˌsɪmptəmə'tɒlədʒɪ). [ad. mod.L. *symptōmatologia*, f. *symptōmat-*, *symptōma* SYMPTOM + *-logia* -LOGY.]

1. The study of symptoms; that branch of pathology which treats of the symptoms of disease; also, a discourse or treatise on symptoms.

1804 *Med. Jrnl.* XII. 564 An abridged Physiology, Pathology, and Sym[p]tomatology. **1822-7** GOOD *Study Med.* (1829) I. 633 Definitions..founded upon a principle of symptomatology rather than of etiology. **1831** J. F. SOUTH tr. *Otto's Pathol. Anat.* 1 So intimately..is pathological anatomy connected with pathology, symptomatology, and surgery. **1869** TANNER *Clin. Med.* (ed. 2) 98 Without a correct knowledge of symptomatology or semeiology—the science which treats of the symptoms and signs of disease—we can know but little of the art of medicine.

2. *transf.* The symptoms of a disease collectively (as a subject of study).

1798 in *Spirit Publ. Jrnls.* (1799) II. 185 To attend the more particularly to the *symptomatologia*, or symptomatology of the disease. **1876** BARTHOLOW *Mat. Med.* (1879) 129 Some cases of acute arsenical poisoning are not distinguishable by their symptomatology or morbid anatomy from cases of epidemic cholera.

So **symptomatological** (ˌsɪmptəmətə'lɒdʒɪkəl) *a.*, pertaining or relating to symptomatology (whence **ˌsymptomato'logically** *adv.*); **symptomatologist** (ˌsɪmptəmə'tɒlədʒɪst), one versed in symptomatology; one who studies or treats of the symptoms of disease.

1843 R. J. GRAVES *Syst. Clin. Med.* xi. 122, I would defy the most accurate symptomatologist to point out any marked distinction. **1859** SEMPLE *Diphtheria* 316 If we glance at the symptomatological picture of Diphtherite. **1876** tr. *Wagner's Gen. Pathol.* (ed. 6) 16 We to-day employ the word crisis rather in a symptomatological way, as an expression for certain appearances. **1889** *Lancet* 12 Jan. 101/1 Alcoholism..exercises on the organism effects manifesting themselves symptomatologically by the diminution of vitality.

†**symp'tomical**, *a. Obs. rare.* [f. SYMPTOM + -ICAL.] = SYMPTOMATIC 1.

1656 J. SMITH *Pract. Physick* 85 If it be symptomical, it must be cured as before. **1676** *Phil. Trans.* XI. 570 A Feaver .., to which the Dysentery and Diarrhœa were only symptomical, not essential.

symptomize ('sɪmptəmaɪz), *v.* [f. as prec. + -IZE; cf. *symbolize*.] *trans.* = SYMPTOMATIZE.

1884 J. TAIT *Mind in Matter* IV. 180 Demoniacal possession..was symptomised by superhuman manifestations. **1908** *Westm. Gaz.* 26 Oct. 8/1 This work symptomises a spirit new in Great Britain's municipal bodies.

symptomless ('sɪmptəmlɪs), *a.* [f. as prec. + -LESS.] Destitute of symptoms; exhibiting no symptoms.

1886 *Brit. Med. Jrnl.* 3 July 9/1 A case of stenosis of the pulmonary artery which was symptomless till the ninth or tenth year. **1889** J. M. DUNCAN *Clin. Lect. Dis. Wom.* xviii. (ed. 4) 140 A limited and otherwise symptomless vaginitis.. may bleed alarmingly.

sympto'mology, shortened form of SYMPTOMATOLOGY.

1868 *Lond. Rev.* 22 Aug. 246/2 The symptomology of brain-disease..Dr. Winslow has been the first to map out. **1913** SIR T. BARLOW in *Times* 7 Aug. 8/2 The ambiguous symptomology which clinical observation reveals.

symtom, -tome, obs. ff. SYMPTOM.

symunt, obs. form of CEMENT.

symylacre, -aker, obs. ff. SIMULACRE.

syn: see SAINT, SIN, SINE¹, SUN.

syn-¹ (sɪn). Latinized form of Gr. συν- (= σύν prep. with), together, similarly, alike, occurring in many modern scientific terms, the more recent or less important of which are collected in this article.

It undergoes assimilation before consonants, before *l* to *syl-*, e.g. SYLLABLE, συλλαβή, SYLLEPSIS, σύλληψις, before labials to SYM- (q.v.), before simple *s* to *sys-*, e.g. SYSSARCOSIS, συσσάρκωσις; before *s* + consonant and *z* it is reduced to *sy-*, e.g. SYSTEM, σύστημα, SYZYGY, συζυγία. The assimilation of (n) to (ŋ) before velars, denoted by γ in Gr., is not represented graphically in L. and Eng., e.g. συγκοπή SYNCOPE.

sy'nacmic *a. Bot.* [Gr. ἀκμή point, culmination, ACME], having the stamens and pistils ripening at the same time; so **sy'nacmy**, simultaneous ripening of the stamens and pistils of a flower (opp. to *heteracmy*); **synadelphic** (-ə'dɛlfɪk) *a. Zool.* [Gr. ἀδελφός brother] (see quot.); ‖**sy'nalgia** *Path.* [Gr. ἄλγος pain; cf. συναλγεῖν to sympathize], sympathetic pain in one part caused by injury in another; so **sy'nalgic** *a.*, of the nature of or affected with synalgia (Dorland); ‖**synandrium** (sɪ'nændrɪəm), **sy'nandry** *Bot.* [Gr. ἀνδρ-, ἀνήρ man, taken as = 'male organ, stamen'], abnormal union of stamens; ‖**synanthema** (-æn'θiːmə) *Path.* (pl. **-mata**) [mod.L., after EXANTHEMA] (see quots.); **synan'thropic** *a.* [ANTHROPIC *a.*], living in habitats made or altered by man; **sy'napomorphy** *Taxonomy* [f. *apomorphy*, f. APO- + Gr. μορφή form], the possession by two organisms of some character (not necessarily the same in each) that is derived from one character in an organism from which they both evolved; also = next; so **sy'napomorph**, any such derived character; **synaposematic** (-næpəʊsɪ'mætɪk) *a. Biol.* [Gr. ἀπό away from, σηματ-, σῆμα mark], applied to different organisms having common warning colours or other characteristics; hence **synapose'maticism, -'sematism**, synaposematic character; **syn'centric** *a. rare*⁻⁰, concentric (Blount *Glossogr.* 1656); ‖**syncerebrum** (-'sɛrɪbrəm) *Zool.* (pl. **-a**) [L. *cerebrum* brain], a term for the compound 'brain' of an insect; hence **syn'cerebral** *a.*, pertaining to a syncerebrum; **syncladous** ('sɪnklədəs) *a. Bot.* [Gr. κλάδος shoot] (see quot.); **syncotyledonous** (-kɒtɪ'liːdənəs) *a. Bot.*, having the cotyledons united; **syncracy** ('sɪnkrəsɪ) *Polit.* [-CRACY] (see quot.); **syncraniate** (-'kreɪnɪət) *a. Zool.* [CRANIUM], applied to that type of skull which includes certain vertebral elements, as in the higher vertebrates; **syncryptic** (-'krɪptɪk) *a. Biol.* [CRYPTIC], applied to the resemblance between different organisms (esp. insects) having common protective coloration by which they are concealed from attack; **syncya'nosis** *Bot.* (pl. **-'oses**) [ad. G. *syncyanose* (A. Pascher 1914, in *Ber. d. Deutsch. Bot. Ges.* XXXII. 340)], the relationship between a unicellular blue-green alga and a host within which it lives symbiotically; also *concr.*, the organisms themselves; **syndiag'nostic** *a. Biol.* [DIAGNOSTIC] (see quot.); **sy'nechthran** *Ent.*, an insect that lives with ants or other social insects as an unwelcome guest in a relationship of synechthry; **synechthry** (-'nɛkθrɪ), erron. **-ecthry**, *Entom.* [ad. G. *synechthrie* (M. E. Wasmann 1896, in *3ème Congr. Internat. Zool.* 412), f. Gr. ἐχθρός hostile], term proposed by Wasmann for the hostile relation between ants and certain other insects which maintain themselves in the ant-colonies as unwelcome guests; hostile commensalism (opp. to *symphily*); ‖**synema** (sɪ'niːmə) *Bot.* [mod.L., erron. for **synnema*, f. Gr. νῆμα thread, filament], a column of united stamen-filaments, as in Orchids, *Malvaceæ*, etc.; **synencephalocele** (-ɛn'sɛfələsiːl) *Path.* (see quot.); **synepigonic** (-ɛpɪ'gɒnɪk) *a. Biol.* [Gr. ἐπίγονος descendant], descended from a common ancestor or ancestors; **synethnic** (-'ɛθnɪk) *a.* [Gr. ἔθνος nation], belonging to the same nation; **'synform** *Geol.*, a fold that is concave upwards, irrespective of the chronological sequence of the strata; cf. SYNCLINE; **synhar'monic** *Math.*, *a.* having a common harmonic relation; *sb.* a locus synharmonic with another (also **synhar'monical**): see quots.; ‖**synkaryon** (-'kærɪɒn) *Biol.* (pl. **-a**) [Gr. κάρυον nut, taken as = nucleus], a pair of nuclei, or a nucleus produced by the fusion of two nuclei, as in fertilization, esp. in certain fungi; hence **synkaryophyte** (-'kærɪəfaɪt) [Gr. φυτόν plant], that stage in the development of a fungus at which synkarya are formed; **synkine'matic** *a. Geol.*, formed or occurring when moving or as an accompaniment to motion; ‖**synkinesis** (-kaɪ'niːsɪs) *Physiol.* [Gr. κίνησις movement], associated movement, esp. reflex muscular movement; so **synkinetic** (-kaɪ'nɛtɪk) *a.*

[KINETIC], pertaining to or of the nature of synkinesis; **syn'neusis** *Petrol.* [Gr. νεῦσις swimming], the clustering together of crystals of a mineral in a rock; freq. *attrib.* in ***synneusis texture***; **synnomic** (-'nɒmɪk) *a. Anthropol.* [Gr. νόμος custom, law] (see quot.); **sy'nocreate** (erron. **-och-**) *a. Bot.*, applied to stipules which unite into a sheath inclosing the stem (Balfour *Man. Bot.*, 1849, §160); **synœkete** (sɪ'niːkiːt) *Ent.* [ad. Gr. συνοικέτης house-fellow, f. συνοικεῖν to live together (f. οἶκος house): cf. G. *synœkie* (M. E. Wasmann 1896, in *3ème Congr. Internat. Zool.* 412)], an insect that lives with ants or other social insects without either benefiting or harming them; **synorchism** (-'ɔːkɪz(ə)m) [Gr. ὄρχις testicle], union or fusion of the testicles; **synoro'genic** *a. Geol.* [cf. G. *synorogenese* sb. (H. Stille *Grundfragen d. vergleichenden Tektonik* (1924) 16)], formed or occurring during a period of orogenesis; **synortho'graphic** *a.*, having the same orthography, spelt alike; **synotic** (sɪ'nɒtɪk) *a.* [Gr. ὠτ-, οὖς ear], characterized by union or fusion of the ears in the middle line of the head; **syn'pelmous**, **syn'petalous** *adjs.*, bad forms of *sympelmous*, *-petalous* (see SYM-); **syn'presbyter**, bad form of *sympresbyter* (see SYM-); ‖**synsacrum** (-'seɪkrəm) *Anat.* [mod.L., f. SACRUM], the composite sacrum, consisting of a number of vertebræ united, in birds and some extinct reptiles; hence **syn'sacral** *a.*, pertaining to the synsacrum; ˌ**synsedi'mentary** *a. Geol.*, formed or occurring at the time of deposition of (the) sediment; **synsepalous** (-'sɛpələs) *a. Bot.*, having the sepals united, gamosepalous; **synspermy** (-'spɜːmɪ) *Bot.* [Gr. σπέρμα seed], abnormal fusion of two or more seeds; so **syn'spermous** *a.*, characterized by synspermy; **syntechnic** (-'tɛknɪk) *a. Biol.* [Gr. τέχνη art, craft], applied to a resemblance between organisms arising from similarity of function; ˌ**syntec'tonic** *a. Geol.*, formed or occurring during a period of tectonic activity; hence **syntec'tonically** *adv.*; **syntelic** (-'tɛlɪk) *a. Anthropol.* [Gr. τέλος end] (see quot. for *synnomic*); '**synteny** *Genetics* [Gr. ταινία band, ribbon], the condition (of genes) of being on the same chromosome; hence **syn'tenic** *a.*; **syntepalous** (-'tɛpələs) *a. Bot.* [see TEPAL], having the tepals united; **synthermal** (-'θɜːməl) [Gr. θερμός heat], *a.* having the same temperature; *sb.* an isotherm connecting places having the same temperature at the same moment of time; **syntoxoid** (-'tɒksɔɪd), a toxoid having the same degree of affinity for the antitoxin as the toxin from which it is derived.

1870 A. W. BENNETT in *Jrnl. Bot.* Oct. 316 In *synacmic plants.. the period of maturity of one organ may frequently exceed in length that of the other, so as to render cross-fertilization easy. **1883** *Science* I. 432/2 In no small number of instances.. the plant is strongly protogynous, while it is sometimes synacmic. **1870** A. W. BENNETT in *Jrnl. Bot.* Oct. 318 *Synacmy, or the contemporaneous maturing of the reproductive organs, is nearly as frequent as protandry. **1887** HARRISON ALLEN in *Science* 11 Mar. 232/2 The action of both wings and feet, since both pairs act together, is what I propose to call *synadelphic. **1890** BILLINGS *Med. Dict.*, **Synalgia*, associated or sympathetic pain. **1897** WILLIS *Flowering Plants* I. 76 Sometimes the union is so complete as to include the anthers, and a *synandrium is formed. **1900** B. D. JACKSON *Gloss. Bot. Terms*, **Synandry*, Morren's term where stamens normally separated are soldered or united. **1899** *Allbutt's Syst. Med.* VIII. 461 The elemental forms present he [*sc.* Auspitz] designated as *anthemata* and the various secondary and later groupings which go to make up the whole *exanthem* as **synanthemata*. **1901** DORLAND *Med. Dict.* (ed. 2), *Synanthema*.., a local eruption consisting of a group of papules. **1936** *Discovery* Mar. 89/2 There can be no question of post-glacial colonisation of Iceland by other than *synanthropic insects. **1971** *Countryman* Summer 187/1 This is probably a yellow slug, *Limax flavus*, a synanthropic species, which lives in and around houses, cellars and old garden walls. **1969** E. MAYR *Princ. Systematic Zool.* x. 202 Derived characters (*synapomorphs of Hennig) shared with a more recent ancestor. **1966** DAVIS & ZANGERL tr. *Hennig's Phylogenetic Systematics* ii. 90 It makes no difference whether the *synapomorphy consists in the fact that an apomorphous character (a′) is present identically in all species..or whether it is present in different derived conditions (a′ and a″). **1979** *Nature* 18 Jan. 176/1 This inference is drawn from the fact that lungfish and cows share derived characters (synapomorphies such as internal nostrils, an epiglottis, a two-chambered auricle and so on..) not found in salmon. **1898** POULTON *Ess. Evolution* (1908) 223 Müllerian Resemblance is not true Mimicry at all, but rather an example of Common Warning Colour,.. the term *Synaposematic was proposed as descriptive of it. **1907** *Nature* 31 Oct. 676/2 As a further illustration of ..'*synaposematism', or the adoption of a common warning badge on the part of distasteful forms, we may take the wonderfully diverse assemblage that centres round the conspicuous and distasteful beetles belonging to the genus Lycus. **1881** E. R. LANKESTER *Stud. Apus*, etc. 32 We distinguish the original ganglion pair of the præstomial region as the archi-cerebrum—it is well to designate by a distinct term the composite ganglion, which may result from the fusion with it of other ganglia—it may be called a *syncerebrum. **1863** M. J. BERKELEY *Brit. Mosses* Gloss. 313 **Syncladous*, used when branchlets grow in tufts from the same point. **1898** *Syd. Soc. Lex.*, **Syncotyledonous*, having its cotyledons joined together. **1861** AUSTIN *Jurispr.* (ed. 2) Note 331 *Syncracy: wherein the executive powers reside in the sovereign one or number; but the legislative powers, in the sovereign one or number, with the active (as distinguished from the passive) portion of the subject citizens. **1902** G. B. HOWES in *Smithsonian Rep.* (1903) 591, I have..proposed to discriminate between the series of terrestrial vertebrates as archæcraniate and *syncraniate... The costal sternum, like the syncraniate skull, is distinctive of the Amniota alone. **1901** *Trans. Entomol. Soc.* 375 Mr. Beddard quotes this..as one of his cases of apparently useless mimicry, but it may be an example of *syncryptic resemblance. **1945** F. E. FRITSCH *Structure & Reproduction of Algae* II. 878 A different relation is seen in the association of certain Myxophyceae of small dimensions with Monads or Bacteria (*syncyanoses of Pascher). **1967** *Jrnl. Phycol.* III. 37/2 *Cyanophora* is one of the few forms among the syncyanoses thus far found which has been thoroughly studied. **1978** *Bio Systems* X. 74/2 Lee suggested that members of the group originated from the union of a non-photosynthetic cryptomonad stock with cyanobacteria, resulting in an early 'syncyanosis' similar to that seen in *Cyanophora paradoxa* today. **1904** POULTON *Ess. Evolution* (1908) 60 Forms having certain structural characters in common distinguishing them from the forms of other groups. Groups thus defined by the Linnaean method of Diagnosis may be conveniently called **Syndiagnostic*. **1910** W. WHEELER *Ants* xxi. 382 In the United States *Megastilicus formicarius*.., which is not uncommon in the large mound nests of *Formica exsectoides*, is..a typical *synechthran. **1967** J. H. SUDD *Introd. Behaviour Ants* vi. 127 Synechthrans are always treated with hostility by the ants and usually they, in turn, prey on the ants. **1899** D. SHARP in *Cambridge Nat. Hist.* VI. 183 '*Synecthry', including those Insects, etc., to which the ants are hostile, but which nevertheless maintain themselves in the midst of their foes. **1859** HENSLOW *Dict. Bot. Terms*, **Synema*, the portion of the Gynostemium corresponding to the position of the combined filaments. **1886** *Buck's Handbk. Med. Sci.* II. 680/2 Encephaloceles arising from abnormal adhesions, or what is technically known as *synencephalocele. **1904** POULTON *Ess. Evolution* (1908) 61 Forms which have been shown..to be descended from common ancestors or from a common parthenogenetic or self-fertilizing ancestor. Such groups may be called *Synepigonic. **1879** *Times* 12 Mar. 4/1 [Dr. Lasker] is, like his *synethnic co-reformer Paul, a man of no great presence. **1937** BAILEY & MCCALLIEN in *Trans. R. Soc. Edin.* LIX. 81 In the following pages: Antiform means a fold that closes upwards. *Synform means a fold that closes downwards. **1978** *Nature* 12 Oct. 539/1 Preserved in a large secondary synform, there occurs a sequence, several hundred metres thick, consisting of ribbon cherts, bedded jasperites, [etc.]. **1850** T. P. KIRKMAN in *Cambr. & Dubl. Math. Jrnl.* V. 102 A..curve ..which..touches the *n* harmonicals (*H*), *synharmonic with *A* in respect of the *n* pairs $(u_e\ v_e)$. *Ibid.* 104 Curves.. which touch alike the three harmonicals..and meet each its synharmonic..at the six angles of the hexagon. *Ibid.* 97 The tangents at the intersection of $p = 0$ and $q = 0$ form with them an harmonic pencil... Let this be denoted by saying that the two branches of [the curve] $R = 0$ are *synharmonicals in respect of [the straight lines] $p = 0$ and $q = 0$. **1904** *Jrnl. R. Microsc. Soc.* Apr. 222 L. Petri..finds the two nuclei (the *synkarion) present in the hyphæ of the trama, as described for other hymenomycetes. **1905** *Brit. Med. Jrnl.* 25 Feb. 442 The male and female nuclei closely combine, forming the synkaryon. **1904** *Jrnl. R. Microsc. Soc.* Feb. 94 That phase in the life-history, the *synkaryophyte, which plays so important a part in the development in the Basidiomycetes. **1932** *Mineral. und Petrogr. Mitt.* XLII. 475 The older Archaean granites of Fennoscandia..belong to characteristically *synkinematic intrusive complexes from an early stage of an orogenic cycle. **1952** T. F. W. BARTH *Theoret. Petrol.* III. 243 Synkinematic granitization is probably responsible for the majority of the large granodiorite and granite batholiths. **1973** J. T. RENOUF tr. *Didier's Granites & their Enclaves* 7 The orogenic granites are classically divided into synkinematic (= synorogenic or syntectonic) and post-tectonic types. **1881** J. ROSS *Treat. Dis. Nervous Syst.* I. v. I. 162 **Synkinesis*. Under this term are generally included certain involuntary movements of paralysed parts; but I shall extend the meaning of the word so as to include also certain motor anomalies which occur in muscles subject to spasm. **1883** ARTHUR *Fernley Lect.* 160 Carpo-genethlic synkinesis of the sexes with other phenomena of the botanic hierarchy. **1901** DORLAND *Med. Dict.* (ed. 2), **Synkinetic*, pertaining to or of the nature of synkinesis. **1921** J. H. L. VOGT in *Jrnl. Geol.* XXIX. 321 The individuals of a mineral, segregated from a magma at an early stage, frequently swam together to assemblings or aggregates, the result of which is a structure, for which I propose the term together-swimming structure or *synneusis structure. **1959** W. W. MOORHOUSE *Study of Rocks in Thin Section* xi. 241 Probably related to the banded character of the basic complexes is a texture, sometimes called 'synneusis' texture, in which the dark minerals..tend to occur as lenticular clumps or aggregates. **1967** *Amer. Mineralogist* LII. 529 The preferential character of synneusis for several common individual minerals and mineral pairs. **1973** J. T. RENOUF tr. *Didier's Granites & their Enclaves* xiv. 368 When two rocks contain the same volumetric percentage of phenocrysts, synneusis is greatest in that with the smaller crystals and thus with the greatest number. **1911** MARETT *Anthropol.* ix. 236 Let us assume, then, that there are two main stages in the historical evolution of society... I propose to term them the *synnomic and the syntelic phases of society. 'Synnomic' (from the Greek *nomos*, custom) means that customs are shared. 'Syntelic' (from the Greek *telos*, end) means that ends are shared. The synnomic phase is, from the psychological point of view, a kingdom of habit; the syntelic phase is a kingdom of reflection. **1910** W. WHEELER *Ants* xxi. 381 The symphiles represent the élite,..and number hardly more than 300 to 400 species, whereas the *synœketes are much more numerous. **1971** E. O. WILSON *Insect Societies* (1972) xx. 390/2 Most of the time..the *Cremastocheilus* have the status of synoeketes, that is, they are simply ignored and allowed to wander through the nest without interference. **1898** *Syd. Soc. Lex.*, *Synorchism. **1936** *Bull Amer. Assoc. Petroleum Geologists* XX. 853 *Synorogenic movements dating from this time are to be recognized everywhere in this continent. **1971** I. G. GASS et al. *Understanding Earth* xx. 292/1 The synorogenic sediments that accompany mountain building. **1974** *Nature* 4 Oct. 382/2 In Africa the Kibaran belt experienced major tectonism about 1,300 Myr BP.. with the subparallel Irumide belt undergoing synorogenic events about 1,100 Myr ago. **1786** PINKERTON *Anc. Sc. Poems* I. p. cxliii, *Synorthographic and Symphonious Words. **1894** W. BATESON *Study of Variation* xviii. 458 The ears of vertebrates..in the *synotic or cephalotic condition are compounded in the middle line to a varying degree. **1903** *Proc. Zool. Soc.* 17 Mar. 282 The pelvis of the Musophagi.., its breadth is due..to the great length of the *synsacral transverse processes. *Ibid.* 273 The most complete *synsacrum is that of *Coua*, and is made up as follows:—1 thoracic, 3 lumbar, 3 lumbo-sacral, 2 sacral, and 4 caudal [vertebræ]. **1960** *Gloss. Geol.* (Amer. Geol. Inst.) (ed. 2) Suppl. 65/1 *Synsedimentary. **1976** *Jrnl. Geol. Soc.* CXXXII. 124 In sheet III the lower contact is a sharp, curved slide plane with occasional synsedimentary striations. **1979** *Nature* 9 Aug. 483/2 This sealing apparently results from a synsedimentary permineralisation caused by colloidal silica. **1847** W. E. STEELE *Field Bot.* p. xxii, Cal[yx] *synsepalous, coloured. Primuleæ. **1900** B. D. JACKSON *Gloss. Bot. Terms*, *Synspermous. **1869** M. T. MASTERS *Veget. Teratol.* 50 *Synspermy, or Union of the Seeds. **1902** POULTON in *Encycl. Brit.* XXVII. 147/1 Resemblances..incidentally caused by functional adaptation, such as the mole-like forms produced in the burrowing Insectivora [etc.]... Such likeness may be called *Syntechnic Resemblance. **1942** M. P. BILLINGS *Structural Geol.* xv. 297 *Syntectonic intrusives are always forcefully injected bodies, because the magma was moving under the influence of orogenic pressures. **1974** *Nature* 22 Mar. 325/2 In coastal Liberia the geological evidence of actual faulting that could definitely be said to be syntectonic with rifting is lacking. **1956** L. V. DE SITTER *Structural Geol.* xxvi. 392 The *syntectonically metamorphosed mica-schists and migmatites. **1979** *Nature* 25 Jan. 290/1 A phase of upright asymmetric folding..with the steep limbs overturned to the north-west took place syntectonically with major brittle thrusting..of all units. **1911** MARETT *Anthropol.* ix. 236 *Syntelic [see *synnomic*]. *Ibid.* 237 That independence of character which is the prime condition of syntelic society. **1971** J. H. RENWICK in *Ann. Human Genetics* XXXV. 80 If the inversion and a marker locus studied in the pedigree are *syntenic (lying on the same chromosome pair), the marker may be on either side of either breakpoint and the linkage..to one of them may be close and may have a good chance of being detected. **1978** *Nature* 13 July 161/1 Five genes in the mouse..are syntenic and their human homologues have been assigned to human chromosome 1. **1971** J. H. RENWICK in *Ann. Human Genetics* XXXV. 83 The prior probability of the hypothesis of *synteny—i.e. that the autosomal marker locus is somewhere on the chromosome pair that bears the inversion —is A/T. **1974** *Sci. Amer.* July 39/1 Assaying a number of clones for various human enzymes therefore provides information on the synteny of genes. **1900** B. D. JACKSON *Gloss. Bot. Terms*, **Syntepalous*, the tepals united. **1839** G. ROBERTS *Dict. Geol.*, **Synthermal*.., having the same degree of heat. Applied to the exterior and interior of the earth, which..are not synthermal, but differ greatly in temperature. **1901** DORLAND *Med. Dict.* (ed. 2), *Syntoxoid. **1903** [see TOXOID].

2. *Chem.* Designating geometrical isomers of organic compounds containing C=N or N=N in which the principal atoms or groups attached to the doubly bonded atoms are on the same side of the plane of the double bond; usu. italicized. Also without hyphen as an independent word. [Introduced in Ger. by A. Hantzsch 1894, in *Ber. Deut. Chem. Ges.* XXVII. 1702.]

1894 *Jrnl. Chem. Soc.* LXVI. I. 454 Such diazo-compounds as exist in the form of rings, due to the formation of inner anhydrides..must be syn-compounds. **1913** T. H. POPE tr. *Molinari's Treat. Gen. & Industr. Org. Chem.* 568 It forms a mixture of phenyldiazonium hydroxide..and syn-diazobenzene hydroxide. **1938** R. L. SHRINER et al. in H. Gilman *Org. Chem.* I. iii. 385 The amine oxide structure does not aid in accounting for the *syn* and *anti* forms of these oximes, but is necessary to account for the tautomerism of these isomers. **1978** *Nature* 9 Feb. 494/2 The intense sweetness of the *a-syn*-oxime of perillartine was first reported in 1920.

syn-[2] (sɪn). Comb. form of SYNTHETIC *a.*, used to form words denoting synthetic products, as '**syncrude**, a synthetic product made from coal in imitation of crude oil; also as *adj.*; '**synfuel**, any fuel made from coal, oil shale, or the like as a substitute for a petroleum product; '**syngas**, a mixture of carbon monoxide and hydrogen, esp. when produced from coal; '**synjet**, jet fuel derived from synthetic crude oil (syncrude); '**synoil**, synthetic oil; '**synroc** [ROC(K *sb.*[1]], any of various synthetic crystalline materials composed chiefly of oxides of metals and semimetals and devised as sufficiently stable to contain radioactive waste in solid solution deep underground.

1971 *Kirk-Othmer Encycl. Chem. Technol.* (ed. 2) Suppl. 189 Both oils are subsequently hydrotreated to produce a syncrude oil. **1976** *Times* 9 Dec. 27 Looking at the alternative power sources for private transport, the survey reckons that the most likely ones are a synthetic liquid fuel (such as methanol or syncrude) derived from coal, or electricity stored in batteries. **1980** *McGraw-Hill Yearbk. Sci. & Technol.* 303/2 Salable by-products of ammonia, sulfur, and phenols are produced by several of the SNG and syncrude processes. **1976** *Dallas Morning News* 22 Sept. 2-D/3 Whatever has happened to all the synthetic fuel we were supposed to get to ease the oil and gas shortage? Now, three years later, we've still done very little towards the development of 'synfuels'. **1980** *Science* 16 May 740 Certain processes for developing some U.S. oil shales may generate more CO_2 per unit of usable energy produced than any other synfuel development. **1982** *Sunday Times* 9 May 54/6 Multi-billion investment—the basic fee to gain entry to the synfuels game—cannot be justified. **1975** *N.Y. Times* 24 Mar. 20/2 Much of the Western coal has been planned for conversion at the mine to synthetic pipeline gas... The 'syn-gas' is to replace natural gas from wells, the fuel that is expected to be in the most critical depletion by 1985. **1980** *Prospects for Petrochemicals in W. Europe* (Shell Internat. Petroleum Co.) 8 By the middle of next century it is possible that the petrochemical industry could even be sustained very largely, if not entirely, on syngas and methanol derived from coal and methane. **1983** *New Scientist* 28 Apr. 207/2 Syn-gas is also made from natural gas..by the related reaction $CH_4 + H_2O = CO + 3H_2$. **1979** *Ibid.* 7 June 818 In the long term, the choice must be between jet fuel derived from synthetic crude (synjet) or a wholly new type of fuel. **1980** *Times* 21 Feb. 20/4 The quick and easy solution, which is 'synjet'—kerosene made from coal, shale or tarsands. **1976** *Time* 1 Mar. 47 So far several plants have been..designed to turn 2,700 tons of high-sulfur Illinois coal into 22 million cu. ft. of 'syngas' and 3,000 bbl. of 'synoil' each day. **1978** *Nature* 3 Aug. 413/1 Whereas glassified waste may devitrify when exposed to ground water at high temperature and pressure, thus exposing a large surface area for the dissolution of the radionuclides in the glass, the new mineral —'synroc'—should be as stable as a natural rock. **1980** *New Scientist* 3 July 9/2 In the Synroc process the radioactive wastes are trapped in the crystal lattices of the minerals of the synthetic rocks and so are completely immobilised. **1982** *Nature* 9 Dec. 470/3 The plant..will make Synroc-C, which consists of 60 per cent titanium dioxide, with an admixture of barium oxide, calcium oxide, zirconia and alumina.

synadelphite (sɪnə'dɛlfaɪt). *Min.* [ad. G. *synadelphit* (Sjögren, 1884), f. Gr. σύν SYN-[1] + ἀδελφός brother + *-it*, -ITE[1]: so named 'because intimately associated with other related species' (Dana).] An arsenate of manganese and aluminium, with some calcium and magnesium, occurring in black or brownish-black monoclinic crystals.

1892 DANA *Syst. Min.* 801.

‖**synæresis** (sɪ'nɪərɪsɪs). Also **syneresis.** [late L. *synæresis*, a. Gr. συναίρεσις a taking or drawing together, contraction, f. σύν SYN-[1] + αἱρεῖν to take.] **1.** *Gram.* Contraction, esp. of two vowels into a diphthong or a simple vowel.

1577 PEACHAM *Gard. Eloquence* E iij, *Synæresis*, when of two sillables in measuring, there is made but one, as when of this word vertuous, which hath .3. Sillables, we pronounce it with two, thus vertues, and likewyse righteous. **1589** PUTTENHAM *Engl. Poesie* II. xiv. [xv.] (Arb.) 139 Contracting a sillable by vertue of the figure Syneresis. **1657** J. SMITH *Myst. Rhet.* 176 Synæresis..is a contraction of two words or syllables into one. **1712** ADDISON *Spect.* No. 470 ¶5 Observing that *Synæresis* which had been neglected by ignorant Transcribers. **1878** G. CONWAY *Versif.* 89 Syllables which by reason of elision, or synæresis, or slurring,..have..no effect on the metre.

2. *Physical Chem.* The contraction of a gel accompanied by the separating out of liquid.

1864 T. GRAHAM in *Proc. R. Soc.* XIII. 336 In the jelly itself, the specific contraction in question, or synæresis, still proceeds. **1937** *Jrnl. R. Aeronaut. Soc.* XLI. 535 The material in tension might be explained by assuming (in accordance with the phenomenon of syneresis) that the solid portion of the isogel is in a state of contraction relative to the less condensed portions. **1974** *Encycl. Brit. Macropædia* IV. 857/2 A flocculated paste, or suspension of very fine particles, often behaves as a gel... The systems are often thixotropic... They show syneresis.

‖**synæsthesia** (sɪnɪs'θiːsɪə). Pl. **-æ** (-iː). Also **synes-.** [mod.L., f. Gr. σύν SYN-[1] + stem αἰσθε- to feel, perceive, after *anæsthesia*.] **1.** *Psychol.* **a.** A sensation in one part of the body produced by a stimulus applied to another part. **b.** Agreement of the feelings or emotions of different individuals, as a stage in the development of sympathy. **c.** Production, from a sense-impression of one kind, of an associated mental image of a sense-impression of another kind: see quot. 1903.

1891 *Cent. Dict.*, *Synæsthesia*, *synesthesia*, the production of a sensation located in one place when another place is stimulated. **1895** *Amer. Jrnl. Psychol.* VII. 90 The study of the varying forms of persisting abnormal association, usually known as 'colored-hearing' and 'forms', but grouped together by Theodore Flournoy, under the convenient name *Synæsthesia*, has hardly..completed the stage of scientific observation. **1897** tr. *Ribot's Psychol. Emotions* II. iv. 231 If..we try to follow the evolution of sympathy..we distinguish three principal phases. The first, or physiological, consists in an agreement of motor tendencies, a *synergia*; the second, or psychological, consists in an agreement of the emotional states, a *synæsthesia*; the third, or intellectual, results from a community of representations or ideas. **1903** F. W. H. MYERS *Human Personality* I. p. xl, Vestiges of the primitive undifferentiated sensitivity persist in the form of *synæsthesiæ*, e.g. when the hearing of an external sound carries with it, by some arbitrary association of ideas, the seeing of some form or colour. **1935** *Brit. Jrnl. Psychol.* XXV. 31 The most interesting phase of M's synaesthesia is the tendency to see the features of people in different colours. Her acquaintances were not only assigned particular colours, but they were remembered in terms of this colour. **1958** *New Scientist* 6 Feb. 29/3 Synaesthesia is not a commonly reported psychiatric symptom. **1971** *Daily Tel.* 21 Aug. 7/3 Synaesthesia (in his case 'colour-hearing') was observed among his blind patients by an English oculist. **1979** C. PRIEST *Infinite Summer* 40 In the morning my synaesthesia seemed to have receded again.

2. *Lit.* The use of metaphors in which terms relating to one kind of sense-impression are used to describe sense-impressions of other kinds; the production of synæsthetic effect in writing or an instance of this.

[**1901** H. OERTEL *Lect. Study of Lang.* v. 327 The second class of metaphors which ought to receive an exhaustive treatment is the transfer of terms from one sense sphere to the other. These..are illustrated by phrases like 'a sharp tone', 'loud colors'... The phenomenon of synaesthesia has received rather full treatment at the hand of the psychologists, but its reflection on language has not yet received adequate treatment by lexicographers.] **1932** G. STERN in *Göteborgs Högskolas Årsskrift* XXXVIII. I. 323 Synaesthesia is especially common among adjectives..but there are numerous instances of nouns..: *The sound and light of sweeter songs* (Swinburne). **1936** W. B. STANFORD *Gr. Metaphor* 59 Synaesthesia..amongst certain schools of poetry became almost a major element in the technique of sense-expression. **1960** E. H. GOMBRICH *Art & Illusion* x. 366 What is called 'synesthesia', the splashing over of impressions from one sense modality to another is a fact to which all languages testify. **1977** *N.Y. Rev. Bks.* 24 Nov. 11/1 No child who has attempted a list like Whitman's or a synesthesia like Rimbaud's or a colloquy with the sun like Frank O'Hara's is likely to forget the parent-poem. **1978** *Times Lit. Suppl.* 1 Dec. 1406/4 Synaesthesia is a common technique, even a theme, in his work. **1982** *N. & Q.* June 194/2 The 'inevitable' complement to the serene synaesthesia of passages like the Hawkshead dedication.

3. *Linguistics.* **a.** The expression of more than one kind of sense-impression in the same word. **b.** The transfer of the meaning of a word from one kind of sensory experience to another. **c.** The relationship between speech sounds and the sensory experiences that they represent.

1946 A. G. ENGSTROM in *Philological Q.* XXV. 10 Traces of synaesthesia are as clear in language as in laboratory records... Hornbostel cites a Negro tribe that has a separate word for seeing, but employs a common term for hearing, tasting, smelling, and touching. **1946** S. D. ULLMANN in *Word* II. 114 What Wundt and his disciples term 'complicative change of meaning' is known to the vast majority of other students as 'synesthesia'. **1956** J. WHATMOUGH *Language* x. 191 There is some evidence to indicate that synesthesia such as associates the meanings of colour and sound under a single word may extend to smaller linguistic units. **1957** S. POTTER *Mod. Linguistics* vii. 154 By *synaesthesia* or *intersensory transfer* a word may be given a new sense. **1972** HARTMANN & STORK *Dict. Lang. & Linguistics* 229/1 *Synaesthesia*, the association of a particular sound or group of sounds with a particular meaning, e.g. *fl-* in *flare*, *flicker*, *flame*, [etc.]. **1977** *Word* 1972 XXVIII. 309 Phonetic symbolism, described as the appropriateness of some phonemes to nonauditory experience, falls under the general heading of synaesthesia or, in psychological terminology, crossmodal association. *Ibid.*, As a result of the clustering, forced-choice testing yields congruent information not only in synesthesia studies but in phonetic symbolism and semantic differential tests as well.

synæsthesis (sɪnɪs'θiːsɪs). [mod.L., a. Gr. συναίσθησις joint perception.] **a.** (See quot.)

1881 MIVART *Cat* 386 *note*, The sum-total of the mental action of a rational animal may be called its *noesis*, which will be the analogue of the *synæsthesis* or sum-total of the felt neural psychoses of an irrational animal.

b. (See quots.)

1922 C. K. OGDEN et al. *Foundations of Aesthetics* 76 Synaesthesis..covers both equilibrium and harmony. **1923** OGDEN & RICHARDS *Meaning of Meaning* vii. 267 We cannot enter here into the details of what, from the standpoint of more or less conventional psychology, may be supposed to happen in these states of synaesthesis. **1943** J. T. SHIPLEY *Dict. World Lit. Terms* 327/2 *Synæsthesis*, the harmonious and balanced concord stimulated by art, as posited in the definition of beauty advanced by Ogden, Richards, and Wood in The Foundations of Aesthetics. **1949** WIMSATT & BEARDSLEY in *Sewanee Rev.* LVII. 40 Among these [types of aesthetic theory] the theory of synaesthesis (Beauty is what produces an equilibrium of appetencies) was the one they themselves [*sc.* Ogden, Richards, & Wood] espoused.

synæsthetic (sɪnɪs'θɛtɪk), *a.* (*sb.*) Also **synesthetic.** **1.** [f. SYNÆSTHESIA, after *anæsthetic*.] Of, pertaining to, or exhibiting synæsthesia. Also *absol.* or as *sb.*, a synæsthetic person. So **synæs'thetically** *adv.*

1910 *Mind* XIX. 296 Sense-experiences synaesthetically aroused. **1920** R. H. WHEELER *Synaesthesia of Blind Subject* 54 Synaesthetic phenomena in the field of imagery..reveal the same characteristics as do the same phenomena in the field of perception. **1925** *Amer. Jrnl. Psychol.* XXXVI. 530 The process of perceiving a synaesthetically colored month as an emotion,—by which we mean that the emotional response is represented in the various qualities of the colored imagery. **1935** *Brit. Jrnl. Psychol.* XXV. 37 Every case of synaesthesia..consists essentially of a parallel arrangement of two gradient series. They may be series of pitches, intensities..or anything else in keeping with the interests..of the synaesthetic. **1936** W. B. STANFORD *Gr. Metaphor* 47 We shall call..transferences from the sphere of one sense to that of another *synaesthetic* or intersensal metaphor. *Ibid.* 61 Writers like Poe..and..Ayala affect the same kinds of synaesthetic phrases. Edith Sitwell has 'creaking light' and 'dawn...whining'. **1942** *Jrnl. Gen. Psychol.* XXVI. 213 Such results emphasize the continuity between synesthetic phenomena and more general phenomena of language and thinking. **1949** KOESTLER *Insight & Outlook* xxiii. 320 It is obvious that such 'synaesthetic' metaphors greatly facilitate the sharing by the reader of the teller's vision. **1951** S. D. ULLMANN *Princ. Semantics* iv. 219 Gombocz developed these distinctions.. redefining the essence of synaesthetic transfer which, contrary to Wundt and Roudet, he included among cases of affective sense-similarity. **1977** *Word* 1972 XXVIII. 306 On investigation, a group of phonetic-symbolism, synesthetic, and semantic-differential studies was shown to have produced two groups of semantic qualities which were internally coherent and mutually exclusive. **1979** C. PRIEST *Infinite Summer* 39, I was still affected by the enemy's synaesthetic gas I had inhaled. My perception was disturbed.

2. [f. SYNÆSTHESIS, after *æsthetic*.] Of or pertaining to synæsthesis.

1922 C. K. OGDEN et al. *Foundations of Aesthetics* 91 What we have called the synaesthetic character of the experience.

synagogal ('sɪnəgəʊgəl), *a.* Also **synagogual.** [f. SYNAGOGUE + -AL[1].] Of, pertaining or relating to, or characteristic of a or the synagogue.

1682–3 *Case Indiff. Things* 10 The Synagogual Worship. **1723** MATHER *Vind. Bible* 298 The reason why the Jews omit the points in their Synagogal copies. **1857** BADEN POWELL *Chr. without Judaism* 151 The whole ecclesiastical system is shown to have originated out of the synagogal, not the sacerdotal. **1887** *Pall Mall G.* 5 May 11/1 Objects used in synagogual and domestic ceremonial. **1892** ZANGWILL *Childr. Ghetto* Proem (1893) 3 The social hierarchy was to some extent graduated by synagogal contributions.

†**syna'gogian**, *a.* *Obs. rare*[−1]. In 7 sin-. [f. late L. *synagōga* or Gr. συναγωγή SYNAGOGUE + -IAN.] = prec.

1632 LITHGOW *Trav.* III. 116 All their Sinagogian or Leuiticall Priests are bred here.

synagogical (sɪnə'gɒdʒɪkəl, -gɒg-), *a.* [Formed as prec. + -ICAL.] = prec.

1621 BP. MOUNTAGU *Diatribæ* 385 The Clarkes of the Chancery..and..Clergy men..would not transferre their name of *Presbyter*, or of *Presbyteratus*, to any such signification, either synagogicall or synodicall, after the Lemannian cut. **1644** J. GOODWIN *Innoc. Triumph.* (1645) 20 Nor were the members of this Assembly, Synod, chosen by the respective Synagogicall Congregations. **1882–3** *Schaff's Encycl. Relig. Knowl.* I. 791 Those synagogical desks from which Jewish rabbins..read.

So **synagogism** ('sɪnəgɒdʒɪz(ə)m, -gɒg-), attachment to a system likened to that of the Jewish synagogue; **synagogist** ('sɪnəgɒdʒɪst, -gɒg-), an adherent of the Jewish synagogue.

c **1662** F. KERBY in *O. Heywood's Diaries*, etc. (1883) III. 27 The Dianists and the contradicting synagogists [cf. *Acts* xix. 1, 8, 9, 27, 34]. **1891** W. TUCKWELL in *Review of Churches* 12 Dec. 175/1 A generation stiffened by three centuries of conventional synagogism.

synagogue ('sɪnəgɒg). Forms: 2–6 **sinagoge,** 3–6 **sinagog, synagog(e,** (4 **sinnagog**), 4–7 **sinagogue,** (5 **synagod**), 5–6 **synagogge,** (6 **synagoog,** 8 **sinegogg, senegog**), 3– **synagogue,** (*U.S.*) **synagog.** [a. OF. *sinagoge* (11th c.), mod.F. *synagogue*, or ad. its source late L. *synagōga*, a. Gr. συναγωγή meeting, assembly, (in LXX.) synagogue, f. συνάγειν to bring together, f. σύν SYN-[1] + ἄγειν to lead, bring.]

1. a. The regular assembly or congregation of the Jews for religious instruction and worship apart from the service of the temple, constituting, since the destruction of the temple, their sole form of public worship; hence, the religious organization of the Jews as typified by this, the Jewish communion.

Rabbinical Heb. *keneseth*, f. *kānaṣ* to collect, assemble.

c **1175** *Lamb. Hom.* 9 Godemen wite ȝe hwet wes sinagoge on þam alde laȝe..Alswa hefden þe giwis heore sinagoge efter moises laȝe alswa we habbet nu cherche efter drihtenes laȝe and efere to þam setteres dei heo comen þa iudeisc folc ..to þan sinagoge. *a* **1300** *Cursor M.* 13615 (Cott.) þe Iuus ..had made..A statut agains Iesum crist, If any wald him leue or lute þair synagoges suld be put vte. **1382** WYCLIF *Acts* ix. 2 Saul..axide of him epistlis into Damaske, to synagogis. **1450–1530** *Myrr. our Ladye* 298 The synagoge ys called the people of the iewes, whiche had knowledge of the comynge of criste by holy prophetes. **1521** FISHER *Serm. agst. Luther* i. Wks. (1876) 315 The lawe of Moyses, & the gouernaunce of the synagoge of the Iewes, was but a shadowe of the gouernaunce of the vnyuersall chirche of christ. *a* **1873** DEUTSCH *Rem.* (1874) 191 What was the attitude of the Synagogue towards all these elements? **1887** *Encycl. Brit.* XXII. 811/2 The synagogue as an institution characteristic of Judaism arose after the work of Ezra. **1909** J. R. HARRIS in *Contemp. Rev.* Apr. 423 The time when the Christian Church had not finally elongated from the synagogue. **1929** *Lit. Digest* 2 Nov. 24/1 New York now has ..the largest synagog in existence—the new Temple Emanu-El on a site overlooking Central Park. **1963** R. I. McDAVID *Mencken's Amer. Lang.* 491 The 1962 Style Book, p. 63 specifies the following:..synagog. **1976** *National Observer* (U.S.) 22 May 16-A/5 Usually he was paid by the synagog and served in various capacities as rabbi, cantor, or schoolteacher.

b. *the Great Synagogue*: a Jewish council of 120 members, said to have been founded and presided over by Ezra after the return from the Babylonian captivity.

1625 T. GODWYN *Moses & Aaron* (1641) 180 That great assembly of Prophets and holy men, called together by Esra, for the reformation of the Church, after their returne from Babylon, is called *Synagoga magna*, Their great Synagogue. **1876** B. MARTIN *Messiah's Kingd.* II. iv. 88 The Great Synagogue, which consisted of 120 members, governed the Jews both in political and ecclesiastical matters for about 110 years, from Nehemiah to Simon the Just, when it was merged in the Sanhedrim. **1881** W. R. SMITH *Old Test. in Jewish Ch.* vi. 156 The Great Synagogue plays a considerable part in Jewish tradition;..we now know that the whole idea..is pure fiction.

2. *transf.* in hostile controversial use, often in phr. ***synagogue of Satan*** (in allusion to Rev. ii. 9).

In quot. 1464 used ignorantly, through a misunderstanding of *sunt synagoga Satanæ*, 'they are the synagogue of Satan', as a personal term of abuse.

1464 in *Academy* 23 Aug. (1890) 151/1 He..affermed that the blessed sacrament of the Auter is a grete devyll of hell, and a Sinagoge. *Ibid.*, He..affermed that oure holy Fadre, the pope of Rome, is a great best, and a devyll of hell, and a Synagoge. **1547** *Bk. Marchauntes* e iij, To be slayne and murdred of them, or at the least excommunicate in their sinagog. **1565** HARDING *Confut. Apol.* IV. 212 b, They can not be the..shining church of Christ... Wherefore it remaineth that it is the synagog of Antichrist, and Lucifer. *Ibid.* VI. 341 b, They resisting the holy Ghost..gather to the synagog of Satan. **1583** in *Cath. Rec. Soc. Publ.* I. 37 To the comforth of them that love Hym and His Spouse the Catholique Church, and to the condemnation of so many that so willingly and wittingly join in the Sinagoge of Satan. **1648** MILTON *Observ. Art. Peace* Wks. 1851 IV. 571 By the incitement..of that unchristian Synagogue [*sc.* Scots Presbytery] at Belfast. **1674** HICKMAN *Quinquart. Hist.* (ed. 2) 133 It were to be wished, that no Arminians had.. forsaken the Church of England, and took sanctuary in the Synagogue of Rome. **1688** HOLME *Armoury* II. 11/2 Where God hath his Church, the Devil will have his Synagogue. **1874** W. P. MACKAY *Grace & Truth* (1875) 233 It is because of the name we bear that the blasphemies of hell are poured upon us. There are the 'synagogues of Satan', in which the blasphemous doctrines of devils are taught.

3. a. A building or place of meeting for Jewish worship and religious instruction.

Rabbinical Heb. *bēth hakkeneṣeth* house of assembly.

[*c* **1175**: see 1.] *c* **1290** *Sancta Crux* 551 in *S. Eng. Leg.* I. 17 Þo þe rode was þare i-founde, alle þe giwes as nome And ladden as forth to heore Synagoge. *c* **1380** *Sir Ferumb.* 2535 To þe Synagoge wan sche cam þe dore heo haueþ oundo. *c* **1400** MAUNDEV. viii. (1839) 93 There besyde was the synagoge where the bysshoppes of Jewes and the sarrazins camen to gidere and helden here conseill. **1577** HOLINSHED *Chron.* II. 776/1 They tooke & sacked the Citie of Lincolne, spoyled the Iewes, and slew many of them, entred their sinagoge, and brent the boke of their lawe. **1596** SHAKS. *Merch. V.* III. i. 135 Goe Tuball, and meete me at our Sinagogue. **1635** A. STAFFORD *Fem. Glory* 224 All of their Religion are enjoyned in solemne Prayer made in their Sinagogues thrice every day. **1721** N. BLUNDELL *Diary* (1895) 197, I was at the Jews Sinegogg by Leadon-Hall Market. **1838** *Civil Eng. & Arch. Jrnl.* I. 327/1 The New Synagogue in Great St. Helen's..has just been completed. **1876** B. MARTIN *Messiah's Kingd.* II. iv. 82 The synagogue was modelled on the temple. Its windows looked towards the holy city. **1887** *Encycl. Brit.* XXII. 812/1 Synagogues were built by preference beside water for the convenience of the ceremonial ablutions.

†**b.** *transf.* A place of worship; a temple. In post-Reformation use applied disparagingly to abbeys or the like. *Obs.*

c **1400** *Destr. Troy* 4467 Thies kynges..turnyt into tempull... Be counsell of the kepers..þat serued þat Synagod. **1490** CAXTON *Eneydos* xiii. 46 Bothe togidre.. wente the two sustres..to the synagoges and temples, where bifore the aulters thei offred sacrifices. **1587** HARRISON *England* II. iii. (1877) I. 74 They..began that synagog [Osney Abbey] 1120, which afterward proued to be a notable den. **1655** FULLER *Ch. Hist.* VI. 326 The Noble Family of the Berkeleys may well give an Abbots Mitre for the Crest of their Armes, because so loving their Nation, and building them so many Synagogues [cf. Luke vii. 5].

c. (See quots.)

1894 *Westm. Gaz.* 31 Dec. 3/2 A large quantity of this fruit ..is bought up by Jews occupying stands in Russell-street. Their quarter is known as the 'Synagogue'. **1909** WARE *Passing Eng.*, *Synagogue*,..shed in the north-east corner of the Garden [= Covent Garden]. So called from this place (erected 1890) being wholly 'run' by Jews.

†**4.** *gen.* An assembly: chiefly as a literalism of biblical translation. *Obs.*

a **1300** *E.E. Psalter* lxxxi[i]. 1 God stode in sinagoge of goddes ma. *a* **1325** *Prose Psalter* vii. 7, & synagoge of folke shal encumpas þe. *a* **1400** *Minor Poems fr. Vernon MS.* xxiii. 650 Whos deore sone stod In þe Synagoge of goddes. **1592** MARLOWE *Mass. Paris* II. ii, There are an hundred Hugonets, and more, Which in the woods doe holde their synagogue. **1881** *N.T.* (R.V.) Jas. ii. 2 If there come into your synagogue [1611 assembly] a man with a gold ring.

5. *attrib.* and *Comb.*

1652 PINCHION (*title*) The Jewes Synagogue; or, a Treatise concerning The ancient Orders and manner of Worship used by the Jewes in their synagogve-Assemblies. *Ibid.*, To Rdr., I thought it necessary to search out, as well as I could, their Synagogue-worship, together with some of their ancient Discipline-practices. *Ibid.* ii. 38 Whiles the Jews lived in their own land, their synagogue discipline did depend upon their Sanhedrin Courts. **1716** PRIDEAUX *Connect. O. & N. Test.* VI. (1718) I. 300 The second part of their synagogue-service is the reading of the scriptures. *Ibid.* 301 Their ordinary synagogue days in every week were Monday, Thursday and Saturday. **1781** COWPER *Truth* 57 A praying, synagogue-frequenting, beau. **1886** CONDER *Syrian Stone-Lore* vii. (1896) 264 The style of the synagogue architecture is very like that of the Roman temples of the same age. The lion, the ram, the hare are carved on the lintels of the synagogue doors—a curious deviation from the law of Moses. **1889** COHEN & DAVIS (*title*) Voice of Prayer and Praise, a Handbook of Synagogue Music. **1910** *Daily Chron.* 1 Feb. 4/7 The proposal that synagogue services should be limited to an hour and a half.

Hence **'synagoguing** *vbl. sb.*, attendance at the synagogue; **'synagoguish** *a.*, showing excessive zeal for the synagogue, fanatical.

1690 D'URFEY *Collin's Walk* I. 37 Your party Synagoguish, Not half so Politique, as Roguish. **1824** MISS FERRIER *Inher.* xliv, The synagogin', the tabernaclin', the psalmin' that goes on in this hoose.

synallactic (sɪnæ'læktɪk), *a. rare.* [ad. Gr. συναλλακτικός, f. συναλλάσσειν to exchange, bring into intercourse, reconcile, f. σύν SYN-[1] + ἀλλάσσειν to change, exchange.] Reconciliatory.

1853 WHEWELL *Grotius* II. xx. II. 252 Retribution [as an end of punishment]..is properly what Aristotle refers to synallactic justice.

synallagmatic (sɪnælæg'mætɪk), *a.* [ad. Gr. συναλλαγματικός, f. συνάλλαγμα covenant, contract, f. συναλλάσσειν (see prec.).] Pertaining to or of the nature of a contract or mutual engagement; imposing mutual obligations; reciprocally binding: esp. in *Civil Law*, of a treaty or the like.

1792 *Ann. Reg.*, *St. Papers* 251/1 These acts..which are synallagmatic acts,..being infringed by the usurping assembly, would be at present annulled. **1818** COLEBROOKE *Obligations* 16 Mutual or synallagmatic contracts are either perfectly or imperfectly reciprocal. **1875** POSTE *Gaius* III. Comm. (ed. 2) 362 The several proffered and accepted promises are called a Bilateral or Synallagmatic Convention. **1898** *19th Cent.* Feb. 234 A synallagmatic contract between two States.

So **synallag'matical** *a.* in same sense; hence **synallag'matically** *adv.*

1871 *Daily News* 20 Apr. 5 Armistice and 'synallagmatical' amnesty... When these terms are mutually—I beg pardon—synallagmatically accepted, then we are told that the peace will be without conquerors and without conquered.

synallaxine (sɪnæ'læksaɪn, -ɪn), *a. Ornith.* [ad. mod.L. *Synallaxinæ* pl., f. *Synallaxis* (Vieillot, 1819), name of the typical genus: see -INE[1].] Belonging to the subfamily *Synallaxinæ* of dendrocolaptine birds, found in tropical America, in habits and appearance resembling tree-creepers.

1862 WOOD *Illustr. Nat. Hist.* II. 260 The Synallaxine birds are generally found upon the trees, which they traverse with great rapidity in search of the various insects on which they feed. **1888** P. L. SCLATER *Argentine Ornith.* I. 195 Nor has it the restless manner of most Synallaxine birds.

‖**synalœpha** (sɪnə'liːfə), **-phe** (-fiː), *sb. Gram.* Also **-le-**. [late L., a. Gr. συναλοιφή, f. συναλείφειν to smear or melt together, f. σύν SYN-[1] + ἀλείφειν to anoint. In F. *synalèphe*, It., Sp. *sinalefa*, Pg. *synalepha*.] The coalescence or contraction of two syllables into one; *esp.* the coalescence (in verse) of two vowels at the end of one word and the beginning of the next, by obscuration of the former (or, *loosely*, by suppression of it, in which case more properly called *elision*). †Also in humorous allusion (quot. 1698).

1540 PALSGR. *Acolastus* E iij b, Whan so euer a worde endeth in a vowel, the nexte word folowyng begynnynge with a vowell..than shall the vowell that the precedent worde ended in, be drouned, and not accounted in scannynge, by this fygure Synalœpha. **1602** CAMPION *Art Engl. Poesie* 38 The Synalœphas or Elisions in our toong are either necessary to auoid the..gaping in our verse..or may be vsd at pleasure, as for *let vs* to say *let's*. **1685** DRYDEN *Sylvæ* Pref., Poet. Wks. (1910) 384 [Ovid] avoids..all Synalœpha's, or cutting off one Vowel when it comes before another, in the following word. **1698** FARQUHAR *Love & Bottle* v. ii, I'll cut off one of his Limbs, I'll make a Synalœpha of him. **1741** J. MARTYN tr. *Virg. Georg.* I. 4 *note* (1811) 2/1 Some editions have *atque*, between *pecori* and *apibus*, to avoid a synalœpha. **1827** TATE *Grk. Metres* in *Theatre of Greeks* (ed. 2) 445 Hegelochus, who acted the part of Orestes..when he came to v. 273, ἐκ κυμάτων γὰρ αὖθις αὖ γαλήν' ὁρῶ, wanting breath to pronounce γαλήν' ὁρῶ with the delicate synalepha required,..stopped between the words, and uttered these sounds instead, γαλῆν ὁρῶ. **1867** BRANDE & COX *Dict. Sci.*, etc. s.v., The synalæpha is commonly.. adopted in Italian and Spanish poetry.

Hence †**synalœpha** *v. trans.* (*nonce-wd.*), to contract by synalœpha (in quot. *fig.*).

1661 FELTHAM *Resolves* II. lvi. (ed. 6) 302 Whatsoever he does well, is presently detracted from, till it be lessened and synalœpha'd [*ed.* **1677** synalœph'd] into nothing.

synamer: see SINAMER.

synamom(e, -mon(d, obs. ff. CINNAMON.

‖**synangium** (sɪ'nændʒɪəm). Pl. **-ia**. Also anglicized **synange** ('sɪnændʒ). [mod.L., f. Gr. σύν SYN-[1] + ἀγγεῖον vessel.]

1. *Anat.* and *Zool.* A collective or common blood-vessel from which several arteries branch; *spec.* the terminal part of the arterial trunk in the lower vertebrates.

1875 HUXLEY in *Encycl. Brit.* I. 763/1 *Pylangium* and *synangium*, together, are the equivalents of that portion of the heart which lies between the ventricle and the anterior wall of the pericardium. **1875** HUXLEY & MARTIN *Elem. Biol.* (1877) 176 The terminal part common to the divergent trunks is the synangium.

2. *Bot.* The oblong mass of coherent sporangia in ferns of the order *Marattiaceæ*.

1881 J. S. GARDNER in *Nature* 13 Oct. 560/1 In the later Carboniferous, Marattioid ferns for the first time occur with the sporangia united in a composite organ called a synangium. **1893** BOWER in *Phil. Trans.* B. CLXXXV. 542 It is difficult to recognize..the exact limits of the sporogenous masses in the synangia.

Hence **synangial** (sɪ'nændʒɪəl), **synangic** (sɪ'nændʒɪk) *adjs.*, pertaining to or constituting a synangium.

1875 HUXLEY in *Encycl. Brit.* I. 765/1 Three thick semi-lunar valves are placed at the ventricular end of this region, and three others..at its synangial end. **1902** C. REID *Ibid.* XXXI. 417/1 Numerous..fern-sporangia occur in the petrified material of the Carboniferous formation; the presence of an annulus is a frequent character.., while synangic sori are rare. *Ibid.*, The genus *Diplolabis* of Renault ..resembles *Corynepteris* in possessing a synangic fructification.

Synanon ('sɪnənɒn). [See quot. 1965[2] for the supposed origin.] The name of a U.S. foundation concerned chiefly with the rehabilitation of drug addicts through group therapy; also (with small initial) the method of psychotherapy practised in its centres (see also quot. 1963). Freq. *attrib.*

1961 *Time* 7 Apr. 33/1 Synanon offers more than a few cures. *Ibid.*, The Synanon system cannot work until the addict really decides..to kick the habit. **1963** *Amer. Jrnl. Sociol.* LXIX. 135/1 The free, unrestricted interaction in small groups called 'synanons'. **1965** L. YABLONSKY *Tunnel Back* p. viii, Synanon is a community of former addicts and criminals. *Ibid.*, The word 'synanon' originated with a newly arrived addict... In his attempt to say two 'foreign' words, 'symposium' and 'seminar' in the same breath, he blurted out 'synanon'. *Ibid.* vi. 137 The small-'s' synanon is the group psychotherapy of the total Synanon social structure. **1969** *Guardian* 16 Aug. 7/3 Synanon's communities are not unlike Socialist communes... Everything is free, everyone 'mucks in'. *Ibid.* 21 Aug. 8/4 Spinrad's latest novel..examines the process by which psychotherapy has become a religious experience, spawning synthetic cults like scientology..and the Synanon game. **1976** J. ROWAN *Ordinary Ecstasy* iv. 44 The essence of the Synanon approach is direct aggressive confrontation of the one group member by one or more other members.

synanthereous (sɪnæn'θɛrɪəs), *a. Bot. rare.* [f. mod.L. *Synanthereæ* pl. (Richard, 1801), f. Gr. σύν SYN-[1] + mod.L. *anthēra* ANTHER: see -OUS.] Belonging to the order *Synanthereæ*, a synonym of *Compositæ*, having the anthers united; syngenesious. Also **synantherous** (-'nænθərəs) *a.*; so **synanthe'rology** [-LOGY], the study of the *Compositæ*; whence **synanthero'logical** *a.*, pertaining to synantherology; **synanthe'rologist**, one who studies or treats of the *Compositæ*.

1859 MAYNE *Expos. Lex.* s.v. *Siphoniphytum*, A *synanthereous plant. **1891** *Cent. Dict.*, *Synantherological. **1881** *Jrnl. Bot.* New Ser. X. 150 The last-named author, *facile princeps* amongst *synantherologists. **1859** MAYNE *Expos. Lex.*, *Synantherologia*..term for a treatise on the plants of the Synanthereæ: *synantherology. **1849** BALFOUR *Man. Bot.* §417 The stamens..may also unite by their anthers, and become syngenesious or *synantherous.

synanthesis (sɪnæn'θiːsɪs). *Bot.* [f. SYN-[1] + ANTHESIS.] Simultaneous ripening of the stamens and pistils in a flower; hence **synanthetic** (-'θɛtɪk) *a.*, exhibiting synanthesis. So **sy'nanthic** *a.* [Gr. ἄνθος flower], characterized by synanthy; **sy'nanthious** *a.*, of leaves, expanding at the same time as the flowers (cf. *synanthous*); **synanthous** (sɪ'nænθəs) *a.*, (*a*) applied to plants whose leaves expand at the same time as the flowers; (*b*) = *synanthic*; **synanthy** (sɪ'nænθɪ), abnormal union or fusion of two or more flowers.

1880 GRAY *Struct. Bot.* vi. §4 (ed. 6) 219 **Synanthesis*, the maturing of the anthers and stigmas simultaneously or nearly so. **1909** *Cent. Dict.*, *Suppl.*, *Synanthetic. **1869** M. T. MASTERS *Veget. Teratol.* 37 *Synanthic flowers of *Campanula medium*. **1845** LINDLEY *Sch. Bot.* viii. (1858) 135 Leaves..*synanthious (i.e. appearing with the flowers). **1832** —— *Introd. Bot.* 401 *Synanthous; when flowers and leaves appear at the same time. **1869** M. T. MASTERS *Veget. Teratol.* 37 *Synanthy may take place without much derangement of the structure of either flower.

synapar, var. SINOPER *Obs.*

‖**synaphe** ('sɪnəfɪ). *Anc. Gr. Mus.* [a. Gr. συναφή connexion, junction, f. σύν SYN-[1] + ἅπτειν to fasten, fix.] The 'conjunction' of two tetrachords (see CONJUNCT B. 6): opp. to DIAZEUXIS.

1740 J. GRASSINEAU *Mus. Dict.* 250 *Synaphe*, a Greek term which signifies, according to Boëtius..conjunction; a chord is said to be conjoint, when so placed between two fourths. **1801** BUSBY *Dict. Mus.* **1898** STAINER & BARRETT *Dict. Mus. Terms* 205/2 After new lyres had been made to carry eight strings the entire octave was included upon the instrument. The old system of tuning the lyre [with seven strings] was then called Synaphe or Conjunction,..and the new, or octave, system was called Harmonia.

‖**synaphea** (sɪnə'fiːə). *Anc. Pros.* [late L., ad. Gr. συνάφεια connexion, f. συναφής connected, united (cf. prec.).] Continuity of rhythm; maintenance of the same rhythm throughout, esp. in anapæstic verse.

1827 TATE *Grk. Metres* in *Theatre of Greeks* (ed. 2) 431 The synaphea (or συνάφεια), that property of the Anapestic system which Bentley first demonstrated, is..scansion continued with strict exactness from the first syllable to the very last, but not including the last itself, as that..may be long or short. **1861** PALEY *Æschylus* (ed. 2) *Supplices* 8 *note*, The law of anapaestic synaphea is violated by a dactyl coming before an anapaest.

synapir, -our, var. SINOPER *Obs.*

synapise: see SINAPIZE.

synapomorphy: see SYN-[1] 1.

synaposematic, etc.: see SYN-[1].

synapse (sɪˈnæps, ˈsaɪ-), *sb. Anat.* [ad. Gr. σύναψις: see SYNAPSIS.] The junction, or structure at the junction, between two neurons or nerve-cells.

1899 *Allbutt's Syst. Med.* VI. 512 A feature of the concatenations of neurons more probably explicative of modification and delay of nerve impulses is the synapse. **1905** McDOUGALL *Physiol. Psychol.* ii. 27 A simple kind of synapse is formed by the division of the end of an axon.. into a number of fine twigs that surround the cell-body of another neurone.

synapse (sɪˈnæps, ˈsaɪ-), *v. Anat.* [f. the sb.] *intr.* Of a nerve-cell or axon: to form a synapse.

1910 *Practitioner* July 98 The rubro-spinal portion (Monakow's bundle) connects the red nucleus with the opposite side of the spinal cord, probably terminating by synapsing round the anterior horn cells. **1963** R. P. DALES *Annelids* vi. 119 The axon is T-shaped, the cell body lying ventrally or ventro-laterally at the bottom of the T and the tips of the arms synapsing with those of the next neuron. **1979** *Sci. Amer.* Sept. 84/1 Many such cells do not themselves make contact with a motor neuron; they synapse instead on yet other neurons of the great intermediate net.

Also **syˈnapsed** *ppl. a. Genetics* [cf. SYNAPSIS 2], (of chromosomes) in a state of synapsis.

1931 *Amer. Jrnl. Bot.* XVIII. 370 The synapsed spireme strands traverse the nucleus freely. **1946** *Nature* 21 Dec. 912/1 Perhaps such chemical agents in the egg help in separating the synapsed X-chromosomes. **1974** *Ibid.* 12 Apr. 566/2 The X element contains three synapsed chromosomes.

synapsid (sɪˈnæpsɪd), *a.* and *sb.* [a. mod.L. *Synapsida* (H. F. Osborn 1903, in *Mem. Amer. Mus. Nat. Hist.* I. 455), f. SYN- + Gr. ἁψίς, ἁψιδ- arch: see -ID[3].] **A.** *adj.* Of or pertaining to the subclass Synapsida, which includes fossil reptiles having a single temporal opening on each side of the skull. So **syˈnapsidan** *a.* **B.** *sb.* A fossil reptile of the subclass Synapsida, showing a skull structure with some mammalian characteristics.

1903 *Mem. Amer. Mus. Nat. Hist.* I. 460 In all Synapsidan types above the Cotylosauria the squamosals and prosquamosals early coalesce. **1910** *Bull. Amer. Mus. Nat. Hist.* XXVII. 114 The Synapsid reptiles.. may conveniently be approached by a cursory review of the reptilian orders. **1933** A. S. ROMER *Vertebr. Paleontol.* vi. 128 Forms with one opening (in which it was presumed that the two openings had fused into one), [were termed] 'synapsid' (fused-arched) reptiles. **1956** —— *Osteol. Reptiles* II. 473 The mesosaurs.. are associated with the synapsid orders. *Ibid.* 474 The synapsids.. seem to be a very natural assemblage. **1974** D. & M. WEBSTER *Compar. Vertebr. Morphol.* v. 102 The presence of this bone in both monotremes, where it is apparently functionless, as well as in metatherians is particularly confusing since there is no indication of a marsupial bone in synapsid reptiles. **1980** *Nature* 24 Jan. 378/2 The mammals arose from advanced synapsids in the Upper Triassic. *Ibid.*, An alternative view of the origin of the synapsid skull is that the ancestral condition of the temporal region consisted of a large supratemporal bone which was in contact anteriorly with the postorbital.

‖**synapsis** (sɪˈnæpsɪs). Pl. synapses (-siːz). [mod.L., ad. Gr. σύναψις connexion, junction, f. σύν SYN-[1] + ἅψις joining, f. ἅπτειν to join.]

†**1.** *gen.* Connexion. *Obs.*

1654 H. L'ESTRANGE *Chas. I* (1655) 88 Some considerable circumstances must not be forgot, by reason of their synapsis, their coherence with this relation.

2. *Biol.* orig. in sense of quots. 1895, 1905; in mod. use, chromosomal pairing during the zygotene stage of meiosis.

1895 J. E. S. MOORE in *Q. Jrnl. Microsc. Sci.* XXXVIII. 296 The transformation of the cells of the first spermatogenetic period into those of the second, which I have termed the synapsis,.. is marked by a peculiar evolution in the chromatin with the formation of peculiar nucleoli.. and by the formation of an archoplasmic constituent round the centrosomes. **1905** *Ibid.* XLVIII. 490 Synapsis represents that series of events which are concerned in causing the temporary union in pairs of pre-maiotic chromosomes, previously to their transverse separation and distribution, in their entirety, between two daughter nuclei. **1908** BOWER *Orig. Land Flora* 50 The nucleus first enters the condition of synapsis, in which a lateral fusion of the chromosomes in pairs, respectively of paternal and maternal origin, is believed to take place. **1912** *Jrnl. Exper. Zool.* XIII. 348 A number of writers have suggested that the term synapsis.. should be abandoned in favour of some less ambiguous word (such as Haecker's term 'syndesis') because it has so frequently been applied to the contraction-figure ('synizesis' of McClung). I am, however, in favor of the retention of the word, for the ambiguity has arisen simply through a misunderstanding of Moore's meaning. He applied the term 'synaptic phase', or 'synapsis', to the series of changes following the last diploid division.. in the course of which the apparent number of chromosomes is reduced to one-half. **1960** L. PICKEN *Organization of Cells* iv. 137 Given the mitotic apparatus, the special features of meiosis might follow from the one act of synapsis—the pairing of homologues. **1978** M. W. FARNSWORTH *Genetics* vi. 123 During the zygotene stage homologous chromosomes begin to pair lengthwise with one another, a process called synapsis.

3. *Anat.* = SYNAPSE *sb.*

1897 FOSTER & SHERRINGTON *Text Bk. Physiol.* III. i. (ed. 7) 929. **1900** *Schäfer's Text-bk. Physiol.* II. 834 The synapses are fewest; in some, perhaps, there intervenes but one synapsis.

synaptase (sɪˈnæpteɪs, -eɪz). *Chem.* [ad. F. *synaptase* (Robiquet, 1838), f. Gr. συναπτός joined together, continuous, with ending as in *diastase.*] An albuminous ferment found in almonds and other oily seeds; also called *emulsin.*

1849 BALFOUR *Man. Bot.* §310 Emulsine, or synaptase, is a nitrogenous compound found in certain oily seeds, as in almonds. **1862** MILLER *Elem. Chem., Org.* (ed. 2) 105 The synaptase of the almond acts upon starch and sugar in a way resembling that in which yeast and gluten act.

†**synaptenic** (sɪnæpˈtiːnɪk), *a. Cytology. Obs.* Also -tænic. [ad. F. *synaptène* (H. von Winiwarter 1900, in *Arch. de Biol.* XVII. 54), f. Gr. συν- SYN-[1]: see -TENE, -IC.] Epithet of the stage of meiosis now known as zygotene.

1900 *Jrnl. R. Microsc. Soc.* 654 The reticulum gives rise to a chromatic thread (deutobroch stage), which at first fills the nuclear cavity (leptotænic stage), and later forms a central dense mass (synaptænic stage). **1922** F. H. A. MARSHALL *Physiol. of Reproduction* (ed. 2) iv. 155 The nucleus enters upon the synaptenic condition, which extends over a somewhat longer time.

synaptic (sɪˈnæptɪk), *a. Cytology* and *Anat.* [In form ad. Gr. συναπτικός connective, copulative; used as the adj. corresponding to SYNAPSIS.] Pertaining to (a) synapsis. Hence **syˈnaptically** *adv.*

1895 J. E. S. MOORE in *Q. Jrnl. Microsc. Sci.* XXXVIII. 287, I therefore propose the term Synaptic phase to denote the period at which this most important change appears in the morphological character of reproductive cells. **1902** A. MACALISTER in *Encycl. Brit.* XXV. 399/2 Connected synaptically with the neurones of other systems. **1913** DORLAND *Med. Dict.*, *Synapse, synapsis*,.. the contact.. between dendrons... Called also synaptic junction. **1974** D. & M. WEBSTER *Compar. Vertebr. Morphol.* ix. 182 Each terminal bouton contains mitochondria and submicroscopic, membrane-bound spheres called synaptic vesicles. **1976** SMYTHIES & CORBETT *Psychiatry* iv. 42 When a nerve-impulse passes down an axon and reaches the terminal a chemical is released which crosses the synaptic cleft and causes depolarization of the next neurone. **1981** *Sci. Amer.* Oct. 122/2 The active form of the transmitter molecule is stored in the sacs called synaptic vesicles until the nerve cell is called on to release it.

‖**synapticula** (sɪnæpˈtɪkjʊlə). *Zool.* Pl. -æ (-iː). Also **synapticulum**, pl. -a. [mod.L., f. Gr. συναπτικός (see prec.) + dim. suffix *-icula, -iculum.*] Each of a number of transverse calcareous processes connecting the septa in certain corals. Hence **synapˈticular** *a.*, pertaining to or consisting of synapticulæ; **synapˈticulate** *a.*, furnished with synapticulæ.

1861 J. R. GREENE *Man. Anim. Kingd., Cœlent.* 155 Septa.. with.. processes, which, in general, meet so as to constitute numerous 'synapticulæ', or transverse props, extending across the loculi like the bars of a grate. **1872** P. M. DUNCAN *Monogr. Brit. Fossil Corals* Ser. II. III. 20 The endotheca.. assumes the synapticular form. **1883** —— in *Jrnl. Linn. Soc., Zool.* XVII. 140 These transversely placed organs.. we have proposed to term *synapticula. Ibid.* 144 Bounded by the synapticulum above. *Ibid.*, A synapticulate structure.

synaptinemal, var. SYNAPTONEMAL *a.*

synapto- (sɪˈnæptəʊ), ad. Gr. συναπτ-ικός, connective, used as comb. form of SYNAPSE, in various terms in *Physiol.*, as **synaptoˈgenesis**, the formation of synapses between nerve cells; **synapˈtology**, the study of the structure and operation of synapses; **syˈnaptosome** [-SOME[4]], a presynaptic nerve ending which, when isolated, seals up to form an intact sac; hence **synaptoˈsomal** *a.*

1967 D. P. PURPURA in A. Minkowski *Regional Devel. of Brain in Early Life* 131 We started this morning with looking at myelinogenesis, moved to cytoarchitectonics, and started talking about the probable growth of dendrites. You have now moved us into a fourth area of maturational considerations—that of synaptogenesis. **1979** *Experientia* XXXV. 207/1 Intracerebellar connections are gradually established as the synaptogenesis proceeds. **1962** *Anat. Rec.* CXLII. 332/2 (*heading*) An electron microscope study of the stratum radiatum of the rat hippocampus.. with emphasis on synaptology. **1965** *Sci. Amer.* Jan. 56/3 Sir Charles Sherrington.. laid the foundations of what is sometimes called synaptology. **1975** *Nature* 8 May 176/2 There have been great advances in knowledge of synaptology from electron microscopic studies of the retina. **1970** *Neurosciences Res.* III. 6 There is more than a sixfold increase in the ATPase activity of the rat brain nerve-ending fraction from prenatal to the 10-day-old animal, the enzyme apparently residing in the synaptosomal limiting membrane. **1978** *Nature* 17 Aug. 706/2 The crude synaptosomal pellet was resuspended in 0·32 M glucose.. and equilibrated.. in a rotary waterbath. **1964** V. P. WHITTAKER et al. in *Biochem. Jrnl.* XC 293/1 The club-like presynaptic nerve endings resist disruption and are snapped or torn off from their attachments to form discrete particles (nerve-ending particles) in which all the main structural features of the nerve ending are preserved. For these particles we propose the name 'synaptosomes' in order to emphasize their relative homogeneity and their resemblance in physical properties to other subcellular organelles. **1973** *Nature* 9 Mar. 122/1 Isolation of intact synaptic nerve endings (synaptosomes) had made it possible to investigate transport across synaptic membranes.

synaptonemal (ˌsɪnæptəʊˈniːməl), *a. Cytology.* Also **synapti-**. [f. Gr. συναπτι-κός connective or SYNAPTO- + Gr. νῆμα thread.] ***synaptonemal complex***: a set of several parallel threads seen adjacent to and coaxial with pairing chromosomes in meiosis.

1958 M. J. MOSES in *Jrnl. Biophysical & Biochem. Cytol.* IV. 637/1 The term 'chromosomal core' was applied to the axial complex when it was first described... A more precise term would.. indicate that the structure is associated specifically with chromosome pairing, and that it is thread-like. Unwieldy though it is, *synaptinemal complex* is more accurately descriptive. **1969** —— in *Genetics* LXI. Suppl. 50 It is proposed that 'synaptonemal complex', because it is similar to the original term and has been employed in the literature to refer to the structure in meiotic bivalents, henceforth be used in place of 'synaptinemal complex'. *Ibid.*, The synaptonemal complex (SC) is a regularly occurring, coplanar set of parallel strands (usually three), coaxial to meiotic bivalent chromosomes. Presence of this linear complex is prerequisite to, but not alone sufficient for chiasma formation (and hence, crossing-over). **1971** *Nature* 3 Sept. 48/1 Chromosome synapsis mediated by the synaptonemal complex seems to be non-specific, for it can also pull together non-homologous chromosomes. **1978** *Bio Systems* X. 111/1 A clear prediction of my phylogeny is that meiotic synaptinemal complex proteins should be homologous in all organisms.

synar, obs. Sc. form of SINNER.

synarchy (ˈsɪnɑːkɪ). *rare.* [ad. Gr. συναρχία, f. συνάρχειν to rule jointly.] Joint rule or sovereignty; participation in government: see quots.

1732 STACKHOUSE *Hist. Bible* VI. iii. (1752) 864 *note*, The Synarchies, or joint Reigns of Father and Son.. have render'd the Chronology a little difficult. **1839** F. LIEBER *Political Ethics* II. xii. 385 Hamarchy, then, signifies something entirely different from the ancient synarchy, which merely denoted a government in which the people had a share together with the rulers proper.

synarthrodial (sɪnɑːˈθrəʊdɪəl), *a.* [f. mod.L. *synarthrōdia* (f. Gr. σύν SYN-[1] + ἀρθρωδία ARTHRODIA) + -AL[1].] Pertaining to or of the nature of a synarthrosis.

1830 R. KNOX *Béclard's Anat.* 279 Bones.. furnished with inequalities which fit into each other,.. invested with a synarthrodial cartilage intimately united to the two articulated parts.

‖**synarthrosis** (sɪnɑːˈθrəʊsɪs). *Anat.* Pl. -throses (-ˈθrəʊsiːz). [mod.L., a. Gr. συνάρθρωσις, f. σύν SYN-[1] + ἄρθρωσις jointing, ARTHROSIS.] A form of articulation in which the bones are firmly fixed so as to be incapable of moving upon one another, as in the sutures of the skull and the sockets of the teeth: distinguished from AMPHIARTHROSIS and DIARTHROSIS.

1578 BANISTER *Hist. Man* 3 b, Not vnder the kynde of Diarthrosis, but Synarthrosis: for asmuch as the mouyng of these bones is most obscure. **1634** T. JOHNSON *Parey's Chirurg.* VI. xlii. (1678) 165 Synarthrosis, or Coarticulation,.. hath.. three kinds. **1841** R. E. GRANT *Comp. Anat.* 125 There are fewer immoveable synarthroses than in birds and mammalia.

synascete (ˈsɪnəsiːt). *Gr. Ch.* [ad. late Gr. συνασκητής, f. σύν SYN-[1] + ἀσκητής: see ASCETIC.] (See quot.)

1850 NEALE *Eastern Ch., Gen. Introd.* IV. ii. 763 The friends of great Saints are described [in the calendar of the Greek Church] as their *synascetes.*

synastry (sɪˈnæstrɪ). *Astrol.* Also in L. form **synastria**. [f. Gr. σύν SYN-[1] + ἀστρ-, ἀστήρ star + -Y.] Coincidence or agreement of the influences of the stars over the destinies of two persons.

1657 W. MORICE *Coena quasi Κοινὴ* xvi. 292 There is some conformity in judgment and affection between them, as they write there is among those, between whom there is a Synastry, and who have the common Stars and influences at their Nativities. **1855** KINGSLEY *Westw. Ho!* xv, That these strange attachments were due to a synastria, or sympathy of the stars, which ruled the destinies of each person. **1860** MOTLEY *Netherl.* I. vii. 366 Born in the same day of the month and hour of the day with the Queen, but two years before her birth, the supposed synastry of their destinies might partly account in that age of astrological superstition, for the influence which he [*sc.* the Earl of Leicester] perpetually exerted.

†**synathˈletic**, *a. Obs. rare*[−1]. [f. Gr. συναθλητής (f. σύν SYN-[1] + ἀθλητής ATHLETE) + -IC.] Pertaining to comrades or allies in a contest.

1671 [R. MACWARD] *True Nonconf.* Pref., If truth do.. require a synathletick zeal.

‖**synaxarion, -ium** (sɪnækˈsɛərɪɒn, -ɪəm). *Gr. Ch.* Pl. -ia. Also in anglicized form **synaxary** (sɪˈnæksərɪ). [eccl. L., a. eccl. Gr. συναξάριον, f. σύναξις SYNAXIS. Cf. F. *synaxaire.*] An account of the life of a saint, read as a lesson in public worship; also, a collection of such accounts. So **synaxarist** (sɪˈnæksərɪst) [Gr. συναξαρίστης], the compiler of a synaxarion.

1850 NEALE *Eastern Ch., Gen. Introd.* IV. iii. 838 *note*, Now follows the Synaxarion, or extracts from the Menology.

Ibid. 890 *The Synaxaria*..are the abbreviated lections from the Menologion, extracted from the Menæa. **1853** SCRIVENER *Collation Grk. MSS. Gospels* p. xxx, There are scattered fragments of a Synaxarion at the end of the book. **1883** SCHAFF *Hist. Chr. Ch., Apost. Chr.* II. xii. §81. 645 In all the existing Greek and Syriac lectionaries or evangeliaries and synaxaries..which contain the Scripture reading lessons for the churches. **1908** J. R. HARRIS *Side-Lights N.T. Research* iv. (1909) 126 The Synaxarist explains this to mean that St. Thomas himself visited China. **1911** *Encycl. Brit.* XXVI. 292/1 The Armenian synaxarium, called the synaxarium of Ter Israël.

‖**synaxis** (sɪˈnæksɪs). *Ch. Hist.* Pl. **synaxes** (sɪˈnæksiːz). [eccl. L., a. eccl. Gr. *σύναξις*, f. *συνάγειν* to gather together.] A meeting for worship, especially for celebration of the Eucharist.

1624 J. FISHER *Answ. Nine Points Controv.* (1625) 235 The whole Church, represented by the Synaxis, or Ecclesiasticall meeting of euery Christian parish. *a* **1638** MEDE *Wks.* (1672) 364 Who knows not that the Synaxis of the ancient Christians consisted of these three parts, Of hearing the Word of God, of Prayers, and Commemoration of Christ in the Eucharist? **1642** JER. TAYLOR *Episc.* xxxvii. (1647) 255 If they will celebrate Synaxes privately, it must be by a Priest, and he must be there by leave of the Bishop. **1682** G. VERNON *Life Heylin* 147 Our Divine built a private Oratory, where he had frequency of Synaxes. *a* **1773** A. BUTLER *Feasts & Fasts* VI. iv. (1839) 215 Theodorus Lector says, Timotheus..first ordered the creed to be recited..at every Synaxis. **1872** MORLEY *Voltaire* v. 244 What was the difference between the synaxis and the mass? **1872** W. E. SCUDAMORE *Notitia Eucharistica* I. i. (1876) 26 This name of Synaxis was given especially to those more solemn assemblies at which the Sacrament was celebrated.

sync, synch (sɪŋk). orig. *U.S.* Also **sink.** Colloq. abbrev. of SYNCHRONISM, SYNCHRONIZATION, SYNCHRONIZE *v.*, etc. Cf. *lip-sync(h)* s.v. LIP *sb.* 7. **a.** In technical senses, esp. in *Cinematogr.* and *Television.* Cf. POST-SYNC(H.

1929 *Photoplay* Apr. 31/2 *In sink*, in synchronism; picture and sound perfectly timed together. **1939** *Reader's Digest* Mar. 41/1 When your [television] set is out of synchronization the image sort of bobs and weaves; it is then 'out of sync'. **1943** *Gloss. Terms Telecomm. (B.S.I.)* 77 *Synchronising signal (Sync pulse)*, a signal sent out periodically by the transmitter in order to keep the receiving system in synchronism. **1945** F. HAMANN *Air Words* 52 *Synch, to*, to synchronize. **1954** *Proc. IRE* XLII. 106/2 With a strong (clean) sync signal, the color-carrier reference signal may be maintained as closely accurate as desired, independent of other factors. *Ibid.* 116/1 The composite system functions as a form of automatic frequency control system when out of sync and as an automatic phase control system when in sync. **1960** *How TV Works* 16/1 A 'line sync' is..the jargon for the timing signal which is given at the end of each separate line of a television picture. **1962** A. NISBETT *Technique Sound Studio* xii. 219 Mixing the output of two gramophone records or tapes playing almost in sync. **1963** MALEY & EARLE *Logic Design of Transistor Digital Computers* x. 275 If they [*sc.* pulsed-circuit flip-flops] are synced with a clock and thus with each other. **1965** *Wireless World* Aug. 389/1 The conditions for direct sync can now be examined. **1966** *Listener* 4 Aug. 160/1 The introduction of new lightweight sync-sound equipment. **1972** M. MUGGERIDGE *Green Stick* ii. 69 The sync frequently went awry, with the words of the song and the movements of the singers lips not tallying. **1973** C. BONINGTON *Everest* xv. 238 Graham and I played with the little synch-sound super 8 mm. cine camera, trying to make a documentary of what life was like at Camp 4. **1977** *Rolling Stone* 5 May 31/1 It was Mercury who would blow a fuse if the lights were out of sync or the PA system malfunctioned. *Ibid.* 16 June 12/3 They wanted it synched to within one frame. **1978** *SLR Camera* Aug. 88/2 For electronic flash the camera is in sync at all speeds from 1/25th sec downwards and with expendable flash bulbs, at all speeds from 1/30th down. **1979** *Mod. Photogr.* Dec. 192/1 Connect an electronic flash to the camera with the proper sync terminal.

b. *gen.* Esp. in phrs. ***in sync, out of sync.*** Also *fig.*

1961 J. STEINBECK *Winter of our Discontent* II. xiv. 278 Something's going on... I just feel it... Everybody's a little out of synch. **1964** 'R. MACDONALD' *Far Side of Dollar* (1965) xxvi. 225 We could step up our schedule and synch our watches, eh? **1966** E. WEST *Night is Time for Listening* vi. 200 No cops, no State Department. Are we in sync? **1968** T. WOLFE *Electric Kool-Aid Acid Test* xi. 147 Somehow this ties in, *synchs*, directly with what Kesey has just said. **1974** *Times Lit. Suppl.* 8 Nov. 1247/4 Worldly success depends on being, as it were, in sync with the contemporary scene, and it was at this point that Fleming began to get out of sync, never to get properly in again. **1977** *Time* 17 Oct. 42/3 The next thing will be to bring the players' uniforms into sync with the floor design. **1978** J. IRVING *World according to Garp* xvii. 352 His watch..was several hours out of sync with the United States; he had last set it in Vienna. **1978** *English Jrnl.* Dec. 50/1 Or is the teaching 'out of synch' with the cognitive development..and the intentions of the learner? **1982** M. MILLAR *Mermaid* x. 110 She..sensed his uneasiness, his awareness that he was out of sync, out of tune.

syncarp (ˈsɪnkɑːp). *Bot.* [ad. mod.L. *syncarpium*, f. Gr. *σύν* SYN-[1] + *καρπός* fruit.] A multiple fruit, i.e. one arising from a number of carpels in one flower: most properly applied when the carpels are coherent (cf. next).

Usually distinguished from an *aggregate* or *confluent* fruit, i.e. one arising from a number of flowers.

1826–34 T. EDWARDS in *Encycl. Metrop.* (1845) VII. 49 Compound fruits or syncarps. **1875** BENNETT & DYER tr. *Sachs' Bot.* 537 Starting from the definition that a fruit is always the product of a single ripe ovary, it follows that several fruits may arise from one flower... The ripe gynæceum has in such cases been termed a multiple fruit, but it would be much better to apply to it the term Syncarp. Thus..the..fruits..of Ranunculus or Clematis or..of Pæonia or Helleborus, form together a syncarp... The syncarp must not be confounded with the pseudocarp resulting from an entire inflorescence, as in..the mulberry and fig..or the pine-apple.

syncarpous (sɪnˈkɑːpəs), *a. Bot.* [f. mod.L. *syncarpus* (f. Gr. *σύν* SYN-[1] + *καρπός* fruit) + -OUS.] Consisting of united or coherent carpels: opp. to *apocarpous.*

1830 LINDLEY *Nat. Syst. Bot.* Introd. p. xxx, Syncarpous [ovaria] are those of which the carpella are compactly combined. **1872** OLIVER *Elem. Bot.* I. iv. 37 The pistil [of Deadnettle] is syncarpous, consisting of two carpels, as indicated by the bifid stigma.

syncarpy (ˈsɪnkɑːpɪ). *Bot.* [Formed as prec. + -Y.] Abnormal union or fusion of two or more fruits.

1869 M. T. MASTERS *Veget. Teratol.* 47 A very remarkable example of Syncarpy.., in which nine strawberries were borne on one stem. **1885** *Athenæum* 5 Dec. 736/2 Some twin apples..were grown at Shepherd's Bush..many of the fruits being good examples of syncarpy.

syncategorem (sɪnˈkætɪgərɛm). *Logic.* Also 7 -eme. [ad. med.L. *syncatēgorēma* (Thomas Aquinas), a. Gr. *συγκατηγόρημα*, f. *συγκατηγορεῖν* (in Logic) to predicate jointly: cf. SYN-[1] and CATEGOREM.] A word which cannot be used by itself as a term, but only in conjunction with another word or words: e.g. a sign of quantity (as *all, some, no*), or an adverb, preposition, or conjunction.

1653 R. BAILLIE *Dissuas. Vind.* (1655) 62 Are not diverse universall propositions even with the Syncatagorem of universalitie of an indefinite nature and sense, which admit the exception of some particulars? **1697** tr. *Burgersdicius' Logic* I. xxix. 116 The Syncategoremes or consignificative Terms..that signifie nothing of themselves but when join'd to other Words, as *every one, all, all that*, &c.

syncategorematic (sɪn,kætɪgɒrɪˈmætɪk), *a.* [ad. Gr. *συγκατηγορηματικός*, f. *συγκατηγόρημα*: see prec. and -IC.] In Logic: of the nature of a syncategorem: opp. to CATEGOREMATIC. Also in extended uses in linguistic analysis.

1827 WHATELY *Logic* (ed. 2) 347 Syncategorematic words are such as cannot singly express a Term, but only a part of a Term. **1843** MILL *Logic* I. ii. §2. **1870** JEVONS *Elem. Logic* iii. 18. **1931** [see AUTOSEMANTIC *a.* (*sb.*)]. **1957** G. RYLE in M. Black *Importance of Lang.* (1962) 159 This is what Mill had said of the syncategorematic words. **1966** J. J. KATZ *Philos. Lang.* v. 312 Since the meaning of 'good' cannot stand alone as a complete concept, we shall say that the meaning of 'good' is *syncategorematic.* **1972** *Language* XLVIII. 351 Syncategorematic features such as abrupt/non-abrupt and strident/mellow... By this term I mean features which necessarily occur only in conjunction with certain other features. Besides the abrupt/continuant vs. strident/mellow example, voiced/voiceless vs. tense/lax appear to be syncategorematic, as do compact/non-compact vs. diffuse/non-diffuse in vowels. **1975** *Ibid.* LI. 32 Russell's contextual or syncategorematic definition of definite descriptions is equivalent to the conjunction of three propositions, one of which embodies a uniqueness claim.

syncategoreˈmatical, *a.* [Formed as prec. + -ICAL.] = prec.

1646 SIR T. BROWNE *Pseud. Ep.* VI. i. 276 The Jews..in their copies expunged the word כל or Syncategorematicall terme *omnis.* *a* **1670** HACKET *Abp. Williams* I. (1693) 76 A cluster of most crabbed Notions, pick'd up out of Metaphysicks and Logic, as Categorematical, and Syncategorematical. **1701** NORRIS *Ideal World* I. vi. 84 A kind of syncategorematical term, such as is not significative by itself. **1935** H. STRAUMANN *Newspaper Headlines* 72 The distinction resembles that of E. Husserl's (categorematical and syncategorematical words).

Hence **syncategoreˈmatically** *adv.*

1600 W. WATSON *Decacordon* (1602) 30 This Elenchiall fallacy (for he will not dare stand syncategorematically to approue it) denies flatly free-will. **1975** *New Left Rev.* Nov.–Dec. 55 Philosophy has no object, in that it is its task to analyse concepts which can only be used syncategorematically, i.e. under some particular description, in science.

‖**syncellus** (sɪnˈsɛləs). *Eccl.* Pl. -i. Also 9 in anglicized form **syncel.** [med.L. *syncellus, sincellus*, lit. one who shares a cell with another, a. Byzantine Gr. *σύγκελλος*, hybrid f. Gr. *σύν* SYN-[1] + *cella* CELL *sb.*] In the Eastern Church, orig. an ecclesiastic who lived continually with a prelate; *esp.* the domestic chaplain of a metropolitan or patriarch; later, a dignitary who was associated with a prelate and succeeded to his office.

Applied by some to ecclesiastics in the Western Church.

1706 PHILLIPS (ed. Kersey), *Syncellus*, a dignify'd Clergy-man in the Greek Church, who was next to the Patriarch; a Bishop's Suffragan. **1728** CHAMBERS *Cycl.* s.v., There were also Syncelli in the Western Church, particularly in France. **1844** KAY *Fleury's Eccl. Hist.* III. 13 *note*, At Constantinople the Syncels possessed a very high rank; in Constantine's time they sat by the side of the Patriarch, taking precedence even of the Metropolitans. **1890** T. W. ALLIES *Peter's Rock* 326 Anastasius, priest and syncellus of Sancta Sophia.

So **synˈcellite** [ad. med.L. *syncellita*: see -ITE[1]].

1720 J. JOHNSON *Collect. Eccl. Laws, etc. Ch. Eng.* anno 679. §7 Your Predecessor Gregory of blessed Memory, and ..St. Augustin his Syncellite.

synch, erroneous form of CINCH *sb.* and *v.*

synch: see SYNC, SYNCH.

synchesis, synchisis, erron. ff. SYNCHYSIS.

synchisite (ˈsɪŋkɪsaɪt, -zaɪt). Also **synchysite.** *Min.* [ad. G. *synchisit* (G. Flink 1901, in *Bull. Geol. Inst. Univ. Upsala* V. 82), f. Gr. *σύγχυσις* confusion + -ITE[1]. (For the reason of the name see quot. 1909.)] A fluocarbonate of cerium and calcium, occurring in minute yellow crystals.

1901 *Jrnl. Chem. Soc.* LXXX. II. 663 Synchysite.—This new name is applied to a mineral from Narsarsuk, in South Greenland. **1909** DANA & FORD *Dana's Syst. Min.* App. II. 102 Synchisite... Crystals minute, often in loose aggregates... Composition, $CeFCaC_2O_6$... From Narsarsuk, So. Greenland... Named from *σύγχυσις*, confounded, in allusion to its being mistaken for parisite. **1965** *Bull. Geol. Survey Dept. Malawi* No. 15. 124 Concentrations of bastnaesite and synchysite occur in the central core of sideritic carbonatite at Chilwa Island. **1975** [see SYNTAXY].

‖**synchondrosis** (sɪŋkɒnˈdrəʊsɪs). *Anat.* Pl. -droses (-ˈdrəʊsiːz). [mod.L., a. late Gr. *συγχόνδρωσις*, f. *σύν* SYN-[1] + *χόνδρος* cartilage: see -OSIS.] The junction of two bones by cartilage; the structure or part in which this takes place; a cartilaginous articulation or symphysis; *spec.* the ***sacro-iliac synchondrosis*** or articulation of the sacrum with the ilium.

1615 CROOKE *Body of Man* 345 A new Synchondrosis or articulation by the mediation of a Cartilage cannot be made. **1732** A. MONRO *Anat. Bones* (ed. 2) 159 On the Chin externally, a transverse Ridge appears in the Middle;..the two Parts, of which this Bone then consists, are joined..in Children by Synchondrosis. **1831** R. KNOX *Cloquet's Anat.* 169 The articulations in which cartilages are employed to keep the bones together are called Synchondroses. **1835–6** *Todd's Cycl. Anat.* I. 249/1 In the sacro-iliac symphysis, or synchondrosis. **1875** HUXLEY in *Encycl. Brit.* I. 753/1 The suspensorium..being, as a general rule, united with some part of the wall of the skull by synchondrosis.

Hence **synchondrosial** (-ˈdrəʊsɪəl) *a.*, of, pertaining to, or constituting a synchondrosis; **synchonˈdrosially** *adv.*, in the manner of a synchondrosis. So **synchondrotomy** (-ˈdrɒtəmɪ) *Surg.* [-TOMY], the operation of cutting through a synchondrosis, esp. the *symphysis pubis* (SYMPHYSIOTOMY).

1866 HUXLEY *Laing's Preh. Rem. Caithn.* 101 Pelves put together without their *synchondrosial cartilages and interpubic ligaments. **1888** HULKE in *Proc. Zool. Soc.* 419 A rough synchondrosial impression. **1902** *Proc. Zool. Soc.* 4 Nov. 291 The pterygials being immovably attached to the scapula and coracoid, either directly or *synchondrosially. **1848** DUNGLISON *Med. Lex.* (ed. 7), *Synchondrotomy.

†**synchrism.** *Obs. rare*⁻⁰. [ad. late L. *synchrisma* (Vegetius) rubbing with liniment, a. Gr. *σύγχρισμα* ointment, f. *συγχρίειν*, f. *σύν* SYN-[1] + *χρίειν* to anoint.]

1656 BLOUNT *Glossogr.* [from Cotgr. *Syncrisme*], *Syncrism* (*syncrisma*), a liquid Medicine, a thin and spreading ointment. **1658** PHILLIPS, *Synchrism.*

synchro (ˈsɪŋkrəʊ). [f. SYNCHRO(NOUS *a.*]

a. = SELSYN. Freq. *attrib.*

1943 *Appl. Electronics* (Mass. Inst. Technol. Dept. Electr. Engin.) vi. 316 When designed so that the rotor may turn or be turned freely, the device is given various trade names, such as *Selsyn, Synchro*, or *Autosyn.* **1958** W. G. HOLZBOCK *Automatic Control* vii. 122 There are different synchro components, such as the synchro transmitter, synchro receiver, synchro control transformer, etc., which are combined in control circuits in various ways. **1980** J. D. LENK *Handbk. Controls & Instrumentation* x. 289 A receiver synchro is limited to light loads such as moving a pointer across a scale to indicate the angular displacement of some device operating a transmitting synchro.

b. Synchronised swimming (see SYNCHRONIZED *ppl. a.*).

1968 G. RACKHAM *Synchronized Swimming* i. 27 Being so diverse in character Synchro provides a wide field of related activities. **1974** *Observer* (Colour Suppl.) 17 Mar. 75/1 A member of the Great Britain Synchronised Swimming Team..has been doing synchro for 11 years.

synchro- (ˈsɪŋkrəʊ), comb. form repr. SYNCHRONOUS *a.* and related words, as in **ˈsynchroflash** *Photogr.*, a flash whose operation is synchronized with the opening of the shutter; **,synchro-ˈsunlight** *Photogr.*, used *attrib.* to designate the use of flash to supplement sunlight; **ˈsynchro-swim(ming)** = *synchronized swimming* s.v. SYNCHRONIZED *ppl. a.*

1940 A. L. M. SOWERBY *Dict. Photogr.* 626 *Synchroflash photography*, the taking of photographs with a flashbulb synchronised to the shutter of the camera. **1952** *Sci. News Let.* 24 Dec. 416/1 Synchroflash testing device enables both the professional and amateur photographer to check his equipment. **1974** *Encycl. Brit. Macropædia* XIV. 324/1 In the early days of *Life* and *Look*, photographers made great use of so-called synchroflash. **1940** F. J. MORTIMER *Wall's Dict. Photogr.* (ed. 15) 316 Synchro-sunlight technique is chiefly of use in connection with figure subjects, where it gives a well-lit figure against a much less well-lit background. **1981** G. L. WAKEFIELD *Beginner's Guide*

Photogr. vii. 137 Synchro-sunlight photography has to be done carefully because if the amount of extra fill-in is excessive the flash takes over from the sunshine and the effect is completely false. **1976** *Star* (Sheffield) 3 Dec. 28/7 Eight Nalgo SC swimmers passed their respective synchro-swim grade examinations at Heeley Baths last night. **1976** *Milton Keynes Express* 11 June 11/1 It is hoped to bring both synchro-swimming and water polo to the city in the near future.

synchrocyclotron (ˌsɪŋkrəʊˈsaɪklətrɒn). *Physics.* [f. SYNCHRO- + CYCLOTRON.] A particle accelerator similar to a cyclotron in which the frequency of the accelerating electric field is decreased as the particles gain energy so as to allow for the concomitant increase in mass and enable greater energies to be achieved.

1947 *Times* 7 July 3/3 One machine being considered for Brookhaven National Laboratory on Long Island, New York, is a huge synchro-cyclotron. **1956** *Nature* 3 Mar. 397/2 These exchanges of views led to the decision to fix the energy of the proposed synchro-cyclotron for the international laboratory at 600 MeV. and that of the proton-sychrotron at greater than 25 GeV. **1971** *New Scientist* 2 Sept. 510/1 The University of Chicago synchrocyclotron.. has been shut down. **1973** L. J. TASSIE *Physics Elem. Particles* 221 In circular accelerators, such as synchrocyclotrons and synchrotrons, the particles are confined to circular or spiralling paths by magnetic guide fields so that they pass one or several radiofrequency sources a large number of times.

synchromesh (ˈsɪŋkrəʊmɛʃ). *Mech.* Also syncro-. [f. *synchronized mesh.*] **a.** A mechanism that facilitates gear-changing in a motor vehicle by automatically causing gearwheels to rotate in synchronism before they engage. Freq. *attrib.*

1929 *Amer. Motorist* Oct. 35/2 (Advt.), Syncro-mesh silent shift transmission. **1931** *Automotive Industries* 24 Oct. 644/1 Constant-mesh gears made synchro-mesh transmissions and free wheeling feasible. **1932** *Oxford Times* 23 Sept. 22/3 Free-wheeling and syncro-mesh gears have for some time been almost universal on cars built in the United States. **1933** *Motor* 10 Oct. 525/3 The Citroën Co. was also early in the field with synchromesh. **1950** *Engineering* 22 Sept. 255/3 Synchromesh engagement is provided for second, third and top gears. **1962** *Which? Car Suppl.* Oct. 129/2 These two cars had no synchromesh on first gear. **1976** P. R. WHITE *Planning for Public Transport* iii. 59 A synchromesh or semi-automatic transmission is quite adequate, as steady running replaces the frequent stopping and starting of urban operation.

b. *fig.*

1966 *Listener* 11 Aug. 204/2 They are vision, sound, decor, lighting, and a sense of style. When all these are in synchromesh, as in a well designed gearbox, the show may be a success. **1977** *Guardian* 5 May 14/2 Somewhere, somewhere, waits the perfect partner, the soul-mate, the sexual syncromesh. **1982** *Church Times* 23 Apr. 7/3 *The Flowers and Fruits of the Bible*..is a lovely book, if slightly out of syncromesh.

Synchromism (ˈsɪŋkrəmɪz(ə)m). [f. SYN-¹ + Gr. χρῶμα colour + -ISM.] A movement in art resembling Orphism, founded by the U.S. painters Stanton Macdonald-Wright (b. 1890) and Morgan Russell (1886–1953), with emphasis on the abstract use of colour. Also, *loosely* = ORPHISM 2. Cf. SYNCHRONISM 4.

1912 M. RUSSELL in G. Levin *Synchromism & Amer. Color Abstraction 1910–1925* (1978) ii. 20 This is cubisme, Futurisme, Synchromisme and any isms possible for many years, perhaps centuries. **1913** *Forum* Dec. 768 This brings us to the latest phase of this chaotic and polyglot age of painting—Synchromism, sired by two Americans, S. Macdonald-Wright and Morgan Russell, which seems destined to have the most far-reaching effects of any art force since Cézanne. **1923** J. GORDON *Mod. French Painters* xiv. 149 Synchromism, Simultaneism..and so on, are merely various more or less pretentious methods adopted by artists..to say that they are going to do just as they like. **1937** T. H. BENTON *Artist in America* ii. 38 My old friend Wright came back to America before the gathering of the war clouds in Europe. He came back, the founder of a new school, synchromism, which he had flung in the face of Paris. **1958** M. L. WOLF *Dict. Painting* 288 Synchromism usually displayed its purposes in pictures of huge size, the colors forming prismatic patterns. **1978** G. LEVIN *Synchromism & Amer. Color Abstraction 1910–1925* ii. 20 The fact that the Delaunays had used closely related terminology, possibly at a slightly earlier date, does not, of course, make Synchromism a direct outgrowth of their art.

Hence **ˈSynchromist** *sb.* and *a.*, **Synchroˈmistic** *a.*

1913 *Forum* Dec. 769 The Synchromists claim to have discovered the secrets of color. **1916** *Ibid.* Apr. 461 His later paintings have undergone somewhat the Synchromistic vision. **1923** [see SIMULTANEIST]. **1936** *Cubism & Abstract Art* (N.Y. Mus. Mod. Art) 74 The first large Synchromist exhibition was held in Munich in June 1913. **1958** M. L. WOLF *Dict. Painting* 202 Known also as the Synchromist School, it [*sc.* Orphism] was essentially an abstract style. **1970** *Oxf. Compan. Art* 1118/2 Arthur Burdett Frost.. helped to spread the ideas of the Synchromists in America. **1974** *Encycl. Brit. Micropædia* VI. 439/3 Although he [*sc.* Macdonald-Wright] denied any connection, his Synchromist theories were also influenced by the contemporary Parisian movement of Orphism.

Synchromy (ˈsɪŋkrəmɪ). Also **synchromy**. [f. as prec. + -Y³, after *symphony*.] An abstract painting of a type characteristic of Synchromism.

1916 *Forum* Feb. 213 Why not hang a Pre-Raphaelite-Moreau work of Claude Buck beside an ultra-modern Synchromy. **1936** *Cubism & Abstract Art* (N.Y. Mus. Mod. Art) 74 The first purely abstract 'Synchromy' was not shown until the exhibition in Paris in the autumn of that year [*sc.* 1913]. **1974** *Encycl. Brit. Micropædia* IX. 737/3 The two artists were living in Paris, painting abstract works they called 'synchromies'.

synchronal (ˈsɪŋkrənəl), *a.* (*sb.*) Now *rare* or *Obs.* [f. late L. *synchronus* SYNCHRONOUS + -AL¹.]

1. = SYNCHRONOUS 1, 1 b. Const. *to.*

1660 H. MORE *Myst. Godl.* v. xv. 182 The things that are found to be Synchronal, have also a natural connexion and complication one with another. **1668** —— *Div. Dial.* v. xxxvii. 513 The Vision of things synchronal to the seven Thunders. **1672** *Mede's Wks.* Gen. Pref. ****j, Those Passages in the Apocalyps which, though dispersed here and there, are Synchronal and Homogenea.. **1837** *For. Q. Rev.* XIX. 416 We, last year, brought before our readers a classical Italian tragedy upon the fall of..Napoleon, although the temerity of such synchronal dramatization was slightly veiled under old Assyrian names. **1856** P. FAIRBAIRN *Prophecy* II. iii. §3. 396 Any other prophetic symbols..that follow, must stand to it in the relation of synchronal, not of continuative and posterior developments.

2. = SYNCHRONOUS 2.

1876 J. ELLIS *Caesar in Egypt* 71 They blithely dance, well-timed by castanets, And cymbals, and the synchronal clap of hands.

†**B.** *sb.* A simultaneous or contemporary event.

1660 H. MORE *Myst. Godl.* v. xvi. 197 The last Synchronals are those that are contemporary to the Seventh Trumpet. **1681** —— *Expos. Dan.* App. i. 257 Those three Synchronals, the restored Beast, the Whore, and the Two-horned Beast. **1685** —— *Paralip. Prophet.* xlii. 364.

synchroneity (sɪŋkrəˈniːɪtɪ, -ˈneɪɪtɪ). Chiefly *Geol.* [f. SYNCHRON(OUS *a.* – *-eity*, after *simultaneity, spontaneity*, etc.] = SYNCHRONISM 1 a.

1909 *Cent. Dict.* Suppl., *Synchroneity*, synchronism; the character or fact of being synchronous; specifically, in *geol.* supposed synchronism in time of deposition of strata. **1945** *Bull. Amer. Assoc. Petroleum Geologists* XXIX. 427 Facts bearing on synchroneity. **1968** R. G. WEST *Pleistocene Geol. & Biol.* xii. 286 There remain very many problems of chronology, in particular the synchroneity of pollen zones. **1979** *Nature* 11 Oct. 431/1 Their data indicate an approximate synchroneity of dinosaur and foram extinctions just below anomaly 29, the maximum error being about 100,000 years.

synchronic (sɪnˈkrɒnɪk), *a.* [f. late L. *synchronus*: see SYNCHRONAL *a.* (*sb.*) and -IC. Cf. F. *synchronique.*]

1. = SYNCHRONOUS 1, 1 b. *rare.*

1833 LAMB *Elia* Ser. II. *Barrenness Mod. Art*, At the interposition of the synchronic miracle. **1887** HEILPRIN *Distrib. Anim.* II. ii. 231 The want of synchronic correspondence..between..closely related assemblages of fossil remains.

2. = next, 2. *rare.*

1892 *Harper's Mag.* Sept. 507 Whose many leaves showed light or dark, synchronic with the breeze.

3. *Linguistics.* [tr. F. *synchronique* (F. de Saussure *a* 1913, in *Cours de linguistique générale* (1916) iii. 117).] Pertaining to or designating a method of linguistic study concerned with the state of a language at one time, past or present; descriptive, as opposed to historical or diachronic. Also *transf.* in Anthropology, etc.

1922 L. BLOOMFIELD in *Classical Weekly* 13 Mar. 142/1 One is glad to see, therefore, that Dr. Sapir deals with synchronic matters (to use De Saussure's terminology) before he deals with diachronic. **1927**, etc. [see DIACHRONIC *a.* 2]. **1937** [see SAUSSUREAN *a.*] **1946** [see ONOMATOPY]. **1954** [see PROCESS *sb.* 5 b]. **1968** *Jrnl. Assoc. Teachers of Russian* XVII. 8 A synchronic study of a language studies the language of a particular period without reference to what went before or came after, and in practice the period in question is generally our own. **1975** *Listener* 20 Mar. 367/3 Though the 'synchronic' approach of the semiologists is for the moment more fashionable, it is impossible not to be interested in the history of social myths.

synchronical (sɪnˈkrɒnɪkəl), *a.* Now *rare.* [Formed as prec. + -ICAL.]

1. a. = SYNCHRONOUS 1. Const. *with*, †*to.*

1652 CHARLETON *Darkn. Atheism* iv. 149 In the year *Æræ Christi nati* 33. (which is synchronical to the 78. of the Julian account). **1677** CARY *Palæol. Caron.* II. II. III. v. 231 Their Beginning and Continuance Synchronical with the Kings of Judah and Israel. **1826** E. IRVING *Babylon* I. III. 179 Which are not successive, but contemporaneous or synchronical. **1838** G. S. FABER *Inquiry* 290 On the strength of evidence, synchronical with the particulars detailed. **1855** MOTLEY *Dutch Rep.* VI. ii. (1866) 801/2 To cast a glance at certain synchronical events in different parts of the Netherlands. **1865** MᶜLAUCHLAN *Early Scott. Ch.* xix. 251 In the MS. containing the synchronical kings of Ireland and Scotland.

b. = SYNCHRONOUS 1 b.

1843 *Florist's Jrnl.* (1846) IV. 252 The attempted synchronical arrangement of the calendar of operations. **1867** J. BURDON SANDERSON in *Phil. Trans.* CLVII. 576 When..great variations of arterial pressure take place.., it is necessary..to adopt some method of marking synchronical points in the two tracings. **1878** H. G. GUINNESS *End of Age* (1880) 140 Rev. xvii, a prophecy which by its synchronical connection with almost all the other predictions..furnishes a most valuable clue.

2. = SYNCHRONOUS 2.

1660 BOYLE *New Exp. Phys. Mech.* Digress. 350 The Systole and Diastole of the Heart and Lungs, being very far from Synchronical. **1664** POWER *Exp. Philos.* I. 65.

3. *Linguistics.* = SYNCHRONIC *a.* 3.

1949 *Oxf. Classical Dict.* 971 If we accept J. B. Hofmann's distinction of the 'diachronical' and the '(idio)synchronical' types of grammar..then Kühner-Blass belongs to the synchronical. **1956** *Archivum Linguisticum* VIII. 174 Particularly out of place in a synchronical book are some assumptions concerning Old Polish.

Hence **synˈchronically** *adv.* = SYNCHRONOUSLY.

1749 HARTLEY *Observ. Man* I. i. §2. 67 Two Vibrations, associated synchronically. **1818** G. S. FABER *Horæ Mosaicæ* I. 305 The question..whether they were..written synchronically with the exodus. **1843** *Civil Eng. & Arch. Jrnl.* VI. 159/1 The simplicity of Greek architecture..is the element which forbids its reproduction synchronically. **1935** *Year's Work in Eng. Stud. 1933* XIV. 48 The seven explanatory aspects include semasiology and morphology treated synchronically or diachronically, and also diachronic phonology. **1947** *Essays & Studies* XXXII. 79 There is, however, one grammar..that feels the need of changing the method, of recording the facts first synchronically, then, in the second part, diachronically. **1968** J. LYONS *Introd. Theoretical Linguistics* i. 46 It does not matter by what route (the number, nature or order of the moves) the players have arrived at the particular state of the game: this state is describable *synchronically* without reference to the previous moves. **1979** *Dictionaries* I. 6 One may wonder whether words like *fro* or synchronically unproductive suffixes like *-ure*..are really indispensable elements of the defining vocabulary.

synchronicity (ˌsɪŋkrəˈnɪsɪtɪ). [f. SYNCHRONIC *a.* + -ITY.] The name given by the Swiss psychologist, C. G. Jung (1875–1961), to the phenomenon of events which coincide in time and appear meaningfully related but have no discoverable causal connection.

1953 *Jrnl. Soc. for Psychical Res.* XXXVII. 28 Synchronicity, he [*sc.* Jung] explains, is not just synchronousness. In a 'synchronicity phenomenon', as he uses the phrase, two contemporaneous events are linked together in a meaningful manner. **1955** R. F. C. HULL tr. *Jung & Pauli's Interpretation of Nature & Psyche* i. 27, I have picked on the term 'synchronicity' to designate a hypothetical factor equal in rank to causality as a principle of explanation. **1963** *Punch* 25 Dec. 910/2 Hauntings..magical coincidence ('synchronicity') the lot. **1974** *Sci. Amer.* Jan. 113/2 The Wilhelm-Baynes volume includes the famous foreword by Jung in which he explains the oracular power of the *I Ching* by his theory of 'synchronicity'. **1980** C. FITZGIBBON *Rat Report* vi. 112 A thought-transference has also no mass, but very considerable energy and therefore 'travels'..through the time element called synchronicity.

synchronism (ˈsɪŋkrənɪz(ə)m). [ad. mod.L. *synchronismus*, ad. Gr. συγχρονισμός, f. σύγχρονος SYNCHRONOUS. Cf. F. *synchronisme*, It. *sincronismo.*]

1. a. The quality of being synchronous; coincidence or agreement in point of time; concurrence of two or more events in time; contemporary existence or occurrence.

1588 J. HARVEY *Disc. Probl.* 21 Is there any greater concordance, or Synchronisme, betweene the prophesie of Elias and this text, than [etc.]? *c* **1624** MEDE *Wks.* (1672) 581 The Apocalypse..hath marks and signs..whereby the Order, Synchronism and Sequele of all the Visions..may be found out. **1697** BENTLEY *Phal.* iv. (1699) 148 The whole tenor of History, confirm'd by so many Synchronisms and Concurrences. **1712** SWIFT *Art Polit. Lying* Wks. 1755 III. I. 123 It is impossible to explain several phœnomena in relation to the celerity of lyes, without the supposition of synchronism and combination. **1802** PLAYFAIR *Illustr. Hutton. Th.* 125 Nor is there any synchronism between the most recent epochas of the mineral kingdom, and the most ancient of our ordinary chronology. **1867** MURCHISON *Siluria* v. (ed. 4) 95 The relative thickness of deposits is no test whatever of their synchronism. **1874** FARRAR *Christ* lviii. II. 342 That Eternity, which is the synchronism of all the future, and all the present, and all the past.

b. *Geom.* The property of being synchronous, as a curve (see SYNCHRONOUS 1 c); *spec.* of a great circle (see CIRCLE *sb.* 2 a), the property that chords starting from the same point of the circumference will be described in equal times by particles descending under the influence of gravity.

1867 BRANDE & COX *Dict. Sci.*, etc. s.v. *Synchronous*, The synchronism of the circle.

2. a. Arrangement or treatment of synchronous events, etc. together or in conjunction, as in a history; agreement in relation to the time of the events described.

1612 SELDEN in *Drayton's Poly-olb.* To Rdr. A 2, Upon weighing the Reporters credit, comparison with more perswading authority, and synchronisme, (the best touch-stone in this kind of triall). *a* **1676** HALE *Prim. Orig. Man.* II. iii. (1677) 143 The coherence and synchronism of all the parts of the Mosaical Chronology. **1837** HALLAM *Lit. Eur.* I. iv. §62 (1847) I. 303 The laws of synchronism..bring strange partners together, and we may pass at once from Luther to Ariosto.

b. (with *a* and *pl.*) A statement or argument that two or more events, etc. are synchronous; a parallel drawn between occurrences, etc. in respect of time; a description or account of different events belonging to the same period; a tabular arrangement of historical events or personages according to their dates.

1593 R. HARVEY *Philad.* 7 Your Synchronisme of Faunus, of Sybilla and Praenestine is to no purpose. **1649** ROBERTS *Clavis Bibl.* 214 Which two Kingdoms..are..described in a continued Synchronisme, or Contemporary Parallel. **1732** BERKELEY *Alciphr.* VI. §21 To range them in synchronisms, and try to adjust them with sacred chronology. **1861** O'CURRY *Lect. MS. Mat. Anc. Irish Hist.* 171 The histories and synchronisms of Erinn. **1888** E. L. CUTTS *St. Augustine* vii. 52 We may make a useful synchronism by noting that the time of his residence was in the year following that in which Symmachus had headed a deputation of senators. **1901** *Temple Bible, Exodus* 136 (*heading*) Synchronism of Ancient History.

c. (*a*) Treatment of details according to identity of period, as in architecture. (*b*) Representation of events of different times together, e.g. in the same picture.

1843 *Civil Eng. & Arch. Jrnl.* VI. 158 The question whether synchronism and uniformity of style are essential to beauty and propriety in architecture. *Ibid.* 160/1 This work is executed with a knowledge of style and detail, with an attention to synchronism..which leaves nothing to be desired. **1854** FAIRHOLT *Dict. Terms Art, Synchronism*, a representation of two or more events at the same time: it was a favourite practice with the mediæval artists to give the entire life of a saint, or history of an event, in one picture.

3. a. Recurrence at the same successive instants of time; the fact of keeping time, i.e. proceeding at the same rate and exactly together; coincidence of period, as of two sets of movements, vibrations, or alternations of electric current.

1854 H. ROGERS *Ess.* (1874) II. i. 90 Exact synchronism and parallelism of movements, as between those of two exactly regulated chronometers. **1869** TYNDALL in *Fortn. Rev.* 1 Feb. 231 The heaping up of motion on the atoms, in consequence of their synchronism with the shorter waves. **1873** JENKIN *Electr. & Magn.* xxii. 323 The synchronism required is in Caselli's instrument obtained by a pendulum at each receiving station;..the one pendulum controls the other by a current which it transmits..through a special circuit. **1902** *Electr. Rev.* 21 Feb. 290/1 A new synchronism indicator for alternators.

b. *spec.* in *Cinematogr.* and *Television.* Cf. SYNCHRONIZE *v.* 2 c.

1904 *Billboard* 27 Aug. 13/4 The motor of the cinematograph is absolutely dependent on the movement of the phonograph axle, and perfect synchronism must be had ..in order to render the illusion as perfectly lifelike as possible. **1928** *Television* Mar. 37 Thus ensuring synchronism between the transmitter and the receiver. **1957** MANVELL & HUNTLEY *Film Music* iii. 75 Nothing..can be more vulgar than music synchronism in films. **1967** *Electronics* 6 Mar. 78/2 (Advt.), The display cathode ray tube on which this output is viewed is scanned in synchronism.

4. = SYNCHROMISM. Cf. SIMULTANEISM 1.

[**1914** M. RUSSELL *Let.* 12 Mar. in G. Levin *Synchromism & Amer. Color Abstraction 1910–1925* (1978) ii. 20 Please don't say Synchronisme which does not apply to painting, the termination is 'chrome', 'color'.] **1961** M. LEVY *Studio Dict. Art Terms* 109 *Synchronism*, an alternative expression for *Orphism*. **1972** C. W. E. BIGSBY *Dada & Surrealism* ii. 10 In some ways it was a part of that artistic re-examination which spawned such schools as impressionism, cubism, futurism and, more exotically, suprematism, rayonism, plasticism, vorticism and synchronism.

5. *Linguistics.* = SYNCHRONY 2.

1962 [see DIACHRONISM 2].

Hence **synchro'nismical** *a.*, belonging to a synchronism or account of synchronous events (see 2 b).

1793 HELY tr. *O'Flaherty's Ogygia* I. 136 The ancient synchronismical account of Flann.

synchronist ('sɪŋkrənɪst). *rare.* Also 8 **sinchronist.** [f. prec.: see -IST. Cf. F. *synchroniste* adj.] One who lives at the same time with another; a contemporary.

1716 M. DAVIES *Athen. Brit.* II. 228 Abhor'd by all their Christian Sinchronists. *a* **1839** GALT *Demon Destiny* v. (1840) 32 When years had pass'd, with beauty bloom'd mature The tended synchronists.

synchronistic (sɪŋkrə'nɪstɪk), *a.* [f. SYNCHRONISM: see -ISTIC.] **1.** Belonging to synchronism; relating to or exhibiting the concurrence of events in time; also *loosely*, involving synchronism, synchronous, simultaneous.

1685 H. MORE *Illustration*, etc. Y j b, Schemes for the more easie understanding, and retaining in memory the synchronistick order of the Visions of the Apocalypse. *Ibid.* Z ij b, The general Synchronistick Table of the Visions of that Book. **1828** [see *symphronistic*, SYM-]. **1854** THIRLWALL *Lett.* (1881) I. 205 The comparative shortness of the interval ..considerably increases the difficulty of the synchronistic view. **1876** S. BIRCH *Rede Lect.* 16 The exact definition of three synchronistic events, the rising of the star, and of the Nile, and the commencement of the normal year of 365¼ days. **1888** A. C. JENNINGS (*title*) Chronological Tables. A synchronistic arrangement of the events of ancient history.

2. *Linguistics.* = SYNCHRONIC *a.* 3.

1937 J. ORR tr. *Iordan's Introd. Romance Linguistics* 284 Internal linguistics is static or synchronistic. **1949** *Archivum Linguisticum* I. 127 On the *synchronistic* plane, homonymy seems..to preclude the existence of any intrinsic link between form and meaning. **1951** [see DIACHRONISTIC *a.*]. **1962** L. J. COHEN *Diversity of Meaning* i. 12 Synchronistic and diachronistic enquiries—studies of a single period and studies through several periods, respectively—can and should complement each other.

3. Pertaining to or having the quality of synchronicity.

1955 R. F. C. HULL tr. *Jung & Pauli's Interpretation of Nature & Psyche* i. 40 Synchronistic events rest on the simultaneous occurrence of two different psychic states. **1972** A. KOESTLER *Roots of Coincidence* iii. 95 Thus precognitive experiences are 'evidently synchronistic.. since they are experienced as psychic images in the present as though the objective event already existed'. **1979** G. ADLER *Dynamics of Self* 10 Synchronistic phenomena, and in particular those of ESP, convinced Jung of the existence of a transcendental 'absolute knowledge'.

So **synchro'nistical** *a.*, now *rare* or *Obs.*, in sense 1; hence **synchro'nistically** *adv.*, in accordance with synchronism, synchrony (sense 2) or synchronicity; *loosely*, synchronously.

c **1624** MEDE *Wks.* (1672) 583, I was once wonderfully pleased with that Opinion..: But now at length the Law of Synchronistical necessity hath beat me from it. **1684** H. MORE *Answ.* 56 The difficult Visions..should..be referred Synchronistically to that Prophecy also. **1685** —— *Refl. Baxter* 5 Without this Synchronistical Skill..to pretend to understand the Apocalypse,..is as fond [etc.]. **1835** (*title*) Annales Antiquitatis. Chronological Tables of Ancient History Synchronistically and Ethnographically arranged. **1860** M. PATTISON *Ess.* (1889) I. 165 Eusebius..undertook a synchronistical compilation of the annals of all known nations. **1878** ZERFFI *Pre-Adamites* 9 We are thus able to trace long periods of an old stone age, a new stone age, and a bronze age, till synchronistically with the historical period we reach the iron age. **1949** *Archivum Linguisticum* I. 128 Is there any intrinsic and synchronistically valid reason for it [*sc.* a name] to have that form and no other? **1980** C. FITZGIBBON *Rat Report* vi. 112 My communication reaches you synchronistically at the same time as all the other rat reports which have been sent out every five hundred years.

synchronize ('sɪŋkrənaɪz), *v.* Also -ise. [f. SYNCHRONISM: see -IZE. Cf. F. *synchroniser.*]

1. a. *intr.* To occur at the same time; to coincide in point of time; to be contemporary or simultaneous. Const. *with.*

c **1624** MEDE *Wks.* (1672) 583 The Second Court.. synchroniseth with the Times of the Beast. **1681** H. MORE *Expos. Dan.* ii. 56 To conceive the times of the little Horn to synchronize with all the middle Synchronals of the Apocalypse. **1791** BURKE *Corr.* (1844) III. 345 To make the invasion synchronize with that bankruptcy, might not be so easy. **1847** DE QUINCEY *Secret Societies* Wks. 1863 VI. 245 The birth and the death..synchronise by a metaphysical nicety. **1859** JEPHSON *Brittany* viii. 115 The degradation of art which synchronized so curiously with the revival of classical learning. **1892** S. LAING *Human Origins* 51 A King of this dynasty, Khudurhagamar, synchronizes with Abraham.

b. *trans.* To cause to be, or represent as, synchronous; to assign the same date to; to bring together events, etc. belonging to the same time. Also *absol.*

1806 LADY MORGAN *Wild Irish Girl* (1867) I. xi. 184 (Funk) He has synchronized heroes who flourished in two distant periods. **1827** *Gentl. Mag.* XCVII. II. 505/2 This little attempt to synchronise the date of all nations with the Mosaic Deluge. **1862** M. HOPKINS *Hawaii* 55 On 'the 25th day of second month of the seventh year of Ansey',—a date difficult for the historian to synchronise with our own era. **1869** RAWLINSON *Anc. Hist.* Introd. 6 Nations accordingly, as the desire of exactness or the wish to synchronise arose, invented eras for themselves.

2. a. *intr.* To occur at the same successive instants of time; to keep time *with*; to go on at the same rate and exactly together; to have coincident periods, as two sets of movements or vibrations.

1867 LEWES *Hist. Philos.* (ed. 3) I. p. xxxiii, So that the movements of Thought may synchronise with the movements of Things. **1869** TYNDALL *Notes Lect. Light* §304 Waves of ether are absorbed with special energy..by atoms whose periods of vibration synchronise with the periods of the waves. **1871** —— *Fragm. Sci.* (1879) II. ii. 31 Small motions which synchronise with the appearance and disappearance of solar spots. **1889** WELCH *Text Bk. Naval Archit.* iii. 60 If the double period of the ship coincides with the period of the wave, the motions of each synchronise, or keep time, with the other.

b. *trans.* To cause to go at the same rate; *spec.* to cause (a timepiece) to indicate the same time as another.

1879 PRESCOTT *Sp. Telephone* 249 The idea of synchronizing the movements of the two instruments..was employed in telegraphy at a very early period. **1881** BIDWELL in *Nature* 10 Feb. 346/1 The two cylinders would be driven by clock-work, synchronised by an electro-magnetic arrangement. **1882** *Society* 18 Nov. 11/1 Unless the clock..was synchronised with Greenwich time.

c. In technical senses: to cause to coincide in time; to operate simultaneously or in synchronization. Also *intr.*

1910 *Chambers's Jrnl.* Mar. 206/1 The movements of the mouths of the characters on the scene synchronise with the utterance of the phonograph. **1922** *Radio News* (U.S.) Nov. 867/1 (*heading*), De Forest demonstrates his invention for synchronizing speech with movies... You..heard the tone which, to a musically trained ear, synchronized perfectly with every movement of the violin bow. **1934** C. LAMBERT *Music Ho!* III. 196 René Clair would not dare to synchronize one of his scenes with the sound of a real bal-musette band. **1940** F. J. MORTIMER *Wall's Dict. Photogr.* (ed. 15) 315 Focal-plane shutters can be well synchronised with the flash on small cameras. **1956** *Focal Encycl. Photogr.* 492/1 The duration of electronic flash discharge is always shorter than the fastest shutter speed with which it can be synchronized. **1957** *Encycl. Brit.* XXI. 912 D/1 It [*sc.* a video signal]..must have added to it the timing pulses needed to synchronize the receiver. **1962** S. A. CHOUDHURY in G. A. T. Burdett *Automatic Control Handbk.* iv. 39 A recent development which enables the receiver to accelerate from rest and automatically synchronise by simply putting the excitation on the selsyns through a three-pole switch. **1977** J. HEDGECOE *Photographer's Handbk.* 34/2 Cheaper cameras which only take bulbs or cubes are synchronized at low speeds, usually around 1/25 sec.

3. *gen.* To combine or co-ordinate.

1973 *N.Y. Law Jrnl.* 3 Apr. 4/5 The law is probably the only profession that must be synchronized with another profession—writing. **1976** *Time* 27 Dec., facing p. 36 (Advt.), Both media synchronize national interests with multinational scope. **1977** *N.Y. Rev. Bks.* 14 July 33/2 Silberman quotes an unreported speech given by the foreign minister, Milos Minic, which alleges not only that Western intelligence is involved with fascist exiles but also that Western press coverage of Yugoslavia is synchronized to discredit the country.

Hence '**synchronizing** *vbl. sb.* and *ppl. a.*; also ˌ**synchroni'zation**, the action of synchronizing, *spec.* in *Electr. Engin.* and in other technical uses.

1828 G. S. FABER *Sacr. Cal. Prophecy* Pref. p. xiii, If the principle of abstract *synchronisation be rejected, the Apocalypse..becomes a mere chaos. **1865** *Pall Mall G.* No. 134. 5/2 The synchronization of the 12th of July with the nomination-day. **1913** *N.Y. Times* 18 Feb. 3/1 Mr. Edison was looking for perfect synchronization of record and film. **1922** *Radio News* (U.S.) Nov. 867/1 Mr. de Forest has solved the secret of the 'talkie movie' with perfect synchronization. **1928** *Manch. Guardian Weekly* 17 Aug. 134/4 The sound is transformed into light and recorded on the margin of the film in automatic synchronisation with the movement of the lips. **1932** *Discovery* July 215/1 Lodge had shown the importance of tuning or 'synchronization'. **1940** *Amateur Radio Handbk.* (ed. 2) xix. 274/1 When the vision signals are..subject to serious interference which tends to upset synchronisation. **1958** *Newnes Compl. Amat. Photogr.* 37 Shutter synchronisation. *Ibid.*, The flash synchronisation may have only an X setting. **1962** S. A. CHOUDHURY in G. A. T. Burdett *Automatic Control Handbk.* iv. 36 If, before the supply is switched on, the rotors are 180 degrees displaced, no synchronisation will take place when the excitation is applied. **1880** *Echo* 24 Dec. 3/4 The *synchronising..of clocks..by means of pneumatic motive power transmitted through tubes..which has been found to answer admirably in Paris. **1882** C. WOOD in *Argosy* XXXIV. 136 We become comparatively intimate; there is a sympathy, a power of 'synchronizing'. **1931** B. BROWN *Talking Pictures* i. 3 The earliest practical attempts at synchronizing, i.e. keeping speech and gesture perfectly in phase. **1943** *Gloss. Terms Telecomm.* (*B.S.I.*) 35 *Synchronising*, the adjustment of the frequency of the time base to bear an integral relationship to the frequency of the phenomenon under investigation. *a* **1727** NEWTON *Chronol. Amended* ii. (1728) 191 Comparing the affairs of Egypt with the *synchronizing affairs of the Greeks and Hebrews. **1839** DE QUINCEY *Mod. Superstit.* Wks. 1862 III. 293 To suppose, that by some synchronising miracle, the constellation had been then specially called into existence. **1889** WELCH *Text Bk. Naval Archit.* iii. 61 If a ship falls in with waves of synchronising period,..her rolling will then be the heaviest. **1901** A. RUSSELL in *Electr. Rev.* 19 July 88/2 The synchronising current. **1926** *Encycl. Brit.* III. 136/1 In the latter case the synchronising signals must be transmitted over a channel separate from the picture channel [in phototelegraphy]. **1928** C. F. S. GAMBLE *Story N. Sea Air Station* iv. 68 The 'synchronizing gear', enabling a machine-gun to fire through the tractor air-screw. **1961** G. MILLERSON *Technique Television Production* ii. 20 (*caption*) The component parts of the video signal..synchronizing level.

synchronized ('sɪnkrənaɪzd), *ppl. a.* [f. prec. + -ED[1].] That has been synchronized or exhibits synchronism; ***synchronized swimming***, a form of swimming which involves a display of ballet-like routines performed to music (often as a competitive sport); hence ***synchronized swimmer***.

a **1919** *N.E.D.*, Synchronized. **1927** *N.Y. Times* 28 Aug. VII. 4/1 During the other portions of the reel there will be a synchronized orchestral score. **1932** *New Yorker* 9 Apr. 51/1 The new Ford has synchronized gear-shifting and a silent second-speed. **1942** *R.A.F. Jrnl.* 16 May 15 The normal armament is two 7·7 mm. synchronised guns. **1950** B. SPEARS (*title*) Beginning synchronized swimming. **1960** C. H. GIBBS-SMITH *Aeroplane* xii. 89 Fokker's monoplane.. with its fixed synchronised gun. **1968** *Courier-Mail* (Brisbane) 1 Feb. 11/8 Both women returned to Brisbane last week from the New South Wales synchronised swimming championships... Synchronised swimming is the initiate's term for water ballet. **1975** *Oxf. Compan. Sports & Games* 1014/1 As well as having the endurance of a trained racing swimmer, the synchronized swimmer must have the skill and artistry of a ballet dancer, and the grace, rhythm, and acrobatic ability of the gymnast. **1979** A. FRASER *King Charles II* (1980) III. xii. 193 There were no fewer than seven clocks in his bedroom (their ill-synchronized chiming drove his attendants mad). **1981** J. BARNETT *Firing Squad* xvi. 221 A synchronized rattle of rifle bolts. **1984** *New Yorker* 19 Mar. 114/2 It is normally very difficult to get a new sport accepted for the Olympics. Synchronized swimming will be on the docket this summer.

synchronizer ('sɪnkrənaɪzə(r)). One who or that which synchronizes; *spec.* a device for synchronizing clocks; also, an apparatus for causing two electric machines to go at the same speed, or for indicating the agreement or difference of their speeds. Also in other technical senses, esp. in *Cinematogr.* and *Photogr.* Cf. SYNCHRONIZE *v.* 2 c.

1883 OGILVIE (Annandale), *Synchronizer*..one who or that which synchronizes; a contrivance for synchronizing clocks. **1916** *Times* 20 May 7/3 At luncheon time to-day the professional clock winders and synchronizers will start the work of advancing by an hour the hands of the clocks under their control. **1924** S. R. ROGET *Dict. Electr. Terms* 253/2 *Synchroniser.* Apparatus for indicating whether two alternating current machines or circuits are in synchronism. **1931** B. BROWN *Talking Pictures* i. 5 The synchronizer itself consisted of a box having a transparent disc, bearing an indicating spot, and coupled by gearing to the mechanism of the cinema projector. **1940** F. J. MORTIMER *Wall's Dict. Photogr.* (ed. 15) 314 A sharp distinction should be drawn between the flashgun and the simpler so-called 'synchronisers' which open the shutter, set at 'Bulb' or a slow snapshot speed, before the flash begins, and allow it to remain open till the flash is over. **1949** *Proc. Inst. Mech. Engin., Automobile Div., 1947–8* III. 98/2 Constant load synchronizers are generally used, except for Vauxhall.. who use the baulked synchronizer. **1957** MANVELL & HUNTLEY *Film Music* i. 17 Throughout the silent period various gramophone synchronizers were developed for use with films. **1970** K. BALL *Fiat 600, 600D Autobook* vi. 53/1 This shaft carries the fourth-speed driven gear and synchronizer ring. **1972** *Times Educ. Suppl.* 21 July 27 The sound.. is first recorded in the usual way. The tape is then passed through the recording head of the synchronizer... Subsequently, when the tape is played back, the control pulses are passed ..to the projector.., and each automatically initiates a change of slide at the predetermined point.

synchronograph (sɪn'krɒnəgrɑːf, -æ-). [irreg. f. Gr. σύγχρονος SYNCHRONOUS + -γραφος -writing, -GRAPH, after *chronograph*.] An automatic recording telegraph worked by an alternating electric current, with a synchronously moving strip of perforated paper.

1897 *Westm. Gaz.* 24 Apr. 7/2 Professor Crehore..has invented a wonderful instrument, called the synchronograph, by which he claims that 3,000 words per minute can be telegraphed, received, and automatically recorded. **1897** *Sci. Amer.* 9 Oct. 231/3 Experiments with the synchronograph, recently conducted in England.

synchronology (sɪŋkrə'nɒlədʒɪ). [f. SYN-[1] + CHRONOLOGY. Cf. F. *synchronologie*.] Combined or comparative chronology; arrangement of events according to dates, those of the same date being placed or treated together. Hence **synchronological** (ˌsɪŋkrɒnə'lɒdʒɪkəl) *a.*, pertaining to or constructed according to synchronology.

1736 BAILEY (folio) Pref., *Synchronology*..Chronology of the same Time. **1836** E. CASWALL (*title*) Pluck Examination Papers,..to which is added A Synchronological Table Of.. Events at Oxford and Cambridge. **1839** CROSTHWAITE (*title*) Synchronology: being a Treatise on the History, Chronology, and Mythology of the Ancient Egyptians, Greeks, and Phœnicians. **1852** G. A. POOLE in *Assoc. Archit. Soc. Rep.* II. 14 A Synchronological Table of the Bishops of the English Sees.

synchronous ('sɪŋkrənəs), *a.* Chiefly scientific and technical. [f. late L. *synchronus*, a. Gr. σύγχρονος, f. σύν SYN-[1] + χρόνος time: see -OUS.]

1. a. Existing or happening at the same time; coincident in time; belonging to the same period, or occurring at the same moment, of time; contemporary; simultaneous. Const. *with*.

1669 GALE *Crt. Gentiles* I. II. v. 56 Hercules, the Tyrian Commander; whom some make synchronous with Moses. **1772** NUGENT *Hist. Fr. Gerund* I. 217 It is affirmed by a coetaneous, syncronous, and faith-worthy author. **1833** LYELL *Princ. Geol.* III. 42 Formations, which, although dissimilar both in organic and mineral characters, were of synchronous origin. **1872** NICHOLSON *Palæont.* 19 Synchronous deposits necessarily contain wholly different fossils, if one has been deposited by fresh water, and the other has been laid down in the sea. **1878** BATES *Centr. Amer.* vi. 78 The rainy season on the coasts is not synchronous with that of the uplands.

b. *transf.* Relating to or treating of different events or things belonging to the same time or period; involving or indicating contemporaneous or simultaneous occurrence.

1823 THOMASINA ROSS *Bouterwek's Hist. Sp. Lit.* I. 499 A synchronous account of all the remarkable productions of the polite literature of Spain. **1843** *Civil Eng. & Arch. Jrnl.* VI. 159/2 Where is the line to be drawn by which different styles ought to have been set apart as worthy to afford a new starting point for synchronous treatment? **1882–3** *Schaff's Encycl. Relig. Knowl.* 1249 The synchronous history of the divided kingdoms of Israel and Judah.

c. ***synchronous curve*** (Geom.), a curve which is the locus of the points reached at any instant by a number of particles descending from the same point down a family of curves under the action of gravity.

1867 BRANDE & COX *Dict. Sci.*, etc.

2. a. Recurring at the same successive instants of time; keeping time *with*; going on at the same rate and exactly together; having coincident periods, as two sets of vibrations or the like. Cf. sense 2 d below.

1677 F. NORTH *Philos. Ess. Mus.* 20 The synchronous motion of the pulses at the mouth of the Pipe with the vibrations of the included Air promote the Sound of the Pipe. **1733** ARBUTHNOT *Ess. Air* (J.), The variations of the gravity of the air keep both the solids and fluids in an oscillatory motion, synchronous and proportional to their changes. **1786** J. PEARSON in *Med. Commun.* II. 98 Pulsation .., synchronous with that of the radial artery. **1866** DK. ARGYLL *Reign of Law* iii. (1867) 173 The beats of a bird's two wings are always exactly synchronous. **1871** TYNDALL *Fragm. Sci.* (1879) I. xiv. 391 Affected by those undulations which are synchronous with their own periods of vibration. **1899** *Allbutt's Syst. Med.* VIII. 42 The spasms of the face and those of the palate were not synchronous. **1972** *Sci. Amer.* Apr. 45/1 In all cases where this effect is significant these same tides will have 'despun' the satellite to synchronous rotation, that is, the satellite's period of rotation around its own axis equals its period of revolution around the planet and it always presents one face to the planet.

b. *Electr.* Applied to alternating currents having coincident periods; also to a machine or motor working in time with the alternations of current.

1897 A. HAY *Princ. Alternate-Current Working* vi. 88 By a *synchronous* motor is meant one whose speed bears a definite ratio to the periodicity of the alternating current. **1901** A. RUSSELL in *Electr. Rev.* 19 July 88/1 The Power Factor of a Synchronous Motor. **1920** *Whittaker's Electr. Engineer's Pocket-bk.* (ed. 4) 219 If..the converter is in parallel with other synchronous machinery. **1930** *Engineering* 25 Apr. 534/3 (*heading*) Hydrogen-cooled synchronous condenser. **1962** J. BELL in G. A. T. Burdett *Automatic Control Handbk.* iv. 7 Torque synchros or synchronous links (Magslips).

¶ *erron.* Of uniform velocity.

1785 REID *Intell. Powers* II. iv. 253 That relation of synchronous vibrations which produces harmony.

c. *Computers* and *Telecommunications*. Of apparatus or methods of working: making use of equally spaced pulses that govern the timing of operations.

[**1947** A. W. BURKS et al. in J. Von Neumann *Coll. Wks.* (1963) V. 68 Since the timing of the entire computer is governed by a single pulse source, the computer circuits will be said to operate as a synchronized system.] **1954** *Trans. IRE Prof. Group Electronic Computers* June 14/2 Because the system being designed was centrally synchronous, overall timing considerations now came to the fore. **1962** Y. CHU *Digital Computer Design Fundamentals* v. 161 The binary state of the signals in logic circuits can be represented by either of two voltage levels or by pulses... A synchronous computer also requires clock pulses. **1971** I. H. GOULD *IFIP Guide Concepts & Terms Data Processing* 76 Synchronous working and asynchronous working often coexist in different parts of a computer system. For example, in many computers the central processor is synchronous, but the operation of peripheral equipment is only initiated by signals from the central processor and thereafter proceeds asynchronously. **1982** HEAP & MARTIN *Introd. Digital Electronics* iii. 73 In the worst case the problem of interfacing two independent synchronous systems which are operating at different clock rates may occur.

d. Of a satellite: rotating round the parent planet at the same rate as the planet rotates. Of an orbit: such that a satellite in it is synchronous.

1961 *N.Y. Times* 30 July IV. 9/8 Synchronous satellites will require bigger boosters to reach their higher altitudes. **1964** *Daily Tel.* 4 Mar. 14/6 Three satellites in this synchronous orbit would give a complete global system of communications except for small regions round the North and South Pole. **1967** *Technology Week* 20 Feb. 4/2 There is substantial agreement that a synchronous satellite is desirable for air traffic control. **1970** *Nature* 9 May 503/1 Only one orbit exists which is at the same time equatorial, circular and synchronous. **1978** *Daily Tel.* 11 July 2/5 'Charon', which brings to 33 the number of known moons in the solar system, appears to have a synchronous orbit around Pluto of 12,000 miles, which means that it always stays over a fixed spot over Pluto.

3. *Linguistics.* = SYNCHRONIC *a.* 3.

1936 [see DIACHRONOUS *a.* 2].

'synchronously, *adv.* [f. prec. + -LY[2].]

1. a. At the same time; simultaneously; contemporaneously.

1793 W. TAYLOR in *Monthly Rev.* X. 375 To mistrust the opinion of our perceiving many ideas synchronously. *c* **1865** *J. Wylde's Circ. Sci.* I. 270/1 The time-balls..are lowered synchronously with that of Greenwich. **1881** J. S. GARDNER in *Nature* 13 Oct. 558/2 Next, almost synchronously, Gymnosperms are met with. **1899** *Allbutt's Syst. Med.* VII. 674 Symptoms of arterial ischæmia may occur synchronously with those of basal meningitis.

b. *transf.* In relation to the same times or periods; in accordance with contemporary conditions.

1843 *Civil Eng. & Arch. Jrnl.* VI. 160/1 Are the architects of the present day alone to be limited to the servile imitation of styles gone before, and their whole intelligence limited to treating them synchronously?

2. (With reference to recurrent or periodic movement): At the same successive instants of time; at the same rate and exactly together; in time *with*.

1822–7 GOOD *Study Med.* (1829) II. 33 That the pulse, if the systole of the heart were the only projectile force, must take place, not synchronously all over the system,..but.. successively through the whole line of the arterial tubes. *c* **1865** in *J. Wylde's Circ. Sci.* I. 214/2 These alternations take place..synchronously with the reversals of the currents. **1893** SIR R. BALL *Story of Sun* 19 The instrument is moved synchronously with the revolution of the heavens.

¶ *erron.* At a uniform rate, uniformly.

1862 R. H. PATTERSON *Ess. Hist. & Art* 67 Sonorous bodies..are those whose parts easily vibrate synchronously, so as to give out clear musical sounds. **1872** COHEN *Dis. Throat* 18 The patient should breathe rather deeply, but quietly, synchronously, and without effort.

3. *Linguistics.* According to the methods or conclusions of synchronic linguistics.

1923 L. BLOOMFIELD in *Mod. Lang. Jrnl.* VIII. 318 At any given time ('synchronously'), the language of a community is to be viewed as a system of signals.

So **'synchronousness,** the quality or condition of being synchronous; synchronism.

In recent Dicts.

synchrony ('sɪŋkrənɪ). [f. Gr. σύγχρονος SYNCHRONOUS: see -Y.] **1.** = SYNCHRONISM 1, 2, 2 b.

1848 W. W. LLOYD in *Numism. Chron.* XI. 105 Very precise arrangement in sequence and synchrony. **1853** MERIVALE *Rom. Emp.* xxx. (1865) III. 417 Orosius,.. anxious..to find or make a synchrony between an epoch so important in the world's history and one of the most signal events recorded in his own creed. **1880** *Athenæum* 18 Dec. 821/1 The relics of the 'Burnt City' of the Troad favour in the most significant manner a synchrony with the graves in the acropolis of Mycenæ.

2. *Linguistics.* A synchronic method of linguistic study; synchronic treatment.

1931 L. H. GRAY in *Amer. Jrnl. Philol.* LII. 77 Synchrony must determine the nature of these categories. **1955** *Word* XI. 630 The Saussurean antinomy between synchrony and diachrony. **1959, 1963** [see DIACHRONIC *a.* 2]. **1972** *Language* XLVIII. 438 It has recently been claimed that Georg von der Gabelentz anticipated a number of Saussurean concepts, in particular his dichotomies of langue-parole and synchrony-diachrony.

synchroscope ('sɪŋkrəʊskəʊp). [f. SYNCHRO- + -SCOPE.] **1.** *Electr. Engin.* An instrument for indicating any difference in frequency or phase between two alternating voltages.

1908 V. KARAPETOFF *Exper. Electr. Engin.* xxi. 494 It only remains..to bring the machine into phase with the voltage at the bus-bars. This is done either by means of properly connected incandescent lamps..or special instruments, so-called synchroscopes. **1952** H. F. BANKS *Electricity* I. xvii. 268/2 A..usually adopted method of paralleling two alternators is by means of the rotary synchroscope. **1981** T. WILDI *Electr. Power Technol.* xix. 364/2 Observe the phase angle between E_0 and E by means of a synchroscope.

2. *Electronics.* (See quot. 1945.)

1945 *Electronic Industries* Sept. 226 *Synchroscope*, an oscilloscope on which recurrent pulses or wave-forms may be observed, which incorporates a sweep-generator that produces one sweep for each pulse, regardless of frequency, thus allowing no more than one cycle to be viewed on the screen. **1947** R. LEE *Electronic Transformers & Circuits* ix. 257 This curve is observed by connecting the vertical plates of a synchroscope..across the transformer output winding. **1953** *Electronic Engin.* XXV. 229/1 Another specialised oscilloscope (synchroscope) is provided to display all details of the television waveform.

synchrotron ('sɪŋkrəʊtrɒn). *Physics.* [f. SYNCHRO- + -TRON.] An accelerator in which electrons or protons gain energy from an alternating electric field as they travel round a closed orbit in a magnetic field, the strength of this field (and in the case of protons, the frequency of the electric field) being increased to keep the radius of the path constant as the particles gain mass relativistically. Also *transf.*

1945 E. M. MCMILLAN in *Physical Rev.* LXVIII. 143/2 (*heading*) The synchrotron—a proposed high energy particle accelerator. **1947**, etc. [see *proton synchrotron* s.v. PROTON 3]. **1950** *Engineering* 24 Mar. 332/2 A new electron synchrotron ..at work on problems of photo-disintegration and pair production. **1971** *Sci. Amer.* July 79/1 The Crab Nebula is a cosmic synchrotron, permeated by electrons with energies of 1,000 billion electron volts or even higher. **1977** J. D. LAWSON *Physics of Charged-Particle Beams* ii. 79 Large synchrotrons consist of a sequence of magnets arranged in a ring separated by 'straight sections', which may not all be of the same length.

2. *attrib.* and *Comb.*, as ***synchrotron emission, mechanism, process***; **synchrotron radiation**, polarized radiation emitted by a charged particle as it spirals at high speed in a magnetic field, as in a synchrotron; the emission of this.

1962 C. SUSSKIND *Encycl. Electronics* 275/2 The visible continuum of the Crab nebula has been accepted as synchrotron emission. **1978** PASACHOFF & KUTNER *University Astron.* xxiv. 594 Continuum radio radiation can be generated by any of several processes. One of the most important is synchrotron emission, the process that produces the radiation from Taurus A. **1956** *Astrophysical Jrnl.* CXXIII. 550 The synchrotron mechanism.. beautifully explains the radiation and polarization of the continuum of the Crab Nebula. **1962** C. SUSSKIND *Encycl. Electronics* 275/2 As few as 10^{-4} relativistic electrons per cubic centimeter, emitting by the synchrotron process in a field of 10^{-5} gauss, can explain the observations. **1975** *Sci. Amer.* Dec. 38/1 When the electrons spiral along the lines of force of the star's magnetic field, they radiate by means of the synchrotron process, emitting radio waves, visible light and X rays. **1956** *Astrophysical Jrnl.* CXXIV. 416 (*heading*) On synchrotron radiation from Messier 87. **1981** J. B. ADAMS in J. H. Mulvey *Nature of Matter* vii. 165 The large size of LEP [*sc.* a synchrotron] is due not to its particle energy but to the need to reduce synchrotron radiation losses and to economize on electrical power consumption.

‖**synchysis** ('sɪŋkɪsɪs). Also *erron.* 6, 9 -chisis, 7–8 -chesis. [late L., a. Gr. σύγχυσις, f. συγχεῖν to mingle, confuse, f. σύν SYN-[1] + χεῖν to pour. Cf. F. *synchyse* in sense 1, *synchysis* in sense 2.]

1. *Gram.* and *Rhet.* A confused arrangement of words in a sentence, obscuring the meaning.

1577 PEACHAM *Gard. Eloquence* G j, *Synchisis*, a confusion of order, in all partes of the construction. **1612** BRINSLEY *Lud. Lit.* 198 They will oft haue a Synchesis, or a disordered confusion of their wordes. **1672** DRYDEN *Def. Epilogue* Ess. (Ker) I. 167 *And be free Not Heaven it self from thy Impiety.* A synchysis, or ill-placing of words of which Tully so much complains in oratory. *a* **1685** KNATCHBULL *Annot. N. Test., Acts* xiii. 27 (1693) 133 The English Translator hath exprest the sence, but not Translated strictly to the words, which by reason of the Synchysis..being not well distinguished, are not..so rightly rendred as they ought.

2. *Path.* Softening or fluidity of the vitreous humour of the eye; called ***sparkling synchysis*** (*s. scintillans*) when minute flakes of cholesterin float in the humour, causing a sparkling appearance in the field of vision.

1684 tr. *Blancard's Phys. Dict.* (1693), *Synchysis*, a preternatural Confusion of the Blood and Humours of the Eye. **1847–9** *Todd's Cycl. Anat.* IV. 99/1 The peculiar softening of the vitreous humour called sparkling synchisis.

synchytic (sɪnˈkɪtɪk), *a.* *rare*⁻¹. [ad. Gr. συγχυτικός, f. συγχεῖν: see prec. and -IC.] Given to commingling or confounding.

1877 *Keightley's Mythol. Anc. Greece & It.* I. i. 11 *note*, Lobeck terms these writers synchytic mythologists, 'who think that the religions of all nations..were the same from the beginning'.

syncipital, synciput, obs. ff. SIN-.

syncke, syncker, obs. ff. SINK, SINKER *sb.*[1]

synckfoly, obs. form of CINQUEFOIL.

1538 TURNER *Libellus, Qvinqve folivm*, synckfoly.

synclastic (sɪnˈklæstɪk), *a.* *Geom.* [f. Gr. σύν SYN-[1] (alike) + κλαστός, taken in the sense 'bent', f. κλᾶν to break.] Of a curved surface: Having the same kind of curvature (concave or convex) in all directions. Opposed to ANTICLASTIC.

1867 THOMSON & TAIT *Nat. Phil.* I. I. §128 We may divide curved surfaces into Anticlastic and Synclastic. A saddle gives a good example of the former class; a ball of the latter. **1875** P. FROST *Solid Geom.* (ed. 2) I. 379 Any point of an ellipsoid is..a point..at which, if a tangent plane be drawn, the surface in the neighbourhood of the point lies entirely on one side of the tangent plane; such surfaces are called Synclastic.

synclinal (sɪnˈklaɪnəl, ˈsɪŋklɪnəl), *a.* and *sb.* [f. Gr. σύν SYN-[1] + κλίνειν to bend + -AL[1].]

A. *adj.* **a.** *Geol.* Applied to a line or axis towards which strata dip or slope down in opposite directions; also said of the fold or bend in such strata, or of a valley, trough, or basin so formed. Opposed to ANTICLINAL.

1833 LYELL *Princ. Geol.* III. 293 A series of anticlinal and synclinal lines, which form ridges and troughs running nearly parallel to each other. **1863** DANA *Man. Geol.* §113. 105 A synclinal valley is a valley formed by strata sloping downward from either side. **1867** MURCHISON *Siluria* viii. (ed. 4) 171 The extension of the..Silurian strata..by..synclinal folds. **1876** PAGE *Adv. Text-bk. Geol.* xix. 376 The synclinal basins of London and Hampshire.

b. *transf.* and *gen.* Inclined or sloping towards each other, or characterized by such inclination.

1880 B. E. FALKONBERG *Desert Life* 320 Narrow avenues of airy palm-trees with their tops of synclinal fan-tracery. **1903** AGNES M. CLERKE *Probl. Astrophysics* I. xi. 126 Synclinal forms (as the petal-shaped structures are called) emerge in both, and the branching effusions round the trapezium seem to mimic details legible in many eclipse-pictures.

B. *sb.* *Geol.* A synclinal line, fold, or depression.

1855 J. PHILLIPS *Man. Geol.* 142 The strata rising and falling in many steep anticlinals and deep synclinals. **1874** RAYMOND *Statist. Mines & Mining* 512 The east shaft..has passed the synclinal and is now cutting through the south-dipping strata.

Hence or so **synˈclinally** *adv.*, in the form of a synclinal fold; **syncline** (ˈsɪŋklaɪn), a synclinal fold or depression; (see also quot. 1972); cf. *synform* s.v. SYN-[1] 1; **synˈclinical** *a.* = SYNCLINAL *a.*; ‖**synclinorium** (sɪŋklɪˈnɔərɪəm), pl. **-ia**, anglicized **synclinore** (ˈsɪŋklɪnɔː(r)), see quots.; whence **syncliˈnorial, -ˈnorian** *adjs.*

1846 WORCESTER (citing ROGERS), *Synclinical*. **1855** J. PHILLIPS *Man. Geol.* 45 The strata are synclinally and anticlinally bent. **1873** J. GEIKIE *Gt. Ice Age* xxi. 266 Diagrammatic view of synclines and anticlines. **1880** DANA *Man. Geol.* (ed. 3) 821 The mountain range, begun in a geosynclinal, and ending in a catastrophe of displacement and upturning, is appropriately named a *synclinorium*... (The word is from the Greek for synclinal, and ὄρος, mountain). *Ibid.* 823 After the last mentioned synclinorial range [of mountains] was completed. **1883** —— *Text-bk. Geol.* 56 (Cent. Dict.) Synclinore. **1883** A. WINCHELL *World-Life* (1889) 331 Geosynclinals are in progress beneath the sea, which will never attain synclinorian crises unless some revolution provides supplies of sediments. **1893** B. WILLIS in *13th Ann. Rep. U.S. Geol. Surv.* II. 219 The two great types of folds are the syncline and the anticline. The syncline..is a depression of the strata from a flat to a basin-shaped form. **1937** *Trans. R. Soc. Edin.* LIX. 81 In common tectonic practice, an anticline has come to be understood as a fold with a core of previously underlying rocks, and a syncline as a fold with a core of previously overlying rocks. **1972** *Gloss. Geol.* (Amer. Geol. Inst.) 718/2 *Syncline*, a fold, the core of which contains the stratigraphically younger rocks; it is concave upward.

synclitic (sɪnˈklɪtɪk), *a.* *Obstet.* [f. Gr. σύν SYN-[1] + κλιτικός, f. κλίνειν to bend, turn, slope.] Having the planes of the fetal head parallel to those of the pelvis. Hence **synˈcliticism** (-sɪz(ə)m), also **synclitism** (ˈsɪŋklɪtɪz(ə)m).

1890 BILLINGS *Med. Dict.*, Synclitic, Synclitism. **1901** DORLAND *Med. Dict.*, Syncliticism.

synclonic (sɪnˈklɒnɪk), *a.* *Path.* [f. mod.L. *synclonus* simultaneous spasm of several muscles: see SYN-[1] and CLONIC.] Applied to clonic spasms affecting a number of muscles at once.

1822–7 GOOD *Study Med.* (1829) IV. 470.

†**syncopa**, *Obs. rare*, repr. F. *cinq pas*, CINQUEPACE, a kind of dance.

1632 LITHGOW *Trav.* IV. 155 So they learne either a French Syncopa, or an Italian Bergamasko.

syncopal (ˈsɪŋkəpəl), *a.* *Path.* [ad. med.L. *syncopālis*, f. SYNCOPE. Cf. F. *syncopal*, †*sin-* (15th c.).] Of, pertaining to, or marked by syncope.

1689 G. HARVEY *Curing Dis. by Expect.* iv. 22 A Patient, decumbent of Leipothymick, or rather Syncopal fits. **1728** CHAMBERS *Cycl.* s.v. *Fever*, The Syncopal Fever is that attended with frequent Swoonings. **1822–7** GOOD *Study Med.* (1829) II. 129 As an associate disease it [*sc.* tertian] is chiefly to be found united with syncopal and soporose affections. **1871** A. MEADOWS *Man. Midwifery* 347 The syncopal condition of the patient. **1893** GASQUET *Gt. Pestilence* 9 *note*, Convulsions alternate with syncopal attacks.

syncopate (ˈsɪŋkəpeɪt), *v.* [f. late L. *syncopāt-*, pa. ppl. stem of *syncopāre* to affect with syncope, f. *syncopē* SYNCOPE.]

1. *Gram. trans.* To cut short or contract (a word) by omitting one or more syllables or letters in the middle; also *pass.* to be produced by syncopation.

1605 CAMDEN *Rem.*, *Surnames* 130 The tyran Time which hath swallowed many names, hath also in vse of speach, changed more by contracting, syncopating, curtelling, and mollifying them. **1848** VEITCH *Grk. Verbs Irreg. & Defect.* s.v. θνήσκω, It is said that τεθνεώς is never syncopated τεθνώς. **1857** JOS. CURRIE *Notes to Horace, Sat.* I. ii. 113 *Soldo* is syncopated for *solido*. **1861** HADLEY *Grk. Gram.* (1884) 47 Δημήτηρ..syncopates all the oblique cases.

2. *Mus.* **a.** *trans.* To begin (a note) on an unaccented part of the bar and sustain it into the accented part; to introduce syncopation into (a passage). **b.** *intr.* To be marked by syncopation.

[**1667, 1752**: see SYNCOPATED 2.] **1776** BURNEY *Hist. Mus.* I. vii. 103 [It] disturbs the metre, and syncopates the music. **1793** *Encycl. Brit.* (1797) XII. 538 *note*, When the treble syncopates in descending diatonically.

3. *fig.* and *transf.* or *allusively*.

1904 BLACKBURN *Rich. Hartley* ii. 17 A succession of shrill yells, and oaths.., syncopated by the swish of the sjambok. **1908** 'IAN HAY' *Right Stuff* xi, A retired Admiral.., whose forty years' official connection with Britannia's realm betrayed itself in a nautical roll, syncopated by gout. **1928** *Sunday Express* 27 May 15 Her eager feet, that used to patter back and forth in happy household duties, now syncopate to the beat of drums and the clashing of cymbals. **1966** *Listener* 28 July 142/3 At the back of Albeniz's mind there is generally..a dancer whose castanets are always syncopating against each other. **1983** P. INCHBALD *Short Break in Venice* xx. 190 They passed a lighthouse syncopating white above with green below.

syncopated (ˈsɪŋkəpeɪtɪd), *ppl. a.* [f. late L. *syncopātus*, pa. pple. of *syncopāre* (see prec.) + -ED[1].]

1. a. *Gram.* Contracted by omission of one or more syllables or letters in the middle.

1665 R. JOHNSON *Scholars Guide* 3 A Circumflex tone, (^) used..over..Words Syncopated and contracted, as, ..*amâsti, tibîcen*. **1877** ABBOTT & MANSFIELD *Gr. Gram.* §51 The syncopated genitive and dative singular of words like πατήρ.

b. *transf.* or *gen.* Cut short, abbreviated.

1897 *Westm. Gaz.* 19 Feb. 3/1 The scrappy history, the political tattle, the syncopated gossip. **1911** J. H. A. HART in *Expositor* Jan. 83 St. Matthew is trying to explain a syncopated report of the original pronouncement.

2. *Mus.* **a.** Characterized by syncopation.

1667 C. SIMPSON *Compend. Pract. Mus.* 156 Of Syncopated or Driving Canon. **1752** CHAMBERS *Cycl.* s.v. *Syncopation*, In syncopated or driving notes, the hand or foot is taken up, or put down, while the note is sounding. **1838** G. F. GRAHAM *Mus. Comp.* 28/2 This legato and syncopated style. **1887** H. C. BANISTER *Mus. Anal.* 165 This bold imitational and syncopated passage.

b. Applied to modern popular music played or composed in the manner typical of ragtime and jazz.

1908 *Catal. Copyright Entries* (U.S. Libr. Congress) 1069/2 Floreine waltz; syncopated, by Ernest J. Schuster. **1929** W. THURMAN *Blacker the Berry* 120 They muddled their words and seemed to impregnate the syncopated melody with physical content. **1969** E. ROTH *Business of Music* x. 247 Apart from syncopated rhythms, jazz proved unfruitful ground for serious music.

c. Designating an orchestra, composer, etc., associated with popular syncopated music.

1927 [see *cross-rhythm* s.v. CROSS- B]. **1928** *Grove's Dict. Mus.* (ed. 3) V. 243/1 Dance bands are frequently spoken of as 'Syncopated Orchestras', less because their music employs syncopation than because their constitution with saxophones, percussive instruments, etc., is designed to emphasize the effects essential to dance music of the American type. **1934** C. LAMBERT *Music Ho!* III. 222 The composer of highbrow jazz must obviously extend his harmonic vocabulary beyond the somewhat narrow range of the syncopated kings.

d. *fig.*

1924 WODEHOUSE *Bill the Conqueror* iii. 62 The breeze was stronger now, and it ruffled the surface of the water, so that the goldfish had for the moment a sort of syncopated appearance. **1950** 'D. DIVINE' *King of Fassarai* xvi. 128 A regular syncopated pattern of shifting light. **1964** E. J. HOBSBAWM *Labouring Men* 133 The oddly syncopated rhythm of the European trade-union 'leaps' between 1889 and 1914. **1974** M. CECIL *Heroines in Love* vi. 155 Eventually Jizabel awoke from her syncopated dreamland. **1979** *Jrnl. R. Soc. Arts* Nov. 751/2 This last element [*sc.* a colonnade] modulates back and forth in a rather jerky and syncopated manner.

3. In a state of syncope. *nonce-use.*

1871 M. COLLINS *Mrq. & Merch.* III. xii. 285 Ethel's smelling-bottle revived one or two syncopated young ladies.

syncopation (sɪŋkəˈpeɪʃən). Also 6–8 **sin-**. [ad. med.L. *syncopātio, -ōnem*, n. of action f. *syncopāre*: see SYNCOPATE.]

1. *Gram.* Contraction of a word by omission of one or more syllables or letters in the middle; *transf.* a word so contracted.

c **1532** DU WES *Introd. Fr.* in *Palsgr.* 898 Syncopation is none other thyng by abreviation of length. **1623** PENKETHMAN *Handf. Hon.* Pref., *Catus* an old syncopation of *Cautus*. **1873** F. HALL *Mod. Eng.* 175 Such syncopations and compressions as gave us *arbalist, governor, pedant*, and *proctor*, from *arcubalista, gubernator, pædagogans*, and *procurator*.

†**2.** *Path.* = SYNCOPE *sb.* 1. *Obs. rare.*

1547 BOORDE *Brev. Health* cccxxiv. (1557) 105 The .324. Chapitre doth shewe of syncopacions or soundynge.

3. *Mus.* **a.** The action of beginning a note on a normally unaccented part of the bar and sustaining it into the normally accented part, so as to produce the effect of shifting back or anticipating the accent; the shifting of accent so produced.

1597 MORLEY *Introd. Mus.* 144 If your base ascende halfe a note..any of the other parts making Syncopation. **1662** PLAYFORD *Skill Mus.* viii. 28 Sincopation is when the striking of Time falls to be in the midst of a Semibrief or Minum, &c. or, as we usually term it, Notes Driven till the Time falls even again. **1694** *Ibid.* (ed. 12) viii. 24 Notes of Syncopation, or Driving-Notes, are, when your Hand or Foot is taken up, or put down, while the Note is sounding. **1730** *Treat. Harmony* 46 The Part of the Cadence which has the Ligature or Sincopation. **1854** *Cherubini's Counterpoint* 17 Syncopation should always have a concord at the unaccented part of the bar. **1880** E. PROUT in Grove *Dict. Mus.* I. 13/1 Another very frequent method of changing the position of the accent is by means of syncopation.

b. Music characterized by a syncopated rhythm, *spec.* dance music influenced by ragtime.

1921 *Chambers's Jrnl.* Jan. 23/1 The pulsating sound [of the drum] heightens excitement to the verge of frenzy, and indicates the direct origin of the orgiastic African syncopation to which the wives and daughters of the conquering Anglo-Saxon race dance with their men-partners, retained by arrangement, in the aristocratic dance-clubs of London and New York. **1928** *Grove's Dict. Mus.* (ed. 3) V. 243/1 Syncopation has become a general term for all that class of 20th-century dance music which has sprung from the American adoption of rag-time. **1962** CHARTERS & KUNSTADT *Jazz* vi. 73 Even the Clef Club Orchestra was advertised as a jazz band, with ''50 Joy Whooping Sultans of High-Speed Syncopation'. **1968** P. TAMONY *Americanisms* (typescript) No. 23. 4 *Syncopation* described 'Alexander's Ragtime Band' and other printed music in the first decade or so of this century, *ragtime* becoming old shoe and pejorative.

c. *fig.*

1979 *Jrnl. R. Soc. Arts* Nov. 777/1 The stained glass and colour syncopations in blues and greens.

syncopator (ˈsɪŋkəpeɪtə(r)). Also **syncopater**. [f. SYNCOPATE *v.* + -OR.] One who performs syncopated jazz music, usu. in a dance band. Freq. *pl.*, in the name of a band.

1926 *Daily Colonist* (Victoria, B.C.) 13 Jan. 6/3 With Professor Hunt's syncopators providing the dance music programme. **1927** *Daily Tel.* 22 Feb. 12/1 You may see (and hear) the first 'Lady Syncopators',..cutting rhythm into jazz patterns with the best of mere male 'syncopators'. **1930** *Dancing Times* Oct. 117/2 The White Star Syncopators, the Cunard Dance Band. **1952** B. ULANOV *Hist. Jazz in Amer.* (1958) ix. 94 The swinging Vendome syncopators took over the stage. **1970** P. OLIVER (*title*) Savannah syncopators.

‖**syncope** (ˈsɪŋkəpɪ), *sb.* Forms: 5 **syn-**, 5–6 **sincopis**, 6 **cincopis** (5–6 **-in**, 6 **-yne**); 6–7 **syncopa**; anglicized 7 **sincop**, 8 **syncop**; 7– **syncope**. [In earliest use, *sincopis*, incorrect nom. inferred from *sincopin* (so in 13th c. OF.), orthographic var. of *syncopēn*, acc. of late L. *syncopē* (also *syncopa*), a. Gr. συγκοπή, f. σύν SYN-[1] + κοπ-, stem of κόπτειν to strike, beat, cut off, weary. The current form is based directly on the Gr. (Cf. It., Sp., Pg. *sincopa*.) For the disyllabic *syncop*, cf. F. *syncope* (sɛ̃kɔp).]

1. *Path.* Failure of the heart's action, resulting in loss of consciousness, and sometimes in death.

In quot. 1750 in extended sense, suspension of vitality.

c **1400** *Lanfranc's Cirurg.* 197 If þere falle ony þing to him as syncopis. *Ibid.* 205 Sumtyme it makiþ a man to haue sincopin. **1525** [see SWOWING *vbl. sb.*]. **1527** ANDREW *Brunswyke's Distyll. Waters* Mj, The same water is very good agaynst fayntnes and dasyng named Sincopis. **1541** *Bk. Properties Herbs* Hiv, Rose water is good for the Syncopyne. *Ibid.* I iv b, It is good for..the Synacop [? *mispr. for* Syncopa]. *c* **1550** LLOYD *Treas. Health* I iv, It doth wonderfully comfort in all kinde syncope. **1612** WOODALL *Surg. Mate* Wks. (1653) 88 Syncope is a solution of the spirits which forsake the heart. *a* **1693** *Urquhart's Rabelais*

III. xxxii. 272 As if she were in a swounding Lipothymy, benumming Sincop. **1713** *Gentl. Instructed* I. (ed. 5) Suppl. ii. p. xi, Some affirm..that she had certainly expired of a Syncop, had she not [etc.]. **1750** *Phil. Trans.* XLVII. 54 They [*sc.* flies and butterflies] came to life after a syncope of longer duration. **1836** MARRYAT *Japhet* lxxix, I found poor Mrs. Cophagus in a state of syncope. **1877** F. T. ROBERTS *Handbk. Med.* (ed. 3) I. 13 Death beginning at the heart is said to be..by syncope. **1899** *Allbutt's Syst. Med.* VI. 543 In Raynaud's disease spasmodic contraction of the arteries occurs in the stage of 'local syncope'.

fig. *a* **1651** SIR J. SKEFFINGTON *Heroe of Lorenzo* (1652) 9 The weaknes of our Wills are the Syncopes of Reputation. **1850** CARLYLE *Latter-d. Pamph.* iv. (1872) 138 Defenders of the hypocrisies, the spiritual vampires..under which England lies in syncope. **1855** MOTLEY *Corr.* (1899) I. vi. 184 Five centuries after the fall of the Western Empire.. lasted the syncope, the comatose trance of Europe.

2. *Gram.* = SYNCOPATION 1. Also *attrib.* and in *Comb.*

1530 PALSGR. 392 In the future indycatyve and present potenciall I fynde somtyme syncopa used, as *pouruoyray*.. for *pouruoyeray*. **1579** E. K. *Gloss Spenser's Sheph. Cal., May* 61 *Nas*, is a syncope, for *ne has*, or *has not*: as *nould* for *would not*. **1679** ALSOP *Melius Inq.* I. i. 45 Augustin (or rather Austin; for his Name as well as his Fame suffers a Syncope). **1764** SWINTON in *Phil. Trans.* LIV. 419 Instances of such a syncope, or extrusion,..are not seldom found in..the Old Testament. **1903** WINBOLT *Lat. Hexam. Verse* 212. **1953** K. JACKSON *Lang. & Hist. in Early Britain* II. 614 A Pr[imitive] W[elsh] syncope-form **Car'dig.* **1972** *Language* XLVIII. 350 The same syncope rule which is optional in Russian /stl/ and /stk/ clusters is obligatory in /stn/ and /zdn/ clusters. *Ibid.*, Maximal distinctiveness, hence retention of the consonant, is manifested in the explicit subcode of contemporary standard Russian; whereas partial absence of distinctiveness, hence syncope of the consonant, is manifested in the elliptic subcode.

†**3.** *Mus.* = SYNCOPATION 3. *Obs.*

1653 LD. BROUNCKER tr. *Des Cartes' Compend. Mus.* 53 In these Tunes Dissonances are frequently used instead of Consonances; which is effected two wayes, viz. by Diminution, or Syncope. *Ibid.* 54 A Syncopa is, when the end of one Note in one voice is heard at the same time with the beginning of one other Note of an adverss part. **1659** C. SIMPSON *Division-Violist* I. 16 A Greater Fourth, or Defective Fifth, hath this priviledge..to be joyned, sometimes, to the Basse, without Syncope, or Binding. **1795** MASON *Ch. Mus.* iv. 249 Syncopes and other foolish artifices.

¶The following explanation (translated from the *Dict. de Trévoux*), which is repeated in some later Dicts., appears to be an error.

1728 CHAMBERS *Cycl.*, *Syncope*, in Music, signifies the Division of a Note; used when two or more Notes of one Part answer to a single Note of the other Part. [Omitted in later edd.]

4. A cutting short; abbreviation, contraction; sudden cessation or interruption. *rare.*

a **1658** CLEVELAND *Common Place* Wks. (1677) 161 Give me lieve by a less Syncope of Time to contract Good Friday and Easter both to a day. **1679** [see 2]. **1784** COWPER *Task* II. 80 Revelry, and dance, and show, Suffer a syncope and solemn pause. **1835** T. MITCHELL *Aristoph., Acharn.* Introd. p. xix, A fourth and fifth campaign, and still no sign of syncope or pause.

†**syncope**, *v. Obs. rare.* Also 5 synkope. [a. OF. *syncoper* (14th c.), or ad. late L. *syncopāre* to SYNCOPATE.]

1. *trans.* **a.** To cut short, cut down, reduce. **b.** To syncopate or slur over (a word or syllable).

c **1412** HOCCLEVE *De Reg. Princ.* 4727 And specialy þat he hir duetee Abrigge naght, ne naght syncope hir wages. *c* **1440** *Jacob's Well* 108 þou hast seyd rechelesly þi seruyse in rape, in syncopyng, in ouyr-skyppyng, in omyttyng. *Ibid.* 115 þe feend seyde: 'J bere in my sacche sylablys & woordys, ouerskyppyd and synkopyd'.

2. *Mus.* **a.** *intr.* To be syncopated. **b.** *trans.* To syncopate.

1728 CHAMBERS *Cycl.* s.v. [with def. of 'syncope'd' note as = dotted note, taken from *Dict. de Trévoux*]. **1752** tr. *Rameau's Treat. Musick* 62 The Bass must always syncope in that case. *Ibid.* 112 That Note is said to be syncoped, and is called a Driving-note. **1801** BUSBY *Dict. Mus.* s.v., In harmony, there are three syncopes: the first is when all the parts syncope at the same time.

syncopic (sɪnˈkɒpɪk), *a. Path.* [f. SYNCOPE + -IC.] = SYNCOPAL.

1889 *Lancet* 27 Apr. 841/2 The local syncopic and asphyxial stages [of Raynaud's disease] were usually well defined. **1897** *Allbutt's Syst. Med.* II. 879 In the last stage [of opium poisoning]..the state may partake of the syncopic character.

syncopist (ˈsɪŋkəpɪst). *nonce-wd.* [f. SYNCOPE + -IST.] One who syncopates a word; *spec.* one who omits vowels or other letters, esp. in proper names or titles, and supplies their places with dashes, dots, or asterisks, as in satirical writing.

1714 ADDISON *Spect.* No. 567 ¶8 In order to outshine all this modern Race of Syncopists,..I intend shortly to publish a Spectator that shall not have a single Vowel in it.

So **ˈsyncopism**, the practice of so writing a word, or a word so written.

In recent Dicts.

†**syncopize** (ˈsɪŋkəpaɪz), *v. Obs.* Also 5 -yse. [a. OF. *sincopiser* intr. to swoon, ad. med.L. *syncopizāre*, f. *syncopē* SYNCOPE. Cf. It. *sincopizzare*, Sp. *sincopizar*.]

1. *intr.* To be affected with syncope; to swoon.

1490 CAXTON *Eneydos* vi. 25 Thenne dydo..bare it moche inpacyently and sorowfully & in suche anguysshe of herte that she swowned, syncopysed, & syghed. **1597** A. M. tr. *Guillemeau's Fr. Chirurg.* 37 b/2 Fearing least he should grow faynt, or syncopize.

2. *trans.* To cut short, 'clip', contract, syncopate.

1642 T. TRESCOT *Zeal. Magist.* 13 Doe not Syncopize.. thy words. **1680** DALGARNO *Deaf & Dumb Man's Tutor* 114 A Poetical humor of Syncopizing and contracting their words.

Hence †**syncopization** (so obs. F.), condition of 'syncopizing', syncope.

1597 A. M. tr. *Guillemeau's Fr. Chirurg.* 51 b/1 The persone must fall into syncopizatione or fayntnes.

syncoptic (sɪnˈkɒptɪk), *a. Path.* [ad. mod.L. *syncopticus*, ad. Gr. συγκοπτικός, f. συγκόπτειν, f. σύν SYN-[1] + κόπτειν to beat, strike, weary.] = SYNCOPAL. So †**synˈcoptical** *a. Obs.*

1656 J. SMITH *Pract. Physick* 142 Another [fever] is syncoptical, which is hot in respect to the Feaver, but cold in respect to the Syncope. **1859** MAYNE *Expos. Lex.*, *Syncopticus*.., syncoptic. **1886** *Nature* 6 May 23/1 The pneumatorectic passed into the 'syncoptic' respiration.

syncotyledonous to **-craniate**: see SYN-[1].

syncranterian (sɪŋkrænˈtɪərɪən), *a. Anat.* [f. Gr. σύν SYN-[1] + κραντῆρες wisdom teeth + -IAN.] Having the teeth in a continuous row, as certain snakes: opp. to DIACRANTERIAN.

In Dicts.

syncretic (sɪnˈkriːtɪk, -ˈkrɛtɪk), *a.* (*sb.*) [f. SYNCRETISM, prob. after *docetic*, *docetism*.]

1. a. Characterized by syncretism; aiming at a union or reconciliation of diverse beliefs, practices, or systems.

1840 F. BARHAM *Alist* 17 The Syncretic Society which we founded for the advancement of literature. **1853** *Fraser's Mag.* XLVII. 293 The philosophy which at the time Minucius was writing arrayed itself against Christianity, was..syncretic. **1884** SAYCE *Anc. Empires East* 204 The syncretic spirit of Phœnician art.

b. *sb.* = SYNCRETIST. (Ogilvie, 1883.)

2. *Psychol.* Relating to or characterized by the fusion of concepts or sensations. Cf. SYNCRETISM 3.

1932 M. GABAIN tr. *Piaget's Moral Judgment of Child* ii. 192 Since every word obtains its meaning as a function of these syncretic schemas, words end by acquiring a substance of their own independently of reality. **1952** WERNER & KAPLAN *Acquisition of Word Meanings* ii. 48 The conclusion can be drawn..that syncretic concepts are more characteristic of the younger children. **1962** I. SARNOFF *Personality Dynamics & Devel.* vi. 126 One variety of syncretic perception..involves a synthesis of sensations that pertain to several different sense modalities. **1969** T. FREEMAN *Psychopathol. of Psychoses* viii. 126 This thinking defect consists in the re-emergence of condensing or syncretic trends, fusing concepts that in normal circumstances are discrete and autonomous.

Hence **synˈcretical** *a.* in sense 1; **synˈcreticism** (-sɪz(ə)m) = SYNCRETISM.

1860 LD. ACTON *Lett.* lxiv. (1906) 145 The representative among Belgian public men of this syncreticism, Dedecker. **1864** tr. *Renan's Life of Jesus* Introd. 18 Asia Minor was.. the theatre of a strange movement of syncretical philosophy.

syncretically (sɪnˈkrɛtɪkəlɪ), *adv.* [f. SYNCRETICAL *a.* + -LY[2].] In a syncretic manner.

1900 W. JAMES *Let.* 10 June in R. B. Perry *Tht. & Char. W. James* (1935) I. 647 Assuming no duality of material and mental substance, but starting with bits of 'pure experience', syncretically taken. **1957** *Times Lit. Suppl.* 27 Dec. 781/3 But he manages to square his religious views.. with a staunch advocacy of anthropology and sociology as ancillary techniques in historical method. To say that this position is syncretically achieved would be something of an understatement.

syncretion (sɪnˈkriːʃən). [Badly f. SYNCRETIC *a.* (*sb.*) or next, after *concretion*.] A combination or synthesis of various tenets or principles.

1872 *Contemp. Rev.* Apr. 664 *note* A loose and vague syncretion of Egoistic and Universalistic Hedonism. **1904** *Month* Jan. 4 A syncretion of incompatible principles.

syncretism (ˈsɪŋkrɪtɪz(ə)m). [ad. mod.L. *syncrētismus* (D. Pareus, 1615), a. Gr. συγκρητισμός, f. συγκρητίζειν to SYNCRETIZE. Cf. F. *syncrétisme*, 'the ioyning, or agreement, of two enemies against a third person' (Cotgr.).

Spelt *syncratism* by Ash (1775), who derives it from κράτος power; the spelling is recorded by some later Dicts.]

1. Attempted union or reconciliation of diverse or opposite tenets or practices, esp. in philosophy or religion; *spec.* the system or principles of a school founded in the 17th century by George Calixtus, who aimed at harmonizing the sects of Protestants and ultimately all Christian bodies: see CALIXTIN 2. (Almost always in derogatory sense.)

1618 *Barnevelt's Apol.* Ded. A4, We may much blush thereat: yea euen as much as we patiently did for your Syncretisme, after it lighted into the hands and style of Moguntinus the Iesuit. [**1651** C. WALKER *Hist. Independ.* III. 26 Independency being a meer complication and Syncretismus, or rather a Sink and Common Sewer of all Errours.] **1653** BAXTER *Meth. Peace Consc.* 274 Flotting a Carnal Syncretism, and attempting the reconcilement of Christ and Belial. **1660** STILLINGFL. *Iren.* I. vi. §3 (1662) 109 Grotius..when hee designed the Syncretism with the Church of Rome. **1778** APTHORPE *Preval. Chr.* 162 This divine light..was..obscured by the prevailing syncretism of true and false religion. **1831** SIR W. HAMILTON *Discuss.* (1852) 409 Their particular dissensions were merged in a general syncretism to resist the novelty equally obnoxious to all. **1839** HALLAM *Lit. Eur.* III. iii. §96 It may be considered as a part of this syncretism, as we may call it, of the material and immaterial hypotheses, that Descartes [etc.]. **1853** *Fraser's Mag.* XLVII. 294 Syncretism, under every possible form—ethical, political, social, and theological, was the favourite policy of the Roman emperors. They would have all the varieties of mankind called in and restamped at the Cæsarean mint. **1887** A. LANG *Myth, Ritual, & Relig.* xv. II. 94 The process of syncretism, by which various god-names and god-natures are mingled, so as to unite the creeds of different nomes and provinces.

2. *Philol.* The merging of two or more inflectional categories.

1909 in WEBSTER. **1933** L. BLOOMFIELD *Language* xxi. 388 Homonymy and *syncretism*, the merging of inflectional categories, are normal results of sound-change. **1949** C. E. BAZELL in E. P. Hamp et al. *Readings in Linguistics II* (1966) 225 It may not always be possible to draw a fast line between syncretism proper and the neutralisation of a morphemic opposition. **1957**, **1963** [see DEFECTIVATION]. **1968** W. J. SAMARIN in J. A. Fishman *Readings Sociol. of Lang.* 664 Planned languages reveal many of the features of pidgin languages, namely, lexical syncretism and reduction of redundancy. **1979** [see SYNTAGMA 4].

3. *Psychol.* The process of fusing diverse ideas or sensations into a general (inexact) impression; an instance of this.

1926 M. WARDEN tr. *Piaget's Lang. & Thought of Child* iv. 130 We can discern in this activity of understanding and invention on the part of the child several of those schemas of analogy, of those leaps to conclusions which are the outstanding characteristics of verbal syncretism. **1963** T. R. & E. MILES tr. *Michotte's Perception of Causality* xvii. 276 It is probable that an extreme 'syncretism' (i.e. an undifferentiated blending) holds sway at this time. **1967** A. L. BALDWIN *Theories Child Devel.* xvii. 501 An example of syncretism in normal adult functioning can be seen in the close relationship between taste and smell.

syncretist (ˈsɪŋkrɪtɪst). [f. prec.: see -IST. Cf. F. *syncrétiste*.] One who practises or favours syncretism; one who attempts to unite diverse beliefs, etc.; *spec.* = CALIXTIN 2. Also *attrib.*

1758 MACLAINE tr. *Mosheim's Eccl. Hist.* Cent. xv. II. i. §5 *margin*, The Platonic Syncretists. **1764** *Ibid.* Cent. XVII. II. II. i. §20 The Syncretists..used their warmest endeavours to promote union and concord among Christians. **1826** C. BUTLER *Life of Grotius* xii. 201 The projects of religious pacification did not cease with Grotius... One description of persons, who engaged in this design, was denominated Syncretists, or Calixtines. **1890** P. H. HUNTER *After the Exile* I. ix. 181 Darius Hystaspes was not a syncretist of the type of Cyrus. **1893** *Tablet* 14 Jan. 61 A syncretist scholastic of the earlier part of the seventeenth century.

syncretistic (sɪŋkrɪˈtɪstɪk), *a.* [f. prec.: see -ISTIC and cf. mod.L. *syncrētisticus* (Calovius 1682).] Belonging to, or having the character of, a syncretist or syncretists; relating to, or characterized by, syncretism. Also = SYNCRETIC *a.* 2. So **syncreˈtistical** *a.*

1764 MACLAINE tr. *Mosheim's Eccl. Hist.* Cent. XVII. II. II. i. §21 *margin*, The rise of the Syncretistical or Calixtine controversies. **1828** PUSEY *Hist. Enq.* I. 57 The signal for the Syncretistic controversy given by Buscher in his work against Calixtus. **1833** J. H. NEWMAN *Arians* I. iv. (1876) 115 Zenobia..succeeded Alexander in her..attachment to the syncretistic philosophy. **1841** *Fraser's Mag.* XXIII. 145 A set of syncretistic legislators. **1864** C. W. KING *Gnostics* 68 The syncretistic sects that had sprung up in Alexandria. **1914** PATRICK *Clement of Alexandria* i. 4 A like syncretistic tendency was exhibited in Gnosticism. **1926** M. WARDEN tr. *Piaget's Lang. & Thought of Child* iv. 132 To this childish form of perception M. Claparède has given the name of *syncretistic perceptions*, using the name chosen by Renan to denote that first 'wide and comprehensive but obscure and inaccurate' activity of the spirit where 'no distinction is made and things are heaped one upon the other'. **1976** S. ARIETI *Creativity* ix. 195 The artist or viewer has a syncretistic grasp of the total object. He abandons precise visualization and experiences an unclear vision of the whole.

syncretize (ˈsɪŋkrɪtaɪz), *v.* [ad. mod.L. *syncrētizāre*, ad. Gr. συγκρητίζειν to combine, as two parties against a third (of uncertain etymology; explained in the 16th and 17th c. as 'to form alliances in the manner of the Cretans').]

1. *intr.* To practise syncretism; to attempt to combine different or opposing tenets or systems; †*loosely*, to agree, accord.

1675 ALSOP *Anti-sozzo* 326 If..we consider which of Christs spiritual Excellencies syncretize with them [*sc.* the types]. *a* **1698** in R. Ferguson *View Eccles.* 55 A Phrase which carrieth an odd sound, and syncretizeth with the Nestorian Gibberish. **1698** S. CLARKE *Script. Justif.* Introd. B 3, Why may not the extending it further be charged as a Syncretising with the Antinomians? **1883** *Encycl. Brit.* XV. 47c/2 Their..syncretizing attitude towards the New Testament.

2. *trans.* To treat in the way of syncretism; to combine, as different systems, etc.

1907 *Hibbert Jrnl.* Jan. 276 One cannot merely syncretise religions.

‖**ˈsyncrisis.** ?*Obs.* [late L., a. Gr. σύγκρισις, f. συγκρίνειν to compound, compare, f. σύν SYN-[1] + κρίνειν to separate.] Comparison; *Rhet.* a figure by which diverse or opposite things are compared.

1657 J. SMITH *Myst. Rhet.* 207 Syncrisis is a comparison of contrary things, and divers persons in one sentence. **1673** *Ess. Educ. Gentlewom.* 38 All Knowledge is increased by Syncrisis. **1674** M. LEWIS *Ess. Educ. Youth* 17 All instruction ought to be by syncrisis, that is, comparing what we are to learn with what we know.

syncromesh, var. SYNCHROMESH.

syncrude: see SYN-².

syncyanosis: see SYN-¹ 1.

‖**syncytium** (sɪnˈsɪtɪəm). *Biol.* Pl. **-ia**. Also anglicized **syncyte** (ˈsɪnsaɪt). [mod.L. (Haeckel), f. Gr. σύν SYN-¹ + κύτος receptacle, vessel, taken as = cell (see -CYTE).] **a.** A single cell or protoplasmic mass containing several nuclei, formed either by fusion of a number of cells without fusion of the nuclei, or by division of the nucleus without division of the cell-substance. **b.** A structure composed of such cells forming the outermost fetal layer of the placenta.

1877 HUXLEY *Anat. Inv. Anim.* iii. 113. **1878** BELL tr. *Gegenbaur's Comp. Anat.* §26. 31 One [group of muscular tissue] consists of cells simple in form, the other of fibres derived from cell-aggregates, or from syncytia; the latter is indicated by the presence of numerous cell-nuclei. **1899** *Allbutt's Syst. Med.* VI. 260 The presence of emboli of placental giant-cells (syncytium) in the pulmonary capillaries in cases of puerperal eclampsia. **1909** J. W. JENKINSON *Experim. Embryol.* 55 The fusion of distinct cells into a syncytium, as in the trophoblast.

Hence **syncytial** (-ˈsɪtɪəl) *a.*, of the nature of or pertaining to a syncytium; **synˈcytiolyse** (-laɪz) *v.* [cf. next], to cause destruction of the syncytium (see b above); **syncytiolysin** (-ˈɒlɪsɪn) [LYSIN] (see quot.); ‖**ˌsyncytiˈoma** [mod.L. after *sarcoma*, etc.], a tumour of the syncytium (sense b); **syncytioˈtoxin** (see quot.); **synˌcytioˈtrophoblast**, the outer, syncytial layer of the trophoblast; also, one of the cells that make up this layer; **synˌcytiotrophoˈblastic** *a.*

1895 *Athenæum* 29 June 842/1 The origin of the ova from syncytial masses of protoplasm. **1903** THAYER *Schmaus' Path. & Pathol. Anat.* 545 Syncytial masses, or trabeculæ of syncytial cells. **1905** *Brit. Med. Jrnl.* 26 Aug. *Epit. Curr. Med. Lit.* 35/1 Syncytiolysing antibodies. **1913** DORLAND *Med. Dict.* (ed. 7), *Syncytiolysin*, a lysin destructive to the syncytium. *Ibid.*, *Syncytiotoxin*, a toxin that has a specific action on the syncytium. **1926** *Jrnl. Anat.* LXI. (*Proc. Anat. Soc.*) 77 The trophoblast consists of a thick folded cellular layer (cytotrophoblast), on the outer surface of which an irregular and as yet thin deeply staining layer of syncytiotrophoblast is in process of differentiation. **1961** *Nature* 29 July 510/1 In human beings, the syncytiotrophoblasts are the fœtal cells in direct contact with the maternal bloodstream. *Ibid.* 511/1 The evidence favours the interpretation of the binding of tagged globulin from post-partum sera by the syncytiotrophoblastic cytoplasm as an immune phenomenon. **1980** *Sci. Amer.* Aug. 82/2 (*caption*) As the invasion proceeds the trophoblast differentiates into two layers, the outer syncytiotrophoblast, which leads the advance into the endometrium, and the cytotrophoblast, which forms a complex system of projections that eventually push through the syncytiotrophoblast into the pools of maternal blood.

synd(e, var. of SIND *sb.* and *v.*

syndactyl (sɪnˈdæktɪl), *a.* and *sb.* Also **-yle**. [a. F. *syndactyle* (Cuvier), f. Gr. σύν SYN-¹ + δάκτυλος finger, DACTYL.] **a.** *adj.* Having some or all of the fingers or toes wholly or partly united, as certain mammals (e.g. kangaroos) and birds (e.g. kingfishers and web-footed birds). **b.** *sb.* A syndactyl animal. So **syndacˈtylic**, **synˈdactylous** *adjs.*; **synˈdactylism**, **synˈdactyly** [F. *syndactylie*], the condition of being syndactyl, esp. as a malformation or deformity; **synˈdactylized** *ppl. a.*, rendered syndactyl.

1836 SWAINSON *Nat. Hist. Birds* I. iv. I. 148 This union of the two outer toes, which, according to M. Cuvier's views, makes them *syndactyle. **1872** COUES *N. Amer. Birds* 178 The middle and outer toes are perfectly coherent for a great distance, constituting the syndactyle..foot. **1835–6** *Todd's Cycl. Anat.* I. 267/1 *note*, The inner toe being deficient; and the two other anterior ones being united as in the other *Syndactyles. **1840** WHEWELL *Philos. Induct. Sci.* I. Introd. p. cxi, To anglicize the terminations of the names which.. Cuvier gives..; thus..the Passerines,..the Syndactyls. **1835** PARTINGTON *Brit. Cycl. Nat. Hist.* I. 441/2 *Syndactylic feet. These [birds] have all the three front toes united. **1889** *Buck's Handbk. Med. Sci.* VIII. 555/1 *Syndactylism in the lower extremity is less rare,..it is not uncommon to see two of the toes united as far as the first interphalangeal joint. **1915** *Man* XV. 176 Photographs and skiographs of members of a family showing hereditary syndactylism and polydactylism. **1908** *Biometrika* Mar. 27 When two fingers are closely *syndactylised the nails are also united. **1835** *Penny Cycl.* IV. 156/2 Bee-eater..one..of the *syndactylous tribe, which have the external toe nearly as long as the middle one, and both joined together up to the penultimate articulation. **1898** *Guide Mammalia Brit. Mus.* 109 The feet [of wombats] show a slight tendency towards a syndactylous structure. **1864** *Reader* 13 Feb. 205/2 Union by integument, or '*syndactyly', of the three middle digits.

syndale, -all, obs. ff. SENDAL.

syndaw: see SINDAW.

synde, obs. form of SHEND *v.*¹

c **1275** LAY. 26569 Bruttus ous wolleþ synde.

syndectomy (sɪnˈdɛktəmɪ). *Surg.* [irreg. f. Gr. σύνδεσμος ligament (cf. SYNDESMO-) + ἐκτομή excision.] Excision of a strip of conjunctiva around the cornea; peritomy.

1869 G. LAWSON *Dis. Eye* (1874) 19 Syndectomy—Peritomy.—This operation was first practised by Dr. Furnari, of Paris, in 1862. It consists in excising a band of conjunctiva and subconjunctival tissue..from around the cornea. *Ibid.* 20, I have on several occasions performed syndectomy as a preliminary to inoculation. **1889** [see PERITOMY].

‖**syndendrium** (sɪnˈdɛndrɪəm). *Zool.* Pl. **-ia**. [mod.L., f. Gr. σύν SYN-¹ + δένδρον tree + *-ium*.] The thick flat quadrate disc suspended from the umbrella by the dendrostyles in rhizostomous hydrozoans.

1859 HUXLEY *Oceanic Hydrozoa* i. 18 In the Rhizostomidæ a complex tree-like mass..is suspended from the middle of the umbrella... The main trunks of the dependent polypiferous tree..unite above into a thick flat quadrate disc, the syndendrium, which is suspended by.. the dendrostyles.

synder, obs. form of CINDER, SUNDER.

‖**synderesis.** *Obs.* Also 5 **synderesys**, 6 **sinderesis**, 6–7 **synderisis**, 7 **synth-**, **sintheresis**. [med.L. *synderesis*, repr. med. (and mod.) Gr. pron. of συντήρησις SYNTERESIS. Cf. F. *syndérèse*, †*sinderese*, It. *sinderesi*, Sp. *sindéresis*, Pg. *synderesis*.] = SYNTERESIS.

c **1400** *Pilgr. Sowle* I. xviii. (1859) 19 [Sathanas loq.] Come forth, thou foule Synderesys, and say what thou knowest of this fals pilgrym. *c* **1420** ? LYDG. *Assembly of Gods* 937 Macrocosme was the name of the felde..In the myddes therof stood Conscience... Synderesys sate hym withyn closyd as in a parke, With hys tables in hys hand her dedys to marke. **1426** —— *De Guil. Pilgr.* 4963 Synderesys..Ys as myche for to seyn,..The hiher party of Resoun; Wherby A man shal best discerne Hys conscience to governe. **1531** *Dial. on Laws Eng.* I. xiii. 31 Sinderesis is a naturall power of the soule sette in the hyghest parte therof, mouynge and sterrynge it to good, & abhorrynge euyll. **1598** MARSTON *Sat.* III. viii. Poems (1879) 172 Returne, returne sacred Synderesis, Inspire our truncks. **1599** B. JONSON *Ev. Man out of Hum.* III. iv, The soules Synderisis. **1600** W. WATSON *Decacordon* (1602) 271 Some sparks of Synderesis, and the lawes of reason. **1603** DEKKER & CHETTLE *Grissil* III. ii, I thought (by the Syntheresis of my soule) I had not been imperished. **1651** J. F[REAKE] tr. *Agrippa's Occ. Philos.* I. lxii. 140 When they [*sc.* passions of the soul] follow the Intellectual apprehension,..they are called intellectuall passions, or synderesis.

b. Remorse or prick of conscience. (Cf. F. *syndérèse*.)

1639 N. N. tr. *Du Bosq's Compl. Woman* I. 39 It is no great priviledg to be exempt from care or unquietnes, as unto stones to be free from maladies, and beasts from a feeling of Synderesis. **1651** HOWELL *Venice* 183 Being perswaded to a moderation of life by that Synedresis [*sic*], that touch of conscience, which coms somtimes by nature.

Hence † **synˈderesize** (sɪnd-) *v. trans.*, to make conscientious; to discharge conscientiously.

1600 TOURNEUR *Transf. Metam.* xxxvi. Wks. 1878 II. 202 Pull off their golden maske, And bid them strait sinderesize their taske.

synderique, error for *syndetique*, SYNDETIC.

syndery, obs. Sc. form of SUNDRY.

†**syndesis** (sɪnˈdiːsɪs). *Cytology. Obs.* [a. G. *syndesis* (V. Häcker 1904, in *Zool. Jahrb.* VII. 200), f. Gr. συν- SYN-¹ + δέσις binding together (f. δεσμός bond, connection).] The pairing of chromosomes in mitosis or meiosis. Cf. SYNAPSIS 2.

1909 *Ann. Bot.* XXIII. 49 Haecker has proposed the word *Syndesis* to apply to the conjugation or association of the homologous parental chromosomes. **1912** [see SYNAPSIS 2]. **1925** E. B. WILSON *Cell* (ed. 3) vi. 503 It is now widely held that reduction is initiated by a preliminary process or synapsis or syndesis in the course of which the chromosomes conjugate.

syndesmo- (sɪnˈdɛsməʊ), before a vowel **syndesm-**, repr. Gr. σύνδεσμος that which binds together, a ligament, in recent terms of anatomy. **syndesˈmitis**, (*a*) inflammation of the ligaments; (*b*) inflammation of the conjunctiva. **syndesmoˈdontoid** *a.* (*sb.*), applied to the articulation formed by the transverse ligament of the atlas vertebra and the odontoid process of the axis. **syndesˈmography**, description of the ligaments (Dunglison 1844). **syndesˈmology**, that branch of anatomy which treats of the ligaments. **synˈdesmophyte** [-PHYTE], a bony outgrowth from an injured joint or vertebra. **syndesˈmosis**, the union of two bones by a ligament; hence **syndesˈmotic** *a.* **syndesˈmotomy**, dissection or surgical section of ligaments.

1848 DUNGLISON *Med. Lex.* (ed. 7) s.v. *Ophthalmia*, *Ophthalmia membranorum* [=] Conjunctivitis, ..*Syndesmitis. *Ibid.*, *Syndesmitis*..inflammation of articular ligaments. **1891** *Cent. Dict.*, **Syndesmodontoid* adj. **1901** DORLAND *Med. Dict.* (ed. 2), *Syndesmo-odontoid*, the posterior of the two atlo-axoid articulations formed between the anterior surface of the transverse ligament and the back of the odontoid process. **1799** *Med. Jrnl.* II. 400 Elements of Myology and *Syndesmology. **1831** R. KNOX *Cloquet's Anat.* 8 The study of anatomy is commonly divided..into several distinct branches,..Osteology..Syndesmology [etc.]. **1957** in *Dorland's Med. Dict.* (ed. 23), *Syndesmophyte. **1966** E. W. BOLAND in J. L. Hollander *Arthritis* (ed. 7) v. xxxix. 648/1 In contrast to the marginal, heavy osteophytes of degenerative disease of the spine, the syndesmophytes of ankylosing spondylitis begin as linear, poorly defined calcifications adjacent to the margins of the vertebral bodies. **1980** BLUESTONE & KATICH in R. Bluestone *Rheumatology* xxiii. 284 (*caption*) Note mature syndesmophytes outlining annulus of several disks and bridging vertebral bodies. **1726** MONRO *Anat. Bones* 321 The Rotula..is connected to the Tibia by a strong *Syndesmosis. **1885** *Buck's Handbk. Med. Sci.* I. 200/1 False, fibrous, or incomplete, anchylosis (syndesmosis) may be either intra-articular or extra-articular. **1844** DUNGLISON *Med. Lex.* (1848), **Syndesmotomy*.., dissection of the ligaments. **1888** *Buck's Handbk. Med. Sci.* VI. 778/1 Syndesmotomy, or the subcutaneous division of ligaments, is employed..in the reduction of old dislocations.

syndetic (sɪnˈdɛtɪk), *a.* [ad. Gr. συνδετικός, f. συνδεῖν to bind together.] **a.** Serving to unite or connect; connective, copulative.

The incorrect form *synderique* in quot. 1621 is due to the Fr. orig. (*nerfs synderiques*, which is copied by Cotgrave).

1621 LODGE *Summary Du Bartas* I. 280 The Tendons.. which the Physicions (after Hippocrates) haue called Synderique [*read* Syndetique] Nerues. **1891** *Cent. Dict.*, Syndetic.

b. *Librarianship.* Pertaining to or designating a catalogue, index, etc., which uses cross-references to indicate links between entries. Also used in automatic data-processing.

1876 C. A. CUTTER *Rules for Printed Dict. Catal.* 15 *Syndetic*, connective, applied to that kind of dictionary catalogue which binds its entries together by means of cross-references so as to form a whole. **1958** T. LANDAU *Encycl. Librarianship* 299/2 *Syndetic*, applied to an alphabetical subject catalogue or dictionary catalogue which includes cross-references as connecting links between subjects. *Ibid.*, Systematic catalogues have no need of such a syndetic apparatus. **1968** T. C. HINES *Vocab. Control in indexing Lit. of Librarianship & Information Sci.* (ERIC doc. No. ED050742) 16 Perhaps because of the concurrent use of shelf classification, library heading lists (although they include a syndetic apparatus which serves some of the same purposes) do not include the kind of classification of the headings themselves found in some thesauri expressed as 'broader terms'. **1974** *Encycl. Brit. Macropædia* X. 869/1 Provision is made for cross-references from unused terms and from one term to a related one. A catalog containing these entries is known as a syndetic catalog. **1977** A. P. JENSEN et al. (*title*) An instructional and research laboratory for syndetic analog-digital computation in science and engineering education. **1981** *Resources in Educ.* Oct. 138/2 This module describes the main subject heading, LC classification numbers which accompany the headings, 'see' references, 'see also' references, subheadings, and other syndetic features of the LC headings.

So **synˈdetical** *a.*; hence **synˈdetically** *adv.*

1891 *Cent. Dict.*, Syndetical. **1895** *Funk's Stand. Dict.*, Syndetically.

syndeton (ˈsɪndɪtən). *Gram.* [Back-formation from ASYNDETON and POLYSYNDETON: cf. SYNDETIC *a.*] (See quots. 1954, 1972.)

1954 PEI & GAYNOR *Dict. Linguistics* 210 *Syndeton*, a phrase or construction in which the elements are linked together by connecting particles. **1971** *Computers & Humanities* V. 262 The frequency distribution enabled us to see also the amount of initial syndeton..in each sample. **1972** HARTMANN & STORK *Dict. Lang. & Linguistics* 230/1 *Syndeton*, a construction, parts of which are linked together by means of conjunctions or joining words, e.g. in *He came and went again.*

syndiagnostic: see SYN-¹.

syndic (ˈsɪndɪk), *sb.* Also 7 **sin-**, **syndique**, (**sin-**, **syndict**), **sindicke**, **syndike**, 7–8 **sin-**, **syndick**, 7–9 **sindic**, (8 **syndac**); also in L. form, 7 **sin-**, **syndicus**. [ad. F. *syndic*, †-*ique* (14th c.), delegated representative, chief magistrate of Geneva, †critic, censor, = Pr. *sendegue*, It. *sindaco* controller, syndic, Sp. *síndico* syndic, recorder, assignee, Pg. *syndico* deputy, delegate, ad. late L. *syndicus* advocate or delegate representing a town, a. Gr. σύνδικος defendant's advocate, f. σύν SYN-¹ + δίκη judgement.]

1. An officer of government having different powers in different countries; a civil magistrate, or one of several such, entrusted with the affairs of a city or community; *spec.* each of four chief magistrates of Geneva.

1601 R. JOHNSON *Kingd. & Commw.* (1603) 88 The towne [*sc.* Geneva] is gouerned by a counsell of two hundred,..out of which is chosen an other counsel, composed of fiue and twentie, and out of these fower especiall men, called Sindiques, who haue the managing of the whole commonwealth. **1654** WHITELOCKE *Jrnl. Swed. Emb.* (1772) I. 142 The three presidents, who are the principal magistrates of the town, with the syndick, who is in nature of recorder. *a* **1700** EVELYN *Diary* 16 Oct. 1644, We got to anker under the Pharos..at the mouth of the Mole of Genoa... Towards evening we..came on shore..where after strict examination by the Syndics, we [etc.]. **1717**

BERKELEY *Tour Italy* Wks. 1871 IV. 577 In Furia they have a syndic for supreme magistrate. **1753** HANWAY *Trav.* (1762) II. I. iii. 15 There are also four sindics, or lawyers, who act as secretaries of the state [at Hamburg]. **1792** A. YOUNG *Trav. France* I. 88 Turned aside to Auvergnac, the seat of the count de la Bourdonaye, to whom I had a letter ..as a person able to give me every species of intelligence relative to Bretagne, having for five-and-twenty years been first syndac of the noblesse. **1812** BRACKENRIDGE *Views Louisiana* (1814) 138 Each district had its commandant, or syndic. These were the judges in civil matters.. and had also command of the militia. **1882** 'OUIDA' *Maremma* I. 18 The little band halted..in the midst of the cathedral square while the captain bade farewell to the syndic of the town.

2. One deputed to represent, and transact the affairs of, a corporation, e.g. a university; *spec.* in the University of Cambridge, applied to members of special committees of the senate, appointed by grace for specific duties.

1607 T. RIDLEY *View Civ. & Eccles. Law* 4 What is the office of a Procurator, Solicitor, or Sindict, or Factor? **1612** DONNE *Let. to Sir H. Goodere* 9 Apr., A Book written against the Popes jurisdiction..by one Richer, a Dr. and Syndique of the Sorbonists. **1662** *Grace Senate Univ. Camb.* 22 July in Kennett *Register* (1728) I. 733 May it please you, that Dr. Gunning and Dr. Pearson may be your legal Syndicks..to treat and conclude with the said Archbishop. **1726** AYLIFFE *Parergon* 427 As a Proctor has the Management of the Business of particular Individuals; so a Syndick manages the Affairs of aggregate Corporations. **1777** *Phil. Trans.* LXVII. 408 Mr. Leyser, syndic of the mines was..at the top of the pit. **1814** *Monthly Mag.* Apr. 293/1 The [printing] machine has been exhibited to the Syndics of the press at Cambridge. **1818** RANKEN *Hist. France* IV. iv. IV. 324 The syndic was the general procurator or agent of the university. **1821** C. BUTLER *Hist. Mem. Engl. Catholics* lv. §2. IV. 13 The greater canons constituted the chapter..with..an officer called a sindic to transact their temporal concerns. **1867** *Chambers' Encycl.* IX. 255/2 The various trading companies in Paris and the university had also their syndics. **1906** W. WALKER *John Calvin* i. 11 The Sorbonne, under the lead of its syndic, Noël Béda, condemned his views in April, 1521.

†**3.** A censor of the actions of another. *Obs.*

1611 COTGR., *Syndic*, a Sindicke, Censor, Controller of manners. **1617** SIR D. CARLETON *Lett.* (1775) 208 To make them sensible..of the wrong..in playing the syndic of the actions of so great a prince. **1638** DRUMM. OF HAWTH. *Irene* Wks. (1711) 165 It is not lawful for a subject to be a syndick of the actions of his prince. **1658** PHILLIPS.

4. *Greek Hist.* The title of various officials at Athens and elsewhere (see quots. and Smith's *Dict. Gr. and Rom. Antiq.*).

1682 WHELER *Journ. Greece* v. 391 Let the Commons chuse Syndicts, that all things which are done against evil doers, may be executed without Reproof. **1745** POCOCKE *Descr. East* II. II. III. xiv. 179 They have two or three Greek syndics on the part of the people, to take care that the antient laws of the island [*sc.* Cephalenia] are observed. **1808** MITFORD *Hist. Greece* v. §4. I. 281 The new law being prepared by this numerous committee, five officers, called Syndics, were appointed to defend the old before the assembly; which then decided between the two.

5. (See quots.) *rare*$^{-0}$.

1728 CHAMBERS *Cycl.* [from *Dict. de Trévoux*], *Syndic*..a Person appointed to solicit some common Affair, wherein he himself has a Share; as happens particularly among several Creditors of the same Debtor, who fails. **1846** WORCESTER, *Syndic*..(*French law*) an assignee. **1847-54** WEBSTER s.v., As in France, syndics are appointed by the creditors of a bankrupt to manage the property.

Hence **'syndicship** = SYNDICATE *sb.* 1.

1706 PHILLIPS, *Syndicate* or *Syndickship*.

†**syndic**, *v.* *Obs.* *rare*$^{-1}$. [ad. F. *syndiquer* to criticize, censure, = It. *sindacare* to look over accounts, censure, Sp. *sindicar* to accuse, ad. med.L. *syndicāre* to examine, f. *syndicus* SYNDIC.] *trans.* = SYNDICATE *v.* 1: cf. prec. 3.

1609 DANIEL *Civ. Wars* III. xc, They, who tooke to Syndicque in this sorte The Actions of a Monarch.

†**syndicable**, *a.* *Obs.* *rare*$^{-0}$. [ad. obs. F. *syndicable*, f. *syndiquer*: see prec.] (See quot.)

1656 BLOUNT *Glossogr.* (from Cotgrave), *Syndicable*.., subject unto examination, censure, or controlment.

syndical ('sɪndɪkəl), *a.* [ad. F. *syndical*, f. *syndic* SYNDIC *sb.*] **a.** ***syndical chamber*** (occas. ***union***) = F. *chambre syndicale*, a union of people engaged in a particular trade, for the protection of their interests; a trade-union.

1864 *Gd. Words* 877/2 Skin-dressers, glovers, whitesmiths, harness-makers, &c., all dwell upon the necessity of forming in France 'syndical chambers,'—i.e., authorised trade societies, for their respective trades... They look to this 'syndical chamber' to extinguish strikes. **1907** *Westm. Gaz.* 19 Mar. 12/1 The Syndical Chamber of Chemical Product Manufacturers.

b. In other collocations: of or relating to syndicalism; organized in unions.

1907 I. ZANGWILL *Ghetto Comedies* 411 Your only remedy is a general strike. You must join the Syndical Anarchists. **1943** G. BRENAN *Spanish Labyrinth* xii. 271 The real strength of the C.N.T. lay..in their powers of syndical resistance. **1955** *Times* 5 Aug. 8/3 General Perón said that the syndical organization of the people fought for ideals and interests.

syndicalism ('sɪndɪkəlɪz(ə)m). [ad. F. *syndicalisme*, f. *syndical*: see prec. and -ISM.] A movement among industrial workers having as its object the transfer of the means of production and distribution from their present owners to unions of workers for the benefit of the workers, the method generally favoured for the accomplishment of this being the general strike.

See Sir A. Clay *Syndicalism & Labour*, 1911, A. W. Kirkaldy *Economics & Syndicalism*, 1914.

1907 *Contemp. Rev.* June 778 'Syndicalism' has a bad odour with the 'respectable' artisan. **1912** J. H. HARLEY in *Contemp. Rev.* Mar. 349 Syndicalism, open or baptised under the name of Industrial Unionism, is one of the unsettling influences in the world of workers.

So **'syndicalist** [F. *syndicaliste*], an adherent or advocate of syndicalism; also *attrib.* passing into *adj.*; **syndica'listic** *a.*

1907 *Nation* 23 Nov. 259/1 The Syndicalists urged a general strike, not only of the railways, but of all workmen, thus hoping to throw the whole country into anarchy. **1907** S. DEWEY in *Atlantic Monthly* Aug. 276/2 The Syndicalist movement—a sort of revolutionary, as distinguished from political, trade-unionism. **1911** G. B. SHAW in *Times* 24 Oct. 9/6 The most dangerous rivals of the Parliamentary Labour Parties in France and England just now are the Syndicalists. **1912** *Daily News* 20 Mar. 1 There was nothing particularly syndicalistic about a request for a minimum wage. **1919** M. BEER *Hist. Brit. Socialism* I. II. x. 286 The organized working class turned syndicalistic. **1962** V. NABOKOV *Pale Fire* 77 We find him next..printing peevish pamphlets, acting as messenger for obscure syndicalist groups. **1974** J. WHITE tr. *Poulantzas's Fascism & Dictatorship* III. iii. 132 At the same time there was the first rupture with the 'left' syndicalist wing of the movement. **1976** *New Yorker* 3 May 89/1 Marcos has said that he wants to encourage trade unionism, but the fact is that, while his government countenances unions, it appears in some ways to be moving toward the creation of a syndicalist state not unlike Mussolini's Fascist corporate state. **1979** *Jrnl. R. Soc. Arts* Nov. 775/2 Here we have then a typical 'vest-pocket utopia' a form of syndicalist and local organization being collaged into the existing fabric, both formally and politically.

‖**Syndicat d'Initiative** (sɛ̃dika dinisjativ). Also with small initials. [Fr.] In France, an association for promoting tourism; a tourist information office.

1911 W. J. LOCKE *Glory of Clementina Wing* ix. 128 The quarter of the town on which the Syndicat d'Initiative prides itself. **1926** E. HEMINGWAY *Sun also Rises* II. x. 92 We went..to the local Syndicat d'Initiative office. **1965** *Harper's Bazaar* Jan. 73/2 The local tourist offices—the *syndicats d'initiative* in France. **1968** F. WHITE *Ways of Aquitaine* 170 Almost all towns and many villages have *syndicats d'initiative*. These are information offices, which will give the tourist local lists of hotels and places of interest. **1972** D. LEES *Zodiac* 85 It's not the sort of thing the Syndicat d'Initiative likes to have get around but it does rain in Antibes every now and again. **1981** C. WATSON *Bishop in Back Seat* xxxvi. 208, I would go to the Gendarmerie, the Syndicat d'Initiative.

syndicate ('sɪndɪkət), *sb.* Also 7 syn-, sindicat. [ad. F. *syndicat* office of syndic, body of syndics, †censure, = Pr. *sendegat*, It. *sindacato* rendering of accounts, order, permission, Sp. *sindicado* syndicate, *sindicato* office of syndic, ad. med.L. **syndicatus*, f. *syndicus* SYNDIC: see -ATE[1].]

1. The office, status, or jurisdiction of a syndic.

1656 BLOUNT *Glossogr* (from Cotgrave), *Syndicat*, the office or degree of a Syndick. **1689** BURNET *Tracts* I. 10 Being of the little Council leads one to the Sindicat. **1728** CHAMBERS *Cycl.* s.v. *Syndic*, The Syndicate comes by Turn to sixteen Persons.

2. A council or body of syndics; *spec.* a university committee appointed for some specific duty (see SYNDIC *sb.* 2); also, a meeting of such a body.

1624 DARCIE *Birth of Heresies* To Rdr., The Venetians.. haue a supreame Magistracie, which they call a Syndicate, that once in a few yeeres, suruey all the Offices and Dignities in their Common-wealth. **1832** tr. *Sismondi's Ital. Rep.* xi. 246 They were obliged to render an account of their administration before a syndicate charged with an examination of their conduct. **1835** in Willis & Clark *Cambridge* (1886) III. 115 The Syndicate appointed 'to consider and report to the Senate, upon..the Library, &c.' ..recommend the appointment of a special Syndicate for making enquiries [etc.]. *Ibid.* 116 A Room for the Vice-Chancellor for holding Syndicates or other uses. **1861** LD. BROUGHAM *Brit. Const.* App. iii. (1862) 429 The office of the Syndicate [in the Dutch Republic] was to watch over the Constitution established by law.

3. a. A combination of capitalists or financiers entered into for the purpose of prosecuting a scheme requiring large resources of capital, esp. one having the object of obtaining control of the market in a particular commodity. Hence, more widely, a combination of persons formed for the promotion of an enterprise; *esp.* a combination for the acquisition of articles, etc. and their simultaneous publication in a number of periodicals; also, a combination of newspapers controlled by such a body. In Gambling, an association of people joined in a gambling or betting enterprise; in Gameshooting, a group of sportsmen who share rented shooting rights; also in Angling.

1865 *Pall Mall G.* 26 Oct. 1 The shares of the promoters ..are thrown into a common stock, and put at the disposal of a secret committee, called by the harmless and, indeed, rather pretty name of a 'syndicate'. Our language owes this term, we believe, to certain French financiers. **1876** *World* V. No. 109. 5 Extensive purchases of railroad stocks were made by Syndicates. **1877** GIFFEN *Stock Exch. Securities* 44 A 'syndicate' may be taken as a general alias for any combination of speculators on the Stock Exchange to force prices in one direction or the other. It is oftenest used in the narrower sense of a combination or partnership to introduce and sell a newly-created security to the public. **1880** *Standard* 29 Nov., The conclusion of the contract with a powerful Syndicate for raising £8,000,000 to complete the Northern Pacific Railway in three months. **1889** *Sat. Rev.* 16 Mar. 300/1 Such a syndicate of quacks and dupes as those who have lately undertaken to run Mr. Parnell. **1889** *Public Opinion* (U.S.) 16 Feb., What are called newspaper syndicates are rapidly extending their field of action. By the establishment of offices not only in America, but at Paris, Berlin, Vienna,..they are able at one stroke to confer world-wide fame on any author whose work is at their disposal. **1890** J. HATTON *By Order of Czar* (1891) 108 It's like a bear transaction against a strong syndicate. **1891** *Athenæum* 12 Sept. 356/3 The first instalment..will appear next month in a 'syndicate' of English and American newspapers. **1934** D. TEILHET *Talking Sparrow Murders* ix. 138 La Roc? He's with von Lindbrulle in a betting syndicate. **1961** C. WILLOCK *Death in Covert* i. 25 The game book for the past three seasons showed an average of 1,200 pheasants, 75 woodcock,..160 hares,..and 30 partridges per season... To hell with any qualms he felt about the members of the syndicate individually. **1964** *New Statesman* 3 Apr. 525/1 The fashion for office syndicates and 'sweeps' for charity. **1978** *Country Life* 27 July 272/1 The syndicates that form the basis of many shoots. **1979** *Angling* July 54/1 Catching good fish from strictly private or syndicate waters would prove nothing.

b. *spec.* (freq. with def. article and capital initial). In the U.S., a network of criminals controlling racketeering and other organized crime; also = COSA NOSTRA. Cf. *The Mob* s.v. MOB *sb.*[1] 5 b.

1929 HOSTETTER & BEESLEY *It's a Racket!* i. 4 Beer and alcohol running, bombing, bank robbery, murder for pay, window smashing, and a score of other crimes that can be carried on successfully only by organized groups or 'syndicates', are all rackets to the police. **1948** E. L. IREY *Tax Dodgers* xiv. 271 The Syndicate was the remnant of the Al Capone mob. **1952** [see ORGANIZED *ppl. a.* 4]. **1962** J. D. MACDONALD *Key to Suite* (1968) i. 7 The smut-shadow of beard gave him somewhat the look of imported syndicate muscle. **1963**, **1964** [see COSA NOSTRA]. **1969** *Guardian* 24 Jan. 7/6 The Syndicate is increasingly entering legitimate business. **1980** S. ALLAN *Dead Giveaway* iv. 38 The Syndicate had not been slow in learning of his involvement ..and using it. **1982** *Amer. Speech* LVII. 244 Some successful criminals escape getting a monicker, for they, especially top-notch con men and syndicate members, think it adds 'class' to be without one.

c. ***Syndicate of Initiative*** = SYNDICAT D'INITIATIVE.

1930 KIPLING *Limits & Renewals* (1932) 325 A syndicate of Initiative has, indeed, approached me to write on the attractions of the district, as well as on the life of Saint Jubanus.

syndicate ('sɪndɪkeɪt), *v.* [In sense 1, f. med.L. *syndicāt-*, pa. ppl. stem of *syndicāre* (see SYNDIC *v.*). In other senses, f. prec.]

†**1.** *trans.* To judge, censure. *Obs.*

1610 DONNE *Pseudo-martyr* 154 Not how hee shall iudge quicke and dead at his second coming, but how his Vicar shall inquire, Examine, Syndicate, Sentence, Depose: yea, Murder Princes on earth. **1627** HAKEWILL *Apol.* IV. ii. §4. 290 Aristotle..vndertooke to censure & syndicate both his Master, and all other Law-makers before him. **1641** MARCOMBES in *Lismore Papers* Ser. II. (1888) IV. 203 Those that haue but mediocre [employments] are soe much obserued and Syndicated. **1822** MRS. NATHAN *Langreath* III. 290 Would that I had to syndicate her oppressors!

2. To control, manage, or effect by a syndicate; *esp.* to publish simultaneously in a number of periodicals (see SYNDICATE *sb.* 3); *spec.* in *Horse-racing*, to sell (a horse) to a syndicate.

1882 *Pall Mall G.* 29 Nov. 5/2 Government loans..are all 'syndicated'—deposited, that is, in the strong boxes of the finance houses interested in their success. **1889** *Ibid.* 20 Feb. 6/2 Mr. W. F. Tillotson..first acclimatized in this country the American system of 'syndicating' fiction. **1891** 'MAX O'RELL' *Frenchm. in Amer.* 240 Dr. Talmage syndicates his sermons, and they are published in Monday's newspapers in all quarters of America. **1892** *Daily News* 13 Feb. 7/2 It is probable that the issue is only syndicated. **1973** *Country Life* 6 Dec. 1897/3 American racing seems to have had a prosperous season with..the prices of bloodstock up. Secretariat was syndicated at $190,000 a share. **1979** D. FRANCIS *Whip Hand* xiii. 161 He buys quite good horses... Then he syndicates them.

3. To combine into a syndicate.

1889 *Pall Mall G.* 3 May 2/1 To underwrite,..syndicate, or otherwise provide working capital for bona fide mining companies. **1892** [see *syndicated* below]. **1916** *Q. Rev.* Oct. 539 A mortgage by bonds, which the bank..will probably share with other banks with whom it is syndicated.

Hence **'syndicated** *ppl. a.* (***syndicated crime***, criminal activities organized by a syndicate (sense 3 b)); **'syndicating** *vbl. sb.*

a **1693** *Urquhart's Rabelais* III. xxvi. 215 Syndicated cock [*orig.* syndicqué]. **1886** *Tinsley's Mag.* July 52 There is time-bargain syndicating for those who prefer a modern road to ruin. **1889** E. M. CLERKE in *Dublin Rev.* Apr. 367 The conditions of trade in the United States under the syndicated system. **1892** *Daily News* 24 Feb. 4/8 Ouida.. has lashed out against agents, syndicates, and the syndicated. **1892** *Times* 14 Oct. 7/2 The proportion of syndicated, or as we should say, of union workmen in France. **1893** *Athenæum* 5 Aug. 193/1 The principles of the syndicating of literary material. **1928** [see GRAMOPHONE *v.*]. **1959** *Times Lit. Suppl.* 11 Dec. 719/2 Mr. Marquis Childs, the well-known syndicated columnist, formerly of the even better-known *St. Louis Post-Dispatch*. **1968** *Globe & Mail* (Toronto) 13 Feb. 8/3 The Roach report..drew a fine distinction between organized crime and syndicated crime. **1972** *Amer. Speech 1968* XLIII. 211 Van Johnson is quoted in Hedda Hopper's nationally syndicated column. **1974** *Howard Jrnl.* XIV. 108 (Advt.), An exposition of the many problems of organized, syndicated or corporate crime. **1976** *Liverpool Echo* 7 Dec. 17/3 The week gave me new experiences of writing. A syndicated article for the country's local newspapers, a particularly difficult article for a sports journal. **1980** *TWA Ambassador* Oct. 85/1 William R. Allen, professor of economics at UCLA, is known nationally for his syndicated radio commentaries.

syndicateer (ˌsɪndɪkəˈtɪə(r)). [f. SYNDICATE *sb.* + -EER[1].] A member of a (financial) syndicate.

1906 *Blackw. Mag.* Jan. 146/1 The syndicateer-in-chief was Mr. Pierpont Morgan. **1908** SIR C. WYNDHAM in *Daily Tel.* 26 Mar. 9/2 The sinews of war are to be provided by millionaires: in other words, our old friends the syndicateers.

syndication (sɪndɪˈkeɪʃən). [In sense 1, ad. med.L. *syndicātio, -ōnem* examination (cf. obs. F. *syndication* censure, criticism, Pg. *syndicação* inquiry), f. *syndicāre* (see SYNDIC *v.*). In senses 2 and 3, f. SYNDICATE *sb.* or *v.*: see -ATION.]

†**1.** The action of judging. *Obs. rare.*

1650 HOBBES *De Corp. Pol.* II. ix. §6. 182 It is therefore necessary, that there be a Power Extraordinary..for the Syndication of Judges and other Magistrates, that shall abuse their Authority.

2. The action or process of forming a syndicate.

1887 *Christian Union* 9 June (Cent. Dict.) The age of syndication, hypothecation, and stock-watering. **1910** *19th Cent.* Aug. 244 The system of syndication has killed free competition at home. **1916** *Times* 8 May 7/6 The German aniline dye companies..announced another important step towards the syndication of practically the whole industry.

3. Publication or ownership by a syndicate. Freq. *attrib.*

1925 A. HUXLEY *Let.* 21 Apr. (1969) 247, I am trying to arrange for syndication of articles in America. **1955** *Times* 2 Aug. 2/5 Syndication is a nuisance to breeders. They have to guess at a horse's ability as a stallion when they take a share in him at the end of his racing days. **1959** R. CONDON *Manchurian Candidate* (1960) ix. 137 The paper..offered Raymond fifty per cent of the syndication money. **1973** K. GILES *File on Death* iv. 97 Once the first instalment hits the street and the syndication rights have been arranged..the Establishment will be chary of proceeding. **1980** *Daily Tel.* 20 Mar. 24/5 (Advt.), Syndication Manager of the Daily Telegraph is looking for a secretary.

syndicator (ˈsɪndɪkeɪtə(r)). [In sense 1, ad. med.L. *syndicātor* examiner (cf. obs. F. *sindicateur* examiner, censor, Sp. *sindicador* informer, prosecutor), agent-n. f. *syndicāre*: see SYNDIC *v.* and -OR[1]. In sense 2, f. SYNDICATE *sb.* or *v.*]

†**1.** One who judges; a judge. *Obs. rare.*

1610 DONNE *Pseudo-martyr* 245 In Capitall matters, saies your great Syndicator, it is lawfull to redeeme the life, *per fas & nefas.* [**1768** BOSWELL *Corsica* iii. 153 The procurators.. choose some persons of high credit and respect, as syndicatori... These make a tour through the different provinces, as our judges in Britain go the circuits... These syndicators are exceedingly beneficial.]

2. One who forms a syndicate. *U.S.*

1891 *Cent. Dict.*, *Syndicator*, one who syndicates, or effects sales. (Recent.) **1896** *Voice* (N.Y.) 12 Nov. 5 A large class of capitalists and 'syndicators'.

syndiotactic (ˌsɪndaɪəʊˈtæktɪk), *a. Chem.* Also (more correctly) **syndyo-**. [f. Gr. σύνδυο two together + τακτ-ός arranged, ordered + -IC.] Having or designating a polymer structure in which the substituent groups alternate on either side of the backbone of the molecule.

1956 NATTA & CORRADINI in *Jrnl. Polymer Sci.* XX. 262 We propose to call all vinyl polymers with alternating D- and L-configurations of their substituents (like 1,2-polybutadiene) 'syndyotactic' polymers. **1966** *McGraw-Hill Encycl. Sci. & Techn.* X. 478/2 Isotactic and syndyotactic (stereoregular) polymers are formed in the presence of complex catalysts. **1972** *Physics Bull.* Nov. 668/3 The cellulose molecule..is syndiotactic and hence able to crystallize. **1978** *Nature* 9 Feb. 508/2 Commercial atactic polystyrene..is 70% syndiotactic.

Hence ˌ**syndioˈtactically** *adv.*; ˌ**syndiotacˈticity**, the property or state of being syndiotactic.

1959 *Jrnl. Polymer Sci.* XXXIV. 9 Syndiotacticity is the corresponding arrangement. We can think of it as composed of positional and structural arrangements identical to those of isotacticity (repetition arrangements) and of a tacticity opposite to that of isotacticity (inversion tacticity). **1964** *Ibid.* B. II. 319 Predominantly isotactic addition may occur on heterogeneous surfaces, accompanied by conversion of the active complexes to form different..catalyst sites, which propagate predominantly syndiotactically. **1974** *Nature* 26 Apr. 758/1 If there is a high degree of syndiotacticity, a structure incorporating four monomer units per fibre repeat may be present.

syndir, syndoc, syndon(e, syndow, syndre, syndri(e: see SUNDER *a.*, SINTOC, SINDON, SINDAW, CINDER, SUNDRY.

syndrome (ˈsɪndrəʊm, formerly ˈsɪndrəmɪ). Also 7 **syndrom.** [mod.L., a. Gr. συνδρομή, f. σύν SYN-[1] + δρομ-: δραμεῖν to run.]

1. *Path.* A concurrence of several symptoms in a disease; a set of such concurrent symptoms.

1541 COPLAND *Galyen's Terap.* 2 B iij, They enquyre the cause prymytyfe as partye of all the syndrome. **1605** DANIEL *Queen's Arcadia* III. ii. (1606) F ij, That so we may preuent the syndrome Of Symtomes. **1670** MAYNWARING *Vita Sana* vi. 75 The syndrom is lethal. **1899** *Allbutt's Syst. Med.* VI. 207 Charcot's syndrome has in a number of reported cases been a precursor of arterio-sclerotic gangrene.

2. †**a.** *transf.* or *gen.* A concurrence, concourse; a set of concurrent things. *Obs.*

1646 SIR T. BROWNE *Pseud. Ep.* II. iii. 66 This motion is termed coition, and that not made by any faculty attractive of one, but a Syndrome and concourse of each. **1651** BIGGS *New Disp.* Pref. 7 A farraginous Syndrome of Knaves and Fools. **1651** CHARLETON *Ephes. & Cimm. Matrons* II. (1668) Pref., Distracted with a syndrome of Remorse, Fear, Anger, and Despair. **1661** GLANVILL *Scepsis Sci.* xxv. (1665) 156 Every single motion owning a dependence on such a Syndrome of præ-required Motors.

b. In recent use, a characteristic combination of opinions, behaviour, etc.; freq. preceded by a qualifying word.

1955 A. HUXLEY *Genius & Goddess* 26 She took a professional interest in caterpillars... It was part of the Gloom-Tomb syndrome. Caterpillars were the nearest approach, in real life, to Edgar Allen Poe. **1958** C. P. SNOW in *Times Lit. Suppl.* 15 Aug. p. iii/2 There is a syndrome of attitudes in literature, nearly all quite modern, apparently unconnected, which spring from the same root. **1965** *Harper's Mag.* Feb. 74 A student.. explained Albuquerque's all-enveloping friendliness in terms of the Luke Short syndrome. Typically in a Luke Short novel, a cowboy, footsore and weary, comes into town carrying a saddle over his shoulders. Nobody asks any questions. Friendliness is simply his for the asking. **1971** C. M. KERMAN *Lang. Behavior in Black Urban Community* i. 16 The demographic statistics of this community, although depicting accurately a cluster of traits which might be labeled those comprising a lower-class poverty syndrome, do somewhat of an injustice to the social structure of the community. **1976** *Globe & Mail* (Toronto) 21 Dec. 7/1 They were working under the old syndrome that we couldn't do anything—the Government would always block us. **1976** J. I. M. STEWART *Memorial Service* xi. 177 His reclusive side—the withdrawn scholar syndrome, it might be called—remained on top. **1980** *West Lancs. Even. Gaz.* 23 Oct. 13 The falling roll syndrome [in schools] was a problem of the greatest magnitude and one never experienced before.

Hence **synˈdromic** *a.*, of or pertaining to the syndrome or combination of symptoms in a disease.

1890 *Smithsonian Rep.* 648 The syndromic episodes, the extreme manifestations of dis-equilibrium.

syndrum (ˈsɪndrəm). [f. SYN(THESIZER + DRUM *sb.*[1]] A drum designed with electronic means of amplification or alteration of pitch, etc.

1979 *Oxford Times* 28 Sept. 22 The drummer used syndrums more inventively than most disco arrangers. **1980** *Musicians Only* 26 Apr. 13/6 There's a Sonor drumkit, syndrums, and a whole range of Latin percussion. **1981** *Guardian* 13 July 9/1 They dressed up the reggae beat with subtle use of electronic 'syn drums' borrowed from the disco world.

syndry(e, obs. forms of SUNDRY.

syndyasmian (sɪndaɪˈæzmɪən), *a. Anthrop.* [f. mod.L. *syndyasmus*, ad. Gr. συνδυασμός coupling, pairing, sexual intercourse, f. συνδυάζειν, f. σύν SYN-[1] + δυάζειν to couple, f. δύο TWO: see -IAN.] Pertaining to or marked by sexual union without exclusive coition or with temporary cohabitation.

1877 L. H. MORGAN *Ancient Society* III. i. 384 The Syndyasmian or Pairing Family..was founded upon marriage between single pairs, but without an exclusive cohabitation.

syndyr, obs. form of CINDER.

syne (saɪn), *adv.* (*conj.*) *Sc.* and *north. dial.* Forms: 4 **seine, syn,** 4–6 (9) **sine,** 5 **seyn(e, syen(e, syon,** (8–9 **saan),** 4– **syne.** [Contracted form of ME. *sethen*, SITHEN, perh. influenced by ON. *síðan*; cf. HYNE, THYNE, WHYNE for HETHEN, THETHEN, WHETHEN. The northern-English spellings with *-ei-* (*-ey-*), riming with *ī*, are common to all four words; their phonological significance is obscure. See also the corresponding form with shortened vowel, SIN *adv.*; cf. SEN *adv.* and SENE *adv.*]

1. Directly or next after that; at the next moment; immediately afterwards; then, thereupon; = SINCE A. 1. (Occas. strengthened by *after.*)

13.. *Gosp. Nicodemus* 1069 (Galba MS.) In aramathi he set me seine [*rimes* hein, fein]. **1375** BARBOUR *Bruce* XI. 216 Valtir, steward of scotland syne, That than wes bot ane berdlas hyne, Com vith a rout of nobill men. *c* **1400** MAUNDEV. (Roxb.) i. 4 Þan men passez thurgh þe land of Pynceras.. and seyne to þe citee of Bradrenople and seyne [*ed.* 1839 aftre] to þe citee of Constantynople. *c* **1400** *Song Roland* 826 All the cursed men to mahoun criene, ledes them on the lond, hold to-gedur seyne. *c* **1425** WYNTOUN *Cron.* III. ix. 1085 And there it wes syne mony day. *c* **1475** *Rauf Coilȝear* 87 First to lofe, and syne to lak, Peter! it is schame. **1513** DOUGLAS *Æneis* I. ix. 78 My fader.. The riche realme of Cyper waistit by weir, And wan it syne. **1561** WINȜET *Four Scoir Thre Quest.* xlvi. Wks. (S.T.S.) I. 106 Be reconcilit with thi brother, and syne cum and offir thi gift. *a* **1568** *Wyfe of Auchtermuchty* 47 (Bann. MS.) And the gudman raiss eftir syne. *a* **1585** MONTGOMERIE *Cherrie & Slae* 515 First spye baith, syne try baith. **1681** COLVIL *Whigs Supplic.* (1751) 37 He empties all the water, syne He fills the place with brandy-wine. **1724** RAMSAY *Tea-t. Misc.* (1733) I. 28 He first speer'd at the guidman, And syne at Giles the mither. **1785** BURNS *Holy Fair* xxiv, In comes a gaucie, gash Guidwife, An' sits down by the fire, Syne draws her kebbuck an' her knife. **1826** R. CHAMBERS *Pop. Rhymes Scotl.* (1870) 283 Jethart justice—first hang a man, and syne judge him. **1891** MORRIS *Poems by Way, Son's Sorrow* 146 Three sons my true-love bore me there, And syne she died who was so dear. **1902** BUCHAN *Watcher by the Threshold* 247 Syne he rebuked her coldness.

†**b.** (with prospective reference): Directly after this, immediately, presently. *Obs.*

c **1420** *Sir Amadace* (Camden) xviii, Go, loke thou diȝte oure soper syne. *c* **1460** *Towneley Myst.* xxx. 534 Nay, tary not so we get ado syne.

c. (in reference to serial order generally): In the next place, next, further, moreover: = THEN 3 b.

c **1400** *Rule St. Benet* (verse) 565 And syen our neghburs sal we luf. **1456** SIR G. HAYE *Law Arms* (S.T.S.) 2 And syne efter sall folowe the principale parties of the buke. *c* **1550** ROLLAND *Crt. Venus* IV. 653 And sine the drink it was sa delicious. *a* **1578** LINDESAY (Pitscottie) *Chron. Scot.* (S.T.S.) I. 4 First to pleis god and syne our nobill king.

2. At a later time, afterwards, subsequently; esp. in phr. *soon or syne*, sooner or later.

1375 BARBOUR *Bruce* I. 450–1 Bot syne our lord sic grace thaim sent, That thai syne, throw thar gret walour, Come till gret hycht & till honour. *c* **1460** *Towneley Myst.* xii. 198 Abyde vnto syne. *c* **1587** MONTGOMERIE *Sonn.* xx. 8 He recompencis, as ȝe play your pairts, Once, soon or syne. *a* **1600** HOOKER *Serm. Nat. Pride* iii. Wks. 1888 III. 627 As verily as God is just, his justice will show itself upon them soon or sine. **1678** *Hist. Indulgence* Ep. to Rdr., Soon or syne he shall be put to it. **1722** W. HAMILTON *Wallace* 318 Each Rogue..Shall be discov'red soon or syne. **1854** MRS. OLIPHANT *Magd. Hepburn* i. I. 19 His fate..waits for him soon or syne. **1899** CROCKETT *Kit Kennedy* vii, We may as well get it over soon as syne!

3. Since that time, since then: = SINCE A. 2.

c **1400** MAUNDEV. (Roxb.) iv. 13 Seyne hiderward myght na knyght see hir. **1513** DOUGLAS *Æneis* I. ix. 79 Evir syne of Troye..The destructioun his bene wele knawin to me. *Ibid.* II. xi. 99 Neuir syne with ene saw I hir eft. **1816** SCOTT *Old Mort.* xlii, I hae seen it mysel mony a day syne. **1854** THACKERAY *Rose & Ring* xii, Marry, indeed am I, my gracious liege—the poor Lord Spinachi, once—the humble woodman these fifteen years syne.

4. (So long) before now; ago: = SINCE A. 4. See also LANGSYNE.

[**14..** *R. Glouc. Chron.* (Rolls) 52 (MS. β) Ȝit is nouȝt longe syne.] **1573** TYRIE *Refut.* in *Cath. Tractates* (S.T.S.) 18 It was Hierusalem ane thousand and fyve hundreth yeir syne. *c* **1620** A. HUME *Brit. Tongue* Ded. (1865) 1, I..set my-selfe, about a yeer syne, to seek a remedie. **1786** BURNS *Twa Dogs* 28 [He] had Luath ca'd him, After some dog in Highland sang, Was made lang syne. **1788** W. H. MARSHALL *Yorksh.* II. 349 'Hoo lang saan?' 'A year saan.' **1818** SCOTT *Hrt. Midl.* v, Ye said a gliff syne it was *quivis*, and now I heard ye say *cuivis* with my ain ears. **1871** C. GIBBON *Lack of Gold* xii, He was here a minute syne.

†**B.** *conj.* = SINCE B. 4. *Obs. rare.*

a **1400–50** *Alexander* 1864 (Dubl. MS.) A sot I hym halde, þat ay hase dene & dispyte of dedes of lityll, Syon [*Ashm. MS.* Sen] oft þe haslokst her is heuen to þe sternes. *c* **1470** HENRY *Wallace* II. 181 Eternaile God, quhy suld I thus wayis de; Syne my beleiff all haile remanys in the?

syne, obs. f. SIN, SIGN; var. SIND.

‖**synecdoche** (sɪˈnɛkdəkɪ). *Gram.* and *Rhet.* Also 4–5 **syn-, sinodoches,** 5 **synadochie,** 6 **sinecdochine, senec(h)doche,** 6–7 **synechdoche,** 7 **sinecdoche, synegdoche, synechdochie.** Also *anglicized* 6 **sinecdoch.** [a. late L. *synecdoche* (in med.L. *sinodoche*, whence obs. F. *synodoche*), a. Gr. συνεκδοχή, f. συνεκδέχεσθαι lit. to take with something else, f. σύν SYN-[1] + ἐκδέχεσθαι to take, take up. Cf. F. *synecdoche, -doque*, It. *sineddoche*, Sp. *siné(c)doque*, Pg. *synecdoche*.

The form *sinecdochine* represents the acc. *synecdochen*, συνεκδοχήν, and *synodoches* is a new nom. formed upon it; cf. *syncopis, -in*, s.v. SYNCOPE.]

A figure by which a more comprehensive term is used for a less comprehensive or *vice versâ*; as whole for part or part for whole, genus for species or species for genus, etc.

Formerly sometimes used loosely or vaguely, and not infrequently misexplained.

1388 *Wyclif's Bible, Prol.* xii. (1850) 47 Bi a figure clepid synodoches [*v.r.* synadochie], whanne a part is set for al, either al is set for oo part. **1432–50** tr. *Higden* (Rolls) IV. 263 Criste was seide to be in the..herte of therthe thre daies and iij. nyȝhtes by a figure callede sinodoches, after Seynte Austyn, sythe Criste reste not in his sepulcre but by xl[ti] howres. **1483** CAXTON *Gold. Leg., Resurr.* (1892) 52 Jhesus was in the sepulcre iii dayes & iii nyghtes. But after saynt austyn the first day is taken by synecdoche, that is, that the last part of the day is taken [etc.]. **1548** R. HUTTEN *Sum of Diuinitie* E ij b, They imagyne a Sinecdoch to be in thys worde. *Ibid.* F viij b, The subtyll cauillacyons, whereby they fayne Sinecdochine. **1551** T. WILSON *Logike* (1580) 75 Therefore, whereas I saie, the Churche doeth not erre, it is called Synechdoche, that is to saie, when the parte is vsed for the whole [*sic*]. **1602** MARSTON *Ant. & Mel.* v. Wks. 1856 I. 55, I did send for you to drawe me a devise, an Imprezza, by Sinecdoche a Mott. **1612** J. MASON *Anat. Sorc.* 56 By these two blessings (to wit) the sunne & raine meaning al other earthly benefits whatsoever, by the figure synechdoche. **1638** CHILLINGW. *Relig. Prot.* I. v. §94. 295 By a Synecdoche of the whole for the part, he might be said to forsake the Visible Church. **1657** J. SMITH *Myst. Rhet.* 44 Of the Grammarians it is called a Synecdoche, or Comprehension, when a common word or name is restrained to a part which is expressed by the Accusative Case..: as, *Æthiops albus dentes*, an Ethiopian white in the teeth; here, white agreeing to the teeth only, is attributed to the whole Ethiopian. **1660** JER. TAYLOR *Worthy Commun.* I. iii. 58 It is by a Metonymy and a Sacramental Manner of speaking, yet it is also a synecdoche of the part for the whole. **1718–31** J. TRAPP tr.

Virg., Eclogues I. 87 *note* (ed. 2) I. 11 *Aristas*, by a Metonymy of the Adjunct, for Harvests; and Those by a Synecdoche, for Years. **1872** MINTO *Engl. Prose Lit.* Introd. 15 Metaphors, personifications, synecdoches and metonymy in almost every sentence. **1900** R. J. DRUMMOND *Apost. Teach.* viii, This ordinance was frequently by synecdoche spoken of as the Breaking of Bread.

synecdochic (sɪnɛk'dɒkɪk), *a.* [ad. mod.L. *synecdochicus*, a. Gr. συνεκδοχικός, f. συνεκδοχή SYNECDOCHE.] **a.** *Gram.* and *Rhet.* = next, a. **b.** *Ethnol.* Involving SYNECDOCHISM (see b).

1787 PINKERTON *Diss. Scythians* I. iv. 69 *note*, Diodorus Siculus remarks the cloudy speech, and intellect, synecdochic phrase, and hyperbolic pride, of the old Celts. **1894–5** *Ann. Rep. Bur. Amer. Ethnol.* 21 Incantation and sorcery through nail-parings, hair-combings, and other parts of the person (the synecdochic magic of Mason).

synecdochical (sɪnɛk'dɒkɪkəl), *a.* [f. mod.L. *synecdochicus*: see prec. and -ICAL.] **a.** *Gram.* and *Rhet.* Involving or constituting synecdoche.

1597 DRAYTON *Heroic. Ep., Shore's Wife to Edw. IV* Note 2, Isis heere is vsed for Thamesis by a Senecdochicall [**1608** synecdochicall] kinde of speech. **1619** SIR J. SEMPILL *Sacrilege Handled* 21 Tremellius..noteth this speech to be both Synecdochicall, in putting Sacrifices for all sorts of Offrings..and Metonymicall. **1637** GILLESPIE *Engl. Pop. Cerem.* III. viii. 165 The first..is the proper signification; the second is metaphoricall; the third synegdochicall. **1650** FULLER *Pisgah* II. v. 134 A cup being taken here by a synecdochicall metonymie for all plentifull provisions. **1702** C. MATHER *Magn. Chr.* VII. i. 5/2 Synecdochical [*mispr.* -doctrical] Pay, being a certain Figure in our avaritious.. Rhetoric, by which there passes, *pars pro Toto*. **1876** J. MARTIN tr. *Keil's Comm. Ezekiel* xl. 38–47 A synecdochical designation aplied to every kind of animal sacrifice.

b. *Ethnol.* = prec. b.

1887 O. T. MASON in *Science* 7 Jan. 17/2 Synechdochical Magic.

synec'dochically, *adv.* [f. prec. + -LY[2]. Cf. late L. *synecdochicē*.] In a synecdochical manner; by synecdoche.

1609 BELL *Theoph. & Remig.* 111 So that Christ vndoubtedly meaneth all the scriptures of the old Testament, when synecdochically he meaneth [*read* nameth] onely the Prophets. **1646** SIR T. BROWNE *Pseud. Ep.* VI. i. 280 So is it said that Christ was three dayes in the grave..which..must be taken Synechdochically, or by understanding a part for an whole day. **1679** C. NESSE *Antichrist* 71 All the world is synecdochically taken for the most parts of it. **1709** CHANDLER *Effort agst. Bigotry* 7 By Meat and Drink are Synecdochically comprehended all other Things of like Nature. **1837** WHEELWRIGHT tr. *Aristoph.* II. 32 *note*, The miseries of war, for which shields are put synecdochically. **1911** H. S. HARRISON *Queed* xvii, The eyes (which you use synecdochically to represent the character).

synecdochism (sɪ'nɛkdəkɪz(ə)m). [f. SYNECDOCHE + -ISM.] **a.** *Gram.* and *Rhet.* Synecdochical style; the use of synecdoche. **b.** *Ethnol.* Belief or practice in which a part of an object or person is taken as equivalent to the whole, so that anything done to, or by means of, the part is held to take effect upon, or have the effect of, the whole.

1854 BADHAM *Halieut.* 463 The surmise of Jovius, though not absolutely impossible is..so unusual a specimen of catachrestic synecdochism as to be scarcely admissible. **1894–5** *Ann. Rep. Bur. Amer. Ethnol.* 23 One or more pieces of the skull (for in synecdochism the piece carries the virtue of the whole) of the slain enemy were used as amulets.

synechalle, -schalle, obs. ff. SENESCHAL.

? *a* **1400** *Morte Arth.* 1871, 1910.

‖**synechia** (sɪ'ni:kɪə, *properly* sɪnɪ'kaɪə). *Path.* Pl. -iæ. [mod.L., ad. Gr. συνέχεια continuity, f. συνεχής continuous, f. σύν SYN-[1] + ἔχειν to have, hold (cf. συνέχειν to hold or keep together).] An affection of the eye, consisting in adhesion of the iris to the cornea (***anterior synechia***) or to the capsule of the lens (***posterior synechia***).

1842 BRANDE *Dict. Sci.*, etc. **1869** G. LAWSON *Dis. Eye* (1874) 53 During the healing.., the pupillary region of the iris..is liable to become engaged in the wound, and an anterior synechia to result. *Ibid.* 81 If..the pupil should become closed..by posterior synechiæ, an iridectomy should be performed. **1884** M. MACKENZIE *Dis. Throat & Nose* II. 481 Synechiae are occasionally symmetrical, being present in both nasal fossae in corresponding situations.

synechism ('sɪnɪkɪz(ə)m). *Philos.* [f. Gr. συνεχής continuous + -ISM: cf. SYNECHIA.] The doctrine that continuity is one of the most important principles in scientific explanation. Hence '**synechist**, an adherent of this doctrine.

1892 C. S. PEIRCE in *Monist* II. 534 The tendency to regard continuity, in the sense in which I shall define it, as an idea of prime importance in philosophy may conveniently be termed *synechism*. **1902** J. M. BALDWIN *Dict. Philos. & Psychol.* II. 657/1 The synechist maintains that the only..justification for..entertaining a hypothesis, is that it affords an explanation of the phenomena. **1909** W. JAMES *Pluralistic Universe* 398 Peirce meets this objection by combining his tychism with an express doctrine of 'synechism' or continuity. **1937** *Mind* XLVI. 394 Book i sets forth the doctrines of *Tychism, Synechism*, and *Agapism*: that is to say, it attempts to explain the universe by the use of Pure Chance, Continuity, and psychological categories. **1976** *Internat. Philos. Q.* XVI. 228 This difficulty is also found in Peirce's notions of tychism and synechism.

synechthran, -echthry: see SYN-[1] I.

synecology (sɪni:'kɒlədʒɪ). Also † synoekology. [ad. G. *synökologie* (Schröter & Kirchner *Die Vegetation des Bodensees* (1902) II. II. 63), f. SYN-[1] + ECOLOGY.] The study of plant or animal communities.

1910 *Proc. 3rd Internat. Bot. Congr.* I. 266 M. Shull... Synoekology of particular regions. **1911** A. TANSLEY *Types Brit. Veg.* 3 The study of synecology is considerably in advance of autecology. **1936** *Nature* 4 Apr. 565/1 Synecology cannot..be properly studied without a good taxonomic knowledge of the local flora. **1957** [see BIOCŒNOLOGY]. **1977** A. HALLAM *Planet Earth* 245 As in ecology, the concern is first with the individual or individual species (autecology), and then investigation proceeds to the assemblage as a whole (synecology).

Hence **syneco'logical** *a.*; **syne'cologist**, a student of synecology.

1922 *Jrnl. Ecol.* X. 14 Up to the present time most ecological work has been of an extensive (synecological) nature. **1938** *Nature* 17 Dec. 1056/1 The synecologist has to name and ecologically to describe and classify the species components of the vegetation. **1940** E. J. SALISBURY in J. S. Huxley *New Systematics* 336 Each [species] has its value for synecological diagnosis. **1974** *Nature* 7 June 599/2 Autecological studies pour out increasing quantities of details for synecologists to work on. **1976** *Ibid.* 22 July p.x (Advt.), Duties: To carry out..synecological studies of aquatic plants in irrigation systems.

synectic (sɪ'nɛktɪk), *a.* [ad. late L. *synecticus*, a. Gr. συνεκτικός, f. συνέχειν: see SYNECHIA and -IC.] **a.** Of a cause: Producing its effect directly, without the intervention of means; immediate; *spec.* in *Old Med.* = CONTINENT *a.* 7. **b.** *Math.* Applied to certain continuous functions: see quot. 1888. So †**sy'nectical** *a.* (in sense a); **synecticity** (-'tɪsɪtɪ), the quality of being synectic.

1697 tr. *Burgersdicius' Logic* I. xvii. 68 A Cause Efficient is said to be next in Species which is so joyned by its Existence to its Effect, as that it is joyned to it without any mediating Virtue... Hitherto appertaineth the Emanative Cause. Likewise the Continent, or Synectical of the Physicians. **1888** B. WILLIAMSON in *Encycl. Brit.* XXIV. 72/1 A function of a complex variable which is continuous, one-valued, and has a derived function when the variable moves in a certain region of the plane is called by Cauchy synectic in this region. **1890** *Cent. Dict.* s.v. *Cause*, The physicians, following Galen, recognized three kinds of causes, the *procatarctic, proëgumenal*, and *synectic*... The *synectic, containing*, or *continent cause* is the essence of the disease itself considered as the cause of the symptoms. **1891** *Ibid.*, Synecticity.

synectics (sɪ'nɛktɪks). orig. *U.S.* Also Synectics. [f. SYNECTIC *a.*, perh. after *dialectics*.] A method of problem-solving, esp. by groups, which seeks to illuminate and utilize the factors involved in creative thinking.

A proprietary term in the U.S. (see quot. 1966).

1961 W. J. GORDON *Synectics* ii. 34 Synectics is an attempt to describe those conscious, preconscious and subconscious psychological states which are present in any creative act. **1965** *Times* 11 Aug. 11 A new philosophy, 'synectics', which is said to liberate the creative instinct and so stimulate inventiveness, is gaining a following among big corporations. **1966** *Official Gaz.* (U.S. Patent Office) 25 Oct. 191 *Synectics*, for teaching services—namely, the teaching to individuals and groups, techniques for arriving at creative new concepts, products and solutions; and advising businesses and individuals [etc.]. **1973** *Times* 22 Jan. 20/7 Synectics, a widely used technique for problem-solving in small groups. **1975** R. H. RIMMER *Premar Experiments* i. 128 The basic thrust of Synectics is joining people together into problem-stating and problem-solving groups. **1976** S. ARIETI *Creativity* xvi. 376 The synectics method started as a group method. But..the occurrence of analogy—that is, the recognition of similarities—is one of the main processes of individual creativity.

synedrial (sɪ'nɛdrɪəl), *a.* [f. SYNEDRION + -AL[1].] = next, b.

1880 *Encycl. Brit.* XIII. 428/2 The respect in which the synedrial president was held.

synedrian (sɪ'nɛdrɪən), *sb.* and *a.* [f. next + -AN.] **a.** *sb.* A member of a synedrion; see also quot. 1606. **b.** *adj.* Of or belonging to a synedrion.

1606 T. WHETENHALL *Disc. Abuses Ch. Christ* 119 [They] call them that desire to have restored againe the auncient order of Parish Synedries, Consistories, or Presbyteries..by the nick names of Synedrians, Consistorians, and Puritans. **1656** BLOUNT *Glossogr.* s.v. *Sanhedrim*, Synedrians (*synedri*) are the Counsellors, Judges, or Members of that Court. **1808** MITFORD *Hist. Greece* xxxix. §4. IV. 448 The Synedrians, resident deputies of the subject states,..met to take the matter into consideration. *Ibid.* 449 It was not probably the purpose of Chares and Demosthenes to injure or offend the Synedrian allies.

‖**synedrion** (sɪ'nɛdrɪən), **synedrium** (-əm). Pl. **synedria.** Also 8 **synhed-**; 7 *anglicized pl.* **synedries;** 8 in forms assimilated to SANHEDRIM, **synhedrim, synedrin.** [mod.L., a. Gr. συνέδριον, f. σύνεδρος: see next.] A judicial or representative assembly, a council, consistory; *spec.* the Jewish SANHEDRIM.

1584 E. PAGET *Calvin's Harm. Evangelists* 5 The Synedrion,..a chosen counsell of the stocke and posteritie of Dauid, whose auctoritie was great. **1590** NASHE *Pasquil's Apol.* I. D j, The Bishoppes..should be throwne downe, and the Iewes Synedrion set vp. **1606** Synedries [see SYNEDRIAN]. *a* **1641** BP. MOUNTAGU *Acts & Mon.* v. (1642) 341 Annas the younger,..calleth a Consistory or Synedrion, and citeth James. **1677** *Howell's Vind.* in *Harl. Misc.* (1810) VI. 128 How..uncapable am I to censure the proceedings of that great senate, that high synedrion, wherein the wisdom of the whole state is epitomized? **1728** CHAMBERS *Cycl.*, *Sanhedrin*, or *Synedrin*, among the Ancient Jews. **1775** ADAIR *Amer. Ind.* 7 In their sweltery town-houses, or supposed synhedria. *Ibid.* 86 If a two-years drought happens, the synhedrim..convene in a body, and make proper enquiry into the true cause of their calamities. **1808** MITFORD *Hist. Greece* xxxv. §1. IV. 238 Seventy-five cities, of importance enough to have each its representative in the congress, or, in the original term synedrium, which assembled at Athens. **1880** *Encycl. Brit.* XIII. 424/1 The [Jewish] synedrium at that time was a political and not a scholastic authority. **1897** R. H. STORY *Apostolic Ministry Scot. Ch.* i. 21 The synedrion held its meetings in the building used by the synagogue for its religious services.

synedrous (sɪ'ni:drəs), *a.* *Bot. rare*[−0]. [f. mod.L. *synedrus*, a. Gr. σύνεδρος sitting with, f. σύν SYN-[1] + ἕδρα seat: see -OUS.] Growing on an angle of the stem, as a leaf-stalk.

1866 *Treas. Bot.*

‖**syneidesis** (sɪnaɪ'di:sɪs). *Theol. Obs.* [Scholastic L., a. Gr. συνείδησις consciousness, conscience, f. συνειδέναι to be cognizant of or privy to a thing, with refl. pron. to be conscious of.

Cf. *Syneide* (personified) in *c* **1620** T. ROBINSON *Mary Magd.* 1245 But still Syneide comforts her againe And tells her, y[t] y[e] lambe, for sinners must bee slaine.]

That function or department of conscience which is concerned with passing judgement on acts already performed. (Contrasted with SYNTERESIS.)

1620 R. CARPENTER *Conscionable Christian* (1623) B j b, Syneidesis-conscience, that is, an actuall application of our knowledge, to this or that particular act or obiect. **1643** HERLE *Answ. Ferne* 2 Consciences synteresis, and syneidesis,..can warrant her to passe her Crisis or conclusive judgement. **1679** J. GOODMAN *Penit. Pard.* I. iv. (1713) 101 That which is called *Synteresis*, and that which is called properly *Syneidesis*, or conscience. By the former of which, man having as it were a standard within himself of good and evil, he may guide himself in the choice of his actions; by the latter he is able to reflect upon himself, and ..pass a judgment upon himself.

synema to **synepigonic**: see SYN-[1].

synenergy (sɪn'ɛnədʒɪ). *rare.* [f. SYN-[1] + ENERGY.] = SYNERGY a, b.

a **1680** GLANVILL *Sadducismus* I. (1726) 98 The Faculty of Union, Motion, and Life, in which all the Sympathies and Synenergies which are found in the World, may be conceived to consist. **1687** H. MORE *Answ. Psychop.* (1689) 114 Whatever Activity, Sympathy, Synenergy,..is found in the World. **1893** *Brit. Med. Jrnl.* 30 Sept. 725/2 Each segment [of the spinal cord] with its corresponding anterior root, represents a functional synenergy.

syneresis: see SYNÆRESIS.

synergetic (sɪnə'dʒɛtɪk), *a.* [ad. Gr. συνεργητικός, f. συνεργεῖν to work together, co-operate.] Orig., working together, co-operative: = SYNERGIC. In mod. use, of or pertaining to synergy (sense c); = SYNERGISTIC *a.* 3. So **syner'getical** *a. rare*; hence **syner'getically** *adv.* (cf. SYNERGISTICALLY *adv.*).

1682 H. MORE *Annot. Glanvill's Lux O.* 120 Acting at two places at once according to its Synergetical vertue. **1836** SMART, *Synergetic*. **1889** DUNMAN & WINGRAVE *Gloss. Anat. Phys. Biol. Terms* App., *Synergetic muscles*..are those which together subserve a certain kind of movement. **1960** R. W. MARKS *Dymaxion World of B. Fuller* 8/1 An illustration of the synergetic effect is the behavior of metallic alloys. *Ibid.* 166 Thus the system joins together 'synergetically' to distribute and inhibit the loads. **1969** R. BUCKMINSTER FULLER *Operating Man. Spaceship Earth* v. 73 Universe is synergetic. Life is synergetic. [*Ibid.* vi. 77 The patron's supine concessions to the nonsynergetical thinking.] *Ibid.* 109 It produced billions of dollars of new wealth through the increased know-how and intelligence thus released, which synergetically augmented the spontaneous initiative of that younger generation. **1975** J. DE BRES tr. *Mandel's Late Capitalism* viii. 251 The so-called synergetic model of company planning—in which the overall result of various programmes exceeds the sum of the partial results foreseen for each individual programme—is..derived from military programmes.

‖**synergia** (sɪ'nɜ:dʒɪə). [mod.L., a. Gr. συνεργία, f. συνεργός working together, συνεργεῖν (see SYNERGETIC *a.*).] **a.** *Physiol.*, etc. = SYNERGY. **b.** *Anthropol.* Agreement in bodily movements or acts, as a hypothetical stage in the development of sympathy: cf. SYNÆSTHESIA.

1859 MAYNE *Expos. Lex.* **1897** [see SYNÆSTHESIA].

synergic (sɪ'nɜ:dʒɪk), *a.* [ad. mod.L. *synergicus*, f. Gr. συνεργός, -εργεῖν: see prec. and -IC.]

Physiol. Working together, co-operating, as a group of muscles for the production of some movement; pertaining to or involving synergy. Also in *Chem.*, with reference to the mutual strengthening of sigma and pi bonds.

1859 MAYNE *Expos. Lex.* **1886** FERRIER *Functions of Brain* vi. (ed. 2) 200 Every form of active muscular exertion necessitates the simultaneous co-operation of an immense assembly of synergic movements. **1899** *Allbutt's Syst. Med.* VII. 61 A failure of synergic action of muscles. **1960** L. E. ORGEL *Introd. Transition-Metal Chem.* ix. 137 We have discussed σ and π bonding independently. While this gives a satisfactory qualitative picture, the synergic interaction between them is most important. **1974** *Encycl. Brit. Macropædia* XVIII. 606/2 Carbon monoxide is able to form carbonyls with transition metals because the bonding of those metals to the carbon monoxide molecule is of a dual or synergic nature.

Hence **sy'nergically** *adv.*, so as to co-operate.
1899 *Allbutt's Syst. Med.* VII. 898 Muscles..which are brought into action synergically.

‖**synergida** (sɪ'nɜːdʒɪdə). *Bot.* Pl. **-idæ** (-ɪdiː). Also anglicized **synergid**. [mod.L., f. Gr. συνεργεῖν to co-operate.] Either of two naked nucleated cells at the apex of the embryo-sac, regarded as co-operating with the oosphere in the production of the embryo.

1882 VINES tr. *Sachs' Bot.* 580 Two of the cells of the egg-apparatus lie nearer the apex..; they are somewhat elongated superiorly, and the nucleus lies in this elongated portion..: these cells have been termed by Strasburger the *Synergidæ*. *Ibid.*, In Sinningia, according to Strasburger, only one synergida is present in some cases. **1898** *Natural Science* June 375 Origin of the embryos from egg-cell, synergids, antipodal cells, or nucellus.

Hence **sy'nergidal** *a.*
In recent Dicts.

synergism ('sɪnədʒɪz(ə)m). [ad. mod.L. *synergismus*, f. Gr. συνεργός working together, συνεργεῖν to co-operate.] **1.** *Theol.* The doctrine that the human will co-operates with Divine grace in the work of regeneration.

1764 MACLAINE tr. *Mosheim's Eccl. Hist.* Cent. XVI. III. II. i. §32 (1833) 488/2 He [*sc.* Strigelius] was accused by Flackius of Synergism at the court of Saxe-Weimar. **1828** PUSEY *Hist. Enq.* I. 23 Even laymen, who would not sign the confutation-book (against Synergism) were excluded from acting as sponsors. **1882–3** *Schaff's Encycl. Relig. Knowl.* III. 2279/2 Synergism is a sublimated type of Semi-Pelagianism.

2. a. *Pharm.* The combined activity of two drugs or other substances, when greater than the sum of the effects of each one present alone.

1910 A. R. CUSHNY *Textbk. Pharmacol. & Therapeutics* (ed. 5) 29 Other examples of synergism are offered by the anæsthetics, for..a mixture of two of these may induce anæsthesia when administered in a dilution far below that necessary if either is employed alone. **1938** [see ANTAGONISM 1 d]. **1961** *Lancet* 12 Aug. 375/2 Combined chemotherapy of acute leukæmia with 6-mercaptopurine plus corticosteroids gave a higher remission-rate than that observed for either of these administered alone... Synergism was not observed with other drug-combinations given for malignant blood diseases. **1972** *Materials & Technol.* V. x. 313 Products of this type are widely used for their ability to work together with other surfactants (synergism), as clarifying and emulsifying agents. **1979** *Buffalo Evening News* 18 May II. 23/2 By combining 2,4-D and silvex, the weed killer became more effective... This is known as synergism.

b. *transf.* and *fig.*

1925 J. LAIRD *Our Minds & Their Bodies* ii. 26 These various arguments..are often so closely allied as scarcely to be distinguished. There is synergism in all their ramifications... Nevertheless, we must try to discriminate between the different steps and stages in these converging arguments. **1941** BEIGEL & KURTH tr. *Reik's Masochism in Mod. Man* i. 30 Freud dropped his attempt to reduce masochism to the assumption of a sexual synergism of pain and discomfort in the infantile organism. **1970** *Nature* 4 July 71/1 We wish to describe synergism between two distinct populations of cells in the production of cellular immunity. **1971** K. CHIN WU in W. O. Dingwall *Survey Linguistic Sci.* (1978) vii. 159 Articulating speech was..a function involving a rather delicate synchronization, synergism to use a more technical term, of many muscular activities that had to be learned. **1974** *Jrnl. Amer. Med. Assoc.* 15 Apr. 290 Thus, it seems that the synergism obtainable by a working together of both professions would, most of all, aid the physicians who read the journals. **1977** *New Scientist* 30 June 767/2 We've done some experiments on cells in culture and you don't get any synergism, you get addition. **1978** *N.Y. Times* 30 Mar. D3/2 (Advt.), The result: a synergism where the results are greater than the sum of the parts.

synergist ('sɪnədʒɪst). Also 7 **sun-**. [f. Gr. συνεργός (see prec.) + -IST.]

1. *Theol.* One who holds the doctrine of synergism. Also *attrib.*

1657 GAULE *Sap. Just.* 11 That the Adamical will, or will from Adams fall,..in the act of Conversion..is thereunto actively cooperating together with God; so the Erasmians, the Sunergists, and Arminians. **1764** MACLAINE tr. *Mosheim's Eccl. Hist.* Cent. XVI. III. II. i. §30. (1833) 488/1 The Synergists..denied that God was the only agent in the conversion of sinful man. **1882–3** *Schaff's Encycl. Relig. Knowl.* III. 2280/1 Strigel,..one of the professors at Jena, and a synergist. **1883** T. M. LINDSAY in *Encycl. Brit.* XV. 85/1 The Synergist controversy, which discussed the nature of the first impulse in conversion.

2. *Med.* and *Physiol.* A medicine, etc., or a bodily organ (*e.g.* a muscle) that co-operates with another or others: cf. SYNERGY b.

1876 BARTHOLOW *Mat. Med.* (1889) 491 Stramonium... Antagonists, Incompatibles, and Synergists, are the same as for belladonna. *Ibid.* 136 [see SYNERGISTIC 2]. **1938** *Brain* LXI. 322 This is not necessarily true for contraction of synergists. **1959** *New Scientist* 13 Aug. 174/3 Chemical research has already provided 'synergists', cheaper materials which, while not insecticidal themselves, are able to make the pyrethrins more effective in greater dilution. **1969** N. W. PIRIE *Food Resources* ii. 67 Substances (called synergists) are added which, though not themselves effective insecticides, prevent those metabolic changes taking place which confer resistance.

synergistic (sɪnə'dʒɪstɪk), *a.* [f. prec. + -IC.] **1.** *Theol.* Of or pertaining to synergism or the synergists.

1818 TODD. **1839** HALLAM *Lit. Eur.* III. ii. §32 Melanchthon espoused the synergistic doctrine. **1864** SHEDD *Hist. Chr. Doctrine* II. IV. ii. 40 Chrysostom's theory of regeneration was firmly synergistic.

2. *Med.* and *Physiol.* Of a substance or procedure: Co-operating with another; exhibiting synergism or synergy.

1876 BARTHOLOW *Mat. Med.* (1888) 136 Synergists. All agents promoting constructive metamorphosis are synergistic to iron. **1962** *New Scientist* 10 May 263/2 Fucidin is 'synergistic' with penicillin and erythromycin—that is, the activity of a mixture is greater than the sum of the individual antibiotics. **1976** *Sci. Amer.* Feb. p. iv/2 (Advt.), The synergistic effect of mixing finely divided titanium dioxide with opacifying dyes permitted us to use a lesser quantity of dyes than if we had used the dyes alone.

3. *gen.* Co-operative, interacting, mutually stimulating.

1965 H. I. ANSOFF *Corporate Strategy* v. 76 This step certainly provides for some of the synergistic interactions. *Ibid.* 83 The synergistic effect can be measured in either of two ways. **1970** *Nature* 26 Dec. 1261/2 The synergistic creativity of Wordsworth and Coleridge which produced *The Lyrical Ballads* in 1798 and began the romantic movement in poetry was over by 1805. **1972** M. CRICHTON *Terminal Man* I. iii. 30 Designing electronic components to be synergistic with the human brain. **1975** J. A. ARGÜELLES *Transformative Vision* i. 7 The ancient *t'ai-chi* of the Chinese..symbolizes not only the synergistic totality of the two modes of consciousness, but also the interaction of day and night, life and death [etc.]. **1980** *Jrnl. R. Soc. Arts* July 497/2 It was intended that..it should consider the synergistic interactions between the different factors.

So **syner'gistical** *a.* (= sense 1); also **syner'gistically** *adv.*

1657 GAULE *Sap. Just.* 5 The Synergistical and the Anabaptistical way of understanding it. **1764** MACLAINE tr. *Mosheim's Eccl. Hist.* Cent. XVI. III. II. i. §30 (1833) 488/1 The synergistical controversy. **1772** TUCKER *Apol. Ch. Eng.* (ed. 2) 60 *note*, The Saxon Divines, with Melancthon at their Head,..adopted another System, viz. The Synergistical. **1876** BARTHOLOW *Mat. Med.* (1879) 502 Combination with agents acting synergistically, as oil of cubebs and sandal-wood. **1968** *N.Y. Times* 8 Jan. 141 By this he meant that science and technology had come to the point where the parts fed upon each other continuously and synergistically to enlarge the whole. **1979** *Logophile* II. v. 8/2 Do the 'principles of acceptance' identified in this study operate synergistically?

synergize ('sɪnədʒaɪz), *v.* [f. SYNERG(IST + -IZE.] *intr.* To act as a synergist, co-operate, as a remedy, or an organ, with another. Hence **'synergizing** *ppl. a.*

a **1919** *N.E.D.*, Synergize. **1954** *Times Lit. Suppl.* 12 Nov. 721/1 The illuminating, synergizing word here, without which the rest is nothing but maundering, is..the word sighs. **1962** *Endocrinology* LXXI. 219/1 Prolactin is well known to synergize with growthhormone in the tibial growth test. **1973** *Nature* 13 Apr. 477/2 Progesterone.. synergizes with oestrogen to enhance sexual receptivity.

synergy ('sɪnədʒɪ). [ad. mod.L. SYNERGIA.] Joint working, co-operation.

†**a.** In general sense. (Cf. SYNERGISM, SYNERGIST 1.) *Obs.*

1660 HEYLIN *Hist. Quinquart.* I. 9 They speak only of such a Synergie, or cooperation, as makes men differ from a sensless stock, or liveless statua, in reference to the great work of his own conversion.

b. In mod. scientific use: Combined or correlated action of a group of bodily organs (as nerve-centres, muscles, etc.); hence, in extended use, of mental faculties, of remedies, etc.

1847 tr. *Feuchtersleben's Med. Psychol.* 88 The transition to the homogeneous is called irradiation (in motor nerves synergy—in sensitive, sympathy). **1867** LEWES *Hist. Philos.* (ed. 3) II. 419 The synergy of organs in producing mental phenomena. **1885** J. MARTINEAU *Types Eth. Th.* (1889) I. 467 The factors of his personality are now a different set of powers, and the product of their synergy cannot therefore be the same.

c. Increased effectiveness, achievement, etc., produced as a result of combined action or co-operation.

1957 R. B. CATTELL *Personality & Motivation* xvii. 791 Immediate synergy through group membership..expresses the energy going into the group life as a result of satisfaction with fellow members. **1960** R. W. MARKS *Dymaxion World of Buckminster Fuller* 8/1 Fuller refers to the integrated behavior patterns as synergy. **1965** H. I. ANSOFF *Corporate Strategy* v. 75 We begin to explore *synergy*... It is frequently described as the '2 + 2 = 5' effect to denote the fact that the firm seeks a product-market posture with a combined performance that is greater than the sum of its parts. **1974** M. B. BROWN *Economics of Imperialism* ix. 228 The world-wide 'synergy' of the trans-national company is ..the logical conclusion of a long historical process of capital accumulation and territorial assimilation. **1981** *Economist* 28 Nov. 19/2 Others, through mergers (eg, research houses into retail brokerage houses), have demonstrated that there is something to be said for synergy.

synester, obs. form of SINISTER.

synesthesia, var. SYNÆSTHESIA.

synesthetic, var. SYNÆSTHETIC *a.* (*sb.*)

synet, obs. form of CYGNET.

1830 ROBSON *Brit. Herald* III. Gloss., *Synettys*, old English for *swans*.

synethnic: see SYN-[1].

synevey, -wey, var. SENVY *Obs.*, mustard.

synew(e, synewi, obs. ff. SINEW, SIN *v.*

synezesis, erron. var. SYNIZESIS 3.

synform: see SYN-[1] I.

synfuel: see SYN-[2].

syng, obs. form of SIGN, SING.

syngameon (sɪn'gæmiːən). *Genetics.* [f. SYNGAMY + -ON[1].] A cluster of species and subspecies between the members of which natural hybridization occurs.

1922 J. P. LOTSY in *Rep. Brit. Assoc. Adv. Sci. 1921* 453 Nature consists of individuals; similar individuals form syngameons, and these have been mistaken for species. **1930** *Svensk Bot. Tidskr.* XXIV. 386, I have..used Lotsy's term 'syngameon' in a rather wide sense, i.e. as a..handy term for any intercrossing population not divided by distinct lines or zones of discontinuity. **1970** *Brittonia* XXII. 335 We realized that syngameon complexes..were currently contributing to the establishment of additional tetraploid populations in neighbouring areas.

syngamete ('sɪŋgəmiːt). *Biol.* [f. SYN-[1] + GAMETE.] The cell produced by the fusion of two gametes in reproduction.

a **1900** C. MACMILLAN in B. D. Jackson *Gloss. Bot. Terms.*

†**syn'gamical**, *a. Obs. rare.* [f. Gr. σύν SYN-[1] + γάμος marriage + -ICAL.] Pertaining to sexual union or copulation.

1669 W. SIMPSON *Hydrol. Chym.* 276 The specifical ferments are..inherent in the syngamical spermatick liquor.

syngamy ('sɪŋgəmɪ). *Biol.* [f. Gr. σύν SYN-[1] + γάμος marriage.] **a.** Free interbreeding between organisms. **b.** The fusion of two cells, or of their nuclei, in reproduction. Hence **syngamic** (sɪn'gæmɪk), **syngamous** ('sɪŋgəməs) *adjs.*

1904 HARTOG in *Q. Jrnl. Microsc. Sci.* Mar. 595, I venture to propose the term 'Syngamy' to replace 'fertilisation' in its modern restricted sense..; and the derivative adjectives 'syngamic' and 'syngamous' follow naturally. **1904** POULTON *Ess. Evolution* ii. (1908) 60 Forms which freely interbreed together..may be..called Syngamic... Free interbreeding under natural conditions may be termed Syngamy.

syngas: see SYN-[2].

synge, obs. form of SIGN, SING, SINGE.

syngen ('sɪndʒən). *Microbiology.* [f. SYN-[1] + GEN(ERATE *v.*] A group of organisms, esp. protozoans, capable of breeding together.

1957 T. M. SONNEBORN in E. Mayr *Species Problem* 201, I propose the term 'syngen' for the potentially common gene pool, for organisms capable of 'generating together'. **1977** *Jrnl. Protozool.* XXIV. 18/1 We have learned so far that there are 'isozymes' of the epiplasmic proteins in *Tetrahymena*; the molecular weights of proteins B and C vary according to species (including syngens).

syngeneic (sɪndʒɪ'niːɪk, -'eɪɪk), *a. Immunol.* [f. SYN-[1] + Gr. γενε-ά race, stock + -IC.]

Immunologically compatible; (of a group of organisms) so closely related that their tissues do not act as antigens when transplanted to one another; = ISOGENEIC *a.*

1961 P. A. GORER et al. in *Nature* 25 Mar. 1025/1 We suggest the introduction of 'syngeneic' as a synonym for 'isogenic'. If one does not wish to refer to 'intra-strain immunity' one could then use 'syngeneic immunity'. **1977** *Lancet* 8 Oct. 743/2 Some syngeneic grafts have failed, sometimes because they were undertaken when the patient was already seriously ill. **1978** *Nature* 17 Aug. 697/2 When tumour cells are inoculated into syngeneic mice their establishment and growth is subject to regulation by the host animal.

Hence **synge'neically** *adv.*

1971 *Nature* 18 June 449/2 The tumour..has been maintained syngeneically as a solid as well as an ascites tumour.

‖**syngenesia** (sɪndʒɪ'niːsɪə). *Bot.* [mod.L. (Linnæus 1730), f. Gr. σύν SYN-[1] + γένεσις production, -GENESIS, with ending as in *Decandria*, etc.: see -IA.] The nineteenth class in the Linnæan Sexual System, comprising plants having stamens coherent by the anthers, and flowers (florets) in close heads or *capitula*; corresponding to the Natural Order *Compositæ*.

Also an order in the classes from the 20th to the 23rd, characterized by similar cohesion of the stamens.

1753 CHAMBERS *Cycl. Supp.* s.v., The *syngenesia* expresses the same class of plants with the compound flowered plants of Ray, and others. **1771** *Encycl. Brit.* I. 648/2 Many flowers, particularly those of the syngenesia class. **1785** MARTYN *Lett. Bot.* ix. (1794) 94 If..the filaments..are free and distinct, but the anthers are connected together, so as to form one body, then your plant will be found in the class *syngenesia*. **1797** *Encycl. Brit.* (ed. 3) XVI. 553/1 *Ruscus*,.. Butcher's Broom: A genus of the syngenesia order, belonging to the dioecia class. **1816** *Encycl. Perth.* V. 638/1 Corn Marigold.. belonging to the syngenesia class of plants.

Hence **syngenese** (ˈsɪndʒɪniːs), a syngenesious plant; **syngenesian** (-ˈniːʃən, -ˈniːsɪən) *a.* = next, a.

1836 Smart, Syngenese. **1840** *Ibid.*, Syngenesian.

syngenesious (sɪndʒɪˈniːʃəs, -ˈiːsɪəs), *a. Bot.* [f. prec. + -OUS.] **a.** Belonging to the class *Syngenesia*; having the stamens united by their anthers. **b.** Of the stamens: United by the anthers so as to form a tube, as in the *Syngenesia* (and in some plants of other classes); also said of the anthers.

1753 Chambers *Cycl. Supp.* s.v. *Syngenesia*, Neither scabious, nor dipsacus, are flosculous, or, as they may much more properly be called, syngenesious plants. **1830** Lindley *Nat. Syst. Bot.* 187 [Lobeliaceæ] Monopetalous milky dicotyledons, with.. syngenesious stamens. **1845** —— *Sch. Bot.* i. (1858) 15 The anthers.. sometimes grow together, when they are called syngenesious. **1896** Henslow *Wild Flowers* 18 In the Compositæ, the so-called syngenesious condition of the anthers is due to a gummy exudation.

syngenesis (sɪnˈdʒɛnɪsɪs). *Biol.* [mod.L.: see SYN-¹ and -GENESIS.] Formation of the germ in sexual reproduction by fusion of the male and female elements, so that the substance of the embryo is derived from both parents.

1836–9 *Todd's Cycl. Anat.* II. 427/2 The theory of Syngenesis or Combination seems to have been applied principally to the explanation of reproduction of quadrupeds and man. **1864** Lewes *Aristotle* xvii. 353 The theory of Syngenesis, which considers the embryo to be the product of both male and female, is as old as Empedocles. **1901** Dorland *Med. Dict.* (ed. 2), *Syngenesis*, the hypothetic principle that each germ contains in itself the germs of every generation that may be derived from it.

syngenetic (sɪndʒɪˈnɛtɪk), *a.* [f. prec.: see GENETIC.]

1. *Biol.* Of or pertaining to syngenesis.

1864 Lewes *Aristotle* xvii. 351 The Syngenetic theory—which makes both parents equally progenitors.

2. *Geol.* Applied to mineral deposits formed at the same time as the enclosing rocks; characterized by or pertaining to a formation contemporaneous with the enclosing or surrounding rock.

1905 J. Geikie *Struct. & Field Geol.* xvi. 225 Ore-formations may be grouped under these two main divisions:—1. Syngenetic or Contemporaneous, and 2. Epigenetic or Subsequent... Syngenetic ore-formations.. are formations of the same age.. as the rocks in which they occur. **1914** [see EPIGENETIC *a.* 2]. **1962** *Geografiska Annaler* XLIV. 382/2 The ice-wedges.. are clearly 'syngenetic'.. i.e. the frost cracks have extended upwards successively as new sediments were deposited on top. **1971** *Nature* 12 Mar. 108/2 It remains to be seen whether the small amounts of racemic amino-acids were syngenetic with the meteorite parent body or were synthesized later. **1978** S. S. Peng *Coal Mine Ground Control* v. 117 Syngenetic anisotropy originates during the formation processes of rock materials. Bedding planes and preferred alignment of pores or mineral grains are examples.

Hence **syngeˈnetically** *adv.*

1951 *Bull. Amer. Assoc. Petroleum Geologists* XXXV. 2226 Apparently the oölites of hematite formed both syngenetically and epigenetically. **1978** *Nature* 19 Oct. 641/1 The Brioverian unicells and colonies are *bona fide* Precambrian fossils:.. they were deposited syngenetically with Precambrian sedimentation.

syngenite (ˈsɪndʒɪnaɪt). *Min.* [ad. G. *syngenit* (Zepharovich, 1872), f. Gr. συγγενής akin, cognate + -ITE¹: so named from 'its close relation to polyhalite' (Dana).] A hydrous sulphate of calcium and potassium, occurring in colourless or white tabular crystals; also called KALUSZITE.

1875 Watts *Dict. Chem.* VII. 1142.

syngil, obs. form of SINGLE *a.*

synglar, -er(e, var. SINGLER *a. Obs.*

synglere, var. SANGLIER, wild boar.

syngnathous (ˈsɪŋgnəθəs), *a. Zool.* [f. mod.L. *Syngnathus* (f. Gr. σύν SYN-¹ + γνάθος jaw) + -OUS.] Belonging to the genus *Syngnathus* or suborder *Syngnathi* of fishes, characterized by the jaws being united into a tubular snout, and including the pipe-fishes and sea-horses.

1871 Darwin *Desc. Man* I. vi. 210 The males of syngnathous fishes receive the eggs of the females in their abdominal pouches.

syngne, syngnefiaunce, syngnett(e, syngnory: see SIGN, SIGNIFIANCE *Obs.*, CYGNET, SIGNET, SIGNORY.

syngraph (ˈsɪŋgrɑːf, -æ-). Also in L. form. [ad. L. *syngrapha, -us*, ad. Gr. συγγραφή, σύγγραφος, f. συγγράφειν to compose in writing, compile, draw up, f. σύν SYN-¹ + γράφειν to write.] A written contract or bond signed by both or all the parties.

1633 Marmion *Fine Comp.* iii. v. F 3 b, I haue here a Syngraphus, a writing with articles, that must be drawn between us. **1656** Blount *Glossogr.*, *Syngraph*.., a Writing or Deed, made or signed with the hand of him that makes a bargain; an Obligation or Bond between two or more; a Specialty of ones own hand. **1830** *Westm. Rev.* July 234 Those enchorial *papyri* in which a registry in Greek happens to be adscribed to the Egyptian syngraph or deed.

†**b.** ? A statement in writing made by several persons jointly. *Obs.*

1662 Evelyn *Diary* 29 Oct., Dr. Basiers.. the greate traveller,.. shew'd me the syngraphs and original subscriptions of divers Eastern Patriarchs.. to our Confession.

syngrene, obs. f. SENGREEN, houseleek.

synharmonic: see SYN-¹.

synhedrion, var. SYNEDRION.

synical, obs. form of SINICAL.

1654 J. Eyre *Exact Surveyor* 70 In all synicall proportions, observe this general rule, that [etc.].

syniper, var. SINOPER *Obs.*

1551–2 in Feuillerat *Revels Edw. VI* (1914) 71 Syniper paper.

‖**synizesis** (sɪnɪˈziːsɪs). Pl. **-ses** (-siːz). [late L., a. Gr. συνίζησις, n. of action f. συνιζάνειν to sink down, collapse, f. σύν SYN-¹ + ἵζάνειν to seat, sit, settle down, f. ἵζειν to seat, sit.]

1. *Gram.* and *Pros.* Fusion of two syllables into one by the coalescence of two adjacent vowels (or of a vowel and a diphthong) without the formation of a recognized diphthong.

1846 Keightley *Notes Virg., Bucol.* vii. 54 If this be the true reading, *sua* is an ablative case contracted by the figure *synizesis*. **1861** Paley *Æschylus, Pers.* (ed. 2) 81 *note*, Κυάνεον... Compare inf... πορφυρέᾳ. In both places Hermann retains the uncontracted form, in which there is synizesis, against κυανοῦν and πορφυρᾷ of later editors.

2. *Path.* Closure of the pupil of the eye.

1820 Good *Nosology* 309.

3. *Cytology.* Also (*erron.*) **synezesis**. A stage of meiosis in some species in which all the chromosomal material is seen tightly contracted into a clump.

1905 C. E. McClung in *Biol. Bull.* IX. 329, I would suggest that.. a new descriptive word be applied to the condition of the nucleus in which the chromatin is found massed at one side of the vesicle, without regard to whether it is a normal phenomenon or not. To carry out this idea I shall call this stage the 'synizesis' of the chromatin. **1921** *Ann. Bot.* XXXV. 367 In this paper the term synizesis is adopted for the tightly contracted phase of the nucleus, following the usage which has become customary in the literature of animal cytology. **1931** *Jrnl. Exper. Zoöl.* LVIII. 299 Synezesis stages were present, but mixed with secondary spermatocytes. **1933** *Cytologia* IV. 270 By the use of the methods employed in the studies reported here, the chromatin is drawn into a tight knot (synizesis) at the stages at which synapsis takes place. **1979** *Hereditas* XCI. 87/1 In the zygotene of the arctic brambles there is a polarised stage called a synizesis. The synizesis is a zygotene bouquet in which mass contraction has occurred.

Hence **syniˈzetic** *a.*

1931 *Amer. Jrnl. Bot.* XVIII. 370 The next stage involves a very rapid shortening of the spireme, the opening out of the spirals, and the transition to an interwoven thread system, which.. persists until toward the climax of synizetic sensitiveness. **1933** *Cytologia* IV. 271 Synizetic stages were studied in asynaptic plants which showed little associations of homologous chromosomes at metaphase.

synjet: see SYN-².

synk(e, synkfoil(e, obs. ff. CINQUE, SINK, CINQUEFOIL.

synkaryon to **-kinetic:** see SYN-¹.

†**synkquatener.** *Obs. rare*⁻¹. Corrupt form repr. F. *cinquantenier* a captain of fifty.

1523 Ld. Berners *Froiss.* I. ccciii. 566 Of the aldermen of the craftes, and of the Synkquateners of the portes [cf. ccclxxv. 623 cinquantenier].

synle, var. SENDLE *adv. Sc.*, seldom.

synnet, var. SENNET¹ *Obs.*

‖**synneurosis** (ˌsɪnnjʊəˈrəʊsɪs). *Anat.* [mod.L., ad. Gr. συννεύρωσις (Galen), f. σύν SYN-¹ + νεῦρον sinew: see -OSIS.] Connexion or articulation of bones by a ligament.

1676 Wiseman *Chirurg. Treat.* vii. ii. 479. **1835–6** *Todd's Cycl. Anat.* I. 257/1.

synneusis: see SYN-¹ 1.

synnewe, -ou, -oun, -ow, obs. ff. SINEW.

synnimone, obs. form of CINNAMON.

c **1580** in *Hist. MSS. Comm., Var. Coll.* (1903) II. 86 Spices spent in one hole yere... Synnimone, ij li.

synnomic: see SYN-¹.

‖**synocha** (ˈsɪnəkə). *Path.* Also 5 **sin-**. [med.L. *synocha*, fem. of *synochus*: see SYNOCHUS.] A continued or unintermitting fever (or a particular species of this: cf. SYNOCHUS).

[**1398** Trevisa *Barth. De P.R.* vii. xli. (Bodl. MS.) lf. 60/2 þis humour is.. Symple whanne blood roteþ in þe veynes & bredeþ contynual feuer þat hatt sinothos & when it roteþ not it cresith in quantite & is ouersette... And þanne comeþ a feuer þat hat Synocha & makeþ swelling. **14..** *Lanfranc's Cirurg.* 298 *note*, Blood.., ȝif it ouer haboundeþ.. & it is hett.. & is corrupt, & neþeles it is not roten, þerof is maad a feuere clepid *synochus continuus*. And ȝif he is roten, þenne is maad þerof a feuere clepid *synocha continua*. **1728** Chambers *Cycl.*, *Synocha*, and *Synochos*... Literally they both signify the same Thing; yet is the former used to signify an intermitting, and the latter a continu'd Fever.]

1801 *Med. Jrnl.* V. 234 Synocha.. much resembles the symptomatic fever attendant upon phlegmon; and therefore, it has.. been termed the inflammatory fever. **1822–7** Good *Study Med.* (1829) II. 222 Of these [names], synocha.. is the worst.. it has been used in different senses by different writers, and approaches so nearly to synochus.. as to create a perpetual confusion in the minds of young students.

synochal (ˈsɪnəkəl), *a.* Also 6 **synocalle**. [f. SYNOCHA, SYNOCHUS + -AL¹.] Of the nature of or pertaining to synocha (or synochus).

1541 Copland *Guydon's Quest. Cyrurg.* M ij b, It is.. better to cut yᵉ veyne, nat onely for the feuers synocalles, but also in all the other that ar of rotten humours. **1727** *Fam. Dict.* s.v. *Fever*, The synochal Fever. **1846** G. E. Day tr. *Simon's Anim. Chem.* II. 282 In variola and varicella.. Urine of a synochal character is.. often met with.

So **ˈsynochoid** (-kɔɪd) *a.*, resembling synocha; **ˈsynochous** (-kəs) *a.*, synochal.

1822–7 Good *Study Med.* (1829) II. 180 The fever.. sometimes assumes a caumatic.. cast, sometimes a typhous, and sometimes a synochous. **1848** Dunglison *Med. Lex.* (ed. 7), *Synochus*... Mixed fever,.. Synochoid fever.

‖**synochus** (ˈsɪnəkəs). *Path.* Also 5 **sin-**. [med.L., a. Gr. σύνοχος, f. σύν SYN-¹ + ὀχ-: ἔχειν to have, after συνέχειν to hold together, be continuous.] = SYNOCHA.

But often distinguished as a different species: see quot. 1848 and the introductory quots. s.v. SYNOCHA.

[**1398, 14..** [see SYNOCHA].] *a* **1412** Lydg. *Two Merchants* 301 The fevere in phisyk is callyd sinochus.]

1625 Hart *Anat. Ur.* i. ii. 27 [He] was.. surprised with that feauer commonly called Synochus. **1657** G. Starkey *Helmont's Vind.* 164 The disease at the first.. was but a plain Diary, though before the Doctors making an end, it be.. changed into a Synochus. **1799** *Med. Jrnl.* II. 409 Persons exposed, without shelter, to the vicissitudes of the atmosphere, have been affected with the synochus. **1813** J. Thomson *Lect. Inflam.* 111 The fever accompanying local inflammation.. is often of a mixed nature like the fever denominated synochus by Dr. Cullen. **1848** Dunglison *Med. Lex.* (ed. 7), *Synochus*, continued fever, compounded of synocha and typhus;—in its commencement often resembling the former; in its progress, the latter.

synocil (ˈsɪnəsɪl). *Zool.* [irreg. f. Gr. σύν SYN-¹ + L. *cilium* (see CILIA): cf. CNIDOCIL, PALPOCIL.] A structure in certain sponges, supposed to be a sense-organ, perhaps analogous to the rods and cones of the retina of the eye: see quot. 1888.

1883 Simmonds *Dict. Trade* Suppl. **1888** Rolleston & Jackson *Anim. Life* 807 A synocil, as yet observed only in a *Sycandra*, is a process of mesoglaea,.. containing a number of fine filaments derived from as many cells situate at its base.

synocreate: see SYN-¹.

synod (ˈsɪnəd). Forms: 4–6 **sinod**, 4–7 **synode**, (6 **senod**), 6–7 **sinode**, 4– **synod**. [ad. late L. *synodus*, a. Gr. σύνοδος assembly, meeting, astronomical conjunction, f. σύν SYN-¹ + ὁδός way, travel; reinforced later by F. *synode* (16th c.). (Cf. It., Sp. *sinodo*, Pg. *synodo*.) L. *synodus* was taken into OE. as *seonoþ, sionoþ, sinoþ, synoþ*; Layamon's *sinað* (25338) may represent contamination of the OE. word with OF. *senat* SENATE. See also SENE.]

1. *Eccl.* An assembly of the clergy of a particular church, nation, province, or diocese (sometimes with representatives of the laity) duly convened for discussing and deciding ecclesiastical affairs. †In early use freq. applied to general councils.

Formerly also, an episcopal or archidiaconal visitation (cf. SYNODAL B. 2).

1387 Trevisa *Higden* (Rolls) V. 41 In þis counsail and synod was þe pope Victor. *Ibid.* 231 þe þridde greet synode [*v.r.* sinod] of þre hondred bisshoppes was i-made at Ephisus. **1485** Caxton *Chas. Gt.* ii. 24 In that synode [of bishops and abbots at Rome] for the grete holynes of charles The pope.. gaf hym power for to ordeyne bisshoppes & archebisshops. **1528** [see SYNODAL *a.* 1]. **1545** *Act 37 Hen. VIII*, c. 17 The Bishopp of Rome and his adherentes.. have in their counsailes & synodes provinciall made.. and decreed diverse ordynances. **1553** Becon *Reliques of Rome* (1563) 213 It was decreed at yᵉ councell of Nice yᵗ euery byshop shoulde twice yearelye haue a Synode or Sene general within hys diocesse. **1591** Lambarde *Archeion* (1635) 8 The two Provinciall Synodes of Canterburie and Yorke. *a* **1600** Hooker *Eccl. Pol.* viii. v. §2 Before Emperours became Christians, the Church had never any generall Synod. **1661** J. Stephens *Procurations* 66 Of Synods there are found sundry kinds, Oecumenical, National, Provincial, and Diocesan. **1677** *Rector's Bk. Clayworth* (1910) 30 By order from my Ld. ArchBp I preachd this day to yᵉ Synod at Southwell. *a* **1700** Evelyn *Diary* 21 July 1641, A stately senate-house, wherein was holden that famous Synod against the Arminians in 1618. **1768** MACLAINE tr. *Mosheim's Eccl. Hist.* Cent. XVII. II. I. ii. §5. IV. 409 [Peter I of Russia] declared himself the supreme pontif and head of the Russian church. The functions of this high and important office were entrusted with a council assembled at Petersburg,.. called the Holy Synod. **1776** GIBBON *Decl. & F.* xv. (1782) I. 586 Towards the end of the second century, the churches of Greece and Asia adopted the useful institutions of provincial synods. **1845** M. PATTISON *Ess.* (1889) I. 17 Bringing him to.. trial before a synod of bishops for his flagrant infraction of the canon law. **1845** S. AUSTIN *Ranke's Hist. Ref.* III. 525 In the year 1533 a provincial synod was established in Strasburg, which included various secular elements, together with the spiritual. **1869** *Act 32 & 33 Vict.* c. 42. §19 Nothing in any Act.. shall prevent the bishops, the clergy, and laity of the said [Irish] Church.. from meeting in general synod or convention, and in such synod or convention framing constitutions.. for the general management.. of the said Church. **1874** GREEN *Short Hist.* i. §3. 30 It was the ecclesiastical synods which by their example led the way to our national parliaments.

b. In Presbyterian Churches: A body or assembly of ministers and other elders, constituting the ecclesiastical court next above the presbytery (see PRESBYTERY 4), and consisting of the members of, or of delegates from, the presbyteries within its bounds.

1593 ABP. BANCROFT *Dangerous Posit.* III. xiii. 109 Assemblies are eyther Classes, or Synods. *Ibid.* 110 A Synode is an assembly of chosen men, from moe Churches, then those that be in one Classis, or conference. **1645** PAGITT *Heresiogr.* 76 The Independents.. teach that everie particular Congregation ought to be governed by its owne particular Lawes,.. without obligation [to] acknowledge Classes or Synods for its government and conduct. *a* **1658** CLEVELAND *Mixt Assembly* I Flea-bitten Synod, an Assembly.. like the rude Chaos of Presbyt'ry, where Laymen guide With the tame Wool-pack Clergy by their side. **1753** *Scots Mag.* XV. 85/1 A provincial synod is a court consisting of all the ministers of a particular number of presbyteries, and one elder chosen.. from each session. They.. judge in all.. appeals from the presbyteries. **1852** EARP *Gold Col. Australia* 79 The Presbyterian Church is under the government of the Synod of Australia, and is divided as follows:—Presbytery of Sydney,.. Presbytery of Windsor,.. Presbytery of Campbelltown,.. Presbytery of Maitland.

2. *gen.* and *transf.* An assembly, convention, or council of any kind. Also *fig.*

1578 H. WOTTON *Courtlie Controv.* 132 The Councell and Sinode of our Genterie. **1580** LYLY *Euphues* (Arb.) 315 A shamelesse Sinod of three thousand greedy caterpillers. **1607** SHAKS. *Cor.* v. ii. 74 The glorious Gods sit in hourely Synod about thy particular prosperity. *a* **1649** CRASHAW *Carmen Deo Nostro* Wks. (1904) 197 An universall Synod of All sweets. **1718** POPE *Iliad* XIII. 662 On golden clouds th' immortal synod sat. **1763** JOHNSON in Boswell *Life*, Sir, we could not have had a better dinner, had there been a Synod of Cooks. **1849** MACAULAY *Hist. Eng.* vi. II. 40 It was not in the power of Jeffreys to overawe a synod of peers as he had been in the habit of overawing common juries.

†**3.** *Astrol.* A conjunction of two planets or heavenly bodies. *Obs.*

1646 CRASHAW *Steps to Temple, Love's Horoscope* 18 How e're Loves native houres were set, What ever starry Synod met. **1651** CULPEPPER *Astrol. Judgem. Dis.* (1658) 30 A Conjunction or Synod.. cannot properly be called an aspect. **1661** BOYLE *Certain Physiol. Ess.* (1669) 30 The Planets.. have (according to Astrologers) in their great Synods or Conjunctions, much more powerful.. Influences .. than are ascrib'd to one or two of them out of that Aspect. **1686** GOAD *Celest. Bodies* II. xii. 329 We speak of Aspects, Synods, and Schematismes, for advantage of Influence Caelestial, and observe, that even they want their Vigour when they want their Friends about them.

4. *attrib.*: †**synod house** (cf. sense 3, and HOUSE *sb.* 8b); **synod-man**, a member of a synod, a synodsman.

1589 GREENE *Tullies Love* Wks. (Grosart) VII. 201 To vnite those loues that Venus in hir Sinod house hath expreslie countercheckt. **1663** BUTLER *Hud.* I. III. 1298 For Bears and Dogs on four Legs go, As Beasts, but Synod-men on Two.

synodal (ˈsɪnədəl), *a.* and *sb.* Also 5–7 **synodall**, **sinodall**, 6 **sinodal**, **-alle**, **synodalle**, **-ole**, 7 **synodale**, **-ol**. [ad. late L. *synodālis*, f. *synodus* SYNOD: see -AL^1. Cf. F. *synodal* (from 14th c.).]

A. *adj.* **1.** Done or made by, or proceeding from a synod (†or general council).

c **1450** *Godstow Reg.* 683 Legatinis of Othon and Octobon and Synodall and other constitucions. **1528** MORE *Dyaloge* IV. Wks. 252/1 It is a law synodall made in the vi Sinode. **1533–4** *Act 25 Hen. VIII*, c. 19 §1 Constitucions ordynance and canons provyncioll or Synodall. **1544** BALE *Chron. Sir J. Oldcastle* 44 The synodall actes of Bysshoppes in theyr dyoceses. **1641** MILTON *Reform.* I. Wks. 1851 III. 15 The whole generall Councel of Nicæa.. determines writing a Synodal Epist[le] to the African Churches to warn them of Arrianisme. **1674** HICKMAN *Quinquart. Hist.* (ed. 2) 107 His subscriptions to the Synodal Determinations. **1756–9** A. BUTLER *Lives Saints, St. Tarasius* (25 Feb.), He was no sooner installed [as pa*t*riarch], but he sent his synodal letters to pope Adrian. **1853** S. WILBERFORCE in R. G. Wilberforce *Life* (1881) II. v. 183 The subjects of inquiry.. touching the synodal action of the Church. **1865** PUSEY *Truth Engl. Ch.* 89 The Synodal decrees of the Council of 214 Bishops at Carthage.

2. Of the nature of or constituted as a synod.

1530–1 *Act 22 Hen. VIII*, c. 15 §13 The Clergy of the provynce of Canturbury in theire Synodall Convocacion. **1572** in *6th Rep. Hist. MSS. Comm.* 636/2 The synodall convention halden at Sanct Andros.. be the haill ministerie the barones, gentelmen and elders of kirkis within Fyf. **1578** *Second Bk. Discipl. Ch. Scot.* xii. (1621) 89 Concerning Provinciall and Synodall Assemblies.., how many and in what places they were to be holden. **1647** *Jus Div. Regim. Eccl.* title-p., The Presbyteriall Government, by Preaching and Ruling Presbyters, in Congregationall, Classicall, and Synodall Assemblies. **1687** *Reply to Reasons Oxford Clergy agst. Addressing* 15 A Synodal Convocation. **1880** McCARTHY *Own Times* lviii, The Irish bishops were to lose their seats in the House of Lords. A synodal, or governing body, was to be elected from the clergy and laity of the Church.

†**b.** *transf.* Connected with or related to church government by synodal assemblies, presbyterian.

1600 W. WATSON *Decacordon* (1602) 94 Cartwrights and Bruses pure synodall ministery. **1640** SIR E. DERING *Sp. on Relig.* 14 Dec. v. 15 You will en-live the same men to bee now Synodall, who were before but Convocationall.

3. Of, belonging to, or connected with, having or characterized by, a synod or visitation.

synodal book (eccl. L. *liber synodalis*): see B. 4. *synodal payment, rent* = B. 2.

1579 FULKE *Confut. Sanders* 687 Charles the King of Fraunce sent a synodall booke into Britane. *a* **1648** LD. HERBERT *Hen. VIII* (1649) 141 That Synodall Judges, going to poore Towns and Villages.., draw Annuall Tribute thence, or Excommunicate them, when they cannot pay. **1661** Synodal payment [see SYNODY 1]. **1695** KENNETT *Par. Antiq.* ix. 649 We find these Synodal witnesses were afterward a sort of impanell'd Jury. **1758** JORTIN *Erasmus* I. 291 Points of Doctrine to be determined by Synodal Authority. **1779** (*title*) A Synodal Charge Delivered to the Clergy of the Diocese of Abo.. by.. C. F. Mennander... Translated from the.. Swedish by.. L. T. Nyberg. **1876** GRANT *Burgh. Sch. Scot.* I. i. 4 Free and quit from all custom, synodal rent, aids, lodgings and conreds. **1910** *Soc. Antiq., Old Sarum Excavation Fund* 6 On synodal and ordination and other solemn days.

B. *sb.* **1.** A synodal decision, constitution, or decree. *Obs.* exc. *Hist.*

1485 CAXTON *Chas. Gt.* 228 He ordeyned bysshops.. & made constytucyons, synodals, and other ordynaunces. *a* **1529** SKELTON *Ware the Hauke* 132 Decrees or decretals, Or holy sinodals. **1660** HEYLIN *Hist. Quinquart.* To Rdr., I have consulted.. the Confessions, the Synodals, and other publick Monuments, and Records of the several parties. **1765** BLACKSTONE *Comm.* I. Introd. iii. 83 All canons, constitutions, ordinances, and synodals provincial.

†**b.** *pl.* Probably, offices or prayers to be used for *festa synodalia* or festivals appointed to be observed by a diocesan synod. *Obs.*

The explanation that it refers to the public recital of synodal or provincial constitutions is given by Sparrow in his *Rationale* (1672) R vij b, and is repeated in Nichols *On Bk. Com. Prayer* (1710) Bj/2, Wheatly *Of Bk. Com. Prayer* (1720) iii. §10. 142 note, Blunt *Annot. Bk. C. P.* (1866) 16 note.

1548–9 (Mar.) *Bk. Com. Prayer* Pref., Vaine repeticions, Commemoracions, and Synodalles.

2. A payment made by the inferior clergy to the bishop, properly on the occasion of a synod, and hence at an episcopal or archidiaconal visitation.

1534 *Lincoln Diocese Documents* 177 The sayd person, and his successours.. shall susteyne.. all proxis and Sinodalles, all dismes and all subsides [etc.]. *c* **1550** *Disc. Common Weal Eng.* iii. (1893) 136 Wheare be theise Synodes nowe kepte? yet they receiue euery yeare theire Synodalles of the poore priestes. **1661** [see SYNODY 1]. **1667** *Answ. West to North* 9 At Easter Visitation the Ministers pay their Pascal Rents, or Synodals. *a* **1679** J. WARD *Diary* (1839) 152 There is a minister in Northamptonshire.. that will not pay the archdeacon synodols, but will pay procurations. **1779** RUDDER *Gloucestersh.* 723 Swell (Upper)... First fruits £7 0 0. Tenths £0 14 0. Procurations £0 6 8. Synodals £0 1 0. **1904** *Daily News* 22 Mar. 3 The Ecclesiastical Commissioners are continuing steadily their work of giving all the Archdeacons a fixed income of £200 a year, instead of a portion being derived from procurations, synodals, visitation or induction fees.

†**3.** A synodal assembly, a synod. *Obs.*

1573 *Reg. Privy Council Scot.* II. 230 Be ordinance of the haill ministeris within Fyff and gentilmen convenit at thair synodall haldin at Sanctandrois. **1596** in *Maitl. Club Misc.* I. 83 Referris the mater.. to the said nixt synodall.

4. A synodal book (see quot., and cf. A. 3).

1844 LINGARD *Anglo-Saxon Ch.* (1845) II. xiv. 339 The new prelate left Rome.. taking with him.. a synodal containing instructions for his personal conduct. *Note*, The synodal was so called, because it was read in the synod.. in which the new bishop was.. installed in his church.

Hence †**syno'dalian** *a.* = SYNODAL *a.* 2b, 3; **'synodalist**, a member of a synodal assembly; **'synodally** *adv.* [cf. med.L. *synodaliter*, F. *synodalement*], by the action or authority of a synod.

1668 *Persec. Ref. Ch. in France* 20 Not admitting to the Lords Supper flagitious persons, Synodally suspended for their scandalous lives. **1702** C. MATHER *Magn. Chr.* IV. iv. 182/2 The Reverend Charles Chancey.. at the time of the Synod,.. opposed the Synodalian Principles. **1902** *Contemp. Rev.* June 895 It had been decided that all the Synodalists should oppose such an institution.

†**synodary.** *Obs. rare*$^{-1}$. [ad. L. **synodārius*, f. *synodus* SYNOD: see -ARY^1.] A member of a synod.

1581 J. BELL *Haddon's Answ. Osor.* III. 359 Doth the Pope want his consistory? hath not this most holy father his synodaryes? [orig. *an sanctissimus pater suos non habet patres conscriptos?*]

†**syno'datic**, *a.* *Obs. rare*$^{-1}$. [ad. med.L. *synodaticus*, f. *synodus* SYNOD.] = SYNODAL *a.* 3.

1661 J. STEPHENS *Procurations* 93 Nor do I think that this Synodatick payment (taken to be the same with the Cathedratick..) was constantly.. paid either *in Synodo*, or at the two Feasts above-named.

†**synodial**, *a.* *Obs. rare*$^{-0}$. [f. SYNOD + -IAL.]

1727 BOYER *Dict. Royal, Eng.-Fr.*, Synodal, Synodical, or Synodial.

†**synodian.** *Obs. rare*$^{-1}$. [f. SYNOD + -IAN.] A member of a synod.

1655 FULLER *Ch. Hist.* x. v. §5 A London Divine, charging the synodians to have taken a previous oath to condemn the opposite party on what termes soever.

synodic (sɪˈnɒdɪk), *a.* [ad. late L. *synodicus*, a. late Gr. συνοδικός (both in sense 2), f. σύνοδος SYNOD.]

1. *Eccl.* = SYNODAL *a.*

1640 R. BAILLIE *Canterb. Self-convict.* Postscr. 16 When the Assemblie of Glasgow had passed this tryall upon them according to our desire, we embraced the Synodick Sentence. **1659** PEARSON *Creed* ii. 282 *note*, They charge all those to whom they write that Synodic Epistle, that they should be satisfied with such expressions as they found in the Scriptures. **1835** I. TAYLOR *Spir. Despot.* v. 210 The synodic system.. is.. named as a principal cause.. of the Spiritual Despotism which.. grasped the Christian world.

2. *Astron.* = next, 2.

1654 T. WHALLEY in *Ussher's Lett.* (1686) 603 A Mean Synodick Month. **1694** W. HOLDER *On Time* i. 11 The Synodic Revolution of the Moon, by which the Month is measured. **1788** *Phil. Trans.* LXXVIII. 419 The lunar month, or mean synodic revolution,.. consists of 29 days, 12 hours, and 792 scruples or parts in 1080; and the year of 354 days, 8 hours, and 864 scruples. **1834** MRS. SOMERVILLE *Connex. Phys. Sci.* v. 29 The synodic motions of the satellites. **1875** TAIT in *Gd. Words* 238 This is the sidereal period of the moon's revolution; not the synodic period, as the time from new moon to new moon is called.

synodical (sɪˈnɒdɪkəl), *a.* [f. as prec.: see -ICAL.]

1. *Eccl.* **a.** = SYNODAL 1.

1561 T. NORTON *Calvin's Inst.* IV. vii. §6 To the Consecration was annexed the sendyng of a Synodicall Epistle. **1612** tr. *Theodoret's Eccl. Hist.* IV. iii. 246 A synodicall epistle concerning the faith, written by Athanasius to the Emperour Iouianus. **1618** HALES *Gold. Rem.* II. (1673) 76 Their answer was that it could not stand with their Conscience to promise Obedience to all Synodical Decrees. **1647** N. BACON *Disc. Govt. Eng.* I. xvi. (1739) 32 In Synodical disputes they would hold with the Canon. **1725** tr. *Dupin's Eccl. Hist. 17th C.* I. v. 69 The synodical or synodal Letters, are those which are wrote in the Name of a Synod, and which contain its Decisions or Regulations. **1820** MILNER *Suppl. Mem. Eng. Cath.* 153 The synodical decision of the Irish Bishops. **1876** *Prayer Bk. Interleaved* 23 Whether or no Edward's First Prayer-book received synodical sanction is a disputed point.

b. = SYNODAL 3.

1565 CALFHILL *Answ. Martiall* 70 The great vertue & profound knowledge of those Synodicall men. **1656** USSHER (*title*) The Reduction of Episcopacie Vnto the Form of Synodical Government Received in the Antient Church. **1736** CHANDLER *Hist. Persec.* 108 He was resolved to have his will, and add synodical authority to his own words and opinions. **1827** HALLAM *Const. Hist.* xi. (1876) II. 315 The presbyterian discipline and synodical government were very partially introduced. **1866** FELTON *Greece, Anc. & Mod.* II. II. iv. 320 Both parties, the Arians as well as the Orthodox, .. resorted to synodical majorities.

c. = SYNODAL 2, 2b.

1593 ABP. BANCROFT *Dangerous Posit.* III. xiii. 110 The Articles of the holy Discipline and Synodicall [*sic*], must alwaies be read [in the synod]. **1600** W. WATSON *Decacordon* (1602) 93 That Synodicall court. **1643** *Ord. Lords & Comm., Westm. Confess.* (1658) 202 Assemblies, which are Congregational, Classical, and Synodical. **1661** *Reg. Privy Council Scot.* Ser. III. I. 29 The assemblieing of ministers in their severall synodicall meittings. *a* **1679** J. WARD *Diary* (1839) 161 Mr. Leigh, the synodical commentator.

2. *Astron.* Pertaining to the conjunction of two heavenly bodies (see CONJUNCTION 3); said *esp.* of the revolution, or period of revolution, of a planet between two successive conjunctions with the sun, or of a satellite between two successive conjunctions with (or occultations or eclipses by) its primary planet. ***synodic month***, the synodic period of the moon, i.e. the time from new moon to new moon; a lunar month, lunation. (Opp. to *sidereal.*)

1669 STURMY *Mariner's Mag.* VI. 95 So twenty nine and half [days] in all, Do make a Month Synodical [*mispr.* Synonidal]. **1696** WHISTON *The. Earth* II. (1722) 177 The Lunar Year was then exactly.. twelve Synodical Revolutions of the Moon. **1761** *Phil. Trans.* LII. 106 The second satellite has a synodical equation of 16′ or 17′ in time, to be subtracted. **1784** HERSCHEL *ibid.* LXXIV. 242 By which means the sidereal is reduced to a proper synodical period. **1788** *Ibid.* LXXVIII. 365 The first satellite performs a synodical revolution round its primary planet in 8 days 17 hours 1 minute and 19·3 seconds. **1812** WOODHOUSE *Astron.* xxviii. 276 The time between conjunction and conjunction, or between opposition and opposition, is denominated, a Synodical period. **1868** LOCKYER *Elem. Astron.* §244. 102 Nineteen synodical revolutions of the node.. are equal to 223 synodical revolutions of the moon.

sy'nodically, *adv.* [f. prec. + -LY^2.]

1. By the action or authority of a synod; synodally.

a **1604** HANMER *Chron. Irel.* (1633) 125 But I may not so leave my Prelates, they synodically decreed as followeth [etc.]. **1618** HALES *Gold. Rem.* II. (1673) 25 Which sentence passed by the major part of Voices, and was Synodically concluded. **1703** W. WAKE *State of Ch.* 507 To be observ'd .. within the Province.. of York too, which had not yet Synodically Agreed to it. **1841** BP. BLOMFIELD *Let.* in A. Blomfield *Mem.* (1863) II. i. 21 There is no intention of passing any episcopal sentence upon Mr. Newman's Tract: that is to say, the Bishops will not do so synodically.

2. In synod, as a synod.

a **1617** BAYNE *Diocesan's Tryall* (1621) 4 If they might meete Synodically. **1687** J. KIRKWOOD *Let. Boyle* B.'s Wks. 1772 I. p. cxciii, The bishop of Ross, with the clergy of his diocese synodically assembled. **1850** S. WILBERFORCE in R. G. Wilberforce *Life* (1881) II. ii. 63 The Bishop and clergy of this diocese synodically gathered in this our cathedral city of Oxford.

†**synodicate**, *v. Obs. nonce-wd.* [f. SYNODIC + -ATE[3].] *trans.* To give out as by synodal authority.

1645 *Arraignm. Persecution* 44 To keep his Holinesse in action, I beseech your Honour, that he may Synodicate a full Resolution to these ensuing Queries.

synodist ('sɪnədɪst). [f. SYNOD + -IST.]

†**1.** A member of a synod. *Obs.*

1626 J. YATES *Ibis ad Cæsarem* I. 5 Arnoldus a great Remonstrant Synodist. **16..** FULLER (Webster 1864), These synodists thought fit in Latin as yet to vail their decrees from vulgar eyes.

2. = next, 3.

1846 WORCESTER cites *Ec. Rev.*

synodite ('sɪnədaɪt). [ad. late L. *synodīta* cœnobite, or late Gr. συνοδίτης (in all three senses), f. σύν SYN-[1] + ὁδίτης traveller (f. ὁδός journey) or f. σύνοδος SYNOD: see -ITE[1].]

†**1.** A fellow-traveller, travelling companion. *Obs.*

1654 H. L'ESTRANGE *Chas. I* (1655) 16 His Councel were his Synodites, and went along with him. **1659** —— *Alliance Div. Off.* 265 Those women, which the Apostles made their synodites and companions in their journeys.

2. (See quot.) *Hist. rare*$^{-0}$.

1862 *Chambers' Encycl.*, *Cœnobites*..or *Synodites*, the name given to those monks who live together, in contradistinction to the Anchorites or hermits.

3. An adherent of a synod; used disparagingly of those who accepted the decrees of the Council of Chalcedon. *Hist. rare*$^{-1}$.

1846 NEWMAN *Developm. Chr. Doctr.* (1878) 313 They disowned the authority of the Council, and called its adherents Chalcedonians, and Synodites.

synodsman ('sɪnədzmən). [f. SYNOD + genitive *-s* + MAN *sb.*[1]]

1. Pseudo-etymological alteration of SIDESMAN, q.v. (sense 1), after med.L. *testis synodalis* lit. synodal witness, a representative of a parish attending a synod.

1680 GODOLPHIN *Repert. Canon.* (ed. 2) 163 *margin*, These Sidemen were called *Testes Synodales* anciently styled Synods-men, thence corruptly called now Side-men. [**1857** TOULMIN SMITH *Parish* 71 It was directed that four, six, or eight, should appear, together with the clergy, to represent the rest, and to be the 'testes synodales', that is, synodsmen.] **1908** *Corringham Ch. Mag.* (cover), Synodsmen;—Mr. —— and Mr. ——.

2. A member of a synod in a church of the Anglican Communion, esp. a member of the General Synod of the Church of England.

1870 *Contemp. Rev.* Sept. 190 The last function of the General Vestry is to elect parochial nominators..and synodsmen to the Diocesan Synod. **1894** *Ch. Times* 16 Mar. 306/4 A large meeting of the lay synodsmen of Belfast. **1970** *Ibid.* 6 Nov. 20/3 Sir John Guillum Scott..read the gospel —the familiar Beatitudes from St. Matthew containing good advice to all synodsmen. **1972** *Times Lit. Suppl.* 20 Oct. 1261/3 Quite beyond the reach of the average synodsman or lay communicant. **1980** *Times* 23 June 18/2 The synodsmen were concerned to see that the new Anglican Liturgy accurately reflected the contemporary face of Anglicanism.

synody ('sɪnədɪ). Also 6–7 **sinody**; *pl.* (*corruptly*) 5 **sinoges**, 6 **sinages**. [ad. med.L. **synodium*, f. *synodus* SYNOD. With the form *sinoges* cf. med.L. *corrogium* for *corrodium* CORRODY.]

1. = SYNODAL *sb.* 2.

1467–73 in *Calr. Proc. Chanc. Q. Eliz.* (1827) I. Introd. 81 [The archdeacons] yerely have payd the seid sinoges and Peter pens..for the churches and parachyns of Bodham, Lympenhowe and Thirkeby. **1542–3** *Act 34 & 35 Hen. VIII*, c. 19 §1 Sinodies Proxies and other Proffettes. **1661** J. STEPHENS *Procurations* 99 All of them make..but one payment..known..by the name *Synodale*, or the Synodal payment, or..the Synody..the said Synody, or Synodal being a Pension certain, is valued in the Kings Books.

2. = SYNOD 1.

a **1548** HALL *Chron.*, *Hen. V* 34 b, At this Sinody [*sc.* the Council of Constance] were assembled (as one authore writeth) ccc xlvj bishoppes.

‖**synœciosis** (sɪniːsɪ'əʊsɪs). *Rhet.* Also **syne-**, **synoi-**, **-cei-**, **-ce-**. [late L., ad. Gr. συνοικείωσις, n. of action f. συνοικειοῦν to associate (persons) as kinsmen or friends, f. σύν SYN-[1] + οἰκειοῦν to make one's own, f. οἰκεῖος domestic, one's own, f. οἶκος house.] A figure by which contrasted or heterogeneous things are associated or coupled, e.g. contrary qualities attributed to the same subject.

1589 PUTTENHAM *Engl. Poesie* III. xix. (Arb.) 216 *margin*, Syneciosis, or the Crosse copling. **1657** J. SMITH *Myst. Rhet.* 120 *Synoeceiosis*... A figure which teacheth to conjoyn divers things, or contraries,..and is, when contraries are attributed to the same thing. **1678** PHILLIPS (ed. 4), *Synoiceiosis*. **1721** BAILEY, *Synoeceosis*.

synœcious (sɪ'niːʃ(ɪ)əs), *a. Bot.* [f. SYN-[1] after DIŒCIOUS, MONŒCIOUS; cf. Gr. συνοικία a community of persons living together.] Having male and female flowers in the same flower-head, as some *Compositæ*, or male and female organs in the same receptacle, as some mosses.

1863 M. J. BERKELEY *Brit. Mosses* ii. 6 Mosses..are..in some rare cases synœcicus.

synœcism (sɪ'niːsɪz(ə)m). *Gr. Antiq.* Also **synoik-**. [ad. Gr. συνοικισμός, n. of action f. συνοικίζειν to cause to dwell with, to unite under one capital city, f. σύν SYN-[1] + οἰκίζειν to found as a colony, to colonize, f. οἶκος house.] The union of several towns or villages into or under one capital city. So **synœcize** (sɪ'niːsaɪz) *v.* [ad. Gr. συνοικίζειν: see above], *trans.* to unite into or under one capital city.

1886 *Eng. Hist. Rev.* I. 636 They always remained separate states and were never synoikised. **1887** A. LANG *Myth, Ritual & Relig.* I. 266 Legends..current before the villages were 'synoecised' into Athens. **1898** J. B. BURY in *Jrnl. Hellenic Studies* XVIII. 15 We would give much to know the details of..the synoecism of Messenia. *Ibid.* 16 If the only purpose of Megalopolis had been to synœcize the Maenalians and Parrhasians. **1902** E. GARDINER in *Encycl. Brit.* XXX. 529/2 When the town was first formed..by the 'synœcism' of the neighbouring villages.

synœkete: see SYN-[1] 1.

synoghe, obs. form of SINEW.

synoicous (sɪ'nɔɪkəs), *a. Bot.* [f. Gr. σύν SYN-[1] + οἶκος house + -OUS.] = SYNŒCIOUS.

1863 M. G. CAMPBELL in *Intell. Observ.* July 412 The barren and fertile flowers are found on the same plant, though not on the same receptacle. To the latter form of growth the term *synoicous* is applied. **1881** *Jrnl. Bot.* X. 98 The synoicous flower of 'Fissidens pusillus'.

synoikise: see SYNŒCIZE.

synoil: SYN-[2].

synomosy (sɪ'nəʊməsɪ). *Gr. Antiq.* [ad. Gr. συνωμοσία, f. συνομνύναι to confederate, f. σύν SYN-[1] + ὀμνύναι to swear.] A political society of men leagued by oath.

1808 MITFORD *Hist. Greece* xix. §4. II. 434 There were at Athens societies called Synomosies, which bore considerable resemblance to our political clubs.

synonym ('sɪnənɪm), *sb.* Forms: see below. [ad. late L. *synōnymum*, *-on*, a. Gr. συνώνυμον, neut. sing. used subst. of συνώνυμος, f. σύν SYN-[1] + -ωνυμ- (as in νώνυμ(ν)ος, ἀνώνυμος nameless, ANONYMOUS) = ὄνομα NAME. Cf. F. *synonyme*, †*sinonime* (12th c.), It., Sp. *sinonimo*, Pg. *synonymo*. The earliest instances are plural (after L. *synonyma*, Gr. συνώνυμα), anglicized *sinonymes*, *synonymes*, in Latin or Græco-Latin form *synonyma*, *synonuma*, incorrectly with addition of pl. *-s*, *synonymas* (whence a rare spurious sing. *synonyma*). The anglicized sing. *synonym(e* scarcely makes its appearance, except in dictionaries, till the close of the 18th century.]

1. Strictly, a word having the same sense as another (in the same language); but more usually, either or any of two or more words (in the same language) having the same general sense, but possessing each of them meanings which are not shared by the other or others, or having different shades of meaning or implications appropriate to different contexts: e.g. *serpent*, *snake*; *ship*, *vessel*; *compassion*, *fellow-feeling*, *sympathy*; *enormous*, *excessive*, *immense*; *glad*, *happy*, *joyful*, *joyous*; *to kill*, *slay*, *slaughter*; *to grieve*, *mourn*, *lament*, *sorrow*. Const. *for*, *of*, †formerly *to*, *with*.

In quot. 1432–50 *sinonymes* is a rendering of the title of Isidore's work *Synonyma de lamentatione animae peccatricis*, where it denotes identical ideas expressed in different ways in the course of the work: cf. OF. *sinonimes* (12th c. in *Romania*, 1876, V. 275).

Plural. α. 5 **sinonymes**, 6–9 **synonymes**, 8 **synonimes**, 8– **synonyms**.

1432–50 tr. *Higden* (Rolls) VI. 51 Isidorus..lefte noble werkes..as the books of his Ethimologies,..of the ordre of creatures, sinonymes, and mony oþer þinges.

1540 PALSGRAVE tr. *Acolastus* Epistle A iij b, Theyr yong scholers..be forced to falle a glosynge..of their latyn bokes ..of dyuers englishe wordes..beinge synonymes..they chuse moste commonly the very worste. **1561** T. NORTON *Calvin's Inst.* I. xiii. §25. 41 b, If the Father and the Sonne were Synonymes or seuerall names signifying one thyng. **1715** BENTLEY *Serm. Popery* 4 Hesychius makes them [*sc.* καπηλεύοντες and δολῶντες] Synonyms. **1783** WALKER 18 Apr. in Boswell *Johnson*, *Walker*. Do you think, Sir, that there are any perfect synonimes in any language? *Johnson*. Originally there were not; but by using words negligently, or in poetry, one word comes to be confounded with another. **1785** REID *Intell. Powers* I. i. 14 Most synonimes have some minute distinction that deserves notice. **1856** MAX MÜLLER *Chips* (1880) II. xvi. 74 The more ancient a language, the richer it is in synonymes. **1863** BAIN *Higher Engl. Gram.* (1879) 73 *Only*, with the synonymes 'solely', 'merely', 'alone'. **1874** SAYCE *Compar. Philol.* i. 27 Another mode of arresting our attention and giving distinctness to the thought which has to be expressed is by setting two synonymes side by side. **1904** H. BRADLEY *Making of English* v. 176 The notion of striking was expressed by the verb now pronounced *slay*, which survives only in a narrowed and developed meaning... Here,..German has kept the old word (*schlagen*), while English has rejected it for more vigorous synonyms.

β. 6–7 **synonoma**, **synonuma**, 6–9 **synonyma**, 7 **synonima**.

1570–6 LAMBARDE *Peramb. Kent* 289 This Horsa, and his Brother Hengist (both whose names be Synonuma, and signifie a Horse). **1573** G. HARVEY *Scholar's Love* in *Letter-bk.* (Camden) 116 Those two, I take it, are Synonoma. **1585** FETHERSTONE tr. *Calvin on Acts* xiii. 1. 290 It may be that they [*sc.* doctors and prophets] are in this place Synonyma, or that they signifie both one thing. **1656** BLOUNT *Glossogr.* s.v. *Marque*, *Marques* and *Reprizals* are used as Synonima. **1668** WILKINS *Real Char.* II. xii. 290 The words *Weal*, *welfare*, are mentioned as Synonoma. **1673** SIR P. LEYCESTER *Hist. Antiq.* I. iii. 97 *Dux* and *Consul* in these Ages were Synonima. **1807** G. CHALMERS *Caledonia* I. II. i. 221 The barrenness of the Anglo-Saxon language may be seen in the fewness of its synonyma.

γ. 6–7 **synonym-**, **-im-**, **-aes**, 6–8 **-a's**, **-as**, (6 **sunonimas**), 6–7 **synonamaes**, 7 **synonemas**, **sinonimaes**.

[**1594** Sunonimas: see 1 c.] **1598** SYLVESTER *Du Bartas* II. ii. II. *Babylon* 368 Better then Greeke with her Synonymaes, Fit Epithetes, and fine Metaphoraes. *a* **1634** COKE *4th Pt. Inst.* (1648) 30 In the statute of 11 H. 4. Customes and Subsidies are used as Synonymaes. **1649** JER. TAYLOR *Gt. Exemp.* I. Sect. vi. 98 All the synonyma's of sadnesse were little enough to expresse this great weeping. **1655** FULLER *Ch. Hist.* VI. i. 269 Nothing more common than to make Monks and Fryers both Synonyma's and reciprocall. **1765** STERNE *Tr. Shandy* VIII. xix, The Corporal, wishing..the word and all its synonimas at the Devil. **1789** G. CAMPBELL *Four Gospels* I. iv. 127 The use of such synonymas [as ἀπιστία and σκληροκαρδία].

Singular. α. 6 **synonomon**, 7 **synonymum**, 7–8 **synonymon**.

In quots. 1583 and 1673 perhaps to be taken as neut. adj.

1583 FULKE *Def. Tr. Script.* i. 11 For them..whiche knowe..that *Simulachrum* is *Synonomon* with *Imago*. **1653** URQUHART *Rabelais* I. v. 26 Give me a synonymon for a gammon of bacon. **1653** H. MORE *Conject. Cabbal.* (1713) 146, I need not note that Μνήμη was added as a synonymon of Μνημοσύνη. **1659** *Termes de la Ley* 352 *Faitour*..an evil doer, or an idle companion,..a Synonymon to Vagabond. **1673** O. WALKER *Educ.* 125 Satyricalnes, (which is almost synonymum to wit).

β. 6 **sinonime**, 8–9 **synonime**, 7– **synonyme(e**.

1598 FLORIO, *Sinomino*, a sinonime, or word of one signification. **1668** WILKINS *Real Char.* III. iv. 314 The last Combination doth consist of such as are..Expositive; either by Synonyme, or by Instance. *Ibid.*, *Dict.*, Synonym. **1727** BOYER *Dict. Royal*, *Synonime*..a Synonym, or Synonyma. **1801** MASON *Suppl. to Johnson*, *Synonyme*, a word of the same meaning as some other word. [Quot. from Reid has *synonimes*.] **1816** COLERIDGE *Lay Serm.* App. p. xvi, *Worth* was degraded into a lazy synonyme of *value*. **1825** MACAULAY *Ess.*, *Milton* (1843) I. 12 Change the structure of the sentence; substitute one synonyme for another; and the whole effect is destroyed. **1828–32** WEBSTER s.v., A name, noun or other word having the same signification as another, is its synonym. **1853** W. GREGORY *Inorg. Chem.* (ed. 3) 25 The term atomic weight is used,..but only as a convenient synonym for the term equivalent. **1869** GLADSTONE *Juv. Mundi* ii. (1870) 69 We have also to consider the word Panachaioi... We cannot take it for a mere synonym of Achaioi.

γ. 7 **synonima**, 8 **synonyma**.

1611 COTGR., *Synonime*, a Synonima. **1727** [see β]. **1776** G. CAMPBELL *Philos. Rhet.* I. I. vi. 172 The stress of the argument lies in a mere synonyma, or something equivalent.

b. *spec.* in *Nat. Hist.* A systematic name having the same, or nearly the same, application as another, esp. as another which has superseded it.

1659 RAY *Corr.* (1848) 2, I shall give the names of all plants..in an alphabetical order, together with their synonyma. **1765** *Museum Rust.* IV. 441 *Gramen typhinum majus, seu primum*... Mr. Hudson then adds, as a synonym, *Gramen typhinum medium* s. *vulgatissimum*. **1833** LYELL *Princ. Geol.* III. Pref. p. xvi, We cannot have too complete a catalogue of all the species..together with their synonyms. **1857** HENFREY *Bot.* §184 We find a distinct generic name given as a synonym.

c. The equivalent of a word in another language.

1594 NASHE *Unfort. Trav.* 27 Bidding a man *boniure* in Germane sunonimas. **1804** ANNA SEWARD *Mem. E. Darwin* 202 Had *life* been used instead of its Latin synonym [*printed* synonism] *ens*.

2. By extension: A name or expression which involves or implies a meaning properly or literally expressed by some other; 'another name *for*'.

1631 MASSINGER *Emperor East* I. ii, *Informer*... As I am the State scout, you may think me an informer. *Mast.* They are Synonima. **1690** C. NESSE *Hist. & Myst. O. & N. Test.* I. 129 Abrahams bosom is made the synonymon (of the same import) with heaven. **1784** R. BAGE *Barham Downs* I. 329 Nor of dishonour neither, which I suppose is the modern synonime with marriage. **1849** MACAULAY *Hist. Eng.* iv. I. 507 His [*sc.* William Penn's] name has..become..a synonyme for probity and philanthropy. **1868** G. DUFF *Pol. Surv.* 229 This region [*sc.* Peru], whose name was so long a synonym for wealth and magnificence. **1874** GREEN *Short Hist.* ix. §1. 602 'Hobbism' became, ere he died, the popular synonym for irreligion and immorality. **1879** LUBBOCK *Sci. Lect.* v. 161 The word *ferrum* was employed in Latin as a synonym for a sword.

3. *transf.* Either of two or more things of like or identical nature but called by different names, e.g. corresponding geological formations in different regions. (Cf. SYNONYMITY b.)

1839 MURCHISON *Silur. Syst.* I. iv. 66 The formation differs essentially both from its type in the North of England, and from its foreign Synonyms.

4. *loosely.* A person of the same name as another; a 'namesake': = HOMONYM 2. *nonce-use.*

1837 SYD. SMITH *Sir J. Mackintosh* Wks. (1850) 650/1 A Scotch cousin, who had mistaken me for my gallant synonym, the hero of Acre.

5. *Comb.*, as (sense 1) ***synonym-pair***; **synonym-compound** (see quot. 1923).

1923 B. KARLGREN *Sound & Symbol in Chinese* iii. 32 The additions were of various kinds, the commonest and by far the most important of which was the formation of what may be called synonym-compounds. This consists in coupling together two simple words with the same or at least analogous meanings, words that formerly had been used alone. **1964** *Language* XL. 104 The Chinese..invented tones to keep the monosyllables apart, and then synonym-compounds, further to clear up the difficulties they were now experiencing with their own language. **1980** *Logophile* IV. I. 28, I have been working for some time on an article about the curious existence in English and French of synonym-pairs.

Hence †**'synonym** *v.* (*rare*), *trans.*, to designate by a synonym.

1761 DA COSTA in *Phil. Trans.* LII. 446 It is truly a kind of crystal, and might with propriety be synonymed *Crystallus viridis columnaris lateribus inordinatis.*

†**sy'nonymal**, *a.* (*sb.*) *Obs.* Also 7 **synoni-**, **sun-**. [f. SYNONYM *sb.* + -AL¹.] **A.** *adj.* Synonymous.

1613 JACKSON *Creed* II. xxx. §19 *margin*, In matters of knowledge or belief, reason and cause are synonymall. **1641** H. L'ESTRANGE *God's Sabbath* 65 In its remotest latitude of signification it is synonymall with what Civilians call *Jus Gentium*, or the Law of Nations. **1659** O. WALKER *Instruct. Oratory* 95 Repetitions..and enlargements by synonymal words.

B. *sb.* A synonym.

1662 J. CHANDLER *Van Helmont's Oriat.* 191 The Fume of Minerals, by reason of its malignity, & an Arsenical poyson, have become Sunonymalls or things of one name: to wit, the Arsenick, and smoakie vapour, and smoak of Metalls fall together or agree in one. **1688** R. L'ESTRANGE *Brief Hist. Times* III. 304 The Synonymals one upon the Neck of Another, savour more of the Skill of the Clark, then of the Faith of the Reporter.

Hence †**sy'nonymally** *adv.*, synonymously.

1630 SPELMAN *De Sepult.* (1641) 16 In this manner the fifth Canon either useth them [*sc.* 'exact' and 'demand'] Synonimally, or [etc.].

synonymic (sɪnə'nɪmɪk), *a.* (*sb.*) [f. SYNONYM *sb.* + -IC, after F. *synonymique*.] **A.** *adj.* Of, relating to, consisting of, or exhibiting synonyms.

1816 W. TAYLOR in *Monthly Rev.* LXXIX. 472 A synonymic table of the geography of Egypt under the Pharaohs. **1857** J. W. GIBBS *Philol. Studies* 220 Synonymic distinctions, however, should not be carried too far in any language. **1871** KIRBY (*title*) A Synonymic Catalogue of Diurnal Lepidoptera. **1881** SHARPE in *Nature* XXIII. 481/2 The intricate windings of synonymic literature. **1899** A. GUDEMAN in *Class. Rev.* XIII. 214/2 *Pulchritudinem ac speciem*. The same synonymic collocation occurs in Firm. Maternus.

¶The meaning 'synonymous' given in mod. Dicts. appears to be unsupported; but cf. next, 1.

B. *sb.* The study of synonyms, as a department of grammar. [Cf. F. *synonymique*, G. *synonymik*.] Also **syno'nymics**.

1857 J. W. GIBBS *Philol. Studies* 220 It is the business of synonymic merely to notice the distinctions actually existing, not to create them, or to anticipate their origin. **1909** *Cent. Dict.* Suppl., Synonymics. **1939** W. E. COLLINSON in *Trans. Philol. Soc.* 54 (*title*) Comparative synonymics: some principles and illustrations. *Ibid.* 58 The first principle I venture to set up in synonymics..[is that] 'one must never be content with studying synonyms as isolated items'. **1962** H. M. HOENIGSWALD in Householder & Saporta *Probl. Lexicogr.* 103 Some works, like Dornseiff's monstrous *Wortschatz* or like other thesauri of synonymics are arranged according to semantic areas.

syno'nymical, *a.* [f. SYNONYM *sb.* + -ICAL.]

†**1.** = SYNONYMOUS 1. *Obs.*

1645 E. CALAMY *Indictm. Eng.* 23 The Apostle reckons up seven synonymicall expressions... The works of the flesh are hatred, variance, emulation, wrath, strife, sedition, envyings. **1690** C. NESSE *Hist. & Myst. O. & N. Test.* I. 89 It being a phrase synonymical.

2. = SYNONYMIC.

1806 DAWSON (*title*) Philologia Anglicana: or a Philological and Synonymical Dictionary of the English Language. **1887** *Amer. Naturalist* XXI. 580 A synonymical and descriptive list.., in which one hundred and seven species..are given. **1895** *Advance* (Chicago) 11 July 62/2 A wonderful Psalm, this [*sc.* the 119th]! Acrostical, synonymical, panegyrical, devotional.

Hence **syno'nymically** *adv.*, as a synonym or synonyms.

1599 *Broughton's Lett.* vi. 20 Συστρατιώτης and ἀκόλουθὸς are all one,..and..synonymically confounded. **1862** H. B. WHEATLEY *Anagrams* 172 The second piece includes some words not synonymically inserted in the first.

synonymicon (sɪnə'nɪmɪkən). [f. SYNONYM, after *lexicon*.] A list or dictionary of synonyms.

1813 W. TAYLOR *Eng. Synonyms* Introd. p. xiv, Blair has deposited in his *Rhetoric*..some further contributions to an english synonymicon.

synonymist (sɪ'nɒnɪmɪst). [f. SYNONYM *sb.* + -IST; cf. F. *synonymiste*.] One who treats of, or makes a list of, synonyms.

1753 *Chambers' Cycl. Supp.*, *Synonymists*, among the botanical writers, such as have employed their care in the collecting the different names, or *synonyma*, used by different authors, and reducing them to one another. **1805** W. TAYLOR in *Monthly Mag.* XX. 18 The German synonimist has produced a work of fuller and sounder information. **1849** SIR J. STEPHEN *Eccl. Biog.* (1850) II. 155 Neither Crabbe, the synonymist, nor even Samuel Johnson, lexicographer, could have discriminated exactly between the senses of two appellations so equivocal.

synonymity (sɪnə'nɪmɪtɪ). [f. SYNONYMOUS: see -ITY.] The quality or fact of being synonymous, or having the same meaning.

1880 J. MORISON in *Expositor* XI. 468 Metaphysical coincidence by no means necessitates the rhetorical synonymity of nomenclature. **1884** *N. & Q.* 6th Ser. X. 43/2 To point out the Germanic origin of his [*sc.* Garibaldi's] name and its synonymity with Shakespere.

b. *transf.* Identity of nature of things having different names (e.g. tones in a musical scale, or geological formations); cf. SYNONYMOUS 1 c.

1875 ELLIS in *Helmholtz's Sensations of Tone* App. 659 To found any harmonic theories on the synonymity of tones in any temperament, when there is known to be no synonymity in nature. **1896** *Naturalist* 210 The synonymity of the Lincoln Carstone and the Norfolk Limestones.

synonymize (sɪ'nɒnɪmaɪz), *v.* [f. late L. *synōnym-um* SYNONYM *sb.* + -IZE.]

1. *trans.* To give the synonyms of. *rare.*

c **1595** CAREW *Excell. Eng. Tongue* in G. G. Smith *Eliz. Crit. Ess.* II. 292 This worde *fortis* wee maye synnonomize after all these fashions, stoute, hardye, valiaunt, doughtye, Couragious, aduenturous, &c. **1697** *Phil. Trans.* XIX. 394 Our Common Garden Kind [of Snail] which I have Synonimized under No. 13.

2. *intr.* To be synonymous *with*. *rare.*

1611 COTGR. s.v. *Rez*, Alluding to the signification of *rez*, wherewith *Tondus* almost synonymizeth.

3. To use synonyms; to express the same meaning by different words. Also in *vbl. sb.* and *ppl. a.* *rare.*

1700 [W. KING] *Transactioneer* 36 He's as successful in his Descriptions as in his Synonymizings. **1805** W. TAYLOR in *Monthly Mag.* XX. 17 To synonimize is to express one thought in different terms. **1851** *Fraser's Mag.* XLIV. 694 The creation of new words, with its synonymizing tendency.

4. *trans.* To furnish with lists of synonyms; to make synonymic. *nonce-use.*

1805 PERRY (*title*) The Synonymous, Etymological, and Pronouncing English Dictionary;..being an attempt to synonymise his [*sc.* Dr. Johnson's] folio Dictionary of the English Language.

5. a. To be synonymous with (a concept, phrase, etc.).

1938 S. LESLIE *Film of Memory* v. 144 The old Baroness was very popular with the crowd and synonymised Victorian charity. **1947** PARTRIDGE *Usage & Abusage* 44/2 *As to* in such senses..is defensible when it synonymizes *in respect of* or *in the matter of*.

b. To regard (terms, concepts, etc.) as synonymous.

1970 *Nature* 5 Sept. 1065/1 Hill's classification is not wholly in line with recent trends in primate systematics, which is to synonymize the species of *Papio*. **1976** *Ibid.* 5 Feb. 360/2 If we were now to start referring to cyanophytes as 'blue-green bacteria', we would implicitly synonymise the words 'prokaryota' and 'bacteria'.

synonymous (sɪ'nɒnɪməs), *a.* Also 7 **synonimus**, 7–9 **synonimous**. [f. med.L. *synōnymus*, ad. Gr. συνώνυμος: see SYNONYM and -OUS.]

1. Having the character of a synonym; equivalent in meaning: said of words or phrases denoting the same thing or idea. Const. *to*, (now usually) *with*.

1610 DONNE *Pseudo-martyr* 389 So doth the law accept it [*sc.* the word 'heresy'] in this oath, where it makes it equiualent, and Synonimous, to the wordes which are ioyned with it, which are *Impious* and *Damnable*. **1678** CUDWORTH *Intell. Syst.* I. iv. 601 That word Substance, being used..as Synonymous with Essence. **1690** *Reasons why Rector of P. took Oath of Allegiance* 11 Lawmakers.. muster up such a number of synonymous Terms, or such as amongst which we can see but small diversity. **1697** *Phil. Trans.* XIX. 398 At one view you have the several Synonimous Names of all precedent Writers of Natural History. **1755** JOHNSON *Dict.* Pref., Words are seldom exactly synonimous. **1813–21** BENTHAM *Ontology* Wks. 1843 VIII. 201/1 Matter, at first sight, may naturally enough be considered as exactly synonymous to the word *substance*. **1816** SINGER *Hist. Cards* 56 The fact appears to be, that Pair and Pack were formerly synonimous. **1872** DARWIN *Emotions* vii. 194 To say that a person 'is down in the mouth' is synonymous with saying that he is out of spirits. **1884** J. TAIT *Mind in Matter* III. 74 If life and mind are not synonymous, neither are brain and mind.

b. Of or relating to synonyms; synonymic. *rare.*

1805 [see SYNONYMIZE 4].

c. *transf.* Said of things of the same nature denoted by different names, i.e. by synonyms; thus = identical. (Cf. SYNONYM 3, SYNONYMITY b.)

1789 BURNEY *Hist. Mus.* III. vii. 439 Two of the five short keys are divided in the middle and communicate to two different sets of pipes so that G♯ and A♭, are not synonimous sounds.

2. In extended sense, said of words or phrases which denote things that imply one another: cf. SYNONYM 2.

1659 T. PECKE *Parnassi Puerp.* 152 Can it be thus, That Tents, and Studies are Synonimous? **1706** ESTCOURT *Fair Example* I. i, Cuckold and Husband are as Synonimous Terms, as Rogue and Attorney. **1769** *Junius Lett.* xv. (1788) 89 Good-faith and folly have so long been received as synonimous terms, that [etc.]. **1777** ROBERTSON *Hist. Amer.* (1778) I. IV. 254 Over all the continent of North America a north-westerly wind and excessive cold are synonymous terms. **1829** CARLYLE *Misc.* (1857) II. 1 Were will in human undertakings synonymous with faculty. **1855** PRESCOTT *Philip II*, I. III. i. 317 The name of soldier was synonymous with that of marauder. **1873** G. S. BADEN-POWELL *New Homes* 431 With many,..going out to Australia is believed to be synonymous with making a fortune.

3. *loosely.* Having the same name; denoted by the same word: = HOMONYMOUS 2.

1734 [see HETERONYMOUS 1]. **1796** KIRWAN in *Trans. R. Irish Acad.* VI. 187 If a magnet be cut in two, in a direction parallel to the axis, the parts before conjoined will now repel each other, because they still retain two synonimous poles. **1876** BESANT & RICE *Gold. Butterfly* xiii, Poor old Abraham Dyson, now lying in a synonymous bosom.

¶ **b.** That may be described in the same terms; of the same description; similar. *Obs.*

1690 D'URFEY *Collin's Walk Lond.* I. 8 'Tis needless to expose His Stockins, or describe, or Shooes, Or Legs, or Feet, since 't may be guessed They were Synonimous to th' rest. **1706** DE FOE *Jure Div.* VII. 142 The Fall of Man having made him a Slave to the Devil, Man grew something Diabolical himself, and strove to practice a synonimous Power over his fellow Creatures.

Hence **sy'nonymously** *adv.*, by or as a synonym, with the same meaning; **sy'nonymousness**.

1659 PEARSON *Creed* i. 100 It [*sc.* creation] is often used synonymously with words which signifie any kind of production or formation. **1671** F. PHILLIPS *Reg. Necess.* 415 The Earls or Counts of England..before the Norman Conquest, were as our learned Selden observed, sometimes Synonimously entituled *Dux* or Dukes. **1688** *Vox Cleri Pro Rege* 47 The King had Sovereign or absolute Power (for our late Prerogative Divines have used both Epiethites Synonimously). **1839** G. ROBERTS *Dict. Geol.*, *Schist*,.. often used synonymously with slate. **1863** MAX MÜLLER *Sci. Lang.* Ser. II. x. (1868) 447 The synonymousness of Sky and God in the Aryan language.

synonymy (sɪ'nɒnɪmɪ). Also 6–9 **synonimy**, 7–9 **synonomy**. [ad. late L. *synōnymia*, a. Gr. συνωνυμία, f. συνώνυμος SYNONYM. Cf. F. *synonymie*, etc.]

†**1.** = SYNONYM 1. *Obs.*

1609 R. BARNERD *Faithf. Sheph.* 27 One word signifying many things, Homonymies: many words signifying againe one thing, Synonymies. **1659** TORRIANO, *Sinònimo*, a Sinonimie. **1730** M. WRIGHT *Introd. Law Tenures* 179 Feud, Fee, and Tenure, are Synonimies, and import but one and the same Policy. **1799** J. SCOTT *Bahar-Danush* Pref. p. iii, The synonymies and compound epithets so abundant in eastern description.

†**b.** *loosely.* A thing of the same name: = HOMONYM 2. *Obs.*

1612 SELDEN *Illustr. Drayton's Poly-olb.* ii. 34 We hauing three riuers of note synonymies with her [*sc.* Isis].

2. The use of synonyms or of words as synonyms; *spec.* a rhetorical figure by which synonyms are used for the sake of amplification.

[**1586** A. DAY *Engl. Secretorie* II. (1625) 91 *Synonimia*, when we bring forth many words signifying of one signification, or sounding to one purpose. **1589** PUTTENHAM *Engl. Poesie* III. xix. (Arb.) 223 When so euer we multiply our speech by many words or clauses of one sence, the Greekes call it *Sinonimia*, as who would say, like or consenting names.] **1657** J. SMITH *Myst. Rhet.* 159 A Synonymie is a commodious heaping together of divers words of one signification. **1880** MASSIE in *Expositor* XI. 147 Ahaz..makes υἱὸς equivalent to δοῦλος... Such sycophantic synonymy St. Paul absolutely repudiates.

3. The subject or study of synonyms; synonyms collectively, a set of synonyms.

a. in grammar.

1683 *Weekly Memorials* 15 Jan. 375 The Synonomie or several Names to the same sense. **1794** MRS. PIOZZI (*title*) British Synonymy; or, an attempt at regulating the choice of words in familiar conversation. **1837** HALLAM *Lit. Eur.* I. iii. §8 The distinctions in Latin syntax, inflexion, and synonymy. **1908** *Expositor* Jan. 73 The best work on New Testament synonymy.

b. in natural history: see SYNONYM 1 b.

1781 *Phil. Trans.* LXXI. 438 Artedi, in his account of this species, has adopted the synonymy of Schonevelde, who describes a fish under the name of *Ophidion imberbe flavum*. **1785** MARTYN *Lett. Bot.* Introd. (1794) 6 A Synonymy, or exact list of the names that every plant bore in all the writers which preceded them. **1854** WOODWARD *Mollusca* II. 162 The synonymy of the genus would fill several pages. **1877** H. SAUNDERS in *Proc. Zool. Soc.* (1878) 156 The comparative simplicity of the synonymy of the *Sterninæ*. **1887** W. PHILLIPS *Brit. Discomycetes* 241 Dr. Cooke has pointed out the fact that two different species have been included by authors under this name... The synonymy is rendered somewhat uncertain by this fact.

4. The quality or fact of being synonymous; identity of meaning; synonymousness.

1794 MRS. PIOZZI *Synon.* I. 182 Yet would such a transposition be no proof of their synonymy. **1815** *Paris Chit-chat* (1816) II. 102 A..philologer established the synonymy of the words *repress* and *prevent*. **1857** H. H. BREEN *Mod. Eng. Lit.* 86 Soane..will have it that Spenser intended the particle 'or' to express synonymy.

synopsis (sɪˈnɒpsɪs). Pl. **synopses** (-siːz). [a. late L. *synopsis* (whence It. *sinossi*, Sp. *sinopsis*, Pg. *synopsis*), a. Gr. *σύνοψις* general view, f. *σύν* SYN-[1] + *ὄψις* view (cf. *συνορᾶν* to see altogether).]

1. A brief or condensed statement presenting a combined or general view of something; a table, or set of paragraphs or headings, so arranged as to exhibit all the parts or divisions of a subject or work at one view; a conspectus.

1611 CORYAT *Crudities* 432 He hath written a synopsis of the history of man. **1644** MILTON *Areop.* (Arb.) 64 The infinit helps of interlinearies, breviaries, synopses, and other loitering gear. **1678** CUDWORTH *Intell. Syst.* Pref. 6 We shall exhibit to the reader's view a brief and general synopsis of the whole following work. **1692** RAY in *Lett. Lit. Men* (Camden) 199, I am now upon a methodical Synopsis of all British Animals except Insects. **1771** BURKE *Corr.* (1844) I. 262, I have now gone minutely through your last tour, and the synopsis, with which you have..closed it. **1844** SIR R. GRIFFITH (*title*) A Synopsis of the Characters of the Carboniferous Limestone Fossils of Ireland. **1856** *N. Brit. Rev.* XXVI. 17 A considerable portion of this Essay consists of summary statements, or abridged recitals of the staple Christian argument... These synopses, or condensed evidences,..are characteristic of Chalmers. **1879** *Cassell's Techn. Educ.* IV. 221/2 Below we give a synopsis of the foregoing, that the painter may have a concise view of the entire process.

transf. **1652** EVELYN *St. France* Misc. Writ. (1805) 50 The Netherlands..which is a perfect encycle and synopsis of whatever one may see elsewhere in all the other countryes of Europe.

2. A general view or prospect, as of a landscape. *rare.*

1844 J. COWELL *Thirty Yrs. passed among Players* I. xxi. 51/2 Snuffed two tallow-candles, and took a synopsis of the floating apartment. **1881** BADDELEY *Highl. Scot.* 68 The Knock of Crieff..commands a synopsis of all that is beautiful around.

3. *Eastern Ch.* A book of prayers for the use of the laity (see quot.).

1850 NEALE *East. Church, Gen. Introd.* IV. iii. 890, I hardly can reckon..The Synopsis, as Office-Books. These are mere compilations..of such prayers as are most likely to be needed in the attendance on the Divine Offices.

Hence **syˈnopsize** (-saɪz) *v. trans.* (orig. *U.S.*), to make a synopsis of, to epitomize.

1882 *Advance* (Chicago) 27 July, Now as for our faith. You have synopsized it. **1890** *Harper's Mag.* Nov. 965/2 The chapter..which we have been here synopsizing. **1959** J. GILL *Council of Florence* p. xv, Very many long speeches occur in the main sources, which I have synopsised. **1974** *Times Lit. Suppl.* 20 Sept. 1018/5 The 'avowal' here is..that of the editors of the volume, in a short preface in which they attempt to synopsize its contents. **1982** *Daily Tel.* 6 Feb. 11/4 Plot is the very least of Hardy. If you were to synopsise the events of this early novel..you would be a laughing-stock.

†**synopsy.** *Obs. rare*$^{-0}$. In 7 -ie. [irreg. ad. late L. *synopsis*: see SYNOPSIS] = SYNOPSIS.

1616 BULLOKAR *Eng. Expos.*, *Synopsie*, a sight or full view of a thing. **1658** PHILLIPS, *Synopsie*, a brief summing up of things contained in a large Treatise.

synoptic (sɪˈnɒptɪk), *a.* (*sb.*) [ad. mod.L. *synopticus* (whence also F. *synoptique*, It. *sinottico*, Sp. *sinóptico*, Pg. *synoptico*), ad. Gr. *συνοπτικός*, f. *σύνοψις* SYNOPSIS (cf. OPTIC).]

1. a. Of a table, chart, etc.: Pertaining to or forming a synopsis; furnishing a general view of some subject; *spec.* depicting or dealing with weather conditions over a large area at the same point in time.

1763 *Phil. Trans.* LIII. 168, I have..computed them again, and they are as in the following synoptic table. **1827** FARADAY *Chem. Manip.* xxii. (1842) 564 The instrument is called a Synoptic Scale of Chemical Equivalents, or more usually Wollaston's Scale. **1851** NICHOL *Archit. Heav.* 193 Madler's synoptic view of what he considers established. [**1861** F. GALTON (*title*) Synchronous weather chart of England.] **1868** *Symons's Monthly Meteorol. Mag.* III. 144 It is now fourteen years since, impressed with the importance of synoptic weather charts,..I attempted to bring out a series of such charts [of the Indian Ocean]. **1887** R. ABERCROMBY *Weather* i. (1888) 8 Such a chart is called a 'synoptic chart' because it enables the meteorologist to take a general view, as it were, over a large area. **1909** A. C. SCOTT *Notes Meteorol. & Weather Forecasting* 1 Within the last 40 years the Synoptic method of weather-charting has been introduced, which has changed the whole aspect of Meteorology. **1939** *Geogr. Jrnl.* XCIV. 135 Synoptic meteorology (i.e. the science of synchronous weather charts). **1963** G. L. PICKARD *Descriptive Physical Oceanogr.* vi. 74 It is..impracticable to obtain a truly simultaneous picture of the ocean, and the synoptic oceanographer has to make the assumption that when he analyses them the data from his cruise or cruises may be considered as simultaneous. **1974** *Nature* 1 Mar. 87/3 Synoptic climatology is essentially a practical subject.

b. Of a mental act or faculty, conduct, etc.: Pertaining to, involving, or taking a combined or comprehensive mental view of something.

1852 J. MARTINEAU *Ess., Unity of Mind in Nature* (1891) III. 105 Without this synoptic progress, the occupation of the intellect would be gone. **1899** *Speaker* 11 Nov. 135/1 That synoptic statesmanship which has done so much for this branch of education in France. **1900** E. HOLMES *What is Poetry?* 28 The poet fuses them [*sc.* phenomena] by the force of his emotion..poetic emotion being essentially a synoptic faculty.

2. a. Applied distinctively to the first three Gospels (viz. of Matthew, Mark, and Luke) as giving an account of the events from the same point of view or under the same general aspect. Also *transf.* pertaining or relating to these Gospels.

1841 MYERS *Cath Th.* III. §17. 45 The Book of Deuteronomy seems to bear something of the same relation to the preceding Four that the Gospel of St. John does to the Synoptic Three. **1861** TRENCH *Comm. Ep. Churches Asia* 163 The words of Christ as recorded in the Gospels, in the three synoptic Gospels above all. **1899** SIR J. C. HAWKINS *Horae Synopticae* Pref. p. v, The origin, mode of composition, and mutual relations of the three Synoptic Gospels form so obscure and so complex a subject of enquiry that it has come to be generally known as the 'Synoptic Problem'.

b. as *sb.* Any one of the Synoptic Gospels (or of their writers = SYNOPTIST 1). Usually in *pl.*

1858 J. MARTINEAU *Stud. Christ.* 257 The Synoptics.. which present only varieties of the same fundamental tradition. **1874** M. ARNOLD in *Contemp. Rev.* Oct. 815 The Fourth Gospel..puts the clearance [of the temple] at the beginning of Christ's career, the synoptics put it at the end. **1875** E. WHITE *Life in Christ* III. xvii, The sublime scenes of His Baptism, and of His Transfiguration..when the synoptics tell us that God spoke of Him as His 'Beloved Son'.

synoptical (sɪˈnɒptɪkəl), *a.* [See prec. and -ICAL.]

1. = SYNOPTIC 1.

1664 EVELYN *Kal. Hort.* Introd., The Observations which ..we have collected together, and here present..as so many Synoptical Tables. *a* **1755** JOHNSON *Plan Dict.* Wks. 1787 IX. 177 In synoptical lexicons, where mutilated and doubtful languages are explained by their affinity to others more certain and extensive. **1826** KIRBY & SP. *Entomol.* III. xxviii. 32 That you may have a synoptical view of the comparative size of the larger insects..I now lay before you a table of the dimensions. **1839** HALLAM *Lit. Eur.* III. III. iii. §134. 117 The ninth chapter of the Leviathan contains a synoptical chart of human science. **1889** *Science-Gossip* XXV. 157 To add to the value of this..useful volume we have also a copious synoptical index and general index.

2. = SYNOPTIC 2. *rare.*

1875 [see SYNOPTIST 1].

Hence **syˈnoptically** *adv.*, in the way of a synopsis; so as to present a general view.

1667 PETTY in Sprat *Hist. R. Soc.* 295, I shall more Synoptically here insert a Catalogue of all Dying Materials. **1882-3** *Schaff's Encycl. Relig. Knowl.* II. 892/2 The best synoptically arranged text.

synoptist (sɪˈnɒptɪst). [f. SYNOPTIC: see -IST.]

1. Any one of the writers of the Synoptic Gospels: see SYNOPTIC 2. (Usually in *pl.*)

1846 GEO. ELIOT tr. *Strauss's Life of Jesus* II. II. vi. 135 The mode in which the synoptists arrange the sayings of Jesus. **1860** WESTCOTT *Introd. Study Gosp.* v. 262 The Synoptists, it is said, describe the public ministry of Christ as extending only over one year. **1875** *Ibid.* iii. (ed. 5) 166 The terms *Synoptist*, *Synoptical*, as applied to the first three Evangelists appear to date from the time of Griesbach, though they were brought into general use by Neander. **1882** FARRAR *Early Chr.* IV. xix. I. 493 Those who hold, in despite of the plain evidence of the Synoptists, and still more of St. John, that our Lord's 'brethren' were among the number of His Apostles.

2. One who compiles a synopsis. *rare*$^{-0}$.

In recent Dicts.

Hence **synopˈtistic** *a.* = SYNOPTIC 2.

1879 E. A. ABBOTT in *Encycl. Brit.* X. 805/2 The author of the Fourth Gospel..speaks of 'the Jews' as an alien race..; but this is not in the manner of the synoptistic tradition.

synoptophore (sɪˈnɒptəʊfɔə(r)). *Ophthalm.* Also -**phor.** [SYN- + OPTO- + -PHORE.] An instrument for measuring the deviations of the visual axes of eyes not properly coordinated for binocular vision.

1934 M. L. HINE *May & Worth's Dis. of Eye* (ed. 7) xxvii. 416 The synoptophore..is an elaborate development of Worth's original amblyoscope. **1955** P. D. TREVOR-ROPER *Ophthalmol.* xviii. 281 Various major amblyoscopes are marketed. The pattern that is perhaps the most generally serviceable is the 'Moorfields Synoptophore'. **1975** *Nature* 17 Apr. 613/2 Binocular interaction was tested on the synoptophor.

synorchism, -orthographic, -orogenic: see SYN-[1].

synosteo-, combining form made up from Gr. *σύν* with + *ὀστέον* bone, and intended (or alleged) to mean 'articulation of bones, joint', in several words instanced only from mod. Dicts.: see quots.

1844 DUNGLISON *Med. Lex.* (1848), *Synosteography*.., the part of anatomy which describes the joints. *Synosteology*.., a treatise on the joints... *Synosteotomy*.., dissection of the joints. **1891** *Cent. Dict.*, *Synosteotome*, in *surg.*, a dismembering-knife.

synosteosis (sɪnɒstɪˈəʊsɪs). *rare*$^{-0}$. [f. Gr. *σύν* SYN-[1] + *ὀστέον* bone + -OSIS.] = SYNOSTOSIS.

1848 DUNGLISON *Med. Lex.* (ed. 7), *Synosteosis, Synostosis* .., union by means of bone.

synostose (ˈsɪnɒstəʊz), *v.* [Back-formation from next.] *pass.* and *intr.* To be affected with synostosis; to be united by a growth of bone.

1878 BARTLEY tr. *Topinard's Anthrop.* iv. 133 The bones become anchylosed, the suture is synostosed. **1904** DUCKWORTH *Stud. Anthropol. Laborat.* 213 The sagittal suture shows no signs of synostosis, nor has the spheno-basilar suture yet synostosed. **1904** —— *Morphol. & Anthropol.* x. 252 Premature synostosis is followed by restricted growth in a direction perpendicular to that of the synostosed suture.

synostosis (sɪnɒˈstəʊsɪs). *Anat.* and *Phys.* Pl. -**oses** (-ˈəʊsiːz). [Contracted from SYNOSTEOSIS.] Union or fusion of adjacent bones by growth of bony substance (either normal or abnormal).

1848 [see SYNOSTEOSIS]. **1864** J. B. DAVIS *Neanderthal Skull* 4 Synostosis, or the premature ossification of one or more of the sutures between the cranial bones. **1898** J. HUTCHINSON in *Archives Surg.* IX. 352 Multiple exostoses, hyperostoses, and synostoses of the vertebral column.

Hence **synostotic** (sɪnɒˈstɒtɪk) *a.*, pertaining to, characterized by, or affected with synostosis.

1864 THURNAM in *Nat. Hist. Rev.* (1865) Apr. 247 The abnormal scaphoid skulls of the African races..seem to fall ..under the definition of what is termed by Welcker, *synostotic dolichocephalism.* **1864** J. B. DAVIS *Neanderthal Skull* 13 The great depression of the frontal and vertical regions in a synostotic skull. **1904** DUCKWORTH *Morphol. & Anthropol.* x. 251 Synostotic deformation..consequent upon..precocious union of two or more cranial bones.

synotic: see SYN-[1].

synou, obs. form of SINEW.

Synousiast, var. SYNUSIAST *Obs.*

synovectomy (sɪnəˈvɛktəmɪ, saɪ-). *Surg.* [f. SYNOV(IA + -ECTOMY.] Total or partial excision of the synovial membrane of a joint, esp. the knee, or of a tendon sheath, esp. to relieve pain.

1903 *Buck's Handbk. Med. Sci.* (rev. ed.) VI. 519/1 The procedures ordinarily employed are *évidement* of the focus, and in the later cases..ablation of the patella, with synovectomy or arthrectomy when necessary. **1923** *Jrnl. Amer. Med. Assoc.* 10 Nov. 1579/1 Synovectomy..was originally recommended as a surgical treatment for synovial tuberculosis. **1940** B. I. COMROE *Arthritis & Allied Conditions* xvii. 222 Synovectomy of the knee is the removal of the synovial tissue of the knee. **1976** *Proc. R. Soc. Med.* LXIX. 930/2 The indications for synovectomy or patellectomy in either rheumatoid or osteoarthritis of the knee are well known and differ little in the elderly.

‖**synovia** (sɪˈnəʊvɪə, saɪ-). Also 8-9 **sin-**. [mod.L. *sinovia*, *synovia*, also *synophia*, an invention, prob. arbitrarily formed, of Paracelsus (died 1541), applied by him to the nutritive fluid peculiar to the several parts of the body, and also to the gout (see quot. in b below), but limited by later physicians to the fluid of the joints.

In mod. dicts. it is derived from Gr. *σύν* SYN-[1] + *ᾠόν*, L. *ōvum* egg, on account of the resemblance of synovia to the white of egg. This is without foundation, and conflicts with Paracelsus's description of synovia as reddish, dark red, grey, etc., according to the part.]

a. *Phys.* The viscid albuminous fluid secreted in the interior of the joints, and in the sheaths of the tendons, and serving to lubricate them; also called *joint-oil* or *joint-water*.

[**1650** *Chymicall Dict.*, *Sinonia* [sic] is white glew of the joints (transl. of **1583** DORNEUS *Dict. Theophr. Paracelsi*, Sinonia est gluten album articulorum). **1693** tr. *Blancard's Phys. Dict.* (ed. 2), *Synovia*, the glutinous Matter betwixt the Joynts.] **1726** MONRO *Anat. Bones* (1741) 59 When the Synovia is not rubbed betwixt the Bones, it inspissates. **1769** *Phil. Trans.* LIX. 44 Without a bursal ligament..to contain the synovia, and keep the bone in its place. **1842** W. ARNOT *Mem. J. Halley* iv. 311 His sprightliness was one reason why his strength lasted so long. It acted like sinovia on the joints of his body. **1872** BRYANT *Pract. Surg.* (1878) I. 59 In some cases the articulation is only filled with an increase of synovia.

†**b.** *Path.* A morbid condition or discharge of this fluid. *Obs.*

Cf. Paracelsus *Paragraphorum* VII. i, De Podagra.. Geminum vero morbi nomen synouia est. Hoc enim ex morbi caussa desumitur.

1661 LOVELL *Hist. Anim. & Min.* 215 The powder used outwardly helps the Synovia, and mundifieth old ulcers. **1758** J. S. *Le Dran's Observ. Surg.* (1771) 296 [He] had an inspissated Sinovia upon his right Foot, which possessed not only the Articulation, but spread over the whole Foot. **1766** *Compl. Farmer* s.v. *Pricking*, If the tendon is wounded, the sole must be carefully drawn, because a sinovia and gleet is discharged. [Cf. quot. **1824** s.v. SYNOVY.]

synovial (sɪˈnəʊvɪəl, saɪ-), *a.* [f. SYNOVIA: see -AL[1].] Pertaining to, consisting of, containing, or secreting synovia.

1756 C. LUCAS *Ess. Waters* I. 184 The Gout is an obstruction of the synovial vessels. **1767** GOOCH *Treat. Wounds* I. 437 Wounds, that enter the joints,..will generally afford a larger synovial discharge. **1808** BARCLAY *Muscular Motions* 436 Had a tendon been substituted, we should naturally suppose..that it would have been surrounded with synovial membrane. **1846** G. E. DAY tr. *Simon's Anim. Chem.* II. 416 The synovial fluid is viscid, transparent, of a yellow or reddish colour, faintly saline. **1864** OWEN *Power of God* 23 A..joint..with the co-adjusted surfaces covered by smooth cartilage, and lubricated by joint-oil, retained and secreted by a synovial capsule.

b. *transf.* Occurring in or affecting a synovial membrane.

1846 BRITTAN tr. *Malgaigne's Man. Oper. Surg.* 83 Synovial cysts. **1879** *St. George's Hosp. Rep.* IX. 776 It is estimated that 85 per cent of the cases of synovial inflammation occur in the knee. **1886** FAGGE *Princ. Med.* II. 529 Synovial rheumatism.

Hence **syˈnovially** *adv.*, by means of synovia, or of a joint containing synovia.

1870 FLOWER *Osteol. Mamm.* x. 135 A small bony nodule ..which is articulated synovially to the upper corner of the outer extremity of the basihyal.

synovin (ˈsɪnəvɪn). [f. SYNOVIA + -IN[1].] The form of mucin occurring in synovia.

1898 in *Syd. Soc. Lex.*

synoviparous (sɪnəˈvɪpərəs), *a.* [f. SYNOVIA + -PAROUS.] Producing or secreting synovia.

1890 BILLINGS *Nat. Med. Dict.*, *Synoviparous crypts*, diverticula from synovial membranes.

synovitis (sɪnəˈvaɪtɪs, saɪ-). *Path.* [f. SYNOVIA + -ITIS.] Inflammation of a synovial membrane.

1835-6 *Todd's Cycl. Anat.* I. 162/2 Acute synovitis of the ankle-joint. **1879** *St. George's Hosp. Rep.* IX. 775 That the pain of synovitis is caused by the distension of the fibrous elements of the joint is generally admitted.

†**synovy.** *Obs.* Anglicized form of SYNOVIA. (Cf. F. *synovie.*)

1684 W. RUSSELL *Phys. Treat.* 92 In every true Gout..the tormenting Pain thereof is only in the Joynt-Water, or Synovy between the Joynts. **1824** R. BOYCE *Fam. Surg.* 28 To stop Synovy, or Joint Oil [in Horses].

synow, obs. form of SINEW.

synroc: see SYN-[2].

syns, synse, obs. ff. SINCE, CENSE *v.*[1]

synsacral to **synspermy:** see SYN-[1].

synsemantic (sɪnsiːˈmæntɪk), *a. Philol.* [ad. G. *synsemantisch* (A. Marty *Untersuchungen zur Grundlegung d. allgemeinen Grammatik und Sprachphilosophie* (1908) II. i. 206): see SYN-[1], SEMANTIC *a.*] Of a word or phrase: having no meaning outside a context; meaningless in isolation; syncategorematic; opp. *autosemantic*. See also note s.v. AUTOSEMANTIC *a.* (*sb.*).

1929, etc. [see AUTOSEMANTIC *a.* (*sb.*)]. **1954** *Archivum Linguisticum* VI. 18 These 'synsemantic' words 'adsignify' or contribute only to the sense of the whole group to which they belong. **1960** *Analysis* XXI. I. 3 According to Brentano 'Paris' is not a genuine constituent of 'I am thinking-of-Paris'. It is in this context, as he sometimes says, a synsemantic expression. As such, it does not refer to anything. **1965** B. COLLINDER in Bessinger & Creed *Medieval & Linguistic Stud.* 28 The definite article is a synsemantic demonstrative pronoun.

syntactic (sɪnˈtæktɪk), *a.* and *sb.* [ad. mod.L. *syntacticus*, ad. Gr. συντακτικός, f. συντάσσειν: see SYNTAX and -IC.] **A.** *adj.* **1.** = SYNTACTICAL. Also *Comb.*, as *syntactic-semantic* adj.

1807 R. KIRWAN *Logick* IV. i. 531 We learn to ascertain the relation of these different parts to each other, according to the syntactic rules peculiar to each language. **1816** P. S. DUPONCEAU *Let.* 31 July in *Trans. Hist. & Lit. Comm. Amer. Philos. Soc.* (1819) I. 402 As I have given to the Chinese and its kindred dialects, the name of *asyntactic*, the opposite name, *syntactic*, appears to me that which is best suited to the languages of the American Indians. **1848** DICKENS *Dombey* xi, The pursuit of stony-hearted verbs, savage noun-substantives, inflexible syntactic passages. **1852** BLACKIE *Stud. Lang.* 7 The grand fundamental types of verbal flexion, and syntactic dependence. **1902** F. E. CLEMENTS in *Univ. Studies Nebraska* III. 19 Syntactic composition is the union under a single accent of two words, one being merely a modifier of the other and in the case demanded by this relation. **1972** G. LAKOFF in *Language* XLVIII. 291 Anaphora..is a syntactic-semantic phenomenon which can, and must, be specified independently of lexical idiosyncrasies. **1978** *Archivum Linguisticum* IX. 79 We will assume that if such commensurability could be established, we would have strong evidence for the existence of a syntactic-semantic component in our overall grammar, rather than separate syntactic and semantic components.

2. Exhibiting or characterized by syntaxy; ***syntactic foam***, a plastic foam made by introducing small hollow spheres into a liquid matrix which then solidifies.

1955 *Sci. News Let.* 2 Apr. 213/3 Called 'syntactic foam', by its developer, the Bakelite Company of New York, the new lightweight material is produced by bonding microscopic hollow spheres made of phenolic resin together with phenolic, epoxy or polyester resins. **1970** *Adv. Chem. Ser.* XCII. 150 Syntactic foams..consist of a dispersion of small hollow glass spheres in a continuous phase or matrix. **1974** *Petroleum Rev.* XXVIII. 675/1 Syntactic foam blocks attached to the top of the frame produce a slight positive buoyancy. **1975** C. A. HARPER *Handbk. Plastics & Elastomers* VII. 44 Syntactic foams, like syntactic crystalline polymers, are characterized by their high degree of order or structure.

B. as *sb. pl.* (const. *sing.*). *Linguistics.* C. W. Morris's term for that branch of linguistics which is concerned with the formal relations of signs to each other.

1937 [see PRAGMATIC *sb.* 4]. **1938** C. W. MORRIS in *Internat. Encycl. Unified Sci.* I. II. 14 Syntactics is, then, the consideration of signs and sign combinations in so far as they are subject to syntactical rules. **1941** A. TATE in *Southern Rev.* VI. 636 The role of syntactics in the semiotic science remains somewhat obscure; it seems to consist in a number of 'transformation rules'—that is, in formulas by which given expressions in words, numbers, or symbols can be changed into equivalent but formally different expressions. **1945** [see *intra-linguistic* s.v. INTRA- 1]. **1964** E. A. NIDA *Toward Sci. Transl.* iii. 35 While semantics deals with the relationship of symbols to referents, syntactics is concerned with the relationship of symbol to symbol; for the meaning of expressions is not to be found merely in adding up symbols, but also in determining their arrangements, including order and hierarchical structuring. For example, the constituents *black* and *bird*, when occurring in juxtaposition, may have two quite different meanings. **1969** [see PRAGMATIC *sb.* 4].

synˈtactical, *a.* [f. mod.L. *syntacticus*: see prec. and -ICAL. Cf. *syntaxical.*] Belonging or relating to grammatical syntax. Also *transf.* in reference to musical composition (quot. 1597) and logic (see SYNTAX 2 d).

1577 PEACHAM *Gard. Eloquence* Bj, A figure is deuided into Tropes & Schemates, Grammatical, Orthographical, Syntactical. **1597** MORLEY *Introd. Mus.* Annot. ¶j b, Musicke is diuided into two parts, the first may be called Elementarie or rudimental, teaching to know the quality and quantity of notes... The second may be called Syntactical, Poetical, or effective; treating of soundes, concordes, and discords. **1755** JOHNSON *Dict.* Pref., The various syntactical structures occurring in the examples. **1846** M. WILLIAMS *Sansk. Gram.* 29 This absence of syntactical auxiliaries leads to the necessity for eight cases. **1852** BLACKIE *Stud. Lang.* 32 To make a regular study of the syntactical laws of the language. **1891** DRIVER *Introd. Lit. Old Test.* (1892) 504 Instances of singular syntactical usages. **1937** A. SMEATON tr. *Carnap's Logical Syntax of Lang.* 2 The difference between syntactical rules in the narrower sense and the logical rules of deduction is the only difference between formation rules and transformation rules, both of which are completely formulable in syntactical terms. **1954** I. M. COPI *Symbolic Logic* vi. 184 To characterize the criterion as 'purely formal' is to say that it is syntactical rather than semantical. **1978** *Jrnl. Symbolic Logic* XLIII. 511 We need first two syntactical transformations on formulae.

Hence **synˈtactically** *adv.*, in relation to, or according to the rules of, grammatical or logical syntax.

1706 BAILEY (*title*) English and Latin Exercises for school-boys, to translate into Latin syntactically. **1858-9** G. P. MARSH *Engl. Lang.* xiii. (1862) 191 They are not syntactically connected. **1940** W. V. QUINE *Math. Logic* vii. 286 The fact that 'Vbl'.., and 'LFmla' are definable in this syntactical notation is perhaps best expressed..by speaking of them as *syntactically definable*. **1967** *Encycl. Philos.* V. 23/1 Deductive systems for sentential logic..serve to characterize logic syntactically. **1971** G. HUNTER *Metalogic* III. 116 PS is syntactically complete..iff no unprovable schema can be added to it..without inconsistency.

syntactician (sɪntækˈtɪʃən). [f. SYNTACTIC + -IAN: see -ICIAN.] **1.** One versed in syntax; a grammarian who treats of syntax. So **syntacticist** (sɪnˈtæktɪsɪst), in same sense.

1900 GILDERSLEEVE *Syntax Classical Greek* Pref., The syntactician of to-day will find ample opportunity to criticise the arrangement. **1904** *Amer. Jrnl. Philol.* XXV. 355 President Wheeler has not been harder on syntacticians than Piron was on grammarians. **1926** [see *rhythm-deaf* s.v. RHYTHM *sb.* 9 a]. **1935** *Punch* 9 Oct. 406/2, I remind myself that the budgerigar is that spiteful little creature known..as the 'lovebird'. I recommend it to future Latin syntacticians as an example of the *lucus a non lucendo*. **1970** *Eng. Stud.* LI. 52 On the whole, present-day syntacticians tend to pay too little regard to the patterning of paradigmatic variables, focusing their attention on syntactic structure on the basis of the theory of grammaticality. **1982** *N. & Q.* Oct. 386/2, I hope the compilers will find a title to express the importance for syntacticians and others of what it will contain.

†**2.** = SYNTAXIAN. *Obs.*

1774 H. T. BLOUNT *Diary* in *Publ. Cath. Rec. Soc.* (1972) LXIII. 358 On the 9th August Jas. Hart, Syntactician, went to England.

syntacticist (sɪnˈtæktɪsɪst). [f. SYNTACTIC *a.* + -IST.] = SYNTACTICIAN I.

1889 W. G. HALE in *Classical Rev.* III. 168/2 The very phrases comparative grammar and comparative philology are commonly used in a way to leave the syntacticist outcast and alien. **1944** *Mind* LIII. 243 What the syntacticist is interested in is, that..these isomorphs are themselves analytic. **1977** *Daily Tel.* 10 Feb. 12/6 Syntacticists, linguists and psycholinguists are turning greedily to the poetics of fiction in 'Winnie the Pooh' and the psychological processes in the reading of 'Alice'.

syntacto- (sɪnˈtæktəʊ), used as combining form of SYNTACTIC *a.*, as **synˌtacto-seˈmantic** *a.* = *syntactic-semantic* adj. s.v. SYNTACTIC *a.* 1; **synˌtactostyˈlistics** *sb. pl.* (const. *sing.*), the study of the stylistic implications of syntactic variation.

1972 *Archivum Linguisticum* III. 7 In particular, I shall show how an adequate grammar must indicate not only a variety of syntacto-semantic features of the noun (such as humanness and inherent duality), but also features of any numeral preceding the noun phrase and certain morphological features of both nouns and adjectives. **1977** *Canad. Jrnl. Linguistics 1976* XXI. 84 The second and third axes represent an arbitrary division of the syntacto-semantic domain of the signal, the motivation for which is discussed below. **1969** Syntactostylistics [see PHONOSTYLISTICS *sb. pl.*].

syntagm (ˈsɪntæg(ə)m). [ad. mod.L. *syntagma*: see next.] †**1.** = next, 1. *Obs.*

In quots. 1621, 1633, 1675, referring to works entitled *Syntagma* or *Syntagmata*.

1621 BP. MOUNTAGU *Diatribæ* 77 In all his [*sc.* Selden's] Syntagmes, he loueth not to tread or goe in common paths. **1633** AMES *Agst. Cerem.* I. 149 Polanus writt his partitions [i.e. *Partitiones Theologicæ*], when he was a young man, and divine, but his Syntagme was his last work. **1658** PHILLIPS, *Syntagme*, an ordering, disposing, or placing of things together. **1672** MARVELL *Reh. Transp.* I. 7 A bulky Dutch-man..contriving those innumerable Syntagmes of Alphabets. **1673** [R. LEIGH] *Transp. Reh.* 107 This is the Syntagm of Calvin's Divinity, and System of our Authors Policy. **1675** J. SMITH *Chr. Relig. Appeal* IV. 43 A Romance hansomly exprest by Peter Rhenensis, as he is quoted by Mr. Selden in his Syntagme *de aureo vitulo*.

2. *Linguistics* = SYNTAGMA 4. Also *transf.* and *fig.*

1947 R. S. WELLS in *Word* III. 8 A compound sign, i.e. an interrupted sequence of morphemes (no two of which occur simultaneously) is called a syntagm. **1959** W. BASKIN tr. *F. de Saussure's Course in General Linguistics* (1960) II. v. 123 In discourse,..words..are arranged in sequence on the chain of speaking. Combinations supported by linearity are *syntagms*. The syntagm is always composed of two or more consecutive units. **1970** E. LEACH *Lévi-Strauss* iii. 48 The term *syntagm*, as applied to an assemblage of non-verbal signs, corresponds to *sentence* in a verbal language. **1973** D. MATIAS tr. C. Metz in *Screen* Spring/Summer 77 The film-maker at each point in the film..has a choice between a limited number of *basic* combinations..the alternating syntagm, the episodic syntagm, the descriptive syntagm, the 'single shot', [etc.]. **1976** *Times Lit. Suppl.* 19 Nov. 1458/3 The syntagm *il ne va pas* is no longer almost identical with *il ne va un pas*. **1978** 'A. BURGESS' *1985* 99 Separate the sexual act from love, and the language of love is devalued. An aspect of our freedom is our right to debase the language totally, so that its syntagms become mere noise.

‖**syntagma** (sɪnˈtægmə). Pl. **-ata** or **-as.** [mod.L., a. Gr. σύνταγμα, f. συντάσσειν (see SYNTAXIS).]

1. A regular or orderly collection of statements, propositions, doctrines, etc.; a systematically arranged treatise.

1644 MILTON *Areop.* (Arb.) 67 All must be supprest which is not found in their Syntagma. **1825** COLERIDGE *Aids Refl.* vii. 198 The Gospel is not a system of Theology, nor a Syntagma of theoretical propositions and conclusions.

2. *Antiq.* **a.** A body of persons forming a division of the population of a country. **b.** A body of troops forming a division of a phalanx.

1813 PRICHARD *Phys. Hist. Man* vii. §2. 333 Diodorus Siculus tells us, that 'besides the priests and military cast, the state [in Egypt] is divided into three syntagmata,..The Herdsmen... The Agriculturists... The Artisans'. **1856** GROTE *Greece* II. xcii. XII. 81 Among these divisions..is the Syntagma, which contained sixteen Lochi.

3. *Bot.* An aggregate of 'tagmata': see TAGMA.

1885 [see TAGMA].

4. *Linguistics.* [ad. F. *syntagme* (F. de Saussure *a* 1913, *Cours de Linguistique Générale* (1916) II. v. 176).] A syntactic unit comprising two or more linguistic signs or elements. Also *transf.*

1937 J. ORR tr. *Iordan's Introd. Romance Linguistics* iv. 286 A syntagma is composed of at least two units in sequence. **1946** *Word* II. 117 To the best of our knowledge, there are three such ultimate and irreducible signs: the phoneme, the word, and the construction or syntagma. *Ibid.* 118 The *syntagma* is defined as the sign of the relations into which the referents of words, enter. **1967** *Ibid.* XXIII. 380 As all composites are syntagmas, i.e., grammatical entities, they must be explainable from an underlying sentence whose syntactic relations they mirror. **1974** M. TAYLOR *Metz's Film Lang.* p. x, A *syntagma* is, consequently, a unit of actual relationship, while a *paradigm* is a unit of potential relationship. **1979** *Trans. Philol. Soc.* 82 The Latin noun declensions provide more than sufficient illustration of syncretism within word paradigms..with the burden of disambiguating relevant properties then being shifted to the syntagma.

syntagmatic (sɪntægˈmætɪk), *a. Linguistics.* [ad. F. *syntagmatique* (F. de Saussure *a* 1913, *Cours de Linguistique Générale* (1916) II. v. 177).] Of or pertaining to the syntactic relationship between linguistic units. Also *transf.*

1937 J. ORR tr. *Iordan's Introd. Romance Linguistics* iv. 333 To the study of the combinations of linguistic signs..he [*sc.* Sechehaye] gives the name of syntagmatic grammar. **1948** J. R. FIRTH in *Trans. Philol. Soc.* 129 We generalize syllabic structure in a new order of abstraction eliminating the specific paradigmatic consonant and vowel systems as such, and enabling the syntagmatic word structure of syllables.. to be stated systematically. **1959** W. BASKIN tr. *F. de Saussure's Course in General Linguistics* (1960) II. v. 123 The syntagmatic relation is *in praesentia*. It is based on two or more terms that occur in an effective series. **1966** T. BENDOR-SAMUEL in C. E. Bazell *In Memory of J. R. Firth* 37 In the grammatical description, as in the phonological, it is not sufficient to speak of units as comprising a structure of elements arranged in place since there are also syntagmatic features whose domain of relevance extends beyond any of the elements of the structure. **1973** MATIAS & WILLEMEN tr. M. Cegarra in *Screen* Spring/Summer 144 Because to Metz, the organisation of the cinema is 'manifestly syntagmatic'.. his criticism of the montage films is in fact no more than reproaching them for being syntagmatically bad. **1981** *Word 1980* XXXI. 243 A hierarchy of phonology, morphology, syntax, and semantics related to each other by paradigmatic and syntagmatic rules.

Hence **syntagˈmatically** *adv.*

1937 J. ORR tr. *Iordan's Introd. Romance Linguistics* iv. 286 The constituent elements of human language, considered at a particular moment,..are related to each other syntagmatically and associatively. **1951** *Essays & Studies* IV. 126 Throughout his poetry Swinburne lays general constructions alongside each other, syntagmatically parallel collocations are a feature of verse-form and stanza-form. **1961** Y. OLSSON *Syntax Eng. Verb* ii. 27 Both collocation and colligation operate syntagmatically, that is, along the line one-after-another. **1973** [see SYNTAGMATIC *a.*]. **1977** *Word 1972* XXVIII. 261 Examples of the alveolarization of the /t/ in word-initial position could be explained syntagmatically (i.e., it might be attributable to the presence of an alveolar consonant in the preceding word).

syntagmeme (sɪn'tægmiːm). *Linguistics.* [f. SYNTAGM(A + -EME.] In tagmemics, a group of tagmemes of one structural level which represents a tagmeme of a higher level (see also quot. 1964).

1958 K. L. PIKE in *Jrnl. Amer. Linguistics* XXIV. 273/2 We have..abandoned the term grammeme and replaced it with Bloomfield's term 'tagmeme'. It also appears probable that we should replace the term 'uttereme' (for 'utterance-eme') with 'syntagmeme'. **1962** E. F. HADEN et al. *Resonance-Theory for Linguistics* iii. 41 This complex of slot and filler constitutes a syntagmeme. **1964** R. E. LONGACRE *Grammar Discovery Procedures* 17 Syntagmemes of one structural level manifest tagmemes of the next higher level; e.g., words manifest phrase level tagmemes. But a syntagmeme may manifest a tagmeme of another syntagmeme on the same level; e.g., one phrase may occur imbedded within another phrase... On occasion, a syntagmeme of a higher level may manifest a tagmeme of a lower level; e.g. a subordinate clause may occur within a phrase. **1971** *Language* XLVII. 739 Syntagmemes are charted for five levels, according to four features: internal constituents, prosody, nucleus and juncture.

syntax ('sɪntæks). Also 7 **syntaxe.** [ad. F. *syntaxe*, †*sintaxe*, ad. late L. *syntaxis*, a. Gr. σύνταξις SYNTAXIS.]

1. a. Orderly or systematic arrangement of parts or elements; constitution (of body); a connected order or system of things.

1605 BACON *Adv. Learn.* II. xix. §1. 69b, Concerning the Syntax and disposition of studies, that men may know in what order or pursuite to reade. **1661** GLANVILL *Van. Dogm.* xii. 116 They owe no other dependence to the first, then what is common to the whole Syntax of beings. *a* **1676** HALE *Prim. Orig. Man.* II. iv. (1677) 157 Perchance..no Man had ever the same Syntax of Phantasie or Imagination that he had. **1696** EDWARDS *Demonstr. Exist. God* II. 124 This single [argument] from the fabrick and syntax of man's body is sufficient to evince the truth of a Deity. **1959** J. D. EVANS *Malta* ii. 67 The decoration [of certain pottery]..derives its general syntax fairly exactly and its patterns in a more general way from the repertoire of the preceding phases. **1965** *Listener* 9 Dec. 965/2 We have to work to reconcile the shiny shoe with the flat red floor or with the absurd loopy shapes of the legs, or the crushed, pulpy mask of the head. For not only is the syntax of the paint disconnected and inconsistent, but the degree of distortion is too. **1967** G. STEINER *Lang. & Silence* 380 A young East German might come to be more at home, in the syntax of his politics and feelings, in Peking or Albania than in Cologne.

†**b.** Physical connexion, junction. *Obs.*

1615 CROOKE *Body of Man* 595 Their articulation doth not differ from the Syntax or coniunction of other parts.

†**c.** Connexion, congruity, agreement. *Obs.*

1656 S. HOLLAND *Zara* (1719) 123 What Syntax is there betwixt a Helmet and a Cap of Maintenance? **1675** BURTHOGGE *Causa Dei* p. vi, I might display the Syntax, Harmony, Connexion, Concinnity of the Notions I employ.

d. That branch of mathematics which deals with the various arrangements of a number of things, as permutations, combinations, and the like.

1861 SYLVESTER *Coll. Math. Papers* (1908) II. 269 The theory of groups.., standing in the closest relation to the doctrine of combinatorial aggregation, or what for shortness may be termed syntax.

2. *Gram.*, etc. **a.** The arrangement of words (in their appropriate forms) by which their connexion and relation in a sentence are shown. Also, the constructional uses of a word or form or a class of words or forms, or those characteristic of a particular author. **b.** The department of grammar which deals with the established usages of grammatical construction and the rules deduced therefrom: distinguished from *accidence*, which deals with the inflexional forms of words as such.

1613 R. CAWDREY *Table Alph.* (ed. 3), *Syntaxe*, construction and order of words. **1636** B. JONSON *Eng. Gram.* II. i, Syntaxe is the second part of Grammar, that teacheth the Construction of words. *Ibid.* II. ii, The Syntaxe of a Noune, with a Noune, is in number, and gender. *Ibid.* v, The Syntaxe of a Verb with a Noune is in number, and person. **1697** BENTLEY *Phal.* (1699) 407 Neither Sense nor Syntax would allow of that Signification. *a* **1700** EVELYN *Diary* 27 Jan. 1658, He..could make congruous syntax, turne English into Latine, and *vice versa.* **1711** GREENWOOD *Eng. Gram.* 29 The Syntax, or Construction of the Noun, is chiefly perform'd by the Help of certain Words call'd Prepositions. **1755** JOHNSON *Dict.*, *Gram.* a, Grammar, which is the art of using words properly, comprises four parts; Orthography, Etymology, Syntax, and Prosody. **1824** L. MURRAY *Engl. Gram.* (ed. 5) I. 217 The English adjective, having but a very limited syntax. **1861** PALEY *Æschylus, Prometh.* (ed. 2) 38 *note*, Ὅτου..being used as if the syntax were δεῖξαι ὑφ' ὅτου, rather than δεῖξαι τὸ βούλευμα ὑφ' οὗ κ.τ.λ. **1885** GROSART *Nashe's Wks.* VI. p. ix, He writes..with uncultured flabbiness, and with irritating syntax.

c. Name of a class in certain English Roman Catholic schools and colleges, next below that called *poetry* (see POETRY 6).

1629 WADSWORTH *Pilgr.* iii. 13 Father Lacy, the Reader of Poetry, and Master of the Syntax. **1655** in Foley *Rec. Eng. Prov. S. J.* (1878) III. 434, I went to the College of St. Omer, where I made one year's syntax. **1679** [see POETRY 6]. **1713** in B. Ward *Hist. St. Edmund's College* (1893) iv. 58 What we call the Accidence they call Figures, which they divide into two years, one for the lower, the second for the higher, the third for grammar, the fourth for Syntax. **1897** W. WARD *Life Cdl. Wiseman* (ed. 2) I. i. 8 Dr. Newsham.. was Wiseman's Professor [at Ushaw] in Syntax (in 1815), and again in Rhetoric.

d. *transf.* in *Logic.* The order and arrangement of the words or symbols forming a logical sentence; the rules operating in formal systems. (See quots.)

1922 tr. *Wittgenstein's Tractatus* 59 The rules of logical syntax must follow of themselves, if we only know how every single sign signifies. **1937** A. SMEATON tr. *Carnap's Logical Syntax of Lang.* 1 By the logical syntax of a language, we mean the formal theory of the linguistic forms of that language—the systematic statement of the formal rules which govern it together with the development of the consequences which follow from these rules. *Ibid.* 2 Thus we are justified in designating as 'logical syntax' the system which comprises the rules of formation and transformation. **1937**, etc. [see METALOGIC]. **1940** W. V. QUINE *Math. Logic.* vii. 286 Discourse which is 'formal' in this sense, and hence translatable into the notation just now described, is called metamathematics, formal syntax, or briefly syntax. **1955** A. N. PRIOR *Formal Logic* iii. 70 But as it happens—this can be shown from outside the system— no set of axioms and rules for a system containing its own syntax ever *is* 'complete'. **1979** J. A. ROBINSON *Logic: Form & Function* ii. 8 The predicate calculus has a simple, systematic basic *syntax*, whose principal feature is the characterization of the class of expressions that are its *formulas*.

e. *Computing.* In extended use (from sense 2 a) with reference to programming languages.

1958 *Communications Assoc. Computing Machinery* Dec. 11 In the sequel explicit rules—and associated interpretations—will be given describing the syntax of the language. **1980** P. CRESS et al. *Structured Fortran with WATFIV-S* i. 8 WATFIV-S not only compiles the FORTRAN program, but detects errors in syntax while doing so. **1981** R. D. TENNENT *Princ. Programming Languages* ii. 25 An abstract syntax tells us what syntactic structures are available in a language, but does not specify which strings of characters are well-formed program texts, nor their phrase structures.

3. *attrib.* and *Comb.*, as ***syntax diagram, table***; ***syntax-directed*** adj.; **syntax language**, the language used to refer to the syntactical forms of an object language; a metalanguage.

1980 L. V. ATKINSON *Pascal Programming* i. 10 The syntax of a programming language can be conveniently illustrated by 'syntax diagrams'. **1961** *Communications Assoc. Computing Machinery* IV. 51 (*heading*) A syntax directed compiler for ALGOL 60. **1972** J. J. DONOVAN *Systems Programming* vii. 228 A syntax-directed compiler uses a data base containing the syntactical rules of a source language to parse..the source-language input. **1935** Syntax language [see OBJECT LANGUAGE 1]. **1956** A. CHURCH *Introd. Math. Logic* 58 The meta-language used in order to study the logistic system..is called the syntax language. **1961** *Communications Assoc. Computing Machinery* IV. 55/1 The descriptions are added to the syntax tables used for the second phase, which invokes DIAGRAM to output the assembly language program.

Syntaxian (sɪn'tæksɪən). [f. prec. + -IAN.] A member of the Syntax class in a Roman Catholic school.

1705 in *Ushaw Mag.* (1903) Dec. 298 Syntaxians 3.. Grammarians 11. **1837** J. C. FISHER *Diary* ibid. (1904) Dec. 242 The Grand Exams. began. The Poets and Syntaxians. **1904** *Ibid.* Mar. 98 Syntax and Grammar played their match on Nov. 17th... The Syntaxians' forwards were soon in evidence.

syntaxic (sɪn'tæksɪk), *a.* **1.** *Cryst.* [f. SYNTAXIS 3 or SYNTAXY + -IC.] = SYNTAXIAL *a.*

1944 [see SYNTAXIS 3]. **1972** *Acta Crystallogr.* A. XXVIII. 509/1 The syntaxic intergrowths of the rare-earth carbonates.

2. *Psychol.* [f. SYN- + TAX(IS + -IC.] A term orig. used by the American psychiatrist H. S. Sullivan (1892–1949), to designate a mode of experiencing or communicating in which objectivity and the use of consensually validated symbols have replaced subjectivity. Cf. PARATAXIC, PROTOTAXIC *adjs.*

1945 P. MULLAHY in *Psychiatry* VIII. 185/2 Consensually validated symbol activity has more recently been called 'syntaxic' thinking by Sullivan. It involves an appeal to principles which are accepted as true by the hearer. *a* **1948** H. S. SULLIVAN *Interpersonal Theory of Psychiatry* (1955) ii. 28, I shall offer the thesis that these modes are primarily matters of 'inner' elaboration of events. The mode which is easiest to discuss is relatively uncommon—experience in the syntaxic mode. *Ibid.* xi. 183 Syntaxic symbols are best illustrated by words that have been consensually validated. **1969** A. NEEL *Theories of Psychol.* xx. 248 The appearance of the syntaxic or reality-oriented period was greatly aided by acquisition of language skills. **1972** L. SALTZMAN in Freedman & Kaplan *Interpreting Personality* vi. 176 Obviously, the capacity for syntaxic thinking requires comfortable amounts of self-esteem. **1975** *Psychol. Abstr.* LIV. 141/1 Sullivan's theory of syntaxic mode is compared with Peirce's concept of symbolic interaction.

syntaxical (sɪn'tæksɪkəl), *a. rare.* [f. SYNTAX + -ICAL. Cf. F. *syntaxique.*] = SYNTACTICAL.

1586 A. DAY *Engl. Secretorie* II. (1625) 81 Schemes Syntaxicall, are Eclipsis... Aposiopesis..Zeugma.. Syllepsis..Prolepsis [etc.]. **1826** SYD. SMITH *Hamilton's Meth. Teach. Lang.* Wks. 1839 II. 325 The case of the substantive, and the syntaxical arrangement in which it is to be placed.

‖**syn'taxis.** Pl. **syntaxes** (-'tæksiːz). Also 7 **sin-**. [late L., a. Gr. σύνταξις, f. συντάσσειν, f. σύν SYN-¹ + τάσσειν (base τακ-) to arrange. Cf. It. *sintassi*, Sp. *sintaxis*, Pg. *syntaxe.*] †**1.** = SYNTAX 2. *Obs.*

In quot. 1632 jocularly used with implication of SYNTAX sense 1. In quot. 1641 = REGIMEN 3.

1540 PALSGRAVE tr. *Acolastus* E ij b, To shew the Syntaxis and the concordance betwene the wordes gouernynge, and them that be gouerned. *a* **1568** ASCHAM *Scholem.* (Arb.) 25 In learninge farther hys Syntaxis, by mine aduice, he shall not vse the common order. **1632** B. JONSON *Magn. Lady* I. i, To wise And well experienc'd Men, words do not signifie; They have no power, save with dull Grammarians, Whose Souls are nought, but a Syntaxis of them. **1641** MILTON *Animadv.* v. 39 If your meaning be with a violent.. Hyperbaton to transpose the Text, as if the Words lay thus in order, neglect not the gift of Presbytery; this were..to make the word gift..start up to governe the word Presbyterie, as an immediate Syntaxis. **1642** HOWELL *For. Trav.* (Arb.) 20 The French tongue..is a bold and hardy speach, therefore the learner must not be bashfull..in speaking any thing,..let it come forth confidently whither true or false Sintaxis. **1749** FIELDING *Tom Jones* II. iii, A young Gentleman..at the Age of Seventeen was just entered into his Syntaxis.

2. *Geol.* An arrangement of fold axes or mountain ranges showing convergence towards a common point. [tr. G. *schaarung* (E. Suess).]

1909 H. B. C. & W. J. SOLLAS tr. *Suess's Face of Earth* IV. 289 In the direction of the syntaxis, i.e. towards the west, their strike bends back in an arc. **1933** W. H. BUCHER *Deformation of Earth's Crust* iv. 84 The abrupt deflections and the repeated syntaxes of the Alpine system of southern Europe and western Asia. **1952** *Q. Jrnl. Geol. Soc.* CVIII. 23 The Upper Assam valley..terminates in one of the most impressive examples of syntaxis which our fascinating world can offer.

3. *Cryst.* = SYNTAXY.

1944 *Amer. Mineralogist* XXIX. 267 Ungemach..has introduced the term *syntaxie* to describe the coalescence of polyptic substances... The best English equivalent is probably 'syntaxis', the adjective being 'syntaxic'. **1951** *Phil. Mag.* XLII. 1020 The commonly observed coalescence or 'syntaxis'..of various types of carborundum.

syntaxist ('sɪntæksɪst). *rare*$^{-1}$. [f. SYNTAX + -IST.] = SYNTACTICIAN.

a **1834** COLERIDGE *Notes & Lect.* (1849) I. 151 The 'it', quite in the genius of vehement conversation, which a syntaxist explains by ellipses and *subauditurs* in a Greek or Latin classic.

syntaxy ('sɪntæksɪ). *Cryst.* [ad. F. *syntaxie* (H. Ungemach 1935, in *Bull. de la Soc. Française de Minéral.* LVIII. 187): see SYNTAXIS and -Y³.] Crystal growth or intergrowth in which the new material has the same orientation as the parent, although it may differ chemically.

1952 M. I. GOLDMAN in *Mem. Geol. Soc. Amer.* L. 7 Although Royer uses 'epitaxie' to designate continuous crystallographic orientation between added material and its nucleus, etymologically it means merely 'orientation upon'. It is desirable to distinguish between the relation of added crystalline material with the same orientation as the nucleus, for which I propose *syntaxy* and *syntaxial.* **1953** G. & J. D. H. DONNAY in *Amer. Mineralogist* XXXVIII. 939 Ungemach's definition of syntaxic intergrowth seems to be unduly restrictive, as this kind of intergrowth is found to occur also with constituent substances that are chemically different. We therefore propose to abandon the condition of identity of chemical compositions. Henceforth we shall use the term *syntaxy* in this extended meaning. **1973** *Jrnl. Solid State Chem.* VI. 396 Ordered syntaxy and polytypism..give a regular repetition of structural or chemical elements over very long crystalline distances. **1975** *Amer. Mineralogist* LX. 351 Intimate syntaxy between parisite, synchisite, roentgenite, and bastnaesite was quite commonly observed even on a very fine scale.

Hence **syn'taxial** *a.*; **syn'taxially** *adv.*

1952 Syntaxial [see SYNTAXY]. **1958** *Liverpool & Manch. Geol. Jrnl.* II. 15 A mosaic of grains can grow by the deposition of material in lattice-continuity with, or syntaxially with..pre-existing free crystal faces. *Ibid.* 27 The syntaxial rim resembles superficially a cement rim. **1972** H. BLATT et al. *Origin Sedimentary Rocks* xiii. 463 Syntaxial overgrowths are large crystals of calcite that have grown in optical continuity with original single crystal grains.

syntechnic: see SYN-¹.

syntectic (sɪn'tɛktɪk), *a.* [ad. late L. *syntēcticus* consumptive, a. Gr. συντηκτικός liquefying, liquefiable, apt to faint, f. σύν SYN-¹ + τήκειν to melt.]

†**1.** *Path.* Having the quality of melting or dissolving: applied to certain wasting diseases. *Obs.*

1651 WITTIE tr. *Primrose's Pop. Err.* II. 90 Those..doe appeare in malignant and burning feavers, which we call syntecticke feavers, seldome in a consumption and hecticke, in which no such melting doth appeare. **1656** J. SMITH *Pract. Physick* 83 Inflammation of the bowels, whence followeth a Syntectick or melting flux.

2. (See quot.)

1908 R. A. DALY in *Amer. Jrnl. Sci.* July 19 The sunken blocks must be dissolved in the depths of the original fluid, magmatic body, with the formation of a 'syntectic', secondary magma. [*Note.*] This name..for a magma rendered compound by assimilation or by the mixture of melts, has been proposed by F. Loewinson-Lessing.

So †**syntectical** *a. rare*$^{-0}$.

1656 BLOUNT *Glossogr.*, *Syntectical*..that sounds [= swoons] often, that is weak or brought low.

syntectonic to **syntepalous:** see SYN-¹.

‖**synteresis** (sɪntɪ'riːsɪs). Pl. **-reses** (-'riːsiːz). [med.L. *syntērēsis* (Thomas Aquinas), a. Gr. συντήρησις careful guarding or watching, preservation, 'scintilla conscientiæ' (Jerome), n. of action f. συντηρεῖν to keep, guard, or observe closely, f. σύν SYN-^{1} + τηρεῖν to guard, keep. Cf. SYNDERESIS.]

1. *Theol.* A name for that function or department of conscience which serves as a guide for conduct; conscience as directive of one's actions: distinguished from SYNEIDESIS. Now *Hist.*

1594 T. B. *La Primaud. Fr. Acad.* II. 576 Although sinne hath greatly troubled the minde.. still there remayned in it some sparkles of that light of the knowledge of God, and of good and euil, which is naturally in men... This remnant that yet remayneth is commonly called by the Diuines *Synteresis.* **1611** W. SCLATER *Key* (1629) 122 A great decay of those naturall syntereses, that is, principles of direction for Morall actions. **1620** R. CARPENTER *Conscionable Christian* (1623) B j b, The Synteresis or treasury of morall principles. **1637** NABBES *Microcosm.* v, Its Synteresis, Or purer part, is th' instigation Of will to good and honest things. *a* **1718** PENN *Lib. Consc.* v. Wks. 1726 I. 453 That Great Synteresis, so much renowned by Philosophers and Civilians, learns Mankind, To do as they would be done to. **1911** E. UNDERHILL *Mysticism* I. iii. 64 The divine nucleus, the point of contact between man's life and the divine life.. has been given many names... Sometimes it is called the Synteresis, the keeper or preserver of his being.

†**b.** Sense of guilt, remorse. (Cf. SYNDERESIS b.)

1650 *Five Philos. Quest. Answ.* v. 1 He whose conscience is tainted with the synteresis of the fact, is troubled in such sort that.. he often bewrayes his owne guiltinesse.

2. *Med.* Prophylactic or preventive treatment. (Probably only a book-term.)

1848 DUNGLISON *Med. Lex.* **1864** WEBSTER.

So †**synteresy** (in 7 -ie). *rare*$^{-0}$.

1616 BULLOKAR *Eng. Expos.*, *Synteresie*, the inward conscience: or a naturall qualitie ingrafted in the soule, which inwardly informeth a man, whether he do well or ill. **1658** PHILLIPS, *Synteresie* (Gr.), a remorce, or sting of conscience.

†**synteretic**, *a.* *Obs.* *rare*$^{-0}$. [ad. med.L. *syntērēticus*, a. Gr. συντηρητικός preservative, f. συντηρεῖν: see prec. and -IC.] (See quot.) So †**synteretics** *sb. pl.* (*rare*$^{-0}$).

[**1684** tr. *Blancard's Phys. Dict.* (1693), *Synteretica*, that part of Physick which gives Rules for the Preservation of Health.] **1704** J. HARRIS *Lex. Techn.* I, *Synteretick* Medicines. **1706** PHILLIPS (ed. Kersey), *Synteretica* or *Syntereticks*.

syntexis (sɪnˈtɛksɪs). *Petrol.* [a. Gr. σύντηξις, f. συντήκειν to fuse together, f. τήκειν to melt: see SYN-^{1}.] The alteration of magma by the melting or assimilation of another rock.

1911 F. LOEWINSON-LESSING in *Geol. Mag.* VIII. 295 When the re-melted portion of the crust is composed of different rocks, eruptive, or sedimentary,.. the process is rather a 'syntexis', as I have called it, an assimilation which is followed by liquation and differentiation. **1932** F. F. GROUT *Petrogr. & Petrol.* III. 230 Syntexis has been appealed to in explaining how the more siliceous and the more alkalic rock clans can be derived from primary basaltic magma. **1966** *McGraw-Hill Encycl. Sci. & Technol.* X. 84/1 In some instances such endomorphic effects are sufficiently intensive to result in modification of the composition of the magma (syntexis).

synth (sɪnθ), colloq. abbrev. of SYNTHESIZER 2 (in sense of musical instrument).

1976 *Liverpool Echo* 24 Nov. 5/4 (Advt.), Crumar String Synth, only one year old, perfect working order, cost nearly £500, accept £270 o.n.o. **1977** *Sounds* 9 July 31/6 They range from a scat slant on 'I Got The Music In Me' through Inter City Disco 'Touch Me Up' to the title cut—a seven minute mutha with heavy southern overtones; brassy, rather stringy, not a synth in sight. **1983** *Yellow Advertiser* (Basildon) 4 Mar. 14/3 Singer-songwriters or synth bands.

synthalin (ˈsɪnθəlɪn). *Pharm.* [a. G. *synthalin* (E. Frank et al. 1926, in *Klin. Wochenschr.* 5 Nov. 2101/1), f. *synth-etisch* SYNTHETIC *a.* + *-a-* + *insu-lin* INSULIN.] A synthetic but toxic aliphatic diguanidine which has the hypoglycæmic effect of insulin when taken orally; decamethylene-diguanidine, $H_2N{\cdot}C(NH){\cdot}NH{\cdot}(CH_2)_{10}{\cdot}NH{\cdot}C(NH){\cdot}NH_2$; also called *synthalin A*; *synthalin B*, an analogous compound in which $-(CH_2)_{10}-$ is replaced by $-(CH_2)_{12}-$.

1927 *Chem. Abstr.* XXI. 772 To produce a molecule of min. toxicity and max. insulin activity, further changes were made in the mol... which resulted finally in a deriv. that is called Synthalin. **1936** HILL & HOWITT *Insulin* ix. 190 The decided differences between the action of both synthalin and synthalin-B and insulin render even these substances doubtful as effective substitutes for the hormone. **1952**, **1961** [see DIGUANIDINE]. **1980** J. CROSSLAND *Lewis's Pharmacol.* (ed. 5) lvi. 878/1 In the early 1920's.. it was found that a number of aliphatic diguanidines such as the Synthalins A and B.. produced hypoglycaemia in man.

synthase (ˈsɪnθeɪz). *Biochem.* [f. SYNTH(ESIS + -ASE.] Any enzyme that catalyses the addition of a group to carbon atoms joined by a double bond, or the converse reaction; also, a synthetase.

1954 COHEN & HIRSCH in *Jrnl. Bacteriol.* LXVII. 182/2 This paper describes an enzyme system synthesizing threonine from homoserine; we have called it threonine synthase. **1961** *Rep. Commission on Enzymes* v. 37 Enzymes removing groups from substrates non-hydrolytically, leaving double bonds (or adding groups to double bonds) will be called 'lyases'... 'Synthetase' will not be used for any enzymes in this class; where it has been customary, 'synthase' will be used instead. **1976** *Ann. Rev. Microbiol.* XXX. 212 An alternate view is that cystspecific RNA synthesis during encystment is not necessary for the formation of cellulose synthase. **1979** *Science* 7 Dec. 1149/3 The ATP synthase is a chemiosmotic membrane-located reversible ATPase.

syntheme (ˈsɪnθiːm). [ad. late L. *synthēma* watchword, permit, a. Gr. σύνθημα collection, connexion, watchword, token, f. συντιθέναι to put together, f. σύν SYN-^{1} + τιθέναι (root θε-) to place.]

†**1.** (See quot.) *Obs.* *rare*$^{-0}$.

1658 PHILLIPS, *Syntheme*, a watch-word; also an intricate sentence; also the same as *Diploma.* [**1904** W. M. RAMSAY in *Expositor* June 421 The Synthêma then was a symbol always with him which spoke direct to him; it was a pledge of success from the god who gave it, and thus filled him with god-given confidence.]

2. *Math.* A system of groups of elements, each of the groups being formed of a certain number of elements, so that each occurs exactly a given number of times among all the groups.

1844 SYLVESTER *Coll. Math. Papers* (1904) I. 91 Let us agree to denote by the word syntheme any aggregate of combinations in which all the monads of a given system appear once and once only... Let us begin with considering the case of duad synthemes. **1879** —— in *Amer. Jrnl. Math.* II. 94.

synthermal: see SYN-^{1}.

synthesis (ˈsɪnθɪsɪs). Pl. **syntheses** (-siːz). [a. L. *synthesis* collection, set or suit, composition (of a medicament), garment (sense 7), hyperbaton, a. Gr. σύνθεσις composition, logical and mathematical synthesis, f. συντιθέναι (see SYNTHEME). In F. *synthèse*, It. *sintesi*, Sp. *sintesis*, Pg. *synthese*, *synthesis*, G. *synthese*.]

1. *Logic, Philos.*, etc. **a.** The action of proceeding in thought from causes to effects, or from laws or principles to their consequences. (Opposed to ANALYSIS 8.)

1611 CORYAT *Crudities* 432 A Sciographie of sacred Theologie according to the three formes of methode, synthesis, analysis, and definition. **1620** [see SYNTHETICAL 1]. **1656** tr. *Hobbes' Elem. Philos.* (1839) 312 Synthesis is ratiocination from the first causes of the construction, continued through all the middle causes till we come to the thing itself which is constructed or generated. **1702** RALPHSON *Math. Dict.* 27 Synthesis or Composition is the Art of searching the Truth or Demonstration, the Possibility or Impossibility of a Proposition, by reasons drawn from Principles, that is by Propositions which demonstrate one another, beginning from the most simple, and so going on to more general and compounded ones,.. till at length you arrive to the last Proposition designed, or Conclusion which is the thing to be demonstrated. **1704** NEWTON *Optics* (1721) 380 The Synthesis consists in assuming the Causes discover'd, and establish'd as Principles, and by them explaining the Phænomena proceeding from them. **1911** CASE in *Encycl. Brit.* XVI. 892/1 Deduction is analysis when it is regressive from consequence to real ground... Deduction is synthesis when it is progressive from real ground to consequence.

[Cf. SIR W. HAMILTON in *Edin. Rev.* (1833) LVII. 236 *note*, 'In one respect,' says Aristotle, 'the Genus is called a part of the Species; in another, the Species a part of the Genus.' (Metaph. L. v. c. 25.) In like manner, the same method, viewed in different relations, may be styled either Analysis or Synthesis. This, however, has not been acknowledged; nor has it even attracted notice, that different logicians and philosophers, though severally applying the terms only in a single sense, are still at cross purposes with each other. One calls Synthesis, what another calls Analysis; and this both in ancient and modern times.]

b. In philosophical systems influenced by Hegelian ideas, the final stage of a triadic progression in which an idea is proposed, then negated, and finally transcended by a new idea that resolves the conflict between the first and its negation.

The process is often represented as that of thesis, antithesis, and synthesis, although the terms are not Hegel's. The term is freq. used in relation to the political philosophy of Marx, where this process is seen as exemplified in the history of man's social development (see *dialectical materialism* s.v. DIALECTICAL *a.* 1 b).

1896 J. MCTAGGART *Stud. in Hegelian Dialectic* i. 2 This idea of the synthesis of opposites is perhaps the most characteristic in the whole of Hegel's system. It is certainly one of the most difficult to explain. **1904** N. I. STONE tr. *Marx's Introd. Critique Pol. Econ.* 288 The two systems by mutually modifying each other may result in something new, a synthesis (which partly resulted from the Germanic conquests). In all of these conquests the method of production.. determines the nature of the new distribution which comes into play. **1936** S. HOOK *From Hegel to Marx* i. 68 A dialectical synthesis is all this and more. Thesis and antithesis are resolved in such a way that.. aspects of each are retained or *conserved* in every new whole or situation; and are reinterpreted or *elevated*. *Ibid.*, For Marx.. the manner of synthesis depends.. upon the shifts and realignments of human interests in time. **1958** P. HEATH tr. *Wetter's Dialectical Materialism* I. i. 4 This third phase then figures in turn as the first step in a new dialectical process, leading to a new synthesis. **1963** F. J. COPLESTON *Hist. Philos.* VII. ix. 177 We have used the word 'synthesis' for the moment of identity-in-difference in the dialectical advance. But.. the terms 'thesis', 'antithesis' and 'synthesis' are more characteristic of Fichte than of Hegel. **1978** P. S. FALLA tr. *Kolakowski's Main Currents Marxism* I. vii. 152 As private property develops it necessarily creates its own antagonist; this negative force is itself dehumanized, and as its dehumanization progresses it becomes the precondition of a synthesis that will abolish the existing opposition together with both its terms.

†**2.** *Gram.* A figure by which a sentence is constructed according to the sense, in violation of strict syntax. *Obs.* (So It. *sintesi.*)

Two kinds were distinguished, *synthesis generis* and *synthesis numeri.*

1612 BRINSLEY *Posing of the Parts* (1615) 44 b, Names of heathenish Gods, men, flouds, moneths, winds [are masculine]. *margin, Albula pota Deo; aqua* is vnderstood by Synthesis. **1657** J. SMITH *Myst. Rhet.* 197 Synthesis.. is a construction made for significations sake, or a speech congruous in sense, not in voyce. **1678** PHILLIPS (ed. 4), *Synthesis*,.. a figure of construction, wherein a noun Collective singular [is] joyned to a Verb plural [etc.]. **1704** J. HARRIS *Lex. Techn.* I.

3. *Surg.* (See quots.) *rare*$^{-0}$.

1706 PHILLIPS (ed. Kersey), *Synthesis*... In Surgery.. that Method whereby the divided Parts are re-united, as in Wounds. **1848** DUNGLISON *Med. Lex.* (ed. 7), *Synthesis of continuity* means the union of the edges of a wound, or the approximation of the extremities of a fractured bone. *Synthesis of contiguity* is the reduction of displaced organs; as in cases of hernia and luxations.

4. a. *Chem.* Formation of a compound by combination of its elements or constituents; esp. applied to artificial production in this way of organic compounds formerly obtained by extraction from natural products. (Opposed to ANALYSIS 3.)

1733 P. SHAW *Chem. Lect.* ix. (1755) 179 We have seen that.. a true Resolution and Recomposition are practicable; and as Chemistry improves, the Business of Analysis and Synthesis must likewise improve. **1859** J. A. WANKLYN in *Proc. Roy. Soc.* X. 4 On the synthesis of acetic acid. **1869** ROSCOE *Elem. Chem.* 299 Alcohol can also be prepared from its elements by synthesis. **1876** tr. *Schützenberger's Ferment.* 6 M. Berthelot.. made the first successful attempt to perform organic syntheses. **1880** *Med. Temp. Jrnl.* 62 The protoplasm of those cells whose function lies in chemical synthesis.

b. *Physics.* Production of white or other compound light by combination of its constituent colours, or of a complex musical sound by combination of its component simple tones. (Cf. ANALYSIS 4.)

1869 TYNDALL *Notes Lect. Light* §263 In reblending the constituent colours, so as to produce the original, we illustrate, by synthesis, the composition of white light. **1879** PRESCOTT *Sp. Telephone* 51 Helmholtz had not only analyzed the vowel sounds into their constituent musical elements, but had actually performed the synthesis of them.

5. In the philosophy of Kant, the action of the understanding in combining and unifying the isolated data of sensation into a cognizable whole.

1817 COLERIDGE *Biog. Lit.* xii. (1907) I. 187 The whole synthesis of our intelligence is first formed in and through the self-consciousness. **1819** J. RICHARDSON *Kant's Logic* Introd. 87 That sort of distinctness, which arises, not by the analysis, but by the synthesis of the marks, is synthetic distinctness. *Ibid.* 88 The making of objects distinct belongs to the synthesis, the making of conceptions distinct, to the analysis. **1839** *Penny Cycl.* XIII. 175/2 Experience proves the possibility of the synthesis of the predicate 'heavy', with the subject 'body'; for these two notions, although neither is contained in the other, are nevertheless parts of a whole, or of experience. **1855** MEIKLEJOHN tr. *Kant's Crit. Pure Reason* 80 But the conception of conjunction includes, besides the conception of the manifold and the synthesis of it, that of the unity of it also.

6. a. In wider philosophical use and *gen.* The putting together of parts or elements so as to make up a complex whole; the combination of immaterial or abstract things, or of elements into an ideal or abstract whole. (Opposed to ANALYSIS 1.) Also, the state of being put so together.

1833 MRS. BROWNING *Prometh. Bound* 534, I.. devised for them Number, the inducer of philosophies, The synthesis of Letters, and [etc.]. *a* **1836** COLERIDGE in *Lit. Rem.* (1838) III. 208 The happiest *synthesis* of the divine, the scholar, and the gentleman was.. exhibited in him. **1836–7** SIR W. HAMILTON *Metaph.* vi. (1877) I. 100 By synthesis.. I view the parts in relation to each other, and finally to the whole..; I reconstruct them. **1842** MRS. BROWNING *Grk. Chr. Poets* Poet. Wks. (1904) 640/2 Disclosing from the analysis of the visible things the synthesis or unity of the ideal. **1855** BROWNING *Cleon* 94 Mankind, made up of all the single men,—In such a synthesis the labour ends. **1855** SPENCER *Princ. Psychol.* II. xxi. 302 To remember that what in the infant is an elaborate synthesis, afterwards becomes an instantaneous.. cognition. **1864** BOWEN *Logic* i. 20 The synthesis of their common Elements into one Concept. **1887** G. T. LADD *Elem. Physiol. Psychol.* II. vi. 388 *note*, The word 'synthesis' for this mental activity is employed and defended by Wundt.. who.. objects to the word 'association'. [For preceding context see SYNTHETIC *a.* 5 a.]

b. A body of things put together; a complex whole made up of a number of parts or elements united.

1865 LECKY *Ration.* (1878) I. 168 A system which would unite in one sublime synthesis all the past forms of human belief. **1870** J. H. NEWMAN *Gram. Assent* I. iii. 31 We fancy that we are doing justice to individual men and things by making them a mere synthesis of qualities. **1882** FARRAR *Early Chr.* II. 100 The Christian life is the synthesis of these Divine graces.

c. *Philol.* Synthetic formation or construction.

1869 FARRAR *Fam. Speech* ii. (1870) 62 The immense victory which has been achieved by the Aryan race, in adopting inflectional synthesis as the basis of their grammatical structure.

7. *Rom. Antiq.* A loose flowing robe, white or bright-coloured, worn at meals and festivities.

1606 HOLLAND *Sueton.* 207 He ware a dainty and effeminate pied garment called Synthesis. **1622** S. WARD *Life of Faith in Death* (1627) 109 At feasts great persons were wont to change their guests ordinary clothes with a white Synthesis. **1891** FARRAR *Darkn. & Dawn* ix, Nero..was dressed in a loose *synthesis*—a dress of light green, unconfined by any girdle.

8. Special Comb.: **synthesis gas**, a gas used as a feedstock in the industrial synthesis of a chemical, *esp.* a mixture of hydrogen and carbon monoxide.

1941 *Thorpe's Dict. Appl. Chem.* (ed. 4) V. 503/1 Synthesis Gas.—There is required for the synthesis of methanol or the Fischer synthesis of hydrocarbons, a gas in which the ratio of carbon monoxide to hydrogen is 1:2. The ratio of CO/H_2 in normal blue water-gas is 1:1·25. **1965** M. SITTIG *Nitrogen in Industry* ii. 31 Synthesis gas, as the term is used here, is the gaseous mixture of one part nitrogen and three parts hydrogen used as a feed material for ammonia manufacture. **1972** *Sci. Amer.* Oct. 28/1 Lurgi has built more than 50 units to provide town gas (for domestic use) or synthesis gas (for making gasoline). **1980** *Prospects for Petrochemicals in W. Europe* (Shell Internat. Petroleum Co.) 8 A more speculative, but nonetheless plausible, prospect..would be the development of a petrochemicals industry based on synthesis gas.

synthesist ('sɪnθɪsɪst). [f. next: see -IST.] One who uses synthesis, or proceeds by a synthetic method. (Opposed to *analyst.*)

1863 J. G. BAKER *N. Yorksh.* 179 The so-called analysts and synthesists of descriptive zoology. **1864** HAMERTON in *Fine Arts Q. Rev.* May 238 Synthesists find continual pleasure in observing the relations of things, but from their largeness of range they constantly miss minute truths, nor do they ever see anything so vividly as the analysts see that which they have analysed.

synthesize ('sɪnθɪsaɪz), *v.* [f. SYNTHES(IS + -IZE. The correct form is SYNTHETIZE.] *trans.* To make a synthesis of; to put together or combine into a complex whole; to make up by combination of parts or elements. Also *absol.* (Opposed to ANALYSE.)

1830 *Fraser's Mag.* II. 393 To analyze is a far easier task than to synthesize. **1851** MRS. BROWNING *Casa Guidi Wind.* I. 813 Soon this leader..will..build the golden pipes and synthesize This people-organ for a holy strain. **1873** SYMONDS *Grk. Poets* i. 9 That Homer had no predecessors, ..no well-digested body of myths to synthesize, is an absurd hypothesis. **1874** MIVART in *Contemp. Rev.* Oct. 793 A Philosophy which as a complement unites in one all other systems, will harmonize with a Religion which as a complement synthesises all other Religions. **1889**—— *Truth* 157 Movements may be synthesized without our will.

b. *Chem.* To produce (a compound, esp. an organic compound) by synthesis.

1865 [see *synthesized* below]. **1897** *Allbutt's Syst. Med.* IV. 316 The kidney is capable of synthesising complex organic substances.

Hence '**synthesized** (-aɪzd) *ppl. a.*, '**synthesizing** *vbl. sb.* and *ppl. a.*

1830 *Fraser's Mag.* II. 393 Experience..is nothing but a continual synthesizing of apprehensions. **1865** *Reader* 8 July 31 The synthesized acids of the lactic series. **1878** T. SINCLAIR *Mount* 30 The synthesising spirit of infinite love in chosen souls alone can create.

synthesizer ('sɪnθɪsaɪzə(r)). [f. prec. + ER[1].]

1. One who or that which synthesizes.

1869 *Contemp. Rev.* X. 287 The competent synthesizer, designer,..theorist. **1980** *Sci. Amer.* Apr. 27/1 The fibrous texture of jade may daunt the synthesizers.

2. *spec.* in *Electronics*, one of various types of instrument for generating and combining signals of different frequencies; esp. a computerized instrument used to create music electronically.

1909 *Cent. Dict.* Supp., *Synthesizer*, in acoustics, an instrument for the production of complex tones of predetermined composition. **1939** H. DUDLEY *U.S. Patent 2,151,091* 21 Mar. 13/2 Control currents are then passed to the speech synthesizer. *Ibid.*, In the synthesizer described in detail above, the element equivalent to the vocal system is entirely electrical. **1943** H. J. FINDEN in *Jrnl. Inst. Electr. Engineers* XC. III. 165 (*heading*) The frequency synthesizer. *Ibid.* 167/2 There is a demand for a precise frequency generator which will give any desired frequency with a pure output. The frequency synthesizer is an attempt to realise this. **1947** *Jrnl. Appl. Physics* July 601 An electronic synthesizer is described for determination of atomic positions in crystals. **1957** *Sat. Rev.* (U.S.) 26 Jan. 56/2 The American school has not yet, so far as I know, made use of the RCA Electronic Music Synthesizer. *Ibid.* 56/3 The perforated tape operates the music synthesizer in much the same way that a music roll 'plays' a player piano. **1958** E. FISCHER-JØRGENSEN in Saporta & Bastian *Psycholinguistics* (1961) 117/2 Of particular interest to the linguist are the various speech *synthesizers* which have been built recently. **1965** *Wireless World* July 62 (Advt.), The new range of MST transistorized receivers uses synthesizers to provide accurate selection of 250,000 frequencies. **1969**, etc. [see MOOG]. **1973** *Melody Maker* 25 Aug. 27 Baker (electronics, bass) came to London from Australia. He's been working with electronics for ten years, concentrating on solo synthesiser performances. **1975** *New Yorker* 5 May 45/1 The synthesizer can produce a ceaseless kaleidoscope of shapes and colors on the screen. **1981** *Oxford Times* 20 Feb. 13/1 He plays acoustic piano as well as imitating steel drums on his synthesiser.

synthetase ('sɪnθəteɪz). *Biochem.* [f. SYNTHET(IC *a.* + -ASE.] = LIGASE; also, a synthase.

1947 COHEN & MCGILVERY in *Jrnl. Biol. Chem.* CLXXI. 132 We wish to suggest the term 'synthetase' for those enzymes creating a new molecule by the elimination of water between two substrate molecules, excluding the formation of phosphote esters and anhydrides. **1961** [see LIGASE]. **1961** [see SYNTHASE]. **1972** *Nature* 15 Dec. 377/1 Aspirin and aspirin-like drugs inhibit..the synthetase which synthesizes prostaglandins from the unsaturated fatty acid, arachidonic acid. **1979** *Sci. Amer.* May 78/2 Interferon also induces the manufacture of a second enzyme, a synthetase that catalyzes the polymerization of adenine nucleotides into a long chain of adenine units called 2,5-oligoadenylic acid.

synthete ('sɪnθiːt). *rare*$^{-1}$. [ad. Gr. συνθέτης composer, agent-n. f. συντιθέναι: see SYNTHEME.] = SYNTHETIST.

1896 *Longm. Mag.* Mar. 473 He was a synthete rather than an analyst.

synthetic (sɪn'θɛtɪk), *a.* and *sb.* [ad. F. *synthétique* (1652 in Hatz.-Darm.), or mod.L. *syntheticus*, ad. Gr. συνθετικός, f. συνθετός, ppl. adj. of συντιθέναι (see SYNTHEME). Cf. It. *sintetico*, etc., G. *synthetisch.*] (In most senses opposed to ANALYTIC.)

A. *adj.* **1.** *Logic, Philos.*, etc. Proceeding from causes or general principles to consequences or particular instances; deductive: cf. SYNTHESIS 1.

1697 tr. *Burgersdicius' Logick* II. 135 Synthetic is that which proceeds from the most simple Principles, to those things which are compounded of those Principles. *Ibid.* 136 The Sciences Theoretical, such as Physicks, Metaphysicks, Mathematicks, &c. are disposed in Synthetick Method. **1798** HUTTON *Course Math.* (1827) I. 3 Synthesis, or the Synthetic Method, is the searching out truth, by first laying down some simple and easy principles, and then pursuing the consequences flowing from them till we arrive at the conclusion. **1832** A. JOHNSON tr. *Tennemann's Man. Hist. Philos.* 33 [Philosophy] proceeds (on general topics) either from principles to consequences (the synthetic order); or from consequences to principles (the analytic order). *a* **1862** BUCKLE *Civiliz.* (1864) II vi. 572 By reasoning from the twofold ideas of action and of sympathy, Hunter constructed the deductive or synthetic part of his pathology. **1869** J. MARTINEAU *Ess.* II. 184 [He] descends into phenomena by Newton's synthetic method.

2. a. *Chem.* Pertaining to or involving synthesis; of organic compounds, produced by artificial synthesis: see SYNTHESIS 4.

1753 CHAMBERS *Cycl. Supp.* **1796** PEARSON in *Phil. Trans.* LXXXVI. 430 It appears from the synthetic experiments that the grain becomes finer as the proportion of tin is increased. **1800** HENRY *Epit. Chem.* (1808) 155 A decisive synthetic proof of the nature of this acid. **1857** MILLER *Elem. Chem., Org.* (1862) i. §3. 69 Synthetic Production of Organic Compounds. **1899** *Allbutt's Syst. Med.* VI. 491 The chromatin (nuclein) in some manner regulates the synthetic metabolism of the cell.

b. Of a substance: made by chemical synthesis in imitation of a natural product (cf. SYN-[2]). Also, esp. of a man-made fibre or fabric: made from synthetic materials rather than natural ones (cf. MAN-MADE *a.*).

1874 *Chem. News* 12 June 265/1 (*heading*) Synthetic cymol obtained from normal bromide of propyl and crystalline bromtoluol. **1907** *Chem. Abstr.* I. 1179 (*heading*) Synthetic resins. **1907** *Nature* 25 Apr. 614/2 Since 'synthetic' indigo was put upon the market in 1897, some uncertainty has existed regarding its tinctorial value as compared with the natural dyestuff. **1909**, etc. [see RESIN *sb.* 3]. **1932** B. HEDWORTH *Foolish Pelican* II. iv. 136 She had discovered.. that synthetic stockings wore better than pure silk. **1941** [see RUBBER *sb.*[1] 11 a]. **1946** A. J. HALL *Stand. Handbk. Textiles* i. 66 The du Pont company..commenced the manufacture of a synthetic fibre which has since become known..as nylon. **1955** J. G. DAVIS *Dict. Dairying* (ed. 2) 1005 Synthetic or imitation cream. **1955**, **1965** [see MAN-MADE *a.*]. **1973** *Materials & Technol.* VI. 485 The cleaning of man-made fibres is usually a relatively simple operation which involves a treatment with a mild soap or a synthetic detergent solution. **1983** *Sci. Amer.* Apr. 73/3 In the 19th century, before the boom in organic chemistry that followed the discovery of synthetic dyes, many prominent chemists had undertaken analyses of inorganic natural substances.

c. *fig.* Artificial, imitation, invented.

1930 *Daily Express* 16 Oct. 5/5 With the synthetic idiot, Harpo, you must have a vein of the ridiculous in your laughter gland if boredom is to be kept at bay. **1932** *Sun* (Baltimore) 29 Aug. 8/2 A printing press upon which were struck off bogus service certificates for 'synthetic veterans'. **1934** *Amer. Speech* IX. 101/2 Even when launched in a preliminary fashion, with say fifty or a hundred users, the synthetic language will not grow of itself. **1948** 'N. SHUTE' *No Highway* iv. 92 The synthetic, phoney film business. **1948** *Newsweek* 10 May 34/2 He has been in London long enough to achieve a synthetic British appearance. **1949** *Hansard Commons* 12 Dec. 2417, I have seldom heard such an outburst of indignation... It seemed to me a little synthetic. **1976** E. FROMM *To have or to Be?* (1979) II. iv. 92 The learned, synthetic smile of the marketplace.

d. *Aeronaut.* Of training, exercises, etc.: simulating on the ground what is performed in the air; also *ellipt.* Similarly of equipment used in such training.

1942 *Tee Emm* (Air Ministry) II. 93 All sorts of gadgets and synthetic devices are used..from the cine-film assessor ..to the Fisher trainer. **1944** *Horizon* Jan. 49 We are now in the middle of 'synthetic'—i.e. doing things on the ground as they will be done from the air. **1948** *Hansard Commons* 15 Mar. 1808 If people can go for an hour or two in the evenings for synthetic training. **1949** *Aircraft Engin.* Apr. 122/2 There is ample mathematical and electric knowledge in existence to-day to construct 'synthetic aircraft' to simulate the flight of any proposed aircraft from the design data. **1956** *U.S. Air Force Dict.* 504/2 *Synthetic*,..artificial or simulated, as in *synthetic combat mission, synthetic training device*, etc. **1976** R. HURST *Pilot Error* 260 Complementary process of behavioural engineering and the selection and training of pilots..Performance prediction. Synthetic flight training. Performance assessment.

†**3.** Pertaining to grammatical construction. *Obs. rare.*

[Cf. **1589** PUTTENHAM *Engl. Poesie* III. viii. (Arb.) 168 That it [*sc.* speech] should cary an orderly and good construction, which they [*sc.* 'the first learned artificers of language'] called Synthesis.]

1778 BP. LOWTH *Transl. Isaiah* Prelim. Diss. p. xxi, The Third sort of Parallels [in Hebrew poetry] I call Synthetic or Constructive: where the Parallelism consists only in the similar form of Construction.

4. In the philosophy of Kant, (*a*) applied to judgements which add to the subject attributes not directly implied in it; (*b*) pertaining to the synthesis of the manifold.

1819 J. RICHARDSON *Kant's Logic* Introd. 80 Analytic or synthetic marks. Those are partial conceptions of the actual conception.., these, partial ones of the merely possible whole conception. **1836** J. W. SEMPLE *Kant's Metaphysic of Ethic* p. lxvii, The synthetic unity of consciousness. **1839** *Penny Cycl.* XIII. 175/2 All speculative *à priori* knowledge ultimately rests upon such synthetic or extending judgments; for though the analytical are highly important and requisite for science, still their importance is mainly derived from their being indispensable to a wide and legitimate synthesis, whereby alone a new acquisition in science can be made. *Ibid.* 177/2 The synthetic activity of the judgment. **1856** FERRIER *Inst. Metaph.* (ed. 2) 25 *note.*

5. a. Of, pertaining to, consisting in, or involving synthesis, or combination of parts into a whole; constructive.

In quots. *a* 1702 and 1798 applied to the logical method properly called *analytical* (the opposite of sense 1); cf. quot. 1833.

a **1702** HOOKE *Disc. Earthquakes* Posth. Wks. (1705) 330 The methods of attaining this end may be two; either the Analytic or the Synthetick. The first is proceeding from the Causes to the Effects. The second, from the Effects to the Causes. **1773** HORSLEY in *Phil. Trans.* LXIV. 280 Both these theorems are so easily derived from the preceeding analysis of the problem, that it is needless to add the synthetic demonstration. **1798** EDGEWORTH *Pract. Educ.* (1811) I. 146 There are two methods of teaching; one which ascends from particular facts to general principles, the other which descends from the general principles to particular facts; one which builds up, another which takes to pieces; the synthetic and the analytic method. *c* **1817** FUSELI in *Lect. Paint.* x. (1848) 523 Analytic or synthetic: from the whole to the parts, or from the parts to the whole. **1833** SIR W. HAMILTON in *Edin. Rev.* LVII. 236 Some..call this mode of hunting up the essence the Analytic; others again, regarding the genus as the whole, the species and individuals as the parts, style it the Compositive, or Synthetic, or Collective. **1873** HAMERTON *Th. about Art* xii. 181 Since painting is.. work emphatically synthetic (being the union of many forms and colours and lights and darks into artistic wholes). **1887** G. T. LADD *Elem. Physiol. Psychol.* II. vi. 388 Its [*sc.* the mind's] activity in combining the sensations into the more complex presentations of sense... This combining activity is best called 'synthetic', or constructive.

b. Concerned with or using synthesis.

1864 HAMERTON in *Fine Arts Q. Rev.* May 238 The synthetic habit of mind. **1877** TYNDALL in *D. News* 2 Oct. 2/4 That vague and general insight..which..was more frequently affirmed by the synthetic poet than by the scientific man.

6. *Gram.* and *Philol.* Characterized by combination of simple words or elements into compound or complex words; expressing a complex notion by a single compounded or complex word instead of by a number of distinct words. (Opposed to ANALYTICAL 1 b.)

1816 P. DUPONCEAU in *Trans. Hist. & Lit. Comm. Amer. Philos. Soc.* (1819) I. 401 The third class [of languages] would..be that in which the principal parts of speech are formed by a synthetical operation of the mind, and in which several ideas are frequently expressed by one word. Such are what are called the Oriental languages, with the Latin, Greek, Slavonic, and others of the same description. These I would call *synthetic.* **1835** G. C. LEWIS *Ess. Rom. Lang.* i. 26 By this change the Latin language of western Europe passed from the synthetic to the analytic class. **1845** *Proc. Philol. Soc.* II. 168 Synthetic forms are not necessarily strictly parallel with the analytic ones of the same import. **1869** FARRAR *Fam. Speech* i. (1870) 27 The synthetic character of ancient languages, compared with the analysis which distinguishes their modern representatives. **1875** WHITNEY *Life Lang.* vi. 105 The loss of formal grammatical distinction by synthetic means.

7. *Biol.* Combining in one organism different characters which in the later course of evolution are specialized in different organisms; having a generalized or undifferentiated type of structure.

1859 tr. *Agassiz's Ess. Classification* 178 Sauroid Fishes and Ichthyosauri are more distinctly synthetic than prophetic types. **1872** H. A. NICHOLSON *Palæont.* 482 Synthetic or generalised plants, having rhizomata resembling those of some ferns, stems having the structure of Lycopodium [etc.].

8. *Math.* Applied to ordinary (as distinct from *analytical*, i.e. algebraic) geometry.

1889 N. F. DUPUIS (*title*) Elementary Synthetic Geometry of the Point, Line and Circle in the Plane.

9. Special collocations: ***synthetic aperture***, a simulated aperture obtained by moving an aerial or detector transversely during reception so as to increase its effective length; usu. *attrib.*, esp.

designating radar employing this; ***Synthetic Cubism***, a type of Cubism involving the combination or reorganization of forms, rather than their analysis (see CUBISM); hence ***Synthetic Cubist*** adj.

1962 *IRE Trans. Military Electronics* VI. 111 (*heading*) Some early developments in synthetic aperture radar systems. *Ibid.* 113/2 Differences between physical and synthetic apertures. **1977** *Sci. Amer.* Oct. 89/1 Since resolution is proportional to the length of the antenna but inversely proportional to the range, for synthetic-aperture radar the two effects compensate for each other... Synthetic-aperture radar thus makes it possible to obtain high-resolution images of terrain many miles away. **1979** *McGraw-Hill Yearbk. Sci. & Technol.* 224/2 Holography has also been applied, in the form of synthetic-aperture techniques, to the B-scan acoustic reflection systems to provide greater detail in the body areas located near the acoustic transducer. **1947** D. COOPER tr. *Kahnweiler's Juan Gris* II. vi. 89 Synthetic Cubism was built on a lasting foundation. Gris..finally gave up presenting the beholder with a great variety of information..about the objects which he displayed. He now offered a *synthesis*: that is to say, he packed his knowledge into one significant form, an emblem. **1981** *Times Lit. Suppl.* 9 Jan. 24/3 When constructed sculpture came, along with Synthetic Cubism in 1912, it did so with suddenness, *éclat*, and in quantity. *Ibid.* 24/4 It is often forgotten that Synthetic Cubist space without collage was potentially the most flexible and exciting pictorial space since the Baroque.

B. *sb.* A product obtained by artificial synthesis rather than from natural sources; esp. a synthetic fibre or fabric. Chiefly *pl.*

1934 in WEBSTER. **1940** *New Statesman* 16 Mar. 361/1 The scientists could see in such synthetics [*sc.* plastics]..the threat of maladjustments in industry. **1943** *Sun* (Baltimore) 10 Feb. 4/2 The company built the new plant at its own expense in an effort to increase supplies of the badly needed synthetic. **1951** P. Z. BEDOUKIAN (*title*) Perfumery synthetics and isolates. **1957** *Times* 12 Nov. (Canada Suppl.) p. v/3 Trapping becomes less and less profitable as synthetics displace furs. **1972** D. BLOODWORTH *Any Number can Play* ii. 10 Lightweight suits cut from one of those shiny Japanese synthetics. **1982** *Sunday Times* 9 May 54/5 There was a sudden scramble to get out of synthetics—those expensive 'fuels of the future'.

synthetical (sɪnˈθɛtɪkəl), *a.* [f. mod.L. *syntheticus*: see -ICAL.] (Opposed to ANALYTICAL.)

1. *Logic, Philos.*, etc. = prec. 1.

1620 T. GRANGER *Div. Logike* IV. ii. 295 Method, is either contextiue, or retextiue. The contextiue is also called Synthesis, or Syntheticall Method. **1673** O. WALKER *Educ.* x. 119 Neither is his Philosophy more notional then all Sciences, which are delivered in a Synthetical, i.e. a doctrinal method, and begin with universal propositions. **1697** tr. *Burgersdicius' Logick* II. 138 It often happens in a Part of a Discipline whose Whole is in Method Synthetical, that the Analytick Order may be kept. **1733** BERKELEY *Th. Vision Vind.* §38 In the synthetical method of delivering science or truth already found. **1827** WHATELY *Logic* Introd. (ed. 2) 16 The synthetical form of teaching is..sufficiently interesting to one who has made considerable progress in any study; and..is the form in which our knowledge naturally arranges itself in the mind..: but the analytical is the more interesting, easy, and natural kind of introduction; as being the form in which the first invention or discovery.. must originally have taken place. **1837** WHEWELL *Hist. Induct. Sci.* VI. vi. §7 II. 100 One consequence of the synthetical form adopted by Newton in the Principia was, that his successors had the problem of the solar system to begin entirely anew. **1864** BOWEN *Logic* x. 321 In descending along its course, the synthetical proof gathers all these accessions into one common trunk.

2. *Chem.* = prec. 2.

1733 P. SHAW *Chem. Lect.* ix. (1755) 169 This Synthetical Chemistry, taken in the strict Sense, for the Recomposition of Bodies from their own Principles. **1796** *Phil. Trans.* LXXXVI. 414, I made the following synthetical observations and experiments. **1877** HUXLEY *Physiogr.* (1878) 111 The discovery of the composition of water was indeed made originally by synthetical, and not by analytical, processes. **1893** W. A. HAMMOND in *N. Amer. Rev.* CLVI. 21 Those medicines which are synthetical, that is, formed in the laboratory by the union of other substances.

3. In the philosophy of Kant: = prec. 4.

1796 F. A. NITSCH *Gen. View Kant's Princ. concerning Man* 76 This act may be called a synthetical act of the reproductive imagination. *Ibid.* 89 A synthetical judgment *à priori*. **1838** [F. HAYWOOD] tr. *Kant's Crit. Pure Reason* 15 That the straight line between two points is the shortest, is a synthetical proposition. For my conception of *straight* contains nothing of quantity, but only a quality. **1839** *Penny Cycl.* XIII. 175/2 Experience, which is itself a synthetical combination of its intuitions. **1884** tr. *Lotze's Logic* 61 Judgments of the form '*S* is *P*' are called synthetical, when *P* is understood to be a mark not already contained in that group of marks which enables us to conceive *S* distinctly; they are called analytical when *P*..belongs essentially to those marks the union of which is necessary to make the concept of *S* complete.

4. a. = prec. 5.

1799 A. YOUNG *Agric. Linc.* 244 This [*sc.* a bog produced by overflow from an artificial channel] Sir Joseph [Banks] calls a synthetical bog; and says, he flatters himself, he shall become master of Mr. Elkinton's mode of drainage soon, as he had succeeded in a synthetical, as well as in an analytical experiment. **1826** KIRBY & SPENCE *Entomol.* xlviii. IV. 461 Though he studied insects analytically with unrivalled success, he was not always equally happy in his synthetical arrangement of them. **1881** ROUTLEDGE *Science* ix. 219 Newton, having thus analysed light, proceeded to arrange experiments for the opposite or synthetical process of recombining the coloured rays.

b. = prec. 5 b.

1812 HAZLITT *On Tooke* Lit. Rem. 1836 I. 360 The difference between the synthetical and analytical faculties. **1829** LOUDON *Encycl. Plants* (1836) 429 The most unreasonable advocate of the exploded doctrines of synthetical botany. **1842** KINGSLEY *Life & Lett.* (1878) I. 71 Synthetical minds are subject to this self-torture.

†**5.** *Gram.* (See quot. and cf. SYNTHESIS 2.)

1656 BLOUNT *Glossogr.*, *Synthetical*, pertaining to the figure Synthesis, which is when a noun collective singular is joyn'd with a verb plural.

synthetically (sɪnˈθɛtɪkəlɪ), *adv.* [f. prec. + -LY[2]: see -ICALLY.] In a synthetic manner; by or in the way of synthesis (in various senses).

1748 HARTLEY *Observ. Man* I. iii. 347 The..making of Hypotheses, and arguing from them synthetically. ?**17..** WALKER (T.), The plan proceeds synthetically from parts to the whole. **1778** BP. LOWTH *Transl. Isaiah* Prelim. Diss. p. xxi, Here the lines..are Synthetically Parallel. **1796** KIRWAN *Elem. Min.* (ed. 2) I. 160, I tried this result synthetically, and found it to resist fusion at 148°. **1812** SIR H. DAVY *Chem. Philos.* 182 Crystals of Glauber's salt may be resolved analytically into Sulphate of Soda and water, or compounded synthetically from these substances. **1873** HAMERTON *Th. about Art* xii. 180 In painting on any one part of your picture you are really painting upon, that is, changing the colour of, the whole canvas at once, and unless you do this always synthetically you will never succeed. **1877** E. CAIRD *Philos. Kant* II. viii. 366, I necessarily represent the manifold as synthetically united in time. **1899** *Allbutt's Syst. Med.* VI. 505 Lecithin..as well as nucleins arise synthetically within the tissues of the body.

syntheticism (sɪnˈθɛtɪsɪz(ə)m). [f. SYNTHETIC + -ISM.] Synthetic character or method.

1863 *Smith's Dict. Bible* III. 1539/2 *note*, The assumption that languages are developed only in the direction of syntheticism.

synthetism (ˈsɪnθɪtɪz(ə)m). [ad. mod.L. *synthetismus*, f. Gr. συνθετίζεσθαι to SYNTHETIZE.] A synthetic system or doctrine.

1832 A. JOHNSON tr. *Tennemann's Hist. Philos.* 463 A new system which he [*sc.* Krug] denominates a Transcendental Synthetism. **1842** SIR W. HAMILTON *Diss.* in *Reid's Wks.* (1846) 797/2.

synthetist (ˈsɪnθɪtɪst). [f. SYNTHETIC or SYNTHETIZE: see -IST.] = SYNTHESIST.

1848 GILFILLAN in *Tait's Mag.* XV. 519 Milton is the synthetist, Dante the analyst of Hell. **1873** HAMERTON *Th. about Art* xii. 167 Synthetists find continual pleasure in observing the relations of things, but from their largeness of range they constantly miss minute truths.

synthetize (ˈsɪnθɪtaɪz), *v.* [ad. Gr. συνθετίζεσθαι, f. συνθετός: see SYNTHETIC and -IZE.] *trans.* = SYNTHESIZE.

1828–32 WEBSTER, *Synthetize, v.t.*, to unite in regular structure. (*Not much used.*) **1854** S. NEIL *Elem. Rhet.* 153 It enables us to synthetize the two prevalent theories of Taste into one. **1888** *Harper's Mag.* Jan. 250 Boucher marked every detail of running movement, and finally synthetized the results of his study in this group. **1904** *Westm. Gaz.* 3 Dec. 16/3 Hennell synthetised alcohol from olefiant gas.

Hence **'synthetized, 'synthetizing** *ppl. adjs.*; also **'synthetizer** = SYNTHESIZER.

1890 *Harper's Mag.* May 838/1 The most gifted of the impressionist painters are analysts and synthetizers. **1892** *Nation* (N.Y.) 17 Nov. 379/3 The grand synthetizing style of [Raphael]. **1918** *Times* 1 May 8/3 The function of the monthly reviews..is to survey things broadly and at a synthetizing distance.

synthol (ˈsɪnθɒl). [a. G. *synthol* (Fischer & Tropsch 1923, in *Brennstoff-Chem.* IV. 281/1), f. *synth-etisch* SYNTHETIC *a.*: see -OL.] (See quot. 1938.)

1924 *Chem. Abstr.* XVIII. 459 The preparation of synthetic oil mixtures (synthol) from carbon monoxide and hydrogen. **1926** J. JOYCE *Let.* 5 Mar. (1966) III. 138 He is now using some kind of new chemical stimulant (not chemical but acting by purely physical means, recently discovered here [in France], I understand, synthol for massaging the temples and brow). **1938** *Thorpe's Dict. Appl. Chem.* (ed. 4) II. 350/2 Using mixtures of carbon monoxide with excess hydrogen..Fischer..obtained a mixture which he termed 'Synthol', consisting of alcohols.., ketones, aldehydes, acids.., and various esters. *Ibid.* 425/2 If, instead of zinc-chromium oxides, an alkalised iron catalyst is employed, the liquid product, 'synthol', obtained is a mixture of alcohols, ketones and hydrocarbons containing from 2 to about 8 carbon atoms per molecule.

synthon (ˈsɪnθɒn). *Chem.* [f. SYNTH(ETIC *a.* + I)ON; cf. -ON[1].] A constituent part of a molecule to be synthesized which readily lends itself to an operation of synthesis.

1967 E. J. COREY in *Pure & Appl. Chem.* XIV. 22 The term 'synthon' is suggested [for such units]. These are defined as structural units within a molecule which are related to possible synthetic operations. **1977** *Jrnl. Chem. Soc.: Chem. Communications* 497 (*heading*) A synthon for epoxyolefin cyclisation. **1980** *Jrnl. Amer. Chem. Soc.* CII. 5979/1 (*heading*) Allyl sulfones as synthons for 1,1- and 1,3-dipoles via organopalladium chemistry.

‖**synthronus** (ˈsɪnθrənəs). *Eccl.* Pl. **synthroni** (-aɪ). [eccl. L., a. eccl. Gr. σύνθρονος, f. σύν SYN-[1] + θρόνος THRONE.] In the early church and the Greek Church, the joint throne of the bishop and his presbyters, usually a semicircular row of seats with the bishop's throne in the middle, placed behind the altar.

1861 NEALE *Notes Dalmatia* 117 The bishop's seat, at the east end of the synthronus, remains with two arms.

syntille, var. SCINTILL *Obs.*

†**syntome.** *Obs. rare.* [ad. Gr. συντομή a cutting short, f. σύν SYN-[1] + τομ-: τέμνειν to cut.]

? Abridgement, brief statement. So †**syntomy** [ad. mod.L. *syntomia* (Puttenham *Engl. Poesie*, 1589, ed. Arber, p. 169), ad. Gr. συντομία], brevity, conciseness.

1641 BRATHWAIT *Penit. Pilgr.* Contents, The Summe, or Graduall Symtome [*sic*] of the Penitent Pilgrim. **1656** BLOUNT *Glossogr.*, *Syntomy*..a cutting away, brevity, or concisenesse.

syntome, -tone, obs. forms of SYMPTOM.

†**syntone**[1]. *Mus. Obs.* [ad. Gr. σύντονος: see SYNTONOUS.] In ***diatonic syntone***, a mistranslation of Gr. διάτονον σύντονον syntonous diatonic (scale), σύντονον being erron. taken as a sb. (see SYNTONOUS).

[Cf. quot. 1694 s.v. DIATONIC 1.] **1784** J. KEEBLE *Harmonics* 30 The diatonic syntone. **1806** KOLLMANN *Theory Mus. Harmony* ii. 6 The first foundation of our modern scale, seems to have been laid in that most antient Tetrachord..of the Greeks, called the Diatonic Syntone, which consisted of four notes, equal to our B C D E.

syntone[2] (ˈsɪntəʊn). *Psychiatry.* [Back-formation from SYNTONIC *a.*[2] 2.] A person having a syntonic temperament.

1940 J. BOWLBY *Personality Types & Mental Illness* ii. 23 Syntones therefore are far from having the 'frank open personalities' commonly attributed to them.

syntonic (sɪnˈtɒnɪk), *a.*[1] *Mus.* [f. Gr. σύντονος (see SYNTONOUS) + -IC.] = SYNTONOUS.

syntonic comma, the common comma (COMMA 3), the difference between a major and a minor tone, or between the major third of the Pythagorean and that of the modern diatonic scale.

1801 BUSBY *Dict. Mus.*, *Syntonic*, the epithet by which Aristoxenus and other ancient musical writers distinguish a species of the diatonic genus, which was nearly the same with our natural diatonic. **1944** W. APEL *Harvard Dict. Mus.* (1946) 166/2 The *Didymic* (Didymos, Greek theorist, b. 63 B.C.) or *syntonic comma* which indicates the difference between E as the fourth tone of the circle of fifths..and the E of just intonation. **1954** *Grove's Dict. Mus.* (ed. 5) IV. 523/1 The comma of Didymus (commonly called a *comma* without qualification, and sometimes a syntonic comma). **1979** *Early Music* Apr. 239/2 The major third produced by tuning four successive perfect fifths..is wider than the pure interval..by a syntonic comma.

syn'tonic, *a.*[2] [In sense 1, f. Gr. σύν SYN-[1] + τόνος TONE + -IC; in sense 2, f. SYNTONY 2 + -IC.]

1. *Electr.* Denoting a system of wireless telegraphy in which the transmitting and receiving instruments are accurately 'tuned' or adjusted so that the latter responds only to vibrations of the frequency of those emitted by the former; also said of the instruments so 'tuned'.

1892 LODGE *Mod. Views Electr.* xvi. 339 The synchronizing of the vibration-period of two things..is well expressed by the adjective 'syntonic' which was suggested to me..by the late Dr. A. T. Myers. That which has been styled resonance I propose, therefore,..to call 'syntony'. **1898** S. P. THOMPSON in *Jrnl. Soc. Arts* XLVI. 457/1 Using ..not merely circuits of wires, but syntonic circuits, which ..are necessarily much more sensitive in their response one to the other. **1898** *Echo* 10 Jan. 2/4 These electrical resonances constitute 'syntonic telegraphy.'

2. *Psychiatry.* Denoting the responsive, lively type of temperament which is liable to manic-depressive psychosis.

1925 A. A. BRILL in *Amer. Jrnl. Psychiatry* LXXI. 592 Bleuler proposed for this reaction the name syntonic. *Syntonic* not only signifies 'equally toned' but also means to be 'attuned' and in 'harmony'... If a person is neither exclusively schizoid, nor entirely syntonic, one can only say that he is preponderatingly schizoid or preponderatingly syntonic... Thus, if a person shows a manic attack, it means that the syntonic components predominate qualitatively and quantitatively to a morbid degree. **1927** [see CYCLOID *sb.* 3]. **1933** *Brit. Jrnl. Psychol.* July 30 Our results would indicate that the connection of cyclothyme or syntonic type with low perseveration..has no experimental support. **1948** NOYES & KOLB *Mod. Clinical Psychiatry* (ed. 3) vi. 98 Bleuler preferred the term 'syntonic' to Kretschmer's 'cycloid' to describe a personality tendency opposed in characteristics to the schizoid. **1969** H. J. & S. B. G. EYSENCK *Personality Structure & Measurement* iv. 23 The large number of persons in the centre of the distribution he would call *syntonic* if they were on the cyclothymic side.

Hence **syn'tonically** *adv.*

a **1919** *N.E.D.* 'In recent Dicts.' **1925** A. A. BRILL in *Amer. Jrnl. Psychiatry* LXXXI. 592 The affectivity of the person reacting for the most part syntonically harmonizes with the people of his environment.

syntonin (ˈsɪntənɪn). *Chem.* [f. Gr. σύντονος SYNTONOUS + -IN.] An acid albuminous substance found in muscular tissue, or produced from myosin by the action of acids.

1859 CARPENTER *Anim. Phys.* i. 33 The substance of which muscles are composed has been commonly considered to be Fibrin, but it differs essentially from fibrin in its properties, and is now distinguished as Syntonin. **1872** HUXLEY *Physiol.* vi. 134 The Syntonin which is the chief constituent of muscle and flesh. **1881** MIVART *Cat* 125 About 15 per cent. of the remaining fourth [of the substance of muscle] is found, after death, to consist of an albuminoid substance called syntonin, or muscle fibrin.

syntonism ('sɪntənɪz(ə)m). *Electr.* [f. Gr. σύν SYN-[1] + τόνος TONE + -ISM.] = SYNTONY 1.
1903 *Rep. Brit. Assoc. Adv. Sci.* 761 The question of 'syntonism', by which it is proposed to assure the secrecy of messages.

syntonize ('sɪntənaɪz), *v. Electr.* [f. SYNTONIC *a.*[2] + -IZE.] *trans.* To make syntonic; to 'tune' or adjust to the same or corresponding frequencies, as a transmitter and receiver in wireless telegraphy. Hence **'syntonized, -izing** *ppl. adjs.*; also **ˌsyntoni'zation**, the action of syntonizing; **'syntonizer**, an apparatus for syntonizing.
1892 LODGE *Mod. Views Electr.* xvi. 355 Vacuum tubes.. attached to an ordinary syntonized receiver. **1898** *Edin. Rev.* Oct. 307 The Marconi apparatus seems to lend itself imperfectly to the 'sharp syntonisation'. **1898** *Engineering Mag.* XVI. 142/1 Lodge's System of Syntonized Wireless Telegraphy. **1900** S. R. BOTTONE *Wireless Telegr.* iv. 107 These [pegs] serve as supports for the rods which are used as 'wings' or syntonizers. **1901** *Munsey's Mag.* June 365/1 A system.. that would be able to syntonize or select its despatches.

syntono- ('sɪntənəʊ), combining form repr. Gr. σύντονος (see SYNTONOUS), as in ***Syntono-Lydian*** adj. [cf. Gr. συντονολυδιστί adv. (Plato)], an epithet of the ordinary (diatonic) Lydian scale in ancient Greek music.
1801 BUSBY *Dict. Mus.*, *Syntono Lydian*, the name of one of the mode in the ancient music. Plato tells us, that the mixo-lydian and syntono-lydian modes were *peculiar to tears.* **1875** STAINER & BARRETT *Dict. Mus. Terms* 209 There was no such enharmonic scale as Syntono-Lydian, nor could such a prefix as Syntono be applied to any enharmonic scale whatever. *Ibid.* 210 The Syntono-Lydian of the manuscript [of Aristides Quintilianus].. is clearly a mistake for Hypo-Lydian... The prefix of 'Syntono' is usually unnecessary, because it means the ordinary Lydian,.. but Plato employs it, because he wishes to distinguish it from the Malakon (or laxly tuned) Lydian.

syntonous ('sɪntənəs), *a. Mus.* [f. Gr. σύντονος strained tight, high-pitched, intense, severe, f. συντείνειν to strain tight, f. σύν SYN-[1] + τείνειν to stretch: see -OUS.] An epithet for the ordinary form of diatonic scale (διάτονον σύντονον) in ancient Greek music, in which the tetrachord was divided into a semitone and two tones, the third note of it being thus tuned to a higher pitch than in the other scales; nearly corresponding to the modern diatonic scale.
1789 BURNEY *Hist. Mus.* III. ii. 164 In describing the diatonic genus, in which the tetrachord is divided into tone major, tone minor, and major semitone:.. for which division, commonly called the syntonous, or intense of Ptolemy, he [*sc.* Zarlino] constantly contends. **1889** W. S. ROCKSTRO in Grove *Dict. Mus.* IV. 502/1 The Syntonous Diatonic of Ptolemy coincided.. with the system advocated by Kepler, Mersenne, Des Cartes, and all the most learned theoretical writers of later date.

syntony ('sɪntənɪ). [f. SYNTONIC *a.*[2] + -Y.] **1.** *Electr.* The condition of being syntonic, or 'tuned' so as to respond to one another, as two electric circuits. Also *attrib.*
1892 [see SYNTONIC *a.*[2] 1]. **1898** *Daily News* 31 Mar. 6/3 True syntony between the sending and the receiving apparatus. **1902** *Westm. Gaz.* 27 Feb. 9/3 For a number of pairs of stations, syntony-constants can be chosen which differ in period or pitch sufficiently to prevent interference.
2. *Psychiatry.* [ad. G. *syntonie* (E. Bleuler 1922, in *Zeitschr. f. d. gesamte Neurol. u. Psychiatrie* LXXVIII. 373).] A syntonic state or condition (see SYNTONIC *a.*[2] 2).
1925 A. A. BRILL in *Amer. Jrnl. Psychiatry* 598 Translating.. syntony into Freudian terms we can say that every transference neurotic has also a fragment of narcistic [*sic*] libido.
3. *transf.* and *fig.*
1958 F. BERRY *Poets' Gram.* ii. 20 [The Towneley pageant] is not a work wherein 'anachronisms' occur but a poetic drama where syntony, or multiplicity of tenses running together, is basic to its conception. **1973** D. MATIAS tr. C. Metz in *Screen* Spring/Summer 55 Pierre Schaeffer's specific propositions towards a classification of the possible interactions between music and image into four categories ('masks', 'opposition', 'synchronism', 'syntony'.) **1978** J. WAINWRIGHT *Jury People* l. 177 There was a link. A basic syntony which each felt for the other. They each recognised in the other a man proud of his own particular skill.

syntoxoid: see SYN-[1].

‖**syntractrix** (sɪn'træktrɪks). *Geom.* [mod.L., f. SYN-[1] + TRACTRIX.] The locus of a point on the tangent to a tractrix at a constant distance from its intersection with the axis. Also **syn'tractory** [TRACTORY *sb.* 3].
1820 G. PEACOCK *Examples Diff. Calc.* I. xxiii. 175 Syntractory. **1852** G. SALMON *Higher Plane Curves* III. (1879) 289 The syntractrix is the locus of a point *Q* on the tangent to the tractrix which divides into portions of given length the constant line *SN*.

syntrierarch (sɪn'traɪərɑːk). *Gr. Hist.* [ad. Gr. συντριήραρχος, f. σύν SYN-[1] + τριήραρχος TRIERARCH.] One of a number of citizens jointly charged with the equipment of a trireme: cf. TRIERARCH. So **syn'trierarchy** [cf. TRIERARCHY], the office of a syntrierarch; the system of syntrierarchs.
1842 *Smith's Dict. Grk. & Rom. Antiq.* 1001/2. **1891** *Athenæum* 25 July 123/1 Under the syntrierarchy there were two trierarchs to one ship.

†**syntrochite.** *Palæont. Obs.* [f. SYN-[1] + TROCHITE.] Name for some kind of fossil: cf. ENTROCHITE, TROCHITE.
1681 GREW *Musæum* III. I. ii. 272 The Syntrochite, as we may name it.

syntrophy ('sɪntrəfɪ). *Biol.* [ad. G. *syntrophie* (E. Wasmann 1897, in *Zool. Anz.* XX. 173), f. Gr. συν- SYN-[1] + τροφή nourishment.] The continuing relationship between the individuals of two different species or strains of organisms in which one, or more usually both, benefit nutritionally from the presence of the other; *spec.* that between two bacterial strains which are dependent on each other for their proliferation. Also **'syntrophism**, in the same sense. Hence **syn'trophic** *a.*
1897 *Jrnl. R. Microsc. Soc.* 283 Wasmann also speaks of the 'syntrophy' of *Lælaps oophilus* Moniez, [a mite] which occurs freely on the surface of the eggs of ants.., but without doing them any damage, apparently depending on the salivary secretion of the ants, which are always licking their eggs. **1946** *Jrnl. Bacteriol.* LII. 503/2 Syntrophism. This is defined as the growth of two distinct biochemical mutants in mixed culture as a result of the ability of each strain to synthesize the growth factor required by the other... Mutants blocked at different steps in the synthesis of the same factor show syntrophism. **1950** *Experientia* VI. 42/2 Other possible explanations of the requirement of intermediate cultivation in the penicillin method include segregation of mutant and non-mutant nuclei from a multinucleate cell, and a syntrophic effect of the non-viable irradiated bacteria, which would promote sterilization of mutants by penicillin. **1971** M. ALEXANDER *Microbiol. Ecol.* x. 242 Mutual feeding by dissimilar auxotrophs is termed syntrophism, a relationship in which two or possibly more populations are able to develop in nutrient-deficient circumstances not suitable for the proliferation, or allowing for the poor development at best, of either. *Ibid.* 243 The extensive distribution of bacteria both exporting and importing growth factors suggests a widespread occurrence of syntrophy in nature.

syntropic (sɪn'trɒpɪk), *a. Anat.* [f. Gr. σύν SYN-[1] + -τροπος turning + -IC; cf. TROPIC.] Forming a series of similar parts pointing in the same direction, as ribs or vertebræ. So (in recent Dicts.) **syntrope** ('sɪntrəʊp), any one of such parts; **'syntropy**, condition of being syntropic.
18.. *New York Med. Jrnl.* XL. 114 (Cent. Dict.).

syntype ('sɪntaɪp). *Nat. Hist.* [f. SYN-[1] + TYPE *sb.* 8 b.] Any one of the original set of specimens from which a species has been described and named.
1909 *Cent. Dict.* Suppl. **1912** *Return Brit. Museum* 172 Echinoids, Asteroids, Ophiuroids, and Crinoids.. including the syntypes of *Millericrinus charpyi* and other specimens. **1918** *Museums Jrnl.* XVII. 112 A brachiopod found at 13,500 feet above sea level... The syntypes of this are in the Peabody Museum of Yale University.

synu, synue, obs. ff. SINEW.

synulotic (sɪnjuː'lɒtɪk), *a.* and *sb. Med. rare*[−0]. [ad. mod.L. *synūlōticus*, ad. Gr. συνουλωτικός, f. σύν SYN-[1] + οὐλοῦν to scar over, f. οὐλή scar.] = CICATRIZANT.
[**1657** *Physical Dict.*, *Synulotica*, medicines to dry up a sore, or to bring it to a cicatrice.] **1704** J. HARRIS *Lex. Techn.* I, Synuloticks. **1859** MAYNE *Expos. Lex.* **1913** DORLAND *Med. Dict.* (ed. 7).

synusia (sɪ'n(j)uːsɪə). *Ecol.* Pl -iae. [mod.L., ad. G. *synusie* (H. Gams 1918, in *Vierteljahrsschr. der Naturforsch. Ges. in Zürich* LXIII. 428), f. Gr. συνουσία society, company.] A group of organisms (usu. plants) of one or more species which have similar life-forms, occupy the same ecological niche, and play a similar role in the community which they form. Also **sy'nusium.**
1924 *Jrnl. Ecol.* XII. 15 An aggregation of plants which belong to the same 'life-form' and make similar demands upon a similar habitat constitutes Gams' conception of a synusium. **1926** TANSLEY & CHIPP *Study of Vegetation* ii. 25 The individuals composing a synusia may belong not only to different species but to different families or even different higher groups. **1930** *Svensk Bot. Tidskrift* XXIV. 496 The method of dividing each sociation into its elementary one-layered units, or synusiae, and grouping the synusiae of each layer independently of those of the other layers to synusiae of higher rank. **1932** FULLER & CONARD tr. *Braun-Blanquet's Plant Sociol.* xii. 302 A cover of crustose lichens, a pure carpet of moss or of dwarf shrubs, the tree layer of a fir stand are ecological synusiae. **1960** [see NICHE *sb.* 3 c]. **1965** B. E. FREEMAN tr. *Vandel's Biospeleology* xvii. 285 Each biotope contains an animal population which is called the synusium. **1975** T. C. WHITMORE *Trop. Rain Forests Far East* ii. 12 Species of very diverse taxonomic affinity make up the synusiae.

†**Synusiast.** *Obs.* Also syno(u)siast. [ad. mod.L. *synūsiasta*, ad. Gr. συνουσιαστής, f. σύν SYN-[1] + οὐσία being, substance. Cf. METUSIAST.] **a.** An adherent of a sect which held that in Jesus Christ there was a commingling of the divine substance and the substance of human flesh. **b.** A believer in consubstantiation.
1585-7 T. ROGERS *39 Art.* xxviii. §4. (1625) 176 The Synusiastes, or Vbiquitaries, which think the Body of Christ is so present in the Supper, as his said Body with bread and Wine,.. of all, and euery communicant, is eaten corporally. **1674** HICKMAN *Quinquart. Hist.* Ep. (ed. 2) a 5 b, Convince a Protestant, that any one place of Scripture must needs be so understood as to assert Consubstantiation, he becomes a Synousiast forthwith. **1728** CHAMBERS *Cycl.*, *Synusiasts*, or *Synosiasts*, a Sect of Hereticks, who maintain'd, that there was but one single Nature, and one single Substance in Jesus Christ.

syn(u)we, obs. ff. SINEW.

synvy, var. SENVY *Obs.*, mustard.

synyght, obs. f. SENNIGHT.

synys: see SINES.

synyster, obs. f. SINISTER.

†**syon.** *Sc. Obs.* Also 6 **syone, syoun.** A kind of coat. Also *attrib.*
1511 *Acc. Ld. High Treas. Scot.* IV. 198 To be the King ane Syone coit xj½ elnis blak satyne. **1526** *Ibid.* V. 273 Aucht ellis of fyne taffeteis to be the King ane gowne, and four ellis .. to be him ane syoun. **1538** *Ibid.* VII. 29, vij elnis of blak satin of Wenis to be the Kingis grace ane syon.

syon, syoun, obs. ff. SCION.

syour(e, obs. forms of SYRE.

sypar(s, obs. forms of CYPRESS[1].
1531 *Rec. St. Mary at Hill* 37 A.. tabull of sypars. **1535** STEWART *Cron. Scot.* (Rolls) II. 569 The sypar tre.

sype, variant of SIPE.

syper(s, var. CYPRESS[3].
1509-10 in Lysons *Environs Lond.* (1792) I. 227 Saten of sypers. **1612** *Pasquil's Night-cap* (1877) 59 His hat.. With treble Syper, and with veluet lin'd.

syph (sɪf). *slang.* Also **siph, siff.** Abbrev. of SYPHILIS. Also with def. article.
1914 *Dialect Notes* IV. 113 *Syph, abbrev.*, syphilis. **1925** *Amer. Speech* I. 24/2 For 'syphilis', 'pox' was used wiedly many years ago, but has given place more recently to the simple abbreviation 'syph'. **1930** J. DOS PASSOS *42nd Parallel* I. 108 He got the siph off 'n her. **1947** *Horizon* Sept. 202 We're going to get the syph. **1947** C. WILLINGHAM *End as Man* ii. 18 Why don't you tell us about that time you got siff from your nigger maid? **1960** D. LYTTON *Goddam White Man* i. 15 Everybody dies of the cough... Or you get syph as well... They say you scream like a hound when you have the syph and the cough together. **1969** P. ROTH *Portnoy's Complaint* 129 I'll come down with the syph from just touching the ticket. **1971** B. W. ALDISS *Soldier Erect* 157 Them mankey whores in yon knocking-shop'll give you a dose as soon as look at you. There's no' a one of them as isn't rotten with siff. **1980** 'D. KAVANAGH' *Duffy* viii. 149 He goes down to the clinic.. and finds he's got the worst case of syph they've seen in years.

syphareit, obs. Sc. f. SEPARATE *a.*
1508 KENNEDIE *Flyting w. Dunbar* 253 Sodomyt, sypharеit fra sanctis celestiall.

sypher ('saɪfə(r)), *v. Carpentry.* [Variant of CIPHER *v.* 9.] To make a lap-joint by overlapping two bevelled or chamfered plank-edges, so as to leave a plane surface. So **sypher-joint.**
1841 DANA *Seaman's Man.*, *Syphering*, lapping the edges of planks over each other for a bulk-head. **1875** KNIGHT *Dict. Mech.*, *Sypher-joint.* (*Carpentry.*) A lap joint for the edges of boards, leaving a flat or flush surface.

sypher, -re, obs. ff. CIPHER *sb.*

syphilide ('sɪfɪlaɪd). *Path.* Also -id. [orig. in pl., ad. F. *syphilides*, f. SYPHILIS, after names of zoological families: see -ID[3].] A generic term for any skin affection of a syphilitic nature.
1829 *Glasgow Med. Jrnl.* II. 327 By syphilide is understood every eruption produced on the skin, by the action of the syphilitic virus. **1879** *St. George's Hosp. Rep.* IX. 476 One married woman.. was admitted covered with secondary syphilides. **1883** F. T. ROBERTS *Handbk. Med.* (ed. 5) 949 The macular syphilide is the commonest eruption. **1897** *Allbutt's Syst. Med.* IV. 807 The papulous syphilide is one of the rarest forms in which syphilis appears in the larynx.

syphilis ('sɪfɪlɪs). *Path.* Also 8 **siphylis**, 9 **siphilis, syphylis.** [mod.L. *syphilis* (*syphilid-*), orig. the title (in full, *Syphilis, sive Morbvs Gallicvs*) of a poem, published 1530, by Girolamo Fracastoro or Hieronymus Fracastorius (1483–1553), a physician, astronomer, and poet of Verona, but used also as the name of the disease in the poem itself; the subject of the poem is the story of a shepherd *Syphilus*, the first sufferer from the disease, the name *Syphilis* being formed on the analogy of *Æneis*, *Thebais*, etc. (The poem was translated in 1686 by Nahum Tate with the title

'Syphilis: or, a Poetical History of the French Disease'.) The term was employed systematically by Fracastoro in his treatise *De Contagione* II. xi. (1546). Cf. F. *syphilis*, It. *sifilide*, Sp. *sifilis*, Pg., G., etc. *syphilis*.

The source of the name *Syphilus* is disputed; it has been suggested that it is a corrupt mediæval form of *Sipylus*, the name of a son of Niobe (so called after a mountain) in Ovid *Metam.* VI. 146 ff. (See F. Boll in *Neue Jahrb. f.d. klass. Altertum*, 1910, XXV. 72 ff., 168.)]

A specific disease caused by *Treponema pallidum* (*Spirochæte pallida*) and communicated by sexual connexion or accidental contact (acquired form) or by infection of the child in utero (congenital form).

Three stages of the disease are distinguished, ***primary***, ***secondary***, and ***tertiary syphilis***; the first characterized by chancre in the part infected, the second by affections of the skin and mucous membranes, the third involving the bones, muscles, and brain.

1718 J. F. NICHOLSON (*title*) The Modern Siphylis: or, the true method of curing every stage and symptom of the venereal disease, etc. **1801** *Med. Jrnl.* V. 85 Surgeons and nurses may by accident inoculate themselves with syphilis, in places appropriated for the reception of venereal patients. **1828–32** WEBSTER, Siphilis. **1845** BUDD *Dis. Liver* 252 A case of great enlargement of the liver, consequent on syphilis and the use of mercury. **1876** BRISTOWE *Theory & Pract. Med.* (1878) 250 Syphilis has occasionally prevailed in the form of widespread and severe epidemics.

fig. **1810** BENTHAM *Packing* (1821) 62 In Rome-bred law.. fiction is a wart, which here and there deforms the face of justice: in English law, fiction is a syphilis, which..carries into every part of the system the principle of rottenness.

attrib. **1891** *Science-Gossip* XXVII. 30 The General Biology of the Microbes of Rabies, Yellow Fever,.. Puerperal Fever, Syphilis-tuberculosis,..&c. **1897** *Allbutt's Syst. Med.* IV. 807 In the syphilis wards of the Berlin Charité Hospital. **1899** J. HUTCHINSON in *Archives Surg.* X. 167 The subsidence of the syphilis-epidemic. **1916** *Nature* 27 Jan. 609/2 Long before salvarsan was proved valuable for killing the syphilis micro-organism.

syphilitic (sɪfɪˈlɪtɪk), *a.* and *sb. Path.* Also 8–9 siphilitic. [ad. mod.L. *syphiliticus* (Sauvages), f. SYPHILIS; the suffix *-itic* is the adj. formative of -ITIS and is strictly inappropriate here.]

A. *adj.* Of, pertaining to, caused by, or affected with syphilis.

syphilitic lobelia, a rendering of *Lobelia syphilitica*, so called as being used as a remedy for syphilis.

1786 ABERCROMBIE *Arrangem.* in *Gard. Assist.* 59 Siphilitic blue lobelia. **1804** *Med. Jrnl.* XII. 505 This affection of his throat might have been owing to some syphilitic virus, which had long lain dormant in the system. **1835–6** *Todd's Cycl. Anat.* I. 184/1 Syphilitic warts..have generally a broad base. **1846** G. E. DAY tr. *Simon's Anim. Chem.* II. 59 Meggenhofen found that the milk of a syphilitic woman reddened tincture of litmus. **1862** M. HOPKINS *Hawaii* 372 A syphilitic ward in the new Queen's Hospital at Honolulu. **1897** *Allbutt's Syst. Med.* II. 1135 Such syphilitic livers..are often immobile on deep inspiration owing to adhesions.

B. *sb.* A person affected with syphilis.

1881 *Physician & Surgeon* III. 138 Whether a syphilitic should ever have professional consent to marry. **1904** *Brit. Med. Jrnl.* 10 Sept. *Epit. Curr. Med. Lit.* 36 The blood..of syphilitics who have been treated with mercury.

syphilize (ˈsɪfɪlaɪz), *v. Med.* and *Path.* [ad. F. *syphiliser*: see SYPHILIS and -IZE.] *trans.* To inoculate with the virus of syphilis, as a means of cure or prevention; also, to infect with syphilis.

1854 H. LEE *Six Lect. Syphilitic Infection* v. 50 He [*sc.* Turenne in 1850] concluded that the third inoculated ulcer bore the same relation to the second as the second did to the first, and so on until the animal became proof against any further inoculation. The animal was then said by M. Auzias [Turenne] to be 'syphilised'. *Ibid.* 51 'It is certain', says Dr. Sperino, 'that of all the women who entered five months ago into the *Syphilicome*, and whom I syphilised to the highest degree, not only have none hitherto been affected with constitutional symptoms, but the health of each of them has gradually improved'. **1871** *Brit. & For. Med.-Chirurg. Rev.* XLVII. 357 Most or all of the European races have already to some extent arrived at the syphilised diathesis. **1873** J. E. MORGAN *Univ. Oars* 83 Alcoholized, syphilized, tainted with scrofula and other constitutional diseases, they become a feeble sickly race.

Hence **syphilization** (ˌsɪfɪlaɪˈzeɪʃən).

1854 H. LEE (*title*) Six lectures on syphilitic infection and syphilisation. **1872** T. BRYANT *Pract. Surg.* (1878) I. 93 Syphilisation originated in 1844 through some experiments of M. Auzias Turenne upon animals to inoculate them with syphilis.

syphilo- (ˈsɪfɪləʊ), used as combining form of SYPHILIS (also with variant **syphilido-**). **ˈsyphiloderm**, ‖**-derma** (pl. **-ata**) [Gr. δέρμα skin], a syphilitic skin-affection = SYPHILIDE; hence **syphiloˈdermatous** *a.* **syphiloˈgenesis**, **-ˈogeny**, production of syphilis (Dorland). **syphiˈlographer** [cf. F. *syphiliographe*], a writer on syphilis; so **syphiˈlography**, the description of syphilis. **syphiˈlologist**, a specialist in syphilology. **syphiˈlology**, the study of syphilis; hence **syphiloˈlogic**, **-ˈlogical** *adjs.* **syphiloˈmania**, a mental derangement in which the person fancies himself affected with syphilis. **syphiˈlopathy**, any syphilitic manifestation. **syphiloˈphobia** (also **syphili-**), morbid fear of syphilis; hence **syphiloˈphobic** *a.*

1852 W. J. E. WILSON *Syphilis* vii. 172 The hereditary erythematous *syphiloderma occurs in three principal forms. **1876** DUHRING *Dis. Skin* 78 In the papular syphiloderm, pustules are at times seen intermingled with the papules. **1857** DUNGLISON *Med. Lex.*, *Syphilographer. **1871** *Brit. & For. Med.-Chirurg. Rev.* XLVII. 357 The last-named distinguished syphilographer [*sc.* Ricord]. **1864–79** BUMSTEAD *Ven. Dis.* (ed. 4) 499 The etiology of cases of this kind should be carefully studied, the subject being one of the most important in *syphilography. **1944** J. H. STOKES et al. *Mod. Clin. Syphilol.* (ed. 3) p. iii, The enormous increase in *syphilologic knowledge.., and the earthquake of penicillin have made the revising of a book at this moment a hazardous undertaking. **1908** E. L. KEYES *Syphilis* p. v, The facts upon which the volume rests are the classified cases from the private office books covering forty years of continuous work by myself along *syphilological lines. **1890** *Lancet* 13 Dec. 1307/1 The Russian Government has appointed a committee, consisting of Professor Tarnovksi and other *syphilologists. **1910** *Practitioner* Feb. 231 Few.. syphilologists..would now venture to give an opinion on a ..lesion without previously examining a scraping. **1890** WEBSTER, *Syphilology. **1893** P. A. MORROW et al. (*title*) A system of genito-urinary diseases, syphilology and dermatology. **1969** J. L. SMITH *Spirochetes in Late Seronegative Syphilis* ii. 9/2 Many practitioners are not aware of even the basic doctrines of classic syphilology. **1848** DUNGLISON *Med. Lex.* (ed. 7), *Syphilomania. **1864–79** BUMSTEAD *Ven. Dis.* (ed. 4) 789 Three sad cases in which syphilomania has led patients..to commit suicide several months after all syphilitic manifestations had disappeared. **1848** DUNGLISON *Med. Lex.* (ed. 7), *Syphiliphobia. **1864–79** BUMSTEAD *Ven. Dis.* (ed. 4) 789 There is a disease worse than syphilis, viz., syphilophobia,..over which remedies have no control. **1906** *Brit. Med. Jrnl.* 13 Jan. 63 The patient's syphilophobia had..increased to such a degree, that it became extremely difficult to manage the case. **1899** *Allbutt's Syst. Med.* VIII. 190 Syphilis causes marked mental disease of various forms, such as *syphilophobic melancholia.

syphiloid (ˈsɪfɪlɔɪd), *a.* (*sb.*) *Path.* [f. SYPHILIS + -OID.] Resembling syphilis.

1813 J. THOMSON *Lect. Inflam.* 435 The syphilitic and the syphiloid are the only new species of ulcers with which..we have become acquainted. **1843** R. J. GRAVES *Syst. Clin. Med.* xxvii. 344 Peculiar forms of diseases which we are forced to look upon as syphiloid.

B. *sb.* A syphiloid disease or affection.

1890 BILLINGS *Nat. Med. Dict.*, *Syphiloids*.., name of a group of endemic diseases due to syphilis in a severe form, with complications. **1897** *Allbutt's Syst. Med.* II. 253 *note*, An attempt has recently been made to claim the Tropical disease Yaws as a malady which while distinct from syphilis, yet resembles it..; and to construct a family of 'Syphiloids'.

syphiloma (sɪfɪˈləʊmə). *Path.* Pl. **-ata**. [f. SYPHILIS + *-oma*, as in *sarcoma*.] A syphilitic tumour. Hence **syphiˈlomatous** *a.*

1864–79 BUMSTEAD *Ven. Dis.* (ed. 4) 645 The syphiloma may form a circumscribed tumor, or may be diffused over a large area. *Ibid.*, Syphilomata of the spinal dura mater. **1898** *Allbutt's Syst. Med.* V. 678 Syphiloma is another cause of hepatic ascites. **1903** *Brit. Med. Jrnl.* 4 Apr. 773 Syphilomatous tissue always forms rapidly.

syphilosis (sɪfɪˈləʊsɪs). *Path.* [f. SYPHILIS + -OSIS.] Syphilitic condition.

1898 *Syd. Soc. Lex.*, *Syphilosis*, syphilitic disease. **1913** *Times* 13 Aug. 3/4 A syphilosis of the lymphatics of the posterior columns of the spinal cord.

syphir, syphyr, obs. Sc. ff. CIPHER *sb.*

1508 DUNBAR *Tua Mariit Wemen* 184 He semys to be sumthing worth, that syphyr in bour. *a* **1520** —— *Poems* lviii. 20 Quha na thing hes, can na thing gett, Bot ay as syphir sett amang thame.

syphon, etc., var. SIPHON, etc.

sypirs, syprees, -es(s, -ys, obs. ff. CYPRESS.

a **1400–50** *Wars Alex.* 3684, þe solers was of Sypirs. **1530** PALSGR. 270/2 Sypres chest, *coffre de cypres*.

syplin, obs. Sc. f. SIPLING, sapling.

syr, syra, obs. ff. SIR, SIRE, SIRRAH.

Syracusan (ˈsaɪərəˌkjuːzən), *a.* and *sb.* [ad. L. *Syrācūsānus*, f. *Syrācūsæ*, Gr. Συράκουσαι Syracuse + -AN.] **a.** *adj.* Of or belonging to Syracuse, a city in Sicily. **b.** *sb.* A native or inhabitant of Syracuse.

1576 FLEMING *Panopl. Epist.* 220 Italian iunkets, and Syracusane deinties. **1611** COTGR., *Petalisme*, a forme..of banishment among the old Syracusans. **1797** *Encycl. Brit.* (ed. 3) XVII. 456/2 The city of Himera was..peopled by the Chalcidians and some Syracusan exiles. **1816** J. SMITH *Panorama Sci. & Art* II. 674 Grape,..red Syracusan. **1839** *Civil Eng. & Arch. Jrnl.* II. 435/2 Syracusan [marble]..was wrought from the *latomia*, which were quarries before Dionysius converted them into prisons. **1875** JEVONS *Money* xvi. 203 Dionysius..obliged the Syracusans to accept his tokens in place of silver coins. **1916** BUCHAN *Hist. War* lxxix. XI. 36 The Syracusan expedition was the death-blow of the Athenian Empire.

So †**Syraˈcusian** *a.* and *sb. Obs.* [cf. L. *Syrācūsius*, Gr. Συρακούσιος].

1590 SHAKS. *Com. Err.* I. i. 14 It hath..beene decreed, Both by the Siracusians and our selues, To admit no trafficke to our aduerse townes. *Ibid.* I. ii. 3 A Syracusian Marchant. **1656** STANLEY *Hist. Philos.* IV. *Bion* iii. (1687) 143/2 A Syracusian wrote of the Art of Rhetorick. **1769** SWINTON in *Phil. Trans.* LX. 85 Whose Greek inhabitants were probably for the most part either Syracusians, or of Syracusian extraction. **1797** *Encycl. Brit.* (ed. 3) XVII. 456/2 The Syracusians built Acræ, Chasmenæ, and Camarina.

Syracuse (ˈsaɪərəkjuːz). [Name of Sicilian city: see prec.] A luscious red muscadine wine made in Italy. See also quots. 1858, 1883.

1768 BOSWELL *Corsica* iii. (ed. 2) 186 At Furiani they make a white wine very like Syracuse, not quite so luscious. **1858** SIMMONDS *Dict. Trade*, *Syracuse*,..the name is also given to a white *vin de liqueur*. **1883** *Ibid.* Suppl., *Syracuse*, an old brown Marsala wine.

syraine, syrang, syranyze, syraphyn, Syrbonian: see SIREN, SERANG, SIRENIZE, SERAPHIM, SERBONIAN.

a **1618** SYLVESTER *Maiden's Blush* 1713 Past Idumæas Palmy Groves, and past Syrbonian Moors.

syrcom-, syrcum-: see CIRCUM-.

syre (saɪə(r)), *sb. Sc.* and *north. dial.* Forms: 6 **scyoure, 7 syour(e, sayer, seyer, 7–9 sire, syer, 8– syre.** [Variant of SYVER.] A gutter, drain, sewer.

1513 *Acc. Ld. High Treas. Scot.* IV. 523 To cast ane scyoure on the est syd of the place. **1601** *Charter* in Dallas *Stiles* (1697) 769 For..upholding of Sinks, Syers, Gutters, Eyes [etc.]. **1610** *Reg. Mag. Sig. Scot.* 142/1 Lie airhoillis, staires, pottis, sinkis, syoures, lang-syouris, eyis, wattergangis. **1643** in *Burgh Rec. Glasgow* (1881) II. 55 To calsey betuixt ther owne lands and the sayer. *c* **1680** [F. SEMPILL] *Banishm. Poverty* 37 in Watson *Coll. Scot. Poems* (1706) I. 12 He and I lap o're many a Syre. *a* **1823** G. BEATTIE *John o' Arnha*, etc. (1826) 95 Let loathsome toads squat in a syre. **1894** *Northumb. Gloss.*, *Sire*, a sewer, a runner of water.

syre, syreen, syren: see SIRE, SAYER[3], SIREEN, SIREN.

Syrette (sɪˈrɛt). Also **syrette**. [f. SYR(INGE *sb.* + -ETTE.] The proprietary name of a disposable injection unit, comprising a collapsible tube with an attached hypodermic needle and a single dose of a drug (esp. morphine).

1941 *Official Gaz.* (U.S. Patent Office) 9 Sept. 280/2 E. R. Squibb & Sons, New York, N.Y. Filed July 29, 1939. Syrette for injection units containing narcotic, hypnotic, sedative, analgesic, and vasoconstrictive preparations. **1947** *Sun* (Baltimore) 7 June 5/5 Morphine-containing Syrettes, used by the armed forces during the war to relieve wounded men, are finding their way into illegal narcotic channels. **1953** *Trade Marks Jrnl.* 12 Aug. 718/2 *Syrette*... Pharmaceutical preparations in collapsible tubes fitted with a hypodermic needle. **1953** [see SHOOT *v.* 23 h]. **1962** L. DEIGHTON *Ipcress File* vi. 40 Dalby put the used morphia syrette tube into a matchbox. **1976** *Interdisciplinary Sci. Rev.* I. 179/1 It would be simple to mass-produce disposable syrettes containing one unit of the anti-soma.

syrge, syrha: see SURGE, SIRRAH.

Syriac (ˈsɪrɪæk), *a.* and *sb.* Also 7 **-aque, -ack.** [ad. L. *Syriacus* = Gr. Συριακός, f. *Syria*, Συρία. Cf. F. *syriaque*, It., Pg. *syriaco*, Sp. *siriaco*.]

A. *adj.* Of or pertaining to Syria: only of or in reference to the language (see B.); written in Syriac; writing, or versed, in Syriac.

1602 T. FITZHERBERT *Apol.* 49 As wel in the Greeke text, as in the Siriac and Caldie. **1635** PAGITT *Christianogr.* I. iii. (1636) 157 The Syriaque tongue, which is composed of the Hebrew, Chalde, Arabique and Greeke tongues. **1659** BP. WALTON *Consid. Considered* ix. 179 Some Syriack Copies of the New Testament. **1683** MOXON *Mech. Exerc.*, *Printing* ii. ¶2 Some Bodies with..the Greek, the Hebrew, and the Syriack Face. **1781** GIBBON *Decl. & F.* xxxiii. (1787) III. 350 *note*, Two Syriac writers..place the resurrection of the Seven Sleepers in the year 736 (A.D. 425), or 748 (A.D. 437), of the æra of the Seleucides. **1867** LADY HERBERT *Cradle L.* iii. 101 A very curious old Syriac copy of the Four Gospels. **1895** J. R. HARRIS *Hermas in Arcadia*, etc. (1896) 45 We have not been in the habit of either studying or trusting Syriac writers in the degree they deserve.

B. *sb.* The ancient Semitic language of Syria; formerly in wide use, = ARAMAIC; now, the form of Aramaic used by Syrian Christians, in which the Peshito version of the Bible is written.

1611 *Bible* Dan. ii. 4 Then spake the Caldeans to the King in Syriacke. *c* **1645** HOWELL *Lett.* (1650) II. 93 Out of that intermixture of Hebrew and Chaldee resulted a third language call'd to this day the Syriac, which also, after the time of our Saviour, began to be more adulterated by admission of Greek, Roman, and Arabic. **1668** WILKINS *Real Char.* 5 Those passages in the Gospel, which are said to be in the Hebrew tongue, as *Talitha Kumi*,..are properly Syriac. **1780** COWPER *Progr. Err.* 499 If stubborn Greek refuse to be his friend, Hebrew or Syriac shall be forc'd to bend. **1781** GIBBON *Decl. & F.* xxxiii. (1787) III. 350 *note*, The narrative [of the Seven Sleepers] which was translated from the Syriac by the care of Gregory of Tours. **1867** WHITNEY *Lang. & Study of Lang.* viii. 298 The ancient Syriac is still the sacred dialect of the feeble bodies of Christians in Asia which represent the Syriac church. **1899** F. C. BURKITT *Early Chr. outside Roman Emp.* 16 The Syriac-speaking subjects of the Christianised Empire.

b. A or the Syriac version (of the Bible).

1644 MILTON *Areop.* (Arb.) 45 As for the burning of those Ephesian books.., tis reply'd the books were magick, the Syriack so renders them. **1692** W. MARSHALL *Gospel-Myst. Sanctif.* x. (1780) 169 The Spirit itself..beareth our spirits witness, as the Syriac and vulgar Latin render it. **1910** *Expositor* May 396 The Latin Vulgate, the two Syriacs, the Gothic.

†**c.** A printers' type of a Syriac letter or character. *Obs. rare.*

1670 R. SCOTT *Let. to Fell* in Hart *Cent. Typogr. Oxf.* (1900) 156 Yᵉ printer..giues mee notice yᵗ they ca[nnot] goe on wᵗʰ yᵉ notes vntill they haue cast a Syriack.

Hence **'Syriacism** (-əsɪz(ə)m) = SYRIASM; **'Syriacist** (-əsɪst), a Syriac scholar; **'Syriacize** (-əsaɪz) *v. trans.*, to turn or translate into Syriac.

1645 MILTON *Tetrach.* Wks. 1851 IV. 237 The New Testament..hath nothing neer so many Atticisms as Hebraisms, and Syriacisms. **1848** *Bagster's Anal. Heb. Conc.* 31 By a Syriacism, the suffixes are sometimes attached, without a union vowel. **1863** LIDDON *Some Words for God* i. (1865) 5 The words actually uttered by our Lord upon the cross, and which He took from a Syriacized version of Ps. xxii.

†**Syriacal**, *a. Obs. rare.* [f. L. *Syriacus* (see prec.) + -AL[1].] Syriac.

1565 HARDING *Answ. Jewel* 52 The Syriacall or Arabike, ..the Egyptian, Ethiopian, Persian, Armenian, Scythian, Frenche or Britaine tonge. *Ibid.* 52 b, Holy Ephrem..wrote many thinges in the Syriacal tonge.

Syrian ('sɪrɪən), *sb.* and *a.* Forms: 5 **Sirien, Syryen,** 6 **Surian, Sirian,** 7 **Sorian,** 6– **Syrian.** [a. OF. *sirien*, mod.F. *syrien*, f. L. *Syrius* (*Surius*) Syrian, or *Syria*: see -AN. Cf. SYRY.]

A. *sb.* A native or inhabitant of Syria, historically a region of Western Asia immediately east of the Mediterranean and since 1946 an independent Arab republic.

a **1400–50** *Alexander* 1447 In þe quilke þe siriens of þis sire so many soroȝes had. **1474** CAXTON *Chesse* II. iv. (1883) 48 The noble knyghtes Ioab and Abysay that fought agaynst the Syryens and Amonytes. **1535** COVERDALE *Dan.* ii. 4 The Caldees answered the kynge in the Syrians speach. **1617** MORYSON *Itin.* I. 233 The Sorians are so called of Syria, in which Prouince they liue, hauing their owne Patriarke. **1656** STANLEY *Hist. Philos.* IV. *Bion* iii. (1687) 143/2 Contemporary with Pherecydes the Syrian. **1770** LANGHORNE *Plutarch* III. 21 The Syrians roamed from town to town without discipline. **1830** H. G. KNIGHT *Eastern Sketches* (ed. 3) Pref. p. xix, The Syrians are, generally speaking, a handsome race.

B. *adj.* **1.** Of, belonging to, or characteristic of Syria or the Syrians.

1537 [COVERDALE] *Orig. & Sprynge of Sectes* 46 The Surian order, or Samaritan faytn. **1560** *Bible* (Genev.) Dan. ii. 4 *margin*, Yᵉ Syrian tongue which differeth not muche from the Caldeans. **1578** H. WOTTON *Courtlie Controv.* 38 A Knight..mounted vpon a mightie Sirian courser. **1667** MILTON *P.L.* I. 421 The Brook that parts Egypt from Syrian ground. **1821** SHELLEY *Hellas* 579 The Christian tribes Of Lebanon and the Syrian wilderness. **1841** LANE *Arab. Nts.* I. 85 He was acquainted with ancient Greek, Persian, Modern Greek, Arabic, and Syrian books. **1850** TENNYSON *In Mem.* lii, The sinless years That breathed beneath the Syrian blue. **1867** M. ARNOLD *Obermann once more* xliv, Now he is dead! Far hence he lies In that lorn Syrian town.

2. In names of plants, animals, and products actually or reputedly coming from Syria, as ***Syrian bear, goat, grape, mastic, oak, pear, rue, thistle, tobacco***: see quots.

1640 PARKINSON *Theat. Bot.* 13 *Marum Syriacum vel Creticum.* The Syrian or Candye Mastick. This Candye or Syrian Marjerome, hath sundry upright stalkes. **1649** OGILBY tr. *Virg. Georg.* II. (1684) 77 The Syrian Pear. **1760** J. LEE *Introd. Bot.* App. 325 Rue, Wild Syrian, *Peganum.* **1780** *Ann. Reg., Chron.* 223/2 A cluster of Syrian grapes, the largest..that ever grew in England. **1812** SHAW *Gen. Zool.* II. II. 374 Syrian Goat... This variety is common in many parts of the East, and is distinguished by the great length of the ears. **1838** *Penny Cycl.* XI. 357/1 The variety of thick-skinned white grape, called the Syrian. **1858** SIMMONDS *Dict. Trade, Syrian Tobacco*, the *Nicotiana rustica*..which furnishes the Turkish, Latakia, and some of the Asiatic tobaccoes. **1866** Syrian thistle [see THISTLE *sb.* 3]. **1879** E. P. WRIGHT *Anim. Life* 116 The Syrian Bear (*U[rsus] Syriacus*) is found on Mount Lebanon, and elsewhere in Western Asia.

Hence **Syri'anic** *a.*, Syriac; **'Syrianism** = SYRIASM; **'Syrianize** *v. trans.*, to make Syrian, to give a Syrian character to.

1828–32 WEBSTER, *Syrianism*, a Syrian idiom, or a peculiarity in the Syrian language. *Paley.* **1873** R. ELLIS *Numerals as Signs of Prim. Unity Man.* 56 The Hungarian *nyoltz*, 'eight', is produced by multiplying the Syrianic *njolj*, 'four', by *tz* for a 'two'. **1893** *Athenæum* 21 Oct. 552/3 'The Gospel according to Peter'..is a Syrianized Greek text. **1915** PETRIE *Handbk. Egypt. Antiq. Univ. Coll. Lond.* 34 Plaster cast of a limestone head of a man, from Thebes, an excellent instance of the delicate Syrianised type of that period.

Syrian, var. ZYRIAN *sb.* and *a.*

Syrianian, var. SIRYENIAN *sb.* and *a.*

Syriarch ('sɪrɪɑːk). [ad. L. *Syriarcha, -archus*, a. Gr. Συριάρχης, f. Συρία Syria + -αρχης ruling, ἄρχειν to rule.] The director of public games in Syria under the Romans, who was at the same time the chief priest.

1840 MILMAN *Hist. Chr.* IV. ii. III. 444. **1893** W. M. RAMSAY *Ch. in Rom. Emp.* xvi. 391 The title Syriarch, applied to the president of the games at Antioch.

Syriasm ('sɪrɪæz(ə)m). [f. SYRIAC, after a Gr. type *Συριάζειν, for Συρίζειν (see SYRISM).

Cf. the earlier SYRIACISM.]

A phrase or construction characteristic of the Syriac language; a Syriac idiom or expression.

1684 N. S. *Crit. Enq. Edit. Bible* xvi. 151 It hath..many Hebraisms and Syriasms. **1725** BLACKWALL *Sacr. Class.* (1727) 27 Hebraisms or Syriasms rather than Grecisms. **1789** G. CAMPBELL *Four Gospels* I. i. 16 Words and phrases, which..might appear to resemble what has been accounted Hebraism or Syriasm in the New Testament. **1818** T. H. HORNE *Introd. Stud. Holy Script.* II. iii. §2. I. 244 The existence of these Chaldaisms and Syriasms, affords a strong intrinsic proof of the genuineness and authenticity of the New Testament. **1907** F. C. CONYBEARE in *Expositor* July 44 It shows none of the Syriasms so frequent in Armenian versions made from Syriac.

Syri'atic, *a. rare.* [ad. L. *Syriăticus*, f. *Syria* (after *Asiăticus*): see -ATIC.] Syrian.

1786 ABERCROMBIE *Arrangem.* in *Gard. Assist.* 50 Syriatic swallow-wort, or Syrian dog's bane.

†**'Syric**, *a. Obs. rare.* In 4 **Sirik**. [ad. L. *Syricus*, f. *Syrus* (Gr. Σύρος) SYRIAN.] Syriac.

1388 WYCLIF *Dan.* ii. 4 Caldeis answeriden the kyng bi Sirik langage.

syringa (sɪ'rɪŋgə). [mod.L. *syringa*, f. Gr. συριγγ-, σῦριγξ pipe, SYRINX. First applied (by Lobel, 1576) to the mock-orange, from its stems being used for pipe-stems, later (by Linnæus, 1735) to the lilac, formerly called also *pipe-tree*, of which it remains the botanical generic name. Cf. SERINGA.] Any of the shrubs of the genus *Philadelphus*, esp. *P. coronarius*, the mock-orange, having creamy-white strongly sweet-scented flowers, cultivated as an ornamental shrub. Also = LILAC 1 a, b.

1664 EVELYN *Kal. Hort.* 67 May..Flowers in Prime, or yet lasting... Syringa's, Sedum's,..Valerian, Veronica [etc.]. **1707** MORTIMER *Husb.* (1721) II. 389 Plant Roses, Lilac, Syringas. **1728** BRADLEY *Dict. Bot., Syringa flore albo simplici*, the single white Pipe-Tree, commonly call'd Syringa by the Gardeners. **1784** COWPER *Task* VI. 150 Laburnum, rich In streaming gold; Syringa, iv'ry pure. **1862** MRS. H. WOOD *Mrs. Hallib.* xxiv, Don't cut too much of that syringa; its sweetness is overpowering in a room. **1904** A. C. BENSON *House of Quiet* xxix, A big syringa which stands above the bowling-green. **1946** T. C. MANSFIELD *Shrubs* 244 Syringa is the botanical name for Lilac. **1974** R. L. FOX *Variations on Garden* 75 The old still try and call it [*sc.* philadelphus] *Syringa* which, of course, is the proper name for lilac.

attrib. **1783** *Phil. Trans.* LXXV. 14 The trifurcated branch of a Syringa bush, or Philadelphus. **1849** BALFOUR *Man. Bot.* §865 *Philadelphaceæ*, the Syringa Family.

syringe (sɪ'rɪndʒ, 'sɪ-), *sb.* Forms: 5 **siryng, syryng,** 5–7 **siring,** 6 **syrring, syrynge, searing,** 6–7 **sirynge, syring, sering,** 7 **cyring, serring(e, sirreng, serrenge, serrindge,** 7–8 **sir(r)inge,** 7–9 **seringe,** 8 **cirenge,** 6– **syringe.** [ad. med.L. *siringa*, *sirynga* (whence OF. *ceringue*, *syringue*, F. *seringue*, It. *sciringa*, Sp. *jeringa*, Pg. *seringa*), to which is due the pronunciation with final (ŋ), which seems to have survived till near the close of the 17th cent. In the 16th cent. the word began to be assimilated to the oblique cases of the classical form *syrinx*, pl. *syringes* (sɪ'rɪndʒiːz), by being spelt with a final *e* and pronounced with (dʒ).]

1. a. A small cylindrical instrument, in its commonest form consisting of a tube fitted with a piston, but in some modern types of a tube with a rubber bulb attached, used to draw in a quantity of water or other liquid, and to eject it forcibly in a stream or jet for making injections, cleansing wounds, etc.; †also used as a catheter.

In quot. 1617 applied opprobriously to a surgeon.

a **1425** tr. *Arderne's Treat. Fistula*, etc. 33, I toke a siryng of siluer and a bleddre y-bounden aboute ful of sanguis veneris, and þe siryng y-putte in þurȝ oon hole and þe bleddre compressed wiþ þe fyngers, þe oile inȝetted went out by al þe holes togidre on boþe sides. *Ibid.* 95 It availeþ mych agayne brynnyng of vryne within in þe ȝerd, If it be cast in wyþ a syryng. **1541** COPLAND *Galyen's Terap.* 2 H iij, A syring of bras yᵗ the grekes call Cathe ring. **1543** TRAHERON *Vigo's Chirurg.* III. x. 99 b, Let thys decoction be spouted into the wounde..wyth a syrynge [orig. *siringa*]. *Ibid.* Interpr., Syrynges, Syryngx signifyeth a pype or spoute. **1561** in *Vicary's Anat.* (1888) App. vi. 189 A sering of siluer, parcell gilte. **1590** BARROUGH *Meth. Phisick* III. lvii. (1639) 192 If urine be gathered in the bladder, let it be brought out with a cyring. **1595** *Widdowes Treas.* E j, With this water with your Searing, squirt it into the Yarde. **1612** WOODALL *Surg. Mate* Wks. (1653) 12 The large Siringe containing one wine pint, commonly called the Glister Siringe. **1615** MARKHAM *Eng. Housew.* (1660) 13 Take old Ale,..adde thereto a pretty quantity of life hony, and as much Allome, and then with a serrindge or such like, wash the sores therewith. **1617** FLETCHER *Mad Lover* III. i, Surgeon, Serring, Dogleach, shall I come fetch ye? **1639** T. DE GREY *Compl. Horsem.* 106 With a pewter or elder sering or squirt inject it into his nose. **1683** SALMON *Doron Med.* I. 92 Water ..cast in with a syring. **1699** GARTH *Dispens.* v. 62 Then, from their level'd Syringes they pour The liquid Volly of a missive Show'r. **1791** *Gentl. Mag.* Jan. 22/2 The use of the syringe is generally recommended by medical practitioners in deafnesses. **1884** PYE *Surgical Handicraft* 480 The Hypodermic Syringe. **1890** *Retrospect Med.* CII. 290 Removing with spoon and syringe the clot itself within the lateral sinus. **1909** *Blackw. Mag.* Jan. 33/1 His subcutaneous syringes for morphia were worn out.

b. A similar instrument used for various purposes, as exhausting or compressing air, squirting water over plants, etc.: see quots.

1659 LEAK *Waterwks.* 3 If the Aire be prest..let it be by means of a Seringe or by a pipe. *a* **1700** EVELYN *Diary* 19 Aug. 1641, By compression of the ayre with a syringe. **1706** PHILLIPS (ed. Kersey), *Syringe*,..an Instrument made of Ivory in use among Confectioners for the making of March-panes. **1710** *New Map Trav. of High Church Apostle* 7 Two Cirenges hanging at his Saddle,..to squirt in the Eyes of his Lowflyers. **1792** *Trans. Soc. Arts* X. 275 A Syringe for watering Plants or Flowers, in imitation of rain. **1805** LOUDON *Improv. Hot-Houses* 162 Giving the whole plants and house a gentle shower with the seringe. **1831** LARDNER *Pneumat.* ii. 228 Two instruments..called syringes, one the exhausting syringe, and the other the condensing syringe. **1867** BAKER *Nile Trib.* xxi. (1872) 366 A quart syringe for injecting brine into fresh meat.

2. Applied to certain natural structures in insects.

1826 KIRBY & SP. *Entomol.* xlvi. IV. 353 *Syringes*..organs situated in various parts of larvæ, from which they ejaculate a watery fluid to annoy or drive away their enemies. **1909** *Century Dict., Suppl., Syringe*..in the head of a hemipterous insect, a chamber beneath the pharynx and extending to the grooves of the setæ in the beak,..supposed to propel the product of the salivary glands towards the tips of the setæ.

3. *Comb.*, as ***syringe-case, -needle, -pipe, -spout, -valve***; **syringe-engine**, a form of hand-pump formerly used as a fire-extinguisher; **syringe-gun**, a syringe used for disabling humming-birds by ejecting water upon them; **syringe passage**, a technique for maintaining a strain of micro-organisms or parasitic protozoans by transferring them through generations of laboratory animals by inoculation with a syringe; also (with hyphen) as *v. trans.*, to subject to this technique; **syringe-passaged** *ppl. a.*

1875 KNIGHT *Dict. Mech.*, Syringe-case. *Ibid.*, Syringe-engine. **1879** GOODE *Catal. Anim. Resources U.S.* 90 Water-guns. Syringe-guns. **1903** *Daily Chron.* 26 Oct. 5/7 To the end of the syringe fitted a needle. The enclosing metal case had apertures for the syringe needle. **1946** *Ann. Trop. Med. & Parasitol.* XL. 270 All the strains [of *Trypanosoma*] having been maintained by syringe passage through small laboratory animals. **1947** *Ibid.* XLI. 29 It is shown from the literature that a strain which is syringe-passaged through mice gradually increases in its sensitivity to arsenicals. **1970** P. J. WALKER in H. W. Mulligan *African Trypanosomiases* v. 89 Syringe passage has certain inherent defects. **1980** *Jrnl. Infection* II. 106 They [*sc.* trypanosomes] had been syringe-passaged from rodent to rodent in the laboratory. **1947** *Ann. Trop. Med. & Parasitol.* XLI. 27 All the trypano-somes present in the syringe-passaged strain were the long heterozygous form of *T[rypanosoma] rhodesiense.* **1971** P. C. C. GARNHAM *Progr. Parasitol.* iii. 28 Such trypanosomes lose their polymorphic morphology, just as they do in syringe-passaged strains in the laboratory. **1653** T. BRUGIS *Vade Mecum* (ed. 2) 147 The holes of the siringe-pipe are like to bee choaked. **1599** MINSHEU *Sp. Dict.* (1623), *Xeringa*..a siring spout to spout into the yard of him that cannot make water. **1875** KNIGHT *Dict. Mech.*, Syringe-valve.

syringe (sɪ'rɪndʒ, 'sɪ-), *v.* Forms: see prec. [f. prec. Cf. F. *seringuer*, It. *sciringare*, etc.]

1. *trans.* To treat with a syringe; to inject or sprinkle fluid into or upon by means of a syringe.

1610 T. COCKS *Diary* (1901) 99 Payde..for seringinge my pursse vj d. **1651** FRENCH *Distill.* iv. 101 Two or three drops being dropped into the Ear, after it is well syringed. **1662** GURNALL *Chr. in Arm.* verse 18. vi. 565 Do with thy soul as the Chyrurgeon with his patients wounds, who seringeth them with some sharp searching water. **1662** R. MATHEW *Unl. Alch.* §92. 159 Being deaf, I employed a man to serrenge my ear. **1747** MRS. GLASSE *Cookery* ix. 82 Your Batter being hot, syringe your Fritters in it. **1842** LOUDON *Suburban Hort.* 453 When the vine is in a growing state the air must be kept moist... This may always be effected by syringing the plants before shutting up the house. **1899** *Allbutt's Syst. Med.* VIII. 780 To syringe out any purulent lesions with carbolic solution.

absol. **1720** PRIOR *Let. to Swift* 4 May, I did not take care of my ears till I knew if my head was my own or not; but am now syringing. **1884** PYE *Surgical Handicraft* 423 Place the patient..with the affected ear downwards, and syringe from below.

2. To inject (liquid) by means of a syringe.

1653 T. BRUGIS *Vade Mecum* (ed. 2) 214 Vineger.. siringed into the eare..is good. **1737** BRACKEN *Farriery Impr.* (1756) I. 299 This Balsam is to be syringed..into the Wound. **1761** *Ann. Reg.* IV. *Usef. Proj.* 128/2 To have some warm milk and water syringed up her nostrils.

Hence **'syringed** *ppl. a.*, **'syringing** *vbl. sb.*

1658 A. FOX *Würtz' Surg.* IV. vi. 335 For pains in the mouth, a strong siringing is necessary. **1676** WISEMAN *Chirurg. Treat.* IV. vi. 326 A flux of bloud from the Nose, Mouth, and Eye, which was stopt by the syringing up of oxycrate. **1747** MRS. GLASSE *Cookery* ix. 82 Syringed Fritters. **1850** *Beck's Florist* 64 *Aristolochia hyperborea*.. requires abundant syringing during the summer, as it is a plant much subject to the attacks of red spider.

syringeal (sɪ'rɪndʒiːəl), *a. Ornith.* [f. L. *syring-*, SYRINX + -AL[1].] Of, pertaining to, or connected with the syrinx in birds.

1872 COUES *N. Amer. Birds* 178 The syringeal muscles are two pairs at most. **1883** MARTIN & MOALE *Vertebr. Dissect.* 141 Cut the trachea across just in front of the attachment of the syringeal muscles.

syringeful (sɪ'rɪndʒfʊl, 'sɪ-). [f. SYRINGE *sb.* + -FUL.] The quantity that a syringe will hold.

1733 A. MONRO in *Med. Ess. Edinb.* I. 98 The Injector.. will be able to throw several Syringe-fulls into the Vessels. **1864** *Daily Tel.* 22 Sept., There is a constant splashing and scrubbing; and if the inquiring traveller issues forth on a Saturday morning into the streets he may very likely get a syringeful of dirty water swished into his face. **1897** *Allbutt's Syst. Med.* II. 885 Shops where injections are to be had at so much the syringeful.

syringin (sɪˈrɪndʒɪn). *Chem.* Also **-ine**. [a. F. *syringine*, f. *Syringa*, generic name of the lilac: see -IN[1].] A white crystalline substance, $C_{17}H_{24}O_9$, obtained from the lilac, *Syringa vulgaris*.

1843 *Chem. Gaz.* 1 Jan. 132 Syringine is insoluble in æther. **1901** DORLAND *Med. Dict.* (ed. 2), *Syringin*.. is used as an antiperiodic in malaria.

syringo- (sɪˈrɪŋgəʊ), combining form of Gr. *σῦριγξ, συριγγ-* SYRINX, in various terms of anatomy, pathology, etc. **syringoˈbulbia**, [L. *bulbus* onion, bulb], the formation of abnormal cavities in the medulla oblongata of the brain (usu. extensions of those of syringomyelia), resulting in symptoms such as paralysis of the palate, pharynx, and larynx. **syˈringograde** *a.* and *sb.* (see quots.). ‖**syˌringoˈmyelia**, ‖**-ˈmyelus** [Gr. *μυελός* marrow, used for 'spinal cord'], dilatation of the central canal of the spinal cord, or formation of abnormal tubular cavities in its substance; hence **syˌringomyˈelic** *a.*, of or pertaining to syringomyelia; so **syˌringomyeˈlitis**, inflammation of the spinal cord producing syringomyelia; **syˌringoˈmyelocele** (see quot.). **syˈringotome** [mod.L. *syringotomus*, Gr. *-τομος* cutting], an instrument for cutting a fistula; so **syrinˈgotomy** [mod.L. *syringotomia*], incision of a fistula.

1908 *Jrnl. Med. Res.* XVIII. 127 The pathological findings have an important bearing upon the explanation of the bulbar symptoms in cases of syringomyelia and *syringobulbia. **1964** S. DUKE-ELDER *Parsons' Dis. Eye* (ed. 14) 545 In syringomyelia cavities form around which secondary gliosis develops in the cervical and upper dorsal cord; in syringobulbia the process extends up to the medulla. **1975** *Neurology* XXV. 875/1 Syringobulbia is an uncommon lesion of the central nervous system, and is particularly rare in children. **1839–47** *Todd's Cycl. Anat.* III. 433/2 *Syringograde animals. Under this denomination we shall include the Holothuria, the Salpæ, and the larvæ of those insects whose progression is effected by the alternate reception and expulsion of water to and from their respiratory organs by an action similar to that of the syringe. *Ibid.* 434/1 The velocity of the Syringogrades is accelerated during the expulsion of the water, and retarded during its reception. **1880** A. FLINT *Princ. Med.* (ed. 4) 759 Cavities of variable size and length and more or less centrally located, may be developed in the spinal cord in various ways. The name *syringomyelus* or **syringomyelia* is given to these pathological canals. **1897** *Allbutt's Syst. Med.* III. 310 In syringo-myelia very copious sweating is often observed. **1908**, **1964** Syringomyelia [see *syringobulbia* above]. **1899** *Allbutt's Syst. Med.* VI. 554 Out of 97 *syringomyelic arthropathies..29 involved the shoulder joint. **1890** BILLINGS *Nat. Med. Dict.*, **Syringo-myelitis*.., central myelitis; the formation in the spinal cord of a fissure or canal which usually lies posterior to the central canal. *Ibid.*, **Syringo-myelocele*.., a variety of spina bifida in which the central canal of the cord is dilated and the nerves run around the cyst. **1880** *Syringomyelus [see *syringomyelia*]. *a* **1883** FAGGE *Princ. Med.* (1886) I. 438 The progressive muscular atrophy due to syringomyelus. **1848** DUNGLISON *Med. Lex.* (ed. 7), *Syringotome. **1753** *Chambers' Cycl. Supp.*, *Syringotomy.

syrinx (ˈsɪrɪŋks). Pl. **syringes** (sɪˈrɪndʒiːz), also **ˈsyrinxes**. [L., a. Gr. *σῦριγξ* pipe, tube, channel, fistula.]

1. An ancient musical instrument: = PAN-PIPE. Also *attrib.*

1606 N. B[AXTER] *Sydney's Ourania* E 2, The Bittour pyping in a Syrinx Reede. **1777** FORSTER *Voy. round World* I. 456 A new musical instrument, consisting of eight, nine or ten slender reeds... Its resemblance to the syrinx, or Pan's flute of the civilized Greeks. **1818** KEATS *Endym.* IV. 686 Pipes will I fashion of the syrinx flag. **1839** T. MITCHELL *Frogs of Aristoph.* 542 *note*, Sharp and piercing syrinx-music. **1850** LEITCH tr. *C. O. Müller's Anc. Art* §387 (ed. 2) 501 Pan appears as.. the teacher of the youthful Olympus on the syrinx.

2. *Archæol. pl.* Narrow rock-cut channels or tunnels, esp. in the burial vaults of ancient Egypt.

1678 CUDWORTH *Intell. Syst.* I. iv. 322 The Former of these Two Hermes.. wrote in Hieroglyphicks upon Pillars, *ἐν τῇ Συριγγικῇ γῇ*, (as the learned Valesius conjectures it should be read, instead of *Σηριαδικῇ*.) Which *Syringes* what they were, Am. Marcellinus will instruct us. **1774** BRYANT *Mythol.* I. 505 Subterraneous passages, consisting of labyrinths cut in the rock, like the syringes in Upper Egypt. **1850** LEITCH tr. *C. O. Müller's Anc. Art* §218 The ground full of syrinxes (tombs of Beni-Hassan).

3. *Ornith.* The organ of voice in birds, also called the lower larynx, at or near the junction of the trachea and bronchi.

1872 COUES *N. Amer. Birds* 178 The syrinx has not more than one pair of intrinsic muscles. **1888** ROLLESTON & JACKSON *Anim. Life* 55 Common Pigeon... The syrinx or lower larynx is simple.

Syriologist (sɪrɪˈɒlədʒɪst). *rare.* [f. Gr. *Σύριος* SYRIAN + -LOGIST.] One versed in the study of Syrian antiquities.

1884 C. R. CONDER in *Contemp. Rev.* Dec. 857 The Egyptologist and the Assyriologist may perhaps be unwilling to allow the Syriologist, as he may be called, an equal footing with themselves.

Syrism (ˈsɪrɪz(ə)m). *rare.* [f. Gr. *Συρίζειν* to speak like a Syrian, f. *Σύρος* Syrian: see -ISM.] = SYRIASM.

1907 J. MOFFATT in *Expositor* Jan. 91 The former.. points to an expression like *ὁμολογειν ἐν τινι*.. as a 'Syrism'.

Syrjenian, var. SIRYENIAN *sb.* and *a.*

syrkett, obs. form of CIRCUIT *sb.*

syrlye, var. SIRLY *a. Obs.*

‖**syrma** (ˈsɜːmə). *Antiq.* [L., a. Gr. *σύρμα*, f. *σύρειν* to drag or trail along.] A long trailing garment, as that worn by tragic actors.

1753 *Chambers' Cycl. Supp.* **1911** R. Y. TYRRELL in *19th Cent.* Apr. 693 He pulls over his stunted shoulders the *syrma* of Attic Tragedy.

‖**syrmæa** (səˈmiːə). *Antiq.* Also **surmaia, surmia**. [mod.L., a. Gr. *συρμαία* radish used as purge-plant, purge, f. *συρμός* vomiting, purging, f. *σύρειν* to drag along, sweep away, purge.] A cathartic said to have been used in some Egyptian forms of embalming.

1833 J. DAVIDSON *Embalming* 8 The third, or common process [of embalming], consisted in passing the Surmaia (supposed a cathartic solution) through the body. **1860** *Smith's Dict. Bible* I. s.v. *Embalming*, The third mode [of embalming].. consisted in rinsing out the intestines with syrmaea, an infusion of senna and cassia. **1885** C. G. W. LOCK *Workshop Receipts* Ser. IV. 41/2 The nature of syrmaea, or, as some spell it, surmia, is not known.

syrmaism (ˈsɜːmeɪɪz(ə)m). *Antiq.* [ad. Gr. *συρμαϊσμός*, f. *συρμαΐζειν* to purge, f. *συρμαΐα* SYRMÆA.] The use of a purgative or emetic.

1842 *Smith's Dict. Grk. & Rom. Antiq.* 608/2 Dogs when indisposed sought the *Triticum repens*, and the same animal taught to the Egyptians the use of purgative, constituting the treatment called Syrmaism.

†**syrˈmatic**, *a. Obs. rare.* [ad. L. *syrmaticus*, a. Gr. **συρματικός*, f. *σύρμα* SYRMA.]

a. ? Uttered in the tone of a tragic actor.

1716 M. DAVIES *Athen. Brit.* II. 74 The Syrmatick Blaze of the Lower-House ran thus.

b. (See quot.)

1748 tr. *Vegetius' Distempers Horses* 280 A Horse or Mule that is syrmatick, or liable to trail his Limbs, is known by these Signs.

syrmountayne, var. SERMOUNTAIN *Obs.*

c **1450** *Alphita* (Anecd. Oxon.) 160/1 *Sagapium* siue *serapium*.. gallice et anglice, syrmountayne.

syrname, obs. form of SURNAME.

Syro- (ˈsɪ-, older ˈsaɪərəʊ), ad. Gr. *Συρο-*, combining form of *Σύρος* a Syrian, used with adjs. or sbs. denoting other peoples, countries, languages, etc., signifying 'Syrian or in a Syrian way', or 'Syrian and..', as ***Syro-Arabian, -Babylonian, -Chaldaic, -Chaldean, -Egyptian, -Galilean, -Græco-Roman, -Hebraic, -hexaplar, -Hittite, -Macedonian, -Mesopotamian, -Palestinian, -Persian, -Philoxenian, -Roman.***

1841 J. C. PRICHARD *Res. Physical Hist. Man* (ed. 3) III. 6 The name of *Syro-Arabians, formed on the same principle as the now generally admitted term of Indo-Europeans, would be a much more suitable expression. *Ibid.*, The Syro-Arabian tribes lost, at an early period, their ascendancy among the civilized nations of the world. **1842** PRICHARD *Nat. Hist. Man* 140 The Syro-Arabian nations, termed by Eichhorn and other German writers Semitic. **1845** KITTO *Cycl. Bibl. Lit.* s.v. *Alphabet*, A remarkable coincidence between the Syro-Arabian alphabet and the phonetic hieroglyphs. *Ibid.*, The earliest monuments of the Syro-Arabians. **1862** tr. *Renan's Age & Antiq. Bk. Nabathæan Agric.* iii. 90 The traditions of the *Syro-Babylonian school. **1835** *Q. Rev.* Sept. 307 A remarkable *Syro-Chaldaic lectionarium in the Vatican library. **1836** N. WISEMAN *Lect. Doctr. Cath. Ch.* II. xiv. 152 In Syro-Chaldaic there is no expression for to accuse or calumniate. **1845** KITTO *Cycl. Bibl. Lit.* s.v. *Zinanion*, The Gospel of Matthew was (as some think) first written in Syro-Chaldaic. **1886** *Encycl. Brit.* XX. 631/1 *Syro-Chaldeans... The language of the mass and church-office is Syro-Chaldaic. **1964** P. F. ANSON *Bishops at Large* vii. 217 Rites and ceremonies were performed like those of the *Syro-Egyptian church. **1808** STOWER *Printer's Gram.* 289 *Syro-Galilean.. Syro-Hebraic [alphabets]. **1824** J. JOHNSON *Typogr.* II. 295 The immediate descendants of the Hebrew [language] were the Samaritan, the Chaldaic, the Arabic, the Egyptian, the Ethiopian, and the Syro-Galilean. **1686** *Ussher's Lett.* 41 From the *Syro-Græco-Roman Month, Elul Gorpiæus and September began. **1808** *Syro-Hebraic [see *Syro-Galilean*]. **1865** J. H. INGRAHAM *Pillar of Fire* I. ix, Another Syro-Hebraic dynasty. **1863** *Smith's Dict. Bible* III. 1629/2 The *Syro-Hexaplar version [*i.e.* Syriac version from Hexaplar Greek Text] was made on the principle of following the Greek, word for word. **1931** *Times Lit. Suppl.* 5 Mar. 176/2 *Syro-Hittite seals. **1962** D. HARDEN *Phoenicians* xiii. 180 Those cylinder-seals and stamp-seals often termed Syro-Hittite, whose motifs and style are so obviously derived from those of Assyria and Babylonia. **1728** CHAMBERS *Cycl.* s.v. *Seleucides*, The Æra of the Seleucides, or the *Syro-Macedonian Æra. **1834** *Mirror of Time* 7 Feb., It corresponds.. with the sixth moons, *Dystrus*, *Sebastus*, and *Dius*, of the Syro-Macedonians, Paphians, and Bithynians. **1840** DE QUINCEY *Essenes* III. Wks. 1890 VII. 161 Under the Syro-Macedonian kings. **1911** G. ELLIOT SMITH *Anc. Egyptians* viii. 143 If Egypt entered into relationship with Sumer by the northern—*Syro-Mesopotamian—route. **1939** L. H. GRAY *Foundations of Lang.* 364 [Arabic] was divided into several dialects, of which only that of Mekkah has survived, this being the parent of a large number of modern vernaculars, notably Arabian.., Irāqian.., *Syro-Palestinian.., Egyptian [etc.]. **1976** *Times* 31 Jan. 13/2 Israeli intervention?.. The mere threat of it headed off Syro-Palestinian intervention in the Jordanian civil war of 1970. **1907** *Edin. Rev.* Apr. 480 Ornaments which may be described as *Syro-Persian. **1818** HORNE *Introd. Study Bible* (1827) 115 The Philoxenian or *Syro-Philoxenian Version derives its name from Philoxenus or Xenayas, Bishop of Hierapolis in Syria, A.D. 488–518. **1686** *Ussher's Lett.* 41 That *æra Dhilcarnaim* is placed by Albategnius in the beginning of the *Syro-Roman Elul or September.

syrocca, syrocco, syrone, syrop: see SIROCCO *sb.*, CIRON, SYRUP.

Syrophœnician (ˌsaɪərəʊfiˈnɪʃ(ɪ)ən), *sb.* (*a.*) *Hist.* [f. L. *Syrophœnix*, *-ic-*, fem. *-phœnissa*, a. Gr. *Συροφοίνιξ*, *-ικ-*, fem. *-φοίνισσα*: see SYRO- and PHŒNICIAN.

OE. versions of Mark vii. 26 have the adj. *sirofenisc*:— *c* **975** *Rushw. Gosp.* Mark vii. 26 *Erat autem mulier gentilis syrophoenissa genere*, wæs wutudlice wif ðæt hæðen ðæs sirophinisca cynnes; *Lindisf.* ðæs cynnes is nemned syrophoenisa; *Ags. Gosp.* sirofenisces cynnes, *Hatton* sy(e)rofeniscas cynnes.]

A native or inhabitant of Syrophœnicia, a Roman province of Western Asia, including Phœnicia and the territories of Damascus and Palmyra. Also *adj.*, belonging to this country or its inhabitants.

1560 *Bible* (Genev.) Mark vii. 26 The woman was a Greke, a Syrophenissian [**1582** *N.T.* (Rhem.) Syrophænician] by nacion. **1840** *C. O. Müller's Hist. Lit. Greece* ii. §4. 15 Aphrodite, whose worship was evidently for the most part propagated over Greece from Cyprus and Cythera by the influence of Syrophœnician tribes. **1860** *Smith's Dict. Bible* I. 856/2 This Syrophoenician worship of the sun and moon.

‖**syrphus** (ˈsɜːfəs). *Entom.* Pl. **syrphi** (ˈsɜːfaɪ). [mod.L. (as generic name in Fabricius, 1775), ad. Gr. *σύρφος* gnat.] A fly of the genus *Syrphus*, typical of the *Syrphidæ*, a large and widely-distributed family of two-winged flies, mostly bright-coloured, feeding on pollen and in the larval state often on plant-lice, etc. Hence **ˈsyrphian, ˈsyrphid** *adjs.*, belonging to this family; also as *sbs.*

1834 MᶜMURTRIE *Cuvier's Anim. Kingd.* 458 In Syrphus, properly so called, the abdomen is gradually narrowed from base to point. **1862** T. W. HARRIS *Insects Injur. Vegetat.* (ed. 3) 608 The Syrphians (Syrphidæ) have a fleshy, large-lipped proboscis. **1876** *Van Beneden's Anim. Parasites* (1883) 122 The banded Syrphus (*Syrphus balteatus*), when in the larva state, seizes the rose aphides, and sucks their blood. **1879** E. P. WRIGHT *Anim. Life* 510 The Syrphi form a pretty family of flies. **1879** *Amer. Naturalist* XIII. 260 Certain syrphus-flies, passionately fond of color, and themselves brightly colored,.. have succeeded in producing certain flowers corresponding to their tastes. **1899** D. SHARP in *Cambr. Nat. Hist.* VI. 502 Syrphid larvae.

syrra(h, syrrha, obs. ff. SIRRAH.

syrreve, obs. form of SHERIFF.

†**syrt.** *Obs.* Forms: 6 **syrte**, 6–7 **sirt**, 7–8 **syrt**. [ad. L. SYRTIS. Cf. F. (pl.) *sirtes*, *syrtes*, It., Sp. *sirte*, Pg. (pl.) *syrtes*.] = SYRTIS.

1575 *Mirr. Mag.*, *Albanact* lvi, As doth the shipman well forsee the storme, And knowes what daunger lyes in syrtes of sande. *Ibid.*, *Madan* vii, As hee that striues in soakte quicke sirts of sand Still sinkes. **1618** BOLTON *Florus* IV. xii. (1636) 328 The Musulamians and Getulians, who border upon the Syrts. **1626** tr. *Boccalini's New-found Politicke* I. 42 They discouered the.. Ocean of the Courts to be all ouer full of flats, shelues,.. quicksands,.. rocks, gulfs, whirl-pools, sirts [etc.]. **1627** MAY *Lucan* IX. 354 These Syrts.. Nature as doubtfull left twixt sea, and land. *c* **1715** YOUNG *Ocean* xvii, The syrt, the whirlpool, and the rock. **1718** ROWE tr. *Lucan* 369 These Syrts shall all be dry and solid Ground.

syrtic (ˈsɜːtɪk), *a.* [ad. L. *syrticus*, f. *Syrtis*: see next and -IC.] Of, pertaining to, or of the nature of a quicksand.

1846 WORCESTER (citing *Ed. Rev.*).

‖**Syrtis** (ˈsɜːtɪs). Pl. **Syrtes** (-iːz). Also 6–7 **sirtis**. [L., a. Gr. *Σύρτις, σύρτις*, f. *σύρειν* to drag along, sweep away.] Proper name of two large quicksands (*Syrtis major* and *minor*) off the northern coast of Africa; hence *gen.* a quicksand.

[**1398** TREVISA *Barth. De P.R.* XV. cl[i]. (Bodl. MS.) lf. 166 b/1 Sirtes beþ places in þe see ful of grauel... Sirtes beþ bi þe see of Egipte and ymedled þerwith in many places.] **1526** TINDALE *Acts* xxvii. 17 Fearynge lest we shulde have fallen into Syrtes [so COVERDALE and *Geneva*; *Great Bible* the Syrtes, *Rheims* the Syrte; 1611 the quicke-sands; Vulg. *Syrtim*, Gr. *τὴν Σύρτιν*]. **1552** ELYOT, *Cyrenaica*.. hath on the west the great Sirtis. **1667** MILTON *P.L.* II. 939 Quencht in a Boggie Syrtis, neither Sea, Nor good dry Land. **1697** DRYDEN *Æneid* IV. 59 Here lies a barren Wast of thirsty Land, And there the Syrtes raise the moving Sand. **1755** *Gentl. Mag.* July 321/2 This prodigious *syrtis*. **1771** SMOLLETT *Humph. Cl.*, *Let. to Sir W. Phillips* 12 Sept., In crossing these treacherous Syrtes with a guide, we perceived a drowned horse.

b. *pl.* used as *sing.*

1646 G. DANIEL *Addresse* 108 Wks. (Grosart) I. 13 The Labour's over If from this Syrte's wee our Sand recover. **1648** —— *Eclog* v. 124 The Syrtes of my Thought confounds my will. **1698** FRYER *Acc. E. India & P.* 58 Somewhat undermined by the beating of the Sea, where it works its self into a Syrtes.

syrup ('sɪrəp), *sb.* Forms: α. 4–6 syrope, 4–7 (9 *arch.*) syrop, (5 cyryppe, 5–7 syr-, sir-, 6–7 syrr-, sirr-, 5 -ip(pe, -yp(pe, -ipe, -epe, 5–7 -op(pe, -ope, -up(pe, -upe), 5- (now *U.S.*) sirup, 6- syrup. β. 4 surrip, surype, 5 surripe, 6 -op, 7 -ope. γ. 5 serop, -ep, 6 -oppe, serrop. δ. 5 soryp, -ippe, 6 -yppe. [a. OF. *sirop*, *cyrop*, *serop* (from 13th cent.), mod.F. *sirop* = It. *siroppo*, *sciroppo*, med.L. *siropus*, *sirupus*, *surupus*, whence MLG. *sirup*, MDu. *syro(o)p*, Du. *siroop*, MHG. *sirop*, *-up*, G., Sw., Da. *sirup*; related to the south-western Romanic forms (with or without Arabic article prefixed) Pr. *eisarop*, *isarop* (cf. MF. *ysserop*, *essyrot*), Cat. *aixarop*, Sp. *jarope* medicinal potion, bitter draught, *jarabe*, †*ajarabe* syrup, Pg. *xarope*, †*enxarope* potion, syrup; all ultimately from Arab. *sharāb* wine or other beverage, syrup, *shurb* drink: see SHRAB, SHRUB *sb.*[2], SHERBET.]

1. A thick sweet liquid; *esp.* one consisting of a concentrated solution of sugar in water (or other medium, e.g. the juices of fruits).

a. Such a liquid medicated, or used as a vehicle for medicines.

1398 TREVISA *Barth. De P.R.* VI. xxi. (Bodl. MS.) lf. 43/2 Some drinke is medicinable [as] surypes [*ed.* **1495** cyryppes], oximel [etc.]. *Ibid.* XVII. xii. 193 b/1 Sirop ymade of wormode helpeþ the lyuoure. *a* **1400–50** *Wars Alex.* 2558 My-self with a serop [*Dubl. MS.* Syrope] sall saue ȝow belyue. *a* **1400–50** *Stockholm Med. MS.* 10 For to makyn surripe þat is stryctyf. *c* **1400** *Lanfranc's Cirurg.* 76 Ȝeue him ..Julep—þat is a sirup maad oonly of water & of sugre. *c* **1450** LYDG. & BURGH *Secrees* 1990 Sorippys bittyr be profitable to the. **1450–80** tr. *Secreta Secret.* 33 It is holsome to take sowre Syrepe fastyng for flewme. **1579** TOMSON *Calvin's Serm. Tim.* 444/1 Physicians.., when they wil giue a sicke man some drinke,..will sweeten it, bycause the medicine of it selfe is vnpleasant, and therefore they mixe some sugar or syrrop with it. **1604** SHAKS. *Oth.* III. iii. 331 Not Poppy, nor Mandragora, Nor all the drowsie Syrrups of the world. **1716** *Poor Robin* Aug. B 4, Patience is as good a Medicine to cure a waspish Woman of Sullenness, as an Ants Egg in Syrup for him that is troubled with the Sciatica. **1811** A. T. THOMSON *Lond. Disp.* (1818) 680 Syrups..are saturated solutions of sugar in water, either simple, or united with some vegetable principle, with the view either to colour, flavour, or medicinal virtue. **1875** H. C. WOOD *Therap.* (1879) 18 Syrups are sugary liquids, the menstruum or basis of which is water, with, in some cases, vinegar or alcohol.

b. As used in cookery, confectionery, etc. as a sweetener, preservative, or article of food; also *gen.* (often in reference to its thick or viscid consistence).

1392–3 *Earl Derby's Exp.* (Camden) 228 Pro sugro et surrip et pro j pot de sitronade, iij duc. *c* **1430** *Two Cookery-bks.* 7 Wardonys in syryp. *Ibid.* 11 Ley it on a dysshe, an caste þe syrip þer-on. *c* **1450** *Ibid.* 87 Peris in Syrippe. **1513** DOUGLAS *Æneis* XII. Prol. 145 Hailsum of smell as ony spicery... Seroppis, sewane, sugour, and synamome. **1601** HOLLAND *Pliny* XX. xix. II. 69 Seeth it a second time with Honie up to the height or consistence of a Syrrup. **1617** MIDDLETON *Witch* I. i, Banqueting stuff, as suckets, jellies, sirups. **1697** DAMPIER *Voy. round World* (1699) 223 Small black Seeds, mixt with a certain red Pulp like thick Syrup. **1769** MRS. RAFFALD *Eng. Housekpr.* (1778) 333 Add four pounds of treble refined sugar, boil it to a thin syrup. **1816** J. SMITH *Panorama Sci. & Art* II. 435 Distil off a part of the acid, till what remains in the retort has the consistence of sirup. **1820** KEATS *Eve St. Agnes* xxx, Lucent syrops, tinct with cinnamon. **1837** M. DONOVAN *Dom. Econ.* II. 229 Molasses..is the syrup which remains after all the sugar has been crystallised from it. **1857** MILLER *Elem. Chem., Org.* (1862) ii. §1. 75 Sugar is largely used as an antiseptic, in syrups and preserves.

c. *spec.* (*a*) = MOLASSES 1. *local* (*U.S.*, etc.). (*b*) In sugar-manufacture, applied to various stages of the liquid.

c **1553** in Hakluyt *Voy.* (1599) II. II. 8 Malassos or sugar Syrope. **1699** *Laws Nevis* xxviii. §3 (1740) 22 Many Persons ..buy Syrups, Sugar, and Melasses, of Negroes who steal the same. **1728** CHAMBERS *Cycl.* s.v. *Sugar*, There are three Kinds of Syrops that run from Sugar. *Ibid.*, Sugars of fine Syrops. **1839** URE *Dict. Arts*, etc. 1204 Syrup intended for forming clayed sugar must be somewhat more concentrated in the teache. **1860** [see 2]. **1889** in *Opelousas* (Louisiana) *Democrat* 2 Feb. 2/3 Outside of Louisiana they usually call syrup molasses.

d. *transf.* A liquid of syrupy consistence.

1838 T. THOMSON *Chem. Org. Bodies* 24 It [*sc.* lactic acid] thickens to a syrup.

2. With qualifying words, indicating the source, or the flavouring or medicinal ingredient, as ***syrup of almonds***, ***s. of diacodium***, ***s. of poppies***, ***s. of rhubarb***, ***s. of roses***, ***s. of squills***, ***s. of vinegar***, ***s. of violets***, etc.; **syrup of figs**, an aperient prepared from dried figs, usu. with senna and carminatives; †**syrup of soot**, humorously for coffee; **syrup of sugar**, molasses (cf. 1 c). Also **golden syrup**, syrup of a bright golden-yellow colour, drained off in the process of obtaining refined crystallized sugar; **green syrup** (see GREEN *a.* 13).

c **1400** *Secreta Secret., Gov. Lordsh.* 83 If he haue þrist, drynke he a syrupe of roses. *a* **1400–50** *Stockholm Med. MS.* 11 For to makyn surripe of violet; it. of wormwode. **1577** B. GOOGE tr. *Heresbach's Husb.* (1586) 147 Some turne it [*sc.* milk] with..syrope of Vinegar. **1663** *Cup of Coffee* (in D'Israeli *Cur. Lit.* (1866) 296/2) A loathsome potion,.. Syrop of soot, or essence of old shoes. **1715** F. SLARE *Vindic. Sugars* 15 Some of the most pleasant Fruits are kept in the Syrup of Sugar..the Revolution of a whole Year. **1728** CHAMBERS *Cycl.* s.v., There are various Kinds of Syrops, denominated from the various Fruits, &c. they are extracted from; as Syrop of Violets, of Elder, of Wormwood, of Poppies, &c. **1741** *Compl. Fam.-Piece* I. i. 18 Take..1 Ounce of Syrup of Diacodium. **1789** W. BUCHAN *Dom. Med.* xl. (1790) 409 Such things as promote expectoration..as the syrup of squills. **1848** DUNGLISON *Med. Lex.* (ed. 7) s.v., Syrups..are chiefly used to render medicines palatable... S. of Almonds..s. of Buckthorn..s. of Garlic..s. of Rhubarb [etc.]. **1849** J. RUSKIN *Diary* Apr. in M. Lutyens *Ruskins & Grays* (1972) xxi. 188 The landlady, who noticed my illness, made me some syrup of violets. **1860** *Ure's Dict. Arts*, etc. III. 825 Crushed sugar..The concentration resembles that of loaf sugar..The first crystallisation is called 'crushed', and the second 'pieces', the drainage from which goes by the name of 'syrup'. When this syrup is diluted, filtered through animal charcoal, and concentrated, it is called 'golden syrup'. **1897** *Allbutt's Syst. Med.* III. 696 Sugar..in the form of honey, golden syrup, or still better the old fashioned black treacle, tends to act as a laxative. **1897** *Sears, Roebuck Catal.* 29/2 Sears' fig laxative (a pleasant syrup of figs for constipation.) **1902** Maple syrup [see TREACLE *sb.* 4]. **1907** *Verney Mem.* I. 9 The fruit syrups, raspberry vinegar, home-made wines..were important drinks when tea, coffee and chocolate were unknown. **1939** A. HUXLEY *After Many a Summer* II. iii. 206 The Baby was acting strange... Acting for all the world like one of those advertisements for Sal Hepatica or California Syrup of Figs. **1981** T. BARLING *Bikini Red North* i. 29 A special diet of laxative chocolate... And syrup of figs.

3. *fig.*

a **1533** LD. BERNERS *Gold. Bk. M. Aurel.* xxix. (1535) 48 b, Lyke maner they of clere vnderstandynge haue nede..to be heled with other syropes than they of grosse vnderstandyng. **1547–64** BAULDWIN *Mor. Philos.* (Palfr.) 86 Vertue..is..a sirrup that forthwith healeth. **1581** PETTIE tr. *Guazzo's Civ. Conv.* III. (1586) 145 Riches..can hardly last, without they be conserued with the sweete sirrope of wisedome. **1589** R. HARVEY *Pl. Perc.* 18 Their rellish is altered so far with the sirope of selfe loue, that Choller is called Zeale, and Melancholy Mortification. **1599** B. JONSON *Ev. Man out of Hum.* II. ii, Why, therein lies the sirrup of the iest. **1600** S. NICHOLSON *Acolastus* (1876) 55 O lend me thy insinuating power, Words steep'd in syrop of Ambrosia. **1679** ALSOP *Melius Inq.* II. iv. 268 They understood nothing of the Modern Curious Arts of Conserving Candying and Preserving Religion in Ceremonious Syrups; and yet Religion kept sweet and Good. **1890** *Spectator* 1 Feb. 170/1 Mr. Gurney's perpetual sweetness is cloying. Spiritual life is not all syrup, and Mr. Gurney's poems are almost all of them syrup.

4. *attrib.* and *Comb.*

1753 *Chambers' Cycl. Supp.* s.v., The business of syrup-making. **1875** KNIGHT *Dict. Mech.* 2191/2 Earthen sirup-jars. *Ibid.*, *Sirup-stand*, an attachment to a soda-water apparatus to supply the tumblers with sirups. **1884** *Ibid.*, *Suppl.* 818/2 The..sirup gage..is a device..for delivering a fixed quantity of sirup and carbonade into bottles at the bottling machine.

'**syrup**, *v.* [f. prec. sb.] Hence **syruped** ('sɪrəpt) *ppl. a.*, '**syruping** *vbl. sb.* and *ppl. a.*

1. *trans.* To cover with or immerse in syrup. Also, in bottling fruit, etc., to fill the bottle with syrup.

1619 DRAYTON *Quest of Cynthia* l, Yet when there haps a honey fall, Wee'll lick the sirupt leaues. **1640** T. CAREW *Complement* vi. Poems (1651) 138 Suger'd sweets, as sirropt berries. **1659** GAUDEN *Slight Healers* (1660) 34 As gilded or syrupped bitter pils. **1859** CHR. G. ROSSETTI *Goblin Market* Poet. Wks. (1904) 7/1 The drip Of juice that syruped all her face. **1875** HOWELLS *Foregone Concl.* 34 Padre Girolamo does not shower these syruped rose-leaves indiscriminately upon visitors. **1885** *Pall Mall G.* 15 Oct. 4/1 The 'syruping' and 'labelling' is..done by boys.

†**2.** To treat with medicinal syrup. *Obs.*

Cf. Sp. *jarop(e)ar*, to medicine.

1671 MAYNWARING *Anc. & Mod. Pract. Physick* 31 No syruping, no apozems, no Barly waters. **1792** W. ROBERTS *Looker-on* No. 29 (1794) I. 418 To be perfumed into health, and syrupped into a sound constitution.

3. To make into or bring to the consistence of syrup.

1847 W. J. EVANS *Sugar-planter's Man.* 174 Moulds.. admit of a..more successful syruping afterwards, should it be desirable to submit the sugar to that operation. *Ibid.* 180 Liquoring or syruping the sugar has for its object the replacing of the dark-coloured molasses by another liquid of greater purity and of lighter colour. *Ibid.* 184 When the sugar after it has been syruped is sufficiently dry, it must be ..put into hogsheads.

†**sy'rupical**, *a.* *Obs. rare*$^{-1}$. [f. SYRUP *sb.* + -ICAL.] = next.

1659 GAYTON *Art Longevity* 58 With candid sugar, Ana, and these all Boyl'd in a Balnec, till Syrrupical.

syrupy ('sɪrəpɪ), *a.* Also 8 syruppy, 9 sirupy. [f. SYRUP *sb.* + -Y.] Partaking of the qualities of syrup; *esp.* having the viscid consistence of syrup.

1707 MORTIMER *Husb.* (1721) II. 344 Apples..that are of a syrupy tenacious nature. **1733** SHAW *Chem. Lect.* xi. (1755) 218 A..rich, syrupy, or treacly Substance. **1740** A. HILL in *Richardson's Corr.* (1804) I. 49 The must, so enriched from its syruppy consistence of body. **1830** M. DONOVAN *Dom. Econ.* I. 281 A sweet and sirupy wine will become improved by keeping on the lees. **1842** T. GRAHAM *Elem. Chem.* III. ii. §2. 774 Phosphovinic acid is a colourless, syrupy liquid. **1897** *Allbutt's Syst. Med.* III. 292 The fluid is evaporated until it acquires a syrupy consistency.

fig. **1832** *Examiner* 663/1 Her voice has lost none of its sirupy richness. **1866** *Contemp. Rev.* II. 186 It is not easy to translate such syrupy sentiment

syrurge, -gery, -gyan: see CHIRURGE, CHIRURGERY, CHIRURGEON.

†**Syry**, *a.* *Obs.* Also 4 Siry, 5 Sire. [ad. L. *Syrius*, a. Gr. Σύριος SYRIAN.] Syrian.

1382 WYCLIF *Dan.* ii. 4 Caldeis answerden to the kyng by Siry [1388 Sirik] speche. *c* **1449** PECOCK *Repr.* IV. iv. 438 Cephas..is..a word of Sire tunge. **1526** *Pilgr. Perf.* (W. de W. 1531) 180 b, After Saynt Bede, in the Syry tonge, Maria is as moche to saye as a lady.

Syryane, Syryen, varr. ZYRIAN *sb.* and *a.*

Syryenian, var. SIRYENIAN *sb.* and *a.*

sys(e: see SEE *v.*, SICE, SITHE *sb.*[1], SIZE.

syser, var. SICER *Obs.*, strong drink.

sysers, sysors, -owrys, etc., obs. ff. SCISSORS.

sysertskite ('sɪsətskaɪt). *Min.* Also sis(s)erskite. [ad. G. *sisserskit* (W. von Haidinger *Handb. der bestimmenden Min.* (1845) IV. 558), f. *Sysert'*, name of a city near Sverdlovsk in Russia: see -ITE[1].] A native alloy of osmium and iridium; iridosmine; (see also quots.).

1850 J. D. DANA *Syst. Min.* (ed. 3) 547 At a high temperature the Sisserskite gives out osmium, but undergoes no further change. **1938** *Mineral. Abstr.* VII. 162 The natural alloys are divided into three groups: (1) iridium group with 0–35% Os, cubic; (2) nevyanskite with 35–50% Os; (3) sysertskite with 50–70% Os. **1963** [see NEVYANSKITE]. **1965** G. J. WILLIAMS *Econ. Geol. N.Z.* x. 155/1 In the other [fraction] consisting of flattened grains of light steel-grey colour, Os was found in excess of Ir, and the Ru proportion is higher—siserskite or ruthenian siserskite. **1973** S. E. LIVINGSTONE in J. C. Bailar et al. *Comprehensive Inorg. Chem.* III. xliii. 1165 Alloys of osmium and iridium occur in placer deposits. These are known as osmiridium or sysertskite—with less than 60% (usually *ca.* 50%) iridium and *ca.* 35% osmium—and iridosmium or nevyanskite—with over 60% (usually *ca.* 70%) iridium and *ca.* 20% osmium.

syskenne, sysme, sysour(e: see SISKIN, SCHISM, SIZER[1].

syss, Sc. pl. of SITHE *sb.*[1] *Obs.*

a **1500** *Lancelot* 3054 And to sir gawan..Me recommend and thonk a thousand syss.

‖**syssarcosis** (sɪsɑː'kəʊsɪs). Also 7–8 sysarcosis. [mod.L., a. Gr. συσσάρκωσις, f. συσσαρκοῦν to unite by flesh, cover over with flesh, f. σύν SYN-[1] + σάρξ flesh.]

1. *Anat.* The union of bones by means of intervening muscle.

1676 WISEMAN *Chirurg. Treat.* VII. ii. 479. **1726** MONRO *Anat. Bones* 267 The Scapula..is connected by Sysarcosis to the Head, Vertebræ, Ribs and Os Hyoides. **1835–6** *Todd's Cycl. Anat.* I. 257.

2. *Path.* and *Surg.* The healing of a wound by granulation or the formation of new flesh.

1753 *Chambers' Cycl. Supp.*, *Syssarcosis*..is also used..to express a method of curing wounds of the head..by means of promoting the granulation, as it is called, or growth of new flesh. **1767** [see SYMPHYSIS 1 c].

sysse, obs. form of SICE.

'**syssel.** *Iceland.* [ad. Icel. *sýsla* business, work, stewardship, prefecture, diocese.] (See quots.) Hence '**sysselman**.

c **1792** *Encycl. Brit.* (ed. 3) IX. 90/2 The governor [of Iceland]..has under him a bailiff, two laymen, a sheriff, and 21 sysselmen, or magistrates who superintend small districts. **1838** *Penny Cycl.* XII. 427/1 These districts [of Iceland] are divided into syssels, or sheriffdoms, a sysselman being a magistrate and receiver of the king's taxes in each of them.

‖**syssitia** (sɪ'sɪtɪə). *Gr. Antiq.* [a. Gr. συσσίτια, pl. of συσσίτιον common meal, or συσσιτία, n. of action f. σύσσιτος eating in common or συσσιτεῖν to mess in common, f. σύν SYN-[1] + σῖτος food.]

a. Meals eaten together in public. **b.** The custom of eating the chief meal of the day at a public mess, as practised in Sparta and Crete. Also **syssition** (-'ɪtɪɒn), a common meal, mess.

1835 THIRLWALL *Greece* I. vii. 287 The most important feature in the Cretan mode of life, is the usage of the *Syssitia*, or public meals, of which all the citizens partook. **1846** GROTE *Greece* II. vi. II. 504 [Lycurgus] constituted..the Syssitia or public mess. **1874** SYMONDS *Sk. Italy & Greece* (1898) I. xiii. 287 Necessity and the waiter drive them all to a sepulchral syssition.

transf. **1885** *Pall Mall G.* 27 May 6/1 As regards the midday meal, I am aware that dinner is provided for the few who elect to do the preparation work at school,..but this is a very different thing from the syssitia that I desiderate.

syst, obs. 2nd sing. ind. pres. of SEE *v.*

systaltic (sɪ'stæltɪk), *a.* [ad. late L. *systalticus*, a. Gr. συσταλτικός, f. σύν SYN-[1] + σταλτός, vbl. adj. f. σταλ-: στέλλειν to place, put (cf. SYSTOLE). Cf. F. *systaltique*.]

1. *Phys.* Contracting; of the nature of contraction; *spec.* applied to movement, as that of the heart, in which there is alternate contraction (*systole*) and dilatation (*diastole*).

1676 *Phil. Trans.* XI. 722 The Systaltick motion of the circumjacent parts, for returning the bloud along the veins to the heart. **1747** tr. *Astruc's Fevers* 156 In such disorders, the sudden systaltic constriction of the skin produces the chilness. **1848** DUNGLISON *Med. Lex.* (ed. 7).

†**2.** Applied to the power of 'materialization' (conceived as contraction or condensation) of a disembodied or unembodied spirit. *Obs.*

1687 H. MORE *Contn. Remark. Stor.* (1689) 411 An eminent Example of this Systaltick Power of Spirits, viz., an Arm seen..striking such a stroke upon the Floor, that it made the very Walls of the House to shake. **1712** *H. More's Antid. Ath.* III. ix. §2. *Schol.* 173 The Devil would so manage himself by the motion..of his body, which by this Systaltick power he could make tangible and palpable.

†**3.** In ancient Greek music applied to a style of melody having the effect of 'contracting' or depressing the mind, or affecting it with tender emotion. *Obs.*

a **1698** W. HOLDER *Princ. Harmony* (1731) 151 The First of these [Keys] is call'd by the Greeks Diastaltic, Dilating; the Second, Systaltic, Contracting; the Last, Hesychiastic, Appeasing. **1776** BURNEY *Hist. Mus.* I. v. 69 *Melopoeia* was divided into three kinds: first, the Systaltic, or that which inspired the..tender passions, as well as the plaintive.

†**systasis** ('sɪstəsɪs). *Obs.* [med. or mod.L., a. Gr. σύστασις composition, collection, union, alliance, f. σύν SYN-¹ + στα- (see SYSTATIC).]

1. The act, or the result, of setting or putting together; combination, synthesis. Also, system.

1605 BACON *Adv. Learn.* II. xvii. §11 Other diversities of Methods..as that of Resolution or Analysis, of Constitution or Systasis, of Concealment or Cryptique. **1658** SIR T. BROWNE *Gard. Cyrus* iv. 68 The three substances..; That is, the indivisible or divine, the divisible or corporeal, and that third, which was the Systasis or harmony of those two, in the mystical decussation. **1710** T. FULLER *Pharm. Extemp.* 201 An..Exultation of the whole Systasis of the Spirits.

2. A political union or confederation. (Cf. SYNCRETISM.)

1790 BURKE *Rev. France* 328 The municipal army..is a worse preservative of a general constitution, than the systasis of Crete, or the confederation of Poland.

systatic (sɪ'stætɪk), *a.* (*sb.*) [ad. med. and mod.L. *systaticus*, a. Gr. συστατικός commendatory, drawing together, compacting, f. σύν SYN-¹ + στα- to place (see STAND *v.*), after συνιστάναι to associate, put together, combine, bring together as friends, introduce.]

1. Pertaining to or involving 'systasis'; synthetic.

1640 G. WATTS tr. *Bacon's Adv. Learn.* VI. ii. 276 Those other Methods, Analytique; Systatique; Dieritique; [etc.].

2. *Path.* Involving several of the sensory powers simultaneously; *sb.* a disease which does this.

[**1820** GOOD *Nosology* 348 Systatica.] In recent Dicts.

3. ***systatic letter*** or ***epistle*** (med.L. *litteræ systaticæ*), an introductory or commendatory letter. *rare.*

a **1919** *N.E.D.* 'In recent Dicts.' **1947** G. EVERY *Byzantine Patriarchate* xiii. 177 The synod decided to ask the Pope for a 'systatic letter'. **1955** S. RUNCIMAN *Eastern Schism* ii. 32 His successor, Sergius IV, sent a Systatic Letter to Constantinople.

†**sy'statical,** *a. Obs.* [Formed as prec. + -ICAL.] Relating to combination or synthesis.

1674 JEAKE *Arith.* 662 Three..is called a Systatical or Substantial Number, because all Sublunary Bodies consist of the three principal Substances, Sal, Sulphur, and Mercury.

system ('sɪstɪm, -əm). Also 7-8 **systeme,** 8 **sistem(e.** [ad. late L. *systēma* musical interval, in med. or mod.L., the universe, body of the articles of faith, a. Gr. σύστημα organized whole, government, constitution, a body of men or animals, musical interval, union of several metres into a whole, f. σύν SYN-¹ + στα-, root of ἱστάναι to set up (see STAND *v.*). Cf. F. *système* (1664, 'le systeme de l'ame', in Hatz.-Darm.), It., Sp. *sistema*, Pg. *systema*, G. *system*, etc.]

I. An organized or connected group of objects.

1. A set or assemblage of things connected, associated, or interdependent, so as to form a complex unity; a whole composed of parts in orderly arrangement according to some scheme or plan; rarely applied to a simple or small assemblage of things (nearly = 'group' or 'set').

a **1638** MEDE *Apostasy Latter Times* (1641) 64 Mans life is a systeme of divers ages... The yeare is a systeme of foure seasons. **1651** HOBBES *Leviath.* II. xxii. 115 By Systemes; I understand any numbers of men joyned in one Interest, or one Businesse. *a* **1676** HALE *Prim. Orig. Man.* I. i. (1677) 15 The Universe, as it comprehends the Systeme, Order and Excellencies of all created Beings. **1729** BUTLER *Serm.* Wks. 1874 II. 31 The body is a system or constitution: so is a tree: so is every machine. **1775** BRYANT *Mythol.* II. 469 The exit from the Ark; when the whole of the animal system issued to light. **1788** PRIESTLEY *Lect. Hist.* III. xiv. 111 The Greeks distributed their years into systems of four, calling them Olympiads. **1802** PALEY *Nat. Theol.* xxv. (1819) 398 The universe itself is a system; each part either depending upon other parts, or being connected with other parts by some common law of motion. **1829** *Chapters Phys. Sci.* 391 The ancients divided the starry sphere into..constellations, or systems of stars.

b. *spec.* (with *this*, a possessive, or the like): The whole scheme of created things, the universe.

1619 SELDEN *Upon Drayton's Bar. Wars* D.'s Poems A iv b, Thy Martiall Pyrrhique, and thy Eqipue straine Digesting Warres with heart-vniting Loues; The two first Authors of what is compos'd In this round Systeme All. **1769** E. BANCROFT *Guiana* 2 The blessings of Nature, have in no part of our habitable system, been dispensed with a more liberal hand. **1816** G. FIELD in *Pamphleteer* (1817) IX. 101 (*title*) Τριτογενεα; or, a Brief Outline of the Universal System.

c. With *the*: (*a*) The prevailing political, economic, or social order, esp. regarded as oppressive; the Establishment; any impersonal, restrictive organization. Freq. with capital initial.

1806 C. WILMOT *Let.* 23 Mar. in Londonderry & Hyde *Russ. Jrnls.* (1934) II. 223 Dozens of Slaves are waiting..to greet the Princess... Her Lenity makes their Lot better perhaps than that of others, but that's saying very little for the System. **1855** *Mechanics' Mag.* LXIII. 542 (*heading*) It is the system. *Ibid.*, I have not heard anything of it from that day to this, and must therefore infer that his Lordship was *instigated* by the 'system'. **1906** U. SINCLAIR *Jungle* xxx. 384 These Western fellows were just 'meat' for Tommy Hinds—he would get a dozen of them around him and paint little pictures of 'the System'. **1911** H. WALPOLE *Mr. Perrin & Mr. Traill* ix. 178 She suddenly..had a revelation..that it wasn't really any one's fault at all—that it was the system, the place, the tightness and closeness and helplessness that did for everybody. **1965** G. JACKSON *Let.* June in *Soledad Brother* (1971) 78 It's frayed nerves, caused by the harsh terms that defeat brought when they went against the system, the same system that runs this place. **1973** *Ottawa Jrnl.* 18 May 16/1 It is the deeply moving, contemporary story of a young man who wouldn't surrender to the System ..and the girl who always stood beside him. **1977** *Gay News* 24 Mar. 20/1 No, I accepted the system wholeheartly—the suit, white stiff collar and tie, night school, the lot. **1981** 'A. CROSS' *Death in Faculty* vi. 65 If I hadn't made it quite to Harvard, I might still have thought there was a chance for me in the system. But Harvard—the oxygen was too pure.

(*b*) *spec.* (See quot. 1945.) *Austral. Hist.*

1874 M. CLARKE *His Natural Life* (1875) III. IV. vii. 194 'You have a future to live for, man.' 'I hope not,' said the victim of the 'system'. **1934** B. PENTON *Landtakers* (1935) I. v. 42 Joe's..not the same as other lags... The System soon breaks them up, but Joe it just sets on fire and leaves him as hard as brick. **1945** BAKER *Austral. Lang.* ii. 43 The prison at Fremantle was the *establishment*, a term which is fit to rank with *the System*—as transportation in general and the maltreatment of prisoners in particular became known—as notable examples of understatement.

2. *Physics.* A group of bodies moving about one another in space under some particular dynamical law, as the law of gravitation; *spec.* in *Astron.*, a group of heavenly bodies connected by their mutual attractive forces and moving in orbits about a centre or central body, as the *solar system* (the sun with its attendant planets, etc.), the *system* of a planet (the planet with its attendant satellites).

1690 LOCKE *Hum. Und.* IV. iii. §24 If we..confine our Thoughts to this little Canton, I mean this System of our Sun. *a* **1704–1842** [see SOLAR *a.* 7]. **1715** tr. *Gregory's Astron.* (1726) I. I. ix. 117 Of the Motion of a System of Bodies revolving about another Body; all which is applied to the System of the Sun, and the Primary and Secondary Planets. **1732** POPE *Ess. Man* I. 25 Observe how system into system runs, What other planets circle other suns. **1816** [see PLANETARY *a.* 1]. **1850** TENNYSON *In Mem.* Concl. 122 Star and system rolling past. **1870** PROCTOR *Other Worlds* xii. 274 First satellite-systems, then planetary systems, then star-systems, then systems of star-systems. **1878** STEWART & TAIT *Unseen Univ.* iii. §103. 114 Taking as our 'system of bodies' the whole physical universe. **1890** C. A. YOUNG *Elem. Astron.* §362 The range of the system [of Saturn] is enormous. Iapetus [the outermost satellite] has a distance of 2,225,000 miles.

3. *Biol.* **a.** A set of organs or parts in an animal body of the same or similar structure, or subserving the same function, as the ***nervous, muscular, osseous,*** etc. ***systems,*** the ***digestive, respiratory, reproductive,*** etc. ***systems***; also, each of the primary groups of tissues in the higher plants.

1740 CHEYNE *Regimen* 168 Accidents that injure the arterial and nervous system. **1838–9** KEMBLE *Resid. Georgia* (1863) 13 The diseases of the muscular and nervous systems. **1841** T. R. JONES *Anim. Kingd.* 302 The generative system appears, at first, to be absolutely wanting in the larva. **1875** BENNETT & DYER tr. *Sachs' Bot.* 77 Forms and Systems of Tissues... We..usually find an Epidermal System, a Fascicular System, and the system of the Fundamental Tissue between them. **1899** *Allbutt's Syst. Med.* VIII. 699 Affections of the pigmentary system.

b. With *the* or possessive: The animal body as an organized whole; the organism in relation to its vital processes or functions.

Occas. extended to include the mind.

[**1683** TRYON *Way to Health* 312 When once the same is wounded, the whole Systeme of Nature is disordered.] **1764** GOLDSM. *Trav.* 347 Till, over-wrought, the general system feels, Its motions stop. **1805** *Med. Jrnl.* XIV. 526 Introducing vaccine virus into the system. **1806** J. BERESFORD *Miseries Hum. Life* XII. xxv, *Ennui* so powerfully predominates over your whole system, mental and bodily, that [etc.]. **1908** R. BAGOT *A. Cuthbert* xxiii. 300 It is extraordinary how long it takes to get those malarial fevers out of the system.

c. In fig. phr. ***to get*** (something) ***out of one's system*** and varr.: to rid oneself of some preoccupation or obsession, esp. by indulging in it to a point of satiety. Cf. quot. 1908, sense 3 b.

1900 H. A. JONES *Mrs. Dane's Defence* IV. 80 I'm rather glad he has taken it [*sc.* a disappointment in love] so violently... It means that in six months it will be out of his system. **1911** G. STRATTON-PORTER *Harvester* xviii. 430 Let me finish... Let me get this out of my system. **1962** P. GREEN tr. *S. de Beauvoir's Prime of Life* iii. 129 She still saw him occasionally, trying, at one and the same time and with equal lack of success, to win him back and get him out of her system. **1970** *New Yorker* 17 Oct. 39/1 By the time I put a couple of drinks under my belt, I worked the whole thing out of my system. **1974** J. GARDNER *Return of Moriarty* 28 We had stayed silent, it was better to let the young fool get it out of his system.

4. In various scientific and technical uses: A group, set, or aggregate of things, natural or artificial, forming a connected or complex whole. **a.** of natural objects or phenomena, as geological formations, mountains, rivers, winds, forces, etc.; also of lines, points, etc. in geometry.

1830 LYELL *Princ. Geol.* I. 125 We may select the great carboniferous series..as the oldest system of rocks of which the organic remains furnish any decisive evidence as to climate. **1831** BREWSTER *Optics* xxviii. 237 If we place a sphere of glass in a glass trough of hot oil, and observe the system of rings, while the heat is passing to the centre of the sphere. **1840** LARDNER *Geom.* 261 Any system of conjugate diameters of an ellipse. **1860** TYNDALL *Glac.* I. vi. 43 We had a good view of the glacier system of the region. **1885** GEIKIE *Text-bk. Geol.* (ed. 2) VI. Introd. 631 We speak of the Chalk or Cretaceous system, and embrace, under that term, formations which may contain no chalk. **1893** H. N. DICKSON *Meteorol.* i. §12 Winds arranged in a rotating system. *Ibid.* iii. §45 Low pressure system or cyclone. **1912** T. G. BONNEY *Work of Rain & Rivers* iv. 95 The History of a River System.

b. of artificial objects or appliances arranged or organized for some special purpose, as pulleys or other pieces of mechanism, columns or other details of architecture, canals, railway lines, telegraphs, etc.

1830 HERSCHEL in *Encycl. Metrop.* (1845) IV. 804 Joint vibrations of a plate and string as a system. **1851** RUSKIN *Stones Venice* (1874) I. viii. 88 Magnificent buildings have been composed of systems of small but perfect shafts. **1855** BAIN *Senses & Int.* I. ii. §8. (1864) 31 A system of telegraph wires. **1868** FREEMAN *Norm. Conq.* II. ix. 318 The system of beacons, which has been traced out over a long range of the hill-tops. **1892** *Daily News* 1 Nov. 6/6 The principal members of the staff are residents upon the company's system and daily travellers upon the line.

c. *Geol.* A major stratigraphic division, composed of a number of series and corresponding to a period (PERIOD *sb.* 4 b) in time; the rocks deposited during any specific period.

1829 A. SEDGWICK in *Trans. Geol. Soc.* III. 121 The previous statements seem to show, that the system of the new red sandstone could not have been produced by any sudden and transitory agency. **1835** —— in *Ibid.* IV. 70 The lowest beds of the carboniferous system of this region. **1835** R. I. MURCHISON in *Phil. Mag.* VII. 48, I venture to suggest ..the term 'Silurian system' should be adopted as expressive of the deposits which lie between the old red sandstone and the slaty rocks of Wales. **1839** —— *Silurian System* xiv. 169, I venture..to apply to it [*sc.* the Old Red Sandstone] the term system, in order to convey a just conception of its importance in the natural succession of rocks. **1882** A. GEIKIE *Text-bk. Geol.* 636 The Geological Record is classified into five main divisions... These divisions are further ranged into systems, each system into series..or formations, each formation into groups or stages. **1898, 1927** [see GROUP *sb.* 4 b (iii)]. **1944** A. HOLMES *Princ. Physical Geol.* vii. 103 Pebbles of Shap granite..occur in the conglomerates at the base of the Carboniferous system in Westmorland. **1961** *Bull. Amer. Assoc. Petroleum Geologists* XLV. 658/2 The system is the fundamental unit of world-wide time-stratigraphic classification of Phanerozoic rocks. .. In the Precambrian, systems still have only local significance. **1971** *Nature* 12 Feb. 480/2 In historical geology, the subdivision of periods into epochs and ages (or systems into series and stages) is usually defined by unconformities.

d. The set of the various phases that two or more given metals are capable of forming at different temperatures and pressures. Usu. with qualifying term, as ***alloy system.***

1911 *Jrnl. Inst. Metals* V. 127 In the year 1897 the late Sir William Roberts-Austen..published the complete freezing-point curve of the copper-zinc alloys... This diagram was the first attempt to construct what would in present-day terminology be the Equilibrium Diagram of the Copper-Zinc System. **1922** *Encycl. Brit.* XXXI. 927/2 In non-ferrous alloys, considerable attention has been given to the alloys of zinc, a portion of the ternary system copper-aluminium-zinc. **1967** A. H. COTTRELL *Introd. Metallurgy* xv. 233 Many alloy systems are complicated by the appearance of several intermediate phases. **1977** *Sci. Amer.* July 82/3 Both cements are based on the ternary system of oxides of calcium, silicon and aluminum (CaO-SiO_2-Al_2O_3).

e. *Linguistics.* A group of terms, units, or categories, in a paradigmatic relationship to one another.

1953 R. H. ROBINS in *Trans. Philol. Soc.* 109 Professor J. R. Firth has recently suggested that the terms 'Structure' and 'System' be kept distinct in the technical vocabulary of linguistic description. 'Structure' might be used to refer to undimensional, linear abstractions at various levels from utterances or parts of utterances... When..categories have been devised by means of which the utterances of the language can be successfully described and analysed, closed systems are formed of these categories. **1956** J. R. FIRTH in *Trans. Philol. Soc. 1955* 91 Neither the Americans nor the Scandinavians have controlled and distinguished the use of *system* and *structure* as we have in the linguistics group at the School of Oriental and African Studies. **1961** Y. OLSSON *Syntax Eng. Verb* ii. 27 Values for the elements are given by *terms* which commute, that is, operate along the line one-instead-of-another; terms constitute *systems*. **1964** R. H. ROBINS *Gen. Linguistics* ii. 49 It is useful to employ *structure* ..specifically with reference to groupings of syntagmatically related elements, and *system* with reference to classes of paradigmatically related elements. **1977** *Canad. Jrnl. Linguistics 1976* XXI. II. 196 Throughout the late 'fifties and early 'sixties he [*sc.* M. A. K. Halliday] extended J. R. Firth's concepts of 'system' and 'structure' and 'modes of meaning' into what came to be known as scale and category linguistics.

f. *Computers.* A group of related programs; *spec.* = ***operating system*** s.v. OPERATING *vbl. sb.* b.

1963 L. SCHULTZ *Digital Processing* xiii. 271 In applications such as were described in Chapter 6, a system of programs rather than a single program is necessary. **1972** *Computers & Humanities* VII. 82 If a package of programs is so tightly integrated that output from one program is automatically input to another program, then it is frequently called a system. **1978** LYNCH & RICE *Computers* ix. 407 A system..handles the manipulation of source programs, language translators, input-output and so on.

g. With reference to business and social organizations and the operations or interactions they involve (see also quot. 1967[2]).

1963 *Brit. Jrnl. Sociol.* XIV. 38 The idea of 'system' has been used to imply that its parts (organizations or institutions) are interdependent with each other: that the performances of the parts have consequences or functions, consequences for the 'performing' part, consequences for other 'parts', consequences for the whole system. **1965** H. I. ANSOFF *Corporate Strategy* (1968) ix. 166 The term 'systems' is becoming popular for describing large-scale non-military industrial projects. **1967** R. WHITEHEAD in Wills & Yearsley *Handbk. Managem. Technol.* iv. 70 The health of the nation is made possible by a number of systems: doctors, nurses, hospitals, pharmaceutical companies, chemists, and, of course, patients. These are not isolated systems but interacting parts of a large and exceedingly complex whole. *Ibid.* iv. 54 The typewriter may be a relatively simple machine but in this context it is a system with a person and a machine coupled together, both interrelated and interacting. **1969** D. C. HAGUE *Managerial Econ.* i. 17 We have been considering models for analysing business problems. These seek to state the set of relationships—what we shall call the system—within which and about which business decisions have to be taken.

h. Colloq. phr. ***all systems go***: everything functioning correctly, ready to proceed; everything fully operational. Chiefly *fig.* (orig. *U.S.*).

1962 [see GO *a.* 1]. **1967** A. LURIE *Imaginary Friends* i. 8 The Seekers were looking for new members, and we should have no trouble making contact. As McMann put it, all systems were Go. **1969** *Times* 22 July (Moon Rep. Suppl.) p. i/1 Neil Armstrong on the porch of the Eagle at 109 hours 19 minutes and 30 seconds to L.O.S., all systems go, over. **1977** *Listener* 7 Apr. 450/1 It was *sportsfest* time again for the BBC last week—all systems go.

i. A prefabricated construction unit used in system building (see *system building*, sense 11 d below).

1963 [see INDUSTRIALIZED *ppl. a.*]. **1969** H. A. FREY tr. *Schmid & Testa's Syst. Building* 26/2 Building with systems is naturally more compatible with team thinking than with the approach of the isolated independent architect. **1974** *Encycl. Brit. Macropædia* III. 455/2 Basically a modular volumetric unit composed of some combination of walls, roof, and/or floor, the box system is usually prefabricated in a plant.

5. *Mus.* **a.** In ancient Greek music, A compound interval, i.e. one consisting of several degrees (opp. to DIASTEM); also, a scale or series of notes extending through such an interval, and serving as the basis of musical composition.

1656 BLOUNT *Glossogr.*, *Systeme*,..the compasse of a song, or (by a metaphor) of any other thing. **1672** T. SALMON *Ess. Adv. Musick* 58 The entire Systeme of an Octave. **1694** HOLDER *Treat. Harmony* vi. 110 Diastem signifies an Interval..; System, a Conjunction..of Intervals. *Ibid.* 111 Thus a Tone was a Diastem, and Diatessaron was a System, compounded of Degrees... And the Scale of Notes which they used, was their Greatest, or Perfect System. **1721** A. MALCOLM *Treat. Mus.* 333 That we may know where each Part lies in the Scale or general System,..which is the true Design and Office of the Clefs. *Ibid.* 335 By this constant and invariable Relation of the Clefs, we learn easily how to compare the particular Systems of several Parts, and know how they communicate in the Scale. **1776** BURNEY *Hist. Mus.* I. i. 12. **1898** STAINER & BARRETT *Dict. Mus. Terms* 207/2 After the time of Ion, the original Greek scale received only one more string, the eleventh... In this..form, it became the 'lesser perfect system' of the Greeks. *Ibid.* 208 The Greater Perfect System.

b. Applied to a stave (*obs.*), or to a set of staves connected by a brace in a score of concerted music.

1672 T. SALMON *Ess. Adv. Musick* 63 A Mean and Treble, which may be..placed upon a Systeme of four or five lines. **1889** GROVE *Dict. Mus.* IV. 45/2 *System*, the collection of staves necessary for the complete score of a piece.

6. *Gr. Pros.* A group of connected verses or periods, esp. in anapæstic metres.

1850 MURE *Lit. Greece* III. 54 A System is a..section of the text of a metrical composition, the numbers of which.. are too extensive to admit of their being comprised in a single verse. **1861** PALEY *Æschylus* (ed. 2) *Agam.* 40 *note*, The chorus of old men.. enter the orchestra..and..sing the following system of anapaests.

†**7.** A pad formerly worn by women to raise up the hair: see TOQUE 1 b, quot. 1817. *Obs.*

II. A set of principles, etc.; a scheme, method.

8. The set of correlated principles, ideas, or statements belonging to some department of knowledge or belief; a department of knowledge or belief considered as an organized whole; a connected and regularly arranged scheme of the whole of some subject; a comprehensive body of doctrines, conclusions, speculations, or theses.

a **1656** HALES *Serm. 2 Pet. iii. 16* Gold. Rem. (1673) 11 Their acquaintance with some *Notitia*, or Systeme of some technical divine. **1678** CUDWORTH (*title*) The True Intellectual System of the Universe. **1699** T. BAKER *Refl. Learn.* i. 4 The moderns.. more pleas'd with their own inventions, than with the dry Systems of the Old Philosophers. *Ibid.* vi. 63 The last Systeme of Logic that I have met with. **1758** C. FLEMING (*title*) A Survey of the Search after Souls,..wherein The principal Arguments for and against the Materiality are collected: And the Distinction between the mechanical and moral System stated. **1781** GIBBON *Decl. & F.* xxvii. III. 59 The humanity of Ambrose tempted him to make a singular breach in his theological system. **1833** TENNYSON *Two Voices* 207 A dust of systems and of creeds. **1845** J. MARTINEAU *Ess.* (1891) II. 341 Morality is not a system of truths, but a system of rules. In other words, it is not a science, but an art. **1850** TENNYSON *In Mem.* Prol. 17 Our little systems have their day. **1875** JOWETT *Plato* (ed. 2) IV. 421 In the Hegelian system ideas supersede persons.

b. *spec.* in *Astron.* A theory or hypothesis of the arrangement and relations of the heavenly bodies, by which their observed movements and phenomena are or have been explained.

1678 CUDWORTH *Intell. Syst.* Pref. A iv, The Word Intellectual, being added, to distinguish it from the other, Vulgarly so called, Systems of the World, (that is the Visible and Corporeal World) the Ptolemaick, Tychonick, and Copernican. **1696** PHILLIPS (ed. 5), *System*... Among Astronomers it is taken for the general Constitution, Fabrick and Harmony of the Universe, or any orderly Representation thereof, according to some noted Hypothesis. **1715** tr. *Gregory's Astron.* (1726) I. 186 To describe the Tychonic System of the World. **1855** BREWSTER *Newton* II. xxiv. 358 The Copernican system is not more demonstrably true than the system of theological truth contained in the Bible. **1870** [see TYCHONIC].

†**c.** In weakened sense: A theory or hypothesis; also, theory (as opposed to practice). *colloq. Obs.*

1728 CHAMBERS *Cycl.* s.v., System and Hypothesis have the same Signification; unless, perhaps, Hypothesis be a more particular System; and System a more general Hypothesis. **1748** CHESTERF. *Let. to Son* 27 Sept., Read and hear..ingenious systems, nice questions, subtily agitated. **1750** *Ibid.* 6 Aug., In the course of the world there is the same difference, in every thing between system and practice. **1756** MRS. CALDERWOOD in *Coltness Collect.* (Maitl. Cl.) 213 A book upon naturall philosiphy, which is much esteemed; it is overturning all the sistem of every thing being produced by generation, and nothing by corruption. **1768** STERNE *Sent. Journ.*, *Mystery*, I could form no system to explain the phænomenon.

†**d.** *transf.* A work or writing containing a comprehensive and regularly arranged exposition of some subject; a systematic treatise. *Obs.* exc. in titles of books.

1658 PHILLIPS, *Systems*,. a Treatise or body of any Art or Science. **1661** J. FELL *Hammond* 6 He presently bought a Systeme of Divinity, with design to apply himself straightway to that study. **1695** in *Fasti Aberd.* (1854) 373 A printed course or systeme of philosophie. **1722** A. NISBET (*title*) A System of Heraldry, Speculative and Practical. **1726** SWIFT *Gulliver* III. iii, Astronomers (who have written large systems). **1727** DE FOE (*title*) A System of Magick; or, a History of the Black Art. **1772** PRIESTLEY *Inst. Relig.* (1782) I. p. xxxii, It will be..advisable, that he give his lectures from a short text or system, written,..that they may have an opportunity of perusing it. **1896** ALLBUTT (*title*) A System of Medicine.

9. An organized scheme or plan of action, esp. one of a complex or comprehensive kind; an orderly or regular method of procedure. Now usually with defining word or phrase.

1663 HEATH *Flagellum* (1672) 17 That there might no vice be wanting to make his Life a systeme of Iniquity. **1734** in *10th Rep. Hist. MSS. Comm.* App. I. 251 The generous system, that his Maty has always pursued. **1746** FRANCIS tr. *Hor., Epist.* I. vi. 99 Farewel, and if a better System's thine, Impart it frankly. **1769** *Junius Lett.* viii. (1788) 63 What system of government is this. **1781** COWPER *Expost.* 91 He found..Their piety a system of deceit. **1790** JEFFERSON *Writ.* (1859) V. 228 The conduct of Spain has proved that the occlusion of the Mississippi is system with her. **1842** TENNYSON *Audley Court* 33 We..discuss'd the farm, The four-field system, and the price of grain. **1873** MORLEY *Struggle Nat. Educ.* 55 Subsidising the denominational system. **1882** *Nature* 9 Feb. 351/1 The system of dredging introduced..on the rivers of France.

b. A formal, definite, or established scheme or method (of classification, notation, or the like).

1753 [see LINNÆAN]. **1760** [see SEXUAL 2 d]. **1797** [see METRICAL *a.*[2] 1]. **1831** [see NOTATION 5 c]. **1849** BALFOUR *Man. Bot.* §719 A natural system endeavours to bring together plants which are allied in all essential points of structure. **1860** [see MORSE *sb.*]. **1864** [see METRIC *a.*[2]]. **1866** WATTS *Dict. Chem.* IV. 136 The system of chemical notation now in use. **1867** [see NUMERATION 1 b]. **1893** *Times* 26 July 12/1 The T.A. system of signalling invented by Admiral Tryon.

c. *Cryst.* Each of the six different general methods in which different minerals crystallize, constituting the six classes of crystalline forms.

1820 *Edinb. Philos. Jrnl.* III. 173 We call every simple form, from which other simple forms are derived, a fundamental form; and the class of figures derived from that fundamental form, a system of crystallisations. **1863** *Fownes' Chem.* (ed. 9) 259–262 All crystalline forms may.. be arranged in six classes or systems:.. 1. The regular system... 2. The square prismatic system... 3. The right prismatic system... 4. The oblique prismatic system... 5. The doubly-oblique prismatic system... 6. The rhombohedral system. **1868** DANA *Min.* (ed. 5) Introd. p. xxi, The systems of crystallization are as follows: 1. Having the axes equal. The Isometric system. 2. Having only the lateral axes equal. The Tetragonal and Hexagonal. 3. Having the axes unequal. The Orthorhombic, Monoclinic, and Triclinic.

d. Any method devised by a gambler for determining the placing of his bets.

1850 THACKERAY *Pendennis* II. xxvi. 262, I won a good bit of money there, and intend to win a good bit more... I've got a system. I'll make his fortune. **1896** *Badminton Mag.* Dec. 708 Straight bets over single events are losing their popularity in favour of 'systems'. A system is a kind of patent safety insurance policy. **1908** CHESTERTON *All Things Considered* 47 His vanity..remains a mere mistake of fact, like that of a man who..thinks he has an infallible system for Monte Carlo. **1965** J. SYMONS *Belting Inheritance* iii. 54 He had all sorts of bright ideas that were going to make a fortune. One was..a racing system, something to do with backing second favourites.

e. ***System D*** [tr. F. *Système D* (also used)], (see quots. 1918, 1970). *slang.*

1918 in C. A. Smith *New Words Self-Defined* (1919) 185 'System D' is coming into play in the United States Army. 'System D' is a bit of French slang. It means to unmix, to disentangle, to go straight through... It comes from the initial letter of the word 'débrouiller'. **1947** M. LASKI in *Vogue* Oct. 63/1 That method called by the French *System D*, the phony medical certificate, the faked-up business journey. **1970** N. FREELING *Kitchen Bk.* v. 45 He was a master of the short cut, the easy way out, the system D. D. stands for dé as in débrouiller or démerder—to extricate, and I suppose that in English it is 'I'm all right, Jack'. **1973** 'TREVANIAN' *Loo Sanction* (1974) 78 MI-6..muddled their way through the Second World War, relying largely on the French organizational concept, 'système D'.

10. In the abstract (without *a* or *pl.*): Orderly arrangement or method; systematic form or order.

1699 T. BAKER *Refl. Learn.* vi. 68 Aristotle is more noted for his order, in bringing Morality into Systeme,..and distinguishing vertues into their several kinds, which had not been handled Systematically before, than for any real improvement he made in this sort of knowledge. **1746** W. HORSLEY *Fool* (1748) II. 47 It [*sc.* government] consists of too many detach'd Parts to be easily reduced into System. **1875** JOWETT *Plato* (ed. 2) I. 426 There is more of system in the Phaedo than appears at first sight. **1876** TREVELYAN *Macaulay* II. xv. 474 Macaulay, even during his hours of leisure, began to read on system.

III. 11. *attrib.* and *Comb.* **a.** *attrib.* Of or pertaining to, or involving a system, systematic, as ***system-name***; belonging to or affecting a system of bodily organs (esp. the nervous system: cf. SYSTEMIC 1 b), as ***system degeneration***, ***disease***, ***tract***. **b.** (i) objective, chiefly in sense 8 or 9 (often with unfavourable implication), as ***system-builder***, ***-building***, ***-destroyer***, ***-maker***, ***-making***, ***-monger***, ***-mongering***, ***-writer***; (ii) in appositive use, as ***system-structure***. See also sense 11 e.

1761 STERNE *Tristram Shandy* IV. xvii. 125 But what it is, I leave to *system builders and fish pond diggers betwixt 'em to find out. **1776** MICKLE tr. *Camoens' Lusiad* VII. 313 *note*, Tristram Shandy tells us, that his father was a most excellent system-builder, was sure to make his Theory look well. **1837** CARLYLE *Fr. Rev.* I. IV. iv, This is the Sieyes who shall be System-builder, Constitution-builder General; and build Constitutions..which shall all unfortunately fall before he get the scaffolding away. **1911** J. DRUMMOND *Paul* vi. 79 There is no attempt at *system-building. **1969** A. MAUDE *Common Problem* v. 94 The difference between this process [*sc.* the construction of a system by a political philosopher] and the determinist system-building of social scientists today is concerned with the making of ethical choices about ends. **1899** *Allbutt's Syst. Med.* VII. 99 The degeneration of the posterior columns of the spinal cord is a *system degeneration. **1905** J. BRIERLEY *Eternal Relig.* vi. 48 The system-maker is by an equal necessity the *system-destroyer. **1899** *Allbutt's Syst. Med.* VI. 494 The chief indication of a *system disease of the neuron is its intrinsic nervous origin. **1717** PRIOR *Alma* III. 330 We *System-makers can sustain The Thesis, which, You grant, was plain. *a* **1721** —— *Cromwell & his Porter* Wks. 1907 II. 267 Your System-Makers and World-wrights. **1749** HARTLEY *Observ. Man* I. Pref. p vi, I think,..that I cannot be called a System-maker, since I did not first form a System, and then suit the Facts to it. **1826** [see METHODIST 2 b]. **1836** H. ROGERS *J. Howe* ii. (1863) 21 Where Scripture speaks, or seems to speak, in consonance with the opinions of the system-maker, well and good. **1884** *Century Mag.* XXVII. 915 There were many independent centers of movement and *system-making. **1750** CHESTERF. *Let. to Son* 6 Aug., A *system-monger, who, without knowing any thing of the world by experience, has formed a system of it in his dusty cell. **1836** H. ROGERS *J. Howe* iii. (1863) 45 There would be no lack of system-mongers and theorists. **1896** *Badminton Mag.* Dec. 711 The system-monger is apt to derive encouragement from the fact that long runs on a colour are rare, the longest known at Monte Carlo being a series of 28 reds. **1940** *Mind* XLIX. 120 Hegel was wrong in his formal *system-mongering which reflects the influence upon his thought of Christian theology. **1978** *N.Y. Rev. Bks.* 23 Feb. 6/1 [Matthew] Arnold frowned on dogmatic religion, puritanism, and system-mongering. **1888** CLODD *Story Creation* iv. 32 The stratified rocks are subdivided into the systems shown on fig. 4..No uniform principle has governed the choice of the *system-names. **1964** P. STREVENS in D. Abercrombie *Daniel Jones* 125 Such disparate bodies of grammatical theory as those which lie behind phoneme-morpheme-syntax grammar..and *system-structure grammar. **1975** M. A. K. HALLIDAY in S. Rogers *Children & Lang.* IV. 225 Prague theory, glossematics, system-structure theory, tagmemics, stratification theory and the later versions of transformation theory are all variants on this theme. **1899** *Allbutt's Syst. Med.* VII. 79, I have seen sclerosis so situated in *system tracts, as to be mistaken for a tract-degeneration. **1711** SHAFTESB. *Charac.* III. Misc. III. ii. 187 A formal and profess'd Philosopher, a *System-Writer.

c. In sense 4 g, as ***system library***, ***technology***, etc.; also ***system contradiction***, ***integration*** (so ***-integrative*** adj.).

1952 T. PARSONS *Social System* 7 The moment even the most elementary system-level is brought under consideration a component of 'system integration' must enter in. **1953** System integrative [see POLAR *a.* 7 b]. **1962** J. RIORDAN *Stochastic Service Systems* iv. 70 As noted previously, this is a system with limited waiting capacity. If the waiting capacity is K − 1, the system capacity is K. **1962** E. GODFREY *Retail Selling & Organization* xi. 120 Many firms now recognize that system training needs to be interspersed with periods of practical selling. **1970** *Gloss. Aeronaut. & Astronaut. Terms (B.S.I.)* x. 4 *System capacity*, the total power available from the power sources under the prescribed operating and environmental conditions in the aircraft. **1973** C. W. GEAR *Introd. Computer Sci.* iv. 156 These built-in subroutines..form part of what is called the system library. **1976** *Time* 20 Dec., facing p. 2 (Advt.), This new aid for a communication-saturated world is one more example of Toshiba's sophisticated system technology, which brings together technology from many different fields to solve complex problems of today. **1977** A. GIDDENS *Stud. in Social & Polit. Theory* ii. 127 By 'system contradiction' I mean a disjunction between two or more 'principles of organization' or 'structural principles' which govern the connections between social systems within a larger collectivity. **1977** *Ibid.* 123 While the notion of function is redundant to the theory of structuration, that of 'social integration' can still be regarded as a basic one—together with the further one of 'system integration'. **1978** J. MCNEIL *Consultant* ix. 108 The details of his past career..appeared to have involved Webb in the study of system efficiency.

d. In pl. *systems*, used esp. in sense 4 g, as ***systems approach***, ***manager***, ***theory***, etc. Cf. also sense 11 e below.

1952 *N.Y. Certified Public Accountant* Oct. 604/2 Principles for acquiring specialized knowledge and experience in the systems field. *Ibid.* 605/2 You can rely on a systems consultant whose business it is to devote more time..than you..can afford to give. **1959** *Economist* 11 Apr. 139/1 The American department is relying increasingly on prime contractors (called 'systems managers') to combine the works of many sub-contractors. **1967** *Ibid.* 28 Jan. 328/3 Airlines in general are shifting toward a 'systems concept' which takes charge of the traveller from door to door, not simply between departure and arrival lounges. **1968** *Sat. Rev.* (U.S.) 23 Nov. 32/3 General Motors and Ford can use a 'systems' approach to their global investments. **1969** *Times* 30 Apr. 23/4 (Advt.), In advanced technology. Systems evaluation engineers. Systems trials engineer. Systems test engineers... We require a number of engineers experienced in the assessment, evaluation and/or trials of complex defence weapon systems. **1970** T. LUPTON *Managem. & Social Sci.* (ed. 2) iii. 80 An example of a practical application of a systems theory of organization. **1975** *Modeling & Simulation* VI. 795 (*heading*) Are systems scientists not scientists? **1976** J. LUND *Ultimate* i. 11 Fernandos was a systems consultant to a group of supermarket owners. **1977** *R.A.F. News* 22 June–5 July 9 (Advt.), Systems test engineers £3,500–£4,000. **1977** A. GIDDENS *Stud. in Soc. & Polit. Theory* ii. 115 Von Bertalanffy counterposes the 'mechanistic' views characteristic of nineteenth-century physical science with the twentieth-century perspective of systems theory. **1978** *Times* 2 Oct. 6/8 A new industry, or sub-industry, has emerged, formed on 'systems houses' which buy in the micro components and other hardware, write the software, and design and market the complete systems. **1978** J. MCNEIL *Consultant* ix. 109 You might have a bit of trouble with my Systems Manager.

e. Special Comb., as **systems** (or †**system**) **analysis**, the rigorous, often mathematical, analysis of complex situations and processes as an aid to decision-making or preparatory to the introduction of a computer; so **systems analyst**; **system building** *vbl. sb.*, a method of construction using standardized prefabricated components (see sense 4 i above); hence **system builder**; **system-built** *ppl. a.*; **system(s) design**, the process or task of matching a computer system to the situation into which it is to be introduced and determining the procedures that are to be used; hence **system(s) designer**; **systems engineering**, the investigation of complex, man-made systems in relation to the apparatus that is or might be involved in them; so **systems engineer**; **system(s) program** *Computers*, a program forming part of an operating system; so **system(s) programmer**, **programming**; **system(s) software** *Computers*, system programs collectively.

1950 in J. H. Batchelor *Operations Research* (1959) 769 Notes on (*m* × 2) evaluation matrices for special system analysis applications. **1953** *Jrnl. Operations Res. Soc. Amer.* I. 191 Sometimes this broad type of operations research is called 'systems analysis', 'systems planning', or 'market research'. **1966** A. BATTERSBY *Math. in Management* i. 26 This field of application of mathematics has been defined as 'systems analysis', which considers the thing-being-managed as a system subject to control and operating within an environment with which it interacts. **1977** *Time* 4 Apr. 50/1 Systems analysis, which is really good common sense on a grand scale, combines the knowledge of mathematical probabilities with the aim of dealing with problems in their entirety rather than just piecemeal. **1955** *Operations Research* III. 470 How does the systems analyst choose the preferred strategy? **1967** D. WILSON in Wills & Yearsley *Handbk. Managem. Technol.* 47 The macro block-diagrams show the main logic for a particular program and may be prepared by the systems analyst. **1982** M. DUKE *Flashpoint* xxvii. 205 From computer programmer to systems analyst. Quite an achievement. **1965** *Times* 4 Dec. 5/7 If you want to give the system-builder a fair chance of developing his system you have got to have continuous production for a number of years. **1973** *Architect* Jan. 4/1 If you require the services of a good system builder... We can manufacture to your own particular design or in a manner which allows the best use of our standard components. **1964** R. M. E. DIAMANT *Industrialised Building* I. p. viii, System building is particularly well suited to the rapid erection of tall, low-cost blocks of flats. *a* **1974** R. CROSSMAN *Diaries* (1975) I. 80 A brilliant group of young men and women actively at work developing two methods of system-building, 5M and 12M. **1968** *Guardian* 13 Nov. 1/4 The Minister of Housing..made strenuous efforts to halt the collapse of confidence in system-built blocks. **1973** *Archit. Assoc. Q.* V. IV. 8/2 Later models [of bungalow] were supplied with what would appear to be system-built furniture. Described by the architect as 'chair-furniture', it consisted of various components which could be assembled into chairs, stools, tables, etc. **1954** *Trans. IRE Prof. Group Electronic Computers* June 8/2 The necessity for effecting compromises and avoiding conflicts of this kind between the rival claims of operational effectiveness and engineering reliability and economy strongly influenced the system design of the SEAC and DYSEAC. **1960** GREGORY & VAN HORN *Automatic Data-Processing Systems* xi. 380 Some analysts with an accounting and systems-design background suggest the straightforward approach—simply asking management people what they must have to control operations. *Ibid.* 396 System design is discussed here in terms of fact finding, developing specifications, meeting specifications, and matching equipment with the system. **1980** *Jrnl. R. Soc. Arts* Feb. 147/1 With the advent of micro-electronics and the growth in the field described nowadays as systems design, there is some danger that..that manager will fail to appreciate the real importance of the design element. **1980** J. MCNEIL *Spy Game* i. 28 Stick to systems design... You make a lousy financial expert. *Ibid.* 22 You're the best systems designer in his Division. **1955** *Business Week* 15 Jan. 164/3 Nowadays, the systems engineer starts a project by wrestling with the abstruse questions of what elements in the system need accurate measurement, which ones are important to control. **1974** *Encycl. Brit. Macropædia* XVII. 972/1 The first task of the systems engineer is to develop as clear a formulation of objectives as possible. **1952** W. H. MARTIN in *Proc. 5th Ann. Conf. Administration of Research 1951* 8/1 In our organization [*sc.* Bell Telephone Laboratories] extensive use is made of an analytical procedure which we call Systems Engineering. **1962** A. BATTERSBY *Guide to Stock Control* i. 9 Two types of specialists concern themselves with the study of these communications networks: we may say broadly that the Organization and Methods experts are responsible for the general layout of the network, whereas the accountants are concerned with the messages which flow along them. The two functions are combined in the new specialism called Systems Engineering. **1973** GOTTFRIED & WEISMAN *Introd. Optimization Theory* i. 5 The techniques of systems engineering (of which optimization techniques constitute an important subclass) are applicable to a very wide variety of physical problems. **1958** *Communications Assoc. Computing Machinery* Aug. 16 System programmers writing in UNCOL can use an existing translator to produce their ML system programs. **1960** *Ibid.* III. 537 (*heading*) A list of computer systems programs for the IBM 650, DATATRON 205, and UNIVAC-SS80. **1973** ABRAMS & STEIN *Computer Hardware & Software* iii. 14 Software may be divided into..applications programs, which are written to solve users' problems, and systems programs, which are concerned with operating the computer service. **1973** C. W. GEAR *Introd. Computer Sci.* ii. 53 These programs, called system programs, will read in our program after it has been punched on cards in a suitable form and arrange for the instruction counter to be set to the address of the first instruction in our program. **1958** System programmer [see *system program* above]. **1970** O. DOPPING *Computers & Data Processing* v. 92 Nowadays, only some very specialized 'system programmers' write programs in machine code. **1958** *Communications Assoc. Computing Machinery* Aug. 12 A minimum of 'system programming' should be required to produce the system initially. **1979** R. BORNAT *Understanding & Writing Compilers* xiv. 240 Most system-programming languages allow stack pointers to be used with even more freedom than in ALGOL 68. **1971** B. DE FERRANTI *Living with Computer* 89 *System software*, those programs, usually prepared by the hardware manufacturer, that provide the link between the programs of the user and the hardware. **1980** PALMER & MORRIS *Computing Sci.* viii. 283 Systems software is written to schedule the various stages in running a program..at the same time making efficient use of the hardware.

systemad ('sɪstɪmæd), *adv. Anat.* [f. SYSTEM + *-ad*: see DEXTRAD.] To or towards the (general) system of the body.

1808 [see PULMONAD].

† **'systemary**, *a. Obs. rare*$^{-1}$. [f. SYSTEM + -ARY.] ? Constituting a system (SYSTEM 2).

1726 DE FOE *Hist. Devil* I. vi. (1840) 76 One devil in a place would be enough for a whole systemary world.

systematic (sɪstɪ'mætɪk, -tə-), *a.* and *sb.* [ad. late L. *systēmaticus*, a. late Gr. συστηματικός (both relating to systems of metres), f. σύστημα SYSTEM. Cf. F. *systématique* (1584).] **A.** *adj.*

†**1.** = next, 1 b. *Obs. rare.*

a **1680** GLANVILL *Serm. Luke xiii. 24* Disc., etc. (1681) 7 All this I must confess,..because Experience constrains me; and I do not know why Systematick Notions should sway more than that.

2. = next, 1. (Passing into sense 3.)

1725 WATTS *Logic* II. iii. §4 (1726) 219 Now we deal much in Essays, and most unreasonably despise systematic Learning. **1812** SIR H. DAVY *Chem. Philos.* 10 The first Arabian Systematic Works on Chemistry are said to have been composed by Geber. *a* **1821** V. KNOX *Ess. Writing* Wks. 1824 I. 5 Systematic books of morality. **1830** HERSCHEL *Study Nat. Phil.* 110 The necessity of saying something learned and systematic, without knowing what to say. **1836** H. ROGERS *J. Howe* ii. (1863) 21 Systematic theology..has..been of questionable benefit. **1847** EMERSON *Repr. Men, Swedenborg* Wks. (Bohn) I. 316 Swedenborg is systematic..in every sentence. **1865** TYLOR *Early Hist. Man.* i. 2 A systematic treatise on the subject.

3. a. *gen.* Arranged or conducted according to a system, plan, or organized method; involving or observing a system; (of a person) acting according to system, regular and methodical.

1789 *Loiterer* 13 June 8 Armour was rarely used in battles where artillery alone could decide..the Day... There was seldom any opportunity of signalizing personal courage amidst the regularity of systematic murder. **1790** BURKE *Rev. France* 84 These gentlemen value themselves on being systematic. **1796** —— *Regic. Peace* ii. Wks. VIII. 244 The systematick proceedings of a Roman senate. **1833** ALISON *Hist. Eur.* (1849) III. xvii. §18. 500 A systematic and uniform line of conduct. **1863** LYELL *Antiq. Man* i. 2 The facts brought to light..during the systematic investigation of the Brixham cave. **1867** DICKENS *Lett.* (1880) II. 273 He is very systematic with the luggage. **1910** *Encycl. Brit.* II. 28/2 Though it will occasionally take a large fly, a worm or other ground-bait, its systematic capture is only essayed with small fish or artificial spinning-baits.

b. Qualifying nouns of action of unfavourable meaning: Carried out with a regularity such as to indicate intention or habitual action; regularly organized (for an evil purpose), or carried on as a regular (and reprehensible) practice. Also said of the agent.

1803 BROUGHAM *Colon. Policy* I. 123 The house of Brandenburg seized this opportunity of prosecuting the systematic views of unprincipled aggrandisement, which have presided over its councils since the name of Prussia was known in Europe. **1828** D'ISRAELI *Chas. I*, I. vi. 163 The systematic intrigues of the Papal Court. **1867** FREEMAN *Norm. Conq.* I. iv. 195 After so many years of systematic devastation. **1874** L. STEPHEN *Hours in Libr.* (1892) I. iii. 106 Pope..was a systematic appropriator..of other men's thoughts. **1874** GREEN *Short Hist.* viii. §3. 489 They turned religion into a systematic attack on English liberty.

c. ***systematic ambiguity*** (*Philos.*) (see quot. 1933). Cf. *systematically ambiguous* adj. phr. s.v. SYSTEMATICALLY *adv.* 1 c.

1910 B. RUSSELL in Whitehead & Russell *Principia Math.* I. Introd. iii. 45 This is due to a systematic ambiguity in the meanings of 'not' and 'or', by which they adapt themselves to propositions of any order. **1933** L. S. STEBBING *Mod. Introd. Logic* (ed. 2) ix. 161 When the same words are used in sentences which express different kinds of propositions, yet in each case the usage is significant, then these words are said to have 'systematic ambiguity'... This ambiguity is *systematic* because it can be formulated according to a rule. **1952** W. V. QUINE *Methods of Logic* p. xi, Systematic ambiguities..are essential to the nature of language. **1979** *Proc. Amer. Cath. Philos. Soc.* LIII. 78 In this paper, I want to argue that there is a systematic ambiguity in the concept of person which explains why it has often been used to favor sexist discrimination.

d. ***systematic error***, an error with a non-zero mean, so that its effect is not reduced when observations are averaged.

1925 R. A. FISHER *Statistical Methods for Research Workers* vi. 169 It is worth while to consider the effects of two classes of systematic errors, which, although of little or no importance when single values only are available, become of increasing importance as larger numbers of samples are averaged. **1981** *Astrophysical Jrnl.* CCXLVIII. 34/2 Although there is a statistically significant deviation from a Planck spectrum, there are serious limitations to the statistical analysis where systematic errors are likely.

4. *Nat. Hist.*, etc. Pertaining to, following, or arranged according to a system of classification; of or pertaining to classification, classificatory. Also of a writer: Composing or adhering to a system of classification.

1796 KIRWAN *Elem. Min.* (ed. 2) I. 23 The distinctive Characters, and systematic Arrangement, of Earths and Stones. **1800** SHAW (*title*) General Zoology or Systematic Natural History. **1829** T. CASTLE *Introd. Bot.* 12 Endeavouring to perfect systematic botany. **1835** J. DUNCAN *Beetles* (Nat. Lib.) 86 Beetles..such as burrow in the earth,..(the *Geodephagi* of some modern systematic writers). **1839** YARRELL *Brit. Fishes* I. Suppl. 11 *Trigla lyra*, the systematic name of our English Piper Gurnard. **1863** HUXLEY *Man's Place Nat.* ii. 102/3 This is a very noteworthy circumstance..but it has little systematic value.

5. Consisting of systems of heavenly bodies. *rare.*

1829 *Chapters Phys. Sci.* 415 Those numerous hosts of systematic universes.

6. = SYSTEMIC 1 b. *rare.*

1899 *Allbutt's Syst. Med.* VII. 3 The 'systematic' lesions [of myelitis].

7. *Chem.* Of the name of a chemical species: constructed in accordance with an agreed set of rules so as to represent the detailed chemical structure of the named species (e.g. N-*methylpent-2-ylamine*); so ***systematic nomenclature***. Cf. TRIVIAL *a.*

1858 *Rep. Brit. Assoc. Adv. Sci. 1857* II. 45 The classification on which the author proposes to base a systematic nomenclature for organic compounds, is a modification of that employed by Gerhardt. **1879** WATTS *Dict. Chem.* Suppl. I. 705 A systematic nomenclature for the hydrocarbons, which are the fundamental compounds of organic chemistry, is a great desideratum. **1892** *Nature* 19 May 57/2 It is clearly an absolute necessity of the times that every compound should bear a systematic name of such a character that it can be at once translated into the corresponding formula. **1959** R. S. CAHN *Introd. Chem. Nomenclature* iii. 39 There is a fundamental disinction between the use of trivial and systematic names: trivial names refer to compounds, systematic names to structures. **1978** *Nature* 31 Aug. 929/2 Natural products with particular molecular features cannot normally be located by the keyword approach, as such compounds usually have trivial, rather than systematic, names. **1982** J. E. FERNANDEZ *Org. Chem.* iv. 59 An international, systematic nomenclature system now exists and is used by organic chemists throughout the world.

B. *sb.* **1.** *Nat. Hist.*, etc. A systematist.

1771 T. PERCIVAL *Ess.* (1777) I. 9 Salt, sulphur, acrimonies, caustics, volatiles, ferments,.. have each.. by different systematics, been received as the..*principia morborum*. **1788** J. BROWN tr. *Elem. Med.* I. 287 *note*, Nothing is more artificial and arbitrary than the arrangements either of Systematics or Nosologists.

2. *pl.* **systematics** [see -IC 2] = TAXONOMY.

[**1840** W. WHEWELL *Philos. Induct. Sci.* I. VIII. ii. 468 A department of the philosophy of natural history which has been termed by some writers (as Decandolle,) Taxonomy.. by some Germans.. has been denominated *Systematik*; if we could now form a new substantive after the analogy of the words Logic, Rhetoric, and the like, we might call it Systematick.] **1888** *Nature* 20 Dec. 177/2 Huxley's classification.. in 1867, marked an epoch in the systematics of birds. **1909** E. B. POULTON in *Q. Rev.* July 14 Many hundreds of naturalists.. devote their lives to systematics—to the study of the differences between species. **1940** J. S. HUXLEY *New Systematics* 1 To-day.. systematics has become one of the focal points of biology. **1951** G. H. M. LAWRENCE *Taxon. Vascular Plants* i. 3 In this text the taxonomy of vascular plants includes the systematics of the taxa known as pteridophytes, gymnosperms, and angiosperms. **1969** E. MAYR *Princ. Systematic Zool.* p. vii, Systematics has had a remarkable renaissance during the last generation.

syste'matical, *a.* Now *rare* or *Obs.* [f. late L. *systēmaticus*: see prec. and -ICAL.]

1. Of a writing or treatise: Containing or setting forth a system or regular exposition of some subject. Of a subject or study: Set forth, or pursued, in the way of a system or regular scheme. Of a writer: Dealing with a subject in this way; cf. 4.

1661 BOYLE *Style Script.* 111 Such Precepts.. are not Express'd and Rang'd in the Bible, as they are wont to be in Systematical Composures. **1698** NORRIS *Pract. Disc.* (1707) IV. 239 But 'tis New Philosophy, and.. he likes the company of his Systematical Divines better. **1767** BLACKBURNE (*title*) The Confessional: or, A Full and Free.. Inquiry into the Right.. Of Establishing Systematical Confessions of Faith and Doctrine in Protestant Churches. **1781** DE LOLME *Const. Eng.* Advt. (1817) p. vi, The book.. met.. with approbation,.. which.. was no small luck for a book on systematical politics. **1782** PRIESTLEY *Corrupt. Chr.* I. I. ix. 124 Anselm, though he writes with wonderful acuteness, is not systematical.

b. Belonging to, or dealing in, a 'system' or theory; theoretical: cf. SYSTEM 8 c.

1748 CHESTERF. *Let. to Son* 25 Mar., They are not the laboured reflections of a systematical closet politician, who, without the least experience of business, sits at home and writes maxims. **1794** R. J. SULIVAN *View Nat.* I. 57 Too much pertinacity in the support of systematical conjecture.

2. *gen.* = prec. 3.

1692 BENTLEY *Boyle Lect.* vii. (1693) 7 A brief account of some of the most principal and systematical Phænomena. **1749** HARTLEY *Observ. Man* I. Pref., Adding such things as were necessary to make the Whole appear more complete and systematical. **1763** J. BROWN *Poetry & Mus.* v. 68 Their [*sc.* the ancients'] Divisions of the Musical Art are precise and systematical. **1804–8** FOSTER *Life & Corr.* (1846) I. 283 A plan of systematical reading. **1820** SCORESBY *Acc. Arctic Reg.* II. 214 The systematical movements of the whales. **1853** RUSKIN *Stones Venice* II. viii. §51. 320 To arrange their ideas in systematical groups.

b. = prec. 3 b.

1750 MISS TALBOT in *Eliz. Carter's Lett.* 26 Nov. (1809) I. 364 Some books of French, Morale Mondaine,.. full of a systematical profligateness, veiled with delicacy of expression. **1755** *Monitor* No. 10. I. 77 The grand systematical corrupter. **1783** BURKE *Rep. Aff. India* Wks. 1842 II. 81 In systematical contradiction to the company's orders. **1816** F. H. NAYLOR *Hist. Germany* I. I. viii. 290 The Jesuits, those systematical foes to every liberal sentiment.

†**3.** Belonging to the system of the universe, or to the solar system; cosmical. *Obs.*

1688 BOYLE *Final Causes Nat. Things* i. 8 These Ends, may,.. be call'd Cosmical or Systematical, as regarding the Symmetry of the great System of the world. **1781** HERSCHEL in *Phil. Trans.* (1782) LXXII. 104 This new kind of systematical parallax, if I may be allowed to use that expression, for signifying the change arising from the motion of the whole solar system. **1797** —— in *Encycl. Brit.* II. 480/2 The greatest.. systematical parallax of the fixed stars will fall upon those that are in the line.. at rectangles to the direction.. of the sun's motion.

4. *Nat. Hist.* = prec. 4. Now *rare* or *Obs.*

1813 SIR H. DAVY *Agric. Chem.* iii. (1814) 118 Some distinctions have been adopted by systematical authors which I have not entered into. **1817** KIRBY & SP. *Entomol.* xvii. (1818) II. 48 Gould.. though no systematical naturalist, was a man of sense and observation. **1829** T. CASTLE *Introd. Bot.* 2 That part of the science, which refers to.. the classification of plants.. is denominated systematical botany.

Hence ˌ**systemati'cality**, the quality of being systematic.

1872 H. NICOL in *Westm. Rev.* XLI. 45 The symbols of foreign [sounds] will, from the systematicality of the alphabet, in most cases explain themselves.

systematically (sɪstɪˈmætɪkəlɪ, sɪstə-), *adv.* [f. prec. + -LY[2]: see -ICALLY.]

1. a. In a systematic manner; according to a system or organized plan; regularly and methodically.

1661 BOYLE *Physiol. Ess.* (1669) 7 Far from having such a stock of Experiments and Observations, as I judge requisite to write Systematically. **1699** [see SYSTEM 10]. **1753** WARBURTON *Princ. Nat. & Rev. Relig.* v. Wks. 1788 V. 71 Urging those truths systematically,.. which the Evangelists proposed singly and without connection. **1809–10** COLERIDGE *Friend* (1818) I. ii 15 The majority of mankind learn nothing systematically, except as schoolboys or apprentices. **1837** LOCKHART *Scott* IV. v. 148 Every case and shelf was accurately lettered, and the works arranged systematically. **1860** MRS. CARLYLE *Lett.* (1883) III. 45 The silence I systematically observe on the shortcomings of servants. **1880** L. STEPHEN *Pope* iv. 93 Pope.. knew the value of independence well enough to be systematically economical.

b. With unfavourable implication: With a regularity indicating (evil) design or habit: cf. SYSTEMATIC *a.* 3 b.

1829 F. GLASSE *Belgic Past.* ii. 39 He systematically gains his ends By sacrifice of principles and friends. **1855** MACAULAY *Hist. Eng.* xviii. IV 144 The enemies of Child had.. accused him of systematically publishing false intelligence. **1858** FROUDE *Hist. Eng.* (ed. 2) II. x. 411 The pope.. had heard.. that abbots and monks in many places were systematically faithless to their vows. **1878** LECKY *Eng. 18th Cent.* I. i. 134 Officers of known Whig tendencies were systematically laid aside.

c. ***systematically ambiguous*** adj. phr. (*Philos.*), having an ambiguity that is systematic (see SYSTEMATIC *a.* 3 c).

1929 C. I. LEWIS *Mind & World-Order* i. 11 The adjective 'real' is systematically ambiguous and can have a single meaning only in a special sense. **1943** I. A. RICHARDS *How to read a Page* iii. 52 There are few important words which are not in varying patterns systematically ambiguous; *say* is typical. These *regular* shifts of sense as a rule give us little trouble in reading. **1967** *Philos.* XLII. 208 'Reality' may be systematically ambiguous

†**2.** By means of a 'system' or theory, theoretically: cf. prec. 1 b. *Obs.*

1749 CHESTERF. *Let. to Son* 19 Dec., This knowledge is not to be gotten systematically; you must acquire it.. by your own observation and sagacity.

systematician (ˌsɪstɪməˈtɪʃən, -stəm-). *rare.* [f. SYSTEMATIC + -IAN, after *mathematician*.] One who constructs, or who adheres (esp. unduly) to, a system.

1886 *19th Cent.* July 73 A 'thought-mathematician', a systematician, a slave to the consistent application of his own theories. **1903** J. C. LAMBERT *Sacraments N.T.* ix. 382 He thinks it necessary to apologise for this lack of consistency on the part of the apostle, by reminding us that Paul was 'no correct systematician'.

systematicity (sɪstɪməˈtɪsɪtɪ, -stəm-). [f. SYSTEMATIC *a.* + -ITY.] The quality or condition of being systematic; systematicness.

1970 CAMPBELL & WALES in J. Lyons *New Horizons in Linguistics* 257 The child first of all does something 'correctly' and then, with every appearance of systematicity, later proceeds to do it 'wrongly'. **1974** R. A. HALL *External Hist. Romance Languages* 239 Meyer-Lübke's work was characterised by sobriety and balance, with exceptional solidity in detail but with an over-all sense of systematicity. **1977** *Language* LIII. 883 He has little time or inclination to follow through his concept of music theory with any thoroughness or systematicity.

syste'maticness. [f. SYSTEMATIC *a.* + -NESS.] The quality of being systematic.

1836 F. W. FABER *Lett.* (1869) 58 To contrast the systematicness of the Primitive Church with.. the modern worship about us.

systematism (ˈsɪstɪmətɪz(ə)m, -stəm-). *rare.* [f. SYSTEMAT-IZE + -ISM. Cf. next.] The practice of systematizing; addiction to system.

1846 W. H. MILL *Five Serm.* (1848) 48 We see harmoniously combined those several aspects of the same great object, in which modern systematism sees only elements of contradiction. **1872** LOWELL *Dante* Prose Wks. 1890 IV. 161 He [*sc.* Dante] combines the.. more abstract religious sentiment of the Teutonic races with the scientific precision and absolute systematism of the Romanic.

systematist (ˈsɪstɪmətɪst, -stəm-). [f. Gr. σύστημα, -ατ- SYSTEM + -IST.] One who constructs, or adheres to, a system, esp. a system of classification in natural history; a classifying naturalist.

In Kirby's use, an advocate of a natural in preference to an artificial system of classification (opp. to METHODIST 2 b).

1700 S. PARKER *Six Philos. Ess.* 46 Your peremptory Systematist boldly distorts Nature. **1753** *Chambers' Cycl. Supp.*, *Systematists*, in botany, those authors, whose works in this science are principally employed about the arranging plants into certain orders, classes, or genera. **1836** *Penny Cycl.* V. 248/2 Grew.. was no systematist; it was reserved for another Englishman [*sc.* John Ray] to discover the true principles of classification. **1840** WHEWELL *Philos. Induct. Sci.* (1847) II. 557 The Fishes, in which province Cuvier has .. been the great systematist. **1902** *Edin. Rev.* Oct. 370 Kaspar Bauhin (1550–1624), the first great botanical systematist.

systematize (ˈsɪstɪmətaɪz, -stəm-), *v.* [f. Gr. σύστημα, -ατ- SYSTEM + -IZE.] *trans.* To arrange according to a system; to reduce to system.

1764–7 LYTTELTON *Hen. II* II. (1769) III. 203 The eastern and western Goths had some general notions of the feudal policy, which were gradually systematised. **1780** HARRIS *Philol. Enq.* II. xii. (1781) 224 Many things have been done in the best and purest taste, long before Rules were established, and systematized in form. **1828** D'ISRAELI *Chas. I* I. viii. 250 His restless ambition.. had systematised intrigue. **1830** MACKINTOSH *Eth. Philos.* Wks. 1846 I. 35 The vast collection of laws enacted or systematized by Justinian. **1899** *Allbutt's Syst. Med.* VIII. 343 Hallucinations, which are systematised into delusions.

b. *absol.* or *intr.* To construct a system (e.g. of philosophy, classification, etc.).

1891 in *Cent. Dict.* **1911** J. OMAN in *Expositor* Oct. 362 The moment he proceeds to systematise,.. he knows, just as little as any other systematiser, what to do with personality.

Hence **'systematized** (-aɪzd) *ppl. a.*, **'systematizing** *vbl. sb.* and *ppl. a.* (in quot. 1827 = 'scheming'); also ˌ**systemati'zation** (-ˈeɪʃən), the action or process of systematizing; a systematic arrangement, statement, etc.; **'systemaˌtizer**, one who systematizes.

1811–13 BENTHAM *Univ. Gram.* Wks. 1843 VIII. 356/2 *Systematization; *i.e.* placing the several denominations.. in systematic order. **1838** [F. HAYWOOD] tr. *Kant's Crit. Pure Reason* 490 The systematization of cognition—that is, the connexion thereof according to a principle. **1864** MAX MÜLLER *Sci. Lang.* Ser. II. iii. 98 *note*, English Phonetics, containing an original systematisation of spoken sounds. **1904** DUCKWORTH *Morphol. & Anthropol.* x. 232 The accompanying scheme.. has been found of practical use in the further systematisation of observations. **1797** BURKE *Regic. Peace* iii. Wks. 1808 VIII. 393 The relations of peace and amity with *systematized regicide. **1827** LYTTON *Pelham* lxxviii, The systematized roguery of London. **1878–9** J. CAIRD *Philos. Relig.* (1880) 106 A living organism is not a mere aggregation of independent parts, but a systematised unity of members. **1884** F. TEMPLE *Relat. Relig. & Sci.* v. (1885) 127 The systematised experience which we call Science. **1780** HARRIS *Philol. Enq.* I. i. (1781) 8 Aristotle.. may be called the *Systematizer of his Master's Doctrines. **1854** R. H. PATTERSON *Ess. Hist. & Art* (1862) 371 Auguste Comte.. is but a systematiser of the doctrines of Confucius and the old philosophers of China. **1828** SEWELL *Oxford Prize Ess.* 18 That mad fondness for *systematizing.. which overthrows all the creations of nature. **1837** WHEWELL *Hist. Induct. Sci.* I. I. ii. §2. 42 The treatises on the various subjects of Natural History.. manifest a wonderful power of systematising. **1827** SOUTHEY in *Q. Rev.* Oct. 312 A cool, crafty, calculating, systematizing knave. **1883** SAYCE in *Contemp. Rev.* Sept. 391 The later age of systematizing philosophy.

systematy (ˈsɪstɪmətɪ, -stəm-). [f. Gr. σύστημα, -ατ- SYSTEM + -Y[3].] Systematic classification; = TAXONOMY.

1912 W. L. BALLS *Cotton Plant in Egypt* 5 In this brief summary of the few available historical facts, it has seemed advisable to evade systematy. **1921** *Oxf. Bot. Mem.* XI (*title*) Elementary notes on the systematy of Angiosperms. **1929** E. M. NICHOLSON *Study of Birds* 20 Mechanical and unfruitful as systematy inevitably is, ornithologists ought to be grateful to those who have plodded through it.

systemed (ˈsɪstɪmd, -t(ə)md), *pa. pple.* and *a.* *rare.* [f. SYSTEM *sb.* + -ED.] Made into a system, systematized; arranged in a system or systems; composed according to system, systematic.

1746 W. HORSLEY *Fool* (1748) II. 47 Men of but middling Genius should keep to plain Rules, system'd to their Hands; acting in right Order by prescrib'd Method. **1807** J. BARLOW *Columb.* x. 275 Social and system'd worlds around him shine. **1836** MRS. BROWNING *Poet's Vow* I. xvii, Hear me forswear man's sympathies... His answering looks, his systemed books.

‖**Système International** (sistɛm ɛ̃tɛrnasjɔnal). Also (*erron.*) **-nationale.** [Fr.] In full ***Système International d'Unités.*** The International System of Units (see INTERNATIONAL *a.* 1 c).

[**1957**: see INTERNATIONAL *a.* 1 c.] **1969** *Symbols, Signs, & Abbreviations* (R. Soc.) 21 (*heading*) The International System of Units (Système International d'Unités—SI). **1971** [see *SI* s.v. S 4 a]. **1972** *Physics Bull.* Aug. 461/3 If the precision of the measurement system can lead us to parts in 10^9, it might be possible to change the way in which the electrical units are defined in the Système Internationale.

systemic (sɪˈstɛmɪk), *a.* (and *sb.*) [irreg. f. SYSTEM + -IC; used for differentiation of meaning instead of the regular *systematic*.]

1. a. *Physiol.* and *Path.* Belonging to, supplying, or affecting the system or body as a whole; orig. and esp. in reference to the general circulation as distinguished from that supplying the respiratory organs (*pulmonary* or *bronchial*).

1803 BARCLAY *New Anat. Nomencl.* 122 Let the vessels which convey it [*sc.* blood] from the lungs to the system be called the Systemic, and those which convey it from the system to the lungs be named the Pulmonic. **1835–6** *Todd's Cycl. Anat.* I. 794/1 The cessation of these actions, and the consequent solution of connection between the various parts of the body, is systemic death. **1841** R. E. GRANT *Comp.*

Anat. 498 The great systemic artery issuing from the left ventricle. **1858** *Blackw. Mag.* LXXXIII. 326 The.. systemic sensation of Hunger. **1889** BARTHOLOW *Mat. Med.* (ed. 7) 489 Systemic effects may be produced by such an application. **1896** NEWTON *Dict. Birds* 1008 The Systemic Circulation.. divisible into Arterial and Venous.

b. Belonging to or affecting a particular system of bodily organs, esp. the nervous system or special parts of it: see quot. 1890.

1887 W. F. REVELL *Ethical Forecasts* 81 Certain molecular movements of nerve-substance marshal themselves, or are marshalled, into such order as..gives rise to orderly sequences of thought... Does there not seem to be..a systemic intelligence, or a systemic grouping of forces which secures the results that intelligence might be expected to secure? **1890** BILLINGS *Nat. Med. Dict.* s.v., *S[ystemic] lesion*, a lesion limited to one set of homologous parts, such as the posterior columns or the anterior cornua of the spinal cord. **1896** *Allbutt's Syst. Med.* I. 181 Systemic sclerosis of a small but defined tract of the spinal cord.

c. Of a herbicide, insecticide, or fungicide: entering the system of a plant or animal and freely transported within its tissues. Also as *sb.*, a systemic agent.

1949 *Ann. Appl. Biol.* XXXVI. 160 The term 'systemic insecticides' refers only to chemical substances which are absorbed by the plant and translocated to all parts of it, rendering it insecticidal. **1961** *New Scientist* 5 Jan. 50/2 The animal systemics ronnel..and CoRal have been in commercial use for some time. **1964** *Which?* Apr. 114/1 Dimethoate and menazon are unlike the other insecticides in being systemics, i.e. they are absorbed into the plant instead of just being deposited on it. **1971** *Exper. Agric.* VII. 2 Four different systemics were used. **1979** *Radio Times* 5–11 May 13/4 The best control is to spray young foliage thoroughly with Benlate systemic fungicide.

2. *gen.* Of or pertaining to a system.

1850 in OGILVIE; hence in later Dicts. **1946** C. MORRIS *Signs, Lang. & Behavior* 104 In the systemic use of signs the aim is simply to organize sign-produced behavior. **1952** A. COHEN *Phonemes of English* 54 It is not as loans, but as residual structural irregularities, which might rather be called 'systemic fragments' than 'coexistent systems'. **1966** S. BEER *Decision & Control* xvii. 439 They will demand that systemic qualities be measured which no-one as yet knows how to measure. **1975** *Times Lit. Suppl.* 17 Oct. 1233/5 A tradition of American political and social thought..that demands social justice without labelling injustice a systemic product. **1977** *Dædalus* Summer 55 Many scholars, especially those whose level of analysis is systemic, implicitly write as if they were addressing themselves to a world government.

3. ***systemic grammar***, a method of linguistic analysis developed by M. A. K. Halliday in 1961 in *Word* XVII, based on the ideas of J. R. Firth and others. Similarly ***systemic linguistics***. Cf. SYSTEM 4 e.

1968 *Computers & Humanities* II. 147 The linguistic description I adopted for my study was systemic grammar. **1971** D. CRYSTAL *Linguistics* iv. 215 More recently, Halliday has developed out of this a concept of *systemic* grammar. **1975** M. BERRY (*title*) Introduction to systemic linguistics. **1978** *Language* LIV. 351 The grammar that assigns to sentences structures like the one in Fig. 1 is generative fusion of elements of American-style immediate-constituent analysis (cf. Nida 1960), European-style dependency theory (cf. Tesnière 1959), and British-style systemic grammar (cf. Halliday 1961).

So †**sy'stemical** *a.* (*obs. rare*), systematic; hence **sy'stemically** *adv.*, (*a*) systematically; (*b*) in relation to the bodily system.

1724 A. COLLINS *Gr. Chr. Relig.* Concl. 273 The commentaries on Scripture, and systemical books of all modern theologues. **1888** *Centen. Confer. Missions* (U.S.) II. 265 What general would dare systemically to fight without reserves? **1889** *Lancet* 4 May 882/1 It seems likely that it [*sc.* corrosive sublimate] acts as much systemically as locally.

'systemist. *rare.* [irreg. f. SYSTEM + -IST.] = SYSTEMATIST.

1796 ELIZA HAMILTON *Lett. Hindoo Rajah* (1811) II. 236 But little pain did the sorrows of the mourners give to the young systemist. **1868** PEARD *Water-farm.* xv. 151 The genus Cyprinus as now restricted by modern systemists contains the common carp and allied species.

systemize ('sɪstɪmaɪz, -tə-), *v.* [irreg. f. SYSTEM + -IZE.] *trans.* = SYSTEMATIZE.

1778 [W. MARSHALL] *Minutes Agric., Digest* 2 He continued to systemize what he thought worthy of his System. **1828–32** WEBSTER. **1846** WORCESTER, *Systemize*, to systematize. *Hiley.* A word rarely used by good writers. **1908** *Westm. Gaz.* 27 June 13/2 Learning made easy and systemised from thirty years' experience.

Hence **'systemized** (-aɪzd) *ppl. a.*, **'systemizing** *vbl. sb.* and *ppl. a.*; also **,systemi'zation**, systematization; **'systemizer**, a systematizer.

1835 I. TAYLOR *Spir. Despot.* v. 204 Nothing cou'd have prevented this systemizing of functions. **1853** *Tait's Mag.* XX. 456 The improved systemization and conduct of Assurance. **1880** RUSKIN *Elem. Engl. Prosody* §8. 9 The whole subject of Prosody has been confused, and its systemization for English readers made virtually impossible, by the want of clearly understanding the difference between accent and time. **1895** *Advance* (Chicago) 370/3 The intellectualism of the reformers asserts itself in the systemizer of the school. **1907** R. J. THOMPSON *Proofs of Life after Death* 34 The amassed, severely tested and systemized knowledge that is..essential to effect a universal conviction.

systemless ('sɪstɪmlɪs, -tə-), *a.* [-LESS.]

1. Devoid of system or orderly arrangement; unsystematic.

1851 RUSKIN *Stones Venice* I. xxv. §20 Dreading to be called upon..to admire a systemless architecture, because it may happen to have sprung from an irrational religion. **1883** *Science* I. 521/2 In upper Swabia, glacial deposits present their peculiar landscape of systemless hills and hollows.

2. *Biol.* Having no differentiated systems of organs; structureless.

1862 DANA *Man. Geol.* 597 If..these simple species existed in the Azoic era, they were systemless life.

system-wise, *adv.* [See -WISE.] In relation to things as they are connected in a system.

1799 LAMB *Let. to Southey* 15 Mar., I never judge system-wise of things, but fasten upon particulars.

systerne, obs. f. CISTERN.

systoflex ('sɪstəʊflɛks). *Electr. Engin.* [f. *systo-*, of unknown origin + FLEX *sb.*[2]] Flexible sleeving for insulating electric wires.

1922 *Wireless World* X. 556/1 One may lose much time trying to push No. 18 wire into systoflex intended for No. 20. **1968** M. WOODHOUSE *Rock Baby* ix. 93 His study..smelled..of soldering fluid, swarf, oil, charred systoflex sleeving..the indefinable smell of home-made electronic gear.

systolated ('sɪstəleɪtɪd), *a. rare*$^{-1}$. [f. next + -ATE[2] + -ED[1].] Contracted by systole.

1820 *Blackw. Mag.* VII. 324, I therefore give him leave to alter my systolated preterites into preterpluperfects.

‖**systole** ('sɪstəli:). Also 6 **sistole**. [mod.L., ad. Gr. συστολή, f. Gr. σύν SYN-[1] + στολ- (:—στέλλειν to place), after συστέλλειν to draw together, contract. Cf. F. *systole*, †*cistole* (*c* 1600), It. *sistole*, Sp. *sístole*, Pg. *systole*.]

1. *Phys.* **a.** The regular contraction of the heart and arteries that drives the blood outward: opposed to DIASTOLE.

1578 BANISTER *Hist. Man* VII. 92 b, Sistole is, when the hart by constriction putteth forth the same [spirit]. **1605** DANIEL *Queen's Arcadia* III. ii. (1606) F j b, The Systole, and Dyastole of your pulse, Do shew your passions most hystericall. **1664** POWER *Exp. Philos.* I. 41 In this Animal [*sc.* lamprey] the heart in every diastole is of a fair purple and ruddy colour, and in every systole pale and wan. **1669** W. SIMPSON *Hydrol. Chym.* 76 The systole of the left ventricle. **1707** FLOYER *Physic. Pulse-Watch* 18 When the Heart is in its Systole, the Arteries are dilated. **1806** H. K. WHITE *Let. to Maddock* 17 Feb., The systole and diastole of my heart seem to be playing at ball—the stake, my life. **1835–6** *Todd's Cycl. Anat.* I. 655/2 The systole of each cavity [of the heart] is immediately followed by its diastole or relaxation. **1877** M. FOSTER *Physiol.* I. iv. (1879) 145 Practically speaking, there is no interval between the auricular and ventricular systole [of the heart].

b. Applied to similar rhythmical contraction in other organs, as the lungs, the intestines, the pulsatile vesicles in protozoans, the contractile vesicles in certain algæ, etc.

1578 BANISTER *Hist. Man* VIII. 99 Not onely to the hart belongeth the same Diastole, and Sistole, but likewise to the brayne. **1657** TRAPP *Comm. Job* x. 8 He was amazed at the manner of the motion of the lungs by Systole and Diastole. **1660** [see DIASTOLE 1]. **1826** KIRBY & SP. *Entomol.* xxxix. IV. 81 A long dorsal vessel, the first step towards a heart, which alternately contracts and dilates with an irregular systole and diastole. **1855** T. R. JONES *Anim. Kingd.* (ed. 2) 306 The contraction or systole in any given [branchial] tuft occurs at frequent but irregular intervals. **1882** W. S. KENT *Man. Infusoria* II. 874 *Systole*, a term applied to the contracting action of the structure known as the contractile vesicle of Infusoria and other Protozoa.

c. *fig.* Also *Comb.*, as ***systole-diastole***.

1831 [see DIASTOLE 1 *fig.*]. **1849** DE QUINCEY *Eng. Mail Coach* i. Misc. (1854) 300 To interrupt the great respirations, ebb and flood, *systole* and *diastole*, of the national intercourse. **1872** GEO. ELIOT *Middlem.* lxiii, There must be a systole and diastole in all inquiry. **1899** W. R. INGE *Chr. Myst.* i. 28 A *systole* and *diastole* of the spiritual life. **1924** C. GRAY *Survey Contemp. Music* 260 The immediate future..will witness a return to tradition... So it always has been... It is the *systole-diastole* of the world of art. **1946** M. LOWRY *Let.* 2 Jan. (1967) 74 Here we come to the heart of the book which..returns..to the uneasy, but healthy, systole-diastole of Hugh.

2. *Pros.* The shortening of a vowel or syllable long by nature or position.

1577 PEACHAM *Gard. Eloquence* E ij b, *Systole*, when a long Sillable is made shorte, contrary to the nature therof, *Darîus* for *Darĭus*, *Diâna* for *Diăna*, *Iosêphus* for *Iosĕphus*. **1639** J. BIRD *Grounds of Gram.* (1641) 183. **1657** J. SMITH *Myst. Rhet.* 176. **1704** J. HARRIS *Lex. Techn.* I, *Systole*, in Grammar, is part of the Poetical Licence, whereby a long Syllable is made short: As in that of Virgil.—*Tulerunt fastidia Menses.*

systolic (sɪ'stɒlɪk), *a.* [ad. mod.L. *systolicus*, f. *systole*: see prec. and -IC. Cf. F. *systolique* (Rabelais).] Pertaining to or marked by systole.

a **1693** *Urquhart's Rabelais* III. iv, The Heart, which by its agitation of Diastolick and Systolick Motions so neatly subtilizeth and inflames it [*sc.* choler]. **1817** tr. *Swedenborg's Heaven & Hell* §445 The systolic motions of the heart. **1853** MARKHAM *Skoda's Auscult.* 158 Systolic murmurs heard in the left ventricle. **1875** H. C. WOOD *Therap.* (1879) 136 The diastole generally becomes imperfect, one portion of the ventricle maintaining its systolic spasm, while the rest dilates. **1877** HUXLEY *Anat. Inv. Anim.* ii. 77 This systolic and diastolic movement usually occurs at a fixed point in the protoplasm. **1899** *Allbutt's Syst. Med.* VII. 241 The cardiac systolic expansion of the brain within the closed cranium is rendered possible by the ebb of the cerebro-spinal fluid.

systren, obs. pl. of SISTER.

systrophe ('sɪstrəʊfi:). *Biol.* [ad. G. *systrophe* (A. F. W. Schimper 1885, in *Jahrb. f. wiss. Bot.* XVI. 221), f. SYN-[1] + Gr. στροφή, turning.] The clumping together of chloroplasts in a cell when exposed to bright light.

1886 *Jrnl. R. Microsc. Soc.* VI. 642 Very strong irritation of light causes the chlorophyll-grains to collect into one or two lumps, a phenomenon for which Schimper proposes the term systrophe. **1936** *Geogr. Jrnl.* LXXXVIII. 48 Diatoms ..sink deeper and display the phenomenon of systrophe. **1966** E. J. STADELMANN in D. M. Prescott *Methods Cell Physiol.* II. vii. 206 Systrophe is a typical and reversible response reaction of the living protoplasm to a variety of stimuli.

systyle ('sɪstaɪl), *a.* and *sb. Arch.* [ad. Gr.-L. *systȳlos* (Vitruvius), a. Gr. σύστῡλος, f. σύν SYN-[1] + στῦλος column, pillar. Cf. F. *systyle*.]

A. *adj.* Applied to architecture in which the columns are close together, viz. at a distance from each other of twice their thickness. **B.** *sb.* A building characterized by such intercolumniation.

[**1563** SHUTE *Archit.* F j, Sistylos,..whose pillers standeth distant one from the other .2. Diameters, or .2. and a halfe at the fourdest.] **1704** J. HARRIS *Lex. Techn.* I, *Systyle*..is a Building where the Pillars stand thick, but not altogether so close as in the Pychnostyle. **1771** W. NEWTON tr. *Vitruvius' Archit.* III. iii. (1791) 52 *note*, The eustyle intercolumns may likewise be two and a half diameters, as the mean between those of the dyastyle and systyle, instead of two and a quarter, which is nearer to the systyle. **1789** P. SMYTH tr. *Aldrich's Archit.* (1818) 147 Whose inter-columniations in the middle are systyle, on each side pycnostyle. **1844** *Civil Eng. & Arch. Jrnl.* VII. 23/2 The Pantheon at Rome is a systyle.

systylous ('sɪstɪləs), *a. Bot.* [f. mod.L. *systylus* (f. Gr. σύν SYN-[1] + στῦλος column) + -OUS.] **a.** In mosses, having the lid permanently fixed to the columella. **b.** Having the styles united into a single column.

1863 M. J. BERKELEY *Brit. Mosses* Gloss. 313 *Systylous*, used when the lid adheres to the columella.

syt: see SET *v.*[1], SIGHT, SIT *v.*, SITE.

sytalle, obs. form of CITOLE.

14.. *Nom.* in Wr.-Wülcker 738/18 *Hic psalmatus*, the sytalle.

syte, obs. form of CITE *v.*

1485 *Acc. St. Dunstan's Canterb.* in *Archæol. Cant.* (1886) XVI. 292 Payde to John Horsley for sytyng of dyuerse personys for the dutis of the Churche viij d.

syte, obs. form of CITY.

1340–70 *Alex. & Dind.* 9 No syte nor no sur stede soþli þei ne hadde. ? *a* **1400** *Arthur* 71 Arthour byseged þat Syte & town. *c* **1440** *Promp. Parv.* 457/1 Syte, *urbs*.

syte: see SIGHT, SITE, SYTH.

†**Syteer.** *Obs.* (?)

1433 *Rolls of Parlt.* IV. 476/2 That the said xxv persones sworen in maner above seid, shall chese vi Men that been called Syteers,..and that they be true Burgeys and resseauntes within the seid Town, to have and occupie..the Office of resceite. **1444** *Ibid.* V. 123/1.

syter, -wurt, obs. var. SETTER *v.*, SETTERWORT.

†**syth**, *sb. Sc. Obs.* Also 6 **syith**, 8 **site**, **syte**. [Aphetic form of ASSYTH *sb.*] Satisfaction, compensation.

to get one's heart's syth of: see quot. 1710.

1567 *Gude & Godlie Ball.* (S.T.S.) 104 ȝour bludie boist na syith can satisfie. **1661** in Cramond *Records of Elgin* (1908) II. 295 The said John wes suire that he wold get his heart syth of everie one that wronged him. **1710** RUDDIMAN *Gloss. Douglas' Æneis* s.v. *Site, syte*, I have gotten my heart's syte on him, i.e. my heart's desire on him, or all the evil I wish'd him.

†**syth**, *v. Sc. Obs.* Also 5 **syþ**, 6 **syith**, **sith**, **cythe**. [Aphetic form of ASSYTH *v.*] **a.** *trans.* To satisfy, give satisfaction to.

c **1425** WYNTOUN *Cron.* v. xii. 3970 (Wemyss MS.) [Scho] gaif þame siluer or payment, Or claiþ to syþ thare entent. **1513** DOUGLAS *Æneis* IX. vii. 116 He mycht do stanche his ire, and syth his thocht. **1536** BELLENDEN *Cron. Scot.* (1821) II. 120 The king was nocht full sithit with his justice. *c* **1550** ROLLAND *Crt. Venus* III. 774 That pane may be in put to Forfaltouris: The Partie sythit, as Law will lat it be.

absol. **1583** *Reg. Privy Council Scot.* III. 599 He forgevis thame..of quhat degre sa evir thay be of. Quhilk as his majestie heir promittis, sa sall he mak it to cythe in gud effect heirefter.

b. ? *intr.* for *pass.* To be satisfied.

1650 in W. ROSS *Aberdour & Inchcolme* (1885) 326 [He had called her] a trumpous [cross-tempered] witch, [and her heart] sythed [glowed with satisfaction, when she saw him coming home in his hurt condition].

syth: see SCYTHE, SEE *v.*, SIGHT, SITH, SITHE.

sythar, var. SIQUARE *Obs.*, moment.

sytharist, obs. f. CITHARIST, player on the cithara; in quot. misused for the instrument.
c **1450** HOLLAND *Howlat* 757 The psaltery, the sytholis, the soft sytharist.

sythe: see SAITHE, SCYTHE, SIGHT, SITH, SITHE.

sythen, -yn, sythence, syther: see SITHEN, SITHENCE, CIDER.

† **'sythment**. *Sc. Obs.* Also 6 **syithment**, 6–7 **sith(e)ment**. [f. SYTH *v.* + -MENT. Cf. ASSYTHMENT.] Satisfaction, compensation, indemnification.
1536 BELLENDEN *Cron. Scot.* (1821) II. 394 In sithement of his ransoun. **1560** ROLLAND *Seven Sages* 58 This is na mendis to me, Howbeit it be ane syithment to my hart. **1572** *Satir. Poems Reform.* xxx. 218 The Lord..send vs ane sythment of yis suddane slauchter. **1633** W. STRUTHER *True Happines* 66 When we seeke a sithment and revenge on our selves for angring him we take Gods part against our selfe. **1667** in Cramond *Ann. Cullen* (1887) 51, £20 to be peyt to the toune for..disturbing the peace theroff with £12 of sythment to the pairtie wronged.

sythol(l, sytole, -olphe, var. CITOLE *Obs.*

sythþe, syth(t)ware: see SITH, SIQUARE.

sythyche, var. of *so thee ich*: see THEE *v.*[1]

sytizin: see CITIZEN.

sytt, variant of SITE *sb.*[1] *Obs.*
c **1560** A. SCOTT *Poems* (S.T.S.) xv. 9 So neides thow nocht now sussy, sytt, nor sorrow.

sytyca, obs. form of SCIATICA.

Syud, var. SAYYID.

syue, var. CIVY *Obs.*, onion sauce.
c **1440** *Anc. Cookery* in *Househ. Ord.* (1790) 449 Turbot, and congur, and plays, and soles in syne [*sic*].

syue, syve, syuer, syun, obs. ff. SIEVE, SURE, SCION.

syver ('saɪvə(r)). *Sc.* Forms: 7–9 **siver**, 9 **syvo(u)r, syver**. [? ad. (north-eastern) OF. *sewiere* SEWER *sb.*[1]] = SYRE.
1606 *Charter* in Dallas *Stiles* (1697) 774 Lie sinks, sivers, guttars, eyes,..airholls [etc.]. **1793** *Statist. Acc. Scot.* VII. 145 The manse..lies in a swamp, the inconvenience of which the present clergyman has..remedied by sivers, as they are here called. **1834** J. WILSON *Noctes Ambr.* Aug., Wks. 1856 IV. 99 She [*sc.* a hare] made for the mouth o' the siver. **1867** J. K. HUNTER *Retrospect Artist's Life* vii. (1912) 66 He has faun wi' a clash in the syvour. **1894** P. H. HUNTER *James Inwick* v. 62 There was Jess an' the kimmers a' stan'in wi' their boynes an' pails at the siver. **1900** J. G. CAMPBELL *Superstit. Scottish Highl.* 209 An opening like the syver of a drain.
attrib. **1889** H. JOHNSTON *Chron. Glenbuckie* 281 These guileless laddie-weans, sitting..by the syver-edge. **1906** N. MUNRO *Daft Days* xiii, He stood on the syver-side. *Ibid.* xvi, The gulls that quarrelled in the syver sand.

sywe, sywester(e, syw(e)te, -yte, obs. ff. SUE, SEWSTER, SUIT *sb.*

syx(e, syxt(e, etc., obs. ff. SIX, SIXTH, etc.

syxt, obs. 2nd sing. ind. pres. of SEE *v.*; obs. f. SEXT.

syyk, obs. f. SICK.

syzygant ('sɪzɪgənt). *Math.* [irreg. f. SYZYGY + -ANT, after *invariant*, etc.] (See quots.)
1882 SYLVESTER in *Amer. Jrnl. Math.* V. 87 Irreducible syzygants and irreducible invariantive derivatives of the same type, to the same quantic cannot coëxist. **1882** HAMMOND in *Amer. Jrnl. Math.* V. 221. **1885** CAYLEY *Math. Papers* XII. 251 A seminvariant may be expressible as a sum of products (of a higher degree) of perpetuants of lower degrees, and of perpetuants of lower degrees, and it is not on this account reducible: a seminvariant so expressible is said to be a 'syzygant'.

syzygetic (sɪzɪ'dʒɛtɪk), *a. Math.* [Loosely f. SYZYGY + *-etic* (cf. Gr. συζυγεῖν to yoke together, be correlative).] Of, pertaining to, or constituting a syzygy (SYZYGY 5). Hence **syzy'getically** *adv.*
1850 SYLVESTER in *Cambr. & Dubl. Math. Jrnl.* V. 276 [*U*, *V*, *W*] are..capable of being connected by integral multipliers *U'*, *V'*, *W'*, such that *U'U* + *V'V* + *W'W* = 0. Any number of functions *U*, *V*, *W* so related, I call syzygetic functions, and *U'*, *V'*, *V''* [*sic*: ? *W'*] I term the syzygetic multipliers. **1852** —— *Ibid.* VII. 75 *note*, Rational integer functions which admit of being multiplied severally by other rational integer functions such that the sum of the products is identically zero, are said to be 'syzygetically related'. **1853** —— in *Phil. Trans.* CXLIII. 407.

† **syzygiacal**, *a. Obs. rare.* [f. Gr. συζυγία or late L. *sӯzygia* SYZYGY + -AC + -AL[1].] = next.
1672 FLAMSTEED in Rigaud *Corr. Sci. Men* (1841) II. 140 Let *MP* be the line of the mean apogæon making an acute angle with the syzigiacal line *SCO*.

syzygial (sɪ'zɪdʒɪəl), *a. Astron.* and *Zool.* [f. late L. *sӯzygia* SYZYGY + -AL[1].] Pertaining to a syzygy or syzygies; having the character of a syzygy (senses 1 b, 3).
1863 FITZ ROY *Weather Bk.* xviii. 253 The moon's greatest tidal action being syzygial, and the least at quadrature. **1873** C. W. THOMSON *Depths of Sea* ix. 452 The first brachial is united to the second by a syzygial joint. **1879** CARPENTER in *Trans. Linn. Soc.* Ser. II. II. I. 48 The number of segments composing the syzygial interval is.. three.

‖**syzygium** (sɪ'zɪdʒɪəm). *Biol.* [mod.L., alteration of *sӯzygia* (see next).] = SYZYGY 3 b.
1885 *Encycl. Brit.* XIX. 855/2 The term 'syzygium' is applied to such a conjunction of two Gregarinidea. **1898** P. MANSON *Trop. Diseases* i. 12 [The crescent body of malaria] is the result of the conjugation of two ordinary plasmodia—a syzygium, in fact.

syzygy ('sɪzɪdʒɪ). Also 7 **sys-, syzigie**, 7–8 **sys-, syzygie**, 8–9 **syzigy**, 9 **syzigee**. [ad. late L. *sӯzygia*, a. Gr. συζυγία yoke, pair, copulation, conjunction, f. σύζυγος yoked, paired, f. σύν SYN-[1] + ζυγ-: ζευγνύναι to yoke. Cf. F. *syzygie* (1584 in Hatz.-Darm.).]
1. *Astron.* † **a.** Orig. = CONJUNCTION 3. *Obs.*
1656 BLOUNT *Glossogr.*, *Sysigie* (*sysigia*), a conjunction, a coupling. The conjunction of the Moone with the Sunne; the new moone. **1686** GOAD *Celest. Bodies* I. xi. 43 The Great and Leading Syzygie, or human Aspect with the ☉. **1690** LEYBOURN *Curs. Math.* 758 So that in every true Syzygy, the Centre of the Deferent agrees with the Centre of the Earth. **1704** J. HARRIS *Lex. Techn.* I, *Syzygie*, in Astronomy, is the same with the Conjunction of any two Planets, or Stars, or when they are both referred to the same Point in the Heavens; or when they are referred to the same Degree of the Ecliptick, by a Circle of Longitude passing through them both.
b. Now extended to include both conjunction and opposition (OPPOSITION 3) of two heavenly bodies, or either of the points at which these take place, esp. in the case of the moon with the sun (new and full moon). Often opposed to QUADRATURE 4 b, c.
1715 tr. *Gregory's Astron.* (1726) I. 123 If the Nodes of the Orbit of the Body *L*, be in the Syzygies of the Body *S*. **1728** CHAMBERS *Cycl.* s.v., On the Phænomena and Circumstances of the Syzygies, a great Part of the Lunar Theory depends. **1749** *Phil. Trans.* XLVI. 150 The greatest Spring-Tides, and least Neap-Tides, are commonly on the third or fourth Day, after the Syzygies and Quadratures. **1833** HERSCHEL *Astron.* xi. 325 Suppose the disturbing body to be fixed in the line of nodes, or the nodes to be in syzygy. **1869** PHILLIPS *Vesuv.* iv. 112 The eruptions were sensibly strengthened at the syzigies and weakened at the quadratures of the moon. **1882** *Nature* 27 July 292/1 The sunspot maxima..are nearly always associated with configurations in which Venus and Earth in conjunction or opposition, have Jupiter in or near syzygy or quadrature.
† **2.** *Anat. pl.* The pairs of cranial nerves. *Obs.*
1681 tr. *Willis' Rem. Med. Wks.* Vocab., *Syzygies*, are the nerves that carry the sense from the brain to the whole body.
3. *Biol.* **a.** A suture or immovable union of two joints of a crinoid; also, the joints thus sutured. **b.** The conjunction of two organisms without loss of identity, as in the genus DIPLOZOON; a syzygium.
1873 C. W. THOMSON *Depths of Sea* ix. 440 The first of the brachial joints..is..split in two by a peculiar kind of joint, called, by Müller, a 'syzygy'. *Ibid.*, When the animal is dying it generally breaks off its arms at these syzygies. **1888** ROLLESTON & JACKSON *Anim. Life* 572 (*Crinoidea*) The lines of union..may be obliterated... The ligamentous connections may become very close... Two joints thus connected are termed a syzygy. *Ibid.* 573 The..ligaments between brachials not united by syzygy appear to be contractile.
4. *Anc. Prosody.* A dipody, or combination of two feet in one metre (METRE *sb.*[1] 4).
[**1706** PHILLIPS (ed. Kersey), *Syzygia*..Among Grammarians, the coupling or clapping of different Feet together in Greek or Latin Verse.] **1836** J. R. MAJOR *Guide Grk. Trag.* 109 Some grammarians, in speaking of anapæstic, iambic, and trochaic verse, use the term *syzygy* (συζυγια) or *dipodia* (διποδια) instead of *metre*.
5. *Math.* A group of rational integral functions so related that, on their being severally multiplied by other rational integral functions, the sum of the products vanishes identically; also, the relation between such functions.
1850 SYLVESTER in *Cambr. & Dubl. Math. Jrnl.* V. 276 The members of any group of functions, more than two in number, whose nullity is implied in the relation of double contact,..must be in syzygy. Thus *PQ*, *PQR*, *QR*, must form a syzygy. **1867** CAYLEY *Math. Papers* VI. 147 While for the degree 5 we obtain 3 covariants and a single syzygy, for the degree 6 we obtain only 2 covariants, but as many as 7 syzygies. **1869** W. K. CLIFFORD in *Proc. Lond. Math. Soc.* 11 Nov. 11 If the 12th powers of the *nil-facta* in the tangential equations of 43 points are connected by a linear syzygy, the 43 points are on a quartic curve. **1886** HAMMOND in *Amer. Jrnl. Math.* VIII. 19 Syzygy Tables for the Binary Quintic.
6. A pair of connected or correlative things; in Gnostic theology, a couple or pair of opposites, or of æons.
1838 SIR W. HAMILTON *Logic* xx. (1866) I. 402 The Greek logicians after Aristotle, looking merely to the two premises in combination, called these Syzygies. **1853** J. MARTINEAU *Ess.* (1891) III. 470 Ourselves and the external world we know..only under relation; of subject, for example, to object;..of phenomenon to cause. Yet, in pursuing this relative course of cognition, we are apt to be struck with the belief that one of the two terms in each of the primary syzygies transcends relation at the very moment of creating it. **1875** LIGHTFOOT *Comm. Col.* 166 The system of syzygies, or pairs of opposites, is a favourite doctrine of this work [*sc.* Clementine Homilies], and in these John stands contrasted to Jesus, as Simon Magus to Simon Peter, as the false to the true. **1890** J. MARTINEAU *Seat Author. Relig.* II. ii. 237 The fourth Gospel..is..itself a Gnosticism, only baptized and regenerate: no longer lingering aloft with the divine emanation in a fanciful sphere of aeons and of syzygies. **1909** GWATKIN *Early Church Hist.* xv. II. 37 Valentinus, says Victorinus, teaches a pleroma and thirty æons, and these he arranges in syzygies or couples.

szaboite ('sæbəʊaɪt). *Min.* [ad. G. *szaboit* (1878), named in honour of Prof. J. *Szabo* of Budapest.] A variety of hypersthene.
1883 *Encycl. Brit.* XVI. 417/1. **1892** DANA *Min.* 350 Szaboite occurs in thin tabular crystals..; it was first described as triclinic and a relation to babingtonite suggested, but its identity with hypersthene was later fixed by Lasaulx.

szaibelyite (seɪ'bɛljaɪt). *Min.* [ad. G. *szaibelyit* (1861), named after *Szajbelyi*, a Hungarian.] A hydrous borate of magnesium, found in nodules in limestone.
1866 BRANDE & COX *Dict. Sci.*, etc. II. 532/1. **1868** DANA *Min.* (ed. 5) 594.

Szechuan (sɛtʃ'wɑːn). Also **Szechwan**. [ad. Chin. *Si-chuān*.] The name of a province in south-western China, used *attrib.* (with reversed stress) to designate the distinctively spicy cuisine originating there. Also *Comb.*, as ***Szechuan-style*** adj. Also *transf.*
1956 BUWEI YANG CHAO *How to cook & eat in Chinese* I. i. 30 Szechwan cooking has a fine balance of flavours except that hot pepper is added freely. **1974** *Times* 23 Aug. (Hongkong Suppl.) p. x/7 The Chinese food in Hongkong is superb..Peking duck and Szechwan smoked duck. **1977** *Harpers & Queen* Nov. 30/2 A new restaurant serving Szechuan food. **1979** *United States 1980/81* (Penguin Travel Guides) 179 Honolulu also has several Mandarin or Szechwan-style Chinese restaurants. **1980** E. BEHR *Getting Even* vii. 89 There was the smell of real Szechuanese cooking, chillies and hot sesame oil... Waiters began serving an elaborate Szechuan meal.

Szechuanese (sɛtʃwɑː'niːz), *a.* and *sb.* Also **Szechwanese**. [f. as prec. + -ESE.]
A. *adj.* Of, pertaining to, or characteristic of Szechuan or its people, or of the Chinese spoken there. **B.** *sb.* **a.** An inhabitant of Szechuan. **b.** The dialect of Szechuan.
1918 *North-China Herald* 19 Jan. 115/2 Szechuanese invasion of Yunnan... It is reported that the Szechuanese have invaded Yunnan. **1937** E. SNOW *Red Star over China* v. 199 The Szechuanese are sentimental about their few bridges. **1947** J. BERTRAM *Shadow of War* x. 336 We gathered for supper at a Szechwanese restaurant and.. tasted..the roast duck of Chengtu. **1947** N. C. SCOTT in *Bull. School Orient. & African Studies* XII. 197 (*heading*) The monosyllable in Szechuanese. **1966** R. & D. MORRIS *Men & Pandas* iv. 65 He not only spoke good English, but also knew the Szechuanese dialect. **1972** 'M. HEBDEN' *Killer for Chairman* II. i. 127, I could hear voices talking in..a Szechwanese dialect... The Szechwanese had a reputation for bloody-mindedness. **1978** A. GREY *Chinese Assassin* xvii. 174 Your Szechuanese accent is a dead give-away. **1980** [see prec.].

Szekel ('sɛk(ə)l), *sb.* (*a.*) Also in Ger. form **Szekler**. [ad. Hungarian *Székely* (also used).] (A member of) a Magyar people living in eastern Transylvania. Also *attrib.* or as *adj.*
1843 *Penny Cycl.* XXV. 164/2 The nation [of Transylvania] in the political sense of the word is composed of three bodies or 'nations', the Hungarians, the Szeklers, and the Saxons, who have the collective name of the 'Uniti'. *Ibid.*, When a Hungarian or Szekler nobleman of Transylvania settles in Hungary, he is entitled to all the privileges of noblemen in Hungary. **1869** A. J. PATTERSON *Magyars* II. xxxi. 354, I started for the little hamlet.. accompanied by a Székel. **1888** E. GERARD *Land beyond Forest* II. xxxviii. 151 The Szekel villages, of a formal simplicity, are as far removed from the Roumanian poverty as from Saxon opulence. **1910** *Encycl. Brit.* X. 392/2 The isolated groups of Hungarians now found in Transylvania and called Szeklers are considered the purest descendants of the invading Magyars. **1920** *Glasgow Herald* 23 Apr. 8 At the very most 1,900,000 Magyars are lost, of whom over 900,000 (including the Szekels) are in Transylvania. **1934** R. W. SETON-WATSON *Hist. Roumanians* ii. 20 Already Koloman and Stephen II in the first three decades of the Twelfth century began to settle Magyar colonists—the so-called Székelys or Siculi. *Ibid.* 21 Transylvania falls into three distinct political groupings—finally crystallised by the events of 1437 into three privileged nations, the Magyars, the Székels and the Saxons. **1956** F. S. PISKY in S. Fischer-Galati *Romania* iii. 54 Although there are no ethnic or linguistic differences, Hungarians make a distinction between the *Szekelys* and *Magyars*. The *Szekelys*, descendants of the free frontiersmen in Transylvania, populate the Odorhei, Cius and Trei Scaune districts. **1974** *Encycl. Brit. Micropædia* VI. 496/3 The Szeklers, meaning Frontier Guards, received their name, it seems, because they were Magyars sent to Transylvania to protect the eastern flank. *Ibid. Macropædia* IX. 31/1 Colonies of Szekels, a people akin to the Magyars who had preceded the latter into the central plains, were settled behind its eastern passes.

Sze Yap (siː jæp). Also **Sze-Yap, Szeyap**. [Chinese.] The name of an area made up of four countries in the south of Guangdong Province

in China (see quot. 1973) used *attrib.* and *absol.* to designate the Chinese dialect spoken there.
[**1948** R. A. D. FORREST *Chinese Lang.* x. 200 Cantonese, with reference also to the dialect of Sze-Yap, to the west of the Canton River delta, generally regarded as a minor variety of Cantonese.] **1964** *Asia Mag.* 12 July 22/3 The Chinese [in Hong Kong]..speak no less than seven tongues —Cantonese, Hoklo, Sze Yap, [etc.]. **1971** K. HOPKINS *Hong Kong* 235 Cantonese is very much the predominant language but there are minorities who speak..Sze Yap. **1973** R. A. D. FORREST *Chinese Lang.* (ed. 3) xi. 235 Usually reckoned a sub-dialect of Cantonese, though, in the opinion of the present writer, showing enough distinctive features to warrant its separation, is the dialect of SzeYap, the 'Four Towns', spoken on the west of the Canton River delta... Like most varieties of Cantonese, Sze Yap has lost all distinction of *s-* and ʃ-. *Ibid.* 328 The Sze Yap dialect has regularly *h-* for *t'*. **1982** *English World-Wide* III. i. 48 Other varieties of Chinese spoken include Szeyap, Chiuchow, Shanghainese, Hokkien and Hakka.

szkippe, obs. f. SKIP *sb.*[1]

‖**szlachta** ('ʃlaxta). *Hist.* [Polish.] The aristocratic or land-owning class in Poland before 1945.
1885 *Encycl. Brit.* XIX. 285/2 We soon find the following divisions of society among the Poles:—(1) the nobility, *szlachta,* who throughout Polish history constitute the nation properly so-called. **1905** *Cambr. Mod. Hist.* (1907) III. iii. 76 Poland was at this time on the threshold of a period of political transition of an almost revolutionary character, the most remarkable feature of which was the elevation to power of the Polish *szlachta,* or gentry. **1969** P. ANDERSON in Cockburn & Blackburn *Student Power* 264 Bronislaw Malinowski, a Polish aristocrat from the Galician szlachta. **1978** W. B. LINCOLN *Nicholas I* iv. 136 The more substantial portions of the Polish *szlachta* (nobility) had done relatively well under fifteen years of Russian rule.

szmikite ('smɪkaɪt). *Min.* [ad. G. *szmikit* (1887), named after *Szmik,* a Hungarian.] A hydrous sulphate of manganese.
1892 DANA *Min.* 933 Szmikite... Amorphous, stalactitic. .. Color whitish, on the fracture reddish white to rose-red.

T

T (tiː), the twentieth letter of the English and other modern alphabets, the nineteenth of the ancient Roman alphabet, corresponding in form to the Greek *T* (*tau*), from the Phœnician (and ancient Semitic) † ✕ ✗ X (*tau*), in Phœnician, and originally also in Greek, the last letter of the alphabet. It represents the point-breath-stop consonant of Bell's 'Visible Speech', or surd dental mute, so called, but in English is gingival or alveolar rather than dental. Several varieties of a *t*-sound occur in different languages, according as the flow of the breath is stopped by bringing the tip or front of the tongue into contact with different points between the edge of the upper teeth and the roof of the palate. Thus, contact of the tip of the tongue with the teeth gives the true dental *t*, which is common in continental European languages, very distinct in Anglo-Irish, and heard in north-western English dialects before *r*, where it is often represented in dialect specimens by spelling *thrue* or *t'hrue* for *true*, and the like (though the consonant is not actually *th* or (θ)). The Indian languages, Aryan as well as Dravidian, distinguish two kinds of *t*, the dental, and the retracted or 'cerebral' (*mūrdhanya*), in Sanskrit त and ट, of which the latter is formed by contact of the retracted tip of the tongue with the roof of the palate. The Engish *t* is formed between these two extreme positions, the contact being with the back of the gum or the front margin of the palate; its sound is much closer to the cerebral than to the dental, and in the Tamil or Telugu representation of English words, the cerebral is regularly put for English *t*. In the Roman transliteration of Indian words it is usual to write *t* for the dental, and to distinguish the cerebral as *ṭ*, as is done in this dictionary. The Semitic languages also distinguish two *t*-sounds, one, the Hebrew *tau* (ת), Arabic *ta* (ت) dental; the other, Hebrew *teth* (ט), Arabic *ṭa* (ط), said to be formed by contact of the blade of the tongue with the palate; this also has been romanized as *ṭ*, though distinguished in Urdū from the cerebral *ṭ*.

In modern English, besides its proper sound as above described, *t* in the combinations *-tion*, *-tious*, *-tial*, *-tia*, *-tian*, *-tience*, *-tient*, after a vowel or any consonant except *s*, has the sound of *sh* (ʃ), in which the following *i* is absorbed, as in *nation* ('neɪʃən), *factious* ('fækʃəs), *partial* ('pɑːʃəl), *militia* (mɪ'lɪʃə), *patience* ('peɪʃəns); but in *-ia*, *-ian*, *i* is sometimes more or less preserved, especially in proper names, as in *inertia*, *Portia*, *Gratian*, *Dalmatian*. In these combinations Latin (t) became (ts), usually written *z*, and then (s), written *c*, in French, as in L. *grātia*, It. *grazia*, F. *grâce*, L. *nātiōnem*, It. *nazione*, OF., Sp. *nacion*. In French and English spelling the Latin *t* was subsequently in most cases restored, e.g. *nation*; but the living sound was (s), and it is this *s* which combining with the following *i* (= *y* consonant) as (sj-), passed in English into (ʃ), in the same way as written *c* or *s* has done in *gracious*, *Asia*, *emersion*: see S the letter, par. 4. Strictly, therefore, what we have is not *ti* pronounced as (ʃ), but (ʃ) derived from *ci*, spelt *ti* after its Latin source. After *s*, the original sound of *t* has remained, as in *bestial*, *Christian*, *Erastian*.

A much more recent change, 'as yet scarcely recognized by orthoepists' (*N.E.D.*, 1910), is the development in southern England of the sound *ch* (tʃ) from *t* followed by *u* with its diphthongal or name sound (juː, jʊ, jʊə), in such combinations as *-tual*, *-tue*, *-tuous*, and especially *-ture*, as in *nature* ('neɪtjʊə(r)), whence ('neɪtjə(r), 'neɪtʃə(r)). In those English dialects in which *u* has not become (juː), the original *t* remains, as in 'critter' = *creature*, 'pictur' = *picture*. In rapid speech *ti* after *s* often passes similarly into (tʃ), as ('kwɛstʃən) for ('kwɛstjən).

T between *s* and syllabic *l* or *n* (*en*), as in *bustle*, *castle*, *epistle*, *christen*, *fasten*, *hasten*, is now usually mute; so between *s* and *m* in *Christmas*, and between *f* and syllabic *n* in *often*, *soften*.

TH is a consonantal digraph representing two simple sounds (θ, ð), for which the Roman alphabet has no simple symbols, and is thus phonetically a distinct letter (or two letters), inserted between TE- and TI-, where see its history and pronunciation.

I. 1. a. The letter and its sound. The plural is variously written t's, *t's*, *ts* (tiːz). See also TEE *sb.*[1]

c **1000** [see B]. *c* **1374** CHAUCER *Boeth.* I. pr. i. 2 (Camb. MS.) Abouen þat lettre in the heyeste bordure a grekyssh t þat singnifieth the lyf contemplatyf. **1487** *Act 4 Hen. VII*, c. 13 Every Person so convicted..for any other Felony..to be marked with a T in the same Place of the Thumb. **1736** AINSWORTH *Lat.-Eng. Dict.* s.v., With a design to hang T on her own gibbet, as Lucian jocosely says. **1847** *Proc. Philol. Soc.* III. 45 Thus the Aztecs of Mexico, though able to pronounce an *l* in the middle of a word, at the commencement find it necessary to prefix a *t*-sound to the liquid. **1859** *Life E. Henderson* vi. 353 Before the little inmate of the Linn could have known a T from a craw's tae. **1861** DICKENS *Gt. Expect.* xvi, Everything producible that began with a T, from tar to toast.

b. In phrase *to cross the* t's: to make the horizontal stroke of *t* (often omitted in hasty writing); *fig.* to be minutely exact or particular in one's account; to make the meaning more distinct; to particularize and emphasize the points. Cf. *to dot the* i's in I (the letter) 1.

1849 [see CROSS *v.* 7 a]. **1865** E. C. CLAYTON *Cruel Fortune* II. 220 To ascertain whether it was..properly spelt, and had all the i's dotted, and the t's crossed. **1882** MRS. HOUSTOUN *Recomm. to Mercy* xx, Please not to cross the t's. **1885** DUNCKLEY in *Manch. Exam.* 15 June 6/2 To dot his i's and cross his t's and polish up his manuscript.

c. Phr. *to a T* (also *to a tee*): exactly, properly, to a nicety.

[The original sense of T here has not been ascertained. Suggestions that it was the *tee* at Curling, or at Golf, or a T square, appear on investigation to be untenable; it has also been suggested that it referred to the proper completion of a *t* by crossing it (see b); or that it was the initial of a word; in reference to this it is notable that *to a tittle* (i.e. to a prick, dot, jot) was in use nearly a century before 'to a T', and in exactly the same constructions: see TITTLE.]

1693 *Humours Town* 102 All the under Villages and Towns-men come to him for Redress; which he does to a T. **1700** *Labour in Vain* VIII. in *Harl. Misc.* (1810) X. 473 Harry cajoled my inquirer, and fitted his humour to a t——. **1771** J. GILES *Poems* 155 I'll tell you where You may be suited to a tee. **1815** *Zeluca* I. 385, I knew my man to a T. **1828** *Life Planter Jamaica* 161, I understand the practice to a tee. **1840** R. H. DANA *Bef. Mast* xxii. 66 The yards were squared 'to a T' by lifts and braces. **1856** MRS. STOWE *Dred* ii, All these old-fashioned goings on would suit you to a T. **1873** K. H. DIGBY *Last Year's Leaves* viii. 302 Then should you scorn such feasts, like me, We've what will suit you to a tee. **1922** JOYCE *Ulysses* 58 Simon Dedalus takes him off to a tee with his eyes screwed up. **1966** *Listener* 29 Sept. 480/1 John Hollis had Walter off to a tee. **1973** *Brit. Printer* May 62/3 Edwin Snell of Yeovil has the direct mail touch to a tee.

2. a. The shape of the letter; an object having the shape **T**. See also TEE *sb.*[1], TAU. Also short for *T beard*, *T iron*, *T rail*: see 3.

a **1619**, *a* **1654** [see 3 b]. **1707** MORTIMER *Husb.* (1721) II. 262 Slit the Bark or Rind about an Inch long, in form of a T. **1733** TULL *Horse-Hoeing Husb.* xxii. 330 Made..with a Head like a T. **1875** SIR T. SEATON *Fret-Cutting* 69 Then see whereabouts to put them through the upright part or T of the bracket. **1891** *Daily News* 27 Apr. 2/5 Plate iron, angles, T's, and bars for railway waggon building are in large request. **1891** *Scott. Leader* 21 Sept. 3 Inquiries for old material are reviving, rails being chiefly in demand. Some holders are now asking 21 dols. for old T's. **1893** F. ADAMS *New Egypt* 237 The tongue of this inverted T, *i.e.*, the entrenchments, had been carried out some two miles.

b. *Electr.* A network of three impedances that can be represented diagrammatically as a T in which the stem and each arm is an impedance. Freq. *attrib.*; so *T-connected* adj.

1909 BEDELL & PIERCE *Direct & A.C. Testing* vii. 248 Transforming from a 2-phase primary circuit to two sets of T-connected secondaries. *Ibid.* 249 The line voltage, thus obtained by the *T*-connection, is accordingly the same as would be obtained by three 3-phase generator coils..in delta. **1934**, etc. [see LATTICE *sb.* 2 d]. **1947** R. LEE *Electronic Transformers & Circuits* vi. 150 In the 'low pass' filter T-section of Fig. 115, the inductance arms shown as *L*/2 and the capacitance *C* are made with losses as low as possible. **1973** J. R. NEUENSWANDER *Mod. Power Systems* iii. 32 For a line of medium length, a better approximation is arrived at through either the π or the T connection. **1975** D. G. FINK *Electronics Engineers' Handbk.* XIII. 30 While many null network configurations are useful (including the bridged-T and twin-T), the Wien bridge design predominates.

c. *Naut.* In phr. *to cross the T*: of a fleet or ship, to cross ahead of another (enemy) fleet's or ship's line of advance approximately at right angles, thus securing tactical advantages.

1916 'TAFFRAIL' *Pincher Martin* xvii. 323 Sir David Beatty..altered course to the east and crossed the enemy's T,..inflicting terrible damage with his heavy fire. **1953** *Hist. Today* Feb. 114/1 The Japanese main force was able to steam across the head of the Russian line... This manoeuvre, known as 'crossing the T', has been the dream of all admirals once steam tactics were introduced. **1968** D. THOMAS *Battle of Java Sea* x. 143 The destroyer *Oshio*..had crossed the Dutch cruisers' T and exchanged a rapid but ineffectual fire with *Java*. **1976** *Oxf. Compan. Ships & Sea* 213/2 The fleet 'crossing the T' has a considerable gunnery advantage.

3. a. *attrib.* (sometimes hyphened): Shaped like the letter **T**; having a cross piece at the top; as ***T bandage***, ***bar***, ***chain***, ***end***, ***fish***, ***handle***, ***head***, ***hinge***, ***iron***, ***joint***, ***key***, ***pattern***, ***piece***, ***spot***, ***tap***, ***tube***, ***wharf***. Also comb., as ***T-formed***, ***-headed***, ***-shaped*** adjs. See also TEE *sb.*[1], TEE-PIECE, etc.

1783 BENTLEY in *Med. Commun.* (1784) I. 257 The canula ..was left in the puncture, secured with a double *T bandage. **1885** W. H. COLEMAN *Hist. Sketch Bk. New Orleans* xviii. 187 The Chevalier appeared in the streets wearing what the surgeons call a T bandage about his face and jaw. **1882** NARES *Seamanship* (ed. 6) 84 Secured by a *T chain. **1841** *Penny Cycl.* XX. 465/2 The *T-formed or arrow-shaped bone [of the Saurians]. **1778** [W. MARSHALL] *Minutes Agric.* 20 Apr. an. 1775, A light beam of seven feet long, drawn by a *T handle, by one man, walking backwards. *a* **1910** *N.E.D.*, *T head. **1913** W. E. DOMMETT *Motor Car Mech.* 42 The arrangement shown at E is the most extensively used, the cylinder being said to have a T-head. **1969** *Jane's Freight Containers 1968–69* 179/3 A new Oil Jetty running 217 m..out into Harwich Harbour.., and having a minimum depth of 33 ft alongside the T-head. **1844** STEPHENS *Bk. Farm* III. 849 They are always attached ..by a *T headed nail and spike. **1844** *Ibid.* I. 198 The inside doors should be hung with *T hinges, 18 inches long. **1838** *Civil Eng. & Arch. Jrnl.* I. 126/1 The roof..is further supported and braced by strutts of *T iron and suspension rods. **1889** *Cent. Dict.*, *T-joint. **1906** *Westm. Gaz.* 16 Mar. 8/1 The main cable..is always connected with the consumer's house by means of a T-joint, which is enclosed in a box filled with bitumen. **1895** PARKES *Health* 54 Lead *T pieces, as they are called [in water-pipes] must be used. **1860** *Biog. & Crit. fr. 'The Times'* 235 *T-shaped traps for the wheatear. **1896** *Farrier's Price List*, *T taps and other tools. **1881** TYNDALL *Floating Matter of Air* III. xviii. 188 One end..of a glass *T-tube was connected with an air-pump.

b. *Special Combs.* (sometimes hyphened). **T account** *U.S. Book-keeping*, a standard form of ledger account (see quot. 1976), or a simplified version of this; **T-bar**, a metal bar with a T-shaped cross-section; a T-shaped fastening on a shoe (cf. *T-strap* below); *spec.* a type of ski-lift consisting of a series of T-shaped bars whereby skiers are towed uphill; † **T beard**, a beard worn in the 17th c., grown or cut in the form of a T; **T-bone steak** orig. *U.S.*, a beef-steak cut from the sirloin and containing a T-shaped bone; also *ellipt.* as ***T-bone***; **T branch**, in piping, a right-angled joint of a small pipe to a main; a T joint; **T cart**, an open phaeton, so called from its groundplan resembling the letter T; **T cloth**, a plain cotton cloth exported to India, China, Africa, etc., so called from the large letter T stamped on it; **T-formation** *U.S. Football*, a T-shaped offensive formation of players (see quot. 1978); **T-junction**, a T-shaped intersection (of pipes, etc.); *spec.* a T-shaped road junction; † **T-light** *Theatr.*, a type of gas lighting-device utilizing a pipe in the shape of a letter T (*obs.*); **T rail**, a railway metal or rail having a T section; **T square**, a square of the form of a **T** or rather ⊢ (with a long stem), used by mechanics and draughtsmen for drawing lines parallel, or at right angles, to each other (see also TEE *sb.*[1]); **T-strap**, a T-shaped instep strap on a shoe; freq. *attrib.*; also *absol.*, a shoe with such a strap; cf. *T-bar* above; **t-totum**: see TEETOTUM. See also T-SHIRT.

1936 OWENS & KENNEDY *Accounting* v. 49 Sometimes 'skeleton' or '*T' accounts are used instead of the regular accounts. **1941** L. O. FOSTER *Introd. Accounting* x. 181 T accounts are accounts without rulings and are used in classroom discussions because of the simplicity of their structure. **1976** D. W. MOFFAT *Econ. Dict.* 270/1 *T account.* In double-entry book-keeping, each account has the name of the account on a horizontal across the top, and then a vertical line separates the debit entries from the credit entries. The lines form a T. **1889** *Cent. Dict.*, *T-bar. **1940** [see *chair-lift* s.v. LIFT *sb.*[2] 10 b]. **1956** [see SECTION *sb.* 2 p]. **1964** *Woman* 18 Jan. 13 Today's chair-lifts and T-bars mean you'll be sitting as much as ski-ing. **1966** A. W. LEWIS *Gloss. Woodworking Terms* 78 (*caption*) T-bar sach cramp. **1972** *Daily Tel.* 24 Jan. 11/7 The little girl's T-bar beach-shoe. **1979** *United States 1980/81* (Penguin Travel Guides) 648 Excellent skiing facilities including a chair lift,..T-bar, beginners' lift, and various snack bars. *a* **1619** FLETCHER, etc. *Q. Corinth* IV. i, Strokes his beard, Which now he puts i' th' posture of a T, The Roman T, your *T beard is the fashion. [*a* **1654** J. TAYLOR (Water P.) *Superb. Flagellum*, [Beards] Some with the hammer-cut, or Roman T.] **1916** *Dialect Notes* IV. 270 *T-steak* or **T-bone-steak*,..

so called from the shape of the bone. **1923** N. ANDERSON *Hobo* I. iii. 34 These bills of fare..displayed..T-Bone Steak. **1934** E. NEWHOUSE *You can't sleep Here* xii. 144 When it's a toss-up between buzzards' gizzards and a t-bone.., me for the t-bone. **1959** *Times* 27 Apr. 7/4 Fillet and T-bone steaks were the order of the hour. **1979** R. RENDELL *Make Death love Me* xi. 98 He got Marty to fetch in three great hunks of T-bone because Joyce said she liked steak. **1873** MISS BROUGHTON *Nancy* II. 24 The butler took the housekeeper a driving-tour in my *T-cart, and threw down one of my best horses. **1882** *Daily News* 30 May 3/1 Stanhope phaetons (generally called by the absurd name of T cart). **1883** F. M. CRAWFORD *Dr. Claudius* xvi, A very gorgeous conveyance, called in America a T-cart, and resembling a mail phaeton in build. **1865** *Manch. Guard.* 2 Mar., *T cloths, 9*d.* and long-cloths, 6*d.* to 1*s.* per piece. **1880** *Plain Hints Needlework* 72 'T cloths' are lengths of 20 yards of calico, specially used as barter with native tribes in Africa. **1930** R. C. ZUPPKE *Coaching Football* vii. 208 The '*T' formation..is at its core a strong formation. **1942** L. O. WALDORF *How to play Football* ix. 112 In 1940, Stanford University used the T formation with great success. **1978** G. WRIGHT *Illustr. Handbk. Sporting Terms* 85/3 *T-formation*, one of the basic offensive formations with the quarterback behind the center and the other three backs behind in a row parallel to the line of scrimmage. **1954** *Gloss. Highway Engin. Terms (B.S.I.)* 56 **T junction*, a junction shaped like a T. **1956** *Nature* 24 Mar. 561/1 The study of the stresses in the T-junction of a branched pipe. **1958** *Listener* 20 Nov. 835/3 The first T-junction that comes along without a signpost of any kind. **1969** E. H. PINTO *Treen* 380/2 The method of making a right-angle turn, or a T junction, is shown in Plate 408, where the tapered short section is driven into a cone socket in the side of the longer length of elm pipe. **1982** S. SPENDER *China Diary* 104 He jumped out of the car ..and walked..till he came to a T-junction where the [traffic] blockage seemed to originate. **1898** A. W. PINERO *Trelawny of 'Wells'* IV. 171 Just below the footlights is a *T-light, burning gas. **1911** [see DU THÉÂTRE]. **1933** J. MARTIN-HARVEY *Autobiogr.* iv. 43 The gloomy underground stage unlit by anything but the 'T' light on which a single jet of gas literally made darkness visible. **1837** *Civil Eng. & Arch. Jrnl.* I. 39/2 The pattern..is by American engineers called the inverted *T rail. **18..** WHITMAN *To Working Men* vi, The strong, clean-shaped T-rail for railroads. [**1701** MOXON *Math. Instr.* 19 *Tee*, a double Square in the form of a T.] **1785** PEACOCK in *Phil. Trans.* LXXV. 369 A common *T square..will answer most purposes. **1861** SMILES *Engineers* II. 76 His trace, his T square, his augers, his gouges, and his engraving tools. **1963** *Times* 1 Feb. 14/5 Some shoes had.. slender *T-straps. **1963** *Harper's Bazaar* Apr. 75 The T-strap sandal shown here in patent leather. **1969** *Sears Catal.* Spring/Summer 7 Dashing T-strap with sparkling patent vinyl upper. **1974** *Country Life* 21 Mar. 687/2 A brogued court with T-strap. **1978** *Detroit Free Press* 5 Mar. A19 (Advt.), Popular T-strap slings with open or closed backs and espadrilles.

II. 4. Used like the other letters of the alphabet to denote serial order: applied e.g. to the twentieth (or more usually the nineteenth) of any series, to the nineteenth sheet of a book, etc.

(*b*) **T-model (Ford)** = *Model T* s.v. MODEL *sb.* 7 e.

1932 [see MODEL *sb.* 7 e]. **1942** Z. N. HURSTON in A. Dundes *Mother Wit* (1973) 28/1 Way after a while a T-model Ford came along full of Negroes. **1962** *John o' London's* 11 Jan. 43/3 Driving a T-model Ford over the roof-tops.

5. A mediæval symbol for the numeral 160, and with a stroke over it (T̄) for 160,000.

6. a. Abbreviations: for various proper names, as Thomas, Timothy, Titus, Theresa, etc.; T *Mus.*, tasto, tempo, tenor, tutti; T officially stamped on a letter, *taxed*, i.e. postage to be paid; T (*Physics*) = TERA-; T (*Physics*) = TESLA; T in a ship's log-book, thunder; T *Math.*, time, terms, etc.; T (*Physics* and *Chem.*) = TRITIUM; t (*Physics*), top or truth, a quark flavour; **TA** (*U.S.*), teaching assistant; **T.A.**, Territorial Army (see also note s.v. *TAVR* below); **T.A.** (*Psychol.*), transactional analysis; **T.A.B.** (*Austral.* and *N.Z.*), Totalizator Agency Board; **T.A.B.** (*Med.*), a vaccine against typhoid, paratyphoid A, and paratyphoid B; usu. *attrib.*; **T. & A., T and A** (*U.S.*), tonsils and adenoids; tonsillectomy and adenoidectomy; **t. and g., t. & g.**, (*Woodworking*), tongued and grooved; **TAT** (*Psychol.*), thematic apperception test; **TAVR**, Territorial and Army Volunteer Reserve (the name given to the restructured Territorial Army in 1967, but replaced by the name 'Territorial Army' in 1979); **T.B.**, torpedo-boat; **T.B.**, Treasury Bill (cf. *T-Bill*, sense 7 below); **T.B., t.b.**, tuberculosis; *T.B.-tested* adj., (of an animal) tested to establish the absence of tuberculosis; also (*U.S. slang*), a confidence trickster (see quot. 1930); **T.B.D., t.b.d.**, torpedo boat destroyer; **TBS**, *t*alk *b*etween *s*hips, a short-wave radio apparatus used for verbal communication between ships at sea; **tbs., tbsp.**, tablespoon(ful); **TCA**, trichloroacetic acid (a herbicide); **TCB** (*U.S. Black slang*), (to) take care of business; **T.C.D.**, Trinity College, Dublin; **TCDD** = *tetrachlorodibenzodioxin* s.v. TETRA- 2 a; **TCNQ** (*Chem.*) [f. T(ETRA- + CN, chemical formula of the cyano group + Q(UINONE], 7,7,8,8-tetracyano-*p*-quinodimethane, an organic compound forming salts of unusually low resistivity; **T.C.P.**, the proprietary name of a disinfectant; **TCP** (*Physics*), time (reversal), charge (conjugation), and parity (conservation); **T.D.** [Ir. *Teachtaí Dála*], a member of Dáil Éireann, the lower house of the Irish parliament; **T.D.**, Territorial Decoration (in the Territorial Army); **TD** (*U.S.* and *Canad. Football*), a touchdown; **T.D.C.**, Temporary Detective Constable; **TDC** (*Mech.*), top dead centre; **TDE** [f. T(WO *numeral a.* + *d*ichlorethane], an organochlorine insecticide (see quot. 1946) formerly used on fruit and vegetables; **T.D.R.**, Treasury Deposit Receipt; **t.d.s.** (*Med.*) [L. *ter die sumendus*], to be taken three times a day; **TEE**, Trans Europ (also Europe, European) Express (train); **TEFL, Tefl** (tɛf(ə)l), Teaching of English as a Foreign Language; **TESL** (tɛs(ə)l), Teaching of English as a Second Language; **TESOL** (ˈtɛsɔl), Teachers of English to Speakers of Other Languages; **TeV**, tera-electron volt; **T.G.**, temporary gentleman (see TEMPORARY *a.* 1 b); **T.G.**, thank God (cf. *D.G.* s.v. D III. 3); **TG** (*Linguistics*), transformational-generative (grammar) (see TRANSFORMATIONAL *a.*); **TGV** [F. *train à grande vitesse*], a type of high-speed French passenger train; **T.G.W.U.**, Transport and General Workers' Union; **THC**, tetrahydrocannabinol; **t.i.d.** (*Med.*) [L. *ter in die*], three times a day; **T.I.G., Tig** (*Engin.*), tungsten inert gas (with reference to welding with a tungsten electrode in an atmosphere of an inert gas); **TIR** [F. *transport international routier*], international road transport (with reference to an international customs agreement: see quot. 1969); **TKO, t.k.o.**, (chiefly *N. Amer.*), in Boxing, a technical knock-out; also *fig.* and as *v. trans.*; **TL**, thermoluminescent (dating technique); also *TL-dating*; **TLC** (*colloq.*), tender loving care; **TLC, t.l.c.** (*Chem.*), thin-layer chromatography; **TLR** (*Photogr.*), twin-lens reflex (camera); **T.L.S.**, *The Times Literary Supplement*; **TM**, trade mark; **TM**, transcendental meditation; **T.M.**, trench mortar (cf. TOC EMMA); **TMV**, tobacco mosaic virus; **T.N.T.** = TRINITROTOLUENE; **T.O.**, turn over (cf. *P.T.O.* = 'please turn over' s.v. P II); **TOEFL**, Test(ing) of English as a Foreign Language; **TOFC** (orig. *U.S.*), trailer on flatcar (with reference to a type of freight container); **TOW**, *t*ube-launched, *o*ptically tracked, *w*ire-guided (missile); **T.P.R.** (*Med.*), temperature, pulse, and respiration; **TR** (*Electronics*), transmit-receive; usu. *attrib.*; **TRF, TRH** (*Biochem.*) = *thyrotropin-releasing factor* or *hormone* s.v. THYRO-2; **tRNA** (*Biochem.*), transfer RNA; also †**T-RNA**; **T.S.** (*U.S. Forces' Slang*), tough shit (also situation, stuff); also used *attrib.* to designate a (real or imaginary) card, etc., allowing the recipient an interview to discuss his grievances with the chaplain; **TS** (*pl.* **TSS**), typescript; **TSA**, Training Services Agency; **TSH** (*Biochem.*), thyroid-stimulating hormone (cf. THYROID *sb.* 2 b); **tsp.**, teaspoon(ful); **TSS**, twin-screw steamer; **TSS** (see *TS* = typescript above); **T.T., t.t.**, teetotal, a teetotaller; **T.T.** (*Comm.*), telegraphic transfer; **T.T.**, Tourist Trophy (freq. used *ellipt.* for *Tourist Trophy Race*); **T.T.** = *tuberculin-tested* ppl. adj. s.v. TUBERCULIN b; also *transf.*; **T.T.F.N.** (*colloq.*), 'ta-ta for now' (a catch-phrase popularized by the 1940s BBC radio programme *Itma*); **T.T.L.** (*Photogr.*), through-the-lens (metering); **TTL** (*Electronics*) = *transistor-transistor logic* s.v. TRANSISTOR *sb.* 3 b; **TV** (*colloq.*, orig. and chiefly *N. Amer.*), a transvestite; **T.V.A.** [Fr., *taxe à la valeur ajoutée*] = V.A.T.; **T.V.A.** (*U.S.*), Tennessee Valley Authority; **TVP**, textured vegetable protein (proprietary name); see TEXTURED *a.*; **TWA** (*U.S.*), Trans World Airlines (formerly, until 1950, Transcontinental and Western Air). See also TAM, TANU, TASS[3], TEWT, TIM, TOPS, T.U.C., TV.

1894 *Westm. Gaz.* 12 Oct. 3/2 'England' stamps these cards with a '*T', an initial which, with St. Martin's-le-Grandiose conciseness stands for 'taxed'. **1951** *Symbols, Signs & Abbreviations* (R. Soc.) 15 Tera (× 10^{12}) *T. **1978** *Guardian Weekly* 27 Aug. 13/3 Sweden's energy requirements..—125 Twh in 1985. **1964** *Internat. System (SI) Units (B.S.I.)* 8 The tesla (symbol *T) is the name given to this unit in Continental literature. **1973** *Physics Bull.* Sept. 555/3 He used pulsed magnetic fields as high as 30 T. **1743** EMERSON *Fluxions* 15, **t* = Number of Terms in V..Continu'd to *t* Terms. **1871** TAIT & STEELE *Dynamics of Particle* (ed. 3) iii. §80 Let *P* be the position of the particle at any time **t*. *Ibid.* §86 If *T* be the time of descent down *AC*. **1978** *Nature* 2 Feb. 407/1 This new quark pair is labelled *t and b for 'top' and 'bottom'. *Ibid.* 407/2 The prudish may care to note that t and b are said to stand for truth and beauty, rather than top and bottom, by some physicists. **1984** *Daily Tel.* 5 July 36/4 Discovery of a sub-atomic particle labelled the 'T-top' quark has been announced by scientists at Cern. **1948** GLASSTONE *Textbk. Physical Chem.* (ed. 2) ii. 172 The ^{3}H isotope, called tritium, symbol *T, has also been obtained by the bombardment of nitrogen by neutrons. **1973** *Nature* 3 Aug. 257/1 The square-root law of mass-dependence does not apply to isotopic variants HDO and HTO. **1724** *Short Explic. For. Wds. in Mus. Bks.*, The Letter *T. is often used as an Abbreviation of the Word *Tutti*. **1969** C. DAVIDSON in Cockburn & Blackburn *Student Power* 357 These considerations make the organization of a radical trade union of *TAs a crucial part of any strategy for change. **1980** *Berkeley Graduate* Oct. 3/4 Matthew Soyster, a Comparative Literature graduate student, is currently a TA in the Rhetoric Department. **1924** *Regulations for Territorial Army* I. iii. 33 An officer appointed to command a brigade.. will..be granted such rank in the *T.A. temporarily. *Ibid.* iv. 53 The senior T.A. officer in the locality. **1939** W. S. CHURCHILL *Let.* 30 Aug. in M. Gilbert *Winston S. Churchill* (1976) V. liii. 1106 Would it not be helpful to call up the reserves and mobilize the TA? **1980** *Whitaker's Almanack 1981* 473/2 The Territorial Army (TA) is designed to provide a reserve of highly trained and well equipped units and individuals. **1972** *N.Y. Times Mag.* 19 Nov. 42 Initial capitals are common in the vocabulary of Transactional Analysis, or *T.A. **1976** *S. Wales Echo* 25 Nov. 16/7 In the group therapy of TA members can see a wider range of ego states than they could on their own, and the collective framework is thought to aid analysis and change. **1957** *Press* (Christchurch, N.Z.) 19 Nov. 16/1 If people want things like the *T.A.B., alcohol and cigarettes. **1969** *Sydney Morning Herald* 24 May 27/1 (*heading*) The Moorebank Handicap, second leg of the TAB double. **1977** *Herald* (Melbourne) 17 Jan. 6/8 A spokesman for the TAB head office. **1929** *Lancet* 9 Feb. 288/1 These *T.A.B. vaccine injections..caused remission in the course of general paralysis. **1970** *Guardian* 24 Jan. 17/3 The Department of Health advises *all* travellers abroad to take the precaution of a TAB vaccination. **1981** *Brit. Med. Jrnl.* 18 Apr. 1313/1 We all lined up, hand on hip, to receive the dreaded TAB. **1942** BERREY & VAN DEN BARK *Amer. Thes. Slang* §532/1 **T.&A.*, tonsils and adenoids. **1960** in *Arch. Otolaryngology* Aug. 183/1 Tonsilloadenoidectomy (T and A) is often classified as minor surgery. *Ibid.* 186/1 Immediate hemorrhage in the first 24 hours post T and A continued to be approximately 3%–4%. **1976** *Amer. Speech 1973* XLVIII. 204 Relatively simple operations like a *T and A*..are considered routine procedures on the hospital's *OR* (operating room) *schedule*. **1948** *Archit. Rev.* CIII. 133 Exterior walls are of two by four studs, four by four posts, faced externally with wood sheathing and *t. and g. vertical boarding. **1949** *Gloss. Terms Timber (B.S.I.)* 41 *t. & g.*, tongued and grooved. **1946** *Jrnl. Presonality* XV. 70 The Thematic Apperception Test (*TAT)..is a projective device which purports to reveal the basic personality characteristics of individuals. **1952** [see GLOBAL *a.* 2]. **1964** M. ARGYLE *Psychol. & Social Probl.* iv. 49 There are various ways of scoring TAT stories for aggressiveness. **1972** *Jrnl. Social Psychol.* LXXXVIII. 191 The standard Murray TATs..were not considered appropriate. **1967** *Army Q.* XCIV. 36 *T.A.V.R. I and II will be adequately equipped with modern weapons and equipment. **1977** *R.A.F. News* 22 June–5 July 18 (*caption*) The Wapinschaw..attracts entries from many regular and TAVR units in the North of Scotland. **1897**, etc. *T.B. = torpedo boat [implied at T.B.D. below]. *a***1912** W. T. ROGERS *Dict. Abbrev.* (1913) 187/1 *T.B.*,..torpedo boat. **1925** R. H. BACON *Naval Scrap-bk.* x. 144 In the 1895 manœuvres, when I was a Lieutenant of just under twelve years' seniority, I was appointed in command of *No. 94 T.B.* **1938**, etc. [see M.T.B. s.v. M 5 a]. **1977** PRESTON & BROWN tr. *Jentschura's Warships Imperial Jap. Navy, 1869–1945* ix. 124 TBs. *1–4* were modelled by Sir Edward Reed on the RN 100ft type. They were assembled in Japan. **1936** *Financial Times* 20 Nov. 1/1, 3 months *T.B.—*£0 10 6·24 pc. **1971** *Financial Mail* (Johannesburg) 26 Feb. 661/1 National has about R25m of TBs on its book. **1912** D. LOWRIE *My Life in Prison* iv. 33 He's doin' 35 years an' has the *T.B. **1921** A. MASON *Flying Bo'sun* ii. 19 Their mother died two years ago... The doctor said it was T.B. **1930** J. LAIT *Big House* i. 7 A confidence (or 'con') man is a 'T.B.', ('con' is short and slang for consumption, and 'T.B.' is ditto for tuberculosis). **1932** U. SINCLAIR *Candid Reminiscences* x. 88 The old captain was ill of TB. **1942** C. HIMES *Black on Black* (1973) 176 Men..of all stages of deterioration—drifters and hopheads and tb's and beggars and bums and bindle-stiffs and big sisters. **1951** J. CANNAN *And all I Learned* x. 180 We've our own cows, T.B. tested and so beautifully kept. **1957** S. SMITH *Coll. Poems* (1975) 336, I lay with my young bride in my arms, A girl with t.b. **1974** M. BUTTERWORTH *Man in Sopwith Camel* ii. 26 They wouldn't take me 'cos I'd had a touch of TB. **1897** KIPLING *Let.* Aug. in C. Carrington *Rudyard Kipling* (1955) xi. 268 Ref: *t.b.d. trials. My attention is at present taken up by one small craft recently lauched from my own works. **1902** —— *Traffics & Discoveries* (1904) 182 The chief engineer o' the *Djinn*, 31-knot T.B.D. **1919** C. P. THOMPSON *Cocktails* 249, I passed an enjoyable day giving a T.B.D. lieutenant a headache. **1978** H. WOUK *War & Remembrance* xx. 200 The TBD is a lot slower. **1944** *TBS [see GRAVELLY *a.* 5]. **1946** *Sat. Even. Post* 26 Oct. 66/3 The astounded admiral grabbed the TBS radio and shouted. **1978** H. WOUK *War & Remembrance* xv. 153 Rear Admiral Spruance, issuing order after order on the TBS, finally regained a semblance of control. **1950** *Good Housek. Picture Cookery* 170/2 Coffee Glacé Icing. 8 oz. icing sugar 2 *tbsps. water. Coffee essence to taste. **1974** J. PAXTON *Everyman's Dict. Abbrev.* 338/1 *tbs., tbsp.*, tablespoon, tablespoonful. **1977** *Times Lit. Suppl.* 1 Apr. 391/2, I only wish my dog *liked* his food sprinkled with the recommended 2 tbs of the product every day. **1960** *Farmer & Stockbreeder* 22 Mar. 136/3 After *T.C.A. treatment 8 weeks should elapse before planting potatoes. **1971** *Arable Farmer* Feb. 15/2 A pre-planting application of TCA to peas may reduce the waxiness of the crop foliage, leading to unexpected damage from dinoseb applied subsequently. **1969** S. E. HENDERSON in Cook & Henderson *Militant Black Writer* 78 These poems were not intended for white readers and white audiences..their purpose was direct address to the black community, to get us together to *TCB. **1973** *New Times* 2 Nov. 41 Where he is always to be found TCB'ing (taking care of business, an old ghetto phrase which originally meant to copulate). **1831** M. C. TAYLOR *Let.* 22 June in J. J. Auchmuty *Sir T. Wyse* (1939) ix. 134 The Scholars of *T.C.D. do not afford a Protestant, a learned or an independent constituency. **1916** H. PLUNKETT *Jrnl.* 29 Apr. in M. Digby *Plunkett* (1949) ix. 212 The firing from the other side of the T.C.D. guards was so fierce that we had to turn back. **1939** JOYCE *Finnegans Wake* 424 Go o'er the sea, haythen from me and leave your libber to TCD. **1979** J. SHEEHAN in J. J. Lee *Ireland 1945–70* 67 A UCD/TCD merger or co-ordination of some sort. **1971** *New Yorker* 14 Aug. 57 The only real question concerning the safety of 2,4,5-T has to do with the *TCDD dioxin with which it is contaminated. **1981** *McGraw-Hill Yearbk. Sci. & Technol.* 199/2 It is impossible to substantiate the charge that TCDD has led to an increase in the number of malformed children in Vietnam. **1960** *Jrnl. Amer. Chem. Soc.* LXXXII. 6408/1, 7,7,8,8-Tetracyanoquinodimethane (*TCNQ) has been synthesized and found to yield a series of stable anion-radical derivatives. **1979** *Sci. Amer.* Oct. 48/2 Many salts in which TCNQ is combined with other atoms or molecules form linear-chain solids. **1934** *Trade Marks Jrnl.* 22 Aug. 1084/1 **T.C.P.*... Antiseptic and germicide solutions (being disinfectants). British Alkaloids Limited, 104, Winchester House, Old Broad Street, London, E.C.2; manufacturing chemists. **1947** J. LEES-MILNE *Diary* 22 Jan. (1983) 128 Cut my mole shaving this morning and thought it would never stop bleeding. T.C.P. finally staunched it. **1959** I. & P. OPIE *Lore & Lang. Schoolch.* ix. 171 Earnestly applying T.C.P... in the privacy of their bedrooms. **1981** G. KAYE *Day after Yesterday* ii. 22 You cried when you only scraped your knee.. a little scrape and a bit of TCP. **1957** *Physical Rev.* CVI. 385/1 According to a general theorem, invariance with respect to the product **TCP* follows for a wide class of field theories from invariance with respect to the proper Lorentz group alone. **1974** FRAUENFELDER & HENLEY *Subatomic Physics* ix. 223 When violation of parity became a possibility the *TCP* theorem suddenly acquired more meaning. **1979** J. C. POLKINGHORNE *Particle Play* iii. 47 We do not know how to write down any theories which are not invariant under TCP. **1947** S. MALONE *Notes on Procedure in Houses of Oireachtas* p. vii, Members of Dail Eirann (Teachtai Dála)—referred to as *T.D.'s or Deputies. **1959** B. CHUBB in D. E. Butler et al. *Elections Abroad* iii. 187 TD—Teachta Dála; the Irish equivalent of Member of Parliament. TDs are addressed as 'Deputy'. **1979** M. MANNING in J. J. Lee *Ireland 1945–70* 51 Its TDs tended to act more as independents than as members of a political party. **1924** *Regulations for Territorial Army* I. x. 145 The letters '*T.D.' will be inserted in the Army List after the name of the officer on whom the decoration is conferred. **1981** *Whitaker's Almanack 1982* 248 *Alport*, Cuthbert James McCall Alport, P.C., T.D. **1953** BERREY & VAN DEN BARK *Amer. Thes. Slang* (1954) §692/2 Touchdown,..**TD, touch.* **1969** *Eugene* (Oregon) *Register-Guard* 3 Dec. 2D/1 Nyseth scored three TDs en route to 137 yards. **1970** *Globe & Mail* (Toronto) 25 Sept. 33/3 Another fumble set up Riverdale's second TD when Bob Nichols recovered the ball in Lions' end zone. **1977** *Detroit Free Press* 11 Dec. 10-D/4 TD passes, home runs, goals or point averages. **1970** G. F. NEWMAN *Sir, You Bastard* ii. 45 *TDC Sneed and DC Lambert to watch on Sloane Square to investigate shoplifting complaint. **1978** B. NORMAN *To nick Good Body* ii. 9 A temporary detective constable..had just brought in the Guv'nor's tea... The Guv'nor waved away the T.D.C. **1938** *Jrnl. R. Aeronaut. Soc.* XLII. 888 *T.D.C. or any other reference marks are marked by the discharge flash of a thyratron circuit, controlled by suitable contacts on the engine crankshaft. **1976** *New Motorcycling Monthly* Oct. 34/2 With piston at TDC, pull barrel up mounting studs. **1946** *Nature* 6 July 22/1 'D.D.D.' or '*T.D.E.' The compound 2.2-*bis*(*p*-chlorphenyl)1,1-dichlorethane..has been shown to be about as toxic as D.D.T. to mosquito larvæ in laboratory tests. **1970** *New Scientist* 1 Jan. 16/1 Much of this case also applies..to the other 'hard' organochlorine insecticides: aldrin,..BHC and TDE (Rhothane). **1948** G. CROWTHER *Outl. Money* (ed. 2) ii. 37 There are four main types of bank assets, which are..bills.., Treasury Deposit Receipts (usually known as *TDRs), investments and loans. **1965** J. L. HANSON *Dict. Econ & Commerce* 383/1 By 1945 T.D.R.s had reached a total of over £1,800 million. **1899** P. G. LEWIS *Nursing* ii. 18 Medicines are ordered to be taken either statim (immediately), or *t.d.s. = ter die sumenda (to be taken three times a day). **1919** *Jrnl. R. Naval Med. Service* V. 93 He was given quinine 15 gr. t.d.s. **1961** *Lancet* 29 July 238/1 The response of our patients to a course of 20 electroshock treatments or to chlorpromazine 100–400 mg. t.d.s **1963** *Times* 23 May 13/7 *TEE trains now link 90 European cities. **1967** R. SAWKINS *Snow in Paradise* iii. 29 The TEE is just about as quick as the plane. **1977** J. PAXTON *Dict. Europ. Econ. Community* 246 *Trans-Europ-Express* (*T.E.E.*). Trans-Europ-Expresses connect major cities in nine European countries by a network of very fast and comfortable trains for which frontier formalities have been reduced to a minimum. **1963** *Language Learning* (Univ. of Michigan) XIII. 225 (*heading*) Reflections on Preparation for *TEFL. **1968** *Language* XLIV. 206 Any gathering of TEFL leaders today will be sure to include a large number who received their initial experience at Michigan. **1977** P. STREVENS *New Orientations Teaching of English* v. 56 The American terms TEFL, TESL, TESOL, TESOLD have no precise counterparts in British usage. **1981** *Guardian* 14 Apr. 21/4 (Advt.), Applications are invited from candidates who have experience in..Tefl. **1967** *Sat. Rev.* (U.S.) 16 Sept. 83 Though a major curriculum emphasis is developing fluency in the English language using the linguistic approach of *TESL (Teaching English as a Second Language), the knowledge of Navaho is still essential to many jobs on the reservation. **1980** *Verbatim* Spring 20/1 A dictionary or international English might have remembered TESL and TEFL 'teaching of English as a Second (or Foreign) Language', however. **1969** *Language* XLV. 171 The two halves of the collection, articles on the description of English and articles on *TESOL, reflect the sad dichotomy between descriptive linguists and language-teaching methodologists the world over. **1956** *Proc. CERN Symposium* I. 64/2 These machines would have equivalent energies of 1340 Gev, or 1·3 *Tev. **1980** *Sci. Amer.* Jan. 32/3 Completion of the full lower ring is now expected toward the end of 1981, and protons at 1 TeV should be delivered to the experimental areas in 1982. **1916** N. MITCHISON *Jrnl.* in *All Change Here* (1975) xv. 147 Last night about half a dozen [officers] came into the salon and started a conversation... They were awful *TGs mostly... Here am I, sitting..in the middle of the stuffy salon of a third-rate French hotel, being as charming as I can to an audience of TGs, all to give them the memory of a pleasant evening to take back to the trenches at Givenchy. **1934** J. RHYS *Voyage in Dark* I. i. 17 'Only three more weeks of this damned tour, *T.G.,' Maudie said. 'It's no life.' **1978** D. MURPHY *Place Apart* xi. 226 Isn't it a tough world to be tryin' to raise twelve boys in? But T.G. so far they're good lads. **1968** B. M. H. STRANG *Mod. Eng. Structure* (ed. 2) 200 The most eminent *TG thinkers are still evolving and modifying parts of their theory. **1971** *Archivum Linguisticum* III. 64 Of recent years it is transformational-generative grammer (TG) that has undoubtedly called the tune. **1977** *Trans. Philol. Soc. 1975* 8 General linguists unsympathetic to TG. **1978** *English Jrnl.* Dec. 52/1 On the other hand, we should not jump indiscriminately into transformational-generative grammar. A full-blown TG grammar is complex. **1980** *N.Y. Times* 19 Nov. 17/1 Among the trains being studied as possible models for Ohio is the French *TGV. [**1924** G. D. H. COLE *Organised Labour* II. i. 20 The Transport Workers' Federation, which..has lost much of its importance since the formation of the *T. and G.W.U.] **1955** *Times* 2 May 12/6 He became general secretary of the T.G.W.U. in 1945. **1957** *Economist* 26 Oct. 292/1 Last July the TGWU, together with the other unions involved, called an official strike of the provincial busmen. **1977** M. WALKER *National Front* vi. 157 It was an American executive who flew to secret talks with the TGWU union negotiators at Llandudno. **1968** *Time* 19 Apr. 79 At a Chicago conference on psychedelic drugs, Dr. Donald R. Jasinski.. reported that he had produced LSD-like symptoms with tetrahydrocannabinol (*THC), one of the purified active ingredients of cannabis. **1974** *Times Lit. Suppl.* 8 Mar. 240/5 Marijuana smokers in the United States are 'playing at cannabis use'—in that their daily ingestion of THC is only one-fifth of that of users in India, Egypt or Morocco. **1885** C. S. WEEKS *Textbk. Nursing* vii. 105/2 **T.i.d., ter in dies*, three times a day. **1941** *Jrnl. R. Naval Med. Service* XXVII. 301 The course of atebrin tablets, one t.i.d. **1976** *Amer. Speech 1973* XLVIII. 198 Referring to the exact times a patient must have a certain medication are *b.i.d.* for *bis in die* 'twice daily', *t.i.d.* for *ter in die* 'three times a day', [etc.]. **1960** *McGraw-Hill Encycl. Sci. & Technol.* XIV. 467/2 Inert gas shielding is essential with tungsten electrodes, hence the term Tungsten Inert Gas (*TIG) welding. **1969** D. K. ALLEN *Metallurgy Theory & Practice* xix. 612 (*caption*) Photomicrograph of a Tig weld with low voltage electron beam weld in center of Tig nugget to show relative width of heat affected zone in each process. **1975** BRAM & DOWNS *Manuf. Technol.* ii. 55 The T.I.G. process differs from the manual metal-arc technique in as much as the electrode is virtually non-consumable. **1968** E. PUGH *Dict. Acronyms & Abbrev.* 169 **TIR*, Transports Internationale Routiers [*sic*]. **1969** *Jane's Freight Containers 1968–69* 141/1 For road transport, the so-called 'TIR' Convention, concluded under the auspices of the ECE, allows the transport of goods under Customs seal in lorries from the Customs office of departure to the Customs office of arrival. **1980** K. HAGENBACH *Fox Potential* xii. 119 We passed a couple of big TIR trucks, each pulling a trailer. **1942** BERREY & VAN DEN BARK *Amer. Thes. Slang* §704/1 Technical knockout,..**T.K.O.* **1956** 'T. BETTS' *Across the Board* xxi. 296 Endocrinology TKO's Freud in the second round. **1968** M. RICHLER in R. Weaver *Canad. Short Stories* 2nd Ser. 164 'You lost by a TKO,' my father said. 'Thanks,' my mother said. **1971** *Weekend World* (Johannesburg) 9 May 1/3 Tulwana's fly weight title which Dlamini took on a third round t.k.o. **1975** J. GORES *Hammett* (1976) iii. 28 Revani TKO'd his Filipino opponent after..using his gut as a workout bag in the fourth [round]. **1972** *Oxf. Univ. Gaz.* CII. Suppl. II. 12 Development and application of *TL at the National Museum, Edinburgh. **1978** *Times* 11 Nov. 3 *TL-dating was developed in the 1960s for dating pottery and other fired materials from archaeological sites. **1960** I. A. STANTON *Dict. for Medical Secretaries* 149/1 **T.L.C.*, abbreviation for tender, loving care. **1973** *Publishers Weekly* 19 Nov. 55/1 The contagious potential of his TLC when he launches a yarn. **1977** *Listener* 12 May 605/3 It is in a nurse's nature and in her tradition to give to the sick what is well called 'TLC', 'tender loving care'. **1961** *Jrnl. Amer. Oil Chemists Soc.* XXXVIII. 316/1 *TLC has a number of features which make it an ideal technique for the analysis of these compounds. **1975** WILLIAMS & WILSON *Biologist's Guide to Princ. & Techniques Pract. Biochem.* iii. 58 Adsorbents used in t.l.c. differ from column adsorbents in that they may contain a binding agent such as calcium sulphate. **1980** *Nature* 8 May 105/1 To determine the sequence of the two amino acids, the active sample was dansylated, hydrolysed and the dansyl derivative examined by TLC. **1965** M. J. LANGFORD *Basic Photogr.* 376/1 (Index), *TLR. **1978** *SLR Camera* Sept. 61/1 Rollei.. originally only manufactured top quality TLR cameras. **1979** *Amat. Photographer* 10 Jan. 110/2 I'd recommend the TLR every time if monochrome prints are the objective, more so when the prints are to over 10 × 8in. **1953** R. CRAWSHAY-WILLIAMS *Let.* 1 Aug. in B. Russell *Autobiogr.* (1969) III. ii. 91 There are a nice lot of sly digs..the *T.L.S. pastiche. **1967** E. COXHEAD *Thankless Muse* i. 18 A little advance something in the TLS never comes amiss, does it? **1977** *Bookseller* 4 June 2704/2 The *Times Literary Supplement* (never called the *T.L.S.* then [in 1952]). **1961** WEBSTER, *TM, trademark. **1964** *Trademarks in Marketplace* (U.S. Trademark Assoc.) 64 We use the term 'trademark' right under the selected word, or we put a little 'TM' in the place where you normally would put the R. **1980** *Sci. Amer.* Oct. 138/1 (Advt.), The Clan of the Cave Bear, Earth's Children™, a novel by Jean M. Auel. **1967** *Listener* 7 Sept. 299/1, I hear you're hostile to drugs now and have taken to *TM. **1977** E. V. CUNNINGHAM *Case of One-Penny Orange* (1978) ix. 110 Topanga Canyon..had..sensitivity centers and nudist camps and TM temples. **1980** *Times* 27 May 1/8 The Home office does not approve the use of TM in borstals or prisons. **1925** FRASER & GIBBONS *Soldier & Sailor Words* 275 T.M. batteries were created for trench warfare and *T.M. schools of instruction were established. **1930** BROPHY & PARTRIDGE *Songs & Slang 1914–1918* 173 When a T.M. battery had fired a few shots it departed with speed. **1960** *Proc. Nat. Acad. Sci.* XLVI. 636 (*heading*) The amino acid composition and C-terminal sequence of a chemically evoked mutant of *TMV. **1974** W. K. JOKLIK in Carlile & Steehel *Evolution in Microbial World* 298 The fascinating work of Klug and his colleagues with TMV. **1915** D. O. BARNETT *Let.* 4 July 203 The yellow muck doesn't choke you, though, like the black greasy smoke (*T.N.T.) which they generally have in the 6 and 8-inch shells. **1962** E. SNOW *Other Side of River* (1963) xxix. 217 A responsible Western physicist's estimate that the world then possessed a nuclear weapons stockpile roughly the equivalent of forty tons of TNT for each person alive. **1979** O. SELA *Petrograd Consignment* 53 The casing contains a pound of TNT and it can be attached to a timing device. **1853** MRS. GASKELL *Cranford* v. 68 However, at the foot of the page was a small '*T.O.', and on turning it over, sure enough, there was a letter to 'my dear, dearest Molly'. **1889** E. C. DOWSON *Let. c* 23 Jan. (1967) 29 When we will proceed to Pinoli or where you will. T.O. Act à votre discretion in the matter of booking seats. **1981** *Oxf. Dict. for Writers & Editors* 412/2 *TO*, turn over. **1964** *Overseas* Jan. 22 On February 17, 1964, a new English-proficiency test for foreign students will be administered overseas. Called *TOEFL for short, this Test of English as a Foreign Language is designed to help..assess the language competence of foreign students. **1972** J. L. DILLARD *Black English* 272 It is of primary importance that all such materials, like all TOEFL materials, take the student's native language (here, dialect) into full account. **1954** *TOFC [see PIGGY-BACK *adv. phr.* (*a.*, *sb.*) b]. **1964** *Economist* 26 Sept. 1243/1 The [US] railways have introduced TOFC service—trailer-on-flatcar, better known as Piggyback. **1969** TOFC [see KANGAROO *sb.* 3 h]. **1972** *Guardian* 22 Aug. 3/1 The missiles [are] called *TOWs... TOW stands for tube-launched, optically tracked, and wire-guided. **1976** *N.Y. Times* 28 Mar. 1 The TOW missile can be used offensively from jeeps or armed cars. **1917** V. BRITTAIN *Let.* 5 Dec. in *Testament of Youth* (1933) viii. 395 Morning work—i.e. beds, *T.P.R.s (temperatures, pulses, respirations), washings, medicines, etc. **1976** *Amer. Speech 1973* XLVIII. 197 His *vitals* 'vital signs' such as temperature, pulse, and respiration (*TPR*). **1945** *Electronic Industries* Sept. 226 **T R switch*, transmit-receive switch. A switch which prevents the transmitted energy from getting to the receiver, but allows the received energy, which is much weaker, to reach the receiver without appreciable loss. This is necessary when the same antenna is used for both transmission and reception. **1975** D. G. FINK *Electronics Engineers' Handbk.* IX. 23 Such limiters are replacing TR gas discharge tubes in radar. **1959** K. SHIBUSAWA et al. in *Endocrinol. Jap.* VI. 31 We found a thyroid stimulating neurohumor in the hypothalamus... It was provisionally designated by us as *TRF (Thyrotropin Releasing Factor). **1972** *Clin. Endocrinol.* (1973) (B.M.A.) 47 Thyrotrophin-releasing factor (TRF), has recently been synthesized. **1968** A. V. SCHALLY et al. in *Rec. Progr. Hormone Res.* XXIV. 449 (*table*) Present name... Thyrotropin-releasing factor. TRF... Proposed name... Thyrotropin-releasing hormone. *TRH. **1977** *Proc. R. Soc. Med.* LXX. 698/1 The chief value of the thyrotrophin releasing hormone (TRH) test has been the diagnosis of dysthyroid eye disease. **1962** *Cold Spring Harbor Symp. Quantitative Biol.* XXVIII. 559 The system consisted of *E. coli* ribosomes and high speed super natant which contained transfer RNA (*T-RNA), the amino acyl-T-RNA synthetases, and the enzymes involved in the final steps of the synthesis of the polypeptide chain. **1966** *Ibid.* XXXI. 587/1 The elution profiles of noninfected-cell and infected cell arginyl tRNA exhibit unambiguous major differences. **1977** *Time* 4 Apr. 39/2 Aaron Klug..first determined the crystalline structure of transfer RNA (tRNA), the molecule that brings amino acids to the ribosome for assembly into protein. **1944** A. M. TAYLOR *Lang. World War II* 69 *TS Cards: Beachhead chaplains are carrying a special 'tough stuff' ticket these days which they issue to guys with complaints about which nothing can be done. **1944** *Yank* 18 Aug. 16/2, I..will be ever grateful for any possible solution, for I have tried everything I know, even prayer. Still TS. **1946** *Amer. Speech* XXI. 249 A *T.S. ticket* is an imaginary form entitling the bearer to sympathy and nothing else. 'All I can do is punch ya T.S. ticket (or slip) for ya.' **1946** *Amer. Jrnl. Social.* Mar. 422 One such expression is 'TS' or 'tough s——'... 'TS', resigned acceptance, said with a bitter smile. **1966** *Sunday Times* (Colour Suppl.) 4 Dec. 73/4 [GI Jargon] *TS*, tough situation. **1942** PARTRIDGE *Dict. Abbrev.* 97/1 **t.s.* or *ts.* or *ts*; also *T.S.*, etc., typescript. **1975** *Record* (Oxf. Univ. Press) xx. 24/1, 11 unsolicited poetry TSS in one week. **1975** *Petroleum Rev.* XXIX. 399/2 The *TSA has been very active since its inception. **1976** *Even. Post* (Nottingham) 15 Dec. 12/7 The TSA's direct training services which include the provision of specially tailored courses to meet individual requirements. **1941** *Trans. Amer. Assoc. Study Goiter* 161 Media, which originally contained *TSH in a concentration equivalent to one unit per cubic centimeter were found to have lost about seven-eighths of their activity. **1983** *Oxf. Textbk. Med.* I. x. 12/2 Hypothyroidism due to TSH deficiency is often mild and easily overlooked. **1950** *Good Housek. Picture Cookery* 161/1 Unboiled fondant. 1 lb icing sugar..tartar..1 *tsp. lemon juice..1 egg white. **1955** R. J. SCHWARTZ *Compl. Dict. Abbrev.* 178/1 *tsp*, teaspoon. **1973** RUBINSTEIN & BUSH *Penguin Freezer Cookbk.* 211, ½ lb. tomatoes, 1 tsp. allspice, 1 tsp. pine kernels. **1935** DUCKWORTH & LANGMUIR *West Highland Steamers* ii. 107 *T.S.S. 'Flowerdale'..came into Mr. MacBrayne's hands as his first twin screw sea-going steamer. **1981** 'J. ASHFORD' *Loss of 'Culion'* viii. 52, I understand you've some information on the sinking of the TSS *Culion*..in the Indian Ocean. [**1841** *Niles' Reg.* 21 Feb. 400/3 *TTT. They have temperance wagons in the west, marked with three Ts, to denote that the owner is a tee-to-taller.] **1922** JOYCE *Ulysses* 159 Selfish those t.t's are. Dog in the manger. **1936** *Punch* 22 July 97/2 Every birthday he gets a magnificent.. Gift Of wine... It is sad To add I've brought him up to be T.T. **1975** J. SYMONS *Three Pipe Problem* v. 35 Can't offer you a beer, strict TT. **1893** R. BITHELL *Counting-House Dict.* (rev. ed.) 292 **T.T.*, telegraphic transfer. **1927** *Financial Times* 3 May 1/4 Kobe, T.T. Yen 24·58d. **1940** *Economist* 11 May 862/2 This compares with..½ per cent. for T.T. redemptions from Palestine. **1966** A. GILPIN *Dict. Econ. Terms* 201 (*heading*) Telegraphic Transfer ('T.T.'). **1913** W. T. ROGERS *Dict. Abbrev.* 192/1 **T.T.* (motor), Tourist Trophy machine. *Ibid.*, *T.T. Race* (motor), Auto-Cycle Tourist Trophy Race. **1914** *Autocar* 16 May 948/2 (*heading*) The T.T. race. **1929** *Motor* 2 July 1060/1 A driver who has, after all, driven at Le Mans and in the T.T. **1976** *Southern Even. Echo* (Southampton) 17 Nov. 21/5 The Isle of Man programme will include the usual classic TT. **1927** *Field* 15 Sept. 413/1 There are now a larger number of farmers producing Grade A (*T.T.) milk. **1958** *Times* 28 July 11/5 A T.T. dairy farm. **1970** A. JENKINS *Drinka Pinta* x. 105 Scots were particularly keen that it should be Grade

'A' (T.T.) milk. **1948** F. Worsley *ITMA* 21 The beloved Cockney Charlady, Mrs. Mopp (played by Dorothy Summers)..did not make her first appearance..until 10th October, 1941... Another of her famous sayings were the letters '*T.T.F.N.'—a contraction of 'Ta-ta for now' with which she made her exit. **1966** A. Hall *Frost* 19 'See you soon then.' 'T.T.F.N.' **1976** *Observer* 11 Apr. 2/6 JY [*sc.* Jimmy Young] said TTFN to Mr Healey. **1968** *Amateur Photographer* 24 Apr. 4/2 (Advt.), The most sought after *T.T.L. camera! **1978** *Ibid.* 2 Aug. 101/1 Landscapes with a lot of sky detail in the shot can often be wrongly exposed, particularly if the camera has TTL metering. **1963** *Electronics* 22 Mar. 54/1 Transistor-transistor logic (*TTL) offers a saturated-transistor logic that is simple, compact, and has a high degree of design flexibility. **1967** *Ibid.* 6 Mar. 123/1 Litton Industries Inc. had developed the 'Phoenix gate' TTL for the Phoenix missile. **1977** *Sci. Amer.* Sept. 79/3 Compared with the previous family of RTL gates, TTL circuits provide greater output power (so that more gates in the next stage of an array can be driven), less stringent tolerances in manufacturing and greater immunity to spurious voltages. **1965** *Realist* Mar. 24 *TVs are not as feminine as they themselves think they are. **1979** J. Hansen *Skinflick* (1980) x. 81 Spence doesn't want to be fooled. He knows I'm a TV. **1983** *The Magazine* Apr. 24/3 We get a lot of TVs in and a few of the leather boys of course. **1963** *Times* 2 Feb. 9/5 When we enter the Common Market,..a *T.V.A. (tax value added) tax will have to be substituted for purchase tax. **1963** *Economist* 17 Aug. 567/2 The probable impact of a TVA tax on different types of industries. **1965** *Listener* 22 Apr. 585/2 The added-value tax is commonly known as the TVA. **1935** *Harvard Law Rev.* XLVIII. 806 It would seem that if the *TVA is in fact unconstitutional, the contracts are subject to rescission. **1936** *N.Y. Herald Tribune* 4 June 36/8 The T.V.A. development. **1943** J. S. Huxley *TVA* 7 TVA stands for Tennessee Valley Authority, and the Tennessee Valley Authority is the outstanding example of democratic planning. **1965** Mrs. L. B. Johnson *White House Diary* 7 Apr. (1970) 256 Lyndon talked about the vast Mekong River project which can provide food and water and power on a scale to dwarf even our own TVA. **1968** *Guardian* 4 July 7/6 What *TVP has been created from is mercifully not revealed. **1969** *Official Gaz.* (U.S. Patent Office) 18 Mar. 120/2 *TVP*... For unflavored and meat and poultry flavored vegetable protein food... First use on or before May 2, 1966. **1974** *Observer* (Colour Suppl.) 24 Feb. 14/1 High-protein mock-meat has been in use in a fairly small way for some years... Known as tvp—textured vegetable protein—it comes in 'extruded' chunks, or minced. **1975** *Trade Marks Jrnl.* 21 May 1049/1 *TVP*... Foods prepared from soya bean derivatives and included in Class 9. Archer Daniels Midland Company.., Decatur, Illinois, United States of America; manufacturers and merchants. **1976** *Times Lit. Suppl.* 13 Feb. 166/1 The chunks of fictionalized, texturized social history (which are to drama as TVP to steak). **1933** *Meccano Mag.* Apr. 270/2 *T.W.A. state that most of the transcontinental air mail is carried by their machines. **1941** B. Schulberg *What makes Sammy Run?* vi. 93 They were flying back again via TWA. **1960** [see *red carpet* s.v. red *a.* 19a]. **1976** *National Observer* (U.S.) 17 Apr. 20/5 Pressed by banks that had lent TWA millions, he sold his TWA stock for $546,549,171.

b. *Biol.* T designates lymphocytes that are derived from or have been processed by the thymus, which are responsible for cellular immune reactions.

1970 *New Scientist* 7 May 271/1 Some of the lymphocytes ..'stray' into the thymus gland, where they are converted.. into a new sort of lymphocyte, called a T cell. **1973** *Sci. Amer.* July 58/1 *T* cells and *B* cells cannot be distinguished by their form. **1974** *Nature* 8 Feb. 387/2 T lymphocytes in human peripheral blood may be identified by their ability to form rosettes *in vitro* with untreated sheep erythrocytes. **1976** *Path. Ann.* XI. 437 During famine the severity and frequency of diseases kept in check by T-cell function, such as tuberculosis, will increase. **1982** Arms & Camp *Biology* (ed. 2) xxxiv. 541 Lymphocytes may be divided into two major groups, T lymphocytes and B lymphocytes.

7. In combinations containing the abbrev. T (or extension, as T.D.) followed by a word, as **T-Bill** [treasury sb.] = *treasury bill* s.v. treasury *sb.* 6 (cf. *T.B.*, sense 6a above); **T.D. pipe** *U.S.* [see quot. 1889], a kind of clay pipe; **T-group** *Psychol.* [training *vbl. sb.*], a sensitivity-training group (see sensitivity 4); **T-man** *U.S. colloq.* [treasury *sb.*: cf. G-man b], a law enforcement officer of the Treasury Department; **T-rule** *Linguistics* [transformational *a.*] = transformational rule (see transformational *a.*); **T scale, score** *Psychol.* [Thorndike-Terman (see quot. 1922)], a method of scaling or scoring a psychological test; **T stop** (*Photogr.*) [transmission], a measured point on a scale of aperture values based on the actual light transmitted through the lens of a camera; similarly ***T number***; **T-unit** *Linguistics* [terminable *a.*], a minimal terminable unit (see quot. 1965).

1982 *Daily Tel.* 27 Sept. 18 Examples..occur in financial futures, with the difference between the futures price and the price of its underlying cash instrument (cf. gold futures and the bullion price, or T-Bill futures and cash *T-Bills). **1880** *Harvard Lampoon* 19 Mar. 26/2 So, after he had taken his breath of fresh air, he filled his *T.D. pipe. **1889** *Amer. N. & Q.* II. 114 'T.D. Pipes.'.. It is said that they took their name from Timothy Dexter, an eccentric capitalist, who in his will left a large sum of money to be expended in the erection of a factory where cheap clay pipes, such as those that now bear the name of 'T.D.'s', were to be manufactured. [**1947** E. H. Paul *Linden on Saugus Branch* 27 Deacon Parker, known to the boys as T.D., because he smoked the one-cent clay pipes of that name.] **1950** *Jrnl. Social Issues* VI. ii. 3 Most of the core staff goes through a 'Practicuum in Group Membership' seminar worked out along the lines of the '*T' group training program at the National Training Laboratory in Group Development. **1967** M. Argyle *Psychol. Interpersonal Behaviour* x. 193 T (training)-groups were first developed in the National Training Laboratories at Bethel, Maine, in 1947... The members of a T-group spend their time studying the group and the processes of social interaction that take place in it. **1977** *N.Y. Times* 15 July c 22/2 We already spend far too much time practicing artificial modes of sociability, such as group encounters, sensitivity training, 'T' groups, Rolfing and the like. **1938** *Sun* (Baltimore) 12 Mar. 10/7 Comparatively little has been heard in late times about the Treasury Department's '*T-men'. **1952** *Daily Progress* (Charlottesville, Va.) 6 Feb. 1/5 T-man William Frank says backdating of tax returns is the major irregularity he found. **1951** G. H. Sewell *Amateur Film-Making* (ed. 2) iii. 32 The *T number indicates the actual light transmission obtained by measuring instruments. **1961** G. Millerson *Telev. Production* iii. 38 Modern lenses are sometimes marked in 'T' numbers rather than f-numbers. **1964** E. Bach *Introd. Transformational Gram.* iv. 60 The difference between PS rules and *T rules can be made clearer..by the following remarks. **1976** *Language* LII. 108 In 1962, Wolfgang Motsch proposed a T-rule for a class of German adjectives. **1922** W. A. McCall *How to measure in Educ.* x. 299 It is a tribute to their genius to call the proposed unit..a Thorndike-Terman, or, for brevity, a T... Every product scales [*sic*] may be transmuted into *T scales, thereby making all scales performance scales. **1954** A. Anastasi *Psychol. Testing* iv. 83 If the normalized standard score is multiplied by 10 and added to or subtracted from 50, it is converted into a **T-score*, a type of score first proposed by McCall. **1970** F. G. Brown *Princ. Educ. & Psychol. Testing* vii. 173 *T* scores were originally defined..with reference to a particular norm group... However, as used today, the *T*-score designation generally applies to any normalized standard score system with $\bar{X} = 50$ and $s = 10$. **1956** J. J. Rose *Amer. Cinematographer* (ed. 9) 133 The new method of calibration will be known as the '*T' Stop system, the T denoting transmission of light and the 'T' stops representing absolutely accurate light measurement. **1977** J. Hedgecoe *Photographer's Handbk.* 344 '*T*' *stops*, more accurate measurement of light entering a lens than 'f' numbers. **1965** K. W. Hunt *Gram. Structure written at Three Grade Levels* iii. 21 These units might be christened 'minimal terminable units', since they would be minimal as to length, and each would be grammatically capable of being terminated with a capital letter and a period. For short, the 'minimal terminable unit' might be nicknamed a '*T-unit'. .. T-unit will be the name used for it in this investigation. **1975** *Language for Life* (Dept. Educ. & Sci.) iii. 39 Writing of high quality can employ a simple style that would not necessarily yield a high score as measured by the T-unit. **1977** *Publ. Amer. Dial. Soc. 1974* lxi/lxii. 30 The transcripts of these interviews (exclusive of garbles and false starts) were marked off into T-units and the mean length of T-units was computed for each informant.

8. Used as a symbol. **a.** *Physics.* [Adopted as being the next letter after S alphabetically (cf. S 7).] *T* is the symbol of the quantum number of iso-spin; = I 7b.

1937 E. Wigner in *Physical Rev.* LI. 110/1 The quantum numbers S_2, Tζ,ζY can be called magnetic quantum numbers. They determine..the μ uniquely. *Ibid.* 117/1 A total isotopic spin T will be a term with the same binding energy for all nuclei with isotopic numbers from −T to T. **1974** *Encycl. Brit. Macropædia* XIII. 339/2 Isospin-equal-one states can exist in the three isobars $^{6}_{2}$He, $^{6}_{3}$Li, and in $^{6}_{4}$Be, whereas the $T = 0$ state can exist only in $^{6}_{3}$Li.

b. *Bacteriology.* [Initial letter of *type.*] T followed by a numeral is the designation of certain strains of phages of the bacterium *Escherichia coli* that have been much used experimentally. So ***T-even***, designating the strains for which the numeral is even.

1944 *Proc. Nat. Acad. Sci.* XXX. 398 The viruses used were the strains α and γ described by Delbrück and Luria and a new strain..which has been determined to be identical with strain *T7* of Demerec and Fano [*reference given to paper* 'in press', *quoted next.*] **1945** Demerec & Fano in *Genetics* XXX. 119 The materials used in our experiments consisted of the same bacterial strain—*E. coli* B—previously used by Luria and Delbrück.., of seven phage strains active on B, and of various strains of bacteria.. resistant to one or more of the phages. The phage strains were indicated as type 1 to type 7 (T1 to T7). **1960** *New Biol.* XXXI. 78 One group of the larger phages..has become the best understood of any kind of virus. These are the closely related T2, T4 and T6, known collectively as the T-even phages. **1968** H. Harris *Nucleus & Cytoplasm* iii. 46 It was known at the time that this work was undertaken that when *E. coli* cells were infected with the T-even bacteriophages net synthesis of bacterial RNA was rapidly inhibited. **1973** R. G. Krueger et al. *Introd. Microbiol.* xiv. 410/2 Studies of T4 mutants have gone a long way towards elucidating the steps by which biological structures, such as the head and tail of the virus, are assembled.

c. *Astronautics.* [Initial letter of *time.*] T represents the time at which a spacecraft is due to be launched.

1959 *Manch. Guardian* 3 Jan. 5 'T-time' is the moment the firing switch is closed to set off a missile. **1970** N. Armstrong et al. *First on Moon* ii. 32 Only in the latter stages of the final countdown does the nomenclature change to T minus hours and minutes.

III. 9. T at the end of a word has sometimes been attached to the word following when this begins with a vowel: hence *the* to, *the* tone, *the* tother; cf. also *'tis*, *'twas*, etc. in 't. The final *t* of *Saint* has in several cases been popularly prefixed to the name, as in ***Tandrew***, ***Tandry*** = St. Andrew; ***Tann*** = St. Ann, hence ***Tanswell***; ***Tantolin*** = St. Antholin; ***Tooly*** = St. Olave; see also tanton, tantony, tawdry.

*c*1450 *Mankind* 75 in *Macro Plays* 4, I gyff no force, by Sent Tanne! **1673** Hickeringill *Greg. F. Greyb.* 264 Our Tantlin Lectures. **1726** F. Howgrave *Stamford* 53 The Corruption that has been made of *St. Anthony* into *Tantony*, and *St. Olave* into *Tooly*. **1872** Hardwick *Trad. Lanc.* 269 Cakes baked for the lace-makers' feasts in honour of St. Andrew..are locally termed '*Tandry Cakes*'. **1880** *W. Cornw. Gloss.*, '*T Andrew's dance*, St. Vitus' dance.

10. In early ME., *t* took the place of initial *þ*, *th*, after a word ending in a dental or *s*, esp. in the demonstratives *the*, *that*, *this*, *tha*, *there*, *then*, *thus*, etc., and the 2nd personal pronoun *thou* and its cases. Already in OE., *þæt þe* became *þætte*, that.

*c*1200 Ormin 325 þiss streon þatt tuss wass sibb Wiþþ preostess & wiþþ kingess. *Ibid.* 12760 Nu shallt tu ben nemmnedd Cefas. *a*1240 *Wohunge* in *Cott. Hom.* 271 Hwa is ta largere þen þu. *c*1400 *Rule St. Benet* 23 þis sais sain benet, þat ta þat ere of elde and vnderstandis, þai sal haue þaire mesur.

IV. 11. 2,4,5-T: a selective herbicide used esp. for controlling brushwood; 2,4,5-trichlorophenoxyacetic acid, $C_6H_2Cl_3{\cdot}O{\cdot}CH_2COOH$.

1947 *Bot. Gaz.* CIX. 194/2 The use of 2,4-dichlorophenoxyacetic acid (2,4-D) has been emphasized in nearly all investigations.., although the possible use of 2,4,5-trichlorophenoxyacetic acid (2,4,5-T) for similar purposes was recognized by Hamner and Tukey. **1956** *Nature* 3 Mar. 418/1 An investigation into the effect of the arboricide 2,4,5-T on freshly cut stumps of thicket suggests that this substance may be of practical value in preventing regeneration. **1977** *New Yorker* 25 July 37/2 The military had withdrawn huge stocks of Agent Orange—a fifty-fifty mixture of 2,4,5-T and 2,4-D, which was principally used in its herbicidal operations—from Vietnam.

t'[1], shortened form of to, before a vowel, formerly in use, often combined with the following word, as *tabandon* to abandon, *tabyde* to abide; so *taxe* to ask, *tescape*, *t'attempt*; also, with omission of *h*, *tave*, *tafe*, to have, *ta* to hae, to have; *tadwellyd* to have dwelt, *talyved* to have lived, etc.

*c*1200 Ormin 3879 þatt doþ uss tunnderrstanndenn. *c*1330 R. Brunne *Chron. Wace* (Rolls) 4334 Ffair folk to fighte, Cesar tabyde. **1426** Lydg. *De Guil. Pilgr.* 1019–22 He gaff to hem.. Talyved euere,.. Neuer tave had necessyte Off deyyng. *Ibid.* 9392 Taxe and lerne, thow art wys. *Ibid.* 9422 And tadwellyd Immutable. *Ibid.* 16962 Tescape Eche Trybulacion. **1559** *Mirr. Mag.* (1563) Bvij, I forced the Frenchemen tabandon theyr bowers. **1592** in Tytler *Hist. Scot.* (1864) IV. 343 Proved cares and assured love aught,.. tafe the upperhand. **1706** E. Ward *Hud. Rediv.* I. iii. 27 T' attempt some Massacre or Treason. **1746** Francis tr. *Hor., Sat.* ii. iii. 117 Staberius thus compell'd his heirs t' engrave On his proud tomb what legacies he gave.

t'[2], north Eng. dial. form of *the*, before a vowel or consonant: as in *t'airm*, *t'bairn*, *t'bottle*, *t'faarm*, *t'heart*, *t'man*, *t'measter*; sometimes also written without apostrophe, *tman*, *tnail*, *trasps*, *twasp*. See the.

't[1], shortened form of *it*, initially or finally, as in *'tis*, *'twas*, *'twere*, *'twill*, *'twould*; *do't*, *see't*, *on't*; formerly often written without apostrophe as one word: see it.

't[2], dial. shortened form of that *relative pron.* or *conj.* Cf. at, 'at *rel. pron., adv., conj.*

1867 *Our Young Folks* Mar. 130 Jest show me that! Ur prove 't the bat Hez got more brains than's in my hat. **1871** W. Alexander *Johnny Gibb* xv. 108, I ance was neepours wi' a chap 't could 'a deen that. **1887** R. T. Cooke *Happy Dodd* xxvii. 286, I didn't feel real cherk this week, so't I didn't go to sewin' s'ciety.

-t, *suffix*[1], formative of the pa. pple. in some weak verbs, for earlier *-d* and *-ed* (see -ed[1]), due usually to the devocalization of *d* after a breath consonant, as in *nipped*, *nip'd*, *nipt*. In some verbs the use of *t* for *-ed* goes back to OTeut., esp. in app. contracted or irregular verbs, as *bought*, *brought*, *might*, *thought*, *wrought* (Goth. *bauht*, *brâht*, *maht*, *þâht*, *waurht*); in others it appears in WGer., as *sought* (Goth. *sôkid*, OS. and OE. *sôht*); in others only in OE. as *laught* (læht), *taught* (tæht, taht). But in the majority of cases the *t* is of later appearance, arising from the reduction of *-ed* to *-'d*, *-d* in Middle or Mod. Engl., with consequent devocalization of *d*, not only after breath consonants, as in *dropt*, *nipt*, *crept*, *slept*, *swept*, *left*, *lost*, *tost*, *past*, but, in certain cases, after liquids and nasals, as in *felt*, *spelt*, *spilt*, *dreamt*, *burnt*, *meant*, *pent*; also in contracted formations, such as *built*, *bent*, *lent*, *sent*, *spent*, *girt*, *cast*. But in many words where the pronunciation has *t*, the current spelling is *-ed*, e.g. *blessed*, *dropped*, *hushed*, *passed* for *blest*, *dropt*, *husht*, *past*. See the article -ed *suffix*[1].

-t, *suffix*[2], formative of the pa. t. of some weak verbs, for earlier *-te*, *-de*, *-ede* (:—*da*, *-ida*, *-eda*). Parallel in formation to the prec., and generally going along with it in ME., and identical in form in mod.E.; but in OE. a pa. t. in *-te* was sometimes used where the pa. pple. retained the fuller *-ed*, as in *cyssan* to kiss, *cyste*, *cyssed*, *settan* to set, *sette*, *seted* (and *sett*). In mod.Eng. on the contrary the spelling in *t* is more frequent in the pa. pple., esp. when used adjectivally, than in the pa. t.: cf. *tempest-tost*, the wind *tossed* the ship; in time *past*, he *passed* his time. In some cases even the form in *-ed* is a mere modern fashion of spelling, at variance with both the pronunciation and the history; thus, *kissed* was in OS. *kusta*, OE. *cyste*, ME. *kist*, as actually pronounced; it has come to be spelt *kissed*, because in other verbs *-ed* is pronounced *-t*.

-t, *suffix*[3]. A formative of sbs. **a.** from verbs, going back to OTeut., and answering variously to the Indo-Eur. suffixes *-tos, -tā, -tis, -tus*, the *t* of which remained in Teutonic, when preceded by a guttural, labial, or *s*; e.g. *draught, drift, flight, frost, gift, heft, might, plight, shaft, shrift, slaught, thirst, thought, thrift, weft*, etc. (in some of which the formation is later and imitative). In a few cases the *t* is a later Eng. change of *-þ* after *h, ȝ*, as in *sight* (OE. *siehþ*), in which *þ* normally represented Indo-Eur. *t*. See -TH[1].

b. from adjs. (or sbs.), changed from earlier *-þ, -th* (in *length*, etc.) after *h, ȝ*, as *height* (Goth. *hauhiþa*, OE. *hiehþo*, ME. *heiȝþe, highth*); *sleight* (ON. *slægþ*, ME. *sleiȝþe*); *theft* (OE. *þiefþ*, ME. *þiefþe*); *dreight* (for *dreighth*, from *dreiȝ*, DREE): here the suffix was OTeut. *-iþô*: *-iðô*: Indo-Eur. *-tā*. See -TH[1]. Also *dought* (OE. *duȝuþ* :—**dugunþ*), *drought* (OE. *drūȝuþ*, Sc. *drouth*), where the OE. suffix *-uþ* was for *-unþ*:—Indo-Eur. *-ntis*.

ta (tɑː), *int.* Also 9 **taa**; **tar**. An infantile form of 'thank-you', now also commonly in colloq. adult use.

1772 Mrs. Delany in *Life & Corr.* (1861) I. 457 You would not say 'Ta' to me for my congratulation. **1807** W. Irving *Salmag.* (1824) 363 How her ten weeks old baby will laugh and say taa! **1892** Zangwill *Childr. Ghetto* I. 117 Give it me. I'll say 'ta' so nicely. **1931** A. Powell *Afternoon Men* xxx. 252 'Will you give him this, Sophy?'.. 'What did he say?' Sophy said: 'He just said, "Tar".' **1946** K. Tennant *Lost Haven* (1947) iii. 47 Grandfather Starbrace shovelled great handfuls of pink prawns... 'Ta, Nathe,' Mr. Thorne said. **1970** 'R. Gordon' *Doctor on Boil* xxiii. 164 'Ta,' he said, slipping the card into the back pocket of his jeans. **1981** D. Clark *Longest Pleasure* vi. 136 'You know your way, don't you?' 'Ta, love.'

ta, obs. and dial. form of THE, THEE, THOU.

1597 Shaks. *2 Hen. IV*, II. i. 63 Thou wot, wot ta? do, do, thou rogue! *a* **1619** Fletcher *Mad Lover* IV. v, Who art ta? **1814** Scott *Wav.* xxix. (*Celt speaks*), 'It was either ta muckle Sunday..or ta little government Sunday that they ca'd ta fast'. *a* **1825** Forby *Voc. E. Anglia* 338 *Ta, te, to, art.* or *pron.* the, this, that, it. **1864** Tennyson *North. Farmer* xi, Done it ta-year I meän 'd.

ta, dial. form of TO *prep.* and sign of *inf.*

1340–70 *Alex. & Dind.* 475 We sen selkouþe þing; þat is ta sain heuene. **1825** Jamieson, *Ta, Ti, To*; the sign of the *inf.* **1898** B. Kirkby *Lakel. Wds.* (E.D.D.), Allus royen an drinken is t'way ta neea spot.

ta, taa, early ME. form of *þa, tha*; see T 10.

ta, taa, in *the ta*, early ME. and north. form of TO *adj.*, in *the to* for *that o* = the one: see T 9.

ta, taa, obs. forms of TOE *sb.*, TAKE *v.*

taa-, in various words: earlier spelling of TA-.

taaffeite ('tɑːfaɪt). *Min.* [f. the name of Edward Charles Richard *Taaffe* (1898–1967), Bohemian-born Irish gemmologist + -ITE[1].] A mauve gemstone similar to spinel, having the composition $BeMgAl_4O_8$ and a hexagonal crystal structure.

1951 B. W. Anderson in *Gemmologist* XX. 76/2 One of the 'spinels' gave a rather high refractive index reading and seemed to show double refraction... The second 'Taaffeite' was found! **1951** —— & Claringbull in *Mineral. Mag.* XXIX. 765 The new mineral..has been named taaffeite in honour of its discoverer. **1967** *Rocks & Minerals* XLII. 803/1 The world's fourth known cut taaffeite was discovered in August of this year. **1974** *Jrnl. Gemmology* XIV. 104 The discovery of the new gem mineral Taaffeite reads like a gemmological fairy tale.

taaibos ('taɪbɒs). *S. Afr.* Also 9 **ta(a)ybosch**; **taaibosch**. [Afrikaans, f. Du. *taai* tough + *bos(ch)* bush.] Any of several shrubs or trees with strong, pliable branches, esp. any of several species of *Rhus*.

1821 C. L. Latrobe *Jrnl. Visit S. Afr.* 559 Taaibosch—a species of Rhus, of which genus several bear the name of Taaibosch. **1833** *S. Afr. Almanac & Directory* p. xlviii, One of the Cape sumachs (Taaybosch) has been recommended for culture. **1834** *Cape Good Hope Lit. Gaz.* Mar. 41 The extract may be procured..if the tree is treated as recommended for the colonial Taybosch. F. G. Stow *Native Races S. Afr.* v. 93 They [*sc.* fish baskets] were composed of reeds and twigs of the taaibosch. **1948** *Cape Times* 5 Aug. 8/7 The safer and more effective plants are reeds and many-stemmed shrubs, such as taaibos. **1974** *Stand. Encycl. S. Afr.* X. 396/1 Taaibos. Name generally applied to plants with tough branches and bark, such as *Passerina vulgaris*..but particularly to shrubby *Rhus* species.

taakhaar, var. TAKHAAR.

taal (tɑːl). *S. Africa.* [a. Du. *taal* language, speech, MDu. and MLG. *tāle* language, speech, tale, = OE. *talu* tale, story, account: see TALE.] The Dutch word for language, speech (*de Nederlandsche taal*, the Netherlands or Dutch language): in English, 'the taal', spec. applied to the Cape Dutch, or Dutch patois spoken in South Africa.

1896 *Westm. Gaz.* 8 Jan. 8/1 He speaks the Taal better than a Hollander can, and can understand the Boers better. **1897** Bryce *Impressions S. Afr.* 480 It [Boer Dutch] differs widely from the cultivated Dutch of Holland,..having become vulgarised into a dialect called the Taal. *Ibid.* 511 Except some of the men from Cape Colony, they could not speak the Boer Taal. **1900** *Spectator* 6 Oct. 460 One of the first results..was to establish the Taal, the Cape patois, as an official language.

attrib. and *Comb.* **1898** *Johannesburg Star* 4 June, Sundry clever and humorous volumes of taal-verse. **1901** *Daily Chron.* 22 July 5/3 An epitome of all the more unattractive qualities of the taal-speaking Dutch.

taal, obs. f. TALE.

taald, obs. pa. pple. of TELL *v.*

taar, obs. f. *tare*, pa. t. of TEAR *v.*; obs. f. TAR.

taarge, taart(e, taas, taast, obs. ff. TARGE, TART, TASS, TASTE.

taas, obs. 2 pers. sing. pres. ind. of TAKE *v.*

tab (tæb), *sb.*[1] Also 7 **tabb**, 8 **tabe**. [Origin obscure. At first a dialect word. Not in Johnson. In some senses it may be short for *tablet*; in others it interchanges with *tag*.]

I. 1. a. A short broad strap, flat, loop, or the like, attached by one end to an object, or forming a short projecting part by which a thing can be taken hold of, hung up, fastened, or pulled; in various applications: see quots.

1607 Markham *Caval.* III. (1617) 83 How the horse is girt ..and by some speciall markes or obseruations about the tabs to know how his garths do hold. **1611** Cotgr., *Contre-sanglot*, a Tab; the leather whereto a girth is fastened; a girth-leather. *Ibid.*, *Crampon de cuir*, a loope, or tab, of leather. **1629** *Pittington Vestry Bks.* (Surtees) 298 For tabbs to the bells, iiij*d.* [Cf. 1628 *Ibid.* 293 For 2 tagges for the belstrings, 6*d.*] **1664** in *Archæol. Æl.* XVII. 127 For broomes and a tab for ye bell 2*d.* **1688** R. Holme *Armoury* III. xviii. (Roxb.) 126/1 The tab at the end of a belt. **1846** Brockett *N.C. Gloss.*, *Tab*..a strap. **1879** Rutley *Stud. Rocks* v. 40 It [a geologist's bag] should have a little tab by which it can be loosely attached to a button. **1894** Maskelyne *Sharps & Flats* 90 The 'tab' or loop at the back of the..boot. **1896** C. D. Waldo *Ban of the Gubbe* 144 If there were tabs to pull up the lid, why should there ever have been a knob or handle? **1904** *Eng. Dial. Dict.*, *Tab*... 5. The loop by which a garment is hung up. *Sc.* **1905** *Daily News* 27 Sept. 6 Strong leather tabs are being fastened to the backs of the volumes of the brobdingnagian catalogues [in the British Museum Library].

b. *spec.* A shoe latchet, for fastening with a buckle, button, or thong. Chiefly *dial.*

1674 Ray *N.C. Words* 47 The *Tab* of a Shooe, the Latchet of a Shooe. **1731** in Bailey. **1775** in Ash. **1904** in *Eng. Dial. Dict.* [from North of Eng. to E. Anglia].

c. A short strap attached at one end to one side of a coat, jacket, vest, etc., and having a buttonhole at the free end for fastening across.

Such a *tab* is often ornamented with a button at the attached end, so as to be symmetrical, and may become purely ornamental as in 2 c.

d. The metal end of a lace, etc.; = TAG *sb.*[1] 3; a shoe-string. *dial.*

a **1825** Forby *Voc. E. Anglia*, *Tab*... 2. The end of a lace, commonly, and perhaps more properly called a *tag*. **1904** in *Eng. Dial. Dict.* [Cumbld. to Oxford, and E. Anglia]. *Ibid.*, *Tab*..a shoe-string [Hampsh.].

e. The tongue of a shoe or boot. *dial.*

1866– in *Eng. Dial. Dict.* from midland counties.

f. = *pull-tab* s.v. PULL- 2: used to open a can of beer, etc.

1963 *Wal. St. Jrnl.* 1 Oct. 16/1 The beer drinker opens the can by pulling off the tab. **1978** O. White *Silent Reach* xi. 108 The fat man..pulled the tab from a can.

2. a. As an ornament of dress: Each of the projecting square pieces formed by cutting out the lower edge of a jacket or other article of dress, or sewn on to its uncut edge, and usually embellished with buttons, embroidery, etc.

c **1880** Mrs. G. M. E. Campbell *Let. to Editor*, A series of small squares cut out of the edge of a cape or sleeve and the intermediate pieces left hanging by way of fringe or ornament, is known by the name of Tabs. **1883** *Truth* 31 May 768/2 This brocade was cut out in deep tabs over a skirt of copper-coloured satin. **1887** *Illustr. Lond. News* 6 Aug. 151/1 The edges of the loose fronts [of the bodice] were.. cut out in tabs.

b. A similar piece sewn by its upper edge on the surface of dress, so as to hang loose; or **c.** in 19th. c. use, sewn on entirely, and variously adorned with buttons, beads, embroidery, etc., smetimes simulating that described in 1 c.

1834 Planché *Brit. Costume* xviii. 275 Towards the close of James [I]'s reign, however,..short jackets or doublets, with tabs and false sleeves hanging behind, succeed to the long-waisted doublets. **1882** *Daily News* 30 Aug. 3/1 Tabs are a favourite trimming for tunics. **1883** C. D. Warner *Roundabout Journ.* 39 Some of them have a black rosette on the shoulder, and a tab hanging from it tipped with ermine. **1909** *Civ. Serv. Store Catal.* 353 [Lady's] coat, 30 inches long, trimmed satin, with satin tabs and buttons.

d. A coloured tab, esp. a red tab or gorget patch, worn by a senior or staff Army officer; hence formerly, in *Army slang*, such an officer.

1916 J. Buchan *Greenmantle* i. 2 'Try my tailor,' said Sandy. 'He's got a very nice taste in red tabs.' **1917** *B.E.F. Times* 20 Jan. 4/2 Realising Men must laugh, Some wise Man devised the Staff: Dressed them up in little dabs Of rich variegated tabs. **1925** Fraser & Gibbons *Soldier & Sailor Words* 275 *Tab, a*, a Staff Officer. **1948** Partridge *Dict. Forces' Slang* 154 *Red tabs*, red gorget patches, worn by Colonels and above. 'Red-tab' was sometimes used for an officer who wore them. **1977** D. James *Spy at Evening* vii. 51 He had red tabs on his collar. He had authority even over my father.

3. *transf.* A small piece of some substance, e.g. of sod or turf.

17.. E. Smith *Compl. Housew.* (1750) 365 Take..three or four tabes of the whitest goose-dung; put all in a quart of strong beer. **1893** Q. [Couch] *Delect. Duchy* 43 The boys.. could toss tabs of turf down her chimney.

4. *techn.* **a.** One of the revolving arms which lift the beaters of a fulling-mill (Knight *Dict. Mech.* 1877). **b.** A narrow projecting strip of metal along the inside of a hollow calico-printing roller to secure it to its mandrel by means of a slot in the latter.

c. *Aeronaut.* A usu. hinged part of a control surface that serves to modify the action or response of the surface.

1934 *Flight* 25 Jan. 75/1 The word 'tab' has been approved by the [U.S.] Department of Commerce as the name for auxiliary control flaps. **1942** 'B. J. Ellan' *Spitfire!* p. x, Winding the bias control one way or the other moves the tab and gives port or starboard bias. **1965** C. N. Van Deventer *Introd. Gen. Aeronautics* iv. 95/2 Controllable or fixed tabs may be attached to any of the control surfaces—the elevators, the ailerons, or the rudder. **1983** D. Stinton *Design of Aeroplane* xi. 397 Often trimming is achieved on the ground by bent plate tabs.

5. A tie-label, a luggage label (cf. TAG *sb.*[1] 8).

1904 *Eng. Dial. Dict.*, *Tab* 3, a label affixed to goods for sale; a luggage label. *Warwick.*

6. An ear. *dial.* and *slang.*

1866 J. E. Brogden *Provinc. Words Lincs.* 202 *Tab*, a piece of leather in the front of a boot, a latchet, the ear. **1959** *New Statesman* 26 Dec. 904/2 Dad was sitting by the fire, behind his paper with one tab lifted. **1977** Scollins & Titford *Ey up, mi Duck!* III. 15 Ah gorra bile be'int me tab.

II. 7. *colloq.* (orig. *U.S.*) A table, an account [cf. TABLET 1 c]; a check; esp. in phr., ***to keep tabs*** (or ***a tab***) ***on***; also *fig.* (cf. TAB *v.* 2). Also, a bill or charge (chiefly *N. Amer.*): see also ***to pick up the tab*** s.v. PICK *v.*[1] 21 m.

1889 *Washington Post* 11 Feb., Every man keeps a mean little tab in his head on his fellows. **1890** *Voice* (N.Y.) 31 July, A generous mother in..Michigan has been keeping tab in her family [on the baking for a year]. **1890** B. Hall *Turnover Club* 19 They knocked off and filed out into the deserted streets, while the Purveyor figured up the 'tabs'. **1897** H. Porter *Campaigning with Grant* x. 159 You can't get away because he [the captain] is always keeping tab on you. **1907** *Daily News* 26 Aug. 7 Being subsequently shown the work tabs with the Salvation Army prices. **1907** W. James *Pragmatism* v. 172 To use this as a tally by which we 'keep tab' on the impressions that present themselves. **1924** [see TAB *v.* 2]. **1929** 'E. Queen' *Roman Hat Mystery* iii. 37 We got to keep pretty close tabs on the time, and I know it was ten minutes because..it was just the part on the stage when [etc.]. **1932** D. L. Sayers *Have his Carcase* xxvi. 348 The one person..likely to have kept tabs on Mr Perkins.. was old Gaffer Gander. **1946** J. O'Hara in *New Yorker* 23 Mar. 25/1 You signed a small tab, sir. **1952** S. Kauffmann *Philanderer* (1953) iii. 52 So all those old ideas are finished and God is dying. There's nobody in Heaven keeping tabs. And there's just going to be less for people to hang on to? **1954** E. B. White *Let.* 9 July (1976) 395, I did a little haying yesterday..and..I am spending today indoors paying the tab. **1963** T. Parker *Unknown Citizen* v. 138 He's antagonistic to anything or anybody who represents authority... He thinks that our main purpose is to keep tabs on him while he's out. **1976** M. Machlin *Pipeline* xii. 144 He started to reach into the pocket of his Arctic down pants for his wallet, but Nick had already paid the tab. **1978** M. Puzo *Fools Die* ii. 18 Jordan knew that Merlyn the Kid kept tabs on everything he did.

8. A cigarette. *north. dial.* and *slang.*

1934 P. Allingham *Cheapjack* iii. 24 ''Ave you got a tab on yer?' The only tabs I knew were connected with the theatre, but I discovered later that 'tab' is a common name in the north for a cigarette. **1948** A. Baron *From City, from Plough* i. 10 'Gie us a tab, Lanky.' He passed his cigarettes round the carriage. **1968** B. Hines *Kestrel for Knave* 71 From various pockets Gryce collected two ten-packets, which rattled when he shook them, a handful of tabs, three lighters and a box of matches. **1980** C. Ross *Case for Compensation* xiv. 68 'Tab?' Duncan looked blank. 'Cigarette?' he said. Duncan accepted. **1983** *New Society* 2 June 333/1 £13.65 a week to pay for..clothes, 'snake bites' (cider and lager), 'tabs' (cigarettes).

9. A tablet or pill, *spec.* one containing LSD or another illicit drug. *slang.*

1961 in Webster. **1968–70** *Current Slang* (Univ. S. Dakota) III–IV. 123 *Tab*, a tablet of sugar or saccharine impregnated with LSD. (Drug users' jargon.) **1971** *Daily Tel.* 18 Sept. 12 Whenever anybody had any money it nearly always went on drugs, with LSD at £1 a 'tab' (tablet). **1973** 'J. Marks' *Mick Jagger* (1974) 137 He presses his palm to his mouth and swallows the tab. **1978** M. Walker *Infiltrator* xii. 136 An order for two tabs of acid.

III. 10. Special combination. **tab collar**, (*a*) a shirt collar whose points are held down by buttons or other fastenings (cf. *button-down* adj. s.v. BUTTON *sb.* 12); (*b*) (see quot. 1957).

1928 *Men's Wear* 21 Nov. II. 5/1 The tab collar is being worn by quite a few of the best dressed eastern university students. It should prove to be an important feature. **1942** B. G. CHAMBERS *Color & Design in Apparel* xv. 498 *Tab collar*. The fronts have loops on the under side with button-holes which fasten on buttons or small rigid stays, that help keep the tie in place at the top of the collar. **1957** M. B. PICKEN *Fashion Dict.* 75/2 *Tab c[ollar]*, collar cut in tabs, often with two at front. **1979** *Time Out* 4 May 65 The Mod revival hits London in force: each day offers a gig at which parkas, tab collars and fox-tailed Lambrettas would be acceptable.

tab (tæb), *sb.*[2] *slang.* [Abbrev. of TABBY *sb.* 3.] **a.** An elderly woman. **b.** *Austral.* A young woman or girl.

1909 J. R. WARE *Passing Eng.* 239/1 *Tabs* (*Theatrical*), ageing women. **1932** H. SIMPSON *Boomerang* x. 276 We don't need to go mackin' round with Chinks and wimmen's earnings. We pay our tabs.. when we want 'em, and tell 'em to get to hell out of it when we don't. **1971** [see MA-IN-LAW].

Tab (tæb), *sb.*[3] *University slang.* [Short for CANTAB.] A member of the University of Cambridge.

1914 C. MACKENZIE *Sinister Street* II. III. iii. 555 He will get his blue next term and show the Tabs that he's a jolly good fellow. **1930** A. ALINGTON *Slowbags & Arethusa* i. 4 Then the morning's play is discussed, the loathly Tabs reviled—for the Slows are Oxford to a man.

tab (tæb), *sb.*[4] *Theatr. slang.* Abbrev. of *tableau curtain* s.v. TABLEAU 6.

1929 J. B. PRIESTLEY *Good Companions* II. vii. 447 The girls here follow him round with their tongues hanging out, as usual—but away from the tabs he's the same as ever. **1936** N. ROYDE-SMITH *All Star Cast* 44 The tab curtains fell together as the girl and the man stood at arm's length from one another. **1946** 'BRAHMS' & 'SIMON' *Trottie True* vii. 164 Down came the crimson tabs. Up went the shouting and the cooing. Out tottered Marie [Lloyd] to the public that idolized her. **1957** P. FRANKAU *Bridge* 59 The dark stage-hand.. came through the tabs. **1983** *Listener* 22/29 Dec. 28/1 When she did the last song, she used to do it in front of the tabs.

tab (tæb), *sb.*[5] *Typewriting* and *Computing.* [Abbrev. of TABULATOR b, TABULAR *a.*, etc.] A tabulator (key); a tabular stop, used to preset the movement of the carriage, cursor, etc., under the direction of the tabulator.

1916 H. ETHERIDGE *Bar-Lock Typewriter Manual* 45 The Tab. key acts exactly in the same manner as the carriage release lever. *Ibid.*, On releasing the Tab. key the carriage remains at the number on the scale where the first stop has been fixed. **1969** *Sears, Roebuck Catal.* Spring/Summer 1195/2 Automatic key-set tabs, clear key. **1982** HARRIS & CHAUHAN *So You want to Buy a Word Processor?* v. 65/1 Not only do tabs have to be set up at appropriate positions, but the facility needs to be reactivated when any of the text involved is subsequently edited.

tab (tæb), *v.* [f. TAB *sb.*[1]]

1. *trans.* To furnish or ornament with tabs: see TABBED.

2. To identify, name, or 'dub'; to label or record. Also, to watch, 'keep tabs on' (formerly also with *up*). *colloq.* (chiefly *U.S.*).

1924 G. C. HENDERSON *Keys to Crookdom* 420 *Tab*, to name. *To keep tabs on*, to keep in touch with. **1926** J. BLACK *You can't Win* xix. 283 You are a burglar; you have put in a week 'tabbing up' a residence. **1946** *Sun* (Baltimore) 18 Feb. 11/5 The Navy has tabbed entertainment with the high-sounding name liaison unit. **1954** 'J. CHRISTOPHER' *Twenty-Second Cent.* 86 The doctors have it all tabbed. It's what they call cumulative stress. **1969** *Eugene* (Oregon) *Register-Guard* 3 Dec. 1D/2 Ken Wiedemann of Cal, tabbed as the best defensive back, was sidelined for a major part of the season with a bad knee. **1978** M. PUZO *Fools Die* ii. 33 He had Jordan tabbed as a degenerate gambler.

tabac (tə'bæk), *a.* (and *sb.*[1]) [f. F. *tabac* TOBACCO.] Of a deep shade of brown; tobacco-coloured. Also as *sb.*

1881 *Queen* 18 June 8/1 *Best felt hats*. For Ladies and Gentlemen. The new 'Vicuna' 'Tabac' Brown, and all Colours. **1886** *Graphic* 30 Jan. 123/2 Colours are Black, Brown, Gold, Geranium, and Tabac. **1894** *Westm. Gaz.* 26 Apr. 3/2 A very stylish costume.. in dark tabac canvas. **1900** *Ibid.* 6 Sept. 3/3 Brown, a dark tabac shade, is by some assigned the place of honour. **1922** *Daily Mail* 18 Dec. 1 (Advt.), In shades of Coral, Champagne,.. Tabac.

‖**tabac** (tabak), *sb.*[2] [Fr.] In French-speaking countries: a tobacconist's shop.

1918 'K. MANSFIELD' *Let.* 11 Jan. (1928) 96 The *tabac* woman did not know me and had no tobacco. **1934** H. MILLER *Tropic of Cancer* 52 We sat in the back of the little *tabac* called *L'Eléphant*. **1965** P. O'DONNELL *Modesty Blaise* vii. 75 He left the boules with the lady who ran the *tabac*. **1980** 'M. HARRIS' *Treasure of Sainte Foy* ii. 18 There is a boulangerie-pâtisserie, a tabac, and the milk bar.

tabaccho, tabacco, tabaco, obs. ff. TOBACCO.

tabachir, var. spelling (properly French) of TABASHEER.

‖**tabacosis** (tæbə'kəʊsɪs). *Path.* [f. mod.L. *tabac-um* TOBACCO + -OSIS.] Disease of the lungs produced by the inhalation of tobacco dust.

1879 BUCK *Hygiene* II. 43 There are but two autopsies of tobacco-workers on record which could be considered cases of tabacosis. **1898** *Syd. Soc. Lex.*, *Tabacosis*,.. produced by the inhalation of dry vegetable fibre (especially cotton). Properly the form due to inhalation of tobacco dust.

tabagane, obs. form of TOBOGGAN.

‖**tabagie** (tabaʒi). [F. irreg. deriv. of *tabac* tobacco (1612 in Hatz.-Darm.).] A group of smokers who meet in club fashion; a 'tobacco-parliament'.

1819 (*title*) The Englishman's Mentor. The Picture of the Palais Royal; describing its spectacles, gaming rooms, coffee houses, restaurateurs, tabagies [etc.]. **1858** CARLYLE *Fredk. Gt.* v. vii. (1872) II. 114 Friedrich Wilhelm.. had his *Tabaks-Collegium*, Tobacco-College, Smoking Congress, *Tabagie*. *Ibid.* 115 Tabagies were not uncommon among German Sovereigns of that epoch. **1885** *Daily News* 28 Nov. 5/3 (Stanf.) A sort of tabagie (to use a word which Mr. Carlyle has made familiar to English readers) or Tobacco Parliament.

‖**taban** ('tæbən). The Malay name of the tree, *Isonandra Gutta* (or *I. Taban*), that yields gutta-percha. Hence ***taban-tree***.

1861 BENTLEY *Man. Bot.* 588 *Isonandra Gutta*, the gutta Percha or Taban-tree.. a native of Singapore, Borneo, and other Malay Islands. **1874** GARROD & BAXTER *Mat. Med.* (1880) 299 Gutta-Percha,.. the inspissated juice of Isonandra gutta, the Gutta-percha or Taban tree.

tabanid ('tæbənɪd), *a.* and *sb.* [f. L. *tabānus* a gad-fly or horse-fly, adopted by Linnæus (1736, in *Acta Soc. R. Scient. Upsaliensis* 31) as a generic name, + -ID[3].] **A.** *adj.* Belonging to the family *Tabanidæ* of flies, of which *Tabanus* is the typical genus. **B.** *sb.* A fly of this family, a gad-fly.

1891 in *Cent. Dict.* **1892** *Insect Life* V. 59 An examination showed it to be a true Tabanid. **1895** *Bulletin Illinois Labor. Nat. Hist.* 197 As restless as a tabanid larva. *Ibid.* 199 It was, perhaps, this that the tabanids were feeding upon. **1931** K. M. SMITH *Textbk. Agric. Entom.* xi. 163 Tabanid larvae are whitish and occur in the water or soil. **1967** V. NABOKOV *Speak, Memory* vi. 137 Because of our ferocious Russian tabanids, one could not leave a horse haltered in a wood for any length of time.

So **ta'baniform** *a.*, having the form of a gad-fly (Mayne *Expos. Lex.* 1860).

tabard ('tæbəd, -ɑːd). Forms: 4- **tabard**; also 4 (9) **tabart, 4-5 tabbard, 4-6 tabarde, 4-8 tabert, 5 taberde, 5-7 taberd, 6 tabarte,** *Sc.* **tawbart, talbart, -ert.** [a. OF. *tabart* (12th c. in Godef.), *tabar* (13-14th c.) = Sp. *tabardo*, It. *tabarro*: ulterior derivation unknown: see Diez.]

†**1.** A garment of coarse material; 'a loose upper garment without sleeves' (Jam.); formerly worn out of doors by the lower classes, also by monks and foot-soldiers. *Obs.*

c **1300** in *Langtoft's Chron.* in *Pol. Songs* (Camden) 303 He haves overhipped, His typeth is typped, hise tabard es tome. **13..** *E.E. Allit. P.* B. 41 His tabarde to-torne and his totez oute. **1362** LANGL. *P. Pl.* A. v. 111 A toren Tabart of twelue Wynter Age. *c* **1386** CHAUCER *Prol.* 541 A Plowman.. In a tabard he rood vpon a Mere. **1389** in *Eng. Gilds* (1870) 81 Noman come be-forn ye alderman.. in tabard ne in cloke. **1513** DOUGLAS *Æneis* I. v. 80 Than with the glitterand volf skyn ouer his array, Cleid in his nwreis talbart glaid and gay. **1523** LD. BERNERS *Froiss.* I. xii. 12 Syr Thomas Wage caused syr Hewe Spencer to be fast bound on ye best and leuiest hors of al ye host, and caused hym to were on a tabarte, suche as traytours and theues were wont to were. **1568** GRAFTON *Chron.* II. 213. [**1866** ROGERS *Agric. & Prices* I. xxii. 582 Tabards, that is short gowns, with or without sleeves, probably without an opening in front, but drawn over the head like a round frock.]

transf. **1423** JAS. I *Kingis Q.* cx, Vnlike the cukkow [is] to the phylomene; Thaire tabartis ar noght bothe maid of array.

2. A short surcoat open at the sides and having short sleeves, worn by a knight over his armour, and emblazoned on the front, back, and sleeves with his armorial bearings. Now only *Hist.*

c **1450** *Brut* cc. 228 (MS. O.), After he lete him vnclo*þ*e of his furrede tabard and of his hood, and.. saide vnto him.. now art *þ*ow no knyȝt, but a knaue. **1562** LEIGH *Armorie* (1597) 96 Gentlewomen vnder the degree of a countesse, haue armes on Taberts. **1603** DRAYTON *Bar. Wars* II. xxiii, Ferrer his Taberd, with rich Verry spred, Well knowne in many a Warlike Match before. **1843** JAMES *Forest Days* I. ii, His sword peeped from under his tabard.

3. a. The official dress of a herald or pursuivant; a coat or jerkin having short sleeves, or none, and emblazoned with the arms of the sovereign.

1598 STOW *Surv.* 238 Now these Tabardes are onely worne by the Heraults, and bee called their coates of Armes in seruice. **1633** B. JONSON *Love's Welcome* Wks. (Rtldg.) 661/1 As witnesseth the brief taberd or coat-armour he carries. **1724** *Lond. Gaz.* No. 6307/1 The Heralds.. invested with Taberts of the Sovereign's Arms. **1808** SCOTT *Marm.* I. xi, Two pursuivants, whom tabarts deck, With silver scutcheon round their neck. **1864** BOUTELL *Her. Hist. & Pop.* xiii. 132 The Tabard remains in use as the Official Habit of Heralds.

b. A fashionable slimly cut ladies' jerkin or similar garment with short (or no) sleeves; *spec.* one used as a beach-robe.

1923 in C. W. Cunnington *Eng. Women's Clothing in Present Cent.* (1952) v. 175 Evening dress with tabard top. **1959** *Housewife* June 49 A beach tabard in.. cotton, over a bikini and bra. **1977** P. D. JAMES *Death of Expert Witness* II. xii. 106 She wore a dress in fine fawn wool, topped with an elaborately patterned, short-sleeved tabard. **1983** *Times* 11 Mar. 8/4 An odd, misshapen tabard, worn with a long slim suede skirt.

†**4.** (?)

1526 *Rutland MSS.* (1905) IV. 264 Leyeng tabardes for your chapell roff, and takyng down the olde ledde.

5. *Comb.* ***tabard-fashion, -wise***; ***tabard-like*** adj.

? *a* **1500** *Assemb. Ladies* 523 In tabard-wyse the slevës hanging doun. **1890** DOYLE *White Comp.* xviii, An air of masterful dignity, which was increased by his tabardlike vesture. **1903** *Daily Chron.* 31 Mar. 9/1 Those [S. African natives] that don a coat wear it behind before, or slung round their shoulders, tabard-fashion.

Hence '**tabarded** *a.*, wearing a tabard.

1837 *Old Commodore* II. 12 The tabarded official most submissively replied, That if such right existed [etc.].

tabarde, obs. var. TABARD, TABRET.

tabarder: see TABERDAR.

tabardillo (tæbə'dɪləʊ, ‖tabar'diʎo). *Path.* [Sp. *tabardillo* (see quot. 1980).] A fever common in Mexico and S. America; now *spec.* a murine typhus (cf. MURINE *a.* b) found in Mexico which, unlike most forms of murine typhus, can occur as an epidemic.

[**1598** W. PHILLIP tr. *Linschoten's Voy. E. & W. Indies* I. i. 2/1 Hee fell sicke of a disease called *Tauardilha*.] **1624** W. ASTON *Let.* 10 Dec. in *Cabala: sive Scrinia Sacra* (1654) I. 166 He hath been held divers dayes with a terrible Calenture, which proved at last a *Tabardillo*. **1853** W. L. HERNDON *Exploration Valley of Amazon* I. v. 113 The most common diseases are pleurisies, rheumatisms, and a putrid fever called *tabardillo*. **1944** R. A. MOORE *Textbk. Path.* xlii. 459 It was shown before 1930 that Brill's disease, tabardillo of Mexico, and endemic typhus of the southeastern United States are all transmitted by the rat flea.. and by the rat louse. **1980** A. L. SMITH *Microbiol. & Path.* (ed. 12) I. xxv. 300/2 The endemic typhus fever of Mexico is known as *tabardillo* (from the Spanish word *tabardo*, meaning a coloured cloak, to designate the mantlelike spotted rash of the disease).

tabaret ('tæbərɪt). [mod. trade name, prob. f. TABBY: cf. TABINET.] A fabric of alternate satin and watered silk stripes used in upholstery.

1790 P. A. ROBB *Let.* in M. Dunsford *Hist. Mem. Tiverton* IV. 235 This year [*sc.* 1752] was introduced to Tiverton the manufacture of.. camblets, tarborates, damasks. **1851** MAYHEW *Lond. Lab. & Poor* I. 427/1 A composition to remove stains from silks, muslins, bombazeens, cords, or tabarets of any kind or colour. **1866** *Times* 23 Apr. Advt., 450 yards rich damasks and tabarets. **1883** [see TABBAREA].

tabaret, obs. form of TABRET.

tabarte, obs. form of TABARD, TABRET.

Tabasco (tə'bɑːskəʊ, -'bæskəʊ). [From Tabasco, name of a river and state of Mexico.] More fully ***Tabasco* (*pepper*) *sauce***: A proprietary name for a very pungent sauce made from the pulp of the ripe fruit of a variety of *Capsicum annuum*. Also *fig.* ***Tabasco allspice***, name for *Pimenta officinalis*, var. *Cumarensis* (formerly *Myrtus Tabasco*), Sp. *Pimienta de Tabasco*.

1876 J. MILLER *First Fam'lies Sierras* 126 The following popular drinks.. were all made from the same decoction of bad rum, worse tobasco, and first-class cayenne pepper. **1878** *Let. to E. McIlhenny* (E. S. Hyatt & Co.) 16 Dec. (MS.), Please send us by return mail your lowest prices and terms on your Tabasco pepper sauce. **1879** E. C. HAZARD *Let. to E. McIlhenny* 30 July (MS.), Would you agree to sell us your entire packing of tabasco sauce? **1898** *Missouri Bot. Garden, 9th Rept.* 59. **1900** *Westm. Gaz.* 5 Dec. 8/2 He.. was ..seized and forced to swallow a large dose of Tabasco sauce mixed with ketchup and cayenne pepper. **1902** *Ibid.* 26 Apr. 2/1 Mix with due assiduity, and finally add from three to six drops of tabasco. **1902** *Trade Marks Jrnl.* 3 Sept. 1010 Tabasco pepper sauce. Pepper Sauce made from Tabasco Pepper. Edward Avery McIlhenny,.. Sauce Manufacturer. —25th July 1902. Mark has been used in respect of the said Goods by the applicant and his predecessors in business since five years before the 13th August 1875. **1903** *Agric. News* (Barbados) XI. 227 There seems to be no reason for supposing that the Tabasco allspice enters into the preparation of Tabasco pepper. **1908** *Times* 30 July 3/3 He had written 'Sultry Stories—Peppery Paragraphs—Tabasco Tales'. Tabasco was a hot sauce. **1923** WODEHOUSE *Inimitable Jeeves* iv. 41 Little as he might look like one of the lads of the village, he certainly appeared to be the real tabasco and I wished he had shown me this side of his character before. **1924** *Trade Marks Jrnl.* 18 June 1385 Tabasco. 439,246. Pepper Sauce made from Tabasco Pepper. McIlhenny Company... 21st July 1923. **1949** *Amer. Speech* XXIV. 34 Tabasco sauce is acid used in breaking a limestone formation. **1979** *Guardian* 19 July 12/3 Fred Jackson in among the saxophones to add a tabasco spice to the disco bids.

‖**tabasheer** (tæbə'ʃɪə(r)). Also 6-7 (fr. Pg.) **tabaxir,** 8 (fr. Fr.) **tabachir.** [Arab., Pers., Urdū *tabāshīr* chalk, mortar.] A siliceous substance, white or translucent, occasionally formed in the joints of the bamboo, also called *bamboo salt*; used medicinally in the East.

1598 W. PHILIP *Linschoten* 104/2 These Mambus have a certain matter within them.. a very medicinable thing..

much sought for by the Arabians, Persians, and Moores, that call it Tabaxiir. **1662** J. Davies tr. *Mendelslo's Trav.* II. 149 A sort of Canes.. in which the Tabaxir is found. **1790** P. Russell in *Phil. Trans.* Abr. XVI. 653 (*heading*) Account of the Tabasheer. **1826** Brewster *Let.* in *Home Life* ix. (1869) 129, I have enclosed some specimens of Tabasheer, a substance of extreme rarity. **1829** *Nat. Philos.* I. Gloss. (Usef. Knowl. Soc.), *Tabasheer*.. is, originally, a transparent fluid in the jointed cavities of the bamboo cane. This fluid thickens,.. until.. it is converted into a white, or a bluish white solid, something like a small fragment of a shell.

Tabassaran (tæbəsə'rɑːn), *sb.* (and *a.*) Also **Tabasaran.** [Native name for a district in S. Daghestan.] A North Caucasian, Lesghian language of Daghestan, known in both written and spoken forms. Also *attrib.* and as *adj.*

1951 W. K. Matthews *Languages U.S.S.R.* v. 89 Agul has twenty-five, Awar thirty, and Tabassaran thirty-five cases. **1968** [see Lesghian *sb.* and *a.*]. **1971** [see Lak[2]]. **1977** C. F. & F. M. Voegelin *Classification & Index World's Lang.* 96 Eleven members of the Caucasian groups have official status as literary languages:.. Tabasaran (35,000).

‖**tabatière** (tabatjɛr). [F. for *tabaquière*, f. *tabac* TOBACCO (Hatz.-Darm.).] A snuff-box. (Rare in Eng. use.)

1823 Scott *Quentin D.* Introd., The marquis was somewhat disconcerted, and had recourse to his *tabatière*. **1841** Lady Blessington *Idler in France* I. xi. 253 A pinch of snuff from the *tabatière* of the Marquise de Rambouillet.

tabbarea (tæbə'riːə). = TABARET.

1843 W. C. Taylor in *Statistical Jrnl.* Dec. 353 It is generally believed that an ancestor of the present.. family of the Latouches commenced the weaving of tabinets or poplins and tabbareas in the liberties of Dublin, about the year 1693. **1883** R. Haldane *Workshop Receipts* Ser. II. 146/1 Tabaret or Tabbarea.—This may be cleaned and finished in the same manner as described for silk damasks.

tabbed (tæbd, 'tæbɪd), *a.* [f. TAB *sb.*[1] + -ED.] Having a tab or tabs; furnished or adorned with tabs, as an article of dress.

1872 J. Drummond in Campbell *Rec. Argyll* (1884) 482 His attendant wears hose tabbed at the top. **1884** G. H. Boughton in *Harper's Mag.* Sept. 533/2 Tabbed jackets, short skirts and buckled shoes. **1901** *Daily Chron.* 5 Oct. 8/3 A pretty blouse, with tabbed fronts bound with stitched white taffetas.

tabber, tabbern, obs. ff. TABOR, TABORN.

tabbied ('tæbɪd), *ppl. a.* [f. TABBY *v.* + -ED[1].] Having a wavy or streaky appearance.

1861 Thornbury *Turner* (1862) I. 279 They have.. a 'tabbied' or 'mackerel' sky.

tabbinet, variant of TABINET.

tabbor, tabborer, obs. ff. TABOR, TABORER.

‖**tabbouleh** (tɑː'buːlɛ). Also **tabbouli, tabbuuli.** [ad. Arab. *tabbūla.*] An Arabic vegetable salad made with crushed wheat.

1955 J. Gulick *Social Structure & Culture Change in Lebanese Village* 42 The other is *tabbuuli*. This has nearly the same ingredients as the salad, but they are chopped up very fine and mixed with cracked wheat which has been soaked in water. **1958** F. Copeland *Land between: Middle East* ix. 99 No picnic is complete without a special salad called *tabbouleh*. **1965** *Times* 31 May 13/6 Tabbouleh is a salad made from crushed wheat known as bourghul, with chopped parsley and mint. **1968** C. Roden *Bk. Middle Eastern Food* 57 *Tabbouleh* is traditionally served in individual plates lined with boiled vine leaves. **1977** C. McFadden *Serial* (1978) lii. 110/2 Marlene must have cooked her head off. The tabbouleh, all that whole-wheat lasagne,.. the brown rice and veggies.

tabby ('tæbɪ), *sb.* and *a.* Also 7 **taby.** [In sense 1, a. F. *tabis*, earlier *atabis* (both 14th or early 15th c. in Godef.), Sp., Pg., It. *tabi*, med.L. *attābi* (M. Devic in Littré), app. a. Arab. *ʿattābiy*, name of a quarter of Bagdad in which this stuff was manufactured, named after *'Attāb*, great-grandson of Omeyya. Of this quarter Yule cites from an Arab writer of the 12th c. 'Here are made the stuffs, called *'Attābīya*, which are silks and cottons of divers colours'.

The connexion of the other senses is not very clear. *Tabby cat*, instanced in 1695, is generally held to have been so named from the striped or streaked colour of its coat. The simple *tabby*, in the same sense, is much later (1774). *Tabby*, old maid, is usually associated with *tabby* a cat; but it appears earlier, and may have originated as the familiar contraction of *Tabitha* (cf. *Abby* for *Abigail*), as an old-fashioned female name, and have become humorously associated with *tabby cat*. It is possible that *tabby* in the sense of she-cat originated in *Tabby* for *Tabitha*; otherwise it is difficult to see any sense-connexion between she-cat and brindled cat, since a tom-cat may also be brindled or striped. Sense 4 of the sb. prob. arose from resemblance to the markings of the tabby cat; the origin of sense 5 is very uncertain, and sense 6 may be a different word, though it may also have originated in a fancied resemblance of colour to that of the tabby cat.]

A. *sb.*

1. a. A general term for a silk taffeta, app. originally striped, but afterwards applied also to silks of uniform colour waved or watered.

1638 [see B. 1]. **1647** Herrick *Noble Numb., New-Yeeres Gift*, Let others looke for pearle and gold, Tissues or tabbies manifold. **1648** —— *Hesper., Life is the Bodies Light* 3 Those counter-changed Tabbies in the ayre, (The Sun once set) all of one colour are. **1654** Whitelocke *Jrnl. Swed. Emb.* (1772) II. 153 The bride and bridegroome were both clothed in white tabby. **1662** J. Davies tr. *Olearius' Voy. Ambass.* 23 One piece of silver'd Taby, with flowers of Gold. **1696** *Lond. Gaz.* No 3228/4 Lost.., a Child's Mantle, of a Sky-colour Tabby. **1720** Swift *Song* Wks. 1755 IV. I. 29 Brocados and damasks, and tabbies and gawses. **1727** Bailey vol. II, *Tabby*, a Sort of Silk, waved or watered. **1736** *Ibid.* (folio), *Tabby*, a kind of coarse Silk taffety watered. **1745** Pococke *Descr. East* II. I. viii. 125 The manufactures they [of Damascus] export, are chiefly burdets of silk and cotton, either striped or plain, and also a plain silks like tabbies. **1760** H. Walpole *Let. to Earl of Strafford* 7 June, The Duke of York, who was dressed in a pale blue watered tabby. **1868** Hawthorne *Amer. Note-Bks.* (1879) II. 61 His lady in crimson tabby. **1888** W. Morris *Arts & Crafts Catal.* 19 A different tone is obtained by the figure and the ground being woven with a longer or shorter twill: the tabby being tied by the warp very often, the satin much more rarely.

b. Short for *tabby gown* or *dress*.

a **1727** Mrs. Delany in *Life & Corr.* (1861) I. 124 To alter my white tabby and my new clothes. **1786** Mme. D'Arblay *Diary* 29 Sept., I wore my memorable present-gown this day... It is a lilac tabby. **1881** Besant & Rice *Chapl. of Fleet* II. 58 A watered tabby would become you.

2. a. Short for *tabby cat* (see B. 2): A cat having a striped or brindled coat.

1774 Goldsm. *Nat. Hist.* (1862) I. IV. iii. 423 The civet varies in its colour, being sometimes streaked, as in our kind of cats called tabbies. **1874** Gordon Stables *Cats* i. 8 *Brown Tabby.* Colour to be rich brown, striped and marked with black... They are the true English cats. *Ibid.* 9 *Blue or Silver Tabby.* Colour to be blue, or silver grey, striped and marked with black. *Ibid.* 12 *Red and White Tabby.* Colour to be reddish or sandy, marked with white. **1903** *Daily Chron.* 28 Oct. 3/1 Among silver tabbies,.. Sweet William and.. Dame Fortune were particularly noteworthy.

b. Also, A she-cat: correlative to *tom-cat*.

1826–8 *Townley's High Life below Stairs* (acting ed.), Your cat has kittened—two Toms and two Tabbies. **1903** *Speaker* 14 Feb. 486/2 Where is the centurion who has ever commanded a tom-cat, the astronomer who predicted the movements of a tabby?

3. a. An old or elderly maiden lady: a dyslogistic appellation; often with a half-humorous attribution of certain qualities of the cat; sometimes applied to any spiteful or ill-natured female gossip or tattler: cf. also CAT *sb.*[1] 2.

[**1748**: see B. 3]. **1761** G. Colman *Jealous Wife* II. iii, I am not sorry for the coming in of these old tabbies. **1782** Eliz. Blower *Geo. Bateman* I. 222 A delightful ground-work, on which the tabbies of Clairfield embroidered a thousand different anecdotes. **1785** Grose *Dict. Vulg. Tongue*, *Tabby*, an old maid; either from Tabitha, a formal antiquated name; or else from a tabby cat, old maids being often compared to cats. **1824** Scott *St. Ronan's* xxxiii, Why should not I pay my respects to Lady Penelope, or any other tabby of quality? **1843** Lever *J. Hinton* xiii, I was playing whist with the tabbies when it occurred. **1894** [see TABLEAU 2 c].

b. An (attractive) young woman or girl; = TAB *sb.*[2] b. *slang.*

1916 C. J. Dennis *Moods of Ginger Mick* 20 Then the tabbies took to screamin'. **1925** Fraser & Gibbons *Soldier & Sailor Words* 275 *Tabby, a*, a girl. **1935** A. J. Pollock *Underworld Speaks* 118/1 *Tabby*, an attractive girl. **1958** J. Wain *Contenders* iv. 88 'I said, is it true what Joe says that you've got yourself fitted out with a tabby?' 'My humble roof,' said Robert.. 'is shared by a distinguished actress.'

4. A collector's name for two Pyralid moths, the Tabby, *Aglossa pinguinalis*, and the Small Tabby, *A. cuprealis*, both with fore wings greyish brown, clouded with a darker colour.

1819 G. Samouelle *Entomol. Compend.* 427 *Pyralis capreolalis*... The small Tabby. *pinguinalis*... The Tabby. *Ibid.* 435 The tea Tabby. **1859** Stainton *Man. Butterfl. & Moths* II. 135 *Aglossa pinguinalis* (Tabby)... Abundant everywhere. *A. cuprealis* (Small Tabby).

†**5.** Padding or quilting to improve the figure. *tabbies*, padded or quilted stays. *Obs.*

1748 Foote *Knights* II. i, Ward, at the Cat and Gridiron, Petticoat-lane, makes tabby all over for people inclined to be crooked; and, if he was to have the universal world for making a pair of stays, he could not put better stuff in them. **1752** —— *Taste* I. i, *Lady Pentweazel.* Bless me, Mr. Carmine, don't mind my shape this bout; for I am only in jumps. Shall I send for my tabbies?

6. A concrete formed of a mixture of lime with shells, gravel, or stones in equal proportions, which when dry becomes very hard. Orig. ***tabby work.***

1802 A. Ellicott *Jrnl.* (1803) 267 A small battery of tabby work (as it is called in that country [Georgia]), which is a composition of broken oyster shells and lime. **1836** Smart, *Tabby*.. a mixture of stone or shell and mortar. **1887** *Cassell's Encycl. Dict.* cites Weale.

B. *adj.* (attrib. use of sb.)

1. Made or consisting of tabby (see A. 1).

1638 T. Verney in *V. Papers* (1853) 197 First, for one good cloth sute, and one taby or good stuff sute. **1661** Pepys *Diary* 13 Oct., This day.. put on.. my false taby waste-coate with gold lace. *a* **1712** W. King *Art of Love* 1043 If she in tabby waves encircled be,.. If by her the purpureal velvet's worn. **1748** H. Walpole *Lett.* (1846) II. 224 A new sky-blue watered tabby coat. **1863** Le Fanu *Ho. by Church-yard* III. 127 Mrs. Sturk.. sat in a dingy old tabby saque.

2. a. Of a brownish, tawny, or grey colour, marked with darker parallel stripes or streaks; brindled: primarily and especially in **tabby cat** or **tabby-cat**, a cat of this coloration, or (by extension) of other colour similarly marked: see A. 2. In quot. 1789 *ellipt.* = tabby coloration.

[**1665**: cf. *tabby-coloured* in C.] *c* **1689** Prior *Ld. Buckhurst playing w. Cat* 21 On her tabby rival's face She deep will mark her new disgrace. **1695** Congreve *Love for L.* II. iii, I can bring witness that.. you suckle a young devil in the shape of a tabby-cat. **1698** Fryer *Acc. E. India & P.* 176 It was a Tigre.. of a light Yellow, streaked with Black, like a Tabby Cat. **1702** Pope *Wife of Bath* 142 The Cat, if you but singe her tabby skin, The chimney keeps. **1747** Gray *Let. to Walpole* in Mason *Life* (1775) 188 Then as to your handsome Cat,.. it must be the tabby one that had met with this sad accident. **1747** —— *Cat* 4 Demurest of the tabby kind. **1789** Mrs. Piozzi *Journ. France* I. 347 Cats.. in the woods are all of the uniformly-streaked Tabby. **1796** Stedman *Surinam* (1813) II. xviii. 62 The spotted cat [fish] is called so from its tabby color and long whiskers. **1903** *Longm. Mag.* Sept. 450 It had been brought up from infancy with a tabby kitten.

fig. (Cf. A. 3). **1874** Mrs. H. Wood *Mast. Greylands* xv, A meddling, tattling, tabby-cat set of women!

b. ***tabby-cat striation***, 'the appearance presented in extreme fatty degeneration of muscle' (*Syd. Soc. Lex.*).

1897 *Allbutt's Syst. Med.* II. 871 The heart.. often shows some fatty degeneration of the myocardium (tabby-cat striation). **1898** *Ibid.* V. 530 The musculi papillares.. are nearly always variegated by wavy whitish streaks—the 'tabby-cat striation' of Quain.

3. Of or pertaining to a tabby, in sense A. 3.

1748 Richardson *Clarissa* (1811) VI. lv. 227 The two antiques only bowed their tabby heads.

C. *attrib.* and *Comb.*, as ***tabby-coloured*** adj.; **tabby-cat** (see B. 2); **tabby-waterer**, one who waters or tabbies silk by a process of calendering; **tabby weave** *Textiles* = *plain weave* s.v. PLAIN *a.*[1] and *adv.* C. c; also ***tabby weaving*** (cf. quot. 1888 at A. 1 above); **tabby work**: see A. 6.

1665 Sir T. Herbert *Trav.* (1677) 304 Cats.. very large they are and tabby-coloured, streakt like those of Cyprus. **1867** Smiles *Huguenots Eng.* (1880) 373 [He] carried on the business of a calenderer and Tabby Waterer. **1879** A. Barlow *Weaving* 89 A piece of plain woven cloth is represented.. as it would be drawn by the designer, and it is generally called 'tabby' or plain weaving. **1906** H. Nisbet *Gram. Textile Design* ii. 6 The 'plain'.. or 'tabby' weave.. is the most simple and elementary combination of two series of threads employed in the construction of textile fabrics. **1957** Simpson & Weir *Weaver's Craft* vii. 77 We may weave a binder thread (a row of plain or tabby weave) of very fine material in between the rows of pattern.

tabby ('tæbɪ), *v.* [f. prec.]

1. *trans.* To give a wavy appearance to (silk, etc.) by calendering. Hence **'tabbying** *vbl. sb.*

1728 Chambers *Cycl.* s.v. *Roll*, Tis also between two Rollers that the Waves are given to Silks, Mohairs, and other Stuffs proper to be tabied. **1839** Ure *Dict. Arts* 1225 Tabbying, or Watering, is the process of giving stuffs a wavy appearance with the calender.

2. To stripe or streak in parallel lines with darker markings. Usually in pa. pple. **'tabbied.**

1860 *All Year Round* No. 37. 260 They [mackerel] were tabbied with indigo tattooings. **1870** Thornbury *Tour Eng.* II. xix. 49 The beautiful fish, shining like solid lumps of rainbow, tabbied with dark veins.

'tabbyhood. [f. TABBY *sb.* + -HOOD.] The condition of being an old maid: see TABBY *sb.* 3.

1793 J. Gifford *Resid. France* (1797) I. 357, I venture to add a word in defence of Tabbyhood. **1824** *Blackw. Mag.* XV. 115 He.. married a wife verging on her tabbyhood.

†**tabe.** *Obs.* [ad. L. *tābēs* (see TABES) or *tābum* corruption, infectious or pestilent disease.] Gradual wasting away; = TABES.

1614 T. Adams *Fatal Banquet* II. Wks. 1861 I. 191 They put a pleurisy into their bloods, a tabe, and consumption into their states. **1633** —— *Exp. 2 Peter* ii. 2 He doth work a tabe and consumption into his fellows' virtues.

tabe, obs. variant of TAB.

†**tabefact,** *a. Obs. rare*$^{-1}$. [ad. L. *tābefact-us*: see next.] Wasted, corrupted.

c **1425** tr. *Arderne's Surgery* (E.E.T.S.) 43, I perceyued þe bone of þe fynger to be tabefacte, i. corrupte.

tabe'faction. *rare*$^{-0}$. [n. of action from late L. *tābefacĕre*, pa. pple. *tābefactus*: see TABEFY.] The action or process of tabefying; the wasting away or consumption of the body.

1658 Phillips, *Tabefaction*, a melting, corrupting, or consuming [1706 (ed. 6) *adds* or wasting away]. **1890** Billings *Nat. Med. Dict.*, *Tabefaction*, emaciation.

tabefical, erron. f. TABIFICAL (infl. by *tabefy*).

tabefy ('tæbɪfaɪ), *v. rare.* [a. obs. F. *tabéfier* (Paré *c* 1570), ad. late L. *tābefacĕre* (Vulgate), to cause to waste (f. *tābē-re* to waste, melt + *facĕre* to make): see -FY; cf. also late L. *tābificāre* (Cassiod.) in same sense (f. *tābific-us* TABIFIC), whence F. *tabifier* (Cotgr., Oudin).]

1. *trans.* To waste away, consume; to emaciate; †to melt down (*obs.*).

1656 Blount *Glossogr.*, *Tabefy*, to corrupt, consume or melt. **1657** Tomlinson *Renou's Disp.* 78 Out of these [Anacards] thus tabefied proceeds a liquor. **1666** G. Harvey *Morb. Angl.* (1672) 79 Meat eaten in greater quantity than what is convenient tabefyes the body.

2. *intr.* To waste away gradually, become emaciated. *rare.*

1891 in *Cent. Dict.*

Hence 'tabefied *ppl. a.*, affected with tabes, decayed, consumptive.

1666 G. HARVEY *Morb. Angl.* i. 4 Whole families.. descended from tabefyed ancestors.

tabel, -ele, -ell(e, obs. forms of TABLE.

Tabele, var. TEBELE.

tabelet(te, tabellet(t, obs. forms of TABLET.

‖**ta'bella.** *Pharm.* Pl. -æ. [L. dim. of *tabula* TABLE.] = TABLET 3.

1693 tr. *Blancard's Phys. Dict.* (ed. 2), *Tabella*, a solid Medicine taken inwardly, made of Powder, and three or four times as much Sugar.. made into little round Cakes upon a Marble Stone. **1706** PHILLIPS (ed. 6). **1890** *Allen & Hanbury's Advt.* in *Lancet* 25 Oct. 74 It..renders our Compressed Tabellæ the most eligible form for the administration of several important medicines.

†**tabe'llarious,** *a. Obs. rare*$^{-0}$. [f. L. *tabellāri-us* (see next) + -OUS.]

1656 BLOUNT *Glossogr.*, *Tabellarious*, belonging to carriers or auditors.

†**tabellary,** *sb. Obs. rare*$^{-0}$. [ad. L. *tabellārius* letter-carrier, courier, f. *tabella* tablet, writing-tablet.]

1656 BLOUNT *Glossogr.*, *Tabellary*, a carrier of letters; an auditor, a scrivener. **1658** in PHILLIPS.

†**'tabellary,** *a. Obs. rare*$^{-1}$. [ad. L. *tabellārius* of or pertaining to voting tablets, f. *tabella* tablet.] Pertaining to the use of voting tablets; ***tabellary liberty***, liberty of voting by tablets.

1613 T. GODWIN *Rom. Antiq.* III. III. v. 142 Cœlius Trib. Pl. established a law, that.. in taintments of treason against any person of State,..or against the Common-weale, this Tabellary libertie should have place, when the people should iudge thereof.

†**ta'bellion.** *Obs.* Also 5 -ioun, -yo(u)n. [ad. L. *tabellio, -ōnem*, one who draws up written instruments, a notary, scrivener, f. *tabella* tablet, letter, etc.] A scrivener, a kind of subordinate notary; *esp.* in the Roman Empire, and in France till the Revolution, an official scribe having some of the functions of a notary. In 17-18th c. used as a recognized designation of a vocation in England and New England.

1413 *Pilgr. Sowle* (Caxton) I. xxi. (1859) 21, I my self wyl only be wryter and tabellyon of al that he wyl sey. **1469** *Sc. Acts Jas. III* (1814) II. 95 His hienes may mak notaris & tabellionis. **1622** MALYNES *Anc. Law-Merch.* 198 A Notarie is called a Tabellion, Scriuenor, or a publike seruant. **1656** in *Thurloe St. Papers* V. 401 We do certify that Rob. Wickenden..is notary and tabellion public in this port of Dover. **1735** in Carol. Hazard *Life T. Hazard* (1893) 229, I Joseph Marion Notary and Tabellion Publick Dwelling in Boston in New England. **1755** MAGENS *Insurances* II. 71 To make the Assurance before a Justice, Notary, Tabellion, or other public Person. **1909** SHARPE *Cal. Let. Bk. I Lond.* p. xxviii *note*, We find him formally appointing a notary public and tabellion throughout the Roman Empire.

taber, taberd, obs. ff. TABOR, TABARD.

taberdar ('tæbədɑː(r)). Also 7 taubator, tabitter, 8 tabiter, 7-8 taberder, 7- tabardar. [f. *taberd*, TABARD.] *lit.* One who wears a tabard; a name formerly given to certain scholars of Queen's College, Oxford, from the gown they wore; still surviving in the name of some of the scholarships at that college.

[**1566** *Register of Queen's Coll.* 5 Apr., Electio Taberdorum habita 5° die mensis Aprilis Anno Elizabethe Regine 8°. **1569** *Ibid.* 29 Jan., Electio Taberdiorum.] **1648** in Burrows *Reg. Visitors Univ. Oxf.* (Camden) 177 Oct. 30 Avery Tompson, Tho. Collinson, Taubators. **1660** WOOD *Life* Dec. (O.H.S.) I. 352 The Taberder sings the aforesaid song. **1691** —— *Ath. Oxon.* I. 348/2 After he [Henry Airay] was Bachelaurs standing, in 1583, he was made *Pauper Puer*, or *Tabardus* or *Tabardarius*; that is, a Tabarder or Tabitter, (so called because anciently they wore Coats or upper Gowns, much according to the fashion of those belonging to Heralds). **1769** *De Foe's Tour Gt. Brit.* II. 243 (Queen's College, Oxford.) The Society consists of a Provost, 16 Fellows, 16 Scholars, 2 Chaplains, 8 Taberders..and 40 Exhibitioners. **1882** *Stat. Queen's Coll.* III. i. in *Stat. Univ. Oxford* 336 The eight holders of Open Scholarships who are highest in seniority from the time of their election shall always be called Taberdars.

†**'tabere.** *Obs.* [perh. var. of TABARD.] A hood for a hawk.

1467 *Mann. & Househ. Exp.* (Roxb.) 431 Paid for a tabere for the hawke, ij.s. iiij.d.

taberer(e, -et(t(e, obs. ff. TABORER, TABRET.

tabergite ('tɑːbəgaɪt). *Min.* [Named (in Ger.) 1847 from Taberg in Sweden: see -ITE[1].] A mineral of the chlorite group.

1868 DANA *Min.* (ed. 5) 496 *Tabergite*, from Taberg, Wermland..is a bluish-green or green chlorite. **1896** CHESTER *Dict. Names Min.*, *Tabergite*...a chlorite-like mineral, classed with both clinochlore and penninite, probably a mixture of one of these with phlogopite.

†**'tabern.** *Obs.* Also 5 tabyrn. [ad. L. *taberna* hut, booth, shop, tavern.] An obsolete doublet of the word TAVERN, variously used in the senses 'shop, tavern, cellar, cupboard'.

14.. *Voc.* in Wr.-Wülcker 729/40 *Hec taberna*, a tabyrn. *c* **1590** MARLOWE *Faust.* viii. 21, I can make thee drunk with ippocras at any tabern in Europe for nothing. **1605** WILLET *Hexapla Gen.* 281 Food..commonly vendible in their tabernes. **1657** TOMLINSON *Renou's Disp.* 472 In the..angle of the kitchin..may be made a Tabern. **1674** RAY *N.C. Words* 47 A *Tabern*, a Cellar.

tabernacle ('tæbənæk(ə)l), *sb.* Forms: 3- tabernacle; also 5-6 taburn-, 6 tabarn-; 4 -acil, 4-5 -akile, 4-6 -akil(l, -akle, 5 -akille, -akyl(le. [a. F. *tabernacle* (12th c. in Hatz.-Darm.), ad. L. *tabernāculum* tent, booth, shed, dim. of *taberna* hut, booth. Used first in special sense 2, from Old Test. history.]

1. A temporary dwelling; generally movable, constructed of branches, boards, or canvas; a hut, tent, booth.

1382 WYCLIF *Num.* xxiv. 5 How feyr thi tabernaclis, Jacob, and thi tentis, Yrael. —— *Mark* ix. 4 Maistir..make we here thre tabernaclis, oon to thee, oon to Moyses, and oon to Helye. **1483** CAXTON *Gold. Leg.* 66/2 Dauid toke the heed of Golye and brought it in to Jherussalem and his armes he brought in to his tabernacle. **1535** COVERDALE *Heb.* xi. 9 By faith was he a straunger in the londe of promes..& dwelt in tabernacles [WYCLIF litel housis]. **1598** HAKLUYT *Voy.* I. 54 Some of these Tabernacles [of the Tartars] may quickely be taken asunder, and set together againe. *c* **1618** MORYSON *Itin* IV. I. (1903) 44 When his Tents were once pitched, then all the Army..pitched their Tents or Tabernacles about him, in a huge Circuite of grounde. **1756-7** tr. *Keysler's Trav.* (1760) II. 433 Frescati..derives its name from the arbours or tabernacles built by the inhabitants of Tusculum, when their city was demolished ..A.D. 1191. **1860** PUSEY *Min. Proph.* 223 The tabernacle was originally a rude hut, formed of intertwined branches. **1864** BURTON *Scot Abr.* I. iii. 109 Some of them..would as soon have sought Kamschatka, as a place wherein to pitch their tabernacle and pursue their fortune.

b. ***Feast of Tabernacles***: a Jewish festival, commemorating the dwelling of the Israelites in tents during their sojourn in the wilderness, held from the 15th to the 23rd of Tisri (October). It was also called the Feast of Ingathering, and was observed as a thanksgiving for the harvest.

1382 WYCLIF *Lev.* xxiii. 34 The fiftenthe day of this seuenthe moneth shulen be the cesynge dayes of the tabernacles [**1388** the feries of tabernaclis]. —— *Deut.* xvi. 13 The solempte of the tabernaclis. —— *Zech.* xiv. 16 That thei..halewe the feest of tabernaclis. **1535** COVERDALE *John* vii. 2 The Iewes feast of Tabernacles [TINDALE the iewes tabernacle feast] was at hande. **1860** PUSEY *Min. Proph.* 79 The feast of tabernacles was the yearly remembrance of God's miraculous guidance and support of Israel through the wilderness. **1896** *Westm. Gaz.* 25 Sept. 3/2 More than any of the other Jewish festivals, Tabernacles claims to be a holyday distinctly commemorative of the harvest.

2. *spec.* in *Jewish Hist.* The curtained tent, containing the Ark of the Covenant and other sacred appointments, which served as the portable sanctuary of the Israelites during their wandering in the wilderness and afterwards till the building of the Temple. Also called ***tabernacle of the congregation*** (or ***meeting***), ***of testimony***, and ***of witness***.

c **1250** *Gen. & Ex.* 3174 Gold and siluer he hauen vt-broȝt, Ðe tabernacle ðor-wið wurð wroȝt. **1340** *Ayenb.* 236 Aaron and his children þet serueden ine þe tabernacle. **1535** COVERDALE *2 Chron.* v. 6 And ye Leuites toke the Arke, & broughte it vp with the Tabernacle of witnesse, and all the holy vessels that were in the Tabernacle. **1642** FULLER *Holy & Prof. St.* III. xxiv. 219 The Tabernacle was a moveable Temple. **1862** STANLEY *Jew. Ch.* (1877) I. vii. 142 The most remarkable vestige of the nomadic state of the nation was the Tabernacle or Tent..the shelter of the Ark.

b. Applied to a portable shrine used in heathen or idolatrous worship.

1382 WYCLIF *Amos* v. 26 And ȝe han born tabernaclis to Moloch, ȝour god. [Also in later versions.]

c. Transferred to the Jewish temple, as continuing the sacred functions and associations of the earlier tabernacle.

1388 WYCLIF *Heb.* xiii. 10 We han an auter, of which thei that seruen to the tabernacle, han not power to ete. **1535** COVERDALE *Ps.* lxxv[i]. 2 At Salem is his tabernacle, & his dwellinge in Sion. **1653** MILTON *Hirelings* Wks. 1851 V. 345 The Levitical and Ceremonial service of the Tabernacle.. which is now abolish'd.

3. *fig.* In phraseology chiefly of biblical origin: A dwelling-place. **a.** *spec.* The dwelling-place of Jehovah, or of God.

Orig. with reference to the Jewish tabernacle or temple.

a **1340** HAMPOLE *Psalter* xiv. 1 Lord wha sall won in þi tabernakile? *Ibid.* xxvi. 9 He hid me in his tabernakill in day of illis. **1382** WYCLIF *Rev.* xxi. 3 Lo! the tabernacle of God [is] with men, and he shal dwelle with hem. **1567** *Gude & Godlie B.* (S.T.S.) 90 O Lord quha sall in heuin dwell with the, In thy tryumphant throne and Tabernakil? **1831** LANDOR *Guzman & Son* 17 Wks. 1846 II. 610 The brave man's breast Is God's pure tabernacle.

b. *gen.* A dwelling-place, a dwelling, a place of abode.

1382 WYCLIF *Job* xii. 6 The tabernaclis of reueres abounden. **1526** *Pilgr. Perf.* (W. de W. 1531) 13 b, For euery good chrysten man and woman a tabernacle of glory. **1635** PAGITT *Christianogr.* I. iii. (1636) 105 They deserue to be receiued into the eternall Tabernacles. **1845** MAURICE *Mor. & Met. Philos.* in *Encycl. Metrop.* (1847) II. 572/1 The portion from the encompassing whole, which hath taken up its tabernacle in these our bodies. **1860** HAWTHORNE *Marb. Faun* (1879) II. viii. 84 How undesirable it is to build the tabernacle of our brief lifetime out of permanent materials. **1891** F. TENNYSON *Niobe* Poems 346 And all The crowned Gods in their high tabernacles Sigh unawares.

c. Applied to the human body regarded as the temporary abode of the soul or of life.

c **1374** CHAUCER *Boeth.* II. pr. iii. 26 (Camb. MS.) Arthow now comen fyrst A sodeyn gest in to the shadwe or tabernacle of this lyf? **1382** WYCLIF *2 Peter* i. 14 The puttyng off of my tabernacle is swift. **1557** N.T. (Genev.) *2 Cor.* v. 1 We knowe that if the tabernacle of this our earthy howse shalbe destroyed, we haue a building geuen of God.. eternal in heauen. **1596** SPENSER *Hymn Hon. Beautie* 142 Many a gentle mynd Dwels in deformed tabernacle drownd. **1671** MILTON *P.R.* IV. 599 True image of the Father,.. enshrin'd In fleshly Tabernacle, and human form. **1746-7** HERVEY *Medit.* (1818) 118 These earthly tabernacles will be transformed into the likeness of Christ's glorious body. **1841** JAMES *Brigand* i, The spirit was busy in its tabernacle dealing with high thoughts.

4. † **a.** An ornate canopied structure, as a tomb or shrine; in quot. *c* 1430, an ornate structure in a pageant. *Obs.*

1297 R. GLOUC. (Rolls) 466 Tours þe gode kniȝt..Brut let bringe an erþe..& let vair tabernacle in honur of him rere. *c* **1394** *P. Pl. Crede* 181 Tombes opon tabernacles tyld opon lofte, Housed in hirnes harde set abouten. *c* **1400** *Destr. Troy* 8813 When this taburnacle atyrit was..Thai closit hit full clanly, all with clene ambur. *c* **1430** LYDG. *Min. Poems* (Percy Soc.) 10 In Cornhille..To do plesaunce to his majesté, A tabernacle surmontyng of beauté Ther was ordeyned. ? *a* **1500** *Maundevile & Sultan of Egypt* 95 in *Rel. Ant.* II. 115 Than the body they bryng unto that place Wher he salle ly armet in his wede, In a tabernacle or a case, Right preciose.

b. A canopied niche or recess in a wall or pillar, to contain an image.

c **1384** CHAUCER *H. Fame* III. 100 But many..Babewinnes and pinacles, Imageries and tabernacles, I saw. **1389** *Eng. Gilds* (1870) 51 An ymage of seynt Wylyam, standyng in a tabernakle, in þe chirche of seynt Margarete of Lenne. **1487-8** *Rec. St. Mary at Hill* 142 Maistres Agnes Breten did do gilte & paynte the tabernacle of owr lady with in þe queer. **1536** *Reg. Riches* in *Antiq. Sarisb.* (1771) 194 A Tabernacle of Ivory, standing upon four feet, with two leaves, and an ymage of our Lady in the middle. **1862** BARING-GOULD *Iceland* (1863) 237 On either side are tabernacles or niches, containing figures.

† **c.** A canopy of tabernacle-work over a throne or stall, esp. the abbot's stall in a choir. *Obs.*

c **1400** *Destr. Troy* 1671 For the souerayn hym selfe was a sete rioll,..Attyret with a tabernacle of Eyntayill fyn. *a* **1400-50** *Alexander* 5645 A tabernacle ouir þe trone tildid vp on loft.

5. *Eccl.* An ornamented receptacle for the pyx containing the consecrated host.

1487-8 *Rec. St. Mary at Hill* 131 Rynges and hookes to henge the clothe for the newe tabernacle. **1546** BALE *Eng. Votaries* I. (1548) 19 b, Pranked vp with tabernacles & lyghtes, sensynges & massinges. *a* **1615** *Brieue Cron. Erlis Ross* (1850) 17 He brought home [for the kirk] an tabernacle. **1716** in J. O. Payne *Recs. Eng. Cath. of* 1715 (1889) 130 A tabernacle of silver belonging to y[e] Altar. **1853** DALE tr. *Baldeschi's Ceremonial* 301 He..opens the Tabernacle, genuflects, and takes out the ciborium. **1885** *Cath. Dict.* 717/1 In most English [R.C.] churches the tabernacle with the Blessed Sacrament is placed over the chief altar.

6. A place of worship distinguished in some way from a church. **a.** A temporary place of worship; esp. applied to the structures temporarily used during the rebuilding of the churches destroyed by the Fire of London in 1666.

1693 EVELYN *Diary* 19 Feb., The Bp. of Lincoln preach'd in the afternoon at the Tabernacle neere Golden Square, set up by him. **1695** SIR J. BRAMSTON *Autobiog.* May (Camden) 389 She [Lady Dyke] was at morninge or euening prayer in the church or tabernacle daily. **1711** *Jrnl. Ho. Com.* XVI. 582 Allowing the 18 chapels or tabernacles to be capable of receiving as many persons as 8 churches. **1739** *Act 12 Geo. II*, c. 7 *Preamble*, The parishioners [of Ealing] were obliged to assemble for Divine worship in a slight Timber Tabernacle.

b. Applied frequently to the meeting-houses or places of worship of Protestant Nonconformists, esp. when not of ecclesiastical architecture.

Sometimes part of the title, as ***Whitefield's Tabernacle*** in Tottenham Court Road, London, and the ***Metropolitan Tabernacle*** built for Mr. Spurgeon; chiefly so used by Baptists and some Methodists. In Scotland, early in the 19th century, commonly applied to the places of worship of the Independents or Congregationalists ('Tabernacle-people'). Otherwise, the name was mostly applied in contempt.

1768 GOLDSM. *Good-n. Man* I. i, I believe she would spread a horse laugh through the pews of a tabernacle. **1796** MORSE *Amer. Geog.* II. 116 A great number of methodist tabernacles. **1805** J. BROWN (Gartmore) *Vind. Presbyt. Ch. Govt.* ii. 13 *note*, The tabernacle-churches in Scotland require their members to stand in singing. **1820** SOUTHEY *Wesley* II. 357 They called it [the shed built as a preaching place for Whitefield] a Tabernacle in allusion to the moveable place of worship of the Israelites. *a* **1878** SIR G. G. SCOTT *Lect. Archit.* (1879) I. 182 Pewing which would disgrace a tabernacle of the last century. *c* **1880** ALLEN *Guide to Nottingham* 33 The next building on the main road of any note is known as *The Tabernacle*..and is a Baptist Chapel.

c. *fig.* Applied to the 'edifice' which for the time enshrines the principles of a party.

1902 SIR H. CAMPBELL-BANNERMAN *Sp. at Leicester* 19 Feb., I do not know down to this moment whether Lord Rosebery speaks to us from the interior of our political tabernacle or from some vantage-ground outside. **1902** LD.

ROSEBERY in *Times* 21 Feb. 6/1 Speaking pontifically within his 'tabernacle' last night, he [Sir H. C.-B.] anathematised my declarations on the 'clean slate' and Home Rule... I remain, therefore, outside his tabernacle, but not, I think, in solitude. **1902** *Westm. Gaz.* 26 Feb. 6/3 Dr. Heber Hart.. is convinced that the principles of the League can be effectively advocated only by those who remain within the tabernacle of the party, whoever may be the Chief Rabbi for the time being.

7. *Naut.* An elevated socket or step for the mast of a river-boat, or a post to which the mast is hinged, that it may be lowered to pass bridges.

1877 in KNIGHT *Dict. Mech.* **1886** *Field* 13 Feb. 209/3 The mizen mast to be stepped in a tabernacle on a false transom in front of the rudder head. **1889** H. M. DOUGHTY *Friesland Meres* 356, I watched the tabernacle anxiously; the strain must be enormous; we must have shrouds set up. **1892** —— *Wherry in Wendish L.* 15 Her one mast, very far forward, is as high nearly as her length, and balanced in a tabernacle with a ton and more of lead.

†**8.** An alleged term for a company of bakers.

1486 *Bk. St. Albans* f vj b, A Tabernacle of bakers.

9. *attrib.* and *Comb.* **tabernacle-niche**, a niche having a canopy of tabernacle-work over it; **tabernacle roof**, a roof which slopes at the ends, as well as the sides, to a central ridge shorter than the side-walls; **tabernacle-spire**, a spire ornamented with many tabernacles or canopied niches; **tabernacle-work**, (*a*) the ornamental carved work or tracery usual in canopies over niches, stalls, or pulpits, and in the carved screens of churches; (*b*) architectural work in which tabernacles form the characteristic feature.

1526 TINDALE *John* vii. 2 Tabernacle feast [see 1 b, quot. 1535]. **1774** PENNANT *Tour Scot. in 1772*, 2 The tabernacle work in the choir is very neat. **1815** J. SMITH *Panorama Sc. & Art* I. 133 The ornamental open work over the stalls is called tabernacle work. **1842** *Civil Eng. & Arch. Jrnl.* V. 121/2 The Tabernacle-spire also is one of which there is no example in this country. **1886** WILLIS & CLARK *Cambridge* III. 286 A central tabernacle-niche, and on each side of it a narrow square-headed window.

'tabernacle, *v.* [ad. med.L. *tabernāculā-re* (1342 in Du Cange: rendering Gr. σκηνοῦν in John i. 14), f. *tabernāculum*: see prec.]

1. *intr.* To occupy a tabernacle, tent, or temporary dwelling, or one that can be shifted about; to dwell for a time, to sojourn: usually *fig.*, in devotional or poetical language, said of the sojourning of Christ on earth or 'in the flesh', and of the indwelling of the Spirit of Christ; also of men as spiritual beings dwelling in the 'fleshly tabernacle' of the body.

1653 COLLINGES *Caveat for Prof.* xiv. 69 The Evangelist Saint John, Joh. i. 14 saith, He tabernacled amongst us. **1667** I. PENNINGTON *Quest. to Prof. Chr.* 20 Is it the flesh and blood of him, who took, tabernacled and appeared in the Body? **1677** GALE *Crt. Gentiles* II. IV. 91 That of Paul 2 Cor. xii. 9.. that the power of Christ might tabernacle or dwel on me. **1847** CHR. ROSSETTI *Face of Deep* (1892) 454 Not with the sparrow building here a house; But with the swallow tabernacling so As still to poise alert to rise and go. **1872** LIDDON *Elem. Relig.* iii. 94 It is.. as personal spirits, tabernacling in bodily forms, that we men are capable of religion. **1876** C. M. DAVIES *Unorth. Lond.* 188 Tabernacling first in a room in Burton Street. **1881** N.T. (R.V.) *John* i. 14 And the Word became flesh, and dwelt [*marg.* tabernacled: Gr. ἐσκήνωσεν] among us.

2. *trans.* To place in a tabernacle; to enshrine.

1822 MILMAN *Mart. Antioch* iii. 116 In thee the light, Creation's eldest born, was tabernacled. **1891** *Tablet* 21 Nov. 825 In any church in this land in which Jesus is tabernacled and has found a home. **1896** *Cath. News* 25 Apr. 6/6 The real presence of God.. tabernacled in yon loving place.

Hence **'tabernacling** *vbl. sb.*, dwelling in a tabernacle or tent; sojourning; temporary abode.

1685 J. SCOTT *Chr. Life* (1699) V. 246 It is no note of distinction between these two dwellings or tabernaclings of Christ. **1856** RUSKIN *Mod. Paint.* IV. v. vi. §9. 89 This tabernacling of the unendurable sun with men. **1866** J. G. MURPHY *Comm. Exod.* xxiii. 16 The feast of tabernacles, because the tabernacling of the people in the wilderness was then commemorated.

'tabernacled (-æk(ə)ld), *ppl. a.* [f. TABERNACLE *sb.* + -ED², perh. after a med.L. **tabernāculātus*.] Made with tabernacle-work, having a carved canopy.

c **1468** in *Archæol.* (1846) XXXI. 333 Over the court gate .. was a riche healme, richelye tabernacled of golde, subtilie gravin things in pinacles. **1905** *Athenæum* 23 Dec. 874/3 A good fifteenth-century tabernacled font cover, 5 ft. high.

'tabernacler. *rare.* [f. TABERNACLE *sb.* + -ER¹.] One who worships in a 'tabernacle'.

1810 COLERIDGE in *Lit. Rem.* (1839) IV. 371 The Ebenezerites.., and their.. fellow Methodists, the Tabernaclers.

tabernacular (tæbə'nækjʊlə(r)), *a. rare.* [f. L. type **tabernāculār-is*, f. *tabernācul-um*: see above and -AR¹.] Of or pertaining to a tabernacle.

1. Of the style or character of an architectural tabernacle; constructed or decorated with open-work and tracery.

1678 WOOD *Life* 28 June (O.H.S.) II. 411 An antient carved peice of tabernacular worke. **1774** WARTON *Hist. Eng. Poetry* (1840) II. xxiii. 300 Cloisters.. fronted with tabernacular or open work.

2. Savouring of the language of a 'tabernacle' or conventicle. *contemptuous.*

1847 DE QUINCEY *Protestantism* Wks. 1858 VIII. 89 The word 'shortcomings'.. being horridly tabernacular, and such that no gentleman could allow himself to touch it without gloves. **1858** BAILEY *Age* 171 But you condemn all verse of solemn vein As canting, tabernacular in strain.

†**taber'naculous**, *a. Obs. rare.* [f. L. *tabernācul-um* TABERNACLE + -OUS: cf. *miraculous.*] = TABERNACULAR.

1696 BROOKHOUSE *Temple Open.* 34 As his [Solomon's] Temple was the Perfection of the Tabernacle, so this City [the New Jerusalem] is the Perfection of the last Tabernaculous Dispensation of [the apocalyptic] Babylon.

†**taber'narious**, *a. Obs. rare*⁻⁰. [f. L. *tabernāri-us* belonging to booths or shops, vulgar, low + -OUS.]

1656 BLOUNT *Glossogr.*, *Tabernarious*, belonging to Shops or Taverns.

taberne, obs. form of TABORN.

taberner, obs. form of TABORNER, TAVERNER.

tabert, tabertte, obs. ff. TABARD, TABRET.

‖**tabes** ('teɪbiːz). [L. *tābēs* wasting away, dissolution, consumption.] **1.** *Path.* Slow progressive emaciation of the body or its parts; consumption.

Common in medical Latin names of specific diseases, as *tabes dorsalis*, locomotor ataxia, *tabes mesenterica*, tuberculosis in the mesenteric glands, etc.

1651 BIGGS *New Disp.* §258 In Tabes, or Consumptions, distempers of the lungs, head, eyes. **1681** tr. *Willis' Rem. Med. Wks.* Vocab., *Tabes dorsalis*, the mourning of the chine; a wasting or consumption of the back. **1706** in PHILLIPS. **1899** *Allbutt's Syst. Med.* VII. 125 General paralysis is a 'tabes of the brain'.

2. Decay of trees or other plants caused by disease or injury.

1832 *Libr. Usef. Knowl., Husb.* III. *Planting* 70 Spontaneous bleeding, or great loss of sap, generally ends in the disease termed *tabes*. *Ibid.* 71 *Tabes*, or the wasting of trees, is brought on not unfrequently by parasitical plants.

tabescent (tə'bɛsənt), *a.* [ad. L. *tābēscentem*, pr. pple. of *tābēscĕre*, inceptive of *tābēre* to waste away: see -ESCENT.] Wasting away.

1890 in BILLINGS *Nat. Med. Dict.* **1898** in *Syd. Soc. Lex.*

So **ta'bescence**, emaciation.

1890 in BILLINGS.

tabetic (tə'bɛtɪk), *a.* and *sb.* [irreg. f. L. *tābēs*, *tābi-*, on false analogy of words etymologically in *-etic*, as *diabetic*.] **A.** *adj.* Of, pertaining to, or affected with tabes or emaciation.

1847 WEBSTER, *Tabetic*, tabid, affected with tabes. **1897** J. HUTCHINSON in *Arch. Surg.* VIII. No. 31. 232 The patient .. has no bladder symptoms, nor any characteristic tabetic pains. **1899** *Allbutt's Syst. Med.* VII. 100, I have met with cases which began with tabetic symptoms and ended in general paralysis.

B. *sb.* One who suffers from tabes.

1899 *Allbutt's Syst. Med* VI. 808 [He] has found the labyrinth and auditory nerve normal in tabetics with defective hearing. *Ibid.* VII. 110 Tabetics, who did not show Romberg's sign.

‖**tabi** ('taːbi). [Japanese.] Also 9 tapie; (anglicized pl.) tabis. Thick-soled Japanese ankle-socks with a separate stall for the large toe, worn by both sexes. Also *attrib.*

1616 R. COCKS *Diary* 23 Jan. (1883) I. 102, 2 peare *tabis* for Jeffrey. **1822** F. SHOBERL tr. *Titsingh's Illustrations of Japan* I. 130 The men leave off the *tapie* on the 1st of the third month, but the women wear them all the year round. **1880** I. L. BIRD *Japan* I. xiii. 131 On her little feet she wears white *tabi*, socks of cotton cloth, with a separate place for the great toe. **1892** H. NORMAN *Real Japan* 193 The costume is completed by a pair of *tabi*. **1895** HOLLAND *Jap. Wife* 18 The curious *tabi* of white cotton, shoes and stockings all in one, with separated toes. **1902** *Daily Chron.* 22 Nov. 3/2 When the whole people celebrate the rites of Shintoism.. men and boys exchange their customary black foot-gear for the white *tabi* of women. **1938** *N. & Q.* 21 May 361/1 The Japanese private.. used to put on his *tabis* and get to work on his arms. **1963** R. GODDEN *Little Plum* 17 'Why, you have made them tanzen—proper Japanese coats—and tabi,' he said, touching the socks. **1975** J. CLAVELL *Shōgun* II. xi. 229 He wore a belted kimono of the Browns and tabi socks and military thongs.

'tabic, *a. rare.* [irreg. f. L. TABES + -IC.] = TABETIC *a.*

1895 in *Funk's Stand. Dict.* **1898** *Syd. Soc. Lex.*, *Tabic*, same as *Tabetic*.

tabid ('tæbɪd), *a.* Now *rare.* [ad. L. *tābidus* wasting, declining, f. *tābēre* to waste: see -ID. Perh. through F. *tabide* (1545 in Hatz.-Darm.).]

1. *Path.* Affected with tabes; wasted by disease; consumptive; marcid. Also *fig.*

1651 BIGGS *New Disp.* §232 Whosoever within fourty daies are not perfectly cured, grow tabid. **1672** SIR T. BROWNE *Let. Friend* §20 Consumptive and tabid Roots sprout more early. **1713** W. CHESELDEN in *Phil. Trans.* XXVIII. 281 A Man, who died Hydropic and Tabid. **1822–34** *Good's Study Med.* (ed. 4) IV. 88 Sinking.. into a premature and tabid old age. **1914** C. MACKENZIE *Sinister St.* II. IV. v. 964 He was disappointed to see no cab.. merely a tabid woman clothed in a cobweb of crape, asleep over her tray of matches. **1947** M. LOWRY *Under Volcano* ii. 58 Outside.. in the backwash of tabid music from the still-continuing ball.

†**2.** Corrupted, decomposed. *Obs.*

1650 BULWER *Anthropomet.* i. (1653) 24 All other Creatures were produced from the tabid Carcasses by the Celestiall influx without seed. **1657** TOMLINSON *Renou's Disp.* 91 These, kept in a moyst place, become tabid.

3. Causing consumption, wasting, or decline.

1671 R. BOHUN *Wind* 140 Dry and tabid mists, which corrupt the lungs. **1895** QUILLER COUCH *Wand. Heath* 92 The tabid Curse Brooded over Pelops' hearse.

4. Of the nature or character of tabes; characterized by wasting away.

1747 tr. *Astruc's Fevers* 136 A simple tabid fever is not so dangerous as a suppurative one. **1765** STERNE *Tr. Shandy* VII. xiv, A gradual and most tabid decline. **1822–34** *Good's Study Med.* (ed. 4) IV. 92 The salacity of age.. often wears away the hoary frame to the last stage of a tabid decline.

Hence **'tabidly** *adv.*, in a tabid manner, consumptively; **'tabidness**, emaciation, tabes.

1672 SIR T. BROWNE *Let. Friend* §4 He that is *tabidly inclined were unwise to pass his days in Portugal. **1668** *Phil. Trans.* III. 699 How it [Sugar] intenerates the flesh, and disposeth to *tabidness. **1700** C. LEIGH *Nat. Hist. Lanc.* II. ii. §2. 62 A tabidness of the Flesh, hot and cold fits alternately succeeding.

†**'tabid**, *v. Obs. rare*⁻¹. [f. prec.] *trans.* To make tabid or consumptive; = TABEFY 1.

1661 FELTHAM *Resolves* II. lxxxv. 374 Slender Hairs.. as nets to catch the dust and moats, which.. we should else draw in, and tabid all our Lungs.

tabific (tə'bɪfɪk), *a. rare.* [ad. L. *tābific-us*, f. TABES: see -FIC. Cf. mod.F. *tabifique* (Littré).] Causing tabes; consumptive, emaciating, wasting.

1669 *Address hopef. yng. Gentry Eng.* 14 Whose souls languish under the irreparable decays of tabific inactivity. **1684** tr. *Bonet's Merc. Compit.* XIV. 492 The Tabifick Matter deposited in the Lungs [in Phthisis]. **1774** T. WEST *Antiq. Furness* p. xvii, The younger sort amongst the fair sex.. have been carried off by tabific complaints.

†**ta'bifical**, *a. Obs.* [f. as prec. + -AL¹: see -ICAL.] = prec.

1608 TOPSELL *Serpents* (1658) 636 So great is the tabifical effect of this poyson of Asps. **1620** VENNER *Via Recta* viii. 192 [They] that are affected with tabefical [*ed.* 1650 tabifical] passions, as sorrow, anxietie of minde [etc.]. **1657** TOMLINSON *Renou's Disp.* 465 When compounded of others, its vertue is more tabifical.

tabil, -ill(e, obs. forms of TABLE.

tabillette, obs. form of TABLET.

†**tabine.** *Obs.* App. the same as TABBY *sb.* 1, the cloth: cf. next.

1611 *Bk. of Rates* (Jam.), Tabins [*ed.* 1670 tabies] of silke, the elle v l. **1626** MIDDLETON *Quiet Life* II. ii. 6 Cloth of tissue or tabine That like beaten gold will shine.

tabinet ('tæbɪnɪt, -ɛt). Also tabb-, -ette. [app. an arbitrary trade-term from TABBY, or perhaps rather from TABINE.] A watered fabric of silk and wool resembling poplin: chiefly associated with Ireland.

1778 *Phil. Surv. S. Irel.* 201 Poplins, some of which, called tabinets, have all the richness of silk. **1796** *Hist. Ned Evans* I. 162 A gown of the most beautiful Irish tabbinet. **1842–3** THACKERAY *Fitz-Boodle's Confess.* Pref., Yonder she marches.. in her invariable pearl-coloured tabinet. **1883** R. HALDANE *Workshop Receipts* Ser. II. 148/1 Irish Poplins and Tabinets are to be cleaned with camphine.

attrib. and *Comb.* **1818** LADY MORGAN *Autobiog.* (1859) 294, I am still in my Dublin tabinette gowns. **1866** *Lond. Rev.* 6 Jan. 6/1 The Lord Lieutenant of Ireland.. holds.. levées which serve to demoralize the middle classes into dire extravagance, and a tabinet gentility. **1886** ROSA MULHOLLAND *Marcella Grace* i, Tabinet-weaving.. is now on the wane.

tabiter, tabitter, obs. forms of TABERDAR.

'tabitude. *rare*⁻⁰. [ad. L. *tābitūdo*, f. stem of *tābēs*, *tābēre*, *tābidus* (see TABES, TABID) + -TUDE.] The state of being affected with tabes; marasmus.

1623 COCKERAM, *Tabitude*, a consumption. **1847** in WEBSTER; and in mod. Dicts.

‖**tabl** (taːbl). Also teboul. [Arab.: see ATABAL.] In the Arab world: a drum (usu. played with the hand).

[**1777** J. RICHARDSON *Arab. & Pers. Dict.* p. xlv, *Tebl* is a drum, *Teblek* a small drum. **1836** E. W. LANE *Acct. Manners & Customs Mod. Egyptians* II. v. 75 Several kinds of drums, of which the most common kinds are the *tub'l bel'edee* (or country drum, that is, Egyptian drum), and the *tub'l Sha'mee* (or Syrian drum).] **1876** STAINER & BARRETT *Dict. Mus. Terms* 415/1 *Tabl*, an Egyptian drum formed from a hollow block of wood, or made of earthenware, with a skin stretched over one end. **1923** *Chambers's Jrnl.* Apr. 307/1 White-collared gentlemen.. play strange instruments—a big guitar, a big drum called a *teboul*. **1976** *Guardian* 16 Dec. 16/3 (Advt.), The *tabl*, the larger wooden drum, probably came [to Qatar] from Africa, though there are obvious etymological links with the Persian *duhul* and the Indian *tabla*.

‖**tabla** ('tabla). Also 9 **tubla**. [Hind., ad. Arab. *ṭabl* (see prec.).] A pair of drums used in Indian music (esp. that of the northern region), of which the left-hand (bass) head is larger than the other (tenor) head; either of these drums separately (see quot. 1969). Also *absol.*, a tabla-player. Cf. MRIDANGAM, PAKHAWAJ.

1865 *Proc. R. Irish Acad.* IX. I. 117 (*Tubla*). These drums, tenor and bass, rank with the pukhraj... The *tubla* drums are made of copper. **1888**, etc. [see MRIDANGAM]. **1914** A. H. F. STRANGWAYS *Mus. Hindostan* ix. 227 The tubla, left and right, are of the shape of a giant tea-cup and coffee-cup respectively. **1927** *Observer* 12 June 14/5 The Hindu drummer's saying that 'the left *tabla* (hand drum) is like the sleeve of my coat, and the right like such embroidery as I may put on it'. **1955** R. P. JHABVALA *To whom she Will* xiii. 92 The musicians.. played with placid expressions.. only the tabla-player smiled. **1969** R. SHANKAR *My Music* i. 40/2 Of the multitude of drums that are found throughout India today, the most popular variety in the North is the *tabla*, which is actually two drums, each with one skin stretched across the top. The smaller of the two drums is the right-hand *tabla*, and the bass, left-hand drum is called the *bonya*, though the two are called collectively *tabla*. **1973** 'D. JORDAN' *Nile Green* xxiv. 99 'No evening Raga tonight?' I asked. 'The tabla has got flu so it's postponed.' **1975** I. MURDOCH *Word Child* 3 Christopher was learning to play the 'tabla', a dreary little oriental drum.

tablature ('tæblətjʊə(r)). Also 6 **tabli-**, 6–9 **table-**, 7–9 **tabulature**. [app. a. F. *tablature* (1553 in Hatz.-Darm.), f. L. *tabula* table; prob. in imitation of It. *tavolatura* 'any kind of Prick-song' (Florio), f. *tavolare* to board, plank, enclose with boards; also 'to set in Musike or Prick-song' (Florio): cf. late and med.L. *tabulāre* to plank, board over (Quicherat *Addenda*; also in Du Cange) and the L. derivatives *tabulātus* boarded, *tabulātio* boarding, flooring, implying the vb.]

1. *Mus.* An old name for musical notation in general, esp. for systems differing from the ordinary staff notation; *spec.* a peculiar form of notation used for the lute and other stringed instruments, in which the lines of the stave denoted the several strings, and letters or figures were placed upon them to indicate the points at which they were to be 'stopped' with the fingers; also, a similar notation for the flute and other wind instruments, in which the lines denoted the several holes, and dots or dashes were placed upon them to indicate those which were to be stopped. Now chiefly *Hist.* exc. in the study and performance of early music.

1574 (*title*) A briefe and plaine instruction, to set all Musicke of 8 diuers Tunes in Tableture for the Lute. **1587** GOLDING *De Mornay* xiv. (1617) 216 The plaine and sweet Harmonie of his [the Lute player's] Tablature, as they terme it. **1596** (*title*) A new Booke of Tabliture.. shewing howe to attain the knowledge to guide and dispose thy Hand to play on sundry Instruments... Whereunto is added, an Introduction to prickesong. **1603** HOLLAND *Plutarch's Mor.* 1046 The propositions described in the Tablature of musicians, which consisteth of five tetrachords. **1641** EVELYN *Diary* Aug., One.. play'd all sorts of compositions [on a chime of bells] from the tablature before him, as if he had fingered an organ. **1724** *Short Explic. For. Wds. in Mus. Bks.*, *Tabulatura*, or *Tablature*, is the old Way of writing Musick with Letters instead of Notes. **1898** STAINER & BARRETT *Dict. Mus. Terms* 426 Organ Tablature was a system of writing the notes without the stave by means of letters... Figured bass has also been called Tablature. **1969** *Daily Tel.* 12 Nov. 14/4 The procuring of music for the lute presented the greatest difficulty: it is not written in staff notation but in tablature, so Dolmetsch had to decipher this from old MSS in the British Museum. **1977** *Listener* 15 Dec. 796/3 Tablatures.. semi-diagrammatic signs that belong to a specific instrument and make no sense in the abstract. **1980** *Early Music* Apr. 250 Our edition includes voice and tablature as well as voice and transcription.

fig. **1649** LOVELACE *Poems* (1864) 121 Sound all my thoughts, and see exprest The tablature of my large brest. **1656** —— *Ibid.* 247 What means this stately tablature, The ballance of thy streins?

2. A tabular formation or structure bearing an inscription or design; a tablet. *Obs.* or *arch.*

1606 FORD *Honour Triumph.* iii. (1843) 25 Whose shames, were they enameled in the tableture of their foreheads, it would be a hideous visour. **1641** *Arminian Nunnery* in R. Brunne *Chron.* (1725) I. p. cxxxi, On the Chimney-peice.. there was a Manuscript Tableture with this Inscription following [etc.]. **1786** MURPHY *Braganza* Prol., A tableture of honour. **1820** MOIR in *Blackw. Mag.* VII. 493 Behind the massy tablatures of death. **1844** *Ibid.* LVI. 586 Ranges of headstones showed, Each on its hoary tablature,.. The sculptured leer of that hyena face.

fig. **1633** FORD *Love's Sacr.* I. ii, You set before you, in the tablature Of your remembrance, the becoming griefs Of a most loyal lady. **1856** DOVE *Logic Chr. Faith* Introd. 15 The .. same method.. would obliterate them from the tablature of human knowledge.

†**3. a.** A painting; a picture; *spec.*: see quot. 1711.

1711 SHAFTESB. *Charact.* (1737) III. 348 In Painting we may give to any particular Work the name of Tablature, when the Work is in reality 'a Single Piece, comprehended in one View,.. which constitutes a real Whole'. **1739** MELMOTH *Fitzosb. Lett.* (1763) 188 Influenced in his censure or applause of the whole tablature, by the predominancy or deficiency of his favorite beauty. **1762** KAMES *Elem. Crit.* (1774) II. xxv. 487 He prefers the Saracen's head upon a sign-post before the best tablature of Raphael. **1767** S. PATERSON *Another Trav.* I. 86 This is the subject of the third tablature.

b. *collectively.* Work consisting or of the nature of paintings or pictures. ? *Obs.*

1714 *Fr. Bk. of Rates* 44 Images painted on Wood or Linen pay as Tableture per 100 Weight. **1762–9** FALCONER *Shipwr.* III. 340 The roof, where storied tablature appear'd. **1819** *Blackw. Mag.* V. 219 To dazzle us with the tablature of splendid hues and imposing forms.

c. *fig.* A 'picture' formed by description or in fancy; (*pl.*) the 'pictures' or representations of memory, or the faculty of retaining these.

1779 SHERIDAN *Critic* I. ii, Yielding a tablature of benevolence and public spirit. **1779** *Hist. Mod. Europe* II. lxx. 490 The transactions of this turbulent period I propose to comprehend in two extensive tablatures. **1860** *Bacon's Mor. & Hist. Wks., Wids. Anc.* (Bohn) 254 How beautifully and elegantly the fable has drawn two reigning characters in human life, and given two examples, or tablatures of them, under the persons of Prometheus and Epimetheus.

4. *Arch.* = ENTABLATURE 1. *rare.*

1869 A. W. WARD tr. *Curtius' Hist. Greece* II. II. iv. 84 The columns rise to bear the tabulature of marble.

†**5.** *Anat.* The tabulate structure of the skull: cf. TABLE *sb.* 16. *Obs.*

1706 PHILLIPS (ed. Kersey), *Tablature*... In Anatomy, it signifies a Division, or parting of the Scull-bones. **1727–41** CHAMBERS *Cycl.*, *Tablature*, in anatomy, a division or parting of the scull into two tables.

table ('teɪb(ə)l), *sb.* Forms: 1 **tabule, tabula**, 3 **tabele**, 5 **tabel, -yl(e, -ule**, 5–6 **-ell(e, -il, -ill(e, -ull(e, -yll(e**, 6 **-ul**; 2– **table**. [In OE. *tabule* wk. fem. (already *a* 900), later also *tabele*, ad. L. *tabula*. In ME. *table* (*a* 1200), a. F. *table* (11th c.), ad. L. *tabula* a flat board, a plank, a board to play on, a writing tablet, a written tablet, a writing, a list, an account, a painted tablet, a painting, a votive tablet, a flat piece of ground, prob. from same root as *taberna* TAVERN.

L. *tabula* became by ordinary phonetic progression in Romanic, *tavola* (as in It.), **tav'la*, *taula* (in Pr.), *tavle*, *taule* (in OF.), *tôle* (F. = sheet of metal); but in most of the langs. these phonetic forms were superseded by others assimilated to the L., as F. *table*, Sp. *tabla*, Pg. *taboa*. The word entered Teutonic at different stages; app. bef. 400 in WGer. as **tabal*, repr. by OHG. *zabal*, ON. *tafl*, board for a game, and OE. *tæfl*, *tæfel* die, tablet, ME. TAVEL[1], q.v.; also later, influenced by L., OHG. *tavala*, *-ela* (MHG. *tavel(e*, MLG., MDu. *tāfele*, *tāvele*, Ger., Du. *tafel*, Da. *tavle*, Sw. *tafel*) table; OE. beside *tabule* had *tabul* masc. and *tablu* fem.]

I. Ordinary senses.

* *A flat slab or board.*

1. A flat and comparatively thin piece of wood, stone, metal, or other solid material (usually shaped by art); a board, plate, slab, or tablet; as a slab forming the top of an altar, or part of a pavement, etc., or a tablet used for ornament or other purpose; also applied to natural formations, as the laminæ of a slaty rock. *Obs.* exc. in special applications: see also senses 2–4.

a **900** tr. *Bæda's Hist.* v. xi. §2 (Camb. MS.; see ed. Miller, pp. 416, 523), Hæfdon hi mid him ʒehealʒode fato and ʒehalʒode tabulan [*MS. B.* ʒehalʒode tablu, *O.* ʒehalʒodne tabul] on wiʒbedes wrixle [L. *tabulam altaris vice*]. **13..** *E.E. Allit. P.* A. 1003 Þe calsydoyne.. In þe þryd table con purly pale. *c* **1440** *Alphabet of Tales* 39 He layed hym downe before þe ya[tt], & knokkid with his tables as lepre men duse. **1447** BOKENHAM *Seyntys* (Roxb.) 35 In tablys of marbyl coryously wrout. **1507** *Acc. Ld. High Treas. Scot.* III. 253 Item, for ane tabil of gold to the Kingis bonet. **1530** PALSGR. 278/2 Table for an auter, *table dautel.* **1585** T. WASHINGTON tr. *Nicholay's Voy.* II. xx. 57 The inner part of the temple is altogether plastered and couered with great tables of Porphyre. **1672** JOSSELYN *New Eng. Rarities* 100 A fair Table curiously made up with Beads likewise, to wear before their Breast. **1687** A. LOVELL tr. *Thevenot's Trav.* II. 75, I observed by the ways side several Rocks of black Stone.. which were all divided into Tables, hardly thicker than blew Slates,.. but joyned very close together. **1730** W. WARREN *Collect.* in Willis & Clark *Cambridge* (1886) I. 225 A Marble Table for y[e] Side-board on a Mohogany Stand. **1849** RUSKIN *Sev. Lamps* iii. §17. 83 The dark, flat, solid tables of leafage. **1889** *Philos. Mag.* May 409 Strata which.. lie in their original horizontal position. These parts are called 'tables' by Suess.

†**b.** A board or plank (in quots., a plank used as a raft after shipwreck); hence *fig.* *Obs.*

1390 GOWER *Conf.* III. 296 He.. broghte him sauf upon a table, Which to the lond him hath upbore. *c* **1440** *Gesta Rom.* lxv. 293 (Harl. MS.) Þerfor seiyth Ierome, *Penitencia est secunda tabula post naufragium*, Penaunce is the secunde table after naufragie. *a* **1533** LD. BERNERS *Huon* lvii. 194 We saued vs on a table of wode. **1617** *Janua Ling.* 6 Contrition of heart is a second table after shipwracke.

2. *spec.* **a.** A tablet bearing or intended for an inscription or device: as the stone tablets on which the ten commandments were inscribed, a memorial tablet fixed in a wall, a votive tablet, a notice-board, etc. *arch.*

c **1050** *Byrhtferth's Handboc* in *Anglia* VIII. 327 Þæra ʒeara ʒetæl hæfð seo tabule þe we mearkian willað. *c* **1175** *Lamb. Hom.* 11 Efter þan drihten him bi-tahte twa stanene tables breode on hwulche godalmihti heofde iwriten þa ten laʒe. *c* **1250** *Gen. & Ex.* 3535 And gaf to tabeles of ston, And .x. bodeword writen ðor-on. *a* **1300** *Cursor M.* 6541 Þe tables þat in hand he [Moses] bare To pees he þam brak right þar. *c* **1400** MAUNDEV. (1839) ii. 10 The table abouen his heued.. on the whiche the tytle was writen, in Ebreu, Greu, and Latyn. **1543** N. HEATH *Injunctions* in Frere *Use of Sarum* II. 236 Certain prayers.. conteyned in Tabylles sett in the grammer scole. **1641** EVELYN *Mem.* 4 Oct., Divers votive tables and relics. **1720** OZELL *Vertot's Rom. Rep.* I. VI. 311 The last Laws of the Decemvirs engraved upon Tables of Brass. **1849** JAMES *Woodman* viii, As stern as the statue of Moses breaking the tables.

†**b.** A small portable tablet for writing upon, esp. for notes or memoranda; a writing-tablet. Often in phr. ***a pair (of) tables***. *Obs.*

rased table = *tabula rasa*: see TABULA 1 b.

a **1300** *Cursor M.* 11087 Þam asked þan sir zachari Tables and a pontel tite. **1382** WYCLIF *1 Macc.* xiv. 17 Thei wryten to hym in brasen tablis. **1387** TREVISA *Higden* (Rolls) VI. 257 Charles.. bare a peyre of tables for to write ynne. **1451** CAPGRAVE *Life St. Aug.* 25 He took a peyre tables, and wroot in þe wax al his desir. **1555** EDEN *Decades* 51 Rased or vnpaynted tables are apte to receaue what formes soo euer are fyrst drawen theron. *a* **1592** GREENE *Jas. IV* Wks. (Rtldg.) 193 Draw your tables, and write what wise I speak. **1614** B. JONSON *Barth. Fair* IV. iii, I saw one of you buy a paire of tables, e'en now. **1656** STANLEY *Hist. Philos.* v. (1701) 184/1 These things are imprinted and form'd in her as in a Table.

c. *fig.* (from a or b). *Obs.* or *arch.*

1382 WYCLIF *2 Cor.* iii. 3 Writun.. not in stoony tablis, but in fleischly tablis of herte. **1599** DAVIES *Immort. Soul* cccxxxv, All these true notes of Immortalitie In our Hearts Tables we shall written find. **1602** LD. MOUNTJOY *Let.* 25 Feb. in Moryson *Itin.* II. (1617) 268, I should.. sooner and more easily.. haue made this Countrey a rased table, wherein shee might haue written her owne lawes. **1693** BENTLEY *Serm.* (J.), The mighty volumes of visible nature, and the everlasting tables of right reason.

d. *Anc. Hist.* (*a*) *pl.* The tablets on which certain collections of ancient Greek and Roman laws were inscribed; hence applied to the laws themselves; esp. ***the Twelve Tables***, drawn up by the decemviri B.C. 451 and 450, embodying the most important rules of Roman law, and forming the chief basis of subsequent legislation. (*b*) ***new tables*** (tr. L. *novæ tabulæ*): see quot. 1727–38.

1726 AYLIFFE *Parergon* 33 By the Law of the twelve Tables, only those were called unto the Legal or Intestate Succession of their Parents, that were in the Parent's power at the time of his Death. **1727–38** CHAMBERS *Cycl.* s.v., *New Tables, Tabulæ novæ*, an edict occasionally published, in the Roman commonwealth, for the abolishing all kinds of debts, and annulling all obligations. **1788** GIBBON *Decl. & F.* xliv. (1790) VIII. 8 In the comparison of the tables of Solon with those of the Decemvirs, some casual resemblance may be found. **1847** GROTE *Greece* II. x. (1849) III. 156 There occurred at Rome several political changes which brought about new tables or at least a partial depreciation of contracts. **1875** MAINE *Hist. Inst.* i. 10 The Roman law.. is descended from a small body of Aryan customs reduced to writing in the fifth century B.C., and known as the Twelve Tables of Rome.

e. ***first, second table***: the two divisions of the decalogue, relating to religious and moral duties respectively, held to have occupied the two 'tables of stone'. Hence *attrib.*

1560 *Maitl. Club Misc.* III. 249 Committing.. adultery brekand the third command of the Second table. **1605** JAMES I *Gunpowder Plot* in *Harl. Misc.* (Malh.) III. 6 All the impieties and sins, that can be devised against both the first and second table. **1672** G. NEWTON in *Life J. Alleine* iv. (1838) 37 He was a second table man, a man of morals. **1873** H. ROGERS *Orig. Bible* i. 21 The great commands of the 'Second Table' are ultimately based on the relations in which all creatures stand to Him who demands our homage in the 'First Table'.

†**3.** A board or other flat surface on which a picture is painted; hence, the picture itself. *Obs.*

1387 TREVISA *Higden* (Rolls) V. 399 Þe baner of þe cros wiþ a crucifix i-peynt in a table [L. *in tabula depicti*]. *a* **1425** *St. Eliz. of Spalbeck* in *Anglia* VIII. 110/5 A tabil, ful wele depeynte with an ymage of oure lorde crucifyed. **1538** STARKEY *England* I. ii. 28 Aftur the sentence of Arystotyl, the mynd of Man fyrst of hyt selfe ys as a clene and pure tabul, wherin ys no thyng payntyd or carvyd. **1538** CROMWELL in Merriman *Life & Lett.* (1902) II. 120 That he may also take the Phisionomie of her that he may ioine her sister and her in a faire table. **1606** PEACHAM *Art Drawing* 7 Cesar.. redeemed the tables of Ajax and Medæa for eighty talents. **1688** R. HOLME *Armoury* III. 145/1 On this Frame [an easel] Painters set their Cloth or Table while it is in working. **1700** T. BROWN *Amusem. Ser. & Com.* 74 My Picture is not yet dry: I will bring you this Table some Months hence.

fig. *c* **1600** SHAKS. *Sonn.* xxiv, Mine eye hath play'd the painter and hath steeld, Thy beauties forme in table of my heart.

4. †**a.** The 'board' on which chess, draughts, backgammon, or any similar game is played. *Obs.*

c **1470** *MS. Ashmole* 344 (Bodl.) lf. 22 This is a Iupertie that may neuer be mated out of the medylle of the table. **1474** CAXTON *Chesse* I. iii. (1883) 14 Then the philosophre began.. to shewe hym the maner of the table of the chesse borde. **1519** HORMAN *Vulg.* lf. 280/1, I have bought a playing tabull, with xii poyntes on the one syde, and chekers on the other syde. **1688** R. HOLME *Armoury* III. 67/2 Those men as break through the other and come to the opposite side of the table, are then made kings. **1801** STRUTT *Sports & Past.* IV. ii. 437 The table for playing at goose is.. divided into sixty-two small compartments arranged in a spiral form.

b. Each of the two folding leaves of a backgammon board (***inner*** and ***outer table***); hence in *pl.* (often ***pair of tables***), a backgammon board (*obs.*). Also, the half of each leaf in relation to the player to whom it belongs.

1483 *Cath. Angl.* 376 A paire of Tabyls *tabelle*. **1573** L. LLOYD *Marrow of Hist.* (1653) 136 The art of dicing and playing divers kinds of games upon tables. **1611** COTGR., *Damier*, a Chesse-boord; or, paire of Tables. **1657** *North's Plutarch, Add. Lives* (1676) 10 Necessitated to cast up the

Cards, to shut the Tables, and to resign the Game. **1745** HOYLE *Backgam.* 22 Two Fours, two of them are to take your Adversary's Cinq Point in his Tables. **1779** MACKENZIE in *Mirror* No. 11 ¶13 [He] snatched up the tables and hit Douglas a blow on the head. **1870** HARDY & WARE *Mod. Hoyle* 141 The object of the game is to bring the men round to your own 'home', or inner table.

c. Phr. ***to turn the tables***: to reverse the relation between two persons or parties, so as to put each in the other's place or relative condition; to cause a complete reversal of the state of affairs. In the active voice, one of the parties is said *to turn the tables* (*upon* the other), in passive, ***the tables are turned*** (sometimes †*the tables turn*).

(A metaphor from the notion of players reversing the position of the board so as to reverse their relative positions.)

1634 SANDERSON *Serm.* II. 290 Whosoever thou art that dost another wrong, do but turn the tables: imagine thy neighbour were now playing thy game, and thou his. **1647** DIGGES *Unlawf. Taking Arms* iii. 70 The tables are quite turned, and your friends have undertaken the same bad game, and play it much worse. **1682** *Enq. Elect. Sheriffs* 31 Whensoever the Tables shall so far turn, as that we have a Mayor who will..drink to one of the contrary and opposite Party. **1713** ADDISON *Guard.* No. 134 ¶4 In short, Sir, the tables are now quite turned upon me. **1889** JESSOPP *Coming of Friars* iii. 165 Suppose the men of the thirteenth century could turn the tables upon us [etc.]. **1893** SELOUS *Trav. S.E. Africa* 33 They had won the first match, though I hoped I might yet turn the tables on them in the return.

** *A raised board at which persons may sit.*

5. An article of furniture consisting of a flat top of wood, stone, or other solid material, supported on legs or on a central pillar, and used to place things on for various purposes, as for meals (see 6), for some work or occupation, or for ornament.

The specific use is often indicated by a qualifying word, as in ***billiard-table***, ***dining-table***, ***writing-table***, ***work-table***, etc.: see these words. ***table dormant***, ***dormant table***: see DORMANT A. 3b. See also ROUND TABLE.

a **1300**, *c* **1330**, etc. [see ROUND TABLE 1a]. *c* **1386** Table dormant [see DORMANT *a.* 3b]. **1393** LANGL. *P. Pl.* C. XIX. 158 Crist..over-turnede in þe temple here tables and here stalles. *c* **1450** *Brut* 446 Next þaim, at the same table syttyng, þe Iustices. *a* **1562** G. CAVENDISH *Wolsey* (1893) 227 My lord's great crosse of sylver accustumably stode in the corner, at the table's end. **1611** COTGR. s.v. *Table*, Round tables take away contention; one being as neere his meat as another. **1625** BACON *Ess., Counsel* (Arb.) 329 A long Table, and a square Table, or Seats about the Walls. **1719** DE FOE *Crusoe* I. 78 To make such necessary things as I found I most wanted, as particularly a Chair and a Table. **1853** W. IRVING in *Life & Letters* (1864) IV. 131, I see you are in the midst of hocus pocus with moving tables [etc.].

b. Phr. ***upon the table***: under consideration or discussion. ***to lay on*** or ***upon the table***: of a legislative or deliberative body, to leave (a report, proposed measure, etc.) for the present, subject to its being considered or called up at any subsequent time; hence, sometimes, to defer its consideration indefinitely (so ***to lie on the table***); more recently also, to present for immediate discussion. Cf. sense 4a of the vb.

1646 R. BAILLIE *Anabaptism* (1647) 163 The question of dipping and sprinkling never came upon the Table. **1730** E. KNATCHBULL in *Camden Soc.* (1963) 3rd Ser. XCIV. 106 So a division for it [*sc.* a Petition] lying on the table, carried by 163 against 144. **1733** in *15th Rep. R. Comm. Hist. MSS.* App. VI. 107 in *Parl. Papers 1897* (C. 8551) LI. 1 The majority, for laying the Petition on the Table..and not hearing it by counsel, was only seventeen. **1744** *Archives New Jersey* (1882) 1st Ser. VI. 191 The House of Representatives..would not commit it [*sc.* a bill] but ordered it to lie on the table. **1817** EVANS *Parl. Deb.* 336 The petition was ordered to lie on the table. **1855** MACAULAY *Hist. Eng.* IV. xix. 343 Shrewsbury laid on the table of the Lords a bill for limiting the duration of Parliaments. **1884** RIDER HAGGARD *Dawn* xlii, The facts are, so to speak, all upon the table, and I will merely touch upon the main heads of my case. **1915** J. LONDON *Let.* 25 Aug. (1966) 458 It is..on the table whether or not we shall say 'it is I' or 'it is me'. **1923** H. M. ROBERT *Parl. Law* (U.S.) 63 It is in order for a mere majority to lay on the table the questions that have not been disposed of. **1958** [see PRAYER[1] 5]. **1977** *Times* 14 Apr. 1/3 While stating that those proposals should 'remain on the table', he [*sc.* Ian Smith] is now prepared to listen to new ideas.

c. *spec.* The table which stands before the Speaker's chair in the House of Commons, at which the Clerk of the House and his assistants receive motions and questions to ministers, etc., and at which new members are sworn in (cf. also prec. sense).

1675 *Grey's Debates* (1769) III. 129 Mr Stockdale, and some others, setting their feet upon the mace, which lay below the table, in the usual place at Grand Committees. **1771** *London Even. Post* 28 Feb.–2 Mar. 3/1 Upon which Mr. Byng and Mr. Buller, seized him by the collar, and brought him up to the table. **1885** *Encycl. Brit.* XVIII. 312/1 Having first taken the oath himself, he [*sc.* the Speaker] is followed by other members, who come to the table to be sworn. **1958** *Spectator* 11 July 47/1 Mr. Gaitskell's head wagged up and down as if he wanted to punch a hole in the Table with his nose.

d. A surgeon's operating-table; also, a table or slab on which a body is laid for post-mortem examination.

1917 T. S. ELIOT *Prufrock* 9 Like a patient etherized upon a table. **1936** G. B. SHAW *Millionairess* II. 166, I should have cut my patients entirely away if the nurse had not stopped me before they died on the table. **1941** A. HUXLEY *Let.* 17 Nov. (1969) 470 The patient will die on the table if operated—off the table, if not operated. **1977** P. D. JAMES *Death of Expert Witness* IV. 226 As for the cause of death..well, you'll have to wait till I get her on the table.

e. Attrib. phr. ***under-the-table***: kept secret, hidden, esp. of clandestine deals or payments. Also (unhyphened) used predicatively and as advb. phr. Cf. *under the counter* s.v. COUNTER *sb.*[3] 4b.

1949 *Sun* (Baltimore) 25 Feb. 19/3 Two home purchasers told a Federal Court jury..that they were required to make under-the-table payments to purchase housing accommodations. **1973** W. H. HALLAHAN *Ross Forgery* vi. 115 Under-the-table freight rebates reached absurd proportions. **1976** *Listener* 5 Feb. 144/1 Some of the sports do check people's bank accounts to see that they have not got too much money under the table. **1976** G. SEYMOUR *Glory Boys* vii. 85 This bomb that the Israelis keep so much under the table..what state is that in? **1980** *Times Lit. Suppl.* 25 July 839/3 The Rheinmetal company for long refused to pay anything, but eventually arranged for an under-the-table payment of DM2,500,000 (which provided $425 for each of its former slaves).

f. A table around which parties (esp. in an industrial dispute) sit to discuss points at issue; a negotiating table. ***round-the-table*** adj. phr., designating such discussions; (***up***)***on the table***: see sense 5b.

1963 [see RECREATIONIST]. **1976** *West Lancs. Evening Gaz.* 15 Dec. 1. 9/4 Transport and General Workers' Union officials want round-the-table talks with the management. **1980** *Times* 6 Feb. 1/1 We hope to get our negotiators around the table as soon as possible.

6. *spec.* An article of furniture as described in 5 upon which food is served, and at or around which persons sit at a meal; often in phr. ***at table***, at a meal or meals; ***for the table***, for eating a meal, for food. (Often passing into c.)

1377 LANGL. *P. Pl.* B. x. 101, I haue yherde hiegh men etyng atte table. *c* **1386** CHAUCER *Prol.* 100 He..carf biforn his fader at the table. *c* **1430** LYDG. *Min. Poems* (Percy Soc.) 67 Nat gredy at the table. *c* **1500** *Doctr. Gd. Servaunts* (Percy Soc.) 8 Ye servauntes that wayte upon the table. **1577** B. GOOGE *Heresbach's Husb.* IV. (1586) 163 They are a very good dishe for the table. **1638** JUNIUS *Paint. Ancients* 164 You doe consecrate your tables, by setting salt-sellers and images of Gods upon the boord. **1706** E. WARD *Wooden World Diss.* (1708) 18 He never deigns to discourse at Table with any below a Brother Captain. **1785** HOLCROFT *Tales of Castle* (ed. 2) I. 65 Just as the family were sitting down to table. **1842** S. LOVER *Handy Andy* ii, He shared in the hospitality of all the best tables in the county. **1855** DELAMER *Kitch. Gard.* (1861) 19 The greening [of potatoes]..renders them unfit for table.

†**b.** A board (cf. sense 1) upon which food is served, placed on trestles or supports (the whole constituting a 'table' in the existing sense), and 'taken up' or removed at the conclusion of the meal. *Obs.*

[**1390** *Earl Derby's Exp.* (Camden) 49/18 Pro j tabula comensali cum j pare tresteles.] *c* **1440** *Promp. Parv.* 485/1 Table, mete boord that ys borne a-wey whan' mete ys doon, *cillaba*. **15..** *Adam Bel* 569 in Hazl. *E.P.P.* II. 162 Take vp the table, anone he bad: For I may eate no more. **1612** SHELTON *Quix.* I. IV. vi. 358 Dinner being ended, and the table taken vp.

c. *transf.* Provision of food for meals; supply of food; fare; = BOARD *sb.* 7; entertainment of a family or guests at table; eating, feasting.

c **1400** *Langl.'s P. Pl.* C. XVII. 322 Hus wone is to wende in pilgrymages, Ther poure men and prysouns beþ, and payeþ for here lyflode [*v.rr.* fode, table]. **1426–7** *Rec. St. Mary at Hill* 67 Also payd for Elymesfordes table ix dayes, euery day ij d. **1602** *2nd Pt. Return fr. Parnass.* II. v. (Arb.) 30 My father..keepes an open table for all kinde of dogges. **1611** COTGR., *Tenir bonne table*, to keepe a good table, to fare well. **1672** SIR C. LYTTELTON in *Hatton Corr.* (Camden) 97 The King allowes mee..10[li] a weeke for a table. **1722** B. STAR tr. *Mlle. de St. Phale's Mem.* i. 4 My Mother..entertained thoughts of placing me in a Convent, paying for my Table. **1882** *Harper's Mag.* LXV. 598 Boarding at four dollars a week, and not a very good table at that.

(*b*) ***the pleasures of the table*** [tr. F. *les plaisirs de la table*], good food and drink, considered as a source of enjoyment.

1769 F. BROOKE *Hist. Emily Montague* IV. 146, I love the pleasures of the table. **1825** SCOTT *Talisman* in *Tales of Crusaders* III. xi. 212 Richard..despised the inclination of the German for the pleasures of the table. **1845** [see SARD *sb.*[2] 1]. **1942** G. M. TREVELYAN *Eng. Social Hist.* xiii. 408 Eighteenth Century Englishmen were much addicted to the pleasures of the table. **1981** T. FITZGIBBON (*title*) The pleasures of the table.

d. Slang phr. (***to put***, etc.) ***under the table***, (to make) drunk to the point of insensibility.

1921 W. S. MAUGHAN *Trembling of Leaf* 28 Walker had always been a heavy drinker, he was proud of his capacity to see men half his age under the table. **1924** D. MARQUIS *Old Soak's Hist. World* vi. 32 By three therty everybody was under the tabil. **1936** V. W. BROOKS *Flowering of New England* v. 95 He was far from sober, or would have been if two tumblers of brandy had been enough to put him under the table.

7. Usually with defining word, as ***the Lord's table***, ***the holy table***: (*a*) In a church, that upon which the elements are placed at the Communion; the communion table: esp. when the rite is not regarded as a sacrifice (cf. ALTAR 2b); (*b*) *transf.* The Communion.

1340 *Ayenb.* 236 Godes table is þe wyeued. Þe coupe is þe chalis. **1526** TINDALE *1 Cor.* x. 21 Ye cannot be parte takers off the lordes table, and off the table off devyls. **1548–9** (Mar.) *Bk. Comm. Prayer, Communion*, Not suffering them to bee partakers of the Lordes table untill he knowe them to bee reconciled. **1550** *Acts Privy Counc.* (1891) III. 170 That it was convenyent to take downe the aultars as thinges abused, and in liewe of them to sett up tables as thinges moste meete for the Supper of the Lorde, and most agreable to the first constitution. **1552** *Bk. Com. Prayer, Communion*, The Table hauyng at the Communion tyme a fayre white lynnen clothe vpon it. **1678** EVELYN *Diary* 22 Mar., Now was our communion table plac'd altar-wise. *a* **1711** KEN *Edmund* Poet. Wks. 1721 II. 203 Just in the midst was th' Holy Table plac'd, Where it the Past'ral Chair directly fac'd. *a* **1751** DODDRIDGE *Hymn*, My God, and is Thy table spread? **1890** BP. W. W. HOW *Holy Communion* II. 66 You will now have some little space of time for private prayer and meditation,..before you go up to the Holy Table. **1902** T. M. LINDSAY *Ch. & Min. in Early Cent.* vi. 254 After the celebration the faithful, who all remained in the church, came forward to the 'Table'.

b. In Presbyterian churches, applied also to each dispensing of the Sacrament on a Communion Sabbath.

Formerly, it was usual to have three or more 'tables', one after another; it is still common to have two. ***to fence the tables***: see FENCE *v.* 9.

1709 [see FENCE *v.* 9]. **1714** T. BOSTON *Mem.* 24 Aug., I communicated at the fourth table. **1840** R. M^CCHEYNE in *Mem.* v. 133 At the last table every head seemed bent like a bulrush while A. B. spoke.

8. *transf.* A company of persons at a table.

c **1330–1485** [see ROUND TABLE 1c]. **1532** MORE *Confut. Tindale* III. 177 Lyke a iugler that conuayeth his galles so craftely, that all the table spyeth them. **1890** DOYLE *White Company* ix, King Arthur and all his table could not have done more.

b. The company at dinner or at a meal.

1602 SHAKS. *Ham.* V. i. 211 Your flashes of Merriment that were wont to set the Table on a Rore. **1750** JOHNSON *Rambler* No. 75 ¶15 He..carries me the first dish, in defiance of the frowns and whispers of the table. **1778** *Phil. Surv. S. Irel.* 424 His flashes of wit and humour keep the table in a roar.

c. An official body of persons who sit at a table for the transaction of business; = BOARD *sb.* 8b. *Obs.* exc. in special connexions.

the Tables in *Sc. Hist.*, the permanent committees formed in 1638, to defend the Presbyterian system, by whom the *National Covenant* was framed. ***Table of Magnates*** and ***of Deputies***, the two divisions of the former Hungarian Diet.

1606 BRYSKETT *Civ. Life* 8, I myselfe can testifie with how good contentment of all the table you did serue so many yeares. **1640–1** *Kirkcudbr. War-Comm. Min. Bk.* (1855) 40 For the foirsaid ryot,..and for the upbraiding of the table, by saying that he was committit to ward without ane fault. **1647** CLARENDON *Hist. Reb.* III. §52 Committees of dexterous men have been appointed out of the Table to do the business of it. **1654** H. L'ESTRANGE *Chas. I* (1655) 149 In despight of the Kings Proclamation, [they] erected Four Tables, one of the Nobility, another of the Gentry, a third of the Burroughs, a fourth of the Ministers; these four were to prepare and digest what was to be propounded at the General Table. **1665** *Nicholas Papers* (Camden) II. 336 Impositions without parliament, committments by councell table. **1673** *Essex Papers* (Camden) 96 There were then two elections in being, one made by y[e] Lord Mayor in y[e] presence & wth y[e] consent of a Table of Aldermen & Sheriffs, & another by y[e] Lord Mayor singly, in y[e] presence of a Table of Aldermen & Sheriffs. **1890** BLAIR *Bellesheim's Hist. Cath. Ch. Scot.* IV. 5 The National Covenant..was framed by four committees called the Tables.

9. a. A table on which some game of chance is played; a gaming-table; also, the company of players at such a table.

1750 JOHNSON *Rambler* No. 15 ¶11, I perpetually embarrassed my partner, and soon perceived the contempt of the whole table gathering upon me. **1770** FOOTE *Lame Lover* II. Wks. 1799 II. 80 Lady Cicely..has six tables every Sunday. **1826** DISRAELI *Viv. Grey* v. xiii, The plan will be for two to bank against the table. **1879** W. COLLINS *Haunted Hotel* iii. 21 A gambler at every 'table' on the Continent.

b. ***to lay, put*** (or ***play with***) (***all***) ***one's cards on the table***: see CARD *sb.*[2] 2d.

c. *Bridge.* The hand belonging to dummy.

1959 *Listener* 7 May 808/2 The lead of the Queen from the table allows East's K 9 x to be smothered. **1960** T. REESE *Play Bridge with Reese* 127, I play low from table. **1974** *Country Life* 28 Feb. 453/2 South won with the Ace, crossed to the Spade Ace on the table, and led a Club.

*** *A tabulated arrangement or statement.*

10. An arrangement of numbers, words, or items of any kind, in a definite and compact form, so as to exhibit some set of facts or relations in a distinct and comprehensive way, for convenience of study, reference, or calculation. Now chiefly applied to an arrangement in columns and lines occupying a single page or sheet, as the multiplication table, tables of weights and measures, a table of logarithms, astronomical tables, insurance tables, TIME-TABLES, etc. But formerly sometimes merely: An orderly arrangement of particulars, a list.

c **1386** CHAUCER *Frankl. T.* 545 Hise tables tolletanes forth he brought Ful wel corrected ne ther lakked nought. *c* **1391** —— *Astrol.* II. §45 So many ȝeris, monythis, & dayes entere in-to thy tabelis of thy mene mote. *c* **1400** *Prymer* (1891) 13 In this table men mowe knowe..what day schal be Ester day. **1553** EDEN *Treat. Newe Ind.* (Arb.) 8 The most parte of Globes and mappes are made after Ptolomeus Tables. **1617** MORYSON *Itin.* To Rdr., A briefe Table expressing the value of the small Coynes most commonly spent. **1660** J. MOORE *Arith.* II. 5 All decimal Arithmetick is brought to that scale or degree..as appears by the Table in the beginning of my other Book. **1674** The multiplication-table [see MULTIPLICATION 6]. **1712** ADDISON *Spect.* No. 421 ¶8 A

Table of the principal Contents in each Paper. **1758** REID tr. *Macquer's Chem.* I. 159 Explanation of the Table of Affinities. **1808** PIKE *Sources Mississ.* III. 221 A statistical table, on which he had in a regular manner taken the whole province of New Mexico,..giving latitude, longitude, and population. **1858** BUCKLE *Civiliz.* (1864) II. ii. 182 Tables of mortality. **1863-72** WATTS *Dict. Chem.* I. 464 Table of Atomic Weights.

†**b.** *absol.* = *table of contents* (CONTENT *sb.*[1] 2 b): a concise and orderly list of contents, or an index; in quot. 1460 applied to a concordance. *Obs.*

1460 CAPGRAVE *Chron.* (Rolls) 154 He was eke the first begynner of the Concordauns, whech is a tabil onto the Bibil. *c* **1550** H. LLOYD *Treas. Health*, The table of this boke. **1583** (*title*) The Newe Testament..with a Table or Concordance, Englished by L. Tomson. **1614** SELDEN *Titles Hon.* Pref. B iij, Out of the Title, Table, and Contents of the Chapters..the Summe and Method discouer themselues. **1707** MORTIMER *Husb.* (1721) I. 393 A Table to the First Volume. **1824** J. JOHNSON *Typogr.* I. 317 The Work contains three Prologues and a Table, which occupy nine leaves.

†**c.** A statement of particulars or details in a concise form, so as to be exhibited at one view, as in a broadside; a synoptical statement; a document embodying such a statement. In quot. *a* 1577 *fig.* a sketch, plan, scheme. *Obs.*

1560 DAUS tr. *Sleidane's Comm.* XVIII. 260 b, *margin*, The Protestauntes answer to the table of outlawery. *a* **1577** SIR T. SMITH *Commw. Eng.* (1609) 134 This being as a project or table of a Commonwealth truly laid before you. **1593-4** (Mar. 20) *Proclam. Privy Counc.* in Arb. *Garner* I. 299 In this brief Table is set down the punishment appointed for the offenders. **1599** MASSINGER, etc. *Old Law* II. i, He bought a table, indeed, Only to learn to die by 't.

†**d.** ***geographical table***: a map or chart. *Obs.*

1610 HOLLAND *Camden's Brit.* (1637) 106 A chorographicall table or mappe of Britaine. **1654** tr. *Martini's Conq. China* A iij b, I thought it good to prefix a little Geographical table of the Countries, and chief Cities, which might serve as a guide to conduct the eye of the understanding.

e. *tables*: the common arithmetical tables, as the multiplication table and those of money, weights, and measures, esp. as learnt at school.

1828 MISS MITFORD *Village* Ser. III. 125 (*Village Schoolmistress*) She is going to be a governess..and it's to be hoped the little ladies will take kindly to their tables. **1893** K. GRAHAME *Pagan Papers* (1894) 127 He had 'gone into tables', and had been endowed with a new slate.

f. = *league table* s.v. LEAGUE *sb.*[2] 5.

1951 *Sport* 6-12 Apr. 10/4 Mr. Drake has been the guiding light behind a remarkable revival that has taken the club soaring up the table. **1972** G. GREEN *Great Moments in Sport: Soccer* v. 62 Around Christmas, they had begun to catch a tide of success as they crept slowly up the table. **1976** *Western Mail* (Cardiff) 27 Nov. 20/2 Newcastle, third in the table thanks to their midweek win over Everton.

II. Special and technical senses (chiefly arising out of sense 1).

†**11.** *pl.* **tables**, formerly the ordinary name of BACKGAMMON (*Obs.* since *c* 1750); app. orig. the 'men' or pieces used in playing early forms of this game: cf. med.L. *tabulæ*, OF. *tables*, ON. *tafla*, pl. *töflur*, in same sense.

Chiefly in the phr. ***to play at (the) tables***, OF. *juer as tables* (*Chans. Rol.* 11th c.). In this application the name has in later use been often associated with sense 4 b.

[*a* **700** *Epinal Gl.* 6 *Alea* teblae. *c* **725** *Corp. Gl.* 110 *Alea* tebl.] **1297** R. GLOUC. (Rolls) 3965 Wiþ pleynge atte tables oþer atte chekere. *a* **1300** *Cursor M.* 28338 (Cott.), I ha me liked..til idel gammes, chess and tablis. **1330** R. BRUNNE *Chron. Wace* (Rolls) 11392 Somme pleide wyþ des & tables. *c* **1386** CHAUCER *Parson's T.* ¶719 Now comth hasardrie with hise apurtenances as tables and Rafles. **1472** *Surtees Misc.* (1888) 25 John Coke suffers men to play in his hous at the tablez for mony by nyghtes. *a* **1548** HALL *Chron., Hen. VIII* 149 b, A proclamacion..against al vnlawfull games..in all places, Tables, Dice, Cardes, and Boules, were taken and brent. **1665** PEPYS *Diary* 21 Sept., After losing a crowne betting at Tables, we walked home. **1700** S. L. tr. *Fryke's Voy. E. Ind.* 10 Tables & Draughts are allowed, yet must they not play at them for Money. **1808** SCOTT *Marm.* I. xxii, Full well at tables can he play, And sweep at bowls the stake away.

12. *Arch.* **a.** A general term for a horizontal projecting course or moulding, as a cornice; a string-course. Usually with defining word, as *base-table*, *bench-t.*, *corbel-t.*, *earth-t.*, *grass-t.*, *ground-t.*, *water-t.*: see these words.

13.. *Gaw. & Gr. Knt.* 789 Ande eft a ful huge heȝt hit haled vpon lofte, Of harde hewen ston vp to þe tablez. **1447-8** Corbel table [see CORBEL *sb.* 3]. **1640** Ground-table [see GROUND *sb.* 18]. **1688** R. HOLME *Armoury* III. 472/1 The Foot Table, is a Square Corner standing out at the bottom, or middle sides of the Gable end. **1845** PARKER *Gloss. Archit.* (ed. 3) 357 The word table, when used separately without any adjunctive term to point out its position, appears to have signified the cornice, but it is very usually associated with other epithets which define its situation, as *base-table*, *earth-table*, or *ground-table*, *bench-table*, *corbel-table*, &c. *Ibid.*, *Earth Table*, or *Ground Table*, and *Grass Table*, the plinth of a wall.., or lowest course of projecting stones immediately above the ground.

b. A member consisting of a flat vertical surface, usually of rectangular form, plain or ornamented, sunk in or projecting beyond the general surface of a wall, etc.; a panel.

1678 MOXON *Mech. Exerc.* No. 6. 113 In Plate 6. *s* is the Table. **1703** MAUNDRELL *Journ. Jerus.* (1721) 37 A large Table plain'd in the side of the Rock. **1727-41** CHAMBERS *Cycl.* s.v. *Pedestal*, The generality of architects..use tables or pannels, either in relievo or creux, in the dyes of pedestals. **1823** P. NICHOLSON *Pract. Build.* 594 Table, projecting or raised. *Ibid.*, Table, raking; one not perpendicular to the horizon. **1876** GWILT *Archit.* Gloss. s.v., When the surface is rough, frosted, or vermiculated, from being broken with the hammer, it is called a *rusticated table*.

13. †**a.** A plot of ground for planting; a bed. Cf. TABLEMEAL. *Obs. rare.*

c **1440** *Pallad. on Husb.* I. 810 Mark oute thi tables [*gloss* beddes], ichon by hem selve. *Ibid.* II. 99 [heading *De tabulis vinearum*] The tables for thi vynes maist thou make..as the list, or as thi lande Wol axe.

b. A flat elevated tract of land; a table-land, plateau; a flat mountain-top; also *Geol.* applied to a horizontal stratum.

1587 HARRISON *England* I. i. 1/2 Albeit the continent hereof..lieth as it were a long table betweene the two seas. **1607** TOPSELL *Four-f. Beasts* (1658) 428 There was a Region, called by Ptolemeus, *Randa marcostra*, wherein he placeth the eleventh Table of Asia. **1634** SIR T. HERBERT *Trav.* 13 The ascent to the Sugar-loafe and Table [Table Mountain], two Hils so named. **1869** TOZER *Highl. Turkey* I. 155 A valley..nearly..filled up from side to side by a level table of land. **1888** J. D. WHITNEY *Names & Places* 181 (Cent. D.) The flat summits of mountains are sometimes called 'tables', and especially in California, where there are several 'table mountains'..capped usually with horizontal or table-like masses of basalt.

c. A flat hedge-bank: see quot. *dial.*

1844 STEPHENS *Bk. Farm* II. 574 The hedger lays them, with the grass side downwards, upon the edges of the set-sods,..pushing them under and as if to support the thorn roots with them. These..are called the *table*.

14. *Palmistry.* The quadrangular space between certain lines in the palm of the hand: see quots., and cf. *table-line* in 22.

c **1460** METHAM *Wks.* 86 The fourthe lyne ys the tabyl lyne, for that parte off the hand ys clepyd the tabyl the qwyche ys be-twene the myd lyne and the tabyl lyne. **1596** SHAKS. *Merch. V.* II. ii. 167 If anie man in Italie haue a fairer table which doth offer to sweare vpon a booke, I shall haue good fortune. **1625** SHIRLEY *Love Tricks* V. i. (1631) 63 In this table Lies your story; 'tis no fable, Not a line within your hand But I easily vnderstand. **1653** R. SANDERS *Physiogn.* 87 This space is called the Table of the hand, which hath on the one side the Mensal Line, on the other the middle Natural Line. **1883** FRITH & HERON-ALLEN *Chiromancy* 138 The Quadrangle is that portion of the human hand comprised between the line of the Head and the line of the Heart, and between the line of Fate and the line of Apollo. It is sometimes called the table of the Hand.

15. †**a.** A small cake of some drug or confection: = TABLET *sb.* 3. *Obs.*

1580 FRAMPTON *Monardi's Dial. Yron* 162 Then take a small table of rosade of a sweete smel. **1621** VENNER *Tobacco* (1650) 410 Tables made with an Ounce or two of fine sugar dissolved in Fennell water.

b. A large flat circular disk, plate, or sheet of crown-glass, being the form in which it is made.

1688 R. HOLME *Armoury* III. 385/2 A *Table* is a broad peece of Glass neere a yard, some more, square, it is also called a Tablet. **1727-41** CHAMBERS *Cycl.* s.v. *Glass*, The number of tables annealed at a time. *Ibid.*, Ratcliff crown glass..the tables being of a circular form, about three foot six inches in diameter. **1823** P. NICHOLSON *Pract. Build.* 420 The glass is bought by the crate, which consists of twelve tables. **1890** W. J. GORDON *Foundry* 144 The 'table' of crown glass is from four to five feet across.

c. A crystal of flattened or short prismatic form.

1796 KIRWAN *Elem. Min.* (ed. 2) I. 362 Crystallized in rhomboidal tables. **1805-17** R. JAMESON *Char. Min.* (ed. 3) 106 Table..is but a very short prism. **1857** MILLER *Elem. Chem.* (1862) III. 542 The acid benzoate of potash..in colourless, pearly tables,..sparingly soluble in water.

d. A sheet (of lead).

1809 BAWDWEN *Domesday Bk.* 294 These manors paid in King Edward's time..five cartloads of lead of fifty tables [orig. *v plaustratas plumbi de l tabulis*].

16. *Anat.* Each of the two dense bony layers of the skull, separated by the diploë.

1612 WOODALL *Surg. Mate* Wks. (1653) 3 If a Fracture happen in the Cranium, with contusion and depression of both the Tables thereof. **1799** HOOPER *Med. Dict.*, *Diploe*..the spongy substance between the two tables of the skull. **1898** *Syd. Soc. Lex.* s.v., The inner or vitreous table is compared to porcelain, and is close-grained and brittle.

17. A flat plate, board, or the like, forming part of a mechanism or apparatus.

†**a.** The face or dial-plate of a clock or watch.

a **1677** HALE *Prim. Orig. Man.* IV. iv. 326 To fit the Table with Divisions suitable to the Hours. *Ibid.* vi. 341 The Wheels, and the Ballance, and the Case, and Table.

b. In various manufactures, A flat metal plate (often movable or adjustable) for supporting something to be operated upon, etc.; the plate with a raised rim on which plate-glass is made.

1727-41 CHAMBERS *Cycl.* s.v. *Glass*, The table of glass is now in its last perfection... When taken out, they lay it on a table of copper. **1832** G. R. PORTER *Porcelain & Gl.* 200 Another essential part of the apparatus consists in flat tables whereon the plates of glass are cast. **1833** J. HOLLAND *Manuf. Metal* II. 238 By turning the wheel, the table E is drawn between the cylinders, the counterpoise F rising accordingly. **1839** URE *Dict. Arts* 590 Whenever the melted glass is poured out, two men spread it over the table. **1877** KNIGHT *Dict. Mech.* 2477/2 The shaping-machine..has two tables for holding work both of which are movable up and down..and longitudinally. **1892** [see *table-loader* in 22].

c. (See quot.)

1763 MILLS *Pract. Husb.* I. 332 M. Duhamel's drill is fastened to the fore-carriage of a common plough. The hind part consists of a plank..at least three inches thick, which is called the table.

d. In an organ: (*a*) The upper part of the sound-board, above the sound-board bars and grooves, perforated with holes for admitting air to the pipes. (In quot. 1852 applied to the sound-board bars.) (*b*) The upper board of the bellows.

1852 SEIDEL *Organ* 52 These partitions are called *grooves*, and the ledges..by which they are separated, *tables*. **1881** C. A. EDWARDS *Organs* 49 The top of the sound-board, technically called the table. **1881** W. E. DICKSON *Organ-Build.* vi. 72 Organ-bellows..consist of three main boards, namely, the middle board, the top board or table [etc.].

e. 'The board or bar in a draw-loom to which the tails of the harness are attached' (Knight, 1877).

f. *Shipbuilding.* = COAK *sb.* 1, q.v.

Cf. TABLE *v.* 6, TABLING *vbl. sb.* 7.

g. ***plain table*** (surveying instrument): see PLANE-TABLE.

18. a. The upper horizontal surface of a table diamond or a brilliant. **b.** Short for TABLE DIAMOND; also applied to other precious stones cut in a similar form.

1530 *Lett. & Pap. Hen. VIII*, IV. No. 6789 (P.R.O.), iiij diamantes wherof ij poynted and ij tables. **1538** *Acc. Ld. High Treas. Scotl.* VII. 14 Ane grete diamand sett in table for the quenis spousing ring. **1703** *Lond. Gaz.* No. 3929/4 Two single Stone Diamond Rings, Tables. **1751** D. JEFFERIES *Treat. Diamonds* (ed. 2) Explan. Techn. Terms, The Table is the large horizontal plane, or face, at the top of the Brilliant. **1861** W. POLE in *Macm. Mag.* III. 184/2 The apex of the upper pyramid is cut off to a considerable extent, and the large facet thus formed is called the *table*. **1904** *19th Cent.* July 136 A necklace of carnelian, 'cut in tables', is deemed worthy of being handed down to posterity as an heirloom.

19. *Perspective.* A name for the perspective plane, or 'plane of the picture': see PLANE *sb.*[3] 1 d. (Cf. sense 3.) ? *Obs.*

1727-41 CHAMBERS *Cycl.*, *Table*, in perspective denotes a plain surface, supposed to be transparent, and perpendicular to the horizon. **1876** in GWILT *Archit.* Gloss.

20. = TABULA 2.

1891 in *Cent. Dict.*

III. *attrib.* and *Comb.*

21. a. Simple attrib.: in sense 5, 'of a table': as ***table-drawer***, ***-edge***, ***-head***, ***-leg***; in sense 6, 'of the dinner-table': as ***table-companion***, ***-fellow*** (***-fellowship***), ***-friend***, ***-guest***, ***-jester***, ***-mate***, ***-parasite***, ***-patron***, †***-peer*** (= -companion), ***-servant***, ***-steward***, ***-waiter***; 'at or round the table': as ***table argument***, ***collection***, ***conference***, ***conversation***, ***fellowship***, ***gratification***, ***philosophy***; of implements, etc. used at table, as ***table cutlery***, ***decoration***, ***-fork***, ***-furniture***, ***-garnish***, ***mat***, ***runner***; of articles of food or drink, consumed or adapted for consumption at table, as ***table ale***, ***beer***, ***bird***, ***cider***, ***dainty***, ***delicacy***, ***drink***, ***fish***, ***fruit***, ***-grape***, ***honey***, ***mustard***, ***potato***, ***salt***; in sense 10: ***table look-up*** (LOOK-UP 2). **b.** Objective, etc., as ***table-jogging***, ***-serving***, ***-setting***, etc.; ***table-thumping*** adj. and sb. **c.** Having the form of a table; having a wide horizontal surface on which things may be placed, as ***table-cabinet***, ***-piano(forte)***, ***-stage***, etc.; ***table-formed***, ***table-like*** adjs.

1547 SALESBURY *Welsh Dict.*, *Ailcwrwf*, *table ale. **1848** DICKENS *Dombey* xviii, Mrs. Wickam..takes more table-ale than usual. **1632** *Star Chamb. Cases* (Camden) 100 It is hard I confesse to call in question for all that is spoaken at table; and yet this should not have been a *table argument. **1643** in *10th Rep. Hist. MSS. Comm.* App. IV. 435, 2 hogsheades of stronge beere, 1 hogshead of *table beere. **1830** M. DONOVAN *Dom. Econ.* I. 207 Table-beer should have the characters of an ale, not of porter. **1884** *St. James' Gaz.* 22 Aug. 4/2 The capercailzie..as a *table bird..will prove a disappointment. **1851** MANTELL *Petrifact.* iii. §1. 136 The floor [of a room in Brit. Mus.] being occupied by twenty-six *Table-cabinets. **1902** *Daily Chron.* 17 May 6/4 There are many families who make it a habit to have a *table collection each week for some religious or philanthropic work. **1656** BLOUNT *Glossogr.*, *Commensal*, a *Table-companion. **1861** THACKERAY *Four Georges* iv. (1876) 107 His next set of friends were mere table companions. **1712** ADDISON *Spect.* No. 495 ¶9 This shuts them out from all *Table Conversation. **1861** *Chicago Tribune* 10 July 1/9 Crockery Ware, *Table Cutlery, Plated Ware, &c. **1946** A. CHRISTIE *Come, tell me how you Live* vii. 116 Civilisation's invention of table cutlery presents a perpetual headache to a worried house-boy. **1802** WOLCOTT (P. Pindar) *Ld. Belgrave & Motions* Wks. 1812 IV. 523 Every *table-dainty, flesh and fish. **1937** C. SPRY *Flowers in House & Garden* 169 Your choice of *table decorations is bound to be influenced by..your guests. **1979** I. WEBB *Compl. Guide Flower & Foliage Arrangement* vii. 97/2 'Frensham' roses and ivy berries combine to make an arresting table decoration. *c* **1813** MRS. SHERWOOD *Stories Ch. Catech.* xvi. 137 To look in the *table-drawer, for a little book. **1817** LADY MORGAN *France* I. (1818) I. 65 The *table-drink of the poorest peasantry. **1935** H. H. BASHFORD *Lodgings for Twelve* 87 George Gedge's Wiltshire guile and a miraculous succession of *table-edge strokes. **1977** F. ORMSBY *Store of Candles* 30 Resumes his beat from table-edge to door, From door to table. **1592** G. HARVEY *Four Lett.* Wks. (Grosart) I. 208 The *Table-fellow of Duke Humfrey, & Tantalus, might learne of him to curse Iupiter. **1863** HAWTHORNE *Our Old Home* (1879) 356, I was meditating in what way this grisly featured table-fellow might..be accosted. **1903** *Hibbert Jrnl.* Mar. 614 James's scruples about *table-fellowship between

Jewish and Gentile believers in Gal. ii. 12. **1770** *Boston Gaz.* 15 Jan. 2/3 **Table fish* warranted the very best, To be Sold at the Store the Corner of Kilby-Street. **1872** F. F. VICTOR *All over Oregon* 63 Besides the salmon of commerce, the Columbia furnishes a great many other species of edible fish ..all of which are excellent table-fish in their proper seasons. **1897** *Outing* (U.S.) XXX. 435/2 Pickerel were better table-fish. **1785** *Daily Universal Reg.* 1 Jan. 3/2 Ivory *table knives and forks. **1842** J. AITON *Domest. Econ.* (1857) 110 The scones should be pricked with a table-fork or small pointed wooden pin. *a* **1843** SOUTHEY *Comm.-pl. Bk.* (1849) IV. 408 The mountains are *table-formed. **1586** T. B. *La Primaud. Fr. Acad.* I. (1594) 135 We must shun such parasites, who are but saluting and *table friends. **1707** MORTIMER *Husb.* (1721) II. 293 The Fig-apple is a good *Table-Fruit. **1861** *Our Eng. Home* 11 The *table garnish was not very extensive, a few wooden platters, some knives and spoons..were the principal articles. **1926** *Zionist Rev.* Apr. 144/2 Splendid prospects exist for good *table-grapes in those parts of Palestine where the Jewish urban population is growing. **1979** *Tucson Mag.* Apr. 20/2 An attractive feature..is the possibility that vineyards will be a 'dryland crop', using considerably less water than table grapes. **1773** MELMOTH *Remarks on Cato* 229 (Jod.) A moderate indulgence..in the *table gratifications. *a* **1592** GREENE *Jas. IV*, Wks. (Rtldg.) 188/1, I found *table-guests to eat me and my meat. **1733** SWIFT *On Poetry* 264 Battus from the *table-head,..Gives judgment with decisive air. **1865** KINGSLEY *Herew.* xix, At the table-head..sat..the new Lord of Bourne. **1571** GOLDING *Calvin on Ps.* xxxv. 16 Y^e *tablejesters, which gave their verdict of his death among the cups. **1891** *Pall Mall G.* 29 Oct. 2/1 There was a certain amount of *table-jogging and spilling of liquors. *c* **1870** TENNYSON in *Daily News* 1 Mar. (1898) 7/5, I am convinced that God and the ghosts of men would choose something other than mere *table-legs through which to speak to the heart of man. **1957** D. D. MCCRACKEN *Digital Computer Programming* xvii. 200 The code number is placed in one of the arithmetic registers and a *table look-up instruction given. **1967** COX & GROSE *Organization & Handling Bibl. Rec. by Computer* VI. 142 These will be linked with 'table-look-ups' within the output programs to translate each symbol into a full form. **1779** in *Dict. Amer. Eng.* (1938) s.v. *Table* n., *Table mat. **1834** DICKENS *Bloomsbury Christening* in *Monthly Mag.* Apr. 380 A front drawing-room, very prettily furnished with a plentiful sprinkling of little baskets, paper table-mats, [etc.]..on the different tables. **1965** A. NICOL *Truly Married Woman* 5 She remembered the wine glasses and the beer-advertising table-mats in time and put those under the sofa. **1624** GATAKER *Mariage Praier* 19 [Woman] was..giuen to man, not to be a play-fellow, or a bed-fellow, or a *table-mate, onely with him,..but to be a yoake-fellow, a worke-fellow, a fellow-labourer with him. **1797** *Encycl. Brit.* (ed. 3) XIII. 192/1 Leaving a cake behind, fit for making the common *table-mustard. **1751** WARBURTON in *Pope's Wks.* (1806) IV. 7 A detected Slanderer, a *Table-Parasite, a Church-Buffoon, and a Party-Writer. **1576** FLEMING *Panopl. Epist.* 14, I knowe you are no *table patrones. **1605** SYLVESTER *Du Bartas* II. iii. *Law* 843 God's pensioner, and Angel's *Table-peer, O Israel! **1576** R. JOHNES (*title*) The Schoolemaster; or Teacher of *Table Philosophie. **1593** G. HARVEY *Pierce's Super.* Wks. (Grosart) II. 34 It is another Table-Philosophy, that I fansie. **1911** *Daily Colonist* (Victoria, B.C.) 27 Apr. 11/7 The hotel furniture consists of.. blankets, sheets, spreads, pillows, toilet sets in 60 rooms, 1 *table piano, card tables, [etc.]. **1952** J. GLOAG *Short Dict. Furniture* 468 Table pianos were designed to conceal the fact that they were musical instruments: when closed they looked like clumsy and ill-proportioned tables. **1976** *Early Music* Oct. 483/1, I find the choice of cover picture oddly revealing: a small table-piano ordered by an aristocrat for his children. **1851** *Official Catal., Gt. Exhib.* III. 1225/1 Patent square and console pianofortes; square and hexagonal *table pianofortes. **1807** VANCOUVER *Agric. Devon* (1813) 200 The produce of the *table potatoe crop seldom falls short of 350 bushels. **1889** *Table runner [see RUNNER 14c]. **1939** W. FORTESCUE *There's Rosemary* xliv. 259, I cut lengths of brocatello, designed cushions and table-runners, &c. **1967** E. SHORT *Embroidery & Fabric Collage* iii. 63 Small mats, table runners, *Radio Times* covers are quite unnecessary. **1878** GURNEY *Crystallogr.* 84 Common *table salt crystallises in this form. **1882** FLOYER *Unexpl. Baluchistan* 163 He had appointed himself *table servant. **1907** *Philippine Education* Sept. 46/1 We had a few lessons in *table-setting. **1867** J. HOGG *Microsc.* I. ii. 88 Below the *table-stage is the secondary or sub-stage. **1963** *Time* 2 Aug. 17/2 The changeover from Stalin, the 'oriental despot', to Khruschev, the *table-thumping but jolly politician. **1964** A. BATTERSBY *Network Analysis* ix. 137 The Esso team..do claim with confidence that resources are utilized more effectively than before,..and that, in general, there is less table-thumping. **1928** D. H. LAWRENCE *Woman who rode Away* 15 The sister was all that could be desired as..an upper parlour-maid, and a *table-waiter. **1975** *Budget* (Sugarcreek, Ohio) 20 Mar. 1/4 Tablewaiters were David F. Yoder, Susie Bontreger, [etc.].

d. Designed to stand on a table, as ***table lamp***, ***lighter***, ***model***, ***stand***.

c **1849** J. S. COYNE *How to settle Accts. with your Laundress* 3 Table at back, L., on which is a table lamp. **1854** C. M. YONGE *Heartsease* I. II. i. 102 A pretty little rosewood work-table, on which was..a table-stand of books. **1907** *Yesterday's Shopping* (1969) 1150/3 Folding Music Stands. .. Table stand... Brass 7/6. **1922** A. BENNETT *Lilian* II. vii. 119 It was the silver table-lamps..that impressed her. **1929** *Radio Times* 8 Nov. 437/1 The table model Columbia is.. the most advanced radio of the day. **1951** *Catal. Exhibits, South Bank Exhib., Festival of Britain* 147/2 Shagreen table lighter. **1954** 'N. BLAKE' *Whisper in Gloom* I. vii. 99 Applying his cigar to a massive table-lighter. **1962** A. NISBETT *Technique Sound Studio* i. 30 There are four types of microphone mounting. These are: (i) The table stand, [etc.]. **1967** P. CHAMBERS *Bad die Young* i. 11 A grateful client had given me a heavy bronze table lighter. **1976** 'W. TREVOR' *Children of Dynmouth* iii. 60 Only a table-lamp burned, its weak bulb not up to the task of fully illuminating the room. **1977** D. E. WESTLAKE *Nobody's Perfect* 10 He'd cased that TV repair shop—he'd even brought in a perfectly good Sony table model and let them charge him for six new tubes.

e. Designating various games played on a table, which simulate more or less closely the action of some sport, as ***table football***, ***hockey***, etc. See also *table-game*, *-tennis*, sense 22 below.

1907 *Yesterday's Shopping* (1969) 1032/2 Wibley Wob or Table Football. A game for 2 or 4 players, to be placed upon an ordinary dining table. **1948** *Sporting Mirror* 21 May 10/3 (Advt.), Send 3d. stamp for full details of *Subbuteo* the game of Table Soccer... Played with 22 miniature men, ball and goals. **1949** S. F. COLLIS (*title*) Proper channels for the distribution of 'table hockey'. **1956** H. & L. EIZENBERG *Omnibus of Fun* xvii. 343 Table Hockey. This ping-pong blow game can have four teams on rectangular table. **1976** DEAKIN & WILLIS *Johnny go Home* i. 27 The biggest amusement arcade he had ever seen..the metropolitan mecca of pinball and table football.

22. Special Combs.: **table-allowance**, an allowance of money for provisions (= *table money* (*a*)); **table-almanac**, an almanac on a single sheet or card; **table-anvil**, 'a small anvil adapted to be screwed to a table for bending plates of metal or wires, making small repairs, etc.' (Knight 1877); † **table balas**: see BALAS, and cf. TABLE DIAMOND, RUBY; **table-bat** [BAT *sb.*^{2} 11], ? a horizontal stratum of 'bat' or shale in a bed of coal; **table bed** see quot. 1773; **table bell**, a small hand-bell placed upon the table for summoning attendants; **table-bit**: see quot.; **table carpet**, a woollen table-cloth (see CARPET *sb.* 1); also, a decorative table-cloth of other material (now *Hist.*); **table-centre**, a piece of embroidery, decorated work, etc., for the centre of a table, placed over the table-cloth; **table centrepiece**, a decorative piece placed at the centre of a table, esp. one arrayed with flowers, etc.; **table-chair** = *chair table* s.v. CHAIR *sb.*^{1} 15; **table-churn**, a churn placed upon a table; **table-clamp**, a clamp for fastening something to a table; **table-clock**, a clock that is or may be placed on a table; **table-couch**, a couch for reclining on a table; **table-counter**, a counter of the form of a table; **table cover**, a cloth of wool or other fabric used for covering a table permanently or when not in use for meals (= TABLE-CLOTH b); † **table-coverer**, an attendant who 'covered' the table, i.e. laid the cloth, etc. for a meal (see COVER *v.*^{1} 2d); **table-crumb**, a crumb that falls from the table at a meal; **table-decker** = *table-coverer*, esp. in the Royal Household (now *rare*); **table desk**, (*a*) a desk with a broad, flat top; (*b*) a kind of folding writing-box that opens to provide a sloping desk-top, for use on a table; **table-discourse**, discourse at table, table-talk; **table-faced** *a.* = TABLE-CUT (see sense 18); **table-flap**, a hinged flap or 'leaf' at the end or side of a table, which can be raised so as to extend the surface; **table game**, a game played on a table or similar surface, usu. with balls, counters, or other pieces (and sometimes distinguished from card- or board-games); † **table-gesture** [GESTURE *sb.* 2], posture or attitude at table, i.e. at a meal; **table-glass**, (*a*) glass made in 'tables' (see 15b), crown-glass; (*b*) a glass (drinking-vessel) for use at table; † **table-gospeller**, one who makes table-talk of the gospel; one whose religion is mere talk; **table-grinder**, 'a form of grinding-bench' (Knight *Dict. Mech.* 1877); **table-ground**, flat elevated ground (cf. TABLE-LAND); **table hand**, (*a*) *N.Z. Sheep-shearing*: in a wool-shed, one who helps the fleece-picker to skirt and roll the fleeces; (*b*) *Printing*, a bindery assistant; **table-hop** *v. intr. U.S. colloq.*, to go from table to table in a restaurant, meeting the diners (cf. *island-hop* s.v. ISLAND *sb.* 4); also **table-hopping** *vbl. sb.*; **table jelly**, a flavoured jelly served at table as a sweet; a commercial preparation for making this; **table-knife**, a knife used at table, esp. one of the shape or size used in cutting the meat small; **table-knight**, a knight who sits at some one's table, *spec.* at the ROUND TABLE; **table-lathe**, a small lathe clamped to a table when in use; **table-leaf** [LEAF *sb.* 12c], (*a*) = *table-flap*; (*b*) any additional piece which can be inserted so as to extend the surface of a table; also *attrib.* **table-leaf joint**, the form of joint, with one part convex and the other concave, used in a hinged table-leaf; **table-lifting**, the lifting of a table by supposed spiritual agency (cf. TABLE-TURNING); **table-line**, in *Palmistry*, a line running from beneath the little finger to the base of the index-finger, forming the upper boundary of the 'table'; **table-linen**, linen for use at table, as table-cloths and table-napkins; **table-loader**, one who loads the hoist-table of a lift; **table-maid**, a domestic servant who lays the table and waits at meals; **table-maker**, a joiner who makes tables; **table manners** *sb. pl.* orig. *U.S.*, behaviour or deportment at table, judged according to accepted standards of propriety; **table-matter** (*Printing*) = *table-work*; **table-money**, (*a*) an extra allowance of money made to the higher officers in the British army and navy for table expenses; (*b*) a charge made in some clubs for the use of the dining-room; also, an extra charge in some restaurants or on board ship; † **table-monument**, a monument consisting of a 'table' (sense 2a); a monumental tablet; **tablemount** *Oceanogr.* = GUYOT; **table-mountain**, a flat-topped mountain; *spec.* the name of the mountain which rises behind Cape Town; **table-moving**, the moving of a table by supposed spiritual agency (cf. TABLE-TURNING); **table-music**, music in parts, so printed (as in some early books of madrigals, etc.) that the performers, sitting at opposite sides of a table, can read their respective parts from the same page or opening; **table-napery** = *table-linen*; **table napkin**, a napkin used at meals to protect the clothes from being soiled, to wipe the fingers, etc.; **Table Office**: in the House of Commons, the office in which the civil servants work whose duties include the preparation of the Notice Paper and the Order Book; by extension, the Office personified by its clerks; **table officer** *Canad.*, any of the principal officers in an organization (cf. BOARD *sb.* 8); **table-pew**, a large pew containing the communion-table, as formerly usual in some Presbyterian and other churches; † **table-picture**, a picture painted on a 'table' (sense 3); **table-plain**, an elevated plain, a table-land; **table-plan**, a seating plan for those attending a formal meal; **table-plane**, a plane for making rule-joints in table-flaps, etc.; **table-plank**, a plank serving as a table when placed upon supports; cf. 6b; **table-plate**, (*a*) articles of plate (PLATE *sb.* 16), for use at meals; (*b*) a plate (usually of earthenware) from which food is eaten at table; (*c*) a flat metal plate on which pulverized gold or silver ore is treated with mercury in the process of amalgamation; † **table-play**, play at 'tables' or backgammon; so † **table-player**, † **tables-playing**; **table-prayers**, a name for the communion service, or a part of it, read at the communion-table, but without administration; † **table-rent**: see quot.; **table rock**, a flat-topped rock; † **table-room**, room or place at table, i.e. at meals; board; **table-saw**, a small saw fitted to a table and worked by a treadle; **table-screen**, (*a*) a trestle table in a wool-shed; (*b*) *Chinese Ceramics* (see quot. 1974); **table-service**, (*a*) the Communion service (in Presbyterian churches); (*b*) service or attendance at table; (*c*) a set of utensils for the table, as a dinner-service; **table-setting**, (*a*) the activity of setting a table: see sense 21b; (*b*) the cutlery, napery, etc., required to set a place at table; **table-shore**, *Naut.*, a low level shore; **table-sod**, in hedging, one of the sods forming the 'table' (sense 13c); **table-song**, (*a*) *Gr. Antiq.*, a song sung by the guests at a banquet in turn; (*b*) a part-song such as is sung in a German *liedertafel* or choral society (*Cent. Dict.*); **table-spar**, a name for WOLLASTONITE, also called *tabular spar*, occurring in 'tables' or flat crystals; **table-sport**, sport or play at table; in quot., an object of sport or mockery at table, the butt or laughing-stock of a company; **table stake** *Poker* (see quot. 1885); **table tape** *Computers*, a magnetic tape containing tabulated numerical information for use in computations; **table-tapping** = TABLE-RAPPING; **table-tennis**, a game resembling lawn-tennis, played upon a table: = PING-PONG; **table-tilting**, **-tipping**, the tilting or tipping of a table by supposed spiritual agency (cf. TABLE-TURNING); so **table-tipper**, one who practises table-tipping; **table-tomb**, a tomb in the Roman catacombs containing a burial-chest with a flat cover; any tomb in some way resembling a table; **table-top**, (*a*) the upper surface of a table; (*b*) a flat top of a hill, rock, etc.; see also TABLE-TOP *a.*; **table-topped** (-tɒpt) *a.*, having a flat top like that of a table; **table-tree**, an adjustable table-like rest mounted on a lathe; **table-turf** = *table-sod*; **table-vessel**, a vessel for use at table; †such vessels collectively (*obs.*); **table-water**, water (*esp.* a mineral water) suitable for drinking at table; **table-wheel**: see quot.; **table wine**, wine suitable for drinking with a meal, esp. plain wine which is not fortified or sparkling; a wine of this class; cf. TAFELWEIN, *vin de table* s.v. VIN 3; **table-work**

(*Printing*), the setting up of tables (sense 10), or of matter between column rules; *concr.* printed matter of this kind, as distinguished from ordinary letterpress. See also TABLE-BOARD, -BOOK, -CLOTH, etc.

1810 Wellington in Gurw. *Desp.* (1838) V. 598, I beg that you will draw a *table allowance of thirty shillings a day. **1621** *Stationers' Register* (Arb.) IV. 11 *Table almanacke on a sheet of paper. **1530** *Lett. & Papers Hen. VIII*, IV. No. 6789 (P.R.O.) A goodly carkeyn with a fayr *table balasse. **1712** F. Bellers in *Phil. Trans.* XXVII. 542 The *Table-Bat, next under the Rubble Iron-Stone. **1714** E. Postlethwayt *Let.* 5 Mar. in E. Pyle *Mem. Royal Chaplain* (1905) 33 Pray take care of putting up the *Table Bed, put nothing in but what belongs to it. **1773** Johnson, *Tablebed*, a bed of the figure of a table. **1779** in *Dict. Amer. Eng.* (1938), *Table bell. **1832** *Chambers's Edin. Jrnl.* I. 236/2 This minikin table-bell, which I must have unconsciously pocketed. **1858** Simmonds *Dict. Trade*, *Table-bell*, a small hand-bell for summoning domestics or office attendants. **1843** Holtzapffel *Turning* II. xxiv. 539 The spoon-bit.. the *table-bit, for making the holes for the wooden joints of tables, [is] of this kind. **1715** J. Chappelow *Rt. Way Rich* (1717) 144 *Table-carpets or bed-coverlets. **1967** E. Short *Embroidery & Fabric Collage* iii. 74 Great families worked their own table carpets in tent stitch on canvas sometimes incorporating their coats of arms into the design. **1901** *Lady's Realm* X. 616 This white satin *table-centre is decorated with ribbon, lace, braid, and embroidery. **1917** *Harrods Gen. Catal.* 882 *Table centre pieces and vases. Finest English hand-made cut crystal. **1979** E. Taylor in I. Webb *Compl. Guide Flower & Foliage Arrangement* viii. 104/3 The table centre-piece holds Norway spruce, variegated holly and berries, pine cones and red ribbons. **1671** in *Farm & Cottage Inventories of Mid-Essex 1635–1749* (1950) (Essex Record Office Publ. No. 8) 120 In The Hall —..one *Table-chaire. **1836** S. S. Arnold in *Proc. Vermont Hist. Soc.* (1940) VIII. 125 Father gave me his old table-chair. **1962** 'K. Orvis' *Damned & Destroyed* v. 35 Shabby men and women sat in white table-chairs. **1844** Stephens *Bk. Farm* III. 906 For this purpose, there is perhaps none better than the *Table-churn. **1774** *Chron.* in *Ann. Reg.* 121/1 A *table-clock, a silver spoon, and a silk gown. **1877** C. Geikie *Christ* lviii. (1879) 704 Lazarus reclined with him on the *table-couch. **1667** in Pettus *Fodinæ Reg.* (1670) 36 One *Table-counter with Cupboards, Shelves, etc. **1848** C. H. Hartshorne *Eng. Med. Embroidery* 126 The manner commonly used in braiding *table covers. **1851** Mayhew *Lond. Labour* I. 388 Sellers of Japanned table-covers... The glazed table-covers. **1864** Webster, *Table-cover*, a cloth for covering a table, especially at other than meal-times. **1737** J. Chamberlayne *St. Gt. Brit.* (ed. 33) II. III. 220 *Table-Coverer to the Chaplains. **1726–46** Thomson *Winter* 255 Till, more familiar grown, the *table-crums Attract his [the redbreast's] slender feet. **1804** J. Grahame *Sabbath* (1808) 34 Where little birds.. Light on the floor, and peck the table-crumbs. **1737** J. Chamberlayne *St. Gt. Brit.* (ed. 33) II. III. 228 *Table-Deckers. **1843** Macaulay *Ess., Mme. d'Arblay* (1887) 755 The whole Palace from Gold Stick in Waiting down to the Table-Deckers. **1983** *Daily Express* 18 Oct. 22/2 Specially trained 'table-deckers' set the places at State banquets. **1904** M. Corelli *God's Good Man* 503 Placed below this, and slightly towards the centre of the room, was the Bishop's *table-desk and chair. **1933** 'A. Armstrong' *Ten-Minute Alibi* I. 9 Right centre is a flat table-desk with two drawers. **1933** *Burlington Mag.* June p. xviii/2 The acquisition from the funds of the Murray Bequest of the table-desk associated with Henry VIII. **1965** J. A. Michener *Source* 799 Gottesmann was surprised, therefore, when this frail child slammed shut the folding table-desk used by the Palmach as its headquarters. **1611** Cotgr. s.v. *Table*, *Table-discourse is an excellent Schoole-maister. **1659** *Burton's Diary* (1828) IV. 395 It is their table discourse that we shall be ruined. **1877** W. Jones *Finger-ring* 366 The other ring is also of gold, with a square *table-faced diamond. **1858** Simmonds *Dict. Trade*, **Table-flap*, the leaf of a folding-table. **1864** *Amer. Boy's Bk. Sports & Games* 455 (*heading*) *Table and toy games. **1905** W. Fiske *Chess in Iceland* 357 We have, as stated, confined ourselves wholly to table-games, that is those which are played on a board or other surface, on which some peculiar design is drawn. **1976** E. Ward *Hanged Man* xxviii. 180 Burnett.. felt helplessness, a toy rabbit running on the magnetized tracks of a table game made for children. **1641** Sanderson *Serm.* (1681) II. 8 They, using the liberty of that power, had appointed sitting or standing, rather than kneeling, as judging either of them a more proper *table gesture than it. **1646** Sir T. Browne *Pseud. Ep.* 241 Many..(though they concede a table-gesture) will hardly allow this usuall way of Session. **1727–41** Chambers *Cycl.* s.v. *Glass*, The same for window, or *table glass, as for round glass. **1815** J. Smith *Panorama Sc. & Art* II. 208 White flint, or English crystal, generally used for table-glasses. **1610** Boys *Wks.* (1630) 374 O that the *table-gospellers of our time..would consider aright this terrible judgement. **1850** R. G. Cumming *Hunter's Life S. Afr.* (1902) 157/1, I had the satisfaction to discover the spoor of three bucks on a piece of rocky *table-ground on the highest summit of the range. **1950** *N.Z. Jrnl. Agric.* Oct. 311/2 Pressing the fleece wool with all the skirtings, bellies, stains, [etc.]..still adhering..costs the farmer far more..than if he had hired one or two *table hands at shearing to skirt his fleece wool for him. **1955** G. Bowen *Wool Away!* vii. 92 A common fault is for a wool-table to be too high, which makes harder work for the table hands and the 'fleeco'. **1972** *Classification of Occupations* (Dept. Employment) III. 172/2 *Bindery assistant.* Performs, by hand or machine, folding, gathering, collating and/or sewing tasks in binding books, periodicals or stationery and assists bookbinders... Other titles include..Table hand. **1979** *West Lancs. Even. Gaz.* 12 Oct. 24 (Advt.), Fully experienced tablehand (SOGAT) required in our Bindery. **1958** *Time* 6 Oct. 16/1 He *table-hopped to shake hands. **1977** *Time* 28 Mar. 28/2 In Charleston, he table-hopped through the cafeteria at the West Virginia State Capitol. **1967** *N.Y. Times Mag.* 20 Aug. 33 The writers' club..is a place for gossip, banter, flirtation, shoptalk, confidences and compulsive *table-hopping. **1895** *Army & Navy Co-op. Soc. Price List* 16 *Table jelly powder. **1917** *Harrods Gen. Catal.* 1224/2 Table jellies (Spring's). **1975** in T. Steel *Life & Death of St Kilda* (1977) xi. 176 She had a few table jellies left. *c* **1460** J. Russell *Bk. Nurture* 334 in *Babees Bk.*, Take a loofe of trenchurs in þy lifft hande, þan take þy *table knyfe. **1810** *Sporting Mag.* XXXV. 282 To work..at his business, as a table-knife cutler. *c* **1865** G. Gore in *Circ. Sc.* I. 235/2 This tendency is sometimes manifested in depositing silver upon table-knives and forks. **1675** J. Smith *Chr. Relig. App.* I. 18 In his erecting of that strange Order of *Table-Knights,..instituted..in contempt of Apollo. **1871** Tennyson *Last Tourn.* 69 Some hold he was a table-knight of thine..the Red Knight, he. **1883** *Proc. Soc. Psych. Research* I. 248 He would have really 'exploded the whole nonsense' of *table-lifting. *c* **1460** *Tabyl lyne [see sense 14 above]. **1611** Cotgr., *Mensale*, the Table-line in the hand; (a tearme of Palmistrie). **1653** R. Sanders *Physiogn.* 45 He that hath the Table-line broad and well-coloured he is jocund and couragious. **1680** *Lond. Gaz.* No. 1500/4 A large black Trunk filled with Diaper-*Table-Linnen and Sheets. **1855** Mrs. Gaskell *North & S.* xxvi, Continuing her inspection of the table-linen. **1892** *Labour Commission Gloss.*, **Table-loaders*, synonymous with 'lift-loaders'. **1862** J. Binny in H. Mayhew *London Labour* Extra vol. 355/2 *Table-maids in aristocratic families or at first-class hotels. **1895** *Cath. News* 16 Nov. 2 She had been tablemaid to a clergyman. *c* **1515** *Cocke Lorell's B.* (Percy Soc.) 10 *Table makers, sylke dyers, and shepsters. **1867** *Harper's Mag.* Sept. 470/1 That upright position which belongs no less to *table-manners than to hygiene. **1904** *Daily Chron.* 28 July 4/7 What the Americans would call his 'table-manners'. **1949** M. Mead *Male & Female* ix. 187 In cultures where table-manners are the insignia of humanity people may be unable to eat their food at the table with some one who eats differently. **1771** Luckombe *Hist. Print.* 283 *Table-matter is generally braced in, when it wants driving out in width. **1835** J. E. Alexander *Sketches in Portugal* vi. 148 A contract was entered into with them.., that they should receive British pay and *table-money during the continuance of the war. **1842** G. Parbury *Hand Bk. for India & Egypt* (ed. 2) 383 Table money, say 25 days, at 3 rupees per diem. **1866** *Cornh. Mag.* Oct. 467 The old screw ..saves half his table-money, and gives you stuff to drink only fit to send down the scuppers. **1901** *Daily News* 13 Dec. 7/1 In the lower-priced restaurants it is called 'table money', and in the higher-priced ones placed under the captivating heading of *couvert.* **1761** *Biogr. Dict.* IV. 200 A handsome *table monument of blue marble was raised over his [Drayton's] grave. **1952** *Procès-Verbaux Assoc. d'Oceanogr. Physique* v. 71 The term guyot seems unnecessary in view of the more satisfactory term *table mount. **1959** Tablemount [see GUYOT]. **1791** *Encycl. Brit.* (ed. 3) VIII. 16/2 On approaching the Cape, a very remarkable eminence may.. be discovered..called the *Table-mountain from its appearance. **1822** G. Young *Geol. Surv. Yorks. Coast* (1828) 67 Extensive flats, nearly level, as in what are called Table mountains. **1886** A. Winchell *Walks Geol. Field* 95 When the erosion cuts the lava-sheet along parallel lines, it gives rise to the forms known as 'table-mountains'. **1853** *Ann. Reg.* 66 The faith in question is termed '*Table-moving'. **1862** B. Taylor *Home & Abr.* Ser. II. vii. 442 Circles began to be formed in my native town, for the purpose of table-moving. **1875** Stainer & Barrett *Dict. Mus. Terms*, **Table music*, compositions intended to be sung by several persons sitting at a table. **1859** Mrs. Gaskell *Round Sofa* 331 Some fine yarn she was having spun for *table-napery. **1564** *Will J. Smyth* (2 Morrison & Crimes, Somerset Ho.), A fine *table napkin with blewe clowdes. *a* **1649** Drumm. of Hawth. *Hist. Jas. IV*, Wks. (1711) 74 Girded about him with a towel or table-napkin, of a comely and reverend aspect. **1828** Scott *F.M. Perth* xxviii, A handful of soft moss served the purposes of a table-napkin. **1882** Caulfield & Saward *Dict. Needlework* 468/1 Tablecloths, table napkins, tray ditto [etc.]. **1917** *Harrods Gen. Catal.* 1448/3, 1 doz. Table Napkins £1 7s. 6d. **1938** *John o' London's Weekly* 18 Mar. 991/3 To plant palm trees and pampas grass on the Devon hills is like calling a table napkin in an Englishman's dining-room a serviette. **1970–1** *Kay's Catal.* Autumn–Winter 585 White cotton tablecloth. .. Matching table napkins available. **1946** *2nd Rep. Sel. Comm. on Procedure* p. iv, in *Parl. Papers 1945–46* IX. 161 Questions received at the *Table Office before the hour of sitting of the House shall be deemed to have been received the day before. **1950** *Erskine May's Law of Parl.* (ed. 15) xii. 243 The Table Office assists the Clerks at the Table particularly in the preparation of the Notice Paper and the Order Book. **1973** *Times* 15 May 7/2 The table office at the House refused, after taking advice, to accept the questions. **1968** *Daily Colonist* (Victoria, B.C.) 9 Nov. 1/6 John Laxton ..confirmed that a..meeting of the caucus of MLA's and the provincial *table officers..had agreed on the convention date. **1973** *Globe & Mail* (Toronto) 8 Sept. 8/5 He's been involved in some of the most complex bargaining in that field..and was one of the table officers when construction workers two years ago rejected a back-to-work order. **1897** Spurgeon *Autobiog.* iv. 26 In front of the pulpit, was the *table-pew, wherein sat the elders of the congregation. **1610** Healey *St. Aug. Citie of God* ii. (1620) 7 Gazing upon a *table picture. **1835** Willis *Pencillings* I. xxiii. 166 A graceful slope..swells up to a broad *table-plain on the mountain. **1911** W. J. Locke *Glory of Clementina Wing* xxiii. 345 Quixtus at the end of the table... Clementina had thus arranged the *table-plan. **1948** G. V. Galwey *Lift & Drop* v. 93 Dance was..fretting over..the way his table plan had been upset. **1982** K. Follett *Man from St. Petersburg* xiv. 252 She sent for Pritchard and made the table plan with him. **1626** in *Mem. Fountains* (Surtees) 365 One bed of wainscott..and also three *table plankes. **1669** W. Montagu in *Buccleuch MSS.* (Hist. MSS. Comm.) I. 446 The Queen's *table plate. **1705** tr. *Bosman's Guinea* 272 As broad as a common Table-Plate. **1877** Raymond *Statist. Mines & Mining* 329 Amalgamation in batteries, on table-plates, in pans, and on a second set of table-plates on a floor below. **1550** Crowley *Last Trump.* 490 Thy tauerne gate, and *table playe, thy cardes, thy dyce. **1586** T. B. *La Primaud. Fr. Acad.* (1589) 317 Plato compared our life to table-play. **1631** R. Byfield *Doctr. Sabb.* 152 Let no Table-play carry away the mind. *c* **1450** *Medulla* (Cath. Angl. 376), *Aliator*, a *tabyl pleyare. **1631** *Celestina* I. 15 Your Table-players, and other Gamesters never lose, but they peale foorth her prayses. **1577** Northbrooke *Dicing* (1579) 55 *Table playing and Chesse playing may be vsed of any men moderately. **1862** *Union* 11 Apr., Anything more dreary than '*Table prayers' at eleven o'clock we cannot conceive. **1701** *Cowell's Interpr.*, **Table-Rents, Redditus ad mensam*, rents paid to Bishops or Religious Prelates, reserv'd or appropriated to their Table or House-keeping. **1817** in *Minnesota Hist. Soc. Coll.* (1860) II. 36 The mode I adopted to ascertain the height of the cataract, was to suspend a line and plummet from the *table rock on the south side of the river. **1853** Mrs. Moodie *Life in Clearings* 365 The fall of that large portion of the table-rock has made the alteration. **1607** Tourneur *Rev. Trag.* IV. ii, For *table-roome, I feed on those that cannot be rid of me. **1881** A. C. Grant *Bush Life Queensl.* I. vii. 85 The fleece, gathered carefully with both hands is conveyed to a long *table-screen. **1971** *Country Life* 10 June 1425/3 Several table screens are on view. A rare example..is made of turquoise matrix carved with an eastern scene. **1972** *Trans. Oriental Ceramic Soc.* XXXVIII. 112 Table screen painted in blue... Chêng-tê period, 1506–21. **1974** Savage & Newman *Illustr. Dict. Ceramics* 282 *Table-screen*, a small rectangular porcelain plaque or tile, usually decorated on both sides, mounted vertically on a stand, and intended to be placed on the scholar's table, probably to protect his work from unwanted sunlight. **1765** J. Wedgwood *Let.* 25 July (1965) 36 Your Brother Josiah's Pottworks were the subject of conversation for some time, the Cream colour *Table services in particular. **1823** Chalmers in Hanna *Mem.* (1849) II. xv. 395 She allowed me..to continue the table-service in the way I had found to be most convenient. **1846** Mrs. Gore *Eng. Char.* (1852) 99 In table-service his attendance was impartial. **1885** *List of Subscribers, Classified* (United Telephone Co.) (ed. 6) 229 (Advt.), Crystal and Demi-Crystal Table Services and Ornaments. **1891** *Cent. Dict.* s.v. *Service*[1], *Table-service*, a set of utensils for the table. **1896** *Daily News* 6 Apr. 2/5 The President..handed to him the handsome table service which he had given to be run for. **1955** *House & Garden* June 74/2 Table mats are a most practical form of *table setting. **1967** E. Short *Embroidery & Fabric Collage* iii. 66 A tablecloth designed with the table setting in mind will enhance the general effect rather than confuse it. **1864** Webster, **Table-shore, Naut.*, a low, level shore. **1871** Tennyson *Last Tourn.* 461 As the crest of some slow-arching wave, Heard in dead night along that table-shore, Drops flat. **1844** Stephens *Bk. Farm* II. 575 The assistant throws the parings of the sides and bottom of the ditch upon the hedge-bank, immediately behind the *table-sod. **1847** Grote *Greece* II. xxix. IV. 109 [Archilochus] was the earliest popular and successful composer of *table-songs or Skolia. **1836** Brande *Chem.* (ed. 4) 860 There are some minerals, and among them *table-spar or Wollastonite.. which are silicates of lime. **1598** Shaks. *Merry W.* IV. ii. 169 Let me for euer be your *Table-sport. **1885** *Encycl. Brit.* XIX. 283/1 The modern usage is to play **table stakes*; i.e., each player puts up such an amount as he pleases at the commencement of each deal, and he cannot be raised more than he has on the table; but he has the option of making good from his pocket a previous raise which exceeds his table stake. **1973** T. Pynchon *Gravity's Rainbow* I. 7 Routine: plug in American blending machine won from Yank last summer, some poker game, table stakes, B.O.Q. somewhere in the north. **1948** *Table tape [see *problem tape* s.v. PROBLEM 7]. **1956** G. A. Montgomerie *Digital Calculating Machines* x. 213 Numbers may also be taken from the table tapes as required. **1854** J. G. MacWalter (*title*) The Modern Mystery of *Table-Tapping. **1887** in *75 Years of Fun* (Parker Bros., Inc.) (1958) 19 *Table Tennis. .. This game is laid out like a lawn tennis court, played and counted just the same, all the rules being observed. **1901** *Daily Chron.* 16 Dec. 8/2 The table tennis or 'ping-pong' tournament..concluded on Saturday night at the Royal Aquarium. **1977** *World Book Encycl.* XIX. 4/2 A British firm manufactured table tennis equipment and registered the name *Ping-Pong* in England in 1900 and in America in 1901. Soon afterward it sold the American rights to Parker Brothers of Salem, Massachusetts. The monopoly of the game by these two companies and their dictation of rules and equipment led to a revolt by internationally organized players in 1921. As a result, the unpatented name *Table Tennis* was adopted. **1903** *Westm. Gaz.* 2 Mar. 7/1 We tried spiritualism..first by *table-tilting. **1865** Lowell *Lett.* I. 386, I translate by direct inspiration of a scholiast turned *table-tipper. **1855** Smedley, etc. *Occult Sc.* 201 If the *table-tipping be made to answer as a code of signals. **1876** E. Venables in *Encycl. Brit.* V. 209/2 In the *table-tomb the recess above, essential for the introduction of the corpse, is square, while in the arcosolium, a form of later date, it is semi-circular. **1807** Vancouver *Agric. Devon* (1813) 293 He reached and ascended the *table top of Haldon. **1886** A. Winchell *Walks Geol. Field* 95 It..projects like a table-top beyond the gravel. **1834** Ld. Houghton *Mem. Many Scenes, Tempe* Introd. (1844) 35 A line of rugged crags, peaked or *table-topped. **1897** *Daily News* 3 May 7/4 A.. valley lying between high, sharply scarped table-topped hills. **1853** O. Byrne *Artisan's Handbk.* 63 A miniature lathe-head mounted on a wooden *table-tree. **1805** R. W. Dickson *Pract. Agric.* I. 119 Care being taken..to raise the ground where they are placed with two or three *table turfs. **1594** Plat *Jewell-ho.* 14 One masse, whereof they make our drinking Glasses, and all sortes of *Table-vessell. **1895** *Westm. Gaz.* 23 Oct. 5/2 The Rosbach *table-water, a fresh sparkling table-water. **1794** *Rigging & Seamanship* I. 57 **Table-wheel*, to lay ropes, from a six-thread rat-line to a two-inch and half rope, is fixed in the wheel-house. **1673** J. Ray *Observations Journey Low-Countries* 340 The red Florence wine is most commended for a *table wine of any in Italy. **1827** Disraeli *Vivian Grey* III. v. iv. 73 Very fair table-wine, I think. **1978** J. Symons *Blackheath Poisonings* I. 40 Roger poured a red table wine that had been decanted. **1771** Luckombe *Hist. Print.* 272 Divisions are used instead of rules, in *Table-work of narrow Columns. **1832** Babbage *Econ. Manuf.* xxi. (ed. 3) 207 Work with irregular lines and many figures, and what the printers call rules,..is called *table-work.* **1879** [see TABULAR 2 c].

table, *v.* [f. TABLE *sb.* In some senses representing F. *tabler* (1544 in Godef.) or med.L. *tabulāre* (Du Cange).]

1. *trans.* To enter in a table or list; to tabulate (*now rare*); †to appoint (a person) to some duty by entering his name in a table or list (*obs.*).

c **1450** in Aungier *Syon* (1840) 324 The secunde and thryd antemes and matens schal be bygon of them that be tabled unto them. **1550** *Rec. Elgin* (New Spald. Cl.) I. 105 That the baillies..tabill certane honest men for gadering of Sanct Gelis lycht. **1611** Shaks. *Cymb.* I. iv. 6 Though the Catalogue of his endowments had bin tabled by his side.

c **1630** SIR T. HOPE *Minor Practicks* (1726) 5 There can be no Protestation granted upon the Copy, till the Copy be tabled. **1838** [implied in TABLING *vbl. sb.* 1].

2. a. To entertain at table as a guest, or for payment; to provide with meals, or *gen.* with food; = BOARD *v.* 8. Now *rare*.

1457-8 *Cal. Anc. Rec. Dublin* (1889) 297 Every of the Baylyfys to tabyll one of them. **1553** in *10th Rep. Hist. MSS. Comm.* App. v. 414 Every Maior..shall tabull and vittaill towe massons or carpinders in his own housse. **1583** STUBBES *Anat. Abus.* II. (1882) 75 They haue..ten pound a yeere..and table themselues also of the same. **1610** HOLLAND *Camden's Brit.* II. 166 He entertained the Freers and tabled them at his owne charge. **1715** BROKESBY *Life Dodwell* 306 Mr. Cherry..procured a Place for him where he might be tabled. **1903** *Westm. Gaz.* 12 Sept. 8/1 At ten o'clock the establishment is closed, after having often tabled between four and five hundred persons.

b. *intr.* (for *refl.*) To have a meal, to dine; to take one's meals habitually (at a specified place or with a specified person); = BOARD *v.* 9. Now *rare*.

1562 *Child Marr.* 139 He came to Schole to Northerden, ..and tablid at Withinshawe, with James Barlowe. **1602** ROWLANDS *Greene's Ghost* 14 Comming to Ordinaries about the Exchange where Merchants do table for the most part. **1748** RICHARDSON *Clarissa* (1810) IV. lvi. 370 O that,..as she boarded there, she had oftener tabled with them! **1857** J. RAINE *Life J. Hodgson* I. 14 It seems to be pretty clear that Hodgson had tabled with this talkative but hearty man.

3. *trans.* **a.** To picture, depict, represent as in a picture: cf. TABLE *sb.* 3. *Obs.* (or *rare arch.*)

1607-8 BACON *Let. to Matthew* in Spedding *Life & Lett.* (1868) IV. 10 This last Powder Treason, fit to be tabled and pictured in the chambers of meditation, as another hell above the ground. **1852** BAILEY *Festus* (ed. 5) xx. 326 That we, in the dark chamber of the heart,..see the world tabled to us.

b. To fix as on a tablet. *rare*[−1].

1852 BAILEY *Festus* (ed. 5) xxxi. 530 Thine the stars Tabled upon Thy bosom like the stones Oracular of light, on the priest's breast.

4. To place or lay upon a table.

a. To lay (an appeal, proposal, resolution, bill, etc.) on the table of a deliberative or legislative assembly; hence, to bring forward or submit for discussion or consideration. In *U.S. Pol.*, to lay on the table as a way of postponing indefinitely; to shelve: cf. TABLE *sb.* 5 b.

1718 *Wodrow Corr.* (1843) II. 378 Another act was passed ..that all appeals should be brought up and tabled before the Bills, within three days after the Assembly sit down. **1726** *Ibid.* III. 245 Provost Campbell's appeal..was tabled, and the President and others moved a committee might be named to take it up. **1862** *Star & Dial* 14 Mar., Mr. Walpole has tabled a set of resolutions devised in the true Conservative spirit. **1866** *Daily Tel.* 30 Jan., To table a resolution has nearly the same effect in America as the order to read a bill 'this day six months' has in England. **1887** *Pall Mall G.* 3 Jan. 11/1 If any more 'Old Residents' wish to be heard they must table their names. **1916** J. B. THOBURN *Stand. Hist. Oklahoma* II. 715 [The bill] was sent to the council where it was considered, amended, and finally tabled. **1931** H. F. PRINGLE *Theodore Roosevelt* I. vi. 71 The resolution had no sooner been offered than..members were ..demanding that it be tabled. **1950** W. S. CHURCHILL *2nd World War* III. II. xxxvi. 609 The British Staff prepared a paper which they wished to raise as a matter of urgency, and informed their American colleagues that they wished to 'table it'. To the American Staff 'tabling' a paper meant putting it away in a drawer and forgetting it. **1974** *Sumter* (S. Carolina) *Daily Item* 22 Apr. 5A/7 Various plans for fundraising were discussed but it was decided to table any such plans until the fall.

b. With other implications: *esp.* to pay down (money); to throw down or play (a card).

1827 CARLYLE *Germ. Rom.* III. 224 Could he tell what to ..table [for the lackey]? **1832** —— *J. Carlyle* 45 A refreshment of ale, for which he too used to table his twopence. **1837** —— *Fr. Rev.* II. III. vi, Royalty has always that sure trump-card in its hand;..yet never tables it, still puts it back again. **1878** BAYNE *Purit. Rev.* v. 177 When the Short Parliament of 1640 refused to grant supplies, Laud's clergy in Convocation tabled their money. **1892** *Gard. Chron.* 27 Aug. 248/2 The nurserymen and florists tabled a large and fine assortment of cut flowers.

5. To furnish (a room) with tables. *nonce-use.*

1844 DICKENS *Mart. Chuz.* xxvii, The offices were.. newly tabled.

6. *Carpentry.* To join two pieces of timber firmly together by means of flat oblong projections (called 'tables' or 'coaks': see TABLE *sb.* 17 f, COAK *sb.* 1) in each alternately, fitting into corresponding recesses in the other. Also *intr.* for *pass.*

1794 *Rigging & Seamanship* I. 23 Cheeks..sometimes table on to the mast-head thus. **1794**-*c* **1850** [see TABLING *vbl. sb.* 7]. **1797** *Encycl. Brit.* (ed. 3) XVII. 402/1 The customary way of putting them together is to table them; and the length of the tablings should be one-half more than the depth of the beam.

7. *Sailmaking.* To make a broad hem or 'tabling' on the edge of (a sail), to strengthen it in that part which is sewed to the bolt-rope (see TABLING *vbl. sb.* 8).

1794 *Rigging & Seamanship* I. 89 *Tabled*, the edges turned over and sewed down. **1797** in *Encycl. Brit.* (ed. 3) XVII. 433/1 That the lower side of the band may be tabled upon or sewed over the end of the buntline pieces. *Ibid.*, The buntline cloths and top-linings are carried up to the lower side of the middle band, which is tabled on them.

8. To sift (shot): see quot.

1858 GREENER *Gunnery* 436 About three different sizes come out through one pan. These are separated by the aid of riddles, or tabled, as the process is termed.

‖**tableau** (tablo, 'tæbləʊ), *sb.* Pl. **tableaux** (tablo, 'tæbləʊz). [F. *tableau* (tablo), OF. *tablel*, dim. of *table*.]

1. A picture; usually *fig.* a picturesque or graphic description.

1699 LISTER *Journey to Paris* 39 The History of Maria of Medicis is Painted by Rubens... The Allegoric assistants in all the Tableaux are very airy and fancifully set out. **1801** FUSELI in *Lect. Paint.* iii. (1848) 429 The Massacre of the Innocents by Baccio Bandinelli..is a complicated tableau of every contortion of human attitude. **1855** H. R. SCHOOLCRAFT in *Longfellow's Life* (1891) II. 301 Exhibiting these fresh tableaux of Indian life. **1886** F. HARRISON *Choice Bks.* iii. 54 They epitomise civilisation in a regular series of striking tableaux of the past.

2. a. A group of persons and accessories, producing a picturesque effect.

1813 SIR R. WILSON *Pr. Diary* II. 458 [In the battle of Leipzig] the whole arrangement and execution were perfect, presenting the grandest tableau ever contemplated. **1867** BAKER *Nile Tribut.* viii. (1872) 130 All now halted, and gazed stedfastly in our direction, forming a superb tableau.

b. = *tableau vivant*: see 4.

1828 W. IRVING *Life & Lett.* (1864) II. 276 We had afterwards a tableau of a Sybil by Mademoiselle F. **1862** BARONESS BUNSEN in Hare *Life* II. vii. 318 After all possible singing and toasting two tableaux were given.

c. *Theatr.* A representation of the action at some stage in a play, created by the actors suddenly holding their positions or 'freezing', esp. at a moment critical to the plot, or at the end of a scene or act; also, as a stage direction. Hence used *transf.* to express the sudden creation of a striking or dramatic situation, a 'scene', which it is left to the reader to imagine.

c **1863** T. TAYLOR *Ticket-of-Leave Man* I. 22 Brierly is overpowered and handcuffed—Guests rush in and form Tableau. **1866** *Black ey'd Susan* ii. 9 fo. 30 The door opens. William enters C. *Susan.* Ah. William! Alive! (*Tableau*). **1881** P. FITZGERALD *World behind Scenes* I. 46 The tableaus at the end of each act..were brought about with admirable simplicity. **1885** *Pall Mall G.* 12 Nov. 11/1 A delay occurs in the working of the machinery [of the guillotine], when in rushes Miss Rorke, and tableau. **1894** *Westm. Gaz.* 18 Oct. 5/2 She overheard a gentleman ask another, pointing to two of the witnesses, 'Which of those old cats is Mrs. C.?' Mrs. C. leaned over and said 'That particular tabby, sir, is behind you'. Tableau! **1982** C. CASTLE *Folies Bergère* vi. 221 There are some 45 sets and tableaux.

d. *Cards.* The arrangement formed by the cards laid out on the table in the game of patience.

1875 A. CADOGAN *Illustr. Game Patience* (ed. 2) 1 Having placed the tableau, take any aces that may appear on the surface of the packets and play them in their allotted spaces. **1913** 'L. HOFFMANN' *Sel. Patience Games* 5 The first step, in the case of most Patience games, is to arrange a certain number of cards face upwards on the table. The cards thus arranged are known as the 'lay-out', or tableau. **1975** *Way to Play* 147/4 Spaces in the tableau (caused by the removal of an entire fan) remain unfilled.

3. A table, a schedule; an official list. (A common use in Fr.)

1798 T. W. TONE *Autobiog.* (1828) 266, I was carried on the tableau of the Armée d' Angleterre. **1863** LEPSIUS *Stand. Alphabet* 75 Comprise the seven classes in a general tableau. **1888** *Harper's Mag.* May 924/1 Those who, belonging to the fourteen grades of the tchin, or official tableaux of rank, are exempt from certain degrading penalties.

4. tableau vivant (tablo vivɑ̃), pl. **tableaux vivants** (same pron.), lit. 'living picture'; a representation of a personage, character, scene, incident, etc., or of a well-known painting or statue, by one person or a group of persons in suitable costumes and attitudes, silent and motionless; *transf.* a picturesque actual scene. (In quot. 1883, applied to a group of statuary.)

1817 MOORE *Lalla R.* Pref. (1850) 15 The different stories ..were represented in *Tableaux Vivans* and songs. **1837** SIR F. PALGRAVE *Merch. & Frier* (1844) 4 The intellectual amusement of a *tableau vivant*. **1844** WARBURTON *Crescent & Cross* (1845) I. xii. 106 The rich colouring, the antique attitudes, the various complexions that continually present themselves, form an unceasing series of *tableaux vivans* in an Eastern city. **1883** C. C. PERKINS *Ital. Sculpt.* 385 Upon canvas the group would be counted a masterpiece, in clay it is a *tableau vivant*.

5. = *simplex tableau* s.v. SIMPLEX *sb.* 4.

1953 A. CHARNES in W. W. Cooper et al. *Introd. Linear Programming* II. vi. 67 The coefficients of the ϵ-polynomial multiplying P_i..are given in due order by the entries in the P_i row of the tableau. **1971** D. C. HAGUE *Managerial Economics* ix. 186 The rule in the Simplex method is that any variable—that is, any *x* or any *s*—which appears on the left-hand edge of the tableau..has a positive value. **1980** A. J. JONES *Game Theory* iii. 165 The artificial variables have performed their function, and we can now drop the columns of the tableau associated with a_5 and a_6.

6. Special combination: **tableau curtain** *Theatr.* (see quot. 1967); cf. TAB *sb.*[4]

1881 W. H. RIDEING *Dramatic Notes* 45 It may here be worth mentioning that the handsome 'tableau curtain' made for this occasion..cost £740. **1967** *Oxf. Compan. Theatre* (ed. 3) 932/1 *Tabs* (short for Tableau Curtain), used originally of an act-drop which parted and rose sideways towards the outer top corners, and by extension to any front curtain or, mistakenly, to curtain settings on the stage.

Hence **'tableau** *v.*, *trans* to put into a tableau.

1903 *Contemp. Rev.* Dec. 873 'Tableaued' year by year in the popular Christmas Crib,..the Ass and the Ox, have become only less familiar than the Shepherds.

'table-board.

†**1.** A board for backgammon or any similar game: = TABLE *sb.* 4 a, BOARD *sb.* 2 c. *Obs.*

1483 *Cath. Angl.* 376/1 A Tabylle burde, *tabella*. **1540** HYRDE tr. *Vives' Instr. Chr. Wom.* F ij, What a foule thing is it, to see a woman in steade of her woolbasket, to handle the tablebourd. **1623** WEBSTER *Devil's Law-Case* II. i, Shaking your elbow at the table-board. **1905** [see TABLEMAN 1].

2. A board forming the top of a table; also a table (*obs.* or *dial.*).

a **1603** in H. Hall *Soc. Eliz. Age* vii. (1886) 99 Table-bordes, formes, and a countinge table. **1668** CLARENDON *Vind.* Tracts (1727) 33 Walnut-tree..of which I made some table-boards and frames for chairs. **1731** W. HALFPENNY *Perspective* p. iv, The Table Board fixed on the three Legs. **1847-78** HALLIWELL, *Table-board*, a table. *Cornw.*

3. Board, i.e. meals, without lodging. *U.S.*

1884 *N. York Herald* 27 Oct. 2/3 First class table Board. **1895-6** *Cal. Univ. Nebraska* 177 Table board ranges from $1.50 to $2.50 per week.

'table-book.

1. A book composed of tablets for memoranda; a pocket note-book or memorandum-book. *Obs.* or *rare*.

1596 NASHE *Saffron Walden* Wks. (Grosart) III. 67 Registers..busie with their Table-books..to gather phrases. **1602** SHAKS. *Ham.* I. ii. 136. **1616** *Trav. Eng. Pilg.* in *Harl. Misc.* (Malh.) III. 332 Writing my notes out of my table-book. **1667** PEPYS *Diary* 10 May, Found in the dead man's pocket..a table-book, wherein were entered the names of several places where he was to go. **1711-12** SWIFT *Jrnl. to Stella* 22 Jan., He thanked me for telling him, and immediately put his name in his table-book. **1816** SINGER *Hist. Cards* 276 He was observed to busy himself by writing in his table book. **1852** THACKERAY *Henry Esmond* II. v. 76 We were off Finisterre on the 31st of July, so Esmond's table-book informs him. **1937** BLUNDEN *Elegy* 11 Might Machiavel Now from his table-book communicate Precept or paradox that could do well In the nerve centres of a modern state?

2. A book of arithmetical or other tables; a Ready Reckoner or the like.

1827 G. DARLEY *Sylvia* 28 He cannot count his fingers Without a table-book.

3. An ornamental book for a drawing-room table.

1845 (*title*) George Cruikshank's Table-Book. **188.** *Lit. World* (Cent. Dict.), The Christmas table-book has well nigh disappeared, and well-illustrated editions of famous works are becoming more and more popular.

Hence †**'table-book-,wise** *adv. Obs.*, in the manner of a table-book (sense 1).

1642 HOWELL *For. Trav.* (Arb.) 27 Some do use to have a small leger booke fairely bound up table-book-wise.

table-cloth ('teɪb(ə)lklɒθ, -ɔː-; for pl. see CLOTH *sb.*). A cloth for covering a table.

a. A cloth, usually of white linen, spread upon a table in preparation for a meal, and upon which the dishes, plates, etc. are placed.

1467 *Mann. & Househ. Exp.* (Roxb.) 409 My mastyr paid there for a tabylle cloth ij.s. vj.d. **1496-7** *Rec. St. Mary at Hill* 34 Item, ij dyapre Tableclothis for the high Auter. **1575** in Willis & Clark *Cambridge* (1886) III. 363 If either fellowe or pensioner do wipe his hande or finger of the table clothe he shall pay for every time j[d]. **1586** B. YOUNG *Guazzo's Civ. Conv.* IV. 185 Y[e] table cloathes wer spread. **1610** HOLLAND *Camden's Brit.* (1637) 481 Table clothes and linnen used at the solemne Coronation. **1855** MRS. GASKELL *North & S.* xxvi, Clothes-basket[s]..full of tablecloths and napkins. **1885** *Manch. Exam.* 9 Sept. 3/1 Equal to the task of instructing a laundress in the ironing of a tablecloth.

b. A cloth, usually of woollen material and often of ornamental design, used to cover a table permanently or when not in use for meals; = *table-cover* (TABLE *sb.* 22).

1610 in *Eng. Wom. Dom. Mag.* (1862) IV. 109 If the green table-cloth be too little I will make a pair of warm stockings of it. **1879** CROCKETT *Kit Kennedy* xlix. 358 The letter was laid down on the tablecloth, with a fast-falling rain of tears falling upon it.

c. *fig.* Name for a cloud covering the flat top and hanging down over the edge of Table Mountain at the Cape of Good Hope.

[**1791** *Encycl. Brit.* (ed. 3) VIII. 16/2 The Table Land or Mountain is sometimes suddenly capped with a white cloud, by some called the 'spreading of the Table-cloth'.] **1836** *Lett. fr. Madras* (1843) 29 When the cloud that they call the Table-cloth comes down, people are often lost in the fog. **1898** *Westm. Gaz.* 13 Oct. 1/3, I had no time to spare for the ascent of Table Mountain, and the tablecloth of clouds indeed forbade me to attempt it.

Hence **'table-,clothing** (-klɒθɪŋ, -ɔː-), linen for table-cloths; **'table-cloth-,wise** *adv.*, in the manner of a table-cloth; **'table-,clothy** (-klɒθɪ, -ɔː-) *a.*, resembling or suggesting a table-cloth.

1859 GEO. ELIOT *A. Bede* xxxi, I'm having linen spun, an' thinking all the while it'll make sheeting and table-clothing for her when she's married. **1891** KIPLING *Life's Handicap, End of Passage* 159 Clouds of tawny dust..flung themselves tablecloth-wise among the tops of the parched trees, and came down again. **1866** HOWELLS *Venet. Life* iii, Where the marble is carven in vast and heavy folds..to simulate a curtain..it has..a harshness decidedly table-clothy.

'table-cut, *a.* (*sb.*) [f. TABLE *sb.*, used adverbially + CUT *ppl. a.* or *sb.*[2]] Of a diamond or other precious stone: Cut in the form of a 'table': see TABLE *sb.* 18 and TABLE DIAMOND.

1688 *Lond. Gaz.* No. 2320/4 Lost.., a Diamond Ring, Table Cut. **1704** *Ibid.* No. 4046/4, 8 Rings, one a Diamond with 7 Stones, Table-cut. **1905** A. LANG in *Longm. Mag.* Apr. 566, I could not tell what stones the table-cut stones were.

b. *sb.* The style of cutting a precious stone as described above.

1891 in *Cent. Dict.*

So **'table-cutter**, a lapidary who cuts precious stones in 'tables'; **'table-cutting** = b.

1877 E. W. STREETER *Precious Stones* iv. 23 A little later [than 1373] the so-called 'table-cutters' at Nürnberg, and all other stone-engravers, formed themselves into a guild. **1877** KNIGHT *Dict. Mech.* 2478/1 Table-cutting is adopted with flat thin gems, which have not sufficient protuberance to be cut as rose diamonds or brilliants.

tabled ('teɪb(ə)ld), *a.* [f. TABLE *sb.* and *v.*]

1. a. Made in or into the form of a table or flat surface; shaped like a table; *spec.* = TABLE-CUT *a.*

1382 WYCLIF *Exod.* xxxv. 11 The tabernacle, and the roof of it, and the coueryng; rynges, and the tablid sides. **1575** LANEHAM *Let.* (Ballad Soc.) 51 Diamons, Emerauds, Rubyes, and Saphyres: poynted, tabld, rok, and roound. **1832** J. BREE *St. Herbert's Isle* 95 Mountains with tabled heads. **1853** M. ARNOLD *Empedocles on Etna* II. 177 Sitting on a tabled stone.

b. Seated at table. *rare*$^{-1}$.

1922 JOYCE *Ulysses* 167 He gazed round the stooled and tabled eaters.

2. ? Pictured, depicted. *rare.*

1848 BAILEY *Festus* (ed. 4) viii. 84 The mornlit revel and the shameless mate, The tabled hues of darkness and of blood.

3. Entered on a list; listed. *Sc.*

c **1630** SIR T. HOPE *Minor Practicks* (1726) 9 The Keeper ..was obliged to affix on the Tolbooth-wall the Roll of the tabled Causes.

4. Having a table or tables: in *comb.*, as ***double-tabled*** adj., having two 'tables', leaves, or tablets (cf. TABLE *sb.* 2 e).

1848 BAILEY *Festus* (ed. 4) xix. 216 The bright universe, The double tabled book of Heaven and earth.

‖**table d'hôte** (tabl dot; anglicized ˌtaːb(ə)l 'dəʊt). [Fr., = host's table.] A common table for guests at a hotel or eating-house; a public meal served there at a stated hour and at a fixed price; an ordinary. Also *attrib.* as ***table d'hôte dinner.***

1617 MORYSON *Itin.* III. 60 Neither at this time was there any ordinarie Table (which they call *Table de l'hoste*, the Hosts table). *a* **1667** COWLEY *Ess. Verse & Prose, Liberty* Wks. (1684) 83 All this is but Tabl'd Host, 'tis crowded with people for whom he cares not. **1759** H. WALPOLE *Let. to H. S. Conway* 19 Sept., Mrs. Howe, who rides a fox-chase, and dines at the *table d'hôte* at Grantham. **1816** *Gentl. Mag.* LXXXVI. I. 198/2 At Dunkirk..I found a good table d'hote, a luxury which foreign travellers do not find in England. **1838** *Murray's Handbk. N. Germ.* 300/1 The table-d'hôte dinner..takes place at 2 o'clock.

'table 'diamond. [f. TABLE *sb.* 18 + DIAMOND.] A diamond cut with a table or large flat upper surface surrounded by small facets; esp. a thin diamond so cut having a flat under surface.

1470 *N.C. Wills* (Surt. 1908) 56 A ringe of gold with table dyamond. **1519** *Lett. & P. Hen. VIII*, III. No. 463 (P.R.O.) A black carkeyn with a syphre..garnysshed with three table diamauntes, oon losenge diamaund, oon great poynted diamaunt. **1607** in *Heriot's Mem.* App. VII. (1822) 212 A ringe, with a table diamond on the head. **1750** D. JEFFRIES *Diamonds & Pearls* 58 The manufacture of Table and Rose Diamonds. **1833** *Encycl. Brit.* VIII. 6 The forms into which the diamond is cut are the brilliant, the rose, and the table. **1877** W. JONES *Finger-ring* 379 A ring with seventy-five table-diamonds, set in gold.

tableful ('teɪb(ə)lfʊl). [f. TABLE *sb.* + -FUL.] The amount or number that a table will hold or accommodate. **a.** As many (persons) as can be seated at a table; a company seated at a table and occupying all the seats around it.

1535 COVERDALE *Mark* vi. 39 He commaunded them all to syt down by table fulles vpon the grene grass. **1774** ABIGAIL ADAMS in *Fam. Lett.* (1876) 35 We make a table-full at meal times. **1858** O. W. HOLMES *Aut. Breakf.-t.* iii, One man who is a little too literal can spoil the talk of a whole tableful of men of *esprit.*

b. As many (things) as a table will hold or is holding, all that is on the table.

1868 H. A. VAUGHAN *Let.* 26 Dec. in *Lett. to Lady Herbert* (1942) 134 Mrs. Vaughan gave us tablefuls of excellent food. **1872** GEO. ELIOT *Middlemarch* II. IV. xxxvi. 228 Lydgate's tableful of apparatus and specimens. **1886** *Philadelphia Times* 9 Jan. (Cent.), Three large tablefuls of housekeeping things. **1977** *Zigzag* June 15/2 He was so pleased to see me that he threw a tableful of drinks over..like in the movies!

†**ta'bleity.** *Obs. nonce-wd.* [f. TABLE *sb.* + -ITY; rendering Erasmus's L. *menseitās* for Gr. τραπεζότης (Diog. Laertes). Cf. CUPPEITY.] The abstract quality of a table.

1542 UDALL *Erasm. Apoph.* 123 b, Hauyng in his mouth.. the said forges vocables of the Idees, as for exaumple, tablietees, for the facion of table. *Ibid.* 124 b [see CUPPEITY]. **1656** STANLEY *Hist. Philos.* VII. (1701) 287/1 Plato answered, it is true indeed, you have Eyes by which the *Table* and *Cup* are seen; but not an Intellect, by which *Tableity* and *Cuppeity* are seen. **1702** LOCKE *Defence* App. *Pers. Identity* (1769) 41 Personality therefore may be ranked among the whole scholastick terms of corporeity, egoity, tableity, etc.

'table-land. [f. TABLE *sb.* + LAND *sb.*[1]] An elevated region of land with a generally level surface, of large or considerable extent; a lofty plain; a plateau.

1697 DAMPIER *Voy.* I. xix. 531 The most remarkable Land at Sea is a high Mountain, steep to the Sea, with a flat even top, which is called the Table Land [at the Cape of Good Hope]. **1774** COOK *Voy. S. Pole* III. iv. (1777) II. 50 At sun-rise we discovered a high table land (an island) bearing E. by S. **1824** MISS MITFORD *Village* Ser. I. 70 (*Lucy*) The common..is one of a series of heathy hills, or rather a high table land, pierced in one part by a ravine or marshy ground. **1899** BARING-GOULD *Bk. of West* I. x. 155 The great irregular tableland of Dartmoor, over a thousand feet above the sea.

b. Without *a* or *pl.*: Elevated level ground.

1836 W. IRVING *Astoria* (1849) 248 These lofty plats of table-land seem to form a peculiar feature in the American continents. **1869** TOZER *Highl. Turkey* II. 190 One long line of table-land.., half mountain, half plain.

c. *fig.*

1820 HAZLITT *Lect. Dram. Lit.* 12 He [Shakspere] indeed overlooks and commands the admiration of posterity, but he does it from the table-land of the age in which he lived. **1876** GEO. ELIOT *Dan. Der.* III. xxii, A healthy Briton on the central table-land of life.

tableless ('teɪb(ə)llɪs), *a.* [-LESS.] Without a table; unfurnished with a table.

1887 H. KNOLLYS *Sk. Life Japan* 183, I am..conducted into the enlarged partition in a doll's house, clean as a match-box, but tableless and chairless. **1895** *Strand Mag.* Oct. 451/1 The tableless, curtainless, carpetless, chestless apartment.

†**'tableman.** *Obs.* Pl. -men.

1. One of the 'men' or pieces used in any game played on a board, esp. backgammon.

1483 *Cath. Angl.* 376/1 A Tabylle man, *scaccus.., calculus.* **1534** *Camden Misc.* (1855) 39 One paire of tables of peerle,..withoute table men. **1626** BACON *Sylva* §158 A Soft Body dampeth the Sound... And therefore..in Colleges they use to line the Tablemen. **1641** HINDE *J. Bruen* xl. 123 He saw everywhere Cards and Dise, Tables and Table-men. **1725** SLOANE *Jamaica* II. 136 The wood [Guaiacum] is..good for bowls, tables, table-men, and cabinets. **1905** FISKE *Chess in Iceld.* 89 The list of chess boards and chess-men, table-boards and table-men in the king's possession.

2. Applied in contempt to a gamester.

1608 DEKKER *Lanthorne & Candlel.* D j b, Knowing that your most selected Gallants are the only Table-men that are plaid withal at Ordinaries. **1609** —— *Gvlls Horne-bk.* Introd. 2 All the painted table-men about you, take you to be heires apparant to rich Midasse.

†**'tablemeal,** *adv. Obs. rare*$^{-1}$. [f. TABLE *sb.* (sense 13 a) + -MEAL: rendering L. *tabulātim.*] By 'tables'; bed by bed.

c **1440** *Pallad. on Husb.* III. 148 Thi vynes olde eke graffe hem table mele.

tablement ('teɪb(ə)lmənt). [f. TABLE *v.* + -MENT, after L. *tabulāment-um*, f. *tabulāre.*]

1. *Arch.* = TABLE *sb.* 12 a; also, a foundation or basement.

a **1300** *Cursor M.* 1678 A schippe be-houes þe to dight... Fiueten [ellen] on heght, þat es þentent, Fra grund vnto þe tabulment. **13..** *E.E. Allit. P.* A. 993 Vch tabelment watz a serlypez ston. **1489** CAXTON *Faytes of A.* II. xxxv. 147 An edyfyce made of grete tymber and of tablementes with many loftes and stallages. **1601** HOLLAND *Pliny* (1634) II. 604 Stones larger than small tablements of pillars or counting-bourds. **1603** —— *Plutarch's Mor.* 1196 We sat us downe upon the tablements on the South side of the temple. **1853** PARKER *Turner's Dom. Archit.* II. v. 218 So that a decent stone tablement be made on the wall.

†**2.** A wooden frontal for an altar: = TABULA 2.

1446 *Yatton Churchw. Acc.* (Som. Rec. Soc.) 86 Payde to W. Stubbe rydyng to Brystowe to see the tabylment. **1500** in *Wiltsh. Archæol., etc., Mag.* (1855) II. 310 Pd. for making of the tabullment of the High Altar. **1552** *Inv. Ch. Goods Berksh.* 24 A clothe to hange before the tablement.

†**3.** A tabulation, list, catalogue. *Obs. rare.*

1551 RECORDE *Pathw. Knowl.* Ep. to King, And thus will I omit this great tablement of vnhappie hap.

†**'tabler**[1]. *Obs.* Also 4 tablere, 5 tabelere. [In sense 1, a. OF. *tablier* (12–13th c. in Godef.) = L. *tabulārium*, in one of its mediæval senses, f. *tabula* table: cf. TABLE *sb.* 4.]

1. A backgammon board; hence, the game of backgammon or 'tables'. Also, a chess-board.

1303 R. BRUNNE *Handl. Synne* 1041 To pley at þe ches or at þe tablere. *c* **1400** *Lanfranc's Cirurg.* 247 Wiþinne a monþe he miȝt se to pleie at þe tabler. **1426** LYDG. *De Guil. Pilgr.* 17272 Squar as ys a Tabler. **14..** *Metr. Voc.* in Wr.-Wülcker 626/13 *Scaccarium* checure, *alea* tabelere, *decius* dyce. **1474** CAXTON *Chesse* IV. i. (1883) 161 Wherfore y^t^ ther ben in the tabler as many poynts wyde as ben full.

2. (? A table-cloth or a towel: med.L. *tablerium.*)

1392 *Earl Derby's Exp.* (Camden) 178 Graunsom bastard pro j tabler per ipsum empt' ibidem pro domino, xij scot. **1393** *Ibid.* 281 Pro iiij lb. cotoni et j matte..pro j tablerio.

tabler[2] ('teɪblə(r)). [f. TABLE *sb.* and *v.* + -ER: in sense 1 = OF. *tableour*; in other senses = OF. *tablier.*]

†**1.** A player at backgammon. Cf. TABLING *vbl. sb.* 2. *Obs.*

1561 BP. PARKHURST *Injunctions* 19 Dycers, tablers, carders, swearers or vehemently suspected therof. **1571** GRINDAL *Injunctions* §23 Rem. (Parker Soc.) 130 Nor any of you shall be..a hunter, hawker, dicer, carder, tabler.

†**2.** Rendering Gr. τραπεζίτης, a money-changer.

c **1550** CHEKE *Matt.* xxv. 27 You schold yeerfoor haav put out mi moni to y^e^ tablers.

3. a. One who gets his meals at another's table for payment; = BOARDER 1. *Obs.* or *rare.*

1598 FLORIO *Ital. Dict.*, *Comensale*, a fellow boorder, a fellowe commoner, a fellow tabler. **1641** HINDE *J. Bruen* iii. 10 He was sent..to be taught and trained up under one James Roe..where he continued a Scholler and Tabler for the space of three yeares. *a* **1714** M. HENRY *Life F. Tallents* Wks. 1853 I. 624 He left off house-keeping, and went to be a tabler. **1755** JOHNSON, Boarder, a tabler; one that eats with another at a settled rate.

†**b.** One who boards persons. *Obs.*

1665 BRATHWAIT *Comment Two Tales* 8 We are to suppose him to be a Lodger or Tabler of Scholars and other Artists, for their Chamber and weekly Commons.

4. In senses 4–8 of TABLE *v.*; as in 'the tabler of the resolution', etc.

a **1910** in *N.E.D.* **1976** H. WILSON *Governance of Britain* vii. 141 If the tablers of each of these questions are called by Mr Speaker, no other question is called.

5. With initial capital. A member of the Round Table organization; a Round-Tabler.

1955 [see SOROPTIMIST *a.* and *sb.*]. **1973** *Scotsman* 21 Feb. 8/4 During lunch with some executives in Rotary and the Round Table..the prominent young Tabler from Lower Yarrow..suggested [etc.]. **1977** *Abingdon Herald* 10 Mar. 2/5 Between them, the 1,215 Tablers are buying an off-shore lifeboat.

'table-ˌrapping, *sb.* (and *a.*) The production of raps or knocking sounds on a table without apparent physical means; by spiritualists ascribed to the agency of departed spirits, and used as a supposed means of communication with them. Also as *adj.*, and **'table-rapper,** one who practises table-rapping.

1856 *Spiritual Herald* Apr. 73 The matter has been explained to us thus... Table-turning and table-rapping are designed to call attention to the existence and presence of super-human powers. **1858** HAWTHORNE *Fr. & It. Note-Bks.* II. 141 He made his communication by means of table-rapping. **1860** *All Year Round* No. 64. 328 His aunt, who almost made a profession of table-rapping, who kept a journal of her spiritual experiences. **1893** *Harper's Mag.* Feb. 377/1, I could not ring a bell when there was none to ring, as spirits do in table-rappers' closets. **1936** M. FRANKLIN *All that Swagger* x. 89 Familiar association with bogus lords and parsons, soothsayers, table-rappers, medical quacks, [etc.]. **1973** T. PYNCHON *Gravity's Rainbow* I. 55 The young statistician is devoted to number and to method, not table-rapping or wishful thinking.

Table Round, = ROUND TABLE *sb.*

'table 'ruby. A ruby cut with a large flat upper surface surrounded by small facets: cf. TABLE *sb.* 18, TABLE DIAMOND.

1529 in *Wills Doct. Com.* (Camden) 18 One ring with a table rubye. **1660** F. BROOKE tr. *Le Blanc's Trav.* 285, I gave a fair table Rubie to my Sister. **1901** *Westm. Gaz.* 31 Dec. 1/1 The Coronation ring..will probably take the form of a plain gold ring set with a large table ruby on which is engraved a plain or St. George's Cross.

'table-spoon. A spoon (larger than a dessert-spoon) used for taking soup, and, in a larger size, for serving vegetables, puddings, etc. at table. Also *loosely*, = TABLESPOONFUL.

1763 *Brit. Mag.* IV. 275 The villain stole two large table-spoons. **1865** DICKENS *Mut. Fr.* I. ii, Like a face in a table-spoon. **1960** E. DAVID *Fr. Prov. Cooking* 506 For 2 lb. of fruit add 6 tablespoons of vanilla sugar. **1981** *Sunday Tel.* 8 Mar. 11/2 Cucumber soup. 1 small onion; 1 clove garlic; 2 tablespoons sunflower oil; [etc.].

Hence **'table'spoonful,** as much as a table-spoon holds; also *fig.*

1772 HIGGINS in *Phil. Trans.* LXIII. 140 Half a table-spoonful of the..solution. **1856** KANE *Arct. Expl.* I. xvi. 198 Brandy..served out in tablespoonful doses. **1880** [see CONTINUED *ppl. a.* 3 b]. **1894** WALSH *Coffee* (Philad.) 240 Add half tablespoonful of powdered chicory to two tablespoonfuls of ground coffee.

'table-stone.

†**1.** *Arch.* A flat stone, a stone tablet; also, a horizontal stone. *Obs.*

c **1467–9** *Durham Acc. Rolls* (Surtees) 641 Pro..nova operacione et posicione tabilstonys [in the walls of a church]. **1554** *Aberdeen Regr.* (1844) I. 281 Findand sufficient hewyn stanes to the haill wark with the tabill stane of the gavillis and makand the said tolbuith vattirthicht.

2. *Archæol.* **a.** A flat stone supported by two or more upright stones; a cromlech or dolmen; also, the horizontal stone forming the top of this.

1840 T. A. TROLLOPE *Summ. Brittany* II. 88 These dolmens, or table-stones, consist..of one large flat mass, supported by several upright stones. **1880** JEFFERIES *Gr. Ferne F.* 150 He crawled right under the table-stone of the dolmen.

b. A small flat round stone supposed to have been used in a game resembling draughts.

1851 D. WILSON *Preh. Ann.* (1863) II. IV. vi. 335 Table-stones, or draughtsmen, are found alongside the weapons and other relics buried with the warrior.

tablet ('tæblɪt), *sb.* Forms: 4–6 **tablette,** 5 **tabulette, -elet(te, (taplet),** 5–6 **tablett, tabellet(t,** 6 **tabillette,** *Sc.* **teblet, tabullatte,** 6– **tablet.** [a. OF.

tablete (13th c.), F. *tablette*, dim. of *table*, = Pr. *tauleta*, Sp. *tableta*, Pg. *taboleta*, It. *tavoletta*, med.L. *tabuleta* (1376 in Du Cange): see TABLE *sb.* and -ET[1], -ETTE.]

1. A small, flat, and comparatively thin piece of stone, metal, wood, ivory, or other hard material, artificially shaped for some purpose; a small slab.

a. A small slab of stone or metal bearing or intended to bear an inscription or carving, *esp.* one affixed to a wall as a memorial; also applied to a flat surface cut in a rock for the same purpose.

c **1315** SHOREHAM iii. 67 Ope two tablettes of ston..He hys [= them] wrot, Moyses by-tok. **1447** BOKENHAM *Seyntys* (Roxb.) 254 A taplet of marbyl [he] held in hys honde. **1649** G. DANIEL *Trinarch., Hen. V* cclxi, His single Honour needs noe Fret of Names..To glimer ore the Tablet. **1700** PRIOR *Carmen Sæculare* 167 When..The pillar'd marble, and the tablet brass, Mouldering, drop the victor's praise. **1851** LAYARD *Pop. Acc. Discov. Nineveh* Introd. 13 The most important trilingual inscriptions hitherto discovered are those..in the rock tablet of Behistun. *Ibid.* vii. 163 Four tablets have been cut in the rock. **1870** F. R. WILSON *Ch. Lindisf.* 30 The mural tablets are also numerous.

b. A slab or panel, usually of wood, for a picture or inscription. ***votive tablet***: an inscribed panel anciently hung in a temple in fulfilment of a vow, e.g. after deliverance from shipwreck or dangerous illness. Chiefly *arch.* or *Hist.*

1581 PETTIE *Guazzo's Civ. Conv.* I. (1586) 30 b, Others, with Tablets and pictures use to represent men and women in some infamous and dishonest act. *a* **1700** DRYDEN (J.), Through all Greece the young gentlemen learned..to design upon tablets of boxen wood. **1782** V. KNOX *Ess.* lxiii. 274 Apelles used to say, that Protogenes knew not when to take his hand from the tablet which he was painting. **1851** D. WILSON *Preh. Ann.* (1863) II. III. ii. 40 A votive tablet in honour of the Legate. **1869** LECKY *Europ. Mor.* I. iii. 382 The votive tablets of those who escaped are suspended in the temple, while those who were shipwrecked are forgotten.

c. A small smooth inflexible or stiff sheet or leaf for writing upon; usually, one of a pair or set hinged or otherwise fastened together; anciently, of wood, or other material, covered with wax, written upon with a style, and used for correspondence, legal documents, etc.; in later times, of ivory, cardboard, or the like, carried in the pocket and used for memoranda; hence sometimes, in pl. ***tablets***, applied vaguely to a note-book. Formerly called *tables* (TABLE *sb.* 2 b).

1611 SHAKS. *Cymb.* v. iv. 109 This Tablet lay vpon his Brest, wherein Our pleasure, his full Fortune, doth confine. **1780** MME. D'ARBLAY *Diary* 29 Apr., Had I not kept memorandums in my tablets, I could not possibly give any account of our proceedings. **1836** MARRYAT *Japhet* xl, I took out my tablets, and wrote down the address. **1860** RAWLINSON *Herodotus* VII. §239 IV. 196 Demaratus..took a pair of tablets, and clearing the wax away from them, wrote what the king was purposing to do upon the wood. **1883** *Chamb. Jrnl.* 28 Apr. 266/2 There were unearthed nearly forty thousand inscribed tablets of unbaked clay. **1885** BIBLE (R.V.) *Isa.* viii. 1 Take thee a great tablet, and write upon it with the pen of a man.

d. In general or various applications, as a slab or tile, used in roofing or flooring, a flat piece in some mechanism, etc.; in quot. 1782 applied to playing-cards. Also, a plaque of pottery; *spec.* one forming the central part of a chimney-piece. Cf. BLOCK *sb.* 12 c.

c **1440** *Pallad. on Husb.* VI. 195 Now brode and thynne Tilette or tabulette of marbul stoon. **1698** FRYER *Acc. E. India & P.* 395 A Bed made..on the Tablets upon the Tops of their Houses. **1768** J. WEDGWOOD *Let.* 6 Nov. (1965) 68, I have lately had a Vision by night of some new Vases, Tablets &c with which Articles we shall certainly serve the *whole World!* **1782** COWPER *Progr. Err.* 170 The painted tablets, dealt and dealt again. **1842** I. WILLIAMS *Baptistery* I. (1874) 1 Quaint tablets rang'd some antique hearth around, Blue Holland porcelain, all rudely wrought. **1775**, **1875** [see BLOCK *sb.* 12 c]. **1970** G. SAVAGE *Dict. Antiques* 462/2 The year 1773 saw the first catalogue of ornamental wares, which included..tablets for chimney-pieces and furniture-mounts.

e. *U.S.* = PAD *sb.*[3] 4. Cf. WRITING TABLET.

1880 *Geyer's Stationer* 12 Aug. (Advt.), The M. & H. Blotter Tablet... Beware of tablets sold by J. C. Blair, as he is manufacturing without a legal right. **1897** *Sears, Roebuck Catal.* 349/2 Everything from a 400 page tablet of fair paper for 4 cents, to one of fine cream laid paper. **1934** *Chain Store Age* (Gen. Merchandise ed.) Jan. 57/2 The customer does not notice that there are three sheets less in a tablet. **1977** *Chicago Tribune* 2 Oct. XII. 39/1 Cadillac boasts in its 1978 Seville that it has made 'provision for a phone installation, writing pad, and pen'. But it's only a provision—you have to supply the phone, pen, and tablet.

f. A small metal disc similar in function to a 'staff' (STAFF *sb.*[1] 9 f), and used for working single-track railways.

1897 W. E. LANGDON *Applic. Electr. to Railway Working* vi. 129 When the instruments are in their normal condition, all tablets being in, the very first ring from the station of whom the permission to withdraw a tablet is made..would ..be equally serviceable for the purpose. **1950** O. S. NOCK *Brit. Locomotives from Footplate* 183 This train was booked non-stop between Arrochar and Crianlarich, but the slack for tablet exchange made it necessary to pass very slowly through Ardline. **1969** *Railway Mag.* Feb. 88 (*caption*) The single-line tablet for the section to Kingussie is being given by the signalman to the driver.

g. A rigid card used in tablet-weaving (see sense 8 below).

1921 M. & H. PEACH tr. *Pralle's Tablet Weaving* 6 The earliest examples found of the little tablets for the weaving were of thin polished wood. **1964** H. HODGES *Artifacts* x. 137 The tablets were generally oval or rectangular with a hole, or a pair of holes, at each end. **1970** J. P. WILD *Textile Manuf. in N. Roman Provinces* vii. 73 Each tablet governs the four (or three) warp-threads which are threaded through its holes..; and the pack of tablets is held in the hand like a pack of cards.

†**2.** An ornament of precious metal or jewellery of a flat form, worn about the person. *Obs.* [Cf. med.L. *tabula* and *tabuletus* in Du Cange.]

c **1400** MAUNDEV. (1839) 234 Euerych of hem bereth a tablett of Iaspere or of Iuory or of cristall. **1504** *Will Goodyear* (Somerset Ho.), My tablet of golde that I was wonte to were abowte my nek. **1542** *Acc. Lord H. Treas. Scotl.* VIII. 58 Chengeis, tabullattis, tergattis, bracelattis, ringis. **1546** *Inv. Ch. Goods* (Surtees) 86 A great tablett of golde havyng in yt the ymage of Our Lady. **1583** GOLDING *Calvin on Deut.* cxxvi. 774 These great lords & braue lads which wil needs weare tablets at their neckes y[t] is to say sumptuous Iewels for folke to gase at a great way off. **1611** BIBLE *Exod.* xxxv. 22 And they came both men and women, ..and brought bracelets, and earerings, and rings, & tablets, all iewels of gold. *c* **1620** Z. BOYD *Zion's Flowers* (1855) 31 The tablets and the rings made for the eare.

3. a. A small flat or compressed piece of some solid confection, drug, or the like; a lozenge of flattened (originally rectangular) form; a flat cake of soap.

1582 HESTER *Secr. Phiorav.* I. xxix. 34 Giuing them euery mornyng one dragme of good Sope in tablettes accordyng to our inuention. **1626** BACON *Sylva* §970 It is yet in use, to wear little bladders of quicksilver, or tablets of arsenic, as preservatives against the plague. **1655** CULPEPPER *Riverius* I. ii. 15 You may often use..these Tablets or Lozenges following. **1704** J. HARRIS *Lex. Techn.* I, *Tablets*, or solid Electuaries, are much the same with Lozenges. **1890** *Lancet* 1 Nov. 39 (Advt., B. W. & Co.) The Bicarbonate of Potash and Bicarbonate of Soda 'Tablets' or 'Tabloids' prove efficacious in dyspepsia. **1898** *Allbutt's Syst. Med.* V. 996 [Trinitrine may be administered] in the form of tablets. **1902** *Times* 30 Mar. 12/3 At this date the plaintiffs had used the word 'tablet' to denote compressed drugs,..but Mr. Wellcome set about finding a new word, and invented the word 'tabloid'. *Mod.* A tablet of chocolate; a tablet of soap.

b. Hence, orig. and chiefly *Sc.* (also **taiblet**), a type of fudge (formerly hardbake or almond toffee) made in tablets; a piece of this.

1736 MRS. MCLINTOCK *Receipts for Cookery* 35 (*heading*) To make Orange Tablets with the Grate. **1850** MRS. DALGAIRNS *Practice of Cookery* 347 Ginger tablet may be made in this way. **1897** *Private Life of Queen* xvii. 140 Among the favourites of the Queen..are..tablets, *petits fours*,..pralines, almond sweets. *c* **1900** *Wee Macgregor* I. 2, I want taiblet. *Ibid.* 5. **1922** 'R. WEST' *Judge* I. ii. 56 Here's some taiblet for you, lassie. **1948** *Good Housek. Cookery Bk.* 643 *Ginger Tablet*, use the same ingredients as for Hazel Tablet, but omit the nuts and vanilla essence and add ½ oz. of ground ginger. **1973** *Times* 13 Dec. 12/2 Tablet, for those who don't know, is a delicious, crumbly fudge that melts in your mouth—it's a Scottish speciality.

c. A piece of compacted powder of standard size, shape, and composition, ready for subsequent moulding.

1935 [see PREFORM *sb.* 1]. **1936** H. W. ROWELL *Technol. of Plastics* xx. 148 A 'tablet' is of the correct weight and density required and is made of suitable diameter and thickness to fit the mould. It is made in a stock size of die and is not preformed to the approximate shape of the moulding. **1947** R. L. WAKEMAN *Chem. Commercial Plastics* v. 76 Tablets and preforms fit freely inside the mold ultimately employed. **1974** *Gloss. Packaging Terms* (*B.S.I.*) III. 9 *Tablet*, a compressed mass of moulding material of prescribed form and mass.

†**4.** Short for *tablet diamond*: see sense 8. *Obs.*

1519 *Lett. & Pap. Hen. VIII*, III. No. 463 (P.R.O.) Having an owche at the eend wherin is sett a fair table balas with iiij fair diamauntes wherof ij great poynted dyamaundes, oon tablet and oon losenge. *Ibid.*, iiij diamauntes wherof ij poynted and ij tablettes.

5. *Glass-making.* = TABLE *sb.* 15 b. ? *Obs.*

1688 [see TABLE *sb.* 15 b].

6. *Arch.* = TABLE *sb.* 12 a, b.

1788 [see GOBELIN 1]. **1823** P. NICHOLSON *Pract. Build.* 444 A Tablet is a projection, fixed in a wall, with one face parallel to the surface. **1875** LEWIS & STREET in *Encycl. Brit.* II. 390/1 The crowning tablet or fillet [of an Egyptian pylon or portico] is quite plain and unornamented.

7. *Anat.* = TABLE *sb.* 16.

1891 in *Cent. Dict.*

8. *attrib.* and *Comb.*: **tablet-book**, a set of tablets for writing on; **tablet check**, in *Telegraphy*: see quot.; †**tablet diamond** = TABLE DIAMOND; †**tablet jewel**, ? = sense 2; **tablet-letter**, an ancient letter written on a tablet; **tablet paper** *U.S.*, notepaper taken from a writing-pad; **tablet tea**, tea made up in tablets (sense 3); **tablet-weaving**, an early method of weaving, in which warp-threads are passed through holes in a number of parallel tablets, which are then rotated to form sheds; **tablet-writing**, writing on tablets.

1896 BOSCAWEN *Bible & Mon.* v. 110 The series of tablets when complete consisted of twelve *tablet-books. **1876** PREECE & SIVEWRIGHT *Telegraphy* 293 Every circuit..is supplied with a form called a '*Tablet check', upon which each message as it goes off is ticked. **1530** *Lett. & Pap. Hen. VIII*, IV. No. 6789 (P.R.O.) Rynges..oon with a *tablet dyamount. [Cf. sense 4 above.] **1598** YONG *Diana* 91 Two iewels curiouslie enchased with tablet Diamonds. **1599** MINSHEU *Sp. Dict., Dial.* 15 Chaines of Ieat, Amber, or such like, *tablet Iewels, girdles [etc.]. **1899** T. NICOL *Archaeol. & Bible* v. 186 Seven of the *tablet-letters are from the Governor of Jerusalem. **1964** MRS. L. B. JOHNSON *White House Diary* 25 Feb. (1970) 73 The file..marked 'particularly appealing'. Those were the letters that were taken to Mrs. Kennedy to read. They came written in poetry, they came in barely legible pencil on *tablet paper. **1891** *Daily News* 5 June 5/6 '*Tablet tea' and 'brick tea', so familiar in Russia,..are apt to be confounded by outsiders. The former..is made of the finest tea-dust procurable... It is manufactured by steam machinery, with the aid of steel moulds, under great pressure. **1921** M. & H. PEACH tr. *Pralle's Tablet Weaving* 6 *Tablet weaving..is considered the origin of all weaving. *Ibid.*, In the Museum at Copenhagen..is a belt which must have been woven by this tablet-weaving method. **1950** *Proc. Prehist. Soc.* XVI. 130 The archaeological material..is then reviewed, with a special note on the curious technique of tablet-weaving. **1979** B. CUNLIFFE *Celtic World* 60/2 Finer weaving to make braid and a form of tablet weaving are also attested. **1905** J. ORR *Probl. O.T.* Notes 525 Cuneiform *tablet-writing probably in some measure continued after the settlement in Canaan.

tablet (ˈtæblɪt), *v.* [f. prec. sb.]

1. a. *trans.* To furnish with a tablet (esp. one bearing an inscription); to affix a tablet to.

1864 *Reader* 11 June 750 A large series of Irish and British fossils, about 17,000 specimens..named and tableted. **1883** G. H. BOUGHTON in *Harper's Mag.* Apr. 698/2 About the square were numbers of..old houses, with elaborately adorned gables, crow-stepped,..and tableted. **1894** *Westm. Gaz.* 28 June 2/2 [The] chapel tableted with the names of some who have died in their country's service.

b. To inscribe on a tablet.

1878 *Masque of Poets* 152 And tableted above Him Still we read 'Love taught the smith to paint'.

2. *trans.* To make into a tablet; ? *intr.* to make tablets.

1889 *Sci. Amer.* 7 Dec. 363/1 A formula for the preparation of liquid glue for tableting purposes, which can be applied cold and which will retain its elasticity. **1936** H. W. ROWELL *Technol. of Plastics* xx. 148 Tableting or preforming or pelleting a powder is generally done on automatic machines. **1963** *Times* 4 May 11/5 In an article in a medical journal some time ago describing the clinical trial of a drug, reference was made to the manufacturer who 'tableted and distributed' the drug. **1973** R. PARKES *Guardians* ii. 59 This heroin is comparable in quality to that being sniffed by U.S. troops in Vietnam and far superior to that being tableted for U.K. distribution.

Hence **ˈtableted** *ppl. a.*, **ˈtableting** *vbl. sb.* and *ppl. a.*

1889 [see sense 2]. **1936** H. W. ROWELL *Technol. Plastics* xx. 148 Tableting machines measure the charge in this way. **1937** *Mod. Packaging* Oct. 110/1 Small powdered, tableted and similar products. **1947** R. L. WAKEMAN *Chrm. Commercial Plastics* v. 76 In compression operations, recourse is often had to tableting and preforming in order to speed up molding. **1972** *Materials & Technol.* V. xxi. 763 The tabletting process consists of feeding free-flowing granules into a..die, and compressing the material. **1983** *Glaxo Group News* Sept. 4/3 The accuracy and efficiency of single punch tabletting machines have been monitored by strain gauges.

table-talk (ˈteɪb(ə)lˌtɔːk). Talk at table; familiar conversation at meals.

In a general sense including ordinary conversation or gossip at the dinner-table; but now usually applied to the social conversation of famous men or of intellectual circles, esp. as reproduced in literary form; cf. the *Colloquia Mensalia* of Luther, first publ. 1567, Engl. transl. 1652, 1846.

a **1569** KINGESMYLL *Godly Advise* (1580) 11 Suche verelie is the Table-talk emongst the Gentiles the gentlemen. **1596** SHAKS. *Merch. V.* III. v. 93 *Ies.* Nay, let me praise you while I haue a stomacke? *Lor.* No pray thee, let it serue for table talke. **1608** BP. HALL *Char. Virtues & V., Busiebodie* Wks. (1627) 188 Himselfe begins table-talke of his neighbour at anothers boord; to whom he bears the first newes, and adiures him to conceale the reporter. **1811** SIR G. JACKSON *Diaries & Lett.* (1873) I. 192 This little episode..started some table talk.

1689 (*title*) Table-Talk: being the Discourses of John Selden Esq.; or his Sence of Various Matters of Weight and High Consequence. **1791** BOSWELL *Johnson* Introd. (1831) I. 55 The small portion which we have of the table-talk and other anecdotes of our celebrated writers. **1838–9** HALLAM *Hist. Lit.* IV. IV. vii. §31. 314 One group has acquired the distinctive name of Ana; the reported conversation, the table-talk of the learned. **1846** (*title*) The Table Talk of Martin Luther, translated and edited by W. Hazlitt.

b. *transf.* A subject for table-talk; a theme for general conversation.

1579–80 NORTH *Plutarch* 775 Antonius commanded him at the Table to tell him what wind brought him thither, he answered, That it was no Table-talk, and that he would tell him to morrow morning fasting. **1781** COWPER *Table Talk* 151 To be the Table Talk of clubs up stairs.

c. *attrib.*

1581 SIDNEY *Apol. Poetrie* (Arb.) 29 Not speaking (table talke fashion..) words as they chanceably fall from the mouth. **1614** JACKSON *Creed* III. xviii. §2 Acquainted with none but table-talke Diuinity.

So **ˈtable-talker**, one who talks or converses at table; esp. a person of high conversational powers.

1846 WORCESTER, *Table-talker*, one who converses at table. *Month. Rev.* **1880** *Q. Rev.* Jan. 101 He was the best of table-talkers.

tabletary ('tæblɪtərɪ), *a. rare.* [f. TABLET *sb.* + -ARY[1]; cf. *planetary.*] Of, pertaining to, or contained in a tablet or tablets.

1880 *Libr. Univ. Knowl.* (N.Y.) II. 186 s.v. *Bank & Banking*, No. 2 dated at Babylon.. 597 B.C., bears tabletary evidence, attested by three witnesses, of the loan of 2 minas.

'table-top, *a.* Also table top, tabletop. [f. *table-top* sb. (see TABLE *sb.* 22).] **1.** Of, pertaining to, or designating photography of subjects which can be contained within the area of a table-top; *spec.* applied to photography of small-scale models which gives the illusion of a larger subject.

1914 S. C. JOHNSON *Saturday with my Camera* xliv. 368 We can all enter the lists of table-top photography,.. and spend our winter evenings counterfeiting, at leisure, many of the most attractive sights of the world. **1923** *Kodak Mag.* Apr. 58 (*heading*) Home-made landscapes—a few words on table-top photography. **1935** *News Chron. Amat. Photogr.* xiv. 176 Flashlight has special application to table-top photography, now becoming so popular, as the illumination is under complete control, and all the work can be done in the evening. **1956** *Focal Encycl. Photogr.* 1151/1 There are three different branches of photography open to the photographer who chooses to work within the limits of a table top studio: still life studies, photography of small scale models and creative composition. The last is the true 'table top photography'. *Ibid.* 1152/2 Most table-top pictures fail either because they include too many items or because they try to represent the subject accurately and in detail instead of simply suggesting it in a broad effect.

2. That is or can be placed, or that takes place, on a table.

1945 F. BROWN in *Astounding Sci. Fiction* Jan. 133/1 There was a boom market in portable and table-top receivers. **1962** *Guardian* 9 July 5/3 He made table top models of the machines. **1971** *Physics Bull.* Sept. 513/2 The total number of installed computers, including table top computers, is expected to be 60 000 in 1975 and 96 500 in 1980. **1979** *Guardian* 31 Oct. 1/8 Fagging.. includes.. retrieving the little red ball when it goes under chairs during games of table-top cricket.

‖**tablette** (tæ'blɛt, 'tæblɪt). [a. mod.F. *tablette*: see TABLET.]

1. = TABLET *sb.* 1 c.

1728 H. HERBERT tr. *Fleury's Eccl. Hist.* I. 536 He came out with the tablette in his hand and read it. **1860** W. COLLINS *Wom. White* ep. i. narr. W. H. vii, I made some entries in my tablettes this morning. Find my tablettes.

2. = TABLET *sb.* 3.

1725 *Bradley's Fam. Dict.*, *Tablette*, or Lozenge, a Term in Pharmacy,.. a solid Electuary.. cut into the form of small, round or square Boards. **1890** *Harper's Mag.* Jan. 230/2 Some *tablettes* of grated cocoa candied in liquid sugar.

3. *Arch.* = TABLET *sb.* 6, TABLE *sb.* 12 a; *spec.* in *Fortif.* (see quot. 1853).

1723 CHAMBERS tr. *Le Clerc's Treat. Archit.* I. 124 Balusters with their Rail, serving as a Tablette or Rest to the Elbows. **1853** STOCQUELER *Milit. Encycl.*, *Tablette*, a flat coping-stone, generally two feet wide and eight inches thick, placed at the top of the revêtement of the escarp, for the purpose of protecting the masonry from the effects of the weather, and also to serve as an obstacle to the besiegers when applying the scaling-ladders.

tableture, obs. or erron. form of TABLATURE.

'table-,turning. The action of turning or moving a table without the use of any apparently adequate means, as by a number of persons placing their hands or fingers upon it; such movements being ascribed by some to spiritual agency (cf. TABLE-RAPPING). So **'table-,turner**, one who practises table-turning.

1853 *Ann. Reg.* 67 When the apparatus was kept in sight it proved to possess a corrective power over the mind of the table-turner. **1855** SMEDLEY, etc. *Occult Sc.* 200 Faraday explains table-turning by involuntary muscular action. **1860** JEAFFRESON *Bk. about Doctors* II. 38 The vagaries of.. electro-biologists, spirit-rappers, and table-turners. **1861** HOOK *Lives Abps.* I. vii. 421 The superstitions of the age, ranking with our mesmerism and table-turning.

tableware ('teɪb(ə)lwɛə(r)). Ware for the service of the table; a collective term for the articles which are used at meals, as dishes, plates, knives, forks, etc.

1772 J. WEDGWOOD *Let.* 10 Sept. (1965) 134, I think he might by that means sell now and then a sett of it in Tableware. **1832** G. R. PORTER *Porcelain & Gl.* 16 The principal inventions of Mr. Wedgwood were—1. His table ware. **1897** *Outing* (U.S.) XXX. 376/2 Each member of the party should provide his own tableware... A cup, plate, and spoon of tin, knife and fork. **1904** *Times* 26 July 7/3 The mayor.. presented him on behalf of the city with a magnificent service of tableware.

tablewise ('teɪb(ə)lwaɪz), *adv.* [f. TABLE *sb.* + -WISE.] In the manner or form of a table: in various senses. †**a.** ? In a rectangular shape. *Obs.*

c **1425** *Found. St. Bartholomew's* 10 The Chirche he made of cumly stoonewerke tabylwyse.

b. In tabular form; tabularly: cf. TABLE *sb.* 10.

1611 SPEED *Hist. Gt. Brit.* v. v. 27 It shal not.. be amisse in this place once for all, tablewise to lay down the same. **1812** G. CHALMERS *Dom. Econ. Gt. Brit.* 463 A Comparative State, tablewise, of our domestic, and foreign trade. **1816** BENTHAM *Chrestom.* Wks. 1843 VIII. 7/2 The matter of the text being thus treated Table-wise.

c. Said in reference to the holy table when placed in the body of the church or chancel with its length in the direction of that of the church; opp. to *altarwise.*

1637 J. WILLIAMS *Holy Table* 10 Your Communion-Table, when it is not used, should stand in the upper end of the Chancell, not Altar-wise but Table-wise. **1654** EVELYN *Diary* 12 July, To Magdalen College [Oxf.], where we saw the Library and Chapell, which was likewise in pontifical order, the altar onely I think turn'd table-wise. *c* **1710** CELIA FIENNES *Diary* (1888) 71 Their alter stood tablewise for ye Comunion just in ye middle of ye Chancell. **1881** W. R. W. STEPHENS *Dioc. Hist. Chichester* 194 In some it [the altar] was placed altarwise, in others tablewise.

d. In reference to a precious stone: Cut as a 'table' (see TABLE *sb.* 18, TABLE-CUT).

1727-41 CHAMBERS *Cycl.* s.v. *Table*, A diamond cut Table-wise.

e. In the form of a table as a piece of furniture, i.e. (placed) horizontally on supports.

1902 *Munsey's Mag.* XXVI. 622/2 It was a flat, plain slab of dark gray stone, placed on pillars tablewise.

‖**tablier** (tablie). [Fr. *tablier*: see TABLER[1].]

†**1.** A chess-board; = TABLER[1] 1. *Obs. rare*$^{-1}$.

1474 CAXTON *Chesse* IV. i. I. vij, For to represente the mesure of this cyte, in whiche this playe or game was founden, the philosopher that fond hit first ordeyned a tablier conteynyng lxiiij poyntes square.

2. A part of a lady's dress resembling an apron; the front of a skirt cut or trimmed in the form of an apron.

1835 *Court Mag.* VI. p. xvii/2 The skirts of these latter are closed before, and trimmed with folds in the form of a *tablier*. **1862** *Eng. Wom. Dom. Mag.* IV. 236/1 The dress.. ornamented in front with a *tablier* of white satin. **1885** *Pall Mall. G.* 29 Jan. 9/1 The bride.. wore a dress of striped white satin with pearl tablier in front and net veil. **1903** *Daily Chron.* 30 May 8/4 At the edge of the tablier skirt that falls loosely over the deep flounce. **1908** *Ibid.* 4 Aug. 7/5 [The gown] has what the French call a 'tablier', that is a plain breadth let in down the front of the skirt.

3. Name for the enlarged *labia pudendi* characteristic of Hottentot women.

1893 *Edin. Rev.* Apr. 294 The tablier is usual among their women and believed to be a mark of race.

tabling ('teɪblɪŋ), *vbl. sb.* [f. TABLE *v.* and *sb.* + -ING[1].]

1. The action of setting down or entering in a table; tabulation. Now *rare.*

c **1450** in Aungier *Syon* (1840) 361 To her settyng hygher or lower,.. tabulyng and assygnementes, alle owe redyly to obey. **1561** *Reg. Privy Council Scot.* I. 179 Without ony continuatioun, dyet or tabling of uther summondis. **1607** COWELL *Interpr.*, *Tabling of Fines*, is the making of a table for euery countie, where his Maiesties writ runneth, conteining the contents of euery fine, that shall passe in any one terme [etc.]. **1624** *3rd Rep. Hist. MSS. Comm.* 30/2 An Act concerning the fees to be taken in cities, boroughs, towns, &c., and the tabling thereof. **1838** W. BELL *Dict. Law Scot.*, Tabling of a Summons. At the institution of the College of Justice (1537), there was appointed a table, in which were set down all summonses, to be called in their turns.

†**2.** Playing at 'tables' or backgammon. Cf. TABLER[2] 1. *Obs.*

1553 *Ord. Voy. Cathay* in Hakl. (1886) III. 19 Neither dicing, carding, tabling, nor other divilish games to be frequented. **1583** BABINGTON *Command.* iv. (1599) 166, I require.. that.. they better weigh whether carding, dising, and tabling.. be exercises commanded of God for the sabaoth day or no. **1608** WILLET *Hexapla Exod.* 411 Vsurie, carding, tabling and such like.

3. The action of providing or fact of being provided with meals; provision of food; boarding, board. Cf. TABLE *v.* 2. Now *rare* or *Obs.*

a **1553** in Cole *Hen. VIII's Scheme Bishopricks* (1838) 117 Borde and tabelyng frely in the late Monasterie to one scole-master. **1587** HARRISON *England* II. vi. (1877) I. 142 To spend their time in large tabling and bellie cheere. *a* **1639** W. WHATELEY *Prototypes* II. xxxiv. (1640) 165 He would have left the matter of his tabling to him. **1725** *Postmaster* 16 Apr. 6 Lodgings, furnish'd or unfurnish'd, with good Tabling or without. **1830** J. HODGSON in J. Raine *Mem.* (1858) II. 154 *note*, You can have a bed and tabling here.

4. Material for table-cloths; table-linen. (Cf. *bedding.*)

1640 in Entick *London* (1766) II. 167 Diaper for tabling. **1721** C. KING *Brit. Merch.* II. 347, 10281 Yards Diaper Tabling, at 2*s.* **1812** J. SMYTH *Pract. of Customs* (1821) 131 Diaper Tabling, of the manufacture of Silesia.

5. Tables collectively; accommodation of tables.

1892 *Gard. Chron.* 27 Aug. 254/3 The length of tabling filled with products must have reached fully half a mile. **1902** *Westm. Gaz.* 21 Mar. 8/1 Supposing we had to put up tabling, the capacity of the hall would be reduced at once from 3,000 to 800.

6. *Arch.* The making of a 'table' or horizontal projecting course (see TABLE *sb.* 12 a); *concr.* such a course itself; *spec.* a coping.

1411 in J. R. Boyle *Hedon* (1875) App. 168 In ij. bussellis calcis emptis pro dictis fenestris et pro tabelyng de les wykes ibidem, iiij. d. **1671** in Holmes *Pontefract Bk. Entries* (1882) 103 Item, for corbells, riggings and tableinge 1. 13. 4. **1870** F. R. WILSON *Ch. Lindisf.* 21 There was the corbel tabling, showing the old height. **1876** GWILT *Encycl. Archit.* Gloss., *Tabling*, a term used by the Scotch builders to denote the coping of the walls of very common houses.

7. *Carpentry* and *Shipbuilding.* See TABLE *v.* 6, and quots.

1794 *Rigging & Seamanship* I. 11 *Tabling* is the uniting of pieces together in a manner similar to the chain-coak, but broader. *c* **1850** *Rudim. Navig.* (Weale) 155 *Tabling*, letting one piece of timber into another by alternate scores or projections from the middle, so that they cannot be drawn asunder either lengthwise or sidewise.

8. *Sailmaking.* A broad hem made at the edge of a sail to strengthen it: see TABLE *v.* 7.

1769 FALCONER *Dict. Marine* (1776), *Tabling, bander*, a sort of broad hem formed on the skirts and bottoms of a ship's sails, to strengthen them in that part which is attached to the bolt-rope. **1794** *Rigging & Seamanship* I. 89. **1882** NARES *Seamanship* (ed. 6) 11 *Tabling*, the double part of a sail, close to the bolt-rope.

9. In hedging: see quot., and cf. TABLE *sb.* 13 c.

1843 J. SMITH *Forest Trees* 24 Give the hedge what is called a tabling, that is to collect the earth.. that has been taken away from the roots,.. and place it again in its original position.

10. *Anat.* = TABLATURE 5.

1891 in *Cent. Dict.*

11. *attrib.*, as †**tabling-den**, a low-class gaming-house; †**tabling school**, a boarding-school.

1886 H. HALL *Soc. Eliz. Age* viii. 105 The towns were flooded with tippling-houses, bowling-alleys, tabling-dens. **1660** C. HOOLE *New Disc. Old Art Teaching Schoole* vi. 282 The shutting of children up.. into a dark room, and depriving them of a meals meat, or the like (which are used in some Tabling Schools).. cannot be commendably.. used in our greater Schooles.

†**'tabling-house.** *Obs.* [f. prec. (sense 2) + HOUSE *sb.*] A house of resort for playing 'tables' or other games; a gambling-house.

The sense 'boarding-house', alleged in mod. Dicts. (app. founded on Halliwell's casual remark in Nares (ed. 1859) on quot. 1577), is not certainly supported by any quot.

1577 NORTHBROOKE *Dicing* (1843) 128 They alledge, that there is none but common gamehouses and tabling houses that are condemned, and not the playing sometimes in their own private houses. **1598** FLORIO *Ital. Dict.*, *Ridotto*,.. a gaming or tabling house. **1605** *Play Stucley* in Simpson *Sch. Shaks.* (1878) I. 165 Gods me, my masters father! Now my master He's at the Tabling-house too!

‖**tablinum** (tə'blaɪnəm). *Rom. Antiq.* Pl. **tablina.** [L. *tablīnum, tabulīnum*, as in definition, also a floored place in the open air, a picture-gallery, f. *tabula* TABLE.] An apartment or recess in an ancient Roman house, opening out of the *atrium* opposite the principal entrance, and containing the family archives, statues, etc.

1828-9 J. NARRIEN *Arch.* in *Encycl. Metropol.* (1845) V. 292/2 The *tablinum*, or repository for the archives and records of the family. **1832** GELL *Pompeiana* I. viii. 159 The tablinum itself, so called from being closed with planks. **1862** E. FALKENER *Ephesus*, etc. II. iv. 259. **1890** *Athenæum* 23 Aug. 265/2 In the central block [of a Roman villa] are the principal rooms, such as the *tabulinum* and *triclinium*.

tabliture, obs. form of TABLATURE.

tabloid ('tæblɔɪd), *sb.* (*a.*) [f. TABL(ET *sb.* + -OID: see sense 1. The figurative, transferred, and sometimes humorous uses derive from the compressed or concentrated form of the drugs sold by the firm under the name.] **1. a.** (With capital initial.) A term registered on 14 March, 1884, by Messrs. Burroughs, Wellcome & Co., as a trade-mark applied to chemical substances used in medicine and pharmacy prepared by them, and afterwards for other goods; held by the Court of Appeal to be a 'fancy word' as applied to the goods for which it is registered, and legally restricted to the preparations of the firm named. Also *loosely*, (with small initial), a small (medicinal) tablet.

1884 *Trade Marks Jrnl.* 23 Apr. 334 *Tabloid*... Burroughs, Wellcome & Company, Snow Hill Buildings, Holborn Viaduct, London, E.C... Chemical substances not included in Class I, used in Medicine and Pharmacy. **1894** *Murray's Handbk. India* (ed. 2) p. xx, For medicine, plenty of quinine in 2 or 4 grain 'tabloids' or pills. **1895** *Army & Navy Co-op. Soc. Price List* 695/1 Tabloids—Ichthyol per bott. 0/7½... Tea per tin 0/5. **1904** *Official Gaz.* (U.S. Patent Office) 18 Oct. 1743/2 Drugs and chemicals for human and veterinary use... *Tabloid.* **1916** 'TAFFRAIL' *Pincher Martin* ix. 161 Morphia tabloids were served out to all the officers of quarters for administration to badly injured men. **1938** E. J. G. FORSE *Ceremonial Curiosities* xxix. 149 It is wise to carry a few simple tabloids with you. **1978** *Daily Mirror* 19 Apr. 24/1, I found a metal box which used to contain 'Tabloid' tea.

b. *fig.*, etc. Freq. *attrib.* or as *adj.*

1898 *Natural Science* Feb. 112 This presumed tabloid condition [of the flints] is brought about by a presumed extreme cold. **1902** *Encycl. Brit.* XXXI. 574/2 The untouched cells below the cut grow larger.. with the formation of tabloid cork-cells. **1903** Nov. 20-Dec. 14 MR. JUSTICE BYRNE in *Repts. Patent & Trade Mark Cases* XXI. 69 The word Tabloid has become so well-known.. in consequence of the use of it by the Plaintiff firm in connection with their compressed drugs that I think it has acquired a secondary sense in which it has been used and may legitimately be used so long as it does not interfere with their trade rights. I think the word has been so applied generally with reference to the notion of a compressed form or dose of anything. **1906** *Westm. Gaz.* 3 Jan. 3/1 Five short tableaux of drama which.. might be described brutally as five tabloids of melodrama. **1909** *Westm. Gaz.* 22 Oct. 5/2 While in literature the trend of taste is all in the direction of tabloids, composers seem ashamed of anything approaching terseness. **1920** R. MACAULAY *Potterism* VI. iii. 232 People might like their science in cheap and absurd tabloid form... The Potter press exulted in scientific discoveries made easy. **1928** *Melody Maker* Feb. 145/2 Mr. Harold Craxton's playing on the piano of the 'Three Blind Mice'..as a tabloid Hungarian Rhapsody by Liszt. **1935** *Brit. Jrnl. Psychol.* July 27 Statements of a vague character, which are condensations of complex propositional wholes... To such propositions I have elsewhere given the name 'tabloids'.

2. a. *R.A.F. slang.* A small Sopwith biplane. (*Disused.*)

1913 *Aeroplane* 11 Dec. 635/2 The small speedy Sopwith biplane has been nicknamed the 'Tabloid' because it contains so many good qualities in such small compass. **1915** *War Illustr.* 20 Feb. 22/2 The 'Tabloid's supreme value lies in its speed and climbing power. **1925** FRASER & GIBBONS *Soldier & Sailor Words* 275 *Tabloid, a,* an Air Force nickname for a type of small Sopwith biplane of high speed and rapid climbing powers, a special favourite from its numerous good points, its, as it were, concentrated excellencies. **1928** C. F. S. GAMBLE *North Sea Air Station* x. 149 In addition to its maximum speed of 92 miles an hour the 'Tabloid' was remarkable in those days for its great speed range.

b. In full *tabloid cruiser*. A small cruising yacht.

1930 *Yachting Monthly* XLIX. 428/1 T's ship, Honora, is, except for her draught, a 'tabloid' cruiser: 19 ft. LOA, with 5 ft. 9 in. beam. **1937** *Ibid.* LXIV. 17/1 Reflections on an unusual little tabloid. **1938** *Ibid.* 452/2 A tabloid cruiser that goes foreign ought to be registered.

3. a. A popular newspaper which presents its news and features in a concentrated, easily assimilable, and often sensational form, esp. one with smaller pages than those of a regular newspaper.

1918 W. E. CARSON *Northcliffe* x. 304 Since 1908 Alfred Harmsworth, like his famous 'tabloid', has disappeared from view. **1926** *Encycl. Brit.* II. 1055/2 The introduction of tabloids may be explained..by the passing remark of Lord Northcliffe, 'If some American does not start one I shall have to come over to do it.' **1928** *Observer* 5 Feb. 18/1 The ..chain now includes 26 papers, in most cases 'tabloids' or papers with a popular appeal. **1934** A. WOOLLCOTT *While Rome Burns* 100, I remembered how confidently, but how inaccurately, the tabloids had prophesied the..divorce. **1949** [see ANGEL *v.* 1]. **1957** *Listener* 31 Oct. 683/2 Newspapers have been allowed to transform themselves into tabloids with gossip columns, adulation of film stars, beauty contests and other requisites of the popular press of the West. **1970** G. F. NEWMAN *Sir, You Bastard* vi. 174, I presume you've read the tabloids? **1978** *Time* 3 July 12/1 The *National Enquirer*, the Florida-based tabloid, dispatched ten reporters and photographers to scour the Riviera in quest of informants on the courtship.

b. *attrib.*, esp. as *tabloid newspaper*.

1901 *Westm. Gaz.* 1 Jan. 9/3 He advocated tabloid journalism. **1902** *Ibid.* 1 Apr. 10/2 The proprietor intends to give in tabloid form all the news printed by other journals. **1918** W. E. CARSON *Northcliffe* x. 299 The New York *World* made its appearance. Harmsworth had issued the paper in what he called 'tabloid form'. **1926** *Amer. Mercury* Dec. 462/1 A tabloid weekly theatrical newspaper, published in New York, and filled with ugly type, heavy black advertisements and the most atrocious English ever put into print, was named as co-respondent by his wife. **1938** [see JAZZ *sb.* 6]. **1949** KOESTLER *Promise & Fulfilment* II. ii. 232 To the distant reader of the tabloid Press..it looked as if history had at last met Metro-Goldwyn-Mayer's most ambitious dream. **1962** V. NABOKOV *Pale Fire* 22 He was back in the car, reading a tabloid newspaper which I had thought no poet would deign to touch. **1977** *New Yorker* 19 Sept. 31/1 Next day, the tabloid *Daily Mail* gave the hearing its entire front page, but the *Guardian* didn't mention it at all.

Hence as *v. trans.*, to express briefly or concisely; to condense. *rare.*

1933 PARTRIDGE *Slang To-day & Yesterday* I. iv. 36 Much of the best wit, the most delectable humour is couched in slang; for, slang offers no compulsion to think *how* the happy thought is phrased or, perhaps, tabloided into an expressive adjective, or a second-sighted noun, an unravelling or illuminating verb. **1934** *Punch* 21 Mar. 329/2 Also there is a certain sketchiness in the tale as tabloided for the two hours' traffic of our stage, and some of the connecting-links seem to have got lost in the process.

tabnab ('tæbnæb). *Naut. slang.* [Origin obscure.] A cake, bun, or pastry; a savoury snack.

1933 M. LOWRY *Ultramarine* v. 212 Perhaps he would be able to speak to Andy when he gave him the tabnabs. **1947** —— *Under Volcano* vi. 172 What the bosun called, with unction, 'afternoon tea'. With tabnabs. The tabnabs were delicate and delicious little cakes made by the second cook. **1962** *Punch* 10 Jan. 98/1 Tea and tabnabs (seafaring for cake). **1978** K. BONFIGLIOLI *All Tea in China* viii. 111 These 'tabnabs' were little gullet-tickling confections... My favourite 'tabnab' was..a little fried potato-cake with a morsel of kari'd mutton inside.

tabo- ('teɪbəʊ), comb. form of TABES, as in **tabopa'ralysis** *Med.* (see quot. 1972); **tabopa'resis** = prec.

1910 F. W. MOTT in Power & Murphy *System of Syphilis* IV. x. 328 An important point to remember is the frequency with which optic atrophy is followed by tabo-paralysis. **1972** R. A. & A. T. WILLIS *Princ. Path. & Bacteriol.* (ed. 3) xvi. 201 The quaternary syphilitic diseases are (1) general paralysis of the insane or dementia paralytica, and (2) locomotor ataxia or tabes dorsalis. A combination of the two, taboparalysis, also occurs. **1910** *Med. Rec.* (N.Y.) LXXVII. 219/1 (*heading*) The pathological prodromes of taboparesis. **1932** W. BOYD *Textbk. Path.* xxx. 829 There is sometimes a combination of tabes and paresis (taboparesis), with degeneration of the posterior columns [of the spinal cord]. **1980** A. KING et al. *Venereal Dis.* (ed. 4) v. 89 This suggests that there is an element of tabes present (taboparesis).

taboggan, tabogmay, var. ff. TOBOGGAN.

taboo, tabu (tə'buː), *a.* and *sb.* Also TAPU, tambu, tabou. [ad. Tongan *tabu* (see A).

'Tabu is also the form in several languages of Melanesia and Micronesia, as in some of the islands of Vanuatu, Kiribati, Papua New Guinea, etc. The general Polynesian and Maori form (also in some of the islands of Vanuatu) is *'tapu* (TAPU), in Hawaiian *'kapu*. Some of the Melanesian langs., as those of Fiji, and some of the Solomon Is., have *'tambu*, New Britain *'tabu* and *'tambu*. Various cognate forms occur in Melanesian and cognate langs. The Tongan form was that first met with by Captain Cook, in 1777, from the narrative of whose voyages the custom with its name became known in England. In Fr. spelt *tabou*. The accentuation *ta'boo*, and the use of the word as sb. and vb., are English; in all the native langs. the word is stressed on the first syllable, and is used only as adj., the sb. and vb. being expressed by derivative words or phrases.]

A. *adj.* (chiefly in predicate). **a.** As originally used in Polynesia, Melanesia, New Zealand, etc.: Set apart for or consecrated to a special use or purpose; restricted to the use of a god, a king, priests, or chiefs, while forbidden to general use; prohibited to a particular class (esp. to women), or to a particular person or persons; inviolable, sacred; forbidden, unlawful; also said of persons under a perpetual or temporary prohibition from certain actions, from food, or from contact with others.

1777 COOK *Voy. to Pacific* II. vii. (1785) I. 286 [At Tongataboo] Not one of them would sit down, or eat a bit of any thing... On expressing my surprize at this, they were all *taboo*, as they said; which word has a very comprehensive meaning; but, in general, signifies that a thing is forbidden. Why they were laid under such restraints, at present, was not explained. *Ibid.* ix. 338 As every thing would, very soon, be *taboo*, if any of our people, or of their own, should be found walking about, they would be knocked down with clubs. *Ibid.* xi. 410 When any thing is forbidden to be eat, or made use of, they say, that it is *taboo*. **1826** SCOTT *Diary* 24 Oct. in *Lockhart*, The conversation is seldom excellent amongst official people. So many topics are what Otaheitians call taboo. **1845** J. COULTER *Adv. in Pacific* xiii. 171 As soon as ever the anchor is down, if the ship is not a taboo or restricted one, she will be at once boarded, not by a few, but hundreds of women. **1888** C. M. WOODFORD in *Proc. Roy. Geog. Soc.* New Monthly Ser. X. 372 The human heads..are reserved for the canoe-houses. These..are tambu (tabooed) for women—i.e., a woman is not allowed to enter them, or indeed to pass in front of them.

b. *transf.* and *fig.*

1826 MISS MITFORD *Village* Ser. II. 63 (*Touchy Lady*) The mention of her neighbours is evidently taboo, since..she is in a state of affront with nine-tenths of them. **1891** *Spectator* 2 May 611/2 A..pledge that that Wednesday should not be absorbed by the Government, but should be taboo. **1901** R. GARNETT *Ess.* viii. 224 The legendary history of Ireland is.. taboo to the serious historian.

B. *sb.* **1.** The putting of a person or thing under prohibition or interdict, perpetual or temporary; the fact or condition of being so placed; the prohibition or interdict itself. Also, the institution or practice by which such prohibitions are recognized and enforced; found in full force in the islands of the Pacific when first visited by Europeans, and still prevailing in some of them, as also, under other forms and names, among many other races in early stages of culture.

The institution is generally supposed to have had a religious or superstitious origin (certain things being considered the property of the gods or superhuman powers, and therefore forbidden to men), and to have been extended to political and social affairs, being usually controlled by the king or great chiefs in conjunction with the priests. Some things, acts, and words were permanently taboo or interdicted to the mass of the people, and others specially to women, while temporary taboo was frequently imposed, often apparently quite arbitrarily.

a. As originally used in Polynesia, New Zealand, Melanesia, etc

1777 COOK *Voy. to Pacific* II. xi. (1785) I. 410 When the *taboo* is incurred, by paying obeisance to a great personage, it is thus easily washed off. *Ibid.*, Old Toobou, at this time, presided over the *taboo*. **1778** KING in *Cook's Voy.* III. xii. (1785) II. 249 The *taboo* also prevails in Atooi, in its full extent, and seemingly with much more rigour than even at Tongataboo. **1779** —— *Ibid.* v. iv. III. 81 The *taboo*, which Eappo had laid on it [the bay at Hawaii] the day before, at our request, not being yet taken off. **1817** SOUTHEY in *Q. Rev.* XVII. 14 This taboo was now to be taken off, by a large slaughter of hogs. **1831** *Tyerman & Bennet's Voy. & Trav.* I. xix. 423 The priests [in Oahu] recommended a ten days' tabu, the sacrifice of three human victims [etc.]. *Ibid.* xx. 440 A pole, ten feet high, on which was suspended a bit of white stick,..having remnants of the bones of a fowl attached to it. This..was a tabu, prohibiting any body from stealing the canes growing there. **1862** M. HOPKINS *Hawaii* 89 One of the great instruments used by both king and priests for maintaining their power and their revenue, was the system of 'tabu' or 'taboo'. **1870** H. MEADE *New Zealand* 319 A tambu has been laid on the trees for a certain number of years.

b. Extended, as a general term of anthropology, to similar customs among other primitive races.

1883 A. LANG in *Contemp. Rev.* Sept. 417 The hero Cuchullain..came by his ruin after transgressing this totemistic taboo. **1896** F. B. JEVONS *Introd. Hist. Relig.* vii. 72 The very conception of taboo, based as it largely is on the association of ideas, is one peculiarly liable to extension by analogy. *Ibid.* viii. 89 The irrational restrictions, touch not, taste not, handle not, which constitute formalism, are essentially taboos. **1905** *Athenæum* 21 Jan. 87/1 Tabus connected with animals and plants are common, and such tabus are part of totemism. **1906** *Ibid.* 17 Mar. 332/1 There are many taboos on food which are certainly not totemic in origin.

c. *Linguistics.* A total or partial prohibition of the use of certain words, expressions, topics, etc., esp. in social intercourse.

1933 [see sense 3 b below]. **1962** S. ULLMANN *Semantics* viii. 205 Taboo is an important cause of semantic change. Language taboos fall into three more or less distinct groups according to the psychological motivation behind them. **1980** R. A. HUDSON *Sociolinguistics* ii. 53 The distinction between conventional and necessary social restrictions is also interesting in view of the strength of feeling which the former arouse. This is particularly clear in the case of *linguistic taboo*, such as the so-called 'four-letter words' of English.

2. *transf.* and *fig.* Prohibition or interdiction generally of the use or practice of anything, or of social intercourse; ostracism.

1833 R. MUDIE *Brit. Birds* (1841) I. 366 There are subjects which appear to be under the taboo of nature. **1852** LYTTON *My Novel* XI. ix, Under what strange taboo am I placed? **1853** S. WILBERFORCE in R. G. Wilberforce *Life* (1881) II. v. 190 To labour hardest as a Bishop is to incur certain taboo. **1894** MRS. FR. ELLIOT *Roman Gossip* 281 French officers..found themselves placed in such a painful taboo at Rome.

3. a. *attrib.* and *Comb.*

1870–4 ANDERSON *Missions Amer. Bd.* II. i. 6 Interwoven with the tabu system. **1896** F. B. JEVONS *Introd. Hist. Relig.* vi. 66 Before a great feast, a taboo-day or days are proclaimed. *Ibid.* vii. 78 They remove their hair before entering on the taboo-state. *Ibid.* viii. 88 The terror..with which he viewed the taboo-breaker. **1897** *Edin. Rev.* July 238 The taboo custom, which is a prohibition with a curse. **1903** R. KIPLING in *Windsor Mag.* 368/2 Remember you're a tabu girl now.

b. *Linguistics.* With reference to an expression or topic considered offensive and hence avoided or prohibited by social custom.

1933 L. BLOOMFIELD *Language* xxii. 396 In America, *knocked up* is a tabu-form for 'rendered pregnant'; for this reason, the phrase is not used in the British sense 'tired, exhausted'... In such cases there is little real ambiguity, but some hearers react nevertheless to the powerful stimulus of the tabu-word. **1978** *Amer. Speech* LIII. 16 It may be that taboo terms form a group which is logically akin to, yet separate from, true slang, since many taboo terms are the only ones available to non-academic speakers. **1980** *Scottsdale* (Arizona) *Progress* 9 Feb. 12 We now have a set of taboo expressions relating to ethnic groups and individuals.

Hence **ta'booism**, the system of taboo; **ta'booist**, one who practises or believes in taboo; **ta'booness**, the state or condition of being taboo.

1885 J. FITZGERALD tr. *Schultze's Fetichism* iii. ad fin., Here is the fetichist become a tabooist, supposing that the description of tabooism heretofore given is correct. **1974** *Verbatim* I. 1. 4/1 The tabooness of *fuck*. **1978** *Maledicta* 1977 I. 236 Tabooness focuses on the speaker and his/her decision about what can or cannot be said in a given context.

taboo, tabu (tə'buː), *v.* [f. prec.]

1. *trans.* To put (a thing, place, action, word, or person) under a (literal) taboo: see TABOO *sb.* 1.

1777 COOK *Voy. to Pacific* II. ix. (1785) I. 359 He had been discovered..with a woman who was *taboo'd*. **1779** KING *Ibid.* v. iv. III. 81 Eappo was dismissed with orders to *taboo* all the bay; and, in the afternoon, the bones [of Captain Cook] were committed to the deep with the usual military honours. **1799** *Naval Chron.* I. 305 Having tabooed one side of the ship in order to get all the canoes on the starboard side. **1831** *Tyerman & Bennet's Voy. & Trav.* II. xxix. 40 There are many houses which, having been built, or occupied, or entered casually by him [King Pomare], are thus tabued, and no woman dare sit down or eat in them. **1865** TYLOR *Early Hist. Man.* vi. 144 In the South Sea Islands, words have been tabued, from connexion with the names of chiefs. **1896** F. B. JEVONS *Introd. Hist. Relig.* vi. 65 On the day of a chief's decease work is tabooed.

2. *transf.* and *fig.* **a.** To give a sacred or privileged character to (a thing), which restricts its use to certain persons, or debars it from ordinary use or treatment; †(*a*) with stress on the privilege: To consecrate, set apart, render inviolable (*obs.*); (*b*) with stress on the exclusion: To forbid, prohibit *to* the unprivileged, or to particular persons.

(*a*) **1832** *Blackw. Mag.* Apr. 582/2 The silks and the veils, &c., which some years ago were as exclusively tabooed, and set apart to the use of the mistress as pearls or rubies, are now familiarly worn by the servant. **1846** R. BELL *G. Canning* viii. 218 Slavery was cruel... But it was a sacred institution..tabooed by the consecrating hand of time.

(*b*) **1825** *Blackw. Mag.* XVII. 161 The 'King's highway' seems Tabooed to these individuals. **1839** T. HOOK in *New Monthly Mag.* LV. 439 There were no splendid couches taboo'd against the reception of wearied feet. **1854** H. MILLER *Sch. & Schm.* xiv. (1860) 151 Such of the gentlemen ..as taboo their Glen Tilts, and shut up the passes of the Grampians. **1870** LOWELL *Study Wind.* 67 That sacred enclosure of respectability was tabooed to us.

b. To forbid or debar by personal or social influence the use, practice, or mention of, or contact or intercourse with; to put (a person, thing, name, or subject) under a social ban; to ostracize, boycott.

1791 [see TABOOED]. **1822** SOUTHEY *Lett.* (1856) III. 305 He has tabooed ham, vinegar, red-herrings, and all fruits. **1850** KINGSLEY *Alton Locke* xxx, The political questions which I longed to solve .. were tabooed by the well-meaning chaplain. **1860** H. GOUGER *Imprisonm. in Burmah* xii. 126, I found myself as strictly tabooed as if I had been a leper. **1862** MAURICE *Mor. & Met. Philos.* IV. x. §18. 664 Their names were tabooed by Whig and Tory coteries. **1888** BRYCE *Amer. Commw.* I. xii. 161 You cannot taboo a man who has got a vote.

Hence **tabooed** (tə'bu:d) *ppl. a.*

1791 BURKE *App. Whigs* Wks. VI. 106 A plain declaration, that the topick of France is *tabooed* or forbidden ground to Mr. Burke. **1841** J. MACKERROW *Hist. Secession Ch.* xxi. 767 Perpetual bickerings between the favoured and tabooed sects. **1849** C. BRONTE *Shirley* xxi. 310 The gentlemen .. regarded me as a 'tabooed woman'. **1906** *Athenæum* 17 Mar. 332/2 We doubt whether M. Reinach is entirely aware of the difficulty and complexity of the problem of the tabooed animals in Leviticus.

‖**taboot**[1] (ta:'bu:t). Also **tabut**. [Hindi, a. Arab. *tābūt* coffin, box, Ark of the Covenant.] A sacred box or coffin; *spec.* a box, representing the tomb of Husain, which is carried in procession through the streets during the Muslim festival of Muharram.

1622 in W. Foster *Eng. Factories India 1622–3* (1908) 94 This daye is heere aryved Sultan (Khus) roues taboots [*sic*] from Brampore, (which to-) morrowe is to bee dispeeded to H(elobass?) there to bee intered by his mother. **1862** MRS. J. B. SPEID *Our Last Yrs. in India* 230 Taboots, or tazzias, the representation of Hosain's mausoleum at Kurbulla. **1879** L. PELLY *Miracle Play of Hasan & Husain* p. xvii, Against the side of the Imambarrah, directed towards Mecca, is set the *tabut*. **1891** *Daily News* 9 Sept. 5/4 Immense sums of money are spent upon the *taboots* .. that, carried in these processions, are broken to pieces and buried at the end of the ceremony. **1958** G. E. VON GRUNEBAUM *Muhammedan Festivals* v. 89 The *ta'ziya*, or Passion play .. became the real climax of the Shī'ite Tenth of Muharram celebrations. The stage requires few properties besides a large *tabut* (coffin), .. and Husain's arms and banner. **1975** *Indian Express* 15 Jan. 5/1 Taboot processions with music will be allowed only on the last day of the Moharrum.

‖**taboot**[2] ('ta:bu:t). Also **tabut**. [Arab., abbrev. of *tābūt raf' al-miyāh* Archimedes screw, or of *tābūt al-sāqiya* scoop wheel: see prec. entry.] A form of water-wheel used in Egypt.

1836 E. W. LANE *Acct. Manners & Customs Mod. Egyptians* II. 25 There is a third machine, called *taboot*, used for the irrigation of lands in the northern part of Egypt. **1841** J. KITTO *Phys. Hist. Palestine* vii. p. ccxcvii, Another machine used for the irrigation of lands, when it is only necessary to raise the water a few feet .. is called the *Taboot*. **1877** *Encycl. Brit.* VII. 708/1 The tâboot .. differs from the sâkiyeh principally in having a hollow wheel instead of the wheel with pots. **1924** *Countries of World* III. 1757/1 The primitive but still effective apparatus known as the 'sakieh', the 'shaduf', and the 'tabut'.

tabor, tabour ('teɪbə(r)), *sb.*[1] Now *rare.* Also 4 **tabre**, 4–5 **tabur**, 5 **-yr**, 5–6 **taboure**, 4–8 **taber**, 6–9 **tabber**. See also TABORN. [a. OF. *tabur* (11th c.), *tabour* (13–16th c.), beside *tanbor*, *tambur* (14–15th c.), *tambour* (16th c.–) = Pr. *tabor*, *tanbor*, Sp. *tambor* (OSp. *atambor*), It. *tamburo*: the relations between the forms in *ta-* and those in *tam-*, *tan-* have not been clearly determined. The word is held to be of Oriental origin, and has been compared with Pers. *tabīrah*, and *tabūrāk*, both meaning 'drum', and with Arab. *ṭanbūr* a kind of lute or lyre. The actual history is uncertain: see Dozy, and Devic in Littré; also Gaston Paris in *Romania*, 1902.]

1. The earlier name of the drum; in later use (esp. since the introduction of the name *drum* in the 16th c.), A small kind of drum, used chiefly as an accompaniment to the pipe or trumpet; a taborin or tabret. Now *Hist.*, *arch.*, or *poetic*.

c **1290** *Beket* 1851 in *S. Eng. Leg.* I. 159 Of bellene and of tabours so gret was þe soun. **1297** R. GLOUC. (Rolls) 8166 Of trompes & of tabors þe sarazins made þere So gret noyse. *c* **1300** *Havelok* 2329 Þe gleymen on þe tabour dinge. **1399** LANGL. *Rich. Redeles* I. 58 Men myʒtten as well haue huntyd an hare with a tabre. **14..** *Voc.* in Wr.-Wülcker 616/28 *Timpanum*, a taber, or a tymbre. **14..** in *Hist. Coll. Citizen London* (Camden) 220 He stode a-pon an hylle wyth hys tabyr and hys pype. *c* **1460** *Emare* 389 Ther was myche menstralse, Trommpus, tabours, and sawtre. **1523** LD. BERNERS *Froiss.* I. cxlvii. 176 Than the kyng mounted on his horse, and entred into the towne with trumpets, tabours. **1587** FLEMING *Contn. Holinshed* III. 1553/2 Singing of psalmes, marching about their fiers with tabber and pipe. **1610** SHAKS. *Temp.* IV. i. 175 Then I beate my Tabor, At which like vnback't colts they prickt their eares. **1624** CAPT. J. SMITH *Virginia* IV. 155 Will any goe to catch a Hare with a Taber and a Pipe? **1693** *Humours Town* 2 The Clamours of a Country-Mob .. is no more than the beating of a Tabour. **1766** GOLDSM. *Vic. W.* iv, The whole neighbourhood came out to meet their minister, .. preceded by a pipe and tabor. **1843** LYTTON *Last Bar.* I. ii, A marvellous horse that beat a tabor with his fore feet. **1880** in Grove *Dict. Music* II. 754/2 The tabor was a diminutive drum, without snares, hung by a short string to the waist or left arm, and tapped with a small drumstick. **1907** *Ibid.* III. 750/2 The pipe and tabor, for a long time very popular throughout Europe, are now obsolete in this country.

fig. **1601** HAKEWILL *Van. Eye* xvii. (1615) 87 The Duke of Vandosme, the common tabour of the French wits. **1624** QUARLES *Job* xi. 69, I am become a By-word, and a Taber, To set the tongues, and eares of men, in labour.

b. *transf.* The drummer (with his drum).

1362 LANGL. *P. Pl.* A. II. 79 Taberes & tomblers & tapesters fele. **1789** BURNEY *Hist. Mus.* III. iii. 254 As a new married couple went out of the church the violins and tabors attended them.

†**2.** The tympanum or drum of the ear. *Obs.*

1594 T. B. *La Primaud. Fr. Acad.* II. 84 The aire .. moueth the litle hammer of the eares, .. and so maketh a sound by meanes of the litle taber, through whose sounde the spirites of hearing are awakened. **1615** CROOKE *Body of Man* 592 The first cauity of the stony bone, which before we called the Tympane, that is the drume or Taber.

3. *attrib.* and *Comb.*, as ***tabor-beating***; ***tabor-like*** adj. or adv.; **tabor-stick**, a drumstick.

13.. *K. Alis.* 2158 (Bodl. MS.) Now rist grete tabor betyng, Blaweyng of pypes, & ek trumping. **1486** *Bk. St. Albans, Hawking* d j b, With yowre hande or with yowre tabur styke becke yowre hawke to come to you. **1698** FRYER *Acc. E. India & P.* 27 The whole Fabrick .. covered atop Taber-like.

‖**'tabor**, *sb.*[2] Also **tabour**. [Boh., Polish, Serb. *tabor*, Magyar *tábor*, a. Turkish *tabor* camp (anciently a camp of nomads formed by a circle of wagons or the like).] An encampment.

1877 *Daily News* 25 Oct. 5/4 At Podgoritza .. 15 tabors of Nizams and four tabors of troops of the reserve are being concentrated preparatory to offensive operations against Montenegro.

tabor, tabour ('teɪbə(r)), *v.* Now *rare.* Forms: see TABOR *sb.*[1] [f. TABOR *sb.*[1], or a. OF. *taborer* (13th c. in Godef.).]

1. *intr.* To perform upon or beat the tabor; to drum. Also *to tabor it.*

13.. *K. Alis.* 924 (Bodl. MS.) Þer was trumpyng & taburyng Lepyng of stedes & nayʒeyng. **1377** LANGL. *P. Pl.* B. XIII. 230, I can noither tabre ne trompe. **1413** *Pilgr. Sowle* (Caxton) II. xliv. (1859) 50 They floyted and they tabered; they yellyd, and they cryed. *c* **1440** *Promp. Parv.* 485/2 Tabowryn, *timpaniso.* **1530** PALSGR. 746/1, I will tabour, play thou upon the flute therwhyles. **1591** NASHE *Pref. Sydney's Astr. & Stella* in G. G. Smith *Eliz. Crit. Ess.* (1904) II. 226 Nor hath my prose any skill to imitate the Almond leape verse, or sit tabring .. nothing but 'to bee, to hee', on a paper drum. **1694** MOTTEUX *Rabelais* IV. xiv. (1737) 56 Trudon Pip'd it and then Taber'd it like mad. **1902** *Speaker* 5 Apr. 10/1 The inevitable 'tambourinaire' fifes and tabors away.

b. *transf.* and *fig.* To beat as upon a tabor; to drum.

1579–80 NORTH *Plutarch* (1676) 72 This brought the common rumor to taber on his [Solon's] head. **1611** BIBLE *Nahum* ii. 7 Her maids shall leade her .. tabring vpon their breasts. **1653** DOROTHY OSBORN *Lett., to Sir W. Temple* (1903) 179 His humour was to rise in the night, and with two bedstaves tabour upon the table an hour together. **1692** L'ESTRANGE *Fables* ccccxvii. (1714) 451 He [the Ass] went .. Tabring with his Feet all the Way. **1719** D'URFEY *Pills* VI. 265 With Hammer on Kettle he tabbers all Day. **1859** F. E. PAGET *Curate of Cumberworth* 356 Mrs. Soaper .. re-echoed her husband's words, and tabbered with her fingers on the table, expectant of my reply.

2. *trans.* To beat (a tune, etc.): cf. DRUM *v.* 8.

c **1385** CHAUCER *L.G.W.* Prol. 354 (Fairf. MS.) In youre courte ys many a losengeour and many a queynt totelere accusour That tabouren [*v.rr.* taboryn, tauburn] in youre eres many a swon.

†**3.** To beat, thump (anything); to thrash. *Obs.*

1624 QUARLES *Job* xviii. 63 Marke with what pride his horny hoofes doe tabor The .. Earth. *a* **1625** FLETCHER *Woman's Prize* II. v, I would tabor her, Till all the legions that are crept into her, Flew out with fire i' th' tails. **1655** tr. *Com. Hist. Francion* III. 55 Beating the Switzers march upon their buttocks; and .. they fell to tabour mine to the same tune.

Hence **'taboring** *vbl. sb.*

13.. [see sense 1]. **1603** HOLLAND *Plutarch's Mor.* 98 Of his drumming, tabouring, and other enormious indignities, under the colour of religion. **1867** MORRIS *Jason* VIII. 360 Bear back the fleece Along our streets .. with much scattered flowers and tabouring.

'taborer. *Obs.* exc. *Hist.* Also 5–7 **taberer**, 6 **tab(b)orer, tabourier, taberer(e**. [f. TABOR *v.* or *sb.* + -ER[1]. Cf. OF. *taboreor* (14th c.).] One who tabors; a drummer; a performer on the tabor.

c **1400** *Song Roland* 918 Trumpetis and taberers, sothe to say. *c* **1430** LYDG. *Min. Poems* (Percy Soc.) 170 Tabourers withe theyr mokkes and false dupplicité Please more these dayes. *c* **1537** *Thersytes* in *Four O. Pl.* (1848) 79 The tryflinge tabborer trowbler of tunys. **1579** SPENSER *Sheph. Cal.* May 22 Before them yode a lusty Tabrere, That to the many a Horne pype playd. **1610** SHAKS. *Temp.* III. ii. 160, I would I could see this Taborer. **1885** *Newcastle Chron.* 25 May, The squire and his dame .. attended by piper and taborer, looking on condescendingly.

taboret, -ete, obs. forms of TABRET.

†**'taborin.** *Obs.* Also 6 **-oryn, taberyne**, 7–8 **tabourin(e**, 9 **-orine**. [a. F. *tabourin* (1482 in Godef. *Compl.*, and in Dict. Acad. 1690), deriv. of *tabour* TABOR; cf. med.L. *taborinus* in sense = *tympanista* taborer (1497 in Du Cange). In mod.F. *tambourin*, Pr. *tamborin*, It. *tamburino.*] A kind of drum, less wide and longer than the tabor, and struck with one drumstick only, to accompany the sound of a flute which is played with the other hand. (In quot. 1871, used for TAMBOURINE.)

c **1500** *Three Kings' Sons* 40 Thorugh all the cristen navee they made to blowe trompettes, claryons & taberynes. **1507** *Justes Moneths May & June* 150 in Hazl. *E.P.P.* II. 119 Of taboryns and of many a douce lute The mynstrelles were proprely clade in sute. **1512** *Helyas* in Thoms *Prose Rom.* (1858) III. 31 Pipes, taborins, doucimers. **1606** SHAKS. *Tr. & Cr.* IV. v. 275 Beate lowd the Taborins, let the Trumpets blow. **1765** STERNE *Tr. Shandy* VII. xliii, 'Tis the fife and tabourin, said I. **1871** R. ELLIS *Catullus* lxiii. 8 With a snowy palm the woman took affrayed a taborine.

Taborite ('tæbəraɪt). [ad. G. *Taboriten* pl., ad. Boh. *taborzhina*, f. *tabor* TABOR *sb.*[2]; so called from their encampment on a craggy height, now the town of Tabor in Bohemia.] A member of the extreme party or section of the Hussites led by Zizska.

1646 BP. MAXWELL *Burd. Issach.* in *Phenix* (1708) II. 313 We might .. add the Remainder of the Waldenses and Albigenses in Piedmont, and the Parts adjoining; or of the Taborites in Bohemia. **1786** A. MACLEAN *Christ's Comm.* III. (1846) 250 Exterminating the Taborites or Vaudois. **1861** J. GILL *Banished Count* vi. 68 The Calixtines might be styled the Gallicans of Bohemia, and the Taborites the Protestants.

†**'taborn, tabroun**, *sb. Obs.* Forms: 4 **taborne**, 4–5 **taburn(e**, 5–6 *Sc.* **taberne**, 6 *Sc.* **tabro(u)n**, **tabberone**, 7 **tabern**, *Sc.* **tabbern**; also *Sc.* 4 **tawburn**, 5 **tawberne**, **talburn**, 6 **tau-**, **tawbron**, **tawbern**, **talbrone**. [A by-form of TABOR, chiefly north. Eng. and Sc., in med.L. *tabornum* (Du Cange). The inserted *n* appears also in OF. *taborner*, *tabourner* vb. (see next). (The Sc. spellings *taw-*, *tal-* stand for a broad *ā*.)] = TABOR *sb.*[1], TABOUR, a drum.

a **1340** HAMPOLE *Psalter* cl. 4 Taburn is made of a dryid scyn. **13..** *E.E. Allit. P.* B. 1414 Tymbres & tabornes, tulket among. *c* **1400** MAUNDEV. (Roxb.) xxxi. 138 Noyse as it ware of trumppes and tawburnez. *a* **1400–50** *Alexander* 1385 Now tynkyll vp taburnes. *c* **1450** HOLLAND *Howlat* 760 The trumpe, and the talburn, the tympane but tray. **1513** DOUGLAS *Æneis* IX. x. 66 Wyth tympanis, tawbronis [*ed.* **1555** tawbernis], ʒe war wont to heyr. **1533** BELLENDEN *Livy* II. xxvi. (S.T.S.) I. 238 With þe noyiss of swasche and tawberon. **1544** *Acc. Ld. H. Treas. Scotl.* VIII. 278 Twa men .. quhilkis had thair tabronis brokin. **1552** LYNDESAY *Monarche* I. 2505 With talbrone, troumpet, schalme, and clarioun. **1561** *Burgh Rec. Edinb.* (1875) III. 114 At the sound of the common bell, trumpet or tabroun. **1559–60** J. WOOD *Let.* in Sir R. Sadler *St. Papers* (1809) II. 156 When they cam nere the towne, hard the commen bell and tabbern. **1688** R. HOLME *Armoury* III. xvi. (Roxb.) 57/1 The pipe belonging to the Tabern is much longer then the whisell or Flajalett.

†**'taborn**, *v. Obs.* Also 5 **taburne**. [f. prec. or ad. OF. *taborner*, *tabourner* (12–14th c. in Godef.) = *taborer*.] = TABOR *v.*, to drum.

13.. *K. Alis.* 1042 (Bodl. MS.) At þe fest was harpyng And pipyng & tabournyng. *c* **1400** *Langl.'s P. Pl.* B. XIII. 230 (MS. C), I can neither taborne ne trompe. **1483** *Cath. Angl.* 376/2 To Taburne, *timpanizare*.

†**'taborner.** Chiefly *Sc. Obs.* [Agent-n. f. TABORN *v.* = OF. *taborneur* (1317 in Godef.).] By-form of TABORER, a drummer.

14.. *Nom.* in Wr.-Wülcker 696/36 *Hic timpanizator*, a taberner. **1483** *Cath. Angl.* 376/2 A Taburner (*A.* Tabernar), *timpanista.* **1518** *Acc. Ld. High Treas. Scotl.* V. 157 To þe Franche Talbanaris and Menstralis .. in aile, viij s. **1560** *Burgh Rec. Edinb.* (1875) III. 74 The sax tabroneris that playit thre sundrie dayis at the parliament. **1688** R. HOLME *Armoury* III. 156/2 *Taberner*, a Man playing on the Tabern and Pipe.

‖**tabot** (ta'bot). [Ge'ez: cf. TABOOT[1].] A box, representing the Ark of the Covenant, which stands on the altar in an Ethiopian church.

1682 J. P. GENT tr. *Ludolphus's New Hist. Ethiopia* III. vi. 294 In the Sanctuary stands the Holy Table, which they call .. *Manbar*... Upon this they place the sacred vessels. First the *Tabot*, or Chest .. an Oblong Quadrangular Table, upon which the Dish and Cup are set. **1710** F. TELLEZ *Trav. Jesuits in Ethiopia* III. x. 242 We restore you the Faith of your Fore-Fathers. The former Clergy-Men may return to their Churches, put in their *Tabotes*, and say Masses. **1834** S. GOBAT *Jrnl. Three Years' Residence in Abyssinia* ii. 243 A church, when there is no 'tabot' in it, is no more to them than a common house. **1923** *Blackw. Mag.* Aug. 256/2 It [*sc.* the Abyssinian Church] venerates an object called the *tabot*, which is the replica of the Ark of the Covenant. **1968** E. ULLENDORFF *Ethiopia & Bible* ii. 83 Criticisms levelled against the Ethiopians on account of their *tabot*-centred worship.

tabougin, var. TOBOGGAN.

tabour, -er, var. TABOR *sb.* and *v.*, TABORER.

tabouret ('tæbərɛt, ‖taburɛ). Also 8 **tabret**. [a. F. *tabouret* (taburɛ), in sense 2 (1442 in Hatz.-Darm.); orig. a small tabor or drum, a TABRET, dim. of *tabour*, TABOR, drum.]

†**1.** The same as TABRET, q.v. *Obs.*

2. a. A low seat or stool, without back or arms, for one person: so called originally from its shape. ***privilege of the tabouret***: see quot. 1656.

1656 BLOUNT *Glossogr.*, *Tabouret*, a pincase; also a little low stool for a childe to sit on. In France the priviledge of the Tabouret is of a stool for some particular Ladies to sit in the Queens presence. **1679** tr. *Marie Mancini's Apol.* 30, I had the priviledge of sitting on a Tabourette in the Queens presence. *a* **1711** KEN *Hymnotheo* Poet. Wks. 1721 III. 191 Soon as a Stranger comes, she'll him embrace, Near her proud Person, on a tabret Place. **1858** MASSON *Milton* (1859) I. 704 A studied slight put upon Lady Scudamore by refusing her the honour of the *tabouret*,—i.e. the right of being seated—on the occasion of a visit of ceremony to the

French queen. **1899** MORROW *Bohem. Paris* 60 He had bought a new easel and two rush-bottomed tabourets.

b. *U.S.* A small table, esp. one used as a stand for house-plants; a bedside table.

1916 *Sears, Roebuck & Co. Catal.* Fall 1244/2 Tabourets or jardinier stands. **1968** J. UPDIKE *Couples* iii. 228 One of his flippers kicked over a tabouret holding a crammed ashtray and a small vase of asters. **1984** M. BABSON *Trail of Ashes* iii. 33 Look in the bedside tabouret for a little nightcap.

†**3.** A pin-case or needle-case. *Obs.*

1656 [see sense 2]. **1891** in *Cent. Dict.*

4. A frame for embroidery, a tambour-frame.

1858 SIMMONDS *Dict. Trade, Tabouret,..* an embroidery frame. **1891** in *Cent. Dict.*

tabourin(e, variant of TABORIN *Obs.*

tabre, tabrer(e, obs. ff. TABOR, TABORER.

tabret ('tæbrɪt). Forms: *α.* 4–5 taberett, 5 -ette, 5–6 -et, 5– tabret, (6 -ette, 7 tabberet, tabaret); *β.* 6 tabertte, -erde, -arte, -arde; *γ.* 5 taborete, 6–7 tabouret. [f. TABOR + -ET[1].]

1. A small tabor; a timbrel. *Hist.* or *arch.*

α. **1464** *Mann. & Househ. Exp.* (Roxb.) 264 Item, for a hedstalle for the taberet iiij d. **1489** CAXTON *Faytes of A.* III. xiv. 198 He had lost hys pype and hys tabret. **1535** COVERDALE *Gen.* xxxi. 27 That I might haue brought the on the waye with myrth,..with tabrettes and harpes. **1607** TOPSELL *Four-f. Beasts* (1658) 134 A Hare..was seen in England..playing with his former feet upon a tabberet. **1683** PETTUS *Fleta Min.* II. 12 Choice Instruments of Musick..also the Tabaret. **1748** RICHARDSON *Clarissa* (1810) IV. xxvi. 147 Not a tabret, nor the expectation of a new joy to animate him on! **1879** STAINER *Music of Bible* 155 The tabret has now been excluded from sacred buildings, having given place to the more solemn and imposing drum.

β. **1556** *Chron. Gr. Friars* (Camden) 27 With trompettes, shalmes, and taberttes in the best maner. **1570** LEVINS *Manip.* 31/1 A Tabarde, *timpanum.* **1575** TURBERV. *Falconrie* 191 The Falconer muste haue with him a little drumme or Taberde fastened to the pommell of his saddle. ? **1600** *Chester Pl., Banns* 118 Get mynstrilles to that shewe, pipe, tabarte, and flute.

γ. **1599** BP. HALL *Sat.* IV. i. 78 Or Mimoes whistling to his tabouret. **1676** DUGDALE *Baronage Eng.* II. 107/2 So shalle they departe the Manoir..with Trompets, Tabouretts, and other manoir of Mynstralce [*orig. c* 1500]. **1885** H. C. McCOOK *Tenants Old Farm* 299 In the katydid..the musical instruments are a pair of taborets.

b. *fig.* **1610** BOYS *Expos. Dom. Epist.* Wks. (1622) 443 Making their infirmities and sinnes our tabret and delight.

†**2.** *transf.* A performer on a tabret. *Obs.*

a **1377** in *Househ. Ord.* (1790) 4 Mynstrelles—Taberett I. **14..** in *Hist. Coll. Citizen London* (Camden) 220 On manly man..that was a taberette..stode a-pon an hylle wyth hys tabyr and hys pype. **1464** *Mann. & Househ. Exp.* (Roxb.) 239, I delyverd my taborete the same day a new gowen, and iij.d. **1540** in *Vicary's Anat.* (1888) App. xii. 241 Item, for John Buntanus, tabret—xljs. iiij d. **1634** SIR T. HERBERT *Trav.* 67 Amongst the horse were aboue fortie Kettle-drummes and Tabrets.

tabret, obs. form of TABOURET.

Tabriz (tə'briːz). The name of a city in north-western Iran, used *attrib.* and *absol.* to designate carpets and rugs made there, the older styles of which often show a rich decorative medallion pattern.

1900 J. K. MUMFORD *Oriental Rugs* xi. 168 The model on which the Tabriz rugs were really designed is the ornamental and richly colored fabric of Kirman in southern Persia. **1911** G. G. LEWIS *Pract. Bk. Oriental Rugs* II. 184 With the Kirman the Tabriz shares the reputation of having the most graceful floral designs. **1931** A. U. DILLEY *Oriental Rugs & Carpets* iv. 104 Modern Tabriz rugs constitute a..revival of weaving that began at least as early as the Caliphate. **1946** *Lancet* 2 Mar. 322/1 The bedside carpet is important and must be gratifying to the bare feet... A subdued Shiraz will fulfil most people's requirements, though leptoforms may require something with a more stimulating pattern, say a Tabriz. **1962** N. FREELING *Love in Amsterdam* II. 79 He bought books and pictures, and had a treasured Tabriz carpet. **1978** S. WILSON *Dealer's Move* iii. 42 A superb Tabriz hung on the wall.

tabro(u)n, tabronar, etc.: see TABORN, -ER.

tab show. *U.S. slang.* [f. TAB(LOID + SHOW *sb.*[1]] A short version of a musical, esp. one performed by a travelling company.

1951 GREEN & LAURIE *Show Biz* 571/2 *Tab show,* tabloid version of a musical. **1953** *Sun* (Baltimore) 30 Sept. 38/6 He traveled in 'tab shows'—vaudeville and musical comedy—through the South. **1983** *N.Y. Times* 12 June XXI. 10/4 Most Broadway musicals are simply streamlined for travel, ranging from the 'tab shows' (short for tabloid) that are the trademark of some resorts, to abridged versions in stock or dinner theaters.

tabu, variant spelling of TABOO.

tabul, obs. form of TABLE.

‖**tabula** ('tæbjʊlə). Pl. **-æ** (iː). [The L. word *tabula* TABLE, used in particular senses.]

1. An ancient writing-tablet; also *transf.* a body of laws inscribed on a tablet: see TABLE *sb.* 2 b, d, TABLET *sb.* 1 c.

1881 E. HÜBNER in *Encycl. Brit.* XIII. 124/1 Instruments or charters, public and private (styled by the Romans first *leges,* afterwards *instrumenta* or *tabulæ*). **1904** C. WORDSWORTH *Old Service Bks.* 264 The Tabula or Wax-brede was of the nature of service-paper rather than of a service-book.

b. *tabula rasa* [L. = scraped tablet], a tablet from which the writing has been erased, and which is therefore ready to be written upon again; a blank tablet: usually *fig.*

1535 LYNDESAY *Satyre* 224 Because I haue bene, to this day, Tanquam tabula rasa. **1607** SIR T. BODLEY in *Cabbala* II. (1654) 76 For that were indeed to become *Tabula rasa,* when we shall leave no impression of any former principles, but be driven to begin the world again. **1662** SOUTH *Serm.* (1727) I. 52 Aristotle..affirms the Mind to be at first a mere *Rasa Tabula.* **1875** JOWETT *Plato* (ed. 2) III. 73 The artist will do nothing until he has made a tabula rasa. **1893** *Nation* (N.Y.) 1 June 403/1 France had become a *Tabula rasa,* and everything had to be reorganized.

2. *Eccl.* A wooden or metal frontal for an altar.

1845 PARKER *Gloss. Archit.* s.v. *Table,* The most remarkable example of the *tabula,* destined for the front of the Altar, is preserved in Westminster abbey; it is formed of wood, elaborately carved, painted, and enriched with a kind of mosaic work of coloured glass superficially inlaid.

3. a. *Anat.* = TABLE *sb.* 16.

1857 DUNGLISON *Med. Dict., Table, Tabula, Tabella, Tabulatum,..* a name given to the plates of compact tissue, which form the bones of the cranium. Of these, one is external; the other internal, and called *Tabula vitrea,* on account of its brittleness.

b. *Palæont.* Name for the horizontal dissepiments in certain corals: cf. TABULATE *a.* 3.

1855 LYELL *Elem. Geol.* xxv. (ed. 5) 407 The *lamellæ* are seen around the inside of the cup;..and large transverse plates, called *tabulæ,* divide the interior into chambers. **1859** MURCHISON *Siluria* (ed. 2) x. 243 The development of the transverse plates or tabulæ, in the body of the coral.

tabular ('tæbjʊlə(r)), *a.* [ad. L. *tabular-is* of or relating to a board or plate, f. *tabula;* now used in reference to many senses of TABLE.]

1. a. Having the form of a 'table', tablet, or slab; flat and (usually) comparatively thin; consisting of, or tending to split into, pieces of this form, as a rock; of a short prismatic form with flat base and top, as a crystal; flat-topped, as a hill.

tabular spar, a name for WOLLASTONITE, as occurring in masses of tabular structure, or rarely in tabular crystals.

1656 BLOUNT *Glossogr., Tabular,* whereof boards, plancks, or tables may be made, long and large. **1688** R. HOLME *Armoury* II. 296/1 The Persian Pye..of a dusky color: the Feet bluish, with black tabular scales. *a* **1728** WOODWARD *Fossils* (1729) I. 34 Nodules..that are tabular and plated. **1796** KIRWAN *Elem. Min.* (ed. 2) I. 36 The tabular [form] which consists of plates that grow thinner and sharp at the extremities. **1802** PLAYFAIR *Illustr. Hutton. Th.* 295 A bed or tabular mass of whinstone..interposed between strata. **1821** JAMESON *Man. Mineral.* 229 Associated with quartz, tabular-spar, and iron-ore. **1826** KIRBY & SP. *Entomol.* IV. xlvi. 332 When it is elevated on a footstalk above the dorsolum, and forms a tabular or flat surface. **1830** LINDLEY *Nat. Syst. Bot.* 210 The apex..is connected by a common tabular dilated stigma. **1850** R. G. CUMMING *Hunter's Life S. Afr.* (1902) 144/2 Mr. Livingstone pointed out to me a range of tabular hills. **1875** HUXLEY in *Encycl. Brit.* I. 130/2 Horizontal plates..which..constitute tabular dissepiments.

b. Painted on a 'table' or panel. *rare.*

1859 GULLICK & TIMBS *Paint.* 305 The uses to which the tabular or wooden pictures were applied.

c. *Geol. tabular (ice)berg,* a flat-topped iceberg which has broken away from an ice shelf.

1840 C. WILKES *Jrnl.* 20 Jan. in *Narr. U.S.A. Exploration Exped.* (1844) II. ix. 315 These tabular bergs are like masses of beautiful alabaster. **1848** C. TOMLINSON *Summer in Antarctic Regions* iv. 114 Westward of this point the *Vincennes* met a remarkable collection of tabular icebergs. **1905** R. F. SCOTT *Voyage of 'Discovery'* I. iv. 118 Cook preserves the name of Ice Island in describing the long tabular berg so typical of the Southern Regions. **1958** [see *ice-shelf* s.v. ICE *sb.* 8]. **1979** C. KILIAN *Icequake* viii. 133 Drifting snow and falling ice masked much of the cliff face, but it did not look like the side of a tabular berg.

2. a. Entered in, or calculated by means of, a table or tables, as a number or quantity.

1710 *Lond. Gaz.* No. 4737/3 In this Book you have above forty thousand Tabular Numbers. **1806** HUTTON *Course Math.* I. 40 Hence, by the rule..1 the tabular height. This being found in the first column of the table, the corresponding tabular area is ·04088. **1837** WHEWELL *Hist. Induct. Sc.* (1857) II. 224 Uranus still deviates from his tabular place.

b. Of the nature of, or pertaining to, a table, scheme, or synopsis; arranged in the form of a table; set down in a systematic form, as in rows and columns.

1816 BENTHAM *Chrestom.* 242 By means of a set of systematic and tabular diagrams. **1830** HERSCHEL *Study Nat. Phil.* II. vi. (1851) 182 A list of them in tabular order. **1832** BABBAGE *Econ. Manuf.* xix (ed. 3) 183 A tabular view of the time occupied by each process. **1876** C. M. DAVIES *Unorth. Lond.* 67 Carefully elaborated tabular statements.

c. *Printing.* (*a*) Applied to matter set up in the form of tables (see *table-work,* TABLE *sb.* 22).

1771 LUCKOMBE *Hist. Printing* 283 The curious method of Tabular Writing..is practised in England to greater perfection than in any other Nation. **1879** *Lond. Compositors' Sc. Prices,* Tabular and Table Work is matter set up in three or more columns and reading across the page. **1899** *Daily News* 11 Sept. 9/5 Compositor.—All-round jobbing, book, and tabular hand.

†(*b*) (Printing) from wooden blocks or tablets, on which the matter is cut. *Obs. rare.*

1816 SINGER *Hist. Cards* II. 75 As far as regards tabular printing, there is no reason to doubt that the Europeans derived their knowledge of printing from the Chinese.

†**tabu'larious**, *a. Obs. rare*[−0]. [f. L. *tabulāri-us* of or belonging to written documents (f. *tabula* table) + -OUS.] (See quot.)

1656 BLOUNT *Glossogr., Tabularious,* pertaining to writings or accounts; also belonging to tables, or good for them.

'tabularize, *v.* [f. TABULAR + -IZE.] *trans.* To put into a tabular form, to tabulate. Hence **,tabulari'zation**.

1853 MORFIT *Tanning & Currying* 332, I have carefully collected and tabularized..the following statistics. **1864** WEBSTER, *Tabularization.*

'tabularly, *adv.* [f. as prec. + -LY[2].] In a tabular form or manner; in a table.

1862 SIR H. HOLLAND *Ess., Meteors* 302 The details..are ..given tabularly. **1875** JEVONS *Money* (1878) 246 The amount of interest being tabularly stated on the form.

tabulary ('tæbjʊlərɪ), *sb. Rom. Antiq.* [ad. L. *tabulārium* a record-office, archives, f. *tabula* table, tablet: see -ARIUM.] A place where the public records were kept in ancient Rome; hence, in other places.

1656 BLOUNT *Glossogr., Tabulary,* a chest or place wherein Registers, or Evidences are kept in a City; the Chancery or Exchequer office. **1835–8** S. R. MAITLAND *Dark Ages* xii. (1844) 196 The charter cited..from the tabulary of the monastery of St. Maur. **1868** in W. SMITH *Dict. Grk. & Rom. Antiq.*

'tabulary, *a.* Now *rare.* [ad. L. *tabulār-is,* f. *tabula* table: see -ARY[2].]

1. Of, pertaining to, contained in, or of the nature of a table: = TABULAR 2 a, b.

1594 BLUNDEVIL *Exerc.* II. (1636) 130 Then subtract the lesser tabulary Sine from the greater. **1674** JEAKE *Arith.* (1696) 104 [The Obolus] is all one with the Sextans, according to the Tabulary Division. **1865** CARLYLE *Fredk. Gt.* XXI. ii. (1873) IX. 268 Much documentary and tabulary raw-material.

†**2.** ? Pictorial. *Obs. rare.*

1716 M. DAVIES *Athen. Brit.* III. 106 Whereunto Fabretti appendicularizes a Tabulary Representation of the Destruction of Troy, and a Description of Fucinus, now call'd the Lake of Celano in the Kingdom of Naples.

†**3.** Made or recorded upon a 'table' or tablet.

1716 M. DAVIES *Athen. Brit.* VI. *Diss. Physick* 29 Even the Original Prescriptions of King Mithridates..were.. thought to be owing chiefly to some of those Empyrical Recipe's recorded in those tabulary Experiences.

tabulate ('tæbjʊlət), *a.* (*sb.*) Also 6 *Sc.* -et. [ad. L. *tabulāt-us* boarded, planked, in med.L. also panelled, f. *tabulāre:* see next.]

†**1.** Formed of 'tables' or panels: panelled. *Obs.*

1596 DALRYMPLE tr. *Leslie's Hist. Scot.* (S.T.S.) I. 295 The inner parte of this tour al of tabulet [L. *tabulato*] Wark curiouslie caruet.

2. Formed like a tablet; thin and flat: = TABULAR 1.

1826 KIRBY & SP. *Entomol.* IV. 349 Postfrænum. I. Tabulate (*Tabulatum*): When it forms a broad pannel or table on each side the postscutellum. Ex. Most *Coleoptera.*

3. *Palæont.* Having *tabulæ* or horizontal dissepiments, as the corals of the group *Tabulata.*

1862 DANA *Man. Geol.* vi. 618 The interior of the coral divided by horizontal partitions (a characteristic called *tabulate* by Edwards). **1879** NICHOLSON (*title*) On the Structure and Affinities of the 'Tabulate Corals' of the Palæozoic Period.

B. *sb.* = TABLET 3. *rare.*

1834 SOUTHEY *Doctor* xxiv. (1848) 58/1 For all faintness.. a cordial was prepared in tabulates, which were called *Manus Christi.*

tabulate ('tæbjʊleɪt), *v.* [f. late L. *tabulāt-,* ppl. stem of *tabulāre* (*Onom. lat. gr.* in Quicherat *Addenda*) to board, plank, floor; in other senses directly from mod. senses of TABLE.]

†**1.** *trans.* (See quot.) *Obs. rare*[−0].

1656 BLOUNT *Glossogr., Tabulate,* to board a floore or other place, to make a thing of boards.

2. To put into the form of a table, scheme, or synopsis; to arrange, summarize, or exhibit in a table; to draw up a table of.

1734 J. KIRKBY tr. *Barrow's Math. Lect.* Pref. 29 That we rightly..tabulate, and calculate scattered ranks of numbers, and easily compute them. **1804** W. TAYLOR in *Ann. Rev.* II. 357 The result of this writer's enquiries and speculations are thus tabulated. **1869** FARRAR *Fam. Speech* ii. (1873) 70 *note,* We may tabulate the Italic family as follows.

†**3.** To enter on the roll. *Sc. Obs.* (Pa. pple. **tabulat(e.)**)

c **1630** SIR T. HOPE *Minor Practicks* (1726) 5 If the principal Cause be of that Nature, which requires to be tabulate.

¶**4.** 'To shape with a flat surface' (Todd). Only in TABULATED *ppl. a.,* q.v.

Hence **'tabulating** *vbl. sb.* and *ppl. a.*

1757 LD. KAMES *Stat. Law Scot.* 357 Tabulating of summons. **1901** *Daily Tel.* 8 Mar. 10/7 The tabulating staff ..are admitted on the ordinary examinations. **1921** J. A. V. TURCK *Origin Mod. Calculating Machines* 124 The carriage in the Ludlum machine..offered no solution to the feature of tabulating. **1979** *Washington Post* 9 June F3 Citizens in West Germany, France, Italy, Belgium and Luxembourg vote Sunday and tabulating begins that night.

tabulated ('tæbjʊleɪtɪd), *ppl. a.* [In sense 1, f. TABULATE *a.* + -ED[1]; in 2, pa. pple. of TABULATE *v.*]

1. Shaped with or having a flat upper surface; flat topped: cf. TABULAR 1. Also, composed of thin parallel layers.

1681 GREW *Musæum* III. I. iv. 282 Many..of the best [diamonds] are pointed with six Angles..and some Tabulated, or Plain, and Square. **1794** SULLIVAN *View Nat.* I. 435 The zoned or tabulated form of the onyx. **1886** A. W. GREELY *Arct. Service* I. vi. 62 The remarkable tabulated masses of land in the neighbourhood of Cape Alexander.

2. Arranged or exhibited in the form of a table, scheme, or synopsis: cf. TABULAR 2.

1802 (*title*) Copy of a Letter from Citizen Talleyrand to Citizen Fauvelet at Dublin, with a Tabulated List of Questions on the Commercial and Maritime Affairs of that Country. **1862** BP. FORBES in *Ecclesiologist* XXIII. 34 We propose giving a tabulated scheme of the different calendars of the Scottish Church. **1862** M. HOPKINS *Hawaii* 369 *note*, A tabulated statement issued by authority.

tabulation (tæbjʊ'leɪʃən). [n. of action from TABULATE *v.*; cf. L. *tabulātio* a flooring over, a floor or story.]

†**1.** See quot. *Obs. rare*⁻⁰.

1658 PHILLIPS, *Tabulation*, (lat.) a fastning together of planks or boards, a making a floor.

2. The action or process of tabulating; arrangement in the form of a table or orderly scheme.

1837 WHEWELL *Hist. Induct. Sc.* (1857) III. 101 The value of such a tabulation was immense. **1867** BRANDE & COX *Dict. Sc.* etc., *Tabulation of chronology*, the arrangement of historical or professedly historical events according to their real or supposed dates is sometimes spoken of under this name. **1883** *Stubbs' Merc. Circular* 10 Oct. 902/1 If the collection and tabulation of these Statistics were entrusted simply to one department.

3. *Arch.* Division into successive stages of height by 'tables' or horizontal mouldings, etc.

1886 WILLIS & CLARK *Cambridge* I. 103 The new design of that front..is..contrived so as to accommodate itself at the angle to the ancient lines of tabulation.

tabulator ('tæbjʊleɪtə(r)). [Agent-n. from TABULATE *v.*: see -OR.] **a.** One who tabulates, or draws up a table or scheme. **b.** A machine or apparatus for this purpose; *spec.* a part of the mechanism of a typewriter (formerly, a separate attachment) for controlling the movement of the carriage in tabular work, indentation, etc.; in *Computing*, a machine that produces lists, tables, or totals from the information in a data storage medium, esp. punched cards or tape.

1885 *Athenæum* 14 Nov. 639/3 This..means a corresponding increase in the work of the tabulators. **1892** *Daily News* 6 June 5/5 It is these cards that are passed through the electrical tabulator, which, by ingenious contrivances, records the answers on a number of dials. **1901** *Phonetic Jrnl.* 28 Sept. 611/1 Mr. F. P. Gorin, inventor of the tabulator bearing his name. **1917** L. R. DICKSEE *Office Machinery* viii. 96 A complete installation, consisting..of three Punches, one Sorter, and one Tabulator, would involve the employment of four operators, none of whom need be skilled accountants. **1922** F. W. PIXLEY *Accountant's Dict.* II. 723/1 Accountants should..consider both systems..The choice will generally depend on the form in which the data is finally required; in other words, the tabulator will usually govern the system adopted. **1949** [see INTERPRETER 5 a]. **1970** O. DOPPING *Computers & Data Processing* iv. 73 A tabulator usually prints around 150 lines per minute, while a normal speed for a computer line printer is 1,000 lines per minute. **1978** J. KELLOCK *Elements of Accounting* xii. 214 The next step is to feed the cards into a tabulator.

tabulatory ('tæbjʊlətərɪ), *a. rare.* [f. L. *tabulāt-*, ppl. stem of *tabulāre* to TABULATE + -ORY[2].] Relating to or consisting in tabulation. Hence '**tabulatorily** *adv.*, in relation to tabulation or tables.

1900 *Daily News* 20 Oct. 7/1 Her occasional historical and tabulatory excursuses may require a skip here and there. **1900** *Words Eyewitness* (1902) 282 The British nation is giving the lie to all history and all rules. Its 'life'—from the insurance-office point of view—is a marvel. Tabulatorily speaking, it is a monstrosity.

tabulature, variant of TABLATURE.

tabule ('tæbju:l). [mod. ad. L. *tabula* table, tablet.] A medicine or drug prepared in a flattened form; = TABLET *sb.* 3.

1893 *Advt.*, Tabules for dyspepsia, headache &c. **1898** *Westm. Gaz.* 28 Nov. 9/2 Witnesses who had been in communication with the prisoner in regard to tabules.

tabule, -ull(e, obs. forms of TABLE.

tabulette, obs. form of TABLET.

tabuliform ('tæbjʊlɪˌfɔ:m), *a.* [f. L. *tabula* table + -FORM.] Having the form of a 'table' or tablet; = TABULAR 1.

1848 LINDLEY *Introd. Bot.* II. 148 A single tabuliform cell of the upper cuticle.

†'**tabulous**, *a. Obs. rare.* [f. as prec. + -OUS.] Divided into compartments by tabulæ.

1733 MASSEY in *Phil. Trans.* XXXVIII. 191 A Tabulous Shell divided into several Cavities.

Tabun ('tɑ:bʊn). Also **tabun**. [Ger., of unkn. origin.] The name of an organophosphorus nerve gas, $(C_2H_5O)(CN)((CH_3)_2N)PO$.

1951 *Acta Physiol. Scandinavica* Suppl. No. 90. 11 The writer's aim has been to synthesize tabun and some of its homologues. **1953** [see SOMAN]. **1967** *New Scientist* 26 Jan. 196/1 The nerve gas Sarin, known as GB, is said to be four times as toxic as the German Tabun of World War II. **1968** [see SARIN]. **1978** A. MELVILLE-ROSS *Blindfold* iv. 26 A single 'Sarin' or 'Tabun' shell of British manufacture found its way to Egypt. **1980** *Sci. Amer.* Apr. 35/1 The first of these compounds, called tabun, was discovered in Germany in 1936 in the course of research on insecticides.

tabur, taburn, obs. ff. TABOR, TABORN.

†'**taburnister.** *Obs. rare.* In 4 -yster, -ystir. [f. *taburn*, TABORN + -STER: feminine corresp. to TABORNER.] A female player on the tabor.

a **1340** HAMPOLE *Psalter* lxvii. 27 Bifor come prynces ioyned til syngand: in myddis of wenchis taburnystirs [L. *iuuencularum tympanistriarum*]. *Ibid.*, Taburnysters.

taby, tabyl, tabyll(e, tabyr, obs. forms of TABBY, TABLE, TABOR.

tac: see TAKE *v.*

tacamahac ('tækəməhæk), **tacamahaca** (ˌtækəmə'hɑ:kə). Also 7–8 **tacamahacca**, 8 **tacamahack**, 8 **taccamahac**, **tacamacha**, **tacka mohacca**. [ad. obs. Sp. *tacamahaca*, in Hernandez 1614 *thecomahaca*, ad. Aztec *tecomahiyac*; mod.Sp. *tacamaca*. Cf. Monardes 1579 'ex Nova Hispania..ab Indis *tacamahaca* vocatum'. In F. *tacamaque*. *Tacamahac* is the more usual form, and that recognized in North America in sense 2.]

1. An aromatic resin, used for incense, and formerly extensively in medicine. **a.** *orig.* That yielded by a Mexican tree, *Bursera* (*Elaphrium*) *tomentosa*. **b.** Extended in the West Indies and S. America to similar resins obtained from other species of *Bursera* and the allied genus *Protium*, and subsequently to resins imported from Madagascar, Bourbon, and the East Indies, chiefly the product of species of *Calophyllum*.

1577 FRAMPTON *Joyful News* I. 3 Gumme called Tacamahaca. **1616** BULLOKAR *Eng. Expos.*, *Tacamahaca*, a Rosin brought out of the West Indies, of great vertue against any cold humours [etc.]. **1703** *Lond. Gaz.* No. 3898/3 The Cargo of the Galeon.., consisting of..Jollop, Gum Elemni, Tacka Mohacca,..&c. **1714** *Fr. Bk. of Rates* 92 Gum call'd Tacamacha *p.* 100 Weight 05 05. **1718** QUINCY *Compl. Disp.* 137 Tacamahack is a resinous Gum, from the West Indies. **1747** WESLEY *Prim. Physick* (1762) 108 Apply to the Cheek Gum Tacamahac spread on Silk. **1802** *Naval Chron.* VIII. 150 (I. of France) Tacamahaca, stinking wood. **1846** LINDLEY *Veg. Kingd.* 460 Tacamahac from *Elaphrium tomentosum*. *Ibid.* 401 The true East India Tacamahaca is produced by *Calophyllum Calaba*.

2. The resin of the buds of the N. American Balsam Poplar, *Populus balsamifera*; hence a name of this tree.

1739 MILLER *Gard. Dict.* (ed. 3) II. *Addenda* s.v., The Tacamahaca. This Tree grows spontaneously on the Continent of America. **1759** *Ibid.* (ed. 7) s.v. *Populus*, The Buds of this Tree are covered with a glutinous Resin, which smells very strong, and this is the Tacamahacca used in the Shops. **1786** J. ABERCROMBIE *Arrangem.* in *Gard. Assist.* 32/1 Tacamahacca, or great balsam poplar. **1842** SELBY *Brit. Forest Trees* 213 The list of Tacamahacs mentioned by Loudon. **1846** LINDLEY *Veg. Kingd.* 255 Poplar buds, especially those of *P*[*opulus*] *nigra*, *balsamifera*, and *candicans*, are besmeared in winter with a resinous.. exudation, which [passes] under the name of Tacamahac. **1881** tr. *Verne's Fur Country* 95 Jaspar also noticed the tacamahac, a species of poplar which grows to a great height.

tacan ('tækən). Also **Tacan**, **TACAN**. [f. the initial letters of *ta*ctical *a*ir *n*avigation.] A navigational aid system for aircraft which measures bearing and distance from a ground beacon. Freq. *attrib.*

1955 *Times* 17 Aug. 6/4 The Defence Department has removed security restrictions from the technical details of Tacan (tactical air navigation system) and the Air Navigation Development Board will reveal them in an announcement on August 19. **1956** *Electrical Communication* Mar. 3/1 Tacan is a system that provides both bearing and distance information on direct-reading instruments in an airplane within 200 nautical miles of a selected ground station. *Ibid.* 26/1 A tacan ground-installed beacon consists of a receiver-transmitter..and either a shipboard or a shore antenna. **1966** [see SHORAN]. **1977** P. WAY *Super-Celeste* III. 129 A small, slim fin broke the smooth underbelly of the plane... 'That's either a UHF antenna or a TACAN aerial,' said Bridge.

‖**tac-au-tac** (takotak). *Fencing.* [F. *tac-au-tac*, lit. clash for clash, f. *tac* echoic word.] In ***tac-au-tac riposte***, the return stroke after parrying with opposition: see quot. 1889 and RIPOSTE *sb.* 1.

[**1889** POLLOCK, etc. *Fencing* (Badm. Libr.) 75 [The riposte] may be delivered in two ways:..[secondly], quitting the steel after a clean, smart parry... This is called..the *riposte du tac-au-tac*.] **1907** *Daily Chron.* 20 Nov. 8/2 The retort was in the nature of the tac-au-tac riposte beloved of the skilled swordsman.

‖**Tacca** ('tækə). *Bot.* [mod.L. a. Malay.] Name of a small genus of tropical herbs with tuberous roots, the type of a natural order *Taccaceæ*. The tubers of *T. pinnatifida* yield the starch known as South-sea arrow-root.

1866 *Treas. Bot.* 1119/1 *Tacca* chiefly differs from its ally *Ataccia* in having a one-celled instead of a three-celled fruit.

Hence '**taccad**, any plant of the N.O. *Taccaceæ*.

1846 LINDLEY *Veg. Kingd.* 149 Order xliii. Taccaceæ.—Taccads. **1855** E. SMITH *Bot.* in *Orr's Circ. Sc.* 187 *Narcissales*..(N.O.) 43 Taccaceæ or Taccads.

‖**taccada** (tə'kɑ:də). [Sinhalese *takkada*.] The Malayan rice-paper plant, *Scævola Lobelia* (or *Königii*), an erect shrub found on the sea-shores of tropical Asia, Australia, and Polynesia; its young stems have a pith resembling that of the rice-paper plant (*Aralia papyrifera*), and are used by the Malays for making artificial flowers, etc.

1866 *Treas. Bot.* 1027/2 *S*[*cævola*] *Lobelia* (alias *S. Königii* and *S. Taccada*), the Taccada of India and Ceylon. **1887** MOLONEY *Forestry W. Afr.* 376 Taccada of India and Ceylon (*Scævola Lobelia*, L.).—Shrubby plant.

‖**tace** ('teɪsi:). [L. *tacē*, imper. of *tacēre* to be silent.] The Latin for 'Be silent'. ***tace is Latin for a candle***, a humorously veiled hint to any one to keep silent about something.

[Cf. **1605** CAMDEN *Rem.* 162 (*Impresses*) Edmund of Langley..asked..his sonnes..what was Latine for a fetter-locke: Whereat when the yong gentleman studied, the father said, '..I will tell you, *Hic hæc hoc taceatis*', as advising them to be silent and quiet.] **1697** *Dampier's Voy.* 356 Trust none of them for they are all Thieves, but Tace is Latin for a Candle. **1752** FIELDING *Amelia* I. x, '*Tace*, Madam', answered Murphy, 'is Latin for a candle; I commend your prudence'. **1821** SCOTT *Fam. Lett.* 24 Feb. (1894) II. 115 *Tace* shall be hereafter with me 'Latin for a candle'.

tace, = *tas*, obs. 3 sing. pres. of TAKE *v.*; obs. form of TASSE.

‖**tacenda** (tə'sɛndə), *sb. pl.* [L., gerundive neut. pl. of *tacēre*: see next.] Things to be passed over in silence; matters not to be mentioned.

1843 CARLYLE *Past & Present* II. x. 125 Willelmus Sacrista, and his bibations and *tacenda* are..softly yet irrevocably put an end to. **1870** S. H. HODGSON *Theory of Practice* I. ii. 217 A greater number of things are classed among tacenda... The French term pudeur seems exactly to express the feeling which is called out painfully or wounded by an lifting of the veil of the tacenda. **1883** *Blackw. Mag.* Feb. 274 Topics..regarded as tacenda by society.

†'**tacent**, *a. Obs. rare.* [ad. L. *tacēnt-em*, pr. pple. of *tacēre* to be silent.] Silent.

1652 KIRKMAN *Clerio & Lozia* 179 There was a fair Tragedy, whose subject I will be tacent of.

‖**tacet** ('teɪsɛt). *Mus.* [L., = 'is silent', from *tacēre* to be silent.] A direction that the voice or instrument is to be silent for a time.

1724 *Short Explic. For. Wds. in Mus. Bks.*, *Tace* or *Tacet*, to hold still, or keep Silence. **1789** REES *Chambers' Cycl.*, *Tacet*, in the Italian Music, is often used to denote a long rest, or pause. **1823** in CRABB *Techn. Dict.*, etc.

tach (tæk), U.S. colloq. abbrev. of TACHOMETER. Cf. TACHO, TACK *sb.*[8]

1966 *Publ. Amer. Dial. Soc.* 1964 XLII. 9 *Tach*.., abbreviation of tachometer. **1974** R. M. PIRSIG *Zen & Art of Motorcycle Maintenance* I. iii. 36 The speedometer needle swings back and forth but the tach reads a steady nine thousand. **1980** *Family Handyman* Sept. 98/2 If you've used a tach/dwell meter for the point adjustment, leave it in place, and attach a timing light.

Tachai ('dɑ:dʒaɪ). Also **Dazhai**. The name of a village in the Shansi Province of the People's Republic of China, used *attrib.* to designate its model commune or the methods of work, etc., associated with it. Also *Comb.*, as ***Tachai-type*** adj.

1969 *Observer* 16 Mar. 2/7 Under the 'Tachai' system, not only are peasants being rewarded with work points instead of hard cash, but the schoolteachers and the 'barefoot doctors' in the communes are also to be paid principally in work points. **1973** J. S. AIRD in Yuan-Li Wu *China Handbk.* I. xviii. 463 Even in the Tachai production brigade in Shansi, the family planning propaganda program at first elicited 'little positive response'. **1975** A. WATSON *Living in China* i. 22 The Communist Party almost always introduces its new policies and goals by putting forward examples for others to copy. One of the most famous of these is Dazhai Commune. **1977** *China Now* June 1 Myriads of such Tachai-type people, Tachai-type cadres, their outlook constantly broadened and deepened by Marxist science. **1979** *Ibid.* Mar./Apr. 3/1 The movement to spread 'Dazhai-type counties' throughout the country is lagging.

tacharanite ('tækərənaɪt). *Min.* [See quot. 1961 and -ITE[1].] A monoclinic hydrated silicate of calcium, magnesium, and aluminium found as white aggregates or masses.

1961 J. M. SWEET in *Mineral. Mag.* XXXII. 750 It is thought that this mineral is sufficiently distinctive to deserve a name of its own and that tacharanite..from the Gaelic *tacharan* (a changeling) would be suitable, both from the nature of its behaviour and the wealth of folklore associated with the island [*sc.* Skye] in which it occurs. **1975** *Ibid.* XL. 113 Tacharanite has been reexamined... The composition approximates to $Ca_{12}Al_2Si_{18}O_{69}H_{36}$. **1978** *Ibid.* XLII. 383/1 Tacharanite in fractures in metagabbroic rocks filled by zeolitic assemblages has been found in the Gruppo di Voltri, Ligurian Alps.

tache († tætʃ; tæʃ, ‖ taʃ), *sb.*[1] Forms: 4 teiche, 4–5 tech(e, tecch(e, techch(e, tacch(e, 4–7 tatch(e, 4–8 tach, 5 tetch(e, taich(e, tachch(e, 6–9 tash, 5– tache. [a. OF. *teche* (11th c.), *tesche, tece, tecce, taiche, teiche, teke, teqe* (Godef.); also F. *tache* (12th c. in Godef. *Compl.*), †*tasche*.

The Fr. word is of uncertain origin, but, according to Hatz-Darm., is to be distinguished from the radical *tac* of TACHE *sb.*[2], ATTACH, etc., with which earlier etymologists have associated it.]

1. †**a.** A spot, blotch, blot. *Obs.* exc. as in b.

13.. *St. Erkenwolde* 85 in Horstm. *Altengl. Leg.* (1881) 268 Wemles were his wedes with-outen any teiche. **13..** *Gaw. & Gr. Knt.* 2436 How tender hit is to entyse teches of fylþe. *a* **1450** *Knt. de la Tour* (1906) 163 A stone so clere and faire that there is no tache therein.

‖**b.** In modern scientific use only as French.

1893 W. R. GOWERS *Dis. Nervous Syst.* (ed. 2) II. 339 The well-known *tache cérébrale*, in which cutaneous irritation is followed by unusually vivid and enduring congestion of the skin [etc.]. **1898** *Syd. Soc. Lex.*, *Tache*, congenital discolorations, or freckles, or spots. Blemish.

c. *spec.* in *Art*, a spot or dash of colour. Also *fig.* Cf. TACHISM.

1957 *Observer* 3 Nov. 14/6 The 'tache' is the mark the painter makes on the canvas with his paint-loaded brush, and an emphasis on the freedom and spontaneity of the creative act itself and on extreme sensitivity towards the actual materials of painting is characteristic of the tachists. **1967** J. N. BARRON *Lang. Painting* 188 *Tachisme*.., a term used to describe a style of painting in which the color is applied in splotches or blots (*taches*) of color. **1978** G. GREENE *Human Factor* II. ii. 67 The simple precise words, with the single tache of colour reminded Castle of the local background so often to be found in primitive paintings.

2. †**a.** *fig.* A moral spot or blemish; a fault or vice; a bad quality or habit; in quots. 1340–70, 1541, a physical blemish. *Obs.*

c **1330** R. BRUNNE *Chron. Wace* (Rolls) 3899 Alle his wykked tecches he left. **1340** *Ayenb.* 32 Vor oþre zix vices ..þet byeþ techches of kuead seriont. **1340–70** *Alisaunder* 282 Hee made a uery uow auenged too beene Of þat teenefull tach [the loss of an eye] þat hee tooke þere. **1377** LANGL. *P. Pl.* B. IX. 146 If þe fader be false and a shrewe, þat somdel þe sone shal haue þe sires tacches. **1422** tr. *Secreta Secret., Priv. Priv.* 188 Vices and ewil taichis thou shalt enchue. *c* **1430** LYDG. *Min. Poems* (Percy Soc.) 256 Snybbyd of my frendys such techechys for t'amende. **1483** CAXTON *Gold. Leg.* 261 b/2 She that neuer had tatche ne spot of corrupcion. **1541** [see TACHE *v.*[1]]. **1577** HELLOWES *Gueuara's Chron.* 106 He had therewith a tache or a fault. **1602** WARNER *Alb. Eng.* XIII. lxxvii. 318 Of whom euen his Adorers write euill Taches many an one.

b. An imputation of fault or disgrace; a stain; a stigma. *Sc. Obs.* or *rare.*

c **1610** SIR J. MELVIL *Mem.* Author to Son (1683) b iij, Her marrying a Man commonly judged her Husbands murtherer would leave a Tash upon her name. **1692** SIR W. HOPE *Fencing-Master* 162 If you can by any means (without puting a tash upon your honour). ? *c* **1716** in Wodrow *Hist. Church Scotl.* (1829) III. 227/1, I have made this reflection, not as a tach upon the persons who suffered. **1723** R. HAY (*title*) A Vindication of Elizabeth More from the Imputation of being a Concubine; and her Children from the Tache of Bastardy. **1862** M. NAPIER *Visct. Dundee* II. 218 The only tache upon his military fame.

†**c.** A smack, slight taste or flavour. *Obs. rare.*

1607 *Barley-Breake* (1877) 28 Their grazing feast will haue a wearish tatch.

3. A distinctive mark, quality, or habit; a trait, a characteristic, good or bad. [So in OF.] *Obs.* exc. *dial.* (tɛtʃ).

a **1400–50** *Alexander* 4390 Oure techis haue we schawid, Oure dedis & of oure disciplyne. **1470–85** MALORY *Arthur* VII. xx. 244 Wel maye he be a kynges sone for he hath many good tatches on hym. **1539** TAVERNER *Erasm. Prov.* (1545) 75 It is theyr owne maners, theyr owne qualities, tetches, condicions, and procedynges that shape them this fortune. **1598** BARRET *Theor. Warres* IV. i. 119 Euery braue man of warre beareth a tatch of ambition and of aspiring minde. **1780** BERRIDGE *Lett.* (1864) 400 Is any tache wanting, you could wish to see in a young man designed for the ministry? **1886** ELWORTHY *W. Somerset Word-bk.*, *Tetch*, habit, gait. 'Tis a tetch her've a-got.

tache, tach (tætʃ), *sb.*[2] Now *rare*. Also 6–7 tatch. [a. OF. *tache* fibula (14th c.), also a large nail: cf. Genevese *tache*, Languedoc *tacho* nail with broad round head, hob-nail, tack, tacket, Sp. *tacha* a kind of nail; also (from OF.) MDu. *taetse*, Du. *taats*, a round-headed nail, an iron pin. A doublet of TACK *sb.*[1] The root is also that of F. *attacher, détacher*, Eng. ATTACH, DETACH. See Diez and Littré. Sense 2 may be in origin a different word.]

1. A contrivance for fastening two parts together; a fibula, a clasp, a buckle, a hook and eye, or the like; a hook for hanging anything on. *Obs.* or *arch.*

14.. *Voc.* in Wr.-Wülcker 583/10 *Fibula*, a tache or a laas [or a botun]. **1452** *Maldon, Essex, Crt. Rolls* (Bundle 31, No. 2 b), A tache of sylver..for a monkis hode. *c* **1500** *Melusine* 304 Thenne geffray cutte the taches of the geant helmet, and after cutte of his heed. **1530** PALSGR. 279/1 Tache for a gowne, *atache*. **1535** in *Ripon Ch. Acts* (Surtees) 359, j tach with j ruby ston. **1535** COVERDALE *Num.* xxxi. 50 Brynge we a present vnto the Lorde what euery one hath,..bracelettes, rynges, earinges and taches. **1582** STANYHURST *Æneis* IV. (Arb.) 99 With gould tache thee vesture purple is holden. **1611** BIBLE *Exod.* xxvi. 6 Thou shalt make fiftie taches [1885 *R.V.* clasps] of gold, and couple the curtaines together with the taches. **1641** EVELYN *Diary* Aug., A lamp..hanging loose upon a tach in the midst of a beame. **1668** WILKINS *Real Char.* II. vii. 184 Hook, Crook, Clasp, Hasp, Tatches. **1867** H. MACMILLAN *Bible Teach.* xiv. (1870) 274 Taches of gold..connecting together the curtains of the tabernacle.

†**b.** A band or strap that may be fastened round anything. *Obs. rare.*

1610 HOLLAND *Camden's Brit.* I. 287 It came into [K. Richard's] mind to draw upon the legs of certaine choise Knights of his a certaine Garter or tach of leather. **1611** SPEED *Theat. Gt. Brit* xiv. (1614) 27/2 K. Richard the First ..girt the legs of certaine choise knights with a tache of leather, which promised a future glory to the wearers.

c. *fig.* A means of attachment, a link, a bond of connexion.

1701 J. LAW *Counc. Trade* (1751) 225 Here is no such bar or tache, as either to hinder or discourage a thief of any sort from returning to his duty. **1860** FARRAR *Orig. Lang.* ii. 47 Finally, the word became a middle term of reminiscence, a tach between the external object and the inward impression.

2. *techn.* A rest for the shank of a punch or drill: see quots. Now *dial.*

1683 MOXON *Mech. Exerc., Printing* xii. ¶9 The Tach is.. to rest and hold the Shank of a Punch steady..while the Work-man Files. *Ibid.* 392 *Tache*, a small Board with Notches in its Fore-edge..to rest the Shank of a Punch in. **1829** in J. HUNTER *Hallamshire Gloss.* **1888–90** *Sheffield Gloss.*, *Tache* (taiche)..has been defined for me as 'a stake or rest used by silversmiths, and fixed in the workbench'.

3. *Comb.*, as †*tach-hook*, †*tach-nail*.

1592 R. D. *Hypnerotomachia* 50 The Veluet brought downe to the frame of the Settles..fastened to the same with tatch Nayles of Golde. **1623** tr. *Favine's Theat. Hon.* II. xiii. 224 Their long Cloak, or Houpe-land,..tied with a Tach-hooke of Wood.

tache (tætʃ), *sb.*[3] Forms: 7–9 tach, tatch, 8 tetch, 8–9 tatche, teach, 9 teache, taych, tache. [app. a. obs. or dial. F. *tache, tèche* plate of iron (Godef.), in Walloon *tak* 'plaque de fer qu'on applique au fond d'une cheminée' (Littré), which in F. dictionaries is usually identified with *tache*, TACHE *sb.*[1]]

1. *Sugar-boiling.* Each pan of the series through which the juice of the sugar-cane is passed in evaporating it; *esp.* the smallest and last of these, called specifically the ***striking-tache***.

1657 R. LIGON *Barbadoes* 84 The Coppers, in which the Sugar is boyled, of which, the largest is called the Clarifying Copper, and the least, the Tatch. *Ibid.* 90 To throw in some of the liquor of the next Copper, to keep the tach from burning. **1740** *Hist. Jamaica* xii. 321 The least is called the Tach, where it boils longest. **1756** P. BROWNE *Jamaica* 131 The juice will often begin to granulate in the second tetch. **1788** P. MARSDEN *Acct. Island Jamaica* 26 The smallest and last copper is called the teach. **1835** in J. H. Ingraham *South-West* I. 240 In the last kettle—the *teach* as it is termed ..the sugar is concentrated to the granulating point. **1839** URE *Dict. Arts*, etc. 1202 The term striking is also applied to the act of emptying the teache. **1862** *Illustr. Catal. Internat. Exhib., Industr. Dept., Brit. Div.* II. No. 6139 Stoves, ranges, sugar pans, teaches, or boilers to any pattern or make. **1871** KINGSLEY *At Last* xi, I flung it, sugar and all, into the tache. **1885** LOCK *Workshop Receipts* Ser. IV. 163/2 The earliest and crudest system of evaporation was the 'copper wall', or 'battery' of open pans called 'teaches' (taches, tayches, &c.). **1887** *Encycl. Brit.* XXII. 626/1 The [cane sugar] juice..is passed from the one [pan] into the other till it reaches the last of the series, the striking teach. **1949** *Caribbean Q.* I. i. 9 The juice, now reduced to a syrup, was ladled into a final copper, the teache, for a last boiling.

†**2.** Applied to the flat iron pan in which tea-leaves are dried. *Obs.*

1701 J. CUNNINGHAM in *Phil. Trans.* XXIII. 1206 The Bing Tea is the second growth in April: and Singlo the last in May and June, both dry'd a little in Tatches or Pans over the Fire. **1802** *Nat. Hist.* in *Ann. Reg.* 764/2 Then they [tea leaves] are tatched; this is done by throwing each time about half a catty of leaves into the tatche, and stirring them with the hand twice, the tatche being very hot. [*Footnote*] Tatche is a flat pan of cast iron.

†**tache**, *sb.*[4] *Obs. rare*$^{-1}$. Also 5 tach, tacche, tasche, tasshe. [Origin obscure.] Touch-wood, tinder.

1393 LANGL. *P. Pl.* C. xx. 211 Bote þou haue tache [*v.rr.* tach, tacche, tasshe, B. XVII. 245 towe] to take hit with tunder and broches, Al þy labour is lost.

tache (tætʃ, taʃ), *v.*[1] Now *dial.* Forms: (4 tass), 5–6 tatch, 6–7 tach(e, 7– *Sc.* tash. [a. F. *tacher*, OF. *tachier* to stain, soil, f. *tache*, TACHE *sb.*[1]] *trans.* To stain or taint, esp. with moral defilement, or with the imputation of guilt or shameful conduct; to stigmatize; rarely (quot. 1541), to infect physically. *Obs.* or *Sc. dial.*

1390 GOWER *Conf.* III. 242 The wyde world merveileth yit, That he [Solomon]..With fleisshly lustes was so tassed [*rime* passed]. **1495** *Trevisa's Barth. De P.R.* VI. v. (W. de W.) m v b, Al chyldern ben tatchyd wyth euyll maners. **1502** ATKYNSON tr. *De Imitatione* III. xxxiv. 223 What shall I say, that am tached thus with tribulacions. **1541** R. COPLAND *Guydon's Quest. Chirurg.* Q ij b, To be scalled, or tached with suche infecte dyseases, or that he bere some tache vpon hym. **1596** WARNER *Alb. Eng.* X. lviii, Otherwise a worthy Prince, nor tache we him but so. *Ibid.* XI. lxv. (1612) 280 Though she did obserue his soone Reuolt..And him thereof had tacht. **1598** BARRET *Theor. Warres* II. i. 28 Infamous, or tatched with foule crimes. *a* **1649** DRUMM. OF HAWTH. *Hist. Jas. V*, Wks. (1711) 104 At the least to leave him suspected and tached with this treason. **1747** in *Ann. Gen. Assemb. Ch. Scot.* (1838) 105 His character ought not to be tashed. **1827** J. WATT *Poems* 101 (E.D.D.) Their frien's gat word an' gather roun' Determin'd sair to tease an' tash.

b. To blemish, deface; to tarnish or spoil slightly by handling or use; to make the worse for wear; ***tashed***, tarnished, worn, weather-beaten. *Sc.*

17.. in Ritson *Sc. Songs* (1794) I. 214 They're tashed like, and sair torn, And clouted sair on ilka knee. **1863** ALEX. SMITH *Dreamthorp* 18 They [books] are tashed as roses are tashed by being frequently handled or smelt. **1895** W. C. FRASER *Whaups* xiii. 189 An indoor face, no tashed wi' the weather, but sair blotched wi' the dram. **1903** GLAISER in *Co-op. News* 16 May 567 (E.D.D.) If thet isna Miss Thorpe's new body slip... Go and get it off afore yo' tash it any worse.

tache (tætʃ), *v.*[2] *Obs.* or *dial.* Also 4–5 tacche, 5–7 tatche, 5–9 tatch. [f. TACHE *sb.*[2], or from the same root. In sense 2 (and sometimes in 1), app. aphetic from *atache*, ATTACH.]

1. *trans.* To fasten, attach, fix, secure (a person or thing). Also *fig.*

a **1310** in Wright *Lyric P.* xxv. 70 Thy love sprenges tacheth me. *c* **1315** SHOREHAM *Poems* ii. 101 Þo þy chyld was an-honge, Itached to þe harde tre Wyþ nayles gret and longe! *c* **1330** R. BRUNNE *Chron. Wace* (Rolls) 12056 Ropes ..to tache & teye. **1483** *Cath. Angl.* 376/2 To Tache, *attachiare*. **1530** PALSGR. 746/1, I tache a gowne or a typpet with a tache. **1575** *Gamm. Gurton* II. iii, To seeke for a thonge Therwith this breech to tatche & tye. **1609** R. BARNERD *Faithf. Sheph.* To Rdr. 7 Tatching matter together with dependancie.

2. To lay hold of (a person); *esp.* to arrest, apprehend by legal authority; = ATTACH *v.* 1 a.

c **1400** *Laud Troy Bk.* 5690 Thei scholde for euere him haue tached, Ne hadde ben duk Menescene. *c* **1440** *Jacob's Well* 24 Alle þat malycyously tachyn, arestyn, or endyten.. men of holy cherch. *c* **1470** HENRY *Wallace* VII. 304 Thar folowed him fyfteyn Wicht, wallyt men..to tach him to the law. **1528** *Tyball's Confess.* in Strype *Eccl. Mem.* (1721) I. App. xvii. 35 The same day..that Sir Richard Fox was tached. **1530** PALSGR. 746/1, I tache a thefe, I laye handes upon hym. ? *a* **1635** FORBES *Disc. Pervers Deceit* 6 (Jam.) A cunning and long covered thiefe tatched with innumerable fanges [plunder].

Hence **'taching** *vbl. sb.* and *ppl. a.* ***taching end***, a shoemaker's waxed thread pointed with a hog's bristle.

c **1440** *Promp. Parv.* 485/2 Tachynge, or a-restynge, *arestacio*. *c* **1485** *E.E. Misc.* (Warton Club) 73 Grynd hem togedyre a longe tyme one a stone, tylle hit be somdele tacchynge. *c* **1535** BYGOD *Impropriations* in *Lever's Serm.* (Arb.) Introd. 13 Snatchynge and scratchinge, tatchynge and patchynge, scrapinge and rakynge togyther of almost all the fatte benefyces. **1611** COTGR., *Ligneul*, shoomakers thread; or, a tatching end. *a* **1763** SHENSTONE *Ess., Men & Manners* (1765) 187 A cobler with ten or a dozen children dependent on a tatching end. **1858** H. AINSWORTH *Mervyn Clitheroe* i. 15 Canes..tied with tatching end to prevent them from splitting. **1881** *Leicestersh. Gloss.* s.v., Every piece of 'tachin-end' used in joining has a hog's bristle fixed at each end so as to act as a kind of flexible needle.

†**tache**, *v.*[3] *Obs.* [Perh. the same in origin as TACHE *v.*[2]; cf. OF. *atachier* in sense 'to attack', It. *attaccare* to attach, to attack, and see note to ATTACH *v.*] *intr.* To make a (hostile) charge or attack; to charge.

a **1400–50** *Alexander* 2622 Kniȝtis on cursours kest þan in fewtire, Taches [*Dubl. MS.* tachyng] in-to targetis tamed þaire brenys [*v.r.* brynnes]. *c* **1400** *Sege Jerusalem* 656 Quarels & arwes..Toysen at þe toures: tachen on þe Jewes. *c* **1400** *Destr. Troy* 6717 Telamon hym tacchit on with a tore speire. *Ibid.* 6783 Deffibus the doughty,..Tachit vpon Teutro, a full tore dynt. *Ibid.* 8297 Then Diamede..On Troiell with tene tachet belyue.

†**tache, tatch**, *v.*[4] *Obs. rare.* [f. TACHE *sb.*[3]] *trans.* To dry (tea) in a 'tache' or shallow pan.

1802 *Nat. Hist.* in *Ann. Reg.* 765/1 Bohea tea is gathered, sunned in baskets, rolled with the hand, and then tatched, which completes it. *Ibid.*, Tatching seems to give the green colour to the leaves of the tea trees.

tache, early ME. var. of TEACH *v.*

'tache, var. TASH.

†**'tached**, *a. Obs.* Also 5 techyd, tacched. [f. TACHE *sb.*[1] + -ED[2].] Having qualities of a specified kind; (well- or ill-) mannered or conditioned.

c **1400** tr. *Secreta Secret., Gov. Lordsh.* 116 He þat hauys a lityll ffface..ys wycked, and euyl-techyd, deceyuant, and dronkelew. *a* **1450** *Knt. de la Tour* (1906) 18 All gentil-women and nobill maydenes..ought to be goodli, meke, wele tached, ferme in estate, behauing, and maners. *c* **1450** *Merlin* 88 The trewest of this londe and beste tacched. **1532** MORE *Confut. Tindale* Wks. 556/2 An euil tached horse shaketh of sometime the bridle and runneth out at large.

†**'tacheless**, *a. Obs. rare*$^{-1}$. In 4 teccheles. [f. TACHE *sb.*[1] + -LESS.] Stainless, faultless.

13.. *Gaw. & Gr. Knt.* 917 Now schal we semlych se sleȝtez of þewez, & þe teccheles termes of talkyng noble.

tacheometer (tækiːˈɒmɪtə(r)). [a. F. *tachéomètre*, f. Gr. ταχε-, obl. stem of ταχύ-ς quick, swift, τάχος swiftness + -METER: see also TACHYMETER.] A name given to instruments (of which there are various kinds) for the rapid location of points on a survey; = TACHYMETER. Hence **tacheo'metric** *a.*, pertaining to a tacheometer or tacheometry; **tache'ometry**, surveying by means of a tacheometer.

1876 *Catal. Sci. App. S. Kens.* 425 The Tacheometer of Gentilli... The means by which it measures the distance is an apparatus which obliges the lunette to traverse an unvarying angle. **1888** B. H. BROUGH *Mine Surveying* 204 The aim of tacheometry is to survey and level simultaneously a tract of ground with the greatest possible accuracy in the least possible time. **1900** *Nature* 11 Oct. 571/2 Suggestions on possible methods of utilising existing transit theodolites for tacheometric work. **1905** MAJOR CLOSE *Test Bk. Surveying* v. 51 Tacheometry (called also in American books Tachymetry or Tachyometry) a system of 'rapid measuring'..includes all the eight variations just mentioned. The system was first largely employed in Italy in 1820, but had been used in the eighteenth century in England. *Ibid.* 55 The term 'tacheometer' is best confined to instruments which have this optical arrangement [a converging lens between the object-glass and the diaphragm of a theodolite].

†**ta'chette.** *Obs. rare*$^{-1}$. [dim. of TACHE *sb.*[1], a spot: see -ETTE.] A stud.

1688 R. HOLME *Armoury* III. xix. (Roxb.) 166/1 *Tachettes*, the buttons or round naile heads which are set about the skirts or the Armour to adorn and set it out, resembling little spots.

tachinid ('tækɪnɪd), *sb.* and *a. Ent.* [a. mod.L. family name *Tachinidæ*, f. generic name *Tachina* (J. M. Meigen 1803, in *Mag. für Insektenkunde* II. 280), f. Gr. ταχινή, fem. of ταχινός swift: see -ID[3].] **A.** *sb.* A small hairy fly of the family Tachinidæ, the larvæ of which are parasitic on other arthropods. **B.** *adj.* Designating an insect of this family.

1888 *Insect Life* I. 44 We also reared an undetermined Tachinid. **1901** *Knowledge* Oct. 234/2 The ants..protect the caterpillars from the attacks of Ichneumon and Tachinid flies. **1925** R. W. G. HINGSTON in E. F. Norton *Fight for Everest* 285 Tachinids were common at the edge of a torrent at 17,000 feet. **1954** BORROR & DELONG *Introd. Study of Insects* xxvii. 636 Tachinid Flies... All the tachinids are parasitic on other insects. **1972** *Nature* 21 Jan. 135/3 Such long-established successes of biological control as that of the ..coconut moth in Fiji by the tachinid parasite. **1979** *New Scientist* 3 May 380/2 Rettenmayer watched the behaviour of the tachinid and conopid flies.

tachist ('tæʃɪst), *sb.* (and *a.*). *Art.* Also ‖**tachiste** (taʃist). [ad. F. *tachiste*, f. *tache* stain, spot + *-iste* -IST.]

†**1.** One who paints by juxtaposing small patches of unmixed colour. *Obs.*

1891 [see *plein-airiste* s.v. PLEIN-AIR]. **1909** C. E. HALLÉ *Notes from Painter's Life* xi. 234 We have even schools which take their names from the manner of using the brush. We have 'Tachists', 'Vibrists', and Heaven knows how many more.

2. a. One who practices tachism (see below).

1954 *New Yorker* 4 Dec. 99/1 Negatively, it can be said that the unknowns are certainly not Cubists and not *tachistes*, and not Mondrianesque or Braqueish either. **1957** [see TACHE *sb.*[1] 1 c]. **1960** *Guardian* 22 Apr. 9/4 The young English tachistes for whom freedom is an engrossing obsession.

b. *attrib.* or as *adj.*

1955 *New Yorker* 31 Dec. 40/3 The car, maybe the vegetables, and certainly the hope of sharing as an artist in the dubious kudos have all been attributed to a *tachiste* French painter. **1956** *Archit. Rev.* CXX. 186/1 In his delectable paintings of trout hovering in light-stained water he uses tachist techniques with a consummate professionalism. **1966** 'H. MACDIARMID' *Company I've Kept* iii. 103 People should not look at his [*sc.* William Johnstone's] paintings with any preconceived ideas and seek for elements in them which can be labelled..'tachist', and the like. **1972** R. QUILTY *Tenth Session* I. 123 An aggressive twenty square feet of tachist canvas. **1982** S. SPENDER *China Diary* 118 The Western artist looks at the model... The first object of his attention is usually the image, even if this is abstract (except for *tachiste* painting).

Hence **'tachism** [cf. F. *tachisme* (also used)] a style of modern painting in which spots or dabs of colour are arranged in apparently random manner to evoke an emotion, scene, etc.; cf. *action painting* s.v. ACTION sb. 16.

1956 *Archit. Rev.* CXX. 333/1 The same Cézanne picture, considered simply as a painted surface, is one of the finest examples of 'tachism' in the history of art. **1957** *Times* 28 Nov. 3/4 The Canadian artist, Mr. Austin Cooper can claim to have been among the first in this country to practise what is now generally known as *tachisme*. **1960** J. COHEN *Chance, Skill & Luck* ii. 42 Nealces may deserve to be described by the historian of art as the founder of Tachism. **1978** *Jrnl. R. Soc. Arts* CXXVI. 696/1 Abstract expressionism and tachisme, dead on time, and an explosion of hard-edged colour, produced, he told me, under the razzamataz influence of New York. **1979** E. H. GOMBRICH *Sense of Order* ii. 62 Any number of Ph.D. theses await being written about the influence of Cubism, of Tachism, of Op or Pop art on fabrics and wall paper.

tachistoscope (tæ'kɪstəskəʊp). [mod. f. Gr. τάχιστο-ς swiftest + -SCOPE.] An instrument by means of which objects may be presented to the eye for a brief measured period, a fraction of a second; one of its principal applications being the measurement of 'the span of apprehension', that is, the amount of detail that can be apprehended by a single act of attention or apperception. Hence **tachisto'scopic** *a.*; **tachisto'scopically** *adv.* (also *fig.*).

1890 BILLINGS *Med. Dict.* II. 641/1 Tachistoscope. **1903** *Psychol. Rev.* X. 393 (*heading*) Tachistoscopic experiments. *Ibid.* 394 The number of separate objects that can be apperceived at once with the tachistoscope is given as varying from four to five. **1909** C. S. MYERS *Text-bk. Exper. Psychol.* 415 The essentials of a good tachistoscope. **1917** *Arch. Psychol.* XL. 3 The material was presented tachistoscopically with a fixed tempo of presentation. **1931** *Brit. Jrnl. Psychol.* XXII. 67 The instrument..embodies an attempt to meet the many theoretical requirements of the perfect tachistoscope by constructing one without moving parts. **1949** *Jrnl. Personality* XVIII. 24 Present tachistoscopically a picture of a love scene, a handsome young Arab leaning yearningly over his beloved on a couch in a Moorish setting. **1969** J. BRUNNER *Plague on Both your Causes* xix. 141, I saw a tachistoscopically rapid glimpse of one of the half-tracks [from a helicopter]. **1979** R. HAWKEY *Side-Effect* vii. 54 I'd like to..have you take the tachistoscopic perception test... Look at a series of images we'd put up on a tachistoscope.

†**'tachment, 'tachement.** *Obs.* [Aphetic f. ATTACHMENT.]

1. Something attached; an appurtenance.

?*a* **1400** *Morte Arth.* 1568, I ʒif the for thy typandez [*MS.* thyʒandez] Tolouse þe riche, The tolle and þe tachementez, tavernez and oþer.

2. A judicial seizure or apprehension of one's person or goods; *ellipt.* the writ authorizing such seizure: = ATTACHMENT 1, 2.

14.. *Customs Malton* in *Surtees Misc.* (1888) 58 Noo othyr Balyffe schal make no tachement nor somond. **1467-9** *Paston Lett.* II. 296 Be the wey of tachements owte of the Chauncer. **1545** BRINKLOW *Compl.* 41 Ye haue a parcyall lawe in making of tachmentys, first come, first seruyd.

tacho ('tækəʊ), colloq. abbrev. of TACHOMETER. Cf. TACH, TACK *sb.*[8]

1964 *Motor* 13 June 9/1 (*heading*) Japanese tachos. **1975** G. J. KING *Audio Handbk.* viii. 195 Now, should the motor speed tend to decrease, owing to an increasing load for example, the tacho output also decreases. **1979** *Truck & Bus Transportation* May 26/1 On the open roads, the rear axle ratio of 4·33:1 made 100 km/h a comfortable cruising speed with a tacho reading of around the 2800 rpm mark.

tacho-'generator (ˌtækəʊ-). [f. *tacho(meter) generator* s.v. TACHOMETER 2.] An instrument that generates a voltage accurately proportional to the rate of rotation of a shaft or the like.

1952 *Electronic Engin.* XXIV. 382/1 Factors affecting the linearity of response with speed of D.C. tacho-generators. **1958** *New Scientist* 4 Sept. 751/1 One such piece of apparatus for keeping watch on the rpm of engines in flight is actuated by a small tacho-generator to measure the rate of rotation and communicate its warning if over-speeding occurs. **1976** *Gramophone* Sept. 510/1 Speed accuracy is controlled by a new system using a tacho-generator.

tachograph ('tækəʊgrɑːf, -æ-). [f. Gr. τάχο-ς speed + -GRAPH.] A device in a motor vehicle for recording its speed, travel time, and other information automatically.

[**1903** *Nature* 26 Nov. 95/2 On the use of the Schrader tacheograph in hydrographic work.] **1909** *Cent. Dict. Suppl.*, *Tachograph*, a recording tachometer applied to shafting or wheels to register rotation-speed; a speed indicator. [*With reference to prec. source.*] **1941** F. D. JONES *Engin. Encycl.* II. 1258 Some of these recording tachometers or tachographs have a dial in addition to the recording charts. **1968** *Guardian* 1 Oct. 5/2 Road tanker drivers..are protesting against the proposal..to install a tachograph in lorries—a device which records speeds, length of time taken on journeys, and periods when the vehicle is stationary. **1976** *Citizen* (Ottawa) 8 Jan. 1/6 The 10 ambulances in Ottawa are equipped with a tachograph that records the speed of the vehicle. **1980** *Times* 24 Jan. 2/3 The Road Haulage Association acknowledged last night that the tachograph, which records speed, mileage travelled, stopping time and the use of brake and accelerator, could open the way to productivity deals if drivers could show that they were operating more efficiently.

tachometer (tæ'kɒmɪtə(r)). [f. Gr. τάχος speed + -METER: cf. *barometer*.] **1. a.** An instrument by which the velocity of machines is measured. *spec.* one that indicates the speed of an engine in r.p.m. **b.** An instrument for measuring the velocity of a moving body of water, a current-measurer.

1810 DONKIN in *Trans. Soc. Arts* XXVIII. 185 An instrument of my invention for indicating the velocity of machines, and which may not improperly be called a Tachometer. **1825** J. NICHOLSON *Operat. Mechanic* 42 The method of putting the tachometer in motion whenever we wish to examine the velocity of the machine. **1864** WEBSTER, *Tachometer*,..(*b.*) an instrument for measuring the velocity of running water in rivers, canals, &c. **1875** L. D'A. JACKSON *Hydraulic Man.* I. 84 The tachometer of Brünings is the best instrument of this type. **1918** *Bull. U.S. Naval Consulting Board* No. 3. 10 Many new instruments have been devised for aircraft. These include..tachometers, which indicate the engine speed. **1953** C. A. LINDBERGH *Spirit of St. Louis* II. vi. 187 The tachometer needle shows 1825 r.p.m. **1975** *Drive* New Year 88/1 This is an important job performed by the rev-counter, or tachometer.

2. Special Comb.: **tachometer generator** = TACHO-GENERATOR.

1946 *Shell Aviation News* No. 103. 24/1 The gearbox is of Rolls-Royce design... It is mounted on the bulkhead and provides drives, on the forward side, for the air pump and the generator, and on the rear side for the tachometer generator. **1958** W. D. COCKRELL *Industr. Electronics Handbk.* II. 254 Tachometer generators are used in systems to generate feedback signals in servoloops or used directly with an indicating instrument.

So **ta'chometry**, the scientific use of a tachometer; the measurement of velocity; also **tacho'metric** *a.*

1891 *Cent. Dict.*, Tachometry. **1931** S. R. ROGET *Dict. Electr. Terms* (ed. 2) 341/1 Tachometric electrometer. **1967** O. I. EGERD *Control Syst. Theory* vii. 238 Tachometric feedback.

‖**ta chuan** (da dʒwan). Also **ta tchuen.** [Chinese *dàzhuàn*, f. *dà* big + *zhuàn* seal character.] In Chinese calligraphy, an early form of script used during the Chou dynasty (*c* 1028–221 B.C.); 'large seal script'.

1894 T. DE LACOUPERIE *Beginnings of Writing in Central & Eastern Asia* 194 The Chinese writing exhibits in its history eight successive styles, viz:..(2) *Ta tchuen* of 820 B.C. **1910** *Encycl. Brit.* VI. 220/1 Authentic specimens of the..*ta chuan*, older or Greater Seal writing, are exceedingly rare. **1958** W. WILLETTS *Chinese Art* II. vii. 566 Those [characters] then substituted..were what Han scholars called *ta chüan* or 'Great Curly', and sometimes *chou wên* after the name of the supposed Annalist. **1966** C. CH'EN *Chinese Calligraphers & their Art* iii. 24 Scholars of a later day have chosen to group all the different scripts before Li Ssŭ's time as the *ta chuan*. **1973** T. C. LAI *Chinese Calligraphy* 12 (*caption*) A ceremonial basin *ta chuan* script.

tachy- ('tækɪ), combining form of Gr. ταχύ-ς swift, used in the formation of some scientific terms. **tachhydrite, tachydrite,** *Min.* [ad. Ger. *tachhydrit* (Rammelsberg 1856), contr. for **tachyhydrit*, f. Gr. ὕδωρ water + -ITE[1]: from its property of deliquescing readily], a chloride of calcium and magnesium found at Stassfurt in Prussian Saxony. **'tachydiˌdaxy** [Gr. δίδαξις teaching]: see quot. **'tachydrome** [Gr. -δρομ-ος -running, -runner, δρόμος a race-course], anglicized form of *Tachydromus*, Illiger's name for the ornithological genus *Cursorius*, a small group of birds allied to the Plovers; = COURSER[3]; so **tachy'dromian**, a bird of this group; **ta'chydromous** *a.*, of the tachydromes; cursorial. **'tachygen,** *Biol.* [-GEN[1]], the sudden appearance of an organ in evolution; the part so appearing (Webster *Suppl.* 1902); so **tachy'genesis** [-GENESIS], acceleration in development by the shortening or suppression of intervening stages; **tachyge'netic** *a.*, of or exhibiting tachygenesis; **tachy'genic** *a.*, appearing or developing suddenly (Webster *Suppl.* 1902). **tachy'glossal** *a.*, *Zool.* [Gr. γλῶσσα tongue], of a tongue: capable of being quickly thrust forth and retracted, as that of the ant-eater; so **tachy'glossate** *a.*, having a tachyglossal tongue; pertaining to the *Tachyglossidæ*, a family of aculeate monotrematous mammals, of which the typical genus *Tachyglossus* contains the Echidna or porcupine ant-eater of Australia; **tachy'glossid**, an animal of this family. **tachy'iater** [Gr. ἰατρός healer], 'one who cures speedily' (*Syd. Soc. Lex.* 1898); hence **tachy'iatry**, the art of quick healing (*ibid.*). **tachyme'tabolism** *Zool.* (see quot. 1973); hence **ˌtachymeta'bolic** *a.* **ta'chypetous** *a.* [πετ-, stem of πέτεσθαι to fly + -OUS], swift-flying (Mayne *Expos. Lex.* 1860). **ˌtachyphy'laxis** *Pharm.* [mod.L., ad. F. *tachyphylaxie* (Champy & Gley 1911, in *Compt. Rend. Soc. de Biol.* LXXI. 161), f. Gr. φύλαξις protection], a rapidly diminishing response to successive doses of a drug. **tachypnœa** (tækɪp'niːə) [Gr. -πνοια, f. πνέ-ειν to breathe], hurried or unusually rapid respiration; hence **tachy'pnœic** *a. Med.*, exhibiting tachypnœa. **'tachyscope** [-SCOPE], a kind of kinetoscope, in which a series of representations of an object in successive phases of motion are rapidly revolved, so as to present the appearance of actual motion. **tachy'thanatous** *a.* [Gr. θάνατος death + -OUS], killing quickly, rapidly fatal. **ta'chytomy, tachy'otomy** [Gr. τομή a cutting], the art of rapid surgical or anatomical operation. **tachy'zoite** *Zool.* [-ZOITE], one form of the protozoon toxoplasma (see quot. 1973).

1866 BRANDE & COX *Dict. Sci.*, etc. II. 532/3 *Tachydrite. **1868** DANA *Min.* 119 *Tachhydrite*... Color yellowish. Transparent to translucent. Very deliquescent on exposure. **1846** WORCESTER, **Tachydidaxy*, a short method of teaching. *Scudamore.* **1842** BRANDE *Dict. Sci.*, etc. **Tachydromians*, the name of a family of wading birds, of which the genus *Tachydromus is the type. **1860** MAYNE *Expos. Lex.* 1247/1 Having the *Tachydromus* for their type: tachydromous. **1893** HYATT in *Proc. Boston Soc. Nat. Hist.* 77 Thus, from Cope's point of view, *tachygenesis is the law of progression, and retardation is the law of retrogression, and they are both essential parts of his law of acceleration and retardation. *Ibid.* 79 Normal types in which tachygenesis occurs in a marked way might be called *tachygenetic. **1891** *Cent. Dict.*, *Tachyglossal, *Tachyglossate. **1974** *Nature* 13 Sept. 143/2 Already at this early age the dog is *tachymetabolic. **1978** *Ibid.* 5 Oct. 441/1 The central nervous system (CNS) is very sensitive to elevated temperatures, and consequently, both bradymetabolic and tachymetabolic terrestrial vertebrates have evolved physiological mechanisms which effect localised cooling of the brain. **1973** BLIGH & JOHNSON in *Jrnl. Appl. Physiol.* XXXV. 954/2 **Tachymetabolism*: The high level of basal metabolism of birds and mammals relative to those of reptiles and other nonavian and nonmammalian animals of the same body weight and at the same tissue temperature... Synonym: *Warm-Blooded.* Antonym: *Bradymetabolism, Cold-Blooded.* **1911** *Index Medicus* IX. Index of Subjects 214/2 *Tachyphylaxis. **1947** F. K. OLDHAM et al. *Essent. Pharmacol.* xi. 132 Its [*sc.* ephedrine's] disadvantages include..the lessened effect of repeated doses (tachyphylaxis). **1979** *Nature* 29 Nov. 515/2 The response to DAEA showed neither desensitisation during a 3-min exposure period nor tachyphylaxis with repeated applications. **1898** *Syd. Soc. Lex.*, *Tachypnœa. **1899** *Allbutt's Syst. Med.* VIII. 109 There is an hysterical dyspnœa, or rather tachypnœa; the respirations are hurried. **1961** WEBSTER, *Tachypneic. **1976** *Lancet* 13 Nov. 1083/1 He was not cyanotic or tachypnœic. **1889** *Sci. Amer.* 16 Nov. 310/1 Mr. Anschuetz has invented apparatus by means of which these [animated] pictures may be exhibited in a very perfect manner. This instrument..is known as the 'electrical *tachyscope'. **1860** MAYNE *Expos. Lex.*, *Tachythanatous. **1890** in BILLINGS *Nat. Med. Dict.* **1898** *Syd. Soc. Lex.*, *Tachyotomy, *Tachytomy. **1973** J. K. FRENKEL in Hammond & Long *Coccidia* 344/1, I am introducing two other terms: '*tachyzoites' for the rapidly multiplying forms of the acute infection, previously called trophozoites, aggregations, and proliferative forms; and 'bradyzoites' for the slowly multiplying encysted forms characteristic of chronic infection, which have been variously called merozoites or just zoites. **1979** *Biol. Abstr.* LXVIII. 7579/1 Probably most toxoplasmosis infections involve the ingestion of cat feces bearing cysts and oocytes

‖**tachycardia** (tækɪ'kɑːdɪə). *Path.* [mod.L. f. Gr. ταχύ-ς swift + καρδία heart.] 'Abnormal paroxysmal rapidity of the heart's action' (*Syd. Soc. Lex.*).

1889 *Lancet* 2 Mar. 442/1 Those nerve cells and fibres which are concerned in the production of the tachycardia. **1891** *Ibid.* 2 May 1012/1 Dr. Wood proposes the restriction of the name 'tachycardia' to those cases in which very violent heart action occurs without obvious reason. **1898** *Allbutt's Syst. Med.* V. 813 Tachycardia..is improperly applied in the sense of mere rate; it is the name of a particular disease.

So **tachy'cardiac** [cf. CARDIAC], (*a*) *adj.*, of or pertaining to tachycardia; (*b*) *sb.* a person subject to or affected with tachycardia.

1898 *Allbutt's Syst. Med.* V. 828 The tachycardiac attacks have been the cause of this disposition. *Ibid.* 832 One of my tachycardiacs began to ride a bicycle two years ago, and with much advantage.

tachygraph ('tækɪgrɑːf, -græf). [a. F. *tachygraphe*, ad. Gr. ταχυγράφος a swift writer, a scribe, f. ταχύ-ς swift + -γράφος writing, writer.]

1. One who practises tachygraphy; a writer of shorthand, a stenographer; *spec.* one of the shorthand writers of the ancient Greeks and Romans.

1810 *Hist. Europe* in *Ann. Reg.* 114/2 If all the speeches.. were faithfully represented by the bench of tachygraphes. **1865** M. PATTISON *Ess.* (1889) I. 87 Of Greek scribes there were two kinds, the tachygraph (ταχυγράφος), and the calligraph (καλλιγράφος). **1895** FARRAR *Gather. Clouds* II. 142 The other tachygraph, Phocas, had also reported this sermon.

2. A tachygraphic manuscript or writing. Also, a tachygraphic sign.

1895 in *Funk's Stand. Dict.* **1965** E. V. K. DOBBIE in *Language* XLI. 153 The inventory of the allographs (including nonalphabetic allographs, such as tachygraphs).

Hence **ta'chygrapher, ta'chygraphist**, a shorthand writer, a stenographer; = sense 1.

1887 *Cassell's Encycl. Dict.*, *Tachygrapher.* **1891** in *Cent. Dict.* **1895** FARRAR *Gather. Clouds* II. 151 That you..may injure my reputation as a tachygraphist.

tachygraphic (tækɪ'græfɪk), *a.* [f. as prec. + -IC: cf. GRAPHIC.] Of or pertaining to the art of tachygraphy or rapid writing; *spec.* applied to a cursive or running handwriting as opposed to one having separate and fully-formed letters, also to writing with many contractions, ligatures, and compendia.

a **1763** BYROM *Robbery Cambr. Coach* xii, 'No Help!' said I, 'No Tachygraphic Pow'r, To interpose in this unequal Hour!' —— *Art Eng. Poetry* vi, To learn the truly tachygraphic Plan. **1852** H. ROGERS *Ecl. Faith* (1853) 38 Amuse yourself (I know your old tachygraphic skill,)..by jotting down some fragments of our absurdities. **1879** RENOUF *Hibbert Lect.* 14 The Egyptians had from the earliest times used a tachygraphic or cursive character which is a rough and abridged form of the hieroglyphic. **1890** E. M. THOMPSON in *Classical Rev.* May 220/1 Thus was introduced into the Greek writing of the middle ages a new set of compendia commonly called tachygraphic signs.

So **tachy'graphical** *a.* [see -ICAL] = prec.

1764 JEFFERSON *Let.* Writ. 1892 I. 356, I will send you some of these days Shelton's Tachygraphical Alphabet, and directions. **1882-3** *Schaff's Encycl. Relig. Knowl.* III. 2556/1 The old character..was altered..and assumed somewhat of a cursive, or tachygraphical form.

tachygra'phometer. [See TACHYGRAPH and -METER.] (See quot. 1900.)

1891 *Rep. U.S. Coast & Geodetic Survey* App. 16. **1900** H. M. WILSON *Topogr. Surveying* xiii. 280 There are two forms of this instrument [Wagner-Fennel Tachymeter]... The first of these..corresponds to a transit, and the second to an alidade. The latter called a tachygraphometer, for use with the plane-table.

tachygraphy (tæ'kɪgrəfɪ). [f. Gr. ταχύ-ς swift + -GRAPHY.] 'The art or practice of quick writing' (J.); variously applied to shorthand, and (in palæography) to cursive as distinguished from angular letters, to the Egyptian hieratic, and to the Greek and Latin writing of the Middle Ages with its many abbreviations and compendia.

1641 SHELTON (*title*) Tachygraphy. The most exact and compendious methode of short and swift writing. **1656** BLOUNT *Glossogr.*, *Tachygraphy*, the art or description of swift writing. **1778** KIPPIS *Biog. Brit.* (ed. 2) I. 538 *note*, Thomas Shelton became famous..for his Tachygraphy; or easy, exact, and speedy short writing. **1826** *Edin. Rev.* XLV. 145 The Hieratic..is immediately derived from the hieroglyphic, of which it is merely a tachygraphy. **1890** E. M. THOMPSON in *Classical Rev.* May 220/1 The twofold system of tachygraphy, if it may be so termed, in use among the scribes of the middle ages.

tachylite, -lyte ('tækɪlaɪt). *Min.* [ad. Ger. *tachylit* (Breithaupt 1826), f. Gr. ταχύ-ς swift + λυτός soluble, in reference to its easy fusibility.] 'A black basaltic glass, formerly regarded as a homogeneous mineral' (Chester *Dict. Min.*).

tachylyte basalt, a variety of basalt having glassy selvages, and a highly microlithic basis.

1868 DANA *Min.* 245 The species may be the same with tachylyte. **1879** RUTLEY *Stud. Rocks* x. 113 A proceeding analogous to that which seems to have taken place in some tachylytes. **1888** G. A. J. COLE in *Q. Jrnl. Geol. Soc.* XLIV. 300 On some additional occurrences of Tachylite. *Ibid.*, This tachylite adhered more firmly to the contact rocks than to the mass from which it was developed.

Hence **tachy'litic, -'lytic** *a.*, of the nature of, composed of, or containing tachylite.

1888 G. A. J. COLE in *Q. Jrnl. Geol. Soc.* XLIV. 303 The vein..showed thin tachylitic selvage.

tachymeter (tæ'kɪmɪtə(r)). Also **tachyometer**. [mod. f. Gr. ταχύ-ς swift + -METER; so F. *tachymètre* (a form more on Gr. analogies than TACHEOMETER).] Name of a surveying instrument, adapted to the rapid location of points on a survey. So **tachy'metric** *a.*, **ta'chymetry**, the use of such an instrument.

1860 MAYNE *Expos. Lex.*, *Tachymeter*, term for an instrument for quickly measuring level surfaces. **1891** BUFF & BERGER *Handbk. Engin & Surv. Instr.* 109 The name Tachymeter, or rapid measurer, has been applied for many years, in Europe, to instruments of this description. *Ibid.*, Tachymetry. **1900** H. M. WILSON *Topogr. Surveying* xii. 236 Tachymetry, or, as it is sometimes called, tachyometry ..enables the operator, by a single observation upon a rod, to obtain the necessary horizontal and vertical data for the determination of the three elements of position of a point on the surface of the earth. *Ibid.*, There are practically two systems of tachymetric measurement: The angular or tangential system; and The stadia, telemeter, or subtend system. *Ibid.* xiii. 282 A most satisfactory tachymeter, both for filling in details on large-scale maps, and for carrying on rough geographic or exploratory surveys.

tachyon ('tækɪɒn). *Physics.* [f. TACHY- + -ON[1].] A hypothetical particle that travels faster than light and has imaginary mass. Hence **tachy'onic** *a.*

1967 G. FEINBERG in *Physical Rev.* CLIX. 1090/1 One description is presented..for noninteracting faster than light particles, which we call tachyons. **1970** *Sci. Amer.* Feb. 70/2 Hence a tachyon that was losing energy by interacting with matter or by radiating light would speed up, whereas a tachyon that was gaining energy from some outside source would slow down, and its speed would approach *c* from above rather than below. **1970** *Physical Rev. D* II. 265/2 (*caption*) *A* and *B* use tachyonic anti-telephones to communicate backwards in time. **1974** *Globe & Mail* (Toronto) 13 Apr. 5/1 The pursuit of the elusive tachyon lures scientists into the realm of complex mathematical abstraction and high-flown theoretical physics. **1978** PASACHOFF & KUTNER *University Astron.* xxvii. 695 So far, there is no experimental evidence that tachyons exist.

tachysterol (tækɪ'stɪərɒl, -'stərɒl). *Biochem.* [ad. G. *tachysterin* (A. Windaus et al. 1932, in *Ann. d. Chem.* CCCCXCIX. 188): see TACHY- and STEROL.] An oily isomer of ergosterol and lumisterol, $C_{28}H_{43}OH$, which will form calciferol when irradiated with ultraviolet light.

1933 *Chem. Abstr.* XXVII. 729 The addn. compd. from irradiated ergosterol and citraconic anhydride (20 g.) and 75 cc. Ac_2O, warmed 2 hrs., give [*sic*] 7 g. of tachysteryl acetate citraconic anhydride... Tachysterol..has not been crystd. **1954** A. WHITE et al. *Princ. Biochem.* I. 1053 Of the series of compounds obtained from the irradiation of ergosterol only calciferol (vitamin D_2) possesses antirachitic activity. However, one of the series, tachysterol, may be catalytically reduced to dihydrotachysterol..which is antirachitic. **1976** H. CAMPION et al. in B. E. C. Nordin *Calcium, Phosphate & Mineral Metabolism* xii. 445 Lythgoe has reported the synthesis of a closely related isomer, tachysterol, by a nonphotochemical pathway.

† **'tacid**, *a. Obs. rare.* [f. L. *tacēre* to be silent + -ID[1]; cf. *acid* from L. *acēre.*] = TACIT.

1651 J. F[REAKE] *Agrippa's Occ. Philos.* 119 Whence also the tacid consents of animals seem to agree with divine bodies. **1659** T. PECKE *Parnassi Puerp.* 38 In the Chest.. lockt up, of your most Tacid Breast.

Hence † **'tacidly** *adv.* = TACITLY.

1640 G. SANDYS *Christ's Passion* III. 255 Nor Loaves, so tacidly increast, Againe so many thousands feast.

tacit ('tæsɪt), *a.* Also 7-8 **tacite**. [ad. L. *tacit-us*, pa. pple. of *tacēre* to be silent. Cf. F. *tacite* (14th c. in Hatz.-Darm.).]

1. Unspoken, unvoiced; silent, emitting no sound; noiseless, wordless.

1605 BACON *Adv. Learn.* I. i. §1 Without the interruption of tacite obiections. **1628** LE GRYS tr. *Barclay's Argenis* 73 With a tacit vpbraiding she put them in mind. **1798** LANDOR *Gebir* II. 238 With a long and tacit step..He looked and tottered on a black abyss. **1824** W. IRVING *T. Trav.* I. 113 A tacit thankfulness in his looks, as if he felt grateful to me. **1854** J. S. C. ABBOTT *Napoleon* (1855) II. xviii. 329 One of those tacit prayers to which no language can give adequate expression.

b. Saying nothing; still, silent.

1604 R. CAWDREY *Table Alph.*, *Tacite*, still, silent, saying nothing. **1651** HOBBES *Govt. & Soc.* xv. §3. 238 Gods lawes are declar'd after a threefold manner: first, by the tacit dictates of Right reason, next by immediate revelation [etc.]. **1804** WELLINGTON in Gurw. *Desp.* (1837) III. 497 If the British Government had remained..a tacit spectator of events. **1866** CARLYLE *Remin.*, *Irving* (1881) I. 221 Edward Strachey was..a man rather tacit than discursive.

2. Not openly expressed or stated, but implied; understood, inferred. ***tacit mortgage***, a lien in the nature of a mortgage created by operation of law. ***tacit relocation***: see RELOCATION.

[*c* **1575** *Balfour's Practicks* (1754) 208 *Tacita relocatio.*] **1637-50** ROW *Hist. Kirk* (Wodrow Soc.) 251 This tacite approveing of these commissioners, men so highlie guiltie, ..argues a great decay of zeall, and courage. **1681** STAIR *Instit. Law Scot.* I. x. §61. 149 In the tacite legal hypothecation, [our custom] hath only allowed a few. **1690** LOCKE *Hum. Und.* III. ii. §8 Common use, by a tacit Consent, appropriates certain Sounds to certain Ideas in all Languages. **1705** ADDISON *Italy*, *Monaca* (1733) 23 A tacit Acknowledgment that Monarchy is the more honourable. **1881** *Spectator* 30 Apr. 573 Locke's doctrine of a tacit social compact.

Tacitean ('tæsɪtiːən), *a.* [f. the name of the Roman historian Tacitus (*c* 54-117): see -AN.] Pertaining to Tacitus, or resembling his pregnant sententious style. So **'Tacitist**, a student or follower of Tacitus; **'Tacitize** *v.*, *intr.* to write in the style of Tacitus.

1890 LOWELL *Milton's Areop.* Lat. Lit. Ess. (1891) 101 He [Milton] is never weary of insisting on the *Tacitean distinction between liberty and license. **1907** *Athenæum* 7 Sept. 265/3 Accurate scholarship, especially in matters of Tacitean diction. **1656** EARL MONM. tr. *Boccalini's Advts. fr. Parnass.* I. xxiii. (1675) 24 He might like a *Tacitist have written the Civil Wars of Flanders. **1833** ROSCOE tr. *Pellico's Ten Years' Imprisonm.* xxxvi, With all my admiration for the genius of Tacitus, I had never much faith in the justice of *tacitising as he does.

tacitly ('tæsɪtlɪ), *adv.* [f. TACIT *a.* + -LY[2].]

1. Without speaking; silently; quietly.

1643 PRYNNE *Rome's Master-Piece* (ed. 2) 24 The secular Iesuites have bought all this street, and have reduced it into a quadrangle, where a Iesuiticall Colledge is tacitly built. **1751** EARL ORRERY *Remarks Swift* (1752) 88 Here a reflection naturally occurs, which..leads me tacitly to admire, and confess the ways of Providence. **1866** GEO. ELIOT *F. Holt* i, To be no longer tacitly pitied by her neighbours for her lack of money.

2. Without stating or expressing it; by implication: cf. TACIT *a.* 2.

1635 EARL STRAFFORD *Lett.* (1739) I. 471 Not tacitely or by way of Consequence, but even in express and binding Terms. **1660** STANLEY *Hist. Philos.* III. I. 30 He tacitely implyed that the rest of mankind were but beasts. **1735** BERKELEY *Free-think. in Math.* §21 There are certain points tacitly admitted by mathematicians. **1825** MCCULLOCH *Pol. Econ.* II. iv. 179 If, as M. Sismondi has tacitly assumed, the machines cost nothing.

'tacitness. *rare.* [f. TACIT *a.* + -NESS.] The quality of being tacit; silence.

1657 W. MORICE *Coena quasi Κοινὴ* xxxii. 298 To instruct ..our brethren, who by our tacitness might be scandalized. **1885** PATER *Marius the Epicurean* I. 15 That inward tacitness of mind esteemed so important by religious Romans.

taciturn ('tæsɪtɜːn), *a.* [ad. L. *taciturn-us*, f. *tacit-us*, TACIT.] Characterized by silence or disinclination to conversation; reserved in speech; saying little; uncommunicative.

1771 SMOLLETT *Humph. Cl.* 26 June, Grieve..was very submissive, respectful, and remarkably taciturn. **1816** *Remarks Eng. Mann.* 61 The people in Europe who partake most with us in this taciturn propensity, are the Dutch. **1849** MACAULAY *Hist. Eng.* vi. II. 68 Godolphin, cautious and taciturn, did his best to preserve neutrality. **1876** BRISTOWE *The. & Pract. Med.* (1878) 875 The patient becomes apathetic, morose or taciturn, or irritable.

Hence **'taciturnist**, one who practises habitual silence or reserve; **'taciturnly** *adv.*, in a taciturn manner; with habitual reserve.

1887 *Congregationalist* (U.S.) 10 Feb. (Cent. Dict.) His [von Moltke's] more than eighty years seemed to sit lightly on 'the great *taciturnist'. **1847** WEBSTER, **Taciturnly*, silently, without conversation. **1902** A. AUSTIN *Ld. Kitchener* in *Standard* 12 July 5/2 Honours he needs not, for about his brow He bears them clustered, taciturnly great.

taciturnity (tæsɪ'tɜːnɪtɪ). Also 5 -te(e, 6 -ty(e, 6–7 -tie. [a. F. *taciturnité* (14th c.), or ad. L. *taciturnitās*, f. *taciturn-us*: see prec. and -ITY.]

1. Habitual silence or disinclination to conversation; reservedness in speech; a taciturn character or state.

c **1450** tr. *De Imitatione* III. xli. 112 Oþer whiles he aunsuerde, lest by his taciturnite occasion of offendynge miȝt haue be yoven. **1491** CAXTON *Vitas Patr.* (W. de W. 1495) I. l. 99b/2 In the sayde monasterie was so grete tacyturnytee and scylence. **1576** FLEMING *Panopl. Epist.* 145, I cannot in this poinct vse taciturnitie and silence. **1606** SHAKS. *Tr. & Cr.* IV. ii. 75 The secrets of nature Haue not more gift in taciturnitie. **1711** ADDISON *Spect.* No. 261 ¶1 My natural Taciturnity hindered me from shewing my self to the best Advantage. **1809** W. IRVING *Knickerb.* III. viii. (1861) 107 Our ancestors were noted as being men of truly Spartan taciturnity. **1856** MISS MULOCK *J. Halifax* ix, After which brief reply John relapsed into taciturnity.

2. *Sc. Law.* The silence of the creditor occasioning the extinction of an obligation in a shorter period than forty years' prescription: it being presumed that the creditor would not have been so long silent if the debt had not been paid or the obligation implemented.

1765–8 ERSKINE *Instit. Law Scot.* III. vii. §29 (1773) 533 No general rule can be laid down, at what precise times actions may be lost by taciturnity. **1838** W. BELL *Dict. Law Scot.* 967/2 The only cases in which extinction by such taciturnity has been recognised were those of bills of exchange, prior to the introduction of the sexennial prescription.

†**taci'turnous**, *a. Obs. rare*$^{-0}$. [f. L. *taciturn-us* TACITURN + -OUS.] = TACITURN.

1727 BAILEY *Dict.* vol. II, *Taciturnous*, silent, saying nothing, making no Noise.

tack (tæk), *sb.*[1] Forms: 4–6 **tak**, **takk(e**, 5–7 **tacke**, 6 **take**, (pl. **tax**), 5– **tack**. [TACK *sb.*[1] and *v.*[1] go together, and are doublets of TACHE *sb.*[2], *v.*[2] (q.v.), though forms in *k* or *q* are not recorded in OF., and the etymological history is obscure. For the ulterior etymology Diez compares Ger. *zacken* prong, MHG. *zacke*, Du. *tak* bough; so also Kluge. (The occurrence of Ir. *taca*, Gael. *tacaid* nail, tack, peg, Breton *tach* small nail, has suggested a Celtic origin for the root *tac-*, but this Thurneysen rejects.) App. most of the senses of the sb., including sense 5, were derived from the vb., but the nautical senses of the vb. arose out of sense 5 of the sb., and in their turn gave rise to senses 6 and 7.]

I. That which fastens or attaches, etc.

1. a. That which fastens one thing to another, or things together: applied to a fibula or clasp, a buckle, a hook or stud fitting into an eye or loop, a nail, or the like. *Obs.* exc. as in senses 2, 3.

13.. *Minor Poems fr. Vernon MS.* lii. 410 He bot a bite þat made vs blak, Til fruit weore tied on treo wiþ tak; O fruit for anoþer. *c* **1440** *Promp. Parv.* 485/2 Takke (*H., P.* or botun), *fibula, fixula.* **1500–20** DUNBAR *Poems* lxxii. 69 Unto the crose of breid and lenth, Syne tyit him on with greit irne takkis. **1617** MINSHEU *Ductor*, A tacke or hooke, vid. *Buckle, Clasp.* **1670** EACHARD *Cont. Clergy* 70 The tackes put into the loops did couple the curtains of the tent, and sew the tent together. **1696** *Lond. Gaz.* No. 3228/4 Lost.., 3 pair of black Stays,..one with black Buckles, in black Tacks and black Loops.

b. The frænum of the tongue (in a tongue-tied person).

1671 LIVINGSTON *Let.* in *Wodrow Soc. Sel. Biog.* (1845) I. 247 The sight of the father's danger brake the tack of a son's tongue who was tongue-tacked from birth.

2. *spec.* **a.** (perh. orig. short for *tack-nail*: see 12 a.) A small sharp-pointed nail of iron or brass, usually with a flat and comparatively large head, used for fastening a light or thin object to something more solid, especially in a slight or temporary manner, so as to admit of easy undoing.

Tacks are distinguished according to their use, as ***carpet-tack***, one used for fixing a carpet on the floor; their action, as ***thumb-tack***, one pushed in with the thumb, as a drawing-pin; their material, as ***brass tack***, ***iron tack***, TIN-TACK. Also in colloq. phr. ***to come*** (or ***get***) ***down to brass tacks***: see BRASS *sb.* 5 b; see also TIN-TACK b.

[**1463**, etc.: see *tack-nail* in 12 a.] **1574** in Feuillerat *Revels Q. Eliz.* (1908) 237 Tackes One Thowsand. *a* **1585** POLWART *Flyting w. Montgomerie* 558 His lugs.. That to the Tron hes tane so many a tacke. **1601** HOLLAND *Pliny* XXXIV. xiv. 514 Yron..for nailes, studs, and tackes, emploied about greeves and leg-harneis. **1688** R. HOLME *Armoury* III. 292/1 Two sorts of tacks used by [shoemakers], the Sole Tack..and the Heel Tack. **1703** MOXON *Mech. Exerc.* 53 Drive in a small Tack on each side. **1745** P. THOMAS *Jrnl. Anson's Voy.* 259 The Scale..is made of Bambo, the Divisions distinguished by small Brass Tacks. **1851** D. JERROLD *St. Giles* xvi. 168 At his work, driving tin tacks into a baby's coffin.

b. (See quot.)

1847–78 HALLIWELL s.v., A wooden peg for hanging dresses on is sometimes called a tack.

3. *Technical uses.* **a.** *Gardening.* A fastening for shoots, etc., consisting of a strip or band secured at each end to a wall or the like. **b.** *Plumbing.* A strip of lead having one end soldered to a pipe, and the other fastened to a wall or support. **c.** *Basket-Making.* A size of willow rod, usu. 3 ft. long.

1545 *Rates of Customs* a vj, Corke takkes the thousande x.*s.* **1615** W. LAWSON *Country Housew. Gard.* (1626) 7 To plant Apricockes, Cheries, and Peaches, by a wall, and with tacks, and other meanes to spread them vpon, and fasten them to a wall. **1658** EVELYN *Fr. Gard.* (1675) 34 They do extreamly ill, when they fagot, and bundle together a great many small twiggs, in one tack. **1693** —— *De la Quint. Compl. Gard.* II. 41. **1823** P. NICHOLSON *Pract. Build.* 408 Two broad pieces of lead, called tacks, are attached to the back lap-joints and spread out, right and left, for fastening the [socket] pipes to the wall by means of wall-hooks of iron. **1877** S. S. HELLYER *Plumber* ii. 33 When there are no chases, and the pipes are fixed on tacks, the tacks should be strong. **1912** T. OKEY *Art of Basket-Making* ii. 6 White and buff rods are sorted into tacks from 2 ft. 6 in. or 3 ft. to 3 ft. 6 in. **1953** [see *long-small* s.v. LONG *a.*[1] A. 18]. **1961** L. G. ALLBON *Basic Basketry* ii. 11 Willow is sold by the bolt... The rods are sorted..on the farm into lengths... Local usage often gives special names to the sizes.., such as Tack or Short Smalls (3 ft.), Smalls (4 ft.),..and so on. **1973** B. MAYNARD *Mod. Basketry from Start* 171 *Tacks*, term used for 3 ft willow rods.

4. a. An act of tacking or fastening together, now esp. in a slight or temporary way; a stitch, *esp.* a long slight stitch used in fastening seams, etc., preparatory to the permanent sewing; a very slight fastening or tie, by which a thing is loosely held, as ***hanging by a tack***.

1705 VANBRUGH *Confed.* V. ii, If dear mother will give us her blessing, the parson shall give us a tack [cf. TACK *v.*[1] 1 c]. **1808** JAMIESON s.v., *It hings by a tack*, it has a very slight hold. **1878** DICKINSON *Cumbld. Gloss.*, *Teck*, *Tack*, a stitch, 'A teck i' time seavvs nine'. *Mod.* Give it a tack, to hold it together until there is time to stitch it.

b. Adhesiveness, tackiness; esp. in *Book-binding*, 'a slight stickiness remaining in leather before the varnish or dressing is quite dry' (C. Davenport).

1908 *Academy* 11 Apr. 656/1 It is very cunningly reproduced, even to the extent of a suggestion of a slight 'tack' belonging to old leather.

II. Nautical and derived senses. (Sense 5 is a special application of 1, and is the origin of sense 7 of the vb., whence again comes sense 6 here.)

5. a. A rope, wire, or chain and hook, used to secure to the ship's side the windward clews or corners of the courses (lower square sails) of a sailing ship when sailing close hauled on a wind; also the rope, wire, or lashing used to secure amidships the windward lower end of a fore-and-aft sail.

to bring, get, haul, or ***put the tacks aboard*** (= to the board), to haul the tacks into such a position as to trim the sails to the wind, to set sail. ***to bring*** or ***have the starboard*** or ***port tacks aboard***, to set the sails to, or sail with, the wind on the side mentioned. Also *transf.* used allusively in reference to travelling by land.

1481–90 *Howard Househ. Bks.* (Roxb.) 111 My Lord paid him for iij. hausers, a peir takkes, a ratling line for Chewdes ..xv.s. **1486** *Naval Accts. Hen. VII* (1896) 13 A payre of takkes & a payr of shets weying DCCXlj lb. **1582** L. WARD in Hakluyt *Voy.* III. 757 Wee brought our tackes aboord, and stoode along West by North and West larboord tacked. **1611** COTGR., *Coytes*, Tackes; great Ropes vsed about the (maine) sayle of a ship. **1626** CAPT. SMITH *Accid. Yng. Seamen* 28 The wind veares, git your star-boord tacks aboord. **1627** —— *Seaman's Gram.* v. 23 Tackes are great ropes which hauing a wall-knot at one end seased into the clew of the saile, and so reeued first thorow the chestres, and then commeth in at a hole in the ships sides, this doth carry forward the clew of the saile to make it stand close by a wind. **1688** J. CLAYTON in *Phil. Trans.* XVII. 984 They must there bring the contrary Tack on Board [*i.e.* to put the vessel on the other tack]. **1747** *Gentl. Mag.* 521 The wind shifted 3 or 4 points, which obliged us to tack, and make more sail, by hauling our main tack on board. **1825** H. B. GASCOIGNE *Nav. Fame* 52 To set each Course the Tacks they Haul on Board, Then drag the Sheets aft, as they can afford. **1846** YOUNG *Naut. Dict.*, *The tack of a fore and aft sail* is the rope which keeps down its lower forward clue; and of a studding sail that which keeps down its lower outer clue. The tack of a lower studding-sail is called the Out-Haul.

transf. **1780** S. CURWEN *Jrnl. & Lett.* 22 June (1864) 277 Discouraged from proceeding further by water,..and taking, as the sailors phrase it, our London tack on board, [we] proceeded the next stage of fifteen miles. **1820** A. GIFFORD *MS. Acc.* 7 Sept., We took our land tacks on board of our waggon, and directed our course west souwest for New London.

b. The lower windward corner of a sail, to which the tack (rope or chain) is attached.

1769 FALCONER *Dict. Marine* (1789), *Aboard main tack!* the order to draw the main-tack, i.e. the lower corner of the main-sail, down to the chess-tree. **1851** KIPPING *Sailmaking* (ed. 2) 5 In all triangular sails and in those four-sided sails wherein the head is not parallel to the foot, the foremost corner at the foot is called the tack. **1904** F. T. BULLEN *Creatures of Sea* xvii. 232 The peak of the sail is dropped and the tack hoisted; in sea parlance, the sail is 'scandalised'.

†**c.** ***tack of a flag***: see quot. *Obs.*

1794 *Rigging & Seamanship* I. 176 *Tack of a Flag*, a line spliced into the eye at the bottom of the tabling, for securing the flag to the haliard.

6. a. An act of tacking (TACK *v.*[1] 7); hence, the direction given to a ship's course by tacking; the course of a ship in relation to the direction of the wind and the position of her sails; a course or movement obliquely opposed to the direction of the wind; one of a consecutive series of such movements to one side and the other alternately made by a sailing vessel, in order to reach a point to windward.

A ship is said to be ***on the starboard*** or ***port tack*** as the wind comes from starboard or port. At each change of tack, the relative positions of the tack and sheet of the courses are reversed.

1614 SIR R. DUDLEY in *Fortesc. Papers* (Camden) 9 Being fare more swyfte then the gallie..(espetiallye uppon a tacke). **1666** PEPYS *Diary* 4 July, Even one of our flag-men in the fleete did not know which tacke lost the wind, or which kept it, in this last engagement. **1676** *Lond. Gaz.* No. 1108/1 Their Admiral was lost by accident, or rather neglect of the Seamen, who omitting upon a Tack to fasten the Guns, they run all to one side, and over-set the ship. **1694** NARBOROUGH, etc., in *Acc. Sev. Late Voy.* I. 165 Before the Ship could Ware and bring to upon the other Tack, She struck. **1749** CAPT. STANDIGE in *Naval Chron.* III. 207 We kept working the Ship in the wind's eye, tack and tack. **1779** KING *Cook's Voy. Pacific* VI. ix. (1785) III. 418 During the afternoon, we kept standing on our tacks, between the island of Potoe, and the Grand Ladrone. **1804** W. LAYMAN in Nicolas *Disp. Nelson* (1845) V. 496 Turning to the Westward, against the wind, some tacks do not exceed one mile. **1836** MARRYAT *Midsh. Easy* xiii, That they should make short tacks with her, to weather the point. **1885** *Law Times Rep.* LIII. 54/1 The *J. M. Stevens* was proceeding under all sail close-hauled on the port tack.

b. *fig.* and *transf.* A zigzag course on land.

1788 J. MAY *Jrnl. & Lett.* (1873) 31, I..advanced as fast as possible to finish my land tacks. **1813** *Salem Gaz.* 22 Oct. 3/2 Saw 2 four horse wagons, standing abreast, upon their larboard tacks, head towards us. **1854** J. L. STEPHENS *Centr. Amer.* 363, I could not walk, so I beat up making the best tacks I could, and stopping every time I put about. **1893** Q. [COUCH] *Delect. Duchy* 305 Bontigo's Van..scaling the acclivity..in a series of short tacks.

7. *fig.* **a.** A course or line of conduct or action; implying change or difference from some preceding or other course.

1675 V. ALSOP *Anti-Sozzo* i. 29 No man more reall when he offers an Injury, nor more complemental in his Courtesies; for he's just now standing upon a Tack. **1697** COLLIER *Ess. Mor. Subj.* II. (1709) 72 His Business will be to follow the Loudest Cry, and make his Tack with the Wind. **1795** BURKE *Let. to Ld. Auckland* Wks. IX. Pref. 22 Through our publick life, we have generally sailed on somewhat different tacks. **1811** T. CREEVEY in *Cr. Papers* (1904) I. vii. 140 They are upon a new tack in consulting publick opinion. **1901** *Scotsman* 8 Mar. 6/5 The bill..seemed to proceed upon the wrong tack.

b. A circuitous course of conduct.

1869 BALLANTYNE *Deanhaugh* 117 (E.D.D.) Your nephew ..canna be up to sae mony shifts an' tacks as you.

III. That which is tacked on or appended.

8. a. Something tacked on or attached as an addition or rider; an addendum, supplement, appendix; *spec.* in parliamentary usage, a clause relating to some extraneous matter, appended, in order to secure its passing, to a bill, esp. a bill of supply.

1705 in Hearne *Collect.* 10 Oct. (O.H.S.) I. 54 All the World's a general Tack Of one thing to another. Why then about one Honest Tack Do Fools make such a Pother? **1712** SWIFT *Jrnl. to Stella* 10 May, The parliament will hardly be up till June. We were like to be undone some days ago with a tack. *a* **1715** BURNET *Own Time* VII. (1823) V. 177 Some tacks had been made to money-bills in king Charles's time. **1768** LD. HILLSBOROUGH in *North Car. Col. Rec.* VII. 868 Appointed by a Law..especially passed for that purpose, and not by way of Tack to a Law for other purposes. **1787** *Minor* I. xiv. 52 My mother to this added the following tack. **1879** MINTO *Defoe* v. 64 The Lords refused to pass the Money Bill till the tack was withdrawn.

b. ***tack-on***: the act of tacking something on, or that which is tacked on or added. *colloq.*

1905 *Outlook* 11 Nov. 664/1 She has not the passion for a tack-on which is general in this country.

9. *dial.* (some doubtfully belonging here). **a.** A hanging shelf: see quot. 1847–78. **b.** Each of the two nibs or handles of a scythe. **c.** *Coal-mining.* A temporary prop or scaffold: see quots.

a. **1446** *Yatton Churchw. Acc.* (Som. Rec. Soc.) 85 It. y payde to Hurneman for ij takys v[d]. *c* **1730** J. POYNTER *Dorset Voc.* in *N. & Q.* 6th Ser. VIII. 45/2 *A tack*, a shelf. **1847–78** HALLIWELL, *Tack*,..a shelf. A kind of shelf made of crossed bars of wood suspended from the ceiling, on which to put bacon, &c. **1862** T. HUGHES in *Macm. Mag.* V. 246/1 An ther wur beacon upon rack An plates to yet it upon tack.

b. *a* **1825** FORBY *Voc. E. Anglia*, *Tack*,..the handle of a sithe. **1892** P. H. EMERSON *Son of Fens* 131 Some on 'em fitting new sticks to the scythes, some on 'em putting in tacks.

c. **1849** GREENWELL *Coal-trade Terms Northumb. & Durh.*, *Tack*, a small prop of coal, sometimes left..to support it until the kirving is finished, except knocking out the tack. **1883** GRESLEY *Coal Mining Gloss.*, *Tack*, ..(Som[erset].) A wooden scaffold put into a pit-shaft for temporary purposes.

IV. As a quality.

10. a. Hold; holding quality; adherence, endurance, stability, strength, substance, solidity. Now *dial.*

1412–20 LYDG. *Chron. Troy* II. 1868 Who þat geynstryueth schal haue litel tak. *c* **1425** *Cast. Persev.* 2987 in *Macro Plays* 166 Tresor, tresor, it hathe no tak. **1573** TUSSER *Husb.* (1878) 168 What tacke in a pudding, saith greedie gut wringer. **1583** GOLDING *Calvin on Deut.* lxvi. 404 There will neuer bee any holde or tacke in it. **1651–66** CARYL *Expos. Job* xxii. 25 (1676) 2255 He should find..that there was tack in it, that it was solid silver, or silver that had strength in it. **1884** *Cheshire Gloss.*, *Tack*,..hold, confidence, reliance. There is no tack in such a one, he is not to be trusted.

b. Adhesive quality, stickiness: cf. TACKY *a.* Used esp. in *Printing*.

18.. *Gilder's Man.* 28 (Cent. Dict.) Let your work stand until so dry as only to have sufficient tack to hold your leaf. **1939** *Printing* Feb. 27/1 Where excess *tack* is attributed to these rollers, it is frequently found that the complainant is.. referring to natural rubber rollers rather than synthetics. **1967** E. CHAMBERS *Photolitho-Offset* xvi. 243 Ink of low tack fills in shadow areas more readily, whilst high tack may pull the surface of a coated paper if the separation is quick. **1971** *Engineering* Apr. 17/1 A suitable adhesive..to give a reasonable tack. **1972** *Physics Bull.* Nov. 665/3 *Tack*, with prepreg materials, the degree of stickiness of the resin. **1979** G. A. GLAISTER *Gloss. Bk.* (ed. 2) 469/1 If an ink has insufficient tack it will not print sharply.

†**11.** Phrases. **a.** ***to hold***, rarely ***have, tack with*** (*to*), to hold one's own with, hold one's ground with, keep up with; to be even with or equal to; to match. *Obs.*

1412-20 LYDG. *Chron. Troy* I. 4259 Here lith on ded, þer a-noþer wounded, So þat þei myȝt with them haue no tak. *a* **1518** SKELTON *Magnyf.* 2084 A thousande pounde with Lyberte may holde no tacke. **1600** W. WATSON *Decacordon* (1602) 71 Secular Priests, whom no English Iesuit is able to hold tacke withall. **1652** URQUHART *Jewel* Wks. (1834) 227 The incomparable Crichtoun had..held tack to all the disputants. **1658** J. HARRINGTON *Prerog. Pop. Govt.* I. xii. Wks. (1700) 317 Fourteen Years had their Commonwealth held tack with the Romans, in Courage, Conduct, and Virtue. *c* **1695** in Curwen *Hist. Booksellers* (1873) 29 To make the parallel hold tack, Methinks there's little lacking.

†**b.** ***to hold*** (a person, etc.) ***tack*** (***to tack***): to be a match for; to hold at bay. *Obs.*

1555 W. WATREMAN *Fardle Facions* II. vi. 150 Thei [Parthians] helde the Romaines suche tacke, that in sondrie warres they gaue them great ouerthrowes. **1606** *Sir G. Goosecappe* III. i, I am sure our Ladies hold our Lords tacke for Courtship, and yet the French Lords put them downe. **1612** DRAYTON *Poly-olb.* xi. 48 Faire Chester, call'd of old Carelegion,..the faithfull station then, So stoutly held to tack by those neere North-Wales men. **1615** HOBY *Curry-combe* i. 3 As if I haue not a good dish of Oysters, and a cold pye at home to hold you tacke. **1706** MRS. CENTLIVRE *Basset-Table* II. Wks. (1723) 221 Ay, give me the woman that can hold me tack in my own dialect. *a* **1825** FORBY *Voc. E. Anglia* s.v. *Hold*, Phr. 'to hold one tack', to keep him close to the point.

†**c.** ***to bear, hold tack***, to be substantial, strong, or lasting; to hold out, endure, hold one's own.

1573 TUSSER *Husb.* (1878) 28 And Martilmas beefe doth beare good tack, when countrie folke doe dainties lack. **1600** W. WATSON *Decacordon* (1602) 164 It serueth to hold tacke, till by inuasion or otherwise the Iesuits may worke their feate. **1663** BUTLER *Hud.* I. III. 277 If this twig be made of Wood That will hold tack. **1673** R. HEAD *Canting Acad.* 19 With good Milk pottage I held tack.

†**d.** ***to hold, keep tack, stand to tack***: see quots.

1611 COTGR., *Ester à vne chose conuenuë*, to keepe touch; hold tacke, stand to a bargaine. **1686** F. SPENCE tr. *Varillas' Ho. Medicis* 305 The correspondence he had in that place not keeping tack at the time prefixt.

†**e.** ***to be half tack with***: (?) to be midway between in position or quality. *Obs.*

1567 MAPLET *Gr. Forest* 60 Reede is halfe tack with the Herbe and tree, but in force or growth, aboue the Herbe. And nothing in strength to the tree his comparison.

V. 12. *attrib.* and *Comb.* **a.** in sense 2: **tack-claw, -extractor, -lifter, -puller**, a tool for extracting tacks or small nails from a carpet, etc.; **tack-comb**, a row of tacks cast in the form of a hair-comb for use in a shoe-making machine; **tack-driver**, a machine which automatically places and drives a series of tacks; also = *tack-hammer*; **tack-hammer**, a light hammer for driving tacks; also as *v. trans.*; **tack-mill**, a factory for making tacks; †**tack-nail**, a tack, tacket, or hob-nail; **tack-rivet**, a small metal rivet; **tack work**: see quot.

1865 *Atlantic Monthly* June 736/2 If she absolutely cannot get a *tack-hammer with a claw on one end, she can take up carpet-nails with an iron spoon. **1889** TALMAGE in *Voice* (N.Y.) 28 Feb., Much [church work] amounts to..a tack-hammer smiting the Gibraltar. **1890** 'R. BOLDREWOOD' *Miner's Right* (1899) 11 Which made the heavy tool tremble in my grasp like a tack hammer. **1908** KIPLING *Bk. of Words* (1928) 36 The meanest collection of packing-cases that was ever tack-hammered together. **1858** SIMMONDS *Dict. Trade*, **Tack-lifter*, a tool for taking up tacks from carpets on a floor. **1884** H. D. LLOYD in *N. Amer. Rev.* June 546 The *tack-mills in the combination run about three days in the week. **1463** in Rogers *Agric. & Pr.* III. 556/3, 1 c. *taknail 4*d.* **1519** HORMAN *Vulg.* 237 Set some tacke naylis or racke naylis arowe. **1591** PERCIVALL *Sp. Dict.*, *Broca*, a shoemakers tacke naile. **1874** THEARLE *Naval Archit.* 71 The side plates, or bars, are connected to the vertical plate by..small rivets, termed '*tack rivets'. **1879** C. HIBBS in *Cassell's Techn. Educ.* IV. 299/2 '*Tack work', which means brass-headed nails, hooks, sash and drawer knobs, and little things of that sort.

b. in sense 5: ***tack-block, -earing, -end, -lashing, -piece*** (see quot.), ***-tackle***; **tack-pins**, belaying pins of the fife-rail (Smyth *Sailor's Word-bk.* 1867).

1777 COOK *Voy.* III. ii. II. 17 When they change tacks they throw the vessel up in the wind, ease off the sheet, and bring the heel or *tack-end of the yard to the other end of the boat, and the sheet in like manner. **1865** MACGREGOR *Rob Roy in Baltic* (1867) 296 The tack end of the boom is made fast to the mast by a flat piece of leather. **1711** W. SUTHERLAND *Shipbuild. Assist.* 164 **Tack-piece*, that to which the Fore-sail is tack'd down. **1769** FALCONER *Dict. Marine* (1776), **Tack-tackle*, a small tackle used occasionally to pull down the tack of the principal sails of a ship to their respective stations. **1882** NARES *Seamanship* (ed. 6) 82 *Tack tackle*..a tackle from the tack of the spanker to the deck.

c. in sense 4: **tack weld** *v. trans.*, to join (materials) at intervals with provisional welds in order to hold them in position for subsequent work; hence as *sb.*

1919 *Chambers's Jrnl.* Jan. 60/2 Up the sides the seams were only welded at intervals, or 'tack welded', as it is called. **1950** B. R. HILTON *Welding Design* ii. 42 If tack welds are not to be removed as the welding proceeds, their section should be equivalent to that of the first weld run. **1964** S. CRAWFORD *Basic Engin. Processes* iii. 82 A tack weld is made by applying the flame to the metal until it melts and then adding a little welding rod. **1979** *Financial Times* 22 Jan. 9/7 The top is tack welded, then the bottom, followed by the sides. Clamps and devices are removed and the weld completed.

d. in sense 10: **tack coat** (see quot. 1954); **tack rag** *U.S.*, an impregnated cloth used for cleaning a surface prior to painting or varnishing.

1949 *Sun* (Baltimore) 17 Oct. 26/3 Workmen spread a 'tack coat' of asphalt on the old pavement. **1954** *Gloss. Highway Engin. Terms (B.S.I.)* 28 *Tack coat*, a coat of liquid (such as bitumen, road tar, or an emulsion thereof) applied as a thin film to a surface to improve the adhesion of a course laid thereon. **1979** *Civil Engin.* Nov. 27/1 The painting on of a grid of levels on the tack coat by engineers. **1958** *Washington Post* 16 Aug. B 3/6 So-called 'tack' rags are used in factories where dust particles are likely to mar freshly painted surfaces. **1979** P. WALLAGE *Restoration Post-W.W. II Cars* ii. 25/2 Go over it with a tack rag.

tack (tæk), *sb.*[2] Chiefly *Sc.* and *north. Eng.* Forms: 4-6 **tak**, 5-6 **takk** (*pl.* **tax**), 6-8 **tacke**, 6- **tack**. [f. *tac, tak*, TAKE *v.*; cf. TAKE *sb.*; also ON. *tak* taking, seizure, etc., *taka* a taking, seizure, capture, revenue, tenure (Vigf.), OSw. *tak* taking, hold, *taka man* collector.]

I. †**1.** A customary payment levied by a ruler, feudal superior, or corporation. *Obs.*

a **1300** *Cursor M.* 28438 Toll and tak, and rent o syse, Withalden i haue wit couettise. **1564** *Reg. Privy Council Scot.* I. 295 To mak and deliver to the saidis Margaret and Alexander infeftmentis of the saidis landis..likwyise..in all pointis without takkis. *a* **1578** LINDESAY (Pitscottie) *Chron. Scot.* (S.T.S.) I. 322 He dressit the said bischope..for certaine teindis and tax that the bischope gaif him.

2. Tenure or tenancy, of land, benefice, etc.: *esp.* leasehold tenure, e.g. of a farm, mill, or the like; the period of tenure. *Sc.* and *north. Eng.* (Cf. ON. *taka* tenure (of land).)

1423 *Charters, etc. of Edinb.* (1871) 55 To have thair corne grundin at the saide millis..durand the saide tak. **1424** *Coldstream Chartul.* (1879) 43 Ye said priores and ye conuent sal enter in ye tak of ye said land at Qwitsonday. **1449** *Sc. Acts Jas. II* (1814) II. 35 Suppos the lordis sel or analy þai landis þ[t] þe takaris sall remayne with þare takis, on to þe ische of þare termes. **1526** *Lanc. Wills* (Chetham Soc.) I. 15, I will that Dorothe my wyff shall have all such takks leysses and graunts as I now have by the graunts of the Abbot of Qhalley. **1571** PLOWDEN *Reports* 169 b, Cesty qe prist lease pur ans dun ferme en le Northe paiz, appelle ceo Tacke. **1671** in *Proc. Soc. Ant. Scot.* (1892) XXVI. 194 We ..Stewart Principall Justiciare and Admirall of Orknay and Zetland, having power be vertue of my tack therof to nominat and appoynt bailyies [etc.]. **1701** J. LAW *Counc. Trade* (1751) 40 That the present farm or tack of the customs be broken, and that the said impositions of foreign excise and entry-money may never hereafter be leased out, or let to farm. **1885** J. G. BERTRAM in *Brit. Alm. Comp.* 77 The 'tack' [of a deer forest] may be for a period of years, or it may be for 'the season'. **1887** *S. Chesh. Gloss.* s.v., 'It's the best tack as ever I seid',..i.e. the farm in question was taken on the best conditions.

b. Sometimes more or less concretely: A leasehold tenement, a farm. *Sc.*

c **1470** HENRYSON *Mor. Fab.* XII. (*Wolf & Lamb*) xviii, How durst thow tak on hand..To put him fra his tak, and gar him thig? **1508** KENNEDIE *Flyting w. Dunbar* 365 Thow has a tome purs, I haue stedis and takkis. **15..** DUNBAR *Poems* xvii. 21 Sum takis vthir menis takkis. **1515** in *Fam. Rose Kilravock* (Spalding Club) 185 Aucht oxin to pleyns ane tak.

c. *fig.* A period, a spell (*of* some condition). *Sc.* Cf. 'lease' of life, etc.

a **1758** RAMSAY *Masque* 189 Thou'lt grant them a lang tack of bliss. **1821** GALT *Ann. Parish* xii, There came on a sudden frost, after a tack of wet weather. **1887** SERVICE *Dr. Duguid* xxi. 138 We had a lang tack of very wat weather.

3. *transf.* An agreement or compact. *Sc.* (Cf. prec. 11 d.)

a **1758** RAMSAY *Clout the Caldron* iv, I've a tinkler under tack, That's us'd to clout my caldron. **1786** BURNS *Earnest Cry & Prayer* vi, In gath'rin' votes you were na slack; Now stand as tightly by your tack.

4. Pasture for cattle let on hire. *dial.*

1804-12 DUNCUMB *Hist. Heref.* I. 214 A *tack*, grass or clover for horses and cattle, hired by the week, month, or quarter. **1863** MORTON *Cycl. Agric.*, *Tack*, hired pasturage. **1873** *Berrow's Worcester Jrnl.* Apr. (E.D.D.), Horses or horned cattle will be taken into Westwood Park to tack or ley. **1877** *Birmingham Weekly Post* 22 Dec. 1/1 It is..a common expression where a farmer turns his cattle out on the lands of another to say they are out at 'tack'. **1879-81** MISS JACKSON *Shropsh. Word-bk.* s.v., 'Yo'n got a power o' stock fur yore farm'..' Aye, I mus' get some out on tack'.

II. 5. A take of fish; a catch, draught, haul: = TAKE *sb.* 5. Also *fig. Sc.* and *north. Eng.*

1596 DALRYMPLE tr. *Leslie's Hist. Scot.* I. 40 Gif in ony place quhair a tak of herring is..ony scheding of manis blude aryse..thay ar said to abhor frome that place. **1597** SKENE *De Verb. Sign.* s.v. *Assisa*, An thousand herring of ilk tack that halds. **1678** W. ADAMS *Dedham Pulpit* 68 Whence a great tack of souls to Christ hath followed. **1772** *Hartford Merc., Suppl.* 18 Sept. 3/2 There is at present the finest tack of herrings ever known, which are now selling on the shore at sixteen-pence the hundred. **1888** VAN HARE *Fifty Years Showman's Life* 2 When they draw their net it's called a tack; if there are plenty of fish in the net they call it a good tack, or if there are very few fish they call it a bad tack.

III. 6. *attrib.* and *Comb.*, as **tack-duty**, the rent reserved on a lease; the rent paid by a tacksman or farmer of the customs; **tack-money**, payment for pannage or pasture; †**tack-swine**, hogs paid in rent; **tack-work**: see quot.

1680 (Dec. 23) *St. Andrew's Town Council Minute-bk.* 86 Impouring him quarterlie to receave from the taxsmen of Costomes the *tak deutie payable for the saidis Costomes. *a* **1722** FOUNTAINHALL *Decis.* (1759) I. 8 Had he not paid the tack-duty for tiends and all. **1809** TOMLINS *Jacob's Law Dict.*, *Tack-Duty*, the rent reserved on a lease. **1876** GRANT *Burgh Sch. Scotl.* II. xiv. 457 In 1680 the council of St. Andrews allocated the tack duties of the customs of the city towards paying the schoolmaster's stipend. **1688** R. HOLME *Armoury* III. 75/1 An Agistor, is an Officer of the Forest, that takes in to Feed the Cattel of Strangers, and receives for the Kings use all such *Tack-Money as becomes due from those Strangers. **1523** FITZHERB. *Surv.* viii. 8 Where as the tenauntes pay *tacke swyne by custome,..or a halfpeny for euery swyne, as the custome is vsed. **1879-81** MISS JACKSON *Shropsh. Word-bk.*, **Tack-work*, work done by contract.

tack, *sb.*[3] *Obs.* or *dial.* [Origin uncertain; in sense 1, it appears to be a doublet of TACHE *sb.*[1]; cf. Picard *taque* = Fr. *tache* spot; but cf. also F. *tac* 'a kind of rot among sheepe; also, a Plague-spot' (Cotgr.), which Hatz.-Darm. think possibly borrowed from L. *tactus* found in the sense of infection, contagious disease. Sense 2 is possibly transf. from 1, but may be of different origin.]

†**1.** A spot, a stain; a blemish; = TACHE *sb.*[1] 1, 2.

c **1425** *Cast. Persev.* 2178 in *Macro Plays* 142 In sory synne had he no tak & ȝyt for synne he bled blody ble. *a* **1603** T. CARTWRIGHT *Confut. Rhem. N.T.* (1618) 467 The witnesse of the other hath often a wrest and tacke of her corruption.

2. A smack, taste, or flavour (*of* something); *esp.* an alien, peculiar, or ill flavour; = TACHE *sb.*[1] 2 c. Also *fig.*

1602 R. T. *Five Godlie Serm.* 146 Superstitious ceremonies, without anie smacke or tacke of anie sound Christian doctrine. **1611** COTGR. s.v. *Piquer*, *Le poisson pique*, begins to haue a tacke, or ill tast. **1622** DRAYTON *Poly-olb.* xix. 130 Or cheese which our fat soil to every quarter sends, Whose tack the hungry clown and plow-man so commends. **1868** ATKINSON *Cleveland Gloss.* s.v., If two articles of food are cooked together, and the stronger flavoured one communicates a taste to the other, it is said to 'have a tak o' t'ither'. **1884** *Cheshire Gloss.* s.v., Ale which has been put into a musty cask is said to have a tack, or a tack of the cask.

†**tack**, *sb.*[4] *Obs. rare.* [Origin uncertain.] A billiard-cue: see quot. 1688.

1688 R. HOLME *Armoury* III. 262/1 On each side [the billiard table] standeth a Man with a Tack in his hand, to push the Ball into an Hassard, or Hole. *Ibid.* xvi. (Roxb.) 69/1 In the base of this quarter, is the figure of the Tack or a Stick used at the Billiard table for the strikeing of an Ivory ball. **1826** J. O'KEEFE *Recollections* I. vii. 268 The young nobleman..when he was the striker, took the nicest pains to place his tack in such a manner, that to hold his adversary's ball seemed a matter of course.

tack, *sb.*[5] [Origin obscure: perh. from TACK *sb.*[1] 10; but cf. also TACKLE *sb.* sense 8.] Foodstuff; chiefly in HARD-TACK, ship's biscuit, SOFT-TACK; also *gen.* stuff, often in depreciatory sense. Cf. TACKLE *sb.* 8.

1833 MARRYAT *P. Simple* xxviii, The..steward..came back with a basket of *soft-tack*, i.e. loaves of bread. **1841** LEVER *C. O'Malley* lxxxviii, No more hard tack thought I, no salt butter. **1864** *Daily Tel.* 5 Nov., Horses stopped to graze, and the men..began quietly munching a hard tack. **1889** D. C. MURRAY *Dang. Catspaw* 129 He knows Lord Byron from beginning to end, but his head's that full of that kind of tack there's no room for anything else. **1894** —— *Making of Novelist* 42, I thought the canteen tack the nastiest stuff I had ever tasted.

tack, *sb.*[6] *rare.* [Echoic. Cf. *tack* sb., clap, *tack* vb., to slap, clap, in *Eng. Dial. Dict.*; F. *tac* in *tac-au-tac.*] The sound of a smart stroke.

1821 SCOTT *Kenilw.* x, Now, hush and listen,..you will soon hear the tack of a hammer.

tack, *sb.*[7] Abbrev. of TACKLE *sb.* †**a.** In sense 1. *dial. Obs.*

1777 in *Eng. Dial. Dict.* (1905) VI. 3/2. **1879** G. F. JACKSON *Shropshire Word-bk.* 428 My tacks bin at Newport, or I'd soon ketch them rots. **1893** J. SALISBURY *Gloss. Words & Phr. S.E. Worcs.* 41 *Tack*,..a collection of tools; a razor-grinder's machine is his tack; a smith's box of tools for shoeing horses is his 'shoeing tack'.

b. In sense 6. Also *Comb.*, as ***tack room***.

1924 I. MADDISON *Riding Astride for Girls* xiv. 226, I will now give a few hints on tack..in the show ring. The tack on a saddle-horse should be as light as possible. **1933** A. BLEWITT *Ponies & Children* iii. 34 Any prize rosettes they win are stuck up on their tack-room wall. **1940** *Evening Sun* (Baltimore) 15 Apr. 21/4 Tack is the name for a rider's equipment—saddle, whip, boots, etc., apparently derived from tackle. **1950** J. CANNAN *Murder Included* iv. 65 Patricia ..was cleaning tack in the stable. **1964** D. FRANCIS *Nerve* xi. 147 It was a tack-room. Every stable has one..the place where the saddles and bridles are kept. **1975** F. KENNEDY *Alberta was my Beat* ix. 111 He stood there like a broke saddle horse as we put the tack on him. **1979** J. JOHNSTON *Old Jest* 100 There was a boy who kept the tack, polished the lovely shiny boots. There was a smell of saddle soap and horse dung. The saddles are flaking now, out in the damp tack room.

tack, *sb.*[8] U.S. colloq. abbrev of TACHOGRAPH, TACHOMETER. Cf. TACH, TACHO.

1963 *Amer. Speech* XXXVIII. 46 *Tack*,..the device in the cab which automatically records miles driven, number of stops, speed, and so on, during a trip; short for *tachometer*. **1971** M. TAK *Truck Talk* 162 *Tack*, short for tachometer or tachograph.

tack, *v.*[1] [Doublet of TACHE *v.*[2]; cf. TACK *sb.*[1]]

I. To attach.

†**1. a.** *trans.* To attach, fasten (one thing to another, or things together). *Obs.* except as in 3.

1387 TREVISA *Higden* (Rolls) III. 173 He..made hem sprede and takkede þe skyn aboute þe chayer [orig. *sellæ judiciariæ circumponi*] þere þe iuge schulde sitte in plee forto deme. *c* **1400** *Brut* 103 Kyng Alurede hade þat boke in his warde, and..lete hit faste bene tackede to a piler, þat men my3t hit nou3t remeve. **1483** *Act 1 Rich III*, c. 8 §16 Without tacking or sowing of any Bulrushes..upon the Lists of the same. **1530** PALSGR. 746/1 Tacke it faste with a nayle. *a* **1616** BEAUM. & FL. *Scornf. Lady* II. iii, Peace, or I'le tack your tongue up to your roof. **1696** BP. PATRICK *Comm. Exod.* xxvi. (1697) 506 The Loops were..tackt to the Selvage of the outermost of them. **1713** STEELE *Englishm.* No. 26. 172 He dried and tacked together the Skins of Goats. **1843** LE FEVRE *Life Trav. Phys.* II. I. xviii. 153 We often tacked on twelve horses to a small vehicle.

b. *transf.* and *fig.* To attach.

a **1533** LD. BERNERS *Gold. Bk. M. Aurel.* xliii. (1535) 83 b, Al the vnderstandynges are tacked to one free wyll. **1653** tr. *Hales' Dissert. de pace* in *Phenix* (1708) II. 376 The Fathers did, with ingenious comments, tack the mysteries of their philosophy to the Word of God. **1695** PRIOR *Taking Namur* ix, With Eke's and Also's tack thy Strain, Great Bard. **1791** GILPIN *Forest Scenery* II. 187 He who works without taste.. tacks one part to another, as his misguided fancy suggests.

†**c.** To join in wedlock. *slang. Obs.*

1732 FIELDING *Debauchees* III. xiv, We will employ this honest gentleman here, to tack our son and daughter together. **1775** SHERIDAN *Duenna* III. iv, I' faith, he must tack me first; my love is waiting. **1821** *Sporting Mag.* VIII. 105 A Curate..Had brought to the altar a pair to be tack'd.

†**2.** To connect or join by an intervening part.

1639 FULLER *Holy War* II. xii. (1840) 65 It [Tyre]..was tacked to the continent with a small neck of land. **1645** EVELYN *Diary* June, The numberless Islands tacked together by no fewer than 450 bridges. **1762–71** H. WALPOLE *Vertue's Anecd. Paint.* (1786) I. 186 They..have tacked the wings to a house by a colonade.

3. a. To attach in a slight or temporary manner; *esp.* to attach with tacks (short nails or slight stitches), which can be easily taken out.

c **1440** *Promp. Parv.* 485/2 Takkyn', or some what sowyn' to-gedur,..*consutulo*. **1642** FULLER *Holy & Prof. St.* III. x. 175 If agitation..jog that out of thy head, which was there rather tack'd then fastned. **1696** J. F. *Merchant's Wareho.* 8 The Hamborough is rowled up very hard, and either tacked with Thred, or tyed about with Tape. **1703** MOXON *Mech. Exerc.* 53 Drive in a small Tack on each side..or you may Tack down two small thin boards on either side. **1830** in Cobbett *Rur. Rides* (1885) II. 348 The wretched boards tacked together, to serve for a table. **1853** KANE *Grinnell Exp.* xxxiii. (1856) 295, I copy the play-bill from the original ..tacked against the main-mast. **1894** *Times* 3 Mar. 11/3 He had 'tacked' the cloth down to the stage. **1896** *Allbutt's Syst. Med.* I. 434 They [jackets] are lined with a layer of cotton-wool neatly tacked in. *Mod.* The sleeves are tacked in to try how they fit.

b. *spec.* †(*a*) *Gardening.* To fasten with tacks (TACK *sb.*[1] 3 a). *Obs.*

1693 J. EVELYN *De la Quint. Compl. Gard.* II. 41 In Tacking for the first time after the Pruning.

(*b*) *Metal-working.* To keep (a metal plate, etc.) in place by small lumps of solder until the soldering is completed.

1886 in *Cassell's Encycl. Dict.*

(*c*) *Plumbing.* To secure (a pipe) with tacks (TACK *sb.*[1] 3 b).

1895 in *Funk's Stand. Dict.*

4. To join together (events, accounts, etc.) so as to produce or show a connected whole; to bring into connexion. (Often implying arbitrary or artificial union.)

1683 DRYDEN *Vindic. Duke of Guise* Dram. Wks. 1725 V. 325 Mr. Hunt has found a rare Connection, for he tacks them together, by the Kicking of the Sheriffs. **1695** J. EDWARDS *Perfect. Script.* 434 Many expositors labour to tack this text to the immediately foregoing one. **1699** BENTLEY *Phal.* 166 The Gentleman..tacks these two accounts together. **1712** J. JAMES tr. *Le Blond's Gardening* 128 The foregoing Practices..being but Things detached and separate,..there is still a farther Difficulty to tack them together, so as to make one Piece. **1720** WATERLAND *Eight Serm.* 221 One might suspect that there had been two Versions of the same words, and Both, by degrees, taken into the Text, and tack'd together. **1844** LINGARD *Anglo-Sax. Ch.* (1858) I. App. B. 326 Traditionary tales, tacked together without regard to place or chronology.

5. To attach or add as a supplement; to adjoin, append, annex; *spec.* in parliamentary usage: see quots. and cf. TACK *sb.*[1] 8. Also const. *on.*

1683 ROBINSON in *Ray's Corr.* (1848) 137 Thus far your queries as to France, to which I will tack an observation to fill up. **1692** LUTTRELL *Brief Rel.* (1857) II. 365 A committee of the lords sat..to search presidents about tacking one bill to another. **1700** EVELYN *Diary* Apr., The greate contest betweene the Lords and Commons concerning the Lords power of..rejecting bills tack'd to the money bill. **1757–8** SMOLLETT *Hist. Eng.* (1759) IX. 296 The lords had already resolved by a vote, That they would never pass any bill sent up from the commons, to which a clause foreign to the bill should be tacked. **1791** 'G. GAMBADO' *Ann. Horsem.* ix. (1809) 107 As it's a fact, you may tack my name to it. **1855** MACAULAY *Hist. Eng.* xxii. IV. 771 A strong party in the Commons..proposed to tack the bill which the Peers had just rejected to the Land Tax Bill. **1863** H. COX *Instit.* I. viii. 114 The return is made by indenture..is signed and sealed, and returned to the Crown office in Chancery, tacked to the writ itself. **1902** L. STEPHEN *Stud. Biog.* IV. v. 179 So prosperous a consummation was never tacked to so dismal a beginning. **1908** L. M. MONTGOMERY *Anne of Green Gables* viii. 83 Marilla was as fond of morals as the Duchess in Wonderland, and was firmly convinced that one should be tacked on to every remark made to a child. **1909** [see TACKING *vbl. sb.* b]. **1960** C. DAY LEWIS *Buried Day* i. 17 My father's family name was originally Day, the Lewis being tacked on by a man who adopted his grandfather or great-grandfather.

6. *Law.* To unite (a third or subsequent incumbrance) to the first, whereby it acquires priority over an intermediate mortgage.

1728 SIR J. JEKYLL in Peere Williams *Reports* (1793) II. 491 If a judgment creditor..buys in the first mortgage..he shall not tack or unite this to his judgment and thereby gain a preference. **1818** CRUISE *Digest* (ed. 2) II. 225. **1841** *Penny Cycl.* XIX. 361/2 Now if..D pays off B, and takes an assignment of his mortgage and of the outstanding term; if, to use the technical phrase, he 'tacks' B's security to his own, he unites in himself equal equity with C, and also the legal right which the term gives him. **1883** *Encycl. Brit.* XVI. 849/1 In addition to the risk of a third mortgagee tacking.

II. Nautical senses. (From TACK *sb.*[1] 5.)

7. a. *intr.* To shift the tacks and brace the yards, and turn the ship's head to the wind, so that she shall sail at the same angle to the wind on the other side; to go about in this way; also ***tack about***. Hence, to make a run or course obliquely against the wind; to proceed by a series of such courses; to beat to windward: often said of the ship itself.

1557 in A. Jenkinson *Voy. & Trav.* (Hakl. Soc.) I. 8 The rest of the shippes shall tacke or take of their sailes in such sort as they may meete and come together, in as good order as may be. **1595** *Drake's Voy.* (Hakl. Soc.) 22 They had the winde of us, but we soone regained it upon them, which made them tacke about. *c* **1600** CHALKHILL *Thealma & Cl.* (1683) 19 His Ketch Tackt to and fro, the scanty wind to snatch. **1748** *Anson's Voy.* II. iv. 163 We tacked and stood to the N.W. **1777** ROBERTSON *Amer.* (1783) III. 217 These.. could veer and tack with great celerity. **1834** *Nat. Philos.* III. *Navigation* II. v. §55. 26 (Usef. Knowl. Soc.) When the wind blows from any point within six points of the bearing of a port for which a vessel is bound, she must tack or ply to windward. **1873** *Daily News* 21 Aug., The little craft was caught by a sudden squall when tacking, or, as sailors say, 'in stays,' taken aback, and capsized in a moment. **1886** E. L. BYNNER *A. Surriage* i. 16 Two or three..ketches were tacking up before the brisk off-shore breeze to make the anchorage.

b. Said of the wind: To change its direction.

1727 *Philip Quarll* (1816) 32, I was hurried on board, the wind having tacked about and fair for our departure. *Mod.* [A sailor said] The wind was tacking all over the place.

8. *intr.* **a.** *transf.* To make a turning or zigzag movement on land.

1700 T. BROWN *Amusem. Ser. & Com.* 34, I Tack'd about, and made a Trip over Moor-fields. **1716** B. CHURCH *Hist. Philip's War* (1865) I. 97 They..tack'd short about to run as fast back as they came forward. **1787** 'G. GAMBADO' *Acad. Horsem.* (1809) 37 [The Massilians] Without a bridle on the bare back, Make with a stick their horse or mare tack. **1854–6** PATMORE *Angel in Ho.* I. ii. IV. (1879) 184 But he who tacks and tries short cuts Gets fool's praise and a broken shin.

b. *fig.* To change one's attitude, opinion, or conduct; also, to proceed by indirect methods.

1637 POCKLINGTON *Altare Chr.* 169 He will..tack about for other considerations..if hee bee well put to it. **1663** PEPYS *Diary* 24 June, He hath lately been observed to tack about at Court, and to endeavour to strike in with the persons that are against the Chancellor. **1791–1823** DISRAELI *Cur. Lit., Dom. Hist. Sir E. Coke*, Bacon..tacked round, and promised Buckingham to promote the match he so much abhorred. **1860–70** STUBBS *Lect. Europ. Hist.* II. ii. (1904) 166 He is not for a moment diverted, although he sometimes consents to tack.

9. *trans.* To alter the course of (a ship) by turning her with her head to the wind (sometimes said of the ship); opposed to WEAR *v.* Also, to work or navigate (a ship) against the wind by a series of tacks. Also *fig.*

1637 POCKLINGTON *Altare Chr.* 152 No man that has not his understanding tackt and the eye thereof turned after the humour of the men of Gr[antham]. **1747** in *Col. Rec. Pennsylv.* V. 115 They then tacked the Ship and stood out to Sea. **1805** *Naval Chron.* XIV. 16 She tacked Ship. **1860** E. STAMP in *Merc. Marine Mag.* VII. 279 All hands were turned up to tack ship. **1906** *Temple Bar Mag.* Jan. 72 It is sung sometimes when tacking ship in fair weather.

tack, *v.*[2] *dial.* [f. TACK *sb.*[2]]

1. *trans.* To take a lease of (a farm, etc.). *Sc. rare.*

1882 JAMIESON, *Tack*, to take, to lease.

2. a. To put *out* (cattle) to hired pasture. **b.** To take (cattle) to pasture for hire.

1839 [SIR G. C. LEWIS] *Heref. Gloss.*, He has tacked out his cattle. **1863** MORTON *Cycl. Agric.*, *Tacking out*, putting cattle upon hired pasturage. **1879–81** MISS JACKSON *Shropsh. Word-bk.* s.v., Mary Cadwallader 'as sent half-a-crown for tackin' the donkey, an' wants to know if you'll tack 'im a week or nine days longer.

tack (tæk), *v.*[3] *Obs.* exc. *dial.* [f. TACK *sb.*[3]: cf. F. *tac* there.] *trans.* To taint, infect; ? to tinge, stain; *dial.* to give a smack or tang to.

1601 HOLLAND *Pliny* XVI. xliv, In case any of the sheep were deeply tackt and infected with the rot. **1643** TRAPP *Comm. Gen.* xxxi. 19 She was somewhat tackt with her fathers superstition. *Ibid.* xxxiv. 28 All the Corinthians were tackt with..the incestuous mans offence. **1868** ATKINSON *Cleveland Gloss.*, *Takt*, adj. Having a marked flavour; usually applied in the case of an acid liquid.

tack, *v.*[4], aphetic f. ATTACK *v.*; cf. *tack* sb. short for *attack* in *Eng. Dial. Dict.*

1720 H. CAREY *Poems* 56 But if they once Tack you, They certainly Back you. **1731** PEYTON *Catastr. Ho. Stuarts* 42 As if a Partridge being near to a Faulcon..might peck and tack her, yet would not she yield to a small Bird.

tack, *v.*[5] *trans.* Abbrev. of TACKLE *v.* 3. Usu. with *up*. Also *absol.* Cf. TACK *sb.*[7] b.

1946 M. C. SELF *Horseman's Encycl.* 395 To tack up a horse means to put the saddle and bridle on him. **1962** W. FAULKNER *Reivers* viii. 178 So we..tacked up and..led the way. **1972** *Islander* (Victoria, B.C.) 26 Mar. 13/1 In addition to being taught how to groom a horse, the new student must learn how to tack-up (that's putting a saddle and bridle on). **1977** *Sunday Tel.* (Colour Suppl.) 1 May 22/3 It is not a bad idea either to acquire a creature that will come when it is called or will at least stand still long enough to get it tacked up for a bit of a ride.

tack, obs. form of TAKE *v.*

tacked (tækt), *ppl. a.* [f. TACK *v.*[1] + -ED[1].] Attached, appended, etc.: see TACK *v.*[1]

1596 WARNER *Alb. Eng.* XII. lxxiii. (1612) 303 Hence Dispensations, Iubilees, Pardons, and such tack't geere, Were had at Rome. **1687** T. LUDFORD in *Magd. Coll.* (O.H.S.) 75 His answer..was drawn up in tacked schedules. **1692** LUTTRELL *Brief Rel.* (1857) II. 363 After a long debate about the tackt clause, [the lords] adjourned it further till Munday. **1693** DRYDEN *Juvenal's Sat.* (1697) p. xxxvi, Laws were also call'd *Leges Saturæ*; when they were of several Heads and Titles; like our tack'd Bills of Parliament. **1904** *Westm. Gaz.* 9 Sept. 3/2 The tacked-on happy conclusion of 'Merely Mary Ann'.

tacker[1] ('tækə(r)). [f. TACK *v.*[1] + -ER[1].]

1. One who tacks: in various senses.

a. *Eng. Hist.* One who favoured the tacking of other bills in parliament to money-bills, in order to secure their passage through the House of Lords; *esp.* in early 18th c., one who advocated tacking the bill against occasional conformity, 1704, to a money-bill.

1704 SIR H. MACKWORTH (*title*) A Letter..Giving a short Account of the Proceedings of the Tackers, upon the Occasional and Self-denying Bills [etc.]. **1705** (*title*) Daniel the Prophet no Conjurer, or his Scandal Club's Scandalous Ballad, called the Tackers, answer'd Paragraph by Paragraph. **1705** HEARNE *Collect.* 27 Oct. (O.H.S.) I. 59 He was a Tacker, and a true Friend of y[e] Church. **1711** *Medley* No. 35. 384 A very bold Attempt was made upon the Civil and Religious Rights of our Fellow-Subjects, by certain Men call'd Tackers or High-Church-men. **1727** *Brice's Week. Jrnl.* 25 Aug. 2 One of the Gentlemen distinguished by the Name of a Tacker in the Reign of King William III. **1859** W. CHADWICK *De Foe* v. 280 Every kind of rascality was attempted to be passed through the Lords by its being tacked to a money bill, and by its being called a money bill; whence the term *tacker*.

b. In various trades, One who tacks or fastens articles or parts of things; also, a machine for putting or driving in tacks.

1727 BAILEY vol. II, *Tacker*, one who fastens or fixes one Thing to another by Tacks, or by Sewing, etc. **1884** E. SIMCOX in *19th Cent.* June 1041 A preparer of collars and wristbands, known as a 'tacker and turner' [in shirt-making]. **1892** *Labour Commission Gloss.*, *Tacker*, one who puts in the tacks used in 'lasting'. **1895** *Daily News* 16 Mar. 6/5 Works..fitted with the latest types of machinery for all purposes, except the magnetic tacker.

2. *dial.* A small child.

1885 *Reports Provinc.* (E.D.D.), Ever since I was a little tacker. **1893** Q. [COUCH] *Delect. Duchy* 220 I've [not] a-zet eyes 'pon the young man since he was a little tacker.

†**tacker**[2], **takkar**. *Sc. Obs.* [f. TACK *sb.*[2] + -ER[1].] One who grants a tack or lease; a lessor.

1551 *Recds. Elgin* (1903) I. 109 All to be eschet to the takkar.

tacket ('tækɪt), *sb.* Now *dial.* Forms: 4–6 taket(e, -ett(e, 5–6 *Sc.* tak(k)at(e, 6– tacket. [f. TACK *sb.*[1] + -ET[1].] A nail; in later use, a small nail, a tack: cf. TACK *sb.*[1] 1, 2; now, in *Sc.* and *north. dial.*, a hob-nail with which the soles of shoes are studded.

1316 in Rogers *Agric. & Prices* II. 524/2 Takets [*ibid.* I. 546 tackets..seem to be cart or strake-nails]. *c* **1330** *Coldingham Priory* Inv. 10 In xviij barres ferri ad fenestras, wegges, et taketes. **1345–6** *Ely Sacr. Rolls* (1907) II. 133 In takettis empt. pro mappis emendandis—4½d. **1483** *Cath. Angl.* 377/2 A Taket, *claviculus*. **1512** *Acc. Ld. High Treas. Scot.* IV. 298 Item, for y[e] takkatis. **1532** *Lett. & Pap. Hen. VIII*, V. 448 Pyne nails and English tacketts for nailing up the said buds and leaves. **1542** *Acc. Ld. High Treas. Scot.* VIII. 132 Twa hankis wyre..to wyre the caisis of the windois..y[e] small takettis deliverit to him thairto. **1617** MINSHEU *Ductor*, A Tacket, or *tache*. Vid. *Naile*. **1698** R. THORESBY in *Phil. Trans.* XX. 207 Curiously nailed with two rows of very small Tackets. **1789** BURNS *Capt. Grose's Peregrinations* vi, Rusty airn-caps and jinglin jackets, Wad haud the Lothians three in tackets. **1859** J. BROWN *Rab & Fr.* (1862) 25 Heavy shoes, crammed with tackets, heel-capt and toe-capt.

attrib. and *Comb.* **1888** GRANT *Keckleton* 63 'The tackit-mackers..can barely supply the deman' for tackits'. **1896** KEITH *Indian Uncle* xvii. 274 He envied the tacket-soled boots that gave his quarry the advantage. **1897** —— *Bonnie Lady* xvi. 171 Wearing his strongest tacket boots.

Hence **'tacket** *v. trans.*, to stud (shoes) with tackets; whence **'tacketed** *ppl. a.*, hob-nailed.

1864 J. BROWN *Let.* Dec. (1912) 234 To-morrow I meant in a pair of tacketed shoon to have explored some Grampian. **1896** SETOUN *R. Urquhart* i, Thick-soled blucher boots tacketed for rough roads. **1899** *Westm. Gaz.* 31 Jan. 1/3 'Tacketed' boots, and clothes,..impervious to the rain.

tackety ('tækɪtɪ), *a. Sc.* [f. TACKET *sb.* + -Y.] Of a shoe: Studded with tackets.

1864 LATTO *Tam Bodkin* ix. (1894) 95 The neb o' Andra's tackety shoe. **1888** BARRIE *Auld Licht Idylls* (1892) 5 My feet encased in stout 'tackety' boots.

tackie ('tækɪ). *S. Afr.* Also **takkie**. [Origin uncertain: perh. rel. to TACKY *a.*² App. not Afrikaans.] A rubber-soled canvas shoe; a plimsoll or sand-shoe. Also, a track shoe with a rubber sole. Usu. *pl.*

c **1902** I. VAUGHAN *Diary* (1958) 60 We all have to wear.. white tackies on the feet. **1913** C. PETTMAN *Africanderisms* 491 *Tackies*, in the border towns of the Eastern Province this is the name given to rubber-soled sand-shoes. **1924** *Ann. Mountain Club S. Afr.* No. 27. 46 Ye who scale with ropes and 'tackies' Cliffs of awe-inspiring grandeur. **1946** *Amer. Speech* XXI. 59 What are known as 'sand shoes' or 'tackies' in English are the same articles which I still backslide into calling 'sneakers'. **1953** M. MURRAY *Fire-Raisers* xi. 108 He padded over the rocks on his tackies. **1955** D. JACOBSON *Trap* I. 20 He wore canvas *takkies* on his feet, his toes poking through the ends. **1961** *Personality* 16 May 27, I have yet to discover why tennis shoes, which are known in England as plimsoles, are called 'tackies' in South Africa. **1981** A. PATON *Towards Mountain* xvii. 134 Hofmeyr was a camper of the first water. He wore an ancient canvas hat, a khaki shirt and shorts, and discoloured sandshoes, known as tackies.

tackifier ('tækɪfaɪə(r)). [f. TACKY *a.*² + -FY + -ER¹.] A substance that makes something sticky; an adhesive agent or ingredient.

1942 *Science Illustr.* Apr. 4/2 As processing aids, naval stores products are numbered among the many plasticizers, softeners, and tackifiers. **1958** *New Scientist* 23 Oct. 1110/2 This pressure-sensitive thermoplastic..is so sticky that a tackifier such as resin need not be added. **1963** H. R. CLAUSER *Encycl. Engin. Materials* 449/2 The liquid nitrile polymer finds use as a tackifier ..in molded rubber parts, cements, friction and calendered stocks. **1970** *New Scientist* 5 Nov. 275 (Advt.), Sometimes it's [*sc.* Lorival liquid rubber] a tackifier in ebonite grinding wheels.

tackily ('tækɪlɪ), *adv.*¹ [f. TACKY *a.*² + -LY².] In a slightly adhesive or sticky manner. (In quot. 1903, *fig.*)

1903 KIPLING *Traffics & Discoveries* (1904) 124 The sea.. drummed tackily to gather my attention, coughed, spat, cleared its throat. **1971** *Sunday Times* 20 June 42 For every loving Mum who has ever wished there was an easier way of preventing nappy-rash than smearing on..petroleum jelly, Johnson & Johnson is introducing ..a melt-on-contact Baby Gel which does the job less tackily.

tackily ('tækɪlɪ), *adv.*² *colloq.* [f. TACKY *a.*¹ + -LY².] In a tasteless or vulgar style; shabbily, dowdily.

1936 M. MITCHELL *Gone with Wind* IV. xxxii. 544 She was ugly and dressed tackily. **1979** P. DRISCOLL *Pangolin* I. xiv. 115 A square little hovel tackily partitioned into two rooms.

'tackiness¹. [f. TACKY *a.*² + -NESS.] The quality of being tacky or slightly adhesive.

1883 R. HALDANE *Workshop Receipts* Ser. II. 184/2 This varnish..retains sufficient tackiness to hold powdered graphite on its surface. **1908** *Installation News* II. 55/1 No doubt the 'tackiness' of the enamel also helps to hold the tube in place.

tackiness². *colloq.* [f. TACKY *a.*¹ + -NESS.] The quality of being cheap or in poor taste.

1977 *Washington Post* 26 Mar. B5 Their visual craftsmanship and polish are compromised by the manifest tackiness of the story material. **1982** J. FOX *White Mischief* i. 19 A provincial tackiness..pervades the residential suburbs of Nairobi.

'tacking, *vbl. sb.* [f. TACK *v.*¹ + -ING¹.] The action of TACK *v.*¹ in various senses.

a. Joining or fastening together, now esp. in a slight or temporary manner; also, that which is tacked or joined on.

1713 DERHAM *Phys. Theol.* IV. viii. (1714) 159 The Muscles, their curious Structure, the nice tacking them to every Joynt. **1880** A. ARNOLD *Free Land* 133 As to mortgages, Mr. Joshua Williams described that nefarious dealing..known as 'tacking'. **1888** MRS. H. WARD *R. Elsmere* xiv, You don't know anything about tacking or fixing, or the abominable time they take. **1887** SAINTSBURY *Hist. Elizab. Lit.* ix. (1890) 351 [In Hobbes's *Human Nature*] the terse phrasing, the independence of all after-thoughts and tackings-on, manifest themselves at once.

b. The attaching to a money-bill in parliament of a measure for some other purpose.

1700 EVELYN *Diary* Apr., This tacking of bills is a novel practice, suffer'd by K. Cha. II. who..let any thing pass rather than not have wherewith to feed his extravagance. *a* **1745** SWIFT *Four last Y.Q. Anne* III. Wks. (Bohn) I. 471/2 The reasonableness of uniting to a money-bill one of a different nature, which is usually called tacking, hath been likewise much debated, and will admit of argument enough. **1909** A. GRANT in *Contemp. Rev.* Nov. 540 The argument that the Finance Bill of this year is an instance of 'tacking', that is, of the inclusion in a Money Bill of clauses not dealing with Finance.

c. *Naut.* The action of making a tack or a series of tacks (TACK *sb.*¹ 6).

1675 tr. *Camden's Hist. Eliz.* III. 414 Ships fit for Fight, Good Sailers, and nimble and tight for tacking about which way they would. **1806** A. DUNCAN *Nelson* 86 The damage.. prevented him from tacking. **1868** E. EDWARDS *Ralegh* I. vii. 111 [The] great galleons..had to encounter the quick fire and the deft tacking of the smaller..ships of England.

d. *attrib.* and *Comb.*, as ***tacking-cotton***, ***-needle***, ***-thread***; **tacking iron** *Photogr.*, a tool used for attaching tissue to a print or mount by the application of heat at chosen points.

1880 *Plain Hints Needlework* 57 'Basting' or 'tacking cotton'. **1898** *Westm. Gaz.* 7 Apr. 3/2 Then run a tacking cotton (no back stitches) all round the four sides... Press the fold of lace till it is nearly dry before you take out the tacking threads. *Ibid.* 8 Oct. 4/1 A sailor's tacking needle. **1973** *Bodl. Libr. Rec.* IX. 2 The work bench is equipped with tacking irons and a pH meter. **1977** J. HEDGECOE *Photographer's Handbk.* 309 (*caption*) Using an electric tacking iron gently touch the center of the tissue, sticking it to the print.

'tacking, *ppl. a.* [f. as prec. + -ING².] That tacks; that joins or connects: cf. prec.

1705 HICKERINGILL *Priest-cr.* II. Wks. 1716 III. 126 If they get..a Tacking Parliament, to make Acts of Uniformity and Conformity to their Models and little Ways. *Ibid.* iv. 40, I never yet in all our Chronicles met with a Parliament stigmatized with the Name of the *Tacking Parliament*.

tackle ('tæk(ə)l), *sb.* Forms: 3–6 takel, 4–6 *Sc.* takil(l, 4–8 tacle, takle, 5 takul(l, 5–6 takell, -yl, -yll, tackyl (tickell), 6–7 tackel, -ell, 6–8 *Sc.* taikle, (8 teakle, *Sc.* -kil), 6– tackle. [app. of Low German origin: cf. MLG. *takel* equipment generally, e.g. of a horseman, spec. of a ship, hoisting apparatus, LG. *takel*, also early mod.Du. *takel* strong rope, hawser, pulley, mod.Ger. *takel*, Sw. *tackel*, Da. *takkel* tackle; f. MLG. *taken*, MDu. *tacken* to lay hold of, grasp, seize, with instrumental suffix *-el*: see -LE 1.]

1. Apparatus, utensils, instruments, implements, appliances; equipment, furniture, gear.

c **1250** *Gen. & Ex.* 883 And tol and takel and orf he [Abram] dede Wenden hom to here oȝen stede. **13..** *Minor Poems fr. Vernon MS.* xxviii. 32 Vr takel, vr tol, þat we on trowe. **1464** *Mann. & Househ. Exp.* (Roxb.) 248 Payd ffor my masterys takelys, ij.d. **1539** *Will L. Godsman* (Somerset Ho.), Item I give all my tickell..to the chapell of Saynt James to the making of the Northe Ille. **1626** B. JONSON *Staple of N.* Epil., We're sorry that haue so mis-spent Our Time and Tackle. **1669** PENN *No Cross* I. iv. §10 To transport themselves, or tackle in a Journey. **1717** DERHAM in *Buccleuch MSS.* (Hist. MSS. Comm.) I. 365, I am sorry my tackle was not ready when you would have favoured me with your company. **1815** MME. D'ARBLAY *Diary* (1876) IV. 295 As I had no writing tackle, I sent him..to procure me proper implements at the stationer's. **1889** J. K. JEROME *Three Men in Boat* 64 George wanted the shaving tackle.

2. a. Freq. with pronunc. ('teɪk(ə)l). The rigging of a ship: in early use often in wider sense of 'equipment' or 'gear' as in 1; in later use *spec.* the running rigging or ropes used in working the sails, etc., with their pulleys; passing into sense 3. ***ground tackle***, anchors, cables, etc., by which a ship is made fast to the ground.

a **1300** *Cursor M.* 24944 Ful fair bicome þat see to sight, And þai bigan þair takel dight. **1390** GOWER *Conf.* I. 312 The reyni Storm fell doun algates, And al here takel made unwelde. **1450–1530** *Myrr. our Ladye* 226 Dresseth surely the ropes and shyp tacle. **1481** CAXTON *Godeffroy* 261 They ..bare away cordes, cables and saylles, and the other takle, and leyde it in the fortresse. **1585** T. WASHINGTON tr. *Nicholay's Voy.* I. xxi. 27 b, Vpon all the gallies..and other vessels all along vpon the takels, yardes, and other ropes and poupes.., aboue 300 candels. **1633** SIR J. BOROUGHS *Sov. Brit. Seas* (1651) 125 To brooke the seas, and to know the use of the tackles, and compasse. **1671** MILTON *Samson* 717 With all her bravery on, and tackle trim, Sails fill'd, and streamers waving. *a* **1687** SIR W. PETTY *Pol. Arith.* (1690) 14 Holland is..for keeping Ships in Harbour with small expence of Men and ground Tackle. **1745** P. THOMAS *Jrnl. Anson's Voy.* 282 The Second Shot..carry'd away..our Fore-stay Tackle. **1885** SIR J. C. MATTHEW in *Law Times Rep.* LII. 265/1 The vessel..was sold as she lay with her gear and tackle.

b. Cordage; a rope used for any purpose.

1529 *Act 21 Hen. VIII*, c. 12 §1 Diuers..persons.. provide Hemp, and thereof make Cables, Ropes,..Traces, Halters, and other Tackle. **1542** *Aberdeen Regr.* (1844) I. 185 For vij stane of takkillis..for bynding of the gunnis. **1570** LEVINS *Manip.* 6/11 A Tackle, *capulum*. **1712** STEELE *Spect.* No. 454 ¶4 The Tackle of the Coach-window is so bad she cannot draw it up again.

fig. **1893** STEVENSON *Heathercat* iii, The circle of faces was strangely characteristic; long, serious, strongly marked, the tackle standing out in the lean brown cheeks.

3. a. An arrangement consisting of a rope and pulley-block, or more usually a combination of ropes and blocks, used to obtain a purchase in raising or shifting a heavy body.

1539–40 in *Devon. N. & Q.* Oct. (1903) 238 Ropys, poleys and other takle to hawse uppe the ledde uppon the Castell. **1626** CAPT. SMITH *Accid. Yng. Seamen* 16 Sheeps feet is a stay in setling a top mast, and a guie in staying the tackles when they are charged with goods. **1722** in *Hist. Brechin* (1867) 133 Item for a big teakil, being double the hight of the small steeple £40 Scots. **1731** DESAGULIERS in *Phil. Trans.* XXXVII. 292 The Machine consists of three Pullies (two upper and one lower, or a Tackle of Three). **1769** K. FITZ GERALD in *Phil. Trans.* LX. 78 It would not be difficult, with a proper teakle, to raise a barometer of this kind..as high as 200 feet. **1796** MORSE *Amer. Geog.* I. 507 The cannon were raised by large brass tacles..from rock to rock. **1830** KATER & LARDNER *Mech.* xv. 198 A combination of blocks, sheaves, and ropes is called a *tackle*. **1859** F. A. GRIFFITHS *Artil. Man.* (1862) 107 A simple tackle consists of one or more pulleys rove with a single rope.

b. A windlass and its appurtenances, used for hoisting ore, etc.; also, generally, the apparatus of cages or kibbles, with their chains and hooks, for raising ore or coal.

1874 J. H. COLLINS *Metal Mining* (1875) 79 The first machine used in mining operations for raising ore or deads is usually the tackle or windlass. **1881** RAYMOND *Mining Gloss.*, *Tackle* (Corn.), the windlass, rope, and kibble.

†**4. a.** Implements of war, weapons; *esp.* arrows; also, a weapon; an arrow. *Obs.*

c **1375** *Sc. Leg. Saints* v. (*Johannes*) 486 It [a bow] suld hafe bene sone out of pyth To schot ony takil vith. *c* **1386** CHAUCER *Prol.* 106 A sheef of pecok arwes bright and kene ..Wel koude he dresse his takel yemanly. *c* **1400** *Rom. Rose* 1729 Shette att me so wondir smert, That thorough myn eye unto myn hert The takel smote, and depe it wente. *c* **1440** *Promp. Parv.* 485/2 Tacle, or wepene, *armamentum*. **1513** DOUGLAS *Æneis* IX. x. 78 His bow..bend hes he, Tharin a takyll set of sovyr tre. *a* **1550** *Christis Kirke Gr.* x, Ane hasty hensure, callit Hary..Tilt up a taikle withouten tary. **1663** BUTLER *Hud.* I. III. 823 This said, she to her Tackle fell, And on the Knight let fall a peal Of Blows so fierce.

†**b.** Phr. ***to stand*** (or ***stick***) ***to one's tackle***: cf. TACKLING *vbl. sb.* 3. *Obs.*

1577–87 HOLINSHED *Chron.* I. 119/1 The Englishmen would in no wise giue ouer, but did sticke to their tackle. **1586** J. HOOKER *Hist. Irel.* in *Holinshed* II. 9/2 To incourage his people to stand to their tackle, and valiently to withstand Mac Morough. **1724** DE FOE *Mem. Cavalier* (1840) 187 Two regiments of country militia..stood to their tackle better than well enough [in defence of a town]. **1828** E. IRVING *Last Days* 230 You would have armed the house against him, and stood to your tackle all the night. **1841** C. BRONTË *Let.* 1 July in Wise & Symington *Brontës* (1932) I. 234 Mrs. White offered me a week..but I demanded three weeks, and stood to my tackle with a tenacity worthy of yourself.

5. Apparatus for fishing; fishing-gear, fishing-tackle.

1398 TREVISA *Barth. De P.R.* XI. viii. (Tollem. MS.), Aristotel sayeþ þat fischeres heldeþ hoot water on here instrumentes and takles, þat þey be þe raþer frore. *Ibid.* XIII. xxix, [The fish] comeþ ofter in to newe tacle þat is set for hem, þan in to olde. **1711** GAY *Rural Sports* I. 181 The Peacock's plumes, thy tackle must not fail. **1783** JOHNSON 20 Apr. in *Boswell*, I indeed now could fish, give me English tackle. **1850** *Act 13 & 14 Vict.* c. 88 §1 The word 'net' shall ..include all descriptions of tackle, trawl, trammel, stake, bag, coghill, eel, haul, draft, and seine nets. **1867** F. FRANCIS *Angling* i. (1880) 27 Use the very neatest tackle which you can afford for roach.

6. The equipment of a horse; harness.

1683 BURNET tr. *More's Utopia* (1685) 115 Take off both his Saddle, and all his other Tackle. **1725** T. THOMAS in *Portland Papers* VI. (Hist. MSS. Comm.) 133 [The] coach ..I thought could hardly have been able to get over.. without some loss either to the poor beasts, or the tackle. **1728** VANBRUGH & CIB. *Prov. Husb.* I. i, Our Tackle was not so tight as it should be. **1890** 'R. BOLDREWOOD' *Col. Reformer* (1891) 102 I've backed two a week since I came, and have three in tackle, in the yard now.

†**7.** A mistress. *Obs. slang.*

1688 SHADWELL *Sqr. Alsatia* IV. Wks. 1720 IV. 85 Oh my dear Blowing, my Convenient, My tackle. *a* **1700** B. E. *Dict. Cant. Crew*, *Tackle*, a Mistress.

8. Victuals; food or drink; 'stuff'. *slang.*

1857 HUGHES *Tom Brown* I. iv, The purl warms the cockles of Tom's heart... 'Rare tackle that, sir, of a cold morning', says the coachman. **1900** G. SWIFT *Somerley* 113 Do you think ladies usually eat that stodgy tackle?

9. [from the vb.] **a.** *Football.* The act of tackling: see TACKLE *v.* 5.

1876 in P. H. Davis *Football* (1911) 462 A tackle is when the holder of the ball is held by one or more players of the opposite side. **1898** A. SPURLING in W. A. Morgan *'House' on Sport* 170 If you are running after an opponent who has the ball, and find he is gaining on you, don't give up, as he may be checked, and you have the pleasure of making a good tackle. **1901** *Scotsman* 11 Mar. 4/8 Neill, by a plucky tackle ..prevented a break away. **1905** *Oxford Mag.* 22 Feb. 215/1 One of his tackles was excellent.

b. In American football: Each of two players (right and left) stationed next to the end rusher or forward in the rush-line.

1891 W. CAMP *Amer. Football* 41 The tackle is an assistant to both end and guard. **1894** *Outing* (U.S.) XXIV. 281/1 Every one knew he had been a famous tackle on one of the football teams. **1905** *McClure's Mag.* (U.S.) June 123/2 Captain and right-tackle of the the Yale eleven.

c. The act of tackling in other sports. Cf. TACKLE *v.* 5 (*c*).

1930 M. POLLARD *Hockey for Women* viii. 106 A defence player can run towards the tackle, but she should never run into it. **1967** J. POTTER *Foul Play* x. 120 Basil was out of the goal in a lightning flash, cutting off the pass with a sliding tackle.

10. *attrib.* and *Comb.*, as ***tackle-box***, ***-chain***, ***-dealer***, ***-hook***, ***-maker***, ***-shop***; **tackle-block**, = BLOCK *sb.* 5; **tackle-board**, a frame, placed at the end of a rope-walk, containing the whirls to which the yarns are attached to be twisted; **tackle-fall**, = FALL *sb.*¹ 26; **tackle-man**, a man who works the tackle, e.g. of a gun; **tackle-room**, a room in which horse tackle is stored; cf. *tack room* s.v. TACK *sb.*⁷ b. See TACKLE-HOUSE, -PORTER.

1793 SMEATON *Edystone L.* §122 A pair of *tackle-blocks. **1902** *Chambers's Jrnl.* Oct. 702/2 This will render carrying a tin *tackle-box unnecessary. 1905 *Daily Chron.* 26 July 4/7 Banks..lined with seedy, quiet, elderly men with tackle-boxes, evening papers, and roach-poles. 1865 S. Ferguson *Lays West. Gael* 119 The windlass strains the *tackle chains, the black mound heaves below. 1698 in *MSS. Ho. Lords* (1905) III. 338 We were forced to unreeve our *tackle-falls to make lanyards for our lower shrouds. 1769 Falconer *Dict. Marine* (1789), *Garant*, a tackle-fall, or the part upon which the labourers pull in hoisting. 1832 *Chambers's Edin. Jrnl.* 7 Apr. 87/1 The lines of the angler may be bought from the *tackle makers. 1857 Hughes *Tom Brown* I. ix, The little tackle-maker..would soon have made his fortune had the rage lasted. 1859 F. A. Griffiths *Artil. Man.* (1862) 207 Traversing *tacklemen..7 and 8. 1873 *Routledge's Yng. Gentl. Mag.* Jan. 79/2 The 'rear tackleman'..held the end of the tackle. 1951 *Chambers's Jrnl.* Oct. 587/1 You enter the *tackle-room, where surgical harness is stored. 1962 A. Fry *Ranch on Cariboo* v. 53 Like all cabins, [it] was kitchen, dining and living all rolled into one, sometimes even tackle room. 1909 *Nation* (N.Y.) 3 Oct. 12/1 Flies..bought at a *tackle-shop.

tackle ('tæk(ə)l), *v.* Forms: see sb. [f. prec. So Da. *takle*, Sw. *tackla* to tackle, to rig a ship.]

[In the following, a MS. variant of *tagild*: see tagle *v.* a1340 Hampole *Psalter, Cant.* 512 þaire affeccioun ere ay takild with sum luf þat draghis þaim fra godis luf.]

†**1. a.** *trans.* To furnish (a ship) with tackle; to equip with the necessary furnishings. *Obs.*

c1400 *Destr. Troy* 12313 To gyffe.. Tho shippes to shilde o þe shyre whaghes,..And tyrn hom to takle, & trusse for the sea. 1486 *Naval Acc. Hen. VII* (1896) 74 The same Ship so takled & aparailled was deliuered..to Rauf Astry. 1530 Palsgr. 752/1 My shyppe is takylled and talowed, and redy to hoyse up the sayle. 1550 Nicolls *Thucyd.* 5 Althoughe the shyppe be..well garnished and tacled with sayle and ballast. 1653 F. G. tr. *De Scudery's Artamenes*, etc. (1655) IV. vii. ii. 99 At the same time, they trimmed and tackled up a great company of Ships. 1686 J. Dunton *Lett. fr. New-Eng.* (1867) 26 He is a pitch'd Piece of Reason, calckt and tackl't, and only studied to dispute with Tempests.

†**b.** To handle or work the tackle of a ship.

1513 Douglas *Æneis* iii. ii. 119 The noyis wpsprang of mony marynair Besy at thair werk, to takilling euery tow Thair feris exhorting. 1549 *Compl. Scot.* vi. 41 Quhen the schip vas taiklit, the master cryit, boy to the top. 1579–80 North *Plutarch* (1676) 7 Scirus..gave to Theseus..another marriner to tackle the sails, who was called Phœas. a1642 Sir W. Monson *Naval Tracts* ii. (1704) 253/2 There are so few Sailors to tackle their Ships, that they will be taken upon the Stays.

†**c.** *intr.* To tack, or sail across the wind. *Obs.*

1632 Lithgow *Trav.* (1906) 288 Seven weekes crossed with Northerly Windes, ever Tackling and boarding from the Affricke Coast, to the Carminian shoare. 1669 in Sturmy *Mariner's Mag.* i. ii. 20 In this unease Of Tackling Boards, we so the way make short.

†**2.** To raise or hoist with tackle. *Obs. rare.*

1711 W. Sutherland *Shipbuild. Assist.* 6 A Portland.. Stone, may be wrought to its exact Shape before it be tackled up on St. Paul's Church.

3. To harness (a horse) for riding or draught. Also *absol.* with *up*.

1714 S. Sewall *Diary* 5 Apr. (1879) II. 432 Our Horses were forced to leap into the Sea. By that time that had tackled them [it] was duskish. 1770 Mrs. E. Smith in *Lett. Jas. Murray* (1901) 130 Wednesday her coach and chaise was tackled for us to take an airing and see all the curiositys of Kelso. 1787 'G. Gambado' *Acad. Horsem.* (1809) 7 How to chuse a horse, how to tackle him properly, in what sort of dress to ride him, how to mount and manage him. 1826 P. Pounden *France & It.* 7 Five untrimmed little horses, tackled to with ropes. 1869 Mrs. Stowe *Old Town Folk* xx, I shall jest tackle up and go over and bring them children home agin. 1890 'R. Boldrewood' *Col. Reformer* (1891) 93 I'll get a spare saddle and bridle, and will tackle him.

4. *colloq.* **a.** To grip, lay hold of, take in hand, deal with; to fasten upon, attack, encounter (a person or animal) physically.

1828 Webster s.v., A wrestler tackles his antagonist; a dog tackles the game. This is a common popular use of the word in New England, though not elegant. 18.. *Dial. Northampton*, The dog tackled the sheep in the field and almost killed one. 1872 Besant & Rice *Ready-Money Mort.* vii, Smith's a big man; but I think I can tackle him. 1887 Jessopp *Arcady* ii. 58 The people seem to have been afraid to tackle them [otters].

b. To 'come to grips with', to enter into a discussion or argument with; to attack; to approach or question on some subject.

1840 Dickens *Barn. Rudge* i, That John Willet was in amazing force to-night, and fit to tackle a Chief Justice. 1858 Masson *Milton* (1859) I. iv. 168 The Respondent having stated and expounded his theses, was then tackled by a series of Opponents. 1887 R. Buchanan *Heir of Linne* iii, I'll tackle the laird myself. 1901 *Scotsman* 13 Mar. 12/2 He too was tackled on the question, but when he explained it..he found the electors..reasonable.

c. To grapple with, to try to deal with (a task, a difficulty, etc.); to try to solve (a problem). Also *transf.*

1847 E. FitzGerald *Lett.* (1889) I. 171 There was no difficulty at all in coming to the subject at once, and tackling it. 1871 L. Stephen *Playgr. Eur.* iv. ii. 320 Learn.. how most effectually to tackle any little difficulty that occurs. 1897 D. Hay Fleming in *Bookman* Jan. 118/1 Has any previous writer ever tackled a work of such difficulty and magnitude among similar surroundings? 1920 *Blackw. Mag.* Jan. 105/2 The sort of road that even a Ford would hesitate to tackle.

d. To attack, fall upon, begin to eat (food).

1884 'Mark Twain' *Huck. Finn* xxx. 313 So the king sneaked into the wigwam, and took to his bottle for comfort; and before long the duke tackled *his* bottle. 1889 J. K. Jerome *Three Men in Boat* xii, We tackled the cold beef for lunch. 1890 'R. Boldrewood' *Col. Reformer* (1891) 132 A strong man gets over it in a day or two, and tackles his bread and meat, and his work, pretty much as usual.

e. *intr.* To set *to*; to grapple *with* something.

1867 Trollope *Chron. Barset* I. xxxii. 273 We'll tackle to? Very well; so be it. 1867 *Country Wds.* No. 17. 262 Tackle to't reet while yo're yung. a1868 S. Lover (Ogilvie), The old woman..tackled to for a fight in right earnest. *Mod. dial.* (E.D.D.) Ah tackled wi' t' badger.

5. (*a*) In *Rugby* and *N. Amer. Football*, To seize and stop (an opponent) when in possession of the ball. (*b*) In *Assoc. Football*, To obstruct (an opponent) with the object of getting the ball away from him. (*c*) In other sports, to obstruct or accost (an opponent) in order to deprive him of the ball or other object of play. Also *absol.*

1884 *Daily News* 23 Dec. 5/5 He..tackled well, kicked judiciously, and as captain of the team gave every satisfaction. 1891 *Lock to Lock Times* 24 Oct. 13/1 (*Association*) He now plays half-back, and is exceedingly useful in that position, tackling and kicking in great style. 1895 H. F. P. Battersby *Hockey* 98 In defence, they [*sc.* the halves] must tackle everything, and stick to it. 1897 *Sportsman* 16 Dec., He was tackled close to his own quarter line. 1899 *Badm. Libr., Football* 121 (*Assoc.*) Practically the best general rule is for the half-back to tackle the man with the ball, and the back to be near up ready to intercept a pass. 1901 *Scotsman* 11 Mar. 4/8 Those who questioned his ability to tackle..must have got a surprise when they saw the manner he dealt with his opponent. 1935 *Encycl. Sports* 701 The referee may also penalise a side if any of the players holds the ball under the water when tackled. 1959 M. Boyd *Lacrosse Playing & Coaching* vi. 70 As soon as their opponents get the ball, attack players must tackle back onto them. 1975 *Oxf. Compan. Sports & Games* 320/2 The supporting backs and line-backers are prepared to tackle the carrier.

†**6.** (?) To enclose or fortify. *Obs. rare*$^{-1}$.

Perh. some error, or a different word.

c1645 Howell *Lett.* i. vi. lviii, The moralist tells us that a quadrat solid wise man should involve and tackle himself within his own vertue, and slight all accidents that are incident to man, and be still the same.

tackled ('tæk(ə)ld), *a.*, *ppl. a.* [f. tackle *sb.* and *v.* + -ed.]

†**1.** Made of tackle or ropes: cf. tackling 6.

1592 Shaks. *Rom. & Jul.* ii. iv. 201 My man shall..bring thee Cords made like a tackled staire.

2. Furnished with a tackle or harness.

1542 *Will Sir C. Storke, Newton Seynt-lo, Somerset* 18 Apr., Wm. Becke a tackled heyfar.

†'**tackle-house.** *Obs.* [f. tackle *sb.* + house.] app. either, A house in which porters employed in loading and unloading ships kept their tackle; or, A house having a tackle or pulley for hoisting heavy goods; a warehouse for lading and unlading merchandise going or coming by sea.

In London each of the twelve great Merchant Companies had formerly the right to have its own tackle-house, with its porter or porters, and in some of them the titular office of 'tackle-house porter' or 'tackle-porter' still survives: see quot. 1851 in b, tackle-porter quot. 1909. The tackle-houses at Southwold were on the quay of a creek, evidently for the loading and unloading of vessels lying there; those at London may have been on the river's brink.

1562 *Will* in T. Gardner *Acc. Dunwich*, etc. (1754) 214 My Tackle House at the Woods-End [Southwold]. 1579 *Act Com. Council London* 15 Aug. (Jrnl. 20, ii. lf. 506), It is thought convenient y[t] no other tacklehouses or companie of porters shall hereafter be erected without the especiell licence of y[e] L. Maior, his brethren, and the Counsell. 1606 *Ibid.* 27 June (Jrnl. 27, lf. 52 b), Complaintes..by freemen porters of the Tacklehouses of the said citie against others streete porters workinge in the said citie, for interdealinge with worke..touchinge shippinge and unshippinge of goodes..with which business the said street porters have not presumed to deal untill of late time. 1607 in *Remembrancia* (City of London) II. 288 The peticion enclosed..by the Porters of the Tackell Houses of this Cittie, prayinge..Assistance for the preventinge of much inconvenience to growe uppon them through the erection of an newe Office to be established for the ladinge and unladinge..of all Marchantes goodes not free of the twelve Companies. [The petition follows, entitled in margin] 'A Peticion concerninge the Tacle Porters'. 1618 in T. Gardner *Acc. Dunwich*, etc. (1754) 215 (*Southwold*) One entire Place, Key or Wharfe, the whole abutting and bounding against..the Tackle-House at the South-East End. 1754 T. Gardner *ibid.* 214 The antient Key stood in the Woods-End-Creek; near thereto were Dwelling-Houses, Warehouses, Tackle-Houses, the Blubber-Pans and Carters-Grounds for Ship-Building. 1842–51 [see b].

b. *attrib.* **tackle-house porter**, *orig.* A porter belonging to or employed at a tackle-house; later (usually shortened to *tackle-porter*: see next) a porter authorized to act as such by one of the London Companies having this right, as distinguished from a *ticket-porter* who was licensed by the corporation.

1606 *Act Com. Council London* 27 June in Mayhew *Lond. Labour* (1861) III. 365/1 Tackle-house porter, porter-packer of the gooddes of English merchants, streete-porter, or porter to the packer for the said citie for strangers' goods. 1646 *Act Com. Council conc. Tackle-house Porters* (1712) 9 Whereas divers Controversies and Differences have heretofore been between the Tacklehouse-Porters of this City, and the Ticket-Porters, otherwise called the Street-Porters of this City in and about several Matters [etc.]. 1842 Pulling *Treat. Laws & Customs London* 502 The Tackle-house Porters, who, with their subordinates the Packers' Porters, originally formed a part of the establishment of the principal trading companies, and were attached to their respective tackle-houses, are employed in lading and unlading goods not subject to metage. *Ibid.* 504 The tackle-house porters are composed of a few persons appointed by the twelve principal companies, to each of which the privilege belonged of having a tackle-house for lading and unlading goods. Each of the companies appoint one person as their tackle-house porter, and some of them two. 1851 Mayhew *Lond. Labour* (1861) III. 366/1 The tackle-house porters that are still in existence, I was told, are gentlemen. One is a wharfinger, and claims and enjoys the monopoly of labour on his own wharf.

'**tackle-ˌporter.** Short for *tackle-house porter*: see preceding.

16.. [see quot. 1607 s.v. tackle-house]. 1648 *Minutes Goldsmiths' Co.* 8 Nov., It was moved by M[r] Ashe that this Company might have some tackle porters waiting at the Customs House as the Fishmongers and other Companies do. 1851 Mayhew *Lond. Labour* (1861) III. 365/2 There were 24 tackle-porters appointed; each of the 12 great city companies appointing two. 1909 Sir W. Prideaux in *Let.* 23 Dec., The [Goldsmiths'] Company used to appoint two tackle porters, but for many years past only one has been appointed. There is no salary or emolument of any kind attached to the office. The present Lord Mayor is tackle porter of this Company.

tackler ('tæklə(r)). [f. tackle *v.* + -er[1].] One who tackles, in various senses. †**a.** (?). *Obs.* **b.** An overlooker of power-loom weavers. **c.** One who tackles in football, etc. **d.** See quot. **e.** See quot.

a. 1686 Blome *Gentl. Recreat.* ii. 62 *Hack Hawk*, that is a Tackler.

b. 1864 Ramsbottam *Phases Distress* 34 Tackler Tom con stond it o'. 1882 *Standard* 7 Sept. 2/3 Power-loom overlookers, or 'tacklers', and carders and strippers followed. 1901 *Speaker* 20 July 439/1 Each 'tackler' or overlooker has a certain number of looms assigned to his care. *Ibid.*, While the tacklers 'drive' the weavers, the manager in turn 'drives' the tacklers.

c. 1891 *Lock to Lock Times* 24 Oct. 13/1 He is a rare tackler, and his famous rushes have warded off many an attack on the Marlow goal. 1955 Doyle & Smith *Lifetime in Hurling* xx. 144 A quick hitter..and a fearless tackler.

d. 1891 *Labour Commission Gloss.*, *Tackler*, one who puts in the tacks used in 'lasting'.

e. 1881 Raymond *Mining Gloss.*, *Tacklers* (Derb.), small chains put around loaded *corves*.

'**tackless,** *a.* [f. tack *sb.*[1] 2 + -less.] Having no tacks; made (as a sewn shoe) without tacks.

1907 *Westm. Gaz.* 4 Nov. 8/4 A boot or shoe..being tackless throughout, is much more flexible than would otherwise be possible. 1907 *Daily Chron.* 5 Nov. 8/2 A patent 'lasting' machine with which boots can be made without the aid of tacks or other metal fastening is shown by the Tackless and Flexible Shoe Machinery Company.

tackling ('tæklıŋ), *vbl. sb.* Also 5–6 tak(e)lyng, 6 taclyng. [f. tackle *v.* + -ing[1].]

†**1. a.** The furnishing of a vessel with tackle. *Obs.*

1486 *Naval Acc. Hen. VII* (1896) 17 The wages of xxx marriners..for the Rigging and takeling of the same Ship.

†**b.** *concr.* The rigging of a ship; the tackle.

c1422 Hoccleve *Jereslaus's Wife* 914 Our takelynges brast and the ship claf In two. 1526 Tindale *Acts* xxvii. 19 The thyrde daye we cast out with oure awne hondes the tacklinge [1885 (R.V.) *marg.* or furniture] of the shippe. 1529 *Act 21 Hen. VIII*, c. 12 §1 The great Cables, Halsers, Ropes, and all other Tackling..for your Royal Ships. c1615 Bacon *Adv. Sir G. Villiers* v. §9 For tackling, as sails and cordage, ..we are beholden to our neighbours for them. 1676 Hubbard *Happiness of People* 12 If the Mast be never so well strengthened, and the Tackline never so well bound together. 1696 *London Gaz.* No. 3176/1 Abundance of Lanthorns were hung upon the Tackling of the Ships. 1769 Falconer *Dict. Marine* (1789) Uu ij b, Unless we adopt the obsolete word *Tackling*, which is now entirely disused by our mariners.

fig. 1601 Sir W. Cornwallis *Ess.* xvi. K iij b, Graue, wise, sober, temperate men,..meete to bee part of the tacklings of a Commonwealth. 1655 Fuller *Ch. Hist.* i. i. §11 A relation as ill accoutred with tacklings, as their Ship;..unrigged in respect of time, and other circumstances.

†**2. a.** Gear, furnishings, fittings, accoutrements, outfit, baggage, etc.; = tackle *sb.* 1. *Obs.*

1558 *Ludlow Churchw. Acc.* (Camden) 86 Takelynges and nayles for the great belle. 1637 B. Jonson *Sad Sheph.* i. ii, Here's Little John hath harbord you a Deere, I see by his Tackling. a1659 *Lond. Chanticleers* ix. in Hazl. *Dodsley* XII. 345 Meet me here two hours hence with all your tacklings. I'll see this bundle shall be safe. 1695 J. Edwards *Perfect. Script.* 120 This sort of country tackling is call'd threshing-instruments. 1718 S. Sewall *Diary* 25 July, I give her two Cases with a knife and fork in each; one Turtle shell tackling; the other long, with Ivory handles. 1749 C. Campbell in *Scots Mag.* Sept. (1753) 454/2 Remember Lady Ardsheil's discharges, and all your other tackling. 1813 Sir R. Wilson *Pr. Diary* II. 244 It is necessary that I should feast myself into a little more *embonpoint*, for otherwise I shall not have sufficient carcase to suspend my tackling upon.

†**b.** A horse's harness. *Obs.*

c1645 Howell *Lett.* (1650) III. 14 If he wanted money to mend his plow or his Cart, or to buy tacklings for his horses. 1726 *Boston News-Let.* 14 July, To be sold..two good carts, four good horses, and tackling compleat for the same. 1787 'G. Gambado' *Acad. Horsemen* (1809) 45 Let me entreat you to examine your tackling well at setting out..: see that your girths are tight.

†**3.** Arms, weapons, instruments; also *fig.*, esp. in phr. ***to stand*** or ***stick to one's tackling***, to 'stand to one's guns', to hold one's ground, to maintain one's position or attitude: cf. tackle *sb.* 4 b; so *to hold tackling* (cf. *to hold tack*, tack

sb. 11); also ***to give over one's tackling***, to 'lay down one's arms', surrender, give in. *Obs.*

14.. *Voc.* in Wr.-Wülcker 565/36 *Armamentum*, takelyng. **1529** More *Dyaloge* IV. Wks. 278/2 Than would he haue them abide by their tackeling like mighty champions. *a* **1548** Hall *Chron., Hen. VI* 160b, Perceiuyng the kentishmen, better to stande to their taclyng, then his imagination expected. **1551** T. Wilson *Logike* (1580) 61 b, Thus the aunswerer..maie..force the apposer to giue ouer his tacklyng, without any aduauntage gotten. **1576** Fleming *Panopl. Epist.* 362 Your brother..tolde me..that you haue forsaken your booke... I wishe you to..sticke still to your tackling: and as you haue begonne, so proceede. **1593** in Abp. Bancroft *Daung. Posit.* IV. iii. 141, I thinke it a great blessing of God, that hath raised vp Martin to hold tackling with the Bishops. *a* **1635** Corbett *Poems* (1807) 23 Reader, unto your tackling look, For there is coming forth a book Will spoyl Joseph Barnisius The sale of *Rex Platonicus*. **1679** *Hist. Jetzer* 29 An ambition to be accounted and Canonized for a Saint, which by standing stoutly to his tackling he hoped for.

†**4.** Fishing tackle. *Obs.*

1548 Elyot *Dict., Alopex marina*..a fysshe of the sea, whyche perceyuynge the hooke to bee fastened in his bealy, byteth of the lyne aboue the taklyng, and so escapeth. **1653** Walton *Angler* 53, I will sit down and mend my tackling. *Ibid.* 105 Sure, Master, yours is a better Rod, and better Tackling. **1727** *Philip Quarll* (1816) 7 Having..caught a..dish of fish, we put up our tackling.

5. The action of the vb. tackle in mod. senses (in quots., in sense 5).

1893 *Daily News* 14 Dec. 2/6 Cambridge's tackling stood them in capital defence. **1900** *Westm. Gaz.* 12 Dec. 7/3 A strong Cambridge attack was foiled by the splendid tackling of the Oxford men.

6. *Comb.* **tackling bag** *U.S.* and *Rugby Football*, a stuffed bag suspended and used for practice in tackling; **tackling dummy** *U.S. Football* = *tackling bag* above; †**tackling-ladder**, a rope-ladder.

1892 *Outing* (U.S.) Jan. 279/2 Their one special piece of apparatus is..the tackling bag, and this is..necessary to the indoor practice of a football team. **1978** *Rugby World* Apr. 25 (Advt.), Order now for 1978–79 pre-season training the new Allander tackling bag. **1904** *Outing* (U.S.) Dec. 367/2 The tackling dummy was used by many squads. **1959** N. Mailer *Advts. for Myself* (1961) 51 The Japs looked like bushes, or like tackling dummies in the evening when practice was over. **1680** Otway *Caius Marius* III. i, My man shall meet thee there; And bring thee cords made like a tackling-ladder.

tackman ('tækmən). *dial.* [f. tack *sb.*[2] 4 + man.] One who looks after horses or cattle which are grazed on tack.

1885 *Athenæum* 10 Oct. 467/2 With constables, tackmen, and pinders we are familiar. **1891** *Sportsman* 14 Feb. 1/1 (Advt.) Wanted, by Young Man, a Situation as Tackman or Helper in a racing stable.

tacksman ('tæksmən). *Sc.* Also 6–9 tax-, 7 taxs-. [f. *tack's*, poss. of tack *sb.*[2] + man.] One who holds a tack or lease of land, a watermill, coal-mines, fisheries, tithes, customs, or anything farmed or leased; a lessee; esp. in the Highlands, a middleman who leases directly from the proprietor of the estate a large piece of land which he sublets in small farms.

1533 *Aberdeen Regr.* (1844) I. 148 Gif thair be ony takkismen of the tovne that dissentis to the paiment of thir settis, that thai salbe dischargit of thair takkis. **1563** *Inchaffray Reg.* (Bann.) 83 Our lait cousing David Lord Drummond and Dame Lilias Ruthven his spous as takismen of the Abbacie of Inchaffray. **1627** *Rep. Parishes Scotl.* (Bann.) 2 William Erle of Angus taxman of the haill personag teinds of the Barronj. **1630** in *Proc. Soc. Ant. Scot.* (1896) XXX. 58 The takismen and custumeris of the saidis impostis of wynnes. **1680** [see tack *sb.*[2] 6] **1775** Johnson *W. Isl., Ostig*, Next in dignity to the laird is the Tacksman. **1791** Newte *Tour Eng. & Scot.* 125 The Tacksmen of the Highlands were usually descendants of those heads of families of whom they held their lands. **1794** *Sporting Mag.* III. 50 Mr. Richard Graham, tacksman of the fishery of J. C. Curwen. **1814** Scott *Wav.* xx, Tacksmen, as they were called, who occupied portions of his estate as..lessees. **1887** *Times* (weekly ed.) 25 Feb. 9/3 In Munster or Connaught, the tacksmen who covenanted directly with the lairds might deal as they pleased with their sub-tenants.

So **'tacks,woman**, a female holder of a tack.

1585 *Exch. Rolls Scotl.* XXI. 583 The dewtie of the kirk of Kinros awand be Agnes Leslie, ledie Lochlewin, taxiswoman thairof.

tacky ('tækɪ), *sb.* and *a.*[1] Also **tackey, tackie.** [Origin obscure.]

A. *sb.* **a.** *U.S.* A degenerate 'weedy' horse: see quot. 1884. **b.** *U.S.* A poor white of the Southern States from Virginia to Georgia.

1800 W. Tatham *Agric. & Commerce* 81 A horse, a cow, or a little *tackie*, &c. (which last term signifies a poney or little horse of low price). **1839** C. F. Hoffman *Wild Scenes* 117 The land pirates had disappeared, without molesting my tackey. **1884** E. Eggleston in *Cent. Mag.* Jan. 444/2 The scrubby little 'tackeys' still taken in the marshes along the North Carolina coast are descendants of the wild horses of the colony. **1888** *Ibid.* Sept. 799/2 If Mr. Catlett will come to Georgia and go among the 'po' whites' and 'piney-wood tackeys'. **1889** Farmer *Americanisms, Tackey*, in the South, a jade of a horse; a sorry beast; and idiomatically a man neglectful of personal appearance. **1896** *Peterson Mag.* Jan. 84/2 Here..is a native of the Virginia wilds, a specimen of the genus 'tacky'.

B. *adj.* Dowdy, shabby; in poor taste, cheap, vulgar. Also *Comb.*, as ***tacky-looking*** adj. *colloq.* (orig. and chiefly *U.S.*).

1862 K. Stone *Jrnl.* 16 Feb. in *Brokenburn* (1955) 89 What a weary, bedraggled tacky-looking set they were. **1883** I. M. Rittenhouse *Maud* 262 Two little cards (with his name printed on them in gilt. Tackey? Ugh). **1893** L. J. Rittenhouse in *Chicago Advance* 22 June, She looks so tacky in her shabby dress. **1937** Hart & Kaufman *You can't take it with You* III. 180 An extremely tacky-looking evening wrap. **1957** M. Kennedy *Heroes of Clone* III. i. 158 He went again to the window to watch for the arrival of the tacky little car. **1967** N. Mailer *Cannibals & Christians* I. 16 All the tacky doings of each small town. **1971** 'O. Bleeck' *Thief who painted Sunlight* (1972) iii. 30 A tacky-looking bulletin board. **1983** *Listener* 10 Feb. 29/3 They were really very good, putting together a fast and lively show, full of cheerfully dreadful jokes and inventively tacky songs.

tacky ('tækɪ), *a.*[2] [f. tack *sb.*[1] 4 b + -y.] Slightly sticky or adhesive: said of gum, glue, or varnish nearly dry.

1788 G. Smith in *Lond. Mag.* 624 The moistened gum..must not be waterish but something tacky or clammy. **1822** Imison *Sc. & Art* II. 244 If left in the damp, it remains tacky..a long time. **1897** *Complete Cyclist* (Isthmian Libr.) 188 Sufficient time must be given to allow the solution to become dry, or, as it is technically known, 'tacky'.

tackyl, tacle, obs. ff. tackle.

‖ **taclobo** (tə'kləʊbəʊ). [Native name in Philippines.] A bivalve mollusc, of great size, the Giant Clam (*Tridacna gigas*) of the Indian and China seas.

1885 Balfour *Cyclop. India* (ed. 3) s.v. *Kima*, The shells of the taclobo, or gigantic Philippine oyster, are used as fonts in the churches of that group. **1885** *Encycl. Brit.* XVIII. 750/2 The 'taclobo' shell sometimes weighs 200 lb., and is used for baptismal fonts.

'tac-,locus. *Geom.* [f. L. *tac-tus* touch + locus.] The locus of the points of contact of two curves of different families, or of two non-consecutive curves of the same family.

1873 Cayley *Math. Papers* VIII. 533.

tacnode ('tæknəʊd). *Geom.* [f. L. *tac-tus* touch + node.] A point at which two parts of the same curve have ordinary contact.

1852 Cayley *Math. Papers* (1889) II. 28 The tacnode is a double point where two branches touch. **1873** Salmon *Higher Plane Curves* 207 Two nodes may coincide, giving rise to the singularity called a tacnode; this is in fact an ordinary (two-pointed) contact of two branches of the curve.

b. *attrib.* **'tacnode-'cusp**, the singularity of a curve which arises when a cusp and an immediately following tangency of the two branches coalesce.

1873 Salmon *Higher Plane Curves* (1879) 207.

taco ('tɑːkəʊ, 'tækəʊ). Chiefly *N. Amer.* [Mex. Sp.] **a.** A Mexican snack comprising a fried, unleavened cornmeal pancake or tortilla filled with seasoned mincemeat, chicken, cheese, beans, etc.

1949 *Amer. Speech* XXIV. 235/2 The *touristas* almost always eat in a Mexican restaurant and bravely attempt to order their meals in Spanish. Such meals are (1) [tækoz], a mispronunciation of the Spanish word *tacos* [takos]. **1957** J. Kerouac *On Road* (1958) xii. 93 We went into a Mexican restaurant and had tacos and mashed pinto beans. **1965** *Austral. Women's Weekly* 20 Jan. 25/1 She would serve up a traditional Mexican dish of unsurpassable excellence, the white meat..rolled up in a delicate crisp pancake, or taco. **1966** *Listener* 4 Aug. 164/2 *Tacos*..are *tortillas* rolled round shredded meat or bird and fried in oil. **1971** *Islander* (Victoria, B.C.) 4 July 2/4 Friends in San Diego had introduced us to tortillas and tacos. **1978** S. Wilson *Dealer's Move* vi. 107 Washing the food down with two strong cups of tea and mopping up with South London's answer to tacos, sliced white loaf.

b. *attrib.*, as ***taco joint***, ***sauce***, ***stand***.

1967 *Trans-Action* Apr. 8/1 Time is alive when and where there is action... During the regular school year it may pick up for an hour in the afternoon when the 'broads' leave school and meet with the set at a corner taco joint. **1977** *Time* 28 Nov. 58/1 Some have about as much feeling for a community's sense of itself and its needs as does the imported manager of a franchised taco joint on the highway outside of town. **1976** *Punch* 11 Aug. 227/1, I took to enchilada mix, tortillas, taco sauce, and all those Mexican delicacies. **1977** *Daily News* (Perth, Austral.) 19 Jan. 13 (Advt.), Taco—a crisp tortilla filled with beef, onions, lettuce, taco sauce and cheese. **1969** D. MacKenzie *Night Boat to Puerto Vedra* (1970) 172 A few seamen were at the taco stands... He bought himself a cone of maize flour filled with peppered ground meat. **1979** R. L. Simon *Peking Duck* ii. 18 Jogging behind a gas station and a taco stand to a nondescript stucco gate.

Taconic (tə'kɒnɪk), *a.* *Geol.* [f. the name of the *Taconic* Mountains in New England and New York State.] **a.** See quot. 1865.

1842 E. Emmons in *Geol. N.Y.* II. vii. 135 It has been deemed advisable to annex to the general account of the group of rocks of the northern district, a brief sketch of the services which constitute the Taconic System. **1849** Lyell *2nd Visit U.S.* (1850) II. 354, I believe the formations called Taconic, in the United States..to be simply Silurian strata much altered, and often quite metamorphic. **1865** Page *Geol. Terms, Taconic*, a term applied by the late Professor Emmons to the rocks east of the Hudson (from the Taconic range lying along the western slope of the Green Mountains),..which consist of slates, quartz-rock, and lime-stones of Lower Silurian or perhaps more properly of Upper Cambrian age.

b. Epithet of an orogeny that occurred in Ordovician times in eastern North America.

1908 *Bull. Geol. Soc. Amer.* XX. 503 The other three [emergences]..were of long duration and of great significance. These are: (1) The Taconic revolution..; (2) the Appalachian revolution.., and (3) the Laramide revolution. **1980** *Sci. Amer.* Oct. 136/1 The southern Appalachians have evolved in a series of collisions of fragments of continental or island-arc material at the eastern edge of North America in the Taconic, the Acadian and the Alleghenian orogenies.

taconite ('tækənaɪt). *Geol.* [f. Tacon(ic *a.* + -ite[1].] **a.** A type of chert used as an iron ore in parts of N. America.

1905 *Econ. Geol.* I. 48 In the Mesabi district the local name 'taconite' is applied to the ferruginous chert. **1951** *Engineering* 22 June 761/2 To be able to take a hard ore, such as taconite, separate the magnetite and silica by grinding the material down to pass a 300-mesh sieve, and agglomerate the concentrates by pelletising, at a price to compete with imported ores, was no mean achievement. **1981** D. R. Coates *Environmental Geol.* v. 104/1 Taconite is a low-grade ore of iron which is the source of most current U.S. iron production.

b. *attrib.*, as ***taconite mine, ore, pellet, tailing***.

1974 *Sumter* (S. Carolina) *Daily Item* 23 Apr. 7B/7 Reserve, which..produces 15 per cent of the iron ore used in the nation's steelmaking blast furnaces, also closed its taconite mine at Babbitt. **1975** *Sci. Amer.* Nov. 52/3 The place of the high-grade ores was then taken by taconite ores containing iron in the form of finely disseminated magnetite. **1958** J. Szarkowski *Face of Minnesota* 270 By 1948 the first mass-produced taconite pellets reached the blast furnaces. **1975** *Telegraph* (Brisbane) 18 Mar. 12/4 The refinery's discharge of taconite tailings.

tacouba (tə'kuːbə). Also **tacooba, tacuba.** [Origin unknown, perh. an Arawakan word.] In Guyana, a tree which has fallen across a river forming a bridge or obstruction. Also *fig.*

1934 E. Waugh *92 Days* ii. 55 In the wet season..you had to crawl across a tacuba leading a swimming horse. **1951** E. Mittelhölzer *Shadows move among Them* II. iv. 196 'What's a *tacooba*?' 'Indian word. Means a fallen tree or any sort of obstruction in a river or creek that constitutes a menace to navigation.' **1959** P. Capon *Amongst those Missing* 124 He had expected rapids every few miles, numerous tacoubas and a cataract or two. **1965** 'Lauchmonen' *Old Thom's Harvest* v. 58 He was a squat negro, a stumpy little piece of a man, a knotty old tacuba tree-stump. **1974** H. MacInnes *Climb to Lost World* vi. 73 The walking itself wasn't difficult, but there were plenty of streams to cross, some of them bridged by slippery tacoubas, or tree jams.

‖ **Tacsonia** (tæk'səʊnɪə). *Bot.* [mod.L. (Jussieu 1789), f. Peruvian name *tacso*.] A genus of West Indian and Central American shrubs, N.O. *Passifloraceæ*, closely allied to the Passion-flowers.

1869 Darwin *Life & Lett.* III. 279 The long pendent tube and valve-like corona which retains the nectar of Tacsonia.

tact (tækt). [ad. (immed. or ult.) L. *tact-us* touch, f. ppl. stem of *tangĕre* to touch: cf. F. *tact* (14th c. in sense 1), Ger. *tact, takt* (1619 in sense 4).]

I. 1. a. The sense of touch; touch. In quot. 1809 *transf.* [So in L.; F. *tact* (14th c. in Littré).]

[*c* **1200** *Vices & Virtues* 17 Ða fif wittes..þat is, *visus, auditus, gustus, ordoratus, et tactus*, þat is ȝesihthe, ȝeherþe, smac, and smell, and tactþe.]

1651 A. Ross *Arcana Microcosm.* II. xxi. 110 Of all the creatures, the sense of tact is most exquisite in man. **1809** Kendall *Trav.* III. 102 Such is the delicacy of their [divining or mineral rods'] tact, that the weakest power is sufficient to determine them. **1865** Grote *Plato* (1867) II. xxvi. 370 The various Percepta or Percipienda of tact, vision, hearing—sweet, hot, hard, light—have each its special bodily organ. **1881** Le Conte *Sight* 77 Sight is a very refined tact.

b. *fig.* A keen faculty of perception or discrimination likened to the sense of touch.

1797 W. Tooke *Life Catherine* II. 206 It was from his genius alone that he had seized the character of other nations, and it shews a niceness of tact exceedingly rare. **1802** Coleridge *Lett., to W. Sotheby* (1895) 397 You..must needs have a better tact of what will offend that class of readers. **1842** Manning *Serm.* ii. (1843) I. 22 To..deaden the keen tact of conscience. **1876** Green *Stray Stud.* 120 The popular voice showed a singular historical tact in its mistake.

2. Ready and delicate sense of what is fitting and proper in dealing with others, so as to avoid giving offence, or win good will; skill or judgement in dealing with men or negotiating difficult or delicate situations; the faculty of saying or doing the right thing at the right time. [a. F. *tact* (Voltaire 1769).]

[**1793** D. Stewart *Outl. Mor. Philos.* I. x. §87 (1855) 48 The use made in the French tongue of the word *Tact*, to denote that delicate sense of propriety which enables a man to feel his way in the difficult intercourse of polished society.] **1804–6** Syd. Smith *Mor. Philos.* xii. (1850) 154 We have begun, though of late years, to use the word *tact*. **1837** Carlyle *Fr. Rev.* (1872) II. I. iv. 22 A most delicate task; requiring tact. **1875** Helps *Ess., Secrecy* 55 Few persons have tact enough to perceive when to be silent, and when to offer you counsel or condolence. **1892** R. B. Brett in *19th Cent.* Jan. 22 That fine instinct in the management of men which is commonly called tact.

†**3.** The act of touching or handling; an instance of this, a touch. *Obs. rare.* [So in L.]

1801 JEFFERSON *Writ.* (1830) III. 467, I judged from a tact of the southern pulse. **1823** J. BADCOCK *Dom. Amusem.* 64 Others that are harmless in tact.

II. 4. *Mus.* A stroke in beating time; = BEAT *sb.*^{1} 4: see also quot. 1891. [= (Germ.) L. *tactus*, Adam v. Fulda 1490; Ger. *tact*, Prätorius 1619.]

1609 J. DOULAND *Ornith. Microl.* 46 *Tact* is a successive motion in singing, directing the equalitie of the measure. **1614** T. RAVENSCROFT *Brief Disc.* 20 Tact, Touch or Time, is, a certaine Motion of the hand (whereby the Quantity of Notes and Rests are directed) by an equall Measure. [**1777** R. DONKIN *Military Coll.* 161 Count Saxe recommends the *tact*, or marching *en cadence*.] **1828** WEBSTER, *Tact*,.. formerly the stroke in beating time in music. **1891** *Cent. Dict.*, *Tact*..in music, a beat or pulse; especially, the emphatic down-beat with which a measure begins; hence, also, a measure.

III. 5. *Psychol.* [Final element of *con*)*tact*.] B. F. Skinner's term for an utterance which is evoked by an object, event, etc., and reinforces the learning of a response. Hence as *v. trans.*, to respond to (a stimulus) with an utterance; *intr.*, to utter words or sounds in this way; so **'tacted** *ppl. a.*; **'tacting** *vbl. sb.* Cf. MAND.

1954 *Brit. Jrnl. Psychol.* Aug. 181 Skinner..describes how a child learns to emit 'tacts' (i.e. verbal responses controlled by properties of objects or situations) under the influence of 'generalized reinforcers', particularly approval. **1957** B. F. SKINNER *Verbal Behavior* v. 81 There is no suitable term for this type of operant... The invented word 'tact' will be used here. The term carries a mnemonic suggestion of behavior which 'makes contact with' the physical world. A tact may be defined as a verbal operant in which a response of given form is evoked (or at least strengthened) by a particular object. **1959**, etc. [see MAND]. **1964** A. W. STAATS *Human Learning* iii. 73/2 The child learns in this manner to tact environmental events as well as objects. **1969** B. F. SKINNER *Contingencies of Reinforcement* viii. 254 The close relation between the topography of behavior and the tacted stimulus. **1977** *Listener* 5 May 597/2 What is nowadays called 'tacting' (i.e., verbal behaviour controlled primarily by its antecedents—in this case the sight of the milk)... Victor was evidently conditioned only to tact.

†**'tactable**, *a. Obs.* [f. L. *tact-* (see TACTIC *a.*^{2}) + -ABLE.] Capable of being touched; tangible.
1611 CHAPMAN *May-Day* I. i. Plays 1873 II. 331 Alas good soules, women of themselves are tractable and tactable enough. **1656** STANLEY *Hist. Philos.* VI. (1701) 257/1 Whatsoever is gustable, is tactable, and humid.

†**tac'tation.** *Obs. rare.* [f. as prec. + -ATION.] The act of touching.
1688 R. HOLME *Armoury* II. 387/1 A Tactation, or a touching, is that whereby we discern the difference of objects, and the nature of things.

tactful ('tæktfʊl), *a.* [f. TACT + -FUL.] Full of or endowed with tact; of actions, displaying or inspired by tact.
1864 *Lond. Soc.* VI. 497, I never heard a better, more tactful speech in my life. **1884** *Macm. Mag.* Nov. 28/1 With a tactful Governor to show them the way. **1894** *Educ. Rev.* VII. 310 An eloquent, tactful and persuasive appeal.
Hence **'tactfully** *adv.*, in a tactful manner.
1880 MISS BIRD *Japan* II. 72 Ito very tactfully neither gave it [the message] nor told me of it. **1889** *Tablet* 21 Dec. 980 To both deputations Mr. Chaplin replied tactfully.

tactic ('tæktɪk), *sb.*^{1} [ad. 17th c. L. *tactic-a*, a. Gr. τακτική (sc. τέχνη) the art of arrangement or tactics, fem. of τακτικός, TACTIC *a.*^{1}, = F. (*la*) *tactique* (sometimes used in Eng.). In sense 2, ad. Gr. τακτικός (sc. ἀνήρ) tactician.]
1. A system of tactics; = TACTICS 1.
[**1570** J. DEE *Math. Pref.* a iv b *margin*, The difference betwene Stratarithmetrie and Tactike [*printed* Tacticie].] **1766** *Misc.* in *Ann. Reg.* 171/2 What is commonly called Tactick, or the formation of battalions. **1801** in Nicolas *Disp. Nelson* (1845) IV. 303 He alluded..to the total want of *tactique* among the Northern Fleets. **1838–42** ARNOLD *Hist. Rome* II. xxix. 143 The arms and tactic of both armies were precisely similar.
b. A piece of military tactics.
1868 FREEMAN *Norm. Conq.* II. ix. 389 Ralph required his men to practise an unusual and foreign tactic.
c. *transf.* and *fig.*
1791 BURKE *App. Whigs* Wks. VI. 206 By a divine tactick. **1817** *Sporting Mag.* L. 8 Great coquettes have another tactic. **1860** M. PATTISON in *Ess. & Rev.* 314 Lord Chesterfield, seeing what advantage the High-church party derived from this tactic, endeavoured to turn it against them.
†**2.** A tactician. *Obs.*
1638 JUNIUS *Paint. Ancients* 128 A Tactike shall never know how to set his men in aray, unlesse he doe first trie the case by designe. *a***1641** BP. MOUNTAGU *Acts & Mon.* ii. (1642) 81 Removes, *ambulante exercitu*, as Tacticks phrase it.
3. *Math.* (See quots.)
1861 SYLVESTER in *Phil. Mag.* 374, I have given the general name of *Tactic* to the third pure mathematical science, of which order is the proper sphere, as are number and space of the other two. **1864** CAYLEY *Math. Papers* V. 294 The two great divisions of Algebra are Tactic and Logistic. **1883** *Ibid.* XI. 433 We have a large enough subject, including the partition of numbers, which Sylvester has called Tactic.

tactic ('tæktɪk), *a.*^{1} [ad. mod.L. *tactic-us* (17th c.), a. Gr. τακτικός of arrangement or tactics, f. τακτός ordered, vbl. adj. of τάσσειν to set in order. Cf. F. *tactique* (1690 in Furetière).]
†**1.** Of or pertaining to military (or naval) tactics; = TACTICAL *a.* 1. *Obs.*
1604 EDMONDS *Observ. Cæsar's Comm.* II. 129 The maner of our moderne training, or tacticke practise. **1635** DAVENANT *Madagascar* (1638) 5 Men so exact, In Tactick Arts, both to designe and act. **1652** C. B. STAPYLTON *Herodian* 141 Skilfull in both parts of War, Tactick and Stratagematick. **1775** *Chron.* in *Ann. Reg.* 107/2 To..follow the tactick rules of the other European powers. **1831** CAMPBELL *Power Russia* vii, The Russ will woo..All murder's tactic arts.
2. Of or pertaining to arrangement or order.
1811–31 BENTHAM *Logic* Wks. 1843 VIII. 218/2 In the works of Aristotle..the tactic was scarcely considered in any other light than that of an instrument employed in carrying on the disputatious branch. **1871** SIR W. THOMSON in *Daily News* 3 May, Visible or invisible..according to circumstances, not only of density, degree of illumination, and nearness, but also of tactic arrangement, as of a flock of birds. **1909** J. W. JENKINSON *Experim. Embryol.* 272 Herbst classifies organic reactions to stimuli as either directive or formative. The former are..tactic when the response is some locomotion of a freer body.
3. *Linguistics.* Of or pertaining to taxemes, their arrangement or order. Cf. TACTICS 3.
1933 L. BLOOMFIELD *Language* x. 166 Combinations of taxemes, or, quite frequently, single taxemes, occur as conventional grammatical arrangements, *tactic forms.* **1962** E. F. HAYDEN et al. *Resonance Theory for Linguistics* iii. 24 Like beads on a string, each entity in phonotactics has a distinct Form, since no two beads can occur in the same place on the string. This is the tactic form, i.e. the structural form in the sequence. **1966** S. M. LAMB *Outl. Stratificational Gram.* 5 This process of isolating recurrent partial similarities is the basis of tactic analysis. *Ibid.* 54 Thus the analysis (*un true*) (*ly*) fits the simplest tactic description. *Ibid.* 58 The description of a stratal system is probably most conveniently presented in two parts: the tactic description and the realizational description. **1968** P. M. POSTAL *Aspects Phonol. Theory* viii. 198 There are four distinct strata, each of which is an independent system with its own generative rules (tactic rules)... The four current properly linguistic strata are..the sememic, the lexemic, the morphemic, and the phonemic. It is apparently the function of the tactic rules on a particular stratum X to generate both the class of X-emes and the possible combinations of X-emes. **1969** *Language* XLV. 303 This tactic fact is that..the low vowels /e a o/ can occur only if accompanied by stress; therefore the only unstressed vowels are /i ə u/.

'tactic, *a.*^{2} (*sb.*^{2}) *rare.* [f. L. *tact-*, ppl. stem of *tangĕre* to touch + -IC; in sense 2 akin to TACT 4.]
1. Of, belonging or relating to touch; tactual.
1625 JACKSON *Creed* v. xii. §3 Touch is but an apprehension or feeling of its own tactick qualities being actually moved by other of the same kind. **1886** T. ARNOLD in *Amer. Ann. Deaf & Dumb* Apr. 125 Exercises to increase the tactic sensibility.
†**2.** Of or pertaining to the beating of time: cf. TACT *sb.* 4. ***tactic song*** (absol. *tactic*), a song to keep rowers in time.
1779 FORREST *Voy. N. Guinea* 25, I found Tuan Hadjee in high spirits, cheering up the rowers with a certain Tactic song, to which a man beat time with two brass timbrels. *Ibid.* 303 In rowing..they have always a song as a kind of tactic, and beat on two brass timbrels to keep time.

tactical ('tæktɪkəl), *a.* [f. Gr. τακτικ-ός (see TACTIC *a.*^{1}, *sb.*^{1}) + -AL^1: see -ICAL. (This appears to be the earliest in use of the words of the group.)]
1. a. Of or pertaining to (military or naval) tactics.
tactical point: a point of place of importance in the disposition of forces. ***tactical unit***: see quot. 1879.
1570 DEE *Math. Pref.* a iv b, Stratarithmetrie..differreth from the Feate Tacticall, *De aciebus instruendis*, bycause, there, is necessary the wisedome and foresight, to what purpose he so ordreth the men: and Skillfull hability, also, for any occasion, or purpose, to deuise and vse the aptest and most necessary order, array and figure of his Company and Summe of men. **1706** PHILLIPS, *Tactical*, belonging to Martial Array. **1777** W. DALRYMPLE *Trav. Sp. & Port.* lvi, Military books had been bought up in all languages for the use of this tactical school. **1836** *Fraser's Mag.* XIV. 453 We have actually seen them form a hollow square..with the most perfect tactical accuracy. **1879** *Soldiering* in *Cassell's Techn. Educ.* IV. 320/1 The largest number of men..to whom one man can issue personal orders..called in infantry the 'tactical unit' or unit of manœuvre. **1884** *Mil. Engineering* (ed. 3) I. II. 14 The first and second lines would be taken from the same tactical unit, each battalion having half a battalion in the front line.
b. Applied to aircraft, bombing, etc., employed in direct support of ground forces. Cf. *strategic bomber*, *bombing* s.v. STRATEGIC *a.* 4.
1916 F. W. LANCHESTER *Aircraft in Warfare* vii. 69 The tactical scout or machine for local reconnaissance will require to be furnished..with both offensive and defensive armament. **1922** *Flight* 24 Aug. 488/1 Tactical bombing and 'trench-strafing', etc., in battles in accordance with the plans and under the command of the naval or military officer in charge of the operations. **1941** A. O. POLLARD *Bombers over Reich* xv. 208 Tactical bombing replaces..the long-range attacks on objectives far behind the lines. **1942** *R.A.F. Jrnl.* 3 Oct. (*recto rear cover*), The transition to low wing monoplane trainers and tactical ships of advanced type. **1955** *Bull. Atomic Sci.* May 192/2 One of the pitfalls of the atomic age is the use of words that becloud important meaning, rather than clarify it. Take the words 'tactical' and 'strategic', in defining two kinds of bombing. **1958** *Listener* 11 Sept. 376/2, I believe that the initiation by the West of the use of small tactical bombs on a battlefield in Europe would prove disastrous to NATO forces. **1977** *R.A.F. News* 11–24 May 6 (Advt.), A two-seater all-weather tactical interdictor and attack bomber.
c. Designating nuclear weapons intended for short-range use against an enemy's forces. Opp. STRATEGIC *a.* 2.
1957 [see STRATEGIC *a.* 2]. **1968** *Observer* 31 Mar. 25/1 Consider the weapons that have become operational for the first time in the past 20 years. They include the H-bomb and the so-called 'tactical' A-bombs. **1970** *Toronto Daily Star* 24 Sept. 22/5 It is estimated that about 20 lbs. or so would be sufficient for one atomic bomb in the one kiloton range, a so-called tactical bomb with mainly localized effects. **1976** LD. HOME *Way the Wind Blows* xii. 167 The balance of argument through the years moved towards a substantial conventional force, but it was gradually rendered somewhat academic by the introduction of the tactical nuclear weapon. **1979** N. CALDER *Nuclear Nightmares* ii. 35 This definition is ..not as sharp as the cynic's version: 'A tactical nuclear weapon is one that explodes in Germany.' *Ibid.*, 'Tactical' nuclear weapons can be let off without necessarily signalling a 'strategic', all-out exchange between the Soviet Union and the United States.
2. a. Of or relating to arrangement, esp. the arrangement of procedure with a view to ends.
1876 TAIT *Rec. Adv. Phys. Sc.* xii. (ed. 2) 302 Each in the same tactical order. **1881** *Nation* (N.Y.) XXXII. 367 With an admirable temper and manners..he combines a good deal of tactical craft. **1893** *Times* 26 Apr. 9/4 To arrive at an understanding upon tactical details.
b. Relating to the construction of a sentence. *rare.*
1698 [see TAGHMICAL].
3. Of a person, his actions, etc.: Characterized by skilful tactics; skilful in devising means to ends.
1883 *Manch. Exam.* 26 Nov. 5/3 The address of the French Ambassador was admirably tactical. **1884** *Ibid.* 20 May 5/1 Those who knew M. Ferry as a practical and tactical statesman. **1899** SIR W. LAWSON in *Daily Chron.* 7 Feb. 4/7 All that we want is..an able, an honest, a tactical leader.
4. *Math.* Of or pertaining to TACTIC (sense 3): opposed to LOGISTICAL.
1864 CAYLEY *Math. Papers* V. 293 A tactical operation is one relating to the arrangement in any manner of a set of things.
Hence **'tactically** *adv.*, in a tactical manner; in reference to tactics.
1871 *Standard* 23 Jan., The Prussians..seem to have out-manœuvred the French both strategically and tactically. **1890** W. STEBBING *Peterborough* ix. 176 The obstinately brave and tactically skilful but uninspired Huguenot [Earl of Galway].

tactician (tæk'tɪʃən). [f. as TACTIC *sb.*^{1} + -IAN. So mod.F. *tacticien* (1812 in Hatz.-Darm.).] One versed or skilled in the science or art of tactics.
1798 LD. AUCKLAND *Corr.* (1862) III. 386 An armed nation, composed, perhaps, of ignorant tacticians, but steady and brave. **1838** *Sparks' Biog.* IX. *Steuben* 23 Trained under so expert a tactician as the great Frederic. **1877** GREEN *Hist. Eng. People* I. 426 Edward..had shewn himself as consummate a strategist in the campaign as a tactician in the field.
transf. **1842** MIALL in *Nonconf.* II. 505 The lubricity of the clever tactician. **1880** 'OUIDA' *Moths* I. 143 She was a clever tactician.
Hence **tac'ticianize** *v. nonce-wd.*, to play the tactician; **tac'titionary** *a.*, **tac'titionist** (bad formations, confusing *-ician* with *-ition*).
1868 *Guardian* 12 Aug. 905 He does not tacticianize morning, noon, and night. **1881** *Philad.* (U.S.) *Record* No. 3467. 2 Mr. Wheeler has never been a tactitionist in his party. **1890** SIR J. FERGUSON in *Standard* 1 May 2/2 But that [legislation] was altogether artificial and tactitionary. **1890** *Sat. Rev.* 3 May 519/2 The possibly useful, but not blessed, word 'tactitionary'.

tacticity (tæk'tɪsɪtɪ). *Chem.* [f. TACTIC *a.*^{1} + -ITY.] The stereochemical arrangement of the units in the main chain of a polymer.
1959 NATTA & DANUSSO in *Jrnl. Polymer Sci.* XXXIV. 4 The rule, or *taxis*, which characterizes an arrangement partially or completely ordered, or tacticity, may be simple or composed by few simple rules. **1967** MARGERISON & EAST *Introd. Polymer Chem.* ii. 63 The tacticity of the chain. **1975** *Nature* 24 Apr. 696/1 Fibrocytes react to some microarchitectural or 'tacticity' difference between homologous copolymeric substrata.

tactics ('tæktɪks). [pl. of TACTIC *sb.*^{1}, rendering mod.L. (17th c.) *tactica* pl., Gr. τὰ τακτικά, lit. 'matters pertaining to arrangement': see -IC^2.]
1. a. The art or science of deploying military or naval forces in order of battle, and of performing warlike evolutions and manœuvres.
As an art or science often construed as *sing.*; as carried out in practice usually as *pl.*
1626 GOUGE *Serm. Dignity Chivalry* §4 Martiall discipline, Artillery tacticks, and Military trainings are matters of moment. **1646** SIR T. BROWNE *Pseud. Ep.* 31 Claudius Ælianus..flourished not long after in the raigne of Trajan, unto whom he dedicated his Tacticks. **1710** J. HARRIS *Lex. Techn.* II, *Tacticks*, is the Art of Disposing any Number of Men into a proper form of Battle. **1782** V. KNOX *Ess.* I. xix. 94 Tactics and fortification..must be studied, as essentially necessary to the military and naval officer. **1853** J. H. NEWMAN *Hist. Sk.* (1873) II. I. iv. 190 Their tactics by sea was a sort of land engagement on deck. **1876** FREEMAN *Norm. Conq.* V. xxiii. 265 At Tinchebrai, though the chiefs are Norman, the tactics are English.
b. *transf.* and *fig.*

1763 SIR W. JONES *Caissa* Wks. 1799 VI. 502 The chief art in the Tacticks of Chess consists in the nice conduct of the royal pawns. **1842** MIALL in *Nonconf.* II. 305 We have seen principle strangled by tactics so often. **1856** EMERSON *Eng. Traits* v. 83 In parliament, the tactics of the Opposition is to resist every step of the Government by a pitiless attack.

†**2.** Arrangement, disposition. *Obs. rare*$^{-1}$.

1650 FULLER *Pisgah* 392 So strange a posture, that scarcely either Jewish or Christian Tacticks of Temple-implements, will admit thereof.

3. *Linguistics.* C. F. Hockett's term for the study of the relation and arrangement of linguistic units, esp. the study of the arrangement of morphemes.

1947 C. F. HOCKETT in *Language* XXIII. 274 We should therefore expect to find the following topics treated in his book..; (4) tactics—stating the arrangements of morphemes... This term seems simpler than 'taxemics' or 'tagmemics' which one might derive more directly from Bloomfield's labels. **1953** F. G. LOUNSBURY in *Yale Univ. Publ. in Anthropol.* XLVIII. 18 Statements describing the occurrences of morphemes constitute the portion of a grammar called *tactics*... Tactics is not concerned with the phonemic forms of morphemes, whether they are constant or variable. **1966** S. M. LAMB *Outl. Stratification Gram.* 1 Each of these systems has its own syntax or tactics, so that a linguistic structure as a whole has a series of tactic components rather than just one.

tactile ('tæktɪl, -aɪl), *a.* [ad. L. *tactilis* tangible, f. *tact-*, ppl. stem of *tangĕre* to touch; cf. F. *tactile.*]

1. Perceptible to the touch; tangible.

1615 H. CROOKE *Body of Man* 717 Beside the Sapour it hath also many Tangible or Tactile qualities. **1706** PHILLIPS (ed. 6) s.v., The chief Tactile Qualities are Heat, Cold, Driness, Moistness, and Hardness. **1898** *Allbutt's Syst. Med.* V. 789 Certain visible and tactile signs.

2. a. Of or pertaining to touch; characterized or influenced by, or relating to the sense of touch. Hence *absol.* as *sb.*, one for whom the sense of touch predominates over the other senses.

1657–83 EVELYN *Hist. Relig.* (1850) I. 34 The tactile, auditory, and olfactory senses. **1855** BAIN *Senses & Int.* II. ii. §2 (1864) 155 That high tactile sensibility distinguishing the tip of the tongue. **1874** CARPENTER *Ment. Phys.* I. i. §10 (1879) 11 Our own Tactile Sense (under which general head may be combined the Sense of Touch, the Sense of Muscular Exertion, and the Mental Sense of Effort). **1876** FOSTER *Phys.* III. iv. (1879) 532 The tactile sensation is..a symbol to us of some external event. **1892** [see MOTILE *a.*]. **1899** *Allbutt's Syst. Med.* VII. 299 Tactile anæsthesia over ..the whole of the left side. **1917** [see AUDILE *sb.*]. **1956** [see AUDILE *a.*]. **1971** A. MONTAGU *Touching* v. 169 Children who are highly tactile but have no accompanying sexual interest in others.

b. Of organs: Endowed with the sense of touch.

1768 TUCKER *Lt. Nat.* (1834) I. 388 The gustatory papillæ of the tongue and tactile papillæ of the fingers. **1859** DARWIN *Orig. Spec.* vii. (1878) 172 The external ears of the common mouse..no doubt serve as tactile organs. **1873** A. FLINT *Nerv. Syst.* i. 39 The name tactile corpuscles implies that these bodies are connected with the sense of touch.

c. *Art. tactile value*: B. Berenson's term for the illusion of tangibility which a painter can create with regard to the figures and objects he represents; the attribute or impression of a tangible quality. Also *transf.*

1896 B. BERENSON *Florentine Painters of the Renaissance* ii. 4 Every time our eyes recognise reality we are..giving tactile values to retinal impressions. **1907** —— *North Italian Painters of Renaissance* 146 In figure painting, the type of all painting, I have endeavoured to set forth that the principal ..sources of life-enhancement are *tactile values, movement,* and *space composition*, by which I mean ideated sensation. **1908** E. M. FORSTER *Room with View* ii. 22 The traveller who has gone to Italy to study the tactile values of Giotto, or the corruption of the Papacy. **1919** A. N. WHITEHEAD *Princ. Nat. Knowl.* 88 This property of 'conveying' an object..is already well-known in the theory of art-criticism, as is evidenced in such phrases as 'tactile-values'. **1938** R. G. COLLINGWOOD *Princ. Art* vii. 146 Mr. Berenson..taught his pupils..to look in paintings for what he called 'tactile values'. **1962** *Listener* 15 Nov. 832/1 It [*sc.* a play] is remarkable because of what one might call, after Berenson, its tactile values. **1970** *Oxf. Compan. Art* 1120/1 Berenson was notoriously incapable of appreciating those schools of modern—and ancient—art which subordinate tactile values to other qualities of pictorial design.

d. *Comb.*, as ***tactile-visual*** adj.

1969 *New Scientist* 27 Mar. 678/1 A tactile-visual system ..should provide valuable information concerning such psychological questions as the nature of sensory processing. **1978** *Verbatim* May 16/1 My point is that the oral-aural mode is intricately combined with the tactile-visual mode.

Hence **'tactilely** *adv.*

1953 A. C. KINSEY et al. *Sexual Behavior Human Female* xiv. 578 Some areas which are tactilely sensitive..are of no especial importance as sources of erotic response. **1977** *Verbatim* Feb. 8/1 It takes some talent and not much money to design and manufacture a book artistically, one that provides as much aestheic pleasure visually and tactilely as it does in its reading.

tactility (tæk'tɪlɪtɪ). [f. after L. type **tactilitās*, f. *tactilis* TACTILE: see -ITY.] The quality or condition of being tactile.

1659 STANLEY *Hist. Philos.* XIII. (1701) 565/2 There are others [qualities] which depend upon these; as Flexility, Tactility, Ductility, and others, from Softness. **1727** BAILEY vol. II, *Tactility*, capableness of being touched. **1899** *Allbutt's Syst. Med.* VIII. 169 Contrast the commonest seat of pain in subjective tactility.

b. Sensitiveness, touchiness. *nonce-use.*

1831 SYD. SMITH *Mem. & Lett.* cccxxi. (1855) II. 331 You have a little infirmity,—tactility, or touchiness.

tactily ('tæktɪlɪ), *adv.* [Irreg. f. TACT + -LY[2].] = TACTFULLY *adv.*

1895 G. MEREDITH *Amazing Marriage* I. iv. 37 She had to warn her brother to preserve his balance. He tactily did so, aware of the necessity. **1929** M. LOWRY *Let.* 13 Mar. (1967) 5 The bewildered parent..would be willing to pay you 5 or 6 guineas a week (I should say six personally, but tactily) if you would tolerate me for any period..as a member of your household.

,tactin'variant. *Math.* [f. L. *tact-us* touch + INVARIANT.] (See quots.)

1856 CAYLEY *Math. Papers* II. 320 The function which, equated to zero, expresses the result of the elimination is an invariant which (from its geometrical signification) might be termed the Tactinvariant of the two quantics. **1873** SALMON *Higher Plane Curves* iii. (1879) 80 The condition that two curves U, V, should touch (which condition is called their tact-invariant).

taction ('tækʃən). [ad. L. *tactiōn-em*, n. of action from *tangĕre* to touch. Cf. F. *taction* (17th c.).] The action of touching; contact.

1623 COCKERAM, *Taction*, a touching. **1668** *Phil. Trans.* III. 689 The First Part of it handles the Taction of Circles. **1726** SWIFT *Gulliver* III. ii, They neither can speak nor attend to the discourses of others, without being roused by some external taction upon the organs of speech and hearing. **1866** SHUCKARD *Brit. Bees* 346 It is possibly from some taction of this instrument that she discerns the sizes of the eggs.

†**tactism** ('tæktɪz(ə)m). *Biol. Obs.* [f. L. *tact-*, stem of *tangĕre* to touch + -ISM.] The motile response of a living organism to an external stimulus.

1902 *Fortn. Rev.* June 1013 By his revelations of the *rôle* of the 'trophisms' and 'tactisms' Dr. Loeb drove boldly into the domain of mental phenomena. **1912** A. TRIDON tr. *Delage & Goldsmith's Theories Evol.* 164 Others..attribute differentiation to the influence of the various tropisms and tactisms.

†**'tactive,** *a. Obs. rare.* [ad. L. type **tactīvus*, f. *tact-*, ppl. stem (see TACT and -IVE).] Of or characterized by touching; = TACTILE *a.* 2.

1634 T. JOHNSON *Parey's Chirurg.* I. x. (1678) 15 That [Spirit] which is carried to the instruments of Touching, as termed the Tactive. **1644** BULWER *Chirol.* 171 Although this touching vertue or tactive quality be diffused through the whole body within and without.

tactless ('tæktlɪs), *a.* [f. TACT + -LESS.] Destitute of tact; awkward.

1847 in WEBSTER. **1875** *Fam. Herald* 17 July 181/2 'But..' laughed Doris, quickly answering this tactless speech. **1886** M. MOORSOM *Thirteen all Told* 26 A glance of warning, which he was too dull and tactless to take.

Hence **'tactlessly** *adv.*, **'tactlessness.**

1893 *Academy* 21 Oct. 333/3 Severe and just, but somewhat tactlessly contrived, measures against the Jewish usurers. **1882** BERESF. HOPE *Brandreths* III. xxxviii. 73, I should not have to blame my own tactlessness for the result.

tactoid ('tæktɔɪd). *Physical Chem.* Also †**taktoid.** [a. G. *taktoid* (Zocher & Jacobsohn 1929, in *Kolloidchem. Beihefte* XXVIII. 167), f. Gr. τακτ-ός ordered (see TACTIC *a.*[1]): see -OID.] A small anistropic, birefringent region in a dilute, isotropic sol, consisting of an aggregate of rod-like particles or macromolecules aligned parallel to one another.

1929 *Chem. Abstr.* XXIII. 2868 In these taktosols..the individual microscopic particles are called taktoids. **1939** *Nature* 14 Jan. 82/1 The formation of tactoids from thixotropic sols,..and the crystallization of proteins are regarded as being typical of unipolar coacervation. **1952** J. T. G. OVERBEEK in H. R. Kruyt *Colloid Sci.* I. viii. 327 The concentrated phase in the tactoids still contains a great deal of dispersion medium which implies that the particles are comparatively far apart. **1953** S. E. LURIA *Gen. Virol.* v. 94 In the liquid phase, the rod-shaped [virus] particles orient themselves sidewise into 'tactoids' which then settle into the liquid crystalline phase. **1978** *Nature* 14 Dec. 666/3 Minton has applied fundamental models for the entropically driven formation of tactoids from long rod-like molecules or particles to the haemoglobin S system.

So **'tactosol** [ad. G. *taktosol* (Zocher & Jacobsohn, *loc. cit.*)], a sol containing tactoids.

1929 [see TACTOID]. **1959** *Lancet* 3 Oct. 513/1 Tactosols are colloidal solutions containing non-spherical particles ('tactoids') which are capable of orienting themselves.

tactor ('tæktə(r)). [a. L. *tactor*, agent-n. from *tangĕre* to touch.] A feeler; an organ of touch.

1817 KIRBY & SP. *Entomol.* xxiii. (1818) II. 312 Some woodlice..use them as tactors, touching the surface on each side with them, as they go along. **1835** KIRBY *Hab. & Inst. Anim.* II. xvii. 113 Cuvier regards them [barbs of some fishes] as a kind of tactors.

tactual ('tæktjuːəl), *a.* [f. L. *tactu-s* touch + -AL[1]: cf. *visual.*] Of or pertaining to touch; of the nature of or due to touch.

1642 H. MORE *Song Soul* II. III. I. xxi, Her sight is tactuall, The sunne and all the starres that do appear She feels them in herself. **1678** CUDWORTH *Intell. Syst.* I. iv. §36. 549 A kind of Tactual Union..with the Centre of the Universe. **1833** CARLYLE *Misc. Ess., Cagiostro* (1872) V. 68 Thy existence is wholly an Illusion and optical and tactual Phantasm. **1871** TYNDALL *Fragm. Sc.* (1879) II. ix. 185 In the lowest organisms we have a kind of tactual sense diffused over the entire body.

Hence **tactu'ality**, tactual quality; **'tactually** *adv.*, in a tactual manner or way.

1858 W. R. PIRIE *Inq. Hum. Mind* vii. 398 It is not improbable that we have even a sense of tactuality, if we may so speak, in the secondary sensations. **1855** H. SPENCER *Psychol.* (1872) I. III. vi. 332 When the combined appliances of touch and muscular sense are fully developed..an immense variety of textures can be known tactually.

†**'tacture.** *Obs.* [ad. L. type **tactūra*, f. *tact-*, ppl. stem of *tangĕre* to touch: see -URE.] Touch, taction, contact.

1597 A. M. tr. *Guillemeau's Fr. Chirurg.* 9 b/1 Yet..with the tacture, or the eyes, we can not espye the fissure or rente. **1650** T. BAYLY *Herba Parietis* 122 Berontus tooke his Amarissa by the hand, whose sprightly behaviour answered the tacture, with like affection. **1727** EARBERY tr. *Burnet's St. Dead* I. 15 The Soul has no Manner of Action either in itself or externally, by Tacture or Impulse, but what proceeds from the force of Thinking.

†**tac'turiency.** *Obs. nonce-wd.* [f. L. type **tactūrīre*, desiderative vb. f. *tangĕre, tact-*, to touch + -ENCY.] The desire of touching.

1652 URQUHART *Jewel* Wks. (1834) 236 The visuriency of either, by ushering the tacturiency of both, made the attrectation of both consequent to the inspection of either.

‖**tactus** ('tæktəs). *Mus.* [L.: see TACT.] = TACT 4.

1740 J. GRASSINEAU *Mus. Dict.* 130 *Metron*, Tactus, Mensura, Battuta,—the beating or measuring the time by a motion of the hand or foot. **1786** BUSBY *Compl. Dict. Mus.* s.v. *Tactus*, ..when the time consisted of a breve in a bar, the time-stroke was called *Tactus-Major*; and when of a semibreve in a bar, *Tactus-Minor*. **1959** *Collins Mus. Encycl.* 644/1 A term used for 'beat' by the theorists of the 15th and 16th cent... The semibreve was the normal *tactus* in the 15th cent.; in the course of the 16th cent. the minim became the normal... With the introduction of bar-lines the semibreve became the unit of a bar and the measuring *tactus* was replaced by the metrical beat. **1980** *Early Music* July 310/2 To sing the passage to a tactus, however, is to miss its *raisson d'être* and obliterate the most vital element of the madrigal's expressive scheme.

tacuba, var. TACOUBA.

Tacully, var. TAKULLI.

tad (tæd). *colloq.* (orig. and chiefly *N. Amer.*) [Orig. uncertain; perh. f. TADPOLE[1].]

†**1.** (See quots.) *Obs.*

1845 in C. Cist *Cincinnati Misc.* I. 240 Among a certain class in the eastern cities,..the word *Tad*, is applied to one who don't nor won't pay. **1851** B. H. HALL *College Words* 297 At Centre College, Ky., there is a society..composed of the very best fellows of the College, calling themselves Tads. **1890** E. B. CUSTER *Following Guidon* 213 These youths [*sc.* graduates from West Point] were called 'tads' and 'plebes'.

2. A young or small child, esp. a boy. Occas. used *joc.* of old men.

1877 BARTLETT *Dict. Amer.* (ed. 4) 688 Tads, *little tads*, small boys. *Old tads*, graybeards, old men. **1896** ADE *Artie* xi. 98 Oh, he's a great old tad. **1901** F. NORRIS *Octopus* I. v. 197 There's a little tad that was just born to be a lady. **1904** W. D. NESBIT *Trail to Boyland* 49 That handle has been broken since he was just a tad. **1928** S. LEWIS *Man who knew Coolidge* I. 55 One of the bell-boys at the hotel, cute little tad, knew the town like a book. **1935** H. DAVIS *Honey in Horn* xxii. 370 I've handled more horses than this tad ever heard of. **1949** O. NASH *Versus* 131 The sea lion loves a loveable lad, An urchin, a gamin, a tyke, a tad. **1974** W. GARNER *Big Enough Wreath* vii. 93 Nowadays young tads think they know it all. **1983** *Sunday Times* 3 Apr. 33/2 The nuns picked me out when I was still a tad, groomed me for a scholarship.

3. A small amount; freq. used *advb.* in the expression ***a tad***, a little, slightly.

1940 *Amer. Speech* XV. 448/1 *Tad*, a very small amount. 'I want to borrow a tad of salt.' **1969** L. MICHAELS *Going Places* 159, I tried to smile. 'You come back later, baby. I'm a tad indisposed.' **1976** *Time* 27 Sept. 39/2 'Pull 'er up a tad, please, mister,' said the nonchalant teen-ager pumping gas. **1977** *Time* 14 Mar. 28/3 White House watchers also think they can glimpse a tad of arrogance showing through the good ole boy pose. **1977** *Globe & Mail* (Toronto) 15 Dec. 8/2 Things are a tad hectic. **1979** D. ANTHONY *Long Hard Cure* xv. 116 Why don't we sit here on the veranda? There's a tad of breeze. **1980** *N.Y. Times* 12 Aug. A18/1 The Mayor's pitch is a tad exaggerated both on the law's certainty and on the roominess of New York's prisons.

tadcheese, tadde, tade: see TOAD.

taddy ('tædɪ). *Sc.* Also Taddy. The name of *Taddy* and Co., of London, used *attrib.* and *absol.* to designate snuff manufactured by them. Also *Comb.*, as **taddy-box**, a snuff-box.

1869 A. MACDONALD *Love, Law & Theology* viii. 118 Tapping his box, and inhaling a large pinch of his favourite Taddy. **1870** J. NICHOLSON *Idylls* 46 Some tea to the auld folk, tobacco or taddy. **1872** 'R. F. BARDINARUS' *Arn at Flail* 9 But John took up the Taddy pouder. **1881** R. FORD *Humorous Sc. Readings* 67 Three or four heapit ladlefu's o' London taddy. **1897** J. WRIGHT *Scenes Sc. Life* 5 Irish blackguard and taddy snuff mixed. **1907** N. MUNRO *Daft Days* xxxiv. 278 The Provost, who had just stepped into P. & A's for his Sunday sweeties, smiled tolerantly and passed his taddy-box. **1939** J. M. DALLAS *Toakburn* 11 He got his best 'sneeshin'' from Johnnie Bickles, who kept the genuine 'taddy'.

taddy, tadee, tadie, obs. forms of TODDY.

Tadjik, Tadzhik, varr. TAJIK.

tadpole[1] ('tædpəʊl). Also 5 **taddepol, tadpolle,** 6 **tadpal,** 7 **tod-, toad-pole, toad-poll.** [f. ME. *tāde, tadde,* TOAD + (app.) POLL *sb.*[1], head, roundhead. The latter element has been questioned, on the ground of the apparent inappropriateness of the name 'toad-head'; but cf. the dialectal synonym *pollhead* or *polehead* (in Sc. and north. Eng. *powheid*), app. = head-head.]

1. The larva of a frog, toad, or other batrachian, from the time it leaves the egg until it loses its gills and tail. Chiefly applied in the early stage when the animal appears to consist simply of a round head with a tail.

14.. *Voc.* in Wr.-Wülcker 569/7 *Brucus,* a taddepol. *c* **1475** *Pict. Voc.* ibid. 766/20 *Hic lumbricus,* a tadpolle. **1519** HORMAN *Vulg.* 277b, This water is full of tadpollys. **1598** SYLVESTER *Du Bartas* II. ii. III. *Colonies* 411 After a sweltring Day, some sultry showr Doth in the Marshes heaps of Tadpals pour. **1605** SHAKS. *Lear* III. iv. 135 Poore Tom, that eates the swimming Frog, the Toad, the Todpole. **1681** HICKERINGILL *Char. Sham-Plotter* Wks. 1716 I. 212 A Sham-Plotter.. is the Spawn of a Papist, as a Toad-Poll of a Toad. **1774** GOLDSM. *Nat. Hist.* IV. 47 The egg, or little black globe which produces the tadpole. **1886** RUSKIN *Præterita* I. ix, 293 Without so much water anywhere as.. a tadpole could wag his tail in.

b. *transf.* and *fig.* (In quot. 1588, a black infant.)

1588 SHAKS. *Tit. A.* IV. ii. 85 Ile broach the tadpole on my Rapiers poynt, Nurse giue it me, my sword shall soone dispatch it. **1881** *Macm. Mag.* XLIV. 475 Such pale tadpoles,.. with listless ways, and few games.

2. Sometimes applied to the tailed larva of a tunicate, the swimming tail of which is afterwards dropped or absorbed.

1880 E. R. LANKESTER *Degeneration* 42 The egg of *Phallusia* gives rise to a tadpole. **1909** W. HATCHETT JACKSON *Let. to Editor,* The ascidian or tunicate tadpole.

3. A local name in U.S. of a water-fowl, the Hooded Merganser, *Lophodytes cucullatus,* apparently from the size of its head, or from the patch of white on its crest.

1891 in *Cent. Dict.*

4. *attrib.* and *Comb.*, as ***tadpole form, state,*** etc.; ***tadpole-like*** adj.; **tadpole fish, -hake,** a ganoid fish of the North Atlantic, *Raniceps raninus.*

1682 DRYDEN *Medal* 304 Frogs and Toads and all the Tadpole Train. **1682** S. PORDAGE *Medal Rev.* 30 The Tadpole-Priests, Shall lift above the Lords, their Priestly Crests. **1768** G. WHITE *Selborne* xvii, Frogs are as yet in their tadpole state. **1832** JOHNSTON in *Proc. Berw. Nat. Club* I. No. I. 7 Of the tadpole fish [*Raniceps trifurcatus,* Flem.], I had the pleasure of exhibiting to you a living specimen. **1847** CARPENTER *Zool.* §980 The young animal [ascidian] has .. a large tadpole-like tail. **1856** GOSSE *Marine Zool.* II. 27 At first it has a tadpole-like form.

Hence (chiefly *nonce-wds.*) **'tadpoledom, 'tadpolehood, 'tadpolism,** the state of being a tadpole; also *fig.*; **'tadpole,ward** *adv.* [see -WARD].

1863 KINGSLEY *Let.* 29 May, in *Life* (1879) II. 157 Little beggars an inch long, fresh from water and *tadpoledom. **1891** C. L. MORGAN *Anim. Sk.* 222 Little Froggies which have just emerged from *tadpole-hood. **1897** G. C. BATEMAN *Vivarium* 296 Many of the Batrachians, during a portion of their tadpolehood, are vegetable feeders. **1897** *Voice* (N.Y.) 8 Apr. 3/1 Degeneration is involution through self *tadpoleward. **1883** BARING-GOULD *J. Herring* III. lix. 293 All previous existence would be *tadpolism.

Tadpole[2]. In *Tadpole and Taper,* names of two political schemers in Disraeli's *Coningsby*; hence allusively, in the sense 'professional politicians, the hacks of a political party'. Hence ***Tadpole and Taperism.***

[**1844** DISRAELI *Coningsby* II. ii, Mr. Tadpole and Mr. Taper were also there; they too had lost their seats since 1832; but being men of business, and accustomed from early life to look about them, they had already commenced the combinations which.. were to bear them back to the assembly where they were so missed.] **1885** *Manch. Exam.* 3 June 5/4 The tadpoles and the tapers of the party demand a cry. **1904** A. BIRRELL in *Contemp. Rev.* Apr. 475 A book further removed from such Tadpole and Taperism is not in the library. **1905** W. CHURCHILL in *Daily Chron.* 13 May 5/6 The Cabinet was packed with nonentities, Tadpoles and Tapers from the Whips' room. **1908** F. HARRISON in *Trans. Roy. Hist. Soc.* Ser. III. III. 45 The reasons why he [Chatham] would never take office again [etc.].. all this has greatly exercised the Tadpoles and Tapers of his age and of our own.

tae, tae'd, Sc. forms of TOE *sb.*, toed.

tae, in *the tae,* Sc. dial. f. TO *adj.* in *the to* = the one, TONE; mod.Sc. dial. form of TO *prep.*

tædium, obs. form of TEDIUM.

‖**tædium vitæ** ('tiːdɪəm 'vaɪtiː, 'viːtaɪ). Also **tedium vitæ.** [L.: cf. TEDIUM.] Weariness of life; extreme ennui or inertia, sometimes regarded as a pathological state.

[**1618** J. CHAMBERLAIN *Let.* 14 Oct. (1939) II. 170 The Lord Clifton.. tooke his paterne from your Secretarie of Utrecht to stab and mangle himself with a penknife.. without any other shew of reason or cause, but even *vitæ tædio* (as he saide himself).] **1759** E. YOUNG *Conjectures on Original Composition* 8 Both These are happy in *this,* that by fixing their attention on objects most important, they escape numberless little anxieties, and that Taedium Vitae which often hangs so heavy on its evening hours. **1796** T. JEFFERSON *Let.* 24 Apr. (1926) 86 My health has suddenly broken down, with symptons which give me to believe I shall not have much to encounter of the *taedium vitae.* **1803** S. OWENSON *St. Clair* xxi. 89 The dreadful oppression of the *tedium vitae.* **1826** *Reg. Deb. Congress U.S.* 30 Mar. 402 *Tedium vitæ* appears in Sunday Schools. **1855** *Newsp. & Gen. Reader's Compan.* 156 That *taedium vitae,* which springs from a consciousness of talents abused and opportunities lost. **1883** T. S. CLOUSTON *Clin. Lect. Mental Dis.* xvii. 560 A cloud of vague depression rests on the man, who shuns society, falls off in fat, becomes restless and hypochondriacal, and feels strongly the *tedium vitæ.* **1891** O. WILDE *Pict. Dorian Gray* xi. 216 That ennui, that terrible *tædium vitæ,* that comes on those to whom life denies nothing. **1920** J. HUNEKER *Painted Veils* vi. 251 Her languour had not been dissipated; 'tædium vitæ', the doctor named it. **1940** 'G. ORWELL' *Inside Whale* 159 Everyone with a safe £500 a year.. began training himself in *taedium vitae.* **1958** L. DURRELL *Mountolive* ix. 187 Even these simple motions of joining with the ordinary world of social habit and pleasure, of relieving the *taedium vitae* of his isolation, were all infected by the new knowledge. **1977** V. S. PRITCHETT *Gentle Barbarian* xii. 201 He.. is suddenly attacked by the *taedium vitae,* the disgust with life, as a man who talks too well may easily be.

‖**tae kwon do** (teː kwɒn doː; teɪ-, taɪ 'kwɒndəʊ). Also **Tae Kwon Do, taekwondo,** etc. [Korean: see quot. 1967.] A Korean system of unarmed combat resembling karate.

1967 *Karate & Oriental Arts* Sept./Oct. 2 Taekwondo, which is just starting in this country.. will be open to the same abuse as karate. *Ibid.* 27/1 Breaking the word Taekwondo down into its three parts we get: Tae—kick, Kwon—fist, Do—art, way, method. **1969** *Melbourne Truth* 12 July 9/4 Rozinsky gained his Black Belt in Tae Kwon Do at the Jidokwan, Seoul, South Korea. **1972** *Sunday Times* (Kuala Lumpur) 18 June 16/7 To unwind and also to keep fit, he sweats it out at tae-kwon-do classes. **1972** C. WESTON *Poor, Poor Ophelia* (1973) xvi. 94 The newcomers to whom Tae Kwon Do seemed an impossible skill. **1976** *Eastern Even. News* (Norwich) 9 Dec. 2/6 Teakwondo (Korean karate) training, Duke Street Centre. **1979** *Sci. Amer.* Apr. 110/1 Karate is just one of a wide variety of martial arts that have evolved in the Orient, including tae kwon do, kempo and kung fu.

tael (teɪl). Also 7 **taile, tayel, tayl,** 7–9 **tale,** 8 **tahel,** 20 **tahil;** 7 **tay, taye,** *pl.* 6 **taes.** [a. Pg. *tael* (pl. *taeis*), ad. Malay *tahil, tail* weight. The early *tay, taes,* etc. represent the Pg. plural.]

1. The trade name for the Chinese *liang* or 'ounce', a weight used in China and the East.

In Chinese use the *liang* varies according to local custom, and to the commodity weighed; but the weight of $1\frac{1}{3}$ oz. avoirdupois is fixed by treaty for commercial purposes.

1598 W. PHILIP *Linschoten* 44 A Tael is a full ounce and a halfe Portingale weight. **1613** J. SARIS *Voy. to Japan* (1900) 222 Bezar stones are there bought by the Taile.. which is one Ounce, and the third part English. **1699** DAMPIER *Voy.* II. I. 132, 5 Tale make a Bancal, a weight so called. **1854** in R. Tomes *Amer. in Japan* (1857) 410 The Japanese have a decimal system of weight, like the Chinese, of catty, tael, mace, candareen, and cash, by which articles in general are weighed; but gold and silver are not reckoned above taels. **1902** *Encycl. Brit.* XXXIII. 813/1 Tahil.. Straits Settlements $1\frac{1}{3}$ oz. av. = 10 chee = 100 hoon. **1908** MORSE *Trade Chinese Emp.* 149 It is necessary always to bear in mind the distinction between the tael of value and the tael of weight. **1947** R. O. WINSTEDT *Malays* vi. 112 Soon after the founding of Malacca Chinese annals under 1416 record.. that, 'tin.. is cast into small blocks weighing 1 *kati* 8 *tahil* or 1 *kati* 4 *tahil* official weight... They use these pieces of tin instead of money.' **1972** *Straits Times* 25 Nov. 15/1 The gold bars, weighing 15 katis seven tahils.

2. a. Hence, A money of account, originally a tael (in weight) of standard silver, the value of which fluctuates with the price of the metal.

The ***Haikwan tael,*** i.e. the tael accepted by the Chinese Foreign Custom-house in payment of duties, is the equivalent of 584·85 grains of pure silver (Morse 152). From 1745 to 1860 its value was between 6*s.* and 7*s.*, in 1864 6*s.* 8*d.*, in 1900 about 3*s.*, in 1904 2*s.* 10*d.*

1588 PARKE tr. *Mendoza's Hist. China* III. iv. 61 They giue him foure million.. Taes. **1598** J. DAVIS *Voy.* (Hakl. Soc.) 152 Foure Masses makes a Perdaw. Foure Perdawes makes a Tayel. **1613** J. SARIS *Voy. to Japan* (1900) 97 Bantam Pepper.. was worth here [Japan] at our comming tenne Tayes the Peecull... A Taye is five shillings sterling with them. **1726** SHELVOCKE *Voy. round World* 457 They demanded 6000 Tahel. **1745** P. THOMAS *Jrnl. Anson's Voy.* 215 Taëls, each of which in our Money comes to about six Shillings and Threepence. **1800** *Chron.* in *Asiat. Ann. Reg.* 62/2 His wealth, which.. is said to have amounted at the lowest computation, to eighty millions of tales, near twenty-seven millions of pounds sterling. **1901** *Empire Rev.* I. 394 The land tax is levied upon the cultivable land, and may be put at half a tael or 1*s.* 6*d.* per acre. **1908** MORSE *Trade Chinese Emp.* 151 The Haikwan tael.. is a purely fictitious and non-existent currency... At no Custom House does any merchant tender Haikwan taels in payment of duties.

b. A Chinese gold coin based on the value of a tael of silver.

1926 E. KANN *Currency China* I. i. 13 Taiping tael gold coin... During the rule of the T'aipings in Nankin a gold coin was issued there.. supposed to represent 25 taels of silver. **1962** R. A. G. CARSON *Coins* 543 A rare tael in gold was also struck in this issue. **1979** *Courier-Mail* (Brisbane) 9 July 4/3 Some Chinese had sufficient savings tucked away in gold taels, the traditional, and sensible, way of saving adopted by many East Asian societies, to bribe officials or simply to pay for the right to escape.

ta'en, contr. f. *taken,* pa. pple. of TAKE *v.*

‖**tænia, tenia** ('tiːnɪə). Pl. **-æ, -as.** [L. *tænia,* a. Gr. ταινία a band, fillet, ribbon.]

1. *Archæol.* A headband, ribbon, or fillet.

1850 LEITCH tr. *C. O. Müller's Anc. Art* §340 (ed. 2) 406 The twisted fillet of the athletes and of Hercules consists of several tæniæ of different colours. **1857** BIRCH *Anc. Pottery* (1858) I. 412 A wreath or branch, which is exchanged on the later vases for the *tainia* or fillet.

2. *Arch.* In the Doric order, A band separating the architrave from the frieze. (So in Vitruvius.)

1563 SHUTE *Archit.* Cj b, The Architraue.. ye shal deuide into 6. parts wherof Tenia, to be the sixte part. **1704** J. HARRIS *Lex. Techn.* I, *Tænia*.. is a Member of the Dorick Capital, which resembles the Shape of a square Fillet. **1817–48** RICKMAN *Archit.* (ed. 5) 32 The fillet of the tenia of the architrave is very nearly as large as the ogee under it.

3. *Surg.* A long narrow ribbon used as a ligature.

1882 in OGILVIE (Annandale).

4. *Anat.* A ribbon-like structure; applied *esp.* to the bands of white nervous matter in the brain and the longitudinal muscles of the colon.

1882 OGILVIE (Annandale), *Tænia hippocampi,* in anat. the plaited edges of the processes of the fornix. **1890** BILLINGS *Med. Dict., Tænia,* a tape; in anatomy applied to tape- or band-like structures.

5. *Zool.* A tapeworm [so in L.]; *spec.* (with capital initial) a genus of cestoid worms, including the common tapeworm. Also *fig.*

[**1693** tr. *Blancard's Phys. Dict.* (ed. 2), *Tænia,* broad Worms.] **1706** PHILLIPS, *Tænia.* **1753** CHAMBERS *Cycl. Supp.* s.v. *Tape-worm,* A fragment of the jointed tænia, sometimes voided.. in separate pieces. **1836–9** *Todd's Cycl. Anat.* II. 121/1 The species of Tænia infesting the intestines of other animals are extremely numerous. **1861** HULME tr. *Moquin-Tandon* II. II. 60 The Tænias and similar animals. **1869** BROWNING *Ring & Bk.* XI. 1606 Unbrokenly lay bare Each taenia that had sucked me dry of juice.

6. *Comb.* **tænia-chain,** the whole series, or a number of the consecutive joints of a tapeworm; **tænia-head,** the scolex of a tapeworm, the worm itself without the proglottides or deutoscolices.

1878 BELL *Gegenbaur's Comp. Anat.* 130 A process of gemmation, the product of which is the Tænia-chain.

Hence **tænian** ('tiːnɪən) *a.*, pertaining to tapeworms; **'tæniate** *a.*, tænioid, tæniiform.

1897 *Allbutt's Syst. Med.* II. 1114 Conditions which favour the entrance of the tænian ova into man or the domestic herbivora. **1860** MAYNE *Expos. Lex., Tæniatus*.. teniate. **1891** *Cent. Dict.*, Tæniate.

tænii- (tiːnɪɪ), combining form of L. *tænia* ribbon, often contracted to **tæni-** (also *erron.* **tænia-**). Also (*U.S.*) **tenii-. tæ'niasis** (pl. **-iases**) *Path.* and *Zool.* [-IASIS], infestation with tapeworms, esp. adult worms in (or formerly in) the genus *Taenia.* **tænii'phobia** [-PHOBIA], morbid fear of tapeworm. **'tæni(i)cide** (also **tæniacide**) [-CIDE[2]], a destroyer of tapeworms, a tænifuge. **'tæni(i)form** *a.* [-FORM], having the form of a tape or ribbon, tænioid. **'tænifuge** (also **tæniafuge**) [-FUGE], *sb.* a substance used to expel tapeworms from the body; *adj.* expelling tapeworms.

1896 F. W. GAMBLE in *Cambr. Nat. Hist.* II. iii. 82 The Jewish observance with regard to swine is the surest preventive measure against *taeniasis. **1900** DORLAND *Med. Dict.* 675/1 Teniasis. **1969** EDINGTON & GILLES *Path. in Tropics* iii. 173 Taeniasis may occur in all countries where beef or pork are eaten. The beef tapeworm—*Taenia saginata*—has a cosmopolitan distribution... The pork tapeworm—*T. solium*—is also widely distributed and its larval stage.. produces cysticercosis in man. **1971** R. A. MARCIAL-ROJAS *Path. Protozoan & Helminthic Dis.* xxxi. 618/1 The pathology and symptomatology of the taeniases in man vary according to the evolutionary stage of the parasite affecting him. **1897** *Allbutt's Syst. Med.* II. 1020 The belief that a worm is present either where no worm had ever existed, or after its complete expulsion—a sort of *tæniaphobia. **1857** DUNGLISON *Med. Dict.* 898/2 *Tæniacide.. Tænicide. **1885** *Lancet* 26 Sept. 568 A Canadian doctor has recently advocated the use of glycerine as a tæniacide. **1872** H. C. WOOD *Fresh-water Algæ* (1874) 101 Conjoined in filiform or *tæniform fascia. **1857** DUNGLISON *Med. Dict.* 898/2 *Tæniafuge.. Tenifuge. **1866** A. FLINT *Princ. Med.* (1880) 575 The male fern (filix mas) is a taenifuge. **1881** tr. *Trousseau & Pidoux' Treat. Therap.* (ed. 9) III. 353 Experiments upon the tænifuge virtues of the [pomegranate-root] bark.

tænio- ('tiːnɪəʊ), combining form of Gr. ταινία ribbon, used in the formation of some zoological terms. **,tænio'branchiate** *a.* [Gr. βράγχια gills + -ATE[2]], having tæniate gills; pertaining to the *Tæniobranchia,* a division of ascidians. **,tænio'glossate** *a.* [Gr. γλῶσσα tongue], in Mollusca, having upon the lingual ribbon one median tooth between three admedian teeth on either side. **tæni'opterine** *a.* [Gr. πτερόν wing + -INE[1]], belonging to the *Tæniopterinæ,* a sub-family of tyrant-birds. **'tæniosome** [Gr. σῶμα body], one of the sub-order *Tæniosomi* of teleocephalous fishes; a ribbon-fish; so **,tænio'somous** *a.*, having a ribbon-like body; pertaining to the ribbon-fishes.

1891 *Cent. Dict.*, *Tæniobranchiate. **1883** E. R. LANKESTER in *Encycl. Brit.* XVI. 660/2 The

Pneumonochlamyda..have..a complex rhipidoglossate or *taenioglossate radula.

tæniodont ('tiːnɪəʊdɒnt). [f. mod.L. order name *Tæniodonta* (E. D. Cope 1876, in *Proc. Acad. Nat. Sci. Philadelphia* XXVIII. 39), f. TÆNIO- + Gr. ὀδούς, ὀδοντ- tooth.] A fossil mammal of the order Tæniodonta, related to the edentates and known from remains found in North America.

1933 A. S. ROMER *Vertebr. Paleontol.* xiv. 278 Taeniodonts..were seemingly never common. **1949** B. PATTERSON in G. Jepsen et al. *Genetics, Paleontol. & Evolution* xiii. 243 (*title*) Rates of evolution in taeniodonts. **1979** M. J. NOVACEK in Fairbridge & Jablonski *Encycl. Paleontol.* 441/1 The taeniodonts..evolved long-clawed feet; ever-growing cheek teeth; short, broad skulls; and deep jaws.

tænioid ('tiːnɪɔɪd), *a.* (Also *erron.* tænoid.) [f. TÆNIA + -OID.] Of a ribbon-like shape; related to the tapeworms.

1836–9 *Todd's Cycl. Anat.* II. 410/2 The Tænioid Sterelmintha furnish us one of the simplest examples of this arrangement. **1867** J. HOGG *Microsc.* 363 The anterior extremity of a taen[i]oid worm is usually called the head. **1875** C. C. BLAKE *Zool.* 327 The name Echinococcus is given to the hydatid cyst filled with the larvæ of tænioid worms.

‖**tæniola** ('tiːnɪəʊlə). *Zool.* Also anglicized 'tæniole. [mod.L. *tæniola*, dim. of *tænia* band, ribbon.] One of the radial partitions in the body of some acalephans.

So '**tæniolate** *a.*, belonging to the division *Tæniolata* of hydroids.

1884 *Proc. Boston Soc. Nat. Hist.* 114 Such a form would differ from a tæniolate Hydrozoon.

tæniolite (tiːnɪ'əʊlaɪt). *Min.* Also tainiolite. [f. Gr. ταινία band, ribbon + -O + -LITE.] A rare colourless mica containing lithium and magnesium but without essential aluminium.

1899 G. FLINK in *Meddelelser om Grønland* XXIV. 116 The name of tainiolite that I have given the mineral is derived from the Greek word ταινία, a band or strip, because the crystals always have the form of bands or strips. **1900** *Amer. Jrnl. Sci.* CLX. 324 Tainiolite (tæniolite) is a kind of mica occurring in elongated colorless crystals. **1938** *Amer. Mineralogist* XXIII. 110 Because of the absence of essential aluminum, taeniolite is unique among the micas. **1962** W. A. DEER et al. *Rock-Forming Minerals* III. 89 A very rare mica, taeniolite (ideal formula $K_2Mg_4Li_2Si_8O_{20}F_4$), has no aluminium... It may be regarded as a magnesian lepidolite although it could be classed also as a lithian phlogopite. **1968** I. KOSTOV *Mineralogy* 361 Tainiolite.

tænite ('tiːnaɪt). *Min.*

†**1.** [f. Gr. ταινία ribbon + -ITE[1]: named 1841.] A variety of feldspar occurring in striped crystals.

1841 E. HITCHCOCK *Rep. Geol. Mass.* II. 676 Some have proposed for it the name *taenite*..on account of its resemblance to a ribbon.

2. [ad. Ger. *tänit*, Reichenbach 1861, f. Gr. ταινία ribbon, from the shape of its crystals.] Nickeliferous iron found in meteorites.

1868 DANA *Min.* 16 Reichenbach has named..that [alloy of iron and nickel] approaching probably the formula Fe_4Ni_3, Tænite. **1883** *Science* I. 464/2 Meteorite fragments are composed of nickeliferous iron, magnetic pyrites, taenite, and silicates.

tafe, = *to have*: see T'[1] and HAVE *v.*

‖**Tafelmusik** ('taːfəlmuˌziːk). Also **tafelmusik**, **tafel musik**. [Ger., lit. 'table music'.] **1.** Music so printed that parts can be read from the same page by two or more persons seated on opposite sides of a table.

1876 STAINER & BARRETT *Dict. Mus. Terms* 420/1 *Tafelmusik*,..table music. **1907** [see sense 2 below].

2. Music intended to be performed at a banquet or a convivial meal, esp. popular in the eighteenth century.

1880 GROVE *Dict. Mus.* II. 400/1 The Tafelmusik, Nachtmusik, etc., [of Mozart] for wind instruments..often present the most extraordinary combinations. **1907** T. S. WOTTON *Dict. Foreign Mus. Terms* 193 *Tafelmusik*,..(1) Music intended to be sung or played at meal times. (2) Music so arranged that two persons seated at opposite sides of a table can sing from the same page. **1961** *Times* 13 Mar. 3/1 Like the more aimlessly gossipy *Tafelmusik* of an eighteenth-century composer. **1969** *Times* 29 May 8/5 The analogy was with contemporary *tafel musik* rather than the wilder shores of radicalism. **1971** G. STEINER *In Bluebeard's Castle* IV. 92 Much of this [eighteenth-century] music was, in fact, conceived as *Tafelmusik* and aural tapestry around the busy room. **1980** *Early Music* July 300/1 If you seek in your Italian madrigal an escape to remote and perhaps picturesque sonorities, then the last thing you want is to understand it well enough to know why it is different from, say, Gregorian chant or rococo *Tafelmusik*. **1980** *Times* 19 Aug. 7/3 One of Telemann's many pieces of *tafelmusik*.

‖**Tafelwein** ('taːfəlvaɪn). Also **tafelwein**. Pl. **-e**. [Ger., lit. 'table wine'.] Wine of less than middle quality, suitable for drinking with an ordinary meal; = *table wine* s.v. TABLE *sb.* 22. Cf. *vin de table* s.v. VIN.

1972 *Times* 27 Nov. (Wines & Spirits Suppl.) p. iii/5 There will be three categories of wine: *tafelweine* for all the *vins ordinaires*; *qualitäswein* for the middle quality wines..; and *qualitätswein mit prädikat*. **1978** W. F. BUCKLEY *Stained Glass* xix. 186 He flashed his light down and saw a half-empty case of white Tafelwein. **1980** A. SCHOLEFIELD *Berlin Blind* III. 183 A bottle of *tafelwein* half empty.

Taff (tæf). Abbrev. of TAFFY[2]. Occas. applied also to women.

1929 F. BOWEN *Sea Slang* 137 *Taff or Taffy*, any Welsh seaman, or one with a Welsh surname. **1943** [see ASDIC]. **1973** M. AMIS *Rachel Papers* 81 She, Nanny, wasn't too bad: a red-faced, fat but strong-looking woman of about sixty-five or seventy. A Taff all right. **1977** *Listener* 25 Aug. 235/1 Taffs and Geordies and Scouses who were barely intelligible.

taffel, -il. *Sc. Obs.* or *dial.* Also 9 tafil. [prob. ad. Du. *tafel*, MDu., MLG. *tafele, taffele*, = Ger. *tafel*, OE. *tæfl* TAVEL[1], TABLE.] A table.

1633 DELL in *Cerem. Coronat. Jas. I* (1685) 16 The Regal, Crown,..and Spurs are laid down on a Taffel besides the Altar. *a* **1670** SPALDING *Troub. Chas. I* (1850) I. 38 The Erll of Erroll sat..at ane four nvkit taffill..coverit with grein claith. **1884** C. ROGERS *Soc. Life Scot.* I. vii. 242 Potatoes were tossed from the saucepan on the tafil or dinner-board.

tafferel ('tæfərəl, 'tæfrəl). Also 7 taffer(r)ell, 8 -eral, -eril, -rill, 8–9 -arel, 9 -aril, -rel. [a. Du. *tafereel* panel, picture, dim. of *tafel* TABLE (for **tafeleel*, with dissimilation of *l..l* to *r..l*). The 19th c. corruption to *taffrail*, with accompanying change of sense, shows confusion of the ending *-rel* with RAIL *sb.*: cf. quot. 1704.]

†**1.** A panel: *esp.* a carved panel. *Obs.*

1622–3 in *Brit. Mag.* (1833) III. 655 Item paid to John James a carver for cutting a Tafferell with a deathes head vpon it which is sett vpp at the entraunce..to our parish Church 00 15 00. **1632** in E. B. Jupp *Carpenter's Co.* (1887) 302 Carpenters..haue allwaies vsed to haue..the cutting of ballesters, hances, tafferrells, pendants and piramides.

2. *Naut.* The upper part of the flat portion of a ship's stern above the transom, usually ornamented with carvings, etc. In later use including, and now applied to, the aftermost portion of the poop-rail, and spelt TAFFRAIL.

1704 J. HARRIS *Lex. Techn.* I, *Tafferel*, is the uppermost Part, Frame, or Rail of a Ship abaft over the Poop. **1705** *Lond. Gaz.* No. 4116/3 Only her Hull from the Taffrill to the Midships remained above Water. **1750** *Minutes Bd. of Admiralty* 1 Jan. (P.R.O.), To cause the Taffarel and Quarter Pieces of the Model of the *Victory* at the Royal Academy at Portsmouth to be carved agreeably to the ornaments of that Ship. **1833** M. SCOTT *Tom Cringle* ix. (1859) 179 He again attempted to drag me away from my hold on the Tafferel. *c* **1850** *Rudim. Navig.* (Weale) 155 *Taffarel* or *taffrail*, the upper part of the ship's stern, usually ornamented with carved-work or mouldings, the ends of which unite to the quarter-pieces. **1857** WILKINSON *Egypt. Pharaohs* 113 Boats had..one rudder turning on the taffrel.

b. *Comb.* **tafferel-rail** = TAFFRAIL.

1846 YOUNG *Naut. Dict.* 244 *Taffrail* or *Tafferel-Rail*, the rail over the heads of the stern timbers.

taffeta, taffety ('tæfətə, -ətɪ), *sb.* (and *a.*) Forms: α. 4 **tapheta**, 4–6 **tafeta**, 4–8 **taffata**, 5–6 **tafata**, 5–7 **taffatas**, 6–7 **taffita**, (6 -yta), 6– **taffeta**, -as. β. 5–8 **taffaty**, 6 **tafete**, -ie, 6 *Sc.* **taffate**, -ati, -atis, -eti, -etti, -ete, -etee, **tapheit**, -ite, -ettye, **taftais**, -teis, **teffites**, 6–7 **taffatie**, -etie, -itie, 6–8 -ity, 6– **taffety**. [a. OF. *taffetas, taphetas* (1317 in Hatz.-D.) or med.L. *taffata*, etc. (Du Cange) = It. *taffetà*, Pg. *tafeta*, Sp. *tafetan*: ultimately a. Pers. *tāftah*, (*a*) silken cloth, (*b*) linen clothing, subst. use of *tāftah*, pa. pple. of *tāftan* 'to shine', also 'to twist, to spin'.] **A.** *sb.* **a.** A name applied at different times to different fabrics. In early times apparently a plain-wove glossy silk (of any colour); in more recent times, a light thin silk or union stuff of decided brightness or lustre. In the 16th c. mention is also made of 'linen taffety'. In recent times the name has been misapplied to various mixtures of silk and wool, and even cotton and jute, thin fine woollen material, etc.

α. **1373** in *Exch. Rolls Scotl.* II. 440 In empcione vnius pecie de taffata. *c* **1386** CHAUCER *Prol.* 440 A Doctour of Phisik..In sangwyn and in pers he clad was al Lyned with Taffata [*Lansd. MS.* tafeta] and with Sendal. *c* **1425** *Cast. Persev.* 239 in *Macro Plays* 84 With tapytys of tafata I tymbyr my towris. **1530** PALSGR. 279/1 Tafata a maner of sylke, *taffetas*. **1561** *Burgh Rec. Edinb.* (1875) III. 122 Sum brawf abulyement of taffate or vther silk. **1604** *Lismore Papers* Ser. II. (1887) I. 106 One ell iij qu[trs] of taffita to line y[e] same Dublett and faice it. **1634** SIR T. HERBERT *Trav.* 182 Taffataes of transparant finenesse. **1650** FULLER *Pisgah* IV. vi. 129 Riddling oracles..like changeable taffata (wherein the woofe and warpe are of different colours), seems of several hues, as the looker on takes his station. **1773** BRYDONE *Sicily* viii. 83 We are melting with heat, in thin suits of taffeta. **1836–41** BRANDE *Chem.* (ed. 5) 156 Trials were made with raw silk, ravelings of white taffeta, and of common sewing silk. **1884** *Girl's Own Paper* Aug. 682/1, I must mention the return of the ancient challis, which is now called a woollen taffetas. **1903** *Times* 12 Feb. 5/3 In silks..it is noted that taffetas are becoming less asked for. **1908** *Let. to Editor, Chiffon-taffeta*, a bright, lustrous, softly finished thin glacé silk, now much worn for ladies' blouses or dresses.

β. **1515** *Acc. Ld. High Treas. Scot.* V. 9 Twa elne of goldin hewit taffity, to be thame quaiffis. **1541** *Ibid.* VIII. 42, v elnis blak teffites of Janis. **1539** *Aberdeen Regr.* (1844) I. 161 Ane blak bonat, with ane typpat of taphite. **1550** LYNDESAY *Sqr. Meldrum* 125 Of yallow taftais wes hir sark. **1573** *Inv. Roy. Wardrobe* (1815) 189 (Jam.) Frenzeit with gold and lynit with reid tafteis. **1583** STUBBES *Anat. Abus.* II. (1882) 108 They must weare silkes..grograms, taffeties, and the like. **1630** CAPT. SMITH *Trav. & Adv.* xvi. 31 A white mares taile with a peece of greene taffity, on a great Pike, is carried before him [the Chan] for a standard. **1766** *Chron.* in *Ann. Reg.* 103/2 An additional duty on the importation of silks, crapes, and taffaties. **1865** E. C. CLAYTON *Cruel Fort.* I. 248 Dressed in the costume of 1827 or 1828—a gown of taffety with gigot sleeves, and a muslin canezon spencer.

b. *fig.* Florid language; = FUSTIAN 2.

1821 BYRON *Jrnl.* 12 Jan. in Moore *Life* III. 102 There is a good deal of taffeta in some of Tom's prefatory phrases.

B. *attrib.* and as *adj.*

1. Of taffeta; of the nature of taffeta.

1552–3 *Inv. Ch. Goods Staffs.* in *Ann. Lichfield* (1863) IV. 38 Itm. ij vestements, on of blewe chamblet, thother of taffeta silke. **1561** *Burgh Rec. Edinb.* (1882) IV. 122 Doubletis of saterne,..tafetie hatis. *a* **1586** SIDNEY *Arcadia* I. (1622) 51 Her bodie..couered with a light Taffata garment. **1602** DEKKER *Satirom.* Wks. 1873 I. 260 Horace did not weare the Badge of gentlemens company, as thou doost thy Taffetie sleeves. *c* **1645** HOWELL *Lett.* (1688) II. 316 Full of Taffity Silks and Sattins. **1725** *Bradley's Fam. Dict.* s.v. *Ointment*, Searce it thro' a Taffety Sieve. **1849** JAS. GRANT *Kirkaldy of Gr.* xxvii, Captain Lambie, he of the taffety standard celebrity. **1883** *Glasgow Herald* 21 Apr. 8/3 Taffeta Silk Gloves. **1903** *Daily Chron.* 26 Sept. 8/6 Evening gowns..made of soft light-blue taffetas silk.

2. *fig.* Florid, bombastic; over-dressed; dainty, delicate, fastidious: ***taffety cream***, a dish of cream and eggs.

1588 SHAKS. *L.L.L.* v. ii. 406 Taffata phrases, silken tearmes precise. **1621** MIDDLETON *Span. Gipsy* IV. iii, Can taffeta girls look plump without pampering? **1653** URQUHART *Rabelais* I. v, O the fine white wine,..it is a kind of taffatas wine. **1719** D'URFEY *Pills* VI. 124 With Taffity-Tarts and Pies. **1723** J. NOTT *Cook's & Confectioner's Dict.* sig. L1, *Taffaty Cream*. Beat the Whites of eight Eggs..with Rose-water,..put it into a Quart of cream. **1773** GOLDSM. *Stoops to Conq.* II. i, A shaking pudding, and a dish of tiff—taff—taffety cream. **1840** MISS YONGE (Heard in Hampshire), The old sow won't eat that stuff, she's so very taffety.

3. *Comb.*, as ***taffeta-bordered***, ***-covered*** adjs.

1889 DOYLE *Micah Clarke* 115 Dame Hobson's best taffeta covered settee. **1908** *Westm. Gaz.* 8 Feb. 13/2 A crown of taffeta with a taffeta-bordered brim of crinoline straw and other such blendings of straw and fabric.

taffey, taffia, variants of TAFIA.

taffrail ('tæfreɪl). *Naut.* Also tafrail. [A 19th c. alteration of TAFFEREL, due to false etymology, the termination *-rel* being taken as RAIL.] The aftermost portion of the poop-rail of a ship.

1814 *Chron.* in *Ann. Reg.* 176/2 We crossed his stern, our jib-boom passing over his tafrail. **1823** SCORESBY *Jrnl. Whale Fish.* 39, I stood on the taffrail as the ship was turned before the wind. **1840** R. H. DANA *Bef. Mast* xxxiii. 126 With her head for the equator, and Cape Horn over her taffrail, she went gloriously on. **1899** BULLEN *Log Sea-waif* 187 She dipped her stern right under, taking a sea in over the taffrail that filled the decks fore and aft.

taffy[1] ('tæfɪ). The earlier form of TOFFEE *sb.*, now Scotch, North Eng., and American.

1. A sweetmeat made from sugar or treacle, with butter, etc.: see TOFFEE *sb.*

1817 R. WILBRAHAM *Cheshire Gloss.*, *Taffy*,..treacle thickened by boiling and made into hard cakes. **1819** R. ANDERSON *Cumbld. Ball.* (*c* 1850) 51 Now heaps o' treagle chaps brong in, An taffey suin they meade us. **1825** JAMIESON, *Taffie*, treacle mixed with flour, and boiled till it acquire consistency; a sweetmeat eaten only on Hallowe'en. **1864** WEBSTER, *Taffy*, a kind of candy made of molasses boiled down and poured out in shallow pans. **1884** W. H. RIDEING in *Harper's Mag.* Mar. 522/1 Is Everton taffy a myth? **1890** S. J. DUNCAN *Social Departure* vii. 57 The steward made almond-taffy, or toffee, as Orthodocia had been brought up to pronounce it.

b. Freq. used in comparisons as a type of something which yields to pressure or can be stretched out into lengths.

1960 R. W. MARKS *Dymaxion World of B. Fuller* 127/2 The wood die rises, actuated by the console controls, while the universal-jointed giant fists stretch the metal gutter piece like *taffy* around the wooden die's elliptical groove perimeter. **1974** K. MILLETT *Flying* (1975) v. 474 Each wonderful swatch of hair like a chunk of taffy stretched. **1979** *Sci. Amer.* Oct. 117/2 Below the interface the lava is a fluid that yields like taffy when a drill probe is pushed into it.

2. *U.S. slang.* Crude or vulgar compliment or flattery; 'soft soap'; blarney.

1878 E. L. WHEELER *Buckhorn Bill* 2/1 Don't try to stuff that kind of taffy down me. *I* know better. **1879** *Tribune* (N.Y.) 16 Sept. (Cent. Dict.), There will be a reaction, and the whole party will unite in an offering of taffy. **1894** HOWELLS *Traveller from Altruria* 180 'If we learn anything at all from him, it will be because you have taught us how.' She could not resist this bit of taffy. **1901** *N. Amer. Rev.* Feb. 172 At this point..we should throw in a little trade-taffy about the Blessings of Civilization.

3. *attrib.* and *Comb.*, as ***taffy stand***, ***stick***; ***taffy-coloured*** adj.; **taffy apple**, a toffee-apple; **taffy-join**, a reunion of young people for the making of taffy to which each contributes; **taffy pull, pulling**, an occasion on which young people assemble to make taffy.

1967 MRS. L. B. JOHNSON *White House Diary* 12 Sept. (1970) 567 Stands dispensing hot dogs, Coca Cola, taffy apples, popcorn, and cotton candy. **1978** A. MALING *Lucky Devil* xxiii. 122, I threw the taffy apple stick away. **1939** L. M. MONTGOMERY *Anne of Ingleside* xxxii. 232 Young Mrs David Ransome, with her taffy-coloured hair. **1970** J. HANSEN *Fadeout* (1972) xi. 89 A taffy-colored cocker spaniel. **1854** Taffy-join [remembered in use]. **1878** *Cumberland Gloss.*, *Taffy joinin'*..young people in the country sometimes assemble on a winter evening and subscribe a few pence each to buy treacle for making 'taffy'. **1883** I. M. RITTENHOUSE *Jrnl.* in *Maud* (1939) 159 We're going to have a taffy pull at our Y.P.T.A. Friday night. **1926** *One Big Union Bulletin* (Winnipeg) 19 Aug. 5/6 We had planned a taffy pull but the ball game was so prolonged that we only succeeded in making fudge. **1982** S. B. FLEXNER *Listening to America* 138 The taffy pulls.. were a suitable face-to-face pastime for courting couples. **1863** M. B. CHESNUT *Diary* 18 Dec. in C. V. Woodward *May Chestnut's Civil War* (1981) xx. 507 General Hood.. wanted me to go to a taffy pulling at the Prestons'. **1912** *Out West* Mar. 166/2 He wrote with beautiful flourishes, little notes of regret.. declining all socials, taffy pullings and croquet parties. **1959** R. CAMPBELL *I Would do It Again* ii. 7 There was taffy pulling and all the other fun that goes with a picnic. **1894** HALL CAINE *Manxman* v. x, Break up every taffy stand in the fair, if you can't find anything better. **1881** T. E. BROWN *Fo'c's'le Yarns* (1889) 151 My lad with the taffystick in his fist.

Taffy[2] ('tæfɪ). [An ascribed Welsh pronunciation of *Davy* or *David*, in Welsh *Dafydd*.] A familiar nickname for a Welshman: cf. *Paddy*, *Sawney*, etc.

a **1700** B. E. *Dict. Cant. Crew*, *Taffy*, a Welshman or David. *Taffy's Day*, the first of March. **1708** *Brit. Apollo* No. 98. 2/2 Welch-men are called *Taffies* from the Corruption of the word *David*. **1893** *Sun* 26 July 2/7 Cheers echoed over the Surrey hills when it was known that for the first time a Taffy had gained the Queen's.

‖**tafia** ('tæfɪə). Also 8 **taffia**, **taffey**, **-fy**. [Origin uncertain: given in 1722 as native name in West Indies (Labat *Voy. aux Iles de l' Amér.* III. 410 L'eau-de-vie qu'on tire des cannes est appelée guildive [see KILL-DEVIL]; les sauvages et les nègres l'appellent *tafia*): but *tāfia* is also given in Malay dicts. as 'a spirit distilled from molasses'. The word appears therefore to be widely diffused in east and west.] A rum-like spirituous liquor obtained from the lower grades of molasses, refuse brown sugar, etc.

1763 tr. *Le Page du Pratz's Hist. Louisiana* II. IV. iv. 266 At night you shall have a cup of *Tafia* (or rum) to give you strength and spirits. **1777** (Apr. 10) in *Illinois Hist. Collect.* (1903) I. 296 The person that intoxicated them with Rum or Taffia. **1779** in W. H. English *Conq. Northwest* (1896) I. 375, 7½ gallons of taffey at sixty-four dollars per gallon. **1779** G. R. CLARK *Campaign Illinois* (1869) 79, I.. gave them.. Taffy and Provisions to make merry on and left them. **1793** TRAPP tr. *Rochon's Madagascar* 189 Over which he poured some *tafia* or rum. **1799** *Naval Chron.* I. 173 A sloop laden with taffia. **1880** G. W. CABLE *Grandissimes* xxviii. 197 From the same sugar-cane comes sirop and tafia. **1889** *Harper's Mag.* Nov. 851 Sugar is very difficult to ship; rum and tafia can be handled with less risk.

tafoni (tæ'fəʊnɪ), *sb. pl. Geol.* [a. G. *tafoni* pl. (F. C. A. Penck *Morph. d. Erdoberfläche* (1894) I. 214), a. Corsican dial. *tafóni* pl., holes, hollows.] Shallow rounded hollows in rock produced by weathering.

1942 C. A. COTTON *Climatic Accidents in Landscape Making* i. 9 Rarely or never are positive signs of sand-blasting found in association with typical tafoni. **1968** R. W. FAIRBRIDGE *Encycl. Geomorphol.* 1103/1 Smaller rounded depressions may diversify the larger tafoni. **1970** R. J. SMALL *Study of Landforms* ix. 294 Cavity weathering, leading to the formation of rounded hollows ('tafoni') in granite, may also be due to chemical decay, since it occurs commonly in shaded areas where moisture is likely to linger.

tafrogenesis, var. TAPHROGENESIS.

taft (tɑːft, tæft), *sb. Plumbing.* A widening-out of the end of a lead pipe into a broad thin flange. Also Comb.: **taft joint**, a joint between two pipes, made by tafting one pipe, shaping the other to fit into it, and soldering them. So **taft** *v. trans.*, to expand and turn outwards at a sharp angle the end of (a lead pipe) so as to form a wide edge or fastening flange.

1877 S. S. HELLYER *Plumber* i. 21 The soil pipe can be 'tafted' at the end. *Ibid.* ii. 33 When the pipe is tafted back at right angles,.. the lower pipe is liable to break away at the taft. **1891** —— *Plumbing* xvii. 91 There is no form of wiped soldered joints so easy to make as a *taft joint*. **1906** GOODCHILD & TWENEY *Technol. & Sci. Dict.* 742/1 *Taft joint*, a blown joint. **1945** W. J. WOOLGAR *Pract. Plumber* iv. 102/2 The taft joints are seldom used in plumbing, because of the low tensile strength. **1972** J. HASTINGS *Plumber's Compan.* 146 A taft joint.. requires little skill in the making. **1976** *Pract. Householder* Nov. 46/1 Plumber's solder can, of course, be used especially with the taft joint and finger wipe joint.

taftais, -eis, obs. Sc. forms of TAFFETA.

tag (tæg), *sb.*[1] Also 5-6 **tagge**, 6 **tagg**, **tage**. [Known shortly after 1400: origin obscure. In senses 1, 2 a, and 3, it is synonymous with DAG *sb.*[1], which appears to have been the earlier form: if so, *tag* may have been influenced by association with TACK. Some compare Sw. *tagg* 'prickle, point, tooth', but evidence of historical connexion is wanting.

The evidence at hand for the early history is deficient, the earliest quot. for the group being *c* 1380 in TAGGED 1, a deriv. of the sb. in sense 1.]

1. Originally, one of the narrow, often pointed, *laciniæ* or pendent pieces made by slashing the skirt of a garment; hence, any hanging ragged or torn piece; also, any end or rag of ribbon or the like.

1402 *Pol. Poems* (Rolls) II. 69 Of suche wide clothing, tateris and tagges, it hirtith myn hert hevyly. *c* **1500** *Rowlis Cursing* 135 in Laing *Anc. Poet. Scotl.*, Ruffy Ragmen [a devil] with his taggis Sall ryfe thair sinfull saule in raggis. **1500-20** DUNBAR *Poems* xxvi. 115 Thae tarmegantis, with tag and tatter, Ffull lowd in Ersche begowth to clatter. **1542** UDALL *Erasm. Apoph.* 313 The skyrtes of his goune all pounced in cuttes and tagges. **1840** THACKERAY *Paris Sk. Bk.* (1872) 7 Crumpled tags of ribbon. **1884** *St. James's Gaz.* 10 May 6/1 The tags of drapery and other accessories. **1889** *Cornh. Mag.* Feb. 124 With tags of ribbon sticking out in unexpected places.

2. A small pendent piece or part hanging from, or attached more or less loosely to the main body of anything. With numerous specific applications, e.g.

a. A matted lock of wool on a sheep; a tag-lock; a twisted or matted lock of hair. **b.** A shred of animal tissue. **c.** A shred of metal in a casting: see quot. **d.** A final curl, twirl, or flourish added to a letter, sometimes used as a mark of contraction. **e.** *fig.* An appendage; the tail-end (of any proceeding).

a. *c* **1640** J. SMYTH *Lives Berkeleys* (1883) I. 157 What money was.. made by sale of the locks, belts and tags of Sheep. **1888** *Harper's Mag.* June 137/2 Her reddish-brown hair, which grew in a fringe below her crown, was plaited into small tags or tails.

b. 1724 RAMSAY *Health* 186 Bones corrupt and bare, Through ulcerated tags of muscles stare. **1897** J. HUTCHINSON *Arch. Surg.* VIII. No. 31. 214 Under atropine the pupils dilated, but shewed numerous tags of adhesion. **1897** *Allbutt's Syst. Med.* III. 716 They [adhesions] are then seen as filamentous tags on the outside of the intestine. **1899** *Ibid.* VII. 612 A small tag of fibrin from the valve.

c. 1863 LYELL *Antiq. Man* ii. 10 Some of the moulds in which the bronze instruments were cast, and 'tags' as they are called, of bronze, which are formed in the hole through which the fused metal was poured.

d. 1867 FURNIVALL *Percy Fol.* I. 18 *note*, To many of the final d's is a tag, which often means nothing, and often means s.

e. 1703 STEELE *Tender Husb.* I. i, Seem to have come into the World only to be Taggs in the Pedigree of a Wealthy House. **1882** HOLLAND *Logic & Life* (1885) 317 Death is but the tag of this life.

3. a. A point of metal or other hard substance at the end of a lace, string, strap, or the like, primarily used to facilitate its insertion through an eyelet-hole, as in a boot-lace or stay-lace, but when externally visible often made ornamental, as on the 'points' in use before buttons; an aglet.

(The first two quots. are of doubtful sense.)

[**1501-2** *Acc. Ld. High Treas. Scot.* II. 33 Item, for taggis to ane Franch sadill and mending of it xij d. **1507** *Ibid.* III. 270 Item, for taggis, bukkilles, and small graith to thaim, xv. s.] **1570** LEVINS *Manip.* 10/19 Yᵉ Tag of a poynt, *ferrētrum*. **1580** HOLLYBAND *Treas. Fr. Tong*, *Vn fer d'aiguillette*, a tagge. **1592** LYLY *Gallathea* v. i. 70 Thy Maister could make silver pottes of tagges of poynts. **1648** GAGE *West Ind.* 56 With long silver or golden Tags hanging down before. *a* **1734** NORTH *Exam.* III. viii. §15 (1740) 593 Now comes the Tag to this fine Lace. **1832** BABBAGE *Econ. Manuf.* iv. (ed. 3) 31 The simple art of making the tags of boot-laces. **1861** WRIGHT *Ess. Archæol.* I. vii. 133 The object.. is part of the metal tag at the end of the belt.

b. *fig.*

c **1572** GASCOIGNE *Fruites Warre* lxi, Is witte nowe wente so wandring from thy minde? Are all thy points so voide of Reasons taggs? **1611** MIDDLETON *Roaring Girl* III. i, Here's the point [*Draws her sword*] That I untruss; 't has but one tag, 't will serve though To tie up a rogue's tongue.

†**c.** Phrases. *to hold tag*, to keep a person engaged in conversation: cf. *to buttonhole*. *to a tag*, to the minutest point, exactly; cf. *to a T. Obs.*

1567 DRANT *Horace, Epist.* v. C vij, Scotfree we may hould tagge In frendly chat this sommers night. **1679** V. ALSOP *Melius Inquir.* Introd. 20 To hang on a string only with those who jump in with our own Points to a Tag. **1682** N. O. *Boileau's Lutrin* IV. 318 At Trent, when Concord in a Bag Came Post from Rome, they hit it to a Tag!

4. a. An ornamental pendant; a tassel; a ribbon bearing a jewel, etc.

1570 LEVINS *Manip.* 10/20 Ye Tag of a purse, *appendix*. **1686** *Lond. Gaz.* No. 2132/4 Lost.., a black laced Palatin with Diamond Tags upon black Ribon. **1762-71** H. WALPOLE *Vertue's Anecd. Paint.* (1786) I. 230 The first lady has tags of a particular form, exactly like those on the dress of my duchess of Suffolk. **1848** THACKERAY *Van. Fair* vi, Our good child.. passed in review all her gowns, fichus, tags, bobbins, laces, silk stockings, and fallals. **1890** *Spectator* 14 June 834/2 The sculptor.. has filled up part of the arch with long heavy tassels hanging from the saddle-cloth. Throughout the work there seems to be an excess of tag and small decoration.

b. *pl.* A footman's shoulder-knots.

1837 J. MORIER *Abel Allnutt* xxx. 175 A stout footman staggering under a long cane and matted tags, and with difficulty waddling in his stiff plushes. **1844** DICKENS *Mart. Chuz.* ix, With such great tags upon his liveried shoulder.

5. A catkin of a tree. *rare.*

1597 GERARDE *Herbal* I. xv. §2. 17 The catkins or tags which grow on nut trees and aller trees. **1878** MRS. STOWE *Poganuc P.* xvii. 147 The tremulous tags of the birches and alders shook themselves gaily out in the woods.

6. The tip of the tail of an animal, esp. when distinct in colour or otherwise; the tail-piece of an angler's fly. (Much earlier in TAGGED *a.* 3.)

1681 CHETHAM *Angler's Vade-m.* xxxv. §1 (1689) 222 Some Red warp'd in for the tag of the Tail. **1787** BEST *Angling* (ed. 2) 106. **1863** KINGSLEY *Water-Bab.* i. 37 A great brown sharp-nosed creature with a white tag to her brush. **1867** F. FRANCIS *Angling* xiii. (1880) 472 Tie on the tag, which is usually a bit of tinsel. **1886** *Field* 27 Feb. 268/1 The fox.. gets the credit of being a vixen; but his snowy tag has only to be seen in order to dispel that notion. **1902** *Encycl. Brit.* XXV. 449/1 Two of the best grayling flies are a very small apple-green dun and the red tag.

7. The strip of parchment bearing the pendent seal of a deed.

1688 R. HOLME *Armoury* III. xv. (Roxb.) 21/1 A writt sealed vp, haueing two taggs or Labells Or, in a feild Gules. **1872** C. INNES *Lect. Scotch Leg. Antiq.* v. 235 A small piece of the seal shall stick at the tag of the brief. **1887** J. B. SHEPPARD in *Lit. Cantuar.* (Rolls) I. 341 *note*, The originals have now both lost their seals, although the slits for the tags remain.

8. a. A tab or tie-label attached by one end to a package, to luggage, etc.; also, a label pinned on as a badge, etc. Also *fig.* = TAB *sb.*[1] 7. orig. and chiefly *U.S.*

1864 WEBSTER, *Tag*.. 2. Any slight appendage..; specifically, a direction card or label. **1891** *Cent. Dict.*, *Tag* .. 2 (c). A strip of leather, parchment, strong paper, or the like, loose at one end, and secured to a box, bag, or parcel, to receive a written address or label. **1908** *Times* 26 Dec. 10/2 A new system of street collecting for public charities by means of tags or labels,.. tried at San Francisco recently on behalf of the Children's Hospital... The advent of 'tag day' is well advertised. *a* **1910** *Mod. Price List*, Tags with strings in packets. Extra large tags with ruled lines. **1961** *Times* 5 Jan. 4/3 After the interval Surrey drafted in extra men to help Prosser keep a tag on Farooq.

b. Sometimes applied to a tab or loop by which a coat or the like is hung up.

c. *Electronics.* A small metal projection to which a wire may be soldered or attached.

1919 R. MORDIN *Strowger Automatic Telephone Exchange* ii. 34 The tags are arranged in ten sets of three rows, and pass completely through holes in the tag board, so that it is possible to wire the tags on either or both sides of the board. **1958** *Practical Wireless* XXXIV. 63/2 All earth leads on the pre-amplifier are taken to one point, actually to a soldering tag on the input coaxial socket. **1971** *Hi-Fi Sound* Feb. 71/1 Never, under any circumstances, solder connections to the tags with them already on the cartridge.

d. (See quot. 1935.) *N. Amer. slang.*

1935 A. J. POLLOCK *Underworld Speaks* 118/1 *Tag*, an automobile license plate. **1971** *Maclean's Mag.* Sept. 34/1 The license plates ('tags'), laws unto themselves, somehow manage to contradict and complement each other at the same time. **1976** *Billings* (Montana) *Gaz.* 18 June 7C/3 [They] observed a Thunderbird with Louisiana tags circling the block.

e. *Computers.* A character or set of characters appended to an item of data in order to identify it.

1948 *Theory & Techniques for Design of Electronic Digital Computers* (Moore School of Electr. Engin., Univ. of Pennsylvania) IV. XXXIX. 1 To introduce.. a new element called a stop order tag which may be attached to the words stored in the memory. **1961** LEEDS & WEINBERG *Computer Programming Fund.* v. 151 Bits 0, 1, and 2 (often called the prefix of the word) and bits 18 to 20 (called the tag) specify the operation. **1963** *IBM Jrnl. Res. & Devel.* VII. 337/2 If it is desired to translate the text with the aid of a microglossary, the text is preceded by a tag specifying the pertinent field. **1978** J. P. HAYES *Computer Archit. & Organization* iii. 149 The processor merely has to inspect the operand tags to determine the specific type of operation to be performed, e.g., a fixed-point double-precision addition.

f. An epithet; a label or popular designation. *colloq.*

1961 in WEBSTER. **1972** *Times* 7 Aug. (Jamaica Suppl.) p. iii/4 The lost goodwill.. and the loss of the tag of still being the safest Caribbean country for investment. **1976** *Daily Tel.* 20 July 3/2 The Black Panther tag, probably coined by the press, was the worst of it. **1982** *Oxford Star* 4-5 Feb. 3/2 Cassells doesn't let the tag of Third Division top scorer bother him too much.

g. A price (cf. *price-tag* s.v. PRICE *sb.* 14); hence, an account or bill. Cf. TAB *sb.*[1] 7.

1968 *Globe & Mail* (Toronto) 3 Feb. B2/3 (*heading*) Petrofind raises fuel oil price, bulk gas tag. **1977** *Modern Railways* Dec. 474/2 BR stresses, too, that if there's a gulf between the price of the basic, low-cost vehicles customers have been using in old-style wagonload working and the tag on a late-1970s air-braked, 75 mile/h vehicle, there's a comparable contrast in the service obtainable. **1979** D. MEIRING *Foreign Body* xviii. 197 Even if they went broke, the bank would pick up Sagr's crude-oil tag and pay it.

9. a. Something appended or added to a writing or speech, esp. by way of ornament or improvement, e.g. the moral of a fable, etc.

a **1734** NORTH *Exam.* II. v. §74 (1740) 360 To avoid the Fastidium of noting all the Author's Tags joined to his Relations of this Time. **1872** MINTO *Eng. Prose Lit.* I. ii. 134 A tag of statistics is very chilling. **1874** L. STEPHEN *Hours in Library* (1892) II. v. 151 [Massinger] is fond of adding little moral tags.. to the end of his plays. **1885** *Manch. Exam.* 13 Oct. 4/7 Each paragraph.. would serve.. as a tag by way of peroration to a debating club harangue.

b. A brief and usually familiar quotation added for special effect; a much used or trite quotation.

1702 S. PARKER tr. *Cicero's De Finibus* I. 5 With Tags of Metre translated from the Greek.. we can dispense well enough. **1866** GEO. ELIOT *F. Holt* xvii, I don't talk in tags of Latin, which might be learned by a schoolmaster's footboy. **1893** JESSOPP *Stud. Recluse* vii. 225 Putting in tags and rags of French.. to conceal poverty of style. **1897** *Sat. Rev.* 18 Dec. 701 The Latin tag holds: 'Quem Deus vult perdere, prius dementat.' **1902** BUCHAN *Watcher by Thresh.* 175 Stories from Procopius and tags of Roman law.

c. The refrain or catch of a song or poem; the last words of a speech in a play, etc.

1717 J. GAY et al. *Three Hours after Marriage* I. 25 The tag of the Acts of a new Comedy. **1755** C. CHARKE *Life* 205 Concluding the Play with Jane Shore's Tag, at the End of the first Act of that Tragedy. **1793** H. WALPOLE *Let. to*

Agnes Berry 18 Oct., They have brought to my recollection the tag of an old song. **1815** SCOTT *Let. to Miss J. Baillie* 12 Nov. in *Lockhart*, I am..anxious to store the heads of my young damsels with something better than the tags of rhymes. **1830** H. LEE *Mems. Manager* II. viii. 104 The tag; which is the technical phrase for the last lines of any play. **1876** *N. Amer. Rev.* CXXIII. 480 And, to borrow the tag of an old story, 'There—my lord—I leave you'.

d. A musical phrase added to the end of a piece in composition or performance (see also quot. 1978). Esp. in *Jazz*.

1929 *N.Y. Times* 20 Oct. IX. 8/6 *Tag*, ending added to a musical composition. **1932** *Melody Maker* June 507/3 The tag..implies that this is a band record. **1943** *Riverboat Jazz* (Brunswick Records) 7 He comes in to play a tag—just a few notes. **1958** P. TANNER in P. Gammond *Decca Bk. Jazz* xi. 130 A tradition has grown up..of concluding with a short drum break and a tag ensemble coda. **1960** H. O. BRUNN *Story Original Dixieland Jazz Band* v. 59 The Dixieland Band's stock ending, the 'dixieland tag', faithfully concluded every number. **1978** *Amer. Speech* 1975 L. 301 *Tag*, added ending of a song, often repeating the final words and designed to make a complete and satisfying arrangement.

e. *Linguistics*. An interrogative formula used to convert statements into questions. Cf. *tag question*, sense 14 below.

1957 *Publ. Amer. Dial. Soc.* XXVIII. 17 An understanding of tags implies an understanding of sentence order and the role of accent. **1963** F. T. VISSER *Hist. Syntax* I. ii. 175 *The type* 'oh, Biffin told you, *did he*? (or *He did*?)'. This type differs from that illustrated in the preceding section in the fact that statement and tag with *to do* are either both positive or both negative. **1973** *Archivum Linguisticum* IV. 69 Tag constructions can convey much to the discriminating listener. **1977** *Language* LIII. 742 An auxiliary verb typically can appear in the tag of tag questions.

†**10. a.** The rabble, the lowest class of people. *Obs.*

1607 SHAKS. *Cor.* III. i. 248 Will you hence, Before the Tagge returne? *a* **1825** FORBY *Voc. E. Anglia*, *Tag*, the rabble.

†**b.** *esp.* in collocation with RAG *sb.*^{1} 3 b: ***tag and rag***, a contemptuous expression for all the components of the rabble, of the lower classes, or of an assemblage of people held in small esteem; all and any, every man Jack, everybody, Tom, Dick, and Harry. *Obs.* See also TAG-RAG.

c **1535** BYGOD *Impropriations* (K.O.), Your fathers were wyse, both tagge and rag. **1553-4** MACHYN *Diary* (Camden) 50 Huntyd, and kyllyd tage and rage with honds and swords. **1566** J. PARTRIDGE *Plasidas* 1041 To walles they go, both tagge and ragge, their Citie to defende. **1610** COOKE *Pope Joan* in *Harl. Misc.* (Malh.) IV. 95 That you have made Levites..of the scurvy and scabbed, of the lowest of the people, tag and rag. *a* **1626** BP. ANDREWES *Serm.* (1641) 181 This is the time when all hypocrites, atheists, tag and rag come. **18..** SOUTHEY *Devil's Walk* xxiii, With music of fife and drum, And a consecrated flag, And shout of tag and rag, And march of rank and file. **1809** W. IRVING *Knickerb.* VI. ix. (1861) 231 Every tag having his rag at his side, to finish his pipe..and laugh at his flights of immortal dulness.

11. In servants' vocabulary: A lower servant.

1857 T. WRIGHT *Dict.*, *Tag*, one who assists another at work in a secondary character. *Northampt.* **1860** *Athenæum* 17 Nov. 664 Servants..with their own distinction of ranks, the 'Pugs' and the 'Tags'.

12. A disease in sheep; = *tag-sore* (14): see quots.

(Cf. TAGGED 5 a, which is evidenced much earlier.)

1741 *Compl. Fam.-Piece* III. (ed. 3) 494 Of the Tag or Belt in Sheep. Sheep are said to be tagged or belt, when they have a Flux, or continued running of Ordure, which lighting upon the Tail, the Heat of the Dung, by its scalding, breeds the Scab. **1756** *Compl. Body Husb.* 694 The Tag is situated in the inner part of the Tail; it consists of Scabs and Sores. **1807** *Essays Highland Soc.* III. 434 A disease..affecting the tail, has been denominated *Tag*.

13. *slang*. A person who follows another as a detective or spy. Cf. TAG *v.*^{1} 4 b, TAIL *sb.*^{1} 6 b.

1966 'A. HALL' *9th Directive* vii. 62 Who were the tags? The thin one, and the one with the splay-footed walk? **1972** J. D. BUCHANAN *Professional* v. 62 Guerin realized he had a tag... Guerin would walk and stop, the tag would do the same. **1979** 'A. HALL' *Scorpion Signal* xii. 139 Ignator went through the lights at yellow... I don't think he was going through on the yellow because he'd discovered the tag.

14. *attrib.* and *Comb.*, as ***tag-like*** adj.; **tag alder**, *U.S. local*, name for some species of alder, esp. *Alnusincana*, *A. serrulata*, and (on the Pacific coast) *A. rubra*; **tag axle** *N. Amer.*, a non-powered set of wheels on a truck, etc., attached so as to support extra weight; **tag-belt**, = *tag-sore*; **tagboard**, (*a*) *U.S.*, a type of strong cardboard, used esp. for making luggage labels; (*b*) *Electronics*, a board of insulating material containing two or more parallel lines of tags (sense 8 c above), so that a component can be mounted between each pair; **tag-boat**, *U.S. local*, a boat towed behind a small steamer or sailing vessel; a tender, cockboat; **tag day** *N. Amer.* = *flag-day* (*b*) s.v. FLAG *sb.*^{4} 7; **tag-end**, the last part or remnant of anything; a remaining scrap or fragment; = FAG-END; **tag-fastener**, **-holder**, a device for attaching tags or labels; **tag line** *U.S.* = PUNCH LINE; **tag-lock**, a matted lock of sheep's wool, esp. one of those about the hinder parts; = DAG-LOCK; **tag-machine**, a machine for making tags or labels; **tag-needle**, a needle for attaching labels to bags, bales, etc.; **tag-phrase**, an automatically repeated or over-used phrase; **tag question** *Linguistics*, a question formed by the appendage of an interrogative formula to a statement; a formula used in this manner (cf. sense 9 e above); **tag-sore**, pustular excoriation of a sheep's tail set up by the irritation of diarrhœal flux; **tag strip** *Electronics*, a strip of insulating material on which are mounted a line of tags (sense 8 c above); **tag-tail**, a worm with a yellow tag or tail; also, a parasite, a hanger-on; **tag-wool**, wool made from tag-locks; **tag-worm**, = *tag-tail*.

1891 *Lancet* 3 Oct. 772/1 *Tag alder. **1971** M. TAK *Truck Talk* 163 **Tag axle*, the hindmost axle of a tandem-axle tractor if that axle serves only to support additional gross weight. **1977** *Telegraph-Jrnl.* (St. John, New Brunswick) 1 June 3/5 He said in an interview that the Motor Vehicles Branch no longer allows extra weight when a third 'tag axle' is added to tandem drive trucks. **1832** BOUCHER *Gloss. Obs. & Prov. Wds.*, **Tagbelt*, excoriation brought on by diarrhoea. **1893** SARAH JEWETT *Deephaven* 128, I got into the schooner's tag-boat quick. **1912** *Walden's Directory of Papers* (Eastern ed.) p. liii, Paper and card board.. translucents, *tag boards, etc. **1952** E. J. LABARRE *Dict. Paper* (ed. 2) 301/1 *Tag paper* or board is a very strong and tough product made on the Fourdrinier (Bristol), used for making the well-known luggage and shipping tags. **1956** *Wireless World* Mar. 125/1 A plain tagboard, carrying resistors and capacitors. **1973** G. DAVEY *Fun with Hi-Fi* iii. 25 (*caption*) Layout and tagboards of Mullard 510 amplifier. **1976** *National Observer* (U.S.) 23 Oct. 20/1 (Advt.), Each issue is 42 or more pages long, bound in sturdy tagboard. **1908** *Tag day [see sense 8 a]. **1916** *Daily Colonist* (Victoria, B.C.) 4 July 6/3 Friday, August 4, is to be tag day for the Italian Red Cross Society. **1949** *Courier-Journal* (Louisville, Kentucky) 3 Sept. 10/1 The conference agreed [upon]..a tag day on which Boy Scouts and Girl Scouts will solicit funds during the Kentucky State Fair. **1807** C. WILMOT *Let.* 15 May in *Russ. Jrnls.* (1934) II. 245, I believe..we have been solemnising..the *Tag end of those very May Day ceremonies which scandaliz'd *ould Cato* near two thousand years ago. **1818** COLERIDGE *Diss. Sc. Method* ii. 40 Not made up of miserable clap-traps, and the tag-ends of mawkish Novels, and endless sermonizing. **1900** *Westm. Gaz.* 8 Nov. 3/2 The mania for gold embroidering and braiding and the gold tag ends of present-day fashions. **1897** *Allbutt's Syst. Med.* IV. 160 Ragged sloughy material, which often projects in *tag-like pieces into the abscess cavity. **1926** G. ADE *Let.* 14 Sept. (1973) 113 The prosecutor asks: 'Do you know him?' She studies him carefully and then pulls the *tag line: 'No, I don't recognize him at all.' **1941** B. SCHULBERG *What makes Sammy Run?* iii. 44 One of those long dirty stories for which the only justification would be the tag line at the climax. **1982** *Fortune* 6 Sept. 53/1 One recent ad. shows a stunning model wearing nothing but a solitaire diamond necklace. 'She can't flaunt a fur on the Côte d'Azur,' reads the tagline. **1615** T. ADAMS *Lycanthropy* 17 They will plucke our fleeces; leave us nothing but the *tag-locks. **1884** *Century Mag.* Feb. 519/2 The tag-locks and pulled wool were mostly worked up in the..small factories into stocking-yarn [etc.] for the farmer's use. **1933** R. TUVE *Seasons & Months* iv. 110 All these uses of the seasons-introduction appear and reappear, sometimes elaborately, sometimes in a mere conventional *tag-phrase. **1963** Tag-phrase [see *goon-like* adj. s.v. GOON 5]. **1933** O. JESPERSEN *Essentials Eng. Gram.* xxviii. 304 Note especially *tag-questions..like: He was angry, wasn't he? **1957** R. W. ZANDVOORT *Handbk. Eng. Gram.* v. ii. 224 A certain type of compound sentence, consisting of a statement followed by an *appended question* (or 'tag question') modelled on the main clause... You are not ill, are you? **1982** *Amer. Speech* LVII. 95 Lakoff..considers tag questions (*He can work, can't he?* and *He is honest, isn't he?*) as declaratives—assertions. **1828** WEBSTER, **Tag-sore*, a disease in sheep. *Cycl.* **1942** *Electronic Engin.* XV. 238/2 Such *tag strips are found in medium wave receivers, as well as in short wave apparatus. **1960** *Practical Wireless* XXXVI. 405/1 A tag-strip provides a convenient anchoring point for leads. **1653** WALTON *Angler* iv. 95 There are..divers other kindes of worms..as the marsh-worm, the *tag-tail,..the gilt-tail. **1681** CHETHAM *Angler's Vade-m.* iv. §5 (1689) 32 Tag-tail is a worm of..a pale Flesh colour, with a yellow Tag on his Tail. **1834** C. A. DAVIS *Lett. J. Downing* 311 You are surrounded by such a raft of snuffle-nose, scabby set of tag-tails, that I can't have nothing more to do with you. **1864** WEBSTER, *Tag-tail*..a person who attaches himself to another against the will of the latter; a dependent; a sycophant; a parasite. **1875** 'STONEHENGE' *Brit. Sports* I. v. xi. §3. 312 The Tagtail is common in good strong clays which are well-manured for turnips, mangold-wurzel, &c. **1602** CAREW *Cornwall* 26 His baites are flies and *Tag-wormes, which the Cornish English terme Angle-touches. **1839** HOFLAND *Brit. Angler's Man.* ii. (1841) 10 The little gilt-tail, or tag-worm, Is of a pale yellow towards the tail.

tag (tæg), *sb.*^{2} (and *a.*) Also 8 **tagg.** [Origin obscure.] **A.** *sb.* **1.** A children's game in which one player pursues the others until he touches one of them, who in turn becomes pursuer; = TIG.

1738 *Gentl. Mag.* VIII. 80/1 In Queen Mary's Reign, Tag was all the Play; where the Lad saves himself by touching of cold Iron. **1760-72** H. BROOKE *Fool of Qual.* (1809) I. v. 67 After they were cloyed with hide and seek, they all played tagg, till they were well warmed. **1864** *Louie's last term* (N.Y.) 179 There's Eva Leonard beckoning to me to come and play Tag. **1903** *Smart Set* IX. 78 The merry hornet played a game Of tag about my head.

2. *Baseball*. The act of putting out a runner by touching him with the ball (or with the gloved hand holding the ball) while he is off base. Also *tag-out*. Cf. TAG *v.*^{2} 2 a.

1941 *Baseball Mag.* Sept. 439/2 A big league infielder.. confessed..'I've made the tag with the empty glove outstretched.' *Ibid.* 439/3 Some stars..use a two-handed tag. **1952** *N.Y. Herald-Tribune* 16 Aug. 11/1 Only Lockman's cut-off of Hartung's throw and the subsequent tag-out of Mathews at third averted further damage to the home forces. **1971** L. KOPPETT *N.Y. Times Guide Spectator Sports* i. 21 The rules forbid a runner to leave the 'base-path'—an imaginary direct line between bases—to avoid a tag.

B. as *adj.* Of, pertaining to, or designating a form of professional wrestling between single alternating representatives of two teams (usu. of two men each).

One team-member cannot enter the ring until the other tags or touches hands with him on leaving it.

1955 *Sun* (Baltimore) 16 May 16/7 (*heading*) 6-man tag bout tops mat card. *Ibid.* For the first time in the history of wrestling, a six-man tag team bout will be staged. **1963** *Economist* 7 Sept. 819/1 The confused spectacle of tag wrestling (four in a ring). **1966** *Times* 28 Feb. (Canada Suppl.) p. xiv/7 The average card in Canada has a tag match (two-man teams with the members taking turns to maul each other). **1972** J. MOSEDALE *Football* viii. 115 He teamed with his old idol Nagurski in tag team matches. **1974** *Greenville* (S. Carolina) *News* 23 Apr. 8/2 In other bouts, Sandy Scott and Johnny Weaver downed Gene Lewis and Bill White in a special tag team event.

‖**Tag** (taːk), *sb.*^{3} [Ger.] = DAY *sb.* 9 c. Usu. *der Tag*.

1914, etc. [see DAY *sb.* 9 c]. **1914** J. M. BARRIE (*title*) Der Tag. **1916** O. SEAMAN *Made in England* 35 For now the psychologic *Tag* has come To put the final lid on Christendom. **1918** *Times* 9 Dec. 9/3 The wonderful day, the great Der Tag, Which Prussians had vow'd with unmannerly brag Should see Old England lower her flag. **1924** J. BUCHAN *Three Hostages* ix. 125 We'll fix the 10th of June for *Der Tag*... The round-up of all must be simultaneous. **1939** C. DAY LEWIS *Child of Misfortune* III. iii. 290 You're saving it up for Der Tag... A time will come when those persons will be very sorry. **1966** P. FLOWER *Fiends of Family* xvi. 187 '*Der tag*,' Maggie said. 'At long last, the day of the great adventure.' **1975** tr. *Melchior's Sleeper Agent* II. 133 When *der Tag* comes, when his usefulness is Kaput, we'll slap him in detention.

tag, var. of TEG, a young sheep.

tag (tæg), *v.*^{1} [f. TAG *sb.*^{1}]

1. *trans.* To furnish or mark with or as with a tag (in various senses).

[**1436**, **1503**: see TAGGING.] **1627** W. HAWKINS *Apollo Shroving* II. i. 20 What did you giue me? Nothing but a dozen of rotten silke points. You must tagge them better ere I trusse vp your request. **1630** DAVENANT *Just Ital.* Wks. (1673) 455, I must e'en go tag Points in a Garret. **1705** *Hudibras Rediv.* IV. vi, Their Hair tagg'd with Pearls of Sweat. **1707** in W. McDowall *Hist. Dumfries* (1873) 461 The expense of tagging, tongueing, transporting and hanging of the said three bells. **1800** WATKINS *Biog. Dict.* s.v. *Bobart*, Mr. Granger says that on rejoicing days he used to tag his beard with silver. **1842** TENNYSON *St. Sim. Styl.* 31 All my beard Was tagg'd with icy fringes in the moon. **1899** CONAN DOYLE *Duet* iv. 41 The dim watery..sunlight..tagged all her wandering curls with a coppery gleam.

b. To furnish with a tag, tab, or label; to label. Also *spec.*, to mark and record (animals) so that their migrations can be traced.

(In quot. 1907 to patch, as with a label.)

1883 *Fisheries Exh. Catal.* 203 Photographs..showing.. the..tagging the fish, and the process of manipulation of the eggs and young fish at the hatchery. **1896** *Daily News* 30 Jan. 3/7 After inspection each animal will be tagged and described so that identification will be easily made upon landing. **1907** *Macmillan's Mag.* May 540 The..cloak of brown sackcloth, sometimes tagged here and there with red and green. **1908** *Daily Chron.* 26 Feb. 8/5 They should be.. wrapped in tissue paper and tagged, so that their covering need not be disturbed in a search for any particular colour. **1953** SCOTT & FISHER *Thousand Geese* vi. 58 The expedition was confined to camp, except for short dashes..to tag a few whooper cygnets. **1974** *Nature* 19 Apr. 642/2 Anglers tagged 954 bass..on the coast of Devon.

c. To furnish (a speech or composition) with a verbal tag, or tags, as quotations; to supply (prose or blank verse) with rimes.

1687 *Reflect. on Hind & Panther* 32 He hath put them into an unusual dress, and hath tagg'd 'em with Rhimes. **1690** *Waller's Poems* II. Pref., Really Verse in those days was but down-right prose, tag'd with rhymes. *a* **1696** AUBREY *Lives* (1898) II. 72 (*Milton*) Dreyden..went to him to have leave to putt his Paradise Lost into a drama in rhymne. Mr. Milton recieved him civilly, and told him he would give him leave to tagge his verses. **1714** POPE *Wife of Bath* 109 And tag each sentence with My life! my dear! **1823** *Examiner* 705/2 Canning tags his speeches with poetry. **1841** D'ISRAELI *Amen. Lit.* (1867) 369 The Scriptures..were tagged with rhymes for ballads.

d. *Biol.* and *Chem.* = LABEL *v.* 2.

1939 *Amer. Jrnl. Physiol.* CXXVII. 557 The radioactivity 'tags' the atoms. **1947** *Ann. Rev. Microbiol.* I. 271 The foregoing method is..not limited to 'tagging' the antigen by means of glucosamine analyses. **1969** *Times* 9 Apr. 7/2 DNA sub-units tagged with radioactive marker atoms were fed to bacteria. **1977** *Sci. Amer.* July 46/3 The antigens were first visualized by tagging their antibodies with a fluorescent dye that could be seen under ultraviolet radiation.

e. *Computers*. To label (an item of data) in order to identify it for subsequent processing or retrieval.

1959 M. H. WRUBEL *Primer of Programming for Digital Computers* iii. 56 We must..tag the instructions to be modified..so that those instructions and no others will be modified by adding the contents of the loop box. **1971** *Computers & Humanities* VI. 43 It is a simple matter to enter and tag automatically categories of information indicated by font and/or format... Such tagging is a part of the Dissly service. **1983** *Trans. Philol. Soc.* 33 This is a program which identifies and tags idioms which it finds in an Idiom list.

2. To append as an addition or afterthought; to fasten, tack on, or add as a tag *to* something. (Chiefly of things non-material.)

1704 SWIFT *Tale Tub* ii. (1709) 39 To this system of Religion were tagged several Subaltern Doctrines. **1785** MARTYN *Rousseau's Bot.* (1794) 10 The barbarous custom.. of tagging new names to the old ones. **1833** M. SCOTT *Tom Cringle* i. 1 Before the time when a gallant action or two tagged half of the letters of the alphabet to a man's name like the tail of a paper kite. **1839–40** W. IRVING *Wolfert's R.* vi. (1855) 87 They could not help expressing their wonder.. why the duke should have tagged this super-numerary day to the end of the year. **1848** THACKERAY *Van. Fair* (Bef. Curtain), I have no other moral than this to tag to the present story of 'Vanity Fair'. **1916** T. MACDONAGH *Literature in Ireland* 150 The first two verses of the better version.. are essential poetry; the three that are tagged on in the song-books are no such thing.

†**3.** To fasten, stitch, or tack together; to join. Also *fig. Obs.* (exc. as in b.)

1681 T. FLATMAN *Heraclitus Ridens* No. 34 (1713) I. 222 He.. has a great share of the Joyner's Trade in tagging Ends of Sedition. **1697** DRYDEN *Æneid* III. 777 His clothes were tagg'd with thorns; and filth his limbs besmear'd. **1706** DE FOE *Jure Div.* VII. 140 Tagging Fig-leaf-Vests, To hide his Body from the Sight of Beasts. **17..** SWIFT (J.), Resistance, and the succession of the house of Hanover, the whig writers perpetually tag together.

b. To join or string together (verses, rimes).

1720 MRS. MANLEY *Power of Love* (1741) p. viii, Adjusted into proper Periods, with necessary Monosyllables to tag them together. **1752** FIELDING *Amelia* VIII. v, I have been sometimes longer in tagging a couplet, than I have been in writing a speech. **1849** C. BRONTË *Shirley* III. vii. 159 He writes verses,—tags rhymes. **1887** LOWELL *Democr.* 207 It shows a pretty knack at tagging verses.

c. *intr.* To serve as a tag (in a verse, etc.).

1878 BROWNING *Poets Croisic* lxxiv, Thetis, who Is either Tethys or as good—both tag.

4. *intr.* To trail or drag behind; to follow closely, follow in one's train. Freq. const. *after, along, (a)round, on.* Also *fig.*

1676 WYCHERLEY *Pl. Dealer* I. i, I hate a harness, and will not tag on in a faction, kissing my leader behind, that another slave may do the like to me. **1768** TUCKER *Lt. Nat.* (1834) I. 596 They range the world with a boisterous rabble tagging at their heels. *c* **1794** *Search after Perfect* I. iv. in *New Brit. Theatre* (1814) III. 55 Why should a nurse and child come tagging after her? **1822** G. F. COOPER *Spy* II. xii. 307 Pooh! Pooh!.. if you tag after a troop of horse, a small bit of a joke must be borne. **1897** KIPLING *Captains Courageous* ix. 214 Don't go taggin' araound after them whose eyes bung out with fatness. **1900** ADE *More Fables in Slang* (1902) 113 The men.. wanted to Tag along, but Clara drove them back. **1902** ELIZ. L. BANKS *Newspaper Girl* 24 I'm an American girl and can take care of myself, and I won't have anybody tagging round after me. **1930** J. DOS PASSOS *42nd Parallel* II. xi. 164 She followed his talk breathless the way she used to tag along after Joe and Alec down to the carbarns when she was little. **1933** D. L. SAYERS *Murder must Advertise* iii. 41 He used to tag round with that de Momerie crowd. **1946** 'P. QUENTIN' *Puzzle for Fiends* (1947) ix. 70 So you're ready to tag along with me, eh, Gordy? **1948** C. DAY LEWIS *Otterbury Incident* 43 Toppy's kid sister.. tagged on, which was rather a bore. **1957** *Economist* 23 Nov. 661/2 There is a Yemeni home public. Its upper crust has been most critical of the recent tendency to tag along with Egypt and do deals, including an arms deal, with Russia. **1960** S. BARSTOW *Kind of Loving* I. vi. 126 Two or three more people sitting outside the room where they actually take the blood. Me and the Old Man tag on to the line. **1960** L. COOPER *Accomplices* I. iv. 37 He was sick of the sight of those damned Batemans... Couldn't we ever go anywhere without them tagging on? **1960** C. DAY LEWIS *Buried Day* ii. 44, I would tag around with him, hardly understanding a word he said because of his thick East-Anglian dialect. **1973** J. PATTINSON *Search Warrant* v. 80, I guess I'll tag along. Just for the ride.

b. *trans.* To follow closely, to dog. Also *spec.*, to follow as a detective or spy. Cf. TAG *sb.*[1] 13, TAIL *v.*[1] 5 b.

1884 C. H. FARNHAM in *Harper's Mag.* Feb. 394/1 The Indians are wandering.., tagged at their heels by death and starvation. **1966** 'A. HALL' *9th Directive* vii. 63 Why did you tag me here? **1975** —— *Mandarin Cypher* viii. 123 If I thought I was tagged here because Chiang had blown me I was wrong.

†**5.** *intr.* To hang down or trail like a tag. *Obs.*

1617 J. MOORE *Mappe Mans Mortalitie* II. viii. 153 They which weare long garments.. doe take and gird them vp, lest they should tag in the way.

6. *trans.* To cut off tags from (sheep).

1707 MORTIMER *Husb.* (1721) I. 243 Before they are shorn, great care ought to be taken to tag them, as they call it, which is to clip away the Wooll of their Tails, and behind, that the Dung may not hang on it. **1853** T. D. PRICE *Diary* 17 Mar. (MS.), Tagged the ewes in the forenoon. **1863** H. S. RANDALL *Pract. Shepherd* iii. 141 Tagging sheep before they are let out to grass. *a* **1890** [implied in TAGGING].

tag, *v.*[2] [f. TAG *sb.*[2]] **1.** *trans.* To touch or hit (a person), as in the game of tag; = TIG *v.*

1878 F. H. HART *Sazerac Lying Club* 166 One of them, who had been 'tagged' seven times in succession, got tired, and proposed to change to playing house. **1891** *Jrnl. Amer. Folk-Lore* IV. 222 One player, who is 'it', attempts to tag, or touch, one of the other players. **1969** I. & P. OPIE *Children's Games* ii. 64 In Monmouthshire, Gloucestershire, and Oxfordshire, they speak of 'tagging' each other.

2. *Baseball* and *Softball.* **a.** To put out (a runner) by touching him with the ball (or with the gloved hand holding the ball) while he is off base. Also with *out.* Cf. TAG *sb.*[2] 2.

1907 'B. L. STANDISH' *Dick Merriwell's Magnetism* xxxviii. 243 He tagged Spratt, and this made the second man out. **1944** E. S. GARDNER *Case of Black-Eyed Blonde* 64 Keep cutting corners, Mason, and I'm going to catch you off first base one of these days, and then I'll tag you out. **1971** L. KOPPETT *N.Y. Times Guide Spectator Sports* i. 21 No one is attempting to tag him. **1976** *Billings* (Montana) *Gaz.* 28 June 1-C/2 (*caption*) Dave Konzen, of Buck's Bar slow pitch softball team, is tagged out as he slides against Heidelberg of Tacoma, Wash. **1982** S. B. FLEXNER *Listening to America* 34 Someone had the bright idea of forcing the runner out by throwing the ball to the base ahead of him or by tagging him with the ball rather than throwing the ball at him.

b. *intr. to tag up*: of a runner to (return to and) touch one's base after a fly ball is caught.

1942 *Baseball Digest* Dec. 52 Fletcher tagged up at third after the catch and then started for the plate. **1971** L. KOPPETT *N.Y. Times Guide Spectator Sports* i. 20 The runner 'tags up', waits at his base until the ball is caught, and still beats the throw to the next base. **1978** G. WRIGHT *Illustr. Handbk. Sporting Terms* 89/2 If the ball is caught.. the base runners, unless tagging up.., may not advance.

c. *trans.* To make a hit or run off (a pitcher).

1961 in WEBSTER. **1974** *Greenville* (S. Carolina) *News* 23 Apr. 8/5 Seaver was taken out of the game after being tagged for hits by the first two batters in the Pittsburgh sixth.

Tagalog (tə'gɑːlɒg), *sb.* and *a.* Also † **Tagal, -la, -lian, -lic, -loc.** [Tagalog, f. *tagá* native to + *ilog* river; cf. Sp. *tagalo.*] **A.** *sb.* **a.** (A member of) a people living in the neighbourhood of Manila in the Philippine Islands. **b.** The Austronesian language spoken by this people, an official language of the Republic of the Philippines.

1704 tr *Careri's Voy. round World* in A. & J. Churchill *Coll. Voy. & Trav.* IV. 430/2 From these are descended the Tagalians, which are the Natives of Manila and the Country about it. *Ibid.* 446/2 The Languages are so numerous, that there are six in the only Island of Manila, which are Tagalian, Pampangan, [etc.]. **1808** *Asiatick Researches* X. 207 The Tagala or rather Tă-Gála or the Gala language is among the Philippines, what the Malayu is in the Malay islands. *Ibid.* 213 With respect to the original literature of the Tăgalás, the accounts of the Spanish missionaries are rather discordant. **1814** J. MAVER *Martinez de Zuñiga's Hist. View Philippine Islands* I. p. xi, In respect to the aboriginal language, or Tagalic, very slight attempts have been made to trace it beyond the quarter in which it was found to prevail. Our author.. draws the conclusion that the Tagalic language and original population of all the islands westward of the coast of South America derive from that continent. **1834** W. MARSDEN *Misc. Wks.* 39 Of these dialects six are considered as meriting distinction..; they are the *Tagala* or *Tagalog* [etc.]. **1840** *Penny Cycl.* XVIII. 88/2 The Malays are divided into a great number of tribes, of which that called Tagala occupies the neighbourhood of Manila. **1885** *Encycl. Brit.* XVIII. 753/1 First among these rank the Tagals... Their language (Tagalog) especially has made extensive encroachments on the other Philippine tongues since the conquest. **1919** F. R. BLAKE in C. F. Hockett *Leonard Bloomfield Anthol.* (1970) 82 This work contains an extended treatment of Tagalog, the most important native language of the Philippine Islands. **1933** L. BLOOMFIELD *Language* vi. 105 Even simpler is the *three-vowel* system which appears in some languages, such as Tagalog. **1974** *Encycl. Brit. Micropædia* IX. 764/3 Most Tagalogs are farmers. **1976** 'G. BLACK' *Moon for Killers* vi. 83 A verbal exchange.. starting in English, shifting to Spanish, and then apparently getting down to the real obscenities in Tagálog.

B. *adj.* Of or pertaining to this people or their language.

1808 *Asiatick Researches* X. 208 The Tăgála alphabet consists of seventeen letters. **1814** [see the sb. above]. **1859** J. BOWRING *Philippine Islands* xiii. 219 What is the Tagáloc language? **1906** *Jrnl. Amer. Folk-Lore* XIX. 191 (*heading*) Philippine (Tagalog) superstitions. **1959** N. MAILER *Advts. for Myself* (1961) 131 Miguel said something to the other Filipinos in the Tagalog language. **1978** M. B. HOOKER *Conc. Legal Hist. South-East Asia* viii. 215 The *Maragtas* text.. is found in a recension dated A.D. 1650 written in the Tagalog script.

'tag-along, *a.* and *sb. N. Amer. colloq.* Also **tagalong.** [f. vbl. phr. *to tag along*: see TAG *v.*[1] 4 a.] **A.** *adj.* **a.** Designating that which is towed or trailed behind something else. **b.** Applied to an uninvited follower.

1944 *Sun* (Baltimore) 21 Jan. 2/3 Evidence of trailed, or 'tag-along', bombs still is scanty. **1960** *Newsweek* 20 June 91/1 The tag-along highway trailers are delivered to.. the bus terminals. **1973** *Islander* (Victoria, B.C.) 10 June 16/1 The small trailer snug beside it like a tagalong pup. **1974** *Spartanburg* (S. Carolina) *Herald-Jrnl.* 21 Apr. C9 (Advt.), Also all types of trucks and truck tractors, all types of trailers including low-boy and tag-A-long.

B. *sb.* An unwelcome, uninvited, or neglected companion.

1961 in WEBSTER. **1967** *Boston Sunday Herald* 2–8 Apr. 45/1 The whole family suffers when Ernie becomes a dreadful tagalong. **1974** *Publishers Weekly* 28 Oct. 46/1 Seems to have spent most of her life as a 'tagalong' to a man who, as test pilot and astronaut, was seldom home. **1977** *Islander* (Victoria, B.C.) 16 Jan. 8/1 (*heading*) Are Victoria women just tag-alongs in motor sports?

tagarene (tægə'riːn). *north. dial.* Also **tag(a)reen.** [Origin uncertain: perh. arbitrary formation on TAG *sb.*[1]] More fully ***tagarene shop***: An old clothes or rag shop; a marine store. Hence **tagarene-man,** the keeper of a marine store, *esp.* one who visits ships in dock or harbour with a boatful of wares for exchange.

1855 ROBINSON *Whitby Gloss.* s.v., 'They keep a tagreen shop', an old clothes store; an old rope and rag depôt. **1894** *Northumb. Gloss.* s.v., A 'tagareen man' has a floating shop which he rows about the tiers of ships, announcing his presence by a bell. **1900** F. W. BULLEN *With Christ at Sea* xi. 285 The skipper arrived with his crony the 'tagarene' man and a large supply of brandy.

tagetes (tə'dʒiːtiːz). [med.L. (L. Fuchs *De Historia Stirpium* (1542) 48), f. *Tages*, name of an Etruscan deity.] An annual or perennial herb of the genus of this name, belonging to the family Compositæ and native to South and Central America; esp. = MARIGOLD 1 b.

1792 *Curtis's Bot. Mag.* V. 150 (*heading*) Spreading Tagetes, or French Marigold. **1895** W. ROBINSON *Eng. Flower Garden* (ed. 4) 780/2 There are also perennial Tagetes, but they are not hardy enough to make satisfactory plants out-of-doors. **1926** *Contemp. Rev.* Feb. 233 A thick mass of petunia and tagetes.. in blossom. **1962** R. PAGE *Educ. Gardener* vii. 220 French gardeners are used to cultivating huge batches of.. several varieties of tagetes. **1975** *Country Life* 13 Feb. 388/2 Tagetes marigolds are not at all bad in shade. **1980** L. MANTELL *Murder or Three* ii. 23 Small shrubs.. and an edging of velvety gold and brown Tagetes.

tagged (tægd, 'tægɪd), *ppl. a.* [f. TAG *sb.*[1] and *v.*[1] + -ED.] Furnished with a tag or tags.

1. a. Of a garment: Slashed. **b.** Tattered. **c.** Bearing or wearing a tag or label; labelled.

c **1380** *Antecrist* in Todd *Three Treat. Wyclif* (1851) 128 Men to kerve here morsellis wiþ tagged cloþes & crakowe pykis. **1570** LEVINS *Manip.* 49/21 Tagged, *laciniatus, infulatus.* **1631** GOUGE *God's Arrows* I. § 57. 98 The Father of the Prodigall seeing his sonne afarre off ragged and tagged. **1908** *Times* 26 Dec. 10/2 By 10 o'clock every man, woman, and child.. were wearing at least one tag, and among the younger men there was competition to be the most 'tagged' person in the city [San Francisco].

d. Of an animal: marked to help study of its habits or migrations.

1927 *Zoologica* IX. 204 Every tagged frog was given a new page. **1979** *Fisherman's Weekly* 21 June 4/3 More than 400 of the tagged brown and rainbow trout released into Draycote Water by fisheries officers of the Severn-Trent Water Authority have already been notified.

e. Fastened *on*, appended. Cf. TAG *v.*[1] 2.

1982 *N. & Q.* Feb. 80/1 A tagged-on chapter on 'Critical History' runs only to six pages.

f. *Computers.* Marked or labelled with a 'tag' (TAG *sb.*[1] 8 e).

1983 *Trans. Philol. Soc.* 29 A tagged corpus.. provides a head start for anyone undertaking more advanced linguistic analyses of the corpus.

2. Of a lace or point: Having a tag or aglet.

1645 EVELYN *Diary* June, Knots of points richly tagged about their shoulders. **1714** *Fr. Bk. of Rates* 45 Laces silk tagg'd per Pound 00 12. **1828** H. BEST *Italy as it is* 228 The tagged ends of the ribs of whalebone by which these [parasols] are distended. *a* **1859** MACAULAY *Biogr., Bunyan* (1860) 37 He learned to make long-tagged thread laces.

3. Of cattle: Having the tail tipped with white (or other distinctive colour); also, furnished with a bob or brush.

1458 *Will* in *Ripon Ch. Acts* 75 Unum bovem vocatum taggyd ox. **1544** in *Knaresborough Wills* (Surtees) I. 42 One taged whye. **1588** *Wills & Inv. N.C.* (Surtees) II. 33 *note*, A black tagged cow. **1640** SIR J. LESSLEY in *Antiq. Rep.* (1809) IV. 436, I maun hae the tag'd tail'd trooper [horse] that stands in the staw. **1680** *Lond. Gaz.* No. 1482/4 One red taged Bullock. **1852** MUNDY *Our Antipodes* (1857) 87 With a white-tagged brush peeping out of his pocket, the dingo's head hanging from the whipper-in's saddle.

4. Of wool or hair: Hanging in matted locks.

1757 DYER *Fleece* I. 369 Skill.. which trims their tails, of filth and tagged wool.

5. a. Of sheep: Having the disease known as tag.

1614 MARKHAM *Cheap Husb.* III. xvii. (1668) 91 A sheep is said to be Tag'd or Belt, when by a continual squirt.. he berayeth his tail in such wise, that.. it scaldeth, and breedeth the scab therein. **1741** [see TAG *sb.*[1] 12].

b. Of wheat: see quot.

1892 *Chamb. Jrnl.* 10 Sept. 591/1 Wheat.. discoloured at the tip of the kernel by smut, 'tagged' as it is called.

6. *Biol.* and *Chem.* = LABELLED *ppl. a.* d.

1945 *Jrnl. Sci. Instruments* XXII. 23/1 Tagged atoms are used to enable the investigator to see where the rest of his material is going. **1955** *Sci. News Let.* 2 July 15/1 When a plant is supplied with isotopically labeled nitrate.. the 'tagged' element rapidly spreads throughout the tissues and is incorporated into all the major nitrogen fractions.

taggeen (tə'giːn). *Anglo-Ir.* [ad. Ir. *taidhgín.*] A small cup or glass (of spirits); a 'dram'.

1899 SOMERVILLE & 'ROSS' *Some Experiences Irish R.M.* i. 10 'There's no bath in the house, sir.. but.. would ye like a taggeen?' This alternative proposal proved to be a glass of raw whisky. **1936** M. FRANKLIN *All that Swagger* iii. 35 Doing the dirty work of some cowardly crawler, who's bought you for a plug of tobacco and a taggeen of rum.

tagger[1] ('tægə(r)). [f. TAG *v.*[1] or *sb.*[1] + -ER[1].]

1. One who tags: see the verb.

1648 *Pair of Spectacles for City* 11 We bound him to a Tagger of Points. **1785** R. GRAVES *Eugenius* I. ii. 6 Our orators are mere praters—and our poets taggers of rhime. **1883** *Sat. Rev.* 12 May 592/1 The Scotch seem to have entertained a mistaken theory that the taggers of rhymes to the prose version of the Psalms were inspired.

†**2.** A tag, a projecting part. *Obs.* ? *misuse.*

a **1687** COTTON *Burlesque Gt. Frost* Poems (1689) 98 Comparing Hedg-hogs, or Porcupine's small Taggers, To their more dang'rous Swords and Daggers.

3. A device for tagging a sheep: see TAG *v.*[1] 6.

1891 in *Cent. Dict.*

4. *pl.* Very thin sheet-iron, usually coated with tin. (Also **taggar.**) Now also *sing.*, chiefly in *attrib.* use. [Probably so called from being used to make tags of laces.]

1834 McCulloch *Dict. Comm.* II. 1160 Taggars 14 by 10 inches, £2 5*s.* **1853** *Lardner's Cab. Cycl., Manuf. Metals* III. 43 Tinned Taggers, Black Taggers. **1858** Simmonds *Dict. Trade, Taggers*, a very thin kind of tin-plates used for coffin-plate inscriptions and tops of umbrellas. **1879** P. W. Flower *Hist. Tin Trade* xii. (1880) 156 A sheet of taggers, as thin as paper itself. **1894** *U.S. Tariff, Schedule Rates* §121 Sheets or plates of iron or steel, or taggers iron or steel, coated with tin or lead..and commercially known as tin plates, terne plates, and taggers tin. **1938** *Shelf Appeal* July 26/1 The tagger-top in its present form, with a cutter in the lid. **1959** *Gloss. Packaging Terms (B.S.I.)* 55 *Lever ring and tagger*, a lever type closure comprising a diaphragm of tagger tinplate or aluminium secured (together with the ring) to the body... *Cutter lid*, an outer lid containing a steel cutter with which the thin tagger tinplate top of the body is pierced and cut away.

tagger[2] (ˈtægə(r)). [f. TAG *sb.*[2] or *v.*[2] + -ER[1].] The pursuer in the game of tag.

1891 in *Cent. Dict.* **1969** I. & P. Opie *Children's Games* i. 23 One person is the tagger and has to count to thirty.

ˈtaggery. *nonce-wd.* [f. TAGGER[1]: see -ERY[1].] The work of a tagger; the tagging of rimes.

1845 *Blackw. Mag.* LVII. 376 Had Milton lived to hear their taggery, wrathful fire would have been in his eyes.

tagging (ˈtægɪŋ), *vbl. sb.* [f. TAG *v.*[1] and *sb.*[1] + -ING[1].] **1. a.** The action of TAG *v.*[1]

1503 *Acc. Ld. High Treas. Scot.* II. 202 For ane curpal and ane tee to the harnes sadill, tagging..of the samyn. **1572** in Feuillerat *Revels Q. Eliz.* (1908) 159 For Tagging of Laces iiij[d]. **1693** Dennis *Imp. Crit.* v. 50 'Tis not the tagging of the Acts with a Chorus, that properly makes a Tragedy one Body, but the Unity of the Action. **1779** Mme. D'Arblay *Diary* 11 Jan., What trouble and tagging we had! *a* **1890** *New Amer. Farm Bk.* 436 (Cent. Dict.) Tagging or clotting is the removal of such wool as is liable to get fouled when the sheep are turned on to the fresh pastures. **1906** *Athenæum* 2 June 664/3 An occasional..tagging-out of a line.

b. The marking of animals as an aid to study of their migrations.

1927 *Zoologica* IX. 201 (*title*) Frog tagging: a method of studying anuran life habits. **1953** Scott & Fisher *Thousand Geese* vi. 65 We worked away in camp at journals, nest records, tagging data. **1960** *Guardian* 25 Oct. 8/4 To study the movement and growth rates there is an elaborate system of fish tagging carried out at sea. **1972** *Even. Telegram* (St. John's, Newfoundland) 24 June 11/1 Tagging studies have shown most salmon intercepted are headed for the northern river spawning beds.

c. *Computers.* The action of TAG *v.* 1 e.

1948 *Theory & Techniques for Design of Electronic Digital Computers* (Moore School of Electr. Engin., Univ. of Pennsylvania) IV. xxxix. 20 This tagging is done by the little cycle..until the sentinel..trips on a coincidence and causes the control to go on to the next stage of computation. **1972** *Computers & Humanities* VII. 5 The study of *Automatic Grammatical Tagging of English*..describes the theory and method of parts-of-speech tags, procedures used in tagging, and the context frame test employed. **1983** *Trans. Philol. Soc.* 33 The tagging of the LOB Corpus is due for completion by September 1983.

2. *attrib.*, as †**tagging iron**, a tailor's tool for tagging cloth.

1436 *Exch. Rolls Scotl.* IV. 681 Certis ferris scissorum dictis taging irynnis.

Taghairm (ˈtœːɣɪrm, ˈtœːɪrm). *Sc.* [Gael.] A method of divination formerly practised in the Scottish Highlands (see quots.).

1774 T. Pennant *Tour in Scotl. & Voy. Hebrides 1772* 311 A vast cataract, whose waters falling from a high rock, jet so far as to form a dry hollow beneath... One of these imposters was sowed up in the hide of an ox, and..was placed in this concavity: the trembling enquirer was brought to the place, where the shade, and the roaring of the waters, encreased the dread of the occasion. The question is put, and the person in the hide delivers his answer, and so ends this species of divination styled *Taghairm*. **1810** Scott *Lady of Lake* iv. iv. 146 Brian an augury hath tried, Of that dread kind which must not be Unless in dread extremity, The Taghairm call'd; by which, afar, Our sires foresaw the events of war. **1906** *Athenæum* 2 June 668/3 Another saying, 'Keep the cat turning', refers to the horrid practice of the Taghairm, or divination by the cat. **1953** *Scots Mag.* Dec. 223 Taghairm was, indeed, a magical means of compelling spiritual presences to grant desirable and valuable boons to the sorcerer who invoked them.

†**ˈtaghmical,** *a. Heb. Gram. Obs. rare.* [f. Heb. *ṭaʿam* taste, discernment, judgement, in later Heb. explanation, meaning, and then the ordinary word for accentual mark (in reference to the functions of the Heb. accents) + -ICAL. (The Heb. ע is here represented by *gh*: cf. *Gaza*, *Gomorrah*.)] Of or pertaining to the Hebrew written accents as determining the syntactical structure and hence the meaning of passages (as understood by the Masoretes).

1698 W. Cross (*title*) The Taghmical Art: or the Art of Expounding Scripture By the Points usually called Accents, But are really Tactical. **1730** T. Boston *Mem.* x. (ed. Morrison) 301 What Mr. Cross calls the Taghmical Art; viz. the sacred stigmatology or accentuation of the Hebrew Bible. **1859** *Life E. Henderson* iii. 119 *note*, The idea broke in upon him when reading Cross's Taghmical Art.

taght, obs. f. *taught*: see TEACH *v.*

tagil: see TAGLE *v.*

tagilite (ˈtægɪlaɪt). *Min.* [f. *Tagilsk* (see def.) + -ITE[1].] A name given by R. Hermann to a hydrous phosphate of copper occurring in monoclinic crystals at Nischni Tagilsk, in the Urals.

1868 Dana *Min.* 567 Hermann's tagilite was in reniform concretions.

†**tagle, tagil, tagyl,** *v.* *Obs.* [Known in northern ME. only in Hampole; app. the same as mod.Sc. TAIGLE, q.v. Prob. of Scand. origin, and cognate with Sw. dial. (Bornholm) *taggla* to disarrange, bring into disorder.

In the quots. from the *Prose Treatises* of Hampole only *tagil*, *tagyl* are cited. In the *Psalter* (ed. Bramley 1884), in Ps. xxxix. 16, 2 MSS. including N., which best represents the original, have *tagild*; 8 later MSS. have *tangild*, *-gyld*, *-glyd*, *-glid*, *-gled*, *-geled*. In *Ibid.*, *Abacuc* 31, MS. N. again has *tagild*; 3 MSS. have *takyld*, *takild*, 2 *tackid*, 2 *tangild*, *tanglid*. Evidently, *tagild* was the original word, *takild* perh. a scribal, and *tangild* a nasalized phonetic variant. *Tagil* appears to be preserved in the Sc. TAIGLE *v.*; the nasalized form remains in TANGLE *v.*, q.v.]

trans. To entangle, to involve or engage in things that embarrass or encumber.

a **1340** Hampole *Ps.* xxxix. 16 (MS. N.) Na man may wit hou many vices ar þat men ar tagild with. [*So MS. S.*; *MSS. U. & L.* tangild; *Laud* 321 tangyld, *Magd. Coll.* 52 *& Laud* 418 tangild, *Bodl.* 953 tanglyd, *Tanner* 1 tangled, *Univ. Coll.* lvi tangeled; *Bodl.* 467 snaryd.] *Ibid.*, *Abacuc* 31 (N.) Swa þaire affecciouns ar ay tagild with som lufe þat drawes þame fra godds lufe. [*MSS. U. & Laud* 286 takild, *S.* takyld; *Tanner* 1 tangild, *Laud* 448 tanglid, *Bodl.* 288 & 877 tackid, *Bodl.* 953 medelid.] *c* **1340** —— *Prose Tr.* 12 All delytes of all thyngez þat mane may be tagyld with in thoghte or dede. *Ibid.* 13 Withowttene tagillynge of oþer thynges.

taglet (ˈtæglɪt). *rare.* [f. TAG *sb.*[1] + -LET.] A small tag: *spec.* **a.** A tendril; **b.** A catkin.

1578 Lyte *Dodoens* v. lxxx. 650 The vine..putteth foorth ..certayne tendrelles, or clasping caprioles, & tying tagglets, wherewith al it taketh hold vpon trees. *Ibid.* 651 The same taggle ttes or clasping tendrelles of the vine. **1698** Fryer *Acc. E. India & P.* 405 Out of Taglets of Willows they make a compound Cool-Water, very sweet smelling and refreshing. **1864** in Webster; and in mod. Dicts.

[**taglia,** the Italian word for a pulley, or system of pulleys: in some recent Eng. dicts. from Brande, but not known in Eng. use.]

tagliacotian: see TALIACOTIAN.

tagliarini (‖taʎʎaˈrini, tæljəˈriːnɪ). [ad. It. *taglierini* sb. pl. (also used); cf. TAGLIATELLE.] Egg noodles cut into very narrow strips.

1846 [see RAVIOLI]. **1899** J. Ross *Leaves from our Tuscan Kitchen* 69 Repeat the alternate layers of tagliarini, cheese and butter, until the dish is full. **1943** A. Simon *Conc. Encycl. Gastron.* IV. 64/1 Italian pastes..known..by different names such as Macaroni, Vermicelli,..Tagliarini, Tagliatelle, [etc.]. **1964** E. H. & M. O. Knopf *Food of Italy* ii. iii. 184 To make tagliarini. Proceed as for lasagne. **1982** G. Bugialli *Classic Techniques Italian Cooking* vi. 138 The finely cut pasta, *taglierini* almost as fine as angel's hair, is appropriate to very delicate sauces and to broths and soups.

tagliatelle (‖taʎʎaˈtɛlle, tæljəˈtɛlɪ). Also tagliatelli (-i). [It., sb. pl., f. *tagliare* to cut.] Egg noodles cut into ribbons. Also *fig.*

1899 J. Ross *Leaves from our Tuscan Kitchen* 69 (*heading*) Tagliatelle with ham. **1926** R. Hall *Adam's Breed* i. iii. 21 There were paste from Naples..Tagliatelle, Gnocchi, [etc.]. **1934** [see PASTA]. **1957** G. Smith *Friends* 9 In Rome, where the *tagliatelli* had disagreed with him. **1967** [see RIGATONI *sb. pl.*]. **1977** *Times Lit. Suppl.* 4 Feb. 120/2 All those tapes, those monstrous forkfuls of magnetized tagliatelle..would lead to definite strangulation. **1980** T. Holme *Neapolitan Streak* 100 She ladled *tagliatelle*..on to the plates of her family. **1983** *Listener* 13 Jan. 5/2 That sentence would have wound up on the cutting-room floor, another piece of inedible Grundig tagliatelle.

†**taglioni** (tɑːˈljəʊnɪ). *Obs.* [Named after a family of ballet-dancers in the early 19th c.] A kind of overcoat in use in the first half of the 19th c.

18.. Scott (Webster), He ought certainly to exchange his *taglioni* or comfortable great-coat for a cuirass of steel. **1837** Thackeray *Ravenswing* iii (1887) 167 A rhubarb-coloured coat of the sort which, I believe, are called Taglionis, and which have no waist-buttons. *a* **1845** Barham *Ingol. Leg.* Ser. iii. *Blasphemer's Warn.*, I've brought to protect myself well, a Good stout Taglioni and gingham umbrella. **1847** *Man in Moon* Apr. I. 201 White Taglioni, with four-in-hand drags on the buttons.

‖**tagma** (ˈtægmə). Pl. **tagmata.** [a. Gr. τάγμα something arranged, f. τάσσειν to set in order.]

1. *Veg. Physiol.* A term applied by Pfeffer (in German, 1877) to the aggregates of molecules of which the structure of a plant is supposed to consist.

1885 Goodale *Physiol. Bot.* §588. 213 *note*, Pfeffer applies a general term, *Tagma*, to all aggregates of molecules, thus bringing under one head the pleon, micella, and micellar aggregate; and he applies the name *Syntagma* to all bodies made up of tagmata. **1889** Burdon-Sanderson in *Nature* 26 Sept. 524 That an element of living material, is not equivalent to a molecule, however big or complex, but must rather be an arrangement or phalanx of molecules of different kinds. Hence the word tagma, first used by Pfeffer, has come to be accepted as best expressing the notion.

2. *Zool.* Each of the morphologically distinct regions, comprising several adjoining segments, into which the bodies of arthropods and some other metamerically organized animals are divided. Chiefly *pl.* Hence **tagˈmosis,** the formation of tagmata.

1902 E. R. Lankester in *Encycl. Brit.* XXV. 691/2 It is convenient to have a special word for..regions of like meres, and we call each a tagma (ταγμα, a regiment). The word 'tagmosis' is applicable to the formation of such regions. **1935** R. E. Snodgrass *Princ. Insect Morphol.* iv. 80 Tagmosis is more variable in the Crustacea [than in insects]; in the Chilopoda and Diplopoda it results only in the formation of a head, including the gnathal segments, and a body. **1980** C. Gillott *Entomol.* iii. 54 The basic segmental structure is frequently obscured as a result of tagmosis. In insects three tagmata are found: the head, the thorax, and the abdomen.

3. *Linguistics.* **a.** A feature of grammatical arrangement or syntax.

1949 *Archivum Linguisticum* I. 1 Such distinctions as that of morpheme and 'tagma' as the constituents of the syntagm provide the necessary correction. But there is a different sense in which morpheme and tagma may share in the expression of the meaning of a syntagm: a feature of meaning may be distributed over both.

b. In tagmemics, the smallest meaningful unit of grammatical substance (contrasted with tagmeme).

1964 R. E. Longacre *Grammar Discovery Procedures* i. 46 Copy the data from the filing slips onto charts: (a) There should be a column for each tagma, i.e. for each tentatively identified function-set correlation. **1969** W. A. Cook *Introd. Tagmemic Analysis* vii. 187 Tagmemics is a grouping process, which involves human judgment, an attempt to group tagmas into units essential to the language, as the language appears to the native speaker.

tagmeme (ˈtægmiːm). *Linguistics.* [f. Gr. τάγμα arrangement (see TAGMA) + -EME.]

1. The smallest meaningful unit of grammatical form.

1933 L. Bloomfield *Language* x. 166 In the case of lexical forms, we have defined the smallest meaningful units as morphemes, and their meanings as sememes; in the same way, the smallest meaningful units of grammatical form may be spoken of as tagmemes, and their meanings as episememes. **1950** S. Potter *Our Language* 86 Beginning with the phoneme, philologists pass on to speak about morphemes, taxemes or tagmemes.

2. The correlate of a grammatical function and the class of items which can perform it.

1943 K. L. Pike in *Language* XIX. 69 Somewhat diffidently I suggest the following classifications and relabelings as perhaps being a bit easier to handle than Bloomfield's... *Tagmeme*, a composite view of the basic composite taxemes of a linguistic form, at any one specific layer of structure. E.g. the total arrangement features of the form *duchess* considered as a single entity. **1957** —— in *General Linguistics* III. 29 In future work, therefore, we are adopting the term *tagmeme*. It should be noted, however, that our definition of this term is sharply different from Bloomfield. **1968** *Language* XLIV. 190 Another basic concept in tagmemic analysis is the consistent distinction observed between obligatory and optional tagmemes. **1969** S. Potter *Changing English* viii. 163 Every sentence is a frame into which syntactic units, or tagmemes, are fitted. When a word is forced into an unusual tagmemic slot, it is said to undergo grammatical conversion or functional shift. **1973** *Amer. Speech 1970* XLV. 135 The highest level tagmeme operates at the level of the T-unit. **1981** *Word 1980* XXXI. 232 The infrastructure of English contains seven slots or tagmemes and that of German six.

tagmemic (tægˈmiːmɪk), *a.* *Linguistics.* [f. TAGMEME + -IC.] Of or pertaining to tagmemes or tagmemics.

1958 K. L. Pike in *Internat. Jrnl. Amer. Linguistics* XXIV. 275 In order to demonstrate another crucial difference between our tagmeme and that of Bloomfield it is necessary to indicate the manner in which slot and distribution class are relevant to our tagmemic view. **1964** R. H. Robins *Gen. Linguistics* p. xx, P. Postal..sets out a vigorous criticism of both immediate constituent and tagmemic analysis. **1968** *Language* XLIV. 190 Tagmemic theory provides a tight hierarchical scheme for grammatical description. **1969** [see TAGMEME 2]. **1978** *English Jrnl.* Dec. 66 A clause analysis technique reflecting a sketch of the core grammatical system of English based on a tagmemic model. **1981** *Word 1980* XXXI. 231 He..adopts the generative tagmemic approach as the basis of his work.

tagmemicist (tægˈmiːmɪsɪst). *Linguistics.* [f. TAGMEMIC(S + -IST.] A student or exponent of tagmemics.

1965 *Language* XLI. 640 It would be easy to go farther and say that transformationists represent the extreme of preoccupation with linguistic theory, while tagmemicists represent the extreme of practical concern. **1972** *Times Lit. Suppl.* 22 Sept. 1116/2 Like the units of the tagmemicists, Saumjan's categories are a combination of form and function. **1977** *Language* LIII. 247 The linguistic study of discourse or intrasentential relations has been carried out by such diverse scholars as..tagmemicists (e.g. Pike 1967).

tagmemics (tægˈmiːmɪks), *sb. pl.* (const. as *sing.*). *Linguistics.* [f. TAGMEME: see -IC 2.] The study and description of language in terms of tagmemes; *spec.* a school of linguistic analysis, based on the work of Kenneth L. Pike (b. 1912), which stresses the functional and structural relations of grammatical units.

1947 C. F. Hockett in *Language* XXIII. 274 This term [sc. *tactics*] seems simpler than 'taxemics' or 'tagmemics', which one might derive more directly from Bloomfield's labels. **1958** K. L. Pike in *Internat. Jrnl. Amer. Linguistics* XXIV. 273 Tagmemics, as I see it, should work with neither of these schematic views by itself. **1964** *Language* XL. 314 The similarity of Firthian linguistics to American slot-and-filler grammatical description, notably tagmemics, has already been noted. **1967** R. H. ROBINS *Short Hist. Linguistics* viii. 212 In thus employing semantics diagnostically, and in severely modifying immediate constituent structures in syntax, tagmemics marks its major divergencies from 'Bloomfieldian' grammatical analysis. **1975** M. A. K. HALLIDAY in S. Rogers *Children & Lang.* IV. 225 With the now general recognition of the basically tri-stratal nature of the linguistic system (and Prague theory, glossematics, system-structure theory, tagmemics, stratification theory and the later versions of transformation theory are all variants on this theme), the semantic perspective has been restored. **1981** *Word 1980* XXXI. 230 He makes use of the slot-and-filler infrastructure, characteristic of tagmemics.

tagmosis: see TAGMA 2.

‖**tagnicati** (taɲi'kati). Also **tañi-**. [a. Guarani and Sp. *tañicati*; in F. *tagnicati*.] The native name in Guarani of the White-lipped Peccary of Paraguay, also called TAYASSU.

1827 GRIFFITH tr. *Cuvier's Anim. Kingd.* III. x. 334 Here may be placed..the Tagnicati, Taitetou, Tajassou, etc. (*Dicotyles labiatus*, Cuv.). **1868** J. E. GRAY in *Proc. Zool. Soc.* 45 *Dicotyles labiatus*. Black-brown, varied with yellowish; no neck-bands; lower jaw white... Tagnicati, Azara, Paraguay i. 25. **1888** WOOD *Illustr. Nat. Hist.* 753 The Tagnicati, or white-lipped Peccary..derives its name from a band of white hairs that crosses the upper jaw, and covers nearly the whole of the lower.

tag-rag ('tægræg), *sb.*, *a.*, *adv.* [Orig. two words, = both *tag* and *rag*: cf. TAG *sb.*[1] 10 b; at length taken as expressing one notion, and hyphened or written as one word, *tag-rag*, *tagrag*.]

A. *sb.* **a.** The rabble, the riff-raff; also (with *pl.*) a member of the rabble; a low or despicable person. Now *rare* exc. as in D.

1609 EBURNE *Maintenance Ministerie* 173 Then the ministerie was filled vp with Tag, rag, such as the time would yeeld. **1638** FORD *Lady's Trial* II. i, Tag, rag, or other, hogen-mogen vanden, Skip-jacks or chouses. **1650** A. B. *Mutat. Polemo* 15 A company of lamentable Tag-rags.. going under the names of Colonels, Majors, and Captains. **1706** E. WARD *Wooden World Diss.* (1708) 85 If ever he prays, it's..to some Tag-Rag, to fetch him a little Ship-Beer. **1826** MOORE *Canonization of St. B-tt-rw-rth* xi, Call quickly together the whole tribe of Canters, Convoke all the serious Tag-rag of the nation. **1870** J. PATRICK *Let.* 10 Nov. in D. O. Hunter *Life Marquess of Bute* (1921) v. 96 At the funeral the Rothesay tag-rag outside cheered me as I left the churchyard.

b. With reference to TAG *sb.*[1], senses 9 and 1, and RAG: A ragged tag or appendage.

1827 CARLYLE *Richter* in *Misc. Ess.* (1872) I. 11 No story proceeds without the most erratic digressions and voluminous tagrags rolling after it. **1831** —— *Sart. Res.* I. iv, Sentences..buttressed-up by props (of parentheses and dashes), and ever with this or the other tagrag hanging from them. **1885** LANG *Custom & Myth* 18 A rude imitation of the human shape..dressed in some tag-rags of finery.

B. *adj.* †**a.** Of or belonging to the rabble. *Obs.* **b.** Consisting of tags and rags of dress, etc.; dressed in rags, ragged.

1601 SHAKS. *Jul. C.* I. ii. 260 If the tag-ragge people did not clap him, and hisse him,..I am no true man. **1675** COTTON *Scoffer Scoft* 90 Tag-rag Plebeans. **1805** W. TAYLOR in *Ann. Rev.* III. 303 Clad in the tagrag garb of democracy. **1897** *Daily News* 1 Nov. 6/3 Love for his dear, tag-rag, genial, happy-go-lucky green isle!

†**C.** *adv.* (for *tag and rag*.) All to tags and rags; also, pell-mell; one and all; in a mingled crowd or heap, promiscuously. *Obs.*

1582 STANYHURST *Æneis* I. (Arb.) 21 Thee northen bluster aproching Thee sayls tears tag rag, to the sky thee waues vphoysing. **1610** B. JONSON *Alch.* v. ii, Men and women, And of all sorts, tag-rag, [have] beene seene to flock here. **1737** OZELL *Urquhart's Rabelais* I. iv. I. 150 After Dinner they all went tag-rag together to the willow-grove.

D. *Phrase.* **a. tag, rag, and bobtail** [orig. an extension of *tag and rag* (TAG *sb.*[1] 10 b): see also BOBTAIL.] Now sometimes **tagrag and bobtail**. A contemptuous term for a number of persons of various sorts and conditions, all and sundry, especially of the lower classes.

1645 *Just Defence John Bastwick* 16 That rabble rout tag ragge and bobtaile. **1660** PEPYS *Diary* 6 Mar., They all went down into the dining-room, where it was full of tag, rag, and bobtail, dancing, singing, and drinking. **1692** L'ESTRANGE *Fables* clxxxv. (1714) 198 Jupiter Invited all Living Creatures, Tag, Rag, and Bob-tail, to the Solemnity of the Wedding. **1728** BYROM *Jrnl. & Lit. Rem.* (1856) I. I. 287 Here's thy good health..and all thy little tag, rag, and bobtails. **1785** WOLCOTT (P. Pindar) *Odes to R.A.'s* II. 1 Tagrags and Bobtails of the sacred Brush. **1840** DICKENS *Barn. Rudge* xxxv, 'We don't take in no tagrag and bob-tail at our house, sir', answered John. **1883** LD. R. GOWER *My Remin.* I. xiii. 251 The mounted police charged the crowd.. and our party had to fly before them along with tag, rag, and bob-tail.

b. *attrib.*

? **1730** *Royal Remarks* 53 The Dramatis Personæ,..a Tag-Rag and Bob Tail Crew. **1849** THACKERAY *Pendennis* vii. (1885) 71 Fancy..your house filled with her confounded tag-rag-and-bobtail relations! **1890** *Guardian* 15 Oct. 1597/1 Inspectors belonging to 'the tag-rag and bobtail class'.

Hence *tag, rag, and bobtailry*; and variations *tag, rag, and long-tail*; *tag, rag, and rascality*.

1701 *New Jersey Arch.* (1881) II. 414 At ye disposall of ye tag, rag, and Rascality. **1719** D'URFEY *Pills* IV. 113 To make a Match with Tag-rag, and Long-tail. **1858** F. E. PAGET *Curate Cumberworth* (1859) 248 A tag, rag, and bobtailry.. gathered together..for electioneering purposes.

ˌ**tag'raggery.** [f. TAG-RAG + -ERY, collective. (Chiefly Carlylese.)] A tag-rag collection or assemblage; a mass of trumpery odds and ends.

1837 MRS. CARLYLE *Lett.* I. 66 When one is delivered from the tag-raggery of printers' devils. **1845** CARLYLE *Cromwell* App. xi. (1871) V. 188 *note*, Antiquarian tagraggeries. **1858** —— *Fredk. Gt.* IV. vii. I. 454 Was there ever seen such a travelling tagraggery of a Sovereign Court before? **1887** *Sat. Rev.* 30 July 139/1 The 'inventing fiend' ....has upset the war-ship so utterly, and has pestered it about with such a tag-raggery of small machines.

‖**tagua** ('tægwə). [Native name in Columbia.] The ivory-palm, *Phytelephas macrocarpa*, which produces the ivory-nut or corozo-nut; also in *Comb.*, as ***tagua-nut, -palm, -plant***.

1830 LINDLEY *Nat. Syst. Bot.* 285 Buttons are turned from the hard albumen of Phytelephas, or the Tagua plant. **1883** JAGO in *Knowledge* July 52/1 Cellulose..occurs in an approximately pure state in the 'tagua-nut'. **1901** KEANE *S. Amer.* I. 132 The tagua, whose melon-shaped pods contain the hard grains known as Vegetable Ivory.

‖**taguan** ('tægwən). [app. native name in the Philippines.

Said by Pallas, *Miscell. Zoolog.* 1766, on the authority of Valentyn *Lettres édif. ex Epist. Jesuit.*, to be so called 'a Philippinensium insularum incolis'.]

The Malayan Flying Squirrel, *Pteromys petaurista*. (Sometimes erroneously applied to other species.)

1807 BARR tr. *Buffon's Nat. Hist.* VII. 169 It was taken upon the Malabar coast, where they are very common, as well as in the Philippine Islands, and other parts of India, where they are called taguans, or great flying squirrels. **1826** SYD. SMITH in *Edin. Rev.* Feb. 309 The taguan knocks you down with a blow of his paw, if suddenly interrupted, but will run away if you give him time to do so. **1901** CORNISH *Living Anim. World* 149 The taguan, a large squirrel of India, Ceylon and the Malacca forests.

‖**tagus** ('teɪgəs). *Gr. Hist.* [Latinized form of Gr. ταγός ruler, leader, f. stem ταγ- of τάσσ-ειν to arrange, order.] A commander, leader, ruler, chief; *spec.* the title of the chief of the confederation of Thessaly.

1839 THIRLWALL *Greece* V. xxxviii. 55 The first step which he had to take was to acquire the title of tagus, and to unite all Thessaly under his legitimate authority. **1846** GROTE *Greece* II. iii. II. 373 A chief or Tagus was nominated to enforce obedience. **1849** *Ibid.* II. liii. VI. 542 The federal authority or power of the tagus, which bound together the separate cities [of Thessaly], was generally very weak.

tah (tɑː), *int.* An exclamation expressing lightness of humour, unconcern, or the like.

a **1688** VILLIERS (Dk. Buckhm.) *Rehearsal* (1714) 73 But you should be light and easie, tah, tah, tah.

tah = *þah*, early form of THOUGH: see T 8.

‖**taha** ('tɑːhɑː), *sb.* [Native (?Bechuana) name.] A South African species of weaver-bird, *Euplectes taha* of Sir A. Smith, now *Pyromelana taha*, the male of which is chiefly yellow and black.

1836 SIR A. SMITH *Rept. of Explor. Exped.* **1906** *Times* 14 Aug. 2/6 Captain B. R. Horsbrugh..serving in the Orange River Colony..presented to the Zoological Society..the taha weaver.

†**ta ha**, *int. Obs.* A derisive exclamation.

a **1529** SKELTON *Replyc.* 75 Se where the heretykes go, Wytlesse wandring to and fro! With, Te he, ta ha, bo ho, bo ho!

‖**tahalli** (tə'hɑːliː). Erron. **tahali**. [Arabic *taχallī* ornamenting.] Decoration.

1833 LONGF. *Outre-Mer* Prose Wks. 1886 I. 166 Moorish knights gayly arrayed..with scarfs of blue and jewelled tahalies. **1904** J. PARKINSON *Lays Love & War* 47 What ho! my spear, My mail, and helm, and gleaming tahali.

‖**taharah** (taha'raː). Also 9 **tohoro**; **tahara**. [a. Heb. *ṭohŏrāh* purification, cleansing.] A Jewish ceremony of washing a corpse before burial.

1819 L. ALEXANDER *Hebrew Ritual* 188 Those who are drawn by lot..to attend, in order to wash the corpse, put on the shrouds... This ceremony is called..*Tohoro*, that is, the cleansing. **1902** *Laws & Bye-laws Burial Soc. United Synagogue* 49 (Index), Tahara men, dismissal of...Tahara women. **1932** C. ROTH *Hist. Marranos* vii. 190 The traditional *taharah*, or ritual laving of the body. **1964** H. RABINOWICZ *Guide to Life* iii. 38 The utmost respect must be shown to the body during *Taharah*... The body is laid on the *Taharah* board... Warm water..must then be poured down the body. **1974** *Jewish Chron.* 1 Nov. 10/1 (*heading*) Tahara helpers required. *Ibid.*, The ministers..had expressed their willingness to be trained in tahara and to help out.

tahil, var. TAEL.

‖**tahina** (tɑː'hiːnə). Also **tahine**, **tahini**, etc. [Arab., f. *ṭaḥana* to grind or crush.] A paste or sauce made of sesame seeds, much eaten in the Middle East.

1950 E. DAVID *Bk. Mediterranean Food* 146 *Tahina* is a thick white oil made from pounded sesame seeds. It is served in a bowl and eaten by dipping bread... You buy the white *tahina* from the grocer, and it is then thinned with water. **1968** C. RODEN *Bk. Middle Eastern Food* 35 *Tahina* itself is a paste made from sesame meal, and can be found in all Greek stores. *Ibid.*, Serve the *tahina* cream in a bowl. **1971** W. TUCKER *This Witch* (1972) ii. 14 The Arab cook had added a small dish of taheena to whet my appetite. **1972** *Vogue* Feb. 33/1 Moroccan tahine dishes with cone lids for couscous, £1.10. **1976** *Ibid.* Jan. 88/2, I like them [*sc.* chick peas] best made into *hummus*, mixed to a smooth paste with *tahini*, lemon juice and garlic. **1976** *Islander* (Victoria, B.C.) 1 Aug. 5/1 They saw a tahina factory where sesame oil is made, the peanut butter of the Middle East. **1979** *Guardian* 8 June 9/4 In Morocco it is either couscous or tajine. **1980** C. SMITH *Cut-Out* xvi. 120 Both Palestinians ate sparingly ....mining modestly into the *hommas* and *tehineh* dips with their *pitta* bread.

Tahiti (tɑː'hiːtɪ). The name of an island in Polynesia used *attrib.* in **Tahiti arrow-root**, a starchy powder made from the tubers of *Tacca pinnatifida*; **Tahiti chestnut** = IVI.

1861 Tahiti arrow-root [see OTAHEITEAN *a.* and *sb.*]. **1884** *Encycl. Brit.* XVII. 664/2 Tahiti chestnut. *Inocarpus edulis*. S. Sea Islands. **1974** G. USHER *Dict. Plants used by Man* 319/1 Polynesian Chestnut, Tahiti Chestnut... The seeds are..eaten raw or cooked. *Ibid.* 564/1 The tuber yields a rather indigestible arrowroot (Fiji Arrowroot, Tahiti Arrowroot,..).

Tahitian (tɑː'hiːʃən, tɑː'hiːtɪən), *a.* and *sb.* Also **Tahitan**, †**Taitian**, †**Taitienne**. [f. TAHITI + -AN; cf. OTAHEITEAN *a.* and *sb.*] **A.** *adj.* Of or pertaining to Tahiti, its inhabitants, or their language.

1822 tr. *Malte-Brun's Universal Geogr.* I. xxiii. 572 Tagalic, Taitienne languages, &c... The Taitian is distributed through all the small islands of the Great Ocean. **1825** W. ELLIS *Jrnl. Tour Hawaii* 244 Both in the Hawaiian and Tahitian languages, every syllable, and every word, ends with a vowel. **1847** *Dublin Rev.* Dec. 357 Numerous other matters of European manufacture..were strewn about among..the ordinary furniture of a Tahitian dwelling. **1852** J. CRAWFORD *Gram. & Dict. Malay Lang.* I. p. cclix, The names of the three plants are exactly according to the Tahitian pronunciation. **1921** tr. *Rathenau's New Society* iv. 26 When a European artist writes or paints in Tahiti, what he produces is not a work of Tahitian culture. **1958** [see CARGADOR]. **1980** *London Mag.* July 23 The ochre Tahitian soil of Gauguin's paintings.

B. *sb.* **a.** A native or inhabitant of Tahiti. **b.** The Polynesian language spoken in Tahiti.

[**1822**: see the adj. above.] **1825** W. ELLIS *Jrnl. Tour Hawaii* 49 He [*sc.* Ellis] could not help stating to them the striking identity between theirs [*sc.* their traditions] and those of the Tahitians. **1854** J. CRAWFURD in C. Bunsen *Outl. Philos. Universal Hist.* I. 427 A sentence in the Maori and Tahitian can be written in words common to both. **1859** N. WISEMAN *Twelve Lect. Sci. & Rev. Relig.* (ed. 6) I. 186 Charlevoix observed it among the Esquimaux,..Wallis among the Tahitans. **1914** R. BROOKE *Let.* Apr. (1968) 572 My Greek is something rusty. Had it been Tahitian now, or Fijian. **1918** L. HUXLEY *Life Sir J. D. Hooker* II. 483 He gratified Banks's philanthropic zeal by leaving in his care two Tahitians and two Maoris. **1957** P. WORSLEY *Trumpet shall Sound* i. 30 Sects including more or less of these elements have also appeared amongst the Tahitians. **1969** J. H. VANCE *Deadly Isles* (1970) iii. 22 He would forget the songs and his few words of Tahitian. **1980** *London Mag.* July 24 Stevenson..and two Tahitians lolling among a pile of coconuts.

‖**tahona** (tə'həʊnə). *U.S.* [Sp.] See quots.

1840 *Civil Eng. & Arch. Jrnl.* III. 129/1 To devise some simple and efficient means of working the 'tahonas', or grinding mills used in the reduction of the silver ore in the mining districts. **1875** J. H. COLLINS *Metal Mining* 113 All the washings..are then ground fine in the 'arrastre' or 'tahona', a rude mill of rough stones worked by mules.

‖**tahr** (tɑː(r)), **tehr** (tɛə(r)). Also **tare**, **tahir**, (**thar**). [Name in the Western Himalayas. (Sometimes confused with *thar*, the Nepālī name of the *gural* or *gooral*, a goat-antelope of Nepāl.)] A wild goat of the genus *Hemitragus*, found in mountainous regions of southern Asia or Arabia, esp. *H. jemlahicus*, which has long brown fur and is native to the Himalayas.

1835 B. H. HODGSON in *Proc. Zool. Soc. Lond.* 492 The Western type of the Himalayan wild goat, called Tehr at Simla and Musuri. **1867** A. L. ADAMS *Wand. Nat. India* 214 Herds of Tare (*Capra jemlaica*, Smith) were often observed during my excursion. The short triangular horns of this species of goat distinguish it from any of its allies. **1867** JERDON *Mammals India* (1874) 286 Tehr. **1885** *Cycl. India* (ed. 3) III. 840/1 *Tehr*, the Himalayan wild goat *Hemitragus Jemlaicus*, Jerdon, pronounced *Tare*, also *Tahir*. It is the Jharal of Nepāl. **1893** LYDEKKER *Horns & Hoofs* 123 The Tahr is found in forest regions. **1902** *Little Folks* Apr. 282/1 The tahrs are true goats, though..they have no beard. Their home is..high up in the Himalaya Mountains. **1939** *Proc. Prehistoric Soc.* V. 52 A muscular development and agility in the feet commonly met with in the chamois,..the tahr and others of their kind. **1959** W. THESIGER *Arabian Sands* xiii. 256 The Arabian tahr had never previously been seen by a European. **1972** T. MCHUGH *Time of Buffalo* xvii. 200 And goats, sheep, and Himalayan tahrs stamp their front hoofs under similar circumstances [*sc.* in rut].

‖**tahsil** (tɑː'siːl). Also **tehsil**, †**tuhseel**. [Urdu; cf. TAHSILDAR.] In India and Pakistan, an administrative division comprising several villages; formerly *spec.* a division made for purposes of revenue administration.

1846 *Directions for Collectors of Land Revenue N.W. Provinces* (India) App. VI. p. xxx, Comparing the tuhseel monthly accounts..with the cancelled dustuks. **1881** *Encycl. Brit.* XII. 769/2 Broadly speaking, the subdivision is characteristic of Bengal..and the *tahsil* of Madras. **1921** *Glasgow Herald* 19 Dec. 12 All district Congress Committees..must send out parties of about 20 Volunteers as a patrol daily in every town, tahsil, and village. **1944** VISCT. WAVELL *Let.* 7 Mar. in *Transfer of Power in India*

(Foreign & Commonw. Office) (1973) IV. 784 Whilst I was at Nagpur I visited a village, a rural tahsil office, and a small irrigation work. **1954** O. H. K. SPATE *India & Pakistan* p. xxiii, The States of India are divided (if large enough) into Divisions and these into Districts... Districts are subdivided into *taluks* (*taluqs*) or *tahsils* (*tehsils*) normally from 3 to 8 to a district. **1962** *Courier-Mail* (Brisbane) 14 Aug. 2/7 The four-tier scheme of basic democracies—at the village, tehsil, district and division levels. **1968** N. MITCHELL *Sir G. Cunningham* v. 100 From 14th to 18th November he was touring on horseback in the Nowshera and Swabi Tahsils. **1971** *Illustr. Weekly India* 18 Apr. 7/2 A very senior and respected elder of our *tehsil* tried to stop me to ask me something. **1975** *Bangladesh Observer* 25 July 4/1 (Advt.), For Tahsil copy in the left hand side of the volume there will be a pocket..for keeping maps.

‖**tahsildar** (tʌxˈsɪldɑː(r)). *E. Indies.* Also 8 **tisheldar**, 9 **tehsildar**, **tuhseeldar**, **tusseeldar**, **taxildar**, 9– **tehsildar**. [Urdū, f. Arab., Pers. *taḥṣīl* collection + Pers. *dār*, agential suffix.] The chief revenue-officer of a subdivision of a district under the Mogul rule; retained by the British; formerly sometimes applied to the cashier in a business house. Also, the chief official of a tahsil.

1799 SIR T. MUNRO *Let.* in Gleig *Life* (1830) I. 215 He [Tippoo] divided his country into 37 Provinces under Dewans..and subdivided these again into 1025 inferior districts, having each a Tisheldar. **1801** WELLINGTON *Suppl. Desp.* (1858) II. 564 Accounts since received from the tahsildar of the Currup talook. **1808** in *5th Rep. Sel. Comm. on E.I. Company* (1812) 583 (Y.) He continues to this hour tehsildar of the petty pergunnah of Sheopore. **1810** CAPT. T. WILLIAMSON *E. Ind. Vade-m.* I. 209 The *sircar*, or *tusseeldar* (cash-keeper) receiving one key, and the master retaining the other. **1849** *Direct. Rev. Off. N.W. Prov.* 188 Great care should be taken to maintain the respectability of the Tuhseeldars. **1871** MATEER *Travancore* 72 [The provinces] are subdivided into thirty-two counties, with a Tahsildar, or magistrate, at the head of each. **1940** *Geogr. Jrnl.* XCV. 426 Khan Sahib Afraz Ghul Khan..is now tehsildar at Gilgit. **1954** J. MASTERS *Bhowani Junction* xxii. 191 That was a message from the tehsildar in Pathoda. **1972** *Times of India* 28 Nov. 1/2 The Mulki rules will apply only to non-gazetted posts and posts of tahsildar and civil assistant surgeons in the Telengana region. **1978** 'M. M. KAYE' *Far Pavilions* vi. 101 Ash had been given lodging for the night in the house of the *tehsildar*.

Tahunian (tɑːˈhuːnɪən), *a.* Also **Tahounian**. [ad. F. *Tahounien* (R. Neuville 1934, in *Revue Biblique* XLIII. 255), f. the place-name *Tahouneh*: see -IAN.] Of, pertaining to, or designating a neolithic culture of Palestine represented by remains found at Tahouneh. Also *absol.*

1936 J. GARSTANG in *Annals Archaeol. & Anthropol.* XXII. 168 There seems to be no doubt that we are in the presence of a distinctive culture of the neolithic period. Whether it will be classed finally as Tahunian II is a matter for experts; meanwhile, as the Tahunian specimens are surface finds..we propose the more descriptive title 'Neo-Tahunian'. **1949** [see MAGLEMOSIAN *a.* and *sb.*]. **1952** V. G. CHILDE *New Light on Most Ancient East* xi. 225 By 1934 assemblages of flints from caves..had enabled Neuville to define a 'Tahunian' industry which could be classified as Neolithic. **1960** K. M. KENYON *Archæol. in Holy Land* ii. 46 The flint industry which has for long been accepted as the classic Neolithic industry of Palestine is called the Tahunian. **1961** G. CLARK *World Prehist.* iv. 82 The lithic industry in the upper Jericho level, with its pressure-flaked tanged arrowheads..compares closely with that of the Tahounian. **1977** *Ibid.* (ed. 3) ii. 51 The Tahunian lithic component shows marked continuity, but one notable innovation in the form of flake arrows with side-notches.

tai (taɪ), *sb.*[1] [Jap.] Also † **tay**. A Pacific sea bream, *Pagrus major*, of the family Sparidæ, eaten as a speciality in Japan.

1620 R. COCKS *Let.* 10 Mar. in *Diary* (1883) II. 311 Dried fish lyke a breame, called heare *tay*, in aboundance. **1727** J. G. SCHEUCHZER tr. *Kæmpfer's Hist. Japan* I. I. 135 *Tai*, is what the Dutch in the Indies call *Steenbrassem*. This is very much esteem'd by the Japanese as the King of Fish. **1795** tr. *Thunberg's Trav.* IV. 39 Among their valuable fishes is what they call the *tay*. **1884** tr. *Rein's Japan* I. vii. 192 The Tai proper is a beautiful deep-red to brown-red gold-bream. **1920** [see SASHIMI]. **1965** W. SWAAN *Jap. Lantern* iii. 41 The deep red and rather bloody-looking *tai* (a type of sea bream).

Tai (taɪ), *sb.*[2] and *a.* Also **T'ai**. [Native name.]

A. *sb.* **a.** (A member of) a group of peoples of southeast Asia which includes the Lao, Shan, and Thai; also *spec.* = THAI *sb.* b. **b.** A group of languages including Thai (Siamese), Lao, Shan, and other languages of southeast Asia, regarded by some as belonging to the Sino-Tibetan family; also *spec.* = THAI *sb.* a. Also *Comb.*, as *Tai Dam*, *Tai-Shan*, *Tai-Chinese* adj. and sb., *Tai Yai*.

1693 A. P. tr. *S. de la Loubère's New Hist. Relation Kingdom of Siam* I. I. ii. 6 The Siameses give to themselves the name of *Tai*, or free, as the word now signifies in their language. **1798** *Asiatick Researches* V. 227 The first dialect is that of the kingdom of Siam, the most polished people of eastern India. They called themselves to me simply Tai. **1811** *Ibid.* X. 241 He divides them into two races, the Tai and the Tai Yai. **1837** *Jrnl. Asiatic Soc. Bengal* VI. 18 The Ahom is a branch of the Tai language, which is spoken, with some variations, by the Khamtis, the Shyáns, the Láos, and the Siamese, all of whom designate themselves by the general appellation of Tai. Among the Ahoms, or the portion of the Tai race inhabiting *Assam*, the language is nearly extinct. *Ibid.*, The sound of the French *u*..is..common in the Tai. **1844** *Chinese Repository* XIII. 169 The inhabitants of this country are not called Siamese but T'ai. **1887** Tai-Shan [see MON-KHMER]. **1902** *Census of India 1901* XII. viii. 119 We are..practically where we were ten years ago in respect of our acquaintance with the early beginnings of the Tai. **1934** WEBSTER, Tai-Chinese, *adj.* **1939** L. H. GRAY *Foundations of Lang.* 389 The group [*sc.* Sino-Tibetan] falls into three great divisions: Yenisei-Ostyak, Tibeto-Burman, and Tai-Chinese. *Ibid.* 390 The other members of the Tai-Chinese family are Si-lo-mo.., Karen.., and Tai, the latter sub-divided into south-eastern, eastern, and northern. To the south-eastern division belong Siamese, Lao, Lü, and Khün. **1948** R. A. D. FORREST *Chinese Lang.* v. 100 There is evidence that T'ai in an older phase used a system of prefixes and infixes in word formation. **1956** J. WHATMOUGH *Language* ii. 32 Note also Tai (Siamese). **1977** Tai Dam [see the adj. below]. **1978** *Amer. Poetry Rev.* Nov./Dec. 15/1 Judith Gautier's informant and lover was a Tai and often himself did not understand the Chinese.

B. *adj.* Of or pertaining to the Tai peoples or languages.

1837 [see the sb. above.] **1883** A. P. PHAYRE *Hist. Burma* i. 12 People of the Tai race were..in the country of the.. river..Sâlwin; and there is evidence of an irruption of that people into the country of the Irâwadi. **1892** *Census of India 1891* IX. viii. 167 The Tai language, of which there are numerous dialects, is essentially a Polytonic language. *Ibid.* 202 A great wave of Tai migration descended. **1902** *Census of India 1901* XII. viii. 119 The classification of the Tai races is a task of far greater magnitude than appeared when the last census was taken. **1933** L. BLOOMFIELD *Language* iv. 69 The second branch of Indo-Chinese is the *Tai* family, which includes *Siamese*. **1948** R. A. D. FORREST *Chinese Lang.* v. 98 The T'ai languages are remarkably uniform over their wide area. **1977** *New Yorker* 5 Sept. 40/3 Of the three groups.. the best off were the Tai Dam..members of a Tai racial group that had settled in China many years ago.

‖**taiaha** (ˈtaiaha). *N.Z.* [Maori.] A long-handled Maori club with a sharp tip. Also *fig.*

1845 E. J. WAKEFIELD *Adventure N. Zealand* I. 140 The *taiaha* is rather a long-handled club than a spear. It..is about six feet long. **1863** A. S. ATKINSON *Jrnl.* 8 Sept. in *Richmond-Atkinson Papers* (1960) II. 61 The first of them was an old man with a handsome taiaha. **1894** *Westm. Gaz.* 29 Aug. 2/1 He looked his best in a picturesque native robe, with lurid feathers in his hair, and a 'taiaha', or spear, in his hand. **1938** R. D. FINLAYSON *Brown Man's Burden* 10 'Ae, we are one people!' he cries, brandishing a taiaha. **1949** P. BUCK *Coming of Maori* (1950) II. xi. 280 The *taiaha* head with its projecting tongue functioned as a stabbing point. **1963** S. ASHTON-WARNER *Teacher* 110 How can I protect my beautiful Matawhero from the taiaha of prejudice? **1974** *N.Z. Listener* 20 July 13/4 The Maori bus driver was 'threatened' with a friendly poke of the taiaha carried by another Maori.

taich(e, obs. ff. TACHE *sb.*[1], spot, stain.

‖**T'ai Chi** (taɪ ˈtʃiː). Also **Tai Chi**, **t'ai chi**, etc. [ad. Chinese *tàijí*, f. *tài* extreme + *jí* limit.]

1. In Taoism and Neo-Confucianism, the Supreme Ultimate (see quot. 1955). Also, the symbol which represents this.

1736 R. BROOKES tr. *Du Halde's Gen. Hist. China* III. 54 They give the first Principle of all things the Name of *Tai ki*. **1845** *Encycl. Metrop.* XVI. 568/2 *T'haï-kĭ* (the Great Summit) the soul of the universe, when in motion.. produced *Yang*, the living principle; when at rest, *Yn*, the dead principle, the one perfect and male, the other imperfect and female; from the union of which the elements sprang. **1914** D. T. SUZUKI *Brief Hist. Early Chinese Philos.* 161 The term, *T'ai Chi*, first appears in one of the Confucian Appendices to the 'Yi Ching' 'In the system of the Yi there is the Great Ultimate (or source or limit, *t'ai chi*).' **1931** A. U. DILLEY *Oriental Rugs & Carpets* (caption to Pl. 63), The centre circle or Tae-keih (Great All) contains Yin (female) and Yang (male). **1955** E. HERBERT *Taoist Notebk.* 3 *T'ai Chi* was presented as the starting-point, which was also the finishing-point, of a cosmic process: a cyclic process of constant change, in the course of which were produced in turn the linked principles of *Yang* and *Yin*..the *Wu Hsing* or Five Elements..and all forms and existences in the material world. **1960** C. WINICK *Dict. Anthropol.* 523/1 *T'ai chi*, in Chinese art, the symbol of the Great Absolute. It consists of a wavy or double curved line bisecting a circle, one half of which is red..and the other black. **1962** E. SNOW *Other Side of River* (1963) I. 338 Tao is the Absolute that contains the total life force, or T'ai Chi.

2. In full *T'ai Chi Ch'uan* [Chinese *quán* fist], a Chinese martial art, believed to have been devised by a Taoist priest in the Sung dynasty (960–1279), promoting meditative as well as physical proficiency.

1962 E. SNOW *Other Side of River* (1963) ii. 24 Servants don't spend their idle time playing mah-jongg now but sit by the bell boards studying English or Russian, or other textbooks, getting ready for after-hours classes; or they do t'ai chi ch'uan calisthenics. **1968** *Times* 22 Nov. 9 Embrace Tiger and Return to Mountain it is called, this being the name of one exercise in T'ai-chi, a Chinese system of callisthenics claimed to produce pliability, health and peace of mind. **1972** DA LIU *T'ai Chi Ch'uan & I Ching* p. v, The movements of T'ai Chi Ch'uan and the hexagrams upon which they are based are both methods of describing the circulation of psychic energy in the body of the meditator. **1979** P. DRISCOLL *Pangolin* I. xx. 147 Kids were doing Tai Chi exercises and playing soccer.

taicoon, taikun, var. ff. TYCOON.

Taig: see TEAGUE 2.

taiga (ˈtaɪgə). [Russ.] The swampy coniferous forest area of Siberia; also, the zone of temperate coniferous forest stretching across Europe and North America.

1888 *Encycl. Brit.* XXIII. 70/2 They [*sc.* the Altai] are chiefly hunters, passionately loving their *taiga*, or wild forest. **1920** J. RITCHIE *Animal Life Scotl.* vi. 329 The typical pine forest region, or taiga. **1946** F. E. ZEUNER *Dating the Past* III. v. 122 Stunted forest of the taiga type may have played a larger part in preglacial Europe than is commonly assumed. **1957** *Times* 12 Nov. (Canada Suppl.) p. xvi/1 Northward..the timber attenuates into sub-Arctic forest (taiga) and finally gives way to the true Arctic tundra. **1964** *Listener* 12 Nov. 747/1 A huge artificial lake has been created, inundating thousands of square acres of the Siberian taiga, the endless forest of birches and firs and pines that covers southern Siberia. **1969** *Beaver* Summer 5/1 Stunted taiga forest, lakes, yellow-green marshes. **1974** T. P. WHITNEY tr. *Solzhenitsyn's Gulag Archipelago* I. I. ii. 24 *Before* it came the wave of 1929 and 1930, the size of a good River Ob, which drove a mere fifteen million peasants, maybe even more, out into the taiga and the tundra. **1980** *Jrnl. R. Soc. Arts* Feb. 140/1 These are generally described in terms of bioclimatic zones—arctic, tundra, taiga, boreal forest, temperate deciduous forests, prairies, desert savanna, and rain forest.

taigle (ˈteɪg(ə)l), *v. Sc.* Also 7 **teagle**. [app. mod.Sc. form of ME. *tagil*, *tagyl*, TAGLE, q.v.]

1. *trans.* To entangle, impede, or hinder in course or action; to keep back, retard, detain, delay.

[*c* **1340**: see TAGLE.]
1635 DICKSON *Writings* (1845) I. 194 He..forgot all things which might teagle him in the way. *Ibid.*, Forget things past that would teagle us. **1684** PEDEN in *Life & Prophecies* (1868) 56 Tell all the Lords people to try by mourning and prayer to teagle Him. **1895** FRASER *Whaups* ii. 23 Others cunningly stretched out their legs to taigle the wrathful dominie. **1895** CROCKETT *Men of Moss-Hags* 64 Ye hae taigled us owerly long already.

2. To 'catch' or entangle in talk; to embarrass.

1865 in *Beeton's Bk. Anecd.* 24 Two graceless young fellows who had determined, as they said, to taigle their minister.

3. *intr.* To linger, tarry, delay; to dally, loiter.

17.. *Laird o Ochiltree Wawis* ix. in Child *Ballads* VII. ccxvii. 196/1 Kind maister, ye've taiglit lang. **1823** GALT *R. Gilhaize* xxvi. (E.D.D.), Robin Brown taigled more than two hours for me. **1895** CROCKETT *Men of Moss-Hags* xi. 87 'Make haste', they said, 'we haena time to taigle wi' ye'.

4. *intr.* To walk slowly or heavily, to drag oneself, to trudge.

1886 STEVENSON *Kidnapped* xviii, Ay, man, ye shall taigle many a weary foot, or we get clear! **1893** —— *Catriona* vii. 74 A man that comes taigling after a Macgregor's daughter. *Ibid.* xix. 223 Her two sisters had to taigle home by theirselves.

‖**taigu** (ˈtaɪguː). [Native name in Guarani.] In **taigu wood**, also called *lapacho wood*: see quots. Hence **taiˈguic** *a. Chem.* in *taiguic acid*, an acid obtained from this wood.

1868 WATTS *Dict. Chem.* V. 655 *Taigu wood*, a wood from Paraguay, resembling guaiacum-wood in appearance and specific gravity. *Ibid.*, *Taiguic acid*..occurs in the cold alcoholic extract of taigu wood. **1892** MORLEY & MUIR *Watts' Dict. Chem.* III. 119 Lapachic acid, $C_{15}H_{14}O_3$; Oxy-amenyl-naphtho-quinone; Taiguic acid..a yellow colouring matter present in the 'lapacho' wood of a genus of the *Bignoniaceæ*.

‖**taihoa** (taiˈhɔa), *int. N.Z.* Also **taiho**. [Maori.] Wait a bit; by and by; presently. Occas. *attrib.*

1842 W. R. WADE *Journey in N.Z.* iii. 66 'Taihoa.' This word has been translated, By and by; but in truth it has all the latitude of directly,—presently,—by and by,—a long time hence,—and nobody knows when. **1851** J. C. RICHMOND *Let.* Apr. in *Richmond-Atkinson Papers* (1960) I. ii. 90 Glad we were to pay off our Maori lad & be done with their provoking 'taiho!' 'waiho' (*presently wait*). **1881** J. L. CAMPBELL *Poenamo* v. 87 That irritatingly provoking word, 'taiho'. **1905** J. M. THOMSON *Bush Boys N.Z.* xii. 170 Taisho, Mac. I'll be there in a minute. [Note] The bush-boy corruption of the Maori 'Taihoa', 'Wait a bit'. **1910** A. A. GRACE *Hone Tiki Dialogues* 4 There is too much taihoa about you Maoris. **1921** H. FOSTON *At Front* 188 Taking twelve years instead of five... It was described as a Taihoa policy. **1965** S. T. OLLIVIER *Petticoat Farm* i. 3 'Taihoa,' Harry said (it was the only Maori word he knew). 'Taihoa, I've not the money yet: wait until I have the money.'

taik(e, obs. forms of TAKE *v.*

taiken, -in, obs. Sc. forms of TOKEN.

taikle, obs. Sc. form of TACKLE.

tail (teɪl), *sb.*[1] Forms: 1 **tæȝel**, **tæȝl**, 3 **teil**, 3– **tail**; also 3–8 **tayl**, 4 **taille**, 4–6 **tayll(e**, 4–7 **taile**, **tayle**, 5–6 **taill**; *Sc.* 4–6 **tale**. [Com. Teut.: OE. *tæȝel*, *tæȝl*, = ON. *tagl* a horse's tail (Sw. *tagel* horse-hair of tail or mane); OHG. *zagel*, MHG. *zagel*, dial. *zail*, *zeil*, tail of animal, etc., mod.Ger. dial. *zagel*, *zâl*, *zael* tail; LG. *tagel* a twisted scourge or whip of thongs or ropes, a rope-end, rope (Brem. Wbch.), Goth. *tagl* hair (of the head, of the camel). Ulterior etymology uncertain; but the evidence appears to show that the primary sense was either 'hair' or 'hairy tail', as of the horse, ox, fox, etc., whence it was extended to the tails of other animals. Already in OE. it was applied to the tails of 'worms' or reptiles, and to the sting of the bee. In OE. the tail was also called *steort*, START. = Du. *staart*.]

1. a. The posterior extremity of an animal, in position opposite to the head, either forming a distinct flexible appendage to the trunk, or being the continuation of the trunk itself behind the anus. Also, a representation or figure of this part.

In most vertebrate animals, consisting of a number of gradually attenuated coccygeal vertebræ covered with flesh and integument; in quadrupeds often clothed with hair, in birds with feathers (see also PEACOCK'S TAIL), and in fishes bearing the caudal fin; in invertebrate animals, sometimes a distinct and well-marked member, at other times not distinctly marked off from the rest of the body.

a **800** *Laws of Ine* c. 59 Oxan tæȝl bið scill[inges] weorð. *a* **1023** WULFSTAN *Hom.* xlii. (1883) 200 Eȝeslice mycele deor ..hi habbaþ tæȝlas ðam wyrmum ȝelice. *c* **1200** *Vices & Virtues* 151 Ðat ðe tail ware on auriche netene. *c* **1205** LAY. 29557 Heo..nomen tailes of rehȝen and hangede on his cape. *a* **1225** *Ancr. R.* 254 Sansumes foxes..weren bi þe teiles iteied ueste..And in euerich ones teile a blase berninde. *c* **1290** *S. Eng. Leg.* I. 363/38 And teiden him sethþe to a wilde hors at þe taile bihinde. **1340** HAMPOLE *Pr. Consc.* 4419–23 He says, 'with his tayle he droghe don even þe thred part of þe sternes of heven,'..Þis was þe taille of þe dragon. *c* **1391** CHAUCER *Astrol.* II. §4 The tail of the dragoun, is in [þe] hows of the assendent. **1413** *Pilgr. Sowle* (Caxton) I. xix. (1859) 19 No body had he under this hede, but only a tayl whiche semyd the tayle of a worme. **1470–85** MALORY *Arthur* v. iv. 165 The bore..whiche was x foote large fro the hede to the taylle. **1483** CAXTON *Gold. Leg.* 174 b/2 Castyng on hym the tayles of thornback or like fisshes. **1486** *Bk. St. Albans* b ij b, The federis of the wynges and of the taylle. *a* **1548** HALL *Chron., Hen. VII* 30 Thinkyng to haue gotten God by the foote, when she had the deuell by the tayle. **1600** J. PORY tr. *Leo's Africa* IX. 341 Others affirmed that they had seene one of those tailes [of a sheep] of an hundred and fiftie pounds weight. *a* **1604** HANMER *Chron. Irel.* (1633) 125 This reformation was but a sweeping of a house with a Foxes tayle. **1626** YATES *Ibis ad Cæsarem* I. 6 Though the head of this Hydra was cut off, yet it had still a frigling taile. **1690** LOCKE *Hum. Und.* III. ii. §3 A Child..applies the Word Gold only to his own Idea of that Colour, and nothing else; and therefore calls the same Colour in a Peacock's Tail, Gold. *a* **1727** NEWTON *Chronol. Amended* i. (1728) 83 The Tayl of the South Fish [constellation]. **1826** KIRBY & SP. *Entomol.* III. xxxiii. 389 *Cauaa* (the Tail). Where the abdomen grows suddenly slenderer, and terminates in a long jointed tail, as in *Scorpio* and *Panorpa*. **1861** HULME tr. *Moquin-Tandon* II. III. iii. 96 The abdomen [of the Crayfish], improperly termed the tail. **1894** NEWTON *Dict. Birds* 701 The so-called 'tail' of the Peacock is formed not by the rectrices or true tail-feathers, but by the singular development of the tail-coverts.

b. The tail of a horse, of which one, two, or three were borne before a pasha as insignia of rank: see PASHA (note), and HORSE-TAIL 1 b.

1717 LADY M. W. MONTAGU *Let. to Abbé Conti* 17 May, The pashas of three tails have those ensigns..placed in a very conspicuous manner before their tents. **1820** HUGHES *Trav. Sicily* II. i. 23 It was governed by beys, and pashas of two tails, sent by the Porte. **1836** *Penny Cycl.* V. 231/1 Bosnia..is governed by a pasha of three tails, to whom the governors of the six sandshaks, who are pashas of two tails, are subordinate.

†**c.** *Contemptuously*: expressing exhaustive clearance: cf. HOOF 3. *Obs.*

c **1330** R. BRUNNE *Chron.* (1810) 214 Of þe aliens ilk taile þe lond voided clere. **1525** LD. BERNERS *Froiss.* II. xlix. 171 There shall not one tayle of them retourne agayne into fraunce.

2. A thing, part, or appendage, resembling the tail of an animal in shape or position.

a. In general sense. **b.** The luminous train usually extending from the 'head' of a comet. †**c.** The germinating sprout of barley; = COME *sb.*[2] *Obs.* **d.** The stalk or peduncle of a fruit (*obs.*); the stalk of a mushroom (*dial.*). **e.** The attenuated part of a muscle at its insertion. **f.** A twisted or braided tress of hair; a queue, pig-tail. **g.** In writing and printing, A stroke or loop forming the lower portion of certain letters and figures, and usually passing below the line. **h.** In musical notation, The line proceeding from the head of a note; the stem. **i.** A kind of wooden lever at the the back of a windmill by which it is turned to the wind; also, a vane for the same purpose. **j.** The long handle of an implement, as a rake. **k.** = QUEUE *sb.* 3; in phrase *in tail* rendering the Fr. *en queue*. **l.** The rear part of an aeroplane or air-balloon. (Except in the case of quot. 1804, the 19th-century examples refer to projected not actual aircraft.) **m.** *Math.* An extremity of a curve, esp. that of a frequency distribution, as it approaches the horizontal axis of a graph; the part of a distribution that this represents. **n.** *Woodworking.* In a dovetail joint: (see quot. 1966).

a. **1523** FITZHERB. *Husb.* §14 The roughe otes..be very lyghte, and haue longe tayles, wherby they wyll hange eche one to other. **1666** G. HARVEY *Morb. Angl.* xxxv. 112 The Distill'd water of those tails that hang on Willow Trees. **1683** TRYON *Way to Health* xix. (1697) 416 To see..a Man, (according to the Vulgar Proverb) appear like an Onion with a Gray Head and a Green Tail. **1776** WITHERING *Brit. Plants* (1796) II. 499 Flowers naked; seeds without tails. **1808** CURWEN *Econ. Feeding Stock* 54 Turnips..with the tops and tails cut off. **1883** R. HALDANE *Workshop Receipts* Ser. II. 255/1 Be careful not to leave clouds or tails where the brush leaves the roof after the stroke. **1883** KNIGHT *Cruise Falcon* (1887) 125 Some tails of strong black tobacco. **1884** W. C. SMITH *Kildrostan* I. iv. 253, I..cannot rise Without it ..More than the kite without its load of tail. **1901** *Daily Chron.* 12 Aug. 3/3 The Kallima butterfly..generally rests upon the trunk of a tree..with the 'tails' on the hind wings directed upwards.

b. [**1297** R. GLOUC. (Rolls) 8604 Þe taylede sterre men clupeþ..Vor þer comþ fram hire a lem suiþe cler & briȝte, As a tayl oþer a launce.] **1572** T. SMITH in Ellis *Orig. Lett.* Ser. III. IV. 7 The new faire Starre, or Comett, but without beard or taile, which hath appeared here this three weekes. **1690** LEYBOURN *Curs. Math.* 451 Kepler is of Opinion, that the Tail of a Comet is only enlightened by the Sun's Beams. **1738** *Gentl. Mag.* VIII. 244/2 They..terrify the gazing Nations, who from their glaring Tail and hideous Aspect forbode the worst of Consequences. **1849** HERSCHEL *Outl. Astron.* §557 The tail is..by no means an invariable appendage of comets.

c. **1594** PLAT *Jewell-ho.* I. 49 The duste and tailes of the malt, which are left in malting. **1763** *Museum Rust.* (ed. 2) I. 114 In what manner to make a profitable use of malt-dust; that is, the dust, tails, &c. which fall off in the screening. **1805** R. W. DICKSON *Pract. Agric.* I. 223 The dust which is screened from malt, mixed with the tails,..may be converted to the purpose of manure.

d. **1613** PURCHAS *Pilgrimage* (1614) 184 If the tayle or wooden substance, whereby it groweth, be on it [an apple].

e. **1719** QUINCY *Lex. Physico-Med.* (1722) 5 The Tendon formed by the Tails of several Muscles. **1877** ROSENTHAL *Muscles & Nerves* (1881) 13 The ends are spoken of as the head and tail, of the muscle.

f. **1799** in *Spirit Pub. Jrnls.* III. 320 Club nor queue, nor twisted tail Nor e'en thy chatt'ring, barber! shall avail. **1840** MARRYAT *Poor Jack* vii, In a minute the tail was off. **1852** MRS. STOWE *Uncle Tom's C.* xx, Her woolly hair was braided in sundry little tails. **1877** A. B. EDWARDS *Up Nile* xxii. 701 They wore their hair..plaited in long tails behind.

g. **1599** MIDDLETON, etc. *Old Law* III. i. 76 The cipher is turned into 9 by adding the tail. **1676** MOXON *Print. Lett.* 16 Describe the Arch for the inside of the Tail of a. **1771** LUCKOMBE *Hist. Printing* 280 The J..should run to the depth of three lines, on account of its tail. **1852** MRS. STOWE *Uncle Tom's C.* iv, Uncle Tom laboriously brought up the tail of his *g* the wrong side out. **1893** FURNIVALL *Capgrave's Life S. Kath.* (E.E.T.S.) p. xxxix *note*, Hart's *e* has a curl or tail under it.

h. *c* **1325** in *Rel. Ant.* I. 292 Ther is a streinant, with to longe tailes. **1597** MORLEY *Introd. Mus.* 9 If your first note lack a tayle. **1674** PLAYFORD *Skill Mus.* I. viii. 28 Semi-quavers are Tyed together by a long stroke on the top of their Tails. **1879** GROVE *Dict. Mus.* s.v. *Crotchet*, But *croche* is a quaver..and is so called on account of the hook at the end of its tail.

i. **1712** J. JAMES tr. *Le Blond's Gardening* 192 Turning themselves to the Wind, by means of a Tail in Form of a Ship's Rudder, which turns about every way. **1892** P. H. EMERSON *Son of Fens* xxxii. 336, I..got hold of the rope and pulled the gripe up, and made that fast round the tail so that wouldn't jerk her off.

k. **1837** CARLYLE *Fr. Rev.* I. VI. iv, Long strings of purchasers, arranged in tail so that the first come be the first served. *Ibid.*, In time we shall see..the art..of standing in tail become one of the characteristics of the Parisian People, distinguishing them from all other Peoples.

l. **1804** G. CAYLEY in C. H. Gibbs-Smith *Sir George Cayley's Aeronautics* (1962) vi. 18 This rod..supported a tail, made of two planes crossing each other at right angles. .. The tail could be set to any angle. **1835** *Nautical Mag.* IV. 612 An internal balloon is fitted for the purpose of ascending and descending at will, and the whole is intended to be propelled by fins, paddles, or wings we may call them. .. Finally the creature enjoys the important appendage of a tail abaft. **1848** *Chambers's Edin. Jrnl.* 6 May 302/2 There was also a tail, which, turning on a joint, was to direct the Ariel's flight. **1909** [see FEATHERING *ppl. a.* c]. **1913** A. H. VERRILL *Harper's Aircraft Bk.* xi. 120 The parts of an aeroplane are mainly the frame, or 'chassis'; the body, or 'fuselage';..the rudder and tail;..and the control system. **1915** D. O. BARNETT *Let.* 13 June 176 Up went his tail, and he began going down in spirals. **1959** *Chambers's Encycl.* I. 99/1 Streamlining eliminates this feature of bluff sections, a narrow wake forming only as the tail is approached. **1978** J. GARDNER *Dancing Dodo* iv. 24 One [body] had been found towards where the tail and elevators should have been... The other had been taken from..the wreckage of the tail cone.

m. **1895** K. PEARSON in *Phil. Trans. R. Soc.* A. CLXXXVI. 397 We require to have the 'tail' as carefully recorded as the body of statistics. Unfortunately the practical collectors of statistics often..proceed by a method of 'lumping together' at the extremes of their statistical series. **1930** E. RUTHERFORD *Coll. Papers* (1965) III. 235 It is seen that the curve is very nearly symmetrical, but that there is a small 'tail' on the low-velocity side. **1980** K. RANDSBORG *Viking Age in Denmark* vii. 157 The Russian and Scandinavian finds of the ninth century have long tails of older coins.

n. **1963** K. WRIGHT *Woodworking* iii. 122 The strongest dovetails are those where pins and tails are equal in size. **1966** A. W. LEWIS *Gloss. Woodworking Terms* 22 *Dovetail*, joint in which the 'tail', shaped like a dove's spread tail, fits between correspondingly shaped pins. This locks the joint and prevents it from being pulled apart in one direction. **1977** *Reader's Digest Bk. of Do-it-yourself Skills & Techniques* 129 Cut down the tails with a dovetail saw, skimming the lines on the waste side.

o. A piece or 'slip' of irregularly bounded land jutting out from a larger piece. *Sc. Obs.*

Represented in med.L. by *cauda*, e.g. 1546–80 in *Regr. of Great Seal of Scotl.* No. 268 Croftam seu caudam; *Exch. Rolls of Scotl.* VII. 169 Cauda de Lekkok *vel* tale de Lekkok.

1472 *Rental Bk. Cupar Angus* (1879) I. 162 With the twa talis of land left and made to ws be the last perambulatioun. **1541** *Records of Elgin* (New Spald. Cl. 1903) I. 64 M[r] Thomas Gaderar..complenit vpon Robert Mawar for cassin ane stank upon ane taill pertynyng to the said M[r] Thomas. **1550** *Ibid.* 100 Ane taill of land lyand on the north syid of the said burgh. **1690** *Ibid.* 349 Croftis, taillis, yairdis and utheris lyabill in paying the teynd scheaff.

3. The train or tail-like portion of a woman's dress (in later use *colloq.*); the pendent posterior part of a man's dress-coat or a peasant's long coat; the loose part of any coat below the waist; (often in *pl.*) the bottom or lower edge of a gown, a skirt, etc., which reaches quite or nearly to the ground; in *pl.*, a tail-coat; a dress suit with tail-coat; *dial.* the skirt of a woman's dress; ***tails***, skirts. Also (in *sing.* or *pl.*), the back part of a man's shirt that reaches below the waist.

1297 R. GLOUC. (Rolls) 2513 Þis maide..side drou hire tail Akne to þe king ȝo sede, Louerd king, washayl. *a* **1450** *Knt. de la Tour* 30 Her hodes, taylles, and sleues be not furred ynowgh after the shape that rennithe now. **1500–20** DUNBAR *Poems* xiv. 73 Sic fowill tailis, to sweip the calsay clene, The dust vpskaillis. **1532** *Acc. Ld. High Treas. Scotl.* VI. 80 Ane doublat with ane taile, to the Kingis grace. **1560** ROLLAND *Crt. Venus* IV. 541 And Venus taill twa Ladeis vp it beiris. **1690** CROWNE *Eng. Friar* v. Wks. 1874 IV. 111 Madam, speak to the ladies now I am here, to let down their trains; 'tis not manners in the presence of a man o' my quality, to cock up their tails. **1762** FOOTE *Lyar* I. Wks. 1799 I. 277 The draggled tail of my tatter'd academical habit. **1845**, etc. [see *shirt-tail* s.v. SHIRT *sb.* 5 c]. **1857** HUGHES *Tom Brown* I. viii, His friends at home..hadn't put him into tails. **18..** *St. Nicholas* (U.S.) XIV. 406 (Cent. D.) Once a boy [at Harrow] has reached the modern remove, he puts on his tails, or tailed coat. **1888** *Century Mag.* May 128/1 He crossed the room, stepping over the tails of gowns, and stood before his old friend. **1890** PARNELL *Sp. Ho. Comm.* 14 Feb., To go about like the traditional Irishman at Donnybrook Fair, and exclaim 'Will nobody tread on the tail of my coat?' **1915** MRS. H. WARD *Eltham House* ii. 23 You made up your mind from the time you got into tails at Eton. **1932** S. GIBBONS *Cold Comfort Farm* i. 10 Charles looked well in tails. **1958** B. NICHOLS *Sweet & Twenties* 110 Young men wore tails and white ties as a matter of course. **1960** *Guardian* 16 Dec. 8/3 At balls, even in the London season, tails are not uncompromisingly de rigueur. **1965** R. P. JHABVALA *Backward Place* iii. 166 He ran after her into the street, the tails of his crumpled shirt flying as he ran.

4. The lower or hinder extremity of anything; the part opposite to what is regarded as the head.

a. in general application.

1362 LANGL. *P. Pl.* A. v. 19 Beches and brode okes weore blowen to þe eorþe, And turned vpward þe tayl. **1731** MORTIMER in *Phil. Trans.* XXXVII. 107 They [packthreads] are all spread on a Cross-piece fastened to two Staples: These are called the Tail of the Mounture. **1778** PRYCE *Min. Cornub.* IV. ii. 234 The stony coarse poorer part settles..on the tail or lower end of the boards. **1805** R. W. DICKSON *Pract. Agric.* I. 296 The tail, or terminating part of the strata. **1859** F. GRIFFITHS *Artill. Man.* (1862) 114 The gun is at the tail of the platform. **1872** ELLACOMBE *Ch. Bells Devon*, etc. ii. 217 Bells are sometimes chimed..by hitching the rope round the flight or tail of the clapper. **1887** D. A. LOW *Machine Draw.* (1892) 6 The head already formed on the rivet, and called the tail, is then held up, and the point is hammered or pressed so as to form another head. **1890** BILLINGS *Nat. Med. Dict.*, *Tail of epididymis*, the lower pointed extremity. **1898** in *Daily News* 8 Nov. 6/1 [Mr. Gladstone] would prefix the address and affix his signature, writing (as he called it) the 'head and the tail'.

b. The terminal or concluding part of anything, as of a text, word, or sentence (cf. HEAD *sb.*[1] 19), of a period of time, or something occupying time, as a storm, shower, drought, etc.

1377 LANGL. *P. Pl.* B. III. 347 And þat is þe taille of þe tixte. *a* **1450** MYRC *Par. Pr.* 1889 Cotte þow not þe wordes tayle. **1579** FULKE *Heskins's Parl.* 258 Here M. Hesk. choppeth off ye taile [of the sentence]. **1613** SIR H. NEVILL in *Buccleuch MSS.* (Hist. MSS. Comm.) I. 131 The tail of this storm fell a little upon my Lord himself. **1771** SMOLLETT *Humph. Cl.* 20 Apr., I now sit down to execute the threat in the tail of my last [letter]. *a* **1774** FERGUSSON *Sandie & Willie* Poems (1789) II. 4 It's wearin' on now to the tail o' May. **1833** HT. MARTINEAU *Loom & Lugger* I. i. 16 At the tail of their conversation. **1872** BLACK *Adv. Phaeton* xx. 278 The tail of a shower sometimes overtaking us.

c. The rear-end of an army or marching column, of a procession, etc. Also *spec.*, the non-combatant personnel of an armed service or of a military unit. (Cf. HEAD *sb.*[1] 18 a.)

1565 COOPER *Thesaurus* s.v. *Agmen*, They cutte of the tayle of the armie, or kyll them that are behynde. **1610** HOLLAND *Camden's Brit.* (1637) 43 They attempted to cut off the taile of our armie. **1800** WELLINGTON in Gurw. *Desp.* (1837) I. 197 Colonel Stevenson is after them, and will cut off part of the tail, I hope. **1858** O. W. HOLMES *Aut. Breakf.-t.* iii. 19 The wit knows that his place is at the tail of a procession. **1899** BALDOCK *Cromwell* 231 The King with the head of his column reached Harborough in safety, the tail quartering as far back as Naseby. **1946** *Hansard Commons* 30 Oct. 690 Our job must be to secure an efficient fighting force in which the tail is kept as short as possible, and the teeth as long and as keen as possible. **1950** *Ibid.* 26 July 555 If one is to provide an operational division,..the tail cannot be avoided, otherwise the division is not operational at all. **1961** B. FERGUSON *Watery Maze* vii. 159 As 'Teeth' troops (to use a phrase which was then [*sc.* in 1942] both new and picturesque, but has long since become a *cliché*) there was little to equal them; but they lacked a 'Tail'—those ancillaries which in modern war virtually wag the dog. **1972** D. BLOODWORTH *Any Number can Play* xiii. 116 When a soldier moves, all his basic needs are looked after by a vast administrative tail that..clothes him, feeds him, transports him. **1977** *R.A.F. News* 30 Mar.–12 Apr. 7/2 It is possible to continue trimming the so-called 'tail' by successive cuts in defence expenditure.

d. The hinder part of a cart, plough, or harrow; = PLOUGH-TAIL . (Cf. HEAD *sb.*[1] 18 c.)

1466 AGNES PASTON *Will* in *P. Lett.* II. 286 Withouȝt they shuld hold the plowe to the tayle. **1526** R. WHYTFORD *Martiloge* 114 b, They were tyed unto the tayles of cartes, & so drawen thrugh bushes, breres, & thornes unto deth. **1547** (15 Nov.) *City of Lond. Rep.* in *Vicary's Anat.* (1888) App. iii. 174 John Launder..& John Croydon..beggers..shall..be whypped naked att A Cartes Taylle. **1563–87**, etc. [see CART'S-TAIL]. **1577** B. GOOGE *Heresbach's Husb.* I. (1586) 21

The partes of the Plowe, are the Tayle, the Shelfe, the Beame [etc.]. **1887** JESSOPP *Arcady* iv. 117 Their sturdy sons will push their way, but not..at the plough's tail.

†**e.** The stern of a ship or boat. (Cf. HEAD *sb.*[1] 21.) *Obs.*

1553 BRENDE *Q. Curtius* T viij, Swimming at the boates tailes. **1645** EVELYN *Diary* June (1827) I. 312 These vessells [gondolas] are built very long and narrow, having necks and tailes of steele. **1709** *Lond. Gaz.* No. 4510/7 The Hoy Burthen 9 or 10 Tun, very full built forward, with a clean Tail.

f. The part of a mill-race below the wheel; the tail-race; the lower end of a pool or stream.

1533–4 *Act 25 Hen. VIII*, c. 7 Any other engine..at the taile of anie mille or were. **1613** J[OHN] D[ENNYS] *Secr. Angling* II. xxvi, See some standing..at the Tayles of Mills and Arches small. **1725** DE FOE *Voy. round World* (1840) 288 The water..had made a pit under it with the fall, like the tail of a mill. **1829** *Nat. Philos.* I. *Hydraulics* iii. 26 (Usef. Knowl. Soc.) To permit a portion of the upper water to flow down into the tail or lower stream immediately in front of the wheel. **1867** F. FRANCIS *Angling* i. (1880) 40 The tail of a pool is a favourite place for them. **1886** *Q. Rev.* Oct. 341 The tail of a swift stream, where it broadens out before another white rapid.

g. The spit or extremity of a reef or sandbank, where it slopes under the water.

1761 *Chron.* in *Ann. Reg.* 149/2 The Actaeon ran aground on the tail of the Pall-Bank. **1799** *Hull Advertiser* 6 Apr. 3/1 The cutter got up as far as the tail of the bank. **1817** *Sporting Mag.* L. 172 At what sailors call the 'Tail' of the land, there is always a turbulent sea, or rather Race. **1858** *Merc. Marine Mag.* V. 225 Ships..should pass as close as possible to the tail of the Reef.

h. The reverse side of a coin; esp. in phr. ***head(s or tail(s***: see HEAD *sb.*[1] 3 b.

1684 OTWAY *Atheist* II. i, As Boys do with their Farthings ..go to Heads or Tails for 'em. **1764** BRIDGES *Burlesque Homer* (1774) 115 (Farmer) 'Tis heads for Greece, and Tails for Troy... Two farthings out of three were Tails. **1801** STRUTT *Sports & Past.* IV. ii. (1810) 296 The reverse of the head being called the tail without respect to the figure upon it. **1884** *Punch* 16 Feb. 73/1 A sovereign, a half sovereign,.. or farthing, so long as it has a 'head' one side, and..a 'tail' the other. **1893** F. ADAMS *New Egypt* 267 The goddess who sits on the 'tails' side of our bronze currency.

i. The lower, inner, or subordinate end of a long-shaped block or brick; the bottom or visible part of a roofing slate or tile.

1793 SMEATON *Edystone L.* §82 The tail of the header was made to..bond with the interior parts. **1856** S. C. BREES *Gloss. Terms*, *Tail*,..the lower end of the slate or tile.

j. *Surg.* Either end of an incision, which does not go through the whole thickness of the skin.

1846 BRITTAN tr. *Malgaigne's Man. Oper. Surg.* 5 The bistoury must be repeatedly passed over the same course, so as to divide layer by layer. Here 'tails' are inevitable; but this inconvenience is light in comparison to the advantages to be sometimes derived from this mode of operating.

k. *Printing* and *Bookbinding.* The lower edge of a page or cover. (Cf. HEAD *sb.*[1] 13.)

1865 HANNETT *Bibliopegia* (ed. 6) 234 The head being cut, the book is taken out of the press, and the quantity to be taken off the tail marked with the compasses. **1895** ZAEHNSDORF *Hist. Bookbinding* 25 *Headbander*, the person who works the fine silk or cotton ornament at head or tail of the book as a finish to the edge.

l. ***tail of the eye***, the outer corner of the eye. ***out of, with the tail of the eye***, with a sidelong or furtive glance.

1802 R. ANDERSON *Cumberld. Ball.* 45 But I only made luive thro' the tail o' my e'e. **1824** GALT *Rothelan* II. v. iii. 203 'Sir Gibrel', cried the lady, at the same time winking to him with the tail of her eye. **1859** READE *Love me little* xiv, Miss Lucy noticed this out of the tail of her eye. **1888** J. PAYN *Myst. Mirbridge* (Tauchn.) II. xvii. 187 Mrs. Westropp watched him with the tail of her eye as she talked to Lady Trevor.

†**m.** A small evening party, subsequent to a dinner or a ball. *Obs.*

1837 C. RIDLEY *Let.* in *Cecilia* (1958) 26 We went to Lady Domville's—the nicest ball I have been at this year... We afterwards went to a tail where we saw a collection of unwashed uncombed philosophers. **1912** G. W. E. RUSSELL *One Look Back* viii. 164 'Tails', as the name implies, were little parties tacked on to the end of big dinners, where a few people looked in, rather cross at not having been invited to dine, or else in a desperate hurry to get on to a larger party or a ball.

n. *Phonetics.* (See quot. 1922.)

1922 H. E. PALMER *Eng. Intonation* iv. 10 Any syllable or syllables following the nucleus in the same Tone-Group is termed the 'Tail' of the group. The Tail-syllable or group of syllables following the Falling Nucleus..is pitched on the low level. **1965** *Amer. Speech* XL. 72 Word order affects intonation in the tail, head, and nucleus.

o. The rear part of a motor vehicle.

1928 E. WALLACE *Double* xiii. 187 Outside he saw five police cars parked bonnet to tail. **1975** *Drive* New Year 106/3 The car's tail tends to drift out of corners at lower speeds than earlier models.

5. a. The lower and hinder part of the human body; the fundament, posteriors, buttocks, backside. ***tail over top*** = ***top over tail***: see TOP *sb.* Now *dial.* and *colloq.* (chiefly *U.S.*, esp. in fig. phrases, as ***to work one's tail off***, to work strenuously).

1303 R. BRUNNE *Handl. Synne* 5416 Þarfor shul þey..Go to helle, both top and tayle. *c* **1330** —— *Chron.* (1810) 70 Into þe waise þam fro he tombled top ouer taile. *c* **1400** *Laud Troy Bk.* 16727 He bar him tayl ouer top, That he lay ther as a sop. ? *a* **1500** *Chester Pl.* (Shaks. Soc.) II. 176 Thou take hym by the toppe and I by the tayle. **1530** PALSGR. 279/1 Tayle or arse, *queue* or *cul.* **1542** UDALL *Erasm. Apoph.* 81 He was forbidden to sitte on his taille & was charged to stand vpon his feete. **1686** tr. *Chardin's Trav. Persia* 97 They go Barefoot, and all in Tattars that hardly cover their Tails. **1889** J. M. DUNCAN *Dis. Wom.* xxxii. (ed. 4) 258 Ever since that time she has had pain, in what she calls her tail. **1935** J. T. FARRELL *Judgment Day* in *Studs Lonigan* (1938) iv. 86 This idea of sweating your tail off with work..is the undiluted crap. **1942** W. FAULKNER *Go down, Moses* 229 This is the first time you've had your tail out of that kitchen since we got here except to chop a little wood. **1969** *New Yorker* 14 June 72/3 Go out there and work your tail off. Don't wake up tomorrow morning regretting that you didn't give a hundred per cent. **1976** *Billings* (Montana) *Gaz.* 1 July 4-E/1, I worked my tail off to help win a pennant for the Dodgers.

b. ***at*** (†***after***) ***the tail of***, at the back of, in the rear of, following; ***in the tail of***, in the train of; so †***to follow the tail of***. Cf. 6.

13.. *K. Alis.* 2142 (Bodley MS.) Siweþ me after [*Weber* at] my taile. **1471** RIPLEY *Comp. Alch.* v. xxviii. in Ashm. *Theatr. Chem. Brit.* (1652) 155 Folys doe folow them at the tayle. **1542** UDALL *Erasm. Apoph.* 283 b, After his taille should come his owne souldyours. *a* **1547** SURREY *Æneid* IV. 207 The skies gan rumble sore, In tail thereof a mingled showr with hayle. **1549** LATIMER *2nd Serm. bef. Edw. VI* (Arb.) 66 That ye wyll geue youre byshoppes charge yer they go home..to se your maiesties iniunctions better kepte, and sende youre visitours in theyr tayles. **1614** RALEIGH *Hist. World* IV. ii. §4. 147 In the taile of these Horses the Regiment of foot marched. **1848** THACKERAY *Van. Fair* xxiii, Peggy with the infantine procession at her tail. **1891** HALL CAINE *Scapegoat* vii, She..had..come to Morocco at the tail of a Spanish embassy.

c. Sexual member; penis or (oftener) pudendum.

1362 LANGL. *P. Pl.* A. III. 126 Heo is Tikel of hire Tayl.. As Comuyn as þe Cart-wei to knaues and to alle. *c* **1450** *Cov. Myst.* (Shaks. Soc.) 134 Suche a ȝonge damesel..Of hire tayle oftetyme be lyght. **1483** *Cath. Angl.* 377/1 A Tayle, *penis equi est.* *c* **1515** *Cocke Lorell's B.* (Percy Soc.) 14 Many whyte nonnes with whyte vayles, That was full wanton of theyr tayles. *a* **1744** POPE *To Mr. J. Moore* iv. **1785** GROSE *Dict. Vulg. T.* s.v. *Cab.* **1972** F. WARNER *Lying Figures* III. 17 Give her her head..and she'll give you her tail. **1977** *Transatlantic Rev.* LX. 78 He had been after her tail for months, but Judy, being an old-fashioned girl, declined his advances.

d. *slang.* †(i) A prostitute (*obs.*); (ii) women regarded collectively (by men) as a means of sexual gratification; sexual intercourse; a sexual partner. Freq. in phr. ***a piece*** (or ***bit***) ***of tail***. Cf. PIECE *sb.* 3 d.

1846 *Swell's Night Guide* 58, I takes my pitch last night on Fleet pave, then..a swell was sweet on me for a tail. **1869** F. HENDERSON *Six Yrs. in Prisons of Eng.* vii. 76 He meant a 'flash-tail', or prostitute who goes about the streets at nights trying to pick up 'toffs'. **1933** M. LOWRY *Ultramarine* ii. 67 It's not as though you were a bloody man who'd been having a bit of tail. **1942**, etc. [see PIECE *sb.* 3 d]. **1951** J. D. SALINGER *Catcher in Rye* xiii. 109 Innarested in a little tail t'night? **1953** H. MILLER *Plexus* (1963) xi. 391 He's at loose ends. Hates his work, loathes his wife, and the kids bore him to death. All he thinks of now is tail. And boy, does he chase it! **1967** J. POTTER *Foul Play* xiii. 157 Where's all the tail today? No Hermione, no Bunty, no Christabel. **1976** 'R. GORDON' *Doctor on Job* vi. 59 Even if it was deciding whether to go out on the booze at night or have a bit of tail off of the wife. **1977** *Transatlantic Rev.* LX. 39 He would yell, 'How y'all doin, chief? Gettin much tail?'

6. a. A train or band of followers; a following; a retinue. Also *fig.*

1297 R. GLOUC. (Rolls) 10774 Hiderward þe kinges conseilors londes hii destruede mid hor tayle. **1362** LANGL. *P. Pl.* A. II. 160, I haue no tome to telle þe Tayl [B. II. 185 taille] þat hem folweþ. *c* **1420** ? LYDG. *Assembly of Gods* 754 Of vngracious gastes he bryngeth a long tayll. **1578** *Reg. Privy Council Scot.* III. 15 To draw eftir thame a large taill of ignorant personis. **1633** B. JONSON *Tale Tub* II. i, Why should her worship lack Her tail of maids? **1675** M. CLIFFORD *Hum. Reason* in *Phenix* (1708) II. 540 If Errors in Belief draw so ill a Tail after them as the Devils and Damnation. **1814** SCOTT *Wav.* xvi, The Chief with his tail on..that is, with all his usual followers. **1838** [MISS MAITLAND] *Lett. fr. Madras* (1843) 180 Everybody has a tail, consisting of poor followers, flappers, and flatterers... When head walks abroad, tail walks after him at a respectful distance. **1862** *Sat. Rev.* 15 Mar. 286 The glorious days when O'Connell's tail supplied Lord Melbourne's Cabinet with the means of protracting a miserable existence.

b. A person (as a detective or spy, etc.) who secretly follows and observes another. Also *collect.*, people in the act of following. Cf. TAG *sb.*[1] 13, TAIL *v.*[1] 5 b. *colloq.* (orig. *U.S.*).

1914 [see TAIL *v.*[1] 5 b]. **1933** A. MERRITT *Burn Witch Burn!* (1934) xii. 181 One of the tails—one of the lads who's been looking—meets up with me. **1940** R. STOUT *Over my Dead Body* xiv. 215 'You were having Miss Lovchen followed?' 'Yes, a double tail... Their instructions are to report in every two hours.' **1955** J. CANNAN *Long Shadows* iii. 63 I'd like to put a tail on the lady. **1962** 'K. ORVIS' *Damned & Destroyed* v. 42, I realized almost at once I'd picked up a tail. The two shadowing me..were..obvious. **1978** M. H. CLARK *Stranger is Watching* xxvi. 112 We'll have a loose tail on you—an agent following you from a distance.

7. a. (Also *pl.*) The inferior, less valuable, or refuse part of anything; foots, bottoms, dregs, sediment. Also *fig.* Cf. TAILING *vbl. sb.*[1] 2.

1542 BOORDE *Dyetary* x. (1870) 256 It [ale] must haue no weft nor tayle. **1642** ROGERS *Naaman* 71 Abandoning the refuse and taile that remained. **1674** RAY *Collect. Words, Prepar. Metals, Tin* 123 The wast Tin that falls hindmost in the Buddle and Wreck, which they call the tail. **1778** PRYCE *Min. Cornub.* IV. i. 221. *Ibid.* Gloss. 329/1 *Tails*, the roughest refuse of stampt Tin thrown behind the tail or end of the buddle. **1890** *Science* 5 Sept. 129 The tails or faints, as well as the still less volatile or ordinary fusel oil, are mixtures of several alcohols and fatty acid ethers.

b. (Also in *pl.*) Short for *tail corn*, etc.: see 12 b, and cf. TAILING *vbl. sb.*[1] 2 a.

1778 [W. MARSHALL] *Minutes Agric.* 14 Oct. an. 1775, Last year, we made a bushel of tail to every fifteen bushels of head. **1801** *Farmer's Mag.* Apr. 215 After grinding [it] produced 483 lb. English of barley meal, 3 lb. and a half of tails, and 40 lb. and a half of bran. **1880** JEFFERIES *Gt. Estate* 110 He had a bushel of the 'tail', or second flour, from the mill.

8. a. The inferior, least influential, or least skilful members of a body; e.g. of a profession, a political party, etc.

1604 HIERON *Wks.* I. 493 Those that are but the refuse, and (as I may so speake) the taile of an honest profession. **1780** BURKE *Corr.* (1844) II. 385, I will say nothing about that tail which draggles in the dirt, and which every party in every state must carry about it. **1855** MACAULAY *Hist. Eng.* xv. III. 553 These Whigs..belonged, not to the main body of the party, but either to the head or to the tail. **1876** GRANT *Burgh Sch. Scotl.* II. xiii. 357 The more talented and industrious scholars are impeded for the sake of the tail of the class.

(*b*) *spec.* in *Cricket*, the lower end of the batting order, comprising the weaker batsmen in a team. Also *fig.*

1851 J. PYCROFT *Cricket Field* xi. 221 Never put in all your best men at first, and leave 'a tail' to follow. **1879** *James Lillywhite's Cricketers' Ann.* 17 The tail was again weak, the last five wickets only adding 16 runs. **1892** *Pall Mall G.* 30 May 1/3 It would seem as if Sussex has a very bad 'tail' indeed this year, the last seven batsmen being good for 35 only in the first innings and for but 37 in the second. **1913** J. B. HOBBS *How to make Century* xii. 82 The fast bowler.. was bowling far too accurately for 'tail' batsmen to do much with him. **1926** C. E. MONTAGUE *Rough Justice* III. ix. 125 They seemed to be talking about the conflict then arising between the House of Lords and the..House of Commons. 'If it comes to a Test Match,' said Wynnant, 'we'll lose. Too long a tail to our team.' **1955** *Times* 4 July 3/2 Due..to the obstinate wriggling of the tail, the last four Cambridge wickets more than doubled the score. **1977** J. LAKER *One-Day Cricket* 67 Marsh, with no support at all from the tail, was left high and dry with 52 not out.

b. *spec.* The inferior animals of a flock or herd.

1844 STEPHENS *Bk. Farm* II. 39 The lambs, dinmonts, or wethers, that are drafted out of the fat stock, are called the sheddings or tails. **1886** C. SCOTT *Sheep-Farming* 88 With overstocking..not only is there a greater 'tail' among the lambs, but the death rate is higher.

9. In various figurative uses.

1340 *Ayenb.* 61 Zuyche byeþ ycleped ine writinge: tayles. Vor hi wreþ þe uelþes of zenne of riche men uor zom timlich guod, hueruore hi byeþ anlicned to þe trayle of þe uoxe. **1382** WYCLIF *Deut.* xxviii. 13 The Lord thi God shal sett thee into heed, and not into tayl [**1388** the tail]. **1579** TOMSON *Calvin's Serm. Tim.* 1036/1 That the worde of God is a truth, a truth without a taile (as wee say). **1630** LENNARD tr. *Charron's Wisd.* I. xx. §8 (1670) 73 To swell and to be puffed up for every good and profitable action, is to shew his tail while he lifts up his head. **1742** *Col. Records Pennsylv.* IV. 555 The names of 'Imposter,..Invader of the Liberties of the People' (with a Tail of et cetera's). **1786** COWPER *Let. to W. Unwin* 24 Aug., I catch a minute by the tail and hold it fast, while I write to you. **1895** MRS. B. M. CROKER *Village Tales* (1896) 64 One of the last joints in the tail of precedence.

10. Short for *tail-ill*: see 14. *Obs.* or *dial.*

1577 B. GOOGE *Heresbach's Husb.* III. (1586) 133 A disease which they call the Woolfe, others the Taile, which is perceiued by the loosenesse or softnesse betwixt the iointes. **1741** *Compl. Fam.-Piece* III. 472 The Disease called the Tail, is by some Farmers called the Wolf.

11. Phrases. †**a.** ***tail on end***, said lit. of some beasts when running with the tail erect; hence *attrib.* headlong; precipitate(ly).

1790 R. TYLER *Contrast* II. ii, I was glad to take to my heels and split home, right off, tail on end. **1850** R. G. CUMMING *Hunter's Life S. Afr.* (ed. 2) I. 98 *note*, Hunted on horseback, and ridden down by a long, severe, tail-on-end chase. *Ibid.* 120 The oryx leading me a cruel long chase due north, tail-on-end, from my waggons.

b. ***with the tail between the legs***, lit. of a dog or other beast; *fig.* with a cowed and dejected demeanour.

c **1400** *Lanfranc's Cirurg.* 59 A wood hound..renneþ hidirward & þidirward..wiþ..his tail bitwene hise leggis. **1842** F. A. KEMBLE *Let.* 6 May in *Rec. Later Life* (1882) II. 218 She has scornfully..departed with her tail over her shoulder, leaving the behind scenes of Her Majesty's Theatre with their tails between their legs. **1884** W. E. NORRIS *Thirlby Hall* xii, We shall have you back here very soon..with your tail between your legs. **1897** *Westm. Gaz.* 22 Jan. 2/3 If this sneaking tail-between-the-legs policy is persisted in no more Church votes for the Union!

†**c.** ***tail and top***, = ***top and tail***: see TOP *sb.*

1558 PHAER *Æneid* v. N j b, Headlong down in dust he ouerturnyd tayle and topp.

d. ***to turn tail*** (orig. a term of falconry), to turn the back; hence, to run away, take to flight.

a **1586** SIDNEY *Arcadia* II. (1629) 109 Would shee..turne taile to the Heron, and flie out quite another way. **1587** GREENE *Euphues his Censure* Wks. (Grosart) VI. 192 To cast out no lure to such a haggarde as would turne taile to a full fist. **1589** PUTTENHAM *Eng. Poesie* III. xxiv. (Arb.) 300 Such as retire from the Princes presence, do not by and by turne tayle to them as we do, but go backward or sideling for a reasonable space. **1611** MARKHAM *Countr. Content.* I. v. (1668) 34 Short winged Hawks..will many times neither kill their Game, nor flie their mark; but will give it over.. and (as Faulconers term it) turn tail to it. **1639** LAUD in Rushw. *Hist. Coll.* (1721) II. II. 899 For him to turn tail against my Lord Deputy must needs be a foul Fault. **1719** DE FOE *Crusoe* (1840) I. xx. 360 The wolves turned tail. **1807** E. S. BARRETT *Rising Sun* II. 128 Ashamed to avow that you are going to turn tail on your former principles.

e. *to get one's tail down* and varr., to become dispirited; *to have one's tail up* and varr., to be in good spirits.

1853 'P. Paxton' *Stray Yankee in Texas* 97 To use an expressive Westernism, 'Dave's tail was up', and every possible preparation was made to preclude a failure. **1874** Hotten *Slang Dict.* 318 *Tail-down*, 'to get the tail down', generally means to lose courage. When a professional at any game loses heart in a match he is said to get his *tail down*. 'His *tail* was quite *down*, and it was all over.' **1917** G. S. Gordon *Let.* 26 Apr. (1943) 75 We were getting jaded till this touch of spring came, and now we have our tails up again, and are prepared to attack anything. **1921** *Punch* 12 Jan. 23, I must try and keep my tail up. **1923** Galsworthy *Captures* 190 He was a Northumbrian .. and his 'tail still up', as he expressed it. **1928** *Sunday Dispatch* 15 July 14, I sincerely hope that .. standard producers .. will not get their tails down over this 'cheap record boom'. **1933** Wodehouse *Mulliner Nights* iii. 93 'Tails up, Uncle Theodore, tails up!' 'Tails up!' repeated the Bishop dutifully, but he spoke the words without any real ring of conviction in his voice. **1941** C. Morgan *Empty Room* ii. 88 May be a snag somewhere. Usually is when one gets one's tail up about an idea. **1960** [see balance *sb.* 15 c]. **1978** R. Mark *Office of Constable* xv. 187 Nevertheless, in dealing with the worst forms of crime our tails were well up.

f. *two shakes of a lamb's tail* (and varr.): see shake *sb.*[1] 2 h.

a **1855** J. F. Kelly *Humors of Falconbridge* (1856) 137 In the wag of a dead lamb's tail. **1901** *Dialect Notes* II. 142 'I'll do it in three jerks of a lamb's tail,' i.e., very quickly. *Ibid.* 429 She got all cleared up in the whisk of a lamb's tail. **1917** *Ibid.* IV. 402 *Two jerks of a lamb's tail, n. phr.*, an instant, a jiffy.

g. *the tail wags the dog*, the less important or subsidiary factor dominates the situation; the proper roles are reversed.

[**1907** M. A. von Arnim *Fräulein Schmidt* xxvi. 84 Isn't it rather weak to let yourself be led round by the nose .. ? It is as though instead of a dog wagging its tail the tail should wag the dog.] **1935** F. Scott Fitzgerald *Let.* 11 Mar. (1964) 260 This letter is a case of the tail (the parenthesis) wagging the dog. **1945** *Jrnl. R. Aeronaut. Soc.* XLIV. 463/1 The aeroplane developing an undamped short period oscillation in which rapid movement of the rudder from side to side plays an essential part—the tail wagging the dog. **1956** W. H. Whyte *Organization Man* ii. 19 The tail wagged the dog in this case and it still often does. **1968** *Listener* 4 Jan. 23/3 Most producers are going to continue resisting .. indulgence in an academic exercise. There's a danger of the tail wagging the dog. **1980** *Truck & Bus Transportation* (Surry Hills, New South Wales) Feb. 26/2 Tractor response during the lane-change manoeuvre shows how the externally-applied force through the fifth wheel induces tractor lateral motion. This is better known as 'tail wagging the dog'.

h. *to be on someone's tail* and varr., to follow or pursue someone closely (see also quot. 1925). Also *fig.*

[**1865** 'L. Carroll' *Alice's Adventures in Wonderland* x. 151 There's a porpoise close behind us, and he's treading on my tail.] **1925** Fraser & Gibbons *Soldier & Sailor Words* 275 *Tail, to get on the*, an Air Force expression for an attack on the rear of an opponent. **1937** Partridge *Dict. Slang* 860/2 *Tail, be—*gen. *shall* or *will be—on a person's*, to look for, to pursue, a person with a view to punishing or severely scolding him: C. 20. **1962** 'J. le Carré' *Murder of Quality* iv. 54, I rather gathered .. that his Chief Constable was treading on his tail, urging him to scour the country for tramps. **1971** B. Malamud *Tenants* 71, I wouldn't want anybody else on my tail or in my hair, with or without cause. **1971** M. Tak *Truck Talk* 154 *Stay on his tail*, to follow another truck closely. **1981** *Sunday Times* 1 Feb. 63/5 Sir Hugh thought the Lonrho boss had put a private eye on his tail.

i. *to chase one's tail*, to indulge in a futile pursuit; to go round in circles.

1963 *Times* 14 May 8/4 'We have been chasing our tails overlong,' he said. 'Given a Labour Government committed to the principles of equity and justice, a coordinated wages policy may be possible.' **1973** *Archivum Linguisticum* IV. 35 Is anything indeed to be gained from hunting for some notion embodying the cumulate surface exponency of .. transitive and perfective .. ? It is all too easy at times to chase our conceptual tail.

j. Also *crag and tail*: see crag *sb.*[1] 1 b. *cut and long tail*: see cut *ppl. a.* 9. *head and (or, nor) tail*: see head *sb.*[1] *to twist the lion's tail*: see lion *sb.* 2 g. *to put salt on the tail*: see salt *sb.*[1] 2 c. *top over tail*: see top *sb.*, and cf. sense 5.

12. *attrib.* or as *adj.* **a.** Forming or situated at the tail, bottom, or rear, hindmost; as *tail decoy, half, hound, van*; coming from the rear, as *tail-wind*. **b.** Forming the lowest or most inferior quality, as *tail barley, corn, flour, meal, wheat*.

a. **1673** S. C. *Rules Civility* 104 Flounders, Place, or the like; .. the tail-half is the best. **1970** T. Hughes *Crow* 15 He stuffed the head half headfirst into woman And it crept in deeper and up to peer out through her eyes Calling its tail-half to join up quickly. **1857** Hughes *Tom Brown* i. vii, The tail hounds all straining to get up with the lucky leaders [in hare-and-hounds]. **1874** J. W. Long *Amer. Wildfowl* xxv. 257 Wait until they are over the 'tail' decoys. **1891** *Daily News* 23 Oct. 5/8 When the last train, with two engines, got through .. the tail van is said to have been floating on the water. **1897** *Westm. Gaz.* 1 Mar. 8/1 With a strong tail wind birds have accomplished more than sixty miles in the hour. **1927** C. A. Lindbergh *We* iii. 39, I left Texarkana with a strong tail wind. **1976** *Evening Times* (Glasgow) 1 Dec. 5/3 Tail winds across the Atlantic knocked up to an hour off the flying times of some transatlantic flights.

b. **1765** *Museum Rust.* IV. lxiii. 282 For tail barley .. *ol.* 14*s.* 3*d.* **1851** *Jrnl. R. Agric. Soc.* XII. i. 133 The light or tail corn goes a considerable length in feeding the horses upon a farm. **1887** O. Crawfurd *Beyond Seas* 35 The enemy's army but riff-raff and tail-corn fellows.

13. General combs.: **a.** attributive, as ***tail-blotch, -cap, -feather, -fur, -plumage, -pocket, -quill, -ring, -spot, -stroke, -temptation, -tip, -tuft***, etc.; **b.** objective and obj. gen., as ***tail-dangler, -raiser, -wagger; tail-buffeting, -chasing, -pulling, -spreading, -switching, -wagging*** sbs. and adjs.; **c.** instrumental and locative, as ***tail-cropped, -decorated, -docked, -joined, -tied*** adjs.; ***tail-fisher, -fishing***; also ***tail-like*** adj.; ***tail-down, -first***, adjs. and advbs.; ***tail-foremost*** adv.

1872 Coues *N. Amer. Birds* 99 *Tail-blotches small or obscure. **1931** *Flight* 30 Jan. 90 To the new phenomenon the subcommittee gives the name '*tail buffeting'. **1947** *Times* 8 Feb. 2/5 There was tail-buffeting within a certain speed range in very bumpy conditions. **1891** Morgan *Anim. Sk.* 198 Each successive moult [of the rattlesnake] leaves an additional *tail-cap of dried skin and these constitute the rattle. **1921** J. D. M. Rorke *Musical Pilgrim's Progress* iii. 49 The excitement and *tail-chasing demonstrations of a dog at the home-coming. **1957** R. H. Smythe *Conformation of Dog* 123 Tail-chasing, spinning and walking in circles. **1892** Kipling *Cleared* xv, *Barrack-r. Ball.* 186 The *tail-cropped heifer's low. **1922** Joyce *Ulysses* 646 It [*sc.* a horse] was a .. *taildangler, a headhanger. **1916** H. Barber *Aeroplane Speaks* 87 An inclinometer .. which will indicate a nose-down position by increase in air speed, and a *tail-down position by decrease in air speed. *Ibid.* 113 If the angle of incidence .. is too great, it will produce an excess of lift, and that way .. result in a tendency to fly 'tail-down'. **1935** P. W. F. Mills *Elem. Pract. Flying* vii. 103 When brought too quickly into tail-down attitude their wings retain an uncomfortable degree of buoyancy for some little time. **1774** Goldsm. *Nat. Hist.* (1776) V. 97 The common eagle .. the *tail feathers white, blackening at the ends. **1886** Stevenson *Kidnapped* xviii. 171 Alan's morals were all *tail-first; but he was ready to give his life for them. **1904** *Blackw. Mag.* June 818/2 A spaniel .. dragged tail-first upstairs and downstairs by a child. **1914** H. M. Buist *Aircraft in German War* v. 101 The latter quality lead to the original example of this tail-first machine being purchased by the Rumanian Army. **1945** *Sun* (Baltimore) 7 Feb. 7-0/4 (*heading*) New 'tail-first' fighter plane appears to fly backward. **1865** Tylor *Early Hist. Man.* xii. 355 To proceed now to the story of the *Tail-Fisher. *Ibid.* 357 The curious mythic art of *Tail-fishing. **1875** Morris *Æneid* viii. 210 Which same .. *Tail-foremost dragged he to his den. **1902** *Daily Chron.* 18 Oct. 8/3 Ermine, spotted with the tips of the *tail-fur. **1649** G. Daniel *Trinarch.* To Rdr. 172 *Tayle-Ioyn'd foxes hurrying Sylla's Nose, A Brand to wast the ffeilds. **1835–6** *Todd's Cycl. Anat.* I. 208/2 The last segment of the *tail-like abdomen. **1849** D. J. Browne *Amer. Poultry Yd.* (1855) 153 A well-developed *tail plumage. **1848** Thackeray *Van. Fair* xiii, The head of the family thrust his hands into the great *tail-pockets of his great blue coat. **1681** Grew *Musæum* i. iv. iii. 75 The two *Tail-Quills of the same [Tropick Bird]. **1894** Newton *Dict. Birds* 705 In some [penguins] the tail-quills, which are very numerous, are also long. **1907** *Macm. Mag.* July 673 His [a tiger's] *tail rings were very finely marked. **1872** Coues *N. Amer. Birds* 101 Wing-bars and *tail-spots ordinary. **1891** Morgan *Anim. Sk.* 138 The vigorous *tail-strokes .. often leave their mark on the smooth surface of the water. **1905** R. Garnett *Shakespeare* 97 *Tail-switching Lucifer, Hell's emperor. **1690** C. Nesse *O. & N. Test.* I. 25 The Son of God .. broke the serpents head, and leaves only *tail-temptations for us. **1904** B'ness von Hütten *Pam* 135 If the proverbial worm had not only turned, but risen on its *tail-tip. **1910** W. de la Mare *Three Mulla-Mulgars* xvii. 224 They sat, with *tail-tufts over their shoulders. *a* **1930** D. H. Lawrence *Last Poems* (1932) 260 The two lions who devoured one another, and left the tail-tufts wagging. **1948** B. Vesey-Fitzgerald *Bk. of Dog* i. 114 Organisations, such as the *Tail Waggers Club, undertake to provide discs that can be attached to the collar. **1952** *Chambers's Jrnl.* Apr. 239/1, I reckon that about 3,000,000 folk would have to look elsewhere for their bread and butter if there were no trawlermen—or fish. We mustn't forget the tail-waggers. **1982** L. Cody *Bad Company* iii. 26 'What's this then? The Tail-Waggers Club? he asked as he .. fended off the retriever's enthusiastic welcome. **1869** Platts tr. *Ikhwanu-s-Safa* 70 If watching, barking, and *tail-wagging are required there, I am the one for it.

14. Special combinations: **tail-area** *Statistics*, an area under the curve of a frequency distribution lying between one end of the curve and any ordinate on the same side of the mode; **tail assembly** [assembly 1 c] *Aeronaut.* = empennage; cf. *tail unit* below; **tailback**: in U.S. football, the player stationed farthest from the forwards; †**tail-band**, = crupper *sb.* 1; **tail-bandage**, a bandage divided into strips at the end; **tail-bay**, (*a*) the space between a girder and the wall: cf. bay *sb.*[3]; (*b*) in a canal-lock, the narrow water-space just below the lock, opening out into the lower pond: see quot.; **tail-beam**, a beam that is tailed in, as to a wall; a tail-piece; †**tail-bearer**, a train-bearer; **tail-binder**: see quot.; **tail-block**, (*a*) *Naut.*: see quot. 1769; (*b*) in a sawmill carriage, a support of the log at the end where the cut ends; (*c*) in a lathe = *tail-stock*; **tail-bond**, *Building*, a stone placed with its greatest length across a wall, serving as a tie to hold the face to the interior; **tail-bone**, any one of the caudal vertebræ in animals; also applied to the coccyx, when anchylosed into one bone; **tail boom** *Aeronaut.*, one of the main spars of the longitudinal framework carrying the tail of an aeroplane when not supported by the fuselage; **tail-box**: see quot.; †**tail-castle**, the poop of a ship; **tail-coat**, a coat with tails; *esp.* a dress or swallow-tailed coat; hence **tail-coated** *a.*; **tail comb**, a comb with a tapering tail or handle used in styling to lift, divide, or curl the hair; **tail cone** *Aeronaut.*, the conical rear end of the fuselage of an aircraft; **tail-coverts** (**-covers**), *sb. pl.*, *Ornith.*, the feathers that cover the rectrices or quill-feathers of the tail in birds; divided into upper and lower, according to their position on the dorsal or ventral surface; **tail-crab** (cf. crab *sb.*[1] 7): see quot.; **tail-cut**: see cut *sb.*[2] 21 a; **tail-dam**, *Sc.*, the tail-race of a mill; **tail-dragger** *Aeronaut.*, an aeroplane that lands and taxis on a tail wheel or tail skid, its nose off the ground; **tail-drain**: see quot. 1805; **tail-ducat** (Ger. *Schwanzdukaten*), a Prussian gold coin of Frederick William I (1713–40), worth about 10*s.* sterling, bearing the king's head with a queue; **tail-dust**: see quot.; **tail-fan**, in macrurous crustacea, the tail-end formed by the sixth pair of pleopods with the telson; **tail fin**, (*a*) the caudal fin of a fish; (*b*) *Aeronaut.* (see quot. 1940); (*c*) an upswept ornamental projection forming a continuation of the fender line at the rear of a motor vehicle; **tail-flap**, (*a*) the tail of a crustacean; (*b*) *Aeronaut.*, an adjustable control surface on the tail of an aircraft; **tail-flower**, a W. Indian araceous plant of the genus *Anthurium*; from its tail-like spicate inflorescence; **tail-fly**, *Angling*, the fly at the end of the leader; a stretcher-fly; **tail gas** (see quot. 1967); **tail-grape**, a name for the species of *Artabotrys*, N.O. *Anonaceæ*, shrubs of tropical Africa and the East Indies; so called from the hook-like form of the flower-stalks, by the aid of which the fruit is suspended; **tail gunner** = *rear gunner* s.v. rear *sb.*[3] (and *a.*[1]) 9; **tail-head**, the root of an animal's tail; **tail-heavy** *a.*, of a motor vehicle, boat, etc.: having a tendency for the rear end to bear down more than the front; hence **tail-heaviness** (used esp. with reference to aircraft); **tail-hook**, *Angling*, the hook of a tail-fly; **tail-hounds**, the hounds in the tail of a pack; **tail-house**: see quot.; **tail-ill**, a name for palsy, supposed to be caused by looseness between the tail-joints; **tail-joist**, a joist tailed into the wall, a tail-piece; **tail-knife**: see quot.; **tail-lamp**, **tail-light**, the (usually red) light or lights carried at the rear of a train, motor-vehicle, aeroplane, etc.; **tail-lobe**, either of the two lobes of the caudal fin present in most fishes; **tail-lock**, a lock at the exit or lower end of a dock; **tail-mill** = *tail-house*; **tail-muscle**, any muscle in the tail of an animal; a caudal or coccygeal muscle; **tail parachute** *Aeronaut.*, a deceleration parachute attached to the tail of an aircraft; **tail-piles**: see quot.; **tail-pin**, †(*a*) some part of an ancient gun or its carriage; †(*b*) a pin for the tail of a woman's gown; (*c*) the centre in the tail-spindle of a lathe; (*d*) *Mus.* (i) (see quot. 1961); (ii) a metal spike attached to the cello and other instruments to support them at the correct height from the ground; **tailplane** *Aeronaut.*, the horizontal stabilizing surface of the tail of an aircraft; **tail-pole**, a wooden lever or turning beam by means of which a post- or windmill is turned to the wind; **tail-rhyme, -rime** = *tailed rime* (tailed[1] 1 d); hence **tail-rimed** *a.*; **tail-rod**, a continuation of the piston-rod, which passes through the back cover of the cylinder, and serves to steady the piston and rod by giving the former a double bearing; **tail-rot** = *tail-ill*; **tail rotor** *Aeronaut.*, an auxiliary rotor at the tail of a helicopter designed to counterbalance the torque of the main rotor; **tail-screw**, in a lathe, the screw which moves the back centre tail-spindle to and fro: the tail-piece; **tail-seed**, the small ill-developed part of a quantity of seed; **tail-shaft**, in screw steamships, that section of the shaft nearest the propeller; †**tail-shot** = *tail-ill* (*obs.*); so †**tail-shotten** *a.*; **tail skid** [skid *sb.* 2 f] *Aeronaut.*, that part of an aircraft's landing gear which supports its tail; **tail-slide** *Aeronaut.* (see quot. 1969); **tail-slip** = *tail-ill*; **tailsman**, *rare*, a ploughman; **tail-soaked** *a.*: see quot.; **tail-spindle**, the spindle in the *tail-stock* of a lathe; **tail-stern**, the tail-piece of a musical instrument; **tail-stock** = dead-head 2 b: see quot.; **tail-tackle**, a handy tackle consisting of a double and a single block, or two double blocks, having the strop of one of the double blocks lengthened as in a tail-block; **tail-trimmer**, *Building*: see quot.; **tail-twisting**, the twisting of a tail or tails; (*a*) *lit.* in the fur-trade; (*b*) in political slang, the act of 'twisting the lion's tail': see lion 2 g; (*c*) in gen. *fig.* use, harassment or malicious annoyance; hence **tail-twist** *v.*, **tail-**

twister; **tail unit** *Aeronaut.* = EMPENNAGE; **tail-valve**, (*a*) the air-pump valve in some forms of condenser; (*b*) = SNIFTING-VALVE; **tail-van**, the last van of a train; **tail-vice**, a small hand-vice with a tail or handle to hold it by (Webster 1864); **tail-walking** , the movement of fish over the surface of water by means of propulsion with the tail; hence (as a back-formation) **tail-walk** *v. intr.*; **tail-water**, the water in a mill-race below the wheel, or in a canal or navigable channel below a lock; **tail wheel** *Aeronaut.* = *tail skid* above; **tail-worm** = *tail-ill*; **tail-worts**, a name given by Lindley to plants of the N.O. *Triuridaceæ*.

1957 KENDALL & BUCKLAND *Dict. Statistical Terms* 290 *Tail area (of a Distribution). **1971** D. C. HAGUE *Managerial Economics* vii. 153 If we want to take the probability of there being less than 2 in of rain, we take the area of the first two bars [of the histogram], and so on. If we do this, we are said to be considering tail areas. **1968** *Globe & Mail* (Toronto) 3 Feb. 1/2 The wreckage was a compacted heap of rubble... Only the *tail assembly was intact. **1977** J. CLEARY *High Road to China* iv. 128 The plane quivered..then the nose came up, the quivering slid out through the tail-assembly. **1930** R. C. ZUPPKE *Coaching Football* vii. 208 The *tail-back is four and one-half yards back of the scrummage line and directly back of the fullback. **1980** *Washington Post* 10 Oct. c6/5 Of the six Rattler touchdowns Keith pointed out FAMU 'earned' only one: the 69-yard first-quarter run by tailback Archie Jones. **1483** *Cath. Angl.* 377/1 A *Taylbande (*A.* Taylle bande), *caudile, subtela.* **1856** S. C. BREES *Gloss. Terms*, **Tail bays*, a name given to common joists when one end is framed in a girder and the other rests on a wall. **1875** KNIGHT *Dict. Mech.* s.v. *Lock*, The tail bay or aft-bay, below the lock-chamber. **1598** MARSTON *Sco. Villanie* II. v, Codrus my well-fac't Ladies *taile-bearer (He that..play'th Flauias vsherer). **1828** *Craven Gloss.*, **Tail-binder*, a long stone..which rests upon the corner stone,..to bind, or give strength to the wall. **1769** FALCONER *Dict. Marine* (1776), **Tail-block*, a small single block, having a short piece of rope attached to it, by which it may be fastened to any object.. either for convenience, or to increase the force applied to the said object. **1829** MARRYAT *F. Mildmay* viii, A tail block was attached to the boom-iron. **1881** YOUNG *Ev. Man his own Mechanic* §591 The tail-block [of a lathe] has a sliding spindle worked by the screw and wheel. **1776** G. SEMPLE *Building in Water* 141 The Headers, Stretchers and *Tail-bonds. **1548–77** VICARY *Anat.* ix. (1888) 74 Three *carti'agiais* spondels of *Ossa caude*, called the *tayle bone. **1898** *Syd. Soc. Lex.*, *Tail-bone*, the coccygeal vertebræ; coccyx, or os coccygis. **1913** *Flight* 23 Aug. 927/1 One of our sketches shows the method of joining the struts to the *tail booms. **1969** K. MUNSON *Pioneer Aircraft 1903–14* 142/1 The three tubular steel tailbooms formed a triangular section, and the tail control wires were led through the uppermost boom, which also acted as a propeller bearing. **1895** RAYMOND *Smoke of War* 22 The *tail-box—one part of that revolving dome at the head of a stone [wind-] mill by which the sails are brought to face an ever-shifting wind. **1585** HIGINS *Junius' Nomenclator* 222/1 *Puppis,..la poupe*, the hind decke, or *taile castell. **1847** ALB. SMITH *Chr. Tadpole* ix. (1879) 86 He was..going to put on a *tail-coat for the first time. **1879** STEVENSON *Trav. Cevennes* (1895) 16 A tall peasant..arrayed in the green tail-coat of the country. **1889** HICKSON *Naturalist in N. Celebes* 10 The visitor must assume a black tail-coat, a white shirt with a black tie,..and, pro forma, a hat. **1850** LYNCH *Theo. Trinal* xi. 211 How he was born, cradled, schooled, *tailcoated, colleged, and the like. **1782** J. WOODFORDE *Diary* 24 Apr. (1926) II. 19 To a *Tail Comb and another Comb for Nancy of Baker p^d. 0. 0. 10. **1855** F. DUBERLY *Let.* 22 July in E. E. P. Tisdall *Mrs. Duberly's Campaigns* (1963) v. 153 Oh, please will you send me a tail comb in the box. **1907** *Yesterday's Shopping* (1969) 110/1 Tail or curling combs—buffalo horn. **1930** V. SACKVILLE-WEST *Edwardians* i. 38 Don't drag my hair back... Give me the tail comb... It wants more fullness at the sides. **1976** J. GRENFELL *Joyce Grenfell requests Pleasure* xvii. 246 Her dark hair was kept neat in a fine net... A tail-comb raised the waves. **1944** H. F. GREGORY *Anything a Horse can Do* xxi. 216 The tail rotor and approximately the last four feet of the *tail cone were broken completely. **1978** Tail cone [see sense 2 m above]. **1861** DU CHAILLU *Equat. Afr.* xvi. 306 Its back, *tail-cover, and very long flowing tail are pure milk-white. **1815** STEPHENS in Shaw *Gen. Zool.* IX. I. 6 *Tail-coverts grey. **1849** D. J. BROWNE *Amer. Poultry Yard* (1855) 21 The wing coverts on the shoulders, and the tail coverts are dark-greyish. **1883** GRESLEY *Coal Mining Gloss.*, **Tail crab*, a crab for overhauling and belaying the tail rope in pumping gear. **1791** *Rep. Nav. Thames & Isis* 12 A *tail Cut from a Lock on River Navigations should be as short as possible. **1903** LUMSDEN *Toorle* v. i. 100 His speech rusht out o' the mou' o' him like water out o' a *tail dam. **1971** *Flying* Apr. 39/2 If you trace the 172 back to the rag-wing 170 *taildragger of 1948. **1981** *R.A.F. News* 14 Jan. 12/3 The Chipmunk is well suited to the unit's role because, as a taildragger, it introduces characteristics that 'sort out the men from the boys'. **1805** R. W. DICKSON *Pract. Agric.* II. 923 **Tail-Drain*, the principal ditch which conveys the water out of the meadow. **1842** J. AITON *Domest. Econ.* (1857) 183 Taking the levels, and laying off the main feeders, the floating gutters, the tail drains,..and the main drain to carry away the whole water. **1864** CARLYLE tr. *Liasenbarth* (1750) in *Fredk. Gt.* XVI. v, A Secretary came..told down on the table five *Tail-ducats (*Schwanz-dukaten*), and a Gold Friedrich under them. **1764** *Museum Rust.* III. lxi. 281 The *tail-dust, which falls through the screen whilst the malt is cleaning before it is put up in sacks,..may be applied to a better use. **1893** STEBBING *Crustacea* xi. 146 Except in the Lithodidæ, that [pair of pleopods] belonging to the sixth segment is always present, this pair with the telson forming the *Rhipidura* or *tail-fan. **1681** GREW *Musæum* I. v. i. 85 The *Tail-Finn, as it were half a Finn, being ½ a foot high. **1835–6** *Todd's Cycl. Anat.* I. 562/2 The horizontal position of the tail-fin..distinguishes the cetacean from the fish. **1940** *Chambers's Techn. Dict.* 333/1 *Fin*, in an aeroplane, a fixed vertical surface giving lateral stability of motion; usually placed at the tail, then sometimes called a tail fin. **1945** W. LANGEWIESCHE *Stick & Rudder* vii. 115 The purpose of the horizontal tail fin is not to hold the tail up, but to hold it down; it is a sort of wing, but a wing set at a negative Angle of Attack. **1954** *Wall St. Jrnl.* 22 Oct. 16/6 Its [*sc.* the car's] high fender-line sweeps backward in a straight line but is slightly lower at the tail fins than at the headlights. **1974** P. DICKINSON *Poison Oracle* i. 22 The plane lay still... The symbol of the rising sun stared from the tall tail fin. **1982** *Quarto* Mar. 7/4 The American family car was a 425-horsepower, twenty-two-foot-long Buick Electra with tail fins in back. **1847–8** H. MILLER *First Impr.* v, Her [female lobster's] dorsal plates curve round from the joint at the carapace till the *tail-flap rests on her breast. **1913** A. E. BERRIMAN *Aviation* p. xxiv, The glide..as the pilot switches on at the last moment and cocks up the tail flap to flatten out ere touching the ground. **1980** J. DITTON *Copley's Hunch* II. i. 115 The tail-flaps were working all right, because he zoomed up and over to gain height. **1884** MILLER *Plant-n.* 161 *Anthurium*, Banner-plant, Flamingo-plant, *Tail-flower. **1883** *Century Mag.* XXVI. 378 For a stretcher or *tail-fly. **1948** *Economist* 31 July 193/2 *Tail gases..carried ..by pipe-line..will replace some of the coke at present used..for the production of ammonia, methanol and petrol. **1967** *Gloss. Terms Gas Industry* (*B.S.I.*) 12 *Tail gas*, refinery gas which is not required for further processing in the refinery. **1884** MILLER *Plant-n.* 163 *Artabotrys*, *Tail-grape. **1939** *War Illustr.* 29 Dec. 539/2 The *tail gunner reported 'Fighters on our tail'. **1971** P. O'DONNELL *Impossible Virgin* xii. 246 A bloke called Worsfold, tail-gunner in a Lancaster during the war..fell over seven thousand feet... Only broke a leg and a few ribs. **1704** *Lond. Gaz.* No. 4018/4 A pretty large white Hound Bitch, with..a Tann'd Spot on her Fore-head, and another on the *Tail-head. **1844** STEPHENS *Bk. of Farm* II. 164 The first point..handled is the end of the rump at the tail head. **1901** *Westmorld. Gaz.* 26 Oct. 5/3 Lost, three Ewes and two Lambs,..ewes marked across tail-head. **1919, 1930** *Tail-heaviness [see *nose-heaviness* s.v. NOSE *sb.* 18]. **1977** D. BEATY *Excellency* vi. 83 The tail-heaviness had been deliberate..this ingenious way of getting rid of him. **1916** H. BARBER *Aeroplane Speaks* 110 The aeroplane will, in flight, be nose-heavy or *tail-heavy. **1923** G. STURT *Wheelwright's Shop* 223 *Tail-heavy*, the opposite fault to fore-heavy. In a tail-heavy cart the tendency was to lift the horse off the ground. **1957** [see SCORCH *v.*[1] 3]. **1978** R. V. JONES *Most Secret War* xvi. 131 The weight of two cameras, about 120 lbs., would pull back the centre of gravity of the aircraft making it 'tail heavy' and dangerous to fly. **1888** GOODE *Amer. Fishes* 8 Use a '*tail-hook' to avoid the risk of losing the minnow without gaining the Perch. **1852** R. S. SURTEES *Sponge's Sp. Tour* (1893) 50 The last of the *tail-hounds are flying the fence out of the first field. **1881** RAYMOND *Mining Gloss.*, **Tail-house, Tail-mill*, the buildings in which tailings are treated. **1824** MACTAGGART *Gallovid. Encycl.* s.v. *Yirb-wives*, When a cow takes the *Tailill, or is Elfshot, these females are sent for to cure them. **1846** J. BAXTER *Libr. Pract. Agric.* (ed. 4) II. 134 This complaint is traced to a most ridiculous cause. The original evil is said to be in the tail; and all maladies of this kind, involving the partial or total loss of motion of the hind limbs of the animal, are classed under the name of *tail-ill*, or *tail-slip*. **1667** PRIMATT *City & C. Build.* 80 Observe that the Carpenter doth pin all his *Tayl-Joynts, they being apt to slip. **1820** SCORESBY *Acc. Arctic Reg.* II. 233 A '*tail-knife',..used for perforating the fins or tail of a dead whale. **1891** *Cent. Dict.*, *Tail-lamp. **1908** *Westm. Gaz.* 17 Nov. 5/2 Side lamps, tail lamp, head-light with separate generator. **1844** *Illustr. Lond. News* 14 Dec. 374 Each train..is provided with..red *tail lights. **1903** *Westm. Gaz.* 28 Jan. 5/1 He did not slow even when the red tail-lights of the standing local train were seen. **1937** *Esquire* Jan. 64/3 He turned and watched the red tail-light sink into the distant darkness. **1946** R. A. MCFARLAND *Human Factors in Air Transport Design* xii. 610 The pilot..had..mistaken the taillight of the stationary D.C.-3 for one of a row of.. boundary lights. **1978** S. BRILL *Teamsters* vii. 286 Only one man was working the night shift, replacing some tail lights on a trailer. **1907** J. E. EWART in *Q. Rev.* Apr. 558 At the base of the long dock there is no vestige of a *tail-lock. **1891** *Cent. Dict.*, *Tail-muscle. **1898** *Syd. Soc. Lex.*, *Tail muscle*, coccygeus, depressor of the tail. **1937** *Jrnl. R. Aeronaut. Soc.* XLI. 731 The Russian plane A N.T.6 which was the first to land at the pole was provided with a *tail parachute, which was released as soon as the skis touched the ice. **1978** A. WELCH *Bk. of Airsports* ii. 29/2 Tail parachutes are 'one-shot' drag producers and are more useful as an emergency aid. **1837** in *Civil Eng. & Arch. Jrnl.* I. 6/1 The component parts of a groin are piles, planking, land-ties,..*tail-piles and keys, and screw-bolts. *Ibid.* 6/2 The relative proportions of the component parts are, four piles, one land-tie with tail-piles and keys [etc.]. **1497** *Naval Acc. Hen. VII* (1896) 84 Lymores with boltes forlokkes kayes lynces and a *taile pynne for the said Curtowe. *c* **1540** HEYWOOD *Four P.P.* in Hazl. *Dodsley* I. 351 The trimming and pinning up their gear; Specially their fiddling with the tail-pin. **1884** E. HERON-ALLEN *Violin-Making* xi. 195 The *Tail-pin*..is the peg of ebony or box-wood, which is firmly fixed into the bottom block..to which is fastened the loop..of the tail-piece. **1887** *Cassell's Encycl. Dict.*, *Tail-pin*, the back-centre pin of a lathe. **1923** E. VAN DER STRAETEN *Technics Violoncello Playing* (ed. 4) iii. 18 The use of the tail pin is now generally adopted, and offers the double advantage of steadying the instrument and strengthening its tone. **1946** R. ALTON *Violin & 'Cello Building* vii. 60 The tail-rest.. over which the tail-gut passes on its way to the tail-pin, must now be inserted. *Ibid.* xv. 147 With a tapered reamer fit the tail-pin into its place, gradually enlarging the hole until the tail-pin fits. **1961** A. BAINES *Mus. Instr. through Ages* 358 *Tailpin*, the button let into the bottom block of a violin, etc., to which the tailpiece is attached by a gut loop. **1978** *Early Music* Oct. 530/2 My own contribution to this debate..is concerned with thicknesses and struttings, lengths and positions of necks, bridge heights and string angles and tailpin hitches. **1909** A. BERGET *Conquest of Air* II. iv. 189 *Tail planes. **1911** [see EMPENNAGE]. **1948** 'N. SHUTE' *No Highway* i. 8 It had only been necessary to break one of these expensive tailplanes for the strength tests for the airworthiness of the machine. **1979** D. KYLE *Green River High* xvii. 219, I tested the tailplane's firmness to be sure it would take my weight. **1945** *Archit. Rev.* XCVIII. 71 This 'winding' of the mill was first accomplished by pushing the whole body of a post mill round by means of the '*tail pole', which projected downwards through the ladder. **1968** J. ARNOLD *Shell Bk. Country Crafts* 170 The problem of keeping the sweeps or sails into the wind was originally met by manual labour at the 'tail-pole', or turning beam. **1838** E. GUEST *Hist. Eng. Rhythms* II. IV. i. 289 This, like the interwoven and *tail-rhime, seems to have been first used by the Latinist. **1916** J. E. WELLS *Man. Writings Middle Eng.* I. 86 Lines 3411 to the end are in tail-rime stanzas. **1945** Tail-rhyme [see RIME *sb.*[1] 2 e] **1982** *N. & Q.* June 242/2 With certain common patterns, of couplets, quatrains, and versions of the tail-rhyme stanza, predominating. **1886** SCHMIRGEL in *Sir Beues* (E.E.T.S.) App. xlv, Romances with *tail-rhymed stanzas. **1894** *Times* 26 June 12/1 Rods, which pass through the covers of the low-pressure cylinders after the manner of a *tail-rod. **1896** KIPLING *Seven Seas* 43 Yon orchestra sublime Whaur-to..the tail-rods mark the time. **1847** W. C. L. MARTIN *Ox* 139/2 Palsy, or paralysis. This disease..bears among farmers and cow-leeches the ridiculous names of joint-yellows, *tail-rot, tail-ill, or tail-slip. **1944** H. F. GREGORY *Anything a Horse can Do* x. 107 The control stick..would decrease the pitch of the blades on the right horizontal *tail rotor. **1979** *Jrnl. R. Soc. Arts* CXXVII. 571/1 The helicopter for replacement of Sea King is rather a noisy beast, in that it has a tailrotor. **1786** *Young's Ann. Agric.* V. 114 (E.D.D.) *Tail-seed from my seed-mill. **1888** KIPLING *Day's Work* (1898) 277 When d'ye ship a new *tail-shaft? **1897** *Westm. Gaz.* 8 July 5/2 The tail-shaft got bent and could not be rectified, consequently the ship became disabled. **1901** *Scotsman* 5 Mar. 7/8 Accidents principally of the kind known as tail-shaft breakages. **1790** J. WOODFORDE *Diary* 5 Feb. (1927) III. 169 My poor Cow rather better this morning, but not able to get up as yet, she having a Disorder which I never heard of before or any of our Somersett Friends. It is called *Tail-shot, that is, a separation of some of the Joints of the Tail about a foot from the tip of the Tail, or rather a slipping of one Joint from another. **1798** *Ibid.* 1 Aug. (1931) V. 130 She is *tail-shotten, & hath something of the Gargut. **1913** A. E. BERRIMAN *Aviation* iii. 25 The *tail-skid is comparatively an insignificant member of the design: provided it serves its purpose as a protection. **1973** J. D. R. RAWLINGS *Pictorial Hist. Fleet Air Arm* ii. 18 The fourth broke his tailskid and had to abort the sortie. **1916** H. BARBER *Aeroplane Speaks* ii. 73 Should the surface tend to assume too large an angle.. the pressure D decreases, with the result that C.P. moves forward and pushes up the front of the surface, thus increasing the angle still further, the final result being a '*tail-slide'. **1969** *Gloss. Aeronaut. & Astronaut. Terms* (*B.S.I.*) II. 2 *Tail slide*, rearward motion of an aircraft along its longitudinal axis from a vertical or near vertical, stalled attitude. **1846** *Tail-slip [see *tail-ill*]. **1867** D. G. MITCHELL *Rural Stud.* 121 Every man who can use a hoe or a pitchfork is supposed to be a competent *tailsman for the plow. **1766** *Compl. Farmer*, **Tail-soaked*, a disease incident to cows, by which the joint of the tail near the rump, will, as it were, rot away. **1864** WEBSTER, **Tail-stock*, the sliding block or support, in a lathe, which carries the tail-screw and adjustable center. **1859** F. GRIFFITHS *Artil. Man.* (1862) 318 If the moveable block of a tackle be strapped with a tail, it is called a *tail*, or *jigger block*: and the tackle a **tail*, or *jigger tackle*. **1823** P. NICHOLSON *Pract. Build.* 594 **Tail-trimmer*, a trimmer next to the wall, into which the ends of joists are fastened. **1898** *Westm. Gaz.* 9 Dec. 7/1 He was..in the hands of clerks and restless explorers who longed to *tail-twist and otherwise annoy. **1887** KIPLING *Plain Tales* (1888) 77 The Colonel's Wife..went away to devise means for 'chastening the stubborn heart of her husband'. Which, translated, means, in our slang, '*tail-twisting'. **1889** EDWARDES *Sardinia* 375 A terrible amount of tail-twisting, kicking and anathematization. **1896** *Westm. Gaz.* 4 Nov. 1/3 If the temper of the British lion is at all affected by the tail-twisting process, he must be in a rage just now and roaring loudly. Tail-twisting seems to be the principal employment of the New York Bryanites. **1902** *Daily Chron.* 13 May 10/6 Fur Trade.—Girls wanted, used to boa and tail twisting. **1937** E. LINKLATER *Juan in China* ii. 58 He had no reason to feel friendly..and the idea of a little tail-twisting was pleasant. **1982** W. J. BURLEY *Wycliffe's Wild-Goose Chase* vi. 110 If there is any attempt at tail twisting you can rely on me to see 'em off. **1926** *Chambers's Jrnl.* Aug. 580/1 In every aeroplane the *tail unit..comprises the rudder [etc.]. **1977** D. BEATY *Excellency* i. 8 A lot of junk..six DC6 wheels, a Viscount tail unit. **1839** R. S. ROBINSON *Naut. Steam Eng.* 131 It will have to pass through the blow-through, or *tail valve. **1885** C. G. W. LOCK *Workshop Receipts* Ser. IV. 99/2 It is usual to fix an extra valve, called a 'tail' valve, to prevent the water from running out of the pipe when not in use. **1971** W. HILLEN *Blackwater River* viii. 72 The trout leaped, *tail-walked, shook himself, leaped again, and ran past the raft for deep water. **1979** *Angling* July 53/2 A fish hits the bait. It runs, leaps, tail-walks. **1946** *Richmond* (Va.) *Times-Dispatch* 16 June 12-B/2 Oh yes, there are certain salt-water fish which do a certain kind of *tail-walking, but the way the bass performs these antics is peculiar to himself. **1970** *Islander* (Victoria, B.C.) 25 Oct. 3/3 Out in the salt-chuck where he [*sc.* a salmon] has a whole ocean to play in you can expect to see some fancy tail-walking. **1759** SMEATON in *Phil. Trans.* LI. 138 An overshot [wheel], whose height is equal to the difference of level, between the point where it strikes the wheel and the level of the *tail-water. **1825** J. NICHOLSON *Operat. Mechanic* 103 When the water in the mill-tail will not run off freely, but stands pent up in the wheel-race, so that the wheel must work or row in it, the wheel is said to be tailed, or to be in back-water or tail-water. **1905** *Westm. Gaz.* 17 Mar. 9/1 At Molesey Lock the tail water was almost five feet above the summer level. **1910** R. FERRIS *How it Flies* xx. 472 **Tail wheel*, a wheel mounted under the rear end of an aeroplane as a part of the alighting gear. **1933** *Jrnl. R. Aeronaut. Soc.* XXXVII. 29 But with the advent of tail wheels, that difficulty should not arise. **1981** *Pilot* Jan. 12/2 A 110 hp tailwheel model. **1811** G. S. KEITH *Agric. Surv. Aberdeen* 491 The *tail-worm is also cured by cutting off a few inches of the tail, which bleeds pretty freely. **1816** TOWNE *Farmer & Grazier's Guide* 67 Tail Worm. In that Part of the Tail which is affected..the Spine appears deprived of Sensibility. **1846** LINDLEY *Veg. Kingd.* 213 *Triuridaceæ.* *Tailworts.

tail (teɪl), *sb.*[2] Forms: 4–6 tayle, tayll, taill, 4–8 taille, taile, 5–7 taylle, (5 tayille, 6 tall), 4– tail. [a. OF. *taille* cut, cutting, division, partition or assessment of a subsidy or impost, tax (12th c. in Hatz.-Darm.), vbl. sb. f. *taillier* to cut, TAIL *v.*[2]

But, in sense 4, OF. *taille* was perh.:—L. *tālea*, med.L. *tālia* stick, rod: cf. TALLY.

Tail in *K. Alisaunder* 2217 (Weber) appears to be a scribal error; MS. Bodley, Laud Misc. 622, has 'among the toyle Hardapilon'.]

I. †1. Shape, fashion, bodily form or appearance. [F. *taille*; cf. CUT *sb.*^{2} 17.] *Obs. rare.*

a **1300** *Cursor M.* 11855 (Cott.) Yee se he has na mans taill [*v. rr.* taille, tale, taile] þar-for yee sai me your consaill. *c* **1325** *Poem Times Edw. II* 282 in *Pol. Songs* (Camden) 336 A newe taille of squierie is nu in everi toun.

II. †2. a. The individual assessment of a subsidy or tallage levied by the king or lord; a tax, impost, due, duty, or payment levied. *Obs.*

1340 *Ayenb.* 38 Kueade lordes..þet be-ulaȝeþ þe poure men: þet hi ssolden loki, be tayles, be tornees. **1375** BARBOUR *Bruce* XII. 320 Gif ony deis in this battaill, His air, but ward, releif, or taill, On the first day his land sall weild. *a* **1450** *Knt. de la Tour* (1906) 89 That quene..dede mani aduersiteez to the pepille, by tailez and subsidiez. **1456** SIR G. HAYE *Law Arms* (S.T.S.) 93 Kirk men suld pay tailles, tributis and imposiciouns to seclere kingis. *c* **1460** FORTESCUE *Abs. & Lim. Mon.* i. (1885) 109 [The king] mey sett vppon thaim tayles and other imposicions, such as he wol hym self, with owt thair assent. *a* **1577** SIR T. SMITH *Commw. Eng.* (1633) 59 The Yeoman or Husbond man is no more subject to taile or taxe in England. **1645** MILTON *Tetrach.* Wks. 1851 IV. 254 Not the drudging out a poore and worthlesse duty forc't from us by the taxe, and taile of so many letters.

‖**b.** Now only as Fr., in form *taille* (tɑj). A tax formerly levied upon the unprivileged classes in France.

a **1533** LD. BERNERS *Huon* lx. 210 He hath reysyd vp in all his londes new taylles & gabeles & impossessyons. **1554** WOTTON *Let.* 29 July in *State Pap. Mary, Foreign* IV. 193 (P.R.O.) The priuiledges of nobilite, emonge the which one is that the gentlemen pay nothing to the ordinarye taylles, which alle Fraunce payeth continuallye to the king. **1682** WARBURTON *Hist. Guernsey* (1822) 48 They should be exempted from all gendarmeries, tailles. **1792** A. YOUNG *Trav. France* 30 The money is raised by tailles, and, in making the assessment, lands held by a noble tenure are so much eased, and others by a base one so burthened, that 120 arpents..held by the former, pay 90 liv. and 400 possessed by a plebeian right..is, instead of that, assessed at 1400 liv. **1863** KIRK *Chas. Bold* I. v. 216 The *taille* and the *gabelle* levied on the villain burghers. **1877** MORLEY *Crit. Misc.* II. 200 The great fiscal grievance of old France was the *taille*, a tax raised..only on the property and income of the unprivileged classes.

III. 3. *Law.* **a.** The limitation or destination of a freehold estate or fee to a person and the heirs of his body, or some particular class of such heirs, on the failure of whom it is to revert to the donor or his heir or assign. [Cf. TAIL *a.*, TAIL *v.*^{2} 5; = TAILYE *sb.* 3.] Hence phrase ***in tail***, as ***estate in tail***, ***tenant in tail***, ***heir in tail***, i.e. within or under the limitation in question.

[**1321–2** *Rolls of Parlt.* I. 394/2 C'est son droit par vertu de la taille avantdit [i.e. an entail to heirs of the body of the spouses].] **1373–5** in *Calr. Proc. Chanc. Q. Eliz.* (1830) I. Pref. 59 An olde dede..comprisynge the wordes of a tayll made in Kynge Edwardes tyme the second. **1439** in *E.E. Wills* (1882) 125 And aftir him and his issue, to Iohn his brother, and his issue in the taile. *c* **1460** FORTESCUE *Abs. & Lim. Mon.* xi. (1885) 136 To some parte þeroff the eyres off thaim þat some tyme owed it be restored; some bi reason off tayles, some bi reason off oþer titles. **1479** in *Bury Wills* (Camden) 52 And after the decess of the seid Alice, I will that the seid maner shall remayne to the issues of my body lawfully begoten accordyng to the tayle therof made. **1523** FITZHERB. *Surv.* 11 If the gyfte were in the tayle and no remaynder in fe euer, nowe the reuercyon resteth styll in yᵉ donor. **1607** COWELL *Interpr.*, *Taile*,..is vsed for the fee, which is opposite to fee simple: by reason that it is so..minced, or pared, that it is not in his free power to be disposed,..but is..tyed to the issue of the Donee... This limitation, or taile, is either generall, or speciall. **1718** PRIOR *Chameleon* 7 As if the Rain-bow were in Tail Settled on him [a Chameleon] and his Heirs Male. **1766** BLACKSTONE *Comm.* II. vii. 115 The incidents to a tenancy in tail. **1796** MORSE *Amer. Geog.* I. 463 All estates given in tail..shall become fee simple estates to the issue of the first donee in tail [cf. quot. 1876]. **1868** ROGERS *Pol. Econ.* xiii. (1876) 177 The defendant a donee in tail, i.e. a person in whose behalf an estate tail had been created. **1876** BANCROFT *Hist. U.S.* V. xv. 516 All donees in tail, by the act of this first republican legislature of Virginia, were vested with the absolute dominion of the property entailed. **1893** MARY CHOLMONDELEY *D. Tempest* iii, You're in the tail, I suppose?

b. With qualifying adjective: ***tail general***, limitation of an estate to a man and the heirs of his body lawfully begotten; ***tail special***, limitation of an estate to a special class of heirs, e.g. to a man and his wife and the heirs of their bodies lawfully begotten; ***tail male*** (or ***female***), limitation of an estate to male (or female) heirs; also *transf.*, the line of descent of dogs or horses, considering either the male or female ancestors.

1495 *Rolls of Parlt.* VI. 485/1 Seised, in his or their Demeane as of Fee, Fee Tayll generall or speciall, or any other astate. **1503** HAWES *Examp. Virt.* xiv. 10 To whome heuen by tayll generall Entayled is by a dede memoryall. **1642** tr. *Perkins' Prof. Bk.* v. §302. 134 If Tenant in generall taile, take a wife and enfeoff a stranger, and take back an estate unto him and his wife in speciall taile. **1710** *Lond. Gaz.* No. 4735/4 Then to his first Son in Tail Male, then to his Daughter in Tail general. **1766** BLACKSTONE *Comm.* II. vii. 113. **1796** MORSE *Amer. Geog.* I. 707 They agreed to grant their lands in tail male in preference to tail general. **1844** WILLIAMS *Real Prop.* (1877) 35 An estate in tail male cannot descend to any but males, and male descendants of males. *Ibid.*, Tail female scarcely ever occurs. **1926** EARL BATHURST *Breeding of Foxhounds* vii. 96 The top line perhaps may be considered important, for it represents the descent in tail-male. *Ibid.* 99 The Bruce-Lowe system..is..the importance of the female line, or 'tail-female'. **1931** *Times Lit. Suppl.* 23 Apr. 325/2 His blood is to be found in most of our 'classic' winners, and in tail female it never waned. **1957** C. LEICESTER *Bloodstock Breeding* ix. 144 This..leaves untouched the tail female line, i.e. the dam, grandam, etc. of the animal under investigation. **1972** *Country Life* 10 Feb. 332/1 One of Whipcord's descendants was the famous Four Burrow Pleader '38, whose ancestry can be traced..on his tail female to Mr. Darley's Damsel..and on tail male (through Whipcord) to the Brocklesby Bumper, 1748.

IV. †4. a. = TALLY *sb.*^{1} 1; hence, a score, an account. ***by tail***, by means of tallies; on credit. (Cf. *on tick*.) *Obs.* [Cf. Cotgr. '*Taille*..also, a tallie, or score kept on a peece of wood'.]

[**1114–18** *Leges Henrici I.* c. 56 §1 Si..controuersia oriatur, siue de taleis agatur siue de supplecione in ipso manerio. **1312** *Rolls of Parlt.* I. 284/1 Les gentz ount diverses acquitaunces, les unes par tailes & par brefs, & les unes par diverses fraunchises.] *a* **1325** tr. *Estatuz del Eschekere* (MS. Rawl. B. 520 lf. 36 b), ȝif ani bringe taille ase of paie imad ate chekere. **1362** LANGL. *P. Pl.* A. IV. 45 He..bereþ awei my whete, And takeþ me bote a tayle [B. IV. 58 taile, taille] of Ten quarter oten. *c* **1386** CHAUCER *Prol.* 570 Wheither that he payde, or took by taille [*v.rr.* taile, tayle]. **1443** HEN. VI *Let.* in Ellis *Orig. Lett.* Ser. III. I. 81 Ther shall be made and delivered..sufficient assignement for your repaiement therof by tailles to be rered at the said Eschequier. **1512** *Earl Northumberland's Househ. Bk.* (1770) 172 The stok of the Tail to be delivert to the Brewar ande the Swatche to the Butler. **1530** PALSGR. 184 *Vnes taylles*, a payre of taylles, suche as folke use to score upon for rekennyng. *Ibid.* 644/1, I nycke, I make nyckes on a tayle, or on a stycke, *je oche*. **1556** WITHALS *Dict.* 56 a/2 A score or tayle to marke the dette vpon, *tessera, vel tessella*. **1607** COWELL *Interpr.* s.v., Taile in the other signification, is what we vulgarly call a Tallie;..a clouen peece of wood to nick vp an accompt vpon. **1647** *City Law London* 49 A Taile of debt ensealed by usage of the city, is as strong as an obligation. **1677** CARY *Chronol.* I. I. I. i. 2 These were the Tailles (as I may so say) by which they marked..the Signal Occurrences of their Life.

†b. *fig.* Account, reckoning. *Obs.*

c **1330** R. BRUNNE *Chron. Wace* (Rolls) 896 Wyþoute seriauntz & oþer pytaille þat ar nought for to sette in taille. *Ibid.* 1316 þre hundred schipes þer was in taille, And foure mo. **1421** *Coventry Leet Bk.* 24 Hit is do the maiour to witt þat tauerners haue sold wyne to certen men of hur alye, be Tailes maid bytwen them, derre than þe maiour hathe ordenyd hit to be sold.

5. *Comb.* **†tail-maker**, (?) one who fashioned the tallies used in the Exchequer; **†tailstick**, a tally-stick. *Obs.*

1235–52 *Rentalia Glaston.* (Som. Rec. Soc.) 217, j porcellum et taylstich' cujuslibet porci necati provenientis de sua custodia. *a* **1577** SIR T. SMITH *Commw. Eng.* (1609) 71 Other officers are Tellers, Auditors, Collectors, rentgatherers, tailemakers.

tail (teɪl), *a.* *Law.* [a. AF. *taylé*, *tailé* = OF. *taillié*, *taillé*, pa. pple. of *taillier* to cut, shape, hence, to fix the precise form of, to limit, TAIL *v.*^{2}; the final *e* having become mute in ME. as in *assign*, *avowe* sbs., and some other legal terms.]

Of a fee or freehold estate (= AF. *fee taylé*, med.Anglo-L. *feodum tāliātum*): Limited and regulated as to its tenure and inheritance by conditions fixed by the donor: thus distinguished from *fee simple* or absolute ownership: see quot. 1592. See also FEE-TAIL, CONDITIONAL *a.* 7.

[**1284** *De Banco Roll*, Mich. 11–12 Edw. I. m. 70 d. Quod predicta Emma non habuit in predictis tenementis nisi feodum talliatum secundum formam donacionis predicte. **1285** *Stat. Westm.* II. (13 Edw. I.) c. 4 Tenentes in maritagium per Legem Anglie, vel ad terminum vite, vel per feodum talliatum. [*tr.* 1543 tenantes in free maryage, by the lawe of Englande, or for terme of lyfe, or in fee taile.] **1292** BRITTON II. iii. §9 Des queus douns aucuns sount condicionels et dount le fee est taylé et en pendaunt jekes autaunt qe cele chose aveigne ou cele. **1294** *Year bks. 21–2 Edw. I* (Rolls 1873) 641 Kar le estatut 'quia emptores terrarum &c.' est entendu la ou home feffe un autre en fee pur, e nent de fee tayle.] **1473** *Rolls of Parlt.* VI. 81/1 That this Acte..extend not..to Sir Thomas Bourghchier Knyght, ne to his heires masles of his body lawfully begoten, ..duryng the seid astate Taille, of, to, or for any Graunte or Grauntes unto hym made. **1473–5** in *Calr. Proc. Chanc. Q. Eliz.* (1830) II. Pref. 58 To make and delyvere unto her a lawefull estate tayle of alle the forseid landes. **1592** WEST *1st Pt. Symbol.* §40 B, A perticuler estate of inheritance, is an estate taile or limited: that is an estate expressing in certaine, whose issue and of what Sexe shall inherite; and it is generall or speciall. **1628** COKE *On Litt.* 26 If lands bee giuen to the husband & the wife, and to the heires which the husband shall beget on the body of the wife, in this case both of them haue an estate taile. **1766** BLACKSTONE *Comm.* II. vii. 112. **1818** CRUISE *Digest* (ed. 2) I. 90 Estates tail, like estates in fee simple, have certain incidents annexed to them, which cannot be restrained by any proviso or condition whatever. **1895** POLLOCK & MAITL. *Hist. Eng. Law* II. II. iv. §1. 19 In 1285 the first chapter of the Second Statute of Westminster, the famous *De donis conditionalibus*, laid down a new rule. The 'conditional fee' of former times became known as a fee tail (Lat. *feodum talliatum*, Fr. *fee taillé*)..and about the same time the term *fee simple* was adopted to describe the estate which a man has who holds 'to him and his heirs'.

tail (teɪl), *v.*^{1} [f. TAIL *sb.*^{1}; in various unconnected senses.]

I. Transitive uses.

1. To furnish with a tail or final appendage. (In early use only in the pa. pple.: see TAILED *ppl. a.*^{1} 1.)

1817 COLERIDGE *Satyrane's Lett.* ii. 211 The cap behind tailed with an enormous quantity of ribbon. **1876** PREECE & SIVEWRIGHT *Telegraphy* 224 A double shackle is fixed, and each side is first 'tailed', that is to say, a wire is passed round the porcelain and bound in the ordinary way, leaving one end projecting to a distance of from eighteen inches to two feet. **1879** BARING-GOULD *Germany* I. ii. 46 In England now anyone adopts arms, and tails his name with esquire, whether he have a right or not to these distinctions.

2. To grasp or drag by the tail.

†*to stave and tail*, to take part in bear-baiting or bull-baiting, by staving the bear or bull, or tailing the dogs.

1663 BUTLER *Hud.* I. II. 163 Lawyers, lest the Bear Defendant, And Plaintiff Dog should make an end on't, Do stave and tail with Writs of Error, Reverse of Judgment, and Demurrer. *Ibid.* III. 134 First Trulla stav'd, and Cerdon tail'd, Until their Mastives loos'd their hold. **1867** F. FRANCIS *Angling* i. (1880) 12 Tailing a fish out is more often employed on salmon. **1892** MRS. J. GORDON *Eunice Anscombe* 177 One..dived forward in a vain attempt to 'tail' the otter. **1893** *Field* 11 Mar. 360/2 Grasp it [the fish] above the tail—'tail it', to employ the technical phrase.

3. To dock the tail of (a lamb, etc.); to cut or pull off that which is regarded as the tail, esp. of a plant or fruit. (Cf. TOP *v.*)

1794 *Rigging & Seamanship* I. 61 Hemp..should be well topt, and tailed; that is, both ends cleared by the hatchell. **1824** L. M. HAWKINS *Mem., Anecd.*, etc. II. 52 A gentleman ..was topping and tailing gooseberries for wine. **1844** STEPHENS *Bk. Farm* II. 42 Another worker..tops and tails the turnips. **1886** C. SCOTT *Sheep-Farming* 88 The number of lambs castrated and tailed.

4. To form the tail or last member of (a procession, etc.); to terminate. (Cf. HEAD *v.* 10.)

1835 *Fraser's Mag.* XI. 465 A male author heads and a male author tails the procession. **1890** *Pall Mall G.* 9 June 4/2 The quaint little procession headed..by the officially-robed Lord Chancellor, and tailed by the blue-gowned Common Councilmen. **1894** R. H. DAVIS *Eng. Cousins* 117 The boat which is to tail the procession.

5. a. In Australia and N.Z.: To follow, drive, or tend (sheep, cattle, or horses).

1844 *Port Phillip Patriot* 5 Aug. 3/6, I know many boys from the age of nine to sixteen years tailing cattle. **1852** MUNDY *Our Antipodes* I. x. 314 The stockman..considers 'tailing sheep' as an employment too tardigrade for a man of action and spirit. **1852** J. R. CLOUGH *Jrnl.* 29 Feb. in J. Deans *Pioneers of Canterbury* (1939) 291, I have had to tail the cattle on foot this five weeks as I have had no saddle. **1871** C. L. MONEY *Knocking about in N.Z.* ix. 133 The horses, after being 'tailed', or shepherded, all day by one of us.., were tied in rows..for the night. **1890** 'R. BOLDREWOOD' *Col. Reformer* (1891) 239 The cattle..being ..'tailed' or followed daily as a shepherd does sheep.

b. To follow someone closely; *spec.* to follow secretly as a detective or spy, etc. Cf. TAG *v.*^{1} 4 b, TAIL *sb.*^{1} 6 b. *colloq.* (orig. *U.S.*).

1907 *Everybody's Mag.* Mar. 341/2 Detectives were assigned to 'tail' him. **1914** JACKSON & HELLYER *Vocab. Criminal Slang* 83 *Tail, verb.* General circulation. To trail; to follow. Used as a noun in the same sense. **1925** E. WALLACE *Strange Countess* ix. 81 'What's your idea in tailing me?'.. '"Tailing"? Oh, you mean following you, I suppose?' **1950** D. HYDE *I Believed* viii. 88 For some months I was tailed by a curious assortment of police agents. **1956** S. PLATH in *Granta* 20 Oct. 22/2 Ben tailed us out to the kitchen, where the black old gas stove was, and the sink, full of dirty dishes. **1966** T. PYNCHON *Crying of Lot 49* v. 130 Oedipa gave him half a block's start, then began to tail him. **1978** S. BRILL *Teamsters* iv. 127 I'm not gonna let you tail me like some kinda cop. **1978** G. GREENE *Human Factor* v. iii. 278 Castle led the way down the stairs to the cellar. Buller followed him and Mr Halliday tailed Buller.

6. *U.S. local.* (See quots.)

1792 BELKNAP *Hist. New Hampsh.* III. 106 In descending a long and steep hill, they have a contrivance to prevent the load from making too rapid a descent. Some of the cattle are placed behind it; a chain..attached to their yokes is brought forward and fastened to the hinder end of the load, and the resistance which is made by these cattle checks the descent. This operation is called *tailing*. **1851** *Harper's Mag.* III. 518 In this manner the load is tailed down steeps where it would be impossible for the tongue-oxen to resist the pressure of the load.

7. To attach to the tail or hind end of something else; to join on behind, annex, subjoin *to*.

1523 LD. BERNERS *Froiss.* I. xci. 113 They toke foure Englysshe shyppes..and tayled them to their shyppes. **1589** PUTTENHAM *Eng. Poesie* II. xii. (Arb.) 128 Wordes monosillables,..if they be tailed one to another, or th' one to a dissillable or polyssillable. **1633** J. CLARKE *2nd Praxis* 44 *Ne* is alwayes tayled to the first word of the Interrogation. **1681** RYCAUT tr. *Gracian's Critick* 224 They met great Mules tailed one to the other. **1685** J. SCOTT *Chr. Life* II. 155 What is this but to tail one folly to another? **1851** MAYHEW *Lond. Labour* II. 161/2 Each new row of houses tailed on its drains to those of its neighbours.

8. *Building.* To insert the tail or end of (a beam, stone, or brick) *into* a wall, etc.; to let in, dovetail.

1823 P. NICHOLSON *Pract. Build.* 365 Party-walls may also be cut into for the purposes of tailing-in stone steps. *c* **1850** *Rudim. Navig.* (Weale) 155 To *tail*, or *dovetail*, to let one piece of timber into another.

9. *passive.* Of a mill-wheel: To be clogged by tail-water (q.v., s.v. TAIL *sb.*^{1} 14, quot. 1825).

10. *slang.* To copulate with (a woman).

1778 in Weis & Pottle *Boswell in Extremes* (1971) 248 When we talk of *pleasure*, we mean sensual pleasure. When a man says he had pleasure with a woman, he does not mean conversation, but that he *tailed* her. **1846** *Swell's Night Guide* 133/2 *Tail*, to cohabit with women. **1973** J. WAINWRIGHT *Devil you Don't* 51 So, I tailed his wife... So what?

II. Intransitive uses.

11. Of a ship: To run *aground* stern foremost.

1725 DE FOE *Voy. round World* (1840) 147 She tailed aground upon a sand bank. **1799** *Naval Chron.* I. 258 The Formidable..tailed on the..mud. *c* **1850** *Rudim. Navig.* (Weale) 117 It is to..preserve the main post, should the ship tail aground.

12. Of water, flame, etc.: To flow or creep back against the current; to run back, recoil.

1799 *Trans. Soc. Arts* XVII. 349 Floods are very apt to dam or tail-back, and thereby impede or clog the..wheel. **1883** GRESLEY *Coal Mining Gloss.* s.v., When fire-damp ignites..and the flame..creeps backwards against the current of air..it is said to tail back into the workings.

13. Of a moving body of men or animals: **a.** To lengthen out into a straggling line, as in hunting, racing, etc.; to drop behind, fall away.

1781 W. BLANE *Ess. Hunting* (1788) 116 [The hounds] not being of equal speed..will be found to tail, which is an inconveniency. **1862** WHYTE MELVILLE *Ins. Bar* x. **1864** TREVELYAN *Compet. Wallah* (1866) 134 As down towards Barton Wold we sail, The Cockneys soon began to tail. **1897** THORNTON *Remin. Clergyman* i. 2 Then straggling, tailing, as the fox-hunters phrase it, up came the field.

b. To move or proceed in the form of a line or tail; to fall into a line or tail.

1859 KINGSLEY *Misc.* (1860) I. 160 If ten men tail through a gap. **1882** MOZLEY *Remin.* I. xix. 128 The congregation.. came down the road in a dense black mass, but obliged to tail a little. **1899** ANNIE E. HOLDSWORTH *Valley Gr. Shadow* x, The procession was tailing to Bergstein.

14. To take a position in which the tail or rear is directed away from the wind, current, etc.

1849 DANA *Geol.* ii. (1850) 115 In more moderate weather the vessel tails out against the wind. **1860** MAURY *Phys. Geog. Sea* ii. 29 Sea-weed always 'tails to' a steady or a constant wind. **1867** SMYTH *Sailor's Word-bk.* s.v., *To tail up* or *down a stream*, when at anchor in a river, is as a ship's stern swings.

15. *Building.* Of a beam, stone, or brick: To have its end let into a wall, etc.: cf. 8.

1842–76 GWILT *Archit.* Gloss. s.v., Where the end of a timber lies or tails upon the walls. **1892** MIDDLETON *Rome* I. 62 Blocks of tufa..tailing 3 to 5 inches into the concrete backing.

16. Of a stream: To flow or fall *into.* (Cf. HEAD *v.* 7.)

1889 *Blackw. Mag.* Apr. 456 *note*, The Dorak canal, which tails into the Jarrahi river. **1900** *Westm. Gaz.* 10 July 2/2 All the channels and spills tailed into the Ziraf.

17. Of a fish: To show its tail at the surface.

1892 in *Daily News* 21 May 5/2 The Man sees there is no fly up. The Man sees the fish are tailing. **1908** *Edin. Rev.* Apr. 391 When trout are 'tailing' they break the surface with their caudal fin as they grub with their noses for water shrimps.

18. *Calico-printing.* Of a colour, etc.: To spread beyond its proper limits in a tail-like blur.

III. With adverbs.

19. tail away. *intr.* To fall away in a tail or straggling line; to die away.

1860 RUSSELL *Diary India* II. xix. 369 They were, however, tailing away fast, as we afterwards discovered. **1905** HICHENS *Garden Allah* vii, The aird, sunburnt tracts, where its life centred and where it tailed away into suburban edges not unlike the ragged edges of worn garments.

20. tail off (out). **a.** *trans.* To cause to fall away gradually towards the end; to taper off.

1827 STEUART *Planter's G.* (1828) 304 They [artificial hillocks] should be well 'tailed out', as the workmen call it, ..letting their hard outline imperceptibly disappear, and, as it were, die away in the outline of the adjoining surface. **1842** S. LOVER *Handy Andy* v, He..finished it in a gentle murmur —tailed it off very taper, indeed.

b. *intr.* To fall away in a tail; to diminish and cease; to come gradually to an end; to subside.

1854 HOOKER *Himal. Jrnls.* I. xvii. 396 It tailed off abruptly at the junction of the rivers. **1862** *Lond. Soc.* II. 86 Already the weaker horses are weeded out, and the poorer spirited are tailing off. **1898** *Allbutt's Syst. Med.* V. 977 The dull sound of valvular tension may be heard to precede it [a cardiac bruit], when it 'tails off' from the first sound. **1905** F. YOUNG *Sands of Pleasure* I. iv, His voice tailed off into a sigh.

c. *intr.* To turn tail, take to flight, go or run off; to withdraw. *colloq.*

1830 A. SEDGWICK *Let.* 21 Nov. in J. W. Clark *Life A. Sedgwick* (1890) I. 366 Many men will tail off, if they have an excuse. **1841** F. E. PAGET *S. Antholin's* vii. 146 Mrs. Spatterdash..tailed off at last to a dissenting chapel. **1868** —— *Lucretia* 102 He ducked his head; made a slouching bow; tailed off to his pigs. **1877** KINGLAKE *Crimea* VI. vi. 376 Some..even tailed off. **1885** RIDER HAGGARD *K. Solomon's M.* xvi, I was tailing out of it as hard as my legs would carry me.

d. *trans.* To pass and leave behind (other competitors in a race, etc.).

1852 BATEMAN *Aquatic Notes* 52 They got close to them at Grassy [corner], but were tailed-off in the Long Reach. **1907** *Times* 6 June 4/3 He was..one of the leaders for half a mile, but afterwards he was tailed off.

21. tail on. **a.** *trans.* To add on as an appendage. **b.** *intr.* To join on in the rear.

1825 (Jan. 3) CAPT. B. HALL in Lockhart *Scott*, Anxious to tail on a branch from Melrose to meet the [projected railway from Berwick to Kelso]. **1862** MAYHEW *Boyhood Luther* i. (1863) 11 As the long train swept by, the peasants and villagers tailed on to the rest. **1874** BURNIE *Mem. Thomas* 451 A superb passenger car which tails on to the trucks. **1880** CLARK RUSSELL *Sailor's Sweetheart* xiv, All hands tailing on, we ran it [a boom] through the bowsprit cap.

22. The vb.-stem in Comb. **tail-back**, a queue of stationary or slowly moving motor vehicles; **tail-off** *colloq.*, a decline or tapering off of demand, etc.; a period of this.

1975 D. LODGE *Changing Places* v. 188 They hit a tailback of rush-hour traffic in the Midland Road. **1978** *Times* 26 July 8/3 One of the worst traffic jams in living memory with tailbacks of several miles. **1975** D. FRANCIS *High Stakes* vii. 109 There would be at first a patch of sporadic success..and then a long tail-off with no success at all. **1984** *Times* 15 Feb. 20/7 Laurie Millbank does not envisage any tail off in demand.

tail (teɪl), *v.*[2] Forms: 4–5 taille, 4–6 taylle, tayle, taile, (6 talle, tale), 6– tail. [ME. *taille*, a. OF. *taillier*, 3 sing. pres. *taille* (S. Leger *a* 1000), to cut, shape by cutting, determine the form of, limit, etc.; in mod.F. *tailler* to cut, etc.; = Pr. *talhar*, *talar*, Cat. *tallar*, Sp. *tajar*, Pg. *talhar*, It. *tagliare*, to cut:—late pop. and med.L. *tāliāre*, *talliāre*, f. *tal(l)ea*, in cl. L. *tālea* rod, twig, cutting: see TALLY *sb.*[1] OF. *taillier* gave *taille* vbl. sb., TAIL *sb.*[2], whence again *taillier* vb. to impose a tax on, to tax: see sense 6 below.]

I. In literal and connected senses.

†**1.** *trans.* To cut, esp. to a certain size or shape; to shape, fashion; ***well tailed***, well shaped or fashioned. See also TAILED *ppl. a.*[2] 1. *Obs.*

c **1400** *Laud Troy Bk.* 3154 Thenne by-gan this clerkes to tayle Parchemyn and lettres dite. **1422** tr. *Secreta Secret., Priv. Priv.* 227 Thay that haue the shuldres hangynge downe-ward and welle taillet, bene fre and lyberall. **1558** *Acc. Fratern. Holy Ghost, Basingstoke* (1882) 9 Paide..for fellinge the oke..Item payde..for tallinge and sawinge of the same.

†**2.** To cut up, cut to pieces, slaughter. *Obs.*

c **1330** R. BRUNNE *Chron. Wace* (Rolls) 14136 Arthur sey þe day gan faille, He bod & stynte his folk to taille.

[*Taile* in *K. Alisaunder* 2133 (Weber) is a scribal error; MS. Bodley, Laud Misc. 622 has (l. 2137) 'Bigynneþ ȝoure fomen coile Alto sleiȝtte & nouȝth to spoyle'.]

†**3.** To put into shape, trim, make ready. (Cf. OF. *metre en taille.*) *Obs.*

c **1330** R. BRUNNE *Chron.* (1810) 115 Dauid of Scotland hasted to þe bataile, Walter Spek ros on hand, þe folk to forme & taile. *c* **1330** —— *Chron. Wace* (Rolls) 12081 Mariners dighte þem..þer takel for to righte & taille. *c* **1375** *Sc. Leg. Saints* xxiii. (*vii Sleperis*) 237 þai..bad malchus he suld hyme taile, & pas tc þe towne fore vitale.

II. [a. AF. *tailler*, OF. *taillier* in sense 'to determine, fix, appoint': cf. the Sc. form TAILYE. But, in sense 5, in later use app. f. TAIL *sb.*[2] 3.]

†**4.** To decide or determine in a specified way; to settle, arrange, or fix (a matter).

[OF. *taillier*: cf. *c* 1250 in Godef. 'Puis fu la pais ensi taillie que..'.]

c **1315** SHOREHAM *Poems* vii. 817 And was þat conseyl so y-tayled, þat hyt ne myȝte habbe faylled To bote of manne. **1375** BARBOUR *Bruce* XVIII. 238 (Edin. MS.) At that tyme he wald him taile, To dystroy wp sa clene the land, That nane suld leve tharin liffand. *Ibid.* XIX. 188 (MS. C) [see TAILYE *v.* 2]. *c* **1425** WYNTOUN *Cron.* VIII. 5309 (Cotton MS.) Had þe Talbot, as talyt [*Wemyss MS.* talȝeit] was, Iustit, he had suelt in þat plasse. **1472–3** *Rolls of Parlt.* VI. 24/1 Yf the seid William Lord Berkeley and Johan his wyfe..cause or suffre any recovere to be had or tayled ayenst theym..by their covyne or assent.

5. *trans. Law.* To limit (an estate of inheritance) to the donee and his heirs general or special; to grant in tail (TAIL *sb.*[2] 3); to tie up by entail; to ENTAIL.

[**1292** BRITTON II. iii. §9: see TAIL *a.*] **1425** in *E.E. Wills* 64 My lande þat is tayled to him. **1425** *Rolls of Parlt.* IV. 274/2 By cause ye name of Duc of Norffolke is tailled to me, and to my heirs males of my body commyng: and ye name of Erel of Norffolke is tailled to me, and to my heirs of my body commyng generaly. **1483** *Ibid.* VI. 253/1 Hereditaments, that were tailled to hym, or to eny other of his Auncesters, by dede or withoute dede. **1501** *Plumpton Corr.* (Camden) 152 If Mr. Eleson can fynd any of your lands talled to the here male, send copies therof: I thinke none be. **1647** N. BACON *Disc. Govt. Eng.* I. xli. (1739) 66 In latter times this estate was also tailed, or cut out some-times to the Sons and Daughters severally. **1864** SERJT. MANNING in *Athenæum* 27 Feb. 302/2 The great land-holders..obtained an Act of Parliament, called the statute *de donis*, which directed that thenceforth the will of the donor should be strictly observed. Upon this the lands so tailed (appointed) became inalienable.

III. Related to *tail* tax, impost (TAIL *sb.*[2] 2).

†**6.** *trans.* To impose a 'tail' or tax upon; to tax. [OF. *taillier*, med.L. *tāl(l)iare*, Du Cange.] *Obs.*

c **1330** R. BRUNNE *Chron. Wace* (Rolls) 2382 þe Duk of Cornewaille, Al þe souþ tyl hym gan tayle. *Ibid.* 16550 Ffro Scotland vntil Cornewaille, Al þe lond gan þey [the Saxons] taille. **1474** *Rolls of Parlt.* VI. 165/1 That the Maier, Bailyfs and Cominalte..to xx li only..shulden be assessed, taxed and tailed. **1525** LD. BERNERS *Froiss.* II. lxii. [lxv.] 210 Nowe they tayle theyr people at theyr pleasure. *a* **1577** SIR T. SMITH *Commw. Eng.* (1633) 263 In France the Lords doe taile them whom they call their subjects at their pleasure and cause them to pay summes of money.

IV. Related to *tail* a tally (TAIL *sb.*[2] 4).

†**7.** *trans.* To mark or record on a tally; to charge (a person) with a debt; *transf.* to make a mark on, to mark. *Obs.*

1377 LANGL. *P. Pl.* B. v. 429 ȝif I bigge and borwe it, but ȝif it be ytailled [*v.r.* tailled, **1393** C. VIII. 35 y-tayled] I forȝete it as ȝerne. ? *a* **1500** *Chester Pl.* vii. 410 Nay, he come by night—all things lafte—Our tuppes with tar to tayle. **1655** FULLER *Ch. Hist.* XI. i. §10 His bond of two thousand pounds wherewith he was tailed continued uncancelled, and was called on the next Parliament.

†**8.** *intr.* To deal by tally, or on credit. *Obs.*

1514 SIR R. JERNEGAN *Let.* in Strype *Eccl. Mem.* (1721) I. App. v. 10 They [of the garrison] had offered the victualers to taylle with them and to set it upon scores:..for mony they had none. **1570** FOXE *A. & M.* (ed. 2) 413/1 He was in great debt..dryuen to tale [*so edd.* 1576–83; *ed.* 1596 tallie] for his owne cates.

†**9.** *trans.* To tally or agree with; to equal; = TALLY *v.*[1] 5. *Obs.*

1638 FORD *Lady's Trial* III. iii, Sure this bulk of mine, 'Tails in the size! a tympany of greatness, Puffs up too monstrously my narrow chest.

tail, *v.*[3] [Local variant of TILL *v.*] *trans.* To set (a trap or snare); to bait (a trap).

1770 G. CARTWRIGHT *Jrnl.* 27 Aug. (1792) I. 30, I tailed a couple of traps for otters, but did not find many rubbing places. **1862** *Telegram* (Yeovil) 15 Feb., The defendant.. proceeded some distance lower, and tailed another trap. **1899** C. K. PAUL *Memories* 250 To tail a trap, to set or bait it. **1901** *Blackw. Mag.* Nov. 691/1 There are the traps to tail.

tail, tailage, obs. ff. TALE, TALLAGE *sb.*[1]

†**'tailard.** *Obs.* In 4 taylard. [f. TAIL *sb.*[1] + -ARD.] One with a tail.

An opprobrious epithet founded on a legend told first of St. Augustine at Dorchester (or Rochester), and later of Thomas a Becket in Kent, in which the people of these places were said to be cursed with tails for indignities done by attaching a tail to these holy men. See Layamon 29535–86, Fuller *Ch. Hist.* II. ii. §22, Lambarde *Kent* 400, Stanley *Hist. Mem. Cant.* (1872) I. 53, and references in the last. On the continent, tails used to be ascribed to Englishmen generally. Cf. TAILED[1] 1 and LONG-TAIL 2 a.

13.. *Coer de L.* 724 The kyng callid Rychard be name, And clepyd hym taylard, and sayde hym schame. *Ibid.* 1996. *Ibid.* 2112 The emperour..cried, as uncourteys: Out, taylards, of my paleys! Now go and say your tayled king That I owe him no thing.

tail-board ('teɪlbɔəd). [f. TAIL *sb.*[1] + BOARD.]

1. The board at the hinder end of a cart, barrow, van, etc.; usually one attached to the bottom by a hinge, and capable of being suspended at various angles for convenience in loading, etc.

1805 *Chron.* in *Ann. Reg.* 376/1 She was crushed between the tail-board of the cart and the house. **1847** ALB. SMITH *Chr. Tadpole* xlvi. (1879) 405 Have you..a shutter, or the tail-board of a cart..you can carry him on? **1881** YOUNG *Ev. Man his Own Mechanic* §1072 The parts which compose the barrow may be enumerated as the two sides, the front, the tail board, the bottom, the wheel, and the legs.

2. (See quot.)

1841 TOTTEN *Naval Textbk.* (U.S.) 411 *Tailboards*, in shipbuilding, the carved work between the cheeks, fastened to the knee of the head.

tailed (teɪld), *a.* and *ppl. a.*[1] Also 4–5 **ytailed.** [f. TAIL *sb.*[1] and *v.*[1] + -ED.]

1. Having, or furnished with, a tail or tails; in *Zool.* and *Bot.* = CAUDATE. Often in parasynthetic comb., as ***long-tailed***, ***white-tailed***, etc.

1297 R. GLOUC. (Rolls) 8821 Men iseie iwis þe tailede sterre, þat gret bodiinge is. *c* **1330** R. BRUNNE *Chron.* (1810) 158 What haf I to do with Inglis tayled kyng? *a* **1400** *R. Glouc.'s Chron.* (Rolls) App. T. 10 Þute libbeþ of þe kunde ytailed maniȝe so. **1413** *Pilgr. Sowle* (Caxton) I. xx. (1859) 20 Thenne answered this tailed worm. **1594** BLUNDEVIL *Exerc.* V. xii. (1636) 556 He is eared and tailed like a Rat. **1601** HOLLAND *Pliny* (1634) I. 352 Panthers are not after the same manner tailed. **1767** GOOCH *Treat. Wounds* I. 147 That called the tailed-bandage, used in compound fractures. **1848** DICKENS *Dombey* v, [A] blue baize tailed coat. **1890** JULIA BALLARD *Among Moths* 17 The hinder wings tailed.

†**b.** Of cattle: = TAGGED 3. *Obs.*

1539 *Will H. Myrth of Puriton, Somerset* 26 Oct. (MS.), To John Hore a taylyd heffer. **1543** *Will J. Popyll, Shapwick, Som.* 9 Jan., ij steyres a taylyd & a sterryd.

†**c.** Of malt: Containing the tails. *Obs.*

1742 *Lond. & Country Brewer* I. (ed. 4) 75 This Caution against using tailed or dusty Malt.

d. ***tailed rime*** (rarely ***tail-rime***), rendering of F. *rime couée*, med.L. *rithmus caudātus* (see COUWEE), applied to a couplet, triplet, or stanza with a tail, tag, or additional short line, either unrimed or riming with another tag further on.

1890 *Cent. Dict.* s.v. *Rime*[1], Tailed rime. **1893** TRAILL *Soc. Eng.* I. iv. 448 [Verses] in *rime couée. Note*, Or tail-rime [ed. **1898** (also called tailed-rime)]: a stanza where some lines, usually the third and sixth, are shorter (*e.g.* Chaucer's Rime of Sir Thopas).

2. *ppl. a.* Deprived of the tail or tails.

1550 *Proclam. Edw. VI* 20 Oct., Wheate..of the meanest sorte, not cleane or tailed. **1844** STEPHENS *Bk. Farm* II. 8 Topped and tailed turnips.

tailed (teɪld), *ppl. a.*[2] [f. TAIL *v.*[2] + -ED[1].]

†**1.** Cut; *esp.* cut to a special shape or size.

c **1430** *Two Cookery-bks.* 55 Take Roysonys of coraunce ..& taylid Datys y-kyt a-long. *a* **1552** LELAND *Itin.* V. lf. 66 Mr. Brainton..dyd fetch much tayled Stone there toward his buildinges.

2. *Law.* Of lands and tenements: Granted, settled, or held in tail (see TAIL *v.*[2] 5); = ENTAILED. *Obs.* or *arch.*

1430–31 *Rolls of Parlt.* IV. 378/1 Toward eny tailled land. *c* **1475** *Harl. Contin. Higden* (Rolls) VIII. 502, I.. condempne..alle thy londes tayled and not tayled to be applyede to the use of the kynge for ever. **1523** FITZHERB. *Surv.* 18 b, Another forme of landes tayled with a remayndre ouer. **1593** *Calr. Laing Charters* (1899) 309 Outwith the teylit land and toftis presentlie occupiit.

tail-end (ˌteɪlˈɛnd). [f. TAIL *sb.*[1] + END *sb.*]

1. a. The hindmost or lowest end of anything; that part which is opposite the head: cf. TAIL *sb.*[1] 4.

1747 H. GLASSE *Art of Cookery* ix. 92 Take a large Eel,.. cut it into four Pieces, take the Tail-end, [etc.]. **1837** M. DONOVAN *Dom. Econ.* II. 277 A tail-end of a rump of beef, weighing 12¾ lb., when boiled gave 1⅝ lb. of bone. **1871** MORRIS in Mackail *Life* (1899) I. 255 Two or three tail-ends of glaciers dribbled over them [cliffs]. **1880** L. WALLACE *Ben Hur* IV. vii, A dray with low wheels and broad axle, surmounted by a box open at the tail-end. **1917** 'CONTACT' *Airman's Outings* viii. 214 V., my pilot and flight-commander, was given to a quick dive at the enemy, ..and another dash to close grips from an unexpected direction, while I guarded the tail-end.

†**b.** *spec.* The backside, rump: = TAIL *sb.*[1] 5.

1377 LANGL. *P. Pl.* B. v. 395 Were I brouȝte abedde, but if my taille-ende it made, Sholde no ryngynge do me ryse, ar I were rype to dyne. **1401** *Pol. Poems* (Rolls) II. 50 Quenching of torches in ȝou tayl-ende.

c. *fig.*; *esp.* the concluding part of an action, period of time, etc.: cf. TAIL *sb.*[1] 4 b.

1845 DARWIN in *Life & Lett.* (1887) II. 31, I am sorry to say I have not even the tail-end of a fact in English Zoology to communicate. **1872** BLACK *Adv. Phaeton* xxii, The tail-end of a shower caught us. **1887** *Spectator* 17 Sept. 1240 At the tail-end of the Session.

d. *Cricket.* = TAIL *sb.*[1] 8 a (*b*). Freq. *attrib.*

1888 A. G. STEEL in Steel & Lyttelton *Cricket* iii. 176 The tail end of a team are usually victims to a good straight fast bowler. **1904** *Westm. Gaz.* 11 Jan. 2/1 Fielder bowled very well indeed at the tail-end men of the Victorian eleven. **1930** *Morning Post* 16 July 11/5 He had batted on three different days, and had shown ability and courage. He can never in future be regarded as a tail-end batsman. **1955** *Times* 13 July 3/2 With the first ball of his next Smales bowled Smith, who had..looked the one man likely to deprive Nottinghamshire of a win with tail-end wickets falling fast. **1976** *0–10 Cricket Scene* (Austral.) 15/1 He..then routed Victoria's tail-end to win another close encounter.

2. The end or tip of a tail. *rare.*

3. = TAILING *vbl. sb.*[1] 2 a.

1859 GEO. ELIOT *A. Bede* vi, Everybody 'ud be wanting bread made o' tail-ends.

4. tail-end Charlie, a tail-gunner; the last aircraft in a flying formation (*Services' colloq.*); also *transf.* and *fig.*, one who comes last or behind, a tail-ender.

1941 *Illustr. London News* CXCIX. 579 (*caption*) The 'tail-end Charlie' of a 'Halifax' gives the 'thumbs up' sign just before his machine takes off. **1942** *Sun* (Baltimore) 8 Aug. 3/1 Lessig crossed the channel with the RAF, flying a Spitfire in the 'tail end Charlie' position—the last plane in a flight of four. **1956** P. SCOTT *Male Child* I. ii. 40 My brother ..was killed in the war... A tail-end Charlie. **1961** *Times* 7 June 5/7 The Spaniard, Goyeneche was *lanterne rouge*, the cyclists' equivalent of tail-end-Charlie. **1976** *Daily Mail* 4 Oct. 3/3 The average lifespan of a 'Tail-end Charlie' was reckoned as ten 'ops.'

transf. and *fig.* **1962** A. SAMPSON *Anat. of Britain* xxxiv. 550 The essential services may, as in America, become regarded as the tail-end Charlies, the forgotten drudges under the pavements and pit-heads. **1969** *Daily National* (Nairobi) 31 Oct. 35 (Advt.), Congratulations to Joginder Singh and Ken Ranyard on their magnificent drive in car No. 46, starting as 'tail end Charlie'. But finishing with the major honours. **1973** *Listener* 15 Nov. 661/3 On tours, when I used to go with my parents..a sort of tail-end Charlie. **1978** A. PRICE *'44 Vintage* x. 131 The jeep behind them was closing up... The Sergeant was taking his tail-end Charlie role..seriously. **1980** *Outdoor Life* (U.S.) (North-east ed.) Oct. 53/3, I found myself on a hillside where the birds were flushing below, but then there was one tail-end Charlie who went up the hill.

Hence **tail-'ender**, one that is at the tail-end (now esp. in *Sport*).

1885 *Sydney Mail* 28 Feb. 451/4 Garrett and Evans, the 'tail-enders', established themselves..firmly at the wickets. **1895** *Outing* (U.S.) XXVI. 31/1 Six teal flew across the water, and I downed the tailender. **1908** *Daily Chron.* 8 Jan. 5/7 The Australians..failed because they could not get our tail-enders out. **1915** *Lit. Digest* 21 Aug. 360/3 The St. Louis Cardinals, whom the writer designates as 'almost chronic tail-enders', are, in regard to the amounts spent for new players, just about the same. **1955** *Times* 23 June 17/1 It has certainly been focused so far on the leaders rather than the tail-enders in the various markets. One possible brake on the rise..is an increase in the corpus of securities. **1961** *Sunday Express* 7 May 1/6 Both men were lapping the tailenders now. **1977** *World of Cricket Monthly* June 24/2 Eric was also the better batsman, Alec being more of the hard-hitting tailender type. **1980** A. CRAWLEY *Dial 200–200* ix. 98 'You might have been killed yourself.' 'Not much chance; the raid had already gone past us. It would have had to be a tail-ender, like the one that got the maid.'

tailer (ˈteɪlə(r)). [f. TAIL *v.*[1] + -ER[1].]

1. *Angling.* A fish that tails: see TAIL *v.*[1] 17.

1899 BUXTON in *19th Cent.* Jan. 120 A moderate performer with the rod..will often..pick up a grubber under the bank, a bulger here, a tailer there. **1899** *Daily News* 22 Apr. 8/3 Now, like a fan, the broad, waving tail of a 'tailer' shows yellow in upper air.

†**2. a.** A follower or hanger-on. **b.** *spec.* on the U.S. Stock Exchange (see quot. 1900). *Obs.*

1838 DISRAELI *Let.* in Monypenny & Buckle *Life Disraeli* (1912) II. i. 20 Two of the greatest ruffians in the House... They are 'Tailers'. **1899** G. B. SHAW *Let.* 30 Dec. (1972) II. 127 Though the old favorites would get in on both sides, there would be a real contest between the outsiders and tailers. **1900** S. A. NELSON *ABC Wall St.* 161 Tailer. Big operators have a following of little traders who tail-on a bull or a bear movement on the theory that to make money it is a good thing to follow in the wake of the successful men. **1903** F. NORRIS *Pit* viii. 269 The 'tailers'—the little Bulls—were radiant.

3. *Austral.* One who follows, drives, or tends sheep or cattle; also, a straggling animal.

1893 K. MACKAY *Out Back* (ed. 2) III. iii. 233 Fitzspats was absent, having gone out with the 'tailers' that morning. **1927** M. M. BENNETT *Christison of Lammermoor* xxvi. 237 The cattle that had come in were watered and handed over to the tailers' mob. **1959** J. WRIGHT *Generations of Men* (1960) ix. 107 Silent dogs at the heels of the tailers.

4. A device with a metal loop used for landing large fish by the tail.

1962 *Times* 31 Mar. 11/5 Some fishermen prefer the tailer to the gaff at all times. **1974** *Country Life* 14 Mar. 599/3, I was not optimistic enough to bring with me a tailer or gaffe or net, but..my fly was taken by an eight-pounder.

5. tailer-out, one who guides timber as it comes off a saw. *Austral.* and *N.Z.*

1907 G. B. LANCASTER *Tracks we Tread* vi. 87 The bench sawyers felt it, and the trolley-men; and each tailer-out and engine driver. **1930** W. SMYTH *Wooden Rails* ii. 32 She came upon the sawyer and his mate, the tailer-out. **1950** *Landfall* IV. 125 The planer..spits out faced boards for the tailer-out to stack by the goose-saw. **1971** *N.Z. Listener* 8 Nov. 15/4 He worked all day as a tailer-out in the mill.

taileron (ˈteɪlərɒn). *Aeronaut.* [Blend of TAIL *sb.*[1] and AILERON.] A horizontal control surface on an aircraft which can function as both elevator and aileron, moving either in unison with its partner or in opposition to it.

1966 D. STINTON *Anat. Aeroplane* viii. 163 The tailerons of the BAC-TSR 2..were slab surfaces that moved either together, as pitch controls, or independently for additional control in roll. **1975** *Flight* 16 Oct. 569 Roll and pitch stabilisation operates by moving the tailplane surfaces as tailerons, leaving the lateral spoilers and ailerons purely under the pilot's control.

tailet (ˈteɪlɪt). *rare.* [f. TAIL *sb.*[1] + -ET[1].] A minute tail or tail-like appendage.

1817 KIRBY & SP. *Entomol.* xxiii. (1818) II. 346 Though the wings are the principal instruments of the flight of insects, yet there are others subsidiary to them... These are winglets, tailets, hooklets.

'tail-gate, *sb.* (and *a.*) [f. TAIL *sb.*[1] + GATE *sb.*[1]]

1. The lower gate or pair of gates of a canal-lock; the aft-gate.

1875 KNIGHT *Dict. Mech.* s.v. *Lock*, The head-gate and tail-gate, which, with the side-walls, inclose the lock-chamber. **1983** G. SWIFT *Waterland* v. 29 The lighters are approaching. Dick is opening the tail-gates.

2. A tail-board or back on a wagon, lorry, etc., hinged or removable to facilitate the loading of goods; a hatchback door on a car. orig. *U.S.*

1868 *Oregon State Jrnl.* 28 Nov. 2/3 The whole charge ..[passed] through the tailgate of the wagon. **1886** E. EGGLESTON *Graysons* xxiii. 345 The two were picking near together and throwing corn over the tail-gate of the wagon. **1909** WEBSTER, *Tail gate*,..a heavy wooden panel pivoted to the end of a railroad car to form an incline from the car bottom to the rails. **1940** W. FAULKNER *Hamlet* IV. i. 246 The wagon moved gradually backward until the head of the first horse was snubbed up to the tail-gate. **1956** *New Yorker* 1 Dec. 196/2 This year's crop of friction-motor automobiles includes..a ten-inch Country Squire station wagon, with a tail gate that can be opened and closed. **1963** *Guardian* 13 Mar. 5/4 The one-piece tailgate, which is counter-balanced, rises to 5 ft. 10 in. from the ground, providing protection for both load and loader against the rain. **1967** *Financial Times* 21 Apr. 9/8 Hi-pope vertical tailgate equipment for fitting to lorries. **1974** *Daily Tel.* 22 Oct. 10/7 The styling is angular, but pleasant, and features a large rear tailgate for access to the luggage compartment behind the rear seats. **1978** J. IRVING *World according to Garp* xv. 309 She felt her way along the truck toward the tailgate. **1980** *Times* 28 May 3/1 BL's long-awaited new small car, the Mini Metro,..is a front-wheel-drive model with two side doors and a tailgate.

B. *attrib.* or as *adj.* **1.** Used to designate a style of jazz trombone playing characterized by improvisation in the manner of the early New Orleans musicians. [From the traditional position of the trombonist at the rear of the wagon in parades, etc.]

1946 R. BLESH *Shining Trumpets* ii. 32 Long glissandi.. heard in the 'tailgate' or circus-style trombone of jazz. **1959** 'R. GANT' *World in Jug* 26 Vic was our trombonist... He had a real tailgate style—that comes from the days when the trombonist sat at the back of the wagon so that he did not push out the eyes of the other bandsmen. **1973** *Times* 25 Jan. 18/6 It needed the utmost in timing and execution, as many would-be tailgate trombonists have since proved by default.

2. Applied to refreshment stops, etc., made during the course of a journey or outing and arranged at the open tail-gate of a parked car.

1970 [see POTLATCH b]. **1980** L. BIRNBACH et al. *Official Preppy Handbk.* 102/2 Tailgate picnics, whiskey sours in the stadium, and the general complexity of the sport guarantee that nobody knows what is going on.

'tail-gate, *v. colloq.* (orig. *U.S.*) Also unhyphened. [f. the sb.] **1.** *intr.* To drive too close behind another vehicle.

1951, **1955** [implied in *vbl. sb.* below]. **1962** 'F. & R. LOCKRIDGE' *Murder has its Points* xiv. 160 The police car they followed knew its way, and Weigand tail-gated. **1964** *Punch* 23 Sept. 442/3 'Don't tailgate!'.. meaning don't drive on the other man's tail. **1976** *Good Motoring* May 32/1 In the dangerous sphere of motorway driving, for example, they would not tailgate at speeds where if the man in front stopped suddenly they could not..help but stop in exactly the same place on the road.

2. *trans.* To follow (a motor vehicle) excessively closely in another vehicle.

1967 *Lebende Sprachen* XII. 73/2 The use of the verb (which is a recent accession) no longer requires that the car ahead does in fact have a tailgate. One can tailgate a VW. **1968** *National Observer* (U.S.) 8 Apr. 5/4 Negro cabbie John W. Smith, whose arrest for 'tailgating' a police car..helped spark five days of rioting.., was found guilty of assaulting a policeman. **1970** *Daily Tel.* (Colour Suppl.) 9 Oct. 25 The cruise cars are programmed on an intricate shuttle, one tailgating the other, so that no more than 20 seconds can.. pass between a radio alarm and the arrival of a car. **1982** H. KISSINGER *Years of Upheaval* vii. 228 We took off in a motorcade traveling at a speed of close to 100 miles per hour with cars tailgating each other.

3. *fig.*

1977 *Times Lit. Suppl.* 20 May 618/3 Pictures tailgate each other, wall to wall, and floor to ceiling, in the authentic eighteenth-century manner. **1978** *Saturday Night* (Toronto) Apr. 5/2 One takeover scenario has tailgated another: in 1969 it was Time Inc. muscling in.

Hence **'tailgater**; **'tailgating** *vbl. sb.*

1951 *Amer. Speech* XXVI. 309/1 *Tail-gating, part. phr.*, a bad practice of following too close to the tail gate of the truck ahead. **1955** *Ibid.* XXX. 93 Twenty-two..[lorry] drivers agreed that tailgating means riding too closely behind the vehicle ahead. **1957** *How to Drive* (Amer. Auto. Assoc.) viii. 71 Expressway 'tailgating' is suicidal. **1968** H. MCCLOY *Mr. Splitfoot* (1969) xvii. 195 Another car passed him and slipped in between his car and Folly's. One of those eager tailgaters who cannot bear to see a few inches between two cars ahead of them. **1970** V. JOHNSTON *Phantom Cottage* xxi. 160 'So if you will just let me keep following your car—'.. 'All right. But no tailgating.' **1976** *National Observer* (U.S.) 13 Mar. 8/6 In informal testing by The Observer, a Cyberlite appeared to reduce 'tail-gating' behind the test vehicle. **1978** *Telegraph* (Brisbane) 18 Jan. 2/1 A spider on the boot is a lot less dangerous than a tailgater on the bumper bar. **1980** *West Lancs. Evening Gaz.* 21 May 1/1 In a statement today the AA said poor driving, including the 'often fatal practice of "tailgating"', was responsible for a big increase in serious accidents.

tailing (ˈteɪlɪŋ), *vbl. sb.*[1] [f. TAIL *v.*[1] + -ING[1].]

1. The action of TAIL *v.*[1], in its various senses.

1703 MOXON *Mech. Exerc.* 267 You must Cement pieces to the ends of your bricks for tailing, or to make them longer. **1781** P. BECKFORD *Hunting* (1802) 70 *note*, The tailing of them [hounds' ears] is usually done before they are put out. **1829** *Nat. Philos.* I. *Hydraulics* iii. 26 (Usef. Knowl. Soc.) The tailing of mill-streams only occurs in the winter seasons, or at times when there is a profusion of water. **1840** HOOD *Up Rhine* 44 Short as the course was, it led to a great deal of what the turfmen call tailing. **1848** H. W. HAYGARTH *Recoll. Bush Life Australia* vi. 56 When cattle are first brought to a new country they are subjected to a process called 'tailing', which consists in watching them with horsemen by day, and driving them into their enclosures every night. **1854** SCOFFERN in *Orr's Circ. Sc., Chem.* 494 Mercury, holding but a slight portion of any impurity, dissolved, loses its property of cohering into globular drops .., and assumes the..appearance designated by the..term *tailing*, that is to say each..aggregation is..an irregularly elongated bar or tail. **1858** O. W. HOLMES *Aut. Breakf.-t.* iv. 86 They will not get up again in the race,..And the rest of them, what a 'tailing off!' **1860** *Merc. Marine Mag.* VII. 327 Moored in 6 fathoms..clear from tailing into shoal water.

2. *pl.* A name for the inferior qualities, leavings, or residue of any product; foots, bottoms.

a. Grain or flour of inferior quality; tail grain, etc. **b.** *Mining.* The residuum after most of the valuable ore has been extracted. **c.** A decomposed outcrop of a vein or bed. **d.** *Tanning*: see quot. **e.** General.

a. 1764 *Museum Rust.* III. xii. 40, I supposed..that they would go to the tailing, or off-fall corn. **1846** *Osborne Times* 24 Aug., For a bushel of best wheat they pay 7s., for first tailings they pay 6s. for second tailings 5s. the bushel. **1883** *Harper's Mag.* June 76/2 All that is left—no longer *wheat*—is divided into 'middlings' and 'tailings'.

b. 1864 WESTGARTH *Colony Victoria* xi. 222 His people were content with 'tailings', and places abandoned by the colonists. **1874** RAYMOND *Statist. Mines & Mining* 20 In the river-beds..are large accumulations of 'tailings', rich in gold, which escaped under the primitive processes of washing formerly in use. **1901** *Scotsman* 3 Apr. 6/7, 1570 tons of tailings produced by cyanide process yielded 138 ozs.

c. 1881 RAYMOND *Mining Gloss.*, *Blossom*, the oxidized or decomposed outcrop of a vein or coal-bed, more frequently the latter... Called..tailing.

d. 1885 C. T. DAVIS *Manuf. Leather* x. (1897) 174 In one of these [methods] the tanning-liquor which has been in use for some time, is made use of under the name of 'tailings', or sour liquor.

e. 1889 *Daily News* 28 Feb. 7/2 We fancy that out of the rejected mass of papers there are very few 'tailings' worth sifting.

3. a. The end or latter part: cf. TAIL *sb.*[1] 4.

1646 SIR J. TEMPLE *Irish Rebell.* II. 53, I shall hope to get the rest of my tailing together, and make such further provision of..materialls as may enable mee to goe through with the same. **1896** KIPLING *Seven Seas* (1897) 30 Good Lord, they slipped behind us In the tailing of our wake!

†**b.** *spec.* = TAIL *sb.*[1] 4 g. *Obs.*

1684 I. MATHER *Remark. Provid.* (1856) 43 The vessel was driven on the tailings of a ledge of rocks, where the sea broke violently.

c. *Arch.* See quot.: cf. TAIL *sb.*[1] 4 i.

1842 GWILT *Archit.* Gloss., *Tailing*, the part of a projecting stone or brick inserted in a wall. **1856** S. C. BREES *Gloss. Terms* s.v., The stone steps of a staircase have a tailing of about 9 inches, in order to support them.

d. *Surg.* = TAIL *sb.*[1] 4 j. *rare.*

1864 in WEBSTER.

4. In calico-printing: A fault of impression, in which the colours are blurred: see TAIL *v.*[1] 18.

5. *attrib.* and *Comb.*, as ***tailing-assay***, ***-barley***, ***-corn***, ***ground***, ***-heap***, ***pile***, ***-sand***, ***-wheat***, ***yard***; ***tailings-man***, ***-mill***; **tailing-mob**, a herd of cattle regularly tailed or herded; **tailing-rope**, *Naut.* = TAIL-ROPE 2 a.

1877 RAYMOND *Statist. Mines & Mining* 106 Yielding..a little over $7.15 per ton, exclusive of their *tailing-assay of $3.76 per ton. **1747** *Gentl. Mag.* 311 The *tailing corn may soon be cleaned. *c* **1830** *Glouc. Farm Rep.* 29 in *Libr. Usef. Knowl., Husb.* III, Their food..in winter [is] raw potatoes, with tailing corn, whey, and skimmed milk. **1878** E. S. ELWELL *Boy Colonists* 67 He had caught sight of a native hanging about the '*tailing-ground'. **1899** *Daily News* 13 Oct. 3/1 The immense *tailing heaps thrown up by the various companies have proved an excellent means of defence, forming earthworks which command the town [Kimberley] from every side. **1885** MRS. C. PRAED *Head Station* 266 The beasts were..made to join what was called the '*tailing mob', or those which had been constantly herded. **1897** 'MARK TWAIN' *Following Equator* lxviii. 687 The gold fields of the world now deliver up to fifty millions dollars' worth of gold per year which would have gone into the *tailing-pile under the former conditions. **1934** I. W. HUTCHISON *North to Rime-Ringed Sun* vi. 54 Across the entrance of the valley..stretched the heaped 'tailing-piles', tippings of the huge gold-dredges. **1495** *Naval Acc. Hen. VII* (1896) 197 *Taylyng Ropes for the Mayne sayle..vj; Crane lynes for the Mayne Toppe..j. **1890** *Goldf. Victoria* 21 Recent assays of the *tailing sand. **1877** RAYMOND *Statist. Mines & Mining* 40 The remainder comprising 9 trammers, 6 mill-men, 1 *tailings-man [etc.]. *Ibid.* 186 The silver or *tailings mill has not undergone any change. **1862** *Q. Rev.* Apr. 286 When..the..*tailing-wheat or 'gristing' is sound and of good quality. **1930** A. W. GROOM *Merry Christmas* xx. 158 The cattle could be seen moving quietly to the *tailing yards. **1963** W. E. HARNEY *To Ayers Rock & Beyond* v. 45 During my early cattle days all mustering was done into drafting yards... They did not alter the method until the drafting-yard' was superseded by the 'tailing-yard' with bronco-panels and twisted greenhide ropes with a leather 'hoonda' for the ring.

†'**tailing**, *vbl. sb.*² *Obs.* Also 4 **-ende**. [f. TAIL *v.*² + -ING¹.] ? Tallying, reckoning.

1362 LANGL. *P. Pl.* A. IX. 74 Ho is..Trewe of his tonge..And trusti of his taylende [B. VIII. 82 tailende, taylyng] takeþ bote his owne.

tailing ('teɪlɪŋ), *ppl. a.* [f. TAIL *v.*¹ + -ING².] That tails.

1899 BUXTON in *19th Cent.* Jan. 121 There is the 'tailing' fish [trout], feeding on caddis snail or shrimp, breaking the surface. **1908** *Edin. Rev.* Apr. 391 Offering the 'tailing' fish a floating fly.

tailism ('teɪlɪz(ə)m). *Pol.* [f. TAIL *sb.*¹ + -ISM.] In Communist jargon, the fault of accommodating policy to the wishes of the masses, thereby following in their wake rather than taking an active revolutionary role.

[**1933** tr. *Lenin's What is to be Done?* ii. 52 It would be more correct to describe its tendency not as opportunism, but *khvostism* (from the word *khvost*)... [Note] *Khvost* is the Russian word for tail.] **1948** J. TOWSTER *Political Power in U.S.S.R.* ix. 180 A double injunction against either 'commanding' or 'tailism' (following, instead of showing initiative). **1957** *Economist* 26 Oct. 320/1 After three months, all the crimes in the jargon book of communist heresy—including such esoteric offences as..'tailism' ('refusal to lead the masses')—have been hurled at the hundreds of eminent non-party rightists uncovered or named during..the recent disharmony. **1966** tr. *Quotations from Chairman Mao Tsetung* xi. 124 The reason why such evils as dogmatism, empiricism, commandism, tailism, sectarianism, bureaucracy and an arrogant attitude in work are definitely harmful..is that they alienate us from the masses. **1971** R. MACFARQUHAR in S. E. Fraser *Educ. & Communism in China* VI. 352 They read aloud the slogans... 'Do you listen to Chairman Mao, or to doctrinairism? Shameful tailism!'

taillable, taillage, obs. ff. TALLIABLE, TALLAGE.

‖**taille.** [F. *taille* (formerly taː, taj, now tɑj) (12th c.) cut: see TAIL *sb.*²]

1. Cut, shape, form; shape of the bust from the shoulders to the waist; figure, build, make. In *Dress-making*, the waist or bodice of a gown; the style or fit of this.

1663 PEPYS *Diary* 13 July, Mrs. Stewart,..with her sweet eye, little Roman nose, and excellent taille, is now the greatest beauty I ever saw. **1697** VANBRUGH *Relapse* IV. vi, You would not think it impossible a person of a worse taille than mine might be a modern man of quality.

2. In old French law, a tax: see TAIL *sb.*² 2 b.

3. *Mus.* (See quot. 1944.)

1842 J. A. HAMILTON *Dict. Two Thousand Musica Terms* 85 *Taille* (French), the tenor voice or part. **1876** STAINER & BARRETT *Dict. Mus. Terms* 420/1 *Taille* (Fr.), (1) the tenor voice or tenor part, (2) the tenor violin, the viola. **1889** GROVE *Dict. Mus.* IV. 52/2 The tenor violoncello clef was originally appropriated to the Taille. **1932** C. S. TERRY *Bach's Orchestra* v. 98 His players were certainly never provided with an instrument capable of sounding g, except the taille. **1944** *Harvard Dict. Mus.* 731/2 *Taille* [F.], old name for a middle voice, particularly the tenor. The term was also used for instruments performing such parts, e.g., *taille de basson*, tenor oboe; *taille de violon* or simply *taille*, viola.

taille, obs. f. TAIL, TALE, TALLY.

‖**taille-douce** (tɑjdus). Also 7 **tale-doux**, 8 **tali-douce**. [Fr., = soft cutting.] Engraving on a metal plate with a graver or burin, as distinguished from work with the dry point, and from etching.

1650 EVELYN *Diary* 21 June, A booke of statues..by which one may discover many errors in the taille douce of Perrier. **1657** in *Burton's Diary* (1828) II. App. 541 That no printers..imprint, or cause to be imprinted any work or works, book or books, taledoux or taledouxes. **1675** *Lond. Gaz.* No. 980/4 He already hath 108 Plates..cut in *Taille Douce.* **1718** A. NISBET *Ess. Armories* Index Terms, *Sable*, Black, is known in Tali-douce by perpendicular and horizontal Hatches. **1810** *Q. Rev.* III. 203 Plates engraved, as Malte-Brun tells us, in *taille douce.* **1897** O. FIRTH *Postage Stamps* ii. 7 The original example of line-engraved stamps, or stamps 'engraved in *taille-douce*'. **1924** F. J. MELVILLE *Compl. Philatelist* vi. 83 Most of the stamps produced after this portrait were surface-printed, but the Falkland Islands and the Turks and Caicos Islands presented it in *taille-douce* engraving. **1955** BOGGS & STRANGE *Foundations of Philately* xi. 128 Line engraving is a classic process which was used for the first adhesive stamps issued in Great Britain in 1840... This process is also known as intaglio, recess printing, or *taille douce.* **1969** F. L. WILDER *How to identify Old Prints* v. 77 Line-engraving (taille-douce) had become the principal form of engraving in France and it was said that the art was almost born and died with him [*sc.* Jacques-Philippe Le Bas], shortly before the Revolution. **1975** W. FINLAY *Illustr. Hist. Stamp Design* ii. 21/2 The paper usually has to be dampened..and then is laid on top of the plate and forced down under great pressure, so that the plate bites into the paper. The paper squeezed into the grooves picks up the ink; this is what gives stamps and banknotes printed in this fashion their characteristic ridged surface. This process is known as *intaglio, taille douce*, recess printing or direct plate printing. Philatelists often use the term 'line engraving'.

tailless ('teɪllɪs), *a.* [f. TAIL *sb.*¹ + -LESS.] Having no tail; deprived of a tail.

15.. *Songs Costume* (Percy Soc.) 88 Elsse our horse and mayres shal be All tayllesse at the Cart. **1781** PENNANT *Quadrupeds* I. 109 Tailless D[eer]. *Ibid.* II. 405 Tailless M[armot]. **1837** MARRYAT *Dog-fiend* xxxvi, He beheld Snarleyyow..tailless. **1854** OWEN *Skel. & Teeth* in *Orr's Circ. Sc., Org. Nat.* I. 189 The frog and other tail-less batrachians. **1874** T. HARDY *Madding Crowd* xxvi, Never did a fragile tailless sentence convey a more perfect meaning. **1887** *Field* 2 July 7/1 Tailless schipperkes. **1893** [see next].

Hence '**taillessness**.

1892 *Pall Mall G.* 24 Feb. 3/1 Our universal taillessness. **1893** *Westm. Gaz.* 22 Sept. 1/2 The little black Schipperkes, the tailless dogs of the Belgian bargees;..their taillessness was a fraud.

‖**tailleur** (tɑjœr). [Fr.] A woman's tailormade suit.

1923 *Weekly Dispatch* 29 Apr. 15 New, indeed, is the sunshade composed of chrome leather, designed specially for use with the morning *tailleur.* **1945** N. MITFORD *Pursuit of Love* xviii. 158 The spring *tailleurs*, the summer *imprimés*, the autumn *ensembles*, and the winter furs. **1982** T. FITZGIBBON *With Love* I. ii. 18, I pressed the black *tailleur*, bought a gay scarf..and went off to look for a job.

‖**tailleur**: see TALLIER.

taillie, variant of TAILYE.

taillour: see next.

tailor ('teɪlə(r)), *sb.* Forms: see below. [ME. a. AF. *taillour* = OF. *tailleor, -eur* (oblique case of *tailler(r)e*); in mod.F. *tailleur* = Pr. *talador* (nom. *talaire*), Cat. *tallador*, Sp. *tallador* engraver, *tajador* cutter, It. *tagliatore* cutter:—late L. or Com. Romanic *tāliātōr-em* (nom. *tāliātor*) cutter, agent-n. from *tāliāre* to cut: see TAIL *v.*² In Fr. the word had, and still has, the general sense of cutter, hewer, sculptor (*tailleur de pierre, de bois, de cuir, d'images*, etc.), but already in the 13th c. was used absolutely for *tailleur d'habits, de robes*, med.L. *tāliātor vestium, robārum*, cutter out or fashioner of clothes, tailor. The latter use is found in Eng. from the 14th c., the general sense 'cutter' being rare and doubtful: cf. 1297, *c* 1412, in sense 1.]

A. Illustration of Forms.

α. 3 [taylur], tailor, 4–5 **taillour**, 4–7 **taylour**, 4–9 **taylor**, 5 **taylere, tayller**, 5–7 **tayler, tailour**, 6– **tailor.**

[**1296** in *Fenland N. & Q.* (1905) July 210 Dilecto nobis in Xpo Ricardo de Masham dicto le Taylur.] **1297** Tailor [see B. 1]. **1318–19** in *Trans. Shropsh. Arch. Soc.* Ser. III. III. 54 Ricardus le taylor de Luytel Shrowardyn. **1362** LANGL. *P. Pl.* A. XI. 181 Trewe tiliers on erþe taillours [*v.r.* taliour] & souteris. **14..** *Voc.* in Wr.-Wülcker 629/1 Taylere, *scissor.* **1484** CAXTON *Fables of Alfonce* xiii, A tayller..as good a workman of his craft, as ony..at that tyme in alle the world. **1573–80** BARET *Alv.* T 10 A Tailour, *sutor vestiarius.* [See also B. 1.]

β. chiefly *north. dial.* and *Sc.* 4–5 **taliour**, 5 **talȝer, -ȝour, -yowr**, 5–6 **tailȝour, taylȝor, -your, -eȝour, taill-, tayllyour**, 6 **talȝear, -yeor, tailȝeour, -eȝour, -yeour, -yeur, telȝ(e)our, -yeour**, 9 *dial.* **taylior, teaylear.**

1415 in *York Myst.* Introd. 26 Taillyoures. *c* **1425** *Voc.* in Wr.-Wülcker 650/20 *Hic sissor*, tayleȝour. **14..** *Nom.* ibid. 685/25 *Hic sissor*, a taylȝor. *c* **1440** *Promp. Parv.* 486/1 Talyowre, *scissor.* **1442** *Aberdeen Regr.* (1844) I. 9 The talȝoures sal fynd [etc.]. **1474** *Acc. Ld. High Treas. Scot.* I. 24 To a tailȝour that makis the Kingis hos. **1483** *Surtees Misc.* (1888) 28 On Breyerton talȝer. **1483** *Cath. Angl.* 377/1 A Taylyour (*A.* Taylȝore), *sartor, scissor.* *c* **1500** *Songs Costume* (Percy Soc.) 62 Tailyeouris and sowtaris, blist be ye. **1530** PALSGR. 279/1 Tayllyour, *cousturier.* **1549** *Compl. Scot.* xvii. 150 Thy father vas ane mecanyc tailȝour. *a* **1568** *Satir. Poems Reform.* xlvi. 64 Ane nobill telȝeour in this toun. **1573** *Ibid.* xxxix. 202 Thay socht na taileȝours for to busc thair breikis. **1580** J. HAY *Cert. Demandes* vii. in *Cath. Tractates* (S.T.S.) 37 Tailyeours, skinnars and wther artisans. **1583** *Leg. Bp. St. Androis* 567 He causit an talyeor turne it.

B. Signification.

1. a. 'One whose business is to make clothes' (J.); a maker of the outer garments of men, also sometimes those of women, esp. riding-habits, walking costumes, etc. See also MERCHANT-TAILOR.

(Although historically the *tailor* is the *cutter*, in the trade the 'tailor' is the man who sews or makes up what the 'cutter' has shaped.)

1297 R. GLOUC. (Rolls) 6391 A robe he let him ssape uerst of blod red scarlet þere þe ssarpe stones bi þe stret is tailors were..þe tailors corue so moni peces uor is robe ne ssolde powȝe. *c* **1412** HOCCLEVE *De Reg. Princ.* 472 The taillours..moot heer-after soone Shape in þe feeld. **1466** *Mann. & Househ. Exp.* (Roxb.) 354 Herry Galle taylour,..axsethe for makenge of a longe gowne of pewke, ij.s. **1504** WRIOTHESLEY *Chron.* (Camden) I. 5 This yeare the Taylors sued to the Kinge to be called Marchant taylors. **1530** PALSGR. 68 A tayllours wyfe or a woman tayllyour. **1595** SHAKS. *John* IV. ii. 195, I saw a Smith..With open mouth swallowing a Taylors newes. **1597** —— *2 Hen. IV*, III. ii. 164 *Shal.* What Trade art thou Feeble? *Feeble.* A Womans Taylor sir... *Fal.* ..But if he had beene a mans Taylor, he would haue prick'd you. **1611** RICH *Honest. Age* (Percy Soc.) 34, I doe see the wisedome of women to be still ouer-reached by Taylers, that can euery day induce them to as many new fangled fashions as they please to inuent. **1663** PEPYS *Diary* 25 May, Into the Coach again, and taking with me my wife's taylor. **1704** J. PITTS *Acc. Mohammetans* iii. (1738) 21 They all sit down cross-legg'd, as Taylors do. **1751** JOHNSON *Rambler* No. 123 ¶5, I..sent for my taylor; ordered a suit..and..staid at home till it was made. *a* **1774** TUCKER *Lt. Nat.* (1834) II. 416 Our London company of tailors have a better title to the dignity of merchant by their magnificent hall. **1845** JAMES *A. Neil* II. i, Did you ever see a tailor cut out a coat?

b. In proverbial and allusive phrases; often implying disparagement and ridicule.

1605 SHAKS. *Lear* II. ii. 60, *Kent.* A Taylor made thee. *Cor.* Thou art a strange fellow, a Taylor make a man? **1607** DEKKER *Northward Hoe* II. i, They say three Taylors go to the making vp of a man, but Ime sure I had foure Taylors and a halfe went to the making of me thus. **1625** B. JONSON *Staple of N.* I. i, Believe it, sir, That clothes do much upon the wit,..and thence comes your proverb, The tailor makes the man. **1651** CLEVELAND *Poems* 23 Like to nine Taylors, who if rightly spell'd, Into one man, are monysyllabled. **1663** BUTLER *Hud.* I. II. 22 Compos'd of many Ingredient Valors Just like the Manhood of nine Taylors. **1819** SCOTT *Let.* 26 July in Lockhart, They say it takes nine tailors to make a man—apparently, one is sufficient to ruin him. **1908** H. B. WALTERS in *Church Bells* 96 'Nine Tailors make a man', is *said* to be really 'nine tellers', 'tellers' being the strokes for male, female, or child, in a funeral knell or passing bell. 3 × 3 for male. [In Dorset these strokes are said to be called tailors: *Acad.* 11 Feb. 1899, 190/1.]

2. A name given to several kinds of fish, as **a.** The tailor-herring and the tailor-shad: see 6. **b.** The Silversides. **c.** The Bleak. **d.** The Australian Skipjack, *Temnodon saltator* (New South Wales).

1676 *Phil. Trans.* XI. 625 In the Creeks are great store of small fish, as Perches, Crokers, Taylors, Eels. **1860** BARTLETT *Dict. Amer.*, *Tailor*, a fish resembling the shad, but inferior to it in size and flavor... On the Potomac, the Blue fish is called a Salt-water tailor. **1880** *Rep. Roy. Comm. Fisheries N.S. Wales* 22 The 'Tailor', is well known in Port Jackson. The young fish are constantly making their appearance in shoals in the summer season. **1883** *Fisheries Exhib. Catal.* (ed. 4) 176 Schnapper, Mullet, Jew-fish, Taylor, Travalley, Black-fish. **1888** [see 6]. **1890** *Fishing Gaz.* 18 Jan. 32/1 All Thames anglers know that bleak are nick-named tailors.

3. Short for TAILOR-BIRD, *proud tailor* (see PROUD *a.* 10).

1848 *Zoologist* VI. 2138 Goldfinches... That bird is in fact here [Leicestershire] known solely as a 'proud-tailor', though for brevity's sake..they..speak of it simply as a teelor.

4. *dial.* **a.** A kind of caterpillar. **b.** A *tipula* or daddy-long-legs.

1682 LISTER *Gœdart Of Insects* 131 A creature furnished with 2 wings and 6 long Feet called by us when boyes, the Tayler. **1816** *Sporting Mag.* XLVIII. 96 The variegated hairy caterpillar called 'the Tailor'. **1840** WESTWOOD tr. *Cuvier's Anim. Kingd.* 619 These insects are well known under the names of *Daddy long-legs, Tailors*, &c.

5. *attrib.* and *Comb.* General, as *tailor-craft, -man, -proprietor, -shears, -shop*; = tailor-made, as *tailor-costume, -frock, -gown, -skirt, -stitching, -suit*; *tailor-built, -cut, -suited* adjs.; also *tailor-like* adj. and adv.; TAILOR-MADE, q.v.

1905 *Daily Chron.* 27 May 3/7 With the hoop, the *tailor-built dress will disappear. **1897** *Westm. Gaz.* 22 Apr. 3/1 A *tailor costume destined for hard wear. *c* **1400** MAUNDEV. (Roxb.) xxvi. 122 All maner of craftez,..*talyour craft and sowter craft and swilk oþer. **1835** J. P. KENNEDY *Horse Shoe Rob.* xxiv, [It] did but little credit to the tailor-craft employed in its fabrication. **1886** G. R. SIMS in *Daily News* 4 Dec. 5/5 Her heavy *tailor-cut walking costume. **1891** 'J. S. WINTER' *Lumley* ix, Mrs. Hope made her appearance in another smart *tailor-frock. **1882** MISS BRADDON *Mt. Royal* III. vi. 106 A well-grown..young woman, in a severe *tailor-gown of undyed homespun. **1630** *R. Johnson's Kingd. & Commw.* 557 Sitting..with their legges acrosse, *Taylor-like. **1882** 'MARK TWAIN' *Prince & Pauper* xiii. 154 Noble large stitches..that do cause these small stingy ones of the *tailor-man to look mightily paltry. **1899** *Daily News* 27 Feb. 6/6 One such costume..which some tailor-man introduced as a novelty this season. **1483** *Act 1 Rich. III*, c. 12 §1 No merchaunt Straungier..brynge..to be sold any manner Gurdels..*Taillourshires, Scisors [etc.]. **1545** *Rates of Customs* cvij, Tayler sheres the dossen vj.s. viij.d. **1916** G. FRANKAU in *Wipers Times* 3 July 7/2 Oh! where is Caw-Caw the Captain bold, The pride of the *tailor-shop?

1979 *Maledicta* III. 20, I played a lot with Mezzrow. And with Sidney Bechet in his tailorshop in Brooklyn. **1896** *Godey's Mag.* Apr. 443/1 Two straight flaps.. finished with several rows of *tailor-stitching. **1907** *Westm. Gaz.* 12 Apr. 13/1 We do not soar beyond the new *tailor-suit for a week or two longer. **1906** *Ibid.* 13 Oct. 13/1 *Élégantes* of Paris who were *tailor-suited.

6. a. Special combinations and collocations: **tailor-fashion** *adv.* = *tailor-wise* adv. below; †**tailor-fly** = sense 4a; **tailor-herring**, a clupeoid fish, *Pomolobus mediocris*, of the Atlantic coast of N. America; also called *fall-herring* and *mattowacca*; **tailor-legged** *a.*, having the knees bent by sitting cross-legged; **tailor-shad** = *tailor-herring*; **tailor tack(ing)** = *tailor's tack*, sense 6b below; **tailor-tartan** *dial.*, a daddy-long-legs or crane-fly; **tailor-warbler** = TAILOR-BIRD; *spec.* the long-tailed tailor-bird, *Sutoria longicauda*; **tailor-wise** *adv.*, in a cross-legged position.

1877 RUSKIN *St. Mark's Rest* II. iv. 45 A curly-haired personage.. sitting in an absurd manner, more or less *tailor-fashion. **1682** LISTER *Gœdart Of Insects* 131 These *Tayler Flyes are very Leacherous. **1767** *Poetry* in *Ann. Reg.* X. 250 A *taylor-legg'd Pompey, Cassius, shall you see, And the ninth-part of Brutus strut in me! **1888** GOODE *Amer. Fishes* 405 [Hickory Shad or Mattowacca] *Clupea mediocris*. In the Potomac the species is called the '*Tailor Shad' or the 'Freshwater Tailor', in contradistinction to the bluefish, which is called the 'Salt-water Tailor' [*Tomatomax saltatrix*]. **1902** R. P. BROWNE *Pract. Work of Dressmaking & Tailoring* iii. 80 '**Tailor Tacking*'—This stitch is used to trace the seams, &c., through to the second side of the cloth—following the lines which have been marked with tailor's chalk. **1979** M. MCCRIRRICK *Better Dressmaking* iv. 35 *Tailor tacker*, for working quantities of tailor tacks on a thick pad of foam rubber... *Marking set*, for transferring single pattern marks to both sides of fabric at the same time as an alternative to tailor tacking. **1896** N. MUNRO *Lost Pibroch* (1902) 64 On the weedy stones the *tailor-tartans leaped like grass hoppers. **1783** LATHAM *Gen. Synops. Birds* IV. 515 *Tailor W[arbler]. This is a small species, being only three inches in length. **1885** *Tailor-wise [see TUCK *v.*[1] 6]. **1913** W. DE LA MARE *Peacock Pie* 20 To see them squatting tailor-wise Around a keg of rum. *c* **1973** J. CHOLERTON *Acrobatic Enchainements* (Assoc. Amer. Dancing) (ed. 7) 3 Lower (side view) to tailor-wise sit.

b. Also with *tailor's* (occas. *tailors'*): **tailor's block, tailor's dummy**, a lay figure on which to fit or display clothes; also *transf.* (*contemptuous*); **tailor's blow**: see quot.; **tailor's chair**, a legless seat with back and knee rest, used by tailors; **tailor's chalk**, hard chalk or soapstone used in tailoring, etc. to make eradicable marks on fabric as a guide to fitting; **tailor's cramp**, 'a spasmodic affection of the muscles of the thumb, forefinger and forearm, occurring in tailors' (*Syd. Soc. Lex.* 1898); **tailor's friend**: see quot.; **tailor's muscle**, the SARTORIUS; **tailor's spasm**, 'a neurosis affecting the muscles of the hands of tailors' (*Syd. Soc. Lex.*); **tailor's tack** (see quot. 1975); usu. in *pl.*; similarly **tailor's tacking** (cf. *tailor tack(ing)*, sense 6a above); **tailor's twist**, stout silk thread used by tailors; **tailor's wagon**: see quot.; **tailor's yard**, the cloth-yard; **tailor's yard (-band)**, a popular appellation of Orion's Belt.

1896 MRS. CAFFYN *Quaker Grandmother* 117 She's a bit too good for that *tailor's block. **1673** HICKERINGILL *Greg. F. Gregb.* 175 A *tailors blow, a knock with a thimble. **1881** C. C. HARRISON *Woman's Handiwork* III. 167 Grass and iris were sketched on the blue surface with *tailor's chalk. **1932** D. C. MINTER *Mod. Needlecraft* 107/2 Almost indispensable to successful dressmaking are.. a yard stick, tailors' chalk. **1966** *Olney Amsden & Sons Ltd. Price List* 36 Tailor's chalk .. Loose boxes of 100 pieces square or triangle. **1889** DOYLE *Micah Clarke* 394 Away, away, you *tailor's dummy! **1977** A. SCHOLEFIELD *Venom* v. 204 A maze of sewing machines and tailors' dummies. **1904** *Woollen Draper's Terms* in *Tailor & Cutt.* 4 Aug. 480/1 **Tailors' Friend*, a rather soft make of canvas used for vest interlining, made in white and black, and colours. **1727–41** CHAMBERS *Cycl., Sartorius*, in anatomy, the *Taylor's muscle. **1758** J. S. *Le Dran's Observ. Surg.* (1771) Cc viij, The Taylor's Muscle, so called because it brings the Legs across. **1894** *Westm. Gaz.* 27 Feb. 6/3 What is known as the 'tailor's muscle' running across the thigh and lifting the leg. **1927** *New Butterick Dressmaker* x. 98 **Tailors' tacks*,—after cutting out a garment.. mark with tailors' tacks the perforations at 'Outlet' or 'Let-Out' seams. **1964** *McCall's Sewing* ii. 32/2 *Tailor's tack*, method of marking pattern symbols. **1975** C. CALASIBETTA *Fairchild's Dict. Fashion* 488/2 *Tailor's tacks*, large stitches taken through two thicknesses of fabric with a loop left between the layers which are later cut apart, leaving tufts in each piece; used for guide marks in tailoring. **1952** E. KING *Successful Home Dressmaking* iv. 22 **Tailor's tacking*, suitable for all fabrics, but specially for woollens, crêpes, lace, velvets and loosely-woven or flimsy goods. **1873** *Young Englishwoman* Mar. 150/2 Work the button-holes with *tailors' twist, which is sold.. at one penny per dozen lengths of one yard. **1818** *Sporting Mag.* II. 232 *Tailors' Waggons, as we used to call.. those great, cumberous, four wheeled chaises. **1547** in Willis & Clark *Cambridge* (1886) II. 727, xx[tie] *taylors yerdes from the northe ende of the old Brewhouse. *a* **1548** HALL *Chron., Hen. VI* 186 b, They came not nere the Southermen by .xl. taylors yerdes. **1827** CLARE *Sheph. Cal.* 111 The *Tailor's Yard-band, which hangs streaming high.

tailor ('teɪlə(r)), *v.* [f. prec. sb.]

1. *intr.* To do tailor's work; to make clothes; to follow the calling of a tailor.

1662 [see TAILORING *vbl. sb.*]. **1719** DE FOE *Crusoe* I. ix. 158, I set to work a Tayloring, or rather indeed a Botching. **1863** W. B. JERROLD *Signals Distr.* 99 Under their superintendence half a dozen boys.. are sewing and tailoring. **1882–3** *Schaff's Encycl. Relig. Knowl.* 2249 [Stilling] taught school two days a week, and tailored four.

2. *trans.* To make or fashion (a garment, etc.) by tailor's work.

1856 KANE *Arct. Expl.* I. xxviii. 366 My buffalo-robes already tailored into kapetahs on their backs. **1888** *Daily News* 30 Apr. 2/7 A coat selling at 2*l.* 2*s.* was sewn and completely tailored for 4*s.* 6*d.*

3. a. To fit or furnish (a person) with clothes; to apparel, to dress. Also *fig.*

18.. BENTHAM *Fragm. Govt.* (ed. 2) Pref., Wks. 1843 I. 249/2 If tailoring a man out with God's attributes.. is blasphemy, none was ever so rank as Blackstone's. **1885** D. C. MURRAY *Rainbow Gold* II. ii, The country tradesmen who tailored him had sleepless nights. **1893** *Westm. Gaz.* 24 July 1/2 He wore a frock coat, and seemed faultlessly tailored.

b. *intr.* To have dealings with tailors; to run up bills with tailors. *colloq.*

1861 HUGHES *Tom Brown at Oxf.* xxviii, You haven't hunted or gambled or tailored much.

4. *trans.* To shoot at (birds) in a bungling manner, so as to miss or merely damage them. *slang.*

1889 *Blackw. Mag.* CXLVI. 475 They ought to wait when a bird rises in this manner and tailor him accordingly. **1903** *Westm. Gaz.* 29 Sept. 4/2 One of them.. letting birds past him untouched, knocking out tail feathers, and generally 'tailoring' his pheasants.

5. *fig.* To design or alter (something) to suit specific needs; to adjust or make suitable. orig. *U.S.*

1942 *Sun* (Baltimore) 23 Oct. 6/2 Maryland farmers will tailor next year's crops to a size which can be worked by their individual families. **1950** *Engineering* 9 June 655/3 To secure maximum performance the apparatus should be 'tailored' for each application. **1951** M. MCLUHAN *Mech. Bride* (1967) 98/2 To the mind of the modern girl, legs, like busts, are power points which she has been taught to tailor. **1959** *Listener* 2 July 35/1 A writer who soberly tailors a piece to fit into sixty minutes. **1961** *New Scientist* 23 Feb. 484/1 Derivatives containing carbon can be 'tailored' to have suitable handling properties. **1964** *Observer* 28 June 23/3 Of course, the story of 'Hiroshima Pilot as Mental Patient' was at once tailored to fit the headlines. **1982** G. F. NEWMAN *Men with Guns* p. vi, The shotguns.. the pair of Luigi Franchi double twelve-gauge.. he had had tailored in London.

'tailorage. *rare.* [See -AGE.] Tailor's work.

1858 CARLYLE *Fredk. Gt.* II. vii. (1873) I. 95 [Ottocar] in great pomp of tailorage. **1865** *Ibid.* XXI. viii. X. 152 A King supremely indifferent to small concerns; especially to that of shirts and tailorages not essential.

tailor-bird ('teɪləbɜːd). [f. TAILOR *sb.* + BIRD *sb.*] One of a number of species of Asiatic passerine singing birds, belonging to the genera *Orthotomus*, *Prinia*, *Sutoria*, etc., which stitch together the margins of leaves with cotton, etc., so as to form a cavity for their nest. Originally applied to a particular species (*Motacilla sutoria* of Pennant, now variously called *Orthotomus sutorius*, *Sutoria longicauda*, or *S. sutoria*) of India and Sri Lanka.

1769 PENNANT *Ind. Zool.* 7 Motacilla Sutoria. The Tailor Bird. **1813** J. FORBES *Oriental Mem.* I. 49 The tailor-bird of Hindostan; so called from its instinctive ingenuity in forming its nest, it.. gathers cotton from the shrub, spins it to a thread by means of its long bill and slender feet, and then, as with a needle, sows the leaves neatly together to conceal its nest. **1870** GILLMORE tr. *Figuier's Reptiles & Birds* 183 The nest of the Tailor Bird is placed in a large leaf, the margins of which are sewn together so as to form a bag. **1876** GRANT *Hist. India* I. xxxii. 170/1. **1895** NEWTON *Dict. Birds* 943 Species of Tailor-birds more or less nearly allied are found throughout the greater part of the Indian Region.

tailordom ('teɪlədəm). [See -DOM.]

1. The state, condition, or fact of being a tailor; *humorously*, the domain or realm of tailors.

1861 G. MEREDITH *E. Harrington* I. iii. 32 Preserve him from tailordom—from all contact with trade—they must. **1873** MAYO *Never Again* iv. 43 With a punctuality unusual in tailordom the clothes were finished. **1901** *Blackw. Mag.* Jan. 44/1 They do for literary art what M. Planché's books .. have done for tailordom.

2. = TAILORING *vbl. sb.* b, TAILORY 3.

1895 RASHDALL *Univ. Europe Mid. Ages* II. 644 The sobriety of hue characteristic of modern clerical tailordom.

'tailored, *ppl. a.* [f. TAILOR *v.* + -ED[1].]

a. Tailor-made.

1862 W. STORY *Roba di R.* (1863) I. iii. 38 He disdains the tailored skirts of a fashionable coat. **1908** *Newspr.*, A tailored suit of tabac brown.

b. *fig.* Made to suit particular needs; adjusted. orig. *U.S.*

1942 *Sun* (Baltimore) 12 Aug. 5/4 Gasoline rationing officials.. said that motorists coming into a rationed area from a non-rationed area on a pleasure trip can be supplied with a 'tailored' ration book to fit their needs. **1954** *Economist* 10 Apr. 141 A specially tailored compound containing the radio-active element. **1956** *B.B.C. Handbk. 1957* 38 The *North American Service* produces specially 'tailored' programmes to be rebroadcast by American and Canadian stations and networks. **1963** *Daily Tel.* 14 Mar. 15 (*heading*) 'Tailored' driving for Sunbeam Alpines.

tailoress ('teɪlərɪs), *sb.* [f. TAILOR *sb.* + -ESS.] A woman who works as a tailor; a woman tailor.

1654 GAYTON *Pleas. Notes* IV. ix. 234 The Protean Tayloresse.. could never be found in the same shape above once. **1771** *Boston Gaz.* 11 Nov. 3/1. **1837** HAWTHORNE *Twice-told T.* (1851) II. i. 9 At one of the back windows I observed some pretty tailoresses, sewing, and chatting. **1860** *Macm. Mag.* II. 46 There are sweaters' dens in London where living wages are utterly out of the reach of the poor tailoress. **1891** *Times* 2 Nov. 5/3.

Hence **'tailoress** *v.*, *nonce-wd.*, *intr.* to follow the occupation of a tailoress.

1865 MRS. WHITNEY *Gayworthys* xxiii. (1879) 231 It's nice to get a glimpse of Eunice when she isn't tailoressing. **1888** [see TAILORING *vbl. sb.*].

'tailorhood. *rare.* [See -HOOD.] The condition of a tailor; tailorly condition.

1847 HELPS *Friends in C.* (1851) I. ii. 32 A creature clipt and twisted and tortured into tailorhood.

tailoring ('teɪlərɪŋ), *vbl. sb.* [f. TAILOR *v.* + -ING[1].] **a.** The action or business of a tailor; the making of garments.

1662 PETTY *Taxes* xv. Tracts (1769) 83 The value of wool, clothing, and tayloring, even to the thread and needles might be comprehended. **1831** CARLYLE *Sart. Res.* I. v, Neither in tailoring nor in legislating does man proceed by mere Accident. **1888** *Queen* 7 Apr. 425 Tailoring for Ladies (and not Tailoressing) is carried on at Ulster House. **1899** *Allbutt's Syst. Med.* VI. 704 Unable to follow her occupation of tailoring.

b. The production of the tailor; tailor's work.

18.. WHITTIER *Pr. Wks.* (1889) II. 239 Priests, stripped of their sacerdotal tailoring, were in his view but men, after all. **1899** WHITEING *5 John St.* xxiv. 246 In all the glory of the best tailoring in town.

c. *fig.* The act of adjusting or producing to suit specific needs. orig. *U.S.*

1943 *Sun* (Baltimore) 5 Feb. 4/5 Thirty-seven ration boards in the State now are completing the tailoring of ration books. **1951** *Times* 21 Sept. 1/5 (Advt.), Highpolymer chemist for applied research on the 'tailoring' of linear macromolecules required by an important, very modern works in S.W. England. **1979** *United States 1980/81* (Penguin Travel Guides) p. xii, Very precise editing and tailoring keeps our text fiercely subjective.

d. *attrib.*

1850 KINGSLEY *Cheap Clothes* in *Alt. Locke* (1881) II. 101 The means of reducing prices in the tailoring trade. **1886** C. E. PASCOE *Lond. of To-day* xli. (ed. 3) 352 The most finished examples of the tailoring art.

tailoring ('teɪlərɪŋ), *ppl. a.* [-ING[2].] That does tailor's work. In quot. *fig.*

1737 M. GREEN *Spleen* 520 These Tayl'ring artists for our lays Invent cramp'd rules, and with strait stays.. Emaciate sense, before they fit.

'tailorism. [See -ISM.] **a.** Tailor's work; a tailor-made dress or garment. **b.** Mode of expression or action characteristic of tailors.

1839 *Fraser's Mag.* XIX. 121 Enrobed in the panoply of unpaid-for tailorism. **1850** L. HUNT *Autobiog.* I. vii. 288 The paternal and inextinguishable tailorism of old Rapid, in a 'Cure for the Heart-Ache'. **1904** *Westm. Gaz.* 14 Apr. 4/2 A short coat with a short skirt and a long coat with a long skirt,.. both being popular tailorisms.

'tailorize, *v.* [See -IZE.] **a.** *trans.* To treat as a tailor; to reduce to tailorhood. **b.** *intr.* To do tailor's work, to act the tailor; to sit cross-legged like a tailor.

1829 SCOTT *Let. to Mrs. Hughes* 24 Aug., Here I am *tailorizing* as my good mother would have said, that is capeing, collaring [etc.]. **1831** CARLYLE *Sart. Res.* I. viii, Our Clothes-thatch, and how.. it tailorises and demoralises us. **1832** *Blackw. Mag.* XXXI. 469 Did not Lord Melbourne—for we have not heard that he had been tailorized into humble submission—did he not kick him? **1873** LELAND *Egypt. Sketch-Bk.* 228 On the bunk where they all seem to be tailorising on their cross legs all day.

Hence **tailori'zation**, acting as a tailor, tailoring.

1853 KANE *Grinnell Exp.* xl. (1856) 365 We have worn out all our flimsy wardrobes, and have of late resorted to domestic tailorization.

'tailorless, *a.* [See -LESS.] Without a tailor.

1876 J. A. H. MURRAY *Let.* in K. H. E. Murray *Caught in Web of Words* (1977) x. 192 We are not quite *tailorless* and so not obliged to go *trouserless*. **1885** MRS. INNES in *Athenæum* 12 Dec. 764 Our butcherless, bakerless, tailorless, cobblerless,.. comfortless jungle. **1889** PROF. HUNTINGTON in *Chicago Advance* 24 Jan., What is barbarism but a tailorless state of society?

'tailorly, *a.* [f. TAILOR *sb.* + -LY[1].] Pertaining to, like, or befitting a tailor; sartorial.

1836 *Fraser's Mag.* XIV. 242 Their boots and their hats, and all tailorly ingredients of appearance,.. are irreproachable. **1887** SMILES *Life & Lab.* 200 Samuel Pepys—a man of gossipy and tailorly turn of mind.

'tailor-,made, *a.* Also tailormade.

1. Made by a tailor; esp. said of women's garments of a heavier type, close-fitting, and plain in style, properly when made by a tailor (as distinguished from a dressmaker); hence ellipt. as *sb.*

1873 *Punch* 20 Sept. 112/1, I shuddered to behold these words, 'Tailor-made costumes for ladies'. **1882** MISS BRADDON *Mt. Royal* II. x. 221 Gowns of dark brown serge which simulated the masculine simplicity of tailor-made garments. **1892** *Daily News* 29 Mar. 2/4 Braid is the favourite trimming for tailor-mades, now that fur is almost out of season. **1906** *Daily Chron.* 1 Sept. 4/7 If 'tailor-made' means anything, it means.. distinct from dressmaker-made on the one hand and factory-made on the other. **1932** AUDEN in *Rev. Eng. Stud.* (1978) Aug. 284 She's been having her tailormades altered. **1981** A. LURIE *Lang. Clothes* viii. 222/1 The ordinary woman.. might wear.. a.. wool or linen suit (the 'tailor-made') with a shirtwaist.

2. a. *fig.* Made such by the tailor, i.e. by one's dress. **b.** *transf.* Dressed in tailor-made garments.

1832 CARLYLE in *Fraser's Mag.* V. 386/1 If such worship for real God-made superiors showed itself also as worship for apparent Tailor-made superiors. **1896** *Westm. Gaz.* 1 May 8/2 Some severely tailor-made ladies were waiting in the entrance-hall. **1904** *Daily Chron.* 28 May 8/1 The 'tailor-made girl', like the 'frilly girl', has her opportunities upon the river.

3. Made to answer a specific demand or requirement; perfectly suited *for* a particular purpose.

1896 G. B. SHAW in *Sat. Rev.* 7 Nov. 494/1 The public were tired of tailormade plays, and were ripe for a revival of colour and costume. **1897** —— in *Ibid.* 1 May 470/2 A theatre which is panelled, and mirrored, and mantelpieced like the first-class saloon of a Peninsular and Oriental liner .. is no place.. for anything except tailor-made drama and farcical comedy. **1938** *Cine-Kodak News* Aug. 10/1 (*heading*) Tailor-made showings. **1946** *Richmond* (Va.) *Times-Dispatch* 24 Nov. 12B The work is another venture in the science of redesigning plants and animals through genetics to bring forth 'tailor-made' species. **1953** *Economist* 30 May (Suppl.) 9/1 The tailormade molecules which form the long fibres used in weaving Terylene. **1958** *Spectator* 14 Feb. 194/3 A seat tailor-made.. for the Liberals to dance further fandangoes on the carefully laid plans of their rivals. **1963** [see PEG *sb.*[1] 1 e]. **1970** G. F. NEWMAN *Sir, You Bastard* i. 14 It's a job almost tailor-made for you. **1972** [see INSIDE *a.* d]. **1980** *Jrnl. R. Soc. Arts* Mar. 185/2 The tailor-made building had arrived.

4. Designating a ready-made (as opp. hand-rolled) cigarette. Freq. *ellipt.* as *sb. slang* (orig. U.S.).

1924 'DIGIT' *Confessions 20th Cent. Hobo* 12 *Tailor-mades*, ordinary ready-made cigarettes. **1930** J. DEVANNY *Bushman Burke* 88 He smoked 'tailor-mades' now. **1945** *N.Z. Geographer* I. 23 The background of all this is tobacco. There are but few pipes, and 'tailor-made' cigarettes are only a luxury. 'Roll your own' is on most lips. **1952** E. WILSON *Equations of Love* 29 Just a match... I don't smoke tailor-mades. **1955** *People* (Austral.) 1 June 8/1 Leopold.. was.. told he had been reported for possessing contraband, a 'tailor-made' cigarette. Leopold didn't even know what a 'tailor-made' cigarette was. **1962** N. FREELING *Love in Amsterdam* III. 145 Martin stayed quiet after distributing his last tailormades. **1974** D. SEARS *Lark in Clear Air* iii. 40, I went and bought a package of Turret tailor-made cigarettes and I lit one.

Hence **'tailor-,madeness**; so **'tailor-make**.

1898 *Daily News* 22 Jan. 6/5 Almost all the gowns of tailor-make were turned back in front with white, red, or cream-colour. **1900** MRS. BANKS in *19th Cent.* XLVIII. 790 A perfectly fitting gown, elegantly 'smooth', though plain in its tailor-made-ness.

'tailor-make, *v.* orig. *U.S.* [Back-formation f. TAILOR-MADE *a.* 3.] *trans.* To design (something) according to specific requirements.

1946 *Sun* (Baltimore) 1 July 8/2 Under ideal weather conditions that seemed to have been tailor made for the occasion, the atom bomb was successfully exploded. **1953** *Ibid.* 14 Apr. 3/4 It may be possible to tailor-make drugs which would prevent each type of dangerous virus from getting the electrical charges it needs in order to attack the target cell. **1959** *Listener* 18 June 1052/2 What will happen when Franco does disappear from the political scene? Some think he is trying to tailor-make a monarchy. **1967** M. CHANDLER *Ceramics in Mod. World* vi. 168 Alumina ceramics can be tailor-made to meet a wide range of industrial requirements. **1973** *Daily Tel.* 9 Aug. 3 (Advt.), If you haven't yet got central heating, an Esso Chartered Installer will tailor-make a complete system to suit your needs. **1981** *Arts Alert* Oct. 3/1 We were asked to tailor-make the hall for the LSO's needs.

'tailorship. [See -SHIP.] The function or performance of a tailor; tailoring.

1830 *Blackw. Mag.* XXVII. 118 Anxious thus early to announce the fact of Tailorship. **1838** *Fraser's Mag.* XVIII. 381 Far better.. had it been to have taken to.. tailorship or cobblership. **1896** *Daily News* 10 Nov. 2/1 From the day they were turned out spick and span with their fine tailorship to this ninth of November.

tailory ('teɪlərɪ). Also 5 talarie, tailloury, 6 (9) tailery, 7 taylorie, -ery. [f. TAILOR *sb.* + -Y: cf. -ORY.]

1. The art, craft, or occupation of a tailor.

c **1449** PECOCK *Repr.* I. x. 49 Euen as sadelarie and talarie been ij dyuerse facultees and kunnyngis. **1598** R. HAYDOCKE tr. *Lomazzo* I. 1 The art of Weauing and Tailery. **1639** in *T. Lechford's Note-Bk.* (1885) 91 Co-partners in the trade of Taylery. **1823** in *Spirit Pub. Jrnls.* 151 A student in tailory, or 'a tailor's apprentice', as the ancients used to say.

2. A tailor's workshop or establishment.

1480 *Wardr. Acc. Edw. IV* (1830) 146 Coleyn threde delivered into the Tailloury. **1897** J. W. CLARK *Observ. Priory Barnwell* p. lxxiv, The Chamberlain is to.. see that they [garments] are properly made in the tailery (*sartrinum*).

3. Tailors' work, tailors' wares; costumery.

1610 GUILLIM *Heraldry* IV. vii. (1611) 205 Heereto we will annex some few examples of Taylorie. **1854** THACKERAY *Leech's Pictures* Wks. 1900 XIII. 489 Mr. Leech has as fine eye for tailory and millinery as for horse-flesh. **1891** *Pall Mall Gaz.* 11 July 2/2 How much time the Kaiser has to spend in the various changes from uniform to uniform... An eighth of his Majesty's time consumed in tailory!! *Sartor resartus*, indeed!

4. *attrib.*

1901 *Westm. Gaz.* 9 May 3/1 What we call the tailory hat. **1906** *Ibid.* 8 Sept. 12/1 The little interregnum till the tailory clothes are ready.

tail-piece ('teɪlpiːs).

1. The piece of anything forming its tail or end; the piece at the end. Also *fig.*

Among technical uses are: the tail-pin of a lathe; in Mining, the perforated end of the tail-pipe of a pump, a snore-piece; in Stereotyping by the paper process, a piece of card-board or the like used to prevent the flow of the metal under the tail-end of the matrix; in Building, a piece inserted by tailing, a floor-timber of which one end rests on the wall; the last sclerite of the pygidium of an invertebrate.

1601 HOLLAND *Pliny* I. 243 In other fishes the taile-peece is in greatest request. **1723** J. NOTT *Cook's & Confectioner's Dict.* sig. K K 3v, Draw your Sturgeon;.. cut your first and second Rand very fair, cutting the Tail-piece least. **1786** BUSBY *Dict. Mus.* s.v. *Tail-piece*, the thin, broad piece of ebony horizontally suspended over the lower end of a violin, and to which one end of the strings is attached. **1843** *P. Parley's Ann.* IV. 282 The chimney ended, as all chimneys do, with the sky for a tail-piece, and when Gibbo put his head out at the top, he.. looked around him, and drew in a few breathings of pure air. **1847** WEBSTER, *Tail-piece*.., in a violin, a piece of ebony at the end of the instrument to which the strings are fastened. **1869** OUSELEY *Counterp.* xxii. 177 It is called the 'coda', or 'tail-piece', of the fugue. **1876** G. F. CHAMBERS *Astron.* 635 A tube sliding easily within the tube to which the rack and pinion is attached, and called the tail-piece, is employed for first getting an approximate focus. **1890** *Spectator* 31 May, Toplady's hymn ['Rock of Ages'] was written as a tail-piece to a controversial article, in which Toplady discussed John Wesley's doctrines in the matter of faith and works.

2. *Printing.* A small decorative engraving placed at the end of a book, chapter, etc.

1707 HEARNE *Collect.* 14 Apr. (O.H.S.) II. 5 In the.. Bible .. are Curious.. tayl-pieces. **1762–71** H. WALPOLE *Vertue's Anecd. Paint.* (1786) IV. 188 Frontispiece and tailpiece to the catalogue of pictures exhibited in 1761. **1862** ANSTED *Channel Isl.* I. vi. (ed. 2) 124 A view of this wreck.. forms a tail-piece to the present chapter. **1895** C. R. B. BARRETT *Surrey* iv. 101 My tail-piece to the last chapter has for its subject the back gables of.. the Hall.

'tail-pipe, *sb.* Also **tailpipe**. **1.** The suction pipe of a pump.

1883 GRESLEY *Coal Mining Gloss.*, *Tail-pipe*. **1889** WELCH *Text Bk. Naval Archit.* xi. 124 A suction-box or valve chest .. is fitted beneath the pump and connected to the bottom thereof by the tail pipe shown.

2. a. *Aeronaut.* (See quot. 1933.) Chiefly *U.S.*

1922 L. S. MARKS *Airplane Engine* xvii. 423 For durability the muffler should be attached to the end of a tail pipe 6 or 8 ft. long which will cool the gases sufficiently. **1933** *Brit. Standards Inst. Specif.* CLXXXV. (Gloss. Aeronaut. Terms) VI. 53 *Tail pipe*, a pipe which leads exhaust gases away from a manifold. **1956** C. W. SMITH *Aircraft Gas Turbines* viii. 167 The exhaust gas pipe from the turbine is conducted to the propulsion nozzle through a duct (often called *tailpipe*). **1956** [see sense 2b below]. **1973** *Physics Bull.* Dec. 728/1 This difference is often referred to as 'excess' or 'tailpipe' noise. Work to date has identified this noise source as being associated with the aerodynamic environment in the core exhaust system.

b. *U.S.* The exhaust-pipe of a motor vehicle.

1956 W. A. HEFLIN *U.S. Air Force Dict.* 511/1 *Tail-pipe* .., an exhaust pipe for escape of gases generated in an internal combustion engine; specif. in a jet engine, the pipelike structure aft of the exhaust nozzle. **1961** E. A. VENK *Automotive Fundamentals* (ed. 2) xi. 179/2 The tail pipe is a long winding pipe which is connected to the muffler... Two tail pipes are used in a dual exhaust system. **1964** S. BELLOW *Herzog* 121 Unless you remembered to bear right the tailpipe would scrape on the rocks. **1973** *Sunday Bulletin* (Philadelphia) 14 Oct. (Parade Suppl.) 16/3 Unfortunately the tailpipe didn't clear the underside of the car. **1979** D. ANTHONY *Long Hard Cure* iv. 33 Lorraine's car was parked .. with the tailpipe backed into a hedge.

'tail-pipe, *v.* [The original implication of the second element seems lost.] *trans.* To tie a tin can or the like to the tail of (a dog, etc.) to distress and frighten him. Hence **'tail-piped** *ppl. a.*

1815 *Sporting Mag.* XLV. 256 A party of men and boys.. having tail-piped a dog for the humane purpose of making sport of its agonies. **1857** KINGSLEY *Two Y. Ago* ii, Even 'the Boys'.. tail-piped not his dog. **1881** BLACKMORE *Christowell* liv, He.. rushed away headlong, like a tail-piped dog, carrying our men after him.

tail-race ('teɪlreɪs). [Cf. RACE *sb.*[1] 8 c.] **a.** The part of a mill-race below the wheel, the tail-water; = TAIL *sb.*[1] 4 f.

1776 C. CARROLL *Jrnl. Miss. Canada* in B. Mayer *Mem.* (1845) 54 The water ran through this passage about as swift as it does through your tail race. **1820** *Aberdeen Jrnl.* 2 Aug. (Jam. s.v. *Hack*), To put proper hecks on the tail-races of their canals. **1873** *Act 36 & 37 Vict.* c. 71 §17 No person shall catch.. any salmon.. in the head race or tail race of any mill.

b. *Mining.* (See quot. 1881.)

1863 *App. Jrnls. House Reps. N.Z.* D. VI. 14 Where the water is heavy, and there are no means of cutting a tail-race, water-wheels have been erected, with Californian pumps attached. **1874** [see PADDOCK *sb.*[2] 3]. **1881** RAYMOND *Mining Gloss.*, *Tail-race*, the channel in which tailings, suspended in water, are conducted away. **1890** *Melbourne Argus* 16 June 6/2 A value of gold equal to the amount now saved was run into the tail-race and lost.

c. The watercourse leading from the turbine of a power-station or dam, etc.

1953 *Times* 4 Aug. 3/4 An electric screen has been devised which is successful in preventing salmon and sea trout from swimming into the tailrace (the outflow from a water turbine) of a power station. **1974** *Progress* (Easley, S. Carolina) 24 Apr. II. 10/2 Rainbows are the most common species stocked into tailrace waters. **1978** *Texas Parks & Wildlife* July 13/3 We've dealt mainly with tailraces below large flood-control and power-generating dams.

tail-rope ('teɪlrəʊp).

† **1.** That part of a horse's harness near the tail, as a breeching or crupper. *Obs.*

c **1325** *Gloss. W. de Bibbesw.* in Wright *Voc.* 168 E à la koue un analuer [*gloss*] a tayl-rop [*Camb. MS.* Vauner, *glossed* taylrop]. *c* **1350** *Nominale Gall.-Angl.* 884 *Esteles, trays, et valuere*, Harnys, trays, taylerope. *c* **1425** *Voc.* in Wr.-Wülcker 665/35 *Hec postela*, taylerape.

2. A rope forming or attached to the tail, or the hinder or lower end of anything; in various technical applications: e.g.

a. *Naut.* (Also *tailing-rope*.) A sheet. (Now *N. Amer.*) **b.** One of several hand-ropes attached to the end of a main rope, as in a bell-rope which requires more than one ringer. **c.** A rope attached to the rear of a train of carriages or wagons to draw them back again, or to retard their speed in running down an incline. **d.** *Coal Mining*: see quot. 1883. **e.** A rope for moving a pulley-case in a slide.

a. 1495 *Naval Acc. Hen. VII* (1896) 206, iij hausers of Normandye.. abought makyng of vj tayle ropes for the Mayne sayle and a craynelyne for the Mayne Toppe. **1916** F. W. WALLACE *Shack Locker* (1922) 81 Make th' tail rope fast. *a* **1932** L. S. TAWES *Coasting Captain* (1967) 27 We had a long tail rope to slack the staysail over with. **1942** *Amer. Neptune* II. 234 'Tail rope' is a short line made fast to the after end of the fore-staysail boom for the express purpose of backing the jumbo.

b. 1656 HEYLIN *Surv. France* 97 There are no lesse then four main ropes, besides their severall tale-ropes, to ring it [a bell at Notre Dame, Paris].

c. *c* **1838** STEPHENSON & BIDDER in *Civil Eng. & Arch. Jrnl.* I. 110/2 We should propose to work this line by what is called a tail rope; that is, a rope attached to the train, by which it is drawn on the return journey. **1867** W. W. SMYTH *Coal & Coal-mining* 157 If the inclination of a down-brow be.. less than 1 in 28, the empty tubs.. must be provided with a tail-rope passing round a sheave at the bottom of the incline, by which they will be hauled down again. **1874** J. H. COLLINS *Metal Mining* 73 In the iron mines of the North of England and South Wales.. 'tail-rope haulage' is exceedingly common. **1900** *Engineering Mag.* XIX. 724 A main rope which pulls the full trams out, and a tail rope which tails after the full trams, and which then becomes the haulage rope to pull out the empty trams.

d. 1883 GRESLEY *Coal Mining Gloss.*, *Tail Rope*,.. 2. A round wire rope attached to cages as a balance. 3. A round hemp rope used for moving pumps in shafts.

e. 1844 STEPHENS *Bk. Farm* II. 293 The pulley-case is moved in the slide, either by a long screw or by a tail-rope, which, when the case is adjusted, is fastened to a cleat.

tailsman, ploughman: see TAIL *sb.*[1] 14.

tailspin ('teɪlspɪn), *sb.* Also **tail spin**, **tail-spin**. [Cf. SPIN *sb.*[1]] **a.** *Aeronaut.* A downward movement of an aircraft in which the tail describes a spiral.

1917 V. W. PAGE *Gloss. Aviation Terms* 23 Tail spin. **1919** in C. A. Smith *New Words Self-Defined* 201, I remember when I thought it was time to try a *vrille* or tail-spin. **1926** *Daily Colonist* (Victoria, B.C.) 17 Jan. 2/5 Collison's airplane went into a tail spin when his motor failed to work. **1953** C. A. LINDBERGH *Spirit of St. Louis* II. vi. 263 He'd tried to land out of a tailspin—that was asking for a crash.

b. *fig.* A state of chaos, panic, or loss of control.

1928 R. E. BYRD *Let.* 24 July in *K. W. Rendell Autograph Catal. No. 34* (Kingston Galleries) (1968) 2, I am pretty much in a tail spin which I don't expect to get out of before the main part of the expedition leaves. **1929** *Times* 2 Nov. 12/6 The cyclic tailspin which has occurred in the 11th year of each of the four great previous periods of commercial prosperity. **1935** WODEHOUSE *Luck of Bodkins* xv. 183 A dashed shame, he considered, that things had gone into a tail spin for him like that. **1954** A. HUXLEY *Let.* 5 Dec. (1969) 717 A child stoked with fats will find it hard, because of adrenalin, to digest and will probably go into a bad psychological tailspin in consequence. **1967** E. S. GARDNER *Case of Queenly Contestant* vii. 84 [He] went into a tailspin. He was afraid of the responsibility. He was afraid his father would find out. *a* **1974** R. CROSSMAN *Diaries* (1977) III. 867 After my denial of the story that appeared in his Manchester lecture, the poor man came along in a terrible tail-spin to see me. **1982** *Daily Tel.* 16 June 19 The Argentine economy was already in a tail-spin before the Falklands invasion.

'tailspin, *v.* Also **tail-spin**. [f. the sb.] *intr.* To perform or go into a tailspin.

1927 [see *barrel roll* s.v. BARREL *sb.* 11]. **1936** F. CLUNE *Roaming round Darling* xvii. 167 We slithered in the mud, barrel-rolled, tail-spinned, sank to our hocks, and became part of the everlasting scenery. **1972** M. J. BOSSE *Incident at Naha* iv. 204, I had never seen Virgil so moved or so bitter. It was unlike him to tailspin into such a downer. **1973** *Daily Colonist* (Victoria, B.C.) 21 June 1/5 The red and white air craft was about 400 feet in the air a mile from the airport when it suddenly went into a nose dive, then tailspun to the pavement.

tailward(s ('teɪlwəd(z), *adv.* [f. TAIL *sb.*[1] + -WARD(S.] Toward the tail; also quasi-*sb.* (with *to*, *from*), the direction in which the tail is.

1617 PURCHAS *Pilgrimage* v. vii. §2. 590 Their faces to the taile-wards. **1665** HOOKE *Microgr.* 162 The finger being rubb'd from the tail-wards towards the head. **1851** MAYNE REID *Scalp Hunt.* l. 384 We were set astride on the bare backs [of the mules], with our faces turned tailwards.

tailwise ('teɪlwaɪz), *adv.* [f. TAIL *sb.*^{1} + -WISE.] In the manner of a tail; also, with the tail foremost, i.e. backward.

a **1845** HOOD *To Dymoke* xi, When he [a horse] waddled tail-wise with the cup to his stall. **1899** WHITING *5 John St.* 33 A ridiculous fag-end..sticks tailwise out behind.

tailye, tailzie, taillie ('telji, 'telɪ), *sb. Sc.* Forms: α. 4–5 talȝe, 5 taylyhe, 5–6 tailȝe, 6 taylie, tailye, tailze. β. 4– taillie, 5– tailyie, tailȝie, 6 talȝie, taillȝie, 6– tailzie. (In Sc. *lȝ* was the regular representative of F. *ll* mouillé (ʎ); this after 1500 was sometimes printed *ly* or *lyh* according to the sound, but more usually *lz* from the similarity of written *z* to *ȝ*.) [In α form *talȝe*, *tailȝe*, *tailyhe*, a. OF. *taille* cutting, = TAIL *sb.*^{2} In β form *tailȝie*, a. OF. *tailliee*, *taillée*, *taillie* (13th c. in Godef.) = Pr. *talhada*, It. *tagliata*:—late L. or Comm. Romanic **tāliāta*, sb. fem. from pa. pple. of *tāliāre* to cut: see TAIL *v.*^{2} and -ADE. In OF., *taille* and *tailliee* were in some senses synonymous, and in Sc. spelling the α and β forms ran together, the β forms in *-ie* at length prevailing.]

†**1.** A cut piece; a cut or slice (of meat). [prop. *tailȝie* = OF. *tailliée*.] *Obs.*

c **1470** HENRYSON *Mor. Fab.* II. (*Town & C. Mouse*) xvi, Muttoun and beif strukkin in tailyeis greit. **1513** DOUGLAS *Æneis* I. iv. 92 Rent furth the entralis, sum in tailȝeis schair. *Ibid.* XIII. ii. 18 Syne hakkin thaime [sacrificial beasts] in talȝeis. **1819** W. TENNANT *Papistry Storm'd* (1827) 185 They denner'd weil, wi' cheirfu' hearts, On tailyies fat and fine.

†**2.** Arrangement, fixture. [prop. *tailȝe* = OF. *taille*.] *Obs.*

c **1425** WYNTOUN *Cron.* IX. 1137 For bathe þai war be certane tailȝe Oblist to do þat deid, sauff failȝe. *Ibid.* 1144 De Lyndissay and de Wellis þa, On hors ane agane a noþir ran, As þar tailȝe was ordande þan.

3. *Sc. Law.* A legal disposition regulating the tenure and descent of an estate or dignity; = TAIL *sb.*^{2} 3, ENTAIL *sb.*^{2} 1. [prop. *tailȝe*.]

1375 BARBOUR *Bruce* xx. 134 (MS. E.) And at this tailȝe [*MS. C.* tale] suld lelely Be haldin, all the lordis swar. *c* **1375** *Sc. Leg. Saints* xxxvi. (*Baptista*) 1038 þane wes antypater wa, þat his fadir sic a talȝe can ma. **1391** in Fraser *The Lennox* (1874) II. 43 To the fulfilling of this taillie the forsaid Erl of Fife sal purches the kingis assent. **1473–4** *Acc. Ld. High Treas. Scot.* I. 6 Certane landis..to be gevin agane to his sone in talȝe. **1535** STEWART *Cron. Scot.* (Rolls) III. 393 And gif of him the airis maill did falze, Robert his bruther the narrest of the tailze. **1578** *Reg. Privy Council Scot.* II. 693 All taillies from the airis generall to the airis maill. **1676** W. ROW *Contn. Blair's Autobiog.* xii. (1848) 452 Desiring that the tailzie of the estate of Buccluch might be broken. **1769** *De Foe's Tour Gt. Brit.* IV. 53 By an Act 20 Geo. II..Heirs of Tailzie are allowed to sell Lands to the Crown [cf. quot. 1747 in TAILYE *v.* 3]. **1814** SCOTT *Wav.* x, In direct contravention of an unrecorded taillie. **1818** —— *Hrt. Midl.* xii, Didna ye get baith liberty and conscience made fast, and settled by tailzie on you and your heirs for ever? **1832** AUSTIN *Jurispr.* (1879) II. li. 865 The fetters of a Scotch deed of tailzie. **1868** *Act 31 & 32 Vict.* c. 101 §104 His heirs, whether of line, conquest, taillie, or provision.

†**4.** An account or reckoning. *Obs.*

1497 *Acc. Ld. High Treas. Scot.* I. 361 Giffin to the quareouris of the est quarel for schort tailȝeeȝ,..xiijs. iiijd. **1508** KENNEDIE *Flyting w. Dunbar* 446 A pak of flaskynnis, fynance for to mak the, Thow sall ressaue, in Danskyn, of my tailye.

tailye, tailzie ('telji, 'telɪ), *v. Sc.* Forms: 4 talȝe, 5 tailȝe, -ȝee, 6 tayllie, 6 tailze, -zee, tailye, 8–9 tailzie (with z for ȝ = y, yh, in print after 1500). [Early Sc. *talȝe*, *tailȝe*, a. F. *taille*, infl. of *tailler* to cut, etc.; = corresp. English TAIL *v.*^{2} The mod. *tailzie* is, as in the sb., an erroneous form for *tailȝe* or *tailye*.]

†**1.** *trans.* To cut; to cut to shape. *Obs.*

1581 *Satir. Poems Reform.* xliv. 200 Thou..I vene, The peperit beif can tailȝe be the threid. **1589** *Reg. Privy Council Scot.* IV. 421 Twa talyeit rubyis in chattonis, and three rubyis caboshon,..being of his Majesteis jowellis.

†**2.** To determine, settle, appoint, arrange. *Obs.*

1375 BARBOUR *Bruce* XIX. 188 And eftir syne war trewis tane Betuix the twa kyngis, that wer Talit [*v.r.* tailȝeit] to lest for thretten ȝheir. *c* **1375** *Sc. Leg. Saints* xxi. (*Clement*) 346 Sic fortone sal ȝe haf nedlinge, As was ȝow talȝet in ȝoure getting. **1456** SIR G. HAYE *Law Arms* (S.T.S.) 269 The bataill be tane under certane condicioun of tayllid strakis.

3. *Sc. Law.* To determine or tie up the succession to (an estate); to entail; = TAIL *v.*^{2} 5.

1536 BELLENDEN *Cron. Scot.* (1821) II. 395 King Robert set ane parliament at Ayre, in the quhilk..he gat the croun of Scotland tailyet to him and the airis male gottin of his body. *a* **1557** *Diurn. Occurr.* (Bannatyne Cl.) 24 The lord Erroll marijt the erle of Lennox sistar, quha bure him ane daughter; his landis was tailyeit. **1747** *Act 20 Geo. II*, c. 50 §14 It shall and may be lawful for any Person..possessed of a Tailzied Estate in Scotland, to sell, dispone, or resign.. any Part thereof, which his Majesty..shall think fit to purchase, for erecting of Buildings, or making Settlements within the same. **1806** FORSYTH *Beauties Scotl.* IV. 150 In 1315 Thomas de Loch Orr is in the parliament at Air that tailzied the crown. **1832** AUSTIN *Jurispr.* (1879) II. li. 864 Proprietors were enabled to tailzie their lands, that is, to make a destination of their estates so as effectually to fetter the power of alienation of future proprietors.

†**4.** To keep account or tally of. *Obs.*

1497 *Acc. Ld. High Treas. Scot.* I. 351 Thome Foret, to remane in Dunbar to resaue and store and tailȝee the lyme, sand and othir gere. **1539** *Ibid.* VII. 217 George Balglavy for awayting and keiping and tailȝeing of the said tymmer, lyme, send, and stane.

Hence **'tailyed, 'tailzied** *ppl. a.*, cut to shape; appointed, fixed, arranged; entailed.

1456 [see 2]. **1589** [see 1]. **1747** [see 3].

tailyeour, -ȝour, obs. ff. TAILOR.

†**tailyevey,** *v. Sc. Obs. rare.* In 6 tailȝevey, taillȝewe. [Origin obscure.] *intr.* To reel from side to side, move to and fro. Hence †**tailȝevey** *sb.*, a reeling or rocking from side to side.

1513 DOUGLAS *Æneis* V. xiv. 77 Quhow that the schip did rok and tailȝevey For lak of a gud sterisman on the se. *a* **1568** in *Satir. Poems Reform.* xlvi. 8 Scho will sale all the wintirnight, And nevir tak a telȝevie. *c* **1579** MONTGOMERIE *Misc. Poems* xlviii. 157 Betuixt the tua [Charybdis and Scylla] we tuik sik taillȝeweis, At hank and buick we skippit syndrie seis.

taim, taime: see THEM, TEAM.

tain (teɪn), *sb.* [a. F. *tain* tinfoil, altered from F. *étain* tin. Cf. also ME. TEYNE.] (See quot.)

1858 SIMMONDS *Dict. Trade*, *Tain*, a thin tinplate; tinfoil for mirrors.

†**tain,** *v. Obs. rare.* In 6 **teyne, taygne**. [Short for *obtain*, or ad. L. *tenēre*, F. *tenir*, on the analogy of the compounds *attain*, *maintain*, *obtain*, etc.] **a.** *trans.* To obtain, get. **b.** *intr.* To obtain, maintain itself, prevail.

1501 *Plumpton Corr.* (Camden) 156 Bryng with you money convenient for your expenses, for as yet..here be now rent teyned. *c* **1530** tr. *Erasmus' Serm. Ch. Jesus* (1901) 21 Enuyes, simulations, and other vicyes, which especyally taygne in olde men.

tain, obs. form of THANE.

tain, taine, obs. ff. *taken*, pa. pple. of TAKE *v.*

tainchell, obs. variant of TINCHEL.

tainct, -ure, obs. ff. TAINT, TAINTURE.

†**'tainder.** *Obs. rare*$^{-1}$. In 5 teyndre. Aphetic form of ATTAINDER.

1469 *Rolls of Parlt.* VI. 231 Afore the seid atteyndre or teyndres.

taing, dial. variant of TANG *sb.*^{1}

taings, Sc. form of TONGS.

†**'taining.** *Obs.* Some kind of device for catching fish in rivers.

1533–4 *Act 25 Hen. VIII*, c. 7 No..persone..shall..take ..in..any..nett, berd net of heare, tainyng, lepe, hyve, crele,..the yonge frye..of any kynde of Salmon. **1558** *Act 1 Eliz.* c. 17 §1 No Person..withe any..Net, Weele, Butt, Tayning, Kepper, Lyme, Crele..shall take..Spawne or Frye of Eeles, Salmon, Pyke or Pyckerell.

tainiolite, var. TÆNIOLITE.

taint (teɪnt), *sb.* Forms: 4–6 **taynte**, 5 **teynt**, 5–7 **taynt**, 6 **tainte, teinte**, 7 **tainct**, 6– **taint**. [Here, as in TAINT *v.*^{1}, two words of distinct origin, being identical in form, appear to have run together in the formation of later senses. The original words are placed under A and B, the blended senses under C.]

A. [Aphetic form of ATTAINT *sb.*]

†**1. a.** A 'hit' in tilting; = ATTAINT *sb.* 1. Also *fig.*

c **1400** *Melayne* 1387 Bot me sall neuer be-tyde that taynte. **1494** in *Letters of Rich. III & Hen. VII* (Rolls) I. 397 Sir Edward A Borough..brake a spere well brokyn, the ij^{de} better, with a teynt. **1543** GRAFTON *Contn. Harding* 596 He ..gaue so many teintes y^t euery man maruayled at his wonderfull feetes. *Ibid.* 599 At euery coursse he brake a speare or gaue a taynt. **1551–2** EDW. VI *Lit. Rem.* (Roxb.) II. 389 Ther was a match..at tilt. Theis [the earl of Warwick, etc.] wane by 4 taintes. **1602** SEGAR *Hon. Mil. & Civ.* III. xxxviii. 168 At the last meeting the French Taint was so strong, as the Englishman was wel-neere borne downe: and so they departed. *c* **1611** CHAPMAN *Iliad* III. 374 This taint he follow'd with his sword, drawn from a silver sheath.

†**b.** *transf.* A knock, a blow. *Obs.*

c **1410** *Master of Game* (MS. Digby 182) vii, If grehoundes gyf hym [the fox] mony tayntes and ouersette hym.

2. A disease in horses; = ATTAINT *sb.* 3.

1565 BLUNDEVIL *Horsemanship* IV. cxix. (1580) 55 Of a nether taint... This is a little bladder full of iellie, much like vnto a wind-gall, not apparant to the eie, but to the feeling, growing in the midst of the pasterne, somewhat aboue the frush. It commeth by a straine, or else by some wrench, or by an ouerreach. **1844** STEPHENS *Bk. Farm* II. 672 His observations are particularly applicable to the *curl*, still they will apply equally well to the *taint*.

†**3.** A conviction; *spec.* the conviction of a jury for having given a false verdict; = ATTAINT *sb.* 4.

1530 PALSGR. 279/1 Taynte, *condamne* [sb.]. **1607** COWELL *Interpr.*, *Taint*..signifieth either substantiuely a conviction, or adiectiuely a person convicted of felonie or Treason &c. See *Attaint.* **1609** SKENE *Reg. Maj.* I. 13 Gif the assisors sall happin to be convict as mensworne in the court, be ane Taynt; that is, be probation of twentie foure loyall men. **1706** PHILLIPS (ed. Kersey), A *Taint*, a Conviction.

†**B.** [a. OF. *teint*, *taint* (12th c.):—L. *tinctu-s* (*u*-stem), and *teinte* (13th c.):—late and med.L. *tincta*, sb. fem. from *tinct-us*, pa. pple. of *tingĕre* to TINGE. Cf. the later doublets TINCT and TINT.] Colour, hue, tint; tinge; dye. *Obs.*

1567 DRANT *Horace, Epist.* II. ii. Hvj, Pearles, stones, iewels, pictures, with costelie kynde of tainte. **1598** PUTTENHAM *Eng. Poesie* III. i. (Arb.) 150 The crimson tainte, which should be laid vpon a Ladies lips, or right in the center of her cheekes. *a* **1592** GREENE *Hexametra Alexis in laudem Rosamundæ* 6 Face rose-hued, cherry-red, with a silver taint like a lily. *c* **1593** EARL OXFORD *Sheph. Commend. Nimph* vii, This pleasant Lilly white, This taint of roseate red.

C. [Senses app. combining A and B.]

1. a. A stain, a blemish; a sullying spot; a touch, trace, shade, tinge, or tincture of some bad or undesirable quality; a touch of discredit, dishonour, or disgrace; a slur.

1601 SHAKS. *Twel. N.* III. iv. 390, I hate ingratitude more in a man, Then..any taint of vice. *a* **1637** B. JONSON *Underwoods* xiii, A hallowed temple, free from taint Of ethnicisme. **1643** CHAS. I. *Proclam.* Wks. 1662 II. 350 Free from the foul Taint of High Treason. **1682** OTWAY *Venice Pres.* II. i, They leave a Taint, a Sully where they've past. **1706** PHILLIPS (ed. Kersey), A *Taint*..a Blur, Spot, or Blemish in one's Reputation. **1742** FIELDING *Jos. Andrews* II. iv, His temper was..without the least taint of moroseness. **1781** COWPER *Expost.* 150 Free from every taint but that of vice. **1819** KEATS *Eve St. Agnes* xxv, She knelt so pure a thing, so free from mortal taint. **1838** PRESCOTT *Ferd. & Is.* (1846) II. xx. 211 A slight taint of pedantry. **1851** BRIMLEY *Ess.*, *Wordsworth* 103 There is no taint upon his robe. **1883** SIR J. BACON in *Law Rep.* 25 *Ch. Div.* 316 For good consideration and without taint of suspicion.

†**b.** A flaw or blemish in the feathers of hawks from improper feeding; = HUNGER-TRACE(S. *Obs.*

1486 *Bk. St. Albans* B ij b, The tayntys that be vppon her tayll and her Wengys wiche tayntys com for lacke of fedyng when thay be Eyes. *Ibid.*, A Taynt is a thyng that gooth ouerwarte the federis of the wynges, and of the tayll lyke as and it were eetyn with wormys.

c. An unpleasant scent or smell. Cf. TAINT *v.* C. 4 c.

1927 H. WILLIAMSON *Tarka the Otter* i. 5 Mingled with the flower odours..was the taint that had given her a sudden shock..; the taint most dreaded by the otters..—the scent of Deadlock, the great pied hound. **1951** 'J. WYNDHAM' *Day of Triffids* xi. 205 On the higher ground there was still little taint in the fresh air.

2. a. A contaminating, corrupting, or depraving influence, physical or moral; a cause or condition of corruption or decay; an infection.

1613 SHAKS. *Hen. VIII*, v. iii. 28 What followes then?..a generall Taint Of the whole State. **1692** LOCKE *Educ.* §68 Keep him from the Taint of your Servants, and meaner People. **1735** BOLINGBROKE *On Parties* ii. 15 That epidemical Taint, with which King James infected the Minds of Men, continued upon us. **1828** MACAULAY *Ess.*, *Hallam* (1887) 93 A deep and general taint infected the morals of the most influential classes. **1832** HT. MARTINEAU *Ireland* vi. 93 The health..was affected by the taint the marsh gave to the atmosphere.

b. A trace or tinge of disease in a latent state.

1615 W. LAWSON *Country Housew. Gard.* (1626) 16 It is a great signe of a taint, and next yeeres death. **1639** T. DE GRAY *Compl. Horsem.* 347 If you doe perceive a taint in his winde. **1804** *Med. Jrnl.* XII. 414 How often does latent venereal taint produce glandular obstructions? **1875** H. C. WOOD *Therap.* (1879) 410 Diseases of the bones, dependent upon or resulting from a scrofulous taint. **1879** *Spon's Encycl. Manuf.* I. 9 It is also essential that there shall be no dry rot or 'taint' present [in the wood]. **1899** *Allbutt's Syst. Med.* VIII. 116 Both diseases own a common origin, namely, hereditary nervous taint.

†**3.** (Also **tant.**) Short for TAINT-WORM; also, a small red spider (see quot. 1646). *Obs.*

1577 B. GOOGE *Heresbach's Husb.* III. (1586) 134 b, If he swell of the taint, or stingworme. **1646** SIR T. BROWNE *Pseud. Ep.* III. xxvii. 176 There is found in the Summer a kind of spider called a Tainct of a red colour... This by Countrey people is accounted a deadly poison unto Cowes and Horses; who, if they suddenly die, and swell thereon, ascribe their death hereto, and will commonly say, they have licked a Tainct. **1656** in BLOUNT *Glossogr.* *a* **1705** RAY *Hist. Insects* (1710) 41 Araneus exiguus coccineus, vulgo Anglicè a *Tant or Taint*.

4. *Comb.* as **taint-free** *a.*, free from taint.

1663 *Flagellum, or O. Cromwell* 205 Nor were most of his Relations taint free of those principles.

†**taint,** *ppl. a. Obs. rare.*

1. [Aphetic form of ATTAINT *ppl. a.*]

a. Attainted, convicted. **b.** Affected, seized, struck. **c.** Exhausted.

c **1330** R. BRUNNE *Chron. Wace* (Rolls) 5164 Recreaunt & teynt. *Ibid.* 10903 Ful of yre, wyþ colour [= choler] teint. *c* **1380** *Sir Ferumb.* 2822 Gyoun þanne was teynt & paal; so longe he hadde yuaste. **1496** *Dives & Paup.* (W. de Worde) II. xvii. 129/1 He sholde be taken as a conuycte and a taynt [*perh.* ataynt] traytour. **1706** PHILLIPS (ed. Kersey), *Taint*, Convicted of a Crime, as Treason, Felony, etc.

2. [Shortened pa. pple. of TAINT *v.*] = TAINTED; infected, corrupt.

1620 QUARLES *Jonah* ix. *Medit.* H ij b, Their seruice is vnsweet, and foully taint. **1743** *Lond. & Country Brew.* IV. (ed. 2) 330 Such casks..will grow furry, taint, and stinking.

taint, *v.*^{1} Forms: 4–6 **taynte**, 5–6 **taynt**, 6–7 **teint**, 5– **taint**. Pa. pple. **tainted**; also formerly contr. **taint (teint,** etc.). [Here, as in the sb., there are two words of distinct origin, A and B, and a series of senses C, in which both appear more or less to blend.]

A. [Aphetic form of ATTAINT *v.*]

I. †**1.** *trans.* To convict, prove guilty; = ATTAINT *v.* 3. *Obs.*

c **1375** *Sc. Leg. Saints* xxxi. (*Eugenia*) 603, & þu with þis dede is wele taynt, þat makis na ansuere to þis plant. *c* **1400** MAUNDEV. (Roxb.) xxvi. 122 All thefez and robbours þat er taynted þeroff. *c* **1400** *Destr. Troy* 8109 Now art þou trewly hor traitour, & tainted for fals. *c* **1440** *York Myst.* xxvi. 6 Traytoures tyte will I taynte. **1603** HOLLAND *Plutarch's Mor.* 485 Apollo commanded them, that if they were all tainted with the said murder, they should all depart out of the citie Chios.

†**2.** To prove (a charge); = ATTAINT *v.* 4. *Obs.*

1424 *Sc. Acts Jas. I* (1814) II. 6/1 And quhar it beis tayntyt þt þai [rukis] bige and þe birdis be flowin and þe nestis be fundyn in þe treis at beltane, þe treis salbe forfaltit to þe king.

†**3.** To subject to attainder; = ATTAINT *v.* 6. *Obs.*

1732–8 NEAL *Hist. Purit.* (1822) I. 71 Elizabeth's blood being tainted by act of parliament.

†**4.** To accuse of crime or dishonour; = ATTAINT *v.* 7. *Obs.*

a **1619** FLETCHER *Bonduca* I. i, 'Tis dishonour, And, follow'd, will be impudence, Bonduca, And grow to no belief, to taint these Romans.

II. †**5. a.** To touch, strike, hit; esp. in tilting; = ATTAINT *v.* 1. *Obs.*

1525 LD. BERNERS *Froiss.* II. clxviii. [clxiv.] 470 They ran togider, & tainted eche other on ye helmes, but their speres grated not. **1582** STANYHURST *Æneis* III. (Arb.) 80, I doe liue, I assure thee, thogh dangers sundrye me taynted. **1583** STOCKER *Civ. Warres Lowe C.* IV. 65 b, The Enemie.. tainted fower of them with the Shot of one Harquebouze. **1590** MARLOWE *2nd Pt. Tamburl.* I. iii, Tilting at a glove, Which, when he tainted with his slender rod, He [etc.].

†**b.** To break (a lance, staff) in tilting, etc. *Obs.*

1599 B. JONSON *Every Man out of Hum.* II. i, He can sit a great horse; hee will taint a staffe well at tilt. **1624** MASSINGER *Parl. Love* IV. iii, Do not fear. I have A staff to taint, and bravely.

B. [a. AF. *teinter* (1409–10), f. *teint*, pa. pple. of OF. *teindre* to dye, colour:—L. *tingĕre* to dye, TINGE; cf. ATTAINT, PAINT.]

†**1. a.** *trans.* To colour, dye, tinge. *Obs.*

[**1409–10** *Act 11 Hen. IV*, c. 6 Qe certeins marchantz aliens.. achatent.. Mill draps de blanket fyne, ou pluis, & les font teintrere [*v.r.* teinter] de lour grayn demesne en Scarlet ou Sangwyne.] **1471** RIPLEY *Comp. Alch.* I. vi. in Ashm. *Theatr. Chem. Brit.* (1652) 130 Able to tayne [? taynt] with colour whych wyll not vade. *a* **1533** LD. BERNERS *Huon* cxxxviii. 513 With the blode of ye dede sarasyns theyr swordys were all tayntyd red. **1589** GREENE *Menaphon* (Arb.) 54 At this, the pore swaine tainted his cheeks with a vermillion die. **1725** *Bradley's Fam. Dict.* s.v. *Butter*, As to that [Butter] which they taint with Eel-pouts, besides that it deceives the Sight it is very often disagreeable to the Taste. [*a* **1839** PRAED *Poems* (1864) II. 57 Bid faith and beauty die, and taint Her heart with fraud, her face with paint.]

†**b.** To dip, bathe. *Obs. rare.*

1594 MARLOWE *Dido* I. i, And Phoebus, as in Stygian pools, refrains To taint his tresses in the Tyrrhene main.

†**2.** To apply tincture, balm, or ointment to (a wound, etc.). *Obs.*

1579 LYLY *Euphues* (Arb.) 65 If it be ripe it shalbe lawnced, if it be broken it shalbe tainted. **1580** —— *Euphues & Eng.* (Arb.) 314 Whether dost thou wade Philautus in launcing the wound thou shouldest taint. **1607** TOPSELL *Four-f. Beasts* (1658) 274 If you slit his [a horse's] fore-head, and loosening the skin from the bone, taint it with Turpentine and Sallet-oyl, it will undoubtedly help him. **1639** T. DE GRAY *Compl. Horsem.* 95 Annoynt, wash, bathe and taint (if need be) the sorance.

C. [Senses in which A and B appear to blend.]

1. *trans.* To affect (esp. in a slight degree); to touch, tinge, imbue slightly (usually *with* some bad or undesirable quality).

1591 SHAKS. *1 Hen. VI*, V. iii. 183 A pure vnspotted heart, Neuer yet taint with loue, I send the King. **1593** —— *3 Hen. VI*, III. i. 40 Nero will be tainted with remorse. **1605** R. CAREW in *Lett. Lit. Men* (Camden) 99, I am tainted with a sparcke of Envye. **1710** BERKELEY *Princ. Hum. Knowl.* Pref., Those who are tainted with Scepticism. **1761–2** HUME *Hist. Eng.* lxix. (1806) V. 198 Nowise tainted with enthusiasm. **1850** LYELL *2nd Visit U.S.* II. 115 The French or Spanish creoles here would shrink.. from inter-marriage with one tainted, in the slightest degree, with African blood. **1884** *Law Rep. 26 Ch. Div.* 124 It does not follow that all the subsequent payments were tainted with the original infirmity.

†**2. a.** To affect injuriously; to cause detriment to; to hurt, injure, impair. *Obs.*

1601 SHAKS. *Twel. N.* III. iv. 13 Sure the man is tainted in's wits. *a* **1623** BEAUMONT *Ode Blessed Trin.* ii, No cold shall thee benumme, Nor darknesse taint thy sight.

†**b.** To sully, stain, tarnish (a person's honour).

1613 SHAKS. *Hen. VIII*, III. i. 56 We come not by the way of Accusation, To taint that honour euery good Tongue blesses. **1710** STEELE *Tatler* No. 182 ¶1 Any Occasion which he thinks may taint his own Honour. **1722** —— *Conscious Lovers* IV. i, The honour of a Gentleman is liable to be tainted by as small a Matter as the Credit of a Trader.

†**3. a.** To affect with weakness; to cause to lose vigour or courage. *Obs.*

1600 HOLLAND *Livy* XXVIII. xv. 679 [They] being thus tainted, as well in courage of heart, as in bodily strength, gave ground and reculed. *c* **1611** CHAPMAN *Iliad* XIII. 449 Fear taints me worthily, Though firm I stand, and show it not.

†**b.** *intr.* To lose vigour or courage; to become weak or faint; to wither, fade. *Obs.*

1605 SHAKS. *Macb.* V. iii. 3 Till Byrnane wood remoue to Dunsinane, I cannot taint with Feare. **1639** HORN & ROB. *Gate Lang. Unl.* xi. §106 Failing of that moisture it flags, tainteth (withereth), and by and by drieth away.

4. a. *trans.* To infect with pernicious, noxious, corrupting or deleterious qualities; to touch with putrefaction; to corrupt, contaminate, deprave.

1573 *Durham Deposit.* (Surtees) 252 The said Bell is a great lyer, and taintyd of his tounge. **1592** SHAKS. *Rom. & Jul.* I. iv. 75 Ladies lips.. Which oft the angry Mab with blisters plagues, Because their breath with Sweet meats tainted are. **1602** MARSTON *Antonio's Rev.* II. ii, Why tainst thou then the ayre with stench of flesh? **1667** MILTON *P.L.* XII. 512 The truth With superstitions and traditions taint. **1770** *Junius Lett.* xxxviii. (1820) 186 The poison of their doctrines has tainted the natural benevolence of his disposition. **1861** THACKERAY *Four Georges* ii. (1862) 116 One.. who tainted a great society by a bad example.

b. *intr.* To become putrefied, corrupted, or rotten; to tarnish.

1601 SHAKS. *Twel. N.* III. iv. 145 Nay pursue him now, least the deuice take ayre, and taint. **1637** T. MORTON *New Eng. Canaan* (1883) 117 Fish and Flesh both will taint in those partes, notwithstanding the use of Salt. **1641** H. L'ESTRANGE *God's Sabbath* 26 The putrefaction which Manna contracted by procrastination on other dayes.. was the greater miracle.. because it tainted against nature. **1766** *Museum Rust.* III. 239 The natural humidity of the plant.. which sometimes.. is retained so long as to cause the heads to taint, and become rotten.

c. *trans.* To drive *out* (rabbits) from their burrows by the introduction of an offensive smell.

1909 O. JONES *Ten Years Game-Keeping* ii. 22 Gipsies are a help to the keeper.. when he has a difficulty in tainting out a colony of rabbits. **1972** *Young's Sporting Appliances* (S. Young & Sons Ltd.) II. 13 Proved to be best after exhaustive tests over many years for tainting out rabbits to lie out for shooting.

Hence **'tainting** *vbl. sb.* and *ppl. a.*

1593 NASHE *Foure Lett. Confut.* Wks. (Grosart) II. 220 Yet tainting is no infamous surgerie for him that hath beene in so many hote skirmishes. **1598** FLORIO, *Macca*, a bruse, a spot, a tainting. **1611** SHAKS. *Cymb.* I. iv. 148 If you buy Ladies flesh at a Million a Dram, you cannot preserue it from tainting. **1632** *Star Chamb. Cases* (Camden) 109 These words were very foule and dishonorable: it is a tainting of all honor. **1842** MANNING *Serm.* xi. (1848) I. 156 All the tainting, stupifying power of its original sin.

'taint (teɪnt), *v.*[2] Also **taint, t'ain't**, etc. Dial. and vulg. contraction of *it ain't*: see AIN'T *v.*; 'T.

1839 [see SNUM *v.*]. **1859** A. J. SYMONDS *Let.* Sept. (1967) I. 206 You will think I am fallen desperately in love. Yet it taint so. **1919** W. DEEPING *Second Youth* xxiii. 194 'Taint like 'im. 'E used to be sensible. **1942** Z. N. HURSTON in A. Dundes *Mother Wit* (1973) 225/1 'T'ain't nothing to you, nohow. **1974** H. R. F. KEATING *Underside* viii. 77 'I'm sure whatever they say's undeserved.' 'No, t'ain't. You ninny.'

taint, obs. variant of TENT *sb.*

taintable ('teɪntəb(ə)l), *a.* [f. TAINT *v.*[1] + -ABLE.] Liable to taint or be tainted.

1864 BLACKMORE *Clara Vaughan* xxxii, We got all that was taintable into the little yard.

tainted ('teɪntɪd), *ppl. a.* [f. TAINT *v.*[1] + -ED[1].]

1. Stained, tinged; contaminated, infected, corrupted; touched with putrefaction or incipient decay; affected with some corrupting influence.

1577 B. GOOGE *Heresbach's Husb.* I. (1586) 43 He thinkes it better to let that [corn] alone that is alredy corrupted, and .. when so euer ye neede to occupie it, to take away that is taynted, and to vse the rest. *a* **1619** FLETCHER, etc. *Knt. Malta* IV. ii, Treason and tainted thoughts are all the gods Thou worship'dst. **1630** B. JONSON *New Inn* II. ii, *Host*... And speakes a little taynted, fly-blowne Latin, After the Schoole. *Bea.* Of Stratford o' the Bow. For Lillies Latine, is to him vnknow. **1709** SWIFT *Adv. Relig.* Wks. 1755 II. I. 99 Women of tainted reputations. **1712** ADDISON *Hymn*, '*How are Thy Servants blest*', Thro' burning Climes I pass'd unhurt, And breath'd in tainted Air. **1821** WORDSW. *Sonn.*, *Virgin*, Woman! above all women glorified, Our tainted nature's solitary boast. **1837** M. DONOVAN *Dom. Econ.* II. 243 In what manner charcoal boiled with tainted meat can affect the interior. **1883** SIR W. B. BRETT in *Law Rep. 11 Q. Bench Div.* 454 That these statements were tainted evidence, because they came from accomplices.

b. Having a taint of disease; infected with latent disease. Cf. TAINT *sb.* C. 2 b.

1596 SHAKS. *Merch. V.* IV. i. 114, I am a tainted Weather of the flocke, Meetest for death. **1697** DRYDEN *Virg. Past.* I. 70 Nor fear a Rott from tainted Company. **1897** *Allbutt's Syst. Med.* II. 924 Children of parents engaged in the manufacture of matches and tainted with phosphorism.

2. Imbued with the scent of an animal (usually a hunted animal). (Cf. BLEMISH *sb.* 4.) *Obs.* or *arch.*

1704 ADDISON *Campaign* 122 So the stanch Hound the trembling Deer Pursues, And smells his footsteps in the tainted dews. **1732** POPE *Ess. Man* I. 214 What modes.. Of smell, the headlong lioness between, And hound sagacious on the tainted green. **1810** SCOTT *Lady of L.* I. ii, [The stag] A moment snuffed the tainted gale.

†**3.** Tinted, stained. *Obs. rare.*

1797 *Encycl. Brit.* (ed. 3) XIII 715/2 They also use a kind of paper for drawing, which is called tainted paper.

tainter, *sb.* and *v.*, obs. f. TENTER.

taint-hook, obs. f. TENT-HOOK.

tainting: see under TAINT *v.*

taintingly (in Shaks.): see TAUNTINGLY.

taintless ('teɪntlɪs), *a.* Chiefly *poet.* [f. TAINT *sb.* + -LESS.] Free from taint; without stain or blemish; immaculate, clean, pure, innocent.

1590 MARLOWE *2nd Pt. Tamburl.* IV. i, To flesh our taintless swords. **1602** MARSTON *Antonio's Rev.* IV. iii, Heaven permits not taintlesse bloode be spilt. **1776** MICKLE tr. *Camoens' Luisad* 333 His loyalty as taintless snow. **1863** KINGSLEY *Water-Babies* i. 44 To the golden sands, and the leaping bar, And the taintless tide that awaits me afar. **1893** in Barrows *Parl. Relig.* I. 725 A pure, taintless, lofty, elevating.. faith.

Hence **'taintlessly** *adv.*, without taint; **'taintlessness**, the quality of being taintless.

1811 SHELLEY *Let.* 26 Nov. (1964) I. 144 The first words you spoke to me.. are eternal earnests of your taintlessness and sincerity. **1846** WORCESTER, Taintlessly. **1963** *English Studies* XLIV. 22 Taintlessness and incorruptibility seem to depend not so much on the predominance of blood stains as on out-look.

'taintment. *rare.* [f. TAINT *v.*[1] + -MENT.]

†**1.** = ATTAINTMENT, ATTAINT. *Obs.*

1613 T. GODWIN *Rom. Antiq.* (1658) 217 Taintments of treason against any person of state.

2. Contamination, defiling tincture.

1633 T. ADAMS *Exp. 2 Peter* ii. 14 That is a rare eye.. that can mingle itself with sordid corruptions, and receive no taintment.

taintor, -our. [Agent-n. from TAINT *v.*[1]]

†**1.** [Cf. TAINT *v.*[1] A.] One who brings legal evidence against another for conviction of some crime; an accuser, informer. *Obs.*

1451 *Sc. Acts Jas. II* (1814) II. 40/2 þat na man haf out of þe Realme gold bulȝeone or siluer vnder þe payn of escheite þareof, þe tane half to þe king & þe toþir half to þe tayntour & þe takar.

2. [a. AF. *teintour* = OF. *teintor, -ur, -eur.*] A dyer. *rare.*

1889 MCANALLY in *Pop. Sci. Monthly* Oct. 812 The cloth .. finished and ready for the Dyer, Litter, or Lister, or the Norman Taintor or Taintur.

tainture ('teɪntjʊə(r)). Now *rare*. Also 5–7 taynt-, 6–7 tainct-.

I. [a. OF. *tainture, teinture* colouring (13th c.), ad. L. *tinctūra* dyeing, TINCTURE; in sense 2 as in TAINT *v.*[1] C.] †**1.** Colouring. *Obs.*

1490 CAXTON *Eneydos* vi. 24 We wryte the grete and firste capytall lettres.. wyth the taynture of reed coloure.

2. Tainting, staining, stain, defilement, infection.

1593 SHAKS. *2 Hen. VI*, II. i. 188 Gloster, see here the Taincture of thy Nest, And looke thy selfe be faultlesse, thou wert best. **1609** RAWLINSON *Fishermen* 11 To keepe it from the corruption and tainture of sin. **1634** T. JOHNSON tr. *Parey's Chirurg.* XVIII. ix. (1678) 419 There are.. three distinct causes of gout: A tainture from the Parents [etc.]. **1645** USSHER *Body Div.* (1647) 126 It shining in him without tainture or blemish. **1681** RYCAUT tr. *Gracian's Critick* 227 Others have always retained some tainture and favour of their former condition. **1854** *Fraser's Mag.* L. 667 Who Neerland's blood feel nobly flow, From foreign tainture free.

II. †**3.** Aphetic form of ATTAINTURE. *Obs.*

1621 G. SANDYS tr. *Ovid's Met.* I. (1626) 20 Asham'd that such a tainture should be lay'd Vpon my blood, that could not be gayn-said.

'taint-worm. *arch.* [f. TAINT *sb.* + WORM.] A worm or crawling larva supposed to taint or infect cattle, etc.: cf. TAINT *sb.* C. 3.

1573 TUSSER *Husb.* (1878) 150 Doo taint wormes good, that lurke where ox should eat? **1637** MILTON *Lycidas* 46 As killing as the Canker to the Rose, Or Taint-worm to the weanling Herds that graze. **1840** BROWNING *Sordello* VI. 158 Study the corpse-face thro' the taint-worms' scurf.

‖**tai-otoshi** (taɪo'tɒʃi). *Judo.* Also Taiotoshi, tai-o-toshi, etc. [Jap., f. *tai* body + *otoshi* the act of dropping.] The body drop throw.

1950 E. J. HARRISON *Judo* iii. 39 The most suitable moment for attempting the Taiotoshi is when your opponent with unbent legs, his body somewhat stiff, has leaned forward a little with his weight resting on his right leg. **1957** TAKAGAKI & SHARP *Techniques Judo* iii. 24 If *tai-otoshi* fails and the opponent pulls back. **1964** LEGGETT & WATANABE (*title*) Championship judo: tai-otoshi and o-uchi-gan attacks. **1978** D. STARBROOK *Judo* iv. 40/2 The tai-o-toshi is a hand throw, and its great advantage over so many other throws is that it can be performed against opponents who are either stationary or moving.

taipan[1] ('taɪpæn). Also 9 taepan, typan. [Dial. var. of Chinese *dàbān*.] **a.** A foreign merchant or businessman in China. **b.** The (foreign) manager or head of a firm in China, esp. Hong Kong. Also *fig.* Hence **'taipanism.**

1834 *Canton Reg.* 28 Oct. 170/2 The election of a temporary Chief for the Superintendence of British affairs, until the appointment of one from England, who must be a *taepan* or Merchant, as before and not a Government Officer. **1892** in K. Lentzner *Dict. Slang-English Austral.* 91 My *typan* must make fun of me, When all his crowd can see —Ah! well, perhaps they do not care For a little clerk like me. **1921** *North-China Herald* 24 Dec. 815/1 What is 'Taipanism as seen in China', which Mr. Ku discusses in a recent issue of the 'Evening Standard'?.. Mr. Ku finds that 'Taipanism' is the spirit of respect for the sacred rights of property and vested interest. **1922** W. S. MAUGHAM *On Chinese Screen* xv. 63 With the elderly, but single, taipan of an important firm, what she simply loved was a game of golf. **1957** R. MASON *World of Suzie Wong* I. i. 9 Chinese taipans, who made the richest Europeans seem like paupers. **1972** *Times* 21 Oct. (Hongkong Suppl.) p. i/4 Opium can no longer be indulged in as it was with restraint by the *taipans*, or merchants, in old Shanghai. **1977** W. TUTE *Cairo Sleeper* i. 14 Ambassadors..mingled with other taipans of the higher civil service... Most members of the club worked in Whitehall. **1983** *Sunday Tel.* 10 Apr. 20/6 The Keswicks of Dumfries married into the Jardines in the middle of the last century. Four of them, including Henry, became *taipan* or head of the house.

taipan[2] ('taɪpæn). Also **Taipan.** [Aboriginal name.] A large dark brown venomous snake, *Oxyuranus scutellatus*, of the family Elapidæ, native to northern parts of Australia.

1933 D. F. THOMSON in *Proc. Zool. Soc.* 858 The name 'taipan', by which *O. scutellatus* is known to the aborigines of Cape York Peninsula, is an excellent vernacular name for the species. *Ibid.*, The taipan frequents the open country of the coast, as well as the inland plains and savannah forests. **1953** P. BRICKHILL in I. Bevan *Sunburnt Country* 96 The long-fanged taipan..grows eleven feet long, and nearly as thick as a man's arm... Only two men are known to have survived a taipan bite. **1966** G. DURRELL *Two in Bush* v. 159 To have kept and bred something as rare and shy as a Taipan is a very great triumph. **1982** *Daily Tel.* 18 Feb. 3/1 A western taipan—one of the world's deadliest snakes—was bitten by a mouse and is fighting for its life in the Darwin Museum, Australia.

‖**Tai-ping** (taɪpɪŋ). Also Taë-ping. [Chinese *T'ai-p'ing*, i.e. *t'ai* great, *p'ing* peace.] The name given to the adherents of a great rebellion which arose in Southern China in 1850, under the leadership of Hung-siu-tsuen, styled *Tien-wang*, Heavenly Prince, and *T'ai-p'ing-wang*, Prince of great peace, who claimed a divine commission to overthrow the Manchu dynasty and establish one of native origin, to be called the *T'ai-p'ing Chao* or Great Peace Dynasty. Also *attrib.* Hence **Tai-pingdom, Tai-pingism.**

The war which ensued devastated some of the most fertile provinces of China for a number of years; partly by means of English help the Tai-pings were finally routed and dispersed in 1865.

1853 *North-China Herald* 7 May 158/1 'Conquering the rivers and mountains', the expression by which the 'holy warriors' of Tae-ping designate their enterprise. **1860** *All Year Round* No. 71. 504 A Taiping's head is paid for, at the rate of one tael. *Ibid.*, He succeeded in forcing back the Taipings when they menaced the Pekin Canal. *Ibid.*, Of these alternatives, piracy pays the best, Taipingism being decidedly the least lucrative. **1883** *Chambers's Encycl.* IX. 274/1 The confusion and expense of the Tae-ping rebellion. **1884** A. FORBES *Chinese Gordon* xi, The Imperialist generals had hemmed Tai-pingdom within certain limits in the lower valley of the Yantsze.

‖**taipo** ('taɪpəʊ). *N.Z.* Also **taepo, Taipo, typo.** [Origin uncertain: see quots. 1891, 1946.]

1. An evil spirit.

1848 R. TAYLOR *Leaf from Nat. Hist. N.Z.* 43 (Morris), *Taipo*, female dreamer; a prophetess; an evil spirit. **1883** W. COLENSO in E. E. Morris *Austral Eng.* (1898) 454/2 Taepo means to visit or come by night,—a night visitant,—a spectral thing seen in dreams,—a fancied and feared thing, or hobgoblin. **1886** *N.Z. Country Jrnl.* X. 262 His wife became seriously affected, declaring that *Taipo* had entered into her. **1891** E. TREGEAR *Maori-Polynesian Comparative Dict.* 440/1 *Taepo*, a goblin, a spectre. Cf. *tae*, to arrive; *po*, night. **1921** H. GUTHRIE-SMITH *Tutira* xi. 91 This crossing has always been known in my time as the 'Taipo'—goblin—crossing, a name probably given because of a totara block which used to lie there hewn roughly to the similitude of a man's head. **1946** *Jrnl. Polynesian Soc.* June 150 *Taipo*, supernatural being; goblin: used by the Maori believing it to be Pakeha, and by the Pakeha believing it to be Maori; often spelt taepo, which also is not a Maori word: so taipo is a word coined by no one knows whom. **1968** *N.Z. Listener* 15 Mar 6/5 He hurriedly looked both ways and took to the scrub as if a taipo were after him. **1971** *Ibid.* 1 Mar. 13/2 As for dreaded taniwhas and taipos, why, I could take you to the home of some.

2. = WETA.

1928 J. DEVANNY *Dawn Beloved* I. vii. 47 The very apogee of excitement would be reached when a 'typo' was discovered. Especially if it happened to be a big fat male. **1946** F. SARGESON *That Summer* 176 But the wetas come out at night... The Maoris call them taipos. **1966** *Encycl. N.Z.* III. 636/2 The tree or ground wetas and the 'taipos' of the West Coast of the South Island, the name of which to the Maori means 'the devil who comes by night'.

tair, obs. Sc. f. TEAR *v.*

taira, var. TAYRA, a Brazilian weasel-like animal.

tairge, obs. and dial. f. TARGE.

tairn, obs. f. TARN.

tairoa, var. TOHEROA.

tais, obs. Sc. f. TASS, *takes* (see TAKE *v.*), *toes* (pl. of TOE).

tais, -e, var. TEISE *sb.* and *v. Obs.*

‖**taisch, taish** (taɪʃ). *Gaelic Folklore.* [a. Gaelic *taibhs* (taivʃ, taiʃ):—OIr. *taidbse*, MIr. *tadhbais*, phantasm.] The phantom or apparition of a living person who is about to die; also, in more general sense, a phantom or vision of second sight.

1775 JOHNSON *Western Isles, Ostig*, By the term *second sight*, seems to be meant a mode of seeing, superadded to that which nature generally bestows. In the Erse it is called *Taisch*; which signifies likewise a spectre, or a vision. **1785** BOSWELL *Tour to Hebrides* 7 Sept., Some women said to him, they had heard two taischs, that is, two voices of persons about to die; and what was remarkable, one of them was an English taisch, which they never heard before. **1792** *Statist. Acc. Scotl., Ross* III. 380 The ghosts of the dying, called *tasks*, are said to be heard, their cry being a repetition of the moans of the sick... The corps follow the tract led by the tasks to the place of interment. [Here *task* appears to be Gael. *tasg* 'ghost', erroneously taken in sense of *taibhs*, taisch.] **1902** J. G. CAMPBELL *Witchcraft & Second Sight* 159 Some time after [the taïsh was seen] a ship was wrecked in the east end of Tiree, and one of the sailors whose dress, when his body was found, corresponded to that of the taish, was taken and buried in Kirkapool.

taisel, taissel, obs. and Sc. ff. TASSEL.

taishes, taisses: see TASSE, thigh-armour.

taist, taister, obs. Sc. ff. TASTE, TESTER.

tait, Sc. variant of TATE.

†**tait,** *a. ME.* and *Sc. Obs.* Also 4 **teyte, tayt.** [a. ON. *teitr* glad, cheerful, corresp. to a doubtful OE. *tǽtan* to gladden, cheer, from an adj. **tát*, and in form to OHG., MHG. *zeiz* tender, dear, pleasing.] Cheerful, lively, active, nimble.

c **1300** *Havelok* 1841 þe laddes were kaske and teyte. **13..** *E.E. Allit. P.* B. 871, I schal biteche yow þo two þat tayt arn & quoynt. **13..** *Gaw. & Gr. Knt.* 1377 Techez hym to þe tayles of ful tayt bestes. *c* **1470** HENRYSON *Mor. Fab.* VII. (*Lion & Mouse*) xiii, Sua come ane trip of myis out of thair nest, Richt tait and trig. **1500–20** DUNBAR *Poems* xiv. 49 Ouir all the gait sa mony thevis sa tait. **1513** DOUGLAS *Æneis* XII. Prol. 184 Litill lammis Full tait and trig socht bletand to thar dammis.

tait (teɪt), *sb. Austral.* [Aboriginal name.] = *honey possum* s.v. HONEY *sb.* (*a.*) 7.

1894 R. LYDEKKER *Hand-bk. Marsupialia* 121 Known to the natives by the name of Tait, and Nulbenger, the Long-snouted Phalanger..is generally found..from Swan River to King George's Sound. **1941** E. TROUGHTON *Furred Animals Austral.* 81 The quaint little animal had quite a variety of names in the native vocabularies.., the one favoured as a popular name being 'Noolbenger', and others including 'Ait' [*sic*] and 'Deed'.

†**taite.** *Obs.* Also 4 **tayt.** [a. ON. *teiti* gladsomeness, joy, cheerfulness, f. *teitr* adj.: see TAIT *a.*] Gladness, alacrity.

13.. *E.E. Allit. P.* B. 889 þenne vch tolke ty3t hem þat hade of tayt fayled, & vchon roþeled to þe rest þat he reche mo3t. *a* **1400–50** *Alexander* 1208 þus 3ede þai furthe..And trottes on toward Tyre with taite [*v.r.* ioy] at þaire hertis.

taith, variant of TATH *sb.* and TATHE *v.*

Taittinger (tatɛ̃ʒe). Also *erron.* Tattinger. The proprietary name of a champagne manufactured and shipped by the firm of Taittinger in Rheims.

1949 *Trade Marks Jrnl.* 6 Apr. 304 Taittinger... Champagne. Etablissements Taittinger Mailly & Cie (a Societe Anonyme organised under the laws of France). **1964** A. LAUNAY *Caviare & After* xv. 106 Unlike other wines, Champagne is known under the name of the shipper... The best known are Boulinger..., Pommery, Taittinger and Veuve Clicquot. **1967** A. ARENT *Gravedigger's Funeral* xii. 189, I will buy you a jereboam of Tattinger. **1971** R. TEMPLE *Schulsinger Affair* i. 12 A bottle of Taittinger Blanc de Blancs, well iced. **1978** R. B. PARKER *Judas Goat* xii. 77 Hawk had filled the sink with ice and put..another bottle of Taittinger champagne in to chill. **1978** D. A. STANWOOD *Memory of Eva Ryker* xxv. 238 A magnum of Tattinger '05.

taiver, taivert, var. TAVER, TAVERT.

Taiwanese (taɪwə'ni:z), *sb.* and *a.* [f. *Taiwan*, the name of a large island off the south-east coast of China + -ESE.] **A.** *sb.* A native or inhabitant of Taiwan. **B.** *adj.* Of or pertaining to the island of Taiwan or its inhabitants.

1942 A. J. GRAJDANZEV *Formosa Today* iv. 53 A rise in the price of Taiwanese rice. *Ibid.* vi. 86 The Taiwanese are a fish-eating people. **1962** E. SNOW *Other Side of River* (1963) lxxi. 549 People talk about giving the Taiwanese a plebiscite on whether they want to join China or not. **1969** *Times* 9 Dec. (Taiwan Suppl.) p. v/8 Sixty-three per cent of local government officials are natives of Taiwan. All local magistrates are Taiwanese. **1970** D. DODGE *Hatchetman* i. 22 We've got Army liaison..Taiwanese liaison, British liaison, Old China hands. *Ibid.* ix. 109 Attempts have been made on my life before, but by Taiwanese; my people, not yours. **1978** *Chicago* June 225/1 The simple storefront does a great job with a menu that includes..unusual Taiwanese squid and cuttlefish dishes. **1979** *Pacific Affairs* LII. 455 There was almost no contact between Red Army units and Taiwanese in this period.

taj (tɑ:dʒ). Also tuj. [Arab. (Pers.) *tāj* crown.] A crown or head-dress of distinction (see also quot. 1877).

1851 *Illustr. Catal. Gt. Exhib.* IV. i. 918/2 Crown, or tuj, as worn by the King of Oude; without jewels. **1877** *Encycl. Brit.* VII. 113/2 The táj, or white cap, with the proper number of terks, or sections, belonging to the order [of dervishes]. **1886** J. ATKINSON tr. *Firdausi's Sháh Námeh* 92 He also gave him a taj, or crown of gold, which kings only were accustomed to wear.

Taj: see TAJ MAHAL a.

tajaçu, tajassu: see TAYASSU.

Tajik (tɑ:'dʒi:k), *sb.* and *a.* Also **Tadjik, Tadzhik,** etc. [a. Pers. *tājik* one who is neither an Arab nor a Turk, a Persian.] **A.** *sb.* **a.** A people of Iranian descent inhabiting Afghanistan and the Turkistan region of Central Asia; now also *spec.* a native or inhabitant of the Tajik S.S.R. **b.** The Persian dialect spoken by this people. **B.** *adj.* Of, pertaining to, or designating this people.

1815 [see HINDKI]. **1836** *Penny Cycl.* V. 71/2 The Tadjicks consider themselves as the aborigines of the country [*sc.* Bokhara], and as the descendants of the ancient Sogdi and Bactrians. **1871**, etc. [see SART *sb.*[2] and *a.*]. **1911** *Encycl. Brit.* XXVI. 365/1 The Tajik population of the richly-cultivated districts north of Kabul. **1920** *Christian World* 26 Aug. 9/2 The fanatical Tadjiks and Sarts of that portion of Turkestan. **1949** F. MACLEAN *Eastern Approaches* I. x. 152, I had no sooner got to sleep than they dug me in the ribs and introduced themselves as Tajiks. **1953** O. CAROE *Soviet Empire* iii. 33 With sedentary and town populations speaking Tajik it can as safely be accepted that they are of Iranian stock-origin. **1959** E. H. CARR *Socialism in One Country* II. xx. 268 The Tajik population, the only non-Turki-speaking group in the area. **1964** H. H. PAPER tr. *Shafeev's Short Gram. Outl. Pashto* 1 Until 1936 the official language of Afghanistan was Kabuli, one of the dialects of Tajik. **1970** *Times* 24 Mar. 7/1 The least emancipated women seem to be found among the Tadjiks, an Iranian people living in the wild mountainous regions at the Soviet Union's extreme south-eastern tip. **1974** *Listener* 17 Oct. 494/2 Travelling through the Hindu Kush..with three Tajik tribesmen. **1977** YIN MING *United & Equal* 4 There is hardly any place along China's long border without its communities of minority nationalities. Among them are.. the Kazakhs, Uighurs, Khalkhas and Tajiks in Sin Kiang. **1978** *Times* 18 Oct. 16/8 [In] Uzbekistan..many..speak Tadzhik..and other Asian languages. **1979** A. HENNING tr. *Myrdal's Silk Road* i. 5 Our hosts..are Tadzhiks... This is the Tashkurghan Tadzhik Autonomous County in the far west of China. *Ibid.* 8 We are sitting on the starkly beautiful, thick, Tadzhik carpet of felted wool. **1980** G. RICHARDS *Red Kill* xxv. 204 Children had come from all corners of the Soviet Union... Azerbaijanis, Tadjiks, Ukrainians.

Taj Mahal (tɑ:dʒ, tɑ:ʒ mə'hɑ:l). [perh. a corruption of *Mumtaz Mahal* (see below) under the influence of TAJ; cf. MAHAL.] The name of a mausoleum built at Agra by Shah Jahan in memory of his wife known as Mumtaz (Pers. 'chosen one') Mahal (d. 1631), used: **a.** *ellipt.* as **Taj.**

1858 W. H. RUSSELL *Diary* 14 Oct. (1860) II. 279, I had seen that Pearl of architecture, the wonder of the world—The Taj of Agra. **1887** KIPLING *Lett. of Marque* (1891) i. 2 He saw from the train the Taj wrapped in the mists of the morning. **1912** E. LUTYENS *Let.* May in M. Lutyens *Edwin Lutyens* (1980) vii. 104 The Taj and some other of the tombs have charm. **1978** 'M. M. KAYE' *Far Pavilions* xiv. 225 Shah Jehan's Empress the lady of the Taj.

b. *fig.* denoting that which is excellent or surpassing of its kind. Also occas. in *transf.* use.

1895 *Q. Rev.* Apr. 353 Stevenson has set up and decorated with every precious stone a building so magnificent, that it deserves to be called the Taj Mahal of our prose literature. **1950** PARTRIDGE *Name into Word* 429 One not seldom meets with such phrases as 'the Taj Mahal of architectural elegance' or 'the Taj Mahal of romantic architecture'. **1980** D. POWNALL *Between Ribble & Lune* i. 20 In 1906..his lordship ordered the structure as a Taj Mahal for his dead wife.

taka ('tɑ:kə). Also **Taka**; pl. (-s). [Bengali *ṭākā.*] The basic monetary unit of Bangladesh, equivalent to one hundred paise; also, a banknote of this value.

Quot. 1975 illustrates the idiomatic use of *taka* with *crore* (= 10 million).

1972 *Guardian* 22 Aug. 10/4 The Bangladesh taka, officially at par with the Indian rupee, is being freely offered ..at 40 per cent discount. **1975** *Bangladesh Times* 21 July 1/3 He said if the factory could produce..30,000 tons of pulp annually that would meet the home demand as well as fetch about Taka six crore in foreign exchange by exporting pulp abroad. To meet with home demand..Bangladesh now had to import pulp worth seven to eight crore Taka annually. **1976** M. S. HOQUE *Hunger* I. i. 7 Nuribow opens the knot at the corner of her sari, takes a Taka therefrom and pays. **1976** *Sci. Amer.* Oct. 32/1–2 (*caption*) The Bengali writing offers a '250-taka prize' (about $17) to anyone who reports a smallpox case to a health office. **1979** *Church Times* 26 Oct. 13/1 Until two years ago, the family's income consisted entirely of Appavo's wage—a princely thirty takas a week (about a pound).

takable: see TAKEABLE.

Taka-diastase (tækə'daɪəsteɪz). Also **taka-.** [f. the name of J. Jokichi *Taka(mine* (1854–1922), Japanese-born biochemist and industrialist + DIASTASE.] A preparation containing a variety of enzymes which is obtained after the treatment of rice or bran with the mould *Aspergillus oryzæ*; now a proprietary name.

1896 *Jrnl. Amer. Med. Assoc.* XXVII. 374 Notes on taka-diastase. **1928** [see PYROPHOSPHATASE]. **1928** *Official Gaz.* (U.S. Patent Office) 6 Nov. 10/2 Takamine Ferment Company, New York... *Taka-diastase...* For koji, moyashi, diastase, ferments, and converting agents. Claims use since 1895. **1955** *Trade Marks Jrnl.* 9 Mar. 258/2 *Taka-diastase...* Diastase for pharmaceutical purposes. **1960** [see

KOJI]. **1969** G. SMITH *Introd. Industr. Mycology* xv. 312 Takamine introduced into commerce..products of high enzymic activity, particularly suitable for the dextrination of starch and the desizing of textiles. These products have been sold under the names 'Taka-diastase'..and 'Oryzyme'. **1976** *Ann. Rev. Microbiol.* XXX. 8 During our studies of adenylate deaminase, we observed that the enzyme from Takadiastase..would deaminate approximately 50% of the adenylate added to the reaction vessel.

takahe ('tɑːkəhiː, ‖'takahe). Also Takahe. [Maori.] = NOTORNIS.

1851 G. MANTELL *Petrifactions* ii. 128 No one had seen such a bird, but all agreed that it was the traditional Moho or Takahé, which they believed was utterly extinct. **1898** *Daily News* 22 Oct. 2/2 The other day a specimen of the takahe..was found in the South Island. **1915** *Chambers's Jrnl.* May 318/2 There are the flightless kiwi, weka, and kakapo parrot; also the very rare takahe. **1966** G. DURRELL *Two in Bush* iii. 103 Then, quite suddenly, from behind a large clump of snow grass, a Takahe appeared... I was imagining something about the size of an English Moorhen ..but there stood a bird the size of a large turkey. **1978** *Nature* 9 Feb. 507/2 Take, for example, the takahe (*Notornis mantelli*), a flightless gallinule endemic to New Zealand.

Takali, var. TAKULLI.

takapu ('tɑːkapʊ). *N.Z.* [Maori.] The Australian gannet, *Sula serrator*.

1842 W. COLENSO in N. M. Taylor *Early Travellers N.Z.* (1959) 54 The natives often take this bird... They call it Takapu. **1882** W. L. BULLER *Man. N.Z. Birds* 91 (*heading*) Gannet. Takapu. **1966** R. A. FALLA *Field Guide Birds N.Z.* 60 Australian Gannet..Local name: Takapu... Mainly white, crown and nape pastel yellow.

takar: see TAKER.

Takayasu (‖taka'jasu). *Path.* [The name of Michishige *Takayasu* (1872–1938), Japanese ophthalmologist, who described the disease in 1908.] *Takayasu's disease*: a chronic arteritis leading to obstruction of blood-flow, esp. in the vessels arising from the aortic arch; pulseless disease.

1952 *Amer. Heart Jrnl.* XLIV. 629 Pulseless or Takayasu's disease is considered by Japanese ophthalmologists to be a rare but definite clinical entity. **1969** EDINGTON & GILLES *Path. in Tropics* viii. 335 At one time Takayasu's disease was thought to affect only young females and the pathological lesions to be restricted to the aortic arch and its major branches. **1978** *Central African Jrnl. Med.* XXIV 144/2 Takayasu's disease (pulseless disease) is a disease of unknown ætiology first described in Japan.

take (teɪk), *v.* Pa. t. took (tʊk); pa. pple. taken ('teɪk(ə)n). Forms: see below. [Late OE. *tacan*, *tóc*, **tacen*, a. ON. *taka*, *tók*, *tekinn* (OSw. *taka*, Sw. *taga*, Da. *tage*), to grasp, grip, seize, lay hold of, take, which appears *c* 1100, in late parts of the OE. Chron., first in MS. D, and then *a* 1150 also in E, and elsewhere, but may have been in use in the Dane-law district *a* 1000. In ME. it gradually superseded the OE. *niman* (see NIM *v.*), and has been, during the later ME. and the whole mod.Eng. period, the simplest and most direct word for the general notion expressed by Da. *tage*, Sw. *taga*, Ger. *nehmen*, Du. *nemen*, Fr. *prendre*, It. *prendere*, Sp., Pg. *tomar*, L. *capĕre*, *sumĕre*, Gr. λαμβάνειν, Russ. *brat'*, *vzyat'*, Heb. *lāqaχ*, etc. ON. *taka* was app. cognate with MDu. and mod.EFris. *tāken* to lay hold of, grasp, seize, catch; it was also in ablaut-relation to Goth. *têkan*, *taitôk*, *têkans* to touch (with the hands, etc.). With the sense in Gothic cf. ON. *taka á*, late OE. *tacan on* to touch.]

A. Illustration of Forms and Inflexions.

Take is, like *shake*, *forsake*, a strong vb. of the 6th ablaut series. In northern ME. the *k* and following short vowel in *take*, *takes*, *taken* were often suppressed, leaving the forms *ta*, *tas*, *tan*, of which *ta*, *tay*, survives in Eng. dialects, *tane* in Sc. and many Eng. dialects, *ta'en* in Eng. poets. The reduction of the pa. t. to *tō* is obs., rare, and doubtful. A weak pa. t. *taked* occurs from 13th c., and is, with *tayed*, *teaed*, *tade*, still dialectal. For the pa. pple *taken*, the pa. t. *took* has been common since 16th c. in vulgar speech and in dialects, which have also *tooken*, *tooked*. In the pa. pple., *ton(e* for the northern *tan(e* occasionally appears. See *Eng. Dial. Dict.*

1. *Infin.*, and *Pres.* α. 2 tacan (tæcen), 3–5 taken, -yn; 4 tac, 4–5 (6– *Sc.*) tak, 5 taake, 6 taik(e, *Sc.* tack; 3– take.

c **1100** *O.E. Chron.* an. 1076 (MS. D) Ac se kyngc.. hine let syððan tacan. *a* **1154** *Ibid.* an. 1140 On þis gær wolde þe king Stephne tæcen Rodbert. *a* **1272** *Luue Ron* 64 in *O.E. Misc.* 95 Al deþ hit wile from him take. **13..** *K. Alis.* 1799 (Bodl. MS.) Þat he shulde of þe werlde & þee Taken tol. **13..** *Cursor M.* 568 (Cott.) Þe god to tak and leue þe ill. *Ibid.* 2812 (Gött.) His mohwes..þat suld his dohutris tac. *c* **1380** WYCLIF *Wks.* (1880) 367 Þai schal taake no þinge ellis. *c* **1400** *Lay Folks Mass Bk.*, *Bidding Prayer* ii. 64 Ensaumpil for to tak. *c* **1440** *Promp. Parv.* 485/2 Takyn, or receyvyn. **1538** KATH. BULKELEY in *Lett. Suppress. Monasteries* (Camden) 230 He..will not taike my answere. **1546** *Yorks. Chantry Surv.* (Surtees) II. 454 No man will taik yt. **1562** WINȜET *Cert. Tractatis* III. Wks. (S.T.S.) I. 34 That this tumult tak rest. **1573** TYRIE *Refut.* in *Cath. Tractates* (S.T.S.) 14 He culd nocht tack tent to sic trifflis. **1785** BURNS *To the Deil* xxi, O wad ye tak a thought an' men'!

β. *contr.* 4 (5–6 *Sc.*) ta, taa, 4–6 (9 *dial.*) tay, tae, 5 tan.

c **1340** *Cursor M.* 1250 (Gött.) Hugat þu sal ta [*Cott.* tak; *Fairf.*, *Trin.* take] þi right way. **1375** BARBOUR *Bruce* x. 610 And thair abaid thair aynd to ta. *c* **1375** *Sc. Leg. Saints* iii. (*Andreas*) 11 Sanct Andrew his way can tay. *c* **1400** *Laud Troy Bk.* 1742 Thelaman..nold her not to his spouse tan. *c* **1560** A. SCOTT *Poems* (S.T.S.) ii. 153 Quhen thay saw Sym sic curage ta. **1570** in J. Redford *Mor. Play Wit & Sc.*, etc. (Shaks. Soc.) 91 Eche swete corde eche ere woolde tay. **1865** WAUGH *Besom Ben* vii, Wheer are yo beawn to tay mo too?

2. *Imper.* α. 3–4 tac, 4–5 (6– *Sc.*) tak, 4– take; *pl.* 3 takez, 4 -es, -is, 5 takeþ. β. *contr.* 4–6 ta, *pl.* tas (4 tatz).

c **1200** ORMIN 8355 Josæp, ris upp & tacc þe child & tacc þe childess moderr. *c* **1230** *Hali Meid.* 7 Tac þe to him treoweliche. **13..** *Cursor M.* 15233 (Cott.) Takes and etes o þis bred. **13..** *E.E. Allit. P.* B. 735 Tatz to non ille, 3if I mele a lyttel more. **13..** *Gaw. & Gr. Knt.* 413 Ta now þy grymme tole to þe. *Ibid.* 1396 Tas yow þere my cheuicaunce. *c* **1386** CHAUCER *Pars. T.* ⁋77 Tak reward of þy value. *c* **1425** *Cursor M.* 661 (Trin.) Beþ war & takeþ good entent. *a* **1510** DOUGLAS *King Hart* II. 149 First witnes thow me ta. **1816** SCOTT *Old Mort.* xliii, This is the way; follow me,..sir, but tak tent to your feet.

3. *Pres. Indic.* (special forms). **a.** *2nd pers. sing.* α. 4 takes, 4–5 -is, 5 -yst, 5– takest. β. *contr.* 4 tas, 5 taas.

13.. *Cursor M.* 18358 (Cott.) Þou þat..fra þi folk þair sinnes take [*Gött.* takis; *c* **1425** *Trin.* takest, *Laud* takyst]. *Ibid.* 27132 (Cott.) Þou þi bising tas be oþer men. *c* **1430** *Christ's own Compl.* 464 in *Pol. Rel. & L. Poems* (1866) 197 No tent þou taas. *c* **1470** HENRY *Wallace* II. 85 To quhom takis thow this thing?

b. *3rd pers. sing.* α. 2 tæcþ, 3–4 takeþ, -eð, 4–5 takith, 4–7 (8– *arch.*) taketh; 4– takes, (6 *Sc.* takis, tekis).

a **1150** *MS.* 303 *Corp. Chr. Coll. Cambr.* 178 (Napier) Swa hwæt swa hit on tæcþ. *c* **1275** LAY. 3361 And takeþ hit his child. *c* **1350** *Will. Palerne* 3193 þe comli quen þan takeþ meliors by þe hande. **13..** *Cursor M.* 29274 (Cott.) On þam þis cursing stede first takes That [etc.]. **1382** WYCLIF *Matt.* x. 38 He that takith nat his crosse. **1484** CAXTON *Fables of Æsop* v. xiii, He is not wyse whiche..taketh debate or stryf. **1571** *Satir. Poems Reform.* xxix. 41 The Duvill..tekis forme of Angell bryte.

β. *contr.* 4–5 tas (4 tath), 4–6 *Sc.* tais, 5 tase, tace.

c **1375** *Sc. Leg. Saints* xviii. (*Egipciane*) 270 Gret dowt in his hart he tais. **1390** GOWER *Conf.* II. 129 He therof his part ne tath. *a* **1400–50** *Alexander* 2666 He..Tas him to his tresory. *c* **1430** *Brut* 406 Tharne Vmfreuyle, his leue he tace [*rime* space]. *a* **1450** *Le Morte Arth.* 956 Sir Gawayne..to conselle he tase [*rimes* was, case, has].

c. *pl.* α. 4 taken, 5 -yn; β. *contr.* 4 tas.

1340–70 *Alex. & Dind.* 566 Of hure tenful tach 3e taken ensample. **1357** *Lay Folks Catech.* 244 What thing so we gete, or tas.

4. *Past Indic.* (and *Subj.*). α[1] ? 1 tóc, 2–3 toc, 3–4 tock, 3–5 tok, 3–6 toke, (4 toek, ? to), 5–7 tooke, 4– took. *pl.* ? 1 tócon, 2 tocan, 3–5 token, 4 tokene, tooken, 5 tokyn.

c **1100** *O.E. Chron.* (MS. D) an. 1075, He..tóc [*MS. E* nam] swilce ȝerihta swa he him gelagade. *c* **1200** ORMIN Pref. 9 Crist toc dæþ o rodetre. *c* **1275** LAY. 54 He..þane hilke boc tock us to bisne. **1297** R. GLOUC. (Rolls) 5864 As me him drinke tok. *Ibid.* 6651 þis erl..toc hire þe castel of bruges. **13..** *Cursor M.* 13152 (Cott.) To þe bure sco tok hir pas. *Ibid.* 16454 Quen þai þe fine gold forsoke, And to [*v.r.* toke] þam to þe lede. **1377** LANGL. *P. Pl.* B. (MS. Rawl.) XVI. 269 + 3 He softe ȝede, þat he toek vs as tit. **1393** *Ibid.* C. IV. 47 Mede..took hym a noble For to be hure bedman. *c* **1420** (?) LYDG. *Assembly of Gods* 421 She toke hym by the hande. *Ibid.* 1888, I..myn hert to me tooke. **1579** LYLY *Euphues* (Arb.) 80 Lucilla..toke him by the hand. **1641** HINDE *J. Bruen* xlviii. 156 A little before hee tooke his Chamber.

c **1100** *O.E. Chron.* (MS. D) an. 1076, And [hi] tócon þær inne mycele æhta. **1154** *Ibid.* (MS. E) an. 1136, þa tocan þa oðre & helden her castles agænes him. *c* **1200** ORMIN 6492 Þeȝȝ tokenn nihhtess reste þær. *c* **1250** *Gen. & Ex.* 3194 Alle ðe bones ðe he ðor token. **1297** R. GLOUC. (Rolls) 3987 A lettre hii toke þe kinge. **13..** *S. Erkenwolde* 57 in Horstm. *Altengl. Leg.* (1881) 267 Quen tithynges tokene to þe tone. *c* **1380** *Lay Folks Catech.* (Lamb MS.) 1211 Whan we tok cristyndom. **1382** WYCLIF *John* i. 5 Derknessis tooken not it. *c* **1400** *Destr. Troy* 4696 Þai..tokyn the tresure. *c* **1449** PECOCK *Repr.* II. ii. 145 To hem whiche token and helden tho ymagis to be her Goddis.

α[2] (*Sc.* and *n. dial.*) 4–9 tuk, 5–9 tuke, (5 twke, 6 twik, tuike), 6– tuik.

c **1375** *Sc. Leg. Saints* i. (*Petrus*) 36 He hym tuk to be hym by In his transfiguracion. *c* **1470** HENRY *Wallace* I. 78 King Eduuard than it tuk in gret greuance. **1533** GAU *Richt Vay* (S.T.S.) 32 The sone..twik apone hyme our natur. *c* **1560** ROLLAND *Seven Sages* (1837) A ij, I..tuke gude nicht. **1596** DALRYMPLE tr. *Leslie's Hist. Scot.* I. (S.T.S.) 100 He tuke thame, he eit thame rawe. *Ibid.* x. 320 His recreatioune he tuike in Caris hous. *Mod. Sc.* We tuik them wi' us.

β. 3 takede, 5– taked. (See *Eng. Dial. Dict.*)

c **1205** LAY. 3333 þe we swa takede him on. **1485** *Waterf. Arch.* in *10th Rep. Hist. MSS. Comm.* App. v. 318 That spoiled, robbed, or taked ony of the Kyngs liege men.

5. *Past pple.* α. 2–4 itaken, 4 ytakyn; 4– taken, (4–5 takin, -yn, 5 -yne, -on, -un, 6 takne, taking; 7 taiken, *Sc.* taikin).

c **1175** Itaken [see B. 14]. *c* **1205** Itaken [see *take on*: 86 i]. *c* **1320** *Cast. Love* 202 Þe blisse of lyf he haþ forsaken, And to deolful deþ him taken. *c* **1330** *Assump. Virg.* (B.M. MS.) 625 When þi lord was ytakyn. *c* **1375** *Cursor M.* 4875 (Fairf.) Qua-so ys takin wiþ stollyn þinge. *a* **1380** *S. Bernard* 612 in Horstm. *Altengl. Leg.* (1878) 51/2 Wiþ seknesse stronge He was itaken. *c* **1400** *Destr. Troy* 1512 His towne was takon. *c* **1449** PECOCK *Repr.* II. iv. 159 Weel takun of wise men. **1537** WRIOTHESLEY *Chron.* (Camden) I. 60 The sayd Halam was takne. **1552** LYNDESAY *Monarche* 5539 Quhilkis salbe taking, but warnyng. **1629** *Reg. Privy Council Scotl.* Ser. II. III. 25 We..have taikin thame.

β. *contr.* 3–5 itake, 4–5 ytake; 4–7 take, 5 (6 *pseudo-Sc.*) tak.

1297 R. GLOUC. (Rolls) 6106 Nou adde heyemen of þe lond itake..His fader ostage god ynou. **1340–70** *Alex. & Dind.* 721 3e schullen..offren to venus A ful derworþe douue on his den take. **1377** LANGL. *P. Pl.* B. XI. 254 So is ..pouerte or penaunce pacientlyche ytake. **1387** TREVISA *Higden* (Rolls) VIII. 79 At Turon he was i-take wiþ a fevere. **1423** JAS. I *Kingis Q.* cxciii, Sche hath me tak, hir humble creature. *c* **1425** *Cursor M.* 928 (Trin.) þat erþe þou were of take. *c* **1440** *Pallad. on Husb.* III. 906 To graffe a quynce is diuers tyme ytake. *c* **1450** *Merlin* 296 And his wif [was] also I-take. **1559** *Mirr. Mag.* (1563) I j, Shortly after was Kyng Henry take, And put in pryson. **1605** Take [see B. 49].

γ. *contr.* 4 y-tan; 4–5 tan, 4–8 tane, (4 tene, 4 (6 *Sc.*) tain, 4–5 tayn, 5–6 *Sc.* tayne, 6 taan, teyne, *Sc.* teine, 6–7 taine, 7 taen), 7–8 ta'ne, 9 (*poet.* and *dial.*) ta'en; (*erron.*) 5 ton, 5 (6 *pseudo-Sc.*) tone.

c **1320** *Sir Tristr.* 1000 Now haþ tristrem y tan Oȝain moraunt to fiȝt. *c* **1340** HAMPOLE *Prose Tr.* (1866) 1 Ihesu the Worde of God has tane manes kynde. **13..** *Cursor M.* 4896 (Cott.) Lok þai alle be tain [*v.rr.* tan, tane, take] and bonden. *Ibid.* 16058 (Cott.) Þai him had tene [*v.rr.* tane, taken] al wit tresun. *c* **1400** *Rule St. Benet* 2112 Þen sall þis rewel eft furth be ton [*rime* gon]. *c* **1470** HENRY *Wallace* II. 400 Wallace..Apon the crag with his suerd has him tayne. **1500–20** DUNBAR *Poems* xlvi. 102 That he..nocht in the feindis net be tone [*rime* allone]. *c* **1520** NISBET *N.T. in Scots, Acts* i. 11 Quhilk is taan vp fra you into heuen. **15..** *Sir A. Barton* in *Surtees Misc.* (1888) 68 Where that Scoott hath teyne frome the a grootte. *a* **1578** LINDESAY (Pitscottie) *Chron. Scot.* (S.T.S.) I. 197 Gif he had teine it. **1597** SHAKS. *2 Hen. IV*, IV. v. 60 The Prince hath ta'ne it hence. **1602** —— *Ham.* I. iii. 107 That you have tane his tenders for true pay. *a* **1631** DRAYTON *Triumph David* 805 The sword taen from the giant's side. *c* **1645** HOWELL *Lett.* v. 30 He hath taine such a habit of it. **1653** *Nissena* 43 From the time she had taen upon her the yoke of marriage. **1875** TENNYSON *Q. Mary* v. v, The Holy Father Has ta'en the legateship from our cousin Pole.

δ. 6–7 tooke, 7–8 (9 *dial.* and *illit.*) took; 7–9 tooken.

1592 KYD *Sol. & Pers.* III. i. 5 My brothers ghoasts.. would now haue tooke their rest. **1610** DONNE *Pseudo-martyr* 353 The Popes haue tooken order..to enact [etc.]. **1633** P. FLETCHER *Pisc. Ecl.* v. ix, Thus many a Nymph is took. *a* **1667** JER. TAYLOR *Rev. to Altar* Wks. 1849 V. 323 God hath tooke seisure of it. **1790** *Cook's Voy.* V. 1808 Having took our departure from Prince William's Sound. **1899** BETHAM-EDWARDS *Lord of Harv.* 155 Mr. Flindell.. has took you up in his gig.

ε. 6 taked.

1512 *Helyas* in Thoms *Prose Rom.* (1828) III. 24 My sonne..hath taked the quene Beatrice..to his wife. **1581** RICH *Farew. Milit. Prof.* (1846) 207 Till he had taked his firste fruites.

B. Signification.

The earliest known use of this verb in the Germanic languages was app. to express the physical action 'to put the hand on', 'to touch'—the only known sense of Gothic *têkan*. By a natural advance, such as is seen in English in the use of 'lay hands upon', the sense passed to 'lay hold upon, lay hold of, grip, grasp, seize'—the essential meaning of Old Norse *taka*, of MDu. *taken*, and of the material senses of *take* in English. By the subordination of the notion of the instruments, and even of the physical action, to that of the result, *take* becomes in its essence 'to transfer to oneself by one's own action or volition (anything material or non-material)'. This becomes then the general or ordinary sense of the verb, which falls into two main divisions, *take* in the sense of 'seize, grip', hence 'appropriate', and *take* in the sense of 'receive or accept what is handed to one'. Subordinate to these are the non-material senses of 'assume, adopt, apprehend, comprehend, comprise, contain'. For the common element of all these notions *take* is the simple and proper term, for which no simpler can be substituted. It is one of the elemental words of the language, of which the only direct explanation is to show the *thing* or *action* to which they are applied.

Take also enters into a great number of idiomatic phrases, which are often difficult to analyse. Many of these are parallel to, and influenced by French phrases with *prendre*: see F. H. Sykes, *French Elements in ME.*, Oxford 1899.

General arrangement of senses: I. To touch. II. To seize, grip, catch. III. Ordinary current sense, i. with material obj.; ii. with non-material obj. IV. To choose, take for a purpose, into use. V. To derive, obtain from a source. VI. To receive, accept, admit, contain. VII. To apprehend mentally, comprehend. VIII. To undertake, perform, make. IX. To convey, conduct, deliver, apply or betake oneself, go. X. Idiomatic uses with special obj. XI. Intransitive uses with preposition. XII. Adverbial combinations = compound verbs. XIII. Idiomatic phrases, and *Phrase-key*.

I. † **1.** To touch (*intr.* with *on*, also *trans.*: = ON. *taka á*, and *taka*). *Obs.*

a **1150** *MS.* 303 *Corp. Chr. Coll. Cambr.* 178 (Napier) Soðlice þæt ilce ele is swa mihtiȝ & swa strange þæt swa hwæt swa hit on tæcþ, þærrihtes hit eall forbærnð. *Ibid.* 179 Sona swa þæt ele toc on þæt wæter, þa aras þær upp swiðe mycel fyr. *c* **1250** *Gen. & Ex.* 3456 Abute ðis munt ðu merke make, If erf or man ðor-one take, It dead ðolen. *c* **1250** *Old Kent. Serm.* in *O.E. Misc.* 31 Ure lord him seide and spredde his hond, and tok his lepre. *a* **1300** *Cursor M.* 10969 (Cott.), I and mi wijf on ald tas. **1340** *Ayenb.* 91 Be zyȝþe, be hyerþe, be smellinge, be zuelȝynge, and be takynge.

II. To seize, grasp, capture, catch, and related senses.

* *in literal and physical sense.*

2. *trans.* To lay hold upon, get into one's hands by force or artifice; to seize, capture, esp. in war; to make prisoner; hence, to get into one's power, to win by conquest (a fort, town, country). Also, to apprehend (a person charged with an offence), to arrest; to seize (property) by legal process, as by distraint, etc. See also *take by* STORM.

c **1100** *O.E. Chron.* an. 1072 (MS. D), Se kyng nam heora scypa & wæpna,..& þa menn ealle he toc, & dyde of heom þæt he wolde. *Ibid.* an. 1076, Ac se kyngc..hine let syððan tacan. **1154** *Ibid.* an. 1140 (Laud MS.), And te Lundenissce folc hire wolde tæcen. *c* **1200** ORMIN 5948, & tatt he siþþenn takenn wass All gilltelæs & bundenn & naȝȝledd uppo rodetre. *a* **1300** *Cursor M.* 4896 Lok þai alle be tain and bonden. *Ibid.* 18554 Als prisun þai him tok for-þi. *c* **1400** *Rom. Rose* 5894 My modir is of gret prowesse; She hath tan many a fortresse. *c* **1450** *Merlin* 13 The Iuges made hir to be taken, and brought hir be-fore them. *c* **1460** *Brut* 524 þei londed & come to Sandwych..& toke the town, & ryfled & dispoyled it. **1526** TINDALE *Matt.* iv. 12 When Iesus had herde that Ihon was taken, he departed in to Galile. **1600** E. BLOUNT tr. *Conestaggio* 184 Hauing quietly taken the other two gallions, they entred within the Porte. **1658** COKAINE *Trappolin* I. i, He is your brothers prisoner..That in the wars of Mantoa was took. **1736** LEDIARD *Life Marlborough* I. 180 The English took about 200 Prisoners. **1803** *Pic Nic* II. No. 8. 61, I was taken into custody. **1854** J. S. C. ABBOTT *Napoleon* (1855) II. 372, I took two guns and retook two.

(*b*) *Criminals' slang.* To break into in order to burgle, to rob.

1926 J. BLACK *You can't Win* xxi. 331 After gathering every scrap of information available, I was sure I could 'take' the spot if I got a fair break on the luck. **1930** D. RUNYON in *Liberty* 8 Nov. 24/2 Someone takes a jewellery store in the town.

b. To catch, capture (a wild beast, bird, fish, etc.); also of an animal, to seize or catch (prey).

c **1200** ORMIN 13504 Rihht alls an hunnte takeþþ der Wiþþ hise ȝæpe racchess. *c* **1250** *Gen. & Ex.* 3323 Ðor miȝte euerilc man fuȝeles taken. *c* **1400** MAUNDEV. (Roxb.) v. 15 þai take wylde bestes riȝt wele. **1509** HAWES *Past. Pleas.* xxxi. (Percy Soc.) 154 Wo worth the beaute which toke me in snare. **1563** B. GOOGE *Sonnets* (Arb.) 82 By hydden hooke, the symple fole is tane. **1648** *Hunting of Fox* 23 They keep packs of dogs, or Beagles, on purpose to take them by hunting. **1801** STRUTT *Sports & Past.* I. ii. 33 The present methods of taking fish. **1892** *Longm. Mag.* Nov. 87 They are readily taken by nets. **1899** RIDER HAGGARD *Swallow* iii, The women and the little ones..were taken by wild beasts.

c. *subj.* in imprecations.

a **1533** LD. BERNERS *Huon* lvii. 192 Mahounde take his soule! **1600, 1749** [see DEVIL *sb.* 17]. **1850** *Tait's Mag.* XVII. 298/1 Here he comes again!—deuce take him. **1856** READE *Never Too Late* l, The devil take the hindmost.

d. In various games, as chess, cards, etc.: To capture (an adversary's piece, card, etc.) so as to put it out of play; also (*Cards*) to gain possession of (a trick): see TRICK *sb.* (Also said of the piece, card, etc., by which the taking is effected).

14.. *Beryn* 1812 The next drauȝt aftir, he toke a roke for nauȝte. *c* **1440** *Gesta Rom.* xxi. 71 (Harl. MS.) Whenne he [the pawn at chess] goth aside, he takith anoþer. **1562** ROWBOTHUM *Play Cheasts* B iv b, Thou shalt take his knight with thy Quene. **1735** BERTIN *Chess* 55 The king takes the queen. **1840** *P. Parley's Ann.* I. 263 A pawn takes the enemy angularly.

e. *Cricket.* To catch (the ball) off the bat so as to put the batsman 'out' (also with the batsman as obj.); of the bowler, To 'capture' (a wicket) by striking it with the ball (or otherwise).

1846 W. DENISON *Cricket* 71 The greatest number of wickets he succeeded in taking in one match was 11. **1870** *Times* 11 July 10/5 Mr. Law was taken easily at the wicket with the score at 22. **1882** *Daily Tel.* 17 May, A minute or two later Walker was smartly taken at the wicket off Garrett. *Ibid.* 24 June, Lucas, who had been fielding at long-off, running at full speed, managed to take it [the ball]. **1883** *Ibid.* 15 May 2/7 He was..taken at cover-point by Woof. **1890** *Field* 10 May 672/2 Studd..was then beautifully taken at long-off.

3. To lay hold of, grasp (with the hand, arms, etc.); to seize and hold. ***to take in one's arms***, to embrace. Often const. *by* the hand, head, horns, tail, etc.: see HAND *sb.* 47, BULL *sb.*[1] 1 c. Cf. also *take hold* in Phrases below (69).

a **1225** *Juliana* 70 He rende his claðes ant toc him seoluen bi þe top. *a* **1300** *Cursor M.* 2364 (Cott.) Ta loth þi broþer sun in hand, To chanaan ȝee most now drau. **1387** TREVISA *Higden* (Rolls) III. 147 To my Crist, whos riȝt hond I haue i-take. **1393** LANGL. *P. Pl.* C. XXII. 170 Crist..took thomas by þe hand. *c* **1425** *Cursor M.* 4357 (Trin.) She toke him aboute þe necke wiþ þis And profered hir mouþ to kis. ?*c* **1500** in *Joseph Arim.* 30 He toke me by the hande and so ledde me in myn house. **1600** W. WATSON *Decacordon* (1602) 117 He tooke him by the sleeve, as they were in going over a stile. **1709** STEELE & ADDISON *Tatler* No. 114 ¶1 He took me by the Hand. **1825** *New Monthly Mag.* XIV. 361, I took her hand and kissed her. **1890** F. BARRETT *Betw. Life & Death* III. 106 He took her in his arms.

4. *intr.* Of a hook, a mechanical device, etc.: To catch, engage: usually const. *into.*

c **1435** *Torr. Portugal* 1608 Sith he pullith at his croke, So fast in to the flesh it toke. **1729** DESAGULIERS in *Phil. Trans.* XXXVI. 197 The Pall or Lever..does so communicate with the Catch, that..the Catch always takes. **1797** *Encycl. Brit.* (ed. 3) IX. 9 The teeth of these four wheels take alternately into the teeth of four racks. **1825** J. NICHOLSON *Operat. Mechanic* 310 The next tooth of the pinion will take into the gap in the end of the rack. *Ibid.* 513 These pins take into holes in the plate, made exactly to fit them. **1856** KANE *Arct. Expl.* II. xxvi. 262 A floe, taking upon a tongue of ice.., began to swing upon it like a pivot.

b. *trans.* Of a mechanical appliance, etc.: To 'lay hold of'; to act upon by contact, adhesion, or the like.

1659 LEAK *Waterwks.* 25 So as the Saws may take the said peece again. **1849** PELLATT *Curios. Glass Making* 94 The punty takes the flat end by adhesion. **1894** *Harper's Mag.* July 191/2 The blades no longer take the water together.

5. *trans.* To strike, hit, impinge upon (a person, etc.), usually *in*, *on* (*across*, *over*, etc.) some part; also with the part as obj.; = CATCH *v.* 11.

[The notion here seems to have been originally to catch or get at a person by means of the part named, which catches the blow that otherwise might have passed.]

c **1400** *Destr. Troy* 8224 Ector turnet with tene, toke hym on þe hed. *c* **1470** HENRY *Wallace* I. 403 Wallas with it [the poutstaff] fast on the cheik him tuk. *Ibid.* III. 175 As he glaid by, aukwart he couth hym ta. **1509** HAWES *Past. Pleas.* xl. (Percy Soc.) 202 Unto me than he came full softely, And with his staffe he toke me on the brest. **1594** SHAKS. *Rich. III*, I. iv. 159 Take him on the Costard, with the hiltes of thy Sword. **1670** COTTON *Espernon* II. v. 201 He was..taken upon the head with a stone. **1719** DE FOE *Crusoe* (1840) I. iii. 52 The blow taking my side and breast, beat the breath, as it were, quite out of my body. **1748** *Anson's Voy.* I. x. 104 A mountainous..sea took us upon our starboard quarter. **1795** *Hist.* in *Ann. Reg.* 70/1 A masked battery took them in flank. **1806–7** J. BERESFORD *Miseries Hum. Life* (1826) VI. Introd., The kick of a horse..took me across the ribs. **1891** *Blackw. Mag.* CL. 651/2 When a sheep runs amuck, he is..a living catapult, that, if he took you fair, would knock the life out of you. **1893** *Chamb. Jrnl.* 3 June 350/1 The ball took him squarely between the eyes.

b. With double obj.: e.g. ***to take any one a blow***.

1448 *Paston Lett.* (1901) IV. 19 He..toke his master on the hepe suyche a stroke that..brake his hepe. *c* **1590** MARLOWE *Faust.* vii. 96 Cursed be he that took Friar Sandelo a blow on the pate! **1596** SHAKS. *Tam. Shr.* III. ii. 165 This mad-brain'd bridegroome tooke him such a cuffe. **1603** —— *Meas. for M.* II. i. 189 If he tooke you a box o'th'eare. **1781** C. JOHNSTON *Hist. J. Juniper* II. 161 Taking him a blow full in the pit of his stomach. *Mod. colloq.* The ball took me an awful whack on the chest.

6. *absol.* or *intr.* **a.** Of a plant, seed, or graft: To 'get hold' of that on which it grows; to take root, 'strike', germinate, begin to grow. Also, in *Med.*, of animal tissue, etc.: to continue in a healthy state after being transplanted.

c **1440** *Pallad. on Husb.* II. 153 In reed erthe ek a vyne is hard to take. *Ibid.* III. 576 But euery day me most hit delue & were Vntil hit take. **1530** PALSGR. 747/1 A yonge plante or sette begynneth to take whan it groweth up. **1661** J. CHILDREY *Brit. Baconica* 14 Fruit fails in one countrey, and takes in another. **1712** J. JAMES tr. *Le Blond's Gardening* 184 The Oak being in its own Nature very difficult to take again. **1802** FORSYTH *Fruit Trees* i. (1824) 2 The cherry and plum will never take upon each other..but the apricot will take upon all sorts of plums. **1875** *Lancet* 23 Jan. 124/3 The transplanted pieces of skin..were found to have 'taken' remarkably well. **1891** *Cosmopolitan* XII. 87/2 Patches where the seed has failed to take. **1892** *Field* 10 Dec. 883/3 We planted a thousand cedars of Lebanon, with shoots 6 in. high, and we have no doubt that they will take well. **1936** *Anat. Rec.* LXIV. 167 Young donors supply material that is more likely to 'take'. **1977** *Time* 7 Mar. 43/2 Odds that a transplanted cadaveric kidney will 'take' are usually no better than 50%.

b. Of ink, etc.: To adhere to the paper, parchment, etc.

1883 R. HALDANE *Workshop Receipts* Ser. II. 192/1 The use of ox-gall, which makes the ink 'take', has also the disadvantage of making it frequently 'run'.

c. Of ice: to form (esp. in a lake, river, etc.). Cf. sense 44 d below. *dial.* and *N. Amer.*

1825 *Kingston* (Upper Canada) *Chron.* 4 Feb. 3/2 On Saturday night last, the ice took between Kingston and Long Island. **1877** E. LEIGH *Gloss. Words used Dial. Cheshire* 206 'The ice is taking' means it is beginning to freeze. **1881** *Edmonton Bull.* 28 Mar. 1/2 Ice took in the Saskatchewan on the 19th of November. **1931** G. L. NUTE *Voyageur* 79 Seines were set in the water just before the ice 'took' on the lake or river.

d. Of a lamb: to be accepted by a foster mother in place of her own dead lamb.

1874 HARDY *Far from Madding Crowd* I. xviii. 204 Mistress and man were engaged in the operation of making a lamb 'take', which is performed whenever an ewe has lost her own offspring, one of the twins of another ewe being given her as substitute.

** *with either the action or the agent non-material.*

7. *trans.* Of a disease, a pain, an injurious or destructive agency, natural or supernatural, magical, etc.; also of a notion, fancy, feeling, etc.: To affect, seize, lay hold of, attack. Also in imprecations, as 'pest' or 'plague take him'.

a **1300** *Cursor M.* 11823 (Cott.) Wit þe crache him tok the scurf [*Trin.* þe ȝicche toke him sikerly]. *a* **1325** *Prose Psalter* xlvii[i]. 5 Drede toke hem. **1450–80** tr. *Secreta Secret.* 31 Than mayst thou ete..as thyn appetit takith the. *a* **1533** LD. BERNERS *Huon* lvii. 194 For a colyke that hath taken me in the ryght syde. *a* **1553** [see MISCHIEF 9 b]. *a* **1566** [see PLAGUE 3 d]. **1581** PETTIE *Guazzo's Civ. Conv.* I. (1586) 12 b, Moued by some sodaine toie which taketh them in the head. **1598** SHAKS. *Merry W.* IV. iv. 32 He blasts the tree, and takes the cattle. **1604** E. G[RIMSTONE] *D'Acosta's Hist. Indies* VII. xxiii. 565 Fire tooke the Temple. **1661** COWLEY *Disc. Govt. O. Cromwell* Wks. 1710 II. 664 Now the Freak takes him. **1707** MORTIMER *Husb.* 173 No Beast will eat sour Grass till the Frost hath taken it. **1889** *Temple Bar Mag.* Dec. 451 An intense weariness of life took him. **1892** *Cassell's Fam. Mag.* Aug. 515/2 What in the name of wonder has taken the girl? **1893** *National Observer* 7 Oct. 542/2 He admired as the humour took him.

absol. **1602** SHAKS. *Ham.* I. i. 163 Then no planets strike, No fairy takes, nor witch hath power to charm.

b. *pass.* To be seized, attacked, or affected (*with* disease, a fit, fancy, etc.); to 'have an attack' of something.

a **1300** *Cursor M.* 8915 (Cott.) Sco es wode and wit warlagh tan [*Trin.* wiþ fende Itake]. **1387** TREVISA *Higden* (Rolls) VI. 157 He was i-take with sikenesse and deyde. *c* **1440** *Promp. Parv.* 261/2 Infectyn..as menne take wythe pestylence. **1526** TINDALE *Matt.* iv. 24 All sicke people, that were taken with diuers diseases and gripinges. *a* **1533** LD. BERNERS *Huon* xlviii. 162 He was taken in loue. **1578** LYTE *Dodoens* 609 The astonied members, or limmes taken with colde. **1680** DRYDEN *Spanish Friar* III. i, I am taken on the sudden with a grievous swimming in my Head. **1865** DICKENS *Mut. Fr.* IV. xiii, Mrs. Boffin was then taken with a laughing fit of clapping her hands, and clapping her knees. **1888** FLORENCE WARDEN *Witch of Hills* I. xiii. 273, I was going to be taken with a fit.

c. *pass.* (*ellipt.*) To have a seizure or attack; to be seized with sudden illness, pain, disease, numbness, or other affection (physical or mental). ? *Obs.* exc. *dial.*

1450–1530 *Myrr. our Ladye* 29 Where the soule was take a non & sore tormented longe tyme togidre. **1568** TURNER *Herbal* III. 40 Good for membres that are num or taken. **1607** MARKHAM *Caval.* VII. (1617) 11 A horse that is taken our common Farriers say to be planet strooke. *c* **1642** LD. HERBERT in *Life* (1770) 45 Others..standing stiff and stark ..seem as if they were taken in their joynts.

d. *pass.* with complemental adj., as ***to be taken ill*** (formerly ***blind, hoarse, lame***), to be seized or struck with illness, etc. Rarely in *active*: see quot. 13... Also humorously (quot. 1838).

13.. *E.E. Allit. P.* A. 1157 No thyng myȝt me dere To fech me bar & take me halte. **1588** PARKE tr. *Mendoza's Hist. China* 48 Whatsoeuer children be borne a creeple..or by sicknes be taken lame. **1657** W. RAND tr. *Gassendi's Life Peiresc* I. 64 Being soon after taken blind. **1662** J. WILSON *Cheats* V. iii, Being taken very ill of a sudden. **1711** STEELE *Spect.* No. 96 ¶2 Master Harry was taken very ill of a Fever. **1802** MAR. EDGEWORTH *Moral T.* (1816) I. iv. 21 She was taken ill in the night. **1838** DICKENS *Nich. Nick.* xxviii, 'Oh, charming!' interrupted Kate's patroness, who was sometimes taken literary. **1891** *Harper's Mag.* Apr. 750/1 He was taken hoarse at the last moment.

e. *intr.* for *pass.*, with *compl.*, as ***to take ill*** = to be taken ill, to fall or become ill. Also humorously (quot. 1890[2]). *colloq.* and *dial.*

1674 N. FAIRFAX *Bulk & Selv.* 131 A woman..who took with child in the very fit of a Third Ague. **1822** J. HODGSON in Raine *Mem.* (1857) I. 400 My father-in-law took ill. **1890** HEALY *Insula Sanct.* 317 He took sick and died in the island. **1890** *Illustr. Lond. News* 29 Nov. 686/3 Then, too, he took studious, and..pored over great tomes and learned things. **1903** TREVELYAN in *Independent Rev.* Dec. 409 Mr. William Pitt..took ill and died after Austerlitz.

f. *intr.* To catch, catch hold: *esp.* of fire, to seize upon combustible substances, to be kindled, begin burning; also of a condition, humour, fancy, etc. (cf. 10 c). Now *rare.*

1523 LD. BERNERS *Froiss.* I. clviii. 192 All the base court was afyre, so that the fyre..toke into the couerynge of a great towre couered with rede. **1634–5** BRERETON *Trav.* (Chetham Soc.) 43 The fire first took in rape-oil. **1639** S. DU VERGER tr. *Camus' Admir. Events* 110 Rottennesse takes sooner in apples, which are bruised. **1700** T. BROWN *Amusem. Ser. & Com.* 52 When any Humour Takes in London. **1803** *Ann. Rev.* II. 189/1 The tinder was ready, and the spark took.

8. *trans.* To 'catch' or come upon (any one) *in* some action or situation; *fig.* to catch or detect *in* (†*with*) a fault or error. ***to take tardy***: see TARDY.

The first two quotations connect this with sense 2.

[**1387** TREVISA *Higden* (Rolls) III. 227 Pomphilia..was i-take into [*v.r.* in] leccherie. *c* **1400** *Apol. Loll.* 6 Many popis han synnyd, and ben snybbid; and sum tan in heresy and deposid.] **1577** HANMER *Anc. Eccl. Hist.* (1663) 85 By reasoning with this old Apelles, I took him with many falshoods. **1597** MORLEY *Introd. Mus.* 95 In which fault you haue beene nowe thrise taken. **1602** *Narcissus* (1893) 91 What was that I tooke you all a gabling tother day? **1607** R. JOHNSON *Pleas. Conceites Old Hobson* (Percy Soc.) 15 His man seeing himselfe so taken napping, for a time stood amazed. **1652** GAULE *Magastrom.* 331 The poore astrologers, who had already been taken with so many lies. **1668** SHADWELL *Sullen Lovers* I. i, I am glad I've taken you within, I come on purpose to tell you the news, d'ye hear it? **1885** MRS. HARRISON ('LUCAS MALET') *Col. Enderby's Wife* VII. ii, The doctor was not easily taken off his guard.

b. To come upon suddenly, overtake, catch. *Obs.* or *arch.* exc. in certain phrases: see *take* SHORT, *take by* SURPRISE, *take at* UNAWARES.

[**13..** *Gaw. & Gr. Knt.* 1811 Iche tolke mon do as he is tan, tas to non ille, ne pine.] *a* **1533** LD. BERNERS *Huon* xlviii. 161 At last a wynd toke them whether they wolde or not. **1568** GRAFTON *Chron.* II. 210 A tempest toke them on the sea, that put them so farre out of their course. **1611** BIBLE *Ecclus.* xxxvi. 26 A man that..lodgeth wheresoeuer the night taketh him. **1890** CLARK RUSSELL *Ocean Trag.* II. xxi. 181 We were at breakfast when the first of the wind took us.

c. *slang.* To swindle, cheat, or deprive of money by extortion. Freq. const. *for*.

1927 [see CLIP *v.*² 9]. **1930** D. HAMMETT *Dain Curse* xii. 122 They landed Mrs Rodman... They took her for one of her apartment buildings. **1956** S. BELLOW *Seize Day* i. 9 They make millions. They have smart lawyers... Whereas I got taken. **1968** 'L. MARSHALL' *Blood on Blotter* xxvii. 183 'How much did you take him for?' 'Slade? Plenty.' **1970** *Washington Post* 30 Sept. B12/4 It looks to me like yo're fixin' to git took for the dollar an' thirty cents, Shuffy. **1978** J. B. HILTON *Some run Crooked* ix. 86 It wasn't enough for Julie just to admit she'd been taken. **1982** 'E. LATHEN' *Green grow Dollars* xiv. 112 'I told Mary to take them for every penny she could get,' he said stoutly.

d. *Motor-racing.* To overtake (a competitor).

1977 *Custom Car* Nov. 14/2 Jimmy Smith..finally took Falcone, who had developed trouble, and stayed ahead to win the race. **1978** *Guardian Weekly* 12 Mar. 23/5 The South African Grand Prix... Peterson (Lotus) shadowed the leader right to the end, taking him on a bend in the last lap for victory.

9. †**a.** To take to task; to reprehend, rebuke. *Obs.* **b.** To check, 'pull up', interrupt. *dial.* (Cf. *take up*, 93 m, n.)

c **1250** *Old Kent. Serm.* in *O.E. Misc.* 32 Þo a-ros up ure lord and tok þane wynd and þo [*MS.* to] see; and al-so raþe hit was stille. *a* **1586** SIDNEY *Arcadia* IV. (1622) 415 And therewith taking himself..said hee. **1637** RUTHERFORD *Lett.* xcviii. (1862) I. 251 But this is my infirmity. By His grace I take myself in these ravings.

10. To catch the fancy or affection of; to excite a liking in; to captivate, delight, charm; to 'fetch'.

1605 [see TAKING *ppl. a.* 2]. **1609** B. JONSON *Sil. Wom.* I. i, Such sweet neglect more taketh me, Than all th' adulteries of art. **1623** B. JONSON *To the memory of Shaks.* 76 Those flights vpon the bankes of Thames, That so did take Eliza, and our Iames! **1656** EARL MONM. tr. *Boccalini, Pol. Touchstone* (1674) 289 With a readiness that much took all the Literati. **1686** W. DE BRITAINE *Hum. Prud.* iv. (ed. 3) 15 Take the Vulgar by your Civilities. **1830** TENNYSON *To the Owl* II. i, Thy tuwhoos..Which upon the dark afloat, So took echo with delight. **1890** F. BARRETT *Betw. Life & Death* II. xxi. 78 You took the whole audience. **1891** GALTON *La Fenton* I. viii. 193 Scarcely the man to take the fancy of a very young girl.

b. *pass.* const. *with*, less usually *by*. Also without const.

1535 COVERDALE *Prov.* vi. 25 Lest thou be taken with hir fayre lokes. **1622** BACON *Hen. VII* 153 King James..taken by Perkins amiable and alluring behauiour..entertained him..as became the person of Richard Duke of Yorke. **1641** W. MOUNTAGU in *Buccleuch MSS.* (Hist. MSS. Comm.) I. 286 The King and Queen seemed to be much taken with..the entertainment. **1798** CHARLOTTE SMITH *Yng. Philos.* IV. 110, I was quite taken with the spirit and beauty of the young gentlewoman. **1867** CARLYLE *Remin.* (1881) II. 23 He was much taken with my little Jeannie, as he well might be. **1969** 'E. FERRARS' *Skeleton Staff* iii. 61 'Not enormously taken, are you?' 'Not bowled over.' **1978** P. H. JOHNSON *Good Husband* iii. 24 But about Ann... you were very taken, weren't you?

c. *absol.* or *intr.* **to take** = to take the fancy, win favour, gain acceptance; *esp.* to win popular favour, become popular.

a **1635** NAUNTON *Fragm. Reg.* (Arb.) 16 It took best with the people. **1654** H. VAUGHAN *Silex Scint.* Pref. (1900) 13 Nothing takes (as they rightly phrase it) like a Romance. **1762–71** H. WALPOLE *Vertue's Anecd. Paint.* (1786) I. 237 The whim took; he repeated the practice. **1817** MISS MITFORD in L'Estrange *Life* (1870) II. i. 4 The new melodrame..takes mightily. **1842** J. A. KASSON *Let.* 22 Nov. in *Virginia Mag. Hist. & Biogr.* (1948) LVI. 418 A person, male or female, that relishes society and can *talk*, will take well. **1858** G. MEREDITH *Let.* 28 Apr. (1970) I. 35 Translate that placard. It would take. **1963** *Listener* 14 Mar. 457/1 Jazz has 'taken' in Africa. **1981** D. MARTIN in Martin & Mullen *No Alternative* ii. 19 The appeal to primitive practices can obscure the pressures of today which make such practices 'take' with a section of the clergy.

d. *trans.* To attract and hold, to 'catch' (a person's eye or attention).

1754 RICHARDSON *Grandison* (1781) V. i. 6 We..took the Bishop's eye. He came to us. **1842** WHEWELL in *Life* (1881) 279, I am not surprised that your attention was taken by the examination papers. **1881** *Scribner's Mag.* XXI. 268/1 Some one took Horton's attention for a moment. **1889** *Eng. Illustr. Mag.* Dec. 268 My eye was taken by something bright.

11. *intr.* Of a plan, operation, etc.: To have the intended result; to succeed, be effective, take effect, 'come off'. (See also 10 c.)

1622 BACON *Hen. VII* 63 The temporarie Fruit of the Parliament in their aide and aduice giuen for Britaine, tooke not, nor prospered not. **1625** MASSINGER *New way* v. i, It may be, Sweetheart, my project took. **1646** H. LAWRENCE *Comm. Angells* 98 This temptation tooke. **1658** *Hist. Christina Queen Swedland* 287 This machine was full of fire-workes, which took very handsomly. **1701** W. WOTTON *Hist. Rome* 356 The design took and the Fellow got away. **1800–24** CAMPBELL *Ritter Bann* xxxi, The treachery took: she waited wild. **1941** B. SCHULBERG *What makes Sammy Run?* xi. 203 She was married... The year she came out. But it didn't take. **1978** D. BLOODWORTH *Crosstalk* xv. 123 [Operation] Crosstalk can do no good whatsoever unless it takes, and..this move against Sviridov..shows it has taken.

†**b.** In weakened or indefinite sense: To have a result of some kind; to turn out, eventuate. *Obs.*

a **1625** FLETCHER *Hum. Lieutenant* III. vii, Did I not tell you how 'twould take? **1648** C'TESS LINDSEY in *Buccleuch MSS.* (Hist. MSS. Comm.) I. 309 My son Paston is in town about a match for his son; how it will take I know not.

c. Of a medicine, inoculation, etc.: To take hold, take effect, prove operative or effective. Also *fig.*

1626 B. JONSON *Staple of N.* v. iii, If all succeed well, and my simples take. **1853** *Jrnl. R. Agric. Soc.* XIV. I. 253 To see if the previous inoculation would still take. **1897** S. L. HINDE *Congo Arabs* 61 The vaccine from Europe,—unfortunately none of it took. **1906** E. DYSON *Fact'ry 'Ands* iii. 29 Fuzzy's love was the mysterious and unhallowed growth of a moment. Sarah..had beguiled him with her Ethiopian grin and glances of matured coyness... In the words of Benno the wise, 'It took like er vaccination'. **1951** G. GREENE *End of Affair* v. iv. 201 'He did it there and then.' .. 'Did what?' 'Baptized her a Catholic... I always had a wish that it would take'. Like vaccination.'

III. Weakened sense of 'seize', with elimination of the notion of force or art: the ordinary current sense. **i.** With a material object.

* *with physical action distinct.*

12. *trans.* To perform the voluntary physical act by which one gets (something) into one's hand or hold; to transfer to oneself by one's own physical act. (Now the main sense.)

a. with the instrumentality of the hand or hands explicitly or implicitly indicated.

c **1200** ORMIN 135 He toc hiss reclefatt onn hand, & ȝede innto þe temmple. *c* **1300** *Cursor M.* 1374 Þou sal tak þis pepins thre, þat I toke o þat appel tre. *c* **1375** *Ibid.* 21529 (Fairf.) Siþen he toke [*Cott.* & *Gött.* nam] a spade in hande. **1387** TREVISA *Higden* (Rolls) VII. 77 Anoon as he hadde i-take þe knyf all þe ymages gonne to grucche and to aryse. *c* **1391** CHAUCER *Astrol.* II. §29 Tak thanne thyn Astrolabie with bothe handes. **1450** W. LOMNER in *Four C. Eng. Lett.* (1880) 4 And toke a rusty sword. **1471** CAXTON *Recuyell* I. Pref., [I] forthwith toke penne and ynke and began [etc.]. *a* **1533** LD. BERNERS *Huon* lix. 207 Take thy vyall, and geue vs a songe. **1608** TOPSELL *Serpents* (1658) 595 If a man take a Snake or a Serpent in to his handling. **1611** BIBLE *John* xxi. 13 Iesus then commeth, and taketh bread, and giueth them. **1799** WORDSW. *Lucy Gray* vi, He plied his work;—and Lucy took The lantern in her hand. **1833** T. HOOK *Parson's Dau.* I. ii, He could take his hat and go.

b. with the instrumentality not expressed or considered.

c **1200** ORMIN 1338 þe preost..toc & snap þatt oþerr bucc Drihhtin þærwiþþ to lazenn. *a* **1300** *Cursor M.* 5646 Þar-for moyses was his nam, For he was o þe water tan. **1470–85** MALORY *Arthur* XXI. v. 849 Syr Bedwere toke the kyng vpon his backe and so wente wyth hym to that water syde. **1584** R. SCOT *Discov. Witchcr.* XII. xviii. (1886) 222 Take a cup of cold water, and let fall thereinto three drops of the same bloud. **1611** BIBLE *Gen.* ii. 22 The rib which the Lord God had taken from man, made hee a woman. **1685** BOYLE *Effects of Mot.* Postscr. 155 Take..of the Arsenical Loadstone well pulverised two ounces. **1771** MRS. HAYWOOD *New Present* 77 Take a quart of shrimps. **1882** SOUTHWARD *Pract. Print.* xi. 444 While the roller [= pressman's assistant] is taking ink, the pressman should employ the time in looking over the heap.

†**c.** To take and put (a garment) *on* one, wrap *about* one. *Obs.*

a **1300** *Cursor M.* 9746 Fader, i sal on me for-þi, O thral tak clething sothfastli. *Ibid.* 10419 Sco tok on hir cleþing o care. **1530** PALSGR. 746/2 Take this mantell aboute you, *affullez ce manteau*. *a* **1604** *Song* in Shaks. *Oth.* II. iii. 99 And take thy awl'd Cloake about thee.

13. To receive into one's body by one's own act; to eat or drink, to swallow (food, drink, medicine, opium, etc.); to inhale (snuff, tobacco-smoke, etc.).

(For tobacco, the ordinary expression is now *to smoke*.)

c **1200** ORMIN 7545 þatt tokenn ȝȝ wiþþ mikell mæþ & ȝȝ unnorne fode. **13..** *Cursor M.* 16762 + 16 He tast it with tonge, Bot þer-of toke he noght. *c* **1400** *Apol. Loll.* 103 þe meyt comendiþ vs not to God,..but frely it may be tan, & frely left. **1509** BARCLAY *Shyp of Folys* (1570) 34 Wine ne ale hurteth no maner creature But sharpeth the wit if it be take in kinde. **1601** HOLLAND *Pliny* XX. iv, The best way to take it [the juice of the radish], is at the end of a meale with the last meat. **1617** MORYSON *Itin.* II. 46 He tooke Tobacco abundantly,..which I thinke preserved him from sicknes. **1654–66** EARL ORRERY *Parthen.* (1676) 683 My Soldiers having.. taken a little refreshment. **1675** BAXTER *Cath. Theol.* II. I. 298 It was then a crime with them to take Tobacco, and now it is none: thus custome changes the matter. **1732** BERKELEY *Alciphr.* v. §7 Those..who take his physic. **1771** FOOTE *Maid of B.* I. Wks. 1799 II. 210 Mr. Flint and I, most evenings take a whiff here. **1784** *Unfortunate Sensibility* II. 40 To take a good drink of raw brandy. **1807** SOUTHEY *Espriella's Lett.* II. 219 We took an early breakfast. **1852** FITZGERALD *Euphranor* (1904) 73 No doubt he took his glass with the rest. **1875** JOWETT *Plato* (ed. 2) I. 429 He died by taking poison. **1879** MORLEY *Milton* 108 He died at Spa, where he was taking the waters, in September 1653. **1891** *Murray's Mag.* Apr. 532 Inordinately given to taking snuff. **1893** *Times* 22 Apr. 7/5 The Queen..took tea at the Cabanon on the sea shore.

b. To expose oneself to (air) so as to inhale it or get the physical benefit of it; chiefly in phr. *to take the air*, to walk out in the open air (now *rare* or *arch.*): see AIR *sb.* 5. So *to take a bath*, to bathe, esp. in a place or vessel prepared for the purpose; but the phrase is also used in sense 52 (cf. BATH *sb.*¹ 6, 1).

1375 BARBOUR *Bruce* VI. 304 The kyng..of his basnet than had tane, To tak the air, for he wes hate. *c* **1450** *St. Cuthbert* (Surtees) 1078 His seruands..Bare him with cute to take þe ayre. **1470–85** MALORY *Arthur* VII. xvii. 239 Eyther of hem vnlaced his helme, and toke the cold wynde. **1594** BARNFIELD *Affect. Sheph.* I. xx Abroad into the fields to take fresh ayre. **1711** ADDISON *Spect.* No. 123 ¶1 As I was Yesterday taking the Air with my Friend Sir Roger. **1777** SHERIDAN *Sch. Scand.* II. ii, Lady Betty..was taking the dust in Hyde Park. **1837** [see BATH *sb.*¹ 1]. **1866** HOWELLS *Venet. Life* 295 When the fair Venetians go out in their gondolas to 'take the air'. **1879** EDNA LYALL *Won by Waiting* xxxi, Her father..was to take a course of baths [in Germany]. **1890** *Cornh. Mag.* July 7 The English people hurry forth to take the morning air.

c. Phr. *not to be taking any..*: not to be in the mood for; to be disinclined for. *slang.*

1900 *Daily News* 10 Mar. 2/1 In the language of the hour, 'nobody was taking any.' **1905** *Daily Chron.* 20 Dec. 3/4 As one of her fellow countrywomen might have said, Frances was not 'taking any' pessimism just then.

** *with physical action subordinated to the relation produced.*

14. To bring, receive, or adopt (a person) into some relation to oneself (e.g. into one's service, protection, tuition, care, companionship, favour). *to take to (into) mercy*: see MERCY *sb.* 5.

c **1175** *Lamb. Hom.* 27 þesne mon ic habbe itaken to mine aȝene bihofþe. *a* **1300** *Cursor M.* 2792, 'I haue', [loth] said, 'doghtres tua, Tas and dos your will wit þaa.' **13..** *Ibid.* 20106 (Gött.) þan tok [*Cott.* nam] þe apostel sone on-ane In-tille his keping, þat maidane. **1388** WYCLIF *Ps.* xxvi[i]. 10 For my fadir and my modir han forsake me; but the Lord hath take me. **1428** in *Surtees Misc.* (1888) 5 þat tha tuke hym to þair grace. *c* **1477** CAXTON *Jason* 17 b, The fayr Myrro..toke Jason so in her good grace that vnto the deth she louyd him. **1531** in *Sel. Cas. Crt. Requests* (1898) 34 The said abbott..was greatly laborid to taike to service the said Roger. **1643** BURROUGHES *Exp. Hosea* (1652) 147 If God takes them to mercy we must be ready willingly to take them into brotherly society. **1654** EARL MONM. tr. *Bentivoglio's Warrs of Flanders* 54 Being then tane into pay by the Princes. **1794** in J. O. Payne *Old Eng. Cath. Missions* (1889) 14 Took into the Church William Fawcett Grange. **1878** *Scribner's Mag.* XVI. 135/1 He would freely take them into his confidence. **1885** *Law Times* LXXX. 6/2 None were allowed to let their rooms or take lodgers. **1891** E. PEACOCK *N. Brendon* I. 120 He took pupils to increase his income.

b. *spec.* in reference to marriage or cohabitation; often in phr. *to take to wife, in marriage.*

c **1200** ORMIN 19593 þat tiss Herode King..haffde takenn all wiþþ woh Filippess wif hiss broþerr. *a* **1300** *Cursor M.* 12667 A man in mariage hir tok, Hight alpheus. *c* **1386** CHAUCER *Melib.* ¶ 590 (Harl. MS.) If a neet-hurdes douȝter ..be riche, sche may cheese of a þousand men which she wol take to hir housbonde. ? *a* **1400** *Punishm. Adultery* 63 in Horstm. *Altengl. Leg.* (1881) 369 He rouȝt not what woman he toke. *c* **1477** CAXTON *Jason* 97 b, That they shold take eche other by mariage. **1560** DAUS tr. *Sleidane's Comm.* 35 b, They bidde him take a Leman lest he attempt to defile honest women. **1687** BURNET *Cont. Reply to Varillas* 77 He professed himself a Lutheran, and took a Wife. **1771** SMOLLETT *Humph. Cl.* 18 July, A young lady..who agreed to take me for better or worse. **1891** *Cornh. Mag.* Dec. 664 He took unto himself a village maid, and settled in Lyndhurst.

c. To possess sexually.

1915 D. H. LAWRENCE *Rainbow* i. 14 Whether he were going to take her out of inflamed necessity. *Ibid.* viii. 216 Even if he did not take her, he would make her relax, he would fuse away her resistance. **1930** A. HUXLEY *Brief Candles* 280 She kissed him again. 'Take me.' **1948** G. VIDAL *City & Pillar* I. vi. 133 He wanted to throw her on a bed and take her against her will, violently. **1962** I. MURDOCH *Unofficial Rose* xiii. 122 'Well, it's up to you too, my queen,' said Randall. 'You want to be—taken, don't you?' **1978** T. ALLBEURY *Lantern Network* viii. 110 She lay with her eyes open as he took her.

15. To transfer by one's own direct act (a thing) into one's possession or keeping; to appropriate; to enter into possession or use of. See also *take in possession*, s.v. POSSESSION *sb.* 1 c; *take possession* in Phrases below (71).

c **1200** *Trin. Coll. Hom.* 167 þe deuel..þan toc his [Job's] oȝen lichame and þer one brohte swo michel sicnesse. *c* **1300** *Harrow. Hell* 103 Heouene ant erþe tac to þe, Soules in helle lef þou me. *c* **1450** *Godstow Reg.* 416 To entre the forsaid tenement and to take and hold all maner of goodes and catallis I-founde in the same. **1535** COVERDALE *Josh.* xix. 47 And the children of Dan..toke it in possession, & dwelt therin. **1611** BIBLE *John* x. 17, I lay downe my life that I might take it againe. **1683** *Pennsylv. Archives* I. 55, I desire thee take the towne of Salem into thy lott. **1795** *Fate of Sedley* I. 189, If he dare to take a bone which they had given to their dogs. **1818** CRUISE *Digest* (ed. 2) IV. 378 The question was, whether the heirs of S. Morris took any estate under this appointment. **1883** *Law Times Rep.* XLIX. 155/1 The undertakers..had power to take lands compulsorily.

b. *absol.* To take possession; *spec.* in *Law*, to enter into actual possession.

c **1407** LYDG. *Reason & Sens.* 6486 The hunger..gredy, and in-saturable Of wommen for to Acroche and take. **1642** tr. *Perkins' Prof. Bk.* i. §52. 24 There is one named in the Lease who may take immediately. **1706** E. WARD *Wooden World Diss.* (1708) 33 But if he gives, he takes too sometimes. **1803** WORDSW. *Rob Roy's Grave* 39 The good old rule..the simple plan, That they should take, who have the power, And they should keep who can. **1818** CRUISE *Digest* (ed. 2) VI. 298 The testator intended, that when Francis was dead without issue, the eldest son should take. **1894** *Daily News* 29 June 5/2 The will of December, 1888, they find, was duly executed... The Royal Academy therefore take.

c. To secure beforehand by payment or contract; e.g. *to take a house*, etc., to engage (a house or other place) for the purpose of occupying it.

1604 E. G[RIMSTONE] *D'Acosta's Hist. Indies* IV. vi. 223 Many Spaniardes..came thither to take mines. **1670** LADY MARY BERTIE in *12th Rep. Hist. MSS. Comm.* App. v. 22 My brother Norreys tooke a box and carryed my Lady Rochester and his mistresse and all us to. **1693** *Humours Town* 8, I have within these few days taken a Lodging. **1743** BULKELEY & CUMMINS *Voy. S. Seas* 196 To take a House in the Country at our own Expence. **1803** *Pic Nic* No. 11 (1806) II. 143 She has now taken a thirty years lease of a house. **1848** THACKERAY *Van. Fair* xli, Colonel Crawley and his wife took a couple of places in the same old Highflyer coach. **1850** *Tait's Mag.* XVII. 719/1 When he took his farm, it was well cultivated.

d. To get or procure regularly by payment (something offered to the public, as a periodical, a commodity). See also *take in*, 84 c.

1593 *Acct. Bk. W. Wray* in *Antiquary* XXXII. 119 May the 28 we begun to take milke of Ann Smith for a halfe penneworth of the day. **1798** J. WOODFORDE *Diary* 6 Jan. (1931) V. 92 Crouse's Norwich Paper which we used to take, did not arrive. **1808** ELEANOR SLEATH *Bristol Heiress* III. 40 A morning paper, which Lady Harcourt constantly took. **1852** DE MORGAN in Graves *Life Sir W. R. Hamilton* (1889) III. 426 You take the Philosophical Magazine, I think. **1897** *N. & Q.* 8th Ser. XII. 354/1 In my boyhood I 'took' the *Penny Magazine*.

ii. With a non-material object.

*** *To take to oneself, assume, an attribute, quality, character.*

16. a. To assume (a form, nature, character, name, or other attribute); sometimes, to assume the part or character of. ***to take on oneself***, to put on.

c **1200** ORMIN 85 He sennde uss.. Hiss Sune.. To takenn ure mennissclezȝe. *a* **1300** *Cursor M.* 14464 Þai said þat crist suld ta manhede Of a maiden and of þair sede. *c* **1385** CHAUCER *L.G.W.* 1142 *Dido*, That Cupido.. Hadde the liknesse of the child I-take. *c* **1440** *Alphabet of Tales* 57 At þe laste he tuke his spiritt vnto hym. **1546** LANGLEY *Pol. Verg. De Invent.* II. xv. 61 God.. toke on him the shape of Man as Abraham sawe him. **1548–9** (Mar.) *Bk. Com. Prayer, Collect Christmas Day*, Almyghtye God, whiche haste geuen us thy onlye begotten sonne to take our nature upon hym. **1605** SHAKS. *Macb.* III. iv. 102 Take any shape but that, and my firme Nerues Shall neuer tremble. **1697** DRYDEN *Virg. Georg.* IV. 329 [They] take the Forms his Prescience did ordain. **1711** ADDISON *Spect.* No. 35 ¶4 An Impostor.. who takes upon him the Name of this young Gentleman. **1810** SCOTT *Lady of L.* III. vii, The mountain mist took form and limb. **1844** *Fraser's Mag.* XXX. 532/2 Liddy was really taking the woman upon her in earnest, since she had attained the matronly age of seventeen. **1887** *Times* (weekly ed.) 9 Dec. 16/2 France cannot take the offensive, but she can paralyse Germany and Italy.

†**b.** To adopt (a law or custom); to undertake or begin to follow or observe. *Obs.*

c **1200** ORMIN Ded. 7 Broþerr min.. Þurrh þatt witt hafenn takenn ba An reȝhellboc to follȝhenn. *a* **1300** *Cursor M.* 19540 Quen þe apostels þan hard sai Samaritans had tan þair wai [*other MSS.* lay]. *c* **1375** *Ibid.* 2700 (Fairf.) Abraham.. was .v. skore bot ane þat day quen þai toke [*Cott.* vnder-fang] þe new lay. **1474** CAXTON *Chesse* II. i. 21 The peple of tarante toke for a custome that the dronken men shold be punysshyd. *a* **1533** LD. BERNERS *Huon* xlv. 151 He thretenethe to slee me by cause I wyll not take on me his law.

c. To assume, adopt (a symbol or badge, or something connected with and denoting a function): in phrases having specific meanings, as:

to take the crown, the throne, to assume sovereignty; ***to take the habit***, to become a monk; ***to take the gown***, to become a clergyman; ***to take the ball*** (at cricket), to assume the position of bowler; ***to take an oar***, to begin to row. See also CROSS *sb.* 4 c, SILK, VEIL *sb.*

c **1330** [see CROSS *sb.* 4 c]. *a* **1380** *St. Bernard* 287 in Horstm. *Altengl. Leg.* (1878) 46 Whon Bernard hed taken his abyt. *c* **1450** *St. Cuthbert* (Surtees) 6620 Þe abyte he toke, as bede of him wryte. **1568** GRAFTON *Chron.* II. 112 He had taken on him a little before the lyuery of the crosse. **1605** CAMDEN *Rem.* (1637) 344 John of Gaunt Duke of Lancaster ..took a red Rose to his device. **1784** J. POTTER *Virtuous Villagers* II. 135, I have now taken the gown. **1855** BROWNING *Protus* 39 John the Pannonian.. Came, had a mind to take the crown. **1860** *All Year Round* No. 66. 384 'Take an oar, sir', said Philip. **1883** *Daily Tel.* 15 May 2/7 The champion took the ball, vice Penn.

**** *To charge oneself with, undertake, discharge.*

17. To assume, charge oneself with, undertake (a function, responsibility, etc.). See also *take charge* (66 below), *take in charge* (CHARGE 13 b), *take in* or *on hand* (HAND 42); also 18 a, b.

c **1200** ORMIN 10896 Sannt Iohann.. toc þatt wikenn þohh þa siþþen, whanne he wisste [etc.]. **13..** *Cursor M.* 12390 Trein beddes was he wont to make And þar-for his seruis to take. *c* **1425** *Ibid.* 4795 (Trin.) Lo I am al redy boun Oure aller nedes to take in place. *c* **1450** *Merlin* 3 This feende that toke this enterprise ne taried not. **1647** JER. TAYLOR *Lib. Proph.* 193 That every man must take his adventure. **1847** MARRYAT *Childr. N. Forest* xviii, I think.. I would take it [the post] on trial. **1863** KINGLAKE *Crimea* I. vi. 88 The plan of taking engagements upon possible eventualities. **1890** TOUT *Hist. Eng. from 1689*, 133 Grenville refused to take office without Fox. **1890** LANE-POOLE *Barbary Corsairs* I. xii. 124 He took service as a boy in the Turkish fleet. **1892** *Speaker* 3 Sept. 279/1 Captain Mayer.. was compelled by circumstances to take the responsibility.

b. To subject oneself to (an oath, vow, pledge, or the like): see also OATH *sb.* 1, DICK *sb.*[5]

1511– [see OATH *sb.* 1]. **1599** SHAKS. *Much Ado* II. iii. 26 Ile take my oath on it. *a* **1715** BURNET *Own Time* an. 1678. III. (1724) I. 435 A bill.. requiring all members of either House ..to take a test against Popery. **1803** *Pic Nic* No. 4 (1806) I. 140 She has taken the monastic Vow. **1897** 'SARAH GRAND' *Beth Bk.* xlvi. (1898) 438 I'll take my dick he'll not trouble us with a bill for the next six months.

(*b*) Phr. ***to take the Fifth Amendment*** (U.S.): to appeal to Article V of the ten original amendments (1791) to the Constitution of the United States, which states that 'no person.. shall be compelled in any criminal case to be a witness against himself'; hence, to decline to incriminate oneself. Usu. *ellipt.*, ***to take the Fifth.***

1955 *U.S. News & World Report* 22 July 36/2 In the armed services, let a man take the Fifth Amendment and his military career is virtually doomed. **1967** *N.Y. Times* 22 Jan. IV. 10/1 (*heading*) Law: taking the Fifth and making a living. **1972** J. G. VERMANDEL *Last seen in Samarra* xx. 133 'You can hardly have in mind to cast me as a villain because of that.'.. Alex nodded. 'Right... If you want to take the Fifth, maybe Derek will settle it for us?' **1976** *Times Lit. Suppl.* 12 Nov. 1413/2 To do what I did not want to do: take the Fifth Amendment. **1978** S. BRILL *Teamsters* Pl. 4 (*caption*) The former gym teacher took the Fifth Amendment when asked about the millions of dollars in insurance he had sold to the Teamsters health and welfare funds.

†**c.** ***to take it***: to make oneself responsible for a statement; to affirm, asseverate. Const. *on* (one's death, honour: see ON *prep.* 12). *Obs.*

1595 SHAKS. *John* I. i. 110 Vpon his death-bed he.. tooke it on his death That this my mothers sonne was none of his. **1598** —— *Merry W.* II. ii. 12, I took't vpon mine honour thou hadst it not. **1631** WEEVER *Anc. Fun. Mon.* 379 Guiltlesse of any offence.. as he tooke it vpon his death.

18. ***to take on*** or ***upon oneself***.

a. To charge oneself with, undertake (an office, duty, or responsibility); to make oneself responsible for. In quot. *c* 1470 *absol.*

a **1300** *Cursor M.* 20790 He wil noght tak þe cark [*MS. F.* charge] on him, Quar [*F.* queþer] þat it be sua soght or nai. **1432** *Paston Lett.* I. 34 The said Erle hath take upon him the governance of the Kinges persone. *c* **1470** HENRY *Wallace* VI. 355 Be caus we wait he is a gentill man, Cum in my grace, and I sall saiff him than, As for his lyff, I will apon me tak. *a* **1533** LD. BERNERS *Huon* xliii. 143 He wyll take on hym this bateyll ayenst the gyant. **1611** BIBLE *Num.* xvi. 7 Yee take too much vpon you [Cov. make to moch a doo], ye sonnes of Leui. *a* **1648** LD. HERBERT *Hen. VIII* (1683) 253 That.. he should persuade her to enter a Monastery, and take on her a Religious life. **1728** in Picton *L'pool Munic. Rec.* (1886) II. 86 Occasioned by.. Mr. Hughes's taking upon him the office of Mayor. **1883** *Century Mag.* XXVI. 608/1 Helen took the blame upon herself.

b. With *inf.* To undertake; to assume the right, presume, make bold (*to do* something).

c **1275** *Passion of our Lord* 619 in *O.E. Misc.* 54 Vre louerd him tok on To schewen his apostles þet he wes god and mon. **1449** *Rolls of Parlt.* V. 151/2 Daren not take uppon hem to labour ayenst suche Felons. *c* **1489** CAXTON *Sonnes of Aymon* xxii. 481, I shall take vpon me to make amendes for hym. **1523** LD. BERNERS *Froiss.* I. cclxxv. 411 To desyre him to take on him to be the Constable of France. **1648** THORPE *Charge at York Assizes* (1649) 26 If any Person take upon him to be a Badger of Corn. **1724** DE FOE *Mem. Cavalier* (1840) 234, I took upon me.. to go to Leeds. **1837** HALLAM *Hist. Lit.* (1847) I. i. §90. 78 Some took on them to imitate what they read. **1885** LD. COLERIDGE in *Law Rep. 14 Q.B. Div.* 825 The judgment, which the plaintiff has taken upon himself to sue out and to enter, is wrong.

†**c.** To profess, claim *to do* something; to assume, presume *that*..(with implication that the claim or assumption is unwarranted). *Obs.*

? *a* **1500** *Wycket* (1828) p. viii, Hypocrites that take on them to make oure Lordes bodye. **1560** DAUS tr. *Sleidane's Comm.* 29 b, As thoughe I toke vpon me that I could not erre. **1653** GATAKER *Vind. Annot. Jer.* 31 The time whereof both of them, contrary to our Saviors avouchment take upon them to determine.

†**d.** To affect, feign, pretend, make believe, *to do* something. *Obs.*

1571 tr. *Buchanan's Detection* E j b, Though thay tuke upon tham as if thay regardit nat these thynges, yet sometyme the rumors.. merely prickit them to the quick. **1597** SHAKS. *2 Hen. IV*, II. ii. 123 How comes that, sayes he that takes vpon him not to conceiue. **1606** —— *Tr. & Cr.* I. ii. 153 Shee takes vpon her to spie a white haire on his chinne.

†**e.** *absol.* or *intr.* To assume authority or importance; sometimes in good sense, to behave bravely or valiantly (quot. *c* 1470), to put oneself forward, assert oneself (quot. 1720); usually in bad sense, = to take too much upon one, to behave presumptuously or haughtily, assume airs. *Obs.*

c **1470** HENRY *Wallace* v. 43 Wallace so weill apon him tuk that tide, Throw the gret preys he maid a way full wide. **1530** PALSGR. 747/1, I take apon me, lyke a lord or mayster, *je fais du grant.* **1581** PETTIE tr. *Guazzo's Civ. Conv.* II. (1586) 109 b, It shalbe the part of a straunger, being in another mans house, not to take vpon him presumptuously. **1637** T. MORTON *New Eng. Canaan* (1883) 306 This man.. tooke upon him infinitely: and made warrants in his owne name. **1667** PEPYS *Diary* 3 June, But, Lord! to see how Duncomb do take upon him is an eye-sore. **1720** DE FOE *Capt. Singleton* xiii. (1840) 233, I found it was time to take upon me a little.

f. *trans.* See 16.

19. a. To undertake and perform, conduct, or discharge (a part, function, duty, service, or the like). See also PART *sb.* 23.

1411 *Rolls of Parlt.* III. 650/1 A Loveday taken bytwen the same parties by William Gascoigne Chief Justice of the forsaid Benche. **1596** [see PART *sb.* 23 b]. **1874** MICKLETHWAITE *Mod. Par. Churches* 60 Each priest.. may take those parts of the service designed to him from time to time. **1885** MARY LINSKILL *Lost Son* iv. 58 Will you favour us by taking the tenor? **1889** *Cornhill Mag.* Dec. 623 The female parts in plays being taken by boys and men. **1890** *Pictorial World* 15 May 616/1 She would take the grammar class at ten and the arithmetic class at eleven. *a* **1910** *Mod.* The assistant master who takes duty also takes preparation. The canon who was taking residence that day.

(*b*) *spec.*, to answer (a telephone call).

1970 P. MOYES *Who saw her Die?* iii. 37 The shrilling of the telephone provided a welcome release... Dolly said, 'I'll take it.' **1976** G. SIMS *End of Web* i. 13 'Sorry, I'll have to take it. Might be a friend I was trying to contact this morning.'.. He picked up the phone. **1979** C. MACLEOD *Luck runs Out* iv. 37 The telephone rang. 'I'll take it,' said Shandy.

b. Phr. ***to take pains, take trouble*** (also formerly ***take labour, toil***, etc.): to take upon oneself and exercise these activities and qualities; to exercise care and diligence: see also PAIN *sb.*[1] 5, 6, TROUBLE *sb.*

13.. *Cursor M.* 4789 (Gött.) Loke quilk of ȝu sal take on hand For vs all take þis trauaile. **1528** *Impeachm. Wolsey* in Furnivall *Ballads from MSS.* I. 360 Whoo hathe þis matyr so playnly declaryd, or hathe the labowur Take. *a* **1533** LD. BERNERS *Huon* lxxxiii. 262 Ye shall not nede to take the laboure. **1600** TOURNEUR *Transf. Metamorph.* lv, But (Knight) believe me, I have t'ane much toile. **1794** MARQ. BUCKINGHAM in *14th Rep. Hist. MSS. Comm.* App. v. 489, I am sure you have taken every pains to do whatever you imagined might best forward my wishes. **1893** LIDDON, etc. *Life Pusey* I. xviii. 420 His unlimited capacity for taking trouble.

***** *To adopt or assume as one's own.*

20. To adopt as one's own (a part or side in a contest, controversy, etc.), to range oneself on, ally oneself with (a side or party); see PART *sb.* 23 c, PARTY *sb.* 5, SIDE *sb.*

c **1420**, etc. [see PART *sb.* 23 c]. **1530** PALSGR. 750/1, I take ones parte, I holde with hym in a mater, *je prens partye.* **1606** G. W[OODCOCKE] *Hist. Ivstine* XXXVI. 114 Shewed in derision to the people that had tooke part with him. **1751** ELIZA HEYWOOD *Betsy Thoughtless* II. 199 To take the party, which would best become his honour and reputation. **1820** L. HUNT *Indicator* No. 15 (1822) I. 118 No wonder that the Queen of France took part with the rebels against.. her husband.

b. *absol.* or *intr.* in same sense: ***to take against***, to oppose; ***to take for***, to support, back up, side with. *rare.* (See also *take with*, 75 d.)

c **1330** R. BRUNNE *Chron. Wace* (Rolls) 15312 And for Englische mennes sake, Ageyn þe oughte we to take. **1770** FOOTE *Lame Lover* II. Wks. 1799 II. 70 A wise man should well weigh which party to take for. **1892** *Longm. Mag.* Mar. 558 'You are not taking against me?' he exclaimed suspiciously.

21. To assume as if one's own, to appropriate or arrogate to oneself (credit, etc.); to assume as if granted, e.g. ***to take leave, liberty***, etc.: see also LIBERTY *sb.*[1] 5 b. ***to take for granted***: see 48.

1525 LD. BERNERS *Froiss.* II. xxi. 46 Wherfore this Kyng Iohan toke tytell to make warr. **1611** BEAUM. & FL. *Philaster* I. i, Kissing your white hand [Mistress] I take leave, To thank your royal father. **1625–** [see LIBERTY *sb.*[1] 5 b]. **1627–77** FELTHAM *Resolves* I. xxxi. 53 Hamans thirst was Honor: Achitophel took the glory of his Counsel. **1820** *Examiner* No. 612. 7/1 We would take leave to recommend ..an alteration. **1850** *Tait's Mag.* XVII. 564/1 Voltaire took all sorts of liberties with his mother tongue. **1870** ROGERS *Hist. Gleanings* Ser. II. 93 He took credit to himself that.. her son remained stanch.

22. *Gram.* Of a word, clause, or sentence: To have by right or usage, either as part of itself or with it in construction (a particular inflexion, accent, case, mood, etc.) as the proper one.

1818 BLOMFIELD tr. *Matthiae's Grk. Gram.* I. 208 Verbs.. which are derived from compound adjectives, take the augment at the beginning. *Ibid.* 472 The following verbs.. take the genitive of the thing. **1860** GOODWIN *Grk. Moods & Tenses* 220 Causal sentences regularly take the Indicative. **1876** KENNEDY *Publ. Sch. Lat. Gram.* §20 All Declensions take the Ending *m* for Masc. and Fem. Nouns. **1881** CHANDLER *Grk. Accentuation* §767 The following take the accent on the penultimate.

IV. Pregnant senses related to III.; usually including a notion of choice, purpose, use, employment, treatment, or occupation.

* *Connoting choice.*

23. To pick out from a number: either by chance, at random; or with intention, to select, choose.

c **1275** LAY. 12176 Ten þusend cnihtes tock Gracien forþrihtes [*c* 1205 he chæs.. ten þusend cnihten]. **1382** WYCLIF *1 Sam.* xiv. 42 Saul seith, Leyeth lot betwix me and Jonathan my sone. And Jonathas is taken. **1535** COVERDALE *ibid.*, Saul sayde: Cast the lot ouer me and my sonne Ionathas. So Ionathas was taken. **1612** *Two Noble K.* II. iii. 70 [*Peasant*] Thou wilt not goe along? *Arc.* Not yet, sir. [*P.*] Well, sir, take your owne time. **1625** BACON *Ess., Ambition* (Arb.) 225 Good Commanders in the Warres, must be taken, be they neuer so Ambitious. **1742** FRANCIS tr. *Hor. Sat.* I. iv. 31 Take me a man, at venture, from the crowd. **1769** JOHNSON 29 Oct. in *Boswell*, I'll take you five children from London, who shall cuff five Highland children.

** *Connoting purpose, use, employment.*

24. To adopt or choose in order to use in some way; to adopt in some capacity (const. *as*, *for*); hence, to employ for a purpose, to have recourse to, avail oneself of, proceed to use (a means or method); to seize (an opportunity, etc.). See also *take day* in Phrases below (67), ADVANTAGE *sb.* 5 b, MEASURE *sb.* 21, OCCASION *sb.*[1] 1.

13.. *Cursor M.* 29177 For a reule þis sal þou take. **1471** SIR J. PASTON in *P. Lett.* III. 15 Thys next terme I hope to take on [= one] weye with hyr or other. **1483–4** *Act 1 Rich. III*, c. 2 §1 That suche exaccions.. afore this tyme takyn be take for no example to make suche or any lyke charge.. hereafter. **1561** [see OCCASION *sb.*[1] 1]. **1579** FULKE *Heskins' Parl.* 316 He taketh times and occasions at his pleasure. **1605** SHAKS. *Macb.* III. i. 23 We should haue else desir'd your good aduice.. In this dayes Councell: but wee'le take to morrow. **1667** DRYDEN *Sir Martin Mar-all* III. i, If thou wilt have a foolish word to lard thy lean discourse with, take an English one. **1686** tr. *Chardin's Coronat. Solyman* 122 He knew.. how to take his Measures to the ruine of his Competitors. **1728** RAMSAY *Bonny Chirsty* iv, He wisely this white minute took, And flang his arms about her. **1729** BP. WADDINGTON in *Lardner's Wks.* (1838) I. p. lxiii, You have certainly took a very proper and christian way with him. **1758** S. HAYWARD *Serm.* Introd. 11 What special methods could be taken to stem the tide of immorality? **1789** *Triumphs Fortitude* I. 101, I shall take the first opportunity of sending the books I promised. **1820** *Examiner* No. 614. 39/1 That great genius is taken as the standard of perfection. **1867** HOWELLS *Ital. Journ.* 118 We raised our sail, and took the gale that blew for Capri. **1890** *Blackw. Mag.* CXLVIII. 442/2 Every possible means is now taken to conceal the truth.

b. To take into use, to use, have recourse to (one's hands, a tool, weapon, etc.) for doing something. ***to take a stick*** (etc.) ***to***, to use it to beat (a person, etc.). (Sometimes with mixture of sense 12.)

1768 STERNE *Sent. Journ.* (1778) II. 25, I took both hands to it. **1888** STEVENSON *Black Arrow* IV. ii. 208 He had ta'en his belt to me, forsooth! **1889** 'LEWIS CARROLL' *Sylvie & Bruno* iv. 53 'Take a stick to him!' shouted the Vice-Warden.

c. *esp.* To take into use or employment, to have recourse to as a means of progression (a vehicle, ship, horse, one's limbs, etc.); to enter or mount for a journey or voyage. Often without article, as ***to take boat, coach, ship***, etc.: see also *take to* (74 b), *take horse* (70 a); HEEL *sb.*[1] 20, LEG *sb.* 2 b, WING *sb.* (Cf. 25.)

c **1450** [see 70 a]. **1517** TORKINGTON *Pilgr.* (1884) 46 We toke our assys at the Mownte Syon, . . and rode the same nyght to Bethlem. **1530** PALSGR. 751/1, I take shyppe or the see, *je monte sur la mer* . . . Where toke they shyppyng, *ou est ce quilz monterent sur la mer.* **1576** [see BOAT *sb.* 1 d]. **1654** tr. *Scudery's Curia Pol.* 19 If the Duke of Guise . . had speedily taken post, and fled from Blois. **1672** SIR C. LYTTELTON in *Hatton Corr.* (Camden) 86, I am . . just taking coach to give his R[ll] Highnesse y[e] paru bien after his late danger. **1721** DE FOE *Col. Jack* (1840) 199, I took the packet-boat, and came over to England. **1844** *Fraser's Mag.* XXX. 603/1 He takes ship for Ireland. **1885** 'ANSTEY' *Tinted Venus* viii. 95 I've a good mind to take the tram to the Archway. **1892** *Monthly Packet* Apr. 444 They . . took train to London.

25. To gain the aid or help of (a place) by betaking oneself to it; to gain, reach, repair to, go into, enter (esp. for refuge or safety); to get into or on to: = *take to*, 74 c. Often in special phrases: see FIELD, GROUND, INN, LAND, REFUGE, SANCTUARY, SEA, WALL, WATER, etc.

c **1205** LAY. 7976 He droh in ane hælue & toc þan [*c* 1275 tock to] herberwe. *c* **1330** R. BRUNNE *Chron. Wace* (Rolls) 5397 Hauene he tok at Porcestre. *c* **1400** *Laud Troy Bk.* 10501 Thei token the toun with mychel spede . . To saue her lyues. **1461** *Paston Lett.* II. 52 The Duc of Excestre and th'erle of Pembrok are floon and taken the mounteyns. **1480** CAXTON *Chron. Eng.* clxx. 155 They that myght take the bridge escaped. **1485** —— *Paris & V.* 43 He took the ryuer wyth hys hors. **1512** *Act 4 Hen. VIII*, c. 2 §2 If any murderer . . hadde taken any Churchy or Churchyerd or murder. **1565** STAPLETON tr. *Bede's Hist. Ch. Eng.* 169 Beinge vysited with syeknesse he toke his bedde. **1583** *Reg. Privy Council Scot.* III. 600 Constraning him to tak his hous for the saifty of his lif. **1618** ROWLANDS *Night Raven* (1620) 12 A cruell Beare, which forc'd him take a tree. **1831** *Examiner* 443/2 Vipers occasionally take the water. **1852** R. F. BURTON *Falconry Valley Indus* v. 61 *note*, The first falcon . . caused the quarry to take the air. **1868** STANLEY *Westm. Abbey* v. 364 But the right of asylum rendered the whole precinct a vast 'cave of Adullam' for all the distressed and discontented of the metropolis who desired, according to the phrase of the time, to 'take Westminster'. **1880** T. STEVENSON in *Encycl. Brit.* XI. 455 A harbour which may be easily taken and left in stormy weather.

b. To adopt and enter upon (a road, way, path, course, etc., *lit.* or *fig.*); to betake oneself to, begin to go along or by: sometimes with mixture of sense 'to choose, select' (23). See also COURSE *sb.* 11 b, 22, WAY *sb.*

a **1300** *Cursor M.* 17643 To ierusalem he tok þe strete. **1375** BARBOUR *Bruce* II. 146 All him alane the way he tais. *c* **1380** *Sir Ferumb.* 3152 þus othere toke þat cors an haste. **1513** DOUGLAS *Æneis* VI. viii. 1 With all his speid fra thens he tuke the gait. *a* **1533** LD. BERNERS *Huon* xxi. 63, I counsell you to take the long way. **1590** SPENSER *F.Q.* I. i. 10 So many pathes, . . That which of them to take in diverse doubt they been. **1697** DRYDEN *Virg. Georg.* III. 459 Pleas'd I am, no beaten Road to take. **1749** FIELDING *Tom Jones* VII. x, Which way must we take? **1827** HALLAM *Const. Hist.* (1876) I. iii. 115 Elizabeth had taken her line as to the Court of Rome. **1895** *Law Times Rep.* LXXIII. 22/1 The court . . left the parties to take their own course.

c. ***to take*** (***a place*** or ***person***) ***in*** (***on***) ***one's way***, to touch at or visit in one's journey; to include in one's route.

a **1622** R. LAYNE in Capt. Smith *Virginia* I. 8, I . . sent Pemissapan word I was going to Croatan, and tooke him in my way. **1676** WOOD *Life* (O.H.S.) II. 342 Wee went home and took Pershore in the way. **1701** W. WOTTON *Hist. Rome, Marcus* vi. 85 He did not take Rome in his way. **1837** LOCKHART *Scott* xliv, Scott . . asked me to walk home with him, taking Ballantyne's printing office in our way.

d. *intr.* ***to take and*** = ***to go and*** s.v. GO *v.* 32 c. *dial.* and *U.S. colloq.*

1836 *Southern Lit. Messenger* II. 388/2 If you do so I will take and tell father. **1859** T. HUGHES *Scouring of White Horse* vi. 129 This here . . maypowl wur the last in all these parts . . but . . the Uffington chaps cum up, and tuk and carried 'un down ther'. **1876** 'MARK TWAIN' *Tom Sawyer* i. 8 I'll take and bounce a rock off'n your head. **1901** J. BARLOW *From Land of Shamrock* 17 Her cherished Nellie 'took and died on her' of some mysterious malady. **1925** W. FAULKNER *As I lay Dying* 44 'She's gone,' Cash says. 'She taken and left us,' pa says. **1977** 'L. EGAN' *Blind Search* viii. 133 Poor soul, this awful cancer. She took and died inside of three months.

*** *Connoting treatment.*

26. *trans.* To proceed or begin to deal with or treat in some way or do something to; hence, to 'take in hand', 'tackle', deal with, treat.

See also *take at advantage* (ADVANTAGE *sb.* 5 c), *take it easy* (EASY B. 4), *take in turns* (TURN *sb.*). (In quot. 1671, to settle, adjust, make up: = *take up*, 93 u.)

1523 [see ADVANTAGE *sb.* 5 c]. **1596** HARINGTON *Metam. Ajax* (1814) 12 He will take a weak man at the vantage. **1607** TOPSELL *Four-f. Beasts* 418 This disease . . , if it be taken in any time, it is easie to be holpen. **1671** H. M. tr. *Erasm. Colloq.* 62 They themselves will better take this difference among themselves. **1720** MRS. MANLEY *Power of Love* (1741) 281 Being taken at such disadvantage; his Valour would have signify'd little. **1734** POPE *Ess. Man* IV. 227 Men in their loose unguarded hours they take, Not that themselves are wise, but others weak. **1737** BRACKEN *Farriery Impr.* (1756) I. 169 The Business is to take the Distemper in its first Stage. **1812** JEFFERSON *Writ.* (1830) IV. 176 To fight two enemies at a time, rather than to take them by succession. **1896** *Law Times* C. 438/2 Admiralty Appeals with Assessors will be taken in Appeal Court I on Wednesday. **1896** *Daily News* 30 May 8/4, I shall not take physiology next year, but I shall give some teaching on the subject in the way of object lessons in hygiene.

b. To use, deal with, or treat (a name or word) in some way. ***to take in*** IDLE, in VAIN.

c **1200** ORMIN 4402 þatt tu ne take nohht wiþþ skarn, Wiþþ hæþinng, ne wiþþ idell þe name off ure Laferrd Crist. *c* **1315** SHOREHAM III. 91 Honury þou schelt enne god . . Take nauȝt hys name in ydelschepe. *c* **1386** [see IDLE B. 1 b].

c. To proceed to deal with mentally; to consider; to reckon. So ***to take into*** or ***under consideration***, to proceed to consider (see CONSIDERATION 2 c). See also *take together*, 92 c.

c **1200** ORMIN 325 Tace nu þiss streon þatt tuss wass sibb Wiþþ preostess & wiþþ kingess. *Ibid.* 335, 339. **1589** PUTTENHAM *Eng. Poesie* III. xix. (Arb.) 236 For example ye may take these verses. **1602** SHAKS. *Ham.* I. ii. 197 He was a man, take him for all in all: I shall not look vpon his like againe. *a* **1635** SIBBES *Confer. Christ & Mary* (1656) 66 Take a good Christian at the worst, he is better than another at the best. **1747** W. HORSLEY *Fool* (1748) II. 319 Take one Man with another now in Prison. **1820** *Examiner* No. 615. 51/1 If the Chamber were to take the petitions into its consideration. **1836** BRANDE *Chem.* (1841) 138 Let us take a fresh-water lake as an example. **1892** *Cassell's Fam. Mag.* Aug. 516/1 This, taken with his secretaryship, . . left him but little leisure.

d. *slang.* To confront, attack; to overcome, defeat; to kill.

1939 'E. QUEEN' in *Blue Bk.* Oct. 17 Seems to me the champ ought to take this boy Koyle. **1956** E. L. PERRY in A. Hitchcock *Stories for Late at Night* (1962) 273 Let's take him . . . That fat guy looks really loaded. **1963** D. CORY *Hammerhead* xi. 161 There were two men now in the doorway, both with pistols. . . One of them Fedora might have taken; but not, he reluctantly decided, both. **1965** I. FLEMING *Man with Golden Gun* vii. 97 It had been damned fine shooting. . . How in hell was Bond going to take him? **1976** *Publishers Weekly* 1 Mar. 93/3 They broke their tie with the Giants and went on to take the Tigers in seven wild World Series games. **1979** E. BERCOVICI *Wolftrap* 41 The man who tried to take me was Martinez. . . Next time I am going to kill him.

**** *Connoting occupation.*

27. To proceed to occupy, enter on the occupation of (a place or position, *lit.* or *fig.*). See also CHAIR *sb.*[1] 9, FLOOR *sb.*[1] 4, GROUND *sb.* 11 c, PLACE *sb.* 13 b, 27, POST *sb.*[3] 2, PRECEDENCE 3, 4, SEAT, STAND, etc.

c **1205** LAY. 7976 He droh in ane hælue & toc þan herberwe. *a* **1300** *Cursor M.* 11443 þai toke þair gesting in þe tun. **1390** GOWER *Conf.* III. 293 This yonge Prince, as seith the bok, With hem his herbergage tok. **1430-40** LYDG. *Bochas* IX. xxxi. (Bodl. MS. 263) lf. 432/2 The ground Itake of wilful pouerte. **1605** SHAKS. *Lear* III. vi. 38 Thou robed man of justice, take thy place. **1711** ADDISON *Spect.* No. 165 ¶5 They took Post behind a great Morass. **1750** GRAY *Long Story* 111 She curtsies, as she takes her chair. **1807-8** W. IRVING *Salmag.* iv. (1811) I. 71 The latter has taken his winter quarters . . in the corner room, opposite mine. **1883** FARGUS *Cardinal Sin* xii, It was soon her turn to take the stage. **1888** *Scottish Leader* 27 July 6/7, I took the chair at a meeting to promote the candidature of a Radical as a member for Parliament.

†**b.** *intr.* ? ellipt. for *take place*, to occur. *rare.*

c **1374** CHAUCER *Troylus* IV. 1534 (1562) And yf so be þat pes her-after take As alday happeþ after anger game.

28. To use, occupy, use up, consume (so much material, space, time, energy, activity, etc.): = *take up*, 93 w (*b*). Sometimes nearly = 'need' or 'require'. Hence (*colloq.*) to require (a person or thing of so much capacity or ability) *to do* something.

to take (*one's*) *time*: to allow oneself sufficient time (to do something); hence (sarcastically), to be 'quite long enough', i.e. too long: to loiter.

a **1578** LINDESAY (Pitscottie) *Chron. Scot.* (S.T.S.) I. 251 This scheip . . tuik so mekill timber that scho waistit all the wodis in Fyfe. **1590** SHAKS. *Mids. N.* I. i. 83 Take time to pause. *c* **1710** CELIA FIENNES *Diary* (1888) 239 At ye ffeete of the bed that tooke ye Length of the roome. **1713** BERKELEY *Hylas & Phil.* i. Wks. 1871 I. 284, I will take time to solve your difficulty. **1753** CHAMBERS *Cycl. Supp.* s.v. *Lime*, Lime-stone generally takes sixty hours in burning. **1788** W. COWPER *Let.* 18 Aug. (1904) III. 303, I took my own time to return, and did not reach home till after one. **1796** [see TIME *sb.* 8 a]. **1858** GLENNY *Gard. Every-day Bk.* 134/1 They take less room on than off. **1873** HARDY *Pair of Blue Eyes* III. i. 21, I don't press you for an answer now, darling. . . Take your time. **1890** *Field* 8 Mar. 364/1 Any ignoramus can construct a straight line, but it takes an engineer to make a curve. **1893** *Nat. Observer* 7 Oct. 541/2 The remainder of the Life will take two more volumes. **1912** W. B. YEATS *Land of Heart's Desire* (ed. 7) 11 It's precious wine, so take your time about it. **1925** W. FAULKNER *As I lay Dying* 246 'Let him take his time,' I said. 'He ain't as spry as you, remember.' **1946**, etc. [see SWEET *a.* 8 d]. **1966** A. HIGGINS *Langrishe, go Down* iii. 28 Taking her time, Helen cycled slowly by the wall of the Charter School. **1981** 'E. FERRARS' *Experiment with Death* iv. 68 Emma suggested that Sam had probably gone to the lavatory. 'If so, he's taking his time,' Roger said.

b. A person is said to *take* a particular size *in* gloves, boots, collars, etc., implying that that is the size which fits.

1897 FLO. MARRYAT *Blood Vampire* ii, [She] informed me the other day that her Mamma took nines in gloves.

c. ***to have*** (***got***) ***what it takes***: to possess the necessary attributes or qualities, esp. those needed for success. *colloq.* (orig. *U.S.*).

1929 *Amer. Speech* IV. 357 To avoid using the word *money*, the well-informed user of slang may use . . *the needful, the wherewithal*, . . or *what it takes.* **1933** F. BALDWIN *Innocent Bystander* ix. 186 Angela, who has planty of what it takes, is the White Hope of the arty crowd which gathers at her penthouse. **1944** M. LASKI *Love on Supertax* iv. 49 Only maturity's got what it takes. **1947** D. M. DAVIN *For Rest of our Lives* 335 The cheap verses had everything it takes to make a soldier's song. **1956** B. HOLIDAY *Lady sings Blues* (1973) iv. 41 Sometimes I wonder how we survived. But we did. If we didn't have what it took at the beginning, we picked it up along the way. **1972** J. WAMBAUGH *Blue Knight* (1973) xiii. 225 He's got everything it takes but guts. **1977** *Zigzag* Apr. 26/1 They've got the right idea and what it takes.

d. ***it takes all sorts to make a world***: see SORT *sb.*[2] 11 d.

e. ***to take one all one's time***: see TIME *sb.* 8 d.

29. To begin or start afresh after leaving off, or after some one else; to resume; = *take up*, 93 r, s. (Also *absol.*) ***to take the word***, to begin to speak, esp. after or instead of some one else: see WORD *sb.*

c **1400** *Destr. Troy* 747 Now turne to our tale, take þere we lefte. **1500** [see WORD]. *a* **1547** SURREY *Æneid* IV. 144 Quene Juno then thus tooke her tale agaíne. **1697** DRYDEN *Virg. Georg.* IV. 219, I must forsake This Task; for others afterwards to take. **1825** SCOTT *Betrothed* xix, Eveline remained silent. The abbess took the word.

b. ***to take it from there***: to take over or continue from the point or situation described.

[**1948** *Radio Times* 19 Mar. 5/3 A new weekly comedy series, *Take It From Here*, will make its appearance . . on Tuesday evening.] **1959** *Internat. Celebrity Reg.* 430/1 Miss Shearer informed the studio of her find. They took it from there. **1960** WODEHOUSE *Jeeves in Offing* xix. 188 His future hangs on this speech, and we've got it and he hasn't. We take it from there. **1973** *Ottawa Jrnl.* 14 July 24/3 They interrupt each other and talk until the breath gives out and then another one cuts in and takes it from there. **1975** N. LUARD *Travelling Horseman* vi. 167 I'd tell him what I'd found out and he could take it from there.

V. To obtain from a source, to derive.

30. To get, obtain, or derive by one's own act from some source (something material or non-material); to adopt, copy, 'borrow' (also *absol.*, quot. 1493); to take example of, 'get' or 'learn' *from* some one (quot. 1544). See also ENSAMPLE *sb.* 2 b, EXAMPLE *sb.* 6 c.

c **1200** ORMIN 14470, ȝiff þu bisne takenn willt Off þise twezȝenn breþre. *c* **1330** R. BRUNNE *Chron. Wace* (Rolls) 5273 þre þousand pound ylka ȝer . . Of alle þe lond gedered & tan. **13..** *Cursor M.* 17288 + 175 Cott. (*insert.*) To haf mercy of synful men Ensaumple at him he toke. *c* **1386** CHAUCER *Wife's Prol.* 183 Rede it in his Almageste and take it there. *c* **1460** FORTESCUE *Abs. & Lim. Mon.* x. (1885) 131 þat we now serch how the kyng mey haue such livelod; but ffirst, off what comodites it mey best be take. **1493** *Festivall* (1515) 145 b, [Luke] loked what Marke and Mathewe had wryten, and so toke at them. **1544** BALE *Chron. Sir J. Oldcastell* in *Harl. Misc.* (Malh.) I. 269 Of them [Annas & Caiaphas] onely haue ye taken it to iudge Chrystes members, as ye do. **1606** G. W[OODCOCKE] *Hist. Ivstine* xxx. 101 Schollers which from him as their tuter had tane theyr practise. **1732** BERKELEY *Alciphr.* III. §9 The proportions of the three Grecian orders were taken from the human body. **1766** GOLDSM. *Vicar W.* xvii, All the ladies of the continent would come over to take pattern from ours. **1878** H. H. GIBBS *Ombre* 8 The Frontispiece . . is taken from Seymour's 'Compleat Gamester'.

b. *spec.* To obtain from its natural source (e.g. stone from a quarry), to get; to pluck, gather (plants, a crop). Now *rare.*

c **1477** CAXTON *Jason* 121 b, And thenne she was . . borne into alle the Regyons of the world where she gadred and toke many herbes of dyuerce facons and condicions. **1585** T. WASHINGTON tr. *Nicholay's Voy.* II. xi. 46 Mines whereof are taken great quantity of stone. **1844** *Jrnl. R. Agric. Soc.* V. I. 174 In taking the crop reaping is universal.

31. To derive, 'draw' (origin, name, character, or some attribute or quality) from some source. Const. *from, in, of.*

c **1200** ORMIN 16340 Adam . . Off whamm I toc mi bodiȝlich. *c* **1205** LAY. 29410 Brutaine hit wes ihaten of Bruttin nom taken. **13..** *Cursor M.* 36 Ilk a frouit . . takes fra þe rote his kinde. *Ibid.* 20085 He þat toke of hir his fless . . hang a tre þar nailed to. **1432-50** tr. *Higden* (Rolls) II. 255 Men of Assiria toke theire name of Assur, men of Hebrewe of Heber. **1474** CAXTON *Chesse* III. i. (1883) 77 We were first formed and toke our begynnyng of the erthe. **1586** W. WEBBE *Eng. Poetrie* (Arb.) 56 Ryme, taken from the Greeke worde Ρυθμος. **1660** BLOOME *Archit.* A j, The . . Columnes called Dorica, taking beginning of Dorus, Prince of Achaia and Peloponnesus. **1772** SIR W. JONES *Ess.* i. Poems, etc. (1777) 186 The Turks . . took their numbers, and their taste for poetry from the Persians. **1855** MACAULAY *Hist. Eng.*

xxii. IV. 776 No English title had ever before been taken from a place of battle lying within a foreign territory.

†**b.** To infer, deduce; to obtain as a result.

c **1380** WYCLIF *Wks.* (1880) 343 But hou shulde men take of þis to roune wiþ prestis & þus to be assoiled? c **1391** CHAUCER *Astrol.* II. §25 Adde thanne thilke declinacion to the altitude of the sonne at noon and tak ther the heuedes of aries & libra & thin Equinoxial. c **1449** PECOCK *Repr.* 54 Of which..text thei taken that whoeuer is a persoon of Saluacioun schal soone understonde the trewe meenyng of Holi Scripture.

32. To get as a result or product by some special process. **a.** To get (information, evidence, etc.), or ascertain (a fact), by inquiry, questioning, examination, or the like; also *transf.* to perform or carry on (an examination or the like) in order to ascertain something (cf. 52).

1460 *Rolls of Parlt.* V. 388/1 By Inquisitions tane uppon ychone of the same Wyrtes. **1511–12** *Act 3 Hen. VIII*, c. 21 Preamble, An untrue Inquysicion taken before your Eschetoure in the seid Countie. **1583** STOCKER *Civ. Warres Lowe C.* I. 68b, Information which was taken by the Inquisitours here aboutes. **1596** SHAKS. *1 Hen. IV*, IV. i. 133 Let vs take a muster speedily. **1600** in *Shaks. Cent. Praise* (1879) 35 The examination of Sr Gelly merick Knyght taken the xvijth of Februarij, 1600. **1697** DRYDEN *Virg. Georg.* IV. 626 Himself their Herdsman, on the middle Mount, Takes of his muster'd Flocks a just Account. **1705** *Lond. Gaz.* No. 4139/5 The King..took a Review of the Forces. **1768** BLACKSTONE *Comm.* III. iv. 59 A commission of assise, directed to the judges and clerk of assise, to take assises; that is, to take the verdict of a peculiar species of jury called an assise. *Ibid.* vii. 101 [The judge] takes information by hearing advocates on both sides, and thereupon forms his interlocutory decree or definitive sentence at his own discretion. **1817** MAR. EDGEWORTH *Harrington* ii. (1832) 21 He hastened down to the country to take the sense of his constituents. **1863** H. COX *Instit.* III. vii. 698 He never disposes of any important preferments without taking the pleasure of the Crown. **1890** *Cornhill Mag.* Sept. 276 Tests are taken to see if the cable has sustained any damage. **1893** *National Observer* 7 Oct. 524/1 A Bill on which it dare not take the country's opinion.

b. To get or ascertain by measurement or scientific observation; also *transf.* to make, perform (a measurement, an observation). See also MEASURE *sb.* 2c, 3a.

c **1430** [see MEASURE *sb.* 2c]. c **1470** HENRYSON *Mor. Fab.* x. (*Fox & Wolf*) v, Bot Astrolab, Quadrant, and Almanak,.. The mouing of the heuin this Tod can tak. **1579** GOSSON *Sch. Abuse* (Arb.) 38 The height of Heauen is taken by the staffe. **1598** PHILIP tr. *Linschoten* I. xciii. 170/1 Taking the hight of the Sunne, we found ourselues to be under 37 degrees. **1622** MASSINGER *Virg. Mart.* III. iii, Misery taking the length of my foot, it boots not me to sue for life. **1663** BUTLER *Hud.* I. I. 122 For he by Geometrick Scale Could take the Size of Pots of Ale. **1697** COLLIER *Ess. Mor. Subj.* I. (1703) 111 The Taylor should take measure of their quality as well as of their limbs. **1847** TENNYSON *Princ.* III. 153 That afternoon the Princess rode to take The dip of certain strata to the North. **1887** WESTALL *Capt. Trafalgar* xviii. 236 Isn't it about time for taking the sun?..it is four days since we knew our position. **1900** LÜCKES *Gen. Nursing* xii. (ed. 2) 147 The temperature has to be taken every hour. *Mod.* The weather was too cloudy to take any observations.

†**c.** To measure off (a length or distance). *Obs.*

1660 BARROW *Euclid* I. ii. Schol., The line AG might be taken with a pair of compasses. **1669** STURMY *Mariner's Mag.* I. ii. 32 Take with your Compasses the Line C. **1831** BREWSTER *Optics* iv. 38 From a scale on which *hm* is 1·500, take in the compasses '1'.

33. a. To obtain in writing, write down, make (notes, a copy, etc.); to write down (spoken words), report in writing (a speech, etc.). Also in phr. ***to take a letter***: to write a letter down in shorthand from another's dictation.

1591–1875 [see NOTE *sb.*² 13b]. **1601** SHAKS. *All's Well* IV. iii. 130 His confession is taken, and it shall bee read to his face. **1653** H. COGAN tr. *Pinto's Trav.* xv. 48 Taking an inventory of this prize. **1708** in *Burton's Diary* (1828) III. 93 His Majesty sent for Mr. Rushworth, the Clerk, whom he observed to take his speech in character. **1712** F. T. *Shorthand* p. vi, 'Tis by Short-Hand that all Speeches, Homilies, Tryals, Sermons, &c. are..taken. a **1715** BURNET *Own Time* ann. 1672 (1823) I. 538 He would not let me take a copy of it. **1732** BERKELEY *Alciphr.* IV. §1 To stand by,.. and take notes of all that passeth. **1776** *Trial of Nundocomar* 22/1 The Monshy took the copy by my directions. **1883** M. D. CHALMERS *Local Govt.* iii. 41 Minutes of the meeting must be taken. **1901** S. PAGET *Mem. Sir J. Paget* iii. (ed. 2) 61 He had no clinical clerks, and his cases were not taken. **1943** K. TENNANT *Ride on Stranger* x. 110 He seated himself at his table... 'Will you take a letter, please?'.. Her pencil travelled quite speedily after his words. **1961** *Times* 7 June 2/5 Director of general publishing house..needs an assistant-cum-secretary. Will be expected to 'take letters'.

b. To obtain by drawing, delineating, etc.; to make, execute (a figure or picture, now esp. a photograph, film, of some object or event); also *transf.* to obtain or make a figure or picture of, to portray; now *esp.* to photograph or film. Occas. *intr.* Also (*colloq.*) *intr.* for *pass.* (with qualifying adv.) of a person: To be a (good or bad) subject for photographing. Cf. TAKE *sb.* 9a.

1607 TOPSELL *Four-f. Beasts* 757 Another picture..which he tooke by another of these Cats in the possession of the Duke of Saxony. **1664** WOOD *Life*, etc. (O.H.S.) II. 20, I went to the castle [Bampton]..and took the ruins thereof. **1751** T. HOLLIS in *Lett. Lit. Men* (Camden) 379 A Scheme for taking and publishing the Antiquities existing at Athens. **1766** GOLDSM. *Vic. W.* xvi, A limner, who travelled the country, and took likenesses for fifteen shillings a head. **1789** MRS. PIOZZI *Journ. France* I. 150 Her portrait..will not be found difficult to take. **1859** REEVE *Brittany* 48 Mr. Taylor took the view three times before he quite satisfied himself as to the quality of the negative. **1889** MALLOCK *Enchanted Isl.* 230, I took a photograph of their church. **1889** BLANCHE HOWARD *Open Door* ix. 145 The photographers..say a woman 'takes' better standing. **1899** F. V. KIRBY *Sport E.C. Africa* xxviii. 310, I wished for my camera, for never was there a better chance of 'taking' one of these animals. a **1910** *Mod.* A snap-shot taken by an amateur. **1917** *N.Y. Times* 25 Feb. 4/1 Two thousand persons participated in the coronation, which required two full days to 'take', despite the fact that it remains on the screen only three minutes. **1929** H. B. ABBOTT *Motion Pictures with Baby Ciné* ii. 4 It has already been stated that the motion picture is made, or 'taken', in a special camera, and that the medium upon which the picture is made is a celluloid film coated with a sensitive emulsion. **1954** N. BAU *How to make 8mm. Films* 99 (*caption*) Hold the camera absolutely steady while taking. *Ibid.* 100 If you are taking a hand-held shot, hold the camera as steady as possible. **1974** *Daily Tel.* 2 May 3/4 Using a friend's projector and screen, he ran a short colour film taken at the wedding.

VI. To take something given or offered; to receive, accept, exact, and related senses.

* *To receive what is given or bestowed.*

34. To receive, get (something given, bestowed, or administered); to have conferred upon one (*spec.* a sacrament, office, order of merit, degree, etc.); to win, or receive as won (a prize, reward); to gain, acquire (experience, etc.; see also ***to take success***, s.v. SUCCESS). Also *absol.*

c **1200** ORMIN 5378 Forr to takenn hæle att himm Off iwhillc unntrummnesse. **13..** *Cursor M.* 12755 (Gött.) In water baptist he alle þa þat come til him baptim to ta. c **1375** *Ibid.* 19531 (Fairf.) Simon..toke þe sacrement of hali kirk. **1382** WYCLIF *Matt.* vii. 8 Eche that axith, takith. —— *1 Cor.* xi. 24 For the Lord Ihesu..took breed..and brak, and seide, Take ȝe and ete ȝe. c **1435** *Torr. Portugal* 2168 And ye now will liston a stound How he toke armes of kyng Calomond. [Cf. ARM *sb.*² 15.] c **1450** *St. Cuthbert* (Surtees) 5412 þar he toke tonsure brade. c **1450** tr. *De Imitatione* III. lix. 250 It is more blessyd to gyue than take. **1617** MORYSON *Itin.* I. 29 In the house where the Doctors, and other Graduates take their degrees. **1689** T. R. *View Govt. Europe* 74 The Nations round about submitted and took Laws from him. **1766** ENTICK *London* IV. 31 The will is to be proved, and administration is to be taken. **1805** SCOTT *Last Minstr.* IV. xxvi, Knighthood he took of Douglas' sword. **1888** MRS. H. WARD *R. Elsmere* iv. 50, I don't feel as if I should ever take orders.

b. To receive (something inflicted); to have (something) done to one; to suffer, undergo, submit to.

c **1200** ORMIN Pref. 90 þatt he toc dæþ o rode. **1303** R. BRUNNE *Handl. Synne* 12626 God graunte vs grace,..for oure synne swyche penaunce [to] take, þat we be neuer more a-teynt. **13..** [see PENANCE *sb.* 2]. **1485** CAXTON *Chas. Gt.* 220 To the ende that they sholde not take deth that day. **1581** RICH *Farewell* (Shaks. Soc.) 212, I will not see her take a manifest wrong. **1663** BUTLER *Hud.* I. II. 947 He took the Blow upon his Arm. **1748** G. WHITE *Serm.* (MS.), He had much rather take, than do, wrong. **1869** FREEMAN *Norm. Conq.* III. xii. 162 The mere senseless love of giving and taking blows without an object. **1879** MISS YONGE *Cameos* Ser. IV. iii. 39 He professed himself ready to take his trial.

c. To receive (something said to one); to receive information of, to hear; in *imper.* often = 'let me tell you'. Somewhat *arch.*

1595 SHAKS. *John* I. i. 21 Then take my Kings defiance from my mouth. **1596** —— *Tam. Shr.* II. i. 191 Take this of me, Kate of my consolation,.. My selfe am moou'd to woo thee for my wife. **1609** HEYWOOD *Brit. Troy* XII. lxiv, After they had tooke and given the Time of Day. **1671** MILTON *Samson* 1570 Then take the worst in brief, Samson is dead. **1805** SCOTT *Last Minstr.* IV. xxvi, Take our defiance loud and high.

d. ***take that!***: (*a*) said as an accompaniment to the delivery of a blow; (*b*) used, with a suggestion of challenge or defiance, to emphasize a foregoing statement.

a **1425** *Cursor M.* 16290 (Trin.) Wiþ his hond a buffet he ȝaf ihesus ful sore..'take þat to teche þe lore'. **1805** C. WILMOT *Let.* 7 Dec. in *Russ. Jrnls.* (1934) II. 209, I don't pity you in the least. Take that for asking me to write you 'beautiful Russian storys'. **1846** W. E. FORSTER in Reid *Life* I. vi. 186 The fact is, they will soon wear nothing. There; take that! **1932** KIPLING *Limits & Renewals* 81 'Then take that!' and he smacked the brute's head. **1942** BERREY & VAN DEN BARK *Amer. Thes. Slang* §158/8 Take that and see how you like it! **1983** A. OLCOTT *May Day in Magadan* xiv. 249 His pride was stung. 'They want me..' he said, with an unthinking 'take that!' tilt of his nose.

35. To enter into the enjoyment of (pleasure, recreation, rest, or the like). See also EASE *sb.* 2, NAP *sb.*² b. (Cf. 13.)

13.. *Cursor M.* 6317 (Gött.) þat niht he ȝede and tok his rest. c **1350** *Will. Palerne* 2488 [þei] hiȝed hem homward fast ..& token redli here rest. **1530** PALSGR. 749/2, I take my rest. **1549** LATIMER *Serm. Ploughers* (Arb.) 38 In the meane tyme the Prelates take theyr pleasures. **1597** BEARD *Theatre God's Judgem.* (1612) 328 Before any other should take tast thereof. **1752** MRS. LENNOX *Fem. Quix.* I. i, Sometimes he took the diversion of hunting. **1779** *Mirror* No. 60 One of the company proposed that they should take a game at cards. **1897** MRS. RAYNER *Type-writer Girl* x. 108 So perforce I took holiday.

** *To receive what is due or owing; to exact.*

36. To receive or get in payment, as wages, etc., or by way of charge or exaction as a fine, tribute; sometimes with connotation 'accept' (cf. 39), or 'charge, exact, demand' (cf. 37, 38).

a **1300** *Cursor M.* 16485 'Tas', he said, 'your penis here A felun folk er yee'. **13..** *Ibid.* 28405 Agains will i lent my thing, And quilum tok þar-for okeryng. **1427–8** *Rec. St. Mary at Hill* 68 Also for a carpenter iiij dayes..takyng vj d & his mete a day. c **1489** CAXTON *Sonnes of Aymon* ix. 216 Straunge knyghtes that were come vnto hym to take wages. **1579** LYLY *Euphues* (Arb.) 133 This olde miser asking of Aristippus what he woulde take to teache and bring vp his sonne. **1684** *Contempl. State Man* I. vi. (1699) 64 What would he now take for all the Honours of this World. **1708** in Picton *L'Pool Munic. Rec.* (1886) II. 83 For takeing greater interest..than by law is allow'd. **1842** BROWNING *Pied Piper* ix, A thousand guilders! Come, take fifty! **1896** *Act 59 & 60 Vict.* c. 59 §2(*b*), Provided always..that no money for admission be taken at the doors.

37. To exact (satisfaction or reparation) for an offence; hence, to execute, inflict (vengeance, revenge; †punishment, †justice). Const. *on*, †*of*.

a **1300** *Cursor M.* 5862 þat suerd apon hus tak na wrak. *Ibid.* 6094 O þam mi wengeance sal i take. c **1330** R. BRUNNE *Chron. Wace* (Rolls) 202 Whan God took wreche of Kaymes synne. **1474** CAXTON *Chesse* II. v. (1883) 68, I wold take vengeance and turmente the. **1533** BELLENDEN *Livy* I. ix. (S.T.S.) 52 þat he mycht Iustlie tak punycioun of all þe Albane pepill. **1607** TOPSELL *Four-f. Beasts* (1658) 127 His fellowes take punishment of him, and fall on him, biting and rending his skin. **1633** [see REVENGE *sb.* 4]. a **1774** GOLDSM. tr. *Scarron's Com. Romance* (1775) II. 118 The counsellor.. had need of all his good sense to prevent him from taking immediate justice on a man, who sought to injure him so capitally. **1779** FORREST *N. Guinea* 313 To take satisfaction ..for the death of Fakymolano's brother at Ramis.

†**38.** To receive, exact, or accept (a promise, engagement, oath, or the like); hence, to administer or witness (an oath). ***to take an oath of, to take*** (any one) ***sworn***: see OATH *sb.* 1, SWORN *ppl. a.*

c **1450**, **1593**, **1599** [see OATH *sb.* 1]. **1560** DAUS tr. *Sleidane's Comm.* 55b, Then began he to take stipulation of them. a **1715** BURNET *Own Time* an. 1672 (1823) I. 538 He took a solemn engagement of her, that, if scruples should arise in her mind, she would let him know them. **1833** *Act 3 & 4 Will. IV*, c. 74 §82 [He] shall be competent to take the acknowledgment of any married woman wheresoever she may reside. **1873** *Act 36 & 37 Vict.* c. 66 §84 Commissioners to take oaths and affidavits in the Supreme Court.

*** *To accept.*

39. To receive (something offered), not to refuse or reject; to receive willingly; to accept. Freq. in phr. ***take it or leave it*** and varr., expressing indifference or a refusal to bargain, compromise, etc. Cf. *take-it-or-leave-it* adj. s.v. TAKE-.

c **1200** ORMIN 4828 ȝiff þatt we takenn bliþeliȝ Att Godd all þatt iss sellþe. c **1330** *Amis & Amil.* 1112 Y schal for the take bataile. c **1400** *Prymer* (1895) 50 Take oure preier, & late þe merci of þi pitee assoile hem þat ben boundun wiþ þe cheyne of synnes. a **1500** in C. Trice-Martin *Chanc. Proc. 15th C.* (1904) 3 To thentent that she shuld not be taken to bayle, but kept still in prisone. **1534** MORE *Treat. Passion* Wks. 1281/1 Such as wil take the benefite. **1576** W. LAMBARDE *Perambulation of Kent* sig. 2D3v, I..doe leaue the Reader to his free choice, to take or leaue the one, or the other. **1591** SHAKS. *Two Gent.* III. i. 100 Take no repulse, what euer she doth say. **1664** T. KILLIGREW *Thomaso* in *Comedies, & Tragedies* I. IV. ii. 361 That is the price, and less I know, in curtesie you cannot offer me; take it or leave it. **1697** in *N. & Q.* 10th Ser. (1908) IX. 378/2 There was not one of the House of Commons but..would take a bribe. **1762** J. WESLEY *Let.* 21 May (1931) IV. 182 As to that particular expression, 'Dying at the feet of mercy', I have only farther to add, I do not care as it is not a scriptural phrase, whether anyone takes or leaves it. **1809** B. H. MALKIN tr. *Le Sage's Gil Blas* x. x. 39, I will give forty [pistoles] at a word; take them or leave them. **1837** DICKENS *Pickw.* ii, Gentleman says he'll not detain you a moment, sir, but he can take no denial. **1848** THACKERAY *Van. Fair* xxii, She held out her hand with so frank and winning a grace, that Osborne could not but take it. **1898** W. S. CHURCHILL in R. S. Churchill *Winston S. Churchill* (1967) I. Compan. II. 917 The tremendous & unchallenged power of the Trust —enabled it to dictate wages to its workmen & prices to its customers. 'Take it or leave it' it said 'This is a free country.' Thereat the oil-mechanic had to accept the offered wage or find another trade and the customer to buy the oil at the offered price or wait in the dark. **1904** STANLEY WEYMAN *Abbess of Vlaye* iii, There's a party ringing at the gate, my lord, and—and won't take no! **1929** D. H. LAWRENCE in *Forum* Jan. p. L/3 The hen knows she is unanswerable... There it is, take it or leave it! **1953** A. UPFIELD *Murder must Wait* xi. 105, I cock a snook at you... You can take it or leave it. **1962** WODEHOUSE *Service with Smile* x. 151 Her air was that of somebody who, where Ickenhams were concerned, could take them or leave them alone. **1977** P. G. WINSLOW *Witch Hill Murder* II. xv. 206, I didn't want to..say I'd gotten married and he could take it or leave it, because I was afraid he'd leave it.

b. Of a female animal: To admit (the male). See also *take horse* in Phrases, 70c. In extended use, of a woman. *rare.*

1577 [see 70c]. **1759** BROWN *Compl. Farmer* 65 Neither can they suckle their young, till they have taken buck. **1845** *Jrnl. R. Agric. Soc.* VI. II. 363, I..set down..the Ewes as they take the ram. **1864** *Ibid.* XXV. I. 254 The number of hours during which they take the bull varies from 24 to 48. **1932** W. FAULKNER *Light in August* x. 212 There were white women who would take a man with a black skin. **1941** N. MAILER *Advts. for Myself* (1961) 36 When I take a man, and I may take him for a lot of reasons, in back of it all is the feeling..that that is something I can do better than any other woman.

c. Of fish (with mixture of sense 2b): To seize (the bait). Also *absol.*

1863 W. C. BALDWIN *Afr. Hunting* vi. 205 They take anything, but we have only crooked pins for hooks, and cannot catch many. **1867** F. FRANCIS *Angling* v. (1880) 162 Sometimes fish rise quickly and take quickly. **1889** MRS. E. KENNARD *Landing a Prize* III. i. 6 Fish always take best after rain.

40. To accept (a wager, or the person who offers to lay the wager). So also in reference to a proposal, etc.: see also *to take any one at his* WORD.

1602 ROWLANDS *Greene's Ghost* 49, I take you, sayd one or two, and the wager being layd, awaie they went. **1719** DE FOE *Crusoe* (1840) II. xiii. 268, I was for taking him at that proposal. **1850** *Tait's Mag.* XVII. 678/2 I'll take ten to one on it. **1890** *Field* 24 May 757/1, 800 to 100 was taken about him. **1890** CLARK RUSSELL *Ocean Trag.* I. vi. 123 He bet me a sovereign... I took him.

b. ***to take one's death*** (upon a thing): to stake one's life upon it.

1533 BECON *Reliques Rome* (1563) 59 He tooke hys death thereon, that he was neuer giltye. **1593** SHAKS. *2 Hen. VI*, II. iii. 90, I will take my death, I neuer meant him any ill.

41. To accept and act upon (advice, a hint, warning, etc.).

c **1300** *St. Margarete* 136 þ^t maide.. seide.. goþ fram me anon; Anoþer consail ich haue itake, ich forsake ȝou echon. *c* **1400** *Destr. Troy* 12869 The troiens full tite token his rede. **1605** [see ADVICE 5]. **1610** SHAKS. *Temp.* II. i. 288 They'l take suggestion, as a Cat laps milke. **1611** [see HINT *sb.* 1]. **1718** LADY M. W. MONTAGU *Let. to Lady Rich* 10 Oct., They.. took the first hint of their dress from a fair sheep newly ruddled. **1877** MISS YONGE *Cameos* Ser. III. xxxiv. 363 Would that France had taken to itself the teaching! **1892** *Punch* 29 Oct. 196/2 [He] begged others to take warning by his fate. **1899** *Tit-Bits* 28 Oct. 109/2 'Come along, dear, take your call', said he, pulling back the heavy curtains.

b. To accept as true or correct; to believe (something told to one). Freq. in phr. ***take it from me***: believe me, take my word for it, be assured. (Cf. 34 c.) Also, to accept mistakenly as trustworthy, to be deceived by (quot. 1728): cf. *take in*, 84 o.

c **1200** ORMIN 2824 Forr þatt tu toc wiþþ trowwþe þatt word. **1587** in W. M. Williams *Ann. Founders' Co.* (1867) 69 He givinge his fayth promyse to Mr. Alderman... Mr. Alderman tooke his worde, and rose, and went his ways. **1605** SHAKS. *Lear* IV. vi. 144, I would not take this from report. **1622** MASSINGER *Virg. Mart.* II. i, We have not been idle, take it upon my word. **1672** WYCHERLEY *Love in Wood* (Dedication) sig. A2^v, Madam, take it from me, no man.. is more dreadful than a Poet. **1728** ELIZA HEYWOOD tr. *Mme. de Gomez's Belle A.* (1732) II. 142 The King seeing that they had took the Feint, said at Night,.. Ghent is invested, and we must go anon to raise the Siege. **1829** G. GRIFFIN *Collegians* I. v. 101 Who should walk in the doore to him, only his dead wife..! Take it from me he didn't stay long where he was. **1889** PHILIPS & WILLS *Fatal Phryne* II. iii. 76 You may take it from me that the pot means what it says. **1902** H. JAMES *Wings of Dove* I. 20 You may take it from me once for all that I won't hear of any one of whom *she* won't. **1938** A. CHRISTIE *Death on Nile* II. xvii. 178, I think you must take it from me, Mr. Pennington, that we have examined all the possibilities very carefully. **1957** D. ROBINS *Noble One* xix. 177 You can take it from me that *I* don't believe a word of it.

42. To accept with the mind or will in some specified way (*well, ill, in earnest*, etc.). See also *to take it on the chin* (CHIN *sb.*[1] 1 d), *to take to heart* (HEART *sb.* 44), *to take it lying down* (LIE *v.*[1] 21 d), *take in good* (etc.) *part* (PART *sb.* 26 b), *take in* SCORN, *take in* SNUFF, *to take it in one's stride* (STRIDE *sb.* 3 d).

c **1200** ORMIN 7390 Biforenn þa þatt täkenn all Onn hæþinng þatt we spellenn. *a* **1300** *Cursor M.* 4619 Nai, sir, tas noght in despite. *Ibid.* 16396 Quen [Pilate] sagh þat al his soigne þai tok it al to ill. *c* **1386** CHAUCER *Wife's T.* 342 To hym that taketh it in pacience. *c* **1450** *St. Cuthbert* (Surtees) 1049 þir wordes cuthbert wysely toke. **1530** PALSGR. 747/1, I take a thyng a mysse, *je mesprens.* **1553** LATIMER *Serm., on Twelfth Day* (1635) 293 b, There is a common saying amongst us.., Every thing is (say they) as it is taken, which indeed is not so: for every thing is as it is, howsoever it be taken. **1577** B. GOOGE *Heresbach's Husb.* IV. (1586) 182 b, They take it ill, and presently leaue working. **1579** W. WILKINSON *Confut. Familye of Loue* B ij, Take this brief.. aunswere.. in good part. **1671** LADY MARY BERTIE in *12th Rep. Hist. MSS. Comm.* App. v. 22 I take it very ill that none of my nephews would drawe mee. **1728** MORGAN *Algiers* I. Pref. 26 Multitudes of People.. would take it in excessive Dudgeon to be thought unfashionable. **1758** JOHNSON *Let. to Miss Porter* 1 Mar., I shall take it very kindly if you write to me. **1872** BLACK *Adv. Phaeton* x. 145 The Lieutenant took the matter very coolly. **1888** MRS. J. K. SPENDER *Kept Secret* III. i. 15, I did not mean you to take me in earnest.

b. To accept without objection, opposition, or resentment; to be content with; to put up with, tolerate, 'stand'. Also ***to take things as one finds them***, also ***to take*** (people) ***as one finds them***: to judge people without preconceptions; to accept people as they are, esp. by expecting no special preparations for one's entertainment, etc.

1470–85 MALORY *Arthur* XX. vi. 805 Ye shalle take the wo with the wele, and take hit in pacyence, and thanke god of hit. **1535** COVERDALE *2 Kings* xiv. 10 Take the prayse, and byde at home. [**1548** E. HALL *Union Lancaster & York* fol. ccxlii^v, Myne aduise is, let all men trust them, as thei fynde them.] **1580** A. MUNDAY *Zelauto* sig. H2^v, In the meane whyle, take as you finde. **1595** MAYNARDE *Drake's Voy.* (Hakl. Soc.) 18 He resolved to departe, and to take the winde as God sent it. **1596** J. HARINGTON *Metamorphosis of Ajax* sig. B4^v, We must now take him as we finde him, with all his faults. **1638** W. CHILLINGWORTH *Relig. Protestants* I. v. 241 But reall externall deeds doe take things in grosse as they find them, not separating things which in reality are joyned together. *c* **1779** R. CUMBERLAND in *Lett. Lit. Men* (Camden) 410, I take events as they fall without murmur or complaint. *c* **1807** J. AUSTEN *Watsons* (1954) 351, I am one of those who always take things as they find them. I hope I can put up with a small apartment for two or three nights. **1809** MALKIN *Gil Blas* v. i. ¶38, I had the good sense to take things as I found them. **1825** in H. Wilson *Mem.* I. 147, I could have been a little romantic about you, it is true; but I always take people as I find them. **1868** DICKENS in *Our Young Folks* May 260 We have but a simple joint.. but if you will take us as you find us it will be *so* kind! **1886** G. B. SHAW *Cashel Byron's Profession* xiv. 148 You can either take me as you find me, or let me alone. **1896** WILLS in *Law Times Rep.* LXXIII. 689/1 If he does not conform to their law, he must take the consequences. **1903** A. BENNETT *Leonora* ii. 47 She's gotten sausages for you.. though I told her you'd take us as you found us. **1912** A. LANG *Shakespeare, Bacon & Great Unknown* xii. 247, I am only taking Ben as I find him and as I understand him. **1943** K. TENNANT *Ride on Stranger* vi. 49 All these go by wearing the peevish expression of a housewife who, not having time to make the beds, grumbles: 'You must take us as you find us.' **1980** T. BARLING *Goodbye Piccadilly* vii. 129 'Do we phone ahead in the name of protocol? 'Hell, no. We take them as we find them.'

c. *to take a joke*: to be able to bear teasing or amusement at one's expense; usu. in negative.

1780 J. WOODFORDE *Diary* 28 Mar. (1924) I. 276 Poor Sam cant take a Joke. I forgot what I said to disoblige him. **1838** C. FOX *Jrnl.* 4 Apr. in *Memories Old Friends* (1882) iv. 27 Speaking of Dr. [John] Dalton, he said he could not take a joke at all. **1863** M. B. CHESNUT *Diary* 14 Dec. in C. V. Woodward *M. Chesnut's Civil War* (1981) xx. 505 When he saw how angry I was, he said, 'Can't you take a joke?' **1921** E. O'NEILL *Diff'rent* I. 223 *Mrs. Crosby*... Shet up your foolin', Jack. *Jack*... Nobody in this house kin take a joke. **1972** D. DELMAN *Sudden Death* (1973) ii. 59 It was a joke. Hell with anybody who can't take a joke.

d. *to* (*be able to*) *take it*: to have the capacity to endure punishment, affliction, etc.

1862 in H. Mayhew *London Labour* (ed. 2) III. 387/2 That first flogging made me ripe. I said to myself, 'I can take it like a bullock.' **1914** O. W. HOLMES *Let.* 24 Sept. in *Pollock-Holmes Lett.* (1942) I. 222, I value everything that shows the quiet unmelodramatic power to stand and take it in your people. **1941** W. S. CHURCHILL in *Unrelenting Struggle* (1942) 190 If the storm is to renew itself, London will be ready, London will not flinch, London can take it again. **1952** *Chambers's Jrnl.* Apr. 196/2 But as soon as I hadn't got Derek—well, I just couldn't take it. **1976** C. BERMANT *Coming Home* I. vi. 87 A slogan, like 'Britain can take it'.

e. ***to take things*** (or *it*) ***as they*** (or *it*) ***come***(*s*): to deal with events as they arise, without anticipating difficulties.

1509 A. BARCLAY tr. *Brandt's Ship of Fools* fo. 266 *recto*, That man folowes hye wysdome Whych takys all thynges lyke as they come. **1611** J. DAVIES *Scourge of Folly* 170 Take all things as they come, and bee content. So many whores do, and yet pay their Rent. **1863** 'OUIDA' *Held in Bondage* I. ix. 203 The true secret is to take things as they come. **1926** [see BOTTOM *sb.* 11 c]. **1979** V. KELLEHER *Voices from River* iii. 34, I was trying not to think... I kept telling myself, take it as it comes.

f. *to take on board*: see BOARD *sb.* 14 e.

43. To face and attempt to get over, through, up, etc. (something that presents itself in one's way), or actually to do so; to clear (an obstacle, as a fence, ditch, wave, space, etc.); to mount (a slope), get round (a corner), clear (the points on a railway line), etc.

1579 TOMSON *Calvin's Serm. Tim.* 912/2 To take hedge and ditch, and go on forwards through brambles and briers. **1632** MASSINGER & FIELD *Fatal Dowry* IV. i, I look about, and neigh, take hedge and ditch. **1838** *Civil Eng. & Arch. Jrnl.* I. 139/2 The tendency to.. friction in passing round curves, and the difficulty of taking the points. **1843** R. J. GRAVES *Syst. Clin. Med.* xxxi. 428 He.. is able to run up, taking two of the large stone stair-steps at each spring. **1859** GEO. ELIOT *A. Bede* xii, Nothing like 'taking' a few bushes and ditches for exorcising a demon. **1864** *Good Words* 628/1 His pony 'takes timber' without asking a question. **1892** *Graphic* 9 Apr. 467/1 The proper course to steer is for Craven Cottage Point, which can be taken rather closely. **1972** M. KENYON *Shooting of Dan McGrew* xxii. 184 He took the corner like a rally driver. **1976** 'B. SHELBY' *Great Pebble Affair* 181, I took the lakeshore S curve designed for thirty mph at fifty-five.

**** *To admit, absorb, include.*

44. a. To admit, let in; to receive something fitted into it (quot. 1793): = *take in*, 84 a.

1674 tr. *Martiniere's Voy. Northern C.* 27 A small hole in the Keel, which took a little water. **1793** SMEATON *Edystone L.* §244 The cavities cut on the under side.. to take the upper half of each cube. **1890** *Temple Bar Mag.* Mar. 371 The *Anonyma*.. several times took more water than we liked.

b. To absorb or become impregnated with (something detrimental, as moisture); to be affected injuriously by; to contract (disease, infection, injury, etc.); to fall into (a fit or trance). See also AIR *sb.* 11, COLD *sb.* 4 a, b, WIND.

13.. *Cursor M.* 23089 (Gött.) Of nakedhede quen i toke [*Cott.* drogh] harm ȝe gaf me clething wid to warm. **1387** TREVISA *Higden* (Rolls) I. 109 þat þe water.. takeþ no defoul, but is clene i-now [etc.]. **1513** *Act 5 Hen. VIII*, c. 4 §1 (3) If the same Worsted.. taketh any Wet, incontinent it will shew spotty and foul. **1530** PALSGR. 747/2, I take colde, *je me morfons.* **1547** *Reg. Privy Council Scot.* I. 78 Personis that.. takis seikness in our Soverane Ladyis army. **1555** EDEN *Decades* 16 The vytayles corrupted by taking water. **1597** SHAKS. *2 Hen. IV*, v. i. 85 As men take diseases, one of another. **1639** N. N. tr. *Du Bosq's Compl. Woman* II. 22 That lampe of the Romans, which.. went out as soone as it tooke Aire. **1712** HEARNE *Collect.* (O.H.S.) III. 301 The Book hath taken wet, and the Letters.. are hardly visible. **1864** *Jrnl. R. Agric. Soc.* XXV. II. 559 Both sheep took the disease. **1885** MRS. LYNN LINTON *Chr. Kirkl.* III. x. 309 A man who takes all the epidemics afloat.

c. To absorb, contract, become impregnated with (a dye, colour, quality, salt, etc.); to receive, become affected by (an impression, a polish, or the like).

1592 SHAKS. *Ven. & Ad.* 354 His tendrer cheeke receiues her soft hands print, As apt as new falne snow takes any dint. **1601** HOLLAND *Pliny* XXXV. vi, It will take colour and be marked verie well. *a* **1642** SIR W. MONSON *Naval Tracts* II. (1704) 264/1 No Flesh in the Indies will take Salt. **1697** COLLIER *Ess. Mor. Subj.* II. (1703) 122 To see the cheeks take the dye of the passions thus naturally. **1727** A. HAMILTON *New Acc. E. Ind.* I. xxii. 260 The Flesh was not so savoury .. nor would it take Salt kindly. **1865** *Reader* 1 Apr. 371/2 It takes dyes admirably—much better than cotton. **1877** W. R. COOPER *Egypt. Obelisks* i. (1878) 3 A granite, or hard sandstone, capable of.. taking a high polish.

d. *absol.* or *intr.* To become affected in the required or desired way: in various applications, as: to catch fire, kindle; to become coated or impregnated with something; to become inoculated; to become frozen; to catch the wind. Occas. *pass.* Cf. sense 6 c above.

1599 SHAKS. *Hen. V*, II. i. 55, I can take, and Pistols cocke is vp, And flashing fire will follow. **1683** MOXON *Mech. Exerc., Printing* xxiv. ¶10 He trys if his Balls will Take, that is..: If he finds the Inck sticks to it equally all about.., it Takes. **1781** *Quebec Gaz.* 11 Jan. 2/1 It has not been known to take so early as the month of December. **1793** *Regal Rambler, or, Devil in Lond.* 40 Our hero laid in a large cargo of fresh fuel, ready to touch and take like phosphorus. **1820** G. SIMPSON *Jrnl. Occurrences in Athabasca Dept.* (1938) 100 This is an unusual late season as the Lake usually takes from the 15th to the 20th Oct. **1830** J. MACMILLAN Let. 15 Dec. in G. P. T. Glazebrook *Hargrave Corr. 1821–43* (1938) 58 We had a very mild fall. The river was not taken before 6th of Decr. **1846** DICKENS *Cricket on Hearth* 30 Vaccinated just six weeks ago-o! Took very fine-ly! **1871** *Scribner's Monthly* II. 458 When the rivers are beginning to 'take' or freeze. **1890** WHITELEGGE *Hygiene* xii. 264 Many [people] 'take' readily within five years [of vaccination].

†**45.** *trans.* To include, comprise; to contain: = *take in*, 84 k. *Obs.*

c **1200** ORMIN 15076 þa fetless tokenn, seȝȝþ Goddspell, Twinne mett, oþerr þrinne. *a* **1637** B. JONSON *Hymn on Nativity* ii, He whom the whole world could not take,.. Was now laid in a manger.

b. Of water: *to take* (one) *up to* (the ankles, knees, shoulders), *over* (the head), to submerge (one) to that depth. Now *Sc.*

1654 Z. COKE *Logick* To Reader, Truths that before delug'd you, will now take you but up to the Ancles. **1818** SCOTT *Rob Roy* xxx, Mountain torrents, some of which took the soldiers up to the knees. **1878** SAXON *Gallovedian Gossip* 15 The sea took him abune the knees. *Mod. Sc.* There's a deep hole there, that will take a man over the head.

VII. Senses related to VI, denoting intellectual action.

* *To apprehend mentally, to conceive, understand, consider.*

46. To receive and hold with the intellect; to grasp mentally, apprehend, comprehend, understand: = *take in*, 84 l. (Now only in reference to the meaning of words.) ***to take*** (*someone's*) ***point*** (and variants): see POINT *sb.*[1] 28 c.

1382 WYCLIF *John* i. 5 And the liȝt schyneth in derknessis, and derknessis tooken [1388 comprehendiden] not it. *c* **1450** *St. Cuthbert* (Surtees) 4656 Goddis wisdome þat none may take [L. *incomprehensibilis*]. **1551** ROBINSON tr. *More's Utopia* II. (1895) 214 Thys kynde of learnynge.. they toke so muche the souner. **1666** PEPYS *Diary* 30 July, The girl do take musick mighty readily. **1737** BRACKEN *Farriery Impr.* (1757) II. 278 The Reader will easily take the Meaning. **1860** THACKERAY *Round. Papers* i. (1899) 170 You take the allegory? Novels are sweets. **1893** *National Observer* 11 Mar. 413/2 An audience.. quick to take his points.

b. *transf.* To apprehend the meaning of, understand (a person, i.e. what he says).

1513 DOUGLAS *Æneis* I. Prol. 318 Quha takis me nocht, go quhair thai haue ado. **1622** BACON *Holy War* Wks. 1879 I. 525/2 You take me right, Eupolis. **1707** J. STEVENS tr. *Quevedo's Com. Wks.* (1709) 350 Do you take me Sir? **1810** CRABBE *Borough* x. iii. Wks. 1834 III. 180, I spoke my thought—you take me—what I think. **1882** STEVENSON *New Arab. Nts.* (1884) 219, I am not in this affair for him. You take me?

47. a. With *adv.* or *advb. phr.* To understand or apprehend in a specified way. Also with person as obj. In quot. *a* 1300, 'to understand to be meant': cf. 48 b.

a **1300** *Cursor M.* 1379 [God] þe fader in cedre þou sal take, A tre of heght, þat has na make. **13..** *Ibid.* 28974 Chastiyng o flex[e]s foure fald to tak In praier, fasting, wand, and wak. *c* **1460** R. ROS *La Belle Dame* 582 And so must he be take in every place. **1552** *Bk. Com. Prayer, Communion* (*ad fin.*), Leste yet the same kneelyng myghte be thought or taken otherwyse. **1642** tr. *Perkins' Prof. Bk.* viii. §522 So was the law taken in Anno 4. H. 3. **1665** BUNYAN *Holy Citie* 164, I the rather take it thus,.. Because [etc.]. **1721** BRADLEY *Philos. Acc. Wks. Nat.* 155 If we take the Story of it right.

†**b.** With *simple compl.* To understand as, suppose to be, consider as: = *take for*, 48; also, to understand to mean: = 48 b. *Obs.*

13.. *Cursor M.* 28121 (Cott.) And titter wald i lesyng make þan man my worde vn-treu to take. *c* **1400** *Apol. Loll.* 35 þo hous of God her is tane þe congregacoun of feiþful men. **1538** *Treat. Bps. Rome Supremacy* i, In times past the Bishop of Constantinople tooke himself highest of all bishops. **1660** MILTON *Free Commw.* Wks. 1851 V. 421 They took themselves not bound by the Light of Nature or Religion to any former Covnant. **1709** STEELE *Tatler* No. 1 ¶9, I take my self obliged in Honour to go on.

c. With *dependent clause*: To suppose, apprehend, assume as a fact, be of opinion (*that* ..). Usually *take it.*

c **1380** WYCLIF *Wks.* (1880) 460 Cristenmen taken ouer þat petre was cristis viker, & suyde hym in maner of lif. **1429** *Rolls of Parlt.* IV. 346/1 So take that the saide Cominaltes been no Cominaltes corporat. **1538** AUDLEY in *Lett. Suppress. Monasteries* (Camden) 240, I take it that your lordshypp ys at appoynt for me to have it. **1596** SHAKS. *Merch. V.* I. i. 63, I take it your owne busines calls on you. **1603** —— *Meas. for M.* IV. ii. 110 As I take it, it is almost day. **1642** tr. *Perkins' Prof. Bk.* v. §354 It is commonly taken, that if a wife run away from her husband.. shee shall loose her dower. **1709** STEELE & ADDISON *Tatler* No. 93 ¶4 Within this Height I take it, that all the fighting Men of Great Britain are comprehended. **1842** TENNYSON *Edwin Morris* 43, I take it, God made the woman for the man, And for the good and increase of the world. **1885** *Law Times* LXXX. 118/2 The learned counsel might take it that this court overruled the objection.

d. With *inf.* To understand, consider, suppose, imagine, assume (*to be* or *to do* something).

1548 UDALL *Erasm. Par. John* 16 b, Men toke him to be mine inferiour. **1663** BUTLER *Hud.* I. II. 889 For Men he [the Bear] always took to be His Friends, and Dogs the Enemy. *a* **1677** BARROW *Serm.* Wks. 1716 III. 72 He that taketh himself to have enough, what doth he need? **1719** DE FOE *Crusoe* (1840) II. vi. 151, I take that man to be a..penitent. **1878** HUXLEY *Physiogr.* 63 It may be taken roughly to represent one inch of rain.

e. *to take* (something) *as done*: to consider an omission not to have occurred; *to take* (something) *as read*: see READ *v.* 11 e.

1893 E. F. BENSON *Dodo* I. i. 9 You haven't congratulated me. Never mind, we'll take that as done.

48. *to take..for.* **a.** To suppose to be, consider as; often, with implication of error, to suppose to be (what it is not), to mistake for; to assume to be; also †to esteem or repute as (*obs.*: cf. 49.) Freq. in phr. *what* or *who(m) do you take me for?* said as a challenge to a derogatory implication, as of foolishness, dishonesty, etc. *take for granted*: see GRANTED 2 b.

c **1435** *Torr. Portugal* 1333 Gret lordys..for a doughty knyght hym tase. *c* **1515** *Cocke Lorell's B.* 3 A man wolde take hym for a shrewe I trowe. **1579** GOSSON *Sch. Abuse* (Arb.) 65, I am not so childishe to take euery bushe for a monster. **1607** TOPSELL *Four-f. Beasts* (1658) 388 We will take it for granted that it pertaineth not to that rank or order. **1632** LITHGOW *Trav.* IX. 396 An Eagle taking his bald pate for a white rocke, let a shell-fish fall on it. **1693** TATE *Juvenal* xv. 178 So soft his Tresses..You'd doubt his Sex, and take him for a Girl. **1712** ADDISON *Spect.* No. 289 ¶1, I have been sometimes taken..for a Parish Sexton. **1847** A. & H. MAYHEW *Greatest Plague* vii. 87, I wanted to ask her who the dickens she took me for. **1889** STEVENSON *Master of B.* x. 267 Do you take me for a fool? **1892** KIPLING & BALESTIER *Naulahka* xvii. 202 'You won't get the chance,' said Tarvin unshakenly... 'What do you take me for?' **1912** C. MACKENZIE *Carnival* xxx. 293 'What do you take me for?' enquired Irene. 'I take you for what you are—a rotter.' **1921** W. J. LOCKE *Mountebank* xiii. 164 'You haven't given me away?' 'My good girl,' I protested, 'what do you take me for?' **1927** W. S. MAUGHAM *Constant Wife* III. 186 But, my poor John, whom do you take us for? Am I so unattractive that what I'm telling you is incredible? **1939** G. B. SHAW *Geneva* II. 32 Then you went to school, did you? *Begonia.* Well, of course: what do you take me for? **1983** 'R. B. DOMINIC' *Flaw in System* xx. 129 What do you take me for? A simp?

b. To understand to mean, to interpret as. Now *rare* or *Obs.* †In quots. *c* 1200, 1340 in converse sense: To reckon or count as, to include in the meaning of (*obs.*).

c **1200** ORMIN 19029 Tacc nu þe sawle forr þatt mann þatt cumeþþ her to manne. **1340** HAMPOLE *Pr. Consc.* 2818 Alle þir four stedes..for helle þai may alle be tane, Of whilk four purgatory es ane. **1596** HARINGTON *Metam. Ajax* (1814) 24 Which word many of the simple hearers and readers take for a precious stone. **1684** J. P. tr. *Frambresarius' Art Physic* iii. 95 Generally the Word Aposteme is taken for any Tumor which is preternatural. **1697** EVELYN *Architects* Misc. Writ. (1825) 379 Otherwhiles it [the astragal] again is taken for the hoop, cincture or collar next the hypotrachelium.

49. To regard, consider, hold, esteem (*as*); to estimate, reckon (*at* so much).

1531-2 *Act 23 Hen. VIII*, c. 3 That any Utlarie..pleded or alleged..shalbe taken but as voide plee. **1534** WHITINTON *Tullyes Offices* I. (1540) 49 He was take as a gret and a famous man. **1605** CAMDEN *Rem.* 36 This is to be take as a granted veritie. **1820** *Examiner* No. 620. 130/2 We are to take the word *liberal*..as a piece of irony. **1893** *Eng. Illustr. Mag.* X. 310/2 An average length of stroke may be taken at about six yards.

†**b.** *pa. pple.* (with qualifying adv.) Reputed, esteemed. *Obs.*

1518 in Ld. Berners *Froiss.* (1812) Pref. 17 Sir John Style ..well beloued and well takyn in theis partes. **1526** TINDALE *Rom.* xvi. 7 Andronicus and Junia my cosyns..which are wele taken amonge the apostles. **1535** COVERDALE *Judith* xvi. 21 Iudith was..right honorably taken in all the londe of Israel. **1597-8** BACON *Ess., Followers & Fr.* (Arb.) 34 A thing ciuile, and well taken euen in Monarchies.

** *To conceive and exercise.*

50. To begin to have or be affected by (a feeling or state of mind); to conceive; hence, to experience, entertain, feel (*delight, pleasure, pride*, etc.).

See also DELIGHT *sb.* 1 b, FRIGHT *sb.* 1, HUFF *sb.* 2 b, INTEREST *sb.* 7, OFFENCE *sb.* 5 c, PET *sb.*[2], PLEASURE *sb.* 5 f, PRIDE *sb.*[1] 4, UMBRAGE, etc.

c **1200** ORMIN 19558 þatt tatt Farisewisshe follc Strang wraþþe takenn haffde. *a* **1300** *Cursor M.* 448 Agains him [God] he tok a pride. **1390-** [see OFFENCE *sb.* 5 c]. **1390** GOWER *Conf.* II. 100 Wherof the king gret hevynesse Hath take. **1470-85** MALORY *Arthur* IV. i. 119 Take none heuynesse, said Merlyn. *Ibid.* VI. xv. 207 She took suche sorou that shee dyed. **1535** COVERDALE *Ezek.* xxxvi. 31 Ye shal take displeasure at youre owne selues, by reason of youre synnes and abhominacions. *a* **1553** [see GRIEF *sb.* 4 b]. **1694** *Acc. Sev. Late Voy.* Introd. 6 Upon some disgust taken at his Master. **1773** *Life N. Frowde* 15 Persons to whom I had taken so much Dislike. **1888** LESTER *Hartas Maturin* III. ii. 41 Women do take prejudices.

b. *absol.* or *intr.* To take a fancy or liking: cf. *take to*, 74 g, *take with*, 75 c.

1600 DYMMOCK *Treat. Irel.* (1841) 6 They are quicke and capable, kind harted where they take. **1874** HARDY *Madding Crowd* xviii, Mistress and man were engaged in the operation of making a lamb 'take', which is performed whenever a ewe has lost her own offspring, one of the twins of another ewe being given her as a substitute.

†**c.** *to take on oneself*: to become distressed or disturbed in mind: = *take on*, 86 j. *Obs.*

1632 J. HAYWARD tr. *Biondi's Eromena* 121 The Prince,.. because he found him not, tooke on him like a mad man.

51. *trans.* **a.** To conceive and adopt with the will (a purpose, resolution, etc.), or with the intellect (an estimate, view, etc.); to form and hold in the mind. See also PURPOSE *sb.* 2 b, REDE *sb.*[1] 2 b.

a **1300** *Cursor M.* 11151 He..tok his redd al for to fle, Priuelik and latt hir be. **1375-** [see PURPOSE *sb.* 2 b]. **1513** DOUGLAS *Æneis* v. i. 10 The Troianis in thare breistis tuk ane ges Quharfor it was. **1652** NEEDHAM tr. *Selden's Mare Cl.* 37 A conclusion [was] taken to refer all to their several Princes. **1660** BARROW *Euclid* Pref. (1714) 2, I took a Resolution to make use of most of the Schemes of the said Book. **1749** FIELDING *Tom Jones* VII. ii, Having taken a resolution to leave the Country. **1891** *Law Times* XC. 462/2 We do not take the alarmist view of our correspondent.

b. To conceive and exercise (*courage, heart*, etc.; †*mercy* (obs.), *pity*, etc.); to form in the mind and exhibit in action. (Sometimes nearly coinciding with sense 16 a, to assume: cf. also branch VIII.) See also COURAGE *sb.* 4 d, HEART *sb.* 49, HEART OF GRACE, PITY *sb.* 2.

13.. *Guy Warw.* (A.) 4656 Now, sir, take þerof pite. **13..**, **1530** [see HEART *sb.* 49]. **13..** *Cursor M.* 27136 Quen þou tas to þe baldhede O gretter mans sinful dede. **1483** CAXTON *G. de la Tour* A viij, Wherfore God took mercy on them. *c* **1490-1841** [see COURAGE *sb.* 4 d]. **1530-1890** [see HEART OF GRACE]. **1593** ABP. BANCROFT *Daung. Posit.* II. vii. 54 They haue taken greater boldnesse, and growen more rebellious. *a* **1715** BURNET *Own Time* an. 1672 (1823) I. 538 No popish priest had ever taken the confidence to speak to her of those matters. **1888** *Times* (weekly ed.) 18 May 3/4 The Arabs would have taken fresh heart.

c. To exercise with the mind, in thought (*note, notice*, †*intent*, etc.), or with the mind and will, in action (*care, heed*, †*diligence*, etc.). Cf. branches VIII, IX. See also CARE *sb.* 3 c, HEED *sb.* 1 b, INTENT *sb.* 2, KEEP *sb.* 1, 2, NOTE *sb.*[2] 20 b, NOTICE *sb.* 6, 7, REGARD *sb.* 6 b, TENT *sb.*[2], THOUGHT *sb.* *to take care of*: see also CARE *sb.*[1] 4 b.

a **1225** *Leg. Kath.* 1379 þe deore Drihtin areaw us, & toc read to ure alde dusischipes. *a* **1300-** [see KEEP *sb.* 1, 2]. *c* **1305-** [see HEED *sb.* 1 b]. **13..** *Cursor M.* 27228 Ilk man þat will ta ȝeme. *c* **1368** CHAUCER *Compl. Pite* 82 But ye the rather take cure To breke that perilouse alliaunce. *c* **1375** *Cursor M.* 12592 (Fairf.) Hamward þai went & to ihesu toke nane entent. *c* **1425** *Ibid.* 7937 (Trin.) Son he seide take good gome ȝyuen þou hast þin owne dome. *c* **1475** *Songs & Carols 15th C.* (Percy Soc.) 54 To here song then tok I intent. **1564-5** *Reg. Privy Council Scot.* I. 320 Quhairunto hir Hienes and hir Counsall mon tak ee and regard. **1588-** [see CARE *sb.* 3 c]. **1592-** [see NOTICE *sb.* 6, 7]. **1596-** [see NOTE *sb.*[2] 20 b]. **1784** R. BAGE *Barham Downs* I. 230, I took no concern about any of them.

VIII. Various senses, nearly = make, do, perform (some action).

(See also senses 19, 37, 51 b, c.)

52. To perform, make, do (an act, action, movement, etc.): usually with some notion of undertaking or taking upon one, and carrying out or carrying on; sometimes with that of getting.

Often it forms with the object merely a periphrastic equivalent of the cognate vb.: e.g. *to take a leap* = *to leap* (*once*), *to take a look* = *to look* (*once*), *to take one's departure* = *to depart.* (See also *take aim* in Phrases, 64; ACTION *sb.* 7, JOURNEY *sb.* 3, STEP *sb.*[1], TURN *sb.*, WALK *sb.*)

c **1380** *Sir Ferumbras* 4029 To-morwe let ous our iorne take, Hamward aȝen to ryde. *c* **1412** HOCCLEVE *De Reg. Princ.* 3400 The kyng took a laghtre, and wente his way. *c* **1449** PECOCK *Repr.* 156 At which men mowe lawȝe and take bourde for her symplenes. **1477** EARL RIVERS (Caxton) *Dictes* 1, I determyned me to take that voyage. **1483** CAXTON *Cato* C vj b, Thou oughtest not to stryue ne take noyse wyth them that ben ful of superfluous wordes. *c* **1489** —— *Sonnes of Aymon* xiv. 341 Thei toke grete debate for me wyth Charlemagn wythin his pavylion. **1491** *Churchw. Acc. St. Dunstan's, Canterb.*, They took an axion ageynst the executores of Wyllyam Belser. **1556** *Chron. Gr. Friars* (Camden) 13 Thys yere the kynge..toke his viage towarde Normandy. **1590** SPENSER *F.Q.* III. xi. 42 Like a winged horse he [Neptune] tooke his flight. **1617** *Acc. Bk. W. Wray* in *Antiquary* XXXII. 214 King James..tooke his progresse towards Scotland. **1678** BUNYAN *Pilgr.* I. 43 How many steps have I took in vain. **1693** *Humours Town* 3 Take a last farewel-look of this overgrown City. *Ibid.* 6 You might take a survey of the Rarities. **1711** BUDGELL *Spect.* No. 77 ¶1 We took a turn or two more. **1719** DE FOE *Crusoe* (1840) II. xiv. 287 Without measuring the windings and turnings it takes. *Ibid.* xv. 315 He takes a great circuit about. **1766** GOLDSM. *Vic. W.* xxviii, My wife, my daughter and herself were taking a walk together. **1845** M. PATTISON *Ess.* (1889) I. 24 When Queen Brunchilde took her departure from Rouen. **1867** AUG. J. E. WILSON *Vashti* xxiv, I came to-day to beg you to take a trip somewhere, by sea or land. **1889** MRS. E. KENNARD *Landing Prize* III. viii. 148 The salmon took a great leap. **1893** J. ASHBY STERRY *Naughty Girl* vii, I'll just take a turn down to the club and see what's going on.

†**b.** *to take beginning*: to begin, start, commence. (See also 31.) *Obs.* [= ON. *taka upphaf*, to begin.]

a **1300** *Cursor M.* 12887 þe ald testament hir-wit nu slakes, And sua þe neu bigining takes. **1557-75** *Diurnal Occurr.* (Bann. Club) 61 Vpoun the first day of August, the Parliament tuke begyning. **1601** DOLMAN *La Primaud. Fr. Acad.* (1618) III. 641 We must all beleeue..that time tooke beginning with the world.

c. *to take five* (or *ten*): to have a five- (or ten-) minute break. Also *loosely*, to relax. *U.S. colloq.*

1929 *Amer. Speech* V. 147 If the miner craves a rest while on the job, he *takes five*, a long enough period for a smoke. **1943** *Yank* 7 May 3 Six members of a reconnaissance group 'take 10' at a railroad station. **1961** G. T. SIMON *Feeling of Jazz* 30 Man, I'm glad they said to take five, because this next arrangement looks rough. **1973** W. SHEED *People will always be Kind* vi. 60 'Could you go a little faster, Fatman?' .. It was difficult making jokes... 'O.K. Fatstuff, take five, I was only kidding.'

d. *to take a fall* (U.S.): (*a*) *slang*, to be arrested or convicted of a crime (cf. FALL *v.* 23 f, g); (*b*) *colloq.*, to suffer a fall; similarly *to take a spill*; also *fig.*, to fall for (cf. FALL *v.* 60).

1942 BERREY & VAN DEN BARK *Amer. Thes. Slang* §353/7 Fall in love...take a fall. *Ibid.* §500/6 Be arrested...take *or* have a fall. **1953** W. BURROUGHS *Junkie* iii. 34 Jack had taken a fall on a safe job and was in the Bronx County jail awaiting trial. **1958** S. J. PERELMAN *Most of S. J. Perelman* 35, I took a rather nasty fall over a wastebasket. **1962** D. LESSING *Golden Notebk.* IV. 474 Molly rang late—says that Jane Bond has 'taken a fall over' Mr Green. **1968** *Globe & Mail* (Toronto) 15 Jan. 29/6 Even the best skier can take a spill. **1973** *Times* 9 Feb. 12/2 Michael Fish took a couple of falls.

53. *to take counsel* († *advice*, † *advisement*): to get advice, to consult, deliberate; †to devise; †to decide: see ADVICE 4, ADVISEMENT 3, COUNSEL 1.

a **1300** *Cursor M.* 4790 þar of es god we ta consail. *c* **1386** CHAUCER *Melib.* ¶760 Thanne Dame Prudence..delibered and took auys in hir self. **1480** CAXTON *Chron. Eng.* cxcvii. 173 The barons token counceyll bytwene hem. **1483** —— *G. de la Tour* D iv b, Withoute takyng ony counceylle of her husbond. **1537** T. CUMPTUN in Ellis *Orig. Lett.* Ser. II. II. 92 After that they had communiked together and taken avisement. **1609** BIBLE (Douay) *Judg.* xx. 32 Who..tooke advise to draw them away from the citie. **1879** M. J. GUEST *Lect. Hist. Eng.* xxxvi. 359 She took counsel with witches and magicians.

†**b.** *intr.* ? ellipt. for *take advisement. Obs.*

c **1400** *Emare* 799 Grete lordes toke hem be-twene, That þey wolde exyle þe quene.

†**54.** *trans.* To arrange, fix, agree upon, conclude (a truce, peace, league, etc.). [Cf. OF. *prendre treve*, 13th c.] *Obs.*

1375 BARBOUR *Bruce* XIV. 96 Quhill trewis at the last tuk thai. *c* **1400** *Laud Troy-Bk.* 8474 It was seyde to the Emperoure..How ffight was taken hem be-twene. *c* **1400** *Destr. Troy* 9072 The Troiens to the tenttes tristy men send, For a tru to be tan. *c* **1470** [see PEACE *sb.* 1 b]. **1523** LD. BERNERS *Froiss.* I. xxxiii. 48 So y[t] they wolde take no peace, nor truse, with y[e] kyng of Englande. *c* **1600** SHAKS. *Sonn.* xlvii. 1 Betwixt mine eye and heart a league is tooke. **1656** S. HOLLAND *Zara* (1719) 135 Having taken a Truce with his Enemy, he would not be the first should break it.

55. *to take adieu, farewell*: to bid farewell, say good-bye, take one's leave. Const. *of*. Cf. *to take leave*: see LEAVE *sb.*[1] 2. So † *to take good night* (*obs.*).

c **1560** ROLLAND *Seven Sages* Prol. ii, I..tuke gude nicht, and said gude schirs adew. **1617** J. TAYLOR (Water-P.) *Trav.* (1872) 2 We all went to the Christopher where we took a Bacchanalian farewell one of another. **1665** PEPYS *Diary* 28 Aug., I think to take adieu to-day of the London Streets. **1700** DRYDEN *Cock & Fox* 256 Last he drew A piteous sigh, and took a long adieu. **1821** SCOTT *Kenilw.* vii, Thus saying, he at length took farewell. **1840** THIRLWALL *Greece* VII. 195 [He] besought Demosthenes to forgive his temporary estrangement,..and took a last farewell of him.

56. To lay hold of, raise, put forth, make (an objection, an exception, a distinction, etc.). See also EXCEPTION *sb.* 7 c, OBJECTION 1 b.

1542- [see EXCEPTION *sb.* 7 c]. **1830** HERSCHEL *Nat. Phil.* 7 The objection which has been taken. **1830** MONK *Life R. Bentley* (1833) I. 303 Instead of doing so, they take a dilemma, and intimate a belief that either by the old statutes, or by the 40th of Elizabeth's, the Master is subject to the jurisdiction of the Bishop of Ely. **1849** MACAULAY *Hist. Eng.* vii. II. 265 Between punishments and disabilities a distinction was taken. *Ibid.* x. 556 The distinction which they took was..ingenious. **1864** BP. WILBERFORCE *Sp. Missions* (1874) 46, I know well the objections men can take.

IX. Senses denoting movement or removal (lead, convey, remove, deliver, etc.), and related senses.

* *To convey, carry, conduct, remove.*

57. a. To carry, convey; to cause (a person or animal) to go with one, to conduct, lead, escort. Also said of a vehicle, etc.: To convey, carry (a person) to some place. Also of a road, way, etc.: = LEAD *v.*[1] 6; so of a journey, etc. Also with *over*, to conduct through or show around (a building, garden, etc.).

c **1200** ORMIN 8355 Josæp, ris upp & tacc þe child, & tacc þe childess moderr. *a* **1300** *Cursor M.* 5117 Tas Ruben þan wit yow. *Ibid.* 23814 Es þar na wai..Cun tak us better. *a* **1400-50** *Alexander* 4886 Syne tas he with him titly his twelue tried prince[s]. **1503** in *Trans. Roy. Hist. Soc.* (1902) 153 Walter Robardes tooke this Alex[r] apart. **1590** SHAKS. *Com. Err.* IV. i. 36 Take the stranger to my house. **1665** MANLEY *Grotius' Low C. Warres* 832 Taking through the marshy Fields of Cazant Twelve hundred Walloons and

Irish with him. **1719** DE FOE *Crusoe* (1840) I. xiv. 246, I took my man Friday with me. *c* **1810** W. HICKEY *Mem.* (1918) II. xix. 251 She..took me over the house, which was a complete a one as ever I saw. **1837** C. FOX *Jrnl.* 15 May in *Mem. Old Friends* (1882) iii. 16 Took them all over the Grove Hill gardens. **1848** THACKERAY *Van. Fair* xlviii, Being obliged to take four of us in his carriage to wait upon His Majesty. **1878** *Scribner's Mag.* XV. 897/1 The second stage of the journey takes the traveler through Egypt. **1880** TROLLOPE *Duke's Children* III. xix. 215, I want to take her all over the house. **1908** *Betw. Trent & Ancholme* 55 A yard or two further takes us to the N.E. corner. *a* **1910** *Mod.* Will this road take me to Abingdon? **1911** *Rep. Labour & Social Conditions in Germany* (Tariff Reform League) III. 166 [He] was able yesterday to take a small deputation..over the 'Triumph' works.

b. To carry or bear (a thing) with one; to carry to some place or person. In quot. 1883, to draw (something) *through* a liquid.

1390 GOWER *Conf.* III. 217 [Eche] hath A pot of Erthe, in which he tath A lyht brennende in a kressette. *a* **1400** *Sir Perc.* 478 He..Tuke with hym his schorte spere. *c* **1470** HENRY *Wallace* II. 85 Thow Scot, to quhom takis thow this thing? **1590** SHAKS. *Com. Err.* IV. i. 37 And with you take the Chaine. **1605** —— *Macb.* v. iii. 19 Take thy face hence. **1768** J. BYRON *Narr. Patagonia* (ed. 2) 221 They will take from the ground a glove or handkerchief. **1858** RAMSAY *Scot. Life & Char.* v. (1870) 118 She went out and did not take the door with her [*i.e.* shut it after her]. **1883** R. HALDANE *Workshop Receipts* Ser. II. 227/1 Take [the yarn] through dilute sulphuric acid, and wash very well.

c. *fig.* To induce (a person) to go; to be the cause of his going. (Cf. BRING *v.* 1 c.)

1848 THACKERAY *Van. Fair* lxvii, 'Particular business', she said, took her to Bruges. **1856** J. H. NEWMAN *Callista* (1890) 114 What takes you into the city this morning? **1883** P. GREG *Sanguelac* II. xi. 223 What took you out so late? *Mod.* The business that took me to London.

d. In colloq. phr. ***you can't take it with you***, in allusion to the impossibility of benefiting from earthly wealth after death.

1841 MARRYAT *Masterman Ready* II. ii. 22 He was very fond of money; but that they said was all the better, as he could not take it away with him when he died. **1923** G. ARTHUR *Let.* 16 Sept. in *Further Lett. Man of no Importance* (1932) 153 Mr. Gladstone, when a dead millionaire was held up for his admiration because he had left large sums for charities, said, 'Thank him for nothing; he was obliged to leave it somewhere as he couldn't take it with him.' **1937** KAUFMAN & HART (*title*) You can't take it with you. **1952** A. CHRISTIE *Mrs. McGinty's Dead* vii. 48 'They inherited a little money when Mrs. McGinty died.'.. 'Well, that's natural enough... You can't take it with you.' **1977** J. PORTER *Who the Heck is Sylvia?* x. 87 You're not short of the odd penny... And you can't take it with you, can you?

58. With *from*, *off* (hence sometimes *simply*): To carry away, to remove; to extract; to deprive or rid a person or thing of (with various shades of connotation): = *take away*, 80 a, *take off*, 85 a, *take out*, 87 a: see also *take out of*, 88.

to take off one's feet: to carry off one's feet by force, as a wind or wave; also *fig.* So ***to take off one's balance***, etc.

a **1272** *Luue Ron* 64 in *O.E. Misc.* 95 Al deþ hit wile from him take. *a* **1300** *E.E. Psalter* i. 5 Als duste þat winde þerthe tas fra. *a* **1400** *Cursor M.* 29546 (Cott. Galba) It takes [*Cott.* steres] his cristendom him fra. *c* **1489** CAXTON *Sonnes of Aymon* 19 Saying, that they should take the head from the body of hym. **1535** COVERDALE *Ps.* l[i]. 11 Take not thy holy sprete fro me. **1567** *Gude & Godlie B.* (S.T.S.) 147 He fra me my Sin hes tane. **1610** HOLLAND *Camden's Brit.* (1637) 73 He..tooke from the towne the benefit of their haven. **1655** SIR E. NICHOLAS in *N. Papers* (Camden) II. 235 His decree is annulled and taken of yᵉ file. **1678** BUTLER *Hud.* III. III. 693 The Law severely contrabands Our taking business off Mens hands. **1818** SCOTT *Hrt. Midl.* xv, The doing so would..take the case from under the statute. **1825** J. NICHOLSON *Operat. Mechanic* 560 A plane, which takes a thin shaving off the surface of the wood. **1867** TROLLOPE *Chron. Barset* i, John did take his eyes off his book. *Mod.* The sea was so rough when I was bathing that the waves took me off my feet.

b. ***to take the life of***: to deprive of life, to kill. Also, ***to take one's*** (***own***) ***life***: to kill oneself, commit suicide.

[**13..** *Cursor M.* 25831 His lijf þan sal be fra him tane.] *c* **1489** CAXTON *Sonnes of Aymon* xii. 306, I praye you..that yourselfe wyl take the liff fro me, and cut of my hede.] **1591** SHAKS. *1 Hen. VI*, III. i. 22 Thou layd'st a Trap to take my Life. **1766** GOLDSM. *Vic. W.* xxx, You imagine, perhaps, that a contempt for your own life gives you a right to take that of another. **1847** TENNYSON *Princ.* v. 397 Take not his life: he risk'd it for my own. **1920** D. H. LAWRENCE *Women in Love* xv. 211 It was not a question of taking one's life—she would *never* kill herself. **1965** *Amer. Speech* XL. 301 This person may indeed take his own life. **1981** *Daily Tel.* 18 June 19/2 A note left by them made it clear that they wanted to take their own lives and also wished to be buried in the same grave.

c. To remove by death. Also *euphem.* in *pass.*, to die.

1552 *Bk. Com. Prayer, Burial of Dead*, Forasmuche as it hath pleased almightie God of his great mercie to take vnto hym selfe the soule of our dere brother here departed, we therefore commit [etc.]. **1593** SHAKS. *3 Hen. VI*, I. iv. 167 Hard-hearted Clifford, take me from the World. **1616** S. MOUNTAGU in *Buccleuch MSS.* (Hist. MSS. Comm.) I. 247 God hath taken to himself my brother Walter Mountagu. **1632** HEYWOOD *1st Pt. Iron Age* v. i. Wks. 1874 III. 338 Since the Fates Haue tane him from vs. **1749** GRAY *Let.* 7 Nov. (1900) I. 204 He who has preserved her to you so many years..has taken her from us to Himself. **1809** J. PORTER *Scottish Chiefs* xxxiv. 257 If all whom I love be lost to me here, take me then to thyself, and let my freed spirit fly to thy embraces in heaven! **1864** TENNYSON *North. Farmer* iii, 'The amoighty's a taäkin o' you to 'issén, my friend', a said. **1920** E. O'NEILL *Beyond Horizon* II. i. 69 It was God's will that he should be taken. **1977** [see PASS *v.* 65 c].

d. To subtract, deduct.

1611 SHAKS. *Cymb.* II. i. 60 This her Sonne, Cannot take two from twenty for his heart, And leaue eighteene. **1806** HUTTON *Course Math.* (1827) I. 8, 6 − 2, denotes that 2 is to be taken from 6. **1876** E. JENKINS *Blot Queen's Head* 28 Every one took 50 per cent. off Bobby's expletives. **1890** *Sat. Rev.* 16 Aug. 192/1 Twopence in the pound was taken off the tea-duty.

e. *absol.* with *from*: To detract from, lessen, diminish. Cf. 80 c, 85 k.

1625 MASSINGER *New Way* IV. i, [Ne'er] sullied with one taint or spot That may take from your innocence and candour. *a* **1700** DRYDEN (J.), It takes not from you, that you were born with principles of generosity. **1891** *Temple Bar Mag.* Oct. 254 It takes greatly from the pleasure.

f. *intr.* for *pass.* (with adv. or advb. phr.) To be capable of being, or adapted to be, taken *off*, *out*, *to pieces*, etc.; to be removable, detachable, etc.

So, by extension, ***to take in and out*** = to be capable of being put in and taken out; so ***to take on and off***.

1669 STURMY *Mariner's Mag.* II. ii. 53 A Brass pair of Compasses..and four Steel Points to take in and out. **1703** MOXON *Mech. Exerc.* 227 The Stop-screw, to take out when the Hollow Axis moves in the Moving-Coller. **1881** GREENER *Gun* 78 Guns..so constructed as to take to pieces and stow away in a small compass. **1892** *St. James' Gaz.* 8 Feb. 6/2 Yours [i.e. hair] takes off at night.

59. in various *fig.* senses. **a.** To carry, draw, or lead in thought, etc.; with *from*, *off*, to distract.

1611 SHAKS. *Wint. T.* IV. iv. 356 Your heart is full of something, that do's take Your minde from feasting. **1670** COTTON *Espernon* II. v. 238 An accident fell out that soon took the Duke off all thoughts of that Solemnity. **1742** *Lond. & Country Brew.* I. (ed. 4) 41 These deluded People are taken into an Approbation of indeed an Ignis fatuus. **1890** *Murray's Mag.* VII. 65 Love..took her out of herself, and soothed her sorrows.

†**b.** ***to take*** (a person) ***with one***: to speak so that (he) can 'follow' or apprehend one's meaning; to enable (him) to understand one; to be explicit. (Usu. in *imper.*) *Obs.*

1592 SHAKS. *Rom. & Jul.* III. v. 142 Soft, take me with you, take me with you, wife. **1695** CONGREVE *Love for L.* v. ii, Ay, but pray take me along with you, sir.

†**c.** ***to take*** (a thing) ***with one***: to bear in mind, keep in remembrance, take note of. *Obs.*

1599 MASSINGER, etc. *Old Law* II. ii, Oh! you are too hot, sir; Pray cool yourself, and take September with you. **1610** HOLLAND *Camden's Brit.* 715 Yet take here with you, that which William Newbrigensis..writeth. **1746** CHESTERF. *Lett.* (1792) I. 295 Take this along with you that the worst authors are always most partial to their own works. **1828** SCOTT *F.M. Perth* v, Take it with you that I will never listen to them.

†**d.** To render, translate. *Obs. rare.*

c **1430** *Syr Gener.* (Roxb.) 25 A clerk itt in to latyn tooke Att hertford out of a booke.

e. To bring or convey to a higher or lower degree; to raise or lower; to advance or put back. See also *take down*, 82; PEG *sb.*[1] 3.

1589- [see PEG *sb.*[1] 3]. **1890** *Field* 24 May 750/3 By steady play the score was taken to 18.

** *To deliver, give, commit, give up.*

†**60.** *trans.* To deliver, hand over; to give; to give in charge, commit, entrust. (= BETAKE 1, 1 b, 2.) Const. to or dative. *Obs.*

[In Layamon, in the early version rarely (2 instances), but in the later very commonly (22 instances), *bitake* is used as equivalent to *bitæche*, *biteche* (BETEACH, to deliver); in 19 cases *biteche* of the earlier text becomes *bitake* in the later. In 4 cases the later version has in the same sense the simple *take*; this became from 1300 to 1530 quite established, and continued in some writers to *c* 1560. This use was not in Norse, and is absent from northern ME. For the history see BETAKE *v.*]

c **1275** LAY. 54 He..wrot..And þane hilke boc tock us to bisne. *Ibid.* 3361 And takeþ [*c* 1205 bitachet] hit his child. *Ibid.* 22378 And ich wolle..To hostage take þe mine sone [*c* 1205 biteche þe mine þreo sunen]. *c* **1290** *S. Eng. Leg.* I. 99/254 To lhesu crist ich habbe al-so al min heorte i-take. **1297** R. GLOUC. (Rolls) 2027 Some sede þat him betere were take is neueu conan þe kinedom of þis lond. **1340** *Ayenb.* 171 þe castel of his herte and of his bodye þet god him heþ ytake to loki. **1377** LANGL. *P. Pl.* B. xv. 575 Owre lorde wrote it hym-selue In stone... And toke it moyses to teche men til Messye com. **1387** TREVISA *Higden* (Rolls) II. 323 Moyses.. took his wif [*uxori tradidit*] þe ryng of forȝetnesse. *c* **1400** *Prymer* (1894) 78 We biseche þee þat þe soule of þi seruaunt ..be not take in-to þe hondis of oure enemy. *c* **1425** *Cursor M.* 15411 (Trin.) In to ȝoure hondes I shal him take [*earlier MSS.* teche]. **1436** *Let.* in Burton & Raine *Hemingbrough* 393, I writte no more..at this tyme, so I tak ȝow to þe Holy Trinite. *c* **1440** *Promp. Parv.* 485/2 Takyn, or delyueryn a thynge to a-nother, *trado*. *c* **1440** *Gesta Rom.* xlvi. 183 (Add. MS.) Take me the Ryng, and I shalle kepe it as my lyf. *a* **1533** LD. BERNERS *Huon* lxvi. 226 Al that ye take me to kepe shalbe sauely kept to your behoue. **1533** MORE *Answ. Poysoned Bk.* Wks. 1063/1 When he tooke them the bread and bode them eate it. *a* **1553** UDALL *Royster D.* I. v. (Arb.) 31 Who tooke thee thys letter?

†**61.** *refl.* **a.** To commit or devote oneself (to God, to Christ, etc.); also, to commit or betake oneself *to* one's legs, heels, weapons, or other means of protection or safety. *Obs.* exc. as in b.

c **1200** ORMIN 356 Aȝȝ fra þatt Adam Godd forrlet & toc himm to þe deofell. *c* **1220** *Bestiary* 98 in *O.E. Misc.* 4 He.. forsaket ðore satanas,..Takeð him to ihesu crist. *a* **1300** *Cursor M.* 23046 þat al þis werld welth for-sok, And enerli to godd þam tok. *c* **1475** *Rauf Coilȝear* 938, I will forsaik Mahoun, and tak me to his micht. **1530** PALSGR. 749/1, I take me to my legges, I flye a waye. **1548** [see HEEL *sb.*[1] 20]. **1606** G. W[OODCOCKE] *Hist. Ivstine* VIII. 38 Which people perceiuing them selues entrapped..fearefully tooke them to their weapons. **1607** TOPSELL *Four-f. Beasts* (1658) 19 The Gyants..took them to their heels and so were overcome.

b. *refl.* To devote or give oneself up; to betake or apply oneself *to* (some pursuit, action, or object).

a **1300** *Cursor M.* 4032 þir breþer tuain þam tok to red To dele þair landes þam bi-tuixs. *c* **1425** *Ibid.* 13429 (Trin.) Of wif forsoke he hondbonde And toke [*earlier MSS.* turned] him to þe better honde. *c* **1440** *Alphabet of Tales* 350 He lefte all his gude and tuke hym to pouertie. **1530** PALSGR. 749/1, I take me to relygyon, or any other Kynde of Lyvynge wherein I must contynue. **1570** T. WILSON tr. *Demosthenes' Olynth.* Epist. *jb, Such are contented..to weare our Countrie cloth, and to take themselues to hard fare. **1576** GASCOIGNE *Steel Gl.* (Arb.) 67 Art thou a craftsman? take thee to thine arte. **1707** *Curios. in Husb. & Gard.* 296 One of these Leaves..took it self to walking as soon as he touch'd it. **1888** SOPHIE VEITCH *Dean's Daughter* I. viii. 155, I..took myself to the Chase. **1890** E. L. ARNOLD *Phra* v, She would not eat and would not speak, and at last took her to crying.

c. *intr.* with *into*: To give oneself up to: = *take to*, 74 e. *rare.*

1756 J. CLUBBE *Misc. Tracts* (1770) I. 105 Men had better read but few books at large, than take into this short and fallacious method of attaining..imperfect knowledge. **1765** *Ibid.* II. 10 Some men taking into life of pleasure, others into an easy chair of sleep and indolence. **1864** CARLYLE *Fredk. Gt.* xv. vi. (1872) VI. 25 Taking deeply into tobacco.

*** *To set oneself, begin, to apply oneself.*

62. *intr.* with *inf.* To set oneself, to begin (*to do* something). [After ON. *taka at*, e.g. *taka at ganga* to begin to go.] *Obs.*

1154 *O.E. Chron.* (Laud MS.) an. 1135, Dauid king of Scotland toc to uerrien him. *c* **1200** ORMIN 223 [Zacariȝe] toc to becnenn till þe follc. *Ibid.* 4772 Swa..þatt hiss bodiȝ toc To rotenn bufenn eorþe. *Ibid.* 8332 Off þa fowwre riche menn þatt tokenn þa to rixlenn. *c* **1320** *Sir Tristr.* 1000 Now haþ tristrem y-tan Oȝain moraunt to fiȝt.

b. In later use, To apply oneself *to* a habitual action (cf. 61 b and 74 e).

1677 YARRANTON *Eng. Improv.* 157 Since the Welsh took to break up their Mountains, and sow them with Corn, they have Corn sufficient for themselves. **1839** *Times* 5 Oct., He took to cultivate his genius by reading political economy. **1856** FREEMAN in W. R. W. Stephens *Life* (1895) I. iv. 232, I have taken to write a little in a penny paper called the *Star*. **1890** *Blackw. Mag.* CXLVII. 262/2 Their taking to smoke tobacco. **1891** G. MEREDITH *One of our Conq.* III. xi. 233 She has taken to like him.

†**c.** *refl.* in same senses. *Obs. rare.*

1489 CAXTON *Sonnes of Aymon* i. 54 The duke Beues toke hym selfe for to wepe strongly. **1605** VERSTEGAN *Dec. Intell.* vi. (1628) 165 They tooke themselues first to rob vpon the sea coastes. *a* **1677** BARROW *Serm.* Wks. 1716 II. 63 A state ..which they took themselves peculiarly to enjoy.

**** *To take one's course, to go.*

63. *intr.* To make one's way, go, proceed; = NIM *v.* 2, FANG *v.* 7. In early use chiefly with *to*; in later use with any prep. or adv. of direction: usually implying prompt action, cf. 'start', 'strike'.

See also *take to*, 74 b; *take away*, 80 d, *take back*, 81 e, *take in*, 84 p, *take off*, 85 n.

c **1250** *Gen. & Ex.* 1751 He toc, and wente, and folwede on. *c* **1330** R. BRUNNE *Chron. Wace* (Rolls) 13566 So harde þe parties to-gidere tok. **13..** *St. Erkenwolde* 57 in Horstm. *Altengl. Leg.* (1881) 267 Quen tithynges tokene to þe tone [= town]. ? **13..** *Cast. Love* 1686 In good tyme the[i] were i-bore, That to that feste mowe takyn [F. *peuent venir*]. *a* **1400** *Gosp. Nicod.* 1122 (Cott. Galba) On þe morn furth gan þai pas, to þaire iorne þai ta. *c* **1435** *Torr. Portugal* 598 A lytyl whyll before the day, He toke into a Ryde Wey. *c* **1489** CAXTON *Sonnes of Aymon* ix. 224 Whan they were all mounted, they toke on theyr way. **1606** G. W[OODCOCKE] *Hist. Ivstine* III. 19 They tooke on their way to seeke a new place of habitation. **1615** G. SANDYS *Trav.* 193 Turning backe, we tooke vp the said streete to the West. **1622** MABBE tr. *Aleman's Guzman d'Alf.* II. 282 They tooke downe through a groue of Alder trees. *c* **1645** T. TULLY *Siege of Carlisle* (1840) 5 Most of the fugatives took streight for Carlisle. **1707** FREIND *Peterborow's Cond. Sp.* 221 My Lord took along the edge of the Hills. **1801** tr. *Gabrielli's Myst. Husb.* III. 74, I took across some fields for the nearest way. **1863** W. C. BALDWIN *Afr. Hunting* vi. 212 He [the elephant] gave chase, and I took up the hill. **1892** MRS. E. STEWART in A. E. Lee *Hist. Columbus, Ohio* I. 264 A gang of wolves took after her.

b. *intr.* Of a road, a river, etc.: To proceed, go, run, strike off (in some direction). *Obs.* or *dial.*

1610 HOLLAND *Camden's Brit.* (1637) 731 Where it [the high road] taketh Northward, it leadeth by Caldwell and Aldburgh. **1865** CARLYLE *Fredk. Gt.* XVIII. ii. (1872) VII. 110 [The river] Moldau..takes straight to northward again. **1894** CROCKETT *Raiders* 175 At this point the drove-road took over the Folds Hill.

c. *refl.* In same sense as a; also = to betake oneself, repair, resort *to*. See also *take off*, 85 c.

1470-85 MALORY *Arthur* I. viii. 45 He took hym to a strong towre with v c good men with hym. *c* **1489** CAXTON *Sonnes of Aymon* xvi. 385 After all thyse wordes, they toke theym selfe on their waye. **1822** BYRON *Werner* I. i. 600 He will take himself to bed. **1865** TROLLOPE *Belton Est.* xxx, I am to pack up, bag and baggage, and take myself elsewhere.

X. In idiomatic phrases with special obj.

64. take aim. To direct a missile at something with intention to strike it; to aim.

1590 [see AIM *sb.* 3]. **1697** DRYDEN *Æneid* x. 479 The Sabine Clausus came, And, from afar, at Dryops took his aim. **1719** DE FOE *Crusoe* (1840) II. iv. 92 He took a sure aim. **1850** *Tait's Mag.* XVII. 546/1 He was in the act of taking aim with a carbine.

65. take alarm. To accept and act upon a warning of danger; hence, to become alarmed or roused to a sense of danger.

1624, 1772 [see ALARM *sb.* 8]. **1689** T. R. *View Govt. Europe* 38 The people took the Alarm, and clamour'd for a

Parliament. **1825** *New Monthly Mag.* XIII. 398 His *amour propre* takes the alarm. **1893** *Nat. Observer* 7 Oct. 535/2 The pirate took the alarm in time.

66. take charge. To assume the care or custody *of*; to make oneself responsible.

1389 [see CHARGE *sb.* 13]. **1495** *Act 11 Hen. VII*, c. 22 §1 A maister Ship Carpenter taking the charge of the werke. **1613** SHAKS. *Hen. VIII*, I. iv. 20 Place you that side, Ile take the charge of this. **1848** THACKERAY *Van. Fair* xli, The Baronet promised to take charge of the lad at school.

†**67. take day.** To appoint or fix a day for the transaction of some business; to make an appointment; to put off to another day. Also *fig.*

a **1400** *Octouian* 1499 They..toke day at the monthys ende Of playn batayle. *c* **1477** CAXTON *Jason* 123 She accorded to her this request and toke daye for to do hit. **1523** LD. BERNERS *Froiss.* I. xxxii. 46 Then they toke day to come agayn a thre wekes after the Feast of saynt John. **1565** STAPLETON tr. *Bede's Hist. Ch. Eng.* 171 To make quick confession of their sinfull actes and not to take dayes with God. **1642** FULLER *Holy & Prof. St.* II. xix.* 126 He had rather disburse his life at the present, then to take day, to fall into the hands of such remorseless creditours.

68. take fire. a. *lit.* To become kindled or ignited; to begin to burn, to kindle, ignite: = *catch fire* (CATCH *v.* 44).

1526 *Pilgr. Perf.* (W. de W. 1531) 263 b, At the last they take fyre & brenne. **1590** SIR J. SMYTH *Disc. Weapons* 21 Through the moystnes of the weather..the powder will take no fire. **1669** STURMY *Mariner's Mag.* v. 89 Dip therein one end of your short Pieces, least they take Fire at both ends together. **1771** SMOLLETT *Humph. Cl.* 4 July, The soot took fire. **1885** *Cent. Mag.* XXIX. 874/1 These..chimneys..often took fire.

b. *fig.* To become 'inflamed' with some emotion or the like; to become excited, esp. with anger; to become enraged, to 'fire up'.

1607 G. WILKINS *Mis. Inforced Marr.* I. in Hazl. *Dodsley* IX. 473 On which tinder he soon takes fire, and swears you are the man. **1608** *Merry Devil of Edmonton* ibid. X. 239 How this jest takes fire. **1761** HUME *Hist. Eng.* III. liv. 171 The Commons took fire, and voted it a breach of privilege. **1844** THIRLWALL *Greece* VIII. lxii. 177 Cleomenes took fire at the affront. **1890** *Temple Bar Mag.* June 17 Lithgow's soul took fire with sympathy.

69. take hold. a. To get something by one's own act into one's (physical) hold; to grasp, seize: = *catch hold* (CATCH *v.* 45), *lay hold* (LAY *v.* 22). Const. *of*; *on*, *upon* (arch.). Also said of things.

1530 PALSGR. 748/2, I take holde apon one, *jempoygne*. **1611** *Vestry Bks.* (Surtees) 161 To picke forth the ould lyme and morter that the new might better take hold. **1613** PURCHAS *Pilgrimage* (1614) 19 [The Indian] Figge-tree..whose branches..doe bend themselves downewards to the earth, where they take holde, and with new rooting multiply. **1754** SHEBBEARE *Matrimony* (1766) II. 193 [She] fell on her Knees..taking hold on the Skirt of his Coat. **1816** [see HOLD *sb.*[1] 2].

b. *fig.* To get a person or thing into its (or one's) 'hold' or power; usually with *of* (*on*, *upon* arch.); of a feeling, a disease, etc.: to seize and affect forcibly and more or less permanently; of fire, to 'lay hold' *of* (something), begin to burn. Also, to seize, avail oneself of (an opportunity).

1577 HARRISON *England* II. vi. (1877) I. 164 A thing latelie sproong vp, when pampering of the bellie began to take hold. **1605** SHAKS. *Lear* IV. vi. 238 Hence, Least that th' infection of his fortune take Like hold on thee. **1708** J. C. *Compl. Collier* (1845) 23 Another dangerous sort of bad Air, but of a fiery Nature like Lightning,..if it takes hold of the Candle. **1725** N. ROBINSON *Th. Physick* 292 When the Disease has taken any Hold of the Patient. **1889** M. GRAY *Reproach Annesley* III. vi, A sense of her bitter bereaval took hold of her.

c. (with *of*) To take possession and management of, take under one's control. ? *U.S.*

1877 RAYMOND *Statist. Mines & Mining* 222 They..know that a company of moneyed men taking hold of their camp will have to spend a considerable amount of money before they can expect to recoup their investment. **1897** KIPLING *Captains Courageous* ix, No, I only capt—took hold of the 'Blue M.' freighters—Morgan and M'Quade's old line—this summer.

†**d.** To attach itself, take root. *Obs. rare*$^{-1}$.

a **1300** *Cursor M.* 9350 It tok neuer in þer hertes hald. **13..** *Ibid.* 10009 (Gött.) þat er four vertus principalys,..All oþer vertus of þaim tas [*Cott.* has] hald.

e. To apply oneself to action; to set to; to take an active part. *dial.* and *U.S.*

1868 ATKINSON *Cleveland Gloss.*, *Tak' hold*, to undertake; an office, or specified performance or duty. **1870** MISS ALCOTT *Old-fashioned Girl* xi, I'm in despair, and shall have to take hold myself, I'm afraid. **1888** BRYCE *Amer. Commw.* III. IV. lxxxvi. 153 To believe that things will come out right whether he 'takes hold' himself or not.

70. take horse. a. To mount a horse; to get on horseback (esp. for a journey): see sense 24 c.

[*c* **1450** *Brut* (E.E.T.S.) 450 On þe morow he toke hys hors and rode to Wyndysore vn-to our Kyng. *c* **1475** *Harl. Contin. Higden* (Rolls) VIII. 544 He toke his hors with a pryvy meyney. *a* **1533** LD. BERNERS *Huon* vii. 18 After masse [they] toke theyr horsses.] **1675** BROOKS *Gold. Key* Wks. 1867 V. 10 Bajazet,..Tamerlane took prisoner,..and used him for a footstool when he took horse. **1743** WESLEY *Jrnl.* (1749) 9 Just as I was taking horse, he return'd. **1889** *Univ. Rev.* Oct. 263 The princes..took horse and fled.

b. *Mining.* (See quot.) *local.*

1855 J. R. LEIFCHILD *Cornwall Mines* 88 When a lode divides into branches, the miners say it has taken horse.

c. Of a mare: see sense 39 b, and HORSE *sb.* 1 c.

1577 B. GOOGE *Heresbach's Husb.* III. (1586) 118 The Mare will not take the Horse. **1688** *Lond. Gaz.* No. 2378/4 A brown bay Filly,..being locked from taking Horse.

71. take possession. a. To get something by one's own act into one's possession; to enter into possession. With *of*: to take into one's possession, make oneself possessor of, take for one's own, appropriate: see POSSESSION *sb.* 1 c.

1535 COVERDALE *1 Kings* xxi. 15 Vp, and take possession of the vynyarde of Naboth the Iesraelite. **1591** SHAKS. *Two Gent.* V. iv. 130 Take but possession of her, with a Touch. *a* **1641** BP. MOUNTAGU *Acts & Mon.* i. (1642) 21 They entred upon, and took possession of the Land of Promise. **17..** *Rem. Reign Will. III* in *Harl. Misc.* (1809) III. 359 The troops..would, in all likelihood, have took possession of White-hall. **1852** MRS. STOWE *Uncle Tom's C.* xxxiv, Then he came, the cursed wretch! he came to take possession.

b. *fig.* (with *of*) To begin to 'possess', dominate, or actuate: cf. POSSESSION *sb.* 5, 6.

1595 SHAKS. *John* IV. i. 32 His words do take possession of my bosome. **1849** MACAULAY *Hist. Eng.* vi. II. 63 Another fatal delusion had taken possession of his mind.

72. In many other phrases, as *to take* ACCOUNT, ACQUAINTANCE, ARMS, BREATH, *the* CAKE, *one's* CHANCE, *the* CHANGE *out of*, CHRISTENDOM, COUNT, *one's* CROSS, EFFECT, END, FLIGHT, FORCE, HEAD, HEELS, *the* INITIATIVE, KNOWLEDGE, *the* LAW, *the* LEAD, LEAVE, ORDER, RECORD, RISE, ROOT, SHARE, STOCK, WITNESS, etc., for which see the sbs. (See also 94.)

XI. Intransitive uses in idiomatic combination with prepositions.

73. take after ——. a. To follow the example of; to imitate; hence, to resemble (a parent, ancestor, predecessor, superior, etc.) in nature, character, habits, appearance, or other quality.

1553 T. WILSON *Rhet.* (1580) 112 If the Nurse be of a noughtie nature, the childe must take thereafter. **1657** HEYLIN *Ecclesia Vind.* Gen. Pref., His Followers all take after him in this particular. **1678** PHILLIPS (ed. 4) s.v. *Imitatives, Patrissare*, to take after the Father, or imitate his actions, humor, or fashion. **1892** *Gd. Words* Nov. 784/2, I take after my mother's family.

†**b.** ? To conceive a desire for or inclination to.

1707 *Curios. in Husb. & Gard.* 6 Men take strangely after this their first Imployment.

take against ——, take for —— (= take part against, with): see 20 b.

74. take to ——. (See also 62, 63.)

a. To undertake, take in hand; to take charge of, undertake the care of. *Obs.* exc. *dial.*

[*Tóc tó þe rice* in quot. 1154 is the equivalent of the earlier *feng tó* (*þam*) *rice* of the Chronicle: cf. anno 488, Her Esc feng to rice; 1066 Her forðferde Eaduuard king, and Harold eorl feng to ðam rice. Cf. also 62 with inf.]

1154 *O.E. Chron.* an. 1140 (MS. E), & te eorl of Angæu wærd ded, & his sune Henri toc to þe rice. *c* **1230** *Hali Meid.* 5 He wile carien for hire þat ha haueð itaken to of al þat hire biheoueð. *c* **1375** *Cursor M.* 5639 (Fairf.) þis wommon bleþely toke þer-to [to þe childe; *Cott. & Gött.* it vnderfang] & fedde hit. *c* **1430** *Freemasonry* 120 That the mayster take to no prentysse, But he have good seuerans to dwelle Seven ȝer with hym. **1863** KINGSLEY *Water-Bab.* v. 199 All the little children whom the good fairies take to, because their cruel mothers and fathers will not. [See *Eng. Dial. Dict.* s.v.]

b. To betake oneself to, have recourse to (esp. some means of progression, as in ***take to the boats, take to flight, take to wing, to one's heels*** (HEEL *sb.*[1] 20); also (now *dial.*) *to* some resource or means of subsistence).

(The intr. use here and in c comes close in sense to the *refl.* use in 61 a, 63 c, and the trans. in 24 c, 25 a.)

c **1205** LAY. 23688 He hit wende þat Arður hit wolde forsaken And nawiht to þan fehte taken. *c* **1400** *Melayne* 1148 At þe laste þay tuke to flyinge. *a* **1450** *Le Morte Arthur* 1380 Madame, how may thou to us take? **1591** SHAKS. *Two Gent.* IV. i. 42 Haue you any thing to take to? *Val.* Nothing but my fortune. **1596** DANETT tr. *Comines* (1614) 32 The King tooke to barge and returned to Paris. **1693** J. DRYDEN, jun. *Juvenal* xiv. 98 The callow Storks..soon as e'er to Wing they take, At sight those Animals for Food pursue. **1708** *Lond. Gaz.* No. 4453/2 They took to their Oars, and got from us. **1761** HUME *Hist. Eng.* II. xxvii. 130 They immediately took to flight. **1786** tr. *Beckford's Vathek* (1883) 121 They all without ceremony took to their heels. **1873** HOLLAND *A. Bonnic.* i. 19, I should have alighted and taken to my feet.

c. To betake oneself to (a place); to repair, resort, or retire to; to take refuge in; to enter.

c **1275** LAY. 7976 He droh to on oþe[r] half and tock to herboreȝe. *c* **1425** *Cursor M.* 2832 (Trin.) No dwellyng here þat ȝe make Til ȝe þe ȝondir feld to take. **1707** FREIND *Peterborow's Cond. Sp.* 211 Take to the Mountains on the right. *a* **1851** MOIR *Bass Rock* iii, The rabbit..Took to its hole under the hawthorn's root. **1879** MISS YONGE *Cameos* Ser. IV. ix. 110 He took to his bed and there lay almost without speaking. [Cf. 25, and BED 6 c.]

†**d.** To attach oneself to, become an adherent of; to direct itself to. *Obs.* (Also with *till*, *unto*.)

c **1205** LAYAMON 29188 Crist seolue he for-soc and to þan wursen he tohc. *c* **1330** R. BRUNNE *Chron.* (1810) 96 þe maistres of þe portes for gyftes tille him toke. *c* **1425** *Cursor M.* 17533 (Trin.) Raþer shulde þei to vs take, þen to ihesu for oure sake. **1625** BACON *Ess.*, *Goodness* (Arb.) 201 If it [goodness] issue not towards Men, it will take vnto Other Liuing Creatures.

e. To devote or apply oneself to; to adopt or take up as a practice, business, habit, or something habitual: cf. 61 b, c. See also ROAD *sb.* 5 b.

a **1300** *Cursor M.* 14114 O mani thing sco [Mary] tok til an, Wit-vten quam es beute nan. **1382** WYCLIF *Gen.* xxxviii. 14 The which, the clothis of widewhed don down, toke to [Vulg. *assumpsit*] a roket. *c* **1430** *Freemasonry* 462 Aȝayn to the craft they schul never take. **1610** HOLLAND *Camden's Brit.* (1637) 692 Clothing (a trade which they tooke to). **1707** J. STEVENS tr. *Quevedo's Com. Wks.* (1709) 319 If you take to Begging, I will take to give nothing. **1834** LYTTON *Pilgr. Rhine* vi, He has since taken to drinking. **1843** *Fraser's Mag.* XXVIII. 203 She..took to wearing caps. **1845** FORD *Handbk. Spain* I. 199 In Madrid..the men have taken to..Parisian *paletots*. **1887** [see DRINK *sb.* 3]. **1893** *Scribner's Mag.* Aug. 227/2 She has taken to society as a duck takes to water.

f. To apply oneself (*well*, *kindly*); to adapt oneself: leading to sense g.

c **1375** *Cursor M.* 8436 (Fairf.) þen was þis childe sette to boke; Ful wele I wis þer-to [*Cott.* þar-wit] he toke. **1625** BACON *Ess.*, *Parents & Childr.* (Arb.) 277 Thinking they will take best to that, which they haue most Minde to. **1766** J. W. BAKER in *Compl. Farmer* s.v. *Turnip*, [The bullock] took kindly to the turnips. **1820** *Examiner* No. 637. 413/2 A tree which is late transplanted seldom takes well to the soil. **1885** in *Manch. Weekly Times* 6 June 5/5 The new members may not take kindly to the work.

g. To take a liking to, conceive an affection for. (For absolute use: see 50 b.)

1748 H. WALPOLE *Corr.* (1837) II. 239, I took to him for his resemblance to you. **1796** LAMB *Let. to Coleridge* 3 Oct., They, as the saying is, take to her very extraordinarily. **1844** LADY FULLERTON *Ellen Middl.* (1884) 23 To use a familiar expression, we took to each other instantaneously. **1885** *Manch. Exam.* 22 July 3/2 When first the idea was suggested, Doré did not take to it.

h. *N.Z. slang.* To attack, usu. with fists.

1911 'KIWI' *On Swag* iii. 9 Take to him, Bill. **1960** N. HILLIARD *Maori Girl* II. xiv. 159 When we got home he really took to me. That was when I lost a lot of my teeth.

75. take with ——. †**a.** To receive, to accept; = sense 39. [= ON. *taka við* to receive.] *Obs.*

1127 *O.E. Chron.* (Laud MS.), þet landfolk him wið toc. *c* **1200** ORMIN 104 To ȝarrkenn follc onnȝæness Crist To takenn wiþþ hiss lare. *Ibid.* 1516 Hu wel he takeþþ aȝȝ wiþþ þa þatt sekenn Godess are. *a* **1300** *Cursor M.* 820 For-þi yett wald he wit him tak. *Ibid.* 5977 Vr lauerd wil tak na wirscip wiþ þat man him dos in cursd kyth. **1456** SIR G. HAYE *Law Arms* (S.T.S.) 68 The barnis..will nocht tak with the doctryne of the faderis. **1538** BALE *God's Promises* in Dodsley *O. Pl.* (1780) I. 9 Yet shall they not with hym take.

†**b.** To take up with; to have to do with. *Obs.*

1597 BACON *Ess.*, *Followers & Friends* (Arb.) 36 It is better to take with the more passable, then with the more able.

c. To be pleased with, put up with. ? *dial.* Cf. 50 b; also *take up with* 93 z (*c*).

1632 RUTHERFORD *Lett.* (1862) I. 97 The silly stranger, in an uncouth country, must take with a smoky inn and coarse cheer. **1638** BRATHWAIT *Barnabees Jrnl.* II. (1818) 59 Thence to Ridgelay, where a black-smith, Liquor being all hee'd take with, Boused with me. **1825** JAMIESON s.v. *Tak with*, 'How does the laddie like the wark?' 'Indeed..he taks unco ill wi't'. **1844** STEPHENS *Bk. Farm* II. 609 In a little time she [a ewe] will take with both [twin lambs].

†**d.** To take part with, agree with. Cf. 20 b.

1654 J. BRAMHALL in *Ussher's Lett.* (1686) 612 Those of the King's Party asking some why they took with the Parliament's side. **1828** SCOTT *F.M. Perth* xxix, I would MacGillie Chattachan would take [*later edd.* agree] with me..instead of wasting our best blood against each other.

†**e.** To admit, acknowledge, own. *Obs.*

a **1653** BINNING *Serm.* (1845) 607 Few of you will take with this, that ye seek to be justified by your own works. **1786** A. GIB *Sacr. Contempl.* I. VII. i. 157 A person is therefore brought to see and take with this sin, only when his conviction issues in conversion.

f. To contract or become affected by; to catch (fire), absorb (water): = 44 b, c (cf. also d). *dial.*

1822 GALT *Steam-boat* xvi. 347 The kill took low, and the mill likewise took wi't,..and nothing was left but the bare wa's. **1847** *Jrnl. R. Agric. Soc.* VIII. II. 380 When it [the flax] begins to ferment, or 'take with the water', the latter becomes turbid and discoloured.

XII. In combination with adverbs, forming the equivalents of compound verbs, chiefly transitive.

76. take aback *trans.*: see ABACK *adv.* 3 (*lit.* and *fig.*).

1748 *Anson's Voy.* II. vii. 215 We were obliged to ply on and off..and were frequently taken aback. **1796** in Nicolas *Disp. Nelson* (1846) VII. p. xxxix, At ¼ past 8 taken flat aback with a strong wind and a high sea from the N.E.b.E. **1829** F. MARRYAT *Frank Mildmay* I. ix. 266, I was so taken aback with the sudden appearance and address of this beautiful vision, that I knew not what to say. **1844** J. T. HEWLETT *Parsons & W.* liii, I never saw a man more 'taken aback' as the sailors say. **1889** J. K. JEROME *Three Men in Boat* xvii, Blest if it didn't quite take me aback.

77. take about. *trans.* To conduct on a round of sight-seeing or on excursions, etc.

1823 P. PANAM *Mem. Young Greek Lady* 117 If you wish for any thing send to him; he will take you about everywhere. **1894** E. FAWCETT *New Nero* Proem 8 He..took him about for almost an hour, showing him a good many places. **1903** A. W. PATTERSON *Schumann* 113 He seems to have taken the Laidlaw ladies about a good deal.

78. take again. a. *trans.* To resume: see simple senses and AGAIN *adv.* †**b.** To withdraw, recall: = *take back*, 81 b: cf. AGAIN *adv.* 3. *Obs.*

1474 CAXTON *Chesse* III. i. (1883) 78 He began to take agayn his vertuous werkis and requyred pardoun and so retourned to god agayn. **1728** RAMSAY *Bob of Dunblane* ii, Lest I grow fickle, And take my word and offer again.

79. take apart. *trans.* **a.** To dismantle or take to pieces; also *fig.*, to search thoroughly; to demolish or wreck.

1936 C. SANDBURG *People, Yes* 60 Let's take it apart to see how it ticks. **1958** M. ALLINGHAM *Hide my Eyes* xv. 150, I am going to take this shed apart if it costs me my ticket. **1968** 'E. PETERS' *Grass Widow's Tale* xi. 140 It has to be somewhere here. Stands to sense. Go take that little front room apart, Skinner. **1969** *Oz* Apr. 25/1 There will be a lobby of Parliament which far from pleading with MPs will probably take Whitehall apart. **1974** D. SEAMAN *Bomb that could Lip-Read* xxiv. 243 There is going to be one God-awful search for the man... They will take this hamlet apart. **1978** M. PUZO *Fools Die* xv. 161 The new kids were wilder and started taking everything apart.

b. To thrash or beat soundly; also *fig.*, to attack with argument or criticism.

1942 N. BALCHIN *Darkness falls from Air* v. 94 Supposing I went round and took him apart? **1963** *Listener* 21 Feb. 350/3 The Labour Party's new leader was taken apart with the sort of cheerful and dedicated venom hitherto reserved for Tory Cabinet ministers. **1969** 'J. ASHFORD' *Prisoner at Bar* xii. 117 And don't get funny with Bladen.. or he'll take you apart at the seams. **1971** S. E. MORISON *European Discovery Amer.: Northern Voy.* vii. 242 Manuel C. Baptista de Lima.. has politely taken me apart and argued for the 1492 date. **1976** *Birmingham Post* 16 Dec. 12/2 League leaders Liverpool were taken apart by the speed, skill and determination of the entire Villa side.

80. take away. a. *trans.* To remove, withdraw, abstract; to remove by death; to subtract: see sense 58 and AWAY *adv.* Also = *put away* s.v. PUT *v.*[1] 38 f (*b*) (*U.S.*).

a **1300** *Cursor M.* 297 If þou ta þe light awai. **1388** WYCLIF *Ps.* I. 13 [li. 11] Take thou not awei fro me thin hooli spirit. **1415** SIR T. GREY in *43 Dep. Kpr. Rep.* 583 A sefenneghte after that Murdok of Fyche was take away. **1477** EARL RIVERS (Caxton) *Dictes* 75 To cut the vynes & take awey the euil branches therof. **1509** HAWES *Past. Pleas.* xliv. (Percy Soc.) 215 Do not I, Tyme, take his lyfe away? **1585** T. WASHINGTON tr. *Nicholay's Voy.* IV. xxxiii. 156 To take away or mittigate some of [these laws]. *c* **1600** *Timon* III. i, Yee theeues, restore what yee haue tane away! **1736** LEDIARD *Life Marlborough* I. 131 It pleased God to take away His Majesty. **1886** AD. SERGEANT *No Saint* ix, It took away his appetite. **1890** *Jrnl. Educ.* 1 June 341/1 Take away 4 cows from 17 cows. **1919** E. O'NEILL *Where Cross is Made* in *Moon of Caribbees* (1923) 16 They say for his own good he must be taken away.

b. *absol.* To clear the table after a meal.

c **1450** *Bk. Curtasye* 820 in *Babees Bk.* 326 Whenne þay haue wasshen and grace is sayde, Away he takes at a brayde. **1768** STERNE *Sent. Journ.* (1775) II. 118 *Mon Dieu!* said Le Fleur,—and took away. **1809** MALKIN *Gil Blas* XI. v. (Rtldg.) 402 The servants.. had taken away and left us to ourselves. **1872** S. BUTLER *Erewhon* viii. 64 She returned in about an hour to take away.

c. *absol.* To detract *from*: = 58 e, 85 k.

1875 FREEMAN *Venice* (1881) 257 The slight touch of Renaissance in some of the capitals.. in no sort takes away from the general purity of the style. **1889** STEVENSON *Master of B.* iv, This takes away from the merit of your generosity.

d. *intr.* To go away, make off: see 63.

1838 C. WATERTON *Ess. Nat. Hist.* p. xxv, After eluding him in cover for nearly half an hour, being hard pressed, I took away down a hedgerow. **1850** R. G. CUMMING *Hunter's Life S. Afr.* (1902) 125/1 They set the dogs after him, when he took away up the river.

81. take back. a. *trans.* To take possession of again, resume: see simple senses and BACK *adv.*

a **1771** GRAY *Dante* 68 Take back, what once was yours. **1908** *Daily Chron.* 26 Oct. 4/6 Molière never said, 'I take my goods where I find them', but 'I take back my goods where I find them'.

b. To withdraw, retract, recall, unsay (a statement, promise, etc.): cf. BACK *adv.* 7.

1775 ABIGAIL ADAMS in *Fam. Lett.* (1876) 86, I had .. made some complaints of you, but I will take them all back again. **1873** M. COLLINS *Squire Silchester* I. ix. 131, I shall take back my yes if you are troublesome.

c. To carry back in thought to a past time; cf. BACK *adv.* 4.

1889 MALLOCK *Enchanted Isl.* 251 These churches took me back to the crusaders. **1890** *Temple Bar Mag.* May 43 The boy's letter has taken me back ten years.

d. = *take aback* (fig.): see ABACK *adv.* 3. ? *dial.*

? *a* **1860** MRS. H. WOOD *Ho. Halliwell* (1890) II. i. 6 Hester was never so taken back in her life. *Ibid.* v. 116 She was 'taken back', as the saying runs.

e. *intr.* To go back, return. ? *Obs.* exc. *dial.*

1674 N. FAIRFAX *Bulk & Selv.* To Rdr., Being quite lost in a wilde and a frightful on and on, I e'en took back again where I was. **1889** STEVENSON *Master of B.* xi. 284 Having ..forgot my presence, he took back to his singing.

82. take down. a. *trans.* To remove from a higher to a lower, or from an upright to a prostrate, position; to lower; to carry down; to cut down, fell (a tree); to pull down (a house, etc.: implying also 'take to pieces'); to distribute (type).

a **1300** *Cursor M.* 11664 'Ioseph', sco said, 'fain wald I rest'... Son he stert and tok hir dun. *c* **1435** *Torr. Portugal* 1426, I rede we take down sayle & rowe. **1548** in E. Green *Somerset Chantries* (1888) 116 One of theis ij churches maye well be spared and taken downe. *a* **1653** BINNING *Serm.* (1845) 425 It taketh down the tabernacle of mortality. **1751** LABELYE *Westm. Br.* 81 Whilst the Arches were unbuilding and taking down. **1818** in Willis & Clark *Cambridge* (1886) I. 573 Taking down three trees. **1886** *Troy* (U.S.) *Daily Times* 2 Jan. 1/3 A boat's crew.. was taken down by a whale near the Cape Verde islands. **1909** R. RENWICK in Marwick *Edinb. Guilds* Pref. 6 The printers, seeing no early prospect of the release of their type.., took it down.

b. With various implications: (*a*) to swallow; †(*b*) to cause (a speaker) to sit down (*obs.*); (*c*) in *Falconry*, to cause (a hawk) to fly down; (*d*) in a school, to get above (another scholar) in class; so of a boat in a race, to get in front of (another boat); (*e*) to lead (a lady) down to dinner at a party.

1607 B. JONSON *Volpone* III. v, I will take down poison, Eat burning coals, do any thing. **1656** in *Burton's Diary* (1828) I. 45 Captain Hatsel was speaking to have the debate put off till Monday, but Colonel Purefoy took him down. **1667** FAIRFAX in *Phil. Trans.* II. 549 Mr. Morley.. was advised by some to take down a spoonfull of good English Honey. **1828** SIR J. S. SEBRIGHT *Observ. Hawking* 36 They are always taken down after having flown unsuccessfully at their game. **1840** M. EDGEWORTH *Let.* 30 Dec. (1971) 573 Sir John Campbell took me down to dinner and I was seated of course beside him. **1844** DICKENS *Mart. Chuz.* xix, I took him down once, six boys, in the arithmetic class. **1848** THACKERAY *Van. Fair* v, Dobbin.. was 'taken down' continually by little fellows. **1887** MRS. J. H. PERKS *Heather Hills* II. xviii. 308 A quiet dinner-party, with a nice, sensible man to take you down.

c. *fig.* To abase, humble, humiliate, abate the pride or arrogance of. In quot. 1562, ? to rebuke, reprimand. *to take* (a person) *down a peg*: see PEG *sb.*[1] 3.

1562 *Child-Marriages* 112 She had spoken to the said Custance, and taken her downe for the same. **1593** PEELE *Chron. Edw. I*, Wks. (Rtldg.) 395 I'll take you down a button-hole. **1608** TOPSELL *Serpents* (1658) 755 For revenge, and taking down the pride of this young man. **1796** MRS. M. ROBINSON *Angelina* II. 27 He seems to experience .. satisfaction in what he calls taking me down. **1857** MAURICE *Ep. St. John* i. 4 Whatever takes down a young man's conceit must be profitable to him.

d. To lower, diminish, lessen, abate, reduce; to lower in health or strength, bring low, depress. Now *Sc.* and *north. dial.*

1697 DRYDEN *Virg. Georg.* III. 209 As for the Females,.. Take down their Mettle, keep 'em lean and bare. **1719** BAYNARD *Health* (ed. 2) 22 By Degrees take down your Heat. **1811** *Self Instructor* 539 Olive colours.. are first put in green, and taken down again with soot. **1836–7** SIR W. HAMILTON *Metaph.* (1877) I. xviii. 342 Taken down with a bilious fever. [See *Eng. Dial. Dict.*]

e. To write down so as to use or preserve (what is said); to take a written report or notes of. Also, with person as obj.: to write down the words of, to take dictation from.

1712 W. ROGERS *Voy.* 248, I took down the Names of those that had any. **1793** *Trans. Soc. Arts* (ed. 2) V. 121 The precision with which you took down their answers. **1883** MORFILL *Slavonic Lit.* iii. 48 These ballads had been taken down about the middle of the eighteenth century. **1883** 'MARK TWAIN' *Life on Miss.* xxii. 247, I enlisted a poet for company, and a stenographer to 'take him down'. **1885** C. H. EDEN *G. Donnington* I. xii. 240 Reporters would take down the speeches. **1928** D. H. LAWRENCE *Woman who rode Away* 18 She certainly didn't want to take him down in short hand.

f. *spec.* To record a contentious statement made in a legislative assembly with a view to invoking disciplinary procedure.

1784 *Universal Mag.* Jan. 45/1 Gen Conway said that he was ready to maintain what he had said. Let the right hon. gentleman move to take down his words, and he would make his charge. **1863** *Illustr. Times* 20 June 422/2 Mr Cox had.. insinuated that.. Lord Ranelagh wished to have power to flog volunteers; and on Monday Mr. Ormsby Gore rose and denounced these words as 'scandalous and unfounded'. Whereupon Sir Robert Jackes Clifton jumped up and moved that the words were taken down. **1934** *Sun* (Baltimore) 3 May 1/4 Representative Pettingill.. threatened to invoke disciplinary procedure against Mr. Britten by means of what is known in the House as 'taking down' his words.

g. To cheat, trick, swindle. *Austral. slang.*

1895 *Argus* (Melbourne) 5 Dec. 5/2 [The defendant] accused him of having 'taken him down', stigmatised him as a thief and a robber.

83. take forth. a. *trans.* To lead forth, conduct out of a place; to bring forth, take out of a receptacle, produce; *fig.* to further, advance.

a **1300** *Cursor M.* 2693 (Cott.) Abram tok forth his men. *c* **1460** *Battle of Otterburn* xxxvi. in Child *Ballads* III. 297/1 The letters fayre furth hath he tayne. **1530** PALSGR. 748/1, I take forthe a man, I avaunce hym. **1890** BESANT *Demoniac* xv, When he [Damien] was taken forth to have his flesh wrenched off with red-hot pincers.

†**b.** *take forth one's way*: to go forth, set forth (see 25 b); also *absol.*, to proceed. *Obs.*

1523 LD. BERNERS *Froiss.* I. x. 10 On the iiii. day they toke forth theyr way. **1674** N. FAIRFAX *Bulk & Selv.* 187 We shall take forth to our last.

†**c.** To learn; *transf.* to teach: = *take out*, 87 f.

1530 PALSGR. 748/1, I take forthe, as a childe, or a scoler dothe a newe lesson, *je apprens*... Take hym forthe a newe lesson. **1549** T. SOME *Latimer's 2nd Serm. bef. Edw. VI* To Rdr. (Arb.) 50 The gettynge of goodes and rytches, before thou hast well learned and taken furth of the lesson, of well vsyng the same. **1581** SAVILE *Tacitus, Hist.* II. lxxxiv. (1591) 102 Taught by ill masters, hee tooke foorth [L. *didicit*] a bad lesson.

84. take in.

* *trans.* **a.** To take, draw, or receive into itself, or into something (see simple senses and IN *adv.*); to admit, absorb, imbibe; to receive as a tributary; to eat or drink, to swallow; to breathe in, inhale; to take on board (a ship). In quot. 1583 *absol.* to admit or let in water, to leak.

13.. *Cursor M.* 6066 (Cott.) Siþen sal ilk hus in take A clene he-lambe, wit-vten sake. *c* **1400** MAUNDEV. (Roxb.) i. 4 It takes in to him xl. oþer ryuers. **1495** *Trevisa's Barth. De P.R.* XVII. ii. (W. de W.) N j b/2 Full of holys to take in ayre. **1583** *Leg. Bp. St. Androis* Pref. 104 in *Sat. P. Ref.* (S.T.S.) 350 He lattis his scheip tak in at luife and lie. **1585** T. WASHINGTON tr. *Nicholay's Voy.* I. x. 12 b, We took in fresh water out of a wel. **1610** HOLLAND *Camden's Brit.* (1637) 547 The River Trent.. taking in the River Soure from the field of Leicester. **1737** BRACKEN *Farriery Impr.* (1757) II. 103 The first of these takes in their Nourishment by their external.. Absorbent Vessels. **1777** HAMILTON *Wks.* (1886) VII. 510 The ships are taking in water and provisions for two months. **1890** *Chamb. Jrnl.* 10 May 292/1 She took in amazingly little water. **1892** *Harper's Mag.* Sept. 596/2 It.. readily takes in and yields moisture.

b. To receive (money) in payment, subscriptions, etc.; to receive and undertake (work) to be done in one's own house for pay.

1699 in *Millington's Sale Catal. Skinner & Hampden Libraries*, Subscriptions are taken in by John Hartley, over against Gray's-Inn in Holborn. **1832** *Examiner* 403/1 She took in washing only for her amusement. **1889** MRS. E. KENNARD *Landing Prize* II. xii. 209 We supported ourselves .. by taking in plain needle-work. **1892** *Idler* June 547 He was taking in more money than he had ever taken in before.

c. To subscribe for and receive regularly (a newspaper or periodical): = sense 15 d.

1712 ADDISON *Spect.* No. 488 ¶2 Their Father having refused to take in the Spectator. **1779** MACKENZIE in *Mirror* No. 2 ¶3 A coffee-house, where it is.. taken in for the use of the customers. **1891** *Blackw. Mag.* CL. 704/1 Many of them take in the French paper just as they buy 'Punch'.

d. *Cards.* To take (a card) into one's hand from the pack.

1879 'CAVENDISH' *Card Ess.*, etc. 69 The holder of the ace of trumps ruffed, i.e. he put out four cards and took in the stock. **1891** *Field* 28 Nov. 843/1 If the non-dealer takes in the king, he ought.. to lead it.

e. To lead or conduct into a house, room, etc. Also *spec.*, to lead in (to dinner). Cf. sense 82 b (*e*), 87 c.

c **1450** *Cov. Myst.* xxvii. (Shaks. Soc.) 268 Take hym in, serys, be the honde. **1863** A. J. MUNBY *Diary* 3 June in D. Hudson *Munby* (1972) 165 The new Lord of the Admiralty ..and his wife: whom I took in to supper. **1887** M. MONKSWELL *Jrnl* fo. 266 *recto*, 25 May in *Victorian Diarist* (1944) 132 We dined with the Dean [of Hereford] that very evening. He took me in. **1893** *Temple Bar Mag.* XCVIII. 469 John took Miss Everard in to supper.

f. To receive or admit as inmate or guest.

1539 BIBLE (Great) *Matt.* xxv. 35, I was herbourlesse, and ye toke me in [WYCL. herboriden me: TINDALE, *Geneva*, lodged me]. **1562** J. MOUNTGOMERY in *Archæologia* XLVII. 231 Hospitalles.. then the poore souldior.. shoulde be taken yn, cured,.. and healed. **1702** ROWE *Tamerl.* IV. i, Why stand thy.. Doors still open To take the wretched in? **1840** *Jrnl. R. Agric. Soc.* I. III. 265 Invalid horses are taken in.. and treated at the hospital. **1849** *Ibid.* X. II. 413 No tenant-cottager shall take in any lodger.

†**g.** To receive or accept into some relation (e.g. into surrender, or as hostage or ally). *Obs.*

1602 LD. MOUNTJOY *Let.* in Moryson *Itin.* II. (1617) 214 By the generall advice of the Counsell I tooke in Turlough mac Henry. **1606** MARSTON *Sophonisba* II. i, Her father.. on suddain shall take in Revolted Syphax.

†**h.** To capture, take prisoner, conquer (in war); to 'take' a town. Cf. sense 2. *Obs.*

1387 TREVISA *Higden* (Rolls) VI. 285 Leo.. wente to Seynt Peter.. wiþ þe letayne, and was i-take in, and his eyȝen i-put out, and his tonge i-kut of. **1535** COVERDALE *Jer.* xlix. 1 Why hath youre kynge then taken Gad in? **1684** *Scanderbeg Rediv.* v. 109 His Majesty took in Raskaw, a Considerable place on the Deinster. **1709** H. FELTON *Diss. Classics* (1718) 10 Open Places are easily taken in.

i. To bring into smaller compass, draw in, reduce the extent of, contract, make smaller; to shorten, narrow, or tighten; to furl (a sail).

take in a reef: to roll or fold up a reef in a sail so as to shorten the sail: see REEF *sb.*[1] 1.

c **1515** *Cocke Lorell's B.* 12 Mayne corfe toke in a refe byforce. **1641** J. JACKSON *True Evang. T.* II. 153 But I must contract my selfe, and take in this saile of speech. *a* **1800** COWPER *Horace* II. Ode x. vi, If fortune fill thy sail.. Take half thy canvas in. **1837** DICKENS *Pickw.* ix, Strapping a buckle here, and taking in a link there. **1841** R. H. DANA *Seaman's Man.* ix. [*heading*] Making and taking in sail. **1848** THACKERAY *Van. Fair* xliii, Sure every one of me frocks must be taken in,—it's such a skeleton I'm growing. **1889** DOYLE *Micah Clarke* xxvii. 281, I took in one hole of my sword-belt on Monday. **1897** *Outing* (U.S.) XXX. 255/1 Take in leaders when about a team's length from corner; then take in wheelers a bit, off-wheeler more than near—in fact, many only take in off-wheel rein a couple of inches.

j. To enclose (a piece of land, etc.); to take into possession (a territory, a common), or into cultivation (a waste); to include; to annex.

c **1539** in G. J. Aungier *Syon Mon.* (1840) 131 To dyche in and take in in our comyn. **1633** G. HERBERT *Temple, Sunday* vi, Christ hath took in this piece of ground, And made a garden there. **1697** in Picton *L'pool Munic. Rec.* (1883) I. 288 Others have a design to take in some Commons near Mosse Lake. **1845** *Jrnl. R. Agric. Soc.* VI. II. 301 Numerous waste patches along the sides of wide roads have been taken in. **1893** *Nat. Observ.* 5 Aug. 290/2 France is determined to take in all Siam. **1897** D. SLADEN in *Windsor Mag.* Jan. 278/1 A new alcove [has been] formed by taking in one of the.. landings.

k. To admit into a number or list; to include, comprise, embrace; *spec.* to include in the consideration, take into account (quot. 1752); to include in a journey or visit; *loosely*, to go to.

1647 HAMMOND *Power of Keys* iii. 23 He hath taken in all the antient Church-writers into his catalogue. **1697** DRYDEN *Virg., Life* (1721) I. 30 Virgil was a great Mathematician, which, in the Sense of those times, took in Astrology. **1752** HUME *Ess. & Treat.* (1777) I. 106 In the former case, many circumstances must be taken in. **1755** in *Essex Inst. Hist. Coll.* (1916) LII. 80 In our way by the Skuylkill rd. took in ye prop[rieto]rs Gardens. **1870** FREEMAN *Norm. Conq.* (ed. 2) I. App. 712 Writers who.. did not understand that his jurisdiction took in Kent. **1879** LUBBOCK *Addr. Pol. & Educ.* iii. 55 Attention will be concentrated on the four subjects taken in. **1880** 'MARK TWAIN' *Tramp Abroad* iii. 42 An owl that come from Nova Scotia..took this thing in on his way back. **1883** BACON *Dict. Boston, Mass.* 359 The out-of-towner who fails to take-in a trip to Taft's. **1925** *New Yorker* 7 Mar. 19/1 There's no use me asking you if you took in all the revues. **1940** 'N. SHUTE' *Landfall* 26 He might pick up Matheson or Hooper and take in a movie. **1968** *Globe & Mail* (Toronto) 17 Feb. 32 (Advt.) Even take in breakfast at Le Drugstore..and head home again on the return flight. **1977** D. BAGLEY *Enemy* i. 12 We took in more theatres, an opera, a couple of ballets.

l. To receive into or grasp with the mind; to apprehend, comprehend, understand, realize; to absorb or imbibe mentally, to learn; to conceive.

a **1677** HALE *Prim. Orig. Man.* I. i. 12 A created Understanding can never take in the fulness of the Divine Excellencies. **1685** BAXTER *Paraphr. N.T.* Matt. xiii. 18–19 By not understanding is meant also, Not considering it to take it in. **1711** STEELE *Spect.* No. 79 ¶5 There is no end of Affection taken in at the Eyes only. **1810** LADY GRANVILLE *Lett.* (1894) I. 16 She plays..on the pianoforte, and takes in science kindly from Mr. Smart. **1877** FREEMAN *Norm. Conq.* (ed. 3) I. App. 731 Writers who do not take in the position of an Earl of the West-Saxons. **1887** BARING-GOULD *Gaverocks* III. li. 140 Sluggish minds..require time to take in new notions.

m. To comprehend in one view (physical or mental); to perceive at a glance.

1727–41 CHAMBERS *Cycl.* s.v. *Eye*, In man..the eye is..so ordered, as to take in nearly the hemisphere before it. **1800–24** CAMPBELL *View St. Leonard's* 18 The eagle's vision cannot take it in. **1878** *Scribner's Mag.* XV. 583/2 We..turned our heads from side to side,..the better to take in the full force of the effect.

n. To believe or accept unquestioningly.

1864 *Spectator* No. 1875. 640 The Undergraduates took it all in and cheered Lord Robert Cecil as their future representative. **1888** FARJEON *Miser Farebrother* II. xiii. 169 Jeremiah listened and took it all in.

o. To deceive, cheat, trick, impose upon. *colloq.*

1740 tr. *De Mouhy's Fort. Country-Maid* (1741) I. 132 The Griparts were never taken in yet, and what's more never will. **1745** FIELDING *True Patriot* No. 9 Wks. 1775 IX. 310 They are fairly taken in, and imposed upon to believe we have..as much money as ever. **1754** E. MOOR in *World* No. 96 III. 234, I am almost of opinion that (in the fashionable phrase) he is 'taking me in'. **1809** W. IRVING *Knickerb.* v. iv. (1849) 277 A contest of skill between two powers, which shall overreach and take in the other. **1846** LANDOR *Imag. Conv.* Wks. II. 228/1 Nobody shall ever take me in again to do such an absurd and wicked thing. **1884** GEO. DENMAN in *Law Rep. 29 Ch. Div.* 473 The Plaintiff has..been taken in and misled.

p. To offer (a subject) for examination.

a **1890** LIDDON *Life Pusey* (1893) I. 20 The poets and historians who, at that time, were taken in by candidates for Classical Honours at Oxford.

q. *Stock Exchange.* To receive contango on (stocks or shares); to accept (stocks, etc.) as security for a loan. Cf. *give on* b s.v. GIVE *v.* 61.

1893 R. BITHELL *Counting-House Dict.* (ed. 2) 292 The term [taken in stock] is applied solely to stocks taken in for fortnightly or monthly loans on the Stock Exchange. **1911** W. THOMSON *Dict. Banking* 503/1 In connection with the Stock Exchange settlements, a 'taker-in' is a broker who lends money against stock (i.e. 'takes in' stock) to a broker who requires to pay for a purchase. **1912** *Q. Rev.* July 102 The dealer says that he will 'take them in', which means that he will lend the money until the settlement following that for which the original bargain was effected. **1928** *Morning Post* 19 Nov. 3/3 If the other man..prefers to take a rate of money rather than to accept the cash which delivery of the shares would produce, he will 'take them in'—the opposite operation to 'giving on'. **1934** F. E. ARMSTRONG *Bk. Stock Exchange* vi. 108 When no 'takers' can be found someone has to provide the cash, and firms known as money brokers frequently agree to 'take in' the securities purely as a money-lending proposition. **1955** *Beginners, Please* (Investors' Chron.) ii. 44 In normal market conditions it is probably easier to 'take-in' shares, i.e., carry over a sale to the next settlement, than to 'give on' shares, i.e., carry over a purchase. This is because generally there are more bulls than bears. Under such conditions the 'giver' pays a rate of interest to the 'taker' for the accommodation provided.

r. *slang.* To take into custody, arrest. Cf. *pull in* s.v. PULL *v.* 26 e.

1942 BERREY & VAN DEN BARK *Amer. Thes. Slang* §500/5 Arrest..take, take in or up. **1978** J. B. HILTON *Some run Crooked* xiv. 138 You can tell me now, or I'm taking you in to help. **1979** J. VAN DE WETERING *Maine Massacre* iii. 26 You're not taking me in, sheriff.

** *intr.* †**s.** To go in, 'put in', enter. *Obs.*

1654 H. L'ESTRANGE *Chas. I* (1655) 88 Taking in at a Cooks shop where he supt. **1677** JOHNSON in *Ray's Corr.* (1848) 127 Great shoals of salmon, which often take in at the mouths of our rivers.

†**t.** *take in with*: to take part with, side with, agree with. *Obs.*

1597–8 BACON *Ess., Faction* (Arb.) 80 It is commonly seene that men once placed, take in with the contrarie faction to that by which they enter. **1646** SIR T. BROWN *Pseud. Epid.* I. vii. (1686) 20 Justinian took in with Hippocrates and reversed the decree. **1647** N. BACON *Disc. Govt. Eng.* I. xxxiv. (1739) 51 Kings doubting to lose their Game, took in with the weaker. *a* **1734** NORTH *Lives* (1826) I. 3 If he had acted in these mens measures, and betraying his master, took in with them.

u. *N. Amer. dial.* To open, begin, *esp.* of a school term. Cf. sense 93 r below.

1876 'MARK TWAIN' *Tom Sawyer* 162 She could hardly wait for school to 'take in'. **1906** *Dialect Notes* III. 160 School takes in early and takes out late, seems to me. **1942** *Post* (Morgantown, W. Va.) 14 Sept. 4 An obligation..upon drivers to be careful of children, esp. in the hours that school takes in and lets out. **1956** W. R. BIRD *Off-Trail in Nova Scotia* iii. 99 One girl turned to me and declared she had seen him with it before school took in.

85. take off. * *transitive senses.*

a. To remove from the position or condition of being *on* (with various shades of meaning); to lift off, pull off, cut off, rub off, detach, subtract, deduct: see simple senses and OFF *adv.*

a **1300** *Cursor M.* 14318 He bad..Of þe tumb tak of þe lidd. **1495** *Ledger-bk. A. Halyburton* 40 Som of that sek, the bat of-tan is 17li. 15s. 2. *c* **1530** H. RHODES *Bk. Nurture* in *Babees Bk.* 67 With your Trenchour knyfe take of such fragmentes. **1644** WINTHROP *Hist. New Eng.* (1825) II. 199 He took off all her commodities, but not at so good rates as they expected. **1703** *Art & Myst. Vintners* 57 Take off the skim, and beat it together with 6 Eggs. **1709** STEELE *Tatler* No. 5 ¶8 A Cannon Ball took off his Head. **1780** COXE *Russ. Disc.* 267 M. Engel..takes off twenty-nine degrees from the longitude of Kamtchatka, as laid down by the Russians. **1852** *Jrnl. R. Agric. Soc.* XIII. I. 80 Repeated crops of hay are taken off without any return. *Mod.* Isn't his name on the list? No, it has been taken off.

(*b*) *spec.* To remove from the person, divest oneself, or another, of, doff (a garment, etc.).

a **1300** *Cursor M.* 9070 (Cott.) 'Tas of', he said, 'mi kinges croun.' **13..** *Ibid.* 8116 (Gött.) Wiþ þis þe king tok of his gloue. **1485** CAXTON *Chas. Gt.* 212 He..took of hys clothes. *a* **1548** HALL *Chron., Edw. IV* 234 He toke of hys cappe, and made a low and solempne obeysance. **1662** J. DAVIES tr. *Olearius' Voy. Ambass.* 140 A little Cap like a Callotte..they never take off. **1736** LEDIARD *Life Marlborough* III. 422 The Armour was taken off. **1850** *Tait's Mag.* XVII. 465/1 She took off her shawl. **1891** *Murray's Mag.* Apr. 531 He never takes off his boots and spurs.

(*c*) To remove or convey (a person) from on shore, from a rock, or from on board ship.

1883 BUCHANAN *Love me for Ever* v. ii. 261 He had arranged..to be taken off one night, and to sail with them right away. **1889** *Eng. Illustr. Mag.* Dec. 267, I might be able to support life on board of her until the *Ruby* took me off. **1890** *Standard* 12 Dec. 5/7 The passengers were taken off and landed safely.

(*d*) *absol.* To clear the table after a meal: = *take away*, 80 b.

1828 J. T. SMITH *Nollekens* I. 91 Nor do I think wine was even mentioned until the servants were ordered to 'take off'.

(*e*) *intr.* for *pass.*: see sense 58 f.

(*f*) *trans. U.S. Blacks.* To rob or burgle; to 'hold up'. Cf. *to rip off* (ii), (iv) s.v. RIP *v.*[2] 6.

1970 C. MAJOR *Dict. Afro-Amer. Slang* 113 *Take off*,..to rob or hurt. **1972** J. HUDSON in T. Kochman *Rappin' & Stylin' Out* 413, I can't go no place expecting to take off some fat sucker if I look like a greaseball. **1973** *Black World* Jan. 56/1 He and Cecil B were to take off a supermarket in San Jose.

b. *trans.* To drink to the bottom, or at one draught; to drink off, 'toss off'.

1613 PURCHAS *Pilgrimage* III. xv. 271 She dranke to him a cup of poysoned liquor: and hauing taken off almost halfe, she reached him the rest. **1662** J. DAVIES tr. *Olearius' Voy. Ambass.* 83 Many Muscovian women took off their Cups as smartly as they [their husbands] did. **1724** RAMSAY *Steer her up*, etc. ii, See that shining glass of claret..Take it aff, and let's have mair o't. **1850** HAWTHORNE *Scarlet L.* iv, And, that thou mayest live, take off this draught.

c. To lead away summarily; *refl.* to go away, take one's departure, be off.

1836 DICKENS *Pickw.* (1837) ii. 7 Here, No. 924, take your fare, and take yourself off. **1838** —— *O. Twist* xxiv, He..took himself off on tip-toe. **1850** *Tait's Mag.* XVII. 609/1 The guilty parties had taken themselves off. **1894** PARRY *Stud. Gt. Composers, Schubert* 230 In dread of being taken off as a soldier. *Mod.* He was arrested and taken off to prison. The child was taken off to bed.

d. To lead away or draw off (in *fig.* sense); to divert, distract, dissuade; †to free, rid (const. *from*); †to remove the opposition of by bribery or corruption, to buy off (*obs.*).

1605 SHAKS. *Macb.* II. iii. 36 It makes him, and it marres him; it sets him on, and it takes him off. *a* **1626** BACON *New Atl.* (1900) 24 And hee..in great Courtesie tooke us off, and descended to aske us Questions of our Voyage and Fortunes. **1670** H. STUBBE *Plus Ultra* 11 This Philosophy..taking us off from the Pedantism of Philology. **1702** tr. *Le Clerc's Prim. Fathers* 27 Having not undertaken to take them off from this Opinion. *a* **1704** *Compl. Servant-Maid* (ed. 7) 58 You must endeavour to take off your Mistress from all the care you can. *a* **1715** BURNET *Own Time* (1823) I. 467 The chief men that promoted this were taken off (as the word then was for corrupting members). **1890** FENN *Double Knot* vii, The conversation took off his attention.

e. To remove or withdraw from office, or from some position or relation; to dismiss; to withdraw (a coach, train, etc.) from running. Also in *Cricket*, to remove (a bowler) after a spell of bowling in order to replace him.

1745 WARD in *Lett. Lit. Men* (Camden) 369 Whom the Emperor had appointed governour..but afterwards..designed to have taken him off. **1768** J. BYRON *Narr. Patagonia* (ed. 2) 189 The centinel was taken off, and we were allowed to look about us a little. **1851** W. BOLLAND *Cricket Notes* iv. 75 Do not..refuse to bowl any more; neither grumble nor growl if you are taken off. **1858** *Jrnl. R. Agric. Soc.* XIX. I. 144 My early calves..I allow to suck the cows for a fortnight, then take them off. **1892** *Field* 28 May 779/3 The coaches..will be taken off for one or more days. *a* **1910** *Mod.* Several trains will be taken off on Bank Holiday. **1921** G. R. C. HARRIS *Few Short Runs* xi. 280 Don't turn sulky because after bowling five consecutive maidens you are taken off. **1977** *Times* 17 Jan. 7/1 When Greig took him off after 95 minutes his figures for the morning were 10-5-7-1.

f. To remove by death, put to death, kill, 'carry off', cut off: said of a person (esp. an assassin), of disease, devouring animals, etc.

1605 [see TAKING *vbl. sb.* 6]. **1608** SHAKS. *Per.* IV. Prol. 14 To take off by treasons knife. **1618** BOLTON *Florus* (1636) 224 Himselfe taken off by sudden death. **1683** BURNET tr. *More's Utopia* Pref., The hiring of Assassinates to take off Enemies. **1701** W. WOTTON *Hist. Rome, Alex.* ii. 487 Diseases..took off very many of them. **1770** LANGHORNE *Plutarch* (1879) II. 828/2 Ptolemy of Cyprus..took himself off by poison. **1832** *Examiner* 6/2 Up to the 20th of November about thirty people had been taken off by cholera. **1840** *Jrnl. R. Agric. Soc.* I. III. 258 The mangold-wurzel was..taken off early by the fly.

g. To remove (something imposed), esp. so as to relieve those subject to it.

1593 SHAKS. *Rich. II*, III. iii. 135 Oh God, oh God, that ere this tongue of mine, That layd the Sentence,..should take it off againe. **1660** INGELO *Bentiv. & Ur.* II. (1682) 147 You think to take off this Inconvenience. **1726** 'PHILALETHES' in J. Ker *Mem.* p. iii, If he would agree to the taking off the Penal Laws. **1737** *Gentl. Mag.* VII. Mar. 172/1 To give immediate Ease to his Majesty's Subjects, by taking off some of the Taxes which are most burthensome to the Poor. **1840** *Penny Cycl.* XVII. 399/2 The ecclesiastical courts may ..take off the penance. **1879** M. J. GUEST *Lect. Hist. Eng.* xiv. 127 He pleased the people greatly by taking off a heavy tax. **1889** M. GRAY *Reproach Annesley* III. ii, The three months' embargo was now taken off.

h. To remove or do away with (a quality, condition, etc.).

1605 SHAKS. *Macb.* v. viii. 71 Who..by selfe and violent hands, Tooke off her life. **1611** —— *Cymb.* v. ii. 2 The heauinesse and guilt within my bosome, Takes off my manhood. **1652** FRENCH *Yorksh. Spa* x. 90 They..should take the water a little warm'd first..the cold being just taken off. **1691** CONSET *Pract. Spir. Crts.* (1700) To Rdr., Which thing..may..take off the Edge of Detraction. **1737** BRACKEN *Farriery Impr.* (1756) I. 227 One or two Purges will take off the Running at his Mouth. **1885** MRS. LYNN LINTON *Chr. Kirkland* II. vi. 189 The smartest and prettiest kind of cap..took off the severity of her smoothly braided hair.

†(*b*) To do away with, disprove, confute. *Obs.*

1630 PRYNNE *Anti-Armin.* 147, I must needs take off two principall daring obiections. **1682** CREECH tr. *Lucretius* (1683) Notes 26 After that I shall take off his exceptions against Providence. **1695** J. EDWARDS *Perfect. Script.* 478 To take off this seeming argument.

i. (*a*) To make or obtain (an impression) from something; to print off. In quot. 1660, to receive as an impression (in *fig.* sense).

1660 tr. *Amyraldus' Treat. conc. Relig.* III. viii. 489 Those [languages] which live..take off better the impression and graces of the language of the Prophets. **1707** HEARNE *Collect.* 24 Jan. (O.H.S.) I. 320 The Stationers were obliged..to take off 200 Copies of any Book. **1817** G. ROSE *Diaries* (1860) I. 19 *note*, He had an impression of 500 taken off. **1825** *New Monthly Mag.* XV. 234/1 The expedient..of taking off an impression in some soft substance.

(*b*) To make (a figure of something); *transf.* to draw a likeness of, to portray: = sense 33 b.

a **1719** ADDISON (J.), Take off all their models in wood. **1835–40** HALIBURTON *Clockm.* (1862) 306 A native artist of great promise..that is come to take us off. **1855** THACKERAY *Newcomes* xliv, Then Clive proposed..to take his head off; and made an excellent likeness in chalk of his uncle. **1890** 'R. BOLDREWOOD' *Col. Reformer* (1891) 182 A young lady who could take off a horse like that—the dead image of him—could do anything.

(*c*) To measure off; to determine or mark the position of: cf. sense 32 c.

1793 SMEATON *Edystone L.* §97 In this way I took off 35..of the most remarkable points,..These 35 primary points having been determined as above.

j. To imitate or counterfeit, esp. by way of mockery; to mimic, caricature, burlesque, parody; to make a mock of. *colloq.*

1750 CHESTERF. *Lett.* (1792) III. 85 He has since been taken off by a thousand authors: but never really imitated by any one. **1760–72** H. BROOKE *Fool of Qual.* (1809) II. 120 He so perfectly counterfeited or took off, as they call it, the real Christian, that many looked to see him..taken alive into Heaven. **1789** MRS. PIOZZI *Journ. France* I. 240 At the hazard of being taken off and held up for a laughing-stock. **1809** MALKIN *Gil Blas* II. vii. ¶20, I can take off a cat to the life: suppose I was to mew a certain number of times? *a* **1845** HOOD *Faithless Nelly Gray* v, She made him quite a scoff; And when she saw his wooden legs, Began to take them off! **1879** MINTO *Defoe* 40 One of the pamphlets which he professed to take off in his famous squib.

k. *absol.* with *from*: To detract from, diminish, lessen: = 58 e, 80 c.

1701 W. WOTTON *Hist. Rome* 264 This gradual Advancement took off from the Obscurity of his Birth. **1753** CHAMBERS *Cycl. Supp.* s.v. *Sal*, A defect or flaw, which took off very much from the value of the gem. **1773** [J. RICHARDSON] tr. *Wieland's Agathon* Pref. 14 There are many allusions in it to modern customs..which take off in a great measure from the antique cast.

l. To close the stitches in knitting; to knit off. Also *absol.*

1849 ESTHER COPLEY *Knitting-bk.* 12 By reversing the right hand pin, so inserting it in two stitches, not in front but at the back of the left hand pin, and knitting them off as one. This [way of reducing the number of stitches] is called 'taking off at the back'.

** *intr.* **m.** To abate, grow less, decrease; (of rain) to cease.

1776 COOK in *Phil. Trans.* LXVI. 447, I judged it was about high water, and that the tides were taking off, or decreasing. **1854** H. MILLER *Sch. & Schm.* xxi. (1858) 463 No sooner had it [the hurricane] begun to take off than I set out for the scene of its ravages. **1878** STEVENSON *Inland Voy.* 20 The rain took off near Laeken. **1899** F. T. BULLEN *Log*

Sea-waif 93 The breeze now began to take off a bit, and more sail was made.

n. To go off, start off, run away; to branch off from a main stream. (Cf. 63, 63 b.)

c **1813** Mrs. Sherwood *Stories Ch. Catech.* xiii. (1873) 112 Dick ran out..and took off into the great bazar. **1825** Waterton *Wand. S. Amer.* iii. iv. 265 The Indian took off into the woods. **1888** *19th Cent.* Jan. 44 The second [headwater of the Hugli] takes off from the Ganges about forty miles eastward from the Bhagirathi. **1959** I. & P. Opie *Lore & Lang. Schoolch.* x. 193 Juvenile language is well stocked..with expressions inviting a person's departure, for instance:..take off, [etc.]. **1968** *Listener* 19 Dec. 809/3 I'm not stopping here,..no matter what they say or do... I'm taking off tonight. **1972** J. Philips *Vanishing Senator* (1973) iii. iii. 147 You'd better take off. I've just got to get some sleep. **1978** M. Duffy *Housespy* vii. 178 Danny Oldfield's taken off. I'll let you know when I find her.

(*b*) To start in leaping; to commence a leap. (Opp. to land *v.* 8 b.)

1814 *Sporting Mag.* XLIII. 287 The spot where the horse took off to where he landed, is above eighteen feet. **1889** *Boy's Own Paper* 7 Sept. 780/3 Competitors should be encouraged to take-off with accuracy. **1892** *Strand Mag.* III. 633/2 The last attitude one would imagine a horse to adopt in 'taking off' for a jump.

(*c*) *Croquet.* To make a stroke from contact with another ball so as to send one's own ball nearly or quite in the direction in which the mallet is aimed: cf. take-off *sb.* 4.

1872 Prior *Notes on Croquet* 48 It were an improvement ..to tether a ball in the centre of the ground, which at starting should be hit by the players from a spot in the middle of the left-hand boundary. Taking off from this tethered ball, they might go to any part of the lawn.

(*d*) *Aeronaut.* Of a pilot, plane, etc.: to perform the operations involved in beginning flight; to become air-borne. Also *transf.* of a bird.

? **1849** G. Cayley *Let.* in C. H. Gibbs-Smith *Sir George Cayley's Aeronautics* (1962) xlii. 136 It is absolutely necessary that the tail be securely braced up a little, and that the centre of gravity be made to act steadily on the bulk of the surfaces so that when weighed up to the weight of the person trying the wings—should it take off, they would skim and not either rise up hill or sink down hill. **1918** *Punch* 3 Apr. 222/2 Yes, he crashed a few days ago—in his first solo flip, taking off. **1927** C. A. Lindbergh *We* ii. 19, I taxied to one end of the field, opened the throttle and started to take off. **1936** G. B. Shaw *Simpleton* ii. 69 All I want is a parapet to take off from. **1951** A. C. Clarke *Sands of Mars* i. 1, I once took-off standing up, just for a bet. **1973** *Sci. Amer.* Dec. 102/1 If the birds are pursued, they take off, but they do not fly far before they land again.

(*e*) *fig.* Of prices, costs, etc.: to rise steeply or suddenly. Of a scheme, project, etc.: to be launched (successfully), to become popular.

1963 J. N. Harris *Weird World Wes Beattie* (1964) xv. 184 Minerva took off, as we say, on a famous Friday the thirteenth... The stock rose from nineteen cents to over a dollar in the last half-hour of trading. **1970** *Melody Maker* 12 Sept. 33/3, I shall be pretty sick if Andy Williams' record takes off and mine dies. **1971** *Physics Bull.* Oct. 590/2 Prof. E. C. Cherry..devised an arrangement which resulted in reduction in bandwidth requirements... This likewise has not taken off so far although much more interest is now being shown in it. **1976** *Ibid.* Sept. 401/1 Production and salary costs 'took off'. **1978** *Detroit Free Press* 5 Mar. B 12/2 They had best seller hopes for the book, but it hasn't really taken off. **1981** *Church Times* 10 Apr. 9/5 Frank Scuffham has hopes of his committee, but acknowledges that it has not taken off yet. **1983** *Times* 20 Jan. 15/3 Sales of existing properties have taken off during the last few months.

o. *U.S. dial.* To absent oneself from work, school, etc.

1935 W. Faulkner *As I lay Dying* 115 You take off and stay in the house today. **1936** W. Greene *Death in Deep South* (1937) 61 She thought she'd be off in the afternoon and she said she'd take off anyway if she wasn't.

86. take on. * *transitive senses.*

a. See simple senses and on *adv.*: in quot. 1877, to take on board (opp. to *take off*, 85 a (*c*)).

c **1579** Montgomerie *Misc. Poems* xlviii. 140 Tak on ȝour babert luif abuird. **1839** Ure *Dict. Arts* 258 (Cards, Playing) The ink or colour..is..laid on the types and blocks..and the impressions [are] taken-on to thick drawing paper by means of a suitable press. **1877** *Scribner's Mag.* XV. 14/1 He took on the passengers who stood clustered on the wharf.

(*b*) †To put on, don (clothing, etc.) *obs.*; to 'put on' or add (flesh, etc.): see put *v.* 46 f (*a*).

1389 in *Eng. Gilds* (1870) 56 þe den xal warn alle þe gylde breþeren þ^t be in toune, for to takyn on here hodis..and comen to messe. *c* **1489** Caxton *Sonnes of Aymon* xxii. 494 Thenne they went, & toke on the beste clothyng that they had. **1583** *Satir. Poems Reform., Life Bp. St. Androis* 1069 On a gray bonnet he tackis. **1847** *Jrnl. R. Agric. Soc.* VIII. ii. 392 Sheep..thrive very well and take on flesh rapidly. **1850** *Ibid.* XI. ii. 600 The animal being thus gradually prepared to take on that increased amount of muscle and fat.

†(*c*) To take up (arms); to arm oneself: see 93 a (*c*). *Sc. Obs.*

1565 *Reg. Privy Council Scot.* I. 355 Thair rebellis ar planelie conspyrit togidder, takin on arms. **1567** *Ibid.* 524 Thai have takin on armes to puneis the authouris of the said cruell murthour.

b. To assume, 'put on' (a form, quality, etc.) = sense 16 a: to assume, begin to perform (an action or function) (cf. 17); to contract, begin to be affected by, 'catch' (cf. 44 b, c).

1799 Kentish in Beddoes *Contrib. Phys. & Med. Knowl.* 258 He took on that peevish irritability so unhappy for the individual. **1842** *Jrnl. R. Agric. Soc.* III. ii. 331 The blanched leaves soon take on the appearance of frost-bitten celery. **1869** G. Lawson *Dis. Eye* (1874) 41 The ulcer..took on a healing action, and soon cicatrized. **1893** M. Gray *Last Sentence* iii. v, The deep, mysterious eyes would take on a deeper charm.

(*b*) To adopt (an idea, etc.); to accept mentally.

1890 *Pict. World* 4 Sept. 298/2 That belonged to the days before its author 'took on religion', as the Methodists term it. **1893** *Nat. Observ.* 23 Sept. 472/2 He is prepared to throw over all his convictions pretty much as he took them on.

(*c*) To apprehend with the senses; to perceive, 'catch'. *rare.*

1827 D. Johnson *Ind. Field Sports* 45, I have heard the natives assert that they take on the scent of the deer many hours after they have passed.

c. To take (a person) into one's employment, or upon one's staff, to engage (also *fig.*); to accept in marriage; to receive into fellowship.

1611 G. Blundell in *Buccleuch MSS.* (Hist. MSS. Comm.) 97 If Holland take any companies on. **1625** Massinger *New Way* ii. iii, I'll not give her the advantage ..To..say she was forced To buy my wedding-clothes, and took me on With a plain riding-suit and an ambling nag. **1826** *Examiner* 631/1 The large manufacturers are about taking on a considerable number of hands. **1893** J. B. Thompson in *Chicago Advance* 20 July, A number of catechumens were taken on during the year.

d. To undertake; to begin to handle or deal with, to 'tackle'.

[*c* **1325** *Spec. Gy Warw.* 267 Allas! what sholen hij onne take, þat wolden here her god forsake þurw sinne of fleschly liking?] **1422** [see taking *vbl. sb.* 6]. **1898** *Daily News* 10 Mar. 7/1 We cannot take on both jobs. **1900** Sir R. Buller *ibid.* 12 Nov. 3/4, I had taken on a task, and I was bound to see it through.

(*b*) To engage (someone) in a fight, contest, argument, etc.

1885 *Graphic* 3 Jan. 11/3 He..so frightened the other.. cowards that..they did not care to 'take him on'. **1915** E. Corri *30 Yrs. Boxing Ref.* 150 Instead of going for what the boxers call the 'easy money', Basham took on Matt Wells. **1928** *Daily Tel.* 24 Apr. 12/6, I saw the Sopwith take him on, and whilst I was changing drums I was attacked again in front by a Roland. **1930** G. B. Shaw *Apple Cart* i. 26 In this conflict we are the challengers. You have the choice of weapons. If you choose scandal, we'll take you on at that. **1976** *Morecambe Guardian* 7 Dec. 8/3 Micky Taylor earned the spotlight with a brilliant, cheeky dribble in which he took on and beat four men.

e. To undertake the management of (a farm, etc.), esp. in succession or continuance.

1861 *Temple Bar Mag.* III. 474 When I was twenty-two, my father died, and I took on the farm. **1889** Mrs. Comyns Carr *Marg. Maliphant* II. xix. 70, I want him to take on another small farm. **1892** *Cornh. Mag.* Oct. 346 It will be quite impossible for me to take on the lease again.

f. †(*a*) To assert, asseverate (cf. 17 c). *Obs. rare.* (*b*) To pretend, affect.

1858 Dickens in *Househ. Words* Xmas No. 20/1 This gent took on not to know me.

1583 Stubbes *Anat. Abus.* ii. (1882) 26 Yet will they sweare, protest, and take on woonderfully, that it is very new, fresh and tender. *Ibid.* 48 If they sell you a cow,..will protest and take on woonderfullie, that hee is but this olde, and that olde.

g. To buy on credit. *Sc.*

1808 Jamieson, *To tak on*, to buy on credit, to buy to accompt. **1866** J. H. Wilson *Our Father in Heaven* (1869) 180, I have heard of young people..going to shops and 'taking on' things, as it is called.

†**h.** To begin, commence (with *inf.*, or *intr.*); = sense 62. *Obs.*

c **1200** Ormin 2553 Ȝho toc onn ful aldeliȝ To fraȝȝnenn Godess enngell. *Ibid.* 11260 Ȝiff þu takesst onn att an & tellesst forþ till fowwre.

** *intransitive senses.*

†**i.** To act, proceed, behave, 'go on'. *Const.* dative, to a person. *Obs.*

c **1205** Lay. 3333 Ȝef ferrene kinges hiherde þa tidinde, þe we swa takede him on. *Ibid.* 5592 Þat word come to Belinne ..heo he hauede itaken on. *Ibid.* 10175 þa þis wes al idon þa token heo oðer weise on. *Ibid.* 31619 Whæt Penda king hafuede iseid and hu he wulle taken on. *c* **1305** *Pilate* 149 in *E.E. Poems* (1862) 115 Ou liþere man,..haþ he itake on so, Assentede he to þe gywes? **1362** Langl. *P. Pl.* A. iii. 76 For toke þei on trewely þei timbrede not so hye. *c* **1450** Lovelich *Grail* lvi. 505 And thus these lyowns Gonnon On to take Til the tyme that Cam Lawncelot de lake.

reflexive. c **1205** Lay. 30680 On alle wissen he toc him on swulc he weore a chepmon.

j. To 'go on' madly or excitedly; to rage, rave; to be greatly agitated; to make a great fuss, outcry, or uproar; now *esp.* to distress oneself greatly. Now *colloq.* and *dial.*

c **1430** *Syr Gener.* (Roxb.) 5200 That yondre knight on the white stede Taketh on as a deuel in dede. **1472** *Paston Lett.* III. 57 My modyr wepyth and takyth on mervaylously. **1530** Palsgr. 750/1, I take on lyke a madde man, *je menrage.* **1535** Coverdale *Num.* xiv. 1 Then the whole congregacion toke on and cryed, and the people wepte. **1600** Holland *Livy* ii. xxvii. 61 All this while Appius raged and tooke on, inveying bitterly against the nicetie and popularitie of his brother Consul. **1668** Pepys *Diary* 8 Apr., Her mother and friends take on mightily. **1767** *Woman of Fashion* I. 157 You'll make me cry too, if you take on in this Manner. **1830** Galt *Lawrie T.* i. ix, He took on like a demented man. **1852** Thackeray *Esmond* ii. i, She took on sadly about her husband.

k. To assume airs; to behave proudly or haughtily; to presume; to take liberties. (Cf. 18 e.)

1668 R. Steele *Husbandman's Calling* vi. (1678) 143 If a worm should take on, lift up itself, and be proud, then anything may be proud. **1851** *Beck's Florist* 180 'Pride goeth before destruction, and a haughty spirit before a fall'. I began to take on; and if the squire gave me any orders, I did not take 'em as I ought to have done.

l. To take service or employment, to engage oneself; to enlist.

a **1670** Spalding *Troub. Chas. I* (1851) II. 335 Diuerss daylie took on [to serve in the army]. **1748** Smollett *Rod. Rand.* xvi, If you take on to be a soldier. **1778** Foote *Trip to Calais* iii. Wks. 1799 II. 377, I am engaged to take on with Miss Lydy. **1890** *Lippincott's Mag.* Mar. 336 At the end of their term of enlistment [they] would refuse to 'take on' again in D Troop. **1892** *Field* 7 May 698/3 'Then', replied one of the men, 'I will take on at 4*s.*'

(*b*) With *with*: to engage oneself to; to begin to associate with, to consort with; = *take up with*, 93 z; to adopt as a practice, etc.

1737 Bracken *Farriery Impr.* (1757) II. 51 Such a Drake has been more used to a Hen when he was young, and..will the sooner take on with her when he grows older. **1844** *Fraser's Mag.* XXX. 104/1 The misthress is going to take on with Mister Jowles the praacher. **1886** M. Gray *Silence Dean Maitland* i, I liked Charlie Judkins well enough before he took on with this love-nonsense. **1894** G. Moore *Esther Waters* 154 His young woman must be sadly in want of a sweetheart to take on with one such as him.

m. To 'catch on', become popular: = sense 10 c. *colloq.*

1897 'Ouida' *Massarenes* xvii, He saw how greatly these musical entertainments 'took on'.

87. take out. *trans.* **a.** To remove from within a place, receptacle, or inclosure; to extract, withdraw, draw forth: see simple senses and out *adv.*

13.. *Cursor M.* 20564 (Gött), I toke þaim vte on [*v.r.* with] mi right hand. **1382** Wyclif *Ps.* lxviii. 15 [lxix. 14] Tac me out fro clei, that I be not inficchid. *c* **1450** *Merlin* i. 1 Whan that oure lorde..had take oute Adam and Eve, and other [from hell]. **1597** Shaks. *2 Hen. IV*, iv. v. 206 Their stings, and teeth, newly tak'n out. **1711** Addison *Spect.* No. 94 ¶9 He had only dipped his Head into the Water, and immediately taken it out again. **1889** F. M. Crawford *Greifenstein* II. xx. 280 Rex took out his purse and gave him a gold piece. *Mod.* I asked for the book at the library, but it had been taken out the day before.

(*b*) To remove, extract (a stain, etc.).

1727 Gay *Begg. Op.* i. ix, Money..is the true fuller's earth for reputation, there is not a spot or a stain but what it can take out. *Mod.* Ammonia will take out the grease-spots.

(*c*) *intr.* for *pass.* See sense 58 f.

b. *trans.* To withdraw from a number or set (actually or mentally); to leave out, except, omit.

c **1200** Ormin 8601 þatt ȝer þatt he wass takenn ut þurrh Drihhtin Godd fra manne. *c* **1315** Shoreham *Poems* i. 552 Þaȝ he ne toke iudas out, þe worste man on erþe. *Mod.* There are 91 festivals in the Prayer Book Calendar; but if you take out those that have no special Collects, there are only 24.

c. To lead or carry out or forth: with various special implications, as: to lead (a partner) out from the company for a dance; to summon (an opponent) to a duel, to 'call out'; to lead (a person or animal) into the open air for exercise; to lead (a woman) in (to a formal dinner), etc. Cf. sense 82 b (*e*), 84 e.

1613 Shaks. *Hen. VIII*, i. iv. 95, I were vnmannerly to take you out, And not to kisse you. **1665** Pepys *Diary* 13 Apr., When the company begun to dance, I came away, lest I should be taken out. **1749** Fielding *Tom Jones* vii. xiii, When a matter can't be made up, as in a case of a blow, the sooner you take him out the better. **1811** Jane Austen *Lett.* 29 May, Mrs. Welby takes her out airing in her barouche. **1876** Trollope *Prime Minister* III. x. 166 John Fletcher took her out to dinner and Arthur did not sit near her. **1877** *Scribner's Mag.* XV. 65/1 He had even promised to take her out on the ice. **1880** Trollope *Duke's Children* ii. xx. 240 It was of course contrived at dinner that Lord Popplecourt should take out Lady Mary. **1893** J. Ashby Sterry *Naughty Girl* ii, It was awfully good of you to take the children out, Charlie. **1905** J. H. Choate *Let.* 27 Jan. in E. S. Martin *Life J. H. Choate* (1920) II. viii. 272 The King took Mama out to dinner. *a* **1910** *Mod.* Take the dog out for a run. **1913** in C. Seymour *Intimate Papers Col. House* (1926) I. vii. 188 He considered taking a duchess or royalty out to dinner was hard sledding.

(*b*) *Cricket. to take out one's bat*: said of a batsman who is 'not out' at the end of the innings.

1890 *Standard* 9 May 3/8 He was batting nearly four hours and eventually took out his bat for 90. **1892** *Sat. Rev.* 16 July 63/2 The captain..took out his bat for 60.

†**d.** (*a*) To give vent to, utter. (*b*) To announce, give out (a text). *Obs.*

1678 Dryden *All for Love* Pref., Ess. (Ker) I. 197 He took out his laughter which he had stifled. **1697** Burghope *Disc. Relig. Assemb.* 6 They will take care to come before the text is taken out.

e. To make a copy from an original; to copy (a writing, design, etc.); *esp.* to extract a passage from a writing or book.

1530 Palsgr. 750/1, I take out a writyng, I coppy a mater of a boke, *je copie.* **1573** *Art of Limming* 11 A pretie deuise to take out the true forme & proporcion of any letter, knott, flower, Image, or other worke. **1604** Shaks. *Oth.* iii. iii. 296, I am glad I haue found this Napkin:..Ile haue the worke tane out. *Ibid.* iii. iv. 180 Take me this worke out..I would haue it coppied. *Mod.* To read a book and take out quotations for the dictionary.

(*b*) To extract from data.

1881 *Times* 10 Nov. 4/2 The surveyor employed..to take out the quantities on the architect's plan—that is, to estimate the quantities of materials and labour which will be required to carry out the proposed plans. **1896** [see quantity 13].

†**f.** To learn (a lesson); *transf.* to teach. (See also 83 c.) *Obs.*

a **1591** H. Smith *Wks.* (1866) I. 499 If we be negligent and slack, and never take out his lessons, but s and at a stay. **1629**

EARLE *Microcosm.* lxv. (Arb.) 89 He hath taken out as many lessons of the world, as dayes. **1642** *Strangling Gt. Turk*, etc., in *Harl. Misc.* (1745) IV. 37 The Discipline of War must take you out other Lessons of Fury.

g. To apply for and obtain (a licence, patent, summons, or other official document) in due form from the proper authority.

1673 *Essex Papers* (Camden) I. 93 Y^{e} vacating their charter, & forcing them to take out a new one. **1687** BURNET *Cont. Reply to Varillas* 76 The Bishops were obliged to take out new Commissions from the King..for holding their Bishopricks. **1726** BERKELEY *Let. T. Prior* 27 Jan., Wks. 1871 IV. 123, I have not yet taken out letters of administration. **1840** *Jrnl. Roy. Agric. Soc.* I. III. 351 Patents have been recently taken out for supposed improvements. **1892** *Sat. Rev.* 30 Apr. 497/1 [He] took out a summons against him.

h. To obtain or enjoy completely. ? *Obs.*

1631 *Celestina* 217, I will goe downe and stand at the doore, that my Master may take out his full sleepe.

i. To obtain, receive, use up, spend, the value of (something) *in* another form. Const. *in*.

1631 HEYWOOD *Fair Maid of West* Wks. 1874 II. 280 Because of the old proverbe, What they want in meate, let them take out in drinke. **1763** FOOTE *Mayor of G.* I. Wks. 1799 I. 168 When he frequented our town of a market day, he has taken out a guinea in oaths. **1828** *Examiner* 794/1 [He] has no objection, when a poor tradesman cannot advance the fee, to take it out in goods. **1891** *Review of Rev.* 15 Sept. 236/2 The prize was one guinea, which had to be taken out in books.

j. *intr.* To go away, make off, start out. *U.S.*

1855 in *Montana Hist. Soc. Contrib.* (1940) X. 137, I took out in order to give them the slip. **1896** 'MARK TWAIN' in *Harper's Mag.* Aug. 355/1 Out jumps four men and took out up the road as tight as they could go. **1929** W. FAULKNER *Sound & Fury* 310 They'll have to hitch up and take out to get home by midnight. **1938** M. K. RAWLINGS *Yearling* i. 11 How come you to take out such a fur piece?

k. *Bridge.* To remove (one's partner) from his situation in the auction by changing the suit of the probable contract or by bidding in response to his double. Also *into* (the fresh suit), with bid as obj., and *absol.*

1917 E. BERGHOLT *Royal Auction Bridge* (1918) 88 How am I to know..whether you are taking me out from strength or from weakness? **1921** A. M. FOSTER *Auction Bridge* 38 If your partner takes you out from weakness into a suit call you are likely to be fined. **1956** MOLLO & GARDENER *Bridge for Beginners* vii. 75 Responder may have a feeble five or six-card suit and nothing else. Then he takes out the double. **1977** *Homes & Gardens* Feb. 17 If..you held hand II, then it would be correct to take out into Two Hearts. *Ibid.* 14 Most players would take their partners out into Four Hearts on both of these hands.

l. To kill, murder; to destroy or obliterate (a specific target). *slang.*

1939 R. CHANDLER *Big Sleep* ii. 26 I'll take him out... He'll think a bridge fell on him. **1955** *Times* 28 June 4/4 The purpose of the attack was to 'take out'—as the strategist's jargon has it— the docks. **1962** L. DEIGHTON *Ipcress File* xviii. 109 In terms of destructive area, this is a bomb that would take out a whole city. **1967** J. M. FOX *Dead Pigeon* 170 'He took out two people who could have involved him'.. 'Took out? You mean he killed them?' **1977** *Times Lit. Suppl.* 15 Apr. 464/4 A sudden air attack, which would take out London, on a scale comparable with the attacks on Dresden or Hiroshima in 1945. **1978** M. DUFFY *Housespy* v. 124 He was taken out yesterday... They ran him down. **1982** *Daily Tel.* 14 June 4/8 For several hours, as a commanding officer and his officers tried to 'take out' the sniper with machine gun, rifle and artillery fire, his bullets ricochetted off rocks above our heads.

m. *Austral.* and *N.Z. colloq.* To accept as a punishment, reward, etc.; to win.

1943 K. TENNANT *Ride on Stranger* xvi. 176 George Benson told her briefly he would see her husband had a lawyer. He would probably get a month at the most and he'd better 'take it out'. **1976** *Australian* 15 July 2 Helen Morse ..takes out the Australian Film Institute's top actress award tomorrow night. **1977** *N.Z. Herald* 8 Jan. I. 6/8 The Games we play..can't..end, till Someone takes them out.

88. take out of. *trans.* **a.** To withdraw or remove from within (*lit.* and *fig.*); to extract (a stain) from: see simple senses and OUT OF *sb.*

to take the words out of one's mouth: see MOUTH *sb.* 3 l.

c **1200** ORMIN Ded. 209 To tākenn ut off helle wa þa gode sawless alle. **1387** TREVISA *Higden* (Rolls) II. 133 While he dwellede longe in Fraunce..Chedde was i-take out of his abbay of Lestynge. *c* **1425** *Cursor M.* 16442 (Trin.) þe monsleer þat barabas was take out of prisoun. **1535** STEWART *Cron. Scot.* (Rolls) II. 660 [He] Out of the erth his deid bodie hes tone. **1659** in *Burton's Diary* (1828) IV. 451 Take heed you take not the thorn out of another's foot, and put it in your own wholly. **1771** MRS. HAYWOOD *New Present* 246 To take Ink out of Linen. **1882** MISS BRADDON *Mt. Royal* III. iv. 59 He took the cartridges out of the case himself.

b. To get, derive, or obtain from.

1579 W. WILKINSON *Confut. Familye of Loue* B iv, Out of their knowledge, whiche they take out of the Scriptures. **1650** J. FRENCH tr. *Paracelsus' Nat. Things* II. 17 Any flint taken out of River water. **1821** SCOTT *Kenilw.* i, There were as good spitchcocked eels on the board as ever were ta'en out of the Isis.

c. To subtract or deduct from. Now *rare.*

1593 FALE *Dialling* 14, I take the complement of the Elevation, which is 38^{d}. out of the reclination of the plat which is 55^{d}., and there remain 17^{d}. **1703** MOXON *Mech. Exerc.* 127 A setting off of 8 Foot broad and 10 Foot long taking out of the Yard.

d. To deprive a person or thing of (some quality, etc.); *spec.* to deprive of (energy or the like); usu. ***to take it out of***, to exhaust, fatigue.

1847 S. WILBERFORCE in *Life* (1879) I. 402 There is so much of interest in a Confirmation, that it takes a great deal out of one. **1858** HAWTHORNE *Fr. & It. Note-Bks.* II. 68 Rome..takes the splendor out of all this sort of thing elsewhere. **1884** H. SMART *Post to Finish* xxxii, Now you say you cannot come, and all the salt is taken out of my holidays. **1890** MRS. LAFFAN *L. Draycott* II. i, The sort of day that takes it out of a man.

e. To remove from the jurisdiction of; to prove not to come under (a statute).

1885 SIR C. S. C. BOWEN in *Law Rep. 29 Ch. D.* 810 The burthen of taking the case out of the Statute of Limitations rests on the Appellant. **1891** *Law Times* XCII. 105/2 All lawyers are familiar with the doctrine of part performance to take a case out of the statute.

f. To take (something) from a person in compensation: ***to take it out of***, to exact satisfaction from.

1851 MAYHEW *Lond. Labour* I. 31/2, I take it out of him on the spot. I give him a jolly good hiding. **1888** M^{c}CARTHY & PRAED *Ladies Gallery* I. iv. 91 What we have to miss in sight-seeing we try to take out of the people in the cars. **1901** *Scotsman* 29 Nov. 8/2 In the olden days the villages 'took it out' of each other with club and spear.

g. ***to take one out of oneself***: to distract one's attention from one's own concerns; to amuse, divert or occupy (a person).

1848 G. JEWSBURY Let. 4 Oct. in *Lett. to Jane W. Carlyle* (1892) 257 There are no bothering algebraical calculations as far as I went, but glimpses, as it were, into the 'everlasting universe of things', till one is taken out of oneself completely. **1908** A. BENNETT *Old Wives' Tale* IV. iv. 531 Dr. Stirling wished to practise his curative treatment of taking the sisters 'out of themselves'. **1929** J. B. PRIESTLEY *Good Companions* II. iii. 301, I haven't enjoyed anything so much, I don't know when..they're so good they've taken me right out of myself. **1941** A. CHRISTIE *Evil under Sun* xii. 218 Poirot had..dwelt on the advantage it would be to Linda to have something to take her out of herself. **1958** P. MARRIS *Widows & their Families* ii. 21 My sister..took me out for walks. It's wonderful how it takes you out of yourself. **1974** [see *outside interest* s.v. OUTSIDE B. 6].

89. take out on. *trans.* In phr. ***to take it out on*** (someone or something): to vent one's anger, frustration, etc., on an object other than the cause of it.

1840 H. COCKTON *Valentine Vox* xxi. 158 P'r'aps you'd like to take it out on me, 'cos if yer would, yer know, why ony say so. **1903** 'C. E. MERRIMAN' *Lett. from Son* vi. 72 Milligan ..came around to take your cussing of him out on me. **1926** G. HUNTING *Vicarion* xviii. 311 Make some records of me, and take it out on them. **1947** A. HUXLEY *Let.* 9 Mar. (1969) 567 He can't associate sex with respectability, but he has to take it all out on tarts or housemaids. **1958** *Daily Sketch* 2 June 12/6 You may be irritable at work, but don't take it out on your colleagues. **1967** *Listener* 11 May 611/2 The country took out its frustrations on Congress. **1978** P. MARSH et al. *Rules of Disorder* ii. 39 My brother..was a troublemaker and now they're taking it out on me.

90. take over. *trans.* †**a.** = OVERTAKE I. *Obs.*

c **1330** *Arth. & Merl.* 7163 The paiens token ouer our men, And fast leyd upon hem then.

b. To take by transfer from, or in succession to another; to assume possession or control of (something) from or after some one else. Also *absol.* Also ***to take over from***: to relieve, take the place of, succeed.

1884 A. FORBES *Chinese Gordon* ii. 36 The army whose command he took over in its headquarters. **1887** WESTALL *Capt. Trafalgar* xiv, [He] took service with us when we took over the *Eureka*. **1890** H. S. MERRIMAN *Suspense* viii, Brenda took over all the smaller household duties. **1891** *Law Reports, Weekly Notes* 43/1 The..company was formed.. for the purpose of taking over the business..carried on by the plaintiff. **1916** 'BOYD CABLE' *Action Front* 182 The colonel was severely wounded and had sent for the second in command to take over. *Ibid.* 234 Riley..explained the position to the subaltern who took over from him. **1946** D. C. PEATTIE *Road of Naturalist* i. 20 A ranker, branching dandelion took over from the desert dandelions. **1978** J. GARDNER *Dancing Dodo* xiv. 101 Terry Makepiece was not going to take over on this. He would see it through himself.

c. To carry or convey across, to transport.

Mod. The ferry-boat will take you over.

91. take to. In passive ***to be taken to*** = to be taken aback: see 76. *dial.*

1865 MRS. H. WOOD *Mildred Arkell* xxxii, Mr. Van Brummel, considerably taken-to at being addressed individually, lost his head completely. **1872** *Argosy* Sept. 183 Mr. T. might possibly have been slightly taken to.., but there was no symptom of it in his voice. [See *Eng. Dial. Dict.*]

92. take together.

a. *trans.* See simple senses and TOGETHER.

†**b.** To collect: cf. PULL *v.* 34 b. *Obs.*

c **1489** CAXTON *Sonnes of Aymon* xix. 429 But he toke togyder his strengthes, & stode vpryghte.

c. To consider or reckon together (cf. 26 c), or as a whole; to reckon as a group or collection.

1678 CUDWORTH *Intell. Syst.* I. iv. §14. 258 Plato in his Cratylus taking these two words, *Zῆνα* and *Διά*, both together, etymologizeth them as one. **1742** RICHARDSON *Pamela* IV. 107 Numps, his Son, is a Character, take it all together, quite of Nature and Probability. *Mod.* Taken together, there cannot be more than a dozen.

93. take up. * *transitive senses.*

a. To lift, raise (from the ground, etc., or from a lying or prostrate position); to pick up; also, to lift or raise (something hanging down) so as to expose what is covered by it. Somewhat *arch.*

a **1300** *Cursor M.* 3064 (Cott.) Drightin has herd þi barn cri, Rise and tak it up for þi. **1382** WYCLIF *John* v. 9 The man is maad hool, and took vp his bed, and wandride. *c* **1420–30** *Prymer* (1895) 9 þi riȝthond took me vp. **1596** SHAKS. *Tam. Shr.* III. ii. 164 The Priest let fall the booke, And as he stoop'd againe to take it vp [etc.]. **1610** HOLLAND *Camden's Brit.* (1637) 278 The garter..which fell from her as she daunced, and the King tooke up from the floor. **1720** DE FOE *Capt. Singleton* v. (1906) 83 Ten men with poles took up one of the canoes and made nothing to carry it. **1844** HOOD *Bridge of Sighs* 5 Take her up tenderly, Lift her with care. **1890** *Univ. Rev.* Feb. 232 Martin..had taken up a stone to throw at him.

(*b*) *spec.* To raise or lift from some settled position, e.g. (plants) out of the ground, (a corpse) out of the grave, (a carpet) from the floor, etc.; to break up the surface of (a field, road, etc.).

† ***to take up the table***: to clear the table after a meal (*orig.* to remove the board off the trestles: see TABLE *sb.* 6 b). *Obs.*

13.. *Cursor M.* 8045 (Cott.) Quen þe king þam [þaa tres] had vp-tan, His ost þam honurd þan ilkan. **15..** [see TABLE *sb.* 6 b]. **1513** MORE in Hall *Chron., Rich. III* (1548) 27 b, Some saye that kynge Richard caused the priest to take them vp,..and to put them in a coffyne. **1585** T. WASHINGTON tr. *Nicholay's Voy.* I. xxi, The table being taken vp, the Ambassador..entred into the pauilion. **1612** [see TABLE *sb.* 6 b]. **1625** MASSINGER *New Way* I. ii, 'Tis not twelve o'clock yet, Nor dinner taking up. **1836–9** DICKENS *Sk. Boz, Sentiment*, The carpet was taken up. **1841** *Jrnl. R. Agric. Soc.* II. II. 229 The turnips were taken up and carted. **1895** *Times* 5 Feb. 8/2 That would mean taking up all the streets in South London.

(*c*) With special obj., implying a purpose of using in some way: as, ***to take up one's pen***, to proceed or begin to write; ***to take up a book*** (i.e. with the purpose to read); ***to take up the*** (or ***one's***) ***cross*** (see CROSS *sb.* 4, 10): ***to take up*** ARMS, *the* CUDGELS, *the* GLOVE, *the* HATCHET (see the sbs.).

c **1420** *Brut* ccxlii. 355 þay waged batayle & cast doun her gloues; & þanne þey were take vp and seled. **1481, 1579** [see GLOVE *sb.* 1 d]. **1590–** [see GAUNTLET *sb.*[1] 1 c]. **1621** T. WILLIAMSON tr. *Goulart's Wise Vieillard* A ij b, I tooke up my Pen againe, and at starts and tymes finished it. **1660** tr. *Amyraldus' Treat. conc. Relig.* II. iv. 216 He took up arms for the conservation of his Country. **1712** STEELE *Spect.* No. 514 ¶ 1 Not finding my self inclined to sleep, I took up Virgil to divert me. **1816** SCOTT *Old Mort.* xxx, That the cause of his country, and of those with whom he had taken up arms, should suffer nothing from being entrusted to him. **1866** G. MACDONALD *Ann. Q. Neighb.* i, A man had to take-up his cross.

(*d*) To raise, lift (one's hand, foot, head, etc.). Now of a horse or other beast.

c **1425** *Cursor M.* 15227 (Trin.) Vp he toke his holy hond & ȝaf þe benesoun. *c* **1489** CAXTON *Sonnes of Aymon* ix. 249 Rycharde that lay a grounde thus wounded..toke up his hede, and sayd [etc.]. **1737** BRACKEN *Farriery Impr.* (1757) II. 73 He steps boldly, and takes up his Fore-Feet pretty high. *Ibid.* 77 A Horse should take up his Feet moderately high.

(*e*) To take (a person) from the ground into a vehicle, or on horseback, etc. Said of a person, or of the carriage, horse, train, etc. Also *absol.* of a vehicle, a train, etc. To take up its occupants.

1689 *Lond. Gaz.* No. 2511/4 A Hackney-Coachman took up 3 Persons at Mark-Lane-end. **1710** *Ibid.* No. 4735/4 A Hackney Coach..that took up his Fair in Southwark. **1831** SCOTT *Ct. Robt.* xiii, We should not criticise the animal [elephant] which kneels to take us up. **1857** TROLLOPE *Barchester T.* x, Carriages..were desired to take up at a quarter before one. **1893** *Eng. Illustr. Mag.* X. 257/2 Our coach..duly took us up, and set us down. **1898** *Westm. Gaz.* 27 June 10/1 All carriages will take up on the Embankment and Savoy-hill. **1909** *Bradshaw's Railway Guide* Aug. 21 Stops to take up 1st class Passengers for London. *Ibid.*, Stops to take up for Reading or beyond.

† (*f*) *fig.* To 'raise' (a siege). *Obs. rare.*

c **1489** CAXTON *Sonnes of Aymon* xxiii. 493 Charlemagne.. receyued theim honourably, and toke vp his siege, and went agen to parys.

b. To lead, conduct, convey, or carry (a person or thing) to a higher place or position.

a **1300** *Cursor M.* 17547 (Cott.) þat helias in ald dais, Was taken up als vnto heuen. **1526** TINDALE *Acts* i. 9 Whyll they behelde he was taken vp, and a cloude receaued hym vp out of their sight. **1748** *Anson's Voy.* II. viii. 219 The taking up oysters from great depths..by Negro slaves. *Mod.* He took me up into the belfry. You needn't walk up the stairs; they will take you up in the lift.

(*b*) *spec.* To bring (a horse, ox, etc.) from pasture into the stable or stall.

1482 *Cely Papers* (Camden) 122 Lette hym [a horse] ron in a parke tyll Hallowtyd and then take hym wpe and ser hym and lette hym stand in the dede of whynter. **1688** R. HOLME *Armoury* III. xix. (Roxb.) 184/2 Take vp your horse, is to take him from grasse to be kept in the stable. **1844** *Jrnl. R. Agric. Soc.* V. I. 75 Calves..are taken up at night about the latter end of October. **1846** *Ibid.* VII. II. 394 Sixteen polled beasts..were taken up.

c. To pull up or in, so as to tighten or shorten; to make fast in this way, as a dropped stitch. In quot. 1882 *intr.* for *pass.* to become shortened, shrink. Also, †to make (a further hole) in order to shorten a strap. Hence, to shorten or tighten (a garment, pattern, etc.), esp. by hemming or tucking.

1804 MAR. EDGEWORTH *Pop. Tales, To-Morrow* 340 This operation of taking up a stitch..is one of the slowest. **1818** C. BROWN *Let.* 7 Aug. in *Lett. J. Keats* (1958) I. 361, I must have another hole taken up in the strap of my Knapsack. **1882** NARES *Seamanship* (ed. 6) 226 The longer the rope the more it takes up. **1891** MISS DOWIE *Girl in Karp.* iii. 33 Each girth was altered to its last hole, the stirrup-leather taken up half a yard, but nowhere could it grip the little beast. **1892** *Field* 8 Oct. 545/3 The direction to the groom would be 'take up' (or 'let down', as the case may be) the near-side horse's coupling rein. **1916** L. I. BALDT *Clothing for Women* ix. 186 To shorten pattern... Lay fold at same point, to shorten length, unless a great deal has to be taken up, in which case some could be taken from the bottom. **1937** P. H. RICHARDS *Dress Creation* XIII. 113 The quantity taken up in the tucks should amount in all to the distance between A and C. **1972** A. ROSS *London Assignment* 28 The trousers were a fraction long, and would need to be taken up.

(*b*) To tie up or constrict (a vein or artery); 'to fasten with a ligature passed under' (J.).

1565 BLUNDEVIL *Horsemanship* IV. iii. (1580) 2 b, Most diseases are healed either by letting of bloud, by taking vp of vaines, by purgation, or else by cauterisation. **1737** BRACKEN *Farriery Impr.* (1757) II. 41 The Absurdity of taking up the Veins for the Cure of Spavins. **1840** *Jrnl. R. Agric. Soc.* I. III. 322 Should any considerable [blood] vessel be opened, it will be necessary to take it up by passing a thread underneath it, and tying it tightly.

d. To take into one's possession, possess oneself of; with various shades of meaning, as: to purchase wholesale, buy up; to get, receive, or exact in payment; to levy; to borrow (at interest); to hire; to apply for or claim. Cf. TAKE-UP *sb.* (*a.*) 6.

1421 *Coventry Leet Bk.* 29 þat no maner of fresche fysher by, ne take up, no maner of fresche fysche of men of the contrey by way of regratry. *c* **1440** *Jacob's Well* 40 And þou apeyryst & lessyst þat tythe in takyng vp þi cost, here þou makyst þe cherche thrall. **1528** *Bill* in R. G. Marsden *Sel. Pl. Crt. Adm.* (1894) I. 41, I Thomas Thorne . . have taken up by exchange of Thomas Fuller merchaunt . . the sum of lx[li] sterling. **1589** PUTTENHAM *Eng. Poesie* III. xii. (Arb.) 179 He that standes in the market way, and takes all vp before it come to the market in grosse and sells it by retaile. **1655** tr. *Com. Hist. Francion* IV. 23, I must buy me a Cloak lined with plush, or take one up at the Brokers. **1760–72** H. BROOKE *Fool of Qual.* (1809) II. 130 He took up all the money he could, at any interest. **1838** T. MITCHELL *Aristoph. Clouds* 6 Strepsiades had for the purchase taken up money with two usurers, Pasias and Amynias. **1890** *Pict. World* 2 Jan. 11/3 The whole of the limited edition . . was taken up by the booksellers on the day of publication. **1971** *Guardian* 15 Apr. 1/1 A major campaign to persuade people to take up their welfare and social security benefits has been launched by the Government.

(*b*) To take (land) into occupation; to begin to occupy, settle upon. Cf. also v (*b*).

1478 *Acta Dom. Conc.* (1839) 6/1 He occupijt and tuke vp sa mekle of þe said landis of þe ȝeris forsaide. **1682** S. WILSON *Acc. Carolina* 16 Rent to commence in two years after their taking up their Land. **1890** 'R. BOLDREWOOD' *Col. Reformer* (1891) 76 Persons . . could 'take up', that is merely mark out and occupy, as much land as they pleased.

(*c*) To accept or pay (a bill of exchange); to advance money on (a mortgage); to subscribe for (stock, shares, a loan) at their original issue.

1832 *Examiner* 283/1 It was not convenient for her husband to take up the bill. **1847** C. G. ADDISON *On Contracts* II. v. §1 (1883) 771 A person who takes up a bill *supra protest* for the benefit of a particular party to the bill succeeds to the title of the party from whom . . he receives it. **1869** *Bradshaw's Railway Man.* XXI. 402 Of 100,000 new 10*l.* shares . . 84,837 have been taken up. **1873** SPENCER *Stud. Sociol.* x. 251 Not one of the thousand shares was taken up. **1888** RIDER HAGGARD *Col. Quaritch* xi. 84, I am disposed to try and find the money to take up these mortgages. **1890** *Chamb. Jrnl.* 10 May 294/1 Sums of money could be remitted for the purpose of taking up bills on the last day of grace. **1891** *Harper's Mag.* Nov. 946/2 He persuaded the citizens to take up the Queen's loans themselves.

(*d*) To make (a collection). *Sc.* and *U.S.* Also *fig.*

1849 E. DAVIES *Amer. Scenes* 42 While they were singing Brother such-a-one would 'take up the collection'. **1880** 'MARK TWAIN' *Tramp Abroad* ix. 88 She became a sort of contribution box. This dear young thing in the theatre had been sitting there unconsciously taking up a collection [of fleas]. **1892** —— in *Idler* Feb. 15 They take up a collection and bury him. **1908** *Daily Chron.* 21 Dec. 4/7 The tambourine . . still serves its notable purpose for 'taking up', as the Scotch say, a collection.

†**e.** To obtain or get from some source; to adopt, 'borrow' (= sense 30); to apprehend with the senses, perceive (quot. 1607); to deduce, infer (= 31 b); to contract, 'catch' (= 44 b). *Obs.*

1607 TOPSELL *Four-f. Beasts* (1658) 454 Presently the wilde beasts take it [the scent] up, and follow it with all speed they can. **1628** EARLE *Microcosm.* ii. (Arb.) 22 Notes of Sermons, which taken vp at St. Maries, hee vtters in the Country. **1662** STILLINGFL. *Orig. Sacr.* III. ii. §5 That the general conclusions of reason . . were taken up from the observation of things as they are at present in the world. **1700** DRYDEN *Pref. Fables* Ess. (ed. Ker) II. 255, I find . . I have anticipated already and taken up from Boccace before I come to him. **1848** *Jrnl. R. Agric. Soc.* IX. II. 360 We can conceive that an animal . . should take up the disease, and afterwards communicate it to others.

†(*b*) ? To receive, get, have accorded to one.

1639 FULLER *Holy War* V. xxvi. (1647) 274 A chronologer of such credit that he may take up more belief on his bare word than some others on their bond.

f. To receive into its own substance or interstices; to absorb (a fluid); to dissolve (a solid); also, to receive and hold upon its surface (quot. 1840). Also *absol.* (see quot. 1974).

1682 *Art & Myst. Vintners* xxxviii. 20 Dip in it [*printed* it in] so many cloaths as will take it up, and put the cloaths in your Hogshead. **1737** BRACKEN *Farriery Impr.* (1757) II. 105 Nutritive Juices, taken up by the absorbent Vessels. **1758** REID tr. *Macquer's Chym.* I. 47 An acid cannot take up above such a certain proportion thereof as is sufficient to saturate it. **1805** W. SAUNDERS *Min. Waters* 29 Water, at a moderate temperature, will readily take up its own bulk of carbonic acid gas. **1840** GOSSE *Canadian Nat.* xvi. 251 Capable of taking up and holding a large quantity of water. **1877** *Scribner's Mag.* XV. 141/2 The elastic roller thus takes up the color from the pores of the wood. **1892** *Cornh. Mag.* Sept. 257 Water will take up 2 lb. 10 oz. of salt to the gallon. **1960** E. L. DELMAR-MORGAN *Cruising Yacht Equipment & Navigation* vii. 86 The planks and timbers will dry out . . . When they are once again waterborne they will leak until the wood 'takes up'. **1974** J. KEATS *Of Time & Island* xi. 177 The [fibreglass] boats did not have to be put into the river to soak, or take up, as the people said.

(*b*) *Engin.* To accept, absorb, or assimilate (by gearing, etc.).

1921 *Conquest* Oct. 510/2 It appears to have solved the problem generally of how gradually and smoothly to take up and transmit the power of a prime mover or motor. **1966** *Listener* 24 Nov. 773/1 Although the paint is applied neatly, there are slight irregularities . . . These slight irregularities help the colours to engage with each other, . . rather as the slightly abrasive surface of a clutch-plate takes up the transmission.

g. To grasp with the mind; to apprehend, understand: = sense 46; *take in*, 84 l. Also with the speaker as obj. (= 46 b). *Obs.* exc. *Sc.* in general sense; now only in restricted sense: To apprehend, appreciate (points in discourse, etc.).

1659 W. GUTHRIE *Christian's Gt. Interest* viii. (1724) 88 A Man may take up his gracious State by his Faith, and the Acting thereof on Christ. **1741** WATTS *Improv. Mind* I. vi. §6 A student should never satisfy himself with bare attendance on the lectures of his tutor, unless he clearly takes up his sense and meaning. **1825** JAMIESON s.v., He taks up a thing before ye have half said it. **1867** N. MACLEOD *Starling* I. v. 55, 'I do not take you up, sir', replied the Sergeant. *Mod.* He is a humorous speaker, and his jokes were well taken up by the audience.

h. To accept. †(*a*) To accept mentally (*upon credit* or *trust*), believe without examination, take for granted. *Obs.* (*b*) To accept (anything offered, esp. a challenge, a bet: also the person who offers it). Cf. 40. See also GAUNTLET *sb.*[1] 1 c, GLOVE *sb.* 1 d: see a (*c*).

1626 BACON *Sylva* §34 It is strange how the ancients took up experiments upon credit, and yet did build great matters upon them. **1662** STILLINGFL. *Orig. Sacr.* I. iv. §8 Greek writers . . took up things upon trust as much as any people in the world did. **1711** ADDISON *Spect.* No. 126 ¶9 Notwithstanding he was a very fair Bettor, no Body would take him up. **1880** G. MEREDITH *Tragic Com.* xviii, Marko . . had taken up Alvan's challenge. **1892** *Sat. Rev.* 8 Oct. 403/2 Mr. Stanley (on taking up the freedom of Swansea) spoke very vigorously on the subject. **1893** *Temple Bar Mag.* XCVII. 21 It don't concern you who takes up the bets.

(*c*) ***to take*** (a person) ***up on*** (something): to accept an offer, invitation, etc. *colloq.*

1914 S. LEWIS *Our Mr. Wrenn* v. 63 'We'll go Dutch to a lodging-house.' . . 'All right, sir; all right. I'll take you up on that.' **1948** 'N. SHUTE' *No Highway* vii. 192 It's just an estimate. . . I didn't want people to take me up to it like this. **1961** J. STROUD *Touch & Go* iv. 45 'Tell her not to hesitate to ask.' 'Thank you. . . I might take you up on that.' **1974** 'E. FERRARS' *Hanged Man's House* xv. 149 I'll go over to see Mrs Bayne and take her up on her invitation to lunch. **1979** B. PARVIN *Deadly Dyke* xxiv. 134, I must be going. I'll take you up on that coffee later.

i. To take (a person) into one's protection, patronage, or other relation; to adopt as a *protégé* or associate; to begin to patronize.

1382 WYCLIF *Luke* i. 54 He, hauynge mynde of his mercy, took vp Israel, his child. **1482** *Monk of Evesham* (Arb.) 35 That worshipfull olde fader the whiche . . had take me vp to be a felow with him of his wey. **1530** PALSGR. 751/2, I take up, as a man taketh up his frende that maketh hym curtesye. *c* **1635** NAUNTON *Fragm. Reg.* (Arb.) 26 The blow falling on Edward late Earl of Hereford, who to his cost took up the divorced Lady, of whom the Lord Beauchamp was born. **1848** THACKERAY *Van. Fair* li, When the Countess of Fitz-Willis . . takes up a person, he or she is safe. **1877** *Scribner's Mag.* XV. 62/2 He is just the man to take up a girl whom everybody neglected. **1892** *Black & White* 10 Dec. 679/1 A great art patron took him up and he became 'the fashion'.

†**j.** To levy, raise, enlist (troops). *Obs.*

1560 DAUS tr. *Sleidane's Comm.* 219 b, He toke vp all that were able to weare armure. **1597** SHAKS. *2 Hen. IV*, II. i. 199 You are to take Souldiers vp, in Countries as you go. **1632** LITHGOW *Trav.* III. 91 He was taken vp as a souldier.

†(*b*) *intr.* for *refl.* To enter (military or naval) service; to enlist; = *take on*, 86 l. *Obs.*

1689 SHADWELL *Bury F.* I. ii, The top of their fortune is to take up in some Troop.

k. *trans.* To capture, seize. †(*a*) *Chess.* = sense 2 d. *Obs.*

c **1440** *Gesta Rom.* xxi. 71 (Harl. MS.) þe rook . . holdith length & brede, and takith vp what so is in his way. *c* **1470** *Treat. Chess* (MS. Ashmole 344 lf. 5), Then he takith hym vpp with his knight.

(*b*) *Falconry.* To bring under restraint (a young hawk 'at hack') in order to train it: see quot. and HACK *sb.*[2] 1. Cf. b (*b*).

1826 J. SEBRIGHT *Observ. Hawking* 8 When . . [Hawks] have omitted to come for their food at the accustomed hour, for two or three successive days, . . it will be necessary to take them up, or they would in a short time go away altogether. **1881** E. B. MICHELL in *Macm. Mag.* Nov. 40 An experienced falconer will 'take up' a young merlin from hack and have him trained in three or four days.

†(*c*) ***to take up for hawks***: (app.) to seize and slaughter (an old or useless horse) as meat for hawks; hence allusively, ***taken up for hawks*** = done for, ruined. *Obs.*

1471 J. PASTON in *P. Lett.* III. 7, I beseche yow, and my horse . . be not takyn up for the Kynges hawkys, that he may be had hom and kept in your plese. *a* **1553** UDALL *Royster Doyster* III. iii, Ye were take vp for haukes, ye were gone, ye were gone. [Cf. **1632** BROME *Northern Lasse* I. iv, 'Slid I'le marrie out of the way; 'tis time I think: I shall be tane up for Whores meat else.]

l. To seize by legal authority, arrest, apprehend; in quot. 1821, to summon as a witness.

1596 SPENSER *State Irel.* Wks. (Globe) 679/1 Though the sherriff have this authoritye . . to take up all such stragglers, and imprison them. **1682** WOOD *Life* 25 Nov. (O.H.S.) III. 31 Duke of York hath brought an action against one Arrowsmith . . upon the statute of *Scandalum magnatum*, who is taken up for it. **1796** SOUTHEY *Lett. fr. Spain* (1799) 303 The Alcayde took up all the inhabitants of the village where it happened. **1821** GALT *Ann. Parish* xii, It was thought she would have been taken up as an evidence in the Douglas cause. **1861** *Temple Bar Mag.* II. 358 [He] was taken up for sacrilege, and brought before a magistrate.

†**m.** To arrest the progress or action of; to check, stop, 'pull up'. *Obs.*

1631 WEEVER *Anc. Fun. Mon.* To Rdr. 7, I haue beene taken vp in diuers Churches by the Churchwardens . . and not suffered to write the Epitaphs. **1699** DAMPIER *Voy.* II. I. iv. 78 For a small piece of Money a man may pass quiet enough, and for the most part only the poor are taken up.

n. *intr.* for *refl.* To check oneself, stop short, 'pull up'; to slacken one's pace; to restrain oneself; to reform, mend one's ways. Now *U.S.*, of a horse; also *intr.* of a rider, to rein in.

1613 FLETCHER, etc. *Captain* IV. iii, Take up quickly; Thy wit will founder of all four else, wench, If thou hold'st this pace: take up, when I bid thee. **1661** PEPYS *Diary* 13 Nov., My expensefull life . . will undo me, I fear, . . if I do not take up. *a* **1700** B. E. *Dict. Cant. Crew* s.v. *Oats*, One that has sown his wild Oats, . . begins to take up and be more Staied. **1832** *Examiner* 611/1 She longs to make her fortune by her trade, that she may 'take up and live godly'. **1868** ATKINSON *Cleveland Gloss., Tak' up*, . . to reform one's ways. **1942** *Sun* (Baltimore) 20 Oct. 15/1 Fogoso . . cut sharply in front of Sunset Boy, causing Jimmy Berger to take up. **1946** *Ibid.* 2 Oct. 15/2 Red Tag ran into tight corners at the head of the stretch and was forced to take up. **1950** *Ibid.* 20 May 11/1 Queen May, ridden by Joe Culmone, was not to get through. . . Culmone was forced to take up.

(*b*) Of weather: To improve, mend, become fair.

1845 *Jrnl. R. Agric. Soc.* VI. II. 570 The weather took up immediately afterwards. **1889** FROUDE *Two Chiefs Dunboy* xiv, On the second evening the weather began to take up.

(*c*) '*Mech.* To close spontaneously, as a small leak in a steam-pipe or water-pipe' (*Cent. Dict.*).

o. *trans.* To check (a person) in speaking; to interrupt sharply, esp. with an expression of dissent or disapproval; to rebuke, reprove, or reprimand sharply or severely. Also ***to take up short***: see SHORT.

1530 PALSGR. 750/1 It pityed my herte to here howe he toke hym up. **1573** L. LLOYD *Marrow of Hist.* (1653) 241 His wife Xantippe began to take her husband up with taunting and opprobrious words. **1645** T. COLEMAN *Hopes Deferred & Dashed* 2 [He] rebukes him sharply, takes him up roundly. **1768** TUCKER *Lt. Nat.* (1834) I. 80 Those, who would find fault with us for attributing colour, heat, and cold, to inanimate bodies, take us up before we were down. **1885** 'ANSTEY' *Tinted Venus* i. 14 'You do take one up so', he complained! 'I never intended nothing of the sort'. **1886** H. CONWAY *Living or Dead* xxv, She wondered why the master took her up so short when she had mentioned his name.

†**p.** 'To oppose, encounter, cope with' (Schmidt *Shaks. Lex.*). *Obs.*

1597 SHAKS. *2 Hen. IV*, I. iii. 73 His diuisions . . Are in three Heads: one Power against the French, And one against Glendower: Perforce a third Must take vp vs. **1607** —— *Cor.* III. i. 244 *Corio.* On faire ground, I could beat fortie of them. *Mene.* I could my selfe take vp a Brace o'th' best of them. **1641** BAKER *Chron.* (1660) 274 King Henry . . in June kept a solemn Just at Greenwich, where he and Sir Charles Brandon took up all commers.

†**q.** (?) To touch up; to urge on, incite. *Obs.*

1565 STAPLETON tr. *Bede's Hist. Ch. Eng.* V. vi. 158 But when I sawe them take their horses vppe with the spurres [*L. concitatis . . equis*].

r. To begin, commence (an action); *esp.* to begin to utter, set up, raise (laughter, lamentation, etc.). In quot. 1689 with *inf.* (obs.); in 1878 *absol.* (*dial.*). *Obs.* exc. *intr.* in *U.S.*, (esp. of a school term) to begin, start up. Cf. sense 84 u above.

c **1400** *Brut* 131 The Kyng his hondes lifte vp an hye, and a grete laughter toke op. *c* **1425** *Cursor M.* 15990 (Trin.) þe cok toke vp his fliȝt. *c* **1500** *Merch. & Son* 103 in Hazl. *E.P.P.* I. 139 The goste toke up a gresely grone, with fendys awey he glode. *a* **1610** HEALEY *Theophrastus* (1636) 70 Then hee would take up a great laughter, as if some prodigy or ominous thing had happened. **1689** AUBREY *Lives* (1898) I. 150 (*2nd Ld. Falkland*) 'Twas not long before he tooke-up to be serious. **1871** E. EGGLESTON *Hoosier Schoolm.* xii. 104 Meetin's took up. **1878** *Scribner's Mag.* XV. 653/1 Meanwhile the 'animal show' at the appointed time 'took up', as the country people expressed it. **1903** J. FOX *Little Shepherd* iii. 42 When school 'took up again', Chad was told to say them aloud in concert with the others. **1949** 'J. NELSON' *Backwoods Teacher* 51 Four other children . . trooped in, having belatedly heard that school was taking up today. **1961** M. BEADLE *These Ruins are Inhabited* (1963) iii. 46 Red's school took up in two days.

†(*b*) To start, raise, or begin a song; hence (*Sc.*) to lead the singing of (a psalm) in church. *Obs.* (Cf. also *to take up one's parable*: PARABLE *sb.* d.)

a **1380** *Minor Poems fr. Vernon MS.* xxiii. 1089 We han taken vp þe song Of Iubilacion. **1577** *Burgh Rec. Edinb.* (1882) IV. 60 The oulklie pentioun of ten schillingis appoynttit to Edwerd . . Hendersoun, for all the dayis of his lyfe for taikin vp of the spalmes. **1637** in Cramond *Ann.*

Cullen (1888) 39 To read in the kirk and take up the psalm every Sabbath. **1825** JAMIESON s.v., 'He tuke up the psalm in the kirk', he acted as precentor.

s. *trans.* To begin afresh (something left off, or begun by another); to enter anew upon; to resume.

1654-66 EARL ORRERY *Parthen.* (1676) 692 With Atasernes I joyfully took up our way to the Camp. **1712** ADDISON *Paraphr. Ps. xix*, Soon as the evening shades prevail, The moon takes up the wondrous tale. **1833** HT. MARTINEAU *Manch. Strike* i. 5 When at last she lost her voice ..he took up the word. **1850** *Tait's Mag.* XVII. 482/2 Mr. Ward's diary takes up the history..just where Lord Malmesbury's memoirs leave it. **1879** M. PATTISON *Milton* xii. 161 He took up all the dropped threads of past years. **1902** O. WISTER *Virginian* xxxii, We took up our journey, and by the end of the forenoon we had gone some distance.

t. To adopt (a practice, notion, idea, purpose, etc.); to assume (an attitude, tone, etc.); to engage in, 'go in for' (a study, profession, business, etc.).

a **1450** *Knt. de la Tour* (1906) 64 She wolde not take hede to abyde unto her neygheboures..haue taken up the guyse or array that she wold haue. **1589** PUTTENHAM *Eng. Poesie* II. xii. (Arb.) 122 They of late yeares haue taken this pastime vp among them. **1611** BIBLE *Transl. Pref.* 6 To haue the Scriptures in the mother-tongue is not a quaint conceit lately taken vp. **1660** tr. *Amyraldus' Treat. conc. Relig.* II. ii. 163 He seem'd to have took up a resolution of trampling upon those superstitions. **1712** ARBUTHNOT *John Bull* I. iv, Lewis Baboon had taken up the trade of Clothier. **1821** SOUTHEY in *Q. Rev.* XXV. 289 Whatever part indeed Cromwell took up would be well maintained. **1890** *Sat. Rev.* 20 Sept. 355/1 Those parts of the Ethics which they are obliged to take up for 'Greats'.

(*b*) To take in hand, proceed to deal practically with (a matter, question, etc.); to interest oneself in, espouse, embrace (a cause).

1502 *Star Chamber Proc.* Michaelm. 18 Hen. VII, The said late Shireffes..caused two of her frendes to take up this haynouse matier betuix theym as arbitrours. **1771** MRS. HARRIS in *Priv. Lett. Ld. Malmesbury* I. 221 This [conflict with the City] was taken up yesterday in the House; the Speaker gave a detail of the fact. **1820** *Examiner* No. 618. 109/1 How generous to take up the cause of the afflicted! **1869** FREEMAN *Norm. Conq.* III. xiii. 312 The cause of William was eagerly taken up. **1892** *Law Times* XCIII. 459/2 Mr. Bros..suggested that the Public Prosecutor should take the matter up.

†**u.** To make up, settle, arrange amicably (a dispute, quarrel, etc.). In quot. 1666, to make up temporarily, 'patch up'. *Obs.*

1560 DAUS tr. *Sleidane's Comm.* 21 b, He had done as much as lay in him that the matter might be taken vp. **1600** SHAKS. *A. Y. L.* v. iv. 104, I knew when seuen Iustices could not take vp a Quarrell. **1605** *Lond. Prodigal* II. ii, If you come to take up the matter between my master and the Devonshire man. **1666** PEPYS *Diary* 24 Oct., The thing is not accommodated, but only taken up.

†(*b*) To make up, make good. *Obs.*

1662 GURNALL *Chr. Arm.* III. 302 If you be hindred of your rest one Night by business, you will take it up the next.

v. To proceed to occupy (a place or position, *lit.* or *fig.*); to station or place oneself in; = sense 27.

1565 STAPLETON tr. *Bede's Hist. Ch. Eng.* 86 Taking vpp his inne, and finding the neighbours of the parish at feast with the oste. **1589** PUTTENHAM *Eng. Poesie* II. v. (Arb.) 88 He taketh vp his lodging, and rests him selfe till the morrow. *a* **1672** WOOD *Life* (O.H.S.) I. 109 When they were going to their..beds, two or 3 houres after he had taken up his rest. **1736** WESLEY *Wks.* (1872) I. 26 Mr. Delamotte and I took up our lodging with the Germans. **1840** THIRLWALL *Greece* lviii. VII. 307 He cleared the defiles and took up his quarters for the rest of the winter at Celænæ. **1888** MCCARTHY & PRAED *Ladies' Gallery* II. ii. 29, I did not accept his invitation to take up my residence in his house. **1893** TRAILL *Soc. Eng.* Introd. 15 We may take up a position from which we can survey the entire array.

†(*b*) To engage or hire (a lodging) for the purpose of occupying; = sense 15 c. Cf. d (*b*). *Obs.*

1602 MARSTON *Antonio's Rev.* I. ii, Twere best you tooke some lodging up, And lay in private till the soile of griefe Were cleard your cheeke. **1709** STRYPE *Ann. Ref.* I. xv. 188 The Bp. of London's palace, and the Dean of Paul's house, ..were taken up for the French ambassadors.

(*c*) ***take up house***: †to take or rent a house (*obs.*); to start housekeeping; become a householder. *Sc.*

1612 *Shetland Act* in *Scotsman* 29 Jan. (1886) 7/2 It sall not be lesum for servile persones not worth..72 punds Scottis to tak up houssis. **1850** *Tait's Mag.* XVII. 13/1 He was unwilling to incur the expense of taking up house. **1876** SMILES *Sc. Natur.* i, John Edward and his wife 'took up house' in the Green, one of the oldest quarters of the city.

†(*d*) *absol.* or *intr.* To take up one's quarters, lodge, 'put up'. *Obs.*

1626 B. JONSON *Staple of N.* IV. ii, How much 'twere better, that my Ladies Grace Would here take vp Sir, and keepe house with you. **1662** PEPYS *Diary* 14 Oct., To Cambridge.., whither we come at about nine o'clock, and took up at the 'Beare'. **1724** DE FOE *Mem. Cavalier* (1840) 14, I was..forced to take up at a little village.

w. *trans.* To occupy entirely; to occupy the whole of, fill up (space, time, etc.); to occupy exclusively (quot. 1615); to occupy so as to hinder passage, to obstruct (quots. 1607, 1631). Cf. 28.

1607 SHAKS. *Cor.* III. ii. 116 My throat of Warre be turn'd ..into a Pipe.., and Schoole-boyes Teares take vp The Glasses of my sight. **1610** HOLLAND *Camden's Brit.* (1637) 633 It tooke up in compasse above a mile. **1615** G. SANDYS *Trav.* 69 The men take them [the public baths] up in the morning, and in the afternoone the women. **1631** WEEVER *Anc. Fun. Mon.* 11 Tombes are made so huge great, that they take vp the Church, and hinder the people from diuine Seruice. **1640** S. D'EWES in *Lett. Lit. Men* (Camden) 167 Some petitions..tooke upp our time a great parte of the morning. **1705** tr. *Bosman's Guinea* 490 The sixteen Red Cliffs, which take up in all about three Miles in length. **1719** DE FOE *Crusoe* (1840) I. v. 85 The 7th..I took wholly up to make me a chair. **1825** *New Monthly Mag.* XIV. 392 The first quatrain..is taken up with a list of rivers. **1885** MRS. LYNN LINTON *Christ. Kirkland* II. ix. 274 It took up his time and bored him.

(*b*) To use up, consume (labour, material): cf. 28. ? *Obs.*

1679 MOXON *Mech. Exerc.* viii. 142 The Fraiming work will take up more labour. **1712** J. JAMES tr. *Le Blond's Gardening* 121 You may fill up the Holes to the Level of the Ground.., to take up the Earth that may possibly remain to be disposed of. **1719** DE FOE *Crusoe* (1840) I. iv. 80 The prodigious deal of time and labour which it took me up to make a plank or board.

(*c*) To occupy or engage fully, engross (a person, his attention, mind, etc.). Chiefly in *pass.* (const. *with*, sometimes *in*); also in *Sc.* and *north. dial.* = to be taken with, take an absorbing or engaging interest in.

1599 B. JONSON *Cynthia's Rev.* v. ii, He is taken up with great persons. *a* **1617** BAYNE *Lect.* (1634) 201 To take our selves up with some behoofefull duty. **1624** MASSINGER *Renegado* IV. i, I am so wholly taken up with sorrow. **1712** BUDGELL *Spect.* No. 301 ¶8, I was wholly taken up in these Reflections. **1832** HT. MARTINEAU *Hill & Valley* v. 76 She is taken up with making her husband comfortable. **1886** RUSKIN *Præterita* I. vi. 174, I was extremely taken up with the soft red cushions of the armchairs. **1892** MRS. H. WARD *D. Grieve* II. vii, I think he feels he must make his way first. His business takes him up altogether.

** *intransitive senses.*

(See also subordinate uses in j (*b*), n, n (*b*, *c*), r, v (*d*).)

x. ***take up for***: to stand up for, take the part of, side with. *U.S.* Cf. *to take for*, 20 b.

1878 *Scribner's Mag.* XV. 769/2 To Amanda's surprise her father took up for Mark. *Ibid.* XVI. 627/2 Twonnet thought..that it was a shame for..Mr. Whittaker to take up for Bonamy. **1936** M. MITCHELL *Gone with Wind* xii. 234, I knew you were doing it just to take up for me. **1977** *New Yorker* 6 June 85/1 'Wouldn't it embarrass *you*, hearing that *your* daddy spent a night in jail?' And Henry said no, it wouldn't—not if he knew his daddy had been taking up for someone.

y. †***take up in***, to interest oneself or itself in, concern itself with, have reference to. *Obs.*

1665 J. SPENCER *Vulg. Proph.* 120 Hath not the World out-grown the follies of Auguries..and took up in the resolves of Reason, as the best Oracle to consult in a civil business? *c* **1666** SOUTH *Serm., John* vii. 17 (1697) I. 246 The former Articles, that took up Chiefly in Speculation and Belief.

z. ***take up with.*** (Cf. *take with*, 75 a-c.) (*a*) To associate with (a person); to begin to keep company with; to consort with (esp. with a view to marriage); to become friendly with, to form a relationship with. Cf. i.

a **1619** FLETCHER *Wit without M.* I. i, He's taken up with those that woo the Widow. **1693** *Humours Town* 28 The man of Mode takes up with a damn'd Jilt. **1815** SCOTT *Guy M.* xi, To see his daughter taking up with their son. **1824** *Examiner* 250/2 Having..absconded and taken up with another woman. **1887** MISS E. MONEY *Dutch Maiden* (1888) 329 If you cannot marry her, you won't care to take up with another. **1957** R. HOGGART *Uses of Literacy* iii. 76 The woman he 'took up with' was likely enough to be married herself and of roughly the same age as his own wife. **1963** *Australasian Post* 14 Mar. 44/1 Miss Dolly has 'taken up' with a poor but respectable cabinet-maker and his wife... She sells her stolen nag to help them out. **1977** *Daily Express* 29 Jan. 7/2 The story is of a poor but pretty girl..who breaks her engagement to a morose butcher..and takes up instead with a feckless punter.

(*b*) To adopt, espouse (esp. as a settled practice); to assent to, agree with, accept. *arch.*

1692 BENTLEY *Boyle Lect.* 58, I could as easily take up with that senseless assertion of the Stoicks. **1724** A. COLLINS *Gr. Chr. Relig.* 275 Taking up with all manner of false proofs in behalf of Christianity. **1825** FROUDE in *Rem.* (1838) I. 178 My lately having taken up with reading sermons. **1885** J. MARTINEAU *Types Eth. Th.* I. 127 We take up at once with the belief that the space around us is empty.

†(*c*) To be satisfied with; to content oneself with, put up with, tolerate. *Obs.*

1609 HOLLAND *Amm. Marcell.* 394 Never doe wee find that he tooke up with any mild correction and punishment. **1633** BP. HALL *Hard Texts* 395 (*Jer.* xxii.) I will not take up with the old and meane buildings of my Ancestors. **1726** BUTLER *Serm., Love God* Wks. 1874 II. 186 Nature teaches and inclines us to take up with our lot. **1736** —— *Anal.* II. viii. ibid. I. 300 The unsatisfactory nature of the Evidence, with which we are obliged to take up. **1825** *New Monthly Mag.* XIII. 588 The book-sellers..buy all the good books, and the joint stock company must take up with the refuse of the market.

†(*d*) To betake oneself to: = *take to*, 74 c. *Obs.*

1785 MISS FIELDING *Ophelia* I. iv, At night he again took up with his Couch.

XIII. 94. In various idiomatic phrases (besides those mentioned under the senses to which they belong), as *take into* ACCOUNT, *in* (*into*) *one's* HEAD, *in* (*to*) PIECES, *to* TASK, *in* TOW, *upon* TRUST, *in* VAIN, *to* WITNESS, *at one's* WORD, *in* WORTH, etc., for which see the sbs.

☛ Key to phrases treated under the senses.

Not including the adverbial combinations 76-93, nor all phrases referred to the sb. or other leading word in them; see also 72, 94.

Take an accent 22, *t* adieu 55, *t* after 73, *t* against 20 b, *t* aim 64, *t* the air 13 b, *t* alarm 65, *t* and 25 d, *t* as it comes 42 e, *t* assizes 32, *t* the attention 10 d, *t* a bath 13 b, *t* beginning 52 b, *t* blind 7 d, *t* one a blow 5 b, *t* buck, bull 39 b, *t* the chair 27, *t* charge 66, *t* in charge 17, *t* cold 44 b, *t* with compasses 32 c, *t* credit 21, *t* at cards, at chess 2 d, *t* the crown 16 c, *t* day 67, *t* one's death 40 b, *t* a degree 34, *t* one's dick 17 b, *t* diligence 51 c, *t* a disease 44 b, *t* as done 47 e, *t* drink 13, *t* in earnest 42, *t* end 72, *t* an examination 32 a, *t* the eye 10 d, *t* a fall 52 d, *t* farewell 55, *t* a fence 43, *t* the Fifth Amendment 17 b, *t* as one finds 42 b, *t* fire 68, *t* five 52 c, *t* flight 72, *t* to flight 74 b, *t* food 13, *t* for 20 b, 48, *t* form 16 a, *t* fright 50, *t* in good part 42, *t* good-night 55, *t* the gown, the habit 16 c, *t* to a habit 74 e, *t* by the hand 3, *t* in *or* on hand 17, *t* a hint 41, *t* hoarse 7 d, *t* hold 69, *t* horse 39 b, 70, *t* house 15 c, *t* in idle 26 b, *t* ill 7 d, e, 42, *t* an inflexion 22, *t* inn 25, *t* inquisition 32 a, *t* intent 51 c, *t* interest 50, *t* into 4, *t* it 17 c, 42 d, 47 c, *t* it from me 41 b, *t* it from there 29 b, *t* a joke 42 c, *t* a journey 52, *t* knighthood 34, *t* labour 19 b, *t* lame 7 d, *t* a lease 15 c, *t* leave 21, 72, *t* or leave 39 a, *t* leg 24 c, *t* a letter 33 a, *t* one's life 58 b, *t* the life of 58 b, *t* in marriage 14 b, *t* medicine 13, *t* mercy 51 b, *t* to mercy 14, *t* minutes 33 a, *t* an oar 16 c, *t* an observation 32 b, *t* an obstacle 43, *t* off one's feet 58, *t* on 50 c, 86, *t* on oneself 16, 18, *t* over 57 a, *t* a paper, periodical 15 d, *t* a photograph, picture 33 b, *t* the points 43, 46, *t* possession 71, *t* punishment 37, *t* a resolution 51 a, *t* salt 13, 44 c, *t* satisfaction 37, *t* ship 24 c, *t* short 8 b, *t* a size (in gloves, etc.) 28 b, *t* snuff 13, *t* in snuff 42, *t* (so much) 28, *t* a spill 52 d, *t* one's stand 27, *t* a step 52, *t* a stick to 24 b, *t* temperature 32 b, *t* ten 52 c, *t* that 34 d, *t* thought 51 c, *t* to 74, *t* one's time 28, *t* toil 19 b, *t* a trip 52, *t* trouble 19 b, *t* truce 54, *t* a turn 52, *t* upon oneself 18, *t* the way 25 b, *t* on one's way 25 c, *t* well 42, *t* (to) wife 14 b, *t* wing 24 c, *t* to wing 74 b, *t* with 75, *t* with one 57 d, 59 b, c.

take (teɪk), *sb.* Also 6 **tayke**, 9 *Sc.* and *north. dial.* **tak**, **takke**: cf. TACK *sb.*² [f. TAKE *v.*]

1. †**a.** = TACK *sb.*² 2, a lease of land or of a farm for a term of years. *Obs.*

1511 *Test. Ebor.* (Surtees) V. 24, I will that my wif & my childre have my take in my fermhold in Kendale. **1542** *Ibid.* VI. 157 Also I give to my wif my take of yeres of the parsonadge of Kellyngton. **1599** *Knaresb. Wills* (Surtees) I. 220 All the tayke of my farmehold to bringe up my children withall.

b. The act of taking or leasing (land); the land taken; a holding; cf. TACK *sb.*² 2 b. *dial.*

1805 DICKSON *Pract. Agric.* I. 80 The quantity of land he must till, would occupy so much of his time, that the *take* would..be injurious to him. *c* **1850** *Northampt. Dialect*, This is my neighbour's take that we are on now, and that yonder is Lord B.'s. **1896** *Daily News* 19 Sept. 2/5 A few new 'takes' have been at less money, but old tenants have had to be content with a 10, 5, and..1 per cent. allowance. **1905** TUCKWELL *Remin. Radical Parson* xi. 157 He..will increase his take, build a cottage on it through a building society [etc.].

2. a. That which is taken or received in payment, or as proceeds of some business or transaction; *pl.* takings, receipts. In quot. 1654, ? impost, contribution imposed. Also *spec.*, personal income or earnings (*U.S. colloq.*).

1654 *Nicholas Pap.* (Camden) II. 41 The take off 200,000 crownes is now sett, and the Emperor declared his present shallbe apart. **1850** N. WISEMAN *Let.* 9 Dec. in *Dublin Rev.* (1919) Jan. 9 On Sunday the church was open... You may judge of the crowds when I tell you that the *take* was £94. **1891** *Daily News* 14 Sept. 2/1 Confident of large 'takes' for to-day and Sunday. **1892** STEVENSON *Across the Plains* 193 [They] depart, if the 'take' be poor, leaving debts behind them. **1905** *Westm. Gaz.* 15 June 11/1 The current [railway] returns include the long-distance Whitsuntide takes. **1937** *Sun* (Baltimore) 9 Feb. 11/2 There is the case of the check-room girl in a hotel, who receives tips for each garment checked, but turns her 'take' over to the management. **1943** *Ibid.* 25 Feb. 12/1 They will seek to increase their take by selling whisky on the side. **1966** P. O'DONNELL *Sabre-Tooth* v. 83 It was a big enough take for her to make a once-only comeback from retirement. **1970** 'B. MATHER' *Break in Line* v. 59 The luggage coolies..who kicked back half of their take to the Pathan hall porter. **1978** *Detroit Free Press* 5 Mar. B7/6 Isley will have to make do with his take from the Tractor Pull.

b. *Criminals' slang* (chiefly *U.S.*). Money acquired by theft or fraud.

1888 J. GREENWOOD *Policeman's Lantern* 69 A tidyish 'take' brought about by what he called the 'sweetstuff lay'. **1927** C. F. COE *Me—Gangster* xiii. 228 After the stick-up.. Carrots..can watch the take till I send the porter over after it. **1934** *Sun* (Baltimore) 14 July 3/5 A self-confessed confidence man..testified that he always handed his take to Graham, who..kept fifteen per cent for providing police protection. **1955** *Publ. Amer. Dial. Soc.* XXIV. 194 The day's *take* is the *knock up*, and the mob usually pools expenses for the day..and this amount is taken off the *top* (the total *take*). **1963** G. J. MCCALL in A. Dundes *Mother Wit* (1973) 422 The multimilliondollar 'take' of the hoodoo complex.

c. *U.S. colloq.* A percentage of a sum of money which is deducted, as for tax or other levies.

1935 *Sun* (Baltimore) 18 Jan. 14/7 Once the mutuel 'take' is raised over 7½ per cent. Maryland no longer can compete with other Eastern tracks. **1942** *Ibid.* 20 Mar. 14/2 What is the whole take of the Lewis dues collectors? How much of that take is a compulsory tribute through strong-arm imposition of closed-shop contracts? **1975** *Lamp* (Exxon Corporation) Winter 11/2 A recent act of Parliament imposes a special tax on revenues from British fields; combined with royalties and corporate income taxes, it raises total government 'take' to as much as 75 per cent, depending on the size of the field.

†**3.** A seizure; a spell of magic or witchcraft; enchantment. *Obs. rare.*

[Cf. TAKE *v.* 7, quot. 1598.] **1678** *Quack's Academy* 7 He has a Take upon him, or is Planet-struck.

4. 'Taking' or captivating quality, charm. *rare.*

1794 MRS. A. M. BENNETT *Ellen* IV. 179 Her face..had that kind of harmony and take in it, which when it has once pleased, will not cease to do so.

5. a. An act of taking or capturing an animal, or (usually) a number of animals (esp. fish) at one time; also the quantity so caught; a catch.

1753 *Scots Mag.* Aug. 422/1 There was a great take of herrings. **1851** MAYHEW *Lond. Labour* (1861) II. 60/1 The yearly 'take' of larks is 60,000. **1854** BADHAM *Halieut.* 339 Of late years.. greater takes have been effected off those of New England alone, than from the great fishery of Newfoundland itself. **1859** BAIN *Emotions* x. 189 The pleasure of each successful throw.. rendering it easy [for the angler] to go on for a long time without a take. **1876** SMILES *Sc. Natur.* vi. 101 The weather.. gave promise of an abundant 'take' of moths. **1883** *Daily Tel.* 25 June 7/1 Small boats being used to ferry the takes of fish to the smacks or steamers.

b. The action or process of catching fish, etc.

1854 H. MILLER *Sch. & Schm.* iii. (1858) 43 We.. became knowing.. about the take and curing of herrings. **1881** A. LANG *Library* 11 The 'take', as anglers say, is 'on' from half-past seven to half-past nine a.m.

6. a. An act, or the action, of taking (in general).

1816- [see GIVE AND TAKE 2, 3]. **1885** *Times* 25 May 9 At each take there is a certain amount of waste.

b. *Chess*, etc. The taking of a piece or pieces.

1870 HARDY & WARE *Mod. Hoyle, Draughts* 107 Such a dashing 'take' as this would not be likely to happen in actual play. **1903** *Times, Lit. Suppl.* 31 July 236/3 A good problem seldom commences with a check or take.

7. a. *Printing.* A portion of copy taken at one time by a compositor to be set up in type; = TAKING *vbl. sb.* 5 c.

1847 J. S. ROBB *Streaks of Squatter Life* 54 Here was a '*take*' in the book of human nature, which was most 'fair copy'. **1853** 'MARK TWAIN' *Let.* 26 Oct. (1917) I. i. 26 When one gets a good agate take, he is sure to make money. **1864** in WEBSTER. **1871** *Printers' Register* 6 Nov., The first 'take' of copy which fell to our share was about two and a half pages of 12 mo Long Primer. **1882** J. SOUTHWARD *Pract. Print.* (1884) 146 The compositor is bound to write his name on his copy, with a mark showing where he began to set... Each of these portions is.. called a 'take'. **1890** W. J. GORDON *Foundry* 192 In the small hours of the morning.. the last speech is coming in on relays of flimsy telegrams, and the compositors are working short 'takes' of half a dozen lines apiece.

b. The amount taken down at one time by each one of a staff of reporters.

1872 J. S. JEANS *West. Worthies* 98 The take of reporters became very much shortened, until they now seldom exceed a quarter of an hour or twenty minutes.

8. a. *Med.* A successful inoculation with a vaccine. **b.** *Agric.* Successful germination and growth of seed. **c.** *Med.* An acceptance by the body of tissue foreign to the site or to the individual.

1909 in *Cent. Dict.* Suppl. **1914** *Q. Jrnl. Med.* VII. 284 Revaccination on an individual who has been vaccinated many years previously usually results in what might be termed a genuine 'take'. **1921** H. GUTHRIE-SMITH *Tutira* xix. 165 Between the isolated plants of the miserable 'take' of seed there was ample space left for the germination of undesirables. **1924** *Surg., Gynecol. & Obstetr.* XXXVIII. 101/2 A temporary take [of grafted skin] occurred but did not thrive well. **1940** R. G. STAPLEDON *Re-grassing* 21 In cases where the 'take' had been exceptionally good, and where there has been no immediate return of undesirable species, excessive early growth is far from disastrous. **1965** *Nursing Times* 5 Feb. 180/1 Persistent negative nitrogen balance results in.. poor graft take. **1977** *Lancet* 13 Aug. 356/2 In studies with live vaccines patients showing serological or virological evidence of virus 'take' are usually compared with the placebo group and/or with vaccine recipients who show no evidence of infection.

9. a. *Cinematogr.* A continuous section of film photographed at one time; an instance of such filming. Also preceding a numeral to distinguish individual sections of film. (In quot. 1922 used *collect.*) orig. *U.S.*

1922 *Opportunities in Motion Picture Industry* (Photoplay Research Soc.) 50 When the daily 'take' is handed in, does Mr. Director look for 'action'; does the technical man look to see how his pet scene photographed? **1928** *Sunday Dispatch* 2 Sept. 5/4 Notwithstanding the fact that the director knows that certain 'takes are useless and need not be printed. **1937** H. G. WELLS *Brynhild* ix. 144 Very few of the players.. realized that a movie take was afoot outside the marquee. **1947** *People* 22 June 5/3 Micky and.. Dave Crowley did the same fight 25 times before the final take was okayed. **1962** *Movie* Sept. 19/1 This conversation occupies part of a long take in a medium shot which favours neither point of view. **1972** *Listener* 22 Dec. 852/1 Sequence of calls before a shot. Production Assistant: 'Quiet. Going for a take.'.. First Assistant: '245, Take 5.' **1976** H. R. F. KEATING *Filmi, Filmi, Inspector Ghote* vi. 53 The scrawled chalk figures on the black board must indicate which scene and 'take' this was.

b. A sound recording; the act of making such a recording. orig. *U.S.*

1926 WHITEMAN & MCBRIDE *Jazz* xii. 248 At 12, a rehearsal or phonograph take. **1946** R. BLESH *Shining Trumpets* ix. 209 The results are.. a tribute to the recording engineer who supervised the 'take'. **1965** *Melody Maker* 3 Apr. 10 Of added interest is the fact that these takes.. have not been issued in Britain before. **1972** *Daily Tel.* (Colour Suppl.) 17 Nov. 9/3 Barkworth once had a one-word voice-over: 'Maltesers', which required 42 takes. Listening to the playback of the tape, he got the giggles. **1977** *Rolling Stone* 13 Jan. 48/2 Still such gems as 'All the Way from Memphis' and 'All the Young Dudes', along with a different take of 'Roll Away the Stone' and two previously unheard cuts,.. give this absorbing group a belated last testament.

10. ***on the take***: taking bribes; capable of being suborned. *slang* (orig. *U.S.*).

1930 *Liberty* 29 Nov. 70/1 There are men and women ready to boost the thief's game. The steer guy finds him work, dicks on the take protect him. **1935** J. O'HARA *Appointment in Samarra* i. 27 There was a councilman who was not on the take. Ed for some reason hadn't been about to get to him with a dime, not a dime. **1942** BERREY & VAN DEN BARK *Amer. Thes. Slang* §374/5 *Bribable*, approachable, fixable, on the take. **1956** B. HOLIDAY *Lady sings Blues* (1973) xxi. 169, I had heard of city cops taking plenty of money, but I never heard of a Treasury agent on the take since long before my time. **1967** *Boston Sunday Globe* 23 Apr. 18/5 In an unguarded public moment [he].. said, 'Half the people in Philadelphia are on the take.' **1975** *Listener* 16 Jan. 67/1 No matter how many Goverment departments were on the take, it was also evident that.. the law enforcers themselves were bent. **1980** R. L. DUNCAN *Brimstone* v. 90 'I'm not on the take,' he said.

[**take**, error for FAKE, a coil of rope.

1658 in PHILLIPS, whence in various later dicts.]

take-, the verb-stem in combinations and phrases used as sbs. or adjs. (mostly *nonce-wds.*): **take-all**, a disease of wheat and other cereals caused by the fungus *Ophiobolus graminis*, which produces a foot rot, yellowing of the plants, and stunted growth; **take-apart** *a.*, capable of being taken to pieces and reassembled; **take-charge** *a. colloq.* (orig. and chiefly *N. Amer.*), pertaining to or characterized by leadership or authority; cf. *take-hold* adj. below; **take-down**, (*a*) an act of taking down (in quot. in sense 82 b (*d*)); (*b*) (a rifle with) the capacity to have the barrel and magazine detached from the stock; usu. *attrib.* or as *adj.*; (*c*) *Austral. slang*, a deceiver, cheat, or thief; **take-downable** *a.*, capable of being taken down; **take-for-granted** *a.*, that takes something for granted, involving unproved assumptions; †**take-heed**, the action of taking heed, caution; a warning to take heed, a caution; **take-hold** *a.* (*U.S. colloq.*) = *take-charge* adj. above; **take-home** *a.* (orig. *U.S.*), that may be taken away home; esp. as ***take-home pay***, that portion of a person's earnings which is left after deductions of tax, insurance, etc.; **take-it-easy** *a.*, that takes things easily, easy-going; adapted for making oneself at ease, comfortable; **take-it-or-leave-it** *a.*, allowing acceptance or rejection; showing indifference; also as *sb.* in various senses (cf. *take it or leave it* s.v. TAKE *v.* 39 a); **take-leave**, *a.* of or pertaining to taking leave, parting, 'farewell'; *sb.* an act of taking leave, leave-taking; **take-on**, a state of 'taking on' (TAKE *v.* 86 j) or mental agitation, a 'taking'; **take-with** *a.* (*U.S. colloq.*), that may be taken along with one; *spec.* (see quot. 1941); also applied to prices; cf. *cash and carry* s.v. CASH *sb.*[1] 2 g. See also TAKE-IN, TAKE-OFF, TAKE-UP.

1880 *Silver's Handbk. Australia* 72 That terrible foe to wheat known as the *take-all in South Australia, has spread beyond the Adelaide plains. **1912** *Bull. Misc. Inf. R. Bot. Gardens Kew* 436 In the condition known as 'Take-all', the plants are attacked seriously at an early stage of growth and become yellow, and often die before the stem is formed. **1950** H. J. MASSINGHAM *Curious Traveller* viii. 150 The weather.. has certainly nursed the spread of take-all. **1978** *Times* 7 Aug. 3/2 'Take-all'.. can make a wheat plant yield a stunted and useless ear. **1966** J. S. COX *Illustr. Dict. Hairdressing & Wigmaking* 147/1 *Take-apart wig. **1979** *Nature* 5 July p. viii/3 Equipment is housed in a practical, take-apart cabinet that provides a support surface and slip-fit vacuum connection for various manifold arrangements. **1954** *Sun* (Baltimore) 1 Apr. 20/4 [The team] lacks a *take-charge guy... Neither.. players.. have those take-charge qualities. **1965** *Economist* 23 Jan. 339/1 Mr Wilson and Mr George Brown, the two take-charge men. **1970** [see PIVOT *sb.* 3 c]. **1976** M. MACHLIN *Pipeline* xlii. 456 Usually that take-charge tone of voice would send the adrenalin racing through Larry's system, setting up deep currents of psychological resistance. **1893** *Westm. Gaz.* 12 June 6/3 In the second division [of Cambridge boat-races] as many as six *take-downs were effected First Trinity III going sandwich boat instead of Christ's [etc.]. **1897** *Sears, Roebuck Catal.* 578/2 All rifles of this model can be furnished with pistol grip, with take down and all other extras. *ibid.* 579/2 No other lengths made in Take Down style. **1901** *Kynoch Jrnl.* Aug.-Sept. 136/1 This is not a 'take-down'.. but the barrel is detachable in the true sense of the word. **1905** A. M. BINSTEAD *Mop Fair* vii. 144 There are more takedowns at this game of racing than are suspected. **1906** E. DYSON *Fact'ry 'Ands* xi. 143 Well, iv she ain't a fair take-down! **1920** G. BURRARD *Notes Sporting Rifles* 15 A rifle on this principle cannot be cleaned from the breech unless it is a take-down model. **1926** J. DOONE *Timely Tips for New Australians* 19 *Take-down*, a slang word for thief. A cheat. **1934** *Bulletin* (Sydney) 31 Jan. 42/2, I could learn something from a cool-headed young take-down like you. **1971** L. KOPPETT *N.Y. Times Guide Spectator Sports* xi. 240 A 'takedown' gives 2 points to the wrestler who puts the other down. **1976** *Shooting Times & Country Mag.* 16–22 Dec. 7/2 (Advt.), Beautiful supple quality leather take down style gun cover... Barrels and action in separate compartments inside. **1977** *Rolling Stone* 24 Mar. 67 It survives the knocks and rough handling of countless loadings, unloadings, road bumps, set-ups, and take-downs. **1815** LAMB *Let. to Southey* 6 May, It will be a *take-downable book on my shelf. **1833** COLERIDGE *Lett., to T. H. Green* (1895) 767, I feel a *take-for-granted faith in the dips and pointings of the needle. **1853** LYNCH *Self-Improv.* ii. 26 You must talk of many things in a take-for-granted style in order to talk at all to the purpose. **1611** COTGR., *Mesgarde*,.. carelesnesse, lacke of good-*take-heed. **1622** FLETCHER & MASSINGER *Span. Curate* IV. v, I know ye want good diets,.. And, in your pleasures, good take-heed. **1648** WARD (*title*) Mercurius Anti-Mechanicus, or the Simple Coblers Boy, with his Lap-full of Caveats (or Take-heeds). **1973** *N.Y. Law Jrnl.* 2 Aug. 16/3 (Advt.), Top salary, benefits for *take-hold person with excellent skills, initiative. **1977** I. SHAW *Beggarman, Thief* I. ii. 21 Your brother Rudy is one hell of a man. A take-hold guy. **1943** *Sun* (Baltimore) 4 Dec. 12/1 (*heading*) Steel workers '*take home' pay rises 55%. **1951** *Manch. Guardian Weekly* 8 Feb. 15/4 It used to be that trainmen were classed first or second in take-home pay. **1968** J. D. WATSON *Double Helix* xvi. 111 Though the theoretical basis for many of their conclusions was shaky, the take-home lesson was obvious. **1973** *Times* 15 Mar. 23/6 Licenses should be granted to 'any retailer whose character and premises satisfy certain minimum standards, at least as far as the take-home trade is concerned. *Ibid.* 23/7 Take-home beer sales. **1976** *National Observer* (U.S.) 28 Aug. 6/3 A total of 823 cadets took the take-home exam.., and many cadets, their attorneys, and others suspect that as many as half the class collaborated. **1977** *R.A.F. News* 11–24 May 1/3 Between £1.68 and £5.29 a week is added to the take-home pay of married men with two children. **1872** *Routledge's Ev. Boy's Ann.* 500/2 The good-humoured *take-it-easy South-Sea Island nature. **1897** *Westm. Gaz.* 24 June 4/2 The walls and roofs of this take-it-easy room were draped with broad stripes of scarlet and white bunting. **1897** MARY KINGSLEY *W. Africa* 251, I affected an easy *take-it-or-leave-it-manner, and looked on. **1902** *Monthly Rev.* Aug. 155 England.. sets out her exhibits with a 'take-it-or-leave-it' air, with a disregard of their possibilities which seems almost wilful. **1933** WODEHOUSE *Heavy Weather* xvi. 280 The gallant nonchalance of that take-it-or-leave-it of his.. had sent Lord Tilbury scrambling for his cheque-book. **1940** C. MORGAN *Voyage* III. v. 267 [He] was a little distinguished among Thérèse's.. adorers.. by.. his attitude of take-it-or-leave-it even towards Thérèse herself. **1942** 'G. ORWELL' *War-Time Diary* in *Coll. Essays* (1968) II. 415, I believe, however, that in spite of the 'take it or leave it' with which our government started off, the terms will actually be modified. **1972** *Adoremus* Jan. 19 Devotion to her.. is more than a matter of personal taste, a take-it-or-leave-it of the Christian religion. **1799** MRS. J. WEST *Tale of Times* II. 93 In his *take-leave visit he made some further discoveries. *c* **1815** JANE AUSTEN *Persuas.* v, Going to almost every house in the parish, as a sort of take-leave. **1837** *Lett. fr. Madras* (1843) 81, I was prevented from finishing this.. by take-leave visits, &c. **1893** *Cornh. Mag.* June 566 The governor is in a dreadful *take on about you. **1894** BARING-GOULD *Kitty Alone* III. 142 Zerah's.. in a fine take-on. **1930** GODLEY & KAYLIN *Control Retail Store Operation* xviii. 214 For a 'cash-*take-with' register transaction, no salescheck is used. **1941** DUNCAN & PHILLIPS *Retailing Princ. & Methods* xx. 720 Sometimes the terms 'take transaction' or 'take-with' are used to identify those sales in which merchandise is given to the customer at the close of the sale rather than having the goods delivered by the store. **1970** *Redbook* Jan. 97/2 Another feature.. of the.. Diet is take-with lunches for the working woman... For five days of each week's menu there are lunches that can be eaten at home or packed to take along to work. **1977** *Chicago Tribune* 2 Oct. IX. B (Advt. Suppl.) 2/2 Chain saws are take-with priced.

takeable, takable (ˈteɪkəb(ə)l), *a.* [f. TAKE *v.* + -ABLE.] Capable of being taken; that may or can be taken; in various senses; in first quot., comprehensible, intelligible (see TAKE *v.* 46).

c **1449** PECOCK *Repr.* I. ii. 11 Which.. is not takeable of mannis witt. **1665** BOYLE *Occas. Refl.* II. vi. (1675) 116 Necessary to the rendring these Medicines takable by me. **1803** *Hist. Europe* in *Ann. Reg.* 21/1 In the last war we had taken every thing that was takeable. **1826** *Examiner* 772/1 Every take-able seat in the house had been taken. **1893** *Temple Bar Mag.* XCVII. 608 It is the only one takable, and I take it.

ˈtake-away, *sb.* and *a.* Also **Take-away, takeaway.** [f. vbl. phr. *to take away*: see TAKE *v.* 80.] **A.** *sb.* **1.** *U.S.* (See quot.) *rare.*

1931 *Amer. Speech* VII. 52 The train that takes the logs to the mill is the 'takeaway'.

2. *Golf.* The initial movement of the club at the beginning of a backswing.

1961 [see *lightning-quick* s.v. LIGHTNING 3 c]. **1976** *Sunday Mail* (Glasgow) 21 Nov. 39/5 Jack Nicklaus.. gives his advice today on another part of a good golf swing—the take-away.

3. A shop which sells take-away food (see sense 1 of the adj. below).

1970 *Cape Times* 28 Oct. 18/1 (Advt.), Are you interested in a take-away.. or supermarket? **1974** *Times* 7 Oct. 8/6 There is just as likely to be a chop suey bar or a chippy or a take-away in.. Bognor Regis.. as in any big city. **1976** J. FRASER *Who steals my Name?* xi. 134 [He] drove to the Chinese Take-Away on the outskirts. **1981** M. HARDWICK *Chinese Detective* xiv. 134 Proprietor of.. a small string of burger eateries and takeaways.

B. *adj.* **1.** That may be taken away; *spec.* designating cooked food sold to be eaten away from the premises of sale.

1964 *Punch* 15 Apr. 572/3 Posh Nosh.. was serving take-away venisonburgers. **1970** *Final Exam. Hons. Eng. Lang. & Lit.* (Univ. Newcastle upon Tyne) 1 (*heading*) Take-away paper. **1971** *Guardian* 27 Mar. 11/1 We sent out to the Chinese restaurant for a Chinese take-away curry. **1974** *Times* 7 Oct. 8/5 British people buy their take-away meals with convenient regularity. **1975** *Times* 18 Aug. 2/4 Second-class travellers will be able to buy a full meal on a take-away tray which will not slip off the tables in their saloons. **1976** *Nature* 18 Mar. 213/2 The takeaway message of the Dunbars' monograph is that superficially similar social systems may be the product of different behavioural arrangements. **1982** *London Rev. Bks.* IV. XXIV. 3/2 As a takeaway sample of what he had in mind, Alvarez contrasted the horses of Larkin's poem 'At Grass'.. with the 'urgent' horses of Ted Hughes's 'A Dream of Horses'.

2. Of, pertaining to, or characterized by the selling of cooked food to be taken away.

1971 *Guardian* 18 June 11/5 Every take-away pieshop and baker sell a Cornish pasty. **1973** *Times* 3 Feb. 13/5 Leslie's also do a take-away service. **1977** *N.Z. Herald* 5 Jan. 2–15/8 (Advt.), Takeaway bar. **1978** *Cornish Guardian* 27 Apr. 14/4 (Advt.), Lucrative beach café.. good take-away business, ice cream servery. **1981** B. Knox *Killing in Antiques* vii. 157 [They] made an expedition.. to the nearest Chinese take-away restaurant and brought back enough food.

take-in (ˈteɪkˌɪn), *sb.* (*a.*) *colloq.* [The verbal phrase *take in* used as sb. or adj.] An act of taking in (TAKE *v.* 84 o); a cheat, swindle, deception; a thing or person that takes one in, a 'fraud'.

1778 Miss Burney *Evelina* (1791) I. xxi. 105, I find it's as arrant a take-in as ever I met with. **1814** Jane Austen *Mansf. Park* v, What is this but a take in? **1818** *Blackw. Mag.* II. 398 There are.. at least twenty take-ins (as they are called) for one true heiress. **1858** Lytton *What will he do* I. xii, Comedians are such takes in.

b. *attrib.* or *adj.* That takes in; deceptive.

1819 *Metropolis* III. 119 Tales of a take-in match and a vicious mother-in-law.

takel, -ell, obs. forms of TACKLE.

Takelma (təˈkɛlmə), *sb.* and *a.* Also 9 **Takilma.** [ad. Takelma *dāᵃgelmâˀn* those dwelling along the river.] **A.** *sb.* **1.** A Penutian language (now extinct) of south-western Oregon. **2.** The North American Indian speakers of this language. **B.** *adj.* Designating this people or their language.

1882 *Mag. Amer. Hist.* Apr. 258 Phonetically, Takilma is more.. vocalic than Kúsa. **1891** J. W. Powell *Indian Linguistic Families* 121 The Takilma formerly dwelt in villages along upper Rogue River, Oregon... They are now included among the 'Rogue River Indians'. **1907** E. Sapir in *Jrnl. Amer. Folklore* Jan.–Mar. 33 The following notes regarding the ideas of the supernatural world held by the Takelma Indians were obtained.. from.. one of the very few full-blood survivors of the Takelmas. **1909** *Publ. Pennsylvania State Univ.: Anthropol.* II. i. 5 The Takelma language represents one of the distinct linguistic stocks of North America. It is.. a source of congratulations that enough of the folk-lore of the Takelmas could be obtained to enable one to assign these Indians a definite place in American mythology. **1912** E. Sapir (*title*) The Takelma language of southwestern Oregon. **1941** C. F. Voegelin in L. Spier et al. *Lang., Culture & Personality* 23 When Sapir studied Takelma in 1906 there were only a few speakers of the language remaining. **1965** *Canad. Jrnl. Linguistics* Spring 124 Some statement should also be made concerning languages for which no speakers were found... Inland, no.. Takelma, Molale, or Cayuse were found. **1974** *Encycl. Brit. Micropædia* VII. 859/2 Six of these [Penutian] languages—Costanoan, Cayuse, Molala, the Yakonan languages.. and Takelma—are extinct.

taken (ˈteɪk(ə)n), *ppl. a.* [pa. pple. of TAKE *v.*, where see Forms.]

a. In various senses corresponding to those of TAKE *v.*, q.v.

a **1340** Hampole *Psalter, Cant.* 522 þe lyknyng of takyn prysuns. **1535** Stewart *Cron. Scot.* III. 430 The tane men als the takaris did exceid. **1561** *Reg. Privy Council Scot.* I. 177 Greit partis of the takin gudis wer disponit in Argyle. **1659** Milton *Civ. Power* Wks. 1851 V. 331 If any man be offended at the conscientious liberty of another, it is a taken scandal not a given. **1742** Young *Nt. Th.* v. 987 Some.. stumble, and let fall the taken prize. **1831** Scott *Ct. Robt.* xxviii, Did not my heart throb in my bosom with all the agitation of a taken bird?

b. With adv. or advb. phr., as ***taken-for-granted, taken-in, taken-on,*** etc.: see TAKE *v.*

a **1586** Sidney *Arcadia* III. (1622) 377 Keeping still her late taken-on grauitie. **1585–7** T. Rogers *39 Art.* (Parker Soc.) 186 Our liturgies.. they call foolishness of taken-on services. **1895** G. B. Shaw in *Liberty* 27 July 2/1 The Impressionist movement.. was evidently destined to improve pictures greatly by substituting a natural, observant, real style for a conventional, taken-for-granted, ideal one. **1901** *Daily Chron.* 24 Dec. 7/1 The bitter cry of the average taken-in tenant, emitted from a chilly residence, mean in furniture. **1907** *Morn. Post* 12 Aug. 2/3 Many of our taken-for-granted notions are seen to be meaningless.

taken, OE. and obs. northern f. TOKEN.

'take-note. A licence empowering the holder to explore for gold in a defined district.

1889 *Daily News* 18 July 7/1 The cost of the take-note amounted altogether to 5*l.* It gave the licensee the right to explore for gold in a certain area for one year. **1895** *Westm. Gaz.* 4 Nov. 6/1 (Gold found in Wales) 'Take notes' of various areas have been secured.

take-off (ˈteɪkˌɒf, -ɔː-), *sb.* and *a.* Also **takeoff.** [The verbal phrase *take off* (see TAKE *v.* 85) used as sb. or adj.]

A. *sb.* **1.** A thing that 'takes off' or detracts from something (see TAKE *v.* 85 k); a drawback.

1826 Miss Mitford *Village* Ser. II. 214 (*French Emigrants*) Notwithstanding these take-offs, our good duchess had still the air of a lady of rank. **1868** Ld. R. Gower *Remin.* (1883) I. xvi. 304 The only take-off to being perfectly happy is the state of my dearest mother's health.

2. An act of 'taking off' or mimicking (see TAKE *v.* 85 j); a mimic; a caricature. *colloq.* Freq. in literary or theatrical use, a skit or parody. Const. *of* or (chiefly *U.S.*) *on.*

1846 *Knickerbocker* XXVII. 457 Whittier will smile at the following 'take-off' of his spirited 'Songs of Labor'. **1855** Robinson *Whitby Gloss.*, A *tak off*, a descriptive burlesque... A mimic, or satirical person. **1884** G. H. Boughton in *Harper's Mag.* Sept. 526/1 He trotted beside the car.., roaring with glee at his 'take off'. **1930** C. Wittke *Tambo & Bones* iv. 157 The take-offs on theatrical stars.. often displayed rare powers of mimicry. **1951** *Manch. Guardian Weekly* 4 Jan. 15/4 Finely written take-off on New York theatre society. **1967** J. Philip et al. *Best of Granta* II. 103 A favourite ploy was to devote a whole issue to a take-off of a national magazine. **1976** *New Yorker* 15 Nov. 4/2 This musical, with the indicated twist, is a foolish takeoff on foolish musicals of the thirties. **1983** *Listener* 30 June 14/3 As well as being a take-off of Italian opera.. *The Beggar's Opera* is a parody of the pastoral mode.

3. a. The act of 'taking off', or springing from the ground, in leaping (see TAKE *v.* 85 n (*b*)); usually *transf.* a place or spot from which one takes or may take off. Also *fig.*

1869 Blackmore *Lorna D.* x, Is she able to leap sir? There is a good take-off on this side of the brook. **1887** M. Shearman *Athletics & Football* v. 153 If the 'take-off' is.. so slippery as to make the jumper nervous of falling, he may.. jump into the bar instead of over it. **1889** *Boy's Own Paper* 7 Sept. 780/3 It.. also encourages the habit of judging the take-off with accuracy. **1904** R. Thomas *Swimming* (ed. 2) 50 *Takeoff*, the board, side of bath or any standing place whether free from spring or not, from which a leap, header, feet first or other spring into water is made or taken. *Ibid.* 409/2 The one 'ready to dive' should have his feet over the edge of the takeoff. **1905** *Westm. Gaz.* 15 May 4/1 The true basis of offensive strategy is to ensure a sound 'take-off'. **1906** *Ibid.* 27 Aug. 4/1 The Great Western adopted Milford Haven as the 'take-off' for its service of steamers to Ireland. **1920** Naylor & Temple *Mod. Physical Educ.* 189 The 'take-off' may be made from one foot. **1951** *Times* 3 Jan. 4/5 Search the rinks of today for a take-off of beauty such as that of Bernard Adams.. and you seek in vain. **1951** *Swimming* (E.S.S.A.) iii. 49 The take-off in the back-crawl is immediate, since there is no over-balancing to contend with as in the front-crawl or the breast-stroke. **1977** *Arab Times* 14 Dec. 10/3 Both high and long jump events were noticeable for their absence of the basic essentials; in the former, jumpers threw themselves at the bar with gay abandon without the slightest modicum of lift at take-off.

b. *Aeronaut.* The act of becoming airborne (see TAKE *v.* 85 n (*d*)). Also *transf.*

1904 *Aeronaut. Jrnl.* VIII. 56/1 The incline is one in two, the lower end forming a curve... The 'take-off' is on an upward incline of one in ten. **1914** in C. F. S. Gamble *Story North Sea Air Station* (1928) 70 That take-off of his was worth going a long way to see. **1918** in *Ibid.* xx. 353 The boat.. taxied slowly along the water until the desired position for the 'take-off' was reached. **1929** *Sat. Even. Post* 14 Dec. 13/2 A group of news camera-men were setting up to catch the take-off of the seaplane. **1942** [see BRIEFING *vbl. sb.* 2]. **1951** [see BLAST-OFF]. **1966** *Electronics* 17 Oct. 107 Lengthy preflight tests increase the probability that the equipment will fail before takeoff. **1974** *Daily Colonist* (Victoria, B.C.) 28 Dec. 4/3 When the [hydrofoil] boat rises on its struts, it is called 'take-off'. **1977** D. Anthony *Stud Game* xii. 69, I have a witness who says you couldn't have made the aeroplane ride... Grant's take-off that night is a matter of record.

4. *Croquet.* A stroke made from contact with another ball so as to send one's own ball nearly or quite in the direction of aim, the other ball being moved only slightly or not at all.

1874 J. D. Heath *Croquet-Player* 39 This is a take-off, and a sharp tap is made. The direction C, in which the mallet is aimed, has approached very near to B, the direction to be taken by the striker's ball Y. *Ibid.* 57 When the latter either is likely to miss his partner, or will have a long take-off to separate you.

5. *fig.* The act of starting off (on a journey, etc.); a departure.

1928 H. Crane *Let.* Dec. (1965) 332 [I] think I'm going to like London entirely too well for an early take-off to Spain. **1965** J. Pollard *Surfrider* ii. 20 Another thing you have to watch is the 'late take-off', catching a wave at the last minute as it begins to break. **1973** *Black Panther* 13 Oct. 17/1 The little green Fiat conveniently parked on the corner for what was to have been a speedy take-off.

6. *fig.* The beginning of (a new phase of accelerated or increased) growth or development. *spec.* in *Econ.*

1953 W. W. Rostow *Process Econ. Growth* i. 17 The term 'take-off' is here used to describe the transition of a society from a preponderantly agricultural to an industrialized basis, or, more generally, a sustained rate of increase in output *per capita.* **1957** *Listener* 10 Oct. 554/2 Development capital and trading conditions which facilitate their take-off into industrialisation. **1964** M. McLuhan *Understanding Media* (1967) II. xiv. 147 'Backward' countries take a long time to reach economic 'take-off'. **1973** *Daily Tel.* 26 Feb. 17/6 The long-expected take-off in the sale of telephone facsimile machines will not happen before next year at the earliest. **1979** *Dædalus* Spring 1 In a country like France, where the postwar 'take-off' was particularly painful.

7. See *power take-off* s.v. POWER *sb.*[1] 18 f.

B. *attrib.* or *adj.* **1. a.** From which one 'takes off' or makes the spring in leaping: cf. A. 3.

1889 *Boy's Own Paper* 7 Sept. 780/3 The ground on the further side of the take-off line. **1896** *Harper's Mag.* Apr. 731 It was a species of hurdle-racing, with the softest of take-off and landing sides [snow].

b. In sense 3 b of the *sb.*, as ***take-off area, run, speed,*** etc.

1943 *Yank* 16 July 10 The planes.. proceed down the roadway to the take-off strip. **1958** *Chambers's Techn. Dict.* Add. 1019/1 *Take-off rocket*, a rocket, usually jettisonable, used to assist the acceleration of an aeroplane. **1958** [see RIGHT OF WAY 3 a]. **1960** *Guide to Civil Land Aerodrome Lighting* (B.S.I.) 7 *Take-off area*, an area on the ground of specified dimensions which abuts the end of a strip. **1968** Takeoff area [see *sand-bar* s.v. SAND *sb.*[2] 10 a]. **1969** *New Yorker* 12 Apr. 100/2 The experiments, after they are set up, will be out of range of the blast of the LM's takeoff rocket. **1973** D. Kyle *Raft of Swords* (1974) II. xv. 162 He made take-off speed bumping disconcertingly. **1976** P. Cave *High Flying Birds* iii. 37 Before strapping in, I walked to the edge of the take-off area and cast my eyes around for any possible snags. **1981** C. Potok *Bk. of Lights* (1982) v. 129 They landed in late afternoon... As they walked, a huge aircraft went into its takeoff run.

c. Of or pertaining to a starting-point or point of development, increase, etc. Cf. senses 5, 6 of the sb.

1947 *Radiology* XLIX. 304/2 Prior to death, the heart may be injured, as shown by a lowering of the take-off level of the T-wave. **1962** M. McLuhan *Gutenberg Galaxy* 79 The great medieval invention of typography that was the 'take-off' moment into the new spaces of the modern world. **1962** E. Snow *Other Side of River* (1963) xxiii. 172 By 1962 natural catastrophes and disastrous mistakes in take-off phases of the communes had cruelly combined to expose fantastic overclaims for agricultural output in 1958. **1965** J. A. Michener *Source* (1966) 840 At eight o'clock all units were in take-off position. **1968** B. Magee *Aspects of Wagner* i. 21 This combination of poetry and symphony that provided the take-off point for Wagner. **1974** *Times* 21 Jan. 6/2 Nineteen sixty-six was the take-off year for population.

2. a. Applied to a part of mechanism for taking something off. Also used of an appliance which removes something. ***take-off board***: see quots.

1896 *British Printer* 138 The sheets should not be allowed to accumulate on the take-off board. **1907** *Cambr. Mod. Hist. Prospectus* 97 So soon as the whole sheet is clear of the take-off drum, flyers.. waft the sheet through a semi-circular arc, and drop it on to the take-off board.. fixed at the end of the press opposite that from which the sheet started. **1945** *Richmond* (Va.) *Times-Dispatch* 8 June 13 For hair-free and satin smooth legs, use take-off hair pads.

b. That may be taken off; designed to be readily put on and taken off.

1950 *N.Y. Times* 29 Nov. 42/6 (*heading*) Take-off attire for spring shown. Bathing suits, town costumes and evening gowns have parts to be removed. **1977** *Lancashire Life* Feb. 20/2 Minty (.. showing their latest range of suites with take-off covers).

'take-out, *a.* and *sb.* Also **take out, takeout.** [f. vbl. phr. *to take out*: TAKE *v.* 87.]

A. *adj.* **1.** Chiefly *N. Amer.* Designed or made to be taken out. **a.** Applied to a mechanical device that may be pulled or folded out as required.

1908 *Sears, Roebuck Catal.* 94 Our new model long body runabout... Very large, roomy seat, small take out seat in rear. **1982** *Motor* 3 July 55/1 A glass tilt or take-out sunroof.

b. Applied to prepared food sold for consumption elsewhere. Cf. TAKE-AWAY *a.* 1.

1968 *Globe & Mail* (Toronto) 17 Feb. 47/4 (Advt.), Soft ice cream and take out food. **1970** *Times* 29 Jan. 27/3 One of New York's finest restaurants will provide gourmet 'take-out' lunches for the hard-pressed executive. **1972** B. Garfield *Line of Succession* (1974) I. 73 Lunch in the office.. had been dreary with takeout food. **1975** *New Yorker* 21 July 83/2 Ken and Eve do a pretty good take-out-sandwich business at noon with people who work in the neighbourhood.

2. Of, pertaining to, or characterized by the sale of prepared food for consumption elsewhere. Cf. TAKE-AWAY *a.* 2. orig. *U.S.*

1941 J. M. Cain *Mildred Pierce* ix. 177 Pies she hoped to sell to the 'take-out' trade. **1947** *Sun* (Baltimore) 2 July 30/1 One chain of sandwich shops, which does a large volume of 'take out' business. **1962** *Advance* Mar. 7/1 If you deliver take-out orders for restaurants, the pay is $20 a week and two meals a day. **1970** *New Yorker* 15 Aug. 22/1 Dialogue overheard in the take-out line of a midtown coffee shop. **1972** J. Wambaugh *Blue Knight* (1973) xi. 183 He boxed some chicken.. for a take-out customer. **1975** *Times* 8 Feb. 7/1 Simple fish-and-chip shops with a take-out counter and a few tables. **1977** *Belfast Tel.* 17 Jan. 15/7 (Advt.), Capable person to organise and run Safari Take-Out Cafe.

3. *Bridge.* Designating a bid or call that takes the bidder's partner out (see TAKE *v.* 87 k); ***take-out double*** = *informatory double* s.v. INFORMATORY *a.* b.

1945 Phillips & Reese *How to play Bridge* 62 When a double is made for that reason it is called an 'informatory' or 'take-out' double. **1959** *Listener* 15 Jan. 146/2 A take-out bid might induce partner to bid too many diamonds. **1962** *Ibid.* 3 May 790/2 The take-out call. **1964** [see INFORMATORY *a.* b]. **1967** R. L. Frey et al. *Bridge Players' Encycl.* 298/2 Negative double, the original name for a take-out double, in general use from 1915 to 1930, about which time the term 'informatory' became current. **1972** *Times* 23 Sept. 9/4 East read more in North's take-out double than in his partner's show of strength.

B. *sb.* **1.** *Bridge.* An act of taking out (see TAKE *v.* 87 k).

1917 E. Bergholt *Royal Auction Bridge* (1918) 88 The 'weakness take-out' or 'rescue' is obligatory in all suits, but the 'strength take-out' only in hearts or spades. **1927** [see DENIAL 6]. **1945** Phillips & Reese *How to play Bridge* 62 If partner has not spoken, or has simply passed, a double of One or Two of a suit is for a take-out. **1962** *Times* 14 Nov. 17/2 The Double which may be either for a penalty or a take-out. **1977** *Times* 10 Dec. 13/4 Opponents double for a take-out whenever they can afford the risk.

2. *U.S.* A tax deducted from winnings on a horse-race.

1946 *Sun* (Baltimore) 18 Aug. 8/3 In some states as much as twelve per cent is deducted from every dollar won to cover breakage, track takeout and state and Government taxes. **1954** *Ibid.* 17 Feb. 20/5 With the present 10-cent take-out Maryland mile tracks are producing the highest revenue in proportion to the population in the area of any state in the nation. **1971** L. Koppett *N.Y. Times Guide Spectator Sports* x. 183 There is a 'take-out'—a tax—that is removed from the pool before winnings are returned. **1978** *N.Y. Times* 30 Mar. D17/4 Plans to reduce the parimutuel takeout at New York Racing Association tracks.

3. In *Bowls*, the knocking of an opponent's wood away from the jack; in *Curling*, the striking of an opponent's stone out of play.

1959 *Times* 19 Aug. 4/5 Either by direct scoring, or through judicious take-outs, he swung the outcome by 15 shots on six of the seven ends. **1961** J. S. SALAK *Dict. Amer. Sports* 441 *Take out* (curling), striking a stone hard enough to remove it from rings. **1962** *Times* 16 Aug. 3/5 A. R. Allen ..successfully essayed take-outs of varying strengths. **1964** [see CANUCK].

4. *U.S.* A special article in a newspaper or journal printed without a break in successive columns or pages so that it can be easily removed.

1961 in WEBSTER. **1980** COLLINS & LAPIERRE *Fifth Horseman* I. 37 When..doing a major take-out on violent crime in the city. **1981** B. GRANGER *Schism* xv. 135 The phenomenon is the story here. UPI already has quite a long takeout on it.

5. A shop selling prepared food or drink for consumption away from the premises. Cf. TAKE-AWAY *sb.* 3. orig. and chiefly *N. Amer.*

1970 *Globe & Mail* (Toronto) 25 Sept. 36/7 (Advt.), Chicken takeout and snack bar, close to city. **1972** *Even. Telegram* (St. John's, Newfoundland) 29 June 22/6 (Advt.), Commercial site. Formerly used as a Pizza Take-Out. **1972** *Guardian* 5 Sept. 17/6 Pizza parlours in Paddington and chop-suey 'takeouts' in Chorlton-cum-Hardy. **1978** *Detroit Free Press* 16 Apr. F 8/10 (Advt.), Bar & Grill. Liquor, beer & wine takeout.

'take-over. orig. *U.S.* Also **take over, takeover.** [f. vbl. phr. *to take over*: see TAKE *v.* 90.]

1. An act of taking over (see TAKE *v.* 90 b). Also, that which is adopted or transferred.

1917 *Acts State New Jersey* xiv. 33 *Take Over*, the action by the department in assuming the control and maintenance of any part or parts of the State Highway System. **1921** W. S. CHURCHILL *Let.* 1 June in M. Gilbert *Winston S. Churchill* (1977) IV. Compan. III. 1489 The whole principle of the 'take over' was to show the actual net cost of Mesopotamia in one vote. **1928** *Amer. Jrnl. Psychiatry* VII. 885 The accessory left ear movement may be a takeover of the same activity during nursing. **1930** J. B. PRIESTLEY *Good Compan.* III. i. 479 They want four thousand, lock, stock, and barrel, except the usual take-overs. **1932** M. JOYNT tr. *Gougaud's Christianity in Celtic Lands* iii. 63 A direct take over of the monastic doctrines of the East. **1946** *Sun* (Baltimore) 10 Aug. 4/7 Special consideration was being given to the planning of a smooth take-over of UNRA facilities. **1954** *Newsweek* 11 Oct. 66/1 A solid hour without the relief of a teammate's take-over..seemed..a strain at times. **1964** M. MCLUHAN *Understanding Media* (1967) I. v. 64 Joyce's Bloom is a deliberate takeover from [Charlie] Chaplin. **1968** *Times* 16 Dec. 7/1 An attempt at a Ministry take-over and a threat to a much valued independence. **1980** *News & Observer* (Raleigh, N. Carolina) 28 Oct. WA-5/8, 3 bedrooms, $1\frac{1}{2}$ baths, good loan takeover, nice patio overlooking woods.

2. A (usu. forcible) assumption of power or government; a military coup.

1957 *Economist* 28 Sept. 1023/2 The change in military personnel in Syria has not been followed yet by any complete communist take-over. **1966** *Listener* 10 Mar. 339/1 It is just over a week since the military take-over in Ghana and the dismissal of Dr Nkrumah. **1977** *Arab Times* 14 Dec. 3/1 The black takeover in Zambia. **1980** *Sunday Times* 21 Sept. 18/1 The military takeover in Turkey nine days ago.

3. *Econ.* The assumption of control or ownership of a business concern by another company, esp. by the acquisition of the majority of its shares, either by agreement or after a take-over bid.

1958 BULL & VICE *Bid for Power* 13 A take-over is intelligible only in the light of subsequent developments. **1959** *Punch* 16 Sept. 177/2 A surge of sentiment for Harrods has set in since the Fraser take-over. *a* **1974** R. CROSSMAN *Diaries* (1976) II. 201 This afternoon Tony Wedgwood Benn made a Statement on the Chrysler take-over of Rootes. **1980** D. WILLIAMS *Murder for Treasure* xvi. 156 The alarms and excursions that could attend the last stages of a take-over.

4. a. *attrib.*, as ***take-over activity, battle, plan,*** etc.

1946 *Sun* (Baltimore) 25 Sept. 12/1 I am giving this 'take-over' plan the pitiless publicity it deserves. **1948** *Times* 13 Mar. 7/2 The discount on the shares narrowed slightly to $2\frac{1}{2}$ per cent. to 2 per cent. below take-over values. **1954** R. SUTCLIFF *Eagle of Ninth* i. 11 After the formal take-over ceremony in the forum, the old garrison marched out. **1957** *Economist* 28 Dec. 1150/2 This is a legitimate dramatic view of a takeover struggle. **1972** *Accountant* 17 Aug. 211/1 Take-over activity serves a dual purpose. **1981** *Times* 13 Oct. 16/4 Takeover fever produced some bright spots in banks.

b. Special Comb.: **take-over bid**, an attempt or offer to gain a controlling interest in a business concern sufficient to take it over (TAKE *v.* 90 b); also *transf.* and *fig.*; hence **take-over bidder.**

1953 *Times* 10 Nov. 5/9 A certain type of financial operation described in general terms by Lord Hacking—the recent epidemic of 'take-over bids'. **1959** *Listener* 24 Sept. 501/1 The take-over bid [for the television audience] was made by A.B.C. who put back their usual production time by an hour. **1965** E. F. RUSSELL *Somewhere a Voice* 88, I could make a takeover bid for the chief of police and preside over the search for myself. **1979** L. MEYNELL *Hooky & Villainous Chauffeur* ii. 27 A whole series of trusts, transfers, holding companies and take-over bids had put him close to his million [pounds]. **1982** *Times Lit. Suppl.* 19 Nov. 1281 There is, after all, no limit to the potential fissiparity of national feeling in a world where the United Nations exists to discourage takeover bids. **1958** *Punch* 27 Aug. 287/1 The voice of the take-over bidder has recently been heard loud, clear and sometimes discordant over the market. **1966** *Observer* 13 Nov. 7/6 With take-over bidders out in force last week, the stock market had more excitement than for some time past.

taker ('teɪkə(r)). Also 4–6 *Sc.* **takar** (5 **-are**, 6 **taikar, takkar**); 6 **takere, tacker.** [f. TAKE *v.* + -ER[1].] One who or that which takes.

1. One who takes, in various senses of the verb.

1486 *Act 3 Hen. VII*, c. 2 Where Wymmen..been oft tymes taken by mysdoers [etc.] and after maried to such mysdoers..Such mysdoers, takers, and procurators to the same [etc.]. **1514** in *Eng. Hist. Rev.* (1900) XV. 450 The payne sessed as well to the Taker as to the gever. **1552** ABP. HAMILTON *Catech.* (1884) 11 Takaris of ouir mekil mail or farme, to the herschipe of the tenentis. **1579–80** NORTH *Plutarch* (1676) 203 We read of Alcibiades, that he was a great taker, and would be corrupted with Money. **1602** MARSTON *Ant. & Mel.* I. Wks. 1856 I. 13 A great tobacco taker too. **1615** G. SANDYS *Trav.* 66 The Turkes are also incredible takers of Opium. **1737** CHAMBERLAYNE *St. Gt. Brit.* (ed. 33) II. 93 Layers and takers of paper on and from the rolling-presses. **1875** JOWETT *Plato* (ed. 2) I. 101 The best taker to pieces of words of this sort. **1885** *Law Times* 7 Feb. 266/1 The taker of a railway ticket must know what is on the face of it.

2. *spec.* †a. One who takes another into his protection, etc.: cf. TAKE *v.* 14. *Obs.*

a **1325** *Prose Psalter* xlv[i]. 7 þe Lord of vertuz ys wyþ vs; our taker [Vulg. *susceptor*] ys God of Jacob. *Ibid.* liii[i]. 4 Our Lord is taker of my soule.

b. One who captures or seizes; a captor, seizer, catcher, apprehender: cf. TAKE *v.* 2.

c **1375** *Sc. Leg. Saints* xxxi. (*Eugenia*) 512 [A lynx] Quhen hir qwhelpis are tan hir fra, To chas þe takaris, þaim to sla. **1454** *Cal. Anc. Rec. Dublin* (1889) 281 Halfe of that ransom to the takerys, and the othir halfe to the courte. *c* **1511** *1st Eng. Bk. Amer.* (Arb.) Introd. 35/1 They be good takers of fysshe. **1611** SPEED *Hist. Gt. Brit.* IX. xv. (1623) 785 The King..had promised a thousand marks to his taker. *c* **1650** DENHAM *Old Age* 196 Takers of cities, conquerors in war. **1807** G. CHALMERS *Caledonia* I. III. iv. 451 A searcher, and taker of thieves, and limmers. **1884** I. BLIGH in *Lillywhite's Cricket Ann.* 7 Principal takers of wickets.

†c. An officer who took or exacted supplies of necessaries for the sovereign: = PURVEYOR 3. *Obs.*

1444 *Rolls of Parlt.* V. 115/1 That no man of this Roialme have Takers but oonlye the Kyng and the Quene. **1519** *Interl. Four Elements* in Hazl. *Dodsley* I. 24 As for capons ye can get none, The king's taker took up each one. **1596** NASHE *Saffron Walden* 62 Let all the droppings of my pen bee seazed vpon by the Queenes Takers for Tarre to dresse ships with. **1619** DALTON *Countrey Just.* xliv. (1630) 103 Offences of Purveyors, Takers,..or other ministers for the King's Majestie.

d. One who takes something from another by force or wrongfully; a robber, thief, plunderer, pilferer; hence, a literary plunderer, a plagiarist. *Obs.* or merged in the general sense.

1500–20 DUNBAR *Poems* xvii. 43 Grit men for taking and oppressioun Ar sett full famous at the Sessioun, And peur takaris ar hangit hie. **1561** T. NORTON *Calvin's Inst.* Pref., As euell as a violent taker or (if you will) a robber. **1609** ROWLANDS *Dr. Merrie-man* 3 Sirrah sayes one, stand, and your Purse deliuer; I am a taker, thou must be a giuer. **1687** M. CLIFFORD *Notes Dryden* ii. 6 Pray hear what Famianus Strada says of such Takers as Mr. Dryden. **1818** SCOTT *Hrt. Midl.* xxix, Robin Hood's dead and gwone, but there be takers yet in the vale of Bever.

e. (*a*) One who takes possession, esp. of land: often with *first* or *next*.

1766 BLACKSTONE *Comm.* II. i. 9 Property, both in lands and moveables, being thus originally acquired by the first taker,..it remains in him, by the principles of universal law, till such time as he does some other act which shews an intention to abandon it. *Ibid.* xviii. 275 The next taker is entitled to enter regularly. **1884** SIR J. W. CHITTY in *Law Rep. 26 Chanc. Div.* 548 The absolute interest which the sixth Earl, as first taker, acquired.

(*b*) One who takes a lease of a farm, a mine, etc.; a lessee or tenant.

1778 PRYCE *Min. Cornub.* 183 When the adventurers thus set a Mine to a farm, they oblige the Taker or Tributor to keep the Mine in good repair. **1805** FORSYTH *Beauties Scotl.* I. 535 The takers grant bill with a surety for the rent.

(*c*) In *Derbyshire Lead Mines*, A miner who takes possession of a mere, after the 'founder' has taken his mere (cf. *taker-mere* in 4 b).

1601 *High Peak Art.* in Mander *Derbysh. Min. Gloss.* (1824) 130 Where any Miner doth take and possess any fresh ground.., and does work the same to the knowledge of any other, who before such takers aforesaid were or pretended to be possessed of the same ground as taker of a Forefield for an old founder. **1747** HOOSON *Miner's Dict.*, *Taker* [is] He that takes a Mear or Mears, from him that is the Founder; several Men may take one after another, if they think it may be worth their while, and then the Mears so taken go by some Name or other, as A's Taker Mear, or B's Taker Mear, or their second or third Taker Mear, to distinguish them from the Founders, and one Taker from another. **1753** CHAMBERS *Cycl. Supp.*, *Next taker*, among miners, is he that hath the next meer in possession.

f. One who accepts a bet. Also in extended use, one who accepts an offer, suggestion, etc.

1810 *Sporting Mag.* XXXV. 245 Two to one were offered ..but there were no takers. **1873** *Standard* 30 Sept., The betting gradually veered round with even money offered on W. Beckwith with no takers. **1897** 'MARK TWAIN' *Following Equator* xxxvii. 333 A youth staked out a claim and tried to sell half for £5; no takers. **1968** *Listener* 25 July 107/3 'If anybody fancies he's better off jumping, he'd better go now.' There were no takers. **1979** J. THOMSON *Deadly Relations* vi. 76 Whoever killed her must have..laid her down fairly carefully. Any takers so far?

g. *foreign taker*: a former officer of the City of London appointed to supervise some of the markets held in the open streets and to attend to their clearing up. *Obs.* exc. *Hist.*

c **1690** in Bohun *Privil. Lond.* (1723) 136 Richard Robinson the present Foreign taker and Yeoman of Newgate Market. **1720** STRYPE *Stow's Surv. Lond.* II. 398 Formerly, before the great Fire..there were these Officers, viz. a Serjeant and Yeoman of the Channel, and Yeoman of Newgate Market, and Foreign Taker, whose Office was to sweep and make clean the said Streets, where the Market People resorted, and to carry away the Soil thereof, and to furnish the Market People with Boards and such like Accommodations... But since Markets are removed out of the Streets..these Officers retain only the Names.

h. *Stock Exchange.* (See quot. 1979.)

1934, 1955 [see TAKE *v.* 84 q]. **1979** G. CUMMINGS *Investor's Guide to Stock Market* 104 *Taker/Taker-In*, a seller of shares previously paid for who is prepared to 'take-in' the shares and receive a rate under a contango instead of delivering in the normal way and receiving payment. Also a speculator who has sold short and is not able to cover his position by the end of the Stock Exchange account by making delivery, and who is ready to take a contango rate from a 'giver'.

†3. Applied to the nippers or claws of a scorpion, etc. *Obs.*

1608 TOPSELL *Serpents* (1658) 752 A flamant Scorpion.. hath tongs and takers very solid and strong, like the Gramnel or Crevish. **1688** R. HOLME *Armoury* II. 199/1.

4. *Comb.* a. With adverbs, forming compound agent-nouns corresponding to adverbial combinations of the verb (see TAKE *v.* 76–93), as ***taker-away, -down, -out,*** etc.: **taker-in**, one who takes in, in various senses (see TAKE *v.* 84); also, an apparatus which takes in or receives something, e.g. the cotton in a carding-machine (quot. 1879); **taker-off**, one who takes off, in various senses (see TAKE *v.* 85); also, an apparatus for taking something off, in a machine (cf. TAKE-OFF, B. 2); **taker-up**, one who or that which takes up, in various senses (see TAKE *v.* 93); *spec.* †(*a*) one who takes another under his charge or protection, a patron, guardian (*obs.*); †(*b*) one who 'raises' the psalm in church, a precentor (*Sc. obs.*); †(*c*) a member of a gang of swindlers: see quot. 1591[2] (*obs.*); (*d*) a purchaser or purveyor of commodities; (*e*) a receiver of money paid, as rent, etc.; (*f*) one who takes possession of an estate; (*g*) a labourer who gathers up the grass just mown; (*h*) something that occupies time, space, etc.

a **1804** W. GILPIN *Serm.* II. xxxvii. (R.), God..the giver, and *taker away of all earthly things. **1848** MRS. GASKELL *M. Barton* xxiii, The taker-away of life. **1836** T. HOOK *G. Gurney* I. 105 A practised *taker-in of credulous men. **1839** C. BRONTË in Mrs. Gaskell *Life* viii. (1857) 127 A straw-bonnet maker, or a taker-in of plain work. **1879** J. ROBERTSON in *Cassell's Techn. Educ.* IV. 273/2 Apart from the slight degree of combing..the only duty required of the 'taker-in' is indicated in its name. **1902** CUTCLIFFE HYNE *Thompson's Progr.* 70 'Who measured the pieces?' 'The taker-in'. **1911** [see TAKE *v.* 84 q]. **1928** *Morning Post* 19 Nov., The operation can be repeated as long as the client, the broker and the taker-in mutually consent. **1979** [see sense 2 h above]. **1825** J. NICHOLSON *Operat. Mechanic* 380 K is the doffer or *taker-off, having affixed to it the steel comb called the doffing-plate. **1830** G. COLMAN *Random Rec., Dr. Graham*, A spurious kind of imitation which may account for the number of takers-off at secondhand. **1888** J. SOUTHWARD in *Encycl. Brit.* XXIII. 706/1 The [printed] sheets are removed singly by an attendant called a taker-off, or by a mechanical automatic arrangement called a flyer. **1883** S. C. HALL *Retrospect* I. 255 A taker-off of peculiarities, he never sought to make a mock of deformity. **1388** WYCLIF *Ps.* xli[i]. 10 [9] Y schal seie to God: Thou art my *takere vp [Vulg. *susceptor*]. **1550** *Act 3 & 4 Edw. VI*, c. 16 § 10 Such childe to be vsed..to what labor..soeuer the said taker vp or M[r] or Maistres shall appointe him. **1578** in Spottiswood *Hist. Ch. Scot.* VI. (1677) 297 Takers up of Psalms, and other Officers of the Church. **1591** PERCIVALL *Sp. Dict.*, *Recogedor*, a gatherer, a taker vp, *collector, receptor*. **1591** GREENE *Disc. Coosnage* (1859) 8 Foure persons were required to performe their coosning commodity. The Taker up, the Verser, the Barnard, and the Butter... The Taker up seemeth a skilful man in al things, who hath by long travail learned..to insinuate himselfe into a man's acquaintance. **1603** *Eng. Mourn. Garm.* in *Select. fr. Harl. Misc.* (1793) 205 One of her own servants, a taker-up of provision. **1620** E. BLOUNT *Horæ Subs.* 120 It is..a taker vp of time that may be better disposed. **1622** MALYNES *Anc. Law-Merch.* 390 The Taker vp of the money at London, payeth for twelue pence the said marke of $13\frac{1}{2}$ pence, at two or three moneths Time in Scotland. *a* **1649** DRUMM. OF HAWTH. *Hist. Jas. III*, Wks. (1711) 50 Taker up of the rents of that earldom. **1715** *Maryland Laws* vi. (1723) 20 The said Commissioners..shall..invest the Taker up, and Builder.. with an Estate of Inheritance, in the said Lot. **1848** *Jrnl. R. Agric. Soc.* IX. II. 501 The takers-up follow the mower.

b. *attrib.* **taker-mere**, in *Derbysh. Lead-mines*, a 'mere' or portion of ground allotted to a 'taker' (2 e (*c*); cf. *founder-meer* s.v. FOUNDER *sb.*[5] 3).

1653 MANLOVE *Lead Mines* 46 But yet a difference may be taken clear, Betwixt a founder, and a taker meer. **1747** [see 2 e (*c*) above]. **1851** TAPPING *Gloss. to Manlove* s.v. *Meer*, A *taker meer* was the meer formerly allotted by custom to any person who chose to have one set out to him after those of the founder and farmer had been allotted.

take-up ('teɪkʌp), *sb.* (*a.*) [The verbal phrase *take up* (see TAKE *v.* 93) used as sb. or adj.] The act of taking up, or a contrivance for taking up.

1. The act of 'taking up' or drawing together the stuff so as to form 'gathers' in a dress; *concr.* one of such 'gathers'.

1825 JAMIESON, *Tak-up, Take-up*, the name given to a tuck in female dress. **1880** *Plain Hints Needlework* 19 The take-up of each gather should be..neatly done.

2. a. A device in a machine for tightening a band, rope, etc. **b.** A device in a sewing-machine for drawing the thread so as to tighten the stitch.

1877 KNIGHT *Dict. Mech.* 2483/2 The independent take-up is one which acts in its own time without being actuated by the needle-bar. **1888** *Sci. Amer.* 3 Mar. 138/2 A sewing machine, and a take up and tension for sewing machines, form the subject of three patents.

3. a. In a loom or other machine, the process of winding up the stuff already woven or treated; *concr.* the part of the mechanism by which this is done. Also *attrib.* or *adj.*, as in ***take-up motion***.

1850 *Rep. Comm. Patents 1849* (U.S.) 186 Improvement in the delivery and take-up motion of Looms. **1877** KNIGHT *Dict. Mech.* 2483/2 The let-off is the paying off of the yarn from the beam, and proceeds coincidently with the take-up. **1884** *Ibid.* Suppl., *Take Up Motion*.., a device for automatically winding the tissue on to the cloth beam.

b. *Cinematogr.* The apparatus for gathering up film after exposure in a projector or camera.

1915 B. E. JONES *Cinematograph Bk.* 162 The take-up or driving mechanism of the bottom spool. **1931** B. BROWN *Talking Pictures* 181 This is threaded through the projector ..and down to the take-up. **1940** *Chambers's Techn. Dict.* 832/2 *Take up, take up reel* (Cinema), the drive and the reel which is necessary to accept the cinematograph film after exposure in the gate of a camera or projector.

4. The part between the smoke-box and the bottom of the funnel of a marine engine boiler.

1838 *Civil Eng. & Arch. Jrnl.* I. 225/1 If the pressure continues..the water rises through the take-up into the fire, and extinguishes it. **1888** A. E. SEATON *Marine Eng.* (ed. 7) 365 The part between the smoke-box and funnel is called the 'uptake' or 'take-up'.

5. *Engin.* The action or process of taking up (see TAKE *v.* 93 f (*b*)).

1912 [see CLUTCH *sb.*[1] 6 a]. **1927** *Daily Tel.* 21 June 7 The clutch too is light in action and positive,..its 'take-up' is smooth and without jerk.

6. The acceptance of something offered; *spec.* the claiming of benefits provided by the Welfare State. Cf. TAKE *v.* 93 d (*a*).

1961 *Economist* 22 Apr. 347/3 Recent studies have suggested a similar social gradient in the use of certain infant welfare services and in the 'take-up' of welfare foods. **1971** *Times* 23 Jan. 18/5 The same low take-up has been shown to apply to free prescriptions. **1975** *Language for Life* (Dept. Educ. & Sci.) xxv. 371 The take-up of longer courses in our sample was very low. **1981** *Daily Tel.* 14 May 36/3 Mr Norman Buchan..put to his 'favourite social services minister'..that not one welfare benefit had 'a take-up' of more than 80 per cent.

7. *spec.* in *Finance*, the action of paying in cash for stock originally bought on margin.

1976 *Glasgow Herald* 26 Nov. 11/9 The market also faced repayment of moderate Bank of England loans.., Treasury Bill take-up, maturing local authority bills in official hands. **1979** *Irish Times* 28 Sept. 15/4 The market had a small net take-up of Treasury Bills to finance.

8. *attrib.*, as ***take-up lever, reel, spool***, etc.

1884 Take-up motion [see sense 3 a above]. **1904** *Dialect Notes* II. 391 *Take-up screw*,..a kind of screw for iron pull-rods or wire rope. **1927** T. WOODHOUSE *Artificial Silk* 123 Then the cloth goes over the emery take-up roller, and finally on to the cloth beam. **1931** B. BROWN *Talking Pictures* 133 Only one spool-carrying spindle is employed, which takes both feed and take-up spools side by side. **1940** Take-up reel [see sense 3 b above]. **1943** *Gloss. Terms Telecomm.* (*B.S.I.*) 85 *Take-up reel*, [on a fire-alarm] a clockwork driven reel, which maintains the tension and winds-up the tape released by the register. **1954** *Trans. IRE Audio* II. 15/1 The tape is fed over another non-rotating tape guide combined with a compliance arm and fed to the take-up reel. **1961** *Which?* Nov. 277 (*caption*) Take up lever. **1972** *Sci. Amer.* Jan. 8/3 The new camera takes the film in a direct line back to the take-up magazine, thus providing an instrument that has only one turn for the film. **1977** J. HEDGECOE *Photographer's Handbk.* 12 The cassette is loaded into a compartment, and film threaded across the back of the camera into a take-up spool. **1978** D. A. STANWOOD *Memory of Eva Ryker* I. xx. 191 The last of the seven hours of tape flipped onto the take-up reel of the recorder.

takhaar ('tɑːkhɑː(r)). *S. Afr.* Also **taakhaar, takhar**, and with capital initial. Pl. **-e** or **-s**. [Afrikaans, f. Du. *tak* branch + *haar* hair.]

A rustic or unsophisticated person (with derog. implication of unkempt appearance). Also *attrib.* or as *adj.* and in *transf.* use.

1899 *Graaff Reinet Advertiser* 20 Nov. (Pettman), There are several other poems, one of which urges the Takhaar Boers to 'Fight, fight, fight!' **1906** A. R. COLQUHOUN *Afrikander Land* 217 With the passing of the old *Taak haare* the little bit of picturesqueness will be gone. **1910** J. BUCHAN *Prester John* ii. 44 The place..gives the ordinary man the jumps... It may be the natives, or it may be the *taakhaars*, or it may be something else. **1931** T. J. HAARHOFF *Vergil in Exper. of S. Africa* 15 The early consuls were described as *capillati*, and the trekkers as *takhare*. **1931** *Times Lit. Suppl.* 3 Dec. 979/2 This motive leads him [*sc.* Haarhoff] to look for special points of resemblance..between the *capillati consules* and the *takhaar* Voortrekkers. **1942** S. CLOETE *Hill of Doves* xxvii. 378 A couple of Takhaars. Two backvelders who said I was a spy. **1971** *Rand Daily Mail* 25 May 11 Commentator X (well known for his scathing comments on British 'takhare'). **1972** *Het Suid-Western* 16 Mar. 2 A political meeting of takhare in the deep north.

‖**takht** (takt). [Pers.] A sofa or bed. So **takhtrawan** (also **taktrevan**) [*rawān* pres. pple. of *raftan* to proceed, travel], a litter or Sedan chair.

1786 S. HENLEY tr. *Beckford's Vathek* 97 Four of the most amiable, placed the Caliph, on a magnificent taktrevan. **1870** R. ANDERSON *Hist. Missions Amer. Board* III. xi. 171 Had not divine mercy stayed them just there, takhtrawan, bearers, and occupant would have been dashed down the precipice. **1979** V. L. PANDIT *Scope of Happiness* vi. 43 There were also low divans called *takhts* in the living rooms. **1981** S. RUSHDIE *Midnight's Children* I. 19 She sips fresh lime water, reclining on a takht.

takil, -ill, obs. Sc. forms of TACKLE.

Takilma, var. TAKELMA.

‖**takin** ('tɑːkɪn). [Native name in Mishmi.] A horned ruminant (*Budorcas taxicolor*) of south-eastern Tibet on the northern frontier of Assam.

1850 B. H. HODGKIN in *Jrnl. Asiat. Soc. Bengal* XIX. 65 The large, massive and remarkable animal, denominated Tákin by the Mishmis, and Kin by the Khamtis, is one of the group of Bovine Antelopes. **1893** LYDEKKER *Horns & Hoofs* iv. 142 No English sportsman has ever shot a takin. **1909** *Daily Chron.* 23 June 5/5 The Zoological Society has just received..a fine young example of the takin, which, next to the okapi, is the rarest and least known of the ruminants... Takins are heavily built and powerful animals, an adult male standing three and a half feet high at the shoulder.

takin, obs. Sc. form of TOKEN.

taking ('teɪkɪŋ), *vbl. sb.* [f. TAKE *v.* + -ING[1].]

I. Simple senses. * *The action or condition expressed by the verb* TAKE.

†**1.** Touching, touch: see TAKE *v.* 1. *Obs. rare.*

1340 [see TAKE *v.* 1].

2. a. Capture, seizure (in warfare, etc.); apprehension, arrest; catching (of fish or other animals): see TAKE *v.* 2, etc.

c **1330** R. BRUNNE *Chron.* (1810) 222 After þe takyng of Kilyngworth castelle. **1456** SIR G. HAYE *Law Arms* (S.T.S.) 53 He herd the newis..of his brothir taking. **1494** *Act 11 Hen. VII*, c. 23 The same herynges..shuld be of on tyme taking and salting. **1534** in *10th Rep. Hist. MSS. Comm.* App. v. 406 If the Kinges Bayleffe be present at the takinge of the same dettor. **1628** SIR S. D'EWES *Jrnl.* (1783) 43 Portsmouth (where he was imprisoned immediatelie upon his taking). **1748** *Anson's Voy.* III. viii. 370 The taking of the Manila galeon. **1869** TOZER *Highl. Turkey* II. 228 The taking of Adrianople by the Turks.

†**b.** A seizure or attack of disease, *esp.* a stroke of palsy or the like; also, enchantment; blasting, malignant influence: see TAKE *v.* 7, *sb.* 3. *Obs.*

1533 ELYOT *Cast. Helthe* (1541) 50 Palseys, called of the vulgare people, takynges. **1559** MORWYNG *Evonym.* 332 The same resisteth the taking, as they cal it, or inchantment. **1605** SHAKS. *Lear* III. iv. 61 Blisse thee from Whirle-Windes, Starre-blasting, and taking. **1639** T. DE GRAY *Compl. Horsem.* 69 The takings, sleeping-evill, madnesse, and the like.

3. a. The physical act of possessing oneself of anything, of receiving, accepting, and related senses: see TAKE *v.* 12, etc.

13.. *Cursor M.* 28578 (Cott.) þirkin sinnes..ar..for-giuen, Wit worthi taking o þe fode O godds aun fles and blode. *c* **1380** WYCLIF *Sel. Wks.* III. 345 Aftir takyng of þe Holi Goost. *c* **1460** FORTESCUE *Abs. & Lim. Mon.* xiii. (1885) 142 Wich maner off takynge is callid robbery. **1500–20** DUNBAR *Poems* xvii. 1, 5 Eftir geving I speik of taking... In taking sowld discretioun be. **1505** *Sel. Cas. Crt. Star Chamber* (Selden) 221 The Town of Glowcestre is fre of all customs and takynges at Worcestre aforeseide. **1526** *Pilgr. Perf.* (W. de W. 1531) 54 Be not dronken through ouermoche takyng of wyne. **1651** HOBBES *Leviath.* II. xxii. 122 A taking of the Sword out of the hand of the Soveraign. **1656** H. PHILLIPS *Purch. Patt.* (1676) 1 The letting and taking of Leases. **1660** WOOD *Life* Dec. (O.H.S.) I. 359 Their taking of notes at sermons. **1714** MANDEVILLE *Fab. Bees* (1725) I. 415 The taking of Snuff and smoaking of Tobacco. **1893** HODGES *Elem. Photogr.* (1907) 115 The taking of portraits. **1896** *Law Times* C. 408/1 The date of the taking of the census..was correctly stated.

b. Mental apprehension or perception (*obs.*); mental acceptance or reception; estimation.

1398 TREVISA *Barth. De P.R.* II. x. (1495) b vj b/1 God.. is aboue vnmateryall & aboue worldly takynge. **1568** in *Liturg. Serv. Q. Eliz.* (1847) 517 With pacient takinge and quiett acceptation of this syckness. *a* **1639** WHATELEY *Prototypes* I. xxi. 253 Manifested in his sorrowful taking of her death.

4. a. Condition, situation, state, plight (in unfavourable sense). Only in phr. *in*, †*at* (*a*) ***taking***, often with defining adj. *Obs.* exc. *Sc.*

1522 SKELTON *Why not to Court* 933 He is at suche takynge. **1542** UDALL *Erasm. Apoph.* 158 Wheras thou art in suche takyng, canst fynd in thyn herte to liue? **1592** LYLY *Midas* I. ii, These boyes be droonk! I would not be in your takings. **1635** R. BOLTON *Comf. Affl. Consc.* iii. (ed. 2) 15 In what a taking was Job. **1662–3** PEPYS *Diary* 12 Jan., The poor boy was in a pitiful taking and pickle. **1715** *Wodrow Corr.* (1843) I. 26 Persons, who have real scruples at oaths, are in a miserable taking. **1837** MRS. CARLYLE *Lett.* (1883) I. 65 We are all in sad taking with influenza.

b. *spec.* A disturbed or agitated state of mind; excited condition, passion. (Const. as in a.)

1577 HANMER *Anc. Eccl. Hist.* (1619) 317 Valens, vnderstanding of this, was in a sore taking. **1581** PETTIE tr. *Guazzo's Civ. Conv.* III. (1586) 159 b, Manie excellent and worthie men..comming before princes..haue plainely shewed in what troublesome taking they haue bene in. **1598** SHAKS. *Merry W.* III. iii. 191. **1676** ETHEREDGE *Man of Mode* III. iii, By this time your Mother is in a fine taking. **1797–8** JANE AUSTEN *Sense & Sens.* xxxvii, Lord! what a taking poor Mr. Edward will be in when he hears of it. **1874** T. HARDY *Madding Crowd* xxx, You must not notice my being in a taking just now.

** *That which is taken.*

5. a. That which is received or gained; *esp.* in *pl.*, the receipts or earnings of merchants, tradesmen, or workmen.

1632 MASSINGER *City Madam* II. i, Some needy shop-keeper who surveys His every-day takings. **1662** GURNALL *Chr. in Arm.* III. verse 18. I. lii. (1669) 417/2 To mend their takings in their shop. **1851** MAYHEW *Lond. Labour* I. 120/2 The weekly 'takings' of the ten thousand men and their families. **1885** G. DENMAN in *Law Rep. 29 Ch. Div.* 469 A charge upon the property, or the takings, or the profits of the concern.

b. That which is captured; *esp.* the fish or other animals caught at one time, a capture, a catch.

1809 MALKIN *Gil Blas* v. i. ¶67 Heyday! madam, your third husband dispatched already? You must be a most deadly taking. **1855** ROBINSON *Whitby Gloss.* s.v., 'A rare takking o' fish', a good catch, or a heavy haul.

c. *Printing.* = TAKE *sb.* 7.

1808 C. STOWER *Printer's Gram.* 467 When the companionship are ready for their first takings of copy. **1875** *Ure's Dict. Arts* III. 640 The MS...is then handed to a clicker, or foreman of a companionship, or certain number of compositors, each of whom has a taking of copy, or convenient portion of MS., given to him, to be set up in type.

II. Combinations.

6. With adv. or advb. phr., expressing the action of similar combinations of the verb in various senses (see TAKE *v.* 76–93): as ***taking away, back, down, for granted, in, off*** (also attrib., esp. in sense 85 n (*b*) of the verb), ***on*** (in quot. = undertaking, enterprise: cf. TAKE *v.* 86 d), ***out, over, up*** (in quot. 1683 *concr.* that which is taken up).

1382 WYCLIF *Isa.* xlii. 22 Thei ben maad in to raueyn,.. in to *taking awei [1388 in to rauyschyng]. **1617** HIERON *Wks.* II. 249 Those gifts..are lyable to taking away. **1629** W. BEDELL in *Ussher's Lett.* (1686) 402 Mr. Usher's sudden taking away,..admonishes me to work while the day lasts. **1487–8** *Durham Acc. Rolls* (Surtees) 651 Pro le *takyng-downe et le riddyng fundi dicti cancelli, xxiijs. iiijd. **1864** *Gd. Words* 317/2 One hour of taking down makes about six hours' work in copying. **1876** LOWELL *Among my Bks.* Ser. II. 174 A childlike simplicity and *taking-for-granted which win our confidence. **1879** CHR. G. ROSSETTI *Seek & F.* 248 Sloth, with its vicious allies of unpunctuality,..half measures, baseless taking for granted, guess-work. **1598** B. JONSON *Ev. Man in Hum.* III. i, The best leaguer that ever I beheld..except the *taking in of—what do you call it? **1603** KNOLLES *Hist. Turks* (1638) 184 Neither is this taking in of the country of Carasina to be accounted a small conquest. **1707** MORTIMER *Husb.* (1721) I. 27 Parcels of Land that would pay well for the taking in. **1902** E. BANKS *Newspaper Girl* 193 They prosper exceedingly and their takings-in at the end of the week are apt to be very large. **1983** *Sunday Tel.* 21 Aug. 11/8 Detection first determines a garment's original shape through successive takings-in and lettings-out. **1605** SHAKS. *Macb.* I. vii. 20 His Vertues Will pleade like Angels, Trumpet-tongu'd against The deepe damnation of his *taking off. **1683** MOXON *Mech. Exerc., Printing* xxii. ¶3 Having Destributed that Taking off he makes another Taking off as before. **1719** DE FOE *Crusoe* (1840) I. iv. 67 Thou art not worth..the taking off of the ground. **1755** *Connoisseur* No. 57 ¶3 Imitations of..well-known characters..to which they have given the appellation of taking-off. **1852** SURTEES *Sponge's Sp. Tour* ix, [The] horse..had scrambled out of the brook on the taking-off side. **1881** *Times* 14 Feb. 4/2 The taking off at the jumps was awkward, and the landing more ugly still. **1894** H. NISBET *Bush Girl's Rom.* 180 If a man or woman was to be spared it was..because their taking off was a waste of powder and lead. **1898** L. STEPHEN *Stud. of Biogr.* I. vii. 230 A mere taking-off place for a flight into the clouds. **1422** tr. *Secreta Secret., Priv. Priv.* 180 That tokenyth hardynesse of herte, grete *takynge on, and stowtesse. **1466** *Paston Lett.* II. 268 To the glaser for *takyn owte of ii. panys of the wyndows. **1924** R. MACAULAY *Orphan Island* xiii. 160 'If you have nothing to contribute, sir,' he whispered, 'kindly pass the plate, which is for puttings in, not takings out.' **1917** *Acts State New Jersey* xiv. 29 For any road in the State Highway System prior to its *taking over as a State Highway [etc.]. **1565** *Taking up [see TAKE *v.* 93 c (*b*)]. *a* **1649** DRUMM. OF HAWTH. *Declar.*, etc., Wks. (1711) 208 The treaty.. discharging all taking up of arms against the kingdom. **1683** MOXON *Mech. Exerc., Printing* xxii. ¶3 Now he has his Taking up in his Hand, with the Face of his Letter towards him. **1798** in Picton *L'pool Munic. Rec.* (1886) II. 224 A constant yearly taking up of money upon new bonds. **1841** *Civil Eng. & Arch. Jrnl.* IV. 318/1 Gearing for producing.. the 'taking-up' or 'traversing motion' of the plank during the operation of sawing.

7. Attributive Combs., as ***taking-day***; ***taking lens, -screen*** (see TAKE *v.* 33 b).

1836 R. FURNESS *Astrologer* I. Wks. (1858) 139 On Takin-days, when wit and ale were free. **1897** *Pop. Sc. Monthly* Nov. 138 The viewing [screens] differ from the taking screens. **1907** *Westm. Gaz.* 24 Aug. 14/2 This positive is then mounted in contact with a viewing-screen ruled in precisely the same way as the taking-screen. **1951** [see FINDER 3 d]. **1961** G. MILLERSON *Telev. Production* iii. 28 (*caption*) Small viewfinder kinescope showing TV picture (optically magnified) seen through taking lens. **1962** M. L. HASELGROVE *Photogr. Dict.* 187 *Taking lens*, the lower lens of a twin-reflex camera, which forms the image actually falling on the film.

'taking, *ppl. a.* [f. as prec. + -ING².] That takes, in various senses; see the verb.

1. Seizing, receiving; getting something into one's possession; rapacious. *rare.*

1483 *Cath. Angl.* 377/2 Takynge, *capax, accipiens, & cetera.* **1598** *Fam. Vict. Hen. V*, ii. 16, I dare not call him theefe, but sure he is one of these taking fellowes. **1835** *Court Mag.* VI. 168/2 There were taking men, who imposed upon him at pleasure; for he did not prosecute.

2. That takes the fancy or affection; captivating, engaging, alluring, fascinating, charming, attractive. (The most usual sense: now *colloq.*)

1605 B. JONSON *Volpone* I. i, That colour Shall make it much more taking. **1665** BOYLE *Occas. Refl.* VI. x. (1848) 376 He will ever consider the taking'st Notions he can frame of vertue, more as Engagements to it, than Arguments of it. *a* **1721** PRIOR *Songs* xv. 11 Phillis has such a taking way, She charms my very soul. **1757** FOOTE *Author* I. Wks. 1799 I. 137 You must provide me with three taking titles for these pamphlets. **1824** DIBDIN *Libr. Comp.* 771 The plates..are bright, spirited, and very 'taking'. **1882** PEBODY *Eng. Journalism* xix. 143 The secret of immediate success in a public writer is said to be mediocre ideas and a taking style.

3. Seizing or affecting injuriously; †blasting, pernicious (*obs.*); infectious, 'catching'. *rare.*

1605 SHAKS. *Lear* II. iv. 166 Strike her yong bones, You taking Ayres, with Lamenesse. *a* **1620** FLETCHER & MASSINGER *False One* IV. iii, I am yet too taking for your company. **1636** FEATLY *Clavis Myst.* xvii. 220 The diseases of the mind are more taking than the diseases of the body.

4. With adverbs, as ***taking-away, -in, -off***, etc.: see TAKE *v.* 76–93. (Here often blending with the vbl. sb.)

1530 PALSGR. 279/1 Takyng away, *ablatif.* **1841** SAVAGE *Dict. Printing* 791 Boys are employed in machine printing to take away the sheets as they are printed..; this is also styled Taking-off, and the boys taking-off boys. **1882** *Worc. Exhib. Catal.* iii. 38 Printing Machine with..automatic taking-off apparatus. **1884** SOUTHWARD *Pract. Printing* 462 When printed,..[the sheets] are deposited in a pile on the taking-off board. **1886** J. PATON in *Encycl. Brit.* XX. 845/1 The twisted twine is drawn off..and is wound on taking-up bobbins.

Hence **'takingly** *adv.*, in a taking manner; engagingly, alluringly, attractively; **'takingness**, taking quality or character, engagingness, alluringness, attractiveness.

1607 BEAUMONT *Woman Hater* IV. ii, I will gather my self together with my best phrases, and so I shall discourse in some sort *takingly. **1681** FLAVEL *Meth. Grace* xxix. 510 This will represent religion very beautifully and takingly to such as are yet strangers to it. *a* **1711** KEN *Psyche* Poet. Wks. 1721 IV. 161 Verse, by which Lust is takingly instill'd. **1656** *Artif. Handsom.* 41 Outward adornings..have something in them of a complaisance and *takingnesse. **1890** J. H. STIRLING *Philos. & Theol.* i. 18 A simple takingness that is divine.

Taki-Taki: see TALKEE-TALKEE I.

takk, takke, obs. forms of TACK *sb.*¹, ², *v.*¹

takkie, var. TACKIE.

takle, takul(l, -yl(l, obs. forms of TACKLE.

taknyn, -ys, -yt, etc.: see TOKEN *v.*

takovite ('tækəʊvaɪt). *Min.* [ad. Serbo-Croat *takovit* (Z. Maksimović 1957, in *Zapisnici Srpskog Geol. Društva za 1955 God.* 219), f. *Tàkovo*, name of a place in Serbia: see -ITE¹.] A bluish green clay-like mineral that is a rhombohedral hydrated basic aluminate and carbonate of nickel.

1957 *Zapisnici Srpskog Geol. Društva za 1955 God.* 224 (*heading*) Takovite, hydrous nickel aluminate, a new mineral... This occurs in Takovo, Serbia, on the contact of limestone and metamorphosed serpentinite. **1977** *Amer. Mineralogist* LXII. 463/1 The formula of the Australian takovite, for which only kaolinite is a significant impurity, is established with greater certainty.

Takulli (tə'kʌlɪ). Also 9 Tacully, Takali, etc. [a. Carrier *dakelne* (pl. of *dakeł*) Carriers, Indians; lit. 'people who go by boat on the water.'] A name for the Carrier Indians of British Columbia: at first used only for the eastern Carrier, but later extended to include the Babine Indians of Babine Lake and the Bulkley River.

1820, etc. [see CARRIER 2 b]. **1846** H. HALE *Ethnol. & Philol.* 201 The country of the *Tahkali* (or Tacullies) includes the region north of the Oregon Territory, termed by the English New Caledonia. **1932** D. JENNESS *Indians of Canada* xxii. 363 The Carrier..had no common name for themselves, only names for the independent sub-tribes into which they were divided. In the nineteenth century, however, they adopted for themselves the obscure title Takulli, bestowed on them apparently by Europeans. **1974** *Encycl. Brit. Micropædia* II. 590/3 They [*sc.* the Carrier] also assumed the name of Takulli (People Who Go Upon the Water), a name of obscure origin.

taky ('teɪkɪ), *a. colloq.* [f. TAKE *v.* (sense 10) + -Y: cf. *shaky*.] = TAKING *ppl. a.* 2.

1854 W. COLLINS *Hide & Seek* I. ix, Those two difficult and delicate operations in art, technically described as 'putting in taky touches, and bringing out bits of effect'.

takyn, -yng, obs. forms of TOKEN.

takyr ('tɑːkɪə(r)). Also **takir**. [a. Turki, Chagatai *takir* f. *tak* smooth.] In Russian Central Asia, any of the wide expanses of clay which are covered with water in the spring and are dry in summer.

1864 A. VÁMBÉRY *Trav. Central Asia* 91 By degrees the sand disappeared, and about midnight we had so firm a clayey soil under us, that the regulated tread of the distant camels echoed as if some one was beating time in the still night. The Turkomans name such spots Takir. **1902** *Encycl. Brit.* XXIII. 511/2 Large areas amidst the sands are occupied by *takyrs.* **1961** L. D. STAMP *Gloss. Geogr. Terms* 444/2 *Takyr*.., area of barren alkaline soil with heavy unstructural clay soil.

tal, obs. f. TALE, TALL.

‖**tala** ('tɑːlə). *Indian Mus.* Also **tal**. [Skr. *tāla*, Hindi *tāl* hand-clapping, musical time.] Musical time or rhythm; one of a series of traditional metrical patterns.

1891 [see JATI, JĀTI]. **1921** [see DHRUPAD]. **1927** *Grove's Dict. Mus.* (ed. 3) II. 704/2 The principle of the time-units within the bar follows the varieties of prosodic feet. These are of one, two, three or four syllables, and the times (*tāl*) are decided by the number of units (*mātra*) in each syllable (*akshara*) or beat (*tāi*). **1961** '*Gramophone*' *Long Playing Classical Record Catal.* Sept. 212/2 *Indian Music..Ragas and Talas.* Indian Instrumentalists. **1967** SINGHA & MASSEY *Indian Dances* v. 65 While the musicians play the syllabic beats, the dancer executes patterns within the tal or time-measure (pronounced 'taal'). **1977** Y. MENUHIN *Unfinished Journey* xii. 258 The *tala* is the rhythm. Dozens exist.

talagalla, var. TALEGALLA.

Talaing (tə'laɪŋ), *sb.* and *a.* Also 8–9 **Talain**; 9 **Talien**. [Native name.] = MON *sb.*² and *a.* Cf. PEGUAN *sb.* and *a.*

1798 F. BUCHANAN in *Asiatick Researches* V. 235 This people are named *Talain* by the *Burmas* and *Chinese* of *Yunan.* **1800** M. SYMES *Embassy to Ava* v. 183 He has abrogated some severe penal laws imposed by his predecessors upon the Taliens, or native Peguers. **1835** *Penny Cycl.* IV. 438/1 Here and there, on the immediate banks of the river, are a few villages of Talain fishermen. **1844** *Jrnl. Asiatic Soc. Bengal* XIII. 43 The city of Puggan was taken, the Talaings were overawed. **1854** *Jrnl. Amer. Oriental Soc.* IV. 282 In its vocables, the Talaing is the most isolated language in Farther India. **1881** C. J. F. S. FORBES *Compar. Gram. Lang. Further India* iv. 51 The British province of Pegu, representing the old Mon or Talaing kingdom, has become practically as Burman..as Ava itself. **1904** G. A. GRIERSON *Linguistic Survey India* II. 1 The Mōn or Talaing spoken in Pegu. **1948** D. DIRINGER *Alphabet* vii. 408 When the ancestors of the modern Burmans came to the Irrawaddy basin, they found the people whom they call Talaings well established in southern Burma. **1957** *Encycl. Brit.* XXI. 759/1 From the Telingas, whose culture they [*sc.* the Mon] took and whose foreign blood they absorbed into their own stock, came the name Talaing. **1973** [see PEGUAN *sb.* and *a.*].

‖**talak** (ta'lɑːk). Also **talaq**. [a. Arab. *ṭalāq* divorce.] In Muslim law: (a method of) divorce by the husband's mere verbal repudiation of his wife in a set form of words (see quots.). Cf. GET *sb.*³

1791 C. HAMILTON tr. *Hedàya* I. IV. 200 Talâk, in its primitive sense, means *dismission*:—in law it signifies the dissolution of a marriage, or the annulment of its legality, by certain words. **1861** in E. F. Moore *Rep. Cases Appeal from E. Indies* VIII. 395 A divorce by *Talâk* is the mere arbitrary act of the husband, who may repudiate his wife at his own pleasure, with or without cause. **1917** *Law Rep. King's Bench Div.* I. 649 In my judgment Dr. Mir-Anwaruddin has made such a marriage, as he was legally entitled to do, to which Talak has no application. **1931** S. VESEY-FITZGERALD *Muhammadan Law* ix. 73 Talaq..is a generic name for all divorce, but is specifically applied to repudiation by or on behalf of the husband. **1962** *Times* 2 Feb. 3/6 A husband domiciled in a Mohammedan country could validly divorce by talak a wife whom he had married in England. **1970** *Daily Tel.* 31 Oct. 3/3 A Pakistani doctor's 'Talaq' divorce was held..to be valid in England. Talaq is the Moslem form which involves saying 'I divorce you' three times... The Talaq was contained in a letter.

taland, -e: see TALENT, TALON.

‖**talapoin** ('tæləpɔɪn). Forms: 6 **tallipoie**, 7–8 **tallapoi(e**, 7 **talapoi, talopoy, talipoy, telapoi**; 8 **talopoin**, 9 **telapoon**, 7– **talapoin**. [ad. Pg. *talapão*, ad. Talaing (Old Peguan) *tala pôi* 'my lord', the title of a Buddhist monk, corresponding (in use) to Burmese *pôngyî*. (Sir R. C. Temple in *Indian Antiq.* XXXIX. 159.)]

1. A Buddhist monk or priest, properly of Pegu; extended by Europeans to those of Siam (Thailand), Burma, and other Buddhist countries.

1586 R. FITCH in Hakl. *Voy.* (1599) II. 261 There are..many goodly houses for the Tallipoies to preach in. **1613** PURCHAS *Pilgrimage* (1614) 462 They..hidde themselues in woods and wildernesses, and some turned Talopoyes: so they call their religious persons. **1634** SIR T. HERBERT *Trav.* 195 The Priests [of Pegu] are called Tallapois. **1696** OVINGTON *Voy. Surat* 593 These Religious they call Telapoi, who are not unlike Mendicant Fryers, living upon the Alms of the People. **1713** BERKELEY *Guard.* No. 3 ⁋3 The Telapoins of Siam have a book of scripture written by Sommonocodom. **1752** HUME *Ess. & Treat.* (1809) II. 463 The excessive penances of the Brachmans and Talapoins. **1800** *Misc. Tr.* in *Asiat. Ann. Reg.* 43/1 Those philosophical begging monks, known under the name of Talapoins, who, in the first century of the Christian æra, emigrated from India, and introduced the religion of Buddha, or Goutama, in Pegu, Siam, China, and Japan. **1858** BP. BIGANDET *Life Gaudama* (1866) 483 The Phongies, or Budhist Monks, sometimes called Talapoins.

2. *Zool.* (In full ***talapoin monkey***.) A small West African monkey, *Cercopithecus talapoin.*

1774 GOLDSM. *Nat. Hist.* (1776) IV. 234 The eighth is the Talapoin;..distinguished..by its beautiful variety of green, white, and yellow hair. **1827** GRIFFITH tr. *Cuvier's Anim. Kingd., Syn. Mam.* 11 The Talapoin Monkey..inhabits Africa. **1868** *Museum Nat. Hist.* I. 30 The mone (*Cercopithecus Mona*) is a species nearly allied to the talapoin. **1896** *List Anim. Zool. Soc.* 7 *Cercopithecus talapoin*... Talapoin Monkey. *Hab.* West Africa.

talar ('teɪlə(r)). [ad. L. *tālār-is*, f. *tālus* ankle: see -AR. So Ger. *talar*.] A long garment or robe, reaching down to the ankles.

1738 [G. SMITH] *Curious Relat.* II. 363 A Blackmore on Horseback, dress'd in white Sattin, with a Scarlet Velvet Talar, embroidered with black Velvet. **1850** LEITCH tr. *C. O. Müller's Anc. Art* §351 *note*, Zeus..has, like an Asiatic monarch, a sceptre and a broad magnificent talar. **1864** ENGEL *Mus. Anc. Nat.* 334 He who led their devotions was a young man in a Polish talar.

‖**talaria** (tə'lɛərɪə), *sb. pl. Anc. Rom. Mythol.* Also 7 in Eng. form **talaries**. [L., neut. pl. of *tālāris*: see prec.; *lit.* things pertaining to the ankles.] Winged sandals or small wings attached to the ankles of some of the deities, esp. Mercury. Hence **ta'laria'd** *a.*, wearing talaria.

1593 G. HARVEY *Pierce's Super.* Wks. (Grosart) II. 253 Euerlasting shooes, like the talaria of Mercury. **1656** BLOUNT *Glossogr.*, *Talaries*, shooes with wings, which Mercury wore, as Poets feigne. **1866** J. B. ROSE tr. *Ovid's Metam.* 26 Doffed the talaria and the helm, retains Caduceus to his aid. *Ibid.* 324 Thence sprung Autolychus, ingenious thief, To the talaria'd god.

†**ta'larian**, *a. Obs. rare.* [f. L. *talāri-s* (see TALAR) + -AN.] Of or pertaining to the ankles; reaching down to the ankles.

1671 H. M. tr. *Erasm. Colloq.* 436 Prelates did ordain that Clergy men should wear Talarian coats, that is, coats hanging down to their ancles. *a* **1693** *Urquhart's Rabelais* III. vii, A colour never used in Talarian garments.

talaric (tə'lærɪk), *a.* [irreg. f. as prec. + -IC.] = prec.

1853 W. B. BARKER *Lares & Penates* 200 A draped female figure, apparently Venus, in a talaric tunic. **1887** B. V. HEAD *Hist. Numorum* 177 A woman clothed in a sleeveless talaric chiton with diplois.

talaunde, talaunt(e, obs. ff. TALON, TALENT.

talayot (tə'lɑːjɒt). *Archæol.* [a. Cat. *talaiot* small watch-tower, ad. Arab. (Muslim Spain) *ṭāli'āt*, pl. of *ṭāli'a* watch-tower; cf. Arab. *ṭali'a* with similar meaning.] A Bronze Age stone tower found in the Balearic Islands, usu. circular with a corbelled roof, used for residential or defensive purposes. Hence **tala'yotic** *a.* Cf. NURAGH.

1893 *Athenæum* 2 Sept. 328/1 Like the Sardinian nuragh, the talayot is essentially a vaulted tower of extra-massive proportions. **1927** *Daily Tel.* 12 July 5/4 The Talayots are round mounds, which appear to have served as sepulchres. **1932** M. MURRAY *Cambr. Excav. in Minorca*: *Trapuco* I. 6 Taulas are always found in connection with *talayots*, circular buildings of rough masonry. **1939** V. F. CHILDE *Dawn Europ. Civilization* (ed. 3) xiv. 249 There is no obvious break between the 'Copper Age' culture represented in the rock-cut tombs and that represented in the 'talayots'. **1950** *Antiquity* XXIV. 154 'Taulas'..occur in association with the strong circular towers known as 'talayots'. **1974** *Encycl. Brit. Macropædia* XIX. 279/1 In the Balearic Isles the Bronze Age corresponds to the 2nd millennium BC and is designated 'talayotic' from the name of the talayot, a megalithic monument in the form of a round or quadrangular tower. **1979** SERVICE & BRADBERY *Megaliths* vii. 131 In Majorca, the talayotic site called Ses Paisses.. includes a central talayot tower, outer walls and four megalithic gateways around the dwellings in the enclosure.

talbanar, talbart, -bert, talberone, obs. Sc. ff. TABORER, TABARD, TABORN.

talbot¹ ('tɔːlbət). [Understood to be derived from the ancient Eng. family name *Talbot*: see quot. 1906 in sense 1; but evidence is wanting.

Chaucer has *Talbot* as the name of an individual dog; and in quot. *c* 1449, John Talbot, Earl of Shrewsbury, is called 'Talbott oure goode dogge' (in allusion to the badge of the family: see sense 2); but it is not clear what is the nature of the connexion between these applications, or which of the senses 1 and 2 was the earlier.

c **1386** CHAUCER *Nun's Pr. T.* 562 Colle oure dogge, and Talbot and Gerland. *c* **1449** in *Pol. Poems* (Rolls) II. 222 He is bownden that oure dore shuld kepe, That is Talbott oure goode dogge.]

1. Name of a variety of hound, formerly used for tracking and hunting; a large white or light-coloured hound, having long hanging ears, heavy jaws, and great powers of scent.

1562 LEIGH *Armorie* 96 b, A Talbot with coller and Lyame, these houndes pursue the fooe of pray, by sente of yᵉ same, orels by yᵉ bloud thereof. **1615** MARKHAM *Country Contentm.* I. 5 The black hound, the black laund,..or the milk white, which is the true Talbot, are best for the string or lyam, for they doe delight most in blood, and haue a naturall inclination to hunt dry-foot. **1654** WASE tr. *Gratii Falisci Cynegeticon* B ij b, Then match them well; and thus a noble seed Derive, these parents will your Talbot [L. *Metagonta*] breed. **1668** CHARLETON *Onomast.* 23 *Sagax*, a Blood-hound, or Talbot. **1706** PHILLIPS (ed. Kersey), *Talbot*, a kind of Hound or Hunting-Dog. **1735** SOMERVILLE *Chase* I. 290 The bold Talbot kind Of these the prime, as white as Alpine snows. **1870** BLAINE *Encycl. Rur. Sports* §1428 The talbot..is supposed to be the original stock from whence all the varieties of the scent hunting hounds are derived. **1906** *Blackw. Mag.* Sept. 381/1 The same white hounds were brought to England by the head of the Talbot family, and rapidly gaining credit for their qualities in the chase of the stag..were known as Talbots.

2. A representation of a hound or hunting-dog; *esp.* in *Her.* that which has been borne for many centuries by the Talbot family.

1491 *N.C. Wills* (Surtees 1908) 62 A standing cupp of silver parcell gilt with talbottes at the fete. **1537** *Will Geo. Talbot, Earl Shrewsbury* Ibid. 145, ij paier of pottes with flatt Talbottes upon the cover, ij paier of pottes with standing Talbottes upon the cover. **1562** [see 1]. **1603** DRAYTON *Bar. Wars* II. xxvii, Behold the Eagles, Lyons, Talbots, Beares, The Badges of your famous Ancestries. **1610** GUILLIM *Heraldry* III. xvi. 147 Hee beareth Or, a Fesse Dauncette, betweene three Talbottes passant, Sable, by the name of Carrick. **1688** R. HOLME *Armoury* II. 184/2 He beareth Gules, a Talbott, (or Blood-hound, or hunting hound) Or. **1884** *Mag. Art* Jan. 102 Another drinking vessel..is in form of a 'talbot', or dog, seated, and richly collared.

†**3.** Name of a dish in cookery. *Obs.*

c **1430** *Two Cookery Bks.* 19 Talbottys.—Take an Hare, an fle hem clene; þen take þe blode, & Brede, an Spycery, an grynde y-fere, & drawe it vppe with þe brothe [etc.].

4. *Comb.* as ***talbot-like*** adj.

1615 MARKHAM *Country Contentm.* I. 5 A large, heauy, slow, true Talbot-like hound.

Talbot[2] ('tɔːlbət). *Optics.* [The name of W. H. Fox *Talbot* (1800–77), English polymath: cf. TALBOTYPE.] ***Talbot's law***, the law that a flickering source of light, varying in either colour or intensity, will be perceived as if it were a constant light source exhibiting the mean value of the varying quantity, provided that the frequency of flickering exceeds the flicker fusion frequency of the eye; also called the ***Talbot-Plateau law*** [J.A.F. *Plateau* (1801–83), Belgian physicist].

1895 E. C. SANFORD *Course Exper. Psychol.* I. vi. 146 (*heading*) The Talbot-Plateau law. **1906** *Bull. Bureau of Standards* (U.S.) II. 2 Talbot's law is thus a statement of physiological rather than of physical phenomena, and depends for its explanation on the action of the eye. **1929** L. T. TROLAND in C. Murchison *Found. Exper. Psychol.* iv. 187 The Talbot-Plateau law..has been established very accurately. **1943** C. T. MORGAN *Physiol. Psychol.* x. 198 As the [flicker] rate is lowered, the subjective brightness of a flickering light may considerably exceed that expected from Talbot's law. **1974** *Sci. Amer.* Apr. 93/1 The law of color fusion, also known as Talbot's law (although it actually goes back to Isaac Newton), enables us to predict what color will be perceived when two colors are mixed.

Talbotype ('tɔːlbətaɪp), *sb.* Also **Talbot-type**. [f. *Talbot* (see prec.) + TYPE *sb.*] The process of photographing on sensitized paper, patented by W. H. Fox Talbot in 1841: = CALOTYPE; also, a picture produced by this process.

1844 *Times* 9 Sept. 1/3 (Advt.), Claudet's Daguerrotype and Talbotype Portraits... Mr. Claudet continues to take portraits by both the above processes... In Talbotype.. persons may be furnished with any number of copies on paper. **1846** *Art-Union Jrnl.* June 143 In September 1840, Mr. Talbot discovered the process first called Calotype (but the name has since been changed by some of his friends into *Talbotype*). **1875** tr. *Vogel's Chem. Light* iv. 35 Thus the Talbot-type, which at first seemed hardly worth notice compared with the process of Daguerre,..ultimately took precedence of Daguerre's. **1883** *Hardwick's Photogr. Chem.* (ed. Taylor) 261 The original Talbotype process, in which the latent image is formed upon Iodide of Silver, produces, next to Collodion, the most stable image.

Hence '**Talbotype** *v.*, to photograph by this process.

1887 FRITH *Autobiog.* I. xx. 246 Photography, or as it was then [1852] called, Talbotyping, was tried.

talboy: see TALLBOY.

talbrone, talburn, variants of TABORN *Obs.*

talc (tælk), *sb.* Also 6–7 **talke**, 7–8 **talck**, 7–9 **talk**. [a. F. *talc* (Palissy *a* 1590) or ad. med.L. *talcum*, = Pg., It. *talco*, Sp. *talco*, *talque*, ad. Arab. *ṭalq*, mentioned A.D. 869 by Jahiz of Bassora, and by Serapion the elder (Syriac and Arabic), Rhazi, Avicenna, Ibn-el-Beithar †1248, etc. Held by Arabic scholars to be from Persian, where the form is *talk*. So Ger., Da., Sw. *talk*; Du. *talk*, *talksteen*.

In med.L., Matth. Silvaticus *Pandectarum Opus*, *c* 1317, has *talk*; later writers have *talcum*; Matthiolus *Comment. in Dioscoridem*, 1549, has *talchus*; Agricola, 1546, *talk*.]

A name applied by the Arabs and mediæval writers to various transparent, translucent, or shining minerals, as talc proper, mica, selenite, etc. Now restricted to the following:

1. a. In popular and commercial use, (loosely) applied to (or including) MICA or Muscovy glass.

1601 HOLLAND *Pliny* XXI. xiv. (1634) II. 95 Many haue made them [bee-hives] of Talc [orig. *speculari lapide*], which is a kind of transparent glasse stone, because they would see through them how the Bees do worke and labor within. **1644** DIGBY *Nat. Bodies* xxviii. 252 The gallery windows of my cabin..were of light moscovia glasse or talke. **1780** COXE *Russ. Disc.* 216 The windows..on account of the dearness of glass and Russian talc are generally of paper. **1866** LIVINGSTONE *Last Jrnls.* (1873) I. vi. 157 Granite with large flakes of talc. **1867** J. HOGG *Microsc.* I. i. 7 He fitted them on a little plate of talc, or thin-blown glass.

b. With *a* and *pl.* A plate of mica used as a microscopic slide.

1761 STILES in *Phil. Trans.* LV. 254 Many of the rings were broke..by some confinement of the talks. *Ibid.* 255 A third observation was made..of some blood dropped upon a single talk. *c* **1790** IMISON *Sch. Art* I. 223 'Tis proper to have some sliders furnished with talcs.

2. *Min.* **a.** A hydrated silicate of magnesium, usually consisting of broad flat laminæ or plates, white, apple-green, or yellow, having a greasy feel, and shining lustre, translucent, and in thin plates often transparent; it exists in three varieties—foliated, massive (*steatite* or *soapstone*), and indurated (*talc slate* or *schist*).

1610 B. JONSON *Alch.* II. v, With the calce of egge-shels, White marble, talck. **1668** WILKINS *Real Char.* 62 Fissil, into Flakes,..Selenite, Muscovia glass, Isingglass, Sparr, Talc. **1681** GREW *Musæum* III. I. v. 308 A piece thus figur'd, I call A Crystal of Talk. **1770** COOK *Voy. round World* II. vi. (1773) 401 Some particular place where they [the Indians] got the green talc or stone of which they make their ornaments and tools. **1811** PINKERTON *Petralogy* I. 177 The mica may pass into talc or steatite, or siderite, as on the summit of Mont Blanc. **1862** DANA *Man. Geol.* §66. 61 Talc.—Infoliated masses; folia flexible but not elastic; also compact, massive, very soft, and having a greasy feel. **1865** BRISTOW *Figuier's World bef. the Deluge* ii. 38 The Serpentine rocks are a sort of compact talc. **1867** BRANDE & COX *Dict. Sci.*, etc., s.v., Talc forms the basis of the rouge used by ladies; it is also employed by tailors for marking lines on cloth, and in a powdered state for making gloves and boots slip on easily, and to diminish the friction of machinery.

b. A species or variety of talc, or a mineral so called.

1794 SULLIVAN *View Nat.* II. 93 We see crystals,..even metals, talks and asbestos, growing from stony substances. **1796** MORSE *Amer. Geog.* I. 460 Talks of various kinds, white, brown, and chocolate coloured crystals.

†**c.** ***oil of talc***, a preparation formerly used as a cosmetic, reputed to be obtained from talc. *Obs.*

1582 HESTER *Secr. Phiorav.* III. lxxxiii. 110 If this [verjuice] bee mixed with Oile of Talke, it will restore the sight vnto those that are almost blinde. **1610** B. JONSON *Alch.* III. ii, You restore [her face] With the oyle of Talck. **1639** J. MAYNE *City Match* II. i. in Hazl. *Dodsley* XIII. 225 Who Do verily ascribe the German War..to curling, False teeth, and oil of talc. [**1678** PHILLIPS (ed. 4), *Talc*, a squamous, white, and lucid stone, of which is made an oil, with which Women that are curious to preserve their beauty use to wash their faces.] **1727–41** CHAMBERS *Cycl.* s.v., Some chymists..pretend to draw from it that precious oil..called Oil of Talc, which is supposed a wonderful cosmetic.

d. [*ellipt.* for *talcum powder* s.v. TALCUM.] Talcum powder, esp. as a cosmetic and toilet preparation. *colloq.*

1938 *Vogue Beauty Bk.* 16 Feb. 24/2 Sifter top talc, 3 at 1s. 6d. **1949** *Heiress* Aug. 82 (Advt.), Fragrant talc cool-silky-perfumed by the master Goya. **1966** P. O'DONNELL *Sabre-Tooth* vii. 105 Two small bars of soap, a tin of talc, and some body mist. **1977** D. CORY *Bennett* ii. 37 Hunter contrived to take a shower..to apply to himself..a dusting of powdered talc.

3. *attrib.* and *Comb.*, as (from 2) ***talc crystal***, ***earth***, ***rock***, ***stone***; ***talc-like*** adj.; esp. in names of mineral substances consisting partly of talc or containing magnesia, as ***talc-alum***, ***-apatite***, ***-chlorite***, ***-garnet***, ***-gneiss***, ***-iron-ore***, ***-ironstone***, ***-spar***, ***-steatite***; **talc powder**, powdered talc, *talcum powder*: see TALCUM; **talc schist**, **talc slate**, a schistose rock consisting largely of talc; (from 1) **talc light**, a window glazed with mica, or a lantern with mica instead of glass; so ***talc-windowed***.

1868 WATTS *Dict. Chem.* V. 656 **Talc-alum*, a term sometimes applied to magnesio-aluminic sulphate. *Ibid.*, **Talc-apatite*, a variety of apatite containing magnesia. *Ibid.*, **Talc-chlorite*, syn. with Clinochlore. **1681** GREW *Musæum* III. I. v. 310 A Diamond-square, i.e. with unequal Angles, and equal sides; whereas in a *Talk-Crystal, both are unequal. **1861** H. W. BRISTOW *Gloss. Mineral.*, *Talc earth, Native. **1868** WATTS *Dict. Chem.* V. 656 **Talc-garnet*, magnesian garnet from Arendal in Norway. *Ibid.*, **Talc-iron-ore*, Magnesian Iron-ore,..an iron-ore..consisting.. of ferrous oxide with much magnesia. *Ibid.*, **Talc-ironstone*, Breithaupt's name for a magnetic iron-ore from Sparta in New Jersey. **1808** PIKE *Sources Mississ.* III. 207 In one or two houses there were *talc lights. **1866** BLACKMORE *Cradock Nowell* li, The rim of dazzled vision whitened to a *talc-like glimmer. **1895** *Syd. Soc. Lex.* s.v. *Powder*, *Talc powder. **1681** GREW *Musæum* III. I. v. 309 A lump of the *Talk-Rock near Spiral, in the upper Carinthia. **1839** URE *Dict. Arts* 747 It is..among the *talc-schists and clay slates, that it usually occurs. **1866** LAWRENCE tr. *Cotta's Rocks Class.* (1878) 244 Talc-schist is almost always stratified, and forms alternating beds with other crystalline schists. **1832** MACGILLIVRAY tr. *Humboldt's Trav.* xxvi. (1836) 392 A primitive clay-slate passing into *talc-slate. **1834–5** J. PHILLIPS *Geol.* in *Encycl. Metrop.* VI. 560/2 Gneiss rocks.. include among them many gradations, chlorite slate, talc slate, hornblende slate [etc.]. **1681** GREW *Musæum* III. I. v. 309 A Green *Talk-Spar..brittle as Glass. **1756–7** tr. *Keysler's Trav.* (1760) IV. 407 A kind of yellow green and whitish *talc-stone dug about Bern. **1888** LEES & CLUTTERBUCK *B.C.* 1887 xix. (1892) 206 An evil-smelling, *talc-windowed American stove.

talc, *v.* Pa. t. and pple. **talcked** (also **talced**). [f. prec. sb.] *trans.* To treat with talc; to coat (a photographic plate) with talc; to dust (the skin) with talcum powder. Hence **talced** (tælkt) *ppl. a.*

1888 *Engineer* LXVI. 334 A glass plate is first cleaned, talced, and collodionized. **1891** *Anthony's Photogr. Bull.* IV. 274 If the wet prints be squeegeed down upon talced glass, a glossy enamelled surface is obtained. **1976** M. NELSON *Crusoe Test* iii. 40 She sprayed and talced her body. **1976** L. DEIGHTON *Twinkle, twinkle, Little Spy* xvii. 175 His..face talced like a..cottage-loaf.

talca, var. TALHA.

talch, obs. form of TALLOW.

talcite ('tælsaɪt). *Min.* [f. TALC *sb.* + -ITE[1] 2.]

a. Kirwan's name for the compact scaly variety of talc. **b.** Name given to a white muscovite from Wicklow. **c.** (See quot. 1888.)

1796 KIRWAN *Elem. Min.* (ed. 2) I. 149 Talcite. Colour, reddish or greenish white, or leek green. **1836** T. THOMSON in *Thomson's Rec. Gen. Sci.* III. 334 The specimens of talcite from Ireland are from the county of Wicklow, where it occurs crystallized in granite. **1888** *Nature* 20 Sept. 506/2 This upper group—that of the talcites (talc-schists)—contains talc only as an accessory constituent.

talcke, obs. form of TALK.

talcky: see TALCY *a.*

talco- ('tælkəʊ), combining form of med. and mod.L. *talcum* talc, in adjs. describing substances of which talc is an element; as ***talcochlo'ritic***, containing talc and chlorite; so ***talcomi'caceous***, ***talco'quartzous***.

1839 DE LA BECHE *Rep. Geol. Cornw.* ii. 29 These talcomicaceous slates of the Lizard. **1860** MAYNE *Expos. Lex.*, *Talcoquarzosus*,..talcoquartzous.

talcoid ('tælkɔɪd), *a.* and *sb.* [See -OID.]

A. *adj.* Resembling or having the form of talc.

1891 in *Cent. Dict.*

B. *sb.* [a. Ger. *talkoid* (Naumann 1859).] A variety of talc: see quot.

1868 DANA *Min.* 454 Talcoid..is a snow-white, broadly foliated talc of Pressnitz.

talcose ('tælkəʊs), *a.* [f. TALC *sb.* + -OSE.] Abounding in or consisting largely of talc.

1796 KIRWAN *Elem. Min.* (ed. 2) I. 382 Talcose Argillite. **1802** PLAYFAIR *Illustr. Hutton. Th.* 224 A schistus, which is talcose rather than micaceous. **1854** F. C. BAKEWELL *Geol.* 22 When talc is an ingredient, the mineral is called talcose granite. **1893** BARKER *Wand. South. Waters* 195 With schist, talcose slate and fragments of quartz.

talcous ('tælkəs), *a.* [f. TALC + -OUS.] Of the nature of talc; talcose.

1735 *Phil. Trans.* XXXIX. 40 Shining Talcous Laminæ are to be seen in the Liquor. **1777** G. FORSTER *Voy. round World* I. 149 A kind of brown talcous clay-stone. **1852** TH. ROSS *Humboldt's Trav.* III. xxv. 65 A gneiss passing into micaceous and talcous slate.

talcum ('tælkəm). Also 6 **talchum**. [med.L.] = TALC. Freq. in ***talcum powder***, a preparation of powdered talc or French chalk; now *spec.* applied to perfumed or medicated talc for general cosmetic and toilet use; also used *absol.*

1558 W. WARDE tr. *Alexis' Secr.* I. 73 b, The poulder of Talchum. **1567** MAPLET *Gr. Forest* 21 Talchum the stone is like to Glasse. **1682** WHELER *Journ. Greece* VI. 451 Some sparkle like Walls of Diamond; which being broken splitteth into Talcum. **1901** *19th Cent.* Oct. 601 The gloves are boiled, then dusted inside with talcum powder. **1908** *Sears, Roebuck Catal.* 797 Violet and white rose talcum powder. *Ibid.*, Just the thing for holding your face powders or talcums. **1927–28** *T. Eaton & Co. Catal.* Fall & Winter 367 Djer-Kiss Talcum Powder is low-priced. *Ibid.*, Pompeian Talcum is a fine white powder with the pleasing Pompeian odor. **1949** *Heiress* June 41 (Advt.), For cool, satin-like Comfort Dubarry Talcum is the dainty woman's necessity. **1968** [see *bath oil* s.v. BATH *sb.*[1] VI]. **1981** *Good Housekeeping* Apr. 166/2 *Talcum powder* is closely related to face powder; the components are similar but the aim of body powder is to provide 'slip', a cooling effect and good absorbency.

Hence as *v. trans.*, to treat with talcum powder; '**talcumed** *ppl. a.*

1923 H. JEROME *Secret Woman* ix. 106 It is only the American man who smells sweet and soapy, as though he had just been shampooed and talcumed. **1943** G. GREENE *Ministry of Fear* I. iii. 47 Her face was talcumed and wrinkled. **1952** C. ARMSTRONG *Black Eyed Stranger* vi. 47 Charles Salisbury had a clean and 'talcumed' look. **1970** *Daily Tel.* 9 Nov. 18/6 Researchers..concluded that the entire traditional marketing approach to toilet paper was wrong. The result is the soft, talcumed, flower-scented creation now on offer.

talcy ('tælkɪ), *a.* Also 7–9 **talky**, 8– **talcky**. [f. TALC *sb.* + -Y: for form with *-ck-* cf. *colicky*.]

a. Pertaining to, of the nature of, or consisting of talc.

1676 *Phil. Trans.* XI. 615 Some are marly..; some bolar, some sandy, some talky, some limy. **1709** *Ibid.* XXVI. 384 A foliated or talky Earth. **1733** *Ibid.* XXXVIII. 66 At last by encreasing the Fire to the highest Degree, there sublimed some white Talcky [*printed* Talckly] Flowers. **1746** DA COSTA *ibid.* XLIV. 405 Most of the talcy Bodies are of a fibrous Nature. **1799** W. TOOKE *Russ. Emp.* I. 118 There rises a talcky micaceous schistus out of the trapp. **1852** TH. ROSS *Humboldt's Trav.* III. xxv. 58 The micaceous and talky slates of his country. **1965** G. J. Williams *Econ. Geol. N.Z.* x. 162/2 A large land-slip extends over a good deal of the lens, and material in the slip contains large blocks of talcy serpentine.

b. Of or pertaining to talcum powder, in toilet and cosmetic use. Cf. talc *sb.* 2 d. *colloq.*

1972 *Daily Tel.* 11 July 13 The faint, talcy smell of babies in the bathroom.

tale (teɪl), *sb.* Forms: 1 talu, *infl.* tale, 2– tale; also 3–5 talle, 3–6 tayle, 4 tayl, taal(e, 4–5 taille, 4–7 tail, 5 tayll(e, 5–6 taill, taile (6 tell(e), 6–9 *dial.* teale. *β.* 1–2, 4 tal, 4 tall. [OE. *talu*, infl. *tale*, = OFris. *tale*, OS. *tala*, MDu., MLG. *tāle*, Du. *taal* speech, LG. *tāl*, OHG. *zala*, MHG. *zal*, Ger. *zahl* number, ON. *tala* talk, speech, tale, number, Da. *tale* speech, discourse; all :—OTeut. **talā* strong fem., from verbal stem *tal-*, in *taljan*, to mention things in their natural or due order, to relate, enumerate, reckon: see tell *v.* The ONorthumb. *tal* and early ME. *tal*, *tall* in sense 6, may represent the ON. *tal* neut. (Sw. *tal* speech, number, Da. *tal* number), or the OE. *ȝetæl* reckoning, number.]

I. †**1. a.** The action of telling, relating, or saying; discourse, conversation, talk. *Obs.*

c **1000** Ælfric *Saints' Lives* (1890) II. 210 Seo modor sæt ȝeornlice hlystende hire tale. *c* **1225** *Ancr. R.* 66 Eue heold ..longe tale mid te neddre. *a* **1250** *Owl & Night.* 3, Iherde ich holde grete tale An hule and one niȝtingale. **13..** *Gaw. & Gr. Knt.* 638 As tulk of tale most trwe. *c* **1400** *Destr. Troy* 1941 He turnyt hym tyte withouten tale more. *a* **1547** Surrey *Æneid* iv. 144 Quene Dino then thus tooke her tale againe. **1592** Shaks. *Rom. & Jul.* ii. iv. 99 Thou desir'st me to stop in my tale against the haire.

†**b.** An enumeration, a list. *Obs. rare.*

c **1050** *Gloss.* in Wr.-Wülcker 437/34 *Laterculus*, talu.

†**2.** Speech, language. *Obs. rare.* (Cf. taal.)

c **1250** *Gen. & Ex.* 450 Bigamie is unkinde ðing, On engleis tale, twie-wifing. *Ibid.* 2526 God schilde hise sowle fro helle bale, Ðe made it ðus on engel tale.

3. a. That which one tells; the relation of a series of events; a narrative, statement, information.

thereby hangs a tale (and such phrases): = 'about that there is something to tell'. *to tell one's tale*: see tell *v.*

a **1060** *Charter of Godwine & Leofwine* in Kemble *Cod. Dipl.* IV. 266 Ða ða him seo talu cuð wæs, ða sende he ȝewrit. *c* **1205** Lay. 24439 Ne mai hit na mon suggen on his tale [*c* **1275** in tale]. *a* **1300** *Cursor M.* 24887 (Edin.) Þe angel þus he tald his talle. **13..** *Ibid.* 8697 (Cott.) O þiskin tall [*Gött.* playnt] him thoght sel-cut[h], Als of a cas þat was vncuth. **1382** Wyclif *Mark* i. 28 And the tale [*gloss* or tything; 1388 fame; Vulg. *rumor*] of hym wente forth anoon in to al the cuntree of Galilee. **1412–20** *Lydg.'s Chron. Troy* (Roy. MS.) Rubric bef. l. 1701 Vlixes taile to Achile. *c* **1460** *Towneley Myst.* xx. 105 Vnto vs he takys no tent, bot ilk man trowes vnto his tayll [*rimes* dayll (= dale), hayll, avayll]. *c* **1470** Henryson *Mor. Fab.* x. (*Fox & Wolf*) ix, Ane leill man is not tane at half ane taill. **1523** Skelton *Garl. Laurel* 1200 Yet, thoughe I say it, therby lyeth a tale. **1535** Coverdale *I Kings* i. 14 While thou..talkest with the kynge, I wyll come in after the, and tell forth thy tayle. **1583** *Leg. Bp. St. Androis* 363 Sua he..brocht the teale bravelie about. **1596** Shaks. *Tam. Shr.* iv. i. 60 *Gru.* Out of their saddles into the durt, and thereby hangs a tale. *Curt.* Let's ha't, good Grumio. **1600** Holland *Livy* v. xxi. 194 But hereto longeth a tale. **1601** Weever *Mirr. Mart.* A iij b, One tale is good, untill anothers told. **1722** De Foe *Col. Jack* i, It was a good while before we ever heard tale or tidings of him. **1878** Browning *La Saisiaz* 181 Then my fellow takes the tale up. **1891** E. Peacock *N. Brendon* I. 117 Mr. Tournay told his tale without comment.

†**b.** The subject of common talk; the 'talk' (of the town, etc.). *Obs.*

c **1230** *Hali Meid.* 33 Vpbrud in uuel muð tale bimong alle. **1596** Drayton *Leg.* iii. 576, I was the Tale of every common Tongue.

c. *pl.* Things told so as to violate confidence or secrecy; reports of private matters not proper to be divulged; idle or mischievous gossip; esp. in *to tell* (*bear, bring, carry*) *tales*; *tales out of school* (see school *sb.*[1] 1 e); proverbial phr. *dead men tell no tales.*

c **1350** *Will. Palerne* 334 Be no tellere of talis but trewe to þi lord. *c* **1450** *Cov. Myst.* (Shaks. Soc.) 353 Now we have golde No talys xul be tolde. **1552** Huloet, Tales to brynge or tell, *perfero.* **1560** T. Becon *Wks.* II. 97 He that hath his body laden with meat & drinke is no more mete to prai vnto god then a dead man is to tel a tale. **1639** Massinger *Unnat. Combat* i. i, Peace, infant! Tales out of school! Take heed, you will be breeched else. **1664** J. Wilson *Andron. Comn.* i. iv. 14 'Twere best To knock 'um i' th' head, and give it out The Soldiers did it... The dead can tell no tales. **1681** Dryden *Span. Fryar* iv. i. 48 There is a Proverb..which saies, that Dead-men tell no Tales; but let your Souldiers apply it at their own Perils. **1702** G. Farquhar *Inconstant* v. 76 Ay, ay, Dead Men, tell no Tales. **1737** L. Clarke *Hist. Bible* (1740) I. i. 73 Joseph..told tales of them to his father. **1838** James *Robber* vi. Dead men tell no tales. **1850** C. Kingsley *Alton Locke* I. iv. 67 Where are the stories of those who have not risen..who have ended in desperation?.. Dead men tell no tales. **1903** *Westm. Gaz.* 12 Feb. 2/3 Telling tales is reprobated by English public-school boys —rightly, in so far as the condemnation is directed against getting others into trouble for your own profit or pleasure. **1974** 'M. Innes' *Appleby's other Story* xv. 122 'There was only one sure way to do it.' 'To kill him?'.. 'Yes. Dead men, they say, can tell no tales.'

d. *in the same tale, in a* (*one*) *tale*, in the same enumeration, statement, or category; hence, in agreement; so *in two tales. arch.*

c **1375** *Cursor M.* 683 (Fairf.) Þe bestes were in samen tale [*Cott.* war samer-tale] Wit-outen hurt in herde ay hale. **1577** Holinshed *Chron.* II. 1656/1 Thou art a false knaue to be in two tales, therfore said he, hang him vp. **1599** Shaks. *Much Ado* iv. ii. 33 'Fore God they are both in a tale. **1642** R. Carpenter *Experience* i. v. 14 Truth must needs be one.. and can never be found in two contrary tales. **1860** Reade *Cloister & H.* lv, Which did accuse heavenly truth of falsehood for not being in a tale with him. **1887** Lang *Myth, Ritual & Relig.* II. 339 The Wesleyan missionary..is in the same tale with the Jesuit.

e. *tale of woe*: see woe *sb.* 1 a.

4. A story or narrative, true or fictitious, drawn up so as to interest or amuse, or to preserve the history of a fact or incident; a literary composition cast in narrative form.

c **1200** *Trin. Coll. Hom.* 101 We nime ȝeme of þre þing on þis tale. *c* **1275** *Passion our Lord* 1 in *O.E. Misc.* 37 Ihereþ nv one lutele tale..As we vyndeþ hit iwrite in þe godspelle. *c* **1290** *Beket* 1 in *S. Eng. Leg.* I. 106 Wolle ȝe nouþe i-heore þis englische tale? **1340–70** *Alex. & Dind.* 190 Tendeþ how þis tale is titeled. **1375** Barbour *Bruce* ix. 576 [He] tald me this taill as I sall tell. *c* **1386** Chaucer *Prol.* 792 That ech of yow, to shorte with oure weye, In this viage shal telle tales tweye. *Ibid.*, *Pard. Prol.* 109 For lewed peple louen tales olde. **1483** Caxton *G. de la Tour* F vij, I wold..that ye knewe..the tale of a quene of Fraunce whiche had to name Brunehault. **1546** J. Heywood *Prov.* (1867) 67 A good tale yll tolde, in the tellyng is marde. **1606** *Sir G. Goosecappe* iii. i. E ij, Indeed Sir the best Tales in England are your Canterburie tales I assure ye. *a* **1771** Gray *Dante* 19 Hates the Tale of Troy for Helen's Sake. **1821** Scott *Kenilw.* xvii, They are spoken in a mad tale of fairies, love-charms, and I wot not what besides.

5. a. A mere story, as opposed to a narrative of fact; a fiction, an idle tale; a falsehood.

c **1250** *Gen. & Ex.* 321 He [Satan]..Wente into a wirme, and tolde eue a tale. **1382** Wyclif *2 Pet.* i. 16 Sotheli we not suynge vnwijse taales, han maad knowun to ȝou the vertu and prescience..of oure Lord Jhesu Crist. **1529** More *Dyaloge* iv. Wks. 269/2 Therfore it is but a tale to saye that faith draweth alway good workes with it. **1553** *Respublica* 727 Vaine woordes beeth but tales. **1619** *Let.* in *Eng. & Germ.* (Camden) 206 The report of the Marquis of Ansbach his having defeated Coronell Fulkes his regiment (which proves altogeather a tale) **1722** De Foe *Plague* 85 There was more of tale than of truth in those things. **1867** *London Herald* 23 Mar. 222/2 If he had had the sense to..pitch them a tale, he might have got off.

b. In phrases, as *a Canterbury Tale, old wives' tales, pipers' tales, travellers' tales, a tale of Robin Hood, of a rocsted horse, of a tub* (see tub), etc.

1532 More *Confut. Tindale* Wks. 576/1 Thys is a fayre tale of a tubbe tolde vs of hys electes. *c* **1549** Cranmer *Serm. Rebellion* Wks. (Parker Soc.) II. 198 If we take it for a Canterbury tale, why do we not refuse it? **1575** Gascoigne *Cert. Notes Instruct.* in *Steele Gl.*, etc. (Arb.) 36 The verse that is to easie is like a tale of a rosted horse. *c* **1590** Marlowe *Faust.* v. 133 Tush, these are trifles and mere old wives' tales. **1591** Harington *Orl. Fur.* xlv. cv, This is a tale indeed of Robinhood, Which to beleeue, might show my wits but weake. **1608** Topsell *Serpents* (1658) 778 To interpret these to be either fables and Canterbury tales, or true historicall narrations. **1611** Cotgr. s.v. *Cicogne*, *Contes de la cicogne*, idle histories; vaine relations; tales of a tub, or, of a rosted horse. *a* **1641** Bp. Mountagu *Acts & Mon.* iii. (1642) 170 Fained leasings and tales of Robin hood. **1724** De Foe *Mem. Cavalier* (1840) 97 Having entertained the fellow with a tale of a tub.

c. A thing now existing only in story; a mere matter of history or tradition; a thing of the past.

1780 Burke *Sp. at Bristol* Wks. III. 413 No power..could have prevented a general conflagration; and at this day London would have been a tale. **1855** B. Taylor *Poems Orient, On the Sea*, The world we leave is a tale untold.

II. 6. a. Numerical statement or reckoning; enumeration, counting, numbering; number.

c **1200** Ormin 4324–5 Þiff þu þise taless kannst Inntill an tale sammnenn. *c* **1205** Lay. 7397 Swa fele þat nuste na man þe tale. **1297** R. Glouc. (Rolls) 8100 Folc also wiþoute tale. *c* **1375** *Sc. Leg. Saints* xxvi. (*Nycholas*) 237 Þe quhet delieuryt hale in quantyte, mesur & tale. *c* **1450** *Hymns Virg.* 122/165 Alle the stonys grett and smale Thatt byth in erthe withoutyn tale. **1594** Carew *Tasso* (1881) 15 Equall in tale, nor lesse in value tride. **1674** N. Fairfax *Bulk & Selv.* 39 Nothing with-holds, but that from an infinite tale of finites there may at length arise an infinite. **1691** Locke *Lower. Interest* Wks. 1727 II. 53 If you make your Money less in Weight, it must be made up in Tale. **1697** Dryden *Virg. Past.* iii. 51 Once she takes the tale of all the Lambs. **1722** De Foe *Plague* 97 An exact tale of the dead bodies. **1780** Johnson *Let. to Mrs. Thrale* 1 May, There were..Lord Monboddo, and Sir Joshua, and ladies out of tale. **1826** G. S. Faber *Diffic. Romanism* (1853) p. liii, The goodly tale of folios..which now decorate or crowd my *penetralê.* **1862** Trollope *N. Amer.* I. xi. 249 By measures of forty bushels each, the tale is kept.

β. c **950** *Lindisf. Gosp.* Matt. xiv. 21 Ðæra etendra..tal [*manducantium numerus*]. *Ibid.* John vi. 10 ȝesetton uutudlice ueras of tal suelce fif ðusendo. *a* **1300** *Cursor M.* 7174 O þat heþen folk he feld A thusand þat wit tal was teld.

b. *by tale*: as determined by counting individual objects or articles; by number; as distinguished from *by weight, by measure.*

c **1205** Lay. 27606 Fif hundred bi tale. *c* **1300** *Havelok* 2026 He weren bi tale sixti and ten. **13..** *Guy Warw.* (A.) 3430 Bi tale .xx. thousend hauberks of stiel. **1470–85** Malory *Arthur* xiii. ix. 623 There fond they by the tale an honderd and fyfty. **1529** More *Dyaloge* iii. iv. Wks. 212 To way them rather then take them by tale. **1594** Plat *Jewell-ho.* iii. 75 Where oysters are..sold by tale. **1776** Adam Smith *W.N.* i. iv. (1869) I. 27 This money..was, for a long time, received at the exchequer by weight and not by tale. **1855** Macaulay *Hist. Eng.* xxii. IV. 695 The second of May had been fixed..as the last day on which the clipped crowns ..were to be received by tale in payment of taxes.

7. The number or amount made up, or to be made up or accounted for; the number all told; the complete sum, enumeration, or list.

a **1225** *Ancr. R.* 42 And siggen þenne hire tale of auez. *c* **1250** *Gen. & Ex.* 2891 Hem-seluen he fetchden ðe chaf,.. And ðo3 holden ðe tiȝeles tale. *a* **1300** *Cursor M.* 18627 Four thusand yere, þat was þe tale, And four hundret and four al hale. **1387** Trevisa *Higden* (Rolls) IV. 427 For Nero somtyme wolde wite þe tale and þe nombre of Iewes þat were at Ierusalem. **1539** Bible (Great) *Exod.* v. 18 Yet shal ye delyuer the hole tale of brycke. **1584** Fenner *Def. Ministers* (1587) 10 In generall and whole tale, we will allowe that, part whereof in the particular and seuerall parcelles wee will gayn-say. **1611** Bible *I Sam.* xviii. 27 They gaue them in full tale to the king. *a* **1732** T. Boston *Crook in Lot* (1805) 98 The one has multiplied the tale of their good works. **1790** Burke *Fr. Rev.* 196 He will hardly be able to make up his tale of thirty millions of souls. **1864** Sir F. Palgrave *Norm. & Eng.* III. 70 They had a fair tale of children. **1884** May Crommelin *Brown-Eyes* xiii, Saddened at the increasing tale of years and months.

†**8.** An account, a reckoning of numbers (of money given and received, etc.). *Obs.*

1401 *Pol. Poems* (Rolls) II. 73 Ȝe wolden that there where oon lesse, Ȝe ȝaue neuer tale. **1483** Caxton *Gold. Leg.* 197 b/1 They moche doubted that they sholde not fynde theyr counte ne tale. **1573** Tusser *Husb.* (1878) 173 Giue tale and take count, is a huswifelie point. **1602** Carew *Cornwall* i. 33 They keepe a iust tale of the number that euery hogshead contayneth. **1755** Smollett *Quix.* (1803) II. 8 The tale and account of what was both sowed and reaped, passed through my hands. **1806–7** J. Beresford *Miseries Hum. Life* (1826) vi. 116 You might just as well require me to deliver in a tale of all the pores in my skin.

†**9.** Reckoning of value; account, estimation, esteem, regard; in phrases, as *to hold* (*make, give, tell*) *no tale of*: to hold of no account. *Obs.*

c **1175** *Lamb. Hom.* 147 Þet he telle swa lutel tale þer of; þet he hit nawicht ne luuie. *c* **1205** Lay. 12764 Þæt nis [*MS.* mis] þer bileued wel neh nan þæt auere beo æi [*c* 1275 eni] tale on. *a* **1300** *Cursor M.* 7554 Quen golias on him bi-held, Ful littel tale of him he teld [*Trin.* litil he set bi him]. *Ibid.* 10980 He sale Bicum a man of mikel tale [*Trin.* a greet mon]. **1362** Langl. *P. Pl.* A. i. 9 Of oþer heuene þen heer holde þei no tale. *c* **1400** *Laud Troy Bk.* 3923 Dyomedes ȝaf no tale Off alle that sat there In that sale. **1496** *Dives & Paup.* (W. de W.) i. vii. 38/2 The goodes of this worlde..they gaaf no grete tale thereof.

III. 10. *attrib.* and *Comb.*: attrib., as *tale-book*, *-faculty*, *-monger*, *-story*; obj. and obj. gen., as *tale-forger*, *-gatherer*, *-maker*, *-writer*; *tale-gathering*, *-spinning*, *-writing* sbs. and adjs.; also **tale-carrier** = talebearer; †**tale-craft**, numeration, arithmetic; †**tale-fish**, a fish of such size as to be sold by tale; **tale-hearer**, a willing listener to scandal or gossip; **tale-master**, the authority for a report; †**tale-money**, money reckoned by the tale, i.e. by counting pieces or coins taken at their nominal value, not by weight; **tale-piet**, a chattering 'magpie'; a tell-tale (*dial.*); **tale-wright**, a constructor or maker of tales. See also talebearer, tale-teller, etc.

1628 Prynne *Brief Suruay* Epist. A ij, For the inhibiting and suppressing of all scurrilous and prophane Play-books, Ballads, Poems, and *Tale-bookes whatsoeuer. **1552** Huloet, Tale bearer or *carier, *rumigerulus.* **1592** Nashe *P. Penilesse* 35 Spirits called spies and tale-carriers. **1643** Prynne *Sov. Power Parl.* App. 32 Common Tale-carriers, and accustomed to talke of trifling matters. **1674** N. Fairfax *Bulk & Selv.* 110 Nothing better is it, than pumping two out of one, or taking the greater number out of the rest, in *Talecraft or Arithmetick. **1677** W. Hughes *Man of Sin* iii. iii. 100 Forraign Authors have not the Monopoly of the *Tale-faculty neither. **1482** *Rolls of Parlt.* VI. 222/1 That *tale fissh shuld not be pakked with the lesse fissh called Grilles,..and that the same tale fissh shuld conteigne in lengeth..xxvi ynches. **1553** Becon *Reliques of Rome* (1563) 198 It is a harde thing for lyers and *taleforgers to agree. **1711** Shaftesb. *Charac.* (1737) I. 350 We may often see a philosopher, or a wit, run a *tale-gathering in those idle desarts. **1647** Trapp *Comm. Matt.* xviii. 16 The tale-bearer and the *tale-hearer are both of them abominable, and shut out of heaven. **1810** *Splendid Follies* I. 183 The variety of grimaces exhibited by the tale-bearer and the tale-hearers. **1483** *Cath. Angl.* 377/2 A *Tale maker, *fabulo.* **1897** *Q. Rev.* July 107 The sale-processes of *tale-makers. *a* **1661** Fuller *Worthies, General* xxiii. (1662) 64, I tell you my Tale and my *Tale-master, which is essential to the begetting of credit to any Relation. **1758** Jos. Harris *Coins* ii. ii. 50 Increasing the quantity of *tale-money, by giving the old names to smaller pieces of silver. *Ibid.* 70 All artificial methods of increasing tale-money are..pernicious. **1613** *Answ. Uncasing of Machivils Instr.* E ij, Rather for thy quiets sake, liue with bread, Then mongst *talemongers seeke to be fed. **1796** W. Marshall *Yorksh.* (ed. 2) Gloss., *Teyl-pyeat*, or *Tel-pie*, a tell-tale..one who divulges secrets; spoken chiefly of children. **1816** Scott *Antiq.* iv, Never mind me, sir, I am no tale-pyet. **1895** Crockett *Men of Moss-Hags* xiii, A Gordon—Covenant or no Covenant—is no tale-piet. *a* **1661** Fuller *Worthies, Wilts.* (1662) iii. 158 Such a Medly Cloth is the *Tale-story of this Clothier. **1570–76** W. Lambarde *Peramb. Kent* (1826) 326 This Clerkly μυθοπλάστης, this *Talewright (I say) and Fableforger. **1845** Poe in *Broadway Jrnl.* 7 June 354/2 If we except..Mr. Hawthorne..and.. one or two others..there is not even a respectably skilful *tale-writer on this side the Atlantic. **1904** *Daily Chron.* 11 May 4/6 A tale-writer who moves through the magazines. **1837** Ht. Martineau *Soc. Amer.* III. 213 *Tale-writing is her forte.

tale (teɪl), *v.* Now *rare.* Forms: 1 talian, 3 talie(n, 4 talen; 3– tale. [OE. *talian* to reckon, impute, enumerate, = OS. *talôn* to reckon (MDu. *tālen* to speak, Du. *talen* to ask), OHG.

zalôn to number, reckon (MHG. *zalen, zaln*, Ger. *zahlen* to pay), ON. *tala* (Sw. *tala*, Da. *tale*) to speak, talk, discourse:—OTeut. **talôjan*, f. stem *tal-*: see TALE *sb.*]

I. †**1.** *trans.* To account, reckon, consider (something) to be (so and so). *Obs.*

c **897** K. ÆLFRED *Gregory's Past. C.* xxxiii. 226 [He] hit ðonne swiðe unaberendlic talað. *a* **900** tr. *Bæda's Hist.* v. xiii. §3 Nis ðis seo hel, swa ðu talest and wenest. *c* **950** *Lindisf. Gosp.* Matt. xxvi. 53 Ðu tales..þæt ic ne mæʒe ʒebidda fader min. *c* **1000** WULFSTAN *Hom.* vii. (Napier) 52 He talaþ ..hine sylfne wærne and wisne. *c* **1000** *Sax. Leechd.* II. 208 Se man..talaþ, þæt he þonne hal sie. *c* **1400** *Cato's Mor.* 100 in *Cursor M.* p. 1670 (Fairf.) þai þat talis miche riches maste in nede and bisines beggis in þis life.

†**2.** To lay to the account of some one, to charge or impute (a thing) *to*. Only OE.

a **900** tr. *Bæda's Hist.* II. ix. §4 Ne tala þu me, þæt ic ne cunne þone intingan þinre unrotnisse. *c* **1000** ÆLFRIC *Hom.* (Thorpe) I. 114 Ne taliʒe nan man his yfelan dæda to Gode.

†**3.** To reckon, enumerate, relate. Only OE.

c **950** *Lindisf. Gosp.* Matt., Pref. (1887) 5/7 Ðæt æt ægiptum..& ða æfterra..to talanna longsum is.

4. To count up; to deal *out* by number.

(In quot. 1626 the sense is not clear: cf. TALLY *v.*[1] I.)

1626 B. JONSON *Staple of N.* I. iii. Stage Direct., He tales the bils, and puts them vp in his pockets. **1828** W. IRVING *Columbus* (1849) III. 135 He..ordered the brawling ruffian to be rewarded with a hundred lashes, which were taled out roundly to him upon the shoulders. **1881** MISS JACKSON *Shropsh. Word-bk.*, *Tale*, to count. 'I tale them ship [= sheep] to forty—'ow many bin a?'

II. †**5.** *trans.* To say, speak, utter, tell. *Obs.*

c **1205** LAY. 787 Nan swa unwitti þat word talie..ær he ihere minne horn. *c* **1420** *Chron. Vilod.* 2157 And when þis blessud virgyn had talyd tys. *Ibid.* 3677 Bot he couthe nowther tale ny telle What þat euer was in his þouʒt. **1593** Q. ELIZ. *Boethius* III. Met. xi. 69 If Platoes Musis tales the trueth.

†**6.** *intr.* To discourse, talk, gossip; to tell (*of*); to tell tales. *Obs.*

c **1205** LAY. 3800 He[o] taleden wið Morgan. *a* **1225** *Leg. Kath.* 795 þis meiden..toc on toward þeos fif siðe tene to talien o þis wise. *a* **1225** *Ancr. R.* 356 þet is eadie scheome þet ich of talie [*MS. T* spekie]. *c* **1374** CHAUCER *Troylus* III. 182 (231) Al þat glade nyght By Troilus he lay with mery chere To tale. **1390** GOWER *Conf.* III. 329 The toun therof hath spoke and taled. *c* **1400** *Laud Troy Bk.* 14524 Priamus ran to halle a-valed, Ther these kynges to-gedur taled. *a* **1500** *Chaucer's Dream* 1896 [They] gan reherse Each one to other that they had seene And taling thus [etc.].

†**b.** To shout. *Obs.*

c **1205** LAY. 20857 Hunten þar talieð; hundes þer galieð. **13..** *K. Alis.* 1415 (Bodl. MS.) þe maryneres crieþ & taleþ, Ancres in to shippe þai haleþ.

tale, variant of TAEL; obs. form of TAIL.

‖**talea** (ˈtɑːliːə). *Mus.* Pl. **taleæ**. [L., lit. stick, cutting.] A repeated rhythmic pattern in late-medieval isorhythmic motets.

1944 W. APEL *Harvard Dict. Mus.* 367/1 The repeated scheme of time-values which is used in the sections A, B, C and..in D, is called *talea* in 14th-century treatises. **1960** *New Oxf. Hist. Music* III. v. 145 The rhythmical pattern of the first section or *talea* serves to determine the formal structure of the whole... The melodic development of the individual *taleae* is now entirely subordinate to a rigid framework dictated by rhythm. **1963** *Listener* 17 Jan. 141/1 The structural skeleton of the movement is sixteen rotations of the melody, containing fifteen rotations of the rhythmic pattern or *talea*. **1974** *Early Music* Oct. 220 In some [motets] the isorhythmic voices are constructed not only with a *talea* (the rhythmic pattern) but also a *color*.

talebearer (ˈteɪlˌbɛərə(r)). [f. TALE *sb.* + BEARER.] One who officiously carries reports of private matters to gratify malice or idle curiosity.

1478 *Maldon, Essex, Court Rolls* (Bundle 50, No. 8), Isabella Aylemer est a talebearer betwyx man and man. **1560** DAUS tr. *Sleidane's Comm.* 21 b, He admonisheth him to gyue no credit to talebearers. **1641** HINDE *Life J. Bruen* lii. 173 He would shut his eares against tale-bearers, being the very seed-men of strife. **1774** MRS. DELANEY in *Life & Corr.* Ser. II. (1862) II. 75 We have heard nothing by the newspapers, but they are false talebearers. **1855** MACAULAY *Hist. Eng.* xii. III. 207 These words were spoken in private; but some talebearer repeated them to the Commons.

talebearing (ˈteɪlˌbɛərɪŋ). The carrying of injurious or malicious reports. Also *attrib.*

1571 GOLDING *Calvin on Ps.* lii. 2 He by his wicked tale-bearing kindled yᵉ Tyrants rage. **1680** ALLEN *Peace & Unity* 27 To forbear all hard speeches..especially tale-bearing, back-biting, and whispering. **1857** HUGHES *Tom Brown* I. iii, He was the great opponent of the tale-bearing habits of the school.

taledge = *t' aledge*: see T'[1] and ALLEGE *v.*

taledoux, obs. var. TAILLE-DOUCE.

taleful (ˈteɪlfʊl), *a.* [f. TALE *sb.* + -FUL 1.] Full of tales; making a long story; talkative.

1726-46 THOMSON *Winter* 90 The cottage-hind Hangs o'er th' enlivening blaze, and taleful there Recounts his simple frolic.

‖**Talegalla** (tælɪˈgælə). *Ornith.* Also **talagalla**, **talegallus**. [mod.L. *talegalla* (F. *talégalle*), arbitrarily formed by Lesson from Malagasy *talèva* the porphyrio, and L. *gallus* cock, as a name for the species *Talegalla cuvieri*, the brush-turkey of Western New Guinea, described by him.

1828 R. P. LESSON *Manuel d'Ornithol.* II. 186 Un oiseau ..qui retrace quelques-unes des formes des talèves ou porphyrions. C'est pour rappeler ces analogies que nous avons forgé le mot hybride *talégalle*. *Ibid.* 295 Talève ou poule-sultane. (Talève, nom malgache usité à Madagascar.)]

A genus of megapod birds inhabiting Australia, New Guinea, etc. As English, chiefly applied to *T. lathami*, the Brush-turkey of Australia.

a **1842** J. GOULD *Birds Australia* (1848) V. pl. 77 *Talegalla Lathami*, Wattled Talegalla; Brush-Turkey of the Colonists. *Ibid.*, The term *Alecturo* having been previously employed for a group of Flycatchers, and the present bird possessing all the characters of M. Lesson's genus *Talegalla* which was published prior to Mr. Swainson's *Catheturus*, I feel that I ought to accept that appellation... It is known to inhabit various parts of New South Wales from Cape Howe on the south to Moreton Bay in the north. **1842** *Penny Cycl.* XXII. 4 Mr. Gould describes *Talegalla Lathami*, or the *Wattled Talegalla* as a gregarious bird. **1890** LUMHOLTZ *Cannibals* 97 The mounds of the jungle-hen are larger than those of the talegalla.

talen, obs. and dial. form of TALON.

Talensi, var. TALLENSI.

talent (ˈtælənt), *sb.* Forms: 1 **talente**; 3- **talent** (4 **taland(e**, 4-6 **-ente**, **-ant**, 6-7 **tallent**). [In OE. *talente, -an*, = OHG. *talenta* str. fem., ad. L. *talenta*, pl. of *talentum*, ad. Gr. τάλαντον balance, weight, sum of money (f. verbal root ταλ-, τλα- to bear). In ME., a. OF. *talent* will, desire, lust, appetite, = Pr. *talant, talen*, Sp., It. *talento* (OSp., Pg. *talante*), med.L. *talentum* (1098 in Du Cange), in a Com. Romanic sense 'inclination of mind, leaning, wish, desire'. Branch III (also in mod.F. and It.) originated in a fig. use of the word in sense 1 b, taken from the parable of the talents, Matt. xxv. 14-30.]

I. An ancient weight, a money of account (L. *talentum*).

1. a. A denomination of weight, used by the Assyrians, Babylonians, Greeks, Romans, and other ancient nations; varying greatly with time, people, and locality.

The Royal Babylonian talent averaged about 29·87 kilograms or 65 lb. 13 oz.; the chief Greek varieties were the Old Æginetan talent of 40·3 kilog. (88 lb. 12 oz.), the later Æginetan or emporetic Attic, 36·4 kilog. (80 lb. 4 oz.), and the Solonic or later Attic, 25·8 kilog. (56 lb. 14 oz., or a little over half a hundredweight).

c **893** K. ÆLFRED *Oros.* IV. vi. §1 Hanna..him ælce ʒeare ʒesealde twa hund talentana siolfres: on ælcre anre talentan wæs lxxx punda. **1382** WYCLIF *Exod.* xxxviii. 26 An hundryd talentes of siluer. —— *Zech.* v. 7 Lo! a talent of lede was born. —— *Rev.* xvi. 21 And greet hayl as a talent cam doun fro heuen. **1494** FABYAN *Chron.* VI. ccvi. 218 There be thre maner of talentes; the firste & grettest is of yᵉ weyghte of .vi. xx. li. weyght. **1552** HULOET, Talent, or certayne poyse or weyght, *talentum*. **1697** DRYDEN *Æneid* IX. 352 With two great Talents of the finest Gold. **1800** *Suppl. to Chron.* in *Asiat. Ann. Reg.* 149/2 They afterwards advanced to deliver their presents, consisting of talents of gold and silver. **1807** ROBINSON *Archæol. Græca* V. xxvi. 551 Grecian weights reduced to English Troy weight:..Talent = 65 lb., 12 dwt., $5\frac{5}{7}$ grains. **1838** THIRLWALL *Greece* III. xix. 121 The statue of Athene in the Parthenon alone contained forty talents weight of pure gold.

b. The value of a talent weight (of gold, silver, etc.): a money of account.

The Babylonian silver talent was equal to 3000 shekels; the Greek talent contained 60 minæ or 6000 silver drachmæ, and the value of the later Attic talent of silver, with pure silver at 4*s.* 9*d.* an oz. troy, has been estimated at £200; at a higher value of silver, at £243 15*s.* (N.E.D.)

c **893** K. ÆLFRED *Oros.* IV. vi. §18 Eac him ʒesealden þæronufan III. M talentana ælce ʒeare. **1382** WYCLIF *Matt.* xviii. 24 Oon was offrid to hym, that owʒte to hym ten thousand talentis. *Ibid.* xxv. 15 As a man goynge fer in pilgrimage, clepide his seruantis, and bitoke to hem his goodis; and to oon he ʒaue fyue talentis, forsothe to an other two. **1387** TREVISA *Higden* (Rolls) III. 5 Of þe whiche richesse..Hircanus þe bisshop ʒaf Anthiochus, Demetrius his sone, þre þowsand talentis. **1530** PALSGR. 279/1 Talent a somme of money, *talent*. **1607** SHAKS. *Timon* II. i. 201 My occasions haue found time to vse 'em toward a supply of mony: let the request be fifty Talents. **1761** RAPER in *Phil. Trans.* LXI. 468 This way of reckoning 100 Drachms to the Mina, and 60 Minas to the Talent, was common to all Greece. **1879** FROUDE *Cæsar* xv. 228 He brought 7,000 talents—a million and a half of English money—to the Roman treasury.

†**c.** *Her.* Used as = BEZANT 3. *Obs.*

1486 *Bk. St. Albans, Her.* E iij, It is not necessari here to expres the colowre of the talentis or besantis: for thay be euer of golde.

†**d.** *fig.* Treasure, riches, wealth, abundance.

a **1400-50** *Alexander* 1666 (Dubl. MS.) Takez hym to hys tresory, talentes hym shewys. *a* **1555** LATIMER in Foxe *A. & M.* (1563) 1311/1 All hayle holy crosse which hath deserued to beare the precious talent of the worlde. **1597** SHAKS. *Lover's Compl.* 204 And Lo behold these tallents of their heir, With twisted mettle amorously empeacht. *a* **1606** *Ballad Stucley* in Simpson *Sch. Shaks.* (1878) I. 146 Many a noble gallant—sold both land and talent. **1635** J. HAYWARD tr. *Biondi's Banish'd Virg.* 66 On her therefore spent he all the talent of his hatred.

II. Inclination, disposition (OF. *talent*).

†**2.** Inclination, propension, or disposition for anything; 'mind', 'will', wish, desire, appetite.

[**1292** BRITTON V. i. §1 Pur doner meillour talent a femmes de amer matrimoigne.] *a* **1300** *Cursor M.* 3913 þan bigan þam tak talent [*v.rr.* talande, taland] To wend in to þair aun land. *c* **1325** *Metr. Hom.* (Vernon MS.) in Herrig's *Archiv* LVII. 263 But hedde he no talent to chase. **1340** HAMPOLE *Pr. Consc.* 8459 To what thyng þe saule has talent, To þat þe body salle, ay, assent. **1375** BARBOUR *Bruce* III. 694 The wynd wes wele to thar talent. **1398** TREVISA *Barth. De P.R.* XII. vi. (Tollem. MS.), To make hem haue talent to mete. *c* **1440** *Promp. Parv.* 486/1 Talent, or lyste,..*appetitus, delectacio*. *c* **1450** *Bk. Hawkyng* in *Rel. Ant.* I. 306 The which schall..make here have a talente to hire mete. *c* **1460** *Towneley Myst.* ix. 157 Yis, lord, I am at youre talent. **1485** CAXTON *Paris & V.* 7 Grete talent and desyre she had to knowe hym. **1530** PALSGR. 279/1 Talent or lust, *talent*.

†**3.** An evil inclination, disposition, or passion; esp. and usually, anger: cf. MALTALENT, 'ill talent', ill-will (which occurs somewhat earlier). *Obs.*

[*c* **1320**: see MALTALENT.] *a* **1380** *St. Ambrose* 698 in Horstm. *Altengl. Leg.* (1878) 19 An officer greued Ambrose sore..And sende word to him wiþ gret talent. *c* **1386** CHAUCER *Man of Law's T.* 1039 Hym ne moeued outher conscience Or Ire or talent or som kynnes affray, Enuye, or pride. *c* **1412** HOCCLEVE *De Reg. Princ.* 2326 Al his angir and his irrous talent Refreyned he. **1622** BACON *Henry VII* 68 One that had of a long time borne an ill Talent towards the King. **1652** EARL MONM. tr. *Bentivoglio's Hist. Relat.* 41 Their tallent is alike evil against the Archduke Albertus and his wife. **1695** TEMPLE *Hist. Eng.* (1699) 581 Several Writers shew their ill Talent to this Prince.

†**4. a.** Disposition or state of mind or character.

c **1330** *Arth. & Merl.* 5882 To geuen the other gode talent. *a* **1400** *Lybeaus Disc.* 612 Elene..ladde her ynto the greves.. Wyth well good talent. **1450-80** tr. *Secreta Secret.* 15 The talent of man takith thereof gret strengthe and corage in alle manhode.

†**b.** *transf.* Quality (of taste or flavour). *rare.*

1562 J. HEYWOOD *Prov. & Epigr.* (1867) 118 The talent of one cheese in mouthes of ten men, Hath ten different tasts. **1606** G. W[OODCOCKE] *Hist. Ivstine* Pref., As with a tun of Wine, which..doth take an euill talent of the Caske.

III. Mental endowment; natural ability.

[From the parable of the talents, Matt. xxv. 14-30, etc.]

5. Power or ability of mind or body viewed as something divinely entrusted to a person for use and improvement: considered either as one organic whole or as consisting of a number of distinct faculties; (with *pl.*) any one of such faculties.

c **1430** LYDG. *Min. Poems* (Percy Soc.) 240 Who shal me save Fro feendys daunger, t'acounte for my talent? **1526** *Pilgr. Perf.* (W. de W. 1531) 12 They be the talentes that god hath lent to man in this lyfe, of the whiche he wyll aske moost strayte accounte. **1574** J. DEE in *Lett. Lit. Men* (Camden) 39 That this florishing Kingdome may long enjoye the great Talent committed to your Lordship (from above). **1586** T. B. *La Primaud. Fr. Acad.* (1589) 353 Hide not this talent, but teach it others, and giue thy selfe an example vnto them of well doing. **1607** HEYWOOD *Fayre Mayde* Wks. 1874 II. 60 His industry hath now increas'd his talent. **1671** WOODHEAD *St. Teresa* II. ii. 10 Our Lord having herein given him an extraordinary talent. **1697** COLLIER *Ess. Mor. Subj.* II. (1709) 178 We should presume People have understood their Opportunities, and managed their Talent, and their Time to advantage. **1781** COWPER *Conversat.* 1 Though Nature weigh our talents, and dispense To every man his modicum of sense. **1842** KINGSLEY *Lett.* (1878) I. 59 Remember that your talents are a loan from God.

6. a. A special natural ability or aptitude, usually for something expressed or implied; a natural capacity for success in some department of mental or physical activity; †an accomplishment (*obs.*).

1600 W. WATSON *Decacordon* (1602) 336 Silly bodies and sorie fellowes of no talent gift or ability. **1635** J. HAYWARD tr. *Biondi's Banish'd Virg.* Ep. Ded., He alone having the talent of both conceiving and expressing himselfe. **1644** EVELYN *Diary* 4 Jan., He would needes perswade me to goe with him..to the Jesuites Colledge, to witness his polemical talent. **1685** DRYDEN *Sylvæ* Pref., Ess. (ed. Ker) I. 266 He is chiefly to be considered in his three different talents, as he was a critic, a satirist, and a writer of odes. **1693** CONGREVE *Old Bach.* IV. xiii, Where did you get this excellent talent of railing? **1774** CHESTERF. *Lett.* I. x. 36 To write letters well.. is a talent which unavoidably occurs every day of one's life. **1846** GREENER *Sc. Gunnery* 398 They seem to possess a 'talent' for this sort of thing. **1849** MACAULAY *Hist. Eng.* ii. I. 199 He had shown..two talents invaluable to a prince, the talent of choosing his servants well, and the talent of appropriating to himself the chief part of the credit of their acts.

b. *pl.* Aptitudes or faculties of various kinds; mental powers of a superior order; abilities, parts.

1654 EVELYN *Diary* 12 July, Mr. Gibbon..giving us a taste of his skill and talents on that instrument [the double organ]. **1656** BLOUNT *Glossogr.* s.v., We say, a man of good talents, i. of good parts or abilities. **1731** FIELDING *Letter Writer* II. i, Love and war I find still require the same talents. **1771** GOLDSM. *Hist. Eng.* II. 259 The duke of Buckingham, a man of talents and power. **1796** MRS. M. ROBINSON *Angelina* I. 69 She is the only unaffected woman of talents I have met with. **1866** WHITTIER *Marg. Smith's Jrnl.* Prose Wks. 1889 I. 92 What avail great talents, if they be not devoted to goodness? **1895** N. W. SIBLEY in *Law Times* XCIX. 476/2 It requires the talents of a Boileau, Molière, or La Fontaine to play the part of a *flâneur* with any success.

c. collective *sing.* (without *a* or *pl.*). Mental power or ability; cleverness.

1622 MABBE tr. *Aleman's Guzman d'Alf.* I. (1623) 193 Other poore rogues of lesse talent. **1670** CAPT. J. SMITH *Eng.*

Improv. Reviv'd 6 As much as their Talent and Capacity will amount to. **1749** MRS. BELFOUR in *Richardson's Corr.* (1804) IV. 259 Your talent may be universal; I believe it is. **1764** GOLDSM. *Trav.* 354 And talent sinks, and merit weeps unknown. **1771** SMOLLETT *Humph. Cl.* 2 June, Without principle, talent, or intelligence. **1800** SOUTHEY *Let. to J. Rickman* 9 Jan., We have men of talent here also. **1809** COLERIDGE *Own Times* 655 The aristocracy of talent. **1821** SYD. SMITH *Wks.* (1850) 313 A work in which great and extraordinary talent is evinced. **1847** EMERSON *Repr. Men, Goethe* Wks. (Bohn) I. 390 In England and in America, there is a respect for talent. **1877** MORLEY *Crit. Misc.* Ser. II. 149 He was a person of no talent, his friends allowed.

d. Talent as embodied in the talented; sometimes approaching or passing into the sense: Persons of talent or ability collectively; as sing., a person of talent. By the sporting press, applied to backers of horses, as distinguished from the 'layers' or bookmakers, the implication being that those whose investments make a horse a 'favourite' are supposed to be 'the clever ones'.

(*Administration of*) *All the Talents* (*Eng. Hist.*), an ironical appellation of the Ministry of Lord Grenville, 1806–7, implying that it combined in its members all the talents.

[**1809** SCOTT *Fam. Lett.* 15 Feb., Yet the aggregate talent from which assistance is expected is very formidable. **1838** MACAULAY *Ess., Temple* (1887) 452 Clarendon..seems to have taken a sort of morose pleasure in slighting and provoking all the rising talent of the kingdom. **1885** J. K. JEROME *On the Stage* 17 Selfish fellows who wanted to keep young talent from the stage.]

1856 G. DAVIS *Hist. Sk. Stockbridge & Southbr.* 213 It summoned to its investigation the first talents of the nation. **1883** *Daily News* 21 July 6/5 Xarifa was the most in demand, and the talent again proved correct in their choice, Mr. Valentine's filly winning a capital race by a neck. **1885** *Field* 3 Oct. 489/1 All the talent were discomfited though; as they often are in Nurseries. **1886** H. HALL *Soc. in Eliz. Age* vii. 100 Throughout the summer there were always two..of the local 'talent' engaged in fishing upon the manor. **1888** H. JAMES in *Fortn. Rev.* May 652 M. Pierre Loti is a new enough talent for us still to feel something of the glow of exultation at his having not contradicted us, but [etc.]. **1928** E. BLOM *Limitations of Music* 139 Honegger is a Swiss and a great talent to boot. **1958** *Spectator* 4 July 14/1 The studio, with its presiding talent, Lee Strasberg. **1977** *Rolling Stone* 24 Mar. 74/1 The record's not great, but the lady's a real talent.

1807 *All Talents in Ireland!* 10 The general impression upon the public mind, relative to the recent change in administration, seems to be, that the downfall of 'All the Talents' was occasioned by the unbending perverseness of my Lord H-w-k..and the deference which Lord G-n-lle paid to Lord H-w-k. **1837** G. W. COOKE *Hist. Party* III. xviii. 460 The administration, which was ironically designated by its opponents as 'All the Talents'. **1861** KNIGHT *Pop. Hist. Eng.* VII. xxvi. 463 The ministry of 'All the Talents' was accepted without any hesitation on the part of the king. **1895** OMAN *Hist. Eng.* xxxviii. 608 The short Fox-Grenville cabinet, which contemporary wits called the ministry of 'All the Talents', on account of its broad and comprehensive character. **1897** MORLEY *Guicciardini* in *Misc.* Ser. IV. (1908) 79 Cabinets of all the Talents have sometimes been cabinets of all the blunders.

e. Frequenters of the underworld. *Austral. slang.* Now *Obs.* or *rare.*

1882 [see FORTY *sb.* 7]. **1928** 'BRENT OF BIN BIN' *Up Country* x. 151 The elder won by telling his son he could use the Waterfall stallion as a saddle-horse in the off season, and have him for his own in place of Black Belle, on condition that he left the talent of Eagle Hawk Gullies strictly alone. **1953** D. CUSACK *Southern Steel* 31 He'd learn responsibility quicker married than he would knocking about the ports with the rest of the talent.

f. The women of a particular locality collectively (as *sing.*), judged according to attractiveness and sexual promise, esp. as *local talent* (see LOCAL *a.* 2d). Also applied occas. to men. *slang.*

1947 [see *local talent* s.v. LOCAL *a.* 2d]. **1950** J. CLEARY *Just let Me Be* 115 [He] looked after her, and Harry grinned at him. 'Not bad, eh?' he said... 'That's a bit of the local talent.' **1963** *Sunday Times* (Colour Suppl.) 1 Sept. 8 You can take a turn on the [sea-]front and see what the talent is like. **1969** J. FOWLES *French Lieut.'s Woman* xxxix. 292 Far duller the customers—the numerically equal male sex, who, stick in hand and 'weed' in mouth, eyed the evening's talent. **1972** 'M. YORKE' *Silent Witness* ii. 24 No chance had come her way... 'Your charms are waning,' Liz had said dryly. 'There isn't any talent,' Sue had answered.

†**7. a.** The characteristic disposition or aptitude of a person or animal. (App. blending 4 and 6.) *Obs.*

1669 DRYDEN *Tempest* Pref., Wks. 1883 III. 105 This is certainly the talent of that nation. **1697** COLLIER *Immor. Stage* i. (1698) 7 Obscenity in any Company is a rustick uncreditable Talent; but among Women 'tis particularly rude. **1697** VANBRUGH *Prov. Wife* II. ii, Besides, 'tis my particular talent to ridicule folks. **1701** SWIFT *Contests Nobles & Com.* Wks. 1755 II. I. 46 It is the talent of human nature to run from one extreme to another. **1741** RICHARDSON *Pamela* I. xxx. 116 Pride is not my Talent. **1774** GOLDSM. *Nat. Hist.* (1776) IV. 159 Its talents are entirely repressed in solitude, and are only brought out by society.

b. The good points or qualities of a horse. ? *Obs.*

1725 *Bradley's Fam. Dict.* s.v. *Horse*, If your Horse's Talent be Speed, all that you can do is to wait upon the other Horse, and keep behind till you come almost to the Stand, and then endeavour to give a Loose by him.

8. *attrib.* and *Comb.*, as *talent-hiding*; **talent agency**, an organization which seeks to place talented amateurs in the world of professional entertainment; **talent money**, a bonus or gratuity given to a professional athlete, etc. for specially meritorious performance; **talent scout** = SCOUT *sb.*[4] 2e; so **talent-scouting** *vbl. sb.*; **talent show**, a show or competition consisting of performances by a series of promising entertainers, esp. ones seeking to enter show business professionally; **talent-spotter** = *talent scout* above; also **talent-spot** *v. trans.* and *intr.*, **talent-spotting** *vbl. sb.*

1956 B. HOLIDAY *Lady sings Blues* viii. 95 Nobody was in a position to push a hotel chain, a broadcasting network, and the talent agency around. **1977** *Rolling Stone* 24 Mar. 48/5 Christine and a girlfriend/singing partner snuck away from their strict parents in Birmingham and visited every talent agency they could find in London. **1623** LISLE *Ælfric on O. & N. Test.* Pref. 7, I thought it a shame, and the great fault also of talent-hiding, to lead all my life in study. **1859** *Bell's Life* 14 Aug. 8/2 When the time arrived for drawing the stumps. Both [players]..were loudly cheered during the presentation of the 'talent' money. **1896** LD. HAWKE in *Westm. Gaz.* 25 Nov. 5/3 Whilst they were pleased to congratulate the one who made 100, [or] a bowler who earned talent money. **1896** *Daily Chron.* 5 May 5/8 Briggs..saw Sugg earn his 'talent money' after the latter had been batting fifty minutes. **1936** *New Republic* 28 Oct. 351/2 Paramount's 'Big Broadcast of 1937'..(Paramount talent-scouts: there's a joker here somewhere.) **1939** N. MONSARRAT *This is Schoolroom* III. xvii. 383 He was appraising the women present, as if he were a talent scout who only recognised one talent. **1952** WODEHOUSE *Pigs have Wings* x. 202, I understand that he's always being approached with flattering offers by the talent scouts of Colney Hatch and similar institutions. **1976** A. POWELL *Infants of Spring* x. 170 Lyall worked intermittently as a film actor, consequence of a talent-scout seeing him making faces in a restaurant. **1934** M. H. WESEEN *Dict. Amer. Slang* 154 *Talent scouting*,..seeking new actors. **1955** F. G. PATTON *Good Morning, Miss Dove* 70 She had won a talent show and gone to New York. **1977** *Detroit Free Press* 11 Dec. 11-B/3 After that he landed parts in the theater productions, ice shows and talent shows. **1937** *Boy's Own Paper* 2 Nov. 80/2 When talent-spotting, the thing he looked out for in a half-back was the ability to deliver an artistic pass. **1968** 'D. TORR' *Treason Line* 69 He had also to prod her into making the best of her mother's party to talent-spot possible agents. **1979** A. BOYLE *Climate of Treason* x. 324 George Blake, a Royal Navy lieutenant whom he had 'talent-spotted' as a possible SIS recruit for counter-espionage work in Germany. **1944** *Gen.* 15 Jan. 27/2 The B.B.C. talent-spotter is touring the Midlands. **1954** I. MURDOCH *Under Net* xiv. 197, I hope that the eye of the talent-spotter has lighted favourably upon you. **1978** L. MEYNELL *Papersnake* vii. 88 It's punk..no action, what you keep these lousy talent-spotters for I can't imagine. **1957** *Observer* 3 Nov. 9/5 Competitions are an effective method for talent-spotting, an encouragement to architects and a means, sometimes, of acquiring a masterpiece. **1978** J. PEARSON *Façades* iv. 69 Thanks to the talent-spotting skill of Richard Jennings..'Drowned Suns' was published in the London *Daily Mirror.*

'talent, *v. rare.* Also 5 -awnt. [f. TALENT *sb.*]

†**1.** *trans.* To fill with desire; = ENTALENT *v.*

1486 *Bk. St. Albans* C j b, That shall talawnt hir wele, and cause her to haue goode appetide.

2. To endow with talent or talents. Chiefly in *pa. pple.* **talented.**

a **1633** ABP. ABBOT in Rushw. *Hist. Coll.* (1659) 449 When one talented but as a common person, yet by the favour of his prince, hath gotten that interest. **1702** C. MATHER *Magn. Chr.* III. 103 So Great an Ability, as that wherewith Mr. Rogers was Talented. *Ibid.* IV. (1853) II. 18 In his peculiar opportunities, with which the free grace of Heaven hath talented him to do good unto the public. *a* **1774** TUCKER *Lt. Nat.* (1834) II. 589 We were neither born nor talented for ourselves alone; we are citizens of the universe.

talent(e, obs. and dial. forms of TALON.

'talented, *a.* [f. TALENT *sb.* + -ED[2].]

I. From obs. senses of TALENT *sb.*

†**1.** Naturally inclined or disposed *to* something.

1422 tr. *Secreta Secret., Priv. Priv.* 228 Tho that haue grete Noosys lyghtely bene talentid to couetise, and bene desposyd to concupiscence.

†**2.** *Her.* = BEZANTY. *Obs. rare.*

1486 *Bk. St. Albans, Her.* E iij, A certan bordure talentit as here, and it is not necessari here to expres the colowre of the talentis or besantis: for thay be euer of golde.

II. From existing sense of TALENT *sb.*

3. Endowed with talent or talents; possessing talent, gifted, clever, accomplished.

[*a* **1633**-: see *talented* as *pa. pple.* in TALENT *v.* 2.]

1827 LYTTON *Falkland* I. 16, I smiled at the kindness of the fathers who, hearing I was talented..looked to my support. **1828** SOUTHEY in *Corr. w. C. Bowles* (1881) 134 Unprincipled people, too many of them talented and clever and most agreeable. **1829** HERSCHEL *Ess.* (1857) 515 Those numerous and talented individuals throughout the continent, and in England. **1830** W. TAYLOR *Hist. Surv. Germ. Poetry* III. 406 His eye, though indicating a talented mind, was restless and unsteady. **1832** COLERIDGE *Table-t.* 8 July, I regret to see that vile and barbarous vocable *talented*, stealing out of the newspapers into the leading reviews and most respectable publications of the day. **1842** PUSEY *Crisis Eng. Ch.* 99 A talented writer, who has been one great instrument in its restoration. **1853** WHITTIER *Prose Wks.* (1889) II. 418 A successful advocate at the bar, talented, affable, eloquent.

talented, obs. variant of TALONED.

†**'talenter.** *Obs. rare.* [f. *talent*, obs. f. TALON *sb.* or *v.* + -ER[1].] A bird of prey with talons, as a hawk.

1620 MIDDLETON & ROWLEY *World Tost at Tennis* Induct., The feather'd talenter to the falling bird.

†**'talentive**, *a. Obs.* In 4–5 -if. [a. OF. *talentif* desirous (12th c. in Godef.), f. *talent*, TALENT *sb.* 2: see -IVE.] Desirous.

13.. *Gaw. & Gr. Knt.* 350 Þaȝ ȝe ȝour-self be talenttyf to take hit to your-seluen. *c* **1450** *Merlin* xx. 352 Thei after that were full talentif hem to sle, yef thei myght hem take.

talentless ('tælǝntlɪs), *a.* [f. TALENT *sb.* + -LESS.] Devoid of talent; not mentally gifted.

1831 *Fraser's Mag.* IV. 180 'Misapplied talent', cry the talentless. **1846** H. W. TORRENS *Rem. Milit. Hist.* 78 The Romans, whose talentless leaders in the early wars of the republic seem to have been prone to depend on the soldier rather than themselves. **1898** *Westm. Gaz.* 11 May 3/2 Dreadful daubs, showing nothing but talentless ambition.

‖**tales** ('teɪliːz). *Law.* [L. pl. of *tālis* such, in the phrase *tales de circumstantibus* 'such (or the like) persons from those standing about', occurring in the order for adding such persons to a jury; whence used as a sb.]

Originally, in plural, Persons taken from among those present in court or standing by, to serve on a jury in a case where the original panel has become deficient in number by challenge or other cause, these being persons *such* as those originally summoned; loosely applied in Eng. as a singular (*a tales*) to the supply of people (formerly even one person) so provided. Also contextually applied to the order or act of supplying such substitutes, as *to pray, grant, award a tales.* In English use now restricted to such summoning of jurors; orig. and still in U.S. of jurors (collectively) and the practice of summoning them.

[*c* **1250** BRACTON 238 b (Rolls IV. 8). **1345** *Year-Bk. 19 Edw. III* (Rolls) 146 Ou le panel par le *Habeas corpora* et *Octo Tales* fuit retourne devant luy. **1346** *Ibid., 20 Edw. III* 490 Par quei il avoit briefe a Vicounte de feire venir præter les deux que furent jurez XII tales. **1370** *Ibid., 44 Edw. III* Mich. pl. 62 f. 25 Pur que il [the counsel] pria XII tales et les serjeants d'autre part disoient que a autrefois il avoit ewe x tales. **1479** *Year-Bk. 18 Edw. IV* Pasch. pl. 31 p. 6 Home n'avera XII tales en nul cas forsque in appeal tantum. **1531** *Registr.omn. Brev. Judic.* (Rastell) 75.]

1495 *Act 11 Hen. VII*, c. 21 Upon every tales graunted, the seid Maire and Aldermen shall impanell the seid Persones. **1607** COWELL s.v., A supply of men empaneled vpon a iury or enquest, and not appearing, or at their apparance, chalenged by..either partie..the Iudge vpon petition graunteth a supply to be made by the Shyreeue of some men there present, equall in reputation to those that were impaneled. And herevpon the very act of supplying is called a *Tales de Circumstantibus. Ibid.*, The first Tales must be vnder [*i.e.* fewer than] the principall panell, except in a cause of Appeale, and so euery Tales lesse then other. *a* **1680** BUTLER *Rem.* (1759) II. 69 He is chosen..like a Tales in a Jury, for happening to be near in Court. **1768** BLACKSTONE *Comm.* III. xxiii. 364 Either party may pray a *tales.* A *tales* is a supply of *such* men as are summoned upon the first panel, in order to make up the deficiency. **1837** DICKENS *Pickw.* xxxiv, It was discovered that only ten special jurymen were present. Upon this, Mr. Sergeant Buzfuz prayed a *tales*; the gentleman in black then proceeded to press into the special jury two of the common jurymen. **1863** H. COX *Instit.* II. iii. 355 In criminal cases it is not the practice to award a *tales.*

b. *Comb.* **tales-book**, a name for the entry-book of persons summoned on a tales: see quots.

[**1604** COKE *Reports* IV. 93 b, Le liuer appel les Tales. **1607** COWELL, *Tales*, is the proper name of a booke in the Kings bench office [citing *Coke*].] **1670** BLOUNT *Law Dict., Tales*, is also the name of a Book in the Kings Bench Office Of such Jury-men as were of the Tales.] **1823** CRABB *Techn. Dict., Tales-book.* Hence in mod. Dicts.

tales, taleshide: see TALLITH, TALSHIDE.

talesman[1] ('teɪliːz-, 'teɪlzmǝn). *Law.* [f. TALES + MAN *sb.*[1]] A member of the tales impanelled to complete a jury: see TALES.

1679 LUTTRELL *Brief Rel.* (1857) I. 18 There was a good jury impanelled, but they were never summoned; so that there were talesmen there ready who did the work. **1770** *Chron.* in *Ann. Reg.* 129/1 Only seven of the special jury attended, so that five talesmen were allowed to be taken out of the box. **1825** *Act 6 Geo. IV*, c. 50 §37 Where a special jury shall have been struck the talesmen shall be such as shall be impanelled upon the common jury panel. **1891** 'OCTAVE THANET' *Otto the Knight, Trusty* 236 One of those court-room hangers-on always ready to the sheriff's hand either for jurors or talesmen. **1906** *Westm. Gaz.* 19 Oct. 14/1 In a murder case now being heard in Albany [N.Y.]. After the expenditure of a whole fortnight in the examination of 522 talesmen, only ten of the number have qualified as jurors.

†**talesman**[2] ('teɪlzmǝn). *Obs.* [f. *tale's*, genitive of TALE *sb.* + MAN *sb.*[1]] The teller of a tale, the author of a story; a relater, a narrator.

a **1568** *Henryson's Credence of Titlaris* 12 (Bann. MS.) Ane worthy lord sowld wey ane taill wyslie..gif the tailis-man [*Maitl. MS.* tellar] abyd at It he wald. **1570–76** LAMBARDE *Peramb. Kent* (1826) 358 Polydore might well have spared to magnifie Becket with this lie,..unlesse he had brought his Talesman with him. **1613** PURCHAS *Pilgrimage* I. ix. 44 Yet the Tales-man shall be Set by the Tale, the Authors name annexed to his Historie. *a* **1700** B. E. *Dict. Cant. Crew*, I tell you my Tale, and my Tales-man, or Author. **1768** Ross *Helenore* 29 Baith tale an' tales-man I to you shall tell.

So † **'tales-,master**, in the same sense: cf. *tale-master*, s.v. TALE *sb.* 10.

1656 HEYLIN *Extraneus Vapulans* 53 Without producing his Tales-master to make it good, he only says that he hath been told.

'tale-,teller. [f. TALE *sb.* + TELLER.]

1. A teller of tales or stories; a narrator.

1387 TREVISA *Higden* (Rolls) I. 337 Beda knew neuere þat ilond wiþ his eyȝe; bot some tale tellere [L. *relator*] tolde hym suche tales. **1530** PALSGR. 279/1 Taletellar, *embouchеur, diseur de fables.* **1623** COCKERAM III, *Bebeus*, a notable Tale-teller. **1728–30** POPE in Spence *Anecd. Bks. & Men* I. (1820) 19 Chaucer.. is the first Tale-teller in the true and enlivened natural way. **1871** MORRIS in Mackail *Life* (1899) I. 263 Thou tale-teller of vanished men.

2. A talebearer; a tell-tale. Also *fig.*

1377 LANGL. *P. Pl.* B. xx. 297 Alle taletellers and tyterers in ydel. **1494** FABYAN *Chron.* VII. ccxxvi. 254 By ill tale tellers.. this brotherlye loue was after desolued. **1583** BABINGTON *Commandm.* ix. (1622) 87 To be a taleteller and false witnesse. **1619** in Ferguson & Nanson *Munic. Rec. Carlisle* (1887) 277 Slandering Robert James to be comon tayle teller to Mr. Chancelor. **1896** BLACK *Briseis* xix, How quick a tale-teller is the expression of your face, to one who has the skill to remark.

3. One who tells a 'tale' or made-up story with the object of deceiving or misleading.

1894 *Daily News* 28 Mar. 5/5 Persons who had not backed horses on the recommendation of a 'tale-teller'.

So **'tale-,telling** *sb.*, the telling of tales, story-telling; *a.*, that tells tales or stories.

1556 OLDE *Antichrist* 116 Thus the harlot bewrayeth him self in his owne tale telling. **1743** FRANCIS tr. *Hor., Odes* I. xviii. 16 The broad-glaring eye of the tale-telling day. **1833** HT. MARTINEAU *Charmed Sea* iv. 54 One is winked at for a tale-telling traveller, if one says what I am saying now. **1898** SAINTSBURY *Short Hist. Eng. Lit.* x. i, The wild stories which float through mediæval tale-telling.

† **tale'vace.** *Obs.* Also 4 **talvace, talvas.** [a. OF. *talevas, talvas* (12th c. in Godefroy), held to be transposed from **tavelas*, ad. It. *tavolaccio* a great table, or target of boards, a wooden buckler, augm. of *tavola*, L. *tabula* table.]

A large shield or buckler, properly of wood.

c **1300** *Havelok* 2323 Buttinge with sharpe speres, Skirming with taleuaces, that men beres. **13..** *Sir Beues* (A.) 3960 And after mete.. þe children pleide at þe taluas. *c* **1400** *Ywaine & Gaw.* 3158 Aither broght unto the place A mikel rownd talvace, And a klub, ful grete and lang.

† **'talewise,** *a. Obs.* Also 4 **talwis, talewys,** 5 **-wijs,** 6 **-wes.** [f. TALE *sb.* + *-wīs*, from OE. *-wīs*, from *wise*, WISE *sb.*, manner, way; cf. *rihtwis* RIGHTEOUS.] Given to tales or talking; addicted to gossip; loquacious, garrulous, blabbing.

c **1200** *Trin. Coll. Hom.* 193 Talewise men þe speches driuen, and maken wrong to rihte, and riht to wronge. **1362** LANGL. *P. Pl.* A. III. 126 Heo is Tikel of hire Tayl, Talewys [**1377** B. III. 130 talwis] of hire tonge. *c* **1430** *How Wise Man tauȝt his Son* 26 in *Babees Bk.* (1868) 49 Be not to tale-wijs bi no wey. **1520** *Treat. Galaunt* (W. de Worde) 17 Talewes and talkynge, and drynkynge ataunte.

talewod, -wood: see TALWOOD.

Talgai (tæl'gaɪ). The name of a farm in Queensland, Australia, used *attrib.* in **Talgai boy, man, skull,** etc., to designate the fossil remains of a form of *Homo sapiens* found there in 1884.

The remains were presented to the University of Sydney in 1914.

1918 S. A. SMITH in *Phil. Trans. R. Soc.* B. CCVIII. 355 A comparison of these radiographs with those of the Talgai skull show that.. an exposure.. was only just sufficient for the bone. *Ibid.* 370 The palate of the Talgai boy approaches that of the reconstructed *Eoanthropus.* **1931** A. KEITH *New Disc. Antiquity of Man* xix. 303 The exact antiquity of the Talgai skull is still a moot point. *Ibid.*, The Talgai canines projected beyond the level of their neighbours. **1931** *Times Lit. Suppl.* 23 Apr. 317/1 Australia, having scored once with the help of the Talgai man, looks.. for a no less successful second innings. **1977** G. CLARK *World Prehistory* (ed. 3) xi. 459 The Talgai group,.. although clearly sapient, retains a number of archaic features.

talgh, -e, obs. forms of TALLOW.

talha ('tælə). Also **talca, talh, talka.** [a. Arab. *ṭalḥa* (collect. pl. *ṭalḥ*).] A small flat-topped spiny tree, *Acacia seyal*, of the family Leguminosæ, native to north-eastern parts of Africa; also, the exudate of this tree, used as a substitute for gum arabic. Also *attrib.*

1857 H. BARTH *Trav. & Disc. N. & Central Afr.* II. xxvii. 224 The forest.. here consisted principally of.. talha-trees. **1867** FLÜCKIGER & HANBURY *Pharmacogr.* 206 Suakin Gum, Talca, or Talha Gum.. is remarkable for its brittleness, which occasions much of it to arrive in the market in a semi-pulverulent state. **1875** [see ITHEL]. **1920** *Nature* 12 Aug. 757/1 The reports.. have references to.. distillation trials with talh wood (*Acacia Seyal*) from the Sudan. **1977** *Time* 3 Jan. 50/1 We bumped along in darkness looking for spots where talha trees or hills would provide protection.

Taliacotian (,tælɪə'kəʊʃ(ɪ)ən), *a. Surg.* Also **Taglia-**, erron. **Tali-**. [f. *Taliacoti-us*, latinized form of It. *Tagliacozzi* + -AN.] Of, pertaining to, or named after Tagliacozzi, a surgeon of Bologna (1546–99); esp. in ***Taliacotian operation***, a plastic operation described by him for restoration of the nose by means of tissue taken from another part.

1656 BLOUNT *Glossogr.*, *Tagliacotian* nose (an inhabitant of Bruxiels had his nose cut off in a cumbate, and a new one of another mans flesh set on in its sted, by *Taliacotius*.. of Bononia), a nose of wax. **1657** W. MORICE *Coena quasi Κοινὴ* x. 120 In a Talicotian way of cure, to.. cut off one mans flesh to salve anothers deformity. **1821** *Blackw. Mag.* IX. 178 The talicotian operation, whereby a nose, almost as good as the old one, lost in battles.., was formed from the skin of the forehead carefully peeled down. **1857** DUNGLISON *Dict. Med.* s.v. *Rhinoplastic*, The Tagliacotian operation.. consists in bringing down a portion of flesh from the forehead, and causing it to adhere to the anterior part of the remains of the nose.

So **Talia'cotify** *v. trans.*, to perform the Taliacotian operation on (a person).

a **1843** SOUTHEY *Comm.-pl. Bk.* (1851) IV. 589/1 The Chev. Saint Thoan found a silver nose so inconvenient that he submitted to be Taliacotified.

taliage, obs. form of TALLAGE.

taliar, variant of TALLIAR, Indian watchman.

† **'taliary,** *a. Obs. rare*[−1]. [f. L. *tāli-s* such, the like (with reference to *tālio*) + -ARY.] Of or pertaining to TALION.

1620 FORD *Linea V.* (1843) 44 So much, it is to bee presumed, the verie taliarie law may require, and obtaine.

† **tali'ation.** *Obs.* exc. *Hist.* [n. of action f. L. *tāli-s* such, the like, as if from a vb. **tāliāre*: cf. late L. *retāliāre* to RETALIATE.] A return of like for like; retaliation; = TALION[1].

[*c* **1485** tr. *Act 37 Edw. III*, c. 18 (MS. Harl. 4999, lf. 67) That ther thei fynden suerte to pursue their Suggestiouns and to incurre and renne the same peyne this that the other shulde have if he were atteynt, in cas that his suggestioun be founde fals and of malice.] **1591** LAMBARDE *Archeion* (1635) 123 The Commons of the Realme assented.. in the Parliament 37. Edward 3. cap. 18. that these Petitioners should put in Suerties of Taliation. **1648** J. BEAUMONT *Psyche* XVII. xxvi, Just Heav'n this Taliation did decree, That Treason Treason's deadly Scourge should be. *a* **1677** HALE *True Relig.* III. 43 If men.. justifie it by the Law of Taliation,.. a Spirit of Revenge, an Eye for an Eye, a Tooth for a Tooth, is.. against the Doctrine of Christ. **1769** BLACKSTONE *Comm.* IV. i. 14 After one year's experience [of 37 Edw. III. c. 18], this punishment of taliation was rejected, and imprisonment adopted in it's stead.

tali-douce, -duce, obs. var. TAILLE-DOUCE.

1683 J. REID *Scots Gard.* I. ii. 7 If your draught be a Talíduce, Mapps or the like.

‖ **taliera** (tælɪ'ɛərə). [Bot. L. f. Bengālī *tālier*, f. Skr. *tālī*, f. *tāla* fan-palm; cf. TALIPOT. (In Hindī *tarra, tara*.)] An East Indian palm, *Corypha Taliera*, allied to and resembling the talipot, but not nearly so high.

1814 ROXBURGH *Hortus Bengal.*, *Corypha Taliera*, Skr. *Talee.* **1837** *Penny Cycl.* VIII. 74/1 The Tara or Talliera, *Corypha talliera*, is an elegant stately species inhabiting Bengal. Its trunk is about thirty feet high... The leaves are used by the natives.. to write upon with their steel stiles.

'taling, *vbl. sb.* Now *rare*. [f. TALE *v.* + -ING[1].] Telling of tales, talking, gossiping; also, a tale.

1382 WYCLIF *Ps.* cxviii[i]. 85 Wicke men tolden to me talingus; but not as thi lawe. *c* **1430** *Pilgr. Lyf Manhode* II. cxxviii. (1869) 124 As flaterye heeld me thus with talinge,.. and told me hire doinges. **1617** HIERON *Wks.* II. 84 Gaming, and taling, and reading of merry stories. **1628** WITHER *Brit. Rememb.* 211 Among the poore are many wicked things.. scolding, fightings, cursings, taleing, lies.

‖ **talio** ('teɪlɪəʊ). [L. *tālio*, f. *tālis* such, the like.] A requiting of like for like, retaliation; = next.

1611 SPEED *Hist. Gt. Brit.* IX. xvi. §2 God obseruing a *talio* and parilitie. **1631** GOUGE *God's Arrows* III. §60. 296 In case of *talio*, or requiting like for like. **1704** HEARNE *Duct. Hist.* (1714) I. 226 *Talio* was a punishment in the same kind, as an Eye for an Eye, a Tooth for a Tooth. **1874** tr. *Lange's Comm. Zeph.* 25 The judgment is talio.

talion[1] ('tælɪən). Also 5 **talyon, talyoune.** [a. F. *talion* (14th c. in Godef. *Compl.*), ad. L. *tāliōn-em*, nom. *tālio*: see prec.] = RETALIATION; *esp.* in the Mosaic, Roman, and other systems of Law, the *Lex talionis*, or † ***talion law***, the principle of exacting compensation, 'eye for eye, tooth for tooth'; also, the infliction of the same penalty on the accuser who failed to prove his case as would have fallen upon the accused if found guilty.

1412–20 LYDG. *Chron. Troy* II. 3066 Vp-on Grekis for her offencioun, To parforme vp þe peyne of talioun. **1456** SIR G. HAYE *Law Arms* (S.T.S.) 273 He suld have the payne of talyoune.., that sik punycioun as the tothir suld have [had] that the crime is put on, sik punycioun sall he have. **1563** J. MAN *Musculus' Commonpl.* 33 b, According to the equitie of the Talion law. **1646** GAULE *Cases Consc.* 174 It is just Talion to deliver such up to Satan that have already given themselves unto him. **1738** WATTS *Holiness of Times* 77 The Talion Law of punishment for injuries received amongst the Jews. **1879** ROLLIN-TILTON tr. *Amicis' Morocco* (1882) 294 She.. demanded that in virtue of the law of talion, he should order the English merchant's two front teeth to be broken. **1880** MUIRHEAD *Gaius* III. §223 By the Twelve Tables the penalties of personal injury were,—for destruction of any of the members, talion.

† **talion**[2]. *Obs. rare*[−1]. [a. OF. *taillon* cutting, deriv. of *taille*, or L. *tālea*: see TAIL *sb.*[2]] A shoot or scion, such as is used in grafting.

c **1440** *Pallad. on Husb.* III. 990 The croppe or talions to graffe is speed, But talions the better me shal fynde On either half maad smoth, vnhurt the rynde.

talionic (tælɪ'ɒnɪk), *a. rare.* [f. L. *tāliōn-em* (see TALION[1]) + -IC.] Of or pertaining to the law of talion, or to the rendering of like for like.

1886 G. MACDONALD *What's Mine's Mine* v, The growing talionic regard of human relations—that, namely, the conditions of a bargain fulfilled on both sides, all is fulfilled between the bargaining parties.

taliped ('tælɪpɛd), *a. Path.* and *Zool.* [f. mod.L. *tāliped-em*: see next.] 'Club-footed, as a result of disease; or as a natural condition, as in the sloth' (*Syd. Soc. Lex.* 1898).

‖ **talipes** ('tælɪpiːz). [mod.L. *tālipēs, -pedem*, f. L. *tālus* ankle + *pēs* foot: cf. *tālipedāre* to walk on the ankles, to be weak in the feet, to walk lamely.]

1. *Path.* Club-foot; clubfootedness. Also *attrib.*

1857 in DUNGLISON *Dict. Med.* **1878** A. M. HAMILTON *Nerv. Dis.* 240 The primary forms are those which are seen in talipes of both kinds. **1879** *St. George's Hosp. Rep.* IX. 615 All cases of talipes have been submitted to subcutaneous tenotomy. **1898** P. MANSON *Trop. Diseases* xiv. 245 Foot-drop should be counteracted by Phelps's talipes splint.

2. *Zool.* A twisted disposition of the feet, occurring naturally in sloths.

1891 in *Cent. Dict.*

talipot ('tælɪpɒt, -pət). Forms: 7–8 **tallipot, -pat,** 7–9 **talipat,** 9 **talipot, -put, talpat.** [a. Sinh. *talapata*, Malayālim *tālipat* = Hindī *tālpāt*:—Skt. *tālapattra*, leaf of the *tāla*, palmyra, or fan-palm, *Borassus flabelliformis*; transferred in Sri Lanka and Southern India to the leaf of *Corypha umbraculifera*.] A South Indian fan-palm, *Corypha umbraculifera*, native in Sri Lanka and Malabar, noted for its great height, and its enormous fan-shaped leaves, which are much used as a material to write on.

1681 R. KNOX *Hist. Ceylon* 15 The first is the Tallipot; It is as big and tall as a Ships Mast, and very streight, bearing only Leaves. **1837** J. MACCULLOCH *Proofs Attrib. God* III. xliv. 162 The Bamboo has been ordained for his dwelling and the Talipot to shelter him from the rains. **1859** TENNENT *Ceylon* I. I. iii. 109 The most majestic and wonderful of the palm tribe is the *talpat* or *taliput*, the stem of which sometimes attains the height of 100 feet, and each of its enormous fan-like leaves, when laid upon the ground, will form a semicircle of 16 feet in diameter.

b. *attrib.*, as ***talipot-leaf, -palm, -tree.***

1681 R. KNOX *Hist. Ceylon* Pref., A Fan made of the Talipat-Leaf. **1720** DE FOE *Capt. Singleton* xviii. (1840) 306 Two great tallipat leaves for tents. **1803** SYD. SMITH *Wks.* (1859) I. 44/2 A leaf of the talipot tree is a tent to the soldier, .. and a book to the scholar. **1834** H. CAUNTER in *Oriental Ann.* vii. 75 [We] had the gratifying opportunity of seeing a talipât palm in blossom.

‖ **taliq** (ta'lik). Also **talik, ta'liq,** etc. [Pers., Arab. *ta'līq*, lit. 'hanging'.] A medieval Persian cursive script characterized by sloping rounded forms and exaggerated horizontal stroke, replaced by NASTALIK in the fourteenth century.

1771 [see NASKHI *sb. pl.*]. **1795**, etc. [see NASTALIK]. **1849** F. MADDEN tr. *Silvestre's Universal Palæogr.* I. 52 In general, especially in fine copies of poetical works, this writing takes a sloping direction, whence it has obtained the name of *taalik.* **1885** T. P. HUGHES *Dict. Islam* 690/2 We now turn to the Oriental style, where we meet again with a bipartition, viz. into the Eastern Naskhī, as it is written in Arabia itself, Egypt, and Syria, and the.. Ta'liq, current in Persia, India, and Central Asia. **1962** D. DIRINGER *Writing* vi. 143 In the course of time the Naskhi script became the parent of innumerable styles and varieties including the *ta'liq* (with its seventy or so secondary forms). **1978** Y. H. SAFADI *Islamic Callígr.* 27 Ta'līq.. became established as a defined script after the invention of Riyāsī in the ninth century.

† **'talish,** *a. Obs.* [f. TALE *sb.* + -ISH[1].] Of the nature of a tale or story; fabulous.

1530 PALSGR. 327/1 Talysshe, full of lyes, *fabuleux.* **1540** —— *Acolastus* Z ij b, All thynges whiche menne telle or reporte of hell, be but talyshe .i. be but fables or tales.

Talisker ('tælɪskə(r)). The name of *Talisker* on the island of Skye, used to designate a variety of Scottish malt whisky manufactured at the distillery there, founded in 1831–32. Also, a drink or glass of this.

1883 *Trade Marks Jrnl.* 9 May 254 Talisker. Roderick Kemp & Co., Talisker Distillery, Syke... Whisky. 31,901. 2nd Apr. 1883. **1926** A. A. MACGREGOR *Over Sea to Skye* xiv. 102 Carbost with its far-famed Talisker distillery is in Bracadale. **1951** R. B. LOCKHART *Scotch* I. ii. 27 He feels.. unable to decide between Talisker and Clynelish, each of which would be put first by its devotees. **1977** D. BAGLEY *Enemy* xxxiv. 278, I ordered two large Taliskers.

† **talisman**[1]. *Obs.* Also 7 **talasumany, talsuman;** pl. 6–7 **talismani, -manni, -mans.** [= F. *talisman*, of uncertain history; occurring in Fr. and Eng. considerably earlier than TALISMAN[2]. It appears to be a corrupt or mistaken form of some Arabic,

Persian, or Turkish spoken word, imperfectly caught by early travellers. See Note below.]

A name formerly applied to a Turk learned in divinity and law, a Mullah; sometimes to a lower priest of Islam, a religious minister, a muezzin.

1599 HAKLUYT *Voy.* II. I. 208 This..Mosquita hath..5 steeples, from whence the Talismani call the people to the Mosquita. **1615** SANDYS *Trav.* 31 Turrets, exceeding high, and exceeding slender..from whence the Talismanni with elated voices (for they vse no bels) do congregate the people. *c***1618** MORYSON *Itin.* IV. (1903) 19 They are instructed by old Talismans called Cozza, as it were doctors of the law. **1632** LITHGOW *Trav.* IV. 142 The Talasumany, which is the chiefe Priest. *Ibid.* VIII. 359 To maintaine them, and a hundred Totsecks and preaching Talsumans..extendeth to two hundred Duccats a day. **1638** SIR T. HERBERT *Trav.* (ed. 2) 267 The Talismanni regard the houres of prayer by turning the 4 hour'd glasse. The Muyezini crie from the tops of Mosques. **1668** RYCAUT *Pres. St. Ottoman Emp.* II. vii. 114 Imams or Priests, Doctours of their Law, Talismans and others, who continually attend there for the Education of youth.

[*Note.* Professor Margoliouth suggests that the word intended may possibly have been *ṭailasān*, a form of hood thrown over the head and shoulders, especially by preachers, but also used by doctors of law and others (see Dozy *Dict. Noms de Vêtements Arabes* 278). The wearer of this might be designated *ṭailasānī*, and this corrupted into *talismānī*. But evidence is wanting.]

talisman² ('tælɪzmən). [= 17th c. F., Sp., Pg. *talisman*, It. *talismano*, ultimately representing Arab. *ṭilsam*, in same sense, ad. Gr. *τέλεσμα* TELESM. The final *-an* is not accounted for.

An Arabic pl. *ṭilsamān*, alleged by Diez s.v., and thence in various recent dictionaries, is an error: no such form exists in Arabic, Persian, or Turkish. The only Arabic form at all similar would be a relative adj. **ṭilsimānī* (one) dealing with talismans, if this were in use. The identity of *talisman* with *τέλεσμα* was first pointed out by Salmasius, *Hist. Augusta* 1620.]

1. A stone, ring, or other object engraven with figures or characters, to which are attributed the occult powers of the planetary influences and celestial configurations under which it was made; usually worn as an amulet to avert evil from or bring fortune to the wearer; also medicinally used to impart healing virtue; hence, any object held to be endowed with magic virtue; a charm.

In quot. 1638 applied to the telesms or consecrated statues set up in Egypt, and later in Greece, to protect the city or community: see TELESM. Among Muslim nations, the potent principle is held to be contained in verses from the Koran engraved on the charm.

1638 JUNIUS *Paint. Ancients* 137 The inaugurated statues, which now adays by them that are curious of such things are called Talisman. **1652** GAULE *Magastrom.* 41 To serve as a Talisman; as their Astrologers think, to aucupate the favour of Venus and the Moon against the influences of Scorpio and Mars. **1656** BLOUNT *Glossogr.*, *Talismans*, images, or figures made under certain constellations. **1663** BUTLER *Hud.* I. I. 530 For mystic learning, wondrous able In magic, talisman, and cabal. **1682** WHELER *Journ. Greece* III. 270 This Inscription is a kind of Talisman, or Charm. **1798** *Loves of Triangles* I. 84 in *Anti-Jacobin* 23 Apr., Each scribbled Talisman, and smoky spell. **1825** SCOTT *Talism.* xviii, Know, then, that the medicine..is a talisman, composed under certain aspects of the heavens. **1875** STUBBS *Const. Hist.* II. xiv. 45 He had stolen from Henry..a Talisman, which rendered its wearer invulnerable.

2. *fig.* Anything that acts as a charm, or by which extraordinary results are achieved.

1784 COWPER *Task* VI. 98 Books are not seldom talismans and spells By which the magic art of shrewder wits Holds an unthinking multitude enthralled. **1834** PRINGLE *Afr. Sk.* xiv. 479 Let us subdue savage Africa by Justice, by Kindness, by the talisman of Christian Truth. **1908** H. A. L. FISHER *Bonapartism* vi. 123 Bonapartism can never again stand as the..talisman of victory.

†**3.** Applied to a person: see quot. *Obs.*

1646 J. GREGORY *Notes & Obs.* (1650) 38 One Debborius a Talisman (*τελεστής*) to prevent the falling of the city in case an earthquake should happen againe, set up this pillar and upon that a marble Pectorall inscribed *ΑΣΕΙΣΤΑ ΑΠΤΩΤΑ*. *Ibid.* 41 Moses the Talisman (so they would account him) sat it up upon a pole in the wildernesse.

†**4.** (? Cf. *tailasān* in note to prec.) *Obs.*

1678 BUTLER *Hud.* III. II. 1555 On whom, in Equipage and State, His Scarecrow Fellow-Members wait,..Each in a tatter'd Talismane, Like Vermine in Effigie slain.

talismanic (tælɪz'mænɪk), *a.* [f. TALISMAN² + -IC. Cf. F. *talismanique* (1625 in Hatz.-Darm.).] Of, pertaining to, or of the nature of a talisman; occult, magical, potent.

1678 BUTLER *Hud.* III. I. 432 Swore you had broke and robb'd his House, And stole his Talismanique Louse. **1761** STERNE *Tr. Shandy* III. xli, The word *siege*, like a talismanic power,..wafting back my uncle Toby's fancy,..he open'd his ears. **1816** T. L. PEACOCK *Headlong Hall* ix, Spellbound by the talismanic influence of the coin. **1877** W. JONES *Finger-ring* 95 A remarkable gold talismanic ring..of Hindu workmanship.

talis'manical, *a.* [See -ICAL.] = prec.

1650 CHILMEAD tr. Gaffarel (*title*) Unheard of Curiosities concerning the Talismanical Sculpture of the Persians. **1661** FELTHAM *Resolves* II. lxi. 313 There is a kinde of Talismanical influence in the soul of such. **1775** R. CHANDLER *Trav. Asia M.* (1825) I. 182 A kind of talismanical protection. **1844** KITTO *Pict. Hist. Palestine* I. iv. I. 110/2 The talismanical scarabæus of the Egyptians.

talis'manically, *adv.* [f. prec. + -LY².] In a talismanic manner; by or as by the influence of a talisman; magically.

1831 *Fraser's Mag.* III. 230 We find the fear talismanically opening heaven's tollgate. **1864** *Realm* 9 Mar. 2 All is talismanically changed.

'talismanist. *rare.* [f. TALISMAN² + -IST.] One who uses or believes in talismans.

1706 PHILLIPS (ed. 6), *Talismanist*, one that makes Talismans or that gives Credit to them. **1720** DE FOE *D. Campbell* Ep. Ded. (1840) 15 Such was even the great Paracelsus,..and such were all his followers..that are talismanists.

talis'mantic, *a. nonce-wd.* [irreg. f. TALISMAN², after *necromantic*, etc.] Talismanic.

1814 *Sporting Mag.* XLIV. 67 The talismantic influence of his pencil.

talit, talith, variants of TALLITH.

talk (tɔːk), *sb.* Forms: see the vb. [f. TALK *v.*] The action or practice of talking.

I. 1. a. Speech, discourse; *esp.* the familiar oral intercourse of two or more persons; conversation (of a familiar kind).

*c***1475** *Rauf Coilȝear* 90 Into sic talk fell thay Quhill thay war neir hame. **1585** T. WASHINGTON tr. *Nicholay's Voy.* I. xvii. 19 The talke betweene them was for this time not very long. **1697** DRYDEN *Virg., Ess. Georg.* (1721) I. 205 Nothing which is a Phrase or Saying in common Talk, shou'd be admitted into a serious Poem. **1728** RAMSAY *Bonnie Chirsty* v, Time was too precious now for tauk. **1783** JOHNSON in *Boswell* (1816) IV. 202 We had talk enough, but no conversation; there was nothing discussed. **1847** HELPS *Friends in C.* I. 1, I do not, however, love good talk the less for these defects of mine.

b. With *a* and *pl.* An instance of this; a conversation.

1548 UDALL, etc. *Erasm. Par. Luke* ix. 88 Their thoughtes and their priuie talkes behynd his backe wer not hydden.. to hym. **1566** ABP. PARKER *Corr.* (Parker Soc.) 268 What speeches and talks be like to rise in the realm. **1658** A. FOX *Würtz' Surg.* I. ii. 3 It is not enough to be full of talks. **1871** L. STEPHEN *Playgr. Eur.* x. (1894) 250 I had many talks with him on the hills. *Mod.* I had a long talk with him on the matter.

c. An informal lecture or address; *spec.* = *radio talk* s.v. RADIO *sb.* 5 b.

1859 A. J. MUNBY *Diary* 2 May in D. Hudson *Munby* (1972) 32 Went to the W. M. College to hear Ruskin's 'talk' about Switzerland... His lecture was historical & geographical chiefly—without book, he standing before the fire. **1900** S. HALE *Let.* 25 Mar. (1919) x. 360 She is giving three 'talks' here in Syracuse. **1923** *Radio Times* 28 Sept. 9/3, 8.45.—A Short Talk by the Rev. W. A. Studdert-Kennedy. **1942** W. WAUGH *Put out More Flags* i. 58 He had ..given the first in what was intended to be a series of talks for the B.B.C. **1962** A. NISBETT *Technique Sound Studio* 273 A 'talk' is a programme or programme segment which consists of one person talking at the microphone, usually from a script. **1977** *Rep. Comm. Future of Broadcasting* (Cmnd. 6753) ii. 12 Radio 3 continued to broadcast some specialised drama, poetry and talks in the evenings.

d. *pl.* Applied *attrib.* to a department of the B.B.C. concerned with the production of radio talks; also to its officials, programmes, etc., and *ellipt.*, the Talks department (with initial capital as a title).

1927 *B.B.C. Handbk.* 1928 124/1 The Talks Department is responsible for the news service, the S.O.S. service,.. Government department talks, and all the sporting, humorous, travel, literary, and general talks. *Ibid.* 125/2 We have evidence..of an increasing demand for the Talks programme and the Talks pamphlet. **1933** J. REITH *Diary* 5 May (1975) ii. 159 He might have done as a talks director ..., but not for the big job. **1938** *Times* 5 Feb. 10/3 Two talks studios, music library, listening hall, [etc.]. **1940** R. S. LAMBERT *Ariel* ii. 49 After the 'hiving off' of Talks, Adult Education and even School Broadcasts, he was left with.. Religion and the Children's Hour. **1942** 'G. ORWELL' *Let.* 16 Oct. in *Coll. Essays* (1968) II. 246 Yours sincerely, (Geo. Orwell) Talks Producer Indian Section. **1954** W. K. HANCOCK *Country & Calling* vii. 189 She became a talks producer on the Overseas Service of the B.B.C. **1962** A. NISBETT *Technique Sound Studio* i. 31 Talks studio tables often have perforated, i.e. acoustically transparent, surfaces. **1978** F. MACLEAN *Take Nine Spies* vii. 228 Guy Burgess.. was appointed to the Talks Department of the BBC. **1980** P. FITZGERALD *Human Voices* ii. 35 No-one could have any [brandy]—a disappointment to everybody except Talks, whose allocation..had already run out.

2. a. A more or less formal or public oral interchange of views, opinions, or propositions; a conference. Also *spec.* in *pl.*, formal discussions, as between representatives of different countries, or between both sides in an industrial dispute; ***talks about talks***: preliminary discussions held before entering into formal negotiations. **b.** A palaver, a pow-wow, as with American Indians; also a verbal message to or from such people.

1550 BALE *Eng. Votaries* II. (1551) 88 At the lattre they came to talkes and to nyghte metynges. **1560** DAUS tr. *Sleidane's Comm.* 229 Themperoure had appoynted a talke of learned men at Regenspurge. *Ibid.* 441 b, Assaied by talcke and conference of learned men. **1760** *St. Papers* in *Ann. Reg.* 231/1 He [Amer. Indian] told the governor he would give his talk the next day; he said he had come with a good talk. **1768** *Chron.* ibid. 89/1 Captain Paterson had sent a talk to the great island, to disclaim the murders, and to pacify the Indians. **1791** W. BARTRAM *Carolina* 210 The talks (or messages between the Indians and white people) were perfectly peaceable and friendly... Bad talks from the Nation is always a very serious affair. **1837** W. IRVING *Capt. Bonneville* III. 114 Indians generally are very lofty, rhetorical, and figurative in their language at all great talks, and high ceremonials. **1952** *Ann. Reg. 1951* 202 The talks broke down on 21 June when it became clear that no agreement was possible. **1971** H. WILSON *Labour Govt.* vi. 78 This time they were more wary, and after some weeks were ready, more for appearances' sake it seemed, to enter into 'talks about talks'. **1977** *Whitaker's Almanack 1978* 590 Greek and Turkish officials began talks in London to try to settle their dispute over rights in the Aegean.

3. Mention (of a subject); making of statements and remarks; rumour; gossip; an instance of this.

1560 DAUS tr. *Sleidane's Comm.* 370 b, In the Emperors court was..no talcke of it, and made as they knew not therof. **1577** *F. de L'isle's Legendarie* A viij b, His brother..who, as the talke went, was sore ouerlayed with Anabaptistes. **1677** WOOD *Life* Apr. (O.H.S.) II. 372 Easter Week, great talk of a comet appearing in England. *a***1768** ABP. SECKER *Serm.*, *Tit. ii.* 6 (1770) III. iii. 68 It will not raise so early or so great a Talk about you. **1866** MRS. GASKELL *Wives & Dau.* xlviii, That would make a talk. **1887** GOLDW. SMITH in *Contemp. Rev.* July 3 A High Commissioner..has been sent to England, and there is talk of sending another to Washington.

4. The subject, theme, or occasion of topical conversation, esp. of current gossip or rumour. Also ***talk of the town*** = TOWN-TALK.

1624 J. CHAMBERLAIN *Let.* 5 June (1939) II. 561 The disgrace that would follow in beeing made *fabula vulgi* and the talke of the towne. **1624** MASSINGER *Parl. Love* IV. v, Live to be the talk Of the conduit and the bakehouse. **1703** CONGREVE *Tears Amaryllis* 107 Wert thou not..The Joy of Sight, the Talk of ev'ry Tongue? **1849** MACAULAY *Hist. Eng.* viii. II. 325 Just when these letters were the talk of all London. **1871** R. ELLIS *Catullus* xliii. 6 Thou the beauty, the talk of all the province? **1912** J. N. MCILWRAITH *Diana of Quebec* xiv. 205 But it would be the talk of the town within twenty-four hours, should even one person chance to see me in pursuit. **1983** *N.Y. Times* 4 Sept. VI. 18/2 The talk of the town this summer, the advertisement was more a lecture than a letter.

II. 5. a. Utterance of words, speaking (to others), speech; = TALKING *vbl. sb.*; also, contemptuously, empty words, verbiage.

big talk, *tall talk*, speaking in a boastful or exaggerated style; see also SMALL TALK.

1539 TAVERNER *Erasm. Prov.* 19 As the man is, so is his talke. **1560** DAUS tr. *Sleidane's Comm.* 363 b, Seldie had the talk, and..propoundeth questions. **1651-7** T. BARKER *Art of Angling* (1820) 6 That is but talk. **1848** THACKERAY *Van. Fair* xxx, But these were mere by-gone days and talk. **1858** LYTTON *What will he do* I. iii, It is I who have all the talk now. **1860** J. G. HOLLAND *Miss Gilbert's Career* x. 173 He sort o' stands round, and spreads, and lets off all the big talk he hears. **1869** [see TALL *a.* 8 b]. **1871** L. STEPHEN *Playgr. Eur.* xiii. (1894) 308 Tall talk is luckily an object of suspicion to Englishmen. **1895** *Pall Mall G.* 8 Oct. 1/3 There is nothing like big talk to draw contributions from a credulous peasantry.

b. Applied to writing of the nature of familiar or loose speech.

1552 ASCHAM in *Lett. Lit. Men* (Camden) 13 Purposing elsewhan to troble yow with the taulk of longer lettres. **1884** *Chr. Commonwealth* 14 Feb. 416/1 Columns of wild, inflammatory, and dangerous talk are appearing in most of our newspapers. **1887** RUSKIN *Præterita* II. i. 1 This second volume must, I fear, be less pleasing... The talk must be less of other persons, and more of myself.

c. *fig.*

1868 HAWTHORNE *Amer. Note-Bks.* II. 218 With so vivid a talk of countenance that it was precisely as if she had spoken. **1879** STEVENSON *Trav. Cevennes* (1886) 130 The indescribable quiet talk of the runnel over the stones.

6. Ordinary manner of speech; way of speaking; native language or dialect; lingo.

*a***1788** T. RITSON in Mrs. Wheeler *Cumbld. Dial.* (1821) App. 2 Yan cudnt tell thare toke be geese. **1890** *Jrnl. Anthrop. Instit.* Feb. 396 [If they do not] speak the same language..the man stays in his own island, and the woman learns his 'talk'.

7. *Comb.*: †**talk-film** *temporary* = TALKIE; **talk-master** *U.S. colloq.*, one who hosts a talk show on radio or television (cf. *quiz-master* (*b*) s.v. QUIZ *sb.*² 2 b); **talk shop** *colloq.* = *talking shop* s.v. TALKING *vbl. sb.* b; **talk show** chiefly *U.S.*, a television programme in which guests are interviewed by the host or 'talk-master'; a television discussion or 'chat' show; also (more *rarely*), a similar programme on radio; †**talk-stuff**, matter for conversation.

1929 *Morning Post* 24 May 12/7 He had been booked..for a talk-film on his voice alone. **1932** *Oxford Times* 23 Sept. 22/5 After a good deal of experimenting I have come to the conclusion that...the best needles to use with a pick-up are those designed for talk-film operation—'talkie' needles. **1975** *Publishers Weekly* 1 Dec. 60/2 Tom Westbrook is the master of radio talkmasters. **1958** *Times* 12 Aug. 7/7 Many Doubting Thomases who regard the United Nations as a mere 'talk shop'. **1973** C. MULLARD *Black Britain* xi. 133 They have broken away from the c.r.c., believing that it is a white man's talk-shop about black immigrant problems. **1965** *Times Lit. Suppl.* 25 Nov. 1042/2 There are now literally thousands of talk-shows. **1977** R. LUDLUM *Chancellor Manuscript* vi. 78 They don't want you giving those interviews or going on talk shows. **1598** MARSTON *Sco. Villanie* III. xi. 22 [He] For want of talk-stuffe, fals to foinery, Out goes his rapier.

talk (tɔːk), *v.* Forms: 3 talkien, -kin, 4 -ken, 4-7 talke, 4- talk, (6 talcke, taulk(e, tawlke; also *Sc.* 5 tawke, 6 tak, 8 tauk, tawk). [ME. *talkien*, *talken*: a deriv. vb. from TALE *sb.* or TELL *v.* Cf. EFris.

talken to talk, chatter, prattle, speak quietly, whisper; also other deriv. vbs. in *-k*, with a diminutive or frequentative force, as *stalk*, *walk*, *lurk*.]

I. Intransitive senses.

1. a. To convey or exchange ideas, thoughts, information, etc. by means of speech, especially the familiar speech of ordinary intercourse; 'to speak in conversation' (J.); to converse.

talk about..., often used *colloq.* to contrast something already mentioned with something still more striking; ***don't talk to me about*** (something), an exclamation against some new topic of conversation of which one has bitter personal experience.

a **1225** *Ancr. R.* 422 Auh talkeð mid ouer meidenes. *a* **1225** *St. Marher.* 13 Ich leote ham talkin ant tauelin of godlec, ant treowliche luuien ham. *a* **1300** *Cursor M.* 11743 (Cott.) Als þai to-gedir talked sua. **1377** LANGL. *P. Pl.* B. XVII. 82 To ouertake hym and talke to hym. *c* **1440** *Promp. Parv.* 486/1 Talkyn, *fabulor, colloquor, confabulor, sermocinor.* **1535** STEWART *Cron. Scot.* (Rolls) II. 123 Thai culd tak and tell of mony thing. **1560** DAUS tr. *Sleidane's Comm.* 125 He hath talked herein with the Dukes of Bavier. **1651** HOBBES *Leviath.* III. xl. 252 The Mountain where God talked with Moses. **1819** *Metropolis* III. 51 My mother and I talked at large on the subject. **1858** HAWTHORNE *Fr. & It. Note-Bks.* I. 180, I doubt whether I have ever really talked with half a dozen persons in my life. **1863** *Fraser's Mag.* Nov. 667 'Talk about women talking!' says a lady of our acquaintance, herself by no means deficient in eloquence. 'Why, look at the debates in the House of Commons, the public dinners, the vestry meetings, and, above all, the gossip, gossip, gossip at those horrid clubs!' **1885** F. ANSTEY *Tinted Venus* xiv. 167 *Well*, Miss Collum, talk about jealousy! **1891** E. ROPER *By Track & Trail* xi. 157 Talk about English people being fond of eating, that Canadian party beat all I had ever seen. **1940** WODEHOUSE *Quick Service* xii. 134 Did she mention her views on poor relations?.. She believes in treating them rough. Talk about oppressed minorities. **1958** P. MARRIS *Widows & their Families* viii. 118 'Don't talk to me about shoes,' said the mother of two small children ruefully. 'My little boy just ripped the sole off one pair.' **1973** W. M. DUNCAN *Big Timer* xxi. 134 Talk about trouble! Goodness knows what Frank will say. **1980** R. HILL *Spy's Wife* vi. 33 'We've had a lot of rain,' said Molly. 'Don't talk to me about rain! You should have been here... I've never seen rain like it.'

b. By extension: To convey information in some other way, as by writing, with the fingers, eyes, etc.

1705 ADDISON *Italy* 459 The Natural Histories of Switzerland talk very much of the Fall of these Rocks.

c. Of a ship, etc.: to communicate by radio.

1912 *Chambers's Jrnl.* Jan. 61/2 When several ships are 'talking' to the shore-station, some delay may arise in getting a message through. **1927** *Pictorial Weekly* 3 Mar. 117/1 Ships of all nationalities 'talking' with shore stations.

2. a. *talk of*: to speak of, about, or in reference to (anything); also, = *talk about* in colloq. use, sense 1 a; often in indirect pass., *to be talked of*. *to talk of* (doing something), to speak somewhat vaguely, so as to suggest a notion, or express one's probable intention, of doing it. *talking of* .., apropos of..; also *joc.* introducing an unconnected subj.

c **1230** *Hali Meid.* 17 ȝif ȝe þrafter þenne speken togedere folliche & talkeð of unnet. *c* **1375** *Cursor M.* 8035 (Fairf.) Hit is meruaile of ham to talke. *c* **1470** HENRY WALLACE I. 295 Tawkand thus of materis that was wrocht. *a* **1555** LATIMER *Serm. in Lincoln* ix. 142 Hearing them taulke of the wonderfull workes which Christ our Sauiour did. **1596** SHAKS. *Merch. V.* I. ii. 45 He doth nothing but talke of his horse. **1661** BOYLE *Style of Script.* (1675) 180 Erostratus, that Fir'd Diana's Temple to be Talk'd of for having done so. **1672**, etc. [see DEVIL *sb.* 22 l]. **1759** JOHNSON *Idler* No. 71 ¶15 [He] talked..volubly of pettifoggers. **1821** SCOTT *Kenilw.* viii, The day was long talked of. **1831** M. EDGEWORTH *Let.* 30 Apr. (1971) 531 'Talking of coincidencies' as Mr. Ward would say.. that was something of a coincidence. **1840** *Spirit of Times* 23 May 133/2 By the way, 'talking of guns', we shall take it as a great favor if our correspondents will send their orders for English Magazines, papers, etc., direct to Messrs. Wiley and Putnam, instead of ordering them from this office. **1851** E. B. BROWNING *Let.* 12 Nov. (1897) II. vii. 29 Talk of English comforts! It's a national delusion. **1857** DICKENS *Let. to Miss Hogarth* 15 Sept., [Wilkie Collins] talks of going to the theatre tonight in a cab. **1876** *Atlantic Monthly* Dec. 684 This gives Pulcheria time to murmer, 'Talk of snub-noses!' **1886** J. PAYN *Heir of Ages* i, Talk of an angel and we hear the flutter of her wings. *a* **1910** *Mod.* Talking of Switzerland —have you ever been there in winter? **1950** F. STARK *Traveller's Prelude* xv. 191 She..asked: 'Were you in a very *small* hospital?' 'I thought so.' Talk of cats!

b. *to talk over*: see 9 c.

3. a. To exercise the faculty of speech; to speak, utter words, say things; often contemptuous: to speak trivially, utter empty words, prate. *to talk to*, to address words to; *colloq.* to rebuke, scold, reprimand; (*U.S.*) *dial.*, to court or woo (a woman); also *to talk up to*. Of a woman: to accept a man's attentions. *to talk at* RANDOM, *at* ROVERS: see these words.

13.. *E.E. Allit. P.* B. 154 þen þe lorde..talkez to his tormenttoures. *c* **1400** *Destr. Troy* 6136 Than Troilus tomly talket agayne. **1508** DUNBAR *Tua Mariit W.* 246 Now tydis me for to talk; my taill it is nixt. *a* **1586** SIDNEY *Ps.* IV. iv, Talk with yor heart and yet be still. **1592** SHAKS. *Ven. & Ad.* 427 What canst thou talke (quoth she), hast thou a tong? **1670** COTTON *Espernon* III. IX. 427 How comes it to pass you are not gone out to meet the Duke of Espernon? he'l talk with you for this when he comes. **1721** RAMSAY *Keitha* 22 Wha 've heard her sing or tauk. **1729** BUTLER *Serm.* Wks. 1874 II. 42 A disposition to be talking for its own sake. **1860** E. M. COWELL *Diary* 17 Feb. in M. W. Disher *Cowells in Amer.* (1934) 18 Arrived there, we were set upon by sleigh conductors, one of whom Sam had also to 'talk to' for using bad language. **1875** JOWETT *Plato* (ed. 2) V. 36 Be assured that I shall be glad to hear you talk as much as you please. **1878** W. S. GILBERT *H.M.S. Pinafore* II. (1881) 295 I'll talk to Master Rackstraw in the morning. **1895** *Dialect Notes* I. 374 Judge Jackson's has been talkin' to my daughter nigh on a year. **1905** in *Eng. Dial. Dict.* VI. 22/2 Pat is talking to Kate this six months, they'll soon be married. **1906** *Dialect Notes* III. 160 *Talk up to, v. phr.*, to court, to woo. 'Bud's talkin' up to her.' **1951** L. CRAIG *Singing Hills* xii. 110 The old man and me are powerful glad Ikey's made up his mind to talk up to a woman. We've been scared he'd be an old bachelor-man. **1951** H. GILES *Harbin's Ridge* xviii. 157 She mentioned that Faleecy John was talking to Jenny Clark a right smart. *Ibid.* 159 I'd not heard of her talking to anybody but Faleecy John.

b. To say something as a rumour or matter of gossip; hence, to indulge in idle or censorious gossip. (Formerly also *trans.* with *obj. cl.*)

1461 *Paston Lett.* II. 7 Item, som men talke Lord Wellys, Lord Wyllouby, and Skales ben on lyve. **1669** LADY CHAWORTH in *12th Rep. Hist. MSS. Comm.* App. v. 12 They talk heere as if the King would goe a northerne progresse this summer. **1719** RAMSAY *Prol. to 'The Orphan'* 15 But let them tauk. **1849** MACAULAY *Hist. Eng.* vi. II. 154 The king said..that it was difficult to prevent people from talking, and that loose reports were not to be regarded.

c. *to talk big, tall*, etc., to talk boastfully; to indulge in inflated language; see also BIG *a.* 8 b; (*colloq.* or *slang*). *to talk down* (*to* an audience), to lower one's discourse to the assumed level of their intelligence; also *transf.* (in quots., of writers). *to talk through one's hat*: see HAT *sb.* 5 c; *to talk through* (*the back of*) *one's neck*: see NECK *sb.*[1] 3 e; *to talk turkey*: see TURKEY[2] 2 d.

1699 R. L'ESTRANGE *Erasm. Colloq.* (1725) 236, I talk big, and wherever I find an hungry Buzzard I throw him out a Bait. **1702** *Eng. Theophrast.* 336 Some people think they need only talk loud and big and be very positive, to make all the World of their Opinion. **1841** THIRLWALL *Lett.* (1881) I. 175 We are able to talk big about light and freedom. **1856** C. M. YONGE *Daisy Chain* II. xiv. 498 'Say it again—what you said about the sea,' said Mary, more comforted than if Ethel had been talking *down* to her. **1888** BRYCE *Amer. Commw.* VI. cx. (1889) 669 On the Fourth of July..the speaker feels bound to talk 'his very tallest'. **1919** H. WALPOLE *Jeremy* ii. 43 He always talked down to us as though we were beings of another and inferior planet. He called it, 'Getting on with the little ones.' **1954** M. F. RODELL *Mystery Fiction* i. 1 This does not mean that mystery fiction need be hack work; nor that the authors of it must 'talk down' to their audiences. **1970** *Sci. Jrnl.* Apr. 84/2 The authors for future titles all seem to be practising scientists. The problem will be whether they can achieve the necessary clarity of style without 'talking down' to their new audiences.

d. *to talk at*, to make remarks intended for some one but not directly addressed to him.

1789 *Loiterer* 14 Feb. 11 Sometimes they talk to me, and sometimes at me. **1837** MARRYAT *Olla Podr.* xxxiii, They talked at us, and not to us. **1838** DICKENS *Nich. Nick.* xxi, Mr. and Mrs. Wititterly, who had talked rather at the Nicklebys than to each other. **1894** MRS. DYAN *All in a Man's K.* (1899) 210 He had had no intention..of..talking at her, but the words had struck home.

(*b*) *to talk over* (another person), to override or talk simultaneously with (another speaker) on a tape recording, broadcast programme, etc.

1962 A. NISBETT *Technique Sound Studio* vii. 126 Superimpositions. Two people talking over each other are irritating. **1975** D. PITTS *Target Manhattan* (1976) xxviii. 111 Would you please announce your name and station first and try not to talk over other people.

e. To say something to the purpose, esp. in colloq. phr. ***now you're talking***. Also *fig.* of money: see MONEY *sb.* 6 a.

1841 DICKENS *Barnaby Rudge* lii, in *Master Humphrey's Clock* III. 238 That's the kind of game... Now you talk, indeed! **1884** J. HAY *Bread-Winners* x. 149 Now you're talkin'. **1920** 'O. DOUGLAS' *Penny Plain* ii. 21 'I'm going to Scotland.' 'Ah,' said James Lauder, 'now you're talking.' **1936** L. HELLMAN *Days to Come* I. 26 'I was in Akron.' That's the job I wanted. 'Now we're talking... That's money for you.' **1952** A. CHRISTIE *Mrs. McGinty's Dead* viii. 59 'A few days later Mrs. McGinty was murdered.' 'Now you're talking.' **1974** M. HASTINGS *Dragon Island* xix. 174 'Now you're talking.' Jukes said approvingly... 'That's the best bit of sense you've spoke today.'

f. In various colloq. phrases stating or implying that someone is in no position to criticize another, exemplified by the types: ***you can't talk!***; (***look, hark***) ***who's talking!***; ***who am I to talk?***; ***I should talk!***

1847 THACKERAY *Van. Fair* (1848) xli. 371 A person can't help their birth... I am sure Aunt Bute need not talk: she wants to marry Kate to young Hooper, the wine-merchant. **1895** KIPLING *Day's Work* (1898) 200 'All you other men think of is to give him an absurd nickname.'.. 'Well, *you* can't talk, William. You christened little Miss Demby the Button-quail.' **1938** N. MARSH *Artists in Crime* ii. 24 You're paying his fare Home, of course. Well, I suppose I can't talk as you've given me the run of your house. **1945** A. KOBER *Parm Me* 62 'Look who's talking!' said Pa Gross, glaring at his wife. **1949** D. SMITH *I capture Castle* ii. 12 She has had that dressing-gown so long that I don't think she sees it any more... But who am I to talk—who have not had a new dressing-gown at all for two years? **1962** J. CANNAN *All is Discovered* i. 11 Anyway Daddy can't talk. Whenever she's out he.. spends hours with Maria. **1968** M. ROSS *Gasteropod* iv. 99 'You should have hated me... Most men would have done.' Max laughed. 'Hark who's talking! What did you do?' **1979** D. GURR *Troika* viii. 55, I was rough on you... And stupid —I should talk!

g. *to talk back*: to answer back; to indulge in 'back-chat'. *N. Amer. colloq.*

1869 'MARK TWAIN' *Innoc. Abr.* xii. 112 There was no 'talking back', no dissatisfaction about over-charging. **1939** L. M. MONTGOMERY *Anne of Ingleside* iv. 22 Dad would never let anyone 'talk back' to Aunt Mary Maria. **1955** L. HUGHES in *Oliphant Q.* Apr.–June 136 All over the world today folks with not even *Mister* in front of their names are raring up and talking back to the folks called *Mister.* **1977** M. FRENCH *Women's Room* (1978) ii. 117, I can't stand it when they start to talk back, be fresh.

h. With alcoholic drink as subj.: used to excuse or explain uncharacteristic sentiments supposedly brought on by the drink consumed. Chiefly in *pres. pple. colloq.*

1922 JOYCE *Ulysses* 742 Paying his compliments the Bushmills whisky talking of course. *a* **1953** E. O'NEILL *Touch of Poet* (1957) I. 42 But you understand, it was the liquor talking, if I said anything to wound you. **1982** R. LEWIS *Gathering of Ghosts* iii. 102 It was all a bit stupid, you know. Beer talking, you know how it is.

i. To disclose information, *spec.* to the police (or another authority), esp. incriminating oneself or others; to confess; to turn informer or 'squeal'. *slang.*

1924 G. C. HENDERSON *Keys to Crookdom* 420 Talk. See squeal, beef, spiel, chew rag. **1952** M. ALLINGHAM *Tiger in Smoke* xv. 216 They've been through it today, but they're not talking. Why should they? **1959** W. GOLDING *Free Fall* vii. 144 'I won't talk. I know nothing.' 'Talk. Yes, that is the word. At some point, Mr. Mountjoy, you will talk.' **1976** *Times Lit. Suppl.* 21 May 605/3 He is, as they say, not talking, and refused to be interviewed by the authors of this book.

j. With advb. accusative. ***to talk one's way in***: to gain admission by persuasion. Similarly with *out*.

1973 *Ottawa Jrnl.* 3 Feb. 6/1 Their length of hospital stays, during which they tried to talk their way out, ranged from seven to 52 days; the average stay was 19 days. **1978** 'D. KYLE' *Black Camelot* xv. 237 If Rasch could talk his way in ..the task would be simple.

4. To utter words, or the sound of words, unconsciously, mechanically, or imitatively, as *to talk in one's sleep*, etc.

1591 SHAKS. *Two Gent.* III. i. 333 Item, she doth talke in her sleepe. **1704** NORRIS *Ideal World* II. iii. 120 That..we may not be supposed to talk like parrots. **1890** *Spectator* 4 Oct., The raven is the largest creature except man that can 'talk'.

5. *fig.* Of inanimate things: To make sounds or noises resembling or suggesting speech. *spec.*, of an anchor which is dragged (see DRAG *v.* 1 c).

1793 WORDSWORTH *Evening Walk* 319 The talking boat that moves with pensive sound. **1832** *Blackw. Mag.* XXXI. 508 She [a ship] began to slip through the water at a rapid rate and to talk. **1883** STEVENSON *Treas. Isl.* v. xxiii, The ship was talking, as sailors say, loudly, treading the innumerable ripples with an incessant weltering splash. **1885** W. L. CARPENTER *Soap & Candles* vi. 161 [The bubbles] make so much noise in their escape that, in the language of the soap-boiler, 'the soap talks'. **1900** *Daily News* 2 Jan. 6/1 It is to be hoped that they will not lose their heads when the rifles begin to talk in earnest. **1914** 'BARTIMEUS' *Naval Occasions* xxiii. 224 'I think the starboard anchor is "talking".'..A dull metallic sound detached itself from the sibilant rushing of water. **1917** J. S. MARGERISON *Sure Shield* 86 It was the ring chain that had worked slightly loose and which was allowing the five-ton mass of cast iron to slide three inches each way as the ship rolled and pitched, and the creaking sound of which had given rise to the phrase 'the anchor's talking'. **1962** W. GRANVILLE *Dict. Sailors' Slang* 118/1 A ship's anchor is said to come home, or 'talk', when it is dragging.

II. Transitive senses.

6. a. To utter or speak in familiar language (words, a tale, etc.); to express in talk or speech (matter, opinions, etc.). †Also with *obj. cl.*: see 3 b. *to talk out*, to utter freely, give full utterance to.

c **1205** LAY. 788 þat nan ne beo so wilde..þat word talie ne talkie mid speche. **13..** *Cursor M.* 17288 + 332 (Cott.) What wordez are þos..þat ȝe to-gedir talk? **13..** *Gaw. & Gr. Knt.* 2133 Bot I wyl to þe chapel..& talk wyth þat ilk tulk þe tale þat me lyste. **1445** in *Anglia* XXVIII. 269 The modrys of eloquence the musys ix..wisely talke dytees ful delectable. **1533** MORE *Debell. Salem* xiv. Wks. 966/2 To heare heresyes talked and lette the talkers alone. **1682** T. FLATMAN *Heraclitus Ridens* No. 52 (1713) II. 78 Let's leave him..and talk a little News that's common to the rest of the World. **1715** DE FOE *Fam. Instruct.* II. i. (1841) I. 174 Why, you talk blasphemy almost. **1775** ABIGAIL ADAMS in *Fam. Lett.* (1876) 115, I have written many things to you that..I never could have talked. **1848** THACKERAY *Van. Fair* xxxiv, They could not talk scandal in any tongue but their own. **1861** HUGHES *Tom Brown at Oxf.* iv, An old friend to whom he could talk out his mind.

b. To use as a spoken language, to speak conversationally: as *to talk French, German, Somerset, slang*. So *to talk sailor* (= to use nautical language), etc. *to talk Greek, Hebrew, Double-Dutch, gibberish*, etc., to use language unintelligible to the hearer.

1859 *Habits of Gd. Society* (new ed.) 89 We..would not have him talk slang. **1869** F. W. NEWMAN *Misc.* 146 A single race, whose ancestors once talked a common language. **1886** *Manch. Exam.* 3 Nov. 5/6 Hundreds of young women who can talk French and German fluently. **1881** *Cent. Mag.* XXIII. 126/2, I..could talk sailor like an 'old salt'. **1903** *Daily Chron.* 12 Feb. 3/1 Englishmen who have visited America will remember their gratification at being invited to 'talk United States'.

7. To discourse about, speak of, discuss. Now *colloq.* ***to talk shop***, to talk about matters pertaining to one's own business or profession.

1387 TREVISA *Higden* (Rolls) IV. 359 He..talkede wiþ hym fiftene dayes þe gospel [*conferens cum eo evangelium*]. **1660** INGELO *Bentiv. & Ur.* II. (1682) 179 He desired to talk some things with him privately. **1667** MILTON *P.L.* III. 483 That Crystalline Sphear whose ballance weighs The Trepidation talkt. **1819** SHELLEY *Julian & Maddalo* 179 Aye, if we were not weak... You talk Utopia. **1821** BYRON *Diary* 29 Jan., They talk Dante—write Dante—and think and dream Dante. **1854** EMERSON *Soc. Aims* Wks. (Bohn) III. 181 Never 'talk shop' before company. **1870** MISS BRIDGMAN *Rob. Lynne* I. ix. 129 He threw all his ardour into talking business. **1871** M. COLLINS *Mrq. & Merch.* I. x. 302 Talking horse, and playing billiards. **1888** *Times* (weekly ed.) 3 Feb. 2/3 'Talking shop'..means talking of the interests of the work which you do, or the profession to which you belong. **1898** P. WHITE *Millionaire's Dau.* xxxi, We talked 'Oxford', the dean addressing his remarks to me.

(*b*) ***to talk a good game***: to discuss a topic convincingly (with implication that no action is taken). Also, ***to talk a great ball game***. *U.S. colloq.*

1972 'H. PENTECOST' *Birthday, Deathday* iv. 39 Hollywood address... Talks a great ball game to the hotel people out there about his big film deals. **1973** *Philadelphia Inquirer* (Today Suppl.) 14 Oct. 171 She still talks a good game. To hear her tell it, she's the Henry Kissinger of consumerism. **1977** *New Yorker* 18 July 52/1 While they talk a good game, their considerations are consolidating their power around the world.

8. To bring or drive (oneself or another) into some specified state by talking.

1599 SHAKS. *Much Ado* II. i. 369 They would talke themselues madde. **1613** —— *Hen. VIII*, I. iv. 45 Talke vs to silence. **1711** POPE *Ess. Crit.* 36 No Place so Sacred from such Fops is barr'd,..Nay, run to Altars; there they'll talk you dead. **1738** JOHNSON *London* 4 And here a female Atheist talks you dead. **1816** SCOTT *Let. to Morritt* 21 Aug. in *Lockhart*, I talked them to death. **1920** R. MACAULAY *Potterism* v. iii. 175 He..used to talk one sick about how little scope he had in his parish.

9. a. With *adv.* or *prep.*: To influence, move, or affect by talking; as ***to talk down***, (*a*) to put down by talking; to out-talk; (*b*) to reduce or diminish by talking; to denigrate or belittle; (*c*) *Econ.*, to depress the value of (a currency) or the price of (a commodity) by making tactical public statements; similarly, ***to talk lower***; (*d*) see sense 9 d below; ***to talk*** (a person) ***into*** or ***out of***, to persuade into, or dissuade from (something) by talking; ***to talk out***, to talk to the end of; to carry on the discussion of (a bill in Parliament, etc.) till the time for adjournment is reached, and so frustrate its progress by preventing its being put to a vote; ***to talk*** (a person) ***over*** or ***round***, to win over, or into compliance, by talking; ***to talk*** (a person) ***through*** (something), to provide with a commentary on (some event); to take through with helpful explanation; ***to talk*** (a thing) ***up***, (*a*) to talk strenuously in support of, to 'crack up'; (*b*) to discuss favourably; to stimulate interest in by talking, esp. exaggeratedly; to praise or advocate (chiefly *U.S.*); to extract from (a person) by persuasion; ***to talk*** (a person) ***up to***, to bring (him) up to the point or level of (something) by talking.

a **1658** FORD, etc. *Witch Edmonton* I. ii, Why Mr. Thorney, d'ye mean to talk out your dinner? **1697** COLLIER *Ess.* II. (1703) 64 A friend who relates his success talks himself into a new pleasure. **1706** VANBRUGH *Mistake* III. i. Wks. (1840) 449/1 [I have] told him the secret, and then talked him into a liking on't. **1719** DE FOE *Crusoe* (1840) II. vi. 152 He talks himself into a..convert. *Ibid.* xii. 262, I would be talking myself up to vigorous resolution. **1722** —— *Col. Jack* (1840) 304, I failed not to talk up the gallantry..of his..majesty. **1797–8** JANE AUSTEN *Sense & Sens.* xxxv, You shan't talk me out of my satisfaction. **1814** —— *Mansfield Park* I. xiii. 269 She started no difficulties that were not talked down in five minutes. **1832** J. S. MILL *Let.* 25 Jan. in *Wks.* (1963) XII. 94 Most men in this country have a strong prejudice against any attempt to *talk them over* as the vulgar say. **1847** TENNYSON *Princ.* v. 284 Her that talk'd down the fifty wisest men. **1862** LATHAM *Channel Isl.* III. xvi. (ed. 2) 377 He..was talked-over by Prince Maurice, whom, unless he meant to be talked-over, he had no occasion to meet. **1863** TROLLOPE *Rachel Ray* I. viii. 151 Mrs. Butler Cornbury..talked her young friend up to the top of the tree. **1865** H. KINGSLEY *Hillyars & Burtons* lvi, He talked over Trevittick, who sulkily acquiesced. **1865** KINGSLEY *Herew.* vi, You need not try to talk this out of my head. **1872** *Rep. Vermont Board Agric.* I. 679 This little conversation led me to talk the matter up with the marble dealers. **1873** *Punch* 19 July 22/2 Mr. Beresford Hope 'talked out' the Bill. **1883** *Cent. Mag.* XXV. 527/2 'Talk him into taking a little rest', said Helen. *a* **1882** TROLLOPE *Autobiogr.* (1883) I. v. 108, I received £20... The money had been 'talked out of' the worthy publisher by..my brother, who made the bargain for me. **1885** C. C. HARRISON in *Harper's Mag.* Mar. 546/1 He must be talked into it. **1894** MISS COBBE *Life* I. 341, I do believe I could walk down anybody and perhaps talk down anybody too. **1900** *Westm. Gaz.* 6 Mar. 9/3 Clever talkers are kept..to 'talk up' the patients to the highest possible fee. **1903** *Speaker* 21 Nov., Suppl. 3 Give Mr. Chamberlain time to talk himself out. **1931** *Daily Express* 5 Sept. 10/5 Amsterdam is taking a bearish view of Royal Dutch and is 'talking' the shares £2 lower. **1932** W. FAULKNER *Light in August* iii. 56 The old men and the old women trying to talk down his gleeful excitement. **1933** *Sun* (Baltimore) 12 July 3/2 Thus far the dollar has been 'talked down'. **1938** *Richmond* (Va.) *Times-Dispatch* 10 Nov. 1/7 (*heading*) Victorious Taft talks down 1940 chances. **1956** H. GOLD *Man who was not with It* (1965) ii. 17 You talk it up like a longtime grifter. **1962** *Spectator* 28 Dec. 999/3 Most professionals [on the Paris Stock Exchange] are talking their market lower. **1967** *Economist* 4 Mar. 797/2 The non-mandatory system..will allow the Government, in American style, to 'talk down' a price. **1970** NEW ENG. BIBLE *Prov.* xix. 26 He who talks his father down vexes his mother. **1976** J. SNOW *Cricket Rebel* 27 A year later when I made my Test debut against New Zealand at Lord's. Ted [Dexter] virtually talked me through the game. **1978** *Daily Tel.* 16 Mar. 11/1, I am fed up with people talking down the NHS, failing to put things into perspective by pointing to the successes as well as the difficulties. **1980** *Times* 28 Jan. 19/2 For years the Silver Users Association..has been successfully talking the price of silver down. **1982** *Nature* 13 May 91/1 True, the Western media are delighted to talk up 'Star Wars' fantasies, the US shuttle, Ariane or Soviet space weapons. But they have overlooked the main substance of the Soviet [space] programme.

b. To spend or pass *away* (time, and the like) in or by talking.

1676 COTTON *Walton's Angler* II. i. (1881) 245 We have already talked away two miles of your journey. **1702** ADDISON *Dial. Medals* Misc. Wks. 1736 III. 12, I am very well content to talk away an evening with you on the subject. **1890** CLARK RUSSELL *Ocean Trag.* III. xxxiv. 242 Thus idly would we talk away the days.

c. ***to talk*** (a thing) ***over, to talk over*** (a matter): to discuss it in familiar conference or conversation.

1734 WATTS *Reliq. Juv.* (1789) 218 When I have talked my diseases all over to them. **1810** SCOTT *Let. to Morritt* 2 Mar. in *Lockhart*, We talked over this subject once while riding on the banks of Tees. **1847** MARRYAT *Childr. N. Forest* xxiii, We will talk over the matter as we go. **1851** FITZGERALD *Euphranor* (1904) 78 They could talk the matter over.

d. ***to talk down***: to provide (an aircraft) with directions by radio communication which enable it to land, esp. in overcast or emergency conditions. Also with *in*: chiefly applied to ships seeking landfall. Hence with the pilot or navigating officer as subj. Occas. with other advbs. and preps.

1943 *Plane Talk* June 28/3 The bombardier talks the pilot 'in', telling him which way to turn. **1945** *Sci. News Let.* 25 Aug. 127/1 A blindfolded pilot..was 'talked-down' to the runway by a control operator. **1946** *Jrnl. Inst. Electr. Engin.* XCIII. III. A. 1–4 124/2 If we make these aircraft carry simple radio receivers, and pin-point them with our accurate radar, it is quite possible to 'talk them down' by giving detailed instructions to the pilot. **1955** *Sun* (Baltimore) 12 June (B ed.) 3/4 The ground controlled approach equipment—through which a plane is 'talked in' to a landing. **1957** *Times* 24 Aug. 4/1 From information telephoned to Ford by police officers it [*sc.* the helicopter] was 'talked' to where two young girls and a young man were clinging to an overturned dinghy. **1960** 'N. SHUTE' *Trustee from Toolroom* 97 They get us on the radar screen and talk us down on to the runway. **1962** J. DILL in *Into Orbit* p. xviii, Shephard was seated before a console..ready to talk John Glenn back to earth. **1967** *Observer* 2 Apr. 10/6 Ships could be advised of optimum routes and speeds as they approach port, and even 'talked in' through fog. **1970** *Daily Tel.* 21 Dec. 2/6 It is a 'blind landing system' in which a ground controller talks down an airliner in bad weather by watching its approach on a radar screen.

10. Colloq. phrases. ***to talk the hind leg off a donkey*** (***horse***, etc.), applied to one who: (*a*) talks with unflagging and wearying persistence, or: (*b*) is said to have the power to persuade another by eloquent or charming speech; ***to talk*** (someone's) ***ear off***: to talk incessantly or until one is tired of listening (*U.S.*).

1808 *Cobbett's Weekly Pol. Reg.* XIII. II. 47 The old vulgar hyperbole of 'talking a horse's hind leg off'..will find its verification in the American Congress. **1861** *Temple Bar* I. 414 One has heard of persons who could 'talk a donkey's hind leg off'. **1879** TROLLOPE *John Caldigate* III. ix. 122 She'd talk the hind-legs off a dog, as we used to say out there [*sc.* in Australia]. **1915** W. S. MAUGHAM *Of Human Bondage* lxxxviii. 459 'Doesn't she look like Rubens' second wife?' cried Athelny. 'Wouldn't she look splendid in a seventeenth-century costume? That's the sort of wife to marry, my boy. Look at her.' 'I believe you'd talk the hind leg off a donkey, Athelny,' she answered calmly. **1935** G. & S. LORIMER *Heart Specialist* i. 9 An American will talk your ear off about his sport with a little encouragement. **1942** G. H. D. & M. COLE *Toper's End* IV. ix. 138 You can talk the 'ind leg off any donkey. **1976** *National Observer* (U.S.) 10 Apr. 9/5 Heck! I could talk your ear off. But let me just say that in all my 40 years of organizing and escorting tours, I haven't found a better one than this one.

talkable ('tɔːkəb(ə)l), *a.* [f. TALK *v.* + -ABLE.] **a.** Of a thing: That can or may be talked of or about. **b.** Of a person: Ready to converse; affable. *rare.*

a **1800** GEN. PAOLI in P. Fitzgerald *Life J. Boswell* (1891) I. viii. 91 So cheerful, so witty, so gentle, so talkable. **1830** *Blackw. Mag.* XXVIII. 893 All speak—talk—whisper..of all the speakable, talkable, whisperable..interesting affairs, incidents and occurrences. **1859** MRS. GASKELL *Lett.* (1966) 546 If Papa gets over-busy; & not talkable as to-day! **1899** H. VAN DYKE *Fisherman's Luck* III. i. 54 A person who has the rare merit of being talkable. 'Talkable' is not a new adjective. But it needs a new definition, and the complement of a corresponding noun...*talkability*. **1963** R. SYMONS *Many Trails* iii. 31 A grown woman yearns for somebody more 'talkable' than a thirteen-year-old.

talkathon ('tɔːkəθɒn). *colloq.* (orig. *U.S.*). [f. TALK *v.* + -ATHON, after *walkathon*.] **1.** An interminable session of talk or discussion; *spec.* a prolonged debate in a legislature or similar body, a filibuster.

1934 *Amer. Speech* IX. 76/2 Apropos of the walkathons,.. a contributor suggests that talkathons will be longer lived, especially in legislative halls. **1948** *Times-Dispatch* (Richmond, Va.) 3 Aug. 1/2 Filibustering Dixie Senators won a major round today in their effort to talk the anti-poll tax bill to death. The presiding officer..decided that an effort to curb the debate was in conflict with Senate rules, and so the talkathon continued. **1957** *Economist* 7 Sept. 820/2 The regular Assembly session..will begin with the annual talkathon, oddly styled the general debate. **1969** *Daily Colonist* (Victoria, B.C.) 3 May 2/7 Rene Matte.. dashed any hopes of government supporters that the Creditistes were tiring of their talkathon. **1978** D. A. STANWOOD *Memory of Eva Ryker* xix. 181 No talkathons tonight, Eva... We'll get a fresh start in the morning.

2. A prolonged broadcast in which a political candidate is interviewed or questioned (*U.S.*). Also applied *transf.* to a lengthy radio or television discussion programme or 'talk show'. Cf. RADIOTHON.

1952 *Economist* 6 Sept. 555/2 The latest American political novelty, the radio 'talkathon', in which..[Mr. Schmitt] answers questions for 25 hours at a stretch. **1961** *N.Y. Times Mag.* 29 Oct. 24/1 (*heading*) Political walkathons and talkathons. **1965** *Punch* 4 Aug. 176/1 The three-hour and twenty-five minute talkathon on BBC 2, was held by chance on the very day that Mr. Callaghan most heavily stamped on the economic brakes.

tal'kation. *nonce-wd.* [f. TALK *v.* + -ATION.] A talking. (Usually dyslogistic.)

1781 H. WALPOLE *Let.* 9 Sept. (1955) XXIX. 152 This is the sum total of what I can learn; matter enough to dissert upon if such were my propensity! but besides not loving talkation, it is painful for me to write. **1800** in *Spirit Pub. Jrnls.* IV. 155 It was no discourse..but a kind of talkation (if I may be allowed the expression). **1898** B. GREGORY *Side Lights Confl. Meth.* 204 A tangled, wearisome talkation then ensued.

talkative ('tɔːkətɪv), *a.* [f. TALK *v.* + -ATIVE.] Given to talking; inclined to talk; chatty, loquacious; garrulous, 'full of prate' (J.).

1432–50 tr. *Higden* (Rolls) VI. 469 Hit is a fowle vice in a kynge to be talkatyve [orig. *dicacem fore*; TREVISA to iangle moche] in a feste. **1529** MORE *Dyaloge* III. Wks. 243/1 The more foole the more talkatife of great doutes and hygh questions of holy Scripture. **1552** HULOET, Talcatiue, or full of talkynge and pratlynge, *fabularis*. **1665** GLANVILL *Def. Van. Dogm.* 51 One Author will not reckon him among the slight and talkative Philosophers. **1866** GEO. ELIOT *F. Holt* ii, [He] became very talkative over his second bottle of port.

b. Said of personal qualities, etc.; also *fig.*

14.. *Craft of Lovers* iv. in *Chaucer's Wks.* (1561) 341 Your peinted eloquence, So gay, so freshe, and eke so talcatife. **1509** BARCLAY *Shyp of Folys* (1570) 54 Sophistrie nor Logike with their arte talcatife. **1644** BULWER *Chirol.* 1 The Hand, that busie instrument, is most talkative. **1719** STEELE *Plebian* Wks. (1790) 293 Nothing is so talkative as misfortune. **1778** MISS BURNEY *Evelina* (1791) II. xxxvii. 257 So little talkative is the fulness of contentment. **1860** TYNDALL *Glac.* I. vii. 47 This..is the most talkative glacier I have ever known.

Hence '**talkatively** *adv.*, in a talkative way.

1589 WARNER *Alb. Eng.* VI. xxx. (1612) 150 For slaunder set on foote, though false, is talkatiuely dome. **1727** BAILEY vol. II, *Talkatively*, after a talkative Manner. **1847** in WEBSTER; and in mod. Dicts.

talkativeness ('tɔːkətɪvnɪs). [f. prec. + -NESS.] The quality or state of being talkative.

1609 W. M. *Man in Moone* (1849) 48 Talkativeness, or much babling. **1674** *Govt. Tongue* vi. 73 We use to call this Talkativeness a Feminine vice. **176.** WESLEY *To Children* 2 Wks. 1811 IX. 92 Talkativeness before any person has the appearance of disrespect. **1840** DICKENS *Old C. Shop* xiv, There was a clinking of wine-glasses and a great talkativeness on the part of everybody.

talk-back ('tɔːkbæk). Also **talkback, talk back.** [f. TALK *v.*] **A.** *attrib.* Designating apparatus and facilities for two-way communication by loudspeaker, usu. between one who gives and one who receives instructions; *spec.* that connecting a studio and a control room.

1933 *B.B.C. Yearbk. 1934* 402 The 'talk back' facilities need setting up to suit the particular conditions of studio, listening point, etc., whereby the person listening to the rehearsal may speak over a microphone circuit and by means of a loudspeaker give instructions to those rehearsing. **1959** H. BARNES *Oceanogr. & Marine Biol.* 197 During the descent instructions are always relayed from the lower laboratory to a man at the winch by a micro-phone and talk-back system, and particular care is taken when nearing the bottom. **1971** M. LEE *Dying for Fun* xxiii. 107 The sound radio producer..put down his talk-back key and said: 'We won't start till you're ready.' **1982** J. SHERWOOD *Shot in Arm* xiii. 126 He pressed the talk-back key. 'Anthea..could you make it a bit lighter and more informal?'

B. *sb.* A talk-back system.

1957 *Listener* 11 July 53 Large numbers mean more widespread buildings and (in spite of a public address system, talkbacks, and so on) it is not always easy to get the people or things one wants as quickly as one wants them. **1962** A. NISBETT *Technique Sound Studio* vi. 107 The studio manager announces over the studio talk-back (which also goes to the recording room), 'We'll be going ahead in ten seconds from...now!' **1979** *Daily Tel.* 23 Apr. 14/4 Next door again is the studio, with Robin Day, that morning's speaker and, between them, a girl wearing headphones who passes on the caller's name and location over the talk back from the cubicle.

talk-down. [f. vbl. phr. *to talk down*: see TALK *v.* 9 d.] The action or process of talking down an aircraft or a pilot. Chiefly *attrib.*

1946 *Engineering Jrnl.* Apr. 233/1 It is felt that the 'talk down' feature will not be well received in airline work. **1948** *Shell Aviation News* No. 123. 11/2 G.C.A. is a 'talk down' system and where such installations are available.. no equipment in the aircraft is needed other than efficient radio telephony. **1955** *Times* 20 June 3/5 The more complicated problems of refuelling in mid-air, baling out on to snowy tundra slopes, and landing at night by 'talk-down'. **1959** K. HENNEY *Radio Engin. Handbk.* (ed. 5) xxvi. 91 (*caption*) Information displayed to operators of precision indicators of GCA 'talk-down' radar landing system. **1963** L. DEIGHTON *Horse under Water* xx. 89 A Viscount came down the GCA talkdown, its white, red and green lights peep-boing the traffic pattern.

talked (tɔːkt), *ppl. a.* [f. TALK *v.* + -ED[1].]

1. Spoken familiarly: chiefly in ***talked-of***, familiarly or vaguely spoken about.

1841 COL. HAWKER *Diary* (1893) II. 208 Our long-talked-of trip. **1865** RUSKIN *Sesame* I. (1897) 16 A book is essentially not a talked thing, but a written thing. **1890** *Spectator* 31 May 764/1 To make himself the observed of all observers, and the talked-of among all talkers.

2. ***talked-about*** (chiefly with qualifying advb.): discussed.

1919 C. S. PARKER *Amer. Idyll* xvi. 178 He was the most talked-about man at the Convention. **1928** *Manch. Guardian Weekly* 7 Sept. 184/3 A striking proof of the reality and significance of the much-talked-about new entente. **1951** *Rochester* (N.Y.) *Democrat & Chron.* 12 Sept. 14/1 The fight, one of the most talked-about in years, will not be on television or radio. **1968** J. D. WATSON *Double Helix* ix. 65 The wine turned the conversation to the currently talked-about Cambridge popsies. **1982** J. FOX *White Mischief* v. 59 She was already a talked-about social success.

talkee. *colloq.* = next 2.

1885 *Illustr. Lond. News* Christmas No. 7/1 Of our five hours' talkee.. a few words are worth recording.

talkee-talkee (ˈtɔːkɪˌtɔːkɪ). [A reduplicated derivative of TALK, with dimin. ending.]

1. The name given to various English-based pidgins or creoles; *esp.* the lingua franca of West Indian Blacks; *spec.* (usu. spelt **Taki-Taki**; also with lower-case initials) an English-based creole language of Surinam; = NINGRE TONGO, SRANAN.

1808 *Edin. Rev.* XII. 413 The *talkee-talkee*, or negro jargon, is now chiefly English. **1810** SOUTHEY *Let. to J. May* 5 Dec., The talkee talkee of the slaves in the Sugar Islands, as it is called, will prevail in Surinam. **1828** *Life Planter Jamaica* 13 Ignorant of the negro corrupted dialect, or the talkee talkee language. **1856** J. H. NEWMAN *Callista* i. (1890) 8 Not without parallel in the talkee-talkee of the West Indian negro. **1932** A. G. BARNETT in *Amer. Speech* VII. 394 In Paramaribo, this speech of former slaves has degenerated into 'Talkee-talkee', which is loaded with a heavy percentage of Dutch. **1933, 1939** [see NINGRE TONGO]. **1955** *Caribbean Q.* IV. II. 167 Translation in the Rural Creole of Surinam (Taki Taki) by Albert Helman. **1961** F. G. CASSIDY *Jamaica Talk* i. 8 It [*sc.* Macca] got into the common speech and has remained in Taki-taki and in Jamaican. **1970** *Language* XLVI. 409 Saramaccan.. is only partly intelligible to speakers of Sranan or Taki-taki.

2. Small-talk; petty or childish talk, chatter; continuous talk or prattle. (*contemptuous.*)

1812 MAR. EDGEWORTH *Vivian* x, There's a woman, now, who thinks of nothing living but herself!—all talkee talkee! **1840** *Fraser's Mag.* XXII. 55 The usual nothings which make up talkee-talkee. **1890** *Nature* 6 Mar. 410/2 That 'talkee-talkee' so often forced into books of this kind.

attrib. **1869** HUXLEY in *Life* (1900) I. xxiii. 309 The discourses are to [be] lessons and not talkee-talkee lectures.

talker (ˈtɔːkə(r)). [f. TALK *v.* + -ER[1].] One who talks or is given to talking; a speaker, a conversationalist; a talkative person.

c **1386** CHAUCER *Pars. T.* ⁋304 Eke if.. he be a talker of ydel wordes of folye or vileynye. **1470–85** MALORY *Arthur* x. lvi. 508 The meryest knyghte.. and the maddest talker. **1648** MILTON *Observ. Art. Peace* Wks. 1851 IV. 564 The overworne objection of every triviall Talker. **1701** W. WOTTON *Hist. Rome* i. 15 Great Talkers should always be mistrusted. **1815** JANE AUSTEN *Emma* xli, I am rather a talker; and now and then I have let a thing escape me which I should not. **1861** CRAIK *Hist. Eng. Lit.* II. 248 Bolingbroke .. was one of the most brilliant orators and talkers.

b. *Comb.*, as **talker-down**, one who talks down; so **talker-out**; **talker-seer**, a seer who is also a talker.

1833 MRS. BROWNING *Prometheus Bound* Poet. Wks. 1889 I. 205 The talker-down Of scorn by scorn. **1884** GOSSE in *Fortn. Rev.* Dec. 784 Such later talker-seers as Coleridge, De Quincey, and Carlyle. **1901** *Daily Chron.* 22 May 7/7 Mr. Banbury, the professional talker out of the House.

'talkfest. *slang* (chiefly *U.S.*). [f. TALK *sb.* or *v.* + FEST.] A session of lengthy discussion or conversation, a 'talkathon'. Cf. GABFEST.

1906 S. FORD *Shorty McCabe* ii. 36 Perhaps it'll be the grand annual ball of the Truck Drivers' Association, or just one of them Anarchist talkfests in the back room of some beer parlor. **1928** W. A. WHITE *Masks in Pageant* 247 He stepped naturally into supremacy at that talkfest [*sc.* a political convention] because he had been training for his famous speech. **1948** *Sun* (Baltimore) 18 June 19/4 (*heading*) County boy, girl win in 4-H 'talkfest'. **1961** B. PIKE *Robert Musil* viii. 167 Action is somehow made to seem irrelevant and trivial in this enormous talkfest. **1972** J. POTTS *Trouble-Maker* vii. 50 She wanted no part of the talkfest that was sure to occupy her fellow guests.

†**'talkful,** *a. Obs. rare.* [f. TALK *sb.* + -FUL.] Full of talk, talkative, garrulous.

1598 SYLVESTER *Du Bartas* II. ii. I. *Ark* 611 Phrenzie that makes.. The talkfull blab, cruel the violent.

talkie (ˈtɔːkɪ). *colloq.* (orig. *U.S.*). Now *Hist.* [f. TALK *v.* + -IE, after MOVIE.] **a.** A talking film, as opp. to a silent film. Freq. in *pl.* (esp. ***the talkies***). Cf. SPEAKIE.

1913 *Writer's Bull.* Mar. 9 The silent 'Movies', so popular to-day, will become tame in comparison with the 'Talkies'. **1921** *Daily Colonist* (Victoria, B.C.) 2 Apr. 12/2 All have seen the movies, now people are to have the opportunity of seeing and hearing the 'Talkies'... The author.. of the remarkable speaking photoplay, 'Shell Shocked' is in the city. **1928** *Daily Express* 6 June 3/1 Marvel of the 'talkies'. **1930** E. WAUGH *Vile Bodies* vi. 94 She said, 'You're much later than you said. It's so boring to be late for a talkie.' **1939** M. S. RICE *Working-Class Wives* v. 110 Another Leeds woman says 'never get out except to shop; have never been to the talkies'. **1955** *Times* 25 May 5/5 It was not until the talkies came that the cinema divorced itself from reading. **1962** *Movie* Dec. 31/3 Part talkie with music and sound effects. **1978** E. MALPASS *Wind brings up Rain* xix. 184 It was about this time that the first Talkies came to Ingerby: a fact that gave Benbow the courage.. to ask Ulrike to go to the pictures with him.

b. *attrib.*

1913 *Technical World Mag.* Aug. 815 One hundred other 'talkie-parties' are beginning in different parts of the city. **1922** *Radio News* (U.S.) Nov. 867/1 Mr. de Forest has solved the secret of the 'talkie movie' with perfect synchronization. **1932** L. GOLDING *Magnolia St.* III. iii. 512 An engagement at a talkie-theatre was about all Wilfred could hope for. **1936** AUDEN *Look, Stranger!* 34 By cops directed to the fug Of talkie-houses for a drug. **1960** *Times* 19 Feb. 5/1 In 1936 he had again the chance to make a feature film—a rather conventional 'talkie' adaptation of a stage success.

'talk-in. [See -IN[3].] **a.** A gathering or meeting for discussion; a conference.

1966 *N.Y. Times* 5 Oct. 46 LeRoi Jones, poet, play-wright and polemicist, sustained each aspect of his reputation.. at a reading at the Village Theater... It was the second in a series of talk-ins presented at that house. **1970** *Times* 7 Sept. 18 At the end of this month the insurance industry starts its talk-in with the Monopolies Commission over fire insurance. **1976** *Cumberland News* 3 Dec. 18/5 Members.. attended a very interesting and comprehensive 'talk-in' on the best way to prepare and present exhibits for showing. **1980** J. DRUMMOND *Such a Nice Family* ii. 16 It's for the patients themselves to choose. Why don't you ask them tonight, at the talk-in?

b. *spec.* as a form of political protest (esp. by students) in which the matter at issue is discussed.

1967 *Time* 30 June 28 Last week 180 Free University students staged a 45-hour hunger strike and talk-in.. to demand the release of a jailed anti-Shah demonstrator. **1977** D. JAMES *Spy at Evening* xx. 159, I was in a student meeting. .. It was a talk-in on Vietnam.

c. A radio or television discussion programme, esp. one broadcast live, and in which the audience may participate.

1971 *Guardian* 14 Dec. 2 Part Two of the Tuesday doomwatch.. charts the putative dangers of spreading nuclear power: then a talk-in asks if we should all keep quiet about it. **1977** D. PARKER *Radio* 154 The first few months of Capitol Radio and LBC (a station mainly concerned with news, but actually including every kind of 'chat' from author-interviews to interminable talk-ins and phone-ins) were dreadful beyond recall.

talking (ˈtɔːkɪŋ), *vbl. sb.* [f. TALK *v.* + -ING[1].]

a. The action of the verb TALK; speaking, discoursing. Also (colloq.) ***talking to***, a reprimand, an admonition; phr. ***to do the talking***.

a **1300** *Cursor M.* 14760 It es bot foli al þi talking. **13..** *Ibid.* 27792 O suernes [*F.* slauþe] cums.. vnnait talckhing. *c* **1386** CHAUCER *Can. Yeom. Prol.* 131 Whil this yeman was thus in his talkyng This Chanon drough hym neer. *c* **1450** tr. *De Imitatione* III. lvii. 134 þi consolacions are not as mannes talkinges or confabulacions. **1503** HAWES *Examp. Virt.* viii. 155 Of whome I oft haue herd grete talkynge. **1667** JER. TAYLOR *Dissuas. Popery* II. II. vi. 144 The superstitious talkings and actings, of their Priests. **1781** COWPER *Conversat.* 8 Words learn'd by rote a parrot may rehearse, But talking is not always to converse. **1873** HARDY *Pair of Blue Eyes* III. iv. 91 Knight did most of the talking along the journey. *c* **1875** 'BRENDA' *Froggy's Little Brother* (new ed.) iii. 35 I'd give him such a talking-to as never he had in his life before! **1884** CLARK RUSSELL *Jack's Courtsh.* xvii, A person capable of giving a seaman a talking to. **1903** *Red Book* Aug. 367/2 The girl did the talking, but for nearly an hour the head of the detective bureau sat silent, impassive as the sphinx. **1948** G. VIDAL *City & Pillar* x. 303 Bob did most of the talking and Jim listened.

b. *attrib.* and *Comb.*, as **talking blues**, a blues song in which the lyrics (usu. narrative) are articulated in a rhythm approaching that of speech; †**talking-craft** (see CRAFT *sb.* 6 c); **talking cure**, colloq. name for psychoanalysis or psychotherapy which relies on verbal interaction; **talking-house**, a house where people meet for conversation; **talking point**, a topic suitable for or inviting discussion or argument; **talking-shop**, a centre for idle and unconstructive talk; (derog.) applied to a parliament, *spec.* the House of Commons; †**talking-stock**, a subject of talk.

1969 *New Yorker* 1 Nov. 25/1 Alice's Restaurant—Arthur Penn's extension of Arlo Guthrie's talking-blues record. **1979** M. BOYCE *I was There!* 10/2 My first attempt at song writing took the form of humorous verse (in 'talking Blues' fashion). **1562** WINȜET *Cert. Tractatis* i. Wks. (S.T.S.) I. 8 Vtheris.. makis of the Gospell ane takin craft. **1910** tr. *Freud's Outl. & Devel. Psychoanal.* in *Amer. Jrnl. Psychol.* XXI. 184 The patient herself, who at this time of her illness .. spoke only English, gave this new kind of treatment the name of 'talking cure'. **1977** R. HOLLAND *Self & Social Context* viii. 240 At first sight nothing would seem more obvious than the dominant role of language in therapy—the talking cure. **1681** OWEN *Apostasy* Wks. 1852 VII. 256 This makes.. misspense of time in talking-houses. **1922** S. LEWIS *Babbitt* iv. 47 A broker.. who understood Talking Points, Strategic Values, Key Situations, Underappraisals. **1979** B. PARVIN *Deadly Dyke* vi. 28 Quite a change of climate.. but a talking point. **1912** C. MACKENZIE *Carnival* xliv. 385 Village! Talking-shop, I should say. **1922** A. M. HYAMSON *Dict. Eng. Phrases* 337/1 *Talking mill* (*shop*), *the*, (contemptuously) the House of Commons. **1942** R. G. COLLINGWOOD *New Leviathan* 213 Contemptuous language about the 'talking-shop at Westminster'. **1944** F. A. HAYEK *Road to Serfdom* v. 46 Parliaments came to be regarded as ineffective 'talking shops'. **1963** V. GIELGUD *Goggle-Box Affair* v. 49, I was an M.P. then... God knows why, damned talking-shop! **1979** R. BLYTHE *View in Winter* i. 72 The forge is the classic talking-shop of the village. **1548** UDALL *Erasm. Par. Luke* xxiv. 189 A common talkyng stocke to all peoples.

talking (ˈtɔːkɪŋ), *ppl. a.* [f. TALK *v.* + -ING[2].]

1. That talks; loquacious.

1562 J. HEYWOOD *Prov. & Epigr.* (1867) 177 One talkyng tung. **1699** R. L'ESTRANGE *Erasm. Colloq.* (1711) 92 This is the talkingst Place that ever I set my Foot in. **1710** STEELE *Tatler* No. 197 ⁋3 The talking Creatures we meet in publick Places. **1770** GOLDSM. *Des. Vill.* 14 The hawthorn bush, with seats beneath the shade, For talking age and whispering lovers made. **1870** M. D. CONWAY *Earthw. Pilgr.* xiii. 171 Man has been defined as the talking animal.

2. a. Comb. ***talking book*** (orig. *U.S.*), a sound recording of a book, for use by the blind; ***talking clock*** = ***speaking clock*** s.v. SPEAKING *ppl. a.* 1; cf. TIM[2]; ***talking doll***, a doll capable of emitting elementary sounds or words when activated; also *transf.* (of a person); ***talking drum***, one of a set of drums, each pitched differently, which are beaten to transmit the words of a message in a tonal language, chiefly in W. Afr. (usu. in *pl.*); ***talking head*** (slang), a television presenter or interviewer who is shown on the screen talking directly in close-up to the camera; freq. in *pl.*; also *transf.*; ***talking machine*** (chiefly *U.S.*), (*a*) a machine designed to imitate human speech; *spec.* (the vocal mechanism of) a talking doll (*rare*); also *fig.*; (*b*) a phonograph; a gramophone which reproduces human speech (now only *Hist.*); ***talking phonograph***: see PHONOGRAPH *sb.* 3 a.

1932 *Ann. Rep. Amer. Foundation for the Blind* 2 The development of books on phonograph records, or 'Talking Books', will be one of the greatest boons ever conferred on the blind. **1960** *Guardian* 22 July 3/4 The blind in Britain are to have 'talking books' incorporating the most advanced tape recording and play-back techniques... The present talking-books are long-playing records. **1978** D. BLOODWORTH *Crosstalk* xxi. 168 Extra-large cassettes.. from the library of the National Institute for the Blind... He examined the talking books. **1936** *Discovery* Oct. 315/1 The 'talking-clock' from which, merely by dialling T-I-M, every telephone user can now learn the exact time. **1969** N. FREELING *Tsing-Boum* xiii. 94 One could phone the talking clock. **1925** C. MORLEY *Thunder on Left* xix. 241 There was the bleat of one of the talking dolls. '*Maaa-Maa!*' it cried. **1974** H. R. F. KEATING *Underside* vii. 66 He had been able to regard her completely in the light of some talking doll, irritating but unconnected.. with the reality of life. **1977** *Detroit Free Press* 11 Dec. 15-A/3 (Advt.), The many phrases this big, beautiful talking doll 'Baby Sez' will make your daughter the happiest kid on the block. **1897** M. KINGSLEY *Trav. W. Afr.* vi. 114 In the street one sees the characteristic standing drum.. and one or two talking-drums besides. **1923** R. S. RATTRAY *Ashanti* iii. 104 The big talking drums were immediately behind him and beat out: The King has sat down. **1966** C. ACHEBE *Man of People* xiii. 166 These were the same people that only the other day.. praise-singers followed with song and talking-drum. **1977** *Rolling Stone* 24 Mar. 48/2 Even drummer Mick Fleetwood finally ventured out from behind his drum kit to play the African talking drum on 'World Turning'. **1983** *Guardian* 19 July 9/4 A talking drums player from Ghana who seemed to have wandered on stage uninvited. **1968** *Punch* 24 Apr. 617/3 Indifference to people who weren't talking-heads?.. If they were so monumentally unmemorable shouldn't they have been skipped altogether? **1976** *Listener* 15 Jan. 52/1, I begin to get very tired of the 'important' interview—indeed, of all talking heads—on television. **1980** *Ibid.* 4 Sept. 299/1, I looked at the talking heads, telling their stories directly to the camera. **1844** *Quincy* (Illinois) *Herald* 9 Feb. 3/2 A German, named Faber,.. in New York, has invented and brought to perfection a talking machine. It is played on by keys like a piano, and can be made to say any thing, in any language, that its inventor desires. **1844** *Picayune* (New Orleans) 18 Mar. 38/2 Why *don't* you go see the Talking Machine, and take little Matilda along with you? **1846** N. P. WILLIS *Compl. Works* III. 674/2, I had a half-hour's interview with the *talking machine* this morning, and found him a more entertaining *android* than most of my wooden acquaintances. **1850** CARLYLE *Latter-Day Pamph.* No. I. 52 A redtape Talking-machine and unhappy Bag of Parliamentary Eloquence. **1891** *Appleton's Ann. Cycl. 1890* 709/1 In 1886, J. S. Taintor, working along the lines followed by Mr. Edison, produced a talking machine, which was called the graphophone, or phonograph-graphophone. **1897** R. STUART *In Simpkinsville* 110 The little talkin' machine inside it has got out o' fix.. an' it don't say 'papa' an' 'mama' any more. **1930** W. FAULKNER *As I lay Dying* 181

Cash aimed to buy that talking machine from Suratt with that money.

b. ***talking film, movie, picture*** (now *Hist.*) = TALKIE a; also formerly ***talking photograph***.

1904 *Science Siftings* 26 Mar. 353/1 The inventor believes that in a short time these talking photographs will supersede the phonograph. **1908** *Variety* 16 May 11/3 (*heading*) Natural voice talking pictures... The idea is to have a capable company behind the screen and take up the cue as each character comes in view. **1921** [see CINEPHONE]. **1927** *N.Y. Times* 28 Aug. VII. 4 If a 'talking movie' throughout were being made, it would be necessary to film a thousand feet at a time. **1978** *Lancashire Life* Oct. 97/3 Talking-pictures were introduced under the management of the late Ignatius Cullen, whose daughters continue to run the Civic Hall Cinema..showing 'wholesome family films' only.

Hence **'talkingly** *adv.*, in a talking manner.

1895 H. B. M. WATSON in *Chap-Bk.* III. 489 At the word, spoken very talkingly, and with such an absence of offense, my dudgeon vanished.

'talk-out. *colloq.* [f. vbl. phr. *to talk out*: see TALK *v.* 9.] **a.** A 'talking out' of a bill in Parliament, a filibuster. (In quot., with pl. *talks out*.) *rare*.

1884 E. W. HAMILTON *Diary* 25 Mar. (1972) II. 583 One cannot help thinking that the Speaker..has missed an opportunity of applying the closure to prevent those purely obstructive 'talks out', which morning sittings are so well adapted to promote.

b. An exhaustive discussion, in which a matter is 'talked out'.

1965 *Listener* 16 Sept. 431/1 The series contained a fair number of..'talk-outs', as I must shudderingly report I have heard them called, on music, drama, poetry. **1967** *Telegraph* (Brisbane) 10 Apr. 7/6 A 'marathon talk-out' or similar scheme for mass support would pressure the Government to solve the present education problem in Queensland. **1978** *New York* 3 Apr. 58/2 At the conclusion of every Wednesday talkout, I was shocked, saddened, and dismayed.

talky ('tɔːkɪ), *a. colloq.* [f. TALK *sb.* + -Y.]

a. Inclined to or abounding in talk; talkative, loquacious.

1815 BYRON *Let.* 31 Oct. (1975) IV. 326 Like other [dinner] parties..it was first silent, then talky, then argumentative,..then drunk. **1862** CARLYLE *Fredk. Gt.* XII. vii. (1873) IV. 172 The King is somewhat talky. **1884** A. A. PUTNAM *Ten Yrs. Police Judge* xii. 101 One of the talky attorneys dispels all their hopes.

b. Of a play, book, etc.: wordy, long-winded; containing verbose or tedious dialogue.

1937 *Partisan Rev.* Dec. 54 The producers, apparently still under the spell of the old superstition that a play cannot be 'talky', proceeded to excise almost all of the hero's connected conversation. **1967** *Times* 23 Nov. 8/7 The action scenes..do a lot to make up for a slow and talky opening. **1976** *Publishers Weekly* 23 Aug. 60/1 Once past the rather talky and confusing opening, readers will find Price's spy novel a corker.

Hence **'talky-'talky** *a.*, abounding in (mere) talk; not rising above the level of talk; *sb.*, trivial conversation; cf. TALKEE-TALKEE; loquacity; similarly, **talky-talk, talki-talk,** trivial conversation, talk for talking's sake.

1870 *Punch* 22 Oct. 173/1 Perhaps this Lighthearted Gallant doesn't have no end of talky-talkies with all the.. six-foot nothings in jack-boots all over the shop. **1883** *Sat. Rev.* 10 Feb. 189/2 These Essays..are very 'talky-talky'. **1884** G. ALLEN *Philistia* II. 301 A social leader, of the ordinary commonplace talky-talky sort. **1884** 'MARK TWAIN' *Huck. Finn* xxvi. 258 All that kind of humbug talky-talk, just the way people always does at a supper, you know. **1907** G. B. SHAW *John Bull's Other Island* IV. 110 Why cant you say a simple thing simply, Larry, without all that Irish exaggeration and talky-talky? **1928** *Daily Express* 16 July 10/2 A..narrative in which motives and character are revealed in deeds and not in talky-talk. **1937** G. M. YOUNG *Daylight & Champaign* 134, I heartily agree that a large part of the talki-talk about influences and relationships could be with great advantage thrown into a single book. **1938** J. CARY *Castle Corner* 546 The poor child had been upset by all the talky-talky. **1953** W. REICH *Murder of Christ* xii. 111 The admirers feel uncomfortable.., not being free ..to engage in small chit-chat and talki-talk. **1965** 'W. HAGGARD' *Hard Sell* xvi. 177 Away with this talky-talk, this stylized sparring between..officials.

talky, variant form of TALCY *a.*

tall (tɔːl), *a.* Also 4–7 tal, 4–6 talle, 6 tawl(l)e. [Of obscure history. Most prob. repr. (with loss of prefix) OE. *ʒe-tæl* (pl. *ʒe-tale*) swift, prompt = OHG. *gizal*, MHG. *gezal* quick. Cf. Goth. *untals* unaccommodating, uncompliant, disobedient, ONorthumb. *untal* evil, improper. For the phonology, cf. *small*:—OE. *smæl*.

The sense-development is remarkable, but is paralleled more or less by that of other adjs. expressing estimation, as *buxom, canny, clean, clever, cunning, deft, elegant, handsome, pretty, proper*; Ger. *klein*, as compared with Eng. *clean*, presents the antithesis to mod. *tall* as compared with *tall* in early ME.

It has been conjectured that in the sense 'high of stature' it is a different word, adopted from Welsh *tal* in same sense; but the latter is, according to Prof. Rhŷs, merely a 16th c. borrowing of the Eng. word (in Owen Pughe's Dictionary erroneously mixed up with the genuine Welsh sb. *tal* end, brow, forehead, with which it has no possible connexion). The 15th c. instance of the adj. cited by Pughe is prob. from sense 2 or 3 below.]

A. *adj.* **I.** †**1.** Quick, prompt, ready, active. *Obs. rare.*

But the sense in both quots. is doubtful; in quot. *c* 1374, *tall* has been taken by some as = 'meek, docile'; quot. 1542 may belong to sense 2.

[*c* **1000** *Ags. Ps.* lvi. 5 (Th.) Wæron hyra tungan ʒetale teonan ʒehwylcre.] *c* **1374** CHAUCER *Compl. Mars* 38 (Harl. MS. 7333) Sche [Venus] made him [Mars] at hir lust [*v.r.* list] so humble & talle [*v.rr.* tal, tall; *Fairf. MS.* humble and calle; *Tan. MS.* humble in alle]. **1530–1600** [see 4]. **1542** UDALL *Erasm. Apoph.* 51 For lesse money..myght I bye a bondeman, that should dooe me tall & hable seruice.

†**2. a.** Meet, becoming, seemly, proper, decent. *Obs.*

[Cf. *c* **1350**–*c* **1440** s.v. TALLY *adv.*] *c* **1400** *Destr. Troy* 3098 Ho tentit not in tempull to no tall prayers, Ne no melody of mouthe made at þe tyme. *c* **1440** *Promp. Parv.* 486/1, Tal, or semely, *decens, elegans*.

†**b.** Comely, goodly, fair, handsome; elegant, fine. Cf. PROPER *a.* 8. *Obs.*

c **1450** *Cov. Myst.* xxiii. (1841) 215 A fayre ʒonge qwene.. Bothe ffresche and gay upon to loke, And a talle man with her dothe melle. **1451** *Paston Lett.* I. 224 On of the tallest younge men of this parysch lyth syke. **1530** PALSGR. 327/1 Talle..*bel*, as *bel home*. *c* **1592** MARLOWE *Jew of Malta* IV. iv, That such a base slave as he should be saluted by such a tall man as I am, from such a beautiful dame as you. **1656** H. MORE *Enthus. Tri.* 31 He was a tal proper man..but of a very pale wasted melancholy countenance.

†**3.** Good at arms; stout or strong in combat; doughty, brave, bold, valiant. Cf. PRETTY 3 a.

c **1400** *Destr. Troy* 8574 Mageron..macchet with Achilles, Wold haue takon the talle kyng, & to toun led. *a* **1518** SKELTON *Magnyf.* 821 *Cou. Ab.* I waraunt you I wyll not go away. *Cra. Con.* By Saynt Mary, he is a tawle man. *Clo. Col.* Ye, and do ryght good seruyce he can. *a* **1529** —— *Agst. Garnesche* I. 5 Syr Frollo de Franko was neuer halfe so talle. *a* **1548** HALL *Chron., Hen. VI* 159 This capitayn [Jack Cade]..assembled together a great company of talle personages. *a* **1553** UDALL *Royster D.* IV. viii, Now sirs, quite our selues like tall men and hardie. **1577** NORTHBROOKE *Agst. Dicing* (1843) 8 If he can kil a man,.. he is called a tall man, and a valiant man of his hands. **1591** GREENE *Art Conny Catch.* III. (1592) 16 He that had done this tall exploit, in a place so open. **1598** J. DICKENSON *Greene in Conc.* (1878) 137 With her tongue she was as tall a warriouresse as any of hir sexe. *a* **1604** HANMER *Chron. Irel.* (1633) 126 Both sides lost many a tall man. *a* **1613** OVERBURY *Ess. Valour in Wife*, etc. (1630) Q vj b, It makes a little fellow to be called a Tall man. **1641** PRYNNE *Antip.* 16 He like a tall fellow, thereupon interdicted the King, with the whole Realme. **1670** MILTON *Hist. Eng.* II. Wks. (1847) 492/2 Telling the tall champions as a great encouragement, that with the Britons it was usual for women to be their leaders. **1820** W. IRVING *Sketch-Bk., John Bull* (1865) 390 The old fellow's spirit is as tall and as gallant as ever. **1825** SCOTT *Betrothed* i, Beloved among the 'tall men', or champions, of Wales.

†**4.** Phrase ***tall of* (*his*) *hand*(*s*:** sometimes, (cf. sense 1) Ready, active, deft, skilful with (his) hands; dexterous, handy; sometimes, (cf. sense 3) Stout of arm, formidable with weapons. So ***tall of tongue***, stout of speech or argument. *Obs.*

1530 PALSGR. 784/1 He is a tall man of his handes,..*cest ung habille homme de ses mains*. **1589** R. HARVEY *Pl. Perc.* (1590) A iij, They were neuer tall fellows of their hands that were such hacksters in the street. **1598** FLORIO, *Manesco*, readie, nimble, or quicke-handed..a tall man of his hands. **1600** HOLLAND *Livy* II. xxxiii. 65 A Noble yoong gentleman, right politicke of advise, active besides, and tall of his hands [L. *promptus manu*]. *Ibid.* III. lxx. 136 Agrippa being a tall man of his handes [L. *viribus ferox*] and young withall,.. caught the ensignes from the ensigne-bearers, advanced them forward his owne selfe. *Ibid.* XXI. xl. 415 Stout in heart, and tall of hand [L. *vigens corpore*]. **1607** MARSTON *What you will* Induct., Goe stand to it; shew thyselfe a tall man of thy tongue. **1632** HOLLAND *Cyrupædia* 46 Swift I am not of foot, nor yet a tall man of my hands.

†**5.** Big, large, bulky. *Obs. rare.*

c **1430** LYDG. *Min. Poems* 200 This fair floure of woman-heed Hath too pappys also smalle, Bolsteryd out of lenghth and breed, Lyche a large campyng balle; There is no bagpipe halff so talle,.. Whan they been full of wynde at alle.

II. 6. a. Of a person: High of stature; of more than average height. Usually appreciative. Also of animals, as a giraffe, stag, or the like. (Cf. ELEGANT *a.* 2 b = tall of stature.)

1530 PALSGR. 327/1 Talle or hye..*hault*. **1538** ELYOT, *Procerus*, longe, talle. **1552** HULOET, Talle or verye hyghe in personage aboue other. **1599** HAKLUYT *Voy.* II. 256 The men are tall and slender. **1697** DRYDEN *Virg. Past.* VII. 54 Fair Galatea,.. Tall as a Poplar, taper as the Bole. **1719** YOUNG *Paraphr. Job* Wks. 1757 I. 215 Will the tall Reem.. Low at the crib, and ask an alms of thee? **1796** H. HUNTER tr. *St.-Pierre's Stud. Nat.* (1799) I. 398 Tall as giants, hairy like bears. **1858** CARLYLE *Fredk. Gt.* V. V. I. 579 One Hohmann, a born Prussian, was so tall, you could not.. touch his bare crown with your hand. **1861** HULME tr. *Moquin-Tandon* I. ii. 14 A man..is called tall when he is above 5.754 feet in height. **1886** RUSKIN *Præterita* I. vii. 210 A tall, handsome, and very finely made girl.

(*b*) In proverbial phr. ***tall, dark, and handsome***, denoting a type of attractive man (see also quot. 1965).

1906 R. E. KNOWLES *Undertow* xi. 135 He was tall—and dark—and handsome. **1940** *Chatelaine* Dec. 55/3 One Squadron Leader tells of filling an 'order' for 'three tall, dark and handsomes to go dancing'. **1958** M. STEWART *Nine Coaches Waiting* vii. 93 Tall, dark and handsome—the romantic cliché repeated itself in my head. **1965** T. WOLFE *Kandy-Kolored Tangerine-Flake Streamline Baby* (1966) ix. 178 It was Cary Grant that Mae West was talking about when she launched the phrase 'tall, dark and handsome' in 'She Done Him Wrong' (1933). **1978** 'H. CARMICHAEL' *Life Cycle* v. 64 If she felt like leaning on his shoulder it was certainly not because he was tall, dark and handsome.

b. Having a specified or relative height; measuring in stature (so much): without implication of great height. (Cf. *big, broad, high*, etc.)

1588 SHAKS. *L.L.L.* IV. i. 47 *Costard.* Which is the greatest Lady, the highest? *Princess.* The thickest, and the tallest. **1685** BAXTER *Paraphr. N.T.* Matt. vi. 27 All your care cannot make you any taller of stature. **1732** MACKY *Mem., Charac.* (ed. 2) 47 [Marquis of Hartington was] taller than a middle Stature. **1744** SARAH FIELDING *David Simple* II. iii, If a Man could make himself happy by imagining himself six Foot tall, tho' he was but three. **1845** JAMES *Arrah Neil* ii, A good deal taller than his companion. **1853** VISCT. S. DE REDCLIFFE in Lane-Poole *Life* II. 242 He is..6 ft. 3 in. tall. *Mod.* How tall are you? He is a little taller than his brother, but both are dwarfs.

c. *absol.* as *sb. nonce-use.*

1903 MAX PEMBERTON *Dr. Xavier* i, They want 'talls' for the first row and she's just the height.

7. a. Of things, as ships (*spec.* square-riggers), trees, mountains: High, lofty; esp. of things high in proportion to their width, as ***a tall chimney, column, house, mast, spire***.

a **1548** HALL *Chron., Hen. IV* 32 b, Talle shippes furnished with vitayles municions and all thynges necessary. **1562** TURNER *Herbal* II. 6 There are two kyndes of ashes [trees], of yᵉ whiche the one is verye high and tawlle. **1582** M. PHILLIPS in Hakl. *Voy.* (1589) 579 Two good tall ships of warre. **1615** G. SANDYS *Trav.* 220 To be imbargued in two tall Ships, and a great Gallion. **1655** STANLEY *Hist. Philos.* III. (1701) 106/1 Above the tallest Hill or Wood. **1702** ROWE *Tamerl.* I. i, Yon tall Mountains That seem to reach the Clouds. **1715** POPE tr. *Homer's Iliad* I. III. 192 When thy tall Ships triumphant stem'd the tide. *Ibid.* XIII. 493 The mountain-oak, or poplar tall, Or pine, fit mast for some great admiral. **1726** —— tr. *Homer's Odyssey* I. IV. 201 From his tall ship the King of men descends. **1784** COWPER *Task* I. 450 Upon the ship's tall side he stands, possess'd With visions prompted by intense desire. **1852** JAMES *Agnes Sorel* i, A tall house in the city of Paris. **1856** KANE *Arct. Expl.* I. xviii. 222 Its tallest summit near the water at thirteen hundred [feet]. *a* **1865** SMYTH *Sailor's Word-bk.* (1867) 674 *Tall ship*, a phrase among the early voyagers for square-rigged vessels having topmasts. **1902** J. MASEFIELD *Salt-water Ballads* 59 All I ask is a tall ship and a star to steer her by. **1908** MISS FOWLER *Betw. Trent & Ancholme* 18 Where ..the Fuchsias grow tall, up to the eaves. **1916** JOYCE *Portrait of Artist* (1969) v. 252 The spell of arms and voices; the white arms of roads..and the black arms of tall ships that stand against the moon. **1975** *Times* 4 July 4/8 The Admiralty Court yesterday granted..an order that the tall ship, Regina Maris, be appraised and sold by the Admiralty marshal to pay a debt... The 137ft-long ship..competed in last year's Tall Ships Race.

b. Of more than average length measured from bottom to top, as a ***tall copy*** of a book, a ***tall folio***. ***tall hat***, a silk hat with high cylindrical crown.

1608 TOPSELL *Serpents* (1658) 747 Very like a small and vulgar Lizard, except..their legs taller, and their tail longer. **1613** SHAKS. *Hen. VIII*, I. iii. 30 The faith they haue in Tennis and tall Stockings, Short blistred Breeches, and those types of Trauell. *a* **1704** T. BROWN *Lett. fr. Dead* II. i. Wks. 1720 II. 160, I..was to write Bills as tall as the Monument. **17..** *John o' Hazelgreen* v. in Child *Ballads* V. 163 Wi arms tall, and fingers small—He's comely to be seen. **1807** SOUTHEY *Lett. from Eng.* I. xxi. 237 The size of the margin is of great importance. I could not conceive what was meant by *a tall copy*, till this was explained to me. If the leaves of an old book have never been cut smooth, its value is greatly enhanced. **1819** SCOTT *Let. to Miss Edgeworth* 21 July in *Lockhart*, A second edition of Walter Scott, a tall copy, as collectors say, and bound in Turkey leather. **1847** L. HUNT *Men, Women & B.* II. vi. 78 The charms of vellums, tall copies, and blind tooling. **1890** 'OUIDA' *Syrlin* xiv, They would go to Eton and wear ridiculous jackets and tall hats.

c. Applied distinctively to species or varieties of plants which grow higher than other species. Cf. *tall-grass* adj., sense C below.

1789 *Ann. Agric.* XII. 441, I was surprized to see no tall oat grass there, the best and most useful of the grasses which meadows can be laid down with. **1835** HOOKER *Brit. Flora* (ed. 3) 50 *Festuca elatior*, Tall Fescue grass. **1846** J. BAXTER *Libr. Pract. Agric.* (ed. 4) I. 371 Tall oat-like soft grass, *Holcus avenaceus*. **1850** KINGSLEY *Alt. Locke* xiv, The tender green of the tall rape, a plant till then unknown to me. **1861** MISS PRATT *Flower. Pl.* IV. 79 Tall Broom-rape.. growing on the roots of the Great Knapweed. **1897–8** BRITTON & BROWN *Amer. Flora*, Tall moss, *Sedum acre*. **1979** *United States 1980/81* (*Penguin Travel Guides*) 763 Now scarcely 1% of the original 400,000 square miles of tallgrass remain.

d. *absol.* as *sb.*

1909 *19th Cent.* Jan. 76 Two thirds gave plants divided into 'talls' and 'dwarfs'.

e. ***tall timber*** (N. Amer.), uninhabited forest. Usu. in phr. ***to break*** (***strike***, etc.) ***for*** (***the***) ***tall timber***; also *transf.*, to run away, escape. Hence ***tall-timbered*** adj.

[**1831** *Boston Transcript* 24 June 2/4 Why didn't Van just go and *tell* the old man he wanted to *break for high timber*?] **1845** *St. Louis Reveille* 22 Jan. 1/6 Knowing the direction of the trees that stood in the grove, I 'broke for the tall timber'. **1877** J. M. BEARD *K.K.K. Sketches* 166 The panic-stricken darkies broke across the landscape with a yearning desire for tall timber that was eloquently depicted on every motion of the supple limbs. **1904** [see SCRATCH *v.* 5 c]. **1914** D. W. ROBERTS *Rangers & Sovereignty* 128 The 'bad men'..began to strike for 'tall timber'. **1921** *Daily Colonist* (Victoria) 22 Mar. 13/1 The northern correspondent of The Colonist has just emerged from the tall timber, where he has been living under canvas for the past two years. **1949** *Skyline Trail* Oct. 18/1, I fell off *three times*; finally the disgusted critter took to the tall timber, leaving me to hike onward and to get across the frigid stream as best I could. **1966** *Times* 28 Feb. (Canada Suppl.) p. ii, Canada is a tall-timbered..rod-and-gun of a country.

f. Of game birds: high-flying. Occas. applied *transf.* to a shot at a bird.

1913 R. Payne-Gallwey *High Pheasants* iv. 37 The tallest pheasants I know of are at Harpton. *Ibid.* v. 45 These high birds.. afford most sporting and tall shots. **1922** H. S. Gladstone *Record Bags & Shooting Rec.* 197 Correct judgment of distance is essential for accurate shooting.. hence the tall stories of tall birds. **1952** J. W. Day *New Yeomen of England* xi. 125 It was all done in the sacred service of King Pheasant, by men who laid out their woods in order to show tall birds. **1962** *Times* 28 Apr. 11/4 But equally tall pheasants can and do come over at shoots on ground as flat as a billiard table. **1976** *Shooting Times & Country Mag.* 18–24 Nov. 28/2 Half a dozen superb tall birds came over the gate.

8. *fig.* †**a.** Lofty, grand, eminent. *Obs.*

1655 Stanley *Hist. Philos.* I. (1701) 45/1 Who in tall Corinth and Pirene dwell. **1686** W. de Britaine *Hum. Prudence* xix. 88 Princes may bestow the tallest Preferments, but they cannot make Men truly Honourable. **1701** Watts *Horæ Lyr.* III. *Death T. Gunston* 187 The tall titles, insolent and proud. **1827** Lamb *Let. to B. Barton* in *Final Mem.* viii. 260 Thine briefly in a tall friendship, C. Lamb.

b. Grandiloquent, magniloquent; high-flown; esp. in ***tall talk*** (talk *sb.* 5). *colloq.*

1670 Eachard *Cont. Clergy* 39 Others.. whose parts stand not so much towards tall words and lofty notions, but consist in.. besprinkling all their sermons with plenty of Greek and Latin. **1864** *Spectator* No. 1884. 911 The somewhat tall title of 'Analysis and Synthesis in Painting'. **1869** *Routledge's Ev. Boy's Ann.* 518 What the Yankees call 'tall talk'. **1876** C. M. Davies *Unorth. Lond.* 55 Then succeeded the minister herself, whose prayer was 'taller' than the young girl's. **1890** *Spectator* 3 May 628/1 The diction is as impetuous as Niagara, as 'tall' as the Eiffel Tower.

c. Exaggerated, highly coloured. *U.S. colloq.*

1846 T. B. Thorpe *Backwoods, Big Bear Arkansaw* (Bartlett), The live Sucker from Illinois had the daring to say that our Arkansaw friend's stories smelt rather tall. **1870** *Zoologist* V. 2350 The producers of what is called 'tall writing'. **1891** *N. York Times* 26 Jan. (Cent. Dict.), A tall yarn about the Jews wanting to buy the Vatican copy of the Hebrew Bible. **1897** *Dublin Rev.* Oct. 267 'Tall stories' are the perquisite of every traveller. **1902** Eliz. L. Banks *Newspaper Girl* 279 Nor do I think that there is anything 'tall' in this statement.

d. Large in amount, big. *slang* (*orig. U.S.*). ***tall order***, something expected to be hard to achieve or fulfil: cf. *big* (*large, strong*) *order* s.v. order *sb.* 24 c.

1842 Dickens *Amer. Notes* (1850) 131/2 We were a pretty tall time coming that last fifteen mile. **1864** F. Lillywhite *Guide to Cricketers* 95 The.. match.. between Surrey and Thirteen of Cambridge University,.. owing to the 'very tall' scoring, was also unfinished. **1884** I. Bligh in *Lillywhite's Cricket Ann.* 4, G. B. Studd's 19 including some tall hits. **1891** W. G. Grace *Cricket* iv. 19 The season, so far, had been dry, and favourable for tall scoring. **1893** F. Adams *New Egypt* 128 It's a tall order, but it's worth trying, isn't it? **1902** *Westm. Gaz.* 13 Feb. 12/2 America is the land of 'tall' things, and this is certainly a 'tall' drink for twenty-five persons. **1905** *Sat. Rev.* 24 June 825 Usurping the functions of the King is rather a 'tall order' for a private M.P. **1920** C. A. W. Monckton *Some Experiences New Guinea Resident Magistrate* xviii. 201, I.. told the police we would make the attempt; clearly they thought we were taking on a devil of a tall order. **1946** *Civil & Milit. Gaz.* 26 May 15 (*heading*) Tall scoring by Indians at Lords. **1950** H. Read *Educ. for Peace* iv. 51 It is, to use our slang expression, 'a tall order', but it has been attempted before. **1976** *Norwich Mercury* 19 Nov. 2/1 'You do not by any chance know of anybody with an old lion's skin?' she asked. A tall order indeed.

†**9.** *fig.* **a.** Great, eminent (*at* something). *Obs.*

1591 Lodge *Diogenes in his Singularitie* (Hunter. Cl.) 29 Verie earnest to prooue himselfe a tall *a b c* Clearke, he read on [etc.]. **1646** G. Daniel *Poems* Wks. (Grosart) I. 83 A hundred Rhiming Fellowes, that have bin Tall Men at Meeter. **1662** Cokaine *Trag. Ovid* IV. vi, Though she's but little, she's a tall woman at a Trencher.

b. Great in quality, excellent, good, first-class. (*U.S. slang.*)

1835–40 Haliburton *Clockm.* (1862) 530 Won't it be tall feedin' at Queen's table, that's all. **1847** Robb *Squatter Life* (Bartlett), I didn't estimate him very tall. **1852** Mrs. Stowe *Uncle Tom's C.* xxxvii, They.. make jist the tallest kind o' broth and knicknacks.

B. quasi-*adv.* In a tall manner; elatedly, proudly; ***to walk tall***, to carry one's head high; to have dignity or self-respect; ***to sit tall***, to sit erect, with a straight back (in quot. *fig.*). Also *comb.*, as ***tall-talking***.

1846 T. B. Thorpe *Myst. Backwoods* 131 (Bartl.), I will walk tall into varmint and Indian. **1860** Thackeray *Round. Papers, De finibus* (1862) 282 The sin of grandiloquence, or tall-talking. **1869** Mrs. Stowe *Oldtown Folks* vi. (1870) 65 I'm 'mazing proud on 't. I tell you I walk tall. **1970** *Guardian* 3 June 20/6 Officials gave the doctors folders entitled, 'Walk Tall in Australia'. *Ibid.* 6 Aug. 9/1 Walk tall, sisters... One woman's distinction adds a tiny bit to the stature of every other woman. **1976** *Billings* (Montana) *Gaz.* 6 July 3D/6 'We need to sit tall in the saddle and ride like hell in the right direction,' the governor added. **1980** *Times* 15 Feb. 16/8 'Walk tall,' say the television commercials [in Hongkong], 'report corruption.'

C. *Comb.*: parasynthetic, as ***tall-bodied*** (having a tall body), ***-elmed, -hatted, -masted, -necked, -sceptred, -stemmed, -tussocked, -wheeled***, etc.; quasi-*advb.*, as ***tall-growing, -sitting***; **tall-grass** *a.*, (esp. of a prairie) characterized by tall grasses (tall *a.* 7 c); **tall poppy**: see poppy *sb.* 1 b; †**tall-sail (tal-sail)** = topsail.

14.. *Siege Jerus.* 289 þey tyȝten vp tal-sail [*v.r.* topsaill], whan þe tide asked, Hadde byr at þe bake, & þe bonke lefte. *c* **1725** Armstrong *Imit. Shaks.* 6 Misc. 1770 I. 147 A blast so shrewd makes the tall-bodied pines Unsinew'd bend. **1825** J. G. Whittier *Poet. Wks.* (1898) 522/2 With tall-masted ships on their broad bosoms riding. **1855** Bailey *Spiritual Leg.* in *Mystic*, etc. 105 Tall-sceptred law, and loin-girt liberty. **1877** Furnivall *Leopold Shaks.* Introd. 117 You ride through Charlecote's tall-elmd park. **1885** Kipling *Departmental Ditties* (1886) 33, I drive no tall-wheeled traps. **1886** P. S. Robinson *Valley Teet. Trees* 63 The tall-tussocked grass of the waste lands. **1897** *Westm. Gaz.* 6 July 2/1 A very tall-sitting lady, with a tremendous matinée hat, sat down in front of me. **1908** Miss Fowler *Betw. Trent & Ancholme* 203 Sun-flowers, and other succulent tall-growing things. **1920** *Carnegie Inst. Washington Publ.* No. 290. 256 The tall-grass prairies are typical of regions in which humid farming prevails. **1922** Joyce *Ulysses* 250 H. halted and four tallhatted white flagons halted behind him. **1925** J. Ferguson in *Oxf. Poetry* 18 The tall-stemmed candles brighten. **1951** *Dict. Gardening* (R. Hort. Soc.) II. 921/1 In the tall-stemmed section, such as *G[rammatophyllum] speciosum*, there are probably six species. **1972** T. McHugh *Time of Buffalo* ii. 16 On the lush eastern half of the tall-grass prairie, one buffalo could have lived for a year on about ten acres. **1972** D. Lees *Zodiac* 27 A tall-hatted chef [was] serving a cold lunch. **1980** *Outdoor Life* (U.S.) (Northeast ed.) Oct. 97/1 Oak thickets, tall-grass ridges,.. and aspen groves.

tall, obs. variant of tail *sb.*^{2}, *v.*^{2}

tallage ('tælɪdʒ), *sb.*^{1} Forms: α. 3–8 **taillage**, 4–5 **taylage**, 4–7 **tailage**, 5 **tayllage** (7–8 **tailliage**). β. 4–5 **taliage**, 4–6 **talage**, 4–9 **talliage**, 5 **tal(l)yage**, 4– **tallage**. γ. 6 **talenge**. [a. OF. *taillage* (1170 in Godef.), f. *tailler*, tail *v.*^{2}: see -age. Hence med.L. *talliagium, tallagium* (*taillagium, taliagium*), *a* 1087 in Du Cange.]

Orig., in *Eng. Hist.*, An arbitrary tax levied by Norman and early Angevin kings upon the towns and the demesne lands of the Crown; hence, a tax levied upon feudal dependants by their superiors; also, by extension, a municipal rate; a toll or customs duty; a grant, levy, imposition, aid.

By the articles of 1297, the Latin version of which is commonly cited as the Statute *De Tallagio non concedendo*, an attempt was made to restrict the right of tallage, which was finally surrendered by the king in the act of 1340.

[**1154–7** *Calr. Charter Rolls* III. 385. **1190** *Pipe Roll 1 Rich. I* (1844) 230 De toto tallagio quod Rex Henricus pater fecit.] *c* **1290** *Beket* 402 in *S. Eng. Leg.* I. 118 A taillage it is, and sumdel with vnriȝte i-take. [**1292** Britton III. vii. §5 Des vileyns, et de villenages.. lour rentes, lour services, lour taillages, et lour custumes. **1302** *Rolls of Parlt.* I. 266/2 Ad assidendos tallagium nostrum in Civitatibus, Burgis, & Dominicis nostris.] *c* **1330** R. Brunne *Chron.* (1810) 44 Now comes Suane.. þe lond leid to taliage so mykelle on ilk a toun. *c* **1374** Chaucer *Former Age* 54 No lord, no taylage by no tyranye. **1387** Trevisa *Higden* (Rolls) II. 97 Hydage, taylage of hydes of lond. Danegeld, taylage i-ȝeue to þe Danes. *c* **1420** *Chron. Vilod.* 224 He granted þo to þe Pope Leo such a talage Offe euery howse in his kyndam a peny by ȝere. **1440** J. Shirley *Dethe K. James* (1818) 7 The saide kynge of Scottes.. ordeynd that tallage.. upon his people. **1481** Caxton *Godeffroy* 277 To helpe.. the cristen men of Iherusalem to paye the cruel taillages that the turkes had sette vpon them. **1534** More *Comf. agst. Trib.* III. Wks. 1212/1 With occasions of his warres, he pilleth them with taxes and tallages vnto the bare bones. **1556** *Chron. Gr. Friars* (Camden) 38 A rysynge in Lyngcolshere of the comons for taske and talenge of ane abbé there. **1610** Holland *Camden's Brit.* II. 141 [The elected chief of every Irish county] had a generall tallage or cutting high or low at his pleasure upon all the inheritance. **1622** F. Markham *Bk. War* v. vi. 183 It is.. the Office of the Treasurer to receiue all Tributs, Taxes, Tailliages and Impositions. **1642** *Declar. Ho. Parlt.* in Rushw. *Hist. Coll.* (1692) III. I. 665 The Law there declared was, That none could be compelled to contribute to any Tax, Tallage, Aid, or other like Charge but by Consent in Parliament. **1762** Hume *Hist. Eng.* I. App. ii. 413 The king.. levied heavy tailliages at pleasure on the inhabitants. **1776** Adam Smith *W.N.* III. ii. (1869) I. 396 The taille, as it still subsists in France, may serve as an example of those ancient tallages. It is a tax upon the supposed profits of the farmer, which they estimate by the stock that he has upon the farm. **1874** Stubbs *Const. Hist.* I. xiii. 585 The donum, auxilium, or tallage, which Henry [II] imposed in lieu of the ancient Danegeld, was assessed by the officers of the Exchequer.

fig. **1303** R. Brunne *Handl. Synne* 9254 Ianglyng longeþ to sacrylage, þar-of takeþ þe fende taylage.

†**tallage**, *sb.*^{2} *Obs.* Also 5–6 **talage**, 6 **-e(d)ge**, 7 **talang**. [app. corruption of tarage *sb.*^{1}] Taste, savour (*lit.* and *fig.*); = tarage *sb.*^{1}

14.. [see tarage *sb.*^{1}]. **1502** Atkynson tr. *De Imitatione* I. xxv. 178 To haue a spirituall tallage in god. **1528** Paynell *Salerne's Regim.* B b, Very nere the talage of water. **1542** Boorde *Dyetary* xii. (1870) 266 Chese.. must be of good sauour & taledge. **1601** Holland *Pliny* VIII. xxxii. 213 Their first milke must haue a taste and talang of those two hearbs. **1617** J. Moore *Map Mans Mortalitie* II. vii. 147 Wherein.. there rests some taste and tallage of the former corruptions.

b. The sense of taste.

1557 *Primer, Prayer after receiving Sacrament*, So to order the talage and taste of my heart, that I never fele other swetenes but thee. **1600** Holland *Livy* V. v. 183 Some kinde of meat or drinke.. to please his palate and to content his talage.

'**tallage**, *v.* [f. tallage *sb.*^{1}] *trans.* To impose tallage upon; to tax.

c **1460** *Godstow Reg.* 102 Whan the kyng tallagith his demaynes thurgh Englond. **1520** *Caxton's Chron. Eng.* VI. 77 b/2 The Archebysshop wolde not graunte hym to talenge the chirches at his wyll. **1523** Ld. Berners *Froiss.* I. ccxxxii. 319 Without taxyng or talagyng any of your subgettes or countre. **1738** *Hist. Crt. Excheq.* ii. 17 None were tallaged, (i.e. taxed by the King or his Justices) but Ancient Demesnes and Burroughs holding of the Crown. **1890** Gross *Gild Merch.* I. 57 The king tallaged his boroughs whenever he pleased. **1898** Maitland *Township & Borough* 66 He was tallaged along with the other men of the town.

tallageable ('tælɪdʒəb(ə)l), *a.* [f. prec. + -able.] Liable to be tallaged or taxed. Hence **tallagea'bility**, liability or ability to be tallaged.

1777 *Misc.* in *Ann. Reg.* 181/1 The other burgesses.. were still talliageable at will. **1888** *Nation* (N.Y.) 31 May 443/3 These lists served to give the King a clue as to the tallageability of the Jews.

†'**tallager.** *Obs. rare*$^{-1}$. In 5 **taylagier.** [f. tallage *sb.*^{1} + -er^2 2: see -er^1 1.] One who assessed or collected tallage; a tax-gatherer.

c **1400** *Rom. Rose* 6811 But se what gold han usurers, And silver eke in garners, Taylagiers, & these monyours, Bailifs, bedels, provost, countours.

†'**tallagie.** *Obs.* [ad. med.L. *tallagi-um.*] = tallage *sb.*^{1}

1444 *Rolls of Parlt.* V. 113/2 Custumes, Subsides, Tallagies. **1488–9** *Act 4 Hen. VII*, c. 5 Gathryng of dismes taxes tallagies or eny other subsidies.

tallance, -and, -aunt, obs. var. talon.

†**tallant.** *Obs.* = filander^1.

1580 Hollyband *Treas. Fr. Tong*, *Filandres*, are certaine stringes sharp as nedles growing in Hauks that are fed with euill meate, and cause him to die; tallants.

tallapoi(e, obs. form of talapoin.

tallat, variant of tallet.

tallboy ('tɔːlbɔɪ). [f. tall *a.* + (app.) boy.]

1. A tall-stemmed glass or goblet. Now *local.*

1676 D'Urfey *Mad. Fickle* II. i, *Bella...* Where shall we meet at night? *Maul.* At Lambs with the Fidles and a Talboy. **1694** Motteux *Rabelais* v. xliii. 195 Cups, Goblets, and Talboys of Gold, Silver, and Cristal. *a* **1700** B. E. *Dict. Cant. Crew*, *Tall-boy*, a Pottle or two Quart-pot full of Wine. **1881** Miss Jackson *Shropsh. Word-bk.* s.v., The Maister wants a jug o' ale.. an' two tumbler-glasses—'e said not to sen' them tall-boys, kigglin' [= tottering].

2. A tall chest of drawers (often raised on legs), usually in two parts, one standing on the other, the lower sometimes projecting beyond the upper; sometimes applied to a chest of drawers or a bureau standing on a dressing-table. Also *attrib.*

1769 *Dublin Merc.* 16–19 Sept. 2/2 Chamber chest, tallboy, dining tables, two side-boards. **1884** *W. Sussex Gaz.* 25 Sept., Mahogany tallboy chest of drawers. **1906** *Westm. Gaz.* 28 June 3/3 Tall-Boys.. those double chests of drawers which are to be found in nearly all old-fashioned houses. **1909** *Civ. Serv. Stores Assoc.* May 451, 18th century Mahogany Tall Boy Chest, with pull-out-tray in centre.

3. A kind of tall chimney-pot.

1884 *Daily Tel.* 28 Jan. (Cassell), Scores of pots, tallboys, cowls.. swept from the chimney-stacks of the Metropolis on Saturday night. **1904** *Daily Chron.* 21 June 3/5, I was fixing her some 'tallboys' on the chimneys.

4. *humorous.* ? A great man, a 'big pot'.

1820 *Examiner* No. 644. 513/2 To play the coxcomb, pedant, and tall-boy. *Ibid.* No. 651. 629/2 The Imperial Tall-boy of Russia.

talld(e, obs. f. *told*: see tell *v.*

talle, obs. f. tail *v.*^{2}, tale, tall.

tallen, tallent, obs. ff. talon.

Tallensi (tə'lɛnsɪ), *sb.* (and *a.*) Also **Talensi, Talenssi**, etc. [Native name.] **a.** An African people of Northern Ghana. **b.** The language spoken by this people, belonging to the Voltaic or Gur group of the Niger-Congo languages. Also *attrib.* or as *adj.*

1920 A. W. Cardinall *Natives N. Territories Gold Coast* I. 1 The area.. is peopled by mixed races, of which the principal tribes are Nankanni, Nabdam, Talansi.. and Builsa. **1936** *Discovery* June 169/1 A Talenssi tribesman of the Gold Coast. **1949** M. Fortes *Web of Kinship among Tallensi* i. 1 The Tallensi are typical of the great congeries of Mole-Dagbane-speaking peoples that occupy the basin of the Volta rivers in the French Ivory Coast. **1951** R. Firth *Elem. Social Organization* vi. 207 In Tallensi ideology filial piety is an important moral principle. **1952** Westermann & Bryan *Lang. W. Afr.* v. 65 *Talensi*, own name talene. Language. Spoken by: Talensi (Tallensi, Tallense, Talansi, Talense), call themselves talis, talensi (Sing. talenja, talenga). Where spoken: Gold Coast, Zuarungu District. **1958** D. Emmet *Function, Purpose & Powers* ii. 33 In the West African Tallensi society.. the important relations in terms of which behaviour is directed are kinship relations. **1963** *Internat. Jrnl. Amer. Linguistics* XXIX. I. 8 An enumeration of the membership of the Niger-Congo family by tentative genetic subfamilies follows.. *Gur*:.. Talensi. **1972** J. Goody in P. Laslett *Household & Family* 106 The Tallensi and the Ashanti of Ghana.

talles: see tallith.

tallet, tallat ('tælət). *dial.* Also 7 **tavelett**, 9 *dial.* **tallot, -ut, -art.** [A West-of-England word, used from Cornwall to Berkshire, from Gloucestersh. to Cheshire, and in English-speaking parts of S. Wales; a. Welsh *taflod* or *taflawd* fem. ('tavlɔd, *dial.* 'talɔd), loft, roof, in OIr. *taibled* a story, ad. med.L. *tabulāta* a boarded structure, a flooring, f. *tabulāre* to board, floor.] A loft formed by laying boards on the joists over a stable, cowshed, or the like, commonly used as a hay-loft (***hay-tallet***); also 'the unceiled space beneath the roof in any building; an attic' (E.D.D.).

1586 *Will I. Palfrye, Ilminster* (Tanner), I..bequeath.. one tallett of barke which is the tallett now over my myll-house. **1607** J. NORDEN *Surv. Dial.* v. 238 Some kind of lofts or hay tallets, as they call them in the West, that are not boorded. **1681** PH. HENRY *Diaries & Lett.* (1882) 307 From yᵉ lower Haybay & Tavelett they pitcht it & carry'd it on Pikehils to yᵉ Carts. **1791** *Life B. M. Carew* (1802) 87 Let me lie and die in some hay-tallet. **1850** SIR T. DYKE ACLAND in *Jrnl. R. Agric. Soc.* XI. II. 745 The humidity of the climate. .. One of the peculiarities resulting from this cause is the building of a second storey or loft over all bullock-sheds; it is called a 'tallat'. **1876** T. HARDY *Ethelberta* II. xlvi, Now up in the tallet with ye..and down with another lock or two of hay.

b. *Comb.* **tallet-ladder**, the ladder giving access to the tallet.

1882 BLACKMORE *Christowell* xv, For the girls there was a tallat ladder.

talliable ('tælɪəb(ə)l), *a.* Now *Hist.* Also 6-7 **taillable**. [a. OF. *taillable* (13th c. in Hatz.-Darm.), f. *tailler*, TAIL *v.*[2]; assimilated to TALLY *v.*] Subject to tallage, liable to be 'tailed' or taxed.

[**1321-2** *Rolls of Parlt.* I. 410/1, Qe lur tenaunz..ne seient geldables ne taillables.] **1531** in W. H. Turner *Select. Rec. Oxford* (1880) 98 They be tallyable with the Burgesses. **1575** *Ibid.* 371 Persons..talliable with scotte, lotte, and other charges as like occupiers. **1554** WOTTON *Let.* 29 July in *State Pap. Mary, Foreign* IV. 193 (P.R.O.) The king [of France] pronounced their sentences..somme..to be degraded from their nobilite.. they were..pronounced to be taillable as anye other villaine. **1600** HOLLAND *Livy* xxxv. xvi. 897 Having..been made tributarie and taillable, he chalengeth of them the auncient rights & duties due from them. **1720** STRYPE *Stow's Surv.* II. v. xxvii. 359/2 They understood, that they of the City of London were not talliable. **1759** HURD *Dialogues* (1760) 270 The great towns and cities that before were royal demesnes, part of the king's private patrimony, and talliable by him at pleasure.

talliage, etc., obs. ff. TALLAGE *sb.*[1], etc.

‖**talliar** ('tælɪə(r)). Also 7 **tarryar, taliar**, 9 *erron.* **taliary**. [ad. Tamil *talaiyāri*.] A village watchman in Southern India.

1680 *Fort St. George Consns.* 10 Feb. (Y.), The Peons and Tarryars sent in quest of two soldiers who had deserted. **1693** in Wheeler *Madras in Old. Time* (1861) I. 267 Taliars and Peons appointed to watch the Black Town. **1707** *Ibid.* II. 74 Resolving to march two hundred and fifty soldiers, two hundred talliars, and two hundred peons. **1858** J. B. NORTON *Topics* 204 The taliary, or watchman, guards it from being taken away by the owners.

talliate ('tælɪeɪt), *v.* [f. med.L. *talliāt-*, ppl. stem of *talliāre* to impose a subsidy or tax: see TAIL *v.*[2] 5.] *trans.* = TALLAGE *v.*; to tax.

1754 HUME *Hist. Eng.* (1761) I. xiii. 316 *note*, The king had not only the power of talliating the inhabitants within his own demesnes, but that of granting to particular barons the power of talliating the inhabitants within theirs. **1826** LINGARD *Hist. Eng.* (ed. 4) III. 190 *note*, It was proved from the records in the chancery and exchequer that they [citizens of London] had been talliated in the years 1214, 1223 [etc.]. **1892** *Yorksh. Inquisitions* I. 81.

†**talli'ation**. *Obs. rare.* [ad. med.L. *talliātio* (Du Cange), n. of action from *talliāre*: see prec.] The action of talliating; tallage.

1531 in W. H. Turner *Select. Rec. Oxford* (1880) 98 So alwey that they be tallyable with the Burgesses of the.. Towne, the same tallyac[i]on to be assessed.

‖**tallicoona** (tælɪ'kuːnə). [corr. of F. *touloucouna* = *tulukuna*, native name in Wolof lang. of Fr. Senegambia; in the cognate Serer lang. *tulukuni*. (Thence by contraction *kunda*, COONDA, also *coondi*.)] A West African tree, *Carapa guineensis*. **tallicoona oil**, a fixed oil expressed from the seeds of this.

[**1832** GUILL. & PERR. *Fl. Seneg. Tent.* I. 128 Vulgo dicitur Touloucouna ab incolis... On obtient par expression de ses amandes une huile fixe connue dans le pays sous le nom d'Huile de Touloucouna.] **1866** *Treas. Bot.* 221 *Carapa guineensis* is a native of Senegal, and scarcely differs from the last [*C. guianensis*, the source of Carap or Crab oil]. Its seeds yield Tallicoonah or Coondi oil, which, besides being used for the same purposes as Crab oil, is employed as a purgative and anthelmintic.

tallied ('tælɪd), *ppl. a.*[1] [f. TALLY *v.*[1] + -ED[1].]

†**1. a.** Cut, scored, marked. *Obs.*

c **1440** *Promp. Parv.* 486/1 Talyyd, *talliatus, dicatus, anticopatus*.

b. Counted, numbered.

1830 *Dublin Even. Post* 17 July 3/2 Not by 'tallied votes' but by acclamation.

2. Made to tally or correspond with each other.

1895 DRIVER in *Expositor* Oct. 289 It is not sufficient for him to show that tallied speeches can exhibit marks of lateness.

tallied *ppl. a.*[2]: see TALLY *v.*[2]

†'**tallier**. *Cards. Obs.* Now only in Fr. form **tailleur** (tɑjœr). Also 8 **talliere, -ieur**. [Agent-n. from TALLY *v.*[3], and from F. *tailler* to deal (at cards).] In rouge-et-noir and similar card-games, the name of the dealer or banker.

1709 *Cotton's Compl. Gamester* 178 (Stanf.) The *Talliere* is he that keeps the Bank. **1715** LADY M. W. MONTAGU *Basset-table* I The Bassette-Table spread, the Tallier come;..Rise, pensive nymph! the tallier waits for you. **1793** *Faro & Rouge et Noir*, Tailleur... The dealer, either the banker or a person he has employed to deal. **1794** *Sporting Mag.* IV. 43 The office of the tallieur is to deal and settle the game of the punters on each side of him. **1825** HOR. SMITH *Gai. & Grav.* II. 243 The Inspector, the Croupier, the Tailleur. **1877** READE *Woman Hater* ix, The *tailleur* dealt, and the croupier intoned.

tallingite ('tælɪŋaɪt). *Min.* [Named 1865 after R. Talling: see -ITE[1].] Hydrous chloride of copper, akin to atacamite.

1865 A. H. CHURCH in *Jrnl. Chem. Soc.* XVIII. 214. **1865** *Athenæum* 25 Mar. 426/2 The new mineral Tallingite.

tallipat, -pot, -put, var. of TALIPOT.

tallish ('tɔːlɪʃ), *a.* [f. TALL *a.* + -ISH[1].] Inclining towards tallness; rather tall.

1748 RICHARDSON *Clarissa* (1810) VI. xxxvi. 132 He is a thin, tallish man. **1858** MASSON *Milton* (1859) I. vi. 467 According to Aubrey, he [Waller] was of tallish and rather slim make. **1882** *Garden* 11 Feb. 90/1 A big clump of tallish trees.

‖**tallith** ('tælɪθ, ‖tal'liθ). Also 7- **talith**, 7 **talles**, 9 **talit, tales**. [Rabb. Heb. *ṭa'llīp*, with Spanish Jews *talīt*, Ger. Jews *tallis*, f. *ṭā'lal*, to cover, shelter, akin to *tsā'lal*, to grow dark, whence *tsēl*, shade (H. Gollancz).] The garment or mantle (in modern times frequently assuming the form of a scarf) worn by Jews at prayer; formerly, and in some countries still, used in place of or in addition to the canopy at weddings, i.e. to cover the heads of bride and bridegroom.

Its religious significance is solely derived from the 'fringes' attached to the four corners in accordance with Numbers xv. 38 and Deut. xxii. 12.

1613 PURCHAS *Pilgrimage* (1614) 194 They call this garment *Talith. Ibid.* 210 The Priest draweth his *Talles* (a large cloth made of haires) before his eyes, and pronounceth the blessing. **1649** PRYNNE *Demurrer to Jews' Remitter* 35 Every Jew after he is past 7. years of age, shall carry a signe ..in his chief garment; that is to say in form of two Talles of yellow taffety. **1839** BEATON tr. *Jews in East* I. v. 152 Every one wore a talit. **1842** BONAR & M'CHEYNE *Mission to Jews* iv. (1843) 237 There were about thirty in the synagogue, all wearing the *Tallith* or shawl with fringes, and the *Tephillin* or phylacteries. **1886** FARRAR *Hist. Interpr.* iii. 126 To unite the Pallium of Japheth with the tallith of Shem. **1892** ZANGWILL *Childr. Ghetto* I. ii. 62, I have not the wherewithal..to make him a Talith-bag.

†'**tallman**. *Obs. Cant.* [f. TALL *a.* + MAN, after HIGHMAN.] In *pl.* Dice loaded so as to turn up high numbers.

1592 KYD *Sol. & Pers.* II. i, *Pist.* Heere are tall men and little men. *Iul.* Hie men and low men, thou wouldst say. **1592** *Nobody & Someb.* I ij b, Fulloms and gourds; heeres tall-men and low-men.

Tallman, var. TOLMAN.

tallness ('tɔːlnɪs). [f. TALL *a.* + -NESS.] The quality of being tall; greatness of stature.

1535 COVERDALE *1 Sam.* xvi. 7 Loke not vpon his countenaunce ner vpon the tallnesse of his person. **1576** FLEMING *Panopl. Epist.* 275 Poplar trees, of notable talnesse. **1630** tr. *Camden's Hist. Eliz.* IV. an. 1592. 41 They soone desisted, being terrified with the tallnesse of the ship. *a* **1661** FULLER *Worthies* (1840) I. xxiv. 101 It plainly proveth the properness of their parts, and tallness of their industry. **1870** SPURGEON *Treas. Dav.* Ps. xliv. 3 What mattered the tallness of the sons of Anak?

†**b.** ***his tallness***, humorous for 'his highness'.

1656 I. S. *Picture New Courtier* 3 An Emissary, employed by his Talnesse to ensnare the plain-hearted.

tallow ('tæləʊ), *sb.* Forms: α. 4 **talȝ, talwgh**, 4-5 **talwȝ**, 5 **talgh(e**; *Sc.* 5-6 **talch**, 6 **tawlche, tawche, tauche, tawcht**, 6-7 **tauch**, 7-8 **taulch**, 9 **taugh**. β. 4 **talowȝ**, 4-6 **talow(e**, 5 **talogh, -ough, -owgh, talwhe, talwe**, 5-6 **talugh(e, talo**, 5-7 **tallo, tallowe**, 6- **tallow**. γ. *Sc.* 5-6 **tallone, -own(e**, 5-7 **-on, -oun(e**, 9 *dial.* **tallan, -in**. [ME. *talȝ, talgh*, known first in 14th c.; corresponds to MLG. *talg, talch*, LG. *talg*, in early mod.Du. *talg, talch* (16th c.), Du. *talk* fem. and Ger. *talg*, in 1572 *talck* masc.; MIcel. (14th c.) *tólg, tólk*, MDa. (13th c.) *talgh, talwh*, MSw. *talgh(er)*, mod.Icel. *tólg*, Norw., Da., Sw. *talg*, Norw. dial. *tolg, taag, taalg, tølg*, Fær. *tálg*.

These forms indicate a common origin, but nowhere has the word yet been found before the 13th c. In the Scandinavian langs. a great diversity of gender suggests that the word is borrowed from MLG.; the ME. may have had a similar origin, but the parallelism of Eng. *sallow*, Sc. *sauch*,:—OE. *sealh*, Anglian *salh*, suggests for Eng. *tallow*, Sc. *tauch*, an OE. **tealh*, **talh*, = OLG. **talg, talh*. Ulterior etymology unknown.]

1. a. The fat or adipose tissue of an animal, esp. that which yields the substance described in 2; suet.

α. **1382** WYCLIF *Ecclus.* xlvii. 2 As talȝ [1388 ynnere fatnesse] seuered fro the flesh. **14..** *Med. Receipts in Rel. Ant.* I. 53 Fresch talgh of a schepe. *c* **1440** *Promp. Parv.* 486/1 Talwhe (*Pynson* talowe), *cepum*. **15..** *Aberdeen Regr.* XXI. (Jam.), Scheip tawcht & nolt tawcht. **1871** WADDELL *Ps. in Scottis* xvii. 10 They're theekit about wi' their ain taugh.

β. **1382** WYCLIF *Exod.* xxiii. 18 [Thow] shal not leeue the talowȝ of my solempnete vnto the morwen. *c* **1400** *Lanfranc's Cirurg.* 60 Take schepis talow [*B.M. MS.* schepys talwȝ]. *c* **1425** *Voc.* in Wr.-Wülcker 660/37 *Hoc sepum*, tallo. **1486** *Bk. of St. Albans* F ij, All beestis that beere talow and stonde vpright. **1518** *Cov. Leet Bk.* 663 That no bocher sell eny of his tallowe aboue ij.s. the ston. **1613** MARKHAM *Eng. Husb.* II. II. vii. (1635) 90 Hee feeds fast, and his tallow wonderfully increaseth. **1787** HUNTER in *Phil. Trans.* LXXVII. 389 Ruminating animals have that species of fat called tallow. **1897** G. H. CLARK in *Outing* (U.S.) XXIX. 338/1 A much needed lunch of delicious reindeer tallow.

†**b.** *fig.* 'Fatness', richness. *Obs.*

c **1380** WYCLIF *Wks.* (1880) 104 For þei [prelatis] ben so chokid wiþ talow of worldly goodis.

2. A substance consisting of a somewhat hard animal fat (esp. that obtained from the parts about the kidneys of ruminating animals, now chiefly the sheep and ox), separated by melting and clarifying from the membranes, etc., naturally mixed with it; used for making candles and soap, dressing leather, and other purposes. In quot. 1590, dripping.

α. **13..** *Coer de L.* 1552 And wex sumdel caste thertoo, Talwgh and grese menge alsoo. *c* **1350** *Usages Winchester* in *Eng. Gilds* (1870) 359 Euerych sellere of grece and of smere and of talwȝ. *c* **1440** tr. *Pallad. on Husb.* I. 444 Thorgh the ston, yf that the water synke, Take picche & talgh, as need is the to spende. **1449** *Aberdeen Regr.* (1844) I. 402 That na man by talch mar than may suffice his houss. **14..** (MS. *a* 1600) *Iter Camerar.* c. 22 in *Scotch Acts* (1844) I. App. iv. 700/1 þai suld gif þair lethir gude oyle and taulch [**1609** SKENE tauch]. **1505** *Burgh Rec. Edinb.* (1869) I. 107 It is.. forbidden that any maner of persoun melt or rynde thair tawlche in fore housis on the hie gaitt. **1544** *Aberdeen Regr.* I. 207 Selling of tauch. **1548** *Burgh Rec. Edinb.* II. 141 [To] by na kitchein fie nor paynsche tawche.

β. **1391** *Earl Derby's Exped.* (Camden) 71 Pro grees et talowe..emptis ibidem. **1413** *Pilgr. Sowle* (Caxton) II. lxi. (1859) 58 Wax shall be wors after it is quenchid, than doth ony talowe. **1496** *Naval Acc. Hen. VII* (1896) 177 Talowgh. Also payed..for DCC weight Talowe. **1529** *Supplic. to King* (E.E.T.S.) 32 A candell (which for lacke of talowe..can not geue light). **1541** *Lanc. Wills* (Chetham Soc.) I. 81 Hole cakes of rendred tallow. **1590** SHAKS. *Com. Err.* III. ii. 100 Her ragges and the Tallow in them, will burne a Poland Winter. **1623** WHITBOURNE *Newfoundland* 98 Diuersities of the ground..that hath come in the Tallo, on the end of the Lead. **1727-41** CHAMBERS *Cycl.* s.v., There are scarce any animals but a sort of Tallow may be prepared from. **1839** URE *Dict. Arts*, etc., *Tallow*..of the ox consists of 76 parts of stearine, and 24 of oleine. **1884** *Harper's Mag.* July 299/1 'Prime' tallow is made from the kidney and caul fat only, while 'regular' tallow is made from the other fat, bones, and trimmings.

γ. **1482** in *Charters, etc. Edinb.* (1871) 169 Buttir, vynagir, flesch, or tallone. **1497** *Acc. Ld. High Treas. Scotl.* I. 349 Item for xxiij pund of talloune to Mons. **1498** *Reg. Privy Seal Scotl.* I. 23/1 Gold, siluer, tallon and al uther gudis that ar forbiddin to be had furth of the realme. **1529** *Rec. Edinb.* (1871) 6 At na candilmakir melt thair tallone on the foirgait. **1542** *Acc. Ld. High Treas. Scotl.* VIII. 77 For viij dusane.. girthis putt upon the talloun punscheonis.

3. a. Applied to various kinds of grease or greasy substances, e.g. those obtained from plants. ***mineral tallow*** = HATCHETTITE: see MINERAL *a.* 5.

1745 P. THOMAS *Jrnl. Anson's Voy.* 185 Of all the Trees that grow in China, that which produces Tallow is in my Opinion the most surprizing. **1860** [see BAYBERRY 2].

b. (See quot.) *local.*

1876 WOODWARD *Geol. Eng. & Wales* vii. 185 Beautiful plumose stalactites are often found in the fissures of the rock, and are called by the workmen..tallow.

4. Elliptical for TALLOW CANDLE.

1819 M. WILMOT *Let.* 21 Dec. (1935) 42 Wax candles are both bad, and dear. We use them of course, and *tallows* in the nursery and Kitchen. **1823** *Blackw. Mag.* XIII. 97 A little pair of tallows unsnuffed before him. **1980** *Times Lit. Suppl.* 22 Aug. 929/3 He would blow out his tallow behind Coloured glass.

5. *attrib.* and *Comb.* **a.** *attrib.* Made or consisting of tallow, as ***tallow-ball, -cake, -dip*** (DIP *sb.* 7), ***-grease, -soap***; of, pertaining to, containing, or dealing in tallow, as ***tallow-can, -crap*** (CRAP *sb.*[1] 3), ***-cup, -leaf*** (LEAF *sb.*[1] 9), ***-light, -man***. **b.** objective, instrumental, similative, etc., as ***tallow-boiler, -melter; tallow-caked*** (obs.), ***-coloured, -hued, -lighted, -like, -pale, -white*** adjs.

1856 KANE *Arct. Expl.* I. xxxii. 448 A few rats chopped up and frozen into the *tallow-balls. **1907** *Westm. Gaz.* 10 Dec. 9/2 The *tallow-boiler, the soap manufacturer, and a vast number of other dependent trades have been hard hit. **1599** *West Riding Sessions Rolls* (Yorks. Rec. Series III.) 135 One *tallowe cake..felonice cepit. **1577** tr. *Bullinger's Decades* (1592) 165 With face of *tallow caked hew. **1877** KNIGHT *Dict. Mech.*, **Tallow-can*, a vessel to hold melted tallow for lubricating purposes. **1822** SCOTT *Nigel* x, His cheek was still pale and *tallow-coloured as before. **1828** *Craven Gloss.*, **Tallow-craps*, the refuse or cracklings of tallow or hog's lard, after being rendered. **1863** HOLME LEE *Annie Warleigh* III. 224 To eat us out o' house an' home, an' keep Magsie doing for iver wi' biscuit, an' tallow-crap. **1877** KNIGHT *Dict. Mech.*, **Tallow-cup*, a lubricating device for journal-boxes, etc., in which tallow is employed as the lubricant. **1835** G. A. MCCALL *Lett. fr. Frontiers* (1868) 274, I set down the *tallow-dip upon the table. **1768** TUCKER *Lt. Nat.* (1834) I. 640 The unhappy negro..is thrown into a stinking hold, kept upon rotten pease besmeared over with *tallow grease. **1824** MACTAGGART *Gallovid. Encycl.* s.v., When an ox or a sheep has a gude *tallow-leaf, it is considered to have fed weel, and to be deep on the rib. **1633** P. FLETCHER *Purple Isl.* VII. xxxvii, *Tallow lights live glitt'ring, stinking die. **1825** CONSTABLE in Lockhart *Scott* lxii, I have hitherto been thinking only of the wax lights, but before I'm a twelvemonth older I shall have my hand upon the tallow. **1879** G. J. ROMANES in *19th Cent.* Sept. 401 The *tallow-lighted blackness of our mines. **1843** R. J. GRAVES *Syst. Clin. Med.* xxv. 326 Frequently they were combined with small *tallow-like sloughs of the mucous membrane at the angles of the mouth. **1860** EMERSON *Cond. Life, Beauty* Wks. (Bohn) II. 435, I have noticed a block of spermaceti lying about..mantelpieces for twenty years.., simply because the tallowman gave it the form of a rabbit. **1815** *Chron.* in *Ann. Reg.* 34/2 A very alarming fire broke out at Mr. Dunkin's, *tallow-melter, in Aldersgate Street. **1596** GOSSON *Pleas. Quippes Upst. Gentlew.* 98 in Hazl. *E.P.P.* IV. 254 But on each wight now are they seene, The *tallow-pale, the browning-bay. **1906** *Daily Chron.* 23 Oct. 5/2 The use of the old-fashioned *tallow soaps. **1853** KANE *Grinnell Exp.* xxxiv. 303 His nose was *tallow-white.

c. Special Combs.: **tallow-berry**, the edible fruit of a small malpighiaceous tree (*Byrsonima lucida*) of the West Indies and Florida Keys; also called *glamberry* (*Cent. Dict.* 1891); also, the tree; **tallow-bush** *U.S.* = *tallow shrub*; **tallow-cut** *a.*, = *tallow-topped*; **tallow-drop**, chiefly *attrib.*, describing a style of cutting precious stones, by which one side is made smooth and convex, the other similarly convex, or flat, or concave; **tallow-gourd**, an E. Indian climbing cucurbitaceous plant, *Benincasa cerifera* (*B. hispida*), so called from the waxy substance which exudes from its fruit when ripe; also called *wax-gourd*, *white gourd*; **tallow-loaf**, †(*a*) a lump of tallow; also *fig.*; (*b*) *attrib.* applied to a kind of cabbage (cf. LOAF *sb.* 5), also called DRUMHEAD (4); **tallow-nut**, a thorny tree, *Ximenia americana* (N.O. *Olacaceæ*), native of tropical America, bearing a plum-like fruit containing a white seed or 'nut'; also called HOG-PLUM, MOUNTAIN-*plum*; **tallow-nutmeg**, a species of nutmeg-tree, *Myristica sebifera*, native of tropical S. America, whose seed yields a concrete oil known as American nutmeg-oil, or virola-tallow; **tallow-oil**, oil expressed from tallow; **tallow pot** *U.S.* and *Austral. slang*, the fireman on a locomotive engine; **tallow shrub**, a N. American shrub, *Myrica cerifera*, also called BAYBERRY (2), CANDLEBERRY (a), or *wax-myrtle*, whose fruit yields a wax-like substance (*bayberry tallow*) used for candles; **tallow-top**, a precious stone cut in *tallow-drop* fashion; also *attrib.*; hence **tallow-topped** adj.; **tallow-wood**, a large Australian tree, *Eucalyptus microcorys*, which yields a very hard greasy wood. See also TALLOW CANDLE, -CHANDLER, etc.

1835 W. G. SIMMS *Partisan* 387 The prisoners..had been made to file into the groves of *tallow bushes. **1855** tr. *Labarte's Arts Mid. Ages* iv. 111 **Tallow-cut*, that is, rounded and polished, in a convex shape, like the modern carbuncle. **1898** *Athenæum* 17 Sept. 391/2 A stone cut *en cabochon*—or tallow-cut, as the old term had it. **1798** GREVILLE in *Phil. Trans.* LXXXVIII. 411 Stones..of the common India polish and form, *en cabochon*, which is often called *tallow drop, from the French..term *goutte de suif*. **1891** KIPLING *Naulahka* vi, It's a tallow-drop emerald. **1483** *Cath. Angl.* 377/2 A *Talghe lafe (*A.* A Tallow lafe), *congiarium*. **1596** NASHE *Saffron-Walden* Wks. (Grosart) III. 183 The verie guts and garbage of his Note-book he hath put into this tallow loafe. **1780** *Lett. & Pap. Bath Soc.* I. 17 The sort principally raised is the tallow-loaf, or drum-head cabbage. **1805** R. W. DICKSON *Pract. Agric.* II. 682 Known in some districts by the name of the tallow loaf cabbage. **1791** W. BARTRAM *Trav. N. & S. Carolina* 94 These shelly ridges have a vegetable surface of loose black mould, very fertile, which naturally produces..*Tallow-nut, or Wild Lime, and many others. **1884** C. S. SARGENT *Rep. Forests N. Amer.* 34 Wild Lime. Tallow Nut... Common and reaching its greatest development in Florida. **1891** *Cent. Dict.*, Tallow-nut. *Tallow-nutmeg. **1914** *Dialect Notes* IV. 164 **Tallow pot*,..the fireman of a locomotive. **1929** *Bookman* July 524/1 I'm surprised to find a student tallow-pot up in the cab takin' orders from the bakehead. **1960** *Listener* 18 Aug. 250/2 Firemen are 'tallowpots' or 'bakebrains'. **1968** *Amer. Speech* XLIII. 289 *Tallow pot*,..originally, before the days of lube oil, a fireman was so-called because he had to get out onto the steam chest of the engine with a can of tallow and hold it so the lubricant would be drawn into the cylinder. **1770** J. R. FORSTER tr. *Kalm's Trav. N. Amer.* I. 192 *Tallow shrub, or Candleberry Tree. **1866** *Treas. Bot.*, Tallow-shrub, *Myrica cerifera*. **1884** F. J. BRITTEN *Watch & Clockm.* 208 Finishers generally use the old English screw head tool for producing the beautiful '*tallow top' screws used in English work. **1865** EMANUEL *Diamonds*, etc. 144 The old English expression, *tallow-topped, which means cut, not in facets, but with a flat or hollow base, and a smooth convex top. **1884** A. NILSON *Timber Trees N.S.W.* 67 *Tallowwood; Mahogany.—A tall tree, with a persistent furrowed fibrous bark. **1889** J. H. MAIDEN *Usef. Plants Australia* 493 In Queensland it is known as 'Peppermint'... But its almost universal name is Tallow Wood... Used..for flooring, *e.g.* in ball-rooms. **1897** *Melbourne Argus* 22 Feb. 5/4 (Morris) That the New South Wales black butt and tallow wood were the most durable and noiseless woods for street-paving.

'tallow, *v.* Forms: see prec. [f. prec. sb.]

1. *trans.* To smear or anoint with tallow; to grease (formerly esp. the bottom of a ship or boat).

a **1400–50** *Alexander* 4208 Quen it [a barge] was done.. pickid & taloghid. **1463** *Mann. & Househ. Exp.* (Roxb.) 220 To the schypmen that talluyd the shyp boot, vj. d. for wyne. *c* **1490** *Promp. Parv.* 486/1 (MS. A) Talwyn (*Pynson* talowyn), *sepo*. **1495** *Naval Acc. Hen. VII* (1896) 225 Talowe occupied abought talowying of the seid ship. **1497** *Acc. Ld. High Treas. Scotl.* I. 378 Item, for pyk to hir and to talloune hir. **1530** PALSGR. 752/1 Tallowe your shyppe or you go, it shall forther you moche on your waye. **1589** WARNER *Alb. Eng., Prose Add.* (1612) 336 Command..that thy Shippes be secretly calked, tallowed, ballaced. **1706** E. WARD *Wooden World Diss.* (1708) 84 There's near as much Stuff drops from his Carcase every Day, as would tallow the Ship's Bottom. **1806** PIKE *Sources Mississ.* (1810) 89 Tallowed my boats with our candles and launched them. **1886** J. K. JEROME *Idle Thoughts* vii, I..tallowed my nose, and went to bed.

†**b.** *intr.* (for *refl.*) *Obs.*

1666 *Lond. Gaz.* No. 28/3 The *Forrester* having washed and tallowed here, is gone to her station. **1720** DE FOE *Capt. Singleton* xiv. (1840) 240 The sloop washed and tallowed also.

2. a. *intr.* Of cattle, etc.: To form, produce, or yield tallow.

a **1722** LISLE *Husb.* (1752) 262 Old cows generally tallowed best withinside. *Ibid.*, Very rarely [for a young cow] to tallow well on the inside. **1796** BURKE *Let. Noble Ld.* Wks. VIII. 63 Their only question will be..how he [the Duke of Bedford] cuts up? how he tallows in the cawl or on the kidneys? *a* **1843** SOUTHEY *Comm.-pl. Bk.* (1851) IV. 400/2 [Cattle] famous for..tallowing within in the first degree.

b. *trans.* To cause (cattle, etc.) to form tallow; to fatten. (Cf. TALLOWED 2.)

1765 *Museum Rust.* IV. xliv. 190 The largest pasture.. will neither skin nor tallow, or, in other words, is fit for nothing but young stock. **1828** WEBSTER, *Tallow*,..to cause to have a large quantity of tallow; as, to tallow sheep.

Hence **'tallowing** *vbl. sb.* and *ppl. a.*

1495 [see sense 1]. **1828** in WEBSTER.

'tallow 'candle, *sb.* A candle made of tallow.

1452 in *Berks, Bucks & Oxon Archæol. Jrnl.* Oct. (1903) 78 Item for j lb. & a hafe of tallowcandell..j d. ob. **1496–7** *Rec. St. Mary at Hill* 33 Item, iiij Candylstykes of laton with braunches for Talough candell. **1545** in *Shropsh. Parish Documents* (1903) 79 For talo candyllys. **1660** BOYLE *New Exp. Phys. Mech.* x. 74 We took a Tallow-Candle of such a size that eight of them make about a pound. **1886** RUSKIN *Præterita* I. vii. 229 My parents..used only tallow candles in plated candlesticks.

Hence **tallow-candle** *v.* (*nonce-wd.*), *trans.* to smear or rub with a tallow candle.

1894 BLACKMORE *Perlycross* 48 The nap of his old velvet-coat where a wicked boy had tallow-candled it.

†**tallow catch**. *Obs.* A phrase applied in Shakspere (so in quartos and folios) to Falstaff, as a very fat man.

By Hanmer taken as = *tallow ketch* 'tub of tallow': see *ketch* 'tub or barrel', a Gloucestershire and West-of-England word, in Eng. Dial. Dict. By Johnson explained as *tallow keech* 'lump or mass of tallow' (see KEECH *sb.*), an explanation adopted by Steevens. See notes in critical editions.

1596 SHAKS. *1 Hen. IV*, II. iv. 252 *Prince*. Thou Knotty-pated Foole, thou Horson obscene greasie Tallow Catch.

'tallow-,chandler. [See CHANDLER 2.] One whose trade is to make or sell tallow candles.

1406 *Close Roll 7 Hen. IV* b, Simon atte Holke, Talogh-chaundeler. **1431** *Cal. Pat. Rolls 9 Hen. VI* 96 Henry Pollard, citizen and talghchaundeler of London. *c* **1515** *Cocke Lorell's B.* 9 Talowe chaundelers, hostelers, and glouers. **1683** TRYON *Way to Health* 595 Neither does a Tallow-Chandler smell those horrible Scents and pernicious Fumes that old Tallow sends forth when it is melted. *a* **1763** LD. GRANVILLE in Boswell *Johnson* an. 1780, A letter, expressed in terms not good enough for a tallow-chandler to have used. **1876** L. STEPHEN *Hist. Eng. Th. 18th C.* I. III. v. 163 He was early apprenticed to a tallow-chandler.

Hence **tallow-'chandlering**, also **tallow-'chandling** (cf. *market-gardening*), the operation or business of a tallow-chandler.

1837–8 THACKERAY *Yellowplush Corr.* i, Her father being a bankrup in the tallow-chandlering way. **1876** L. STEPHEN *Hist. Eng. Th. 18th C.* I. III. v. 163 The exception to his tallow-chandling was a short residence with Sir Joseph.

'tallow-,chandlery. [f. prec.: see -ERY.]

a. The business or trade of a tallow-chandler. **b.** The place of work of a tallow-chandler.

1815 *Niles' Reg.* VIII. 141 There are..6 tallow chandleries [in Pittsburgh]. **1846** H. MELVILLE *Typee* xxv. 203 Mehevi..looking as if he had..undergone the process of dipping in a tallow-chandlery. **1864** in WEBSTER. **1866** *Routledge's Every Boy's Ann.* 71 His own tallow-chandlery business.

tallowed ('tæləʊd), *a.* Forms: see TALLOW *sb.* [f. TALLOW *sb.* and *v.* + -ED.]

1. Smeared or anointed with tallow, greased: said esp. of a ship's bottom.

c **1440** *Promp. Parv.* 486/2 Talwyd, *cepatus*. **1513** DOUGLAS *Æneis* IX. ii. 97 The tallownit burdis kest a pyky low [= the tallowed boards emitted a pitchy flame]. *a* **1547** SURREY *Æneid* IV. (1557) F j b, Now fleetes the talowed kele. **1716** *Lond. Gaz.* No. 5412/2 A clean-tallowed French Snow. **1804** NELSON in Nicolas *Disp.* (1846) VI. 283 She would require a clean tallowed bottom every six weeks.

†**2.** Of cattle, etc.: (Well) furnished with fat or tallow; in grease. *Obs.*

1523 FITZHERB. *Husb.* §57 And se the oxe haue a greate codde,..for than it shulde seme, that they shulde be wel talowed. **1613** MARKHAM *Eng. Husbandman* II. II. vii. (1635) 81 A..signe that the beast is very well tallowed within.

'tallower. *rare*. [f. TALLOW *sb.* and *v.* + -ER[1].] (See quots.)

1828 WEBSTER, *Tallower*, an animal disposed to form tallow internally. *Cyc.* **1882** OGILVIE (Annandale), *Tallower*, a tallow-chandler. **1946** E. ST. J. BROOKS *Sir C. Hatton* ii. 26 She married..John Farrington, a tallower of the same town.

'tallow-face. Now *rare* or *Obs.* A pale, yellowish-white face; hence, a person having such a face: a term of contempt.

1592 SHAKS. *Rom. & Jul.* III. v. 158 Out you baggage, You tallow face. **1616** R. C. *Times' Whistle* v. 2237 O, 'tis Fumoso with the tallow-face. **1638** SIR T. HERBERT *Trav.* (ed. 2) 127 The entrance..neer which is hung a mirrour whether to admire their tallow faces in, or internal deformities, I know not.

So **'tallow-faced** *a.*, having a tallow-face.

1592 GREENE *Disput.*, etc. 17 The Paynters coulde not.. make away theyr Vermiglion, if tallowe facde whoores vsde it not for their cheekes. **1621** BURTON *Anat. Mel.* III. ii. IV. i. (1651) 519 Every Lover admires his Mistress, though she be..pale, red, yellow, tand, tallow-faced. **1681** W. ROBERTSON *Phraseol. Gen.* (1693) 446 A deformed, thin, tallow-faced fellow, he looks like a Ghost. **1883** STEVENSON *Treas. Isl.* II. viii, It was the tallow-faced man.

'tallowiness. [f. TALLOWY + -NESS.] The quality of being tallowy.

1832 S. WARREN *Diary Physic.* I. xiii. 291 The tallowiness of her complexion.

tallowish ('tæləʊɪʃ), *a.* [f. TALLOW *sb.* + -ISH[1] 2.] Of the nature of or resembling tallow; tallow-like, tallowy.

1552 HULOET, Tallowyshe, or lyke to tallow, *seuiosus*. **1598** FLORIO, *Songioso*, fattie, lardie, greasie, tallowish. **1731** MEDLEY *Kolben's Cape G. Hope* II. 65 The Fat [of Cape sheep] is not so tallowish as that of European Mutton; and the poorer Sort..use it in the Place of Butter. **1838** GRANVILLE *Spas Germ.* 378 The cheeks, formerly tallowish and saffrony, became ruddy.

tallow keech, ketch: see TALLOW CATCH.

'tallow-,tree. A name given to various trees yielding substances resembling tallow; *spec.* **a.** *Stillingia sebifera*, a euphorbiaceous tree of China, cultivated also in India and the warmer parts of America for the fatty covering of its seeds; **b.** *Pentadesma butyracea*, a guttiferous tree of Sierra Leone, also called *butter and tallow tree* (BUTTER *sb.*[1] 5); **c.** *Vateria indica* (N.O. *Dipterocarpaceæ*) of Malabar; **d.** = *tallow-wood* (TALLOW *sb.* 5 c).

1704 PETIVER *Gazophyl.* IV. xxxiv, *Ricinus Chinensis Sebifera*..China Tallow-tree. **1851** *Art Jrnl. Illustr. Catal.* II. p. vi/1 The tallow-tree of China, the seeds of which furnish a fatty matter manufactured..into candles. *c* **1865** LETHEBY in *Circ. Sc.* I. 95/1 A solid oil..is obtained from the tallow-tree of Java—probably a species of *Bassia*. **1887** MOLONEY *Forestry W. Afr.* 279 Butter or Tallow tree of West Africa (*Pentadesma butyracea*, Don).—Fruits yield a yellow greasy juice when cut, which is mixed by the Negroes with their food.

tallowy ('tæləʊɪ), *a.* Also *Sc.* **taughy**. [f. TALLOW *sb.* + -Y.]

1. Having the nature or properties of tallow; sebaceous.

c **1440** *Promp. Parv.* 486/1 Talwy, *ceposus*. **1530** PALSGR. 327/1 Talowye, *grasseux*. **1594** T. B. *La Primaud. Fr. Acad.* II. 112 Oyle, or some other tallowy and moyst matter. **1771** SMOLLETT *Humph. Cl.* 8 June, The tallowey rancid mass called butter. **1904** FARRER *Garden Asia* 130 The tallowy noisomeness of the temple smells.

b. Smeared with tallow; greasy.

1867 N. MACLEOD *Starling* xxiv, I assure you he has a taughy fleece to scoor in this parish!

2. Resembling tallow in colour or complexion.

1832 [implied in TALLOWINESS]. **1847** LE FANU *T. O'Brien* 170 A tallowy sensual face. **1883** STEVENSON *Treas. Isl.* I. ii, He was a pale, tallowy creature. **1899** *Allbutt's Syst. Med.* VIII. 677 The integument became dense, tallowy in colour and otherwise changed.

3. Of a beast: Abounding in tallow, fat.

1495 *Trevisa's Barth. De P.R.* IX. xix. (W. de W.) 357 In Nouembre beestes wexen fatte and talowy and namely swyne. **1818** *Blackw. Mag.* III. 528 The bullock..lays himself down, with a lengthening groan, once more into his tallowy laziness.

tally ('tælɪ), *sb.*[1] Forms: 5–6 **taly(e**, 6 **tallye**, **tallee**, **tale**, 6–7 **talie**, **tallie**, **talle**, 7–9 **talley**, 6– **tally**. [In 15th c. *talye* = AF. (14th c.) *tallie* = Anglo-L. *tālea*, *tālia*, *tallia*, in same sense, L. *tālea*, cutting, rod, stick. The doublet *taille*, *taile*, TAIL *sb.*[2], from French *taille*, was in earlier use, and did not become obsolete till 17th c.]

1. a. A stick or rod of wood, usually squared, marked on one side with transverse notches representing the amount of a debt or payment. The rod being cleft lengthwise across the notches, the debtor and creditor each retained one of the halves, the agreement or tallying of which constituted legal proof of the debt, etc. Cf. TAIL *sb.*[2] 4.

[**1189** (Aug.) GERVASE OF CANT. *Op. Hist.* (Rolls) I. 453 Videlicet ut conventus Monachos tres vel quatuor ad custodiendas villas ordinaret, qui redditibus omnibus thesaurariis a conventu constitutis per taleas responderent. **1203** in *Placit. Abbrev.* (1811) 38/2 Eustacius..inde producit sectam et talliam ostendit quam fecerunt. **1321–2** *Rolls of Parlt.* I. 401/1 Illoques pristrent des biens .. pur lour sustenaunce saunz paiement fere ou tallie al gardeyn du dit leu.]

c **1440** *Promp. Parv.* 486/1 Taly, or talye, .. *talia, tallia.* **1545** BRINKLOW *Compl.* vi. (1874) 19 Ye shal not haue hir redy mony neyther, but a taly. **1552** HULOET, Talye or tale vsed in receypte, *tessera*, .. *tesserula*, .. *dimin.* a lyttle or shorte tallye. **1557** *Order of Hospitalls* H ij, The Tallyes of the same Baker and Bruer shalbe in the custodie and keping of the Thresorer. *a* **1628** PRESTON *New Covt.* (1634) 323 There is a law in the mind within, answerable to the law of God without; .. it answers as Tallie answers to Tallie. **1756** *Gentl. Mag.* XXVI. 606/1 Harry, who ought to have minded the Tallies of the milk-score. **1790** PALEY *Horæ Paul.* xiv, It is like comparing the two parts of a cloven tally. **1881** WHITEHEAD *Hops* 62 In some cases the very old fashioned method prevails of cutting notches upon wooden tallies, one part kept by the picker, the counterpart by the measurer.

b. Such a cloven rod, as the official receipt formerly given by the Exchequer for a tax, tallage, etc. paid, or in acknowledgement of a loan to the sovereign.

[**1166** *Pipe Rolls 12 Hen. II* (1888) 2 Et x. li. in 11 talliis. **1178** *Dialogus de Scaccario* v, Quid ad factorem talearum. **1284** *Provis. Exch.* (St. Rec. Comm. I. 69/1), Omnes illi qui habent tallias de scaccario de debitis suis vel antecessorum suorum.] *a* **1604** HANMER *Chron. Irel.* (1633) 208 Calmagh burnt all the rolles and tallyes of that countie. **1626** CHAS. I in *Buccleuch MSS.* (Hist. MSS. Comm.) I. 264 Acquittances to be given you, which shall be your warrant for striking tallies and for repayment hereafter. *a* **1692** POLLEXFEN *Disc. Trade* (1697) 70 When any Tax or Imposition is granted by Parliament, Tallies, Exchequer Notes or Bills, issued out upon the same, for the supplying of the Government with Ready Money till the Duties be paid. **1697** *Lond. Gaz.* No. 3328/4 Lost .. a Talley of 300 l. on Wines and Tobacco, Dated the 11th of March, 1695, No. 2329. **1738** *Hist. Crt. Excheq.* v. 91 To pay in their Rents into the Exchequer, and take Tallies from thence. **1776** ADAM SMITH *W.N.* II. ii. (1869) I. 319 In 1696, tallies had been at forty, and fifty, and sixty per cent. discount, and bank notes at twenty per cent. **1847** J. FRANCIS *Hist. Bank Eng.* iv. 59 Tallies lay bundled up like Bath faggots in the hands of brokers, and stock-jobbers. **1848** WHARTON *Law Lex.* s.v., The use of tallies in the Exchequer was abolished by 23 Geo. III c. 82, and the old tallies were ordered to be destroyed by 4 & 5 Wm. IV c. 15. **1896** ANSON *Law & Cust. Constit.* II. vii. II. i. 329 *note* 2, In 1834 .. orders were given to destroy the tallies. They were used as fuel in the stoves which warmed the Houses of Parliament; they overheated the flues and burned down the Houses.

†**c.** ***tally of pro*** (i.e. *pro*, for or in favour of some one), ***tally of sol*** (i.e. *solutum*, paid): see quot. 1843. *Obs.*

1691 W. LOWNDES *Acc. Revenue Eng.* 88 (MS.) The Tally of Pro called also the Tally of Assignement Imports on the same Stick both a Receipt and payment. **1696** *Lond. Gaz.* No. 3157/4 Lost .. a Tally of Pro, dated the 18th of May 1695, in the Name of John Richards, Esq; for 300 l. struck on the Commissioners of His Majesty's Hereditary and Temporary Revenues of Excise. *Ibid.* No. 3244/4 Lost a Talley of 100 l. upon the Temporal Excise, struck the 5th of Aug. 1696, pro Edvardo Nicholas. **1697** *Ibid.* No. 3308/4 Lost .., a Talley of Pro No. 90. struck Aug. 6, 1696, in the Name of Edward Nicholas Esq; for 100 l. in part of 35000 l. by him Lent the 2d of July, 1696, upon the Hered' and Temp' Excise. **1703** *Ibid.* No. 3933/4 The Tallies of Pro, levied upon the Surplus of the Duties on Malt. **1843** *Fourth Rep. Dep. Kpr.* App. II. 166 The Tally of *Sol* .. whereon the word *sol* was written, to show that the money .. had been paid into the Exchequer. *Ibid.*, The Tally of Pro .. operated as a modern cheque on a banker, being given forth in payment from the Exchequer, as a charge upon some public accountant, for him to pay the sum expressed thereon, out of the revenues in his hands. **1896** ANSON *Law & Cust. Constit.* II. vii. II. i. 329.

d. *transf.* Any tangible means of recording a payment or amount.

1863 FAWCETT *Pol. Econ.* II. x. (1876) 258 Each customer, when he makes a purchase, receives certain tin tickets or tallies, which record the amount of his purchases.

2. a. The record of an amount due; a score or shot, an account. *Obs.* Also, the record of a number.

1573 TUSSER *Husb.* (1878) 170 In buieng of drinke, by the firkin or pot, The tallie ariseth, but hog amendes not. **1828** *Life Planter Jamaica* 55 Keep tally of their number. **1833** HT. MARTINEAU *Brooke Farm* vii, To measure the milk and keep the tally. **1951** 'J. WYNDHAM' *Day of Triffids* xi. 201 He had taken a tally of the livestock and the number of blind among it. **1976** H. WILSON *Governance of Britain* iii. 55 The prime minister usually keeps a tally of those for and against.

†**b.** †*Naut.* ***petty tally***, a petty account kept of a ship's provisions, orig. of a certain portion; hence *transf.* provisions. *Obs.*

1626 CAPT. SMITH *Accid. Yng. Seamen* 39 How to keep his Petty Tally. **1627** —— *Seaman's Gram.* xv. 74 A Commander at Sea should doe well .. to consider .. how to .. prouide his petty Tally. *Ibid.* 75 There is neither .. Grocer, Poulterer, .. nor Butchers shop, and therefore the vse of this petty Tally is necessary. *a* **1642** SIR W. MONSON *Naval Tracts* VI. (1704) 519/2 Beer, Cask, Bread, and Petty-Talley .. 12*l.* **1678** PHILLIPS (ed. 4), *Petty-Tally*, in Navigation is a competent proportion of edible and potable commodities in a Ship, according to the number of the Ships company. **1823** in CRABB *Technol. Dict.* **1847** in CRAIG.

†**c.** ***upon the tally***: on credit, 'on tick'; by running up a score. *Obs.*

1807 *Sporting Mag.* XXIX. 185 To buy goods upon the Tally. (This term Tally, Mr. Garrow said, was not much known to the public.)

d. *spec.* in sporting use, a total score; also in *Baseball*, a single run.

1856 *Spirit of Times* 27 Dec. 276/3 One of these swiftly-delivered balls, when stopped by a skillful batsman, is sure to give the .. striker time to go his rounds in safety, and score one tally as he reaches home. **1868** H. CHADWICK *Game of Baseball* 46 *Tally*, this term applies to the total score of the single innings played, or of the even innings, or of the totals at the close of the match. **1875** *Chicago Tribune* 29 July 5/4 [They] were only two tallies behind at the beginning of the ninth inning. **1949** *Marshfield* (Wisconsin) *News-Herald* 19 July 9/1 Phil Satkowiak homered with none on in the fourth and his teammates added two more tallies. **1976** *Liverpool Echo* 23 Nov. 17/1 Ainsdale marksman Alex Blakeman took his tally to nine goals from his last four games with a brilliant hat-trick. **1977** *Guernsey Weekly Press* 21 July 8/5 They shocked their opponents by scoring four runs on four hits in the top of the first and .. holding the red-and-blacks to only one tally in the bottom half.

e. *Austral.* and *N.Z.* (See quot. 1965.)

1881 A. BATHGATE *Waitaruna* xii. 173 There was a rivalry among them [*sc.* shearers] as to who would have the biggest tally. **1908** D. FERGUSON *Bush Life Austral. & N.Z.* (ed. 4) v. 39 Not only did his tallies of 170, 180, and even 190 place him beyond the reach of the keenest competitor, but the quality of his work was far above that of shearers in ordinary. **1930** L. G. D. ACLAND *Early Canterbury Runs* 1st Ser. vii. 170 The combined shearing tally was .. 115,000 sheep. **1965** J. S. GUNN *Terminol. Shearing Industry* II. 31 *Tally*, a specialised alternative term for a number of sheep. Each shearer has his personal tally for .. the day, progressively to date, and his final tally for the shed... At one time a notch was cut on a tally stick on the call of 'tally' or 'hundred', which indicated a hundred sheep counted.

3. *fig.* (from 1 and 2). Reckoning, score, account. Now *rare.*

1614 RALEIGH *Hist. World* II. (1634) 214 Ordinary occurrences, that are to be numbred by a shorter Tally [than by the year]. **1628** WITHER *Brit. Rememb.* IV. 1807 Left they upon thy Tally all that sin. **1648** C. WALKER *Hist. Independ.* I. 96 He that hath a Tally of every mans faults but his own hanging at his Girdle. **1649** G. DANIEL *Trinarch., Rich. II*, xxxviii, He threatened To weare it worthy, and a Tally make Of slaughter, to outvye his shop-board's Chalke. **1822** HAZLITT *Table-t.* (1870) I. i. 14 It is stamped on his brain, and lives there thenceforward, a tally for nature, and a test of art. **1950** J. AGEE *Morning Watch* (1951) II. 61 Hell of a saint I'd make, he said to himself; and added with cold and level weary self-disgust to the tally of the sins he must soon confess, I swore in Lady Chapel in the presence of the Blessed Sacrament.

4. a. Each of the two corresponding halves or parts of anything; a thing, or part, that exactly fits or agrees with another thing or corresponding part; a counterpart; *fig.* an agreement, correspondence.

1651 CLEVELAND *Mixt Assembly* 35 Whose Members being not tallies, they'. not own Their fellows at the Resurrection. *a* **1700** DRYDEN (J.), So suited in their minds and persons That they were fram'd the tallies for each other. **1816** JEFFERSON *Writ.* (1830) IV. 297 If histories so unlike .. can .. be brought to the same tally, no line of distinction remains between fact and fancy. **1833** J. HOLLAND *Manuf. Metal* II. 266 The bit of which key is so cut or shaped as to form a complete tally with the interior machinery. **1906** *Edin. Rev.* Jan. 207 Here he will find again the tally between proportion and thought.

b. ***to live (on) tally***, to live in concubinage, to cohabit without marriage. *slang.*

1864 HOTTEN *Slang Dict.* 253 *Tally*, 'to live *tally*,' to live in a state of unmarried impropriety. **1867** B. BRIERLEY *Traddlepin Fold* 174 Aw'd advise thi t'live tally .. if theaw con mak' it reet wi' some cwd damsel. **1877** *5 Years' Penal Servitude* iii. 246, I never took to a moll except on tally. *Ibid.* vi. 377 A man she was then living 'tally' with. **1890** *N. & Q.* 7th Ser. X. 297/2 To 'live tally' is quite a common expression amongst the working classes in Lancashire, as is also tally-woman. **1901** MABEL PEACOCK in *Folk-Lore* June 174 He had for years been 'living tally' with a woman—that is in cohabitation without marriage.

5. a. A number, group, series, lot, tale; *esp.* a certain number or group (of things or persons) taken as the unit of computation. Also, 'a company or division of voters at an election' (*Eng. Dial. Dict.*): see quot. 1774.

1674 N. FAIRFAX *Bulk & Selv.* 56 Every tally by which we tell things must be either even or odd. **1683** KENNETT tr. *Erasm. on Folly* 102 When they tone out their daily Tally of Psalms. **1725** *Bradley's Fam. Dict.* s.v. *Wall*, Some Bricks .. are broken, in every Load or 500 Bricks; and the Tally or Tale, is, for the most part, .. too little. **1774** BURKE *Sp. Concl. Poll* Wks. III. 16 Mr Brickdale opened his poll, it seems, with a tally of those very kind of freemen, and voted many hundreds of them. **1843** LEVER *J. Hinton* xvii. (1878) 123 We told them off by tallies as they marched on board. **1886** *Pall Mall. G.* 4 June 14/1 Some few years ago .. Victoria was well ahead of New South Wales in the tally of her people. **1889** *19th Cent.* Nov. 755 Though we had three deaths during the passage, as we also had three births, our tally remained correct. **1890** *Science* 12 Dec. 323 All the Indians .. were drawn up in tallies, and arranged according to families. **1892** *Labour Commission Gloss.*, *Tally*, a check account made by a person receiving goods; .. used for the number of bricks or tons of other goods carried on canal boats and river barges.

b. *spec.* In market-gardening, Five dozen (cabbages, bunches of turnips, etc.).

1851 MAYHEW *Lond. Labour* I. 92, I buy turnips by the 'tally'. A tally's five dozen bunches. **1883** *Daily News* 6 Sept. 2/7 Cauliflowers, 5s. per tally. **1891** *Times* 28 Sept. 4/2 Cabbages, 1s. 6d. to 2s. 6d. per tally; .. marrows, 2s. 6d. to 3s. 6d. per tally.

c. *spec.* In hop-picking, A specified number of bushels that have to be picked for one shilling: see quot. 1904, and cf. quot. 1881 in 1.

1868 *A Hop-sketch* in *Derby Mercury* 12 Feb., Back at the 'tally' to play your part. **1891** *Scott. Leader* 24 Sept. 7 A strike has occurred among the hop-pickers .. owing to alleged 'excessive measure and high tally'. **1904** *Daily Chron.* 29 Aug. 8/3 The pay is .. at the rate of 1s. for a certain number of bushels, called the 'tally', which varies from five to eight or nine, according to the growth of the hops.

d. The last of a specified number forming a unit of computation, on the completion of which the tally-man calls 'tally' and notes it down.

1886 P. CLARKE *New Chum in Australia* xii. 175 As a 'hundred' is called, one of us calls out 'tally', and cuts one notch in a stick. **1894** *Northumbld. Gloss.* s.v., If the articles are counted singly, they are called out up to the nineteenth; but instead of .. 'twenty', the word tally is substituted; thus 'eighteen, nineteen, *tally*'... In counting articles that can be lifted in groups the tale is thus made—'five, ten, fifteen, *tally*'.

†**6.** A mark (such as the notch of a tally) representing a unit quantity, or a series or set of units.

1719 D'URFEY *Pills* (1872) III. 314 In Courts had all their Heart's desire, For every Kiss a Tally. *Ibid.* IV. 264 He notcht his Arse with Tallies. **1807** CRABBE *Parish Reg.* I. 252 Where chalky tallies yet remain in rows.

7. a. A distinguishing mark on a bale or case of merchandise, etc., corresponding to one in a list, for the purpose of comparison or identification; hence, a mark, label, ticket, or tab, used for this purpose, or to denote the weight and contents, etc.

1851 H. MELVILLE *Moby Dick* I. xli. 303 Tying a lettered leathern tally round its neck. **1860** MAURY *Phys. Geog. Sea* vi. §324 But the air is invisible; and it is not easily perceived how either marks or tallies may be put on it, that it may be traced. **1865** *Morning Star* 27 Jan., I entered the weights in the landing-book, and marked them in the tallies .. and I saw a great number of the tallies afterwards put on the bales.

b. *Coal-mining.* (See quots.)

1883 GRESLEY *Coal Mining Gloss.*, *Tally*, a mark or number placed by a collier upon every tub of coals loaded. .. They are usually little bits of tin having a number stamped upon them. **1890** *N. & Q.* 7th Ser. X. 297/2 At many pits it is customary to send the tubs of coals to bank with tin tallies attached... This tally is so that the banksmen and weighmen may place the coals to the credit of the men working in the banks below, the banks and tallies bearing the same numbers.

c. *spec.* in *Gardening*, A tab or label of wood, metal, etc., on which are inscribed the name, class, etc. of the plant or tree to which it is attached, or beside which it is stuck in the ground.

1822 LOUDON *Encycl. Gard.* III. IV. 1190 Every plant [in a Botanical Garden] ought to have its name painted on strong cast-iron talleys. **1842** *Penny Cycl.* XXIV. 17/1 Many different kinds of tally are used in gardens and arboretums, to bear either numbers referring to a catalogue, or the names of the plants near which they are placed. **1870** THORNBURY *Tour Eng.* I. i. 23 The .. gray stone, the tally to mark a seed plot in Death's neglected garden. **1881** *Encycl. Brit.* XII. 234/2 Tallies of wood [in horticulture] should be slightly smeared with white paint and then written on while damp with a black-lead pencil.

d. A tie-label, tab, or tag for luggage, etc.

1909 *Advt.*, Temple Tower Tallies, 1*d.* per packet, strung ready for use.

e. *Naut. slang.* (See quots 1929, 1946). Also ***cap-tally*** = ***tally ribbon***, sense 9 c below.

1929 F. C. BOWEN *Sea Slang* 138 *Tally*, a name or name-plate of any description. **1945** 'TACKLINE' *Holiday Sailor* i. 9 We queued-up before him to have our cap-tallies—*not* cap-ribbons, we now discovered—secured about our caps with the authentic sailor's-knot. **1946** J. IRVING *Royal Navalese* 172 *Tally*, a sailor's name is his 'tally'—e.g. 'Answer your tally!'

¶**8.** Used as = TAIL *sb.*[2] 2 b. *Obs.*

1609 OVERBURY *Observ. St. France* Wks. (1856) 238 The gentrie are the onely entire body there, which participate with the prerogatives of the crowne; for from it they receive .. supply to their estates, by governments and pensions, and freedome from tallies upon their owne lands. **1642** HOWELL *For. Trav.* (Arb.) 74 When one hath seene the Tally and taillage of France, .. the Assise of Holland, the Gabels of Italy, .. hee will blesse God, and love England better ever after.

9. *attrib.* and *Comb.* **a.** Simple attrib. and obj. gen., as (from 1 a, 1 b) ***tally-broker***, ***-court***, ***-cutter***, ***-office***, ***-stick***; (from 2 a, 2 b, 2 e) ***tally-book***, ***-check***, ***-keeper***, ***-table***; **b.** in reference to the instalment or petty credit system (cf. 2 c) worked by the TALLYMAN, as ***tally-business***, ***-draper***, ***-master***, ***-packman***, ***-room***, ***-shop***, ***-system***, ***-trade***. **c.** Special combs.: **tally band** *Naut.* = *tally ribbon* below; **tally-board**, a board on which an account is notched or chalked; e.g. one on which the record of a weaver's work is kept (*Eng. Dial. Dict.*); **tally card** *U.S.*, a score-card; **tally-clerk**, one who checks merchandise with a list in loading or discharging cargo; also (*U.S.*), one who assists in counting and recording votes; **tally-husband** (*slang*), a man who 'lives tally' (4 b) with a woman; **tally-mark** = sense 7; **tally-pot**, a vessel in which records of a counting or voting are placed (*Funk's Stand. Dict.* 1895); **tally ribbon** *Naut.*, a sailor's cap-ribbon bearing the name of his ship (cf. sense 7 e above); **tally-room** (Ireland), a committee-room at an election; **tally-sheet**, a score-sheet, esp. (*U.S.*) in recording votes; **tally-shouter** (*Mining*), see quot.; **tally-stick**, a stick used as or like a tally (sense 1); **tally-writer**, formerly, the clerk who wrote the description and amount of the payment on two opposite sides of the exchequer tallies. See also TALLYMAN, WOMAN.

1977 *Times* 7 Jan. (Royal Navy Suppl.) p. ii/6 That dear little pancake hat with its silk *tally band;.. I believe that it was because of that little hat that I had joined the WRNS in the first place. **1965** J. S. GUNN *Terminol. Shearing Industry* II. 31 **Tally book*, the official record of what every man has shorn in each run of the day. **1972** T. A. BULMAN *Kamloops Cattlemen* xxxi. 178 Our tally books showed that we were short a bull and six head of cattle. **1849** JAMES *Woodman* vii, You have not got the *tally board so completely in your hand, my friend. *a* **1716** SOUTH *Serm.* (1717) IV. 154 Such a Money-Monger, such a *Tally-Broker, and Cheater of the Publick. **1851** *Tally-business [see *tally-master*]. **1862** MISS BRADDON *Lady Audley* xxvii, You're not connected with—with the tally business, are you, sir? **1909** *Cent. Dict.* Suppl., *Tally card. **1928** *Publisher's Weekly* 14 July 172 Allied with these are tally cards, playing cards, novelties and party favors. **1884** *Times* (weekly ed.) 10 Oct. 13/4 Rudely inscribed potsherds..*tally-checks scrawled with entries of time-labour and food-wages. **1890** *Daily News* 13 Sept. 6/4 A large number of ships' *tally clerks,.. have not had a day's work for weeks. **1902** *Westm. Gaz.* 25 Feb. 2/1 There is a duplicate of this board, but on a small scale, placed on the desk of the tally-clerk, so that the record of the votes is constantly before his eyes. **1684** E. CHAMBERLAYNE *Pres. St. Eng.* II. (ed. 15) 105 In the *Tally Court—the *Tally-cutter attends. **1786** *St. Paper* in *Ann. Reg.* 193/1 The tally writer ..takes an account of the sum, and writes it on both sides of the tally delivered to him, with the sum cut upon it in notches by the tally-cutter. **1880** 'MARK TWAIN' *Tramp Abroad* v. 55 The *tally-keeper..tallied one for the opposition in his book. **1883** GILMOUR *Mongols* xviii. 247 Ocher..threw up his office of tally-keeper. **1851** MAYHEW *Lond. Labour* I. 383/2 The 'travellers'..are occasionally shopmen, for a 'large' *tally-master not unfrequently carries on a retail trade in addition to his tally-business. **1631** SIR S. D'EWES *Jrnl. Parlt.* (1783) 52 That unjust and rare recorde called Domesdei in the *tallie-office of the Exchequer. **1851** MAYHEW *Lond. Labour* I. 381/1 The pedlar or hawking tallyman travels for orders... The great majority of the *tally-packmen are Scotchmen. **1919** W. LANG *Sea Lawyer's Log* 14 Those three caps, too, look very smart, with the neat, white canvas cover which we wear during the summer months, and the *tally ribbon with its tricky little bow on the left side. **1842** S. LOVER *Handy Andy* xvii, The popular tunes..in the *tally rooms, while the fellows are waiting to go up. **1910** *Daily News* 24 Jan. 8 Mr. Wood could neither show himself in the place nor get a tally-room, as they call their committee-rooms there [Lisburn]. **1889** *Century Mag.* Feb. 622/1 The growing dispositon [in U.S.] to tamper with the ballot-box and the *tally-sheet. **1893** *Scribner's Mag.* June 779/2 To call her attention to a tally-sheet, covering a period of three calendar months. **1851** MAYHEW *Lond. Labour* I. 32/1 The poor,.. pawnbrokers, loan-offices, *tally-shops, dolly-shops, are the only parties who will trust them. **1870** *Public Opinion* 16 July, [He] described from personal inspection the low quality of the provisions supplied in the tally-shops. **1883** GRESLEY *Coal Mining Gloss.*, **Tally-shouter*, one who shouts out the numbers on the tallies to the weigher. **1830** *Virginia Lit. Museum* 27 Jan. 526/2 A 'negro boy, with a *talley stick was a statesman complete in his school'. *a* **1861** T. WINTHROP *Canoe & Saddle* (1863) vii. 153 She could not tell how many [years], having dropped her tally-stick in the fire..that very day. **1895** HOFFMAN *Beginnings of Writ.* 140 Several tribes of Indians, in California, employed a variety of tallysticks to record transactions in business. **1897** MARY KINGSLEY *W. Africa* 49 They hopefully notched away the moons on their tally-sticks. **1850** J. R. PLANCHÉ *Island of Jewels* II. i. 21 Is it all a trick, you make this mighty splash on, Or, is the *tally system here in fashion? **1851** MAYHEW *Lond. Labour* I. 372/2 Some had been unsuccessful as tallymen when shopkeepers, or travellers for tally-shops, and have resorted to hawking or street-trading,.. blending the tally system with the simple rules of sale for ready money. **1829** COBBETT *Adv. Yng. Man* ii. 60 The '*Tally-trade' by which household goods, coals, clothing, all sorts of things are sold upon credit, the seller keeping a tally, and receiving payment..little by little. **1851** MAYHEW *Lond. L.* I. 383/1 Establishments, 'doing largely' in the tally-trade. **1786** *Tally writer [see *tally-cutter*].

†**tally**, *sb.*[2] *Cards. Obs.* [f. TALLY *v.*[3]: cf. F. *taille* from *tailler* to deal.] At faro, basset, etc., A deal.

1706 MRS. CENTLIVRE *Basset Table* IV. 53 *Captain*... Pray count the Cards, I believe there's a false Tally. *Sir James*. .. No, they are Right, Sir (Sir James counts em). **1760** FOOTE *Minor* III. (1781) 65 A most infernal run. Let's see (Pulls out a card) Loader a thousand, the Baron two, Tally—Enough to beggar a banker.

'**tally**, *sb.*[3] *rare.* Short for TALLY-HO. So **tally** *v.*[4], to signal with *tally-ho!*

1886 FORTESCUE *Stag Hunting on Exmoor* (1887) 180 Another hundred yards of slow hunting, and then a loud tally proclaims a fresh find. *Ibid.* 182 The farmer is half inclined to fear he has tallied a fresh hind.

tally ('tælɪ), *v.*[1] Forms: see TALLY *sb.*[1] [f. TALLY *sb.*[1] Cf. also med.L. *talliāre* to cut (wood); also, to conform or cause to correspond in number or measure: see Du Cange.

(Some of the uses may have been influenced by association with L. *tālis* such, *tālio* giving like for like.)]

I. 1. a. *trans.* †To notch (a stick) so as to make it a tally (*obs.*); hence, to mark, score, set *down* or enter (a number, etc.) on or as on a tally; *transf.* to record, register.

c **1440** *Promp. Parv.* 486/1 Talyyn, or scoryn' on taly, *tallio, dico.* **1632** *Star Chamb. Cases* (Camden) 94 Mrs Jennet Carrier had a knife in her hand,.. to tally a stické to shewe how many dishes full there were. **1633** FORD *Broken H.* IV. i, So provident is folly in sad issue, That afterwit, like bankrupt's debts, stands tallied, Without all possibilities of payment. *a* **1640** W. FENNER *Sacr. Faithf.* (1648) 53 There is not one of them that God tallies down, or reckons for a praier. **1706** E. WARD *Wooden World Diss.* (1708) 18 At every tenth Call perhaps you may tally down a Sailor. **1890** *Century Mag.* June 205/2 These [field judges] measure and tally the trials of competitors in jumps, pole vaults [etc.].

b. *spec.* To identify, count, and enter each bale, case, article, etc. of a cargo or lot of goods in loading or discharging.

1812 J. SMYTH *Pract. of Customs* (1821) 7 Goods paying Duty by Tale, are, at the delivery, to be tallied at 1, 10, 20, &c. according to the nature thereof. **1886** *Pall Mall G.* 29 Jan. 5/2 Upon the mates of ships..falls the bulk of the work and responsibility entailed in getting a ship ready to receive cargo, in 'tallying' the cargo, in preparing her to leave port [etc.]. **1899** F. T. BULLEN *Log Sea-waif* 226 No pretence was made of tallying in the cargo.

c. To furnish (a bale of goods, etc.) with a tally or identifying label; to distinguish, mark, or identify by or as by a tally: see TALLY *sb.*[1] 7.

1837 MARRYAT *Dog-Fiend* xxxiv, Leaving his people to mark and tally the bales. **1860** MAURY *Phys. Geog. Sea* (Low) vi. §332 We have tallied the air, and put labels on the wind. **1865** *Morn. Star* 27 Jan., If a number of bales were tallied as having arrived by a vessel called the Onwards, the label with the mark 'Onwards' on it was taken off and another marked the 'City of Dublin' placed in its stead.

d. *Sport* (chiefly *N. Amer.*). To score (a run, goal, etc.). (*a*) *intr.*

1867 *Ball Players' Chron.* 14 Nov. 2/4 Taylor took his first on a muff by Banker and tallied on passed balls. **1903** *N.Y. Times* 18 Aug. 5/2 The home players tallied only five times during the entire contest. **1931** *Randolph Enterprise* (Elkins, W. Va.) 9 July 5/3 The nine from Randolph had tallied five times in the same frame. **1947** *Sun* (Baltimore) 8 Nov. 12/2 The visitors tallied for the first time in the opening minutes of the game when Ann Worthington sent a hard shot into the corner of the cage. **1968** [see PERIOD *sb.* 4 f]. **1974** *Cleveland* (Ohio) *Plain Dealer* 13 Oct. C.2/3 Terell tallied on a two-yard run and took a pass from Jeff Starrett 70 yards for a second score.

(*b*) *trans.*

1875 *Chicago Tribune* 24 Aug. 5/6 A furious overthrow by Beals at second..tallied three unearned runs. **1966** *Telegraph* (Brisbane) 22 Jan. 5/2 He started racing in November, and in five starts has tallied a win, second, and a third. **1976** *Billings* (Montana) *Gaz.* 6 July 1-c/6 The Angels tallied their fifth run in the third inning as Bob Brenly came on a Young single to short center.

2. a. To count or reckon *up*, to number.

1542 BECON *Pathw. Prayer* vi. C viij, Some..vpon theyr bedes taly vp I cannot tel howe many lady Psalters. **1586** W. WEBBE *Eng. Poetrie* (Arb.) 62 The first or the first couple hauing twelue sillables, the other fourteene, which versifyers call Powlters measure, because so they talle their wares by dozens. **1598** *Wills & Inv. N.C.* (Surtees) II. 335 Two men, to serve..att the pitt, to take the reckoninges, the one..who doth tallee the horses. **1648** BP. HALL *Breath. Devout Soul* iv. 5, I have not kept even reckonings with thee; I have not justly tallied up thy inestimable benefits. **1660** *Col. J. Okie's Lament.* 10, I must not tally the Account of our State Stinking Beer. **1885** A. MUNRO *Siren Casket* (1889) 85 They anchor'd at morning to tally their spoil.

b. *fig.* To reckon, estimate (with *obj. cl.*). *colloq. rare.*

1860 HOLLAND *Miss Gilbert* xix, You can't hardly tally how she's coming out because she ain't exactly a woman yet.

†**3.** *intr.* To deal on tally or credit; to open or have a credit account *with* any one. *Obs.*

1596 [see TAIL *v.*[2] 8, quot. 1570]. **1724** SWIFT *Drapier's Lett.* Wks. 1755 V. II. 25 Several gentlemen have been forced to tally with their workmen, and give them bits of cards sealed and subscribed with their names.

II. †**4.** *trans. fig.* To cause (things) to correspond or agree; to 'match'; *pa. pple.* matched, suited, adapted. *Obs.*

1627 BP. HALL *Holy Observ.* Wks. 50 Morall philosophy [teacheth] that tallying of iniuries is iustice; diuinitie, that good must be returned for ill. *c* **1717** PRIOR *Epitaph* 16 They seem'd just tallied for each other. *a* **1745** POPE (J.), They are not so well tallied to the present juncture. **1812** JEFFERSON *Writ.* (1830) IV. 177 Peculiarly tallied in interests, by each wanting exactly what the other has to spare.

†**5. a.** To compare, as tallies, for the purpose of verifying an account, etc. *Obs.*

1702 *Lond. Gaz.* No. 3827/4 These are to give Notice to all the Fortunate in Sydenham's Land-Lottery..to bring their Prize Tickets, in order to have the same Tallied. **1703** *Ibid.* No. 3963/4 All Persons, whose Tickets in the late Land-Lottery have not been tallied and reported.

†**b.** *fig.* To bring into comparison, compare.

1773 J. ROSS *Fratricide* VI. 478 (MS.) What but a shadow is this mortal life When tally'd with eternity?

6. *intr.* To agree, as one half of a cloven tally with its fellow; to correspond or answer exactly; to accord, conform, fit. Const. †*to* (obs.), *with*. (The chief current sense.)

1705 ADDISON *Italy* 227, I found pieces of Tiles that exactly tally'd with the Channel. **1720** *Lett. Lond. Jrnl.* (1721) 64 The Courage and Understanding of her [the High Church's] Passive Sons Tally to each other. **1727** SWIFT *Gulliver* IV. xii, Neither shall I ever be able to comprehend how such an animal [Yahoo], and such a vice [pride], could tally together. **1738** WARBURTON *Div. Legat.* I. 271 A Theory that does not exactly tally with fact. **1757** DA COSTA in *Phil. Trans.* L. 229 The impressions of ferns, grasses, &c. are easily recognizable, they so minutely tally to the plants they represent. **1779** J. MOORE *View Soc. Fr.* (1789) I. xxiv. 188 High hills, whose opposite sides tally so exactly. **1891** E. PEACOCK *N. Brendon* II. 82 It tallies exactly with what the others have said.

III. (? Connected with TALES.)

7. *trans.* (?) To summon or empanel as a juryman.

1776 in Stonehouse *Axholme* (1839) 145 None of the Lord's tenants, either freehold or copyhold, to be tallied out of the Manor, to the Assizes, Sessions, or Sheriff's Court.

'**tally**, *v.*[2] *Naut.* Now *rare.* [Origin obscure.]

1. *trans.* To haul taut (the fore or main leesheets). Hence **tallied** *ppl. a.*[2]

c **1450** *Pilgrim's Sea-Voy.* 19 in *Stacions Rome* (1867) 37 A boy or tweyn Anone up styen, And ouerthwart the sayle-yerde lyen;—'Y how! taylia!' the remenaunt cryen, And pulle with alle theyr myght. *a* **1625** *Nomenclator Navalis* (Harl. MS. 2301), When they hale aft the Sheate of Maine or Fore-Saile, they saie Tallee aft the Sheate. **1627** CAPT. SMITH *Seaman's Gram.* ix. 39 Get your Starboord tacks aboord, and tally and hale off your Lee-Sheats. **1762–9** FALCONER *Shipwr.* II. 212 Taught aft the sheet they tally, and belay. **1769** —— *Dict. Marine* (1789), *Border les écoutes tout plat*, to tally the sheets flat aft. **1836** E. HOWARD *R. Reefer* xxx, By hauling along tallied bights of rope.

2. *intr.* To catch hold or 'clap' *on* to a rope.

1840 R. H. DANA *Bef. Mast* xxviii. 97 All hands tallied on to the cat-fall. *Ibid.* xxxv. 133 All hands tally-on to the main tack. **1896** KIPLING *Seven Seas* 93 Heh! Tally on. Aft and walk away with her! Handsome to the Cathead now; O tally on the fall!

†**tally**, *v.*[3] *Cards. Obs.* Also 8 (taillé), tailly. [ad. F. *tailler* to cut, esp. to deal at faro, etc.: see TAIL *v.*[2]] *intr.* At faro, basset, and similar games, To be banker (i.e. to deal).

[**1701** FARQUHAR *Sir H. Wildair* I. i, The French marquis, you know, constantly taillés. *Ibid.* II. ii, I relied altogether on your setting the cards; you used to taillé with success.] **1706** MRS. CENTLIVRE *Basset Table* IV. 52 *Lady R.* Sir James, pray will you Tally? *Sir J.* With all my Heart, Madam. (Takes the Cards and shuffles them.) **1715** LADY M. W. MONTAGU *Basset-table* 68 Wretch that I was, how often have I swore When Winnall tally'd, I wou'd Punt no more? **1716** —— *Let. to C'tess of Mar* 17 Dec., The duke taillys at basset every night. **1748** H. WALPOLE *Let. to Mann* 26 Dec., I don't know whom your Highness will get to tally to you; you know I am ruined by dealing.

tally, *v.*[4]: see TALLY *sb.*[3]

tally ('tɔːllɪ), *adv.* Now *rare* or *Obs.* [f. TALL *a.* + -LY[2].] In a tall manner.

†**1.** In a seemly manner; becomingly, elegantly; fairly, well; bravely. *Obs.*

c **1350** *Will. Palerne* 1706 Sche..borwed boiȝes cloþes, & talliche hire a-tyred tiȝtli þer-inne. *c* **1400** *Destr. Troy* 8813 When this taburnacle atyrit was tally to end, Thai closit hit full clanly, all with clene ambur. *c* **1440** *Promp. Parv.* 486/1 Tally,..in semely wyse, *decenter, eleganter.* **1450** *Anc. Deed* A. 8559 (P.R.O.) in *Catalogue* IV. 327 [Proctour should come to the] Hall of Broghton and ther tawly besek John of Broghton [es]qwier to be his gode master.

2. Highly, loftily.

1611 COTGR., *Hautement*, highly, tally. **1613** FLETCHER, etc. *Captain* II. ii, You Ludovick That stand so tally on your reputation You shall be he shall speake it.

tallydiddle, variant of TARADIDDLE.

tally-ho (ˌtælɪˈhəʊ), *int.* and *sb.* Also 8–9 **tallio**, 9 **tally-o**, **-oh**, **talleyho**. [app. an altered form of the Fr. *taïaut* (Molière, *Les Fâcheux* 1662), *tayau, tayaut* (Furetière), used in deer-hunting; earlier Fr. equivalents were *taho, tahou, theau, theau le hau, tielau, thialau*, and *thia hillaud* (Godef.).

The various Fr. forms appear to be meaningless exclamations. Much conjecture has been spent in vainly trying to put a French meaning into the English form by finding in it *taillis* coppice, *est allé* is gone, *hors* out, etc.]

1. The view-halloo raised by huntsmen on catching sight of the fox. **a.** as *int.*

[Cf. **1756** FOOTE *Englishman returned fr. Paris*, Sir Toby Tallyho (name of a roistering character).]

1772 R. GRAVES *Spir. Quixote* (1783) I. 68 Jerry..with the utmost vociferation, in the fox-hunters' language, cries out, 'Tallio! Tallio! Tallio!' **1815** W. H. IRELAND *Scribbleomania* 19 Then at it, my Pegasus, here's whip and rein, Tally ho! Tally ho! dash it bold o'er the plain. **1835** *Encycl. Brit.* (ed. 7) XI. 752 The view holloa of the hare is, 'Gone away'; of a fox, 'Tallyho'. **1859** *Art Taming Horses*, etc. x. 168 When a fox breaks cover near you,..don't be in a hurry to give the 'Tally-a-e-o!' *Ibid.* 169 When he [the fox] is well away through the hedge of a good-sized field, halloo..'Tally-o aw-ay-o-o!' giving each syllable very slowly... If the fox makes a short bolt and returns, it is 'Tally-o *back*!' with the '*back*' loud and clear. If the fox crosses the side of a wood when the hounds are at check, the cry should be 'Tally-o over!'

b. as *sb.* Also *fig.*

1787 *Generous Attachment* I. 115 One of his tallios would have sent them screaming out of their senses. **1830–83** R. EG.-WARBURTON *Hunt. Songs* (ed. 7) XXVII. i, Beasts of the chace that are not worth a Tally-ho! **1860** *All Year Round* No. 71. 485 How the glad tally-hos, triumphant who-whoops,..come from the very hearts of the farmers. **1955** *Times* 9 Aug. 9/2 Even the eminent scholar and social worker Liang Shu-ming has been cast out... Throughout China the tally-ho of the party hacks is echoing.

c. *attrib.*

1825 H. WILSON *Mem.* (ed. 2) III. 96 A drunken man, in a dashing light green coat, a red waistcoat, and large tally oh! pin in his shirt. **1857** H. BREEN *Mod. Eng. Lit.* 138 Perhaps the most characteristic style of all is the tally-ho, or Nimrodian style. **1922** JOYCE *Ulysses* 571 A pack of bloodhounds led by Hornblower of Trinity brandishing a dogwhip in tallyho cap, and an old pair of grey trousers, follows from far.

2. a. Originally, the proper name given to a fast day-coach between London and Birmingham, started in 1823; subsequently appropriated by other fast coaches on this and other roads, and treated somewhat as a common noun. Also *tally-ho coach*.

1831 T. ATTWOOD 9 Oct. in *Life* xii. (1885) 184, I prefer your coming by the Safety Tally ho, because it puts up at the most convenient inn. **1857** HUGHES *Tom Brown* I. iv, Tally-ho coach..don't wait for nobody. *Ibid.*, His father..had resolved that Tom should travel down by the Tally-ho, which..passed through Rugby itself. **1866** GEO. ELIOT *F. Holt* Introd., The mail still announced itself by the merry notes of the horn; the hedge-cutter..might still know the exact hour by the..apparition of the pea-green Tally-ho or the yellow Independent. **1903** C. G. HARPER *Stage-coach & Mail* II. ix., x., xiii. [much historical information].

b. *U.S.* A large four-in-hand coach or drag.

1882 HOWELLS in *Longm. Mag.* I. 55 There was a tally-ho coach which had been driven out from Boston. **1885** W. P. BREED *Aboard & Abroad* 127 Who could..not take a tour of eight or ten hours in tallyho or wagonette? **1895** *Nebraska State Jrnl.* 18 June 4/2 A talleyho ride was taken by a large party of young people Friday afternoon.

tally-'ho, *v.* [f. prec.]

1. *trans.* To salute or make known the presence of (a fox) by the cry of 'tally-ho'.

1812 *Sporting Mag.* XXXIX. 230 A fox was tallyho'd breaking covert, and the dogs laid on him. **1825** *Ibid.* XV. 363 The servant..tallyho'd the fox.

2. *intr.* To cry or utter 'tally-ho' or a similar call.

1826 J. WILSON *Noct. Ambr.* Wks. 1855 I. 137 A troop o'..tallyhoin' 'wild and wayward humourists'. **1829** HOOD *Epping H.* lxxiv, And milkmen tally-ho'd! **1904** H. SUTCLIFFE in *Westm. Gaz.* 1 Dec. 2/3 Oh, up to the saddle, the horn tally-ho-ing, Up to the tops of the hills o' Craven!

tallying ('tælɪɪŋ), *vbl. sb.* [See -ING[1].] The action of TALLY *v.*[1], in various senses.

c **1440** *Promp. Parv.* 486/1 Talyynge, *talliacio.* **1632** LE GRYS tr. *Velleius Paterc.* 168 The tallying up of the names of these able wits. **1893** *Daily News* 14 Apr. 5/7 Superseding ship's officers in the work of tallying.

b. *spec.* Exact correspondence.

1845-6 TRENCH *Huls. Lect.* Ser. I. iv. 69 The curious tallying of the Old with the New. **1895** STALKER in *Expositor* Sept. 203 The tallying of events with the..predictions.

'tallying, *ppl. a.* [See -ING[2].] That tallies; corresponding.

1854 OWEN *Skel. & Teeth* in *Orr's Circ. Sc.* I. *Org. Nat.* 179 Such names, when applied to the tallying bones in lower animals, losing that significance.

tallyman ('tælɪmən). [f. TALLY *sb.*[1] + MAN.]

1. a. One who carries on a tally-trade, or supplies goods on credit, to be paid for by instalments.

1654 GAYTON *Pleas. Notes* IV. xi. 242 Brewers, Clerks, Bakers, and all Tally-men. **1678** *Four for Penny* in *Harl. Misc.* (ed. Park) IV. 148 The unconscionable Tally-man..lets them have ten-shillings-worth of sorry commodities,..on security given to pay him twenty shillings by twelve-pence a week. *a* **1700** B. E. *Dict. Cant. Crew, Tally-men,* Brokers that let out Cloths at moderate Rates to wear per Week, Month, or Year. **1851** MAYHEW *Lond. Labour* I. 380/2 The pedlar tally-man is a hawker who supplies his customers with goods, receiving payment by weekly instalments, and derives his name from the tally or score he keeps with his customers.

b. (See quot.)

1889 *Academy* 29 June 440/1 In the tailoring trade the worst paid work is that of the 'tallyman', who takes orders direct from the actual wearer without the intervention of any contractor.

2. One who tallies, or keeps account of, anything; *spec.* a clerk who tallies or checks a cargo in loading or discharging.

1857 *Spirit of Times* 23 May 190/3 The tallymen were: Olympic, E. W. Cody; Bay State, W. W. Bragg, jr. **1867** 'T. LACKLAND' *Homespun* ii. 155 It may be the vote is very close; in that case the outside counters and tall-ymen are as much in the dark as the rest. **1888** ROOSEVELT in *Century Mag.* Apr. 862/1 With the voice of a stentor the tally-man shouts out the number and sex of each calf. **1889** DOYLE *Micah Clarke* 190, I reckon them to be..mayhap five thousand two hundred foot. I have been thought a good tally-man on such occasions. **1897** KIPLING *Capt. Courageous* ix, I'm tally-man for the schooner.

3. One who 'lives tally' with a woman. *slang.*

1876 J. READ *They all do It* (song) 3 Mrs Brown says it's a sin, that Mrs Smith drinks gin And harbours tally-men from day to day. **1890** *N. & Q.* 7th Ser. X. 297/1 The terms *tally-man* and *tally-woman*, indicating a man and woman living together without marriage, are used in mining districts.

¶**4.** Erroneously for TALESMAN. *Obs.*

1682 *Enq. Elect. Sheriffs* 10 A company of Mercenary fellows, that used to serve as Tallymen in Guild-hall for their Groats a Cause; who..would, to recover their Four-pence a Trial, sell the Charter and all the Priviledges of this honourable Corporation.

Hence **'tallymanning, 'tallymanship** (*nonce-wds.*), the business or occupation of a tallyman.

1844 J. T. HEWLETT *Parsons & W.* xxxiv, The nature and objects of tallymanship. *Ibid.*, He talked of nothing but tally-maning.

'tallywoman. [f. TALLY *sb.*[1] + WOMAN.]

a. A woman who sells goods on credit: cf. TALLYMAN 1. **b.** *slang.* A woman who 'lives tally' with a man (see TALLY *sb.*[1] 4 b): correlative to TALLYMAN 3.

1727 GAY *Begg. Op.* III. v, Mrs. Diana Trapes, the Tally-Woman. **1890** *Leeds Mercury* 11 Aug., in *N. & Q.* 7th Ser. X. 229/1, I thought she was his tally-woman lately. **1890** [see TALLYMAN 3]. **1894** *Daily Chron.* 11 June (Funk), Her dress she gets by paying a small weekly sum of 2*d.* or 3*d.* to what is called a 'tallyman' or 'tallywoman'.

talm, *v.* *Obs.* exc. *dial.* Forms: α. 4-5 **talme.** β. 6-7 **tawme,** 7-9 **tawm,** 8-9 **taum.** [Akin to ON. *talma* to hinder, obstruct, MLG. *talmen* to trouble with speaking, LG. *talmen* to be slow in speech and at work, to linger, dawdle (*Brem. Wbch.*), EFris. *talmen* to plague, worry, solicit tiresomely, Du. *talmen* to linger, dawdle, loiter.] *intr.* To become exhausted; to fail, tire, faint, swoon.

α. *c* **1325** *Song on Learning Music* in *Rel. Ant.* I. 292, I donke upon David til mi tonge talmes. ? *a* **1400** *Morte Arth.* 2581 Thow trowes with thy talkynge þat my harte talmes! *c* **1440** *Le Bone Florence* (Ritson) 769 Hur fadur nere hande can [= gan] talme, Soche a sweme hys harte can swalme.

β. **1566** DRANT *Wail. Hierim.* K iv, (*Lam.* ii. 11) My babes dyd faynt, And sucklynges tawmed in the streetes. **1674** RAY *N.C. Words* 47 To *Tawm*; to swoon. **1684** MERITON *Yorksh. Dial.* 169 Ise like to tawme, this day's seay [= so] varry warme. **1787** GROSE *Provinc. Gloss.* Suppl., *Taum*, To swoon. **1828** *Craven Gloss.*, *Taum*, to swoon, to fall sick; generally, 'to taum over'.

Hence **talm** *sb.*, faintness, exhaustion; in mod. dial. **(tawm),** 'a fit of faintness or sickness' (E.D.D.).

c **1375** *Cursor M.* 20758 (Fairf.) Ga to þa men þat lijs in talme [*Cott. & Gött.* sualm(e, *Trin.* qualm], And touche ham..And þai salle baþ haue hele & witte.

talma ('tælmə). Pl. **-as.** [Named after François Joseph Talma, French tragedian (1763–1826).] A cape or cloak worn by men, and also by women in the 19th c.

1852 P. S. G. TEN BROECK *Let.* 1 Apr. in T. Donaldson *Moqui Pueblo Indians* (1893) 26 The most beautiful part of their dress is a talma.., which is thrown over the shoulders, fastened in front, and, hanging down behind, reaches halfway below the knee. **1860** HAWTHORNE *Marb. Faun* i, If a lion's skin could have been substituted for his modern talma. **1894** *Times* 17 Aug. 9/3 [U.S. tariff] On cloaks, dolmans, jackets, talmas, ulsters, or other outside garments for ladies and children's apparel.

talman, variant of TALISMAN[1] *Obs.*, mullah.

talmessite (tæl'mɛsaɪt). *Min.* [a. F. *talmessite* (Bariand & Herpin 1960, in *Bull. de la Soc. franç. de Min. et Crist.* LXXXIII. 120/1), f. *Talmessi*, name of a mine near Anarak, Iran: see -ITE[1].] A hydrated arsenate of calcium, magnesium, and barium, $Ca_2(Mg,Ba)(AsO_4)_2.2H_2O$, found as triclinic crystals.

1961 *Chem. Abstr.* LV. 8186 Analysis of an arsenate of Ca and Mg discovered in 1955..permits the definition of this new mineral as an isomorph of β-roselite... The name talmessite is proposed for the mineral. **1977** *Mineral. Abstr.* XXVIII. 229/2 White fibrous radiating aggregates of talmessite occur linked with the baryte.

talmi ('tælmɪ), **talmi-gold.** [a. Ger. *talmigold*, a fancy designation for trade purposes.] An alloy of copper, zinc, and tin, plated with gold, used for cheap jewellery.

(See *Monatsblatt des Gewerbe-Vereins für Hannover* July-Aug. 1863, *Deutsche Industrie-Zeitung*, 28 Sept. 1871.)

1868 WATTS *Dict. Chem.* V. 657 *Talmi gold*, an alloy used for the manufacture of trinkets, contains..86·4 per cent. copper, 12·2 zinc, 1·1 tin, and 0·3 iron. **1890** A. H. HIORNS *Mixed Metals* 109 §31 Talmi or Talmi Gold.—Also termed Abyssinian gold.

‖**Talmid Chacham** ('talmɪd 'xɔxam). Also **talmid chocham, hakham,** etc., and with small initials. [Heb., lit. 'disciple of a wise man'.] One well versed in the Jewish Law; a wise man (see also quot. 1962[1]). Cf. HAHAM.

1863 *Chambers's Encycl.* V. 720/2 *Rabbi* (Master), *Talmid Chacham* (Disciple of Wisdom), were titles of honour given to those expert in a knowledge of the law. **1905** *Jewish Encycl.* XI. 678/2 *Talmid Ḥakam*..Honorific title given to one well versed in the Law... The talmide ḥakamim formed in Jewish society a kind of aristocracy having many privileges. **1959** D. D. RUNES *Conc. Dict. Judaism* 217/1 *Talmid Chakham*, student of true knowledge as interpreted by the Talmudic sages. **1962** *New Jewish Encycl.* 475/1 *Talmid Ḥakham*, originally this Hebrew term referred to a disciple of a learned man (that is, a teacher of the Oral Law), as its literal meaning implies. Later it applied to any Talmudic scholar of high reputation, and in its present usage it applies to any individual of high Jewish scholarship. **1962** B. ABRAHAMS tr. *Life of Glückel of Hameln* ii. 22 God ... does not desert a Talmid Cocham. [*Note*] A wise and clever man, one well versed in the Torah and Talmud. **1973** *Jewish Chron.* 19 Jan. 42/3 A native of Czechoslovakia, he studied at Miskolc, Galanta, and other yeshivot, and was a man of scholarship—a *talmid chacham* in the truest sense of the word.

†**tal'mouse.** *Obs.* [a. obs. F. *talmouse* (talmuz), also *talemouse* (14th c. in Hatz.-Darm.), of uncertain origin; see conjectures in Littré.] 'A Cheese-cake; a Tart, or cake made of egges, and cheese' (Cotgr.); a piece of sugared pastry, containing cream, cheese, and eggs (Littré).

1600 SURFLET *Countrie Farme* V. xxii. 723 Some make with butter, cheese and yolkes of egges,..cheese cakes, talmouses and little lenten loaues.

‖**Talmud** ('tælmʊd, tæl'muːd). Also 6 **Thalmood,** 6-8 **Thalmud** [a. late Heb. *talmūd* instruction (*c* 130 A.D.), f. *lāmad* to instruct, teach. So med.L., F., Ger., etc. *talmud.*

From its primary sense of 'teaching, instruction, learning', the word was applied to the teaching or instruction contained in a biblical text, and to the body of traditional learning possessed by a particular Rabbi; but it came to be applied distinctively to the discussion, explanation, and illustration of the body of traditional law contained in the Mishnah, and so to the concrete collection of this teaching.]

In the wide sense, The body of Jewish civil and ceremonial traditionary law, consisting of the MISHNAH or binding precepts of the elders, additional to and developed from the Pentateuch, and the later GEMARA or commentary upon these, forming a complement, explanatory, illustrative, and discursive, to the Mishnah. The term was originally applied to the Gemara, of which two recensions exist, known respectively as the Jerusalem (or Palestinian) and the Babylonian Talmud; to the latter of which the name is in strictest use confined.

The precepts of the Mishnah were collected and codified about A.D. 200; the redaction of the Jerusalem Talmud had reached almost its present form by A.D. 408; that of the Babylonian Talmud extended from A.D. 400 to 500.

1532 MORE *Confut. Tindale* Wks. 679/2 As the Iewes had set vp a boke of their Talmud to destroye the sense of the scripture. **1580** G. GILPIN *Beehive Rom. Ch.* 74 The Iewes Rabbines..with their Caballa and with their Thalmood. **1636** WEEMSE *Treat. 4 Degenerate Sons* 349 They say that the text of the Scriptures is like water, and Mishna like wine, and the Talmud like spiced wine... So they compare the Law to salt, Mishna to pepper, and the Talmud to spices. **1665** BOYLE *Occas. Refl.* V. vii. (1848) 322 He must devour the tedious and voluminous Rhapsodies that make up the Talmud, in many of which he can scarce learn any thing but the Art of saying nothing in a multitude of words. **1727-41** CHAMBERS *Cycl.* s.v., When they [the Jews] say simply the Talmud, they always mean this [the Babylonian Talmud]. **1867** DEUTSCH in *Q. Rev.* Oct., Between the rugged boulders of the law which bestrew the pass of the Talmud there grow the blue flowers of romance and poetry, in the most catholic and Eastern sense.

attrib. **1892** ZANGWILL *Childr. Ghetto* I. 123 Mr. Moggid, you're a saint and a Talmud sage.

Talmudic (tæl'muːdɪk, tæl'mʌdɪk), *a.* (*sb.*) [f. prec. + -IC.] Of or pertaining to the Talmud.

1611 H. BROUGHTON *Require Agreement* 73 My next demaund, Rabbi, shall trie your Thalmudique skill. **1618** J. PAGET *Arrow agst. Brownists* Title-p., An Admonition tovching Talmudique and Rabbinical allegations. **1677** GALE *Crt. Gentiles* II. III. 167 Corrupt imitamens of Pythagorean and Talmudic Traditions and Canons. **1831** CARLYLE *Sart. Res.* I. v, Its..depth of Talmudic and Rabbinical lore. **1854** MILMAN *Lat. Chr.* IV. i. *note*, Sale has traced..the fables in the Korân to their Talmudic or Rabbinical sources.

†**B.** *sb.* = TALMUDIST. *Obs. rare.*

1624 R. SKYNNER in *Ussher's Lett.* (1686) 351 It is observable how Christ disputing against the Jews about the Resurrection, doth prove the Resurrection out of the sayings of their own Talmudicks. *a* **1656** BP. HALL *Revelation Unrevealed* viii. Wks. 1837 VIII. 540 Those carnal pleasures ..dreamed of by those sensual Turks and Talmudiques [*printed* -iges].

Hence †**Talmu'dician,** *sb.* = TALMUDIST c.; as adj., = TALMUDIC. *rare.*

1575 T. ROGERS *Sec. Coming Christ* 6/1 Many things in those Thalmudician books.

Tal'mudical, *a.* [f. as prec. + -AL[1].] Of, pertaining to, or contained in the Talmud; of the nature of or characteristic of the Talmud.

1605 CAMDEN *Rem.* (1637) 169 Whether this Cabala is more ancient than the Talmudicall learning. **1693** J. EDWARDS *Author. O. & N. Test.* 352 The wisest of all the Talmudical doctors. **1748** HARTLEY *Observ. Man* II. ii. 122 There are many Passages in the Talmudical Writings which afford Confirmation to the New Testament. **1867** *Q. Rev.* Oct. 437 Household words of talmudical Judaism, to which Christianity gave a higher and purer meaning.

'Talmudism. *rare.* [f. TALMUD + -ISM.]

1. Belief in or practice of the teaching of the Talmud.

1883 *Illinois Mission News* Nov. 132 The temporal effects of Talmudism may be..judged upon its own merits. **1896** *Nation* (N.Y.) 16 July 54/1 Talmudism and ritualism and Christian exclusion and repression have endowed him [the Jew] with a second nature which is mistaken for his fundamental character.

2. *fig.* in *Pol.* use [tr. Russ. *talmudízm*], (see quot. 1957). Cf. next.

1957 R. N. C. HUNT *Guide to Communist Jargon* xviii. 65 Dogmatism—or Talmudism, as Stalin at times called it—is defined..as 'the uncritical acceptance of dogma without considering the conditions of its application'. **1965** P. O'DONOVAN et al. *United States* iii. 56/1 Is this the victory of pragmatism over Constitutional talmudism?

Talmudist ('tælmədɪst, tæl'muːdɪst). [f. TALMUD + -IST.] **1. a.** One of the authors of the Talmud. **b.** One who accepts or believes in the authority of the Talmud. **c.** One learned in the Talmud; a Talmudic scholar.

1569 J. SANFORD tr. *Agrippa's Van. Artes* 6 b, There is a great contention of the Hebrewe tounge and Carracter, betwene the Thalmudistes. *c* **1645** HOWELL *Lett.* (1650) II. 10 The Jews at this day are divided to three sects. The first, which is the greatest, are call'd the Talmudists, in regard that, besides the holy scriptures, they embrace the Talmud. **1742** BISCOE *On Acts* (1829) 86 The Talmudists frequently speak of the transmigration of the souls of good men. **1882** *American* III. 186 Dr. Joseph Barclay, Bishop of Jerusalem, an eminent Talmudist. **1882** *Century Mag.* XXIV. 49 All [orthodox] Jews with whom Americans and Europeans are acquainted are Talmudists.

2. *fig.* in *Pol.* use (see quot. 1957). Cf. prec.

1957 R. N. C. HUNT *Guide to Communist Jargon* xviii. 65 The second edition of the *Large Soviet Encyclopædia*.. defines *Talmudist* (figuratively) as 'a pedant, dogmatist, formalist, doctrinaire'. **1965** *New Statesman* 14 May 772/2 Soviet Russia is described as a 'filthy shed'... Its inhabitants are 'slaves' and its rulers 'blockheaded talmudists'.

Hence **Talmu'distic**, **Talmu'distical** *adjs.* = TALMUDICAL. So **'talmudize** *v. trans.*, to make Talmudic; to allegorize or mix with fable; hence **talmudi'zation**.

1593 NASHE *Christ's T.* (1613) 76 With Th' almudisticall dreames. **1642** CUDWORTH *Disc. Lord's Supper* 30 Besides these Talmudisticke Jewes, there is another Sect..that reject all Talmudicall Traditions. **1781** WARTON *Hist. Eng. Poetry* lx. (1840) III. 386 The name Ariel came from the Talmudistic mysteries. **1839** R. PHILIP *Life W. Milne* ix. (1840) 246 There are facts in his itinerary although Talmudized. **1860** W. W. WEBB in *Med. Times* 1 Dec. 537/1 Talmudistical commentators on clinical medicine, whose patients seem to be immortal. **1927** V. BURCH *Jesus Christ & his Revel.* 13 If the Talmud depraves the values of Jesus Christ with cynicism, and the Kûran talmudises Him so that he becomes an inferior Jewish prophet, then we are guilty of a double talmudisation of the One we are said to follow. **1931** *Times Lit. Suppl.* 19 Mar. 228/2 Extraneous influences, historical development, Talmudization, do not trouble him.

‖**Talmud Torah** ('tælmuːd 'təʊrə, 'tɔərə). [Heb., 'study of the (Jewish) Law'; cf. TALMUD, TORAH.] The study of the Jewish Law. Also freq. used *attrib.* and *absol.* to designate a school run by the community for the instruction of children in the Jewish religion (see also quot. 1962). Cf. CHEDAR.

1844 *Jewish Chron.* 18 Oct. 7/1 Mr. L. A. Green.. received the rudiments of his education at the 'Talmud Torah School', Bell Lane, Spitalfields. **1881** *Encycl. Brit.* XIII. 686/2 Besides the schools of the Alliance, there are 2287 pupils in the wretched Talmud Torah schools. **1907** I. ZANGWILL *Ghetto Comedies* 387 'We can meet and practise in your Talmud-Torah Hall!' 'The holy hall of study!' gasped the Rabbi. **1932** C. ROTH *Hist. Marranos* 391 A secret society for the purpose of studying the Law—*Talmud Torah*. **1960** L. P. GARTNER *Jewish Immigrant in Eng. 1870–1914* viii. 221 The Jews' Free School in Spitalfields... In its early days..was a Talmud Torah..for poor children. **1962** *New Jewish Encycl.* 477/1 *Talmud Torah*, the literal meaning of this Hebrew term is 'the study of the Torah' or the 'teaching of the Torah', but it is commonly used as a designation for an elementary Hebrew school. Whereas the traditional *Heder* was a private religious school, the *Talmud Torah* was a public institution maintained and administered by the community in order to provide education for orphans or children of parents who could not afford private teaching. In America, Talmud Torah generally refers to a school which meets in the afternoon after the secular school session is over. Its curriculum includes the study of the Bible, Hebrew, Jewish history, customs and ceremonies, and other phases of elementary Jewish knowledge. **1964** W. MARKFIELD *To Early Grave* (1965) ix. 151 When he wanted he had a marvellous head for Talmud Torah, except that he very seldom wanted and gave the *rebbe* trouble. **1968** M. RICHLER in R. Weaver *Canad. Short Stories* 2nd Ser. 155 My mother came home from her Talmud Torah meeting. **1976** B. WILLIAMS *Making of Manchester Jewry* xii. 322 The ten Corfiote families..contribute[d] collectively in 1872 to the languishing Talmud Torah of their home town.

talnakhite (tæl'nækaɪt). *Min.* [ad. Russ. *talnakhit* (Bud'ko & Kulagov 1968, in *Zap. Vsesoyuznogo Min. Obshchestva* XCVII. 63), f. *Talnakh*, name of a locality near Dudinka in northern Siberia: see -ITE[1].] A sulphide of copper and iron, $Cu_9Fe_8S_{16}$, found as yellow, usu. iridescent, crystals of the cubic system.

1969 *Mineral. Abstr.* XX. 148/1 (*heading*) The new mineral talnakhite—the cubic variety of chalcopyrite. **1978** *Canad. Mineralogist* XVI. 29 The talnakhite structure has a broad range of possible compositions including both $Cu_9Fe_8S_{16}$ and $Cu_9Fe_9S_{16}$... The relatively restricted compositions found for natural talnakhite are the result of a change in kinetics of the ordering transformations with composition.

talo- (teɪləʊ), combining form of L. *tālus* ankle-bone, forming a few adjectives in anatomy, in sense 'pertaining to the ankle-bone', as **talo-cal'caneal**, **talocal'canean** *a.* [CALCANEAN, heel-bone], **talo-'fibular** [FIBULA], **talo-'scaphoid** [SCAPHOID], **talo-'tibial** [TIBIA]. **ˌtalocalˌcaneona'vicular** *a.*, applied to the joint comprising the rounded head of the talus and the corresponding concavity formed by the navicular bone and calcaneus; **talona'vicular** *a.*, applied to the ligament joining the talus and navicular bone, and also to the joint between these bones (part of the talocalcaneonavicular joint).

1887 *Cassell's Encycl. Dict.*, Talo-scaphoid. **1890** BILLINGS *Nat. Med. Dict.*, *Talo-calcaneal*,.. *Talo-calcaneal articulation*... *Talo-fibular ligaments*,..anterior and middle fascicles of external lateral ligament of ankle-joint... *Talo-scaphoid articulation*.. *Talo-tibial ligaments*,..passing between the internal malleus and astragalus. **1900** DORLAND *Med. Dict.* 668/1 Talocalcanean. **1907** MORRIS & MCMURRICH *Treat. Human Anat.* (ed. 4) III. 304 The articulations of the anterior and posterior portions of the tarsus..consist of two separate joints, viz., (i) an inner, the talo-navicular, which communicates with the anterior talo-calcaneal articulation; and (ii) an outer, the calcaneo-cuboid. **1913** *Gray's Anat.* (ed. 18) 402 (*heading*) Talocalcaneonavicular articulation. **1962** *Ibid.* (ed. 33) 559 The lateral talocalcanean ligament..passes downwards and backwards from the lateral process of the talus to be attached to the lateral surface of the calcaneus. **1977** *Bone & Joint Diseases* (Brit. Med. Assoc.) 3 The talo-navicular joint has been replaced experimentally. *Ibid.*, 113 Talipes equinovarus or clubfoot is a limb anomaly that is best regarded as a congenital dislocation at the talo-calcaneonavicular joint. **1979** R. H. FREIBERGER et al. *Arthrography* xi. 238/1 The most commonly injured of the lateral supporting ligaments of the ankle is the anterior talofibular ligament. **1979** *Brit. Med. Jrnl.* 15 Dec. 1594/2 Simple rigidity of the talocalcaneal joint increases oxygen consumption during walking by up to 20%.

talon ('tælən), *sb.* Forms: α. 4–5 **taloun(e**, 5 **-owne**, 5–7 **tallon**, 7 **tal(l)en**, *pl.* **tallance**, 5– **talon**. β. 5–6 **talente**, **talaunt(e**, **tala(u)nde**, 5–7 **talland**, 6 **tallaunt(e**, 6–7 **talant(e**, **tallent**, 6–7 (9 *dial.*) **tallant**, 6–8 (9 *dial.*) **talent**. [ME. a. OF. *talon* heel of a man, or of a shoe, hinder part of the foot of a quadruped = Pr. *talo*, Sp. *talon*, Pg. *talão*, It. *talone* heel, heel-piece:—late pop. L. or Com. Romanic *tālo*, *tālōn-em* heel, deriv. form of *tālus* ankle. With the β forms *talant*, *talent*, cf. *ancient*, *margent*, *parchment*, *peasant*, *tyrant*, etc.: see -ANT[3]. The sense-development shows the stages: ankle; heel of man (of a shoe, etc.); heel or hinder part of the foot of a beast; hinder claw of a bird of prey; any claw (usually in pl. the claws) of a bird, a dragon, an ungulate beast, an insect, etc. The extension to a bird of prey, and subsequent stages, are peculiar to English.]

I. † **1. a.** The 'heel' or hinder part of the foot of certain quadrupeds, as swine and deer, or of the hoof of a horse. *Obs.*

c **1410** *Master of Game* (MS. Digby 182) xxiv, A gret boore shall haue longe traces and þe clees rounde before and brode sooles of þe feete and a good talowne and longe bones. **1611** COTGR., *Argot*,..the deaw-clawe of a dog, &c.; the heele, or talon of a hog. **1639** T. DE GRAY *Expert Farrier* II. xvii. 298 [The Quitter-bone] causeth a hard round swelling upon the cronet of the hoofe, betwixt the heele and the quarter of the long talent. [**1688**, **1725**: cf. *talon-nail* in 5.]

† **b.** The hallux or hinder claw of a bird. *Obs.*

1486 *Bk. St. Albans* a viij, The grete Clees [of a hawk] behynde..ye shall call hom Talons. **1530** PALSGR. 279/1 Talant of a byrde the hynder-clawe, *talon*, *argot*. **1552** HULOET, Talent or clawe of a hawke, *vngula*. **1577** B. GOOGE *Heresbach's Husb.* IV. (1586) 157b, Let therefore your Henne be of a good colour, hauing..her tallons euen. *Ibid.* 158 Your Cockes..of colours, as I tolde you for the Hennes, and the like number of tallons.

2. *pl.* The claws (or less usually in *sing.* any claw) of a bird or beast. **a.** *spec.* The powerful claws of a bird of prey, or of a dragon, griffin, etc.

α. ? *a* **1400** *Morte Arth.* 800 The dragone..Towchez hym wyth his talounez, and terez hys rigge. *c* **1400** MAUNDEV. (1839) xxvi. 269 [The Griffon] hath his talouns so longe and so grete as þough þei weren hornes of grete oxen. *a* **1661** HOLYDAY *Juvenal* 250 Lubin..understands not how the pygmie should be snatch'd-up by the crane.. in his crooked talens, when as the crane's talents are not crooked. **1671** MILTON *P.R.* II. 403 With sound of Harpies wings, and Talons heard. **1727** SWIFT *Gulliver* II. v, A kite..would have certainly carried me away in his talons. **1884** PAE *Eustace* 137 We must see and take the Falcon from the talons of the French eagle.

β. **1432–50** tr. *Higden* (Rolls) II. 369 Bryddes hauenge wynges and talandes. *Ibid.* VIII. 37 Thre [young eagles].. did bete the egle with theire talauntes and wynges. *a* **1533** LD. BERNERS *Gold. Bk. M. Aurel.* xxviii. (1535) 47b, He sawe two kytes ioninge to gyther with their talantes. **1579** GOSSON *Sch. Abuse* (Arb.) 20 The Harpies haue Virgins faces, and vultures Talentes. **1635** R. JOHNSON *Hist. Tom a Lincolne* (1828) 104 The nailes of his fingers were as the tallents of eagles. **1760–72** H. BROOKE *Fool of Qual.* (1809) IV. 151 What would become of my..dove, within the talents of such a vulture? **1893** SALISBURY *S.E. Worc. Gloss.*, *Local Pronunc.*, *Talents*, talons.

b. The claws (or in *sing.* any claw) of a wild beast, of an insect, etc.

α. *a* **1591** H. SMITH *Jonah's Punishm.* II. (1602) B viij, Like Lions, which will be gentle vntill their tallons grow. **1664** POWER *Exp. Philos.* I. 5 The other four legs are cloven and arm'd with little clea's or tallons (like a Catamount). *a* **1667** COWLEY *Sylva, Ret. out of Scotl.*, Let spotted Lynces their sharp Talons fill, With Chrystal fetch'd from the Promethean Hill. **1873** HOLLAND *A. Bonnic.* xi. 184 Sheathed within the foot of velvet was hidden a talon of steel.

β. **1432–50** tr. *Higden* (Rolls) I. 83 Men hauenge hedes lyke dogges, whiche be callede Cynocephali,..y-armede with teithe and talaundes, lyffenge by hawkenge and huntenge. **1571** GOLDING *Calvin on Ps.* x. 10 The talantes and teethe of the Lyon. **1628** GAULE *Pract. The. Panegyr.* 47 It sufficeth, that wee discerne this Lyon, by his Talent.

c. Allusively applied to the grasping fingers or hands of human beings. (Cf. CLAW.)

1588 SHAKS. *L.L.L.* IV. ii. 64 If a talent be a claw, looke how he clawes him with a talent. **1594** ? GREENE *Selimus* Wks. (Grosart) XIV. 264, I can scarce keep her talents from my eies. **1600** J. PORY tr. *Leo's Africa* III. 142 They haue.. neither kniues or spoones but only their ten talons. **1818** SCOTT *Hrt. Midl.* xviii, An I had ye amang the Frigate Whins, wadna I set my ten talents in your wuzzent face for that very word? **1860** HAWTHORNE *Marb. Faun* xvi, Still he washed his brown, bony talons.

d. *fig.*

1586 MARLOWE *1st Pt. Tamburl.* II. vii, Now doth ghastly Death With greedy talents gripe my bleeding heart. **1600** SURFLET *Countrie Farme* III. xxxiv. 497 The oliue tree being once seased in his tallance of a good peece of ground, contenteth it selfe. **1748** JOHNSON *Van. Hum. Wishes* 168 Rebellion's vengeful talons. **1751** —— *Rambler* No. 113 ¶7 Nothing should have torn me from her but the talons of necessity. **1774** BURKE *Corr.* (1844) I. 451 That they may yet be able to save something from the talons of despotism.

II. 3. *transf.* A heel-like part or object. [In a, b, c = F. *talon*.] **a.** *Naut.* The curved back of a ship's rudder. ? *Obs.* **b.** *Arch.* An ogee moulding: = OGEE 2. **c.** The 'heel' of a blade, as of a sword. **d.** A part of the shell of a bivalve; cf. HEEL *sb.*[1] 7h. **e.** The projection on the bolt of a lock against which the key presses (Knight *Dict. Mech.* 1877). **f.** (See quot.)

a. **1485–6** *Naval Acc. Hen. VII* (1896) 14 For a pece of tymbre..spent in makyng of a talland for the same Rother. **1867** SMYTH *Sailor's Word-bk.*, *Tallant*, the upper hance, or break of the rudder abaft.

b. **1704** J. HARRIS *Lex. Techn.* I. s.v., The Talon consists of two Portions of a Circle, one without, and the other within; and when the Concave Part is uppermost, it is called Reversed Talon. **1753** HOGARTH *Anal. Beauty* xii. 172 That ornamental member called by the architects 'cyma recta', or talon. **1810** *Rudim. Anc. Archit.* (1821) 41 The ovolo and talon are always employed as supporters to the essential members of the composition, such as the modillions, denteles, and corona. **1842–76** GWILT *Archit.* Gloss., *Talon*, the name given by the French to the ogee.

c. **1854** WOODWARD *Mollusca* II. 276 Umbones elongated, progressively filled up with shell, and forming an irregular 'talon' in front of the fixed valve.

d. **1869** BOUTELL *Arms & Arm.* ix. (1874) 180 From the *talon*, or heel of the blade, on the opposite side, is a hollow indent, intended to hold the thumb.

f. **1898** *Syd. Soc. Lex.*, *Talon*, a heel or low cusp of a tooth.

4. *fig.* **a.** *Cards.* The remainder of the pack after the hands have been dealt. *Cent. Dict.* 1891. **b.** *Comm.* See quot. 1882. (So both in Fr.)

a. **1862** C. C. MEEHAN *Law & Practice of Game of Euchre* v. 86 *Talon*, the eleven cards remaining in the pack after the dealer has distributed five to each player and turned up the twenty-first card for the trump. **1921** M. C. WORK *Auction for Two or Three* III. 78 *Talon*..is, in fact, a sort of secondary *Stock* in Russian Bank and a distinguishing term must be used to describe it. **1977** *Jrnl. Playing-Card Soc.* May 25 When the discard is complete, everyone should have 11 cards and the four face-down cards remaining are called the talon.

b. **1882** BITHELL *Counting-Ho. Dict.* (1893) s.v., A Talon, as most commonly known in commerce, is the last portion of a sheet of coupons.., and contains on its face an intimation that if it is presented at the house or office indicated, a new sheet of coupons will be given in exchange for it... The Talon is also a name applied to the marginal appendage of a Spanish coupon, and..payment of the coupon is refused if such talon or appendage happens to have been cut off. **1932** *Daily Tel.* 8 Oct. 2/3 Provision was made on May 3 for the conversion of the Austrian share of liability..into new 4 per cent. bonds. Bonds, Talons, or coupons must now be presented at the Staatszentralkasse, Singerstrasse 17, Vienna, before Dec. 31. **1964** *Lebende Sprachen* IX. 99/2 A *coupon sheet*, consisting of *dividend coupons* and a *talon*, is attached to each share warrant. The dividend coupons are used by the holder to collect dividends. When the last coupon has been cashed, the talon is exchanged for a new coupon sheet. **1979** *Daily Tel.* 26 Nov. 24/6 The Bank of England give notice that new *coupon* sheets for the above-mentioned Loan will be available on and after 17th January 1980 in exchange for *talons*.

5. *attrib.* and *Comb.*, as ***talon-like***, ***-tipped*** adjs.; † **talon-nail**, in *Farriery*, a shoeing-nail driven into the back part of the hoof.

1688 R. HOLME *Armoury* III. 89/2 *Tallon Nail*, is that Nail driven in the shooe towards the Horse heel. **1725** *Bradley's Fam. Dict.* s.v. *Shoeing of horses*, The two Talon nails must be drove first, then look whether the shoe stands right or not. **1883** 'MARK TWAIN' *Life on Mississippi* xxxi. 339 His hand ..was talon-like, it was so bony and long-fingered. **1894** *Outing* (U.S.) XXIV. 195/1 And talon-tipped hands toss him kisses. **1897** *Allbutt's Syst. Med.* II. 52 The nails are often split and break, or are changed into talon-like appendages.

Hence † **'talon** *v. trans.*, to tear with the talons; to claw. In quot. *fig.*

1685 F. SPENCE tr. *Varillas' Ho. Medicis* 306 When they came to talon them with an usurpation.

taloned ('tælənd), *a.* Also 7 **ta(l)lented**. [f. TALON *sb.* + -ED[2].] Furnished with talons.

1611 COTGR., *Empieté*, pawed, pounced, clawed, talented. **1611** BIBLE *Jer.* xii. 9 A speckled [*marg.* tallented] bird. **1706** WATTS *Horæ Lyr.* II. *To Mitio* I. 119 A speedier prey To talon'd faulcons. **1838** S. BELLAMY *Betrayal* 164 One talon'd hand appear'd. **1840** CARLYLE *Heroes* v. (1858) 315 As if you should overturn the tree, and..show us ugly taloned roots turned-up into the air.

talonid ('tælənɪd). *Zool.* [f. TALON *sb.* 3f + -ID[5].] A flattened cusp on a mammalian lower molar tooth, corresponding to the talon on an upper molar.

1897 H. F. OSBORN in *Amer. Naturalist* XXXI. 1002 It [*sc.* the talon] invariably appeared first in the lower molars (where we may distinguish it as the 'talonid'). **1919** [see HYPOCONID]. **1922** W. K. GREGORY *Orig. & Evol. Human Dentition* I. 38 The premolars..already possessed incipient talonid spurs. *Ibid.* 39 The talonids had not yet acquired basins or fossæ. **1968** [see HYPOCONID]. **1979** *Nature* 20 Sept. 213/2 The isolated lower second molar of the right side ..has the basic tribosphenic pattern with an elevated trigonid and a low talonid.

talook, -dar, etc.: see TALUK, TALUKDĀR.

‖**Talpa**[1] ('tælpə). [L. *talpa* mole.]

1. *Zool.* The genus typified by the common mole (*Talpa europæa*).

[**1398** TREVISA *Barth. De P.R.* XVIII. cii. (Bodl. MS.), The wonte [*v.r.* molle] hi3t *Talpa*.] **1706** PHILLIPS (ed. 6), *Talpa*, (Lat.) the Mole or Want.

2. *Path.* An encysted cranial tumour; a wen.

1693 tr. *Blancard's Phys. Dict.* (ed. 2), *Talpa*, a Tumor, so called, because that as a Mole . . creeps under ground; so this feeds upon the Scull under the Skin. **1726** QUINCY *Lex. Phys.-Med.* (ed. 3), *Talpæ* and *Nates*, are Tumours generally confined to the Head. **1857** DUNGLISON *Med. Lex.*, *Talpa*, . . a tumour on the head, which has been supposed to burrow like a mole. **1890** BILLINGS *Nat. Med. Dict.*, *Talpa*, . . abscess in superior and posterior part of head.

talpa[2] ('tælpə). *U.S.* Var. CATALPA.

1926 J. MASEFIELD *Odtaa* xvii. 283 Hi could see the fronds of the talpas moving above him. **1933** *Amer. Speech* VIII. 53/1 Talpa, n. Catalpa. This tree . . has been planted in some Ozark towns.

talpat, variant of TALIPOT.

†**talpe.** *Obs. rare*[−1]. [f. L. *talpa*, or a. OF. *talpe*, *taulpe* (F. *taupe*) mole.] A mole.

c **1440** *Pallad. on Husb.* I. 931 Either shall thees talpes voide or sterve.

talpi-, combining form of L. *talpa* mole, as in †'**talpicide** [see -CIDE 2], the killing of moles; '**talpiform** *a.*, mole-shaped; '**talpify** *v. trans.* (*nonce-wd.*), to make mole-like (in allusive use). So '**talpid** *Zool.* [f. mod.L. *Talpid-æ*], an animal of the family *Talpidæ*, a mole; '**talpine** *a.*, pertaining to the moles, of the sub-family *Talpinæ*; '**talpoid** [-OID, so F. *talpoïde*], *a.* having the form or structure of a mole; *sb.* an animal allied to the mole.

1656 BLOUNT *Glossogr.*, **Talpicide*, the taking or killing moles or woants. **1660** S. FISHER *Rusticks Alarm* Wks. (1679) 326 But J. O. is so totally *talpified, that . . he can't see that Jewish Idolatry nearer home. **1860** MAYNE *Expos. Lex.*, *Talpiformis*, applied by Latreille to a Family . . which resemble the Talpa: *talpiform. **1890** BILLINGS *Nat. Med. Dict.*, *Talpiform*, shaped like a mole. **1860** MAYNE *Expos. Lex.*, *Talpinus*, . . *talpine.

tal qual (tæl kwæl), *adv. phr. Newfoundland.* Also **talqual.** [Shortened from L. *talis qualis* such as, of which sort or quality.] 'Just as they come': used with reference to fish sold without sorting.

1732 in *Calendar State Papers, Amer. & W. Indies* (1939) 282 And by carrying a mixt cargoe which is all sold at markett for marchantable fish, when it's only (what in the stile of the fisherman is called Tal Qual) to the shoarmen. *c* **1894** in *Dict. Newfoundland Eng.* (1982) 557/1 Tal qual, sometimes called *all qualls*, fish bought without culling is clearly the Latin *talis qualis*, 'such as it is'. **1928** in *Ibid.* 557/1 [He] said that tal qual fish was $8.20. **1930** W. F. COAKER *Hist. Fishermen's Protective Union of Newfoundland* 30 Fish would not have advanced beyond $5.30 taqual [*sic*] this season if the F.P.U. did not exist. **1934** *Rep. Newfoundland R. Comm.* 105 in *Parl. Papers 1933–4* (Cd. 4480) XIV. 357 During the war years, quantity rather than quality became the ruling consideration; the 'cull' was therefore dispensed with and fish were bought on what is known as the 'talqual' system, viz. an average price was fixed for the whole of a fisherman's catch without any exact regard to the varying qualities of the fish comprising the catch.

†'**talright**, *a. Obs. rare*[−1]. [f. TALL *a.* + RIGHT *a.*] Upright and tall; lofty.

1582 STANYHURST *Æneis* I. (Arb.) 34 On back her quiuer shee bears, and highlye the remnaunt Of Nymphs surpassing with talright quantitye mounting.

'**talshide.** *Obs.* exc. *Hist.* Also 5 **talschide, -shed,** 6–7 **taleshide,** 7 **talshid.** [f. OF. *tail* cutting, cut + SHIDE: cf. TALWOOD.] A shide or piece of wood of prescribed length, either round, or split in two or four, according to thickness, for cutting into billets for firewood.

Talshides were classed from No. 1 to No. 7 according to girth: No. 1 contained round timber of 16 in. girth, half-round of 19 in., quarter-cleft of 18¾; No. 2 contained round 23 in., half-round 27 in., quarter-cleft 26 in.; No. 3 round 28 in., half-round 33 in., quarter-cleft 32 in.; No. 4 round 33 in., half-round 39 in., quarter-cleft 38 in., and so on: see Act 43 Eliz. c. 14.

1444–5 in Willis and Clark *Cambridge* (1886) I. 391 In prostracione, fissura, et factura CCC di Talschides apud Langley. **1447–8** *Ibid.* 388 Pro prostracione, sicatione, fissura, et factura, xiiij[m] Talshides apud Snowdenhill. **1502** ARNOLDE *Chron.* (1811) 98 Item euery taleshide of one be in gretnes in the middis xx. ynches of assise. **1526** in *Househ. Ord.* (1790) 162 A Duke or a Dutchess for their Bouche of Court . . [was to have] one torch, one pricket, two sises, one pound of white lights, ten talshides, eight faggotts. **1664** EVELYN *Sylva* 99 Every Taleshide to be four foot long, besides the carf; and if nam'd of one, marked one, to contain 16 inches circumference, within a foot of the middle.

‖**taluk, taluq** (tə'lu:k). *East Ind.* Also 8–9 **talook,** 9 **talooka, -ah,** 9– **taluka.** [a. Urdū *ta*ʿ*alluq* estate, tract of proprietary land, f. Arab. ʿ*alaqa* to adhere, be affixed.] *orig.* A hereditary estate belonging to a native proprietor; also, more usually, a subdivision of a *zillah* or district, comprising a number of villages, placed for purposes of revenue under a native collector; a collectorate. Also *attrib.*

1793 *Bengal Permanent Settlement Reg.* in *Bengal Code* (1913) I. 9 Dependent *taluk*. **1799** WELLINGTON *Suppl. Desp.* (1858) I. 370 He may hereafter plunder the remainder of that talook. **1802** CLOSE in Owen *Wellesley's Desp.* (1877) 235 Such exchanges of talooks or lands shall be made hereafter . . as the completion of the said purpose may require. **1839** *Lett. fr. Madras* (1843) 258 Let there be four schools at Madras . . one, at the principal station of every Zillah; and one in every Talook. *Ibid.* 259 In the Talook schools English would be unnecessary. **1880** C. R. MARKHAM *Peruv. Bark* 352 The taluq or district of Wainad is a plateau, averaging an elevation of 3000 feet above the sea. **1891** *Rep. Administration Local Boards in Bombay Presidency 1889–90* 1 There are . . 39 Taluka Local Boards, presided over by the Assistant and District Deputy Collectors in charge of the tálukas. **1905** A. ANDREW *Indian Probl.* 21 It is not possible for the President of a Taluk Board to attend to the schools in his charge. **1931** *Times Educ. Suppl.* 4 Apr. 123/2 The local municipal *taluka* or district board. **1977** *Lancet* 2 July 39/2 We have in fact already prepared a plan for the treatment of rabies in the taluka (somewhat bigger than a village).

‖**talukdār, taluqdār** (tə'lu:kdɑ:(r)). *East Ind.* [f. prec. + *-dār*, Pers. agential suffix.] The holder of a taluk or hereditary estate, or the officer who has charge of the district so called. Hence **talukdārī, -daree (talookdarry),** the office or position of a talukdār.

1793 *Bengal Permanent Settlement Reg.* in *Bengal Code* (1913) I. 9 Dependent *talukdar*. **1798** WELLESLEY in Owen *Desp.* (1877) 170 Orders shall . . be issued to all talookdars on the frontiers. **1801** R. PATTON *Asiat. Mon.* 116 By acquiring a larger extent of the same species of hereditary possession, they became what are called talookdars. *Ibid.* 147 A grant of talookdarry of thirty-eight villages 'which lay contiguous to their factory in Bengal'. **1893** *Nation* (N.Y.) 27 July 70/2 The 'landlords' (or 'talookdars', as they were called in that district). **1904** *Times* 5 Oct. 8/6 Proposals respecting the education and training of the Oudh taluqdars put forward by Raja Ali Mahomed.

talus[1] ('teɪləs, ‖taly). Also 7 **talu, talud.** [a. F. *talus* (16th c.), in Dict. Acad. 1696 *talut*, OF. (12th c. in Hatz.-Darm.) *talu* slope:—late pop. L. **tālūt-um*, deriv. of *tālus* ankle (taken in sense of F. *talon* heel): cf. next.]

1. A slope; *spec.* in *Fortification*, the sloping side of a wall or earthwork, which gradually increases in thickness from above downwards.

1645 N. STONE *Enchiridion Fortif.* 3 On the inward side they gave them [the walls] a *Talud* or slooping which increased them in thicknesse towards the bottom. **1672** *Phil. Trans.* VII. 4081 The first Wall . . being much broader below by reason of the *Talu* or slope. **1704** J. HARRIS *Lex. Techn.* I, *Talus*, or *Talut*, properly signifies any Thing that goes sloping, as the Talus of a Wall in Masonry. . . In Fortification, the Talus of a Bastion or Rampart, is the Slope allowed to such a Work whether it be of Earth or Stone. **1762** STERNE *Tr. Shandy* VI. xxi, To determine the depths . . of the ditches,—the talus of the glacis, and the precise height of the . . parapets. **1862** WRAXALL tr. *Hugo's Misérables* III. vii, The enemy's guns had opened a break from the parapet to the talus.

†**b.** The sloping side of a trench or the like.

1727 *Bradley's Fam. Dict.* s.v. *Garden*, There must be one on the Brink of the Trench to spread the Dung upon the Talus.

2. *Geol.* A sloping mass of detritus lying at the base of a cliff or the like, and consisting of material which has fallen from its face; also, the slope or inclination of the surface of such a mass.

1830 LYELL *Princ. Geol.* I. II. xx. 266 It is only at a few points that the grassy covering of the sloping talus marks a temporary relaxation of the erosive action of the sea. **1863** —— *Antiq. Man* xvii. 343 Huge taluses of fallen drift. **1865** LIVINGSTONE *Zambesi* vii. 171 The talus of each portal, keeping close together northwards, makes a narrow, upright-sided trough from the cataract up to Pajodze. **1876** PAGE *Adv. Text-bk. Geol.* xv. 275 The cemented fragments of a terrestrial talus or scree. **1881** DARWIN *Veg. Mould* 279 An old talus of chalk-fragments (thrown out of a quarry) which had become clothed with turf.

attrib. and *Comb.* **1867** H. MACMILLAN in *Macm. Mag.* No. 99. 256/2 Great talus-heaps of débris. **1904** *Daily Chron.* 24 Mar. 3/1 There was no stratification as might be expected if it were a talus-formation. **1906** *Ibid.* 20 Feb. 4/2 The water getting into the talus rock, a mass of soft stuff without any regular drainage.

b. A descending slope of a mountain, etc., without reference to its mode of formation.

1830 SIR T. D. LAUDER *Moray Floods* 230 We found an extensive marl bank reposing on the inclined talus at the foot of the hill. **1853** KANE *Grinnell Exp.* xv. (1856) 108 One of these bergs presented a long inclined talus, which was evidently part of an original slope, unaltered by after changes in equilibrium. **1856** —— *Arct. Expl.* I. xv. 169 A slide down an inclined plane, whose well-graded talus gave me ample time to contemplate the contingencies at its base. **1865** LIVINGSTONE *Zambesi* ii. 61 One point of view on the talus of mount Morumbwa. **1868** LOCKYER tr. *Guillemin's Heavens* (ed. 3) 100 Beyond the second ridge a talus slopes gradually down northwards to the general level of the lunar surface.

‖**talus**[2] ('teɪləs). Pl. **tali.** [L. *tālus* ankle.]

1. The ankle-bone or astragalus; also applied to an analogous part in birds and insects.

1693 tr. *Blancard's Phys. Dict.* (ed. 2), *Talus*, see *Astragalus*. **1706** PHILLIPS (ed. 6), *Talus*, (lat.) the Ancle or Huckle-Bone, otherwise call'd Astragalus; the Pastern of a Beast; also a Die to play with. **1826** KIRBY & SP. *Entomol.* III. 385 *Talus* (the Ankle), the apex of the Tibia [of an insect], where it is united to the Tarsus. **1899** *Allbutt's Syst. Med.* VI. 556 The capsule of the ankle-joint was loose and lax, the talus smooth and oblique.

2. *Path.* A variety of clubfoot in which the toes are drawn up, the heel resting on the ground.

1864 in WEBSTER. **1887** in *Cassell's Encycl. Dict.*

3. A nodular concretion somewhat resembling an astragalus bone.

a **1728** WOODWARD *Nat. Hist. Fossils* (1729) I. I. 81 Of the Septa, or Partitions, that parcel out this Body into various Masses or Tali.

talvace, -vas, variants of TALEVACE *Obs.*

talvett, variant of TOVET, two-peck measure.

talwar: see TULWAR, Indian sabre.

talweg, var. THALWEG.

'**talwood.** *Obs.* exc. *Hist.* Also 4–5 **talwode, tallwod(e, (taleghwode, tallowood),** 5–9 **tallwood,** 6 **tal(e)wod, talewood, tallwodde, tallewode,** 6–7 **tall wood.** [A rendering of OF. *bois de tail* 'bois en coupe' (Godef.), f. *tail* cutting, cut.] Wood for fuel, cut up usually to a prescribed size: cf. TALSHIDE.

[**1268–** Tallwood: cited in Rogers *Agric. & Prices* I. 393 et seq.] **1350** in Riley *Mem. Lond.* (1868) 254 Talwode. **1373** *Ibid.* 369 Taleghwode. **1424** *Will Stawell* (Somerset Ho.), Centum de talwode. **1497** *Naval Acc. Hen. VII* (1896) 227 M[l] tallowood occupyed & spent abought hetyng of pitche Talowe Tarre & Rosyn. **1502** ARNOLDE *Chron.* (1811) 97 The Ordinaunce for the Assise of Talewod and Belet in the Cyte of London. **1530** PALSGR. 279/2 Tallwodde pacte wodde to make byllettes of, *taillee*. **1552–3** *Act 7 Edw. VI*, c. 7 All talwoode, billet, fagot and coles . . shall kepe thassises hereafter expressed. [A statement of sizes and prices follows.] **1573** TUSSER *Husb.* (1878) 133 Pile tallwood and billet, stacke all that hath band. **1674** JEAKE *Arith.* (1696) 68 Fuel contains Billets, Cordwood, Faggots, Talwood, and Coals. **1859** PARKER *Turner's Dom. Archit.* III. iv. 101 It was the duty of the grooms of the chamber to procure a regular supply of tallwood and fuel for the fire.

TAM (tæm). Also **Tam,** etc. [f. the initial letters of *t*elevision *a*udience *m*easurement (see below).] Used in *Comb.*, usu. as ***TAM rating***, to denote a measure of the number of people watching a particular television programme as estimated by the company Television Audience Measurement Ltd. Also *absol.*, the company itself.

1958 *Observer* 14 Dec. 15/1 In the telly-dominated world, where everybody from a philosopher to a flat-catcher is judged by his tam-rating, it was encouraging to see originality break through the crust of diffidence. **1959** *Listener* 24 Sept. 501/1 Head-hunting rivalry is understandable, but why does the type of head matter? Egg-shaped or with forehead villainous low, all are equal in the sight of TAM. **1960** *Spectator* 14 Oct. 565 Processed and packaged . . down to strip-cartoon versions compatible with the maximum Tam ratings. **1963** *Daily Tel.* 17 Oct. 16/2 According to TAM figures published last Friday, [etc.]. **1966** *Punch* 24 Aug. 302/3 The first episode topped the Tamratings. **1975** LD. HAILSHAM *Door wherein I Went* xxv. 158 They have their own fish to fry, their TAM ratings, their circulations, their Charters, their editorial policies, even their advertisers.

tam, abbreviation of TAM-O'-SHANTER.

1895 *Daily News* 8 Apr. 6/7 The 'Tams' as the Tam O'Shanters are now universally called by shopkeepers, are favourites for windy weather. **1896** *Godey's Mag.* Feb. 224/2 The headgear is a coquettish white Tam with a white quill. **1899** ANNIE E. HOLDSWORTH *Valley Gt. Shadow* x, I'll put on your tam—there!

tamable, variant spelling of TAMEABLE.

Tamachek, var. TAMASHEK.

tamahauke, obs. form of TOMAHAWK.

tamain, var. TAMEIN.

‖**tamal** (ta'mal). Also **tamaul,** *erron.* **tamale.** [Mexican Sp. *ta'mal*, pl. *tamales* (-'ales).] A Mexican delicacy, made of crushed Indian corn, flavoured with pieces of meat or chicken, red pepper, etc., wrapped in corn-husks and baked.

1856 OLMSTED *Texas* (Bartl.), This [crowd] attracts a few sellers of whiskey, tortillas, and tamaules. **1860** BARTLETT *Dict. Amer.*, Tamal, or Tamauli. **1884** *Boston* (Mass.) *Jrnl.* 16 Feb. 2/2 A queer article of food, known as 'tamales', is sold in the streets of San Francisco at night by picturesquely clad Spaniards. **1893** KATE SANBORN *Truthf. Wom. S. California* 29 A *tamale* is a curious and dubious combination of chicken hash, meal, olives, red pepper, and I know not what, enclosed in a corn-husk.

‖**tamandua** (tə'mændʊə). Also 7 **tamendoa.** [Pg. *tamandua* (in Gandavo *Historia*, 1576, *tamendoa*), a. Tupi *tamanduà*. (See J. Platt in *Athenæum* 19 Oct., 1901, 525.) So F. *tamandua* (1694 in Hatz.-Darm.), Sp. *tamándoa*.]

†**a.** Originally, a name for the Brazilian ant-eaters generally, including the great ant-eater or ant-bear, *Myrmecophaga jubata* (in Tupi *tamandua guaçu*).

1614 PURCHAS *Pilgrimage* IX. iv. (ed. 2) 835 The Tamendoas are as big as a Ram, with long and sharp snouts, a taile like a squirrell, (twice as long as the body and hairy). **1693** *Phil. Trans.* XVII. 851 The *Tamandua* or Ant-bear.

[1753 CHAMBERS *Cycl. Supp., Tamandua*,.. called in English the ant-bear, and by the Brasilians *tamandua-guaçu*.] **1774** GOLDSM. *Nat. Hist.* (1776) IV. 338 The larger tamandua, the smaller tamandua, and the ant eater.

b. Now generally restricted by naturalists to the smaller *Tamandua tetradactyla*, and its congeners.

1834 *Penny Cycl.* II. 65/1 The *Tamandua* (*Myrmecophaga tamandua*, Cuvier,) or second species of ant-eater, is an animal much inferior to the great ant-bear in point of size, being scarcely so large as a good-sized cat. **1849** [see next]. **1851** OWEN in *Phil. Trans.* CXLI. 744 In the Tamandua (*Myrmecophaga Tamandua*)..all the cervical vertebræ have spinous processes except the atlas. **1896** *List Anim. Zool. Soc.* 198 *Tamandua tetradactyla*, Tamandua Ant-eater. **1903** *Westm. Gaz.* 17 Feb. 10/2 A new and interesting arrival at the Zoological Gardens is the Tamandua ant-eater,..a native of the forests of tropical America, where it leads an entirely arboreal life.

‖**tamanoir** (tamanwar). [F. corrupt form of Carib *tamanoà*, = Tupi *tamanduà*: see prec.] The French name of the ant-bear: see prec. a.

1785 T. JEFFERSON *Notes on Virginia* vi. 85 Aboriginals of ..America..Tamanoir. **1849** *Sk. Nat. Hist., Mammalia* IV. 212 In the general plan of its osteology the tamandua agrees with the tamanoir, but the bones of the muzzle are shorter than the cranial portion. *Ibid.* 213 In its manners the tamandua agrees with the tamanoir, with this difference, that it often climbs trees.

‖**tamanu** ('tæmənuː). Also **-no.** Tahitian name of the tree *Calophyllum Inophyllum* (see POON *sb.*[1], TACAMAHAC); also *attrib.*, as ***tamanu-resin, -tree.***

1839 T. BEALE *Nat. Hist. Sperm Whale* 349, I..engraved my name in the bark of a large tamanu tree. **1866** *Treas. Bot.*, *Tamanu*, a green heavy resin from the Society Islands, obtained from *Calophyllum Inophyllum*. **1897** *Daily News* 22 Mar. 8/2 The mountain forest of 'tamanu'. **1902** R. LOVETT *Chalmers* v. 142 A fine tamano tree grew close by.

tamarack ('tæməræk). Also 9 **-ac, -ach** (*erron.* **tamarisk**), **tamerack, temerack.** [app. a native Indian name in Canada.] **a.** Any of several North American larches, esp. the red larch, *Larix laricina*; = HACKMATACK. **b.** The shore pine, *Pinus contorta*, or the lodgepole pine, *P.c.* var. *latifolia*, of western North America; also, the timber of any of these trees.

1805 W. CLARK *Jrnl.* 14 Sept. in *Orig. Jrnls. Lewis & Clark Exped.* (1905) III. 66 The Mountains..thickly Strowed with falling timber & Pine Spruce fur Hackmatak & Tamerack. **1810** F. A. MICHAUX *Histoire des Arbres Forestieres* I. 29 American larch..Hacmatack..Tamarack par les Hollandois du New-Jersey. [*a* **1817** T. DWIGHT *Trav. New Eng.*, etc. (1821) I. 36 Hacmontac, or Tamarisk.] **1817** W. KEYES *Jrnl.* 25 Aug. in *Wisconsin Mag. Hist.* (1920) III. 351 Crossed a large meadow, a temerack swamp &c. **1841** F. COOPER *Deerslayer* xxiii, The tamarack is healthiest in the swamp. **1842** G. BARSTOW *Hist. N. Hampsh.* 453 Boughs of the tamarac and spruce overhang the road. **1855** LONGF. *Hiaw.* VII. 48 Give me of your roots, O Tamarack! **1874** COUES *Birds N.W.* 152 Nesting in the tamarack swamps and windfalls of Minnesota. **1894** *Outing* XXIV. 94/1 By vigorous working of three paddles we got up a 'tamarack breeze' that carried us rapidly along. **1947** R. PEATTIE *Sierra Nevada* 160 Lodgepole pine..is plain tamarack to many Californians. **1979** J. VAN DE WETERING *Maine Massacre* xix. 225 The only decorations, hanging from hooks on the low, handhewn tamarack beams, were tools and weapons.

‖**tamarau** ('tæmərau). Also **tamarao, timarau.** [Native name.] A diminutive black buffalo, *Bubalus mindorensis*, peculiar to the island Mindoro, in the Philippines.

1898 *Guide Mammalia* 68 Attention may likewise be directed to the small Philippine Buffalo.., or Tamarau. **1898** WORCESTER *Philippine Isl.* xvi. 364 We had been tempted to visit the island [Mindoro] by stories of a strange animal called the '*timarau*', which was said to abound in the interior. **1902** *Geogr. Jrnl.* XIX. 622 The Tamarao, the remarkable anoa-like animal peculiar to Mindoro.

tamari (tə'mɑːrɪ). [Jap.] A Japanese variety of rich soy sauce. Freq. *attrib.*, as ***tamari (soy) sauce.***

1977 *Spare Rib* Jan. 36/3 For protein use soya bean paste (miso) or tamari soy sauce. **1978** G. DUFF *Vegetarian Cookbk.* 14 Tamari is the genuine traditional Japanese soy sauce made only by natural methods from a mixture of wheat and whole soya beans. **1981** *Times* 22 Jan. 10/8 Root vegetables can be stir-fried..and flavoured with..soy or tamari sauce.

tamaric, -ice, -i(c)k, obs. forms of TAMARISK.

tamarillo (tæmə'rɪləʊ). *N.Z.* [Artificial name (see quot. 1966); cf. Sp. *tomatillo*, dim. of *tomate* TOMATO.] = *tree tomato* s.v. TOMATO 2 b.

1966 *N.Z. Herald* 6 Sept. 5 The familiar tree tomato will go under the name of tamarillo after January 31, next year. *Ibid.*, It is hoped that export markets for both raw and processed fruit may be more successful with the use of this new, sub-tropical-sounding name. **1969** *N.Z. News* 23 July 4/5 Oranges, lemons,..tamarillos and chinese gooseberries are now in their shortest supply for several years. **1979** *Times* 17 Nov. 26/4 Specialities from New Zealand, including..tamarellos [*sic*].

tamarin ('tæmərɪn). [a. F. *tamarin* (La Condamine 1745), a. native name in the Galibi or Carib dial. of Cayenne.] A name for several species of the genus *Midas* of South American marmosets or squirrel-monkeys.

[**1745** LA CONDAMINE *Relat. Voy. Amér. Mérid.* 165 On les nomme *Pinches* à Maynas, et à Cayenne. *Tamarins*.] **1780** SMELLIE tr. *Buffon's Nat. Hist.* (1791) VIII. 203 *note*, In Cayenne, there are very small monkeys called *tamarins*, which are extremely beautiful. They exceed not the size of a squirrel. **1797** *Encycl. Brit.* (ed. 3) XVII. 500/1 The tamarin, *Sagoinus Midas*, or great-eared monkey. **1854** H. G. DALTON *Brit. Guiana* (1855) II. 452 The Marakina or Silky Tamarin. **1881, 1896** Negro tamarin [see NEGRO 7]. **1882** Red-handed tamarin [see RED-HANDED *a.* 2]. **1899** *Daily News* 21 Nov. 5/1 The exceedingly rare monkey from South America, known as the red-bellied tamarin.

tamarind ('tæmərɪnd). Forms: 6–7 **tamarinde,** 7 **-ynd, tamerind, thamarind,** 8 **tamarinth,** 7– **tamarind;** also 6 (from Pg.) **tamarindo,** *pl.* **-os,** 6–7 (It.) *pl.* **tamarindi,** 7 (from F.) *pl.* **tamarines.** [= Sp., Pg., It. *tamarindo*, med.L. *tamarindus*, ultimately ad. Arab. *tamr-hindī*, i.e. date of India, whence in the early herbalists and physicians *tamar indi*, in Marco Polo (Fr. version) *tamarandi*; in 13th c. F. *tamarindes* pl. (Hatz.-Darm.), mod.F. *tamarin* (15th c. in Hatz.-Darm.).]

1. The fruit of the tree *Tamarindus indica* (see 2), a brown pod containing one to twelve seeds embedded in a soft brown or reddish-black acid pulp, valued for its medicinal qualities, and also used in cookery as a relish, etc. In *Commerce, Med.*, etc. ***tamarinds*** means this pulp.

1533 ELYOT *Cast. Helthe* (1539) 60 Pourgers of choler... Tamarindes, halfe an ounce in a decoction. **1582** N. LICHEFIELD tr. *Castanheda's Conq. E. Ind.* I. xl. 94 They haue greate store of Ginger, Cardamomon, Tamarindos.. and such lyke. **1612** WOODALL *Surg. Mate* Wks. (1653) 165 The Tamarinds brought from the Indies. **1652** FRENCH *Yorksh. Spa* ix. 82 Some Lenitive, as..Manna, Tamarines, ..syrop of Roses. **1732** ARBUTHNOT *Rules of Diet* in *Aliments*, etc. 244 Tamarinds, cooling, astringent, yet laxative to the lower Belly. **1812** J. SMYTH *Pract. of Customs* (1821) 252 The Tamarind is a pod resembling a bean-cod, containing two, three, or four seeds. **1872** OLIVER *Elem. Bot.* II. 166 Tamarinds, as imported, are the pulp of the fruit of *Tamarindus*, preserved in syrup.

2. A large tree, *Tamarindus indica*, N.O. *Leguminosæ*, supposed to be a native of the E. Indies, but now cultivated in warm climates generally, bearing dark-green pinnate leaves and racemes of fragrant yellow flowers streaked with red, and producing the fruit described in 1, also a hard and heavy timber.

1614 PURCHAS *Pilgrimage* V. vii. (ed. 2) 483 Ouer the said Temple grow many Tamarinds. **1698** FRYER *E. India & P.* 126 A Grove of Mangoes and Thamarinds. **1727–46** THOMSON *Summer* 667 Lay me reclined Beneath the spreading tamarind. **1753** HANWAY *Trav.* (1762) I. VII. xcv. 438 A table of tamarinth,..half the diameter of the tree which produced it. **1872** OLIVER *Elem. Bot.* II. 165 The streaked wood of the Tamarind..used in cabinet work.

3. Applied to various trees (or their fruits) which resemble the tamarind in some respect; e.g. in New South Wales and other parts of Australia, a species of *Cupania*; usually with defining words.

bastard tamarind, *Acacia trichophylloides*, of Jamaica (Miller *Plant-n.* 1884). **black, black-crown, brown,** or **velvet tamarind**, a small leguminous tree, *Codarium acutifolium* or *Dialium guineense*: see quots. **Manilla tamarind**: see quot. 1866. **wild tamarind**, applied to various leguminous trees or shrubs, as, in the W. Indies, *Pithecolobium filicifolium*; in Jamaica, *Acacia arborea*; in Trinidad, *Pentaclethra filamentosa* (Miller). **yellow tamarind** of tropical America, *Acacia villosa*.

1833 M. SCOTT *Tom Cringle* vii. (1859) 130 Overshadowed by a magnificent wild Tamarind. **1857** HENFREY *Bot.* 280 The Tamarinds of Sierra Leone,..are species of *Codarium*. **1866** *Treas. Bot.* 898/2 P[*ithecolobium*] *dulce*, a large tree native of the hot regions of Mexico..is now planted..in the Madras Presidency, where the fruit is known as Manilla Tamarinds. *Ibid.* 397/2 D[*ialium*] *acutifolium*, the Velvet Tamarind of Sierra Leone..The pod, about the size and form of a filbert, is covered with a beautiful black velvet down. **1887** MOLONEY *Forestry W. Afr.* 332 Velvet Tamarind of Sierra Leone, Black Tamarind... The pulp surrounding the seeds is pleasantly acid and commonly eaten.

4. *attrib.* and *Comb.*, as ***tamarind-pod, -pot, -pulp, -seed, -stone, -tree***; also **tamarind-fish**, a relish made from various kinds of Indian fish preserved with the acid pulp of the tamarind fruit; †**tamarind-palmetto**, some species of palmetto; **tamarind-plum**, an E. Indian tree, *Dialium indicum*, or its fruit: see quots.; **tamarind tea, tamarind water**, an infusion of tamarinds, used as a cooling drink; **tamarind-whey**: see quot.

1858 SIMMONDS *Dict. Trade*, *Tamarind-fish. **1865** FR. DAY *Fishes Malabar* Introd. 9 The best Tamarind fish is prepared from the Seir fish and from the *Lates calcarifer*. **1698** FRYER *Acc. E. India & P.* 16 [The island of Johanna] The outwart Coat of which is embroidered with *Thamarind Palmetto. **1846** LINDLEY *Veg. Kingd.* 549 *Dialium indicum*, also called the *Tamarind Plum. **1857** HENFREY *Bot.* 280 Besides the Tamarind, other fruits, less acid, are eaten, as the Tamarind Plum. **1866** *Treas. Bot.* 1121/1 The *tamarind-pods imported from the East Indies vary in length from three to six inches, and are slightly curved. They consist of a brittle brown shell, within which is a soft acid brown pulp, traversed by strong woody fibres. **1850** THACKERAY *Pendennis* li, He knew the way to the *tamarind-pots. **1836** BRANDE *Chem.* (ed. 4) Index, *Tamarind pulp, 1062. **1844** H. H. WILSON *Brit. India* II. II. iv. 163 The Hindus endeavoured to appease the cravings of nature with..bruised *Tamarind stones, and the leaves of trees. **1883** *Chambers' Encycl.* IX. 283/1 *Tamarind tea is made by infusing tamarinds in boiling water. **1681** R. KNOX *Hist. Ceylon* IV. i. 118 [He] sat down under a *Tamarind Tree. **1825** *Hone's Every-day Bk.* I. 678 According to some botanists, the tamarind-tree enfolds within its leaves the flowers or fruit every night. **1885–8** FAGGE & PYE-SMITH *Princ. Med.* (ed. 2) I. 150 For beverages he may be allowed to choose among barley-water, toast-and-water, lemonade, *tamarind-water,..and cold weak tea. **1883** *Chambers' Encycl.* IX. 283/1 *Tamarind whey is prepared by boiling one ounce of tamarinds with a pint of new milk, and straining.

†**tamarine.** *Obs. rare*[−1]. Some kind of cloth.

1691 *Lond. Gaz.* No. 2675/4 A Piece of Ash-coloured woolly Tamarine striped with black.

tamarisk ('tæmərɪsk). Forms: α. 5 **thamarike, -yke,** 6 **tamarice,** 6–8 **-ic, -ik, tamerick,** 7 **tamricke.** β. 5–7 (in L. form) **tamariscus,** pl. **-i;** 6– **tamoriscke** 6–7 **tamar-,** 7 **tameriske, tamriske,** 6– **tamarisk.** [ad. late L. *tamariscus* (Palladius), var. of *tamarix, -icem*, whence F. *tamaris* (13th c.), also in 16th c. *tamarisc, tamarix*. Ulterior source of the L. name unknown.]

A plant of the genus *Tamarix*, esp. *T. gallica*, the common tamarisk (called in L. *myrica*, in Gr. μυρίκη), a graceful evergreen shrub or small tree, with slender feathery branches and minute scale-like leaves, growing in sandy places in S. Europe and W. Asia, and now much planted by the seashore in the south of England. Several other species, some with trunks 6 or 7 feet in girth, occur in the Mediterranean region.

German tamarisk, the allied *Myricaria germanica*.

c **1400** *Lanfranc's Cirurg.* 220 Make him a gargarism of liquiricie, yreos, & tamarisci. *c* **1440** *Pallad. on Husb.* XII. 316 Atte gynnyng of this moone, of thamarike And other floures wilde, useth the bee Hony..to pike. **1548** TURNER *Names of Herbes* s.v. *Myrica*, The scholemaisters in Englande haue of longe tyme called myrica heath, or lyng, but so longe haue they bene deceyued al together. It maye be called in englishe, Tamarik. **1562** —— *Herbal* II. 59 Y[e] Cypres tre and the Tamarisk haue carnose or fleshy leues. **1599** HAKLUYT *Voy.* II. I. 165 The Archbishop of Canterburie Edmund Grindall, after he returned out of Germany, brought into this realme the plant of Tamariske from thence. *c* **1611** CHAPMAN *Iliad* XXI. 18 On the shore, the Worthy hid, and left his horrid lance Amids the Tamriskes. **1715–20** POPE *Iliad* VI. 49 His headlong steeds..Rush'd on a tamarisk's strong trunk, and broke The shatter'd chariot from the crooked yoke. **1794** MRS. RADCLIFFE *Myst. Udolpho* iv, They sauntered over hillocks covered with lavender, wild thyme, juniper, and tamarisk. **1827** *Gentl. Mag.* XCVII. II. 34 Say, wilt thou court the tamarisk's lowly shade, And tune to strains of love thy dulcet reed? **1864** GILBERT & CHURCHILL *Dolomite Mount.* 68 Clumps of alder and willow, interspersed with bushes of the tamarisk (*Myricaria germanica*).

†**b.** A decoction or other preparation of the leaves of this plant, formerly used in medicine. *Obs.*

1579 LANGHAM *Gard. Health* (1633) 627 Tamariske: it is a medicine of excellent power and vertue against the stopping & hardnes of the milt, if it be but drunke out of, being made into a vessell to drinke it. **1621** BURTON *Anat. Mel.* II. iv. I. v. (1651) 374 The wines ordinarily used to this disease are Wormewood-wine, Tamarisk and Buglossatum. **1718** QUINCY *Compl. Disp.* 139 Tamarisk..attenuates, opens and absterges.

c. *attrib.* and *Comb.*, as ***tamarisk-bough, -branch, -bush, -jungle, -stem, -tree, -twig; tamarisk-fringed, -grown*** adjs.; **tamarisk salt**, salt found adhering to the trunk of *Tamarix orientalis* in edible quantity (*Cent. Dict.*); hence ***tamarisk-salt-tree***; **tamarisk ware**, vessels or dishes made from the wood of the tamarisk.

c **1611** CHAPMAN *Iliad* X. 395 He hung them vp aloft, vpon a *Tamricke bow. **1863** M. L. WHATELY *Ragged Life Egypt* xx. 202 The school-room had been swept neatly and decorated with tamarisk-boughs and a few flowers. **1816** H. G. KNIGHT *East. Sk.* Pref. (1830) 36 *Tamarisk bushes, stunted acacia trees,..complete the produce of the choicest spots in the Deserts [of Arabia]. **1899** F. C. GOULD in *Westm. Gaz.* 6 Sept. 1/3 The *tamarisk-fringed white-dusted road. **1712** tr. *Pomet's Hist. Drugs* I. 64 From this Wood is made a white Chrystal Salt, called *Tamarisk Salt. **1578** LYTE *Dodoens* VI. xv. 677 Swine which haue bene dayly fedde out of a trough..made of *Tamarisk tree or timber, haue bene seene to haue no milt at al. [Cf. PLINY *N.H.* 24. 9. 41.] *c* **1611** CHAPMAN *Iliad* VI. 37 Low-growne Tamricke trees. **1876** *Oxford Bible-Helps* 116 Of the tamarisk-tree seven species exist in Palestine. **1614** PURCHAS *Pilgrimage* IV. vii. (ed. 2) 371 Muttering their prayers, holding a bundle of small *Tameriske-twigs. **1712** tr. *Pomet's Hist. Drugs* I. 64 They..make little Casks, Cups, and Dishes of it, which are call'd *Tamarisk Ware.

¶ Erron. used for TAMARACK, q.v. (quot. *a* 1817).

tamarugite (tə'mæruːgaɪt). *Min.* ['f. the pampas del Tamarugal' (Chester); see -ITE[1] 2 b.] Hydrous sulphate of aluminium and sodium; a sodium alum.

1890 *Amer. Jrnl. Sci.* Ser. III. XL. 258 One of these [sulphates] is *tamarugite*: this occurs in massive forms, colourless and with a radiated structure.

tamarugo (tæmə'ruːgəʊ). Also *erron.* **tamarugal.** [Chilean Sp.] A small evergreen tree, *Prosopis tamarugo*, of the family Leguminosæ, native to the salt deserts of northern Chile and used to provide fodder in arid regions.

1972 *World Crops* XXIV. 297/1 The tamarugal is a thin-branching tree of 20–25 ft average height, yielding a leaf and a seed which are both nutritious and palatable. **1975** *Underexploited Trop. Plants* (Nat. Acad. Sci., U.S.) 128 In salt-devastated regions of suitable climate, tamarugo, an evergreen plant, could become a year-round fodder supply. *Ibid.* 129 Tamarugo pods need extensive leaching before they can be eaten by humans. **1977** *New Scientist* 17 Mar. 638/1 The leguminous tamarugo tree from Chile..can supply forage in dry, salty regions. **1980** *Times* 5 June 26/9 Where few economic plants could grow, the Tamarugo flourishes and provides good fodder all the year round.

‖**tamasha** (tə'mɑːʃə). *East Ind.* Also †**tomasha, -shaw, -sia,** †**tumasha.** [a. Arab., Pers., Urdū *tamāʃā* walking about for recreation or amusement, an entertainment, f. 6th conj. of *maʃa(y)* to walk.]

1. An entertainment, show, display, public function.

1623 in Foster *Eng. Factories Ind.* (1908) II. 274 Nothing done more then a tomashaw. [**1687** A. LOVELL tr. *Thevenot's Trav.* II. 90 They stop at the meanest thing, to do that which they call *Tamacha*, (that's to say,) to consider and admire it.] **1698** FRYER *Acc. E. India & P.* 159 Two Englishmen were come to the Tomasia or Sight. **1863** TREVELYAN *Compet. Wallah* (1866) 104 He had invited all the English residents to a grand tumasha at his camp. **1872** MRS. VALENTINE *Let.* in *Mem.* viii. (1882) 135 The usual tamashas went on. **1888** *United Presbyt. Mission. Rec.* Sept. 293 They had appointed pioneers to discover what the tomasha was to be. **1889** *Pall Mall G.* 9 May 7/1 The people say to the Christian missionaries: 'Yours is a very dull religion; there is not enough tamasha (that is, show or function) about it'. **1892** *Sat. Rev.* 18 June 700/2 That very funny tamasha which is called a Convention in American politics. **1904** *Blackw. Mag.* June 835, I thought the tamasha had begun and turned out to look. **1906** *Athenæum* 26 May 635/1 The serious business of life..at..Khapallu..seems to be polo and tamashas.

2. *transf.* A fuss, a commotion.

1882 F. M. CRAWFORD *Mr. Isaacs* x. 213 Mr. Ghyrkins.. wanted to know 'what the deuce all this *tamāsha* was about'. **1923** KIPLING *Land & Sea Tales* 226 Why is there this *tamasha* (fuss)? **1964** A. SWINSON *Six Minutes to Sunset* ii. 24 Stewart..asked 'What's all the *tamasha* about?' **1981** S. RUSHDIE *Midnight's Children* I. 30 Enough of this tamasha! No more of this..tomfoolery!

Tamashek ('tæməʃɛk). Also **Tamachek.** [Berber: see quot. 1896.] The Berber language spoken by the Tuaregs.

1885 *Encycl. Brit.* XVIII. 778/2 The principal dialects [of Berber] are the Kabyle, the Shilha, and the Tuarek or Tamashek, corresponding nearly to the ancient Numidian, Mauretanian and Gætulian respectively. **1896** A. H. KEANE *Ethnol.* xiv. 384 This word [sc. *Tamahu*] still exists under various dialectic forms (*Tamaheeg, Tamashek, Tamazigt*) applied collectively to the Hemitic languages of the Sahara and Mauritania. The form T-amazig-t, when stripped of its fem. prefix and postfix particle *t*, is seen to be identical with the *Maxyes* of Herodotus (later *Masices, Mazices*), i.e. Amzigh, pl. Imazighen, 'freemen', the most general name of the Mauritanian Berbers. **1908** T. G. TUCKER *Introd. Nat. Hist. Lang.* 173 Thus old Egyptian *annuk*.. = 'I', for which the Berber Tamashek has *nek*... 'He' is an old Egyptian *entuf*, in Tamashek it is *enta*. *Ibid.* 174 Berber languages are still spoken in the Western Sahara (where is to be found the *Tamashek*, which is usually treated as the most representative dialect). **1974** *Encycl. Brit. Macropædia* VIII. 596/2 Tamashek has several verbal tenses. **1978** D. BAGLEY *Flyaway* xiii. 94 Assekrem is a Tamachek word—it means, 'The End of the World'.

‖**tambac,** a native Indian name of agalloch or aloes wood.

1727–51 CHAMBERS *Cycl.* s.v. *Aloes*, The heart, or innermost part [of Aloes] called *tambac*..is more valued by the Indians than gold itself.

tambac, tambayack, obs. var. TOMBAC.

‖**tambagut** ('tæmbəgʌt). [Native name, from its cry, in the Philippines.] The Crimson-breasted Barbet of the Philippines (*Megalæma hæmacephala*). (*Cent. Dict.*)

tambala (tæm'bɑːlə). Also **tambola**; pl. **tambala, -s.** [Nyanja, lit. 'cockerel'.] A currency unit in Malawi, equal to 1/100 of a kwacha. Also, a coin of this value.

1970 *Compton Yearbk.* 188 Malawi's decimal currency was to be introduced in March 1971; the new unit, the kwacha, is divided into 100 tambolas. **1970** *Whitaker's Almanack 1971* 982 Malawi. *Malawi Kwacha* of 100 *Tambala* (from Feb. 15, 1971)... [Coins] *Tambala* 20, 10, 5, 2, 1. **1983** *Times* 19 Dec. 11/2 The Africans think we're mad ..but really it wouldn't seem right without..the five-tambala pieces in the pudding.

†**Tambaroora** (tæmbə'rʊərə). *Austral. Obs.* The name of a town in New South Wales, used to designate a bar game in which the winner buys drinks for the players. Also in *Comb.*, as *Tambaroora muster*.

1882 A. J. BOYD *Old Colonials* 63 It may be that the exciting game of Tambaroora is not familiar to all my readers... Each man of a party throws a shilling, or whatever sum may be mutually agreed upon, into a hat. Dice are then produced, and each man takes three throws. The Nut who throws highest keeps the whole of the subscribed capital, and out of it pays for the drinks of the rest. The advantage of the proceeding lies in this: Where drinks are charged at sixpence, the subscription is double that amount for each... Thus if ten Nuts go in for a Tambaroora, with nobblers at sixpence, the winner pockets five shillings by the transaction. **1895** C. CROWE *Austral. Slang Dict.* 84 *Tambaroora*, a game of a shilling each in the hat and the winner shouts. **1897** *Bulletin* (Sydney) 18 Dec. (Red Page), The essence of a present-day tambaroora is a sweep for the purchase of drinks—frequently on the principle that more liquor can be purchased wholesale for 1s. 6d. than six thirsty people can buy for 3d. each. Hence 'tambaroora muster', when the droughty party musters all the coin it's possessed of, and one individual goes and bargains for the beer. **1901** *Bulletin Reciter* (Sydney) 202 (*poem-title*) Tambaroora. **1945** BAKER *Austral. Lang.* ix. 172 Just as the *shout* is an institution in this part of the world so are the..*Tambaroora muster* and a few other variations on the theme, all of which concern the creation of a jack-pot, usually with the object of buying drinks. The *Tambaroora* —taken from the name of an eastern township—dates from the early 1880s. The idea behind these expressions..is that everyone pays for himself.

tamber ('tæmbə(r)). Phonetic respelling of TIMBRE *sb.*[3], used *spec.* in *Linguistics*.

[**1920** *S.P.E. Tract* III. 11 Our English form of the French sound of the word would be approximately *tamber*; and this would be not only a good English-sounding word like *amber* and *clamber*, but would be like our *tambour*, which is *tympanum*, which again is *timbre*.] **1923** *Ibid.* XII. 60 Those enchanting qualities, the rhythm, the phrasing, the tamber, and accent of the living voice. **1937** J. R. FIRTH *Tongues of Men* iii. 36 In chiming reduplications you get..likeness of repeated articulation with difference of vowel quality or *tamber difference*—e.g., *see-saw*. **1950** D. JONES *Phoneme* iii. 12 An alphabetic system of phonetic transcription consists of letters representing sound-qualities (tambers) or phonemes. **1973** J. C. WELLS *Jamaican Pronunc. in London* iv. 56 The tamber of nonprevocalic /l/ has been shown only when 'dark'. *Ibid.* 130 Chomsky and Halle call this feature 'tense' rather than 'long', thereby emphasizing the tamber differences.

tamberbase: see TAMBOUR *sb.* 1 b.

Tamberlaine, -lane: see TAMERLANE.

'**tambo**[1]. [Negro abbrev. of *tambourine*: cf. BANJO.] The tambourine-player in a negro minstrel troupe. Also, the tambourine played by such a musician.

1848 *New Negro Forget-me-not Songster* 32 We plaid dis song, 'on de banjo', Wid de fiddle and de bones, and ole tambo. **1870** T. A. BROWN *Hist. Amer. Stage* 70/1 George Christy took the bone end, with Lansing Durand as tambo. **1884** *Sat. Rev.* 7 June 740/1 A single row of negro minstrels seated on chairs..at the ends are Bones and Tambo. **1952** [see QUILL *sb.*[1] 1 c]. **1958** P. OLIVER in *Decca Bk. Jazz* i. 22 The 'nigger minstrel' troupes comprising banjo players and 'end men' playing 'tambo and bones' being popular in the North throughout the nineteenth century.

‖**tambo**[2] ('tæmbəʊ). [Sp., ad. Quechua *tampu* wayside hostelry.] In the Andean countries, esp. Peru, a lodging house or inn.

1830 E. TEMPLE *Trav. Var. Parts Peru* ii. 65, I went from *tambo* to *tambo* in search of a lodging. **1854** W. L. HERNDON *Amazon* I. 60 We stopped at four, at the tambo of Acchahuarcu. **1902** *Encycl. Brit.* XXV. 377/1 One of the most interesting topics of study is the trails along which the seasonal and annual migrations of tribes occurred, becoming in Peru the paved road, with suspension bridges and wayside inns or tambos. **1959** G. WOODCOCK *Incas & Other Men* I. iii. 45 Primitive shelters, still called tambos, which were maintained..where no hotels existed. **1978** D. P. WERLICH *Peru* ii. 36 The Incas constructed granaries to supply the army..and maintained *tambos* to serve travellers.

Tamboekie, var. TAMBOUKI *sb.* and *a.*

tamboetie, var. TAMBOTI(E.

tambola, var. TAMBALA.

tamboo[1] (tæm'buː). *Mil. slang.* Also **tambu.** [ad. Pers., Hindi *tambū* tent.] In the war of 1914–18, a temporary rough shelter in a trench.

1916 *Sphere* 19 Feb. 188 b/1 The 'Tamboo', as the sleeping apartment [in a dug-out] is called. **1918** W. OWEN *Let.* 28 Sept. (1967) 579 Am still sitting on straw under our Tamboo, for it is raining again. *Ibid.* 10 Oct. 582 The corrugated iron wall of my Tamboo. *Ibid.* 31 Oct. 591 My servant & I ate the chocolate in the cold middle of last night, crouched under a draughty Tamboo, roofed with planks. **1925** [see BIVVY, BIVY].

tamboo[2] ('tæmbuː). Also **tambou.** [Blend of TAMBO or TAMBOUR *sb.* + BAMBOO *sb.*] In full *tamboo-bamboo*. In the West Indies, a small drum made of bamboo. Freq. *attrib.* Hence **tamboo-bamboolst,** one who plays the tamboo.

1942 H. C. GORDON *West Indian Scenes* II. iii. 57 The chief of these [instruments] for beating time was the *tambou*, a small drum. **1955** *New Commonwealth* 28 Nov. Suppl. p. xviii/2 They were not..allowed to make tambour (tamboo) bamboo bands. **1956** *Caribbean Q.* IV. III. & IV. 195 Five to twenty stickmen formed a band..accompanied by drummers and/or tamboo bamboo bands. **1959** W. A. SIMMONDS '*Pan*'—*Story of Steelband* 8 'Hell-yard', traditional headquarters of the Tamboo-bambooists of downtown Port-of-Spain. **1960** *Times* 17 Sept. 7/6 The three major influences on the development of the modern steel orchestra of Trinidad are the 'tamboo-bamboo' drum, the 'bottle and spoon', and the Indian drum and music of the Hosein festival. *Ibid.*, The tamboo-bamboo requires careful fashioning.

tamboo, variant of TABOO.

Tambookie, var. TAMBOUKI *sb.* and *a.*

tamboora, var. TAMBOURA.

tambor ('tæmbə(r)). [var. of TAMBOUR *sb.*]

a. See TAMBOUR *sb.* 3. **b.** *tambor-oil*: see quot.

1890 BILLINGS *Nat. Med. Dict.*, *Tambor oil*, an oil obtained from the seeds of *Omphalea oleifera*..of Central America; said to be purgative without griping.

tamboritsa, var. TAMBURITZA.

tamboti(e (tæm'buːtɪ). *S. Afr.* Also **tamboetie, tambootie,** etc. [ad. Xhosa *um-Thombothi*.]

1. A deciduous tree, *Spirostachys africana*, of the family Euphorbiaceæ, native to southern Africa and with dark, rough bark and short spikes of tiny flowers. Freq. *attrib.*

1852 J. S. CHRISTOPHER *Natal* 32 The yellow, assegai, iron,..and Tamboote wood, grow in abundance. **1859** R. J. MANN *Colony of Natal* 157 A dark brown, very hard wood, distinguished by the Kafirs as 'tamboti-wood'..is employed in the construction of axles. **1871** J. MACKENZIE *Ten Years N. Orange River* xxiv. 460 The tall and resinous tambootie tree, which I selected for beams and rafters, was easily split. **1951** *Cape Argus* 27 Oct. (Mag. Sect.) 2/4 Our site was pitched in the shade of a glorious tambotie tree. **1963** H. C. BOSMAN *Unto Dust* 43 Inside were tamboetie wood trestles for the coffins. **1973** PALMER & PITMAN *Trees S. Afr.* II. 1157 The tamboti is widely known for three reasons—its fine wood, its toxic properties, and its 'jumping beans'.

¶**2.** *tambotie grass* = *tambouki grass* s.v. TAMBOUKI *a.*

1866 T. GEAST *S. Afr. Diaries* 42, I observed that almost every stem of the long tambootie grass had a silken filament flying from it. **1899** ALICE WERNER *Capt. of Locusts*, etc. 80 Open glades with bushes and clumps of tambootie-grass scattered about. **1939** tr. *E. N. Marais's My Friends the Baboons* iii. 31 The footpath here passed through a stretch of high tambotie grass.

tambou, var. TAMBOO[2].

Tambouki (tæm'buːkɪ), *sb.* and *a.* Also **Tamboekie, Tambookie, Tambuki,** etc., and with small initial. [S. Afr. Du., f. *Tembu*, tribal name + dim. ending *-kje*.]

†**A.** *sb.* The Tembu people. Cf. TEMBU *sb. Obs.*

1786 G. FORSTER tr. *Sparrman's Voy. Cape of Good Hope* II. 147 On the other side of Zomo dwells another nation, who, by the Snese-Hottentots, are called Tambukis. **1792** E. RIOU tr. *J. van Reenan's Jrnl. Journey from Cape of Good Hope* 24 The country of the Tamboekies. *Ibid.* 42 The country of Captain Joobie the Tambookie. **1801** J. BARROW *Trav. Interior S. Afr.* I. iii. 201 With the Tambookies they live on friendly terms. **1824** [see AMAPONDO]. **1874** *Friend* (Bloemfontein) 2 Apr., We were not sure but that the Tambookies would join the confederacy against us. **1902** *Encycl. Brit.* XXX. 3/1 The Ama-Tembu nation, popularly called Tambookies.

B. *adj.* †**1.** Designating or pertaining to the Tembu people. *Obs.* Cf. TEMBU *a.*

1827 G. THOMPSON *Trav. S. Afr.* (ed. 2) II. 336 The *Tambookie* or *Amatymba* tribe. **1835** N. ADAMS *Let.* 5 June in D. J. Kotzé *Lett. Amer. Missionaries* (1950) 75 There is a good waggon road to Natal through the Tambookie country. **1846** J. C. BROWN tr. *Arbousset & Daumas's Explor. Tour N.E. Colony Cape of Good Hope* xii. 93 Lekoro..undertook a military expedition to the Tambuqui country. **1860** W. SHAW *My Mission in S.E. Afr.* 486 The Rev. John Ayliff, the resident Missionary, was constrained to escape with his family, accompanied by the native inhabitants of the Mission village, and take refuge in the Tembookie country. **1875** *Handbk. S. Afr.* (S.W. Silver & Co.) 460 *Tambookieland*, the country formerly inhabited by the Tambookie tribes of Kaffirs.

2. Of or belonging to Tembu-land, as in *tambouki grass*, one of several tall coarse grasses of southern Africa, esp. one of the genus *Cymbopogon* or *Hyparrhenia*; *tambouki wood*, tamboti wood (see TAMBOTI(E 1).

1837 J. KIRKMAN in F. Owen *Diary* (1926) 158 The mother and child had hidden under the long Tambookie grass. **1858** SIMMONDS *Dict. Trade*, *Tambookie-wood*, a hard handsome furniture-wood: when powdered it is used by the Zulus of Africa as an emetic. **1885** RIDER HAGGARD *K. Solomon's Mines* iv, Dry tambouki grass..is made into a bed. **1905** *Blackw. Mag.* Sept. 382/1 [The grass] was dashed aside by some large object that came rapidly towards him, but was concealed beneath the long tambouki. **1910** J. BUCHAN *Prester John* xiv. 230, I was..into a piece of parkland with long, waving tambuki grass. **1963** H. C. BOSMAN *Unto Dust* 119 Her hair was bleached the yellow of tamboekie grass in winter.

tambour ('tæmbʊə(r), -bə(r)), *sb.* [a. F. *tambour* drum: see TABOR.]

1. a. A drum; *spec.* the great or bass drum.

1484 CAXTON *Fables of Æsop* (1889) 95 Of his skynne he dyd doo make tambours, whiche ben euer bete. **1706** PHILLIPS (ed. 6), *Tambour*, a Drum, an Instrument of Martial Musick. **1745** POCOCKE *Descr. East* II. I. xvi. 156 One of them played on a tambour, and sung a Curdeen song. **1810** SOUTHEY *Kehama* I. xiv, And still with overwhelming din The tambours and the trumpets sound. **1812** —— *Lett.* (1856) II. 307 A tambour is an outlandish drum, not such as soldiers use. **1879** STAINER *Music of Bible* 140 As they [cymbals] became reduced in size it was found possible to insert several pairs under the rim of the tambour.

‖**b. tambour de basque** (also 7 **tamber de base, tamberbase,** 9 **tamborbasque**) [F. *tambour de basque*, †*de Biscaye*], a tambourine.

1688 R. Holme *Armoury* III. xvi. (Roxb.) 85/1 He beareth sable, a Tamber de Base, or Tamber-base, Or... This is a kind of Instrument, vsed among the auncient Jews, and now by the Turkes. **1780** Beckford *Italy* (1834) I. iv. 34 *Tambours de basque* at every corner. **1840** *Encycl. Brit.* (ed. 7) XXI. 72/2 *Tambour de Basque*, a well-known kind of small drum, commonly called a tambourine. It is much used among the Biscayans.

2. An instrument for recording pulsations, as in respiration: see quots.

1877 Foster *Phys.* I. iv. §2 Each bag communicates by a separate air-tight tube with an air-tight tambour on which a lever rests; so that any pressure on either bag is communicated to the cavity of its respective tambour, the lever of which is raised in proportion. *Ibid.* II. ii. §1 The movements of the column of air in the trachea are transmitted to the tambour, the consequent expansions and contractions of which are transmitted by means of a lever resting on it to the recording drum. **1890** Billings *Nat. Med. Dict.*, *Tambour*, drum; used to collect and transmit movements in graphic registering apparatus.

3. (Also **tambor.**) A fish which makes a drumming noise, or which resembles a drum in form; as a fish of the genus *Pogonias*, a drum-fish; a globe-fish, swell-fish, or puffer; also the red rock-fish, *Sebastodes ruber*, of the coast of California.

[**1683-4** Robinson in *Phil. Trans.* XXIX. 480 Many Tamburo's or Drum-Fishes.] **1854** Bushnan in *Orr's Circ. Sc.* I. *Org. Nat.* 151 The pogonias, on account of the sounds which it produces, has been named the tambour. **1891** *Cent. Dict.*, Tambor.

4. a. A circular frame formed of one hoop fitting within another, in which silk, muslin, or other material is stretched for embroidering. Cf. tambouring-*machine*.

1777 Sheridan *Sch. Scand.* II. i, When I saw you first sitting at your tambour, in a pretty figured linen gown. **1781** Mme. D'Arblay *Diary* Mar., Portraits of the three beautiful Lady Waldegraves,..at work with the tambour. **1818** Todd, *Tambou'r*. **1841** Borrow *Zincali* I. viii. §1. 131 Intertwining with their sharp needles the gold and silk on the tambour.

b. A species of embroidery in which patterns are worked with a needle of peculiar form on material stretched in a tambour-frame; now superseded by pattern-weaving; in recent use = *tambour-lace*: see 8.

1813 *App. to Chron.* in *Ann. Reg.* 252/1 A bounty upon the exportation of stuffs, of silk ornamented with embroidery, tambour, needle work, lace or fringe. **1859** Green *Oxf. Stud.* ii. §7 (O.H.S.) 94 A French master of tambour and similar accomplishments. **1883** *Standard* 26 June 3/3 The.. Limerick production is of four kinds: Tambour, the simplest and commonest. **1898** *Cent. Mag.* Jan. 365/1 My sisters and I covered it [the frock] with embroidered buds and roses, done in tambour. **1908** *Westm. Gaz.* 25 Apr. 13/2 Then there is the imitation of old Tambour.

c. A kind of fine gold or silver thread.

1848 [see passing *vbl. sb.* 3]. **1899** W. G. P. Tounsend *Embroidery* v. 82 Gold and Silver Passing and Tambour.—Fine kind of threads. *Ibid.* vi. 106 How tambour gold is used over cardboard. **1901** Day & Buckle *Needlework* xxix. (ed. 2) 245 For stitching through, there is a finer [gold] thread, called 'tambour'.

5. *Arch.* **a.** The core of a Corinthian or Composite capital. **b.** Any one of the courses forming the shaft of a cylindrical column. **c.** The wall of a circular building surrounded with columns. **d.** A round exterior building surrounding the base of a dome or cupola; also the circular vertical part of a cupola. **e.** A lobby or vestibule enclosed with folding doors and ceiling, as within the porch of a church, to prevent the direct passage of air, etc. **f.** A projecting part of the wall of a tennis court: see quot. 1816.

1706 Phillips (ed. 6), *Tambour*... In Architecture, the Vase or Ornament in the Chapiter of Pillars of the Corinthian Order: Also the Name of part of a Tennis-Court. **1727-41** Chambers *Cycl.*, *Tambour*, in architecture,.. applied to the Corinthian and Composite capitals, as bearing some resemblance to a drum... *Tambour* is also used for a little box of timber-work, covered with a cieling, withinside the porch of certain churches... *Tambour* also denotes a round course of stone, several whereof form the shaft of a column, not so high as a diameter. **1816** *Encycl. Perth.* XXII. 220/2 On the right hand side of the [tennis] court from the dedans is the tambour, a part of the wall which projects, and is so contrived in order to make a variety in the stroke. **1823** P. Nicholson *Pract. Build.* Gloss., *Tambour*, ..also the wall of a circular temple, surrounded with columns. **1838** *Civil Eng. & Arch. Jrnl.* I. 338/2 An iron clamp was fastened on the shoulder of the capital, and another on the lowest tambour of the column. **1841** *Penny Cycl.* XX. 73/1 If the dome [of the Pantheon] had sprung immediately from the upper cornice, so as to present a perfect hemisphere on the outside, the rotunda itself would have looked merely as a tambour to it. **1864** *Athenæum* 27 Feb. 304/2 Above the roofs will rise (in the centre) a bold tambour pierced with windows and inclosing the lower portion of the dome.

6. *Mil.* A small defensive work formed of palisades or earth, usually in the form of a redan, to defend an entrance or passage.

1834 J. S. Macaulay *Field Fortif.* 91 These small redoubts or tambours, though weak in themselves, are of use when nothing better can be done. *Ibid.* 140 Tambours are constructed with timbers 10 feet long, and about 6 inches square, which are planted touching each other, and sunk 3 feet into the earth. **1853** Stocqueler *Milit. Encycl.*, *Tambour*,..a work formed..so that, when finished, it may have the appearance of a square redoubt cut in two... Tambours are also solid pieces of earth which are made in that part of the covert-way that is joined to the parapet. **1895** *Chapters in Adventurous Life* 340 There was a chapel of St. George some little distance inland of this point, around which a tambour of loose stones had been raised.

7. A sliding, flexible shutter or door on a piece of furniture, made by sticking narrow strips of wood to a backing of canvas.

1940 *Chambers' Techn. Dict.* 833/1 *Tambour* (*Furn.*), a panel of slat-work or pleated textile material. **1952** J. Gloag *Short Dict. Furnit.* 469 The tambour is used for desk tops and occasionally for doors. **1970** D. Ash *Dict. Eng. Antique Furnit.* 147/1 Tambours were introduced from France where they had been in use since about 1750, and were chiefly popular in England in the last quarter of the 18th century.

8. *attrib.* and *Comb.*, as (in sense 1) ***tambour-peal***; (in sense 4) ***tambour-cotton, -embroidery, -school, -sprig, -waistcoat, -work, -worker***; (in sense 7) ***tambour construction, cupboard, desk, door, front, shutter, slide, top, writing-table***; ***tambour-fronted*** adj.; also **tambour-frame**, = sense 4; **tambour hook** = *tambour needle*; **tambour-lace**, a modern lace resembling tambour (4 b), consisting of needlework designs on machine-made net; **tambour-needle**, the needle used in tambour-work, a small steel hook set in a handle; **tambour-stitch**, the loop-stitch used in tambour-work; also a stitch used in crochet, by which a pattern of ridges intersecting at right angles is produced; so **tambour-stitcher**.

1934 *Burlington Mag.* Sept. 213/2 The origin of the *tambour construction of doors, roll-tops, etc., which appeared in Europe about the middle of the eighteenth century; the bamboo sticks were split and the halves fastened on a piece of strong canvas, the whole being fitted into grooves. **1918** *Heal & Son Catal.: Cottage Furnit.* 26 Mahogany Inlaid Sideboard, bow front with *tambour cupboard in centre. **1797** *Prices Cabinet Work* 57 A *Tambour Desk, Three feet long, four long drawers in front. **1803** T. Sheraton *Cabinet Dict.* 316 *Tambour doors are often introduced, in small pieces of work, where no great strength or security is requisite, as in night tables, and pot cupboards. **1973** 'K. Royce' *Spider Underground* ix. 139 The room was a library with an incongruous television set in one corner... Tambour doors were pulled across the ugly eye of the screen. **1781** in H. M. Brooks *Olden Time Series* (1886) IV. 52 Isaac Greenwood..makes Flutes,..Tea-Boards, Bottle-Stands, *Tamboy [*sic*] Frames. **1782** J. Byng *Jrnl.* 24 Aug. in *Torrington Diaries* (1934) I. 74 The long gallery is furnish'd with modern frippery, as tambour frames, &c. **1798** Tambour-frame [see *tambour-needle*]. **1803** Mar. Edgeworth *Emilie de Coulanges* (1832) 157 She would rather see Emilie guillotined at once, than condemned..to work like a galley-slave at her tambour-frame for her bread. **1884** *Bookseller* 6 Nov. 1190/1 She.. added to their slender earnings by her skill at the tambour frame. **1952** J. Gloag *Short. Dict. Furnit.* 469 A *tambour front is shown on the Harlequin Table illustrated on page 283. **1979** *Country Life* 30 Aug. 589/1 The compartment below, tambour-fronted, contains two drawers. **1880** L. Higgin *Handbk. Embroidery* v. 52 Irish or Limerick lace.. is made on net in the old tambour frames, and with a *tambour or crochet hook. **1899** *Westm. Gaz.* 28 Dec. 3/2, I would recommend the charming and inexpensive *Tambour lace for this design. **1798** Edgeworth *Pract. Educ.* (1811) I. 103 A lady who is learning to work with a *tambour needle puts her head down close to the tambour frame. **1863** Janet Hamilton *Poems & Ess.* 196 The daughter plied the tambour-needles. **1823** Mrs. Hemans *Siege Valencia* v, The Moor is on his way! With the *tambour-peal and the tecbir-shout. **1799** J. Robertson *Agric. Perth* 382 At Callander the weaving of cotton goods and a *tambour-school have been lately introduced. **1962** *V. & A. Mus. Internat. Art Treasures Exhib.* 18/2 A George III satinwood secretaire bookcase banded with tulip and kingwood..in the centre a writing desk enclosed by a *tambour shutter. **1973** *Country Life* 11 Jan. 91/3 Early-19th-century satinwood bedside cupboard..[with] tambour shutters. **1975** *Ibid.* 9 Oct. (Suppl.) 42/1 Sheraton Period Mahogany Work Table... The top section..is fitted with..two *Tambour slides. **1779** Sheridan *Critic* I. i, Tropes and flowers suit the general coarseness of your style, as *tambour sprigs would a ground of linsey woolsey. *c* **1840** Lady Wilton *Art of Needlework* xx. 317 There are *tambour-stitch, satin—chain—and queen-stitches. **1953** M. Powys *Lace & Lace-Making* xi. 179 The outline may be made with tambour or chain stitch. **1883** *Art Jrnl.* 150/2 Done by Turkish workers, and Chinese and Indian *tambour-stitchers. **1797** *Prices Cabinet Work* 57 A Library Writing Table with *Tambour Top. **1944** G. Heyer *Friday's Child* vi. 68 They laid the foundations of their future home by purchasing..a tambour-top writing-table, a crystal lustre, and a shaving-stand. **1778** Mme. D'Arblay *Diary* 23 Aug., A *tambour waistcoat, worked in green silk. **1806-7** J. Beresford *Miseries Hum. Life* (1826) II. Sigh xiii, After having consumed three years on a piece of *tambour-work. **1879** *Temple Bar Mag.* Oct. 218 Her needle went to and fro through her tambour work. **1780** *Chron.* in *Ann. Reg.* 201/2 They were *tambour workers. **1794** *Cabinet Maker & Upholsterer's Guide* (ed. 3) pl. 69 (*caption*) *Tambour Writing Table and Bookcase.

tambour ('tæmbʊə(r), tæm'bʊə(r)), *v.* [f. prec. sb.]

1. *trans.* To work or embroider in a tambour-frame; to ornament with tambour-work.

1774 *Westm. Mag.* II. 166 The waistcoats tamboured with coloured silks only, or interspersed with gold and silver. **1840** Mrs. Gaugain *Lady's Assist. Knitting*, etc. I. 189 Join it up..by tambouring it together about 2¼ inches at each side, and draw it up at each end. **1885** *Birmingham Daily Post* 5 Jan. 6/6 Some [fabrics] are embossed, and some tamboured in gold, or otherwise treated.

fig. **1830** *Blackw. Mag.* XXVII. 171 A coarse..web of words..—tamboured with clusters of fantastic figures.

2. *intr.* To work at a tambour-frame; to do tambour-work.

a **1845** Barham *Ingol. Leg.* Ser. III. *Knight & Lady*, She sat herring-boning, tambouring, or stitching. **1863** Janet Hamilton *Poems*, *Tambourer*, She who tambours, tambours, tambours for fifteen hours a day Would have shoes on her feet and dress for church, had she a third of our pay.

Hence **tamboured** *ppl. a.*, ornamented with tambour-embroidery; worked, as a design, on the tambour-frame.

1799 *Hull Advertiser* 30 Nov. 1/1 Some remarkably elegant..tamboured..muslins. **1830** Scott *Demonol.* i. 30 This personage, with tamboured waistcoat. **1885** *Manch. Exam.* 2 Mar. 4/6 Business..in tamboured cloths for Spain is also dull.

‖**tamboura** ('tæmbərə, tæm'bʊərə). Also 6 **tambora**, 7 **tamera**, 9 **tumboora**, **tamboora**, **tambur(a)**, **tanpoora**, etc. [app. ad. Pers. *ṭanbūr*, Arab. *ṭunbūr*, in same sense.]

a. A long-necked lute of the Near East and Balkans, with a pear-shaped body and a fretted neck. Cf. pandora[2], tamburitza.

1585 T. Washington tr. *Nicholay's Voy.* III. i. 69 b, A thing very like vnto a Cittern, which they call Tambora. **1662** J. Davies tr. *Olearius' Voy. Ambass.* 276 He would needs play on the *Tamera*,..an Instrument us'd by the Persians instead of the Lute. **1828** *Asiatic Costumes* 13 The tumboora in shape resembles the guitar more than any other instrument. **1909** M. E. Durham *High Albania* vi. 141 A man..came in with a tamboora and played.., his fingers plucking strange trills..from the slim, tinkling instrument. **1937** P. Thornton *Dead Puppets Dance* i. 19, I contented myself with drumming on the floor..and clapping the rhythms of the tambora players. **1975** L. Picken *Folk Musical Instruments of Turkey* III. 220 This orientation.. corresponds to one of the orientations adopted in preparing blocks of wood for Bulgarian *tambura*. **1983** *Listener* 20 Oct. 29/1 Saturday night's programme of Turkish music..was a continuous performance by the burbling, throaty flute called *ney* and the harsh, plucked instrument called the *tanbur*.

b. A long-necked fretless instrument of the lute family with a round body and usu. four wire strings plucked by the fingers, and used to provide a drone accompaniment in Indian music.

1864 Engel *Mus. Anc. Nat.* 51 The tamboura..is at present in use, especially in Persia, Hindoostan, and Asiatic Turkey. **1875** —— *Musical Instruments* v. 47 The Hindus.. have also the divinity Ganesa, the god of Wisdom, who is represented as a man with the head of an elephant, holding a *tamboura* in his hands. **1891** C. R. Day *Music & Mus. Instruments S. India* vii. 103 The vina, the tamburi or tamburu-vina, and the kinneri still remain just as they are described in the ancient books. **1921** H. A. Popley *Mus. India* vii. 110 The *Tambūr* is perhaps the most common stringed instrument in India. **1966** *Punch* 23 Nov. 770/2 The uncanny buzzing drone of a tambura, a four-stringed Indian instrument that looks like a bloated outsize wooden barometer. **1970** *Daily Tel.* 21 Sept. 9/1 She was singing.. meanwhile plucking steadily at the drone-strings of her tanpoora. **1971** *Illustr. Weekly India* 25 Apr. 35/1 With Lata Mangeshkar sitting holding the *tanpura*, these inspirations would be shaped and sung and recorded. **1977** *N.Y. Times Mag.* 4 Dec. 41/3 Ram Dass had disembarked barefoot, wearing a long white robe and carrying a tamboura for chanting. **1980** A. Desai *Clear Light of Day* iv. 178 The *tanpura* player..strummed the *tanpura* strings as if in a mesmerised state. **1981** Ld. Harewood *Tongs & Bones* xvii. 264 He was surrounded by two other vocalists (one also playing the tambura).

tambourer (see the verb). [f. tambour *v.* + -er[1].] One who does tambour-work.

c **1810** Malthus in *Trav. Diaries* (1966) 225 Much deb.[auchery] prevails among the weavers, tambourers and master manufacturers. **1833** Brewster *Nat. Magic* xi. 287 A tambourer of ordinary skill could not..earn more than five or six shillings a week by constant application. **1845** *New Statist. Acc. Scotl.* VI. 294 English women taught the tambourers here the art. **1863** Janet Hamilton *Poems*, *Tambourer*, Still the tambourer bends wearily over the frame.

tambouret ('tæmbʊrɛt). ? *Obs. rare*. Also 7 **tamburet**. [f. tambour + -et[1]: cf. tabouret.]

†**1.** = tabouret 2. *Obs. rare*$^{-1}$.

1658 tr. *Hist. Christina A.Q. of Swedland* II. 75 The tamburet [orig. *tamburetto*], which is a less seat, granted usually by Queenes to Princesses of great quality, was given to the Dutchesses of Ascot, of Auray, and the Princess of Ligni.

2. A small drum; a tabret or taborin. ? *Obs.*

1776 Hawkins *Hist. Music* I. II. ix. 248 The *Tympanum leve*, an instrument yet known by the name of the *Tambouret*. **1839** Adm. Paget *Autobiog.* ii. (1896) 59 This stirring [Bohemian] song, accompanied..with guitars and tambourets.

tambourin (‖tɑ̃burɛ̃, 'tæmbʊrɪn). [mod.F. (Voltaire 1769) = Pr. *tamborin*, It. *tamburino*, dim. of *tambour* drum: the earlier Fr. form down to 1700 was *tabourin*: see taborin.]

1. The long narrow drum or tabor used in Provence (see taborin); applied also to 'a bottle-shaped drum used in Egypt' (*Cent. Dict.*).

1833 Brewster *Nat. Magic* viii. 205 He holds in one hand a flageolet, and in the other the stick with which he beats the *tambourin*. **1907** Rickert *Gold. Hawk* xxxix. 296 The music was pipe and tambourin, of course, how else should one dance in Provence?

2. A Provençal dance, originally accompanied by the tambourin. **b.** A piece of music for such a dance, in duple rhythm and quick time.

1797 *Encycl. Brit.* (ed. 3) XVIII. 305/1 *Tambourin*,.. name of a dance performed on the French stage. The air is lively, and the movements are quick. **1884** W. B. SQUIRE in Grove *Dict. Mus.* IV. 55 *Tambourin*, an old Provençal dance, in its original form accompanied by a Flute and Tambour de Basque [*error for* Tambourin].

Hence **'tambourin** *v.*, to play on the tambourin; **,tambouri'nade** [after *serenade*, etc.; see -ADE], a performance on the tambourin.

1884 J. PAYNE *Tales fr. Arabic* II. 234 They gave not over .. tambourining and piping till the night waned. **1893** E. H. BARKER *Wand. South. Waters* 27 Every morning at five the tailor..awoke the echoes of the gorge with a long and furious tambourinade.

tambourinate (tæmbə'ri:neɪt), *v.* [f. TAMBOURINE *sb.* + -ATE³.] *trans.* To beat (a rhythm) as on a tambourine. (Only in the works of C. Mackenzie.)

1913 C. MACKENZIE *Sinister Street* I. I. iv. 47 He tambourinated upon the window-pane a gay little tune. **1928** —— *Extremes Meet* 63 Waterlow tambourinated with his knuckles on the shop-door the rhythm of the soldier's chorus from *Faust*.

tambourine (tæmbə'ri:n), *sb.* Forms: 6 **tamburin**, 7 **-ine**, **timburine**, 9 **tambourin**, **-borine**, 8- **tambourine**. [app. ad. F. *tambourin*, dim. of *tambour* (see TAMBOURIN), but used not in the sense of that word, but in that of F. *tambour de basque*.]

1. A musical instrument consisting of a wooden hoop having skin or parchment stretched over one side, and pairs of small cymbals, called jingles, placed in slots round the circumference, small bells being sometimes fastened to the edge. It is played by shaking, striking with the knuckles, or drawing the fingers across the parchment.

The earlier names for this or a similar instrument mentioned in the Bible were *timbre* and *timbrel*. It is not clear what Spenser and Jonson meant by *tamburin*, *timburine*; the word was known to Blount 1661 only from Spenser; the modern use was unknown to Bailey, to Johnson, and to Ash (1775); it is certain in quot. 1782; but as it does not agree with that of F. *tambourin* it is difficult to know how it arose.

1579 SPENSER *Sheph. Cal.* June 59, I sawe Calliope wyth Muses moe..Theyr yuory Luyts and Tamburins forgoe. *Ibid.* Gloss., *Tamburines*, an olde kind of instrument, which of some is supposed to be the Clarion. **1637** B. JONSON *Sad Sheph.* I. iii, Though all the Bels, Pipes, Tabors, Timburines ring. **1661** in BLOUNT *Glossogr.* [giving Spenser's gloss]. **1791** WALKER *Dict.*, *Tambarine*, a tabour, a small drum.

1782 W. F. MARTYN *Geog. Mag.* I. 17 The tambourine.. which is well known in the streets of this metropolis,..being a hoop covered with parchment, and furnished with small pieces of metal hanging to the edges of it. **1821** CLARE *Vill. Minstr.* I. 38 To join the dance where gipsy fiddlers play, Accompanied with thumping tambourine. **1884** V. DE PONTIGNY in Grove *Dict. Mus.* IV. 55 *Tambourine* (Fr. *Tambour de Basque*)..consists of a wooden hoop, on one side of which is stretched a vellum head, the other side being open. **1899** KIPLING *Absent-Minded Beggar* i, Will you kindly drop a shilling in my little tambourine For a gentleman in khaki ordered South? [Refers to its use as a collecting dish.]

Comb. **1840** DICKENS *Barn. Rudge* xli, Some black tambourine-player, with a great turban on.

2. tambourine pigeon (also ellipt. *tambourine*): an African species of pigeon, so called from the resonance of its note.

1891 *Cent. Dict.*, Tambourine. **1896** *List Anim. Zool. Soc.* 466 *Tympanistria bicolor*, Tambourine Pigeon.

Hence **tambou'rine** *v. intr.*, to play the tambourine.

1891 *Daily News* 5 Sept. 3/3 The jingle of the tambourining poke-bonnetted lass [i.e. member of the Salvation Army].

tambouring, *vbl. sb.* [f. TAMBOUR *v.* + -ING¹.] The action of the verb TAMBOUR; embroidery done by this method. Also *attrib.*, as ***tambouring-engine***, ***-machine***, a machine for doing this work.

1775 ASH Suppl., *Tambouring*, the act of ornamenting with a kind of particoloured needlework. **1815** SIMOND *Jrnl. Tour Gt. Brit.* I. 285 The tambouring or embroidering mill. **1830** GALT *Lawrie T.* III. i, His wife had been bred to the tambouring. **1833** *Encycl. Brit.* (ed. 7) VII. 407/2 *margin*, Tambouring machine. **1872** *Routledge's Ev. Boy's Ann.* 223/2 The movements of the tambouring engine. **1908** *Daily Chron.* 21 Oct. 7/5 Some of the finer embroidery, called tambouring, is still worked by hand on a frame.

‖**tambreet** (tæm'bri:t). [Mallangong lang. of New South Wales.] A native name of the duckbilled platypus.

1840 *Penny Cycl.* XVII. 28/1 The Duckbill, or Duckbilled Platypus..; Mallangong, Tambreet,..Watermole of the English colonists. **1864** in WEBSTER; and in mod. Dicts.

tambu, var. TAMBOO¹.

Tambuki, var. TAMBOUKI *sb.* and *a.*

tambur(a, var. TAMBOURA.

‖**tamburitza** (tæm'bʊrɪtsə). Also **tamboritsa**, **tamburica**, etc. Pl. **-n**, **-s**. [Serbo-Croat.] A stringed musical instrument of the Balkans resembling a guitar or mandoline. Cf. TAMBOURA a.

1941 N. BESSARABOFF *Anc. Europ. Mus. Instruments* IV. 219 The *Tanbourica*, as used by the southern Slavs, belongs to a family of instruments similar to the Arabian-Persian *tanbur*. **1961** A. BAINES *Mus. Instruments* ix. 212 The pandoura, or 'long-necked' lute, remains a popular instrument from Persia..to the Balkans (*tamboritsa*). **1969** *Daily Tel.* 5 Nov. 13/6 Dancers from the Northern region of Barania..danced with joyful abandon to the music of tamboritzan—plucked instruments resembling guitars and mandolines. **1970** *Daily Colonist* (Victoria, B.C.) 14 Nov. 22/4 She first played on tamburitzas, Balkan instruments made by her father. **1972** DEAN & SMITH *Wisconsin* 32/2 Then the band starts banging on tamburitzas, and the patrons explode into an intricate folk dance. **1972** *Times* 21 Oct. 7/4 A choir sang Slavonian songs accompanied on the national instruments, *brim* and *tamburica*, like small mandolines. **1979** *United States 1980/81* (Penguin Travel Guides) 263 This is a Serbian restaurant where you can dine to the tune of tinkling tamburitzas.

Tamburlain(e: see TAMERLANE.

tame (teɪm), *a.* Forms: 1, 4 **tam**, 3- **tame**, 4-5 *Sc.* **tayme**; 1 **tǫm**, 2-3 **tom**, 4 **tome**. [OE. *tam* (*tǫm*) = OFris. (EFris.) *tam*, OLG. **tam* (MLG., LG., MDu., Du. *tam*), OHG., MHG. *zam* (Ger. *zahm*), ON. *tamr*:—OTeut. **tamo²* (evidenced in Goth. only by the deriv. *vb. tamjan* to tame). The Teut. stem *tam-* is cognate with that of L. *domāre*, Gr. δαμ-ᾶν to tame, subdue. The OE. variant *tǫm* was retained in southern Early ME. down to *c* 1300; the existing *tame* represents the inflected forms of *tam*: cf. also TAME *v.*¹]

1. a. Of animals (rarely of men): Reclaimed from the wild state; brought under the control and care of man; domestic; domesticated. (Opp. to *wild*.)

c **888** K. ÆLFRED *Boeth.* xxxv. §6 Wildu ðior..woldon.. standon swilce hi tame wæron. *c* **1000** ÆLFRIC *Saints' Lives* (1900) II. 326 Se wulf folȝode..swylce he tam wære. *c* **1000** *Ags. Gloss.* in Wr.-Wülcker 481/22 *Subjugalis*, tam. *c* **1250** *Gen. & Ex.* 174 He made on werlde al erue tame. *Ibid.* 1482 Esau wilde man huntere, And Iacob tame man tiliere. *a* **1300** *Cursor M.* 25430 (Cott.) Of al þin sandes wild and tam, Man þou scop and gaf him nam. *c* **1375** *Sc. Leg. Saints* xxix. (*Placidas*) 318 Wyld hors & tayme. **1526** TINDALE *2 Pet.* ii. 16 The tame and dom beast speakynge with mannes voyce. **1653** WALTON *Angler* ii. 44 I'll try if I can make her [a young otter] tame. **1660** F. BROOKE tr. *Le Blanc's Trav.* 166 They have also tame Lions. **1698** FRYER *Acc. E. India & P.* 271 From a Salvage Prince rendred himself a tame Follower of the Patriarch. **1772** PRIESTLEY *Inst. Relig.* (1782) I. 32 Small and tame animals breed fast. **1844** H. H. WILSON *Brit. India* II. 372 The beasts of the forest, or the scarcely tamer human beings. **1859** H. KINGSLEY *G. Hamlyn* xxviii, A tame black belonging to us. He is great at all sorts of hunting.

b. *humorously*, of a person: Domestic; kept or supported for domestic or private use.

1711 ADDISON *Spect.* No. 47 ⁋2 It was formerly the Custom for every great House in England to keep a tame Fool dressed in Petticoats. **1895** *Westm. Gaz.* 13 Mar. 8/1 At the Treasury..A tame bookbinder receives £105 a year. *Mod.* They endow 'tame professors' to advocate their views.

2. a. Applied to plants, also (in *U.S.*) to land: Cultivated, improved by culture; garden- as opposed to *wild*; now restricted to U.S. use.

tame hay, hay made from specially sown grasses or forage plants; cf. *wild hay*. (Western U.S.)

1551 TURNER *Herbal* I. C v b, I haue not sene yet the right tame Anemone. **1562** —— *Herbal* II. 112 Tame or gardin radice. **1578** LYTE *Dodoens* III. lix. 399 The tame Hoppe hath rough branches. **1604** E. G[RIMSTONE] *D'Acosta's Hist. Indies* IV. xxxi. 295 Cherries, both wilde and tame have not prospered well at the Indies. **1629** PARKINSON *Paradisus* (1904) 420 Any Rose either wilde or tame. **1838** H. W. ELLSWORTH *Valley Upper Wabash* iv. 39 It is very desirable ..to get the tame grasses..set as soon as possible. **1857** *Trans. Illinois Agric. Soc.* II. 382 Where tame pasture is resorted to something more needs to be done. **1881** *Rep. Indian Affairs* (U.S.) 107 Some few have raised tame grapes. **1885** tr. *Hehn's Wand. Plants & Anim.* (1887) 94 Herodotus makes the oracle speak of the tame olive. **1887** *Buck's Handbk. Med. Sc.* V. 9/2 The careful pioneer..had his corral..where the land had become 'tame'. **1936** *Sun* (Baltimore) 15 Sept. 26/8 Tame hay production..is estimated at 355,000 tons. **1962** A. FRY *Ranch on Cariboo* x. 106 In conjunction with his store, he..put up a big field of good tame hay. **1976** *Billings* (Montana) *Gaz.* 20 June 8-D/8 (Advt.), 320 acres, 148 tillable now in tame grass.

fig. **1855** THACKERAY *Newcomes* xlviii, His lordship sowed tame oats now after his wild ones.

3. a. Having the disposition or character of a domesticated animal; accustomed to man; not showing the natural shyness, fear of, or fierceness to man; familiar; also of persons, their disposition, etc.: made tractable, docile, or pliant.

c **888** K. ÆLFRED *Boeth.* xxv. §1 Seo leo, ðeah hio wel tam se. *a* **1000** *Gnom. Verses* 142 Til mon tiles & tomes meares. *a* **1225** *Ancr. R.* 144 Noðing ne awildeð wilde uleschs ne ne makeð hit tommure þen deð muche wecche. *a* **1225** *Leg. Kath.* 1318 þet he ne talde him al tom ear he turnde from us. *a* **1250** *Owl & Night.* 1444 Hwich beo þe gome þat of þe wilde makeþ tome. *a* **1300** *Cursor M.* 11628 Al þe bestes þat ar wild For me most be tame and mild. *c* **1302** *Pol. Songs* (Camden) 194 Alas! thou seli Fraunce, for the may thunche shome, That ane fewe fullaris maketh ou so tome. *c* **1374** CHAUCER *Compl. Mars* 278 The pruddest of yow may be made ful tame. *c* **1430** *Hymns Virg.* (1867) 63 Y wole þee leere To make þi lord to þee tame. **1526** *Pilgr. Perf.* (W. de W. 1531) 39 Go home mekely & tame to thy place. **1785** GROSE *Dict. Vulg. Tongue* s.v., To run tame about a house, to live familiarly in a family with which one is upon a visit. **1908** *Betw. Trent & Ancholme* 26 It [a gull] became tame enough to watch its food being dug.

b. ***tame cat***: One who is on the footing of the domestic cat; a person who is made a convenience by his friends. So †***tame-fellow***, †***tame goose*** (*obs.*). (Cf. 1 b.)

1605 *Case is Altered* (Halliw.), Utterly cast away upon a noddy, a ninny-hammer, a tame-goose. *a* **1700** B. E. *Dict. Canting Crew*, *Tame-fellow*, tractable, easy, manageable. [**1878** MRS. H. WOOD *Pomeroy Abb.* I. 255 Here has he been in the house continually like a tame cat.] **1885** *World* 9 Sept. 9 It sheds the gentle glamour of romance over the tame cat himself and the household where he is always welcome. **1900** *Daily News* 16 Jan. 3/2 He is the tamest of tame cats amongst local officials.

†**c.** *poet.* applied to a thing with which one is familiar. *Obs.*

1606 SHAKS. *Tr. & Cr.* III. iii. 10 All That time, acquaintance, custome and condition, Made tame, and most familiar to my nature.

4. Subdued as by taming; submissive; meek; poor-spirited, pusillanimous; servile.

1563 B. GOOGE *Eglogs*, etc. (Arb.) 87 The countnaunce sad The drowping Courage tame. **1654** WARREN *Unbelievers* 235 They are a company of tame Souldiers. **1715** POPE *Iliad* I. 168 Shall I my prize resign With tame content, and thou possess'd of thine? **1761-2** HUME *Hist. Eng.* (1806) V. lxx. 269 They should expose themselves..to public contempt, on account of their tame behaviour. **1769** *Junius Lett.* xi. (1820) 47 Never hope that the freeholders will make a tame surrender of their rights. **1849** MACAULAY *Hist. Eng.* ix. II. 422 The tribunal lately so insolent, became on a sudden strangely tame.

5. a. Lacking animation, force, or effectiveness; deficient in striking features; weak, spiritless, insipid, dull.

1602 SHAKS. *Ham.* III. ii. 18 Be not too tame neyther: but let your owne Discretion be your Tutor: suit the action to the word. **1651** JER. TAYLOR *Serm. for Year* I. v. 63 He that is cold and tame in his prayers, hath not tasted of the deliciousness of Religion, and the goodnesse of God. **1766** GOLDSM. *Vic. W.* xv, The tame correct paintings of the Flemish school. **1850** ROBERTSON *Serm.* Ser. I. xvi. (1866) 266 These words fall short: they are too tame and cool. **1860** TYNDALL *Glac.* I. xxvii. 217 My delight..was tame compared with that of my companions. **1894** PARRY *Stud. Gt. Composers*, *Schubert* 232 The tamer style of his instrumental works was probably owing to the same causes which made his song-writing so very remarkable.

b. Of scenery: Wanting boldness; having no striking features.

1807 SIR R. C. HOARE *Tour Irel.* 186 On descending..the scenery..becomes tamer. **1894** MRS. H. WARD *Marcella* I. 16 A broad expanse of tame arable country.

6. *Comb.*, as ***tame-spirited***, ***-witted***, etc.

1596 NASHE *Saffron-Walden* Wks. (Grosart) III. 72 Poore tame-witted silly Quirko. *Mod.* One could not expect the nation to be so tame-spirited.

tame (teɪm), *v.*¹ [ME. *tamen*, f. TAME *a.*, taking in the 14th c. the place of the earlier TEME:—OE. *tęmian*, f. *tam* adj.]

1. *trans.* To bring (a wild animal) under the control or into the service of man; to reclaim from the wild state, to domesticate. Also *fig.*

c **1315** SHOREHAM *Poems* vi. 65 þat vnicorn þat was so wyld ..þou hast y-tamed [hyt], and i-styld. **1390** GOWER *Conf.* II. 161 Hou men hem scholde ryde and tame. *c* **1440** *Promp. Parv.* 486/2 Tamyn, or make tame, *domo*. **1593** SHAKS. *Lucr.* 956 To tame the vnicorne, and Lion wild. **1710** STEELE *Tatler* No. 222 ⁋3 As People tame Hawks and Eagles, by keeping them awake. **1863** LYELL *Antiq. Man* 24 At a later period..the lake-dwellers succeeded in taming that formidable brute the *Bos primigenius*, the Urus of Cæsar. **1877** E. R. CONDER *Bas. Faith* i. 23 Or tames the lightning to be his newsmonger and his lamplighter.

†**b.** To bring (a wild plant) under or into cultivation; to reclaim or improve (land) by cultivation.

1601 DOLMAN *La Primaud. Fr. Acad.* (1618) III. 795 Many great personages..haue taken paines to tame them, and cause them to grow in gardens. **1697** DRYDEN *Virg. Georg.* I. 144 For he with frequent Exercise Commands Th' unwilling Soil, and tames the stubborn Lands. *a* **1722** LISLE *Husb.* (1757) 100 (E.D.D.) By that time the ground will be tamed. **1746** W. DUNKIN in Francis *Horace, Ep.* II. ii. 280 Another shall..tame the savage Soil.

2. To overcome the wildness or fierceness of (a man, animal, or thing); to subdue, subjugate, curb; to render gentle, tractable, or docile.

1382 WYCLIF *Dan.* ii. 40 Hou yrun brekith to gydre alle thingus, and dauntith [*gloss* or tamith]. *c* **1400** *Destr. Troy* 2294 Soche tyrandes to tame, þat vs tene wirkes. **1526** TINDALE *1 Cor.* ix. 27 But I tame my body and brynge hym into subjeccion. *a* **1548** HALL *Chron.*, *Hen. IV* 23 The prince ..had tamed & brideled the furious rage of the wild and sauage Welshemen. **1667** MILTON *P.L.* XII. 191 This River-dragon tam'd at length submits To let his sojourners depart. **1748** GRAY *Alliance* 43 Industry and gain..Command the Winds, and tame th' unwilling Deep. **1783** CRABBE *Village* II. 165 To tame the fierce grief and stem the rising sigh. **1838** DICKENS *Nich. Nick.* ix, She hoped she had tamed a high spirit or two in her day. **1852** MRS. STOWE *Uncle Tom's C.* xix, I took him in hand, and in one fortnight I had him tamed down as submissive and tractable as heart could desire. **1859** *Art Taming Horses*, etc. i. 20 Mr. Rarey had tamed Cruiser, the most vicious stallion in England. **1863** [see sense 1].

b. *intr.* To become tame; to grow gentle, submissive, or sedate. Also with *down*.

1646 SHIRLEY *Narcissus* lxxiii, All wilde shall tame before thee as thou go'st. **1655** H. VAUGHAN *Silex Scint.* I. *Disorder & Frailty* iii, My weak fire..after all my height of flames, In sickly expirations tames. **1853** MISS YONGE *Heir of Redclyffe* xii, She had..tamed down into what gave the promise of a sensible woman.

3. *trans.* To reduce the intensity of; to tone *down*; to temper, soften, mellow; also, to render dull or uninteresting.

?*a* **1500** *Chester Pl.* vii. 78 Hemlockes, and herif..With Tarboyst most bene all tamed. **1697** DRYDEN *Virg. Georg.* III. 836 Nor cou'd Vulcanian Flame The Stench abolish, or the Savour tame. **1700** —— *Baucis & Philemon* 69 This in the pot he plung'd without delay To tame the flesh, and drain the salt away. **1847** H. ROGERS *Ess.* I. v. 221 The first editors had tamed down some of the more startling statements of Pascal. **1871** PALGRAVE *Lyr. Poems, Brecon Bridge*, Manhood's colours tamed to gray.

4. Combs. (sb. or adj.) of the verb-stem with a sb. (as obj.), as **tame-grief**, *sb.* that which subdues grief, or *adj.* that subdues grief; **tame-horse** = tamer of horses (tr. Gr. ἱππόδαμος); **tame-poison**, a name of *Vincetoxicum officinale* (also called *Asclepias* or *Cynanchum Vincetoxicum*), the root of which was used as an antidote to poisons.

1605 SYLVESTER *Du Bartas* II. iii. I. *Vocation* 151 Soule's remedy! O contrite heart's restorer! Tears-wiping tame-griefe! *c* **1611** CHAPMAN *Iliad* II. 16 Sleepes the wise Atreus-tame-horse sonne? **1785** MARTYN *Rousseau's Bot.* xvi. (1794) 216 Common Swallow-wort or Tame poison. **1866** *Treas. Bot.* 1217 The root..was formerly in some repute as a medicine;..as an antidote to poisons—whence it has been named Contrayerva Germanorum and Tame-poison.

Hence **tamed, 'taming** *ppl. adjs.*

1552 HULOET, Tamed, *domesticus*,..*domitus*. **1582** STANYHURST *Æneis* II. (Arb.) 55 Tamde men haue one saulfty. **1697** DRYDEN *Virg. Georg.* III. 227 Let 'em run at large; and never know The taming Yoak. **1836** J. H. NEWMAN in *Lyra Apost.* (1849) 217 Time hath a taming hand! **1894** A. WHYTE *S. Rutherford* xi. 87 Tamed and softened..by that taming and softening book.

tame (teɪm), *v.*[2] Now *dial.* Also 6 **tayme**. [Aphetic f. ATTAME, ENTAME *v.*]

1. *trans.* To pierce, cut into (in fighting or carving); to cut or break into, so as to use.

c **1400** *Laud Troy Bk.* 7405 Her woundes bledde, her flesch was tamet, The holest of hem ful sore was lamet. **1470–85** MALORY *Arthur* II. xviii. 97 Balan..smote hym thorow the shelde and tamyd his helme. **1513** *Bk. Keruynge* in *Babees Bk.* (1868) 265 Tayme that crabbe. **1642** FULLER *Holy & Prof. St.* II. xviii. 118 Then he tameth his stacks of corn, which..providence hath reserv'd for time of need. **1840** H. AINSWORTH *Tower Lond.* xxxix, In the old terms of his art, he leached the brawn,..tranched the sturgeon,..tamed the crab, and barbed the lobster. **1847–78** HALLIWELL, *Tame*, to cut; to divide. *West.* **1904** in *Eng. Dial. Dict.* s.v., *S. Dev.* We shall have to tame the rick.

†**b.** To broach (a cask, bottle, etc.); also with the liquor as obj. *Obs.*

?*a* **1412** LYDG. *Two Merchants* 701 Who that wil entren to tamen of the sweete, He mvst as weel..To taste the bittir. *c* **1440** *Promp. Parv.* 486/2 Tame, or attame vessellys wythe drynke.., *attamino*. **1483** *Vulgaria abs Terentio* 15 b, I haue tamed or set a broche all my pypys or tunnys. **1681** W. ROBERTSON *Phraseol. Gen.* (1693) 1205 To tame a vessel, i.e. to tap or broach it.

†**2.** *fig.* To enter upon, broach (a subject); to take upon oneself; to begin upon; begin *to do* something. *Obs.*

c **1386** CHAUCER *Nun's Pr. Prol.* 52 (Harl. MS.) And right anoon he haþ his tale tamyd [*v.r.* attamed]. *c* **1407** LYDG. *Reson & Sens.* 5636 He wolde ha tamyd Tan [= t'han, *i.e.* to have] touched yonge Rosis new.

†**3.** To injure, hurt. *Obs.*

c **1430** *Hymns Virg.* (1867) 55 þouȝ ȝe drinke poisoun, it schal not ȝou tame. *c* **1480** *Life St. Kath.* (MS. Cott. Titus A xxvi) 180 Neyþer clothys ne theyr here was tamyd with þe fire.

tameable, tamable ('teɪməb(ə)l), *a.* [f. TAME *v.*[1] + -ABLE.] Capable of being tamed.

1552 HULOET, Tameable, *domitalis, e.* **1576** FLEMING *Caius' Dogs* Preamble, In the second Order of milde and tamable beasts. **1648** WILKINS *Math. Magick* II. *Dædalus* vii. (1707) 118 Great Fowl, of a strong lasting Flight, and easily tameable. *Mod.* Tameable if taken young.

Hence **'tameableness, tamea'bility (tama-)**, the quality of being tameable.

1821 SYD. SMITH in Lady Holland *Mem.* (1855) II. 213 The kingdom is in the hands of an oligarchy, who..are too cunning, and too well aware of the tameability of mankind to give it up. **1828** WEBSTER, Tamableness. **1898** E. P. EVANS *Evol. Ethics* vi. 218 The tamability of an animal is simply its capability of adapting itself to new relations in life.

†**'tamehed.** *Obs. rare*⁻¹. [f. TAME *a.* + -HEAD.] Tameness, domesticity, docility.

c **1250** *Gen. & Ex.* 1485 Ðe fader luuede esau wel,..ðe moder, iacob for tamehed.

‖**tamein** (tæ'maɪn). *Burma.* Also 9 **tamehn, te-mine; tamain.** [Burmese.] A draped garment resembling a sari, worn usu. by women.

1839 H. MALCOLM *Trav. S.-E. Asia* I. II. iii. 214 Women universally wear a te-mine, or petticoat. **1858** C. T. WINTER *Six Months Brit. Burmah* vii. 56 The *te-miné* is a very scant garment. *Ibid.* viii. 73 The woman's tamehn is a simple piece of cotton or silk. **1863** *Leisure Hour* Oct. 667/1 With their shaven heads..and their scant tameins (petticoats). **1888** *Bow-Bells Weekly* 11 May 293/2 Burmese women..wear of evenings or when visiting religious places, gay-coloured silk 'tameins'. **1908** LADY R. CHURCHILL *Reminisc.* (1973) xiii. 272 As we drove by I saw half a dozen priests in their yellow 'tamains', or robes. **1926** *Chambers's Jrnl.* Feb. 66/1 An old *tamein* of blue cotton check..covered her from armpit to calf. **1950** J. H. WILLIAMS *Elephant Bill* x. 164 She wore her blue *tamain* girdled above her breasts, leaving her beautiful pale shoulders bare. **1984** J. COLENBRANDER *Portrait of Fryn* ix. 133 Mademoiselle Denigré, the blind French silk-weaver of the Royal *tameins*.

tameless ('teɪmlɪs), *a.* [f. TAME *v.*[1] + -LESS.] That has never been tamed; that cannot be tamed; untamed, untameable.

1597–8 BP. HALL *Sat.* II. i. 49 The tame-lesse steed could well his wagon wield, Through downes and dales of the vneuen field. *a* **1604** HANMER *Chron. Irel.* (1809) 369 The bones of him they Noble Meler call, Who was the tamelesse tamer of the Irish nation all. **1801** SOUTHEY *Thalaba* v. vii, And Tigris bore upon his tameless stream Armenian harvests to her multitudes. **1890** 'R. BOLDREWOOD' *Col. Reformer* (1891) 129 A playful touch with the spurs..caused that tameless steed to jump on one side.

Hence **'tamelessness.**

1815 BYRON *Parisina* xiii, From thee—this tamelessness of heart. **1883** JEFFERIES *Story of my Heart* i. 9 The age, tamelessness, and ceaseless motion of the ocean.

tameletjie (tamə'lɛcɪ, -tʃɪ). *S. Afr.* Also **tammeletje, tommelaitje,** etc. [perh. f. Afrikaans *tabletje* small cake of chocolate, sugar, etc.] A hard toffee, sometimes containing pine nuts.

1838 T. SHONE *Diary* 6 Aug. in *Voorloper* (1976) 788 In the evening I made the Children some tommelatche as a treat on my birthday. **1862** —— 18 June in *Ibid.*, Made some Tommy Larche for the children. **1862** —— 17 July in *Ibid.*, Mrs. K. gave me a bason of sugar, to make Tomelah. **1904** H. DUCKITT *Hilda's Where is It? of Recipes* 237 *Tamelijtjes* (a favourite Cape sweet). **1926** P. SMITH *Beadle* (1929) 181 Jantje brought with him, secreted about his person, a horrible sticky mess of almond tommelaitjes. **1947** L. G. GREEN *Tavern of Seas* 65 For the children there would always be tameletjies, the sweets made of sugar, water, eggs, naartjie peel and dennebol pits—sweets that were typical of an earlier Cape Town, but which are not made so often now. **1953** *Cape Argus Mag.* 28 Feb. 3/7 Under a large oak in the main avenue sat a friendly, fat Coloured woman selling sweets—the 'Tammeletje Woman' we called her. **1974** *Cape Times Weekend Mag.* 12 Jan. 7 We searched among the pine needles for pips and collected cones. The highlight of our excursions was the tameletjies, a delicious sweet made with butter, brown sugar, syrup, vinegar and water, and the addition of the pips, which my elder sister made for us.

tamely ('teɪmlɪ), *adv.* [f. TAME *a.* + -LY[2].] In a tame manner, in any of the senses of TAME *a.*; e.g. like a tame animal; submissively, tractably, quietly, passively; without resistance; without spirit or animation; without bold features.

1597 SHAKS. *2 Hen. IV*, IV. ii. 42 True Obedience..[may] Stoope tamely to the foot of Maiestie. *a* **1631** DONNE *Annuntiation & Passion* 1 Tamely fraile flesh, abstaine to day; to day My soule eates twice. **1651** JER. TAYLOR *Serm. for Year* I. v. 63 Our prayers upbraid our spirits when we beg coldly and tamely for those things for which we ought to dye. **1770** *Junius Lett.* xxxvi. (1820) 172 The English people will not tamely submit to this unworthy treatment. **1839** DARWIN *Voy. Nat.* i. (1879) 2 A kingfisher, which tamely sits on the branches of the Castor-oil plant. **1869** PHILLIPS *Vesuv.* vii. 172 Slopes not tamely identical but harmoniously diverse. **1885** *Manch. Exam.* 28 Jan. 3/4 An example rather of tamely edifying expatiation than of penetrative or stimulating thought.

tamendoa: see TAMANDUA.

tameness ('teɪmnɪs). [f. TAME *a.* + -NESS.] The quality or condition of being tame, in any sense; e.g. domesticated condition, absence of wildness; lack of spirit or courage; absence of animation or variety; commonplace quality.

1530 PALSGR. 279/1 Tamenesse, *priueur*. **1585** T. WASHINGTON tr. *Nicholay's Voy.* II. viii. 41 b, These Partriges..become wild, forgetting their tamenes. *a* **1633** AUSTIN *Medit.* (1635) 152 So that they lose not their fervour in Tamenesse, nor in preposterous zeale forget their Gentlenesse. **1655** *Nicholas Papers* (Camden) II. 177 Iff our dull countrymen will not fly to theire swords, they will suffer the deserved punishment of theire tameness. **1759** JOHNSON *Idler* No. 47 ¶ 12 He laughs at the letters..for their tameness of expression. **1774** GOLDSM. *Nat. Hist.* (1776) II. 310 The difference between animals in a state of nature and domestic tameness is so considerable, that [etc.]. **1781** COWPER *Alex. Selkirk* ii, They are so unacquainted with man, Their tameness is shocking to me. **1851** *Beck's Florist* 195 The monotony and tameness of a villa-garden. **1855** MACAULAY *Hist. Eng.* xix. IV. 370 This tameness was merely the tameness with which a tiger, caught, caged, and starved, submits to the keeper who brings him food.

tamer ('teɪmə(r)). [f. TAME *v.*[1] + -ER[1].] One who or that which tames.

1530 PALSGR. 279/1 Tamar of a horse, *courtier de chevaulx*. **1610** HEALEY *St. Aug. Citie of God* 139 Scipio..the tamer of Carthage. **1742** GRAY *Adversity* 2 Thou tamer of the human breast. **1859** *Art Taming Horses*, etc. vi. 77 The moment the horse moves the tamer draws the strap tight round the body of the horse.

tamera, tamerick, obs. ff. TAMBOURA, TAMARISK.

tamerack, obs. var. TAMARACK.

'Tamer'lane, 'Tambur'laine. European corruptions of *Timur lenk* = lame Timur, appellation of Timur, the great Tartar conqueror 1335–1405, the title-character of Marlowe's tragedy *Tamburlaine* 1586, and of Rowe's *Tamerlane* 1702. Used allusively for a person like Timur, a conqueror, a scourge, a despot. Also *attrib.* and *comb.*, as ***Tamerlane-like*** adj. or adv. Hence **'Tamerlanism** *nonce-wd.*

a **1579** T. HACKET tr. *Amadis of Fr.* XII. 306 (Stanf.) A number of Califes, Souldans, Tamberlanes. **1593** G. HARVEY *New Letter* Wks. (Grosart) I. 297 The graund Dissease..smiling at his tamberlaine contempt, Sternely struck-home the peremptory stroke. **1596** NASHE *Saffron-Walden* Wks. Siv b, Tamburlain-like, hee braues it indefinently in her behalfe. **1598** E. GILPIN *Skial.* (1878) 32 It is the scourge, the Tamberlaine of vice, The three square Tyborne of impieties. *c* **1618** MORYSON *Itin.* IV. (1903) 322 The German language..sounding better in the mouth of Tamberlin, than of a Civill man. **1632** MASSINGER *Maid of Hon.* II. ii, *Page*... I'll make Thy back my footstool. *Sylli.* Tamberlane in little! **1843** CARLYLE *Misc.* (1872) VII. 30 Out of it had come Napoleonisms, Tamerlanisms.

Tamil, ('tæmɪl). Also 8 **Tamoul,** 8–9 **Tamul.** [ad. *Tamir, Tamiḷ*, native name (known in 8th c.) of the people and language; in Pālī and Prākrit *Damiḷa, Daviḷa, Daviḍa*, Sinhalese *Demaḷa*, Skr. *Dramiḷa, Dramiḍa, Draviḍa* (whence Dr. Caldwell's term *Dravidian* for the Tamulic or Tamil family of languages). So Pg., Du., Ger. *Tamul*, F. *Tamoul*.]

a. One of a non-Aryan race of people belonging to the Dravidian stock, inhabiting the south-east of India and part of Sri Lanka. **b.** The language spoken by this people, the leading member of the Dravidian family. Also *attrib.* or as *adj.*

[**1579** (*title*) Doctrina Christam..feita em Portugal.. Tresladada em lingua Malavar ou Tamul. [Cochin].] **1734** (*title*) A Grammar of the Damul or Tamul Language. [Tranquebar.] **1778** (*title*) A Grammar for learning the Principles of the Malabar Language, properly called Tamul or the Tamulian Language. (Wepery.) **1788** *Encycl. Brit.* (ed. 3) I. 494/1 s.v. *Alphabet*, From this Shanscrit are derived the sacred characters of Thibet, the Cashmirian, Bengalese, Malabaric, and Tamoul. **1807** F. BUCHANAN *Jrnl. fr. Madras* II. 441 In the Tamul language it is called *Shuri cull*, or itch-stone. **1811** T. S. MOODELLIAR (*title*) A Tamil Expositor. [Madras.] **1842** W. C. TAYLOR *Anc. Hist.* xviii. (ed. 3) 575 By the persecution of the Buddhists..a great portion of the literature of India has been lost, and in particular,..all the ancient literature of the people that speak the Tamul language. **1864** M. C. SWAMY in *Reader* 12 Mar. 336/2 The Tamils [of Ceylon belong]..to the Dravidian race... Their religion is Sivaism, and their language the Tamil. **1869** *Chambers's Encycl.* IX. 285/1 The earliest history of the Tamil' country is still involved in obscurity. **1902** *Daily Chron.* 30 Aug. 8/1 To expel from the British Empire the Tamil-speaking tribes who presume to influence its policy. **1911** *Encycl. Brit.* XVII. 478/2 There has been a great development in agricultural enterprise,..the estates being mainly in the hands of Europeans, and the labour mostly Tamil. **1971** *Ceylon Daily Mirror* 4 Oct. 2/2 There should be healthy rivalry and peaceful co-existence of political parties in Tamil areas.

Hence **Ta'milian (Ta'mulian)** *a.*, Tamulic; *sb.* a member of the Tamil people; **Ta'mulic** *a.*, pertaining to the Tamils or their language, Tamil.

1764 *Ann. Reg.* 114 Dr. Francke, in Germany had sent them a number of Tamulian types..the government having erected a printing-office in the city of Madrass. **1788** *Asiatick Researches* I. 146 The *Tamulians* (or *Malabars*) having no *h* in their alphabet. *Ibid.*, In their language, which is the *Tamulic*..the place is called *Mâvalipuram*. **1800** *Misc. Tracts* in *Asiatic Ann. Reg.* 81/1 The Tamulic termination *en*..creates a striking resemblance between Pooden and the Wooden of the Goths. **1854** [see MUNDA *sb.* and *a.*]. **1856** [see MALAYALI]. **1863** LEPSIUS *Standard Alph.* 226 The four letters..which the Tamulians have added to the Sanscrit alphabet. **1872** MORRIS *Eng. Accidence* i. 12 The Dravidian or Tamulic [groups], including Tamul, Telegu, Malabar, Canaries. *a* **1881** [see BANDYMAN]. **1959** V. CRONIN *Pearl to India* vi. 89 Among the Tamilians *Védam* means both the three collections of hymns known as the Vedas, and also religion in general. **1968** P. LAL *Indian Recipes* 57 Pongal.. is the Tamilian New Year. **1971** *Illustr. Weekly India* 25 Apr. 4/2 The Tamilian is well known for his remarkable adaptability to his surroundings.

†**tamin.** *Obs.* Also 7–8 **-ine.** [app. aphetic deriv. of F. *étamine* (in OF. *estamine*) STAMIN.] A thin woollen stuff: = STAMIN. Also *attrib.*

1552 in J. C. Jeaffreson *Middlesex County Rec.* (1886) I. 8 Unum par manicarum de serico vocato tamin [*pr.* tawin] damaske ad valenciam v.*s.* **1611** COTGR., *Estamine*, the stuffe Tamine; also, a strayner, searce, boulter, or boulting cloth. **1625** MASSINGER *New Way* III. ii, I took her up in an old tamin gown. **1653** URQUHART *Rabelais* I. lvi, Their stockins were of tamine [F. *estamet*] or of cloth-serge. **1714** *Fr. Bk. of Rates* 366 Cloth-Rash and Tamine common. [**1822** NARES, *Tamine*, a sort of woollen cloth; probably the same that is now called *tammy*.]

¶**b.** A strainer or bolter, of this stuff; = TAMIS 1.

1847 in WEBSTER. Hence in later dicts; perh. never in use.

taming ('teɪmɪŋ), *vbl. sb.* [f. TAME *v.*[1] + -ING[1].] The action of TAME *v.*[1] Also *attrib.* **'taming-stick**, a kind of yoke for newly captured slaves.

c **1440** *Promp. Parv.* 486/2 Tamynge fro wyyldenesse, *domesticacio*. *a* **1533** FRITH *Disput. Purgat.* (1829) 137 What thou shalt do to the profit of thy neighbour, and taming of thy flesh. **1596** SHAKS. *Tam. Shr.* IV. ii. 54 Faith he is gone vnto the taming schoole..and Petruchio is the master. **1866** LIVINGSTONE *Last Jrnls.* (1873) I. iv. 107 Nearly all were in the taming-stick.

†**taminy.** *Obs.* Prob. a misprint or misreading of TAMIN or TAMMY *sb.*

1737 *Ochtertyre House Bk.* (1907) 77 For six yeards of yellow taminy £o. 6. o. **1755** JOHNSON, *Taminy*, a woollen stuff. Hence in ASH, and recent Dicts.

†ˈ**tamis.** *Obs.* Also 7 **tamise**, 9 **tammis**: see also TAMMY *sb.*[2] [a. F. *tamis* (tami) a sieve (of wire, silk, hair, etc.) (12th c. in Littré) = Pr. *tamis*, Sp. *tamiz*, It. *tamigio*, Ven. *tamiso*, med.L. *tamisium* (Du Cange), identical in origin with WGer. **tamisjo-*, the source of OE. and MLG. *tęmes* sieve, MDu. *tęmse*, OHG. *zemisa*: see TEMSE.]

1. A sieve; a strainer or bolting-cloth; also ***tamis-bolter, -cloth.***

1601 HOLLAND *Pliny* XVIII. xi. I. 567 The best bread is of the finest wheat floure, which hath passed through a small tamis bulter. *Ibid.* XXII. xxv. II. 142 If they be halfe sodden in water..then let passe through a tamise, that the brans might be separate. **1698** M. LISTER *Journ. to Paris* (1699) 141 This Stone is beat to Powder, and sifted through a fine Tamis. **1801** MOLLARD *Art of Cookery* (1836) 169 Rub them through a tamis cloth or sieve. **1817** W. KITCHINER *Cook's Oracle* (1818) 244 Strain it through a tammis into a clean stewpan. *Ibid.* 280 *note*, A *Tammis* is a worsted cloth,.. made on purpose for straining sauces. [Cf. p. 230, a tammy, or fine sieve.]

2. A name for an anther. (? from its scattering pollen.)

1665 REA *Flora* I. ix. 51 Six chives [in the tulip], tipt with pendents (which are those after the French we call Tamis). **1688** R. HOLME *Armoury* II. 65/1 The Agot Tulip is of a sad Isabella colour, with..a dark bottom, and large black Tamis. **1725** *Bradley's Fam. Dict.* s.v. *Tulip*, The bottom and Tamis blue. **1775** ASH, *Tamis* [erroneously explained].

3. *attrib.*, as ***tamis-bolter, -cloth*** (see 1); **tamis-bird**, the guinea-fowl (? from its speckled or powdered appearance).

1774 GOLDSM. *Nat. Hist.* (1862) II. III. vi. 75 They [Guinea-hens] are by some called the Barbary-hen: by others the Tamis bird.

tamisage (ˈtæmɪsɪdʒ). *Math.* [ad. F. *tamisage* sifting: see TAMIS and -AGE.] Applied by Sylvester to a method of finding invariants.

1882 CAYLEY *Math. Papers* XI. 409 *heading*, Note on an exceptional case in which the Fundamental Postulate of Professor Sylvester's theory of Tamisage fails.

‖**tamizdat** (ˈtæmɪzdæt). [Russ., f. *tam* there + *izdat*, abbrev. of *izdat'el'stvo* publishing house, after SAMIZDAT.] Russian writings which are published abroad and smuggled back into the U.S.S.R.; also this system of publication.

1974 MOORE & PARRY *Twentieth-Cent. Russ. Lit.* viii. 157 *Tamizdat*, a Russian word of later coinage and less spread than *samizdat*..refers to printed (not typed) material smuggled into the USSR from outside. *Ibid.* viii. 161 Plain mail is frequently used by people sending *samizdat* items out of the Soviet Union and *tamizdat* literature being sent into that country. **1975** *Economist* 11 Oct. 60/1 The volume of *samizdat* (unofficial and uncensored literature) has diminished, but this has been compensated for by the brisk circulation of publications known as *tamizdat* (from *tam*, 'there') printed abroad. **1978** *Observer* 1 Jan. 4/7 The era of *samizdat* is ending, he [*sc.* Georgy Vladimov] says. In its place has arrived the era of what he calls '*tamizdat*'—publication abroad of Russian writings that are then smuggled back into Russia. **1982** *Times Lit. Suppl.* 3 Sept. 950/1 It is thus a combination of *samizdat* and *tamizdat* (i.e., both unofficial Soviet and émigré publications).

tamka, var. TANGA[1]

tamkin, obs. var. TAMPION, plug.

Tamla Motown (ˈtæmlə ˈməʊtaʊn). The name of two U.S. record labels, *Tamla* and *Motown*, launched in 1960 by Berry Gordy Jr., used *attrib.* and *absol.* to designate a style of music characterized by a heavy beat and influenced by gospel music, which was made popular by the Black artists he employed. Also *ellipt.* as **Tamla**. Cf. MOTOWN.

[**1964** *Melody Maker* 6 June 13/6 So far, the Tamla-Motown operation has subsisted almost entirely on single record hits.] **1968** P. OLIVER *Screening Blues* ii. 46 Rhythm and blues, rock 'n roll, the Tamla-Motown sound and the techniques of the gospel singer. **1970** *Melody Maker* 3 Oct. 25/1 The new record is directly in between reggae and Tamla Motown. *Ibid.* 25/2 I've always wanted to try to get a Jimmy Cliff sound, so I am bound to aim in a Tamla direction. **1977** *Time Out* 28 Jan.–3 Feb. 62/1 (Advt.), All types of sounds wanted—progressive/rock/oldies/middle of the road/jazz/blues/tamla-soul/classical/easy listening/ films/shows/budget.

Tammany (ˈtæmənɪ). **a.** The name of the central organization of the Democratic party in the City (formerly also in the State) of New York, located in *Tammany Hall*, in 14th Street, New York. In English use the name has become esp. associated with the political and municipal corruption which at various times has characterized the government of New York. Also applied *transf.* to any similarly corrupt political organization or situation.

Tamanen, Tamene, Taminent, Taminy was the name of an Indian chief with whom W. Penn had transactions for land 1683 and 1697. Some time prior to 1771 the name became 'canonized', and from 1772 for about twenty years 'Saint' (or 'King') *Tamina, Tamany, Tammany* (generally identified with the chief of Penn's time) was regarded as the tutelar saint of Pennsylvania and other northern colonies or States, and the day assigned to him, May 1st (Old Style), May 12th (New Style), appropriated to popular celebrations, festive gatherings (often with some benevolent object), etc. From 1782 the name became associated with Societies established on a more or less permanent basis, of which that organized in New York is mentioned in 1787. The one which in 1790 is recorded as the 'Society of St. Tammany' and 'the Sons of St. Tammany and Columbian Order', and which in its constitution is claimed to be 'founded on the true principles of patriotism, and has for its motives charity and brotherly love', soon developed strong political activity, and by *c* 1810 had become the head-quarters of the Democratic Party (then called the Republican Party) in the State and City of New York. (From notes supplied by Mr. A. Matthews, Boston, Mass.)

1683 in *Pennsylv. Archives* (1852) I. 62, I, Tamanen..for me and my heirs and assignes doe graunt and dispose of all my Lands Lying betwixt [etc.]. **1683** PENN *Wks.* (1782) IV. 305. **1771** W. EDDIS *Lett. fr. Amer.* (1792) 115 The Americans on this part of the continent have..a Saint..The first of May is.. set apart to the memory of Saint Tamina. **1772** *Pennsylv. Chron.* 4 May VI. 63/2 On Friday..a number of American Gentlemen, Sons of King Tammany, met at the House of Mr. Bryn, to celebrate the Memory of that truly noble Chieftain... It is hoped..a Society may be formed of great Utility to the Distressed; as this meeting was more for the purpose of promoting Charity and Benevolence, than Mirth and Festivity. *Ibid.* 15 June VI. 85/1 The Sons of St. George, St. Patrick, St. Andrew, St. David, and King (or Saint) Tamany. **1773** in *Pennsylv. Mag. Hist. & Biogr.* (1902) XXV. 446 The natives..have adopted a great warrior sachem and chief named Tammany ..to be the tutelar Saint of this Province [Pennsylvania]. **1779** *New Jersey Jrnl.* 4 May in *N.J. Archives* Ser. II. III. 310 Saturday last being the anniversary of St. Tamany, the titular St. of America. **1785** WASHINGTON *Diary* 2 May in *Pennsylv. Mag.* (1893) XVIII. 412 Accepted an invitation to dine with the Sons of Saint Taminy [at Richmond, Virginia]. **1787** *New York Jrnl.* 3 May 3/1 Tuesday last, being St. Tammany's Day [the Tutelar Saint of America] the St. Tammany Society of this City held their Anniversary Meeting, at the Wigwam at Halls. **1790** *Ibid.* 11 May 3/3 To-morrow..the annual feast of St. Tammany will be celebrated by the Sons of St. Tammany and Columbian Order, at their wigwam on the banks of the Hudson. **1805** (*title*) An Act to incorporate the Society of Tammany, or Columbian Order, in the City of New York. Passed April 9, 1805. **1838** W. IRVING in *Life & Lett.* (1866) III. 126 Yesterday I had a full deputation from Tammany Hall.. informing me that I had been..nominated as Mayor. **1850** WHITTIER *W. Leggett* Pr. Wks. 1889 II. 200 The democratic committee issued its bull against him from Tammany Hall. **1901** 'MARK TWAIN' *Speeches* (1910) 114 Great Britain had a Tammany and a Croker a good while ago. **1910** *Encycl. Brit.* II. 142/2 The spectacle of a Clerico-anti-Semitic tammany in Vienna had strengthened the resistance of the better elements in the country. **1980** J. BARNETT *Palmprint* xiii. 137 You're been out in the Caribbean before... Politics here are pure Tammany Hall circa 1900.

b. *attrib.* and *Comb.*, as ***Tammany-organization, -ring, -tariff, -ticket; Tammany-ridden*** adj.; **Tammany tiger**, the symbol of the New York Tammany Society.

1871 *Harper's Weekly* 11 Nov. XV. 1056 The Tammany Tiger Loose.—What are you going to do about it? **1872** O. W. HOLMES *Poet Breakf.-t.* vi. (1885) 155 The Tammany Ring..is to take the place of the feudal lord. **1872** RUSKIN *Fors Clav.* II. xiv. 10 A complete Tammany Ring and lowest circle in the Inferno of the Worst. **1887** J. CHAMBERLAIN in *Times* (weekly ed.) 14 Oct. 3/1, I cannot accept as desirable ..the degradation of the great city of Belfast and the province of Ulster to a Tammany ring in Dublin. **1894** *Daily News* 5 July 5/6 'The Tammany Tariff'..appears to refer to the rates at which certain abuses and violations of the law have in that city been able to enjoy a practical immunity. **1899** *Ibid.* 29 May 6/7 Even Tammany-ridden New York has made up its mind to construct a new underground system. **1901** *Scotsman* 7 Nov. 4/2 His opponent..was backed by the immensely powerful Tammany organisation. **1953** *Manch. Guardian Weekly* 12 Nov. 2 Wagner, son of the late New Dealer swallowed up his opponents..leaving a broad smile on the face of the Tammany tiger.

Hence (chiefly *nonce-wds.*) **Taˈmmanial** *a.*, of or belonging to (St.) Tammany; **ˈTammanify, ˈTammanize, ˈTammany** *vbs.*, *trans.* to influence or dominate by, or as by, Tammany; whence **ˈTammanied** *ppl. a.*, **ˈTammanifiˈcation, Tammaniˈzation**; also **ˈTammanyism**, the system or principles of Tammany; **ˈTammanyite**, one who adopts the methods and principles of Tammany, an adherent of Tammany.

1791 J. PINTARD in *Amer. Daily Reg.* (N.Y.) 16 May, Before them was borne the cap of Liberty; after following seven hunters in Tammanial dress, then the great standard of the society. **1793** (May 15) in G. Meyers *Hist. Tammany Hall* (1901) 10 At Tammanial Hall in Broad street. **1882** *Tribune* (N.Y.) 5 Apr., A resolution striking the names of the Tammanyites from the caucus roll. **1893** in *Westm. Gaz.* 1 Nov. 3/1 For a section of the Press to Tammany London in the interests of the contractors and themselves. **1898** *Daily News* 28 Mar. 7/2 The charge brought against the Progressives of Tammanyfying London. **1899** *Westm. Gaz.* 14 Feb. 2/3 From all accounts Tammanied New York is anything but an ideal place in which to live. **1903** *Daily Rec. & Mail* 11 Nov. 4/3 A charge of paving the way for Tammanyism. **1909** *Sat. Rev.* 24 Apr. 518/1 To prevent the Tammanisation of London.

tammar (ˈtæmə(r)). Also **tamma.** [Aboriginal name.] A greyish-brown scrub wallaby, *Thylogale eugenii*, found in south-western parts of Australia. Cf. PADDYMELON.

[**1892** A. ZIETZ in *Trans., Proc., & Rep. R. Soc. S. Austral.* 1891–92 XV. 18 *Macropus eugenii.* Dama or Kangaroo Island Wallaby. **1924** F. W. JONES *Mammals S. Austral.* II. 240 The Dama Wallaby group was widely spread over the southern portion of Australia.] **1926** K. S. PRICHARD *Working Bullocks* iii. 27 The great days they had spent together, as youngsters, hunting..tammas, in the Paper Bark swamps. **1941** E. TROUGHTON *Furred Animals Austral.* 193 Dama Pademelon; Tammar. **1970** W. D. L. RIDE *Guide Native Mammals Austral.* v. 48 Tammars are able to survive on food containing little water. **1979** *Nature* 5 Apr. 549/2, I therefore examined the role of the neural pathway from the mammary gland in tammar wallabies carrying diapausing embryos.

†ˈ**tammel.** *Obs. rare.* App. an alteration of STAMMEL, on analogy of *tamin* for *stamin.*

1616 *Trial C'tess Somerset* in *Relat. Poysoning Sir T. Overbury* (1651) 106 The Prisoner..being attired in black Tammel, a Cyprus Caperoon, a Cobweb Lawn Ruff and Cuffs. **1668** *Flemings in Oxford* 9 Apr. (O.H.S.) I. 437 Paid unto Dr Smith which my Lady had disbursed for Tammell for my wife 01 05 00.

tammeletje, var. TAMELETJIE.

tammie (ˈtɑːmɪ). *Sc.* [Sc. f. TOMMY.]

1. Name of a loaf of home-baked bread, used in Edinburgh and the surrounding district.

1828 MOIR *Mansie Wauch* xviii, Their usual rations of beef and tammies. **1890** *Anent Old Edinburgh* 83 The pay was [1807] 6*d.* a day and a coarse roll called a 'tammie'.

2. tammie-norie. A local name in Scotland for the Puffin, *Fratercula arctica*; also *Tommy Noddy.*

1701 J. BRAND *Descr. Zetl.* viii. (1703) 119 Each kind or sort do Nestle by themselves; as the Scarfs by themselves, so the Cetywaicks, Tominories, Mawes, etc. **1816** SCOTT *Antiq.* vii, 'Did I not hear a halloo?' 'The skreigh of a Tammie Norie', answered Ochiltree, 'I ken the skirl weel'. **1841** R. CHAMBERS *Pop. Rhymes Scotl.* (1870) 190 The Puffin. Tammie Norie o' the Bass Canna kiss a bonny lass. **1896** NEWTON *Dict. Birds* 943 *Tammy-Norie*, a northern form of Tom-Noddy, and a name for the Puffin.

Tammuz: see THAMMUZ, TAMMUZ.

tammy (ˈtæmɪ), *sb.*[1] Also 7 **tammey**, 8 **tamy.** [Appears to be identical with obs. F. *tamise* 'étoffe de laine lustrée' cited by Littré from a letter patent of 22 July, 1780 (cf. *cerise, cherry*); but this may have been an adaptation of the Eng. word, which was in use a century earlier. It has also been suggested to be a corruption of TAMIN, or a deriv. of F. *estame* worsted, *estamet* cloth-rash (Cotgr.).] A fine worsted cloth of good quality, often with a glazed finish.

Much mentioned in 17th and 18th centuries, but app. obs. before 1858. The name was revived as a trade-term in the late 19th c.: see quot. 1876.

1665 in Strype *Stow's Surv.* (1754) II. v. xviii. 380/2 All other Kersies, Bayes, Tammies, Sayes, Rashes [etc.]. **1675** OGILBY *Brit.* 146 Stow market... Its chiefest Trade is making of Tammeys, and the Town affords several good Inns for Entertainment. **1706** PHILLIPS (ed. Kersey), *Tamy*, a kind of Stuff. **1730** BAILEY (folio), *Tammy*, a Sort of Worsted-Stuff, which lies cockled. **1757** DYER *Fleece* III. 481 Cheyney, and bayse, and serge, and alepine, Tammy, and crape, and the long countless list Of woollen webbs. **1758** *Chron.* in *Ann. Reg.* I. 119/1 Her riding dress a light drab, lined with blue tammy. **1770** *Gentl. Mag.* XL. 221 An account of a new loom, for weaving tamies, serges, stuffs and worsted cloaths. **1797** *Monthly Mag.* III. 34 Bradford is a manufacturing town for tammies, and other worsted stuffs. **1812** J. BIGLAND *Beauties Eng. & Wales* XVI. 805. **1858** SIMMONDS *Dict. Trade*, *Tammies*, a commercial name formerly given to Scotch camlets; a worsted fabric resembling bunting, but closer and finer. **1876** T. C. ARCHER *Wool & Applications* 46 Tammies are now made of wool with cotton warp. They are highly glazed and dyed in bright colours, and are still favourite fabrics.

b. *attrib.*, as ***tammy gown, lining, warp.***

1666 WOOD *Life* June (O.H.S.) II. 80, I bought of Mr. Fifield an English Tammy gowne which cost me, out of the shop, 2*li.* 4*s.* I had 18 yards and an half, at 2*s.* (a) yard. **1678** *Lond. Gaz.* No. 1329/4 A brown cloth wastecoat, a red tammy petticoat. **1719** J. ROBERTS *Spinster* 346 Many woollen stuffs..are quite lost,..such as..worsted tammy draughts. **1835** URE *Philos. Manuf.* 159 The hardest twisted worsted is called tammy warp. **1883** R. HALDANE *Workshop Receipts* Ser. II. 147/1 Tammy lining may also be cleaned with camphine.

ˈ**tammy**, *sb.*[2] [app. a. F. *tamis* (tami) TAMIS, assimilated to prec., perh. with the notion that it was made of that material.] A strainer.

1769 J. SKEAT *Art Cookery* 27 Then strain or rub them through a tammy into another clean stewpan. **1796** MRS. GLASSE *Cookery* v. 44 Strain it off through a tammy. **1883** 'ANNIE THOMAS' *Mod. Housew.* 49 These vegetables can.. be boiled to pulp and passed through a tammy.

attrib. **1839** URE *Dict. Arts* 106 It must be equalised still more by passing through a tammy cloth, or a sieve.

Hence ˈ**tammy** *v.*, *trans.* to strain through a tammy.

1903 *Daily Chron.* 14 Mar. 8/5 Then tammy or rub through a fine sieve with a wooden spoon.

tammy (ˈtæmɪ), *sb.*[3] Short for *Tammy Shanter*, corruption of TAM-O'-SHANTER.

1894 MRS. L. B. WALFORD *Matchmaker* xliv, The letter was found inside the inner brim of his 'Tammy'. **1896** *Westm. Gaz.* 26 Sept. 7/2 The Burns Statue... The poet stands in an easy attitude... He wears the 'tammy', the ploughman's coat and breeches, and the rough Scotch stockings.

tamongoong, var. TEMENGGONG.

tam-o'-shanter (ˌtæməˈʃæntə(r)). Also 9- **Tam o' Shanter**. [f. the name of the hero of Burns's poem of that name (i.e. *Tom of Shanter*).] In full, *Tam o' Shanter bonnet, cap*: A soft woollen bonnet with flat circular crown, the circumference of which is about twice that of the head, formerly worn by Scottish ploughmen, etc.; introduced, in a modified form, *c* 1887 as a head-dress for girls and young women. Abbreviated TAM, TAMMY.

1840-50 [Remembered in use]. **1884** *West. Daily Press* 29 May 3/7 The Tam o' Shanter is still occasionally worn [by men]. **1887** *Scott. Leader* 24 Sept. 5 Mr. O'Brien..was wearing an overcoat and a Tam o' Shanter, for the morning air was chilly. *Ibid.* 19 Oct. 4 The head-dress [adopted by Dundee factory girls] is the modest one of either a single or double-peaked cap or a Tam o' Shanter bonnet, and those workers who have adopted this..have been jeered at, and in some cases mobbed, while passing along the street. **1887** J. ASHBY STERRY *Lazy Minstrel* (1892) 26 Or if you think it right or wrong—I'll wear my Tam o' Shanter. **1888** BLACK *Adv. House-Boat* vi, A grey Tam o' Shanter..impervious to the wet. **1895** [see TAM].

Hence **tam-o'-shantered** *a.*, wearing a tam-o'-shanter.

1894 DU MAURIER *Trilby* I. 81 He married the..tartaned and tam-o'-shantered barmaid at the Montagnards Ecossais.

tamoure, var. TAMURE.

tamoxifen (təˈmɒksɪfɛn). *Pharm.* [f. *t* (perh. f. T(RANS) + AM(INE + OXY- + PHEN(OL, with alteration of *y* and *ph*.] An œstrogen antagonist, $(CH_3)_2N(CH_2)_2{\cdot}O{\cdot}C_6H_4{\cdot}(C_6H_5)C{:}C(C_6H_5){\cdot}CH_2CH_3$, used to treat breast cancer and infertility in women.

1972 *Approved Names 1970* (Brit. Pharmacopœia Comm.) Suppl. IV. 6 Tamoxifen. **1972** *Clin. Endocrinol.* I. 275 A derivative of triphenylethylene was examined by Harper & Walpole (1967a,b) for its anti-oestrogenic activity in rats. This compound..was subsequently named tamoxifen. **1980** *Brit. Med. Jrnl.* 29 Nov. 1459/1 Lung metastases then enlarged and tamoxifen was substituted but discontinued after only two months because of progressive disease.

tamp (tæmp), *v.* [app. a 19th c. workmen's word; perh. a back-formation from *tampin* (var. of TAMPION) taken as = *tamping*.]

1. *trans. Mining.* **a.** To stop up (a bore-hole) with clay, sand, etc., rammed in upon the charge before firing the shot; also, to pack up (a gallery of a military mine) before firing it, in order to concentrate the effect. **b.** To ram home (the charge) in a bore-hole. Also *absol.*

1819 FARADAY in B. Jones *Life* (1870) I. 301 Men.. employed in making holes, tamping and blasting the rock. **1834** J. S. MACAULAY *Field Fortif.* 203 Then tamp strongly and carefully the ends of the gallery, leaving the space intended to be demolished void. **1838** *Civil Eng. & Arch. Jrnl.* I. 292/1 The hole is tamped with dry clay to the top. **1843** *Ibid.* VI. 165/1 To form these chambers the rock was perforated.., and the different proportions of powder were introduced..and 'tamped up' close. **1860** RUSSELL *Diary India* I. 199 The mines will soon be tamped, and the whole nest of temples [over the river at Cawnpore] will leap into the air amid fire and thunder. **1899** *Westm. Gaz.* 4 Dec. 2/1 All charges should be 'tamped'—that is, pressed or secured in position with stones or other material wedged around them—wherever possible.

2. To stop up with clay or loamy earth the issues of a blast-furnace (Knight *Dict. Mech.* 1877).

3. a. To ram down hard, so as to consolidate (earth, gravel, etc.); to pun; = POUND *v.*[1] 6; also to pack (anything) round with earth so rammed down.

1879 L. STOCKBRIDGE *Investig. Rainfall* (Boston, U.S.) 5 [The lysimeter] was finished by throwing back and tamping in the earth which had been excavated on three sides. **1890** T. C. CLARKE in *Railways Amer.* 38 The track is raised, the gravel tamped well under the ties, and the track is ready for use. **1909** *Installation News* III. 63 If the conductor is tamped round with granulated carbon.

b. To pack or consolidate tobacco in (a pipe or cigarette) by a series of light taps. Also with tobacco as obj. and const. *down*. orig. *U.S.*

1920 in WEBSTER. **1939** R. P. WARREN *Night Rider* ii. 42 The Captain took out his pipe, tamped it, and with an excess of care lighted it. **1940** *Sun* (Baltimore) 14 Aug. 8/6 The pipe stoppers used to tamp tobacco in the pipe bowl will be on view. **1941** 'A. MACDONALD' in *Astounding Sci. Fiction* Oct. 18/2 The man..took out another cigarette, tamped it on one end, turned it and tamped the other. **1959** J. CARY *Captive & Free* xxx. 134 Syson settled himself more comfortably and tamped his pipe with the end of a pencil. **1979** *PN Rev.* No. 9. 35/1 A pipe-smoker Tamps tobacco Down to the base of the pipe bowl. **1981** *Guardian* 12 Oct. 10/4 A local soul, resting from his labours, tamping the dottle in his pipe.

4. *transf.* and *fig.* To oppress or constrict as by ramming; to subdue or contain by force. Also const. *down*. *U.S.*

1959 N. MAILER *Advts. for Myself* 19 We've all been flattened by the dead air of this time, dinched and tamped into a flat-footed class. *a* **1963** S. PLATH *Ariel* (1965) 74 Perfection... Cold as snow breath, it tamps the womb. **1976** *Time* 27 Sept. 27/2 While inflation has been tamped to just over 6%, unemployment is still high. **1977** *Time* 18 Apr. 53/2 Carter may be gambling that..he can tamp down the debate over the safety of nuclear power.

5. *Comb.*, as **tamp-work**, a surface made hard by tamping.

1855 R. F. BURTON *El-Medinah* I. xiii. 370 He sees a plain like tamp-work, where knobs of granite act daisies.

Hence **tamped** (tæmpt) *ppl. a.*, made hard and solid by pounding.

1875 R. F. BURTON *Gorilla L.* (1876) II. 204 The flooring is hard, tamped clay. **1878** H. M. STANLEY *Dark Cont.* II. iii. 83 The compact clay and tamped floor.

‖**ˈtampan.** Also **tanpan**. [? Sechuana name.] A blood-sucking tick of the genus *Ornithodorus*, esp. *O. moubata*, the vector of African relapsing fever.

1861 D. LIVINGSTONE *Pop. Acct. Trav. S. Afr.* viii. 120, I dreaded the '*tampans*', so common in all old huts. **1880** P. GILLMORE *On Duty* 295 Bitten all over by 'tampans', an insect synonymous to the 'jigger' of the West Indies. **1883** J. MACKENZIE *Day-dawn in Dark Places* 157 The mother was annoyed in her house by 'tanpans', insects whose bite is more distressing than that of mosquitoes. **1937** *Handbk. for Farmers S. Afr.* 522 The fowl tick, often called 'tampan', is an oval-shaped, slate-coloured tick with light yellow legs. **1971** D. J. POTGIETER et al. *Animal Life S. Afr.* 222/1 To control the tampan, the floors of native huts should be well dusted with BHC powder.

Tampax (ˈtæmpæks). Also **tampax**. The proprietary name of a sanitary tampon for women; also applied *loosely* to any variety of tampon, and in fig. contexts. Cf. TAMPON *sb.* 1.

1932 *Official Gaz.* (U.S. Patent Office) 29 Mar. 1063/2 Tampax. For sanitary absorbent tampons. **1935** *Trade Marks Jrnl.* 13 Feb. 187/1 Tampax... Sanitary absorbent tampons. **1955** W. GADDIS *Recognitions* III. v. 884 When we launched the customs almost arrested me, they thought my Tampax was incendiary bombs. **1975** J. MCCLURE *Snake* iii. 35 '*Ach*, come on, Klip—what's got your Tampax in a twist?'..'It's nothing,' he muttered... 'I'm just pissed off.' **1977** M. DRABBLE *Ice Age* II. 159 She went to the lavatory: there, for the first time for weeks, she found a Tampax machine. **1979** [see TAMPON 1].

tampeon, obs. form of TAMPION, plug.

tamper (ˈtæmpə(r)), *v.*[1] Also 4-7 **temper**. [Before 1600 mostly spelt *temper*, and app. originating in TEMPER *v.*, as used in reference to clay. The trans. use *to temper clay* appears to have become absol. *to temper*, and then intr. *to temper in clay*; hence fig. *to temper* or *tamper in* or *with* any business or matter. *Tamper*, which appears in reference to clay in 1573, was prob. a dial. or workmen's pronunciation, which became at length established, so as to differentiate this vb. from TEMPER.

For a development of sense very similar to that shown in *temper* and *tamper*, cf. MEDDLE *v.*]

I. †**1. a.** *intr.* To work in clay, etc. so as to mix it thoroughly. **b.** *trans.* To temper (clay). *Obs.*

1573 TUSSER *Husb.* (1878) 37 A fork and a hooke, to be tampring in claie, A lath hammer, trowel, a hod, or a traie. **1766** *Compl. Farmer* s.v. *Spiky-roller*, Where..the clay grows dry, and will not admit of being duly tampered for use without great pains in breaking it.

II. 2. *intr.* To work or busy oneself for some end; to machinate, scheme, plot. Const. *in* some practice, *for* something, *to do* something.

α. **1596** DRAYTON *Leg.* iv. 289 Here first to worke my busie brayne was set,..To temper in so dangerous assayes. **1611** SPEED *Hist. Gt. Brit.* VIII. vii. §17. 404 Howsoeuer Edward and he had tempered for the Kingdome.

β. **1613** FLETCHER, etc. *Captain* IV. ii, You have been tampring any time these three days, Thus to disgrace me. *a* **1661** FULLER *Worthies, Yorks.* (1662) II. 191 Tampering too soon and too openly, to derive the Crown in his wives right to himself. **1674** *Essex Papers* (Camden) I. 196 Yt I might discover whether Ormond was tampering, wth ye assistance of Duke, to give Essex his place. **1678** BUTLER *Hud.* III. II. 269 Others tamper'd For Fleetwood, Desborough, and Lambert. **1709** STRYPE *Ann. Ref.* I. xxxii. 328 The provost of Paris, being here in London, was especially tampering in treasonous practices against the Queen. **1736** CHANDLER *Hist. Persec.* 355 He tamper'd..to introduce some ceremonies bordering upon superstition. **1768** H. WALPOLE *Hist. Doubts* 77 The queen dowager tampered in this plot. **1823** SCOTT *Peveril* vii, You shall ..[not] tamper..amongst my servants, with impunity.

3. *intr.* To try to deal or enter into clandestine dealings *with* (a person), *about* or in order *to* some design; often with the connotation of meddling or interfering improperly with a person.

α. **1567** HARMAN *Caveat* 70 For often hee hath bene tempering with me [a woman], and yet haue I sharpely sayde him naye. **1584** R. SCOT *Discov. Witchcr.* II. ii. (1886) 16 If they should first be committed to prison the divell would temper with them and informe them what to doo. **1599** SANDYS *Europæ Spec.* (1632) 108 After that the Pope was once againe admitted, and had libertie to temper with his partie at pleasure. **1603** KNOLLES *Hist. Turks* (1621) 71 Shortly after he began also to temper with Guy, perswading him to resigne unto him that little right.

β. **1649** MILTON *Eikon.* iii. 23 Tampering both with the English and the Scotch army to come up against the Parlament. **1683** KENNETT tr. *Erasm. on Folly* 65 Another had been tampering with his neighbours wife. **1741** RICHARDSON *Pamela* (1824) I. 58 When he withdrew, I began to tamper with the farmer and his wife. **1748** —— *Clarissa* (1811) III. vii. 60 Joseph,..by tampering with Will, got all my secrets. **1790** BEATSON *Nav. & Mil. Mem.* II. 2 A small squadron..was detached after them, who found them busy in tampering with the natives. **1840** DICKENS *Barn. Rudge* xxxii, She has been tampered with, and most treacherously deceived. **1852** MISS YONGE *Cameos* II. ii. 17 He was trafficking with her enemies and tampering with her friends. **1870** DISRAELI *Lothair* ix, Their secret organisation is tampering with the people and tampering with the priests.

4. *intr.* To have to do or interfere *with* improperly; to meddle *with* (a thing).

α. **1601** HOLLAND *Pliny* II. 220 Hee would needs be handling and tempering with the weapons of his said guest.

β. **1636** *Divine Tragedie lately Acted* 12 [He] spied a Gun over the chimney..and fell a tampearing with it, and first levelled at the mayds. **1655** FULLER *Ch. Hist.* I. ii. §11 Humane Policy seldome proves prosperous, when tampering with Divine Worship. **1684** BUNYAN *Pilgr.* II. 85 This Boy has been tampering with something that lies in his Maw undigisted. **1789** W. BUCHAN *Dom. Med.* x. (1790) 119 There is no passion with which people are so ready to tamper as love. **1826** SCOTT *Jrnl.* 29 Dec., The son.. tampers with phrenology. **1868** FARRAR *Silence & V.* ii. (1875) 40 What was first tampered with, then yielded to, then persisted in, is next justified.

†**b.** *spec.* To meddle *with* medically. *Obs.*

1655 CULPEPPER *Riverius* Printer to Rdr., Not that every Fool should turn Physition, or that every Reader should tamper with him or her self. **1677** G. MOUNTAGU in *Buccleuch MSS.* (Hist. MSS. Comm.) I. 326, I beseech you tamper not too much, nor let blood too much this cold season. **1706-7** FARQUHAR *Beaux' Strat.* IV. i, I have been a tampering here a little with one of your Patients. **1784** COWPER *Task* v. 668 Vain tamp'ring has but foster'd his disease.

5. *intr.* To meddle or interfere *with* (a thing) so as to misuse, alter, corrupt, or pervert it.

α. **1593** SHAKS. *3 Hen. VI*, IV. vi. 29 Your Grace..may seeme as wise as vertuous, By spying and auoiding Fortunes malice, For few men rightly temper with the Starres. **1641** 'SMECTYMNUUS' *Answ.* Post (1653) 89 Peckam Archbishop of Can. in a Synod was tempering with the Kings liberties.

β. **1610** COOKE *Pope Joan* 38 Some paltry fellow hath bene tampering with his writings. **1722** DE FOE *Moll Flanders* (1840) 302 To have her up for tampering with the evidence. **1769** SIR W. DRAPER in *Junius Lett.* xxvi. (1820) 122 It is highly unbecoming the dignity of peers to tamper with boroughs. **1860** *All Year Round* No. 65. 354 His pistols, which Marcel had previously tampered with, miss fire. **1862** MAURICE *Mor. & Met. Philos.* IV. vii. §80. 413 Those had in his judgment tampered with truth. **1888** BRYCE *Amer. Commw.* v. lxxxviii. 379 A large number of persons accused of..tampering with ballot boxes.

b. *trans.* To put *off* or do away with by tampering or clandestine dealing. *rare.*

1817 KEATINGE *Trav.* II. 217 No putting off trials..until prosecutions are wearied off, or tampered off.

†**6.** *trans.* To bias, affect, influence, sway (a person, his mind, passions, etc.); to disaffect. *Obs.*

? for *tamper with*, or = TEMPER *v.* 6.

1687 R. L'ESTRANGE *Answ. Diss.* 43 The Worst Way of Tampering Peoples Minds, and Spiriting away their Hearts from their Sovereign. **1692** —— *Josephus, Antiq.* XIV. xx. (1733) 381 If he could but steal him away into Judæa, the Jews might be tamper'd to a Revolt.

Hence **'tampered** (also *tampered-with*), **'tampering** *ppl. adjs.*

1681 DRYDEN *Abs. & Achit.* I. 809 The tampering world is subject to this curse, To physic their disease into a worse. **1856** MRS. BROWNING *Aur. Leigh* IV. 474 And kept her safe from tampering hands. **1869** *Daily News* 30 Aug., You have allowed yourself to be tampered with... You appear before us as a tampered witness. **1895** G. TYRRELL in *Month* Nov. 361 The tampered-with fragments in the Christian Fathers.

†**ˈtamper**, *v.*[2] *Obs. rare.* [Known only in Ph. Holland; ? suggested by L. *temperāre*.] *intr.* To beat lightly, to tap; to continue tapping, to TABOR.

1606 HOLLAND *Sueton.* Annot. 15 The maner of these priestes..was to beat the Taber or tamper upon the Timbril, which is expressed here in these words, *Orbem digito temperat*. *Ibid.* 29 It will sound like a taber or drum, if one tamper upon it.

ˈtamper, *sb.* [f. TAMP *v.* + -ER[1].]

1. One who tamps a boring, etc.; also, a tamping-bar; an instrument or machine used for tamping.

1864 WEBSTER, *Tamper*, 1. One who tamps, or prepares for blasting... 2. An instrument used in tamping; a tamping-iron. **1954** *Highway Engin. Terms* (*B.S.I.*) 49 *Tamper*, a wooden or metal template, beam or frame used for compacting road materials and for shaping the surface. It is manipulated by hand and may or may not carry mechanical means for tamping or vibrating. **1956** *Railway Mag.* May 344/2 It is a four-wheel caravan, painted yellow, providing living accommodation for the two men who operate the Matisa ballast tamper. **1967** *Boston Sunday Globe* 23 Apr. B 63/1 You will also need..a tamper that you can make by nailing handles to a short section of a log. **1976** *Jrnl.* (Newcastle) 26 Nov. (Advt.), Welding equipment, bench drill, bench grinder, wacker tampers, traffic light set.

2. A casing around an atomic bomb which increases its efficiency and decreases the critical mass required for an explosion.

1945 H. D. Smyth *Gen. Acct. Devel. Atomic Energy Mil. Purposes* xii. 126 While the effect of a tamper is to increase the efficiency both by reflecting neutrons and by delaying the expansion of the bomb, the effect on the efficiency is not as great as on the critical mass. **1961** *New Scientist* 26 Oct. 231/1 A tamper, a heavy casing whose inertia resists dispersion in the early stages. **1977** N. Freeling *Gadget* ii. 75 If the criticality isn't right then your whole exercise in cores and tampers..stays the way it is.

tamperer ('tæmpərə(r)). [f. tamper *v.*[1] + -er[1].] One who tampers; a schemer; a meddler.

1599 Sandys *Europæ Spec.* (1632) 88 Yea there are not wanting some temperers among them, that have beene talking a long while..of a Generall solemne Conference. **1681** H. More *Exp. Dan.* Pref. 93 Unfaithful Tamperers with the Souls of men. **1854** Dickens *Child's Hist. Eng.* xxxii. III. 157 He..was surrounded in the Tower by tamperers and traitors. **1906** *Athenæum* 3 Feb. 131/3 Modern tamperers with the ecclesiastical architecture.

'tampering, *vbl. sb.* [f. tamper *v.*[1] + -ing[1].] The action of the verb tamper, in various senses: †plotting; meddling, improper interference.

a **1625** Fletcher *Nice Valour* v. i, There is no tampering with these Cupids longer. **1738** Birch *Milton* M.'s Wks. I. 32 By reason of his continual Studies and the Head-ach,.. and his perpetual tampering with Physic, his Eyes had been decaying for twelve Years before. **1822** W. Irving *Braceb. Hall* xx, There is something strangely pleasing in these tamperings with the future. *a* **1854** H. Reed *Lect. Eng. Lit.* iv. (1878) 153 It has come down from a remote antiquity, and has..escaped the tampering of modern hands.

'tamperproof, *a.* Also **tamper-proof**. [f. tamper *v.*[1] + proof *a.*] Proof against being tampered with; not susceptible to misuse. Esp. of mechanism.

1886 *Time* July (Advt., rear cover), An indicator which records the hours your day or night watchman remains on duty, and is absolutely tamperproof. **1954** *Federal Suppl.* (U.S.) CXVIII. 182/2 Armstrong in part claims a tamper-proof feature on Cel-O-Seal bands since they must be destroyed before being taken off the bottle. **1960** *Times* 3 Oct. (Advt. Suppl.) 1/2 A tamper-proof seal. **1967** D. C. Cooke *c/o American Embassy* (1968) xiii. 129 Timber locks are virtually tamperproof. **1970** *New Yorker* 3 Oct. 41/1 Not altogether tamperproof waiting lists. **1979** C. McCarry *Better Angels* iv. xv. 310 The computer had been designed to be absolutely tamper-proof.

tampicin ('tæmpɪsɪn). *Pharm. Chem.* [f. *Tampico* + -in[1]: in F. *tampicine*.] The resin, $C_{68}H_{108}O_{28}$, obtained from Tampico jalap, the tuberous root of *Ipomæa simulans*.

1890 in Billings *Nat. Med. Dict.* **1898** in *Syd. Soc. Lex.*

tampin, obs. variant of tampion.

tamping ('tæmpɪŋ), *vbl. sb.* [f. tamp *v.* + -ing[1].] The action of the verb tamp: the plugging or filling up of a blast-hole above the charge; the packing of the part of a military mine nearest the charge with earth or other material.

1828 J. M. Spearman *Brit. Gunner* (ed. 2) 301 The stoppage or tamping of a mine. **1845** *Encycl. Metrop.* XVI. 303/1 The sand-bags used for tamping should not be filled up to the top.

b. *concr.* The material used for this purpose.

1828 in Webster. **1843** *Civil Eng. & Arch. Jrnl.* VI. 120/2 It would have found vent by blowing out the tamping. **1909** *Installation News* III. 63 The upper casting, to which the cable or tape is electrically connected by lead tamping.

c. *attrib.* and *Comb.*, as *tamping material*; **tamping-bar, -iron**, = stemmer: see quot. 1877; **tamping-machine**: see quot.; **tamping-plug**, a plug or stopper used to block up a bore-hole.

1838 *Civil Eng. & Arch. Jrnl.* I. 292/1 Drawings of the jumpers, the *tamping bar, the needle, and the discharging reed. **1891** C. Roberts *Adrift Amer.* 75 It was pick and shovel and tamping bar day in and day out. **1864** Webster, **Tamping-iron*. **1877** Knight *Dict. Mech.*, *Tamping-iron*, a tool, prudently made of copper, by which the tamping is wadded down upon the cartridge or charge in a hole, for blasting. *Ibid.*, **Tamping-machine*.., a machine for packing clay or the material for artificial stone into a mold. **1839** Ure *Dict. Arts* 836 Dry sand is sometimes used as a *tamping material. **1877** Knight *Dict. Mech.* **Tamping-plug*,..it usually consists of a cone with barbs, or of a set of wedge-shaped blocks, which jam by the pressure from beneath. **1884** *Mil. Engineering* (ed. 3) I. ii. 116 Sandbags ready filled for *tamping purposes should be provided.

tampion, tompion ('tæmpɪən, 'tɒmp-), *sb.* Forms: α. 5 tampyne, 5–6 -on, -ond, -yon, 6 -ioun, 6–8 -in, 7 -eon, 5– tampion; 6–7 tampkin, 7–8 tamkin; (7–9 tampoon). β. 7 tomping, 8–9 -ion, 9 -eon; 7 tomking, 7–8 -kin, tompkin. [a. F. *tampon*, in same senses (1440 in Godef. *Compl.*), a nasalized var. of F. *tapon* (1382 in Hatz.-Darm.) a piece of cloth to stop a hole, etc., deriv. of *tape* plug; cf. *tamper*, nasalized var. of *taper* vb. to plug. The original form *tampon* has undergone many corruptions in Eng.: cf. *pompon*, pompion, pumpkin. The form *tampoon* (cf. *dragoon*, etc.) appears to be confined to dictionaries (from Phillips downwards). *Tompion* is a frequent form in all senses. See also tampon.]

†**1.** A plug for stopping an aperture: e.g. a bung for a cask, etc. *Obs.*

c **1460** J. Russell *Bk. Nurture* 68 in *Babees Bk.* (1868) 121 With fawcet & tampyne redy to stoppe when ye se tyme. **1504** *Cal. Anc. Rec. Dublin* (1889) 393, viii. *d.* to hym that skowre the tamponds of the pypes. *Ibid.*, The skowryng of the tampones of the pypes. *c* **1512** in *Archæologia* (1902) LVIII. 302 A susp[i]rall with a tampioun to clense the home pype. **1594** Plat *Jewell-ho.* i. 37 You must suffer the water to passe away by some tampion. **1658** Phillips, *Tampoon*, or *Tampkin*, a small piece of wood serving for a bung. **1729** Shelvocke *Artillery* iv. 174 The Globe..shall be filled.. and then stopped with a Tompion that has been steeped in hot Pitch. [**1882**: see 3 *fig.*]

†**b.** *Farriery.* A seton; a tent; a pessary: cf. tampon *sb.* 1. *Obs.*

1565 Blundevil *Horsemanship* iv. lxvi. (1580) 27 Make two stiffe long rowles, or tampins, of linnen clowtes, or such like stuffe, sharpe pointed like Suger loues:..thrust them vp into the Horses nostrils. **1610** Markham *Masterp.* ii. cxi. 395 Put therto a tampin made of the inner rinde of Elder barke. *Ibid.* clvii. 464 Take a tampin of horse haire twound together.

†**2.** A disk-shaped or cylindrical piece of wood made to fit the bore of a muzzle-loading gun, and rammed home between the charge and the missile, to act as a wad. *Obs.*

1481–90 *Howard Househ. Bks.* (Roxb.) 40 Item ij. c. tampons xvj. d. **1485** *Naval Acc. Hen. VII* (1896) 69 Gonne Tampyons..ccc. **1497** *Ibid.* 105 Tampons for gonnes..xj[ml] c. *Ibid.* 340 Tampiones..ccc shotte. **1489** Caxton *Faytes of A.* ii. xxvi. 139 Cartes laden with Elme wode for to make the said tampons. **1530** Palsgr. 279/1 Tampyon for a gon, *tampon*. **1582** Stanhurst *Descr. Liparen* in *Æneis*, etc. (Arb.) 137 Slinging Stoans, and burlye bulets, lyke tamponds. **1588** *Acts Privy Counc.* (1897) XVI. 25 Arrowes for the said muskettes with tampkines of eche 1,000. **1688** R. Holme *Armoury* iii. xviii. (Roxb.) 142/1 Of charging..a Morter peece..put in the Tampkin..a round peece of soft wood put into the mouth of the chamber. **1692** *Capt. Smith's Seaman's Gram.* ii. iii. 92 Wedges, Tomkings, Priming-Irons. *Ibid.* xxi. 134 Draw out the Ladle, and with the Tampion at the other end of the Staff, thrust home the Powder. **1727–41** Chambers *Cycl.*, *Tampion, Tompion, Tamkin*, or *Tomkin*, a kind of plug or stopple..to keep down the powder in a fire-arm. **1828** Spearman *Brit. Gunner* (ed. 2) 307 In the larger mortars,..the chamber should be filled with powder, a tompeon of wood placed over it, and both the tompeon and shell surrounded with sifted earth or sand.

†**b.** Applied to the bottom plate of grape-shot, which serves as a wad to the charge. *Obs.*

1802 James *Milit. Dict.* (1816), *Tampions*, in sea-service artillery, are the iron bottoms to which the grape-shot are fixed. **1823** Crabb *Techn. Dict.*, *Tompions.* [Hence in various later Dicts.]

3. A block of wood fitting into the muzzle of a gun, and serving to exclude rain, sea-water, etc.

a **1625** *Nomenclator Navalis* (Harl. MS. 2301), Tampkin is a small peece of Wood turned fitt for the mouth of anie peece which is putt in..to keepe out the raine or Sea water, from washing in, when the Peeces lie without Bord. **1627** Capt. Smith *Seaman's Gram.* xiv. 68 A Tomkin is a round peece of Wood put into the Peeces mouth and couered with Tallow. **1662** J. Davies tr. *Olearius' Voy. Ambass.* 27 The Tampion, which they had forgotten to take out of one of the pieces, pass'd very near me. **1748** Smollett *Rod. Rand.* lxv, He commanded..the tompions to be taken out of the guns. **1835** Marryat *Pirate* xiv, Clear away the starboard guns, and take out the tompions. **1904** Fitchett *Commander of Hirondelle* 157 The wooden tompions were still lying harmlessly within their iron lips.

fig. **1756** *Gentl. Mag.* XXVI. 398 Take out the tompkin of your mouth, and fire away loud as thunder. **1864** Blackmore *Clara Vaughan* lxxiii, She commenced an active bombardment, pulling out the tompions from every gun of mock religion. **1882** G. Macdonald *Castle Warlock* xv. (1883) 83 No sooner did the..note of the discharge of its [bottle of claret's] tompion reach his ear [etc.].

4. In the organ: see quots.

1864 Webster, *Tampion*,..a plug used to stop closely the upper end of an organ-pipe. **1865** *Chambers' Encycl.* VII. 111/2 (*Organ*) A mouth-pipe may be stopped at the upper end by a plug called a *tompion* the effect of which is to lower the pitch an octave.

†**5.** (See quot.) *Obs. rare*[−1].

1611 Cotgr., *Pivot*,..the Piuot, or (as some call it) the Tampin of a gate, or great doore.

6. = tampon 2.

1877 Knight *Dict. Mech.*, *Tompion*..2 (Lithography) the inking pad of the lithographic printer; *Tompon.* [Hence in mod. Dicts.]

Hence **'tampion, tompion** *v. trans.*, to insert in the manner of a tampion or plug.

1897 *Daily News* 3 Feb. 5/3 London..is not without its trophy lamp-posts, for..in front of the house once occupied by Admiral Boscawen, are two which are tompioned into old cannon captured from the French in a naval fight.

tampkin, obs. variant of tampion.

tampon ('tæmpən, -ɒn), *sb.* Also **tompon**. [ad. F. *tampon*: etymologically a doublet of tampion, introduced anew from mod. French.]

1. A plug or tent inserted tightly into a wound, orifice, etc., to arrest hæmorrhage, or used as a pessary (*Surg.*). Esp. one inserted into the vagina; now *spec.* one made commercially and bought to provide sanitary protection during menstruation. Also *attrib.*

1848 C. D. Meigs *Females & their Diseases* xxxiii. 432 Having confidence in the power of the tampon to suppress *such* a flooding [*sc.* menorrhagia], I would let her go very far towards a dangerous state rather than subject her to the mortification of the surgical intervention. **1860** Mayne *Expos. Lex.*, *Tampon*..*Obstet.*, a less inelegant term for the plug, whether made up of portions of rag, sponge, or a silk handkerchief..in cases of hemorrhage. **1872** T. G. Thomas *Dis. Women* (ed. 3) 61 [To] keep the displaced and congested uterus out of the cavity of the pelvis by a tampon of medicated cotton. **1888** *Scott. Leader* 14 June 4/1 The new species of cannula employed..is provided with a tampon, and is constructed [so] as to prevent hæmorrhage. **1896** *Allbutt's Syst. Med.* I. 438 Tampons are pear-shaped with the thread attached to the lower end. **1921** B. M. Anspach *Gynecology* xxxix. 709 Tampons are made by placing over a strip of absorbent cotton a smaller strip of lamb's wool, and binding them together. **1932, 1935** [see Tampax]. **1957** T. N. A. Jeffcoate *Princ. Gynaecol.* xliii. 635 Proprietary tampons of various kinds are available but this method of applying antiseptics [to the vagina and cervix] is now rarely used. **1964** *Which?* Mar. 84/1 Medical opinion has always been divided over the use of tampons instead of external towels. **1970** G. Greer *Female Eunuch* 50 The success of the tampon is partly due to the fact that it is hidden. **1979** *Guardian* 27 Mar. 9/4 The tampon market is worth about £14 millions a year. Tampax has 62 per cent.

2. The dabber or inking ball used in lithography and copperplate printing. (So also in French.)

1877 Knight *Dict. Mech.*, *Tompon*, the inking-pad of the lithographic printer. **1882** G. Reid in *Encycl. Brit.* XIV. 701/1 (*Lithography*) An engraved stone is printed by using a small wooden tapper or tampon, either round at the sides, flat below, with handle at top, or square, with the corners rounded off.

3. Special Comb. **tampon-screw**, an instrument used for inserting or withdrawing a tampon from a wound, etc.

1884 Knight *Dict. Mech.* Suppl., Tampon-screw.

'tampon, *v. Surg.* [f. prec. sb.: cf. F. *tamponner* (15th c. in Hatz.-Darm.).] *trans.* To fill or stop (a wound, cavity, etc.) with a tampon; to plug.

1860 J. M. Carnochan *Operat. Surg.* 279 (Cent. Dict.) The hemorrhage was stopped by tamponing the bony aperture [gunshot wound in head]. **1898** *Syd. Soc. Lex.*, *Tamponing*, in Surgery the operation of plugging a wound or natural orifice with a tampon or tampons.

So **'tamponage, 'tamponment** [F. *tamponnement*], the employment or application of a tampon.

1902 *Cassell's Encycl. Dict., Suppl.*, Tamponment.

tampon, -pond, -poon, obs. var. tampion.

tampo'nade.

1. *Surg.* The application of a tampon or tampons.

1890 Billings *Nat. Med. Dict.*, *Tamponade*, the application of tampons. **1900** *Lancet* 27 Oct. 1191/1 He suggested free opening and curetting with patient and prolonged flushing and subsequent gauze tamponade.

2. *Path.* Interference with the action of the heart by an excessive accumulation of blood or other fluid in the pericardial sac.

[**1930** Beck & Cox in *Arch. Surg.* XXI. 1039 The tamponade effect produced by atmospheric pressure may be excited in various types of operation... In the selection of cases for operation, the heart should possess a certain reserve power capable of withstanding this tamponade effect.] **1932** *Southern Med. Jrnl.* (U.S.) XXV. 785/1 Blood is trapped in the pericardial sac, producing heart tamponade. **1962** *Lancet* 8 Dec. 1195/2 In view of the poor response to external massage and the probability of cardiac tamponade, left anterior thoracotomy was undertaken. **1974** Thornton & Levy *Techniques Anaesthesia* vi. 170 Tamponade may develop following open heart surgery.

†**tampoy.** *Obs. rare.* [? Malay.] (See quots.)

1656 Blount *Glossogr.*, *Tampoy*, a curious sort of drink in the Moluccaes and Philippines made of a kind of Gilliflowers. **1823** Crabb *Technol. Dict.*, *Tampoy*, a sort of drink made of gilliflowers. **1909** *Daily Chron.* 23 Aug. 4/7 The mention of British wines..has set an octogenarian sighing for a beverage called 'tampoy', which was highly esteemed in Early Victorian days.

tampyne, -pyon, obs. ff. tampion.

tamquam: see tanquam.

tamricke, -riske, obs. ff. tamarisk.

tam-tam ('tæmtæm). *Mus.* [Echoic, app. of Creole origin: cf. Fr., Ger. *tam-tam*.] A metal gong of oriental origin, *spec.* a Chinese gong, now used in western orchestras.

1839 Ure *Dict. Arts* 333 Cymbals, gongs, and the tamtam of the Chinese are made of an alloy of 100 of copper with about 25 of tin. **1856** Mrs. C. Clarke tr. *Berlioz' Instrument.* 229 The gong, or tam-tam, is employed only in funereal compositions and dramatic scenes where terror is carried to its height. **1859** R. Hunt *Guide Mus. Pract. Geol.* (ed. 2) 210 The tam-tams and cymbals of bronze of the Chinese are forged with the hammer. **1900**, etc. [see gong[2]]. **1933** M. D. Calvocoressi tr. *H. Scherchen's Handbk. Conducting* iii. 132 The tone of the gong does not differ from that of the tamtam but is definite in pitch. Sometimes composers prescribe a gong when they obviously mean a tamtan. **1947** *Penguin Music Mag.* May 85 There is a passage for tubular bells, cymbal, tam-tam, triangle. **1951** E. Paul *Springtime in Paris* vii. 131 The gyrations of a near-eastern dance, to the beat of inaudible tam-tams. **1961** *Radio Times* 20 July 18/3 Six players, their instruments including bongos and maracas..a whip, temple block, four tam-tams, and crotales. **1978** P. Griffiths *Conc. Hist. Mod. Music* xi. 164 A large tam tam (a kind of gong) is activated by two performers with various objects. **1983** *Listener* 15 Sept. 31/4 His orchestra (enlarged by two harps, piano, organ, celesta and a big percussion battery including tam-tam and bells) is handled with extreme refinement and virtuosity.

tam-tam, var. tom-tom.

Tamul, -ulian, -ulic: see Tamil.

‖**tamure** (ta'mure). Also **tamoure**. [Tahitian.] A Tahitian dance, the *ori Tahiti*.

1964 *Wanganui Photo News* 4 July 5 (*caption*) Nurse Anna Paotonu danced the tamoure for the floor. **1970** J. H. VANCE *Deadly Isles* iii. 25 Ah! the *tamure*! which was to the hula as whisky to milk. **1976** *Sat. Rev.* (U.S.) 30 Oct. 30/2 Palm trees and girls dancing the sexy *tamure*.

Tamworth ('tæmwəθ). The name of a town in Staffordshire, used *absol.* or *attrib.* to designate a pig of the breed of this name, usually red or brown in colour, lean and large in build, and used to produce bacon; also, the breed itself, first developed in the area.

1860 S. SIDNEY *Youatt's Pig* (ed. 2) iii. 34 The cross of the Berkshire with the Tamworth produces the most profitable bacon pigs in the kingdom. *Ibid.*, The Tamworth Breed is a red, or red-and-black pig,—hardy, prolific,.. but slow in maturing. **1886** J. LONG *Bk. Pig* ix. 161 A cross between the Tamworth and the Berkshire was considered most valuable. **1897** S. SPENCER *Pigs* i. 17 The mahogany or grizzled pig.. has acquired the name of the Tamworth. **1950** CARROLL & KRIDER *Swine Production* vi. 83 The Tamworth is a strictly bacon breed and the oldest of domesticated breeds of hogs. *Ibid.* 84 Tamworths are large, rugged hogs. **1967** M. KENYON *Whole Hog* viii. 93 Most of your Tamworths you call Duroc. They're the red ones—reddish-brown. **1977** *Jrnl. R. Soc. Arts* CXXV. 702/2 Tamworth pigs.., although still relatively scarce, have increased in numbers dramatically. *Ibid.* 704/2 The Tamworth.. can adapt itself to a wide range of climatic conditions.

tamy, obs. form of TAMMY *sb.*[1]

tan (tæn), *sb.*[1] (*a.*) Also 7 **tann(e**. [prob. a. F. *tan* (13th c. in Littré, also in Cotgr. 1611 '*tan*, the barke of a young Oake, wherewith, being small beaten, leather is tanned') = med.L. *tannum*, app. of Celtic origin: cf. Breton *tann* masc., oak, Cornish *glas-tannen* evergreen oak, ilex (Thurneysen). Thence the vb., med.L. *tannāre*, OF. *tanner* to tan; cf. also Du. *taan*, late MDu. *tāne* tan, *tānen* to tan.]

A. *sb.* **I. 1. a.** The crushed bark of the oak or of other trees, an infusion of which is used in converting hides into leather.

[**1604**: implied in *tan-mill*; **1611** in *tan-pit*: see C.] **1674** JEAKE *Arith.* (1696) 69 Tann, 1 Load must be 60 yards long, 1 yard high, 3 Rinds thick. **1706** PHILLIPS (ed. 6), *Tan*, the Bark of a young Oak, beaten small and us'd.. for the tanning ..of Leather. **1727–41** CHAMBERS *Cycl.* s.v., Not only the bark, but every part of the oak-tree.. makes good Tan. **1840** *Encycl. Brit.* (ed. 7) XXI. 73/2 The word tan is sometimes, though improperly, used for the bark itself, which is the chief ingredient in the tanning of leather. **1852** MORFIT *Tanning & Currying* (1853) 38 The name *tan* is applied to coarsely-powdered bark containing a principle which is the active agent in the tanning of hides.

b. Spent bark from the tan-pits, used by gardeners, and for riding-courses, etc.

1739 MILLER *Gard. Dict.* II. s.v., The best Sort of Tan for Hotbeds, is, that which is ground of a midling Size, neither too small nor too large. **1766** *Ann. Reg.* 108 A melon raised ..in Southwark upon tan was sold in Covent-garden Market. **1812** *New Botanic Gard.* I. 54 A thin covering of tan or some other substance. **1849** LONGF. *Kavanagh* xix. 101 Circus,—with its tan and tinsel. **1887** *Morn. Post* 8 July (Sport. Notes), After the usual canter [she] galloped him a mile and a quarter on the tan.

2. The astringent principle contained in oak-bark, etc.; tannin; also the solution of this, tan-liquor, 'ooze'.

1800 HENRY *Epit. Chem.* (1808) 289 Until very lately, tan had been known only as a production of nature. **1810** —— *Elem. Chem.* (1826) II. 284 Tan exists abundantly in the bark of the oak, the willow, &c., and in the gall-nut. **1866** ROGERS *Agric. & Prices* I. xxiv. 612 To preserve them, the nets were soaked in tan.

II. 3. a. The brown colour of tan; tawny.

1888 *Daily News* 17 July 5/8 Simplicity is the word of command as regards outlines, and tan is the special colour of this season. **1888** *Lady* 25 Oct. 378/1 [Gloves] in the beautiful shades of brown, chocolate, oak, tans, and black.

b. *esp.* The bronzed tint imparted to the skin by exposure to the sun or the weather.

1749 J. CLELAND *Mem. Woman Pleasure* II. 233 The tan of his travels, and a beard.. had.. given it [*sc.* his face] an air of becoming manliness. **1827** CLARE *Sheph. Cal.* 48 And scare the tan from summer cheek. **1851** HAWTHORNE *Ho. Sev. Gables* v, The clear shade of tan, and the half-a-dozen freckles. **1885** *L'pool Daily Post* 7 May 5/3 With the tan of a southern sun upon his face.

c. *pl.* Short for *Black and Tans* (see BLACK *a.* 14 c). Also *sing.*, a member of this organization. Usu. with capital initial.

1932 S. O'FAOLÁIN *Midsummer Night Madness* 19 The Tans in their roaring Lancia patrol cars. *Ibid.* 227 'Shut up, you,' said the Tan angrily. **1951** C. LYNCH-ROBINSON *Last of Irish R.M.s* x. 161, I am sure that even amongst this class of the Tans.. there were a number of quite decent fellows. **1962** E. O'BRIEN *Lost Girl* xii. 132 God Almighty, it reminded me of the tans.. the night they burst the door in. **1978** F. BURTON *Politics of Legitimacy* iii. 69 Mrs Johnson sees the British troops of today.. as latter-day Tans.

4. *pl.* [ellipt. use of the adj.] Articles of dress, etc., of a tan colour; *esp.* tan shoes or boots.

1902 *Daily Chron.* 17 Sept. 5/2 Please say.. where these boots can be bought. I always buy my tans in the cheapest market. **1904** *Ibid.* 2 July 8/5 Tans are in far greater demand than has been known for years.

B. *adj.* Of the colour of tan or of tanned leather; of a yellowish or reddish brown; tawny; bronzed, sunburnt. Also *euphem.* (*rare*), black, negro.

1665 WOOD *Life* 6 May (O.H.S.) II. 35 A pair of tan leather gloves. **1845** DISRAELI *Sybil* IV. vii, Beautiful black and tan spaniels. **1887** W. S. GILBERT *Ruddigore*, I kept guinea pigs.. and a small black and tan [dog]. **1896** *Monthly Packet* Christm. No. 61 The daintiest of tan shoes. **1896** EDITH THOMPSON *ibid.* 98 Too well-fitting tan boots.. only adapted to mountain excursions of the picnic order. **1908** *Betw. Trent & Ancholme* 218 The white or tan sails pass by. **1950** *Sun* (Baltimore) 13 Sept. 14/2 He has written an article in the 'tan' national magazine *Ebony*. **1963** *Pix* 28 Sept. 63 Her hair should be blonde and bunched and her figure trim and tan. **1974** S. SHELDON *Other Side of Midnight* xiv. 275 He looked tanner and leaner than when she had last seen him.

C. *attrib.* and *Comb.*

1. from the sb. (in senses 1 a, 1 b) [some perhaps partly from the verb-stem: cf. TAN-HOUSE], as ***tan-colour***, ***-liquor***, ***-mill***; ***tan-burning***, ***-strewn***, ***-trodden*** adjs.; **tan-ball**: see quot.; **tan-bark**, = sense 1 a; **tan-bath**, a bath containing an infusion of oak-bark in water (*Cent. Dict.* 1891); **tan-bay**, the loblolly bay, *Gordonia Lasianthus* (ibid.); **tan-bed**, a hot-bed made of spent tan; a bark-bed; **tan-extractor**, a device for extracting the tannic acid and astringent principles from bark (Knight *Dict. Mech.* 1877); **tan-fat**, = TAN-VAT; **tan-fork**, a gardener's hand-fork for lifting tan; **tan-gallop**, = *tan-ride*; **tan-loft**, the loft of a tan-house; **tan-ooze**, **-pickle**, the liquor of a tan-vat: = OOZE *sb.*[1] 2; **tan-pit**, (*a*) = TAN-VAT; (*b*) in gardening, a tan-bed; **tan-pot** (see quot. 1978); **tan-press**, a machine for expressing moisture from the spent tan (*Cent. Dict.*); **tan-ride**, a riding-track covered with tan; cf. RIDE *sb.*[1] 2 a; **tan-spud**, a curved chisel for peeling the bark from oak or other trees; a peeler; **tan-stove**, a bark-stove; also, a hot-house with a bark-bed; † **tan-tub**, = TAN-VAT; **tan-turf**, spent tan pressed into bricks for fuel; = *tanners' turf* (TANNER[1] b); **Tan war** *Ir. Hist.*, the conflict between the Black and Tans and the Irish Republican Army in 1921; **tan-work**, **-yard**, a place where tanning is carried on; a tannery.

1882 OGILVIE (Annandale), **Tan-balls*, the spent bark of the tanner's yard pressed into balls or lumps, which harden on drying and serve for fuel. **1799** W. TOOKE *View Russian Emp.* I. I. ii. 34 The *tanbark-tree.. and many others. **1891** *Cent. Dict.*, Tan-bark. **1903** *Smart Set* I. 140/1 She had ridden her first horse over the tanbark of Durland's. **1739** MILLER *Gard. Dict.* II. s.v., There are some Persons who make their *Tan-beds much wider than what is here mentioned. **1812** *New Botanic Gard.* I. 81 The pots should be plunged into a tan-bed. **1882** PATON in *Encycl. Brit.* XIV. 382/2 'Spent tan', usually to be burned in a special form of *tan-burning furnace for raising steam. **1811** *Self Instructor* 539 Dark browns, minims, and *tan-colours. **1859** THOMPSON *Gard. Assist.* 124 *Tan-fork. **1856** 'STONEHENGE' *Brit. Sports* II. I. x. §2. 357/2 A *tan-gallop.. made permanently on a course three-quarters of a mile in circumference. **1882** PATON in *Encycl. Brit.* XIV. 382/2 One of the commonest plans for ascertaining the strength of the *tan liquor technically called ooze, or wooze, is by means of a kind of hydrometer called a barkometer. **1852** HANNA *Chalmers* IV. xxi. 404 Dr. Chalmers opened the *tan-loft for public worship. **1604** E. G[RIMSTONE] *D'Acosta's Hist. Indies* IV. xii. 243 Instruments, which beat this stone like vnto *tanne milles. **1839** URE *Dict. Arts* 1195 (*Sugar*) The first machines employed to squeeze the canes, were mills.. somewhat like tan-mills. **1901** F. ADAMS in *N. & Q.* 9th Ser. VII. 412/1 '*Tan ouse', tanner's ouse, or oak bark, an infusion of which is employed for tanning hides. **1820** T. MITCHELL *Aristoph.* I. 259 On him fell *tan-pickle, and nectar on you. *a* **1859** MACAULAY *Hist. Eng.* (1861) V. 181 The drink tasted like tanpickle. **1611** COTGR., *Coudroir*, a Tanfat, or *Tanpit. **1707** MORTIMER *Husb.* I. 123 What improves it to that Value is the emptying of the Town Tann-pits on it. **1810** BOSWELL *Edinburgh* Poet. Wks. (1871) 48 Neighbouring tan-pits scent the passing gales. **1858** GLENNY *Gard. Every-day Bk.* 34/1 Although a tan-pit is not absolutely necessary to make a hot-house, it is necessary to have bottom-heat at command. **1946** K. TENNANT *Lost Haven* (1947) vii. 96 They could mend nets, boil *tan-pots, play football. **1978** *Regional Lang. Stud.-Newfoundland* VIII. 18 A tan-pot or barking kettle is a large cauldron used for 'barking' a fisherman's nets with tan to prevent them from rotting in the salt water. **1863** LAWRENCE *Border & Bast.* iv. 70 In the centre is a large fountain of white marble, round which is a broad *tan-ride. **1884** YATES *Recoll.* II. ii. 81 A tan-ride furnished with various obstacles for leaping experiments. **1828** WEBSTER, **Tan-spud*,.. **Tan-stove*. **1904** *Blackw. Mag.* June 796 Chilcote glanced over the *tan-strewn ride. **1887** J. ASHBY STERRY *Lazy Minstrel* (1892) 42 What studies of man and of woman and horse Here pass up and down on the *tan-trodden course! **1586** J. DAVIS *Voy.* (Hakl. Soc.) 17 They found bags of trayne oyle,.. seale skinnes in *tan tubs, with many other such trifles. **1799** *Hull Advertiser* 2 Mar. 2/1 Tan-yard, bark-mill,.. tan-tubs, vats and materials. **1851** MAYHEW *Lond. Labour* II. 87/2 *Tan-turf is oak bark made into turf after its virtues have been exhausted in the tan-pits. **1968** 'N. BLAKE' *Private Wound* iii. 41 Flurry and I'd had enough of it after the *Tan war. **1981** J. WRIGHT *Devil's Parole* ii. 27 His tales of the Tan War ..his often cruel sketches of the Irish. **1822** J. FLINT *Lett. Amer.* 125 An iron foundery.. a *tan-work, a glass-house. **1711** *Customs Notice* in *Lond. Gaz.* No. 4862/4 Any Tan-house, *Tan-yard, Work-house. **1777** J. ADAMS in *Fam. Lett.* (1876) 241 A mill to grind bark for the tanyard. **1878** Tan-yard [see *hound-pup* s.v. HOUND *sb.*[1] 7 a]. **1911** J. MASEFIELD *Everlasting Mercy* 18 The tan-yards stank of bitter bark.

2. adjs. from A. 3, or B, chiefly parasynthetic, as ***tan-coloured***, ***-faced***, ***-sailed***, ***-skinned***, ***-tinted***.

1630 J. TAYLOR (Water P.) *Proclamation* Wks. II. 252/2 The Sunburnt tanskind Indians. **1685** *Lond. Gaz.* No. 2037/4 A black-brown Gelding.. Tan mouth'd. **1861** L. L. NOBLE *Icebergs* 63 Scudding under their tan-colored canvas. **1869** *Routledge's Ev. Boy's Ann.* 454 A tan-faced digger. **1888** *Dict. Nat. Biog.* XIII. 142/2 The tan-sailed barges sailing through the flats. **1892** *Daily News* 29 Mar. 2/4 An Eton jacket of the tan-tinted cloth, with sleeves to match.

tan, *sb.*[2] Short for FAN-TAN, a Chinese gambling game.

1883 STEVENSON *Silverado Sq.* 189 Where he might.. lose his little earnings at the game of tan.

‖**tan** (tan), *sb.*[3] [Jap.] A Japanese unit of arable land or forest, equal to 300 *bu*; in modern use equivalent to approximately 0·245 acres (9·92 ares).

1871 A. B. MITFORD *Tales of Old Japan* II. 2 Rice land is divided into three classes; and,.. it is computed that one *tan* (1,800 square feet).. should yield to the owner.. five bags of rice per annum. **1914** F. BRINKLEY *Hist. Jap. People* xxxvi. 527 In Hideyoshi's system,.. the rule of 360 *tsubo* to the *tan* (a quarter of an acre) was changed to 300 *tsubo*. **1931** G. B. SANSOM *Japan* I. v. 98 The area was two *tan* (1 *tan* is 1,000 square yards). **1964** *Japan* (Unesco) (rev. ed.) i. 19/2 The Imperial Proclamation of the Taika Reformation was announced at the end of the year 646... Taxes shall comprise two large bundles and two small bundles of rice crop on one *tan* (about 0.245 acre). **1970** J. W. HALL *Japan* vi. 54 Strips of one *tan* each (at that time approximately .3 acres).

‖**tan** (tan), *sb.*[4] [Jap.] A Japanese unit used for measuring cloth, equivalent to about ten yards in length and just over one foot in width; also, a piece of cloth of this size.

1876 W. E. GRIFFIS *Mikado's Empire* (1877) II. 609 A *tan*, or piece of cloth, varies in length from 25 to 30 or more feet. **1909** *Westm. Gaz.* 23 Oct. 13/1, I sentence each one to bring within three days one tan (about twenty-five yards) of cotton cloth. **1931** G. B. SANSOM *Japan* III. x. 187 Princes of the blood and ministers of the first rank were restricted to 500 *tan* of cloth. *Ibid.*, One *tan* is about ten yards.

‖**tan** (dan), *sb.*[5] Also **dan**. [Chinese.] A female character in a Chinese drama or opera; an actor of such a role.

1886 *Jrnl. R. Asiatic Soc.* (N. China Branch) XX. 208 *Tan* is a female character, and varies also according to age and.. circumstances. **1917** S. COULING *Encycl. Sinica* 149/1 There are five classes of characters in a play.. *shêng*.. *tan*.. *ching*.. *mo*.. and.. *ch'ou*. **1937** ARLINGTON & ACTON *Famous Chinese Plays* p. xxiv, *Tan*, subdivided into *laotan*, elderly dames with orange bandeau but no make-up; *ch'ing-i*, virtuous maidens and dutiful matrons; and *hua-tan*, vivacious and temperamental—often a courtesan or a piquante little maidservant. **1973** R. F. S. YANG in Yuan-li Wu *China* 739 The 'four great *tan* actors', namely, Mei Lan-fang, Ch'eng Yen-ch'iu, Shang Hsiao-yün, and Hsün Hui-sheng (all were female impersonators). **1975** C. P. MACKERRAS *Chinese Theatre in Mod. Times* xii. 199 The list of actors who took part in the festival of 1959 is an impressive one. Among exponents of the Peking Opera were three of the 'four great *tan*'. **1978** *Nagel's Encycl.-Guide: China* 201 There exist series of *dan*, or feminine roles, *sheng*, or chief masculine roles, *jing*, or heroic characters with painted faces, and *zhou* or fools.

‖**tan** (dan), *sb.*[6] [Chinese.] A Chinese unit of weight equivalent to approximately 110 lb. or 50 kg. (formerly approximately 133 lb., 60 kg.)

1911 *Encycl. Brit.* XXVIII. 494/1 *Tan*, China = 25 gallons. Also 133⅓ lb. weight. **1965** T. R. TREGEAR *Geogr. of China* iii. 108 In terms of food this meant a loss of 250 million *tan* (1 *tan* equals 133 lb.) since one *mow* produces an average of 2½ *tan*. **1973** *Genius of China* 104/2 It is calculated that the price recorded.. would in the reign of Wu Ti be approximately the equivalent of over 20 *tan* of grain.

tan (tæn), *v.* Also 5–6 **tanne**, 6–7 **tann**. Pa. t. and pple. **tanned** (tænd). [Late OE. *tannian*, evidenced *c* 1000 in pa. pple. *ȝetanned*, and agent-n. *tannere*, prob. f. med.L. *tannāre* (*tanare* in Erfurt Gl. *a* 900) to tan (whence pa. pple. *tannālus*, in Du Cange), f. *tannum* TAN *sb.* Cf. also OF. *tanner*, *taner* (13th c. in Littré), whence app. the ME. and modern vb. Cf. also Du. *tānen* to tan, generally held to be from Fr.]

1. a. *trans.* To convert (skin or hide) into leather by steeping in an infusion of an astringent bark, as that of the oak, or by a similarly effective process.

c **1000** [see TANNED 1]. [**1321–2** *Rolls of Parlt.* I. 415/2 Et xiiii li. pur quirs tannés de faire Barhides, & Sakes as draps.] *c* **1350** [see TANNED 1]. **14..** *Rule Syon Monast.* ix. in Aungier *Syon Monast.* (1840) 272 Withe hosen and schone tanned. *c* **1440** *Promp. Parv.* 486/2 Tannyn, or barkyn, *frunio*. **1481** CAXTON *Godeffroy* clxviii. 249 There was seint peter herberowed in a tanners hows, that tanned leder. **1503–4** *Act 19 Hen. VII*, c. 19 *Preamble*, No corryour ..[shall] cory any hyde of Leyther but such as afore be sufficiantly tanned. **1630** *Tom Thumbe* 56 in Hazl. *E.P.P.* II. 179 His bootes and shoes a mouses skin, there tand most curiously. **1768** BOSWELL *Corsica* iii. (ed. 2) 195 In the island of St. Kilda they tan with the tormentil root. **1875** URE *Dict. Arts* III. 85 About three months is usually occupied in tanning calf-skins.

b. *transf.* To treat (fishing-nets, sails, etc.) with tanners' ooze or some preserving substance; also, to act upon as an astringent.

1601 J. Keymor *Dutch Fishing* (1664) 7 Shee [the Herring Buss] imployeth..at Land..Tanners to Tan their Nets and Sayles. **1615** [see tan-vat]. **1889** J. M. Duncan *Clin. Lect. Dis. Wom.* xii. (ed. 4) 82 The styptic may pass into the uterine veins in the broad ligament, and produce changes there—tanning the parts. **1905** *Daily News* 26 July 6 'Drink less tea', says he, 'but, above everything, mind the infusing'. .. The British interior will continue to be tanned until the sun of Albion shall set.

c. In the manufacture of artificial marble, to steep (the composition) in a hardening and preservative preparation: cf. tannage 1.

1891 in *Cent. Dict.*

2. a. To make brown (the face or skin), esp. by exposure to the sun or weather; to embrown, sunburn; hence, to make dark or tawny in colour.

1530 Palsgr. 752/2, I tanne in the sonne, or am sonne brente... You shall tanne your selfe more upon the see than upon lande. **1590** Spenser *F.Q.* I. vi. 35 His..face all tand with scorching sunny ray. **1601** Holland *Pliny* I. 127 The neerer they approch to the riuer Indus, the deeper coloured they are and tanned with the Sun. **1660** F. Brooke tr. *Le Blanc's Trav.* 102 The people are..of a good stature, but a little tann'd. **1746–7** Hervey *Medit.* (1767) I. 262 Heat, whose burning Influence..tans into Soot the Ethiopian's Complexion. **1812** Byron *Ch. Har.* II. lxix, In war well season'd, and with labours tann'd. **1853** Mrs. Gaskell *Cranford* xv, His face was deep brown, as if tanned and re-tanned by the sun.

fig. *c* **1645** Howell *Lett.* (1650) II. 17 All Egypt and Barbary, with Lybia and the Negro's Country, are tainted and tand with this black Religion. **1979** *Internat. Jrnl. Sociol. of Law* VII. 230 Ehrlich was not interested in the social life but in the 'legal life' of the Bukowina and..his picture of 'legal life' is heavily tanned by the traditional pattern of the Bukowinian society.

b. *intr.* (for *refl.*) To become sunburnt or darkened by exposure.

1530 [see 2]. **1884** *Illustr. Lond. News* 26 Jan. 91/2 One advantage you swarthy people have over us—you don't tan. **1889** *Nature* 24 Oct. 633/2 The capacity to tan, or become darker by exposure, varies much.

3. *trans.* ***to tan** (a person's) **hide***, also simply ***to tan*** (a person): to thrash soundly. *slang* or *colloq.* (Cf. hide *v.*[2] 2.) Occas. *intr.*

c **1670** *Expost. Let. Men Buckhm.* 2/2 Let not your Worships thick skin be too sensible that we thus Tan your Hide. **1731** Coffey *Devil to Pay* iv. (1733) 13 Come, and spin, you lazy Drab, or I'll tan your Hide for you. **1835–40** Haliburton *Clockm.* (1862) 120 I'll tan your hide for you, you may depend. **1862** Mrs. H. Wood *Channings* II. ix. 137 'I'll tan you too, Mr. Bywater.'.. 'Tan away,' coolly responded Bywater. 'I can tan again.' **1890** J. Curtin tr. *Sienkiewicz' With Fire & Sword* xli. 475 To-day you tan people, to-morrow they tan you. **1903** *Spectator* 14 Feb. 245 Midshipmen, who are boys, are 'tanned', but not Lieutenants of twenty-five.

4. *Photogr.* To harden (gelatin) chemically in proportion to the amount of exposure.

1899 C. F. Townsend *Chem. for Photographers* (ed. 2) iv. 75 Formaldehyde is not the only aldehyde capable of tanning gelatine. **1957** R. W. G. Hunt *Reproduction of Colour* v. 43 Gelatin, in its usual state, is soluble in hot water. But by suitable chemical treatment it can be hardened, or tanned, so that it becomes insoluble. **1979** G. Haist *Mod Photogr. Processing* I. v. 225 Images produced in the presence of such oxidation products are also tanned.

tan, = *to han*, to have: see t'[1] and have.

c **1407** [see tame *v.*[2] 2].

tan, obs. inf. and pa. pple. of take *v.*; obs. phonetic var. of *þan* then.

tan., *Math.* abbreviation of tangent B. 1.

tana, *Zool.*: see Tupaia.

tana(h, tanadar, varr. thana, thanadar.

†**tanacles**, *sb. pl. Obs. rare*[−0]. Also 6 -**akles**, 7 -**ackels**. [app. var. tenacle, ad. L. *tenāculum*, modified after It. *tanaglie* pl. pincers, tongs:—L. *tenācula*.] (See quots.) Hence †**tanacle** *v. Obs. rare*[−0].

1598 Florio, *Tanaglie*, toongs, pincers, tanakles, mullets. *Tanagliare*, to torture, to pinch, to tanakle with toongs, pincers or tanakles. **1623** Cockeram, *Tanackels*, Pincers for tortures. **1656** Blount *Glossogr.*, *Tanacles*. **1721** Bailey, *Tanacles*,.. Instruments of Torture like Pincers.

tanager ('tænədʒə(r)). *Ornith.* Also 7- **tangara**. [ad. mod.L. *Tanagra* (Linnæus 1758), for Tupi *tangara* (used by Brisson 1760).] A bird of the genus *Tanagra* or family *Tanagridæ* of passerine birds, of Central and South America.

There are numerous species, named from their colour, as ***black-headed, green-headed; red, scarlet, spotted, variegated, yellow tanager***; from other characteristics, as ***crested, grand hooded, silent t.***; from their native locality, as ***Brazilian, Mississippi t.***; from resemblance to other birds, as ***bullfinch, oriole t.***; from their discoverer, as ***Cooper's t.***, etc.

1614 Purchas *Pilgrimage* ix. iv. 843 The Tangara which haue the falling-sicknes, the rest dancing about that which is fallen, with a noise, from which they will not be skarred till they haue done. [**1648** Marcgrave *Hist. Nat. Brasil.* 214 *Tangara* Brasiliensibus; (reperiuntur ejus aliquot species colore variantes).] **1688** R. Holme *Armoury* II. 243/1 The Brasilian Tangara [hath] Legs and Feet cinereous, inclining to dusky. **1825** Waterton *Wand. S. Amer.* (1882) 26 A numerous species of bird called Tangara. **1844** *Zoologist* II. 444 The occurrence of the Red-breasted Tanager near Cheltenham. **1857** Mayne Reid *War Trail* xlv, The sweet warbling voices of the silvias, finches, tanagers, that..adorn the American woods with their gorgeous colours. **1863** Thoreau *Excursions* 31 The tanager flies through the green foliage as if it would ignite the leaves. **1893** W. H. Hudson *Idle Days Patagonia* x. 156 It is impossible to say of many species which are finches and which tanagers. **1896** Newton *Dict. Birds* 943 *Tanager*..adapted from the quasi-Latin *Tanagra* of Linnæus,..an adaptation, perhaps with a classical allusion, of *Tangara*, used by Brisson and Buffon.

Hence **'tanagrine** *a.*, of or pertaining to tanagers; belonging to the family *Tanagridæ*, or subfamily *Tanagrinæ* (*Cassell's Encycl. Dict.* 1887); **'tanagroid** (**tangaroid**) *a.*, resembling the tanagers; akin in structure to the tanager family.

1879 E. P. Wright *Anim. Life* 254 The Tangaroid Perchers.

Tanagra ('tænəgrə). The name of a city of Boeotia in ancient Greece, used *attrib.* and *absol.* to designate terra cotta statuettes of the 5th to 3rd centuries B.C. found in the neighbourhood. (See also quot. 1899.)

1878 C. Schreiber *Jrnl.* 29 Aug. (1911) II. 195 M. Grean was resettling some of his Greek (Tanagra) specimens. **1890** O. Wilde *Pict. Dorian Gray* (1891) 112 She had all the delicate grace of that Tanagra figurine that you have in your studio. **1899** C. A. Hutton *Greek Terracotta Statuettes* ii. 17 That aspect of individuality which is the great charm of the Bœotian statuettes from the Tanagra district, and which is so characteristic of them that any specially pretty figure, whatever its provenance, is popularly known as a 'Tanagra'. **1915** V. Horsley in S. Paget *Sir V. Horsley* (1919) 309 Some wonderful Greek sculptures small scale, and large Tanagras. **1927** *Glasgow Herald* 22 June 10 The style of the Tanagra heads of ancient Greece. **1960** R. G. Haggar *Conc. Encycl. Continental Pott. & Porc.* 469/1 Tanagra figures have been much admired..and much faked,—many of the fakes appearing..in the late 1870s and early 1880s not many years after the first discoveries of genuine Tanagra statuettes. **1978** 'M. M. Kaye' *Far Pavilions* II. xv. 240 Shushila-Bai was as small and exquisite as a Tanagra figurine.

tanaid ('tænəɪd), *a* and *sb. Zool.* [f. mod.L. *Tanaidæ*, f. generic name *Tanais*.] **a.** *adj.* Of or pertaining to the *Tanaidæ*, a family of cheliferous isopod crustaceans, typified by the genus *Tanais*. **b.** *sb.* A member of this family.

1893 Stebbing *Crustacea* xxi. 327 The marital Tanaid frequently sacrifices his mouth-organs to the enormous development of his chelipeds.

tanaist, Tanakin, obs. ff. tanist, Tannakin.

tanaiste ('tɔːnɪʃtə). [a. Ir. *tánaiste*: see tanist.] The deputy prime minister of the Republic of Ireland.

1938 *Éire: New Irish Constitution: Citizen's Manual* 22 The Taoiseach nominates a member of the Government as Tánaiste to act in his place for all purposes, should the Taoiseach die or become permanently incapacitated, or be temporarily absent. **1975** *Irish Times* 10 May 5/4 A tribute to the work of the former members..was paid by the Tanaiste and Minister for Health, Mr. Corish. **1982** M. Wallace *Brit. Govt. in N. Ireland* v. 94 The Labour *Tanaiste* or Deputy Prime Minister.

tanakaha: see tanekaha.

tanalized ('tænəlaɪzd), *a.* [f. *Tanal(ith*, proprietary name of a water-borne preservative for wood + -ize + -ed[1].] Of timber, treated with Tanalith preservative or a similar compound.

1964 *Weekly News* (Auckland, N.Z.) 29 July 42/4, I built in tanalised or creosoted exotic timber which is everlasting and grown for the purpose by our Forest Service. **1967** *Daily Tel.* 15 Apr. 19/7 (Advt.), Garden frames. Made from tanalised timber, never need painting or maintenance. **1980** *Amateur Gardening* 18 Oct. 1c/1 To this end, one of the most useful stock items you can keep is a bundle or two of tanalised batten.

Tancook ('tænkʊk). *New Hist.* The name of an island at the mouth of Mahone Bay, Nova Scotia, used *attrib.* in ***Tancook whaler***, a double-ended schooner, about 45 feet long of a type formerly built there. Also ***Tancook schooner***.

1933 *Yachting* Feb. 102/2 It will be the last model of a real Tancook whaler made in Nova Scotia. **1947** *Sun* (Baltimore) 18 Sept. 23/7 The Scotia schooner built to slide over rocks is Nicholas G. Schlegel's Windstark. The type is called a 'Tancook schooner', from the locality in Nova Scotia where she was built. **1951** H. I. Chapelle *Amer. Small Sailing Craft* iii. 166 The Tancook whaler was one of the most handsome of the double-enders used on the Atlantic Coast. **1967** H. F. Pullen *Atlantic Schooners* 33 The Tancook whaler was somewhat similar to the pinky, but with much sharper lines.

tand, obs. f. *tanned*, pa. pple. of tan *v.*

tandava ('tɑːndəvə). Also **tandav**. [a. Skr. *tāṇḍava*.] The dance of Shiva; a traditional style of dancing in India, of a vigorous and masculine character. Cf. lasya.

1924 Ld. Ronaldshay *India: Bird's-Eye View* xxi. 272 A dance of Shiva called Tandava, performed in cemeteries and burning-grounds. **1937**, etc. [see lasya]. **1967** Singha & Massey *Indian Dances* 22 Tandav was first danced by the god Shiva, Lord of the Dance, who then conveyed this art to mortals through his disciple Tandu. Shiva is the symbol of procreation and it is because of this that tandav is often regarded as a male dance. **1969** *Weekly Mail* (Madras) 26 July 10/4 The same movements performed with the vigour of males is tandava while it becomes lasya when performed by women possessing feminine grace. **1978** G. Vidal *Kalki* vii. 162 Indeed, there is a legend that the end will come when Siva begins the Tandava Dance, or dance of eternity.

tandem ('tændɛm, -əm), *sb.*[1] and *adv.* Also 8–9 *erron.* **tandum**. [app. L. *tandem* at length (of time) used punningly.]

A. *sb.* **1. a.** A two-wheeled vehicle drawn by two horses (or other beasts of draught) harnessed one before the other.

1785 Grose *Dict. Vulg. T.*, *Tandem*, a two wheeled chaise, buggy, or noddy, drawn by two horses, one before the other, that is *at length*. **1789** *Loiterer* No. 42. 12, I have not the smallest desire to ride in Mr. Whirligig's Tandem. **1807** Byron *Let. to Miss Pigot* 11 Aug., We shall..proceed in a tandem..to Inverary. **1821** A. Hodgson *Lett. fr. N. Amer.* (1824) II. 110 Painted sleighs..are dashing along [Broadway, New York] in all directions,..some with two horses abreast; some harnessed as tandems, and others with four in hand. **1850** *N. & Q.* 1st Ser. I. 382/1 We have a practical pun now naturalized in our language in the word 'tandem'. **1861** Hughes *Tom Brown at Oxf.* i, They drove tandems in all directions, scattering their ample allowances ..about roadside inns.

b. *transf.* A pair of carriage-horses harnessed one before the other. Also *fig.*

1795 W. Felton *Carriages* (1801 II. 120 A Tandum..is ..two horses in a team, or one before the other, to draw a two-wheeled chaise. *a* **1805** A. Carlyle *Autobiog.* (1860) [449 In the end of summer [of 1764] I went again with Mrs. Carlyle to Harrogate,..I got an open chaise with two horses —one before the other, and the servant on the first. *Ibid.*] 458 Blackett's horse was very heavy, and my tandem far outran them. **1859** Cornwallis *New World* I. 104, I.. equipped a dog-cart and tandem, for a drive to the diggings. **1885** *Pall Mall G.* 14 Jan. 3/2 The old political tandem, in which the poor man with talent and the rich man without it pulled together, is no longer possible.

2. Short for *tandem bicycle* (*tricycle*), *canoe*, *engine*: see C.

1884 *Daily News* 19 Sept. 3/3 Cycling on a 'tandem' in Norway... When our tandem..was placed upon the pier, we were surrounded by an eager crowd. **1888** *Encycl. Brit.* XXIII. 560/1 For nearly every make of single tricycle there is a corresponding tandem. **1900** *Engineering Mag.* XIX. 778/1 Triple-expansion engines,..having 1 high, 1 intermediate and 2 low pressure cylinders arranged as twin vertical tandems.

B. *adv.* One behind the other, in single file; originally of a team of two horses. Also *fig.*

1795 W. Felton *Carriages* (1801) II. Gloss., *Tandum*, the manner of driving two horses in a team. **1818** T. L. Peacock *Nightmare Abbey* i, His fellow-students..drove tandem and random in great perfection. **1837** *Chron.* in *Ann. Reg.* 1 Jan. 1/2 The letters are conveyed daily from Canterbury to Dover on sledges drawn by three and four horses, tandem. **1893** *Atlantic Monthly* Feb. 196/1 Three logs chained tandem constituted the load, and we vaulted upon the last log for a ride to the boom. **1897** *Outing* (U.S.) XXX. 135/1 The patient mules, driven tandem, were dragging a heavy barge down the canal.

b. ***in tandem***, arranged one behind the other; also *fig.*, together, in partnership.

1930 [see Corliss]. **1949** [see scaling *vbl. sb.*[3] 2]. **1957** I. Asimov *Naked Sun* (1958) ii. 30 There were two seats in tandem, each of which could hold three. **1964** S. Lieberson in J. A. Fishman *Readings Sociol. of Lang.* (1968) 553 These measures, used in tandem, provide an instrument for a quantitative approach to a basic sociolinguistic problem. **1974** *News & Press* (Darlington, S. Carolina) 24 Apr. 8/7 Management and labor are learning to work in tandem, as has been evidenced by the sharp drop in strikes.

C. *attrib.* and *Comb.* **1. a.** *gen.* as ***tandem-curricle, -drag*** (drag *sb.* 1 d), ***-driving, -horse, -sleigh, -team, -whip***; ***tandem-wise*** adv.; **tandem axle** (see quot. 1969); usu. *attrib.*; **tandem bicycle** (**tricycle**), **canoe**, a bicycle (tricycle) or canoe for two persons, one seated behind the other; **tandem duplication** *Genetics*, an atypical form of duplication (duplication 1 e) in which the repeated segments lie immediately adjacent to one another on the same chromosome; **tandem formation** *Tennis*, the position of partners in a doubles match in which server and netman occupy the same half of the court at service; **tandem garage**, a garage with space for two vehicles to be parked one behind the other rather than side by side; **tandem-paced** *a.*, in cycle-racing: involving the use of a tandem for pacing; **tandem-play**: see quot.

1956 in E. Molloy *Automobile Engineer's Ref. Bk.* xxx. §7 The Eaton type *tandem axle unit has been developed as a method of increasing the proportion of payload to gross vehicle weight. **1969** Baker & Stebbins *Dict. Highway Traffic* 230 *Tandem* (*axles*),..an assembly of two axles for the support of the rear of a truck trailer. **1977** 'D. Rutherford' *Return Load* ii. 29 I'd suggest you have one of these new tandem axle Taskvans... They have air-bellow suspension. **1896** G. B. Shaw *Let.* 5 July (1965) I. 634, I will get a *tandem bicycle; and we shall ride along over the celestial plains. **1899** *Daily News* 11 Jan. 2/4 In the Soudan they used a small dynamo driven by means of a tandem bicycle. **1867** J. MacGregor *Thousand Miles in Rob Roy Canoe* (ed. 5) ii. 37 In the Canoe Club we have three '*tandem' canoes, each for two paddles. **1815** *Reviewers Reviewed* 18 Even Doctor Solomon..is ready with his *tandem curricle to invite him to Gilead Hall. **1817** J. Palmer *Jrnl. Trav. in U.S.* etc. (1818) 217 [At Montreal] I have seen a *tandem dog cart, the dogs harnessed and belled the same as horses. **1825** C. M. Westmacott *Eng. Spy* I. 86 Since she put down her *tandem drag. **1850** Thackeray *Pendennis* xix, Riding and *tandem-driving were the fashions of the ingenuous youth. **1959** C. M. M. Begg

Introd. Genetics x. 137 A *tandem duplication can result from unequal crossing over. **1981** L. L. MAYS *Genetics* xii. 529 Tandem duplication of a short region of one chromosome is thought to result from inaccurate crossing over processes. **1830** LYTTON *P. Clifford* xxxi, A light cart drawn by two swift horses in a *tandem fashion awaited the fugitives. **1890** W. J. GORDON *Foundry* 73 They are being built with the high-pressure above the low-pressure, tandem fashion, with a piston-rod common to both. **1967** P. METZLER *Advanced Tennis* ix. 116 When first confronted with the *tandem formation..the left-hander is likely to continue hitting his return in its usual direction. **1976** *Tennis Today* Oct. 12/1 The American juniors played the whole match using what they call the Tandem Formation, more normally referred to as the Australian Formation in this country. **1968** *Globe & Mail* (Toronto) 3 Feb. 41/2 (Advt.), Executive home. Seven room solid brick bungalow with *tandem double garage. **1974** *Country Life* 7 Mar. (Suppl.) 32 *l*, 2 reception rooms, kitchen/breakfast room. Tandem garage. **1801** FELTON *Carriages* II. App. 6 When loaded, a leading or *Tandum horse, is mostly applied. **1895** *Baily's Mag.* May 353/2 A useful house-of-call, at which you could pop on a *tandem leader. **1929** *Star* 21 Aug. 17/1 F. W. Southall is expected to make an attack on the one mile *tandem-paced record. **1955** *Times* 11 July 5/7 D. Marsh (Shaftesbury C.C.) won the 12-hour tandem-paced cycle race at Herne Hill on Saturday. **1895** *Funk's Stand. Dict.*, **Tandem-play* (Football), a play in which the man running with the ball is preceded or followed, or both preceded and followed, by other men of his own side..to assist him in breaking through the opposing line. **1863** 'OUIDA' *Held in Bondage* (1870) 31 Dashing on with his *tandem-team too quickly for identification. **1835** WILLIS *Pencillings* I. xxxiii. 230 It might have been touched from the deck with a *tandem whip. **1860** *All Year Round* 496 The two horses which he has..had harnessed to it *tandem-wise.

b. With reference to systems of work, machines, etc., which involve the use of two or more elements operating together or in series; **tandem engine**, a steam engine with two cylinders one in front of the other, the two pistons working on a common piston-rod.

1878 *Engineer* XLVI. 23 (Paris Exhibition), 60 Horse Power Compound Tandem Engine. **1901** *Feilden's Mag.* IV. 413/1 The fan engines, which were tandem-compound, were afterwards fitted with low-pressure relief-valves, in addition to those fitted in the high-pressure cylinders. **1921** *Telegr. & Telephone Jrnl.* VII. 79/2 With a machine switching tandem exchange large groups..can be established between each local exchange and the tandem exchange. **1923** HARBORD & HALL *Metallurgy of Steel* II. xiv. 290 Splitting up the mill into a breaking-down mill, which is placed in front of, and feeds, the smaller finishing mill (the arrangement being usually known as a tandem mill) is preferable where there is a sufficient output to justify employing two sets of men. **1924** W. AITKEN *Automatic Telephone Systems* III. 79 Tandem working through a tandem office will be introduced into London as quickly as possible. **1933** K. B. MILLER *Telephone Theory & Pract.* III. iv. 243 In large cities..tandem operation is especially useful. *Ibid.*, The cost and inconvenience of using the tandem routing must be balanced against the trunk saving which it produces. **1955** *Archit. Rev.* CXVII. 141/2 A motor assembly known as a Two-speed Tandem Motor combines a squirrel cage and slip-ring motor within a single frame. **1959** *Wall St. Jrnl.* 3 July (Eastern ed.) 5/5 The New York State Thruway Authority has approved the use of tandem-trailers over its 559-mile highway system. The tandem vehicles—which consist of a heavy duty truck tractor hitched to two regular size trailer units—have been in experimental use. **1967** *New Scientist* 16 Feb. 397/1 Although the majority of larger telephone exchanges in Britain have direct connections with all other exchanges, many have to route their outgoing calls through central switching exchanges known as tandem exchanges. **1970** *Gloss. Aeronaut. & Astronaut. Terms (B.S.I.)* VI. 2 *Tandem boost*, a boost rocket motor assembly which is located at the rear of the missile and co-axially with it. **1971** W. K. V. GALE *Iron & Steel Industry: Dict. Terms* 54 *Continuous mill* (*tandem mill*), any rolling mill in which the stands are arranged in tandem. **1976** *NBR Market-place* (Wellington, N.Z.) III. 3/4 Tandem blades clog up with shaving foam and don't give as even a shave as the single blade. **1978** *Detroit Free Press* 14 Apr. 16D/2 Carrying 22 extra bolts and a new coupling device, a tandem tanker rumbled down a test track.

2. Passing into *adj.* **a.** In various uses with reference to the occurrence of one thing behind or after another.

1926 *Daily Tel.* 7 Aug. 7/4 Someone has given the appropriate name 'tandem' system to a form of curriculum in which students were limited to one main subject, and one subject only, at a time. **1952** *Mind* LXI. 356 Is minding what one is doing, then, after all, a tandem occurrence? **1968** E. A. POWDRILL *Vocab. Land Planning* iii. 54 Two-tier, or tandem, development is merely the utilisation of backland to place one or more houses behind another. **1980** *Archaeology* Nov.-Dec. 37 We took a series of tandem camera exposures from the 300 meter level.

b. Co-operative, joint, dual; involving two persons, organizations, etc.

1962 *Economist* 24 Mar. 1094/1 The future is seen..in terms of a 'tandem' economic partnership between two continental common markets. **1963** *Times Lit. Suppl.* 18 Jan. 44/4 The tandem authors of this study merely add to the confusion. **1976** *National Observer* (U.S.) 21 Feb. 1/5 These tandem operations, Totera and Schuler explain, involve every aspect of IRS forms. **1977** *Time* 26 Sept. 37/3 Kepesh recalls a tandem tantrum he had with his wife.

Hence **'tandem, 'tandemize** *vbs.*, *intr.* to drive a tandem; *trans.* to harness or drive (a horse, etc.) tandem fashion; **'tandemer, 'tandemist,** one who rides a tandem bicycle or tricycle.

1828 *Sporting Mag.* XXII. 132 We *tandem'd on to Melton for a finishing treat. **1898** *Speaker* 16 July 87 They tandemed the donkey to drag their impedimenta up the slope of 1,200 feet. **1894** *Daily News* 3 May 8/6 At 5 miles the *tandemers had cut the record by a good deal over 2 min. **1885** *Cyclist* 5 Aug. 1026/2 The silken fetters of matrimony convert a happy bicyclist into..an equally happy *tandemist. **1824** *Blakw. Mag.* XV. 115 Reginald..drinks—games—hunts—*tandemizes. **1840** *New Monthly Mag.* LIX. 492 Tandemizing, cricketizing, boatizing,..is not to be carried on without a considerable expenditure.

† **tandem,** *sb.*[2] *U.S. Obs.* [Origin unascertained: perh. from a place-name.] Name of some kind of linen, in 18th c. classed among Silesia linens.

1747 *Boston* (U.S.) *Even. Post* 18 May 2/2 To be sold cheap..Lloyd's Garlets, Tandems, Cambricks, Taffatees. **1754** *Boston Gaz.* 31 Dec. 3/2 Just Imported from London, And Sold By Samuel Abbot,..3-4th and yard wide garlix's, tandems, hollands, cambricks. **1755** *Boston Even. Post* 26 May 4/2 Ten Pieces yard wide Tandems,..three Pieces Osnabrigs. **1783** *Circular from Hamburg* in *Pennsylv. Gaz.* 26 Nov. 3/1 German cloth of every quality and colour.. Silesia linens..Rough dowlas, Quadruple tandems, Brown Silesias.

tandemly ('tændəmlı), *adv.* Chiefly *Genetics.* [f. TANDEM *sb.*[1] and *adv.* + -LY[2].] End to end.

1968 *Jrnl. Molecular Biol.* XXXII. 328 Cairns' (1966) hypothesis that the long DNA fibers are composed of many tandemly joined replication sections is proved. **1974** [see REPLICON]. **1978** *Nature* 5 Oct. 364/3 The histone genes of *Drosophila* represent a tandemly repeated gene family. **1980** *European Jrnl. Cell Biol.* XXII. 430 As Hensen's node regresses, paraxial somitomeres are added tandemly.

tandle, tanle ('tand(ə)l, 'tan(ə)l). *Sc.* and *north. dial.* Also 8–9 **taanle, tawnle,** 9 **taunle, tannel.** [perh. an altered form of ON. *tandr, tandri* fire = OHG. *zantaro, zantro,* MHG. *zanter, zander*: but the history is incomplete.] A large fire in the open air, a bonfire; esp. one made at certain seasons in the year, as on May Day, Midsummer Eve, or the first of November.

1788 PICKEN *Now-a-days* Poems 62 Thae flirds o' silk.. Had I our doghter's at a candle, They'd mak' a been an' rowsan tandle. **1793** *Statist. Acc. Scotl.* VII. 622 An antient practise..of kindling a large fire, or tawnle as it is usually termed, of wood. **1802** SIBBALD *Scot. Poetry* Gloss. s.v., The custom of kindling large fires or Taanles, at Midsummer, was formerly common in Scotland. **1845** *New Statist. Acc. Scotl.* V. 223 The custom of the baal-fire or Tannel is still observed on the last day of July, St. Margaret's Day. **1887** J. SERVICE *Dr. Duguid* iv. 28 Bigging great taunles on the holms o' the Garnock.

tandoori (tæn'dʊərı), *a.* (*sb.*) Also **tanduri.** [Adj. form of next (sense 2).] Of, pertaining to, or designating food cooked in a tandour (sense 2), or this style of cooking. Also *absol.* as *sb.*

1958 R. HOWE *Cooking from Commonwealth* 484 Since partition the most popular form of restaurant cooking in India's capital, Delhi, has been tanduri cooking. *Ibid.* 540 Tanduri chicken is always eaten with the fingers. **1961** MRS. B. SINGH *Indian Cookery* I. 18 A tandoor is used for the preparation of tandoori chicken, tandoori fish, seekh kabab, tandoori roti, nan, sheermal etc. **1966** *Daily Tel.* 24 Oct. 11/3 The fabulous *tandoori* cooking from the north-west of India: charcoal-heated clay-oven cooking which ensures food of distinction. **1969** *Guardian* 2 Oct. 17 The restaurant specialises in exclusive Indian cuisine: Tandoories—meat and chicken grilled in clay ovens over a charcoal fire. **1969** *Enact* (Delhi) Nov. 18/2 Bring out the *tanduri* fish. **1970** D. SINGH *Indian Cookery* 30 *Tandoori* is food cooked on the spit in a clay oven. *Ibid.* 32 The various kebabs and kaftas used in tandoori, grills and roasts. **1975** *Indian Express* 1 Aug. 4/4 Multipurpose gadget for tandoori cooking. **1977** D. JAMES *Spy at Evening* viii. 53 Dinner..at..my favourite Tandoori house on Sidney Street. **1979** *Daily Tel.* 11 June 8/8 More rice is being eaten in Britain. Not in the old-fashioned rice pudding, but with curry, chop-suey and tandoori dishes.

‖ **tandour, tandoor** ('tændʊə(r)). Also 7 **tenur, tenner,** 8–9 **tendour,** 9– **tan-, tendoor, tandur.** [In sense 1, = F. *tandour*, a. *tandūr*, Turkish pronunc. of Pers. and Arab. *tannūr* oven, portable furnace, a. Aramaic *tannūrā*, Heb. *tannūr*, Assyrian *tinūru* furnace, oven; in sense 2, ad. Urdu or Punjabi *tandūr* oven; cf. Turkish *tandır* clay oven, ult. as above.]

1. A heating apparatus consisting of a square table with a brazier under it, round which persons sit for warmth in cold weather in Persia, Turkey, and adjacent countries.

1662 J. DAVIES tr. *Olearius' Voy. Ambass.* 294 They [Persians] call this kind of Stoves *Tenner. Ibid.* 303 In Winter they have their *Tenurs* against the Cold. **1718** LADY M. W. MONTAGU *Let. to Mrs. Thistlethwayte* 4 Jan., Warming themselves..neither by chimney nor stoves, but a certain machine called a *tendour*, the height of two feet, in the form of a table, covered with a fine carpet or embroidery. This is made only of wood, and they put into it a small quantity of hot ashes, and sit with their legs under the carpet. **1802** *Edin. Rev.* I. 51 The tandour supplies the want of grates and chimnies.

2. Usu. **tandoor.** A clay oven used in northern India and Pakistan; a shop that sells food cooked in this. Also *Comb.*, as ***tandoor-cooked*** adj.

1840 FRASER *Trav. Koordistan*, etc. I. vi. 150 A sort of oven called a *tendour*. *Ibid.* II. ix. 200 *Tendoor.* **1925** M. L. DARLING *Punjab Peasant* viii. 166 A significant change is that, when the cultivator goes to town, he is not as content as he was with the low-class *tandur*, but has begun to put up at the hotel. **1947** *Civil & Milit. Gaz.* 8 Apr. 11/1 Some 'tandur' shops were partially affected by the fire. **1957** C. RAND *Twain shall Meet* 77 They complain too that there is no room for *tandoors*, special jarlike ovens for baking *chapatis*—wheat pancakes—a Punjab staple. **1967** *Guardian* 8 Dec. 6/4 North Indian or Pakistani [cooking] depends on the clay oven called a tandoor, into which kebabs, chickens marinated in yoghourt and spices, and the special bread called nan are lowered and rapidly cooked. **1974** [see NAN[3]]. **1977** *Sunday Times* (Colour Suppl.) 27 Nov. 35/3 The tandoor is the traditional oven used in Indian villages. It is fashioned out of clay and left to dry for two days. Then it is seasoned with yoghurt, spinach and oil to smooth it and prevent it from cracking. It is this, combined with the tremendous even heat of the burning coals, that gives tandoor-cooked meat its mild aromatic flavour.

tandrec, variant of TANREC.

‖ **tandstickor** ('tænd,stıkə(r)). [a. Swed. *tändstickor* matches, pl. of *tändsticka*, f. *tända* to light, kindle + *sticka* splinter, spill. The Eng. popular use was taken from the word 'Tändstickor', i.e. 'matches', on boxes of matches made in Sweden.] More fully, ***tandstickor match***, a cheap kind of lucifer match imported from Sweden.

1884 *Pall Mall G.* 19 July 20/1 Who ever sees the Tändstickors nowadays except in Continental hotels? **1889** RIDER HAGGARD *Allan's Wife*, etc. 313 It was a 'tandstickor' match, and burnt slowly and dimly. **1898** *Westm. Gaz.* 3 June 4/3 The public which purchases the ordinary or tandstickor match.

† **tandy,** ? obs. form of TAWNY.

1496 *Fysshynge with an Angle* (1883) 34 The tandy flye at saynt Wyllyams daye, the body of tandy wull & the wynges ..of the whitest mayle of þe wylde drake.

tane, obs. pa. pple. of TAKE *v.*; Sc. and north. dial. f. TONE, in *the tone* = the one.

‖ **tanekaha** (tɑːne'kaha). Also **tana-.** [Native Maori name.] A New Zealand conifer, the Celery-topped Pine, *Phyllocladus trichomanoides.*

1875 T. LASLETT *Timber Trees* xxxviii. 306 The Tanakaha Tree..is found scattered over a large portion of the northern island of New Zealand. **1883** J. HECTOR *Handbk. N. Zealand* (1886) 101 Tanekaha, Celery-leaved Pine. A slender, handsome tree, 60 ft. high.

tanewa, obs. var. TANIWHA.

tang (tæŋ), *sb.*[1] Forms: α. 4–7 **tange,** 7–8 **tangue,** 8–9 *dial.* **taing,** 5– **tang.** β. 5–6 **tong(g)e.** [Known in literature from 14th c., but prob. in much earlier use in northern Eng.: a. ON. *tange* point, spit of land, tang of a knife, etc., Norw., Da. *tange*, Sw. *tång(e*, Færoese *tangi*.]

I. 1. A projecting pointed part or instrument.

a. The tongue of a serpent, formerly thought to be the stinging organ; the sting of an insect. (Now *dial.*)

a **1350** *St. Matthew* 58 in Horstm. *Altengl. Leg.* (1881) 132 Men þat þai [serpents] bifore had biten And with þaire tanges ful sare smetyn. *c* **1440** *Promp. Parv.* 496/2 Tongge, of a bee, *aculeus*. *c* **1440** STAUNTON *St. Patrick's Purg.* (1900) 61 þei maden to me an hudious noyse..with blaryng owt of here brennyng tanges. **1483** *Cath. Angl.* 378/1 A Tange of A nedyr, *aculeus, acus, pugio.* **1530** PALSGR. 281/2 Tonge of a bee, *esguillon.* **1787** GROSE *Provinc. Gloss., Tang*,..a sting. **1876** *Whitby Gloss., Tang*, a sting or point. **1877** *N.W. Linc. Gloss., Tang*,..the tongue of a snake, with which people believe it has the power of stinging... The sting of an insect.

b. *fig.* A 'sting', a pang.

1724 RAMSAY *Health* 156 The flagg'd embrace, and mercenary squeeze, The tangs of guilt, and terrors of disease. **1868** LANIER *Jacquerie* I. 73 Oh, sharper tangs pierced through this perfumed May.

c. *dial.* A sharp point or spike; the pin of a buckle; one of the prongs or tines of a fork; a prong or tine of a stag's horn.

The sense 'leg of a pair of tongs' in R. Holme may have been derived from the tang of a fork.

1688 R. HOLME *Armoury* II. 132/2 [Of a horn] The lower Tang [is] the Brow-Antlier. [*Ibid.* III. xiv. (Roxb.) 7/1 He beare[th] Sable, a paire of Tonges closed in ye tanges Argent.] **1781** J. HUTTON *Tour to Caves* (ed. 2) Gloss., *Tang*, a pike. **1828** *Craven Gloss., Tang, Teng*,..the prong of a fork. 'A fork wi three tangs'. **1843** *Civil Eng. & Arch. Jrnl.* VI. 147/1 On the lower edge [of the excavator or shovel] are four tangs or points, which serve to penetrate and loosen the soil. **1868** ATKINSON *Cleveland Gloss., Tang*, the tongue of a buckle, the prong of a fork. **1877** E. PEACOCK *N.W. Linc. Gloss., Tang*, the tongue of a buckle.

d. †The barb of a hook (*obs.*); the tongue of a Jew's-harp (also *fig.*).

1688 R. HOLME *Armoury* III. xvi. (Roxb.) 80/1 The tongue of the hooke is that little tang or slip on the inside of it, which ..hinders the hooke from comeing out. Some call it the barbe. **1887** *Suppl. to Jamieson, Tang o' the trump*,..the tongue of the Scottish trump or Jew's harp;..the chief or most important person in a company.

e. (See quot.) *dial.* (So in Old Norse.)

1822 HIBBERT *Shetl. Isles* 518 A narrow stripe of land stretches out that is named the Taing of Torness. The word Taing expresses the character of the low projecting cape. [Cf. p. 479 Ting of Torness.]

2. a. An extension of a metal tool or instrument, as a chisel, file, knife, axe, coulter, pike, scythe, sword, etc., by which it is secured to its handle or stock. Also in certain firearms.

Originally a spike or rod to thrust into the stock; hence extended to a piece of any shape or form having the same function: see quots. Now the chief literal sense.

c **1440** *Promp. Parv.* 496/2 Tongge of a knyfe, *pirasmus*. **14..** *Nom.* in Wr.-Wülcker 735/19, 20 *Hoc tenaculum, Hic spirasmus*, a tang. **1483** *Cath. Angl.* 378/1 A Tange of A knyfe, *parasinus*. **1649** BLITHE *Eng. Improv. Impr.* (1653) 67 The Stayl must be plated with Iron,..through which, as also the Wood, the tange of the Coulter must come. **1688** R.

HOLME *Armoury* III. 321/2 The Cheeks, or Plates, or Tangs [of a hammer are] the Irons which hold the Head on. *Ibid.* xxii. (Roxb.) 284/1 The handle is neere a yard long, with an Hoop at the end for the Tang of the Trowell to be fastned in. **1805** C. JAMES *Milit. Dict.* (ed. 2), *Tang*, the upper part of the plug, or breech pin. **1831** J. HOLLAND *Manuf. Metal* I. 281 The tang, or part by which it [a penknife blade] is to be held during grinding, and ultimately to be fixed in the haft. **1837** WHITTOCK *Bk. Trades* (1842) 226 In forming the tangs of most files, it is necessary to make the shoulders perfectly square and sharp. **1864** R. F. BURTON *Dahome* 44 African battle-axes with..the tangs set in the hafts. **1869** V. D. MAJENDIE *Milit. Breech-Loading Rifles* 62 The locking arrangements consists of the following parts:—Steel bolt.. Recess in breech tang for bolt. **1884** W. H. RIDEING in *Harper's Mag.* June 78/2 The blade..is welded, in the case of a dinner-knife, to a piece of iron, which forms the 'tang' or the part that is inserted in the handle. **1904** BUDGE *Guide 3rd & 4th Egypt. Rooms Brit. Mus.* 7 Two bronze ribbed spear-heads, with tangs. **1909** *Text Bk. Small Arms* I. iv. 35 The rear end of the body is in the form of a tang with sides. **1918** E. S. FARROW *Dict. Milit. Terms* 605 *Tang*, the projecting portion of the breech of a musket, by which the barrel is secured to the stock. **1929** *War Office Textbk. Small Arms* i. 12 On the underside of the cocking-piece is a projection..which travels in a groove, cut for it in the tang of the body. **1965** H. L. BLACKMORE *Guns & Rifles of World* 100 Butt tang engraved with Royal arms of France. **1976** *Shooting Mag.* Dec. 61/1 (Advt.), Mode 801 Luxus O/U shotgun..10 mm wide ventilated barrel rib, sling swivels, top tang safety, double trigger.

b. A root or fang of a tooth; a root or branch of a tree. Now chiefly *dial.*

1715 MOLYNEUX in *Phil. Trans.* XXIX. 372 Strong Tangs or Roots,..by which the Tooth receives its sense and Nourishment. **1886** HOLLAND *Chester Gloss.*, *Tangs*, (2) the principal roots or branches of a tree.

3. = *surgeon-fish* s.v. SURGEON *sb.* 3 b.

1734 MORTIMER in *Phil. Trans.* XXXVIII. 317 *Turdus rhomboïdalis.* The *Tang.* This Fish hath on each side the Tail a sharp pointed Bone, which it can erect in its own Defence. **1902** WEBSTER Suppl., *Tang*,..any West Indian species of surgeon fish, as the common tang (*Teuthis hepatus*), the blue tang (*T. cæruleus*), and the ocean tang (*T. Bahianus*). **1925** D. S. JORDAN *Fishes* (rev. ed.) xxxviii. 618 In the next family, *Acanthuridæ*, the surgeon-fishes or tangs, the scales remain small. **1965** MRS. L. B. JOHNSON *White House Diary* 3 June (1970) 281 These were lots of little bright yellow fish, young blue tang, they called them—as they grow up they change color. **1980** R. E. THRESHER *Reef Fish* xx. 147 The surgeonfish, or tangs, are high-bodied, laterally compressed fish.

4. a. *Stereotyping.* The piece of superfluous metal formed at the end of the plate; the pour-piece. **b.** *Stereotyping.* That part of the papier-maché flong or mould which overlaps the tail end of the matrix so as to prevent the metal from flowing under the end of the mould in the casting-box; the tail-piece. **c.** *Typefounding.* The projection at the bottom of a piece of type which is formed by superfluous metal cooling in the opening of the mould.

a. 1880 F. J. F. WILSON *Stereo- & Electrotyping* 43 When the casting is sufficiently cool the superfluous metal at the head, called the 'tang', or 'pour-piece', may be removed by the circular saw or sharp-pointed hook. *Ibid.* 65 The 'pour-piece', or tang, is removed from the top end of the plate, and the bevel formed at the same time.

b. 1891 in *Cent. Dict.* **1910** H. HART *Let. to Editor*, Occasionally the tang is lengthened, for use in a large casting-box, by pasting on to it a piece of thick paper or thin cardboard.

c. 1908 *Proc. Institution Mechanical Engineers* Dec. 1034 The gate through which the metal passes into the mould becomes also filled with type-metal and forms a projecting *tang* which must be broken from the type. **1921** W. H. SLATER *What Compositor should Know* I. 23 Finishing means breaking off the 'tang' or 'jet' left at the bottom of each letter when this is not done on the machine. This tang occurs on all types cast by hand and all large sizes cast by machine. **1951** S. JENNETT *Making of Bks.* ii. 32 When type is cast a fragment of metal, the tang, is left adhering at the base from the orifice in the mould through which the molten metal is injected. This tang is broken off and the resulting roughness of the fracture ground down.

II. 5. a. A penetrating taste or flavour; usually (but not always) an after-taste, or a disagreeable or alien taste from contact with something else.

c **1440** *Promp. Parv.* 496/2 Tongge, or sharpnesse of lycure yn tastynge, *acumen.* **1582** BRETON *Floorish upon Fancie* (Grosart) 41/2 At first, me thought the tast was reasonable good: But..it left (alas) a bitter tang behinde. **1598** FLORIO, *Piccante*, a tartenes vpon the toong, a tang left vpon the toong. **1624** A. WOTTON *Runne from Rome* 3 (As new vessels doe) keeping a tang of the first liquor wherewith I was seasoned. **1660** FULLER *Mixt Contempl.* (1841) 225 The best oil is said to have no taste, that is, no tang. **1736** BAILEY *Househ. Dict.* 100 Brandy either French or English, that has no burnt tang or other ill taste. **1806–7** J. BERESFORD *Miseries Hum. Life* (1826) IX. xv, A strong tang of tallow or onion in your bread and butter. *a* **1825** FORBY *Voc. E. Anglia*, *Tang*, a strong flavour; generally, but not always, an unpleasant one. **1883** MRS. E. H. ROLLINS *New Eng. Bygones* 180 Apples..picked freshly fallen from the earth had a keen spicy tang.

fig. **1612** T. TAYLOR *Comm. Titus* i. 15 The sweetest sinnes would carry a bitter tang, if we would but remember what sweete comfort of the creatures we haue forfeited for them.

b. A pungent odour, a penetrating scent.

1858 GEN. P. THOMPSON *Audi Alt.* I. xxx. 117 All places smell of hangman, it is everywhere the same tang; we might as well be hooped up with the body of a deceased felon on a gibbet of the olden style. **1883** STEVENSON *Silverado Sq.* 163 Like the smell of a washing-house, but with a shrewd tang of the sea salt. **1899** CROCKETT *Kit Kennedy* xxvii. 262 The tang of the cottage peat reek hangs like the peculiar incense of home. **1903** *Sat. Rev.* 14 Nov. 607 The air has a tang of its own, recognisable even in the closest lanes.

c. ? A pungent or stinging effect; 'something that leaves a sting or pain behind it' (J.).

But the meaning here is disputed: cf. TANG *sb.*[2] Shakspere may in this use have associated the two words.

1610 SHAKS. *Temp.* II. ii. 52 But none of vs car'd for Kate. For she had a tongue with a tang, Would cry to a Sailor, goe hang!

6. *fig.* **a.** A slight 'smack' *of* some quality, opinion, habit, form of speech, etc.; a 'suspicion', a suggestion; a trace, a touch *of* something.

1593 HARVEY *New Letter* Wks. (Grosart) I. 285, I cannot but..conceiue as it were a tang of pleasure in mine owne displeasure. *a* **1625** FLETCHER *Hum. Lieut.* I. i, Before I thought ye To have a little breeding—some little tang of Gentry. **1645** PAGITT *Heresiogr.* (1662) 137 The teachers have a strong tange of Pelagius. **1651** *Life Father Sarpi* (1676) 37 He had always kept a tang of the Neapolitan Dialect. **1657** AUSTEN *Fruit Trees* II. 153 Although the graft changes the sap of the wild stock into its owne nature, yet.. a tang of the wild nature remains. **1751** GRAY *Wks.* (1825) II. 162 The language has a tang of Shakespear that suits an old fashioned fable very well. **1854** H. ROGERS *Ess.* II. i. 74 A still more serious fault in Locke is what we may venture to call a tang, if not of materialism, of something that displays a latent tendency towards it.

b. Distinctive or characteristic flavour or quality.

1868 ALEX. SMITH *Last Leaves* 242 You cannot touch the tang of any literary coterie. **1900** H. HARLAND *Cardinal's Snuff-box* xv. 122 His speaking-voice..was sweet, but with a kind of trenchant edge upon it, a genial asperity, that gave it character, tang. **1903** *Daily Chron.* 8 Oct., Such a phrase as 'Food-taxers' has no the requisite tang.

tang (tæŋ), *sb.*[2] A word sometimes app. purely echoic, denoting the strong ringing note produced when a large bell or any sonorous body is suddenly struck with force, or a tense string is sharply plucked; but often denoting a sound of a particular tone, esp. (? under the influence of TANG *sb.*[1]) one of an unpleasant kind; a twang.

(Some place here Shakspere's 'tongue with a tang' (see TANG *sb.*[1] 5 c), which has prob. influenced some of the later uses here quoted.)

1669 HOLDER *Elem. Speech* 78 There is a pretty affectation in the Allemain, which gives their Speech a different Tang from ours. **1686** BUNYAN *Country Rhymes* xxix. 37 Nor is there anything gives such a tang When by these Ropes these Ringers ring them well. **1866** LOWELL *Study Wind.* 120 But he had hoped for a certain tang in the down-come of the bell. **1871** P. H. WADDELL *Ps. in Scotch* Pref. 2 Mony a tang o' his [David's] harp had its ain sugh eftirhen' in Gethsemane. **1880** [see TANKARD 3]. **1885** *Century Mag.* XXVI. 888 A sort of fever which lent a petulant tang to her speech. **1892** *Star* 9 Aug. 1/7 The organist has..a hard task in eradicating the awful Cambridgeshire tang from the voices of his raw material. **1897** MISS BROUGHTON *Dear Faustina* xiv, Faustina is still fondly smiling, but in her tone there is the slight tang of displeasure. **1899** CROCKETT *Kit Kennedy* iii. 20 A..voice..with the snell Scottish scolding 'tang' in it, which is ever more humorous than alarming to those whom it addresses.

b. quasi-*adv.* As an imitation of the sound of a vibrating string.

1812 H. & J. SMITH *Rej. Addr.*, *Theatre* 25 Tang goes the harpsichord, too-too the flute.

tang (tæŋ), *sb.*[3] *dial.* [Of Norse origin; = Norw., Da., Færoese *tang*, Sw. *tång* seaweed, Icel. *þang* fucus. The Norns of Orkney and Shetland had also, like Norwegian, *tang.*] A collective name for large coarse seaweeds, esp. species of *Fucus*; tangle, sea-wrack; also called *sea-tang.*

black tang, the bladder-wrack, *Fucus vesiculosus.* **prickly tang**, *F. aculeatus.* **yellow tang**, *F. nodosus.*

1547 SALESBURY *Welsh Dict.*, *Dylysc*, Tang. **1655** BP. J. RICHARDSON *Observ. O.T.* 11 The likeliest reason is from the Hebrew appellation, calling it the sea of weeds, or sedge, *mare algosum*, of flag, or rush, or tange. *a* **1733** *Shetland Acts* 33 in *Proc. Soc. Ant. Scot.* (1892) XXVI. 201 That none take bait nor cast tang in another man's ebb. **1769** PENNANT *Zool.* III. 169 Lying under the stones among the tang on the rocky coasts of Anglesea. **1796** *Statist. Acc. Scotl.* XVII. 233* The sea-oak (*Fucus vesiculosus*, Lin.), which we denominate black tang. **1809** EDMONDSTON *View Zetland Isl.* II. viii. 6 Before 1808, the yellow tang and the black tang were the only species used in the manufacture of kelp. **1810** *Edin. Rev.* XVII. 146 The prickly tang..often grows intermixed with the bladder-wrack. **1859** H. KINGSLEY *G. Hamlyn* xxxiv, Wet-footed and happy, dragging a yard or so of sea-tang behind her.

b. *Comb.*, as *tang-covered* adj.; **tang-fish**, the seal; **tang-sparrow**, the rock pipit (*Anthus obscurus*); **tang-whaup**, the whimbrel (*Numenius phæopus*).

1888 JESSIE M. E. SAXBY *Lads of Lunda* 122 The *tang-covered crown of the Skerry. **1809** EDMONDSTON *Zetland* II. 292 Seals are seen..[on] the coast of Zetland, and are vulgarly known by the name of *tang-fish. **1822** HIBBERT *Shetl. Isl.* 586 The smaller seals or Tang-fish, so named from being supposed to live among the Tang. **1880** JAMIESON, **Tang-sparrow.* **1885** SWAINSON *Provinc. Names Birds* 46 Rock pipit..called from being exclusively confined to the sea shore..also..Tang sparrow (Shetland Isles). **1808–18** JAMIESON, **Tang-whaup*, the whimbrel, Orkn. **1833** *Montagu's Ornith. Dict.* 534 Whimbrel... *Provincial.* Curlew knot... Tang-whaup.

tang (tæŋ), *sb.*[4] Also **tangue**. [f. native name.] = TANREC.

1891 in *Cent. Dict.*

Tang (tæŋ), *sb.*[5] Also T'ang, Tanga. [Chinese *táng.*] **a.** The name of a dynasty which ruled in China from A.D. 618 to *c* 906; a ruler belonging to this dynasty.

1669 J. OGILBY *Nieuhoff's Embassy from E.-India Co. to Emperor of China* I. xviii. 282 At last having miserably worried and weakened each other, they were all subdued by the seventh Race called *Tanga*, which seized upon the whole Empire, and reigned with his Posterity till the Year of Christ 618. **1738** J. B. DU HALDE *Descr. Empire China & Chinese Tartary* I. 194 (*heading*) The Thirteenth Dynasty, call'd Tang, which had Twenty Emperors, in the Space of Two hundred eighty nine Years. **1788** tr. *Grosier's Gen. Descr. China* II. VI. iii. 209 Under the *Tang*, this superstition still continued. **1837** *Penny Cycl.* VII. 81/1 Ly-yuen..in A.D. 622 founded the dynasty of Tāng. **1925** B. RACKHAM in R. Fry et al. *Chinese Art* 15 When the classic period of T'ang is reached, the potters are working with the easy mastery of artists in their craft. **1940** E. POUND *Cantos* xiv. 41 Tang rising. And the first Tang was Kao Tseu, the starter. **1979** MILLS & MANSFIELD *Genuine Article* iii. 62 Ming, Sung and T'ang have become names synonymous with the finest ceramics. T'ang was the dynastic name of the pottery of China in the eighth century AD.

b. *attrib.* or as *adj.* Freq. used to designate artefacts, etc., of this period.

1831 *Canton Miscellany* IV. 246 The Tang Dynasty was founded at the commencement of the Seventh century. **1854** *North-China Herald* 17 June 184/1 The first emperor of the T'ang dynasty. **1910** *Encycl. Brit.* VI. 213/2 It is in fact from the early religious schools of Japan that we can best conjecture the grandeur of the T'ang style. **1924** M. BORDEN *Three Pilgrims & Tinker* ii. 21 The van was full of the favourite belongings of each member of the family: their mother's Tang horses. **1935** *Burlington Mag.* Jan. p. xiii/2 The T'ang and Sung ceramics..should arouse much interest. **1943** D. WELCH *Maiden Voyage* xviii. 153 Chou bronzes, T'ang grave figures and Sung porcelain. **1955** *Times* 6 Aug. 7/6 Eight Bodhisattvas, typical of early T'ang painting, and clearly owing their inspiration to Indian models. **1962** E. SNOW *Other Side of River* (1963) xviii. 130, I..remembered the description of the scene by the T'ang poet Chen Chang. **1976** 'M. DELVING' *China Expert* xiii. 179 How many T'ang horses..really came from T'ang graves? **1980** *Times* 1 Mar. 13/6 Two hours' drive north-west of Xian is the tomb complex of the Tang emperor.

tang (tæŋ), *v.*[1] Also 5 taang, 7–9 *dial.* teng. [f. TANG *sb.*[1]]

1. *trans.* †To pierce; to prick (*obs.*); to sting as a serpent or an insect. Also *absol.* (Now *dial.*)

a **1400–50** *Alexander* 4798 At opir time of oure tulkis was tangid to dede And slayn with þa serpents a sowme out of noimbre. *c* **1400** MAUNDEV. (Roxb.) xxxi. 141 Þai had within þam nedders, þat taanged þe husbands. *c* **1440** *Alph. Tales* 473 A serpent..tanged hym hugelie. **1684** MERITON *Praise Ale* 149 Hee [an ox]'s teng'd, hee'l dee; Let's stick him. **1788** W. MARSHALL *Yorksh.* II. Gloss., *Teng*, to sting, as the bee or the adder. **1888** *Sheffield Gloss.* s.v., That bee has tanged me.

†**b.** *fig.* To pierce with grief or compunction.

a **1400–50** *Alexander* 3637 Þan was he tangid with tene & turbled vnfaire.

2. To furnish with a tang, spike, flange, etc.

1566 in *Invent. R. Wardr.* (1815) 169 Item sex pair of brasin calmes tangit with irne serving for battertis, moyanis, falconis. **1608** SYLVESTER *Du Bartas* II. iv. III. *Schisme* 122 But I will have your carrion shoulders goar'd With scourges tang'd with rowels [orig. *garnez de cloux*]. **1839** BYWATER *Sheffield Dial.* 33 He mood'st blade... Then he tangs it. **1879** *Cassell's Techn. Educ.* IV. 298/1 The end of the tube is bent and hammered over..and is afterwards 'dubbed' or 'tanged'.

†**b.** *fig.* To give point or effective force to. *Obs.*

a **1518** SKELTON *Magnyf.* 2234 Tushe! these maters that ye moue are but soppys in ale; Your trymynge and tramynge by me must be tangyd.

3. To affect with a tang or (unpleasant) taste.

1686 F. SPENCE tr. *Varillas' Ho. Medicis* 330 They tang'd the good and added to the bad. **1742** *Lond. & Country Brew.* I. (ed. 4) 36 The Liquor suffers, and will be tanged with a noxious Taste.

tang (tæŋ), *v.*[2] [Mainly echoic, like TANG *sb.*[2] (cf. TING *v.*, TONG *v.*); but in some instances affected by TANG *sb.*[1]]

1. *trans.* To strike (a bell or the like) so as to cause it to emit a sharp loud ringing note.

1556 OLDE *Antichrist* 10 Is it ynough for him to tang the watchebell? **1841** C. H. HARTSHORNE *Salop. Antiq.* Gloss. 590 *Tang*, to make a harsh discordant noise by striking against a piece of metal: chiefly used in reference to the swarming of bees. Ex. 'Tang the fryingpan'. **1842** AKERMAN *Wilts. Gloss.* s.v., 'To tang the bell' is to pull it.

2. To utter with a tang or ringing tone.

1601 SHAKS. *Twel. N.* II. v. 163 Let thy tongue tang arguments of state; put thy selfe into the tricke of singularitie. **1863** COWDEN CLARKE *Shaks. Char.* ii. 54 Touchstone..can tang out a sarcasm with any professor of cynicism.

b. To impart a tang or twang to. *nonce-use.*

a **1849** H. COLERIDGE *Young & Contemp.* Poems (1851) II. 328 So long shall Gray, and all he said and sung, Tang the shrill accents of the school-girl's tongue.

3. *intr.* To emit a sharp and loud ringing or clanging sound; to ring, clang.

[**1601** SHAKS. *Twel. N.* III. iv. 78 Let thy tongue langer [**1767** CAPELL tang] with arguments of state.] **1686** BUNYAN *Country Rhymes* xxix. 36 When ringers handle them with Art and Skill, They then the Ears of the observers fill, With such brave Notes they ting and tang so well As to out strip all with their ding, dong, Bell. **1842** AKERMAN *Wilts. Gloss.*, *Tang*, to make a noise with a key and shovel at the time of swarming of a hive. *a* **1845** HOOD *Tale of Trumpet* xxxvi,

The smallest urchin whose tongue could tang, Shock'd the Dame with a volley of slang.

4. *trans. dial.* To affect (swarming bees) with a clanging noise, so as to make them settle: = TING *v.*

1881 MISS JACKSON *Shropsh. Word-bk.* s.v., Mak' 'aste an' fatch the warmin'-pon an' the kay o' the 'ouse to tang the bees.

5. *intr.* To move *on* with a tang.

1906 *Daily Chron.* 7 June 4/7 The car 'tanged' on.

‖**tanga**[1] ('tæŋgə, ‖'tʌŋa). *East Ind.* Forms: 6– **tanga**; 6–7 **tango**, 7 **tang**, **tanghe**, 8 **tange**, 9 **tungah**, **tanja**, **tank**, **tanka**; 20 **tamka**, **tangka**, **tenga**. [app. a. Pg. *tanga*, ad. *ṭaṅka* in various Indian vernaculars:—Skr. *ṭaṅka*, a weight = 4 māshās (beans), a coin; also, *ṭaṅkaka*, a stamped coin: see Note below.] A name (originally of a weight) given in India, Persia, and Turkestan to various coins (or moneys of account), the value of which varied greatly at different times and places; it is still applied in certain places to a copper, in others to a silver coin. **a.** in Goa, and on the Malabar coast: see quots.

1598 W. PHILLIP *Linschoten* xxxv. 69/1 There is also a kinde of reckoning of money which is called Tangas, not that there is any such coined, but are so named onely in telling, fiue Tangas is one Pardaw,..foure Tangas good money are as much as fiue Tangas bad money. *Ibid.* xcii. 161/2 Foure Tangoes. **1615–16** R. STEELE in Purchas *Pilgrimes* (1625) I. IV. xiii. 523 Their moneyes in Persia..are..of Copper, like the Tangas and Pisos of India. **1662** J. DAVIES tr. *Mandelslo's Trav.* 107 Five *Tanghes* make a Serafin of silver, which..is set at 300. Reis, and six *Tanghes* make a *Pardai*. **1698** FRYER *Acc. E. India & P.* 207 [Coins in Goa], 60 Rees make a Tango. **1700** S. L. tr. *Fryke's Voy. E. Ind.* xii. 180 Some Chests of Tanges and Larines, (which is a certain Money of that Country). **1766** GROSE *Voy. E. Ind.* (1772) I. 283 (Y.) Throughout Malabar and Goa, they use tangas, vintins, and pardoo xeraphin. **1858** SIMMONDS *Dict. Trade*, *Tanga, Tanja*, a money of Goa on the Malabar coast, worth about 7½*d.* [**1886** YULE *Hobson-Jobson* 682 The name still survives at Goa as that of a copper coin equivalent to 60 reis or about 2*d.*]

b. in Turkestan, Persia, Tibet, etc.

1740 THOMPSON & HOGG in Hanway *Trav.* (1762) I. IV. lii. 242 Their coin [at Khiva] is ducats of gold,..also tongas, a small piece of copper, of which one thousand five hundred are equal to a ducat. *Ibid.* 244 Their money [at Bokhara] is ducats of gold,..also a piece of copper, which they call *tongas*, that pass at fifty to eighty to a ducat, according to their size. **1815** MALCOLM *Hist. Persia* II. xx. 250 One tungah..a coin about the value of five pence. **1876** C. MARKHAM *Narr. Mission George Bogle to Tibet* xiii. 129 The following memorandum of weights used in Tibet is among Mr. Bogle's papers..5 *tanks* make one *nega*. **1889** G. N. CURZON *Russia in Central Asia* vi. 189 At the time of my visit the silver *tenga* was worth about fivepence. **1892** W. W. ROCKHILL *Jrnl.* 23 July (1894) IV. 253 The chief inquired if I had any Chinese silver or rupees to exchange for Lh'asa tankas. **1904** *Times* 19 Sept. 12/6 (*Tibet*) The official rate of exchange is three tankas to a rupee. **1904** A. T. DE MATTOS tr. *Grenaud's Tibet* viii. 301 The commonest coin within the limits of the kingdom of Lhasa is the tangka. **1924** *Glasgow Herald* 30 June 12 Every time I rode through the city [of Bokhara] one of the Cossacks carried a purse with silver 'tengas' (a metal coin worth about sixpence), and distributed them to the..poor. **1970** R. D. TARING *Daughter of Tibet* iv. 44 The *tamka* was then worth about ninepence. **1972** G. MULLER tr. *Schön's World Coin Catal. Twentieth Cent.* 826 Tibet..15 skarung = 1 tangka..3 tangka = 1 Indian rupee. **1974** D. NORBU *Red Star over Tibet* i. 34, 670 silver coins called *tamka*.

[*Note.* Under the Mogul sovereigns, the silver *ṭaṅka* was the chief silver coin, the same as the silver dinar or later rupee; mention is also made in 14th c. of a *ṭaṅka* or dinar of gold, worth 10 silver dinars. About 1500 there were black or copper *ṭaṅkas*, of which 20 went to the old silver *ṭaṅka*. In the end of the 16th century, the *tanga* was a money of account, and afterwards a copper coin, at Goa, where it is still in use: see quot. 1886. The name also survives, in derived forms, in most of the Indian vernaculars, as that of a copper coin, and in Urdū, in its Sanskrit form and sense, as that of a weight. The identity of the Turkī *tanga*, *tonga* with the Sanskrit word has been disputed, and the word attributed to a Chagatai Turkī origin.]

tanga[2] ('tæŋgə). [a. Pg., ad. Quimbundo *ntanga* loincloth.] **a.** (See quot. 1960): the garment is also worn by men. **b.** A bikini made of triangles of material joined by thin ties; *spec.* the lower half of this. Cf. STRING *sb.* 6c.

1912 T. A. JOYCE *S. Amer. Archeol.* xii. 265 The so-called *tangas*.., triangular in shape, and convex in section,..are found in the burial-urns of women... It has been suggested that they are the 'translations' into pottery of the small triangular leaf coverings worn by many of the women of primitive Brazilian tribes in historical times. **1921** *Museum Jrnl.* (Univ. of Pennsylvania) Sept. 146 Nothing whatever was found on the inside of the burial urns except the so-called 'tangas' or fig leaves supposed to have been worn by the women... The tangas were always well made, hard burned, highly polished, and either in bright red monochrome or painted designs. **1948** B. MEGGARS in J. H. Steward *Handbk. S. Amer. Indians* III. 157 Tangas, which are found in abundance, are thought to have been worn by the women as a pubic covering. **1948** A. MÉTRAUX in *Ibid.* 670 Women..wore a short apronlike (tanga) cotton fringe..or a cotton skirt. **1960** C. WINICK *Dict. Anthropol.* 525/1 *Tanga*, a pubic covering worn by Indian women, especially in tropical South America and the West Indies. The most common form of tanga today is a beaded apron. Others consist of a small triangle of inner bark. **1975** *Times* 5 June 12/1 Nylon jersey tanga (or string). **1976** R. CONDON *Whisper of Axe* I. x. 60 She had the sort of body that should not..wear anything but a *tanga*, that wonderful Brazilian string bikini.

tanga, var. of TONGA, an Indian cart.

‖**tangalung** ('tæŋgəlʌŋ). Also **tangga-**. [Malay *tanggālung*.] The civet cat of Sumatra and Java, *Viverra tangalunga*; the Sumatran civet.

1820 SIR S. RAFFLES in *Trans. Linn. Soc.* (1822) XIII. 251–2. **1824** T. HORSFIELD *Zool. Researches Java*, etc. s.v. *Viverra Rasse*, A very perfect specimen of the Viverra Zibetha, the Tanggalung of the Malays, forwarded from Sumatra by Sir Stamford Raffles... The Tanggalung is two feet six inches long; the head measures six inches and three-fourths, and the tail eleven inches. **1843** *Penny Cycl.* XXVI. 406/2.

tangana (tæŋ'gɑːnə). Also **Tangana**. [Origin unknown.] A type of rhythm used in jazz music (see quot. 1952).

1926 A. NILES in W. C. Handy *Blues* 24 The Habañera or tango rhythm... Both the justification for its use in Negro music, and the explanation of its subsequent popularity among the Negroes themselves, are supplied on acceptance of the plausible theory that this is an African rhythm (the native word is *tangana*) and Spanish only by adoption through the Moors. **1952** B. ULANOV *Hist. Jazz in Amer.* (1958) iv. 31 In 1914 Handy published his 'St. Louis Blues' with its provocative Tangana rhythm, which is a kind of habanera or tango beat consisting of a dotted quarter, an eighth-note, and two quarter-notes. **1959** 'F. NEWTON' *Jazz Scene* iii. 41 An admixture of certain rhythms such as the tangana, or the habanera which..roused a particularly vivid response among continental negroes.

Tanganyikan (tæŋgə'njiːkən), *a.* (*sb.*) [f. *Tanganyik(a* (see below) + -AN.] Of or pertaining to Tanganyika, now the continental part of the E. African republic of Tanzania. Also as *sb.*, a native or inhabitant of Tanganyika. Cf. TANZANIAN *sb.* and *a.*

1905 *Rep. Brit. Assoc. Adv. Sci.* 430 The total number of Tanganyikan species of fishes amounts to eighty five. **1957** *African Affairs* LVI. 304 He went on to ask..whether the tsetse fly experiments were providing a hope that the scourge of the fly would be overcome... It would make for a great development in Tanganyikan agriculture. **1962** *Sunday Express* 21 Jan. 5/8 We who live in Tanganyika must think of ourselves as Tanganyikans and work for our country. **1971** *Standard* (Dar es Salaam) 7 Apr. 4/5 They could not cope with the then Tanganyikan education curriculum.

tangara, tangaroid: see TANAGER.

‖**tangata** ('taŋata). [Maori: see KANAKA.]

a. In Maori parlance, a person, a human being. **b.** *tangata whenua* (fɛ'nʊa), lit. 'people of the land', local people (e.g. as opp. to *nga manuhiri* the visitors).

1840 W. DEANS *Let.* 30 Oct. in J. Deans *Pioneers of Canterbury* (1939) 29 He says they will take no other white man with them and they all want me to go and live there, calling me the *tangata* Widerup or the proprietor of it. **1949** P. BUCK *Coming of Maori* (1950) I. v. 65 The Maori people who were in occupation of New Zealand at the time of European contact were the descendants of the intermixture of three successive groups of immigrants: the moa-hunters and the early *tangata whenua* [etc.]. **1974** *N.Z. Listener* 20 July 13/1 The body was lying in state on the stage at the end of the hall and the tangata whenua were seated. **1974** [see MOA-HUNTER].

tange, obs. form of TANG, TANGA[1], TONG.

tanged (tæŋd), *a.* [f. TANG *sb.*[1] and *v.*[1] + -ED.] Having a tang; furnished with a tang to fix in a handle; barbed; forked.

1888 *Sheffield Gloss.*, *Tanged*, forked. **1891** R. DAY in *Proc. Soc. Antiq.* 22 Jan. 226 A small tanged chisel. **1896** KIPLING *Seven Seas* 125, I left my views of Art, barbed and tanged below the heart Of a mammothistic etcher at Grenelle. **1899** R. MUNRO *Prehist. Scotl.* v. 167 Arrow points may be divided into tanged and untanged. **1904** BUDGE *Guide 3rd & 4th Egypt. Rooms Brit. Mus.* 8 Iron javelin-head, tanged... Barbed and tanged arrow-heads of iron.

tangeite ('tæŋgeɪaɪt). *Min.* [ad. Russ. *tangeít* (A. Fersman 1925, in *Priroda* No. 7–9. 239), f. the name of the *Tange* Gorge, Tyuya-Muyun, Fergana, central Asia: see -ITE[1].] An orthorhombic basic vanadate of copper and calcium, $CuCa(VO_4)(OH)$, that is a secondary mineral found as green or greenish yellow crystals; calciovolborthite.

1927 *Mineral. Abstr.* III. 234 For the crystalline varieties the name tangeite, from the Tange gorge, is proposed, and for the colloidal variety the term 'Turkestan volborthite' is retained. **1951** C. PALACHE et al. *Dana's Syst. Min.* (ed. 7) II. 816 Tangeite appears to be identical with calciovolborthite. **1971** *Mineral. Mag.* XXXVIII. 488 The writers..now place on record an occurrence in Leicestershire of tangëite, $CuCaVO_4OH$, and volborthite, $Cu_3(VO_4)_2.3H_2O$, not hitherto described from Britain.

tangelo ('tændʒələʊ). [f. TANG(ERINE *sb.* 2a + POM)ELO.] A hybrid citrus fruit resembling a thick-skinned orange, produced by crossing the tangerine, *Citrus reticulata*, and the pomelo, *C. grandis*; also, the tree bearing this fruit.

1904 *Cosmopolitan Mag.* XXXVII. 262 Under the auspices of the United States Department of Agriculture has been evolved the 'tangelo'. **1905** WEBBER & SWINGLE in *Yearbk. U.S. Dept. Agric. 1904* 235 The term 'tangelo' is suggested by the writers as a name for this group of loose-skinned fruits, which lie midway between the pomelo and tangerine. **1932** SWINGLE & ROBERTSON in *Proc. 6th Internat. Congr. Genetics* II. 385 The exhibit shows..tangelo fruits preserved in fluid. **1939** *Times* 23 Feb. 17/4 The basket [of Jamaican fruit] contained uglis, tangelos, grapefruit, oranges, [etc.]. **1969** *Oxf. Bk. Food Plants* 88/2 Tangelos are hybrids between the tangerine and grapefruit. **1970** *Harrod's Summer Food News* 8/1 Canadian tangelo juice. **1977** *N.Z. Herald* 8 Jan. 1–5/6 (Advt.), Fruit trees..tangelos.

tangena: see TANGHIN.

tangence ('tændʒəns). *rare.* [a. F. *tangence* (1835 in Dict. Acad.), f. *tangent* adj.: see -ENCE.] The act or fact of touching, touch; point of contact.

1840 *Blackw. Mag.* XLVIII. 275 They [Correggio's paintings] stand betwixt passion—the tangence of mentality and materiality, and the distinctly intellectual and moral.

tangency ('tændʒənsɪ). [f. L. type *tangentia, f. *tangent-em* TANGENT: see -ENCY.] The quality or condition of being tangent; state of contact.

problem of tangencies, in old *Geom.*, a problem in which it is required to describe a circle passing through given points, and touching straight lines or circles the position of which is given, the data being limited to three.

1819 *Pantologia* s.v., Problem of Tangencies. *Ibid.*, The treatise of tangencies was restored by Vieta. **1867** F. H. LUDLOW *Little Brother* 34 The wildest point of tangency which Man's railroads make with Weaver's woods. **1895** H. P. STOKES in *Athenæum* 16 Nov. 690/1 Points of tangency between certain Elizabethan celebrities.

tangent ('tændʒənt), *a.* and *sb.* [ad. L. *tangens*, *tangent-em*, pr. pple. of *tang-ĕre* to touch; used by Th. Fincke, 1583, as sb. in sense = L. *līnea tangens* tangent or touching line. In F. *tangent*, *-e* adj., *tangente* sb. (Geom.), Ger. *tangente* sb.]

A. *adj.*

1. a. *Geom.* Of a line or surface in relation to another (curved) line or surface: Touching, i.e. meeting at a point and (ordinarily) not intersecting; in contact. Also as quasi-*adv.*

A surface may also be tangent to another surface along a *line* (e.g. a plane in contact with a cylinder). In quot. 1869, Taking place along a tangent. Cf. B. 1 b.

1594 BLUNDEVIL *Exerc.* II. (1597) 48b, Our moderne Geometricians haue of late inuented two other right lines belonging to a Circle, called lines Tangent, and lines Secant. **1644** DIGBY *Nat. Bodies* xiii. §8. 114 The reflexion must follow the nature of tangent surfaces. **1713** BERKELEY *Guard.* No. 126 ¶2 Hence..the earth,..without flying off in a tangent line, constantly rolls about the sun. **1866** PROCTOR *Handbk. Stars* 33 The cone, instead of being a tangent-cone, is supposed to be a secant-cone, intersecting the sphere. **1869** TYNDALL in *Fortn. Rev.* 1 Feb. 245 All the vibrations tangent to the little circle..are reflected perfectly polarized. **1876** *Catal. Sci. App. S. Kens. Mus.* §102 Model exhibiting the simultaneous transformation..of the tangent paraboloid of the conoid into the tangent plane of the cylinder. **1936** A. W. CLAPHAM *Romanesque Archit.* viii. 167 The subsidiary towers..at Mainz and Laach..are set axially and tangent at the ends of the transept. **1977** *Sci. Amer.* Aug. 37/1 The radiation is emitted tangent to these trajectories.

†**b.** *Cryst.* Applied to a plane replacing an edge or solid angle of a crystal (which is more properly a *secant* plane). *Obs.*

1823 H. J. BROOKE *Introd. Crystallogr.* 109 Edges replaced by tangent planes. **1851** RICHARDSON *Geol.* v. 88 Crystals often present the appearance of having lost their edges and solid angles, which are then said to be replaced by tangent planes.

c. *transf.* Said of the wheel of a bicycle or tricycle having the spokes tangent to the hub.

1886 *Bicycling News* 6 Aug. 664/1 Laced tangent wheels, hollow rims, Hancock's tyres.

2. *fig.* 'Flying off at a tangent' (see B. 1c); divergent, erratic.

1787 BURNS *Let. to Moore* 23 Apr., If once this tangent flight of mine were over, and I were returned to my wonted leisurely motion in my old circle. **1799** E. DU BOIS *Piece Family Biog.* I. 152 The voluble loquacity and tangent style of reasoning of their new companion.

3. In general sense. **a.** Touching, contiguous.

1846 ELLIS *Elgin Marb.* I. 107 Beaten together till the tangent surfaces were fitted to each other.

b. Of or pertaining to touch; ***tangent sense***, sense of touch. *nonce-use.*

1802 E. DARWIN *Orig. Soc.* III. 424 Say, did these fine volitions first commence From clear ideas of the tangent sense?

B. *sb.*

1. *Math.* (ellipt. for *tangent line.*) [= Fr., Ger. *tangente.*] **a.** *Trigonometry.* One of the three fundamental trigonometrical functions (cf. SECANT, SINE), originally considered as functions of a circular arc, now usually of an angle (viz. that subtended by such arc at its centre): *orig.* The length of a straight line perpendicular to the radius touching one end of the arc and terminated by the *secant* drawn from the centre through the other end; in mod. use, the ratio of this line to the radius, or (equivalently, as a function of the angle) the ratio of the side of a right-angled triangle opposite the given angle (if acute) to that of the side opposite the other acute angle (the tangent of an obtuse angle being numerically equal to that of its supplement, but of opposite sign). Abbrev. *tan*.

Tables of tangents and cotangents were constructed and used by the Arab mathematicians of the 9th and 10th c. (see Nallino *Al Battani, Opus astronomicum*, Milan 1903, I. 182); but began to be constructed in Christendom late in the 15th c. The names *tangens* and *secans*, introduced by Thos. Fincke (Finkius) in 1583, had no connexion with the names used by the Arabs.

[**1583** FINCKE *Geometriæ Rotundi* v. 64 De semicirculi sinibus, tangentibus, secantibus. *Ibid.* 73 Recta sinibus connexa est tangens peripheriæ aut eam secans.] **1594** BLUNDEVIL *Exerc.* II. (1597) 57 b Of which Arke the line AD is the Tangent, and the line CD is the Secant thereof. **1635** [see COTANGENT]. **1658** PHILLIPS, *Tangent*, .. a Mathematical Term used chiefly in Astronomy, .. signifies, a right line perpendicular to the Diameter drawn by the one extream of the given Arch, and terminated by the Secant. **1690** LEYBOURN *Curs. Math.* 397 Which Scales of Tangents .. let be extended to 75 deg. at least. **1728** PEMBERTON *Newton's Philos.* 366 The refracting powers .. will be in the duplicate proportion of the tangents of the least angles, which the refracted light can make with the surfaces of the refracting bodies. **1828** HUTTON *Course Math.* II. 3 As the arc increases from o, the sines, tangents, and secants, all proceed increasing, till the arc becomes a whole quadrant .., and then the sine is the greatest it can be ..; and both the tangent and secant are infinite.

b. *Geom.* A straight line which touches a curve (or curved surface), i.e. meets it at a point and being produced does not (ordinarily) intersect it at that point. *spec.* in *Surveying*, a tangent to a curve at a point (***tangent point***) where the curve starts or finishes; freq. *attrib.*, as ***tangent distance, length***, the length of such a tangent from the tangent point to its intersection with the other tangent.

In Higher Geometry a tangent is regarded as the limiting position of a line intersecting a curve when the two (or more) points of intersection coincide, and is hence defined as a straight line passing through two (or more) consecutive points of the curve. If the curve be conceived as traced by a moving particle, the tangent at any point of it represents the direction of motion at that point; hence a body moving in a curve, when the restraining force is withdrawn, flies off *at a tangent*, i.e. along the tangent (cf. the *fig.* use in c). At a point of inflexion, where the curvature (i.e. deviation from the straight line) changes its direction, the tangent intersects as well as touches the curve.

1655 T. GIBSON *Syntaxis Math.* xiii. 142 To draw a tangent [cf. 1551 RECORDE *Pathway*, touche line] to any point assigned in any section, or from any point without the section. **1704** J. HARRIS *Lex. Techn.* I, *Tangent*, of a Parabola, (or other Conick Section, or Geometrical Curve) is a Right Line Drawn, cutting the Ax Produced, and touching the Section in one Point without cutting it. **1706** W. JONES *Syn. Palmar. Matheseos* 221 A Tangent to any point of the Circumference [of a circle] is Perpendicular to the Radius drawn to that Point. **1832** *Nat. Philos.* II. *Introd. Mech.* p. xvi. (Usef. Knowl. Soc.). If a stone, whirled round in a sling, gets loose at the point A .., it flies off in the direction AB: this line is called a tangent. **1850** T. BAKER *Rudimentary Treat. Land & Engin. Surveying* II. ii. 171 Find the radii, as BO, CO'; the tangent point, as C'; and the junction point, as C, with the position of the common tangent at the junction point. **1862** W. J. M. RANKINE *Man. Civil Engin.* I. v. 111 The places where permanent marks of the course of the line are chiefly required are on the tangents of curves. **1902** R. E. MIDDLETON et al. *Treat. Surveying* II. v. 61 Find length of tangent for a 3° curve with central angle of $35^\circ 42'$. **1978** J. G. MCENTYRE *Land Survey Systems* x. 329 An easement curve is a transition curve utilized to increase the degree of curvature gradually from the tangent point to the circular portion of a curve. **1983** J. C. MCCORMACK *Surveying Fundamentals* xxi. 384 The tangent distances are taped from the *P.I.* [*sc.* point of intersection] down both tangents to locate the *P.C.* and *P.T.*

c. In general use, chiefly *fig.* from b, esp. in phrases (***off***) ***at, in, upon a tangent***, i.e. off or away with sudden divergence, from the course or direction previously followed; abruptly from one course of action, subject, thought, etc., to another.

1771 SMOLLETT *Humph. Cl.* (1815) 219 After having twelve times described this circle, he lately flew off at a tangent to visit some trees at his country-house in England. **1815** *Paris Chit-Chat* (1816) II. 92 The passengers on the roof, being at the highest point of projection flew off in a tangent, and were precipitated .. into a field of new-mown hay. **1825** BENTHAM *Ration. Reward* 393 That manner which they have .. of flying off in tangents when they are pressed. **1865** LECKY *Ration.* (1878) I. 284 *note*, Flying off at a tangent from his main subject. **1875** WHITNEY *Life Lang.* viii. 150 To abandon the established habits of speech and go off upon a tangent. **1879** MISS BRADDON *Clov. Foot* x, Smoking his cigar, and letting his thoughts wander away at a tangent every now and then.

2. The upright pin or wedge fixed at the back of each of the keys of a clavichord, which on the depression of the key pressed up against the string and caused it to sound, acting also as a bridge to determine the pitch of the note. [= Ger. *tangent*.]

[**1614** PRÆTORIUS *Syntagma Musicum* III. 68 Es hat aber ein solch Geigenwerk an statt der Tangenten [etc.].] **1878** A. J. HIPKINS in Grove *Dict. Mus.* I. 367 The tangents .. not only produced the tones but served .. to measure off the vibrating lengths required for the pitch of the notes. **1896** C. W. NAYLOR *Shaks. & Music* 68 *note*, The German clavichord had 'tangents' of brass at the ends of the key levers.

3. Short for *tangent scale, tangent galvanometer*: see C.

1861 W. H. RUSSELL in *Times* 14 May, His guns were without screws, scales, or tangents. **1905** PREECE & SIVEWRIGHT *Telegraphy* 404 Perhaps the most useful galvanometer for general testing purposes is the Tangent.

4. A straight section of railway track. *U.S. colloq.*

1895 in *Funk's Stand. Dict.*

C. Combinations and special collocations.

(Some of these are examples of the adj. qualifying a sb.)

tangent backsight, = *tangent scale* (*a*); **tangent balance**, a balance in which the weight is shown on a graduated arc by a pointer attached to the beam; the bent-lever balance, common as a letter-balance; **tangent compass** = *tangent galvanometer*; **tangent galvanometer**, a galvanometer in which the tangent of the angle of deflection of the needle is proportional to the strength of the current passing through the coil; **tangent scale**, (*a*) in *Gunnery*, a kind of breech-sight in which the heights of the steps or notches correspond to the tangents of the angle of elevation; (*b*) a graduated scale indicating the tangents of angles (see quot. 1902); **tangent screw**, a screw working tangentially upon a toothed circle or arc so as to give it a slow motion for delicate measurements or adjustments; **tangent sight**, = *tangent scale* (*a*).

For *tangent cone, line, plane, surface*, etc., see A. 1; for *tangent distance, length, point*, see B. 1 b.

1862 *Catal. Internat. Exhib.* II. XI. 23 The *Tangent back-sight is elevated by a rack and pinion, the latter having a micrometer wheel for finer readings than the divisions on the tangent stem allow. **1873** MAXWELL *Electr. & Magn.* (1881) II. 325 The current is .. proportional to the tangent of the deviation, and the instrument is therefore called a *Tangent Galvanometer. **1876** PREECE & SIVEWRIGHT *Telegraphy* 267 The insulation resistance is the only test which is taken by means of the tangent-galvanometer. **1859** F. A. GRIFFITHS *Artil. Man.* (1862) 51 A *Tangent scale is affixed to the breech of Guns, and Howitzers, by means of which the requisite elevation may be given. **1902** SLOANE *Stand. Electr. Dict.*, *Tangent scale*, an arc of a circle in which the number of graduations in any arc starting from zero are proportional to the tangent of the angle subtended by such arc. The system is for use with tangent galvanometers. **1862** *Catal. Internat. Exhib.* II. XIII. 5 Circumferenter or miner's dial, with *tangent screw adjustment. **1877** KNIGHT *Dict. Mech.*, *Tangent-screw*, an endless screw tangentially attached to the index-arm of an instrument of precision, enabling a delicate motion to be given to the arm after it has been clamped to the limb, and permitting angular measurements to be made with greater exactness than could be done were the movement entirely effected by hand. **1908** *Treat. Serv. Ordn. Roy. Artill.* 513 The *tangent sights consist of triangular nickel-plated steel bars graduated on the rear face.

'tangent, *v. rare.* [f. the sb.] *intr.* To go off or away at a tangent (see TANGENT *sb.* 1 c); to fly off at an angle.

1920 F. NIVEN *Tale that is Told* vii. 44 They are always tangenting away, not from what I have said, but from what they imagine I have said. **1940** 'GUN BUSTER' *Return via Dunkirk* II. i. 85 The empty sardine tin that the Babe pitched, tangented off the side of his tin hat into the long grass. **1974** K. MILLETT *Flying* (1975) II. 201 She chuckles and then tangents off to some article .. she read.

tangental (tæn'dʒɛntəl), *a.* [f. TANGENT *sb.* + -AL[1].] Of, pertaining to, or of the nature of a tangent; = next, 1. Hence **tan'gentally** *adv.*

1849 H. MILLER *Footpr. Creat.* x. 109 Nor are the openings of the medullary rays frequent in the tangental section. **1856** DOVE *Logic Chr. Faith* I. ii. II. §1. 91 These motions .. are the result of two somethings, one of which is tangental, the other centripetal. **1867** J. HOGG *Microsc.* I. iii. 207 They are sometimes called the horizontal, vertical and tangental. **1891** *Cent. Dict.*, Tangentally.

tangential (tæn'dʒɛnʃəl), *a.* (*sb.*) [f. L. type **tangentia* (see TANGENCY) + -AL[1].]

A. *adj.* Of or pertaining to tangency or a tangent.

1. a. Of, pertaining to, or of the nature of a tangent; identical with, or drawn at, a tangent to a curve or curved surface.

1630 R. DELAMAINE *Grammalogia* App. 62 If the Declination be above 38. gr. 3. m. you may move the Tangent of 45. softly alonge by the Tangentiall degrees of Declination in the fixed, untill 45. gr. in the moveable be opposite to 45. gr. in the fixed. **1763** *Phil. Trans.* LIII. 68 The proposed demonstration of this tangential property. **1828** J. M. SPEARMAN *Brit. Gunner* 265 The apparent level is a straight line tangential to the surface of the earth, or true level. **1881** TAIT in *Nature* XXV. 128 The glass is extended in a radial and compressed in a tangential direction.

b. Of motion or force: Acting along a tangent to a curved line or surface.

1709 STEELE *Tatler* No. 43 ¶7 The Tangential and Centripetal Forces, by their Counter-struggle, make the Celestial Bodies describe an exact Ellipsis. **1768** TUCKER *Lt. Nat.* (1834) I. 413 He might give the heavy planets their tangential motion by one strong and exactly poised stroke. **1880** BESSEY *Botany* 129 The tangential growth of the surrounding cells. **1883** *Science* I. 523/1 The tangential tension of the bark increases with the growth of the stem.

c. Of a thing: That lies in a tangent to a curved surface.

1854 J. SCOFFERN in *Orr's Circ. Sc., Chem.* 388 One part [of a globular box] is furnished with a tangential jet. **1899** *Allbutt's Syst. Med.* VIII. 331 The tangential fibres of the cortex. **1901** A. J. EVANS in *Oxf. Univ. Gaz.* 12 Feb. 339/2 A small vase with incised returning spirals and tangential leaves. **1905** BOND *Goth. Archit.* 164 The ambulatory with tangential chapels.

d. *spec.* (*a*) Of the spokes of a wheel (as in a bicycle): Arranged as tangents to the hub. (*b*) Of a fabric (as a tyre-cover): Having layers of thread lying diagonally from edge to edge, so as to distribute the strain.

1898 *Cycling* 63 The best results are obtained from a fabric which .. consists of layers of independent threads running diagonally from edge to edge of the cover and not interwoven. This is called a 'tangential' fabric because the pull travels lengthwise along the threads (as in a tangent spoke) and not across them.

(*c*) Of the pick-up of a record-player: so mounted that it is kept at a tangent to the groove by a rectilinear motion of the arm.

1937 *Electronics* X. 9/2 The whys and wherefores of the 'tangential' type pick-up mount and its effects on distortion and record wear. **1977** *Time* 10 Oct. 43/1 (Advt.), The Beogram 4002 has an electronically controlled tangential arm which plays records in the same way that they were cut: tracing a straight line from the edge of the record to its centre instead of tracing an arc.

2. a. *fig.* Going off suddenly 'at a tangent'; erratic; divergent; digressive.

1867 F. H. LUDLOW *Genre Pict., Little Briggs & I*, 199 A remedy to this day sovereign .. for all tangential aberrations from the back of a colt or the laws of society. **1876** T. HARDY *Ethelberta* (1890) 297 Those devious impulses and tangential flights which spoil the works of every would-be schemer who instead of being wholly machine is half heart. **1903** *Spectator* 31 Jan. 184/2 A collection of mixed and tangential information.

b. That merely touches a subject or matter.

1825 HAZLITT *Spirit of Age, Coleridge* (1886) 46 Our author's mind is (as he himself might express it) tangential. There is no subject on which he has not touched, none on which he has rested. **1885** O. W. HOLMES *Emerson* 165 Emerson had only tangential relations with the experiment.

c. ***tangential energy***: in the writings of P. Teilhard de Chardin, the form of energy that is manifest in the workings of the physical world and is described by the laws of thermodynamics. Cf. *radial energy* s.v. RADIAL *a.* 6. [tr. F. *énergie tangientielle*, introduced *c* 1938 by P. Teilhard de Chardin (*Le Phénomène Humain* (1956) I. ii. 62).]

1959, **1965** [see RADIAL *a.* 6]. **1969** A. RICHARDSON *Dict. Christian Theol.* 332/2 Tangential energy links units at the same level of organization.

B. *sb. Geom.* ***tangential of a point*** (in a curve of the third or higher order), the point at which a tangent at the given point meets the curve again.

1858 CAYLEY *Coll. Math. Papers* II. 558 A derivative which may be termed the 'tangential' of a cubic, viz. the tangent at the point (x,y,z) of the cubic curve $(*)(x,y,z)^3 = 0$ meets the curve in a point (ξ, η, ζ), which is the tangential of the first-mentioned point. **1859** *Ibid.* IV. 188. **1879** G. SALMON *Higher Plane Curves* v. (ed. 3) 130.

Hence **tangentiality** (-ʃɪ'ælɪtɪ), the quality or condition of being tangential.

1889 *Philos. Mag.* Apr. 335 The perpendicularity of E and the tangentiality of H to the surface.

tangentially (tæn'dʒɛnʃəlɪ), *adv.* [f. prec. + -LY[2].] In a tangential way; in the manner, position, or direction of a tangent; at a tangent.

1839 URE *Dict. Arts* 479 The fusees are fixed obliquely and not tangentially to their peripheries. **1854** J. SCOFFERN in *Orr's Circ. Sc., Chem.* 269 A force acting .. tangentially to the circle. **1884** BOWER & SCOTT *De Bary's Phaner.* 620 They are connected one with another in their longitudinal course by numerous anastomoses both radially and tangentially. **1903** *19th Cent.* July 82 The rapidly moving fragment flies away tangentially.

'tangently, *adv. rare.* [f. TANGENT *a.* + -LY[2].] At a tangent.

1903 *Times* 6 Feb. 9/6 Some of them were occasionally thrown off tangently.

tanger ('tæŋə(r)). Also **tenger**. [In sense 1, f. TANG *v.*[1] + -ER[1]; in sense 2, f. TANG *sb.*[1] 2.]

1. *dial.* A person who has a noticeable effect on another (see also quot. 1886).

1886 W. CUDWORTH *Rambles round Horton* 237/1 *Tenger*, a deceiving person. **1914** D. H. LAWRENCE *Prussian Officer* 221 She looked a tanger sitting there, all like statues, her and the geese. **1922** —— *England, my England* 269 She's a tanger——'s driven the gel to what she is.

2. One who furnishes implements with a tang.

1921 *Dict. Occup. Terms* (1927) §279 *Tanger, saw tanger*, places saw blade against gauge in semi-automatic machine, which marks and purchases tang hole in blade and rivets on tang. **1960** *Classification of Occupations* (Gen. Register Office) Index 107/2 Tanger—*cutlery mfr.* ... *razor mfr.* ... *saw mfr.*

Tangerine (tændʒə'ri:n), *a.* and *sb.* Also 8 -een, 9 -ene. [f. *Tanger, Tangier* + -INE[1].] **A.** *adj.* Of or pertaining to, or native of Tangier, a seaport in Morocco, on the Strait of Gibraltar. ***Tangerine orange***, a small flattened deep-coloured variety of orange orig. from Tangier, *Citrus nobilis* var. *Tangeriana*.

1710 ADDISON *Tatler* No. 250 ¶3 An old Tangereen Captain with a Wooden Leg. **1841** TILLERY in *Gard. Chron.* 781 The Tangerine Orange.—I beg to draw attention to the cultivation of this as a fruit for the dessert. **1882** *Garden* 18 Feb. 122/2 Two dishes of Tangerine Oranges.

B. *sb.* **1.** A native of Tangier.

1860 *All Year Round* No. 71. 491 Winterfield was sold to a Tangarene.

2. Now with lower-case initial. **a.** A Tangerine orange: see A.

1842 *Gard. Chron.* 6 The Tangerine I suspect to be only a variety of it [the Mandarin Orange]. **1891** *Daily News* 26 Dec. 5/4 There is an unusually good supply of tangerines. **1908** R. W. CHAMBERS *Firing Line* vi, Please get me a few tangerines—those blood-tangerines up there.

b. A deep orange colour; also *attrib.* and *Comb.*, as ***tangerine-coloured*** adj.

1899 *Daily News* 16 Sept. 7/3 Ruddy pink and tender amethyst, tangerine, orange, mist-grey [etc.]. **1904** *Ibid.* 6 Oct. 8/4 Taking as the colour key-note, the fashionable tangerine shade. **1977** M. KENYON *Rapist* iii. 31 Shovelling sugar into his tangerine-coloured tea.

tanges, obs. form of TONGS.

tanggalung: see TANGALUNG.

tanggyl, var. of TANGYL *a. Obs.*

‖**tanghan, tangun** (ˈtɑːŋghən, ˈtæŋgʌn), **tānyan** (ˈtɑːnjan). *East Ind.* [Hindi *ṭāṅghan*, f. Tibetan *rTañān*, f. *rTa* horse (Yule).] The native horse of Tibet and Bhutān, a strong and sure-footed little pony. Also *tanghan horse*, *pony*.

1774 in Aitchison *Treaties*, etc. (1876) I. 155 That..the Deb Rajah shall pay an annual tribute of five Tangun horses to the Honorable Company. *c* **1774** BOGLE *Narr.* in Markham *Tibet* (1876) 17 We were provided with two tangun ponies of a mean appearance. **1793** HODGES *Trav. India* 31 These horses are called tanyans, and are mostly pye-bald. **1840** *Penny Cycl.* XVI. 143/2 The small horses, the *Tanguns*, are noted for their hardihood and activity, but they are not natives, but introduced from Tibet, and..they degenerate on the south of the Himalaya Mountains.

tanghe, obs. form of TANGA[1].

tanghicin: see after next.

‖**tanghin** (ˈtæŋgɪn). Also 8 **tanguin**, 9 **tanquen**, **tangkin**, **tangena**, **-gina**. [a. F. *tanghin*, ad. Malagasy *tangena*, *tangen'*.]

1. A poison obtained from the kernels of *Tanghinia venenifera*, N.O. *Apocynaceæ*, a shrub of Madagascar, the fruit of which is a large purplish drupe. The kernels were formerly used by the natives to test the guilt of a suspected person. Also *attrib.*, as ***tanghin poison***; ***tanghin camphor*** = *tanghinin* (see below).

1788 tr. *Sonnerat's Voy.* III. 44 The tanguin is one of the most terrible poisons in the vegetable world. **1842** *Penny Cycl.* XXIV. 31/1 This name [*Tanghinia*] was given by Aubert du Petit Thouars to the plant which produces the celebrated Tanghin poison of Madagascar. *Ibid.*, He..insisted that the Tanghin should be administered to himself. **1860** R. F. BURTON *Centr. Afr.* II. 357 The Tangina poison of the Malagash. **1880** J. SIBREE *Gt. African Isl.* xiv. 282 The chief use of the tangena ordeal was for the detection of witchcraft, by which the African races understand the use of poisonous drugs for evil purposes.

2. The shrub itself: more properly *tan'gena* or *tan'gina*. Also *attrib.*

1866 *Treas. Bot.* 1123/1 Tanghin or Tanquen is the only plant belonging to a genus which botanists have named Tanghinia. **1880** J. SIBREE *Gt. African Isl.* xiv. 281 The tangena is a small and handsome tree growing in the warmer parts of the island, and the poison is procured from the nut of its fruit. **1889** AGNES MARION *Tangena Tree* xiii, Horror-stricken, she flung the Tangena-fruit away.

Hence †**ˈtanghicin**, †**ˈtanghin**, **ˈtanghinin**, the poisonous principle of tanghin, tanghin camphor.

1838 T. THOMSON *Chem. Org. Bodies* 926 A peculiar crystallized matter is extracted, to which they have given the name *tanghicin*. **1868** WATTS *Dict. Chem.* V. 658 The kernels..contain..a crystallisable substance called tanghin-camphor or tanghinin... Tanghinin is very poisonous.

‖**tangi**[1] (ˈtæŋɪ). *N. Zealand.* [Maori, = lament, dirge.] A formal lamentation; a dirge, a coronach. Also *transf.* and *fig.*

1836 J. A. WILSON *Missionary Life & Work in N.Z.* (1889) III. 34 Here we found many wailing over a dead body... As we passed some left the *tangi* and joined us. **1844** S. SELWYN 10 Apr. in A. Drummond *Married & Gone to N.Z.* (1960) 113 Nothing to disturb us but the incessant tangi of the children at night. **1845** E. J. WAKEFIELD *Adv. N. Zealand* I. vii. 194 They..bore it [a corpse]..to the village, where the usual *tangi* took place. **1883** RENWICK *Betrayed* 41 'Tis the tangi floats on the sea-borne breeze, In its echoing notes of wild despair. **1901** *Scotsman* 9 Apr. 6/5 The..Agent-General for New Zealand recently received from the Maori inhabitants of his colony a 'tangi' or 'lament' on the death of Queen Victoria. **1905** W. BAUCKE *Where White Man Treads* 278 Our college graduate arrives; the home-coming tangi and nose-greeting is over; the guest meal set out on the floor. **1941** BAKER *N.Z. Slang* vi. 56 When we refer to *holding a tangi* about a setback or problem we are putting another Maori term into colloquial use. **1959** TINDALE & LINDSAY *Rangatira* xviii. 172 The tangi mourning ceremonies. **1963** B. PEARSON *Coal Flat* ii. 42 She said to me, 'Come on Joe, we'll have a *tangi* together.'

Hence as *v. intr.* to lament, to mourn; also *transf.* and *fig.*

1844 M. WILLIAMS 17 Oct. in A. Drummond *Married & Gone to N.Z.* (1960) 39, I could not think how I had consented, and tangied over his preparations. **1864** A. S. ATKINSON *Jrnl.* 19 Apr. in *Richmond-Atkinson Papers* (1960) II. 107 She sat down, began tangi-ing,..& so they remained for some minutes. **1873** J. H. H. ST. JOHN *Pakeha Rambles through Maori Lands* x. 168 The old man,..enumerating the different degrees of relationship he stood in to the deceased, and his appreciation of his virtues, '*tangied*' again to such an extent, that another relation, affected at his extreme grief, presented him with a horse. **1881** J. L. CAMPBELL *Poenamo* vii. 201 Those who had *tangied* over Ngatai had to come and *tangi* over Te Pirete. **1943** N. MARSH *Colour Scheme* xiii. 224 'She's going to *tangi*.' 'To wail..to lament the dead.'

‖**tangi**[2] (ˈtaŋgi). [Pashtu *tangai*, pl. *tangī*, f. (Pers.) *tang* narrow, *tanga* mountain pass.] A gorge or defile in north-western Pakistan.

[**1854** *Q. Jrnl. Geol. Soc.* X. 467 Mr. Loftus..explains the great clefts or 'Tangs' (as they are termed in Persian) which pass through the elongated limestone saddles. These tangs are very numerous.] **1901** *Mem. Geol. Survey India* XXXI. 188 Narrow gorges or rifts locally called 'tangi'. **1923** *Blackw. Mag.* Feb. 221/2 The river emerged through a narrow Tangi in the hills. **1954** O. H. K. SPATE *India & Pakistan* xvi. 425 Tangis or transverse clefts, often only a few yards wide, by which the streams penetrate the longitudinal ridges. **1983** J. MASTERS *Man of War* x. 125 The Wazirs will try to ambush us... I've been marking my map with every likely gully and *tangi*.

tangibility (tændʒɪˈbɪlɪtɪ). [f. as TANGIBLE: see -ILITY.] The state or quality of being tangible; perceptibility to the touch; tangibleness.

1665 NEEDHAM *Med. Medicinæ* 99 As if they did touch after the gross manner of tangibilitie. **1678** CUDWORTH *Intell. Syst.* I. v. 770 Tangibility and impenetrability, were elsewhere made by him the very essence of body. **1823** COLERIDGE *Table-t.* 3 Jan., Define a vulgar ghost... It is visibility without tangibility.

b. With *a* and *pl.*: A tangible thing or matter.

1849 H. MILLER *Footpr. Creat.* xiv. 255 Cut off..from all the tangibilities of the real waking-day world.

tangible (ˈtændʒɪb(ə)l), *a.* [ad. L. *tangibilis* that may be touched, f. *tangĕre* to touch: see -BLE. So F. *tangible* (16th c. in Littré).]

A. *adj.* **1. a.** Capable of being touched; affecting the sense of touch; touchable.

1589 PUTTENHAM *Eng. Poesie* II. i. (Arb.) 78 Of the things that haue conueniencie by relation, as the visible by light colour and shadow: the audible by stirres, times and accents: ..the tangible by his obiectes in this or that regard. **1678** CUDWORTH *Intell. Syst.* I. v. 769 That body, or that which is tangible and divisible, is the only substantial thing. **1825** MACAULAY *Ess., Milton* (1887) 11 The..desire of having some visible and tangible object of adoration. **1886** MYERS *Phantasms of Living* I. Introd. 59 These sounds, these movements, these tangible apparitions.

b. Hence, Material, externally real, objective.

1620 T. GRANGER *Div. Logike* 56 Whereof externall, and tangible workes are produced. **1827** HARE *Guesses* Ser. I. (1873) 3 The threatenings of Christianity are material and tangible. **1874** L. STEPHEN *Hours in Library* (1892) I. iii. 117 He would not have had much chance of winning tangible rewards. **1875** FORTNUM *Maiolica* i. 1 From a very early period of human existence, known to us only by the tangible memorials of primitive inhabitants.

(*b*) ***tangible assets***, physical and material assets which can be precisely valued or measured.

1930 [see INTANGIBLE *sb.*]. **1977** *Time* 8 Aug. 39/3 Recognizing that shares of many companies are selling at far less than the replacement value of their tangible assets, a number of chief executives have been using corporate cash to buy the assets of other companies at a discount. **1982** *Daily Tel.* 2 Sept. 19/2 Alexander Howden's net tangible assets were overstated..according to the audit of the British insurance company.

2. That may be discerned or discriminated by the sense of touch; as ***a tangible property*** or ***form***.

1664 JER. TAYLOR *Dissuas Popery* i. 5 This method..is the best, the most certain, visible and tangible. **1684** J. P. tr. *Frambresarius' Art Physic* i. 14 [They have] so many real Agreements of Tangible Qualities. **1709** BERKELEY *Th. Vision* §45 Certain ideas perceivable by touch—as distance, tangible figure, and solidity. **1814** CHALMERS *Evid. Chr. Revel.* viii. 211 The only way to learn its tangible properties is to touch it.

3. *fig.* That can be laid hold of or grasped by the mind, or dealt with as a fact; that can be realized or shown to have substance; palpable.

1709 BERKELEY *Th. Vision* §96 Tangible ideas. *a* **1763** BYROM *Crit. Rem. Horace* Poems 1773 I. 310 That none of you touch a most tangible Blunder. **1839** JAMES *Louis XIV*, II. 284 These proposals assumed a more tangible form.. after the arrival of Turenne. **1852** GROTE *Greece* II. lxxiii. (1862) VI. 415 Without any tangible ground of complaint.

4. Capable of being touched or affected emotionally.

1813 L. HUNT in *Examiner* 11 Jan. 22/2 He..is like the.. Executioner,..tangible neither by groan nor by indignation.

B. as *sb.* A thing that may be touched; something material or objective. Also *fig.*

1890 W. JAMES *Princ. Psychol.* II. xix. 77 Those things are *tangibles*; their real properties, such as shape, size, mass, consistency, position, reveal themselves only to touch. **1962** Y. MALKIEL in Householder & Saporta *Probl. Lexicogr.* 5 Range, i.e. the volume and spread of the material assembled, represents..the most obvious criterion [for classifying dictionaries]; it is also the most objective, involving by definition tangibles alone. **1965** *Economist* 21 Aug. 697/2 He also had some tangibles to offer, in particular a request to Congress to eliminate the import fee on sugar. **1980** I. ST. JAMES *Money Stones* II. i. 39 Financial operators like me deal in paper and rarely have first-hand contact with tangibles.. reducing..a new jumbo jet or a sugar crop to one common denominator..Money.

Hence **ˈtangibleness**, the quality or state of being tangible; **ˈtangibly** *adv.*, in a tangible manner.

1727 BAILEY vol. II, **Tangibleness*, capableness of being touched or felt by the Touch. **1843** MILL *Logic* I. ii. §4 When only one attribute..is designated by the name; as visibleness; tangibleness; equality; squareness; milkwhiteness; then the name can hardly be considered general. **1893** C. A. WINGERTER in Barrows *Parl. Relig.* II. 1410 We have not appreciated it [duty to the poor] fully unless we recognize its tangibleness. **1847** WEBSTER, *Tangibly. **1858** MACDONALD *Phantastes* v. (1878) 73 The human forms appeared..more tangibly visible.

tangina, tangkin: see TANGHIN.

tangis, obs. Sc. form of TONGS.

tangiwai (ˈtæŋɪwaɪ). *Min.* [Maori, = tear-water.] A translucent kind of bowenite serpentine found in New Zealand that has droplet-shaped markings when polished.

1863 F. E. MANING *Old New Zealand* 321 This particular *mere* must have been made of the lovely translucent *tangiwai*. **1880** [see KAWA-KAWA[1] 2]. **1911** [see BOWENITE]. **1935** *Trans. & Proc. R. Soc. N.Z.* LXV. 201 All the talc-epidote-bearing serpentines examined by the writer are typical *tangiwais*.

tangka, var. TANGA[1].

tangle (ˈtæŋg(ə)l), *sb.*[1] [= Norw. *taangel*, *tongul*, Færoese *tongul*, ON. and Icel. *þöngull* (:— *þangulr*) 'the stalk of *Laminaria digitata*', app. deriv. of *þang* bladder-wrack, TANG *sb.*[3]

The etymological history is not clear; *tangle* cannot have come down from ON., because ON. *þ* remains in Sc. and Eng. as *th*: cf. *Thurso*, *Thorpe*, *Thwaite*, *Thoresby*, etc.; it must therefore either have spread south from Orkney and Shetland, where ON. *þ* had become *t*, or be a later adoption from Norwegian or other lang. having *t* for ON. *þ*. (The name 'tangle' is not mentioned among the Algæ in Lightfoot's *Flora Scotica*, 1778.)]

1. A general term for the larger seaweeds, species of *Fucus* and allied genera; = TANG *sb.*[3] Often *sea-tangle*. (Prob. orig. an inaccurate use; cf. 2.)

1536 BELLENDEN *Cosmogr.* xiv. in *Cron. Scot.* (1821) I. p. xlix, Maister Alexander Galloway..liftet up ane see-tangle, hingand full of mussill schellis fra the rute to the branchis. **1596** DALRYMPLE tr. *Leslie's Hist. Scot.* (S.T.S.) I. 62 He saw bred of a sey tangle, mussilis. **1603** HOLLAND *Plutarch's Mor.* 676 It hath gotten about the keele a deale of mosse, reits, kilpe, and tangle. **1664** *Phil. Trans.* I. 13 Upon which ..Rock-weed or Sea-tangle did grow a hand long. **1744** PRESTON *ibid.* XLIII. 61 There are Plenty of Sea-weeds, called Tangle, growing on the Rocks, of which might be made Kelp. **1895** CROCKETT *Men of Moss-Hags* lii, Certain ..persons were carrying away sea-tangle from his foreshore.

2. *spec.* Either of two species of seaweed, *Laminaria* (*Fucus* L.) *digitata* and *L. saccharina*, having long leathery fronds, the young stalk and fronds of which are sometimes eaten. (This is the Norse sense, and prob. the proper one.)

1724 RAMSAY *Tea-t. Misc.* (1733) I. 91 Scrapt haddocks, wilks, dulse and tangle. **1807** THOMPSON *Cat. Plants Berwick-on-Tweed* 112 *Fucus digitatus*, Fingered Fucus; Tangle. **1820** SCOTT *Monast.* Answ. Introd. Epist., I never saw it cast ashore any thing but dulse and tangle. **1845** EDMONSTON *Flora of Shetland* 54 *Laminaria digitata* is by them [the Orcadian peasantry] termed Tangle. **1846** LINDLEY *Veg. Kingd.* 21 The young stalks of Laminaria digitata and saccharina are eaten under the name of 'tangle'. **1875** J. H. BALFOUR in *Encycl. Brit.* I. 508/2 Dulse and tangle was formerly a common cry in the streets of Edinburgh.

3. *Comb.*, as ***tangle-strewn***, ***-tasselled*** adjs.; **tangle-fish**, a popular name of the needle-fish or pipe-fish, *Syngnathus acus*; **tangle-picker**, a bird, the Turnstone (*Strepsilas interpres*); **tangle-tent**, in surgery, a tent or pledget of sea-weed; **tangle-weed**, **tangle-wrack**, = sense 1.

1838 PARNELL in *Mem. Werner. Soc.* VII. 394 *Syngnathus acus*, *Tangle-Fish, Scotland, [so called] by the fishermen, in consequence of its being found under seaweed, which they call tangle. **1882** YARRELL *Hist. Birds* (ed. 4) III. 290 Searching among sea-weed for its food: whence its appropriate Norfolk name of '*Tangle-picker'. **1882** *Good Cheer* 41 Cool sea scented breezes came up from the *tangle-strewn sands. **1812** W. TENNANT *Anster Fair* I. xxvi, Upropp'd from sea, a *tangle-tassell'd shape. **1889** J. M. DUNCAN *Clin. Lect. Dis. Women* v. (ed. 4) 17 The cervix [uteri] was dilated by a *tangle-tent. **1825** G. F. LYON *Brief Narr. Attempt to reach Repulse Bay* 65 The sea was much agitated, a great quantity of *tangle weed floating about. **1834** M. SCOTT *Cruise Midge* (1863) 20 Far down amongst the tangleweed and coral branches at the bottom of the deep green sea. **1870** J. LAUDER *Warblings of Caged Bird* 37 Whaur the stanes are green wi' moss And the tangle weeds are plenty. **1890** W. PATER *Wks.* (1901) VIII. 23 All around the gulf there is but an expanse of *tanglework. **1721** RAMSAY *Prospect of Plenty* 228 Wild shores..Plenish'd with nought but shells and *tangle-wreck.

tangle (ˈtæŋg(ə)l), *sb.*[2] [f. TANGLE *v.*[1]]

1. a. A tangled condition, or *concr.* a tangled mass; a complication of threads, hairs, fibres, branches, boughs, or the like, confusedly intertwined or interlaced, or of a single long thread, line, or rope, involved in coils, loops, and knots; a snarl, ravel, or complicated loose knot. Also *transf.* of streams, paths, etc. similarly intertwisted or confused.

1615 W. LAWSON *Country Housew. Gard.* (1626) 20 That it [the soil] may run among the small tangles [of the roots] without straining or bruising. **1637** MILTON *Lycidas* 69 To sport with Amaryllis in the shade, Or with the tangles of Neæra's hair. **1667** —— *P.L.* IX. 632 Hee [the serpent] leading swiftly rowld In tangles, and made intricate seem strait, To mischief swift. *a* **1774** TUCKER *Lt. Nat.* (1834) II. 35 If upon combing his head he meets with a tangle that tears off two or three hairs **1842** DARWIN in *Life & Lett.* (1887) I. 321 This bow became covered with a tangle of creepers. **1856** KANE *Arct. Expl.* I. xxix. 378 The rise and fall of the tides always breaks up the ice..in a tangle of irregular, half-floating masses. **1861** D. COOK *P. Foster's D.* vii, One of a small tangle of courts between Long Acre and New Street, Covent Garden. **1873** HALE *In His Name* v. 26 In a tangle of low, scrubby oaks. **1879** M. D. CONWAY *Demonol.* I. III. ix. 386 The Gorgon's head..with its fearful tangle of serpent tresses. *Mod.* This string is all in a tangle.

b. *spec.* A dredger for sweeping the sea-bed, consisting of a bar to which are attached a number of hempen 'mops', in the fibres of which the more delicate marine specimens are entangled.

1882 D. C. BEARD *Amer. Boy's Handy Bk.* xi. 88 The Tangle, a name given to tassels of hemp that are often attached to the bottom of the dredge itself or used separately. **1883** LESLIE tr. *Nordenskiöld's Voy. Vega* 97 The hempen tangles were used, and brought up a very abundant yield of large, beautiful animal forms. **1884** *Science* IV. 227/2 The true province of the tangles is a very rocky bottom, where neither the dredge nor trawl can be safely used.

2. *fig.* A complicated and confused assemblage; a muddle, jumble, complication, medley, puzzle; a confused network of opinions, facts, etc.; also, a perplexed state.

1757 DYER *Fleece* II. Poet. Wks. (1761) 110 And silent, in the tangles soft involv'd Cf death-like sleep. **1800** COLERIDGE *Death Wallenst.* 183 Where's he that will unravel This tangle, ever tangling more and more? **1858** SEARS *Athan.* III. x. 330 The tangles of metaphysics in which they sought to involve the great Apostle. **1866** J. H. NEWMAN *Gerontius* v. 42 Methinks I know To disengage the tangle of thy words. **1873** MORLEY *Rousseau* II. 126 The complex tangle of the history of social growths. **1883** SIR T. MARTIN *Ld. Lyndhurst* xi. 285 The skill with which he reduced into method and compass the enormous tangle of facts and figures.

3. *Comb.* = in a tangle, tangled, as ***tangle-twine***, ***-twist***, ***-wood***; ***tangle-haired***, ***-headed***, ***-tailed*** adjs.; also **tangle-swab**, one of the mops of a tangle for dredging (sense 1 b).

1861 L. L. NOBLE *Icebergs* 68 They were a russet, *tangle-haired and shaggy-bearded set. **1884** 'MARK TWAIN' *Huck. Finn* xv. 131, I think you're a *tangle-headed old fool, Jim. **1908** *Westm. Gaz.* 15 Aug. 15/3 A gipsy woman, with tangle-headed children, carrying faggots on their backs. **1884** *Science* IV. 148/1 Several *tangle-swabs were generally attached to the hinder end of the bag. *Ibid.* 227/2 The use of hempen tangle-swabs attached to the dredge was introduced by the English exploring-steamer Porcupine in 1868 or 1869. **1883** W. G. COLLINGWOOD *Philos. Ornament* v. 121 The builders of early Italian cathedrals..now run wild with the northern *tangle-tailed mysteries. **1878** BROWNING *La Saisiaz* 94 The wreaths, *Tangle-twine of leaf and bloom. **1889** *Chicago Advance* 6 June, 'Twould take ten miles o' this here *tangletwist to make one. **1894** *Ibid.* 26 Apr., He scuttled off in a wild panic through the thick *tanglewood.

'tangle, *sb.*[3] *Sc.* and *north. dial.* [Of uncertain origin: perh. belonging to TANGLE *sb.*[1] or [2], or due to a vague combination of the two notions, or to some association with *dangle*.]

1. A pendent icicle. *Sc.*

1673 *Wedderburn's Voc.* 34 (Jam.) *Stiria*, a tangle of yce. **1813** E. PICKEN *Misc. Poems* I. 77 (E.D.D.) Frae ilk buss, the tangles gay, Hang skinklin' in the mornin' ray. **1888** BARRIE *Auld Licht Idylls* i, The waterspout that suspends its 'tangles' of ice over a gaping tank.

2. A tall and limp or flaccid person. *Sc.*

1789 ROSS *Helenore* (ed. 3) 21 She's but a tangle, tho' shot out she be.

3. Anything long and dangling, as a tress of hair, a long root-fibre, a torn loosely-pendent strip of cloth, etc.

1864 S. BAMFORD *Homely Rhymes*, etc. 148 Her bonny tangles Were hung wi star-spangles. **1892** M. C. F. MORRIS *Yorksh. Folk-talk* 386 When t' tang'ls is brokken they [potatoes] can't taatie. **1904** *Eng. Dial. Dict.* s.v. (W. Yks.), Her gown was all rives and tangles.

4. Applied to plants having long, winding, and often tangled stalks, as the species of *Myriophyllum* (Water Milfoil) and *Potamogeton* (Pondweed); and to plants of tangled growth, as ***blue tangle(s*** (U.S.), ***red tangle***: see quots.

1857 DUNGLISON *Med. Lex.*, Tangles, Blue, *Gaylussacia dumosa*. **1866** *Treas. Bot.*, *Blue Tangle*, an American name for *Gaylussacia frondosa*. **1886** BRITTEN & HOLL. *Eng. Plant-n.*, Tangle, Red, *Cuscuta Epithymum*.

b. *Comb.* **tangle-berry** = *blue tangles* (see 4), DANGLE-BERRY.

'tangle, *a. Sc.* [f. TANGLE *sb.*[3]] Long and limp; tall and loose-jointed. Also in comb., as ***tangle-backed***.

c **1817** HOGG *Tales & Sk.* I. 291 She was perfectly weak and tangle, her limbs being scarcely able to bear her weight. **1825** JAMIESON, *Tangle*, tall and feeble, not well knit..as, 'a lang tangle lad'. **1896** L. KEITH *Ind. Uncle* x. 172 Yin o' the tangle-backit kind.

tangle ('tæŋg(ə)l), *v.*[1] Also 4–5 **tangil, -yl,** 4–6 **-el(e,** 6 **-ell.** [Known first in later 14th and early 15th c. MSS. of Hampole's *Psalter* (*a* 1340), as a variant reading for *tagil, -yl*, the form in the earliest MSS., used also in other works attributed to Hampole: see TAGLE *v.*, of which *tangle* was app. a nasalized variant.

The vb. thus appears a century and a half earlier than TANGLE *sb.*[1] seaweed, from which some have suggested its derivation. It is however possible that the later senses 4 and 5 may have been associated with and influenced by that sb. TANGLE *sb.*[2] was a direct derivative of the vb.]

†**1.** *trans.* To involve or engage (a person) in affairs which encumber and hamper or embarrass, and from which it is difficult to get free; = ENTANGLE *v.* 2. Chiefly *refl.* and *pass.*; also, to embarrass, confuse (the brain, mind, conscience, etc.).

a **1340** HAMPOLE *Psalter* xxxix. 16 (MS. U.) Na man may wit how many vices ere þat men ere tangild with. [*So* 8 *MSS.*: tangild, -gyld, -glyd, -glid, -gled, -geled; 2 *earliest MSS.* tagild.] —— *Ibid.*, *Abacuc* 31 [see TAGLE *v.*]. **1526** *Pilgr. Perf.* (W. de W. 1531) 63 b, With the whiche he wyll tangle theyr myndes and trouble theyr conscyences. **1526** TINDALE *1 Tim.* vi. 10 Coveteousnes.., which whill some lusted after, they..tangglyd them selves with many sorowes. **1530** PALSGR. 752/2, I am tangled in busynesse, and can nat tel howe to wynde me out. **1561** NORTON & SACKV. *Gorboduc* IV. ii, O happie wight, that suffres not the snare Of murderous minde to tangle him in bloode. **1577–87** HOLINSHED *Chron.* III 1133/2 The queene tangling hir selfe contrarie to promise in hir husbands quarrell. **1671** MILTON *Samson* 1665 Not willingly, but tangl'd in the fold Of dire necessity.

2. To involve in material things that surround or wind about, so as to hamper and obstruct; also, to cover or wreathe with intertwined growth or with something that obstructs. Also *fig.*

1506–11 SIR R. GUYLFORDE *Pylgr.* (Camden) 60 We were soo tangled in among the sayde deserte yles that we coude not gette oute frome amonges them. **1593** DRAYTON *Eclogues* vi. 167 See where yon little..Lambe of mine It selfe hath tangled in a crawling Breere. **1727** DE FOE *Hist. Appar.* iv. (1840) 44 But hang..upon the mere thread, and choose to hamper and tangle themselves. **1829** SIR W. NAPIER *Penins. War* II. 255 He could not, alone, force his way to Lisbon,..through a country tangled with rivers. **1853** G. JOHNSTON *Nat. Hist. E. Bord.* I. 144 The sloes and brush-wood that tangle the brae. **1856** KANE *Arct. Expl.* I. xx. 250 His journal-entry referring to the 23d, while tangled in the ice. **1867** LADY HERBERT *Cradle L.* x. 280 Beautiful gardens..tangled over with ipomeas and other bright creepers. **1885** R. BUCHANAN *Annan Water* v, The hedges were tangled with wild rose bushes.

3. To catch and hold fast in or as in a net or snare; to entrap. Chiefly, in early use always, *fig.*

1526 TINDALE *Matt.* xxii. 15 The farises..toke counsell howe they myght tangle him in his wordes. —— *1 Cor.* vii. 35 This speake I..not to tangle you in a snare: but for that which is honest and comly vnto you. **1540–1** ELYOT *Image of Gov.* 20 They woorke theyr nette so finely,..that in one meishe or other he shall be tangled. **1592** SHAKS. *Ven. & Ad.* 67 Looke how a bird lyes tangled in a net. **1593** —— *2 Hen. VI*, II. iv. 55 [They] Haue all lym'd Bushes to betray thy Wings, And flye thou how thou canst, they'le tangle thee. **1635** BARRIFFE *Mil. Discip.* i. (1643) 5 They doe but tangle themselves in their owne snares. **1806** J. GRAHAME *Birds Scotl.* 43 May never fowler's snare Tangle thy struggling foot.

4. To intertwist (threads, branches, or the like) complicatedly or confusedly together; to intertwist the threads or parts of (a thing) in this way; to put or get (a long thread or a number of threads, etc.) into a tangle. Also *fig.*

1530 PALSGR. 752/2, I tangell thynges so togyther that they can nat well be parted a sonder... You have tangled this threde so that it is marred. **1577** B. GOOGE *Heresbach's Husb.* II. (1586) 54 They come vp as it weere to one roote, and tangled together. **1665** *Phil. Trans.* I. 35 Those insects ..tangled together by their long tailes. **1671** GREW *Anat. Plants* iii. App. §9 As we are wont to tangle the Twigs of Trees together to make an Arbour Artificial. **1850** SCORESBY *Cheever's Whalem. Adv.* ix. (1858) 117 As the different coils run from the tub, they sometimes, when not well laid down, get 'foul' or tangled. **1855** MACAULAY *Hist. Eng.* xxii. IV. 798 He had cut the knot which the Congress had only twisted and tangled.

5. a. *intr.* for *refl.* To be or become tangled or confusedly intertwined. In quot. 1908, to have a tangled course, to twist about confusedly.

1575 TURBERV. *Falconrie* 175 The falcon bating this way and that way, she shall never twinde nor tangle bicause the ring followeth hir still. **1623** WEBSTER *Duchess Malfi* III. ii, My hair tangles. **1657** W. COLES *Adam in Eden* cci, It [dodder] tangleth about it like a net. **1713** J. PETIVER in *Phil. Trans.* XXVIII. 204 The whole Plant is clammy, and its branches tangle much. **1902** *Westm. Gaz.* 3 Sept. 3/1 Above them [graves] tall grass grows and tangles, as if it were holding them together. **1908** *Sat. Rev.* 26 Sept. 392/1 She wandered..Down lanes that tangled through the countryside.

†**b.** *fig.* To become involved in contention. *Obs.*

1535 *St. Papers Hen. VIII*, II. 249 Perceyving that thErle of Ossorie soo stedfastely and ernestly tanglid against the same traictors. **1536** *Ibid.* 330 OConor his he that now moste begynneth newly to tangle ageinst the army.

c. *transf.* To fight, to engage in conflict or argument (*with* or *up with*); also *fig.* and *loosely*, to associate or become involved with. *colloq.* (orig. *U.S.*).

1928 *Amer. Speech* III. 29 Fistic action in large and copious quantities is expected..tonight when Dave Shade tangles with Maxie Rosenbloom. **1929** D. HAMMETT *Red Harvest* xxiv. 242 While we're tangling, them bums will eat us up. **1929** D. RUNYON in *Hearst's Internat.* July 58/2, I remember reading in the paper about a lot of different guys who are considered very sensible until they get tangled up with a doll. **1942** *Sun* (Baltimore) 13 May 15/4 (*heading*) Preakness victor will tangle with old rivals if he runs at Belmont. **1945** L. R. GRIBBLE *Battle Stories of R.A.F.* xxv. 64 There's no better fun in the world than tangling with the Hun. **1953** E. S. GARDNER *Case of Green-Eyed Sister* (1959) ii. 17 You tangle up with Brogan..and you'll learn something about the noble art of shake-down. **1957** R. LAWLER *Summer of Seventeenth Doll* I. i. 17, I dunno why I always have to get tangled up with little men, just the same. Even Wallie, he was shorter than me. **1958** B. BEHAN *Borstal Boy* III. 185, I don't like tangling with anyone, but Ickey Summers was the sort of little bastard that would pick a fight with you until he lost and the best thing to do with him was to make sure that he lost the first time. **1960** M. STEWART *My Brother Michael* ix. 118, I didn't particularly want to tangle with Danielle. **1966** P. O'DONNELL *Sabre-Tooth* xviii. 244, I fancy we'll tangle in the long run, Willie. But not for a while. **1978** J. B. HILTON *Some run Crooked* xi. 116 There were men here who had nothing particular to hide, but who had learned..that it was better not to tangle with Kenworthy. **1982** *Times* 10 Dec. 11/5 The mood of the House was sombre, and he had no desire to tangle with the Secretary of State.

6. *Comb.* of the verb-stem with an object, as **tangle-leg(s**, that which tangles the legs: a popular name of an American shrub, the Hobble-bush, *Viburnum lantanoides*; also for strong beer or spirits; cf. TANGLEFOOT b; **tangle-toad**, a name for the creeping buttercup, *Ranunculus repens* (*Eng. Dial. Dict.*).

1860 BARTLETT *Dict. Amer.* s.v. *Hobble Bush*, A straggling shrub, also called Tangle-Legs and Wayfaring. **1880** R. JEFFERIES *Gt. Estate* iv. 68 Some more 'tangle-legs'—for thus they called the strong beer. **1882** SALA *Amer. Revisit.* (1885) 285 The particular kind of whiskey known as 'tangle-leg'.

†**'tangle,** *v.*[2] *Obs.* [freq. of TANG *v.*[2]: see -LE 3.] *intr.* To give out a quick succession of ringing sounds. Cf. TWANGLE, TINKLE. Hence †**'tangling** *vbl. sb.*[2]

c **1580** JEFFERIE *Bugbears* Epil., Song ii. in *Archiv Stud. Neu. Spr.* (1897), With janglynges, with banglynges, with tanglynges, A sprityng go we! *a* **1652** BROME *Queene's Exchange* II. ii, The great Bells of our Town, they tingle they tangle, They jingle they jangle, the Tenner of them goes merrily.

tangled ('tæŋg(ə)ld), *ppl. a.* [f. TANGLE *v.*[1] + -ED[1].] Interlaced or intertwined in a complicated and confused manner; matted, mixed up confusedly; *fig.* complicated, intricate.

1590 SHAKS. *Mids. N.* v. i. 125 His speech was like a tangled chaine: nothing impaired, but all disordered. **1634** MILTON *Comus* 181 The blind mazes of this tangl'd Wood. *a* **1717** PARNELL *Health* 45, I lead where Stags thro' tangled Thickets tread. **1750** SHENSTONE *Rural Elegance* 204 The tangled vetch's purple bloom. **1808** SCOTT *Marm.* VI. xvii, Oh what a tangled web we weave When first we practise to deceive! **1874** M. CREIGHTON *Hist. Ess.* i. (1902) 20 The tangled thread of Italian politics.

tanglefoot ('tæŋg(ə)lfʊt), *a.* and *sb.* [f. TANGLE *v.*[1] + FOOT *sb.*] **a.** *adj.* That tangles or entangles the foot. **b.** *sb.* That which tangles or entraps the foot; *spec. U.S. slang*, an intoxicating beverage, esp. whisky. Also *attrib.* So **'tangle-footed** *a.*, having tangled feet, stumbling.

1860 BARTLETT *Dict. Amer.*, *Tangle-foot*, one of the Western figurative terms for whiskey. **1871** *Hartford Courant* 17 Mar. (Farmer *Slang*), He proceeded..toward a neighboring saloon in quest of tangle-foot. **1881** 'MARK TWAIN' *Innoc. at Home* ii, He could..hold more tangle-foot whisky without spilling it than any man in seventeen counties. **1888** *Voice* (N.Y.) 27 Dec., [Stories] of this tanglefooted variety, which trip up and throw themselves by their absurdity and self-contradiction. **1893** *Chicago Advance* 28 Sept., The tangle-foot complications in which it was sure to involve its defenders. **1900** *Daily News* 11 Apr. 3/2 The poisonous 'Cape Smoke', or 'tanglefoot', which they [soldiers] get in too great abundance out here. **1908** W. R. HEARST in *Westm. Gaz.* 2 Oct. 5/1 The deeper he sinks into the tangle-foot of corruption and contradiction.

tangle-leg(s: see TANGLE *v.*[1] 6.

tanglement ('tæŋg(ə)lmənt). [f. TANGLE *v.*[1] + -MENT.] The fact or condition of being tangled; an instance of this; a tangle.

1831 J. WILSON *Unimore* ii. 199 All matted thick with briery tanglement Like Indian Jungle. **1879** J. MORISON in *Expositor* IX. 122 A little tanglement of phraseology. **1892** *Chambers's Jrnl.* 6 Aug. 508/2 We lay utterly helpless amidst this tanglement of weeds.

tangler ('tæŋglə(r)). [f. TANGLE *v.*[1] + -ER[1].] One who or that which tangles.

c **1520** M. NISBET *N. Test. in Scots, Jas.* ii. 21 *margin*, Abraham was nocht a wayne tangler of faith.

'tanglesome, *a.* [f. TANGLE *sb.*[2] or *v.*[1] + -SOME.] Full of tanglement, tangled, confused. Also *dial.* (see quot. 1823).

1823 E. MOOR *Suffolk Words & Phr.*, *Tanglesome*, discontented—obstinate—fretful—not essentially different from *Tankersome*. **1888** *Engineer* LXV. 317 Things are in such a tanglesome condition.

'tangling, *vbl. sb.*[1] [f. TANGLE *v.*[1] + -ING[1].] The action of TANGLE *v.*[1]; complicated or confused intertwining; complication; †contention.

[*c* **1340**: see TAGLE *v.*] **1535** *St. Papers Hen. VIII*, II. 272 Which had bene wele forwardes by this tyme, yf this wilful tangeling with OConour had not bene. **1538** in *Lett. Suppress. Monasteries* (Camden) 169 Many leasses grauntede oute by the olde prior,.. with muche tangullyng and besines. *a* **1633** AUSTIN *Medit.* (1635) 282 When wee thus let slip these heavenly Thred Lines..wee fall to tangling, tying, and knitting. **1868** *Rep. U.S. Commissioner Agric.* (1809) 289 The silk skeins are tied to prevent tangling.

b. *concr. pl.* Things that tangle or entangle.

1575 TURBERV. *Venerie* 138 Me thinkes I see the Toyle, the tanglings and the stall Which are prepared and set full sure, to compasse me withall. **1591** PERCIVAL *Sp. Dict.*, *Cazcarias*, tanglings about chickins feete. **1904** *Daily News* 26 Nov. 6/8 Clinging tanglings of the thorny briar.

tangling, *vbl. sb.*[2]: see TANGLE *v.*[2]

'tangling, *ppl. a.* [f. TANGLE *v.*[1] + -ING[2].] That tangles, in various senses of the verb.

a **1586** SIDNEY *Ps.* XXV. x, This Lord..will set free My feet from tangling net. **1667** MILTON *P.L.* IV. 176 The undergrowth Of shrubs and tangling bushes. **1756** H. JONES *Earl of Essex* 17 Amidst thy tangling snares involv'd. **1801** BLOOMFIELD *Rural T., Walter & Jane* 115 When to these tangling thoughts I've been resigned.

Hence **'tanglingly** *adv.*, in a tangling manner.

1847 in WEBSTER.

tangly ('tæŋglı), *a.*[1] [f. TANGLE *sb.*[1] + -Y.] Strewn with, full of, or consisting of tangle.

1762-9 FALCONER *Shipwr.* III. 777 Helpless, on the tangly beach he lay. *a* **1851** MOIR *Old Seaport* iii, Far beneath the surf upheaved The sea-weed's tangly arms.

'tangly, *a.*[2] [f. TANGLE *sb.*[2] + -Y.] Abounding in tangles; tangled.

1813 J. C. HOBHOUSE *Journey* (ed. 2) 655 A tangly flat, overrun with low shrubs. **1887** C. L. PIRKIS *Dateless Bargain* I. ii. 44 More limp and tangly than a skein of silk. **1899** *Westm. Gaz.* 12 June 1/3 Plunge in the jungle's tangly growth.

'tangly, *a.*[3] *Sc.* and *north. dial.* [f. TANGLE *sb.*[3] + -Y.] Long and limp, or flaccid; feeble, flabby: = TANGLE *a.*

1812 P. FORBES *Poems* 57 (E.D.D.) Tanglie taperin' tails. **1855** ROBINSON *Whitby Gloss.*, *Tangling* or *Tangly*, untidy in dress, ragged or hanging in shreds. 'A lang tangly lass', having the well-known meaning of 'long and lazy'. **1904** *E. Dial. Dict.* s.v., (N. Yks.) He's a great tangly lad.

tango ('tæŋgəʊ), *sb.*[1] Pl. **tangoes, tangos** (*preferred*). [a. Sp., orig. a Negro or gypsy dance festival.]

1. a. A Spanish flamenco dance.

1896 H. C. C. TAYLOR *Land of Castanet* 103 The girls.. dance again, not the vulgar flamenco or tango, but the charming dance of the province. **1931** [see FARRUCA]. **1967** 'LA MERI' *Spanish Dancing* (ed. 2) vi. 83 The Tango (Tango Gitano, Tango Flamenco) is of Arabic origin... It might be well to observe here that the Tango Gitano has nothing whatever in common with the Argentine tango save the name.

b. A syncopated ballroom dance in 2/4 or 4/4 time introduced into Europe and N. America from Argentina, related to the Cuban Habanera but probably of African origin, characterized by a slow gliding movement broken up by pointing positions; a piece of music for this dance.

1913 G. GROSSMITH in *Daily Graphic* 12 May 9/1 'A Peeress' talks about the Tango. This is a most graceful and beautiful dance. **1915** T. BURKE *London Nights* 254 Music, gaiety, sparkle, fine dresses, costume songs, tangos, smart conversation and faces, and all the rest of it. **1921** *Spectator* 19 Feb. 236/3 Instead of a stately waltz at an even pace, Myers had no sooner taken the magnificent lady round the waist, than they were covering the floor with a glorified tango. **1925** C. CONNOLLY *Let.* 8 Apr. in *Romantic Friendship* (1975) 67 Someone is playing tangoes on a guitar. **1947** [see GUAJIRA]. **1962** *Melody Maker* 7 July 7/5 Kid Thomas..leads his septet through standards, pops and tangoes. **1976** BOTHAM & DONNELLY *Valentino* iv. 34 This arrogant and deliciously handsome Continental who danced the tango as though it had been invented for him. **1981** E. NORTH *Dames* viii. 138 The music..played..a tango... He regarded better dancers tangoing.

2. *attrib.* and *Comb.*, as (sense 1 b) ***tango band, -dancer, -dancing, foxtrot, music, rhythm, step***; **tango tea**, a thé dansant, usu. at a hotel or other gathering place, arranged for the purpose of dancing the tango (*disused*).

1927 C. CONNOLLY *Let.* 13 Feb. in *Romantic Friendship* (1975) 255 This is a very grand hotel, all lights and carpets and a melodious tango band. **1932** Tango band [see RUMBA *sb.* 1 a]. **1974** M. BUTTERWORTH *Man in Sopwith Camel* I. 11 Norman the demon tango-dancer of the Palais. **1918** G. FRANKAU *One of Them* XXXI. 243 She..knew how wise she'd been to countermand Breastplate and shield which, though they looked entrancing, Would both have been a bore for tango-dancing. *c* **1925** 'H. NICHOLLS' (*music title*) Sunny Havana: tango foxtrot. **1913** *Sheffield Daily Tel.* 5 Sept. 6/4 Tango music is also expected to rival the popularity of ragtime. **1966** A. CAVANAGH *Children are Gone* II. v. 45 The Muzak was dispensing tango rhythms, loud and sinuous. **1977** 'F. CLIFFORD' *Ten Minutes on June Morning* 90 The music came again, tango rhythm. **1981** E. WARD *Baltic Emerald* ix. 64 A new tango step. **1913** *Punch* 6 Aug. 125 No tango-teas shall be given in *this* drawing-room. **1918** G. FRANKAU *One of Them* I. 14 What time we sang of guns and gore and trenches, Instead of oysters, tango-teas and wenches.

tango ('tæŋgəʊ), *sb.*[2] (*a.*) [f. TANG(ERINE *sb.* 2 + -O[2], perh. influenced by prec. sb. or by TAN *sb.*[1] 3.] A colour shade of deep orange.

1913 *Vanity Fair* Sept. 59/3 The one shown is of sand color and tango. **1933** *Archit. Rev.* LXXIII. 70 The colour scheme of the shopfront is tango-red throughout. **1958** B. NICHOLS *Sweet & Twenties* x. 126 Jade green, cerise, tango. **1976** *Burnham-on-Sea Gaz.* 20 Apr. 18/3 (Advt.), 1974 Hillman Hunter GLS 4-door saloon, tango.

'tango, *v.* [f. TANGO *sb.*[1]] *intr.* **a.** To dance the tango.

1913 *Punch* 10 Dec. 486/1 'Do you tango?' she asked me as soon as we were comfortably seated. **1925** C. DODD *Farthing Spinster* III. iii. 299 Young Jellis tangoed up to the two ladies. **1941** B. SCHULBERG *What makes Sammy Run?* xi. 206 Sammy didn't know how to tango. **1952** M. LASKI *Village* ii. 42 She..watched her father tangoing..with Daisy Bruce. **1975** *Times* 4 Sept. 14/6 You have to count anxiously like one learning to tango. **1981** [see TANGO *sb.*[1] 1 b].

b. *fig.* Freq. in proverbial phr. ***it takes two to tango***.

1952 HOFFMAN & MANNING *Takes Two to Tango* (*song*) 2 There are lots of things you can do alone! But, takes two to tango. **1965** *Listener* 24 June 923/2 The President would like to know whom to negotiate with... On this score, the President has a firm, and melancholy, conviction: it takes two to tango. **1970** B. CONACHER *Hockey in Canada* (1972) x. 116 Despite all the problems I had had with Imlach, and believe it or not I realize it takes two to tango, I wouldn't have missed playing in the best league in the world. **1973** *Houston* (Texas) *Chron.* (Texas Mag.) 14 Oct. 2/1 An upcoming film of such explicit sexuality it'll have to tango with the new pornography rulings. **1977** *Time* 31 Oct. 48/1 Ellis Rabb can tango with words and he is a sly devil at milking an audience dry of laughter. **1979** *Guardian* 4 Apr. 12/3 It takes two to tango... Mrs Thatcher has turned Mr Callaghan down.

Hence **'tangoing** *vbl. sb.*; **'tangoist**, an exponent of the tango.

1913 G. B. CROZIER *Tango & How to dance It* i. 8 The Parisian version of the Tango..has so much to recommend it that one may..predict for it a permanent place in our affections long after the present craze for 'Tangoing' is over. *Ibid.* ii. 28 Embryonic 'Tangoists' cannot do better than bear that graceful animal [*sc.* the tiger] in mind while attempting to follow their advice. **1928** *Daily Express* 6 July 3/3 This tango is so slow, so smooth, so syrupy. Caterpillars skating over egg-shells could not move more gracefully, more softly, than the contemporary tangoists. **1976** U. HOLDEN *String Horses* vii. 81 They'd show the Camp what real tangoing was.

tango, var. TANGA[1], East Indian coin.

tangoreceptor ('tæŋgəʊrı,sɛptə(r)). *Zool.* [f. L. *tang-ĕre* to touch + -O + RECEPTOR.] A sensory receptor which responds to touch or pressure.

1906 C. S. SHERRINGTON *Integrative Action Nervous Syst.* ix. 335 The sessile creature retains..only some gustatory (?) receptors round the mouth, and some tangoreceptors..in the tegument. **1937** L. V. HEILBRUNN *Outl. Gen. Physiol.* xl. 506 In man and mammals, in addition to ordinary free nerve endings, special types of tangoreceptors are found in the skin and in the viscera. **1980** L. H. CHAPPELL *Physiol. Parasites* ix. 165 The sensory papillae of cercariae are thought to be tangoreceptors.

‖**tangpu** (daŋbu). Also **Tang Pu.** [Chinese *dǎngbù*, f. *dang* party + *bù* office.] The headquarters of the Kuomintang at the central, and various local, levels.

1941 E. SNOW *Scorched Earth* VI. ii. 206 The *tangpu* system in China is a product of 'natural' political evolution. **1943** J. T. PRATT *War & Politics in China* xii. 200 Borodin impressed upon Dr. Sun the importance of securing the assent of the people at large to the revolutionary programme... This was to be effected by organizing local branches of the Kuomintang—Tang Pu—and by systematic propaganda. **1972** A. DESTENAY tr. *Guillermaz's Hist. Chinese Communist Party 1921–1949* vi. 79 Party offices (Tangpu) existed at the provincial, district and local levels.

tangram ('tæŋgræm). [Origin obscure: second element app. -GRAM.] The name given to a Chinese geometrical puzzle consisting of a square dissected into five triangles, a square, and a rhomboid, which can be combined so as to make two equal squares, and also so as to form several hundred figures, having a rude resemblance to houses, boats, bottles, glasses, urns, birds, beasts, men, etc.

(The Chinese name is *Ch'i ch'iao t'u* 'seven ingenious plan'. The name *tangram* seems to have been given in England, or perhaps in U.S. but some have conjectured for the first element Chinese *t'an* 'to extend', or *t'ang* commonly used in Canton for 'Chinese'. Others have conjectured *Tan* to be the name of the inventor; but no such person is known to Chinese scholars.)

1864 WEBSTER, *Tangram*, a Chinese toy made by cutting a square of thin wood, or [the like] into seven pieces. **1874** [see PUZZLE *sb.* 3 b]. **1908** H. E. DUDENEY *Tales with Tangrams* in *Strand Mag.* Nov. 581 It is probable that Tangrams were originally designed not as a pastime, but as a means of instruction... Professor Max Müller said that 'the science of Tangrams gave evidence of a higher state of civilization than now exists in China'.

tangs, northern and Sc. form of TONGS.

tangue, obs. f. TANG *sb.*[1], [4].

tanguin: see TANGHIN.

tangun, var. TANGHAN, Tibetan horse.

Tangut ('tæŋgu:t), *sb.* (and *a.*). Also 8–9 **Tangout.** [App. a. Mongol, f. Chinese *Tanghsiang* (tribal name): (see also quot. 1979).] A Tibetan people who inhabited north-western China and western Inner Mongolia, and formed the independent kingdom of Hsi Hsia from the eleventh to the thirteenth centuries A.D.; the country or language of this people. Also *attrib.* or as *adj.* Also **Tan'gutan** *a.* and *sb.*

1598 HAKLUYT tr. W. de Rubruquis in *Voy.* I. 116 Between the foresaid mountaines Eastward inhabiteth the nation of Tangut, who are a most valiant people. **1613** PURCHAS *Pilgrimage* IV. ix. 337 There were of them divers nations, called by one common name Mogli, which were divided into seven principal tribes, whose names were Tatar, Tangut, Cunat, Talair, Sonich, Monghi, Tebeth. **1795** W. WINTERBOTHAM *Hist. & Geogr. View Chinese Empire* 182 Thibet is known under different names, the Chinese call it Tsang; the Tartars, Barantola, Bouttan, and Tangout. **1827** H. E. LLOYD tr. *Timkowski's Trav. through Mongolia to China* I. xii. 442 Tangout is a Mongol word, designating the country which at present forms the whole of the western frontier of China, and is inhabited by the eastern Tibetans. **1876** H. H. HOWORTH *Hist. Mongols* I. i. 5 This town [*sc.* Ninghia]..was called in the Tangutan language Eyirkai. **1876** E. D. MORGAN tr. *Prejevalsky's Mongolia, Tangut Country & Northern Tibet* II. iv. 109 The Tangutans, or the Si-fan as the Chinese call them, are of the same race as the Tibetans. *Ibid.* 119 In the Tangut country ..the price of brick tea has considerably risen. **1888** *Encycl. Brit.* XXIII. 343/2 The Tang-chang and Peh-lang tribes boasted also of being descended from a monkey; they were the two great divisions of the Tang-hiang or Tangut, offsets of the same Sien-pi stock as that of the conquerors of Tibet. **1908** J. CURTIN *Mongols* iv. 75 The subjection of the Kirghis and this new victory over Tangut secured the position of Jinghis in Northeastern Asia. **1934** K. S. LATOURETTE *Chinese* I. iv. 159 The Later Chao was succeeded in the Northwest by a state established by a Mongol people, formerly supposed..to be Tanguts. **1954** PEI & GAYNOR *Dict. Linguistics* 214/1 *Tangut*, an Asiatic language, a member of the Eastern group of the Mongol branch of the Altaic sub-family of the Ural-Altaic family of languages. **1979** L. KWANTEN *Imperial Nomads* v. 72 This fails to explain how and when the inhabitants of Hsi Hsia became known as Tangut. *Ibid.*, Most scholars remain convinced that the Tangut language is a member of the Sino-Tibetan linguistic family, although..recent linguistic research indicates that there is a distinct possibility that Tangut is either a Turkic dialect or a language heavily influenced by a Turkic dialect.

tangy ('tæŋı), *a.* Also †**tangey.** [f. TANG *sb.*[1] + -Y[1].] **a.** Having a sharp, distinct, or spicy taste. Also, characterized by a disagreeable tang or flavour (*rare*).

1875 *Ure's Dict. Arts* (ed. 7) III. 189 There is a perceptible deficiency in that fine, clean flavour, which is the perfection of a glass of good beer, its place being usurped by a flavour coarse and tangey. **1931** B. STARKE *Touch & Go* xii. 193 The meal was strong and tangy and tough and stringy. **1946** C. S. FORESTER *Lord Hornblower* iii. 37 A bite of red cheese, tangy and seasoned. **1958** *People* 4 May 7/4 (Advt.), You will find Tango the tastiest, tangiest whole orange drink ever! **1966** *Woman's Own* 22 Jan. 29/1 What all my friends like is its sharp, tangy flavour. **1976** *National Observer* (U.S.) 17 July 1/3 After a tangy dinner of sausage creole, everybody is lounging about the living room. **1979** J. WAINWRIGHT *Home is Hunter* xxi. 71 The iced cider was a pleasant surprise; tangy, cool.

b. *transf.* and *fig.* Cf. SPICY *a.* 7.

1948 *Sun* (Baltimore) 3 Dec. 14/2 (*heading*) The tangy story of the frozen-orange juice industry. **1953** J. MASTERS *Lotus & Wind* x. 137 This was heavier, tangier stuff, and it reminded him more of animals than of flowers. **1967** *Punch* 4 Oct. 520/2 Despite a twinkly fondness for waggish puns.. his style isn't exactly tangy. **1978** H. WOUK *War & Remembrance* viii. 78 She knew a tangy tale or two about Madge Knudsen!

†**tangyl,** *a. Obs.* (See quot.)

c **1440** *Promp. Parv.* (E.E.T.S.) 473 Tangyl [*v.r.* tanggyl], or froward and angry, *bilosus*.., *ffelleus*.

tanh (tæn'eıtʃ). *Math.* Abbrev. of *hyperbolic tangent*.

1879 *Encycl. Brit.* IX. 819/2 Similarly we have the hyperbolic tangent tanh *x*, &c. **1968** E. T. COPSON *Metric Spaces* vii. 107 The restriction..can be removed by considering for example the function tanh *f*(*x*).

tan-house. [f. TAN *v.* and *sb.*[1] + HOUSE.]

1. A building in which tanning is carried on.

14.. *Voc.* in Wr.-Wülcker 585/7 *Frunitorium*, a tanhous. **1529** *Act 21 Hen. VIII*, c. 13 §32 Be it enacted..That no Spiritual Person..have..any Manner of Tan-house. **1626** *Knaresb. Wills* (Surtees) 102 All the barke in the tann house ..all the tubbes and seasterans in the tanhouse. **1791–1823** D'ISRAELI *Cur. Lit.*, *Bibliomania*, I [Bruyere] as little..care to visit the tan-house, which he calls his library.

2. [f. TAN *sb.*[1]] A building for storing tan-bark.

1858 SIMMONDS *Dict. Trade*, *Tan-house*, a deposit place for tanners' bark.

tania, tanier, varr. TANNIA.

tanin, obs. form of TANNIN.

tanist ('tænıst). *Anc. Irish* and *Gaelic Law.* Also 6 **taniste, tanistih, tanest, taynist,** 9 **tanaist;** cf. TANISTER. [ad. Irish and Gael. *tánaiste*, OIr. *tanaise, -aiste*, anything parallel or second to another; the next heir to an estate.] The successor apparent to a Celtic chief, usually the most vigorous adult of his kin, elected during the lifetime of the chief: see TANISTRY.

1538 *St. Papers Hen. VIII*, III. 56 Murghe Obreene, the said Obrenes broder, being the tanest, or successour to Obreene. **1543** *Ibid.* 481 He have restored this berer, his eldist brother, to the office or rombe of Taniste. **1596** SPENSER *State Irel.* Wks. (Globe) 612/1 The Tanistih hath also a share of the countrey allotted unto him. **1646** SIR J.

TEMPLE *Irish Rebell.* 9 *note*, In every Irish country there was a Lord or Chieftain, and a Tanist, who was his successor apparent... He that was most active, of greatest power, and had most followers, alwayes caused himself to be chosen Tanist. **1761–2** HUME *Hist. Eng.* (1806) III. xlvi. 690 The chieftains and the tanists, though drawn from the principal families, were not hereditary, but were established by election, or, more properly speaking, by force and violence. **1813** SCOTT *Rokeby* IV. vi, The Tanist he to great O'Neale. **1861** PEARSON *Early & Mid. Ages Eng.* xxx. 373 Any one of the reigning family might succeed the chief. The heir-apparent was nominated by election among the tribe in the chief's lifetime, and called 'tanist'.

b. *Comb.*, as **tanist-abbot** (see quot.); **tanist-stone**, a name given to some large monoliths, popularly supposed to mark the spot where tanists were formerly elected.

a **1627** C. MAGEOGHEGAN tr. *Ann. Clonmacnois* 147 He was called in Irish tanaise abbaid, tanist [*lit.* second] of the abbot, or seenab [= secundus abbas], in anglo-irish, tanist-abbot. **1851** D. WILSON *Preh. Ann.* (1863) I. v. 140 The Tanist-Stones, where the new chief or king was elected. **1885** *Blackw. Mag.* July 116/1 The Scotland, Tanist stones .. have been frequently found.

Hence **'tanistship**, the office or dignity of a tanist. So **ta'nistic** *a.*, of, pertaining to, or proceeding by the system of tanistry.

1585 in Hardiman *O'Flaherty's Iar-Connaught* (1846) 313 That the .. titles of captayneships, taynistships .. be utterlie abollyshed. **1590** SIR J. PERROT in *Carew MSS.* (1869) 28 The captainries and tanistships. **1881** *Athenæum* 29 Jan. 157/3 The ancient earldoms were not partible, and the succession was tanistic.

'tanister. *rare.* [ad. Irish and Gael. *tanaistear*, f. *tanaiste* (see prec.) + *fhear* man.] = prec.

1612 DAVIES *Why Ireland*, etc. (1787) 182 For every theft under fourteen pence, a fine of five marks should be paid; forty-six shillings and eight pence to the Captain, and twenty shillings to the Tanister. **1937** *Burke's Landed Gentry* (ed. 15) 1496/1 Hugh Vernon Macleod, 11th Chief-tain of Talisker, and apparent Tanister of Macleod of Macleod.

tanistry ('tænɪstrɪ). *Anc. Irish* and *Gaelic Law.* Also 6 **-istrye**, 7 **-estry**, 7–8 **thanistry**. [f. TANIST + -RY.] A system of life-tenure among the ancient Irish and Gaels, whereby the succession to an estate or dignity was conferred by election upon the 'eldest and worthiest' among the surviving kinsmen of the deceased lord.

1596 SPENSER *State Irel.* Wks. (Globe) 611/2 All the Irish doe hold theyr landes by Tanistrye. *a* **1604** HANMER *Chron. Irel.* (1633) 17 The two sonnes were put beside, and the eldest of the sept (after the Irish Tanistrie) tooke place. **1617** MORYSON *Itin.* II. 6 The Irish Law of Tanistry (by which a man is preferred to a boy, and the Vncle to that Nephew whose Grandfather ouerliues the Father, and commonly the most actiue Knaue, not the next Heire, is chosen). **1663** SIR R. GORDON *Govt. Scotl.* in *Macfarlane's Geogr. Collect.* (S.H.S.) II. 391 The law of Tanistrie wes that a Prince dying and leaving behind him children in minority .. the neerest male of the blood royall .. tooke the government upon him. **1778** *Phil. Surv. S. Irel.* 396 Him they called Thanist, and the Custom Thanistry. **1827** HALLAM *Const. Hist.* (1876) III. xviii. 344 The law of tanistry, of which the principle is defined to be that the demesne lands and dignity of chieftainship descended to the eldest and most worthy of the same blood. **1904** *Times, Lit. Supp.* 22 July 229/1 Despite tanistry .. Scotland managed to have real Monarchs when Ireland had none.

b. The office of a tanist (= Gael. *tanaisteachd*).

1813 SCOTT *Rokeby* IV. vi, Against St. George's cross blazed high The banners of his Tanistry.

‖**taniwha** ('tænɪwɑː, ‖'tanifa). *N.Z.* Also †**tanewa**, **taniwoa**, and with capital initial. [Maori.] A mythical monster supposed to reside in deep water.

1840 J. S. POLACK *Manners & Customs New Zealanders* II. xiii. 126 The additional name of *Taniwoa* is added, (a water god). **1842** W. R. WADE *Journey in N.Z.* i. 34 One of our boatmen quickly repeated that the place was tapued for the tanewa (a water demon). **1863** F. E. MANING *Old N.Z.* ii. 26 Down, villain! down to .. the Taniwha cave! **1882** W. D. HAY *Brighter Britain!* II. 214 They [*sc.* the Maori] have a tale of these taniwha .. somewhat parallel to our nursery stories of dragons. **1905** [see NGARARA]. **1921** H. GUTHRIE-SMITH *Tutira* x. 70 They felt the net being dragged away from them by the *taniwha* known to haunt the bay. **1938** R. FINLAYSON *Brown Man's Burden* 56 The carved taniwha monsters of the meeting-house. **1948** J. K. BAXTER *Blow, Wind of Fruitfulness* 37 Riding the logs upstream, and waiting for the taniwha. **1966** *Encycl. N.Z.* I. 48/2 Places along the sea shore were feared because they were the haunts of the *taniwha*, awesome water monsters with man-killing tendencies.

tanja, var. TANGA[1], East Indian coin.

tanjib: see TANZIB.

tank (tæŋk), *sb.*[1] Forms: 7 **tanke, tanque, tancke, tanck**, 7– **tank**. [In sense 1, perh. immediately from an Indian vernacular: cf. Guz. *tānkh* an underground reservoir for water (Shakespear), *ṭānki* a reservoir of water, a small well (Wilson); Marāthi *ṭānken, ṭāken*, a reservoir of water, a tank (Wilson); *ṭānkā* a cistern of stone inside a house, etc., a reservoir for rain-water: words which some would connect with Skr. *taḍāga* pond, lake, pool; others think that they are all derived from Pg. *tanque* pond = Sp. *estanque*, F. *étang*:—L. *stagnum* pond, pool, with which at least the Indian words were identified by the Portuguese, who even in the *Roteiro de Vasco da Gama* and through the 16th c. applied *tanque* to the Indian reservoirs, called also in Fr. *estang* (Pyrard de Laval *c* 1610). The 17th c. Eng. forms *tanque* and *tanke* appear to be taken from the Pg.; *tanck, tank*, on the other hand, with It. *tancho* (Varthema 1510), may have been from Guz. *tānkh*. As to the Eng. use in senses 1 b and 2, it is not clear whether this came from Anglo-Indian usage, or was immediately related to Pg. *tanque*. It could scarcely arise out of earlier Eng. or Sc. *stank* 'pond, fish-pond, stagnant pool, ditch', since this never in sense approached that of *tank*.]

1. a. In India, A pool or lake, or an artificial reservoir or cistern, used for purposes of irrigation, and as a storage-place for drinking-water.

c **1616** TERRY *Voy. E. Ind.* (1655) 105 Besides their Rivers, .. they have many Ponds, which they call Tanques, .. fill'd with water when that abundance of Rain fals. **1634** SIR T. HERBERT *Trav.* 51 Tancks or couered ponds of water, fild by the beneficiall raines, for the vse and drink of Trauellers. **1638** W. BRUTON in Hakluyt *Voy.* (1807) V. 50 (Y.) A very faire Tanke, .. a square pit paved with gray marble. **1698** FRYER *Acc. E. India & P.* 159 Oblong stone Tank... In this all of both Sexes Wash (this Solemnity being called the *Jatry*, or Washing). **1799** SIR T. MUNRO in G. R. Gleig *Life* (1830) I. iv. 241 One crop under a tank, in Mysore or the Carnatic, yields more than three here. *c* **1813** MRS. SHERWOOD *Stories Ch. Catech.* xxiv. (1873) 258 Near to the mosque were many trees, and a stone tank, full of clear water. **1877** G. CHESNEY in *19th Cent.* Nov. 610 The greater part of the irrigation in southern India is effected by means of tanks... These tanks in fact resemble the reservoirs for water-works now to be found in most parts of England... Artificial lakes .. they more properly deserve to be called. **1886** *Daily Tel.* 16 Jan. (Cassell), The tank covers seventy-two acres, and is one of the largest in India.

(*b*) In Australia, an artificial reservoir designed to hold water for livestock; *U.S. dial.*, an artificial pond or lake.

1898 D. CARNEGIE *Spinifex & Sand* 81, I append a table showing cost and contents of Government tanks excavated at the base of granite rocks between Southern Cross and Coolgardie. **1903** 'T. COLLINS' *Such is Life* 265 On a well-managed station .. a tank is, whenever possible, excavated on the margin of a swamp. **1911** C. E. W. BEAN *'Dreadnought' of Darling* i. 7 There is only one boundary rider's hut in it and one 'tank' of water. The tank may have dried up. **1915** *Dial. Notes* IV. 229 *Tank*, an artificial lake. 'Most west Texas towns get their water from *tanks*.' **1936** F. CLUNE *Roaming round Darling* xiv. 121, I strongly object to the back country habit of calling holes scooped out of the ground tanks. **1955** W. FOSTER-HARRIS *Look of Old West* ix. 273 Tank is cow country [language] for a small pond, made by damming a ravine or fixing a hollow to catch and hold rain water. **1965** *Austral. Encycl.* I. 133/2 In Australia, every farmer is interested in constructing and maintaining tanks and dams.

b. A natural pool or pond; a 'stank'. *dial.* and *U.S.* (Quot. 1678 perh. belongs to 1.)

1678 PHILLIPS (ed. 4), *Tank*, (old word) a little Pool or Pond. **1825** BROCKETT *N.C. Words*, *Tank*, a piece of deep water, natural as well as artificial. **1867** LADY HERBERT *Cradle L.* vii. 169 They took a walk .. to the 'Pool of David', a square tank at the bottom of the valley full of rain water. **1890** *Amer. Antiquarian* July 201 Here and there great hollows filled with rain-water. These places are called 'tanks' by the ranchmen. **1896** *Dialect Notes* (Amer.) I. 426 (E.D.D.) Drive your horse into the tank.

2. a. An artificial receptacle, usually rectangular or cylindrical and often of plate-iron, used for storing water, oil, or other liquids in large quantities. Also *spec.* a water receptacle (with transparent sides) in which to keep fish; an aquarium.

1690 DRYDEN *Don Sebast.* II. ii, Here's plentiful provision for you, Rascal, sallating in the Garden, and water in the tanck. **1706** PHILLIPS, *Tank*, .. a Cistern to keep Water in. **1835** SIR J. ROSS *Narr. 2nd Voy.* xxiv. 234 The ice in the tanks was this day reduced. **1837** GORING & PRITCHARD *Microgr.* 197 The stop-cocks .. being opened, the water from the tank will flow freely into the vessels O and H. **1854** P. H. GOSSE *Aquarium* i. 3 The tanks in the new Fish House just erected in the [Zoological] Society's Gardens in the Regent's Park. **1869** E. A. PARKES *Pract. Hygiene* (ed. 3) 12 Tanks to hold rain-water require constant inspection. **1871** *Young Gentleman's Ann.* Dec. 28 Other engines .. carry their water in a tank (called a saddle-tank) which rests on the top of the boiler. **1881** RAYMOND *Mining Gloss.*, *Tank*, a subterranean reservoir into which a pump delivers water for another pump to raise. **1890** G. C. BATEMAN *Fresh-Water Aquaria* i. 6 The ordinary oblong tank .. containing four glass sides, is both ornamental and useful. **1891** *New York Tribune* 17 Oct. 12/3 (Funk) The gas tank was fifty feet in diameter. **1936** M. G. ELWIN *First Steps in Aquarium Keeping* iv. 27 The tank will look unfinished without a couple of the beautiful Angel fish. **1971** R. F. O'CONNELL *Freshwater Aquarium* 127 The breeding tank should be cleaned thoroughly and filled with seasoned water to a depth of 8 inches. **1982** I. PETROVICKÝ *Trop. Aquarium Fishes* 13 If an aquarium is to be purely ornamental, it is better to select one larger tank.

b. The fuel container of a motor vehicle.

1902 A. C. HARMSWORTH *Motors & Motor-Driving* vii. 117 With the gravity-fed carburetter the tank is fitted in the body of the car. **1944** L. D. KITCHIN *Road Transport Law* 19/1 Not more than 60 gallons of petroleum spirit, including that contained in any vehicle fuel tank, may be kept in any one storage place. **1978** K. AMIS *Jake's Thing* xxiv. 244 'Are we low on petrol, Ivor?' 'No, I had a full tank when I picked you up.'

3. Short for *tank-engine, -steamer*, etc.

1891 *Daily News* 23 Sept. 3/3 They were picked up in a very exhausted condition by a German oil tank from New York to Rotterdam. **1903** *Westm. Gaz.* 31 Dec. 3/2 Trains hauled .. by a mammoth tank.

4. *U.S. slang.* A cell in a police station, *spec.* one in which several prisoners (esp. drunks) are held.

1912 D. LOWRIE *My Life in Prison* iii. 30, I glanced at the number on the cell door. It was .. 34 Tank. **1933** 'J. SPENSER' *Limey* xvii. 256 In our tank .. there were three Chicago gangsters waiting to be returned to that city. **1947** A. R. BOSWORTH *San Francisco Murders* 264 The day a police reporter had to pick him out of the collection in the drunk tank. **1951** *Life* 8 Jan. 24 (*caption*) Still relatively blissful but due for an unhappy awakening, some of the 1,200 Angelenos charged with drunkenness sleep it off in the tank. **1964** WODEHOUSE *Frozen Assets* iii. 50 It gets boring after a while being thrown into the tank, always with that nervous feeling that this time the old man won't come through with the necessary bail. **1981** L. DEIGHTON *XPD* xxv. 210 And then tossed into the drunk tank like a common criminal.

5. *attrib.* and *Comb.*, as *tank-head, -maker, -room, -sinker, -storage, -work*; *tank-like* adj.; *spec.* in sense 1, as *tank-cultivation, -silt, -system, -water*; *tank-watered* adj.; in sense 2, constructed as or fitted with a tank for conveying liquids, etc., esp. mineral oils in bulk, as *tank-barge, -boat, -car, house, -ship, -steamer, -train, -truck, -van, -vessel, -wagon*; **tank bag**, a receptacle for carrying luggage which fits on to the petrol tank of a motorcycle; **tank circuit** *Electronics*, a resonant circuit placed in the anode circuit of a valve oscillator in order to supply energy to an aerial for transmission; **tank-engine**, a railway engine which carries the fuel and water receptacles on its own framing and not in a separate tender; **tank farm** orig. *U.S.*, a collection of tanks for the large-scale storage of oil; **tank furnace**, (see quot. 1970); **tank-iron**, plate-iron of a thickness suitable for making tanks; **tank-locomotive** (*U.S.*) = *tank-engine*; **tank-man, tank-pipe**: see quots.; **tank-plate** = *tank-iron*; **tank-runner**, the pheasant-tailed Jacana, or Water-pheasant, *Hydrophasianus chirurgus*, of India and Sri Lanka, so called from its ability to run over floating lotus-leaves, etc.; **tankstand** *Austral.* and *N.Z.*, a stand or support for a tank in which water is stored; **tank-station**, a station or place where a tank or tanks are provided, e.g. on a railway for supplying water to the engines or for storing oil, in a mine for storing water; **tank suit** *U.S.*, a (ladies') one-piece bathing-suit with scooped neck (cf. MAILLOT 2); **tank top**, (*a*) the top of a tank; (*b*) a sleeveless upper garment with round neck and deep armholes, freq. of knitted material and similar to the top of a one-piece bathing-suit, worn by men or women; cf. *tank suit* above; **tank town** *U.S.*, a small, unimportant town, orig. one at which trains stopped to take on water; **tank-valve**: see quot.; **tank-waste**, the insoluble sediment from the dissolving tanks in alkali works; **tank-worm**, a nematoid worm inhabiting the mud of Indian tanks, and believed to be the young of the guinea worm.

1974 *Cycle World* June 24 (Advt.), Rain-proof cycle luggage... *Tank bag—straps to gas tank. **1980** *Guardian* 28 Apr. 8/6 A set of good bike luggage—panniers and top box —is the best solution... A cheaper alternative is a pair of carriers to sling over the seat and a good tank bag. **1894** *Labour Commission* Gloss., **Tank-barges*, .. used specially for conveying tar and oil in bulk in large tanks fitted or built in the barges. **1889** *Daily News* 2 Jan. 2/4 The .. recent explosion of a *tank-boat near Calais. **1874** KNIGHT *Dict. Mech.* 457/2 *Tank-car. **1877** *Ibid.*, *Tank-car*, a large tank mounted on a platform-truck for carrying petroleum or other liquid. **1904** *Daily Chron.* 23 Mar. 7/3 The railway provides tank cars and tank stations along its route for Russian oil only. **1928** L. S. PALMER *Wireless Princ. & Pract.* vi. 183 A slightly different method is that of using a '*tank' circuit, which consists of a low impedance oscillatory circuit connected from the earth end of the aerial inductance to earth. **1959** K. HENNEY *Radio Engin. Handbk.* (ed. 5) xviii. 14 Resonant tank circuits are used in .. power amplifiers to remove the effects of tube and circuit stray capacitances. **1971** *Gloss. Electrotechnical, Power Terms* (*B.S.I.*) III. vii. 22 *Tank circuit*, tuned circuit in the anode circuit of the final stage of a transmitter which supplies the radio-frequency energy to the aerial or aerial feeder. **1875** *Madras Revenue Board Rep.*, The *tank cultivation suffered most. **1850** *Pract. Mech. Jrnl.* III. 33 The centre of the boiler .. is $3\frac{1}{2}$ inches lower in the *tank engine. **1864** WEBSTER, Tank engine. **1902** *Westm. Gaz.* 4 July 12/1 A tank-engine of absolutely novel type and colossal dimensions. **1932** *Amer. Speech* VII. 271 **Tank-farm*, a group of storage tanks. **1941** *Sun* (Baltimore) 7 Nov. 17/1 Chemical flames prevented anyone from getting into the explosion area, which Sears described as a 'tank farm', the storage area of the vinylite or plastics producing section. **1974** *Daily Tel.* 30 May 8/6 Huge 'tank farms' may be needed in parts of Scotland to store the oil. **1879** *Encycl. Brit.* X. 659/1 Mr Archibald Stevenson of Glasgow has patented a *tank furnace fired by common coal from one end, with working holes on the other three sides. **1908** W. ROSENHAIN *Glass Manufacture* iv. 72 The tank furnace utilises the heat of the flame more efficiently. **1970** *Gloss. Industrial Furnace Terms* (*B.S.I.*) 20 *Tank furnace*, a furnace in which glass is melted in a refractory bath. **1895** *Funk's Standard Dict.*, **Tank-head*, the head or end of a metal tank. **1941** *Sun* (Baltimore) 15 Oct. 19/2 It is an unwatched light showing quick red flashes,.. 28 feet above water, on a white skeleton tower and *tankhouse on concrete piers. **1978** *Jrnl. R. Soc. Arts* CXXVI. 693/1 An important application is that of titanium blanks for the production of the starting sheets used in copper refinery tankhouses. **1864** Webster, *Tank-iron. **1897** *Daily News* 18 June 8/4 Round in shape, but flat and *tank-like on the top. **1905** *Westm. Gaz.* 21 May 1/3 It consisted of three terraces and a tank-like pond on the basement floor. **1877** Knight *Dict. Mech.*, **Tank-locomotive*,.. one having a tank or tanks enabling it to carry a supply of water sufficient for its own consumption without a tender. **1858** Simmonds *Dict. Trade*, **Tank-maker*, a manufacturer of iron cisterns for ships, or of slate, or well-secured plank cisterns on shore. **1909** *Westm. Gaz.* 21 May 4/1 The tank-makers in Germany cannot buy their raw material from abroad. **1891** *Labour Commission* Gloss., **Tank-men*, men employed in large steamers to look after the water tanks. **1894** *Ibid.* s.v. *Pipes*, **Tank pipes*, pipes used for filling or emptying the water ballast or fresh water tanks. **1892** *Daily News* 4 July 9/7 *Tank-plates are quoted £6 10s, and rods £7. **1901** *Scotsman* 2 Mar. 9/1 The circulation of sea-water in the *tank-room [of the zoological station]. **1945** *Sun* (Baltimore) 23 Aug. 9-0/1 More than 100 *tankships, many of which had been torpedoed.. have been cleaned and made free of gas. **1978** M. Dewis *Law Health & Safety at Work* i. 5 The crew of a British tankship. **1905** A. Andrew *Ind. Problems* ii. 51 In most places *tank silt can be got. This is a valuable manure. **1900** H. Lawson *On Track* 37 Bush-fencers, *tank-sinkers, rough carpenters, &c.— were finishing the third and last culvert of their contract. **1941** *Coast to Coast* 146 Then she crept off the veranda and went down under the *tankstand. The soil under the tank was a rich chocolate brown, and there were drips of water coming from the tap. **1965** S. T. Ollivier *Petticoat Farm* v. 66 Emma carefully retraced her steps down the windmill until she reached the.. corner of the tank-stand. **1977** C. McCullough *Thorn Birds* vi. 116 A drover whose cross said only *Tankstand Charlie he was a good bloke*. **1889** *Daily News* 2 Jan. 2/4 The *tank steamer Oka.. represents the advance so far made towards perfection in the building of ships designed for the carriage of [petroleum]. **1959** P. Roth *Goodbye Columbus* ii. 20 She wore a black *tank suit and went barefooted. **1979** *Dancemagazine* Feb. 108/3 In *Moth Dance*, the lines of Hermans' tensed, slender body, in tanksuit and reflecting sunglasses, become clearer as the semidarkness grows lighter. **1902** S. Smith *Life-Work* xxii. 214 In Southern India the *tank system prevails. **1900** *Engineering Mag.* XIX. 678 The margin plates of the *tank top are put on, and the tank-top plating itself. **1968** *New Yorker* 27 Jan. 25 Miss Farrell—a tall, pretty ballerina dressed in a purple tank top and baggy rubber warm-up pants. **1971** *Observer* 1 Aug. 22/3 A favourite Paris idea is to put little woolly vests or tank tops over shirts and under suit jackets. **1977** Miller & Swift *Words & Women* 157 Even the latter have given up whalebone corsets and starched winged collars without assuming they have to switch to miniskirts or tank tops. **1906** J. F. Kelly *Man with Grip* 11 *Tank towns are big ones, compared to our route. **1940** R. Chandler *Farewell, my Lovely* v. 38 You would find them in tanktown vaudeville acts. **1978** *Times* 25 Mar. 14/4 When vaudeville was in its final death throes, young Donald O'Connor was.. going—as the show biz legend decreed he should—from 'one tank town to another'. **1901** *Munsey's Mag.* XXV. 749/1 Racks for the loading of *tank trains. **1904** *Blackw. Mag.* May 609/1 A crowd of Wadaruma women.. rushed out to fill their gourds from the *tank-truck behind the engine. **1976** *New Yorker* 9 Feb. 66/8 It was solved by designing a tank truck that intermittently travelled around the array and sprayed the mirrors with a cleaning solution. **1877** Knight *Dict. Mech.*, **Tank-valve*, (Railway Engineering) a form of valve used in locomotive water-supply tanks, for admitting water to the discharge-pipe. **1887** *Daily News* 27 July 6/3 The commoner fish brought in *tank vans was sold by the consignees from the vans. **1877** Knight *Dict. Mech.*, *Tank-vessel. *c* **1890** *Nature*, Disasters during the discharge of cargoes from tank-vessels. **1886** *Pall Mall G.* 10 June 14/1 [He] has invented a system of delivering oil in bulk by means of a street *tank-waggon. **1889** *Ibid.* 3 Aug. 7/1 A new process for the manufacture of soda.. recovers the sulphur of the *tank waste. **1905** A. Andrew *Ind. Problems* ii. 53 Cultivator of *tank-watered land. **1898** *Engineering Mag.* XVI. 133/1 A Notable Piece of Lead *Tank Work. **1883** *Chambers's Encycl.* s.v., There is extreme probability that these *tank-worms are the origin of the guinea-worm.

†**tank**, *sb.*[2] *Herb. Obs.* [ME. *tanke*; origin obscure.] The wild carrot; according to Gerarde, the wild parsnip.

a **1400–50** *Stockh. Med. MS.* 181 Bryddys neste or tanke: *daucus asininus*. *Ibid.* 182 þe lesse tank: *daucus creticus*. **14..** *MS. Arundel* 272, lf. 46 (Halliw.) Brydswete or tank. Hit hath leves like to hemlok, and a quite flower. **1597** Gerarde *Herbal* App., Tanke is wild Parsnep.

†**tank**, *sb.*[3] *Obs.* Erroneously shortened from *copped tank*: see copintank.

1688 R. Holme *Armoury* ii. 55/2 Like long Hatters Blocks, or capped tanks, *i.e.* Hats with Brims. *Ibid.* iii. 271/1 A Womans Head couped.. on her Head a Capped Tank Embowed, and Tied under her Chin. *Ibid.* 395/2 Mens heads are.. covered with.. Caps, Cowles, Tankes, Morions, Insulas, Hats and Hoods.

tank, *sb.*[4] *rare*$^{-0}$. = tang *sb.*[1]

1858 Simmonds *Dict. Trade*, *Tank*,.. the end of a file, etc. inserted in a socket.

‖**tank**, *sb.*[5] [Cf. tanga[1].] (See quots.)

1698 Fryer *Acc. E. India & P.* 206 (jewel weights) 1 *Miscall* is 1 *Tank*. **1858** Simmonds *Dict. Trade*, *Tank*.. a small Indian dry-measure, averaging 240 grains in weight; a Bombay weight for pearls, of 72 grains.

tank, *sb.*[6] *dial.* In 7 tanck. [Echoic.] 'A blow, a knock' (E.D.D.).

1686 Plot *Staffordsh.* 30 The Operators in Iron.. are all awakened with a little blow (or tanck) upon a pair of their tongues (which is the common means they use for that purpose). [**1904** in *Eng. Dial. Dict.* from Yorksh. to Northampton and Worcestersh.]

tank, *sb.*[7] [Special use of tank *sb.*[1] adopted in Dec. 1915 for purposes of secrecy during manufacture.]

1. a. An armoured military vehicle moving on a tracked carriage and mounted with a gun, designed for use in rough terrain.

First put into commission on 15 Sept. 1916.

1916 *Times* 18 Sept. 9/6 'Tanks' is what these new machines are generally called, and the name has the evident official advantage of being quite undescriptive. **1917** A. Machen *Terror* i. 19 Last summer there were very few people outside high official circles who knew anything about the 'Tanks', of which we have all been talking lately. **1918** *Review of Reviews* (N.Y.) Oct. 383 The British tanks, as first produced, were of two types, male and female. The male tank was armed with two six-pounder, rapid-fire Hotchkiss guns, and four Lewis machine guns... The female type carried a lighter armament. **1926** *Daily Colonist* (Victoria, B.C.) 10 Jan. 5/2 Voltaire is said to be the real inventor of the armored war tank. In 1756 he designed what was called the 'Assyrian Chariot', which was armed like the tank. **1940** *Richmond* (Va.) *Times-Dispatch* 10 Aug. 1 (*heading*) Army irked as news leaks of plans for monster tank. **1957** *Encycl. Brit.* XXI. 791/2 In 1940.. the French alone possessed about 3,600 tanks.. superior in armour and fire power to those of the Germans. **1970** *Sunday Times* (Colour Suppl.) 16 Aug. 13/4 For security purposes the cumbersome metal machines needed a code-name: 'water carriers' was rejected in favour of 'tanks'. **1977** C. McCullough *Thorn Birds* xv. 344 Went through them big buggers of tanks like a dose of salts.

b. In pl., *ellipt.* for Tank Corps.

1943 J. B. Priestley *Daylight on Saturday* iv. 21 Her husband was abroad, in the Tanks. **1967** L. Deighton *Only when I Larf* (1968) vii. 85, I could see that the war had to come, so I.. got a commission in the tanks. **1981** A. Price *Soldier no More* vii. 97 He was in the tanks during the war.

2. *attrib.* and *Comb.*, as ***tank battle***, ***Corps***, ***crew***, ***driver***, ***officer***, ***raid***, ***warfare***; ***tank-like*** adj.; also used of naval vessels designed to transport and put ashore tanks, as ***tank-landing craft***, etc. (cf. *landing craft*, *ship* s.v. landing *vbl. sb.* 8); **tank buster** *slang*, an aircraft or other device designed to combat tanks (cf. -buster); also *fig.*; **tank-destroyer** *U.S.*, a highly-mobile armoured fighting vehicle equipped with a field gun, designed to combat tanks; **tank-man**, a member of a military tank crew; **tank transporter**, a wheeled vehicle for the transportation of a tank; **tank trap**, an obstacle placed or constructed so as to impede or prevent the progress of a tank; **tank turret**, the rotating structure on a tank on which the gun is mounted; **tank watch**, a gold watch designed by Cartier of Paris, decorated with gemstones, and usu. regarded as a status symbol [designed in 1917; the gold side-panels were held to resemble the wide tracks of the new armoured tanks (see sense 1 a)].

1944 C. Milburn *Diary* 7 June (1979) 217 A tank battle was raging in one spot and an air battle not far away. **1978** A. Melville-Ross *Blindfold* xxii. 130 The great tank battles of the Second World War. **1941** *Illustr. London News* 29 Nov. 691/1 The Hawker 'Hurricane' is.. proving its superiority in the battle of the Libyan Desert.. as a dive-bomber and 'tank-buster'. **1942** J. Sweeney in Murdock & Drake-Brockman *Austral. Short Stories* (1951) 384 No sooner does the gong go for the third than Irish walks into.. a rip-snorting tank-buster that Big Joe had been saving up for a secret weapon. **1967** *Electronics* 6 Mar. 311/2 (Advt.), Tiny tankbuster. **1917** *Army Order 239* 28 July, We deem it expedient to authorize the formation of, and to provide rates of pay for, a corps to be entitled 'Tank Corps'. **1976** *Listener* 20 May 633/3 He had joined the Tank Corps... He was lying in bed in barracks one night, listening to the flow of unremitting obscenity from his fellow tankmen. *a* **1944** K. Douglas *Alamein to Zem Zem* (1946) 14 As soon as this was finished I began to make the acquaintance of my tank crews. **1973** A. Price *October Men* v. 71 Tales of stranded tank crews parboiled. **1941** *Sun* (Baltimore) 28 Aug. 24/1 The army today demonstrated.. the type of unit it hopes is the answer to *panzer* attack, a 'tank-destroyer' battalion of fast-moving, self-propelled field guns protected to a certain extent by armor. **1961** W. Vaughan-Thomas *Anzio* v. 76 The American 894th Tank-Destroyer Battalion.. attacked again. The tank-destroyers advanced line ahead like battleships of old. **1928** Tank driver [see caterpillar *v.*]. **1980** J. Ditton *Copley's Hunch* i. ii. 42 'You [*sc.* the RAF] go into action sitting down.' 'So do tank drivers.' **1917** W. S. Churchill in M. Gilbert *Winston S. Churchill* (1977) IV. Compan. i. 87 In addition a number (say) 50 tank-landing lighters would be provided, each carrying a tank or tanks. **1945** Tank landing ship [see landing *vbl. sb.* 8]. **1969** *Listener* 4 Sept. 304/2 In January 1956 I thought I was going to a reserve fleet, but rather to my delight I was appointed to another command. This was to a tank landing-craft called *HMS Redoubt* in Malta. **1977** *Navy News* June 23 Audemer, a Royal Corps of Transport tank landing craft, is in the Review lines. **1916** E. Montagu *Let.* 31 Oct. in M. Gilbert *Winston S. Churchill* (1972) III. Compan. ii. 1580 Cannot the idea of the Tank be so extended as to use a Tank-like machine to protect our Infantry. **1977** C. Fremlin *Spider-Orchid* xvii. 111 A sort of monstrous arrogance.. driving tank-like over all concerns other than its own. **1934** *N. & Q.* CLXVI. 73/2 In the tank-man we shall have the steel-clad mediaeval knight back again. **1976** Tankman [see *Tank Corps* above]. **1949** R. Chandler *Let.* 24 Jan. (1981) 145 At one [table] sat.. a demobbed tank officer with his mother. **1978** A. Price *'44 Vintage* xi. 136 He certainly didn't intend to let any bloody tank officer.. out-crawl him. **1917** 'Contact' *Airman's Outings* 135 Farther along the road was the scene of the first tank raids. **1943** *Times* (Weekly ed.) 24 Nov. 6 'Tank Transporter.' To save wear and tear of tracks and to save petrol, tanks are transported over hard roads by huge tank-carrying lorries. **1972** D. Bloodworth *Any Number can Play* xvi. 149 A respray job. .. What ran into it, a tank-transporter? **1925** *Scribner's Mag.* Sept. 234/1 Tank traps, trenches so wide that the little fellows went nose-down into them and stuck, and direct fire from Boche artillery stopped the most of them. **1977** *Time* 10 Jan. 22/2 The Chileans, bracing for a possible invasion, are mining the desert, implanting tank traps and building fortifications. **1946** E. Linklater *Private Angelo* xi. 131 Romans.. tossed flowers into jeeps and tank-turrets. **1979** D. Graham in K. Douglas *Alamein to Zem Zem* 10 Sufficient of its character remained, however, for it to move into action .. with tank turrets open and umbrellas up. *a* **1944** K. Douglas *Ibid.* (1946) 14 It is low-built, which in.. tank warfare, is a first consideration. **1977** B. Freemantle *Charlie Muffin* ii. 29 His absorption in the history of tank warfare. **1976** *Vogue* Dec. 216 Cufflinks and watches all from Cartier... Tank watch edged with diamonds, £1,800. **1978** T. Gifford *Glendower Legacy* (1979) 119 She looked at her Cartier tank watch with the sapphire on the stem.

Hence **'tanker**[2] *colloq.* = *tank-man*, sense 2 above.

1919 *W.R.A.F. on Rhine* July 27 Little boys with.. tanks .. asking the girls to come and play... What jolly boys those Tankers were! **1940** *Sun* (Baltimore) 23 Sept. 11/4 There are tankers who long ago served in the same regiment when it was fully horsed. **1961** W. Vaughan-Thomas *Anzio* v. 79 Italian geography is unfriendly to the tank, and there were moments when tankers must have felt that the whole country was one enormous, endless anti-tank ditch. **1974** C. Ryan *Bridge Too Far* iii. ix. 187 Taylor had hoped for the support of the tankers' guns along the fifteen-mile stretch of corridor the Screaming Eagles must control.

tank, *sb.*[8] *slang.* [Prob. abbrev. of tankard.] The amount held by a drinking-vessel; hence *loosely*, a drink (usu. of beer). Cf. jar *sb.*[2] 2 c, tank *v.*[1] 5 a.

1936 O. Nash *Primrose Path* 46 What can a man.. Ask.. More than a pipe.. And a modest tank of beer? **1941** Baker *Dict. Austral. Slang* 75 *Tank*, a pint of beer. **1958** *Spectator* 7 Feb. 171/1 Their carousals over a few friendly tanks at the neighbouring Whitehall milk bar.

tank, *v.*[1] [f. tank *sb.*[1]]

1. *trans.* To lift or measure in a tank.

1886 *Sci. Amer. Suppl.* 9130 If this [water] can be tanked or weighed, no material error should occur. **1890** *Colliery Advert.*, The water pumped or tanked out.

2. To store or preserve in a tank. Also, to put into a tank.

1900 *Lancet* 22 Sept. 873/2 Sailors.. who have had to drink tanked and often impure water. **1960** Koestler *Lotus & Robot* i. i. 42 The driver-owners are so poor that they only tank one or two gallons at a time.

3. To treat in a tank or tanks.

1906 U. Sinclair *Jungle* iii. 43 To another room came all the scraps to be 'tanked', which meant boiling and pumping off the grease to make soap and lard.

4. To immerse in a tank; to duck. *dial.*

1863 Reade *Hard Cash* xxxviii. III. 68 They tanked her cruel, they did; and kept her under water till she was nigh gone.

5. Chiefly *to tank up*. **a.** *intr.* for *refl.* To fill oneself with drink, to drink heavily. Also *refl.* Cf. tanked *ppl. a.* 1. *slang.*

1902 A. H. Lewis *Wolfville Nights* xv. 236 Bowlaigs would reepair back ag'in to the Major [with the bottle], when they'd both tank up ecstatic. **1920** C. L. Stagg *High Speed* viii. 142 Both of 'em are tankin' up next door, and layin' for you and the whole bunch. **1925** F. Scott Fitzgerald *Great Gatsby* (1926) ii. 28, I think he'd tanked up a good deal at luncheon, and his determination to have my company bordered on violence. **1939** A. Huxley *After Many a Summer* ii. iii. 208 She.. made him feel good, like you felt when you'd tanked up a bit on Scotch. **1951** W. C. Williams *Autobiogr.* xxv. 148 Perhaps he was insubordinate or tanked himself up or did something otherwise improper. **1959** A. Christie *Cat among Pigeons* 18 On Sports Day.. Lady Veronica arrived completely sober. .. But there were times when Lady Veronica tanked herself up. **1974** D. Ramsay *No Cause to Kill* ii. 132 Jessie's a lush. .. Hardly ever leaves the house.. except to tank up at the neighbourhood hangouts. **1980** I. Hunter *Malcolm Muggeridge* xii. 216 Behan arrived for the interview 'somewhat full' and proceeded to tank up further in the BBC hospitality room.

b. *trans.* To fill the tank of (a vehicle) with fuel; to refuel. Also *absol.*, and *intr.* for *pass. colloq.*

1933 [implied in tanking *vbl. sb.*[1]]. **1944** 'N. Shute' *Pastoral* ii. 37 The Bowser was waiting to tank up the Wellington. **1948** —— *No Highway* ix. 244, I guess we'll make Ivanhoe by sundown... Tank up there, 'n have plenty up at the lake. **1959** Halas & Manvell *Technique Film Animation* v. 65 A cartoonist may want to give an automobile the characteristics of a dog in its attitude to the fuel that its owner offers it... It shakes its shaggy head in refusal to tank up with the wrong brand of spirit. **1963** D. Irving *Destruction of Dresden* iii. iii. 139 The whole force [of aircraft] had been tanked up with maximum fuel loads, 2,154 gallons of petrol each. **1977** N. Freeling *Gadget* i. 5 The four cars.. stopped once to tank up. **1978** —— *Night Lords* xxx. 140 At the edge of the service area he stopped.. while the car was tanked.

c. *transf.* and *fig.*

1942 *Tee Emm* (Air Ministry) II. 145 It's no good tanking up on them [*sc.* vitamins] and hoping you'll be able to detect a black cat at midnight in a Bremen cellar from 10,000 feet. **1959** *Word Study* Oct. 2/2 We are grateful for them, 'tank up' on their detailed and highly useful messages, and perhaps put them away for future reference. **1975** R. Butler *Where All Girls are Sweeter* ii. 15 She was twiddling the empty glass... I tanked her up and waited.

6. *intr.* In Lawn Tennis, to lose or fail to finish a match deliberately; to default. *slang.*

1976 *Times* 30 Sept. 11/5 Too many..singles players do not enter for the doubles. Either that, or they scratch or 'tank' (in boxing parlance, 'take a dive'). **1979** *Guardian* 13 Jan. 11 But it is ironic that Connors, a player generally considered too honest to 'tank' to anyone, should be the one to suffer.

Hence **'tanker³**, a heavy drinker; **'tanking** *vbl. sb.*¹ (in the senses of the vb.).

1891 *Cent. Dict.*, *Tanking*, the operation or method of treating in tanks, as fish for the extraction of oil, by boiling, settling, etc. **1918** H. Bindloss *Agatha's Fortune* iv. 40 When you get the tanking habit such things happen. **1930** *Aberdeen Press & Jrnl.* 31 Jan. 7/5 Tanking consists of salting ungutted herrings into big tanks for future use. **1932** H. Crane *Let.* 16 Feb. (1965) 400 Especially with Luz around, who Lisa says is a great little tanker. **1933** *Flight* 16 Feb. 157/1 Petrol-filling installations, *i.e.* hand pumps, are now available on all important aerodromes, and the average time spent in tanking is only 45 min. **1935** J. O'Hara *Appointment in Samarra* ii. 49 But the rest of them! God, what a gang of tankers they were.

tank, *v.*² [f. tank *sb.*⁷] **1.** *intr.* To proceed or make one's way in a tank. Also *fig.*

1939 H. G. Wells *Holy Terror* iii. ii. 271 The city crowds cheered, the armies went tanking forward. **1945** A. Thirkell *Miss Bunting* ix. 192 He tanked right over her without so much as noticing her. **1972** R. Poole *Towards Deep Subjectivity* i. 4 The Russians..shot their way in, they tanked their way in.

2. *trans.* To defeat convincingly, to beat, thrash, or overwhelm. Hence **'tanking** *vbl. sb.*² Cf. tonk *v. Sc. dial.*

1973 'J. Patrick' *Glasgow Gang Observed* vi. 60 We were to play football... ('Uzz Young Team always tank them.'). **1976** *Sunday Mail* (Glasgow) 26 Dec. 2/1 They..had just come from a party for Rangers F.C., who tanked the local Clachnacuddin side 8–0. **1982** P. Turnbull *Dead Knock* iii. 56 Glasgow..[is] a good city... The reputation for violence comes from the gangs who give each other tankings.

‖**Tanka**¹ ('tæŋkə). Also **tankia, tanchia.** [a. Chinese (Cantonese), f. Chinese *tan*, lit. 'egg', + Cantonese *ka*, in South Mandarin *kia*, North Mandarin *chia*, family, people.] The boat-population of Canton, who live entirely on the boats by which they earn their living: they are descendants of some aboriginal tribe of which *Tan* was apparently the name. ***Tanka boat***, a boat of the kind in which these people live.

1839 *Chinese Repository* VII. 506 The small boats of Tanka women are never without this appendage. **1848** S. W. Williams *Middle Kingd.* I. vii. 321 The *tankia*, or boat-people, at Canton form a class in some respects beneath the other portions of the community. *Ibid.* II. xiii. 23 A large part of the boats at Canton are *tankia* boats, about 25 feet long, containing only one room, and covered with movable mats, so contrived as to cover the whole vessel; they are usually rowed by women. **1909** *Westm. Gaz.* 23 Mar. 5/2 The Tankas, numbering perhaps 50,000 in all, gain their livelihood by ferrying people to and fro on the broad river with its creeks.

‖**tanka**² ('tæŋkə). Also **Tanka.** [Jap., f. *tan* short + *ka* song.] A form of Japanese verse which consists of thirty-one syllables, the first and third lines containing five and the other three lines seven syllables.

1877 W. G. Aston *Gram. Jap. Written Lang.* (ed. 2) x. 197 *Tanka*..or *mijika-uta*, i.e. 'short poetry', so-called to distinguish it from *naga-uta* or 'long poetry', is by far the commonest Japanese metre. **1899** —— *Jap Lit.* I. ii. 29 The Tanka is the most universal and characteristic of the various forms of poetry in Japan. **1923** Jun Fujita (*title*) Tanka; poems in exile. **1940** W. de la Mare *Pleasures & Speculations* 201 A Japanese tanka..on the prolification on the exquisite little cups of the lichen. **1968** *Encycl. Brit.* XII. 886/1 From the raw material of Chinese poetry came the exquisite haiku and tanka forms. **1982** *PN Rev.* No. 26. 60/1, I do not think that haiku and tanka are translatable... Fortunately, there is a great deal more to Japanese poetry than tanka and haiku.

‖**tanka**³ ('tæŋkə). Also **thang-ka, thanka,** etc. [a. Tibetan *t'án-ka, t'án-ga* image, painting.] A Tibetan religious (scroll-)painting on woven material, hung as a banner in temples and carried in processions.

1925 G. Roerich *Tibetan Paintings* 17 The most characteristic production of Tibetan pictorial art is the so-called than-ka, a word which is commonly interpreted as 'banner'. **1928** 'Ganpat' *Magic Ladakh* vii. 129 From the beams of the flat ceiling depend painted banners of silk—the gift of various donors. These *tankas*, as they are called, are often very beautiful. **1939** M. Pallis *Peaks & Lamas* I. vi. 68 We were also shown a scroll-painting of the type found universally in Tibet, and called a t'hanka. **1952** A. K. Gordon *Tibetan Relig. Art* 15 Thang-kas are paintings or, occasionally, embroidered pictures, usually called 'banners'. They..are hung in the temples and at family altars in homes... They portray a deity..or scenes from the life of Buddha. **1969** R. Farre *Beckoning Land* xx. 242 Thankas are similar to Chinese scroll paintings but the Tibetan ones are always on some religious theme. **1979** *Financial Times* 7 July 2/2 The imposing Potala Palace is uninhabited with its thousands of priceless gold Buddha statues, rare 'tankas', innumerable Buddhist scrolls and scrips.

tanka, var. tanga¹, East Indian coin.

'tankage (-ɪdʒ). [f. tank *sb.*¹ or *v.*¹ + -age.]

1. Tanks collectively; a provision or system of storage-tanks, sometimes with special reference to its capacity. Also *attrib.*

1866 J. E. H. Skinner *After the Storm* I. xvii. 226 There was more fencing in and a greater show of tankage about the wells at Pithole Run... Huge tanks, like brewers' vats surrounded '54'. **1883** *Century Mag.* XXVI. 332 A tankage capacity of over thirty millions of barrels. **1892** *Daily News* 21 July 2/3 The Baltimore Electric Refining Company..has already contracted to double its tankage. **1893** *Westm. Gaz.* 27 Mar. 6/1 The Russian firms have an extensive tankage system in England. **1904** *Daily Chron.* 2 June 7/5 A depôt.. will be secured..for the purpose of erecting several big tankages, warehouses, and the necessary plant for the unloading of the company's own tank steamers.

2. The act or process of storing liquid in tanks; the price charged for this.

1891 in *Cent. Dict.*

3. The residue from tanks in which fat, etc. has been rendered, used as a coarse food, and as manure.

1886 *Sci. Amer.* LV. 149 A new drier adapted for drying ..tankage, sewage, clay, fertilizers, etc. **1887** F. H. Storer *Agric.* (1892) I. xiv. 388 Under the name of tankage, a kind of flesh-meal is prepared in this country [U.S.] from the refuse meat, entrails, and other offal that accumulate in slaughter-houses. **1898** *Engineering Mag.* XVI. 128/1 The receiving tanks,..each receiving the cooked garbage, called tankage, from four digesters.

4. The fuel-carrying capacity of an aircraft.

1942 W. S. Churchill in *Second World War* (1951) IV. I. vii. 114 We intend to increase petrol tankage of some Liberator aircraft to give an operational range of 2,300 sea-miles. **1950** *Times* 17 Feb. 8/5 The maximum still air range with full tankage of 300 gallons and 1,750 lb. of payload will be 1,250 miles and the practical stage length about 850 miles. **1966** M. Woodhouse *Tree Frog* v. 38 'What really shook me was the tankage.'.. 'How much fuel does that thing hold?'

tankard ('tæŋkəd). Also 4–5 (8) tancard, 5–7 -kerd, 6 -(c)karde, -ckerd, *Sc.* -kert, 7 (9 *Sc.*) tanker. [= MDu., Du. *tanckaert* = *kitte*, L. *obba*, *cantharus* (= sense 2 below), (Kilian); also F. *tanquart*, pl. *tanquars* (Rabelais). Ulterior history unknown: ? transposition of **kantar*(*d*, *cantharus*.]

†**1.** A large open tub-like vessel, usually of wood hooped with iron, etc. (sometimes of leather); *spec.* such a vessel used for carrying water, etc.; often used to render L. *amphora*. *Obs.*

1310 *Acc. Exors. T. Bp. of Exeter* (Camden) 10 De iijs. de xij tancardis ferro ligatis debilibus. **1341–2** *Ely Sacr. Rolls* (1907) II. 118 In ligatura unius tankard cum ferro. **1352** *Acc. Excheq. Q.R.* (Bundle 20 No. 27 Publ. Rec. Office), Pro quadam [*sic*] magno vase..vocato 'tankard'. **1382** Wyclif *Zech.* v. 6 This is an amfer [*gloss* or a vessel that sum men clepen a tankard] goynge out. *c* **1440** *Promp. Parv.* 486/2 Tankard, *amphora*. *c* **1475** *Pict. Voc.* in Wr.-Wülcker 771/31 *Hec amphora*, a tancard. **1551–2** *Act* 5 & 6 *Edw. VI*, c. 15 §2 Such as make Males,..Leather Pottes, Tanckardes, Barehides or any other Wares of Leather. **1573–80** Baret *Alv.* T 56 A Tankerd of nine gallons, *amphora*. **1688** R. Holme *Armoury* III. xxi. (Roxb.) 253/2 He beareth Vert, a Dary womans Tankerds, or Milk Tankerds, or two Tankerds of Milk.

2. a. A drinking-vessel, formerly made of wooden staves and hooped; now *esp.* a tall one-handled jug or mug, usually of pewter, sometimes with a lid: used chiefly for drinking beer.

1485 *Naval Acc. Hen. VII* (1896) 51 Drynkyng bolles of tree..xx, Tankerdes..viij. **1495** *Ibid.* 260 Tankardes of a galon apece. **1513** Douglas *Æneis* III. viii. 30 A mekle tankert [L. *magnum cratera*] with wyne fillit to the throt. **1515** Barclay *Egloges* iv. (1570) C vj/1 Talke he of tankarde, or of his boxe of tarre. **1530** Palsgr. 279/1 Tankard a vessell, *brocq, pot, broc.* **1566** *Eng. Ch. Furniture* (Peacock) 91 A penny tanckerd of wood. **1601** F. Tate *Househ. Ord. Edw. II*, §47 (1876) 29 Thei shal wash the tankers, cups, and al manner of vessel which thei have custody of. **1710** Hearne *Collect.* (O.H.S.) III. 99 Charlett then order'd a Tankard of Ale to be fetch'd. **1819** Wordsw. *Waggoner* II. 58 What tankards foaming from the tap. What store of cakes in every lap. **1873** 'Ouida' *Pascarèl* I. 53, I have seen a good many of our people with their noses buried in the tankards.

b. *transf.* in cool tankard, q.v.

3. Applied to a sheep-bell, from its shape. *dial.*

1880 R. Jefferies *Gt. Estate* vi. 123 'It's Johnson's flock; I know the tang of his tankards'. The flat-shaped bells hung on a sheep's neck are called tankards.

4. *attrib.* and *Comb.*, as ***tankard-cup, -lid***; ***tankard-shaped*** adj.; **tankard-turnip**, a variety of turnip with a long tuber; †**tankard-woman**, a female tankard-bearer; †**tankard-yeoman** = tankard-bearer.

1729 Swift *Direct. Servants, Butler*, When any one calls for ale..fill the largest *tancard cup topfull. **1642** Milton *Apol. Smect.* Wks. 1851 III. 263 No marvell, if he brought us home nothing but a meer *tankard drollery. **1852** Wiggins *Embanking* 85 Such sluices..have what are called *tankard-lid doors, working on a bar with rounded ends in a cheek, attached to each side of the sea end of the 'gutter', as it is there called. **1744** W. Ellis *Mod. Husbandman* Jan. ii. 34, I saw a Farmer transplanting his biggest green *tankard Turneps. **1796** W. Marshall *Midland Counties* II. Gloss., *Tankard-turnep*, the pudding, or longrooted turnep. **1828–32** Webster, *Tankard-turnep*, a sort of turnep that stands high above the ground. *a* **1667** Cowley *Ess. in Verse & Pr.*, *Of Obscurity*, He had taken great pleasure in hearing of a *Tanker-woman [*aquam ferens muliercula*, Cicero *Tusc.* 5. 36. 105] say as he past, This is That Demosthenes. **1553** Becon *Reliques of Rome* (1563) 52 That theyr Patrone was some good *tankerd yeoman.

'tankard-ˌbearer. One who bears a tankard; *spec.* †**a.** One employed in drawing and carrying water from the public pumps and conduits (*obs.*); **b.** A cup-bearer.

c **1515** *Cocke Lorell's B.* 10 Tankarde berers, bouge men, and spere planers. **1532** More *Confut. Barnes* viii. Wks. 738/2 King or subiect, carter or cardinal, butcher or bishop, tanckerdberer or kennel raker. **1538** Elyot, *Amphorarius*, he that beareth the potte, a tankarde bearer. **1598** B. Jonson *Ev. Man in Hum.* I. ii, Like a tankard-bearer at a conduit. **1601** *Ibid.* (Qo.) III. iii, What? a tankard-bearer, a thread-bare rascall, a begger. **1675** Brooks *Gold. Key* Wks. 1867 V. 164 He begs water of a poor tankard-bearer to refresh himself in his weariness and thirst: John xix. 28.

So **'tankard-ˌbearing** *a.*

16.. Marvell *Tom May's Death*, For a tankard-bearing Muse must we, As for the basket, Guelphs and Ghibelines be.

tankdrome, var. tankodrome.

tanked (tæŋkt), *ppl. a.* [f. tank *v.*¹ 5 + -ed¹.]

1. *slang.* Filled with (alcoholic) drink; intoxicated; occas. *transf.*, drugged. Freq. with *up*. Also in phr. ***tanked to the wide*** (cf. wide *sb.*) and in developed uses: completely intoxicated.

1893 [see pub *sb.* 1]. **1899** A. M. Binstead *Gal's Gossip* 97 When my male parent, who was a free and frequent librator [*sic*], came home tanked up. **1917** [see blotto *a.*]. **1932** H. Simpson *Boomerang* ix. 183 Dawlish wrote poetry, and caused acute discomfort by reciting it aloud on starry nights when he was tanked up. **1964** Wodehouse *Frozen Assets* iv. 77 If a fellow raised from rags to riches at the breakfast table isn't tanked to the uvula by nightfall, it simply means he hasn't been trying. **1968** [see eyebrow 1 d]. **1977** J. McClure *Sunday Hangman* xv. 178 He'd arrived half-tanked already.

2. *colloq.* Filled *up*, fuelled. Also *fig.*

1954 A. Huxley *Let.* 5 Dec. (1969) 717 A child tanked up with sugar or glucose is likely to get through a party without untoward incidents. **1968** R. Clapperton *No News on Monday* v. 49, I got the Riley tanked up and started the long haul from Sydney. **1973** J. Drummond *Bang! Bang! You're Dead* xxxi. 107 We may need the trucks at any time, keep them tanked up.

tanker¹ ('tæŋkə(r)). [f. tank *sb.*¹ + -er¹.]

1. a. A sea-going vessel fitted with tanks for carrying oil or other liquids in bulk. Cf. *tank-boat, -steamer, -ship* s.v. tank *sb.*¹ 5.

1900 *Boston Herald* 17 Jan. 1/3 The wreck was a tanker. **1905** *Daily News* 20 Mar. 7 A tanker stood ready in the bay to take the English residents to a place of safety. **1920**, etc. [see oil *sb.*¹ 6 e]. **1923** R. D. Paine *Comrades of Rolling Ocean* iv. 73 There was only four of us floated ashore on a capsized boat after the blessed tanker turned turtle. **1950** *Sun* (Baltimore) 19 Oct. (B ed.) 4/3 It was in 1878 that he [*sc.* Gustav Conrad Hansen] first put his idea into practice, converting two sailing ships into tankers. **1962** R. H. Brown *Dict. Marine Insurance Terms* 281 A loaded tanker is usually low in the water. **1977** *R.A.F. News* 11–24 May 4/4 Two.. dinghies attended by a Swedish tanker.

b. A road or rail vehicle with a container designed for transporting fluids in bulk. (Freq. with qualifying word.) Cf. *tank-truck, -wagon* s.v. tank *sb.*¹ 5.

1927, etc. [see oil *sb.*¹ 6 e]. **1947** *Times* 8 Mar. 4/2 Milk tankers carrying supplies for 400,000 Londoners from creameries in Shropshire. **1951** 'J. Wyndham' *Day of Triffids* xvii. 300 With a hose from the tanker which held our main petrol supply I filled the half-track's tanks to overflowing. **1960** *Farmer & Stockbreeder* 2 Feb. 74/1 [He] received fatal injuries..when his car was involved in a collision with a petrol tanker. **1978** J. Sherwood *Limericks of Lachasse* iii. 35 There were two big road tankers..in the car park. It was used as a safe overnight compound for tankers.

c. An aircraft used for carrying fuel in bulk, esp. for the aerial refuelling of other craft.

1931 *Jrnl. R. Aeronaut. Soc.* XXXV. 1145 It is..possible that aircraft which had become obsolete as passenger carriers might be utilised as tankers..although..recent experiments indicate that refuelling in the air will best be accomplished by the use of tankers specially designed for their duty. **1950** C. H. Latimer-Needham *Refuelling in Flight* i. 1 Two aircraft were equipped as tankers..and... were fitted with a 50-ft. length of hose. **1979** J. Barnett *Backfire is Hostile* xiii. 145 The Russian carrier *Kiev* has flown off a number of strike aircraft at present refuelling from aerial tankers at low level.

2. a. *attrib.* and *Comb.*, as ***tanker aircraft, load, train***, etc.

1938 *Jrnl. R. Aeronaut. Soc.* XLII. 389 The aeroplane would then take off with a small quantity of fuel in the tanks ..and the tanks would be filled in the air from the tanker aircraft. **1945** G. Millar *Maquis* iv. 57 What they don't booze they send off to their factories in tanker wagons to make explosives with. **1953** *Times* 31 Oct. 11/1 The tanker drivers' strike is out of the way. **1958** *Ann. Reg. 1957* v. i. 360 The rise in tanker freights, and the greater use of the Cape route. **1965** D. Francis *Odds Against* xi. 150 We might not find Smith, the tanker driver. **1973** *Country Life* 29 Mar. 873/3 A 3,000-hen battery laying unit produces weekly a 600-gallon tanker load of cage manure. **1978** *Times* 16 Aug. 2/6 The tanker train ran out of control. The tanker guard is blamed. **1981** 'D. Rutherford' *Porcupine Basin* vii. 126 Two tanker-loading jetties pushed their long arms..out into the water. **1982** *Daily Tel.* 15 Dec. 24/4 Six TriStar aircraft are to be ordered from British Airways for use as strategic tanker aircraft for the RAF.

b. Special Comb.: **tanker man**, a seaman who is a member of the crew of a tanker (sense 1 a above).

1932 *Times* 9 Mar. 15/6 What can be done to help these tanker-men to bear or to enrich their isolation? **1974** J. DYSON *Prime Minister's Boat* xxx. 179 Come sun-up, the tanker men could pick them off at their leisure.

Hence as *v. trans.*, to transport in tankers; **'tankering** *vbl. sb.*, the putting (of oil, etc.) into tankers.

1928 *Daily Express* 20 Feb. 13 Port Said, where the tankering costs the.. Company £1,000,000 annually. **1980** *Times* Jan. 15/4 Airlines.. use a complicated logistics operation to 'tanker' fuel around the world to avoid particular airports where it is scarce and expensive.

tanker[2]: see TANK *sb.*[7]

tanker[3]: see TANK *v.*[1]

tanker, obs. form of TANKARD.

tankette (tæŋ'kɛt). *Mil. disused.* [f. TANK *sb.*[7] + -ETTE.] A small armoured vehicle designed to facilitate the movement of infantry across rough country.

1927 [see DRAGON[1] 10]. **1927** *Observer* 13 Nov. 19/5 The War Office sent a few tanks, tankettes and six-wheelers to perform. **1931** G. LE Q. MARTEL *In Wake of Tank* xi. 120 He produced a two-man machine with armour protection... These machines were called Tankettes at this time, and they were required to act as scouts. **1942** *Times* (Weekly ed.) 2 Dec. 12 German barbarians pillaged Mikhailskoye collective farm, while they tied its chairman, an ardent Soviet patriot, to tankettes and tore him to pieces.

tankful ('tæŋkfʊl). [f. TANK *sb.*[1] + -FUL.] As much as a tank will contain. Now usu. with reference to the fuel tank of a car.

1887 J. ASHBY STERRY *Lazy Minstrel* (1892) 19 Anemone-hunters roam over the rocks, All hoping to fish up a tankfull. **1890** *Mission Herald* (Boston) June 237 The teacher had his tankful [of water] stored up. **1968** 'E. TREVOR' *Place for Wicked* ii. 23 He'd.. taken her away with the seat-belt on and a warm engine and half a tankful on the dial. **1971** A. PRICE *Alamut Ambush* viii. 96 Give him a car and a tankful of petrol. **1978** *Detroit Free Press* 5 Mar. (Parade Suppl.) 26/1 The result is your average miles per gallon for the previous tankful. The cumulative average, after a few tankfuls, will be an accurate measure of your car's mileage efficiency.

tankia, variant of TANKA[1].

'tankle, *sb.* The second element in the reduplicated TINKLE-TANKLE, sometimes used by itself to express a less acute sound than TINKLE. So **'tankle** *v.*, **'tankling** *vbl. sb.*

1864 WEBSTER, *Tankling*, a ringing noise; a tinkling. **1894** WISTER in *Harper's Mag.* Sept. 514 The flat can-like tankle of the square bell. *Ibid.* 518 The bell.. tankled.

tankless ('tæŋklɪs), *a.* [f. TANK *sb.*[1] + -LESS.] Without a tank.

1894 H. D. LLOYD *Wealth agst. Commw.* 237 The donors might drive the churches, which have no tank-cars, out of the business, as they have done the tankless refiners [of oil].

†tankodrome ('tæŋkəʊdrəʊm). *Obs.* Also tankdrome, tanko-drome. [f. TANK *sb.*[7] + -O + -DROME, after AERODROME 2 b.] An area where military tanks are kept.

1918 *Illustr. London News* 27 July 98 A 'tankdrome' on the Western Front. **1919** C. P. THOMPSON *Cocktails* 250, I left the tankodrome and went down with him to the machine. **1920** J. C. FULLER *Tanks in Great War* 58 A tankodrome (Tank Park) was established at Acheux.

tanky ('tæŋkɪ). *Naut. slang.* Also **tankie**. [f. TANK *sb.*[1] + -Y[6], -IE.] The navigator's assistant; the captain of the hold (see quot. 1945).

1909 J. R. WARE *Passing Engl.* 241/1 *Tanky* (Navy), foreman or captain of the hold—which looks like a tank. **1921** *Blackw. Mag.* July 50/1 I'm hanged if I do Tankie any more. **1944** J. MALLALIEU *Very Ordinary Seaman* vi. 91 Draw the meat, spuds, bread, butter, and vegetables from Tanky. **1945** *Times Lit. Suppl.* 9 June 271/3 The nickname 'Tanky' belonged to his [*sc.* a navigator's] Yeoman and derived from this man's incidental duty of looking after the freshwater tanks... When refrigerated storage for meat was introduced.. it was the practice.. to turn the care of these spaces over to 'Tanky'... Thus the lower deck came to connect 'tanky' with fresh meat... There are now, in consequence, at least two 'Tankies' in most ships: the officers' 'Tanky' who provides their bathwater and.. the matlows' 'Tanky' who issues the meat and spuds. **1956** H. TUNSTALL-BEHRENS *Pamir* ix. 114 The sharp-witted Amigo had the job of Mate's Tanky.

'tanling. *rare.* [f. TAN *a.* + -LING[1].] One tanned by the sun's rays; a person of dark skin.

1611 SHAKS. *Cymb.* IV. iv. 29 To be still hot Summers Tanlings, and The shrinking Slaues of Winter. **1830** TENNYSON *Dualisms* Poems 146 Mid May's darling golden-locked Summer's tanling diamond-eyed. **1877** BLACKIE *Wise Men* 41 Behind the march Of some barbarian tanling, cradled now Behind the Oscan hills.

†tanmerack. *Sc. Obs. rare.* [Corruption of Ir. *tarmanach*, var. of *tarmachan*.] = PTARMIGAN.

1792 *Trans. Antiq. Soc. Scotl.* II. 70 Here also is the Tanmerack, a fowl of the size of a dove, which always inhabits the tops of the highest mountains.

tanna ('tɑːnə). Also with capital initial. Usu. in pl. **tannaim** ('tɑːnəɪm); also **†tanaim, tannain.** [a. Aramaic, = teacher, f. *tĕnā* to repeat, learn, cogn. w. Heb. *šānāh*: see MISHNAH, MISHNA.] One of the Jewish doctors of the law of the first two centuries A.D. whose opinions are recorded in the Mishnah and Baraita. Occas. as **tannaite** ('tɑːneɪaɪt) (also as adj., = *tannaitic*); **tannaitic** ('tɑːneɪˌɪtɪk, ˌtɑːneɪ'ɪtɪk) *a.*, of or pertaining to the tannaim.

1718 [see MISHNICAL *a.*]. **1845** *Encycl. Metrop.* IX. 639/2 He [*sc.* Antigonus of Socho] was the founder of the school of the tannain or mishnical doctors, by which name all the doctors of the Jewish law are distinguished, who lived between the death of Simon [the Just] and the middle of the second century after Christ. **1888** *Encycl. Brit.* XXIII. 36/1 The Mishnic doctors.. were and are called *Tannaim*. **1905** *Jewish Encycl.* X. 633/1 In rabbinical literature careful discrimination must be made between the tannaitic period and that of the Amoraim. **1911** *Encycl. Brit.* XXVI. 399/1 The term *tanna* is used in the Talmud of those teachers who flourished in the first two centuries of the Christian era. **1919** H. A. A. KENNEDY *Theol. Epistles* i. 17 These were due to the wisdom of many teachers, of whom the most famous were the so-called Tannaites. **1941** G. G. SCHOLEM *Major Trends in Jewish Mysticism* ii. 51 The tradition of Tannaitic mysticism and theosophy was really alive among them [*sc.* the later Merkabah mystics]. **1950** L. S. THORNTON *Revelation & Mod. World* ix. 283 The rabbinical teacher was known as a *tanna*, that is a 'repeater' of the tradition. *Ibid.*, There was a '*tannaite*' succession of teachers which traced its genealogy back through successive pairs of rabbis to the men of the Great Synagogue. **1957** *Encycl. Brit.* XV. 458/1 The Midrash of the schools, often called Halakhic or Tannaite (i.e. Mishnaic) Midrash. **1969** D. DAUBE *Roman Law* iii. 158 Tannaitic law, that is to say, the early Talmudic law of, say, 100 BC to AD 200. **1977** *New Yorker* 17 Oct. 48/3 Rabbi Gabriel used to remind her that, even according to the strictest letter of the law, kissing and embracing are permitted and that tannaim and amoraim frolicked with their spouses in bed.

tanna(h, tannadar, var. THANA, THANADAR.

tannable ('tænəb(ə)l), *a.* [f. TAN *v.* + -ABLE.] Capable of being tanned.

1879 in WEBSTER *Suppl.*

tannage ('tænɪdʒ). [f. TAN *v.* + -AGE; or perh. a. F. *tannage* (14th c. in Hatz.-Darm.).]

1. The art or process of tanning; also *concr.* the produce of tanning. (With quot. 18.. cf. TAN *v.* 1 c.)

1662 J. DAVIES tr. *Olearius' Voy. Ambass.* 42 They are as yet unacquainted with Tannage. **1778** *Phil. Trans.* LXVIII. 128 The leather.. is of a superior quality to that of the old tannage. **18..** *Marble-Worker* §129 (Cent. D.) The most important operation in the composition of artificial Marbles is that of tannage, without which it would be impossible for the cabinet maker to scrape and polish the material. **1893** *Times* 13 Dec. 3/5 Up-country tannages had a fair market throughout... Bombay tannages were in fair request at about last sales prices. **1901** *Daily Chron.* 18 Nov. 3/7 The sterling quality of English sole leather—good, honest, oak-bark tannage—has passed into a proverb.

attrib. **1732** Tannage bill [see TANNERY 2].

b. *transf.* The tanning or sunburning of the skin.

1845 BROWNING *Flight of Duchess* iii, They should have got his cheek fresh tannage.

2. A tannery. *Sc.*

1799–1812 [A tannery known as 'the Tannage' existed in Hawick in the lane still called *Tannage Close*]. **1867** D. BLACK *Hist. Brechin* 185 A piece of ground formerly occupied as a cornyard and tannage was purchased.

†'Tannakin. *Obs.* Also 6 **tannikin**, 7 **tanakin**. A diminutive pet-form of the name Ann or Anna (cf. *Tann* = *St. Ann*, *Ted* = Edward); *spec.* used for a German or Dutch girl.

1557 P. HOBY *Let. to Cecil* in Burgon *Gresham* (1839) I. 227, I praie ye, desire my Lady to come, and to bringe Tannikin [Cecil's daughter Anne] with her. **1596** NASHE *Saffron Walden* 130 Like a Germane, that neuer goes to the warres without his Tannakin. **1605** MARSTON *Dutch Courtezan* I. i, A pretty nimble eyd Dutch Tanakin. **1608** ARMIN *Nest Ninn.* (1880) 47 Like a Dutch Tannakin, sliding to market on the ise.

tannase ('tæneɪz). *Biochem.* [a. F. *tannase* (A. Fernbach 1900, in *Compt. Rend.* CXXXI. 1214): see TANNIN and -ASE.] An enzyme that hydrolyses ester linkages in tannins.

1901 J. R. GREEN *Soluble Ferments* (ed. 2) x. 169 Tannase attacks not only tannin but the compound of tannin and gelatin, as well as other tannates. **1929** R. P. WALTON tr. *Waldschmidt-Leitz's Enzyme Actions & Properties* 122 Tannase.. must be regarded as a specific esterase having a special affinity for the esters of phenol carboxylic acids. **1979** *Jrnl. Chromatogr.* CLXX. 446 The use of tannase (tannin acylhydrolase..) in localization procedures for enzymatic activity has never been studied.

tannate ('tænət). *Chem.* [a. F. *tannate* (Proust 1798), f. TANN-IC + -ATE[4].] A salt of tannic acid.

1802 *Nicholson's Jrnl.* II. 72 The small quantity of tanin dissolved in this water would combine with the lime.. and would form a tanate of lime. *Ibid.* 198 The tannate of tin. **1808** HENRY *Epit. Chem.* 240 The gallate and tannate of iron are.. essential constituents of inks. **1882** *Encycl. Brit.* XIV. 385/1 [It] gives up its dissolved gelatin to the tan of the stronger solution outside to form tannate of gelatin.

tanné, -ee, obs. forms of TAWNY.

tanned (tænd), *ppl. a.* [f. TAN *v.* + -ED[1].]

1. a. Converted into leather; preserved by tanning.

c **1000** ÆLFRIC *Gloss.* in Wr.-Wülcker 118/7 ȝetannede hyd. *c* **1350** *Usages Winchester* in *Eng. Gilds* (1870) 358 Euerych cart þᵗ bereþ y-tanned leþer to selle. **1497** *Naval Acc. Hen. VII* (1896) 102 Tanned hides. *a* **1548** HALL *Chron., Hen. VII* 4 b, Their brest plates.. were made of tanned lether. **1666** WOOD *Life* Jan. (O.H.S.) II. 98 For a tan'd paire of gloves, 1*s.* **1837** M. DONOVAN *Dom. Econ.* II. 54 Herodotus says the tanned human skin excels all others in whiteness and brilliancy.

b. *slang.* Beaten, thrashed.

1905 *Dundee Advertiser* 8 July 6 Away back in boyhood's happy days.. 'a tanned hide' had a significance all its own.

2. a. That has been rendered brown or tawny, esp. by exposure to the sun; sunburnt.

1564–78 BULLEYN *Dial. agst. Pest.* (1888) 29 A Lackey clothed in Orenge Taunie and White, with a paire of bare tanned legges. *c* **1600** SHAKS. *Sonn.* lxii, Beated and chopt with tand antiquitie. **1632** MILTON *L'Allegro* 90 If the earlier season lead To the tann'd Haycock in the Mead. **1709** O. DYKES *Eng. Prov. & Refl.* (ed. 2) 190 As diligent as any toiling tann'd Hay-maker in the Field upon a Sunshiny Day. **1859** JEPHSON *Brittany* ix. 137 The healthy tanned complexions which mark a seafaring population.

b. Of a reddish brown or tawny colour.

1575 TURBERV. *Venerie* 10 Such [deer] as be dunne on the backe hauing their foure quarters redde or tanned, and the legs of the same coloure, as it were the coloure of a hares legs. **1616** SURFL. & MARKH. *Country Farme* 675 The white hound, the fallow or taund hound, the grey-hound, and the blacke hound. **1719** LONDON & WISE *Compl. Gard.* VII. vi. 166 A certain tann'd and red Colour which covers all the Rind. **1863** W. C. BALDWIN *Afr. Hunting* iii. 76 [The inyala] is of the bush buck species,.. with spiral horns, tanned legs, very long hair on his breast and quarters.

3. Spread or covered with tan.

1870 *Daily News* 6 June, The thoroughbreds were led round the well-tanned enclosure. **1891** *Ibid.* 6 Mar. 3/5 A thick ring of spectators surrounded the tanned enclosure.

4. *humorous nonce-use.* Made or governed by Kett the tanner.

1549 CHEKE *Hurt Sedit.* 8 The other rable of Norfolke rebelles, ye pretend a common welth... A marueylous tanned common welth.

5. Immunol. ***tanned-(red-)cell***, used *attrib.* to designate a test in which antibodies can be detected by observing the agglutination of red blood cells that have been coated with tannic acid which has then bound with the appropriate soluble antigen.

1956 *Jrnl. Immunol.* LXXVI. 409/1 The tanned cell hemagglutination test.. was also applied to the problem. **1962** *Lancet* 5 May 951/2 In a series of 78 patients with pernicious anæmia, the tanned-red-cell agglutination test was positive in 24% of males. **1980** *Canad. Jrnl. Zool.* LVIII. 245 One group [of cattle] infected with only *H*[*ypoderma*] *lineatum* was followed using the tanned-cell hemagglutination technique.

tanner[1] ('tænə(r)). Also ? 1 **tannere**, 2–3 **tanur**, 4 **tannere**, 4–5 **-our**, 5 **-ar(e**, 6 **-ar**, **tanyer**. [The form corresponds with a rare OE. *tannere* from *tannian* to tan, and with OF. *tanere* (1226 in Godef. *Compl.*), nom. case of *taneör*, *tanour*:—L. *tannātor*, *tannātōr-em*, but perh. actually represents the French word. The form *tanyer* appears to be assimilated to words like *sawyer*, *hosier*, *farrier*; but cf. OF. *tanière* (1280 in Godef.).]

1. a. One whose occupation is to tan hides or to convert them into leather by tanning.

a **975** *Grant by K. Eadgar* in Kemble *Cod. Dipl.* II. 411 Be eastan ea and tannera hole [*lit.* tanners' hole]. ? *a* **1189** in *Rep. Hist. MSS. Comm.*, *Var. Coll.* IV. 50 Deorlingno tanur, Iordano cordwaner. **1226** in J. T. Gilbert *Hist. & Munic. Doc. Irel.* (Rolls) 83 Willelmus, filius Iohannis tanur. *c* **1350** *Usages Winchester* in *Eng. Gilds* (1870) 359 Euerych tanner þᵉ halt bord in þᵉ heyestret of Wynchestre. **1393** LANGL. *P. Pl.* C. I. 223 Taylours and tanners and tyliers of erthe. **1415** *Ordo paginarum* in *York Myst.* Introd. 19 Tannours. [*In heading of Play* (*c* 1435) *called* The Barkers.] **14..** *Customs of Malton* in *Surtees Misc.* (1888) 63 A tannar schall not use nor ocupy schomakar crafte. **1526** TINDALE *Acts* ix. 43 He taryed many days in Joppa with one Simon a tanner. **1565** *Old Order Bk. in the Tower* 39 Also we present, all the Tanyers that wash their skins within the Tower Ditch. **1739** MILLER *Gard. Dict.* II. s.v. *Tan*, I find there are several Degrees of Fineness, to which the Tanners do grind their Bark. **1868** FREEMAN *Norm. Conq.* II. viii. 177 In every form which the story has taken.., the mother of the Conqueror appears as the daughter of a tanner at Falaise.

b. *Comb.* **tanner eagle**, a rendering of Gr. βυρσαίετος (*lit.* hide-eagle), as a designation of Cleon, who was a tanner. Also compounds of *tanner's*, *tanners'*, as ***tanner's*** or ***tanners' bark, hair, mill, ooze, waste, water***; **tanners' sumac**, the tree *Rhus Coriaria*, the dried and chopped leaves and shoots of which are used in tanning; **tanners' tree**, *Coriaria myrtifolia*, a low deciduous shrub of Southern Europe used in tanning; also = *tanners' sumac*; **tanners' turf**, tan-turf.

1820 T. MITCHELL *Aristoph.* I. 179 Your snake—and snake, so runs the prophecy, Shall beat the *tanner-eagle. **1837** WHEELWRIGHT tr. *Aristoph.* I. 304 This Paphlagonian is the tanner-eagle. **1731** MILLER *Gard. Dict.* s.v. *Acacia*, The third, sixth, and seventh Sorts.. should have a Hot-bed of *Tanner's Bark. **1707** MORTIMER *Husb.* (1721) II. 254 A stock of Clay well mix'd with Horse-dung to prevent its freezing, and with *Tanner's Hair to prevent its cracking. **1611** COTGR. s.v. *Tan, Moulin à tan*, a *Tanners mill. **1587–1725** *Tanners owze, etc. [see OOZE *sb.*[1] 2 *a*, *β*]. **1858** HOGG *Veg. Kingd.* 222 *Tanners' sumach. **1884** MILLER *Plant-n., Sumach*, Tanner's, *Rhus Coriaria. Ibid.*, *Tanner's tree, *Coriaria myrtifolia* and other species. **1688** R. HOLME *Armoury* III. 86/2 **Tanners* [*Turfe*],..the Bark cast out of the Tan-Pits,..wrought into Turfes, which dried is good fire Fuel. **1815** J. SMITH *Panorama Sc. & Art* II. 608 The bark of oak, or *tanners' waste, when completely putrefied ..greatly improves cold, stiff heavy soils. **1552** HULOET, *Tanners water, *nautea, æ.*

2. [f. TAN *v.* 2 a.] A lotion, cream, etc., designed to promote a sun-tan when applied to the skin on exposure to the sun; ***artificial, man-made tanner***, one which colours the skin brown without the aid of the sun.

1969 *Daily Tel.* 2 July 15/8 People with sensitive..skins should be wary of all artificial tanners. It's advisable to try any man-made tanner on a small patch of skin. **1972** *Vogue* June Special 40/2 The new tanners: something here for every kind of skin... Rub your tanner right up into the hairline. **1979** *Country Life* 31 May 1776/1 There are many artificial tanners on the market; the Charles of the Ritz Self Tanning Foam, £3.95, claims to..tan the skin in a similar way to the sun.

tanner[2] ('tænə(r)). *slang* (now *Hist.*). [Origin uncertain: see hearsay account in B. Hooper *Leather Manufact.* (1891) 65.] A sixpence. Also *attrib.*

1811 *Lex. Balatr., Tanner*, a sixpence. **1812** J. H. VAUX *Flash Dict., Tanner*, a sixpence. Three and a tanner. **1844** DICKENS *Mart. Chuz.* xxxvii, 'How much a-piece?' The man in the monument replied, 'a Tanner'. It seemed a low expression, compared with the monument. **1908** *Daily Express* 3 Feb. 1/1 Seventeen tannercabs [sixpenny cabs] made their appearance in the streets on Saturday, and were in great demand.

tannery ('tænərɪ). [f. TANNER[1] + -Y: see -ERY. Cf. F. *tannerie* (13th c. in Hatz.-Darm.).]

1. A place where tanning is carried on.

[**1396–1401** *Rolls of Parlt.* I. 228/2 Coreum, cortices et utensilia in tanneria sua.] **1736** J. M'URE *View Glasgow* 285 There is a stately Brewarie..adjacent to the above great Tannarie. **1839** *Penny Cycl.* XIV. 437/1 The tanneries of Marocco. **1856** STANLEY *Sinai & Pal.* vi. 269 A tradition.. describes the premises to have been long employed as a tannery.

attrib. **1852** HANNA *Chalmers* IV. xxi. 401 Never was the true work of school and church done better than in that old tannery-loft.

2. The process or trade of tanning; tannage.

14.. *Beryn* 3237 And I shall tech hym, as I can,..Tyll it be abill of prentyse to crafft of tan[e]ry. **1732** *Rec. Convent. Roy. Burghs* V. 529 A propper clause in the tannage bill for saving the rights of the cordiners cf..royal burghs as to their priviledge of tannery. **1837** CARLYLE *Fr. Rev.* III. v. vii, Gun-boring, Altar-burning, Saltpetre-digging, and miraculous improvements in Tannery!

attrib. **1887** *Pall Mall G.* 12 Sept. 8/2 A great fire broke out..in the extensive tannery works.

‖**tannia, tanier, tannier** ('tænjə(r), ‖'tanja). Also tania, tanier, tannier. [a. Tupi *taña, taya*, Carib *taya*.] A species of *Caladium* or *Xanthosoma* (*X. sagittifolium*), N.O. *Araceæ*, cultivated in Brazil, the West Indies, and tropical Africa, for its farinaceous tuberous root; it is closely allied to the EDDOES.

[**1625** PURCHAS *Pilgrims* IV. 1310 There are certaine Taiaobas, that are like Cabiges.] **1756** P. BROWNE *Jamaica* 332 The purple Cocco and Tannier. **1766** J. BARTRAM *Jrnl.* 10 Feb., in W. Stork *Acc. E. Florida* (1790) 32 Breakfasted on a mess of tanniers, a species of eddo. **1792** MAR. RIDDELL *Voy. Madeira* 84 The *arum virginiana*, or *tannier*, and the *arum esculentum*, or *eddoe*, are two excellent farinaceous vegetables. **1871** KINGSLEY *At Last* vi, His patch of provision-ground..gives him..yam, tania, cassava, and fruit too. **1898** L. CROOKALL *Brit. Guiana* vi. 83 Then there are white yams and buck yams,..tannias and eddoes. **1953** *Caribbean Q.* III. II. 103 In 1811, Charles Edmonson.. reported..: 'The quantity of rice the Bush Negroes have just rising out of the ground is very considerable independent of yams, tannias, plantains, tobacco, &c.' **1955** *Ibid.* IV. II. 112 Grated tannia fritters..fried in deep fat on a coalpot. **1968** [see DASHEEN]. **1979** *West Africa* 8 Jan. 51/1 In Cameroon..the other, *tannia* sort [of cocoyam] is called *macabo*.

tannic ('tænɪk), *a. Chem.* [f. TANN-IN + -IC.] In tannic acid, a name introduced in 1834 by Pelouze instead of TANNIN, in recognition of its acid character and reactions; originally applied to the tannin principle obtained from oak-galls, a white amorphous strongly astringent substance, $C_{14}H_{10}O_9$, now more particularly distinguished from other forms of tannin as GALLOTANNIC *acid*. Now chiefly used in a general sense to include a great number of allied substances, which differ in the proportion of their elements.

These are distinguished by compound names indicating their source, as *quercitannic acid*, that obtained from oak-bark, $C_{15}H_{12}O_9$; also *caffetannic* ($C_{15}H_{18}O_8$), *catechutannic* ($C_{17}H_{17}O_9$), *cincho-* or *quinotannic* ($C_{14}H_{16}O_9$), *fraxitannic, kinotannic, ratanhiatannic acids*, obtained from coffee, catechu, cinchona, ash-leaves, kino, and ratanhia respectively.

[**1834** (Feb. 17) PELOUZE in *Ann. de Chimie* LIV. 337 La place du tannin, qu'il serait plus convenable d'appeler *acide tannique*, est marqué à côté de l'acide gallique lui-même.] **1836** BRANDE *Chem.* (ed. 4) 925 A peculiar proximate principle, designated *tannin*... It has been obtained in a distinct form by Pelouze, and its characters are such that it may be appropriately termed *tannic acid*. **1869** ROSCOE *Elem. Chem.* (1871) 405 Tannin, or Tannic Acid,..is contained widely diffused in certain parts of plants. **1874** GARROD & BAXTER *Mat. Med.* (1880) 281 The cincho-tannic and red cinchonic acids are powerfully astringent—like tannic and gallic acids.

tannie ('tanɪ). *S. Afr. colloq.* Also **Tannie**. [Dim. of Afrikaans *tante*: see TANTE 2.] **a.** An informal mode of address used to an aunt or any older woman. **b.** A prim elderly woman. Also *transf.*

1958 L. VAN DER POST *Lost World Kalahari* i. 16 'Old tannie sea-cow' was our endearing way of naming the hippopotamus, so called because it was there in the surf of the sea to welcome my people when they first landed in Africa. **1958** R. COLLINS *Four-Coloured Flag* 16 'Good afternoon, Tannie,' he mumbled, from a distance of twenty feet. **1958** *Cape Times* 10 Dec. 11/3 The radiologist told him of the shrieks from alarmed *tannies* in from the country when they found themselves being elevated on high. **1969** I. VAUGHAN *Last of Sunlit Years* ix. 77, I am finding that most Afrikaans children call one 'Aunty', or 'Tannie', and are most charmingly co-operative. **1980** *Rand Daily Mail* 15 Apr. 8/3 So tasteful one feels sure one's most uptight Victorian tannie from Tweetackie-slippersfontein would be pleased to receive her

tanniferous (tæ'nɪfərəs), *a.* [f. TANNI(N + -FEROUS.] Yielding or abounding in tannin.

1878 URE *Dict. Arts* IV. 897 The most advantageous tanniferous substance is an extract of the chestnut, costing about 3*d.* per lb.

tannigen ('tænɪdʒɛn). *Pharm.* [f. TANNI(N + -GEN.] A compound of tannin and acetyl, used as an intestinal astringent; acetyl-tannin.

1898 in *Syd. Soc. Lex.* **1905** H. D. ROLLESTON *Dis. Liver* 297 If this [diarrhœa] is troublesome, bismuth, aromatic chalk and opium mixture, dilute sulphuric acid, tannigen.. should be given.

tannikin, variant of TANNAKIN.

tannin ('tænɪn). *Chem.* [a. F. *tanin*, 'le principe tannant' (1798 Proust in *Ann. de Chimie* XXV. 225), f. *tan* TAN *sb.*[1] + -IN[1].] Any member of a group of astringent vegetable substances, the *tannins*, which possess the property of combining with animal hide and converting it into leather.

The first member of this group isolated and so named was the tannin of gall-nuts, subsequently also called TANNIC *acid*; and to this the names *tannin* and *tannic acid* are still often specifically applied. But the discovery that the astringent principles of other vegetable substances were not chemically identical with that of gall-nuts made it needful to distinguish the various tannins. The original or 'ordinary tannin' became distinctively GALLOTANNIN, other members of the group being named *caffetannin, catechutannin, kinotannin, quercitannin*, etc. (cf. TANNIC), or particularized as *oak-bark tannin, alder, beech, hop, horse-chestnut, larch, rhatany tannin*, according to their source.

1802 *Nicholson's Jrnl.* II. 198 Abridgment of a Memoir of Mr. Proust on Tanin and its Species. **1804** *Phil. Trans.* XCIV. 210 The effects which it produced on gelatin, also demonstrate the presence of tannin. **1836** BRANDE *Chem.* (ed. 4) 928 *note*, The tannin of catechu is said to contain less oxygen than that of galls. **1838** T. THOMSON *Chem. Org. Bodies* 109 Pure tannin is colourless. **1867** BAKER *Nile Tribut.* viii. (1872) 123 It is rich in a hard gum, which appears to be almost pure tannin. **1895** MUIR & MORLEY *Watts' Dict. Chem.* V. 632/1 The origin of tannin in plants has given rise to much debate.

b. *attrib.* and *Comb.*, as ***tannin drop, pill, treatment; tannin-like*** adj.; **tannin-glycerol**, glycerin of tannic acid; **tannin-sac**, a vessel in plants which secretes tannin.

1874 GARROD & BAXTER *Mat. Med.* (1880) 357 Tannin Lozenges. **1875** BENNETT & DYER *Sachs' Bot.* 628 Tannin-like compounds are formed in particular cells. **1879** *St. George's Hosp. Rep.* IX. 800 It soon passed off again with rest and the opium and digitalis and tannin pills. **1884** BOWER & SCOTT *De Bary's Phaner.* 153 We may here introduce these organs as Tannin-sacs. They occur as elongated sacs, especially near to the vascular bundles, in the parenchyma of the stem and petiole of many Ferns (Marsilia, Polypodiaceæ, Cyatheaceæ, Marattiaceæ, &c.). **1898** P. MANSON *Trop. Diseases* vi. 121 The tannin treatment..might also be tried.

Hence **'tannined** (-ɪnd) *a.*, charged or impregnated with tannin; **tannin'genic** *a.*, in ***tanningenic acid***, a synonym of CATECHUIC *acid* and CATECHIN.

1898 E. F. SPENCE in *Westm. Gaz.* 6 Sept. 3/3 For breakfast we had undrinkable coffee, which we exchanged for tannined tea. **1852** MORFIT *Tanning & Currying* (1853) 69 Catechuine or tanningenic acid.

tanning ('tænɪŋ), *vbl. sb.* [f. TAN *v.* + -ING[1].] The action of the verb TAN; an instance of this.

1481 in *Eng. Gilds* (1870) 332 As in tannyng, coryyng, cuttyng, or sowyng. *c* **1515** *Cocke Lorell's B.* 2 A tanner for euyll tannyng of lether. **1598** FLORIO, *Adustione*,..a tanning in the sunne. **1794** *Rigging & Seamanship* I. 85 The tanning of sails in the royal navy has been tried. **1863** SIR G. G. SCOTT *Glean. Westm. Abb.* (ed. 2) 65 Witnessing the 'tanning' of the rascal's 'hide'. **1899** C. F. TOWNSEND *Chem. for Photographers* (ed. 2) iv. 75 The 'tanning' of the gelatin or rendering it insoluble. **1935** *Discovery* July 190/1 Wash-out gelatine relief by development tanning, used for making matrices for obtaining 'imbibition'. **1944** J. S. HUXLEY *On living in Revolution* 70 Lamarckism..the inheritance of characters acquired by an individual as a result of changes in the environment, like tanning due to sun. **1980** B. H. CARROLL et al. *Introd. Photogr. Theory* xi. 227 Tanning development involves the formation of an image in the form of insolubilized gelatin.

attrib. **1727–41** CHAMBERS *Cycl., Tan*, the bark of the oak, chopped, and ground, by a tanning-mill, into a coarse powder. **1887** J. E. TAYLOR *Tourist's Guide Suffolk* 61 Combs..is distant 1 m., well known for the extensive tanning-works of Messrs. Webb. **1963** *Listener* 17 Jan. 138/1 From winter resort patronized by the pre-1914 crowned heads of Europe to tanning-factory for bikini-clad campers.

'tanning, *ppl. a.* [-ING[2].]

a. That tans.

a **1717** PARNELL *Health* 35 Her hardy face repels the tanning wind. **1828** P. CUNNINGHAM *N.S. Wales* II. 75 If our..tanning barks, and bark extracts, do not continue to pay. **1857** MILLER *Elem. Chem.* III. xi. 672 Sewing up the hide, filling it with the tanning infusion.

b. *spec.* in *Photogr.* Cf. TAN *v.* 4.

1930 G. E. BROWN *Clerc's Photography* xxviii. 224/2 The localized tanning of the gelatine gives rise to unequal contractions of the film during drying... Tanning developers are not used in astronomical work. **1959** *Chambers's Encycl.* X. 686/2 Most fixing solutions also contain a tanning or hardening agent which unites with the gelatin of the emulsion layer, increases its melting-point and reduces its swelling in water. **1973** D. A. SPENCER *Focal Dict. Photogr. Technol.* 617 A typical tanning developer contains little if any sulphite.

tannish ('tænɪʃ), *a.* [f. TAN *a.* + -ISH[1].] Somewhat tan-coloured.

1935 J. T. FARRELL *Judgment Day* xiii. 287 He glanced at a squat fellow in a crimson jersey and tannish knickers. **1947** D. M. DAVIN *Gorse blooms Pale* 53 It [*sc.* the calf] had Rosy's colouring, only at the ends the hair deepened into the Jersey's tannish black. **1961** M. BEADLE *These Ruins are Inhabited* (1963) iii. 40 We ambled into..a tiny Saxon church. Of tannish stone..it was thick-set..and sheltering. **1965** *Amer. Philos. Q.* II. 320/2 A deep olive green..would be more beautiful..against a tannish pink.

tanno-. *Chem.* Combining base of *tann-ic, tann-in*, used in forming names of tannin compounds, etc., and also in compound substantives, e.g. ***tannometer*** for *tannin-meter*. **tannoca'ffeic acid**, = CAFFETANNIC *acid*. **'tannoform**, $C_{29}H_{20}O_{18}$, a product of gallotannic acid and formaldehyde; a reddish white, light powder, insoluble in water, but soluble in alkaline solutions. **tanno'gallate, tanno'gallic** *a.* = GALLOTANNATE, -TANNIC. **tanno'gelatin**, a mixture of gelatin with a solution of tannin.

c **1865** in *Circ. Sc.* I. 351/1 *Tanno-caffeic acid, when roasted, develops the agreeable smell of coffee. **1899** *Allbutt's Syst. Med.* VIII. 726 Powders of *tannoform, salicylic acid, talc, bismuth, or lycopodium may be employed. **1819** BRANDE *Chem.* 394 The *tannogallate of iron is of the utmost importance, as forming the basis of writing ink, and of black dyes. **1836** —— *Chem.* (ed. 4) 928 Tannin forms a white precipitate in solution of gelatin (**tannogelatin*), which, when carefully dried, becomes hard and tough. **1877** KNIGHT *Dict. Mech.*, **Tannometer*, a hydrometer for determining the proportion of tannin in tanning liquor.

tannoid ('tænɔɪd), *a. Chem.* [f. TANN-IN + -OID.] Of the nature of, or akin to, tannin.

1898 *Naturalist* 186 The choking influence exerted by the tannoid compounds.

Tannoy ('tænɔɪ). Also **tannoy**. A proprietary name for electrical apparatus concerned with sound reproduction and amplification. Now used generally, esp. to denote a form of public address system.

1928 *Trade Marks Jrnl.* 18 Apr. 605 Tannoy 488,958. Electrical Instruments and Apparatus for use in connection with Wireless Telegraphy and Telephony and Electrical Conductors... Guy Rupert Fountain, trading as the Tulsemere Manufacturing Co... 28th February 1928. **1942** *Ibid.* 21 Oct. 433/1 Tannoy. Electric signalling and alarm apparatus, telephone systems.. television..radio apparatus,..sound reproducing and sound amplifying instruments..; public address apparatus; electric amplifiers. **1944** 'N. SHUTE' *Pastoral* ii. 36 He was lighting his pipe..when the Tannoy sounded metallically above his head. **1954** G. SMITH *Flaw in Crystal* xx. 215 The tannoy blared, telling the passengers to go aboard. **1958** M. K. JOSEPH *I'll soldier No More* ix. 158 A tannoy-loudspeaker on the deck brought them the hourly news bulletins. **1969** A. GLYN *Dragon Variation* i. 11 Above them the hoarse voice of the muezzin crackled through the Tannoy, calling the faithful to prayer. **1977** G. SCOTT *Hot Pursuit* iii. 34 A call in the Tannoy system drowned my words. **1980** *Daily Tel.* 12 Nov. 19/3 They were furious after missing a train because of a wrong announcement on the station tannoy.

Hence as *v. trans.*, to call (someone) by public address system; *intr.*, to use a public address system; **'tannoyed** *ppl. a.*, transmitted by public address system; **'tannoying** *ppl. a.*

1966 *Punch* 20 Apr. 564/1 The President spoke, and his tannoyed voice boomed back off the blighted trees and the peeling architecture. **1970** B. TURNER *Another Little Death* ii. 14 He held the line while Chief Inspector Rillie was Tannoyed out of the basement. **1976** *Times* 24 Apr. 4 The Portuguese Socialist leader arrives behind a convoy of tannoying cars and almost bounces into the crowd. **1978** *Times* 2 Oct. 4/3 A great crowd..being ordered around by Tannoyed voices.

tanny(e: see TAWNY.

Tanoan (tə'nəʊən), *sb.* and *a.* [f. Sp. *Tano*, ad. Southern Tewa self-designation '*tʰánu*, + -AN.]

A. *sb.* A family of languages spoken in parts of New Mexico and Arizona by Pueblo Indians; also, the group of people which speaks these languages. **B.** *adj.* Of, pertaining to, or designating this linguistic group.

1891 J. W. POWELL *Indian Linguistic Families of Amer.* 121 Tañoan. **1909** *Amer. Anthropologist* XI. 564 The Keres (Queres) are introduced among tribes speaking languages of the Tanoan family. **1925** [see KERES]. **1928** J. P. HARRINGTON *Vocab. Kiowa Lang.* 1 A brief text [has]..been included, as well as Tanoan etymologies taken from the Tewa dialect spoken at San Juan Pueblo near Santa Fe, New Mexico. *Ibid.* 11 In the Tanoan languages, several of the consonants have a hard and a soft form. **1941** C. F. VOEGELIN *Language, Culture & Personality* 28 Only fragmentary notes and word lists for Tanoan were available. Taos was taken as a type for Tanoan phonetics and morphology. **1950** F. EGGAN *Social Organization of Western Pueblos* 314 The Tanoan groups in the Rio Grande. **1959** G. L. & E. L. TRAGER in *Amer. Anthropologist* LXI. 1078 (*title*) Kiowa and Tanoan. **1974** *Encycl. Brit. Micropædia* IX. 810/2 *Tanoan languages*, the family of Aztec-Tanoan languages spoken in the valley of the Rio Grande in..New Mexico, U.S., including Northern Tiwa, Southern Tiwa, Piro, Tewa, Tano (the type language), and Towa; spoken by about 5,000 people (24,500 in 1680).

tan-pit: see TAN *sb.*[1] C.

tanpoora, tanpura, varr. TAMBOURA.

‖**tanquam** ('tænkwæm). *Obs.* Also (in sense 3) **tam quam**. [L. *tam quam*, *tanquam* so much as, as much as, as if, as it were.]

1. Something that has only an apparent existence; a mere seeming; an 'as it were'.

1654 WHITLOCK *Zootomia* 537 He sheweth the Visibles, or Things of this World to be but *tanquams*, only *as it weres*.

2. In the University of Cambridge [from L. *tanquam socius*, 'as if a fellow']: see quots.

a **1661** FULLER *Worthies* (1662) II. 207 Thomas Dove D.D. was born in this City,..bred a Tanquam (which is a Fellowes Fellow) in Pembroke-Hall in Cambridge. **1706** PHILLIPS (ed. 6), *Tanquam*..In the Universities..is taken for a Person of Worth and Learning, that is fit Company for the Fellows of Colleges, &c.

3. *Law.* = QUI TAM: see quot. 1907. (From the words *tam...quam...*, beginning the two clauses.)

c **1570** *Pride & Lowl.* (1841) 47 For I declare (quod he) in the *Tam quam* How so the matter goe, they gette no cost [i.e. because costs are not given against the Crown]. **1592** GREENE *Upst. Courtier* Wks. (Grosart) XI. 258 Suppose some be so stuborne as to stand to the triall, yet can this cunning knaue declare a *Tamquam* against them, so that though they be cleered, yet can they haue no recompence at all, for that he doth it in the courts behalfe. **1809** in TOMLINS *Law Dict.* [**1907** *Encycl. Laws of Engl.* VII. 239 s.v. *Informer*, Actions by common informers are termed *qui tam* actions, or popular actions, when the informer recovers the statutory penalty (*tam pro domino rege quam pro se ipso*).]

‖**tanrec, tenrec** ('tæn-, 'tɛnrək). Also 8 **tondruck, tendrac**. [= F. *tanrec*, ad. Malagasy *tàndraka*, dial. form of *tràndraka*, the native name.] An insectivorous mammal, *Centetes ecaudatus*, allied to the hedgehog, and covered with spiny bristles intermixed with silky hairs; the Madagascar hedgehog. Also any species of the genus *Centetes* or family *Centetidæ*.

1729 R. DRURY *Madagascar* (1890) 81 A creature which I call a ground-hog, and which in their language is called 'tondruck'. **1785** SMELLIE tr. *Buffon's Nat. Hist.* (1791) VII. 86 The Tanrecs or Tendracs are small East Indian animals, which have some resemblance to our hedgehog. **1835** KIRBY *Hab. & Inst. Anim.* II. xxiv. 514 The hedgehog and tenrec present..something more than an analogy to the porcupines and some of the rats. **1852** TH. ROSS *Humboldt's Trav.* II. xvii. 134 The tanrecs, or Madagascar hedgehogs,..pass three months of the year in lethargy. **1879** E. P. WRIGHT *Anim. Life* 69 The Spiny Tanrec (*Ericulus spinosus*) is considerably smaller than the previously-mentioned species [*Centetes ecaudatus*]. **1900** *Westm. Gaz.* 8 Sept. 8/2 Two curious little creatures,..called Tenrecs.., have just been added to the Zoo.

‖**tansu** ('tansu). [Jap.] A Japanese chest of drawers.

1886 E. S. MORSE *Japanese Homes & their Surroundings* iv. 196 The *tansu*—a chest of drawers not unlike our bureau—is often placed within the closet. **1936** K. NOHARA *True Face of Japan* x. 141 The *tansu*, or chest, consists of two, three, or at the most four drawers above each other, which fit exactly into the wall recesses. **1958** M. JOYA *Things Japanese* III. 82 There are unpainted *tansu* or chests, tables, trays and boxes. **1970** P. ZELVER *Honey Bunch* (1971) iv. 16 There was a good modern couch, a Japanese tansu, the art nouveau desk. **1977** *South China Morning Post* (Hong Kong) 15 Apr. 31/7 Happy Joss has just received a new shipment of tansu, Imari, hibachi and fabrics from Japan.

tansy ('tænzɪ). Forms: 5 **tanesey**, 5–8 **tansie**, 5–9 **tansey**, 6 **-sye, -say, taunsey**, 7–8 **tanzy, -zey**, 5– **tansy**. [a. OF. *tanesie* (13th c.), *tanoisie*, *tenasie*, mod.F. *tanaisie*, aphetic form of *athanasie* 'the hearbe Tansie' (Cotgr.), ad. med.L. *athanasia* tansy, a. Gr. ἀθανασία immortality. Cf. also It. *atanási* 'Tansie or siluerwort' (Florio 1611), *atanásia* the herb tansy (Baretti 1824), Pg. *atanasia* or *athanasia*, the herb tansy. Hatz.-Darm. mention also a med.L. *tanasia*, but without reference. But apart from this it seems clear that OF. *tanesie* was aphetic for *atanesie*, the name prob. referring to the long persistence of the flowers: cf. quot. 1597; also EVERLASTING and F. *immortelle*.

Med.L. had also the name *Tanacētum* (now the botanical generic name) with the variants *tanesetum*, *tansetum*, *tanicetum*. *Tanezatum* and *athanacetum* (*c* 1250) are also cited by Burgess. These seem to show that *athanacetum* and *tanesetum* were latinized formations from OF. *tanesie*, although the force of the suffix is not clear.]

1. An erect herbaceous plant, *Tanacetum vulgare*, N.O. *Compositæ*, tribe *Corymbiferæ*, growing about two feet high, with deeply cut and divided leaves, and terminal corymbs of yellow rayless button-like flowers; all parts of the plant have a strong aromatic scent and bitter taste.

Formerly much used in medicine as a stomachic, and in cookery. ***curled tansy***, a variety with curled leaves, is used, like parsley, for garnishing dishes.

[*c* **1265** *Names of Plants* in Wr.-Wülcker 556/17 *Tanesetum*, [AFr.] *tanesie*, [Eng.] helde.] *c* **1420** *Liber Cocorum* (1862) 50 Þen grynde tansy þo iuse owte wrynge, To blynde with þo egges with owte lesynge. *c* **1425** tr. *Arderne's Surgery* (E.E.T.S.) 74 Porcelane, bursa pastoris, rede rose, tanesey, wormode, horsmynt. **14..** *Nom.* in Wr.-Wülcker 712/33 *Hoc tansetum*, tansaye. *c* **1450** *Alphita* 16/1 *Atanasia*..tanacetum idem. Hanc utuntur Salerniani et Hispanni similiter, tansie. **1538** TURNER *Libellus*, *Athanasia* que grece tagetes, latine tanacetum, anglice dicitur Tansey. **1549** *Compl. Scot.* vi. 67, I sau tansay, that is gude to purge the neiris. **1597** GERARDE *Herbal* II. cxcix. 526 Tansie..in Latine *Tanacetum* and *Athanasia*, as though it were immortall; because the floures do not speedily wither. **1599** A. M. tr. *Gabelhouer's Bk. Physicke* 124/1 Take the herbe Tansy. **1688** HOLME *Armoury* II. 89/1 Curled Tansy, the leaves are..somewhat crumpled together. **1743** *Lond. & Country Brew.* II. (ed. 2) 101 Tanzy..or any other bitter Herbs. **1770** *Phil. Trans.* LX. 10, I observed quantities of juniper and tanzey. **1785** MARTYN *Rousseau's Bot.* xxvi. (1794) 385 Of the first section, with discoid flowers, you have the Tansy. **1838** T. THOMSON *Chem. Org. Bodies* 478 Oil of tansey..is extracted from the leaves and flowers of the *tanacetum vulgare*, or common tansey... It has the peculiar flavour of tansey. **1885** RUSKIN *Præterita* I. iii. 103, I passed my days much as the thistles and tansy did.

2. a. Applied to other plants, esp. the Silverweed or Goose-grass, *Potentilla anserina*, often distinguished as ***wild tansy*** and ***dog's*** or ***goose tansy***; also locally to Yarrow, *Achillea Millefolium*, and Ragwort, *Senecio Jacobæa* (Britten and Holl.).

[*c* **1440** *Promp. Parv.* 486/2 Tanze, herbe (*K.*, *P.* tansy), *tanasetum domesticum, quia tanazetum silvestre dicitur* gosys gresse, *vel* cameroche.] *c* **1530** *Pol., Rel. & L. Poems* (1866) 36 Take wylde tansey, and grynde yt, and make yt neshe, & ley it therto, and it wyl bryng it owght. **1605** TIMME *Quersit.* III. 181 Infused in water of silverweed, called wilde tansey. **1671** SALMON *Syn. Med.* III. xxii. 391 Argentina, Ἀθανασία ὑλόεσσα, wilde-Tansie, stops all Fluxes whatsoever. **1707** MORTIMER *Husb.* (1721) I. 312 Goose-grass or Wild-tansie is a Weed that strong Clays are very subject to. **1860** MAYNE *Expos. Lex.*, *Tansy, Wild*, a common name for the *Potentilla anserina*, or silver-weed.

b. With distinctive additions: **Cape tansy**, *Athanasia capitata* var. *glabrata*; **maudlin tansy**, *Achillea Ageratum*; **shrubby tansy**, *Tanacetum suffruticosum*; **white tansy**, (in Lyte) *Achillea nobilis* of Southern Europe; erroneously applied to other plants.

c **1711** PETIVER *Gazophyl.* ix. Tab. 81 Box-leaved *Cape Tansey... Leaves pale green, and thick set round the Stalk. **1668** WILKINS *Real Char.* II. iv. 84 *Ageratum*. *Maudlin Tansy. **1855** DUNGLISON *Dict. Med.* (ed. 12), M[audlin] Tansey, *Achillea ageratum*. **1578** LYTE *Dodoens* I. x. 17 There be two sortes of Tansie. The one great and yellow, the other small and white... *Tanacetum minus*, *White Tansie..The second groweth in some places of Italie; in this countrey ye shall not finde it but in the gardens of certayne Herboristes. **1688** R. HOLME *Armoury* II. 72/1 The White Tansie, or Agrimony..is a short shrub of no height.

3. a. A pudding, omelet, or the like, flavoured with juice of tansy: see also 5. *arch.* or *dial.*

Said to have been eaten at Easter in memory of the 'bitter herbs' of the Passover.

c **1450** *Two Cookery-bks.* 86 Tansey. Take faire Tansey, and grinde it in a morter; And take eyren, yolkes and white, And drawe hem thorgh a streynour, and streyne also þe Iuse of þe Tansey..; and medle the egges and the Iuse togidre [etc.]. **1513** *Bk. Keruynge* A vj b, A tansye fryed, & other bake metes. *c* **1530** *Caroll* in *Anglia* XII. 588 At Easter commeth alleluya With butter cheese and a tansay. **1561** HOLLYBUSH *Hom. Apoth.* 18 Let him take Neppe that cattes delite in..and make a taunsey thereof. *a* **1601** ? MARSTON *Pasquil & Kath.* I. 154 There's but two Lambs,..three tartes, and foure tansies, for supper. **1621** FLETCHER *Pilgrim* III. vi, They [eggs] shall be all addle, And make an admirable tanzey for the devil. **1634–5** BRERETON *Trav.* (Chetham Soc.) 69 A dainty tansy of gooseberries. **1652** CULPEPPER *Eng. Physic.* 17 A Tansie or Caudle made with eggs and the juyce thereof while it is young, putting to it some Sugar and Rose-water. **1666** PEPYS *Diary* 20 Apr., And there spent an houre or two with pleasure with her, and eat a tansy. **1748** MRS. SARAH HARRISON *Housekpr.'s Pocket-Bk.* iii. (ed. 4) 11 Trotters, To be served up as a Tanzey. **1754–6** *Connoisseur* No. 48 (1767) II. 95 Mince-pie..is as essential to Christmas, as..tansy to Easter. **1787** BEST *Angling* (ed. 2) 60 If you can catch enough of them they make an excellent tansy, their heads and tails being cut off; and fried in eggs. **1837** DISRAELI *Venetia* I. iv, A Florentine tourte, or tansy.

b. A merrymaking or festive gathering; a village feast held on Shrove Tuesday. *dial.* See *Eng. Dial. Dict.*

†**4.** Phrase. *like a tansy*: properly, fittingly, perfectly; perfect. *Obs.* [Origin unascertained.]

1611 BEAUM. & FL. *King & No K.* v. i, To have a Leg broken, or a Shoulder out, with being turn'd o' th' Stones like a Tansie. **1694** MOTTEUX *Rabelais* IV. xxii, That's well said,..now this is something like a Tanzy [orig. *C'est bien dit et advisé*]. **1738** SWIFT *Pol. Conversat.* I. 89 *Miss.* Look, Lady Answerall, is it not well mended? *Lady Ans.* Ay, this is something like a tanzy. **1759** STERNE *Tr. Shandy* II. vi, I would work..like a horse, and make fortifications for you something like a tansy.

5. *attrib.* and *Comb.*, as ***tansy flower, leaf, tea***; ***tansy-leaved*** adj.; **tansy-cake, tansy-pudding**, culinary preparations appropriate to Easter; **tansy-faced** *a.*, having a yellow complexion; **tansy mustard**: see quot.; **tansy oil**, the essential oil of tansy.

c **1420** *Liber Cocorum* (1862) 50 For a *tansy cake. Breke egges in bassyn..þen grynde tansy [etc.]. **1725** BOURNE *Antiq. Vulg.* xxiv. 198 Recreations and Diversions on Easter Holy Days,..playing at Hand-Ball for a Tanzy-Cake. **1777** BRAND *Pop. Antiq.* 253 The winning a Tanzy Cake at the Game of Hand-Ball, depends chiefly upon Swiftness of Foot. **1894** O. HESLOP *Northumb. Gloss.*, *Tansy-cake*, a girdle-cake flavoured with tansy. **1624** MIDDLETON *Game at Chess* v. iii, A sun-burnt, *tansy-fac'd belov'd. **1905** *Daily Chron.* 18 Oct. 4/5 A pond, lying deep among *tansy flowers. **1822** *Hortus Anglicus* II. 181 *S*[*isymbrium*] *Tanacetifolium*, *Tansey leaved Wild Rocket. **1882** *Garden* 12 Aug. 145/3 The Tansy-leaved Thorn. **1856** A. GRAY *Man. Bot.* (1860) 36 *S*[*isymbrium*] *canescens*,..*Tansy Mustard. **1894** MUIR & MORLEY *Watts' Dict. Chem.* IV. 638/1 *Tansy Oil, the essential oil obtained by distillation of the tansy contains 1 p.c. of a terpene $C_{10}H_{16}$, 26 p.c. of an alcohol $C_{10}H_{18}O$, and 70 p.c. of tanacetyl hydride $C_{10}H_{16}O$. **1769** MRS. RAFFALD *Eng. Housekpr.* (1778) 177 A *Tansey Pudding of ground Rice. **1771** H. WALPOLE *Let.* 5 Aug., There are three or four very high hills,..exactly in the shape of a tansy pudding. **1908** *Daily Chron.* 18 Apr. 7/5 Chester still clings to its Tansy pudding, symbolical of the bitter herb commanded at the paschal feast. **1893–4** R. O. HESLOP *Northumberland Words* II. 718 **Tansy-tea*, an infusion of the herb. **1902** *Spectator* 12 Apr. 546/1 Patent pills and soothing syrups have taken the place of calamint and tansy tea. **1965** M. THOMAS *Grannies' Remedies* 26 *Hysterics*... Strong tansy tea, taken cold and in small quantities, is good.

tant, var. TAINT *sb.* (C. 3); obs. f. TAUNT.

tant, tanta, varr. TANTE 2.

tan'tadlin, tan'toblin. *slang* or *dial.* Also 7 **tantaublin**, 7–9 **-ablin**, 9 **-ablet**; **-addling**, 20– **-af(f)lin.**

1. A tart or round piece of pastry. Now *dial.*

1630 J. TAYLOR (Water P.) *Gt. Eater Kent* Wks. I. 146/1 Pancake, or Fritter,..Mackeroone, Kickshaw, or Tantablin. *a* **1825** FORBY *Voc. E. Anglia*, *Tantablet*, a sort of tart, in which the fruit is not covered by a crust, but fancifully tricked and flourished, with slender shreds of pastry. **1876** T. M. BOUND *Hereford. & Shropsh. Provinc.* (E.D.D.), *Tantadlin*, an apple dumpling made in circular form. **1905** in *Eng. Dial. Dict.* VI. 29/1 (S. Not.) She made cakes an' tantaflin sorts o' things. A bit o' that beef for me; a don't care for non o' yer tarts an' tantaflins. **1911** D. H. LAWRENCE *White Peacock* iii. 38 I'm sure you like tantafflins, don't you, Georgie?

†**2.** A lump of excrement, a turd. *Obs.*

1654 GAYTON *Pleas. Notes* III. ii, But our Don could not distinguish a Tantoblin from a Pancake. *Ibid.* IV. iv. 191 Such odour breath'd, and such strong airs were hobling, As use to ascend from a new laid Tantaublin. **1785** GROSE *Dict. Vulg. T.*, *Tantadlin tart*, a sirreverence, human excrement.

3. *attrib.* or *adj.* (?)

1871 COWDEN CLARKE in *Gentl. Mag.* Aug. 336 Horace Walpole (who, by the way, seems to have been a tantaddling old eaves-dropper) has recorded that he [Addison] died drunk with brandy.

tantalate ('tæntələt). *Chem.* [f. TANTAL(UM + -ATE[4].] A salt of tantalic acid.

1849 D. CAMPBELL *Inorg. Chem.* 275 Tantalates of the alkalies, obtained when a solution is evaporated, or by boiling, are acid insoluble salts. **1873** WATTS *Fownes' Chem.* (ed. 11) 495 In all these minerals tantalum exists as a tantalate of iron and manganese.

Tantalean (tæn'teɪliːən), *a.* Also **-ian.** [f. L. *tantale-us* (f. TANTALUS) + -AN.] Of or pertaining to Tantalus; like that of Tantalus; tantalizing.

a **1618** DAVIES *Wittes Pilgr.* Wks. (Grosart) II. 24 Men ouertoild in Common-Wealth affaires Gett much Tantalian wealth by wealthie paines. **1671** H. M. tr. *Erasm. Colloq.* 540 The Lord will take away the Tantalean stone [orig. *Dominus tollet saxum Tantaleum*, i.e. the rock that threatened to fall on Tantalus; hence, the impending punishment for sin]. **1866** J. B. ROSE tr. *Ovid's Met.* 157 Niobe With tongue Tantalian reprobate and free.

tantalian (tæn'teɪlɪən), *a. Min.* [f. TANTAL(UM + -IAN 2.] Of a mineral: having a (small) proportion of a constituent element replaced by tantalum.

1930 W. T. SCHALLER in *Amer. Mineralogist* XV. 572 Tantalum—tantalian. **1959** [see FERRIAN *a.*].

tantalic (tæn'tælɪk), *a.*[1] *Chem.* [f. TANTAL(UM + -IC.] Of or derived from tantalum; in names of chemical compounds in which tantalum is pentavalent, as ***tantalic chloride, fluoride***;

tantalic oxide, anhydride, Ta_2O_5; ***tantalic acid, hydrated tantalic oxide***, $H_2O.Ta_2O_5$.

1842 PARNELL *Chem. Anal.* (1845) 70 After having been heated to redness, alone, tantalic acid is insoluble in all liquids. **1849** D. CAMPBELL *Inorg. Chem.* 273 A compound of this metal [tantalum] with oxygen—namely, tantalic acid—is found in the minerals *tantalite* and *columbite* of Bavaria and North America. **1877** WATTS *Fownes' Chem.* I. 466 Tantalum, in its principal compounds, is quinquivalent, the formula of tantalic chloride being $TaCl_5$..and that of tantalic oxide (which, in combination with bases forms the tantalates) Ta_2O_5.

Tantalic (tæn'tælɪk), *a.*[2] [f. TANTALUS + -IC.] = TANTALEAN; tantalizing.

1882 H. C. MERIVALE *Faucit of B.* I. I. vi. 96 One of those Oxonian breakfasts which..haunt like Tantalic phantoms the egg and bacon of later years. *Ibid.* III. II. xx. 187 He..sketched Tantalic pictures of wealthy homes.

tantaline ('tæntəlaɪn), *a. Ornith.* [f. TANTAL-US 3 + -INE[1].] Of or pertaining to the *Tantalinæ* or wood storks, a sub-family of the *Ciconiidæ* or stork family, typified by the genus TANTALUS.

†**Tantalism** ('tæntəlɪz(ə)m). *Obs. rare.* [f. TANTAL-US + -ISM.] Punishment or torment like that of Tantalus; tantalization.

c **1614** FLETCHER, etc. *Wit sev. Weapons* II. ii, Think on my vengeance, choak up his desires, Then let his banquetings be tantalisme. **1711** ADDISON *Spect.* No. 90 ¶6 A Person lying under the Torments of such a kind of Tantalism, or Platonick Hell. **18..** JOS. QUINCY (Webster, 1828), Is not such a provision like tantalism to this people?

tantalite ('tæntəlaɪt). *Min.* [ad. Ger. and Sw. *tantalit* (named 1802 by Ekeberg), f. TANTALUM (of which it is a source): see -ITE[1].] Native tantalate of iron or ferrous tantalate, found in black lustrous crystals.

1805 NISBET *Dict. Chem.*, Tantalium..constitutes a component part of tantalite and yttrotantalite. **1809** WOLLASTON in *Phil. Trans.* XCIX. 246. **1868** WATTS *Dict. Chem.* V. 666 Ferrous Tantalate, $FeO.Ta_2O_5$..occurs native as tantalite..rarely however quite pure, the iron being generally more or less replaced by manganese, and the tantalum by niobium, tin, and zirconium.

†**tantalium** (tæn'teɪlɪəm). *Chem. Obs.* An early variant of the name TANTALUM (after other names of metals in -IUM).

1805 NISBET *Dict. Chem.*, *Tantalium* is a new metal, which has lately been discovered by Mr. Ekeberg, a Swedish chemist. **1812** SIR H. DAVY *Chem. Philos.* 50. **1839** URE *Dict. Arts* 309 It is also called Tantalum.

tantalization (ˌtæntəlaɪ'zeɪʃən). [f. next + -ATION.] The action of tantalizing or fact of being tantalized.

1654 GAYTON *Pleas. Notes* IV. xv. 253 Poor Rosinant..whose paines and Tantalizations..were more irksome to the beast, than all his other out-ridings. **1821** *Blackw. Mag.* X. 729 The delay and tantalization is horrific. **1849** C. BRONTË *Shirley* I. viii. 225 Rose had no idea of tantalization, or she would have held him awhile in doubt. **1931** H. S. WALPOLE *Judith Paris* IV. 678 From that misery of tantalization he had died. **1983** *Listener* 28 July 32/3 The human frame is just not conditioned to support such stupendous tantalisation.

tantalize ('tæntəlaɪz), *v.* [f. TANTAL-US + -IZE. So mod.F. *tantaliser* (Littré *Suppl.*).]

1. *trans.* To subject to torment like that inflicted on Tantalus; to torment by the sight, show, or promise of a desired thing which is kept out of reach, or removed or withheld when on the point of being grasped. Also *absol.*

1597 TOFTE *Laura* III. xii, Ah doo not still my soule thus Tantalize, But once (through grace) the same imparadize. **1646** TRAPP *Comm. John* vi. 55 Our Richard II. was starved at Pomfret Castle by being tantalized. **1784** KING *Cook's Voy. Pacific Ocean* VI. ix. III. 432, I should otherwise have felt exceedingly tantalized with living under the walls of so great a city, full of objects of novelty, without being able to enter it. **1803** WELLINGTON in *Gurw. Desp.* (1837) II. 461, I was tantalized all the morning with the sight of the enemy's camp, pitched at the distance of twenty miles. **1860** TYNDALL *Glac.* I. iv. 36 The mirage..which so tantalized the French soldiers in Egypt.

b. *fig.* To tease or torture into an artificial form.

1807 CRABBE *Parish Reg.* III. 217 Where those dark shrubs that now grow wild at will, Were clipt in form and tantaliz'd with skill. **1897** *Westm. Gaz.* 25 Mar. 3/2 Chiffon tantalised into a hundred tucks bristling all over the brim and the crown.

†**2.** *intr.* To act Tantalus, to suffer like Tantalus.

1640 FULLER *Joseph's Coat, Comm. 1 Cor.* xi. 20 The poor people in Corinth did see, and smell, what the rich men tasted; Tantalizing all the while, and having their penury doubled by the 'antiperistasis' of other's plenty. **1648** E. SPARKE *Pref. to Shute's Sarah & Hagar* b j b, But, not to tell you of a Banquet, and make you Tantalize. **1673** *Ess. Educ. Gentlewom.* 25 Men are very cruel..; to make any thus to tantalize is a great torment.

Hence **'tantalized** *ppl. a.*, **'tantalizing** *vbl. sb.*

1640 NABBES *Bride* IV. iii, To have seen this wench and not to enjoy her is such a tantalizing to me. **1659** *Gentl. Calling* v. (1696) 64 A sort of Tantalized creatures, not peculiar only to this latter age. **1694** MOTTEUX *Rabelais* v. xvi. (1737) 72 Without any long..Tantalizing in the Case.

tantalizer ('tæntəlaɪzə(r)). [f. prec. + -ER[1].] One who or that which tantalizes.

1792 G. WAKEFIELD *Mem.* (1804) I. i. 16 Alas! this episcopal tantalizer was only gratifying his facetious propensity at the expence of an unsuspecting child of simplicity and innocence. **1844** WARDLAW *Lect. Prov.* (1869) I. 50 The blessed God is no tantalizer. **1889** *Pall Mall G.* 11 July 6/1, I have received a puzzle of the 'Pigs in Clover' kind. .. 'Penning the Lambs' is the name by which the latest variation of the original tantalizer has been christened.

'tantalizing, *ppl. a.* [f. as prec. + -ING[2].] That tantalizes; tormenting by exciting desires which cannot be satisfied.

1657–83 EVELYN *Hist. Relig.* (1850) I. 206 Tantalizing and horrible torments. **1754** MRS. DELANY in *Life & Corr.* (1861) III. 271 It was a tantalizing sort of entertainment to those who love dancing or eating. **1873** HOLLAND *A. Bonnic.* iii, Answering all inquiries concerning it, with the tantalizing statement that it was 'a secret'.

Hence **'tantalizingly** *adv.*; **'tantalizingness**.

1847 WEBSTER, *Tantalizingly*. **1864** *Q. Rev.* CXVI. 151 There are few things in history more tantalisingly obscure. **1889** *Scribner's Mag.* Nov. 555/2 Imagine the tantalizingness of this.

Tantall, obs. anglicized form of TANTALUS.

tantalous ('tæntələs), *a. Chem.* [f. TANTALUM + -OUS.] Applied to compounds containing a greater proportion of tantalum than those called *tantalic*, as ***tantalous oxide***, tantalum dioxide, TaO_2.

1868 WATTS *Dict. Chem.* V. 665 Dioxide of Tantalum, or Tantalous Oxide..is a dark-grey mass, which scratches glass, and acquires metallic lustre by burnishing.

tantalum ('tæntələm). *Chem.* Also TANTALIUM. [f. TANTAL-US, with the ending *-um* (more usually *-ium*), appropriate to metallic elements: cf. *aluminum* and *aluminium*; see quot. 1802.] One of the rare metals, occurring in combination in various rare minerals, and in certain metallic ores; discovered in 1802 by Ekeberg in two minerals, one from Finland and the other from Sweden, which he named tantalite and yttrotantalite. It has been isolated as a solid greyish-white colour and metallic lustre, and has been used for the incandescent filament in electric lamps. Atomic weight 182; symbol Ta. Also *attrib.*, as ***tantalum lamp***, etc.

[Cf. **1802** EKEBERG in *Kongl. Vetenskaps Acad. Handl.* XXIII. 80 (tr.) This new recruit among the metals I call TANTALUM, partly following the custom which favours names from Mythology, partly in allusion to its incapacity, when immersed in acid, to absorb any and be saturated.] **1809** WOLLASTON in *Phil. Trans.* XCIX. 246 The Swedish metal has retained the name of Tantalum given to it by M. Ekeberg. **1810** HENRY *Elem. Chem.* (1826) II. 69 The oxide of tantalum, ignited with charcoal, melts and agglutinates. **1906** *Price Sheet*, Siemens Tantalum Lamps for continuous current... The Tantalum Lamp differs from the ordinary glow lamp in having a filament of the rare metal Tantalum instead of carbon. **1907** *Outlook* 23 Mar. 378/1 Tantalum..is so hard and brittle that no ordinary metallurgical process was able to turn it into wire.

Tantalus ('tæntələs). Also anglicized 4 **Tantale**, **Tantaly**, 7 **Tantall**. [L., a. Gr. Τάνταλος.]

1. Name of a mythical king of Phrygia, son of Zeus and the nymph Pluto, condemned, for revealing the secrets of the gods, to stand in Tartarus up to his chin in water, which constantly receded as he stooped to drink, and with branches of fruit hanging above him which ever fled his grasp; a rock is also said to have hung over him threatening to fall. Hence *allusively*.

c **1369** CHAUCER *Dethe Blaunche* 709, I haue more sorowe than Tantale. **1390** GOWER *Conf.* II. 139 Ther is a peine.. Benethe in helle, which men calle The wofull peine of Tantaly. **1580** LYLY *Euphues* (Arb.) 396 As the Apples that hang at Tantalus nose. **1599** HAKLUYT *Voy.* (1809) 642 He gathereth fruits as they say, out of Tantalus his garden. **1738** GRAY *Propertius* III. 89 The long thirst of Tantalus allay. **1767** B. THORNTON tr. *Plautus, Miser* v. vi, The masters of our age..I call them Gripe-alls, Harpies, Tantalusses. **1835** SIR J. ROSS *Narr. 2nd Voy.* xlvii. 610 It was now long since it had been but the water of Tantalus. **1853** KANE *Grinnell Exp.* xliii. (1856) 397 It seems like our cup of Tantalus: we are never to reach it. **1897** *Westm. Gaz.* 21 July 7/2 It serves as a veritable tantalus to the market.

2. A stand containing usually three cut-glass decanters which, though apparently free, cannot be withdrawn until the grooved bar which engages the stoppers is raised.

1888 G. GROSSMITH *Society Clown* 178, I sent him a small souvenir in the shape of a 'Tantalus'. **1898** *To-Day* 5 Nov. 1/2 He crossed to a recess, and touched the spring of a tantalus. It flew back with a harsh click. **1904** *Strand Mag.* Mar. 246/2 A tantalus containing brandy and whiskey. **1904** *Daily News* 30 Aug. 8 The winner of the sack race received a two-bottle tantalus.

3. *Ornith.* A genus of storks, including *T. ibis* (formerly erroneously identified with *Ibis religiosa* of Egypt); the wood stork or wood ibis.

1824 STEPHENS in Shaw *Gen. Zool.* XII. 1 The Tantali in many respects resemble the Storks. *Ibid.* 2 The White-headed or Ceylonese Tantalus, is the largest of the genus. **1827** R. JAMESON tr. *Cuvier's The. Earth* 313 M. Macé also sent us a tantalus. *Ibid.*, The Tantalus ibis of naturalists. **1896** *List Animals Zool. Soc.* 423 American Tantalus. *Ibid.* 424 African Tantalus..Indian Tantalus.

4. *attrib.* and *Comb.*, as ***tantalus-draught***; ***tantalus-like*** adj.; **tantalus-case**, **-stand** = sense 2; **tantalus-cup**: see quot. 1842; also *fig.*

1601 YARINGTON *Two Lament. Trag.* v. ii. in Bullen *O. Pl.* IV, Yet Tantall-like, he shall but glut his eye Nor feede his body with salubrious fruite. **1842** BRANDE *Dict. Sc.*, etc., *Tantalus's cup*, a philosophical toy which amusingly exhibits the principle of the siphon... The legs of the siphon are concealed by the hollow figure of a man whose chin is on a level with the bend of the siphon; so that the figure stands like Tantalus in the fable,—up to the chin in water, but unable to quench his thirst. *a* **1850** MARG. F. OSSOLI *Life Without & Within* (1860) 30 Tantalus-like, he makes this world a Tartarus. **1884** RIDER HAGGARD *Dawn* vii, No misadventure came to mock them, dashing the Tantalus cup of joy to earth before their eyes. **1899** DOYLE *Duet* viii. (1909) 46/2 The Tantalus spirit-stand stood upon the walnut sideboard. **1905** *Daily Chron.* 11 July 7/1 Presents, including..a tantalus case, a diamond pin, and other trifles. **1908** *Edin. Rev.* July 101 The Tantalus-draught escaped his thirsty lips.

†**'tantamount**, *sb. Obs.* Also 7 **tant amount**, **tantamont**, 8 **tant'amount**. [app. from TANTAMOUNT *v.*; perh. influenced by *amount* sb. beside *amount* vb.] That which amounts to as much, or comes to the same thing; something equivalent (*to*); an equivalent.

1637 HEYLIN *Brief Answ.* 26 You come very neare it, to a tantamont. **1641** PRYNNE *Disc. Prel. Tyr.* II. 216 He pronounced no particular sentence..but he did tant amount or more. **1642** W. PRICE *Serm.* 40 Anger, and rancored envy, which..are a Tantamount to murder. **1646** BP. MAXWELL *Burd. Issach.* 41 Letters of caption (that is..the tant'amount of the Writ *De Excommunicato capiendo*).

tantamount ('tæntəmaʊnt), *a.* Also 7 **tant a mount, tanta-mount, tantamont,** 7–8 **tant'amount**. [app. from the sb. The earlier quots. under a. are scarcely distinguishable from quot. 1641 in the *sb.* Perh. influenced by *paramount*.] As much; that amounts to as much, that comes to the same thing; of the same amount; equivalent.

†**a.** In predicate without construction. *Obs.*

1641 O. ST. JOHN *Argument of Law*, etc. 24 If a man take the broad Seale from one Pattent, and put it to another, here he is counterfeiting, it's tantamount, and therefore Treason. **1686** GOAD *Celest. Bodies* I. xv. 80 Conjunction, Opposition, and Quadrate go for Tant-amount in the Meteorological Part. **1769** BURKE *Corr.* (1844) I. 169 Provided instructions (or thanks, which are tantamount but more respectful,) should be the mode proposed. **1826** SOUTHEY *Vind. Eccl. Angl.* 224 You..avoid the word, and speak of the Real Presence, as if the terms were tantamount.

†**b.** Const. *as*, *with*. *Obs.*

1644 BP. MAXWELL *Prerog. Chr. Kings* 10 Howsoever their tenets by deductions and consequences are tant'amount as theirs. **1644** J. GOODWIN *Innoc. & Truth Triumph.* (1645) 11, I utterly renounce the consequence, conceiving it to be tantamount with an absolute mistake. **1684** T. BURNET *Th. Earth* I. 256 For this is tantamount with the former. *a* **1692** POLLEXFEN *Disc. Trade* (1697) 57 Tant a mount, as if carried from us in Money.

c. Const. *to*. The current use.

1652 HEYLIN *Cosmogr.* Introd. 7 That saying of Berosus will prove tantamount to a Text of Scripture. **1659** —— *Certamen Epist.* 389 They are tantamount to a plain acknowledgement. *a* **1692** POLLEXFEN *Disc. Trade* (1697) 93 They..laid such Impositions on our Woolen Goods, as was tant a mount to a Prohibition. **1777** J. LOVELL in Sparks *Corr. Amer. Rev.* (1853) I. 411 Is not this..tantamount to a disavowal of the first treaty? **1874** CARPENTER *Ment. Phys.* I. i. §18 Is not this tantamount to saying that they go on by a force of their own?

d. attributively. *rare.*

1692 BP. PATRICK *Answ. Touchstone* 17 Giving us express Words, and not words Tantamount. **1798** WASHINGTON *Let. Writ.* 1893 XIV. 29 The President; to whom I have expressed tantamount sentiments in more concise terms. **1868** ROGERS *Pol. Econ.* i. (1876) 3 A tantamount service should be given in exchange for them.

†**'tantamount,** *v. Obs.* Also 7 **tant amount, tant-amount, tant'amount**. [a. AF. *tant amunter*, or perh. (in 17th c.) ad. It. *tanto montare* to amount to as much.

Cf. **1292** *Year-bk. Trin.* 20 *Edw. I* (Rolls) 31 Tant amunte qe Adam neyt pas plus procheyn heyr. **1303** *Year-bk. Mich.* 31 *Edw. I* 335 Herle dist..qe tant amunte qil ne entra pas dans soun baroun.]

1. *intr.* To amount to as much, to come to the same thing; to be or become equivalent. Const. *to* or *unto* (something).

1628 COKE *On Litt.* I. i. §1. 10 They doe tant amount to a feoffment or grant. *Ibid.* 391 It ought to be pardoned specially, or by words which tant amount. **1642** JER. TAYLOR *Episc.* ix. (1647) 36 Yet this will not tant'-amount to an immediate Divine institution for Deacons. **1659** FULLER *App. Inj. Innoc.* III. 7 His not denying tant-amounteth to the affirming of the matter. **1699** SALMON *Bate's Dispens.* (1713) a vij, Those Things..which may tantamount to more than an hundred times its Value. **1716** M. DAVIES *Athen. Brit.* II. 211 Tant-amounting, in a more reform'd Perfection, to the different Religious Orders.

2. *trans.* To amount or come up to (something); to equal.

1659 T. PECKE *Parnassi Puerp.* 132 Account Hercules Labours; they Twelve tantamount. **1683** *Vind. Case relating to Green-Wax-Fines* 65 Your peaceable Subjects..whose indearment in that Case will tant-amount the Profits falling short.

Hence †'**tantamounting** *ppl. a.* (*obs. rare*⁻⁰); whence †'**tanta,mountingly** *adv.*, 'equivalently, in effect' (Davies).

1655 FULLER *Ch. Hist.* II. ii. §28 Did it not deserve the Stab of Excommunication, for any dissenting from her practice, tantamountingly to give her the Lie?

tan-tan ('tæntæn). [In quot. 1653 a. obs. F. *tantan* 'the bell that hangs about the necke of a cow' (Cotgr.): in earlier F. also *tentan, tenten, -tent*; in quot. 1893 purely echoic.] Name for a bell; also applied to the sound of a kettle-drum.

1653 URQUHART *Rabelais* I. xvii, They would serve very well for tingling Tantans and ringing Campanels. **1893** J. HOWLAND in *Mission. Herald* (Boston) Aug. 341 The droning sound of.. a rude kind of flute, and the monotonous tan-tan of a drum.

tantany, obs. form of TANTONY.

tantara ('tæntərə, tæn'tɑːrə), *int.* and *sb.* Also extended **tanta'rara, 'tantara-'rara, 'tantara'tara.** (Cf. TARATANTARA.) [Echoic.]

A. *int.* Imitative of the sound of a flourish blown on a trumpet, or sometimes of a drum.

c **1537** W. GRAY '*Hunt is up*' iv. in W. Chappell *Popular Music* I. 60 The woddes rejoyce at the mery noise Of hey tantara tee ree! **1580** H. GIFFORD *Gilloflowers* (Grosart) 60 Tantara, tantara, the trumpets sound, Which makes our hearte with joy abound. **1589** *Love & Fortune* C iij b, Then, tantara tara, we shall haue good play. **1590** NASHE *Pasquil's Apol.* I. B iv, Tantara, tantara, is he fled indeede? let me sende a Sakar after him. *a* **1600** *Winning of Cades* Chorus, in Percy *Reliques* (1765) II. 224 Dub a dub, dub a dub, thus strike their drums, Tantara, tantara, the Englishman comes. **1644** Z. BOYD *Gard. Zion* in *Zion's Flowers* (1855) App. 12/1 The trump of war doth still Tantara blow. **1680** OTWAY *Caius Marius* III. ii, Tantarara go the Trumpets. **1846** A. BECKETT *Comic Nursery Tales* 35.

B. *sb.* A fanfare, or flourish of trumpets; hence, any similar sound.

1584 *Reg. Stationers' Co.* 19 July (Arb.) II. 434 [License to print a ballad entitled] The saylers newe tantara. **1605** SYLVESTER *Du Bartas* II. iii. III. *Law* 1009 A Heav'nly Trump, a shrill Tantara blowes. **1641** EARL MONM. tr. *Biondi's Civil Warres* III. 118 There should want instruments to outdoe the Tantaraes of the enemies contemptible Campe. **1750–51** MRS. DELANY in *Life & Corr.* (1861) Ser. I. III. 17, I heard a tantararara at the door, and in walked my Mrs. Hamilton. **1843** LEVER *J. Hinton* lv, Amid a cheer.. and a tantarara from the trumpets.

attrib. **1800** WORDSWORTH *Andrew Jones* i, I wish the press-gang or the drum With its tantara sound would come And sweep him from the village!

tantarum, var. TANTRUM.

tantaublin: see TANTADLIN.

‖**tant bien que mal** (tɑ̃ bjɛ̃ kə mal), *adv. phr.* [Fr., lit. 'as well as badly'.] With indifferent success; moderately well, after a fashion.

1765 LD. CHESTERFIELD *Let.* (1774) II. 490 They amuse me, *tant bien que mal*, for an hour or two every morning. **1843** THACKERAY *Irish Sk.-Bk.* II. v. 97 Sketching, *tant bien que mal*, the bridge and the trees.. the writer became an object of no small attention. **1890** W. JAMES *Princ. Psychol.* II. xxvi. 494 We explain the mystery *tant bien que mal* by our evolutionary theories. **1939** *Scrutiny* VIII. 42 Thus his fleshly desires are satisfied, *tant bien que mal*.

‖**tante** (tɑ̃t, 'tantə). Also **Tante. 1.** [Fr., Ger.: cf. AUNT.] An aunt; also, an older woman who stands in a close relationship. Freq. prefixed to a proper name or as a form of address.

1815 F. BURNEY *Let.* 13–18 May (1980) VIII. 129 'My tante' made me a long agitated visit. **1929** E. M. BRENT-DYER *Rivals of Chalet School* i. 18 It was a smiling small face .. that was raised to 'Tante Marguérite's' when Mrs Russell drew her close for a kiss. **1932** G. HEYER *Devil's Cub* i. 15 Aunt Fanny has already warned Tante against your nobody. **1935** Z. N. HURSTON *Mules & Men* II. vi. 287 Ah don't have five nickels, Tante Celestine, but Als'll send a boy to get them. **1941** M. TREADGOLD *We couldn't leave Dinah* viii. 130 I lived in Nuremberg.. Grandmother and Tante Anna and Tante Frieda were very good to me. **1943** H. T. KANE *Bayous Louisiana* viii. 166 A nonc and tante.. seem far closer than the usual American uncle and aunt. **1964** S. BELLOW *Herzog* 146 Come here, little Moses, and sit on your old *tante's* knee. **1981** B. DE BREFFNY *My First Naked Lady* III. 147 Anna's mother, tante Rachel, was Turkish.

2. *S. Afr.* With pronunc. ('tantə). Also **Tant** (usu. preceding a proper name which begins with a vowel), **tanta.** [Afrikaans, from Du.] = sense 1 above. Also more widely, a term of respect for any elderly woman. Cf. TANNIE.

1845 S. DENNISON *Let.* 12 Apr. in D. R. Edgecombe *Lett. Hannah Dennison* (1968) 205 Pray give my love to Miss Gush and Mrs G and remember me kindly to your good Tant. **1871** H. H. DUGMORE *Reminisc. Albany Settler* (1958) iii. 33 Powers of persuasion had to be employed with oude Tante Nieuwkerk. **1872** *Cape Monthly Mag.* Sept. 230 And then, does it not sometimes guard the slumbers and share the dreams of our beloved 'tantas'? **1883** [see OOM]. **1900** H. BLORE *Imperial Light Horseman* 162 If a Boer were to be presented at Court he'd offer to shake hands with Queen Victoria, and address her as 'Tante'. All women to whom one wishes to pay respect are called 'Tante'. **1923** O. SCHREINER *Thoughts on S. Afr.* vii. 260 Oom and Tante, I will whisper to you a secret! **1937** C. R. PRANCE *Tante Rebella's Saga* 63 Each homestead on a circuit has its own special call.. so that every Tante on the line knows.. if.. someone has something to say to Tant' Emmerentia. **1950** *Cape Times Mag.* 5 Aug. 3/3 Tanta Theodora thought that her kettle.. was not as dazzling as it might be. **1969** *Personality* 5 June, Always there is the contrast between past and present.. the austere black dress of the old tante and the bright miniwear of a visiting granddaughter. **1974** *Panorama* Apr. 21 Imagine the surprise of old Tant Alida Prinsloo at finding the contents of her voorhuis (living room) described.

tante: see TAUNT, ATAUNT 1.

tanten: see TANTON.

†**tanterueale.** The name of some bird.

1575 E. HAKE *Newes Powles Churchyarde* D iij b, Stent, Stockard, Stampine, Tanterueale, and Wigeon of the best.

tanteuxenite (tæn'tjuːksɪnaɪt). *Min.* [f. TANT(ALUM + EUXENITE.] A titanotantalate of yttrium, $Y(Ta, Ti)_2O_6$, found as brownish or black, tabular or prismatic, orthorhombic crystals.

1928 E. S. SIMPSON in *Jrnl. R. Soc. W. Austral.* XIV. 45 Whilst normal euxenite.. is a titanoniobate of yttrium, the mineral here described differs from it in being essentially a titanotantalate of yttrium... A new name being required for the species, Tanteuxenite is suggested. **1970** *Neues Jahrb. für Mineral.: Abhandl.* CXII. 131 Tanteuxenite has been found in rough flat prisms in the alluvials of Liha, together with columbite, euxenite and uranium microlite. **1974** [see STRUVERITE 2].

‖**tanti** ('tæntaɪ). [L. *tantī* 'of so much (value)', gen. of *tantum*, neut. of *tantus* so much.] Of so much value, worth so much; worth while. Formerly also as an exclamation of contempt or depreciation: So much *for*...!

1590 MARLOWE *Edw. II*, I. i, *Tanti*; I'll fawn first on the wind That glanceth at my lips, and flieth away. **1633** J. FISHER *Fuimus Troes* III. vii. F iij, No kingly menace or censorious frowne Doe I regard. Tanti for all your power! **1639** T. LECHFORD *Note-Bk.* (1885) 89 If the State & the Elders thinke that the matters I treate on are not tanti or that they are just occasion of Disturbance. *a* **1640** DAY *Parl. Bees* Prol., That slights your errant or his art that penn'd it, Cry *Tanti*: bid him kisse his Muse and mend it. **1757** WARBURTON *Let. to Garrick* 25 Jan., in *Garrick's Corr.* (1831) I. 78 Is it *tanti* to kill yourself, in order to leave a vast deal of money to your heirs? **1888** *Athenæum* 29 Sept. 415/2 Was it quite *tanti* to write a fresh small monograph so soon after Mr. Froude's 'Bunyan'.

‖**tantième** (tɑ̃tjɛm). *rare.* [Fr., f. *tant* so much + *-ième*, ending of Fr. ordinal numerals.] A percentage or share, esp. of profits, royalties, etc.

1897 G. B. SHAW *Let.* 8 Sept. (1965) I. 804 You would simply be robbing the deserving poor if you cut off my tantième. **1911** —— *Lett. to Granville Barker* (1956) 175 Where should I be if I had to live on my tantiemes.

†**tanti'llation.** *Obs. nonce-wd.* [f. L. *tantillum* a trifle, dim. f. *tantus* so great + -ATION (here irregularly used).] A trifling space (of time).

1651 BIGGS *New Disp.* ¶ 237 As if in such a tantillation or moment of time.

†**tan-tin.** *Obs. nonce-wd.* Imitation of the sound of a bell: in quot. advb.

1721 AMHERST *Terræ Fil.* No. 41 (1754) 217, I scarce had slept: at six, tan tin The bell goes: servitor comes in.

tantiny, obs. form of TANTONY.

tantipartite (tæntɪ'pɑːtaɪt), *a. Math.* [f. L. *tantus, -um* as much + *partītus* divided.] Homogeneous and of the first degree in each of a number of sets severally, and so of total degree equal to the number of the sets.

1858 CAYLEY *Math. Papers* II. 517 Such covariants may be termed *tantipartite* covariants. **1860** *Ibid.* IV. 604 A function which is linear in respect to several distinct sets of variables separately is said to be tantipartite... Thus a determinant is a tantipartite function of the lines or of the columns.

'**tantity**, *nonce-wd.*, a rendering of mod.L. *tantitās*, 'the fact of being or having so much', f. L. *tāntus* so much.

[Attributed in some recent dictionaries (from Annandale's Ogilvie, 1882, onward) to James Mill, who used only the Latin (*Elem. Human Mind*, 1829, II. xiv. §2, 50) '*Quantitas*, if it was kept to its original meaning, would still connote *tantitas*; just as *paternity* connotes *filiality*'.]

tantivy ('tæntɪvɪ, tæn'tɪvɪ), *adv., sb., a., int.* Now *rare* or *arch.* Also 7 **tantivie, -vey, -ve,** 8 **-vee, -vi, tantwivy.** [Origin obscure: ? echoic, representing the sound of a horse's feet.]

†**A.** *adv.* At full gallop; swiftly; headlong.

1641 BROME *Jov. Crew* IV. i, Up at five a' Clock in the morning.. And Tantivy all the country over, where Hunting, Hawking, or any Sport is to be made. **1648** *Fraction in the Assembly* 7 Till her Tongue travel'd tantivie, and more then a Canterbury pace. **1690** *Pagan Prince* xxi. 58 (*heading*) How he rode Tantivy to Papimania. **1705** HICKERINGILL *Priest-Cr.* II. A ij b, (Like so many Asses) to let Hypocrisy bestride them,.. and ride them—Tantivee. **1785** GROSE *Dict. Vulg. Tongue* s.v., Away they went tantwivy, away they went full speed. **1823** SCOTT *Peveril* xxxiii, There are those amongst us who ride tantivy to Rome, and have already made out half the journey.

B. *sb.* **1.** (from the adverb.) A rapid gallop; a ride at this pace. Also *transf.* and *fig.*

a **1658** CLEVELAND *Reply Parlt.-Officer* Wks. (1687) 93, I expected to hear from you in the Language of.. the Prodigal Son, and not in such a Tantivy of Language. **1680** V. ALSOP *Mischief Imposit.* xi. 94 Jogging on their own pace, neither the high-trot nor the Tantivey. **1721** CIBBER *Refusal* IV, Ah! poor Soul! piteous bad! All upon the Tantivy again! **1854** THOREAU *Walden* iv. 125 The Tantivy of wild pigeons, flying by twos and threes athwart my view.. gives a voice to the air.

2. A nickname given to the post-Restoration High-Churchmen and Tories, esp. in the reigns of Charles II and James II.

This arose 1680–81, when a caricature was published in which a number of High Church clergymen were represented as mounted upon the Church of England and 'riding tantivy' to Rome, behind the Duke of York. Cf. **1681** *Trial of S. Colledge* 25 *Dugdale.* And there is one Picture that I have not shewed yet... *Jefferies.* There are some Churchmen; what are they a doing? *Dugdale.* They are a parcel of Tantivy men riding to Rome, and here's the Duke of York, half Man, half Devil, trumpeting before them. *Ibid.* 59 *Mr. Charlett.* It was the pictures of the Tantivies and the Towzer [Roger L'Estrange], and he told me they were made by Colledge, he was a very ingenious man. *a* **1734** NORTH *Exam.* I. ii. §130 About Half a Dozen of the Tantivies were mounted upon the Church of England, booted and spurred, riding it, like an old Hack, Tantivy to Rome.

1680–81 G. HICKES *Spirit of Popery* 23 The Clergy.. called them Priests, and Bishops, which in these days would pass for Episcopal tantivies. **1681** LUTTRELL *Brief Rel.* (1857) I. 124 The former are called by the latter, tories, tantivies, Yorkists, high flown church men, &c. **1706** PHILLIPS (ed. 6), *Tantivy*... Also a Nick-name given by the Dissenters to a Worldly-minded Church-man, that bestirs himself for Preferment. **1707** HEARNE *Collect.* 24 Feb. (O.H.S.) I. 336 Hei! day! What in the High-Rope! a high-Flyer and a Tantivi! **1730** SWIFT *Vind. Ld. Carteret* 27 Favouring none but High-Church, High-flyers,.. Tip-top-gallon-men, Jacobites, Tantivyes, Anti-Hanoverians [etc.]. **1841** MACAULAY *Ess., Comic Dramatists* (1887) 613 Collier.. was a Tory of the highest sort, such as in the cant of his age was called a Tantivy. **1849** —— *Hist. Eng.* ii. I. 256.

3. *erron.* applied to a blast or flourish on a horn.

1785 GROSE *Dict. Vulg. Tongue* s.v., Tantwivy was the sound of the hunting horn in full cry, or that of a post horn. **1834** MEDWIN *Angler in Wales* II. 97 A schoolboy put an end to all the Childe Harolding by a tantivy on a bugle.

C. *adj.* ? orig., in ***tantivy men*** and the like, attrib. use of B. 1; afterwards often of B. 2.

1681 T. FLATMAN *Heraclitus Ridens* No. 7 (1713) I. 42 In favour of the Tory and Tantivy Party. **1682** MRS. BEHN *City Heiress* 30 Perverted with Ill Customs, Tantivie-Opinions, and Court-Notions. **1682** *New News fr. Bedlam* 26 Whereas you say it was a high Presbyterian Trot, I rather believe it was a Tantivy Gallop. **1691** *Andros Tracts* II. 246 Had King Rehoboam kept his Tantivy Doctrine of Passive Obedience and Non Resistance to himself,.. the poor People had been his Servants for ever. **1715** *State Quacks* 21 High Tantivee Scaramouches make Choice of a vast Heap of Epithets as unintelligible.. as impertinent. **1826** SCOTT *Woodst.* xx, Master Wildrake is one of the old school—one of the tantivy boys. **1884** *Q. Rev.* July 32 Birmingham itself.. to become as great a stronghold of 'tantivy' politics as it was in the days when it rabbled Priestley.

D. *int.* An imitation of the sound of galloping or scudding feet; later (*erron.*) of the sound of a horn.

1697 VANBRUGH *Æsop* II. i, *Æsop*.. But (like some of our friends) they found 'Twas safer much to scour. *Rog.* Tantive! Tantive! Tantive! **1719** D'URFEY *Pills* (1872) II. 188 Tantivee, tivee, tivee, tivee, High and Low. Hark, hark how the merry merry Horn does blow. **1821** *Sporting Mag.* VIII. 156 Tantivy! tantivy! the hunting-horn blew.

†**tantivy,** *v. Obs. rare.* [f. prec.]

1. *intr.* To ride full tilt; to hurry away.

1681 T. FLATMAN *Heraclitus Ridens* No. 29 (1713) I. 186 You will Tantivy then out of Town. **1796** MME. D'ARBLAY *Camilla* III. viii, Pray where are they gone, tantivying?

2. *trans.* ? To call 'tantivy'; to 'give it him' for calling one 'tantivy'.

1681 T. FLATMAN *Heraclitus Ridens* No. 34 (1713) I. 218 Never a word said to them for Torying, Tantivying and Masquerading his Majesty's most loyal and dutiful Subjects. **1711** SWIFT *Jrnl. to Stella* 10 Oct., I'll 'tantivy' him with a vengeance.

†**tantivyism.** *Obs.* [f. as prec. + -ISM.] The practice or principles of tantivies: see TANTIVY *sb.* 2.

c **1680** HICKERINGILL *Hist. Whiggism* II. Wks. 1716 I. 100 He was afterwards made Bishop of Chichester, and then Bishop of Norwich, just as Mr. Mountague leapt, and perhaps upon the same rise and advantage of the ground, Tantiviisme. **1681** T. FLATMAN *Heraclitus Ridens* No. 7 (1713) I. 40 A Church of England Man maintaining the necessity of the words *As by Law now Establish'd*, which you know is Tantivyism and Toryism in the highest degree. *Ibid.* No. 20 I. 135 To profess sincere Loyalty to his Majesty's Person and Government, to give him humble Thanks for his Gracious Promises in his Declaration.. is now become perfect Toryism, Tantivyism, and *tantum non* Abhorrism.

[**tantling**, in Johnson (whence in subsequent dictionaries), a suggested alteration of TANLING in Shaks. *Cymb.* IV. iv. 29.]

‖**tant mieux** (tɑ̃ mjø). [Fr.] So much the better. Cf. TANT PIS.

1754 LD. CHESTERFIELD *Let.* 8 Mar. (1774) II. 354, I really believe [he] will be your friend upon my account; if you can afterwards make him yours, upon your own, *tant mieux*. **1791** H. WALPOLE *Let.* 26 May (1944) XI. 272, I am rich in letters from you... You tell me mine entertain you; *tant mieux*; it is my wish, but my wonder. **1830** M. EDGEWORTH *Let.* 8 Dec. (1971) 444 He.. promised to do all he can for him... If that should be while I am here—tant mieux. **1876** C. M. YONGE *Three Brides* I. xii. 188 'She seems absolutely repellent.' '*Tant mieux*,' muttered Raymond. **1929** [see next]. **1972** M. KAYE *Lively Game of Death* (1974) xiii. 74 If your boss can pin his death on somebody, *tant mieux*.

‖**tant ne quant**, *adv. phr. Obs. rare.* Also 4 **taunt ne caunt.** [OF. (*ne*) *tant ne quant.*] In no wise, not at all.

13.. *S. Eng. Leg.* (MS. Bodl. 779) in Herrig's *Archiv* LXXXII. 341/256 He ne tornyd one his þouȝt noþer taunt ne caunt. **1390** GOWER *Conf.* I. 241 Mi goode Sone, as of Supplant Thee thar noght drede tant ne quant.

†**'tanto,** *sb. Obs. rare.* [app. erroneous form and use of Sp. *tanteo* computation, calculation, number of counters for marking a game: perh. *tantoes* is mispr. for *tanteos.*] A counter used in gaming.

1646 EARL MONM. tr. *Biondi's Civil Warres* IX. 196 Honours are the Alchimy of Princes, which like Gamesters Tantoes, are worth as much, as they are made to be worth.

‖**tanto** ('tanto), *adv. Mus.* [It.:—L. *tantum* so much.] So, so much: as ***allegro non tanto***, fast, but not too much so.

1876 STAINER & BARRETT *Dict. Mus. Terms.*

tantoblin: see TANTADLIN.

†**tanton.** *Obs.* [Short for *Saint Anthon*: cf. T 7, and next.] In ***tanton man***: an inmate of a hospital, or the like, dedicated to Saint Anthony.

1515 *Test. Ebor.* (Surtees) V. 65 To every Tanten man ther dwellyng iiij d., to pray for my sowll.

tantony ('tæntənɪ), *sb.* Also 7 **-any**, 8 **-iny**. [f. T 7 + ANTHONY.] A shortened form of *St. Anthony*, chiefly used *attrib.* in reference to the attributes with which the saint was represented (cf. Mrs. Jamieson *Sacred & Legendary Art* (1848) II. 367–379), as ***tantony crutch, tantony pouch.*** *spec.* **b.** (more fully ***tantony bell***) a hand-bell; a small church bell: see quots. **c.** (more fully ***tantony pig***) [St. Anthony being the patron of swine-herds, and represented as accompanied by a pig], the smallest pig of a litter; also *fig.* said of one who very closely or obsequiously follows another: cf. context of quot. 1598, and quot. 1662 s.v. ANTHONY.

a. 1594 LYLY *Moth. Bomb.* II i, The dudgen dagger, by which hanges his tantonie pouch.

b. 1567 *Gude & Godlie B.* (S.T.S.) 175 The Paip He had to sell the Tantonie bell And Pardonis thairin was. **1854** MISS BAKER *Northampt. Gloss.*, *Tantony*, the small bell over the church-porch, or between the chancel and the nave: the term is also applied to any small hand-bell. 'Ring the tantony' is evidently a corruption of St. Anthony, the emblem of that saint being a bell at his tau-staff, or round the neck of his accompanying pig. **1872** ELLACOMBE *Ch. Bells Devon*, etc. ix. 497. **1904** in *Eng. Dial. Dict.* (Hunts.), *Tantony*, the name given to a bell which is rung at the entrance gate of the grounds at Kimbolton Castle to give notice of the arrival of visitors. [See *N. & Q.* 8 Feb. 1851, 105/1; 14 June 484/1.]

c. [**1598** STOW *Surv. Lond.* (1603) 185 Whereupon was raysed a prouerbe, such a one will follow such a one, and whine as it were an Anthonie pig.] **1659** GAUDEN *Tears of Ch.* 595 Some are such Cossets and Tantanies that they congratulate their Oppressors and flatter their Destroyers. **1738** SWIFT *Pol. Conversat.* 76 She made me follow her last Week through all the Shops like a Tantiny Pig. **1765** BICKERSTAFFE *Love in Village* I. ix, To see you dangling after me every where, like a tantony pig. **1891** BESANT *St. Katherine's by the Tower* I. 148 They run the same way—like Tantony pigs.

Hence †**'tantony, 'tantany** *v.*, to follow constantly or closely like a tantony pig.

1675 CROWNE *Country Wit* v, Do not follow and tantany us, Mr. Ramble, for, I declare positively, thou shalt never have my daughter.

‖**tant pis** (tɑ̃ pi). Also **tant-pis**. [Fr.] So much the worse. Cf. TANT MIEUX.

[**1768** STERNE *Sentimental Journey* I. 92 *Tant pis* and *tant mieux* being two of the great hinges in French conversation, a stranger would do well to set himself right in the use of them.] **1782** H. WALPOLE *Let.* 25 Mar. (1955) XXIX. 207 The new cabinet are to be Lord Thurlow, Chancellor, (*tant pis*), [etc.]. **1855** A. THACKERAY *Jrnl.* 10 June in H. Ritchie *Lett. A. T. Ritchie* (1924) v. 68 But tant-pis, when I'm older I hope I shall do it better. **1929** A. HUXLEY *Let.* 24 Nov. (1969) 319 If you happen to find people constituted like yourself, tant mieux. If you find them differently constituted, tant pis. **1979** N. SLATER *Falcon* ix. 160 If Hudson wouldn't play ball when the crunch came, then—*tant pis*. Too bad.

‖**'Tantra.** [Skr. *tantra* loom, warp, hence groundwork, principle, system, doctrine, f. *tan* to stretch, extend.] One of a class of Hindu religious works in Sanskrit, of comparatively recent date, chiefly of magical and mystical nature; also, of a class of Buddhist works of similar character.

1799 *Asiatic Researches* V. 53 The Tantras form a branch of literature highly esteemed, though at present much neglected. *Ibid.* 62, I am informed, that the Tantras collectively are noticed in very ancient compositions. **1901** *Mission. Rec. U.F. Ch. Scotl.* Sept. 411/2 The Tantras, the sacred books of the Shakti worshippers.

Hence **'Tantrism**, the doctrine or principles of the Tantras; **'Tantrist**, an adherent of tantrism.

1877 Tantrism [see SAKTA]. **1882** OGILVIE (Annandale), Tantrism. **1891** tr. *De La Saussaye's Hist. Sc. Relig.* lxxv. 622 Tantrism..is common to Buddhist and Hindu communities. **1891** *Cent. Dict.*, Tantrist.

'Tantric, *a.* Also **tantric, tantrik.** [f. TANTRA + -IC.] Of or pertaining to the Tantras; characteristic of Tantrism. In Western use, also *loosely* denoting the association of spiritual and erotic practices. Occas. as *sb.* (in form *Tantrik*), (*a*) a practitioner of Tantrism; (*b*) a Tantra.

1905 *Q. Rev.* July 201 The Buddhist worship of these deities is undoubtedly due to Tantric influence. **1920** WEBSTER, Tantrik. **1927** A. HUXLEY *Proper Studies* 181 The Tantric reformation introduced worship of goddesses, together with a rich collection of magical and erotic rites. **1937** M. COVARRUBIAS *Island of Bali* (1972) vii. 174 It was Erlangga who instituted Javanese as the official language of Bali. Tantric black magic seems to have played an important part in Erlangga's time. **1954** W. NOYCE *South Col* iv. 61 Erotic paintings of tantric gods and goddesses adorn the walls. **1956** A. HUXLEY *Adonis & Alphabet* 59 The Tantriks of northern India and Tibet. **1959** *Times Lit. Suppl.* 20 Feb. 96/2 It contains elements..which belong to the Tantric Buddhism of India. **1961** A. HUXLEY *Let.* 8 Jan. (1969) 902 Pure perceptual receptivity is the basis, incidentally, of many Tantrik exercises. **1966** L. COHEN *Beautiful Losers* III. 241 An entire cult of Tantric lore perfectionists turned excocentric in their second chance at compassion. **1969** *Cultural News from India* Nov. 16 But his oils showed an innate understanding of Tantric motifs as well as the..use of material within an arbitrarily fixed boundary. **1977** *Time Out* 28 Jan.–3 Feb. 65/2 (Advt.), Student of energy release, seeks tantric adept, female. **1977** *It* May 17/1 The Vak.. develops in the course of its manifestation into the seed-sounds of the Tantriks. **1980** *Dædalus* Spring 103 Repressed Hindus rejoice in myths of extreme forms of..erotic Tantric orgiasticism.

Tantricism ('tæntrɪkɪz(ə)m). [f. prec. + -ISM.] = TANTRISM; also *spec.* Tantric yoga.

1959 *Times Lit. Suppl.* 20 Feb. 96/2 The secret of Tantricism lies in the control of nervous centres. **1969** *Newslet. Tibet Soc. U.K.* June 2 Gyudto and Gyudmed, the Upper and Lower Colleges of Tantricism, in its reorganised form.

tantrum ('tæntrəm). *colloq.* Also 8–9 **tantarum**. [Origin unascertained.

(In Wallis's *Room for the Cobbler of Gloucester* (1668) 4 *tantrum* appears as a Welshman's mispronunciation of *anthem*, but apparently has no connexion with this word.)]

An outburst or display of petulance or ill-temper; a fit of passion. Freq. in *pl.* Now often *spec.* a fit of bad temper in a young child.

1714 E. VERNEY *Let.* 30 Oct. in M. M. Verney *Eighteenth Cent. Memoirs* (1930) II. xxi. 18 Our lady has had some of her tanterums as Vapors comeing out etc. **1748** FOOTE *Knights* II. Wks. 1799 I. 84 None of your fleers!..Your tantrums!—You are grown too headstrong and robust for me. **1754** SHEBBEARE *Matrimony* (1766) I. 122 Where did the Wench get these Tantarums into her Head? **1776** MRS. DELANY in *Life & Corr.* Ser. II. (1862) II. 206 Treating him with some contempt when he is in his tantrums. **1824** W. IRVING *T. Trav.* I. 217 An author, who was always in a tantrum if interrupted. **1837** DISRAELI *Venetia* I. vi, He goes into his tantarums at the abbey. **1884** *Times* 12 Mar. 3 The defendant told him not to get into a tantrum. **1927** A. CONAN DOYLE *Case-Bk. Sherlock Holmes* xi. 283 Sir Robert was in one of his tantrums. **1966** M. FRAYN *Russian Interpreter* xxii. 103 'Let's put all these books away in the case again,' she said coaxingly, as if Proctor-Gould had thrown his toys about in a tantrum. **1979** N. GORDIMER *Burger's Daughter* 329 If we'd still been children, I might have been throwing stones at him in a tantrum.

Tantum ergo ('tæntəm 'ɜːgəʊ). [First two words of the penultimate stanza, which begins 'Tantum ergo sacramentum Veneremur cernui' (Therefore we, before him bending, This great sacrament revere), of the hymn of St. Thomas Aquinas 'Pange lingua gloriosi Corporis mysterium'.] The last two stanzas of this hymn sung at Benediction; also, a setting of these.

1709 A. BUSBY in B. Jarrett *Eng. Dominicans* (1921) ix. 188 Tantum ergo was sung by the Cannons accompanied with Musick wich fild our hearts with joy. **1897** ADDIS & ARNOLD *Cath. Dict.* (ed. 5) 84/1 Next the Te Deum..or some other canticle..is sung, followed by the 'Tantum Ergo'. **1905** J. H. HARTING *Hist. Sardinian Chapel* 38 A *Tantum Ergo* was composed by Alessandro De Angioli for the Sardinian Chapel. **1922** JOYCE *Ulysses* 355 Then they sang the second verse of the *Tantum ergo*. **1976** N. ROBERTS *Face of France* vii. 82 The procession to the Altar of Repose, when the *Tantum Ergo* comes rolling out in Gregorian and sonorous Latin.

†**'tantuple,** *a. Obs.* [f. L. *tantus* so great, after QUADRUPLE, etc.] That is so many times another quantity; equimultiple.

1656 HOBBES *Six Lessons* iii. Wks. 1845 VII. 240 The antecedents are of their consequents totuple or tantuple, that is, equimultiple.

TANU ('tɑːnuː). Also **Tanu.** [Acronym f. the initial letters of *T*anganyika *A*frican *N*ational *U*nion.] The name of a former political party in Tanganyika (now Tanzania).

1957 *Times* 15 Feb. 7/2 Speeches made recently by the president of the T.A.N.U. **1957** J. NYERERE *Let.* in *Times* 18 Sept. 9/4 For the last three years T.A.N.U. has been trying to get from the administering authority a statement that it intends to develop Tanganyika to become a democratic African state. **1959** *New Statesman* 12 Sept. 300/1 TANU now has 800,000 members, each of whom pays two shillings entrance fee and six shillings a year. **1967** *Economist* 18 Feb. 613/1 The constitution of the Tanganyika African National Union (Tanu) lays down [etc.]. **1971** *Standard* (Dar es Salaam) 7 Apr. 1/4 He asked all members of the corporation to study well the new Tanu Guidelines during their discussions. **1977** *Jrnl. Commonwealth & Compar. Politics* XV. 247 TANU and the Afro-Shirazi Party of Zanzibar officially merged in February 1977 to form Chama cha Mapinduzi (the Revolutionary Party of Tanzania), abbreviated to CCM. **1978** S. NAIPAUL *North of South* II. iii. 163 The peasants here displayed little or no understanding of TANU policies.

tan-vat ('tænvæt). Also 6–8 **-fat.** [f. TAN *v.* or *sb.* + VAT.] The receptacle, a tub, cistern, pit, or the like, containing the 'ooze' in which the hides are laid in tanning.

1592 GREENE *Upst. Courtier* Wks. (Grosart) XI. 261 Howe comes this to passe? by your tanne-fats for sooth. **1615** E. S. *Britain's Buss* in Arb. *Garner* III. 630 Every net must be tanned in a tan-fat. **1655** FULLER *Ch. Hist.* VI. ii. §1. **1779** E. BEATTY in J. L. Hardenbergh *Jrnl.* (1879) 65 There was a tanfat farm with several Hides at a tannery which the soldiers got. **1828** WEBSTER, Tan-vat. **1895** S. R. HOLE *Little Tour Amer.* 86 Grant tried that [tanning], but found no gold in the tan-vat.

tany, tanya, var. TAWNY, TANIA.

tanyan, var. TANGHAN, Tibetan horse.

†**'tanystome.** *Ent. Obs.* [a. F. *tanystome*, f. Gr. τανύ-ειν to stretch + στόμα mouth.] A fly of Latreille's second family of Diptera, *Tanystomata*, including the gad-flies and their allies. Hence †**ta'nystomate**, †**ta'nystomine**, †**ta'nystomous** *adjs. Obs.*

1860 MAYNE *Expos. Lex.*, *Tanystomus*..long-mouthed; applied to a Family..of the *Diptera*: tanystomous.

Tanzanian (tænzə'niːən), *sb.* and *a.* [f. *Tanzania* (see below) + -AN, -IAN.]

A. *sb.* A native or inhabitant of Tanzania, an E. African state formed in 1964 by the union of the republics of Tanganyika and Zanzibar. **B.** *adj.* Of or pertaining to Tanzania.

1965 *Economist* 23 Jan. 332/3 Mr Nyerere..apparently decided he must at any cost assert Tanzanian independence from this supposed American intrigue. *Ibid.* 6 Feb. 519/1 Whatever in the world, Tanzanians are asking, have they done. **1970** *Drum* (E. African ed.) Feb. 22/3 A gradual increase in standards of health, education and housing..will mean in the end healthier, wealthier, better-fed and happier Tanzanians. **1973** *Listener* 6 Sept. 301/1 The Chinese-built Freedom Railways reached the Zambian border, its Tanzanian section having been completed. **1978** S. NAIPAUL *North of South* II. ii. 158, I watched the Swedish girl weighing the babies... 'We cannot get well-off and educated Tanzanians to come and help us out.' *Ibid.* vi. 248 The Immigration Officer (Tanzanian) poked a grinning head through the doorway.

tanzanite ('tænzənaɪt). *Min.* [f. as prec. + -ITE[1].] A highly pleochroic violet-blue gemstone that is a variety of zoisite in which some of the aluminium is replaced by vanadium.

1968 *Wall St. Jrnl.* 14 Oct. 4/1 Tiffany & Co. disclosed discovery of a rare gemstone that the firm's vice president, Henry B. Platt, has named tanzanite. The gem, discovered last year in Africa's Tanzania, has the blue coloring and relative transparency of a sapphire. **1975** *Nat. Geographic* Apr. 490/1, I take a dusty detour to see the mining of glorious gems of transparent purplish blue. Tiffany's has named them tanzanites.

tanzey, tanzie, tanzy, variants of TANSY.

‖**tanzib** (tæn'ziːb). Also 8 **tanjeeb**, 9 **tanjib**. [Persian f. *tan* body + *zīb* adornment.] A fine kind of Indian muslin made chiefly in Oudh.

1727–41 CHAMBERS *Cycl.* s.v. *Muslin*, There are various kinds of muslins brought from the East-Indies; chiefly Bengall; betelles, tarnatans,..tanjeebs. **1864** J. S. BUCKLE *Manuf. Compend.* p. xi, 49 inches wide Tanjib, 38 yards long 14 × 10—i.e., 14 picks or threads in ¼ inch of the warp, and 10 picks or threads in ¼ inch of the weft. **1880** BIRDWOOD *Ind. Arts* II. 85 A tanzib or tanjib muslin.

‖**tao** (taʊ, d-). Also **Dao, Tao, taou, tau.** [Chinese *dào* (Wade-Giles *tao*) way, path, right way (of life), reason.]

1. a. In Taoism, an absolute entity which is the source of the universe; the way in which this absolute entity functions.

1736 R. BROOKES tr. *Du Halde's Gen. Hist. China* III. 30 Among the Sentences [of Lao Kiun] there is one that is often repeated..: Tao, says he, or Reason, hath produced one, one hath produced two, two have produced three, and three have produced all things. **1797** *Encycl. Brit.* IV. 676/1 *Tao* is one by nature: the first begot the second; two produced the third; the three created all things. **1868** J. CHALMERS *Lau-Tsze's Specul. Metaph.* p. xii, Existence is..said to be produced from nonexistence, and *Tau* is the union of the two. **1904** W. G. OLD tr. *Laotze's Simple Way* iv. 30 Tao is without limitation; its depth is the source of whatever is. **1934** A. D. WALEY *Way & its Power* 50 *Tao* is the way that those must walk who would 'achieve without doing'. But *tao* is not only a means, a doctrine, a principle. It is the ultimate reality in which all attributes are united. **1950** A. HUXLEY *Themes & Variations* 172 In China and Japan mountains were taken more seriously. The aspiring artist was advised ..to contemplate them lovingly until he could understand the mode of their being and feel within them the workings of the immanent and transcendent Tao. **1957** J. KEROUAC *On Road* (1958) 251 He was reaching his Tao decisions in the simplest direct way. **1963** D. C. LAU *Lao Tzu* 23 In the *Lao tzu*, the *tao* is no longer 'the way of something', but a completely independent entity, and replaces heaven in all its functions. But the *tao* is also the way followed by the inanimate universe as well as by man. **1971** F. MANN *Acupuncture* (ed. 2) iv. 47 The root of the way of life (Dao or Tao), of birth and change is Qi. **1980** M. H. KINGSTON

China Men (1981) 96 Bak Goong thought he understood the Tao, which is everywhere and in everything, even in our excrement.

b. = TAOISM, TAOIST *a.*

1745 tr. J. F. Gemelli Careri in A. & J. Churchill *Coll. Voy. & Trav.* (ed. 3) IV. II. iv. 313/2 In some of these *Pagods*, religious men and women live in community to serve them; of which there are two sorts, the one of the sect of *Foe*, and the other of that of *Tao*. **1747** *New Gen. Coll. Voy.* IV. I. v. 214/1 The Sectaries say..that the great Doctrine of *Fo* and *Tau* swallows up all in nothing. **1831** *Canton Miscellany* I. 28 Hwuy-tsung, an Emperor of the Sung Dynasty, was fond of being a Priest of the Taou Sect. **1959** *Listener* 26 Feb. 388/2 Tao and Zen. **1980** *Jrnl. R. Soc. Arts* Feb. 137/2 The garden was seen as the most powerful metaphysical symbol for Tao, Shinto and Zen.

2. In Confucianism and in extended uses, the way to be followed, the right conduct; doctrine or method.

1934 A. D. WALEY *Way & its Power* 30 Each school of philosophy had its *tao*, its doctrine of the way in which life should be ordered. **1943** C. S. LEWIS *Abolition of Man* iii. 30 In the older systems both the kind of man the teachers wished to produce and their motives for producing him were prescribed by the *Tao*—a norm to which the teachers themselves were subject and from which they claimed no liberty to depart. **1966** F. SCHURMANN *Ideology & Organization in Communist China* i. 50 The Chinese Communists speak of the forces of world history which are universal and cosmic. Though this belief clashes with traditional Confucian beliefs of *tao* (something akin to 'natural law'), it bears certain similarities to the Taoist belief in Heaven as a real force. **1970** H. G. CREEL *What is Taoism?* i. 2 Tao at first meant 'road' or 'path'. From this it developed the sense of a method, and of a course of conduct. As a philosophical term it appears first in the Confucian *Analects*. For the Confucians *tao* is the way, the method, of right conduct for the individual and for the state. **1972** F. FITZGERALD *Fire in Lake* i. 11 In analyzing these disasters the emperor blamed them on his deviation from Tao, the traditional way, which was at once the most moral and the most scientific course. **1980** *Dædalus* Spring 34 A Tao of Physics in which the details of modern macrophysics and microphysics are matched to those of the mystical tradition.

Taoiseach ('tiːʃəx, -ax). [a. Ir., lit. 'chief, leader'.] The Prime Minister of the Republic of Ireland.

1938 *New Irish Constitution: Citizen's Man.* 17 Dail Eireann is dissolved by the President on the advice of the Taoiseach. **1941** G. B. SHAW *Matter with Ireland* (1962) 285 The Irish Taoiseach (Premier), Mr de Valera, made no move. *a* **1966** 'M. NA GOPALEEN' *Best of Myles* (1968) 128 You pick up the receiver and say 'Who? The Taoiseach? Oh very well. Put him on.' **1973** *Irish Times* 2 Mar. 9/1 Whoever is going to be Taoiseach is going to have to sweat and work every minute of every day. **1981** *Listener* 1 Jan. 4/2 Mrs Thatcher..permits herself to follow very much the kind of approach the Taoiseach, Mr Charles Haughey, was hoping for.

Taoism ('tɑːəʊɪz(ə)m, 'daʊɪz(ə)m). Also **taou-, tau-, tavism, Daoism.** [f. TAO + -ISM.] A system of religion, founded upon the doctrine of the ancient Chinese philosopher Laotsze (or Lao-tzŭ), born 604 B.C., set forth in the work *Tao tê king*, 'Book of reason and virtue', attributed to him. It ranks with Confucianism and Buddhism as one of the three religions of China.

1838 GÜTZLAFF & REED *China Opened* II. xv. 209 (*heading*) Taouism. **1839** *Chinese Repository* VII. 511 We have all this time been working through the mazes of Taouism..merely to give a better explanation of the notions of this sect. **1858** MAX MÜLLER *Chips* (1880) I. ii. 51 The religious system of Laotse, or the Tao-ism of China. **1903** *Rev. Missions* Mar. 539 Taoism, an older religion than Buddhism—dating indeed from before the teachings of Confucius—was so purely beautiful as delivered by Lao-tsze, its great teacher. **1948** *Mind* LVII. 535 Dr. Fung..shows how Buddhist philosophy..influenced both Confucianism and Daoism. **1981** *Times* 22 June 6/8 It is not the Vatican which bothers China's leaders most in religious matters—but Daoism (formerly known as Taoism), the only religion truly native to China. *Ibid.* 11 Nov. 6/7 The ancient Chinese religion of Daoism.

Taoist ('tɑːəʊɪst, 'daʊɪst), *sb.* (*a.*) Also **taou-, Dao-.** [f. as prec. + -IST.] **a.** An adherent of Taoism.

1838 GÜTZLAFF & REED *China Opened* II. xv. 209 Such are the better description of Taouists in China. **1839** *Chinese Repository* VII. 520 The Taouists are by no means behind in referring to an abode of lasting bliss, which does however still exist on earth. **1863** ALCOCK *Capital Tycoon* I. 392 [To] feel, or affect, great contempt for any creed but that of Taouists. **1885** *Athenæum* 17 Oct. 500/3 It [the 'Taou-tih-king'] may be considered, therefore, as the Bible of the Taouists. **1971** *Ink* 12 June 8/3 There were many non strict Daoist farmers there who could have been VC. **1981** *Times* 22 June 6/8 Unlike the Buddhists, the Daoists have been granted no licence to continue or revive their practices.

b. *attrib.* or as *adj.* Of or belonging to the Taoists or to Taoism.

1839 MALCOLM *Trav.* II. III. v. 184 Great officers, and even the emperor himself, build and endow Boodhist and Taouist temples. **1882** *Athenæum* 16 Sept. 361/2 With the exception of Laou-tsze, the early Taouist philosophers have found no place in English literature... Though professing to be followers of Laou-tsze, they never perfectly understood him, and perverted his doctrines into childish babblings.

Hence **Tao'istic** *a.*

1856 MEADOWS *Chinese* 440 Representatives of a Buddhistic or Taouistic element that is struggling with the Confucian element to assert for itself a place in the new religion. **1884** *Brit. & For. Evangelical Rev.* Apr. 367 The Taoistic, or Rationalistic system is about as old as Confucianism.

Tao Kuang (daʊ gwæŋ). Also **Daoguang.** The title of the reign of Xuan Zong (Min-Ning), emperor of China 1821–50, used *attrib.* and *absol.* to designate the period of his reign or pottery and porcelain made at this time.

1927 W. B. HONEY *Later Chinese Porcelain* 59 A considerable part of Tao Kuang porcelain was made in revived Yung Chêng patterns. **1951** R. S. JENYNS *Later Chinese Porcelain* ii. 20 A series of 1662 to 1675 wares, often with K'ang Hsi marks, and some marked Shên-tê t'ang, a hallmark which does not occur only on Tao Kuang pieces. **1960** H. HAYWARD *Antique Coll.* 277/1 *Tao Kuang period*, (1821–50). Characteristic Chinese porcelain wares of this reign are those minutely painted in *famille rose*..style, employing low-toned enamels, and *graviata*, coloured grounds. **1973** *Country Life* 7 June 1680/2 A pair of reticulated ruby ground hexagonal vases..famille rose 19⅝ in, Tao Kuang. **1976** SCOTT & KOSKI *Walk-In* (1977) ii. 16 A shabby reproduction, made..in Hong Kong, of a Tao Kuang teapot. **1980** *Catal. Fine Chinese Ceramics* (Sotheby, Hong Kong) 90 Seal mark and period of Daoguang (Tao Kuang).

Taos (taʊs, 'tɑːɒs). The name of a town in New Mexico, used *attrib.* (occas. *absol.*) to designate members of a Pueblo Indian people living there, or the language of this people, a variety of Tiwa.

1844 J. GREGG *Commerce of Prairies* I. 86 A Taos Indian who formed one of the Mexican escort, seeing a gun levelled at his commander, sprang forward and received the ball in his own body, from the effects of which he instantly expired! **1887** *Scribner's Mag.* II. 510 Then the saddle-blanket is laid over his withers, with sometimes a *tilpah*, or parti-colored rug, woven and dyed by the Navajo or Taos Indians. **1939** *Language* XV. 51 The Taos language forms with that of Picurís..the northern branch of Tiwa. *Ibid.*, The old people..speak Taos and Spanish. **1944** B. JOHNSON *As much as I Dare* 287 Adobe walls around the garden and various nooks and vistas were being built by Taos Indian labor. **1964** *Language* XL. 202 He has published an article describing the application of his system to the Taos language and culture. **1973** A. H. WHITEFORD *N. Amer. Indian Arts* 28 Taos and Picuris make only unpainted gold-tan pottery. **1978** *Language* LIV. 233 'About the nearest he ever came to having fun' was making charts of the Taos pronoun. **1978** G. A. SHEEHAN *Running & Being* viii. 111 A Taos Indian chief had once told him that white men were covered with wrinkles because they were crazy.

‖**taotai** ('taʊtaɪ, d-). *Hist.* Also **Taotai, tautai,** etc. [Chinese *dàotái*.] The title given to the Chinese provincial officer responsible for the civil and military affairs of a district, abolished shortly after the establishment of the Republic in 1911.

1747 *New Gen. Coll. Voy.* IV. I. vi. 253 To every District there also belongs a Mandarin, called Tau-ti. **1835** *Chinese Repository* Oct. 279 The class of officers next in rank to these are called taou or taoutae: they are not under the orders of the 'two sze', but of the governor and lieut.-governor, and it is their duty to take part in the 'protection' and 'circuit-supervision' of portions of the province. **1848** S. W. WILLIAMS *Middle Kingdom* I. vii. 345 The gabel and commissariat are mostly under the direction of officers called *tau*, or *tautai*, sometimes termed intendants of circuit, who have other functions in addition. *Ibid.* 346 The *tautai*..are a kind of deputy of the governor-general and lieutenant-governor, residing in the *tau*, or circuits, into which each province is divided. **1895** *Daily News* 19 Jan. 6/6 A number of Chinese guerilla troops recently tried to enter Neuchwang. The taotai of the city closed the gates, and offered an armed resistance to their entry. **1926** *Blackw. Mag.* Nov. 629/1 A mandarin named Liang was sent to the island as Taotai. **1943** J. T. PRATT *War & Politics in China* xii. 193 When the Revolution came to Shanghai the Taoti—the chief Chinese official—requested the consular body to take temporary charge of the court. **1959** P. FLEMING *Siege at Peking* iii. 42 Henceforth Bishops would rank with Governors-General and Governors, Provicaires with Treasurers, Judges and Taotais, and so on down the respective hierarchies.

‖**t'ao t'ieh** (taʊ tjə). Also **taotie, tao-tieh.** [Chinese *tāotiè*.] The name of a mythical monster, or a mask-design showing its face, found esp. on metalware of the Chou period (1122–221 B.C.). Freq. *attrib.*

1915 R. L. HOBSON *Chinese Pottery & Porcelain* II. xvii. 290 This is the face of the t'ao t'ieh (the gluttonous ogre) supposed originally to have represented the demon of the storm. **1933** *Illustr. London News* 9 Dec. (Suppl.) p. i/1 This bell has a *t'ao-t'ieh* design on the upper part. **1958** W. WILLETTS *Chinese Art* I. iii. 161 *T'ao-t'ieh*..is a device in which two confronting zoomorphs in profile form the left and right sides of an animal mask seen in full face. *Ibid.* 162 Karlgren analyses the *t'ao-t'ieh* motive into six different types. **1965** *New Statesman* 20 Aug. 257/1 Eloquent prose passages like René Grousset's dramatic evocation of the *t'ao-t'ieh* on the sides of Chou vessels. **1973** *Genius of China* 47/2 It is notable that the convention of the face painted on this bowl shows no relation to the *t'ao-t'ieh*, an evil-averting monster mask which pervades the later bronze-age art of central China. **1978** *New Archaeol. Finds in China* II. 29 Some broken pieces of the outer coffin remain; they are carved with a *tao-tieh* (ogre-mask) design in the form of an ox head. **1980** *Catal. Fine Chinese Ceramics* (Sotheby, Hong Kong) 80 A further frieze of upright acanthus leaves around the neck.., the shoulders set with moulded *taotie* (*t'ao t'ieh*) mask and ring handles.

‖**taovala** (taʊvɑlə). [Tongan.] In Tonga, a piece of fine matting worn round the waist over a *vala* or Tongan kilt (and without which one is not considered properly dressed).

Traditionally worn by the male (with the exception of the Queen as monarch). It should be torn in several places, to show that the wearer does not set himself above his fellows.

1947 *Pacific Islands Monthly* Sept. 60/3 (*caption*) He wears the 'Taovala' (mat tied with coconut fibre) which is a 'must' with all Tongans who would show respect to their chiefs. **1953** *News Chron.* 2 June 7/1 With him rides a Queen—Queen Salote Tupon of the Tonga Islands. Her ceremonial dress includes a loose blouse and ankle-length skirt, round which is draped a tao-vala—a mat made from brown pandana leaves. **1977** *Daily Tel.* 15 Feb. 17/4 Pretty Tongan girls in white with the Taovala (traditional belts made from tree bark) round their waists kept the Royal party as cool as they could with fans made from the prickly-leaved pandanus tree.

tap (tæp), *sb.*[1] Forms: 1 **tæppa**, 4 **teppe**, 5–7 **tappe**, 7 **tapp**, 5– **tap**. [Com. Teutonic: OE. *tæppa* (wk. masc.) = OLG. **tappo* (MDu., MLG., LG. *tappe*, EFris. *tappe*, *tap*, Du. *tap*, NFris. *tâp*), OHG. *zapfo* (MHG. *zapfe*, Ger. *zapfen*), ON. *tappi* (Sw. *tapp*, Da. *tap*):—OTeut. **tappon-*, orig. a tapering cylindrical stick or peg (cf. *tap-root*).]

1. a. A cylindrical stick, long peg, or stopper, for closing and opening a hole bored in a vessel; hence, a hollow or tubular plug through which liquid may be drawn, having some device for shutting off or governing the flow; used especially in drawing liquor from a cask, or water from a pipe, and for regulating the flow of gas, steam, etc.; a cock, a faucet.

c **1050** in *Techmer's Int. Zeitschr. für allg. Sprachwissensch.* II. 120 Đonne þu win habban wille, þonne do þu mid þinum twam fingrum, swilce þu tæppan of tunnan onteon wille. *Ibid.*, Tæppan teon. **1340** *Ayenb.* 27 Vor hit behoueþ þet zuich wyn yerne by þe teppe ase þer is ine þe tonne. *c* **1440** *Promp. Parv.* 486/2 Tappe, of a vessel, *ductillus, clipsidra*. **1530** PALSGR. 279/1 Tappe or spygote to drawe drinke at, *chantepleure*. **1588** *Marprel. Epist.* (Arb.) 38 Sir Ieffry..tooke such vnkindenes at the alehouse, that he sware he would neuer goe againe into it..the tap had great quietnes and ease therby. **1688** R. HOLME *Armoury* III. xx. (Roxb.) 231 The Cock or Tapp, letting out the hot water. **1768** COOK *Voy. round World* I. ii. (1773) 17 It was impossible..to draw out any of its contents by a tap. **1874** MICKLETHWAITE *Mod. Par. Churches* 185 A few taps only are turned, and all is ready for lighting.

b. *fig.*

c **1386** CHAUCER *Reeve's Prol.* 36 As many a yeer as it is..Syn that my tappe [*v.r.* tap] of lif began to renne. **1599** *Broughton's Let.* xi. 37 This whole tractate of yours,..is but the droppings of other mens taps. **1658** GURNALL *Chr. in Arm.* II. verse 16. viii. (1669) 203/2 Labour to take the advantage of thy present relenting frame,..now the Ordinance hath thawed the Tap. **1907** *Daily Chron.* 18 Apr. 5/6 There was certainly a 'tap on', as the vulgar phrase is, in the market yesterday, and much scrip was thrown out at ½ to ⅝ premium.

c. *on (in) tap*, on draught, ready for immediate consumption or use (*lit.* and *fig.*); also *spec.* in *Stock Exchange* use, applied to securities which are the subject of a large issue. Cf. quot. 1907, sense 1 b. †*to sell by tap* (*Sc. Obs.*), to sell in small quantities, to retail.

1483 *Seill of Caus, Edin.* 2 May (Jam.), That no common cremaris of the toune wse to sell be tap ony hammermans work. **1862** LOWELL *Biglow P.* Ser. II. 54 Who is he that..has eloquence always on tap? **1890** R. L. STEVENSON *Vailima Lett.* (1895) 35 The moon is on tap again. **1891** T. HARDY *Tess* i, There's a pretty brew in tap at the Pure Drop. **1908** [see CONCERTINA *v.*]. **1923** *Westm. Gaz.* 8 Jan. 4/2 It is some time since 'additional' Treasury Bills have been on 'tap' at so low a rate as..1⅞ per cent. **1926** L. R. ROBINSON *Investm. Trust Organization & Managem.* 71 Whether the investment trust should raise its funds by keeping 'on tap' its offerings to the public and 'feeding' them out in response to demand..depends upon a number of factors. **1931** J. GREENHILL in *Westm. Bank Guild Lectures 1930–1* III. 105 We have not seen Bills 'on tap' for some considerable time past. **1935** A. HUXLEY *Let.* 5 June (1969) 396 His own left organizations in France will of course be on tap. **1958** *Times* 2 Oct. 3/3 Anything offered by television is on tap. **1965** J. L. HANSON *Dict. Econ. & Commerce* 371/2 Securities are said to be on 'tap' when they are issued in unlimited quantities (though the amounts permitted to each individual may be restricted) and are available for purchase direct from the issuing authority at any time. **1975** J. F. BURKE *Death Trick* (1976) v. 82 We'll look into those alibis. Meanwhile, I want you both on tap. Understand?

d. *Electr. Engin.* = TAPPING *vbl. sb.*[1] 2 b.

1900 M. A. OUDIN *Standard Polyphase Apparatus & Systems* ix. 173 The secondary of each interchangeable transformer has two taps, giving 50 per cent and 86·7 per cent of the full voltage, so that either transformer can serve as the teaser, or supplementary one, by using the proper terminals. **1947** R. LEE *Electronic Transformers & Circuits* viii. 214 To improve the closeness of voltage control, a variable autotransformer has been developed in which the moving tap is a carbon brush which slides over exposed turns of a winding. **1974** C. C. WOODWARD *Cable Television* vi. 121 A complete new installation..from the tap to the subscriber's television set.

e. *Stock Exch.* A security which is available 'on tap' (see sense 1 c above).

1948 *Economist* 8 July 772/2 £24½m...was perhaps acquired by original conversion of Local Loan or through the tap; but the additional £55m. was presumably bought on the market. **1960** *Ibid.* 8 Oct. 167/2 The issue price is nominal, since no one expected more than a small fraction of Wednesday's issue of £500 million would be taken by the public. The rest goes into the official tap, and the tap price can of course be adjusted as events dictate. **1967** *Ibid.* 4 Feb. 444/1 Supplies of the long tap (Treasury 6¾% 1995/98), issued only last October 28th, had already run out. **1976**

Southern Even. Echo (Southampton) 12 Nov. 24/6 Gilts managed to push forward by $\frac{1}{4}$ to $\frac{3}{8}$ taking the new Treasury 14 per cent. 1982 'tap' up 1/16 to 98 5/16. But the new long 'tap' Treasury $15\frac{3}{4}$ 1996 stays at $97\frac{1}{2}$. **1980** *Times* 15 Jan. 18 It would not surprise them to see the authorities issue another tap at the end of this week.

2. a. A tap-room or tap-house. *colloq.* Also *spec.* at *Eton College*: (†*the*) *Tap*, a place where beer is sold to pupils at Eton.

1725 *New Cant. Dict.* s.v. *Tape*, The Renters of the Tap ..in Newgate. **1771** SMOLLETT *Humph. Cl.* II. 11 June, Rabbit him! the tap will be ruined. **1837** J. D. LANG *N.S. Wales* II. 102 He had been drinking in the Tap over-night. **1857** HUGHES *Tom Brown* I. iv, Guard emerges from the tap, where he prefers breakfasting. **1865** *Etoniana* 23 The 'Tap' and the Christopher had their earlier prototypes. **1917** A. HUXLEY *Let.* 30 Sept. (1969) 134 They were regrettably caught at the time just entering Tap. **1980** *Sunday Times* (Colour Suppl.) 14 Dec. 94/3 On the other days I'm free and I go for a drink to Tap.

b. A pit in which tan-liquor is mixed; = LEACH *sb.*[2] 2. ? *Obs.*

1797 *Encycl. Brit.* (ed. 3) XVIII. 307/1 Strong liquor called ooze or wooze prepared in pits called letches or taps kept for the purpose, by infusing ground bark in water.

3. a. The liquor drawn from a particular tap; a particular species or quality of drink. Also *fig.* a particular strain or kind of anything. *colloq.*

1623 tr. *Favine's Theat. Hon.* I. i. 1 Such a one was called a Gentleman of the first Tappe. **1832** L. HUNT *Redi Bacchus in Tuscany* 75 Those Norwegians and those Laps Have extraordinary taps. **1848** THACKERAY *Van. Fair* xxxiv, I wish my aunt would send down some of this to the governor; it's a precious good tap. **1872** O. W. HOLMES *Poet Breakf.-t.* vi. (1885) 139 Sentiment wasn't his tap. **1902** A. BIRRELL *W. Hazlitt* iv. 55 His [Hazlitt's] 'tap' was too bitter, his stride too long.

b. Short for *tap-cinder*: see 8.

1878 URE *Dict. Arts* IV. 493 Using such purple ore in the ordinary way, as fettling in conjunction with 'tap', pottery mine, etc.

4. *Mech.* A tool used for cutting the thread of an internal screw, consisting of a male screw of hardened steel, grooved lengthways to form cutting edges, and having a square head so that it may be turned by a wrench.

1677 MOXON *Mech. Exerc.* ii. 31 Turn about the tap in the hole, and make grooves and threds in the Nut. **1816** [see *screw nut*: SCREW *sb.*[1] 24]. **1875** *Carpentry & Join.* 81 A tap ..to cut the requisite thread inside the nut. **1884** F. J. BRITTEN *Watch & Clockm.* 232 Taps for watch makers' use are made by running a piece of steel through a screw plate.

5. An object having the shape of a slender tapering cylinder, as an icicle; *esp.* a tap-root.

1658 PHILLIPS, *Isicle*,..a tappe of ice, a drop of water frozen. **1796** C. MARSHALL *Garden.* xix. (1813) 318 The tap of the oak will make its way downward, in a direct line, through the hardest soils. **1857** H. MILLER *Test. Rocks* xi. 497 The central axes of the trees do not elongate downwards into a tap but throw out horizontally on every side a thick net-work of roots.

6. a. A device by means of which a telephone conversation may be listened to secretly by a third party. Cf. TAP *v.*[1] 2 c.

1923 E. WALLACE *Missing Million* xxiii. 181 How did you know where the 'tap' was? **1959** *Washington Post* 26 Oct. A2/1 Law enforcement agencies use the taps even where prohibited by law. **1967** *Times Rev. Industry* Aug. 76/1 Telephones can be tapped so that it is virtually impossible for physical search to locate the tap, and if a searcher came near to it, the tap would automatically destroy itself without trace.

b. The act of listening secretly to a telephone conversation by means of a connection to the wire. Cf. *phone-tap* s.v. PHONE *sb.*[2] 3; *telephone tap* s.v. TELEPHONE *sb.* 3.

1950 *Sun* (Baltimore) 24 Jan. 12/3 The Holmes view has been accepted by the Supreme Court in a series of decisions steadily narrowing the use to which wire-tap material may be put in court. But there is still a shadow-land within which the Justice Department feels safe in authorizing use of the wire tap. **1968** W. GARNER *Deep, Deep Freeze* iii. 35 He'd made a phone tap, a successful tap, and overheard a reference to an agent..who was being sent to England. **1973** B. MURPHY *Business of Spying* viii. 134 As well as being 'bugged', a telephone can be 'tapped'. This permits the recording and/or monitoring of both sides of the conversation. The most basic and easy way to monitor a telephone conversation is to carry out a direct line tap. **1979** *Guardian* 1 Mar. 1/3 There had to be good grounds for suspecting that a tap would be productive.

c. A recording made secretly from a telephone conversation.

1969 L. SANDERS *Anderson Tapes* (1970) xxix. 73 Tape SEC. 25 JUN 68... This is a telephone tap. **1978** S. BRILL *Teamsters* ii. 62 Telephone taps were played on tape recorders in court.

7. *on the tap*, begging, making requests for loans. Cf. TAP *v.*[1] 3. *slang.*

1932 A. GARDNER *Tinker's Kitchen* III. i. 217 Bob the journalist was, like everyone else at the Cross,..out to get what he could...,in plain words 'on the tap'. **1977** P. CARTER *Under Goliath* xii. 61 She was a real moaner and always on the tap, borrowing sugar and milk.

8. *attrib.* and *Comb.*, as, in sense 1, *tap-dropping* (also *taps-droppings*), *-maker*, *-spirits*; in sense 1 e, *tap bill*, *bond*, *issue*, *price*, *rate*, *sale*, *stock*; in sense 2, *tap-boy*, *-man*; also **tap-auger**, an auger for boring tap-holes; **tap-bar**, a testing bar placed in a cementation furnace and withdrawn for inspection during the process (*Cent. Dict.* 1891); **tap-bolt**, a threaded bolt which is screwed into a part, as distinguished from one that penetrates it and receives a nut; **tap-borer**, a tapering instrument for boring bung-holes or tap-holes; **tap-changing** *Electr. Engin.*, the process of changing the connection to a transformer from one tap to another so as to vary the turns ratio and hence control the output voltage under a varying load; so **tap-changer**, an apparatus for accomplishing this; **tap-cinder**, the slag or refuse produced in a puddling furnace; **tap-dressing**, decoration of wells at Whitsuntide, a Derbyshire custom; †**tap-lead**, = *tap-trough*; **tap-plate**, a steel plate having holes, wormed and notched, for cutting external threads, a screw-plate (Knight *Dict. Mech.* 1877); **tap-rivet**, **tap-screw**, = *tap-bolt* (hence **tap-rivet** *v. trans.*, to secure by tap-rivets; **tap-riveting**, the use of tap-rivets); †**tap-shackled** *a.*, 'fettered' by drink, drunk; †**tap-staff**, a staff used to stop the tap-hole of a mash-tub; †**tap-stone**, (?); **tap-tool**, = sense 4; †**tap-tree**, = *tap-staff*; †**tap-trough**, a leaden trough used in brewing; †**tap-waiter**, a waiter in a tap-room or tap-house (*obs. rare*); **tap-water**, water drawn through a tap; *spec.* water supplied by a system of pipes and taps for household use; †**tap-whips**, **tap-whisk**, dialect variants of TAP-HOSE; †**tap-wort**, the dregs of ale or beer; **tap wrench**, a wrench for turning a tap-tool. See also TAP-HOLE, TAP-HOSE, etc.

1688 R. HOLME *Armoury* III. 317/2 (Coopers' Instruments) *Tap Auger. **1957** A. C. L. DAY *Outl. Monetary Econ.* xxxv. 443 The British Exchange Equalization Account started operations with large quantities of sterling assets, which it holds in the form of '*tap' Treasury bills. **1864** WEBSTER, **Tap-bolt*. **1942** *Sun* (Baltimore) 9 May 16/1 (*heading*) About $4,500,000 '*tap' bonds sold here. **1877** KNIGHT *Dict. Mech.*, **Tap-borer*. **1801** G. HANGER *Life* II. 97 A *tap-boy at a public-house. **1931** S. R. ROGET *Dict. Electr. Terms* (ed. 2) 342/2 *Tap changer. **1962** *Newnes Conc. Encycl. Electr. Engin.* 748/2 Where possible, the tap-changer has minimum voltage to earth, and on most high-voltage line transformers it is at the neutral point. **1979** *Railway Gaz. Internat.* Jan. 49/1 As compared with the equivalent..tap-changer loco, maintenance was halved. **1929** W. T. TAYLOR *Electr. Supply Transformer Systems* ii. 21 For station and distribution types of transformers, voltage control is now effected by *tap-changing on load; several satisfactory designs have been produced which enable tap-changing to be carried out directly on tappings from the main transformers. **1962** *Newnes Conc. Encycl. Electr. Engin.* 748/1 Tap-changing may be done when the transformer is out of circuit. **1861** *Lond. Rev.* 16 Feb. 167 In the process of making malleable iron, which is called 'puddling', there is a large quantity of refuse, known as '*tap-cinder'. **1894** *Daily News* 23 Apr. 8/4 Some time ago it was discovered that this tap-cinder contained an amount of phosphorus which rendered it of sufficient service for basic steel-making as to justify the cost of its transmission for that purpose to the continent. **1851** in *N. & Q.* 2nd Ser. IX. 431/1 A great deal of taste and fancy is exhibited in the..'*tap-dressing'. **1860** *Ibid.* 430/2 [He] was collecting [flowers] for the Pilsley 'Well' or 'Tap' dressing. **1892** *Daily News* 22 Sept. 3/1 The Rev. G. S. Tyack's account of the curious custom of well-dressing, or 'tap-dressing', as it is called. **1608** MIDDLETON *Fam. Love* IV. iii, How rank the knave smells of grease and *taps-droppings! **1678** *Quack's Academy* 4 Vials filled with Tap-droppings. **1926** L. R. ROBINSON *Investm. Trust Organization & Managem.* 71 '*Tap issues' are better fitted for a market in which the investor is learning for the first time the advantages of participation in investment trusts. **1973** *Daily Tel.* 3 Feb. 21/1 During the past fortnight, despite the exhaustion of two sizeable tap issues and the successful launching of a new $9\frac{1}{2}$ p.c. long-dated stock, the [gilt-edged] market has lacked impetus. **1429** in Rogers *Agric. & Pr.* III. 550/1 *Vas plumbeum* called *tapled. **1892** *Pall Mall G.* 23 Mar. 6/3 One of his former friends,..a *tap-maker. **1907** *Month* July 7 Not but what priests doctor their stuff and give short measure like any *tap-man. **1958** *Times* 21 June 11/3 The strong demand for Funding Five-and-a-Half per Cent., 1982–84,..enabled the '*tap' price (the price at which Government departments are prepared to sell the stock they took up when the original issue was made) to be raised by 1–16 twice during the day. **1922** *Daily Tel.* 12 June 2/1 New second-hand Treasuries were dealt in at $2\frac{1}{4}$ per cent., the '*tap' rate now being $2\frac{1}{2}$ per cent. **1869** SIR E. J. REED *Shipbuilding* ii. 43 They are each composed of two angle-irons, *tap-riveted or screwed (and not through riveted) to the bottom plating. **1874** THEARLE *Naval Archit.* 79 It is connected to the stem, either by angle-irons on each side, through riveted, and tap riveted to the stem. *Ibid.* 129 In riveting the angle-irons of bilge keels to the bottom plating *tap rivets are used. *Ibid.*, *Tap riveting is employed in securing plates to forgings. **1926** L. R. ROBINSON *Investm. Trust Organization & Managem.* 71 '*Tap' Sales, and occasional flotations. **1958** *Times Rev. Industry* Dec. (London & Cambridge Econ. Bull.) p. x/2 Tap sales have reduced bank liquidity. **1891** *Cent. Dict.*, **Tap-screw*. **1604** J. MORRIS *Commpl.-bk.* (Brit. Mus. Roy. MS. 12 B v) lf. 6 b, A scholler of Cambridge being somewhat *tap-shackled walking in the streete met a blacke bull. *c* **1608** HEALEY *Disc. New World* 82 [He] being truely tapp-shackled, mistooke the window for the dore. **14..** *Voc.* in Wr.-Wülcker 572/13 *Ceruida*, a *tapstaf. **1688** R. HOLME *Armoury* III. 319/2 The Brewers Thorn with the Tap Staff through the middle of it. **1703** J. MORE *Engl. Interest* (ed. 2) 66 After this, you must lift up your Tap-staffe, and let out about a Gallon [from the mash-vat]..and put it up again, stopping your Tap-hole. **1966** *Punch* 9 Nov. 710/3 The Bank will not allow anything like a boom in gilt-edged to develop—and it has *tapstocks of its own to sell. **1980** *Times* 15 Jan. 15 Without tap stocks to deter them, gilts climbed briskly. **1522** *Wills & Inv. N.C.* (Surtees 1835) 106 Also I bequeth to my son John Trollop ..the brewehouse..a brewelede with a mashefatt and a *tap-stone with a boltong arke and the bras pottes called Thornley Pottes. **1874** THEARLE *Naval Archit.* 127 Screwing the rivet into a screw hole previously prepared for it by means of a '*tap tool'. **1483** *Cath. Angl.* 378/1 A *Tap tre, *ceruida, clipcidra*. **1743** R. MAXWELL *Sel. Tr. Soc. Improv. Agric. Scot.* 284 Take out your Cork, or Tap-tree, and have a Tub below to receive the Lee that comes off. **1335** in Riley *Lond. Mem.* (1868) 194, 1 *tappetroghe [of lead]. **1835** DICKENS *Sk. Boz* (1836) 1st Ser. II. 179 You leave your bag and repair to 'The Tap'... The *tap-waiter finds himself much comforted by your brandy-and-water. **1881** TYNDALL *Float. Matter Air* 81 Ice-water, distilled water and *tap-water..deprived of their powers of infection. **1898** P. MANSON *Trop. Diseases* i. 32 Wash in tap water and then in distilled water, dry and mount in zylol balsam. **1743** *Lond. & Country Brew.* IV. (ed. 2) 267 In [a Mash-Tub] fix a Brass Cock of three Quarters of an Inch Bore in a *Tapwhips, or do it by Plug and Basket. **1854** MISS BAKER *Northampt. Gloss.*, *Tap-whisk. **1881** *Leicester. Gloss.*, *Tap-whisk*,..the wicker strainer placed at the back of the tap inside a mash-vat, &c. **1582** BRETON *Toyes Idle Head* Wks. (Grosart) 26/2 A cuppe of small *Tap worte. **1815** J. SMITH *Panorama Sc. & Art* I. 40 The *tap-wrench is simply a lever, with a hole..to admit the rectangular head of the tap, for the purpose of turning it round. **1956** H. TOWNSEND in D. L. Linton *Sheffield* xvi. 299 Sheffield plays a large part in the production of drills and tipped cutters,..bit gauges, tap wrenches, pin vices,..and so on. **1964** S. CRAWFORD *Basic Engin. Processes* i. 26 As its name implies the tap-wrench is required to provide a convenient method of revolving the tap in the drilled hole.

tap (tæp), *sb.*[2] Forms: 4 tap(p)e, 5 tapp, 6– tap. [f. TAP *v.*[2] So OFris. *tap*; cf. F. *tape* slap.]

1. a. A single act of tapping; a light but audible blow or rap; the sound made by such a blow.

13.. *Gaw. & Gr. Knt.* 406 ȝif I þe telle trwly, quen I þe tape haue. *Ibid.* 2357 At þe þrid þou fayled þore, & þer-for þat tappe ta þe. *a* **1466** CHAS. DK. ORLEANS *Poems* (Roxb.) 7 As strokis grete not tippe, nor tapp, do way The rewdisshe child so best lo shall he wynne. *a* **1577** GASCOIGNE *Adv. F. I.* Wks. (Roxb.) I. 463 Much greater is the wrong that rewardeth euill for good, than that which requireth tip for tap. **1597** SHAKS. *2 Hen. IV*, II. i. 206 This is the right Fencing grace (my Lord) tap for tap and so part faire. *c* **1614** FLETCHER, etc. *Wit at Sev. Weapons* III. i, But when a man's sore beaten o' both sides already, Then the least tap in jest goes to the guts on him. **1720** JENYNS *Art Dancing* II. Poems (1761) 21 Let them a while their nimble feet restrain, And with soft taps beat time to ev'ry strain. **1794** MRS. RADCLIFFE *Myst. Udolpho* vii, A gentle tap at the chamber-door roused her. **1862** SALA *Seven Sons* II. vii. 194 The convicts were called off by the tap of a drum. **1877** *Encycl. Brit.* VII. 609/2 Rolling croquet..is made by trailing the mallet after the balls as soon as the stroke or tap is made.

b. **tap-tap**, a repeated tap; a series of taps; also *adv.*

1837 THACKERAY *Ravenswing* ii, Mr. Tressle's man.. ceased his tap-tap upon the coffin. **1840** MARRYAT *Poor Jack* xxiii, The water went tap, tap, tap against the bends. **1905** E. CHANDLER *Unveiling of Lhasa* xii. 212 The tap-tap of the Maxim, like a distant woodpecker, in the valley.

c. = TAP-DANCING.

1944 N. STREATFEILD *Curtain Up* viii. 97 The same sandals do for everything except tap. **1950** BLESH & JANIS *They all played Ragtime* (1958) iii. 57 Chauvin had a fine tenor voice and sang and danced superbly, buck and wing, regular and eccentric tap. **1952** A. LOMAX *Mister Jelly Roll* v. 202 Well, I did my tap numbers in a lot of shows after that. **1972** *Guardian* 13 Dec. 9/1 It was quite bad enough doing tap—all the kids at school used to tease me.

d. *Phonetics.* A single momentary contact between vocal organs in the production of a speech sound; the sound produced by such contact.

1952 [see *one-tap* s.v. ONE *a.* 34 a]. **1954** PEI & GAYNOR *Dict. Linguistics* 214 The Spanish *pero* is pronounced with a *tap r*, but *perro* with a *trill r*. **1964** W. JASSEM in D. Abercrombie et al. *Daniel Jones* 339 The assumption that two 'taps' are sufficient for a sound to be labelled 'rolled'. **1977** *Language* LIII. 861 The individual closures of a trill are much more rapid than the single closure of a tap.

e. In fig. phr. ***a tap on the wrist***, a mild reprimand. Cf. SLAP *sb.*[1] 2 a.

1973 *Black Panther* 20 Oct. 2/1 Forty pages of charges gathered by the Justice Department, and he gets off with a tap on the wrist for income tax evasion. **1974** *Anderson* (S. Carolina) *Independent* 23 Apr. 4A/1 Disrespect for the law and the courts stems from instances.. in which the accused have been found not guilty or have received a mere tap-on-the-wrist sentence when it was obvious that all evidence pointed to guilt.

2. Pl. **taps** (*U.S. Milit.*): a signal sounded on the drum or trumpet, fifteen minutes after the tattoo, at which all lights in the soldiers' quarters are to be extinguished. Sounded also, like *last post* (POST *sb.*[8]) over the grave of a soldier. Also *fig.*, the end.

1824 *H.R. Doc. 18th U.S. Congress 1 Sess.* No. 111. 35 It is his [*sc.* the orderly's] duty..to visit his rooms, at the taps; see that the lights are extinguished; the fires properly secured; the occupants present, and in bed. **1862** *Index* (U.S.) 25 Sept., I well remember how 'at taps' we were wont to huddle together in our narrow quarters, each man's knapsack serving for his pillow. **1869** T. W. HIGGINSON *Army Life* (1870) 34 The mystic curfew which we call 'taps'. **1891** *Cambridge* (Mass.) *Tribune* 10 Jan. 8/5 The customary volleys were fired over the grave, and Bugler Fitzgerald sounded 'taps', the soldier's last sad farewell. **1904** J. A. RIIS *Roosevelt* viii. 199 Taps had been sounded long since. **1917** A. G. EMPEY *Over Top* 258 Then it was taps for me.

3. A piece of leather with which the worn-down heel or sole of a boot is made up and repaired or 'tapped' (*U.S.*); a plate or piece of iron with which the heel is shielded; also, the sole of a shoe (*Eng. dial.*). (Cf. TAP *v.*[2] 3.)

on one's taps, on one's feet; on the move; busy.

1688–*c* **1850** [see HEEL-TAP *sb.* 1]. **1743** J. HEMPSTEAD *Diary* 12 Dec. (1901) 418 Nailed on a pr of Tapps on a pr of New Shoes for adam. **1844** W. BARNES *Poems Rural Life* Gloss., *Tap*, the sole of a shoe. **1855** HALIBURTON *Nat. & Hum. Nat.* II. 332 They have to be on their taps most all the time. **1864** WEBSTER, *Tap*.. the piece of leather fastened upon the bottom of a boot or shoe in tapping it, or in repairing or renewing the sole or heel. **1882** JAGO *Cornw. Gloss.*, *Tap*, the sole of a boot or shoe. Also the iron..'scute' of the heel, 'heel tap'. **1954** J. STEINBECK *Sweet Thursday* 33 Brown calf shoes (heel taps a little run over). **1965** E. TUNIS *Colonial Craftsmen* iv. 107 The thick leather for the tap (sole) soaked all day in water. **1976** *National Observer* (U.S.) 6 Mar. 14/6 Amazing polyurethane taps keep heels perfect for months. Attach in seconds to any heel, and no one can tell you're wearing taps.

4. In negative context: the slightest amount *of work*. Cf. STROKE *sb.*[1] 11 a. *colloq.*

1887 *Lantern* (New Orleans) 22 Jan. 2/2, I understand that Eddie never done a tap of work in his life. **1946** F. SARGESON *That Summer* 185 For several weeks Jack hadn't done a tap of work in the garden. **1952** E. O'NEILL *Moon for Misbegotten* I. 10 He's nothing but a drunken bum who never done a tap of work in his life.

5. *Comb.* **tap-in** *Basketball*, a goal scored by tapping the ball into the basket, usu. when following up an unsuccessful shot; **tap-kick** *Rugby Football*, a light kick given to the ball whereby play is re-started from a penalty and possession retained; also as *v. trans.*; **tap pants** *U.S.*, a type of fashionable ladies' knickers; **tap penalty** *Rugby Football*, a penalty taken with a tap-kick; **tap-piece** = 3; hence **tap-piece** *v.*, to repair with a tap-piece; **tap shoe**, a shoe worn for tap-dancing, having a specially hardened sole or attached metal plates at toe and heel to make a tapping sound.

1948 *Daily Progress* (Charlottesville, Va.) 4 Feb. 9/3 Counting a tap-in one point would help equalize the height advantage, he said, but as in the case of the delayed whistle, what would constitute a tap-in? **1976** *Cumberland & Westmorland Herald* 4 Dec. 12/5 Coward netted a brace with a powerful long-range shot and a tap-in from Martin's cross. **1960** T. MCLEAN *Kings of Rugby* xi. 120 When Hewitt after a tap-kick penalty in the Lions' 25 set off with a tremendous burst of speed..the audience rose to him in wonderment and delight. **1978** *Rugby World* Apr. 6/1 After he had given an indirect free-kick against the French, the Scotland captain, Doug Morgan, dropped a goal direct from hand, without bringing it into play with a tap-kick first. *Ibid.*, Mr. Thomas's explanation was that he had been telling the French why the kick had been awarded and that his back was half-turned when Morgan began the run-up to his kick. 'I assumed Morgan had tap-kicked the ball first,' he said. **1977** Tap pants [see TEDDY 3]. **1982** *Penthouse* July 26, I..have bought pretty tap pants and knickers from various lingerie establishments. **1976** *Sunday Post* (Glasgow) 26 Dec. 36/3 It only took Gala five minutes to score. From a tap penalty Dickson tore a gash in the defence, and Telfer accepted his scoring pass in the corner. **1978** *Rugby World* Apr. 33/1 He ..carries particularly fond memories of the six tries he recorded last season, almost all from tap penalties at close range. **1903** R. WATSON *Closeburn* xiv. 235 Mony a day I hae tappieced and heeled your auld shoon. **1932** *Boot & Shoe Recorder* 20 Feb. 62/3 A four style range of toe, ballet, acrobatic and tap shoes covers the usual store's requirements. **1936** 'ISOLDE' *Tap Dancing Made Easy* 9 You can practise in an ordinary pair of shoes, but much better results can be obtained when wearing proper Tap shoes. **1980** *Daily Tel.* 10 Mar. 12/6 The musical..brings out the best in the most bashful of bathroom singers and puts imaginary tapshoes on confirmed wall-flowers everywhere.

tap, *sb.*[3] [app. short for TAPNET; cf. also TOP *sb.*[3]] A rush-basket (usually containing *c* 28 lbs.) in which figs of an inferior quality are imported. *Comb.* **tap-figs** (colloq. shortened to *taps*), figs of the quality imported in taps.

c **1860** [Recollected in use]. **1909** *Wholesale Grocer's Price-list*, Figs..Layers 40/-..50/-per cwt. Taps, 19/-... Naturals 25/6. **1910** *Produce Mark Rev.* 19 Feb. 155 Figs.. Layer Figs..Pulled figs..Naturals..Comadra, Taps.

‖**tap** (tæp), *sb.*[4] *East Ind.* [a. Pers. *tap* fever, heat; = Skr. *tapa* heat, *tāpa* heat, pain, torment.] Malarial fever.

1882 F. M. CRAWFORD *Mr. Isaacs* xii, Unless I feared the *tap*, the bad kind of fever which infects all the country at the base of the hills.

tap (tæp), *v.*[1] Forms: 1 tæppian, 5–6 tappe, 6 tape, 7–8 tapp, 5– tap; also *Sc.* (in sense 4, 4 b) 5–7 top(pe, 6 talp, 6–7 tope, 7 taip, (topt). [Com. Teutonic: OE. *tæppian*, from *tæppa* TAP *sb.*[1] = MLG., MDu., LG., and Du. *tappen*, MHG., Ger. *zapfen*, ON., Sw. *tappa*, Da. *tappe*, all from the cognate sbs. Cf. F. *taper*, to plug, from OLG.]

I. To open (a cask, reservoir).

1. *trans.* To furnish (a cask, etc.) with a tap or spout, in order to draw the liquor from it.

c **1050** in *Techmer's Int. Zeitschr. für allg. Sprachwissensch.* (1885) II. 125 ʒyf þe ʒedryptes wines lyste, þonne do ðu mid þinum swyþran scytefingre on þine wynstran hand, scytlce þu tæppian wille, and wænd þinne scytefinger adune. **1483** *Cath. Angl.* 378/1 To Tappe, *ceruidare*. **1570** LEVINS *Manip.* 27/22 To Tappe, *fistulum addere*. **1696** PHILLIPS (ed. 5), To *Tapp a Vessel*, to fix a Tapp in the Bung-hole..thereby to draw out the Liquor. **1832** LYTTON *Eugene A.* III. iii, I will tap a barrel on purpose for you. **1880** *Act 43 & 44 Vict.* c. 24 §90 The rectifier must not..tap, open, alter, or change any cask..containing any such spirits.

2. a. To pierce (a vessel, tree, etc.) so as to draw off its liquid contents; to broach; to draw liquid from (any reservoir); *slang*, to draw blood from the nose.

e.g. To bore into (a tree) so that sap may exude; to allow the molten metal to run from (a furnace); to pierce the wall of (a reservoir), to drain (a marsh).

1694 WESTMACOTT *Script. Herb.* 12 It [the Quicken] will yield a liquor, if tapt as we do birch in the spring. **1792** BELKNAP *Hist. New Hampsh.* III. 114 The season for tapping the [maple] trees is in March. **1809** *Nat. Hist.* in *Ann. Reg.* 843/1 The maple tree..the oftener it is tapped the better. **1832** HT. MARTINEAU *Hill & Vall.* iv. 60 He was just going to tap the furnace, i.e. to let out the fused iron. **1840** DICKENS *Barn. Rudge* li, Perhaps, sir, he kicked a county member, perhaps sir he tapped a lord..blood flowed from noses, and perhaps he tapped a lord. *c* **1865** J. WYLDE in *Circ. Sc.* I. 419/2 The tree is 'tapped'; that is, a hole is cut into it.., and the resin exudes. **1868** CARLYLE *Fredk. Gt.* (1872) X. App. 199 What bogs he has tapped and dried, what canals he has dug. **1878** HUXLEY *Physiogr.* 27 The natural reservoir being thus tapped, a spring of water flows out. **1900** G. C. BRODRICK *Mem. & Impr.* 315 The Braemar air..coming across treeless granite mountains which tap the rain-clouds as they sweep over.

b. *spec.* in *Surg.* To pierce the body-wall of (a person) so as to draw off accumulated liquid; to drain (a cavity) of accumulated liquid.

1655 [see TAPPING *vbl. sb.*[1]]. **1709** STEELE *Tatler* No. 62 ¶11, I have ever since my Cure been..dropsical; therefore I presume it would be much better to tap me. **1778** LATHAM in *Phil. Trans.* LXIX. 56, I tapped her once in a fort-night. **1807–26** S. COOPER *First Lines Surg.* (ed. 5) 527 If any of the viscera protruded..he used to reduce them, and then tap the hydrocele in the common manner. **1869** G. LAWSON *Dis. Eye* (1874) 71 Tapping the anterior chamber with a fine needle, and letting off the aqueous, will often do good. **1898** *Allbutt's Syst. Med.* V. 788 The peritoneal cavity and pleura become repeatedly full of fluid and have to be tapped again and again.

c. ***to tap an electric wire*** or ***cable***: to divert part of the current, esp. so as to intercept a telegraphic communication. So ***to tap a call, line, message, telephone***, etc.

1869 *Cornh. Mag.* XIX. 759 A favourite plan of the raiders was to 'tap' the wire. **1871** *Q. Jrnl. Sci.* I. 117 For days the unconscious French were sending [telegraphic] messages, which were 'tapped' by the Prussians. **1874** J. H. BUNNEL in J. E. Smith *Man. Telegraphy* (ed. 10) p. xv, The means employed to 'tap' a Telegraph line..are very simple. **1878** A. PINKERTON *Strikers, Communists, Tramps & Detectives* xvi. 199 The strikers certainly had some experienced telegraphers..capable of tapping the lines. **1879** PRESCOTT *Sp. Telephone* 108 The telephone presents facilities for the dangerous practice of tapping the wire. **1892** *N.Y. Tribune* 15 Jan. 7/5 (Funk) By tapping the wire for a message from Guttenburg the operator could interrupt communication with all three. **1897** *Westm. Gaz.* 3 Apr. 9/3 It would be an unheard of thing for any casual merchant steamer to 'tap' a company's cable out at sea in order to gratify a private whim for news. **1897** *Daily News* 14 July 3/4 Extraordinary allegations of 'tapping' telegraph wires were made yesterday in a case heard at the Liverpool County Court. **1909** G. B. SHAW *Press Cuttings* 3 Why didnt you telephone? *Balsquith.* They tap the telephone. **1911** *World's Work* XVIII. 588/2 Hundreds of amateur installations erected in the vicinity of either station, whereby messages might be tapped or confused. **1957** *Times* 7 June 10/5 (*heading*) Calls tapped on barrister's telephone. Home Secretary questioned. **1972** *Ibid.* 19 Dec. 2/7 He could not prove beyond all reasonable doubt that the call he made to Mr Hope on December 1 had been tapped. **1978** G. A. SHEEHAN *Running & Being* ii. 32 There is no need to tap my phone or open my mail.

3. *fig.* To open up (anything) so as to liberate or extract something from it; to open, penetrate, break into, begin to use. Also *absol.*

e.g. To open up (a country, district, trade, mineral vein, etc.); to extract money or elicit information from (a person); to rob (a till or house), pick (a pocket); to break (money) (BREAK *v.* 2 e); to broach (a subject).

1575 *Gamm. Gurton* II. iii, Ye see..that one end tapt of this my short devise, Now must we broche t'other to, before the smoke arise. **1750** H. WALPOLE *Lett.* (1846) II. 358 How does *cet homme là*..dare to tap the chapter of birth? **1768** —— *Hist. Doubts* 43 Dr. Shaw no doubt tapped the matter to the people. **1781** —— *Let. to W. Mason* 22 May, After tapping many topics, to which I made as dry answers as an unbribed oracle, he vented his errand. **1828** *Craven Gloss.* s.v., To tap a note or sovereign, to get it changed. **1840** DICKENS *Old C. Shop* lxiii, Here I am—full of evidence—Tap me! **1864** *Home News* 19 Dec. 19/2 So well had the interior of India been tapped by new roads. **1872** RAYMOND *Statist. Mines & Mining* 268 It is the intention of the owner to tap the vein by a tunnel. **1878** W. J. THOMS in *Folk Lore Rec.* I. Pref. 16 Mr. Gomme has 'tapped'—(I thank thee, Horace Walpole, for teaching me that word)—has tapped a subject which is, I believe, new in this country. **1879** A. PINKERTON *Criminal Reminiscences* xiii. 212 In the act of 'tapping' the till of a North Side [of Chicago] German grocery. **1901** *Essex Weekly News* 29 Mar. 5/1 The first gentleman who was tapped for a subscription generously promised £30. **1903** F. W. H. MYERS *Human Personality* I. 315 While he was entranced, we endeavoured to 'tap' Mr. Browne. *c* **1926** [see MARBLE *sb.* 4 c]. **1929** W. R. BURNETT *Little Caesar* i. 10 They only bank once or twice a week. They're careless, get that; because they've never been tapped. **1931** T. HORSLEY *Odyssey of Out-of-Work* xxiii. 247 We'll tap these mansions. **1931** 'G. ORWELL' *Coll. Ess.* (1968) I. 57 Ginger tapped the local butcher, who gave us the best part of two pounds of sausages. **1935** —— *Clergyman's Daughter* ii. 105 They were begging..'tapping' at every..likely-looking cottage. **1939** J. WORBY *Spiv's Progress* iii. 17 Every night he would put on his plimsolls and go tapping. **1979** *Tucson* (Ariz.) *Mag.* Mar. 46/1 Many of the big plush resorts that tap you for $80 to $100 a day.

II. To draw off (liquid, etc.).

4. a. To draw (liquor) from a tap; to draw and sell in small quantities. Also *fig.*

1401 *Pol. Poems* (Rolls) II. 95 Me thynkith ʒe ben tapsteres in alle that ʒe don: ʒe tappe ʒour absoluciones that ʒe bye at Rome. **1589** NASHE *Anat. Absurd.* 20 These Bussards thinke knowledge a burthen, tapping it before they haue halfe tunde it. **1621** *Sc. Acts Jas. VI* (1816) IV. 669/2 Four pundis..of ilk Tune of wyne To be toppit, ventit, and sauld in smallis within the said burgh. **1665** *Phil. Trans.* I. 46 The boyled liquor..is tapp'd out of the said Kettles, through holes beneath. **1677** *Act 29 Chas. II*, c. 2 §1 Any.. person or persons who doe or shall sell or tap out Beere or Ale publiquely or privately. **1737** (*title*) An Act for laying a Duty of Two Penies Scots upon every Scots Pint of Ale and Beer brewed for Sale, brought into, vended, tapped, or sold within the Town of Aberbrothock. **1743** *Lond. & Country Brew.* III. (ed. 2) 236 The Beer or Ale in a Week after should be tapt. **1871** B. TAYLOR *Faust* I. ii. (1875) II. 13 The City Council too must tap their liquor. **1872** YEATS *Techn. Hist. Comm.* 126 On festive occasions, these lords alone possessed the privilege of tapping wine.

†**b.** *transf.* To retail (any commodity). *Sc. Obs.*

1478–9 *Burgh Rec. Edinb.* (1869) I. 37 That na regratour by nor tap any vittale to regrate agane vnder the payne of pvnissing be the baillies after the tenour of the first act. *Ibid.*, Top [see TAPPER[1] 1 b]. **1538** *Aberdeen Regr.* XVI. (Jam.), For the spilling of the merkat in bying of wittail in gryt, & topping tharof befor none. **1573–4** *Burgh Rec. Glasgow* (1876) I. 450 To pas to Dunbertane to arreist schippis for talping of greit salt. **1605** in Gross *Gild Merch.* (1890) I. 222 To tapp tar, oil, butter, or to tapp eggs. **1615** *Stirling Council Rec.* in *Trans. Nat. Hist. & Archæol. Soc. Stirling* (1902) 61 Na craftsman [sal] buy, top, nor sell any merchand wairis.

c. *absol.* To draw liquor; to act as tapster.

a **1597** PEELE *Jests* Wks. (Rtldg.) 619/1 Those bomborts that live by tapping, between the age of fifty and three-score. **1598** SHAKS. *Merry W.* I. iii. 11, I will entertaine Bardolfe: he shall draw; he shall tap. **1625** MASSINGER *New Way* IV. ii, For which gross fault I here do damn thy license, Forbidding thee ever to tap or draw.

5. a. To draw off (liquid) from any source.

1597 [see TAPPING *vbl. sb.*[1]]. **1825** J. NICHOLSON *Operat. Mechanic* 357 When the fluid lead is tapped, or drawn off. **1853** 'C. BEDE' *Verdant Green* I. xi, He told Verdant, that his claret had been repeatedly tapped. **1873** TRISTRAM *Moab* xviii. 361 Little rills tapped from the springs. **1894** BOWKER in *Harper's Mag.* Jan. 417 [It] floats on the top, and is easily tapped off.

†**b.** *intr. fig.* To 'turn on the tap' of gifts; to open the purse or pocket; to spend or 'bleed' freely. *slang. Obs.*

1712 ADDISON *Spect.* No. 550 ¶1 A certain Country Gentleman begun to tapp upon the first Information he received of Sir Roger's Death. **1713** STEELE *Guard.* No. 58 ¶6, I design to stand for our borough the next election, on purpose to make the squire on t'other side tap lustily for the good of our town.

III. Technical uses.

6. *Mech.* **a.** To furnish (a hole) with an internal screw-thread, or (any part) with a threaded hole.

1808 HENRY in *Phil. Trans.* XCVIII. 287 The lower orifice..is tapped internally, for the purpose of receiving a small screw. **1825** J. NICHOLSON *Operat. Mechanic* 131 A screw..is cut on the gudgeon..and a piece of iron..is tapped to fit it. **1833** HOLLAND *Manuf. Metal* II. 105 The [gun] barrel having been tapped at the stouter end, and being fitted with the breech screw. **1902** MARSHALL *Metal Tools* 32 Holes of varying sizes..are drilled and tapped.

b. To furnish with an external screw-thread; to convert (a bolt or rod) into a screw.

1815 J. SMITH *Panorama Sc. & Art* I. 40 The bolt or pin intended to be tapped, either with a screw-plate or stocks, is tapered in a small degree at the extremity. **1837** *Civil Eng. & Arch. Jrnl.* I. 48 The lower part of the king-bolt is tapped with a screw and nut. **1888** RUTLEY *Rock-Forming Min.* 23 Each rod is tapped with a [screw-]thread.

c. To cause to pass through or in by screwing.

1869 SIR E. J. REED *Shipbuild.* ii. 44 The angle-irons..are secured to the plating by 1 inch screws tapped through it. **1885** C. G. W. LOCK *Workshop Receipts* Ser. IV. 341/2 The hook should be 'tapped' in very tight.

7. To deprive (a plant) of its tap-root.

1792 *Trans. Soc. Arts* X. 6 Young Oaks..are for the most part tapped at the time of removal.

Hence **tapped** (tæpt), *ppl. a.*[1]

c **1670** W. SIMPSON *Hydrol. Ess.* 111, I caused a tap'd vessel to be filled. **1839** URE *Dict. Arts*, etc. 158 Two tapped holes in the bar. **1874** THEARLE *Naval Archit.* 79 Four of the rivets..are through, and four are tapped. **1880** C. R. MARKHAM *Peruv. Bark* 459 Regularly tapped trees do not exceed 60 feet in height. **1881** W. E. DICKSON *Organ-Build.* viii. 95 Tapped Wires..are pieces of wire about $3\frac{1}{2}$ inches in length..and cut with a screw-thread upon about half their length. **1902** MARSHALL *Metal Tools* 63 The thread should be tried into a nut or tapped hole of the right size from time to time until a proper fit is arrived at. **1925** P. J. RISDON *Crystal Receivers & Circuits* 9 In the case of a tapped inductance coil, the wire is tapped at every turn for so many turns, for fine adjustment, and then once every few turns for coarse adjustment. **1964** L. DEIGHTON *Funeral in Berlin* v. 37 Transcripts of tapped phone calls. **1978** D. MURPHY *Place Apart* ii. 22 He called in a disguised message over the tapped phone that he would be over that evening.

tap (tæp), *v.*[2] Forms: 3 tep, 5 tappe, 9 tapp, 5– tap. [ME. *tapp-en*, of echoic origin, either immediately in Eng. (cf. RAP *v.*), or through F. *taper* in same sense (12th c. in Godef.).]

1. a. *trans.* To strike lightly, but clearly and audibly; rarely applied by meiosis to a sharp knock or rap. ***to tap up***, to rouse, cause to get up by tapping at the door. ***to tap out***, to mark or signify by a tap or series of taps; to cause to be produced thus; *spec.* to type out (a letter, etc.).

a **1225** *Ancr. R.* 296 Ne ȝif him neuer inȝong, auh tep him oðe schulle, uor he is eruh. *c* **1440** *Promp. Parv.* 487/1 Taspyn, *palpo*... Taspynge (*K., P.* tappynge), *palpacio, palpitacio.* **1603** KNOLLES *Hist. Turks* (1621) 971 Tapt the said Resuan once or twice about the pate. **1761** STERNE *Tr. Shandy* IV. Introd., This faithful slave..has carried me.., continued he, tapping the mule's back, above six hundred leagues. **1777** COOK *Voy. Pacific* II. xi. (1784) I. 409 The person who is to pay obeisance, squats down before the Chief, and bows the head to the sole of his foot;..having tapped, or touched it with the under and upper side of the fingers of both hands, he rises up, and retires. **18..** MOORE *Song, The Woodpecker*, Every leaf was at rest, and I heard not a sound, But the wood pecker tapping the hollow beech tree. **1839** URE *Dict. Arts* 517 s.v. *Founding*, Before lifting off the frame, we must tap the pattern slightly, otherwise the sand enclosing it would stick to it. **1840** MARRYAT *Poor Jack* xxiv, I went to bed, was tapped up..by Bessy. **1848** THACKERAY *Van. Fair* xxvi, He sate there tapping his boot with his cane. **1888** BURGON *Lives 12 Gd. Men* I. i. 71 He tapped my fingers in the way which was customary with him. **1903** R. LANGBRIDGE *Flame & Flood* i. 4 He was tapping out a cautious progress towards the women with a stick, letting himself down with a surprised bump upon each step. **1904** W. E. NORRIS in *Longm. Mag.* Dec. 168 A parchment-visaged priest..taps his insistent gong. **1912** *Red Mag.* Mar. 427/2 The clock of the Royal Exchange began to tap out the hour of nine. **1944** in B. A. Botkin *Treas. S. Folklore* (1949) III. i. 447 He..tapped out '73', which is the telegrapher's traditional symbol for goodby. **1952** M. LASKI *Village* xviii. 248 Gerald tapped out a formal letter on the old typewriter. **1976** J. MCCLURE *Rogue Eagle* ii. 27 Buchanan put down his cup where the writer carriage wouldn't bump it..and..tapped out the name of his freelance agency.

b. To strike (the foot, hand, etc.) lightly upon something.

a **1500** *Ragman Roll* 131 in Hazl. *E.P.P.* I. 75 And your foot ye tappyn, and ye daunce. **1820** W. IRVING *Sketch Bk., Rip Van Winkle*, The bystanders began now to..tap their fingers against their foreheads. **1847** TENNYSON *Princ.* Prol. 149 Upon the sward She tapt her tiny silken-sandal'd foot.

c. To arrest (someone). Also in phr. ***to tap on the shoulder***. *slang.*

[**1785** GROSE *Dict. Vulgar T.* sig. Z3, *A tap on the shoulder*, an arrest.] **1859** G. W. MATSELL *Vocabulum* 89 *Tap*, to arrest. **1894** J. G. LITTLECHILD *Reminiscences of Chief-Inspector Littlechild* xix. 193 We instructed him..to hint darkly that he was going to be 'tapped'—i.e. taken into custody on charges connected with the forged cheques. **1968** [see DO *v.* 11 l].

2. a. *intr.* and *absol.* To strike a light but distinct blow; to make a sound by so striking, e.g. on a drum; *esp.* to knock lightly *on* or *at* a door, etc. in order to attract attention. Also in reduplicated form **tap-tap** and varr., to tap repeatedly (usu. as pres. pple.).

c **1425** *Cast. Persev.* 2111 in *Macro Plays* 140 Putte Mankynde fro þi castel clere, or I schal tappyn at þi tyre. **1791** MRS. RADCLIFFE *Rom. Forest* x, She tapped gently at the door. **1831** POE *Raven* iv, So faintly you came tapping. **1873** BLACK *Pr. Thule* xix, He tapped with his stick on one of the panes. **1888** F. HUME *Mme. Midas* I. ii, Tapping with his wooden leg on the floor. **1891** T. HARDY *Tess* xliv, They heard her footsteps tap along the hard road as she stepped out to her full pace. **1922** JOYCE *Ulysses* 284 A stripling, blind, with a tapping cane, came taptaptapping by Daly's window. **1977** *New Yorker* 6 June 38/2 Two reels of thread escaped from it, rolled along the landing, and went tap-tapping down the stairs. **1982** R. TIMPERLEY *Face in Leaves* iv. 34, I heard her typewriter tap-tap-tapping.

†**b.** *spec.* of a hare or rabbit: To make a drumming noise with the feet in rutting-time. *Obs.*

1575 TURBERV. *Venerie* 238 A hare and a conie beateth or tappeth. **1650** [see TAPPING *ppl. a.* below]. **1706** PHILLIPS (ed. 6) s.v., Among Hunters, a Hare is said to Tap or Beat, i.e. to make a Noise. **1711** PUCKLE *Club* (1817) 90 And told us..a goat rats, a boar freams, a hare tapps.

c. To walk with sharp light steps.

1749 FIELDING *Tom Jones* XI. ii, Old England for ever!..my brave lad! I am going to tap away directly.

d. To sound, esp. as a signal.

1887 A. J. WILSON *At Mercy of Tiberius* xxxiii. 576 Somewhere in the apartment, a bell tapped. *Ibid.* 577 The time has come; the drum taps, I must march away. **1915** C. JOHNSON *Battleground Adventures* liv. 419 A bell would tap for a waiter to come and take the team.

3. *trans. dial.* and *U.S.* To add a thickness of leather to the sole or heel of (a shoe) in repairing; cf. TAP *sb.*[2] 3. Also *absol.*

1746 J. HEMPSTEAD *Diary* 1 Jan. (1901) 453, I tapt & nailed Jont. Pierpoints Shoes. **1781** in *Narragansett Historical Reg.* (1882) I. 284 Tapped a pair of shoes. **1818** J. KITTO in Eadie *Life* ii. (1861) 44 Set to tapping leather shoes to-day. **1846** WORCESTER *Dict.*, *Tap*, to add a new sole or heel to a shoe. **1847–78** HALLIW., *Tap* to sole shoes. **1852** *Knickerbocker* XL. 149 There is also the shoemaker..who 'taps' for half the city price. **1880** *W. Cornw. Gloss.* s.v., The tap of your shoe is wearing; it wants tapping.

4. To designate or select (a person) for a task, honour, or membership of an organization. *U.S. colloq.*

1952 E. O'NEILL *Moon for Misbegotten* I. 55 He was tapped for an exclusive Senior Society at the Ivy university to which his father had given millions. **1972** J. MOSEDALE *Football* ii. 13 *Sports Illustrated* magazine tapped him..as its 'Sportsman of the Year'. **1977** *Time* 23 May 13/3 Britain's youthful Foreign Secretary David Owen announced last week that he had tapped Jay, at 40, to serve as Ambassador to Washington.

Hence **'tapping** *ppl. a.*

1650 FULLER *Pisgah* III. ix. 338 Here..the beating Hares [are said] to forme, the tapping Conies to sit. **1816** *Sporting Mag.* XLVII. 177 The Oilman is a tapping and inoffensive hitter. **1890** 'R. BOLDREWOOD' *Col. Reformer* (1891) 240 Far and faint..whips resound..like a tapping-bird or the snapping of dried sticks.

tap, Sc. dial. form of TOP.

‖**tapa**[1] ('tæpə). Also **tappa**. [Com. Polynesian *tapa* (in dialects which substitute *k* for *t*, *kapa*).] A kind of unwoven cloth made by the natives of Polynesia from the bark of the Paper Mulberry (*Broussonetia papyrifera*).

1823 BYRON *Island* II. ii, In summer garments be our limb array'd; Around our waists the Tappa's white display'd. **1845** J. COULTER *Adv. Pacific* xvii. 268 The beating out of the tappa or native cloth. **1898** F. T. BULLEN *Cruise Cachalot* 296 All..were furnished only with a 'maro' of 'tapa', scanty in its proportions, but still enough to wrap round their loins.

b. *attrib.* and *Comb.*, *as* ***tapa-cloth***, ***-kilt***, ***-mallet***, ***-mat***; ***tapa-shrouded*** adj.

1853 *Househ. Words* VII. 135/2 This tappa cloth is made by beating a part of the bark..with a sort of wooden mall. **1866** *Treas. Bot.* 172/2 An exceedingly tough cloth, called tapa or kapa cloth. **1870** MEADE *N. Zealand* 305 The unpleasant sound of the tappa mallet. **1891** STEVENSON *Vailima Lett.* iv. (1895) 47 With blacked faces, turbans, tapa kilts, and guns, they looked very manly. **1899** *Blackw. Mag.* Nov. 671/2 The tapa-shrouded, slumbering forms of the few native passengers. **1906** *Macm. Mag.* Apr. 479 Sitting cross-legged on the tappa-mats.

‖**tapa**[2] ('tapa). [Sp., lit. 'cover, lid'.] Usu. *pl.* In Spanish bars or cafés, a savoury snack or hors d'œuvre of sausage, cured ham, seafood, potato salad, etc., typically served with glasses of wine or sherry.

The slices of sausage, etc., were originally put on top of the glasses as 'lids'.

1953 C. SALTER *Introducing Spain* iv. 36, I should like to draw attention to..the admirable habit of the 'tapa'. In Spain, when you order a drink in a bar.., you will always be given..something to eat. **1959** W. JAMES *Word-bk. of Wine* 186 *Tapas*, small dishes served gratis in boat-shaped saucers with every glass of wine ordered..in a Spanish bodega or café. **1964** C. ROUGVIE *Medal from Pamplona* vi. 79 Must be a pub there with tapas..these bits of food they give you free with the booze. **1978** J. HYAMS *Pool* vi. 74 She had *tapas* and white wine at Café Monaco with a friend. **1982** D. SERAFÍN *Madrid Underground* 63 It was the hour to take *tapas* or pre-dinner snacks.

‖**tapaculo** (tapa'kulo). Also **tapacolo**. [Sp., f. *tapa* cover + *culo* backside.] A South American passerine bird, *Pteroptochus albicollis* (*megapodius*), which carries its tail inclined towards its head, also called in Chile *tualo*; the Chilean rock-wren.

1839 DARWIN *Voy. Nat.* xiv. 329 It is called Tapacolo, or 'cover your posterior'. *Ibid.* 330 The tapacolo is very crafty. .. It is also an active bird. **1896** NEWTON *Dict. Birds* 947 The true Tapaculo, *P. albicollis*,..rarely flies, hops actively ..with its tail erect or turned towards its head.

‖**tapadero** (tapa'dero). Also 9 **-daro**, **-dera**, **tapi-**. [Sp. *tapadero* cover, lid, stopper, f. *tapar* to stop up, cover.] A heavy leather housing for the front of the stirrup, used in California and elsewhere in North America to protect the foot against thorny undergrowth and keep it from slipping forward.

1844 J. GREGG *Commerce of Prairies* I. 213 The stirrups..over which are fastened the tapaderas or coverings of leather to protect the toes. **1872** 'MARK TWAIN' *Roughing It* xxiv. 178 It was a Spanish saddle, with ponderous *tapidaros*. **1879** *Cimarron* (N. Mexico) *News & Press* 20 Nov. 3/4 New Saddler Shop... Stirrups, Tapaderos, Saddle Bags, etc. **1891** *Cent. Dict.*, Tapadera. **1897** *Westm. Gaz.* 8 Oct. 2/1 Tapideros, or leather coverings for the stirrups, avoid the danger of the foot going right through the stirrup. **1933** J. STEINBECK *To God Unknown* xxv. 321 Joseph lifted the heavy saddle, and as the tapadero struck the horse's side, it reared. **1975** F. KENNEDY *Alberta was my Beat* p. vi, It [*sc.* a saddle] was complete with Tapadero covered stirrups.

tapalpite (tə'pælpaɪt). *Min.* [Named 1869 from Sierra de Tapalpa (Mexico): see -ITE[1].] Sulphotelluride of bismuth and silver, found in grey metallic masses (Chester).

‖**tapas** ('tapas). [Skr., lit. 'heat'.] In Hinduism and Jainism, (the practising of) religious austerity or bodily mortification. Also **tapa'sya** [Skr., religious austerity.]

1810 J. MALCOLM in *Asiatic Res.* XI. 267 Na'nac was celebrated for the manner in which he performed *Tapasa*, or austere devotion. **1815** M. ELPHINSTONE *Acct. Kingdom of Caubul* II. xii. 318 The Tapasya, or ascetic devotion of Gurug. **1924** W. B. SELBIE *Psychol. Relig.* 50 The ascetic methods of tapas and yoga, physical practices which belong to a debased mysticism not far removed from magic. **1962** A. HUXLEY *Island* ix. 137 The real thing only comes to people after years and years of meditation and *tapas* and..well, you know—not going with women. **1969** *Indo-Asian Culture* Oct. 53 In this art form..there is less of the austerity of *tapasya* in the artist's way of working. **1974** *Encycl. Brit. Macropædia* II. 137/1 In India, in the late Vedic period.., the ascetic use of *tapas* ('heat', or austerity) became associated with meditation and *yoga*, inspired by the idea that *tapas* kills sin.

‖**tapayaxin** (tæpə'jæksɪn). [Native Mexican.] The orbicular horned lizard, *Phrynosoma orbiculare*, incorrectly called the *horned frog* or *toad*.

[**1615** F. HERNANDEZ *Cuatro Libr. Naturaleza* 188 Del animal que llaman tapayaxin y los Españoles camaleon. **1693** RAY *Syn. Quad.* 263.] **1753** CHAMBERS *Cycl. Suppl.*, *Tapayaxin*,..a very remarkable species of lizard, called by Hernandez the *lacertus orbicularis*. **1858** BAIRD *Cycl. Nat. Sci.* s.v. *Agamidæ*, The Tapayaxin, *Agama orbicularis*.

tapcery, var. TAPISSERY *Obs.*, tapestry.

'tap-dancing. [f. TAP *sb.*[2]] A form of exhibition dancing characterized by rhythmical tapping of the toes and heels.

1928 *Daily Express* 27 June 9 The inventor of tap dancing. **1934** *Evening News* 1 Mar. 11/2 If the working girl doesn't do her bending and stretching, then she joins a tap-dancing class. **1953** R. LEHMANN *Echoing Grove* 33 She wished to study tap-dancing, and to broaden the mind. **1972** *Guardian* 29 Jan. 9/4, I started as a dancer: tap dancing, acrobatic dancing, funny dancing. **1977** D. MACKENZIE *Raven & Ratcatcher* ii. 19 Tap-dancing schools.

Also **'tap-dance** *sb.*; also *fig.* and as *v. intr.* (occas. *trans.*); **'tap-dancer**.

1927 *New Republic* 12 Oct. 210/1 That fair singer, good tap-dancer, born-to-the-purple, bred-in-the-bone, works-while-she-sleeps comedian, the plump May Barnes. **1929** D. RUNYON in *Hearst's Internat.* July 56/2 Miss Billy Perry is worth a few peeks, especially when she is out on the floor of Miss Missouri Martin's Sixteen Hundred Club doing her tap dance. **1931** G. CADWELL (*title*) How to tap dance. **1941** *Penguin New Writing* X. 17 The sergeant..had been a tap-dancer in civilian life. **1946** R. CAMPBELL *Talking Bronco* 25 The tap-dance of the morning stars. **1950** J. D. MACDONALD *Brass Cupcake* (1955) i. 11 He stood up and tap-danced me out to the gate. **1963** A. LUBBOCK *Austral. Roundabout* 100 The moths tap-danced on the fly-screens. **1972** *Guardian* 28 Jan. 9/1 The lacquered, ringletted monsters who tap-danced their way into the weepies. **1974** *Listener* 17 Jan. 92/2 Old-fashioned, out-dated routines: middle-aged black tap-dancers, a middle-aged blonde. **1977** N. ADAM *Triplehip Cracksman* xvii. 171 A larger one [*sc.* table] which would have made a good one-shot tap-dance floor. **1978** W. F. BUCKLEY *Stained Glass* xxi. 209 He could be tap dancing on it and still he'd be a goner.

tape (teɪp), *sb.*[1] Forms: 1 tæppe, (5 tappe, 6 tapp); 4– tape. [OE. *tæppe* or *tæppa* (nom. not found); origin unascertained. The lengthening of the vowel from ME. *tappe* to *tāpe* is unexplained.]

1. a. A narrow woven strip of stout linen, cotton, silk, or other textile, used as a string for tying garments, and for other purposes for which flat strings are suited, also for measuring lines, etc.

c **1000** *Ælfric's Voc.* in Wr.-Wülcker 107/33 *Tenia*, tæppan (pl.), *uel* dolsmeltas. *c* **1386** CHAUCER *Miller's T.* 55 The tapes of hir white voluper Were of the same suyte of hir coler. *c* **1425** *Voc.* in Wr.-Wülcker 655/15 *Hec tenea*, tappe. **1519** *Churchw. Acc. St. Giles, Reading* 5 For tapis for iij° Amys i[d] ob. **1573–80** BARET *Alv.* T 60 A Tape, to knit the apron about with. **1690** *Lond. Gaz.* No. 2529/4 Lost.., a black Box..tied about with a white Tape. **1805** *Trans. Soc. Arts*, etc. XXIII. 119 A measuring tape..having inches on one side. **1833** HOLLAND *Manuf. Metal* II. 225 When the rollers revolve, the motion of the tapes carry the sheet of paper with them, and deliver it over another roller,..where it is taken up by two sets of endless tapes. **1879** JAS. GRANT in *Cassell's Techn. Educ.* IV. 270/1 A partner in the manufactory of inkles and tapes.

b. Without article, as name of the material or substance. Also *fig.*: see RED-TAPE.

1537–8 *Rec. St. Mary at Hill* 378 Paid for silke tape iijs iiijd. **1546** in W. H. Turner *Select. Rec. Oxford* (1880) 184 For viij yardes and a half of tape. **1653** WALTON *Angler* vii. 158 A convenient quantitie of tape or filiting. **1714** GAY *Sheph. Week* Monday 37 This pouch, that's ty'd with tape of reddest hue. **1856** READE *Never too late to mend* xxv, Twenty years gone in tape and circumlocution. **1898** J. BERWICK *Philos. Romance* iv. 46 Reams of blue paper tied with pink tape.

c. A piece of tape suspended across the course at the finishing point in a race, or (formerly) between the goal-posts in Association football; in *Horse-racing*, a tape or set of tapes suspended across the course at the starting-point of a race; also *fig.* Also used *lit.* or *fig.* in phrases: ***to breast the tape***, to reach the finishing-line in a race; ***on the tape***, at the very end of a race.

1867 *Routledge's Handbk. Football* 54 Football Association Rules... A goal shall be won when the ball passes between the goal-posts under the tape. **1868** H. F. WILKINSON *Mod. Athletics* 17–18 The Goal..should consist of a piece of stout white tape tied to the post at one side..and held loosely by the judge across the course, so that when the winner passes the post he may carry the tape away. **1880** *Times* 12 Nov. 4/5 The ball is shot under the tape or over the bar, and the call of time immediately afterwards proclaims the game at an end. **1903** *Punch* 11 Feb. 103/1 Though a toughish task remains Before I breast the tape, J. Chamberlain, of Birmingham, Will round (or square) the Cape. **1916** J. B. COOPER *Coo-oo-ee* xvii. 270 'They've got me on the tape!' he cried; 'but I'm satisfied.' **1922** JOYCE *Ulysses* 608 Judge of his astonishment when he finally did breast the tape and the awful truth dawned upon him anent his better half, wrecked in his affections. **1937** 'P. WENTWORTH' *Case is Closed* vii. 72 He was running in his school sports, winning the hundred yards again, breasting the tape, hearing the applause break out. **1955** *Times* 13 Aug. 4/2 Wheeler..regained the ground he had lost and just robbed the Hungarian of victory on the tape. **1957** D. FRANCIS *Sport of Queens* vi. 122 The six or seven stranded starting tapes familiar in flat racing are not used for National Hunt racing. A single strand across the course is pulled down to a catch at shoulder level, and when this is released..the tape flies up at an oblique angle. **1963** *Times* 21 Feb. 4/5 They were described by an official observer after the last N.E.D.C. meeting as 'just coming up to the tapes'.

d. *Army* and *R.A.F. slang.* A chevron indicating rank worn by a non-commissioned officer on the upper part of the coat-sleeve; a stripe (STRIPE *sb.*[3] 2).

1943 HUNT & PRINGLE *Service Slang* 64 *Tapes*, the stripes worn by Corporals, Sergeants, and Flight Sergeants in the R.A.F. and by Lance-Corporals or Lance-Bombardiers, Corporals or Bombardiers, and Sergeants in the Army. **1944** *Gen* 15 Jan. 9/2 That binder's working for his tapes. **1944** *R.A.F. Jrnl.* Aug. 258, I wouldn't leave this unit for three tapes.

2. a. A long, narrow, thin and flexible strip of metal or the like; *esp.* such a strip of steel used as a measuring line in surveying.

1884 *Health Exhib. Catal.* 77/2 Solid Copper Tape Lightning Conductor. **1884** *Edin. Rev.* July 48 The main stem of the conductor shall consist of a copper rod or tape. **1900** H. M. WILSON *Topogr. Surv.* xxi. 500 The steel tape is capable of giving a precision indicated by a *probable error* of one 2,000,000th part of a measured line. *Ibid.*, Base measurement with steel tapes.

b. The paper strip or ribbon on which messages are printed in the receiving instrument of a recording telegraph system. Also used in computing and data processing; = *paper tape* s.v. PAPER *sb.* 12.

1884 *Pall Mall G.* 27 Dec. 5/2 This 'tape' is supplied by a telegraphic company, and automatically records in dozens of different offices in the City the variation of prices from hour to hour inside the House. **1888** BESANT *50 Years Ago* 213 Now we watch the tape, day by day, and hour by hour. **1905** PREECE & SIVEWRIGHT *Telegraphy* 171 Punching and feeding the tape forward is performed by an electro-magnet. *Ibid.* 172 To produce a type-printed page from the record perforated on the tape. **1945** J. VON NEUMANN in B. Randell *Origins of Digital Computers* (1973) 355 These instructions must be given in some form which the device can sense. Punched into a system of punchcards or on teletype tape, magnetically impressed on steel tape or wire, [etc.]. **1948** *Math. Tables & Other Aids Computation* III. 8 Orders to the machine..are represented on tape by all combinations of three holes out of six. **1960** M. G. SAY et al. *Analogue & Digital Computers* ix. 266 The only problem in fast photoelectric reading arises when the tape has to be set in motion and stopped so rapidly that [etc.]. **1978** D. D. SPENCER *Data Processing* v. 105 Data are often hand-sorted before being punched into the tape.

c. = *magnetic tape* s.v. MAGNETIC *a.* 5. Cf. *steel tape (b)* s.v. STEEL *sb.*[1] 18.

1932 *Radio Times* 29 July 239/3 The Blattnerphone is an invention for recording magnetically upon steel tape. **1942** *Jrnl. R. Aeronaut. Soc.* XLVI. Abstr. Sci. & Technical Press 68 It consists of recording a sound pattern magnetically on steel tape. The signal is picked up from the tape at frequent split-second intervals. **1953** *Newsweek* 11 May 28/1 It was recorded on tape and was broadcast later that day. **1964** M. MCLUHAN *Understanding Media* xviii. 295 Tape and the l.p. record suddenly made the phonograph a means of access to all the music and speech of the world. **1982** *Times* 26 Oct. 15/7 Access to specific pieces of information is far faster on a compact, rapidly spinning disk than on a long ribbon of tape.

d. A length or reel of (magnetic or paper) tape; a recording on tape.

c **1946** [see SUBROUTINE]. **1952** W. STEVENS *Let.* 13 May (1967) 750, I read at Cambridge a week or two ago and apparently someone in the audience took a tape. **1956** G. A. MONTGOMERIE *Digital Calculating Machines* x. 213 The instructions are punched in the tapes in a very simple notation. **1966** *Listener* 25 Aug. 287/2 This production came via a tape from the Holland Festival. **1977** *New Yorker* 22 Aug. 56/3 Most thefts of computer tapes are probably not reported to the police. **1978** D. D. SPENCER *Data Processing* v. 105 Both the tapes and the tape-producing equipment require less space than punched cards and card-producing equipment. **1983** D. DUNNETT *Dolly & Bird of Paradise* v. 54 Kim-Jim loved telly films... I had brought a lot of tapes with me.

e. Used in names designating (paper, transparent film, etc.) tape coated with adhesive and used for fastening packages, etc.; usu. as the final element of a Comb., as ***adhesive tape***, ***Scotch tape***, SELLOTAPE, ***sticky tape***: see under first element.

1966 A. W. LEWIS *Gloss. Woodworking Terms* 99 *Tape*, gummed paper strip used to hold the edges of veneer together while the glue dries.

3. *slang.* Spirituous liquor, esp. gin (***white tape***); ***red tape***, brandy. Cf. RIBBON *sb.* 4c.

1725 *New Cant. Dict.*, *Tape*, *Red* or *White*, Geneva, Aniseed, Clove-Water, &c. so called by Canters and Villains, and the Renters of the Tap..in Newgate, and other Prisons. **1755** *Connoisseur* No. 53 ¶4 Every night-cellar [will] furnish you with Holland Tape, three yards a penny. **1830** LYTTON *P. Clifford* x. (1854) 80 Red tape those as likes it may drain. **1837** THACKERAY *Ravenswing* vi, Gin.., under the name of 'tape', used to be measured out pretty liberally in what was..his Majesty's prison of the Fleet.

4. *attrib.* and *Comb.*, as, in sense 1, ***tape-length***, ***-maker***, ***-making***, ***-moulding***, ***-purl*** (PURL *sb.*[1] 2), ***-ribbon***, ***-seller***, ***-string***, ***-stripe***, ***-weaver***, ***-work***; ***tape-like***, ***-slashing*** adjs.; in sense 2b, 'of, or recorded by, the telegraphic tape', ***tape-price***, ***boy***, ***-report***, ***-system***; ***tape-printing*** adj.; in senses 2c, d ***tape editing***, ***editor***, ***eraser***, ***head*** [HEAD *sb.* 11g], ***speed***, ***splicing***; ***tape-controlled***, ***-playing*** adjs.; (in sense 2e) ***tape dispenser***. Also **tape-bound** *a.*, bound with tape; = *tape-tied*; **tape-carrier**, a frame in which a tape sprinkled with powdered corundum is mounted as a cutting or filing instrument; **tape cartridge** = *tape cassette* (see also quot. 1983); **tape cassette** = CASSETTE d; **tape-check** *Mus.*: in an upright pianoforte, a type of check (CHECK *sb.*[1] 10d) developed by Robert Wornum (1780–1852) and incorporating a tape; also *attrib.* in ***tape-check action***; **tape deck** (see DECK *sb.*[1] 3f); **tape-delay**, the use of a tape recorder to introduce an interval between recording and playing back or transmitting (cf. DELAY *sb.* 1c); **tape drive**, a tape transport or tape deck for use in computing; **tape-fish**, an eel-like fish having a flat elongated body, a ribbon-fish; **tape-fuse**, a ribbon-like fuse, very rapid in action; **tape-grass**, an aquatic herb, *Vallisneria spiralis*, with narrow grass-like leaves; **tape guipure** *Lace-making* (see quots. 1865, 1881); **tape hiss**, extraneous high-frequency background noise during the playing of a tape recording; **tape-line**, a line of tape; *spec.* a strip of linen or steel marked with subdivisions of the foot or metre, sometimes coiling in a cylindrical case with a winch or spring; **tape loop** = LOOP *sb.*[1] 4k; **tape-machine**, *(a)* the receiving instrument of a recording telegraph system, in which the message is printed on a paper tape; *(b)* = *tape-sizing machine* (*Cent. Dict.*, *Supp.* 1909); **tape-man**, in Surveying, each of the two men who measure with the tape-line; **tape-measure**, a measuring line of prepared tape, marked with feet and inches, etc., esp. one of five or six feet long used by tailors, dressmakers, etc.; also as *v. trans.*, to measure with a tape-measure; hence **tape measurement**; **tape-needle**, an eyed bodkin for inserting tape; **tape player**, a machine for playing (cassette) tape recordings; cf. *record player* s.v. RECORD *sb.* 14; **tape-primer**, an obsolete primer for fire-arms, consisting of a flexible paper or other band containing small fulminating charges at equal distances; **tape punch** *Computers*, a device which punches holes in paper tape in patterns that represent coded information; also **tape-punching**; **tape reader** *Computers*, a device for sensing information recorded by sequences of holes or magnetized areas on computer tape (see READER 7); also **tape reading**; **tape reproducer**, a machine that plays or reads tapes but does not record or punch them; **tapescript** [after *transcript*, *typescript*, etc.], a tape recording of the spoken word, esp. in the form of a lesson, interview, etc.; a transcript or text of this; **tape-sizer**, a man in charge of the machine (***tape-sizing machine*** or *tape-machine*) for sizing the cotton warp threads to be used in weaving; = TAPER *sb.*[3]; **tape-stretcher**, a contrivance to maintain a uniform tension of the measuring line in surveying; **tape-ticker** = *tape-machine*; **tape-tied** *a.*, tied with tape; also *fig.* bound by 'red-tape', restricted by officialism; so **tape-tying** *a.*; **tape transport**, a mechanism which controls the movement of recording tape past a stationary head; also, a tape deck. See also TAPE RECORDER.

1900 *Westm. Gaz.* 5 July 5/2 Should the *tape-bound authorities in Pall Mall blankly refuse to equip..the 320 extra men. **1969** *Listener* 2 Jan. 12/1, I was in the Newsroom:..where..*tape boys..bore in huge foaming trays of paper strip to the duty editors. **1961** *High Fidelity Trade News* Sept. 55/3 Foley Electronics offers..an automatic *tape cartridge playback unit employing the endless loop principle. **1972** *Observer* (Colour Suppl.) 22 Oct. 53/2 Tape cartridges are plentiful, even if cassette material is strangely lagging. **1983** D. H. SANDARS *Computers Today* vi. 159 *(caption)* Magnetic tape cartridges are used in minicomputers and data entry stations. This tape is ¼ inch wide and varies from 140 to 450 feet in length... Magnetic tape cassettes are used in microcomputers and data entry stations. This tape is either 150 or 300 feet long. **1972** G. V. HIGGINS *Friends of Eddie Coyle* xv. 88 He opened the glove compartment and removed a *tape cassette. **1983** Tape cassette [see *tape cartridge* above]. **1929** *Evening News* 18 Nov. 2/6 Pianette... Iron frame. *Tape check action. **1954** *Grove's Dict. Mus.* (ed. 5) VI. 739/1 We must now turn our attention to an action known as the 'tape-check'. **1966** W. L. SUMNER *Pianoforte* iii. 66 A later model anticipated the tape-check action, which prevented the hammer from giving unwanted repetition. **1962** *Gloss. Terms Automatic Data Processing* (*B.S.I.*) 98 *Tape-controlled carriage. **1949**, etc. *Tape deck [see DECK *sb.*[1] 3f]. **1967** *Oxf. Computer Explained* 7 A new configuration..consisting of twelve 30 kc tape decks, a high speed printer, a paper-tape reader, and a monitor printer. **1977** 'E. CRISPIN' *Glimpses of Moon* xii. 242 His stereo tape-deck only a few seconds away from the enormous climax of *Also Sprach Zarathustra*. **1968** *Listener* 12 Dec. 802/3 The music dissolves again, surmounted by quiet seagull sounds produced by high squeaks of feed back multiplied by means of *tape-delay. **1982** *Ibid.* 18 Aug. 27/1 The catalyst which sets *Clocks and Clouds* in motion is the gradual de-synchronisation of identical melodic patterns—the classic 'tape-delay' device of electronic music. **1975** *New Yorker* 10 Mar. 31/1 An automatic *tape dispenser. **1952** *Proc. Electronic Computer Symp., Los Angeles* (IRE Prof. Group Electronic Computers) 4 *(heading)* Survey of *tape drive systems. **1978** J. MCNEIL *Consultant* x. 114 The computers..showed little signs of life beyond the occasional twitch from the tape drives. **1983** D. H. SANDARS *Computers Today* vi. 163 Before the data on a magnetic tape can be processed by a computer, the tape must be placed in a machine called a tape drive or tape transport. **1961** *Times* 17 Apr. 3/1 Knowledge of radio-production and *tape-editing. **1973** G. TALBOT *Ten Seconds from Now* xix. 239 A wonderland of recording rooms and tape-editing suites. **1959** 'F. NEWTON' *Jazz Scene* x. 169 Recording supervisors, sound engineers and *tape editors. **1958** *Oxf. Mail* 27 Aug. (Suppl.) 4/6 (Advt.), The..*tape eraser will erase the contents of a spool of tape of any size up to ten inches at one operation. **1885** C. F. HOLDER *Marvels Anim. Life* 101 The band or *tape-fishes, from their snake-like appearance, are first worthy of notice. **1857** GRAY *First Lessons Bot.* (1866) 167 This may be..seen..in the leaves of the Freshwater *Tape-Grass (*Vallisneria*), under a good microscope. **1865** F. B. PALLISER *Hist. Lace* iii. 35 In that class called by the lace-makers '*tape guipure', the outline of the flowers is formed by a pillow or hand-made braid about the eighth of an inch in width, the middle filled in with the needle. **1881** C. C. HARRISON *Woman's Handiwork* I. 94 Tape-guipure, made of linen tape twisted and folded into a pattern, held together with bars and then filled in and enriched with needlework. **1882** CAULFEILD & SAWARD *Dict. Needlework* 246/2 An embroidery worked in imitation of the Tape Guipure Laces. **1960** *Practical Wireless* XXXVI. 401/2 (Advt.), Luxury model with press-button inputs to suit any pick-up or tuner and most *tape-heads. **1980** *Sunday Times* 24 Aug. 14/7 Magnetic patterns on the tape are translated by a tape-head into electrical impulses. **1962** A. NISBETT *Technique Sound Studio* ii. 38 There may be *tape hiss due to setting the gain too low. **1977** *Gramophone* Oct. 638/2 The tape hiss seems now to be higher too. **1900** H. M. WILSON *Topogr. Surv.* xxiii. 533 Both tapemen keep a record of the number of *tape-lengths between stations. **1880** BARWELL *Aneurism* 6 Broad, *tape-like ligatures were used. **1897** *Allbutt's Syst. Med.* III. 838 The passage of pipe-like or tape-like motions is..due merely to the action of the sphincter. **1847** WEBSTER, *Tapeline. **1858** in SIMMONDS *Dict. Trade.* **1893** SELOUS *Trav. S.E. Africa* 91 A few measurements..taken on the spot with a tape-line. **1962** *Tape loop [see LOOP *sb.*[1] 4k]. **1976** W. H. CANAWAY *Willow-Pattern War* xx. 199 The signal would be going out from a tape-loop. **1891** *Daily News* 9 Apr. 7/1 Some twenty or thirty men, who were crowding round a '*tape machine'..waiting for the result of the second race of the day to come through. **1900** H. M. WILSON *Topogr. Surv.* xxiv. 532 The *tapemen measure the distance with the steel tape, which is stretched by a twenty-pound tension on the front end by the fore tapeman with a spring-balance. **1873** *Young Englishwoman* Mar. 151/2 Pin your *tape-measure down on one of the fronts. **1877** KNIGHT *Dict. Mech.*, Tape-measure. **1907** *Westm. Gaz.* 20 Mar. 10/1 As tested by the tape-measure..the..giantess might make an excellent claim to be the 'greatest' woman who has ever lived. **1962** L. DEIGHTON *Ipcress File* xxv. 158 Birth marks..were photographed and *tape measured. **1971** LAVER & COLLINS *Educ. Tennis Player* i. 19 Dave Anderson..tape-measured me..and reported that my left forearm is twelve inches around. **1922** JOYCE *Ulysses* 523 *Tape measurements will be taken next your skin. **1863** *Archæol. Cantiana* V. 14 A portion of the old *tape moulding or parallel band. **1852** MRS. STOWE *Uncle Tom's C.* xv, I'll look your box over.—Thimble, wax,..scissors, knife, *tape-needle; all right. **1880** *Plain Hints Needlework* 68 Tape-needle is generally used in the North of England instead of this word [bodkin]—and..would be better if more generally used, to describe what it really is, a needle to run a piece of tape into a hem, or caseing. **1961** *High Fidelity Trade News* Sept. 55/3 *(heading)* Foley presents 'endless loop' *tape player. **1977** *New Yorker* 24 Oct. 112/3 Such misdeeds as..having a tape player on too loud. **1962** *Times* 5 July 15/6 *Tape-playing equipment to the value of some £160 altogether was being used. **1889** *Hints to Speculators* (G. Gregory & Co.) (ed. 5) 20 Deal at *tape prices. **1895** *Daily News* 14 June 5/2 The machines set up in the offices record the prices on the familiar strips of paper from which the name of 'tape prices' is taken. **1903** *Q. Rev.* Jan. 106 Tape-prices do not represent actual transactions. **1877** KNIGHT *Dict. Mech.* 2495/2 The *tape-primer required a peculiar lock, having a recess for containing the tape and mechanism for advancing each primer successively to the nipple. **1903** *Westm. Gaz.* 25 Aug. 2/3 The fee charged for maintaining and superintending the *tape-printing telegraph machine which supplies the Peers with news in the Prince's Chamber. **1947** *Tape punch [see *tape reader* below]. **1967** A. BATTERSBY *Network Analysis* (ed. 2) viii. 134 The sheets are then passed to a tape-punch operator who converts the information on them into a punched tape. **1951** M. V. WILKES et al. *Preparation of Programs for Electronic Digital Computer* 42 *(heading)* *Tape punching and editing facilities. *a* **1652** BROME *Queen & Concub.* IV. i, *Lol.* Can you handle the Bobbins well, good Woman? Make statute-Lace? you shall have my Daughter. *Pogg.* And mine, to make *Tape-Purles. **1947** *Math. Tables & Other Aids to Computation* II. 355 In addition to these parts there are..a drum commutator for operating the relays, a *tape reader and a tape punch. **1964** C. DENT *Quantity Surveying by Computer* iii. 26 The program is all ready to be read by the input tape-reader at 300 characters per second. **1972** M. WOODHOUSE *Mama Doll* x. 143 It's frequency-coded for a tape-reader. **1970** O. DOPPING *Computers & Data Processing* xv. 237 *Tape reading and tape writing can go on partly simultaneously, if the design of the computer allows it. **1901** *Westm. Gaz.* 20 June 6/3 The '*tape' report..said there was no opposition to the Charing Cross, Euston, and Hampstead Railway scheme. **1961** *Tape reproducer [see REPRODUCER 2]. **1962** *Gloss. Terms Autom. Data Processing* (*B.S.I.*) 97 *Tape reproducer*, a machine used to copy and edit paper tape. **1962** A. NISBETT *Technique Sound Studio* 246 *Control cubicle* (BBC), the soundproof room equipped with control desk, gramophone and tape reproducers and high quality loudspeaker. **1647** CLARENDON *Hist. Reb.* VIII. §128 He commanded every Man to tye a white *tape Ribban, or Handkerchief above the Elbow of their right Arme. **1961** J. S. HOLTON et al. *Sound Lang. Teaching* 248 **Tapescript*, term used to describe the written program (exercises and instructions) that the teacher has prepared for recording a language laboratory lesson. **1969** *John Edwards Mem. Foundation Q.* V. I. 10 These tapescripts..are resumés of interviews of artists. **1983** *Financial Times* 16 Apr. 14 It is telly docu-drama at its most truth-honouring; based on real tapescripts, speeches and official records. **1835** WILLIS *Pencillings* I. ii. 20 The Marseilles *tapeseller. **1897** S. WEBB *Indust. Democ.* I. IV. iv. 105–6; II. II. x. 478 *Tape-sizers. **1891** *Labour Commission* Gloss., The machine used by the taper is called the *tape-sizing machine. **1882** *Standard* 7 Sept. 2/3 The enormous *tape-slashing machines,.. followed. **1954** *Gramophone Record Rev.* Jan. 139/1 With a *tape speed of 7½ ins. per second the capstan thus makes about 80 revolutions per second. **1956** *Language* XXXII. 281 These experiments served as a test for two *tape-splicing techniques. **1900** H. M. WILSON *Topogr. Surv.* xxi. 501 *Tape-stretchers. **1871** *Figure Training* 57 The ladies.. prohibit all restriction of the waist except by the aid of a broad band and *tape-strings. **1865** CARLYLE *Fredk. Gt.* xx. v. (1873) IX. 78 These long lanes, or *tape-stripes of the Torgau Forest. **1904** *Daily News* 6 July 7 Mr. Francis E. Macmahon, inventor of the *tape ticker, died very suddenly at Newmarket yesterday morning. **1732** POPE *Ep. Bathurst* 301 A flock-bed..With *tape-ty'd curtains, never meant to draw. **1748** THOMSON *Cast. Indol.* I. 502 Whose desk and table make a solemn show, With tape-tied trash. **1900** *Daily News* 1 Aug. 3/1 Good scouts..of more importance to an army in the field than all the tape-tied intelligence officers out of Hades. **1954** *Trans. IRE Audio* II. 23/1 The overall design of a *tape transport for a professional tape recording system is very complex. **1981** *Hi-Fi Answers* Nov. 117/1 The tape transport is press button controlled, and operation appears to be achieved by a combination of mechanical and electrical means. **1983** Tape transport [see *tape drive* above]. **1832** *Fraser's Mag.* Oct. 382 The *tape-tying crew who had wriggled themselves into office. **1725** *Lond. Gaz.* No. 6380/12 Robert Johnson,..*Tape-weaver. **1890** W. J. GORDON *Foundry* 208 The paper supports itself all through the machine, and the *tapework is reduced to a minimum.

tape (teɪp), *sb.*² *dial.* [var. of TALPE, *taupe*: cf. *chafe* from Fr. *chauffer*.] The mole.

1847–78 HALLIW., *Tape*, a mole. *South.* **1881** *Isle of Wight Gloss.*, *Tape*, or *Teype*, a mole, or want. *Tape-taker*, a mole-catcher.

tape (teɪp), *v.* [f. TAPE *sb.*¹]

1. a. *trans.* To attach a tape or tapes to; to supply with a tape; to fit with tapes; to tie *up*, fasten, bind, or wind with tape (also *fig.*); *spec.* in *Bookbinding*, to join the sections of (a book) with tape. Also, to affix or fasten (*up*) with adhesive tape.

1609 T. COCKS *Diary* (1901) 85 Given nursse for tapinge & starching my cuffes ijd. **1854** H. MILLER *Sch. & Schm.* xv. (1857) 347 Of that accessible store-house in which the memories of past events lie arranged and taped up. **1854** E. MAYHEW *Dogs* (1861) 241 [He] first, by way of precaution, tapes the animal; that is, he forms a temporary muzzle, by binding a piece of tape thrice firmly round the creature's mouth. **1859** THACKERAY *Virgin.* lxxxiv, Every scrap of paper which we ever wrote, our thrifty parent..taped and docketed and put away. **1894** BOTTONE *Electr. Instr. Making* (ed. 6) 115 The armature must also be most carefully taped and varnished. No part of the iron, where the wire has to be wound, should be left uncovered. **1956** A. H. COMPTON *Atomic Quest* iv. 259 Alvarez taped three copies of this note to instrument boxes. **1972** *Daily Colonist* (Victoria, B.C.) 18 Jan. 17/1 Every girl..should clip it out and tape it to her bedroom mirror. **1979** R. JAFFE *Class Reunion* (1980) I. i. 36 Daphne had taped up small museum reproductions of famous paintings and prints.

b. *spec.* to bind or gag (a victim, etc.) with adhesive tape. Also with *up*.

1932 'SPINDRIFT' *Yankee Slang* 60 *Tape a guy*, gag a victim with adhesive plaster. **1950** 'P. QUENTIN' *Follower* xix. 135 Once they'd taped his wrists, all hope would be gone. **1962** 'H. HOWARD' *Double Finesse* vi. 69 It shouldn't take Alan longer than that to tape the night-watchman's mouth. **1977** D. ANTHONY *Stud Game* xiv. 84 He knocks you out..tapes you up neatly, and calls us to come and get you. **1981** P. MALLORY *Killing Matter* xv. 157 Tie her and tape her.

2. a. *trans.* To measure with a tape-line.

1886 [implied in TAPING *ppl. a.* below].

b. *Gunnery.* To get the range of (a position), by means of a tape-line used in conjunction with a range-finder; hence, to hit and silence (a target).

See also sense 5 below.

1917 A. G. EMPEY *From Fire Step* xi. 65 Our artillery had taped or silenced them [*sc.* the trench mortars]. *Ibid.* xxi. 146 The German artillery..had us taped (ranged) for fair; it was worth your life to expose yourself for an instant. **1919** J. B. MORTON *Barber of Putney* iii. 45 There's a sniper got that corner taped. **1919** G. K. ROSE *2/4th Oxf. & Bucks L.I.* 36 The Pozières ridge, whose crest was well 'taped' by the German guns. **1927** E. THOMPSON *These Men thy Friends* iii. 70 'He tried them at sixteen hundred yards, and got nowhere near them—lengthened the range a thousand, and was still short. But Johnny [Turk] had *us* taped' he added. 'No bothering about mirage for him. He knew the land and the distance of every blotch and pimple on it.'

3. *intr.* To appear (of such a size) on measurement with a tape; to measure (so much).

1895 J. G. MILLAIS *Breath fr. Veldt* (1899) 237 *note*, A good Mashonaland head seldom tapes more than 12 inches.

4. *trans. Sc.* To measure *out* in tape-lengths; to deal out slowly or sparingly; to use sparingly.

1721 RAMSAY *To R.H.B.* vii, Then let us grip our Bliss mair sicker, And tape our Heal and sprightly Liquor. **1818** SCOTT *Hrt. Midl.* xii, Ye sall hae a' my skill and knowledge to gar the siller gang far—I'll tape it out weel.

5. Colloq. phr. *to get* or *have* (someone or something) *taped*: to size up, ascertain, or understand fully (someone or something).

The development of this phrase is unclear. It may have arisen as a figurative use of sense 1 with the idea of 'tying up, having under control or in order' (cf. quot. 1854) or of sense 2 with the idea of 'measuring, assessing'.

1914 JOYCE *Dubliners* 210, I never saw such an eye in a man's head. It was as much as to say: *I have you properly taped, my lad.* He had an eye like a hawk. **1919** *War Slang* in *Athenæum* 18 July 632/2 'I got you taped,' an N.C.O. may say to a man, meaning 'I know what you are up to.' **1929** J. B. PRIESTLEY *Good Companions* I. iv. 114 We've made a 'ell of a bad break if we tell 'er co we are and then there's nothing doin'. Got us taped then. **1944** A. E. COPPARD in *Wine & Food* XLIII. 153, I want to get off the land. Can you find a boat? Not a motor-boat, that's noisy and they've got the harbour taped for sure. **1959** *Times Lit. Suppl.* 13 Mar. 142/4 The main part of the book, with its cold effort to get Mencken 'taped'. **1977** *Evening Post* (Nottingham) 27 Jan. 6/5 And so say all of us. Let's hope Portland have illiteracy 'taped'.

6. To record on (magnetic) tape; to make a tape recording of. Also *absol.*

1950 *Senior Scholastic* 1 Mar. 25T (*heading*) We tape it. Recorders produce a transformation in the classroom. **1958** S. ELLIN *Eighth Circle* (1959) II. ii. 41 He's being taped Sunday, so have one of the girls make a transcript of the tape. **1960** *Guardian* 9 Nov. 11/1 One [teenager] with a tape recorder can tape a pile of 'pop' records. **1966** E. MCGIRR *Funeral was in Spain* 20 Okay, men, let's hear his verbal run through. I understand you didn't tape. **1975** R. H. RIMMER *Premar Experiments* (1976) i. 130 I've tried taping sober, high on alcohol, and stoned on grass. **1978** R. NIXON *Mem.* 501, I was not comfortable with the idea of taping people without their knowledge.

Hence **taped** *ppl. adj.*, also with *out*, measured or sized up; fully ascertained (cf. senses 2 b, 5); **'taping** *vbl. sb.* and *ppl. adj.*

1886 *Blackw. Mag.* Sept. 337 Temporary taping-boys [employed on Ordnance Survey]. **1892** *Daily News* 13 Oct. 7/2 Two large taped frames in the centre. **1929** *Papers Mich. Acad. Sci., Arts & Lett.* X. 329/1 *Taped out*, an expression applied to a strip of land upon which the German gunners had accurately registered distances. **1933** WODEHOUSE in *Sat. Even. Post* 30 Dec. 58/2 Didn't I tell you that I had everything taped out? **1953** POHL & KORNBLUTH *Space Merchants* (1955) v. 55 What..have you got to back that statement up with? Letters? Memos? Taped calls? **1955** I. A. RICHARDS *Speculative Instruments* x. 122 The study of language, even in the most elementary stages, has to be a dependant of that highest generic taping which may be called ethics. **1960** *Daily Mirror* 23 Apr. 18/3 Bobby Darin ..left behind a taped Saturday Spectacular... This will be shown on ITV tonight. **1968** H. WAUGH *Con Game* xii. 109 A few of the people connected with the show had got together after the taping. **1972** R. PRAWER JHABVALA *New Dominion* I. 58 He kept turning on the taped music and the concealed lighting.

tape, obs. form of TAP.

tapecer, -ere, -ery, var. TAPISSER, -ERY *Obs.*

tapeinocephalic, etc.: see TAPINO-.

tapeism, tapeist: see TAPISM, -IST.

tapeless ('teɪplɪs), *a.* [f. TAPE *sb.* + -LESS.] Without tape, without the use of tapes.

Mod. A tapeless printing machine; a machine giving a tapeless delivery of printed sheets.

tapen ('teɪpən), *a. rare.* [f. TAPE *sb.*¹ + -EN⁴: cf. *oaken*, *silken*.] Composed of tape. In quot. *fig.*

1856 READE *Never too Late* xxv, His heart broke..its tapen bonds, and the man of office came quickly to the man of God.

‖**tapénade** (tapenad). Also **tapenade**. [Fr., f. Prov. *tapéno* capers.] A Provençal dish, usu. served as an hors d'œuvre, made principally from black olives, capers, and anchovies.

1952 G. MAUROIS *Cooking with Fr. Touch* iii. 56 Here is a southern (Nice) recipe for *tapenade*, which uses eggs, olives, and anchovies. *Ibid.*, *La tapenade* used always to figure on the list of hors d'œuvres at the old Hotel Victoria in Cannes. **1960** E. DAVID *Fr. Provincial Cooking* 142 To make the *tapénade*, called after the capers (*tapéno* in Provençal) which go into it. *Ibid.*, The *tapénade* is served pressed down into little deep yellow earthenware pots, like a pâté. **1966** P. V. PRICE *France: Food & Wine Guide* 299 Tapenade or tapanda. Pounded black olives served on toast or as an *hors d'œuvres*. **1978** *Times* 20 May 10/2 Regular dishes such as tapénade (a Provençal purée of capers, black olives, anchovies, and sometimes tunny fish).

†**'tapener.** *Obs. rare.* [Derivation obscure.] A kind of clothworker; ? a weaver of burel.

a **1400** *Usages of Winchester* in *Eng. Gilds* (1870) 350 Þe Tapeners þat worcheþ þe burelles..shullen take for þe cloth xviij d. *Ibid.* 352 Þe chaloun of foure ellen and o quarter of langnesse, shal habbe tweye ellen and an halfe to-fore þe tapener in þe werke.

taper ('teɪpə(r)), *sb.*¹ Also 1 tapor, -ur; 3–5 tapere, 4–5 tapre, -ur, -ir, 5 -yr, 5–7 tapper, 6 tapar, -ire, 7 tapor, -our. [OE. *tapur*, *-or*, *-er*: not in the cognate langs. According to Kluge, *Engl. Stud.* XX. 335, a dissimilated form of **papur*, ad. L. *papyrus*, which in glossaries (*a* 1100) is rendered 'taper', and in some Romanic forms has the sense 'wick of a candle', for which the pith of the papyrus was used. See Körting No. 6852.]

1. a. Originally, A wax candle, in early times used chiefly for devotional or penitential purposes; now *spec.* a long wick coated with wax for temporary use as a spill, etc. *to hold a taper to the devil*: cf. CANDLE *sb.* 5 b.

c **897** K. ÆLFRED *Gregory's Past. C.* xxxvi. 258 He hiene onælð mid ðæm tapore [*Hatton MS.* tapure] ðæs godcundan lieȝȝes. *c* **1000** *Sax. Leechd.* III. 202 Wex oððe taperas, ȝesihð blisse hit ȝetacnat. *a* **1100** *Voc.* in Wr.-Wülcker 267/12 *Lampas*, leohtfæt. *Candela*, candel. *Papirus*, taper. *c* **1200** *Trin. Coll. Hom.* 47 On ure honde beren candele berninde, taper oðer candele. *c* **1290** *S. Eng. Leg.* I. 19/12 Seint Dunstones moder taper a fuyre werth a-non. **1377** LANGL. *P. Pl.* B. XVII. 203 To a torche or a tapre þe trinitee is lykned. *c* **1460** *Brut* 508 She was enioyned to open penaunce, forto go thrugh Chepe, bering a tapere in hir hand. *a* **1512** FABYAN *Will* in *Chron.* (1811) Pref. 4 That they doo purvay for .iiii. tapers of iii lb. evry pece, to brenne aboute the corps and herse for the forsaid .ii. seasons. **1530** PALSGR. 279/1 Tapar of waxe, *cierge.* **1601** SHAKS. *Jul. C.* IV. iii. 275 How ill this Taper burnes. **1635** A. STAFFORD *Fem. Glory* 153 Very many Tapours were burning in the Church. **1653** GATAKER *Vind. Annot. Jer.* 36 To stoop so low, as to bear a taper before the Divel. **1696** PHILLIPS (ed. 5), *Taper*, a long and large siz'd Light made in form of a Pyramid made of Wax, and made use of in Churches for the most part. **1742** YOUNG *Nt. Th.* v. 720 Our birth is nothing but our death begun; As tapers waste, that instant they take fire. **1869** TOZER *Highl. Turkey* II. 115 The number of tapers, which, ..on festivals, were lighted in all parts of it [a church]. **1878** HUXLEY *Physiogr.* 79 A glowing taper bursts into flame when plunged into oxygen.

b. *fig.* Something that gives light or is figured as burning; in modern use esp. a thing that gives a feeble light.

a **1000** *Phœnix* 114 in *Codex Exon.*, Sweȝles tapur. **1588** SHAKS. *L.L.L.* v. ii. 267 Tapers they are, with your sweete breathes puft out. **1635** A. STAFFORD *Fem. Glory* 8 The Apostles, those holy Tapours of the primitive Church. **1646** J. HALL *Horæ Vac.* 8 The Tapour of Devotion burnes but dimly. **1646** JENKYN *Remora* 22 God may suffer the taper of the opportunity to burn out. **1699** POMFRET *Poems* (ed. 11) 44 The twinkling Tapers of the Night. **1770** GOLDSM. *Des. Vill.* 87 To husband out life's taper at the close. **1808** SKURRAY *Bidcombe Hill* 23 Whilst from the sky, the new-born moon display'd Her feeble taper, twinkling thro' the gloom. **1821** SHELLEY *Adonais* v, And happier they..Whose tapers yet burn through that night of time In which suns perished.

2. *attrib.* and *Comb.*, as *taper-candlestick*, *-flame*, *-fly*, *-light*, *-spark*, *-stand*, *-stick*; *taper-bearer*, *-holder*, *-maker*; *taper-lighted* adj.; †**'taperwort**, the Great Torch Mullein (*Verbascum Thapsus*).

c **1450** in Aungier *Syon* (1840) 342 They schal reuerently holde them styl in ther handes, ȝe also the *taperebererars as moche as they may,..in to tyme they haue offred hem at autyr to the preste. **1847** GOUGH & PARKER *Gloss. Terms Heraldry* 70 The **taper-candlestick*, borne in the arms of the Founders' Company..has a spike, or..a pricket, upon which the taper is placed. **1818** KEATS *Endymion* III. 116 Like *taper-flame..He rose in silence. **1616** DRUMM. OF HAWTH. *Song* Poems (1656) 60 Like a *Taper-fly there burne thy Wings. **1907** *Daily Chron.* 11 Apr. 3/7 A little pierced *taper-holder, with gadrooned edge, dated 1764. **1577** tr. *Bullinger's Decades* (1592) 103 Let..no man sette pearchers or *taper light before the Gods. **1595** SHAKS. *John* IV. ii. 14 With Taper-light To seeke the beauteous eye of heauen to garnish, Is wastefull, and ridiculous excesse. **1814** SCOTT *Ld. of Isles* III. viii, A taper light gleams on the floor. **1913** W. DE LA MARE *Peacock Pie* 119 Lantern-light, taper-light, Torchlight. **1850** ALLINGHAM *Poems*, *Light[house]* ii, Our fire and *taper-lighted room. **1396–7** *Abingdon Acc.* (Camden) 66 Johannes *Tapermaker 'pro Rectore de Appleton'. **1877** ALLINGHAM *Songs, Ball. & Stories, Pilot Boat* ii, A cottage by the strand With its feeble *taper-spark. **1837** LOCKHART *Scott* vi. (1839) I. 253 His first fee..was expended on a silver *taper-stand for his mother. **1546** in Hardiman *O'Flaherty's Iar Connaught* (1846) 230 Two candell or *tapire styckes of Shylver. **1956** G. TAYLOR *Silver* v. 114 *Taper Sticks.* Examples do not occur in silver until the later part of the period, and are generally miniature candlesticks. **1982** *Nat. Art-Coll. Fund Ann. Rep. 1981* 39/1 Taper-sticks were made to hold tapers for lighting candles or pipes, and generally have flat circular bases and narrow sockets. **1601** HOLLAND *Pliny* II. 274 The great Mullen or *Taperwort. [Cf. **1578** LYTE *Dodoens* 118 The whole top with his pleasant yellow floures sheweth like to a waxe candell or taper cunningly wrought.]

taper ('teɪpə(r)), *sb.*² [In sense 1, app. f. TAPER *sb.*¹; in other senses, app. from the vb. or adj.]

I. 1. A spire or slender pyramid; a figure which tapers up to a point.

1589 PUTTENHAM *Eng. Poesie* II. xi. (Arb.) 108 Of the Spire or Taper called Pyramis. The Taper is the longest and sharpest triangle that is, and while he mounts vpward he waxeth continually more slender, taking both his figure and name of the fire, whose flame..is alwaies pointed.

II. 2. Gradual diminution in width or thickness in an elongated object; continuous decrease in one direction; *spec.* in *Forestry* (see quot. 1957); *fig.* gradual decrease of action, power, capacity, etc.

1793 SMEATON *Edystone L.* §81 From thence its taper diminishing more slow, its sides by degrees come into a perpendicular. *Ibid.* §303 Iron plugs..upon a very gentle taper. **1840** J. BUEL *Farmer's Comp.* 145 They should be square, with a gradual taper to the point. **1875** R. F. MARTIN tr. *Havrez' Winding Mach.* 22 To try and manufacture steel ropes with a continuous taper. **1893** P. J. CARTER *Treatise Mensuration Timber* i. 5 Long logs should be measured in two or more sections..the sections increasing..with the taper of each log. **1945** G. B. GRUNDY *Fifty-Five Years at Oxford* vii. 132 A scale of taper which means the number of inches a tree decreases in girth between its base..and a point in its circumference ten or twenty feet above that. **1957** *Brit. Commonwealth Forest Terminol.* II. 194 *Taper*, the decrease in diameter of a tree bole or log from the base upwards.

3. Anything that gradually diminishes in size towards one extremity, as a tapered tube.

1882 *Worc. Exhib. Catal.* iii. 16 Sanitary tubes, bends, junctions, tapers, sluice valves.

4. *Comb.*, as **Taper-Lock, taper-lock** *Mech.*, a proprietary name in the U.S. for a type of tapered bush (BUSH *sb.*^{2} 1 b) inserted into a pulley, sprocket, etc., to enable it to be mounted rigidly on a shaft; **taper tap** *Mech.*, a tap (TAP *sb.*^{1} 4) tapered lengthways for about two thirds of its length, used to begin the process of cutting a screw thread in a hole; **taper-vice**, a vice adapted to hold objects which have not parallel sides.

1954 *Official Gaz.* (U.S. Patent Office) 4 May 31/1 Dodge Manufacturing Corporation, Mishawaka... **Taper-Lock.* .. For machine elements to be mounted on shafts and bushings therefor. **1971** *Engineering* Apr. 4/2 Pulleys.. complete with Taper-Lock bushes for fast, easy fixing. **1971** *Power Farming* Mar. 75/2 The new pulley illustrated incorporates the quick-fit taper-lock centre. *a* **1877** KNIGHT *Dict. Mech.* III. 2495/1 The process of screw-cutting was greatly improved by Maudslay, who introduced the practice of having three cutting edges, and using three taps, the entering *taper tap, the middle tap, and the plug tap. **1964** S. CRAWFORD *Basic Engin. Processes* i. 24 The taper tap has a chamfer or tapered lead for a length of 8–10 threads. **1877** KNIGHT *Dict. Mech.* 2495 *Taper-vise.

taper ('teɪpə(r)), *sb.*^{3} *Cotton-weaving.* [f. TAPE *v.* + -ER^1.]

a. (See quot. 1891.) Also *tape-sizer.*

1881 *Instructions to Census Clerks* (1885) 68 *Looming and Taping Room* [in Cotton Manufacture]:..Taper. Beam Flanger. Beamer. **1891** *Labour Commission* Gloss., *Tapers*, those in the cotton mills who take a number of 'beams' or bobbins as they come from the warper,..and run them through the 'size' upon another beam (called the weaver's beam). When this process is complete the produce is called a 'warp'. **1904** *Dundee Advert.* 5 July 10 The late Mr. Eli Higham, originally a taper at a cotton mill at Sabden.

b. One who tapes or deals with tape in other occupations.

1921 *Dict. Occup. Terms* (1927) §304 Coil taper,..binds coils with tape. **1927** *Daily Express* 2 Dec. 2/4 Taper,..[an] operator in charge of the insulation of armature.

taper, *sb.*^{4}: see TADPOLE^2.

taper ('teɪpə(r)), *a.* Also 5 tapre. [f. TAPER *sb.*^{1}: perh. through the earlier TAPERWISE: cf. quot. 1496.] **a.** Diminishing gradually in breadth or thickness towards one extremity (originally, upward); becoming continuously narrower or more slender in one direction; tapering.

1496 *Bk. St. Albans, Fishing* h j b, Thenne shaue your staffe & make hym tapre wexe [*a* **1450** *Fysshynge with an Angle*, 'tapur wyys waxing']. *a* **1625** *Nomenclator Navalis* (Harl. MS. 2301), *Taper bore*, is when a Peece is wider at the Mouth than towards the Breech. **1649** BLITHE *Eng. Improv. Impr.* v. (1653) 24 Make thy Drain, or Trench, somewhat Taper (*viz.*) Narrower and Narrower downwards. **1678** MOXON *Mech. Exerc.* vi. 113 All sorts of Stuff or work that are smaller at one end than at the other, and diminish gradually from the biggest end, is said to be *Taper*. **1688** R. HOLME *Armoury* III. 318/1 The lower part [of a drawing iron is] Taper, ending in a point. **1697** DRYDEN *Virg. Past.* VII. 54 Fair Galatea,..Tall as a Poplar, taper as the Bole. **1706** PHILLIPS (ed. 6), *Taper* or *Tapering*,..like a Cone, or Pyramid. **1758** *Vacation* in Dodsley *Collect. Poems* VI. 151 If Marian chance to shew Her taper leg and stocking blue. **1770** *Chron.* in *Ann. Reg.* 152/1 The body runs taper to the tail. **1821** COMBE *Wife* III. (Chandos ed.) 330 To the fine taper fingers' ends. **1888** HASLUCK *Model Engin. Handybk.* (1900) 38 The piston-head has a taper hole through it, into which the tapered end of piston-rod is forced.

b. *fig.* Of resources: Diminishing, becoming more and more 'slender'. *colloq.* or *slang.* †Also, of a person: reduced in funds, short (of money).

1789 J. BYNG *Torrington Diaries* (1935) II. 88 So now, being taper of the said necessary commodity [*sc.* cash], I was obliged to recruit from M. Oliver. **1851** MAYHEW *Lond. Labour* I. 224/1 Just in the critical time for us, as things was growing very taper. *Ibid.* (1861) II. 237/1 That sort of thing soon makes money show taper.

c. *Comb.*, chiefly parasynthetic in -ED^2, as ***taper-bored, -headed, -limbed, -moulded, -pointed*** (but in some of these *taper* may be sb.); also with a participle, as ***taper-grown***; **taper roller bearing**, a roller bearing in which the rollers are tapered slightly and lie at an angle to the axis of the bearing, so as to provide resistance to thrust along the axis as well as at right angles to it.

1626 CAPT. SMITH *Accid. Yng. Seamen* 32 To know whether she be equally bored, camber, taper, or belbored. **1634–5** BRERETON *Trav.* (Chetham) 165 They are called drakes. They are taper-bored in the chamber. **1664** POWER *Exp. Philos.* I. 13 Bristles or prickles like whin-pricks perfectly taper-grown. **1678** PHILLIPS (ed. 4), *Taper-board*, in Gunnery, is when a piece is wider at the mouth than towards the breetch. **1725** PHILIPS *To Miss Carteret* 41 Then the taper-moulded waist With a span of ribbon brac'd. **1828** J. E. SMITH *Eng. Flora* II. 12 Leaves broad, taper-pointed, angular rather than toothed. *c* **1843** CARLYLE *Hist. Sk.* (1898) 270 The taper-limbed Apollo figure. **1930** *Engineering* 7 Feb. 169/3 The driving wheels..are mounted on taper-roller bearings. **1971** *Power Farming* Mar. 50/1 The Benedict Soilmaster takes care of seed bed cultivations —and your tractor... No gears, no cranks and adjustable taper-roller bearings result in minimal maintenance.

taper ('teɪpə(r)), *v.* [f. TAPER *sb.*^{1}: cf. also TAPER *sb.*^{2} 1, of same date.]

1. a. *intr.* To rise or shoot up like a flame, spire, or pyramid (*obs.*); *fig.* to rise or mount up continuously in honour, dignity, rank, etc. *Obs.*

1589 PUTTENHAM *Eng. Poesie* II. xi. (Arb.) 109 Like as this faire figure Of tall comely stature By his kindly nature Endeuors soft and faire To Taper in the ayre. *c* **1645** HOWELL *Lett.* I. I. ii, Sir George Villiers..tapers up apace, and grows strong at Court. **1697** *Wars Eng. & Fr.* in *Harl. Misc.* (1810) X. 298 The Black Prince, having now won his spurs, and being tapered up to his full growth. **1887** *Pall Mall G.* 7 Mar. 2/1 Might it interest him..to watch the workings of Synods all over Prussia, tapering up (if I may use the term) by a process of elimination into a General Synod and its standing committee?

†**b.** (?) *nonce-use.* ? To talk loftily. *Obs.*

1683 E. HOOKER *Pref. Pordage's Mystic Div.* 103 How magnificously soever wee bragg and vapor and taper of our Reason, or Faith, Intellect, intelligibl Ideas and æternal Verities.

2. a. *intr.* To narrow or diminish gradually in breadth or thickness towards one end; to grow smaller by degrees in one direction. Const. *away*, *off*, etc.

1610 [see TAPERING *vbl. sb.*]. **1687** A. LOVELL tr. *Thevenot's Trav.* II. 27 The Castle,..situated on a little hill of an oval figure, that tapers from the bottom to the top. **1797** S. JAMES *Narr. Voy.* 164 A beautiful river, which tapers away..into a pleasant rivulet. **1815** ELPHINSTONE *Acc. Caubul* (1842) I. 127 Peaks of great height and magnitude, which do not taper to a point. **1884** BOWER & SCOTT *De Bary's Phaner.* 420 The bundles taper off gradually and terminate below the apex of the leaf. **1886** *Law Rep. 32 Chanc. Div.* 72 A strip [of land] tapering from a width of twelve inches to a point.

b. *fig.* ***to taper off*** (***away, down***): To become gradually less in intensity, etc.; also *colloq.* to leave off a process or habit by degrees, *esp.* to diminish gradually the quantity or potency of one's drink.

1848 J. F. COOPER *Oak-Openings* I. iv. 66 It's hard to give up old habits, all at once. If I could only taper off on a pint a day, [etc.]. **1848** WEBSTER *Let.* 18 Sept., in *Corr.* (1857) II. 285 My catarrh has been..severe. I hope it will soon begin to taper off. **1860** RUSSELL *Diary India* II. xii. 218 We saw him tapering away till he appeared a mere speck, as he went down the mountain-side, and finally disappeared altogether. **1871** NAPHEYS *Prev. & Cure Dis.* I. iii. 109 He makes..an unavailing effort to 'taper off' [from the use of ardent spirits]. **1898** *Allbutt's Syst. Med.* V. 947 If [the murmur] begin with the diastole of the heart and taper off during the pause, it is an easy sign to interpret. **1903** *Smart Set* IX. 12/2, I had been drinking hard for six months, and there was no such thing as clipping it short all at once. I had an idea of tapering off. **1960** *Wall St. Jrnl.* 18 Nov. 13/1 Carloadings 'taper down' starting in mid-November, when the bulk of Christmas shipping has been completed. **1971** *Daily Tel.* 4 Aug. 2/7 The deal is worth nearly £4-a-week more to the lower grades tapering down to £2 at the top end.

3. a. *trans.* To reduce gradually and regularly in breadth or thickness in one direction; to make tapering.

1675 HOBBES *Odyssey* 106 They smooth'd and taper'd it, as I would have it. **1771** LUCKOMBE *Hist. Print.* 315 This Bar..is tapered away. **1802** BEDDOES *Hygëia* VII. 42 As if the narrow chest had been lengthened or tapered out into neck. **1860** *All Year Round* No. 57. 159, I taper the point of my pencil. **1875** R. F. MARTIN tr. *Havrez' Winding Mach.* 26 A specimen of this sort of rope..was tapered in a length of 25 metres from ·30 metre at one end down to ·18 at the other.

b. *fig.* To reduce gradually in quantity; to diminish by degrees: esp. with *off*, *down*.

1899 *Allbutt's Syst. Med.* VIII. 419 The best method.. would be to 'taper off' the daily amount of drink. **1971** *Daily Tel.* 2 Aug. 7/8 There is speculation that the Government investment..in tracked hovercraft is to be tapered off. **1977** *Lancet* 23 Apr. 909/2 Oral prednisolone, 1 mg/kg/day, was resumed and rapidly tapered down to 0·5 mg/kg/day.

tape 'record, *sb. rare.* [f. TAPE *sb.*^{1} + RECORD *sb.*] A record(ing) on magnetic or other tape.

1905 *Talking Machine News* III. 57/1 A tape record could be made to be reproduced by either the cylinder of [*sic*] disc type of machine. **1914** *Sci. Abstr.* B. XVII. 372 The author submits some tape records which are reproduced. **1961** Y. OLSSON *Syntax Eng. Verb* ii. 17 Speech in its natural environment or in tape-record tapping. **1968** *Listener* 6 June 733/2 Fuzzy telephones or muzzy tape records.

'tape-record, *v.* [Back-formation from next.] *trans.* To record (sounds, etc.) on magnetic tape by means of a tape recorder.

1950 *Aviation Week* 6 Mar. 35 (*heading*) Plane-tower talk tape-recorded. **1955** E. WARNER *Trial by Sasswood* ix. 177 As though your thoughts..had been tape-recorded and played back to you. **1967** A. HENRI in *Penguin Mod. Poets* X. 25, I sit here..trying to taperecord the sound of windflowers and celandines. **1978** N. J. CRISP *London Deal* vii. 110 Could we tape record this?

Hence **'tape-recorded** *ppl. a.*

1951 *Time* 25 June 23/2 Testimony continued—part of it played scratchily from long, tape-recorded interviews with addicts. **1973** S. TRUEMAN *Fascinating New Brunswick* xvi. 125 Her tape-recorded folksongs have left a priceless heritage to New Brunswick.

'tape re,corder. Also with hyphen. [f. TAPE *sb.*^{1} + RECORDER^1.] †**1.** A device which records data on 'ticker' tape. *Obs.*

1892 W. P. LOMBARD in *Jrnl. Physiol.* XIII. 4 The labour of measuring the curves and of computing the total work was so great..that it was found necessary to devise an apparatus which would record automatically the total height to which the weight was lifted. This apparatus, which may be called a tape recorder, consisted of an endless tape. **1922** *Science & Invention* Feb. 935 The accompanying diagram shows a very interesting special arrangement with relay for operating a tape recorder, klaxon or telegraph sounder.

2. An apparatus for recording sounds, etc. on magnetic tape and afterwards reproducing them.

1932 *B.B.C. Techn. Tables & Gloss.* 65/2 Steel Tape Recorder. **1949** *Consumer Reports* Feb. 68/2 The three tape models all proved..substantially more convenient than earlier tape recorders and better than..the wire recorders tested. **1949** *Electronic Engin.* XXI. 369 There will be a selection from the very wide range of G.E.C. sound equipment..and the new G.E.C. Tape Recorder. **1953** M. MCCARTHY *Groves of Academe* xiii. 252 The psychology student with the tape-recorder. **1964** M. MCLUHAN *Understanding Media* (1967) v. 63 Radio and gramophone and tape recorder gave us back the poet's voice. **1978** J. A. MICHENER *Chesapeake* 854 From the moment Amos discovered what those newfangled tape recorders could do, he was satisfied that his..problems were solved.

Also **tape recordist**, one who makes tape recordings.

1960 *Guardian* 9 Nov. 11/1 The tape recordists were clearly making money out of their activities. **1970** J. EARL *Tuners & Amplifiers* iii. 70 If you are a keen tape recordist then the amplifier should certainly be equipped with at least source sockets for tape replay.

'tape re,cording, (*vbl.*) *sb.* [f. TAPE *sb.*^{1} + RECORDING *vbl. sb.*, after prec.] A record (of sounds, etc.) on magnetic tape; the process of making such a recording.

1940 *Electronics* May 16 (*heading*) Photo-electric tape recording. *Ibid.* 17/1 The editor of such tape recordings has considerable freedom in arranging the material. **1946** *Electronic Engin.* XVIII. 54 (*heading*) German tape-recording equipment. **1954** A. HUXLEY *Let.* 12 Dec. (1969) 718, I listened to the tape recording and the foreign language certainly doesn't sound like the gibberish of ordinary glossolalia. **1962** A. LURIE *Love & Friendship* xiv. 286 His voice sounded funny to him, like a tape-recording. **1977** P. STREVENS *New Orientations Teaching Eng.* xiii. 163 A set of specialized tape recording/replay machines.

tapered ('teɪpəd), *a.* [f. TAPER *sb.*^{1} + -ED^2.] Lighted by, or accompanied by the use of, tapers.

1745 WARTON *Pleas. Melanch.* 196 The taper'd choir, at the late hour of pray'r. **1792** S. ROGERS *Pleas. Mem.* II. 325 The chanted hymn, the tapered rite. **18..** CAMPBELL *On Poland* 49 The taper'd pomp—the hallelujah's swell.

tapered ('teɪpəd), *ppl. a.* [f. TAPER *v.* + -ED^1.] Made to taper; diminished in breadth or thickness by degrees; tapering, taper.

1669 STURMY *Mariner's Mag.* V. xii. 63 If you will make for tapered bore Guns, your Forms must be accordingly tapered. **1783** JUSTAMOND tr. *Raynal's Hist. Indies* I. 141 Ten or twelve pinnated leaves, tapered towards the top, very broad at their basis. **1839–40** W. IRVING *Wolfert's R.* (1855) 49 A lady's glove, of delicate size and shape, with beautifully tapered fingers. **1882** NARES *Seamanship* (ed. 6) 75 The fore and main tacks are tapered ropes.

taperer ('teɪpərə(r)). [f. TAPER *sb.*^{1} + -ER^1.] The bearer of a taper in a religious ceremony.

c **1450** in Aungier *Syon* (1840) 276 The taperers schal holde the tapers, turnyng westwarde, whilst the seyd herse is in sensyng. *Ibid.* 307 The ij taperers..schal take the two torches, and folowe the banerer al thre in surplys. **1901** W. H. ST. J. HOPE in *Archæol. Jrnl.* Mar. 6 The cross-bearer and taperers, followed by the censer-bearer. **1905** *Daily News* 24 Apr. 2 Behind him comes the cross, with its attendant taperers, next the banners.

†**'taper-fashion,** *a.* and *adv. Obs.* [f. TAPER *sb.*^{1} + FASHION *sb.*] Of or in the fashion or form of a taper; taper-like in shape; tapering, tapered.

1545 ASCHAM *Toxoph.* (Arb.) 126 Those [stales, i.e. stems of arrows] that be lytle brested and big toward the hede called by theyr lykenesse taperfashion, reshe growne. **1551** RECORDE *Cast. Knowl.* (1556) 147 Then doth the shadow [in an eclipse] growe lesser and lesser in spyre forme, or taper fashion.

†**'tapering,** *sb. Obs. nonce-wd.* [f. TAPER *sb.*^{1} + -ING^1.] The using of tapers.

1599 SANDYS *Europæ Spec.* (1632) 140 Willing by his Testament to bee buried in the night without their attending, tapering, censing or singing.

'tapering, *vbl. sb.* [f. TAPER *v.* + -ING^1.] The action of the verb TAPER in various senses; *concr.* a thing or part that tapers. Also ***tapering-off.***

1610 W. FOLKINGHAM *Art of Survey* I. iii. 6 The boaling, spreading,..and tapering of trees. **1677** MOXON *Mech. Exerc.* ii. 30 The Screw-plate will, after it gets a little below the tapering, go no further, but work and wear off the thred again it made about the tapering. **1884** BOWER & SCOTT *De Bary's Phaner.* 485 Those [cells]..must further show a conical tapering. **1890** L. C. D'OYLE *Notches* 186 It will take you months of steady tapering down. **1890** W. JAMES *Princ. Psychol.* I. iv. 124 The question of 'tapering-off', in abandoning such habits as drink and opium-indulgence, comes in here. **1955** KOESTLER *Trail of Dinosaur* 136 The Jews alone among the varied European immigrant population have resisted this 'tapering off' process.

'tapering, *ppl. a.* [-ING^2.] That tapers; taper.

a **1625** *Nomenclator Navalis* (Harl. MS. 2301) s.v., I have seene in Flemings the Top saile Tapering. **1665** *Phil. Trans.* I. 35 Insects with large Heads and small tapering Bodies. **1787** A. CLARKE in *Life* iv. (1863) 33 After the tapering thread of life is spun out. **1807** HUTTON *Course Math.* II. 267 A piece of tapering timber. **1893** LIDDON, etc. *Life Pusey* I. i. 5 Long hands and tapering fingers.

Hence **ˈtaperingly** *adv.*, in a tapering manner.

1878 H. S. Wilson *Alp. Ascents* iii. 92 As a champagne bottle has to be taperingly elongated. **1883** C. Robson in *Science Gossip* May 106 The posterior portion of the abdomen beyond the cornua prolonged taperingly considerably.

ˈtaperly, *adv. rare.* [f. TAPER *a.* + -LY[2].] In a tapering manner, taperingly, slenderly.

1802 *Sporting Mag.* XX. 292 A small dog, taperly and elegantly formed.

taperness (ˈteɪpənɪs). [f. TAPER *a.* + -NESS.] The condition of being taper; tapering shape.

1741 *Compl. Family-Piece* II. ii. (ed. 3) 330 Fine Sprouts ..that will answer for Taperness to one another. **1818** Keats *Endymion* I. 783 Fold A rose-leaf round thy finger's taperness, And soothe thy lips. **1871** *Figure Training* 76 A waist of remarkable taperness.

taperwise (ˈteɪpəwaɪz), *adv.* [f. TAPER *sb.*[1] + -WISE: cf. TAPER-FASHION.] In the manner of a taper; with gradual diminution of thickness towards one end.

a **1450** *Fysshynge wyth an Angle* (1883) 8 Then shaue the stafe and make hyt tapur wyyȝ waxing [1496 *Bk. St. Albans* tapre wexe]. **1575** Laneham *Lett.* (1871) 6 Eache with hiz syluery Trumpet of a fiue foot long, foormed Taper-wyse. **1601** Holland *Pliny* I. 392 The scape or stalk..not aboue 10 cubits in height, growing taper-wise, small and sharp in the top. **1609** C. Butler *Fem. Mon.* v. (1623) Mj, A handfull..of Boughes with hearbs, bound taper-wise together. **1727** *Bradley's Fam. Dict.* s.v. *Dog.* His tail or stern strong set on, waxing Taper-wise towards the top.

taperwort: see TAPER *sb.*[1]

†**ˈtapery.** *Obs. nonce-wd.* [f. TAPE *sb.*[1] + -ERY, after *napery, drapery.*] Tape and the like.

1657 Howell *Londinop.* 90 Weavers of divers sorts, to wit, of Drapery or Tapery, and Nappery.

tapes, tapes(ch)er: see TAPIS *v.*[3], TAPISSER.

‖**tapesium** (təˈpiːsɪəm). *Bot.* [mod.Lat. for med.L. *tapēcium, tapētium*, ad. Gr. ταπήτιον, dim. of τάπης carpet.] A carpet or layer of mycelium on which the receptacle is seated in discomycetous fungi (Phillips *Brit. Discomycetes*, Gloss.).

1887 W. Phillips *Brit. Discomycetes* 42 Seated on a distinct tapesium. *Ibid.* 279 Cups 200 to 300μ broad, seated on a dark radiating tapesium.

tapessarie, -erie, var. TAPISSERY *Obs.*

†**tapester, -ister.** *Obs. rare.* Also 5 tapster. [Corruption of *tapeser* TAPISSER, prob. by association with trade names in *-ster*; cf. TAPESTRY.] = TAPISSER. Also *attrib.*, as *tapester-work.*

1472-3 *Rolls of Parlt.* VI. 37/2, xii Quyssions of Tapster-work. **1594** R. Ashley tr. *Loys le Roy* 29 b, Smithes, glasiers, tapisters, painters. **1609** Bible (Douay) *Exod.* xxxv. 35 To make the workes of a carpenter, a tapester, an embroderer of hyacinth and purple. [**1859** Parker *Turner's Dom. Archit.* III. iii. 62 The most lucrative trade of the fifteenth century was that of a 'tapister'.]

tapester, obs. form of TAPSTER.

tapestry (ˈtæpɪstrɪ), *sb.* Forms: 5 tapstery, 5–6 tapestrye, 5–8 tapistry, 6 tapstry, -ye, tappistre, 6–7 tapes-, tapis-, tapstrie, 6– tapestry. [Corruption of *tapesry, tapesserie, tapisry*, or other form of TAPISSERY. The *t* may have developed phonetically between *s* and *r*, or may have been aided by words in *-istry*: cf. TAPESTER. (In Milton and Dryden a disyllable.)]

1. a. A textile fabric decorated with designs of ornament or pictorial subjects, painted, embroidered, or woven in colours, used for wall hangings, curtains, covers for seats, to hang from windows or balconies on festive occasions, etc.; especially, such a decorated fabric, in which a weft containing ornamental designs in coloured wool or silk, gold or silver thread, etc., is worked with bobbins or broaches, and pressed close with a comb, on a warp of hemp or flax stretched in a frame. Often loosely applied to imitative textile fabrics.

1434 [implied in TAPESTRY-WORK]. **1467** *Mann. & Househ. Exp.* (Roxb.) 387 My mastyr bowte of Skukborow of Cornelle, xij. peces of curse tapstery. **1500-20** Dunbar *Poems* lxxvii. 49 The streittis war all hung with tapestrie. **1513** Douglas *Æneis* IX. vi. 120 Prowd tapystry, and mekle precius ware. **1545** *Rates of Custom* C vij, Tapistry wyth sylke the ell xx d. **1570** Levins *Manip.* 106/13 Tapstrye, *tapêtum.* **1573-80** Baret *Alv.* T 62 Tapestrie, or hangings, in which are wrought pictures of diuerse colours. **1590** Shaks. *Com. Err.* IV. i. 104 In the Deske That's couer'd o're with Turkish Tapistrie. **1633** G. Herbert *Temple, Church Porch* xlv, I care not though the cloth of state should be Not of rich arras, but mean tapestrie. **1649** Milton *Eikon.* xxvii. Wks. 1851 III. 513 To be struck as mute and motionless as a Parlament of Tapstrie in the Hangings. **1700** Dryden *Pal. & Arc.* III. 104 Rich tapestry spread the streets, and flowers the posts adorn. **1777** Watson *Philip II* (1839) 47 Arras was famous for tapestries, which still retain the name of that place. **1835** *Penny Cycl.* IV. 68/1 *Bayeux Tapestry*, a web or roll of linen cloth or canvass, preserved at Bayeux in Normandy, upon which a continuous representation of the events connected with the invasion and conquest of England ..is worked in woollen thread of different colours. **1842** Brande *Dict. Sc.* etc. s.v., In Painting, *tapestry* is applied to a representation of a subject in wool or silk..worked on a woven ground of hemp or flax. **1858** Hawthorne *Fr. & It. Note-Bks.* I. 162 Gobelin tapestry..brilliant as pictures.

b. *transf.* and *fig.*

1581 Sidney *Apol. Poetrie* (Arb.) 25 Nature neuer set forth the earth in so rich tapistry, as diuers Poets haue done. *c* **1630** Risdon *Surv. Devon* §175 (1810) 184 A bridge, whose chiefest tapestry is Ivy. **1693** Evelyn *De la Quint. Compl. Gard.* II. 179 Squares covered with Green Herbs, compleat the tapestry, that adorns the Ground. **1831** Carlyle *Sart. Res.* I. x. (1858) 38 Looking at the fair tapestry of human life. **1845** Stocqueler *Handbk. Brit. India* (1854) 215 The rich tapestry of the jungles. **1875** Lowell *Under Old Elm* II. iii, Present and Past..inseparably wrought Into the seamless tapestry of thought.

c. Now freq. applied to (pieces of) canvas embroidery executed typically with wool in tent stitch.

1882 Caulfeild & Saward *Dict. Needlework* 473/2 Tapestry worked by the needle..differs but slightly from Embroidery. The stitches are made to lie close together, so that no portion of the foundation is visible. **1955** *Stitchcraft* Mar. 9 The design [for a picture] is worked in tent-stitch by the counted thread..; the chart includes instructions for tent-stitch and hints on stretching tapestry. **1971** *Harrods Magical Christmas* 9 Tapestry Cushion Pack of tramme canvas, wools and needle. *Ibid.*, If desired, we will stretch and mount the finished tapestry on velvet. **1976** P. Clabburn *Needleworker's Dict.* 263/3 Nowadays in Britain, any piece of canvas work, large or small, is called tapestry work, which is a misnomer, while America, although not falling into that particular trap, calls canvas work needlepoint, which is also confusing as that word should apply to lace made with a needle.

2. Short for *tapestry-carpet, needle*: see 3.

1879 *Cassell's Techn. Educ.* IV. 390/1 In the Brussels the coloured wools make up the bulk of the carpet, while in the 'tapestry' the wool..is..all on the surface. **1895** *Montgomery Ward Catal.* Spring & Summer 88/1 Needle Case... Contains—..Crewel..Tapestry..Bodkin. **1968** J. Ironside *Fashion Alphabet* 94 *Tapestry*, a needle which has a blunt point and large eye, used for embroidery with wool.

3. *attrib.* and *Comb.*, as ***tapestry artist, covering, hall, -hanging, -maker, -making, -man, room, table-cover, wool; tapestry-covered, -like***, adjs.; **tapestry beetle**, a dermestid beetle, *Attagenus piceus*, the larva of which is destructive to tapestry, woollens, etc.; **tapestry-carpet**, a carpet resembling Brussels, but in which the warp-yarn forming the pile is coloured so as to produce the pattern when woven; **tapestry-cloth**, a piece of tapestry; *spec.* a corded linen prepared for 'tapestry-painting' (*Cent. Dict.*); **tapestry-moth**, a species of clothes-moth, as *Tinea tapetzella*; cf. *carpet-moth*; **tapestry needle**, a blunt needle with a large eye used in tapestry-making and canvas embroidery; **tapestry-painting**, painting on linen in imitation of tapestry; material thus prepared; **tapestry-stitch**, properly = GOBELIN *stitch*; also applied to the cross- and tent-stitch work on fine canvas (*tapisserie au petit point*); **tapestry-weaver**, one who weaves tapestry; also, a species of spider; **tapestry-weaving**, the weaving of tapestry the method of weaving by bobbin and comb, used in making tapestry, as distinct from weaving in a loom with a shuttle. See also TAPESTRY-WORK.

1908 *Times, Lit. Suppl.* 3 Sept. 286/3 Designs prepared by a *tapestry artist from bird's-eye views specially drawn by William Van de Velde the Elder. **1858** Simmonds *Dict. Trade*, **Tapestry-carpets*, the name generally given to a.. two-ply or ingrain carpet, the warp or weft being printed before weaving, so as to produce the figure in the cloth. **1579** Tomson *Calvin's Serm. Tim.* 656/2 Long and large *tapistrie clothes. **1552** Huloet, *Tapestry couerynge, *instratum.* **1634** Milton *Comus* 324 Honest-offer'd courtesie Which oft is sooner found in lowly sheds With smoaky rafters, than in *tapstry Halls And Courts of Princes. **1552** Huloet, *Tapestrye hangynges for noble mens houses. **1700** Congreve *Way of World* II. vi, Like Solomon at the dividing of the Child in an old Tapestry Hanging. **1884** J. Tait *Mind in Matter* (1892) 95 *Tapestry-like designs. **1611** Cotgr., *Tapissier*, a *Tapistrie-maker. **1876** Rock *Text. Fabr.* 95 The art of *tapestry-making. **1727-41** Chambers *Cycl.* s.v., The design, or painting the *Tapestry-man is to follow, is placed underneath the warp. **1815** Kirby & Sp. *Entomol.* viii. (1818) I. 233 *T[inea] tapetzella*, or the *tapestry moth, not uncommon in our houses, is most injurious to the lining of carriages. **1888-9** *T. Eaton & Co. Catal.* Fall & Winter 64/2 The Household Needle Case contains darners, glovers, square-carpet, yarn, chenille, *tapestry,..and crewel needles. **1967** E. Lemarchand *Death of Old Girl* xvii. 196 Tim Pollard watched her..as she plied a tapestry needle. **1817** M. Edgeworth *Harrington* xviii. 496 Mr. Montenero..asked, in particular, about a *tapestry room,—a picture of Sir Josseline. **1977** R. Player *Month of Mangled Models* vi. 105 The casements of the Tapestry Room were wide span, and the Camelot curtains had been pulled back. **1859** W. Collins *Q. of Hearts* (1875) 23 A rugged *tapestry table-cover. **1796** Morse *Amer. Geog.* II. 345 The Flemings formerly engrossed *tapestry-weaving to themselves. **1889** Alan S. Cole *Cantor Lect., Egyptian Tapestry* I. 8 The process [anciently] employed is the same as that which was used by the great Flemish weavers..for making their splendid war tapestries, and is now commonly known as the tapestry weaving or Gobelins process. **1880** L. Higgin *Handbk. Embroidery* i. 4 **Tapestry Wool* is more than twice the thickness of crewel... Tapestry wool is not yet made in all shades. **1960** G. Lewis *Handbk. Crafts* 36 The most usual wool for this work is that with a slight twist to it called 'tapestry' wool, but other kinds may be used according to the mesh of the canvas.

tapestry (ˈtæpɪstrɪ), *v.* [f. prec. sb. See also TAPISTER.]

1. *trans.* To cover, hang, or adorn with, or as with, tapestry. (Chiefly in *pass.*)

c **1630** Risdon *Surv. Devon* §192 (1810) 206 The ruins.. is..tapestried with ivy. **1798** Charlotte Smith *Yng. Philos.* II. 102 The hardiest plant that tapestries the rude bosom of the North. *Ibid.* 165 My walls..were tapestried with the rock lichen. **1881** Mrs. C. Praed *Policy & P.* II. 14 The grape-leaves with which the verandah was tapestried.

2. To work or depict in tapestry.

1814 Scott *Wav.* lxiii, Remnants of tapestried hangings. **1876** T. Hardy *Ethelberta* II. xl, Where Elizabethan mothers and daughters..had tapestried the love-scenes of Isaac and Jacob.

Hence **ˈtapestried** *ppl. a.*, adorned with tapestry; woven in the manner of tapestry.

1769 Sir W. Jones *Pal. Fortune* 24 Some tap'stried hall, or gilded bower. **1794** Southey *Retrospect* 104 Still with pleasure I recall The tapestried school, the bright brown-boarded hall. **1814** [see 2]. **1848** Thackeray *Bk. Snobs* xlii, Making covers of..net-work for these tapestried cushions.

ˈtapestry-work. = TAPESTRY *sb.* 1.

1434 *N.C. Wills* (Surtees 1908) 43 Lectum meum de tapstriwerke cum leonibus et pelicano. **1459** in *Paston Lett.* I. 479 Item, j testyr of blewe tapistry warke. **1587** Fleming *Contn. Holinshed* III. 1332/1 The feast was excellentlie well furnished of all things, & speciallie of tapistrie worke & other deuises of sugar. **1601** Holland *Pliny* VIII. xlviii. 227 The course rough wool..hath been of auncient time highly commended and accounted of in tapestrie worke. **1812** Mar. Edgeworth *Vivian* viii, Miss Strictland [followed] bearing her ladyship's tapestry work.

Comb. *c* **1515** *Cocke Lorell's B.* 9 Borlers, tapstry worke, makers, and dyers.

So **ˈtapestry-worked** *a.*, tapestried; **ˈtapestry-worker**, one who works or makes tapestry.

1727 (*title*) The Practice of Perspective..a work highly necessary for Painters, Embroiderers, Jewellers, Tapestry Workers. **1883** Ld. R. Gower *Rec. & Remin.* xxi. II. 60 Two large tapestry-worked screens. **1908** H. Pentin *Judith* iv. 77 'Judith and Holofernes' was also a favourite subject for tapestry-workers.

†**tapet**, *sb. Obs.* (exc. *Hist.*). Forms: 1 tęped, tæpped, tæppet; 3–4 (9) tapit, 4–5 tapyt, 4–6 tapite, -yte, -ete (also 9), 5 tapytt, -e, (tepit), 5–6 tapett, -e, tappet, 6 -ett, -e, *Sc.* tapeit, taphet, 4– tapet. [The OE. *tęped* was WGer. ad. late L. *tapētum*: cf. OHG. *tęppid, tęppith* (more usually *tęppih*, Ger. *teppich*). The later OE. *tæpped, -et* (cf. also MLG. *teppet*) may have been re-influenced by Latin. ME. *tapet, tapit*, etc. perh. came down from OE.; but the word may have been introduced anew in 13th c. from L., or from Prov. *tapit* or other Romanic form: cf. MDu. *tapijt*, and see TAPIS.] A piece of figured cloth used as a hanging, table-cover, carpet, or the like.

a **900** *Kentish Glosses* in Wr.-Wülcker 61/1 *Tapetibus pictis*, ȝemetum tepedum. *c* **1000** Ælfric *Voc.* in Wr.-Wülcker 152/1 *Sipla*, an healfhruh tæppet. *c* **1050** in Thorpe *Charters* (1865) 429, VII ofbrædelsas and II tæppedu.

a **1300** *Cursor M.* 11240 Was þar na pride o couerled [*v.r.* couerlite] Chamber curtin ne tapit [*v.rr.* -ite, -yte]. **13..** *Gaw. & Gr. Knt.* 858 Tapytez tyȝt to þe woȝe, of tuly & tars, & vnder fete, on þe flet, of folȝande sute. **1382** Wyclif *2 Sam.* xvii. 28 Couerynge clothis, and tapetis [**1388** tapitis]. **1398** Trevisa *Barth. De P.R.* v. lxii. (Bodl. MS.), The flesche þat lieþ in þe vtter parties of bones..is as it were a nedeful tapet and esement. **1425** *Rolls of Parlt.* IV. 298/1 Þere was on a nyght [a man] taken by hynd a tapet in ye said Chambre. *c* **1477** Caxton *Jason* 97 b, Medea..brought him into the chambre where they satte vpon a moche riche tapyte. **1513** Douglas *Æneis* I. xi. 8 Amang prowde tapeitis and miche riche apparale Hir place sche tuik. *a* **1562** G. Cavendish *Wolsey* (1893) 227 Leanyng ayenst the tappett or hangyng of the chamber. **1585** T. Washington tr. *Nicholay's Voy.* II. v. 35, 4. tapites floured, of pinsed satten. **1591** Spenser *Muiopotmos* 276 Each doth chuse What storie she will for her tapet take. [**1859** Parker *Turner's Dom. Archit.* III. iv. 104 The bed..consisted of a selour, a testor, a counterpoint, six tapits of arras [etc.]. **1875** Pollen *Anc. & Mod. Furn.* 31 Carpets, *tapete*, blankets, or other woollen coverlids for sofas or beds, were made at Corinth.]

b. In figurative and allusive uses: cf. CARPET *sb.* 2 b and 3.

c **1380** Wyclif *Wks.* (1880) 246 Summe ladies ben menys to haue a daunsere, a trippere on tapitis, or huntere or haukere. *c* **1430** Lydg. *Compl. Bl. Knt.* 51 The soyle was.. oversprad with tapites that Nature Had made her selfe. *c* **1470** Harding *Chron.* cxv. vii. (MS. Ashm. 34) lf. 90 God sette neuer Kynge to be a Ryotoure To trippe on tapites and leue in Idilnesse. **1563** *Mirr. Mag.* Induct. i, The gladsom groves that nowe laye overthrowen The tapets torn, and every blome downe blowen.

c. *attrib.* †**tapet-hook**, a hook for hanging 'tapets' or tapestry-hangings to the wall.

1480 *Wardr. Acc. Edw. IV* (1830) 121 Crochetts and tapethooks for the hangyng of the same verdours.

†**ˈtapet**, *v. Obs.* [f. prec. sb.] *trans.* To hang with 'tapets' or tapestry; to adorn with tapestry. Also *fig.*

c **1369** Chaucer *Dethe Blaunche* 260 Hys hallys I wol do peynte with pure golde And tapite hem ful many folde. *c* **1407** Lydg. *Reson & Sens.* 2766 The launde rounde aboute ..Tapited al the large pleyn Of herbys and of fressh[e] flours. **1412-20** —— *Chron. Troy* I. 1659 [Medea] koude.. in wynter with flowris fresche of hewe, Araye þe erþe and tapite hym in grene.

tapet, -ette: see TAPPET.

tapetal (tə'piːtəl), *a. Bot.* [f. TAPET(UM + -AL[1].] Of or pertaining to the TAPETUM (2).

1882 VINES *Sachs' Bot.* 480 These divisions produce a tapetal layer at an early stage which surrounds each group of spore-mother-cells. **1882** —— in *Nature* 19 Oct. 595/2 The surrounding protoplasm which is derived from the disorganised tapetal cells.

‖**tapeti** ('tæpətɪ). Also 7 tapati. [Tupi.] The Brazilian rabbit, *Lepus brasiliensis.*

1613 PURCHAS *Pilgrimage* (1614) 842 The Tapati also barke like Dogges. **1774** GOLDSM. *Nat. Hist.* (1776) IV. 54 The Tapeti, or the Brasilian rabbit, is in shape like our English ones, but is much less.

‖**tapette** (tapɛt), *sb.* (and *a.*). [F. *tapette* pederast, homosexual (*slang*), f. *taper* to tap, hit + *-ette*, fem. suffix.] A passive male homosexual; an effeminate man or 'pansy'. Also as *adj.*

1930 E. WAUGH *Vile Bodies* ii. 22 My dear, he looks terribly *tapette.* **1936** 'R. WEST' *Thinking Reed* xiii. 455 'It will make my room look as if I were a *tapette*!' exclaimed Marc. **1949** A. WILSON *Wrong Set* 174 She replied '..you do look madly tapette when you're drunk.' **1960** J. BALDWIN *Another Country* (1963) II. i. 183 Yves had lived by his wits in the streets of Paris, as a semi-*tapette*, and as a *rat d'hôtel.* **1978** J. SHERWOOD *Limericks of Lachasse* xv. 181 My mother ..wondered if you were perhaps *tapette*, but my brothers assured her that..you were perfectly masculine.

‖**tapetum** (tə'piːtəm). [Late and med.L. *tapētum* (pl. *tapēta* in Probus), for L. *tapēte* carpet.]

1. *Comp. Anat.* An irregular sector of the choroid membrane in the eyes of certain animals (e.g. the cat), which shines owing to the absence of the black pigment; also *tapetum lucidum* or *t. choroideæ.*

1713 DERHAM *Phys. Theol.* IV. ii. 102 This Illumination he speaks of, is from the Tapetum in the bottom of the Eye. **1799** *Monthly Rev.* XXX. 146 The posterior half of a cat's eye..was immersed in a bason of water, and examined. The tapetum appeared very bright, the retina not having acquired sufficient opacity to become visible. **1869** H. USSHER in *Eng. Mech.* 3 Dec. 270/3 A..shining appearance at the bottom of the eye, called the 'tapetum' or 'carpet'.

2. *Bot.* The layer of epithelial cells which lines the inner wall of the sporangium in ferns, etc., or of the pollen-sac in flowering-plants.

1882 VINES *Sachs' Bot.* 437 The inner cell again forms four tabular segments which are parallel to the outer parietal cells and which constitute the tapetum. **1885** GOODALE *Physiol. Bot.* (1892) 171 *note*, The epithelium which lines the pollen-sac has been termed the *Tapetum.*

tapeworm ('teɪpwɜːm). [f. TAPE *sb.*[1] + WORM; from its flat ribbon-like form.] A cestoid worm (e.g. *Tænia solium*), which when adult infests the alimentary canal of vertebrates; = TÆNIA 5.

1752 J. HILL *Hist. Anim.* 15 The flat Tænia. The Tapeworm..is found in the human intestines, and in those of many other animals. **1799** *Med. Jrnl.* I. 277 Successful experiments, not only to discover that unwelcome visitor the tape worm, but likewise to destroy and expel it. **1860** G. H. KINGSLEY in *Vac. Tour.* 163 The trout in some of the lakes have been infested with tapeworm.

b. *fig.* A parasite.

1824 W. IRVING *T. Trav.* II. x. (1849) 246 They were absolute tape-worms to my little theatre; the more it took the poorer it grew. **1860** EMERSON *Cond. Life, Culture* Wks. (Bohn) II. 369 Can we never extract this tape-worm of Europe from the brain of our countrymen?

c. *attrib.* and *Comb.*, as ***tapeworm infection***; ***tapeworm-shaped*** adj.; **tapeworm-plant**, an Abyssinian tree, *Brayera anthelmintica* (N.O. *Rosaceæ*), the pistillate inflorescence of which is used as a vermifuge (*Cent. Dict.* 1891).

1839 G. ROBERTS *Dict. Geol., Tænianus*,..tape worm shaped. **1897** *Allbutt's Syst. Med.* II. 1019 In many instances of tape-worm infection, the parasite appears to give rise to no inconvenience whatever.

tapheit, -eta, -ettye, -ite, obs. ff. TAFFETA.

taphiser, variant of TAPISSER *Obs.*

tap-hole ('tæphəʊl). [f. TAP *sb.*[1] + HOLE *sb.*]

1. The hole in a cask, vat, or the like, in which the tap is inserted.

1594 PLAT *Jewell-ho.* III. 10 These halfe tubs hauing tap-holes within. **1707** MORTIMER *Husb.* (1721) II. 322 Put it back again, stopping your Tap-hole.

2. A small opening in a furnace, through which the metal, or slag, or both, may be run out; also, a hole in a cementation furnace in which tap-bars (see TAP *sb.*[1] 8) are inserted.

1825 J. NICHOLSON *Operat. Mechanic* 341 Each pot has also small openings in its end, through which the ends of two or three of the bars are left projecting in such a manner, that by only removing one loose brick from the external building, the bars can be drawn out..; these are called the tap-holes. **1839** URE *Dict. Arts* 320 In the melting furnaces, the metal is run out by a tap-hole in the side. **1861** FAIRBAIRN *Iron* 101 The fluid iron, as it flows from the tap-hole, is fully white hot, and perfectly limpid.

taphonomy (tæ'fɒnəmɪ). *Palæont.* [f. Gr. τάφος grave + -NOMY.] The study of the processes by which animal and plant remains become preserved as fossils. Hence **tapho'nomic, -ical** *adjs.*; **ta'phonomist**, a specialist in taphonomy.

1940 J. A. EFREMOV in *Pan-Amer. Geol.* LXXIV. 93, I propose for this part of palaeontology the name of 'Taphonomy', the science of the laws of embedding. *Ibid.*, Taphonomical research allows us to glance into the depth of ages from another point of view. **1971** *Nature* 8 Oct. 391/2 There seem to be neither palaeoecological nor taphonomical features of the formation that would preclude *Hipparion* being represented in the assemblage. **1974** *Times* 2 Mar. 14/2 Russian scientists have brought together a team of geologists..and a group of taphonomists: the last belong to a speciality created in Russia for studying the way animals and plants are preserved in their burial sites. **1974** *Nature* 8 Mar. 100/3 Sessions were devoted to..patterns of diversity and implications of taphonomic evidence for behaviour patterns. **1977** LEAKEY & LEWIN *Origins* i. 12/2 Any scientific meeting on our origins nowadays might be attended by archeologists..[and] taphonomists. **1981** *Nature* 10 Dec. 598/3 Palaeontologists are..bringing their subject out of the museum through studies of the processes by which the fossil record forms (taphonomy). *Ibid.*, Much of the book concentrates on the principles, methods of study and results of taphonomic studies of (mainly) African vertebrates.

tap-hose ('tæphəʊz). Now *dial.* Also 7 tapwaze, 8 -owze, 9 -ooze, -wees. [f. TAP *sb.*[1]

The precise sense in which *hose* is used in the second element is not clear; in later use it has been associated with other words, esp. OOZE, WASE, bundle of straw.]

A strainer placed over the tap-hole in a mash-tub or the like, to prevent any solid matter from passing into or through the tap.

14.. *Voc.* in Wr.-Wülcker 606/28 *Quaxillum*, a tappehose. **1480** *Maldon, Essex, Court Rolls* (Bundle 51, No. 3 b), i vatte, I taphose, I rother. **1609** C. BUTLER *Fem. Mon.* (1634) 157 But first provide..a Tub or Kive, with a Tap, and Tap-waze. **1707** MORTIMER *Husb.* (1721) II. 322 Till it [wort] runs clear, which it will not do at first tho' your Tap-hose be never so well adjusted. **1736** BAILEY *Househ. Dict.* 232 Having an open headed cask with a tap, and tap-owze. **1854** MISS BAKER *Northampt. Gloss., Tap-ooze, Tap-whisk*, the wicker strainer placed over the mouth of the tap in a mash-vat when brewing, to allow the wort to ooze through, and to prevent the grains passing. [See also TAP *sb.*[1] 8.]

'tap-house. [f. TAP *sb.*[1] + HOUSE *sb.*[1]] A house where beer drawn from the tap is sold in small quantities; an ale-house; sometimes in connexion with a brewery. Also, the tap-room of an inn. Also *fig.*

1500-1 in Swayne *Sarum Churchw. Acc.* 55 In emendando hostium de le Taphouse, iiijd. **1591** NASHE *Prognostication* Wks. (Grosart) II. 153 That their Hoffes and tappe houses shall be more frequented, then the Parishe Churches. **1603** SHAKS. *Meas. for M.* II. i. 219. **1642** MILTON *Apol. Smect.* vi. Wks. 1738 I. 120 To creep into every blind Tap-house that fears a Constable more than a Satyr. **1764** *Low Life* 35 Some Gentlemens Coachmen at the Tap-Houses of the Inns. **1896** *Daily News* 20 May 5/6 'Tap-houses' of breweries; licences to enable distilleries to sell two gallons of spirit, more, but not less, for home consumption.

attrib. *c* **1639** R. DAVENPORT *Surv. Sciences* Poems (1890) 328 That Tap-house trick of ffidling. **1883** S. C. HALL *Retrospect* I. 120 He got drunk like a tap-house sot.

‖**taphrenchyma** (tæ'frɛŋkɪmə). *Bot.* [mod.L. (Morren), f. Gr. τάφρος pit + ἔγχυμα infusion.] Pitted tissue; = BOTHRENCHYMA.

1876 J. H. BALFOUR in *Encycl. Brit.* IV. 87/1 The names of *bothrenchyma* and *taphrenchyma* have been given to a tissue composed of such cells.

taphrogenesis (tæfrəʊ'dʒɛnɪsɪs). *Geol.* Also tafro-. [ad. G. *tafrogenese* (E. Krenkel *Die Bruchzonen Ostafrikas* (1922) v. 181), *taphrogenese* (—— *Geologie Afrikas* (1928) II. 636), f. Gr. τάφρος pit: see -GENESIS.] The formation of large-scale geological structures by high-angle or block faulting, esp. as the result of tensional forces in the crust. Hence **taphro'genic** *a.*

1923 *Bull. Geol. Soc. Amer.* XXXIV. 200 Faulting through tension [in East Africa] has gone on in compensation for the orogeny elsewhere. Therefore tafrogenesis (from the Greek for rifts or graben) is the counterpart of orogenesis, and East Africa is the type area for tafrogenic structures. **1963** E. S. HILLS *Elem. Structural Geol.* xi. 315 Taphrogenic movements—The necessity to recognise a third type of movement is indicated by the tectonic importance of major belts of block faulting, notably the rift valley and graben zones... The term was coined for the East African rifts, and is largely descriptive. In general, however, it implies tensional forces as opposed to horizontal compression for orogeny and differential vertical movements for epeirogeny. **1978** *Nature* 9 Mar. 158/2 Sedimentation has been controlled by NW-SE trending faults in close relationship to the taphrogenesis of the SW-NE trending Benue trough. **1979** *Ibid.* 7 June 478/3 There may be a long time interval between initial taphrogenic activity ('rifting') and creation of ocean floor by spreading ('drifting').

‖**tapia** ('tɑːpɪə). [Sp. *tapia* mud-wall: see Diez.] Clay or mud puddled, rammed, and dried: used for walls. Also *attrib.*

1748 *Earthquake of Peru* iii. 268 The Walls are of Clay ramm'd between two Planks, which they call Tapias. **1834-47** J. S. MACAULAY *Field Fortif.* (1851) 146 Loop-holes, when they can be given a regular form, as in mud or tapia walls. **1878** HOOKER & BALL *Marocco* 322 The remains of massive walls of tapia. **1883** *Sunday Mag.* 689 Strengthened by an unbroken ring of solid walls built of tapia or concrete.

tapice, tapicer, var. TAPIS *v.*[1], TAPISSER.

tapidaro, tapidero, varr. TAPADERO.

†**tapinage.** *Obs.* Also 4 tapy-, tapnage. [a. OF. *tapinage* place of concealment, f. *tapin* a concealed or disguised person, f. *tapir*: see TAPIS *v.*[1]] Hiding, concealment, secrecy.

13.. *K. Alis.* 7116 (Bodl. MS.), Whiles þe kyng in his Tapynage [*Weber* tapnage] Sent after Antioche þe Ostage. **1390** GOWER *Conf.* II. 187 This newe tapinage of lollardie. *c* **1400** *Rom. Rose* 7363 That they wolde gone in tapinage, As it were in a pilgrimage. [**1616** BULLOKAR *Eng. Expos.*, *Tapinage*, secrecie, slilinesse. **1656** BLOUNT *Glossogr.*, *Tapinage*, secrecy, a lurking, or lying close.]

taping: see TAPE *v.*; also, the occupation or work of a tape-sizer: see TAPE *sb.*[1] 4 and TAPER *sb.*[3]

tapinocephalic, tapeino- (tə,paɪnəʊsɪ'fælɪk), *a. Anthrop.* [f. Gr. ταπεινός low + κεφαλή head + -IC: see CEPHALIC.] Of the nature of, or having, a low flattened skull. So **ta,pino'cephalism, ta,pino'cephaly**, the condition of being tapinocephalic.

1878 BARTLEY tr. *Topinard's Anthrop.* I. v. 176 Tapinocephalic. *Ibid.* Index, Tapinocephaly. **1886** *Jrnl. Anthrop. Inst.* XVI. 150 The skulls thus agree with the ordinary Bushman skull in most respects being microseme, platyrhine, tapeinocephalic. **1897** *Ibid.* XXVII. 281 The former inclining to tapeinocepahlism. **1898** A. C. HADDON *Study of Man* ii. 47 The East Anglians have a form of skull slightly different to that of the South Saxons. It is rather broader, less tapeinocephalic (i.e. less low in the crown).

†**tapinophoby.** *Obs. nonce-wd.* [f. Gr. ταπεινός low, base + *-phoby*: see -PHOBIA.] (See quot.)

1772 R. GRAVES *Spir. Quixote* I. vi. (1783) I. 18 Such readers as are possessed with the modern tapino-phoby, or dread of every thing that is low..in writing.

†**tapi'nosis.** *Rhet. Obs.* [ad. Gr. ταπείνωσις lowness (of style).] (See quots., and cf. DIMINUTION 2 b.) Hence †**tapi'notically** *adv.*, by way of tapinosis.

1589 PUTTENHAM *Eng. Poesie* III. xvii. (Arb.) 195 If ye abase your thing or matter by ignorance or errour in the choise of your word, then is it by vicious maner of speach called *Tapinosis.* *c* **1600** *Timon* II. iv. (1842) 35 *Pseud.*.. They did obscure the sunne beames with wette clothis. *Demeas.* A *tapinosis* or diminution. **1652** URQUHART *Jewel* Wks. (1834) 292 Words diminishing the worth of a thing, tapinotically. **1657** J. SMITH *Myst. Rhet.* 57 In Meiosis, the speaker ought to take care that he fall not into that fault of speech, called *Tapinosis*, humility, that is when the dignity or majesty of a high matter is much defaced by the basenesse of a word; as to call the Ocean a stream, or the Thames a brook.

tapioca (tæpɪ'əʊkə). Forms: 8-9 tipioca, 9 tabiaca, (tapiaca), tapioca. [a. Pg., Sp., F. *tapioca*, a. Tupi-Guarani *tipioca*; f. *tipi* residue, dregs, + *og*, *ók* to squeeze out. (Cavalcante in Skeat.)] **a.** A starch used for food, the prepared flour of the roots of the CASSAVA plant. Also *attrib.*

[**1612** CAPT. SMITH *Map Virginia* 13 The chiefe roote they haue for foode is called *Tockawhoughe*... Raw it is no better then poison, and being roasted except it be tender..it will prickle and torment the throat extreamly. **1648** MARCGRAVE *Hist. Nat. Brasil.* 67 Fecula albissima, quam indigenæ vocant Tipioja, Tipiaca & Tipiabica.] **1707** SLOANE *Voy. Jamaica* I. 131 The juice evaporated over the fire gives the Tipioca meal. **1753** CHAMBERS *Cycl. Supp.*, *Tipioca*, a name given..to a sort of cream or flower made from the yucca or manihot-root..after expressing the juice. **1792** *Encycl. Brit.* (ed. 3) IX. 79/2 Starch, which the Brasilians export in little lumps under the name of *tapioca.* **1812** J. SMYTH *Pract. of Customs* (1821) 253 Tapioca is the farina, obtained by subsidence in a very fine state, after washing the pulp of the root of the Cassava, which grows in South America. **1837** W. TAYLER *Diary* 14 May in J. Burnett *Useful Toil* (1974) II. 181 They had two soles fried with saws..a tabiaca pudding, cheese and butter. **1859** D. BUNCE *Travels with Dr. Leichhardt* 107 Christmas day..tapioca pudding, each man having as much as he could eat. **1869** R. F. BURTON *Highl. Brazil* II. 39 The sediment of the juice that comes from the mass is called tipioca (our tapioca) and the liquor is thrown away. **1891** KIPLING *Life's Handicap* vii. 169 Smoked tapioca pudding.

b. In generalized application.

1856 *Farmer's Mag.* Nov. 409 Properly granulated and dried, potato meal forms an excellent tapioca.

tapiolite ('tæpɪəlaɪt). *Min.* [ad. Sw. *tapiolit* (A. E. Nordenskiöld 1863); named after *Tapio*, a Finnish deity: see -LITE.] 'Columbo-tantalate of iron, resembling tantalite, but containing no manganese' (Chester).

1868 DANA *Min.* (ed. 5) 518 Tapiolite..occurs near the Kulmala farm, in the village of Sukula, in the parish of Tammela, Finland.

tapir ('teɪpə(r), -ɪə(r)). Also 8 tapyr. [ad. Tupi *tapira* or *tapyra*, now usually called *tapyra-ete* 'true' or 'real tapir', and *tapir-ussu* 'great tapir', to distinguish it from European cattle, to which the name *tapira* was also given by the aborigines.] An ungulate mammal of tropical America of the genus *Tapirus* or family

Tapiridæ, somewhat resembling the swine (but more nearly related to the rhinoceros), having a short flexible proboscis.

Originally applied to the species *Tapirus americanus* of Brazil; thence extended to the two Central American species, *T. Dowii* and *T. Bairdi* (also *Elasmognathus*), and the Malay Tapir, *T.* (or *Rhinochœrus*) *indicus*.

[**1568** tr. *Thevet's New Found Worlde* 78 (*heading*) Tapihire, a beaste. **1580** De Lery *Voyage au Brésil* 312 Tapiroussou, une beste qu'ils nomment ainsi. **1648** Marcgrave *Hist. Nat. Brasiliae* vi. vi. 229 Tapiierete Brasiliensibus, Lusitanis Anta. **1693** Ray *Syn. Quad.* 126 Tapiierete. **1753** Chambers *Cycl. Supp.*, *Tapijerete*..the name of an animal found in some parts of America, and called by the Portuguese *anta*.] **1774** Goldsm. *Nat. Hist.* (1776) IV. 331 The tapir may be considered as the hippopotamos of the New Continent. **1796** Stedman *Surinam* II. xxiii. 176 The flesh of the tapira is delicate, being accounted superior to the best ox-beef. *Ibid.* (*Plate*), Tapir. **1834** *Nat. Philos.* III. *Phys. Geog.* 55/2 (Usef. Knowl. Soc.) In America, the only representative of these large pachydermatous animals is the tapir. **1865** Tylor *Early Hist. Man.* xi. 305 The snout of the tapir..protrudes a little more than that of our pigs.

b. *attrib.* and *Comb.* **tapir mouth**: see quot.

1891 *Syd. Soc. Lex.* s.v. *Mouth*, *Tapir mouth*, Landouzy's term for the peculiar tapir-like expression of mouth produced by wasting of the muscles of the face in myopathic atrophy. **1902** P. Fountain *Mts. S. America* iii. 87 Tapir-beef is the best meat to be obtained in South America.

So **tapi'ridian**, *a.* belonging to the family *Tapiridæ*; *sb.* an animal of this family; **'tapirine** *a.*, of or pertaining to the tapirs; **ta'pirodont** *a.* [Gr. ὀδούς, ὀδοντ- tooth], marking a dentition similar to that of the tapirs (*Cent. Dict.* 1891); **'tapiroid** *a.*, allied to or resembling the tapirs.

1880 *Libr. Univ. Knowl.* (N.Y.) VII. 474 The herbivora will contain the suborders proboscidians,..*tapiridians, having long noses but not prehensile or only very slightly so, as the rhinoceros and tapir. **1891** C. F. Holder *Darwin* 206 Animals without the peculiar *tapirine teeth. **1849-52** *Todd's Cycl. Anat.* IV. 926/1 In the transverse divisions of the crown we perceive the affinity to the *Tapiroid type. **1880** Dawkins *Early Man* ii. 30 In France [the tapir] is associated with two tapiroid genera.

tapis ('tæpɪs, ‖tapi), *sb.* Forms: 5 tappes, 6 *Sc.* tapeis, 7- tapis. [a. F. *tapis*, OF. *tapiz* (12th c.) = Sp., Pg. *tapiz* (pl. *tapices*):—pop. L. type **tappētium*, for late L. *tapētium* (-*ēcium*), ad. Gr. ταπήτιον, dim. of τάπης (acc. τάπητα) cloth wrought with figures in various colours, tapestry.

Late L. *tapētium* might also be inferred from *tapētia*, pl. of cl. L. *tapēte*, neuter; L. had also *tapēta* pl., as from **tapētum*, and *tapētæ* pl., as from **tapēta*; also (immed. from Gr.) acc. sing. masc. *tapēta*, pl. *tapētas*, as from **tapēs* masc. In later and med.L., Isidore has pl. *tapēta*; later forms cited by Du Cange are *tapēcius*, *tapēsium* (from *tapētium*), and *tapētiæ* pl. Beside the forms mentioned above, It. has *tappeto*, Sp. and Pg. *tapete*, Pr. *tapit*. From late L. and Rom. came also OE. *tęped*, *tæpped*, *-et*, and the cognate forms mentioned under TAPET.]

†**a.** A cloth worked with artistic designs in colours, used as a curtain, table-cloth, carpet, or the like.

1494 Fabyan *Chron.* vi. cxli. 129 Beholde now this house, where are now the ryche tappes & clothis of golde. **1539** *Inv. R. Wardrobe* (1815) 50 Item four grete pece of tapis of Turque, off the quhilkis ane is of silk. Item fiftene litle tapis of Turque. *a* **1600** in Pinkerton *Anc. Scott. Poems* (1786) I. 257 Thy beddis soft, and tapeis fair. **1800** J. Hurdis *Fav. Village* 134 What loom e'er furnish'd for imperial floor Tapis more rich, or grateful to the foot.

b. Phrase. ***on* (*upon*) *the tapis*** [from F. *sur le tapis*], on the table-cloth, under discussion or consideration. Cf. CARPET *sb.* 1 b.

1690 Clarendon *Diary* 2 May, Lord Churchill and Lord Godolphin went away, and gave no votes in the matter which was upon the tapis. **1782** *Europ. Mag.* I. 248 Several marriages are adjusted, and many others are on the tapis. **1809** Han. More *Cœlebs* II. xxxiv. 128, I had..been trying to bring Lucilla on the tapis. **1865** *York Herald* 18 Mar., The question of the legitimate claimant has for a long time been upon the *tapis*. **1880** *Manch. Guardian* 23 Nov., This view was held by Mr. Stansfield when his successor's bill was on the *tapis*.

‖**c.** ***tapis vert***, a long strip of grass-covered ground; a grass walk. Cf. CARPET *sb.* 3.

1960 O. Manning *Great Fortune* iii. 215 They were walking down the main path beside the *tapis vert*. **1965** Mrs. L. B. Johnson *White House Diary* 9 Mar. (1970) 248 He wants to..preserve the tapis vert, the long green ribbon that stretches..from the Capitol to the Lincoln Memorial. **1976** D. Wood *Pract. Garden Design* ii. 42 Two steps down..to the enclosed gardens on either side of the *tapis vert*—'green carpet'.

tapis, tapish ('tæpɪs, -ɪʃ), *v.*[1] *Obs.* or *arch.* Forms: 4-7 tapis (4 tapise, -ice), 6-7 tappas, 6-8 tapish, 7 tappish, tappes, 7-9 tappis, 9 tappice. [f. OF. (*se*) *tapir*, *tapiss-* (12th c. in Hatz.-Darm.); ulterior origin uncertain: see -ISH[2].] *intr.* To lie close to the ground, lie low so as to be hid; to lurk, skulk, lie hid. (The *pa. pple.* is commonly used in intransitive sense: cf. *fallen*, *risen*.)

c **1330** R. Brunne *Chron.* (1810) 3 With joy alle at ons þei went tille Snawdone On Iuor & Ini, þat tapised by þat side, To purueie þam a skulkyng, on þe Englis eft to ride. *c* **1330** —— *Chron. Wace* (Rolls) 11529 þou schal nought tapice a night to slepe. **1592** Warner *Alb. Eng.* vii. xxxvi. (1612) 175 Now tappas closely, silly Heart,..The Huntsmans-selfe is blind. **1599** A. Hume *Hymns, Day Estivall* 126 The hart, the hynd, and fallow deare, Are tapisht at their rest. **1611** Markham *Countr Content.* i. iv. (1668) 25 Hee will tappish oft, that is, he will ever and anon be lying down and lurking in dark holes and corners. **1613** Drumm. of Hawth. *Cypress Grove* Wks. (1711) 119 The spider; that pitcheth toyls, and is tapist, to prey on the smaller creatures. **1659** *Lady Alimony* ii. vi. in Hazl. *Dodsley* XIV. 322 Sir Reuben..like a ranger may tappis where he likes. **1688** Shadwell *Sqr. Alsatia* v. i, You'l find him tappes'd in some Ale-house. **1823** Scott *Peveril* xxxiii, Your father..is only tappiced in some corner. *a* **1825** Forby *Voc. E. Anglia*, *Tappis*, to lie close to the ground. A sportsman's phrase... 'It is so wet the birds cannot tappis'.

b. *trans.* (and *refl.*) To hide, conceal. *arch.*

a **1660** *Contemp. Hist. Irel.* (Ir. Archæol. Soc.) II. 127 If you yett insiste to see the disposition of man to the quicke discouered, and take of the veile wherwith [it is] tapissied. **1831** Scott *Cast. Dang.* xi, Having tappiced herself behind the little bed.

Hence †**'tapised** (**tapist, tapiced**) *ppl. a.*, hidden, concealed; †**'tapissing** *vbl. sb.*, in quot. *concr.* a hiding-place.

a **1340** Hampole *Psalter* xvii. 13 He sett myrknesis his tapissynge [L. *latibulum*]. **1621** Lady M. Wroth *Urania* 35 Wee..made them as fearefully rush vp, as a tapist Buck will doe, when he finds his enemies so neere.

tapis, tapish ('tæpɪs, -ɪʃ), *v.*[2] Now *dial.* Forms: 4 tapis, 8-9 tapish, 9 tappish. [perh. for **tabish*, f. L. *tābēscere* to waste away, decline.] *intr.* (*a*) To languish, pine away; (*b*) to be mortally sick or diseased. (Often in *pa. pple.* in intrans. sense.)

c **1375** *St. Aug.* 499 in Horstm. *Altengl. Leg.* (1878) 70, I ..þat sum tyme was a bitter berkere..Ayeynes lettres goode and mete..And I tapissed [L. *tabescebam*] vndur such lettring. **1747** Hooson *Miner's Dict.* Vj, When Miners are troubled in the Mines by Damps,..yet..are preserved by being timely helped, and escape with Life; such a one we say, is Tapish'd, or more or less. **1865** Sleigh *Derbysh. Gloss.* s.v., Hur tappish'd yes' morn. **1875** *Manch. Guard.* 1 Mar. (E.D.D.), His brother said he thought he was 'tappished' with a decline. *Ibid.* 29 Mar., 'This arm's tappished', ..'This wood's tappished'. **1891** *Sheffield Gloss.* Suppl. 58 *Tapish*, to waste or pine away... 'He tapished and died'.

†**tapis**, *v.*[3] *Obs.* Forms: 6 tappes, 6-7 tapes, 7 tapis. [a. F. *tapisse-r* (15th c. in Hatz.-Darm.), in OF. *tapissier*, f. *tapis*: see TAPIS *sb.*] *trans.* To hang, cover, or adorn with tapestry; also, to adorn with figures, as tapestry.

1528 Lyndesay *Dreme* 325 That myrke Mansioun is tapessit with stynk. **1562** Leigh *Armorie* (1597) 122 Chamber, richly arrayed and tappesed with Arras. **1601** Holland *Pliny* xix. iv, The windowes beautified with green quishins, wrought and tapissed with floures of all colours. **1602** Carew *Cornwall* 111 b, Onely there remaine the Iuie-tapissed wals of the keepe.

tapism ('teɪpɪz(ə)m) [f. TAPE *sb.*[1] + -ISM.] Official formality or routine; = RED-TAPISM.

1852 *Q. Rev.* Mar. 418 There affection bursts the cold priggery of tapeism—she vents her sorrows at his departure.

†**tapisser.** *Obs.* exc. *Hist.* Forms: 4-5 tapycer, tapecer, -e, tapicer, tapesere, taphiser, 5 tapiser, tapser, 5-6 tapisser, *Sc.* tapescher. [a. AF. *tapicer* = OF. *tapicier* (13th c.), mod.F. *tapissier*, f. OF. *tapiz*, F. *tapis*, figured cloth: see TAPIS *sb.* and -ER[2].] A maker or weaver of figured cloth or tapestry.

c **1386** Chaucer *Prol.* 362 A Webbe, a Dyere, and a Tapycer [*v.rr.* taphiser, tapecer(e)]. **1388** Wyclif *Exod.* xxxviii. 23 A tapesere and a broderere of iacynt, purpur, vermyloun and bijs. **1439** in *Ancestor* July (1904) 17 A coverlit and a testre of tapicers werk. **1541** *Acc. Ld. High Treas. Scotl.* VIII. 42 Given to the tapescher for his warkmanschip. **1591** Sparry tr. *Cattan's Geomancie* 225 He shall be a tapisser or spinner of cloth of golde. **1883** M. E. Haweis in *Contemp. Rev.* Sept. 426 Chaucer describes the fat dyer and tapiser in his prologue. **1892** Besant *London* 194 When certain tapicers were charged with selling false blankets.

Hence †**tapisser-work** *Obs.*, tapestry-work.

1459 *Test. Ebor.* (Surtees) II. 227 Hengyng for ye halle and parlor of tapisserwerk.

†**'tapissery.** *Obs.* Also 5 tapecery(e, tapcery, tapisery, -yssere, 5-6 -ery(e (tapserye), 6 tapycerye, -esserie, -essarie (*Sc.*), tappyssery, tapissary, -arie, tapisry, -issrie, 7 -issry. [a. F. *tapisserie* (14th c. in Hatz.-Darm.), f. *tapissier* a tapestry-worker, or *tapisser* to cover with carpet, f. *tapis* carpet, table-cloth: see TAPIS *sb.* and -ERY.] The early form of the word TAPESTRY. Also *attrib.*

1426 *E.E. Wills* (1882) 76 A blewe bedde of Tapecery. *c* **1430** Lydg. *Min. Poems* (Percy Soc.) 6 Clothis of gold, silk, and tapcery. *c* **1430** *Brut* 460 Alle the stretes..were hanged with clopes of arras and with clothes of tapissery werk. **1497** *Caxton's Chron. Eng.* vii. (W. de W.) S vj b/1 The stretes were coueryd ouer his heed wyth sylk of tapisery. **1525** Ld. Berners *Froiss.* II. li. 181 Chambres hanged with tapyceryes and curteynes. **1530** Palsgr. 279/1 Tappyssery werke, *tapisserie*. *a* **1548** Hall *Chron., Hen. VI* 115 b, Riche clothes of Arras and Tapissrie. **1555** W. Watreman *Fardle Facions* ii. xi. 260 The grounde couered and garnisshed with natures Tapesserie. **1578** T. N. tr. *Conq. W. India* 183 Rich Mantels, Tapissary Targats, tuffes of feathers. **1683** Evelyn *Diary* 4 Oct., The new fabriq of French tapissry. **1697** —— *Numismata* viii. 285 Clemens Alexandrinus in the Tenth Book of his Tapisseries.

tapist ('teɪpɪst). [f. TAPE *sb.*[1] + -IST.] = RED-TAPIST.

1852 Jerdan *Autobiog.* II. 41, I do not think he could leave the amount of a tapist's quarter's salary behind him.

†**'tapister, -tre**, *v.* *Obs.* [f. *tapister*, TAPESTER *sb.*] = TAPESTRY *v.*

1587 Harmar tr. *Beza's Serm.* 263 Flowers with which the earth is tapistred. **1592** Greene *Upst. Courtier* B j, A vale all tapistred with sweet and choice flowers. **1644** Evelyn *Diary* 7 Nov., The room..is tapisstred with crimson damasq embrodred with gold.

tapister, var. TAPESTER *Obs.*, tapestry-worker.

†**'tapiter.** *Obs. rare.* [f. *tapit*, TAPET *sb.* + -ER[1].] = TAPISSER. Also *attrib.*

c **1440** *York Myst.* xxx. 270 (*title*) The Tapiteres and Couchers. **1485** *York Civic. Rec.* (Yorks. Archaeol. Soc.) (1939) I. 115 It was determyned that the tapiters, cardemakers and lynwyves of this Citie be togader annexid to the bringing furth of the padgeants of the tapiter craft and cardmaker.

tap-lash ('tæplæʃ). Now *dial.* Also 7 -lush. [f. TAP *sb.*[1] + LASH *v.*[1]]

1. The 'lashings' or washings of casks or glasses; dregs or refuse of liquor; very weak or stale beer.

1623 J. Taylor (Water P.) *Disc. by Sea* B vij, To murder men with drinking, with such a deale of complementall oratory, As, off with your Cup, winde vp your bottome, vp with your taplash, and many more eloquent phrases. **1681** W. Robertson *Phraseol. Gen.* (1693) 597 Very tap-lash; dead drink. **1813** *Sporting Mag.* XLII. 118 Liquors of all denominations from champagne to humble tap-lash. **1828** *Craven Gloss.*, *Tap-lash*, thick small beer; poor, vapid liquor of any kind.

fig. **1672** Marvell *Reh. Transp.* I. 227 This the Tap-lash of what he said. **1769** Colman *Prose Sev. Occas.* (1787) III. 157 Thou..draw'st the taplash of another's brains.

b. *attrib.* or *adj.*

1642 in J. B. Williams *Eng. Journalism* (1908) 36 They have filled the City..with the fruits of their taplush inventions. **1673** Bp. S. Parker *Repr. Reh. Transp.* 197 Bandied up and down by the School-men in their taplash disputes. **1682** Hickeringill *Mushroom* Wks. 1716 II. 366 Stale Taplash droppings, old and sowr.

†**2.** Applied contemptuously to a publican. *Obs.*

c **1648** *Eng. Ballad*, '*No Money, No Friend*' (Farmer), Each Taplach..would cringe and bow, and swear to be My Servant to Eternity. **1719** D'Urfey *Pills* (1872) IV. 320 Thus is it not evident Tap-lashes don't thrive?

Tapleyism ('tæplɪɪz(ə)m). [f. the name of Mark *Tapley*, a character in Dickens's *Martin Chuzzlewit* (1843-4) + -ISM.] Optimism in the most hopeless circumstances, as expressed by Tapley's determination always to remain 'jolly'. Also **'Tapleyan** *a.*

1857 B. Smith *Let.* in W. James *Mem. & Stud.* (1911) ix. 246, I have a good share of Tapleyism in me and come out strong under difficulties. **1900** F. W. Maitland *Let.* 22 Jan. (1965) 209 Your letter..told me more than I had learned from any newspapers about the gloom of England, though I had read something between lines which seemed to me Tapleyan. **1972** *Scots Observer* 12 Mar. 2/2 What impressed me..was the grim way they held on to optimism... If that is Tapleyism..then Tapleyism is a fine thing.

†**'taplin, tapling.** *Obs.* (See quots.)

1748 Brownrigg *Making Salt* ii. ii. §1. 54 The pan..is placed over the furnace, being supported at the four corners by brick work; but along the middle, and at the sides and ends, by round pillars of cast iron called taplins, which are placed at three feet distance from each other, being about eight inches high, and at the top, where smallest, four inches in diameter. **1753** Chambers *Cycl. Supp.*, *Taplings*, in the English salt-works, the name given to certain bars of iron which support the bottom of the pan in which the brine is boiled. **1797** *Encycl. Brit.* (ed. 3) XVI. 626/2 [as in quot. 1748].

'taplings, *sb. pl.* 'The strong double leathers made fast to the ends of each piece of a flail'; the middle-band. (Halliwell 1847-78.)

tapnage: see TAPINAGE.

'tapnet, †**topnet.** [In 16th c. *topnet*, app. altered from TOPPET (*tappet*) q.v. Cf. TAP *sb.*[3]] A basket made of rushes, in which figs (formerly also raisins, etc.) are imported; also a conventional measure of quantity; = FRAIL *sb.*[1]

α. **1524** in Rogers *Agric. & Prices* III. 535/4 [Figs] Topnets. **1537** in J. H. Blunt *Myrr. oure Ladye* Introd. 31 Dyuerse sortes of Spices and fruyttes..Nutmygges.. Corans..Gynger..Isonglas..Figge doodes v Topnettes ij lb.—xj s. ix d. *c* **1550** *Customs Duties* (B.M. Add. MS. 25097), Figgs dodes, the topnet, xx d. **1882** Rogers *Agric. & Prices* IV. 671 Between 1516 and 1540 the price of figs by the toppet or topnet is a little over 2*s.* 3*d.*... Such a price.. suggests..that the toppet contained about 30 lbs., and that it corresponds to the earlier frail... In 1533 figs are bought by the topnet at Cambridge and by the frail at Stonor, at the same price, 2*s.* 6*d.*

β. **1553** W. Cholmeley *Request & Suite true-hearted Eng.* in *Camden Misc.* II. 17 Fyggis at xx*d* the tapnet. **1556** W. Towrson in Hakluyt *Voy.* (1589) 99 Three Tapnets of figges, two pots of oyle. **1682** *Privil. Citizens Lond.* 71 For Tapnets and Frails of Figs per Ton..xx d. **1812** J. Smyth *Pract. of Customs* (1821) 88 Frails, or Tapnets, are baskets made of rushes. **1858** in Simmonds *Dict. Trade.* **1910** *Grocer, Diary* 47/1 *Figs*, Faro, tapnets, 28 lbs.

attrib. **1578** Lyte *Dodoens* v. lxxxi. 652 Currantes or Raysens of Corinthe, do not much differ in vertue, from tapnet or frayle Raysens.

†**'tapon.** *Sc. Obs.* Also 6 **tappone, tawpon, talpoun,** 7 **tapoun.** [a. F. *tapon* (1382 in Hatz.-Darm.), earlier form of *tampon* plug, etc., f. *taper* to plug (of OLG. origin: see TAP *v.*¹).] A word having the general sense 'plug, peg, pin', in various applications.

1. A peg in a drinking-vessel, a pin; = PEG *sb.*¹ 2 b, PIN *sb.*¹ 1 f.

1543 *Burgh Rec. Edinb.* (1871) II. 112 That all nichtboures..sendand for wyne..haif thair pynts of just mesure merkett with the townis merk, and that the samyn haif ane talpoun as vse is in vther pairts. **1543–4** *Ibid.* 115 Stowppis of mesour with tawponis in the hals, merket with the townis merk. **1551** *Ibid.* 161 That the samyn haue ane tappone as vs is in vther pairtis.

2. A peg acting as a tappet (TAPPET¹).

1640 A. MELVILLE in *Extracts fr. Comm.-pl.* (1899) 29 The said quheill hath of taponis that liftis ye hamer 8.

3. A main branch or ramification of the root of a tree or plant; a subsidiary root.

1641 R. BAILLIE *Lett., to Mrs. Baillie* 6 Feb. (1841) I. 298 We trust God will putt them [the Bishops] doun, bot the difficultie to gett all the tapouns of their roots pulled up are yet insuperable by the arme of man.

4. ***tapon staff***, ? the stave containing the vent-peg.

1661 *Sc. Acts Chas. II* (1820) VII. 230/2 That no barrell be sooner made and bloune, but the Coupers birne be set theron, on the tapon staff thairof.

tap-ooze, -owze, etc.: see TAP-HOSE.

tapotement (tə'pəʊtmənt). *Med.* [a. F. *tapotement*, f. *tapoter* to tap: see -MENT.] Percussion, esp. as a part of the treatment in massage.

1889 *Lancet* 2 Mar. 423/1 Best attained by certain manipulations which include circular movements, kneading, and *tapotement*. **1896** *Allbutt's Syst. Med.* I. 374 Tapotement is the application of rapid blows delivered with the ulnar edge of the hand.

tapp, obs. f. TAP.

tappa, variant of TAPA¹.

'tappable, *a.* [f. TAP *v.*¹ + -ABLE.] Capable of being tapped or pierced for juice; fit for tapping.

1910 *Westm. Gaz.* 13 Apr. 10/1 [The estate] already possesses no fewer than 40,780 [rubber] trees, with 14,700 at a tappable age. **1910** *Morning Post* 22 Apr. 1/3 [The] C. Rubber Company..having over 100,000 tappable trees between four and 10 years old.

‖**tappal, -aul** (tə'pɔːl). *Anglo-Ind.* [Of obscure and uncertain origin: see Yule.] The transmission of letters, etc. by relays of runners; the organization by which this is carried on; the postal matter or conveyance, the mail; one who carries the post; an arrival or dispatch of letters.

1791 JAS. ANDERSON *Corr.* 64 A letter by the Tappal or Dawk. **1799** WELLINGTON in Gurw. *Suppl. Desp.* (1858) I. 303, I have sent orders to the postmaster at Seringapatam to run a tappall from thence to Nuggur. **1809** LD. VALENTIA *Voy.* I. vii. 385, I might go by tappaul the whole way to Seringapatam. **1889** *Blackw. Mag.* Feb. 199 Farewell to telegrams and tappals for a fortnight.

Hence ‖**tappal-wallah** [cf. *competition-wallah*], a runner who carries the post in S. India.

1865 *Daily Tel.* 12 Dec. 7/2 The tappal-wallah does not turn up with the letters at the proper time.

tappas, var. TAPIS *v.*¹ to lie hid.

tappe, obs. form of TAP, TAPE.

tapped *ppl. a.*¹: see TAP *v.*¹

tapped, *ppl. a.*² [f. TAP *v.*² + -ED¹.]

a. *Phonetics.* Pronounced with a tap (see TAP *sb.*² 1 d). **b.** ***tapped penalty*** (Rugby Football), a penalty taken with a tap-kick (see TAP *sb.*² 5).

1964 R. H. ROBINS *Gen. Linguistics* 101 A flapped or tapped /r/..when the tongue tip lightly and momentarily touches the alveolar ridge is common between two vowels (as in *merry*). **1966** R. E. ASHER in C. E. Bazell *In Memory of J. R. Firth* 17, *r* is a tapped alveolar consonant. **1977** *Observer* 22 May 23/3 Bevan took a tapped penalty 15 yards from his own line.

‖**tappen** ('tæpən). [Sw. and Norw. *tapp-en* the plug.] The plug by which the rectum of a bear is closed during hibernation.

[**1830** L. L. LLOYD *Field Sports N. Europe* I. v. 89 His bowels and stomach become quite empty, and..the extremity of them is closed by an indurated substance, which in Swedish is called *tappen*. **1835** *Penny Cycl.* IV. 85/1 *note*, The plug (in Norway termed the *Tappen*), found in the rectum of fat hybernating bears.] **1865** WOOD *Illustr. Nat. Hist.* I. 393 The 'tappen' is almost entirely composed of pine-leaves, and the various substances which the Bear scratches out of the ants' nests.

tapper¹ ('tæpə(r)). Forms: 1 **tæppere,** 2 **-are,** 6– **tapper,** *Sc.* **tappar, topper.** [OE. *tæppere*, f. *tæppa*, TAP *sb.*¹, *tæppian*, TAP *v.*¹: see -ER¹.]

†**1. a.** One who taps casks or draws liquor; a tavern-keeper; = TAPSTER 2. *Obs.*

a **1000** *Ags. Gloss.* in Wr.-Wülcker 202/14 *Caupus, i. tabernarius qui uinum uendit.* tæppere. *a* **1050** *Liber Scintill.*, etc. (1889) 226 Na byþ ȝerihtwisud tæppere [L. *caupo*] fram synnum welera. *c* **1537** *Thersites* in *Four O. Pl.* (1848) 82 The tapper of Tauystocke & the tapsters potte. **1618** D. BELCHIER *Hans Beer-pot* B j b, Ioaske Flutterkin, a Tapper.

†**b.** A retailer; cf. TAP *v.*¹ 4 b. *Sc. Obs.*

1478–9 *Burgh Rec. Edinb.* (1869) I. 37 The provest and counsale of the towne ordanis the meilmen topperis fremen of the towne and [to] top his meill daylie. **1580** *Burgh Rec. Glasgow* (1876) I. 82 That na topparis of small salt..by ony salt in greit..quhill ix houris of the daye. **1605** in Macgregor *Hist. Glasgow* xviii. (1887) 157 Tappers of woollen and linen cloth.

2. a. One who or that which taps, in various senses; e.g. one who taps trees for the sap or juice; a machine for milking cows.

1884 C. G. W. LOCK *Workshop Receipts* Ser. III. 309/1 The tapper then goes round provided with the bark scraper. **1884** J. SCOTT *Barn Implements* xvii. 157 Tube-milkers, or tappers; Sucking-machines; and Mechanical hand-milkers, or squeezers and strippers. **1908** *Westm. Gaz* 2 Mar. 5/2 The ruthless destruction of date palms by 'tappers' is said to be most evident in Madras.

b. One who 'touches' another for money; a beggar. Cf. TAP *v.*¹ 3. *slang.*

1930 G. SMITHSON *Raffles in Real Life* xiv. 189 He was a hanger-on, a common cadger, a 'tapper'. **1939** J. WORBY *Spiv's Progress* iv. 32, I didn't have time to light a cigarette before I was accosted by a tapper. **1962** *John o' London's* 25 Jan. 82/2 One who lives by cadging or begging is a *bummer*, *knocker* or *tapper*.

c. One who taps (TAP *v.*¹ 2 c) telegraph or telephone wires; a phone-tapper, a wire-tapper.

1973 P. TAMONY *Americanisms* (typescript) No. 33. 7 Thirty three states legislated total wiretap bans.., while six created partial bans which allowed police to tap.., but forbidding private tappers under any conditions. **1976** *Time* 27 Dec. 42/2 Halperin..was furious at learning that the FBI had tapped his telephone... Last week Morton Halperin won a resounding victory that could cost his tappers, starting with President Nixon, nearly $1 million in damages. **1980** E. BEHR *Getting Even* xv. 170 He delivered an oblique message in Chinese... The tappers might not even tell the difference.

3. One who works a screw-cutting tap for threading holes or orifices: cf. TAP *v.*¹ 6.

1909 in *Cent. Dict. Suppl.*

tapper² ('tæpə(r)). [f. TAP *v.*² + -ER¹.]

1. One who taps or lightly strikes: e.g. one who taps at a door, etc.; one who taps the wheels of railway carriages, to test their soundness; a shoemaker who rivets on soles and heels; a dialect name of the lesser spotted woodpecker.

1810 *Splendid Follies* III. 89 If the young gentleman did not immediately return to town, and satisfy their urgent demands, a tapper would..make his appearance at Mistley. **1837** DICKENS *Pickw.* xxxii, A low tap was heard at the room door. Mr. Bob Sawyer..bade the tapper come in. **1883** *Macm. Mag.* Feb. 269 The honest tapper of every wheel [of a railway train]. **1885** SWAINSON *Provinc. Names Birds* 99 Lesser Spotted Woodpecker (*Dendrocopus minor*). Also called..Wood tapper... Tapperer,..or Tapper. **1903** *Daily Chron.* 11 Sept. 8/4 Boot Trade, repairs.—Smart tapper to finish on machines.

2. That which taps or lightly strikes, as a hammer for striking a bell; *spec.* a key in an electric telegraph which is depressed (with a tapping sound) to complete the circuit, a telegraph key; in wireless telegraphy, a device for restoring the filings to their original condition; also ***tapper-back***.

1876 PREECE & SIVEWRIGHT *Telegraphy* 43 There are two forms of the single needle instrument in general use, viz. the drop-handle and the pedal or tapper form. *Ibid.* 47 The sending portion of the 'pedal' or 'tapper' form of single needle. **1898** *Edin. Rev.* Oct. 306 The restoration to the coherer of its defective efficacy is brought about by the automatic action of a 'tapper'. **1903** *Sci. Amer.* 26 Dec. 483/2 In 1894 he [Sir O. Lodge] exhibited at Oxford his first 'tapper-back', or automatic system of decohering the iron filings after each impulse.

tapper, tappes, obs. ff. TAPER, TAPIS.

Tappertitian (tæpə'tɪʃən), *a. rare.* [f. the name of Simon *Tappertit*, a conceited apprentice in Dickens's *Barnaby Rudge* (1841) + -IAN.] Characteristic of or resembling Tappertit, esp. in his amorous approaches to Dolly Varden.

1895 G. B. SHAW in *Sat. Rev.* 19 Jan. 94/1 One's gorge rose at the Tappertitian vulgarity and infamy of the thing. **1903** —— *Man & Superman* p. xxviii, I have been proof against the garish splendors and alcoholic excitements of the ordinary stage combinations of Tappertitian romance with the police intelligence. **1949** ST. J. ERVINE *Craigavon* II. lxi. 287 Had they been, there would not have been any procession of Tappertitian playboys.

tappet ('tæpɪt). Also 8–9 **tapit,** 9 **tapet, tappit, tabbot.** [app. f. TAP *v.*² + -ET¹; but the use of the suffix is abnormal. Cf. mod.F. *tapette* a flat piece of wood for driving in corks.]

A projecting arm or part in a machine, which by the movement of the latter comes intermittently into contact with another part, so as to give or receive motion.

1745 *Specif. Kay & Stell's Patent* No. 612 There are likewise fixed in the sliding beam or hollow rowler, at proper distances, sundry tapits. **1824** R. STUART *Hist. Steam Engine* 114 The pins or tappets [are] fixed on the plug-frame (or tappet rod)..: at the ascent or descent of these pins, they strike on the ends of the levers or spanners..connected with the valves,..and open or shut them. **1831** J. HOLLAND *Manuf. Metal* I. 241 As the wheel shaft revolves, the tappits successively strike the hammer tail. **1839** URE *Dict. Arts*, etc. 1287 *T* is the shaft of the eccentric tappets, cams, or wipers, which press the treddle levers alternately up and down. **1870** J. M. NUTTER in *Eng. Mech.* 4 Mar. 610/2 Much depends upon the description of loom and make of tabbots in treading motion. **1907** *Westm. Gaz.* 28 Nov. 4/1 The inclined valves and new valve tappets..mark it [a motor car engine] with a distinctiveness all its own.

b. *attrib.* and *Comb.*; appositive, 'that is a tappet', as ***tappet-arm, -lever, -pin, -plate***; 'of a tappet or tappets', as ***tappet action, -bevel, -bowl, motion***; 'having or worked by a tappet or tappets', as ***tappet-port, -rod, -valve, -wheel***.

1824 Tappet rod [see above]. **1837** H. STANSFELD in *Civil Eng. & Arch. Jrnl.* I. 54/2 Certain Machinery of a Tappet and Lever Action. **1839** URE *Dict. Arts*, etc. 1287 Heddle leaves, actuated by the tappet wheels upon the axis Q. **1895** *Model Steam Engine* 46 Simply altering the position of the tappet lever by means of two screws. **1908** *Westm. Gaz.* 28 Apr. 4/2 The valve-stems may be lengthened or the tappet-ports enlarged.

tappet, 16th c. var. TOPPET, basket.

tappet, -ett, -ette, variants of TAPET.

†**tappette.** *Obs. rare.* [? dim. of TAP *sb.*¹: see -ETTE.] A catkin.

1561 HOLLYBUSH *Hom. Apoth.* 34 b, Take the tappettes or flouringe of Walnuttes and Filberts when they florishe, new gathered after that they be fallen from yᵉ trees.

tappice, var. TAPIS *v.*¹ to lie hid.

tappil, tapple, tappit, var. (chiefly *Sc.*) of TOPPLE, TOPPED.

tappin, Sc. f. TOPPING.

tapping ('tæpɪŋ), *vbl. sb.*¹ [f. TAP *v.*¹ + -ING¹.]

1. a. The action of TAP *v.*¹ in various senses.

1597 A. M. tr. *Guillemeau's Fr. Chirurg.* 20 b/2 In the drawing or tappinge of the water. **1655** CULPEPPER *Riverius* VII. v. 164 The Opening or Tapping for the Dropsie. **1713** CHESELDEN *Anat.* III. x. (1726) 228 This kind of dropsie is sometimes cured by tapping. *c* **1865** J. WYLDE in *Circ. Sc.* I. 410/2 They are..obtained from the tree.., by the process of 'tapping'. **1905** H. D. ROLLESTON *Dis. Liver* 171 A woman ..eventually died after her sixtieth tapping. **1909** *Installation News* II. 172/1 Alternating current..is carried into one side of the transformer giving 50 volts on the secondary at one tapping for lighting purposes, and three other tappings at 7, 12½ and 20 volts for cooking and heating.

b. *concr.* That which is drawn by tapping, or runs from a tap; a means of tapping.

1597 A. M. tr. *Guillemeau's Fr. Chirurg.* 53 b/1 His drinck, harshe and noughtye tappinges of wyne. **1686** PLOT *Staffordsh.* 17 It smelt just like the soure tappings of dead beer in a Cellar. **1862** DANA *Man. Geol.* 648 All wells and springs are tappings of these subterranean waters.

c. *attrib.* and *Comb.*, as ***tapping-apparatus*** (Knight *Dict. Mech.* 1877); **tapping-bar,** a sharp-pointed crowbar used in opening the tap-hole of a furnace; **tapping-clay,** plastic clay used to close a tapping-hole; **tapping-cock,** a cock having a taper stem, which allows it to be driven firmly into an opening; **tapping-drill,** a drill for boring holes in water-pipes; **tapping-gouge,** a gouge used in tapping the sugar-maple; **tapping-hole,** (*a*) a tap-hole in a furnace; (*b*) a hole drilled in metal to be tapped or furnished with an internal screw-thread; **tapping-iron** = *tapping-gouge*; **tapping-machine,** (*a*) a machine for cutting internal screw-threads; (*b*) a machine for tapping water- or gas-mains, a tapping-drill; **tapping-pot,** a pot to receive liquid metal from the tap-hole; **tapping-tool,** (*a*) = TAP *sb.*¹ 4; (*b*) any implement for tapping the sugar-maple.

1861 FAIRBAIRN *Iron* 133 The fire is to be carefully raked out at the *tapping hole, which is again to be made good with loam. **1894** BOWKER in *Harper's Mag.* Jan. 418 A channel known as the tapping-hole, taps the metal from the crucible. **1840** GOSSE *Canadian Nat.* vi. 68 A semicircular incision is made [in the tree] with a large iron gouge, called a *tapping iron.

2. (In senses 2 c, 3 of the vb.)

1931 T. HORSLEY *Odyssey of Out-of-Work* xxiii. 243 You do the tapping; I'll wait for you at the gate. **1955** 'E. CRISPIN' *Fen Country* (1979) 54 A line from your special switchboard..could be made safe from tapping. **1966** *Times* 14 Nov. 10/6 Mr. Russell Kerr..is to ask the Home Secretary..on how many occasions warrants have been issued for the tapping of M.P.s' private telephones.

b. *spec.* in *Electr. Engin.*, an intermediate connection made in a winding.

1903 K. EDGCOMBE *Whittaker's Electrical Engineer's Pocket Bk.* 244 The secondary of one of the transformers is wound to give a voltage equal to the required three-phase line-to-line voltage, and is divided into two equal parts by a middle tapping. **1934** *Discovery* Oct. 301/2 Twelve tappings are fitted to give an impedance range of 1·6 to 25,000 ohms. **1950** *Engineering* 22 Sept. 245/3 Tappings from the secondary and filament windings are connected to the electrodes. **1975** G. J. KING *Audio Handbk.* iii. 71 A tapping on the resistive element facilitates coupling of the loudness filter.

c. *attrib.* and *Comb.* (sense 2 b), as ***tapping point***; **tapping coil** *Electr. Engin.*, a coil which acts as a tapping.

1933 P. KEMP *Alternating Current Electr. Engin.* (ed. 4) xiv. 188 In order to permit of a slight variation in the secondary terminal voltage, it is usual to provide a number of tapping coils in the L.T. winding. **1958** J. SHEPHERD et al. *Higher Electr. Engin.* xiv. 344 The tapping coils are placed physically in the centre of the transformer limb to avoid unbalanced axial forces acting on the coils. *Ibid.* 343 If.. contact with position 2 is made before contact with position 1 is broken, the coils connected between these two tapping points are short-circuited, and will carry damagingly heavy currents.

'tapping, *vbl. sb.*^{2} [f. TAP *v.*^{2} + -ING^1.]

a. The action of TAP *v.*^{2}; the sound made by this action; †in *Etching*: see quot. 1688 (*obs.*); also *spec.* tap-dancing. Also reduplicated, **tap-tapping**, repeated or continued tapping.

c **1440** [see TAP *v.*^{2} 1]. **1688** R. HOLME *Armoury* III. 151/1 *Tapping*, is wip[ing] or sliding ones hand upon the Varnish to make it smooth and even on the Plate. **1786** MME. D'ARBLAY *Diary* 6 Nov., I heard a tapping from a window upstairs. **1860** RUSSELL *Diary in India* II. xvii. 321, I was informed that the tents were going to be struck immediately, and the tap-tapping of the kelassees confirmed the fact. **1872** BLACK *Adv. Phaeton* xxxi, Here a tapping all round the table greeted the orator. **1944** J. JOHNS *A.B.C. Tap Dancing* 2 'Tapping' has few stable rules but limitless variations.

b. The soling or heeling of boots and shoes. *dial.* and *U.S.*

1857 EADIE *J. Kitto* ii. (1861) 44 Revelations about list and leather, tapping and closing.

c. *attrib.* and *Comb.*, as ***tapping test***; **tapping key** *Electr.* = KEY *sb.*^{1} 12 a; **tapping-room**, a room in which tapping or boot-soling, etc. is done.

1895 *Westm. Gaz.* 17 Apr. 2/3 So the tapping test for railway carriage axles is a fraud. **1905** *Ibid.* 21 Sept. 7/1 An adjoining factory used.. as a tapping room. **1916** 'BOYD CABLE' *Action Front* 173 These [orderlies].. brought them long screeds to be translated to the tapping keys. **1938** *Brit. Jrnl. Psychol.* XXIX. 41 Two tapping keys.. were placed below the handles.

tappis, tappish, variant of TAPIS *v.*^{1}, ^{2}.

tappit ('tæpɪt), *ppl. a. Sc.* = TOPPED *ppl. a.*; *esp.* crested, tufted; chiefly in the collocation **tappit hen,** (*a*) a hen having a crest or topknot; (*b*) a drinking-vessel having a lid with a knob; *spec.* one containing a Scotch quart.

1721 RAMSAY *Ode to the Ph——* iii, That mutchkin stoup it hauds but dribs, Then let's get in the tappit hen. **1794** BURNS *Lines on Tumbler* ii. **1814** SCOTT *Wav.* xi, A huge pewter measuring-pot, containing at least three English quarts, familiarly denominated *a tappit hen.* **1821** GALT *Ann. Parish* ii, His head powdered and frizzled up like a tappit-hen. **1906** *Athenæum* 30 June 803/3 Of genuine old pewter.. here are.. flagons, tappit-hens, toddy-ladles.

tapple up tail: see TOPPLE *v.*

†tappy, *v. Obs. rare*$^{-0}$. = TAPIS *v.*^{1}

1706 PHILLIPS (ed. 6), To *Tappy*, (among Hunters) to lie hid as a Deer does.

'tap-room. [f. TAP *sb.*^{1} + ROOM *sb.*^{1}] A room in a tavern, etc., in which liquors are kept on tap.

1807 *Sporting Mag.* XXIX. 78 Gore was in the doorway between the tap room and the bed room. **1838** DICKENS *O. Twist* viii, [He] turned into a small public-house, and led the way to a tap-room. **1855** MACAULAY *Hist. Eng.* xii. III. 184 The ambassador was put one night into a miserable taproom full of soldiers smoking.

tap-root ('tæpru:t), *sb.* [f. TAP *sb.*^{1} + ROOT.] A straight root, of circular section, thick at the top, and tapering to a point, growing directly downwards from the stem and forming the centre from which subsidiary rootlets spring.

1601 HOLLAND *Pliny* XVI. xxxi. 477 The Fir and Larch have one tap root and no more; for upon that one maine maister-root they rest and are founded. **1733** TULL *Horse-Hoeing Husb.* i. 1 The Tap-Root commonly runs down Single and Perpendicular, reaching sometimes many Fathoms below. **1815** J. SMITH *Panorama Sc. & Art* II. 597 Such plants have no tap-roots, but strike their fibres horizontally in the richest part of the soil. **1851** GLENNY *Handbk. Fl.-Gard.* 160 It has a tap-root like a carrot, but small.

fig. **1825** COLERIDGE *Aids Refl.* (1836) 349 Its fibres are to be traced to the tap-root of humanity. **1887** LOWELL *Democr.* 36 This sentiment, which is the very tap-root of civilization and progress.

attrib. **1890** *Eng. Illustr. Mag.* Christm. No. 158 That's a tap-root idea, Fraser.

Hence **'tap-root** *v. intr.*, of a plant, to send down a tap-root (whence **'tap-rooting** *ppl. a.*); **'tap-rooted** *a.*, having a tap-root.

1725 *Bradley's Fam. Dict.* s.v. *Ilex*, These, like our English Oak, are tap-rooted, and therefore delight in deep Soil. **1769** L. EDWARD in *Hist. Line.* (1834) I. 20 The oak roots stand upon the sand, and tap-root into the clay. **1805** R. W. DICKSON *Pract. Agric.* I. 12 In loosening the ground for carrots, or other tap-rooted plants. **1897** WILLIS *Flower Pl.* I. 185 Tap-rooting plants.. would not be able to cling to their supports in time to prevent falling off.

†'tapsail, -seil. *Obs. rare.* Some kind of East Indian cotton material.

1725 *Lond. Gaz.* No. 6388/2 The following Goods, viz... Negannepants, Tapseils,.. Arrangoes. **1851** in HILPERT *Eng.-Germ. Dict.* **18..** in FLÜGEL.

tapsal-, tapsie-teerie, *Sc.*: see TOPSY-TURVY.

†'tapsebarbe. *Obs. rare*$^{-1}$. [? obs. F., ad. med.L. *T(h)apsus barbatus*, former name of *Verbascum Thapsus*.] The Great Torch Mullein.

[*c* **1450** *Alphita* (Anecd. Oxon.) 182/1 *Tapsus barbatus maior masculus*,.. g[allice] molayne, an[glice] catesteyl, *uel* feldwrt.] **1526** *Grete Herball* ccccvii. (1529) Y ij b, Tapsebarbe is a maner of herbe called moleyne, wherof is made a maner of torches whan it is greased.

tapsell ('tæps(ə)l). [Origin uncertain.] ***tapsell gate***, a type of churchyard gate peculiar to Sussex, which turns about a central post.

1922 H. ALLCROFT *Downland Pathways* 114 You approach the building through a 'tapsel-gate'. **1947** E. MEYNELL *Sussex* vi. 134 One of those curious gates, swinging on a central post, known as tapsell gates. **1957** H. HALL *Some Sussex Sayings & Crafts* 181 *Tapsell gate*, this ingenious gate is peculiar to Sussex, but nothing is known of its origin or its designer. Its special use is to prevent cattle entering churchyards and to make room for coffin bearers to pass through easily... Today there are only six in the country. **1969** *Daily Tel.* 27 Feb. 21/8 Tapsell gates sometimes have a hook or spring-catch or even are chained and padlocked. **1979** *Country Life* 15 Mar. 726 Tapsell gates, which turn on a central pivot, are peculiar to Sussex. It has been suggested that they are so-called after one Tapsell, a Sussex iron-master.

tapser, -erye, var. TAPISSER, -ERY *Obs.*

tapsia, obs. form of THAPSIA.

†'tapsimel. *Obs. Old Med.* [med.L. *tapsi mel*, lit. honey of THAPSUS or Mullein (*Verbascum Thapsus*).] A plaster made of mullein and other herbs with honey.

c **1425** tr. *Arderne's Surgery* (E.E.T.S.) 31 Þat confeccion ..þat receyueþ Smalache, wormode, moleyne, sparge, &c., wiþ clarified hony soþen togidre at þe fire and kept by itself in a vessell is called 'Tapsimel'. *Ibid.* 35 Þat he take þe ȝolke of an ey to whiche be added þe half parte of tapsimell. *Ibid.* 73 Þis oyntment is called tapsimel, of tapsibarbati. **1658** ROWLAND tr. *Moufet's Theat. Ins.* 912, I might here set down the.. Tapsimel of Arden, and all syrups that were anciently made of honey.

†tapskin. *Obs. nonce-wd.* [f. TAP *v.*^{2} + SKIN *sb.*] A drumstick.

1605 *Play Stucley* in Simpson *Sch. Shaks.* (1878) I. 196 Drum [= Drummer], thump thy tapskins hard about the pate [*Stage direct.* Drum sounds] And make the ram-heads hear that are within.

tapster ('tæpstə(r)). Forms: 1 tæppestre, 4 tappester, 4–6 tapester, 5 tap(p)estere, tapstere, 5–6 tappyster, *Sc.* and *n. dial.* tapstare, 6 -ar, 5– tapster. [OE. *tæppestre*, fem. of *tæppere*, TAPPER^1: see -STER.]

†**1.** *orig.* A woman who tapped or drew ale or other liquor for sale in an inn; a hostess. *Obs.*

c **1000** ÆLFRIC *Gram.* ix. (Z.) 36 *Caupona*, tæppestre. *c* **1386** CHAUCER *Prol.* 241 He knew.. euerich Hostiler and Tappestere. *c* **1440** *Promp Parv.* 486/2 Tapstare, *ducillaria, propinaria, clipsidraria.* **1474** CAXTON *Chesse* III. vi. h vj b, That I haue sayd of the seruauntes beyng men, the same I say of the women as chamberers and tapsters. *c* **1485** *Digby Myst.* III. 495 With sum praty tasppyster wold I fayne rown. *a* **1518** SKELTON *Magnyf.* 420 A tappyster lyke a lady bryght. **1568** *Satir. Poems Reform.* xlviii. 100 Thre lassis.. That tyme that thay wer tapstaris.

2. A man who draws the beer, etc. for the customers in a public house; the keeper of a tavern.

The word in the first three quots. may be feminine.

c **1400** *Destr. Troy* 1594 Tauerners, tapsters, all the toune ouer. *c* **1450** *Mankind* 267 in *Macro Plays* 11, I haue be sethen with ȝe comyn tapster of Bury. **1530** PALSGR. 279/1 Tapster, *boutelier, boutiliere.* **1570** LEVINS *Manip.* 77/4 A Tapster, *promus.* **1598** SHAKS. *Merry W.* I. iii. 17 An old Cloake, makes a new Ierkin: a wither'd Seruingman, a fresh Tapster. **1612** W. PARKES *Curtaine-Dr.* (1876) 26 Ther's Tom the Tapster peerelesse for renowne, That drank three hundred drunken Dutch-men downe. **1676** *Lond. Gaz.* No. 1103/4 John Bowman, late Tapster at the Bear Inn in Bath. **1720** SWIFT *Stella's Birthday* 9 Though the treach'rous tapster Thomas Hangs a new angel two doors from us. **1871** SMILES *Charac.* i. (1876) 14 The decayed serving-men and tapsters who filled the Commonwealth's army.

†**3.** One who sells by retail or in small quantities.

1402 *Pol. Poems* (Rolls) II. 95 Me thynkith ȝe ben tapsteres, in alle that ȝe don; ȝe tappe ȝour absoluciones that ȝe bye at Rome. *c* **1450** *Godstow Reg.* 101 The abbesse graunted that her men of Wycombe shold be tempters or tapsters of brede and ale in the fee of the same abbesse.

4. *Comb.*, as ***tapster-like*** adj.

1607 R. C[AREW] tr. *Estienne's World of Wonders* A iv b, Leauing inkhorne phrases and tapsterlike termes for the tauerne. **1842** F. HOWES *Horace's Sat.* I. 2 This tapster-like retailer of the laws.

Hence **'tapstering** *ppl. a.*, acting as a tapster; **'tapsterly** *a.*, characteristic of or befitting a tapster; **'tapstership**, the office of a tapster; †**'tapstry**, a tap-room.

1861 SALA *Dutch Pict.* xii. 187 Is he going to scour the country with his marauding, *tapstering butchers? **1589** NASHE *Pref. Greene's Menaphon* (Arb.) 9 In anie *tapsterlie tearmes whatsoeuer. **1598** BARRET *Theor. Warres* I. i. 5 Honest and valiant men, not tapsterly praters. **1597** *1st Pt. Return fr. Parnass.* v. ii. 1538 As for youre *tapstershipp in hell, it were a good office in soe whott a place. **14..** *Beryn* 299 The Pardoner.. Stalkid in to the *tapstry.

tapstery, -strie, -stry, -e, obs. ff. TAPESTRY.

'tapstress. [f. TAPSTER + -ESS; formed after *tapster* had ceased to be feminine: cf. *seamstress, songstress.*] A female tapster.

1631 HEYWOOD *1st Pt. Maid of West* I. Wks. 1874 II. 269 You are some tapstresse. **1667** SIR C. LYTTELTON in *Hatton Corr.* (Camden) 52 Hee has married a dirty tapstresse. **1839** H. AINSWORTH *J. Shepherd* III. xiii, The tapstress was full of curiosity.

tap-tap, tap-tapping: see TAP *sb.*, TAPPING *vbl. sb.*

tap-tap, tap-tapping: see also TAP *v.*^{2} 2.

taptoo, taptow, obs. ff. TATTOO *sb.*^{1}

tapu ('tɑ:pu:), *a.* and *sb.* [Var. TABOO, TABU *a.* and *sb.* (Largely a regional variation, esp. in *N.Z.*: see note at TABOO.] **A.** *adj.* **a.** = TABOO *a.* Also (*rarely*) *fig.*

1832 H. WILLIAMS *Jrnl.* 18 Jan. in H. Carleton *Life H. Williams* (1874) 114 The canoe was *tapu*, having conveyed the body of Heagi.. to his former place. **1849** W. T. POWER *Sketches in N.Z.* p. xliv, A barbarous murder was committed by some of the natives under the protection of Rangihaeta, who refused to give them up; moreover, making the road 'tapu' which communicated between the coast and Wellington. **1873** TROLLOPE *Austral. & N.Z.* II. 419 Priests are *tapu*. Food is very often *tapu*, so that only sacred persons may eat it, and then must eat it without touching it with their hands. Places are frightfully *tapu*, so that no man or woman may go in upon them. **1902** G. B. SHAW *Mrs. Warren's Profession* p. xiii, Mrs Warren's profession must be either tapu altogether, or else exhibited with the warning side as freely displayed as the tempting side. **1936** *Discovery* Jan. 14/1 The Maoris had found out that the Morioris were a very *tapu* people. **1967** A. & D. REID *Paddle Wheels on Wanganui* iv. 33 The bodies were recovered and laid in the old house which was then declared tapu. **1978** P. GRACE *Mutuwhenua* ix. 56 Those hills, there are tapu places in them.

B. *sb.* = TABOO, TABU *sb.* 1 a. Also (*rarely*) *fig.*

1833 H. WILLIAMS *Let.* July in H. Carleton *Life H. Williams* (1874) 134 Some proposed Paihia, but this we declined, fearing it might bring the *tapu* upon a considerable portion of the land. **1851** MRS. R. WILSON *New Zealand*, etc. 24 But chiefly thou, mysterious Tapû, From thy strange rites a hopeful sign we draw. **1872** A. DOMETT *Ranolf & Amohia* 89 His sole 'tapu' a far securer guard Than lock and key of craftiest notch and ward. **1902** G. B. SHAW *Mrs. Warren's Profession* p. xiii, Each nation has its particular set of tapus in addition to the common human stock. **1938** R. FINLAYSON *Brown Man's Burden* 41 Uncle Tuna.. disapproved of joking about matters of tapu. **1971** *N.Z. Listener* 29 Mar. 11/1 In old New Zealand there were two main causes of sickness and disease. One was the violation of tapu or a tapu place.

Also as *v. trans.* = TABOO, TABU *v.* 1. Now *rare.*

1837 in R. McNab *Old Whaling Days* (1931) xxi. 335, [I] tapued a piece of land of the proprietors, two respectable chiefs, for some blankets and fish-hooks. **1851** V. LUSH *Jrnl.* 16 Dec. (1971) 94 A native burial place which the Tryces had been obliged to fence in before the natives would allow them to dwell in peace—so great is the natives' dread lest a spot they have *tapued* should be desecrated by man or beast. **1863** F. E. MANING *Old New Zealand* i. 14 A good gun... I must have this; I must *tapu* it before I leave the ship. **1890** *Jrnl. Anthrop. Inst.* XIX. 100 Tapu is an awful weapon. I have seen a strong young man die the same day he was tapued.

Tapuia (tə'pu:jə), *sb.* (and *a.*) Also 7 Tapui; 9 Tapuio; Tapuya. [a. Pg. *Tapuia*, Sp. *Tapuya*, ad. Tupi-Guaraní *tapua* savage, slave.] (A member of) a Brazilian Indian people not of Tupi stock. Also *attrib.* or as *adj.*

1613 PURCHAS *Pilgrimage* IX. vi. 712 Towards the East dwell the Itatini people, which call themselves Garay, that is, Warriours; and others, Tapuis or Slaues. **1860** MAYNE REID *Odd People* 44 Farther down the river, the 'Indio manso' is a 'tapuio', a hireling of the Portuguese, or, to speak more correctly, a *slave. Ibid.* 46 By such name is his house (or village rather) known among the *tapuios* and traders of the Amazon. **1910** *Encycl. Brit.* I. 783/2 The name Amazonas arises from the battle he had with a tribe of Tapuya savages. **1944** S. PUTNAM tr. *E. da Cunha's Rebellion in Backlands* i. 44 The hiding-places of the Tapuia. *Ibid.* ii. 83 The predominance of Tapuia terms in the geographic names of these places—terms that have resisted absorption by the Portuguese and Tupi languages.

†tapul. *Obs.* [Of uncertain origin: perhaps orig. an error.] A name applied by Hall (*a* 1548) to some part of the body-armour; thence, by modern antiquaries taken as a name for the vertical central ridge of the breastplate.

a **1548** HALL *Chron., Hen. IV* 12 One company had the plackard,.. the tasses, the lamboys, the backpece, the tapull, and the border of the curace all gylte. [MEYRICK *Anc. Armour* (1824) II. 258 commenting says 'Perhaps the projecting edge perpendicularly along the cuirass, from the French *taper*, to strike'. Hence the following:] **1834** PLANCHÉ *Brit. Costume* 243 The breast-plate was still [reign of Hen. VIII] globose, but towards the end of this reign rose to an edge down the centre called the tapul—a revival of an old fashion. **1869** BOUTELL *Arms & Arm.* ix. (1874) 155 A ridge (in England called the *tapul*) which divides the breast-plate and cuirass into two compartments, and is carried out to a point.. over the middle of the body. **1870** C. C. BLACK tr. *Demmin's Weapons of War* 226. **1896** E. J. BRETT *Anc. Arms & Armour* Plate 1. **1909** ASHDOWN *Arms & Armour* 283.

tap-waze, etc.: see TAP-HOSE.

†tapyn, obs. f. TAPON, TAMPION plug.

14.. *Voc.* in Wr.-Wülcker 569/40 *Calopodium*, a tapyn.

taqua-nut, (erron.) var. of TAGUA-*nut*.
a **1864** S. F. Baird in Webster. Hence in mod. Dicts.

tar (tɑː(r)), *sb.*[1] Forms: α. 1 **teru, teoru (-o)**, (**-tearo**); 3–5 (6– *Sc.*) **ter**, 4 (*Sc.* 4–) **terr**, 4–6 **terre**, 4–5 **teer**, (5 **tere**). β. 4–7 **tarre**, 4–8 **tarr**, 5 **taar**, 6– **tar**. γ. 1 **tyrwe**, 2 **tirwe**. [OE. *teru* (gen. *terw-es*), *teoru* (*-o*):—**terwo-* neut. = MLG. *ter. tere*, LG. and (thence) mod.Ger. *teer*, Du. *teer*; also ON. *tjara* fem. (Norw. *tjøra*, Sw. *tjära*, Da. *tjære*). OE. had also the deriv. form **tierwe*, *tyrwe*:—**terwjōn*. Generally considered to be a deriv. of OTeut. **trewo-*, Goth. *triu*, OE. *treow* tree (Indo-Eur. *derw-*: *dorw-*: *dru-*): cf. Lith. *darvà* pine-wood, Lett. *darwa* tar, ON. *tyr-viðr* pine-wood. Thus *terwo* may have meant orig. 'the product (pitch) of certain kinds of trees'.]

1. a. A thick, viscid, black or dark-coloured, inflammable liquid, obtained by the destructive distillation of wood (esp. pine, fir, or larch), coal, or other organic substance; chemically, a mixture of hydrocarbons with resins, alcohols, and other compounds, having a heavy resinous or bituminous odour, and powerful antiseptic properties; it is much used for coating and preserving timber, cordage, etc. See also COAL-TAR. Also formed in the combustion of tobacco, etc.

In some early quots. used for BITUMEN: cf. 2.

α. *a* **700** *Epinal Gloss.* 677 (Sweet *O.E.T.*) *Napta*, blaecteru. *Ibid.* 858 *Resina*, teru. *c* **725** *Corpus Gloss.* 1360 *Napta*, blaec-teoru. *Ibid.* 1716 *Resina*, teoru. *c* **1000** *Sax. Leechd.* II. 76 Meng wiþ sote, sealt, teoro, huniȝ, eald sape, smire mid. *c* **1050** *Voc.* in Wr.-Wülcker 412/6 *Gluten*, lim, oððe tero. *c* **1250** *Gen. & Ex.* 662 To maken a tur, wel heȝ & strong, Of tiȝel and ter, for water-gong. *a* **1300** *Cursor M.* 11899 Þai..drund him in pike and terr. **1436** *Libel Eng. Policy* in *Pol. Poems* (Rolls) II. 171 Peltre-ware, and grey pych, terre, borde and flex. **1483** *Cath. Angl.* 380/2 Ter, *bitumen*. **1508** Kennedie *Flyting w. Dunbar* 335 Thou salbe brynt, With pik, fyre, ter, gun puldre, or lint. **1522** More *De Quat. Noviss.* Wks. 74/1 Thei had leuer eate terre than tryacle. **1720** in *Jrnl. Derbysh. Archæol. Soc.* (1905) XXVII. 215 Ter and oile.

β. **1355–6** *Abingdon Rolls* (Camden) 9 In tarr et rubea petra xx d. *c* **1440** *Pallad. on Husb.* XII. 239 Rubrike and taar [L. *pix liquida*] wormys & auntis sleth. ?*a* **1500** *Chester Pl.* vii. 33 Heare is tarr in a pot. **1555** Philpot in Foxe *A. & M.* (1583) 1835/1 He that toucheth tarre, can not but be defiled therby. **1610** Shaks. *Temp.* II. ii. 54 She lou'd not the sauour of Tar nor of Pitch. **1681** *Patent Specif.* (1856) No. 214. 1 A new way of makeing pitch and tarre out of pit coal. **1813** Davy *Agric. Chem.* iii. (1814) 98 Tar and pitch principally consist of resin in a partially decomposed state. **1872** Oliver *Elem. Bot.* II. 247 Tar is distilled from faggots of Pine, chiefly Scotch Fir, in the North of Europe. **1921** *U.S. Patent 1,398,734* 2/1 The catch basins..are adapted to concentrate the heavier particles of tar from smoke. **1932** *Amer. Jrnl. Cancer* XVI. 1513 The tar of cigarette smoke contains nicotine, phenolic bodies, pyridine bases, and ammonia. **1974** M. C. Gerald *Pharmacol.* viii. 155 Some of these are polycyclic hydrocarbons, commonly referred to as 'tars', and are undoubtedly responsible for the disproportionately greater incidence of lung cancer among cigarette smokers.

γ. *c* **1000** Ælfric *Hom.* I. 20 ȝeclæm ealle þa seamas mid tyrwan. *a* **1175** *Cott. Hom.* 225 Iclem hall þe seames mid tirwan.

b. Proverb. ***to lose the sheep*** (dial. ***ship***) ***for a ha'p'orth of tar***: see HALFPENNYWORTH b.

c. Applied *fig.* in derogatory reference to someone of mixed Black (or Indian, etc.) and white origin: cf. TAR-BRUSH b.

1897 Anne Page *Afternoon Ride* 68 There was a touch of tar in this buxom dame.

d. ***to beat*** (***knock,*** etc.) ***the tar out of***: to beat unmercifully, to reduce to a state of helplessness. Cf. SHIT *sb.* 1 g. *U.S. slang.*

1884 *National Police Gaz.* 6 Sept. 11/1 (*heading*) The celebrated New York dubs get the tar knocked out of them. **1916** 'Texas' *Trav. Tourist 'Typo'* 46 The newsboy..whose chief occupation is..to wallop the tar out of smaller newsboys. **1939** D. Trumbo *Johnny got his Gun* ii. 35 Naturally you..wanted Germany to get the tar kicked out of her. **1973** Wodehouse *Bachelors Anonymous* vii. 80 She is a fine upstanding woman, fully capable of beating the tar out of you.

e. Colloq. abbrev. of TARMAC *sb.* or TARMACADAM; a road surfaced with this.

1934 Dylan Thomas *18 Poems* 26 Nor city tar and subway bored to foster Man through macadam. **1971** *E. Afr. Standard* (Nairobi) 13 Apr. 6/5 He thought the tarmac was dangerous anywhere. Next year he wanted to see less tar and higher speeds elsewhere. **1980** G. Lord *Fortress* iii. 26 Both roads were dirt... The tar ended miles back.

2. Applied, with distinctive epithets, to natural substances resembling tar, as petroleum or bitumen: see quots. 1796, 1875, and MINERAL *a.* 5.

1747 Wesley *Prim. Physick* (1762) 37 Half a teaspoonful of Barbadoes Tar. **1796** Morse *Amer. Geog.* I. 558 A spring, on the top of which floats an oil, similar to that called Barbadoes tar. **1875** *Ure's Dict. Arts* III. 397 In a great number of places..a more or less fluid inflammable matter exudes. It is known as Persian naphtha, Petroleum, Rock-oil, Rangoon tar, Burmese naphtha, &c.

3. A familiar appellation for a sailor: perh. abbreviation of TARPAULIN. Cf. JACK-TAR.

1676 Wycherley *Pl. Dealer* II. i, *Nov.* Dear tar, thy humble servant. **1695** Congreve *Love for L.* IV. xiv, You would have seen the Resolution of a Lover,—Honest Tarr and I are parted. **1706** Swift *To Peterborough* xi, Fierce in war, A land-commander, and a tar. **1709** Steele *Tatler* No. 31 ¶2 A Boatswain of an East-India Man..like a true Tar of Honour. **1820** Scoresby *Acc. Arctic Reg.* I. 514 The chief mate..a resolute and noble tar. **1862** Baring-Gould *Iceland* (1863) 179 The jolly tars seize the horses and ride them helter skelter up hill and down dale.

4. *attrib.* and *Comb.* **a.** *attrib.* Made of, from, or with tar; consisting of, containing, or derived from tar; as ***tar-bath***, ***-creosote***, ***derivative***, ***-dye***, ***-lotion***, ***-mark***, ***-oil***, ***-ointment***, ***-pill***, ***-plaster***, ***product***, ***-salve***, ***-soap***, ***-spring***, ***-tincture***, ***-vapour***, ***-varnish***, ***-wash***; covered or impregnated with tar, as ***tar-bandage***, ***-cloth***, ***-cord***, ***-neckcloth***, ***-paving***; used for holding, or in making, tar, as †***tar-boist*** (= TAR-BOX 1), ***-bucket***, ***-can***, ***-copper***, ***-funnel***, ***-horn***, ***-kettle***, ***-pit***, †***-pough***, †***-stoup***, ***-trough***, ***-tub*** (in quot. *fig.*). **b.** objective, instrumental, etc., as ***tar-burning***; ***tar-bind***, ***-brand***, ***-mark***, ***-paint*** vbs., ***tar-bedaubed***, ***-clotted***, ***-laid***, ***-painted***, ***-paved***, ***-roofed***, ***-scented***, ***-smelling***, ***-soaked***, ***-streaked*** adjs.; ***tar-spraying***, ***-sprinkling***; ***tar-like*** adj. **c.** Special Combs.: **tar acid**, any of numerous phenolic constituents of coal-tar distillates that react with dilute caustic soda to give water-soluble salts; **tar acne**, *Path.*, an inflammatory disease of the skin produced by rubbing with tar, etc.; **tar and feathers** *U.S.* (with reference to the practice of tarring and feathering: see TAR *v.*[1] b); **tar-baby**, (*a*) the doll smeared with tar, set to catch Brer Rabbit (see quot. 1881); hence *transf.*, *spec.* an object of censure; a sticky problem, or one which is only aggravated by attempts to solve it (*colloq.*); (*b*) a derog. term for a Black (*U.S.*) or a Maori (*N.Z.*); **tar ball**, (*a*) see quot. 1735; (*b*) a ball of crude oil found in or on the sea; **tar base**, any of numerous cyclic, nitrogen-containing bases present in coal-tar distillates; **tar-beer**, a mixture of tar and beer, used medicinally (cf. TAR-WATER 1); **tar-board**, see quot.; 'a building-paper saturated with tar' (*Cent. Dict.*); **tar-boiler**, (*a*) a boiler used for tar; †(*b*) *U.S. slang* = TARHEEL (*obs.*); **tar-boy** *Austral.* and *N.Z.*, an assistant hand in a shearing shed who treats injured sheep with tar or other disinfectants; † **tar-breech** *a.*, wearing tarry breeches: epithet for a sailor (cf. *tarry-breeks*); **tar-bush**, one of several aromatic shrubs of western N. America, esp. one of the genus *Eriodictyon*, of the family Hydrophyllaceæ, which includes several sticky or tomentose evergreens; **tar kiln**, a covered heap of wood or coal from which tar is obtained by burning; **tar-lamp**, a lamp in which tar is used as the illuminant (Knight *Dict. Mech.* 1877); **tar-lubber**, contemptuous name for a sailor (cf. 3); **tar-marl**, **-marline** (*dial.*), tarred twine used in thatching; **tar-paper** chiefly *N. Amer.*, paper saturated with tar; often used as a building material; freq. *attrib.*; **tar-pavement**, **-paving**, a form of surfacing for roads, pathways, etc., composed mainly of tar; † **tar-pitch** (*terpiche*) = sense 1; **tar-pot**, (*a*) a pot containing tar; (*b*) humorously applied to a sailor (cf. 3); (*c*) an opprobrious name for a Black (*U.S.*) or a Maori (*N.Z.*) (cf. *tar-baby* (*b*) above); **tar-putty**, a viscid substance made by mixing tar and lamp-black; **tar-sand**, a deposit of sand impregnated with bitumen; **tar-weed**, *U.S.*, name for plants of the genera *Madia*, *Hemizonia*, and *Grindelia*, from their viscidity and heavy scent; **tar-well**, a receptacle in gas-works for collecting the tarry liquid which separates from the gas; **tar-wood**, resinous wood from which tar is obtained; **tar-work, -s**, a place for making tar; **tar-worker**, a workman employed in making tar; **tar-yard**, a yard in which tar is made. See also TAR-BARREL, -BOX, -BRUSH, etc.

1909 *Chem. Abstr.* III. 1079 (*heading*) Hydrocarbons obtained from the *tar acids of petroleum. **1951** M. McLuhan *Mech. Bride* (1967) 91 (Advt.), Coal-Tar Chemicals—Benzol, toluol, naphthalene, tar acids, tar bases, solvents, [etc.]. **1974** Tar acid [see *tar base* below]. **1899** *Allbutt's Syst. Med.* VIII. 918 A form of eruption very similar to this occurs in workers in creasote and tar—'*tar acne'. **1775** P. V. Fithian *Jrnl.* 8 June (1934) II. 25 He hears many of his Townsmen talking of *Tar and Feathers—These mortifying Weapons. **1834** *Southern Lit. Messenger* I. 87 If he remained longer, he was in danger of tar and feathers. **1954** J. Steinbeck *Sweet Thursday* xxxviii. 261 He left town, and just as well. There was talk of tar and feathers. He must have heard. **1982** W. Mankowitz *Mazeppa* vi. 97 The Vigilance Committees..had asserted law summarily with fast necktie parties, rail-rides and tar and feathers. **1881** J. C. Harris *Uncle Remus* ii. 20 Brer Fox..got 'im some tar, en mix it wid some turkentime, en fix up a contrapshun what he call a *Tar-Baby. *a* **1910** 'Mark Twain' *Autobiogr.* (1924) II. 18 For two years the *Courant* had been making a 'tar baby' of Mr. Blaine, and adding tar every day—and now it was called upon to praise him. **1924** Kipling *Debits & Credits* (1926) 97 Number Five Study..were toiling inspiredly at a Tar Baby made up of Beetle's sweater, and half-a-dozen lavatory towels;..and most of Richard's weekly blacking allowance for Prout's House's boots. **1948** S. Lewis *Kingsblood Royal* 334 'I didn't know she was a tar-baby.'.. 'Don't be so dumb. Can't you see it by her jaw?' **1959** M. Shadbolt *New Zealanders* 140 'What a hide, though—' 'Those tar-babies and that fellow in the sweater.' **1976** *National Observer* (U.S.) 29 May 15A/3 The troubled U.S. Postal Service is fast becoming the political tar baby of the year. **1978** J. Updike *Coup* (1979) iv. 135 She was one of those white women who cannot leave black men alone... Some questing chromosome within holds her sexually fast to the tarbaby. **1735** Bracken in Burdon *Pocket Farriery* 39 *note*, There is a Ball under the name of *Tar Ball. **1972** *Science* 16 June 1258/2 Crude oil lumps ('tar balls') are now universal constituents of the surfaces of the world oceans. **1891** *Cent. Dict.*, **Tar bandage*, an antiseptic bandage made by saturating a roller bandage, after application, with a mixture of 1 part of olive oil and 20 parts of tar. **1921** *Jrnl. Amer. Chem. Soc.* XLIII. 1936 Crude coal *tar bases vary greatly..in the nature and in the proportion of the bases which they contain. **1951** [see *tar acid* above]. **1974** *Encycl. Brit. Micropædia* II. 1017/2 Tar bases are the basic constituents of the distillate oils, present after tar acids have been removed. **1899** *Allbutt's Syst. Med.* VIII. 605 A *tar bath..has not only an anti-pruritic but also a curative action. **1906** *Daily Chron.* 31 Aug. 3/2 In his patched and very much *tar-bedaubed punt. **1857** Dunglison *Med. Lex.* s.v. *Pinus sylvestris*, Tar water..is employed chiefly in pulmonary affections... A wine or beer of tar, *Tarbeer, Jews' beer, has been employed in Philadelphia in similar cases. **1909** *Westm. Gaz.* 30 Aug. 2/1 There are two distinct methods of *tar-binding the surface of our roads. **1877** Knight *Dict. Mech.*, **Tar-board*, a strong quality of mill-board made from junk and old tarred rope. **1845** *Cincinnati Misc.* I. 240 The inhabitants of..N. Carolina [are called] *Tar-boilers. **1885** W. Whitman in *N. Amer. Rev.* Nov. 433 Among the rank and file..[in the Civil War] it was very general to speak of the different States they came from by their slang names. Those from..North Carolina [were called] Tar Boilers. ?*a* **1500** *Chester Pl.* vii. 78 With *Tarboyst most bene all tamed, Penigras, and butter for fat sheepe. **1888** 'R. Boldrewood' *Robbery Under Arms* I. x. 123 There wasn't a man of the lot in the shed, down to the *tarboy, that wouldn't have done the same. **1936** A. Russell *Gone Nomad* iii. 19 Then I found myself a tar-boy in the shearing-shed. **1956** G. Bowen *Wool Away!* (ed. 2) 157 *Tar-boy*, the hand who walks the board where sheep are subject to the fly and who puts a smear of tar on the cuts made on sheep. **1977** C. McCullough *Thorn Birds* x. 231 Luke took himself off on the shearing circuit as a tar boy, slapping molten tar on jagged wounds if a shearer slipped and cut flesh as well as wool. **1878** E. S. Elwell *Boy Colonists* 205 It took a good month to muster and *tar-brand all the sheep. **1890** 'R. Boldrewood' *Col. Reformer* (1891) 120 Flock..to be counted, or drafted, or shifted, or tar-branded. **1582** Stanyhurst *Æneis* IV. (Arb.) 108 A runnagat hedgebrat, A *tarbreeche quystroune dyd I take. **1723** *Amer. Weekly Mercury* 23–30 May 2/1 The forced Men..carryed the Brigantine into Curacao, with the Captains Head in a *Tarr Bucket. *a* **1909** *Joseph W. Caldwell: Mem. Vol.* (1909) 66 There were a brindled cur dog under the wagon, keeping company with the tar bucket that swung from the coupling pole. **1931** *Sun* (Baltimore) 28 Oct. 13/4 Tall 'tar-bucket' helmets with the black plumes. **1864** Carlyle *Fredk. Gt.* xv. i. (1873) V. 270 Mankind..took to ..*tar-burning and *te-deum*-ing on an extensive scale. **1884** W. Miller *Dict. Eng. Names Plants* 134/2 *Tar-bush, Californian. *Eriodictyon californicum.* **1902** *Out West* Oct. 452 There were the innumerable cacti with their brilliant flowers, and the tar bush. **1949** *Chicago Tribune* 20 Feb. 30/3 Cedar and mesquite alone are costing Texas ranchers 115 million dollars a year. Add the..blue oak, creosote, tarbush ..and prickly pear and the toll is terrific. **1888** J. Shallow *Templars' Trials* xi. 24 He approached..as cautiously as a boy with a *tar can does a wasp's nest. **1899** T. Hardy in *Academy* 18 Nov. 599/1 Great guns were gleaming there —Cloaked in their *tar-cloths. **1900** H. G. Graham *Soc. Life Scotl. 18th C.* xv. (1901) 513 Thin, short *tar-clotted fleeces of the sheep. **1768** *Chron.* in *Ann. Reg.* 113/2 A fire broke out in a tar-yard..by the *tar-copper boiling over. **1879** Jefferies *Wild Life in S.C.* 47 A couple of flakes fastened together with *tar-cord. **1868** *Q. Rev.* Apr. 346 A very singular product called *tar-creosote or carbolic acid. **1896** *Allbutt's Syst. Med.* V. 45 Among the *tar derivatives [may be specially mentioned] creosote and guaiacol. **1894** *Westm. Gaz.* 8 Mar. 3/3 The stockings..are dyed with *tar-dyes, which are perfectly harmless. **1573** Tusser *Husb.* (1878) 38 A sheepe marke, a *tar kettle. **1755** *Gentl. Mag.* XXV. 551/1 A sufficient crop of these old knots (which are full of rosin) for the *tar-kilns. **1943** H. Parkes in C. Goerch *Down Home* xx. 99 Any one who has ever seen a tar kiln in operation or been around a turpentine distillery will realize what sticky and dirty work it is. **1856** Kane *Arct. Expl.* II. i. 26 We have been using up our *tar-laid hemp hawsers. **1683** Robinson in *Ray's Corr.* (1848) 137, I have observed the inhabitants of Languedoc get a *tar-like like substance out of the Juniperus. **1899** *Allbutt's Syst. Med.* VIII. 521 The use of tar soaps, followed by *tar lotions, is sometimes more efficacious. **1610** Healey *St. Aug. Citie of God* 707 Another *Tarre-lubber bragges that hee is a souldiour. **1844** Stephens *Bk. Farm* III. 1282 The letter P..on the rump to shew the *tar-mark of the farm on which..it had been bred. **1825** Jamieson Suppl. II. 86/1 An old Angus laird,..on observing that one of the young ladies had both earrings and patches, cried out..in obvious allusion to the means employed by store-farmers for preserving their sheep; 'Wow, wow! Mrs. Janet, your father's been michtilie fleyd for tyning you, that he's baith *lug-markit* ye and *tar-markit ye.' **1918** *Chrons. N.Z.E.F.* 30 Aug. 61 Tar-marking and branding cattle. **1863** *Stamford Mercury* 27 Sept., He got some *tar-marline and tied the horse's mouth. **1713** Steele *Englishman* No. 47. 303, I stood by just now, when a Fellow came in here with a *Tar Neckcloth. **1891** *Cent. Dict.*, **Tar-oil*, a volatile oil obtained by distilling tar. **1895** *Outing* (U.S.) XXVI. 365/1 The little black bottle of tar-oil. **1787** P. F. Freneau *Journey from Philadelphia* ii. 14 You *tar-painted [*Poems* (1795) vii. 343: Tar-smelling] monster!.. If Snip should be drownded, and lost in the sea, You never once think what a loss it would be! **1906** *Westm. Gaz.* 13

Sept. 10/2 The cost of *tar-painting a road eight yards wide averages about £60 a mile. **1891** H. Campbell *Darkness & Daylight* xxxi. 611 If he ventures to charge more, except for a dress..or for *tar-paper..he is liable to lose the license. **1907** *Putnam's Monthly* July 482/1 A whole house covered with tar paper and studded with brass tacks sat complacently upon a hay wagon. **1919** S. Lewis *Free Air* 122 Then a lonely, tight-haired woman in the doorway of a tar-paper shack waved to her. **1966** D. F. Galouye *Lost Perception* ix. 89 The plane..taxied up to a frame building with a tarpaper roof. **1978** R. Ludlum *Holcroft Covenant* xxxii. 370 The tar paper..bulged slightly next to the wall. **1883** *Proc. Assoc. Munic. Engin.* X. 53 The tar macadam roadways and *tar paved footways..I found in good..order. **1883** *Proc. Assoc. Municipal Engin.* X. 53 My first experience in *tar pavement was in 1850. *Ibid.*, *Tar paving had been used to some extent for footways previous to..March 1881. **1967** *Gloss. Highway Engin. Terms (B.S.I.)* 47 *Tar paving*, a surfacing of tarmacadam laid in one or two courses for footpaths, playgrounds, and similar areas for pedestrian or very light vehicular traffic. **1728** E. Smith *Compl. Housewife* (ed. 2) 304 *The *Tar Pills for a Cough.* Take Tar and drop it on Powder of Liquorish, and make it up into Pills. **1808** *Med. Jrnl* XIX. 225 Tar pills made up with magnesia were also administered. **1839** Ure *Dict. Arts* 963 A considerable quantity is distilled over into the *tar-pit. *a* **1387** *Sinon. Barthol.* (Anecd. Oxon.) 34 *Pix liquida*, ..*terpiche. **1899** *Allbutt's Syst. Med.* VIII. 582 A *tar plaster is better than one of chrysarobin. **1573** Tusser *Husb.* (1878) 30 With tar in a *tarpot. **1641** Best *Farm. Bks.* (Surtees) 23 One of the girles is to keepe fire under the tarr-potte. **1903** F. T. Bullen in *Daily Chron.* 8 June 3/3 Like many other old tar-pots, I have been intensely annoyed and disgusted by the so-called 'real' sea-books put forward. **1944** H. L. Mencken in *Amer. Speech* XIX. 174 *Pickaninny* was..used..affectionately. So..was *tar-pot*..signifying a Negro child. **1949** F. Sargeson *I saw in my Dream* xiii. 120 He'd never let the tarpots inside the shed with their lousy sheep. *c* **1394** *P. Pl. Crede* 618 Þei may trussen her part in a *terre powȝe! **1903** *Westm. Gaz.* 16 Sept. 2/1 The value of the annual output of *tar products is over ten millions. **1888** *Engineer* LXVI. 521 '*Tar-putty'..a viscous mixture of tar and well calcined lampblack. **1896** Howells *Impressions & Exp.* 282 A *tar-roofed shanty. **1844** Stephens *Bk. Farm* III. 1118 Applying *tar-salve to sheep. **1899** *Nature* 15 June 159/1 Great trouble has been experienced in the effort to penetrate the '*tar-sands' at the base of the Cretaceous strata. **1978** *Ibid.* 29 June 703/3 The heavier oils will also have to be used as chemical feedstocks in the future: for example, Canada's 'tar sands', now the subject of a multi-million dollar project in Alberta. **1973** R. Adams *Watership Down* (ed. 2) xxiv. 173 He sat..on the bank above the *tar-smelling road. **1892** *Pall Mall G.* 22 Sept. 14/2 The *tar-soaked logs burn with a peculiar brilliance. **1899** *Allbutt's Syst. Med.* VIII. 584 To take frequent baths with *tar soap. **1909** *Westm. Gaz.* 30 Aug. 2/1 Roads..treated by the cheaper method of *tar-spraying them on the surface. **1775** R. Chandler *Trav. Greece* (1825) II. 367 The *tar-springs of Zante are a natural curiosity deserving notice. **1782** J. Trumbull *M'Fingal* iv. 70 Adown his *tar-streak'd visage, clear Fell..th'indignant tear. **1939** S. Spender *Still Centre* iv. 94 You stood once In the tar-streaked drizzling street. **1899** *Allbutt's Syst. Med.* VIII. 605 To paint the skin with a strong *tar tincture. **1534** *Acc. Ld. High Treas. Scotl.* VI. 235 For the lane of ane *tar troch, viij d. **1697** tr. *C'tess D'Aunoy's Wks.* (1715) 375 He ran to his nasty *Tar-tub of a Mistress. **1805** Dickson *Pract. Agric.* I. 48 The outside..properly payed over with pitch or *tar-varnish. **1898** J. Hutchinson in *Arch. Surg.* IX. No. 36. 373, I prescribed a *tar wash and it suited admirably. **1884** Miller *Plant-n.*, *Tar-weed, Californian, the genera *Madia* and *Hemizonia.* **1909** *Daily Chron.* 8 Mar. 4/6 The unjustly named 'tar-weed'..scattered over great tracts of wild country..California smells of it, and smells very pleasantly. **1857** Miller *Elem. Chem.* III. 558 The tar, as it accumulates..flows over into the *tar wells. **1856** Emerson *Eng. Traits* iv. 65 King Hake..sets fire to some *tar-wood. **1791** *Trans. Soc. Arts* IX. 132 The iron-masters furnish the *Tar-works with coal. **1906** *Westm. Gaz.* 10 Aug. 10/2 The average life of *tar-workers is eighty-six. **1768** *Tar-yard [see *tar-copper* above].

‖**tar** (tɑː(r)), *sb.*[2] *Anglo-Ind.* [Hindi *tār.*] A telegram.

1893 Kipling in *Harper's Weekly* 30 Dec. 1246/3 My father is at the *tar*-house sending *tars.* **1901** —— *Kim* xi. 286 Therefore I did not send a *tar* (telegram) to any one saying where the letter lay. **1978** 'M. M. Kaye' *Far Pavilions* iv. xxviii. 411 It would have been a simple matter for the Rana ..to arrange for a *tar* (telegram) to be dispatched.

tar (tɑː(r)), *v.*[1] Pa. t. and pple. **tarred** (tɑːd). Forms: 1 **tierwian, tyrwian;** 3–5 **terren,** 4 **tere;** 5–7 **tarre,** 6–8 **tarr,** 6– **tar.** [f. OE. *teoru, teorw-,* TAR *sb.*[1]]

a. *trans.* To smear or cover with tar. Also *absol.*

[*a* **1000** *Beowulf* 295 Niw tyrwydne [= new-tarred] nacan on sande arum healdan.] *c* **1250** *Gen. & Ex.* 2596 In an fetles of riȝesses wroȝt, Terred ðat water dered it noȝt, Ðis child wunden ȝhe wiðle don. *c* **1300** *Havelok* 707 Hise ship..He dede it tere, an ful wel pike. *c* **1440** *Promp. Parv.* 489/2 Terryn, wythe terre, *colofoniso.* **1495** *Naval Acc. Hen. VII* (1896) 214 Hawsers olde & ffeble Tarred—iij; New Hawsers nott tarred—j. **1600** Shaks. *A.Y.L.* iii. ii. 63 Our hands..are often tarr'd ouer, with the surgery of our sheepe. **1689** *Lond. Gaz.* No. 2483/3 They had Tarr'd the Bridge, and laid Combustible Stuff in order to burn it. **1783** M. Cutler in *Life*, etc. (1888) I. 94 Tarred apple-trees to keep the millers from going up. **1840** Longf. in *Life* (1891) I. 361 The canker-worms have begun their journey up the trees, and to-morrow I shall tar. **1884** *Act 47 & 48 Vict.* c. 76 § 5 A person shall not, without due authority,..paint or tar any post office,..telegraph post, or other property.

b. To smear (a person's body) over with tar; esp. in phr. *to tar and feather*, to smear with tar and then cover with feathers: a punishment sometimes inflicted by a mob (esp. in U.S.) on an unpopular or scandalous character. Also *fig.*

(The practice was imposed by an ordinance of Richard I in 1189 as a punishment in the navy for theft: see Rymer *Foedera* (1704) I. 65/2, Hakluyt *Voy.* (1599) II. 21, Holinshed *Chron.* (1807) II. 213; in Howell's *Fam. Lett.* (1650, I. iii. xxvii. 81) it is said to have been applied in 1623 by a bishop of Halverstade to a party of incontinent friars and nuns; but in neither case is the specific term used.)

1769 *Boston* (Mass.) *Chron.* 30 Oct. 3/2 A person..was stripped naked, put into a cart, where he was first tarred, then feathered. **1774** J. Adams in *Fam. Lett.* (1876) 12 Pote ..railed away at Boston mobs, drowning tea, and tarring Malcom. **1774** T. Hutchinson *Diary* 1 July, K[ing George III].—I see they threatened to pitch and feather you. H[utchinson].—Tarr and feather, may it please your Majesty. **1774** Burke *Amer. Tax.* Wks. II. 374 You must send the ministers tarred and feathered to America. **1774** *Chron.* in *Ann. Reg.* 127/2 Mr. John Malcomb, an officer of the customs at Boston, who was tarred and feathered, and led to the gallows with a rope about his neck. **1784** Dk. Rutland *Corr. w. Pitt* (1890) 37 Persons are daily marked out for the operation of tarring and feathering. **1846** Hare *Mission Comf.* ii. (1876) 61 [We] tar and feather our feelings with the dust and dirt of earth. **1850** N. Hawthorne in Bridge *Pers. Recoll.* (1893) 114 If I escape from town without being tarred and feathered, I shall consider it good-luck. **1925** A. Huxley *Those Barren Leaves* ii. iii. 113 Miss Carruthers, who has a short way with dissenters, would like to see them tarred and feathered—all except pacifists, who, like strikers, could do with a little shooting. **1960** N. Annan in *Victorian Stud.* June 331 The individualist, the eccentric, the man who offends against the trivial rules of the club, are tarred and feathered with gleeful brutality. **1977** *Daily News* (Perth, Austral.) 19 Jan. 6/5 The victims were stripped naked, tarred and shorn of their hair. **1981** A. Price *Soldier no More* 161 The Russians..wouldn't have cared less if we'd tarred and feathered Nasser and run him out of Suez on a rail.

c. *fig.* To dirty or defile as with tar; esp. in phr. ***tarred with the same stick*** (or ***brush***), stained with the same or similar faults or obnoxious qualities. (In quot. *a* 1612, ? to darken, obscure; in quot. 1622 in allusion to the protective and curative use of tar by shepherds, etc.)

a **1612** Harington *Epigr.* (1633) i. lxviii, To purge the vapours that our cleare sight tarres. **1622** Fletcher & Massinger *Span. Curate* iii. ii, I have nointed ye, and tarr'd ye with my doctrine, And yet the murren sticks to ye. **1818** Scott *Rob Roy* xxvi, They are a' tarr'd wi' the same stick—rank Jacobites and Papists. **1823** Cobbett *Rural Rides* (1885) I. 283 'You are all tarred with the same brush', said the sensible people of Maidstone. **1860** Reade *Cloister & H.* xl, Now this Gerard is tarred with the same stick. **1881** W. E. Forster in Reid *Life* (1888) II. viii. 368 My replacement by some one not tarred by the coercion brush.

tar, †**tarre,** *v.*[2] *Obs. or arch.* Forms: α. 1 **tyrw(i)an,** 5 **terw-yn;** 4–5 **terre(n,** 4 **ter,** 4– Sc. **terr.** β. 4–7 **tarre,** 5– **tar.** [ME. *terren*, app. representing OE. **tęrw(i)an* (**tierw-, tyrw-*), collateral form of *tęrȝan* (*tierȝ-, tyrȝ-*) to vex, irritate, provoke. For the phonology cf. TAR *v.*[1] See also TARY *v.*

OE. *tęrȝan* (WSax. **tierȝ-, tyrȝan*), **tęrw(i)an* (**tierw-, tyrw(i)an*) = OLG. **tęrgan*, MLG. *tergen, targen*, LG. and EFris. *targen*, Da. *tærge*, MDu., Du. *tergen*, to provoke, irritate, exasperate, vex, tease (Kilian, '*terghen* irritare, lacessere, infestare, vexare, provocare ad iram, exacerbare'), mod.Ger. *zergen*; pointing to an OTeut. **targjan.* The phonology of the OE. by-form *tęrw(i)an* has not been satisfactorily explained. Relationship to Russian *dergat'* 'to pluck, pull, tweak' has been suggested.]

1. *trans.* To irritate, vex, provoke. Now only in ***tar on*** (Shaks. *tarre on*), to incite, hound on.

a **1000** *Guthlac* 259 (288) Beoð þa ȝebolȝne þa þec breodwiað, tredað þec and terȝað and hyra torn wrecað. *a* **900** *Kentish Gl.* 508 Tirhþ, *inridet.* **10..** *Lambeth Ps.* lxxiii. 10 Usque quo deus improperabit inimicus: *gl.* hu longe tyrweþ fynd. *Ibid.* lxxxvii. 8 Generatio praua et exasperans: *gl.* þweor mæȝþ & tyrwiende *vel* þurhbitter. *Ibid.* 40 Quotiens exacerbaverunt eum: *gl.* hu ȝelome hiȝ tyrwedon hine. *Ibid.* 41 Hiȝ tyrwadon *vel* gremedon. *Ibid.* 55 Hiȝ costnadon & tyrwodan god þane healican.

c **1380** Wyclif *Serm.* Sel. Wks. II. 44 To terre [*v.r.* ter] men for to fiȝte. **1382** —— *Deut.* iv. 25 That ȝe terren [*v.r. MSS. a* 1400 tarre] hym to wraþþe. —— *Eph.* vi. 4 ȝe fadris, nyle ȝe terre ȝoure sones to wraþþe. **1387** Trevisa *Higden* (Rolls) V. 355 Þe kynges..sone..gan to tarry [*v.r.* terre] and to angre [*probrosis verbis lacessivit*] Þe Longobardes. **1395** Purvey *Remonstr.* (1851) 18 Thei blasfemen God and terren him to wraththe.

β. *a* **1400** Tarre [see quot. 1382 above]. **1561** in *Three 15th Cent. Chron.* (Camden) 119 They came unto me rounde aboute my chamber,..stearde me, and tarde me, and so vexed me as I was never in my lyffe so soore troubled. **1595** Shaks. *John* iv. i. 117 And, like a dogge,..Snatch at his Master that doth tarre him on. **1602** —— *Ham.* ii. ii. 370 The Nation holds it no sinne, to tarre them to Controuersie **1606** —— *Tr. & Cr.* i. iii. 392 Pride alone Must tarre the Mastiffes on, as 'twere their bone. **1837** Carlyle *Fr. Rev.* I. ii. ii, The cries, the squealings of children,..and other assistants, tarring them on, as the rabble does when dogs fight. **1859** Kingsley *Misc.* II. v. 225 The selfishness of the memorialists led them to tar on the rival selfishness of the water companies.

†**2.** To weary, fatigue. *Obs. rare.*

[Known only in form *terw-yn*. The sense in *Promp. Parv.* corresponds rather to the trans. use of OE. *téorian* to tire, but was possibly an offshoot from that of 'vex, harass'. The same sense-development appears also in the cognate TARY *v.* 2.]

c **1440** *Promp. Parv.* 489/2 Terwyn, or make wery or weryyn, *lasso, fatigo.* Terwyd, *lassatus, fatigatus.* Terwynge, *lassitudo, fatigacio. Ibid.* 522/2 Weryyn, or make wery or terwyn, *fatigo, lasso.*

†**3.** *intr.* ***tar and tig, tig and tar***, to act forcefully or wantonly; to use force and violence. *Sc.*

c **1470** Henryson *Mor. Fab.* v. (*Parl. Beasts*) i, [The fox] That luifit weill with pultrie to tig and tar [*Bann. MS.* tere]. *a* **1568** Balnaves in *Bannatyne Poems* (Hunter. Cl.) 391 To tar and tig, syne grace to thig, That is ane petouss preiss. *Ibid.* 392 To tig and tar, syne get the war, It is evill merchandyiss.

Hence †**tarring** (**terring**) *vbl. sb.*, provocation.

1382 Wyclif *2 Kings* xxiii. 26 The Lord is not turned aweye fro the wrath of his grete woodnes..for the terryngis in the whiche Manasses hadde terred hym. —— *Ps.* xciv. 9 As in the terring [**1388** the terrying to wroþþe], after the day of tempting in desert.

tar, obs. f. *tare, tore*, pa. t. of TEAR *v.*[1]

‖**tara** (ˈtɑːrə), *sb.* [? Native name in Tasmania.] The edible fern of Tasmania and New Zealand, a variety of the common brake, *Pteris aquilina* var. *esculenta.* Also ***tara fern.***

1834 Ross *Van Diemen's Land Ann.* 129 (Morris *Austral Eng.*) The most extensively diffused eatable roots..are those of the tara fern..[which] greatly resembles *Pteris aquilina*, the common fern, brake,..or brackin, of England, ..it is known among the aborigines by the name of tara.

tara, *int.*[1] An exclamation. (Cf. F. *tarare*; also TARATANTARA.)

In quot. 1672, it occurs in a passage burlesquing a scene in Dryden's *Tyrannic Love* iv. i.

1672 Villiers (Dk. Buckhm.) *Rehearsal* v. i. (Arb.) 113, *1 King.* Tara, tara, tara, full East and by South. *2 King.* We sail with Thunder in our mouth. **1922** Joyce *Ulysses* 166 Tara tara. Great chorus that. Tara. Must be washed in rainwater. Meyerbeer. Tara: bom bom bom. *Ibid.* 503 Exercise your mnemotechnic. *La causa è santa.* Tara. Tara.

tara (təˈrɑː), *int.*[2] Also **tarra(h,** etc. Colloq. (mainly North.) alteration of TA-TA, in familiar use.

1958 A. Sillitoe *Saturday Night & Sunday Morning* ii. 27 'See yer't dinnertime, Arthur.' 'Tarr-ar, Dad.' **1967** E. Williams *Beyond Belief* i. i. 6 They are off arm in arm to Belle Vue. Ta-ra-for-now, they call out, the warm casual Lancashire way of saying goodbye, 'ta ra!' **1973** B. Bainbridge *Dressmaker* iii. 39 'Tarrah, Valerie!' called Rita up the stairs. 'Thank you very much for having me.' **1981** B. Hines *Looks & Smiles* 121 'I'm off now, Mum, ta-ra.' 'Ta-ra, love. See you tonight.'

tarabagan, var. TARBAGAN.

‖**tarada** (taˈraːda). [ad. Arab. *tarrāda* cruiser, swift war canoe.] A canoe used by the Marsh Arabs of Iraq.

1960 G. Maxwell *Ring of Bright Water* i. vi. 75 We spent the better part of those two months [in Southern Iraq] squatting cross-legged in the bottom of a *tarada* or war canoe. **1964** W. Thesiger *Marsh Arabs* iii. 23 The top part of the ribs was..studded with five rows of flat, round nail-heads two inches across. These decorative nails were the distinguishing mark of a *tarada*..which only a sheikh may own. Years later, in Oslo, I saw the Viking ships preserved there and was at once reminded of the *taradas* in the Marshes. **1974** *Blackw. Mag.* Oct. 341/1 There is a bigger canoe called a *tarada*, graceful and swift, with a fine upsweep prow.

taradiddle, tarradiddle (ˌtærəˈdɪd(ə)l; *main stress shifting*), *sb. slang* or *colloq.* Also 9 **tarri-, tally-.** [cf. DIDDLE *v.*[3] 2, *sb.*[2]: the first element is obscure: cf. TARA *int.*[1]] A trifling falsehood, a petty lie; a colloquial euphemism for a lie; a 'fib'.

1796 Grose *Dict. Vulg. Tongue* (ed. 3), *Taradiddle*, a fib, or falsity. **1844** J. T. Hewlett *Parsons & W.* xliv, Telling a tarradiddle or two. **1865** Mrs. Gaskell *Wives & Dau.* xlvii, Oh, don't call them lies, sister; it's such a strong, ugly word. Please call them tallydiddles, for I don't believe she meant any harm. **1882** J. Payn *Thicker than Water* i, Our widow paid..the compliment of telling a 'tarradiddle' or white lie. **1885** Huxley *Let.* 23 Feb. in *Life* (1900) II. 97 Everybody told us it would be very cold, and, as usual, everybody told taradiddles.

ˌ**taraˈdiddle, tarradiddle,** *v. slang* or *colloq.* [f. prec.] **a.** *intr.* To tell taradiddles or fibs. **b.** *trans.* To impose upon, or bring into some condition, by telling fibs. Hence ˌ**taraˈdiddler**, one who taradiddles, a petty liar.

1828 *Examiner* 658/1 His enemies..squibbed, and paragraphed, and taradiddled him to death. **1847–78** Halliwell, *Tarra-diddled*, imposed upon, generally by lies. **1880** *Society* 29 Oct., Perhaps there is not a more facile..tarradiddler than the London correspondent of the provincial newspaper. **1909** *Athenæum* 6 Mar. 281/1 A barefaced tarradiddler or a prophet.

†ˈ**tarage,** *sb.*[1] *Obs.* Also 5 **tarrage**: see also the collateral form TALLAGE *sb.*[2] [app. of F. origin; etymology unascertained.] Taste, flavour; quality, character; esp. as derived or communicated.

c **1407** Lydg. *Reson & Sens.* 3943 Swich is the tarage of the roote, Somtyme as any sugre soote And bitter sodeynly as galle. **1429** *Pol. Poems* (Rolls) II. 141 Of all these thy grene tender age,..Of manly prowesse shal taken tarage. *c* **1430** Lydg. *Min. Poems* (Percy Soc.) 180 Ner the vyne his holsome fressh tarage, Whiche yeveth comforte to al maner age. *Ibid.* 192 Thus every thing,..As frute and trees, and folke of every degré, Fro whens they come thei take a tarage. *c* **1450** Lydg. & Burgh *Secrees* 1886 Watrys that renne be many diuers londys,..Which tarage haue of foreyn dyvers sondys. **14..** *Epiphanye* in *Tundale's Vis.* 119 Thys day he turned water into wyne..of tarage [*MS. Soc. Antiq.* 134 lf. 26 talage] inly gud and fyne.

† **tarage**, *sb.*[2] *Obs.* [app. variant form of TERRAGE.] ? A ground in artistic representation.

1439 in *Archæologia* XXI. 37 An Image of Seynt George beyng upon a grene tarage, wt a damasell knelyng. *c* **1468** *Ibid.* XXXI. 336 On every tarage a tree of gold.

† **'tarage**, *v. Obs.* [f. TARAGE *sb.*[1]] To have a character or quality *of* some kind, to 'taste of', 'smell of' (*intr.* and *trans.*). So † **'taraged** *a.*, having a (specified) quality or character.

c **1407** LYDG. *Reson & Sens.* 3378 Hyr tayl ys werray serpentyne, And hir bely eke Capryne,.. whan she is hoot, Rammysh taraged as a goot. *c* **1430** —— *Min. Poems* (Percy Soc.) 217 Frut fet fro fer tarageth of the tre. **1430–40** —— *Bochas* IV. xv. (MS. Bodl. 263) lf. 243/2 How man and beeste & euery creature Tarageth the stok of his natyvite. *Ibid.* VIII. xxiv. lf. 402/1 Eche werm sume parti taragethe of his brood.

† **taragmite** (tə'rægmaɪt), *a. Geol. Obs. rare.* [f. Gr. τάραγμα disturbance, f. ταράσσειν to disturb + -ITE[1].] (See quots., and cf. PHANERITE.)

a **1857** J. FLEMING *Lithol. Edinb.* v. (1859) 50 The first or Taragmite series, have been formed subsequently to the dressings, and, where present, repose upon them. **1859** PAGE *Geol. Terms, Taragmite Series*.. a term employed by Dr. Fleming in his 'Lithology of Edinburgh' to embrace the Boulder Clay, or lowest stage of the modern epoch, as 'having been formed when violent aqueous movements were taking place, and probably at a period when the state of our island was widely different from the present'.

taragon, var. of TARRAGON.

Tarahumara (,tærəhu:'mɑ:rə), *sb.* and *a.* Also Tarahumar(e. [a. Sp., of uncertain origin.]

A. *sb.* **a.** (A member of) an Uto-Aztecan people of north-western Mexico. **b.** The language of this people. **B.** *adj.* Of, pertaining to, or designating this people.

1874 H. H. BANCROFT *Native Races Pacific States* I. v. 609 The *Tarahumares* inhabit the district of Tarahumara in the state of Chihuahua. *Ibid.* III. v. 666 The Tarahumara, which is a more polished language than its neighbors, contains words similar to the Aztec. **1911** J. G. FRAZER *Golden Bough: Magic Art* (ed. 3) I. iii. 150 The Tarahumares of Mexico are great runners. **1912** C. LUMHOLTZ *Unknown Mexico* I. viii. 168 Tarahumare pottery is exceedingly crude. **1934** A. L. KROEBER *Uto-Aztecan Lang. Mexico* 13 Varohío .. is in all most similar to Tarahumar. But it can hardly be .. merely a provincial dialect of Tarahumar. **1963** C. W. PENNINGTON *Tarahumar of Mexico* i. 5 Zapata's résumé of the Tarahumar missions in 1678.. indicate that Coyáchic.. was an important Tarahumar center. **1964** E. A. NIDA *Toward Sci. Transl.* iii. 35 The Tarahumara in northern Mexico have five basic color words, including one term *siyonomi*, which covers both green and blue. **1975** *Language* LI. 798 In Tarahumara, *-tu/-ru* retains the sense 'become' in its use as a derivational suffix. **1979** *Tucson* (Ariz.) *Mag.* June 48/2 Several Tarahumara dwellings and farm buildings have been reconstructed for the exhibit.

‖ **tarairi** (tə'raɪrɪ). Also taraire. [Maori name.] A timber tree of New Zealand, *Beilschmiedia Tarairi*, N.O. *Lauraceæ*: see quots.

1873 *Catal. Vienna Exhib.* (Morris), Tarairi. Used for most of the purposes for which sycamore is applied in Europe. **1883** J. HECTOR *Handbk. N. Zealand* (1886) 106 Tarairi. A lofty forest tree, 60 ft. to 80 ft. high, with stout branches. Wood white, splits freely, but not much valued.

tarakihi (tara'kihi). *N.Z.* Also **terakihi** (tɛrə'ki:). [Maori.] A marine fish, *Cheilodactylus macropterus*, silver in colour with a black band behind the head, belonging to the morwong group and found off the coasts of New Zealand.

1873 J. H. H. ST. JOHN *Pakeha Rambles through Maori Lands* II. x. 173 Our best fish are the tarakihi, patiki or sole, and whitebait. **1937** *Nature* 7 Aug. 223/1 Tarakihi.. flesh was found to contain appreciable amounts of vitamin A. **1959** A. H. MCLINTOCK *Descr. Atlas N.Z.* 48 Tarakihi.. second only in importance [as a commercial catch] to snapper, is trawled off the east coast.. [and] also caught in quantity in deep water along the west coast. **1960** N. HILLIARD *Maori Girl* II. v. 96 She.. was preparing to fry a piece of *terakihi* for their tea.

taramellite (tærə'mɛlaɪt). *Min.* [a. It. *taramellite* (E. Tacconi 1908, in *Atti dell' Accad. Naz. dei Lincei: Rendiconti, Classe di Sci. Fisiche*, etc. XVII. I. 814), f. the name of T. *Taramelli* (1845–1922), Italian geologist: see -ITE[1].] An orthorhombic borosilicate of barium and other metals, chiefly iron and titanium, and usu. containing some chlorine.

1908 *Jrnl. Chem. Soc.* XCIV. II. 863 The author describes a new mineral, taramellite, occurring in radiating, fibrous, acicular aggregates or slender veins in the calcareous zone of Candoglia-Ornavasso (Val Toce). **1973** *Mineral. Abstr.* XXIV. 433/2 More than 50 minerals have been identified in rocks of this quarry of the Pacific Limestone Products Co. [in California]. They include.. 15 silicates three of which, celsian, pabstite, and taramellite, are Ba-bearing.

taramosalata (,tærəməsə'lɑ:tə). Also **taramasalata**. [a. mod.Gr., f. ταραμᾶς preserved roe (ad. Turk. *tarama* soft roe, red caviare) + σαλάτα SALAD.] A Greek fish pâté made (traditionally) from the roe of the grey mullet or from smoked cod's roe, mixed with garlic, lemon juice, olive oil, etc. Also *ellipt.* as **tarama**.

1910 Z. D. FERRIMAN *Home Life in Hellas* iv. 181 Red caviar.. is pounded with garlic and lemon juice into what is called *tarama salata*. **1958** R. LIDDELL *Morea* II. iii. 70 A vinegary *taramosalata*, a preparation of salted fish eggs and oil, which is always Lenten food in Greece. **1964** *Spectator* 8 May 645/1 A Greek fish pâté, *taramasalata*. **1972** *Harper's & Queen* Apr. 92/1, I quite often add tarama to go with the avocado. **1978** *Chicago* June 233/1 Dinnertime favorites include saganaki,.. taramosalata, red caviar, etc.

‖ **taran** ('tarən). *Sc.* [Gael. *taran.*] The ghost of an unbaptized child.

1775 L. SHAW *Hist. Moray* VI. iv. 307 It was likewise believed.. that Children dying unbaptized (called *Tarans*) wandered in woods and solitudes, lamenting their hard fate, and were often seen. **1776** PENNANT *Tour Scotl. in 1772* II. Addit. 13. **1813** ELLIS *Brand's Pop. Antiq.* (1849) II. 73.

Taranaki (tærə'nækɪ). The name of a province in New Zealand, used *attrib.* in **Taranaki gate**, a gate made of wire strands attached to upright battens (see quot. 1966).

1937 M. E. C. SCOTT *Barbara Prospers* 27 She.. had the 'Taranaki' gate open in a twinkling. **1948** R. FINLAYSON *Tidal Creek* 205 Mind you get the taranaki gate properly up. **1953** J. W. BRIMBLECOMBE *Shear Nonsense* 110 He can now open a Taranaki gate without rolling himself up in it. **1966** G. W. TURNER *Eng. Lang. Austral. & N.Z.* ii. 31 The province gives its name to the *Taranaki gate*, a moveable piece of a wire fence held by a loop of wire at one end to form a makeshift gate. **1968** *Landfall* XXII. 390 Sure enough, we found someone had taken down the Taranaki gate on the side that led to the Oteranika Road.

taranakite (tærə'nɑ:kaɪt). *Min.* [f. prec.: see -ITE[1].] A hydrated basic phosphate of potassium (partly replaced by ammonium) and aluminium, found as a soft, whitish or grey clay-like substance composed of minute rhombohedral crystals.

1866 HECTOR & SKEY in *Rep. & Awards of Jurors N.Z. Exhib., 1865* 423 Taranakite, a new Phosphatic mineral.. presented by H. Richmond.. This singular mineral was mistaken for Wavellite. **1882** *Trans. N.Z. Inst.* XV. 385 Taranakite.. a double hydrous phosphate of alumina and potash, part of the alumina being replaced by ferric oxide, was first discovered by H. Richmond, Esq., at the Sugar Loaves, Taranaki. **1976** *Mineral. Abstr.* XXVII. 256/2 Aluminian strengite.., vivianite.., and taranakite..(small yellowish white aggregates) from the Castellane caves, Apulia, southern Italy, occur embedded in small 'terra rossa' deposits, near the contact with superimposed layers of bat guano.

† **'tarand, ta'randre.** *Obs.* Also **tarandule**, and in L. forms **tarandus, -andrus**. [a. F. *tarande*, obs. *tarandre*, ad. med.L. *tarand-us*, L. *tarandr-us* (Pliny), name of a northern beast, supposed to be the reindeer.] A name given to some northern quadruped, at length identified with the reindeer.

1572 BOSSEWELL *Armorie* II. 57 The fielde is of the Topaze, a Tarandre tripping, Rubye, unguled Diamonde. Tarandrus is a beaste in bodye like a great Oxe, hauing an head like to an harte, and hornes full of branches. *Ibid.* III. 22 b, The Tarandule is a beaste commonly called a Buffe, which is like an Oxe, but that he hath a bearde like a Goate. **1613** PURCHAS *Pilgrimage* (1614) 559 The Tarandus is a Beast somewhat resembling an Oxe, in quantitie, a Hart in shape. **1753** CHAMBERS *Cycl. Supp., Tarandus*, in zoology, a name given by Agricola and some other authors, to the rein-deer.

b. Said to have, like the chameleon, the power to 'change himselfe into the thing he toucheth or leaneth vnto' (Florio); so Rabelais IV. ii. Also *fig.*

It is not certain that *tarand* (applied scurrilously to Christ) in quot. *c* 1440, is the same word.

c **1440** *York Myst.* xxxiii. 381 (*iii Miles*) All þin vntrew techyngis þus taste I, þou tarand. **1642** R. CARPENTER *Experience* II. xi. 218 Like the Tarrand, which walking in a Garden, represents the colour of every flower in his skin. **1694** MOTTEUX *Rabelais* IV. ii. I. **1702** *Eng. Theophrast.* 363 As the tarand changes its colour with every plant that it approaches so the wise man adapts himself to the several humours and inclinations of those he converses with.

'tarantant. *rare.* [See -ANT.] = TARANTATO.

1883 *Chamb. Jrnl.* 1 Dec. 761/1 When the tarantant had by this means recovered, he or she remained free from the disease until the approach of the warm weather in the next year.

tarantara: see TARATANTARA.

‖ **tarantass** (,tarən'tas). Also **-as**. [ad. Russ. *tarantas*[ъ].] A four-wheeled Russian travelling-carriage without springs, on a long flexible wooden chassis.

1850 (*title*) The Tarantas, travelling impressions of Young Russia, by Count Sollogub. **1876** BURNABY *Khiva* xxxvi. 342 The tarantass.. resembled a hansom cab without the wheels,.. fastened in a brewer's dray. **1882** H. LANDELL *Through Siberia* I. 135 A roofless, seatless, springless, semi-cylindrical tumbril, mounted on poles which connect two wooden axle-trees.. called by the general name of *tarantass*.

‖ **tarantato** (taran'tato). *rare.* Pl. **-ati** (-'ati). Also fem. **taran'tata**, *pl.* **-ate**. [It. *taran'tato* 'bitten with a tarantula' (Florio), affected with tarantism, f. *Taranto* name of the town: see -ISM.] One who has been bitten by a tarantula; one suffering from tarantism.

1685 BOYLE *Effects of Mot.* vi. 76 Narratives of the effects of Music upon the *Tarantati*. **1717** BERKELEY *Tour Italy* Wks. 1871 IV. 544 The tarantato that we saw dancing in a circle paced round the room. *Ibid.* 545 None danced but the tarantata. Her father certainly [was] persuaded that she had her disorder from the tarantula.

‖ **tarantella** (tærən'tɛlə). Also 9 **tarent-**, and from F., **tarent-, tarantelle**. [It. *tarantella* (in F. *tarentelle*, Sp. *tarantela*), dim. formation from *Taranto* the town of *Tarentum* in southern Italy. Popularly associated with *tarantola, tarantula* the spider, also a deriv. of *Taranto*. (Etymologically, *tarantella* might be a further dim. of *tarantula*: cf. L. *fabula, tabula, fabella, tabella*.)] A rapid whirling South Italian dance popular with the peasantry since the fifteenth century, when it was supposed to be the sovereign remedy for tarantism.

1782 *Char.* in *Ann. Reg.* II. 11/2 The Tarantella is a low dance, consisting of turns on the heel, much footing and snapping of the fingers. **1844** DISRAELI *Coningsby* IV. xi, He could dance a Tarantalla like a Lazaroni. **1866** ENGEL *Nat. Mus.* vii. 259 According to popular belief, a person bitten by the venomous spider Tarantula can be recovered from the state of nervous disorder which the poison produces, only by dancing the Tarantella until complete exhaustion compels him to desist from the vehement exercise. **1894** *Times* 3 Mar. 11/2 While the plaintiff was dancing a tarantella with a tambourine her foot slipped, owing, as she alleged, to the negligent stretching of the carpet, or 'stage cloth'.

b. The music for such a dance, or composed in its rhythm, formerly quadruple, but now always in 6–8 time, with whirling triplets, and abrupt transitions from the major to the minor.

1833–5 BABINGTON tr. *Hecker's Epidemics* (1859) 113 The Italians.. have retained the Tarantella, as a particular species of music employed for quick lively dancing. **1884** C. F. WOOLSON in *Harper's Mag.* Jan. 216/1 A gay Tarantella, which set all the house-maids dancing.

tarantism ('tærəntɪz(ə)m). Also 9 **tarent-**, and (in L. form) **tarant-, tarentismus**. [ad. mod.L. *tarantismus* = It. *tarantismo*, F. *tarentisme*, from It. *Taranto* name of the town (see prec.); but popularly associated with *tarantola* the tarantula spider, whence sometimes called *tarantulism*.] A hysterical malady, characterized by an extreme impulse to dance, which prevailed as an epidemic in Apulia and adjacent parts of Italy from the 15th to the 17th century, popularly attributed to the bite or 'sting' of the tarantula.

The dancing was sometimes held to be a symptom or consequence of the malady, sometimes practised as a sovereign cure for it.

1638–56 COWLEY *Davideis* I. Notes §32 We should hardly be convinced of this Physick, unless it be in the particular cure of the Tarantism, the experiments of which are too notorious to be denyed or eluded. **1770** *Phil. Trans.* LX. 237 People.. get a little money, by dancing when they say the tarantism begins. *Ibid.*, In Sicily, where the summer is still warmer.. the Tarantula is never dangerous, and music is never employed for the cure of the pretended tarantism. **1822–34** *Good's Study Med.* (ed. 4) III. 338 This form of the disease appears to be a near relation to the tarantismus of Sauvages. **1833–5** BABINGTON tr. *Hecker's Epidemics* ii. (1859) 106 The origin of tarantism itself is referrible.. to a period between the middle and the end of this century, and is consequently contemporaneous with that of the St. Vitus's dance (1374). **1883** *Chambers's Encycl.* IX. 296/2 *Tarantism* may be defined a leaping or dancing mania, originating in, or supposed to originate in, an animal poison. .. The gesticulations, contortions, and cries somewhat resembled those in St. Vitus's Dance, and other epidemic nervous diseases of the middle ages. **1883** *Chamb. Jrnl.* 1 Dec. 760/2 The earliest mention of *tarantismus* is found in the works of Nicolas Perotti, who died in 1480.

tarantula (tə'ræntjʊlə). Also 6 **tarentula**, 7 **-entola, tarantule**. [a. med.L. *tarantula* (*Onomast. Lat. Græc.*), It. *tarantola*, f. *Taranto* a town in modern Apulia:—L. *Tarentum*, ad. Gr. Τάρας (Τάραντα). Cf. F. *tarentule* (16th c. in Littré; in OF. only *tarente*).]

1. a. A large wolf-spider of Southern Europe, *Lycosa tarantula* (formerly *Tarantula Apuliæ*), named from the town in the region where it is commonly found, whose bite is slightly poisonous, and was fabled to cause TARANTISM.

1561 T. HOBY tr. *Castiglione's Courtyer* I. (1577) C v b, Them that are bitten with a Tarrantula. [*margin*] A kind of spiders, which being diuers of nature cause diuers effectes, some after their biting fal a singing, some laugh [etc.]. **1584** LYLY *Sappho* IV. iii, I was stung with the flye Tarantula. **1592** GREENE *Philom.* (1615) G iij b, Such as are stung by the Tarentula, are best cured by Musicke. **1601** R. JOHNSON *Kingd. & Commw.* (1603) 113 In this countrey is bred the Tarantola, whose venom is expelled with the fire and musick. **1630** J. TAYLOR (Water P.) *Bawd* Wks. I ij/1 Saint Vitus or Vitellus,.. an excellent patron or proctor to cure those that are bitten of a Spider called Tarrantulla, or Phallanx. **1658** J. ROWLAND *Moufet's Theat. Ins.* 1061 All those that are stung with the Tarantula, dance so well, as if they were taught to dance, and sing as well as if they were musically bred. **1711** *Let. to Sacheverel* 20 Such a Frenzy ran thro the Nation, as if they had been all bitten with Tarantulas. **1771** D. CIRILLO in *Ann. Reg.* 85/1 Several experiments have been tried with the Tarantula; and neither men nor animals, after the bite, have had any other complaint, but a very trifling inflammation upon the part. **1861** HULME tr. *Moquin-Tandon* II. v. ii. 263 The Common Tarantula.. is about an inch in length... A number of fabulous tales, all of them equally absurd, have been related of the Tarantula.

b. Popularly applied to other noxious spiders, esp. to the great hairy spiders of the genus *Mygale*, natives of the warmer parts of America.

1794 MORSE *Amer. Geog.* 597 Scorpions and tarantulas are found here [Dutch Guiana] of a large size and great venom. **1834** PRINGLE *Afr. Sk.* ii. 142 The terror of snakes, scorpions, tarantulas, and other noxious creatures of the African clime. **1871** KINGSLEY *At Last* xvii, The chief engineer exhibited a live 'Tarantula', or bird-catching spider. **1893** KATE SANBORN *Truthf. Wom. S. California* 107 Tarantulas never come out at night... Mr. Wakely, who has caught more of these spiders than any living man, does not seem to dread the job in the least.

†**c.** By confusion, mistaken for or applied to some (supposed) venomous reptile: see quots. *Obs.*

[**1598** FLORIO, *Tarantola*, a serpent called an eft or an euet, some take it to be a flye whose sting is.. deadly, and nothing but diuers sounds of musicke can cure the patient. Also a fish so called.] **1615** G. SANDYS *Trav.* 249 Hereabout.. are great store of Tarantulas: a serpent peculiar to this countrey. **1616** BULLOKAR *Eng. Expos.*, *Tarantula*, a little beast like a Lizard, hauing spots in his necke like starres. **1753** CHAMBERS *Cycl. Supp.*, *Tarantula*, in zoology, a name given by the Italians to a peculiar species of lizard. [**1896** *List Anim. Zool. Soc.* 577 *Tarentola mauritanica*.. Moorish Gecko.]

2. Contextually, The bite of the tarantula; hence, erroneously, = TARANTISM.

a **1586** SIDNEY *Arcadia* I. ix. (1590) 38 b, This word, Louer, did not lesse pearce poore Pyrocles, then the right tune of musicke toucheth him that is sick of the Tarantula. **1633** G. HERBERT *Temple, Dooms-day* ii, Peculiar notes and strains Cure Tarantulaes raging pains. **1651-3** JER. TAYLOR *Serm. for Year* I. xix. 250 He dies with a Tarantula, dancing and singing till he bowes his neck, and kisses his bosome with the fatall noddings and declensions of death.

fig. **1828** *Lights & Shades* II. 278 My wife's tarantula is never cured, her fingers are never out of her harpsichord.

3. *fig.* from 1 and 2.

1608 MIDDLETON *Trick to Catch Old One* I. i, Hence, courtesan, round-webb'd tarantula. **1652** URQUHART *Jewel* Wks. (1834) 280 Stung with the tarantula of a preposterous ambition. **1666** R. WILDE *Poems* (1870) 103 May he resume King David's harp, and play The tarantule of discontent away. **1685** *Answ. Dk. Buckhm. on Lib. Consc.* 4 Stung with the Tarantula of his Paper, which may make me dance and caper. **1721** PRIOR *Dial. Dead* (1907) 268 You find others bit with the same Tarantula. **1837** CARLYLE *French Revolution* II. I. vi. (*Je le jure*), Saw the sun ever such a swearing people? Have they been bit by a swearing tarantula?

¶**4.** Erroneously for TARANTELLA, the dance.

1698 FRYER *Acc. E. India & P.* 111 They labour as much as a Lancashire Man does at Roger of Coverly, or the Tarantula of their Hornpipe. **1865** *Daily Tel.* 14 Dec. 7/3 All the dances of the civilised world, from the tarantula to the *trois temps*.

5. *attrib.* and *Comb.*, as ***tarantula bite, dance, dancer, spider, sting***, etc.; ***tarantula-stung*** adj.; **tarantula-hawk, -killer**, any of several species of spider wasp of the genus *Pepsis* that occur in the south-western U.S. and kill tarantulas; **tarantula-juice** *U.S. slang*, inferior whisky.

1647 HARINGTON in *Nugæ Ant.* (1779) II. 92 We grasp but airy blisses, and thus, tarantula-stung, dye amidst laughing fits. **1688** R. HOLME *Armoury* II. 215/2 The Tarantula Spider.. of Apulia.. hath only six legs, and a stretched out tail. **1833-5** BABINGTON tr. *Hecker's Epidemics* ii. (1859) 110 The excitement which the Tarantula dancers felt at the sight of anything with metallic lustre. **1861** *Harper's Mag.* Jan. 147/2 Little to drink, except old-fashioned tarentula-juice, 'warranted to kill at forty paces'. **1867** *Amer. Naturalist* I. 137 The large, red-winged 'Tarantula Killer'.. is, as far as I know, the largest of the dauber group. **1878** B. F. TAYLOR *Between Gates* 198 The tarantula hawk.. pounces upon his victim and makes a needle-cushion of him. **1899** D. SHARP in *Camb. Nat. Hist.* VI. iii. 105 *P[epsis] formosus*, Say, is called in Texas the tarantula-killer; according to Buckley, its mode of attack on the huge spider is different from that made use of by its European ally. **1902** *Westm. Gaz.* 12 Aug. 10/1 In Orsuna [Spain].. there is a 'Guild of Tarantula-players'.. who earn considerable fees by sending round their members to heal the sufferers from the tarantula bite. **1932** *Sun* (Baltimore) 8 June 9/1 A large wasp, known.. as a 'tarantula hawk', was victor over a tarantula in a battle. **1939** C. W. TOWNE *Her Majesty Montana* 38 In the saloons, poisonous liquors are vended to all comers under the name of 'tangleleg', 'forty-rod', 'lightning', 'Tarantula-juice', etc. **1980** F. H. WAGNER *Wildlife of Deserts* 148 Formidable as the tarantula is, it has its own enemies. The large tarantula hawk wasp (*Pepsis*) feeds the spiders to its young.

Hence **ta'rantular, ta'rantulary, ta'rantulous** *adjs.*, of or pertaining to the tarantula (in quots. *fig.*); **ta'rantulate** [cf. It. *tarantolato*], †**ta'rantulize** *vbs.*, *trans.* to affect with tarantism; **ta'rantulism** = TARANTISM.

1857 *Chamb. Jrnl.* VIII. 227/1 Seized with the *tarentular phrensy. **1781** E. POULTER *Peripatetics* 14 In Bath.. Perpetual Dancing's our disorder here. Gronovius proves them, to the plainest sense, Under *Tarantulary influence. **1737** M. GREEN *Spleen* 146 Motions unwill'd its powers have shown *Tarantulated by a tune. **1774** 'JOEL COLLIER' (Bicknell) *Mus. Trav.* 14, I drove away the evil spirit, and cured her of her *tarantulism that night. **1652** BENLOWES *Theoph.* III. lix. 44 In Saul, disguis'd When Satan oft *Tarantuliz'd, The Psalming Harp was 'bove thy swaying Scepter priz'd. **1895** *Lit. World* 23 Aug. 141/1 The reputation.. will survive the *tarantulous bites of envious detractors.

†**Tarantulle** (tærən'tu:l). *Obs.* [Cf. TULLE.] The proprietary name of a kind of cotton fabric.

1890 *Trade Marks Jrnl.* 3 Sept. 878 Tarantulle 89,034. Cotton piece goods of all kinds. Tootal Broadhurst Lee Company.. Manchester.. Manufacturers.—10th April 1889. **1915** *Official Gaz.* (U.S. Patent Office) 16 Mar. 1033/1 Tarantulle... Cotton piece goods—viz. Nainsooks, Cambrics, and Madapolams. **1923** *Daily Mail* 9 Jan. 1 (Advt.), Ladies' Night-dress, in standard Tarantulle, trimmed strong Embroidery. **1932** D. C. MINTER *Mod. Needlecraft* 253/2 Tarantulle. Dorcas cambric or fine longcloth.

tarapin(e, obs. form of TERRAPIN.

tarara (tə'rɑːrə). Also *redupl.* [Echoic.] = TARANTARA 1.

1891 KIPLING *Light that Failed* ii. 18 Ridin', ridin', ridin', two an' two, Ta-ra-ra-ra-ra-ra-ra, All the way to Kandahar. **1892** —— *Barrack-Room Ballads* 57 You can't refuse when you get the card And the widow gives the party. (*Bugle*: Ta—rara—ra-ra-rara!) **1980** D. BLOODWORTH *Trapdoor* v. 25 The situation was.. saved in the nick of time—tarara, *tarara*—by a little old lady.

taras, -asse, obs. forms of TERRACE.

Tarascan (tə'ræskən), *sb.* and *a.* [f. Sp. *Tarasco*, name of a Meso-American Indian language of S.W. Michoacán, Mexico + -AN.]

A. *sb.* **a.** A member of an Indian people of the mountain area about lake Pátzcuara in Michoacán. **b.** Their language. **B.** *adj.* Of or pertaining to this people or their language.

[**1874** H. H. BANCROFT *Native Races Pacific States* I. vi. 643 The Michoacagues or Tarascos are warlike and brave. *Ibid.* III. x. 744 The Tarasco, the principal language of Michoacan, can be placed almost upon an equality with the Aztec, as being copious and well-finished.] **1911** C. THOMAS *Indian Lang. Mexico & Central Amer.* 51 The Tarascan language is now well known as constituting a separate family. **1914** R. J. MACHUGH *Mod. Mexico* i. 2 One hundred and thirty-three separate Indian tribes recognized in Mexico.. are arranged under sixteen language groups—the Athapascan.. Piman, Tañoan, Tarascan, [etc.]. **1931** S. CHASE *Mexico* ii. 31 There was only one basic culture in Mexico and Central America, in which the Mayas, the Toltecs, the Aztecs, the Tarascans, the Zapotecs and various other nations shared. **1948** R. C. WEST (*title*) Cultural geography of the modern Tarascan area. **1964** E. A. NIDA *Toward Sci. Transl.* v. 94 Tarascan, a language of Mexico which has a number of metaphors, does not readily admit new ones. **1974** *Encycl. Brit. Macropædia* XII. 164/2 The relative isolation created by the mountains permitted the Tarascans to work out their own cultural variant.

‖**tarata** (ta'rata). [Maori.] Native name in New Zealand of a small evergreen tree (*Pittosporum eugenioides*), also called *lemon-wood*.

1876 W. N. BLAIR in *Trans. N. Zeal. Inst.* IX. 143. **1879** J. B. ARMSTRONG *ibid.* XII. 329 (Morris) The tarata or Lemon-wood, a most beautiful tree, also used for hedges.

taratantara (tɑːrə'tæntərə, -tæn'tɑːrə). Also 6 **taratauntara**, 7 **taratantarra, tarratantara, taratantaro (taratamara)**; also, 6-7 **taratantar**, 7-9 **tarantara**, 9 **tarantarrara**. Cf. TANTARA. [Echoic: cf. L. *tara'tantara* (Ennius) sound of the trumpet (so It. *taratan'tara* in Florio), and med.L. *taratantarum* a sieve or winnowing machine (*Cath. Angl.*, s.v. *Tempse*); It. *taratan'taro* a mill-clack (Florio).]

1. A word imitating, and hence denoting, the sound of a trumpet or bugle (in quot. 1620, of a drum). Also *attrib.*

1553 T. WILSON *Rhet.* 92 b, Or when one is lustye to saye Taratauntara, declaringe therby that he is as lustye, as a Trumpette is delitefull, and styrringe. **1557** GRIMALD *Death Zoroas* in *Tottell's Misc.* (Arb.) 120 Now clattering arms.. Gan passe the noyes of taratantars clang. **1620** T. GRANGER *Div. Logike* 66 The Drum soundeth taratantara. **1621** BURTON *Anat. Mel.* II. iii. VII. (1652) 354 Let drums beat on, trumpets sound Taratantarra, let them sack cities. **1638** RANDOLPH *Hey for Honesty* I. ii, I would have blown a Trumpet Tarantara. **1660** Z. CROFTON *Fastening St. Peter's Fetters* 72 The Tarratantara murmur of the Lincoln-shire and York-shire men in their rebellious holy pilgrimage. **1667** DENHAM *Direct. Paint.* II. vii, To raise it, we must have a Naval War, As if 'were nothing but Tara-Tan-Tar. **1698** VANBRUGH *Æsop* II, *Æsop*. To boot and saddle again they sound. *Rog.* Ta ra! tan tan ta ra! ra ra tan ta ra! **1873** 'OUIDA' *Pascarèl* I. 121 Their Tirolean postilions roused the echoes.. with a tarantarrarara upon their tassellated bugles.

†**2.** *fig.* High-flown, loud, extravagant, or pretentious talk. Also *attrib.* *Obs.*

1599 *Broughton's Let.* ii. 11 To coyne an epistle.. with such Taratantara fictions and applauses. **1670** EACHARD *Cont. Clergy* 43 Making a high rant about a shittle-cock, and talking tara-tantaro about a feather. **1674** R. GODFREY *Inj. & Ab. Physic* 29 [To] please himself in talking Tara-tan-tara about the Philosophers stone and Horizontal Gold.

Hence **tara'tantar, tara'tantarize** [= med.L. *taratantarizāre*] *vbs.*, *intr.* to sound, or imitate the sound of, a trumpet; *trans.* to sound with a loud noise like the blare of a trumpet.

1656 BLOUNT *Glossogr.*, *Tarantarize*,.. to sound a trumpet, to sing or sound *taratantara*. **1840** G. RAYMOND in *New Monthly Mag.* LIX. 244 She taratantared a dozen bells.

taraxacin (tə'ræksəsɪn). *Chem.* [f. next + -IN[1].] A bitter crystalline substance obtained from the juice of dandelion-root. So **tara'xacerin**, resin of taraxacum.

1858 HOGG *Veg. Kingd.* 462 A peculiar crystallizable principle was discovered in the juice by M. Polex, which he called *taraxacin*. **1868** WATTS *Dict. Chem.* V. 671 The bitter substance of the root [of the dandelion], the so-called taraxacin, and the resin, have been examined by Polex (Arch. Pharm. xix. 50). **1890** THORPE *Dict. Applied Chem.* I. 646/1 From that part of the coagulum left undissolved by the water alcohol extracts *taraxacerin* $C_8H_{16}O$ (Kromayer).

‖**taraxacum** (tə'ræksəkəm). [med.L. from Arabic, ultimately Persian. The *Synonymia Arabo-Latina* of Gerard of Cremona (died 1189) has '*Tarasacon*, species cichorei'. This appears to have been a corruption or misreading of the Arabic name *ṭarakhshaqōq* or *ṭarkhshaqōq*, itself according to the Burhan-i-Kāti (native Persian lexicon), originally an arabicized form of the Persian *talkh chakōk* 'bitter herb'.

Many corrupt forms of the name (due chiefly to misreading of unpointed similar consonants in a foreign word) are given by Ibn Baithar. 'The reading *ṭarakhshaqōn*, with ن for ق, appears in the glossary of Ibn al Hashsha on the work of Razi' (Devic in Littré *Supp.*), and appears to be the source of Gerarde's *tarasacon*.]

a. *Bot.* Name of the genus of Composite plants (by Linnæus included in *Leontodon*) including the dandelion (*T. Dens-leonis*, *T. officinale*, or *Leontodon Taraxacum*). **b.** *Pharm.* A drug prepared from the root of the dandelion, used as a tonic and in liver complaints.

1706 PHILLIPS (ed. 6), *Taraxacum* or *Taraxacon*, (Gr.) the Herb Dandelion, or Sow-Thistle. **1845** BUDD *Dis. Liver* 36 Some principles of rhubarb and taraxacum might pass off in it likewise. **1857** G. BIRD *Urin. Deposits* (ed. 5) 436 Taraxacum, a popular cholagogue, owes its diuretic action.. to a similar cause. **1875** H. C. WOOD *Therap.* (1879) 425 Diuretic properties have also been ascribed to taraxacum.

tarbagan ('tɑːbəgən). Also **tarabagan**. [a. Russ. *tarbagán*.] A large long-haired marmot, *Marmota bobak* or *M. sibirica*, found in the steppes of eastern and central Asia; also, the pelt of this animal.

1928 in *Funk's Stand. Dict.* **1930** M. BACHRACH *Fur* xii. 156 The other variety [of marmot pelts] is called Tarbagans, or Tarbaganas. **1947** *New Biol.* II. 11 It [*sc.* the germ of plague] is present.. in.. tarbagans in China. **1951** WHITBY & HYNES *Med. Bacteriol.* (ed. 5) xviii. 303 The more important reservoirs of sylvatic plague include.. tarbagans in China. **1962** P. MANSON-BAHR *Patrick Manson* xix. 168 The giant marmot.. was being hunted for its fur, known as tarabagan skins. **1971** P. C. C. GARNHAM *Progress in Parasitol.* iii. 32 The infection primarily occurs in a variety of wild rodents.. such as the tarabagan in Mongolia.

tar-barrel ('tɑː,bærəl). A barrel containing or that has contained tar: esp. as used for making a bonfire; formerly also in the carrying out of capital punishment by burning.

c **1450** *B.M. Add. MS.* 10036 (Destr. Jerus. by Vespasian) lf. 24 With bowes schot and with arblast, With tarbarelle and with wilde fyre. **1580** *Vestry Bks.* (Surtees) 120 Item paid for a tarbarrell at cronation day, vj d. **1685** *Lond. Gaz.* No. 2080/3 A large Bonfire or high Piramid of Tar-barrels, being erected in the said Market place. **1725** RAMSAY *Gentle Sheph.* v. i, Till in a fat tar-barrel Mause [a witch] be burnt. **1850** CARLYLE *Latter-d. Pamph.* i. 2 The European populations everywhere hailed the omen; with shouting and rejoicing, leading-articles and tar-barrels.

†**b.** Applied opprobriously to a person. Cf. TAR-BOX b. *Obs.*

1695 CONGREVE *Love for L.* III. vii, If I were a man, you durst not talk at this rate,.. you stinking tar-barrel.

tarbet ('tɑːbət). *Sc. local.* Also **tarburt**. [ad. Gael. *tairbeart* peninsula, isthmus.] A neck of land, an isthmus; hence, a portage between two lochs or navigable channels. (Also, a proper name of villages, etc. so situated.)

1843 *Statist. Acc. Scotl.* VII. 136 A narrow isthmus or tarburt over which boats were drawn. **1875** W. MCILWRAITH *Guide Wigtownshire* 64 Advantage was taken of the conformation of the land to form a tarbet.

tarboggin, -bogin, var. TOBOGGAN.

‖**tarboosh** (tɑː'buːʃ). Also 8 **tarpous**, 9 **tarboush, -bouch, -bush**. [a. Arabic *ṭarbūsh*; so called in Egypt (Freytag); in F. *tarbouch*.] A cap of cloth or felt (almost always red) with a tassel (usually of blue silk) attached at the top, worn by Muslims either by itself or as part of the turban; the *fez* is the Turkish form.

1702 W. J. tr. *Bruyn's Voy. Levant* xx. 91 This Tarpous, which serves the Women as a sort of a Head-dress, is a large Cap of Six or eight Quarters, made of Cloth of Gold. **1839** LANE *Arab. Nts.* (1859) I. iv. 256 He took the turban with its tarboosh,.. and kept them himself. *Ibid.* 288 *note*, The Tarboosh is a woollen skull-cap, of a deep blood-red colour, having a tassel of dark blue silk attached to the crown. It is worn by most Arabs of the higher and middle classes. **1884** J. COLBORNE *Hicks Pasha* 105 The tarboosh, or fez—as it is called in Turkey—.. is adopted by Mussulmans, as it allows for the fulfilment of the Mahommedan observance in prayer of touching the earth with the forehead. **1885** LADY BRASSEY *Trades* 291 Turks Islands derive their name from a beautiful scarlet cactus, in shape like a fez or tarbouch.

Hence **tarbooshed, tarbushed** (-'buːʃt) *a.* [-ED[2]], wearing a tarboosh.

1873 LELAND *Egypt. Sketch-Bk.* viii. 106 Through them tarbushed or turbaned and dark men peered curiously at the strangers.

tar-box ('tɑːbɒks). A box formerly used by shepherds to hold tar as a salve for sheep.

c **1420** ? LYDG. *Assembly of Gods* 326 The rewde god Pan.. Clad in russet frese, & breched lyke a bere, With a gret tar box hangyng by hys syde. **1523** FITZHERB. *Husb.* §41 And a shepeherde shoulde not go without his dogge, his shepe hoke, a payre of sheres, and his terre boxe. **1602** *2nd Pt. Return fr. Parnass.* v. ii. 2088 A shepards hooke, a tarbox, and a scrippe. **1658** OSBORN *Jas. I*, Wks. (1673) 514 (Spight of his Tarbox) he died of the Scab.

†**b.** Applied contemptuously to a person: = 'stinking fellow'. *Obs.*

a **1592** GREENE *Jas. IV*, III. i, Such as rub horses do good service in the commonweal, ergo, tarbox, master courtier, a horse-keeper is a gentleman. **1687** SETTLE *Refl. Dryden* 12 Tarbox Muly Lahas is not the Fool this bout.

tar-brush ('tɑːbrʌʃ). **a.** A brush used for smearing anything with tar. ***knight of the tar-brush***, allusively applied to a sailor: cf. TAR *sb.*[1] 3.

1711 W. SUTHERLAND *Shipbuild. Assist.* 135 Tarr Brushes—2. **1865** KINGSLEY *Herew.* vi, Do any of you knights of the tar brush know whether we are going to be drowned in Christian waters?

b. *fig.*, esp. in such derog. phrases as ***a dash*** or ***touch of the tar-brush***, applied to someone of mixed Black (or Indian, etc.) and white origin, as shown in the colour of the skin. (In first quot. applied to a Negro.)

In quot. 1895 ***touched with the same tar-brush*** = 'tarred with the same brush': see TAR *v.*[1] c.

1796 GROSE *Dict. Vulgar Tongue* (ed. 3), *Blue-skin*,..any one having a cross of the black breed, or, as it is termed, a lick of the tar brush. **1835-40** HALIBURTON *Clockm.* (1862) 179, I great opinion of you, Pompey; I make a man of you, you dam old tar brush. **1859** LANG *Wand. India* 50 The mother must have been very fair, if she were a native, the boy is so very slightly touched with the tar-brush. **1864** TREVELYAN *Compet. Wallah* (1866) 198 Brunette! I should rather think she is! There's a strong touch of the tar-brush in that quarter. **1895** *Month* Aug. 547 On this occasion all alike were touched with the same tar-brush. **1899** C. J. CUTCLIFFE HYNE *Further Adv. Capt. Kettle* viii. 189 Those snuff-and-butter coloured ladies..ignore their own lick of the tar-brush. **1928** J. BUCHAN *Runagates Club* i. 18 The Du Preez family had lived..close up to the Kaffir borders, and somewhere had got a dash of the tar-brush. **1970** D. M. DAVIN *Not Here, Not Now* VII. iii. 340 If he hadn't been an Irishman you'd think he had a touch of the tar-brush himself. **1975** 'S. MARLOWE' *Cawthorn Jrnls.* (1976) xix. 163 She was beautiful... High yellow. Some places they would have said she had just a touch of the tar-brush.

So **'tar-brusher**, one who uses a tar-brush; *fig.* one who 'blackens' a reputation, a defamer.

1884 *Pall Mall G.* 5 June 5/1 Mr. Brewer was neither a whitewasher nor a tar-brusher: he had very few fads.

Tarbuck knot ('tɑːbʌk nɒt). *Mountaineering.* [f. the name of the British mountaineer Kenneth *Tarbuck* (b. 1914), who invented it.] An adjustable loop knot (see quots.).

1947 K. TARBUCK in *Wayfarers' Jrnl.* No. 8. 52 The practical advantages of the Tarbuck knot lie in its adjustability. It can easily be slid up or down the standing rope by hand in order to vary the size of the loop. **1950** tr. *Mountaineering Handbk.* (Assoc. Brit. Members Swiss Alpine Club) App. 167 The end of the rope..is tied..with a Tarbuck knot... Although in its general action this knot is similar to the Prusik knot, it has in addition a remarkable shock-absorbing run when subjected to a severe shock load. **1968** P. CREW *Encycl. Dict. Mountaineering* 114/2 Most knots bend the rope into a sharp angle, which reduces the strength of the rope by quite a high percentage—this is avoided in the Tarbuck knot.

tarbuttite ('tɑːbətaɪt). *Min.* [f. the name of P. C. Tarbutt (1874-1943), English mining engineer + -ITE[1].] A basic zinc phosphate, Zn_2PO_4OH, found as faintly coloured or colourless triclinic crystals.

1907 *Nature* 27 June 215/1 L. J. Spencer exhibited a suite of beautifully crystallised minerals, presented to the British Museum by Mr. Percy C. Tarbutt, from the Rhodesia Broken Hill mines in north-western Rhodesia... The crystals of this new species, for which the name *tarbuttite* is proposed, are anorthic. **1955**, **1974** [see *parahopeite* s.v. PARA-[1] 2c].

tarcat, obs. Sc. form of TARGET.

†**tar'cays.** *Obs. rare*⁻¹. [a. OF. *tarquais* (13th-16th c.) = It. *turcasso*, med.L. *turcasia*, med.Gr. *ταρκάσιον*, a. Pers. *tarkash* quiver: see Devic in Littré Suppl. s.v. *Carquois*.] A quiver.

1490 CAXTON *Eneydos* xv. 54 She hadde a fayr tarcays, coueréd wyth fyne cloth of damaske, alle fulle of arowes.

tarcel, obs. f. TARSEL, TERCEL.

tarcelet, obs. f. TERCELET.

tarche, tarchon, obs. ff. TARGE *sb.*[1], TARRAGON.

tard, obs. f. TARRED.

†**'tardance.** *Obs.* [a. obs. F. *tardance* (1307 in Godef.), f. *tarder* TARDE *v.*: see -ANCE.] Delaying, delay. Also †**'tardancy (-ency)**.

1595 *Q. Eliz. & Levant Co.* (1904) 53 Whose [ambassador] playnly excuseth the tardance thereof by reason thatt his maysters treasury..is exhausted. **1635** J. HAYWARD tr. *Biondi's Banish'd Virg.* 227 If any tardance of mine bee the occasion of your Highnesse sufferings. **1654** COKAINE *Dianea* IV. 340 Dorcone arrived just upon that time there, when tardency could not but be perilous.

†**tar'dation.** *Obs.* [ad. late L. *tardātiōn-em*, n. of action f. *tardāre* to delay. Cf. OF. *tardation* (14th c. in Godef.).] The action of delaying, delay; slackening of speed, retardation. (In quot. 1601, want of motion, or stagnation.)

1500-20 DUNBAR *Poems* lxxi. 35 Thy tardatioun caussis ws to think lang. **1601** DOLMAN *La Primaud. Fr. Acad.* III. lix. 271 Raine-water..doth putrifie through tardation and slownes. **1674** PETTY *Disc. Dupl. Proportion* 113 The degrees of Tardation, which Bullets make in..their way. **1727** BAILEY vol. II, *Tardation*, a Loitering, Lingering.

†**'tardative,** *a. Obs.* [f. L. *tardāt-*, ppl. stem of *tardāre* to delay, tarry + -IVE.] Tending to slacken speed, retarding.

1665-6 *Phil. Trans.* I. 274 Whatever effect (accelerative or tardative).

†**tarde,** *a.* (*adv.*) *Obs.* [ad. L. *tard-us* slow.]

1. Slow: = TARDY *a.* 1 a.

1547 BOORDE *Brev. Health* §321 If naturally a mans memory is tarde of wyt and knowlege. **1624** HEYWOOD *Gunaik.* VII. 334 They neither speed, Nor doth their pace seeme tarde.

b. Late: = TARDY *a.* 1 b. *rare*⁻⁰.

1613 R. CAWDREY *Table Alph.* (ed. 3), *Tarde*, late.

2. *to take tarde*, to overtake, surprise; = 'to take tardy' (TARDY *a.* 2).

1547 SALESBURY *Welsh Dict.*, *Dala ar y gamfa*, take tarde. **1578** TIMME *Caluine on Gen.* iii. II. 102 But God shall alwayes take vs tarde in the sinne of Adam. **1584** R. SCOT *Discov. Witchcr.* XV. xxiii. (1886) 369 They were convicted, and..almost taken tarde with the deed doing.

B. *adv.* **a.** Late. **b.** Slowly. [F. *tard* adv.]

1557 in *Rep. Hist. MSS. Comm.*, *Var. Collect.* IV. 223 Forasmoche as Mr. John Hooper [and 5 others]..came into this house tarde, after nyne of the clocke this day, therefore they..are amerced in 12*d.* a peece. **1597** A. M. tr. *Guillemeau's Fr. Chirurg.* 11/1 The winter, when as the corruptione goeth somwhat tarder or sloer forwarde.

†**tarde,** *v. Obs. rare.* [a. F. *tarde-r* (12th c. in Godef.):—L. *tardāre.*] *trans.* To retard, delay.

1524 *St. Papers Hen. VIII*, VI. 364 The said Duke and his armye was so tarded and retracted, that [etc.].

tardency, erron. f. TARDANCY *Obs.*

Tardenoisian (tɑːdə'nɔɪzɪən), *a. Archæol.* [ad. F. *Tardenoisien*, f. *Tardenois* (see below): see -IAN.] Of, pertaining to, or resembling the mesolithic culture remains of which were first discovered in Tardenois, dept. of Aisne, France. Also *absol.*, this culture.

[**1912** R. MUNRO *Palæolithic Man* xi. 277 (*heading*) *Tardenoisien* flint industry.] **1921** *Glasgow Herald* 16 Feb. 13 Tribes..characterized in their industry by little geometric flints called Tardenoisian. **1939** C. S. COON *Races of Europe* iii. 56 The cultures of the Mesolithic period may be divided into two elements... One was the intrusive Tardenoisian with its advanced microlithic technique, which came in from the south across the straits of Gibraltar. **1948** A. L. KROEBER *Anthropology* (ed. 2) xvi. 63 As early as 1887, Piette discovered an Azilian period after the Magdalenian, and in 1896 de Mortillet added the Tardenoisian to this. **1951** *Field Archaeol.* (Ordnance Survey) (ed. 3) 13 'Pigmy' flints of the type known as Tardenoisian from the site at Fère-en-Tardenois in Northern France. **1975** J. G. EVANS *Environment Early Man Brit. Isles* v. 103 Features of a third group, considered to reflect the continental Tardenoisian, were also incorporated, in particular the use of the chisel-ended..arrowhead.

†**tardi'dation.** *Obs. rare*⁻¹. [irreg. ? for *tardation* or *tarditation*.] = TARDATION.

1647 HERRICK *Noble Numb.*, *Salutation* 49 Avoid all snares Of tardidation in the Lords Affaires.

tardie, tardife, obs. forms of TARDY.

tardigrade ('tɑːdɪgreɪd), *a.* (*sb.*) [a. F. *tardigrade* (*a* 1615 in Godef. *Compl.*), or ad. L. *tardigrad-us* walking slowly, f. L. *tardus* slow + *-gradus* stepping, going.]

1. Walking or going slowly; slow-paced.

1623 COCKERAM, *Tardigrade*, a slow goer. **1656** BLOUNT *Glossogr.*, *Tardigrade*, that goeth slow or hath a slow pace. **1852** MUNDY *Our Antipodes* (1857) 185 The *Deborah* proved a marine hackney-coach of the most tardigrade order. **1875** W. HOUGHTON *Sk. Brit. Insects* 145 The Meloë..a bloated, tardigrade, wingless beetle upon the meadow.

b. *fig.* Sluggish in thought or action, unprogressive, 'slow-going'.

1883 *Pall Mall G.* 28 Dec. 4/2 Even in our tardigrade West Country the farmer has begun to discover,..that he, too, is an economical power.

2. *Zool.* **a.** Belonging to the sub-order (*Tardigrada*) or family (*Bradypodidæ*) of edentate mammals, comprising the sloths.

1799 CARLISLE in *Phil. Trans.* XC. 101 The habits of life among the tardigrade animals, give occasion for the long continued contraction of some muscles in their limbs. **1892** W. H. HUDSON *Natur. La Plata* xxii. 350 Tardigrade mammals of arboreal habits.

b. Belonging to the group *Tardigrada* of Arachnids, comprising the minute aquatic animals called water-bears or bear-animalcules.

1847-9 *Todd's Cycl. Anat.* IV. 415/1 Doyere states that he has found zoospores in the tardigrade Infusoria. **1891** *Cent. Dict.* s.v., *Tardigrade rotifers* [obs.], the *Tardigrada Arctisca*; bear-animalcules.

B. *sb.* **a.** An edentate mammal of the sub-order *Tardigrada*; a sloth.

1827 GRIFFITH tr. *Cuvier's Anim. K.* III. 251 The tardigrades will form the first class [of the Edentata]... Their name is derived from their excessive slowness. **1835** KIRBY *Hab. & Inst. Anim.* II. xvii. 208 The last family..in the present Order [Edentates] is very well distinguished by the name of *Tardigrades*.

b. An arachnid of the group *Tardigrada*; a water-bear.

1860 *All Year Round* No. 43. 387 The tardigrades dwell in the same localities as the rotifers. **1872** DARWIN in *Life & Lett.* III. 169 On this view, a Rotifer or Tardigrade is adapted to its humble conditions of life by a happy accident; and this I cannot believe.

tardigradous (tɑː'dɪgrədəs), *a.* [f. L. *tardigradus* + -OUS: see prec.] = TARDIGRADE *a.*

1658 SIR T. BROWNE *Pseud. Ep.* III. xxviii. (ed. 3) 227 [The tiger] is but a slow and tardigradous animal. **1848** JOHNSTON in *Proc. Berw. Nat. Club* II. No. 6. 310 Mite about a line in length,..tardigradous. **1866** *Pall Mall G.* 17 Sept. 4 Meanwhile Dissent does not wait for the tardigradous action of superior authorities.

†**tar'diloquent,** *a. Obs. rare*⁻⁰. [f. L. *tard-us* slow + *loquent-em*, pr. pple. of *loqui* to speak: cf. L. *tardiloquus*.] Speaking slowly, slow-speaking. So †**tar'diloquy** *Obs. rare*⁻⁰.

1623 COCKERAM, *Tardiloquie*, slow speech. **1656** BLOUNT *Glossogr.*, *Tardiloquent*, that speaks slowly, or draws his speech out at length.

tardily ('tɑːdɪlɪ), *adv.* [f. TARDY *a.* + -LY[2].] In a tardy manner. **a.** Slowly; with slow movement or progress.

1597 SHAKS. *2 Hen. IV*, II. iii. 26 For those that could speake low, and tardily, Would turne their owne Perfection, to Abuse. **1791** COWPER *Retired Cat* 67 The night rolled tardily away. **1793** SMEATON *Edystone L.* §219 *note*, I found it [cement] to set very tardily. **1872** MORLEY *Voltaire* (1886) 10 The great tides of circumstance swell so tardily, that whole generations wait in vain for the full flood on which the race is borne to new shores.

b. After the proper or expected time; after delay; late, lately. **c.** Sometimes implying 'not readily, reluctantly'.

1821 JOANNA BAILLIE *Met. Leg.*, *Columbus* xlviii, Four small vessels..yet granted tardily For such high service. **1839** JAMES *Louis XIV*, IV. 198 Those motives were somewhat tardily felt, and were..soon forgotten. **1855** MACAULAY *Hist. Eng.* xxii. IV. 744 Harcourt..had with difficulty reconciled his conscience to the oaths, and had tardily and unwillingly signed the Association.

tardiness ('tɑːdɪnɪs). [f. as prec. + -NESS.] The quality of being tardy. **a.** Slowness of movement or action.

1605 SHAKS. *Lear* I. i. 238 A tardinesse in nature, Which often leaues the history vnspoke That it intends to do. **1751** JOHNSON *Rambler* No. 111 ¶4 Something of the tardiness and frigidity of age. **1802** PALEY *Nat. Theol.* xvi. (1817) 138 The tardiness of his pace seems to have reference to the capacity of his organs. **1863** KINGLAKE *Crimea* II. 247 They ..conformed with great care to the tardiness of our advance.

b. Delay in time; lateness.

1752 JOHNSON *Rambler* No. 200 ¶6 The tardiness of his return, gave me reason to suspect that time was taken to deliberate. **1781** COWPER *Retirement* 475 He chides the tardiness of every post, Pants to be told of battles won or lost. **1825** J. NEAL *Bro. Jonathan* II. 201 Hence the tardiness of our information.

c. Lateness in arriving, esp. at a meeting or assembly, a class or school, etc. *U.S.*

1828 WEBSTER, *Tardiness*,..lateness; as, the tardiness of witnesses or jurors in attendance; the tardiness of students in attending prayers or recitation. **1902** J. CORBIN *American at Oxford* 17 All this brings recollections of the paternal roof, where tardiness at breakfast meant the loss of dessert. **1930** *Randolph Enterprise* (Elkins, W. Va.) 2 Oct. 5/4 No business enterprise would tolerate the percentage of absence and tardiness experienced in the schools.

†**'tardious,** *a. Obs. rare*⁻¹. [irreg. f. TARDY *a.* + -OUS.] = TARDY *a.*

?*c* **1580** T. HACKET *Treas. Amadis de Gaule* 159, I never shewed my selfe to be tardious nor slouthfull.

'tarditude. *rare*⁻¹. [ad. L. *tarditūdo*, f. *tardus* slow: see -TUDE.] = next; in quot. 'slowness' or unwillingness *to do* something.

1794 COLERIDGE *Lett.*, *to Southey* (1895) 85 My inconsistencies have given me a tarditude and reluctance to think ill of any one.

tardity ('tɑːdɪtɪ). Now *rare*. Also 5 -ee, 6-7 -ie. [a. OF. *tardité* (1420 in Godef.), earlier *tardeté*, ad. L. *tarditās*, f. *tard-us* slow: see -ITY.]

1. Slowness of movement or action: = TARDINESS a. In later use, a technical term of *Physics*, opp. to *velocity*.

[*c* **1386** CHAUCER *Pars. T.* ¶644 The synne that men clepen Tarditas, as whan a man is to laterede or tariyng er he wole turne to god.] *c* **1450** *Mirour Saluacioun* 4410 Wightlayke delyvrenesse with out ony tarditee. **1586** B. YOUNG *Guazzo's Civ. Conv.* IV. 178b, For his rude simplicitie and tarditie. **1603** SIR C. HEYDON *Jud. Astrol.* xxiii. 514 [He] confesseth velocitie, and tarditie, in the Moone. **1656** S. HOLLAND *Zara* (1719) 2 The Champion began to tax himself of tardity. **1714** DERHAM *Astro-Theol.* VII. v. (1769) 180 The tardity of the periodic motion in their respective orbits. **1852** DE MORGAN in Graves *Life Sir W. R. Hamilton* (1889) III. 353 In every semicircle, the intension of the breadth [ordinate] begins from the utmost degree of velocity, and terminates at the utmost degree of tardity in the middle of the arc.

2. The fact of being late; lateness.

1599 NASHE *Lenten Stuffe* 33 [They] furrowe vp the rugged brine and sweepe through his tumultuous oous [ooze]..rather then in tendring their allegeance they should be benighted with tardity. **1601** BP. W. BARLOW *Defence* 41 For tarditie and suspence of the assent, may arise by some obstacle not remooued. **1638** WOTTON *Let.* in *Reliq.* (1651) 486, I beseech you..not to conceive by the tarditie of my Answer unto you, any faintnesse in the acknowledgment of your favors.

tardive ('tɑːdɪv), *a.* [mod. a. F. *tardif*, *-ive*: see TARDY.] **a.** Characterized by lateness, or tending to appear late; of late appearance or development.

1905 H. D. ROLLESTON *Dis. Liver* 320 A case of tardive hereditary syphilis with stricture of the hepatic duct.

b. Path. ***tardive dyskinesia***, a neurological disorder, usu. a late-developing side-effect of long-term treatment with anti-psychotic drugs, which is characterized by involuntary movements of the face and jaws.

1964 A. FAURBYE et al. in *Acta Psychiatrica Scandinavica* XL. 12 Tardive dyskinesia is first and foremost characterized by the occurrence of dyskinetic movements. **1979** *Nature* 1 Mar. 59/1 Of all the side effects of drugs used to treat psychotic illness such as schizophrenia, chronic tardive dyskinesias are the most disturbing.

So †**tar'divity** [F. *tardiveté*], lateness of development or maturity. *Obs. rare.*

1725 *Bradley's Fam. Dict.*, *Tardivity*, a Term, says Monsieur Chomel, which may and ought to be made use of, tho' at present obsolete, when such a Fruit is mention'd on the account of its becoming late ripe.

tardle ('tɑːd(ə)l). *dial.* A tangled mass, a tangle.

Cf. *tardle* vb. to entangle (Dorset) in Eng. Dial. Dict.

1898 T. HARDY *Wessex Poems* 204 While her great gallied eyes, through her hair hanging loose Sheened as stars through a tardle of trees.

tardon, var. TARDYON.

tardy ('tɑːdɪ), *a.* (*adv.*) Forms: α. 5 **tardyve**, 6 **tardife**. β. 6 **tardye**, **-dee**, 6–7 **tardie**, (7 **tar'de**), 6– **tardy**. [a. F. *tardif*, *-ive* (12th c. in Littré) = Sp. *tardio*, It. *tardivo*:—pop.L. type **tardīvus*, f. *tardus* slow: see -IVE. In the β forms the ending *-ive* is reduced to *-ie*, *-ye*, *-y*: see -IVE, par. 3.]

1. Slow: in various senses. **a.** Slow in motion, action, or occurrence; making little progress in a comparatively long time; of slow nature, sluggish.

α. **1483** CAXTON *Gold. Leg.* 23b/2 We ought to gyue thankynges to the dyuyne dyspensacion, for the tardyue creaunce of holy faders to us necessarye. ?*c* **1580** T. HACKET *Treas. Amadis de Gaule* 155 Trusting that..ye wil not be tardife in so good a worke. **1600** F. WALKER tr. *Sp. Mandeville* 59 The chollerick man is commonly hasty and heedelesse..and the flegmatick more slowe and tardife.

β. **1590** SHAKS. *Com. Err.* II. i. 44 Say, is your tardie master now at hand? **1594** —— *Rich. III*, II. i. 89 Some tardie Cripple bare the Countermand. **1713** YOUNG *Last Day* III. 176, I faint, my tardy blood forgets to flow. **1751** JOHNSON *Rambler* No. 169 ¶1 Thus the firmest timber is of tardy growth. **1866** G. MACDONALD *Ann. Q. Neighb.* xxviii, To watch the gradual and tardy awakening of the intellect.

b. Not acting, coming, or happening until after the proper, expected, or desired time; late, behind-hand; delaying, or delayed; dilatory; sometimes, delaying through unwillingness, reluctant, 'slow' (*to* some action, or *to do* something).

1667 MILTON *P.L.* x. 853 On the ground Outstretcht he lay,..oft Curs'd his Creation, Death as oft accus'd Of tardie execution. **1742** WEST *Let.* in *Gray's Poems* (1775) 147 O join with mine thy tuneful lay, And invocate the tardy May. **1749** JOHNSON *Van. Hum. Wishes* 160 See nations slowly wise, and meanly just, To buried merit raise the tardy bust. *a* **1822** SHELLEY *Chas. I*, II. 355 Oh be our feet still tardy to shed blood. **1849** MACAULAY *Hist. Eng.* ii. I. 191 Then, at length, tardy justice was done to the memory of Oliver. **1908** *Betw. Trent & Ancholme* 47 When a girl used to think her admirer rather tardy in asking for the wedding-day.

c. Late for a meeting, assembly, class, school, or appointment. *U.S.*

1638 in *Archives of Maryland* (1883) I. 6 Such as did appeare thoughe tardie should be pardoned. **1843** *Yale Lit. Mag.* VIII. 240 We were '*tardy*' at our matins. **1904** *Minneapolis Times* 29 May 6 Don't shoot your husband when he is two hours tardy for supper. **1948** *Daily Ardmoreite* (Ardmore, Okla.) 4 July 21/4 During this time he had been neither absent nor tardy.

†**2. a.** Phr. ***to take*** (also rarely ***catch, find***) a person ***tardy***: to overtake (? orig. on account of slowness of advance); to surprise; to come upon unprepared or unawares; hence, to detect, 'catch' in a crime, fault, error, etc.: often merely synonymous with TAKE *v.* 8. *Obs.*

1530 PALSGR. 554/1 s.v. *Forage*, As we went a foragynge the laste daye, we were almoste taken tardy of a bande of horse men. **1542** UDALL *Erasm. Apoph.* 253 He tooke her tardie with a plaine lye. **1579** FULKE *Refut. Rastel* 725, I haue taken him tardye alreadie in falsifying the scripture. **1594** SHAKS. *Rich. III*, IV. i. 52 Be not ta'ne tardie by vnwise delay. **1601** DENT *Pathw. Heaven* 355 So shall the comming of the sonne of man to iudgement, take the world tardy and unprepared. **1620** ROWLANDS *Night Raven* 16 A Drunkard, (whom the cup did tardy catch). **1640** BRATHWAIT *Boulster Lect.* 94 Who, being found tardy, said he was troubled with a Spirit. **1677** *Conn. Col. Rec.* (1852) II. 499 Pawbequenuck ..being found tardy of inticeing the surrenderers to depart from the English..was sent to prison. **1690** C. NESSE *O. & N. Test.* I. 306 To sing morning hymns..from which exercise this angel must not be taken tardy, much less be absent.

†**b.** *ellipt.* for 'taken tardy': Detected in a fault, caught tripping. *Obs.*

1591 R. TURNBULL *Exp. Jas.* 150b, Adulterie, a grieuous euill,..yet David (the man of God) was tardie therein. *a* **1643** J. SHUTE *Judgement & Mercy* (1645) 118 Montanus, in whose heresie Tertullian (though else a good man) was tardie. **1705** tr. *Bosman's Guinea* 358 A Negroe, who had been tardy with one of the King's Wives. **1706** PHILLIPS (ed. 6), *Tardy*,..also guilty, found tripping, or in a Fault.

3. quasi-*adv.* Behind time, late. Phr. ***to come tardy off***, to fall short, to be done or carried out inadequately (*obs.* or *arch.*: cf. COME *v.* 61 i).

1586 WARNER *Alb. Eng.* II. xiii. (1589) 54 When Troy was ouer stoute,..and tardie lookt aboute. **1592** SHAKS. *Rom. & Jul.* II. vi. 15 Too swift arriues as tardie as too slow. **1718** HICKES & NELSON *J. Kettlewell* I. vi. 23 He never..incurred the least Censure, as by Neglect of..Prayers, or coming Tardy to them. *a* **1836** LEVERETT *Lexicon Lat.-Eng.* Pref., In such a case, the work is better overdone than come tardy off.

4. *Comb.*, as ***tardy-gaited***, ***-moving***, ***-rising*** adjs.

1599 SHAKS. *Hen. V*, IV Prol. 20 The confident and ouer-lustie French, Doe..chide the creepple-tardy-gated Night, Who..doth limpe So tediously away. **1719** YOUNG *Busiris* 63 How like the dyal's tardy moving Shade! **1757** DYER *Fleece* I. Poems (1761) 82 Thither crowds Each greedy wretch for tardy-rising wealth, Which comes too late.

†**tardy**, *v.* *Obs.* [f. prec. adj.] *trans.* To make tardy; to delay, retard, keep back.

1611 SHAKS. *Wint. T.* III. ii. 163 Which had been done, But that the good mind of Camillo tardied My swift command. **1623** tr. *Favine's Theat. Hon.* VI. ix. 153 So much tardied and neglected by the miserable estate and condition of France. **1972** AUDEN *Epistle to Godson* 10 We've had it, are in for a disaster that no four-letter words will tardy.

tardyon ('tɑːdiːɒn). *Physics.* Also **tardon** ('tɑːdɒn). [f. TARDY *a* (*adv.*) + -ON[1].] A sub-atomic particle that travels at less than the speed of light.

1969 BILANIUK & SUDARSHAN in *Physics Today* May 47/2 Let us refer to all subluminal particles as tardyons. **1970** *New Scientist* 10 Sept. 521/1 The number of tachyons in a system may vary from observer to observer—yet another deviation from the conventional world of tardons. **1972** *Nature* 7 Jan. 10/3 This assumes that 'ordinary' particles (called tardyons in this sort of discussion) have a mass *m* such that m^2 is greater than zero. **1975** J. TAYLOR *Superminds* (1976) vi. 114 Tardons (slower-than-light particles) and tachyons can never interchange roles.

tare (tɛə(r)), *sb.*[1] Forms: 4– **tare**, *pl.* 4 **taren**, 4–5 **taris**, 5– **tares**; also 5 **thare**, 6 **taar(e**, **terre**, **ter(e**, 9 *dial.* **tar**, **tor**. [A word of obscure origin and history: known first *c* 1330 in sense 1, also *c* 1400 in *wiilde tare*, a vetch of some kind, and in the later Wycliffite N. Test., 1388, used to render Gr. L. *zīzania*. For the form Kluge compares ODu. **taruwe*, MDu. *terwe*, *tarwe*, a name of wheat, cogn. with Lith. *dirva* a wheat-field. But no satisfactory explanation has been offered of the transference of sense.]

1. a. The seed of a vetch: usually in reference to its small size. (Probably familiar in early times, as too frequently present in seed-corn.)

c **1330** *Arth. & Merl.* (Kölbing) 7354 þei our folk tohewen waren To smale morsels, so be taren. **1530** PALSGR. 279/1 Taare a corne lyke a pease, *lupins*. **1555** EDEN *Decades* 9 Many of them [grains of gold]..were as bygge as tares or fytchis. **1576** BAKER *Jewell of Health* 185 Take of this masse vnto the quantity of three Tares. **1657** R. LIGON *Barbadoes* 65 This vermine will get..under the nayl of your Toes, and there make a habitation..as bigge as a small Tare. **1808** *Med. Jrnl.* XIX. 287 A globule, about the size of a small tare, being thrown on paper moistened. **1876** BRISTOWE *The. & Pract. Med.* (1878) 669 The follicles enlarge to the size of a tare or pea.

†**b.** Taken as a type of a very small particle; a whit, a jot, an atom. *Obs.*

c **1386** CHAUCER *Reeve's T.* 80 But ther of sette the Millere nat a tare.

2. A name given to some species of vetch: **a.** in early times, esp. to those occurring as weeds in corn-fields. (Lyte, 1578, uses it only of these, applying 'vetch' or 'fitch' to *Vicia sativa* (sense b); with Gerarde, Ray, and later writers, 'tare' and 'vetch' become synonymous.)

Still entering into the names of the 'Hairy or Rough-podded Tare', *Vicia hirsuta* (*Ervum hirsutum*), and 'Smooth Tare', *V. tetrasperma* (*E. tetraspermum*), cornfield weeds: see also STRANGLE-*tare*, TINE-*tare*. In quots. 1573–78, applied (after Dodoens) to *Lathyrus Aphaca*, now a rare 'colonist' in English corn-fields, but perhaps then more common, being imported with dirty seed-wheat. Formerly also applied vaguely to other plants of these and allied genera, or to weeds resembling them in their habit.

c **1400** *Lanfranc's Cirurg.* 88 Orabum þat is wiilde tare. *c* **1450** *Alphita* (Anecd. Oxon.) 131 Orobus, *gall.* uesche, *anglice* thare uel mousepese. *Ibid.* 186 *Trifolium acutum*, wildetare *uel* tintare. **1523** FITZHERB. *Husb.* §20 There be diuers maner of wedes, as thistyls, kedlokes, dockes,..dog-fenell, mathes, ter, and dyuers other small wedes. *Ibid.*, Terre is the worste wede,..and groweth mooste in rye, and it groweth lyke fytches, but it is moche smaller, and it wyll growe as hyghe as the corne, and with the weyght therof, it pulleth the corne flatte to the erth, and freteth the eares away. **1573–80** BARET *Alv.* T 63 Tares which commonlie growe amongst corne, are temperate in heat, *aphaca*. **1578** LYTE *Dodoens* IV. xxviii. 485 The Tare groweth in feeldes, & is found growing in this Countrie, in fertil groundes amongst wheat & Rye. **1598** SYLVESTER *Du Bartas* II. i. III. *Furies* 166 Cockle, wilde Oats, rough Burs, Corn-cumbring Tares.

b. Now, in general agricultural use, applied to the cultivated vetch, *Vicia sativa*, grown (often with oats, etc.) as fodder. In a collective sense, or as name of a crop, used in *plural* form (cf. *oats*, in like use).

1482 *Cely Papers* (Camden) 109 Yowre yonge horsse.. wull ete noo mete yett bot grasse and grene tarys. **1530** PALSGR. 278/2 Taars a kynd of corn, *dragee*. [See DREDGE.] **1552** HULOET, Tares or vetches, a kinde of pulse or grayne, *eruila, eruum, orobum, i.* **1577** HARRISON *England* II. vi. (1877) I. 153 Horssecorne, I meane, beanes, peasen, otes, tares, and lintels. **1697** DRYDEN *Virg. Georg.* I. 110 Where Vetches, Pulse, and Tares have stood. **1760** R. BROWN *Compl. Farmer* II. 87 Tares are of as great advantage to land as other pulses are. **1801** MASON *Suppl. to Johnson*, *Tare*, a name frequently given to the common vetch. **1846** J. BAXTER *Libr. Pract. Agric.* (ed. 4) II. 312 Tares will do well on any rich or good soil. **1887** BOWEN *Virg. Eclogue* III. 100 Lean my bull, though he feeds on the richest tares.

c. *Angling.* (See quot. 1971.)

1971 *Angling Times* 10 June 12/1 Tares: a cereal bait used for roach fishing. **1976** *Reading Chron.* 19 Nov. 26/7 Kennet-style hemp groundbait and caster on the hook failed to get him a bite for the first 90 minutes. Then he switched to floated tares and the roach came thick and fast.

3. a. *pl.* Used in the later Wycliffite (or Purvey) version of the N.T. (*Matt.* xiii. 25), also in some MSS. of the earlier text, and thence in Tindale's and subsequent 16–17th c. versions, to render L. *zīzania* (Vulg.), Gr. ζιζάνια, as name of an injurious weed among corn, which in the first Wyclif version had been rendered 'dernel or cokil', the latter going back in translations and quotations to Old English, the former to Early ME.: see DARNEL, COCKLE. *Obs.* exc. as a biblical use, and as in b.

Evidently Purvey and his co-revisers adopted *tares* as in their opinion more intelligible than the earlier 'dernel' or 'cokil'. Probably they thought of *Vicia hirsuta* the Strangle-tare, or other species of wild vetch, as familiar noxious weeds in English cornfields.

1388 WYCLIF *Matt.* xiii. 25 Whanne men slepten, his enemy cam, and sewe aboue taris [1382 dernel; *gloss* or cokil] in the myddil of whete. **1526** TINDALE *ibid.*, Whyll men slepte ther cam his foo and sowed tares amonge the wheate. **1594** HOOKER *Eccl. Pol.* III. i. §9 His Church he compareth unto a field, where tares manifestly known and seen by all men to grow intermingled with good corn. **1611** BIBLE *Matt.* xiii. 36 Declare vnto vs the parable of the tares [1388 WYCLIF taris, TINDALE tares] of the field. *a* **1674** CLARENDON *Surv. Leviathan* (1676) 307 These are the men who..watched the tares..and pulled them up.

b. Hence in allusive and fig. uses.

a **1711** KEN *Direct. Prayers* Wks. (1838) 354 The tares of sedition have been industriously sown among you. **1806** JEFFERSON *Writ.* (1830) IV. 64 They will not suffer friend or foe to sow tares among us. **1816** SOUTHEY *Lay Laureate* lxvii, The heart of man is rich in all good seeds; Neglected, it is choak'd with tares and noxious weeds. **1818** BYRON *Ch. Har.* IV. cxx, Weeds of dark luxuriance, tares of haste, Rank at the core, though tempting to the eyes. **1878** STUBBS *Const. Hist.* III. xxi. 615 In the new world, as in the old, the tares are mingled with the wheat.

4. *attrib.* and *Comb.*, as ***tare hay***, ***seed***, ***verdage***; **tare-grass** (*dial.* **tar-grass**), some species of wild tare or vetch ('*Vicia hirsuta* or perh. *V. Cracca*', Britten & Holland); **tare-thistle**, ? the sow-thistle (*Sonchus arvensis*), a prickly plant growing as a weed in corn; **tare-sown** *a.*, sown with tares (sense 3); **tare-vetch** (**-fitch**, **tarvetch**, **-fitch**), name for *Vicia hirsuta* and other wild or weedy species of vetch and allied plants.

1686 PLOT *Staffordsh.* 204 The wild Vetch, here call'd *Tar-grass. **1694** W. WESTMACOTT *Script. Herb.* 192 These wild sorts [of Tares] are called by some Tar-grass. **1763** *Museum Rust.* (ed. 2) I. 225, I had last summer a crop of *tare-hay that was astonishing. **1578** LYTE *Dodoens* IV. xxviii. 486 The *Tare seede is of a restringent vertue like y[e] Lentil. **1797** T. PARK *Sonn.* 110 The *tare-sown plains of age we feebly reap. **1753** CHAMBERS *Cycl. Supp.* s.v. *Rabbit*, The general cure is the keeping them low, and giving them the prickly herb, called *tare-thistle, to eat. **1778** [W. MARSHALL] *Minutes Agric., Digest* 44 Horses require very little corn when they are on a *tare-verdage. **1530** PALSGR. 279/1 *Tarefytche a corne, *lupyn*. **1813** T. DAVIS *Agric. Wilts* Gloss., *Tare-vetch*, withwind, the red and white striped convolvulus, these two plants are the plague of a weak wheat-crop in the sand-lands. **1886** BRITTEN & HOLLAND *Eng. Plant-n.*, Tar-fitch.., *Vicia hirsuta*.—*Salop.* Blue Tar-fitch, *Vicia Cracca*.—*Cheshire.* Yellow Tar-fitch, *Lathyrus pratensis*.—*Chesh.*.. Tar Vetch (or Tar-Vatch), *Vicia hirsuta*.—*Dorset.*

tare (tɛə(r)), *sb.*[2] [a. F. *tare* (15th c. in Hatz.-Darm.) waste or deterioration in goods, deficiency, imperfection, also as in Eng., = med.L., It., Pr., Sp., Pg. *tara*, OSp. *atara* (Littré), ad. Arab. *ṭarḥah* that which is thrown away, f. *ṭaraḥa* to reject.]

a. The weight of the wrapping, receptacle, or conveyance containing goods, which is deducted from the gross in order to ascertain the net weight; hence, a deduction made from the gross weight to allow for this; also (esp. as ***tare weight***), the weight of a motor vehicle or aircraft without its fuel and other equipment.

1486 *Naval Acc. Hen. VII* (1896) 13, ij barrelles Gonne-powdre conteyning in weight besides the tare Diij lbs. *Ibid.* 14 A barrell of gonnepoudre weying the tare abated cclb. **1598** FLORIO, *Tara*, the tare, waste or garbish of any marchandise or ware. **1599** HAKLUYT *Voy.* II. 274 Note y[t] in Ormuz they abate tare of all sorts of commodities. **1617** SIR D. CARLETON in *Buccleuch MSS.* (Hist. MSS. Comm.) I. 190 The reducing the matter of Tare to the same terms as it was. **1670** BLOUNT *Law Dict.*, *Tare* and *Tret*, the first is the weight of Box, Straw, Cloaths, &c. wherein Goods are packed. The other is [etc.]. **1674** JEAKE *Arith.* (1696) 639 If 132 lb. abate 12 lb. for Tare, then 1 C. shall be but 120 lb. **1812** J. SMYTH *Pract. of Customs* (1821) 11 The Tares on several sorts of Goods were ascertained by the Farmers of his Majesty's Customs, in the year 1667, a Table whereof was then published by their order. **1882** *Mechanical World* 4 Mar. 137/1 The method of weighing is to ascertain the weight of load and truck combined, and then deduct the tare of the latter from the total. **1892** *Labour Commission* Gloss., The *tare* of the tub is the weight of the empty tub or hutch used in conveying the coals. **1903** *Motor. Ann.* 64 A steam lorry, which will carry any weight up to seven tons, and has a tare of scarcely three tons.

attrib. **1900** *Engineering Mag.* XIX. 738 Dependent.. upon the total useful load it is possible to carry on a vehicle of a given tare weight. **1901** *Westm. Gaz.* 16 Nov. 2/1 It is difficult to see why in the case of motors there should be a tare-limit of three tons. **1944** C. A. ZWENG *Aviation Dict.* 329/1 In weighing an aircraft.. the weight of any incidental equipment needed, and whose weight is included in the final weight, must be subtracted to obtain the correct weight. This is called the tare weight. **1950** *Gloss. Aeronaut. Terms* (*B.S.I.*) I. 43 *Tare weight*, for design purposes: the standard weight of a type of aircraft complete in flying order but without crew, fuel, oil, removable equipment or payload. **1967** *Times Rev. Industry* May 78/2 Reductions of more than 50 per cent in tare weight.. can often be made by using a particular new material. **1977** *Mod. Railways* Dec. 480/2 All timing loads in the working timetables are now calculated for tare weights in tonnes.

b. *Chem.* The weight of a vessel in which a substance is weighed, or of another vessel equal to it, deducted in ascertaining the weight of the substance.

1888 *Amer. Chem. Jrnl.* X. 319 The difference between the weights of the crucibles plus the oxide and those of their tares was then determined.

c. *fig.* (Cf. F. *tare* defect, vice, blemish.)

1630 LENNARD tr. *Charron's Wisd.* I. xiv. §17 The Spirit hath its maladies, defects, tares or refuse. **1896** VERN. LEE in *Contemp. Rev.* June 822 Is there not in this case a tare —a diminution of aesthetic value to our detriment?

d. *tare and tret*: the two ordinary deductions in calculating the net weight of goods to be sold by retail: see TRET; also, the rule in arithmetic by which these are calculated.

1670 [see above]. **1692** COLES, *Tare and tret*, (allowance for) the weight of box, bag, &c. and waste on emptying, &c. **1709** STEELE *Tatler* No. 46 ¶1 He gave diurnal Audiences concerning Commerce, Politicks, Tare and Tret, Usury. **1844** DICKENS *Mart. Chuz.* xix, We learnt Tare and Tret together, at school.

fig. c **1838** DE QUINCEY *Pope* Wks. 1863 XV. 121 The allowance for tare and tret as a discount in favour of Pope.

e. *Comb.* †**tare-master** = TARER. *Obs.*

1625 *Laws Stannaries* xi. (1808) 21 The poiser, the tare-master and their deputies, ought to be sworn in the stannary-court.

tare (tɛə(r)), *v.* [f. TARE *sb.*[2]] *trans.* To ascertain, allow for, or indicate the tare of.

1812 J. SMYTH *Pract. of Customs* (1821) 168 Two Jars tared three pounds each. *Ibid.* 247 It is the practice at the West India Docks to make a memorandum of the packages which are tared, on the back of the blue book. **1880** LOMAS *Alkali Trade* 246 It is usual not to tare the casks at all, but to invoice the gross weight as soda. **1890** *Pall Mall G.* 29 Sept. 8/2 The Custom House authorities have given notice that on and after October 1 their officers will have instructions to weigh and tare packages of tea to the half-pound instead of to the pound, as heretofore.

Hence **tared** *ppl. a.*, of which the tare or weight when empty has been ascertained.

1854 J. SCOFFERN in *Orr's Circ. Sc., Chem.* 333 Being collected on a tared filter, its weight may be estimated. **18..** *U.S. Dispensatory* 575 (Cent. Dict.) The neck of a bottle.. marked for the quantity of liquid to be percolated,.. or of a tared bottle, if the percolate is to be weighed.

tare, obs., arch., and dial. f. and pa. t. of TEAR *v.*[1]; var. TEAR *sb.* fine flax; var. TAHR, Himalayan goat; obs. f. THERE: see T 8.

tare (in phr. *tare and ages*, *wounds*): see TEAR *sb.*[2] 3 d.

taree: see TODDY.

tarentaal (tærən'tɑːl). *S. Afr.* Also **tarantal(l)**. [a. Afrikaans.] Either of two guineafowl of the family Numididæ, the crowned guineafowl, *Numida meleagris*, or the crested guineafowl, *Guttera edouardi*, both found in southern Africa.

[**1822** W. J. BURCHELL *Trav. Interior S. Afr.* I. xv. 364 The missionaries have a few domestic fowls.. and Guinea hens or Pintadoes, which are called by the quaint name of *Jan Tadentaal*.] **1827** T. PHILIPPS *Scenes & Occurrences in Albany* 99 Ten guinea-fowl.. called here, by the Hottentots, *tarentalls*. **1906** W. L. SCLATER *Birds S. Afr.* IV. 228 Crowned Guinea-fowl... 'Tarantal' of Dutch. **1948** H. V. MORTON *In Search of S. Afr.* ix. 282 We would walk over the veld watching the guinea-fowl, the tarentaal, pour away into the mealies. **1953** U. KRIGE *Dream & Desert* vii. 187 Great Oupa, whose ear was so acute he could hear from the front stoep the call of a tarentaal against the ridge, slowly opened his eyes. **1958** MCLACHLAN & LIVERSIDGE *Roberts' Birds of S. Afr.* (rev. ed.) 100 Crowned Guinea-Fowl. Tarentaal. *Numida meleagris*.. The only Guinea-fowl in our area with a casque on the head.

Tarentine ('tærəntaɪn), *a.* and *sb.* [ad. L. *Tarentīn-us* of Tarentum.] **a.** *adj.* Of or pertaining to Tarentum. †**Tarentine spider**, the Tarantula. †**b.** *sb.* Name of some herb.

c **1440** *Pallad. on Husb.* II. 372 And yf thou wolt ha nuttis Tarentyne. **1668** *Phil. Trans.* III. 660 The structure of the body of this Tarentin Spider. **1698** FRYER *Acc. E. India & P.* 119 Herbs for Salading are Purslain, Sorrel, Lettice, Parsley, Tarentine, Mint, and Sog, a sort of Spinach.

c. *sb.* A native or inhabitant of the ancient city of Tarentum (now Taranto), in SE Italy.

1579 T. NORTH tr. *Plutarch's Lives* 443 Pyrrhus.. arrived at the length in the city of Tarentum, with twenty thowsand footemen.. ioyning thereto to the choycest pyked men of the Tarentines. **1720** H. EELBECK tr. *Cicero's First Oration Archias* 11, I am of Opinion that the Rheginians, or.. the Tarentines, would not have refused the Privilege to this Poet. **1812** C. KELSALL tr. *Cicero's Last Pleadings against Verres* 97 What remuneration.. could compensate.. the Tarentines, if they were to lose their Europa on a bull.. and other works [of art]? **1978** M. GRANT *Hist. Rome* III. v. 77 The Tarentines were governed by a democracy, which.. displayed.. relative stability.

tarentism, variant of TARANTISM.

‖**tarentola** (tə'rɛntəʊlə). [It.: see TARANTULA.] A harmless lizard, *Tarentola* (*Platydactylus*) *mauritanica*, the Moorish Gecko, found in southern Europe and northern Africa. Also the genus to which this belongs. So **tarente**.

[**1838** *Penny Cycl.* XI. 104/2 Those lizards which the Italians called *Tarentola*.] **1883** in *List Anim. Zool. Soc.* (1896) 577.

tarentola, -tula, obs. ff. TARANTULA.

†'**tarer**. *Obs.* [f. TARE *sb.*[2] + -ER[1].] An assay-officer of the stannaries, who ascertained the amount of dross or foreign matter in the tin.

1625 *Laws Stannaries* ix. (1808) 20 If the tin be not found faulty to the value assessed by the tarer [etc.]. *Ibid.* x, If any man.. hide worse matter than tin within his.. blocks of tin, which the tarer by his outward essay with his chizel cannot come at.

†**ta'rette**. *Obs. rare.* Also 4 'tarrit. [a. OF. **tarete*, = *taride* (13th c. in Godef.), = med.L. *tarīda*, *tarēta* 'navis onerariæ species, eadem quæ Tartana vocitata, ut quidam volunt' (Du Cange), a. Arab. *tarīdah* 'actuaria navis'; cf. med. Gr. ταρίδος = δρόμων (ibid.).] A kind of ship of burden or merchant vessel of the Middle Ages. Cf. TARTAN *sb.*[2]

a **1352** MINOT *Poems* iii. 80 Eight and forty galays and mo, And with them als war tarettes two. [**1354** in Rymer *Fœdera* (1825) III. I. 274/1 Sciatis quod suscepimus in protectionem.. tres taritas, diversis bonis & mercimoniis carcatas, quæ juxta insulas nostras.. jacent ancoratæ.] **1362** *Ibid.* (1830) III. II. 641 Quædam magna navis, vocata Tarrit, et tres aliæ grossæ naves.

†**tarf**, *sb. Obs.* [A deriv. of TIRVE *v.* to turn: cf. TURF *sb.*[2]] The turn or facing of a cap.

1545 *Rates of Customs* A viij, Cappes with syngle tarfs the dossen xiii. s. iiii d. **1555** WATREMAN *Fardle of Facions* II. xi. 245 Then aftrewarde are thei [Janizarie] chosen into souldie, and haue giuen them.. a white cappe, with a tarfe tourned vpwarde.

Hence †'**tarfed** *a.*, having a tarf. See also TURFED.

1545 *Rates of Customs* A viij, Cappes double tarfed & necked, and all other of frenche makyng.

‖**tarfa** (tar'fɑː). Also **tarfah**. [a. Arab. *ṭarfā*.] The tamarisk, *Tamarix gallica*, which exudes a gum called manna. Also *attrib.*

1858 BONAR *Hymns Faith & Hope* 216 Creeping through the wiry boughs Of these tarfas. **1859** MARTIN tr. *Kurtz's Hist. Old Covt.* III. 31 The manna produced on the tarfah shrub is caused by the prick of an insect. **1870** JAS. HAMILTON *Moses* xiii. 216 Jehovah did not ignore the few drops which already trickled from the tarfah-trees.

targat(e, -gatt, obs. forms of TARGET.

targe (tɑːdʒ), *sb.*[1] Now *arch.* and *poet.* Forms: 3- targe; also 4 tarche, 5 taarge, 6 terge, *Sc.* 6- tairge. [In late OE. *targe* fem., *targa* masc., ME. *targe*, = OF. *targe* (11th c. in *Roland*) = It. *targa*, Pr. *targua*, ad. ON. *targa* fem. (c 950 in Vigf.), shield, cogn. with OHG. *zarga* fem., 'edging, border'. OE. *targe* fem., *targa* masc. were prob. from ON.; ME. *targe* from OF.; the Pr. and Sp. *tarja*, MHG. *tartsche*, early mod.Du. *tartsche*, *targie*, also from French. (The OCat. *darga*, Sp. and Pg. *adarga*, appear to be from Arab. *al-darqah* the shield of leather and wood.)]

1. A shield; *spec.* a light shield or buckler, borne instead of the heavy shield, esp. by footmen and archers.

[c **997** *Charter of Æ-deric* in Kemble *Cod. Dipl.* III. 304 Twa targan and twegen francan. c **1015** *Charter of Æðelstan Æðeling* ibid. 363 Ic ʒeann Ælmere minen discðene.. mines taregan.] **1297** R. GLOUC. (Rolls) 7462 Wiþ stronge targes hom biuore þat archers ne dude hom noȝt. **13..** *Sir Beues* (A.) 4214 Þo Beues seȝ is strokes large, He kepte his strokes wiþ is targe. c **1386** CHAUCER *Prol.* 471 On hir heed an hat As brood as is a bokeler or a targe [*rime* large]. c **1470** HENRY *Wallace* VIII. 799 Feill Inglismen.. With schot was slayn, for all thar targis strang. **1549** *Compl. Scot.* vi. 42 Tua handit sourdis and tairgis. **1569** STOCKER tr. *Diod. Sic.* I. xiii. 22 His footemen which carried the terges and scaling ladders. **1667** MILTON *P.L.* IX. 1111 Those Leaves They [Adam & Eve] gatherd, broad as Amazonian Targe,.. To gird thir waste. **1715-20** POPE *Iliad* XIII. 513 The spacious targe (a blazing round, Thick with bull-hides and brazen orbits bound). **1810** SCOTT *Lady of L.* V. xv, Ill fared it then with Roderick Dhu, That on the field his targe he threw. **1894** GLADSTONE *Odes Horace* II. vii, Philippi's headlong rout we shared, I parted from my targe, not well.

b. *fig.*

a **1300** *Cursor M.* 9972 (Cott.) Maria maiden, mild o mode.. standes vs for sceild and targe [*Laud* tarche]. **1536** BELLENDEN *Cron. Scot.* (1821) II. 181 Knawing weill that devine helpe is the only targe and sicker munition of kingis and realmes. a **1578** LINDESAY *Chron. Scot.* (S.T.S.) I. 127 Ane faithfull subiect and sicker tairge to the commone weill. **1599** JAS. I Βασιλ. Δωρον (1682) To Rdr., To which hydra of diverslie enclined spectators, I have no targe to oppone.

†**2.** A name applied in the reigns of the first three Edwards to the King's private or privy seal (perh. bearing a shield as its device). *Obs.*

[**1309** *Rolls of Parlt.* I. 444/2 Quant as Brefs de la targe, le Roy voet, qe l'Ordenance soit gardee, qe en fust fait en temps le Roy son pere, laquele est en Chancellerie. a **1315** *Lib. de Antiq. Leg.* (Camden) App. 252 Ces lettres desuz son prive seal de la targe. **1315** *Rolls of Parlt.* I. 339/1 Par Bref de la targe. **1347** *Ibid.* II. 193/1 Briefs soutz le grant Seal, & Letres soutz la targe.] c **1492** *Gest Robyn Hode* ccclxxxv. in Child *Ballads* III. 75/1 He toke out the brode targe [*v.r.* seale], And sone he lete hym se.

†**b.** (See quot.) *Obs. rare.*

c **1440** *Promp. Parv.* 487/1 Targe, or chartyr, *carta*.

3. *attrib.* and *Comb.*: **targeman**, a man armed with a targe.

?**17..** *Battle of Sheriff-Muir* (Cent. Dict.), He stoutly encounter'd the targemen. **1895** *Daily News* 29 Oct. 6/5 The twin targe brooch that clasps her robe.

†**targe**, *sb.*[2] *Obs.* [f. TARGE *v.*[1]] Tarrying, delay.

13.. *Coer de L.* 2790 Whenne that ilke man hadde hys charge, Home they wolden, withouten targe.

targe, *sb.*[3] *Sc.* [f. TARGE *v.*[3]] = TARGER.

1887 SERVICE *Dr. Duguid* ix. 67 Bessie Graham was a terr'ble tairge, and had a tinkler tongue in the heid of her. **1896** J. HORNE *Canny Countryside* iv. 40 Fat wud ye do wi' a targe lek her?

†**targe**, *v.*[1] *Obs.* [a. OF. *targier*, *targer* (11th c. in Godef.) to tarry:—pop.L. type **tardicāre*, deriv. of L. *tardāre* to be late, to tarry, f. *tardus* slow. (For Fr. form cf. *juger*:—L. *jūdicāre*.) See also TARRY *v.*] *intr.* To delay; = TARRY *v.* Hence †**targing** *vbl. sb.*

c **1250** *O. Kentish Serm.* in *O.E. Misc.* 36 Ne solde no man targi for to wende to godalmichti ne him to serui. c **1290** *S. Eng. Leg.* I. 350/177 Þo he [Askebert] targede a luyte þis luþere dede to done. **1297** R. GLOUC. (Rolls) 2363 War-to [= why] targe [*MSS.* 1400- tarie, tarye] we so long to quelle him atten ende? a **1330** *Otuel* 833 Þo wenten þei forþ wiþouten targing. c **1400** *Laud Troy Bk.* 7588 So weri thei ben and ouer-charged, Here socour foule fro hem targed. c **1440** *Pallad. on Husb.* III. 1075 Fructifying wodes.. Wherof sum fruit wol targe & sum wol hie.

†**targe**, *v.*[2] *Obs. rare.* [f. TARGE *sb.*[1], or a. OF. *targier*, *targer* (13th c. in Godef.) to protect, defend (cf. mod.F. *targuer*, a. It. *targar*(*si*)), f. *targe*: see TARGE *sb.*[1]] *trans.* To protect or defend as with a targe or shield; to shield.

c **1430** *Pilgr. Lyf Manhode* I. cxxviii. (1869) 68 This targe targede him as longe as he bar it with him. **1489** CAXTON *Faytes of A.* I. i. 2 Couenable to couure & targe the body of man agaynst the strokes of dartes.

targe, *v.*[3] *Sc.* Also **tairge**, **terge**. [Origin and, hence also, the sense development uncertain. Jamieson and E.D.D. start with the sense 'to beat, strike, thrash', but quote no instances before 1833. (L. *tergere* to rub, wipe, cleanse, correct, has been suggested.) The 'soft' *g* (dʒ) suggests Romanic origin.]

1. *trans.* To question closely, cross-examine.

1786 BURNS *Inventory* 41, I on the questions tairge them tightly. **1819** W. TENNANT *Papistry Storm'd* (1827) 213 Tairge them about it now.. O' sic ane styk untill this day We never heard a cheep! **1869** TROLLOPE *Phineas Finn.* (ed. Tauchn.) II. iii, He.. had on this occasion targed two or three commissariat officers very tightly with questions respecting cabbages and potatoes.

2. To keep in strict order, look after strictly.

1814 SCOTT *Wav.* xlii, Callum Beg.. discharging the obligation, by mounting guard over the hereditary tailor of Sliochd nan Ivor; and, as he expressed himself, 'targed him tightly' till the finishing of the job. **1868** TROLLOPE *Linda Tressel* i. 13 Linda.. was.. targed more strictly in the reading of godly books.

3. To reprimand, scold loudly; to beat, thrash.

1825 JAMIESON, To *Targe*, *Tairge*, to beat, to strike, *Perths.* **1833** J. S. SANDS *Poems* Ser. I. 105 (E.D.D.) Targed him tightly till he fell. **1861** R. QUIN *Heather Lintie* (1866) 165 Targe him tichtly wha debases Frail human nature.

targer ('tɑːdʒə(r)). *Sc.* Also **tairger**, **terjer**. [f. TARGE *v.*[3] + -ER[1].] One who targes; a termagant; a scold.

1822 CARLYLE *Early Lett.* (1886) II. 104 Where is the targer? **1886** MURDOCH *Sc. Readings* Ser. II. 59 Happily rid o' his awfu' terjer o' a mither-in-law. **1899** CROCKETT *Kit Kennedy* xxix, O, she's a tairger.

target ('tɑːgɪt), *sb.*[1] Forms: α. 5 tergett, 5-7 targett, 4- target; β. 5-6 targat, 6 -gatt, tergat(e, -guette, *Sc.* tergatt, tarcat, 6-7 targuet. [dim. of

TARGE *sb.*[1]: cf. F. *targete, -ette*, also 15–16th c. *targuet(t)e*, It. *targhetta*.

The actual history is uncertain, chiefly from the ambiguity of the spelling *target*. The current pronunciation with 'hard *g*' (g) is carried back to 15th c. by the spelling *targat* (so in 16th c. *-guet*), but the early spelling *target* might be ('tɑːrdʒɛt), which would have been the natural English diminutive of TARGE. In French also, the ordinary form was *targete, targette* (-ʒɛt); but, alongside of this, *targuete* (-gɛt), is cited of 1494, and *-guette* in 16th c. (possibly after Pr. *targuetta* or It. *targhetta*). It is possible that Eng. *target* had at first 'soft *g*' (dʒ) after *targe* and OF. *target(t)e*, but that this was at an early date changed to the present pronunciation with 'hard *g*', after F. *targuet(t)e*, and the Prov. and Italian forms.]

1. A light round shield or buckler; a small targe. Also *fig.* Now chiefly *Hist.*

a. **c 1400** MAUNDEV. (Roxb.) xxi. 97 Þai bere a grete target, with whilk þai couer all þaire body. *a* **1400–50** *Alexander* 2622 Taches in-to targetis tamed þaire brenys. *c* **1440** *Promp. Parv.* 487/1 Ta(r)get, or defence,..*scutum, ancile.* **1483** *Cath. Angl.* 380/1 A Tergett, *pelta.* *a* **1548** HALL *Chron., Hen. VIII* 2 The kynges banner and courser, his coate of armes, his sworde, his target, and his helme. **1633** T. STAFFORD *Pac. Hib.* I. iv. (1821) 55 At whom hee discharged his Pistoll, which lighted upon his Targett. **1724** DE FOE *Mem. Cavalier* (1840) 147 [The highlanders] carried great wooden targets, large enough to cover the upper part of their bodies. **1791** BOSWELL *Johnson* 17 Oct. an. 1773, He strutted about the room with a broad sword and target. **1869** BOUTELL *Arms & Arm.* ix. (1874) 164 The Scots auxiliary troops, who took a part with the French forces at the battle of Fontenoy, appeared with shields or targets.

β. **14..** *Voc.* in Wr.-Wülcker 615/27 *Targia*, a targat, or a pavys. **1507** *Acc. Ld. High Treas. Scot.* III. 394 To Simon Glasfurd buklarmakar, for hornyng of foure tergatis,..iij li. **1508** *Ibid.* IV. 121 Item, payit..for ane sicht of ane tarcat, thre lokkis to basnetis, xij bukkilles. **1513** DOUGLAS *Æneis* VIII. vii. 146 The horrible tergate, bustuus Egida, Quhilk is the grevit Pallas grysly scheild. **1542** UDALL *Erasm. Apoph.* 314 The image of the same Quintus made with his terguette. **1556** *Chron. Gr. Friars* (Camden) 93 Havyng their targattes on their sholderes.

†**2. a.** A shield-shaped ornament or plaque of precious metal, often jewelled, worn esp. as a decoration in the head-dress. *Sc. Obs.*

1507 *Acc. Ld. High Treas. Scot.* IV. 15 Tua targetis for bonetis hornyt with gold for bonetis. **1542** *Inv. Roy. Wardrobe* (1815) 68 Item ane bonet of blak velvott with ane tergat of the marmadin, hir taill of dyamonttis. **1556** LAUDER *Tractate* 439 Nocht haueand respect..To Tergats, Chenis, nor goldin Ryngis. *a* **1578** LINDESAY (Pitscottie) *Chron. Scot.* (S.T.S.) I. 368 He gaif hir great giftis of cheinzeis targattis and tablattis and ringis. ? *a* **1600** *Johnie Armstrong*, Ther hang nine Targats at Johnys Hat, And ilk an worth Three hundred Pound.

†**b.** A piece of money: app. a scudo, an écu.

[Cf. med.L. *scutum, scutatum* a coin of the early French kings (Du Cange).]

1671 H. M. tr. *Erasm. Colloq.* 79 What price dost thou set upon thyself? At ten targets [orig. *Decem scutatis*].

3. a. A shield-like structure, marked with concentric circles, set up to be aimed at in shooting practice; hence, any object used for the purpose, and *transf.*, *spec.* (*a*) a place or object selected for military attack, esp. by aerial bombing or missile assault; (*b*) a part of the body at which a boxer directs his attack.

1757 E. PERRONET *Mitre* I. cxxxix, The Target of the Muse. [*Note.* This word is here used in the military sense, and signifies a But or mark to be shot at.] **1801** STRUTT *Sports & Past.* II. i. §17, I have seen the gentlemen who practise archery in the vicinity of London, repeatedly shoot from end to end, and not touch the target with an arrow. **1802–16** C. JAMES *Milit. Dict.*, *Target*,..a mark for the artillery, &c. to fire at in their practice. **1859** *Musketry Instr.* IV. 51 The targets are to be six feet in height and two in breadth, constructed of iron of sufficient thickness to be rifle-bullet proof. **1871** TYNDALL *Fragm. Sc.* (1879) I. xvi. 423 In firing a ball against a target the projectile, after collision, is often found hot.

transf. **1902** *Encycl. Brit.* XXXIII. 380/2 Taking range and size of target together, the most advantageous position is to be on the bow of the enemy while he bears abaft your beam. **1914** HAMEL & TURNER *Flying* xvi. 285 A pilot will have to make three or four attempts before..a bomb can be released in any hope of getting near the target. **1921** J. DRISCOLL *Text-bk. Boxing* 70 The 'jaw' target is..preferable, if it should happen to be exposed. **1958** F. C. AVIS *Boxing Ref. Dict.* 112 *Target*, that part of the boxer's body which may properly be punched, namely, the entire front and side parts of the body above the belt and the head. **1959** *Chambers's Encycl.* XIII. 430/1 The bomber force was sent out and so timed as to converge upon the target and complete the entire attack within a few minutes. **1971** H. MACMILLAN *Riding Storm* viii. 272 The R.A.F. carried out a number of rocket attacks on military targets.

fig. **1900** LD. ROBERTS in *Daily News* 27 July 5/3 The enemy were strongly entrenched, fought stubbornly, and gave no target.

b. *fig.* Something aimed at or to be aimed at; *esp.* a person who is the object of general abuse, scorn, derision, or the like; = BUTT *sb.*[4] 5.

1757 [see 3]. **1842** TENNYSON *Locksley Hall* 146 They to whom my foolish passion were a target for their scorn. **1889** *Tablet* 14 Dec. 947 A target for the abuse of the prejudiced, the ignorant and the profane. **1906** *Times* 24 July 8/5 A target for popular ridicule.

c. A shooting match; the score made at such a match.

1825 *Sporting Mag.* XVI. 426 A grand target of the Reedwood Foresters took place the middle of August at Blithfield. **1858** GREENER *Gunnery* 313 A comparison between the largest 'target' of to-day, and the best that Colonel Hawker ever made with his crack Joe Manton, will show a progressive improvement of nearly 100 per cent., not only in closeness of shooting, but also in penetration. **1884** *Pall Mall G.* 26 July 8/2 The Artists' team have made a magnificent target, and are scarcely likely to be beaten.

d. *Physics.* The object or material at which a beam of atomic or sub-atomic particles is directed, as in a cathode-ray tube or particle accelerator.

1915 *Chambers's Jrnl.* Sept. 593/1 This anti-kathode (or target), enabling us to focus the rays, was introduced by Herbert Jackson. **1932** *Proc. R. Soc.* A. CXXXVII. 230 A target, A, of the metal to be investigated is placed at an angle of 45 degrees to the direction of the proton stream. **1953** AMOS & BIRKINSHAW *Television Engin.* I. x. 217 The action of television camera tubes is dependent on an electron beam which is focused on the target and deflected so as to cover it in a series of scanning lines. **1961** G. R. CHOPPIN *Exper. Nuclear Chem.* viii. 111 In a cyclotron, only one target at a time may be irradiated. **1975** D. G. FINK *Electronics Engineers' Handbk.* xi. 61 The target becomes positively charged in proportion to the light intensity.

e. *Biol.* and *Med.* A region in a cell which is especially sensitive to radiation.

1936 D. E. LEA et al. in *Proc. R. Soc.* B. CXX. 56 The hypothesis that the bacterium is uniformly sensitive to radiation throughout its volume raises..difficulties, and attention will therefore be turned to the alternative hypothesis that a target exists which is specially sensitive. **1968** *Brit. Med. Bull* XXIV. 244/2 The curve can be represented by a model in which each of several targets in the organism must interact with radiation. **1979** I. M. LEAHY et al. *Nurse & Radiotherapy* iii. 30 Targets are necessarily very small and are usually assumed to be within the nucleus or the DNA material itself.

f. *colloq.* An amount set as a (minimum) objective, esp. in fund-raising; a result (i.e. a figure, sum of money, etc.) aimed at. Phr. *on target*, on the right track, as forecast. Hence *loosely*, any goal which one strives to achieve.

1942 *N. & Q.* CLXXXIII. 256/1 *Target.* Who invented the ingenious use of this word for the amount aimed at in a public subscription? I think the use has been extended to things like coal consumption. **1943** *Ann. Reg. 1942* 307 The London Warship Week resulted in 146,065,225*l.* being raised as against the original target of 125,000,000*l.* **1951** E. GOWERS *ABC of Plain Words* 133 If target was to have all the stimulating force it was capable of, it would not do to treat it as a live metaphor, and exhort people to do nothing more exciting..than merely to hit it. So we were offered a great variety of things that we might meritoriously do to our targets. We might reach them, achieve them, attain them or obtain them; we were to feel greatly encouraged if we came in sight of the target to which we were trying to do whatever we were trying to do, and correspondingly depressed if we found ourselves either a long way behind it or (what apparently amounts to the same thing) a long way short of it. **1952** *Sat. Rev.* 20 Sept. 9/2 There are legislative targets, crop targets, charity targets, gross national product targets. **1964** F. CHICHESTER *Lonely Sea & Sky* xxxii. 333, I had failed to beat my 30 day target by 3 days, 15 hours, 7 minutes. **1967** *Time* 18 Aug. 88 Diddy is sure he did it; yet a blind girl near by who hears all and who proves to be on target about everything else, says he never left his seat. **1977** *Times* 10 Aug. 5/5 There has been unrealistic targeteering; the 1960s building target of 500,000 was never required. **1981** *Times* 23 Oct. 22/1 First-half results from Jeavons Engineering are on target at £306,000 pre-tax.

g. *Linguistics.* = OUTPUT *sb.* 1 e.

1970 J. HILL in *Linguistic Inquiry* I. 539 The formal statement of the HAB formation rule of Cupeño..is not going to be like the usual..rule involving description of input..; it can instead be visualized as involving first a statement of the target or output, and then a statement for reaching the target. **1977** *Language* LIII. 209 This constraint is a target; i.e., a number of rules of various types conspire to keep the verb in sentential second position.

4. Applied to various objects resembling a target or shield. †**a.** A cymbal. *Obs.*

1696 tr. *Du Mont's Voy. Levant* xxi. 275 They have a kind of Violin, with three Strings,..and several little Brazen Targets, which..they knock against one another.

b. *Cookery.* The neck and breast of lamb as a joint; the fore-quarter without the shoulder.

1756 GRAY *Let. to W. Mason* 19 Dec., Lord Surrey loved buttered lyng and targets of mutton for breakfast. **1872** MARY JEWRY *Every-day Cookery* 72/2 Roast Target of Lamb. *Ibid.*, Target is only the breast and neck joints not separated.

c. The sliding sight on a levelling staff; a vane.

d. A disc-shaped signal on a railway switch, etc., indicating its position. *U.S.*

1877 KNIGHT *Dict. Mech.*, *Target*,..the sight, sliding on a leveling-staff. Also called a vane. **1884** *Ibid.* Suppl. 810/1 Two targets, generally a round and an oblong one, and generally painted red and white respectively, are set at right angles to each other on a revolving shaft. *Ibid.*, A common form of ordinary switches is an upright pivoted lever with target on top. **1900** H. M. WILSON *Topogr. Surveying* xv. 311 Leveling rods are of two general types: 1 Target rods; and 2 Speaking of self-reading rods. *Ibid.* 313 The Boston [leveling] rod has a fixed target, and all readings upon it are obtained by extending the rod.

5. *attrib.* and *Comb.*, as (sense 3) *target-firing, -practice, -range, seeking, -shooting, -shot*; *target-like, -proof, -shaped* adjs.; *target-practise* vb.; (appositively) designating an object of attack, as *target area, boat, vehicle*, etc.; (see also *target ship*); *transf.*, esp. of a particular group over which influence is sought, as *target audience, company, group, population*; (sense 3 d) *target nucleus, volume*; (sense 3 f, passing into adj.) by which the desired goal is specified, as *target date, figure, output, prize, size*, etc.; **target-card**: see quot.; **target cell** *Biol.* and *Med.*, an abnormal form of red blood cell which appears as a dark ring surrounding a dark central spot in stained blood films; hence *target cell anæmia*, descriptive of any anæmia in which target cells are abundant; **target dialect**, the variety of a language learned as a second dialect; †**target-fence**, a protective fence or covering formed by targets or shields; a testudo; **target indicator**, an object, as a flare, dropped in order to illuminate or delimit a target for aerial bombing; **target-lamp, -lantern**, *U.S.*, a lamp or lantern attached to a signal-target (see sense 4 d), the function of which it discharges at night; **target man**, †(*a*) a man armed with a target (*obs.*); (*b*) *U.S.* a signal-man who works signalling targets: see sense 4 d; (*c*) *Assoc. Football* (see quot. 1978); **target organ** *Biol.*, any organ which responds to a particular hormone or hormones in the body (cf. *target tissue* below); **target program** *Computers* = *object program* s.v. OBJECT *sb.* 10; **target-rifle**, a rifle adapted to target-shooting; †**target-roof**, a testudo (= *target-fence*); **target-ship**, a condemned ship used as a target; **target theory** *Biol.* and *Med.* (see quots. and cf. sense 3 e above); **target tissue** *Biol.*, any tissue which responds to a particular hormone or hormones within an organism (cf. *target organ* above). See also TARGET LANGUAGE.

1936 *Proc. R. Soc.* B. CXX. 57 To prove that the target is a biological reality..the obvious experiment..is to use several different intensities of alpha rays and beta rays and to calculate the *target area in each experiment. **1939** W. S. CHURCHILL in *New Statesman* 7 Jan. 6/2, I think a great mistake has been made in spreading our A.R.P. efforts over the whole country, instead of concentrating on what I should call the target areas. **1958** F. C. AVIS *Boxing Dict.* 77 *Off the target*, not connecting the opponent in the target area. **1980** J. MCCLURE *Blood of Englishman* xxv. 232 'Target area coming up,' he said, picking up the line of a wriggling dirt road... They were down to about 600 feet above the ground. **1956** *U.S. Air Force Dict.* 513/2 **Target audience*, in psychological warfare, the people at whom propaganda is directed. **1982** *Underground Grammarian* Sept. 2/2 In order to broaden the 'target audience' of your newsletter..I might suggest that such material be written at a lower level of readability. **1934** T. E. LAWRENCE *Let.* 8 June (1938) 805 At the moment we are all up to the teeth in 5 more *target boats. **1875** *Encycl. Brit.* II. 378 (*Archery*) **Target-card*, a card coloured in the same manner as the target, containing the names of the shooters, and used for scoring their respective hits. [**1938** A. M. BARRETT in *Jrnl. Path. & Bacteriol.* XLVI. 603 They will here be called 'target types of red blood corpuscle', or more briefly, 'target corpuscles'. I have deliberately chosen a name which refers only to their appearance in stained films and not to their three-dimensional form.] *Ibid.* 605 Often the frequency of *target cells appeared to be affected by the thickness or thinness of the film. **1940** W. DAMESHEK in *Amer. Jrnl. Med. Sci.* CC. 445 Since an outstanding abnormality was the presence of large numbers of peculiar erythrocytes designated as 'target cells' by Barrett, the name 'target cell anemia' was adopted for this previously undescribed condition. **1969** EDINGTON & GILLES *Path. in Tropics* x. 353 Excluding films obtained from persons homozygous or heterozygous for haemoglobin C, a high percentage of target cells in normal blood films has been observed in Ghana, Nigeria, and from East Africa. **1977** *Time* 17 Oct. 58/3 The firm that eventually acquires the *target company. **1945** W. S. CHURCHILL *Victory* (1946) 108 Full hutting..is nearing completion, the *target date for which is May. **1977** *Whitaker's Almanack 1978* 595 The Rhodesia conference in Geneva became deadlocked when leaders of White and Black delegations failed to agree on a target date for legal independence. **1972** J. L. DILLARD *Black Eng.* vii. 293 The Network Standard dialect, for which both white and Black speakers have shown marked preferences, is obviously the preferable *target dialect. **1598** GRENEWEY *Tacitus, Ann.* XIII. ix. (1622) 191 Hauing deuided his armie into foure parts, he [Corbulo] lead some close and thicke ranked together, for a *target fence to vndermine and beate downe the rampire. **1653** H. COGAN tr. *Pinto's Trav.* lxix. (1663) 280 The Elephants withall setting their Trunks to the target fences..tore them down in such sort, as not one of them remained entire. **1978** J. IRVING *World according to Garp* viii. 163 Roberta was a *target figure; she had made some people very angry. **1832** G. DOWNES *Lett. Cont. Countries* I. 138 A shooting-establishment, where *target-firing is practised. **1972** *Times* 13 Dec. 4/7 It made no discriminations among *target groups. **1979** *Bull. Amer. Acad. Arts & Sci.* Mar. 33 The programs to be undertaken in reaching these target groups were to involve workers in both the public and private sectors of health, agriculture, and education. **1944** *Times* 11 Apr. 4/4 The attack began with the dropping of *target-indicators through cloud. **1555** EDEN *Decades* 55 He browght furth al his *target men for feare of theyr venemous arrowes. **1884** KNIGHT *Dict. Mech.* Suppl. s.v. *Signaling Target*, Turned by the target-man by means of a hand-lever. [**1974** *Times* 23 Feb. 14/8 Even eight, nine and ten-year-olds these days are taught by games masters in terms of 'striker', 'target player'..and the rest.] **1975** *Times* 14 Oct. 10/2 (*caption*) Stuart Pearson, a target man with Manchester United. **1978** *Sunday Times* (Colour Suppl.) 28 May 34/4 *Target man*, forward, usually a large one, used in central positions where colleagues can find him with long passes, usually to his head. **1955** FRIEDMAN & WEISSKOPF in W. Pauli *Niels Bohr* 134 According to this model the effect of the *target nucleus upon an incident particle can be described, at least as a first approximation, by an attractive potential. **1947** H. SELYE *Textbk. Endocrinol.* 17/1 The so-called '*target organs' or 'end organs' do not necessarily react to hormones under all conditions. **1972** *Sci. Amer.* Nov. 24/1 The pituitary secretes several complex hormones that travel through the bloodstream to target organs, notably the thyroid gland, the gonads and the cortex of the adrenal glands. **1944** *Hutchinson's Pict. Hist. War.* 27 Oct. 1943–11 Apr. 1944. 441 Once more the merchantship *target output was achieved. **1971** *Computers & Humanities* V. 292 SPIRES is based on a behavioral science analysis of the information needs of a *target population. **1844** *Regul. & Ord. Army* 288 The Surgeon, or Assistant-Surgeon, is to attend all Field Days, and invariably at *Target-practice. **1902** *Bible Student* Oct. 198 They may safely tolerate attacks as the target practice of children. **1949** H. PREECE in B. A. Botkin *Treas. S. Folklore* II. iv. 341 The rumbling underground is Britt Bailey *target-practising for a million years of shooting in hell. **1982** *Sunday Sun-Times* (Chicago) 8 Aug. 9 A witness..allegedly saw Hartmann's widow, Debra, target practicing at a suburban gun shop. **1962** *Target price [see *off-farm* s.v. OFF- 4 b]. **1969** P. B. JORDAIN *Condensed Computer Encycl.* 516 The process begins with a source-language program..and ends with a *target program. **1979** *Personal Computer World* Nov. 84/1 Any areas of data must be excluded from both and left intact as they are used by both the target program and the trace routine. **1895** *Outing* (U.S.) XXVI. 79/1 The State owns two large *target ranges which are also used as camp grounds. **1901** *Westm. Gaz.* 23 Dec. 4/3 As a *target-rifle the Lee-Metford is by no means in the front rank. **1601** HOLLAND *Pliny* I. 189 The vse..of the pauois, mantelets, *targuet-roofs, for the assault of cities. **1610** —— *Camden's Brit.* I. 36 The Romans with a Testudo, or targuet-roofe.. tooke the place. **1947** *Britannica Bk. of Year* 841/2 **Target-seeking missile*, a missile, equipped with a target-seeking mechanism, which is attracted toward its target when it approaches its vicinity. **1977** *R. Air Force Yearbk.* 4/2 (*caption*) A Harrier GR Mk 3..with laser-ranging and target-seeking equipment in the nose. **1837** P. KEITH *Bot. Lex.* 200 The pedicle..supports a *target-shaped substance. **1901** *Pall Mall G.* 23 July 1 A *target ship, on board of which every new type of armour was tested. **1855** GEO. ELIOT in *Fraser's Mag.* LI. 706/2, I will tell you of Weimar fairs and *target-shooting. **1905** *Blackw. Mag.* May 646/2 It is foolish for an indifferent *target-shot to go lion-hunting. **1966** *Observer* 17 Apr. 10/3 Is there any magic in the figure of 30—the *target size for classes? **1936** D. E. LEA et al. in *Proc. R. Soc.* B. CXX. 62 That regions of special sensitivity to radiation do exist..has been demonstrated and the additional postulate of the *target theory, namely that there is only one such region, in an individual organism, is not improbable for bacteria. **1979** I. M. LEAHY et al. *Nurse & Radiotherapy* iii. 30 One theory that has proved to be applicable to radiation biology experimentation is known as target theory. Briefly stated, this theory proposes that if alterations are produced within certain critical molecules in the cell, the loss of vital function that would result would lead to the death of the cell. **1960** JENSEN & JACOBSEN in Pincus & Vollmer. *Biol. Activities Steroids* iii. 162 Information concerning the chemical fate—in the specific *target tissues—of physiological amounts of steroid sex hormones should prove of value. **1974** M. C. GERALD *Pharmacol.* xxiii. 409 Whereas growth hormone and thyroid hormone are capable of influencing virtually all the cells of the body, most hormones act rather selectively on specific tissues referred to as target tissues. **1975** *Sci. Amer.* July 94/1 Where trees are concerned one of the target tissues for auxin is the cambium. **1965** *New Scientist* 18 Mar. 701/2 The spacecraft will be manoeuvred by the pilots to approach the *target vehicle closely, and finally to dock with it in a firm, mechanical manner. **1946** D. E. LEA *Actions of Radiations* iii. 91 That dose..produces an average of one cluster in a volume equal to the *target volume.

'target, *sb.*[2] *Sc.* [Etym. uncertain; Jamieson compares Sw. *targa* to tear.] A tatter, a shred.

1773 R. FERGUSSON *Compl. Plainstanes* 86 The weight o' ilka codroch chiel, That does my skin to targets peel. **1789** D. DAVIDSON *Th. Seasons* 120 Until her apron was sae stent, The strings in targets, flew.

b. *targets of skate*, 'long slices of this fish dried' (Jam.).

'target, *v.* [f. TARGET *sb.*[1]]

†**1.** *trans.* To protect with or as with a target; to shield. *Obs.*

1611 G. H. *Anti-Coton* 18 [He] targets himselfe with the authoritie of Siluester. **1686** F. SPENCE tr. *Varillas' Ho. Medicis* 337 The garrison of Florence..was not sufficient to ward and target it from insult.

2. To use (a person) as a target. Also *fig.*

1837 *Fraser's Mag.* XVI. 244 If you doubt my word, load and target me again. **1844** W. H. MAXWELL *Sports & Adv. Scotl.* iii. (1855) 49 To be targetted through..the..newspapers and executed afterwards in effigy.

3. *U.S.* To signal the position of (a railway switch, etc.) by means of a target (TARGET *sb.*[1] 4 d).

1893 *Columbus* (Ohio) *Dispatch* 17 Nov., The crews of both trains claim to have had the crossing targeted.

4. To plan or schedule (something) to attain an objective. Chiefly in *Econ.*

1948 *Observer* 14 Mar. 3/6 Even herrings have targets now: 175,000 tons of fish are being 'targeted' to yield 17,000 tons of oil a year. **1959** *Time* (Atlantic ed.) 17 Aug. 53 Exports of heavy goods..are targeted to rise this year some 40%. **1972** *Newsweek* 7 Aug. 43/3 With test flights now targeted for 1976, the Shuttle is expected to be ready for operational missions in 1978. **1973** *Daily Tel.* 8 Dec. 23/2 Investment income..is targeted to reach £1 million in two years.

5. To aim (a nuclear weapon) at a target. Freq. const. *on.*

1964 *Financial Times* 23 Mar. (Defence Suppl.) 17/4 The Soviet presence..comprises..a force of about 100 MRBMs targeted on Japan. **1972** *Sci. Amer.* Nov. 21/1 Each missile launches a 'bus', which has on board a large number of reentry missiles, each of which can be accurately and independently targeted. **1978** *Observer* 25 June 21/3 There were enough warheads to target some on China as well.

transf. **1973** *Times* 2 Nov. 4/2 The scheme is targeted at those wanting to buy an older property. **1974** *Nature* 1 Mar. 1/1 Research money should be targeted on problems whose solution would have the greatest benefit for society. **1983** *New Scientist* 21 July 208/1 Practical conservation can rarely preserve an entire fauna: rather it is targeted at particular species.

6. To mark out or identify (a place, person, etc.) as a target. Chiefly *U.S.*

1966 *Guardian* 30 Dec. 14/8 US policy is to target North Vietnamese military targets only. **1976** *National Observer* (U.S.) 27 Nov. 5/1 He has no worlds left to conquer, for NCEC has captured all the 'marginal' conservative seats it had targeted. **1978** S. BRILL *Teamsters* vii. 297 The airline industry was being targeted for a recruiting drive. **1983** *Listener* 25 Aug. 4/3 They've targeted 22 airlines for special treatment.

7. To direct or aim on a course. Freq. const. *to.*

1974 *Nature* 1 Mar. 16/3 Temperature profiles of the moons of those planets will be helpful in targeting the spacecraft to take a look at the most interesting features. **1976** *Sci. Amer.* June 74/1 The second spacecraft will be targeted to fly past Saturn and on toward Uranus. **1976** *National Observer* (U.S.) 21 Aug. 3/3 Then allocations are made with about one-third going to state governments and two-thirds to local governments, targeted to those jurisdictions with the highest unemployment. **1980** *Sci. Amer.* Aug. 88/2 Highly specialized transport systems that are in effect independent of the tissue through which they convey substances might be exploited as a means of 'targeting' therapeutic drugs for particular organs or tissues. **1981** *New Scientist* 6 Aug. 343/2 Later perhaps it will be possible to target liposomes or red cells..to whatever part of the body they are needed [*sic*].

Hence **'targeting** *vbl. sb.*

1961 *Guardian* 24 Oct. 8/4 Being forced to rely on so much inspection..that targeting information would be given away to the other side. **1963** *Newsweek* 11 Feb. 23 Planners have recently put forward the notion of city-avoidance, a tacit agreement between potential enemies to arrange their targeting so that missiles are aimed at military objectives rather than civilian populations. **1968** *Economist* 8 June 65/2 A general complaint is that consultants sometimes stick too much to their business precepts, such as 'targeting' and do not bend enough to the particular needs of the company. **1976** *National Observer* (U.S.) 27 Nov. 5/1 NCEC laid out $350,000 for candidates in 1976. That paid for 64 polls in 32 separate congressional districts and for computerized precinct targeting and analysis in more than 40 districts. **1977** *Time* 21 Nov. 24/2 None of these possess as sophisticated a targeting system as the new Soviet model's [*sc.* a T-72 tank]. **1982** *Financial Times* 13 Mar. 14/1 In terms of targeting ability.

targetable ('tɑːgɪtəb(ə)l), *a.* [f. TARGET *v.* + -ABLE.] **a.** Of nuclear missiles or warheads: capable of being aimed at a target. **b.** Of military installations or equipment, etc.: that may be picked out as a target.

1968 *N.Y. Times* 8 Apr. 46 The United States will in the next few years add to its arsenal missiles capable of putting into space a number of individually targetable warheads. **1968** *Economist* 6 July 10/2 Both in submarine-borne and land-based missiles the Americans have established a lead over the Russians in the development of MIRVs (multiple independently targetable re-entry vehicles). **1972** *Sci. Amer.* June 15/3 Land-based intercontinental ballistic missiles..can readily be located with the aid of surveillance satellites, so that they must be regarded as 'targetable' in the event of an enemy first strike. **1981** *Ibid.* Feb. 20/3 Silos are targetable. **1982** M. DUKE *Flashpoint* xxi. 151 Minuteman-III, with its multiple independently targetable warheads.

targeted ('tɑːgɪtɪd), *a.* [f. TARGET *sb.*[1] + -ED[2].] Furnished with a target or shield, or with something resembling one.

1653 GAUDEN *Hierasp.* 527 Not rough and targetted as the Rhinoceroes, but soft and gently clothed as the sheep. **1848** CLOUGH *Bothie* Poems (1892) 202 The Marquis's targeted gillies.

'targeted, *ppl. a.* [f. TARGET *v.* + -ED[1].]

1. Designated or chosen as a target.

1965 *Economist* 20 Feb. 733 We must..have a short take off and landing (STOL) capability; otherwise the aircraft is tied to targeted concrete and will be destroyed on the ground by the enemy. **1971** *Nature* 22 Oct. 517/3 He labelled sickle cell anaemia a targeted disease for concentrated research. **1974** *Spartanburg* (S. Carolina) *Herald-Jrnl.* 21 Apr. A8/3 Light industry was just meeting a targeted 4 per cent increase. **1979** *Sci. Amer.* Aug. 139/2 In the late 1960's the U.S. Government's 'Operation Shamrock' intercepted international Telex communications to and from 'targeted' individuals, including antiwar activists. **1983** D. WILLIAMS *Treasure Preserved* i. 8 Anyone..who detected Louella engaged in private ombudsman activity had a duty immediately to alert the targeted department.

2. Aimed, directed; given a target.

1969 *Guardian* 23 June 10/2 MIRV (Multiple Independently Targeted Re-Entry Vehicle). **1974** L. THOMAS *Lives of Cell* 116 We need more targeted research, more mission-oriented science. **1978** *Dædalus* Spring p. xiv, The distinction between basic and applied or targeted knowledge becomes crucial.

targeteer (tɑːgɪ'tɪə(r)). *Obs.* exc. *Hist.* Also 6–7 **targe(t)tier**, 7 **targatier**, **-tyer**, **targuattier**, **targue(t)tier**, **targueteere**. [prob. ad. It. *targhettiere* (Florio), f. *targhetta* target: see -EER[1].] A foot-soldier armed with a target; a peltast.

1586–8 in Hakluyt *Voy.* (1600) III. 812 Our General himselfe with certaine shot and some targettiers went ouer into the maine. **1590** MARLOWE *Edw. II*, III. ii, A band of bow-men and of pikes, Brown bills and targeteers, four hundred strong. **1600** HOLLAND *Livy* XXVIII. v. 670 A thousand targuattiers called Peltati. **1601** R. JOHNSON *Kingd. & Commw.* (1603) 18 He [Chas. VII of France].. adioined to them Targatiers, Harbengers, Mustermasters. **1676** HOBBES *Iliad* 53 He found him out With many targetiers environed. **1824** MACAULAY *Misc. Writ.* (1860) I. 176 The targeteers of Iphicrates. **1881** JOWETT *Thucyd.* I. 147 The Chalcidian hoplites..were assisted by a few targeteers.

†**targeter**. *Obs.* In 4 **tergeter**. [f. TARGET *sb.* + -ER[1].] A shield-maker, or a shield-bearer.

1382 WYCLIF *2 Chron.* xii. 10 The golden tergetis..for the whiche the kyng made brasen, and toke hem to the princis of the tergeteris [1388 scheeld makeris; Vulg. *scutariorum*]. *Ibid.* 11 Whanne the kyng schulde goone in to the house of the Lord, the tergeters [Vulg. *scutarii*] camen, and token hem.

†**'targeting**. *Sc. Obs. rare.* [f. TARGET *sb.*[1] 2 + -ING[1] 1 f.] Work consisting of targets; target-like trimmings of women's dresses.

1563 KNOX *Hist. Ref.* IV. Wks. 1848 II. 389 The seally sowll..can neather cary with it gold, garnassing, targatting, pearle, nor pretious stanes. *a* **1651** CALDERWOOD *Hist. Kirk* (1843) II. 216 The preachers spake freelie against the targetting of weomen's tailes, and the rest of their vanitie.

target language. [f. TARGET *sb.*[1] + LANGUAGE *sb.*] **a.** The language into which a translation is made.

1953 *Philos. Sci.* XX. 217 Imagine an utterly moronic student without the slightest knowledge of either the source-language or the target-language, i.e., the language into which the given text is to be translated. **1959** [see LANGUAGE *sb.* 1 d]. **1969** P. B. JORDAIN *Condensed Computer Encycl.* 515 In assembly and compiler operations, a programmer-oriented language is converted to a target language for execution on the computer. **1976** *Canad. Jrnl. Linguistics* Spring 96 A translator needs to have deciphered the ambiguity in a given sentence..in order to be able to translate it, provided of course that this sentence does not have a syntactic homonym in the target language.

b. A foreign language which it is aimed to learn or acquire.

1965 P. STREVENS *Papers in Lang. & Lang. Teaching* viii. 103 The difficulties..vary according to the learner's mother-tongue as well as his target-language. **1973** K. A. SEY *Ghanaian English* ii. 22 Lacking the native speaker's linguistic intuitions, the L_2 speaker has to depend on his limited acquaintance with the target language. **1976** *Word 1971* XXVII. 351 Integratively oriented students are more strongly motivated and more successful in learning the target language than instrumentally oriented students.

tar-grass: see TARE *sb.*[1] 4.

Targum ('tɑːgəm, ‖tar'gum), *sb.* Also 6–7 **thargum**. [a. Chaldee *targūm* interpretation, f. *targēm* to interpret: see DRAGOMAN.] Each of several Aramaic translations, interpretations, or paraphrases of the various divisions of the Old Testament, made after the Babylonian captivity, at first preserved by oral transmission, and committed to writing from about A.D. 100 onwards.

The extant Targums together comprise all the books except Ezra, Nehemiah, and Daniel.

1587 GOLDING *De Mornay* xxvii. (1592) 427 The Thargum of Hierusalem and the Onkelos which are bookes of cheefe authoritie among the Iewes. **1613** PURCHAS *Pilgrimage* (1614) 174 This the Hebrewes call *Targum*, that is, the Translation, which hath with them no lesse credit then the Text it selfe. **1646** SIR T. BROWNE *Pseud. Ep.* V. x. 249 Jonathan who compiled the Thargum, conceives the colours of these banners to answer the pretious stones in the breastplate, and upon which the names of the Tribes were engraven. **1706** A. BEDFORD *Temple Mus.* viii. 159 We find the Targum of Onkelos to be mark't with the Accents. **1776** BURNEY *Hist. Mus.* I. 228 *note*, The Targum, or Chaldee Paraphrase, mentions an instrument not to be found in the original, or in any of the translations. **1864** *Reader* 16 Jan. 74/1 The Targums are versions of the Old Testament in what has been called Chaldee, but which is, in fact, the language of Aram or Syria.

Hence **Targum** *v. trans.*, to interpret or paraphrase (Scripture) in the manner of the Targums (also *absol.*); **Targumic** (tɑː'guːmɪk), **Tar'gumical**, *adjs.*, of or pertaining to the Targums; **Tar'gumically** *adv.*, in the manner of the Targums.

a **1873** DEUTSCH *Rem.* (1874) 361 The authenticity of the Targumic Texts. **1883** F. DELITZSCH in *Athenæum* 26 May 668/3 A considerable number of Targumic and Talmudic words..occur in the Assyrian and Babylonian language. **1883** EDERSHEIM *Life & Times Jesus* I. II. viii. 206 At that time each one Targumed for himself... The New Testament writers..when it seemed necessary, literally or Targumically rendered a verse. *Ibid.* II. v. xiv. 574 S. Matthew, Targuming this prophecy in form as in its spirit.

Targumist ('tɑːgəmɪst, tɑː'guːmɪst). [f. TARGUM *sb.* + -IST.] **a.** One of the translators and commentators who compiled the Targums. **b.** 'One versed in the language and literature of the Targums' (Ogilvie).

1642 MILTON *Apol. Smect.* i. Wks. 1851 III. 282 Then we must conclude that Jonathan, or Onkelos the Targumists were of cleaner language then he that made the tongue. **1695** J. EDWARDS *Perfect. Script.* 482 It can't be expected that these Targumists should render the Hebrew word for word. **1851** M. A. DENHAM *Slogans N. Eng.* p. ix, The Targumists state that the banners were distinguished by their colours. **1891** T. K. CHEYNE *Orig. Ps.* viii. 444 Is the Targumist altogether wrong in his general view?

Hence **Targu'mistic** *a.*, of or pertaining to the Targumists.

1890 *Andover* (U.S.) *Rev.* VII. 101 (Cent. Dict.) Showing the prevalence of the Targumistic exegesis.

'Targumize, *v.* [f. TARGUM *sb.* + -IZE.] *trans.* To make a Targum of or upon.

1671 LIGHTFOOT *Horæ Hebr.*, *John* viii. 59 The Book of Job..Targumised; (that is, renderd into the Chaldee

Tongue). *a* **1873** DEUTSCH *Rem.* (1874) 399 The Book of Esther..has been targumised many times.

tarheel ('tɑːhiːl). *U.S. colloq.* Also **Tar Heel, Tar-heel, tar-heel.** [f. TAR *sb.*[1] + HEEL *sb.*] A nickname for a native or inhabitant of North Carolina, in allusion to tar as a principal product of that State. Also *attrib.* Hence **'tar-heeled** *a.*

1864 R. E. PARK *Diary* 9 Dec. in *Southern Hist. Soc. Papers* (1876) II. 232 A poor, starving Tar Heel at Elmira. **1869** *Overland Monthly* III. 128 A brigade of North Carolinians..failed to hold a certain hill, and were laughed at by the Mississippians for having forgotten to tar their heels that morning. Hence originated their cant name, 'Tar-heels'. **1878** *Scribner's Monthly* Apr. 833/1 A little fellow from North Carolina..announced to the convention he was from 'the tar-heeled state'. **1888** *American Humorist* 2 June (Farmer *Americanisms*), A little volume of North Carolina sketches, written by a talented young friend of mine, in the genuine tarheel dialect. **1889** *Jrnl. Amer. Folk-Lore* II. 95 The mountain 'tarheel' gradually drifted into a condition of dreary indifference to all things sublunary but hog and hominy. **1942** S. KENNEDY *Palmetto Country* 260 North Carolina became known as the Tar-heel State. **1959** [see REDNECK 1 a].

'tarhood. *nonce-wd.* [f. TAR *sb.*[1] 3 + -HOOD.] The general body of sailors; sailors collectively.

1749 H. WALPOLE *Lett.* (1846) II. 264 This circumstance ..has been so ridiculed by the whole tar-hood, that the romantic part has been forced to be cancelled.

tarie, obs. f. TARRY *sb.* and *v.*, var. TARY *v.*

tarier, obs. form of TARRIER[1].

tariff ('tærɪf), *sb.* Forms: 6–8 **tariffa,** 7 **terrif,** 8 **terif,** 8–9 **tarif,** 7– **tariff.** [a. It. *tariffa* 'arithmetike or casting of accounts' (Florio), 'a book of rates for duties' (Baretti), = Sp., Pg. *tarifa*, ad. Arab. *taʿrīf* notification, explanation, definition, article, f. *ʿarafa* in 1st conj. to notify, make known. So F. *tarif.*

The word came into general use as a technical term (sense 2), and this character it long retained in English use, being hardly found, except as applied to the Customs 'tariff'; its more general application (sense 3), found earlier on the Continent and in U.S., has become more common in Great Britain only since *c* 1890.]

†**1.** An arithmetical table or statement; a table of multiplication, a ready reckoner, or the like.

1591 *Garrard's Art Warre* 224 So that helping your memorie with certain *Tablei* or *Tariffas* made of purpose to know the numbers of the souldiers that are to enter into ranke. **1704** J. HARRIS *Lex. Techn.* I, *Tarif*, (in *Arithmetick*) is either a small Table..to expedite Multiplication; or else a Proportional Table contrived for the expediting a Question in the Rule of Fellowship. **1726** COLSON in *Phil. Trans.* XXXIV. 170 Reduce the Dividend and Divisor to small Figures, and form a Tariffa or Table of all the Multiples of the Divisor as far as 5. **1727** BAILEY vol. II, *Tariff* (with Arithmeticians) a proportional Table contrived for the speedy resolving Questions in the Rule of Fellowship;.. Also a Table framed to shew..any Multiple or Divisor, taken any Number of Times under ten. **1770** *Monthly Rev.* 507 That a tariff or table may be established of these proportions.

2. An official list or schedule setting forth the several customs duties to be imposed on imports and exports; a table or book of rates; any item of such a list, the impost (on any article); also the whole body or system of such duties as established in any country.

1592 WOTTON *Lett., to Ld. Zouche* 3 Oct. (1907) I. 288 The book that I put to be copied for your Honour is not yet ended, nor the *tariffa* of all the towns in the Grand Duke's territories, in my hands. *a* **1700** B. E. *Dict. Cant. Crew*, *Tariff*, a Book of Rates or Customs. **1713** *Treaty Utrecht* in Magens *Insurances* (1755) II. 495 The general Tariff made in France the 18th Day of September in the Year 1664, shall take place again. *a* **1719** ADDISON (J.), A tariff, or declaration of the duties of import and export. **1725** *Lond. Gaz.* No. 6414/2 The putting..into Execution the new Tarif or Book of Rates. **1816** (Feb. 12) SEC. DALLAS in *Ann. Congress* (1854) 1674 A statement of the general principles for reforming the tariff of the United States. **1845** MCCULLOCH *Taxation* II. v. (1852) 238 The duties in this tariff mostly vary from 40 to 5 per cent. *ad valorem.* **1868** M. E. G. DUFF *Pol. Surv.* 25 The kingdom's wealth might be economized by the adoption of a free-trade tariff. **1879** ROGERS in *Cassell's Techn. Educ.* IV. 128/2 A tariff..of a highly protective character, in the interest of employers or manufacturers.

3. A classified list or scale of charges made in any private or public business; as, a hotel tariff, a railroad tariff (*U.S.*).

a **1751** BOLINGBROKE *Fragments* xxx. Wks. 1754 V. 246 Even in times less antient, the church of Rome found it necessary to publish a tariff, or book of rates, which I have seen in print, wherein the price is set over against every sin, lest purchasers should be imposed upon. **1837–9** HALLAM *Hist. Lit.* I. iii. §147 The university of Paris proceeded to establish a tariff, according to which every edition was to be sold. **1838** *Murray's Hand-bk. N. Germ.* 428 Tariff per post of 2 German miles. **1867** HOWELLS *Ital. Journ.* 204 Show me the tariff of fares. **1881** *Chicago Times* 12 Mar., The following is the present railroad tariff on flour, grain, and boxed meats from Chicago to the eastern points named.

4. *attrib.* and *Comb.*; **a.** attrib., as ***tariff-act, -bill, -duty, -legislation, -monger, -movement, -office, -party, -preference, -question, -treaty, war***; **b.** instrumental, as ***tariff born, -bound, -fed, -protected, -raised, -ridden*** adjs.; **c.** objective and obj. gen., as ***tariff adjustment, -maker; tariff-cutting, -mongering, -raising, -regulating, -tinkering*** adjs. **d.** Special comb., **tariff wall,** a national trade barrier in the form of a tariff; hence **tariff-walled** *a.* See also TARIFF-REFORM.

1816 *Ann. Congress* (1854) 1137 The provisions of the proposed new tariff duties. **1821** J. Q. ADAMS *Mem.* (1875) V. 309 The revival at the next session of Congress of Mr. Baldwin's tariff bills. **1824** *Ibid.* VI. 282 There had been sharp words in the tariff debate this day in the House. **1831** *Ibid.* (1876) VIII. 438 The Free-Trade and Tariff Conventions. **1832** PRES. JACKSON *Message Congr. U.S.*, A mistaken view of the considerations which led to the adoption of the tariff system. *c* **1843** GLADSTONE in Morley *Life* (1903) I. II. viii. 267 Endeavouring to make tariff treaties with foreign countries. **1862** *Macm. Mag.* Sept. 413 Stories about tariff grievances. **1884** S. E. DAWSON *Handbk. Dom. Canada* 288 As promoters of private legislation, or as tariff-doctors, or as volunteer advisers, interested or disinterested. **1889** *Puck* (U.S.) XXV. 248 (*heading*) High tariff-wall. **1891** *Century Dict.*, *Tariff-ridden*, burdened with a tariff or tariffs; carrying an excessive burden of indirect taxation. **1897** *Daily News* 21 Sept. 2/3 American tariff-tinkering. **1898** *Ibid.* 8 Aug. 8/2 A little tariff-card [of a hotel] enclosed showed that the sum stated was liable to some little expansion. **1900** *Jrnl. Sch. Geog.* (U.S.) Apr. 147 There have been twenty-five tariff acts prescribing, modifying or regulating tariff duties, the first being the Calhoun Act, 1816. **1904** *Daily News* 3 Mar. 8 A warning against tariff-mongers, tariff-meddlers, and tariff-muddlers of all denominations. **1904** J. DENNEY *Let.* 4 Aug. (1920) 50 We..have nothing to offer..like a Free Trade Government dealing with tariff-walled nations. **1904** JUDGE PARKER (U.S.) in *Daily Chron.* 11 Nov. 5/5 To prevent the tariff-fed Trusts and illegal combinations from absorbing the nation's wealth. **1909** H. W. V. TEMPERLEY in *Cambr. Mod. Hist.* VI. ii. 49 The tariff-war was often the precursor of the trade-war. **1932** *Sun* (Baltimore) 17 Sept. 8/3 The proposed policy is variously known as a bargaining or trade-building policy of tariff adjustment. **1934** A. HUXLEY *Beyond Mexique Bay* 85 Symptoms, such as tariff-wars and armaments. **1935** E. WINGFIELD-STRATFORD *Harvest of Victory* I. ii. 19 The combined handicaps of tariff-walled markets, ruined customers, slackening demand for..coal, [etc.]. **1962** *Daily Tel.* 16 Jan. 20/4 The agreement nearing completion in Brussels on a tariff-cutting agreement with the Common Market is satisfactory on the whole. **1964** *Ann. Reg. 1963* 70 Feelings were ruffled by..the Secretary of Commerce's denunciation of a Canadian tariff-adjustment scheme. **1973** *Times* 3 Jan. (Forward into Europe Suppl.) p. xi/2 The tariff walls begin to crumble. **1977** *Whitaker's Almanack 1978* 978 The CET is based on the arithmetical average of those national tariffs it replaced, and after two international tariff-cutting rounds now stands at an average of 6 per cent.

Hence (chiefly *nonce-wds.*) **'tariffable** *a.*, that can be subjected to a tariff; **tari'ffade** [after *crusade*], an agitation in favour of a tariff; **ˌtariffi'cation,** (*a*) the fixing of a tariff; (*b*) conversion to a pro-tariff party; **'tariffism,** the principle or system of imposing a tariff, advocacy of a (high or low) tariff; **'tariffist,** an advocate of a tariff; **'tariffite,** = prec.; also *attrib.*; **'tariffize** *v.*, *trans.* to subject to a tariff or system of tariffs (in quot. in sense 3); **'tariffless** *a.*, without a tariff.

1895 *Funk's Stand. Dict.*, **Tariffable*, subjectable to a tariff. **1904** P. GEDDES in *Ideals Sc. & Faith* 201 To play his patriotic part in the approaching, ever-victorious *Tariffades by which the megalopolitan wealth and imperial greatness are to be assured. **1892** *19th Cent.* Dec. 940 Sir B. Samuelson's proposal to make compulsory the method of *tariffication..which has been optional with railway companies for forty years past. **1908** *Westm. Gaz.* 29 May 2/3 The complete tariffication of the Unionist Party. **1903** *Daily Chron.* 25 Sept. 4/5 The chief apostle of high *tariffism. **1901** *Westm. Gaz.* 3 Apr. 2/3 Taking the two bodies together the Low *Tariffists are in a majority of one. **1905** *Daily Chron.* 8 Sept. 4/4 The tariffists and purblind economists see the chief reason of Germany's industrial prosperity in its protective system. **1830** *Western Monthly Rev.* III. 376 She is a true *tariffite, a hearty and staunch advocate for the genuine American system. **1906** *Daily Chron.* 12 Jan. 5/2 This has excited great indignation on the part of the Tariffite candidate. **1848** *Tait's Mag.* XV. 319 This would *tariffize the world. **1891** MISS DOWIE *Girl in Karp.* 271 A total stranger condescended to..make a *tariffless hotel of their house.

'tariff, *v.* [f. prec. sb. So F. *tarifer.*]

†**1.** *intr.* To have to do with a tariff. *nonce-use.*

1756 MRS. CALDERWOOD *Jrnl.* (1884) 292 A tariff of fixed duties [was] to have been settled at the treaty of Utrecht, but ..was referred to commissaries; of this number was Blair's uncle, John Drummond, who tariffed all his days... Andrew Mitchell..who tariffed at Bruxells for some years.

2. *trans.* To subject to a tariff-duty; to fix the price of (something) according to a tariff; in quot. *a* 1868, to rate (a person) according to a tariff.

1828 WEBSTER, *Tarif* v.t. to make a list of duties on goods. **1864** TREVELYAN *Compet. Wallah* (1866) 169 If the Sidonians..had paid five per cent. on Madapollams tariffed at nine-pence. *a* **1868** M. J. HIGGINS *Ess.* (1875) 158 A slow sulky conductor he silently endures, and tariffs him accurately on reaching the end of the stage. **1870** *Daily News* 6 Oct., If the siege lasts long enough, dogs, rats, and cats will be tariffed. **1887** *Westm. Rev.* June 362 In 1583 the best Gascony wine was tariffed in London..at £13 the tun. **1904** MRS. DAUNCEY *Englishw. Philippines* vi. (1906) 49 For these schools and..schoolmasters this pastoral country [the Philippines] is taxed and tariffed to breaking point.

3. To make into a pro-tariff party. *nonce-use.*

1909 *Westm. Gaz.* 2 Mar. 2/2 The way in which the Tory Party has been tariffed.

Hence **tariffed** ('tærɪft) *ppl. a.*, priced by or subjected to a tariff.

1874 SYMONDS *Sk. Italy & Greece* (1898) I. xiv. 299 The pay is reduced to its tariffed medium. **1903** *Westm. Gaz.* 17 Aug. 2/1 The ingenious device of buying highly tariffed foreign coffee and sending it to Cape Colony, whence it was reshipped as preferred East Indian coffee.

'tariff-re'form. *gen.* The reform of a tariff, or of existing tariff conditions; *spec.* (*Hist.*) in U.S. politics, 'a reform favouring a general reduction of import duties, and in general a movement away from Protection' (*Cent. Dict.* 1891); in early-20th c. British politics (usually with capitals, *Tariff Reform*), the extension of the tariff on imports, as opposed to 'Free Trade'. Also *attrib.*, as ***Tariff Reform League, movement, party, policy,*** etc.

1859 R. COBDEN *Let.* 8 Nov. in F. A. Wellesley *Paris Embassy during Second Empire* (1928) ix. 193 There is no Imperial road to tariff reform, and if he [*sc.* Napoleon III] goes to work à la Villafranca, he will find himself in a supplement of vexations and troubles. **1891** in *Cent. Dict.* **1895** *Funk's Stand. Dict.*, *Tariff-reform*,..applied in the United States to a movement away from the policy of protection. **1903** MORLEY *Gladstone* I. II. viii. 264 It was by the principles of free trade that Peel and his lieutenant justified tariff-reform. **1903** J. CHAMBERLAIN *Sp.* Introd. 8 They [speeches] have..been..supplemented by statistics and details..which it is the function of the Tariff Reform League and the Imperial Tariff Committee to supply in their publications. **1908** E. E. WILLIAMS in *Westm. Gaz.* 20 Feb. 2/3 [Formed May 14, 1903 as the Protection League] A fortnight later it changed the name to the Tariff League, and again a fortnight later to that of the Imperial Tariff League ..[after] some six or seven weeks it was formally amalgamated with an inchoate body (comprising chiefly members of Parliament in sympathy with the new movement) under the title of the Tariff Reform League. **1908** *Westm. Gaz.* 24 Aug. 2/2 If [Mr. Bryan's] declaration means anything, it is a notable advance in what Americans call 'Tariff Reform'—i.e., a change of the Tariff in the direction of Free Trade.

Hence **tariff-reformer,** an advocate or supporter of tariff-reform; in British politics from 1903, an advocate of an extended tariff on imports.

1903 J. CHAMBERLAIN *Sp.* Introd. 9 The Tariff Reformers ..believe that..by re-arming ourselves with the weapon of a moderate tariff, we may still defend our home market against unfair competition.

tariment: see TARRYMENT.

taring ('tɛərɪŋ). [f. TARE *sb.*[2] and *v.* + -ING[1].] The calculation and abatement of the tare on goods; †abatement for defective goods (*obs.*).

1622 MISSELDEN *Free Trade* ii. 51 To haue drawne the Taring [*margin*, That is, abating for the faults thereof] of Cloth into Holland, where the Buyers are in some sort, Iudges and Parties. **1882** BITHELL *Counting-ho. Dict.*, *Taring*, is the process of calculating and making the Tare. **1883** *Times* 2 Apr. 4 The planter..can..put a stop to..the taring of the chest of tea by the Customs.

taris, obs. form of TERRACE.

'tarish, *a. rare.* [f. TARE *sb.*[1] + -ISH[1].] Having the nature or character of tares (in allusion to the parable of the tares: see TARE *sb.*[1] 3).

1601 BP. W. BARLOW *Defence* Pref. 6 Pregnant natures, are like lustie groundes,..neglected and vntilled, [prove] tarish and weedy. **1610** J. ROBINSON *Justif. Separat.* iii. § 6 Wks. 1851 II. 125 A singular spirit of..discerning, by which they do discover..this tarish disposition under the veil of holiness.

tarisum: see TARRYSOME.

‖**tarkashi** (tɑːˈkæʃiː). Also **tar-kashi.** [Hindi *tār-kaśī*, lit. 'wire-drawing'.] The Indian craft of inlaying wood with brass wire; the artefacts so produced.

1878 G. C. M. BIRDWOOD *Handbk. Brit. Indian Section* (Paris Universal Exhibition) 79 In Mynpuri work,..we find ..wood inlaid with brass wire in various geometrical.. patterns... At Mynpuri,..it goes by the name of *tarkashi*, or 'wire work'; a word which suggests the possible etymology of the word *tarsia*. **1910** E. R. NEAVE *mainpuri: Gazetter* 73 Mainpuri has long been noted for its beautiful wood work inlaid with brass wire, known as *tarkashi* (lit. wire-drawing). The best dark *shisham* is the only wood employed... There are about twenty artisans in the town engaged in the trade. **1979** *Inside-Outside* (Bombay) June–July 51 That was 1963, which you could say was the year that *tarkashi* arrived—in its new incarnation. *Ibid.* 54 The raw material of *tarkashi* used to be brass sheet.

tarlatan ('tɑːlətən). Also 8 **tarnatan,** 9 **tarlatane, tarleton.** [a. F. *tarlatane*, dissimilated from *tarnatane* (1723 in Hatz.-Darm.: cf. quot. 1727–41); prob. of Indian origin.] A kind of thin open muslin, used esp. for ball-dresses. Freq. *attrib.* Also *absol.*, to designate a dress made of this fabric.

1727–41 CHAMBERS *Cycl.* s.v. *Muslin*, There are various kinds of muslins brought from the East-Indies; chiefly Bengal; betelles, tarnatans, mulmuls [etc.]. **1844** *Lexington* (Kentucky) *Observer* 25 Sept. 1/6 Tarlatan Muslin..will be sold. **1849** *Trelawny* (Jamaica) 24 Apr. 1/2 Rich colored gingham, and tarleton plaid. **1852** MRS. STOWE *Uncle Tom's Cabin* I. xviii. 309, I was just dying to know whether you would appear in your pink tarletane. **1853** LOWELL *Lett.* (1894) I. iii. 219 The cheapening of a tarlatan muslin. **1858** SIMMONDS *Dict. Trade*, *Tarlatan*, a kind of book-muslin principally made in Scotland. **1873** MISS WOOLSEY *What Katy Did at Sch.* x. 166 Cecy has got some beautiful new dresses,—a white muslin, a tarlatan, and a pink silk. **1873** *Young Englishwoman* Jan. 51/3 Does she never go to a ball or dance, and require the extra dress in the shape of a white tarlatan or something of that sort? **1903** *Daily Chron.* 3 Oct. 8/4 Tarlatan is another old-world material now being resuscitated for evening dresses. **1936** M. MITCHELL *Gone with Wind* 175 Maybelle Merriwether went toward the next booth..in an apple-green tarlatan so wide that it reduced her waist to nothingness. **1936** N. STREATFEILD *Ballet Shoes* iv. 50 When you start on Monday you're having rompers, two each, black-patent ankle-strap shoes, and white tarlatan dresses, two each, with white sandal shoes. **1975** *New Yorker* 29 Dec. 23/3 Sleptsov also found..a tarlatan bag on a collapsible hoop (and the muslin still smelled of summer and sun-hot grass).

†**'tar,leather**[1]. *Sc. Obs.* Also 6 -ledder, 7 -ladder. [app. a. Gael. *tarr-leathar* belly-leather, f. *tarr* belly + *leathar*, ad. Eng. LEATHER.] 'A strip of raw sheep-skin (cut from the belly of the skin when it was newly flayed), salted and dried, and cut up into thongs for ties or mid-couples of flails' (*Suppl.* to Jamieson, 1887).

1566 *Burgh Rec. Edinb.* (1875) III. 226 The saidis flescheouris..cuttis ane tarledder of the skyn thairwith, diminisching thairby bayth the skynnis and the woll in lenth and breid. *Ibid.*, Nor yit to diminische the samyn be cutting of ony sic pairt as thai call the tarledder. *a* **1585** POLWART *Flyting w. Montgomerie* 571 His shaven shoulders shawes the marks, no dout, Of teugh tarladders, tyres, and other tawes.

Hence †**tarleathered** (**-letherit**, etc.) *ppl. a.*, *Sc. Obs.*, applied to a sheep-skin from which a tarleather has been cut.

1570 *Rec. Convent. Roy. Burghs* I. 21 [To] be presentitt.. with the skyn and byrn vn tarletheritt, and plukkitt or powitt. **1585** *Burgh Rec. Edinb.* (1882) IV. 407 That na merchants tak vpoun hand to by any skynns quhilk ar plukket and tarletherit as said is, vnder the pain foresaid.

†**tarleather**[2]. *Obs. rare*[−1]. A term of opprobrium applied to a woman.

1575 *Gamm. Gurton* III. iii. C iij b, Comst behynd me thou withered witch; & I get once on foote, Thouse pay for all, y^u old tarlether.

†**'Tarltonize,** *v. Obs. nonce-wd. intr.* To act or speak like Tarlton, a celebrated comic actor of the latter part of the 16th century.

1592 G. HARVEY *Four Lett.* Wks. (Grosart) I. 168 His vaine-glorious and Thrasonicall brauinge: his piperly Extemporizing, and Tarletonizing. *Ibid.* 202 The very Timpanye of his Tarltonizing wit.

'Tarmac, *sb.* [Abbrev. f. TAR MACADAM.] The registered trade-mark of a kind of tar macadam consisting of iron slag impregnated with tar and creosote; also designating a surface made of tar macadam. Now freq. with small initial. ***the tarmac*** (colloq.), the airfield or runway.

1903 *Trades Mark Jrnl.* 1 July, Class 17. Tarmac. **1904** *Westm. Gaz.* 13 Dec. 4/2 Mr. Montagu suggested..the making of all roads..by the Tarmac process. **1905** *Chambers's Jrnl.* 14 Jan. 110/2 The road surveyor..appears to have almost solved the problem of finding a dustless, a rainproof, and a cheap material by the employment of an iron-slag mixed with tar. This material he calls tarmac. **1905** *Times* 1 Aug. 14/2 He suggests that the club..should entirely remake some..stretch of road near London with Tarmac. **1919** C. ROBERTS *Training Airmen* v. 37 An open, wind-swept place... A broad strip of tarmac on which various aeroplanes are receiving the solicitous attention... That is the sight which quickens the cadet's pulse. **1921** *Flight* 11 Aug. 544/2 Aerodrome improvements..are now being carried out on the tarmac. Work has been commenced on the laying of a tarmac road from the sheds to the Customs enclosure. **1931** *Observer* 10 May 5 The lanes that he once used to choose have now been straightened out into fine, noble tarmac highways. **1948** 'N. SHUTE' *No Highway* iv. 109 Samuelson met them on the tarmac. **1970** *Drum* (E. Afr. ed.) Feb. 31/3 One travels on tarmac the whole way to the Kenya border on some of the finest road surfaces on the continent. **1976** *Sunday Telegraph* (Colour Suppl.) 28 Nov. 57/2 A speed establishd with the car on dry Tarmac. **1979** J. RABAN *Arabia through Looking Glass* iii. 67 People in gold-trimmed robes stepped off aeroplanes and were embraced by similarly robed officials who stood in waiting on the tarmac.

'tarmac, *v.* [f. the sb.] To cover with tar macadam. Chiefly *pass.* or as *ppl. a.*, with spelling ***tarmac(c)ed, tarmacked.*** Hence **'tarmacing** *vbl. sb.* Cf. TARMACADAM *v.*

1966 C. WILSON *Glass Cage* II. 90 It was a row of small, semi-detached modern houses with front gardens, and the road had not yet been fully tarmacced. **1972** 'R. GORDON' *Doctor on Brain* xiv. 97 All that lies before me is a well-tarmacked dead straight motorway leading to the grave. **1974** *New Society* 14 Mar. 627/3 Ponds which are filled in and reclaimed by farmers, or tarmacked for car parking by the local pub. **1975** *Ibid.* 18 Dec. 663/3 The aesthetic and environmental objections to the tarmacing of 15 odd acres of land. **1977** *Belfast Tel.* 28 Feb. 13/1 (Advt.), Now's the time to have your driveways Bitmaced or Tarmaced. **1981** E. NORTH *Dames* vii. 129 The tarmacked runway.

,tarma'cadam. Also **tar macadam.** [f. TAR *sb.*[1] + MACADAM *sb.*] A mixed material for making roads, consisting of some kind of broken stone or ironstone slag in a matrix of tar alone, or of tar with some mixture of pitch or creosote.

1882 (June 17) *Proc. Assoc. Municipal Engineers* VIII. 91 In Barnsley we have tarred macadam, and the cost of it was 1*s.* 2*d.* *Ibid.* 92, I should have liked to have heard more about the cost of the tar-macadam roads. **1883** (Sept. 28) *Ibid.* X. 53 Tar macadam for roadways was first introduced in Sheffield. **1909** J. W. SMITH *Dustless Roads* i. 10 The macadamised road construction of the future is to be found in the use of tar: that is to say, in what is termed tar macadam. **1959** *Chambers's Encycl.* XI. 724/2 A modification of the tarred macadam road is that known as 'tarmacadam', in which all the pieces of road metal are coated with tar before being spread on the road and rolled. **1965** P. WAYRE *Wind in Reeds* xvi. 229 Concrete or tarmacadam paths..were out as far as we were concerned. **1980** *West Lancs. Even. Gaz.* 6 Mar. 17 (Advt.), Tarmacadam—concrete and flagging.

Hence **tarma'cadam** *v.* (in quots. as *pa. pple.* and *ppl. a.*). Also *attrib.* Hence Cf. TARMAC *v.*

1910 *Times* 23 July 8/6 The tar-macadamed Madeira-road ..proved them to have been pioneers in this matter. **1976** *Glasgow Herald* 26 Nov. 2/7 (Advt.), Driveways excavated, slabbed, tarmacadamed, trees pruned and lopped. **1978** *Morecambe Guardian* 14 Mar. 22/1 (Advt.), Partly tarmacadamed playground.

tarmac(c)ed, tarmacked: see TARMAC *v.*

tarmachan, -michen, obs. ff. PTARMIGAN.

tarmagon, tarmegant, obs. ff. TERMAGANT.

tarmaret, -rick, obs. erron. ff. TURMERIC.

tarn (tɑːn). Forms: 4–5 terne, 5–6 tarne, 7 tearn, (8 *Sc.* tairn), 7– tarn. [ME. *terne*, a. ON. **tarnu, tjorn, tjörn*; = Swed. dial. *tjärn, tärn*, Norw. *tjörn*, Da. *tjern.*]

A small mountain lake, having no significant tributaries. (Originally local northern English, now generally used by geologists and geographers.)

[**1256** *Assize Roll* 979 m. 10 d (Westmorland), Agnes.. appellat..Edelinam filiam Ricardi de Blaterne [= Blea-tarn] quod ipsa dederat ei potum mortiferum bibere.] **13..** *E.E. Allit. P.* B. 1041 Þer ar tres by þat terne of traytoures. *c* **1420** *Avow. Arth.* x, Gauan, with any more, To the tarne con he fore, To wake hit to day. **14..** (*heading*) The Awntyrs off Arthure at the Terne Wathelyne. **1587** HARRISON *England* I. xv. in Holinshed I. 95/1 The Air or Arre riseth out of a lake or tarne south of Darnbrooke. **1674** RAY *N.C. Words*, A *Tarn*, a Lake or Meer-pool, a usual word in the North. **1797** COLERIDGE *Christabel* I. Concl. 28 By tairn and rill, The night-birds all that hour were still. **1810** WORDSW. *Scenery Lakes* i. (1823) 24 Tarns are found in some of the vales, and are numerous upon the mountains. **1813** SCOTT *Trierm.* I. x, Though never sun-beam could discern The surface of that sable tarn, In whose black mirror you may spy The stars, while noon-tide lights the sky. **1880** HAUGHTON *Phys. Geog.* v. 235 The largest river in the world takes its most remote origin among the Andean Highlands, in a little inky tarn.

b. *attrib.* and *Comb.*

1873 M. COLLINS *Miranda* II. 83 Miranda, whose aureate hair and tarn-brown eyes had something unique about them. **1884** SWINBURNE *W. Collins* Misc. (1886) 59 A picture of upland fell and tarnside copse in the curving hollow of a moor. **1886** BURTON *Arab. Nts.* (abr. ed.) I. 72 The sorceress took in hand some of the tarn-water. **1903** *Smart Set* IX. 133/2 Hers is one of those clear, tarnlike natures which one gauges quickly.

tarn, obs. and dial. form of TERN, the sea-bird.

tarnal ('tɑːnəl), *a.* (*adv.*) *slang*, chiefly *U.S.* Aphetic dial. pronunciation of *eternal*, vulgarly used as an expression of execration, passing into a mere intensive: cf. ETERNAL *a.* 7. Hence **'tarnally** *adv.*

1790 R. TYLER *Contrast* II. ii. (1887) 39 The snarl-headed curs fell a-kicking and cursing of me at such a tarnal rate, that..I was glad to take to my heels. *Ibid.* 90 Laugh by rule! Well, I should like that tarnally. *a* **1821** [J. W. MASTERS] *Dick & Sal* lxii. (E.D.D.), Dare was a tarnal sight of meat. *a* **1828** J. BERNARD *Retrospections Amer.* (1887) x. 241 May I be 'tarnally starved down for mutton broth, if [etc.]. **1828** *Craven Gloss.*, *Tarnal*, eternal. **1848** LOWELL *Biglow P.* II. 72, I darsn't skeer the tarnal thing fer fear he'd run away with 't. **1922** JOYCE *Ulysses* 419 Tarnally dog gone my shins if this beent the bestest puttiest longbreakyet.

tarnatan, variant of TARLATAN.

tarnation (tɑː'neɪʃən), *sb.*, *a.*, *adv. slang*, chiefly *U.S.* A variant of *darnation*, DAMNATION *sb.* 3; app. associated with TARNAL.

A. as *sb.*

1790 R. TYLER *Contrast* v. i. 68 Tarnation! That's no laughing matter though. **1801** COL. G. HANGER *Life* II. 151 The Americans say, Tarnation seize me, or swamp me, if I don't do this or that. **1830** W. CARLETON *Traits Irish Peasantry* I. 49 Tare-nation to the rap itself's in my company. **1832** *New England Mag.* (Boston) III. 380 We have 'Tarnation' and 'darnation' for damnation. **1922** JOYCE *Ulysses* 183 Wall, tarnation strike me! **1938** M. K. RAWLINGS *Yearling* v. 49 Git away, you blasted bacon-thieves!.. Git to tarnation! **1983** C. MACLEOD *Bilbao Looking-Glass* xix. 175 Tarnation! Here comes another o' them mobile camera units.

B. as *adj.* Damned, damnable, execrable.

1784 W. WILSON in *Mem.* (1896) 47 They only came to look at the 'tarnation Tories' from Canada. **1835–40** HALIBURTON *Clockm.* (1862) 54 Now, says he, I'm in a tarnation hurry. **1857** MRS. CARLYLE *Lett.* (1883) II. 329 After having been all but asphyxiated with tarnation folly.

C. as *adv.* Damnably, desperately, execrably.

1790 R. TYLER *Contrast* v. i. (1887) 88 What the rattle makes you look so tarnation glum? **1830** GALT *Lawrie T.* II. i, Which is tarnation bad. **1890** GUNTER *Miss Nobody* vi, People..don't call me 'my *good* man', for they know I'm a tarnation *bad* one when I'm riled, sonny!

'tarn-cap. *rare.* [ad. Ger. *tarnkappe.*] A magic cap, securing the invisibility of the wearer.

1856 R. A. VAUGHAN *Mystics* (1860) I. 3 Rings of Gyges, coats of darkness, tarn-caps, and other means of invisibility. **1863** C. M. YONGE *Hist. Christian Names* II. 312 Siegfried, by means of his tarn cap, invisibly vanquished the Valkyr.

tarne, var. THERNE, *Obs.*, girl.

'tarnhelm. Also **Tarn-helm, tarn-helm.** [Ger.; cf. TARN-CAP and DERN *a.*] In Wagner's opera *Der Ring des Nibelungen*, a magic helmet which either secures the invisibility of the wearer or enables him to change his appearance at will; = TARN-CAP. Also *fig.* Hence **'tarn-helmed** *a.*

1877 A. FORMAN tr. *Wagner's Nibelung's Ring: Rhinegold* 45 (*stage direction*) He puts the..'Tarn-helm' on his head... His figure disappears; in his place a pillar of cloud is seen. *Ibid.* 57 (*stage direction*) He puts the tarn-helm on again... He disappears; the gods perceive..a toad creeping towards them. **1896** G. B. SHAW in *Star* 22 July 1/7 The magical strangeness of the wishing cap or 'tarnhelm'. *a* **1930** D. H. LAWRENCE *Sex, Literature & Censorship* (1955) 84 It is something in her *will*. It is her tarnhelm. **1971** *Daily Tel.* 4 Oct. 13/3 The fateful ring is grabbed by the tarnhelmed Siegfried.

tarnish ('tɑːnɪʃ), *sb.* [f. TARNISH *v.*] The fact of tarnishing or condition of being tarnished; loss of brightness, discoloration; stain, blemish; also *concr.* the substance of such discoloration; the tarnished coating. Also *fig.*

1713 *Gentl. Instr.* II. ix. (ed. 5) 182 Care is taken to wash over the Foulness of the Subject with a pleasing Tarnish. **1738** *Gentl. Mag.* VIII. 580/2 The same Thing again is to be said of Tarnish, Discolouring, &c. from Time, the Air, &c. **1865** DICKENS *Mut. Fr.* II. xiii, Effacing the old rust and tarnish on the money. **1877** DANA *Text-bk. Min.* II. (1891) 190 A surface possesses the steel tarnish, when it presents the superficial blue color of tempered steel. **1878** HUXLEY *Physiogr.* 75 There are many metals, such as gold, which never exhibit rust or tarnish.

tarnish ('tɑːnɪʃ), *v.* [ad. F. *terniss-*, extended stem of *ternir, ternissant* (15th c. in Godef.) (see -ISH[2]), f. *terne* adj. dull, dark; of doubtful origin.

Referred by Diez and others to OHG. *tarnan*, MHG. *ternen* (= OS. *dernjan*, OE. *diernan*) to conceal, hide, f. OHG. *tarni* (OS. *derni*, OE. *dierne, derne*) hidden, secret, obscure. But there are difficulties, arising from the late appearance of the Fr. word, as well as from the form and sense. The change from *tern-* to *tarn-* appears to have taken place in English; but no example of *ternish* has been found.]

1. *trans.* To dull or dim the lustre of, to discolour (as a metallic surface by oxidation, etc.); to cause to fade; to spoil, wither.

1598 FLORIO, *Ternire*, to tarnish, to darken any glasse with breathing vpon it [**1611** to tarnish or darken and mist-ouer, as burnished plate or glasse will be being breathed vpon]. **1709–10** ADDISON *Tatler* No. 121 ¶1 Her Clothes were very rich, but tarnished. **1726** *Adv. Capt. R. Boyle* (1768) 103 The Sun's tarnishing my Complexion. **1858** LARDNER *Hand-bk. Nat. Philos.*, etc. 367 Whatever tarnishes or roughens the surface of metal, increases its radiation.

b. *fig.* To take away from the purity of, cast a stain upon; to sully, taint; to bring disgrace upon.

1697 COLLIER *Ess.* II. *Value of Life* (1698) 31 Nothing that may..tarnish the Glory, and weaken the Example of the Suffering. **1786** W. THOMSON *Watson's Philip III* (1839) 355 Unwilling that his reputation should be tarnished. **1884** L. J. JENNINGS *Croker Papers* I. ii. 44 The naval glory of England was tarnished by the successes of the American naval force.

2. *intr.* To grow dull, dim, or discoloured; to fade, wither; *esp.* of metals, to lose external brightness or lustre.

1678 PHILLIPS (ed. 4) s.v., Any thing that is Gilded, is said to Tarnish, when it begins to lose its Luster [**1706** to grow dull, to lose its Gloss, Lustre, or Brightness]. **1696** TATE & BRADY *Ps.* cii. 27 And, like a Garment often worn Shall tarnish and decay. **1758** JOHNSON *Idler* No. 35 ¶9 The brass and pewter..are only laid up to tarnish again. **1878** HUXLEY *Physiogr.* 75 Many metals rapidly rust or tarnish when exposed to even the driest air.

b. *fig.* To become dull, dim, or sullied.

1681 DRYDEN *Abs. & Achit.* 249 Till thy fresh glories, which now shine so bright, Grow stale, and tarnish with our daily sight. **1789** MRS. PIOZZI *Journ. France* II. 102 Travellers who seek for images that never tarnish, and for truths that never can decay. **1810** *Splendid Follies* II. 95 The frailties of your nature predominated the glare of your riches,..from that hour they tarnished.

Hence **'tarnishing** *vbl. sb.* and *ppl. a.*; also **'tarnishable** *a.*, that may tarnish or be tarnished; **'tarnisher**, one who or that which tarnishes.

1858 SIMMONDS *Dict. Trade*, *Tarnishing*, a process of giving gold or silver a pale or dim cast, without either polish or burnish. **1864** WEBSTER, *Tarnisher.* **1885** *Proc. Roy. Soc.* 7 May 340 A means of rendering tarnishable metals and alloys less tarnishable. **1894** DU MAURIER *Trilby* II. 22 A tarnishing breath had swept over the reminiscent mirror of his mind.

tarnished ('tɑːnɪʃt), *ppl. a.* [f. prec. + -ED[1].] Having lost purity or lustre, faded; also *fig.* sullied, dishonoured.

1716 LADY M. W. MONTAGU *Let. to C'tess Bristol* 22 Aug., Like a poor town lady of pleasure..with tarnished silver-laced shoes. **1726–46** THOMSON *Winter* 182 The..forest.. sheds What of its tarnished honours yet remain. **1855** MACAULAY *Hist. Eng.* xxii. IV. 765 He had ceased to be called by the tarnished name of Monmouth.

tarnowitzite (ˈtɑːnəʊvɪtsaɪt). *Min.* [a. G. *tarnowitzit* (Breithaupt 1841): see def.] A variety of Aragonite containing about 4 per cent. of carbonate of lead, found at Tarnowitz in Silesia.

1866 BRANDE & COX *Dict. Sci.*, etc. II. 532/2. **1867** *Ibid.* III. 703/2. **1868** DANA *Min.* (ed. 5) 696 Tarnovicite.

taro (ˈtɑːrəʊ, ˈtærəʊ). Also 8 **tarrow**, 9 **tara, tarro.** [Native Polynesian name, found by Cook in the Sandwich Islands.] **a.** A food-plant, *Colocasia antiquorum*, N.O. *Araceæ*, cultivated in many varieties (*C. esculenta, macrorhiza*, etc.) in most tropical countries for its starchy root-stocks, or its succulent leaves or stems, which in a raw state are acrid, but lose their acridity by boiling.

1769 S. PARKINSON *Jrnl.* 1 Oct. in *Jrnl. Voy. South Seas* (1773) II. 97 Adjoining to their houses are plantations of Koomarra and Taro. **1779** COOK *Voy. Pacific* (1784) III. v. iv. 79 Each man carrying..bread-fruit, *taro*, and plantains in his hand. *Ibid.* vi. 106 These plantations consist of the tarrow or eddy root, and the sweet potatoe [etc.]. **1802** *Brookes' Gazetteer* (ed. 12) s.v. *Ranai*, It produces very few plantains and bread-fruit trees, but abounds in yams, sweet potatoes, and taro. **1894** *Dublin Rev.* Oct. 460 Yams and taros are cultivated.

b. *attrib.*, as ***taro-patch, -plain, -plant, -plantation, -root, -swamp.***

1814 W. BROWN *Hist. Propag. Chr. among Heathen* II. 400 A large piece of ground stocked with breadfruit, cocoa nuts, and tarro roots. **1846** LUNDIE *Mission. Life Samoa* xxii. 141 All are busy building houses and clearing for taro-patches. **1847** WHITTIER *Dan. Wheeler* 79 Amidst Owyhee's hills of blue And taro-plains of Tooboonai. **1894** *Daily News* 11 Sept. 6/1 Streams of water..fertilising thousands of taro plantations. **1894** B. THOMSON *S. Sea Yarns* 111 The taro swamp was hard and fissured.

taroc (ˈtærɒk). Also 7-9 **tarok, tarock.** [ad. It. **tarocco*, in pl. *tarocchi*, of unknown origin. Also Ger. *tarock*, F. *tarot*: see TAROT.]

a. = TAROT a. **b.** (also in *pl.*) = TAROT b.

a. 1611 FLORIO, *Tarocchi*, a kind of playing cardes called Tarocks or Terestriall triumphs

b. 1739 GRAY *Let. to R. West* in Mason *Mem.* (1807) I. 211 Play at Ombre and Taroc, a game with 72 cards all painted with suns, and moons, devils and monks. [**1816** SINGER *Hist. Cards* 236 The pack of cards with which *Tarocco* is played, consists of two parts; the first is fifty-six cards of the usual Italian suits, *Spade, Coppe, Bastoni*, and *Denari*... The other part consists of twenty-two cards,..twenty-one of these are called *Tarocchi*, and the twenty-second *Il Matto*, or the fool.] **1887** BEATTY-KINGSTON *Music & Manners* II. 318 Skilful players of écarté and tarok.

tarogato (ˈtarogato). Also **tárogató.** [a. Hungarian *tárogató*.] A Hungarian woodwind instrument with a conical bore, orig. a double-reeded instrument resembling a shawm, but in the 1880s reconstructed with a single reed and fitted with keys. (Now obsolescent in Hungary, and treated as a historical national instrument.)

1907 T. S. WOTTON *Dict. Mus. Terms* 195 *Tárogató*, an instrument which has been used in Paris and Brussels etc. to take the *cor anglais* part at the end of Scene 1 Act III *Tristan und Isolde*. **1935** *Swing Music* Mar. 18/2, I had schemes for original instruments—among them the harpsichord..and a Hungarian reed-instrument called a tárogató. **1965** *Listener* 24 June 940/3 The *tárogató*, resembling the clarinet, but essentially an oboe family instrument. **1974** *Encycl. Brit. Micropædia* IX. 828/3 *Tárogató*, single-reed wind instrument, widely played in the folk music of Romania and, especially, Hungary.

tarot (tɑːrəʊ). [F. *tarot* (also 16th c. *tarault, tarau*), ad. It. **tarocco* (pl. *tarocchi*): see TAROC.]

a. One of a set of playing-cards, first used in Italy in the 14th c. (Also used in fortune-telling.) Also *attrib.* **b.** *pl.* The game played with these.

The tarots, strictly speaking, are a series of 22 figured cards (21 of which are numbered), all being trumps, which are added to a set of 56 (in four suits), forming a pack of 78.

1598 G. DE LA MOTHE *French Alph.* (1639) 148 Will you play at Tables, at Dyce, at Tarots, and Chesse? **1872** W. SKEEN *Early Typogr.* 55 A single pack of 'tarots', admirably painted about 1415 by Marziano,..cost the enormous sum of 1500 golden crowns (about £625). **1888** *Chambers' Encycl.* II. 763/1 No Spanish *tarots* are known to exist. **1899** *Fortn. Rev.* Oct. 611 Piot..was..the first to collect 'Tarots', those valuable playing cards, which now fetch such a high price. **1900** *Pall Mall G.* 18 Aug. 2 (Cassell *Suppl.*) As fall the Tarot cards, so fell Each rose-page of the Oracle. **1928** D. BYRNE *Destiny Bay* vii. 319 An old woman crazed by gambling and tarot cards. **1957** L. DURRELL *Justine* III. 180 Justine..would sit cross-legged on the bed and begin to lay out the little pack of Tarot cards. **1972** *Time* 19 June 26/2 The Center also presents tarot-card readings. **1977** *Jrnl. Playing-Card Soc.* May 3 Some Milan card makers reached a high degree of technical and artistic quality, including specialisation in a particular type of Tarot pack, usually with a narrow format.

tarow, obs. f. TARROW *v. Sc.*, to tarry.

tarp (tɑːp). Orig. *U.S.* abbrev. of TARPAULIN *sb.*

1906 *Out West* Apr. 319 The men had unrolled their 'tarps' and spread their beds for the night on the ground in front of the little shack. **1919** W. H. DOWNING *Digger Dial.* 49 *Tarp*, a tarpaulin. **1941** *Times* (Weekly ed.) 15 Oct. 7/3 The gunner had taken the tarp off the seven-pounder forward and was adjusting the sights and oiling the gun. **1964** F. O'ROURKE *Mule for Marquesa* (1967) ii. 33 Saddles, blankets, pack cushions, sweat cloths, tarps, ropes. **1971** C. BONINGTON *Annapurna South Face* 249 Coated nylon tarps ..Plastic tarps. **1980** *Christian Sci. Monitor* (Midwestern ed.) 4 Dec. B 32/1 Caked with ice from the violent waves, the tarps were almost unmanageable.

‖**ˈtarpan.** *Zool.* [According to Pallas, *Zoogr. Rosso-Asiatica* 1831, called Tarpàn by the Kirghiz Tatars. (So F. *tarpan*, Littré 1874.)] The wild horse of Tartary: see quots.

1841 C. HAMILTON SMITH *Nat. Hist. Horses* 160 The Tahtar or even the Cossack nations..assert that they can distinguish a feral breed from the wild by many tokens; and ..denominate the real wild horse *Tarpan* and *Tarpani*. *Ibid.* 163 Real Tarpans are not larger than ordinary mules, their colour invariably tan, Isabella, or mouse. *Ibid.* 164 There is always a certain number of expelled Tarpan stallions among them [feral herds]. **1905** W. RIDGEWAY *Origin of Thoroughbred Horse* 34 It would appear that Prejvalsky's horse is nothing more than the Tarpan of the older writers. **1910** DR. P. CHALMERS MITCHELL *Let. to Editor*, I think it is clear that the name Tarpan belongs to a genuine wild horse, a true species, but that it has been subsequently applied to the progeny of escaped domestic horses.

†**tarpaulian,** *sb.* and *a.* *Obs.* Forms: 7 **tarpailian, -paulian, -pollian,** 8 **-polian, -pawlian.** [from next, after adjs. and sbs. in *-ian*.]

a. *sb.* = next, 2. **b.** *adj.* = next, 3 b.

a **1656** USSHER *Ann.* vi. (1658) 124 The number of horse-boyes, and foot-boyes, and of hangers-on, and the tarpailians in the corn-ships,..he thinks to be greater..than that of the souldiers came unto. *c* **1660** W. G. *Ode to Gresham College* in Weld *Hist. Roy. Soc.* (1848) I. 80 Every Tarpaulian shall then with ease Saile any ship to the Antipodes. **1673** HICKERINGILL *Greg. F. Greyb.* 140 Shall not your pilot, holla, whoop? And rowze Tarpollians that lye sleeping. **1719** D'URFEY *Pills* II. 60 Hear the noise of the Tarpawlian Boys; Port, Fort, Port.

tarpaulin (tɑːˈpɔːlɪn), *sb.* Forms: 7 **tarpaulling, tarr pawlin, tarrpawling, tarpolin, -paling, -palin, (-pallion),** 7-8 **-pawlin,** 7-9 **-pawling, -pauling,** 7- **tarpaulin.** [Generally thought to be f. TAR *sb.*[1] + PALL *sb.*[1] + -ING[1] 1 f, g (as in *netting, grating*, and cf. AWNING).

The blackness of tarred canvas may have suggested its likeness to a funeral pall; though, in the absence of any instance of *tar-pall*, this origin must remain conjectural.]

1. a. A covering or sheet of canvas coated or impregnated with tar so as to make it waterproof, used to spread over anything to protect it from wet. Also, without *a* or *pl.*, canvas so tarred; sometimes applied to other kinds of waterproof cloth.

1605 B. JONSON *Volpone* IV. i, On the one [wall] I strain me a fair tarpauling, and in that I stick my onions, cut in halves. *a* **1625** MANWAYRING *Nomencl. Naval.* (Harl. MS. 2301), *Tarpawling*, is a peece of Canvas that is tar'd all over to Lash upon a Deck or Grating to keepe the Raine from Soaking through. **1626** CAPT. SMITH *Accid. Yng. Seamen* 30 A trar-pawling [*sic*] or yawning. **1652** ASHMOLE *Theat. Chem. Brit.* Prol. 12 To Hang a Presence Chamber with Tarpalin, instead of Tapestry. **1719** DE FOE *Crusoe* I. 68, I made me a large Tent,..and cover'd the uppermost with a large Tarpaulin which I had sav'd among the Sails. **1800** COLQUHOUN *Comm. Thames* 639 Each Lighter is furnished with a Tarpaulin to protect the Cargo from damage. **1890** W. J. GORDON *Foundry* 150 In the days when the London and Birmingham Railway considered it so beneath their dignity to carry coals to London that they introduced tarpaulins for the purpose of hiding the vulgar freight of which they were ashamed.

b. A sailor's hat made of tarpaulin.

1841 in TOTTEN *Naval Text-Bk.* (Webster). **1845** S. JUDD *Margaret* II. xi, A burly fellow in a tarpauling and blue jacket. **1858** in SIMMONDS *Dict. Trade.*

2. a. *transf.* A nickname for a mariner or sailor, esp. a common sailor. Now *rare* or *arch.* (Cf. TARPAULIAN, TAR *sb.*[1] 3.)

1647 CLEVELAND *Char. Diurnal-maker* Wks. (1687) 82 He is a perfect Sea-man, a kind of Tarpawlin. **1660** HOWELL *Parly Beasts* 12 To be a Mariner, or Tarpaling, is one of the most servile and slavish condition of life that can be. **1687** SETTLE *Refl. Dryden* 21 He was too blame for making his Hametalhaz a Courtier and no Tarpolin. **1722** DE FOE *Col. Jack* i, Every tarpawling, if he gets but to be lieutenant of a press smack, is called captain. **1849** DICKENS *Dav. Copp.* xxi, What does this here blessed tarpaulin go and do? **1893** STEVENSON *Catriona* xxx. 366 The seamen pursued us... They were but bandy-legged tarpaulins after all. **1922** JOYCE *Ulysses* 610 Chews coca all day long, the communicative tarpaulin added. **1963** *Australasian Post* 14 Mar. 44/1 All the 'tarpaulins' had abandoned their lives of near slavery at sea and with fine wisdom had scattered inland.

b. Formerly applied to a sea-bred superior officer (captain, etc.) as contrasted with the military officers often appointed to command men-of-war. (Cf. 3 b.) In quot. 1909 erron. taken as = 'ranker'.

c **1690** R. GIBSON (B.M. Add. MS. 11602, lf. 40), Upon the Different Conduct between Seamen and Gentlemen Commanders in ye Navy (not bredd Tarr Pawlins) since 1652. **1855** MACAULAY *Hist. Eng.* xvi. III. 716 There was an end of privilege if an Earl was to be doomed to death by tarpaulins seated round a table in the cabin of a ship. **1894** C. N. ROBINSON *Brit. Fleet* 347 Drake and his brother tarpaulins. **1909** *Naval Warrant Officers' Jrnl.* Dec. 138/2 It would have been deeply interesting had Mr. Hannay *en passant* designated those Admirals and Captains who were called 'Tarpaulins' because of their ranker origin. *Ibid.*, Captain James Cook, the explorer, Captain C. Askew, and Captain J. Coglan are three of many names of 'Tarpaulins' which might be cited.

3. *attrib.* **a.** in sense 1: Made of tarpaulin.

1627 CAPT. SMITH *Seaman's Gram.* xiii. 61 A plug lapped in Okum, and well tarred in a tarpawling clout. **1688** in *Daniell's Catal. Autograph Lett.* (1904) July 30/2 Yesterday my Ld. Chancellour was taken at Wapping in a tarpalin habitt. **1832** C. M. GOODRIDGE *Voy. South Seas* 25 Carefully secured from the damp in a tarpawling bag. **1833** MARRYAT *P. Simple* xliii, There's many a clear head under a tarpaulin hat.

b. in sense 2 or 2 b: Of, belonging to, or that is, a mariner or sailor; sea-bred. Now *rare*.

1647 WARD *Simp. Cobler* 16 A shamefull sliding into other such tarpauling tenets. **1654** WHITLOCK *Zootomia* 221 A learned vote that any Tarpawlin Marriner might have nulled. *c* **1690** R. GIBSON (B.M. Add. MS. 11602, lf. 47), I finde many Accidents to have happened for want of Tarrpawling Commanders or Gentlemen throughly acquainted with Maritime Affaires. **1692** LUTTRELL *Brief Rel.* (1857) II. 354 Divers tarpawlin masters of ships recommended by the Trinity house, have passed examination in order to be received into the King's service. **1696** in *Ab. De la Pryme's Diary* (Surtees) 278 Chattam, a small tarpaulin town, joyning to Rochester. **1836** W. IRVING *Astoria* III. 222 John Young, the tarpawling governor of Owyhee. **1889** DOYLE *Micah Clarke* 23 He was one of the old tarpaulin breed, who had fought..against Frenchman, Don, Dutchman, and Moor.

4. *Comb.*, as ***tarpaulin-maker, -covered*** adj. **tarpaulin muster** [MUSTER *sb.*[1]], a collection or pooling of money among seamen; also *transf.* and *fig.*

1858 SIMMONDS *Dict. Trade*, *Tarpaulin-manufacturer*, one who oils or tars canvas for covers. **1889** in *Cent. Dict.* **1897** *Outing* (U.S.) XXX. 261/2 A tarpaulin-covered box of tackle belonging to Harry. **1904** E. S. EMERSON *Shanty Entertainment* 26 Each one in the room to sing, recite, or shout all round, and..a tarpaulin muster every half-hour for drinks, or smokes. **1907** *Daily Chron.* 25 Oct. 7/2 A young tarpaulin-maker of nineteen. **1907** J. MASEFIELD (*title*) A tarpaulin muster. **1920** P. L. WALDRON *Afloat & Ashore* vii. 83 The crew had a tarpaulin muster to have a last evening ashore. **1945** E. GEORGE *Two at Daly Waters* 102 As she had not brought a town outfit, Daly Waters had what we call in the bush a tarpaulin muster (the loan of everybody's best clothes). **1954** H. W. EDWARDS *Under Four Flags* xxiv. 125 With the generosity proverbial among sailors, they had a 'tarpaulin muster'.

Hence **tarˈpaulin** *v.*, *trans.* to cover with a tarpaulin; *intr.* to shelter oneself under a tarpaulin; **tarˈpaulined** *a.*, covered with a tarpaulin.

1882 'F. ANSTEY' *Vice Versâ* xvi, Some tarpaulined cattle-vans. **1891** CONST. MACEWEN *3 Women in 1 Boat* 85 We discussed whether we would 'tarpaulin' there for the night. **1894** *Outing* (U.S.) XXIV. 376/2 We had another boat, but it was housed and tarpaulined on deck.

Tarpeian (tɑːˈpiːən), *a.* [f. L. *Tarpei-us*, or ad. L. *Tarpeiān-us* adj., f. proper name *Tarpeius* or *Tarpeia*.] Denoting a rock-face on the Capitoline Hill at Rome over which persons convicted of treason to the state were thrown headlong. Also *Comb.*, as ***Tarpeian-fast*** adj. *poet.*

1607 SHAKS. *Cor.* III. i. 213 Beare him toth' Rock Tarpeian, and from thence Into destruction cast him. *Ibid.* III. iii. 88 Let them pronounce the steepe Tarpeian death. **1671** MILTON *P.R.* IV. 49. **1746** FRANCIS tr. *Hor. Sat.* I. vi. 51 From the Tarpeian rock's tremendous height, Or to the hangman Cadmus give their fate. **1843** MACAULAY *Horatius* xvi, Now, from the rock Tarpeian, Could the wan burghers spy The line of blazing villages. **1876** G. M. HOPKINS *Wreck of Deutschland* xxix, in *Poems* (1967) 61 The Simon Peter of a soul! to the blast Tarpeïan-fast, but a blown beacon of light.

tarpon (ˈtɑːpɒn). Forms: 7 **tarpom,** 8 **-oen,** 9 **-um,** 9 **tarpon.** [So Du. *tarpoen*: origin not ascertained.] The Jew-fish, *Megalops atlanticus*, a giant representative of the herring tribe found in the warmer waters of the western Atlantic: see JEW-FISH and ELOPS. Sometimes extended to the E. Indian species *M. cyprinoides* (*M. thrissoides*).

1685 L. WAFER *Voy.* (1729) 321 Of these they make nets for fishing, but only for great fish, as Tarpoms, or the like. **1699** DAMPIER *Voy.* II. II. 12 The Tarpom is a large scaly Fish, shaped much like a Salmon, but somewhat flatter.. with Scales as big as a Half Crown. **1796** STEDMAN *Surinam* II. 229 A large fish..called tarpoen..which is white, about 2 feet 6 inches. **1888** GOODE *Amer. Fishes* 406 The sailors' name for this fish,..is 'Tarpum' or 'Tarpon'. **1901** *Scotsman* 4 Oct. 5/1 The largest tarpon ever captured.. weighed 205 lb., and measured 8 ft. and 2 in. in length.

b. *attrib.* and *Comb.*

1887 *Sporting Life* 22 June 2/6 Tarpon fishing is not half so exciting as catching man-eating sharks with a hand-line. **1888** GOODE *Amer. Fishes* 412 Tugging at a tarpum-line in the Gulf of Mexico. **1895** *Blackw. Mag.* Aug. 281 He has made a special study of tarpon-tackle during his annual visits to the best tarpon-waters.

Tarquinian (tɑːˈkwɪnɪən), *a.* [f. L. *Tarquini-us* + -AN: ult. Etruscan.] Of or pertaining to either of two kings of ancient Rome traditionally named Tarquinius, or to the dynasty to which these kings belonged.

1600 Index to *P. Holland's Romane Hist.* sig. 6Dv[v], Tarquinien gentlemen beheaded in Rome. **1740** J. DYER *Ruins of Rome* 4 Such the Sewers huge, Whither the great Tarquinian Genius dooms Each wave impure. **1849** D. SPILLAN tr. *Livy's Hist. Rome* I. II. iii. 82 Only with the Tarquinian race will kingly power depart hence. **1977** G. CLARK *World Prehistory* (ed. 3) IV. 198 The Roman republic dates from the expulsion of the Tarquinian (Etruscan) dynasty in 510 B.C.

tarrace, obs. form of TARRAS, TERRACE.

tarradiddle, tarrage: see TARA-.

tarragon (ˈtærəgən). Also (6–8 **tarchon**), 6–9 taragon. [Given in 1538–48 as the English for med.L. *tragonia* and *tarchon*: cf. 16th c. F. *targon* (Rabelais, Cotgr. 1611), It. *taracone*, *tarcone* (Florio 1598, 1611), Sp. *taragontia*, *-goncia* (Matthioli 16th c., Percival, Minsheu). *Tarchon* appears in the Latin version of Symeon Sethus *De Cibariis* (Basle 1538), repr. Byzantine Gr. ταρχών. Sethus compiled from Arab sources, and his ταρχών represented Arab. *ṭarkhōn* (in Ibn Beithar, Avicenna, Razi), *altarcon* in Gerard of Cremona, *a* 1187; according to Arabic lexicographers a foreign word: some think ad. Gr. δράκων (Devic), by an early association, similar to what is found in the 16th c., with the Gr. δρακόντιον, *-οντία* (Hippocr., Diosc.), the name of *Arum Dracunculus*.

The two plants were included by Matthioli, 1565, under *Δρακοντία*, *Dracunculus*, the Tarragon being distinguished as *Hortensis Dracunculus*; he also gives, as including both, It. *dragontéa*, Sp. *taragontia*, F. *serpentine*, all originally names of *Arum Dracunculus*. This association is commemorated in the botanical names *Artemisia Dracunculus* and *Arum Dracunculus* (now *Dracunculus vulgaris*), as well as in 16–17th c. applications of the name DRAGON, DRAGONS. The 16th c. herbalists' L. *Tragonia*, and the Sp. *estragon*, Pg. *estragão*, F. *estragon*, are all derived from *tragon*, *targon*, *tarchon*; the 16th c. Sp. *taragoncia* and mod.Sp. *taragona* show the nearest relationship to the Eng. name.]

1. A plant, *Artemisia Dracunculus*, N.O. *Compositæ*, of the wormwood genus, a native of Southern Russia and Eastern Europe, the aromatic leaves of which are used to flavour salads, soups, etc.

1538 ELYOT, *Tragonia*, an herbe nowe callid Taragon, late sene in this realme, whiche hath a tast like gynger. **1548** TURNER *Names of Herbs*, *Tarchon*..is called wyth vs Tarragon. **1579** LANGHAM *Gard. Health* (1633) 630 Tarragon is good in Sallads with Lettuse as Rocket is. **1693** EVELYN *De la Quint. Compl. Gard.* II. 202 Tarragon is one of the perfuming or Spicy Furnitures of our Sallets. **1706** PHILLIPS (ed. 6), *Tarchon*, Taracon, or Garden-Dragon, an Herb. **1767** ABERCROMBIE *Ev. Man his own Gard.* (1803) 668/1 Tarragon: fine flavoured aromatic plant, to improve the flavour of soups and sallads. **1882** *Garden* 21 Jan. 50/1 Keep up good supplies of Tarragon and small salads.

†**2.** Sometimes applied (by confusion of names) to the Garden Dragon, *Dracunculus vulgaris*, N.O. *Araceæ*, or the Green Dragon, *Arisæma Dracontium*, N.O. *Orontiaceæ*: see DRAGONS. *Obs.*

1591 PERCIVALL *Sp. Dict.*, *Taragontia*, taragon, *Draguntea*. **1598** FLORIO, *Taracone*,..the hearbe Taragon or garden Dragon.

3. *attrib.*, as ***tarragon leaf***; **tarragon vinegar**, vinegar flavoured with the leaves or oil of tarragon.

1845 E. ACTON *Mod. Cookery* v. 163 Tarragon vinegar... Gather the tarragon late in July,..put it into small stone jars ..pour in..vinegar to cover. **1855** DELAMER *Kitch. Gard.* (1861) 138 Tarragon vinegar, pickled tarragon leaves, and sometimes the fresh green leaves in salad, are..powerful agents in the hands of a skilful and judicious cook. **1883** W. WILLIAMS in *Knowledge* 20 July 35/2 Stock broth, tarragon vinegar, ketchup, &c.

Tarragona (ˌtærəˈgəʊnə). The name of a town and a province in north-eastern Spain, used *attrib.* and *absol.* to designate any of various wines produced there (see quot. 1958).

1888 *Encycl. Brit.* XXIV. 607/2 In Catalonia there is a much more important wine industry, the district producing what is known in England as Tarragona or Spanish red. **1926** F. H. BUTLER *Wines & Wine Lands of World* v. 50 From the Catalan country, on the same sea-board but much to the north, come the abundant Tarragona wines. **1958** A. L. SIMON *Dict. Wines* 153/2 Tarragona..is also, the name given to the best fortified wines of Catalonia, wines very dark in colour, naturally very sweet, and the fermentation of which is checked by added Brandy—as with Port. Tarragona was for many years the poor man's Port. Its chief merits were its deep colour, its great sweetness, its high alcoholic strength and its low price. **1967** A. LICHINE *Encycl. Wines* 504/2 The wine actually named Tarragona is sweet... The appellation is restricted to the dessert and fortified red and white wines produced within a delimited area and matured or prepared in the cellars of Tarragona, or of Reus close by.

tarra(h), var. TARA *int.*[2]

tarrapin, tarrar, varr. TERRAPIN, TERRIER *sb.*[1]

tarras (ˈtærəs), *sb.* ? *Obs.* Also 6–8 **tarrace**, 7–8 **tarris**, 8 **terrace**, 8–9 **terras**, 9 **tarrass**. See also TRASS. [ad. early mod.Du. *ta'rasse*, *te'rras*, *ti'ras* (Kilian), Du. *tras* neut., Ger. *trasz* masc. (17th c., Kluge), also *tarrasz* (Sanders 1865); of Romanic origin: cf. OF. *terrace* (12th c.), *-asse*, *tierasse*, *-aisse* fem., 'torchis, terre à foulon, trass' (Godef.), It. *terraccia*, *-azza* fem., 'rubble or rubbish' (Florio 1611):—late L. **terrācea* earthy, earthen: cf. TERRACE.]

A kind of rock, allied in composition to pozzolana, consisting largely of comminuted pumice or other volcanic substance; it is found along the Rhine between Cologne and Mainz, and was formerly imported from Holland for making a mortar or hydraulic cement. Hence, the mortar or cement made of this, used for pargeting, lining cisterns, etc.; also applied to other similar cements.

1612 STURTEVANT *Metallica* xiii. 95 Part or appurtenance in buildings,..made either of Bricke, Tile, Lead, Wood, Tarras, or Free-stone. **1662** *Stat. Irel.* (1765) II. 416 Tarras, the barrel 6s. 8d. **1698** LISTER *Journ. Paris* (1699) 52 Which I make no doubt are set in Cement or Tarras, that is, the *Pulvis Puteolanus*. **1735** J. PRICE *Stone-Br. Thames* 5 All the Joints set in Tarris. **1765** *Museum Rust.* IV. lviii. 244 To make it almost as hard as terras. **1775** SMALL in *Phil. Trans.* LXVI. 444 By laying the ground-floor with terrace. **1786** *Projects* in *Ann. Reg.* 96/1 Dutch terras is a *tufa* stone, found on the rocky banks of the Rhine. **1800** *Hull Advertiser* 5 Apr. 1/3 Mortar..mixed..with a due proportion of Terrace or other Water Cement. **1813** SIR H. DAVY *Agric. Chem.* (1814) 327 Taras, which was formerly imported in considerable quantities from Holland, is a mere decomposed basalt. **1822** G. YOUNG *Geol. Surv. Yorks. Coast* (1828) 139 The manufacture of terras, or Roman cement. **1838** *Civil Eng. & Arch. Jrnl.* I. 412/2 Tarras, or trass, is a bluish black cellular trap or lava, quarried at Andernach on the Rhine into mill-stones. *Ibid.*, Of late years, these stones [*septaria*], burnt and reduced to powder, ..have entirely superseded the employment of puzzolana and of Dutch tarras. **1842–76** GWILT *Archit.* Gloss., *Tarras*, a strong cement, useful formerly in water-works.

b. *attrib.* and *Comb.*, as ***tarras mortar***, ***work***; ***tarras-layer***.

1596 LODGE *Wits Miserie* (Hunter. Cl.) 33 His nose sticks in the midst like an embosement in Tarrace worke. **1741** SYMPSON in *Phil. Trans.* XLI. 856 Strong Cement composed of Lime, Sand, Brick-dust, &c. which the Masons of that Country [Lincoln] call Terrace-mortar. **1819** W. S. ROSE *Lett.* I. 54 Many Venetian tarrass-layers have set out, upon invitation, to Russia. **1838** *Civil Eng. & Arch. Jrnl.* I. 413/2 Tarras mortar, made of white lime and tarras, requires long and repeated beating to bring it to perfection.

tarras, *v.* ? *Obs.* Forms: see prec.; also 5 **terys**, 8 **terass**. [In later use app. f. TARRAS *sb.*; but in earlier use prob. f. F. *terracer*, *terrasser* in some of its senses: see TERRACE *v.*] *trans.* To cover, coat, or lay with plaster; in later use, with tarras. Hence **tarrassed** *ppl. a.*

1485 *Churchw. Acc. St. Mary at Hill* (Nichols 1797) 94 Paid the Dawber for terysing of floris per day 8d. **1611** FLORIO, *Pauimentare*, to paue, to terrace. **1615** tr. *De Monfart's Surv. E. Indies* 7 The houses..are lowe enough, vaulted under, and tarassed on the top. **1705** *Lond. Gaz.* No. 4163/1 His Royal Highness has ordered the Towers of the old Castle..to be vaulted and terrassed, to prevent the Effect of the Bombs. **1764** HARMER *Observ.* I. iii. 89 An upper-story, which is flat on the top and either terraced with hard plaister, or paved with stone. **1789** *Trans. Soc. Arts* (ed. 2) II. 235 The plants were..put in a stone cistern, well terassed. **1795** *Statist. Acc. Scot.* XVI. 4 [The] space under the tarrass'd floor was filled with earth. **1796** MORSE *Amer. Geog.* II. 492 [Great Wall of China] being terrassed and cased with bricks. **1819** W. S. ROSE *Lett.* I. 117 Collecting the rain on tarrassed roofs, as at Malta.

tarras, tarrass(e, obs. ff. TERRACE.

tarred (tɑːd), *ppl. a.* Also 7 **tard**. [f. TAR *v.*[1] + -ED[1].] Smeared or covered with tar. (In quot. 1688, marked or formed with tar.)

1615 MARKHAM *Eng. Housew.* II. v. (1649) 167 With a pair of sheeres..she shall cut away all the course locks, pitch, brands, tar'd locks, and other feltrings. **1688** *Lond. Gaz.* No. 2377/4 A Tarr'd P. on her Rump. **1828** J. M. SPEARMAN *Brit. Gunner* (ed. 2) 147 Tarred cordage is chiefly useful for cables and ground tackle, which are constantly soaked in water. **1887** *Pall Mall G.* 29 Sept. 6/1 The erection and re-erection of tarred barricades.

tarrer (ˈtɑːrə(r)). [f. TAR *v.*[1] + -ER[1].] One who tars. (In quots. in reference to tarring and feathering: see TAR *v.*[1] b.)

1784 MRS. R. B. SHERIDAN *Let.* in T. Moore *Mem. Life R. B. Sheridan* (1825) xv. 485 You mistake, if you suppose I am a friend to your tarrers and featherers:—it is such wretches that always ruin a good cause. **1894** *Columbus* (Ohio) *Dispatch* 8 Aug., The cases of the tarrers have not been passed upon yet.

tarrer(e, tarres, obs. ff. TARRIER[2], TERRACE.

† **'tarriage**. *Obs. rare*[−1]. In 5 **taryage**. [f. TARRY *v.* + -AGE.] Tarrying, delay: = next, 1.

c **1470** HENRY *Wallace* x. 416 Than for to fle he tuk no taryage.

tarriance (ˈtærɪəns). *arch.* Also 5 **tary-**, 5–7 **tari-**, 6–7 **tarry-**; 5–6 **-ans**, 5–7 **-aunce**, 6–7 **-ence**. [f. TARRY *v.* + -ANCE.]

1. The action of tarrying; delay, procrastination.

1460 *Paston Lett.* I. 527 Besechyng your maistership not to be dysplesed with my long taryans. **1542** UDALL *Erasm. Apoph.* 295 b, To make no ferther delaie ne taryaunce. **1563** GOLDING *Cæsar* v. (1565) 137 Fabius..making no long tarience in hys iorney, met hym with hys Legion. **1576** FULWEL *Ars Adulandi* vii. (1579) G iij, Better is a litle tariance then a raw dinner. **1591** SHAKS. *Two Gent.* II. vii. 90, I am impatient of my tarriance. **1694** S. SEWALL *Diary* 6 Apr. (1878) I. 390 Sawing and fitting this board made some inconvenient Tarriance. **1808** SOUTHEY *Chron. Cid* 173 The tarriance that had been made. **1898** T. HARDY *Wessex Poems* 90 Worn with tarriance I care for life no more.

2. Temporary residence or continuance in a place; sojourn, abiding.

1530 PALSGR. 279/2 Taryaunce, abyding, *demourance*. **1681** R. KNOX *Hist. Ceylon* II. vi. 56 Making these Tents stronger or slighter, according to the time of their tarriance. **1721** STRYPE *Eccl. Mem.* III. vi. 66 After a year or two's tarriance in London. **1885** T. HODGKIN *Italy & Inv.* III. IV. viii. 307 It may have been during this tarriance at Rome that Theodoric commenced..draining the Pontine Marshes.

†**3.** Abiding in expectation; awaiting, waiting.

1561 T. NORTON *Calvin's Inst.* II. 105 To confirme them in loking for him, that they should not waxe faint with long tarriance. **1599** ? SHAKS. *Pass. Pilgr.* vi, Cytherea..A longing tariance for Adonis made. **1646** TRAPP *Comm. John* xx. 6 The good ground brings forth fruit with patience or tarriance.

†**4.** The causing of delay; hindrance. *Obs.*

1598 R. BERNARD tr. *Terence*, *Andria* V. v, Neither is there any let or tarriance, but that I may marry her out of hand.

tarriar, obs. form of TERRIER.

tarrididdle, variant of TARADIDDLE.

tarrier[1] (ˈtærɪə(r)). *arch.* Also 4 **tariere**, 4–6 **tarier**, 5 **teryar**, **-iar**, 6 **tar(r)yer**, **-iar**. [f. TARRY *v.* + -ER[1].]

1. One who tarries or delays; a lingerer, procrastinator; one who stays or remains.

1382 WYCLIF *Jer.* Prol., God is redi to ȝyue good, to punshen a tariere. *c* **1440** *Promp. Parv.* 489/2 Teryar, or longe lytare (*P.* teriar or longe bidar). **1530** PALSGR. 317/2 Longe taryer. **1531** ELYOT *Gov.* I. xxiv, Called of them *Fabius cunctator*, that is to saye the tariar or delayer. **1577** NORTHBROOKE *Dicing* (1843) 95 Saint Paule admonisheth women..to be byders and tariers at home. **1581** J. BELL *Haddon's Answ. Osor.* 496 There be behind yet many tarryers, I will not say Traytors to the Common weale. **1665** BRATHWAIT *Comment Two Tales* (Chaucer Soc.) 29 This Chanterer was a notable Tarrier. **1845** BROWNING *Glove* 91 Sound the trumpet, no true knight's a tarrier!

†**2.** One who (or that which) delays some one; a hinderer, obstructor; an obstruction. *Obs.*

1614 B. JONSON *Barth. Fair* I. v, Why doe you stop, am I your Tarriars? **1622** J. RAWLINS *Fam. Recovery Ship of Bristol* E j b, To catch the soules of mortall men, and entangle frailty in the tarriers of horrible abuses, and imposturing deceit.

tarrier[2] (ˈtærɪə(r)). Forms: 5 **tarrer(e**, 6 **tarryour**, 7–8 **terrier**, 9 **tarrier**. [In 15th c. *tarrer(e*, a. OF. *tarere* (*c* 1200 in Godef.), mod.F. *tarière*:—late L. *taratrum* (Isidore XIX. xix. 15, '*taratrum* quasi *teratrum*'): cf. Gr. τέρετρον borer, gimlet.] A boring instrument, an auger; now, an instrument for extracting a bung from a barrel.

c **1460** J. RUSSELL *Bk. Nurture* 65 Looke þow haue tarrers two a more & lasse for wyne. *Ibid.* 71 So when þow settyst a pipe abroche... With tarrere or gymlet perce ye vpward þe pipe ashore. **1513** *Bk. Keruynge* in *Babees Bk.* (1868) 266 Than loke ye haue two tarryours, a more & a lesse. **1611** COTGR., *Terriere*, a Terrier, or Augar. **1706** PHILLIPS (ed. Kersey), *Terrier*..a sort of Awger to bore with. **1904** *Daily Chron.* 19 Feb. 3/2 A London cellarman asks for his 'tarrier' to take out a bung from the barrel.

†**tarrier**[3], **tarriour**. *Obs.* [f. **tarry* vb. in *tarrying-iron* + -ER[1], -OUR.] A pair of tiring-irons.

1601 DEACON & WALKER *Answ. to Darel* To Rdr. 4 The very frame itselfe..resembleth fitlie a paire of tarriours, or tyring yrons.

tarrier, obs. or vulgar form of TERRIER *sb.*[2] (dog).

tarriness: see TARRY *a.*

tarring (ˈtɑːrɪŋ), *vbl. sb.* [f. TAR *v.*[1] + -ING[1].] The action of coating or smearing with tar.

1473–4 in Swayne *Sarum Churchw. Acc.* (1896) 15 For the tarryng of the hempon cabul. **1542** *Acc. Ld. High Treas. Scotl.* VIII. 132 Mending and tirring of lxx ald somes. **1589** *Pappe w. Hatchet* E j b, I thinke them woorth neither the tarring, nor the telling. **1669** J. OWEN in *State Papers, Dom.* 576 We spend 2 [lasts of tar] at a tarring. **1774** T. HUTCHINSON *Diary* 1 July (1883) I. 164 The committee for tarring and feathering blamed the people for doing it. **1784** [see TAR *v.*[1] b]. **1844** DICKENS *Martin Chuzzlewit* xxxiii. 390 He..invariably recommended..the 'tarring and feathering' of any unpopular person who differed from himself. **1861** *Illustr. Lond. News* 17 Aug. 152/1 The tarring and feathering of defenceless individual Northerners.

attrib. **1851–4** TOMLINSON *Cycl. Arts* (1867) VI. 468/1 The tarring-house is separated from the other buildings by a second partition.

tarris, obs. form of TARRAS, TERRACE.

tarrish (ˈtɑːrɪʃ), *a. rare.* [f. TAR *sb.*[1] + -ISH[1].] Resembling tar; having a taste or consistency like that of tar. **b.** [f. TAR *sb.*[1] 3.] Of or belonging to sailors; nautical.

1681 R. KNOX *Hist. Ceylon* I. vi. 25 They are small like a Fly, and black,..their honey somewhat tarrish. **1841** *Fraser's Mag.* XXIV. 307, I saw there were swabs opposite me. (This is the tarrish tongue for officer or epaulette.)

tarro, variant of TARO, the plant.

tarrock (ˈtærək). [Of uncertain origin; the ending *-ock* is app. diminutive, as in *puttock*, etc.] A name applied locally to various sea-birds: in the Shetland Islands, to the Arctic Tern; elsewhere to the Kittiwake, to the young of the Common Gull, and to the Common Guillemot.

1674 RAY *Collect. Words, Water Fowl* 94 The Tarrock: Cornub: *Larus cinereus Bellonii.* **1678** —— *Willughby's Ornith.* 346 Bellonius his ash-coloured Gull, called in Cornwal, Tarrock. **1768** PENNANT *Zool.* II. 424 Linnæus.. makes this species [winter mew] synonymous with the *Larus tridactylus* or *Tarrock.* **1771** —— *Tour Scot. in 1769*, 36 Kittiwakes, or Tarrocks. **1774** GOLDSM. *Nat. Hist.* (1776) VI. 79 It is.. the tarrock, and the terne, that venture to these dreadful retreats, and claim an undisturbed possession. **1833** *G. Montagu's Ornith. Dict.* 505 *Tarrock*, a name for the Gull in its immature plumage. *Ibid.* 508 Common Tern, *Sterna hirundo. Provincial*... Tarrock, or Tarret. **1880** J. SKELTON *Crookit Meg* iv. 48, I promised to get a tarrock's wing for Eppie.

tarrow ('tærəʊ), *v. Sc.* [app. a parallel form to TARRY *v.* (sense 3): cf. *harrow* and *harry*, *worow* and *worry*.] *intr.* To delay, hesitate, show reluctance. (Nearly = TARRY *v.* 3.)

c **1375** *Sc. Leg. Saints* xxxiii. (*George*) 133, & gyf þu tarowis it to do.. we sal bryne þe & al þine. *c* **1470** HENRYSON *Mor. Fab.* XIII. (*Frog & Mouse*) xxii, And it to cun perqueir se thow not tarrow. *a* **1568** in *Bannatyne Poems* (Hunter. Cl.) 268 On twenty schilling now he tarrowis To ryd the he gait by the plewis. **1637** RUTHERFORD *Lett.* (1862) I. 295, I am sure it is sin to tarrow at Christ's good meat, and not to eat when he saith, 'Eat, O well beloved'. **1666** J. LIVINGSTONE in *Sel. Biog.* (Wodrow Soc.) I. 282 Tarrow not of this my dealing. **1725** RAMSAY *Gentle Sheph.* I. ii, Like dawted wean that tarrows at its meat. **1786** BURNS *Dream* xv, I hae seen their coggie fou, That yet hae tarrow't at it. **1899** SPENCE *Shetland Folk-Lore* 216 The mair he tarrows the less he gets.

Hence **'tarrowing** *vbl. sb.* and *ppl. a.*; **'tarrowingly** *adv.*, reluctantly.

c **1375** *Sc. Leg. Saints* xxxix. (*Cosme & Damyane*) 60 He It tuk tarowandly. *c* **1598** D. FERGUSON *Sc. Prov.* §42 (1785) 4 A tarrowing bairn was never fat. **1632** RUTHERFORD *Lett.* (1862) I. 91 Let your soul, like a tarrowing and misleared child, take the dorts. **1832** A. HENDERSON *Sc. Prov.* 131 Lang tarrowing taks a' the thanks awa.

tarrow, variant of TARO.

tarry ('tærɪ), *sb.* Also 4–6 tary, 6 tarie, *Sc.* tairrie. [f. TARRY *v.*]

†**1.** The act of tarrying; spending or loss of time; delay, procrastination. *Obs.*

c **1375** *Sc. Leg. Saints* xxvii. (*Machor*) 485 þane machore .. reprowyt þe mastir man of his tary & his slawnes. **1451** CAPGRAVE *Life St. Gilbert* (E.E.T.S.) 113 He, with-oute ony tary, mad calle all þe court of Rome. *c* **1510** BARCLAY *Mirr. Gd. Manners* (1570) Ev, In tary is no trust, but ieopardy mortall. **1562** SIR R. MAITLAND *Poems* (1830) 17 To cheis and tak ane husband without tarie. *a* **1578** LINDESAY (Pitscottie) *Chron. Scot.* (S.T.S.) I. 142 The king determinat to compell them that was within the house, be lang tairrie to rander and gif it ower. **1745** WRIGHT in *N. Eng. Hist. & Gen. Reg.* (1848) II. 207 We made no tarry but set forward for Fort Dummer.

2. Temporary residence, sojourn; a 'stay'. Now chiefly *U.S.*

c **1375** *Sc. Leg. Saints* xviii. (*Egipciane*) 1272 Vith hym na langer tary scho vald ma. **1516** ALLEN in Lodge *Illustr. Brit. Hist.* (1791) I. 11 He sayth his tarry is but short her. **1589** *Reg. Privy Council Scot.* IV. 425 In cais our tary sal happin .. to be langair. **1786** M. CUTLER in *Life*, etc. (1888) II. 273 To.. make provisions for a much longer tarry. **1817** *London Courier* 7 July, The Duke of Wellington was on his arrival received by a guard of honour, and the band of the 88th continued to play during his Grace's tarry. **1866** WHITTIER *Marg. Smith's Jrnl.* Pr. Wks. 1889 I. 89 He is to make some little tarry in this town.

tarry ('tɑːrɪ), *a.* [f. TAR *sb.*[1] + -Y.]

1. Consisting or composed of tar; of the nature of tar.

1552 HULOET, Tarrye, or of tarre, *piceus.* **1782** J. TRUMBULL *M'Fingal* 65 From nose and chin's remotest end, The tarry icicles depend. **1841** *Civil Eng. & Arch. Jrnl.* IV. 12/1 Its change from.. a solid to that of a tarry, viscous, semifluid. **1899** *Allbutt's Syst. Med.* VIII. 517 All tarry and resinous substances absorb oxygen rapidly or slowly.

b. Resembling tar; having the consistence, colour, or flavour of tar.

1880 M. MACKENZIE *Dis. Throat & Nose* I. 154 The blood [of the heart] is [in certain cases of diphtheria] fluid and tarry. **1896** C. E. RYAN *With Ambulance thro' Franco-German War* v. 63 A small patch of blood-stained earth beside him—not red, but tarry-black. **1904** *Daily News* 27 Dec. 10 The Souchong teas.. have a special flavour.. which the trade describe as 'tarry'.

2. Covered, smeared, soiled, or impregnated with tar; tarred; black as if smeared with tar.

a **1585** POLWART *Flyting w. Montgomerie* 745 Tary tade [= toad], thous defate. **1641** BEST *Farm. Bks.* (Surtees) 23 Such [locks of wool] as are hairy and tarry. **1686** *Lond. Gaz.* No. 2201/4 [He] had.. an old black Tarrey Hat on his head. **1753** *N. Jersey Archives* XIX. 283 A Pair of tarry Duck Trowsers. **1824** MCCULLOCH *Highl., etc. Scot.* I. 382 In contact with her tarry sides. **1840** DICKENS *Old C. Shop* v, Two or three tarry boys.

b. *fig.* Thievish. (Cf. *tarry-fingered* in 4.)

1822 GALT *Sir A. Wylie* II. xvii. 158 The gipsies hae tarry fingers, and ye would need an ee in your neck to watch them.

3. *fig.* ? Foul, unclean; ? rude, uncultured.

1579 W. WILKINSON *Confut. Familye of Loue* 57b, Poysoned speaches, and tarrye Rhetorick. **1779** J. ADAMS *Diary* 11 May, Wks. 1851 III. 200 Dr. W. told me of Tucker's rough, tarry speech about me, at the navy board.

4. *Comb.*: **tarry-breeks** (orig. *Sc.*), **-jacket**, **-John**, humorous nicknames for a sailor (cf. TAR *sb.*[1] 3); **tarry-fingered**, **-fisted** *adjs.*, having the fingers or hands smeared with tar; *fig.* thievish.

1786 BURNS *Dream* xiii, Young royal *Tarry Breeks [Prince William], I learn, Ye've lately come athwart her. **1855** KINGSLEY *Westw. Ho* xxx, No old tarry-breeks of a sea-dog. **1825** JAMIESON, **Tarry-fingered, Tarry-handit*, dishonest, disposed to carry off by stealth. **1906** *Daily Chron.* 4 Aug. 8/4 All the gold that has ever been gathered by *tarry-fisted gentry of the Bragwell and Rudge order. **1822** SCOTT *Nigel* iv, My husband must be the slave of every *tarry jacket that wants but a pound of oakum. **1888** STEVENSON *Black Arrow* IV. vi, Long-headed *tarry-Johns, that fear not fire nor water.

Hence **'tarriness**, tarry condition or quality.

1892 WALSH *Tea* (Philad.) 193 This smokiness and 'tarriness' does not develop until after the teas have left China.

tarry ('tærɪ), *v.* Now chiefly *literary* in Gt. Brit., still *colloq.* in U.S. Forms: 4–6 **tarye**, 4–7 **tarie**, **tary**, (5 **tery**, **tare**), 6 **tarrye**, 6–7 **tarrie**, 5– **tarry**. [Of obscure origin: some would identify it with TARY *v.* to irritate, or with TAR *v.*[2], *tarre*, OE. *tęrgan* to vex; to both of which the sense is an obstacle. See *Note* below.]

†**1.** *trans.* To delay, retard, defer, put off (a thing, an action); to protract, prolong. *Obs.*

c **1320** R. BRUNNE *Medit.* 597 Thos howndes were lothe hys deþ for to tarye. *c* **1386** CHAUCER *Reeve's Prol.* 51 Sey forth thy tale, and tarie nat the tyme. **1388** WYCLIF *Ecclus.* iv. 3 Tarie thou not [Vulg. *non protrahas*] the ȝifte to a man that is set in angwisch. **1398** TREVISA *Barth. De P.R.* XI. vii. (Bodl. MS.) lf. 109/2 ȝif is yuel and distemperat.. it.. tarieth and letteþ repinges of corne and of fruyte. **1494** FABYAN *Chron.* VII. ccxxxviii. 278 That he shulde for no mede tary rightfull sentence. **1583** STOCKER *Civ. Warres Lowe C.* IV. 52b, Which Citie not meanyng to tarrie the siege, rendred to the saied Count.

†**2.** To detain, delay, retard, keep back (a person or agent) for a time; to keep waiting; to hold in check, impede, hinder. *Obs.*

1340 HAMPOLE *Pr. Consc.* 3921 þat he may.. In purgatory qwyte alle þe dett, þat hym fra blis may tary or lett. *c* **1386** CHAUCER *Sqr.'s T.* 65, I wol nat taryen yow for it is pryme. **1387** TREVISA *Higden* (Rolls) VII. 235 Duke William and his men were longe y-taried in Seynt Valerik his haven. **1470–85** MALORY *Arthur* XVIII. vii. 735 Sir kyng, he sayd, tary me noo lenger for I may not tary. **1571** GOLDING *Calvin on Ps.* xxix. 7 So many stops tary us and stay us back. **1609** SKENE *Reg. Maj.* I. 114b, But gif.. the parties wald set them to tary the court, with exceptions frivolous.

3. *intr.* To delay or be tardy in beginning or doing anything, esp. in coming or going; to wait before doing something; to linger, loiter.

c **1350** *Will. Palerne* 3128 I coniure þe.. þatou titli me telle & tarie nouȝ no lenger **1382** WYCLIF *Ecclus.* xiv. 12 Be thou myndeful for deth shal not tarien [Vulg. *mors non tardat*]. *c* **1400** *Rule St. Benet* 60/445 Bot chaistese þam & tery noght. *c* **1440** *Promp. Parv.* 489/2 Teryyn [*MS. S.* tarryyn] or longe a-bydyn, *moror, pigritor.* **1489** CAXTON *Faytes of A.* III. xii. 193 Yf he had taried to the morn after. *a* **1586** SIDNEY *Arcadia* III. (1622) 238 Not daring to tary long about it. **1611** BIBLE *Judg.* v. 28 Why tarie the wheeles of his charets? **1693** CONGREVE *Old Bach.* IV. i, Nothing can be done here till I go, so that I'll tarry, d'ye see? **1756** C. LUCAS *Ess. Waters* I. 32 The waters cannot tarry long in their passage, but.. run towards the.. level grounds. **1849** MACAULAY *Hist. Eng.* v. I. 610 He saw that if he tarried the royal cavalry would soon be in his rear. **1892** *Nation* (N.Y.) 27 Oct. 318/2 The good monks.. were.. going to attend high mass.., so we had no time to tarry.

b. To linger in expectation of a person or occurrence, or until something is done or happens; to wait. Const. *till*, *for*, Sc. *on*, *upon* (with *indirect passive*).

1390 GOWER *Conf.* I. 187 This false knyht.. Hath taried til thei were aslepe. **1515** BARCLAY *Egloges* iv. (1570) Dj b/2 What, tary man a while till better fortune come. **1526** TINDALE *John* xxi. 23 Yf I will have hym to tary [WYCLIF dwelle, **1611** tarry] tyll I come what is that to the? **1535** COVERDALE *Tobit* v. 7, I praye the, tary for me, tyll I haue tolde my father. **1560** DAUS tr. *Sleidane's Comm.* 274, I.. would tary to se the ende. **1580** LYLY *Euphues* (Arb.) 427 Euphues knowing the tyde would tarrye for no man. **1609** SKENE *Reg. Maj.* I. 124* He quha is challenged sall be taried vpon, vntill he returne hayme. **1765** M. CUTLER in *Life*, etc. (1888) I. 9 Then the sacrament was administered (which I did not tarry to see). **1816** SCOTT *Antiq.* i, Time and tide tarry for no man. **1870** E. PEACOCK *Ralf Skirl.* I. 167 They had not long to tarry for the coming of their host.

†**4.** *intr.* To remain, stay, abide, continue (in some state or condition). *Obs.*

c **1450** LOVELICH *Merlin* 452: Thus it Taryede jn-to pentecost feste. **1480** *Robt. Devyll* 25 in Hazl. *E.P.P.* I. 219 Wyueles longe, said the duke, haue I taryed. **1551** T. WILSON *Logike* (1580) 38 If the generall woorde be taken awaie, the kinde tarieth not. **1597** A. M. tr. *Guillemeau's Fr. Chirurg.* 17b/2 Els the ioyncte might be criple, and tarrye lame. **1637–50** ROW *Hist. Kirk* (Wodrow Soc.) 488 Pardoned by the King, provyding they tarie weill in tyme comeing. **1776** R. KING in *Life & Corr.* (1894) I. 24 Few of the men now with Genl. will tarry longer than the expiration of their enlistments. **1814** SCOTT *Wav.* xii, Declining the Baron's invitation to tarry till after dinner [etc.].

b. To abide temporarily, to sojourn; to stay, remain, lodge (in a place). *arch.* exc. in *U.S.*

13.. *E.E. Allit. P.* C. 87, I schal tee in-to Tarce, & tary þere a whyle. **1432–50** tr. *Higden* (Rolls) VI. 127 The Danes taryenge in wynter at Repyndoun. **1538** ELYOT, *Pernocto*.., to tarye all the nyghte. **1599** MASSINGER, etc. *Old Law* IV. i, As long as she tarried with her husband, she was Ellen. **1611** BIBLE *Ps.* lxviii. 12 She that tarried at home, diuided the spoile. **1741** RICHARDSON *Pamela* (1824) I. cii. 499 Miss Cope came.. and tarried with me three days. **1766** J. INGERSOLL *Lett. Stamp-Act* 62, I tarried that Night at Mr. Bishop's. **1820** W. IRVING *Sketch Bk., Leg. Sleepy Hollow*, Ichabod Crane.. sojourned, or, as he expressed it, 'tarried', in Sleepy Hollow, for the purpose of instructing the children of the vicinity. **1850** HAWTHORNE *Scarlet L.* viii, I must tarry at home, and keep watch over my little Pearl. **1871** R. ELLIS *Catullus* lxv. 2 Ortalus, I no more tarry the Muses among. **1877** FREEMAN *Norm. Conq.* (ed. 3) II. x. 469 There they were to tarry [*earlier edd.* remain] through Lent.

5. *trans.* To wait for, wait in expectation of; to await, expect; †to stay for (a meal). †*tarry out*, to stay till the end of. *to tarry* a person's *leisure*: see LEISURE *sb.* 3c. *arch.*

1432–50 tr. *Higden* (Rolls) VI. 23 Messias whom þe Iues taryede. **1579** G. HARVEY *Let. to Spenser* Wks. (Grosart) I. 20 The Tyde tarryeth no manne, but manye a good manne is fayne to tarry the Tyde. **1654** EVELYN *Diary* 10 July, On Monday, I went again to the schools,.. and.. tarried out the whole Act in St. Mary's. *a* **1662** HEYLIN *Laud* (1668) 176 He caused me to tarry Dinner with him. **1829** LYTTON *Devereux* I. viii, I pressed him.. to tarry your coming. **1868** MILMAN *St. Paul's* xi. 283 The Lord Mayor tarried the sermon, which lasted into the night.

†**b.** To outstay, stay over (a given time). *Obs.*

?*a* **1500** *Symmye & Bruder* 66 in *Bannatyne Poems* (Hunter. Cl.) 416 Bot or thay twynd him and his dudis, The tyme of none wes tareit; Wa worth this wedding, for be thir widis, The meit is al miskareit.

[*Note.* It cannot be disputed that the ME. forms of this verb are identical with those of TARY 'to provoke, irritate, harass, vex, excite', both being in ME. *tery-*, *tary-* (the spelling *tarry* being rare before 1500). Original identity with *tary*, and thus derivation from OE. *tęrgan*, would also account for the apparent identity of *tarry* and TARROW, since both could go back to the OE. variant types *tęrgan* (*tærȝan*), *tęrw(i)an* (*tærw(i)an*), with phonetic development according to the position of the *ȝ* and *w* in different inflected forms: cf. HARROW and HARRY, *worow* and WORRY. The consequent identification with OF. *tarier* might also help to explain the existence of the derivatives *tarriage*, *tarriance*, *tarryment*, with French suffixes (although it is to be noted that these appear as derivatives of *tarry* and not of *tary*).

But no sense in the least approaching 'tarry' occurs in OE. *tęrgan*, *tęrw(i)an*, or in OF. *tarier*, and the difficulty of deriving this sense from that of 'provoke, vex, harass' seems almost insurmountable. Some have suggested an influence upon *tarry* of the synonymous TARGE *v.*[1], OF. *targier*; but this seems impossible. Others, seeing that ME. *terwen*, *terre*, TAR *v.*[2] and TARY had both a (rare) sense (2) 'to weary, fatigue, tire' (as if influenced by OE. *téorian*, ME. *tiere*, *tere*, TIRE) have thought that this sense provided a connecting link between the notions of 'vex' and 'delay, retard'; but there is nothing in the quotations to confirm this view, and the actual history of *tarry* in its existing sense remains unascertained.]

tarryer, obs. form of TARRIER[1], TERRIER *sb.*[2]

tarryhooting (tærɪ'hu:tɪŋ), *vbl. sb.* Chiefly *U.S. dial.* [Prob. var. of *callyhooting* (*Dict. Americanisms*) in same sense.] Going about with much noise and motion; gallivanting. Freq. const. *around*. Also as *v. intr.* (chiefly *pres. pple.*).

1940 *N.Y. Jrnl. & American* (*Amer. Weekly*) 16 June 4/3 Her husband was 'tarryhootin'' around payin' court to gals on both cricks. *Ibid.* 4/4 He took to disappearing & 'tarryhootin'' during the ninth year of the marriage. **1950** R. MOORE *Candlemas Bay* iv. 219 'Hi,' Grampie said. 'You're quite a feller for tarryhooting around the woods.' 'Apparently,' Mr. Raymond said. 'Was you chasing Evelyn?' 'Yes... Yes, by God, I was.' **1959** *Spectator* 27 Nov. 779/2 The pundits in Vigo Street.. turned this new venture [sc. *The Wind in the Willows*] down... After a certain amount of tarry-hooting around, Mr. Mole.. was deposited in the amiable bosom of Sir Algernon Methuen.

tarrying ('tærɪɪŋ), *vbl. sb.* [f. TARRY *v.* + -ING[1].]

1. The action of the verb TARRY, q.v.; delaying, delay, waiting, loitering, etc.

1340–70 *Alex. & Dind.* 818 Wiþ-oute tariynge tid þis tiþingus come. *c* **1350** in *Eng. Gilds* (1870) 357 þey shoide, at here aȝe-comynge, ȝelde trewe a-counte.. by-þowte taryȝynge. *c* **1440** *Promp. Parv.* 489/2 Teryynge, or longe a-bydynge, *mora, pigricia.* *a* **1450** MYRC *Festial* 18 This þe taryng of Thomas byleue broght vs yn full byleue. **1535** COVERDALE *Ps.* xxxix. 17 Make no longe tarienge, o my God. **1596** DALRYMPLE tr. *Leslie's Hist. Scot.* x. (S.T.S.) 395 Tha wald tyne waichtie materis,.. throuch thair Absense, or lang tarieng. **1865** W. G. PALGRAVE *Arabia* I. 86 We determined to march on without further tarrying.

2. Abiding, sojourning: see TARRY *v.* 4b.

1445 in *Anglia* XXVIII. 271 In the she had a restyng place or taryng ony while. **1577–87** HOLINSHED *Chron.* III. 826/2 If he of his noble courage would giue him tarieng and abode. **1607** R. JOHNSON *Pleas. Conceites Old Hobson* (Percy Soc.) 14 During the time of his taring there.

†**3.** (See quots., and cf. BUNDLE *v.* 5.) *U.S.*

1775 A. BURNABY *Trav.* 83 A very extraordinary method of courtship, which is sometimes practised amongst the lower people of this province, and is called Tarrying. **1778** ANBUREY *Trav. Amer.* xlix. (1791) II. 87 That custom [bundling].. is in some measure abolished; but they still retain one something similar, which is termed *tarrying*.

'tarrying, *ppl. a.* [f. as prec. + -ING[2].] That tarries: **a.** Delaying, lingering, tardy; **b.** Remaining, abiding.

c **1386** CHAUCER *Pars. T.* ¶644 The synne that men clepen Tarditas, as whan a man is to laterede or tariynge er he wole turne to god. **1422** tr. *Secreta Secret., Priv. Priv.* 223 Tarynge of speche, the voyce ful and stronge. **1483** *Cath. Angl.* 378/1 Taryinge, *morosus* (A.). **1654** Z. COKE *Logick* 38 Action is either Immanent and tarrying [or] Transient and passing.

Hence **'tarryingly** *adv.*, lingeringly, tardily.

1450–1530 *Myrr. our Ladye* 26 The systers fulfyll the offyce of theyr seruyce somwhat more tareyngly.

tarrying-iron: see TIRING-IRON.

† **'tarryment.** *Obs. rare*⁻¹. In 6 **tariment.** [f. TARRY *v.* + -MENT.] Delay, tarrying.

1560 ROLLAND *Crt. Venus* I. 804 Withouttin tariment It salbe done.

tarryour, obs. form of TARRIER².

† **'tarrysome,** *a. Sc. Obs. rare.* In 6 **tari(e)sum.** [f. TARRY *sb.* or *v.* + -SOME.] Characterized by tarrying; slow, lingering; wearisome.

1513 DOUGLAS *Æneis* IV. xii. 100 Haffand rieuth,.. Off hir lang sorow and tarisum deid. **1535** STEWART *Cron. Scot.* (Rolls) II. 6 It war ouir lang and tariesum to tell.

† **tars, tarse.** *Obs.* Also 5 **tarsse.** [a. OF. *tarse* (1345 in Godef.); in med.L. *pannus Tarsicus*; formerly held to be the same word as *Tarse*, Tarsus in Cilicia (either because fabricated at or imported by way of Tarsus); but probably referring to Tarsia or Tharsia, described in Maundeville (xxiv, Roxb. xxvii) as 'the kingdom of Tarse', upon which the land of Cathay 'marcheth toward the west', app. Turkestan; hence prob. the same as TARTAR *sb.*³, and TARTARIN¹ 2, q.v.] A rich and costly stuff of Oriental origin, used in the West in the 14th and 15th c. Also *cloth of tars*.

[**1295** *Visitatio Thesaur. S. Pauli Londin.* (Du Cange), Casula de panno Tarsico, Indici coloris.] **13..** *Gaw. & Gr. Knt.* 571 Dubbed in a dublet of a dere tars. **1377** LANGL. *P. Pl.* B. xv. 163 As gladde of a goune of a graye russet As of a tunicle of tarse or of trye scarlet. ?*a* **1400** *Morte Arth.* 3190 In toges of tarsse fulle richelye attyrde. *c* **1400** MAUNDEV. (Roxb.) vi. 20 Cledd in clathe of gold or tars, or in chamelet. *a* **1400-50** *Alexander* 1515 [He] arais all þe cite, Braidis ouire with bawdkyns all þe brade stretis, With tars & with tafeta þar he trede sulde. *Ibid.* 4673 Doubeletis of damaske & sum of dere tars. [**1834** PLANCHÉ *Brit. Costume* 105 The rich stuff called 'cloth of tars' is mentioned in this reign [Edw. I]. It was latinized *tarsicus* and *tartarinus.* **1880** BIRDWOOD *Indian Arts* II. 74 Cloth of Tars is from Tarsus, or perhaps from Tabriz.]

tarsal ('tɑːsəl), *a.* (*sb.*) [ad. mod.L. *tarsāl-is*, f. L. *tars-us*: see TARSUS and -AL¹.]

1. Of or pertaining to the tarsus of the ankle or foot, in its various senses.

1817 KIRBY & SP. *Entomol.* (1818) II. xxiii. 328 The grasshoppers with setaceous antennæ..have four tarsal joints. **1826** *Ibid.* III. xxxv. 670 The tibia or shank is the fourth joint of the leg, which..is the analogue..of the tarsus or tarsal bones of vertebrate animals. **1840** G. V. ELLIS *Anat.* 712 The tarsal artery..gives branches to the extensor, to the bones of the tarsus and their articulations. **1851** RICHARDSON *Geol.* viii. (1855) 314 The foot, like the hand, [consisting] of three ranges of bones, tarsal, metatarsal, and phalanges. **1875** C. C. BLAKE *Zool.* 94 The number of tarsal scales is a specific test in most birds. **1875** CAMBRIDGE in *Encycl. Brit.* II. 295/2 The third, or inferior tarsal claw [of spiders]. **1883** THOMPSON tr. *Müller's Fertil. Fl.* 51 The carrying-power of the tarsal brushes is increased.

2. Of or pertaining to the tarsi of the eyelids.

1839 T. BEALE *Nat. Hist. Sperm Whale* 119 The eyelids are without cilia and tarsal cartilages. **1889** G. A. BERRY *Dis. Eye* i. 2 An oily secretion is formed in the tarsal, or Meibomian glands. **1890** WEBSTER, *Tarsal tetter*,..an eruptive disease of the edges of the eyelids.

B. *sb.* Short for *tarsal bone, joint*, etc.

1881 MIVART *Cat* 341 The tarsals each ossify from one centre, as do the carpals. **1888** *Athenæum* 17 Mar. 344/3 A paper..'On the Carpus and Tarsus of the Anura.'..In the hind foot they recorded the discovery of a fourth tarsal. **1889** E. D. COPE in *Amer. Naturalist* Oct. 863 Carpals and tarsals not distinct in form from metapodials.

tarsalgia: see TARSO-.

tarsall, obs. form of TERCEL, hawk.

† **tarse**¹. *Obs.* Also 6 terse. [OE. *teors* = OHG., MHG. *zërs*, MDu. *teers, teres.*] The penis.

c **1000** *Sax. Leechd.* I. 358 Wið hærþena sare & teorses bares bræᵹen meng wið huniᵹ. *c* **1000** *Voc.* in Wr.-Wülcker 265/33 *Calamus*, teors, þæt wæpen *uel* lim. **1382** WYCLIF *1 Sam.* xviii. 25 No sposeilis, but oonli an hundrid tersis [1388 prepucies] of Philisteis. **14..** *MS. Porkington x* (Halliw.) Now ȝe speke of a tarse. **1500-20** DUNBAR 7 *Deidly Synnis* 88 Tersis. **1530** PALSGR. 279/2 Tarse of a man or beest, *uit.* **1730-6** in BAILEY (folio).

tarse² (tɑːs). *rare*⁻⁰. [a. F. *tarse*, ad. L. TARSUS.] = TARSUS 1.

1842 in BRANDE *Dict. Sc.*, etc. Hence in later Dicts.

tarse, variant of TARS *Obs.*

'tar-sealed, *a. N.Z.* (and *Austral.*). [f. TAR *sb.* + SEALED *ppl. a.*] Of a road, etc.: surfaced with asphalt. Also as *v. trans.* (chiefly *pa. pple*).

1928 R. G. STAPLEDON *Tour in Austral. & N.Z.* i. 12 Practically every mile of the road so traversed is 'tar sealed'. **1936** 'R. HYDE' *Passport to Hell* iii. 68 The oakum comes in little short rope-lengths, ship-ropes tarsealed, greasy, and hard. **1959** A. H. MCLINTOCK *Descr. Atlas N.Z.* 62, 10,384 miles of roads and highways are tar-sealed or concreted. **1960** I. CROSS *Backward Sex* i. 14 Across a tarsealed yard was the New Wing. **1963** A. LUBBOCK *Austral. Roundabout* 10 The bitumen, or tar-sealed, roads are only made over the most frequented highways, and through towns. **1966** G. W. TURNER *Eng. Lang. in Austral. & N.Z.* viii. 172 Roads are still 'tar-sealed'. **1977** *N.Z. Herald* 8 Jan. 4-1/3 (Advt.), Situated at Ola Point on the Whangaroa Harbour and gently sloping from tarsealed road frontage to the reserve at Harbour edge.

Hence **'tar-seal** *sb.*, a road surface made with asphalt; a road so surfaced; also **'tar-sealing**.

1957 *Numbers* Mar. 14 The tar-seal led purposefully to a wall of..stiff pale grasses. **1959** M. SHADBOLT *New Zealanders* 88 They descended..into a lonely part of country. Tar-seal gave way to a road of clay and pumice. **1963** N. HILLIARD *Piece of Land* 91 They'd brought in a lot of land around here since the new tarseal went through. **1964** *Evening Post* (Wellington, N.Z.) 10 Mar. 9/4 'Tar-sealing originated in Taranaki,' said Mr. Daniell [of Akura, Masterton]. 'Metal for the roads in the New Plymouth area had to be carted all the way from the Patea River and was, of course, expensive. Traffic threw much of the metal off the roads and one day a New Plymouth councillor suggested that they 'seal the metal on the roads' with tar, and so 'tarsealing' was born.' **1972** M. GEE *In my Father's Den* 26 Her sandals made a clacking noise on the tar-seal. **1977** *N.Z. Herald* 8 Jan. IV. 5/1 (Advt.), Situated on corner of 600 acres. This is very private yet adjacent to tarseal.

tarsectomy, -ectopia: see TARSO-.

† **tarsel, tarcel.** *Obs.* Also 5-6 -ell; 6 tersele. Apparently a corrupt variant of TASSEL.

1459 *Paston Lett.* I. 487 Item, j. prikkyng hat, covered withe blake felwet. Item, ij. tarcellys on hym be hynde. **1558** in Feuillerat *Revels Q. Eliz.* (1908) 92, v dd. of tarsells by him made of ye same sylver. **1570** LEVINS *Manip.* 57/11 A Tarsel, *appendix.* **1578** *Richmond Wills* (Surtees) 278, j grose of statut lace vᵉ. viijᵈ. iiij gernesh tersele xijᵈ.

Hence † **tarcelled** *a.* = TASSELLED.

1558 in Feuillerat *Revels Q. Eliz.* (1908) 39 Clothe of sylver tarcelled with cullen sylver.

tarsel, -ell, -elet, obs. ff. TERCEL, -ELET.

‖ **tarsia** ('tɑːsɪə). Also 7 **tersia.** [a. It. *tarsia* 'marquetry or small inlaid workes of diuers colours of bone, horne, wood or Iuorie' (Florio).] A kind of mosaic inlaid work in wood of various colours and shades. Also *attrib.* as *tarsia-work*.

1665 SIR T. HERBERT *Trav.* (1677) 138 But if Mosaick be in wood 'tis called *Tersia*: the several pieces of which are boil'd and dyed into what colour the workman fancies. **1875** POLLEN *Anc. & Mod. Furn.* 28 The wood veneered or inlaid with marquetry or tarsia work of ivory, ebony, box, palm. **1883** FR. M. PEARD *Contrad.* I. 228 Cortina..with its great schools of filigree and tarsia work. **1901** *J. Black's Carp. & Build., Home Handicr.* 61 Tarsia..was a species of wood inlay or mosaic of which the Italians of the late Mediæval period were the great exponents.

Tarsian ('tɑːsɪən), *a.* and *sb.* [f. *Tars(us* (see below) + -IAN.] **A.** *adj.* Of or pertaining to Tarsus, a Cilician city in south-eastern Asia Minor, and the birthplace of St. Paul. **B.** *sb.* A native or inhabitant of Tarsus.

1895 W. M. RAMSAY *St. Paul Traveller* i. ii. 31 Paul was careful to keep within demonstrable law..when he claimed to be a Tarsian citizen. **1914** W. R. INGE in *Q. Rev.* CCXX. 50 The Emperor showed great favour to the Tarsians. **1920** J. A. ROBERTSON *Hidden Romance N.T.* iv. 69, The Tarsian, a diminutive youth, nervous and awkward in manner. **1928** J. P. ARENDZEN *Men & Manners in Times of Christ* viii. 128 Did St. Paul, by claiming Tarsian citizenship, mean to imply that..he was a man of means?

tarsier ('tɑːsɪə(r)). *Zool.* [a. F. *tarsier*, f. *tarse* TARSUS. So named by Buffon from the structure of the foot: see quots.] A small lemuroid quadruped, *Tarsius spectrum*, of Sumatra, Borneo, Celebes, and the Philippines, called also malmag or spectre, related to the aye-aye of Madagascar.

1774 GOLDSM. *Nat. Hist.* (1776) IV. 248 The last animal of this class is called by Mr. Buffon, the Tarsier... The bones of..the Tarsus, are..so very long, that from thence the animal has received its name. **1785** SMELLIE *Buffon's Nat. Hist.* (1791) VII. 171 The Tarsier, or Woolly Jerboa.. is remarkable for the excessive length of its hind legs. The bones of the feet, and particularly those which compose the upper part of the tarsus, are prodigiously long. **1882** A. R. WALLACE in *Contemp. Rev.* Mar. 427 The Tarsier, or spectre-lemur, of the Malay islands.

tarsioid ('tɑːsɪɔɪd), *sb.* and *a.* *Palæont.* [f. TARSI(ER + -OID.] **A.** *sb.* A fossil primate belonging to the suborder Tarsioidea, of which tarsiers are the only living members. **B.** *adj.* Of, pertaining to, or resembling a fossil tarsioid or a tarsier.

1913 G. E. SMITH in *Rep. Brit. Assoc. Adv. Sci. 1912* 585 It may have been the case that the original habitat of the Tarsioids ranged from North America to South-eastern Europe. *Ibid.* 590 The factors that..have transformed a Tarsioid Prosimian into an Ape. **1925** *Bull. Geol. Soc. China* IV. 142 Primitive lemuroid and tarsioid fossil remains are widely known from England eastwards to the Carpathians. **1929** F. W. JONES *Man's Place among Mammals* xl. 359 We have further grounds in analogy with the jaws of the known tarsioids. **1968** W. LE GROS CLARK *Chant of Pleasant Exploration* iii. 76 A rich assortment of extinct 'tarsioids'.. extended their range over considerable areas. **1973** B. J. WILLIAMS *Evolution & Human Origins* ix. 124/1 It has been suggested that the higher primates did go through a tarsioid stage of evolution.

tarsiped ('tɑːsɪpɛd), *sb.* (*a.*) *Zool.* [ad. Zool. L. generic name *Tarsipēs, -ped-em*, f. L. TARSUS + *pēs, ped-* foot.] A small marsupial mammal, *Tarsipes rostratus*, the *tait* of West Australia. **b.** *adj.* Of or belonging to the family *Tarsipedidæ*, of which this animal is the type. So **tar'sipedid, -ine, -oid** *adjs.*, belonging to the family *Tarsipedidæ*.

‖ **tarsitis** (tɑː'saɪtɪs). *Path.* [mod.L., f. Gr. ταρσός the rim of the eyelid + -ITIS.] Inflammation of the tarsus of the eyelid.

1890 in BILLINGS *Nat. Med. Dict.*

† **'tarso.** *Obs.* [a. It. *tarso.*] A white siliceous stone found in Italy, formerly used in glass-making.

1662 MERRETT tr. *Neri's Art of Glass* viii, Tarso..makes ..fairer glass than any sand that is in Tuscany. **1712** tr. *Pomet's Hist. Drugs* I. 105 Beat..finely and searse your Tarso, Crystal, &c. **1799** G. SMITH *Laboratory* I. 171 The fluxes used in the other are salts, or arsenic, and the body consists of tarso, white river pebbles, and such stones.

tarso- (tɑːsəʊ), before a vowel **tars-**, comb. form of Gr. ταρσός, TARSUS, a formative of technical terms of anatomy, pathology, and surgery.

‖ **tar'salgia** [Gr. -αλγια, ἄλγος, pain], (*a*) a general term for pain in the tarsus; (*b*) see quot. **tar'sectomy** [Gr. ἐκτομή excision], excision of one or more of the tarsal bones. ‖ **tarsec'topia** [ECTOPIA], displacement of the tarsus. ‖ **tar'soclasis** [Gr. κλάσις fracture], (*a*) rupture of the tarsal cartilages (*Syd. Soc. Lex.* 1899); (*b*) rupture of the fibrous tissue forming the basis of the eyelids (Cassell *Suppl.* 1902). ‖ **tarsomalacia** (-'eɪʃ(ɪ)ə) [Gr. μαλακία softness], a softening of the palpebral cartilages (*Syd. Soc. Lex.* 1899). **tarsopha'langeal** *a.*, pertaining to or connecting the tarsus and the phalanges. ‖ **tarso'phyma** [Gr. φῦμα tumour], a swelling or tumour of the tarsus (Dunglison, 1857). **'tarsoplasty** [-PLASTY], plastic surgery of the eyelid (*Syd. Soc. Lex.*). **tar'sorrhaphy** [Gr. ῥαφή seam], plastic suture of the eyelid. **tarso'tarsal** *a.*, = *medio-tarsal* (see MEDIO-). **tarso'tibial** *a.*, = TIBIOTARSAL. **tar'sotomy** [Gr. τομή cutting]: see quot. 1857.

1890 BILLINGS *Nat. Med. Dict.*, **Tarsalgia*,..peculiar neuralgic affection of the foot, often with some flattening of the arch and contraction of the plantar muscles; observed in policemen, soldiers, etc. *Ibid.*, **Tarsectomy.* **1891** *Lancet* 28 Feb. 491/1 A case in which Syme's amputation had been performed on one foot and tarsectomy on the other for severe talipes. **1860** MAYNE *Expos. Lex.*, **Tarsectopia.* **1890** in BILLINGS *Nat. Med. Dict.* **1871** HUXLEY *Anat. Vertebr. Anim.* viii. 333 The *tarsophalangeal synostosis above described is freely movable on the astragalus. **1846** BRITTAN tr. *Malgaigne's Man. Oper. Surg.* 277 In the second case are employed excision of the conjunctiva, excision of the tarsal cartilage, V shaped excision of the lid, *tarsoraphy. **1898** P. MANSON *Trop. Diseases* xxvi. 421 Tarsorraphy for ectropion of the lower lid..may sometimes have to be performed. **1857** DUNGLISON *Dict. Med. Sc.*, **Tarsotomy*,..the section or removal of the tarsal cartilages. **1893** *Brit. Med. Jrnl.* 18 Feb. 341/2 Tarsotomy..is of service where the varus is the chief defect.

tarso-metatarsal (ˌtɑːsəʊmɛtə'tɑːsəl), *a.* and *sb.* *Comp. Anat.* **a.** *adj.* (*a*) Of or pertaining to the tarsus and the metatarsus, as 'the tarso-metatarsal ligaments'; (*b*) Of or pertaining to a tarso-metatarsus. **b.** *sb.* Short for *tarso-metatarsal bone* or *ligament*.

1835-6 *Todd's Cycl. Anat.* I. 288/1 In the Grallatores.. the tarso-metatarsal bone is remarkably elongated. **1851** MANTELL *Petrifact.* ii. § 1. 79 There are also tarsometatarsals of a remarkable extinct genus named *Aptornis. Ibid.* § 3. 116 The longest tarso-metatarsal bones I have seen are eighteen inches and a half in length. **1872** HUMPHRY *Myology* 28 Near the insertion of the middle portions of the tarso-metatarsals. **1875** SIR W. TURNER in *Encycl. Brit.* I. 841/2 The configuration of its tarso-metatarsal joint and the attachment of the transverse metatarsal ligament prevent the great toe from being thrown across the surface of the sole as the thumb is thrown across the palm.

‖ **tarso-metatarsus** (ˌtɑːsəʊmɛtə'tɑːsəs). *Comp. Anat.* Also in Fr.-Eng. form **ˌtarso-'metatarse.** The bone formed by ankylosis of the tarsus and the metatarsus in birds and early reptilian types.

1854 OWEN *Skel. & Teeth* in *Orr's Circ. Sc.* I. *Org. Nat.* 224 The period at which these several constituents of the 'tarso-metatarse' coalesce is shorter in the birds that can fly than in [the others]. **1870** ROLLESTON *Anim. Life* 18 The fibula never articulates with the tarso-metatarsus.

tarsonemid (tɑːsə'niːmɪd), *a.* (and *sb.*) [f. mod.L. family name *Tarsonemidæ*, f. generic name *Tarsonemus* (Canestrini and Fanzago 1876, in *Atti Soc. Veneto-trentina Sci. Nat.* V. 14), f. TARSO- + Gr. νῆμα thread: see -ID³.] Of or pertaining to a mite of the family Tarsonemidæ. Also as *sb.*

1922 *Nature* 20 Mar. 396/1 A Tarsonemid mite..feeds on the blood of the bee. **1951** *Dict. Gardening* (R. Hort. Soc.) IV. 2082/1 Tarsonemid mites..are of great economic importance owing to the injury caused by them to cultivated plants. **1959** T. E. HUGHES *Mites* v. 73 Many other tarsonemids are plant parasites.

tarsse, variant of TARS *Obs.*

‖**tarsus** ('tɑːsəs). *Anat.* Pl. -i. [mod.L., a. Gr. *ταρσός* the flat of the foot between the toes and the heel; also the rim of the eyelid; in F. *tarse.*]

1. The first or posterior part of the foot: a collective name for the seven small bones of the human ankle, arranged in two transverse series, the proximal or tibial, consisting of the astragalus and os calcis (or calcaneum), and the distal, or metatarsal, consisting of the naviculare (centrale, or scaphoides), the cuboides, and the three ossa cuneiformia; also, the corresponding part in mammalia generally, and in some reptiles and amphibia.

1676 WISEMAN *Chirurg. Treat.* VII. ii. 479 The Conjunction is called *Synarthrosis*; as in the joyning..the Tarsus to the Metatarsus. **1693** tr. *Blancard's Phys. Dict.* (ed. 2), *Tarsus*..also eight backward Bones of the Foot, ordered like Grates. **1704** J. HARRIS *Lex. Techn.* I, *Tarsus*, is the Space between the lower end of the two Focils, and the beginning of the Five long Bones which sustain, and are articulated with the Toes. **1872** NICHOLSON *Palæont.* 305 The small bones of the ankle, known as the tarsus. **1875** HUXLEY & MARTIN *Elem. Biol.* (1883) 225.

b. In birds, the third segment of the leg, the shank (which is rarely fleshy or feathered), corresponding to the mammalian tarsus and metatarsus conjoined: = TARSO-METATARSUS.

1828 STARK *Elem. Nat. Hist.* I. 253 (Birds, *Bucco*) Tarsus shorter than the exterior toe; the anterior toes united to the second joint. **1874** COUES *Birds N.W.* 321 Tarsi nearly naked, the feathers extending but a little way below the heel-joint. **1880** A. R. WALLACE in *19th Cent.* XXXV. 100.

c. In insects and other *Arthropoda*, a series of small articulations forming the true foot; in spiders, the last joint, forming, with the preceding joint or metatarsus, the foot.

1826 KIRBY & SP. *Entomol.* III. xxviii. 48 [In insects] the foot or Tarsus, is almost universally monodactyle. **1828** STARK *Elem. Nat. Hist.* II. 155 (Crustacea, *Cryptopoda*) None of the tarsi are fin-shaped. **1834** McMURTRIE *Cuvier's Anim. Kingd.* 311 (Arachnides, *Clotho*) The tarsi, only, are furnished with spines. **1867** J. HOGG *Microscope* II. iv. 587 The tarsus, or foot of the Fly consists of a deeply bifid, membranous structure.

2. The thin plate of condensed connective tissue found in each eyelid. Now *rare* or *Obs.*

1691 RAY *Creation* II. (1692) 119 The side of the Triangle, which is toward the little Corner of the Eye, and is moveable, was reinforced with a Border, which supplies the place of the Tarsus. **1727–41** CHAMBERS *Cycl.*, *Tarsus* is also a name given by some anatomists to the cartilages which terminate the palpebræ, or eyelids.

tart (tɑːt), *sb.* Also 4–6 **tarte**, 5 **taarte, tartt**, 6 **tairte**, 9 *Sc.* **tairt, teart.** [a. F. *tarte* (13th c.), an open tart, in our sense 1 b (*a*), = med.L. *tarta* (1103 in Du Cange); of uncertain origin.

F. *tarte* was held by Diez to be altered from OF. *torte*, F. *tourte*, a disc-shaped cake or loaf, also a pasty, a pie, late L. *torta panis*, a kind of loaf or bread (Vulg.): and the two words certainly sometimes run together in use: cf. It. (Florio) *torta, tortara* 'a tart' (Baretti), *torta* 'a pasty'; Sp. (Minsheu) *torta, tarta* 'a tart', mod.Sp. *torta* a covered pasty, *tarta* a tart; but there are phonetic difficulties in the identification, which is rejected by Hatz.-Darm. Du. *taart*, tart, is from Fr. The Welsh *torth*, Breton *tors* round loaf, are from L. *torta* or OF. *torte*.]

1. Name for various dishes consisting of a crust of baked pastry enclosing different ingredients; †**a.** formerly with meat, fish, cheese, fruit, etc.: the same or nearly the same as a *pie*. **b.** In current use restricted to (*a*) a flat, usually small, piece of pastry, with no crust on the top (so distinguished from a pie), filled with fruit preserve or other sweet confection; (*b*) a covered fruit pie: = PIE *sb.*² 1 (*c*): in this application formerly chiefly *dial.* or *local*, now in polite or fashionable use.

a. ? *a* **1400** *Morte Arth.* 186 Tartes of Turky, taste whane þeme lykys. *c* **1400** *Rom. Rose* 7041 With tendre gees, & with capons, With tartes, or with chesis [*MS.* cheffis] fat, With deynte flawnes, brode & flat. **14..** *Voc.* in Wr.-Wülcker 565/44 *Artocrea*, *ance* a tart. *c* **1430** *Two Cookery-bks.* (E.E.T.S.) 47 Tartes de chare... Tartes of Fyssche. *c* **1440** *Promp. Parv.* 487/1 Taarte, bake mete.., *tarta*. **1523** SKELTON *Garl. Laurel* 1245 The Balade also of the Mustarde Tarte; Suche problemis to paynt it longyth to his arte. **1552** HULOET, Tarte or march pane, *chanona*. **1598** *Epulario* H iij, To make Tarts..of Creuisses. *Ibid.* H iij b, To make Tarts of Eeles. **1771** MRS. HAYWOOD *New Present* 192 A Tart [made of veal suet, seasoning, bread, eggs, veal sweetbreads, ..etc. made in a dish].

b. *c* **1430** *Two Cookery-bks.* (E.E.T.S.) 48 Tartes of Frute in lente. **1562** TURNER *Herbal* II. 119 b, The tartes made onlye of Heppes serue well to be eaten of them that vomit to much. **1580** in *Hist. MSS. Comm., Var. Collect.* (1903) 444 b, Dinner. To my Master... A boild meat of mutton [etc.]. Second course. Rabytes roste. Chickins roste [etc.]. .. Arttigoges, and strobarye tairte. **1584** COGAN *Haven Health* cvii. (1636) 108 Boyle them [fruit]..till they be soft, then to draw them, as yee doe a tart. **1668–9** PEPYS *Diary* 24 Feb., A mighty neat dish of custards and tarts. **1696** PHILLIPS (ed. 5), *Tart*, a sort of Baked Dish, consisting of Summer Fruits bak'd in Paste. *c* **1710** CELIA FIENNES *Diary* (1888) 218 One of ye West Country tarts..its an apple pye with a Custard all on the top. **1725** *Bradley's Fam. Dict.* s.v., When the Tart is made, you must cover it at top with some Bands of Paste, and having sugar'd it, bake it in the Oven. **1737** *Gentl. Mag.* VII. 307/2 Need I the currant sing, or goosberry praise, Prepar'd in tarts which artful females raise? **1769** MRS. RAFFALD *Eng. Housekpr.* (1778) 215 To preserve Currants for Tarts. **1899** W. H. MALLOCK *Individualist* xix. 187 Her rejection of a nice little jam tart ..'she never touched *patisserie*'.

2. *fig.* **a.** Applied, *gen.* (orig. often endearingly) to a girl or woman; freq. in Australia and N.Z. Also in Liverpool dial. (with def. article or possessive pron.): a wife or girl-friend. *slang.*

1864 HOTTEN *Slang Dict.* 254 *Tart*, a term of approval applied by the London lower orders to a young woman for whom some affection is felt. The expression is not generally employed by the young men, unless the female is in 'her best'. **1898** in M. Davitt *Life & Progr. Austral.* xxxv. 192 And his lady love's his 'donah', Or his 'dinah', or his 'tart'. **1916** [see DINKUM *a.*]. **1918** *N.Z.E.F. Chrons.* 5 July 252/2, I blushes like a 14-year old tart. **1931** 'G. ORWELL' *Coll. Essays* (1968) 71 This word [*sc.* tart] now seems absolutely interchangeable with 'girl', with no implication of 'prostitute'. People will speak of their daughter or sister as a tart. *a* **1943** L. ESSON in *Penguin Bk. Austral. Ballads* (1964) 233 All the tarts iz waitin'..In their flashest clobber. **1959** I. & P. OPIE *Lore & Lang. Schoolch.* xv. 327 In the south of England a girl is often spoken of as a 'tart' (referred to as such by boys aged 11), and..no disrespect is implied by the word. A 'posh tart' is indeed a general term of admiration for a well-dressed, nice-looking girl. **1962** *Guardian* 24 Dec. 4/2 It's the little things at home that start nagging, and the tart's not well. **1966** [see JUDY]. **1980** V. S. PRITCHETT *Tale Bearers* 84 His mother, a decent, now elderly tart found living with her black servant.

b. A female of immoral character; a prostitute. Also *loosely* as a term of abuse. *slang.*

1887 *Morn. Post* 25 Jan., The paragraph..referred to the young ladies in the chorus at the Avenue and spoke of them as 'tarts'. It was suggested on the part of the prosecution that the word 'tart' really meant a person of immoral character. **1894** *Daily News* 5 Feb. 2/7 Some of the women described themselves as 'Tarts'..and said that they got their living in the best way they could. **1903** FARMER *Slang*, *Tart* (common). Primarily a girl, chaste or not; now (unless loosely used) a wanton, mistress, 'good-one'. **1922** E. O'NEILL *Hairy Ape* v. 57 I see yuh, yuh white-faced tart, yuh! **1936** G. GREENE *Gun for Sale* ii. 37 A woman policeman kept an eye on the tarts at the corner. **1951** S. LONGSTREET *Pedlocks* II. v. 93 Real fancy night[-gown], pink drawers, black lace... Nothing cheap for us like the grimy tarts on Mercury Street. **1965** E. J. HOWARD *After Julius* ix. 133 People don't..call other people tarts because they go to bed with people without marrying them. **1979** J. COOPER *Class* 17, I evolved a new way of dressing: five-inch high-heeled shoes, tight straight skirts, very very tight cheap sweaters, and masses of make-up... I looked just like a tart.

c. The young favourite of an older man; a catamite. Also *loosely*, a male prostitute. *slang.*

1935 I. MILLER *School Tie* II. ix. 110 Being a tart. The sort of thing you were getting up to with Black last Easter term. **1943** D. WELCH *Jrnl.* 23 Feb. (1952) 43 A week afterwards I had a letter from this old boy—quite elaborately romantic. .. As Geoffrey approached I held the letter down, against me. 'What are you engrossed in?' he jeered... 'A tart-note I bet. You've had a tart-note.' **1952** A. WILSON *Hemlock & After* I. v. 95, I can usually manage a tart's holiday at Cannes or Ischia. **1976** *Times Lit. Suppl.* 30 Jan. 100/3 He nearly loses the boy to a male tart in the city. **1977** *Ibid.* 1 Apr. 401/4 The boys that Isherwood and his friends picked up were not professional tarts only out for what they could get.

3. *attrib.* and *Comb.*, as ***tart-dish, -maker, -seller***; †**tart-stuff**, a confection of fruit for making tarts (*obs.*); **tart-woman**, a woman who sells tarts.

1782 WITHERING in *Phil. Trans.* LXXII. 329 Vessels.. made like a common *tart-dish, with a spreading border. **1886** *Pall Mall G.* 15 May 3/2 Verses, eulogizing the *tart-maker and her handiwork. **1851** MAYHEW *Lond. Labour* I. 199/1 I've been a cake and a *tart-seller in the streets for seven or eight years. **1623** *Althorp MS.* in Simpkinson *Washingtons* (1860) p. xlvii, Lumpe sugar for *tarte stuffe. **1848** THACKERAY *Van. Fair* l, When he was rich he would buy Leader's pencil-case and pay the *tart-woman. **1851** —— *Eng. Hum.* iii. (1863) 126 This boy went invariably into debt with the tart-woman.

tart, *a.* Forms: 1 **teart**, 6–7 **tarte**, 4, 6– **tart.** [OE. *teart*; ulterior derivation obscure: by some referred to root of *ter-an* to TEAR.

The sense-history is also deficient. *Teart* appears in OE. only in reference to punishment, pain, or suffering, which use of *tart*, after many centuries, reappears late in 16th c. In the ME. period, the word is known only by a single instance in Chaucer (if this is the adj.), continued after 1500, in sense 'of a sharp, pungent, or sour taste'. In 1500 it is also applied to a sharp or pungent weapon; and about 1600 to sharp, bitter, caustic, or stinging words. It is difficult from these data to infer the sense-development; and the order here followed is provisional.]

†**1.** Of pain, punishment, suffering, discipline, law: Sharp, severe, painful, grievous. *Obs.*

In OE.; not known in ME.; in mod.Eng. possibly newly developed from sense 2.

c **1000** in Napier *O.E. Glosses* 52/1946 *Acerrimo*, *i. asperrimo*, on þære teartestan. *Ibid.* 168/218 *Acra*, i. tearte. *c* **1000** ÆLFRIC *Hom.* II. 344 Ac beo hem gesæd, ær he ʒewite, ða teartan witu, þæt his heorte mid ðære biternysse beo ʒehrepod.

1577 HANMER *Anc. Eccl. Hist.* v. xvi. 89 Themison.. tasted not of the tarte conyzance of confession. before the tyrant. **1579** GOSSON *To Gentlew. Cit. Lond.* in *Sch. Abuse* (Arb.) 61 My Schoole is tarte, but my counsell is plesaunt. **1602** FULBECKE *Pandectes* x. 81 And Iustinian his Law is tarte; *Si quis..auserit, capitali pœna feriatur.* **1605** SHAKS. *Lear* IV. ii. 87 Another way The News is not so tart.

2. Sharp to the sense of taste; †bitting, pungent (*obs.*); now *esp.* sour, acid, or acidulous.

(The sense in the Chaucer quot. is not quite clear.)

c **1386** CHAUCER *Prol.* 381 To boille the chiknes with the Marybones And poudre Marchant tart and galyngale. *a* **1529** SKELTON *El. Rummyng* 435 Myghty stronge meate For the deuyll to eate; It was tart and punyete. **1601** HOLLAND *Pliny* II. 219 The Patient is to eat tart and sharp meats and poignant sauces [*margin* As Radish roots and oxymell]. **1626** DEAN *Spadacrene Angl.* Title-p., A Brief Treatise of the Acid Tart Fountain in the Forest of Knaresborough.

1530 PALSGR. 327/1 Tarte, sharpe in taste as vinagre is, *aigre, poignant*. **1552** HULOET, Tarte, *acidus*. *Ibid.*, Tarte or somewhat eyger, *subacidus*. **1652** CULPEPPER *Eng. Physic.* (1809) 356 If you love tart things, add ten drops of oil of vitriol to your pint. **1772–84** COOK *Voy.* (1790) I. 139 Cherries..the juice of which was agreeably tart.

†**b.** Of the sense of taste: Keen. *Obs. rare*$^{-1}$.

1605 B. JONSON *Volpone* II. i, Would you ever be fair and young? Stout of teeth, and strong of tongue? Tart of palat? quick of ear?

†**3.** Sharp, keen (as an edge, point, or weapon).

c **1500** MEDWALL *Nature* (Brandl) 777, I bought thys dagger at the marte, A sharp poynt and a tarte. **1600** MARLOWE & CHAPMAN tr. *Hero & Leander* v. K iij b, Thin like an iron wedge, so sharpe and tart, As t'were of purpose made to cleaue Loues heart.

4. *fig.* Of words, speech, a speaker: Sharp in tone or tendency, biting, cutting, acrimonious, caustic.

1601 BP. W. BARLOW *Serm. Paules Crosse* Pref. 10 Here I renounce all tart and soure speach. **1615** BRATHWAIT *Strappado* (1878) 35 Where wilt thou begin With thy tart phrase, to stinge and nettle him? **1669** GALE *Crt. Gentiles* I. III. x. 106 The Cynics..were very tart and satyric in their Declamations against this..kind of Oratorie. **1691** HARTCLIFFE *Virtues* 185 Sometimes a tart Irony goes for Wit. **1710** ADDISON *Tatler* No. 157 ⁋6 Entertaining the Company with tart ill-natured Observations. **1822** W. IRVING *Braceb. Hall* xxix, Her mind was made up, and she grew tart on the least contradiction. **1855** MACAULAY *Hist. Eng.* xxii. IV. 719 Ill humour..might sometimes impel him to give a tart answer.

5. *Comb.*, as ***tart-tongued***.

1602 FULBECKE *2nd Pt. Parall.* 26 b, Being a tart-tounged detractor.

tart, *v.*^{1} *rare.* ? *Obs.* [f. prec. adj.: cf. *to sour*.]

1. *trans.* To make tart, to sour; †to make pungent, give pungency to (*obs.*).

1616 T. SCOTT *Christ's Politician* 32 One sponefull of vineger will soone tart a great deale of sweete milke. *a* **1634** RANDOLPH *Poems* (1668) 28 To walk on our own ground.. The best of sawce to tart our meats.

2. *intr.* To become tart or sour.

1629 GAULE *Holy Madn.* 244 An ill Liquor that being kept too long, hath tarted and tainted the Caske.

tart, *v.*^{2} *slang.* [f. TART *sb.* 2.] **1.** *trans.* To treat in the manner of a catamite or tart; to favour. *nonce-use.*

1930 AUDEN *Poems* 31 For where are Basley who won the Ten, Dickson so tarted by the House, Thomas who kept a sparrow-hawk?

2. To dress *up* or adorn (a person), usu. in a showy or gaudy manner; to titivate; also *refl.* and *intr.* for *refl.* Freq. *trans.* and *fig.*

1938 [implied at TARTED *ppl. a.* a]. **1952** *Archit. Rev.* CXII. 371/2 Unfortunately these devices to prevent the neighbourhood's slip from showing, have been 'tarted-up' with a variety of recessed panels, pipe ends, exposed brick heads and so forth, which seem to have no function. **1959** *Times Lit. Suppl.* 29 May p. xix, There seems nowadays a disposition to tart up Shakespeare as if he cannot be taken straight. **1961** [see PRETTY *v.*]. **1967** *Spectator* 1 Dec. 690/3 Peacetime seems to have been passed in seducing the daughters of the local townsfolk..or tarting up one's uniform with more feathers or buttons. **1972** J. WILSON *Hide & Seek* ii. 35 You won't be able to tart yourself up like a teenager much longer, Rose. **1976** J. COOPER *Harriet* II. xiv. 115 They were tarting up in the Ladies. **1978** *Observer* 16 Apr. 38/1 American dealers would tart up the junk and sell it at suburban auctions at three times the English price.

3. *intr.* **a.** To meet or pursue women. **b.** Of a girl or woman: to behave like an immoral woman or a 'tart'; freq. const. (*a*)*round*.

1948 D. BALLANTYNE *Cunninghams* 30, I bet he's been tarting. **1949** J. B. PRIESTLEY *Home is Tomorrow* II. i. 47, I know I've behaved badly tarting around. **1959** K. WATERHOUSE *Billy Liar* ii. 33, I would fall to wondering whether she was tarting round the streets with some American airman. **1960** *Spectator* 18 Nov. 784 The boy would now turn soft and the girl start tarting. **1981** P. VANSITTART *Death of Robin Hood* IV. v. 206 All had tales of adventure... Some claimed to have been tarting. **1983** J. WAINWRIGHT *Their Evil Ways* II. 66 Her mother was tarting around with this other bloke.

tartan ('tɑːtən), *sb.*^{1} orig. *Sc.* Also 6–7 **tartane, tertane,** (6 **teartane**). [Of uncertain origin: in use early in 16th c.

It has been conjectured to be a. F. *tiretaine* (1247 in Godef. *Compl.*) 'a kind of cloth, half wool, half linen or cotton', for which a variant *tertaine* is quoted by Godefroy of date 1487: cf. the 16th c. Sc. spelling *tertane*. Another conjecture would identify the cloth with that called *tartar* or *tartarin* (q.v.) of which the 16th c. forms *tartarne, tarterne*, somewhat approach *tartane*. But the quots. for TARTAR and TARTARIN point to a richer and more costly stuff.]

1. a. A kind of woollen cloth woven in stripes of various colours crossing at right angles so as to form a regular pattern; worn chiefly by the Scottish Highlanders, each clan having generally its distinctive pattern; often preceded by a clan-name, etc. denoting a particular traditional or authorized design. Also, the pattern or design of such cloth, and applied to silk and other fabrics having a similar pattern. ***shepherds' tartan***, shepherds' plaid: see quot. 1882. In quot. 1810 *pl.* tartan garments.

?*a* **1500** *Symmye & Bruder* 22 in Sibbald *Chron. Sc. Poetry* (1802) I. 360 Syne schupe thame up, to lowp owr leiss, Twa tabartis of the tartane. **1533** *Acc. Ld. High Treas. Scotl.* VI. 79 For fresing of ane tartane galcot. *Ibid.* 80 Ane uthir tartane galcoit gevin to the King be the Maister Forbes. **1538** *Ibid.* 436 Item, for iij elnis of heland tertane to be hois to the Kingis grace, price of the elne iiij s. iiij d. **1546** *Aberdeen Regr.* (1844) I. 236 Item, ane vob of tartane, contenand x ellis, the price of ell iiij s. *Ibid.*, Ane blankat of tartane. **1548–51** *Ibid.* XX. (Jam.), Ane gelcoit of quhit tertane. **1630** J. TAYLOR (Water P.) *Pennilesse Pilgr.* Wks. I. 135/1 Stockings (which they call short hose) made of a warme stuffe of diuers colours, which they call Tartane. **1806** *Gazetteer Scotl.* (ed. 2) 395 Of late the greater part of the tartan for the army has been manufactured in this parish [St. Ninians]. **1810** SCOTT *Lady of L.* III. xxvii, Their feathers dance, their tartans float,..A wild and warlike groupe they stand. **1821** D. STEWART *Sk. Highlanders Scotl.* I. III. i. 229 The pipers wore a red tartan of very bright colours, (of the pattern known by the name of the Stewart tartan). **1855** MACAULAY *Hist. Eng.* xiii. III. 354 Men wearing the same tartan, and attached to the same lord, were arrayed against each other. **1862** 'SHIRLEY' *Nugæ Crit.* vi. 239 Dressed in a bodice and kirtle of shepherd tartan. **1882** OGILVIE (Annandale), *Shepherd's..tartan*, a kind of small check pattern in cloth, woven with black and white warp and weft; (b) a kind of cloth..woven in this pattern—generally made into shepherd's plaids. **1891** *Cent. Dict.* s.v., *Silk tartan*, a silk material for women's dresses and men's waistcoats, woven in the style of the Scottish clan tartans. **1897** *Private Life of Queen* xxv. 209 The writing-room is hung entirely with the Balmoral tartan. **1905** *Times* 7 Sept. 5/4 Considerable success has followed the bringing out of quite a variety of tartans for next spring. **1906** *Athenæum* 2 June 671/2 The whole question of the date of clan tartans is difficult. **1949** 'J. TEY' *Brat Farrar* xiii. 114 A frayed Stewart tartan ribbon off a box of Edinburgh rock. **1981** *Times* 3 Feb. 17/6 Streaming from her helmet were two lengths of Colquhoun tartan from the clan of which her father was chief.

b. *transf.* Applied to one who wears tartan; a Highlander; collectively, those who wear tartan; the body of Highlanders; the men of a Highland regiment.

1817 CANNING in Hanna *Mem. Chalmers* (1849) II. v. 102 The tartan [so runs the speech attributed to him, i.e. Canning, regarding Dr. C.] beats us all. **1859** COLIN CAMPBELL in A. Forbes *Life* v. 127 [Then Sir Colin called to Colonel Ewart,] 'Ewart! Bring on the tartan!'..[and the seven companies of the Ninety-Third dashed from behind the bank].

c. Used to denote young people who are members of Protestant gangs in Northern Ireland, from their traditional support of Glasgow Rangers Football Club.

1972 *Guardian* 17 Mar. 1/3 The local Protestant street gangs, mainly known as 'Tartans' because of their traditional association with the Rangers Football club. **1974** *Listener* 14 Mar. 324/2 Until recently these streets were terrorised by Tartan Gangs. Now their place has been taken by these youngsters, acting in the name of the Loyalist cause... Their behaviour is modelled on the Tartans. **1977** P. CARTER *Under Goliath* iii. 15 Most of the kids were in tough Prod gangs, like the Tartans.

2. *Angling.* Name of an artificial salmon-fly.

1837 J. KIRKBRIDE *Northern Angler* 73 What is called the tartan-fly kills well in the Highlands at the clearing of the water. **1847** T. T. STODDART *Angler's Compan.* xiii. 240 Salmon flies... The Tartan. Mottled black and white tail feather from turkey. **1867** F. FRANCIS *Angling* x. 315 The Tartan is a strange looking fly. [Description follows.]

3. Short for *tartan-purry*: see 5 b. *Sc.*

1893 HENDERSON *Old World Scotl.* 80 Of oatmeal we have tartan—a pudding made chiefly of chopped kale and oatmeal.

4. (Properly with capital initial.) The proprietary name of a synthetic resin material used for surfacing running tracks, ramps, etc. Usu. *attrib.*, as *Tartan track*.

1964 *Official Gaz.* (U.S. Patent Office) 14 Jan. TM 60/1 Tartan. For synthetic resin material for application to various surfaces..To provide a resilient surface theron. First use Aug. 28, 1962. **1968** *Listener* 10 Oct. 485/2 The 100-metre final is also on Day Three. A fast time with thin air, the 'tartan' track and, maybe, the new brush spike, is inevitable. **1969** *Trade Marks Jrnl.* 22 Oct. 1732/1 *Tartan.* .. Synthetic resins for use as floor and road surfacing materials. **1972** *Radio Times* 1 June 13/3 Britain's sprint hope..says..'I've got a good coach, there's a tartan track two minutes up the road.'

5. *attrib.* **a.** Made of tartan; having a chequered pattern like that of tartan.

1533 [see 1]. **1549** *Fragm. Ayr Burgh Rec.* (Gen. Reg. Ho., Edinb.), Item for teartane claith, aucht lib. **1721** RAMSAY *Tartana* 78 Who 'midst the snows the best of limbs can fold In Tartan Plaids, and smile at chilling cold. *c* **1750** in Ritson *Sc. Songs* (1794) II. 107 O! to see his tartan trouze, Bonnet blue, and laigh-heel'd shoes! **1853** 'C. BEDE' *Verdant Green* I. vii, A gentleman clad in tartan-plaid. **1869** E. A. PARKES *Pract. Hygiene* (ed. 3) 403 One pair of tartan trousers in rifle regiments.

b. tartan-purry (*Sc. local*): see quots.

c **1746** FORBES *Dominie* II. (1785) 35 Tartan-purry, meal and bree, Or butt'ry brose. **1790** SHIRREFS *Poems* Gloss., *Tartan purry*, a sort of pudding made of red colewort chipped small, and mixed with oatmeal. **1819** W. TENNANT *Papistry Storm'd* (1827) 52 Some ran to parritch, some to kail;..And some to tartan-purry. **1866** T. EDMONDSTON *Gloss. Shetl. & Orkn.*, *Tart-and-purrie*, porridge made with the water in which cabbage has been boiled.

c. Used *loosely* in various *transf.* and *fig.* collocations to designate something pertaining to Scotland or which evokes Scottish nationalist fervour.

1954 J. P. BARTER (*title*) Ritchie; or, behind the Tartan Curtain. **1975** *Globe & Mail* (Toronto) 27 Sept. 6/6 The British press has taken extreme care to avoid the suggestion that the activities of the 'Tartan Army' are linked to the legitimate national movement embodied in the Scottish National Party. **1976** *Listener* 28 Oct. 555/2 Radio 3's *Scottish Evening*... Overall there was a blessed absence of.. Tartan Romanticism. **1982** *Times* 9 Jan. 6/1 Almost all Scottish MPs..are Scots by birth... It is not simply raw xenophobic tartan nationalism.

tartan, tartane ('tɑːtən, ‖tartan), *sb.*[2] Also 7 tartain. [a. Fr. *tartane* (1632 in Hatz.-Darm.), a. It., = Sp., Pg. *tartana*, supposed by Diez to be derived from Arab. *tarīdah*: see TARETTE. But connecting evidence is wanting.] A small one-masted vessel with a large lateen sail and a foresail, used in the Mediterranean; = TARTANA[1].

1621 *Admiralty Crt. Exam.* No. 43. 24 Aug., A small vessel called a tartain flotinge and driveinge to and fro in the sea. **1666** *Lond. Gaz.* No. 77/2 A small Tartane arrived here two daies since from Provence. **1697** DAMPIER *Voy. round World* (1699) 30 Captain Wright..had taken a Spanish Tartan, wherein were 30 men, all well armed. **1756–7** tr. *Keysler's Trav.* (1760) IV. 119 A Turkish tartane, with red colours, emblazoned with three crescents, &c. was performing quarantine. **1805** WILKES in *Mem.* II. 171, I could not go in a small tartan without some one friend. **1896** VIZETELLY *Zola's Rome* 295 The few tartanes which brought wine from Sicily, never came higher than the Aventine.

tartan, *sb.*[3] *rare*$^{-0}$. = TARTANA[3].

1858 SIMMONDS *Dict. Trade, Tartan*,..a long covered carriage.

‖**tartan,** *sb.*[4] [Assyrian. See 2 Kings xviii. 17, Isa. xx. 1.] The ancient Assyrian commander-in-chief.

1880 CHEYNE *Isaiah* (1884) I. 16 No Satraps nor Tartans are necessary. **1893** SAYCE *Higher Crit.* (1894) 427 The 'tartan' of Sargon entered Jerusalem and forced Hezekiah to become his tributary. **1899** T. NICOLL *Rec. Archæol. & Bible* vii. 255 The Tartan fought against Ashdod and took it.

'tartan, *v.* [f. TARTAN *sb.*[1]] *trans.* To clothe or array in tartan; also *fig.* So **tartaned** ('tɑːtənd) *a.*, clothed in tartan, wearing tartans.

1813 HOGG *Queen's Wake* 283 Tartaned chiefs in raptures hear The strains, the words, to them so dear. **1875** A. SMITH *Aberdeenshire* I. 656 The crested chief led on his tartaned band. **1881** J. F. CAMPBELL in Ld. A. Campbell *Rec. Argyll* (1885) 441, I was first tartaned, more than fifty years ago.

‖**tartana**[1] (tar'tana). [It. *tartana*: see TARTAN *sb.*[2]] = TARTAN *sb.*[2]

1588 *Ancaster MSS.* in *Hist. MSS. Comm.* (1907) XLV. 113 They have almost two hundred Tartanars, which are a kind of fish boats they use in the Straits. **1617** LD. CAREW *Lett.* (Camden) 92 They have allso 200 tartenas, which are a kind of flat-bottomde boates. **1773** *Phil. Trans.* LXV. 1, I hired a fishing vessel, called a *tartana*, with eighteen men in her. **1884** W. SIME *To & Fro* 17 Here are tartanas waiting the voyager.

†**tartana**[2] (tɑː'tɑːnə). *Obs. rare.* [Pseudo-latinized form of TARTAN[1].] = TARTAN *sb.*[1] 1.

1721 RAMSAY *Tartana* 82 Bright Tartana's waving in the wind. *Ibid.* 315 A bright Tartana veiled the lovely fair.

‖**tartana**[3]. [Sp. *tartana*.] A covered vehicle used in Spain, esp. in Valencia.

1829 W. IRVING in *Life & Lett.* (1864) II. 408 We made our journey..in a kind of covered cart called a Tartana, drawn by a mule. **1845** FORD *Handbk. Spain* I. 438 A *Tartana*, the common Valencian vehicle... It may be compared to a Venetian gondola on wheels. **1882** *Harper's Mag.* Sept. 564 In summer it is covered with tartanas, bouncing little covered waggons lined with crimson curtains.

tartane: see TARTAN *sb.*[1] and [2], TERTIAN.

tartar ('tɑːtə(r)), *sb.*[1] Also 4 tartre, 5 tarter, -are, (6 tartarum, 7–8 tartarus). [a. F. *tartre* = Sp., Pg., It. *tartaro*, med.L. *tartarum* (*tartharum*), med.Gr. τάρταρον; perh. of Arabic origin: Simon of Genoa (fl. 1292), *Synonima* (ed. 1473), has '*Tartar* arabice, tartarum quod ex uino in lateribus uegetis generatur'.

But there is some doubt as to this, the usual Arabic term being *durdī*, from Pers. *durd* sediment, dregs; *tartīr*, found in mod.Arabic lexicons from 1639, is held by Dozy to be borrowed from European langs. The med.L. *tartarum* appears in the *Dictionarius* of Joh. de Garlandia, *c* 1225.]

1. *Chem.* Bitartrate of potash (acid potassium tartrate), present in grape juice, deposited in a crude form in the process of fermentation, and adhering to the sides of wine-casks in the form of a hard crust, also called *argal* or ARGOL, which in the crude state varies from pale pink to dark red, but when purified forms white crystals, which are ***cream of tartar***.

(†In quot. *c* 1425 applied to the dregs of malt liquor.)

c **1386** CHAUCER *Can. Yeom. Prol. & T.* 260 Of Tartre, Alum glas, berme, wort and argoille. **1398** TREVISA *Barth. De P.R.* XVI. xcix. (Tollem. MS.), Tartar is wyn drastes [*tartarum est vini fæculentia*], and like to a softe ston cleuynge harde to þe sides of þe tonnes. *c* **1425** tr. *Arderne's Surgery* (E.E.T.S.) 49 Ffirst I made hym ane emplastre of tartare of ale, i.[e]. dreggez. *c* **1550** LLOYD *Treas. Health* B vij, Wyne Lyes called Tartarum..menglid in oyle and Veniger is verye good. **1679** V. ALSOP *Melius Inquir.* Introd. 32 Like Tartar, [it] is so baked and crusted to the sides of the Vessel, that till you knock off the Hoops and take the frame in pieces, no Art of Man will free the Cask from a tang at least of the old mustiness. **1732** ARBUTHNOT *Rules of Diet* in *Aliments*, etc. 259 Small Wines with little Oil and much Tartar. **1797** *Encycl. Brit.* (ed. 3) IV. 495/2 The tartar of the white wines is of a greyish white colour, called white tartar; and that of red wine has a red colour, and is called red tartar. **1883** *Hardwich's Photogr. Chem.* (ed. Taylor) 96 Tartaric Acid..is derived from a substance called Tartar, deposited from the juice of the Grape during fermentation. This Tartar is an Acid Tartrate of Potash.

b. Hence, 'A generic name for salts of tartaric acid' (Watts).

c. Commercially, applied not to the argol or original deposit, but to a product that has undergone partial purification: see quot.

1893 THORPE *Dict. Applied Chem.* III. 783 The crust is known as 'argol', and when recrystallised produces 'tartar', which by further crystallisation is converted into 'cream of tartar', technically known as 'cream'.

d. *fig.*

1590 MARLOWE *2nd Pt. Tamburl.* IV. i, A soul Created of the massy dregs of earth, The scum and tartar of the elements. *a* **1631** DONNE *Serm.* (1649) II. xix. 153 Impatience in affliction..a leaven so kneaded into the nature of man, so innate a tartar, so inherent a sting. **1683** BURNET tr. *More's Utopia* Pref. (1684) 4 Our Language has, like a rich Wine, wrought out its Tartar. **1824** LANDOR *Imag. Conv.*, *Ld. Brooke & Sir P. Sidney*, Desire of lucre... It is the tartar that encrusts economy.

2. *transf.* Any calcareous or other incrustation deposited from a liquid upon bodies in contact with it. (With quot. 1605 cf. TARTARER, TARTAROUS 2.)

1605 TIMME *Quersit.* III. 161 Of the congelations of these salts comes goutes..and diuers kinds of obstructions, according to the diuersitie of tartars and of salts which are ingendred and procreate to nature in our bodie. **1756–7** tr. *Keysler's Trav.* (1760) III. 151 This water is impregnated with tartar, so that the bottom and pillars..are incrusted with it. **1789** MRS. PIOZZI *Journ. France* I. 427 [It] incrusted a stick with its tartar in two minutes.

b. *spec.* A deposit of calcium phosphate from the saliva, which tends to harden and concrete upon the teeth. (So F. *tartre*; cf. Ger. *weinstein*.)

1806 *Med. Jrnl.* XV. 30 We find that this coagulum has the greatest similarity with the tartar adhering to the teeth. **1822–34** *Good's Study Med.* (ed. 4) I. 65 The teeth are always subject to be covered over with layers of an earthy material secreted as a constituent part of the saliva, and denominated tartar. **1897** *Allbutt's Syst. Med.* IV. 743 The concretions of tartar that gather round the teeth.

3. Phrasal combinations:

a. cream of tartar: see 1 and CREAM *sb.* 4; †**magistery of tartar** = *vitriolated tartar*: see b; **oil of tartar**, old name for a saturated solution of potassium carbonate; †**salt of tartar**, an old name of potassium carbonate; **spirit of tartar**, the liquid obtained by dry distillation of tartar; it contains pyrotartaric acid and other substances.

1584 R. SCOT *Discov. Witchcr.* XIV. i. (1886) 295 These things are of necessitie to be used; namelie..claie made with horsse doong, mans haire, *oile of tartre, allum, glasse, woort, yest, argoll. **1660** BOYLE *New Exp. Phys. Mech.* xxiv. 189 As strong a solution of Salt of Tartar in fair Water as could be made (we having no Oyl of Tartar *per deliquium* at hand). **1706** PHILLIPS, *Oil of Tartar per Deliquium*, the fixt Salt of Tartar dissolved by being expos'd to the Air in a Cellar, or other cool moist place. **1707** *Curios. in Husb. & Gard.* 67 Spirit of Vitriol and Oil of Tartar..mingled together, are surprizingly hot. **1646** SIR T. BROWNE *Pseud. Ep.* 87 A pint of *salt of tartar exposed unto a moist aire untill it dissolve, will make far more liquor, or as some tearm it oyle, then the former measure will contain. **1794** SULLIVAN *View Nat.* I. 339 Moisture drawn from it [the air] by dry salt of tartar, in such quantity, as to make the salt become intirely fluid. **1832** G. R. PORTER *Porcelain & Gl.* 83 Precipitating with salt of tartar (sub-carbonate of potass). **1860** MAYNE *Expos. Lex.*, **Spirit of Tartar*, a name for pyrotartaric acid. [**1868** WATTS *Dict. Chem.* V. 402.]

b. †**chalybeate tartar, tartar chalybeated,** potassio-ferric tartrate, $C_4H_4K(FeO)O_6$; †**regenerated tartar**, acetate of potassium, $C_4H_6O_3.K_2O$; †**soluble tartar**, neutral potassium tartrate, $C_4H_4K_2O_6$; also applied to ammonium potassium tartrate, $C_8H_4(NH_4)KO_6$; †**vitriolated tartar, tartar vitriolate**, sulphate of potassium, K_2SO_4.

1727–41 CHAMBERS *Cycl.* s.v. *Crystal*, Crystal of *tartar chalybeated, is when it is impregnated with the most dissoluble parts of iron. **1860** MAYNE *Expos. Lex.* s.v. *Tartar*, **Chalybeate Tartar*.., a name for the *Potassio-tartras ferri*. **1753** CHAMBERS *Cycl. Supp.* s.v., The good effects of *regenerated tartar in the cure of obstructions of the bowels. **1860** MAYNE *Expos. Lex.*, *Regenerated Tartar*, term for the *Acetas potassæ*. **1704** J. HARRIS *Lex. Techn.* I, **Soluble Tartar*, is made by boiling in 3 Pints of Water, 8 Ounces of Cream of Tartar, and 4 Ounces of the Fix'd Salt of Tartar. **1860** MAYNE *Expos. Lex.*, *Soluble Tartar*, a term for the *Tartras potassæ*. **1704** J. HARRIS *Lex. Techn.* I, **Tartar Vitriolate*, is made by pouring Spirit of Vitriol on Oil of Tartar *per Deliquium*, by little and little. **1727–41** CHAMBERS *Cycl.* s.v., Vitriolated Tartar, which some call Magistery of Tartar, is oil of Tartar mixed with rectified spirit of vitriol. **1820** T. THOMSON *Syst. Chem.* II. 435 Known by the name of *vitriolated tartar*, till the French chemists called it *sulphate of potash*..in 1787.

c. 'tartar-e'metic, †***emetic tartar***, common name in pharmacy of potassio-antimonious tartrate, $C_4H_4K(Sb.O)O_6 + \frac{1}{2}H_2O$, a poisonous substance, used in medicine to excite vomiting. Hence **'tartar-e'meticize** *v.* (*nonce-wd.*), *trans.* to dose with tartar-emetic.

1704 J. HARRIS *Lex. Techn.* I, *Tartar Emetick.* See *Emetick Tartar. Ibid., Emetick Tartar*, is only Cream or Crystal of Tartar poudred and mixt with a quarter part of *Crocus Metallorum*, and..the Mixture..boil'd in an earthen Pan in a sufficient quantity of Water, for about 8 or 9 Hours. **1758** J. S. tr. *Le Dran's Observ. Surg.* (1771) 334 A Dose of Tartar Emetic. **1795** GAITSKELL in *Memoirs Med.* IV. 79 (heading) Observations and Experiments on the external absorption of Emetic Tartar and Arsenic. **1846** MRS. CARLYLE *Lett.* (1883) I. 383 Dosing me with tartar-emetic and opium. **1844** J. T. HEWLETT *Parsons & W.* vi, Tartar-emeticising the establishment at breakfast.

Tartar, Tatar ('tɑːtə(r)), *sb.*[2] (*a.*). Also 6 *pl.* **Tartaries,** 7, 9 **Tâtar, Tahtar.** [a. F. *Tartare* (OF. also *Tartaire*, 13th c.), or ad. med.L. *Tartarus*, pl. *Tartari*, ethnic name; in Sp., Pg., It. *Tartaro*; Du. *Tartaar, Tarter*, Ger., Da. *Tartar*, Sw. *Tartar, Tartarer*; Polish *Tatar*, Turk., Pers. *Tātār*. In OF. more usually *Tartarin*, med.L. *Tartarīnus*, TARTARIN; cf. Russ. *Tatarin*ᵘ.

The original name (by which the people in question either called themselves or were designated by their neighbours) is generally held to have been, as in Persian, etc., *Tātār*, as to the language and meaning of which various conjectures have been put forth; but in Western Europe, they appear from the first as *Tartari, Tartares*, or *Tartars*, their name being apparently associated with *Tartarus*, hell. See the saying attributed by many historians to St. Louis of France *a* 1270, in Littré, s.v. *Tartare*, and a translation in quot. 1842 below. The form *Tâtar* and its derivatives are now often used in ethnological works in sense 1, but the long-established *Tartar* is always used in the derived senses, and is also held by some to have been the original name: see quot. 1885, and its context.]

A. *sb.*[2] **1.** A native inhabitant of the region of Central Asia extending eastward from the Caspian Sea, and formerly known as Independent and Chinese Tartary. First known in the West as applied to the mingled host of Mongols, Tartars, Turks, etc., which under the leadership of Jenghiz Khan (1202–1227) overran and devastated much of Asia and Eastern Europe; hence vaguely applied to the descendants of these now dwelling in Asia or Europe; more strictly and ethnologically, to any member of the Tâtar or Turkic branch of the Ural-Altaic or Turanian family, embracing the Turks, Cossacks, and Kirghiz Tartars. (In all these uses, but esp. the last, now often written *Tatar, Tâtar.*)

c **1386** CHAUCER *Sqr.'s T.* 20 This noble kyng this Tartre, Cambynskan. *Ibid.* 258 This Tartre kyng. **1474** CAXTON *Chesse* IV. iii. (1883) 170 Therfore the tartaris haue their wyues in to the felde with hem. **1525** LD. BERNERS *Froiss.* II. ccxxiii. 363 The dealyng of the turkes and tartaries with yᵉ portes and passages of the kynges, soudans and miscreantes. **1585** T. WASHINGTON tr. *Nicholay's Voy.* III. x. 86 Moores, Indians, or Tartares. **1588** PARKE tr. *Mendoza's Hist. China* 18 It [the great wall] was for his defence against the Tartaries, with whome he had warres. **1590** SHAKS. *Mids. N.* III. ii. 101 Looke how I goe, Swifter then arrow from the Tartars bowe. **1600** HAKLUYT *Voy.* (1810) III. 55 They be like to Tartars, with long blacke haire, broad faces, and flatte noses. **1612** BREREWOOD *Lang. & Relig.* (1614) 94 It is alleaged that the word *Tatari*, or *Totari*, (for so indeed they are rightly called, as learned men obserue, and not *Tartari*) signifieth in the Syriaque and Hebrew tongues, a Residue or Remainder such as these Tartars are supposed to bee of the Ten Tribes. **1745** P. THOMAS *Jrnl. Anson's Voy.* 241 Since the Tartars have been Emperors of China, the Lamas have succeeded the Chinese Bonzes in the Direction of Religious Affairs. **1837** CARLYLE *Fr. Rev.* III. I. i, Into the body of the poor Tatars execrative Roman History intercalated an alphabetic letter; and so they continue Tartars, of fell Tartarean nature, to this day. **1842** *Penny Cycl.* XXIV. 73 The name of Tatar is still given to the Turkish inhabitants of southern and eastern Russia... The Tatars call themselves Turks, and feel highly offended by being called Tatars, a name which in their idiom signifies 'robbers'. **1842** tr. *Let. S. Louis* (*a* 1270) ibid., In the present danger of the Tartars either we shall push them back into the Tartarus whence they are come, or they will bring us all into heaven. **1885** E. PEARS *Fall Constantinople* 15 *note*, I write Tartar instead of Tatar because I agree with Dr. Koelle that the first is the form which the Tartars themselves used until they came into contact with foreigners, like the Chinese and Russians, who had changed the form of the word.

2. Transferred uses. **a.** A military valet. [So in F.]

1747 *Gentl. Mag.* Dec. 570/2, 13,421 Convents of monks ..which may be called the Field regiments, and, together with the brother servitors, invalids, tartars and scullions, may amount to 160,000. **1839** tr. *Lamartine's Trav.* 168/1 Our moukres, Tatars, and horsemen, bivouacked in the orchards.

†**b.** An old cant name for a strolling vagabond, a thief, a beggar. Cf. BOHEMIAN *sb.*, GIPSY *sb.*, TARTARIAN *sb.* b. *Obs.*

1598 SHAKS. *Merry W.* IV. v. 21 Here's a Bohemian-Tartar taries the comming down of thy fat-woman: Let her descend. **1697** VANBRUGH *Relapse* IV. vi, Here, pursue this Tartar, bring him back.

c. As an opprobrious appellation.

1590 SHAKS. *Mids. N.* III. ii. 263 Thy loue? out tawny Tartar, out. **1828** *Craven Gloss., Tartar* a covetous, griping person.

3. *fig.* **a.** A savage; a person supposed to resemble a Tartar in disposition; a rough and violent or irritable and intractable person: when applied to a female, a vixen, a shrew, a termagant.

1663 DRYDEN *Wild Gallant* II. i, I never knew your grand-mother was a Scotchwoman: Is she not a Tartar too? **1771** SMOLLETT *Humph. Cl.* (1815) 146 He is generally a tartar at bottom; a sharper, a spy, or a lunatic. **1778** JOHNSON in *Mme. D'Arblay's Diary* 23 Aug., They will little think what a tartar you carry to them. **1818** BYRON *Juan* I. clxxxiv, His blood was up: though young, he was a Tartar. *a* **1845** HOOD *Tale of Temper* i, However, cooks are generally Tartars. **1865** DICKENS *Mut. Fr.* I. viii, The old man was a awful Tartar. **1891** *Athenæum* 11 Apr. 469/2 When provoked he proved a tartar.

b. *slang.* One hard to beat or surpass in skill, an adept, a 'champion'. (Cf. slang use of 'bully'.)

1785 GROSE *Dict. Vulg. T.* s.v., He is quite a tartar at cricket, or billiards.

4. Phrase: ***to catch a Tartar***: to get hold of one who can neither be controlled nor got quit of; to tackle one who unexpectedly proves to be too formidable. Also in allusive expressions.

1663 BUTLER *Hud.* I. III. 865 Now thou hast got me for a Tartar, To make me 'gainst my will take quarter. **1678** DRYDEN *Kind Keeper* V. i, What a Tartar have I caught! **1690** J. MACKENZIE *Siege London-Derry* 39/2 As it happily fell out, they Catcht a Tartar. **1700** S. L. tr. *Fryke's Voy. E. Ind.* 96, I rather hug'd my self that I had let my Tartar go. **1720** DE FOE *Capt. Singleton* xvi. (1906) 260 Tell him, if he should try, he may catch a Tartar. **1725** *New Cant. Dict.* s.v., *To catch a Tartar*, is said, among the Canting Varlets, when a Rogue attacks one that he thinks a Passenger, but proves to be of this Class.., who, in his Turn,..robs,..and binds him. **1850** SCORESBY *Cheever's Whalem. Adv.* vi. (1858) 80 Many an old whaler..has been compelled to give in as beaten when fast to one of these 'North-west Tartars' [whales]. **1897** FLOR. MARRYAT *Blood Vampire* xiv, You must give up flirting, my boy, or if I mistake not, you'll find you've caught a Tartar.

5. (*absol.* use of B.) The language of the Tartars.

1668 [see SCYTHIAN *sb.* 2]. **1862** *Jrnl. Amer. Oriental Soc. 1861* VII. 272 They have by some been designated the 'Tartar', by others the 'Finnish', 'Ural-Altaic', 'Mongolian', and 'Turanian'. **1884** G. SMITH *Short Hist. Chr. Missions* ix. 109 He [Monte Corvino, 1305] translated the New Testament and Psalter into Tartar.

B. *adj.* **1.** Of or pertaining to the people referred to in 1 above, or their country. Also noting animals, plants, etc., belonging to Tartary. **Tartar bread**: see TARTARIAN *a.*[1] b.

1731 *Hist. Litteraria* III. 250 He settles wherever he comes, and like a Tartar-Hord, never quits the Ground while there is a bit of green Herbage left. **1811** PINKERTON *Mod. Geog.* (ed. 3) 346 A beautiful Tatar girl astride on a cow. **1815** ELPHINSTONE *Acc. Caubul* (1842) II. 202 Their features..refer them at once to the Tartar stock. **1842** J. B. FRASER *Mesopot. & Assyria* xv. 369 There were also the shore-lark..and the Tartar lark (*A[lauda] tartarica* of Pallas). **1866** *Treas. Bot.* 158/2 *Tartar Bread*, the fleshy root of *Crambe tatarica*. **1868** *St. Paul's Mag.* July 485 Scratch an amateur actor as you would a Russian, and the Tartar vanity will come through. **1883** MORFILL *Slavonic Lit.* i. 6 The Russian language is hemmed in on..the east by Finnish and Tatar dialects.

2. *fig.* Tartar-like; rough and violent, savage.

1809 MALKIN *Gil Blas* II. vii. ¶22 Little do you fathom my character, to be deceived..by my Tartar contour! **1880** J. NICOL *Poems & Songs* 23 The winter came with all its Tartar rigour.

C. *Comb.*, as ***Tartar-like*** adj.; **Tartar-nosed** *a.*, snub-nosed like a Tartar; **tartar** (‖**tartare**) **sauce** [tr. Fr. *sauce tartare*], a sauce made of mayonnaise and chopped gherkins, capers, etc., usu. served with fish.

1827 T. L. MCKENNEY *Tour Lakes* 380 [The Chippeway Indians] Their tents and belts are all Tartar-like. **1837** *Boston Advert.* 17 Jan. 4/4 Miss Stevens was a tartar-like looking lady, very long and unbending. **1855** E. ACTON *Mod. Cookery* (rev. ed.) vi. 143 Tartar sauce. (Sauce à la Tartare.)... Tartar-mustard..is to be preferred to English for this sauce. **1889** C. OWEN *Choice Cookery* 48 Tartare sauce is mayonnaise with the addition of mustard, chives, pickles, and tarragon, chopped. **1897** MRS. RAYNER *Type-writer Girl* xiv, He..called you a Tartar-nosed imp. **1951** *Good Housek. Home Encycl.* 677/1 *Tartare Sauce*..is served with fish, salads, and such vegetables as globe artichokes. **1959** *Good Food Guide* 292 Seafood pilaf with tartare sauce. **1973** 'D. JORDAN' *Nile Green* xxiii. 93 The waiter..nearly tipped the tartare sauce down Mara's neck.

Hence †**Tarta'resque** *a.* Tartar (language) (*obs. rare*); **'Tartarism,** a Tartar state or condition.

1693 P. GORDON *Geog. Gram.* II. vii. (1725) 184 The language of the Crim-Tartars is the Scythian or pure Tartaresque, which hath such a Resemblance to the Turkish as the Spanish to the Italian. **1892** *Harper's Mag.* July 255/1 A line which divides the Tartarism of Russia from the civilization of Europe.

†**'tartar,** *sb.*[3] *Obs.* Also 5 **tarter, -yr, -or,** 5–6 **-ir,** (6 **tarterus, tartarium**). [= OF. *tartare, tartaire* (*c* 1300 in Godef.), med.L. *tartarium, tartareus* (*pannus*) 'cloth of Tartary'. Cf. TARS, TARTARIN[1] 2, and quot. 1880.] A rich kind of cloth, probably silk, used in 15th and 16th centuries; the same as TARTARIN[1] 2.

1473 *Acc. Ld. High Treas. Scotl.* I. 16 Item, for v. elne of tartar to lyne a gowne of clath of gold to the King. **1488** *Ibid.* 85 Item, a couering of variand purpir tartar, browdin with thrissillis and a vnicorne. **1494** *Ibid.* 224, j ell of tartor to lyne the hud. **1496** *Ibid.* 298 Item, for viij elne of tartyr, to the Kingis jakat of clath of gold,..vi li. iiijs. *c* **1500** *Flower & Leaf* 212 On every trumpe hanging a brood banere Of fyn tartarium, were ful richly bete. **1501** *Acc. Ld. High Treas. Scotl.* II. 28 Item, for half an elne tartir to the tothir scarlet hos to bordour thaim with. **1502** ARNOLDE *Chron.* 73 Item of carde, bokram, fustian, clothes of gold and of silke, veluet, damask, sateyn, taffata, tarterus, couerchis,..the same broker shall haue for the valur of euery xx. s. iij. d'. **1602** SEGAR *Hon. Mil. & Civ.* II. xi. 71 One Knight shall giue him his shirt, another his hose, the third his dublet, another shall apparell him in a kertle of red Tartar. [**1880** BIRDWOOD *Ind. Arts* II. 73 Tartariums, Colonel Yule believes, were so called 'not because they were made in Tartary, but because they were brought from China through the Tartar dominions'.]

b. Comb. ***tartar-satin.***

1483–4 in Swayne *Sarum Churchw. Acc.* (1896) 35 Pro tribus le nailes de tartersaten' pro emendacione vestamenti.

†**'Tartar,** *sb.*[4] *Obs.* Also 6 **Tartare.** [a. F. *tartare*, or ad. L. *Tartarus*, a. Gr. Τάρταρος.] = TARTARUS; the infernal regions; hell. Also *attrib.*

1500–20 DUNBAR *Poems* lxxxvi. 20 Tryumphand tempill of the Trinite, That turned us fra Tartar eternall. **1590** SHAKS. *Com. Err.* IV. ii. 32. **1591** SPENSER *M. Hubberd* 1294 His snakie wand, With which the damned ghosts he governeth, And furies rules, and Tartare tempereth. **1601** SHAKS. *Twel. N.* II. v. 225 If you wil see it follow me. *To.* To the gates of Tartar, thou most excellent diuell of wit.

†**'tartar,** *v. Obs. rare*[−1]. [f. TARTAR *sb.*[1]] trans. To treat with tartar-emetic.

(In quot. with play on TARTAR *sb.*[1], Tartarus.)

1647 WARD *Simp. Cobler* (1843) 19 When I want physick for my body, I would not have my soule tartared, nor my Animal Spirits purged.

Tarta'ræan, *a. rare*[−1]. [Cf. Gr. Ταρτάρειος.] = TARTAREAN[1].

1872 K. H. DIGBY *Ouranogaia* xii. I. 264 The monster.. Whom Tartaræan sisters even hate.

'tartarated, *a. Chem.* [f. TARTAR *sb.*[1] + -ATE + -ED.] Combined with tartar; as in ***tartarated antimony, iron, soda.***

1863 W. AITKEN *Sc. & Pract. Med.* (1866) II. 67 Tartarated iron (*Ferrum tartaratum*) is also a useful remedy. **1868** GARROD *Mat. Med.* (ed. 3) 139 Tartarated Soda. Tartrate of Soda and Potash. **1876** HARLEY *Mat. Med.* (ed. 6) 164 Tartarated Soda was discovered in 1672. **1899** *Allbutt's Syst. Med.* VIII. 578 Tartarated antimony has been praised..in the acute stages of the disease [psoriasis].

†**Tar'tareal,** *a. rare.* [f. as next + -AL[1].] = next.

1602 F. HERING tr. *Oberndorf's Anat.* 6 Trying their Tartareall conclusions, by more then Tragicall Deaths.

Tartarean (tɑː'tɛəriːən), *a.*[1] [f. L. *Tartareus* of or pertaining to TARTARUS + -AN.] Of or belonging to the Tartarus of the ancients; hence, pertaining to hell or to purgatory; infernal.

1623 COCKERAM, *Tartarean*, belonging to hell. **1667** MILTON *P.L.* II. 69 Mixt with Tartarean Sulphur, and strange fire. **1702** POPE *Thebais* 435 Drives the dead to dark Tartarean coasts. **1759** W. WILKIE *Epigon.* IV. 110 Many still, who yet enjoy the day, Must follow down the dark Tartarean way. **1870** LOWELL *Among my Bks.* Ser. I. (1873) 125 The tartarean impostor and his companions at once vanished.

b. *fig.* (cf. *infernal*).

1806–7 J. BERESFORD *Miseries Hum. Life* (1826) IV. xxxii, Your ear is..engaged by the Tartarean yell of its driver. **1851** CARLYLE *Sterling* I. iii. (1872) 14 At a safe distance.. lie the tartarean copper forges of Swansea.

†**Tartarean,** *a.*[2] *Obs.* = TARTARIAN *a.*[1]

1759 GOLDSM. *Bee* No. 6. 11, The other offered himself up as a sacrifice to the Tartarean enemy. **1804** C. B. BROWN tr. *Volney's View Soil U.S.* (Philad. ed.) 364 A distinct race, with no Tartarean features.

tartaren, -ene, variants of TARTARIN[1].

tartareous (tɑː'tɛərɪəs), *a.*[1] [f. mod.L. *tartareus* (f. *tartarum* TARTAR *sb.*[1]) + -OUS.]

†**1.** *Path.* Of the nature of a tartar, or calcareous or earthy deposit; characterized by such deposits. (Cf. TARTAROUS 2.) *Obs.*

1625 HART *Anat. Ur.* II. x. 119 From whence do they [Paracelsists] inferre a great number of such tartareous diseases, as they call them? *Ibid.*, Abundance of a tartareous or terrestrious substance. **1658** A. FOX *Würtz' Surg.* III. xi. 249 This moisture..doth join with the gluten of the joint, and groweth tartareous. **1677** PLOT *Oxfordsh.* 211 A Tartareous humor got together in the veins under the tongue.

†**2.** Like tartar in consistence or formation; of the nature of a concretion or crust; gritty. *Obs.*

1669 W. SIMPSON *Hydrol. Chym.* 131 Every tartareous recrement fastened to the sides of the said vessels. **1671** J. WEBSTER *Metallogr.* xvi. 238 Mingled with other metals, as lime and tartareous stones, in which black floats and slats do break. **1677** GREW *Anat. Seeds* i. §1 The Tartareous Stone of a Plum. **1683** A. SNAPE *Anat. Horse* v. i. (1686) 195 A Bone is said to be..made of the most earthy and tartareous part of the Seed in the Womb.

†**3.** *Chem.* Having the quality of tartar or argol; containing or derived from tartar; ***tartareous acid***, early name of tartaric acid. (Cf. TARTAROUS.) *Obs.*

† *tartareous acidulum* (F. *acidule tartareux*), an old name of tartar.

1663 BOYLE *Usef. Exp. Nat. Philos.* II. v. xix. 283 Meats that are Salt and Tartareous. *c* **1790** tr. *De Morveau's*, etc. *Table Chem. Nom.* (*Encycl. Brit.* ed. 3 IV. 598 a), Radical principle of the tartareous acid. **1800** tr. *Lagrange's Chem.* II. 198 When exposed to heat in contact with the air, the tartareous acidulum is decomposed, fuses, swells up. **1822**

IMISON *Sc. & Art* II. 183 The tartareous acid dissolves the oxide of tin.

4. *Bot.* Of a crust-like structure like tartar: descriptive of certain lichens.

1845 LINDLEY *Sch. Bot.* ix. (1858) 155 Thallus thick, granular and tartareous, greyish-white. **1861** H. MACMILLAN *Footn. fr. Page Nat.* 75 We have no data from which to ascertain the age of tartareous species, which adhere almost inseparably to stones.

† **Tar'tareous**, *a.*[2] *Obs.* [f. L. *tartare-us* (f. TARTARUS) + -OUS.] Of or pertaining to Tartarus; Tartarean, infernal, hellish, very wicked.

1619 BAINBRIDGE *Descr. Late Comet* 37 Never was there more need of circumspection, then in this fæculent and tartareous age. [Here perh. a fig. use of prec.] **1667** MILTON *P.L.* VII. 238 The Spirit of God..downward purg'd The black tartareous cold infernal dregs Adverse to life.

† **'tartarer.** *Obs. rare*[−1]. [f. TARTAR *sb.*[1] + -ER[1].] One who attributed diseases to the presence of tartar.

1662 J. CHANDLER *Van Helmont's Oriat.* 230 What things I have read out of many Books, which Paracelsus writeth concerning Tartarers, I will contract into a brief tract.

tartaret ('tɑːtərɪt). [a. obs. F. *tartaret*, also *tartarot* (16th c. in Godef.), f. TARTAR *sb.*[2]: app. because supposed to come from TARTARY.] In full **tartaret falcon**: the Barbary Falcon, *Falco barbarus*.

1575 TURBERV. *Falconrie* 26 That falcon which is called the Tartaret or Barbary Falcon, whome they doe chiefly vse in Barbary. **1860** H. AINSWORTH *Ovingdean Grange* 61 Gallant to behold was the Barbary or tartaret falcon. **1867** 'OUIDA' *C. Castlemaine* (1879) 11 She would stroke, half sadly, the smooth feathers of her tartaret falcon Gabrielle.

Tartarian (tɑː'tɛərɪən), *sb.* and *a.*[1] Also 5–6 **Tartarien**, 9 **Tatarian**. [*c* 1400 (see A) a. OF. *Tartarien* (13th c. in Godef.); later f. med.L. *Tartaria* TARTARY + -AN.]

A. *sb.* = TARTAR *sb.*[2] 1.

c **1400** MAUNDEV. (1839) xxiii. 247 Of the lawe & the customs of the Tartarienes, duellynge in Chatay. *Ibid.* 252 Alle the Tartarienes [*Roxb.* xxvi. 124 Tartarenes] han smale eyen. **1538** Tartarien [see RUSSIAN *sb.*[1]]. **1599** THYNNE *Animadv.* (1875) 54 The Tartarians obteyned the kingdome of Syria in the yere 1240. **1708** E. COOK *Sot-weed Factor* (1900) 10 My Friend suppos'd Tartarians wild, Or Chinese from their Home exiled. **1835** K. H. DIGBY *Mores Catholici* VI. ii. (1846) II. 27/2 Fitter for those hordes of Tartarians than for a commonwealth of Christians.

b. 'A cant word for a thief' (Nares).

1608 *Merry Devil Edmonton* in Hazl. *Dodsley* X. 212 There's not a Tartarian nor a carrier shall breathe upon your geldings. **1640** *Wandering Jew* 3 (Nares) If any thieving Tartarian shall break in upon you, I will, with both hands nimbly lend a cast of my office to him.

B. *adj.* Of or pertaining to Tartary or its people; = TARTAR *a.*

1590 WEBBE *Trav.* (Arb.) 18 The Tartarian Souldiers had wonderfull greate and rich spoyles. **1603** KNOLLES *Hist. Turks* (1638) 196 Tamerlane the great Tartarian prince,..in a great battell at mount Stella, abated the Othoman pride. **1634** W. WOOD *New Eng. Prosp.* (1865) 30 As swift as arrow from Tartarian Bow. *a* **1725** LD. WHITWORTH *Acc. Russia in 1710* (1758) 9 Casan and Astracan were Tartarian kingdoms. **1839** *For. Q. Rev.* XXII. 109 Interesting to the readers of Tartarian tales. **1845** *Proc. Philol. Soc.* II. 171 The Tartarian class of languages..furnishes a valuable confirmation of this theory.

b. In names of things of actual or supposed Tartar origin; as **Tartarian bread** (see quot. 1829); **Tartarian lamb**, the 'Scythian' or 'vegetable lamb', a polypodiaceous fern, *Cibotium Barometz*, from the resemblance which its woolly root-stock, inverted, bears to a lamb: see BAROMETZ, and cf. Maundeville (1839), ch. xxvi (Roxb. xxix). Also *Tartarian cherry, honeysuckle, maple, motherwort, oat*, etc., for which see the sbs.

1805 DICKSON *Pract. Agric.* I. 578 In the Siberian or Tartarian oat the grains are thin and small. **1811** PINKERTON *Mod. Geogr.* (ed. 3) 346 The..Tartarian honey-suckle, Tatarian mulberry, and the Daourian rose, form thickets of exquisite beauty. **1817** SHELLEY *Rev. Islam* VI. xix, A black Tartarian horse of giant frame Comes trampling o'er the dead. **1823** CRABB *Technol. Dict.*, Tartarian lamb. **1829** LOUDON *Encycl. Plants* 557 [Crambe] tatarica is called by the Hungarians *Tatar-Kenyer* or Tartarian bread, and its root stripped of the bark and sliced is eaten with oil, vinegar, and salt. **1836** *Penny Cycl.* VI. 431/2 The Tartarian cherries of the English gardens. **1866** *Treas. Bot.* 280/2 C[*ibotium*] *Barometz*, sometimes called *C. glaucescens*, is believed to be the Baranetz, *Agnus Scythicus*, or Tartarian Lamb, about which travellers have told so wondrous a tale. **1882** *Garden* 13 May 322/2 The ordinary white-flowered form of the Tartarian Honeysuckle [*Lonicera tatarica*].

Tar'tarian, *a.*[2] *rare.* [f. L. TARTAR-US + -IAN.] Pertaining to Tartarus; infernal; = TARTAREAN *a.*[1]

1864 KINGSLEY *Rom. & Teut.* xi. 297 (tr. *Ep. to Pepin* an. 755) Lest your bodies and souls be torn and tormented for ever, in inextinguishable and Tartarian fire with the devil and his pestiferous angels. **1875** JOWETT *Plato* (ed. 2) III. 33 Cocytus and Styx,..and the rest of their Tartarian nomenclature.

tartaric (tɑː'tærɪk), *a.*[1] *Chem.* [f. TARTAR *sb.*[1] + -IC; in mod.L. *tartaric-us*, F. *tartarique*.] Of the nature of, related to, or derived from tartar or argol. ***tartaric acid*** (formerly *tartareous* or *tartarous acid*), an organic acid, $C_4H_6O_6$ = $C_4H_2O_2$ + $(OH)_4$, or $CO_2H{\cdot}(CHOH)_2{\cdot}CO_2H$, of which there are five isomeric forms, differing in their optical properties, viz. *dextrotartaric* acid (dextrorotary), *lævotartaric* acid (lævorotary), *paratartaric* acid (distinctively called RACEMIC acid), *mesotartaric* acid (optically inactive), and *metatartaric* acid; specifically, the first of these, a colourless crystalline compound, occurring largely in the vegetable kingdom, esp. in unripe grapes, and as a potassium salt in argol or tartar of wine, from which it is commercially prepared. So ***tartaric amide, anhydride, ether***, an amide, anhydride, or ether of tartaric acid.

1790 KERR *Lavoisier's Elem. Chem.* 190 Tables of the combinations of Oxygen with the compound radicals. Name of radical: Tartaric. Name of resulting acid (new nomencl.): Tartarous acid. Unknown till lately. **1794** G. PEARSON tr. De Morveau, etc. *Table Chem. Nomencl.* 28 The radical Tartaric yields only the tartareous Acid in which the basis is conceived to predominate. **1810** HENRY *Elem. Chem.* (1826) II. 227 The tartaric acid is generally obtained from the bi-tartrate of potassa (purified cream of tartar). **1813** SIR H. DAVY *Agric. Chem.* (1814) 107 The tartaric acid may be obtained from the juice of mulberries and grapes. **1827** FARADAY *Chem. Manip.* vi. 189 Tartaric acid or tartrates have an extraordinary power in rendering many metallic oxides soluble. **1876** HARLEY *Mat. Med.* (ed. 6) 729 Tartaric acid—the acid of tartar—was discovered by Scheele in 1770. **1868** WATTS *Dict. Chem.* V. 690 Tartaric Amides. *Ibid.* 691 Insoluble Tartaric Anhydride, $C_4H_4O_5$. *Ibid.* 692 The acid tartaric ethers are formed by the direct action of tartaric acid on the alcohols. *Ibid.*, Ethylic Tartrate, or Tartaric Ether, $C_8H_{14}O_6$..is decomposed by sodium, with evolution of hydrogen.

Tartaric (tɑː'tærɪk), *a.*[2] Also Tataric. [f. TARTAR *sb.*[2] + -IC.] Of, pertaining to, or connected with the Tartars or Tartary.

1811 PINKERTON *Mod. Geog.* (ed. 3) 335 Europe can in future have little to apprehend from the Tataric swarms. **1834** *Penny Cycl.* II. 478/1 The Tartaric region, as it is next the Siberian, so it resembles it in most respects. **1855** MAX MÜLLER *Lang. Seat of War* 96 Tataric has become the name of that class of Turanian languages of which the Turkish is the most prominent member.

† **'tartarin, -ine**, *sb.*[1] *Obs.* Forms: 4 **tarterine**, 5 **-yn(e, -en, -on**; 4–5 **tartaryn(e**, 5 **-en(e, -on(e, (-yan), tarturyn, (tatterine), tarturne**; 6 **tartarne, -erne, -orn(e, tartron**, 6–7 **tartern**, 7 **tartarin, -ine**. [a. OF. *Tartarin* = med.L. *Tartarīn-us*, f. *Tartar-us*, TARTAR *sb.*[2] and [3], with suffix -INE[1], as in *Tarentine*, etc. (med.L. pl. *Tartarīnī* also embodying the notion 'people of Tartarus'); in OF. also in sense 2.]

1. = TARTAR *sb.*[2] 1; in *pl.* = med.L. *Tartarīnī*.

a **1400–50** *Alexander* 5484 Of terands of þir tartaryns twa & twenti kyngs. *c* **1400** MAUNDEV. (1839) xxi. 224 Tartarynes [*Roxb.* xxiv, folk of Tartre] & þei þat duelle in the grete Asye, þei camen of Cham. *c* **1400** *Three Kings Cologne* 148 þe wich pepil cleped hem-self Tartaryns.

2. A rich stuff, apparently of silk, imported from the East, prob. from China through Tartary; = TARTAR *sb.*[3] Cf. SARSENET. [OF. *tartarin*, earlier *drap tartarin* (1295 in Godef.).]

1343 *Enrolled Acc.* (W. & H.) 3 m. 38 b, ij vlnis panni serici ix peciis Tartaryn et j pecia Samitell. **1345–9** *Wardr. Acc. Edw. III* in *Archæologia* XXXI. 72/2, j. frontale de tarteryn. *Ibid.* 85/2, vj. vln. de Tartaryn. *c* **1400** MAUNDEV. (1839) xxiii. 255 Cloþes of gold, & of Camakaas, & tartarynes [*Roxb.* xxvi. 125 tartarene, *F. text* tartaires]. **1407** *Nottingham Rec.* II. 50 Pro dimidia virga de viridi tarteren, xviij d. **1411** in *Somerset Medieval Wills* (1901) 50 [One hanging of black and white] 'Wyrsted' 'cum penna de Tatterine'. **14..** *Epiph.* in *Tundale's Vis.*, etc. (1843) 114 Wer ther of gold any clothes fownde Of sylke damaske or of tartryn. **1444** *Test. Ebor.* (Surtees) II. 110 Myn aulter-clothe of reed tarteryn with ye corteyns. **1455** *Coventry Leet Bk.* 283 To make a newe pensell in Tarturne xvj d. **1459** in *Somerset Medieval Wills* (1901) 191 Curteynes of tarteron. **1512** *Acc. 4 Hen. VIII*, c. 6 *Preamble*, Saten, sarsenet, tartron, chamblet, and every other Cloth of Silke. *c* **1530** LD. BERNERS *Arth. Lyt. Bryt.* (1814) 381 Florence layd her downe in her bedde in a lyghte kyrtell of chaungeable vyolet tartorne. **1538** in *Lett. Suppress. Monasteries* (Camden) 268, ij. copes of redd tartarne. *a* **1548** HALL *Chron., Hen. VII* 1 b, Yᵉ third [standard] was of yelowe tarterne, in the which was peinted a donne kowe. **1661** MORGAN *Sph. Gentry* IV. i. 5 Having Mantles of silk over a Kirtle of red Tartarin. **1688** R. HOLME *Armoury* III. 55/2 Another puts on him a Kirtle of red Silk or Tartarine.

fig. *c* **1430** LYDG. *Min. Poems* (Percy Soc.) 30 Thi chekes hangen, thyn eyene wax read as wyne, And wel belyned with good read tartaryne.

attrib. *a* **1400–50** *Alexander* 1547 (MS. D) Tyrett alle in tonacles of tartaren webbys. [**1861** *Our Eng. Home* 92 The rich taffeta, the velvets, and Tartaren silks, were often worn without a shred of underclothing.]

† **'tartarin**, *sb.*[2] *Obs.* [f. TARTAR *sb.*[1] + -IN[1].]

1. A name given by Kirwan to potash.

1796 KIRWAN *Elem. Min.* (ed. 2) II. 5 Vegetable Alkali (which I call Tartarin). **1799** —— *Geol. Ess.* v. 150 The tartarin lately discovered in clays and many stones.

2. 'Native sulphate of potassium, also called Arkanite and Glaserite' (Watts *Dict. Chem.* V. 696).

Hence **'tartarinated** *a.*, combined with tartarin.

1796 KIRWAN *Elem. Min.* (ed. 2) II. 311 The Acido Tartarinated Calx is fusible *per se*.

Tartarin, ('tɑːtərɪn, ‖tartarɛ̃), *sb.*[3] Name of a bombastic character, 'Tartarin of Tarascon', created by A. Daudet; hence, used allusively as sb. or adj.

1903 *T.P.'s Weekly* 11 Sept. 459/3 In his vivid red sash he carried two enormous pistols—tartarin pistols,..that not alone did not, but could not fire a shot. **1905** *Blackw. Mag.* May 643/1 There are too many loquacious Tartarins abroad without the engaging ways of the man of Tarascon. **1906** *Academy* 17 Nov. 492/1 Its Gasconing is in the Tartarin vein.

† **'tartarine**, *sb.* *Obs.* [a. F. *tartarin.*] (See quot.)

1607 TOPSELL *Four-f. Beasts* (1658) 10 There was at Paris another beast called a Tartarine, and in some places a Magot (much like a Baboun),..being as great as a Gray-hound.

tartarine, variant of TARTARIN *sb.*[1]

† **'tartarine**, *a.*[1] *Obs.* [f. TARTAR *sb.*[1] + -INE[1].] = TARTAROUS *a.*

1731 S. HALES *Stat. Ess.* I. 198 The like tartarine concretions are also frequently formed in some fruits. **1775** SIR E. BARRY *Obs. Wines* 193 These concretions from spring water are of a Tartarine kind.

† **'Tartarine**, *a.*[2] *Obs. rare*[−0]. = TARTAREAN *a.*[1]

1656 BLOUNT *Glossogr.*, *Tartarine, Tartarean*,..of hell, hellish, terrible.

tartarish ('tɑːtərɪʃ), *a.*[1] *rare.* [f. TARTAR *sb.*[1] + -ISH[1].]

a. Of wine: Inclined to deposit tartar. **b.** Of the eyes: Inclined to form concretions (cf. TARTAROUS 2).

1757 A. COOPER *Distiller* II. ii. (1760) 118 Without the peculiar Taste and Flavour of the Plant, but generally somewhat tartarish and limpid. **1807** SOUTHEY *Lett.* (1856) II. 4 My son is rather ailing just now..His eyes are as Tartarish as his sister's.

† **'Tartarish**, *a.*[2] *Obs. rare*[−1]. [f. TARTAR *sb.*[2] + -ISH[1]: cf. *Turkish*.] = TARTAR *a.* 1.

1670 *Lond. Gaz.* No. 431/2 The Tartarish Envoye in this Court, presented the Count de Montecuculi with an excellent Tartarian Horse.

tartarite, variant of TARTRITE.

tartarium: see TARTAR *sb.*[3]

† **'tartarizated**, *ppl. a.* *Chem. Obs.* [f. mod.L. *tartarizāt-us* tartarized + -ED[1].] Tartarized.

1651 FRENCH *Distill.* vi. 187 Pour upon them rectified Spirit of Wine tartarizated. *Ibid.* 196 Adde the tartarizated quintessence. **1794** G. PEARSON tr. De Morveau, etc. *Table Chem. Nom.* §14 Tartarisated Bases.

tartari'zation[1]. *Chem.* [f. TARTARIZE *v.*[1] + -ATION.] The action or process of tartarizing.

1720 S. PARKER *Biblioth. Bibl.* I. 438 By Sublimation, and Precipitation or Tartarisation.

Tartarization[2], [3]: see TARTARIZE *v.*[2] and *v.*[3]

tartarize ('tɑːtəraɪz), *v.*[1] *Chem.* [f. TARTAR *sb.*[1] + -IZE.] *trans.* To treat or impregnate with tartar; to rectify by means of the salt of tartar. (Usually in *pa. pple.*: see TARTARIZED *pa. pple.*[1])

1706 PHILLIPS (ed. 6), To *Tartarize*, (in Chymistry) to refine, or purify by the means of Salt of Tartar. **1727–41** CHAMBERS *Cycl.*, *Tartarizing*, a term used by some writers, for the act of refining or purifying, by means of salt of Tartar. **1755** JOHNSON, *Tartarize*, to impregnate with tartar.

'Tartarize, *v.*[2] Also Tatarize. [f. TARTAR *sb.*[2] + -IZE.] *trans.* To convert or transform into a Tartar. Hence **'Tartarized** *ppl. a.*[2]; also **Tartari'zation**[2], the process of Tartarizing, the condition of being Tartarized.

1877 D. M. WALLACE *Russia* xxii. 347 The Khans never for a moment dreamed of attempting to Tartarize their Russian subjects. **1878** H. A. WEBSTER in *Encycl. Brit.* VIII. 702/2 The Tchuvashes are a Tatarized branch of the Finns of the Volga. **1889** J. ABERCROMBIE *East. Caucasus* 210 To the west of Derbend I found Tāts who..are in process of becoming wholly Tatarized.

'Tartarize, *v.*[3] *rare.* [f. L. TARTAR-US + -IZE. (Representing Gr. ταρταροῦν, 2 *Pet.* ii. 4.)] *trans.* To consign to Tartarus; to condemn to punishment in hell. Hence **Tartari'zation**[3].

1675 R. BURTHOGGE *Causa Dei* 32 So..doth Peter speak, when..he saith God did Tartarize the Angels in Chains of Darkness, or put them in Chains of Darkness in Tartarus. **1819** G. S. FABER *Dispensations* (1823) I. I. vii. 422 We may collect that the precipitation of the messengers into Tartarus bore a strong resemblance to the overthrow of Sodom and Gomorrah..though the very agent employed in their tartarization might be used also as an instrument in God's hand of bringing on the deluge.

tartarized ('tɑːtəraɪzd), *ppl. a.*[1] [f. TARTARIZE *v.*[1] + -ED[1]; cf. F. *tartarisé*, mod.L. *tartarizatus*.]

1. Rectified by treatment with cream of tartar.

a **1648** DIGBY *Chym. Secr.* (1683) 70 Tartarised S[piritus] V[ini]. **1694** SALMON *Bate's Dispens.* I. ii. (1713) 60/2 This Tartaris'd volatile Spirit, is highly deobstructive. **1758** REID tr. *Macquer's Chym.* I. 115 Ardent spirits may be freed from much of their phlegm by means of these salts thoroughly dried... When rectified in this manner it is called Tartarised

Spirit of Wine. **1844** J. T. HEWLETT *Parsons & W.* xxv, Fiery, tartarized, brandied products of Spain.

2. Mixed or impregnated with tartar; holding tartar in solution.

1694 SALMON *Bate's Dispens.* II. vi. (1713) 593/1 A Tartarised Julep. **1710** T. FULLER *Pharm. Extemp.* 83 Elixir Proprietatis Tartarised 4 scruples. **1784** M. UNDERWOOD *Dis. Childr.* (1799) I. 27 The tartarised wine of antimony is a very proper [emetic]. **1802–3** tr. *Pallas's Trav.* (1812) I. 353 The tartarised spirit of sal ammoniac rendered the water white as milk.

3. Combined with tartaric acid, so as to form a tartrate: = TARTRATED.

1732 *Hist. Litteraria* IV. 27 A tedious way of preparing Tartarised Tartar. **1758** REID tr. *Macquer's Chym.* I. 126 Soluble Tartar. It is also called the Vegetable Salt, as being obtained from vegetables only, and again Tartarized Tartar, because it consists of the acid and the alkali of Tartar combined together. **1788** WALKER in *Phil. Trans.* LXXVIII. 398 Tartarized natron (Rochelle salt). **1796** KIRWAN *Elem. Min.* (ed. 2) II. 470 Tartarised Iron being more soluble than Tartarised Uranite. **1857** MILLER *Elem. Chem.* III. 330 A solution of tartarized antimony acts as a violent emetic and cathartic poison.

Tartarized, *ppl. a.*[2]: see TARTARIZE *v.*[2]

Tartarly (ˈtɑːtəlɪ), *a. nonce-wd.* [f. TARTAR *sb.*[2] + -LY[1].] Tartar-like; rough and fierce.

1821 BYRON *John Keats* i, Who kill'd John Keats? 'I', says the Quarterly, So savage and Tartarly, "Twas one of my feats'. **1894** A. BIRRELL *Ess.* v. 49 It was enough to sting Scott to fury, and make him fall upon the old man in a manner somewhat too savage and tartarly.

tartarne, -taron(e, variants of TARTARIN[1].

Tartaˈrology. [f. Gr. Τάρταρο-ς TARTARUS + -LOGY.] A doctrine as to Tartarus; hence, a doctrine of hell and future punishment.

1867 KINGSLEY *Water of Life*, etc. vi. 93 The Middle Ages, when men really believed in that same Tartarology, with the same intensity with which they now believe in the conclusions of astronomy or of chemistry. **1868** *Contemp. Rev.* VII. 158 The ordinary Tartarology flows far more directly from the sixth book of the Æneid than from anything in Holy Scripture.

†**tartarous** (ˈtɑːtərəs), *a. Obs.* [f. TARTAR *sb.*[1] + -OUS; = F. *tartareux.*]

1. Of the nature of, consisting of, or containing tartar or argol.

1655–87 H. MORE *App. Antid.* (1712) 215 The tartarous parts of Wine, that are driven outward to the sides of the vessel. **1658** R. WHITE tr. *Digby's Powd. Symp.* (1660) 81 Tartarous lees, which fall to the bottom. **1710** T. FULLER *Pharm. Extemp.* 214 By reason of a delicate Tartarous Acidity. **1768** *Woman of Honor* II 196 A jollitry, raised by a wretched tartarous wine.

2. *Path.* Said of indurations, inspissated fluids, phlegms, etc., attributed to the presence of tartar in the body. (Much employed in 17th and early 18th centuries by the followers of Paracelsus.)

1605 TIMME *Quersit.* I. xiii. 64 The oile of pepper doth attenuat..and cut tartarus matters in the body. **1657** *Physical Dict.*, *Tartarous matter*, congealed hard substances of an acrimonious sharp nature.., being coagulated in the joynts, it's the principal cause of the gout. **1718** QUINCY *Compl. Disp.* 123 In Tubercles and Tartarous Indurations of the Lungs. **1744** BERKELEY *Siris* §86 The asperity of tartarous salts, and the fiery acrimony of alkaline salts irritating and wounding the nerves, produce nascent passions and anxieties in the soul.

3. *fig.* Having elements of acerbity, unrefined, rough. *rare.* (? with play on TARTAR *sb.*[2])

1601 B. JONSON *Poetaster* v. i, I iudge him of a rectified spirit,..refin'd From all the tartarous moodes of common men.

4. In early Chemistry: **a.** Of the appearance, consistency, or supposed character of tartar or argol.

1707 *Curios. in Husb. & Gard.* 66 Air..contains some.. tartarous and metallick Parts. *Ibid.* 327 When the Fern was burnt, it was between dry and wet: thus the Salt was as it were Tartarous and Substantial.

b. Of the nature of or derived from tartar; *tartarous acid*, an earlier name of TARTARIC *acid.*

1790 Tartarous acid [see TARTRITE]. **1794** G. ADAMS *Nat. & Exp. Philos.* I. xii. 502 Obtained by distillation..from tartar, from all tartarous salts. **1812** SIR H. DAVY *Chem. Philos.* 121 The tartarous acid is entirely separated from lime, and the oxalic acid from oxide of lead, by quantities of sulphuric acid, merely sufficient to saturate the two bases.

Hence †ˈ**tartarousness**, tartarous quality, acerbity. *Obs.*

1657 R. LIGON *Barbadoes* Index 84a, The salt and tartarousnesse of this Temper, causes it to turn, as Milk does, when any soure or sharp liquor is put into it.

‖ˈ**tartarum, ˈtartarus** [mod.L.], early synonyms of TARTAR[1].

‖**Tartarus** (ˈtɑːtərəs), *sb.* [L. *Tartarus*, a. Gr. Τάρταρος.] The infernal regions of ancient Greek and Roman mythology, or the lowest part of them; hence sometimes used for hell.

[**1508** KENNEDIE *Flyting w. Dunbar* 552 Spynk, sink with stynk ad Tertara Termagorum.] **1586** SIR E. HOBY tr. *Cognet's Pol. Disc. Truth* xxxi. 146 The strange kinde of punishmentes..prepared for the wicked in the gayle of vengeance, which he calleth *Tartarus*, a place of darkenesse and torments. **1651** HOBBES *Leviath.* III. xxxviii. (1839) 445 For example, that they [the damned] are in Inferno, in Tartarus, or in the bottomless pit. **1658** SIR T. BROWNE *Hydriot.* iv. 60 Condemned unto the Tartara's of Hell. *a* **1774** TUCKER *Lt. Nat.* (1834) II. 321 The enjoyments of Elysium and punishments of Tartarus. **1895** SALMOND *Chr. Doctr. Immort.* I. vii. 146 The incurably corrupt are hurled into Tartarus.

b. A place likened to Tartarus, in situation or character.

1821 DE QUINCEY *Confess.* I. (1822) 42 She never emerged from the dismal Tartarus of the kitchens, &c. to the upper air. **1853** KANE *Grinnell Exp.* xxxi. 271 The temperature and foulness of air in the between-deck Tartarus can not be amended. **1887–8** tr. *Hugo's Notre-Dame* VIII. ii, This Tartarus was called simply The Question Chamber.

Hence **ˈTartarus** *v. nonce-wd.*, *trans.* to consign to Tartarus (repr. Gr. ταρταροῦν, 2 *Pet.* ii. 4).

1856 S. R. MAITLAND *False Worship* 31 The apostle's statement respecting the sinning Angels is, that, having been tartarus'd,..they have been reserved unto Judgment.

Tartary (ˈtɑːtərɪ). [a. F. *Tartarie*, ad. med.L. *Tartaria*, land of the Tartars: associated with TARTARUS: hence sense 2.]

1. a. The country of the Tartars: see TARTAR *sb.*[2]

c **1369** CHAUCER *Dethe Blaunche* 1025 Ne sende men..into Tartarye..ne in-to Turkye. **1500–20** DUNBAR *Poems* xxxiii. 5 Me thocht a Turk of Tartary Come throw the boundis of Barbary. **1719** DE FOE *Crusoe* (1858) 575 A part of the Great Karakathy, or Grand Tartary. **1886** KINGTON OLIPHANT *New English* I. 536 From Tartary came *hordas*.

†**b.** = TARTAR *sb.*[3]

c **1400** MAUNDEV. (1839) xxiii. 247 Þei ben cloþed with precious cloþes of Tartarye & of cloþes of gold.

†**2.** Tartarus, as a region. *Obs.*

c **1588** SPENSER *Virg. Gnat* 543 Lastly the squalid lakes of Tartarie, And griesly Feends of hell him terrifie. **1591** *Troub. Raigne K. John* (1611) 59 Let the blacke tormentors of deep Tartary Vpbraide them with this damned enterprise. *c* **1620** T. ROBINSON *Mary Magd.* 735 Amonge ye blacker sonnes of Tartary, Seu'n hideous fiery sprights shee euocates.

3. *attrib.* **Tartary oat**, a wild oat, *Avena fatua*, which has a loose inflorescence.

1790 S. DEANE *New-England Farmer* 193/2 I have lately met with the Tartary oats, which..differ in their manner of growing. **1891** R. WALLACE *Rural Econ. Austral. & N.Z.* xviii. 260 The straw is not so long or of such good quality as the straw of the Tartary Oat.

tartaryn(e, variant of TARTARIN[1] *Obs.*

tarted (ˈtɑːtɪd), *ppl. a.* [f. TART *v.*[2] 2 + -ED[1].]

a. Of a person: dressed *up* in a showy manner, gaudily adorned. Also without *up*.

1938 E. BOWEN *Death of Heart* I. iii. 61 After dark, she [*sc.* London] is like a governess gone to the bad, in a Woolworth tiara, tarted up all wrong. **1952** D. ADAMS *Murder, Maestro, Please* xvi. 113 These tarted-up hags! **1972** 'R. CRAWFORD' *Whip Hand* I. viii. 49, I know your natures, you tarted-up toffs. **1979** *Even. Standard* 13 Sept. 19/6 Prostitutes..are of the conventional kind, in high heeled shoes and characteristically 'tarted' both cosmetically and sartorially.

b. *transf.* and *fig.*

1958 K. AMIS *I like it Here* ii. 21 A collection of tarted-up reviews. **1967** *Spectator* 20 Oct. 455/3 The tarted-up village inn, remodelled with the single aim of attracting motor trade from a distance. **1972** *Where?* Mar. 96/3 ROSLA enthusiasts for tarted-up curricula need to heed the warning. **1981** J. SCOTT *Distant View of Death* xiv. 182 The tarted panda reversed..and drove in the wake of the quarry. **1983** *Listener* 21 July 33/2 At the other end of the spectrum of the Higher Rubbish—defined for the moment as tarted-up junk..—is Elizabeth Taylor in the vastly enjoyable, utterly brainless *The VIPs*.

tarten (ˈtɑːt(ə)n), *v. rare.* [f. TART *a.* + -EN[5].]

1. *trans.* To make tart or sharp; = TART *v.*[1]

1882 BLACKMORE *Christowell* III. iii. 49 There was no such apple on the place, to bring out and tarten up the flavour of the gentle ones in cider.

2. To affect with sharpness or acidity. *rare*[−1].

1925 W. DE LA MARE *Broomsticks* 58 Hardly had its juice tartened my tongue.

Tarter, obs. f. TARTAR.

tarteran, -terine, -tern(e, -teyn, -tian, etc., var. TARTARIN[1] *Obs.*

tarterus: see TARTAR *sb.*[3]

tartillo, obs. f. (or ? mispr. for) TORTILLA.

‖**tartine** (tɑːrˈtiːn). [F. *tartine* (Oudin, 1642) little tart, bread and jam, bread and butter (also fig. as in b), f. *tarte*, TART *sb.*] **a.** 'A slice of bread spread with butter or preserve' (Stanf.).

1804 F. BURNEY *Jrnl.* 1 Oct. (1975) VI. 477, I have given no more medicine—plenty of tisanes &c, & tartines of Honey & salad are all he has taken. **1826** [H. BEST] *Four Years France* 237 The tea equipage, with its usual accompaniments of tartines and toast. **1842** THACKERAY *Fitz-Boodle Papers* ii, She placidly handed out this decoction, which we took with cakes and tartines. **1885** WARREN & CLEVERLY *Wand. Beetle* 15 Bread and butter was better than nothing, so we got her to cut us some enormous tartines.

b. *fig.* A big article of commonplace character.

1907 *Athenæum* 13 July 48/2 In a first glance through the galleries you stop before the huge 'tartines', the more.. sensational pictures which aim at attracting the crowd.

tartir, variant of TARTAR *sb.*[3]

tartish (ˈtɑːtɪʃ), *a.*[1] [f. TART *a.* + -ISH[1].] Somewhat tart, slightly pungent or acid; also *fig.*

1712 E. COOKE *Voy. S. Sea* 338 Another Sort like a Curan ..eats tartish. **1747** *Gentl. Mag.* Oct. 488/2 Let spirit of vitriol be mixed therewith..in such quantity as to give the tartish taste. **1828** J. WILSON in *Blackw. Mag.* XXIV. 511 The Monthly [Magazine] so smartish—the Westminster, so tartish. **1890** STANLEY *Darkest Afr.* I. ix. 212 The tartish, crimson, and oblong fruit of the amoma.

Hence **ˈtartishly** *adv.*, somewhat tartly.

1823 J. WILSON *Trials Marg. Lyndsay* xxxii, Snuffy-nosed maiden aunts..sourishly and tartishly disposed.

tartish, *a.*[2] *colloq.* [f. TART *sb.* 2b + -ISH.] = TARTY *a.* (and *sb.*)

1929 C. CONNOLLY *Let.* Nov. in *Romantic Friendship* (1975) 327 We both felt that you thought she was tartish. **1944** E. BOWEN in *Penguin New Writing* XX. 62 Collie was wearing that tartish house-coat. **1956** E. GRIERSON *Second Man* xiv. 249 A brocade house-coat and mules of a pink, tartish shade. **1972** *Daily Tel.* 4 Oct. 13/2 His mother is snappish, tartish and neglectful.

tartlet (ˈtɑːtlɪt). Forms: 5 tartlote, tartlett, tartelat, 8– tartlet. [a. F. *tartelette* (14th c. in Littré), dim. of *tarte*, TART *sb.*; in 18th c. perh. formed anew on TART *sb.*]

1. A small tart.

c **1420** *Liber Cocorum* (1862) 41 Tartlotes. Take porke sothun, and grynde hit wele... Kover hit with lyddes, and pynche hit fayre,..And bake hit forthe. *c* **1460** J. RUSSELL *Bk. Nurture* 521 Iusselle, tartlett, cabages, & nombles of vennure. *c* **1475** *Pict. Voc.* in Wr.-Wülcker 789/6 *Hec artocria*, a tartelat. **1788** V. KNOX *Winter Even.* (1790) II. xxix. 194 The puffs and tartlets of the pastry-cook. **1836–9** DICKENS *Sk. Boz, Mistaken Milliner*, Plum-pudding and apple-pie and tartlets without number. **1837** T. HOOK *Jack Brag* xiv, Three raspberry tartlets. **1889** STEVENSON & OSBOURNE *Wrong Box* v. 79 He returned with a large bag of the choicest and most tempting of cakes and tartlets. **1965** [see SALPICON].

2. A young woman of immoral character, a young 'tart'.

a **1890** in Barrère & Leland *Dict. Slang* (1890) II. 337/1 E'en tartlets are stale, be they ever so tasty—The magic has fled from their langourous looks. **1961** *Spectator* 3 Mar. 304/3 Love for a tartlet in Florence.

tartly (ˈtɑːtlɪ), *adv.* [OE. *teartlíce*: see TART *a.* and -LY[2].] In a tart manner; sharply; with acidity; usually *fig.* with asperity of tone. In quot. 1599, 'with sourness of aspect' (J.).

c **1000** in Napier *O.E. Glosses* 81/3011 *Acriter*, teartlice. *Ibid.* 122/4730 *Acrius*, teartlicor. **1599** SHAKS. *Much Ado* II. i. 3 How tartly that Gentleman lookes, I neuer can see him, but I am heart-burn'd an howre after. *a* **1661** FULLER *Worthies* (1662) III. *Worc.* 169 One jeeringly saluted him, 'Good morrow, Bishop quondam', to whom Bonner as tartly returned, 'Good morrow, Knave semper'. **1791** BOSWELL *Johnson* 19 Apr. an. 1773, Johnson, offended,..answered tartly, 'No, Sir; do you read books through?' **1876** MISS BRADDON *J. Haggard's Dau.* II. 163 'You may as well wait till tea's finished', exclaimed Judith tartly.

tartness (ˈtɑːtnɪs). [OE. *teartnysse*: see TART *a.* and -NESS.] The quality of being tart.

†**1.** Severity; painfulness. *Obs.* (In later quots. fig. from 2.)

c **1000** in Napier *O.E. Glosses* 85/3158 *Acerbitatem*, teartnesse. *a* **1602** W. PERKINS *Cases Consc.* (1619) 61 The sweetnesse of comfort..if it bee alaied with some tartnesse of the Law. **1647** TRAPP *Comm. Matt.* x. 24 Sweeten me the tartness of all our sufferings with this sentence, as with so much sugar.

2. Sharpness of taste; †pungency (*obs.*); acidity.

1530 RASTELL *Bk. Purgat.* III. vii. F iij b, That eyer wyll.. vapour out the tartnes and sowernes of that humour. **1538** ELYOT, *Acrimonia*, tartnes, which biteth the tunge, and perceth the heed, as in the taste of garlyke, oynions, and other lyke thynges. **1562** TURNER *Herbal* II. 58 b, Vnrype mulberries besyde theyr tartnes they haue also a sournes. **1634** T. JOHNSON *Parey's Chirurg.* XXVI. vii. (1678) 632 Acidity or tartness is also in verjuice. **1770** COOK *Voy. round World* III. i. (1773) 501 The juice had an agreeable tartness, though but little flavour.

3. *fig.* Sharpness of disposition, language, etc.; biting or caustic manner or character; acerbity, pungency, acrimony, asperity of tone.

1548 UDALL, etc. *Erasm. Par. Mark* ix. 67 Which with the tartenesse of truth byteth awaye. **1579** GOSSON *Sch. Abuse* (Arb.) 31 The bitternesse of rebukes, and..the tartenesse of euery taunt. **1607** SHAKS. *Cor.* v. iv. 18 The tartnesse of his face, sowres ripe Grapes. **1709** HEARNE *Diary* in *Remains* (O.H.S.) II. 196 The Plowman's Tale... If it were Chaucer's, it was left perhaps out of his Canterbury Tales, for yᵉ Tartness against the Popish Clergy. **1748** SMOLLETT *Rod. Rand.* xliv, I told him with some tartness,..he might have chosen a more convenient opportunity. **1866** *Lond. Rev.* 3 Mar. 242/1 Lord Russell with a good deal of tartness declared that before February was out the Bill should be before the house.

tartor, variant of TARTAR *sb.*[3]

†ˈ**tartora, ˈtartorary.** *Obs.* [? corruptions of It. *tartaro* TARTAR[1].] ? = TARTAR *sb.*[1]

1545 *Rates of Customs* C vij b, Tartorary the pounde xij.d. **1586** *Ibid.* E viij, Tartora the pound xii.d.

tartorne, variant of TARTARIN[1] *Obs.*

tartralic (tɑːˈtrælɪk), *a. Chem.* [ad. F. *tartralique* (Frémy 1838), arbitrarily formed on *tartr-ique* (f. *tartre* TARTAR[1] + *-ique*), to indicate derivation from tartaric acid: cf. TARTRELIC. (*Annales de Chimie* LXVIII. (1838).)] In *tartralic acid* (also called *ditartaric* or *isotartaric acid*), $C_8H_{10}O_{11} = 2C_4H_6O_6-H_2O$, an amorphous deliquescent substance obtained by heating tartaric acid. Its salts are **tartralates**.

1857 MILLER *Elem. Chem.* III. 332 If tartaric acid be heated to 374°, it fuses; two equivalents of the acid lose one equivalent of water, and thus become converted into a new acid, termed by Fremy the *tartralic*. If tartaric acid be kept longer in fusion half its basic water is expelled, and tartrelic acid is formed. *Ibid.*, A soluble tartralate of this base is formed. **1868** WATTS *Dict. Chem.* V. 691 *Ditartaric Acid*,.. called *Tartralic acid* by Frémy, *Isotartaric acid* by Laurent and Gerhardt.

tartramic (tɑː'træmɪk), *a. Chem.* [f. TARTR(O- + AM(MONIUM) + -IC.] In ***tartramic acid***, $C_4H_7NO_5$, an amidated derivative of tartaric acid. Its salts are **'tartramates**. Also ***tartramic ether***, a name of *ethylic tartramate*, obtained by the action of alcoholic ammonia on tartaric ether; also called **tartra'methane**.

1857 MILLER *Elem. Chem.* III. 318 It is they [the dibasic acids] only that can furnish the amidated acids, such as the oxamic, tartramic, and lactamic acids. **1868** WATTS *Dict. Chem.* V. 697 Tartramate of calcium..is very soluble in water..and forms large tetrahedral crystals.

'tartra,mide. *Chem.* [f. TARTR(O- + AMIDE.] The amide of tartaric acid, $C_4H_4(NH_2)_2O_4$, a crystalline body produced by passing dry ammonia gas into an alcoholic solution of tartaric ether.

1868 WATTS *Dict. Chem.* V. 697.

'tartranil. *Chem.* [f. TARTR(O- + ANIL 3.] A granular compound, $C_{10}H_9NO_4$, = *phenyl-tartrimide*, produced by dehydration of acid tartrate of aniline by expulsion of $2H_2O$. Hence **tar'tranilate**, a salt of tartranilic acid; **tartra'nilic** ***acid***, $C_{10}H_{11}NO_5$, obtained by boiling tartranil with aqueous ammonia; **tar'tranilide**, $C_{16}H_{16}N_2O_4$, a substance produced by the action of heat on neutral tartrate of aniline, by expulsion of $2H_2O$.

1868 WATTS *Dict. Chem.* V. 698 Tartranil..separates, on cooling from hot solutions, as a white granular powder, or in nacreous laminæ. *Ibid.*, Tartranilide crystallises in colourless, nacreous, slender, interlaced needles. *Ibid.* 697 The tartranilic acid separates in light red warty masses and shining laminæ. *Ibid.*, *Tartranilate of Barium*..crystallises in shining spangles.

tartrate ('tɑːtrət). *Chem.* [a. F. *tartrate*, f. *tartre*, TARTAR *sb.*[1]: see -ATE[1].] A salt of tartaric acid ($CO_2H.(CHOH)_2.CO_2H$) formed by substituting a metal or radical for the hydrogen of the carbonyl groups (CO_2H).

These salts are very numerous, and are *acid* or *neutral*, according as one or both of the hydrogen atoms are replaced; thus, ***acid potassium tartrate*** is $CO_2H.(CHOH)_2.CO_2K$; ***neutral potassium tartrate***, $CO_2K.(CHOH)_2.CO_2K$. The H atoms can also be replaced by two different metals or radicals, forming double salts, as ***sodium potassium tartrate***, $CO_2.Na.(CHOH)_2.CO_2K$, ***potassium antimonyl tartrate***, $CO_2K.(CHOH)_2.CO_2SbO$.

1794 G. ADAMS *Nat. & Exp. Philos.* I. App. 547 Tartrats—the earthy insoluble in water, the alkaline soluble. **1815** J. SMITH *Panorama Sc. & Art* II. 436 Tartaric acid..unites with the alkalies, and most of the earths. The salts formed with it are called tartrates. **1869** ROSCOE *Elem. Chem.* (1871) 200 Potassium Carbonate can be obtained perfectly pure by heating pure potassium tartrate to redness.

'tartrated, *ppl. a. Chem.* [f. prec. + -ED.] Made into a tartrate; tartarated.

1879 *St. George's Hosp. Rep.* IX. 162 Treatment with a calomel purge and an emetic of tartrated antimony and ipecacuanha. **1899** CAGNEY tr. *Jaksch's Clin. Diagn.* vii. (ed. 4) 318 An alkaline solution of tartrated soda.

tartrazine, tartre: see TARTRO-, TARTAR[1].

tartrelic (tɑː'trɛlɪk), *a. Chem.* [ad. F. *tartrélique* (Frémy 1838), arbitrarily formed, along with TARTRALIC, q.v., to indicate derivation from tartaric acid by further heating; the *a* and *e* indicating the order of production of these modifications. (*Annales de Chimie* LXVIII. (1838).)] In ***tartrelic acid***, soluble tartaric anhydride, $C_4H_4O_5 = C_4H_6O_6-H_2O$, obtained as a yellowish deliquescent mass by quickly heating small quantities of tartaric acid. Its salts are **'tartrelates**. See TARTRALIC.

1838 R. D. THOMSON in *Brit. Ann.* 319 Tartrelic acid. **1857** MILLER *Elem. Chem.* III. 332 [see TARTRALIC]. **1868** WATTS *Dict. Chem.* V. 691 Chloride or acetate of calcium added to the solution [of tartrelic acid] throws down tartrelate of calcium.

tartrethylic, etc.: see TARTRO-.

†**'tartrite.** *Chem. Obs.* Also **tartarite.** [a. F. *tartrite* (1787), f. F. *tartre*, TARTAR[1] (whence the earlier *tartarite*): see -ITE[1].] A salt of tartarous or tartareous acid. (As this is now *tartaric* acid, the tartrites are now called *tartrates*.)

1790 KERR tr. *Lavoisier's Elem. Chem.* 255 As the acid from tartar is not fully saturated with oxygen, we call it tartarous acid, and the neutral salts formed by its combinations with salifiable bases tartarites. *Ibid.*, Cream of tartar..in our new nomenclature is named acidulous tartarite of potash. **1794** G. PEARSON in *Phil. Trans.* LXXXIV. 396 From the precipitation of tartrite of pot-ash ..this acid might be supposed to be the tartareous.

tartro-, before a vowel **tartr-** [f. F. *tartre*, TARTAR[1]], in names of chemical compounds containing or derived from tartaric acid; as **'tartrazine** [AZO- + -INE[5]], a fast and brilliant dye-stuff of rich orange yellow; **tartre'thylic** ***acid*** [ETHYLIC] = *ethyltartaric acid*, $C_6H_{10}O_6$: see quot. 1868; its salts are **tar'trethylates**; **tartrome'thylic** ***acid*** [METHYLIC] = *methyl-tartaric acid*, $C_5H_8O_6$: its salts are **tartro-'methylates; tartro'vinic** ***acid*** = *tartrethylic acid*. So ***tartrocarbhydric***, ***tartroglyceric***, etc.

1894 *Times* 15 Aug. 12/1 *Tartrazin, a colour noteworthy not only for its fastness to light, but also because of its brilliancy and purity. **1857** MILLER *Elem. Chem.* III. 318 Vinic or ethylic acids, such as sulphethylic, oxalethylic, and *tartrethylic. **1868** WATTS *Dict. Chem.* V. 694 *Tartrethylic* or *Tartrovinic acid*..crystallises in elongated prisms, with oblique bases; it is colourless, inodorous, tastes both sweet and sour. **1837** R. D. THOMSON in *Brit. Ann.* 342 When tartaric and racemic acids are treated..with pyroxylic spirit ..similar acids are formed which may be termed *tartro carbydric and racemo carbydric acids. **1838** T. THOMSON *Chem. Org. Bodies* 182 *Tartromethylate of potash may be obtained in the same way as tartrovinate of potash. *Ibid.* 180 *Tartromethylic acid..was also discovered by M. Guerin-Varry. **1837** R. D. THOMSON in *Brit. Ann.* 340 **Tartrovinic acid*, M. Guerin Varry..obtained it by boiling tartaric acid with absolute alcohol for a considerable time [etc.]. **1838** T. THOMSON *Chem. Org. Bodies* 174 A dilute solution..left exposed to an atmosphere of 77°, lets fall some..crystals of tartrovinic acid.

tartron, variant of TARTARIN[1] *Obs.*

tartronic (tɑː'trɒnɪk), *a. Chem.* [ad. F. *tartronique* (Dessaignes 1854), arbitrarily f. *tartrique* (perh. with *ni-* of *nitro-*). (*Comptes Rendus* XXXVIII. 44.)] In ***tartronic acid***, a dibasic acid, $C_3H_4O_5$, produced by the spontaneous decomposition of nitro-tartaric acid, crystallizing in large prisms. Its salts are **'tartronates**.

1866 ODLING *Anim. Chem.* 133 Mesoxalic acid is convertible by deoxidation or hydrogenation into tartronic acid. **1868** WATTS *Dict. Chem.* V. 698 The tartronates of the alkali-metals are soluble in water. **1873** RALFE *Phys. Chem.* p. xxix, Uric acid..is often represented as consisting of one radical of tartronic acid and two of urea.

'tartrous, *a.* [ad. F. *tartreux*, f. *tartre* TARTAR *sb.*[1] + -OUS.] Encrusted with (dental) tartar.

1904 *Brit. Med. Jrnl.* 20 Aug. 369 Tongue heavily coated, teeth tartrous.

'tartryl. *Chem.* [f. TARTR(O- or F. *tartre* + -YL.] The radical $C_4H_2O_2$ of tartaric acid. Hence **tar'trylic** *a.*, a synonym of *tartaric*.

1868 WATTS *Dict. Chem.* V. 698.

tartryn, -yne, variants of TARTARIN[1] *Obs.*

‖**Tartuffe, Tartufe** (tartyf, tɑː'tuːf). Also 7–8 **tartuff.** [F. *Tartufe*, *Tartuffe*, name of the principal character (a religious hypocrite) in a comedy by Molière (1664): app. = OF. *tartuffe*, It. *tartuffo* truffle, as a concealed production.

Littré cites It. *Tartufo*, name of a character in the Malmantile of Lippi, as app. Molière's source.]

A hypocritical pretender to religion, or, by extension, to excellence of any kind.

1688 *Pulpit Popery, True Popery* 72 Well, let Schoolmen and Cardinals..be call'd in, they are but Tartuffs; for Exposition and Representation are now the Standard of Romish Doctrine. **1738** WARBURTON *Div. Legat.* I. Ded. 24 Tartufes without Religion. **1765** STERNE *Tr. Shandy* VIII. ii, The arrantest *Tartuffe* in science, in politics,—or in religion. **1878** J. PAYN *By Proxy* I. xii. 138 A touch of the Tartuffe or the Joseph Surface.

Hence **Tar'tufferie, -ery** [F. *tartuferie*], **Tartuf(f)ism,** the character or conduct of a Tartuffe, hypocrisy; **Tar'tuffian, Tar'tuf(f)ish** *adjs.*, pertaining to or characteristic of a Tartuffe, hypocritical, pretentious; hence **Tar'tuffishly** *adv.*; **Tar'tuffily** *adv.* (*nonce-wd.*).

1851 *Fraser's Mag.* XLIII. 151 Her national *Tartuffery augmented and became more offensive. **1906** *Sat. Rev.* 13 Oct. 450/1 That incorrigible 'Tartufferie' which marks all our conquests. **1872** *Routledge's Ev. Boy's Ann.* 672 In such a very *Tartuffian way. **1915** *Tartuffily [see PECKSNIFF]. **1768** STERNE *Sent. Journ.* (1778) I. 66 God help her!..she has some mother-in-law, or *tartufish aunt..to consult upon the occasion. **1824** *Examiner* 594/1 That Alliance so *tartuffishly termed 'holy'. **1688** *Pulpit Popery, True Popery* 72 The *Tartuffism of Deposition of Princes, and Adoration of Images, and the rest of the once old and new Pulpit-Popery. **1891** *Sat. Rev.* 10 Oct. 403/1 The victim of Tartufism of the most disgusting kind.

tarturne, tartyr, variants of TARTARIN[1], TARTAR *sb.*[3]

tarty ('tɑːtɪ), *a.* (and *sb.*) *colloq.* [f. TART *sb.* 2 b + -Y[1].] Resembling or suggestive of a 'tart', or woman of immoral character; cheap, gaudy. Occas. *absol.* as *sb.*

1918 G. FRANKAU *One of Them* xxi. 163 Of that barred citadel whose mincing misses Persuade the chaste to emulate the tarty. **1929** D. H. LAWRENCE *Pansies* 123, I suppose most girls are a bit tarty to-day So that's why so many young men have long faces. **1944** M. LASKI *Love on Supertax* ix. 85 Some very tarty South American perfume. **1956** L. MCINTOSH *Oxford Folly* xiv. 231 A fat middle-aged woman with henna'd hair and clothes that managed to be at once tatty and tarty. **1978** M. DICKENS *Open Bk.* ix. 78 Frank, who was respectably married, was half afraid of Jean, but half delighted. Her tarty teasing made him feel shockingly male.

tarve (tɑːv). [app. the same as TARF.] A turn; a bend, a curve.

1848 F. COOPER *Bee-hunter* ii, I can't say much for your axe, stranger, for this helve has no tarve to 't.

tar-vetch: see TARE *sb.*[1] 4.

Tarvia ('tɑːvɪə). Chiefly *N. Amer.* [f. TAR *sb.* + L. *via* road.] The proprietary name of a road-surfacing and binding material made from tar. Also (irregularly) **'tarviate** *v. trans.*; hence **'tarviated** *ppl. a.*

1912 *Official Gaz.* (U.S. Patent Office) 23 July 1125/1 Tarvia..Pitch prepared from natural or manufactured bituminous oils and tars for road and pavement construction, roofing, waterproofing, and insulating. Claims use since June 1, 1903. **1926** *Daily Colonist* (Victoria, B.C.) 23 July 18/1 There has been a saving, over contract price, of $12,000, in tarviating the twenty-six miles of Island Highway. **1928** *Trade Marks Jrnl.* 18 Jan. 82 *Tarvia*... Raw or partly prepared mineral substances, for use in the manufacture of road-making materials. **1940** *Chambers's Techn. Dict.* 835/1 *Tarviated*.., a term applied to macadam road surfacings in which the stone is bound together with tar. **1947** *Archit. Rev.* CI. 163 A tarvia floor was chosen because of its cheapness and its acoustical properties. **1952** *Jrnl. Acoustical Soc. Amer.* XXIV. 662/1 It is..necessary to record on the identical stretch of tarvia road. **1966** R. H. RIMMER *Harrad Experiment* (1967) 25 A one lane tarvia road between two stone pillars. **1972** *Islander* (Victoria, B.C.) 23 Jan. 16/2 My feet got so sensitive I could sense the difference between tarvia, gravel, or concrete immediately.

'tar-,water. [f. TAR *sb.*[1] + WATER *sb.*]

1. An infusion of tar in cold water, formerly in repute as a medicine.

1740–1 BERKELEY *Let. T. Prior* 8 Feb., I believe tar-water might be useful to prevent..such an evil [a felon]. **1744** —— (*title*) Philosophical Reflexions and Inquiries concerning the Virtues of Tar-Water [*ed.* 2 Siris, a Chain of Philosophical [etc.]]. **1744** GRAY *Let. to Wharton* 26 Apr., Mr. Trollope and I are in a course of Tar-Water. **1756** H. WALPOLE *Let. to Mann* 8 Dec., He [Sir H. Mann's brother] has been drinking tar-water since the middle of November. **1840** E. FITZGERALD *Letters* (1889) I. 60, I have also just concocted two gallons of Tar water under the directions of Bishop Berkeley. **1891** SYDNEY *Eng. in 18th C.* I. 311 No remedy was more popular during the second half of the eighteenth century than tar-water.

2. 'The ammoniacal water of gas-works' (Simmonds *Dict. Trade*, 1858).

‖**tarwhine** ('tɑːhwaɪn). Also **tarwine.** [? Native name.] An Australian fish, *Chrysophrys sarba*, used for food.

1880 INGLIS *Austral. Cousins* 298 In the brackish waters near Lake Macquarie, are most plentiful supplies of black bream, tarwine, flathead, whiting, river gar-fish and others. **1883** E. P. RAMSAY *Food Fishes N.S. Wales* 12 (Fish. Exhib. Publ.) The black bream (*Chrysophrys australis*) and the tarwhine (*Ch. hasta*) are both valuable food-fish,..they attain a weight of 4 to 5 lbs.

tarwinie, var. of TAUHINU.

†**tary,** *sb. Obs.* Also 6 **tarie, -ye.** [f. TARY *v.*] Vexation, trouble, annoyance.

1528 LYNDESAY *Dreme* 277 For to rehers thare lyffis vitious, It wer bot tarye to the auditouris. **1533** GAU *Richt Vay* (S.T.S.) 66 We haiff mekil tarie of it [our body] heir in ye wardil. *c***1576** MAITLAND *Poems* (1830) 40 And tak ane wyf to bring him selffe in tarye, For fresche Maii and cauld Januarij Agreeis nocht upon ane sang in tune.

†**'tary,** *v. Obs.* Forms: 4–5 **tarien,** 5 **teryyn,** (**tarry**), 5–6 **tarie, -ye,** (**tarrie**), **tary.** [ME. *tery-yn, tari-en* appears to represent in form and sense both OE. *tęrȝan*, **tærȝ(e)an*, *tyrian*, **tęrian*, to provoke, and OF. *tarier* to provoke, excite, in F. dial. to vex, irritate, torment, tease (of doubtful origin). In so far as *tary* was of OE. origin, it was a doublet of TAR *v.*[2] See Note.]

1. *trans.* To provoke, vex, worry, harass.

*a***1300** *E.E. Psalter* cv[i]. 8[7] Þai taried [*irritaverunt*] vpsteȝ and in se, Rede se. *a***1325** *Prose Psalter* ibid., Tariden. **13..** *Cursor M.* 28153, I womman haue vn-buxum bene And tarid myn husband to tene. **1340** HAMPOLE *Pr. Consc.* 1189 Þa þat wille him folow, he..scornes and taries in his nedes. **1387** (MS. *c***1410**) TREVISA tr. *Higden* (Rolls) V. 355 Þe kynges..sone..gan to tarry [*v.r.* terre; orig. *lacessivit*] and to angre Þe Longobardes wiþ despitous wordes. *c***1400** *Destr. Troy* 7287 He was tarriet with the Troiens, & tenit full euyll. *c***1440** *Promp. Parv.* 489/2 Teryyn, or ertyn. [Ertyn, *irrito.*] *c***1440** *Psalmi Penit.* (1894) 38 Yn this world ys no scharpur arwe, Than the turment [*MS.* turnement] that me gan tarie [*rime* marie]. **1567** *Gude & Godlie B.* (S.T.S.) 176 Kingis to marie, and sum to tarie, Sic is his power and mycht.

2. To weary, tire, fatigue. (Cf. TAR *v.*[2] 2.)

*c***1375** in T. Wright *Rel. Antiq.* I. 9 *Fatigatus*, y-taried.

Hence † **tarying, teryynge** *vbl. sb.*, provoking; † **taryer, teryare**, a provoker, vexer; † **taryingness**, provocation.

a **1300** *E.E. Psalter* xciv. 9 [xcv. 8] Als aftre dai in taryingnesse Ofe fandinge in wildernesse. *a* **1400** Hylton *Scala Perf.* (W. de W. 1494) II. xxii, Of tarienges & temptacions that Soules fele bi her ghostly enmyes. *c* **1440** *Promp. Parv.* 489/2 Teryare, or ertare, *irritator*... Teryynge, or ertynge, *irritacio*.

[*Note.* The form *teryyn* (= *tery-en, teri-en*) in Promp. Parv., with its derivatives *teryare, teryynge*, points to OE. *tergan*, with the palatal *g* reduced to *y* consonant or *i*, as in the actually recorded late OE. form *tyrian* (imper. *tyrie*, pa. t. *tyrgde, tyrigde, tyride*), giving a ME. *teri-en* (*tery-yn*), with a variant *tary-en, tari-en*, perh. from an Anglian **tærg(e)an*, as in *weryen, warien*, from OE. *wergean, wærgean, wiergan, wyrgean, wyrian*, WARRY, to curse. The coincidence of *tarien* in form and meaning with OF. *tarier* would tend to reinforce it as the leading form. It is noteworthy that ME. examples of *tary-* are not known before *c* 1300, and that *tery-* is cited only from *Promp. Parv.* As to possible connexion with TARRY see Note to that vb.]

tary, taryance, -ans, etc., obs. ff. TARRY, TARRIANCE.

taryar, -er, obs. ff. TERRIER *sb.*[2]

Tarzan ('tɑːzən). The name of a character in a series of novels by the American author Edgar Rice Burroughs (1875–1950), and in subsequent films and television series, who is orphaned in West Africa in his infancy and reared in the jungle by a mother-ape, used *transf.* to designate a person distinguished by physical strength or agility.

[**1914** E. R. Burroughs (*title*) Tarzan of the apes.] **1921** *Glasgow Herald* 25 Oct. 5/5 At fruit picking time there is a regular colony of Tarzans disporting themselves in the branches. **1938** M. Allingham *Fashion in Shrouds* vi. 78 Ramillies was ruddy pleased... Saw 'imself a Tarzan. **1946** Koestler *Thieves in Night* 150 Their bodies [are] those of a horde of Hebrew Tarzans roaming in the hills of Galilee. **1960** *John o' London's* 14 Apr. 436 The tough 'Tarzan's' relationship with his landlady..is tenderly portrayed. **1974** H. MacInnes *Climb to Lost World* vi. 85 It wasn't a normal four hour walk—more like an obstacle course for budding Tarzans. **1981** R. Barnard *Mother's Boys* i. 15 Gordon began his morning liturgy of exercises... 'Bloody Tarzan,' said Brian.

b. Allusively in *attrib.* use.

1932 R. Knox *Broadcast Minds* vii. 161 Though the Tarzan-stuff may make snappy reading. **1941** A. Cotterell *What! No Morning Tea?* 103 Not hothouse gymnasium overdevelopment, but sheer Tarzan physical wellbeing. **1961** M. Jones *Potbank* xxvi. 114 A remarkably handsome young man with a Tarzan physique. **1974** V. Canning *Painted Tent* ix. 189 Nearly killed myself on the tower ladder today. Saved by a Tarzan act.

Hence ˌ**Tarza'nesque** [-ESQUE], '**Tarzan-like** *adjs.*

1933 *Punch* 27 Dec. 712/1 Taken in conjunction with my Tarzanesque agility, They constitute a clue to my athletic versatility. **1943** *Copper Camp* (Writers' Program, Montana) 214 Butt Block gazed pridefull at his partner, smiled and then with brawny fists pounded, Tarzan-like, upon his hairy chest. **1973** C. Bonington *Next Horizon* xi. 158 He loved being the centre of attraction, dropped easily into Tarzanesque poses, and enjoyed showing off the odd feat of strength. **1980** T. Holme *Neapolitan Streak* 160 He had to perform a Tarzan-like operation, lowering himself.. and then swinging down.

tas, obs. f. TASS.

tas = *takes*: see TAKE *v.* A.

Tasaday (tə'sɑːdaɪ, 'tæsədaɪ), *sb.* [a. *Tasaday*, prob. f. *tau* person + *sa* (place marker) + *dâya* inland.] **a.** (A member of) a people living on the Philippine island of Mindanao (see note). Also *attrib.* **b.** The Manobo language of this people.

The Tasaday were said to have isolated themselves (allegedly in flight from a plague epidemic) some eight hundred years ago, forsaking their skills in rice-agriculture, metallurgy, etc., and taking up a less advanced form of existence (see quots.). Their 'discovery' and identification as a separate ethnic group were subsequently shown to be fraudulent.

1971 *Guardian* 19 July 3/1 Dark skinned, fruit-eating men, known as Tasadays..near Lake Sebu, in Cotabato Province..south of Manila. The tribesman..number about sixty... Their isolation was total until 1966. **1971** *Philippine Jrnl. Linguistics* II. 3 A comparison of the lexical items of Tasaday..reveals that the language has most cognates with ..B'lit Manobo. **1972** *National Geographic* Aug. 232/2 Igna ..translated from T'boli.. to Tasaday. *Ibid.* 239 (*caption*) The staple of the Tasaday diet..is a wild yam. **1973** E. Hyams *Final Agenda* ix. 118 The pacific and gentle manners of the Tasaday people, a Stone Age vestige still living on Mindanao. **1975** *New Society* 4 Dec. 559/2 In the early 1960s, Dafal, a wandering hunter, came across a small and timid band of food-gatherers, calling themselves Tasaday, living deep in the forest reaches of southern Mindanao in the Philippines. **1988** *Daily Tel.* 23 Aug. 29/3 The world's press flocked to the remote rain forests of the Philippines to meet the gentle Tasaday tribe, which seemed untouched by civilisation... But now they have been exposed as an elaborate fraud cooked up by a playboy millionaire and a friend of ex-president Marcos.

‖ **tasajo** (ta'saxo). Also 8 **tassajo**, 9 **tassago**. [Sp. *tasajo* a slice of dried meat, in Pg. *tasalho*; cf. Cat. *tasco*. Of uncertain origin: see Diez 490.] Buffalo meat cut into strips and dried in the sun.

[**1760–72** tr. *Juan & Ulloa's Voy.* (ed. 3) II. 244 The flesh after having been cut into thin slices, is salted, and this is what they call Tassajear.] **1783** Justamond tr. *Raynal's Hist. Indies* V. 365 The inhabitants [of Trinidad] shoot them [wild cattle], and cut their flesh into slips..which they dry. .. This provision, which is called Tassajo, is sold in the French settlements. **1851** Mayne Reid *Scalp Hunt.* xxvi, Those who remain cut the [buffalo] meat into long thin strips, and hang it over the lines already prepared for this purpose. It is thus left to be baked by the sun into '*tasajo*'. **1858** Simmonds *Dict. Trade*, *Tasajo*, a name in New Granada for dried meat; hung beef. **1891** *Cent. Dict.*, Tassago.

tasar, var. TUSSER, TUSSORE, an Indian silk.

† **tascal.** *Sc. Obs.* exc. *Hist.* [a. Gael. *taisgeal* the finding of anything that was lost, f. *taisg* a treasure, *taisg* to deposit, hoard, bury.] In *tascal money*, a reward formerly paid in the Scottish Highlands for information regarding stolen cattle.

c **1730** Burt *Lett.* (1754) II. xxiv. 243 Sending Persons into the Country suspected, and by them offering a Reward (which they call Tascal Money) to any one who should discover the Cattle, and those who stole them. **1827** J. Anderson *St. Soc. & Knowl. Highl.* 70 He who..received tascal money as informer, met scorn, perhaps death. **1907** A. Lang *Hist. Scot.* IV. xv. 368 Tascal money used to be paid to traitors among the robbers.

† '**tasco**, '**tascony.** *Obs. rare*[−0]. [ad. It. *tasconio* 'a kind of white clay or marble, whereof goldsmiths pots...were made' (Florio 1598), ad. L. *tasconium* (Pliny).] (See quots.)

1726 Bailey, *Tasco*, a sort of Clay, for making Melting-Pots. **1730** —— (folio), *Tascony*, a sort of white Earth like Chalk, and is the only Earth that endures the Blast of the Bellows and Heat of the Fire and running Metal. **1823** Crabb *Techn. Dict.*, Tasco.

tase, obs. form of *takes*, inflexion of TAKE *v.*

tase, var. TEISE *v.*, *Obs.*, to stretch, bend (a bow).

tasel, -ell(e, obs. ff. TEASEL.

taseometer (tæsɪ'ɒmɪtə(r)). [f. Gr. τασε-, stem of τάσις tension + -METER.] (See quot.)

1880 *Telegraphic Jrnl.* VI. 126. **1884** Knight *Dict. Mech.* Suppl., *Taseometer*, invented by Steiner, of Vienna, for measuring the strains of structures. It depends upon the tone given out by a wire or strip when stretched. The wire being attached the variation in length of the bar causes a change in the tone.

Taser ('teɪzə(r)). orig. and chiefly *U.S.* Also taser. [f. the initial letters of *T*om *S*wift's *e*lectric *r*ifle (a fictitious weapon), after LASER[2].] A weapon which fires barbs attached by wires to batteries, and causes temporary paralysis. Hence '**Tasered** *a.*, paralysed by means of a Taser.

Developed by Taser Systems Inc., Los Angeles.

1972 *Science* 12 May 615/2 A taser is an instrument that fires a cluster of electrified barbs which become snagged in the victim's clothing and paralyze him until the current is switched off. **1973** *Guardian* 16 Apr. 11 A pan-lethal weapon called the Taser, developed by a California manufacturer... Two electrical wires lash out... The suspect stiffens from shock. His muscles are paralysed. **1975** *Globe & Mail* (Toronto) 4 Oct. 10/1 The Taser Public Defender, as it's called, can penetrate nearly two inches of clothing and give up to a 50,000-volt charge. Taser Systems Inc. of Los Angeles, the manufacturer, says it is not lethal but is designed to stop attackers in their tracks. **1976** *N.Y. Times Mag.* 4 Jan. 13 A powerful transformer within the Taser generates 50,000 volts when a trigger is pressed. This jolt, sent through the wires into the darts, which have been shot into the skin or clothing of the victim, cause him to become 'Tasered'. **1977** *Observer* 21 Aug. 2/7 There was the taser that fired barbs attached to wires into demonstrators to paralyse them with electric shocks.

tases, obs. f. *tasses* thigh-armour: see TASSE *sb.*[1]

tash (tæʃ). Also **'tache**. Colloq. abbrev. of MOUSTACHE, MUSTACHE *sb.* 1 a.

1893–4 R. O. Heslop *Northumberland Words* II. 719 *Tash*, a moustache. 'Him wi' the *tash*.' **1943** Hunt & Pringle *Service Slang* 64 *Tash*, moustache. **1965** R. Simons *Dead Reckoning* iv. 56 'E 'ad a little tash, just under 'is nose. **1968** A. Diment *Great Spy Race* viii. 123 He was.. spluttering through his straggly 'tache. **1973** A. MacVicar *Painted Doll Affair* vi. 70 A wee runt wi' a Mexican 'tache. **1980** *Home & Country* Nov. 602/1 (Advt.), 12" male dolls.. Painted hair and tash.

tash, *dial.*, blemish: see TACHE *sb.*[1]

tashed, tarnished: see TACHE *v.*[1]

Tashi Lama ('tæʃɪ 'lɑːmə). Also 8–9 **Teshoo Lama, Teshu Lama**; 9 **Tishu Lama**, etc. [f. *Tashi* Lhunpo, the name of the monastery ruled by the Tashi Lama, + LAMA[1].] A title of the Panchen Lama (see PANCHEN).

1774 G. Bogle *Mission to Tibet* (1876) p. xlvii, There have been two great incarnations of equal rank: the Dalai Lama at Potala..; and the Teshu Lama at Teshu Lumbo, the incarnation of the Buddhisatwa Amitabha. **1784** S. Turner *Let.* 2 Mar. in *Acct. of Embassy to Court of Teshoo Lama in Tibet* (1800) III. 366 He will ratify the promises made to the former Teshoo Lama, the moment the present Lama is capable of renewing the application. **1811** W. Kirkpatrick *Acct. of Kingdom of Nepaul* 341 Some persons of rank on the part of the Teeshoo Lama, and Sankia Lama, came into the Goorkha camp. **1819** F. Hamilton *Acct. of Kingdom of Nepal* I. i. 57 Still more celebrated is the Tishu Lama, who resides at Degarchi, and is the spiritual guide of the Chinese emperors. **1876** [see LAMA[1]]. **1923** *Daily Mail* 18 Apr. 5 The Tashi Lama is of equal rank with the better-known Lama Guru of Lhassa, but he rules over a smaller area, and has not nearly so much temporal power as the latter, though he is regarded as a holier person. **1950** A. De Riencourt *Lost World* viii. 96 His new name was Panchen Rimpoche or Precious Great Sage and his successors became known all over the world as Panchen or Tashi Lamas.

‖ **tashlik, tashlich** (taʃ'liːk). [Heb. *taʃlīk* 'thou shalt cast', future Hiphil of *ʃālak* to cast.] A symbolical custom, popularly in vogue among Jews, of repairing, on New Year's Day, to a stream of running water, and repeating certain biblical verses indicative of sin and forgiveness, specially Micah vii. 19, 'Thou wilt cast all their sins into the depths of the sea'.

1880 *Jewish World* 30 Sept., Tashlich..a simple fad of mediæval rabbinism, of late date and origin, and wholly unknown to our ancient sages. **1902** *Daily Chron.* 2 Oct. 7/1 They have imported with them from their native ghettos the singular practice known as 'Tashlikh', which is performed by the side of a stream of running water or on the seashore. .. A favourite resort for the purpose of 'Tashlikh' is the Custom House Quay, and the front walk of the Tower.

Tasian ('tɑːsɪən, 'teɪʃ(ɪ)ən), *a.* and *sb. Archæol.* [f. Deir *Tasa*, the name of a village in Upper Egypt, + -IAN.] **A.** *adj.* Of, pertaining to, or designating the pre-Dynastic Neolithic culture represented by remains found at Deir Tasa. **B.** *sb.* A person of the Tasian culture; the culture itself.

1929 G. Brunton in *Antiquity* III. 459 This new cultural phase we have named Tasian from the village of Deir Tasa where the graves were first located. *Ibid.* 466 It may be premature to say definitely that the Tasians preceded the Badarians, but all the evidence points in that direction. **1931** [see BADARIAN *a.*]. **1934** V. G. Childe *New Light on Most Anc. East* iii. 52 Remains found at Deir Tasa and other sites on the east bank of the Nile in Middle Egypt..belong to a people who have been termed Tasians. **1939** —— *Dawn Europ. Civilization* (ed. 3) xii. 218 Beaker-like vases decorated with zones of incision which might be clay translations of such basketry vessels occur in Egypt in the early 'Tasian' phase of culture. **1961** G. Clark *World Prehist.* v. 103 Although no radiocarbon or absolute dates are available for the Tasian it is generally held on not very impressive evidence to have preceded the Badarian.

tasil(l, obs. ff. TEASEL.

tasimeter (tə'sɪmɪtə(r)). [f. Gr. τάσι-ς tension + -METER.] An electrical apparatus for measuring minute variations of temperature, length, moisture, etc. by means of changes in the electrical conductivity of carbon resulting from alterations of pressure caused by these variations.

1878 *Nature* 25 July 329/2 An account..of Edison's Tasimeter. **1879** H. W. Warren *Recr. Astron.* iv. 62 If the temperature of a summer morning rises ten or twenty degrees we scarcely notice it; but the magnetic tasimeter measures $\frac{1}{5000}$ of a degree. **1881** *Nature* 25 Aug. 390/2 No satisfactory results have been obtained in the attempt to measure the heat of the stars with the tasimeter. **1893** *Review of Rev.* Dec. 606 A little machine called the tasimeter, which measures degrees of heat, of moisture..of odours and sound.

Hence **tasi'metric** *a.*, of or pertaining to the tasimeter or to tasimetry (*Cassell's Encycl. Dict.* 1888); **ta'simetry**, the measurement of pressures (*Funk's Standard Dict.* 1895).

task (tɑːsk, -æ-), *sb.* Also 4–7 **taske**, 5–7 **tasque**. [a. ONF. *tasque* (13th c. in Godef.) = OF. *tasche*, F. *tâche*; or ad. med.L. *tasca* (*taschia*) (*c* 800 in Du Cange), according to Diez, by metathesis for *taxa*, f. L. *taxāre* to rate, estimate, value, in med.L. to impose or assess a tax.]

I. † **1.** A fixed payment to a king, lord, or feudal superior; an impost, tax; tribute. *Obs.*

[**1114–18** *Laws Hen. I*, c. 78 § 5 Persoluantur uel in taschis uel huiusmodi suggerendis, sicut de b[a]st[ar]dis est institutum.] *c* **1400** *Laud Troy Bk.* 17918 This is the somme that Gregays aske, That thei wole haue vnto her taske: Ten hundrid thousand pound of golde. **14..** in *Wars Eng. in France* (1864) II. 525 Tasques, taylles, inposicione of the comyns. *c* **1440** *Promp. Parv.* 487/1 Taske, or talyage, *taliagium, taxa*. *c* **1475** *Harl. Contin. Higden* (Rolls) VIII. 454 Grete exaccions and taskes. **1530** Palsgr. 279/2 Taske that a prince gadereth, *taulx*. **1624** *Maldon, Essex, Borough Deeds* (Bundle 108 lf. 12), xxd. payd the collectors of the taske for twoe fifteenes and tenths. *a* **1625** Sir H. Finch *Law* (1636) 298 High Collectors of any Taske, Subsedie, or lone. **1766** Blackstone *Comm.* II. v. 75 By statute 25 Edw. I. c. 5 & 6..it was enacted, that the king should take no aids or tasks but by the common assent of the realm.

2. a. A piece of work imposed, exacted, or undertaken as a duty or the like; originally, a fixed or specified quantity of labour or work imposed on or exacted from a person; later, the work appointed or assigned to one as a definite duty.

a **1300** *Cursor M.* 5872 And taron sett he men at ask Of ilk dai to yeild þair task [*v.r.* taske]. **13..** *Ibid.* 29000 Has he

[Christ] sett vs certain task Quilk ar þai bones for to ask. *c* **1400** *St. Alexius* (Laud 622) 675 Nouȝth as a Man of task. **1530** TINDALE *Exod.* v. 14 Wherfore haue ye not fulfilled youre taske in makinge brycke? **1549** COVERDALE, etc. *Erasm. Par. Rom.* 8 The Iewes..whiche hauyng..become christian men, & worke no longer now, as it wer by tasque, but vnfainedly & purely put theyr trust in him. **1573–80** BARET *Alv.* T 79 The Taske, or worke that one is appointed to do. **1645** MILTON *Tetrach.* Wks. 1851 IV. 237 A task we know is a proportion of work, not doing the same thing absolutely every day, but so much. **1699** BURNET *39 Art.* xxv. (1700) 283 Prayers gone through as a Task can be of no value. **1711** ADDISON *Spect.* No. 111 ¶6 The silk-worm, after having spun her task, lays her eggs and dies. **1758** JOHNSON *Idler* No. 13 ¶6 She..appoints them a task of needle-work. **1856** OLMSTED *Slave States* 435 In getting fuel from the woods..one cord is the task for a day. **1892** WESTCOTT *Gospel of Life* 272 Each age has its own task, and we can dimly see our own.

b. *spec.* A portion of study imposed by a teacher; a lesson to be learned or prepared; *spec.* (*Winchester College slang*) an essay or composition to be written. Now *arch.*

1742 SHENSTONE *Schoolmistress* 155 Eftsoons the urchins to their tasks repair, Their books of stature small they take in hand. **1760** FRANKLIN *Ess.* Wks. 1840 II. 126 These lessons might be given every night as tasks. **1811** BYRON *Hints fr. Hor.* 231 Fines, tutors, tasks, conventions threat in vain. **1900** J. S. FARMER *Public School Word-Bk.* 201 *Task*, (*subs.*) (Winchester), all kinds of composition other than an Essay or Vulgus. **1901** *Northern Whig* 8 May (E.D.D.), An Ulster lad, when at school, gets his 'tasks'. **1980** 'T. HINDE' *Sir Henry & Sons* xv. 151 The weekly essay..called a task, is written by every boy in the school.

c. *Psychol.* A piece of work or an exercise given to a subject in a psychological test or experiment. Cf. AUFGABE.

1913 H. MÜNSTERBERG *Psychol. & Industrial Efficiency* xviii. 237 We know how the consciousness of the task to be performed has an organizing influence on the system of those psychophysical acts which lead to the goal. **1951** G. HUMPHREY *Thinking* 99 The energy [for mental operations] may..conceivably originate in..the task or motive. **1972** *Jrnl. Social Psychol.* LXXXVII. 96 Sixty males received..electric shocks of varying magnitude from a confederate during a 10-trial probability estimation task.

3. In more general sense: Any piece of work that has to be done; something that one has to do (usually involving labour or difficulty); a matter of difficulty, a 'piece of work'. Cf. JOB *sb.*[2] 4.

1593 SHAKS. *Rich. II*, II. ii. 145 Alas poore Duke, the taske he vndertakes Is numbring sands, and drinking Oceans drie. **1637** T. MORTON *New Eng. Canaan* (1883) 182 My taske..is to intreat of the naturall indowments of the Country. **1641** BROME *Jov. Crew* II. Wks. 1873 III. 384 Alass poor Knave! How hard a tasque it is to alter Custome! **1754** *Connoisseur* No. 42 ¶7 To rescue our Native Language..is a task worthy those who are accounted Ornaments of our Seats of Learning. **1841** W. SPALDING *Italy & It. Isl.* III. 101 Never had sovereigns been called upon to perform a task more difficult than that which lay before the restored princes of Italy. **1858** FROUDE *Hist. Eng.* III. xvii. 525 He had taken upon himself a task beyond the ordinary strength of man.

II. Phrases. †**4. a.** *at task*: (*a*) at so much for a specified amount or piece of work, by the piece; (*b*) ? taken to task, blamed (a doubtful sense, the reading being uncertain). **b.** *by task, to task*, by the piece. **c.** *under task*, under the command of a taskmaster; by compulsion. *Obs.*

a. 1477–8 in Swayne *Sarum Churchw. Acc.* (1896) 364 Helyng and poyntyng in dyvers places atte Taske. **1605** SHAKS. *Lear* I. iv. 366 (Fol. 1) Yet vnder pardon You are much more at task [*Qo.* 1 attaskt] for want of wisedome, Then prai sd for harmefull mildnesse.

b. 1601–2 in Willis & Clark *Cambridge* (1886) II. 628 Item for caruing the eight beastes by taske. **1803** *Naval Chron.* XV. 58 A job note..an actual statement of the work performed by job and task. **1476–7** in Swayne *Sarum Churchw. Acc.* (1896) 363 Swaryng of timber to carpenters to taske viijd.

c. 1671 MILTON *Samson* 35 To grind in Brazen Fetters under task With this Heav'n-gifted strength.

5. *to take to task*: †(*a*) to undertake as one's task or special piece of work; †(*b*) to challenge (a person) to a task; †(*c*) to take (a person or thing) in hand, to deal with; (*d*) *esp.* (in current use), to deal with or tackle in the way of fault-finding or censure, to call to account about a matter: cf. TASK *v.* 5, TAX *v.* 6.

1546 *Accts. Osney & St. Frideswyde's* (MS. Wood, D. 2, p. 585), To a laborer pulling downe stone at Osney church, for yᵉ masons yᵗ took yᵉ walle to taske at frideswides. **1570** J. DEE *Math. Pref.* a iv b, Geographie did principally take the Element of the Earthes description..to taske. **1589** PUTTENHAM *Eng. Poesie* III. xix. (Arb.) 253 He..would take any common souldier to taske at wrastling, or weapon, or in any other actiuitie..of armes. **1649** BP. HALL *Cases Consc.* (1650) 265 Apollos..knew nothing but the Baptisme of John: till Aquila and Priscilla took him to task, and more perfectly expounded to him the way of God. **1682** WOOD *Life* 31 May (O.H.S.) III. 19 George Royse..took his principles to take and exposed them very smartly. **1740** tr. *De Mouhy's Fort. Country-Maid* (1741) I. 84 What is the Matter, my pretty Girl?..has any one been taking you to Task? **1760–72** H. BROOKE *Fool of Qual.* (1792) I. 81 [He] shut the door, and called him to task. **1822** *Examiner* 365/1 The *Quarterly* is taken to task for neglecting its duty. **1890** DOYLE *Capt. 'Polestar'*, etc. 205 My employer took me severely to task.

III. 6. *attrib.* and *Comb.*, as, †(in sense 1) *task-book, -cope, -gatherer, -money, -roll* (obs.); (in senses 2 and 3), *task assignment, -book, -house, -labour, -labourer, -lord, -officer, performance, -reading, role, -verse; task-directed, -like, -orientated, -oriented, -related* adjs.; **task force** orig. *U.S.*, an armed force organized for a special operation under a unified command; hence *transf.*, any group of persons organized for a special task, esp. an investigative committee; **task group**, a naval task force, or a subdivision of such a force; **task-man**, an officer who sets a task, a taskmaster; **task-note**, a memorandum of work done by the piece, a job-note: see quot. 1803 in 4b; **task-system**, the system of working by the piece. See also TASKMASTER, etc.

1964 *Task assignment [see ASSIGNMENT 13]. **1624** *Maldon, Essex, Borough Deeds* (Bundle 108 lf. 8), xs. payd to Samwell Chese for new writing of the *taske booke (in parchment) this yere. **1882** J. PARKER *Apost. Life* I. 17 Some men hardly can open the Bible..because they remember that in early days it was the task-book. **1463** in *Bury Wills* (Camden) 21 To aquyte the said Seynt Marie preest of the *taske Abbot's cope and alle manner charges generally at ony [time] askyd by ony manner of mene. **1971** J. S. BRUNER *Beyond Information Given* (1974) xvii. 302 The picture of development drawn thus far is much too *task-directed, too playless to be characteristic of the first year of life. **1941** *Time* 23 June 41/3 A division of Marines and one of infantry ..as a potential A.E.F. '*task force'—for action overseas. **1942** *Jrnl. R. Aeronaut. Soc.* XLVI. 340 Low speed battleships are useless as a constituent of so-called 'task' forces. **1949** *Richmond* (Va.) *Times- Dispatch* 1 Mar. 1/1 The work stoppage resulted from an attempt by the city to try out a 'task force' system of collections. Under this plan, workers are assigned a certain route to be covered each day. When they complete their route, they can go home, regardless of how long it has taken. **1954** *Economist* 9 Jan. 97 The task force appointed..to examine the civil service. **1966** [see PROJECT *sb.* 5 d]. **1971** *Nature* 24 Dec. 435/3 A task force set up under the auspices of the National Heart and Lung Institute. **1980** *Birds* Autumn 13/3 The problem [of bird smuggling] has become so serious in the USA that the Justice Department has been ordered to establish a special task force. Over a period of 12 months, nearly 1,000 birds have been seized by Customs officers. **1982** *Times* 3 June 8/6 The work of getting the components of the task force to sea has often been swift. **1552** HULOET, *Taske gatherer, *exactor*. **1943** *Daily Tel.* 23 Oct. 1/4 Capt. Mackintosh, as the senior commanding officer, commanded a *Task Group, which included one of the latest battleships and American destroyers. **1952** [see KAMIKAZE *sb.* 2]. **1979** *Navy News* Feb. 2/1 Ships in a Royal Navy task group broke off from their work surveying the coast of Iran last month to ferry British and American dependants away from the troubled country. **1847** LD. LINDSAY *Hist. Chr. Art* I. Introd. 168 There was my place of prayer, there the *task-house of my most wretched flesh. **1812** *Gen. Hist.* in *Ann. Reg.* 161/2 The working of mines, and other *task labour. **1838–9** FR. A. KEMBLE *Resid. in Georgia* (1863) 28 In the part of Georgia where this estate is situated, the custom of task labour is universal. **1897** A. DRUCKER tr. *Ihering's Evol. Aryan* 116 The Egyptians knew no mercy for their *task-labourers. **1830** FR. A. KEMBLE *Let.* in *Rec. Girlhood* (1878) II. iv. 115 With what *task-like feeling I set about most of my work. **1605** SYLVESTER *Du Bartas* II. iii. III. *Law* 137 They labour hard, eat little, sleeping lesse, No sooner layd, but thus their *Task-Lords presse. **1856** OLMSTED *Slave States* 435 One cord is the task for a day... The *taskman selecting the trees ..that he judges will split easiest, one hundred a day. **1593** *Jack Straw* I. in Hazl. *Dodsley* V. 379 Thou hast thy *task-money for all that be here. **1803** *Naval Chron.* XV. 58 Is there any particular form of job or *task note? **1865** J. H. INGRAHAM *Pillar of Fire* (1872) 135 Enrolling them under *task-officers. **1953** *Jrnl. Abnormal & Soc. Psychol.* XLVIII. 401 (*heading*) Coding noise in a *task-oriented group. **1971** J. Z. YOUNG *Introd. Study Man* xx. 273 Both social and task-oriented behaviours are relatively consistent for both boys and girls from about 4 to 12 years. **1974** tr. *Wertheim's Evolution & Revolution* i. 38 Equally, modernity in political structure is positively related to a task-oriented bureaucracy and a recruitment on the basis of skills. **1970** *Jrnl. Gen. Psychol.* Jan. 91 The findings of this study that the *task performance of internals was better. **1956** J. KLEIN *Study of Groups* viii. 112 If a member proposes that the group shall rehearse a play and another says that he hates play-acting, that is a *task-related contribution. **1972** *Accountant* 21 Sept. 357/2 A more task-related analysis might be used. **1967** M. ARGYLE *Psychol. Interpersonal Behaviour* iv. 71 The *task roles of providing 'fuel', putting the 'threads' of the discussion together, and clarification, were generally performed by the same person; the social roles of making tactful comments to heal hurt feelings, and joking, were performed by others. **1577** in *10th Rep. Hist. MSS. Comm.* App. IV. 439 A *taske rowle made for the manor of Romseley. **1863** P. BARRY *Dockyard Econ.* 57 Examined as to the operation of what is known as the *task and job system. **1875** LOWELL *Wks.* (1890) IV. 360 At school Wordsworth wrote some *task-verses on subjects imposed by the master.

task (tɑːsk, -æ-), *v.* [f. TASK *sb.* Cf. *to fine*, etc.]

I. †**1.** *trans.* To impose a tax upon; to tax; to exact tribute from. *Obs.*

1483 CAXTON *Gold. Leg.* 64b/2 He shal taske and dyme your corn and sheues. *a* **1500** in *Arnolde's Chron.* (1811) p. xix, This yere lost the Kinge Normandy and Angeoy, and euery plough land [was] tasked at iij. s. for to gete it ageyne. **1530** [see 2]. **1596** SHAKS. *1 Hen. IV*, IV. iii. 92 Hee..in the neck of that, task't the whole State. **1598** W. PHILLIP *Linschoten* I. xcii. 152/1 All the townes men [were] tasked euery one at a certaine summe of mony. **1642** ROGERS *Naaman* 424 He taskes thee not to the cost of Jewish worship, or Popish wast.

2. a. To force, put, or set (a person) to a task; to impose a task on; to assign a definite amount of work to.

1530 PALSGR. 753/1, I taske, I put or sette one to his taske what laboure he shall do or what he shall paye, *je tauxe.* **1588** SHAKS. *L.L.L.* II. i. 20 But now to taske the tasker. **1667** WOODHEAD *St. Teresa* II. xi. 93 Let her task, and employ them in..Exercises. **1784** COWPER *Task* II. 23 Thus man devotes his brother, and destroys;..Chains him, and tasks him, and exacts his sweat With stripes. **1828** *Life Planter Jamaica* 154 The negroes complained more of the [fact] of being tasked, than..of the additional labour.

b. Const. *to, with*, with *sb.* or *inf.* Often *fig.*

c **1590** GREENE *Fr. Bacon* xiv. 53 To task yourself to such a tedious life As die a maid. **1596** SHAKS. *1 Hen. IV*, IV. i. 9 Nay, taske me to my word; approue me Lord. *c* **1600** —— *Sonn.* lxxii, O least the world should taske you to recite, What merit liu'd in me that you should loue. **1607** —— *Cor.* I. iii. 39 A Haruest man, that ['s] task'd to mowe Or all, or loose his hyre. **1726** POPE *Odyss.* xx. 134 Twelve female slaves..Task'd for the royal board to bolt the bran From the pure flour. **1809** W. IRVING *Knickerb.* v. iv, Man alone..tasks creation to assist him in murdering his brother worm! **1975** *Sentinel* (Ottawa) III. II. 3/2 Capt. Ditter was tasked to help prepare this issue. **1980** *Oxf. Star* 20 Nov. (Advt.), A small engineering team tasked with the design, building and commissioning of high volume production lines.

3. *transf.* and *fig.* **a.** To occupy or engage fully or burdensomely; to subject to severe burden, labour, or trial; to put a strain upon; to put in a condition of stress or difficulty; to put to the proof; = TAX *v.* 4.

1598 SHAKS. *Merry W.* IV. vi. 30 Doctor Caius..Shall shuffle her away, While other sports are tasking of their mindes. **1599** —— *Hen. V*, I. ii. 6 Some things of weight, That taske our thoughts. **1647–8** COTTERELL *Davila's Hist. Fr.* (1678) 28 At length he resolved to task the King's inclinations. **1742** RICHARDSON *Pamela* IV. 61 You must not task me too high. **1850** W. IRVING *Goldsmith* i. 22 He tasked his slender means to the utmost in educating him. **1872** YEATS *Growth Comm.* 115 It tasked his diplomatic skill to effect his departure in safety.

b. *spec.* To test the soundness of (a ship's timbers, a plank, etc.).

1803 *Naval Chron.* X. 259 That..frigate is..to be, what is called in the language of the dock yard, tasked, to see if her timbers are sound. **1867** SMYTH *Sailor's Word-bk.*, *Tasking*, examining a vessel to see whether her timbers are sound.

4. To give or portion *out* (work) as a task.

a **1641** BP. MOUNTAGU *Acts & Mon.* vii. (1642) 438 They have their work for the day tasked out unto them. **1812** [see TASKER 3 b].

II. 5. To take to task; to censure, reprove, chide, reprehend; = TAX *v.* 6. Now const. *with.*

1580 G. HARVEY *Let. to Spenser* Wks. (Grosart) I. 87 If it lyke you in the meane while..to see howe I taske a young Brother of myne. **1608** TOPSELL *Serpents* (1658) 721 There is another pretty fable in Esop, tasking discontented persons under the name of Frogs. **1614** J. COOKE *Tu Quoque* F j, I call thee vp, and taske thee for thy slownesse. **1632** MASSINGER & FIELD *Fatal Dowry* I. ii, To say 'the late dead Marshal, The father of this young lord here, my client, Hath done his country great and faithful service' Might task me of impertinence. **1965** K. GRAHAM *Eng. Criticism of Novel* iv. 117 Trollope is another offender who is frequently tasked with endangering the wholeness of his novels. **1976** *Times Lit. Suppl.* 20 Feb. 197/1 He tasks Taylor with suggesting that Hegel reappeared in Anglo-Saxon thought at the turn of the century.

Hence **tasked** (tɑːskt, -æ-) *ppl. a.*; ˈ**tasking** *vbl. sb.* and *ppl. a.*

1543 *Harding's Chron.* CXVI. viii. P vj b, Saint Edmundes landes he hurt by great taskyng [*Bodl. MSS.* taxinge] And tallage. **1812** Tasked work [see TASKER 3 b]. **1848** LOWELL *Vision Sir Launfal* I. Prelude 28 Bubbles we buy with a whole soul's tasking. **1852** D. G. MITCHELL *Dream Life* 199 The fruits..hanging heavily from the tasked trees. **1856** OLMSTED *Slave States* 435 It is the driver's duty to make the tasked hands do their work well. **1872** J. S. BLACKIE *Ascent Cruachan* v. in *Lays Highl.* 103 We have done our tasking bravely, With the thews of Scottish men.

ˈ**taskage.** *nonce-wd.* [f. TASK *sb.* or *v.* + -AGE.] Tasking; imposed labour; tasks collectively.

1830 W. TAYLOR *Hist. Surv. Germ. Poetry* II. 73 Sisyphus also I saw, with unwelcomest taskage tormented.

tasker (ˈtɑːskə(r), -æ-). [f. TASK *v.* (or *sb.*) + -ER[1].]

†**1.** One who assesses or regulates a rate or price (e.g. of lodgings, things brought to market, etc.).

1538 ELYOT, *Agoranomus*, he that setteth the pryce of vyttayle, a tasker. **1577** HARRISON *England* II. iii. (1877) I. 82 Vicechancelors are changed euerie yeare, as are also the proctors, taskers, maisters of the streates and other officers. **1614** PURCHAS *Pilgrimage* II. ii. (ed. 2) 113 They had ten Aediles, Taskers or Iudges of the Market. [Cf. TAXER 1 b.]

2. One who imposes or sets a task; a taskmaster.

1588 SHAKS. *L.L.L.* II. i. 20 But now to taske the tasker. **1654** WHITLOCK *Zootomia* 297 This Avaricious Plenty is its own Tasker, its owne Pharaoh. **1678** DRYDEN & LEE *Œdipus* III. i, Hear, ye sullen powers below: Hear, ye taskers of the dead. **1827** W. KENNEDY *Poems* 63 It may not be, My taskers call me to the sea.

3. One who works or is paid by the task or piece, as distinct from a day-labourer, etc. (*dial.*).

1621 BURTON *Anat. Mel.* Democr. to Rdr. 12 If our greedy Patrons hold vs to such hard conditions..they will make some of vs at last turne Taskers, Costermongers, sell Ale..or worse. **1623** R. CARPENTER *Conscionable Christian* 3 A due Tasker and Day-labourer for the appointed wages and gaine. **1794** T. DAVIS *Agric. Wilts.* 90 In cutting the lent corn, few 'taskers' are employed, the resident labourers being generally sufficient.

b. *spec.* One who threshes corn with a flail, as TASK-WORK or piece-work: see quot. 1792.

[**1375** (MS. 1487) BARBOUR *Bruce* v. 318 (Cambr. MS.) He suld..haf..A flaill, as he a taskar [*Edinb. MS.* (an. 1489), thresscher] ware.] **14..** *Nom.* in Wr.-Wülcker 697/19 *Hic triturator*, a tasker. *c* **1575** *Balfour's Practicks* (1754) 377 He that is tasker in ony man's barn. **1744–50** W. ELLIS *Mod. Husb.* IV. IV. 125 (E.D.S.) A tasker who threshes out his quota of grain. *Ibid.* 131 Tasker-servant. **1792** *Statist. Acc. Scotl.* II. 353 The taskers are those, who are employed in threshing out the corn; and they receive..the twenty-fifth part for their labour; and this has been their fixed and stated wages, as far back as can be remembered. **1812** SIR J. SINCLAIR *Syst. Husb. Scot.* I. 82 The tasker, (or thresher who worked by tasked work), had to take it from the heap, ..to lay it on the floor, to shake it well, and then to thresh it.

'task,master. [f. TASK *sb.* + MASTER *sb.*¹] One whose office is to allot tasks and see to their performance; an overseer; a middleman; *spec.* in plastering (see quot. 1892); also *fig.* one who allots a duty, or imposes a heavy burden or labour.

1530 TINDALE *Exod.* i. 11 And he [Pharao] sette taskemasters ouer them. *Ibid.* 14 And the officers of the children of Israel which Pharaos taskmasters had sett ouer them, were beaten. **1631** MILTON *Sonn.*, '*How soon hath Time*', All is, if I have grace to use it so, As ever in my great task Masters eye. **1797** GODWIN *Enquirer* I. viii. 67 There is no equality between me and my Task-master. **1869** W. P. MACKAY *Grace & Truth* (1875) 212 The task-master's whip held over his head. **1892** *Labour Commission* Gloss., *Taskmaster*, one who takes work from the original contractor in the plastering industry, and sets a given quantity of work to be done in a certain time.

Hence **'task,mastership**, the office or position of a taskmaster.

1815 *Zeluca* I. 70 All the arts, and all the sciences..all conned in submission to taskmastership. **1898** *Daily News* 12 Nov. 3/6 Having..passed through both the terrible ordeal of a lower boy's life at Eton and..having enjoyed the delights of cruel taskmastership.

'task,mistress. [f. as prec. + MISTRESS *sb.*] A woman (or something personified as female) who assigns tasks, or apportions labour.

1603 H. CROSSE *Vertues Commw.* (1878) 150 His taskemistresse Iuno was faine to crie out, *Defessa sum iubendo.* **1741** RICHARDSON *Pamela* (1824) I. ix. 245 You will consider yourself as the task-mistress, and the..female servants as so many negroes. **1817** SHELLEY *Rev. Islam* XI. xvii, For which, O willing slaves to Custom old, Severe taskmistress, ye your hearts have sold. **1899** CROCKETT *Kit Kennedy* 212 Kit knew that his task-mistress was listening.

'task-work. [f. TASK *sb.* + WORK *sb.*]

1. Work performed as a task; forced labour; hence, oppressive or burdensome work.

1582 STANYHURST *Æneis* I. (Arb.) 34 Shee frams firmlye statuts, and task wurcks equalye parteth. **1814** JEFFERSON *Writ.* (1830) IV. 241 It was the heaviest task-work I ever went through. **1827** SCOTT *Jrnl.* 14 Jan., I feel a dislike to order and to task-work of all kinds. **1849** GROTE *Greece* II. xxxviii. V. 28 The canal-cutting..was..distributed under their measurement as task-work among the contingents of the various nations. **1885** BIBLE (R.V.) *Prov.* xii. 24.

2. Work done by the piece; piece-work.

1486–7 in E. B. Jupp *Carpenters' Co.* (1887) 349 That no persone of the said crafte hereafter make any foreign carpenter his fellows..in any taske werke takyng. **1581** in Feuillerat *Revels Q. Eliz.* (1908) 344 a, Tasque work viz. to John Rose for a Mount. **1721** PERRY *Daggenh. Breach* 77 They work'd two or three Times as much by Task-work as by the Day, or by the Tide. **1855** J. R. LEIFCHILD *Cornwall Mines* 142 In Cornish mines, the sinking of shafts and the driving of levels is paid by tut-work or task-work, at so much per fathom.

Taslan ('tæslən). [Invented word.] The proprietary name of a process for bulking or texturing synthetic yarns; also, a yarn which has been subjected to this process.

1954 *Trade Marks Jrnl.* 31 Mar. 328/2 Taslan 726,376. All goods included in Class 23. **1954** *Official Gaz.* (U.S. Patent Office) 13 July 263/2 E.I. du Pont de Nemours and Company, Wilmington, Del... *Taslan* for thread and yarn. Use since Jan. 4, 1954. **1957** *Times* 14 Jan. 11 *Taslan*, a process for 'texturing', or 'bulking' synthetic yarns such as acetate, nylon or Terylene to give softer handle and improve draping qualities. **1959** A. J. HALL *Stand. Handbk. Textiles* (ed. 5) iii. 131 Bulk yarns can be produced in various ways ..but much success has attended the method used for the production of Taslan yarns. **1960** *Skinner's Silk & Rayon Rec.* Oct. 994/2 Car upholstery is another field in which *Taslan* has found a good reception in the U.S. **1963** A. J. HALL *Textile Sci.* iii. 130 There are various types of textured yarns which have now become available for weaving and knitting into fabrics under branded names such as Agilon, Banlon, Taslan, etc.

tasle, tasler, obs. ff. TEASEL, TEASELER.

taslet ('tæslɪt). *Sc. arch.* Usually in pl. **taslets**, in 6 **teslottis, teslettis, tasletis.** [A deriv. of TASSE *sb.*¹ (or its French original), with dim. suffix -LET; perhaps from TASSET with suffix-change. Cf. also OF. (Picard) *tasselet*, dim. of *tassel* plastron or frontlet of a lady's dress (1507 in Godef.), Rouchi *tasselet* 'petite plaque de plomb'.] *pl.* Tasses, tassets: see TASSE *sb.*¹, TASSET.

1507 *Acc. Ld. High Treas. Scotl.* III. 391 For vj quartaris rede to covir the Kingis tasletis,..xx s. **1541** *Ibid.* VIII. 33 Deliverit..to lyne the teslottis of harnes maid to his Grace, vij quarteris blak sating..lvj s. **1542** *Ibid.* 54 Ane lycht harnes with doubill teslettis..to the Kingis grace. **1819** SCOTT *Leg. Montrose* ii, Thigh-pieces of steel, then termed taslets, met the tops of his huge jack-boots. **1870** *Athenæum* 22 Jan. 126 Over his trunk-hose are steel thigh-pieces or taslets.

Tasmanian (tæz'meɪnɪən, tæs-), *a.* and *sb.*

A. *adj.* Of or pertaining to Tasmania in Australasia. In names of animals, plants, etc., native to Tasmania, as ***Tasmanian devil*** (see DEVIL 7), *T.* ***wolf*** (see WOLF). Also ***Tasmanian cranberry, currant, honeysuckle, ironwood,*** etc.: see the sbs.

1851 *Illustr. Catal. Gt. Exhib.* IV. I. 998/3 Many Tasmanian plants bloom throughout the winter months. **1874** M. CLARKE *His Natural Life* II. v. 104 'And what books do you read?'..'"Blair's Sermons," and "The Tasmanian Almanack".' **1920** *Glasgow Herald* 23 July 6 He..attended the royal meeting of the Tasmanian Racing Club in the afternoon. **1964** W. L. GOODMAN *Hist. Woodworking Tools* 157 The Sanderson Brothers & Newbould catalogue has a variation of this called the 'Tasmanian' tooth. **1975** *Listener* 7 Aug. 172 The remnants of the four Tasmanian tribes, the last of the 5,000 Tasmanians who were there when the Europeans landed.

B. as *sb.* **a.** A member of the aboriginal people of Tasmania, now extinct.

1842 *Penny Cycl.* XXIV. 90/2 That courage was rewarded by the appointment of Mr. Robinson to the office of 'civilizing' the Tasmanians at Flinders' Island. **1899** J. MILNE *Romance of Pro-Consul* viii. 79 The Tasmanians have now been extinct for years. **1918** L. HUXLEY *Life J. D. Hooker* I. 106 A meagre record of the thousands of native Tasmanians. **1935** HUXLEY & HADDON *We Europeans* iv. 120 Of all existing men the Arctic Eskimo is the most leptorrhine and the equatorial negro one of the most platyrrhine, but the Tasmanians, who lived in a temperate climate, were also platyrrhine. **1978** *Nature* 18 May 185/2 Within a few decades they were nearly exterminated by European settlers, until the scattered survivors were removed in 1834 to Flinders Island, where the last full-blooded Tasmanian died in 1876.

b. A native or inhabitant of Tasmania.

1934 T. WOOD *Cobbers* xiii. 163 Tasmanians, I found, grumble. **1974** *Country Life* 7 Nov. 1388/2 Although.. whaling had started in its adjacent waters, the Tasmanians themselves were prohibited from engaging in the industry. **1978** A. WAUGH *Best Wine Last* x. 118 One of my two uncles ..married a Tasmanian.

tasmanite ('tæzmənaɪt). *Min.* [f. *Tasmania* + -ITE¹.] A resinous hydrocarbon containing sulphur, occurring in reddish-brown scales on the Mersey river, Tasmania.

1864 A. H. CHURCH in *Phil. Mag.* XXVIII. 465 On Tasmanite, a new Mineral of Organic Origin. *Ibid.* 467 When Tasmanite is heated in the air, it burns readily with a very smoky flame and offensive odour.

Tasmanoid ('tæzmənɔɪd), *a.* [f. TASMAN(IAN *sb.* + -OID.] Resembling or allied to the ethnological type of the aborigines of Tasmania.

1938 *Skr. Norske Videnskaps-Akademi (Mat.-Nat. Kl.)* 1937 153 It is not inconceivable that an original Tasmanoid population in Australia was driven south. **1943** *Mem. Nat. Mus. Melbourne* XIII. 44 The evidence..strongly suggests that the earliest migrants belonged to a Tasmanoid (Negrito) race..and that this race..found its way to Tasmania. **1958** F. E. ZEUNER *Dating the Past* 281 Wunderly comes to the conclusion that the skull combines Australoid and Tasmanoid characteristics in about equal proportions.

tasol, tasque, obs. ff. TEASEL, TASK.

tasp, tasping: see TAP *v.*² 1, quot. *c* 1440.

tass¹ (tɑːs, -æ-). Now only *dial.* Also 4 **tas,** 4–5 **tasse,** 5 (7) **taas.** [a. OF. *tas* masc. (Wace, 12th c.), also *tasse* fem. (13th c. in Godef.), = Pr. *tatz*; generally held to be of Low German origin: cf. Du. *tas*, MDu. also *tass* heap (not known elsewhere in Teut.): see Franck.] A heap, pile, stack.

c **1330** *Arth. & Merl.* 6719 Thei lay of paiens mani tasse, Wide and side more and lasse. *c* **1386** CHAUCER *Knt.'s T.* 147 To ransake in the taas of the bodyes dede. **1412–20** LYDG. *Chron. Troy* IV. 2397 Worþi knyȝtes..In þe feld on ouþer part y-lorn, Which in þe taas ful besely þei souȝt. *c* **1440** *Promp. Parv.* 487/1 Tasse, of corne, or oþer lyke, *tassis.* **1577** B. GOOGE *Heresbach's Husb* (1586) 42 Bestowe your Corne in severall tasses and moowes. **1616** BULLOKAR *Eng. Expos.*, *Taas*, an heape. **1735–6** PEGGE *Kenticisms* (E.D.S.), *Tass-cutter*, that utensil or implement with which they cut hay in the stack. *Ibid.*, An hay-tass is an hay-mow. **1887** *Kentish Gloss.*, *Tas*, or *tarse*, a mow of corn.

tass² (tæs). Now chiefly *Sc.* Forms: 5–9 **tasse,** 6 **tais, tas,** 6– **tass.** [a. OF. *tasse* goblet (1380 in Godef.), in mod.F. cup = Pr., Cat., med.L. *tassa* (1337 in Du Cange), Sp. *taza*, Pg. *taça*, It. *tazza*, app. a. Arab. *ṭass*, *ṭassah* basin, usually held to be ad. Pers. *tast* cup, goblet.] A cup or small goblet, esp. one of silver or the like; the contents of this; a small draught of liquor.

c **1483** CAXTON *Dialogues* 21 Pawteners, tasses [Fr. *Aloyeres, tasses*], Coffyns and penners. **1513** DOUGLAS *Æneis* XIII. ix. 25 The cowpis greit and drynkyn tassis fyne. **1549** *Compl. Scot.* xvii. 145 To drynk vattir..in ane glas, or in ane tasse of siluyr. **1583** *Leg. Bp. St. Androis* Pref. 136 We toome a tass of wyne. **1653** URQUHART *Rabelais* I. li, Great antick vessels, huge pots,..big tasses. **1725** RAMSAY *Gentle Sheph.* III. ii, Elspa, haste ye,..And fill him up a tass o' usquebæ. **1818** SCOTT *Rob Roy* xviii, A tass of brandy or aquavitæ, or sic-like creature comfort. *a* **1825** FORBY *Voc. E. Anglia*, *Tass*, a dish or a dram; as a tass of tea, or a tass of brandy. **1859** THACKERAY *Virgin.* liv, A little tass of Cherry-brandy! **1899** CROCKETT *Kit Kennedy* 321 Scottish stone-ale, 'virulent as a tass of raw brandy'.

Tass³ (tæs). Also **TASS.** [a. Russ., acronym f. the initial letters of *Telegrafnoe agentstvo Sovetskogo Soyuza.*] The official Soviet news agency.

1925 *Times* 27 Aug. 11/7 A decree ratified by the Soviet authorities changes the name of Rosta (Russian Telegraph Agency) to Tass (Telegrafnoye Agenstvo Sovietskovo Soyuza = Telegraph Agency of the Soviet Union), as from August 1 next. **1942** *Nature* 25 Apr. 475/1 It is announced by the Tass Agency that [etc.]. **1950** A. HUXLEY *Themes & Variations* 52 Not..that he had the faintest premonition of Harmsworth or Hearst,..of Goebbels or Tass. **1958** *Spectator* 27 June 824/1 The new Tass statement on the Lebanon. **1974** T. P. WHITNEY tr. *Solzhenitsyn's Gulag Archipelago* I. I. i. 9 Several days later TASS will issue an angry statement to all the papers. **1981** *Guardian* 27 Apr. 5/2 Tass, reporting from Warsaw, said..that 'revisionist elements in the party' were trying to paralyse it.

tass, obs. form of TACHE *v.*¹, to stain.

tassago, tassajo, var. TASAJO, dried meat.

tassal, variant of TASSEL *sb.*²

tassar, var. TUSSER, TUSSORE, an Indian silk.

tasse (tæs), *sb.*¹ *Obs.* exc. *Hist.* Only in pl. **tasses** ('tæsɪz), in 6 **taisses,** 6–7 **tases, taces,** 7 **taishes.** [In form the same word as OF. *tasse* purse, holster; in sense = F. *tassette*, obs. *tassete*, a small pocket or pouch, a steel plate intended to guard the thigh, dim. of *tasse*.

The connexion of sense is not clear; but cf. It. *scarsella* a pocket; *scarselloni* bases or tasses for a horseman (Florio 1611); Sp. *escarcela*, 'escarcelle, gibier, bourse; aussi la tassette' (Oudin 1660); *escarcela*, a satchel, pouch, or bag; the armour from the waist to the thighs (Stevens 1706).]

pl. A series of articulated splints or plates depending from the corslet, placed so that each slightly overlapped the one below it, forming a sort of kilt of armour to protect the thighs and the lower part of the trunk.

a **1548** HALL *Chron., Hen. IV* 12 One company had..the tasses, the lamboys, the backpece, the tapull and the border of the curace all gylte. **1579–80** NORTH *Plutarch* (1676) 212 Their legs were armed with Greaves, and their thighs with Tases. **1581** STYWARD *Mart. Discipl.* II. 165 To haue good curates for their bodies, taces for their thighes. **1596** WARNER *Alb. Eng.* XII. lxix. (1612) 291 The Taishes, Cushies, and the Graues, staffe, Pensell, baises. **1598** BARRET *Theor. Warres* Gloss. 253 Taisses, a French word, and is the arming of the thighes, annexed vnto the forepart of the Corslet. **1688** R. HOLME *Armoury* III. xix. (Roxb.) 166/1 Armour for the thighes, of the French called Cuissets, and Taces or Tasses, because they are tached or tacked on with straps of leather to the corslett. **1869** BOUTELL *Arms & Arm.* x. (1874) 203 Below the waist, and there connected with the bottom of the breastplate, the body was protected by a series of narrow overlapping plates..denominated taces. **1888** F. COWPER *Capt. of Wight* (1889) 337 The taces of his armour had saved his thigh.

† **tasse,** *sb.*² *Obs. rare*⁻¹. app. the same as TASSEL *sb.*¹: perh. an erroneous form.

1570 LEVINS *Manip.* 34/33 Yᵉ Tasse of a purse, *appendix.*

† **tasse,** *v. Obs. rare*⁻¹. [a. OF. *tasser* (12th c. in Godef. *Compl.*), going with *tas, tasse* heap, TASS¹.] *trans.* To heap, pile.

a **1400** *Octouian* 695, I woll vpon thy body tasse [*rimes* masse, passe] Well many a dent.

tasse, variant of TASS², a cup.

tassel ('tæs(ə)l), *sb.*¹ Also 5 **tasshel, tasselle,** 6–9 **tassell,** 7 **tastle, tossell,** 8 **tossel** (also 9 *dial.*), -**il,** *Sc.* **taisel.** See also TARSEL. [a. OF. *tasel, tassel* clasp (*c* 1150 in Godef.): cf. It. *tassello* the collar of a cloak, a label; med.L. *tassellus, tacellus*: see Du Cange. Referred by Diez to L. *taxillus* small die (cf. next): but this is doubtful. The sense-development in Italian, French, and English has not been clearly made out: see Diez, Godefroy, Du Cange. The variant *tossel* (now *dial.*) suggests some association with TOSS *v.*]

† **1.** A clasp or fibula by which the two sides of a cloak or the like are held together. *Obs.*

a **1300** *Cursor M.* 4389 He drou, sco held, þe tassel brak, þe mantel left, he gafe þe bak. **13..** *Guy Warw.* (A.) 5736 Gij bi his mantel drouȝ so, þat þe tassels brosten ato. *c* **1420** *Anturs of Arth.* xxviii. (Irel. MS.), Monli in his mantille he sate,..The tassellus were of topeus. [**1876** PLANCHÉ *Cycl. Costume* I. 503 *Taselle, tasseau*, Fr... Also used for the clasp or fibula through which the cords passed which secured the mantle on the shoulder.]

2. a. A pendent ornament consisting of a bunch or thick fringe of threads or small cords hanging in a somewhat conical shape from a solid rounded knob or mould, or from a knot formed by their junction with a cord. Frequently attached to a curtain, cushion, walking-cane, umbrella, etc., or forming the pull of a blind-cord or bell-cord.

13.. *Gaw. & Gr. Knt.* 219 A lace..Wyth tryed tasselez þerto tacched in-noghe. *c* **1440** *Promp. Parv.* 487/1 Tassel, *tassellus.* **1480** *Wardr. Acc. Edw. IV* (1830) 125 For the makyng of xvj laces and xvj tasshels for the garnysshing of divers of the Kinges bookes. **1530** PALSGR. 279/2 Tassel that hangeth at a thyng of sylke or golde, *houppe doree.* **1590** SPENSER *F.Q.* I. viii. 3 An horne of bugle small, Which hong adowne his side in twisted gold And tasselles gay. **1624**

CAPT. SMITH *Virginia* II. 35 All their tailes meete in the toppe of their head like a great Tassell. *a* **1625** FLETCHER *Nice Valour* II. i, And smile, and wave a chair with comely grace too, Play with our tastle gently. **1706** PHILLIPS (ed. 6), *Tassels of a Coach*, certain Silk-cords fasten'd on each Side the Doors, which serve for a Stay to those that ride in it. **1718** *Free-thinker* No. 44 ¶ 10 A young Damsel.. tied a Gold Cord with two large Tossels of Gold to his Sword. **1755** *Connoisseur* No. 97 ¶ 1 The fellow-commoners, noblemen, and other rich students, whom.. the courtesy of the University [of Cambridge] has honoured with a cap adorned with a gold tossel. **1792** in *Hist. Broughton Place Ch. Edin.* (1872) 20 A' their taisels, vain an' gay To mak us stare. *a* **1815** in G. Rose *Diaries* (1860) II. 438 He put out his hand to pull the bell, but could not catch the tassel. **1849** LAYARD *Nineveh & Rem.* I. iii. 49 A knotted girdle, ending in tassels, encircled the loins. **1886** RUSKIN *Præterita* I. vii. 233 A cushion of crimson velvet.. with gold tassels at the corners.

†**b.** *Univ. slang.* One who wears a cap with a tassel; an undergraduate. Cf. TUFT. *Obs.*

1828 *Sporting Mag.* XXI. 428 A capital front rank of 'tassels'.. all eager for a 'slap at a snob'.

3. Anything resembling or suggesting a tassel: **a.** In a tree or plant, a pendent catkin, blossom, flower, or bud; *spec.* the staminate (terminal) inflorescence of the maize-plant (*U.S.*): see also *tassel-hyacinth* in 5.

1646 WINTHROP *New-Eng.* (1826) II. 267 Great harm was done in corn.. by a caterpillar... They eat up first the blades of the stalk, then.. the tassels, whereupon the ear withered. **1755** *Gentl. Mag.* Sept. 408/2, I found a fine stalk of Indian corn..; I cut off the male tossil as soon as it appeared, and there was produced a large ear, but no good grains upon it. **1824** MISS MITFORD *Village* Ser. I. (1863) 61 In early spring, when the fragrant palms were on the willow, and the yellow tassels on the hazel. *a* **1835** MRS. HEMANS *Voice of Spring* iii, The larch has hung all his tassels forth. **1863** KINGSLEY *Water-Bab.* i. 15 The bird-cherry with its tassels of snow. **1894** E. EGGLESTON in *Century Mag.* Apr. 850 Our country people, when speaking of the male flower of the maize, preserve the broad vowel of their ancestors: 'tossell' it will remain in spite of the schoolmaster.

†**b.** A tuft; a fringe. *Obs.*

1609 C. BUTLER *Fem. Mon.* i. (1623) B iij, Besides their Soueraigne, the Bees haue also subordinate Gouernours... For difference from the rest they beare for their crest a tuft or tossell, in some coloured yellow, in some murrey, in manner of a plume. **1672** JOSSELYN *New Eng. Rarities* 35 The other is nothing but Bones with Tassels hanging from their Jaws, with which they [whales] suck in their prey.

¶**4.** In med. (Anglo-) Latin, *tassellus* is given by Du Cange as used = *fimbria*, fringe of a cope or chasuble. Dr. Rock, *Church of our Fathers* (II. 32–), explains Du Cange's quots. otherwise, and holds that *tassellus* had the following uses: **a.** The large thin sheet of gold or silver hanging behind on the cope; **b.** Any piece of gold or silver plate fastened to a vestment (copes and chasubles having 'their *tasselli* sparkling with gems, hung all about them'); **c.** The ornaments on the back of episcopal gloves, when not done in embroidery, but made of silver or gold plate. By Dr. Rock himself, and some writers after him, the English word *tassel* has been used in senses b and c.

[*c* **1188** GERV. CANT. in Dugdale *Monast. Angl.* (1655) I. 21 Duas capas de pallio cum tassellis auro paratis. *c* **1250** MATT. PARIS *Vitæ Abb. S. Albani* (1639) 55 Capam unam purpuream, morsu et tassellis charissimis redimitam. *a* **1252** *Visit. Churches St. Paul's* 14 in *Camden Misc.* (1895) IX, Item capa chori crocea cum duobus tassellis brusdatis Majestate et Maria.] **1849** ROCK *Ch. our Fathers* II. 161 *note*, These tassels, as we said before, were thin plates of beaten gold or silver. **1887** *Archæologia* L. II. 448 Upon the 'tassels' of the cope of Richard Ruffus were depicted the martyrdoms of St. Stephen and St. Thomas.

5. *attrib.* and *Comb.*, as ***tassel-board, -drop, -maker, -making***; ***tassel-hung*** adj.; **tassel-cock**, a game-cock which has a tuft of feathers in place of the comb; **tassel-corn**, (*U.S.*) the grain of maize borne abnormally on the 'tassel' (see 3 a); **tassel-fish**, an Australian fish, *Polynemus quadridactylus*, the pectoral fins of which terminate in a number of long threads; **tassel-flower**, (*a*) a tassel-like flower; *spec.* the orange, scarlet, or yellowish blossom of *Emilia sagittata* (*Cacalia coccinea*), N.O. *Compositæ*, or the plant itself; (*b*) a shrub or tree of the genus *Inga* (*Cent. Dict.* 1891); **tassel-grass**, (*a*) a grass or (?) sedge with pendent spicules; (*b*) *Ruppia maritima*, an aquatic herb of which the seed-vessels are borne on clusters of lengthened pedicels; **tassel hyacinth**, *Muscari comosum*, the stalk and flower of which resemble a tassel; also called *purse-tassel, purple tassels* (Miller *Plant-n.* 1884); **tassel-pondweed** = *tassel-grass* (*b*) (ibid.); **tassel-stitch**, an embroidery stitch used in forming a fringe, loops of thread being left, which are afterwards cut; **tassel-tree** = TASSEL-BUSH (*Cent. Dict.* 1891); **tassel-worm**, a grub which feeds on the tassel of the maize-plant.

a **1639** SPOTTISWOOD *Hist. Ch. Scot.* VI. (1677) 407 Every Chair had a *Tassel-boord covered with fine Velvet. **1898** *Pall Mall G.* 3 Feb. 9/1 'Henny' cocks.. have won more battles.. than any other birds, except it be the '*tassel' cock. **1883** E. L. STURTEVANT in *Science* I. 234/1 (Variability of Maize) *Tassel-corn,—some of the kernels heavily, others slightly husked. **1852** R. S. SURTEES *Sponge's Sp. Tour* (1893) 150 A chased and figured fine gold brooch, with two pendent *tassel-drops. **1898** MORRIS *Austral Eng.*, **Tassel-fish*, a thread-fish of Queensland, of the genus *Polynemus*. **1902** J. T. CRITCHELL in *Encycl. Brit.* XXXII. 110/2 Several species of the tassel fish (*Polynemus macrocohoir*), from which isinglass is procured, have been taken by fishermen. **1836** A. LINCOLN *Familiar Lect. Bot.* (ed. 5) 83 *Tassel-flower; from the East Indies. **1863** 'G. HAMILTON' *Gala-Days* 10 The scarlet tassel-flower utterly refuses to unfold his brave plumes. **1885** G. ALLEN *Babylon* vi, Do you know the tassel-flower? **1957** C. O. BOOTH *Encycl. Ann. & Biennial Plants* 261/2 *E*[*milia*] *sagittata*.. is the popular Tassel Flower, or Flora's Paintbrush, a charming half-hardy annual. **1810** SOUTHEY *Kehama* XIII. xi, *Tassel-grass, whose silvery feathers play O'ertopping the young trees. **1861** MISS PRATT *Flower. Pl.* V. 336 Sea Ruppia or Tassel-grass.. has slender, much-branched stems.. and long slender bristly leaves with sheaths. **1850** TENNYSON *In Mem.* cii, The low love-language of the bird In native hazels *tassel-hung. **1790** *Curtis's Bot. Mag.* IV. 133 (*heading*) Two Coloured, or *Tassel Hyacinth. **1865** M. EYRE *Lady's Walks in S. France* xxiii. 251 The starch, and the tassel-hyacinth,.. and many others.. are all common flowers about Bagnères. **1961** R. GENDERS *Miniature Bulbs* II. 165 The 'Tassel Hyacinth' grows a foot high. **1902** *Daily Chron.* 9 Sept. 3/6 A number of the *tassel-makers were independently interviewed in their own homes while at work... *Tassel-making is one of the three worst paid of the various home industries open to sweating. **1882** CAULFEILD & SAWARD *Dict. Needlework* 194/2 **Tassel Stitch*, a stitch used to make a looped fringe as an edging to Embroideries.

tassel, torsel ('tæs(ə)l, 'tɒs(ə)l, 'tɔːs(ə)l), *sb.*[2] *Arch.* Also 7–9 **tossel**, 9 **tassal**. [a. OF. *tassel*, mod.F. *tasseau*, = It. *tassello* a bit of stone or wood to stop a hole:—L. *taxillus* a small die. The form *torsel* app. arises from workmen's lengthening of the vowel in *tossel*.] A short board or 'templet' placed under the end of a beam or other timber where it rests on brickwork or stonework.

1632 in E. B. Jupp *Carpenters' Co.* (1887) 301 The making of all mantletrees tassels and footepaces of timber. **1654** *Ibid.* 316 That no Timber.. be laid in Chimneys except the mantle trees Tassells and Discharges. **1667** PRIMATT *City & C. Build.* 82 Allow six foot of Timber for every Chimney, for Mantle-trees and Torsels. **1703** MOXON *Mech. Exerc.* 264 When you lay any Timber on Brick-work, as Torsels for Mantle-Trees to lye on. **1823** P. NICHOLSON *Pract. Build.* 595 *Torsel*, a piece of wood laid into a wall for the end of a timber or beam to rest on. **1842–76** GWILT *Archit.* Gloss., *Tassal, Tassel, Torsel*, or *Tossel*, the plate of timber for the end of a beam or of a joist to rest on.

tassel ('tæs(ə)l), *v.* Also 4 **tassil**, 5 **tacel**, 8 **tassel**. [f. TASSEL *sb.*[1]]

1. *trans.* To furnish or adorn with or as with a tassel or tassels.

In *pa. pple.* in *Her.* indicating that the tassel or tassels are of a tincture different from that of the rest of the bearing.

? *a* **1366** CHAUCER *Rom. Rose* 1079 A robe.. With orfrays leyd was everydel,.. And with a bend of gold tasseled. *c* **1386** —— *Miller's T.* 65 By hir girdel heeng a purs of lether Tasseled with grene and perled with latoun. **14..** *Sir Beues* (MS. N.) 3777 + 7 Tacellid wiþ rosys off syluyr bryȝt. **1572** BOSSEWELL *Armorie* II. 92 He beareth Argente, a pursse gules, doble tasseled d'azure. **1724** *Lond. Gaz.* No. 6290/2 A Velvet.. Cushion edged and tasselled with Gold. **1894** *Blackw. Mag.* Sept. 317/2 The blond sallow tasselled itself with gold.

2. *intr.* Of maize and sugar-cane: To form 'tassels', to flower, bloom. Chiefly *U.S.* Also ***tassel out***.

1757 in C. R. Woodward *Ploughs & Politicks* (1941) 278 Just before it Tossles it should be plowed & hoed again. **1774** P. V. FITHIAN *Jrnl.* (1900) 212 The Corn is beginning pretty generally to tassel. **1785** WASHINGTON *Writ.* (1891) XII. 227 It [Indian corn] should be kept clean and well worked.. till it shoots and tassels at least. **1843** *Amer. Pioneer* II. 83 Corn, if planted, grows a foot high, tassels out and dies. **1881** NICHOLSON *Fr. Sword to Share* xxii. 153 Cane grew.. almost everywhere.. at altitudes up to 3,000 feet above sea-level, at half that height it ceased to blossom or tassel. **1887** M. E. WILKINS *Humble Romance* 29 His corn tasselled out.. as soon as anybody's. **1966** R. G. TOEPFER *Witness* v. 34 Mr. Davis Miller's corn was starting to tassel out and you could pretty near see it grow.

Hence **'tasselling, 'tasseling** *vbl. sb.* (also *concr.* work composed of tassels) and *ppl. a.*

1829 *Anniversary, Beatrice* 232 She couches in the pleached bower Which tasselling honeysuckles deck. **1881** NICHOLSON *Fr. Sword to Share* xxix. 222 In November the cane tops will throw out a feathery, dove-coloured blossom, called tasselling. **1902** *Westm. Gaz.* 12 July 7/3 The sides of the stairs.. are.. finished off with gold tasselling.

tassel, obs. form of TEASEL, TERCEL.

'tasselated, *ppl. a. rare*[−1]. [f. assumed vb. **tasselate* (f. TASSEL *sb.*[1] + -ATE[3]) + -ED[1]: cf. *tessellated, castellated, foliated*, etc.]

= TASSELLED.

c **1860** B. HARTE *My Otherself* in *Fiddletown*, etc. (1873) 127 There was no rustle of the tasselated corn.

tassel-bush ('tæs(ə)lbʊʃ). [f. TASSEL *sb.*[1] + BUSH *sb.*[1]] The common name in America of an evergreen shrub, *Garrya elliptica*, a native of California, Mexico, Cuba, and Jamaica: so called from its elegant long drooping catkins.

1891 in *Cent. Dict.* **1900** *Field* 22 Dec. 972/1 The Tassel Bush.. is an evergreen bush from California, the tip of every young growth being now laden with clusters, or bunches of soft-grey tassels or catkins, that give to it a very distinct and ornate appearance.

tasselet ('tæsəlɪt, -ˌɛt). [f. TASSEL *sb.*[1] + -ET[1].] A diminutive tassel.

1577 HARRISON *England* II. v. (1877) I. 121 Two mantels.. with laces, tasselets, and knops of blue silk.

tassel-gentle, tassel-hawk: see TERCEL.

tassell, obs. form of TEASEL, TERCEL.

tasselled, -eled ('tæs(ə)ld), *ppl. a.* [f. TASSEL *sb.*[1] or *v.* + -ED.] **a.** Furnished or adorned with or as with a tassel or tassels; of a person, wearing a tassel or tassels. **b.** Formed into, or resembling in some way, a tassel or tassels; of a fern, having divisions like tassels at the apex of each frond.

a. 1611 COTGR., *Houpé*.. tufted, or tasselled. *c* **1633** MILTON *Arcades* 57 Ere the.. tasselld horn Shakes the high thicket, haste I all about. **1784** COWPER *Task* II. 749 The tasseled cap and the spruce band. **1808** SKURRAY *Bidcombe Hill* 49 Not long ago, on Cherwell's banks we rov'd, Link'd arm in arm, like other tassell'd youths. **1841–4** EMERSON *Ess.* Ser. I. xi. (1876) 263 You shall still see.. the tasselled grass, or the corn-flags.

b. 1882 *Garden* 29 Apr. 301/3 A very elegant Hare's-foot Fern, having the long graceful fronds tasselled at the tips.

tasseller, -eler ('tæs(ə)lə(r)). [f. TASSEL *v.* + -ER[1]; cf. OF. *taseleor*.]

†**1.** One who makes tassels. *Obs. rare.*

1301 *Rolls of Parlt.* I. 248/2 Matilda la Taselere. *Ibid.* 255/2 Gilbert le Taselere.

2. One who wears a cap with a tassel; †***gold tasseller***, a nobleman who is a member of a university, distinguished by his academic cap having a tassel of gold thread: cf. TASSEL *sb.*[1] 2, quot. 1755.

1846 LANDOR *Citation Shaks.* Wks. II. 285/2 The worst question to any gold tasseller is, 'How do you do?'

'tasselly, -ely, *a.* [f. TASSEL *sb.*[1] + -Y.] Characterized by or abounding in tassels.

1611 COTGR., *Houpelu*.. lockie, tassellie, tufted. **1901** *Elizabeth & Germ. Gard.* 164 Four little podgy, buttony, tasselly red chairs.

tasset. *Archæol.* Only in pl. **tassets** ('tæsɪts). [ad. F. *tassette*, in OF. *tassete*: see TASSE *sb.*[1]]

In *pl.* = *tasses*: see TASSE *sb.*[1] (App. only in modern archæological or romantic use.)

1834 PLANCHÉ *Brit. Costume* 241 Tassets and cuishes, composed of several plates instead of one, are seen upon the thigh. **1872** LONGF. *Wayside Inn* III. *Charlemagne* 49 His greaves And tassets were of iron. **1876** H. AINSWORTH *Leaguer of Lathom* (1878) 32 Both were accoutred in steel breastplates and tassets.

‖**tassette** (tasɛt). [Fr. dim. of *tasse*, TASS[2]: see -ET[1].] A small pointed infusible earthenware cone, used in sets of three to support objects in a kiln or muffle, in place of a stilt or triangle.

1891 in *Cent. Dict.*

tasshel, obs. form of TASSEL *sb.*[1]

tassie[1] ('tæsɪ). *Sc.* [dim. of TASS[2]: see -IE.] A small cup or 'tass'.

17.. *Homely Ballad* (in *Burns' Poems* (1834) II. 229 *note*), Ye'll bring me here a pint of wine, A server and a silver tassie. **1788** BURNS *My Bonie Mary* i. *a* **1810** in Cromek *Rem. Nithsdale Song* 94 But here's my Jean's health i' the siller-lipped-tassie!

Tassie[2] ('tæsɪ). Also ¶**Tassi, tassie**. The name of James *Tassie* (1735–99), Scottish gem engraver, used *attrib.* and *absol.* of replicas of ancient engraved gems or original portrait reliefs made in glass paste by him or by his nephew William Tassie (1777–1860) who succeeded him.

1819 KEATS *Let.* 13 Mar. (1958) II. 45 On looking at your seal I cannot tell whether or not it is done with a Tassi—it seems to me to be paste. **1894** J. M. GRAY *James & William Tassie* viii. 65 The Shadford Walker Sale included.. over a hundred large Tassie medallions of contemporary personages. **1942** E. BLUNDEN *Romantic Poetry & Fine Arts* 10 His [*sc.* Keats's] own particular Tassie was 'a lyre with the strings broken'. **1972** *Times* 1 Aug. 11/5 (Advt.), A collection of paintings.. Tassi medallions. **1979** MILLS & MANSFIELD *Genuine Article* vii. 109 Many people fail, when encountering what might be a 'Tassie', to.. see if the alleged diamond is backed by metal. **1981** 'J. GASH' *Vatican Rip* iii. 36 That glimpse of Mrs Culpepper's 'tassie', as we call such incised semiprecious carvings. *Ibid.* v. 46 The silly bitch laughingly refused to sell me her tassie ring.

Tassie[3] ('tæzɪ). *Austral. slang.* Also **Tassey, Tassy**. [Hypocoristic, f. *Tasmania* or TASMANIAN *sb.* b: see -IE.] **a.** Tasmania. **b.** A Tasmanian.

1894 *Argus* (Melbourne) 26 Jan. 3 Today Tassy—as most Victorian cricketers and footballers familiarly term our neighbour over the straits—will send a team into the field. **1905** in A. B. Paterson *Old Bush Songs* 51 Once more the Maorilander and the Tassey will be seen Cooking johnny cakes and jimmies on the plains of Riverine. **1915** H. LAWSON *Coll. Verse* (1969) III. 154 Fighting hard for little Tassy, where the apple orchards grow. **1936** F. CLUNE *Roaming round Darling* xix. 188 The Poet says that's the area of Tasmania. I'll take his word for it, as I haven't time to go and measure Tassie. **1938** N. MARSH *Artists in Crime* vi. 76 'Aussie', 'Tassie', 'a goodee', 'a badee'. Pray spare me these bloody abbreviations. **1956** S. HOPE *Digger's Paradise* 77 The Hobart–Launceston express has the advantage of allowing the customer to see Tassie's beautiful countryside. **1977** *Herald* (Melbourne) 17 Jan. 14/2 (Advt.), Come to 'Tassie' the Casino State.

tassil, -ill, obs. forms of TEASEL, TERCEL.

tasso ('tæsəʊ). [perh. f. TASAJO: cf. Louisiana French *tasseau* jerked beef.] = TASAJO.

1841 *Southern Lit. Messenger* VII. 77/2 The evening banquet of gumbo, tasso, and beef, in every variety of form, was shortly served up by their attendants. **1934** E. WAUGH *Handful of Dust* vi. 336 Mr. Todd..gave him farine and *tasso* and sent him on his journey. **1958** J. CAREW *Wild Coast* viii. 106 Enough food to last Hector for a week—unleavened bread and bits of jerked pork in it, strips of tasso, cassava bread. **1959** P. CAPON *Amongst those Missing* 168 He bought two sacks of farine, two of tasso, one of Brazil nuts and one of cashew nuts.

tastable: see TASTEABLE.

taste (teɪst), *sb.*[1] Forms: 4–8 **tast,** 4–5 **taast,** 4–6 (*Sc.* -7) **taist,** (6 *Sc.* **test**), 5– **taste.** [a. OF. *tast* touching, touch, = It. *tasto* a feeling, a touch, a trial, a taste (Florio); f. OF. *taster* (mod.F. *tâter*), It. *tastare*: see TASTE *v.* Cf. also OF. *taste*, It. *tasta*, a surgical probe.]

I. †**1.** The sense of touch, feeling (with the hands, etc.); the act of touching, touch. *Obs.*

[**1292** BRITTON III. ii. §13 Et puis soynt chargez qe eles.. enquergent de la femme qe se fet enceynte par tast de soen ventre et de ses mameles.] **13..** *Cursor M.* 542 (Cott.) Þis vnder wynd him gis his aand, þe erth þe tast, to fele and faand. **1422** tr. *Secreta Secret., Priv. Priv.* 208 The taste is a commyn witte, Spraden throgh the body, but hit Shewyth hym most by the handys..; by that witte we knowen hote, colde, dry, moyste, and other Suche thynges. *c* **1430** *Pilgr. Lyf Manhode* I. lxxii. (1869) 42 At the taast, and at the sighte, at the smellinge, and at the sauouringe, bred and wyn it may seeme.

†**2. a.** A trying, testing; a trial, test, examination.

1377 LANGL. *P. Pl.* B. XII. 131 Kynde witte cometh of alkynnes siȝtes,..of tastes of treuthe, and of deceytes. **1586–7** Q. ELIZ. in *Four C. Eng. Lett.* (1880) 30 To make tast of the greatest witz amongs my owne, and then of French and last of you. **1605** SHAKS. *Lear* I. ii. 47, I hope for my Brothers iustification, hee wrote this but as an essay, or taste of my Vertue. **1663** *Flagellum, or O. Cromwell* (1672) 155 To appoint a Tast or Recognition of the Government.

†**b.** A trial, an attempt. *Obs. rare*$^{-1}$.

c **1330** R. BRUNNE *Chron. Wace* (Rolls) 5400 He wende haue taken þe toun in hast, Bot he failled of his tast.

II. †**3. a.** The act of tasting, or perceiving the flavour of a thing with the organ of taste (sense 4); the fact of being tasted. *Obs.*

13.. *Coer de L.* 3075 When he has a good tast, And eeten weel a good repast. **1340–70** *Alex. & Dind.* 357 Þere-of we taken a tast what time þat vs nede. **1393** LANGL. *P. Pl.* C. I. 228 Tauerners 'a tast for nouht' tolden þe same. **1579** LYLY *Euphues* (Arb.) 176 For before the tast of the Gospel I was worse then a beast. **1592** SHAKS. *Rom. & Jul.* II. vi. 13 The sweetest honey Is loathsome in his owne deliciousnesse, And in the taste confoundes the appetite. **1667** MILTON *P.L.* I. 2 The Fruit Of that Forbidden Tree, whose mortal tast Brought Death into the World, and all our woe. **1766** ENTICK *London* IV. 367 They obtained a grant of..the taste and assize of bread.

b. *transf.* The means of tasting; hence, such a small quantity as admits of being tasted; a very small quantity (esp. of alcoholic drink), a sip; *spec.* (*U.S. slang*), an alcoholic drink; alcohol.

1530 in W. H. Turner *Select. Rec. Oxford* (1880) 91 He sent for the tast of wyne..dew to him of every hoggshed. **15..** *Aberdeen Reg.* (Jam.), And send one taist of the wyne to the yerll of Rothes. **1723** S. SEWALL *Diary* 4 Apr., My wife sent them a Taste of her Dinner. **1888** 'R. BOLDREWOOD' *Robbery under Arms* xxxviii, Bring me a taste of grog, will ye? **1904** in *Eng. Dial. Dict.* [from Scotl., Irel., N. Engl.]. **1919** E. O'NEILL *Rope in Moon of Caribbees* 202 Will ye have a taste? It's real stuff. **1966** *New Yorker* 25 June 33 Why don't you stop up Wednesday, and we'll have a taste. **1973** T. KOCHMAN *Rappin' & Stylin' Out* 162, I view such terms as 'pluck' for wine and 'taste' for liquor as embodying an action element retained from its more conventional use as a verb. **1976** *New Yorker* 1 Mar. 84/2 He said, 'Take me for a taste.' We went into a bar, and I thought he'd settle down for a few, but he only had two shots. **1978** *Maledicta* 1977 I. 224 Had a complete and unabetting weakness for *taste* (liquor).

c. *fig.* A slight experience, received or given; a slight show or sample *of* any condition or quality.

1390 GOWER *Conf.* II. 373 Whanne I beclippe hire on the wast, Yit ate leste I stele a tast. **1526** *Pilgr. Perf.* (W. de W. 1531) 234 That is none other thynge but a taste how swete our lord Jesu is. **1586** DAY *Eng. Secretary* I. (1625) A ij b, Socrates in his cradle had no taste of his after-wise-dome. *c* **1595** CAPT. WYATT *R. Dudley's Voy. W. Ind.* (Hakl. Soc.) 40 Most of them havinge some little tast of the Spanish tounge. **1669** PENN *No Cross* xxi. §39 A soul Mortified to the World, and quickned to some Tasts of a Supernatural Life. **1825** LAMB *Elia* Ser. II. *Superannuated Man*, Where was.. the promised rest? Before I had a taste of it, it was banished. **1897** A. MORRISON *Dorrington Deedbox* i, My first taste of grouse-shooting was a complete success.

d. *a taste* (advb.): *colloq.* to a small but perceptible degree; slightly; a little. Cf. BIT *sb.*[2] 5.

1894 HALL CAINE *Manxman* I. v, Aisy! Your legs a taste higher, sir, just to keep the pickle off your trousers. *Ibid.* III. xii, 'Nancy will tidy the room a taste', she said coaxingly.

4. a. The faculty or sense by which that particular quality of a thing described in 5 is discerned, the organs of which are situated chiefly in the mouth; one of the five bodily senses.

c **1380** WYCLIF *Serm.* Sel. Wks. I. 87 Whan þer tast is freishe, for to juge þe goodnesse, and after whan þei ben drunken and þer taast failiþ, þanne he puttiþ wers wyn. *c* **1394** *P. Pl. Crede* 537 Þanne haue y tynt all my tast touche and assaie! **1398** TREVISA *Barth. De P.R.* III. xx. (1495) d vj b/2, The taast is a wytte of knowynge sauours. **1587** MASCALL *Govt. Cattle, Horses* (1627) 111 Sometimes a horse will loose his tast, which commeth of sorrow. **1600** SHAKS. *A.Y.L.* II. vii. 166 Second childishnesse, and meere obliuion, Sans teeth, sans eyes, sans taste, sans euery thing. **1680** MORDEN *Geog. Rect., Germany* (1685) 119 Fruits more pleasant to the sight or tast. **1861** HULME tr. *Moquin-Tandon* II. I. 49 Taste is a species of touch of still more delicate character. **1884** *Cornh. Mag.* Dec. 620 Taste..is not equally distributed over the whole surface of the tongue alike.

b. *out of taste*, not able to distinguish flavours.

a **1541** WYATT *Sonnets* xviii, And if I have, after such bitterness, One drop of sweet, my mouth is out of taste. **1646** JENKYN *Remora* 20 The palat..is put out of taste. **1729** SWIFT *Direct. Servants, Footman* ¶28 Your mistress will confess that her mouth is out of taste.

5. a. That quality or property of a body or substance which is perceived when it is brought into contact with certain organs of the mouth, etc., esp. the tongue; savour, sapidity; the particular sensation excited by anything in this manner.

1382 WYCLIF *Jer.* xlviii. 11 Therfore abod stille his tast in hym, and his smel is not chaungid. *c* **1400** MAUNDEV. (1839) xxvii. 273 Full gode fissch..of right goode tast. *c* **1430** LYDG. *Min. Poems* (Percy Soc.) 15 Damysyns wiche withe her taste delyte. **1535** COVERDALE *Wisd.* xvi. 2 A new & straunge taist. **1594** PLAT *Jewell-ho.* II. 11 A far more liuely & penetratiue tast. **1605** TIMME *Quersit.* I. v. 19 Diuers kindes of saltes..haue diuers tastes. **1702** J. PURCELL *Cholick* (1714) 87 The acid Taste of this Recrement, and its coagulating of Milk, are undoubted. **1800** tr. *Lagrange's Chem.* II. 74 Iron..has a styptic taste, very sensible. **1857** MILLER *Elem. Chem.* (1862) III. 161 Sometimes a wine acquires a peculiar flavour known as the 'taste of the cask'.

fig. **14..** HOCCLEVE *Compl. Virgin* 213 Ther-in fynde I a bittir taast; For now the taast I feele & the streynynge Of deeth. **1579** LYLY *Euphues* (Arb.) 176 How comfortable is the feeling and tast of grace. **1605** SHAKS. *Macb.* v. v. 9, I haue almost forgot the taste of Feares. **1720** MRS. MANLEY *Power of Love* (1741) III. 187 All the Favours upon Earth, from the greatest Beauties could have no Taste for Roderigo.

†**b.** Odour, scent, smell. *Obs.*

c **1400** *Destr. Troy* 1668 Þat smelt is & smethe, smellis full swete, With taste for to touche the tabull aboute. ?*c* **1475** *Sqr. lowe Degre* 850 Frankensence and olibanum That whan ye slepe the taste may come.

c. In fig. phr. *a bad* (or *nasty*) *taste in the mouth* and varr., a lingering feeling of repugnance or disgust left behind by a distasteful or unpleasant experience.

1857 MRS. GASKELL *Life C. Brontë* II. viii. 186 They [*sc.* Balzac's novels] leave such a bad taste in my mouth. **1899** R. WHITEING *No. 5 John St.* II. xxv. 255 Never before have I heard such a speech... 'Sort o' gives yer a nasty taste in the mouth,' says Low Covey. **1904** *Daily News* 14 Dec. 5 The poems leave a nasty taste in the mouth; the taste of a snarl and a sneer. **1943** *Sun* (Baltimore) 22 Apr. 18/1 A decidedly sour taste was left by the opening number. **1969** R. HARPER *World of Thriller* ii. 71 When all the characters are corrupt or shoddy, the reader goes away with a bad taste in his mouth. **1979** R. PERRY *Bishop's Pawn* iv. 70 It had taken me nearly an hour to go through the dossier and when I'd finished reading I had a nasty taste in my mouth.

III. †**6.** Mental perception of quality; judgement, discriminative faculty. *Obs.* exc. as in 8.

13.. *Cursor M.* 11327 (Cott.) Þis symeon þat had his tast Toched o þe hali gast. *a* **1425** *Ibid.* 18889 (Trin.) Þe salmes seiþ bi good taast His wonynge shulde be wilde & waast. **1502** ATKYNSON tr. *De Imitatione* I. xxii. 171 Thou hast no spirituall tast. **1692** DRYDEN *St. Euremont's Ess.* 350 If so be they demand of me..more than discretion in Commerce, and a taste in Confidence.

7. a. The fact or condition of liking or preferring something; inclination, liking *for*; †appreciation.

c **1477** CAXTON *Jason* 72 Therfore wille thou..employ thy corage after the taste of our desires. **1552** *Godly Prayers* in *Liturg. Serv. Q. Eliz.* (1847) 253 That we..may have some taste and feeling for it in our hearts. ?*c* **1580** T. HACKET *Treas. Amadis* 236 She hath somewhat a regarde to things that are agaynst my owne taste. **1635** N. R. *Camden's Hist. Eliz.* II. 153 From the time that I had any tast of Religion. **1711** ADDISON *Spect.* No. 93 ¶13 A Man that has a Taste of Musick, Painting, or Architecture. **1727** POPE, etc. *Art of Sinking* 73 The taste of the bathos is implanted by nature itself in the soul of man. **1728** SWIFT *Intelligencer* No. 3 ¶3 Whoever hath a taste for true humour. **1791** MRS. INCHBALD *Simp. Story* III. v. 70 She had acquired a taste for those amusements. **1838** LYTTON *Alice* I. ix, The other girl is more amusing, more to my taste. **1880** L. STEPHEN *Pope* iv. 86 Every opportunity for the indulgence of his favourite tastes.

†**b.** Enjoyment, pleasure, 'relish'. Const. *in*, *of*.

1604 E. G[RIMSTONE] *D'Acosta's Hist. Indies* III. ix. 150 He found not in himselfe any disposition to goe to any other place, nor to take any taste in any thing. *a* **1716** BLACKALL *Wks.* (1723) I. 15 The Happiness of a Man's life consists not in the Abundance of the things that he possesses..But in the taste and relish that he has of them.

c. *transf.* The object of one's liking or preference.

1739 G. STONE in *Buccleuch MSS.* (Hist. MSS. Comm.) I. 392 White beauties..are the taste of the Irish nation.

8. a. The sense of what is appropriate, harmonious, or beautiful; *esp.* discernment and appreciation of the beautiful in nature or art; *spec.* the faculty of perceiving and enjoying what is excellent in art, literature, and the like.

1671 MILTON *P.R.* IV. 347 Sion's songs, to all true tasts excelling Where God is prais'd aright. **1694** CONGREVE *Double Dealer* I. ii, No, no, hang him, he has no Taste. **1712** ADDISON *Spect.* No. 409 ¶1 Rules..how we may acquire that fine Taste of Writing, which is so much talked of among the Polite World. **1768** W. GILPIN *Ess. Prints* 160 There is a fine taste in his landskips. **1776** SIR J. REYNOLDS *Disc. Art* (1778) 311, I have mentioned taste in dress, which is certainly one of the lowest subjects to which this word is applied. **1784** J. BARRY in *Lect. Paint.* ii. (1848) 108 The word Taste, as applied to objects of vision,..means..that quick discerning faculty or power of the mind by which we accurately distinguish the good, bad, or indifferent. *a* **1834** COLERIDGE *Treat. Method* i. (1849) 16 A fine Musical taste is soon dissatisfied with the Harmonica, or any similar instrument of glass or steel. **1835** URE *Philos. Manuf.* 254 Taste is displayed both in the forms and grouping of the figures, and the disposition of the colours. **1850** W. IRVING *Goldsmith* xxvii. 268 The latter part of the year 1768 had been made memorable in the world of taste by the institution of the Royal Academy of Arts. **1872** MINTO *Eng. Prose Lit.* Introd. 29 The word *taste*..in its wider sense is equivalent to artistic sensibility,..in its narrower sense it may be expressed as artistic judgment.

b. Style or manner exhibiting æsthetic discernment; good or bad æsthetic quality; the style or manner favoured in any age or country.

1739 LABELYE *Short Acc. Piers Westm. Br.* 44 The People who design'd and executed London-Bridge, and other Bridges in the same Taste. **1755** *Compl. Lett.-writer* (1759) 227 Her own old-fashioned breast-plate in the taste of the last century. **1819** SCOTT *Ivanhoe* xxviii, A rich habit, which partook more of the Eastern taste than that of Europe. **1826** DISRAELI *Viv. Grey* II. xii, Nothing could be more moderate, or, as Miss Gusset said, 'in better taste'. **1843** BORROW *Bible in Spain* xxxvi. (Pelh. Libr.) 256 It was..built something in the Moorish taste.

IV. 9. *attrib.* and *Comb.*, as ***taste-area, -centre, -fibre, -leader, -maker, -meter, -organ; taste-pleasing*** adj.; **taste-beaker, -bulb, -goblet,** former names for the *taste-bud*; **taste-blindness** *Biol.* (see quot. 1934); so **taste-blind** *a.*; **taste-bud,** a group of cells in the epithelium of the tongue etc., through which the faculty of taste operates; also *fig.*; **taste-cell**: see quot.; **taste-corpuscle** = *taste-cell*; **taste-cup, -pit,** one of the minute pits found on the epipharynx of an insect, having in the centre a peg, the termination of a nerve; **taste-hair,** one of the setæ or bristles, near the mouth of an insect or other arthropod, supposed to be organs of taste; †**taste-paper,** in the (old) Greats examination at Oxford, the paper in which passages were set from the classical authors for critical and exegetical treatment; **taste-test** *v. trans.*, to test (something) by tasting it, to test the taste of (something); also *absol.*; so **taste-tested** *a.*; **taste-tester.**

1901 E. B. TITCHENER *Exper. Psychol.* I. iv. 64 Each papilla carries a number of *taste-beakers, clusters of taste-cells and supporting cells, which constitute the specific end-organs of taste. **1934** *Jrnl. Heredity* XXV. 189/2 There is less likelihood of finding a group entirely *taste blind. **1975** *Nature* 6 Feb. 442/1 The designation 'tasters' for the more sensitive individual and 'non-tasters' or 'taste blind' for the less sensitive. **1934** *Jrnl. Heredity* XXV. 190/1 *Taste blindness is an inherited inability to taste certain thiocarbamides as crystals or in cold diluted solutions as bitter. **1965** M. A. AMERINE et al. *Princ. Sensory Evaluation Food* ii. 112 Based on studies of families and twins, 'taste blindness' was first reported to be a simple recessive character. **1879** J. FULTON *Text Bk. Physiol.* (ed. 2) xiv. 365 Peculiar structures, known as *taste buds, or taste goblets, have been discovered in the circumvallate papillæ. **1951** V. NABOKOV *Speak, Memory* ii. 30 It is..to the lowly and ugly agarics, that nations with timorous taste-buds limit their knowledge and appetite. **1963** *Listener* 3 Jan. 40/1 Vested interests and pressure-groups work upon everything from our political opinions to our taste-buds. **1970** T. S. & C. R. LEESON *Histology* (ed. 2) xiv. 274/2 A few taste buds are found also in the palate and epiglottis. **1883** *Science* I. 232/2 The *taste-bulbs, numbering 700 or more, lying in the papillary wall of the valla. **1888** J. G. M'KENDRICK in *Encycl. Brit.* XXIII. 79/2 The terminal organs of taste consist of peculiar bodies named taste-bulbs or taste-goblets. **1890** BILLINGS *Nat. Med. Dict.* s.v. *Taste*, **Taste-cells*, spindle-shaped or staff-shaped cells in the interior of the taste-bulbs. **1891** *Cent. Dict.*, **Taste-center*, the gustatory nervous center, located by Ferrier in the gyrus uncinatus of the brain. **1898** PACKARD *Text-bk. Entomol.* 45 The structure and armature of the epipharyngeal surface even besides the *taste-pits, *taste-cups, and rods, is very varied. **1899** *Allbutt's Syst. Med.* VI. 793 Whether the *taste-fibres pass by the second or third divisions of the nerve. **1879** *Taste-goblet [see *taste-bud*]. **1905** *Jrnl. R. Micros. Soc.* Apr. 180 *Taste-hairs, homologous with Kræpelin's taste-hairs in Muscidæ, are found in various orders of insects. **1952** D. RIESMAN *Individualism Reconsidered* (1954) 207 The problem..of becoming a possible *taste-leader. **1961** *New Left Rev.* Jan.–Feb. 34/2 These areas of work are excluded, by the *tastemakers, from the concept of 'serious' art. **1978** *Jrnl. R. Soc. Arts* CXXVI. 725/2 Federigo's artistic patronage did prove a tastemaker, though of a limited kind. **1814** COLERIDGE in Cottle *Remin.* (1837) II. 211 This *taste-meter to the fashionable world, gives a ludicrous portrait of an African belle. **1927** HALDANE & HUXLEY *Animal Biol.* i. 25 A number of very small *taste-organs are scattered over certain parts of the tongue [of the frog]. **1970** G. ORDISH tr. *Chauvin's World of Ants* vii. 175

The taste organ is situated in the antennae. **1860** HUGHES *Tom Brown at Oxf.* xxiv, In the *taste paper.., as they compare notes, he seems to have almost struck the bull's eye in his answers. **1898** *Taste-pit [see *taste-cup*]. *a* **1586** SIDNEY *Arcadia* I. (1622) 8 A place cunningly set with trees of the most *tast-pleasing fruits. **1979** *Wichita* (Kansas) *Eagle* 23 May 1-B/4 If you've never cooked with fresh ginger ..*taste-test before adding more. **1980** D. WILLIAMS *Murder for Treasure* xx. 198 He found himself staring into the eyes of a gargantuan dog whose giant tongue was taste-testing his chin. **1960** *Time* (Atlantic ed.) 11 Apr. 58 Critically *taste-tested piles of free cigarettes. **1969** *Listener* 24 July 127/3 Game would be virtually tasteless if *taste-testers succeeded in eliminating all its off-flavours.

taste (teɪst), *sb.*[2] *U.S. local.* [Origin unascertained.] A kind of narrow thin silk ribbon used for edge-binding: now commonly called taffeta-binding. See also WIRE-*taste*.

1847 in WEBSTER. *a* **1889** F. A. P. BARNARD in *New Haven* (Conn.) *Palladium* 18 Apr., If..Mrs. S. has any taste she will oblige me by sending me half a yard, no matter of what color, so it be not black.

taste (teɪst), *v.* Forms: 3-5 **tasten,** (3 **tasti,** 4 **tasty, taaste,** 4-6 **taast,** 4-8 **tast,** 4-7 **taist,** 6 *Sc.* **test,** 7 **teast),** 4- **taste.** [ME. *tasten*, a. OF. *taster* to touch, feel (12th c.), in 13-14th c. also to taste, mod.F. *tâter* to feel, touch, try, taste, = Pr., OSp. *tastar*, It. *tastare* to feel, handle, touch, grope for, try (Florio):—Com. Romanic or late pop.L. **tastare*, app. from **taxāre* :—**taxitāre*, freq. of *taxāre* to touch, feel, handle (Gellius, etc.): see TAX *v.*]

I. Of touch, feeling, or experience generally.

†**1.** *trans.* To try, examine, or explore by touch; to feel; to handle. *Obs.*

c **1290** *St. Michael* 312 in *S. Eng. Leg.* I. 308 With þat finguer he wole hit tasti ȝif it is a-riȝt i-wrouȝt. *c* **1330** R. BRUNNE *Chron. Wace* (Rolls) 9011 He tasted his pous,..He seide he knew his medycyn. *c* **1330** *Amis & Amil.* 1401 Leches..That gun to tasty his wounde. **1390** GOWER *Conf.* III. 315 This noble clerk, with alle haste Began the veines forto taste. **1480** CAXTON *Ovid's Met.* x. vii, She toke hardynes for the derknes, and tasted the waye on the ryght side & lyft. **1525** LD. BERNERS *Froiss.* II. xxxviii. 115 The men of armes entre into the dykes,..and tasted the dyke with their speares, and passed ouer to the fote of the wall. **1648** CRASHAW *Delights Muses, Music's Duel* 112 With a quiv'ring coynesse tasts the strings.

†**b.** *intr.* To feel, touch; to grope. *Obs.*

1377 LANGL. *P. Pl.* B. XVII. 147 þe fyngres..Bitokneth sothly þe sone..þat toched and tasted atte techynge of þe paume. *c* **1450** *Merlin* xxxiii. 681 She be-gan to taste softly till he fill on slepe. **1481** CAXTON *Reynard* xii. (Arb.) 27 Isegrym..crope a lityl in, and tasted here and there, and at laste he sayde..what I seche I fynde not. **1483** —— *G. de la Tour* F ij b, He tasted aboute & founde well that the dede was trewe.

†**c.** *trans.* To come into contact with, to touch.

1634 SIR T. HERBERT *Trav.* 18 Such as haue the Scuruy.. so soone as they taste the shore..eat three-leafed-grasse.

†**2.** *trans.* To put to the proof; to try, test. *Obs.*

13.. *Cursor M.* 12934 (Gött.) þe warlou wili..wold him tast wid sin, To witt if he had part him in. *c* **1450** LOVELICH *Grail* lii. 603 He lyht Adown..and tasted his harneis In that stede, þat it scholde not faille whanne he hadd nede. **1585-6** SIR T. SHERLEY in *Leycester Corr.* (Camden) 174, I thowght to tast her affectyon unto your lordship. **1615** CHAPMAN *Odyss.* XXI. 211 And he now began To taste the bow. **1670** COTTON *Espernon* II. v. 206 Him he first tasted by Lafin, the same who had made himself a Mediator betwixt the Duke of Espernon and l'Esdiguieres in Provence.

b. *spec.*: see quots.

1711 W. SUTHERLAND *Shipbuild. Assist.* 164 *Tasting of Plank or Timber*, chipping of it with an Addice to try the Defects. *c* **1850** *Rudim. Navig.* (Weale) 155 *Tasting of plank or timber*, chipping it with an adze, or boring it with a small augur, for the purpose of ascertaining its quality.

†**c.** To attempt, try *to do* something. *Obs. rare.*

c **1330** R. BRUNNE *Chron. Wace* (Rolls) 13834 On many manere ilk oþer tasted Ilk oþer to slo, ilk oþer to wounde. *c* **1450** *Merlin* xxxii. 649 He caste a-wey his clubbe and tasted to chacche the kynge in his armes.

3. *fig.* To have experience or knowledge of; to experience, feel; to have a slight experience of.

Often (in later use perh. always) *fig.* from 4.

a **1300** *Cursor M.* 18940 Als gaf to þaim þe haligast Alkin wiit to tuche and tast. *c* **1380** WYCLIF *Serm.* Sel. Wks. I. 126 He shal not taaste þe longe deþ. **1576** FLEMING *Panopl. Epist.* 35 In ciuil commotions all thinges are miserable:.. this our present age also hath oftentimes tasted. **1630** *R. Johnson's Kingd. & Commw.* 138 [The Gaules] who from Caesars time till then, had not tasted the force of a forren power. **1693** *Humours Town* A ij b, You have tasted the Pleasures of the Town. **1717** OCKLEY in *Lett. Lit. Men* (Camden) 353, I enjoy more repose here than I have tasted these many years. **1864** BURTON *Scot Abr.* I. iv. 207 John Knox, who was just returned from tasting the tender mercies of France as a galley-slave.

†**b.** To have carnal knowledge of. *Obs.*

1611 SHAKS. *Cymb.* II. iv. 57 If you can mak't apparant That you have tasted her in Bed; my hand, And Ring is yours. *a* **1639** T. CAREW *Poems* (1651) 32 So shalt thou be despis'd, fair Maid, When by the sated lover tasted. **1752** YOUNG *Brothers* IV. i, What, see, talk, touch, nay taste her!

II. Of the special sense that resides in the tongue and palate.

4. *trans.* To perceive by the sense of taste; to perceive or experience the taste or flavour of.

1340-70 *Alex. & Dind.* 952 In menskinge of mouþ mirþe we hauen, In tendere touchinge of þing, & tastinge of swete. *c* **1375** *Cursor M.* 23456 (Fairf.) In þis werlde has men liking ..squete spiceri to tast [*Cott.* fell] & smelle. *c* **1430** LYDG. *Min. Poems* 14 Wellys most holsom of savour, For to be tasted of every governour. *c* **1440** *Promp. Parv.* 487/1 Taastyn, *gusto.* **1535** COVERDALE *2 Sam.* xix. 35 This daye am I foure score yeare olde. How shulde I..taist what I eate or drynke? **1592** SHAKS. *Rom. & Jul.* I. iii. 30 When it did tast the Worme-wood. **1774** GOLDSM. *Nat. Hist.* (1776) VI. 242 When once it has tasted human flesh, it never desists from haunting those places where it expects the return of its prey. **1909** *Daily Chron.* 17 Nov. 8/4 She said the smells were so bad that they could be tasted as well as smelt.

†**b.** *fig.* To perceive or recognize as by the sense of taste. *Obs.*

1583 BABINGTON *Commandm.* i. 10 Euen a world it is to see how all, as dead, doo tast no sinne in it. **1591** HARINGTON *Orl. Fur.* Pref. ¶ viij b, Three syllabled wordes..which who mislike, may tast lamp oyle with their eares. **1616** B. JONSON *Devil an Ass* I. vi, Nay, then I taste a Trick in 't.

c. *absol.* or *intr.* To experience or distinguish flavours; to have or exercise the sense of taste.

1387 TREVISA *Higden* (Rolls) II. 181 þey..mowe noþer see ne hire, ne taste, ne smelle. *c* **1560** A. SCOTT *Poems* (S.T.S.) xxxi. 18 No wit salbe degest, To heir, se, smell, nor test. **1601** SHAKS. *Twel. N.* I. v. 98 O, you are sicke of selfe-loue, Maluolio, and taste with a distemper'd appetite. *Mod.* I have got a very bad cold, and can neither taste nor smell.

5. *transf.* (*trans.*) To perceive by some other sense, esp. smell. Now only *poet.* or *dial.*

1656 EARL MONM. *Advt. fr. Parnass.* 380 Would you have men taste the odoriferousness of those Aromaticks which you..have brought from the Indies? **1674** RAY *N.C. Words*, To *Tast*; i.e. to smell in the North. **1796** PEGGE *Derbicisms* (E.D.S.), *Taste*, to smell, in the North. See Ray. You commonly ask a person to *taste* your snuff. **1819** KEATS *Isabella* ix, I must taste the blossoms that unfold In its ripe warmth this gracious morning time. **1844** KINGLAKE *Eöthen* ii. (1878) 25 To taste the cold breath of the earliest morn.

6. To try the flavour or quality of by the sense of taste; to put a small quantity of (something) into the mouth in order to ascertain the flavour, etc.; *spec.* to test the quality of by tasting, for trade purposes. Also *absol.*

a **1300** *Cursor M.* 13403 (Cott.) þai fild a cupp þan son in hast, And gaf it þe architricline to tast. *Ibid.* 16773 (Gött.) þat bitter drinc..He tasted it, bot noght he dranc. **1388** WYCLIF *Rom.* xi. 16 If a litil part of that that is tastid be hooli, the hool gobet is hooli. **1535** COVERDALE *Job* xxxiv. 3 For like as the mouth tasteth [1382 WYCLIF bi tast demeth] the meates, so the eare proueth & discerneth the wordes. **1552** HULOET, Taste afore or fyrste, *prolibo.* **1604** in *Eng. Gilds* (1870) 435 The ale teaster to teast the ale before they sell it. **1769** COOK *Voy. round World* I. iii. (1773) 44 Having tasted the liquor, they returned it, with strong expressions of disgust. **1837** WHITTOCK, etc. *Bk. Trades* (1842) 441 This system of tasting constitutes the acme of the great Teaman's trade.

b. *intr.* with *of*: see 12 a.

c. *spec.* (*trans.*) To test or certify the wholesomeness of (food provided) by tasting it; also *absol.* to act as taster *to* a person. Also *fig.*

1595 SHAKS. *John* v. vi. 28 How did he take it [poison]? Who did taste to him? **1600** J. PORY tr. *Leo's Africa* Introd. 32 He [the emperor] is tasted vnto, not before, but after he hath eaten and drunke. **1678** DRYDEN *All for Love* I. i. 15 Thou and I, Like Time and Death, marching before our Troops, May taste fate to e'm; Mowe e'm out a passage. **1682** SOUTHERNE *Loyal Brother* I. i, True, I make bold To taste their letters to 'em, as they pass Through my Employment.

d. *fig.* To make trial of as by the sense of taste; to try the quality of. Also with *obj. cl.*, and *absol.* or *intr.* Cf. sense 2.

1382 WYCLIF *Ps.* xxxiii. 9 [xxxiv. 8] Tastith, and seeth, for sweete is the Lord. **1390** GOWER *Conf.* II. 395 Mi fader, nay; bot I have tasted In many a place as I have go, And yit love I nevere on of tho. **1597** MORLEY *Introd. Musicke* Annot., Who hath tasted the firste elements of musicke. **1601** B. JONSON *Poetaster* v. iii, Then come home, And taste a piece of Terence. **1819** KEATS *Isabella* xlix, O turn thee to the very tale, And taste the music of that vision pale. **1896** MRS. CAFFYN *Quaker Grandmother* 294 She waited breathlessly to taste the quality of her mercy.

7. To have or take a taste of (food or drink); to take only as much as is sufficient to try or perceive the taste of, to eat or drink a little; but often by meiosis, simply for 'eat' or 'drink'. Negatively, ***not to taste*** = not even to taste, not to eat or drink at all. Also *fig.* to get a 'taste' of.

a **1300** *Cursor M.* 12559 (Cott.) Noþer durst þai drinc ne ete, Ne brek þair brede, ne tast þair mes Til he war cummen til þair des. **1382** WYCLIF *Luke* xiv. 24, I seie to ȝou, for noone of tho men that ben clepid, schal taaste my souper. **1596** DALRYMPLE tr. *Leslie's Hist. Scot.* (S.T.S.) I. 69 Of mony things we sal taist a few as we may. **1624** QUARLES *Job* xi. Medit. 35 Wisdom digests, what knowledge did but tast. **1653** WALTON *Angler* i. 2, I often..taste a cup of Ale there. **1700** ASTRY tr. *Saavedra-Faxardo* I. 31 It will suffice therefore for a Prince to tast the Arts and Sciences. **1754** GRAY *Pleasure* 60 She eyes the clear crystalline well [of Pleasure], And tastes it as it goes. **1853** KINGSLEY *Hypatia* x, He had tasted no food since noon the day before.

b. *absol.* or *intr.* ellipt. for 'taste wine or alcoholic drink'; to take a little drink. *Sc.*

1823 GALT *R. Gilhaize* v. (E.D.D.), He pressed my grandfather to taste. **1901** S. MACNAUGHTON *Fortune of Chr. M'Nab* ii, 'Thank you', said Christina, 'I do not taste'. *Mod. Sc.* Will you not taste? Do you never taste?

8. To like the taste of (usually *fig.*); to relish, approve of, enjoy, like, take pleasure in; in earlier use sometimes in neutral sense: to appreciate. Now *arch.* or *dial.*

1605 EARL OF SALISBURY in *Buccleuch MSS.* (Hist. MSS. Comm.) 81 This [proposal] was at first but little tasted by them. *a* **1617** BAYNE *On Eph. i.* (1634) 244 Many..taste their pottage, like Esau, better than their birthright. **1624** BEDELL *Lett.* iv. 81 A more sensible proofe how the Pope tastes these Titles. **1751** CHATHAM *Lett. Nephew* ii. 6, I hope you love and taste those authors [Homer and Vergil] particularly. **1768** EARL HARDWICKE *Let.* 17 May, The king seemed to taste the Duke of Grafton, and commended his parts. **1791** BOSWELL *Johnson* 2 Apr. an. 1775, If I wondered at Johnson not tasting the works of Mason and Gray, still more have I wondered at their not tasting his works. **1805** MRS. R. TRENCH in *Rem.* (1862) 170 Mad. de Sévigné, whom for the first time I really taste and admire. **1879** GEO. ELIOT *Theo. Such* i. 10 The work..I am told is much tasted in a Cherokee translation. **1896** 'IAN MACLAREN' *Kate Carnegie* 33 The story was much tasted by our guard's admirers.

9. *intr.* Of a substance: To have a taste of a specified or implied kind; to produce a certain taste in the mouth; to have a taste or flavour *of*.

1552 HULOET, Tastyng or castynge an yll taste or sauoure, *virosus.* **1615** G. SANDYS *Trav.* 66 Blacke as soote and tasting not much unlike it. **1653** WALTON *Angler* iii. 73 It looks well, and tastes well. **1655** FULLER *Ch. Hist.* I. ii. §11 This new Wine, put into old Vessels, did in after-Ages taste of the Caske. **1681** CHETHAM *Angler's Vade-m.* xxxix. §1 (1689) 253 It will make him to tast very sour. **1729** SWIFT *Direct. Servants, Cook* ¶ 26 If your butter tastes of brass, it is your master's fault. **1871** CALVERLEY *Proverb. Philos.* in *Verses & Transl.* (ed. 4) 95 Let him drink deeply.., nor grumble if it tasteth of the cork. *Mod.* The milk has begun to turn; it tastes rather sour.

b. *fig.* To produce a particular effect upon the mind or feelings; to partake of the nature, character, or quality *of*; to savour *of*.

1559 W. CUNNINGHAM *Cosmogr. Glasse* 5 All other artes (whiche taste of the Mathematicalles). *c* **1575** J. HOOKER *Life Sir P. Carew* (1857) 19 His behaviour tasting after the French manner. **1613** SHAKS. *Hen. VIII*, II. iii. 89 How tasts it? Is it bitter? **1621** SANDERSON *Serm.* I. 179 This ungodly king Ahab; see how all that come of him, taste of him. **1840** CLOUGH *Dipsychus* Poems (1892) 109 The place, the air Tastes of the nearer north.

†**c.** *trans.* To savour of. *Sc. Obs.*

1596 DALRYMPLE tr. *Leslie's Hist. Scot.* x. 417 Ony thing ..of him said that taisted not Ill talk, haitred, and Invie.

†**10.** To cause a pleasant taste in (the mouth); to affect (the palate) agreeably; hence *fig.* to please, suit, be agreeable to. (Orig. *intr.* with dative obj.; in quot. 1672 with *to.*) *Obs.*

a **1586** SIDNEY *Arcadia* III. (1622) 352 Bitter griefs tastes mee best, pain is my ease. **1624** HEYWOOD *Gunaik.* VIII. 383 When wholesome foode would not tast their mouths, they devised sweet meates to realish their pallats. **1631** —— *Maid of West* III. Wks. 1874 II. 299 Call for what wine best tasts you. **1672** MARVELL *Reh. Transp.* I. 184 Nothing less will taste to your palate.

11. To impart a taste or flavour to; to flavour; also *fig.* Now *rare.*

a **1577** GASCOIGNE *Flowers* Wks. (1587) 40 A salad or a sauce, to tast your cates withall. **1598** B. JONSON *Ev. Man in Hum.* I. iv, We will have a bunch of radish and salt to taste our wine. **1904** J. WELLS *J. H. Wilson* xxi. 293 All his teachings were coloured and tasted by the channel through which they ran.

12. taste of, a construction used in several senses, sometimes simply = taste, sometimes = take a taste of, eat or drink a little of. So ***taste on*** (now *dial.*), † ***taste to*** (obs.).

In some cases, as in quots. 1526 in b and c, perhaps a literalism of translation (not found in the Vulgate, Wyclif, or Rhemish N.T.); but see OF 29 a, and cf. *take a taste of.*

a. To make trial of by tasting, to try the taste of; = 6. Also *fig. arch.*

a **1400-50** *Alexander* 2074 þan pullis him vp þe proude kyng & on þe pepire tastis. *c* **1491** *Chast. Goddes Chyld.* 11 The bee goth and tasteth of many fair floures. *c* **1550** CHEKE *Matt.* xxvii. 34 When he had taasted on it [TINDALE therof], he wold not drink. **1604-63** *Inscr. on Ch. Bells* in North *Ch. Bells Linc.* (1882), I sweetly toling men do call to taste on meats that feeds the soule. **1807** SOUTHEY *Espriella's Lett.* II. 196 We tasted of this bread: it was dry, but not unpleasant. **1848** J. H. NEWMAN *Loss & Gain* 154, I taste of every thing, I depend on nothing.

b. To eat or drink only a little of; with negative, not to eat or drink at all; = 7. Also *fig.*

13.. *K. Alis.* 5070 (Bodl. MS.) The kyng..forbed..þat non ne shulde..Of þe water drynk ne taste. *c* **1400** *Destr. Troy* 6427 The tydis not to taste of þis triet meite. **1526** TINDALE *Luke* xiv. 24 None of those men which were bidden shall tast of my supper [μου τοῦ δείπνου]. **1591** SHAKS. *1 Hen. VI*, II. iii. 79, I craue..that we may Taste of your Wine. **1607** TOPSELL *Four-f. Beasts* (1658) 19 Asses are subject to madness when they have tasted to certain herbs growing neer Potnias. **1667** MILTON *P.L.* IX. 651 Of this Tree we may not taste nor touch. **1699** DRYDEN *Epist. to J. Dryden* 61 For age but tastes of pleasures, youth devours. **1765** T. HUTCHINSON *Hist. Mass.* I. ii. 232 They had but tasted of the words..of the gentlemen.

c. To have experience or knowledge of; to feel, experience; = 3.

1526 TINDALE *Matt.* xvi. 28 Some there be a monge them that here stonde, whych shall nott taste of deeth [οὐ μὴ γεύσωνται θανάτου], tyll they shall [etc.]. **1552** LATIMER *Serm. 4th Sund. Epiph.* (1584) 315 b, He himself hath tasted of al trouble. *a* **1562** G. CAVENDISH *Metr. Vis., Earl of Essex* vi, I ame tastyng on the payn. **1599** MASSINGER, etc. *Old Law* II. ii, So contentedly, You cannot think unless you tasted on't. **1667** MILTON *P.L.* IX. 476 Hope here to taste Of pleasure. **1742** GRAY *Adversity* 6 The Proud are taught to taste of pain. **1832** HT. MARTINEAU *Ireland* v. 75 Wherever the population had tasted of oppression.

†**d.** = 3 b. *Obs.*

1607 TOURNEUR *Rev. Trag.* II. ii, I do embrace this season for the fittest To tast of that yong Lady.

e. See 9, 9 b.

tasteable, tastable (ˈteɪstəb(ə)l), *a.* Also 6 **tastible**. [In ME. a. OF. *tastable* having the capacity of feeling, f. *taster* to feel, touch; in mod.Eng. f. TASTE *v.* + -ABLE.]

I. †**1.** Capable of feeling or perceiving by the sense of touch. *Obs. rare*⁻¹.

c **1400** tr. *Secreta Secret., Gov. Lordsh.* 98 Þe wyttys þat er yn þe hondes ys in a touchable & tastable stryngh [F. *li sens qi est en la main est en force touchable e tastable*; L. *palpatiua*].

II. 2. Capable of being tasted. Also *fig.*

1572 J. JONES *Bathes of Bath* II. 18 The fittest instrument, the truest touchestone, of all properties, trying both toucheable and tasteable qualities. **1589** PUTTENHAM *Eng. Poesie* II. i. (Arb.) 78 Things that haue conueniencie by relation, as the visible by light..: the tastible by sauours to the rate: the tangible by his objectes in this or that regard. **1627–77** FELTHAM *Resolves* II. xliv. 245 Pleasures are not truly tastable, but in the solid tracts of Temperance. **1755** MILLER in *Phil. Trans.* XLIX. 163 This juice has no other tasteable quality but that of heating without turning sour. **1829** JAS. MILL *Hum. Mind* (1869) I. 13 We should have no idea of objects as seeable, as hearable, as touchable, or tasteable.

†**3.** Pleasant to the taste; savoury, 'tasty'. *Obs.*

a **1641** BP. MOUNTAGU *Acts & Mon.* vii. (1642) 443 Esseni are those that live the life of Monks, eating no pleasant or tasteable meat at all. **1791** *Gentl. Mag.* Feb. 127/1 The fruit was tasteable.

tasted (ˈteɪstɪd), *ppl. a.* and *adj.* [f. TASTE *v.* and *sb.*[1] + -ED.]

A. *ppl. a.* [f. TASTE *v.*] Perceived by the taste, etc.: see the verb.

c **1403** ? LYDG. *Crt. Sapience* Proeme vii, As tasted bytternesse All swete thynge maketh be more precyous.

B. *adj.* [f. TASTE *sb.*]

1. Having a specified taste (with adj. or adv.).

1604 JAS. I *Counterbl.* in *Ess. Poesie*, etc. (Arb.) 107 The miraculous omnipotencie of our strong tasted Tobacco. **1607** TOPSELL *Four-f. Beasts* (1658) 208 They are much fatter and better tasted. **1682** WHELER *Journ. Greece* IV. 295 The white..is very well tasted. **1684** BUNYAN *Pilgr.* II. 133 They were very good tasted Fruit. **1707** MORTIMER *Husb.* (1721) II. 297 A pleasant tasted Perry. **1725** DE FOE *Voy. round World* (1840) 328 The water..was very sweet, wholesome, and good tasted. **1812** SOUTHEY in *Q. Rev.* VII. 69 *note*, The milk..is ill tasted. **1836** W. IRVING *Astoria* (1849) 409 Mountain mutton..extremely well tasted.

2. Having taste or critical discernment (of a specified kind).

1802 H. C. ANDREWS *Bot. Rep.* I. 255 The late elegantly tasted Mrs. North.

tasteful (ˈteɪstfʊl), *a.* Also 7–8 **tastful**. [f. TASTE *sb.*[1] + -FUL.]

†**1.** Having the capacity of tasting or trying.

1647 CRASHAW *Poems, Flaming Heart* 50 What is't your tasteful spirits do prove In that rare life of her and love?

2. Having an agreeable taste; palatable, toothsome, tasty. Now *rare*.

1611 COTGR., *Savoureux*, sauorie, tastfull, tart, well smacking. **1621** BP. MOUNTAGU *Diatribæ* 358 Stolne waters are sweet,..no Bread so tastefull as that of the Sanctuarie. **1707** *Curios. in Husb. & Gard.* 217 The tasteful Cider. **1747** *Gentl. Mag.* May 243/2 With Temp'rance came, delightful guest! Health,—tasteful food, and balmy rest. **1887** HISSEY *Holiday on Road* 177 Sheep that live upon such a pasturage should yield a tasteful dish.

†**b.** *fig.* Mentally pleasant or agreeable. *Obs.*

a **1659** OSBORN *Ess.* iii. Wks. (1673) 562 Since nothing is more tasteful to Humanity, than Understanding. *a* **1701** MAUNDRELL *Let. to Sir C. Hedges* in *Journ. Jerus.* (1732) Pref., An Affectation, which however tastful it may be to the Persons who use it [etc.].

c. Full of taste; highly-flavoured. *rare.*

1881 SALA in *Illustr. Lond. News* 14 May 467/3 Punch is too strong and tasteful with turtle soup.

3. Having or showing good taste, as a person; displaying good taste, as a work of art, etc.

1756 *Connoisseur* No. 120 ¶6 These are the poets who favour us with..tasteful compositions. **1816** SINGER *Hist. Cards* 213 They were drawn on the blocks by the tasteful pencil of Stothard. **1849** *N. & Q.* I. 28/2 The tasteful publisher of the 'Aldine Poets'. **1863** LYELL *Antiq. Man* ii. 10 The pottery..is of a more ornamental and tasteful style.

b. Of or pertaining to taste; æsthetic.

1851 J. HAMILTON *Royal Preacher* x. (1858) 134 Conceding..the same right to exert his tasteful and intellectual faculties when listening to a sermon as when perusing a..book.

Hence **ˈtastefully** *adv.*, in a tasteful manner, with good taste; **ˈtastefulness**, the quality or state of being tasteful (in various senses).

1611 COTGR., *Savoureusement*, sauorily, *tastfully, tastingly, with a good stomacke. **1808** MRS. KEMBLE *Day after Wedding* 3 A Lady's Dressing-room tastefully furnished. **1900** *Westm. Gaz.* 22 Oct. 4/2 The tastefully-arranged gardens which are to be found at many stations on that railway. **1727** BAILEY vol. II, **Tastefulness*, Relishableness, Palatableness. **1844** DICKENS *Mart. Chuz.* ix, Mr. Pecksniff's delight in the tastefulness of the house.

tasteless (ˈteɪstlɪs), *a.* Also 7–8 **tastless**. [f. TASTE *sb.*[1] + -LESS.]

1. Destitute of the sense of taste; unable to taste. Also *fig.* Now *rare*.

1591 SYLVESTER *Du Bartas* I. iv. 148 When wilfully his taste-less Taste delights In things unsavory to sound appetites. *a* **1631** DONNE *Funeral Elegy* Poems (1654) 219 As aged men are glad Being tastlesse grown, to joy in joyes they had. **1704** CIBBER *Careless Husb.* v. (1705) 60 Won't you think me tastless to the Joy you've given me? **1713** ROWE *Jane Shore* v. i, My tasteless Tongue cleaves to the clammy Roof. **1820** C. R. MATURIN *Melmoth* (1892) III. xxvii. 104 Every thing that could tempt the tasteless palate of age.

2. Without taste or flavour; exciting no sensation of taste; insipid.

1611 FLORIO, *Insapcrito*, vnsauorie, tastelesse. **1661–79** BOYLE *Scept. Chem.* IV. Wks. 1772 I. 533 He never was able to make them [chymical oils] tasteless. **1748** *Anson's Voy.* II. xii. 267 Very dry and tasteless food. **1831** J. DAVIES *Manual Mat. Med.* 329 A powder of an orange yellow colour, inodorous, and tasteless.

3. *fig.* Exciting no interest; dull, insipid, uninteresting.

1603 FLORIO *Montaigne* (1634) 143 Enterludes and commedies rejoyce and make us merry, but to players they are tedious and tastelesse. **1781** COWPER *Conversat.* 715 The song of Sion is a tasteless thing, Unless when rising on a joyful wing. **1814** WORDSW. *Excurs.* I. 612 A while on trivial things we held discourse, To me soon tasteless. **1822** LAMB *Elia* Ser. I. *Distant Corr.*, If it [sentiment] have time to cool, it is the most tasteless of all cold meats.

4. Devoid of good taste; of persons, lacking in discrimination, or in critical discernment and appreciation; of things, showing want of good taste.

1676 ETHEREDGE *Man of Mode* III. ii, Nature..puts sophisticate dulness often on the tasteless multitude for true wit and good-humour. **1709** SWIFT in *Lett. Lit. Men* (Camden) 342 Your Lordship is universally admired by this tastless People. **1791** GILPIN *Forest Scenery* II. 75 It not only shews the hand of art; but of the most tastless art. **1843** PRESCOTT *Mexico* I. ii. (1864) 17 As different from their ancestors as are the modern Egyptians from those who built,—I will not say, the tasteless pyramids. **1853** KINGSLEY *Hypatia* vii, The tasteless fashion of an artificial and decaying civilization.

Hence **ˈtastelessly** *adv.*, in a tasteless manner; without taste.

1854 *Tait's Mag.* XXI. 386 Even that comes tastelessly on the ear of the player on the world's stage, unless it is accompanied with a bouquet. **1880** *Daily News* 30 Nov. 3/1 Their houses..are solidly if tastelessly furnished.

tastelessness (ˈteɪstlɪsnɪs). [f. prec. + -NESS.]

1. Lack of the sense of taste; *fig.* lack of relish or appreciation. Now *rare*.

1626 DONNE *Serm.* iv. (1640) 38 Our palate dead in a tastlesnesse. **1713** BERKELEY *Guard.* No. 49 ¶9 A secret indignation at the tastelessness of mortal men, who, in their race through life, overlook the real enjoyments of it. *a* **1774** TUCKER *Lt. Nat.* (1834) II. 404 Such austerities and labours of devotion, such a tastelessness of all innocent enjoyments.

2. Absence of taste or flavour; insipidity. Also *fig.*

1600 SURFLET *Countrie Farme* III. lxi. 567 Their sharpnes, sowrenes, tartnes, harshnes, eagernes, sweetenes, and tastlesnes. **1875** H. C. WOOD *Therap.* (1879) 468 On account of its tastelessness, this preparation..is sometimes employed as a purgative for children.

3. Absence or want of æsthetic discernment.

1778 MALONE *Note on Tit. A.* in *Shaks.'s Wks.* VIII. 561 One of their own fraternity, (who cannot well be suspected of asinine tastelessness, or Gothic prepossessions). **1825** *Blackw. Mag.* XVIII. 240 Others assign it to the nonchalance and tastelessness of managers. **1855** DORAN *Hanov. Queens* II. i. 30 Garrick, considering he was a man of taste, displayed great tastelessness on this occasion.

†**ˈtasten**, *v. Obs. rare*⁻¹. [f. TASTE *sb.*[1] + -EN[5].] *trans.* To produce a sensation of taste in.

1579 LODGE *Def. Poetry* 15 The receipt is bitter, therfore I would wysh you first to tasten your mouth with the Sugar of perseuerance.

taster[1] (ˈteɪstə(r)). Forms: 4–6 **tastour**, 5 **-ar**, **taastowre**, 6– **taster**. [a. AF. *tastour* = OF. *tasteur*, f. OF. *taster*: see TASTE *v.* Later treated as agent-n. of the Eng. vb.: see -ER[1].]

1. a. One who tastes, or tries the quality of a thing by tasting; *spec.* one whose office, business, or employment is to test the quality of victuals sold to the public, as ale, wine, tea, etc. by taste; hence in comb. ALE-TASTER, TEA-TASTER, q.v. Also *fig.* In quot. 1596, the mouth.

c **1440** *Promp. Parv.* 487/1 Taastowre, *gustator, ambro.* *c* **1450** in *Surtees Misc.* (1888) 62 Two ale tastars, yᵉ qwhyche two tastars..schall taste the ale of all common brewers every weke. **1526** *Pilgr. Perf.* (W. de W. 1531) 274 b, To be vynteners, discerners, and tasters of the same. **1596** HARINGTON *Metam. Ajax* (1814) 36 Riding on a great sow and holding before her taster a dirty pudding. **1633** G. HERBERT *Temple, Odour* i, As Amber-greese leaves a rich sent Unto the taster. **1756** C. LUCAS *Ess. Waters* I. 79 Judicious tasters dilute hot liquors. **1854** LOWELL *Jrnl. in Italy* Pr. Wks. 1890 I. 115, I reckon myself a good taster of dialects. **1866** CARLYLE *Remin., E. Irving* (1881) 314, I..demanded back my poor MS. from Murray, received with it some apologetic palaver (enclosing an opinion from his taster..), and much hope [etc.]. **1905** *Sat. Rev.* 17 June 816/1 On the whole the first literary 'taster' of the MS. was, we think, justified in rejecting Coryat.

b. *transf.* A device which tests as by tasting.

1837 WHEWELL *Hist. Induct. Sc.* (1857) III. 24 Which thus acted as a sort of electric taster.

2. A domestic officer whose duty it is to taste food and drink about to be served to his master, in order to ascertain their quality, or to detect poison.

1387 TREVISA *Higden* (Rolls) VIII. 197 A monk..made a drink of venym,..and drank to þe kyng as it were his tastour. **1580** HOLLYBAND *Treas. Fr. Tong* s.v. *Eschanson*, A taster of meates to kinges or other. **1602** T. FITZHERBERT *Apol.* 31 The Emperour Claudius, poysoned by his taster. **1662** HIBBERT *Body Div.* I. 206 Princes have their tasters before they eat, lest there should be poison in the dish. **1738** SWIFT *Pol. Conversat.* i. 13 What, Miss, Will you be my Taster [of a dish of tea]? **1895** *Westm. Gaz.* 30 Oct. 3/2 Not a morsel or a drop ever passes the Sultan's lips, they say, until he has tried it first on a taster.

fig. **1640** REYNOLDS *Passions* xvii. 179 Knowledge is Appetites Taster.

3. An implement by which a small portion of anything is taken for tasting.

a. A small shallow cup of silver, often with an embossed or corrugated bottom which reflects the light through the liquor, for tasting wines.

1420 *E.E. Wills* (1882) 46 A tastour of seluer with myn owne merke ymade in þe bottom. **1530** PALSGR. 279/2 Tastour a lytell cuppe to tast wyne, *tasse a gouster le uin.* **1681** *Lond. Gaz.* No. 1665/4 One Silver Brandy Taster, marked with R. H. A. **1704** *Ibid.* No. 4055/4 Two long footed Silver Cups, one Taster. **1858** [see b].

b. An instrument by which a small portion is taken from the interior of a cheese; a skewer for testing the condition of hams.

1784 TWAMLEY *Dairying* 79, I told her Cheese of that countenance always was sweet. I put my taster into one and gave it her to taste. **1811** [see *cheese-taster*, CHEESE *sb.*[1] 7]. **1858** SIMMONDS *Dict. Trade, Taster*,..a scoop for tasting cheese; a skewer for trying hams; a dram cup.

4. A small portion of food, etc., or of anything, for a sample; a taste; *spec.*, a portion of ice cream served in a shallow glass.

1826 SYD. SMITH *Granby* Wks. 1867 II. 90 It shall be the taster of the cheese, and we are convinced it will sell the whole article. **1891** *Daily News* 28 July 7/2 He went to the defendant's [an ice-cream vendor] stall in London-wall and asked him for a 'taster'. **1899** *Westm. Gaz.* 20 May 2/1 The 'taster', a free gift bestowed of yore in order to retain the..goodwill of regular but temporarily impecunious customers. **1901** *Daily Tel.* 21 May 10 The irate signor..produced—not a half-penny taster for the policeman but a tattered copy of a work called 'Law without Lawyers'. **1927** W. E. COLLINSON *Contemp. Eng.* 16 The Italian often known as an ice-cream Jack with his ice-cream barrow still follows his calling and no doubt the youngsters still ask for wafers and tasters.

‖**taster**[2] (ˈtɑːstə(r), -æ-). *Zool.* [G. *taster* feeler, antenna, f. *tasten* to feel, touch.] In certain Hydrozoa, A modified zooid situated on the polypstem, and somewhat resembling the polypites, but having no mouth; a hydrocyst or feeler.

1884 *Stand. Nat. Hist.* I. 100 Alternating with the polypites at intervals along the polypstem are found very curious bodies called tasters, which have a close likeness to the flask-shaped zoöids. [**1888** ROLLESTON & JACKSON *Anim. Life* 770 *Siphonophora*... The various parts..(1) The polypite or gastrozooid... (2) Hydrocysts or feelers (= Taster of German writers)... These structures are polypites in which the distal or oral extremity is imperforate and usually armed with cnidoblasts. The pedicle is absent or short.]

†**ˈtastesome**, *a. Obs. rare.* [f. TASTE *sb.*[1] + -SOME.] Pleasant to the taste; 'tasty', toothsome.

1598 FLORIO, *Gusteuole*, smacking, tastesome, tasting well.

‖**tastevin** (tastəvɛ̃, tat-). [An earlier form of mod.Fr. *tâte-vin*, lit. 'wine-taster', revived as in the title of the *Confrérie des Chevaliers du Tastevin* (founded 1933).]

1. a. = TASTER[1] 3 a. **b.** (With capital initial.) In France, a member of an order or guild of wine-tasters.

1952 A. LICHINE *Wines of France* viii. 79 Most tasters use the *tastevin* in Burgundy. **1966** P. V. PRICE *France: Food & Wine Guide* 147 The three top sketches show a Burgundy tastevin, with irregularly patterned indentations and a thumb-rest. **1969** DOROZYNSKI & BELL *Wine Bk.* 280 Wine-tasting orders, associations, fraternities and clubs are born almost every year... The Tastevins de Bourgogne..are among the best known in France. **1971** *Esquire* July 22/4 The enthronement of the Tastevins takes place in nearby Clos de Vougeot. **1979** *Homes & Gardens* June 129/1 We moved on to the splendid Beaune Boucherottes, its dusky red lights twinkling in the tiny silver *tastevin* that Andre always uses to assess colour.

2. *attrib.* (in sense 1 b), signifying approval by a special committee of wine-tasters.

1964 H. JOHNSON *Encycl. Wine* 290 System of labelling certain Burgundy wines... Upon payment of a certain sum per bottle, these wines may carry a special, rather elaborate Tastevin label. **1968** *Times* 3 Sept. 20/5 An invitation to attend the Tastevin banquet at the Château Clos de Vougeot. **1977** W. M. SPACKMAN *Armful of Warm Girl* 109 This was a Tastevin bottling which he'd never found before outside of France.

tastily (ˈteɪstɪlɪ), *adv.* [f. TASTY *a.* + -LY[2].] In a tasty manner; tastefully.

1799 R. WARNER *Walk* (1800) 80 The slope..is tastily managed and appropriately ornamented. **1809** PINKNEY *Trav. France* 24 The fruits were in plates very tastily painted in landscape. **1845** M. J. HIGGINS *Ess.* (1875) 216 Tastily but inexpensively dressed.

tastiness (ˈteɪstɪnɪs). [f. as prec. + -NESS.] The quality or state of being tasty.

1882 HOWELLS in *Longm. Mag.* I. 44 Lexington has escaped the ravages alike of 'tastiness' and of enterprise. **1902** MARY E. MANN *Fields Dulditch* iii. 39 He ain't to comparison in tastiness to th' gage.

tasting (ˈteɪstɪŋ), *vbl. sb.* [-ING[1].]

1. The action of the verb TASTE.

a. In a general sense, trying, testing; †esp., in early use, touching, feeling; also the sense of touch (*obs.*).

13.. *K. Alis.* 4031 (Bodl. MS.) It is ywrite þat euery þing Hym self sheweþ in þe tastyng. *c* **1375** *Sc. Leg. Saints* vi. (*Thomas*) 407 Wittis four,..sycht, heryngе, gustyne, tastyne. *c* **1430** *Pilgr. Lyf Manhode* I. cxxi. (1869) 63 Alle tastinges generalliche is vnderstonde bi the hondes. **1711**, **1850** [see TASTE *v.* 2 b].

b. Now, the action of TASTE *v.* II; †also formerly, the faculty or sense, and the quality of a substance so apprehended: = TASTE *sb.*[1] 4, 5 (*obs.*).

1390 GOWER *Conf.* III. 33, I take of love my fiedinge Withoute tastinge or fielinge. **1426** AUDELAY *Poems* 7 Thi heryng, thi seyng, as I the schewe, Thi sy3t, thi smellyng, here be iij. Thi touchyng, thi tastyng, here v. ther be. *c* **1460** J. RUSSELL *Bk. Nurture* 1199 Credence is vsed, and tastynge, for drede of poysenynge. **1530** PALSGR. 279/2 Tastyng with the mouthe, *gouster*. **1774** GOLDSM. *Nat. Hist.* (1776) II. 183 The sense most nearly allied to smelling is that of tasting. **1841-4** EMERSON *Ess.*, *Exper.* Wks. (Bohn) I. 178 Intellectual tasting of life will not supersede muscular activity. **1898** 'IAN MACLAREN' in *Woman at Home* Oct. 56/1 If Thomas takes to tasting [i.e. tippling, drinking]..it's all over with him.

2. a. quasi-*concr.* A small portion taken to try the taste; a taste (esp. of spirituous liquor). Also *fig.*

1526 *Pilgr. Perf.* (1531) 49 For they be but tastynges, shadowes, or tokens of the gloryous fruytes to come. **1830** CUNNINGHAM *Brit. Paint.* II. 69 He gave them a tasting of his spirit in two or three sarcastic sentences. **1893** J. SKINNER *Autobiog. Metaphysician* vii. 48 He got a glass from Mr. Reed and another tasting from another neighbour.

b. A gathering for the purpose of tasting and comparing various kinds of drink, usu. wine. See also *wine-tasting* s.v. WINE *sb.*[1] 9.

1959 I. ROSS *Image Merchants* viii. 128 'Cognac and coffee' tastings which Kaduson persuaded leading hotels.. to hold. **1963** *Harper's Bazaar* Feb. 22/3 The Lebègue tastings usher in the autumn wine season. **1977** T. HEALD *Just Desserts* i. 23 It's their annual tasting..for one or two of the better known wine and food writers. **1978** *Times* 4 Mar. 10/7 The Malmaison Wine Club..holds sit-down tastings, which are often attended by wine trade trainees.

3. *attrib.* and *Comb.*, as ***tasting party, power, room***; **tasting-bone**, a bone put into the broth to give it a taste or flavour; **tasting-knife**, a cheese-taster (see TASTER 3 b); **tasting-order**, an order to visit stores of wine, etc., and to taste or sample them.

1850 MRS. CARLYLE *Let. to Carlyle* 8 Sept., It [Kingsley's *Alton Locke*] seems to me..a mere..broth of *Morning-chronicle-ism*, in which you play the part of the *tasting-bone of Poverty Row. **1757** H. WALPOLE tr. *Hentzner's Trav.* 52 At last came an unmarried Lady..and along with her a married one, bearing a *tasting-knife. **1859** SALA *Gas-light & D.* xiv, Quite gone in liquor and overcome with the *tasting-orders of years. **1978** *Times* 4 Mar. 10/3 The '*tasting parties' offered by many [wine] firms..are social rather than studious occasions. **1599** DAVIES *Immort. Soul* ccxv, Therefore the Soule doth vse the *tasting power. *a* **1966** 'M. NA GOPALEEN' *Best of Myles* (1977) 122 Gallantry and distinguished conduct in the [ice-cream] *tasting room. **1970** *Country Life* 1 Oct. 837/3 It is distinctly cool..in the subterranean tasting room where red and white ..wines are sampled.

'tasting, *ppl. a.* [-ING[2].] That tastes.

1598 [implied in next]. **1907** *Contemp. Rev.* Oct. Lit. Suppl. 2 The tasting sense is soon ruined.

'tastingly, *adv.* [f. prec. + -LY[2].] In a tasting manner.

1598 FLORIO, *Saporitamente*, sauourly, smackingly, tastingly, hungerly. **1894** BARING-GOULD *Kitty Alone* II. 150 The fire..sending the tips of its flames tastingly towards him.

†**'tastive**, *a. Obs. rare*⁻¹. [f. TASTE *sb.*[1] or *v.*: see -IVE.] Having the quality of taste; sapid.

1644 DIGBY *Nat. Bodies* xxvii. §6. 246 The same thinges that yield also tastiue particles.

tastle, obs. form of TASSEL.

tasto ('tasto). *Mus.* [It., = touch, key.]

a. The key of a piano or the finger-board of a stringed instrument. **b.** Phr. ***sul tasto*** [lit. 'over the finger-board']: a direction in a musical score that the stringed instrument is to be played with the bow over the finger-board; ***tasto solo***: a direction that the bass notes are to be played alone without any harmony.

1740 J. GRASSINEAU *Mus. Dict.* 268 *Tasto*, the touch or part of an instrument whereon, or by means of which its notes are made to sound, be it on the neck, as lutes..; or the front of organs. **1772** W. TANS'UR *Elements of Mus.* v. 221 *Tasto*, the Touches or Keys of Organs &c. *Tasto solo*, to strike such Sounds till other Words, or Parts come on. **1876** STAINER & BARRETT *Dict. Mus. Terms* 421/2 *Tasto*,..(1) A key of a pianoforte. (2) The touch of a pianoforte or organ. **1889** GROVE *Dict. Mus.* IV. 63/2 'Tasto solo', the key alone, is in old music written over those portions of the bass or continuo part in which the mere notes were to be played by the accompanyist, without the chords or harmonies founded on them. **1946** E. BLOM *Everyman's Dict. Mus.* 600/1 *Sul tasto* (It.), a direction indicating that a passage of string mus. is to be played with the bow over the finger-board. **1974** *Sci. Amer.* Jan. 93/2 Farthest from the bridge..the timbre has the gentle character that composers seek by designating *sul tasto*: 'bow over the fingerboard'. **1980** *Early Music* Apr. 150/2 In Rameau's day the single harpsichordist either did not play during the purely orchestral music and choruses or at most played the bass line only, either *tasto solo* (at pitch) or *all'unisono* (doubling an octave above or below).

tasty ('teɪstɪ), *a.* Now *colloq.* and *dial.* Also †**tastey.** [f. TASTE *sb.*[1] + -Y.]

1. a. Pleasing to the taste; appetizing, savoury.

1617 HIERON *Wks.* II. 203 Sowre herbs, with which that tastie meat, the paschall lambe..was to be eaten. **1795** in *Spirit Pub. Jrnls.* IV. 220 A tasty bird, that pheasant. **1849** CURZON *Visits Monast.* 144 A famous pie, or pilau, with rice and a tasty sauce. *a* **1862** BUCKLE *Misc. Wks.* (1872) I. 381 The arts of compounding a pleasant pudding or combining a tasty pie.

b. *fig.* Pleasant, agreeable, attractive.

1796 MRS. M. ROBINSON *Angelina* III. 179 'Here you are, my tasty ones!' exclaimed Sir Edward. 'Why, you played us a trick'. **1821** CLARE *Vill. Minstr.* I. 201 Pausing o'er each tasty flower. **1899** R. WHITEING *No. 5 John St.* vii. 61 'Nice and tastey,' observes my friend..as he points to a leg that seems to fear nothing on earth..not even Lord Campbell's Act. **1976** *Sounds* 11 Dec. 41/5, I couldn't help wishing Can'd..pump out a tasty three minute song like their last single,..'I Want More'.

c. (See quots.). *slang.*

1975 *Observer* 11 May 2/7 'I got the impression that he with a bit tasty' (i.e., had a criminal record). **1980** *Daily Mail* 21 Mar. 7/2 A 'tasty villain' (a known criminal).

2. a. Characterized by or displaying good taste; tasteful, elegant. Now *rare.*

1762 GOLDSM. *Cit. World* lxxvii, [The silk] is at once rich, tasty, and quite the thing. **1784** *New Spectator* No. 16. 5 [Ranelagh] This region of taste was visited on Friday evening, by a great number of tasty people indeed. **1813** J. C. HOBHOUSE *Journey* (ed. 2) 501 The head-dress of the younger girls is tasty; their hair falls down their backs in profusion. **1821** COLERIDGE in *Blackw. Mag.* X. 254, I wish I could find a more familiar word than *aesthetic*... To be sure, there is *tasty*; but that has been long ago emasculated for all unworthy uses by milliners, tailors, and..dandies. **1862** THACKERAY *Philip* xxiv, My..waistcoat..is a much more tasty thing than these gaudy ready-made articles.

b. Fastidious. *rare.*

1905 A. ADAMS *Outlet* 102 The two strangers were rather tasty, but Siringo ate ravenously.

3. *Comb.*, as ***tasty-looking.***

1867 F. FRANCIS *Angling* x. (1880) 375 This is a very tasty-looking fly. **1888** F. COWPER *Capt. of Wight* (1889) 50 Some tasty-looking rolls, fresh butter, and cheese.

tasul, tasyl, -yll, -ylle, obs. ff. TEASEL.

tat (tæt), *sb.*[1] *slang.* Also **tatt.** [Origin unascertained.] **1. a.** *pl.* **tats**: Dice; *esp.* false or loaded dice. **b.** *Comb.* as **tat-box**, a dice-box; **tat-monger**, a sharper who uses false dice. See also TATSMAN.

1688 SHADWELL *Sqr. Alsatia* I, *H*... Pox o' the Tatts for me! I believe they put the Doctor upon me. *B.* Tatts and Doctor! what's that? *S.* The tools of Sharpers, false dice. *Ibid.*, He was but a Sharper, a tat-monger. *a* **1700** B. E. *Dict. Cant. Crew*, *Tatts*, false Dice. *a* **1809** J. PALMER *Like Master* (1811) I. xv. 215 He ransacks every house in St. James's parish, where the tats are at work, to punish those for what he, himself, practised. **1812** J. H. VAUX *Flash Dict.*, *Tatt-box*, a dice-box. **1887** HENLEY *Villon's Straight Tip* ii, Rattle the tats, or mark the spot.

2. *pl.* **tats, tatts.** Teeth; now usu. with ref. to a set of false teeth. *slang* (chiefly *Austral.*).

1919 W. H. DOWNING *Digger Dialects* 49 *Tats*, teeth. **1935** A. J. POLLOCK *Underworld Speaks* 119/2 *Tats*, teeth. **1962** *Coast to Coast 1961-62* 131 He'd lost his 'tatts' in a brawl in Townsville the night before we left Australia. **1976** *Express* (Austral.) 3 Nov. 2/3 Talking of 'tats' a dental standards official said false teeth for animals are nothing new.

tāt (tɑːt), *sb.*[2] *East Ind.* Also **taut.** [Hindī *ṭāṭ* a strip of very thick hemp-canvas, about 10 inches wide, of which several are sewn together to make a mat or screen.]

a. Coarse canvas made from various fibres, esp. jute, and used as sacking.

1820 *Trans. Lit. Soc. Bombay* III. 244 (Y.) Made into coarse cloth taut, by the Brinjaries and people who use pack bullocks, for making bags (gonies) for holding grain, &c. **1858** SIMMONDS *Dict. Trade*, *Tat*, a name in India for cloth made from the fibre of the *Corchorus olitorius*. Hence **1864** in WEBSTER; and in later Dicts.

b. In tea-drying: a tray or shelf, freq. of hessian, on which green tea leaves are spread to wither.

1922 H. J. MOPPETT *Tea Manuf.* 14 Withering tats must present a smooth even surface free from corrugations or pockets. *Ibid.* 15 Insufficient tat space is a bad fault. **1935** W. H. UKERS *All about Tea* II. 515/1 *Tat*, a shelf made of wire or Hessian..on which green tea leaves are spread for withering. **1957** *Encycl. Brit.* XXI. 863/2 After plucking, the leaf is withered by being spread on bamboo trays in the sun, or on withering tats within doors. **1958** T. EDEN *Tea* xiii. 150 Some factories have 'mobile tats'. They are slung from pulleys travelling on overhead rails such that each individual bank of tats can be removed from its internal location and brought to a loading and weighing platform at any time.

tat, tatt, *sb.*[3] *Anglo-Ind.* Short for TATTY *sb.*

1812 MARIA GRAHAM *Jrnl. Resid. India* 125 (Y.) During the hot winds tats (a kind of mat), made of the root of the koosa grass,..are placed against the doors and windows. **1837** *Lett. fr. Madras* (1843) 77, I have a tatt, or thick mat, at my window, which excludes the sun, and men sit outside pouring water on it all day, so that the wind..blows always cooled through the water.

tat, tatt, *sb.*[4] *Anglo-Ind.* Short for TATTOO *sb.*[3], a native pony of India.

c **1840** in Parker *Bole Ponjis* (1851) II. 215 With its bright brass patent axles, and its little hog maned tatts. **1845** STOCQUELER *Handbk. Brit. India* (1854) 109 The pony (familiarly called *tat*—corruption of the native name for the small animal, *tattoo*). **1891** *Blackw. Mag.* May 684 Cantering his tat up to the door.

tat, *sb.*[5] *slang.* Also **tatt.** [Origin uncertain: cf. OE. *tættec* a rag, and TATTY *a.*[1]]

a. A rag; also (in *sing.*), poorly made or tasteless clothes. Hence, a shabby person, a slut.

1839 [see POSH *sb.*[2] 1]. **1851** MAYHEW *Lond. Labour* I. 424/2 I'll tell you about the tat (rag) gatherers; buying rags they call it. **1882** *Sydney Slang Dict.* 9/2 The paper makers get the tats. **1936** N. COWARD *To-Night at 8.30* I. 93 You should have seen the company: a couple of old tats got up as Elizabethan pages. **1947** N. MARSH *Final Curtain* iv. 53 Do they think it's any catch living in a mausoleum with a couple of old tats? **1972** D. GODDARD *Blimey!* (1974) iv. 43 King's Road beckons the well-heeled traveller into a cloud-cuckoo land of high-priced tat and gear. **1977** M. DRABBLE *Ice Age* II. 212 She was dressed..in a horrible collection of tat—a long shiny maroon skirt, a baggy flowered blouse, a grey cardigan, and a green cardigan on top of that.

b. Rubbish, junk, worthless goods. Also *transf.* and *fig.*

1951 W. SANSOM *Face of Innocence* iv. 55 He was talking of his business in Georgian and early Victorian objets d'oeil. He called it tat. **1958** A. WILSON *Middle Age of Mrs Eliot* II. 151 It was filled..with a jumble of pleasing, valuable antique furniture and hideous, worthless bric-a-brac... 'I like tatt,' he had said. **1967** N. MARSH *Death at Dolphin* ii. 40 A small shop in Walton Street where they sold what he described as: 'Very superior tatt. Jacobean purses, stomachers and the odd codpiece.' **1970** 'D. HALLIDAY' *Dolly & Cookie Bird* iv. 52 Are they selling tat medals as well? **1971** D. LEES *Rainbow Conspiracy* iii. 38 Oh no! Not that load of old tat. We threw it out at afternoon [news] conference. **1976** *New Musical Express* 12 Feb. 26/3 That long deleted album..sounds like a heap of prissy irrelevant whimsical lysergic tat with Disney lyrics. **1981** *Times Lit. Suppl.* 18 Sept. 1060/1 New ways of getting the johns to spend their money on previously unsellable old tat.

tat, *sb.*[6] Also **tatt**, (*erron.*) **taut, tawt.** [Origin obscure: cf. TATTY *a.*[1]] (See quot. 1887.)

1887 JAMIESON *Suppl.*, *Tat, taut, tawt*, a tangle, matted tuft or lock of wool or hair. **1922** JOYCE *Ulysses* 423 A slut combs out the tatts from the hair of a scrofulous child. **1968** *Saturday Night* Mar. 34/3 The hair was full of tats so it was easy to find places to stick the flowers.

tat, *sb.*[7], in phr. *tit for tat*: see TIT.

Tat (tɑːt), *sb.*[8] Also **Tât.** [a. Russ., from Turkish.] (A member of) an agricultural people perh. related to the Tajiks and living in Azerbaijan and Dagestan; also, the Iranian language spoken by this people.

1834 A. BURNES *Trav. Bokhara* II. 265 We find as great a variety among the citizens of Toorkistan as in the subdivisions of the Tartars. The aborigines of the country are the Tajiks or Tats. **1888** *Encycl. Brit.* XXIII. 25/1 The Tajaks are known as Tâts on the west side of the Caspian. **1939** H. FIELD *Contrib. Anthropol. Iran* iii. 157 While.. these elements cannot be considered pure Iranian there remain the Talych (91,000), Tat (74,000) and Persian (50,000), all of which are clearly Iranian dialects. **1951** W. K. MATTHEWS *Lang. U.S.S.R.* vii. 104 The Tat of Azerbaijan, north of Baku, is like Talysh, a divergent variety of Persian. **1981** *Jewish Chron.* 24 Apr. 6/5 A Tat, a mountain Jew from Daghestan in the Caucasus, Mr Irmiya Rabayev, 31, has been a refusenik for seven years.

tat, *v.*[1] [Origin uncertain: ? echoic; cf. *tap, pat.*] *trans.* **a.** To touch lightly, pat, tap. *dial.* †**b.** A euphemism for To flog. *Obs. slang.*

1607 DEKKER & WEBSTER *Northw. Ho* II. i, Come tit me, come tat me, come throw a kiss at me. **1812** J. H. VAUX *Flash Dict.*, *Tat*, to flog, or scourge. **1847-78** HALLIWELL, *Tat*... (3) To touch gently. *Hants.*

tat, *v.*[2] Also **tatt.** [Origin unknown: cf. TATTING *sb.*] **a.** *intr.* To do tatting. **b.** *trans.* To make by tatting.

[**1842**: see TATTING *sb.*] **1882** MRS. ALEXANDER in *Belgravia* July 104 Winnie produced her tatting, and applied herself to it... At the mention of his mother Laura involuntarily clasped her hands, and Winnie ceased to tatt. **1905** MRS. E. GLYN *Viciss. Evangeline* 123 They knitted ties and crocheted comforters, and one even tatted.

tat, *v.*[3] *slang.* [f. TAT *sb.*[5]] *intr.* To gather rags.

1851 MAYHEW *Lond. Labour* I. 417/1 He goes tatting and billy-hunting in the country (gathering rags and buying old metal). **1910** *Nottingham Guardian* 2 June, The prisoner.. told the police that he came in possession of the lead when he went round 'tatting'.

tat, *v.*[4] *Sc.* and *north. dial.* [Goes with TAT *sb.*[6]] *trans.* and *intr.* To tangle, or make tangled or matted: see TAUT *v.*

1829 BROCKETT *N.C. Gloss.* (ed. 2), *Tat*, to mat, to entangle. **1887** in JAMIESON *Suppl.* **1894** *Northumb. Gloss.*, *Tat*, to mat together.

ta-ta (ˌtɑː'tɑː, 'tætɑː, tæ'tɑː), *int.*, *sb.*, and *a.* Also **tata, ta ta**, etc. **A.** *int.* A nursery expression for 'Good-bye'; now also in gen. colloq. use. Cf. TATTY-BYE *int.* and *T.T.F.N.* s.v. T 6.

1823 S. HUTCHINSON *Let.* Sept.-Oct. (1954) 261 Baby I believe has not learnt any new words since Mrs M. wrote last, but she has the old ones very perfect—'Gone'—'Ta ta'—'By bye'. **1837** DICKENS *Pickw.* xxvii, 'Tar, tar, Sammy', replied his father. **1878** F. C. BURNAND *Strapmore* i. 15 Ta-ta, little one *très cher*! Bye-bye. **1891** MRS. WALFORD *Mischief of Monica* III. 171 'Ta-ta'; and the speaker slipped behind backs and vanished. **1901** 'M. FRANKLIN' *My Brilliant Career* xxxii. 272 (*heading*) Ta-Ta to Barney's Gap. **1922** T. S. ELIOT *Waste Land* II. 26 Goonight Bill. Goonight Lou. Goonight May. Goonight. Ta ta. Goonight. **1934** —— *Rock* i. 69 Well, tar, tar, boys. **1949** G. B. SHAW *Buoyant Billions* IV. 52, I must go now to see about Father's lunch. Tata. **1951** R. BRADDON *Naked Island* II. vi. 153 'All right, Mr. McLeod, fall out.'.. 'Ta-ta, Rod—see you in Australia.' **1960** L. REID BANKS *L-Shaped Room* xxiii. 297 Charlie'll come up in a few minutes and see how you're getting on. Tata for now. **1983** P. INCHBALD *Short Break in Venice* vii. 68 Sod off!.. We'll talk later... Tata.

B. as *sb.* A nursery or playful term. **a.** A walk or outing. Also *fig.* **b.** A hat, bonnet, etc.

a. 1886 J. SULLY *Teacher's Handbk. Psychol.* x. 185 A child of eighteen months will mentally rehearse a series of experiences, as those of a walk: 'Go tata, see geegee.' **1912** D. H. LAWRENCE *Let.* 28 Mar. (1962) I. 104 In the evening Diddler took me a tat-tar, and of course got lost. **1930** —— *Nettles* 9 Want to go a little tattah? So it shall... If it's good! .. It shall go a tattah with its Auntie In a motor. **1958** 'N. BLAKE' *Penknife in my Heart* iii. 45 Sharp at 10.45 every night.. he takes his dog out for a ta-ta. **1969** J. WAINWRIGHT *Take-Over Men* vii. 121 They're a con man's dream. They're taken for a ta-ta every market day.

b. *c* **1910** F. W. LEIGH in *Francis & Day's Album of Famous Old Songs* (1956) VIII, Put on your tat-ta, little girlie. **1912** C. MACKENZIE *Carnival* iii. 21 The tying on of her 'ta-ta'—at first a frilled bonnet, later on a rakish Tam o' Shanter. **1920** 'K. MANSFIELD' *Lett. to J. M. Murry* (1951) 506, I put on my ta-ta. **1949** M. STEEN *Twilight on Floods* IV. viii. 644 How about having the ta-tas ready to show her?

C. *attrib.* or as *adj.* ***ta-ta theory*** (Philol.), the theory that language originated in an attempt to imitate the body's gestures with the vocal organs.

1930 J. R. FIRTH *Speech* i. 7 According to the *ta-ta* theory of Sir Richard Paget, the tongue makes the same gesture while saying *ta-ta* or *hither* as would be made by the hand with similar intention. **1939** L. H. GRAY *Foundations of Lang.* 40 Language has been traced.. by others to sounds produced by the vocal organs when half-consciously imitating the movements of the body in performing some activity (the ta-ta theory). **1972** HARTMANN & STORK *Dict. Lang. & Linguistics* 160/1 R. Paget (1869–1955) claimed that language comes from the combination of certain gestures and tongue movements (*ta-ta theory*).

‖**tatami** (ta'tami). Also 7 **tatamee, tattami.** [Jap.] A rush-covered straw mat which is the usual floor-covering in Japan and the size of which (approx. six feet by three feet) functions as a standard unit in room measurement.

1614 R. WICKHAM in *Trans. Asiatic Soc. Japan* (1898) XXVI. 209, I.. made Tatamee of Meaco 15⅝. *Ibid.*, I sold it per 14 Tatamees at 120 Mas per tatamee. **1616** R. COCKS *Diary* 23 Jan. (1883) I. 103, 20 *tattamis* for Matingas howse. **1625** PURCHAS *Pilgrimes* II. v. 326 Hee caused at Ozaca a Hall to bee erected, with a thousand Tatami (very elegant mats). **1880** I. L. BIRD *Unbeaten Tracks in Japan* I. ix. 89 Japanese house-mats, *tatami*, are as neat, refined, and soft a covering for the floor as the finest Axminster carpet. **1886** A. C. MACLAY *Budget of Lett. from Japan* 42 *Tatamis* are heavy padded mats about seven feet long, three feet wide, and about two inches thick. They are the only covering that the Japanese ever use for their floors... They are manufactured of soft rushes, and are bordered with silken edges. **1909** *Cent. Dict.* Suppl., *Tatami*.. 2. A Japanese measure of surface, that of a mat 6 shaku in length by 3 shaku in width, or nearly 6 feet by 3 feet. **1924** *Public Opinion* 28 Nov. 527/2 It is a strict rule that tatamis must be kept clean. **1933** R. V. C. BODLEY *Japanese Omelette* xii. 116 The dining room floor, instead of being matted with *tatami* as in Japan, was made of some kind of oilcloth. **1957** *New Yorker* 23 Nov. 120/2 *Tatami* cover the floors of nearly all Japanese houses. **1960** B. LEACH *Potter in Japan* iii. 68 In twenty years' time, won't the Japanese room with 'tatami' (the thick compressed straw matting) become a luxury as the foreign style is today? **1974** *Encycl. Brit. Micropædia* IX. 837/3 The standardized size of the mat has created an important modular unit in the development of Japanese architecture; for example the *shōji* .. are approximately as high as the tatami are long. **1976** P. QUENNELL *Marble Foot* v. 182 No less beautiful.. were the *tatami* that lined our floors, long greenish slabs, that turn with age a dull gold, of finely woven rush-matting. **1981** G. MACBETH *Kind of Treason* ix. 92 He relaxed on the *tatami* and spoke with polite approval of the cousin's *tsuba*.

2. Freq. *attrib.*, as ***tatami mat, matting, room.*** Also *Comb.*, as ***tatami-floored, -matted*** adjs.

1947 J. BERTRAM *Shadow of War* VI. 200 Each man had some two and a half feet by six feet of *tatami* mat. **1962** *Times* 25 Jan. 13/4 The man who comes to lay the *tatami* matting in his house. **1979** S. COE in I. Webb *Compl. Guide to Flower & Foliage Arrangement* xvii. 231/2 The room.. is quite small, about 3 × 3 m (10 × 10 ft) or four and a half *tatami* mats. **1979** *Jrnl. R. Soc. Arts* Nov. 749/1 The interior spaces provide everything that the harsh exterior rejects: complex flowing geometries, traditional tatami room, lush furnishing and peaceful, controlled nature. **1980** J. MELVILLE *Chrysanthemum Chain* 127 The tatami-matted floor of Yamamoto's room. **1981** C. POTOK *Bk. of Lights* (1982) v. 162 He had a fish dinner in a lovely tatami-floored Japanese restaurant. **1982** *Nature* 20 May 181/1 Thus the popular, but erroneous, Japanese view that they have grown taller by adopting the habit of sitting on Western chairs rather than sitting with legs folded underneath the body on a *tatami* mat.

tataow, obs. f. TATTOO *v.*[2]

Tatar: see TARTAR[2].

tatarwagge: see TATTER *sb.*[1] 3.

tatch, tatche: see TACHE.

tatchy, dial. f. TETCHY.

tate (tet, tɪət), *sb.*[1] *Sc.* and *north. dial.* Forms: 7–9 **tait,** 8 **teat, tet, tett,** 6– **tate.** [Origin obscure; prob. Norse: cf. Icel. *tæta* to tear to shreds, to tease, *tæta* a shred; also, fluff of wool, etc., a particle of anything.]

1. A small tuft or lock of hair, wool, or other fibrous material, consisting of only a few fibres; a small handful of grass, hay, or corn.

1513 DOUGLAS *Æneis* VI. v. 11 Apon his chin feill cannos haris gray, Lyart feltat tatis. **1570** LEVINS *Manip.* 39/14 A Tate, *fibra.* **1618** *Trial Marg. Barclay*, etc. in Scott *Demonol.* ix. (1831) 318 He was found.. strangled and hanged [in his cell].. with a *tait* of hemp, or a string supposed to have been his garter. *a* **1774** FERGUSSON *Iron Kirk Bell* Poems (1845) 43 Auld Reekie's childer now Maun staup their lugs wi' teats o' wool Thy sound to bang. **1782** BURNS *Death of Mailie* 34 Wi' teats o' hay an' ripps o' corn. **1818** SCOTT *Hrt. Midl.* xxii, There's a chield can spin a muckle pirn out of a wee tait of tow! **1856** R. SIMPSON *Covenanters of South* 332 The wool.. was to be found here and there in handfuls, or in tates, as they are called, lying on the heath. [In *Eng. Dial. Dict.* Northumb., to N. Lanc. and Yorks.]

2. *gen.* A small piece; a particle or morsel (of anything); in quot. 1722 *advb.* = 'a bit', a little.

With *tate* of meal, etc., cf. the common Sc. *a hair* of meal, of salt, etc. in same sense.

1722 RAMSAY *Three Bonnets* I. 143 Observing Jouk a wee tate tipsy. **1805** G. M'INDOE *Poems, Million of Potatoes*, But to disperse them a' in taits, Through different hands, at different rates,.. I ne'er could wi' be troubled. **1891** H. HALIBURTON *Ochil Idylls* 68 O' winter snaw there's but a tate remainin'. *Mod. Sc.* No a tate o' meit was left.

†**tate, tath,** *sb.*[2] *Obs.* Also 7 **tathe.** [In Irish *taite*; but held to be a borrowed word: cf. Joyce *Ir. Names of Places* I. 246. Some think it derived from prec.] A measure of land formerly used in Ireland, equal to 60 Irish acres.

1607 DAVIES *Lett. Earl Salisb.* i. Tracts (1787) 229 Every ballybetagh.. containeth sixteen taths; every tath containeth three-score English acres or thereabouts. *a* **1660** *Contemp. Hist. Irel.* (Ir. Archæol. Soc.) I. 339 Every ballyboe, quarter, pole, or tathe of land. *Ibid.* 349 Twoe tates of the three tates of Ballagh. **1842** S. C. HALL *Ireland* II. 354 The lesser divisions were known by the various appellations of quarters, half quarters, ballyboes, gneeves, tates, &c. **1861** REEVES in *Proc. Roy. Ir. Acad.* VII. 484.

†**tate,** *a. Sc. Obs. rare*$^{-1}$. ? variant of TAIT *a.* in sense 'wanton, brisk, untamed'.

c **1375** *Sc. Leg. Saints* iv. (*Jacobus*) 328 For scho had bulis wilde and tate, þat scho nocht trewit mycht ȝokkit be In carte, na wane, be ony degre.

tate, obs. form of TEAT.

tater ('teɪtə(r)). Also **tator, tatur.** [Dial. variant of POTATO *sb.* 2. Cf. TATIE; TATTIE.]

1. = POTATO *sb.* 2.

1759 L. WOOD *Jrnl.* 27 May in *Essex Inst. Hist. Coll.* (1882) XIX. 65 We travelled.. 9 miles to Capt Curtises and there we Dined upon codfish and taters. **1815** *Sporting Mag.* XLV. 2 A piece of taters or a few turnips. **1833** MARRYAT *P. Simple* xiv, Officers who boil their 'tators in a cabbage-net hanging in the ship's coppers. **1848** THACKERAY *Bk. Snobs* xiv, Baked 'taturs. **1884** *Gd. Words* May 333/2 The other man.. plied a vigorous trade in 'taters and trotters. **1911** F. H. BURNETT *Secret Garden* xxiv. 252 Anything'll grow for him. His 'taters and cabbages is twice th' size of anyone else's. **1939** F. THOMPSON *Lark Rise* i. 11 Mother spent hours boiling up the 'little taturs'. **1943** W. STEVENS in O. Williams *New Poems 1943* 236 (*title of poem*) No possum, no sop, no taters. **1977** *New Yorker* 27 June 76/3, I et 3 lbs. of taters.

2. *attrib.* and *Comb.* ***tater-trap*** *slang* = *tattie-trap* s.v. TATTIE 2.

1845 W. T. PORTER *Big Bear Arkansas* 22 Them ar 'Indian mounds' ar tater Rills. **1846** *Swell's Night Guide* 133/2 *Tater trap*, the mummer, mouth. **1847** J. R. LOWELL *Biglow Papers* 1st Ser. iii. 34 He draws his furrer ez straight ez he can, An' into nobody's tater-patch pokes. *c* **1869** TAYLOR & DUBOURG in M. R. Booth *Eng. Plays of 19th Cent.* (1973) III. 303 The coal and 'tatur shed where he worked all the week. **1876** I. BANKS *Manchester Man* III. i. 12 Shut up his tater-trap fur him! **1890** P. H. EMERSON *Wild Life* 38, I adwised them fellers at the pub ter keep their tater-traps shut. **1902** W. N. HARBEN *Abner Daniel* 198, I got up on the head of a tater-barrel behind the counter. **1917** 'H. H. RICHARDSON' *Fortunes R. Mahony* I. ii. 20 From the back of the hall came the curt request to him to shut his 'tater-trap'. **1930** *Dialect Notes* VI. 89 *Tater jack*, variety of fermented liquor, made in [lumber] camp from potatoes.

tater, obs. form of TATTER.

tath (taθ), **tathe** (teθ), *sb. Sc.* and *dial.* Also 5 **taht,** 9 **taith, teath.** [a. ON. *tað* dung, manure, whence *taða* fem. the manured home-field, hay from this field, *teðja* to dung, manure. In Norw. and Sw. dial. *tad* dung.]

1. The dung of cattle, sheep, etc. left for manure on land on which they have been pastured.

1492 *Act. Dom. Conc.* (1839) 289/2 Þe saidis personis sall content & pay.. for þe wanting of þe taht & fulȝe of þe said nolt & scheip. **1545** *Acct.* in *Paston Lett.* VIII. (B.M.), Itm. for the tathe of ccvj Shepe at Beekham, due att Myddesomer.. lxvj s. vj d. **1611** SPEED *Theat. Gt. Brit.* xviii. (1614) 35/1 These heaths by the compasture of the sheepe (which we call Tathe) are made so rich [etc.]. **1854** *Jrnl. R. Agric. Soc.* XV. I. 100 To mix the teath with the soil. **1867** *Ibid.* III. II. 534 [Geese] eat far cleaner than sheep, and, in fact, leave nothing but their 'taith', which answers admirably as a preparation for the next wheat-crop.

b. (See quot. 1701.)

a **1641** SPELMAN *Icenia* in *Posth. Wks.* (1698) 162 Stercorationem *Tath*.. appellant. **1701** *Cowell's Interpr.*, *Tath*, in Norfolk and Suffolk the Lord of each Mannor had the Privilege of having their Tenants Flocks of Sheep brought at Night upon their own Demesne Ground, there to be foulded for the benefit of their Dung, which liberty of so improving their Land is called *Tath.*

2. *transf.* Rich or rank grass growing where the land has been manured in this way, or, by extension, where it has been flooded (***water-tath***). ? *Obs.*

1807 *Ess. Highl. Soc.* III. 468 All grasses which are remarkably rank and luxuriant, are called *tath*, by the stock farmers, who distinguish two kinds of it; *water tath*, proceeding from excess of moisture, and *nolt tath*, the produce of dung.

3. ***sea-tath***: a sea-bottom covered with sediment.

1796 *Statist. Acc. Scotl.* XVII. 70 Oysters are found on a strong clay bottom, on rocks and stones, and sometimes, though but thinly, in what is called by the fishers *sea tathe.* These last are of a very inferior quality.

4. *attrib.* and *Comb.*, as **tath-field, -fold,** a field or fold in which cattle or sheep are confined in order to manure it.

1752 MACCOLL in *Scots Mag.* (1753) Aug. 394/1 They were harrowing the tath-field. **1795** *Statist. Acc. Scotl.* XIV. 143 The spots thus manured are called tath-fields. **1825** JAMIESON, *Tath-fauld, tath-faud*, a fold in which cattle are shut up during night, to manure the ground with their dung.

tath, obs. f. *taketh*: see TAKE *v.* A. 3 b β.

tath, tathe, variants of TATE *sb.*[2]

tathe, tath, *v. Sc.* and *dial.* Also 5 **taþin,** 8 **taith,** 8–9 **teath.** [f. TATH *sb.*: cf. ON. *teðja* to manure.]

1. *trans.* To manure (land) by turning sheep or cattle upon it (usually said of the cattle); also, by extension, by flooding it (***to water-tathe***).

c **1440** *Promp. Parv.* 487/2 Tayin [*v.r.* tathyn] londe wythe schepys donge,.. *rudero*,.. *stercoro.* **1628** COKE *On Litt.* 57 As if I lend to one my Sheepe, to tathe his land. **1743** MAXWELL *Sel. Trans. Soc. Improv. Agric. Scot.* 38 It has.. been in Pasture these twelve Years... It is well tathed. **1799** J. ROBERTSON *Agric. Perth* 64 The out-fields lying farthest from the townships, were taithed or dunged by confining the cattle in folds, over night, during summer and autumn, upon that particular portion.. which was to be ploughed next spring. **1808** J. WALKER *Econ. Hist. Hebr. & Highl. Scot.* (1812) I. 167 There is yet another way in which the sediment of water may be applied as a manure,.. this is, by .. Water-tathing. *Ibid.* 168 When a field has been water-tathed.. but for one winter, the growth of grass upon it is more early. **1843** *Jrnl. R. Agric. Soc.* IV. I. 122 Teathing the barley-stubble which is intended for turnips will cause the anbury.

2. *intr.* Of cattle, etc.: To drop dung *upon* land so as to manure it.

1743 MAXWELL *Sel. Trans. Soc. Improv. Agric. Scot.* 123 The Dung of Horses is not proper for sandy Grounds, being too hot, as may be observed from the Ground they tathe upon in Summer.

Hence **'tathing** *vbl. sb.* (also *concr.*).

c **1440** *Promp. Parv.* 487/2 Taynge [*v.r.* tathing] of lond, *ruderacio.* **1529** *Anc. Deed* A. 13557 (P.R.O.) To fynd the tenauntz.. tathyng to ther londes. **1792** *Statist. Acc. Scot.* II. 404 A priest.. who had a right to every seventh acre of Ladifron, and to the tathing (dung as left on the ground) every seventh night. **1793** *Ibid.* VI. 268.

Tatianist ('teɪʃ(ɪ)ənɪst). [f. *Tatian* (name of a Christian apologist of the 2nd century, who afterwards became a Gnostic) + -IST.] A follower of Tatian; a member of the ascetic sect of Encratites; also incorrectly **Tatian** in same sense. So **Tatianic** (teɪʃɪ'ænɪk) *a.*, of or pertaining to Tatian, or to his DIATESSARON or harmony of the Gospels.

1585–7 T. ROGERS *39 Art.* vi. (1628) 32 Some accepted onely the Acts of the Apostles, as the Tatians. **1635** PAGITT *Christianogr.* III. (1636) 60 Heretiques as the Tatians,.. teaching against Marriage. **1754–8** BP. NEWTON *Obs. Dan.* xiii. 200 The mystery of iniquity continued to work very strongly in.. the Tatianists. **1862** G. H. TOUNSEND *Man. of Dates* s.v. *Encratites*, Tatian flourished about A.D. 173. His followers were called in addition to Encratites, Tatianists, Apotactites, and Hydroparastates. **1907** MOFFATT in *Expositor* July 62 The Tatianic arrangement reflects the original order [of the N.T. books].

tatie ('teɪtɪ). Also **'tato, taty, tautie, tauty.** [Dial. variant of POTATO *sb.* 2: see *Eng. Dial. Dict.* Cf. TATER; TATTIE.]

1. = POTATO 2.

1788 E. PICKEN *Poems* Gloss., *Tawties*, potatoes. **1793** R. BROWN *Comic Poems* (1817) 118 Sawt herrings, tawties, water kale. **1805** G. M'INDOE *Million of Potatoes* Poems (1805) 145 It's lang ere I the taties need. **1809** T. DONALDSON *Poems* 19 'Tatoes travel slawly down The throat. **1812** P. FORBES *Poems* 31 A charger's just a muckle pig, For ha'din' kail or 'tatoes. **1870** D. J. KIRWAN *Palace & Hovel* xiv. 214 Guv us a taty, Jenny. **1894** J. MENZIES *Our Town* 240 We div look at our tauties on Saubbath. **1920** W. DE LA MARE *Poems 1901–1919* II. 170 There's goose, baked taties and cabbage. **1979** *Bull. Yorks. Dial. Soc.* Summer 15 The wor acres o gowden corn, taties an sugar beet, pearce an quiet.

2. *attrib.* and *Comb.*, as ***tatie pot***; **tatie-bogle** = *tattie-bogle* s.v. TATTIE 2.

1838 J. M. WILSON *Hist. Tales Borders* IV. 306 Ye look mair like a tauty bogle than a Christian man. **1853** S. R. WHITEHEAD *Nelly Armstrong* I. i. 24 It was fitter for a tatie-bogle's back than a leddy's. **1871** J. RICHARDSON *Cummerland Talk* 1st Ser. 7 A dish consisting of beef or mutton, cut into pieces, and put into a large dish along with potatoes, onions, pepper, salt, etc., and then baked in the oven,..is called in Cumberland *taty-pot*. **1893** *West Cumberland Times* (Holiday No.) 5/4 'Begok, it's tatie pot!' says Ben. **1974** *Times Lit. Suppl.* 1 Mar. 215/1 Mr Wyatt soon made friends among the woodmen and farm workers, enjoyed a tatie-pot supper at the nearest inn. **1976** *Cumberland News* 3 Dec. 24/2 Lazonby Methodist Church raised over £70 with a 'tatie-pot' supper. **1978** R. HILL *Pinch of Snuff* xxiii. 234 Going off home for a tatie-pot supper and an early night. **1982** *Sunday Tel.* 21 Feb. 16/7 There await you, in all their rich goodness, leek pie and Mendip snails, Cumbrian tatie pot and tripe,..Dorset sausage and Somerset apple cake.

tato, tatoo, obs. forms of TATTOO.

'tato, var. of TATIE.

‖**tâtonnement** (tatɔnmɑ̃). Also **tatonnement.** [Fr., f. *tâtonner* to feel one's way, proceed cautiously.] Experimentation, tentative procedure; ***tâtonnement process***, a process of trial and error.

1847 A. DE MORGAN *Formal Logic* II. 324 M. Gergonne's complex propositions..requiring a separate *tâtonnement* for many things the analogues of which appear as connected results of my system. **1964** W. S. VICKREY *Metastatics & Macroeconomics* i. 21 The postulate that an equilibrium would be reached by a series of adjustments through recontracting, or 'tâtonnements'. **1975** *Jrnl. Econ. Theory* X. 122 W. Neuefeind, A tatonnement process for *N*-person games, *CORE Discussion Paper* 7136. **1978** S. WEINTRAUB *Capitalism's Inflation & Unemployment Crisis* ix. 176 Unbounded pathological Wicksellian-Hayekian cases can be discounted, though some minor (*tatonnement*) imbalances are inevitable.

‖**tatou, tatu** ('tætuː). Also 6 **tattou,** 8 **tattu,** 9 **tatoo, tattoo.** [Native name in Tupi. So F. *tatou*, Sp. *tato*, Pg. *tatu*.] An armadillo.

1568 tr. *Thevet's New Found Worlde* 84 There are founde great number of Tattous, that are beasts armed. **1613** PURCHAS *Pilgrimage* (1614) 842 The Tatu or Armadilla, which digs as much as many men with mattocks. **1766** E. BANCROFT *Guiana* ii. (1769) 145 The Tattu, or Armadillo, of Guiana, is the largest of that species of animals. **1805** T. LINDLEY *Voy. Brazil* 134 He was waiting for tatoos, or armadilloes, which seldom appear before dusk. **1894** *Outing* (U.S.) XXIV. 176/2 In Brazil, where he is called the 'tattoo', his flesh is much prized.

b. In combination with defining words, applied (in Tupi and Guarani) to various species, as ˌ**tatou'ay (tatou-áiba),** the wounded armadillo; **tatouete (tatuete),** [-*ete* true] Tatusia verdadeira; ˌ**tatou'hou,** ˌ**tatou-'peba,** = PEBA; ˌ**tatou-'poyou,** = POYOU: see quots.

[**1648** MARCGRAVE *Hist. Nat. Brasil.* VI. viii. 231 Tatv & Tatv-peba Brasiliensibus, Armadillo Hispanis, Encuberto Lusitanis. *Ibid.*, *Tatv-ete* Brasiliensibus,..priori est minor. **1693** RAY *Quadrupeds* 233 *Tatuete* Brasiliensibus, Armadilli secunda species.] **1753** CHAMBERS *Cycl. Supp.*, *Tatuete*,..a species of tatu, or armadillo, smaller than the common one. **1774** GOLDSM. *Nat. Hist.* IV. iv. 132 The third [kind of Armadillo] is the Tatuette, furnished with eight bands. **1834** *Penny Cycl.* II. 352/1 The peba (*D*[*asypus*] *peba*), called by the Guaranis *tatouhou*, or *black tatu*, is extremely common in Paraguay. *Ibid.* 352/2 The peba, or, as it is commonly called in Brazil, tatu-peba, has thirty-two teeth. *Ibid.* 353/2 The *poyou*..or yellow-footed armadillo (for thus Azara interprets the name)... The *tatu-poyou* is easily distinguished..by the unusual flatness and broadness of its body. *Ibid.* 354/2 The *Tatouay* (*D. Tatouay*, Desmarest), or wounded armadillo, is so called by the Indians in allusion to its tail, which is naked, or as it were rudely deprived of the crust or bony tube which covers this organ in all the other species.

‖**tatpurusha** (tæt'pʊrəʃə). *Philol.* Also **tatpuruṣ(h)a** and with capital initial. [Skr., lit. 'his servant'.] A compound in which the first element qualifies or determines the second, while the second retains its grammatical independence as noun, adjective, or participle.

1846 M. WILLIAMS *Elem. Gram. Sanscrit* ix. 157 Native grammarians class compound nouns under five heads: the 1st they call *Tatpurusha* or those composed of two nouns. **1872** [see BAHUVRIHI]. **1901** A. A. MACDONNELL *Sanskrit Gram.* vi. 159 The past part...gata, 'gone to', is often used at the end of Tatpuruṣas in the sense of 'relating to', 'existing in'. **1946** *Trans. Philol. Soc. 1945* 86 From this combination we get the tatpuruṣa compounds *śilõñcha-* and *śilõñchana-*. **1957** S. POTTER *Mod. Ling.* iv. 91 *Bookcase* consists of substantival attribute + substantive. It belongs to that class of compounds known as *tatpurusha* to Indian grammarians because the first component determines or qualifies the second. **1969** —— *Changing English* ii. 58 It [*sc.* 'year-book'] is a tatpurusha type of compound that has been in use in English for hundreds of years, written solid by Anglo-Saxon scribes.

tatsman ('tætsmən). *slang.* [f. *tats* dice, pl. of TAT *sb.*[1] + MAN *sb.*[1]] A dice-player, or a sharper who cheats with dice.

1825 C. M. WESTMACOTT *Eng. Spy* (1907) I. 211 *note*, A *tats man*, a proficient with the bones, one who knows every chance upon the dice.

tatt: see TAT.

tattami, obs. var. TATAMI.

tattaow, obs. f. TATTOO *v.*[2]

tattarrattat (ˌtætəræ'tæt). *nonce-wd.* [Echoic.] = RAT-A-TAT.

1922 JOYCE *Ulysses* 732, I knew his tattarrattat at the door.

tat-tat ('tæt'tæt). [Echoic: cf. TAT *v.*[1]] = RAT-TAT.

1786 MME. D'ARBLAY *Diary* 17 July, A tat-tat at my door followed, and a lady entered.

tattee, variant of TATTY *sb.*

tatter ('tætə(r)), *sb.*[1] Also 5–6 **tater,** (5 **tatar**), 7 **tattar (totter),** 8 *Sc.* **tetter.** [Known only from *c* 1400, but evidenced in earlier use by TATTERED *a.* Of Scandinavian origin: cf. ON. **taturr* (later Icel. *tǫturr*, *töturr*), pl. *tötrar* tatters, rags, in Norw. dial. *totra*, pl. *totror*. In OF. an instance of *tatereles* rags, tatters ('a ces vies tatereles vestues') occurs in *Aucassin et Nicolette* vi.

(Notwithstanding similarity of sense, the Norse and Eng. word has no known etymological or phonetic connexion with MLG. and LG. *talter*, pl. *talteren*, *taltern*, tatters, rags (Brem. Wbch.), whence app. Norw. dial. *taltra*, pl. *taltrar*.)]

1. a. An irregularly torn piece, strip, shred, or scrap of cloth or similar substance, hanging loose from the main body, esp. of a garment; more rarely applied to the separate pieces into which a thing is torn; a rag. In *pl.* often = tattered or ragged clothing; rags.

In early quots. applied in contempt to the 'dags' or projecting pieces of a slashed garment; in quot. 1470–85 to the sharp points or jags in a dragon's tail.

1402 *Pol. Poems* (Rolls) II. 69 Of suche wide clothing, tateris and tagges, It hirtith myn hert hevyly. **1470–85** MALORY *Arthur* v. iv. 165 A dredeful dragon..his hede..enameled with asure.., his taylle ful of tatters. **1520** *Treat. Galaunt* 137 in *Ballads fr. MSS.* I. 450 With longe taters downe to the ars behynde. **1612** ROWLANDS *Knaue of Harts* 23 A suite of ragges and tatters on my backe. **1621** T. WILLIAMSON tr. *Goulart's Wise Vieillard* 172 To goe woolward, in sackcloth, and haire cloth, in totters and ragges. **1686** tr. *Chardin's Trav. Persia* 97 They go Barefoot, and all in Tattars. **1791** MRS. RADCLIFFE *Rom. Forest* ii, The remains of tapestry hung in tatters upon the walls. **1840** R. H. DANA *Bef. Mast* xxv. 82 Furl the sail before it blows to tatters. **1873** 'OUIDA' *Pascarèl* I. 25 What does a tatter or two in the dress signify? **1884** BOWER & SCOTT *De Bary's Phaner.* 216 Thin very obscure tatters of the ruptured tissue clothe the walls of the mature passage.

b. *fig.* or in fig. context.

1576 FLEMING *Panopl. Epist.* 81 Torne to tatters with a thousand tempests of troubles. **1602** SHAKS. *Ham.* III. ii. 11 To see a robustious Pery-wig-pated Fellow, teare a Passion to tatters, to verie ragges. **1607** *Barley-Breake* (1877) 5 Then Hate, and Enuie, all to totters went. **1792** COWPER *Let. to W. Hayley* 4 June, Returned from my walk, blown to tatters. **1875** JOWETT *Plato* (ed. 2) I. 189 Philosophers,..who tear arguments to tatters.

†**2.** *transf.* A person wearing tattered or ragged clothes; a tatterdemalion. *Obs.*

c **1600** DAY *Begg. Bednall Gr.* v. (1881) 110 How, mary with a Beggar? mix the blood of Strowds with a tatter? *a* **1635** RANDOLPH *Hey for Hon.* III. i, Well spoke, my noble English tatter, Lead up the vanguard. **1637** HEYWOOD *Roy. King* II. viii, What Tatter's that that walkes there?

3. *attrib.* and *Comb.*, as †***tatter-rag***; ***tatter-eared, -fudded*** (Sc.: see FUD), ***-skinned, -tailed, -tangled*** adjs.; †**tatter-wag** (**tatar-wagge**), **tatter-wallop** (*Sc.* and *n. dial.*), a fluttering tatter or rag; also, a person in ragged clothes.

1953 R. GRAVES *Poems* 18 *Tatter-eared and slinking alley-toms. **1880** J. NICOL *Poems & Songs* 29 The dirty *tatter-fudded Poor stowaway. **1570** LEVINS *Manip.* 10/36 *Tatterraggs, *panniculi*. **1924** R. CAMPBELL *Flaming Terrapin* ii. 26 And like a leper, faint and *tatter-skinned, The wan moon makes a ghost of every tree. **1876** G. M. HOPKINS *Poems* (1967) 177 *Tatter-tangled and dingle-a-danglèd Dandy-hung dainty head. *c* **1600** RUGGLE *Club Law* (1907) III. ii, This is some *tattertaild Athenian. *c* **1400** *Rom. Rose* 7257 And grey clothis not ful clene But fretted full of *tatarwagges. *c* **1400** *Laud Troy Bk.* 9247 He hewys his mayles res by res, He hewys hem alle In taterwagges, His hauberk heng alle In ragges. **1808** JAMIESON, **Tatter-wallops*, tatters, rags in a fluttering state. **1819** W. TENNANT *Papistry Storm'd* (1827) 204 Hood..cowl and clout, In tatter-wallops flew about. **1828** *Craven Gloss.*, *Tatter-wallops*, a woman with ragged clothes. **1910** *Chambers's Jrnl.* Jan. 30/1 Ye're aye tearin' yer clothes, ye wee tatter-wallops!

tatter, *sb.*[2] *rare.* [f. TAT *v.*[2] + -ER[1].] In *Needlework*: One who tats or does tatting.

1881 *Faith & Unfaith* I. iv. 54 Miss Peyton..confronts this eminent tatter.

tatter, *sb.*[3] *slang.* [f. TAT *v.*[3] + -ER[1].] A refuse-gatherer, a rag-collector. Cf. TOTTER (s.v. TOT *sb.*[5]). Also **tatterer.**

1890 BARRÈRE & LELAND *Dict. Slang*, *Tatter* (tramps), a rag-gatherer. **1910** *Church Times* 15 July, Their occupations being largely that of 'Tatterers' —*i.e.* rag and bone and bottle-gatherers, and casual labourers. **1921** *Dict. Occup. Terms* (1927) §970 Tatter,..collects [waste] with a hand-pushed barrow or cart. **1969** *Telegraph & Argus* (Bradford) 16 Oct. 9 He was wearing a dark jacket, and light drill trousers. He is believed to be a rag tatter.

tatter, *a. dial.* [?] Cross, peevish, testy.

1579 TWYNE *Phisicke agst. Fort.* I. xv. 17 b, His two wiues, most tatter and testie olde women. *Ibid.* cx. 139 When a man maketh hym selfe seruiceable and subiect to a tatter olde foole. **1736** LEWIS *Isle of Thanet* Gloss., *Tatter*, ragged, cross, peevish, 'he is a very tatter man'. **1887** *Kentish Gloss.* s.v., The old 'ooman's middlin' tatter to-day, I can tell ye.

'tatter, *v.*[1] Also 4 **tater.** [app. a back-formation from TATTERED.] **a.** *trans.* To tear or reduce to tatters; to make ragged; to tear in pieces, mangle. Also *fig.* ***to tatter a kip*** (slang): see KIP *sb.*[3] 1.

(The ppl. adj. *tattered* and vbl. sb. *tattering* are known before the simple vb.)

[*c* **1380**: see *tattering* vbl. sb. below.] *c* **1440** *York Myst.* xlvi. 44 (Of Christ scourged and crowned with thorns) Ilk tag of þat turtill so tatterid and torne es.] **1608** SYLVESTER *Du Bartas* II. iv. v. *Decay* 342 A Lion, that hath tatterd heer A goodly Heifer, there a lusty Steer. **1652** *Persuasive to Compliance* 6 A Nation so exhausted and tattered by divisions. **1766** GOLDSM. *Vic. W.* xx, To assist at tattering a kip, as the phrase was, when we had a mind for a frolic. **1837** C. LOFFT *Self-formation* I. 34, I tattered some good poetry to rags, expressly for her gratification. *a* **1845** HOOD *Forge* II. xvi, Shrieking for flesh to tear and tatter.

b. *intr.* To be or become tattered. *rare.*

1595 [see *tattering* ppl. adj. below]. **1934** DYLAN THOMAS in *New Verse* Apr. 12 Our strips of stuff that tatter as we move.

Hence **'tattering** *vbl. sb.*[1] (in quot. *c* 1380, slashing of garments) and *ppl. a.*[1]

c **1380** WYCLIF *Sel. Wks.* III. 124 Men deformen hor body by hor foule atyre..and tatering of clothes. *c* **1580** JEFFERIE *Bugbears* Epil., Song ii. in *Archiv Stud. Neu. Spr.* (1897), With battrynges, with plattrynges, with tattrynges. **1595** SHAKS. *John* v. v. 7 After such bloody toile, we bid good night, And woon'd our tott'ring colours clearly vp, Last in the field, and almost Lords of it.

'tatter, *v.*[2] *Obs.* exc. *dial.* In 4–5 **tater.** [Appears before 1400: = MDu. and Du. *tateren* to stammer, MFl., Fl., to speak imperfectly or inarticulately, MLG., LG., and EFris. *tateren*, *tatern*, *tattern* to babble, speak nonsense; to chatter. From the same (prob. echoic) stem as TATTLE.] *intr.* **a.** To talk idly, chatter, prate, tattle. **b.** 'To scold; to chide; to be furious or cross' (E.D.D.). Hence **'tattering** *vbl. sb.*[2] and *ppl. a.*[2]

c **1380** WYCLIF *Wks.* (1880) 192 Oure fleschly peple haþ more lykynge in here bodely eris in sich knackynge & taterynge þan in herynge of goddis lawe. *c* **1440** *Promp. Parv.* 487/1 Tateryn, or iauerყn, or speke wythe owte resone (*K.* or iangelyn,..*P.* iaberyn). *Ibid.*, Taterynge, or iauerynge (*S.* iaperynge, *P.* iaberinge), *garritus*. **1888** ELWORTHY *W. Somerset Gloss.* s.v., Come now, there's to much tatterin' by half, let's have less noise and more work!

'tatter, *v.*[3] *dial.* [Origin obscure: the form is frequentative; cf. *patter*.] *intr.* To move or bestir oneself actively; to go or run at a great rate.

a **1825** FORBY *Voc. E. Anglia*, *Tatter*, *v.* to stir actively and laboriously... 'He is a very pains-taking man; always *towing* and *tattering* after his business'. **1828** T. C. CROKER *Fairy Leg.* II. 127 Away they went tattering along the road making the fire fly out of the stones at no rate. **1842** S. LOVER *Handy Andy* xiv, The bell rang violently. 'There, do you hear him tattering?' **1897** CROCKETT *Lochinvar* v. 68 Running fleet-foot..as though the devil himself had been tattering at his tail.

tatter, erron. variant of TOTTER.

tatterdemalion, -demallion (ˌtætədɪ'meɪlɪən, -'mælɪən). Forms: α. 7–9 **tatterdemallion,** (7 **tatter-, totter-de-mallion, -timallion).** β. 7–9 **tatterdemalion,** (7 **tatter-, totter-demalian, -dimalian, -demalean,** 8 **-demelon).** [f. TATTER *sb.*[1], or more prob. TATTERED *a.*, with a factitious element suggesting an ethnic or descriptive derivative. The earlier pronunciation rimes with *battalion*, *Italian*, *stallion*, as shown by the frequent doubling of *l*.]

A person in tattered clothing; a ragged or beggarly fellow; a ragamuffin.

α. **1611** B. JONSON *Introd. Verses* in *Coryat's Crudities*, This Horse pictur'd showes that our Tatter-de-mallian Did ride the French Hackneyes and lye with th' Italian. *a* **1626** MIDDLETON *Mayor of Queenb.* v. i, He's not so wise as he ought to be, to let such tatterdemallions get the upper hand of him. **1630** CAPT. SMITH *Trav. & Adv.* xvi. 30 Yet those tattertimallions [Tartars] will have two or three horses, some foure, or five. **1642** HOWELL *For. Trav.* (Arb.) 37 Great numbers of poore French tatterdimallians, being as it were the Scumme of the Countrey. **1693** *Oxford-Act* 2 Loyal Oxford..Soon form'd in Squadrons and Battalions To Swinge the Duke's Tatterdemalions. *a* **1700** B. E. *Dict. Cant. Crew*, *Tatter-de-mallion*, a ragged, tatter'd Begger,..having better Cloths at Home. **1879** *Scribner's Mag.* XIX. 296/1 It is rare to see a tatterdemallion in Paris.

β. **1608** DEKKER *Belman Lond.* (1640) 3 Rector Chory (the Captain of the Tatterdemalions). **1622** DEKKER *Virg. Mart.* III. i, Among so many millions of people, should thou and I onely be miserable totterdemalions? **1637** HEYWOOD *Roy. King* II. vii, A Tatterdemalean, that stayes to sit at the Ordinary to day. **1650** HOWELL *Giraffi's Rev. Naples* I. 7 A few poore Tatterdimalians had made all that noise. **1771** SMOLLETT *Humph. Cl.* 24 May, Mrs. Bramble..said, she had never seen such a filthy tatterdemalion. **1858** O. W. HOLMES *Aut. Breakf.-t.* xi. 108 A group of young tatterdemalions playing pitch-and-toss.

b. *attrib.* or as *adj.*

1614 J. COOKE *Greene's Tu Quoque* K j b, Puh, the Italian fashion? the tatterd-de-malian fashion hee meanes. **1651** BIGGS *New Disp.* §53 That Tatterdemalion Linostema of Peripatetical and Galenical predicaments. **1837** CARLYLE *Fr. Rev.* I. IV. iii, Saint-Antoine..reinforced by the unknown Tatterdemalion Figures, with their enthusiast complexion and large sticks. **1855** CHAMIER *My Travels* II. vi. 85 The most beggarly remnants of tatterdemalion garments. **1893** *Spectator* 25 Nov. 738/1 These tatterdemalion scraps and fragments of political discontent.

Hence (*nonce-wds.*) ˌ**tatterde'malionism**, the style or practice of a tatterdemalion; ˌ**tatterde'malionry**, the body of tatterdemalions.

1840 *Blackw. Mag.* XLVIII. 491 Hungarian, Croatian, and Wallachian tatterdemalionry. **1884** *Dumbarton, Vale of Leven*, etc. 27 The tatterdemalionism with which we usually associate the abodes of such. **1887** *Blackw. Mag.* CXLI. 821 His coat was out at both elbows... It was..a kind of defiant tatterdemalionism that the Colonel liked to hug.

tattered ('tætəd), *a.*, *ppl. a.* Forms: *α.* 4 tatered, tatrid, tatird, 5 tatyrd, tatterid, 5–7 tatterd, 6– tattered, -r'd. *β.* See TOTTERED. [app. orig. f. TATTER *sb.*[1] + -ED[2]: cf. RAGGED *a.*; subseq. treated as pa. pple. implying a vb.: see TATTER *v.*[1]]

†**1.** Having 'tatters', jags, or long pointed projections; denticulated, jagged; slashed or laciniated, as a garment. *Obs.*

c **1394** *P. Pl. Crede* 753 His syre a soutere.., His teeþ wiþ toylinge of leþer tatered as a sawe. **1470–85** MALORY *Arthur* v. iv. 165 His [a dragon's] taylle whiche is al to tatterd sygnefyeth the noble knyghtes of the round table. **1501** DOUGLAS *Pal. Hon.* I. xxv, Dragouns,..With mouthis gapand, forkit taillis tatterit.

2. Torn or rent so as to hang in tatters; ragged. (See also TOTTERED *ppl. a.* 1.)

1596 SPENSER *F.Q.* v. xii. 28 Their garments yet, Being all rag'd and tatter'd. **1600** HOLLAND *Livy* II. xxiii. 58 His apparrell was all to tattered, foule and loathsome. **1709** ADDISON *Tatler* No. 100 ¶3 Crowds of People in tattered Garments. **1791** COWPER *Odyss.* IX. 80 Our tatter'd sail-cloth crackled in the wind. **1905** R. GARNETT *Shaks.* 26 The last year's tattered foliage That long ago has rustled to the earth.

3. *transf.* †**a.** Clad in jagged or slashed garments (*obs.*). **b.** Having tattered or ragged garments.

1340 HAMPOLE *Pr. Consc.* 1537 Som has þair clethyng hyngand als stoles Som gas tatird als tatird foles. *c* **1380** WYCLIF *Wks.* (1880) 148 In here gaye pellure & precious cloþis & wast festis & tatrid squeyeres & oþere meyne. **1596** [see TOTTERED *ppl. a.* 1]. **1623** MASSINGER *Dk. Milan* III. i, To see the tattered'st rascals of my troop Drag them out of their closets. ? *a* **1750** *Nursery Rime, House that Jack Built* viii, This is the man all tattered and torn. **1883** *Century Mag.* July 419/2 An aged and tattered negro was the mule's ring-master.

†**4.** Having unkempt dishevelled hair, of irregular length; shaggy. Cf. TATTY *a.*[1] *Obs.*

1340 [see 3]. *c* **1460** *Towneley Myst.* i. 137 Now ar we waxen blak as any coylle, And vgly, tatyrd as a foylle. **1709** STEELE & SWIFT *Tatler* No. 70 ¶10 A..French Mongrel, that was..in a tatter'd Condition, but has now got new Hair.

†**5.** Of a ship, building, or other solid structure: Dilapidated, battered, shattered. *Obs.* (See also TOTTERED *ppl. a.* 2.)

1599 NASHE *Lenten Stuffe* Wks. (Grosart) V. 277 Nothing of that Castle saue tattered ragged walles nowe remaines. **1666** DRYDEN *Ann. Mirab.* cxxxiv, [He] warns his tattered fleet to follow home. **1700** S. L. tr. *Fryke's Voy. E. Ind.* 30 To mend our tattered ships. **1797–8** JANE AUSTEN *Sense & Sens.* xviii, I do not like ruined, tattered cottages.

†**b.** Of troops: Routed and broken up, shattered, disintegrated. *Obs.*

1675 OTWAY *Alcibiades* III. i, Their tatter'd troops are scatter'd o'er the plain. **1728** MORGAN *Algiers* I. iii. 40 Where he continued till he had recruited his tattered army.

Hence '**tatteredly** *adv.*

1673 E. BROWN *Trav. Germ.*, etc. (1677) 126 The Windows..being of Glass, looked not so tatterdly as the ragged Paper Windows of Florence.

tattering, *vbl. sb.* and *ppl. a.*: see TATTER *v.*[1], [2].

†'**tatterly**, *a. Obs. rare.* [f. TATTER *sb.*[1] + -LY[1].] Of the nature of tatters; tattered.

1739 MACHIN in Rigaud *Corr. Sci. Men* (1841) I. 354 Impudently sending them in such tatterly rags a begging to your worship.

Tattersall ('tætəsəl), *sb.* (and *a.*) [The name of Richard *Tattersall* (1724–95), horse-auctioneer.]

1. Used chiefly in the possessive (occas. abbrev. **Tatt's, Tatts**) to denote: **a.** The horse-auction market established by him in 1766 at Hyde Park Corner. Also *transf.* and *fig.*

1795 *Sporting Mag.* VI. 5/1 The gentlemen of the turf assembled every sale day..at Tattersalls. **1825** *Monthly Mag.* 1 Mar. 129/2 The sale days, at Tattersall's, formerly on Monday and Thursday. **1834** CARLYLE *Sartor Resartus* I. iv. 12/1 He burst forth like the neighing of all Tattersall's. **1846** 'SYLVANUS' *Pedestrian & Other Remin.* xxv. 241 They've three or four working the oracle at Tatt's. **1880** *Illustr. Sporting & Dramatic News* 4 Dec. 282/1 There has lately been opened at Christchurch, New Zealand a new 'Tattersall's', the want of which has long been felt. **1882** C. M. YONGE *Unknown to History* II. v. 64 'Paul's Walk' was the Bond Street, the Row, the Tattersall's, the Club of London. **1893** *Cassell's Family Mag.* Aug. 646/1 Ponies and donkeys are here too, for the costermongers. Indeed we might call it the costermonger's horse fair, the Tattersall's of the poorer classes. **1973** *Country Life* 15 Nov. 1547/3 Tattersall's..moved from Hyde Park Corner in 1865, to Knightsbridge Green... Tattersall's continued selling bloodstock and hunters..for some years after the ring of carriage horses' hooves had ceased. **1982** *Daily Tel.* 4 Mar. 18/3 The [Hunters' Improvement and National Horse Breeding] society..based..for the past 16 years at Tattersalls.

b. The principal betting enclosure on a racecourse. Also ***Tattersall's Ring.***

1836 T. HOOD *Let.* 12 Jan. (1973) 211 Tattersall style of betting. **1843** *Illustr. London News* 17 June 418/1 The winners have been haunting Tattersall's..in search of a settlement. **1863** *Observer* 18 Jan. 2/4 The lobby of the hall is like the betting-room at Tattershall's in a low way. **1865** *Once a Week* 28 Oct. 523/1 At one time..rarely did the flood of speculation overflow the dykes of 'The Corner'. Now we have an *al fresco* Tattersall's at nearly every open space in London. **1901** *Cassell's Mag.* Sept. 368/2 Tattersall's Ring at race-meetings and the committee of Tattersall's which rules the betting world, have now no connection with the firm..at Albert Gate. **1922** *N. & Q.* 9 Sept. 206/2 *Outside*, all other enclosures on a racecourse save Tattersall's, which is 'inside'. **1951** E. RICKMAN *Come racing with Me* xvi. 151 The customary reference to the chief betting 'ring' on any racecourse as 'Tattersalls' or 'Tatts' is a relic of the rough-and-ready days when it was an enclosure used principally by bookmakers and backers who were members of Tattersalls' Subscription Room. **1962** [see RAIL *sb.*[2] 2 f]. **1973** [see *silver ring* s.v. SILVER *sb.* and *a.* 21 a]. **1983** 'F. PARRISH' *Bait on Hook* v. 68 He had no real idea what class of man they were looking for—a denizen of the Members' Enclosure] at £6, Tattersalls at £3.50, the Silver Ring for £1, the course for nothing.

c. The name of a lottery which originated in Sydney in 1881, moved to Tasmania in 1896, and since 1954 has operated from Victoria. Freq. abbrev. in *colloq.* use.

1895 N. GOULD *On & off Turf in Austral.* vi. 52 (*heading*) 'Tattersalls' and 'Oxenhams'. *Ibid.* 61 Mr. George Adams ..runs his consultations, or sweeps, under the name of 'Tattersall', and they are very popular all over the Colonies. **1945** BAKER *Austral. Lang.* xv. 264 *To take a ticket in Tatt's* is to buy a ticket in Tattersall's sweepstakes, Tasmania. *Safe as Tatt's* is synonymous with perfect safety. **1951** J. FRAME *Lagoon* 57 His fingers search an envelope for the pink sheet that means Tatts results, ten thousand pounds first prize. **1957** —— *Owls do Cry* xvii. 73 The Art Union? There was a theory that if you bought a ticket up north where the population was thickest you were sure to win a prize. The raffle? Tatts? **1965** *Austral. Encycl.* V. 371/2 The oldest continuing public lottery in Australia is 'Tattersall's',.. established at Sydney in 1881... It took its name from Richard Tattersall's horse-auction mart in London. **1969** *Australian* 24 May 40/4 My man asked if he would abolish Tatts, seeing gambling was such a reprehensible thing.

2. *attrib.* or as *adj.* (freq. with small initial). Designating (a fabric with) a small and even check pattern or garments made from such a material. Hence ***tattersall-checked*** adj. Also *absol.*

From the traditional design of horse blankets.

1891 *Cassell's Family Mag.* Dec. 58/1 All those curious checked cloths which rejoice in the name of 'Tattersall' because, I suppose, they resemble horse cloth. **1951** J. D. SALINGER *Catcher in Rye* xii. 103 This..guy, in a grey flannel suit and one of those flitty-looking tattersall vests. **1958** *Vogue* Jan. 35 Tattersall checks of black and caramel. **1963** *Guardian* 2 Oct. 8/5 Simpsons have Tattersall check shirts of woollen fabric. **1967** [see *gun club* s.v. GUN *sb.* 17]. **1972** *New Yorker* 7 Oct. 12/1 (Advt.), Snuggle yourself.. inside our tattersall-checked robe. **1976** *National Observer* (U.S.) 2 Oct. 3/3 (Advt.), Also available in neat tattersall checks of rust/green on camel ground. **1978** *N.Y. Times* 30 Mar. C11/1 The collection's subdued neutral colors, sedate tattersalls and similarly classic patterns. **1980** U. CURTISS *Poisoned Orchard* xi. 126 Fawn corduroys and a yellow tattersall shirt. **1981** *Daily Tel.* 14 Sept. 13/2 Viyella Tattersall check shirt.

tattertimallion, obs. f. TATTERDEMALION.

tattery ('tætərɪ), *a.* [f. TATTER *sb.*[1] + -Y.] Full of tatters; tattered, ragged. Also *Comb.*, as ***tattery-clothed*** adj.

c **1843** CARLYLE *Hist. Sk.* (1898) 242 Deluges of tangled tattery hair. **1867** —— *Remin.* (1881) II. 21 Books in tattery, ill-bound or unbound condition. **1941** S. O'CASEY *Let.* Jan. (1975) I. 874 The half-fed, tattery-clothed, lice-lorn children scattered now over England by the falling bombs.

tattie ('tætɪ). [Dial. variant of POTATO *sb.* 2. See dialect dicts. for fuller documentation. Cf. TATER; TATIE.]

1. = POTATO *sb.* 2. Also *fig.*, a stupid person.

c **1800** in F. P. Hett *Mem. S. Sibbald* (1926) 203 Then there's champit tatties, after they are boiled, the water is poured off them then they ar' champet wi' the champer in the pot. **1879** *Forfar Poets* 139 Gae hame, ye simple tattie. **1901** G. DOUGLAS *House with Green Shutters* 234 I'll feenish the tatties at ony rate. **1921** A. S. NEILL *Carroty Broon* xv. 202 I'm at the tatties wi' achteenpence a day. **1973** *Stornoway Gazette* 27 Jan. 10/4 Tatties and herrings for supper. **1976** *Sunday Mail* (Glasgow) 26 Dec. 18/1 A tractor ran over her leg as she was picking tatties from a field on the outskirts of Monifeith.

2. *attrib.* and *Comb.*, as ***tattie-field***; **tattie-bogle** = *potato-bogle* s.v. POTATO *sb.* 7; also *fig.*, a simpleton; **tattie-trap** *slang* = *potato-trap* s.v. POTATO *sb.* 7.

1865 *Scotsman* 28 June, First then come the trades' unions and strikes,..as a tattie-bogle..to scare the black and croaking denizens of the wood. **1922** J. BUCHAN *Huntingtower* xii. 240 There's..me..no more use than a tattie-bogle. **1969** M. PUGH *Last Place Left* xii. 73 The gasworks doctor, you tattie bogle There's only one doctor. **1979** L. DERWENT *Border Bairn* xi. 128 Others I dredged up from somewhere in my head, about tattie-bogles, bubblyjocks and real adventures. **1891** BARRIE *Little Minister* III. xxxv. 64 The Retery's in flood..; T'now-dunnie's tattie field's out o' sicht. **1983** *Listener* 18 Aug. 23/2 *Another Time, Another Place* includes a vivid background of wet and windy tattie fields. **1894** J. B. SALMOND *My Man Sandy* 175 Juist you keep your tattie-trap steekit. **1899** A. L. SALMON *West-Country Ballads* 74 Cureit's tattie-trap an' muzzle, Like a bwoy's be smooth an' bare.

tattie, var. TATTY *sb.*; obs. f. TATTY *a.*[1]

tatting ('tætɪŋ), *sb.* [Origin unknown: perh. an arbitrary formation. It has the form of a verbal sb. from TAT *v.*[2]; but that verb is of more recent appearance, as if merely a back-formation from *tatting.*] **a.** *sb.* A kind of knotted lace, netted with a small flat shuttle-shaped instrument from stout sewing-thread; used for edging or trimming, and sometimes for doyleys, parasol covers, etc. (called in F. *frivolité*, Ger. *frivolitäten*). **b.** *vbl. sb.*[1] The action or process of making this. Also *attrib.* as ***tatting-cotton, -edging, -net, -shuttle, -stitch, -work.***

(Tatting-shuttles exist which are said to have been used before 1820.)

1842 MRS. GAUGAIN *Lady's Assist. Knitting*, etc. II. 411 Common Tatting Edging. *Ibid.* 412 If the Tatting has not been properly worked, this scollop will not draw. All Tatting stitches must be formed with the loop round the fingers. **1864** *Sat. Rev.* 22 May, It retires to talk scandal over her tatting with any fashionable old maid with whom the party may be tormented. **1865** *Reader* 28 Oct. 479/3 In 1851 the Census showed a return of 902 pupils in the various arts of crochet laces, point lace.., pillow lace,..plain sewing, knitting and tatting. **1877** KNIGHT *Dict. Mech.*, *Tatting-shuttle*, a small shuttle used in tatting. **1895** *Times* 2 Jan. 13/2 Orders for cotton embroidery edgings, trimmings, and tattings have been disappointing. **1901** CLARA MORRIS *Life on Stage* 46 The 'tatting' craze was sweeping over the country [U.S.A.] then [*c* 1863]; everybody wore tatting, and almost everybody made it.

tatting ('tætɪŋ), *vbl. sb.*[2] [f. TAT *v.*[3] + -ING[1].] Rag- or scrap-collecting (see also quot. 1926). Cf. TOTTING (s.v. TOT *sb.*[5]).

1926 *Glasgow Herald* 14 Dec. 10/7 The word 'tatting'.. appears..to mean the annexation by dustmen..of stray articles of small value found in dustbins. **1969** *Listener* 6 Feb. 169/2 Now,..scrap-collecting and dealing are the biggest stand-by, with 'tatting' (rag-collecting), [etc.]. **1977** SCOLLINS & TITFORD *Ey up, mi Duck!* III. 52 *Tattin'*, going round collecting scrap, as a scrap-merchant does.

tattle ('tæt(ə)l), *sb.* Also 6 tatle: see also TITTLE-TATTLE. [f. next. Cf. LG. *tätel* in same sense.] The action of tattling; idle or frivolous talk; chatter, gossip.

a **1529** Tyttel tattyll [see TITTLE-TATTLE]. **1589** GREENE *Menaphon* (Arb.) 40 Amidst other tattle, they prattled of the beautie of Samela. **1654** WHITLOCK *Zootomia* 57 At Gossipings, Funeralls, at Church before Sermons, and the like opportunities of tattle. **1713** SWIFT *Cadenus & Van.* 320 They..told the tattle of the day. **1869** DIXON *Tower* I. xviii. 215 All this tattle was repeated..to the Queen. **1895** C. GORE *Dissert.* I. vi. 60 The reserve of the canonical and the vulgar tattle of the apocryphal Gospels.

b. with *a* and *pl.* A fit of tattling; a 'gossip'. Now *rare.*

1583 BABINGTON *Commandm.* vii. (1590) 309 The dalying tatles of these courting dayes,..and the wanton greetings in euery place now vsed. **1612** tr. *Benvenuto's Passenger* II. i. §16 Like olde wiues tales, or tattles. **1783** *Priv. Lett. Ld. Malmesbury* (1870) I. 485, I understand there have been some little tattles going between us. *c* **1824** PRAED *Pol. & Occ. Poems, Coronat. Chas. X*, Three dukes were very nearly slain, Which would have made a tattle For many a day.

c. *attrib.* and *Comb.*, as ***tattle-basket*** (cf. *chatterbox*), ***-monger.***

1736 AINSWORTH *Lat. Dict.* II, *Lingulaca*,..(2) A prating gossip, a tattle-basket. **1848** THACKERAY *Bk. Snobs* iv, She knew..how all the tattle-mongers..watched the movements of the Snobkys with interest. **1874** LISLE CARR *Jud. Gwynne* I. ix. 272 A prosaic friendship, that has nothing in it at which the tattlemongers of this place may chatter.

tattle ('tæt(ə)l), *v.* Also 8 tattel; *pr. pple.* and *gerund* 5–6 tatelyng(e, 5–7 tatling. [Appears in Caxton's 'Reynard the Fox', 1481, where it reproduces MFlem. *tatelen*, a parallel form to the more usual MFlem., MDu., MLG., also Flem., Du., EFris. *tateren* (see TATTER *v.*[2]), with exchange of frequentative suffixes *-er*, *-el*. LG. has also *tateln*, *täteln* to gabble, cackle (whence *tatelgos* gabbling goose), Brem. Wbch. Cf. also TITTLE *v.*, and TITTLE-TATTLE, in LG. *titeltateln.* Ultimately onomatopœic.]

†**1.** *intr.* To speak hesitatingly, falter, stammer; *esp.* to prattle as a young child; to utter baby-talk.

1481 [see TATTLING *vbl. sb.* 1]. **1579** LYLY *Euphues* (Arb.) 129 When the babe shall now begin to tattle and call hir Mamma. **1586** DAY *Eng. Secretary* I. (1625) 68 A childe.. whose infancy tatling with a pleasant lisping sound, shall become an incredible delight to the Parents hearing. *a* **1719** ADDISON tr. *Ovid, Birth Bacchus* 40 In her trembling gate she [Juno] totters on, And learns to tattle in the Nurse's tone.

2. To utter small talk; to talk idly or lightly; to chatter, babble, prate; to chat, gossip.

1547 [see TATTLING *vbl. sb.* 2]. [**1550**: see TATTLER 1.]. *a* **1568** *Bannatyne Poems* (Hunter. Cl.) 1082 Louers must be tatling; Go to, good sir, you ar ane foole, yow dull me with your pratling. **1581** J. BELL *Haddon's Answ. Osorius* 490 To tattle and clatter without Judgement of matters of Divinitie. **1668** DRYDEN *Evening's Love* III. i, I must tell you, sir, you have tattled long enough. **1751** JOHNSON *Rambler* No. 153 ⁋14, I was tattling with my former freedom. **1838** LYTTON *Alice* III. vii, She tattled on, first to one,.. then to all.

b. *transf.* and *fig.*

1576–1881 [see TATTLING *ppl. a.* b]. **1600** J. LANE *Tom Tel-troth* 37, I seeme to heare resounding Ecchoes tatling, Of misdemeanors raigning heere and there. *a* **1603** T. CARTWRIGHT *Confut. Rhem. N.T.* (1618) 581 The merite of this reliefe, whereof your by-note in the margent tatleth.

3. To talk without reticence so as to reveal secrets or private affairs; to blab, 'tell tales'. (Now usually with mixture of sense 2.)

1581 [see TATTLING *ppl. a.*]. **1639** S. DU VERGER tr. *Camus' Admir. Events* 211 To have exposed her to the tatling of tongues, was a thing he feared like death. **1652** J. WRIGHT tr. *Camus' Nat. Paradox* v. 93 People of that Nature have never a greater itch to bee Tatling, than when they are commanded to be Silent, and the greater the danger is, the more are they tempted to reveal it. **1710** PALMER *Proverbs* 197 When one of the gang tattles, confesses, and accuses the rest. **1876** HOLLAND *Sev. Oaks* xx, She had always been one whom they could have in their families..she never tattled.

4. *trans.* To utter, say, or tell over in tattling. Now *rare*.

1588 SHAKS. *Tit. A.* IV. ii. 168 Then let the Ladies tattle what they please. **1593** *Tell-troth's N.Y. Gift* (1876) 11 They will tatle tales. **1649** MILTON *Eikon.* xvii. 159 This intricate stuffe tattl'd here of Timothy and Titus and I know not whom thir Successors. **1729** T. COOKE *Tales, Proposals*, etc. 57 What from the Frankness of your Soul you say, The Fool may tattel, and the Knave betray.

5. With advb. extension: To get or bring into some condition by tattling.

1751 JOHNSON *Rambler* No. 108 ⁋10 Lest the hours.. should be tattled away without regard to literature. **1838** LYTTON *Alice* III. vii, She tattled on..till she had tattled herself out of breath.

Hence **'tattlement**, tattling, chatter.

1837 CARLYLE *Misc.* (1872) VI. 225 Poor little Lilias Baillie; tottering about there, with her foolish glad tattlement.

tattler ('tætlə(r)). Also 6 tatyllar, 6–9 tatler. [Agent-n. f. TATTLE *v.* + -ER¹. So LG. *täteler.*]

1. One who tattles; an idle talker, a chatterer; a gossip; a talebearer, telltale.

1550 CROWLEY *Last Trump.* 1609 Vaine tatyllars, That do vse false rumoures to sowe. **1611** BIBLE *1 Tim.* v. 13 Not onely idle, but tatlers also, and busibodies, speaking things which they ought not. **1682** BUNYAN *Holy War* xi. (Cassell) 249 Mr. Prywell..a sober and judicious man, a man that is no tattler, nor raiser of false reports. **1781** COWPER *Friendship* xvii, Whoever keeps an open ear For tattlers, will be sure to hear The trumpet of contention. **1847** L. HUNT *Men, Women, & Bks.* II. x. 252 As great and scandalous a tattler as anybody.

2. *slang.* A striking watch, a repeater; a watch in general.

1688 SHADWELL *Sqr. Alsatia* II. Wks. 1726 IV. 47 Here's a Tatler, gold, all gold, you rogue. *a* **1700** B. E. *Dict. Cant. Crew, Tattler*, an Alarm, or Striking Watch, or (indeed) any. **1844** W. H. MAXWELL *Sports & Adv. Scot.* viii. (1855) 85 He carries his 'tatler' in the waistband of his unmentionables.

3. *Ornith.* Any of the sandpipers of the genus *Totanus* or subfamily *Totaninæ*; so called from their vociferous cry.

1831 RICHARDSON & SWAINSON *Faun. Bor.-Amer.* II. 388 *Totanus semipalmatus* (Temm.), Semipalmated Tatler. **1872** COUES *N. Amer. Birds* 250 The *Terekia cinerea*..stands between the godwits and tattlers. **1892** A. E. LEE *Hist. Columbus* (Ohio) I. 17 *note*, Yellow-legged snipe, or tattler, ..common in autumn on western rivers.

So **'tattlery** (*rare*$^{-0}$), 'idle talk or chat' (Webster 1847).

tattle-tale ('tæt(ə)lteɪl), *sb.* (and *a.*) *colloq.* (orig. and chiefly *U.S.*). [f. TATTLE *sb.* (or *v.*), after *tell-tale.*] **1.** = TELL-TALE *sb.* (*a.*) 1 a. Occas. *attrib.* or as *adj.* (cf. TELL-TALE *sb.* (*a.*) 3 b).

1889 'C. E. CRADDOCK' *Despot of Broomsedge Cove* 429 I'd strangle that tattle-tale with a mighty good will. **1918** J. G. THOMPSON *Lest we Forget* 230 An American boy was expelled from a German gymnasium in Berlin, because he refused to 'tattle-tale' on the pupils in his class. **1929** W. FAULKNER *Sound & Fury* 91 'I already told on her,' Jason said... 'And see what you got by it,' Caddy said. 'Tattletale.' **1946** C. MCCULLERS *Member of Wedding* I. 45 'Frankie ain't no tattle-tale,' said Berenice. **1962** 'K. ORVIS' *Damned & Destroyed* xiii. 89 Helen's tattle-tale scars. **1964** D. MACARTHUR *Reminiscences* I. 26 Come what may, I would be no tattletale. **1977** D. BAGLEY *Enemy* v. 37 Nellie *is* a tattle-tale, isn't she? Too bloody gossipy.

2. A tachograph; also in oil-well drilling (see quot. 1942).

1942 BERREY & VAN DEN BARK *Amer. Thes. Slang* §516/5 *Tattletale*, an instrument recording the pressure of the bit on the bottom and the work done during a shift. **1949** *Amer. Speech* XXIV. 35 Another characteristic of oil-field language is the predominance of compound words... Compound nouns coined from a verb and its object are *bore hole*..*swamp pole*, and *tattle tale*. **1962** *Ibid.* XXXVII. 272 *Tattletale*,.. a complex device used on trucks, buses, and locomotives which records exact time, distance, and speed on a cylinder, and is used to check on how much speed and how many stops a vehicle made. **1971** M. TAK *Truck Talk* 165 *Tattletale*, a sealed tachograph in a tractor that simultaneously records a truck's speed and the time of day; thus producing a record of driving hours and stops. Installed by large companies to check on driver efficiency and running time, tattletales are, needless to say, unpopular with drivers.

3. *Comb.* **tattle-tale grey**, an off-white colour resulting from inadequate laundering. Also *fig.*

1943 D. W. BROGAN *Eng. People* 11 If the victory of the United Nations is a good thing for all..a member of this alliance may be well advised to put up with the fact that the other members' records are not snowy white, but at best tattle-tale grey. **1973** *Houston* (Texas) *Chron. Mag. People, Places, Pleasures* 14 Oct. 11/4 In case all this still leaves the tattle tale grey, one must begin it all over again.

Hence (*rarely*) as *v. intr.*, to tell tales or 'sneak' on (somebody).

1918 J. G. THOMPSON *Lest we Forget* 230 An American boy was expelled from a German gymnasium in Berlin, because he refused to 'tattle-tale' on the pupils in his class.

tattling ('tætlɪŋ), *vbl. sb.* [f. TATTLE *v.* + -ING¹.] The action of the verb TATTLE.

†**1.** Faltering, stammering; prattling; baby-talk.

1481 CAXTON *Reynard* xxvii. (Arb.) 65 But who can gyue to his lesynge a conclusion, and pronónce it without tatelyng [*orig.* ende seit sine woerden sonder tatelen]. **1749** FIELDING *Tom Jones* XVIII. xiv, He declares the tattling of his little grand-daughter, who is above a year and a half old, is sweeter music than the finest cry of dogs in England.

2. Idle talking; chattering, prating; gossiping; blabbing, tale-telling.

1547 in Strype *Eccl. Mem.* (1721) II. iv. 24 [Barlow, bishop of S. Davids..preached at court..urging..a redress of several abuses in religion... The Bishop of Winchester.. was mightily disturbed at it, calling it] his tattling. **1598** SHAKS. *Merry W.* IV. i. 26 Peace, your tatlings. **1673** *Lady's Call.* I. i. §12 When 'tis remembred that St. Paul makes tatling the effect of idleness. *a* **1693** *Urquhart's Rabelais* III. xiii. 106 The..tatling of Jackdaws,..kekling of Hens. *a* **1720** SEWEL *Hist. Quakers* (1795) I. IV. 364 We do it in private to keep you from tattling. **1825** T. HOOK *Sayings* Ser. II. *Man of Many Fr.*, So that no discovery..might be made by any tattling amongst the servants.

'tattling, *ppl. a.* [f. as prec. + -ING².] That tattles; chattering; gossiping; tale-telling.

1581 J. BELL *Haddon's Answ. Osor.* 28 Blowen abroad.. amongest tattlyng women, foolishe children. **1664** BUTLER *Hud.* II. I. 77 This tattling Gossip knew too well What mischief Hudibras befell. **1712** ARBUTHNOT *John Bull* III. v, Tattling people that carried tales. **1841** HOOD *Tale Trumpet* 92 In the prattling, tattling village of Tringham.

b. *transf.* and *fig.*: cf. *babbling*; sometimes = 'tell-tale'.

1576 GASCOIGNE *Philomene* 35 The tatling Awbe doth please some fancie wel, And some like best, the byrde as Black as cole. **1652** BENLOWES *Theoph.* IV. lxviii, When keen breath'd winds..glaze tatling stream. **1731** SWIFT *Cassinus & Peter* Wks. 1755 IV. I. 165 Nor whisper to the tattling reeds The blackest of all female deeds. **1881** E. ARNOLD *Ind. Poetry* 91 Let him hear the tattling ripple Of the bangles round thy feet.

Hence **'tattlingly** *adv.*

1847 in WEBSTER.

tatto, Sc. dial. or vulgar corr. of POTATO.

tattoo (tæ'tu:), *sb.*¹ Forms: *α.* 7 **tap-too, tap too, tapp too,** 7–8 **taptow,** 7–9 **taptoo.** *β.* 7 **tat too, tato,** 8 **tatoo,** 9 **tattoe,** 7– **tattoo.** [In 17th c. *tap-too*, a. Du. *taptoe* in same sense; f. *tap* the tap (of a cask), + *toe* = *doe toe* 'shut'. So Sw. *tapto*, Sp. (1706) *tatu*. Cf. Ger. *zapfenstreich*, LG. *tappenslag*, Da. *tappenstreg*, with the first element the same, and second element meaning 'stroke, beat'.

Although Du. *tap toe* was in military use in our sense 1 in the 17th c., there is reason to doubt if this was its original use. *Tap toe = doe den tap toe* 'put the tap to', 'close or turn off the tap', was app. already in colloquial use for 'shut up! stop! cease!'; Dr. Kluyver points out, in a play of 1639 from Emden, *Doch hier de tap van toe* = 'but here we shut up', or 'say no more'.]

1. *Mil.* A signal made, by beat of drum or buglecall, in the evening, for soldiers to repair to their quarters in garrison or tents in camp.

α. **1644** *Col. Hutchinson's Orders* in T. C. Hine *Nottingham*, etc. (1876) App. §8 If anyone shall bee found tiplinge or drinkinge in any Taverne, Inne, or Alehouse after the houre of nyne of the clock at night, when the Tap-too beates, hee shall pay 2*s.* 6*d.* *Ibid.* §10 After the houre of nyne of the clock at night, after the taptoo hath beaten, untill the Revelly hath beaten the next morninge. **1645** N. DRAKE *Siege Pontefr.* (Surtees) 65 Not to stay there any longer but till tapp too beate, which was about 10 a clock. **1675** *Lond. Gaz.* No. 1014/4 The third night, after..the Taptow had beaten, we made a very good Retreat, without the loss of a Man. **1706** PHILLIPS (ed. 6), *Tat-too* or *Tap-too*, the beat of Drum at Night for all Soldiers to repair to their Tents. **1736** AINSWORTH *Lat. Dict.*, Taptow, tattoo. **1803** COLLINS *Gen. & Garrison Orders* (1879) 30 After the beating of the taptoo. **1833** SIR C. J. NAPIER *Colonies* 190 The soldiers are just able to hear the 'taptoo' beat.

β. **1688** R. HOLME *Armoury* III. xix. (Roxb.) 153/2 The drummer is to beat all maner of beats, as a Call, a Troope, a March,..a Retreit, a Tato, and a Revally. **1698** FRYER *Acc. E. India & P.* 74 None but Christians lodge within the City [Bacein], the Banyans repairing to the Suburbs upon Tattoo. **1767** in R. Rogers *Jrnls.* (1883) 238 *note*, Your memorialist must further inform you that Rum was let out of the Fort after tatoo. **1814** SCOTT *Wav.* lxvii, I question if the red-coats hae beat the tattoo yet, and we're not safe till then. **1844** *Regul. & Ord. Army* 259 The Tattoo is to beat at Eight o'clock in the Winter, and at Nine o'clock in the Summer Season. **1884** GROVE *Dict. Mus.* IV. 63/2 The Tattoo concludes by the 'Second Post' or 'Last Post'.

b. A military entertainment consisting of an elaboration of the tattoo by extra music and performance of exercises by troops, generally at night and by torch or other artificial light. (So G. *zapfenstreich.*)

1742 H. WALPOLE *Lett.* (1903) I. 216 You know one loves a review and a tattoo. **1904** *Daily News* 8 Aug. 7 The Sherwood Foresters..carried out the tattoo under the direction of Lieut. Parkinson. **1907** *Standard* 19 Jan. 6/7 After dark there was a torchlight tattoo, in which 800 men took part.

c. A drum-beat in general, as a means of raising an alarm, attracting attention, etc.

1688 in Boys *Sandwich* (1792) 760 The news..caused us ..to keep a strong watch, and the tattoo was sent about. **1709** STEELE *Tatler* No. 109 ⁋3 A young Lady cannot be married, but all the Impertinents in Town must be beating the Tattoo from one Quarter of the Town to the other, to show they know what passes. **1717** PRIOR *Alma* I. 454 All those, whose hearts are loose and low Start if they hear but the tattoo. **1872** C. GIBBON *For the King* i, The drum beat a reckless tattoe.

fig. **1579** DILWORTH *Pope* 87 Every such advertisement is a tattoo for all the mercenary scribblers in a nation.

2. *transf.* A beating or pulsation as of a drum; the action of beating, thumping, or rapping continuously upon something.

1755 H. WALPOLE *Lett.* (1846) III. 136 Can I help feeling a tattoo at my heart, when the Duke of Newcastle makes as great a figure in history as Burleigh or Godolphin? **1820** *Sporting Mag.* VI. 178 He..played such a tattoo upon his antagonist's head, as rendered him almost senseless. **1840** THACKERAY *Bedford-Row Conspir.* iii, Beginning to play a rapid tattoo with her feet. **1878** *Masque Poets* 97 The hail begins to beat outside A tattoo for the storm.

b. ***devil's tattoo***: the action of idly tapping or drumming with the fingers, etc. upon a table or other object, in an irritating manner, or as a sign of vexation, impatience, or the like.

1803 MAR. EDGEWORTH *Belinda* xvii, Mrs. Freke beat the devil's-tattoo for some moments. **1826** DISRAELI *Viv. Grey* II. ii, The Peer sat in a musing mood, playing the Devil's tattoo on the library table. **1855** H. SPENCER *Princ. Psychol.* (1872) II. VIII. iv. 544 Beating the 'devil's tattoo' with the fingers on the table, is a recognized mark of impatience.

tattoo (tæ'tu:), *sb.*² Forms: 8 **tat(t)aow,** 8–9 **tattow, tatoo,** 9 **tatto, tatu,** 8– **tattoo.** [In 18th c. *tattaow, tattow* (ta'taʊ), a. Polynesian (Tahitian, Samoan, Tongan, etc.) *'tatau* (in Marquesan *'tatu*) sb. denoting the markings. (For the vb. the expression is *ta 'tatau* to strike or stamp tattoo.)

The word is recorded from Tahiti as *tataou* in Bougainville's *Voyage autour du Monde* 1766–9 (Paris 1771), and as *tattow* in Capt. Cook's *First Voyage* July 1769. The current Eng. *tattoo* and F. *tatou* are perversions of the native name.]

a. The act or practice of tattooing the skin (see TATTOO *v.*²); the mark or design made by tattooing.

[**1769** COOK *Jrnl. 1st Voy.* July (1893) 93 Both sexes paint their Bodys, *Tattow*, as it is called in their Language. This is done by inlaying the Colour of Black under their skins, in such a manner as to be indelible.] **1777** G. FORSTER *Voy. round World* I. 390 The punctuation which the natives call tattow. **1803** J. BURNEY *Discov. S. Sea* I. ii. 61 They [natives of the Philippines] had the custom of marking their bodies in the manner, which, to use a word lately adopted from the language of a people more recently discovered, we call tattow. **1863** R. F. BURTON *Abeokuta* I. iii. 104 There was a vast variety of tattoos and ornamentation. **1906** *Athenæum* 17 Mar. 334/2 The Kenyahs and Sea-Dayaks also appear to have borrowed the practice of tatu very largely from the Kenyans; but most of the Indonesian tribes have all had.. a distinctive tatu.

b. *attrib.* and *Comb.*, as ***tattoo mark***.

1845 J. COULTER *Adv. in Pacific* xiv. 209 Then entered the tatoo-men. **1892** 'MARK TWAIN' *Amer. Claimant* xvi. 164 His horny hands and wrists were covered with tattoo-marks. **1899** WERNER *Capt. of Locusts* 9 His teeth are not filed, and he has strange tattoo-marks on his face.

'tattoo, *sb.*³ *East Ind.* Also 8 tatoo, 9 tatto, tattu, (tut-hoo). [a. Hindī *ṭaṭṭū*.] A native-bred Indian pony. Also *attrib.* as ***tattoo horse, mare***. Abbreviated TAT (*sb.*⁴).

1784 in Seton-Karr *Select. fr. Calcutta Gaz.* (1864) I. 15 On their arrival at the Choultry they found a miserable dooley and 15 tattoo horses. **1800** *Misc. Tr.* in *Asiat. Ann. Reg.* 171/2 A man mounted on a tattoo came forward to tell us, that [etc.]. **1809** BROUGHTON *Lett. Mahratta Camp* xiv. (1892) 117 These tut,hoos are a breed of small ponies, and are the most useful and hardy little animals in India. **1814** SOUTHEY in *Q. Rev.* XII. 200 A Mahratta wife..frequently rides astride..upon a bullock, an ass, or a little *tattoo* horse. **1886** *Blackw. Mag.* Sept. 365/1 Drawn by tattoos and bullocks.

ta'ttoo, *v.*¹ [f. TATTOO *sb.*¹]

1. *trans.* To beat (a drum, etc.); to strike (something) with a succession of blows, to thump.

1780 S. J. PRATT *Emma Corbett* (ed. 4) II. 51 A little drum tattoo'd by the timber instrument that served him for an arm. **1863** COWDEN CLARKE *Shaks. Char.* xvi. 402 Then let us hope he may not have his head tattooed.

2. *intr.* To beat as upon a drum; to thump, tap, or rap upon something with a succession of blows.

1806 WOLCOTT (P. Pindar) *Tristia* Wks. 1812 V. 235 There Folly rushes with his dirty boots, Tattoos, and nearly thunders down the dwelling. **1832** HT. MARTINEAU *Ireland*

iii. 39 Her father..tattooing with his brogues upon the threshold. **1883** DUTTON COOK *P. Foster's D.* iv, Don't tattoo with your fingers, it fidgets me.

b. *trans.* To cause (something) to rap in this way (*upon* something else).

1810 *Splendid Follies* I. 57 Miss Betty..sat tattooing one of her shoe-heels upon the hearth.

Hence **ta'ttooing** *vbl. sb.* (also *attrib.*).

1871 B. HARTE *2nd Review Grand Army* ii, The wandering night-winds seemed to bear The sounds of a far tattooing. **1884** ALLBUTT *Visceral Neuroses* i. 23 Some little blinking, twitching, or tattooing trick which quickens as thoughts and words come faster.

ta'ttoo, *v.*[2] Forms: see TATTOO *sb.*[2] [f. TATTOO *sb.*[2]; already used as a vb. by Capt. Cook.]

1. *trans.* To form permanent marks or designs upon the skin by puncturing it and inserting a pigment or pigments: practised esp. by many Malayo-Polynesian peoples; also by some ancient nations, and by individuals (e.g. seamen) in developed countries since the 18th c. **a.** with the person or part as obj.

1769 COOK *Jrnl. 1st Voy.* July (1893) 93 This method of Tattowing I shall now describe... As this is a painful operation, especially the Tattowing their Buttocks, it is performed but once in their Life times. *Ibid.* 27 Nov. 164 Few of these people were Tattow'd or marked in the face,.. several had their Backsides Tattow'd. **1774** MME. D'ARBLAY *Early Diary* (1889) I. 325 His hands are very much tattooed. **1774** *Charac.* in *Ann. Reg.* 61/2 His hands are tattaowed, according to the mode in his native country. **1835** SIR J. ROSS *Narr. 2nd Voy.* xvi. 251 All were tattooed to a greater or less extent. **1846** BRITTAN tr. *Malgaigne's Man. Oper. Surg.* 88 We know that soldiers tattoo their arms and breasts, and impress and trace on them words and figures that neither lotions nor even blisters can efface. **1847** GROTE *Greece* II. xxv. IV. 5 They [Illyrians] shared with the remote Thracian tribes the custom of tattowing their bodies. **1852** MUNDY *Our Antipodes* x (1855) 247 [The Maori women] tattoo the under-lip a deep blue. **1887** W. S. GILBERT *Ruddigore* I, Look at his arms—tattooed to the shoulder.

b. with the mark or design as object.

1809 A. HENRY *Trav.* 248 The women..usually tatoo two lines, reaching from the lip to the chin. **1857** HUGHES *Tom Brown* II. ii, His long skinny arms all covered with anchors and arrows and letters, tattooed in with gunpowder like a sailor-boy's. **1877** W. H. DALL *Tribes N.W.* 89 The.. practice of tattooing perpendicular lines on the chin of women. **1902** *Man* II. 99 That a totem should be tatued on a body is a widespread practice.

2. *transf.* and *fig.* To mark, spot, or stain, esp. in a permanent way; to affect or characterize permanently as if by marking; to defame, vilify, 'blacken' (quot. 1884).

1774 *Westm. Mag.* II. 145 Well I remember when tataow'd you stood, In all the dignity of H——'s blood. **1806–7** J. BERESFORD *Miseries Hum. Life* (1826) VI. *Miseries Stage C.* xi, A Harridan with a face tattooed with wrinkles. **1847** LONGF. in *Life* (1891) II. 86 Proof-sheets of Evangeline all tattooed with Folsom's marks. **1884** *Tribune* (N.Y.) June, Mr. Blaine is tattooed... So was Abraham Lincoln... As soon as any man gains public confidence, malignant and envious creatures are found to revile him. **1886** RUSKIN *Præterita* I. vi. 177 The pleasure of tattooing myself with tar among the ropes.

Hence **tattooed** (-'u:d) *ppl. a.*, **ta'ttooing** *vbl. sb.* (also *concr.*; also *attrib.*, as ***tattooing-needle***); also **ta'ttooage** (*nonce-wd.*), a tattooed design [= F. *tatouage*]; **ta'ttooer**, one who practises tattooing; **ta'ttooist**, a professional tattooer; **ta'ttooment**, the action or process of tattooing.

1846 THACKERAY *Cornhill to Cairo* xiii, Above his *tattooage of the five crosses, the fellow had a picture of two hearts united. **1789** MRS. PIOZZI *Journ. France* II. 17 The accounts given us in Cook's Voyages of *tattowed Indians. **1791** GILPIN *Forest Scenery* II. 261 The Indian..doting on her black teeth, and tattooed cheeks. **1846** KEIGHTLEY *Notes Virg., Georg.* III. 25 The wild-looking tattooed Britons. **1897** P. WARUNG *Tales Old Regime* 168 Tattooed anchor on right forearm. **1906** *Athenæum* 17 Mar. 334/2 To classify the tatued peoples of Borneo. **1789** *Loiterer* 18 July 7 The most famous *Tataower in the Country. **1837** *Fraser's Mag.* XVI. 641 The azure dye of the tattooer is lastingly imprinted in the face of an Otaheitan. **1883** *Daily News* 26 Oct. 5/2 The great tattooers among European peoples are French soldiers and French criminals. **1773** *Charac.* in *Ann. Reg.* 3/2 They have a custom of staining their bodies..which they call *Tattowing. **1830** MARRYAT *King's Own* iii, The practice of tattooing is very common in the navy. **1859** JEPHSON *Brittany* xii. 211 Scored..to resemble the tattooing of a New-Zealander. **1877** KNIGHT *Dict. Mech., Tattooing-needle* (Surgical), an instrument for inserting a pigment beneath the epidermis. Used..for coloring white spots on the cornea. **1894** *Pall Mall G.* 5 Dec. 2/1 *Tattooists vied with each other in their efforts to invent new designs. **1885** J. H. DELL *Dawning Grey, Mind* 35 At best But rude *tattooment of embellishment.

tattoo, tattou, variants of TATOU, armadillo.

Tatt's: see TATTERSALL *sb.* (and *a.*)

tattu, variant of TATOU, TATTOO *sb.*[3]

‖**tatty** ('tætɪ), *sb. East Ind.* Also **tattie, tattee, tatti.** [a. Hindī *ṭaṭṭī*.] A screen or mat, usually made of the roots of the fragrant cuscus grass, which is placed in a frame so as to fill up the opening of a door or window, and kept wet, in order to cool and freshen the air of a room. Abbreviated TAT (*sb.*[3]).

1792 WILLIAMS in *Phil. Trans.* LXXXIII. 131 Tatties.. are affixed to the door or window frames, and kept constantly sprinkled with water. **1809** BROUGHTON *Lett. Mahratta Camp* x. (1892) 83 The hot winds have set in, and we are obliged to make use of *tattees*, a kind of screens made of the roots of a coarse grass called Kus. **1811** H. MARTYN in *Mem.* III. (1825) 342, I got a tattie made of the branches of the date tree, and a Persian peasant to water it. **1901** *Indian Standard* 16 Mar. 1/1 Those who..have neither Khas Tatties nor thermantidotes will pant..for want of fresh air.

attrib. **1848** tr. *Hoffmeister's Trav. Ceylon*, etc. vii. 277 [Rooms with] but one external entrance, and that closed up by means of a tatty-frame.

Hence **tattied** ('tætɪd) *a.*, furnished with a tatty or tatties.

1894 *Blackw. Mag.* Sept. 387/2 The Anglo-Indian is a close prisoner within the kus-kus tattied walls.

tatty ('tatɪ), *a.*[1] *Sc.* Also 6 **taty, tawty, tattie,** 9 **tawtie, tautie.** [app. related in form and sense to OE. *tættec* a rag, a tatter; cf. also TAT *sb.*[4], which is not evidenced so early, and may be a back-formation.] Of hair tangled, matted; of an animal or skin, shaggy with matted hair.

1513 DOUGLAS *Æneis* VII. xii. 63 A felloun bustuus and gret lyoun skyn, Terrible and rouch, wyth taty lokyrand haris. **1533** BELLENDEN *Livy* II. xi. (S.T.S.) I. 166 The hare of his berde was lang and taty [*v.r.* tawty]. **1818** SCOTT *Rob Roy* xxxiv, Wha wad hae thought there had been as muckle sense in his tatty pow. **1834** CARLYLE in Froude *Life* (1882) II. xviii. 428 Old pollarded..lime trees standing there like giants in tawtie wigs (for the new boughs are still young).

tatty ('tætɪ), *a.*[2] *colloq.* [f. TAT *sb.*[5] + -Y[1].]

1. Of a person, an animal: untidy, disreputable, 'scruffy'. Cf. TATTY *a.*[1]

1933 N. COWARD *Design for Living* II. iii. 67 Going round in a troupe, with all those tatty old girls. **1951** J. CANNAN *And All I Learned* x. 165 You mustn't call Brownie a tatty old trout. **1967** N. FREELING *Strike Out* 38 I've seen the painter..rather a tatty chappy by their standards. **1978** *Lancashire Life* Apr. 36/2 A widower living with his one son and a tatty collie dog, he had been a soldier for many years.

2. Of clothes, decoration, etc.: shabby, tawdry, cheap.

1940 N. MITFORD *Pigeon Pie* vii. 117 The 'King's' tatty striped wall-papers. **1951** 'A. GARVE' *Murder in Moscow* vii. 84 Ivan pushed up his tatty fur hat. **1959** H. R. F. KEATING *Death & Visiting Firemen* xv. 195 You're a man, I can see that, in spite of your tatty old clothes. **1963** *Times* 4 June 14/2 Nineteenth-century-style songs, played by a jaunty orchestra before tatty red-plush curtains and even tattier scenery, accompany the high jinks. **1976** *Sunday Post* (Glasgow) 26 Dec. 29/4 It [sc. the car] was a tatty green, so a pal and I painted it navy blue.

3. Of a place or a building: badly cared for, neglected, run down.

1956 L. MCINTOSH *Oxford Folly* iv. 53 This is Oxford's latest coffee-bar... The others are getting so tatty. **1966** *Listener* 12 May 686/1 Some distance from the edge of the Falls a sizeable crack has opened up... Neither the Americans nor the Canadians can afford to have Niagara looking so tatty. **1978** L. HEREN *Growing up on The Times* iii. 63 The car drove through the rather tatty outskirts of Tel Aviv.

4. *transf.* In other miscellaneous uses.

1957 *Listener* 19 Dec. 1026/1 Look what we did to that tatty second act. **1959** *Economist* 28 Mar. 1153/2 The Prime Minister's reply looks like a foretaste of the tattier tactics that will be used by the less inhibited Tories in the election. **1965** *New Statesman* 9 Apr. 585/2 The entire vision's too enormous for accommodation within the tatty ingenuities of the stage. **1975** in R. Crossman *Diaries* I. 376 This was a somewhat tatty account of Labour's first year in Government, prepared in Transport House as a diatribe against the Tories.

Hence **'tattily** *adv.*; **'tattiness.**

1952 A. WILSON *Hemlock & After* I. v. 93 He rejected the 'tattiness' of dead mullion and withered sycamore berries. **1957** *Observer* 29 Sept. 12/1 The keynote of these tattily exotic revues is imitation. **1959** S. GIBBONS *Pink Front Door* ix. 118 I've got you the rooms. Four of them, furnished rather tattily. **1973** J. WAINWRIGHT *Pride of Pigs* 8 The impression of tarted up tattiness. **1980** *Times Lit. Suppl.* 3 Oct. 1118/5 The novel is firmly set in the very recent past.. and rock music, fashion, the death of Elvis, the tattiness of London are described in detail.

tatty-bye (tætɪbaɪ; stress variable), *int.* [Fanciful formation: cf. TA-TA *int.* and GOODBYE.] A colloquial form of farewell.

1971 A. MORICE *Murder in Married Life* vi. 56 'Ta-ta for now, then.' 'Tatty-bye, Sandy darling.' **1974** M. BABSON *Stalking Lamb* xv. 113 I'll say tatty-bye for now then... And we'll see you soon. You know the way, don't you?

tatu: see TATOU, TATTOO *sb.*[2]

tatuete (erron. -ette): see TATOU.

†**tatuite,** = *t' atwite*, to twit, taunt: see T'[1] and ATWITE *v.*

c **1315** SHOREHAM *Poems* i. 1132 For for-ȝetene sennes, þat oure foman aredy haueþ..Tatuite.

tatusiid (tə'tu:sɪɪd), *a.* and *sb. Zool.* [ad. mod.L. *Tatusiidæ*, pl., f. *Tatusia*, f. Tupi *tatu*: see TATOU and -ID[3].] **a.** *adj.* Belonging to the family *Tatusiidæ* of armadillos, typified by the genus *Tatusia*. **b.** *sb.* An armadillo of this family.

taty, tatyllar, obs. ff. TATTY *a.*[1], TATTLER.

‖**ta tzu-pao** (da: dzəbau). Also **dazebao, dazibao, tatzepao, ta-tzu-pao.** [Chinese *dàzìbào*, f. *dà* big + *zì* character + *bào* newspaper, poster.] In the People's Republic of China, a wall poster written in large characters that expresses a (political) opinion or other message.

The posting of *ta tzu-pao* is no longer encouraged in China.

1960 *Peking Rev.* 5 Apr. 8/2 Criticism and self-criticism through large-scale airing of views and opinions, big debates and putting up *dazibao* (posters in large characters) are carried out in government and people's organizations. **1962** E. SNOW *Other Side of River* (1963) xlviii. 368 Around the basketball court and a stage which prisoners had built were bulletin boards posted with *ta tzu-pao* such as you see before any Chinese factory: essays, rhymes, praise and mutual criticism, lists of model workers and their awards. **1967** S. KNIGHT *Window on Shanghai* lviii. 250 Four foreigners in Peking put up a 'dazebao' criticizing the treatment given us by the Chinese. **1968** *Globe & Mail* (Toronto) 5 Feb. 10/2 A tatzepao (big-character poster) reproduced by the Shanghai newspaper claimed that the handful of party leaders now accused of being capitalist roaders exaggerated the role played by technical knowledge. **1973** T. R. TREGEAR *Chinese* iii. 58 Walls everywhere were covered with *ta-tzu-pao*, big-character newspapers. **1979** *Globe & Mail* (Toronto) 4 Apr. 1/2 Some students at Peking University told Western journalists that the repression was wrong as far as the poster or dazibao writers at Xidan democracy wall were concerned.

tau (tɔ:, taʊ). Also 4, 6 **taue,** 4 **tav,** 4–8 **taw,** 5 **tayu, tayewe.** [a. Gr. ταῦ, name of the letter **T** in the Greek alphabet, as in the Semitic whence the Greek was derived: see T, the letter.]

1. The name of the letter T in the Greek, Hebrew, and ancient Semitic alphabets. Often in the sense 'last letter', as *tau* was orig. in Greek, and continued to be in Hebrew, etc.

a **1300** *Cursor M.* 12199–12204 Þe letters fra alpha to taw [*Gött.* tau, *F.* taw, *Tr.* tayu], Wit sundri sight man mai þam knau [*Tr.* sew]. Quat es taw, sai first to me, And i sal vndo alpha to þe; For he þat alpha can noght se, Hu sal he wijt quat tav mai be? **1838** JACKSON tr. *Krummacher's Elisha* ix. 199 Set a mark upon them..a Tau, the last letter of the Hebrew alphabet, upon their foreheads. **1883** I. TAYLOR *Alphabet* I. 239 The letters *he*, *lamed*, and *tau* are almost the same in the Siloam inscription as on the Moabite stone, which is older by a century and a half. *Ibid.* II. 106 The persistency in the shape of *tau*, which varies less than any other letter, our modern capital **T** hardly differing from the [Phœnician] Baal Lebanon form.

2. a. A mark of the shape of the letter **T**, a St. Anthony's cross; a figure of this as a sacred symbol (also in *Heraldry*). Also formerly applied to the sign of the cross as made with the hand.

a **1300** *Cursor M.* 6078 (Cott.) On aiþer post þer hus to smer, A takin o tav on þair derner [*Gott.* On ilk derner, A sine of tau T [*Trin.* thayu] make ȝe þer]. *Ibid.* 21711–6 Þe signe o tav in ald laies Bitakens cros nu in vr daies... Tau and cros bath er als an, Bot tav has yerd a-bouen nan. *c* **1446** LYDG. *Nightingale Poems* ii. 318 This banner is most myghti of vertu,..Most noble signe and token of Tau. **1700** ASTRY tr. *Saavedra-Faxardo* II. 316 It is by the Tau they are stampt with, that they are assured of their real Value. **1704** J. HARRIS *Lex. Techn.* I, *Taw*, the Heralds have an Ordinary which they reckon among the Crosses, called by this Name, and of this Figure. **1895** *Q. Rev.* July 213 Tradition may conceive that the Tau was the mark of Cain. **1908** *Ibid.* July 142 Little images of bad silver, with the Saint's bell, his 'Tau' and the notorious pig.

b. Applied to the *crux ansata* of ancient Egyptian symbolism, the *ankh* ☥.

1785 [see ANSATED *ppl. a.*]. **1841** J. G. WILKINSON *Manners & Customs Ancient Egyptians* 2nd Ser. II. xv. 283 The sacred *tau*, or sign of Life, was presented to him. **1857** WILKINSON *Egypt. Time Pharaohs* 133 The gods hold in one hand the sacred Tau, or sign of life. **1877** A. B. EDWARDS *Up Nile* ix. 238. **1886** C. R. CONDER *Syrian Stone Lore* 253 *note*, The emblems of the..phœnix, the tau, the labarum, and the fylfot occur, but not the cross.

3. A **T**-shaped pastoral staff.

1855 tr. *Labarte's Arts Mid. Ages* xiii. 381 Pastoral staff called..a Tau. **1875** MASKELL *Ivories* 84 The Tau..is but a form of the pastoral staff, adopted in more than one country of Western Europe early in the middle ages.

4. A name, or part of the name, of various animals having markings resembling the letter **T. a.** The toad-fish (*Batrachus tau*) of the Atlantic coast of N. America. **b.** A kind of moth: see quot. 1832; also, a kind of beetle, and of fly.

1832 J. RENNIE *Conspect. Butterfl. & Moths* 36 *Bombycidæ* (Stephens)... The Tau Emperor [Moth] (*Aglaia Tau*, Ochsenheimer). Said to be British on doubtful authority.

5. *Particle Physics.* Freq. written τ. **a.** A meson that decays into three pions, now identified with the kaon. Also ***tau meson.***

1949 *Nature* 15 Jan. 86/2 We have considered the possible relations of the present results to the particles..referred to as τ-mesons, evidence for which has been recently reported by Bradt and Peters. **1955** *Proc. Glasgow Conf. Nucl. & Meson Physics 1954* 347 The striking similarity of the masses of the θ^0 and $\tau\pm$ mesons. **1968** M. S. LIVINGSTON *Particle Physics* vii. 138 The θ decayed into two pions while the τ decayed into three pions. **1973** L. J. TASSIE *Physics Elem. Particles* vii. 61 The solution to the θ–τ puzzle was that the θ and τ particles were the same, now called the *K*-meson, and the parity was not conserved in the decay of *K*-mesons.

1974 FRAUENFELDER & HENLEY *Subatomic Physics* ix. 205 The decays of the tau and the theta were so slow that they were known to be weak.

b. An unstable heavy charged lepton which has a spin of ½ and a mass of approximately 1780 MeV (3490 times that of the electron) and which decays into an electron or muon or into hadrons, in every case with one or more neutrinos. Also ***tau lepton, particle.***

1977 M. L. PERL in *Proc. Internat. Symposium Lepton & Photon Interactions at High Energies* 146 All..data..agree on the following points... c. The behavior of these [leptonic] events is consistent with the hypothesis that a new charged lepton, τ, exists with a mass of 1.9 ± 0.1 GeV/c^2. **1978** PERL & KIRK in *Sci. Amer.* Mar. 50/3 We shall relate here the story of the discovery of the new heavy lepton and its antiparticle, which we have named the tau and the antitau. **1979** *McGraw-Hill Yearbk. Sci. & Technol.* 240/1 It was first discovered through reaction (1), in which a positron (e^+) and electron (e^-) annihilate and produce a pair of τ-leptons of opposite electrical charge. **1980** *Sci. Amer.* July 60/1 More recently a third neutrino flavor has been added to accompany the newly discovered tau particle, which is a massive sibling of the electron and the muon. **1981** D. H. PERKINS in J. H. Mulvey *Nature of Matter* iv. 79 The neutrino is a muon-type neutrino and in subsequent interactions will always produce a charged μ, not an e or τ.

6. *attrib.* and *Comb.*, as ***tau-shaped*** adj. (= **T**-shaped); **tau-bone**, a **T**-shaped bone, as the INTERCLAVICLE; **tau-cross**, a **T**-shaped cross (= sense 2); so **tau-crucifix**; **tau-ring**, ? a ring inscribed with the letter **T**; **tau-staff**, a **T**-shaped staff (= sense 3).

1474 *Will Ld. Mountioye* (Somerset Ho.), A *Tayewe crosse. **1562** LEIGH *Armorie* 60b, Ouer all a crosse Taue. **1885** *Blackw. Mag.* July 129/2 The tau cross, crux ansata, St. Anthony's cross,..is the commonest of all primitive symbols. **1888** F. G. LEE in *Archæologia* LI. 356 There are ..no less than five heads of tau-crosses preserved in the South Kensington Museum. **1877** W. JONES *Finger-ring* 155 A very interesting collection of so-called *Tau (T) rings were exhibited. **1888** F. G. LEE in *Archæologia* LI. 356 A figure of a bishop or abbot..bearing a *tau-shaped staff. **1905** *Athenæum* 10 June 727/2 A tau-shaped central chamber. **1885** M'CRIE *Sk. & Stud.* 37 The other carries a cross-headed or *tau-staff. **1888** F. G. LEE in *Archæologia* LI. 356 Head of a tau-staff of the eleventh century.

tau, taubator, obs. ff. TAW *sb.*[2], TABERDAR.

tau, obs. var. TAO.

‖**taua** (ˈtaʊa). [Maori.] A Maori army or war party.

1858 J. WHITELEY *Let.* 19 Apr. in *Richmond-Atkinson Papers* (1960) I. 390 The taua seemed to be mustering their forces last night from the south. **1882** W. D. HAY *Brighter Britain!* I. x. 254 Instead of leading a ferocious taua, he finds himself the venerated pastor of a little community. **1921** H. GUTHRIE-SMITH *Tutira* x. 69 Two *tauas* or war-parties. **1959** TINDALE & LINDSAY *Rangatira* viii. 79 A taua of fighting-men, about fifty strong, was advancing towards them. **1978** [see RANGATIRA].

‖**taubada** (taʊˈbɑːdə). [Local word.] On the island of New Guinea, used to refer to anyone in a position of authority, esp. as a respectful form of address.

1891 W. D. PITCAIRN *Two Years among Savages of New Guinea* iii. 58 If he be a 'Taubada' that is to say a person of importance. **1924** 'R. DALY' *Outpost* xii. 116 Did the Taubada want to make them the laughing-stock of their enemies? **1945** *Coast to Coast 1944* 101 A native voice said, 'One more come, taubada.' **1963** *Times* 3 Dec. 8/1 Some *taubadas* and *mastas* have forsaken the hotels for clubs to which natives are not yet admitted.

Tauberian (taʊˈbɪərɪən), *a.* *Math.* [f. the name of Alfred *Tauber* (1866–?1942), Slovak mathematician + -IAN.] Applied to theorems in which the behaviour in the limit of a series or function is deduced from a weaker limiting property together with some additional condition, esp. theorems in which convergence is deduced from summability.

1913 HARDY & LITTLEWOOD in *Proc. London Math. Soc.* XI. 411 The general character of the theorems which it [*sc.* this paper] contains is 'Tauberian': they are theorems of the type whose first example was the beautiful converse of Abel's theorem originally proved by Tauber. **1962** D. R. COX *Renewal Theory* i. 14 A result of this type, enabling the limiting behaviour of $k(x)$ to be deduced from that of $k^*(s)$, is called a Tauberian theorem. **1979** *Nature* 24 May 358/1 Rau is well known and remembered for his valuable contributions to the theory of Tauberian theorems, function-theory and the theory of Dirichlet series.

taubron, -er, var. TABORN, -ER, *Obs.*

tauch, -e, taugh, obs. or arch. Sc. ff. TALLOW.

Tauchnitz (ˈtaʊknɪts, ˈtaʊxnɪts). The name of Christian Bernhard, Baron von *Tauchnitz* (1816–95), publisher of Leipzig, used *attrib.* and *absol.* with reference to volumes in the Collection of British and American Authors, a series begun by him in 1841 for sale on the continent.

1856 MRS. GASKELL *Let.* 26 Dec. (1966) 430 For 'North & South' I received 600£..having the Tauchnitz profit... I suppose however you would allow me to retain the profits arising from the American & Tauchnitz edit:. **1863** J. MORREL *Jrnl.* 10 July (1963) iii. 94 In a twinkling all our 'Tauchnitzes' became pocket editions. **1895** *Daily News* 15 Aug. 5/1 The excitement lest the Customs' officer were to find the Tauchnitz in the trunk. **1901** *Ibid.* 5 Jan. 7/4 Desolate dwellings, strewn with a few sixpenny magazines and smuggled Tauchnitzes. **1902** H. JAMES *Wings of Dove* III. v. 102 The uncut but antiquated Tauchnitz volume of which, before going out, she had mechanically possessed herself. **1920** JOYCE *Let.* 12 May (1966) II. 464 The head of the firm would like to have a copy with a view to including it in the Tauchnitz edition. **1936** E. AMBLER *Dark Frontier* vi. 88 A Tauchnitz edition of Butler's *Erewhon* purchased hastily from a station bookstall. **1960** *Times* 7 July 14/7 A library of 'Tauchnitz' books. **1975** T. ALLBEURY *Special Collection* iv. 125 A handful of Tauchnitz pocket editions.

taucht, obs. f. *taught*, pa. t. and pple. of TEACH *v.*

taudr(e)y, obs. ff. TAWDRY.

taught (tɔːt), *ppl. a.* [pa. pple. of TEACH *v*, which see for earlier Forms.]

1. Of a person: Instructed, trained; †learned (*obs.*). Now usually *absol.*, 'the taught', or in comb. with adverbs, as ***ill-taught, well-taught.***

1382 WYCLIF *Eccl.* ii. 16 The taȝt man dieth also and the vntaȝt. ?*a* **1400** *Morte Arth.* 178 Alle with taghte mene and towne in togers fulle ryche. **1483** *Cath. Angl.* 377/1 Tawght, *doctus, instructus.* **1552** HULOET, Taught or newlye instructed, *catechizatus.* **1831-3** E. BURTON *Eccl. Hist.* iv. (1845) 72 The mere necessity of instruction would give to the teachers a superiority over the taught. **1860** PUSEY *Min. Proph.* 283 Truth of knowledge is the same in the Teacher and the taught.

2. Of a subject, art, etc.: Conveyed by instruction: see TEACH *v.* 5.

1909 *Westm. Gaz.* 4 May 5/1 This, we are assured, was not a taught trick, but a perfectly natural demonstration.

Hence †**ˈtaughtly** *adv.*, learnedly, skilfully.

1382 WYCLIF *Wisd.* xiii. 11 If any crafti man..hewe of the wode an euene tree, and of this taȝtli [**1388** perfitli; Vulg. *docte*] pare awei al the rinde.

taught, pa. t. and pple. of TEACH *v.*; var. TAUT *a.*

tauhinu (taʊˈhɪnʊ). *N.Z.* Also **tarwinie**. [a. Maori.] An evergreen shrub, *Pomaderris phylicifolia*, of the family Rhamnaceæ, native to New Zealand and southeastern Australia and bearing downy leaves and clusters of small yellow flowers. Also *attrib.*

1848 R. TAYLOR *Leaf from Nat. Hist. N.Z.* 25/2 *Tauhinu*, a shrub. **1903** B. E. BAUGHAN in Chapman & Bennett *N.Z. Verse* (1956) 54 Briar, tauhinu, an' ruin. **1927** J. DEVANNY *Old Savage* 47 Behind her, tough shrubs, tarwinie and gorse, mantled the terrace leading back to the low hills. **1950** *N.Z. Jrnl. Agric.* Oct. 297 (*caption*) Note the prevalence of tauhinu scrub. **1964** *Weekly News* (Auckland) 15 Apr. 37/3 Tauhinu was the worst scrub to plough, for it grew outward along the ground.

Tauism, var. TAOISM.

tauk, taulke, obs. ff. TALK.

‖**taula** (ˈtaʊlə). *Archæol.* [Cat., f. L. *tabula* table.] A Bronze Age stone structure found on Minorca in the Balearic Islands, consisting of two slabs forming a T-shaped column, freq. enclosed by a horseshoe-shaped wall and believed to be a place of worship.

1881 R. L. PLAYFAIR *Handbk. Mediterranean* II. 459/2 A bi-lithon, or altar, composed of two immense monoliths,.. carefully dressed, called *Altar* or *Taula*, altar or table. **1911** M. S. BOYD *Fortunate Isles* xvi. 192 Just behind the talayot ..stands another relic of prehistoric times in the shape of a *taula*. **1932** *Discovery* July 238/2 Minorca possesses a form of megalithic structure which does not occur elsewhere. This is the *taula*, a table consisting of a slab of stone set upright in a groove in the flat rock-floor. **1950** *Antiquity* XXIV. 154 These excavations might have solved the problems of the date and purpose of the constructions known as 'taulas'. **1979** SERVICE & BRADBERY *Megaliths* vii. 134 The largest taula (the name means 'table' in Catalan..) ..is beside the talayot of Trepuco. *Ibid.*, As with all taulas, it is very broad in one dimension, very narrow in the other.

taulch, obs. Sc. f. TALLOW.

tauld(e, Sc. f. *told*: see TELL *v.*

taum (tɔːm). *Sc.* and *north. dial.* Also **tawm, towm, toum, tome, tom, tam**, etc. [a. ON. *taumr* a cord, rein, line, etc., in Norw. *taum* string, line, e.g. on a fishing-rod (Aasen), in Færoese *teymur* (*ey* = ON. *au*) a short string at the end of a fishing line to which the hook is secured. Cognate with OE. *téam* line, team, OHG. *zoum*, Ger. *zaum*, OS. *tôm*, Du. *toom* rein, bridle: see TEAM *sb.*] A fishing-line, usually one of horse-hair twisted. Locally, also, a string of other kinds (*E.D.D.*).

a **1733** *Shetland Acts* 11 in *Proc. Soc. Antiq. Scot.* (1892) XXVI. 198 All lines and tomes made of horse-hair. **1802** SIBBALD *Chron. Scot. Poetry* Gloss., Towm. **1818** HOGG *Brownie of Bodsb.* etc. I. ix. 158 [He] cleekit a hantle o' geds and perches [out of the loch] with his toum. **1825** BROCKETT *N.C. Words, Tawm, Tam*, a fishing line. 'A lang twine tam'. **1828** *Craven Gloss., Taum*, a fishing line. **1851** *Cumbld. Gloss., Tome*, a hair line for fishing. **1855** ROBINSON *Whitby Gloss., A Tawm*, a fishing line and rod. 'A fishing tawm'. **1904** *Daily Chron.* 19 Feb. 3/2 When a Scotch fisherman speaks of his line as a 'taum', he makes rather a fine use of the Old Norse word for 'bridle'.

taum(e, obs. and dial. ff. TALM *v.*, to faint.

taune, variant of TAWNE *v.*[1] *Obs.*

Taung (taʊŋ). Also **Taungs**. The name of a town in the northern Cape Province, South Africa, used *attrib.* in ***Taung child, skull***, etc., to designate the remains of a fossil hominid, *Australopithecus africanus*, found in a limestone cliff there in 1924. Cf. AUSTRALOPITHECUS.

1931 A. KEITH *New Discoveries Antiquity Man* iii. 61 How does the brain development of the Taungs skull fit into the human scheme of growth? **1962** G. H. R. VON KOENIGSWALD *Evol. Man* iii. 61 (*caption*) Front view of original Taungs skull. **1973** B. J. WILLIAMS *Evol. & Human Origins* ix. 136/1 The Taung child had an endocranial capacity of approximately 405 cc. *Ibid.* 136/2 Judging the Taung specimen from tooth eruption to be around five years of age, the adult individual would have had a cranial capacity of 440 cc. **1978** P. V. TOBIAS in C. J. Jolly *Early Hominids in Africa* 45 The *prima facie* case for the likely taxonomic affinities of the Taung skull rests on the concept that two main hominid lineages..existed side by side in Africa.

‖**taungya** (ˈtaʊŋjə). Also **taunggya**, †**toungya**. [Burmese, f. *taung* hill + *ya* plot, field.] A temporary hillside clearing. Usu. *attrib.*, designating a method of shifting cultivation practised in Burma, and a system of forest management based on this (see quot. 1938) and employed in tropical countries.

1876 *Encycl. Brit.* IV. 560/2 The system of cultivation known in Bengal as the *jûm*, that is clearing virgin soil by burning, cultivating it for one or two years, and then leaving it again to the jungle, is here [*sc.* in Burma] extensively practised under the name of *toungya* cultivation. **1904** [see KUMRI]. **1921** *Times Lit. Suppl.* 8 Sept. 574/3 The best system of raising teak is in taungya plantations. **1926** TANSLEY & CHIPP *Study of Vegetation* xi. 257 Plant succession in deserted taungyas or cultivated land. **1938** H. G. CHAMPION in Champion & Trevor *Man. Indian Silviculture* I. vi. 182 *Taungya* plantation procedure.. depends on getting the cultivator to plant or sow a new forest crop with his food crop, so that when he moves on, useful trees and not weeds will restock the area. **1946** [see JOOM]. **1952** [see *shifting cultivation* s.v. SHIFTING *ppl. a.* 1 b]. **1975** *Daily Tel.* 6 Oct. 9/3 Dr. Earl commends the 'taungya' method of managing eucalyptus plantations in Uganda.

taunt (tɔːnt), *sb.*[1] Forms: 6 **taunte, tawnte**, 6–7 **tant**, 6– **taunt**. [*Taunt sb.*[1] and vb.[1] are not found before 1500; origin obscure.

The most likely suggestion is that the sb. arose from the Fr. phrase *tant pour tant*, 'one for another, tit for tat', lit. 'as much for so much', englished in 16th c. as *taunt pour taunt* and *taunt for taunt*; hence, as primary sense, 'a return thrust, an effective rejoinder'. But the chronology of the sb. and vb. makes this doubtful.

Other suggestions, for vb. or sb., are OF. *tanter*, variant of *tenter* to try, prove, tempt; MHG. *tant* empty talk; and Du. *tanden* 'impetere, invadere aliquem' (Kilian), none of which seem adequate.]

†**1.** In phrase ***taunt for (pour) taunt***, like for like, tit for tat, in reply or rejoinder. *Obs.*

1542 UDALL *Erasm. Apoph.* 311 Cicero for that he had separated & deuided hymself from Piso, who had marryed his doughter, gaue Pompeius again taunte pour taunte, for yᵉ same kept warre against his owne father in lawe. **1548** —— *Erasm. Par. Luke* iii. 48b, Answer taunt pour taunt the one contrarie to the other. *c* **1550** CROKE *XIII Ps.* (Percy Soc.) 13 When they rebuked me so sore, I wold not render taunt for taunt. **1620** T. GRANGER *Div. Logike* 124 Regestion is commonly termed like for like, pin driuing out a pin, tint for taunt.

†**2.** A smart or clever rejoinder, a jesting quip or witty gibe; banter. *Obs.*

1571 *Damon & Pithias* in Hazl. *Dodsley* IV. 24 Ready to answer, quick in taunts, pleasant to jest. **1579** LYLY *Euphues* (Arb.) 33 Fine phrases, smooth quippes, merry tauntes. *a* **1625** FLETCHER *Hum. Lieutenant* IV. i, She's as wanton as a Kid to th' out side, As full of Mocks and Taunts.

3. a. An insulting or provoking gibe or sarcasm; a mocking or scornful reproach or challenge; a casting of something in any one's teeth.

a **1529** SKELTON *Bowge of Courte* 70 Her chyef gentylwoman..Gaue me a taunte, and sayde I was to blame. **1548** UDALL *Erasm. Par. Luke* ii. 25b, There was in hym no malapertenesse of cockyng or geuyng tauntes. **1552** HULOET, Tawnte, *morsus*,..*pipulum.* *a* **1572** KNOX *Hist. Ref.* Wks. 1846 I. 12 Many tantis war gevin thame in thair teith. **1591** SHAKS. *1 Hen. VI*, I. iv. 39. **1598** —— *Merry W.* v. v. 151 Haue I liu'd to stand at the taunt of one that makes Fritters of English? **1603** HOLLAND *Plutarch's Mor.* 354 True it is that a man of government may otherwhiles give a taunt and nipping scoffe, he may cast out also a merrie jest to moove laughter. **1680** C. NESSE *Church Hist.* 146 Many a taunt was cast on the old king. **1725** POPE *Odyss.* III. 179 With ireful taunts each other they oppose. **1871** B. TAYLOR *Faust* (1875) I. xix. 168 With sneers and stinging taunts disgrace me.

†**b.** *transf.* An object of insulting or scornful gibes. *Obs. rare.*

1611 BIBLE *Jer.* xxiv. 9, I will deliuer them..to be a reproch and a prouerbe, a taunt and a curse.

4. *Comb.*, as **taunt-song**, used to refer to certain passages in the Old Testament, *spec.* as a rendering of Heb. *māšāl.*

1906 S. R. DRIVER *Habakkuk* (Cent. Bible) 78 'Parable' in these passages [*sc.* Habakkuk 2: 6] suggests a wholly incorrect idea; and the best rendering is probably *taunt-song.* **1928** C. GORE et al. *New Commentary on Holy Scripture* 444/1 In that day of relief from sorrow and fear a taunt-song will be sung against the King of Babylon. **1959** G. W. ANDERSON *Crit. Introd. O.T.* v. 109 The second contains a striking taunt-song over the descent of a tyrant.. to the abode of the dead.

†**taunt**, *sb.*² *Obs. rare.* [Origin unascertained.] A branch, a twig.

1567 GOLDING *Ovid's Met.* VII. 91 And all the Pismeres creeping still upon his tawnts and sprigs [*Lat.* totidemque animalia ramis Ferre].

taunt (tɔːnt), *a.* (*adv.*) Also tant. [Origin and history obscure: perhaps two words; sense 2 evidently goes with TAUNT *v.*² and ATAUNT *adv.* 2.]

1. (?) Haughty; 'high and mighty'; 'stuck-up'. In *mod. dial.* saucy, pert.

*c***1500** MEDWALL *Nature* (Brandl) 823 Thys boy ys passyng taunte [*rime* avant]. *a***1550** *Image Ipocr.* II. 198 in *Skelton's Wks.* (1843) II. 425/1 He is so hault and taunt That he dare hyme avaunt, All erthly men to daunt. **1880** *W. Cornw. Gloss.*, *Taunt*, pert. 'A taunt piece of goods.' **1882** JAGO *Gloss. Cornw. Dial.*, *Taunt*, pert, 'high and mighty', saucy.

2. *Naut.* Of masts: Excessively tall or lofty.

[*c***1579**: implied in TAUNT *v.*²] **1622** R. HAWKINS *Voy. S. Sea* lix. 138 Neither can the ship be so strong with a decke and a halfe..: nor carry her Mastes so taunt: nor spread so great a clue. *a***1625** *Nomenclator Navalis* (Harl. MS. 2301), *Taunt* is when a mast is very high for the proportion of the shipp, wee saie it is a Taunt-mast. **1627** CAPT. SMITH *Seaman's Gram.* iii. 15 For a man of warre, a well ordered Taunt-mast is best. *Ibid.* 17 If your Masts be taunt, your yards must be the shorter. *a***1700** B. E. *Dict. Cant. Crew*, *Tant, Tantest*, Mast of a Ship or Man, Tall, Tallest. **1736** LEWIS *Hist. Thanet* Gloss., *Taant*, tall, or too high for its breadth or bigness, 'a taant mast, house'. **1831** *Examiner* 740/2 With a deep keel and sharp run, taunt sticks and spanking sails. **1851** KIPPING *Sailmaking* (ed. 2) 189 *Taunt*, an epithet, at sea, signifying high or tall. It is particularly expressed of the masts, when they are of extraordinary length. **1863** ROBSON *Bards Tyne* 397 Tant ships, that come with rampant rig, Against its sides are rested. **1898** F. T. BULLEN *Cruise Cachalot* 370 The 'crow's nests' are dismantled, taunt topgallant-masts sent up, and royal yards crossed.

†**b.** Phr. ***with taunt sail(s)***, also ***bearing a taunt sail***, with all sail set: cf. ATAUNT 2. *Obs.*

1622 R. HAWKINS *Voy. S. Sea* liii. 124 With much winde, and a chapping Sea, bearing a taunt-sayle. **1632** LITHGOW *Trav.* v. 177 Shippes were wont to passe vnder with taunt sayles. *Ibid.* x. 502 A gallant ship, puft with taunt saile.

c. *Comb.*, as ***taunt-masted, -rigged.***

1627 CAPT. SMITH *Seaman's Gram.* iii. 15 Taunt-masted. **1704** J. HARRIS *Lex. Techn.* I, *Taunt*, when the Masts of a Ship are too tall for her, they say she is *Taunt-masted*, or that her Masts are very *Taunt*. **1825** H. B. GASCOIGNE *Nav. Fame* 70 Taunt rigg'd she seems, and like a Privateer.

†**B.** *adv.* (?) To the full, thoroughly: cf. ATAUNT 1. *Obs.*

*a***1550** *Hye Way to Spyttel Ho.* 542 in Hazl. *E.P.P.* IV. 49 And there they prate, and make theyr auaunt Of theyr deceytes, and drynk adew taunt.

taunt (tɔːnt), *v.*¹ Also 6–7 tant. [See TAUNT *sb.*¹]

†**1.** *intr.* To make a smart or effective rejoinder; to answer back in equivalent terms; to exchange banter. *Obs.*

1513 MORE *Rich. III* in Hall *Chron.* (1548) 16 b, [Jane Shore] had a proper wytte..somtyme tantyng without displeasure, but not without disporte. *a***1529** SKELTON *Agst. Garnesche* ii. 37 To turney or to tante with me ye ar to fare to seke. **1548** THOMAS *Ital. Dict.* (1567), *Motteggiare*, to taunt pretely, or to cutte another mans woordes wittily or finely.

†**2.** *trans.* To answer (a person) with a bantering or mocking rejoinder; to 'chaff', banter. *Obs.*

1515 BARCLAY *Egloges* II. (1570) Biv/1 If thou call for ought by worde, signe or becke, Then Jacke with the bushe shall taunt thee with a chek. **1568** GRAFTON *Chron.* II. 58 The king receyued him..taunting him iestingly and merily, as though one Realme were not able to holde them both. **1596** DALRYMPLE tr. *Leslie's Hist. Scot.* VII. (S.T.S.) 8 This man tane in the feild the Bruse mirrilie tantis, and sayis, Welcome father, says he.

b. *dial.* (See quot.)

*a***1825** FORBY *Voc. E. Anglia*, *Taunt v.* to teize, to pester with silly questions, importunate entreaties, or any mode of minute vexation.

3. To reproach (a person) *with* something in a sarcastic, scornful, or insulting way.

1560 DAUS tr. *Sleidane's Comm.* 363 b, Than waxed he also more angry, and..taunted them with sore rebukes. **1565** COOPER *Thesaurus*, *Increpare probris*, to taunte with reprochful woordes. **1601** HOLLAND *Pliny* II. 571 Mamurra, whom the Poet Catullus..so tanted and reuiled in his verses. **1722** DE FOE *Plague* (1840) 66 Taunting him with want of courage to leap into the great pit. **1802** MAR. EDGEWORTH *Moral T.* (1816) I. xiii. 103 It ill became a person..who did not dress nearly as well as themselves, to taunt his betters with poverty. **1879** FROUDE *Cæsar* xxii. 386 They taunted him with cowardice.

b. *intr.* To utter taunts or stinging reproaches.

1560 DAUS tr. *Sleidane's Comm.* 306, I am not so cleane without experience, but I could taunte againe. **1577** FULKE *Conjut. Purg.* 370 You taunt at the author of that booke. *a***1688** BUNYAN *Israel's Hope Encouraged* Wks. (ed. Offor) I. 613 Those very men that are pleased to taunt at this kind of inference. **1802** MARIAN MOORE *Lascelles* II. 21 Mr. Richards was taunting at the disappointed Miss le Gros. **1833** MRS. BROWNING *Prometh. Bound* i. 91 Here, now, taunt on!

c. *trans.* with *obj. cl.* To say tauntingly. *rare.*

1873 BROWNING *Red Cott. Nt.-cap* II. 462 Folk may taunt That half your rock-built wall is rubble-heap! **1878** —— *La Saisiaz* 299 Taunt not 'Human work ape work divine?'

4. *trans.* To drive or get by taunting; to provoke.

1813 BYRON *Bride Abydos* II. xviii, Proscribed at home, And taunted to a wish to roam. **1837** W. IRVING *Capt. Bonneville* III. xlix. 253 But the Blackfeet were not to be taunted out of their safe shelter. **1888** *Pall Mall G.* 31 July 11/2 Viscount Wolmer probably repented of having helped to taunt it out of Mr. Morley.

Hence **'taunted** *ppl. a.*

1818 SCOTT *Battle Sempach* xii, 'Shalt see then how the game will fare', The taunted knight replied. **1882** *Sat. Rev.* 6 May 567/1 When the taunted victim..has drunk deep enough of the bitterness of death.

†**taunt**, *v.*² *Naut. Obs. rare*⁻¹. [app. f. TAUNT *a.* 2.] *trans.* To hoist, raise, elevate.

*c***1579** MONTGOMERIE *Misc. Poems* xlviii. 93 Vp uent our saillis, tauntit to the huins [= hunes], The trumpits soundit tuentie mirrie tuins.

taunter ('tɔːntə(r)). [f. TAUNT *v.*¹ + -ER¹.] One who taunts: see the verb.

1552 HULOET, Tawnter, *nasutus.* **1558** *Cranmer's Confut. Vnwritten Verities* Pref. Bviij, Taunters & fault finders with others, rather then menders of themselfes. **1579–80** NORTH *Plutarch* (1676) 291 Socrates..was a plain simple man to them that knew him but outwardly, or else a pleasant Taunter or Mocker. **1822** *Examiner* 688/1 Cold-blooded taunter of the suffering people.

†**'tauntful**, *a. Obs. rare*⁻¹. [f. TAUNT *sb.*¹ + -FUL.] Full of taunts; reproachful.

1715 TICKELL *Iliad* I. 15 Be all thy Rage in tauntful Words exprest.

taunting ('tɔːntɪŋ), *vbl. sb.* [f. TAUNT *v.*¹ + -ING¹.] The action of TAUNT *v.*¹

1563 WINȜET *Four Scoir Thre Quest.* Wks. (S.T.S.) I. 57 The erroneous assault me be [= by] tanting and mockrie. **1563** *Homilies* II. *Matrimony* (1859) 502 How few matrimonies there be without chidings, brawlings, tauntings, repentings. **1791** COWPER *Odyss.* XVII. 476 A tongue accustom'd much To tauntings. **1809–11** COMBE *Syntax* XXVI. 356 'Tis thus I..foil their tauntings with a joke.

'taunting, *ppl. a.* [f. as prec. + -ING².] That taunts, or reproaches provokingly.

*a***1548** HALL *Chron.*, *Hen. IV* 19 Railyng rimes, malicious meters and tauntyng verses. **1649** ROBERTS *Clavis Bibl.* 491 Their taunting Proverb against God is propounded. **1796** BURKE *Regic. Peace* i. Wks. VIII. 106 They accompanied their notice..with every kind of insolent and taunting reflection. **1844** THIRLWALL *Greece* VIII. lxii. 155 Cleomenes insulted his disappointment by a taunting letter.

'tauntingly, *adv.* [f. prec. + -LY².] In a taunting manner; with derisive or insulting reproach.

1549 COVERDALE, etc. *Erasm. Par. 1 Peter* 10 Not disdeynfully, nor tauntynglye as though you were offended at them. **1607** SHAKS. *Cor.* I. i. 114 (Fol. 2) The belly.. tantingly replyed To' th' discontented Members. **1646** J. WHITAKER *Uzziah* 13 [It] was tauntingly spoke of Christ, He saved others, himself he cannot save. **1876** MOZLEY *Univ. Serm.* v. (1877) 116 The question has often been asked tauntingly—Why has not Christianity done away with war?

So **'tauntingness.** *rare*⁻⁰.

1727 BAILEY vol. II, *Tauntingness*, a sharp, haughty, biting Reproachfulness. **1731** *Ibid.*, *Tauntingness*, Raillery.

'tauntless, *a. nonce-wd.* [f. TAUNT *sb.*¹ + -LESS.] Lacking or without a taunt (sense 3).

*c***1879** G. M. HOPKINS *Poems* (1967) 82 Tongue true, vaunt- and tauntless.

taunt ne caunt: see TANT NE QUANT.

Taunton ('tɔːntən, locally 'tɑːntən). Name of a town in Somersetshire; hence short for *Taunton cloth*, a woollen cloth formerly made there.

1499 in *Somerset Medieval Wills* (1901) 379 To William Busshop halfe a packe of Tauntons. **1607** *Act 4 Jas. I*, c. 2 §7 Every Broade Cloth..called Tauntons, Bridgwaters, and Dunsters made in the Westerne partes of Somersetsheire.

Taunton turkey ('tɔːntən 'tɜːkɪ). *U.S.* The name of *Taunton*, Massachusetts, used *attrib.* to designate the ale-wife, *Pomodorus pseudoharengus*, a fish resembling a herring found in marine or fresh water in eastern North America; = ALE-WIFE².

1851 A. ALLIN *Home Ballads* 13 'Taunton turkeys' are so thick, We sell them by the rod! **1950** *Chicago Tribune* 17 Jan. 14/3 In Massachusetts..the spring herring is known as 'Taunton turkey'.

'tauntress. *rare.* [f. TAUNTER + -ESS.] A female taunter, a taunting woman.

1557 *Agst. Vnstedfast Woman* in *Tottell's Misc.* (Arb.) 177 O temerous tauntres, that delightes in toyes..Ianglyng iestres, depraueres of swete ioyes.

tauny, obs. f. TAWNY.

tauorsay: see TAV-.

taupata ('taʊpətə). *N.Z.* [a. Maori.] An evergreen shrub or small tree, *Coprosma repens*, of the family Rubiaceæ, native to New Zealand, and bearing shiny leaves and clusters of small white flowers followed by orange-red berries.

1864 J. D. HOOKER *Handbk. N.Z. Flora* 268/1 Taupata *Coprosma retusa.* **1906** LAING & BLACKWELL *Plants N.Z.* 392 C[*oprosma*] *Baueri* is much used for hedges in Wellington and Melbourne. In the former place it is generally known as *taupata.* **1946** *Jrnl. Polynesian Soc.* LV. 159 *Taupata*, a tree ..with dark green leaves shining as if varnished. **1960** N. HILLIARD *Maori Girl* III. vi. 215 And there's the lights on the leaves of the taupata. **1966** G. DURRELL *Two in Bush* ii. 68 The list of plants used in this nest building reads like something out of Lewis Carroll: taupata twigs, scurvy grass and mesembryanthemum. **1982** F. BREAM *Island of Fear* 6 The graves..under the taupata trees.

taupe (təʊp, tɔːp). [a. Fr., f. L. *talpa* mole.] A brownish shade of grey resembling the colour of moleskin. Also *Comb.*, as ***taupe-coloured*** adj.

1911 *Daily Colonist* (Victoria, B.C.) 5 Apr. 24/1 (Advt.), Important silk purchase..in colors of rose, Persian blue.. taupe, purple, mauve. **1921** *Glasgow Herald* 18 June 4 Pearl, smoke, taupe, mouse and other soft becoming shades of grey. **1955** W. GADDIS *Recognitions* II. ix. 714 The hole in the roof had, of course, been repaired; and the interior done over in taupe and white. **1967** *Boston Sunday Herald Mag.* 26 Mar. 21/1 Use taupe powder to create depth. **1976** L. ST. CLAIR *Fortune in Death* xxi. 215 The subdued taupe of her suit. **1982** M. MCMULLEN *Better off Dead* (1983) I. iii. 19 The velvet was taupe-coloured.

taupie, variant of TAWPIE.

†**taur.** *Obs.* [ad. L. *taur-us* or OF. *tor, taur, thaur*, bull.] A bull; the constellation Taurus.

*c***1386** CHAUCER *Wife's Prol.* 613 Myn Ascendent was Taur and Mars ther-Inne. *c***1425** WYNTOUN *Chron.* II. 1269 A taur, þat is a buyl..Scho saw ner by hir on þe greyn.

†**taure.** *Obs. rare*⁻¹. Corruption of TOUR, a fringe of hair worn on the forehead, by association with *taurus* bull: cf. BULL-HEAD 3, quot. 1688.

1688 R. HOLME *Armoury* II. 464/2 Women wear Hair..in Taures when the hair on the forehead is curled and standeth out. *Ibid.*, Bull-heads, when the said curled forehead is much larger than the Taure.

Taurean ('tɔːriːən), *a.* (and *sb.*) [f. L. *taure-us* adj. (f. *taurus* bull) + -AN.]

a. Of or belonging to a bull. *rare.*

1656 BLOUNT *Glossogr.*, *Taurean, Taurine*, of or belonging to a bull. **1900** LEWIS & SHORT *Lat.-Eng. Dict.*, *Taureus*, of a bull or ox,..[*taurea*] *vincla*, i.e. taurean bands (a poet. expression to denote glue), Lucr. 6, 1071.

b. Of or pertaining to the constellation or zodiacal sign of Taurus. Cf. TAURIAN *a.* b.

1924 C. E. O. CARTER *Conc. Encycl. Psychol. Astrol.* 105 Obedience is generally regarded as a Taurean virtue. **1928** W. H. SAMPSON *Zodiac* iii. 25 The Pleiades are part of the constellation Taurus..more Taurean in nature. **1974** *Woman* 4 May 56/1 A Taurean mother will help her Piscean children to develop their own talents.

B. as *sb.* = TAURUS 1 c.

1911 I. M. PAGAN *From Pioneer to Poet* ii. 31 The burlesque Taurean is fat, thick-necked, gross and overfed looking, and often has a great love of low comedy. **1916** K. T. CRAIG *Stars of Destiny* 37 Mental exactness and persistence are attributed to Taureans. **1969** 'V. PACKER' *Don't rely on Gemini* (1970) xiv. 118 Brahms was a Taurus. .. Fred Astaire, Bing Crosby, and Perry Como are all Taureans, too. **1976** *Sunday Mail* (Glasgow) 26 Dec. 27/6, I always believed Taureans were home-lovers.

taureau ('tɒrəʊ). *Canad. Hist.* Also †toreau. Pl. taureaux. [a. Canad. Fr., a. Fr. *taureau* bull.] A bag of buffalo-hide for carrying pemmican; also *transf.*, the pemmican itself.

1794 J. MACDONNELL *Jrnl.* 14 Jan. in L. E. R. Masson *Les Bourgeois de la Compagnie du Nord-Ouest* (1889) I. 287, I cut 20 sacks or *taureaux* to put pemican in and gave them to Minie to sew. **1795** —— *Jrnl.* 28 Apr. in *Ibid.* 294 Started them for the Forks with 138 + 137 taureaux of pemican. **1807** W. F. WENTZEL *Let.* 27 Mar. in *Ibid.* 90 This is our staple article of provisions when travelling, it is called *taureau* or *Pimecan.* **1821** G. SIMPSON *Jrnl. Occurrences Athabasca Dept.* (1938) 278 It may be well to have the Toreau in Store. **1890** *Trans. R. Soc. Canada* VIII. II. 104 A sack or 'toreau' of pemmican, as it was called, consisted of nearly equal quantities of tallow and dried meat. **1911** K. HUGHES *Father Lacombe* iii. 32 They pounded dried meat to powder in wooden bowls, mixing hot grease and dried berries with it, packing the whole into large sacks of buffalo-hide, called by the Metis—*taureaux*... This was *pimik-kan*, the manna of the Canadian prairies. **1927** A. P. WOOLLACOTT *Mackenzie & his Voyageurs* 52 It [*sc.* pemmican] was a staple food among the fur-traders on long journeys, when..game could not be had. Also known as 'taureaux'. **1931** G. L. NUTE *Voyageur* 213 The train wound its slow way back to Pembina laden with..228 *taureaux*, or leather bags of pemmican. **1951** W. O'MEARA *Grand Portage* xxiv. 139 The pemmican [had been] mixed and stored in shaggy taureaux.

tauri-, combining form of L. *taurus* bull, in TAURICIDE, etc.; see TAURUS, and cf. TAURO-.

'Taurian, *a.* [irreg. f. L. *taur-us* bull + -IAN.]

a. = TAUREAN, TAURINE *a.*

1882 *Harper's Mag.* Sept. 563/1 Three days of bull-fighting..with eight taurian victims each day.

b. Of or pertaining to the constellation Taurus; characteristic of a person born under the zodiacal sign of Taurus. Cf. TAUREAN *a.* b. Occas. as *sb.*, = TAURUS 1 c.

1909 WEBSTER, *Taurian*..Of or pert. to Mount Taurus, or the constellation Taurus. **1928** W. WILSON *Astrology* iii. 53 The Taurian life has been spoken of as happier at the end than at the beginning. **1938** D. ANRIAS *Man & Zodiac* vii. 69 Afflicted Taurians rarely trust men or circumstances. **1972** D. LEES *Zodiac* 15 Zodiac..predicted that Julius would make a tremendous coup on the stock market, provided he got off his lazy Taurian arse and acted immediately. **1972**

Vogue 1 Mar. 144/4 He's a Gemini... I'd be much better off with a Taurian.

tauric (ˈtɔːrɪk), *a.* [f. Gr. ταῦρος or L. *taurus* bull + -IC.] Pertaining or relating to, or of the nature of, a bull; taurine.

1816 G. S. FABER *Orig. Pagan Idol.* I. 406 The tauric Jupiter was the parent of the Cretan Minos. **1818** —— *Horæ Mosaicæ* I. 314 He set up at Bethel two calves of gold in apparent imitation of the tauric Cherubim of the temple. **1882** R. BROWN *Law Kosmic Order* 43 In the tauric and bovine form.

tauricide (ˈtɔːrɪsaɪd). *rare.* [f. L. *taur-us* bull: see TAURI- and -CIDE.] **a.** A bull-slayer; a matador. **b.** The slaughter of a bull.

1845 E. WARBURTON *Crescent & Cross* I. ix. 169 Cambyses, the tauricide,..and the desert..have left little trouble to the tourist. **1852** *Fraser's Mag.* XLV. 536 The great tauricide still hesitated. **1882** *Pall Mall G.* 11 Sept. 2 If you kill him you are guilty of felony or tauricide.

†**tauriˈcornous,** *a. Obs. rare*[−1]. [f. as prec. + L. *cornu* horn + -OUS.] Having horns like those of a bull.

1646 SIR T. BROWNE *Pseud. Ep.* v. ix. 247 Their descriptions must be relative, or the Tauricornous picture of the one, perhaps the same with the other. **1656** BLOUNT *Glossogr., Tauricornous,* horned like a Bul.

Taurid (ˈtɔːrɪd). *Astron.* [f. TAUR-US, after LEONID, PERSEID. In F. *taurides* pl. (Littré 1877).] In *pl.* A system of meteors which appear to radiate from a point in the constellation Taurus, about the 20th of November.

1888 *Cassell's Encycl. Dict.,* Taurides.

tauridor, obs. form of TOREADOR.

†**tauˈriferous,** *a. Obs. rare*[−0]. [f. L. *taurifer* (f. *taurus* bull) + -OUS: see TAURI- and -FEROUS.]

1656 BLOUNT *Glossogr., Tauriferous,* which beareth or nourisheth Buls or neat. **1721** in BAILEY.

tauriform (ˈtɔːrɪfɔːm), *a.* [ad. L. *tauriform-is,* f. *taurus* bull: see TAURI- and -FORM.] Having the form of a bull.

1721 BAILEY, *Tauriform,*..in the Shape of a Bull. **1803** G. S. FABER *Cabiri* I. 347 Bud-Arc, the tauriform god of the Arc. **1809** E. DAVIES *Mythol. Druids* 170 The usual residence of the tauriform god. **1877** A. W. WARD in *Encycl. Brit.* VII. 403/2 The tauriform sun-god whom his worshippers adored with loud cries.

taurine (ˈtɔːraɪn), *sb.*[1] *Chem.* Also -in. [f. *tauro-* in *taurocholic* + -INE[5].] A neutral crystallizable substance, $C_2H_7NSO_3$, *amido-ethyl-sulphonic acid,* obtained in 1826 by L. Gmelin from ox-bile, and contained in the bile of most other animals, resulting from the transformation of taurocholic acid under the influence of acids and alkalies.

1845 G. E. DAY tr. *Simon's Anim. Chem.* I. 47 Taurin forms colourless regular six-sided prisms, terminated by four- or six-sided pyramids. **1868** WATTS *Dict. Chem.* V. 701 Taurocholic acid..when boiled with water, or with alkalis, ..is resolved into taurine and cholic acid. **1869** ROSCOE *Elem. Chem.* (1871) 438 A peculiar substance termed taurin is obtained by the action of acids on bile.

taurine (ˈtɔːraɪn), *a.* (*sb.*[2]) [ad. L. *taurīn-us,* f. *taurus* bull: see -INE[1].] **A.** *adj.* Of, pertaining to, of the nature of, or resembling a bull; bovine. Also *spec.,* pertaining to bull-fighting.

1613 HEYWOOD *Brazen Age* I. Wks. 1874 III. 176 Hadst thou not stoopt thy horrid Taurine shape I would haue peece-meale rent..thy tough hide. **1809** E. DAVIES *Mythol. Druids* 173 The wounding of this bull, who represented the taurine god. **1818** R. P. KNIGHT *Symbolic Lang.* (1876) 79 The taurine figures of Bacchus and the Rivers have more or less of the original bull. **1876** M. COLLINS *Fr. Midnight to M.* III. v. 57 Immovable as a taurine statue of Nineveh. **1932** R. CAMPBELL *Taurine Provence* 28 Every village westward of Martigues has three or four fêtes a year all accompanied by taurine ceremonies. Nearly every village has its small arena. **1977** *Monitor* (McAllen, Texas) 3 July 6B/3 Longinos Mendoza is also slated to appear on the card having shown exceptional taurine skill during his last performance [*sc.* a bullfight].

B. *sb.* A taurine beast, a bull. *nonce-use.*

1888 *Harper's Mag.* Apr. 783 Sturdy and stocky as a Jersey bull, and with not a little of that taurine's pugnacity.

tauriscite (ˈtɔːrɪsaɪt). *Min.* [ad. G. *tauriszit* (Volger 1855), from the Latin name of its locality, *Pagus Tauriscorum* (Canton Uri, Switzerland): see -ITE[1].] Native ferrous sulphate, like copperas, but occurring in acicular crystals.

1868 DANA *Min.* 644. **1896** CHESTER *Dict. Names Min.* 266.

†**tauˈrize,** *v. Obs. nonce-wd.* [f. L. *taur-us* bull + -IZE.] *intr.* To play the bull, to take the form of a bull.

1727 SOMERVILLE *Wife* 12 What form great Jove would next devise, And when his godship would again Taurise?

tauro-, repr. Gr. ταυρο-, combining form of ταῦρος (= L. *taurus*) bull, occurring in a few words derived from Greek and modern chemical terms, and in rare nonce-formations. **ˈtaurobole** [cf. TAUROBOLY], a bull-slayer; also **tauroˈbolic** *a.,* of the nature of tauroboly. (Both *rare.*); **tauˈrolatry** [-LATRY], worship of a bull (in quot. with allusion to 'John Bull'). **tauroˈmorphous** *a.* [Gr. ταυρόμορφος, f. μορφή form], having the form of a bull. **tauro-ˈserpentine** *a.,* relating to a bull and a serpent. See also below.

1934 R. CAMPBELL *Broken Record* viii. 183 These two great horsemen are superior equestrian *tauroboles to any of the Portuguese, Spanish or Mexican. *Ibid.* iii. 67 A truly *taurobolic and Mithraic sensation. **1901** *Speaker* 8 June 278/2 Is not *Taurolatry the religion of Englishmen? **1891** *Cent. Dict.,* *Tauromorphous. **1855** BAILEY *Mystic* 58 As told in mysteries *tauro-serpentine.

tauroboly (tɔːˈrɒbəlɪ). *Gr. Antiq.* [ad. L. *taurobolium* (also in Eng. use), f. Gr. ταυροβόλος striking or slaughtering bulls, f. ταῦρος bull + stem of βολή cast, stroke, wound. So F. *taurobole.*] The slaughter of a bull or bulls; *spec.* a pagan sacrifice of a bull in honour of Cybele, with its attendant rites, including a bath in bulls' blood; also, the representation of such a slaughter or sacrifice in sculpture, etc.

1700 tr. *Danet's Dict. Grk. & Rom. Antiq., Tauropolium,* or *Tauropolion* [sic], Sacrifices of Bulls, which were offered to Cybele,..to render Thanks..for her teaching Men the Art to tame those Animals. **1845** *Encycl. Metrop.* XVI. 114/1 They offered a sacrifice of a bull or ram, (whence the terms *Taurobolium* and *Ariobolium,*) in the blood of which the hierophant was also sprinkled. **1879** FARRAR *St. Paul* (1884) I. xviii. 187 *note,* Such were the taurobolies and kriobolies —hideous blood baths. **1882** [see KRIOBOLY]. **1889** FARRAR *Lives Fathers* I. ix. 562 He [Julian] washed away the lustral waters of baptism in the reeking horrors of a Tauroboly. **1891** *Smith's Dict. Grk. & Rom. Antiq.* II. 762/2 A temple of the Magna Mater where these rites of *taurobolium* were celebrated stood on the Vatican.

taurochenocholic (ˌtɔːrəʊkiːnəʊˈkɒlɪk), *a. Chem.* [f. next, by insertion of *-cheno-* from Gr. χήν goose.] In ***taurochenocholic acid,*** a sulphuretted acid ($C_{29}H_{49}NSO_3$) found in goose-bile.

1868 WATTS *Dict. Chem.* V. 700.

taurocholic (tɔːrəʊˈkɒlɪk), *a. Chem.* [f. TAURO- + Gr. χολή gall, bile + -IC: cf. CHOLIC.] In ***taurocholic acid,*** an acid ($C_{26}H_{45}NSO_7$) found in the bile of the ox and of most other animals, mostly together with glycocholic acid. Hence **taurocholate** (tɔːˈrɒkəʊlət), a salt of taurocholic acid.

1857 MILLER *Elem. Chem.* III. xii. §2. 702 Both of these resinous acids (the *glycocholic* and the *taurocholic*) contain nitrogen. The taurocholic acid also contains sulphur. *Ibid.* 706 The taurocholates of the alkalies are very soluble in water and in alcohol. **1872** THUDICHUM *Chem. Phys.* 17. **1872** HUXLEY *Phys.* v. 122 The taurocholate and glycocholate of soda, or bile salts, as they are sometimes called.

ˈtaurocol(l. *rare.* Also in L. form -colla. [ad. Gr. ταυρόκολλα, f. ταῦρος bull + κόλλα glue.] Glue made from bulls' hides.

1678 PHILLIPS, *Taurocolla,* a glutinous substance made out of Bulls Hides, and therefore so called, though oft times it is made of the Ears and Feet of fourfooted Creatures. **1753** CHAMBERS *Cycl. Supp., Taurocolla,* bull-glue, a sort of glue much used among the antients in works that required strength. **1847** WEBSTER, *Taurocol.* **1882** OGILVIE (Annandale), *Taurocoll, Taurocolla.*

taurodont (ˈtɔːrəʊdɒnt), *a.* [f. TAURO- + Gr. ὀδούς, ὀδοντ- tooth.] Of mammalian molar teeth: having large broad crowns and short roots.

1915 A. KEITH *Antiquity of Man* viii. 148 Molar teeth [in Neanderthal man] are large in crown and body and extremely short in root... To [*sic*] this peculiar form of molar tooth..I have proposed the name of 'taurodont'. **1927** PEAKE & FLEURE *Hunters & Artists* 18 This condition of the teeth, known as taurodont, has been found among some representatives of Neanderthal man. **1948** *New Biol.* V. 84 The teeth [of Neanderthal man]..are often of that specialised kind called 'taurodont'—they are stumpy with short roots. **1971** *Nature* 5 Feb. 409/2 The frequent lack of incisors and well worn flattened taurodont molars superficially suggest the crateriform decay of Moon's mulberry molars. **1973** B. J. WILLIAMS *Evolution & Human Origins* x. 159/2 The molars and premolars are 'Taurodont', meaning that they have an enlarged pulp cavity.

taurodontism (tɔːrəʊˈdɒntɪz(ə)m). [f. as prec. + -ISM 3.] In certain mammals, the condition of having taurodont teeth.

1913 A. KEITH in *Proc. R. Soc. Med.* (Odontol. Sect.) VI. 103 For this condition or tendency Professor Keith proposed the name of 'taurodontism'. **1939** *Nature* 23 Dec. 1055/2 In some peculiarities of the teeth he [*sc.* Sinanthropus] approaches the gorilla..and..the female orang in 'taurodontism'. **1959** J. D. EVANS *Malta* i. 36 They are molars, but the roots, instead of being separate, as in normal human teeth, are fused together. This is a phenomenon known technically as *taurodontism,* and it is particularly characteristic of the primitive type of human known as Neanderthal man. **1982** *Times* 27 Nov. 4/1 The molar exhibits marked taurodontism, an enlargement of the pulp cavity extending down into the roots, which..is characteristic of early Neanderthals.

tauromachy (tɔːˈrɒməkɪ). Also sometimes in foreign forms. [ad. Gr. ταυρομαχία, f. ταῦρος bull + μάχη fighting (see -MACHY): so F. *tauromachie.*] The practice or custom of bull-fighting; also (with *a* and *pl.*) a bull-fight.

1846 THACKERAY *Cornhill to Cairo* ii, It was not a real Spanish tauromachy—only a theatrical combat. **1846** *Times* 17 June 5/6 The art of tauromachy has just sustained an irreparable loss by the death of Montes, the Spanish matador. **1892** *Cornh. Mag.* Sept. 292 In the interests of civilisation and progress, it declares against the tauromachies. **1902** *Munsey's Mag.* XXVI. 524/2 Under the Bourbons, it [bull-fighting] went out of royal fashion, though it was still practised, and it was restored by Ferdinand VII, who established a college of tauromachy. [**1910** *Encycl. Brit.* IV. 789/1 *Bull-fighting,* the national Spanish sport. The Spanish name is *tauromaquia.*] **1923** W. J. LOCKE *Moordius & Co.* xi. 147 After public renunciation of *tauromachie,* gracefully made among a circle of Spanish friends. **1967** MCCORMICK & MASCAREÑAS *Compl. Aficionado* ii. 35 One has only..to read certain of the early manuals of tauromachia..to realize that..a good deal has been gained through modern changes. **1969** C. IRVING *Fake!* (1970) viii. 99 He was to do over two hundred of them [*sc.* drawings], the best of which are probably in the Picasso *Tauromachia* series.

So **tauromachian** (-ˈmeɪkɪən), **tauromachic** (-ˈmækɪk) [F. *tauromachique*] *adjs.,* of or pertaining to tauromachy; **tauroˈmachics** [-IC 2], the business of bullfighting.

1845 FORD *Handbk. Spain* I. 146 A tendency to gitanesque and tauro-machian slang. **1846** —— *Gatherings fr. Spain* (1906) 233 The beloved monarch shut up the lecture rooms forthwith, opening..by way of compensation, a tauromachian university. **1887** *Daily Tel.* 17 June (Cassell), The matador is forbidden by the laws of tauromachic etiquette to attack the bull. **1894** *Westm. Gaz.* 13 June 2/1 There are about fifteen special tauromachic newspapers..in France. **1934** F. M. FORD *Let.* 14 Sept. (1965) 234, I don't know why I should deluge you with..tauromachics.

‖**Taurus** (ˈtɔːrəs). [L. *taurus* bull.]

1. *Astron.* **a.** The second of the zodiacal constellations, the Bull, in which are included the groups of the Pleiades and Hyades. **b.** Also, the second of the divisions or signs of the Zodiac, into which the sun enters on or near the 21st of April: originally identical with the constellation (cf. CANCER 2). Symbol ♉.

c **1391** CHAUCER *Astrol.* I. §21 As aries hath [respect to] thin heued, & taurus thy nekke & thy throte, gemyni thyn armholes & thin armes. **1398** TREVISA *Barth. De P.R.* VIII. x. (Bodl. MS.), Taurus..is an erþy signe..And he is þe hous of substaunce and of ryches and possessioun of fonging & of ȝeuynge. **1588** SHAKS. *Tit. A.* IV. iii. 69 See, see, thou hast shot off one of Taurus hornes. **1664** BUTLER *Hud.* II. III. 904 Some say the Zodiack-Constellations Have long since chang'd their antique Stations Above a Sign, and prove the same In Taurus now, once in the Ram. **1667** MILTON *P.L.* I. 769 As Bees In spring time, when the Sun with Taurus rides. **1868** LOCKYER *Elem. Astron.* §94. 36 In 1861 it was found that a small nebula, discovered in 1856 in Taurus.. had disappeared.

c. A person born under the zodiacal sign of Taurus. Also *attrib.* or as *adj.*

1901 C. A. WALKER *Under a Lucky Star* 84 The head-workers of humanity could accomplish but little without assistance from the practical, executive Taurus. **1927** G. SULLY *First Princ. Astrol.* iii. 24 Taurus and Gemini make good mates when they set out to help one another unselfishly. **1943** D. POWELL *Time to be Born* xi. 272 Her astrologer..failed her by promising a new man, a Taurus with a heart condition. **1964** L. MACNEICE *Astrol.* v. 147 A 19th-century astrologer's idea of a Taurus woman. **1971** V. CANNING *Firecrest* iii. 35 Henry Martin Dilling, born 1927, the same age as himself; though Dilling was a Leo and he Taurus. **1979** S. RIFKIN *McQuaid in August* (1980) ix. 85 I'm Sagittarius. If you're Taurus..we can get a big thing going.

†**2.** *Zool.* An obsolete genus including the common ox (now *Bos taurus*).

taurylic (tɔːˈrɪlɪk), *a. Chem.* [f. L. *taur-us* bull + -YL + -IC.] In ***taurylic acid,*** a colourless oil (C_7H_8O) obtained together with phenol from human urine and that of cows and horses.

1868 WATTS *Dict. Chem.* V. 701 Taurylic acid..isomeric with anisol, benzylic alcohol, and cresol—perhaps identical with the latter. **1873** RALFE *Phys. Chem.* 56 Taurylic acid is a colourless, oily liquid, fluid at 18°.

tau-staff: see TAU.

Tau Sug (taʊ sʊg), *sb.* (and *a.*) Also **Tao Sug, Tausug, Taw Sug.** [Tau Sug, f. *taw* person + *sug, sulúg* current.] One of the Islamic groups inhabiting the Sulu Archipelago in the Philippine Islands, whose ancestors can be traced back to the Butuan area of north-east Mindanao; the Austronesian language spoken by this people. Also *attrib.* or as *adj.* Cf. SULU[1].

1923 [see SULU[1]]. **1964** P. G. GOWING *Mosque & Moro* i. 1 Ninety-two percent of all Muslim Filipinos belong to the Tau Sug, Maranao,..and Samal groups. *Ibid.* 2 A vigorous and proud people, the Tau Sug are the backbone of the historic Sultanate of Sulu. **1964** E. A. NIDA *Toward Sci. Transl.* ix. 207 In the expression 'sat and begged' as rendered into Tau Sug, a language of the Philippines, one must specify one of these actions as primary and the other as secondary. **1973** J. A. BRUNO (*title*) The social world of the Tausug. **1977** [see SULU[1]].

taut (tɔːt), *a.* Forms: α. 3–4 **toȝt, -e,** 4 **toght, touht, towt, -e,** (**tout**); 5 **towght,** 5–7 (9 *dial.*) **tought** (7 **toft**). β. 5–9 **taught.** γ. 7–9 **tort.** δ. 8–

taut. [The history of this word is in many points obscure. Though the form *taught* (now spelt *taut*) is known to us only after 1600, there is little doubt that it is the same word as the ME. *toȝt*, *toght*, *tought*, used also by Capt. Smith 1612 (and in Forby). The etymology of *toȝt*, *toght*, is doubtful; but it is generally held to be related in some way to the ablaut-grade *tog-*, *toȝ-* of OE. **téohan*, *téon*, TEE *v.*[1], Goth. *tiuhan* to draw. See Note below.]

† **1. a.** Tense, as a surface; tight, distended, full to distention. *Obs.*

α. *c* **1325** *Poem Times Edw. II* 160 in *Pol. Songs* (Camden) 331 He maketh his mawe touht off the beste. *Ibid.* 238 ibid. 334 The best he piketh up himself, and maketh his mawe touht. *c* **1380** *Sir Ferumb.* 4390 þat ech of hem ne drof forþ on, With pakkes y-charged euerechon, Wyþ harneys y-fillid toȝte. *c* **1386** CHAUCER *Sompn. T.* 559 Than shul this cherl with bely stif and toght As any Tabour, hither ben ybrought. *c* **1450** *Songs, Carols*, etc. (E.E.T.S.) 118/24 Your brest is so towght, Tyll ye haue well cowght. **1612** CAPT. SMITH *Map Virginia* 28 They haue a great deepe platter of wood. They couer the mouth thereof with a skin, at each corner they tie a walnut,..with a small rope they twitch them togither till it be so tought and stiffe, that they may beat vpon it as vpon a drumme.

δ. **1878** H. M. STANLEY *Dark Cont.* I. xvii. 456 Their rounded bodies were as taut as a drumhead.

† **b.** *fig.* (?) Firm, firmly fixed or settled, clinched. (See also TOUGHT *a.*)

13.. *E.E. Allit. P.* A. 521 Gos in-to my vyne, dotz þat ȝe conne. So sayde the lorde & made hit toȝt.

2. a. Tightly drawn, as by longitudinal tension; stiff, tense, not slack. Chiefly in nautical use.

α. **1604** *Peele's Tale Troy* 256 Away they fly, their tackling toft [*ed.* 1589 teft] and tight. *a* **1825** FORBY *Voc. E. Anglia*, *Taught*, *tought*, tight.

β. *a* **1625** *Nomenclator Navalis* (Harl. MS. 2301), We saie sett taught ye shrowdes y[e] staies or anie other Roape when it is to slack. **1627** CAPT. SMITH *Seaman's Gram.* ix. 42 Cast of that Boling.., and hale vp taught the other. **1669** STURMY *Mariner's Mag.* I. ii. 18 Hawl them taught and belaye them. **1793** SMEATON *Edystone L.* §259 We..fixed our great tackle to it..and hove all taught. **1816** SCOTT *Antiq.* viii, Haul taught and belay! *c* **1820** G. BEATTIE *John o' Arnha'* 55 (Jam.) Ilk tendon, taght like thairm, was lac'd. **1828** WEBSTER, *Taught* [pron.] *taut*, stretched; not slack. **1833** MARRYAT *P. Simple* xxx. II. 174 The yards carefully squared, and the ropes hauled taught.

γ. *a* **1687** PETTY *Treat. Naval Philos.* I. ii, Setting of the Shrowds loose or tort as the Condition of Sailing of the Vessel requires. **1806** W. TAYLOR in *Ann. Rev.* IV. 773 Tort and smooth threads of flax and hemp. **1847** EMERSON *Poems* (1857) 99 Yet holds he them with tortest rein.

δ. **1727-41** CHAMBERS *Cycl.*, *Taught*, or *Tau't*,..in the sea language, is the same as stiff, or fast. **1796** NELSON in Southey *Life* (1813) II. vi. 1 My complaint is as if a girth were buckled taut over my breast. **1840** R. H. DANA *Bef. Mast* xxvii, The land-breeze set in, which brought us upon a taut bowline. **1883** STEVENSON *Treas. Isl.* v. xxiii, The hawser was as taut as a bowstring.

transf. **1748** SMOLLETT *Rod. Rand.* xxiv. (1760) I. 191 Many a taught gale of wind has honest Tom Bowling and I weathered together.

b. Tightly or trimly done up; put into good order. Of a person: Neat in appearance. Esp. in phr. ***taut ship***, a disciplined or strictly run ship; also *attrib.* and *fig.* Cf. sense 2 c below.

1829 D. JERROLD *Black-Ey'd Susan* III. ii. 43 The trimmest sailor as ever handled rope..give me taut Bill before any able seaman in his Majesty's fleet. **1870** *Daily News* 1 Dec., Shops ran up shutters, everything was made taut. **1871** WHITTIER *Sisters* xii, In the tautest schooner that ever swam He rides at anchor in Annisquam. **1880** CLARK RUSSELL *Sailor's Sweetheart* vii, By breakfast-time the ship was clean and taut fore and aft. **1881** *Scribner's Mag.* XXI. 271/1 [She appeared] in Miss B——'s shop, taut and trim. **1887** BESANT *The World went* i, A fair wind, and the ship taut and trim. **1941** *Time* 29 Dec. 8/1 The promoted admirals were 'taut ship' commanders (meaning rigid disciplinarians, as opposed to 'happy ship' officers). **1970** H. WAUGH *Finish me Off* (1971) 106 Yesterday she had been haughty and taut-ship, but today..Mrs. Hardell's position had suddenly become tenuous. **1974** *Progress* (Easley, S. Carolina) 24 Apr. 2/2 His language was salty and he ran a taut ship. He demanded discipline, accuracy, integrity and honesty, as well as good writing. **1977** *Navy News* July 20 All the taut-ship zeal for a tip-top navy, which gave Whale Island its fame as one of the best-known of service establishments, has been redirected. **1980** *Globe & Laurel* July/Aug. 250/1, I found the first half of the book, which describes Trevelyan's efforts to create a taut ship, as he takes Icarus through a NATO exercise, a ship's fire, and a funeral at sea, sketchy and unsatisfactory.

c. *fig.* Of a person: Strict or severe as to duty.

1833 MARRYAT *P. Simple* xii, He was considered to be the taughtest (that is, the most active and severe) boatswain in the service. **1851** KINGSTON *Pirate Medit.* (1860) 4 What sort of a chap is our skipper? He looks like a taut hand.

d. *fig.* Of music, literature, etc.: concise, controlled; of the human voice: strained.

1966 *Listener* 10 Feb. 219/2 The music..did not seem to have quite the structural control or clarity of texture one discerned in the piano concerto, where..the thought seems more taut and the tension is therefore more easily maintained. **1972** *Observer* 16 Apr. 33/6 A short, taut, yet circumstantially detailed account. **1976** M. MACHLIN *Pipeline* lv. 557 Coutts voice was taut with worry. **1978** *Internat. Herald Tribune* 24 July 14/4 Among reviewers, the favored adjectives of the past—trenchant and ironic for books, taut, pert and luminous for theatrical productions—have been overtaken by sentimental.

3. Used adverbially and parasynthetically in *Comb.*, as ***taut-necked***, ***-rigged***, ***-stretched*** adjs.

1829 D. JERROLD *Black-Ey'd Susan* I. i. 15 There's not so fine, so noble, so taut-rigged a fellow in His Majesty's navy. **1943** D. GASCOYNE *Poems 1937–42* 42 The sky's a faded blue and taut-stretched flag Tenting the quadrangle. **1948** L. MACNEICE *Holes in Sky* 31 The taut-necked donkey's.. lamenting.

[*Note.* For the interchange of *taught*, *tought*, cf. *aught*, *ought*; *naught*, *nought* (where however *au* is the earlier), and the falling together in sound in mod. Eng. of *bought*, *sought*, *wrought*, *brought*, *thought* (OE. *bohte*, *sóhte*, *worhte*, *brǫ́hte*, *þǫ́hte*) with *caught*, *distraught*, *raught*, *taught* (ME. *cahte*, *distraught*, OE. *rǽhte*, *tǽhte*, *táhte*), where the two sounds remain distinct in Sc. (*bocht*, *thocht*, *cauwcht*, *tauwcht*) and northern Eng. *Toȝt*, *toght*, has been suggested to be:—an OTeut. **tohto[z]* (from ablaut-grade *tog-*), which is improbable, since no trace of such a form appears in OE. or any of the cognate languages; also, to be a syncopated form of ME. *toȝed*, now *towed* (see TOW *v.*[2]); this seems impossible. With more probability it has been viewed as an altered form of ME. *tiȝt* TIGHT, under the influence of *toȝed*, or more prob. of *toȝen* 'drawn', pa. pple. of TEE *v.*[1] It is noticeable that *toȝt*, *touȝt*, *tought*, occur also in ME. and Sc. as variants of TOUGH *a.*]

taut (tat, tɑt), *v. Sc.* Also **tawt**, **tat**. [Origin obscure: cf. TATTY *a.*[1]; also TATTER *sb.*[1]]

a. *trans.* To tangle or mat together (hair or wool). **b.** *intr.* To become tangled or matted, as hair or wool. Hence **'tauted (tautit)** *ppl. a.*, tangled, matted; having the hair tangled.

1782 BURNS *Poor Mailie's Elegy* vi, She was nae get o' moorland tips, Wi' tawted ket, an' hairy hips. **1786** —— *Twa Dogs* 20 Nae tawted tyke, tho' e'er sae duddie. **1853** J. CRAWFORD in *Whistle-Binkie* (1890) II. 224 While frae the bairnie's tautit hair The frozen crystals hung. **1882** JAMIESON Supp. s.v. *Tat*, Dinna taut your hair sa. **1893** STEVENSON *Catriona* xx, God's truth, it's the tautit laddie!

taut, var. f. TAT *sb.*[2], a coarse Indian cloth.

taut, **taute**, obs. ff. *taught*: see TEACH.

tautaug, variant of TAUTOG.

tautegorical (tɔːtɪˈgɒrɪkəl), *a. nonce-wd.* [f. TAUT(O-, after ALLEGORICAL.] (See quot. 1825.) So **tautegory** (ˈtɔːtɪgərɪ) [after ALLEGORY].

1825 COLERIDGE *Aids Refl.* 199 The base of Symbols and symbolical expressions; the nature of which as always tautegorical (i.e. expressing the same subject but with a difference) in contra-distinction from metaphors and similitudes, that are always allegorical (i.e. expressing a different subject but with a resemblance). **1825** —— in *Rem.* (1836) II. 352 This part of the *mythus* in which symbol fades away into allegory but..never ceases wholly to be a symbol or tautegory. **1846** JOWETT in *Life & Lett.* (1897) I. v. 146 In one word he [Coleridge] had comprised a whole essay, saying that mythology was not allegorical but tautegorical. **1862** STANLEY *Jew. Ch.* (1863) I. vi. 136 The wilderness, as it intervenes between Egypt and the Land of Promise..is, as Coleridge would have said, not allegorical, but tautegorical, of the events which..we designate by those figures.

tauten (ˈtɔːt(ə)n), *v.* Also 9 **taughten**. [f. TAUT *a.* + -EN[5].]

1. *trans.* To make taut, or to cause to become taut; to tighten.

a **1814** C. DIBDIN *Song, Sailor's Jrnl.*, While taught'ning the forestay, I saw her faint **1880** CLARK RUSSELL *Sailor's Sweetheart* III. ii. 57 The warp sang out as we tautened the bight of it. **1886** SHELDON tr. *Flaubert's Salammbo* xiii. 310 [Catapults] were tautened with levers, pulleys, capstans, or drums. **1903** L. BECKE in *Pall Mall G.* 28 Mar. 2/2 In another moment or two your line is tautened out.

2. *intr.* To become taut, as a rope under tension.

1849 *Blackw. Mag.* LXVI. 732 The dip of the hawser scarce tautening at each strain. **1879** BEERBOHM *Patagonia* v. 66 The shock, as the lasso tautened, threw his horse on its haunches. **1896** *Strand Mag.* XII. 350/2 The life-line tautened, and I was soon lifted from my feet.

Hence **'tautened** *ppl. a.* (also *fig.*); **'tautening** *vbl. sb.*

1840 R. H. DANA *Bef. Mast* xxiii, Our ship being very good upon a tautened bowline. **1879** *Man. Artill. Exerc.* 633 Wedges, oak, small..20 Tautening lashings. **1906** E. K. ROBINSON *Relig. Nat.* 28 The sudden tautening of the muscles. **1929** E. CARFRAE *Guarded Heights* xxiii. 202 Carey's voice had a queer little tautened note when he spoke again.

tauthrie, obs. f. TAWDRY.

tautie, var. TATTY.

tautly (ˈtɔːtlɪ), *adv.* [f. TAUT *a.* + -LY[2].] In a taut manner; with tautness.

1882 NARES *Seamanship* (ed. 6) 182 The bunt..will not allow the parrel to be passed tautly. **1882** O'DONOVAN *Merv Oasis* I. i. 20 A very thick cable..is drawn as tautly as possible across the stream.

tautness (ˈtɔːtnɪs). [f. as prec. + -NESS.] The state or quality of being taut.

1861 E. S. KENNEDY in *Peaks, Passes & Gl.* Ser. II. I. 166 The taughtness of the rope unavoidably makes it difficult to retain a foothold. **1889** J. M. DUNCAN *Clin. Lect. Dis. Wom.* xxix. (ed. 4) 233 There being only a little tautness left on one side.

tauto- (tɔːtəʊ), before a vowel properly **taut-**, repr. Gr. ταὐτο-, combining form of ταὐτό, contraction of τὸ αὐτό, the same (cf. AUTO-[1]); occurring in TAUTOLOGY, TAUTOMERISM, and their derivatives; also the following technical words, mostly of rare occurrence. **'tauto,baryd**, *Math.* [irreg. f. Gr. βαρύς heavy], that curve upon which the pressure of a heavy particle moving under gravity is the same at every point (cf. TAUTOCHRONE). **tauto'graphical** *a.* [Gr. γραφικός descriptive], presenting the same geographical features throughout, monotonous in form. **tauto'hedral** *a.*, *Cryst.* [Gr. ἕδρα base], having the same face or side in common: see quot. **tauto'metric**, **tauto'metrical** *adjs.*, *Pros.* [late Gr. ταὐτόμετρος, f. μέτρον measure], of the same metre; having the same arrangement of syllables in the verse, or occupying the same position metrically. **tauto'morphous** *a.*, *Cryst.* [Gr. μορφή form], applied to a symmetrical form such that corresponding points or faces of it can be brought into congruence by revolution about an axis. **'tautonym**, *Nat. Hist.* [Gr. ταὐτώνυμ-ος *a.*, f. ὄνυμα, ὄνομα name], a scientific name in which the same word is used for genus and species; so **tauto'nymic** *a.*, pertaining to or constituting a tautonym; **tau'tonymy**, the use of tautonyms. **tauto'ousian** (**tautousian**), **-ious** *adjs.*, *Theol.* [f. eccl. Gr. ταὐτοούσιος (Epiphanius), f. οὐσία essence], having absolutely the same essence. † **tau'topathy** [Gr. ταὐτοπάθεια, f. πάθος suffering], suffering caused by the same thing as was habitually used previously. **'tautophone** = SUMMATOR 2. **tau'tophony** [med. Gr. ταὐτοφωνία (Eustathius), f. φωνή voice], repetition of the same (vocal) sound; so **tauto'phonic**, **-ical** *adjs.*, repeating the same sound. **tau'topody**, *Pros.* [Gr. ταὐτοποδία, f. πούς, ποδ- foot], repetition of the same metrical foot; a double foot or dipody consisting of the same foot repeated twice; so **tauto'podic** *a.*, belonging to or constituting a tautopody. **,tautosy'llabic** *a.*, belonging to the same syllable. **tauto'zonal** *a.*, *Cryst.*, belonging to or situated in the same zone; hence **tautozo'nality**, the quality of being tautozonal.

1891 *Cent. Dict.*, **Tautobaryd*. **1860** *Temple Bar Mag.* I. 121 Syria is the most wearying, sun-baked, *tautographical place in the world,..blinding limestone ridges, limestone mule-paths, limestone valleys, limestone everything and everywhere. **1895** STORY-MASKELYNE *Crystallogr.* iii. §36 When two zones have a face in common, that is to say when their zone-circles intersect in a pole, they will be spoken of as **tautohedral* in that face or pole. **1894** FENNELL in *Class. Rev.* Feb. 49/1 *Tautometric responsion of single words is as a rule without significance and may sometimes be due to chance. **1892** *Athenæum* 16 July 92/1 Mr. Bury has either failed to detect, or neglected to notice,..κεινοῦ σὺν ἀνδρός, v. 9, *tautometrical with ἀνδρὸς φιλοξεῖν-, v. 20. **1895** STORY-MASKELYNE *Crystallogr.* vi. §150 It is not difficult to determine whether in any particular case correlative mero-symmetrical forms are enantiomorphous or *tautomorphous; i.e. cannot be brought into congruence, or can be so brought by revolution round one or more zone-lines. **1901** *Ibis* Oct. 722 We cannot agree with Señor Berg that everyone ought to call..the Night-Heron *Nycticorax nycticorax*, for we do not ourselves recognise the obligations of the new system of *tautonyms. **1896** *Ibid.* July 364 This repeating of the specific name seems specially awkward in the cases of the unavoidable *tautonymic names. **1908** *Athenæum* 18 Mar. 342/1 He concluded with a proposal to get rid of *tautonymy—as in *Trutta trutta*, *Apus* (*Apus*) *apus*, or other comical arrangements—by a plan distinguishing what was legal in the past from what is to be legal in the future. [**1678** CUDWORTH *Intell. Syst.* I. iv. §36. 611 That the ancient orthodox fathers, who used the word *Homoousios* against Arius, intended not therein to assert the Son to have one and the same singular or individual essence with the Father, appeareth plainly from their disclaiming and disowning those two words, Ταυτοούσιον and Μονοούσιον. Concerning the former of which, Epiphanius thus;..'We affirm not the Son to be *Tautoousion*, (one and the same substance with the Father) lest this should be taken in any way of compliance with Sabellius'.] *Ibid.*, Athanasius.. disclaimeth a monoousian Trinity, as Epiphanius did before a *tautoousian; both of them a Trinity of meer names..they alike distinguishing them from the homoousian Trinity, as a Trinity of real Hypostases or Persons. **1846** WORCESTER, *Tautoöusian*, **Tautoöusious*, having the same identical essence. **1882** OGILVIE, *Tautoöusian*, same as *Tautousian*... *Tautousian*, *Tautousious*, in *theol.* having absolutely the same essence. **1652** N. CULVERWELL *Treat.* I. xvii. (1661) 152 Anacreon..by a most emphatical *Tautopathy, was choak'd with the husk..of a Grape. **1940** *Character & Personality* VIII. 216 (*title*) The use of the *tautophone ('verbal summator') as an auditory apperceptive test for the study of personality. **1847** WEBSTER, **Tautophonical* ..**Tautophony*. **1881** G. W. MOON *Revisers' Eng.* xxiv. (1882) 64 They say 'That ye may be sons of your Father which is in heaven: for he maketh his sun to rise'.. tautophony, suggestive of a pun. **1898** F. HARRISON in *19th Cent.* June 942 If your ear does not hear the false note, the tautophony or the cacophony in the written sentence as you read it. **1891** *Cent. Dict.*, **Tautopodic*..**Tautopody*. **1888** J. WRIGHT tr. *Brugmann's Elem. Compar. Gram. Indo-Gmc. Lang.* I. 92 Before the Christian era *tautosyllabic *ai̯* became *ē* in Latin. **1953** *Archivum Linguisticum* V. 22 The lengthening of short vowels before tautosyllabic *s* or [z]. **1978** *Language* LIV. 193 A tautosyllabic consonant. **1878** GURNEY *Crystallogr.* 21 They are also said to be *tautozonal, by which is meant that they all lie in one and the same zone. **1895** STORY-MASKELYNE *Crystallogr.* iii. §36 Two or more poles (or their faces) are said to be tautozonal or heterozonal with a third, according as they lie in the same or different zone-circles (or zones) with it. **1880** L. FLETCHER in *Philos. Mag.* Feb. 84 The property of *tautozonality is a permanent one.

tautochrone ('tɔːtəkrəʊn). *Math.* [f. TAUTO- + Gr. χρόνος time: cf. F. *tautochrone* (Dict. Trévoux 1771).] That curve upon which a particle moving under the action of gravity (or any given force) will reach the lowest (or some fixed) point in the same time, from whatever point it starts. So **tautochronism** (tɔː'tɒkrənɪz(ə)m), the property of a tautochrone; **tau'tochronous** *a.*, having the character of a tautochrone; occupying the same time, isochronous.

*a*1774 GOLDSM. *Surv. Exp. Philos.* (1776) II. 142 The time spent in determining the figure of a tautochrone might have been more usefully employed in this research. 1842 BRANDE *Dict. Sc.*, etc. s.v., Newton and Hermann also determined the tautochrone in a vacuum, when gravity is supposed to be directed towards a given centre. Newton likewise showed that the cycloid is also the tautochrone in a resisting medium, when the resistance is proportional to the velocity. 1842 *Exam. Papers* 47 (*Dubl. Univ. Cal.* 1843), Prove that the cycloid is the only plane curve possessing the property of tautochronism. 1846 SMART Suppl., *Tautochronous*, arriving at the same time; having the property of the tautochrone.

tautoclin ('tɔːtəʊklɪn). *Min.* [ad. Ger. *tautoklin* (Breithaupt 1830), f. Gr. ταὐτό (TAUTO-) + κλίνειν to bend, incline; so called 'because it has the same rhombohedral angle as dolomite' (Chester).] A greyish-white variety of ANKERITE.

1868 DANA *Min.* (ed. 5) 685.

tautog (tɔː'tɒg). Also **tautaug, tetaug.** [ad. Narragansett *taut-auog*, pl. of *taut* name of the fish: see quot. 1643.] A labroid fish, *Tautoga americana* (*T. onitis*), also called *black-fish* or *oyster-fish*, abundant on the Atlantic coast of N. America, and esteemed for food.

1643 ROGER WILLIAMS *Key to Lang. of America* xix. 115 Of Fish and Fishing. *Taut-aûog.* Sheeps-heads. 1828–32 WEBSTER, *Tetaug*, the name of a fish on the coast of New England; called also black fish. 1848 BARTLETT *Dict. Amer.*, *Tautaug.* 1851 HAWTHORNE *Ho. Sev. Gables* xviii, Real turtle, we understand, and salmon, tautog, canvass-backs, pig, English mutton. 1888 G. B. GOODE *Amer. Fishes* 288 'Tautog' would consequently seem to be a word from the dialect of the Narragansett Indians.

tautographical, -hedral: see TAUTO-.

†**'tautolite.** *Min. Obs.* [ad. Ger. *tautolit* (Breithaupt 1826); 'adapted from [Gr.] ταὐτόμετρος of the same measure, referring to a supposed axial relation, and λίθος' (Chester); see TAUTO- and -LITE.] An obsolete synonym of ALLANITE.

1828 *Philos. Mag.* May 398 The tautolite seems to be related to the chrysolite, as the ceylanite to the spinelle. 1868 DANA *Min.* (ed. 5) 286 *Bucklandite* is anhydrous allanite in small black crystals... *Tautolite*..is probably the same species.

tautologic (tɔːtəʊ'lɒdʒɪk), *a. rare.* [f. Gr. ταὐτολογία TAUTOLOGY + -IC: cf. the adv. ταὐτολογικῶς in Eustathius *c* 1160.] = next, 1.

1828 *Blackw. Mag.* XXIV. 906 Dr. Johnson..he charges ..with a plethoric and tautologic tympany of sentence. 1858 CARLYLE *Fredk. Gt.* VII. v. (1872) II. 287 No end of florid inflated tautologic ornamental balderdash.

tautological (tɔːtəʊ'lɒdʒɪkəl), *a.* [f. as prec. + -AL[1]: see -ICAL.]

1. a. Pertaining to, characterized by, involving, or using tautology; repeating the same word, or the same notion in different words.

1620 T. GRANGER *Div. Logike* 387 Lest thy discourse be tedious, Tautologicall, erroneous. 1670 BLOUNT *Law Dict.* s.v. *Alnager*, Measurer, and Alneger, which last, though it be a Tautological expression (Aulnage and Measure, being the same thing denoted in two Languages) yet long usage and custom have brought them to distinct Offices. 1800 in *Four C. Eng. Lett.* (1880) 355 Now and then, in the career of declamation, he becomes tautological and ineffective. 1869 INGLEBY *Introd. Metaph.* II. ii. 176 One writer..desperately declares that the Laws of Motion are mere truisms, or tautological judgments.

b. *Mod. Logic.* Characterized by or involving tautology (in sense f).

1922 tr. *Wittgenstein's Tractatus* 97 In the one case the proposition is true for all the truth-possibilities of the elementary propositions. We say that the truth-conditions are *tautological.* 1926 F. P. RAMSEY in *Proc. London Math. Soc.* XXV. 341 The idea to be defined is one of the essential sides of mathematical propositions, their content, and their form. Their content must be completely generalized, and their form tautological. 1933 *Mind* XLII. 41 Each postulate functions in limiting the ranges of the variables in such a manner that any change is one postulate..involves a reciprocal change in its other parts, which change causes it to remain analytic or tautological. 1950 R. CARNAP *Logical Found. Probability* iv. 289 With respect to the tautological evidence '*t*'. 1971 G. HUNTER *Metalogic* III. 171 Suppose that A is an instance of a tautological schema of Q.

2. Of an echo: Repeating the same sound several times. ? *Obs.*

1677 PLOT *Oxfordsh.* 7 These return syllables and words, the same oftentimes repeated, and may therefore be stiled Tautological Echo's. 1807 JOYCE *Sci. Dial.* xiii. (1846) 232 Called tautological or babbling echoes.

†**3.** *loosely.* Of the nature of a repetition, identical (*with*). *Obs. rare*[−1].

1689 G. HARVEY *Curing Dis. by Expect.* xvi. 125 Compound Waters..tautological the one with the other.

Hence **tautologi'cality**, the quality of being tautological.

1936 J. R. WEINBERG *Exam. Logical Positivism* ii. 80 The formal property of certain combinations of symbols, which is called tautologicality, is solely responsible for the unconditional truth of the truths of logic.

tautologically (tɔːtəʊ'lɒdʒɪkəlɪ), *adv.* [f. prec. + -LY[2].] In a tautological manner, with tautology.

1620 T. GRANGER *Div. Logike* 292 Handle the same matter (homogeneously, not tautologically). 1820 COLERIDGE *Let. C. A. Tulk* 17 July (in *Pearson's Catal.* (1894) 14) At once superfluous and defective, tautologically superfluous in the point of co-equality, and dangerously defective in that of the subordination. 1840 HOOD *Up Rhine* 61, I join with Dr. Watts' sluggard in wishing tautologically, for 'a little more sleep and a little more slumber'. 1979 J. A. ROBINSON *Logic: Form & Function* iii. 43 We can extend this idea to the case when infinitely many sentences together tautologically imply a given sentence.

So **tauto'logicalness** (Bailey 1727 vol. II).

tautologism (tɔː'tɒlədʒɪz(ə)m). *rare.* [f. TAUTOLOGIZE: see -ISM.] The use or practice of tautology; an instance of this. Used by Farrar *spec.* for the combination of two synonymous words or syllables for the sake of precise expression of the meaning, as in Chinese.

1815 *Sporting Mag.* XLVI. 117 Hard and callous, form a tautologism. 1816 BENTHAM *Chrestom.* 293 The reproach of tautologism,—incurred..by the observation. 1869 FARRAR *Fam. Speech* iv. (1873) 122 This chaos [of homonyms in Chinese]..is reduced to order and meaning..partly by what may be called tautologism, i.e. by using a *second* synonym to define the word which is vague; in point of fact, by making two vague words into one definite word.

tautologist (tɔː'tɒlədʒɪst). [f. as prec. + -IST.] One who practises tautology.

1702 STEELE *Funeral* I. 14 Oh! that Damn'd Tautologist too—That [Mr.] Puzzle and his Irrevocable Deed! 1727 BAILEY vol. II, *Tautologist*, one who says the same Things over and over. 1805 W. TAYLOR in *Ann. Rev.* III. 649 All such literary tautologists are proper objects of epitomization.

tautologize (tɔː'tɒlədʒaɪz), *v.* [f. TAUTOLOGY + -IZE. (The Gr. equivalent was ταὐτολογεῖν.) Cf. APOLOGIZE.] *intr.* To repeat the same thing in the same or different words; to use tautology. Also with *it* (quot. 1656).

1607 TOPSELL *Serpents* (1658) 761 To take occasion to tautologize, or to speak one thing twice. 1615 JACKSON *Creed* IV. iv. §1 Even the most acute amongst the school-men whiles they seek to clear this doubt do but falter and tautologize. 1656 S. H. *Gold. Law* 1 We are constrained.. to Tautologize it in repetitions, even to a wearying of our selves and the world with words. ?16.. *Plutarch's Mor.* IV. 220 (L.) The tautologizing babler, if he be a physitian, certainly is more troublesome than the disease.

Hence **tau'tologizer**, one who tautologizes; a tautologist.

1657 J. WATTS *Vind. Ch. Eng.* 241 A vain babler, a tautologizer and a vain repeater.

tautologous (tɔː'tɒləgəs), *a.* [f. Gr. ταὐτολόγ-ος repeating what has been said (f. ταὐτό the same + -λογος saying, f. λέγειν to say) + -OUS.] = TAUTOLOGICAL 1.

1714 J. FORTESCUE-ALAND *Pref. Fortescue's Abs. & Lim. Mon.* 67 The County of Devon, in the old way of Speaking ..called the County of Devonshire, which is the constant Expression in old Deeds, and signifies the same thing tho' it be tautologous. 1786 H. TOOKE *Purley* I. ix. 406, I have been purposely tautologous, that by my indifferent application of the two words *of* and *for*..the smallest..opposition between these prepositions might be done away. 1853 *Fraser's Mag.* XLVII. 358 The circuitous jargon—the tautologous gabble ..of special pleading. 1884 SIR W. B. BRETT in *Law Times Rep.* 10 May 315/2, I have come to the conclusion..that the Legislature intended in this case to be verbose and tautologous, and to say the same thing twice over. 1935 *Mind* XLIV. 195 The tautologous '*p* or not *p*'. 1940 W. V. O. QUINE *Mathematical Logic* i. 50 Statements which are true by virtue solely of the truth-functional modes of composition will be called *tautologous.*

Hence **tau'tologously** *adv.* = TAUTOLOGICALLY.

1865 J. P. COLLIER *Bibl. Catal.* I. 109 It begins thus tautologously: 'The present plagues that now we fele'. 1904 *Westm. Gaz.* 22 Oct. 3/2 'Fraud-pilfered'—the indictment is tautologously complete.

tautology (tɔː'tɒlədʒɪ). [ad. late L. *tautologia* (*c* 350 in Mar. Plotin. Sacerd.), a. Gr. ταὐτολογία, f. ταὐτολόγος: see TAUTOLOGOUS; in F. *tautologie.*]

a. A repetition of the same statement. **b.** The repetition (esp. in the immediate context) of the same word or phrase, or of the same idea or statement in other words: usually as a fault of style.

1587 FLEMING *Contn. Holinshed* III. 1533/1 This ambassage is reported in the historie of Scotland, wherevnto (for the auoiding of tautologie) we refer the reader. *a* 1653 GOUGE *Comm. Heb.* (1655) 99 To shew that there is no tautology, no vain repetition of one and the same thing therein. 1686 GOAD *Celest. Bodies* I. xii. 56 The Taedium of Tautology is odious to every Pen and Ear. *a* 1748 WATTS *Improv. Mind* II. ii. §4 By securing you from an appearance of tautology, or repeating the same words too often. 1790 WESLEY *Wks.* (1872) IV. 487 That villanous tautology of lawyers, which is the scandal of our nation. 1869 FARRAR *Fam. Speech* iv. (1873) 134 One leading syllable thrusting itself with the most obtrusive tautology through a whole sentence.

c. With *a* and *pl.* An instance of this; a tautological phrase or expression; †a repetition *of* something already said (quot. 1599).

1579 FULKE *Confut. Sanders* 644 It is a foolish tautologie, for you sayed the same immediatly before. 1599 *Broughton's Let.* ix. 32 Euery later paperwork of yours is but a Tautology of the former. 1698 WANLEY in *Lett. Lit. Men* (Camden) 258, I called the library a venerable place; the Books sacred reliques of Antiquity, &c.; with half a dozen tautologies. 1844 LD. BROUGHAM *Brit. Const.* xix. §1 (1862) 309 Repetitions and tautologies are used.

d. Applied to the repetition of a statement as its own reason, or to the identification of cause and effect.

1659 PEARSON *Creed* ii. (1839) 157 To assign any thing as the cause or reason of itself, is a great absurdity, and the expression of it a vain tautology. 1662 H. MORE *Philos. Writ.* Pref. Gen. (1712) 15 The resolution of such Phaenomena as we experience in ourselves..into this vital oneness,..is no vain Tautology, or the mere saying a thing is so because it is so. 1836–7 SIR W. HAMILTON *Metaph.* (1859) II. xxxix. 377 There is thus conceived an absolute tautology between the effect and its causes. We think the causes to contain all that is contained in the effect; the effect to contain nothing which was not contained in the causes.

e. *transf.* A mere repetition of acts, incidents, or experiences; in quot. 1650, used for the sending of a thing to its place of origin.

1650 FULLER *Pisgah* II. v. 128 Some wil object it was a real tautology to bring purples to Tyre, seeing the best of the world were made in that place. 1657 W. DILLINGHAM *Contn. Siege of Ostend* in *Sir. F. Vere's Comm.*, It was so thick stuck with bullets, that the Ordnance could scarcely shoot without a tautologie, and hitting its former bullets. 1687 NORRIS *Coll. Misc.* (1699) 324 Our whole Life is but a nauseous Tautology. 1863 COWDEN CLARKE *Shaks. Char.* i. 14 The poet has avoided a dramatic tautology (if I may so use the term) in bringing about the death of two worthy men immediately upon the heels of each other.

f. *Mod. Logic.* A compound proposition which is unconditionally true for all the truth-possibilities of its elementary propositions and by virtue of its logical form.

1919 B. RUSSELL *Introd. Math. Philos.* xviii. 203 The characteristic of logical propositions that we are in search of is the one which was felt..by those who said that it consisted in deducibility from the law of contradiction. This characteristic we may call *tautology.* *Ibid.* 205 The importance of 'tautology' for a definition of mathematics was pointed out to me by..Ludwig Wittgenstein, who was working on the problem. 1922 tr. *Wittgenstein's Tractatus* 97 The tautology..is unconditionally true. 1933 *Mind* XLII. 37 So taken, a postulate is a tautology and cannot be denied. 1959 *Listener* 19 Mar. 510/1 The simplest rigorous proof is tautology. This consists, essentially, of showing that some statement covers all possibilities. 1964 M. BLACK *Compan. Wittgenstein's Tractatus* xliii. 231 Johnson's ..'formal truth' and 'formal falsity'..seem to correspond exactly to W.'s 'tautology' and 'contradiction'. 1979 J. A. ROBINSON *Logic: Form & Function* iii. 42 A..general decision procedure for determining whether or not a sentence is a tautology.

tautomerism (tɔː'tɒmərɪz(ə)m). *Chem.* [f. Gr. ταὐτο-, TAUTO- + μέρος part, after ISOMERISM; rendering Ger. *tautomerie* (Laar 1885).] The property exhibited by certain organic compounds of behaving in different reactions as if they possessed two (or more) different constitutions, that is, as if the atoms of the same compound or group were arranged in two (or more) different ways, expressible by different structural formulæ (e.g. the group $-CH{:}C(OH)-$, or $-CH_2.CO-$, in ethyl acetoacetate); *esp.* such a property due to the reversible migration of an atom (esp. of hydrogen) or group within a molecule (see also quots.).

[1885 CONRAD LAAR in *Ber. Dtsch. Chem. Ges.* XVIII. 652 Um die gegenseitige Beziehung gleichberechtigter Formeln ..kurz bezeichnen zu können, schlage ich hierfür den Ausdruck 'Tautomerie' vor.] 1890 NEF in *Jrnl. Chem. Soc.* LVIII. 983 A discussion of the alleged cases of tautomerism in ethyl succinosuccinate and analogous compounds. 1901 DIXON *ibid.* LXXIX. 543 Hitherto no isomerism (or tautomerism) has been established amongst mineral derivatives analogous to that subsisting between the normal and *iso*thiocyanates of organic radicles. 1927 T. M. LOWRY in *Chem. Rev.* IV. 233 The necessity for a new definition of tautomerism arises from the fact that Laar embodied in his original definition a theory which is now universally recognized as being incorrect,..namely, that the various formulae which can be assigned to a tautomerism compound represent 'not isomeric but identical substances'. The new definition has the advantage that there is no theory behind it, since it is limited to a mere statement of the fact of dual reactivity. 1927, 1936 [see *keto-enol* s.v. KETO- b]. 1937 H. B. WATSON *Mod. Theories Org. Chem.* ix. 117 Until a relatively recent date..'tautomerism' was used exclusively to denote the migration of hydrogen. The similar migration of anionic atoms or groups is now recognized, however; this .. is included under .. 'tautomerism'. 1964 [see PROTOTROPY]. 1969 C. K. INGOLD *Structure & Mechanism Org. Chem.* (ed. 2) xi. 795 Laar's interpretation was that two such structures did not represent distinct and potentially separable species, but only the end-phases of an intramolecular oscillatory situation in a single chemical species. *Ibid.* 799 Since 1911 there has been no question but that the concept of tautomerism, in terms of which Conrad Laar had incorporated so many scattered observations into a phenomenon, has to be redefined..as meaning reversible isomeric change. Problems of isolation and proof of identity of tautomers are dependent simply on temperature and the available techniques.

So **tautomer** ('tɔːtəmə(r)), any one of the forms of a tautomeric compound in relation to another; **tautomeric** (tɔːtəʊ'mɛrɪk) *a.*, pertaining to or exhibiting tautomerism; **tau'tomerize** *v. intr.*, to change into another tautomeric form; **tau,tome'rizable** *a.*, capable of being changed into a tautomeric form; **tau,tomeri'zation**; **tautomery** (tɔː'tɒmərɪ) [ad. Ger. *tautomerie*], = tautomerism.

1886 tr. *Richter's Organic Chem.* (1899) I. 55 Laar.. assumes that such compounds consist of a mixture of structural isomerides, in that an easily mobile hydrogen atom oscillates between two positions in equilibrio, and thereby the entire complex becomes mobile. He designates the phenomenon as *tautomery*. **1890** GOLDSCHMIDT & MEISSLER in *Jrnl. Chem. Soc.* LVIII. 499 Assuming that in the reactions of tautomeric compounds which take place under the influence of electrolytes, the intramolecular change is brought about by the free ions. **1903** *Amer. Chem. Jrnl.* May XXIX. 406 It [thio-urea] may react with the metal [silver] to form a sulphide, or its tautomer may form an insoluble silver compound. **1904** *Ibid.* Dec. 606 There are ten possible tautomeric formulas for this phenylacetylurazole, and four possible positions for the acetyl group. **1905** WALKER *Chem. Soc. Annual Rep.* 9 It is suggested that an absorption band appears wherever there is tautomeric change within the molecule. **1934** WEBSTER, Tautomerize... Tautomerizable... Tautomerization. **1938** H. ADKINS in H. Gilman *Org. Chem.* I. ix. 820 Unsaturated acids tautomerize in the absence of added reagents at temperatures near their boiling points. *Ibid.*, There is little or no correlation between the rate of tautomerization (mobility) and the extent of the reaction. **1962** Tautomerizable [see RAMAN]. **1972** R. A. JACKSON *Mechanism* iv. 60 This could plausibly lose carbon dioxide to give the carbanion 82 which would rapidly tautomerize to pyridine 83 by a proton shift. **1978** *Jrnl. Amer. Chem. Soc.* C. 4627/2 Activation of the catalyst by tautomerization to a rhodium (I) complex.

tautometric to **tautozonal**: see TAUTO-.

tava(h), var. TAWA².

tavarish, var. TOVARISH, TOVARICH.

tavarn, obs. form of TAVERN.

† **Ta'vasco.** *Obs.* Variant of TABASCO.

1652 WADSWORTH *Chocolate* 14 Some doe put into it [chocolate] black Pepper, and also Tauasco.

Tavastian (tə'væstɪən), *sb.* (and *a.*) [f. *Tavast(ehus*, Sw. name of the Finnish town of Hämeenlinna in the province of Häme + -IAN.] A member of one of the major ethnic groups of the Finnish people. Also *attrib.* or as *adj.* Also **'Tavastlander.**

[**1891** A. FEATHERMAN *Social Hist. Races Mankind* IV. 417 The Finns call themselves in their own language Suomalainen (swamp men)... From the dialects which they speak they are divided into two tribes: the Tawaster and the Karelian... The Tawasters..inhabit the central part of Finland.] **1898** J. ABERCROMBY *Pre- & Proto-Historic Finns* I. i. 3 The Finns of Finland (*Suomi*) call themselves *Suomalaiset*, and are broadly divided into two branches, the Tavastlanders (Hämäläiset) and the Karelians (*Karjalaiset*). **1911** WEBSTER, *Tavast*,.. *Tavastian*..*n.*, a Finn of a type characterized by broad, thickset figure and blond complexion. **1934** *Ibid.*, Tavastian, *adj.* **1935** HUXLEY & HADDON *We Europeans* vi. 181 These characters are seen among Finns, White Russians and..the Tavastians of Finland. **1957** *Encycl. Brit.* IX. 257/2 The *Finns* proper... There are two principal subdivisions, the Tavastlanders or Hämäläiset in the south and west and the Karelians or Karjalaiset in the east and north. The Tavastlander has a round head, a broad face, concave nose, fair complexion. **1965** E. JUTIKKALA in Glass & Eversley *Pop. in Hist.* xxiii. 569 The growth was by no means proportional to that of the 11 Tavastian parishes mentioned. **1966** L. DEIGHTON *Billion-Dollar Brain* ix. 79, I am a typical Tavastian... We are Tavastian people from the south and centre of Finland. **1974** *Encycl. Brit. Micropædia* IV. 145/3 The Finns proper, the Tavastlanders (or Tavastians), and the Karelians..had their own chiefs.

tave (teɪv), *v.* Now *dial.* Also 7 **tauve**, 8–9 **taave**, 9 **teave**. [app. of Norse origin: cf. Norw. dial. *tava* to toil or struggle without much effect, to fumble, be exhausted.] *intr.* To move the limbs ineffectually; to sprawl; to strike out at random with the arms or legs; to throw oneself about, as a person in a passion, in a fever, etc.; to act violently in any way; to strive, toil, labour, or struggle in work, difficult walking, etc.

c **1350** *St. Mary Magd.* 401 in Horstm. *Altengl. Leg.* (1881) 85 Sethin it [the child] swelid and turned & tauyd. **14..** *Beryn* 2061 Sith yee of hym be sesid, howe evir so yee [? hee] taue, Let hym nevir pas. **1566** DRANT *Horace* A iv, Where now and then (O just rewarde) in raginge surge sum taves. **1674** RAY *N.C. Words* 47 To *Tave*; Lincoln. to rage. **1691** *Ibid.* 73 Sick People are said to *tave* with the Hands when they catch at any thing. **1681** HICKERINGILL *Black Non-Conf.* Postscr., Wks. 1716 II. 168 Him that bespoke a Picture of a Horse lying (tauveing) upon his Back. **1790** MRS. WHEELER *Westmld. Dial.* (1821) 40, I wur sae teerd wie maanderin up an dawn an teaavin ith ling, I laaid me dawn on a breaad Scar, an sean fel asleep. **1825** BROCKETT *N.C. Words, Taving*, irregular motion; picking the bed-clothes in febrile delirium. **1828** *Craven Gloss.*, *Tave*, to kick with the feet like a distracted person. **1855** ROBINSON *Whitby Gloss.*, To *Teeave*, to paw and sprawl with the arms and legs. **1891** T. HARDY *Tess* xii, See how I've got to teave and slave, and your poor weak father with his heart clogged like a dripping-pan.

tave = *to have*: see T'¹ and HAVE *v.*

† **tavel**, *sb.*¹ *Obs.* Forms: 1 **tæfl**, **tæfel**, 3 **tævel**, **tavel**. [OE. *tæfel* fem., = WGer. **tabal*, ON. *tafl*, OHG. *zabal*, ad. late L. or Com. Romanic *tav(o)la*:—L. *tabula* table, board, esp. board to play on, in which sense it was taken app. bef. 400 into WGer. See TABLE.] A die for playing with; also, a game of chance, or the board on which it is played. Also *attrib.* Hence (in OE.) **tæfl-stán**, a piece or 'man' for playing with, a die; (ME.) **tævelbred** = TABLE-BOARD 1, ON. *taflborð*; (OE.) **tæflere**, a player at tavel or with dice.

a **800** *Erfurt Gloss.* 6 *Alea*, tefil. *c* **1000** ÆLFRIC *Voc.* in Wr.-Wülcker 150/21–5 *Alea*, tæfel. *Aleæ*, tæfelstanas. *Aleator*, tæflere. *Pirgus* cyningstan on tæfle. *Tessere, uel lepusculæ*, feðerscite tæfel. *c* **1000** in Thorpe *Codex Exon.* 331/19 Dryhten..dæleð sumum tæfle cræft, bleo-bordes gebregd. *Ibid.* 345/2 Hy twegen sceolon tæfle ymb sittan.. habban him gomen on borde. *c* **1205** LAY. 8133 Summen pleoden on tæuelbrede. *c* **1275** *Ibid.*, Somme pleoide mid tauel.

Tavel (tavɛl), *sb.*² The name of a commune on the Rhône (department of Gard, France), used *attrib.* and *absol.* to designate a rosé wine produced there.

1875 H. VIZETELLY *Wines of World* I. iii. 28 Of the rose-colour wines of the Côtes du Rhône, such as the dry and insidious Tavel,..and the robust Roquemaure,..the majority made default. **1926** P. M. SHAND *Bk. Wine* v. 178 On the opposite bank of the Rhône..is the little village of Tavel, which produces the delicious Tavel Rosé (Ancien Vignoble). **1934** J. I. DAVIS *Beginner's Guide to Wines* 49 Tavel..is a most delicious table wine. **1951** R. POSTGATE *Plain Man's Guide to Wine* iv. 90 Tavel is both dry and fruity... All rosés are a pretty colour; Tavel is perhaps the prettiest. **1963** N. FREELING *Gun before Butter* III. 153 They drank a Tavel wine from near Avignon. **1974** *Guardian* 24 Jan. 13/5 The best rosé in the world is probably Tavel. **1980** 'M. HARRIS' *Treasure of Sainte Foy* xviii. 229 He goes on through the small town of Tavel—this is where Tavel rosé comes from.

† **'tavel**, *v. Obs.* [OE. *tæflian*, f. *tæfel*, TAVEL *sb.*¹] *intr.* To play at dice.

a **1100** *Voc.* in Wr.-Wülcker 267/8 *Cotizo*, ic tæfle. *a* **1250** *Owl & Night.* 1666 Riȝt swa me gred þe manne a schame, þat tauelep & forleost þat game.

tavel, early var. of TEVEL *v. Obs.* or *dial.*

tavelett, obs. form of TALLET.

† **'tavelin.** *Obs.* Also 5–6 **tavelyn**, 6 **-yng**, **-ing**, **tavalyn**. [app. ad. It. *tavolino* 'any little boord, table, tablet' (or some cognate word), dim. from *tavola* 'a table, planke, or flat boorde' (Florio).] Formerly, with furriers, (in *pl.*) app. the boards between which small packages of skins were imported; hence, a small package of skins or certain portions of fur (usually or always four), put up between two boards. (Cf. TIMBER, applied to a package of forty skins between two stout boards of timber (Skene).)

1439 *Inv. T. Burgh* (Comm. Crt., Lond., Prowet 22). xxx lose tavelyns xv d. **1503** *Privy Purse Exp. Eliz. of York* (1830) 89, iiij tavelyns of shankes for the coler and fent of the said gowne, ijs. **1505** *Acc. Ld. High Treas. Scot.* III. 42 Item, for xiiij tavalyns of ermyng to the samyn goun, brocht be the Quenis maister of wardrob; ilk pece ij s. iiij d, summa..vi li. x s. **1545** *Rates of Customs* C vij b, Tauelynges the hundreth vj s. viij d. **1586** *Ibid.* E viij, Taueling the c, xiij s. iiij d.

† **'tavell.** *Silk-weaving. Obs.* exc. as Fr. **tavelle** (tavɛl). Also 6 **tavel**, **tavyll**, **tavil**. [a. F. *tavelle* (in sense 2), app. ad. L. *tabella* tablet.]

† **1.** The bobbin on which silk is wound for use in the shuttle. *Obs.*

1523 SKELTON *Garl. Laurel* 791 To weue in the stoule sume were full preste, With slaiis, with tauellis, with hedellis well drest. *a* **1529** —— *Agst. Comely Coystrowne* 34 Wele sped in spyndels and turnyng of tauellys. **1530** PALSGR. 279/2 Tavell an instrument for a sylke woman to worke with. **1538** ELYOT, *Liciatorium*, a weauers shyttel, or a sylke womans tauell, wheron sylke or threde beinge wounden, is shot through the web or lome. **1620** THOMAS *Lat. Dict.* s.v. *Liciatorium*.

‖ **2.** (mod. Fr. tavelle.) A large drum or bobbin on which the silk is wound off the cocoons.

1868 *Rep. U.S. Commissioner Agric.* (1869) 286 These [machines] consisted of, 1st, a series of tavelles to wind, clean, and equalize the threads during their automatic winding off [etc.].

taver ('teɪvə(r)), *sb. Sc.* Also 9 **taiver**. [app. of Norse origin: cf. Norw. *tave* clout, rag, any torn piece of stuff, Da. *tave* fibre, filament of tow, wool, etc.] A mere shred or filament; a 'rag' (of meat).

1808 JAMIESON, *Taivers*, s. pl. tatters; as, boiled to taivers, Fife. **1819** TENNANT *Papistry Storm'd* (1827) 15 Sorrow gin Paip was boil'd to taivers, And I'd a platefu' o' the bree! **1822** GALT *Steam-boat* xii. 288 They don't know how to cook yonder..they boil the meat to tavers.

taver ('teɪvə(r)), *v. Sc.* Also 9 **taiver**. [freq. of TAVE *v.*] *intr.* To wander vaguely or aimlessly; to wander mentally, to talk incoherently as one delirious; to talk idly and foolishly. Hence **'tavering** *vbl. sb.* and *ppl. a.*, wandering, etc.; **'tavert** *ppl. a.*, fatigued or exhausted with wandering, or with toil or struggle; incoherent, confused, stupefied, stupid; also **'taversome** *a.*, fatiguing, exhausting.

1535 STEWART *Cron. Scot.* (Rolls) III. 420 Fra hill to hill rynnand as tha war hyrit, In mure and mos so tavert war and tyrit. *a* **1598** ROLLOCK *Serm.* Wks. 1849 I. 435 He callis our warkis tavering, going out of the way. *Ibid.* 436 His actiounis ar taverings, all wandring out of the way. [*So ed.* **1599**; *ed.* **1616** wauering, wauerings.] **1808–18** JAMIESON, *Taiver*, to wander;..to rave as mad... *Taiversum*, tiresome, fatiguing. *Taivert.* **1822** GALT *Sir A. Wylie* xxx, Ye wouldna hae me ..to sit till I'm taiver't?.. I fin' the wine rinnin in my head already. **1823** —— *Entail* xviii, I would na trust the hair o' a dog to the judgment o' that tavert bodie, Gibby Omit. **1887** J. SERVICE *Dr. Duguid* xxii, The taivert tenets of the Antiburgher Kirk.

tavern ('tævən), *sb.* Forms: 3–7 **taverne**, (4 **tavarn**, 5 **tawern**, 6 **taverin**, *Sc.* **taveroun**), 7– **tavern**. [a. OF. *taverne* (1256 in Littré):—L. *taberna* a shed constructed of boards, a hut, booth, stall, shop, workshop, also a tavern or inn (so in earliest French and Eng. examples). Cf. TABERN.]

1. In early use, A public house or tap-room where wine was retailed; a dram-shop; in current use = PUBLIC HOUSE 2 b.

See also humorous use (word-play on name *New Inn Hall*) in quot. 1854.

[**1286** *Memoranda K.R. 14 & 15 Edw. I* 3 b, Tauernes ke sunt en meimes la Meisun ke est assise par entre la Meison Thomas le Vineter vers le Su.] **1297** R. GLOUC. (Rolls) 4024 Hor ydelnesse hom ssal bringe to sunne of lecherye, To tauerne & to sleuþe, & to hasardrie. **1303** R. BRUNNE *Handl. Synne* 1025 Tauerne ys þe deuylys knyfe Hyt sleþ þe, oþer soule or lyfe. **1340** *Ayenb.* 56 Þe tauerne ys þe scole of þe dyeule huere his deciples studieþ. *c* **1440** *Jacob's Well* 147 Þe tauerne is welle of glotonye, for it may be clepyd þe develys scolehous. **1570** B. GOOGE *Pop. Kingd.* IV. 53 This done, they to the Taverne go, or in the fields they dine. **1593** SHAKS. *Rich. II*, V. iii. 5 Can no man tell of my vnthriftie Sonne?.. Enquire at London, 'mongst the Tauernes there. **1611** COTGR., *Tavernier*,..a Victualler, of whom (as in our Tauernes of London) one may haue meat, and drink for his money. **1693** *Humours Town* 108 The Taverns are the Nurseries of Profaneness and Treason. **1710** SWIFT *Lett.* (1767) III. 14, I dined to-day at a tavern with Stratford. **1785** TRUSLER *Mod. Times* III. 76 When we reached London..we put up at one of those taverns called hotels. **1809** KENDALL *Trav.* III. lxxii. 128 The doctor keeps a public house, or, as the term is, a tavern. **1840** DICKENS *Barn. Rudge* ii, This tavern would seem to be a house of call for all the gaping idlers of the neighbourhood. **1854** 'C. BEDE' *Verdant Green* II. xi. 103 He seemed to feel that the Dons of his college would look shy upon him, and he expressed his opinion that it would be better for him to migrate to the Tavern... A name given to New Inn Hall, not only from its title..but also because the buttery is open all day, and members of the Hall can call for what they please at any hour. **1904** *Westm. Gaz.* 11 May 1/2 Richard Shute —the only first-class man ever produced by the defunct 'Tavern', as New Inn Hall [Oxford] used to be called.

† **2.** A shop or workshop attached to or under a dwelling-house; often under ground, a cellar. Cf. CELLAR 2, WINE-CELLAR. *dial. Obs.*

1521 in *Test. Ebor.* (Surtees) VI. 4 Al my tymber and bordes in the Taverne, except a kilnehouse of x postes that lieth in the laithe and in the gaitehouse. **1566** in S. O. Addy *Evolution Eng. House* (1905) 96 William Tomson for his taverne stare, iiij d. **1575** *Ibid.* 95 Payd to ij dykers for casting earth furth of the taverne iiij daies, ij s. viij d. **1583** *Will Myles Fox* (Somerset Ho.), My Shop with two undershops or Taverins. **1703** THORESBY *Let. to Ray* (W. Yorksh. Words), *Tavern*, a cellar. **1905** ADDY (as above) 94–5 In England shops in front of town houses were sometimes known as 'taverns',..and were below the surface of the streets, like cellars... These 'taverns' were entered by stairs.

3. As a rendering of L. *taberna*: see the etymology.

1382 WYCLIF *Acts* xxviii. 15 Whanne bretheren hadden herd, thei runnen to vs til to the cheping of Appius, and to a place that is clepid Thre tauernes [*Vulg.* tres Tabernas]. **1611** BIBLE ibid., They came to meet vs as farre as Appii forum, and the three Tauernes.

4. *attrib.* and *Comb.* **a.** Attributive, as ***tavern-bill***, ***-boy***, ***-bully***, ***-bush*** (BUSH *sb.*¹ 5), ***-chair***, ***-discourse***, ***-door***, ***-drawer*** (DRAWER *sb.*¹ 2), ***-fellow***, ***-house***, ***-lady***, ***-lantern***, ***-man***, ***-music***, ***-quarrel***, ***-reckoning***, ***-restaurant***, ***-score***, ***-song***, ***-supper***, ***-talk***, ***-wine***, etc. **b.** Objective and obj. gen., as ***tavern-frequenter***, †***-ganger***, ***-goer***, ***-haunter***, ***-hunter***, ***-hunting***, ***-keeper***, ***-tracer***. **c.** Instrumental, locative, etc., as ***tavern-gotten***, ***-tainted*** adjs. **d.** Special combs.: † **tavern-fox**, in phr. ***to hunt a tavern-fox***, to get drunk: see FOX *sb.* 1 d and *v.* 2; **tavern-token**, a token given in change by a tavern-keeper, which he will again accept in payment; † ***to swallow a tavern-token***, to get drunk (*obs.*).

1611 SHAKS. *Cymb.* V. iv. 161 You shall..fear no more *Tauerne Bils. **1796** H. HUNTER tr. *St.-Pierre's Stud. Nat.* (1799) III. 286 The appellation of 'good man', so frankly bestowed on him by the *tavern-boy. **1852** THACKERAY *Esmond* II. i, A *Tavern-bully beaten. **1570** FOXE *A. & M.* (ed. 2) 1206/1 Seeing good wyne nedeth no *tauerne bushe to vtter it. *a* **1668** DAVENANT *News fr. Plymouth* Wks. (1673) 2 In the Metropolis,.. Where still your Taverne Bush is green and flourishing. **1787** SIR J. HAWKINS *Johnson* 87, I have heard him assert, that a *tavern-chair was the throne of human felicity. **1660** R. COKE *Justice Vind.* Pref. 12 The subject of all *tavern-discourses. **1474** *Coventry Leet Bk.* (E.E.T.S.) 400 Yf he sell any feetiff wyn his *Tauerne durre to be sealed Inne, and he to make a fyne at the kynges wyll. *a* **1704** T. BROWN *Lond. & Lacedem. Oracles* Introd., Wks. 1709 III. III. 124 The Oyster-wench in her lawful Occupation at the Tavern-door. **1721** CIBBER *Rival Fools* I. i, Can't you practise.. upon a *Tavern-Drawer, or a Box-keeper at the Play-House? **1899** *Month* June 613 The roystering joviality of Prince Harry's tavern-fellow. **1635** J. TAYLOR (Water P.) *Old Parr* C ij b, Nor did hee ever hunt a *Taverne Fox. **1483** *Cath. Angl.* 378/2 A *Tawern ganger, *attabernio*. **1797** T. PARK *Sonn.* 82 Meeting with some *tavern-goer. **1538** ELYOT, *Circumcelliones*, *tauerne haunters, or raylers aboute. **1583** GOLDING *Calvin on Deut.* li. 305 These Tauernhaunters or Alehouse Knightes which counterfeit the preachers. **13..** *Cursor M.* 28462 (Cott.) Til *tauerne huse my-seluen was wont, And draun men þer-til vmstont. **1553** BECON *Reliques of Rome* (1563) 28 The aforesayd pope made.. a decree, that priestes should be no *tauern-hunters. **1641** MILTON *Animadv.* xiii. Pr. Wks. (1847) 69/2 Their laziness, their *tavern-hunting, their neglect of all sound literature. **1611** COTGR., *Tavernier*,.. a *Tauerne-keeper. **1779** *Mirror* No. 46 ⁋ 23 Familiar.. to the very tavern-keepers of this city. **1763** MRS. F. SHERIDAN *Discovery* II. i, I don't doubt but he is going to some of his *tavern-ladies. **1664** ETHEREDGE *Love in Tub* IV. ii, Go with a *Tavern-Lanthorn before me at Noon-day. **1755** JOHNSON, **Tavernman*, one who keeps a tavern. **1643** SIR T. BROWNE *Relig. Med.* II. §9 That vulgar and *Taverne-Musick. **1979** *Listener* 30 Aug. 275/2 The best *tavern music in South London is.. jazz. **1820** HAZLITT *Lect. Dram. Lit.* 30 Marlow was stabbed in a *tavern quarrel. **1880** W. D. HAY *Doom of Gt. City* 46 One place I knew slightly, a *tavern-restaurant, where I had occasionally dined. **1973** *Washington Post* 13 Jan. A 3/6 Mr. and Mrs. Harry Grenwalt .. were celebrating their 42nd wedding anniversary at the tavern-restaurant. **1714** MANDEVILLE *Fab. Bees* (1724) I. 19 Those, that remain'd,.. when they paid their *Tavern Score, Resolv'd to enter it no more. **1823** BYRON *Don Juan* VIII. lxiii. 142 Without which Glory's but a *tavern song. **1917** J. MASEFIELD *Lollingdon Downs* 90 Within the tavern-song, hid in the wine. **1959** I. & P. OPIE *Lore & Lang. Schoolch.* xvi. 346 This jingle may be compared with the tavern song which was printed in *Vinculum Societatis*. *a* **1680** BUTLER *Rem., Charac.* (1759) II. 439 He is the Whores Jackal,.. and at Night has his Share in a *Tavern-Supper. **1760** *Cautions to Officers Army* 124 Tavern-Suppers are generally expensive. **1609** *Ev. Woman in Hum.* III. i. in Bullen *O. Pl.* IV, Urge no more, 'tis *Taverne talke. **1638** FORD *Lady's Trial* II. ii, You are grown a tavern-talk, Matters for fiddlers' songs. **1598** B. JONSON *Ev. Man in Hum.* I. iii, Drunk sir?.. perhaps he swallow'd a *tauerne token, or some such deuise sir. **1604** *Meeting Gallants* 17 Indeed he had swallowed downe many Tauerne-tokens, and was infected with the plague of drunkennes. **1604** DEKKER *Hon. Wh.* I. iv, If he have but.. a spleene not so big as a taverne token.

Hence (mostly *nonce-wds.*), ˈ**tavernize** *v. intr.*, to frequent taverns; ˈ**tavernless** *a.*, devoid of taverns or inns; ˈ**tavernly** *a.*, smacking of the tavern; ˈ**tavernous** *a.* [after *cavernous*], tavern-like; ˈ**tavernry**, tavern-expenses; ˈ**tavernwards** *adv.*, towards a tavern.

1851 *Fraser's Mag.* XLIV. 425 The frequent *tavernising, if we may coin a word, is another peculiarity. Pepys was a giant in this way, and sang and roystered.. in the public houses of the day. **1897** 'MARK TWAIN' *More Tramps Abroad* lxxi, The Bishop.. was once making a business-progress through the *tavernless velt. **1612** SHELTON *Quix.* (1746) I. III. ii. 119 So returning him Thanks with *Tavernly Phraze for his large Offers. **1866** LD. HOUGHTON *Sp.* in *Life* (1890) I. ii. 75 The low.. ill-lit, cavernous, *tavernous gallery. *a* **1670** SPALDING *Troub. Chas. I* (1851) II. 102 Thay comptit and reknit for thair *tavernrie with ther mistressis. **1892** *Daily News* 10 Mar. 2/4 Thirty young fellows.. were promptly on the 'double' *tavernwards.

ˈ**tavern**, *v.* Now *rare* or *Obs.* [f. prec. sb., as a rendering of med.L. *tabernāre*, f. *taberna* (common in 14–15th c.).]

†**1.** *trans.* Of a leaseholder or copyholder: To subdivide his tenement; ? *orig.* to erect a cottage (*taberna*) on his holding, and apportion a piece of land to it. *north. Obs.*

[**1365** *Durham Acc. Rolls* (Surtees) I. 38 Idem Johannes illud [tenementum] tabernavit sine licencia. *Ibid.* 42 De Johanne Anderson pro licencia tabernandi unum cotagium. **1402** *Charta* (Du Cange), Ne scolaribus detur occasio mercandi seu Tabernandi.] **1534** *Augm. Off., Convent. Leases, Yorks.* No. 888 That the said Thomas and Roger his sonne.. shall not taverne the said fermhold nor no parcell therof bot to dwell and remane of the said fermhold apon payn [etc.]. **1551** *Richmond Wills* (Surtees) 72 If it happ my wife to latt or taverne any parte of said fermehold, (not beyng of habilitie to occupie the same) then I will that Roland my eldest sonne have it. **1575** [see TAVERNING 1]. **1577** *Eccl. Proc. Bp. Barnes* (Surtees) 18 And doe not let out, lease out, or taverne out, their livings.

2. *intr.* To frequent taverns; also ***to tavern it***.

1580, etc. [see TAVERNING 2]. **1610** *Histrio-m.* VI. 209 Each .. taverns it with drunken suppers still.

†**b.** *trans.* with *out*: To spend in 'taverning'.

1628 FELTHAM *Resolves* II. [I.] lvii. 164 When, like Nero, thou should'st Taverne out thy time with Wantons.

taverna (təˈvɜːnə). [a. mod.Gr. ταβέρνα tavern.] A Greek eating-house.

1914 L. M. J. GARNETT *Greece of Hellenes* xii. 151 The typical 'public house' of Greece is a small tavern... Adjoining many of these humble wayside *tavérnas* are gardens roofed with spreading vines. **1952** [see BOUZOUKI]. **1963** *Harper's Bazaar* Jan. 59/2 Food in *tavernas* is.. not always very good. **1972** *Daily Tel.* (Colour Suppl.) 24 Nov. 20/4 Multitudes of rather second-rate tavernas and pizza-houses [in Australia]. **1977** B. PYM *Quartet in Autumn* xviii. 160 Not Greece of course..—one could hardly imagine Marcia in a taverna, eating octopus. **1978** *Chicago* June 34/2 Penny Evans.. is the best taverna singer we've ever heard. **1980** R. TINE *State of Grace* (1982) xix. 169 They won't respect you. In every corner *taverna* [in Sicily] they'll be laughing at you.

taverner (ˈtævənə(r)). Also 4 **tavernyer, tavarnere,** 5 **tawerner, -yrner, tavernere,** 6 **-ar,** *Sc.* **-eir,** 7 **-o(u)r;** (5 **taberner**). [a. AF. *taverner* = OF. *tavernier* used in senses 1 and 2 below (*c* 1200 in Godef. *Compl.*), f. *taverne*, TAVERN, or:—post-cl. L. *tabernārius* shopkeeper.]

1. One who keeps a tavern; a tavern-keeper. *arch.*

13.. *Sir Beues* (A.) 4357 He askede at þe tauarnere, þat armede folk, what it were. **1340** *Ayenb.* 44 And zelleþ ontreweliche, ase doþ þise tavernyers þet uelleþ þe mesure myd scome. **1382** WYCLIF *Ecclus.* xxvi. 28 The tauerner shal not be iustified fro synnes of lippis. **14..** *Nom.* in Wr.-Wülcker 688/19 *Hic tabernarius*, taberner. **14..** *Lytyll Thanke* 19 in Ritson *Anc. Songs* (1792) 78 They callyd the tawyrner to ffyll þe quarte, And lette note for the coste. **1500–20** DUNBAR *Poems* xxxiv. 46 (R. MS.) 'Be Godis bluid', quod the taverneir, 'Thair is sic wyne in my selleir As neuir come in this cuntrie'. **1530** PALSGR. 279/2 Tavernar a wyne sellar, *tauernier*. **1603** HOLLAND *Plutarch's Mor.* 46 Are you become indeed a Tavernour, Whose father was a woorthy governour? **1720** STRYPE *Stow's Surv.* II. 194/1 This Company anciently consisted of.. The Vinteners, who were the Merchants that imported Wine.., and the Taverners, who kept Taverns for them, and sold it out by Retayl. **1760** J. ADAMS *Diary* Wks. 1850 II. 85 [He] may.. multiply taverns and dram shops, and thereby secure the votes of taverner and retailer. **1868** E. EDWARDS *Ralegh* I. iv. 66 Under the powers of the assigned patent, [he] considerably increased the number of licensed taverners.

†**2.** One who frequents a tavern or taverns; a tippler. *Obs.*

1340 *Ayenb.* 51 Vor alþeruerst he becomþ tauernyer, þanne he playþ ate des. **1579** TWYNE *Phisicke agst. Fort.* II. xc. 278 b, There is.. nothyng more vayne then typplers and Tauerners. **1612** T. TAYLOR *Comm. Titus* i. 7 (1619) 129 So should I be a swearer? a taverner? a drunkard?

ˈ**taverning**, *vbl. sb.* Now *rare* or *Obs.* [f. TAVERN *v.* + -ING[1].] The action of the verb TAVERN.

†**1.** See TAVERN *v.* 1. *Obs.*

1575 SIR J. FORSTER in *St. Papers Eliz., Borders* XIX. 81 (P.R.O.) When anye Inhabitant here hath.. a Tenement.. scant sufficient for the meinteignaunce of one person, yf he chaunce to dye havinge two sonnes, he devydeth the said Tenement betwixt them bothe, and thus the taverninge of the Queynes lande ys hinderance for kepinge of hors and armor.

2. The action or practice of frequenting taverns.

1580 in *Liturg. Serv. Q. Eliz.* (Parker Soc.) 574 The Sabboth days.. is spent full heathenishly, in taverning, tippling, gaming, playing and beholding of Bear-baiting and Stage plays. **1597–8** BP. HALL *Sat.* II. i, Or wicked Rablais dronken revellings, To grace the mis-rule of our tavernings. **1654** WHITLOCK *Zootomia* 503 Another cries out on the ones Taverning (where he would not spend a six pence, he never knew any come to good that did).

attrib. **1837** *New Monthly Mag.* LI. 41 No wonder that, with these taverning habits, Jonson lived poor and died no richer.

3. The keeping of a tavern.

1774 J. WENTWORTH in F. Chase *Hist. Dartmouth Coll.* (1891) I. 264 Inquiring into the reasons of granting license to Mr. Payne for taverning and retailing.

tavert, *ppl. a.*: see TAVER *v.*

Tavgi (ˈtævgɪ), *sb.* (and *a.*) Also **Tavghi, Tavghy, Tavgy.** [a. Russ.] **a.** (A member of) a Finno-Ugric people (now called Nganasan) living between the Yenisey and Khatanga rivers in north-west Siberia. **b.** The language of this people. Also *attrib.* or as *adj.*, esp. in ***Tavgi-Samoyed***.

1886 *Encycl. Brit.* XXI. 251/2 The Tavghi Samoyedes may number about 1000. **1888** *Ibid.* XXIV. 1/1 *Ural-Altaic languages.. Tavghi*, between lower Yenisei and Khatanga rivers. **1934** WEBSTER, *Tavgi*, var. of *Tavghi*. **1951** W. K. MATTHEWS *Lang. U.S.S.R.* iii. 17 Tavgi (Nganasan) in Taimyr. **1954**, **1967** [see NENETS]. **1975** G. F. CUSHING tr. *Hajdu's Finno-Ugrian Lang. & Peoples* iii. 216 The Nganasans are called Tavgi-Samoyeds. **1977** C. F. & F. M. VOEGELIN *Classification & Index World's Lang.* 343 Yenisei Samoyed.. appears to be transitional between Yurak and Tavgy Samoyed.

Tavism, variant of TAOISM.

†ˈ**Tavistock**. *Obs.* In 6 **Tave-**. A woollen cloth formerly made at the town of Tavistock.

1535–6 *Act 27 Hen. VIII*, c. 12 §3 Any clothes called Tavestockes, Westerne doseyns, Friseys, Kendalles, Cottons, and all manner of course clothes made for lynynges. **1545** *Rates of Customs* d iij b, vj. Tauestockes for a clothe. [**1551–2** *Act 5 & 6 Edw. VI*, c. 6 §29 Any Clothe or Clothes made in the Towne of Tavestoke in the Countie of Deuon.. commenlye called Tavestoke Clothes.]

tavistockite (ˈtævɪstɒˌkaɪt). *Min.* [Named by Dana, 1868, from *Tavistock*, a town in Devonshire, where found: see -ITE[1].] 'Hydrous phosphate of aluminum and calcium, found in microscopic acicular crystals' (Chester *Names Min.*).

[**1865** A. H. CHURCH in *Jrnl. Chem. Soc.* 264 Our present mineral is from Tavistock, Devonshire.] **1868** DANA *Min.* 582 Tavistockite.

†**tavorsay**. *Old Cookery. Obs.* [?] A dish of spiced cod's head and liver.

c **1450** *Two Cookery-bks.* 114 *Tauorsay.* Nym ye hed of ye codlyng & ye liuere, & pike out ye bones, cast therto goud poudre of piper & gyngiuer, and gif forth.

†**taw**, *sb.*[1] *Obs. rare.* [f. TAW *v.*[1]]

1. Tawed leather; white leather.

c **1562** in J. T. Gilbert *Calr. Anc. Rec. Dublin* (1891) II. 23 Gloves, purses, whit tawe and suche like wurke apperteyninge to thoccupacion of glover.

2. A thong, whip, lash.

Perh. a different word; app. the sing. of TAWS, TAWSE (which is evidenced much earlier).

1787 GROSE *Provinc. Gloss.*, *Taw*, a whip. N. **1853** W. WATSON *Poems* 28 (E.D.D.) The nippy taw Comes whiskin' whiles athort us a'. [**1864** WEBSTER, *Taw*,.. (*pl.*). A whip or instrument of punishment used by a schoolmaster.]

taw (tɔː), *sb.*[2] Also 8 **tau**, 9 **tor**. [Origin unascertained, and order of senses uncertain: perh., like *alley*, ALLY *sb.*[2], an abbreviation.]

a. A large choice or fancy marble, often streaked or variegated, being that with which the player shoots.

1709 STEELE *Tatler* No. 30 ⁋ 1 He is hiding or hoarding his Taws and Marbles. *a* **1761** CAWTHORN *Wit & Learn.* Poems (1771) 48 He minded but his top, or taw. **1807**, **1833** [see ALLY *sb.*[2]]. **1837** DICKENS *Pickw.* xxxiv, After enquiring, whether he had won any alley tors or commoneys lately. **1843** THACKERAY *Irish Sk. Bk.* xxiv, Large agate marbles or 'taws'. *a* **1845** HOOD *Clapham Acad.* xiv, Five who stoop The marble taw to speed. **1857** HUGHES *Tom Brown* I. iii, His small private box was full of peg-tops, white marbles (called 'alley-taws' in the Vale), [etc.]. **1876** GRANT *Burgh Sch. Scotl.* II. v. 179 A still greater favourite is shooting a 'taw', which requires no small dexterity.

b. *transf.* A game played with such marbles.

1709 STEELE *Tatler* No. 112 ⁋ 3 A Game of Marbles, not unlike our modern Taw. **1784** COWPER *Tiroc.* 307 To kneel and draw The chalky ring, and knuckle down at taw. **1798** *Sporting Mag.* XII. 169 At cricket, taw, and prison-bars, He bore away the bell. **1840** THACKERAY *Paris Sk.-bk.* (1869) 45, I would lay a wager that.. their school learning carried them.. only to the game of taw.

c. The line from which the players shoot in playing the game. Hence in phrases: see quots.

1740 DYCHE & PARDON s.v. *Knuckle*, They frequently say, *Knuckle down to your taw*, or fit your hand exactly in the place where your marble lies. **1840** *Spirit of Times* 7 Mar. 6 We have understood that Boston.. will be *en route* for the stable.. at Columbia, South Carolina—that is, if Wagner 'comes to taw'. **1854** MISS BAKER *Northampt. Gloss.* s.v., 'Shoot from taw'. 'You don't stand at taw'... 'If you don't do so and so I'll bring you to taw'. **1868** in *Amer. Speech* (1965) XL. 132 He smiles at all the girls he meets, And you smile at him on the crowded streets, Why don't you make him 'come to taw', I know he wants a mother-in-law. **1881** *Leicesters. Gloss.* s.v., A ring is scratched on the ground, and at some distance from it a straight line called taw. *Ibid.*, We thus get the phrases.. 'come up to scratch' and 'come up to taw'. **1904** W. N. HARBEN *Georgians* xxxii. 292 His wife's a bully woman; she fetched 'im to taw. **1934** D. RUNYON in *Collier's* 3 Mar. 41/1 Georges takes a wonderful liking to Princess O'Hara right from taw. **1935** H. DAVIS *Honey in Horn* ix. 113 The only way Mrs. Yarbro could tell anything was to start from taw. **1956** *Coast to Coast* 183 Starting off from taws with a big load to carry. **1969** *Sunday Truth* (Brisbane) 5 Oct. 14/4 Without a share of overseas star shows, Seven has been battling from taws, but.. is.. getting stuck into the other networks with a 'super-specials' policy change.

†**taw**, *sb.*[3] *Obs. rare.* [Derivation unascertained.] A rootlet, a fibre of a root.

1615 W. LAWSON *Country Housew. Gard.* (1626) 16 Though they get some hold in the earth with some lesser taw, or tawes, which giue some nourishment to the body of the tree. *Ibid.* 24 To dresse the roots of trees, to take away the tawes, and tangles, that lap and fret and grow superfluously. **1670** CAPT. J. SMITH *Eng. Improv. Reviv'd* 58 A Plant by its Roots and Tawes, or Fibres, sucks in the Juice of the Earth. **1765** *Museum Rust.* V. 117 Its root.. is round, and thick set with taws.

taw (tɔː), *v.*[1] Forms: 1 **tawian**, 3 (*Orm.*) **tawwenn**, 3–4 **tauwen**, 4–6 **tawe**, 6– **taw**. [OE. *tawian* = MLG., MDu., Du. *touwen*, LG. *tauen*, *töwwen* to prepare (leather), to tan, to curry, OHG. *zawjan*, *zowjan* (MHG. *zouwen*, *zöuwen*) to prepare, make, Goth. *taujan* to do, make:—OTeut. **tawôjan* and **tawjan*; from a stem *taw-*, *tôw-*, not certainly found in pre-Germanic.]

1. *trans.* To make ready, prepare, or dress (some raw material) for use, or for further manipulation; e.g. to soften (hides) by beating, to heckle (hemp), etc.; †in early use, to till (land).

a **900** tr. *Bæda's Hist.* IV. xxix. (1890) 366 Þa bæd se Godes man þæt him man isern ʒeloman mid hwæte ðyder brohte þæt land mid to tawienne. *c* **1200** ORMIN 15903 All swa summ þe nowwt i ploh þe turrnenn erþe & tawwenn. **1545** *Rates of Customs* C v, Sylke tawe[d] and died the pounde viii s. **1555** W. WATREMAN *Fardle Facions* II. ix. 193 He.. taweth the skinne betwixte his handes, vntill it become very souple and soft. **1628** *Robin Goodfellow* II. (1841) 28 And whilst that they did nimbly spin, The hempe he needs must taw. **1651** BIGGS *New Disp.* Pref. 7 Being tawed open by wedge after wedge. **1861** *Jrnl. Brit. Archæol. Assoc.* Mar. 20 A slick-stone for tawing or softening hides by friction.

2. *spec.* To make (skins) into leather by steeping them, after suitable preparation, in a solution of alum and salt; the product is white and pliant, and is known as *alum, white*, or *Hungarian leather*.

(In early quots., not separable from sense 1.)

a **1225** *Ancr. R.* 418 Þet heo [ower cloðes] beon unorne & warme, & wel i-wrouhte—uelles wel i-tauwed. *a* **1300** *Sat. People Kildare* ix. in *E.E.P.* (1862) 154 Daþeit þe sotter þat tawiþ ȝure leþir. *c* **1410** *Master of Game* (MS. Digby 182) vi, þe furrure..is not feyre; and also it stynketh euer, but if hit be wele ytawede. **1474** *Coventry Leet Bk.* (E.E.T.S.) 401 The sise of a whittawer is that he make nor tawe no maner of lether but Shepes lether, Gettes lethir, deris ledur, horse-lethir, or houndes-lether. **1560** *Let.* in Hakluyt *Voy.* (1598) I. 307 If you send 100 of them [seal skins] tawed with the haire on, they will bee solde, or else not. **1607** TOPSELL *Four-f. Beasts* (1658) 45 The hides..being tawed and wrought artificially they make garments of them. **1613** FLETCHER, etc. *Captain* III. iii, Yes if they taw him as they do whit-leather Upon an iron. **1711** *Lond. Gaz.* No. 4862/4 Mills..where they shall Tan, Taw or Dress..any such Hides. **1877** KNIGHT *Dict. Mech.*, *Tawing*, a process of tanning in which mineral agents are substituted for vegetable extracts. **1879** *Cassell's Techn. Educ.* IV. 88/1 Carefully-prepared goat-skin, tanned, tawed, dyed, and grained.

†**3.** *fig.* To treat (a person) abusively or with contumely; to vex, torment; to harass, afflict; to abuse, outrage, profane. *Obs.*

c **893** K. ÆLFRED *Oros.* IV. i. § 1 Þa þe þær ȝefongne wæron, hie tawedan mid þære mæstan unieðnesse. *c* **1000** ÆLFRIC *Saints' Lives* (1890) II. 102 Forðan ðe he godes templ tawode to bysmore. *c* **1000** —— *Hom.* II. 486 And se deofol eow tawode þurh his drymen. *a* **1023** WULFSTAN *Hom.* xxxiii. (Napier) 162 [Hi] scendað and tawjað to bysmore þæs þeȝnes cwenan and hwilum his dohtor. **13..** *Minor Poems fr. Vernon MS.* liv. 76 To a piler I was I-piht, Togget and tauwed al þe niht. **1549** CHALONER *Erasm. on Folly* G ij, To be briefe, they are not tawed nor plucked asunder with a thousand thousand cares.

b. To whip, flog, thrash. *Obs.* exc. *dial.*

1600 HOLLAND *Livy* VIII. xxviii. 301 He caused him to be stripped naked, and whipping cheare to be presented unto him. The poore stripling thus pitteously tawed and torn, ran forth into the open street. **1614** B. JONSON *Barth. Fair* IV. iv, You know where you were taw'd lately, both lash'd, and slash'd you were in Bridewell. **1682** D'URFEY *Butler's Ghost* 43 Truss'd on her Knee she'd briskly taw him, And, like Virago, clapperclaw him. **1863** SALA *Capt. Dangerous* viii, I grew sick of being tawed for offences I had never committed. **1883** CLELAND *Inchbracken* xvi. 126, I would have her tawed through the town at the cart's tail.

taw (tɔː), *v.*[2] Chiefly *dial.* [f. TAW *sb.*[2]] *intr.* To shoot or aim with a taw or marble.

1863 MRS. TOOGOOD *Yorks. Dial.*, You don't taw fairly. **1883** *Almondbury & Huddersf. Gloss.* s.v. *Hundreds*, When ..the one who is on for his pizings manages to taw into the hole, the game is concluded. **1898** [see TAWER[2]].

taw, obs. form of TAU, TOW.

‖**tawa**[1] ('tawa, *colloq.* 'taʊə). [The Maori name.] A tall and handsome forest tree of New Zealand, *Beilschmiedia* (*Nesodaphne*) *Tawa*, N.O. *Lauraceæ*, with damson-like fruit; allied to the Taraire, but inferior as timber.

1839 [see BILLY[3]]. **1866** *Treas. Bot.* 786/1 Called Tawa by the natives. **1883** J. HECTOR *Handbk. N. Zealand* (1886) 106 *Tawa*, a lofty forest tree 60 ft. to 70 ft. high, with slender branches. The wood is light, and soft, and is used for making butter-kegs.

tawa[2] (tɑː'wɑː). Also **tava(h)**. [a. Hindi, Punjabi *tavā* frying-pan, griddle.] A circular griddle used in the Indian subcontinent for cooking chupattis and other food.

c **1843** H. LAWRENCE *Jrnls.* (1980) viii. 134 The *tavah* a convex iron plate on which are [*sic*] baked the thin unleavened bread of the people. **1963** *Guardian* 1 May 6/4 Iron 'tawa' (a baking utensil like the Scots girdle for oatcakes). **1969** *Eve's Weekly* (Bombay) 20 Dec. 65/3 Make a gash in the flat side of each chestnut and dry roast in the oil in a large tava for a few minutes. **1971** *Femina* (Bombay) 16 Apr. 55/1 Roll out into *chappatis* and bake on a *tawa* on a very low fire till it cooks through.

†**tawak**, = to awake: see T'[1].

c **1315** SHOREHAM *Poems* i. 1412 Ta-wak Hy þet slepeþ ine senne slep.

Tawarek, var. TUAREG *sb.* and *a.*

tawbern, -bron, -burn, Sc. var. TABORN *Obs.*

tawche, tawcht, obs. Sc. forms of TALLOW.

tawcht, obs. Sc. f. *taught*: see TEACH *v.*

tawd, obs. Sc. f. *told*, pa. t. and pple. of TELL *v.*

†**tawder**, *v. Obs. nonce-wd.* [f. TAWDRY *a.*] *trans.* To deck *out* in tawdry garments.

1716 LADY M. W. MONTAGU *Let. to C'tess of Bristol* 22 Aug., A sort of shabby finery, a number of dirty people of quality tawdered out.

tawdrily ('tɔːdrɪlɪ), *adv.* [f. TAWDRY *a.* + -LY[2].] In a tawdry manner; with cheap finery.

1736 PULTENEY *Let. to Swift* 21 Dec., A rabble of people ..seeing her very oddly and tawdrily dressed, took her for a foreigner. **1816** *Sporting Mag.* XLVIII. 189 A lady observing her neighbour in a public room, dressed very tawdrily. **1879** FROUDE *Short Stud.* (1883) IV. v. 351 The two figures..are tawdrily coloured in white and red and gold.

tawdriness ('tɔːdrɪnɪs). [f. as prec. + -NESS.] The quality of being tawdry.

1670 *Moral State Eng.* 161 There was a kind of tawdriness in their Habits. **1753** HOGARTH *Anal. Beauty* vi. 35 That tawdriness may not destroy the proper effect of variety. **1841** GALLENGA *Italy* (1848) I. 139 The tinsel and tawdriness of an imitative dauber.

†'**tawdrum.** *Obs. nonce-wd.* [f. TAWDRY, with L. ending: cf. *nostrum*.] A tawdry decoration.

1680 BETTERTON *Revenge* V. iv. 65 No matter for Lace and Tawdrums.

tawdry ('tɔːdrɪ), *sb.* and *a.* Also 6 **tauthrie, tawdrie** (see next); 7 **taudrey, tawdery**, 7–8 **taudry**. [As sb. short for TAWDRY LACE, q.v.; hence referring to the showy but cheap quality of these in the 17th century.]

A. *sb.* †**1.** Short for TAWDRY LACE. *Obs.*

1612 DRAYTON *Poly-olb.* ii. 46 Of which the Naides, and the blew Nereïdes make Them Taudries for their necks. *Ibid.* iv. 50 Not the smallest Beck But with white Pebles makes her Taudries for her neck.

2. Cheap and pretentious finery.

a **1680** BUTLER *Rem.* (1759) I. 223 Applaud th' outsides of Words, but never mind, With what fantastic tawdery th'are lin'd. **1747** RICHARDSON *Clarissa* (1811) II. xx. 139 Only for the sake of having a little more tawdry upon his housings. **1831** *Examiner* 390/1 A dress circle!..look at the tawdry and the ennui! **1867** SMILES *Huguenots Eng.* (1880) 349 A poor bedizened creature, clad in tawdry.

B. *adj.* **1.** Of the nature of cheap finery; showy or gaudy without real value.

1676 ETHEREDGE *Man of Mode* II. ii, A Woman that Can doat on a senseless Caper, a Tawdry French Riband, and a Formal Cravat. **1686** BURNET *Lett.* (1708) 288 A Tawdry Imbroidery of Gold and Silver. **1711** STEELE *Spect.* No. 80 ¶3 A gay West Indian, who appeared in all the Colours which can affect an Eye that could not distinguish between being fine and taudry. **1805** REPTON *Landscape Gard.* 160 The lavish profusion of tawdry embellishment. **1859** JEPHSON *Brittany* ii. 14 The high altar is wretchedly tawdry.

†**b.** Untidy; slovenly; ungraceful. *Obs. rare.*

1671 GREW *Anat. Plants* v. §3 A Flower without its Empalement, would hang as uncouth and taudry, as a Lady without her Bodies. *c* **1820** JOANNA BAILLIE *Summer's Day* 83 His awkward..lad, Who trails his tawdry armful [of hay] o'er the field.

2. *transf.* Of persons or their condition: Tawdrily dressed or decked out; cheaply adorned.

1676 WYCHERLEY *Pl. Dealer* v. i, Taudry affected Rogues, well drest. **1706** PHILLIPS (ed. 6), *Taudry* or *Tawdry*,.. tricked up with such tinsel Stuff, or Lace as is usually sold at Audery-Fair in Cambridge-shire. **1851** HELPS *Comp. Solit.* vii. (1874) 133 Like one of those tawdry girls who pass by me. **1862** MISS BRADDON *Lady Audley* xxvii, An aspect of genteel desolation and tawdry misery not easily to be parallelled in wretchedness.

3. *fig.* esp. of style, diction, etc.; hence of a speaker or writer: Trumpery.

1696 R. L'ESTRANGE *Seneca's Mor.* (ed. 6) Afterth. 12 With-out forcing the Design of the Author, or intermixing any Tawdry Flowrishes by the By. *a* **1718** PENN *Maxims* §126. Wks. 1726 I. 850 'Tis but Taudry Talk, and next to very Trash. **1764** GOLDSM. *Traveller* Ded., Him they dignify with the name of poet: his tawdry lampoons are called satires. **1808** SCOTT *Let. to Lady L. Stuart* 19 Jan. in *Lockhart*, His language is too flowery and even tawdry.

†**tawdry lace.** *Obs.* [See T (the letter) 7.] In the earliest quotation *St. Audrey's lace*, i.e. lace of St. Audrey, Etheldrida, or Æþelðryþ (daughter of Anna king of East Anglia, and patron saint of Ely): A silk 'lace' or necktie, much worn by women in the 16th and early 17th c.; sometimes taken as a type of female adornments.

[As to the origin of the name, it is told, originally by Bæda (*Eccl. Hist.* IV. ix.), and after him by Ælfric in the Life of St. Æþelðryth, Virgin (*Ælfric's Lives of Saints*, ed. Skeat, 1885, xx. ll. 49–60), that St. Audrey died of a tumour in her throat, which she considered to be a just retribution, because in her youth she had for vain show adorned her neck with manifold splendid necklaces, 'forðan þe ic on iuȝoðe frætwede mine swuran mid mæniȝfealdum swurbeaȝum'. In the 16th century, N. Harpsfield, Archdeacon of Canterbury under Philip and Mary (died 1588), after relating the story in his (Latin) *Historia Anglicana Ecclesiastica* (Douay 1622), adds 'Our women of England are wont to wear about the neck a certain necklace [*torquem quendam*], formed of thin and fine silk, perchance in memory of what we have told'. See also, more particularly, quot. 1674 below. Skinner in his *Etymologicon* (licensed 1668), explains *Tawdry lace* as 'Ties, fringes, or bands, bought at the fair held at the fane of St. Etheldreda, as rightly points out Doctor Th. Henshaw'. There is no discrepancy between the two statements. 'St. Audrey's laces' would naturally be largely offered for sale at her fair, and though this did not give the article its name, it doubtless made it more widely known, and led to the production of cheap and showy forms for the 'country wenches' (see Nares s.v.), which at length gave to *tawdry* its later connotation.]

[**1530** PALSGR. (ed. 1) 63/2 Seynt Audries lace, *cordon.*] **1548** PATTEN *Exped. Scotl.* Pref. c iv b, Pardon Beades, Tanthonie belles, Tauthrie laces, Rosaries, Collets. **1579** SPENSER *Sheph. Cal.* Apr. 135 Binde your fillets faste, And gird in your waste, For more finesse, with a tawdrie lace. **1593** *Jack Straw* III. D iv, *Queen*... I will speake for thee. *T. M.* Will you in faith, and I will give you a tawdrie lace. **1610** FLETCHER *Faithf. Sheph.* IV. i, The Prim-Rose Chaplet, taudry-lace and Ring, Thou gavest her for her singing. **1611** SHAKS. *Wint. T.* IV. iv. 253 Come you promis'd me a tawdry-lace, and a paire of sweet Gloues. **1674** BLOUNT *Glossogr.*, *Taudrey Lace*, so called from St. Audrey (Ethelreda) who thought her self punished for wearing rich Necklaces of Jewels; and therefore women after that wore Necklaces of fine silk, called Taudrey Laces. *c* **1750** SHENSTONE *Elegies* xi. 18 To deck my native fleece with tawdry lace!

†'**tawdryne.** *Obs. nonce-wd.* [App. an arbitrary formation on *tawdry*.] = prec.

1586 W. WEBBE *Eng. Poetrie* (Arb.) 84 See ye not your selues doo demeane too rudely: Bynd the fillets: and to be fine the waste gyrt Fast with a tawdryne [Webbe's rendering in sapphics of Spenser's stanzas: see quot. 1579 in prec.].

tawed (tɔːd), *ppl. a.* [f. TAW *v.*[1] + -ED[1].] Made, as white leather, by the process of tawing. Also *transf.* (cf. *tanned*).

1545 *Rates of Customs* b iv, Graye tawed, the tymber vi. s. viii. d. **1563** *Mirr. Mag.*, *Induct.* xxxix, With tawed handes, and hard ytanned skyn. **1642** T. LECHFORD *Plain Dealing* (1867) 115 For the Winter they have boots, or a kind of laced tawed-leather stockins. **1711** *Lond. Gaz.* No. 4862/4 Hides and Skins, Tanned, Tawed or Dress'd. **1852** MORFIT *Tanning & Currying* (1853) 412 The tawed leather is the raw skin combined with subchloride of aluminium. **1879** *Cassell's Techn. Educ.* I. 150/2.

tawer[1] ('tɔːə(r)). Forms: 4–5 **tawier(e**, 4–7 **tawyer**, (5 **toyar**, 6 **tawhear**, 8 **tawar**), 5– **tawer.** [f. TAW *v.*[1]: see -ER[1]. With the earlier *tawyer*, cf. *lawyer, sawyer*.] One who taws; one who prepares white leather; = WHITE-TAWER.

[**1311** *Letter Bk. D. Lond.* lf. 127 Walterus le Whitawyer. **1346** *Ibid. F.* lf. 126 b, Les bones gentz Megucers appellez Whittawyers.] **1382** WYCLIF *Acts* ix. 43 Many dayes he dwellide in Joppe, at Symound, sum coriour [*gloss* or tawier, *v.rr.* tawer, tawiere]. **1480** [see TAWING 1]. **1481–90** *Howard Househ. Bks.* (Roxb.) 505 Payd to the toyar for iiij. boke skynnys. **1559** MACHYN *Diary* (Camden) 208 A tawhear of skynnes. **1570** LEVINS *Manip.* 74/44 A Tawer, *alutarius.* **1607** TOPSELL *Four-f. Beasts* (1658) 169 The skins of this Beast are dressed by Tawyers, with the fat of fishes and Alum. **1658** R. FRANCK *North. Mem.* (1821) 280 There live the tanners, tawyers, fell-mongers, parchment, and vellum-dressers. **1795** *Statist. Acc. Scotl.* XIV. 552 There are 17 tanners, 18 curriers, and 13 tawers. **1883** *Century Mag.* XXVII. 75 In this part of Paris live all tanners and tawers and their kindred.

'**tawer**[2]. [f. TAW *v.*[2]] One who aims a taw.

1898 ALICE B. GOMME *Games* II. 113 If one player knocks out a marble, he is entitled to 'taw' at the rest in the ring until he misses; and if a sure 'tawer' not one of the others may have the chance to taw.

tawern, obs. form of TAVERN.

tawery ('tɔːərɪ). *rare.* [f. TAWER[1] or TAW *v.*[1]: see -ERY.] An establishment where skins are tawed.

1830 MAUNDER *Dict. Eng. Lang.*, Tawery, a manufactory in which skins are dyed with alum. **1885** C. T. DAVIS *Manuf. Leather* 656 (Cent. Dict.) In Parisian taweries calves' brains, intimately mixed with wheat flour, are used as a substitute for yelk of egg.

tawes, obs. form of TAWS.

tawght, tawhte, obs. ff. *taught*: see TEACH *v.*

‖**tawhai** ('tafai, 'tɑːwaɪ). Also **tawai**. [Maori.] The native name in New Zealand of several species of beech, called by the settlers *birches*.

1873 *Catal. Vienna Exhib.*, *Tawhai*, large and durable timber, used for sleepers. **1883** J. HECTOR *Handbk. N. Zealand* (1886) 102 *Tawhai*, Red-birch (from the colour of the bark). A handsome tree, 80 ft. to 100 ft. high.

‖**tawhiri** (tɑː'firi, ta'wiːrɪ). Also **tawiri**. [Maori.] Native name of the New Zealand tree *Pittosporum tenuifolium*, noted for its fragrant white blossoms.

1872 A. DOMETT *Ranolf* VI. i. 108 Its floor..with faint tawhiri-leaves besprent. **1884** T. BRACKEN *Lays Maori* 21 The early breeze that..stole the rich Tawhiri's sweet perfume.

tawie ('tɔːɪ), *a. Sc. dial.* [? f. TAW *v.*[1] + -Y, in sense 'easy to taw': cf. *wieldy*.] Tractable, docile, easy to manage.

1786 BURNS *To Auld Mare* v, Ye ne'er was donsie; But hamely, tawie, quiet, an' cannie, An' unco sonsie.

tawing ('tɔːɪŋ), *vbl. sb.* [f. TAW *v.*[1] + -ING[1].]

1. The action or process of preparing white leather: see TAW *v.*[1] 2.

1408 *Litt. Red Bk. Bristol* (1900) II. 99 Qe nulle homme ..ne vse ascun manere tawing de ascuns pealx en lez ditz schopes. **1480** *Wardr. Acc. Edw. IV* (1830) 121 And to Joh'n Massy tawyer for tawing of a tymbre of hole sables iiij s. **1517–18** in Swayne *Sarum Churchw. Acc.* (1896) 59 For Tawynge of Buckys skynnys to couer ij Mase Bokys, xij d. **1711** *Lond. Gaz.* No. 4862/4 Their Places of tanning, tawing, or dressing of such Hides. **1884** KNIGHT *Dict. Mech.*, *Tawing*, tanning a lamb-skin with the wool on it.

attrib. **1588** L. M. tr. *Bk. Dyeing* 49 Take your tawing stocke, and taw it [black leather] well therewith. **1882** PATON in *Encycl. Brit.* XIV. 389/2 They receive..a second treatment with the tawing mixture.

b. (*pl.*) *concr.* (See quot.)

1611 COTGR., *Megis*, tawings; the offals, or peeces cut from skinnes in tawing.

†**2.** The action of flogging or punishing. *Obs.*

1620 SHELTON *Quix.* (1746) IV. vii. 54 Fearing least the Whipping-task and Tawing might light upon him. **1622** MABBE tr. *Aleman's Guzman d'Alf.* I. 240 He would willingly haue the tawing of mee. **1642** ROGERS *Naaman* 30 The Lords own tawing of him [Job]..to wring this speech from him.

tawk(e, tawlke, obs. forms of TALK.

tawlche, obs. Sc. f. TALLOW.

tawld, obs. Sc. f. *told*: see TELL *v.*

tawle, obs. f. TALL.

tawm, dial. f. TALM *v.*, to faint.

† **tawn,** *v. Obs. rare*$^{-1}$. [app. an alteration of TAN *v.* under the influence of TAWNY *a.*] *trans.* To make tawny; to bronze, 'tan'. So (*rare*) **tawn** *sb.*, the bronzing of the skin produced by exposure; occas. as *adj.*, tan or tawny-coloured.

1721 RAMSAY *Tartana* 94 While scorching Titan tawns the shepherd's brow. *a* **1734** NORTH *Lives* (1826) III. 96 It was a considerable time before this upper lip having been long shaded..took the same tawn as the rest of his face. **1851** H. MELVILLE *Moby Dick* I. v. 48 This young fellow's.. cheek is like a sun-toasted pear in hue... That man..looks a few shades lighter... In the complexion of a third still lingers a tropic tawn. **1920** E. POUND *H. S. Mauberley* 27 Tawn fore-shores. **1939** JOYCE *Finnegans Wake* 540 Redu Negru may be black in tawn.

† **tawne, taune,** *v.*[1] *Obs.* [Early ME. *tawne(n*, *taun-e(n*, aphetic form of **at-awne(n*, *at-aune(n*, f. AT- *pref.*[1] + *awne(n*, in Ormin *awwnenn*, AWN(E *v.*[2], to show, exhibit. OE. **awnian* has not been found, but ME. *t-awnen* is parallel to MLG., MDu., LG. *t-ônen*, Du. *t-oonen*, MHG. *z-ounen* to show. These point to an OTeut. **at-awnôjan*, as a by-form of Goth. *at-augjan* (OS. *t-ogian*, OE. *æt-eowan*, *æt-iewan*) to bring before the eyes, to show, f. OTeut. **augon-*, *augn-*, *awn-*, stems of *augon-* eye. See Feist *Got. Etymol.*, s.v. *Augō*, Brugmann ed. 2, §165, §681, Schade s.v. *zougan*, Franck s.v. *toon*, *toonen*.]

trans. To show, manifest, exhibit.

c **1220** *Bestiary* 767 Ful wel he [Christ] taunede his luue to man. *c* **1250** *Gen. & Ex.* 636 God..Taunede him in ðe walkene a-buuen Rein-bowe. *Ibid.* 1022 Ðis time oðer ȝer Sal ic me to ðe taunen her. *Ibid.* 2034 To tawnen ðe ðe soðe her-bi. *Ibid.* 3444 On oðer daiȝes morȝen quile, God tauned moysi quat he wile.

† **tawne,** *v.*[2] *Sc. Obs. rare*$^{-1}$. [? Deriv. of TAW *v.*[1]; ? for *taw-en.*] *trans.* To tame, subdue, soften.

1606 BIRNIE *Kirk-Buriall* xv. D iv, The sore sight of that saint his syres death, did so tawne the truculent turke.

tawniness (ˈtɔːnɪnɪs). [f. TAWNY *a.* + -NESS.] The quality or condition of being tawny.

c **1550** LLOYD *Treas. Health* F viij, Coluer dounge ground in vyneger and smeared ouer thy face putteth away al morphewe & tawnines. **1623** MIDDLETON *More Dissemblers Besides Wom.* v. ii, She's the sun's masterpiece for tawniness. **1727** BAILEY vol. II, *Tawniness*,..the Being of the Colour of tanned Leather. **1875** BROWNING *Aristoph. Apol.*, *Herakles* 406 He spread The tawniness behind—his yellow head Enmuffled by the brute's.

† ˈ**tawnish,** *a. Obs. rare.* [f. TAWN(Y *a.* + -ISH[1].] Somewhat tawny; tanned.

1675 *Lond. Gaz.* No. 1020/4 Having black strait hair, a tawnish complexion. **1684** *Ibid.* No. 1972/4 A tall slender Man,..of a Tawnish Complexion.

tawnt(e, obs. forms of TAUNT.

tawny (ˈtɔːnɪ), *a.* and *sb.* Forms: α. 4–7 **tauny,** 5– **tawny**; also 4 **tawne,** (4–5 **taunde**), (6 **tawneye,** 6–7 **-ie,** 6–9 **-ey**). β. (chiefly *north.* and *Sc.*) 5 **tannye, tannee,** 5–6 **tanne, tany,** 5–7 **tanny**; see also TENNE. [ME. *tauny*, *tawne*, a. AF. *taune*, OF. *tané* (12–13th c. in Godef. *Compl.*), later *tanné*, 'foncé comme le tan', f. *tan*, TAN *sb.*[1] The *au*, *aw* appears to have arisen from the OF. pronunciation, in which the *a* before *n* was nasalized, *tãne* (tɑ̃ne): cf. *pawn*, *aunt*, †*demaund*, †*Fraunce*.]

Name of a composite colour, consisting of brown with a preponderance of yellow or orange; but formerly applied also to other shades of brown.

A. as *adj.* Having, or being of, this colour.

α. **1377** LANGL. *P. Pl.* B. v. 196 Þanne cam coueytise..in a tauny tabarde of twelue wynter age. **1395** *E.E. Wills* (1882) 5, I deuyse to..my doughter a tawne bed of silk. **1487** in *Surrey Archæol. Soc. Collect.* (1865) III. 163, I bequeathe my tawny velvet gowne to be made a chesible thereof. **1538** *Test. Ebor.* (Surtees) VI. 85 My tawney chamlett dublett. **1578** LYTE *Dodoens* I. xxi. 32 Peruincle..The floure most commonly is blew, & sometimes white, & tawnie, but very seldome. **1599** DAVIES *Immort. Soul* clxxxviii, As the World's Sun..Makes the Moor black, the European white; Th' American tawny. **1601** B. JONSON *Poetaster* III. iv, We must haue you turne fiddler againe,..get a base violin at your backe, and marche in a tawnie coate. **1632** LITHGOW *Trav.* IV. 162 The other Turkes which are borne in Asia major and Ægypt..are of a greater stature, tauny. **1706** PHILLIPS (ed. 6), *Tawny*, that is of a tanned, or yellowish, or dusky Colour. **1791** COWPER *Iliad* x. 211 A lion's tawny skin Around him wrapp'd. **1844** DICKENS *Mart. Chuz.* xii, That port, being a light and tawny wine. **1856** DELAMER *Fl. Gard.* (1861) 60 *Hemerocallis flava.*—Day Lily; a plant with yellow or tawny flowers. **1904** *Blackw. Mag.* July 2 The patched old tawny sails.

β. *c* **1425** tr. *Arderne's Surgery* (E.E.T.S.) 27 Puluer of gallez and psidie and puluer tanny. **1564** *Reg. Privy Council Scot.* I. 308 Sex pece of broun and tanne clayth. *a* **1585** POLWART *Flyting w. Montgomerie* 736 Tanny cheeks, I think thou speiks with thy breeks. **1638** JUNIUS *Paint. Ancients* 270 They resemble the similitude of a tanie or a white man. **1652** J. WRIGHT tr. *Camus' Nat. Paradox* 362 Her complexion (which is somewhat tanny by beeing much exposed to the Sun).

B. as *sb.* **1.** Tawny colour. In *Her.* = TENNE.

a **1400–50** *Alexander* 4335 Nouthire to toly ne to taunde transmitte we na vebbis, To vermylion ne violett ne variant littis. *c* **1410** *Master of Game* (MS. Digby 182) xiii, þe best hue of rennynge houndes whiche be goode, is cleped broune tanne. **1493** *Mem. Ripon* (Surtees) III. 164 Pro xij virgis panni coloris de tawne pro vestura choristarum. **1601** HOLLAND *Pliny* XXIV. iv. 178 Without forth of a light tawnie or yellowish red. **1610** GUILLIM Heraldry I. iii. (1660) 20 Tawny (saith Leigh) is a Colour of Worship, and of some Heralds it is called Bruske. **1641** G. SANDYS *Paraphr. Song Sol.* I. i, This Tawney from the Sun I took. **1756** C. LUCAS *Ess. Waters* I. 103 The bright red is reduced to somewhat of a tawny. **1848** THACKERAY *Van. Fair* xxiv, I ain't particular about a shade or so of tawny.

†**2. a.** Cloth of a tawny colour. [Cf. OF. *tanné*.]

α. **1416** in *Somerset Med. Wills* (1901) 75, j joup de Taune furr[ata] cum nigro. **1462** *Mann. & Househ. Exp.* (Roxb.) 149 Ffor a ȝerd and di. off tawny, vj.s. vj.d. **1566** in Hakluyt *Voy.* (1598) I. 358 Some blacks for womens garments, with some Orenge colours and tawneis. **1572** in Feuillerat *Revels Q. Eliz.* (1908) 187 Of Satten Tawnie twelve yardes. **1587** FLEMING *Contn. Holinshed* III. 1338/1 Clothed in white, yellow, & orange tawnie.

β. **1462** *Paston Lett.* II. 103 Your son wolle haue to hys jakets murry and tany. **1494, 1502** Rowane tanne [see ROWAN[3]]. **1497** *Acc. Ld. High Treas. Scot.* I. 343 For iij elne and ane half of Rowane tannee. **1501** *Ibid.* II. 49, iiij elne Franch tanne.

†**b.** *pl.* Garments made of this cloth. *Obs.*

c **1800** R. CUMBERLAND *John de Lancaster* (1809) III. 116 The..livery-men brushing up their orange tawnies.

3. A brown-skinned person; = TAWNY-MOOR. *arch.*

1660 F. BROOKE tr. *Le Blanc's Trav.* 347 There are Tawnies amongst them, they weare in their eares rings of gold and silver. **1681** *Lond. Gaz.* No. 1672/4 Run away..a Tall slender Indian Tawney. **1751** FRANKLIN *Observ.* Wks. 1887 II. 234 In America, where we have so fair an opportunity, by excluding all blacks and tawnys, of increasing the lovely white and red. **1850** SMEDLEY *Frank Fairlegh* xxx, Rajah somebody or other..on his elephant, attended by a train of tawnies.

†**4.** A sweet beverage, so called from its colour.

β. *c* **1430** *Two Cookery-bks.* 26 Take almaunde Mylke, & Sugre, an powdere Gyngere, & of Galyngale, & of Canelle, and Rede Wine, & boyl y-fere: & þat is gode tannye.

5. A local name for the common bullfinch, from the colouring of the female.

1847–78 HALLIWELL, *Tawny*, a bullfinch. Somerset. **1885** SWAINSON *Provinc. Names Birds* 67 The same parts in the female are reddish-brown; hence Tawny (Somerset).

6. = *tawny port*, sense C. c below.

1929 J. B. PRIESTLEY *Good Companions* II. i. 278 'Waiter, I want a bottle of port.'.. 'Well, we've the Tawny at three-and-nine the bottle.' **1959** W. JAMES *Word-Bk. of Wine* 148 The commonest style of port is tawny, a blend of several vintages between four and ten years old. *Ibid.*, White port is simply port made from white grapes, and is sometimes blended with young red port to make the cheaper sorts of tawny. **1976** *Times* 6 Nov. 13/2 Prices are around £3 for a fine old tawny, about £4 to £5 for a vintage.

C. Combinations and special collocations. **a.** Parasynthetic, etc., as ***tawny-coloured***, ***-eyed***, ***-faced***, ***-haired***, ***-necked***, ***-skinned***, ***-stained***, ***-tanned***, ***-throated***, ***-visaged***, ***-whiskered***.

1572 in Hakluyt *Voy.* (1600) III. 465 The people of the countrey are of a good stature, tawny coloured, broad faced, flat nosed. *a* **1618** SYLVESTER *Spectacles* x, When the Leaves in Autumn wither With a tawny-tanned Face. **1687** *Lond. Gaz.* No. 2298/3 A tawny visaged Man. **1740** PINEDA *Span. Dict.* s.v. *Denostar*, A tawny fac'd Woman dress'd up, reviles the fair one. **1839** BAILEY *Festus* v. (1852) 65 Red, black or white, olive, or tawny-skinned. **1853** M. ARNOLD *Philomela* in *Poems* (new ed.) 64 Hark! ah, the nightingale! The tawny-throated! **1859** GEO. ELIOT *A. Bede* v, Some tawny-whiskered, brown-locked, clear-complexioned young Englishman. **1862** BURTON *Bk.-Hunter* I. 18 He was not a black-letter man..or a tawny-moroccoite [collector of books bound in tawny morocco]. **1930** E. BLUNDEN *Poems* 42 And tawny-stained with ruin [the brook] trolls across The tiny village battered into dross. **1940** C. DAY LEWIS tr. *Virgil's Georgics* IV. 90 A laminated dragon or lioness tawny-necked. **1952** R. CAMPBELL tr. *Baudelaire's Poems* 87 Like angels fierce and tawny-eyed, Back to your chamber I will glide.

b. With other names of colour, expressing a modification by tawny, as ***tawny-brown***, etc.

1502 *Privy Purse Exp. Eliz. of York* (1830) 9, iiij yerdes.. of sarcenet of tawny grene. **1725** DE FOE *Voy. round World* (1840) 121 The people were black, or rather of a tawny dark brown. **1751** *Affect. Narr. of Wager* 97 Their Colour a Tawney Olive. **1812** SIR H. DAVY *Chem. Philos.* 280 It.. becomes of a tawney yellow colour. **1839** URE *Dict. Arts* 619 For..tawny-gray,..the stuff must receive a previous blue ground by dipping it in the indigo vat. **1905** *Westm. Gaz.* 4 Mar. 2/3, I looked across the desert, tawny-gold beneath the pitiless sun.

c. In special collocations, esp. in names of particular species of animals of a tawny colour, or plants with tawny flowers, as ***tawny bunting***, ***monkey***, ***thrush***, ***vulture***; ***tawny day-lily***, ***sedge***; also in collectors' names of moths, as ***tawny pinion***, ***wave***, etc.; † **tawny-coat**, an ecclesiastical apparitor, from the colour of his livery; **tawny eagle**, *Aquila rapax*, found in Africa and western Asia; **tawny emperor**, collectors' name for *Apatura herse*, a large butterfly (cf. EMPEROR 4); **tawny frogmouth** = PODARGUS; **tawny owl**: see OWL *sb.* 2 b; **tawny port**, a port wine made from a blend of several vintages matured in wood (see quot. 1951).

1766 PENNANT *Zool.* I. 112 *Tawny Bunting. **1591** SHAKS. *1 Hen. VI*, I. iii. 56 Out *Tawney-Coates, out Scarlet Hypocrite. **1634** HEYWOOD *Mayden-head Lost* I. Wks. 1874 IV. 114 Though I was neuer Tawny-coate, I haue playd the summoners part. **1859** *Ibis* I. 88 The claim of the *Tawny Eagle..to be considered European rests at present solely upon a trophy of the Russian war. **1912** J. STEVENSON-HAMILTON *Animal Life Afr.* xvii. 286 The tawny eagle is of mottled brown colour above, and tawny chestnut beneath, with yellow legs. **1979** G. & D. LLOYD *Birds of Prey* 82 The Tawny Eagle..of Africa and Asia is 26 to 31 inches in size and is the world's commonest eagle. **1901** A. J. CAMPBELL *Nests & Eggs Austral. Birds* II. 539 (*heading*) *Tawny frogmouth. **1933** [see PODARGUS]. **1968** BREEDEN & SLATER *Birds Austral.* 69 (*caption*) The yawn of this Tawny Frogmouth reveals its enormous gape. **1768** PENNANT *Zool.* I. 158 The *Tawny Owl... The color of this kind is sufficient to distinguish it from every other. **1848** THACKERAY *Van. Fair* xliii. 382 The particular *tawny port was produced when he dined with Mr. Osborne. **1951** R. POSTGATE *Plain Man's Guide to Wine* viii. 116 Tawny port is port of various years, blended and matured in cask... Tawny port..soon loses the rich purple colour of vintage port, and is ready to drink much sooner. **1979** *Country Life* 4 Jan. 40/1 (Advt.), Old Tawny Port wines by *Quinta do Noval*..Portugal. **1859** MISS PRATT *Brit. Grasses* 35 C[arex] fulva (*Tawny Sedge). **1783** LATHAM *Synopsis* III. 28 **Tawny Thrush*, Arct. Zool... Head, back, and wing coverts tawny. **1891** *Cent. Dict.* s.v., *Tawny thrush*, the veery, or Wilson's thrush, *Turdus fuscescens*, one of the four song-thrushes which are common in eastern parts of North America. **1781** LATHAM *Synopsis Birds* I. 19 *Tawny Vulture... Inhabits Falkland Islands.

Hence † ˈ**tawny** *v. trans.*, to make tawny; to tan. *Obs. rare.*

1602 BRETON *Mother's Blessing* (Grosart) 9/1 The Sunne so soone, the painted face will tawny. **1613** HEYWOOD *Brazen Age* II. ii, He smels all smoake, and with his nasty sweate Tawnies my skinne.

† ˈ**tawny-moor.** *Obs.* [f. TAWNY + MOOR *sb.*[2]: cf. BLACKAMOOR.] A name given to the tawny or brown-skinned natives of foreign lands; prob. originally to natives of northern Africa.

1603 OWEN *Pembrokeshire* v. (1892) 42 They seeme more like tawney Moores, then people of this lande. **1650** R. STAPYLTON *Strada's Low C. Warres* I. 22 Military Revells: wherein the Emperour himself ran a tilt, habited like a Tauny-moor. **1686** J. DUNTON *Lett. fr. New-Eng.* (1867) 27 Tho' he was a Tawney-more Indian, yet he was a Converted one. **1717** MRS. CENTLIVRE *Bold Stroke for Wife* I. i. (1749) 14 There's a Black, a Tawnymoor, and a Frenchman. [**1849** A tawny Moor: see MOOR *sb.*[2] 1.]

tawpie, tawpy (ˈtɔːpɪ), *sb.* and *a. Sc.* Also 9 **taupy, taupie, tawpee.** [Prob. from Norse: cf. Norw. *taap* 'half-witted person, chiefly of women' (Ross), Da. *taabe* fool, simpleton, Sw. *tåp* simpleton, *tåpig* foolish, weak-minded.]

A. *sb.* A foolish, senseless, or thoughtless girl or woman; ***idle tawpie***, a slattern.

1728 RAMSAY *Monk & Miller's Wife* 135 'Pottage', quoth Hab, 'ye senseless tawpie!' **1787** BURNS *Verses at Selkirk* iv, Gawkies, tawpies, gowks, and fools, Frae colleges and boarding-schools. **1824** MISS FERRIER *Inher.* xl, That light-headed tawpee [a servant] is off to a sick mother. **1834** *Tait's Mag.* I. 610/2 Many of his female friends were very accomplished, whom he thought useless tawpies for all that. **1902** *Ardrossan & Saltcoats Herald* 5 June 2 The word *taupie* meaning a foolish petted person.

B. *adj.* Foolish, senseless, empty-headed. (Said in reference to a girl or woman.) Now *rare.*

1814 *Saxon & Gael* I. 46 (Jam.) Comin' to his table wi' my tawpy dochter in her auld gown. **1823** GALT *Entail* xvi, The tawpy taunts of her pridefu' customers. **1826** J. WILSON *Noct. Ambr.* Wks. 1855 I. 174 Great langlegged, tawdry and tawpy limmers standin at closes. *a* **1836** AFFLECK *Poet. Wks.* 80 (E.D.D.) Taupie Meg is just as bad, A common limmer.

tawridore, obs. form of TOREADOR.

taws, tawse (tɔːz), *sb.* Chiefly *Sc.* Forms: 6 **tawis, -es,** 8 **tawz, taz,** 8– **tawse,** 9– **taws.** [app. plural of TAW *sb.*[1] 2 (but evidenced much earlier); sometimes treated as a singular.]

1. A whip for driving a spinning top; esp. one made of a thong: see quot. 1892. (In quot. 1513 prob. *pl.* as in 2.)

1513 DOUGLAS *Æneis* VII. vii. 91 As..the round top of tre [wooden top] Hit with the twynit quhyp, dois quherle, we see..smyttin wyth the tawis dois rebound, And rynnis about, about, in cirkill round. **1892** *Ballymena* (Antrim) *Observer* (E.D.D.), *Tawse*, a few strips of leather tied to a shaft, used by boys in spinning tops.

2. *spec.* An instrument of family or school discipline, used in Scottish and many English schools, consisting of a leathern strap or thong, divided at the end into narrow strips. Also *transf.* and *fig.*

In Sc. const. as plural, and in phrase ***a pair of taws***.

a **1585** POLWART *Flyting w. Montgomerie* 57 In thy teeth bring mee the tawes, With beckes my bidding to abide. *Ibid.* 571. **1719** RAMSAY *2nd Answ. to Hamilton* vi, I've kiss'd the tawz, like a good bairn. **1721** —— *Lucky Spence* ix, Vild hangy's taz ye'r riggings fast Makes black and blae. **1725** —— *Gentle Sheph.* v. iii. Prol., The tawz Was handled by revengefu' Madge. **1825** BROCKETT *N.C. Words*, *Taws*, a *pair of taws*, a leather strap used by schoolmasters for chastising children. **1825** CARLYLE *Early Lett.* (1886) II. 329 A pedagogue called Fate; he is an excellent teacher, but his fees are very high, and his tawse are rather heavy. **1834** M. Scott *Cruise Midge* (1863) 207, I took out the Tawse, and laid them on the closed Bible as a terror to evil doers. **1865** R. Chambers *Ess.* Ser. II. 79 He carried a pair of short but impressive taws. **1892** *Schoolmaster* 31 Dec. 1165/2 Nottingham School Board. The Board authorises assistants to administer corporal punishment to the extent of a light stroke with a cane or tawse. *Mod. Sc.* Behave yoursel', or you'll get the taws.

Comb. **1865** G. Macdonald *A. Forbes* 49 The smile, which, in spite of pain, had illuminated his tawse-waled cheeks. **1885** 'S. Mucklebackit' *Rural Rhymes* 142 The ancient tawse-swasher pled weariness.

Hence **tawse** *v. trans.*, to chastise with the taws.

1790 Shirrefs *Poems* Gloss., *Taz*, to whip, scourge, belabour. **1883** *Mem. A. Maclean* 240 He was tawsed for his obstinacy.

tawt, var. taut *v.*

tawte, tawth, obs. ff. *taught*: see teach *v.*

tawyer, obs. var. tawer.

tawz, obs. f. taws.

tax (tæks), *sb.*[1] Also 4–7 **taxe**, *Sc.* 5–7 **taxt** (6 **taxte**). [app. f. tax *v.* Appears earlier than F. *taxe* (1405 in Godef. *Compl.*; rare bef. 16th c.), f. *taxer* vb.; also earlier than med.L. *taxa* in Du Cange. In ME., *taxe* and *taske*, task *sb.*, were at first almost synonymous; but in their sense-development they were differentiated, *tax* following that of the corresponding verb, as an assessed *money* payment.]

1. a. A compulsory contribution to the support of government, levied on persons, property, income, commodities, transactions, etc., now at fixed rates, mostly proportional to the amount on which the contribution is levied.

'Tax' is the most inclusive term for these contributions, esp. when spoken of as the matter of *taxation*, and in such phrases as *direct* and *indirect tax* (see direct *a.* 6 e, indirect 2 c), including also similar levies for the support of the work of such local or specific bodies as county or municipal councils, poor law or school boards, etc. But in British practice few of the individual imposts are called by the name, the most notable being the income tax, land tax, and property *tax* (also *dog-tax, match-tax, window-tax*), the rest being mostly styled 'duties', as *excise, import, export, estate, house, stamp, death duties*, etc. The 'taxes' levied by local bodies are usually called 'rates', e.g. *borough, county, poor, school, water rate*, etc. In U.S. 'tax' is more generally applied in ordinary language to every federal, state, or local exaction of this kind: cf. the combs in 7.

†*to pay double taxes* (quot. 1759), i.e. to have two residences on which the assessed taxes were paid.

a **1327** *Pol. Songs* (Camden) 151 Mo then ten sithen told y my tax. *c* **1330** R. Brunne *Chron.* (1810) 247 þe lerid & þe lay granted þat þei said, & assigned a day, þat taxe to be laid. *c* **1380** Wyclif *Sel. Wks.* III. 298 Oure clergie schal paie no subsidie ne taxe. *c* **1420** *Brut* 382 þere was grawnted vnto þe King, to maynetayne his warres, bothe of spiritualte & temporalte, an hole taxe and a dyme. *c* **1430** *Syr Gener.* (Roxb.) 5537 Taxe geteth he noon of Perse lond. **1480** Caxton *Chron. England* cxlix, Kyng Iohan..let arere an huge taxe thurgh oute all englond, that is to say xxxv. M. marc. **1483** *Cath. Angl.* 378/2 A Taxe, *tallagium*. **1533** *Acc. Ld. High Treas. Scotl.* VI. 129 Lettrez to Dunde, Perth [etc.] to inbring thair taxtis for furnesing of wageouris. **1535** Coverdale *1 Kings* ix. 15 The summe of the taxe, that kynge Salomon raysed to the buyldinge of the house of the Lorde. **1552** Huloet, Taxe or subsidye graunted. **1607** Cowell *Interpr.*, *Task*, alias *Taxe*,..is such a kinde of tribute, as being certainly rated vpon euery towne, was wont to be yearely paide... Now is it not paide, but by consent giuen in Parlament, as the Subsidie is. **1651** Hobbes *Leviath.* II. xx. 106 Men ought to pay such taxes as are by Kings imposed. **1752** Hume *Ess. & Treat.* (1777) I. 344 A tax on German linen encourages home manufactures. **1759** Dilworth *Pope* 116 Pope..was able to pay double taxes, and lived like a man in a genteel independance. **1765** Blackstone *Comm.* I. viii. 308 The land tax, in it's modern shape, has superseded all the former methods of rating either property, or persons in respect of their property. **1776** Adam Smith *W.N.* v. ii. (*heading*) Part II, Of Taxes. *Ibid.* (1869) II. 461 A direct tax upon the wages of labour,..though the labourer might perhaps pay it out of his hand, could not properly be said to be even advanced by him. **1801** Hamilton *Wks.* (1886) VII. 192 There is, perhaps, no item in the catalogue of our taxes which has been more unpopular than that which is called the direct tax. **1840** McCulloch in *Encycl. Brit.* (ed. 7) XXI. 95 A tax may be either *direct* or *indirect*. It is said to be *direct* when it is immediately taken from income or capital; and *indirect* when it is taken from them by making their owners pay for liberty to use certain articles, or to exercise certain privileges. **1846** (*title*) The Local Taxes of the United Kingdom. **1878** Jevons *Prim. Pol. Econ.* xvi. §97. 129 In England the taxes amount to something like ten per cent., or one pound in every ten pounds.

†**b.** The rate at which anything is charged.

1455 *Rolls of Parlt.* V. 308/2 Eny Dismes or Subsidies.. aftir the taxe or quantite of an hole Disme.

c. *the taxes*, the tax-collector. *colloq.*

1874 W. S. Gilbert *Charity* 111, Nobody calls on him except the taxes. **1888** Stevenson *Popular Authors* 11, Even the Rates and Taxes..have actually read your tales.

2. *fig.* Something compared to a tax in its incidence, obligation, or burdensomeness; an oppressive or burdensome charge, obligation, or duty; a burden, strain, heavy demand.

a **1628** F. Grevil *Let. to Hon. Lady* iv. Wks. 1870 IV. 267 When Nature..foresaw this distresse or taxe, like to fall vpon her freedome. **1691-8** Norris *Pract. Disc.* (1711) III. 65 Sleep, that great Tax and Custom of Nature upon the life of man. **1713** Steele *Guard.* No. 85 ¶1 To suffer scandal.. is the tax which every person of merit pays to the publick. **1727** De Foe *Eng. Tradesman* xix. (ed. 2) 258 A young beginner has such a tax upon him before he begins, that he must sink perhaps..half..his stock in painting and gilding, wainscoting and glazing, before he..can open his shop. **1826** Disraeli *Viv. Grey* II. xiv, You great men must pay a tax for your dignity. I am going to disturb you. **1862** H. Spencer *First Princ.* I. i. §8 The greatness of the question.. justifies even a heavier tax on the reader's attention.

†**3.** = task *sb.* 2, 2 b. *Obs. rare.*

1390 Gower *Conf.* I. 94, 'I bidde nevere a betre taxe' Quod sche, 'bot ferst, er thou be sped, Thou schalt me leve such a wedd, That [etc.]'. **1559** *Mirr. Mag.* (1563) Oj, A certayne taxe assygnd they have To shyne, and tymes divyde. **1564** *Advertmts.* in Cardwell *Doc. Ann.* (1839) I. 294 The archedeacon shall appoynte the curates to certaine taxes of the Newe Testamente to bee conde without booke. And at theire nexte synode to exact a rehearsall of them.

†**4.** The action or an act of taxing or charging a person with some offence; a charge, accusation; censure. *Obs.*

1611 Beaum. & Fl. *Knt. Burn. Pestle* Induct., Flie far from hence All private taxes, immodest phrases, What e'r may but shew like vicious. **1621** Venner *Tobacco* in *Via Recta*, etc. (1637) 354 They shall not passe without my tax. **1634** Jackson *Creed* VII. xiv. §6 It was not a prophecy but a sharp reproof or tax. **1642** *Declar. Lords & Com.* 7 Nov. 4 After many high taxes of Us and Our Government.

†**5.** A price-list, tariff. [So F. *taxe.*] *Obs. rare*⁻¹.

1625 D. Gordon (*title*) Pharmaco-Pinax, or a Table and Taxe of all the Pryces of all usuall Medicaments.

†**6.** Phr. *to have in tax*, to have laid upon one, to have in hand. *to take in tax*, to take to task.

1635 *Voy. Foxe & James to N.W.* (Hakl. Soc.) 422 They being pertinent to the purpose I have in taxe. **1667** Pepys *Diary* 16 May, Sir Edward Savage did take the said Moyer in tax about it.

7. *attrib.* and *Comb.* **a.** General: attributive, as *tax bill, bracket, -claim, consultant, -defaulter, dodge* (also as *v. intr.*), *fiddle* (colloq.), *-law, -levy, -master, -mistress, -money, -paper, -rate, -return, -revenue, -system, year*; objective and obj. gen., as *tax-assessor, -collector, -controller, -dodger, -dodging, -extortioner, -farmer, -farming, -fiddler* (colloq.), *inspector, -layer, -levying* adj., *-receiver*; instrumental, etc., as *tax-born, -bought, -burdened, -free, -laden* adjs. **b.** Special combs.: **tax allowance**, a sum that is to be deducted from gross income in the calculation of taxable income; **tax avoidance**, the arrangement of financial affairs so as to reduce tax liability within the law; so **tax-avoider, -avoiding** *ppl. a.*; **tax bite** *U.S. colloq.*, a deduction in the form of tax; **tax-bond** (*U.S.*), a state bond receivable as taxes (*Funk's Stand. Dict.* 1895); **tax-book**, a list of property subject to taxation, with the amount of the taxes; **tax break** *colloq.* (orig. *U.S.*), a tax advantage or concession allowed by government; **tax-certificate** (*U.S.*), a certificate given to a purchaser at a tax-sale by the authorized official, entitling the holder to a tax-deed at a certain date (*Funk*); **tax code**, a code number representing the tax-free part of an employee's income, assigned by tax authorities for use by employers in calculating the amount of tax to deduct under the PAYE system; **tax credit**, a sum that can be offset against a tax liability; *spec.* one that results in a payment to any person whose liability is less than this sum; **tax-deductible** *a.*, allowable as a tax deduction; so **tax-deductibility**; **tax deduction** chiefly *U.S.*, an expense that can be deducted from gross income in calculating taxable income; **tax-deed** (*U.S.*), a conveyance made and delivered by the authorized official to a purchaser of land at a tax-sale (*Cent. Dict.* 1891); **tax disc**, a circular label displayed in the window of a motor vehicle showing the date up to which motor vehicle excise duty has been paid; **tax dollar** *U.S.*, a dollar paid as tax; **tax-duplicate** (*U.S.*), a duplicate record of all tax-assessments, furnished to a tax-collector (*Funk*); **tax-eater**, one who is supported from the public revenue; so **tax-eating** *sb.* and *a.*; **tax evasion** orig. *U.S.*, the reduction of tax payments by misstatement of income or other illegal means; so **tax-evader, -evading** *vbl. sb.*; **tax-exempt** *a.*, free from a liability to be taxed; *sb.*, a tax-exempt security; so **tax exemption**; **tax exile**, one who lives in a country chosen for its lower taxes on personal income; the state of doing this; **tax haven**, a country that attracts companies or individuals by its low taxes; **tax holiday** *colloq.*, a period of tax exemption or tax reduction, esp. one of fixed duration; **tax-lien** (*U.S.*), the lien held by the state on property subject to taxation, which has priority over all other claims (*Funk*); **tax-list** = *tax-book*; **tax-loss**, a loss that can be offset against taxable profit earned elsewhere or in a different period; also *transf.* and *attrib.*; **taxman**, a tax-collector; also, an inspector of taxes or similar official; (with *the*) the Board of Inland Revenue, personified; **tax point**, the date upon which value added tax becomes chargeable in any particular transaction; **tax relief** = relief[2] 7; **tax-roll** = *tax-book*; **tax-sale** (*U.S.*), a sale of the property of a delinquent tax-payer, made in order to defray the taxes due by him (*Cent. Dict.*); **tax shelter**, an opportunity for incurring expenses so that they can be used to reduce tax liability; so **tax-sheltered** *a.*, providing such an opportunity; **tax threshold**, the level of income at which tax begins to be payable; **tax-title** (*U.S.*), the title conveyed to the purchaser of property sold for taxes (*Funk*). See also tax-cart, tax-gatherer, tax-payer, etc.

[**1935** *Times* 16 Apr. 9/3 The cost of these various amendments in income-tax allowances will amount to £10,000,000.] **1950** *Economist* 22 Apr. 903/2 Statisticians have allowed an increase..to reflect the increase in initial *tax allowances on plant purchased from April. *a* **1974** R. Crossman *Diaries* (1976) II. 174 The Chancellor's only votes were gained from those who shared his male views and in particular objected to taking away money from middle-class families by tampering with their children's tax allowances. **1892** *Daily News* 20 Feb. 6/7 Any one who has had dealings with *tax assessors will not easily be convinced that they are men to be hoodwinked in this simple way. **1927** *Hansard Commons* 4 July 961, I think that all these devices for *tax avoidance ought to be stopped. **1951** L. H. Seltzer *Nature & Tax Treatment Capital Gains & Losses* ii. 43 Wide openings for tax avoidance through so-called reorganization provisions were soon discovered. **1972** *Accountant* 28 Sept. 401/2 This amendment was designed to counteract certain tax avoidance schemes. **1960** *Guardian* 9 July 10/2 Every word of this was fascinating to all tax-payers and *tax-avoiders. **1980** *Listener* 1 May 578/3 The *tax-avoiding English who have arrived [on the Isle of Man] since the war. **1720** in *Mass. House of Representatives Jrnl.* (1921) II. 284 A Petition..Complaning of the Proceedings of the Court..in their Nulling Three *Tax-Bills by them made..[was] Sent up. **1850** R. W. Emerson *Let.* 6 Mar. in R. B. Perry *Thought & Char. W. James* (1935) I. 68 If a good bookseller thinks that such readings in New York will pay my taxbills and bad gardening in Concord, I shall try the experiment. **1978** W. White *W. Whitman's Daybks. & Notebks.* I. p. xii, Tax bills, water bills, subscriptions to daily papers. **1954** *Sun* (Baltimore) 26 Jan. (B ed.) 1/4 The Iowa senator called for ..legislation by Congress to put a *tax bite on foreign coffee traders operating in this country. **1976** *National Observer* (U.S.) 22 May 2/4 The upshot of the committee's action is a proposal to enlarge the tax bite for some wealthy individuals and contract it for others. *c* **1630** Risdon *Surv. Devon* §76 (1810) 78 So I find it in the *tax-book of England. **1846** McCulloch *Acc. Brit. Empire* (1854) II. 211 A certificate..that this portion was entered in the public tax-books, for an amount of land-tax entitling the possessor to a vote. **1823** Byron *Juan* XI. xli, If he found not this spawn of *tax-born riches. **1831** E. Elliott *Corn-Law Rhymes, Caged Rats* i, But ye are fat,..And fill'd with *tax-bought wine. **1975** R. Stout *Family Affair* (1976) xviii. 189, I am already in an uncomfortably high *tax bracket for the year and would take no jobs anyway. **1968** *Nation* 4 Nov. 463/1 What better way to entice private enterprise than with a tax credit or some other sort of *tax break? **1969** *N.Y. Times* 4 Sept. 6/1 Companies will not get the tax breaks they formerly got on amortization of new equipment. **1982** *Economist* 18 Dec. 17/2 Governments should cease to shower capital with tax breaks that artificially lower capital's price. **1904** *Q. Rev.* July 182 Plunging his *tax-burdened people into the horrors of a sanguinary and needless war. **1899** *Daily News* 24 Nov. 4/7 Dr. Robert refused as Mayor to sign the *tax-claims. **1961** M. Kelly *Spoilt Kill* III. 163 Writing paper, annual notice of *tax code, medical card. **1976** *Star* (Sheffield) 3 Dec. 6/7 We have reached a ludicrous state of taxation when a man on state aid receives enough to exceed his tax allowance but this does not prove that the social security payments are too high, but rather, that wage rates, and especially tax codes are far too low. **1833** J. S. Mill in *Monthly Repos.* VII. 581 These taxes..throw electioneering influence into the hands of the *tax-collectors. **1862** Miss Braddon *Lady Audley* xxi, Does she still take me for a tax collector? **1976** J. R. L. Anderson *Redundancy Pay* i. 10 He had..developed a shrewd ability as a *tax consultant, particularly in the property market. **1946** H. M. Groves *Postwar Taxation & Econ. Progress* vii. 227 This could be done readily by permitting the taxpayer [with a fluctuating income] to sum his taxes over a period of years, calculate what his tax bill would have been if his income had been distributed evenly among these years, determine the difference between the two, and claim the difference as a refund or *tax credit. **1973** *Guardian* 24 Jan. 14 The Green Paper proposes first that most tax allowances ..should be replaced by tax credits... Anyone whose tax liability was less than their tax credits would be paid the difference. **1974** *Nature* 10 May 103/3 A company can obtain 'foreign tax credits' (which can be offset against United States tax) in respect of taxes paid to foreign governments. **1980** *Daily Tel.* 23 Feb. 19/2 A final of 8p a share payable on April 3, makes 14.25p net against 10.15p net or 20.36p including the related tax credit compared with 15.15p. **1972** *Accountant* 5 Oct. 422/1 Many captives are established to take advantage of this *tax deductibility of insurance reserves. **1954, 1965** *Tax-deductible [see deductible *a.*]. **1977** D. Anthony *Stud Game* vii. 45 Most of Grant's calls were on business, tax-deductible items. **1942** F. W. Marshall *Legitimate Deductions* vi. 40 In enacting provision for income *tax deductions, Congress is only interested in determining what part of a company's [or person's] gross income it believes should be treated as net income for the purpose of income taxation. **1971** 'O. Bleeck' *Thief who painted Sunlight* (1972) xiv. 122 He can contribute fifty percent of his income each year and claim it as a tax deduction. **1979** *Guardian* 5 July 3/4 The tax deduction for having a company car is a tiny fraction of its real value. **1951** AUDEN *Nones* (1952) 28 Agents of the Fisc pursue Absconding *tax-defaulters through The sewers of provincial towns. **1972** *Times* 3 Oct. 2/8 (*heading*) 'Scrap *tax discs' call. **1962** J. BRAINE *Life at Top* xxiii. 254 The usual *tax dodge... It makes me sick to the stomach. **1972** *Listener* 21 Dec. 865/1 He hasn't killed himself yet... He's waiting till 5 April... Some sort of tax dodge. **1976** *Morecambe Guardian* 7 Dec. 17/2 With that film is '*The Swiss Conspiracy*' which is all about people who tax dodge, and blackmail, are blackmailed, and murdered, not necessarily in that order. **1876** *Nation* (N.Y.) 30 Mar. 202 The *tax-dodger is one who, finding that the rate of taxation in Boston is too high for his means, flies..to some rural town. **1895** *Westm. Gaz.* 4 Sept. 2/3 What the Tax-Dodger thinks he is doing is to defraud Sir William Harcourt's successor at the Exchequer of the gains of a tyrannical impost. *Ibid.*, [Those] who practise the gentle art of *tax-dodging in this respect are in the long run defrauding their own order. **1976** *Billings* (Montana) *Gaz.* 17 June 2-E/1 The fate of a plan to use *tax dollars to improve off-street parking in downtown Bozeman will be decided July 7. **1818** COBBETT *Pol. Register* XXXIII. 350 If you were to see one of my sons now becoming a *tax-eater, as a commissioned officer in the army. **1965** MRS. L. B. JOHNSON *White House Diary* 12 Aug. (1970) 310 We hope for fewer dropouts thirteen years from now, for children able to grow up with a prospect of being responsible citizens, taxpayers, not tax-eaters. **1817** COBBETT *Wks.* XXXII. 25 Who look upon the poor as rivals in the work of *tax-eating. **1822** —— *Rur. Rides* (1885) I. 151 Some one of the tax-eating crew had.. called me an 'incendiary'. **1936** *Sun* (Baltimore) 30 Jan. 1/1 The time has come for a direct attack on the attempt at Washington to substitute a tax-eating bureaucracy for a liberal democratic system. **1927** *Hansard Commons* 4 July 955 What is to be done with the *tax evader meanwhile? **1960** Tax-evader [see SNOBOCRACY]. **1971** 'G. BLACK' *Time for Pirates* iv. 78 If this deal went all right..the Hydes could be on their *tax-evading boat in a couple of years. **1922** *Hansard Commons* 27 June 1920 That type of company must be perfectly well identifiable when it is seen. You notice the stigmata of *tax evasion about it when you see it, not in the mere registration, but in the conduct and carrying on of its business. **1977** WARREN & PONSE in Douglas & Johnson *Existential Sociol.* x. 277 It is stigmatized..in the courts of law..and (unlike tax evasion) it is stigmatized morally in the courts of public opinion. **1925** *Contemp. Rev.* June 703 He has a deep resentment against their taking refuge in *tax-exempt securities. **1933** *Business Week* 22 Feb. 4/1 Elimination of tax exempts is the object of an amendment to the Constitution offered by Senator Hull of Tennessee. **1966** *Economist* 30 Mar. 78/3 These industrial bonds..have so dogged the market as to increase all borrowing costs for tax-exempts. **1977** *New Yorker* 19 Sept. 27/2 One way to do this is to float a municipal-bond issue, which traditionally pays tax-exempt interest. **1978** G. VIDAL *Kalki* v. 117 Any bona fide religion is tax-exempt in the United States. **1927** BOWLEY & STAMP *Nat. Income 1924* v. 42 Incomes above the *tax-exemption limit. **1975** *N.Y. Times* 28 Nov. 37/4 One example of the use of incentives to attract investment is the tax-exemption on municipal bond income. **1969** *Manch. Guardian Weekly* 22 Nov. 11 Has Anthony Grey..joined the ranks of the *tax exiles? **1978** J. R. L. ANDERSON *Death in Greenhouse* ii. 27 Neither of us was attracted by the prospect of living in tax-exile. **1903** D. M'LEAN *Stud. Apost.* x. 141 Palestine..fell under this *tax-farming system. **1959** 'M. INNES' *Hare sitting Up* I. i. 27 *Tax fiddle of some kind? I don't like that sort. **1961** *Times* 31 May 10/4 Inclined to see in every taxpayer a more or less skilful..*tax-fiddler. **1704** ADDISON *Italy* (1733) 126 The Fowl and Gibbier are *tax free. **1917** W. S. CHURCHILL 9 Sept. in M. Gilbert *Winston S. Churchill* (1977) IV. Compan. I. 156, I do not however exclude the possibilities of a special bonus, presumably tax free. **1960** *Business Week* 24 Dec. 32/2 Interest in *tax havens is largely due to the fact that U.S. tax law permits a company to accumulate profits abroad tax-free. **1964** A. WYKES *Gambling* x. 241 Tax-free prizes. **1973** *Times* 18 May 29/6 The Briton wanting to minimize his taxes through getting paid in a tax haven. **1950** *Times* 24 Apr. 5/7 The stimulation of enterprise is essentially best organized on a regional footing. At present it is undertaken with varying determination by different colonies. Some grant free import of capital equipment and '*tax holidays' for pioneer industries. **1977** *Time* 10 Oct. 60/1 Haughey's notion of a permanent tax holiday for artists has at least stopped the drain of home-grown talent. **1978** *Jrnl. R. Soc. Arts* CXXVI. 224/2 There was firstly a three-year tax holiday followed by a period allowing accelerated depreciation and gradually increasing rates of tax. **1959** J. WOOD *Simple Guide for Taxpayer* iii. 28 Once the form has been completed it must be sent back to the *Tax Inspector who sent it out. **1842** MIALL in *Nonconf.* II. 201 The *tax layers and the tax payers. **1892** GRIFFITH tr. *Fouard's St. Peter* 45 To exempt them from the *tax levies every seventh year. **1902** *Westm. Gaz.* 5 June 4/2 Representation in the law-making and *tax-levying assembly. **1898** ANTROBUS tr. *Pastor's Hist. Popes* VI. 91 The *tax-list..has been preserved, and is interesting. **1959** *Times* 24 Dec. 7/4 (*heading*) *Tax-loss farming. *Ibid.*, Sir,—The so-called tax-loss farmer is generally speaking a man who carries on two businesses, one profitable and the other unprofitable. As a matter of taxation machinery he pays tax in respect of his profitable business and afterwards claims a refund of tax in respect of his unprofitable farming business. **1965** I. FLEMING *Man with Golden Gun* vii. 100 Others would want to buy in..cheaply, and use it [*sc.* a hotel] as a tax-loss to set against more profitable enterprises elsewhere. **1970** *Money Which?* Mar. 64/3 Don't wait until the very end of the tax-year before selling shares for tax-loss purposes. **1975** *Times* 14 Jan. 12/6 (Advt.), *Wanted.* Large run-down school... High tax losses an inducement to purchase. **1803** G. COLMAN *John Bull* I. i. 3 She had disgraced her family by marrying herself to a *tax-man. **1830** MRS. BRAY *Talba* x. 83 The griping taxman, and the conquered and taxed Moor. **1891** R. DOWLING *Isle Surrey* 21 The taxman and the gasman and the waterman. **1968** *Guardian* 22 June 5/5, I don't know what the taxman would say if you tried to get that as an expense allowance. **1970** *Money Which?* Mar. 43/2 You are allowed free of tax.. family allowances, most pensions and some other social security benefits. The taxman views all these as earned income. **1796** MORSE *Amer. Geog.* II. 549 Plundered by collectors and *tax-masters. **1738** *Gentl. Mag.* VIII. 193/1 [Fashion] keeps them perpetually busy in doing and undoing; and Folly is her Prime Confident and *Taxmistress. **1610** *Histrio-m.* VI. 205 Soft, sirs, I must talk with you for *tax-money, To relieve the poor. **1658** J. HARRINGTON *Oceana* 77 The Parishes having Levied the Tax money,..shall return it unto the Officers of the Hundreds. **1858** E. B. RAMSAY *Remin.* v. (1870) 102 The provost sends me a *tax paper. **1972** *Accountant* 21 Sept. 369/2 It might be of interest..to mention the special rule for the *tax point of barristers' services. **1876** BANCROFT *Hist. U.S.* VI. xxxix. 207 In proportion to the general *tax-rates. **1886** W. J. TUCKER *E. Europe* 57 As long as..he is able to keep pace with his tax-rates, which..are daily becoming more exorbitant. **1830** COBBETT *Rur. Rides* (1885) II. 343 Your petitioners are the bees, and..the *tax-receivers are the drones. **1916** *Tax relief [see INCOME-TAX.] **1931**, etc. [see RELIEF[2] 7]. **1980** *Times* 9 Aug. 16/4, I have been offered remortgage, but my accountant says it will not qualify for tax relief. **1870** 'MARK TWAIN' *Sketches New & Old* (1875) 319 A wicked *tax-return..calculated to make a man report about four times his actual income to keep from swearing to a falsehood. **1888** BRYCE *Amer. Commw.* II. xliii. (1889) I. 498 Apt to turn their property into these exempted forms just before they make their tax returns. **1891** GRIFFITH tr. *Fouard's Christ* I. 225 Engaged in farming out the *tax-revenue of the provinces. **1545** *Reg. Privy Council Scot.* I. 21 To bring in with him the *taxt roll. **1841** SPALDING *Italy & It. Isl.* I. 399 In Campania..Honorius was compelled in the year 395 to expunge from the tax-roll, as become utterly waste, more than three hundred thousand acres of land. **1961** *Guardian* 20 Feb. 16/7 If all the *tax shelters were eliminated..the income tax yield would be increased by a third. **1982** *Financial Times* 13 Mar. 14/3 Investors will be seeking to use up the effective tax shelter offered by an appreciation of their assets each year in line with inflation. **1959** *Wall Street Jrnl.* 17 Sept. (Eastern ed.) 21 (Advt.), *Tax-sheltered investment. **1976** *National Observer* (U.S.) 17 Jan. 9/6 And how to defer income tax on the interest you get. Plans that offer marvelous tax-sheltered advantages. **1976** F. ZWEIG *New Acquisitive Society* II. iv. 108 The *tax thresholds in real terms have been substantially lowered over the years. **1970** *Tax year [see *tax-loss* above]. **1971** *Money Which?* Mar. 4/1 These taxes are charged for a particular year of assessment, which always starts on 6 April and ends on 5 April in the following year. This is commonly called a tax year.

†**tax**, *sb.*[2] *Obs.* Also in 6 taxe. [ad. L. *tax-us* yew.] The yew-tree (also *tax-tree*); *transf.* a bow made of the wood of the yew.

1541 *Act 33 Hen. VIII*, c. 9 §6 No bowyer shall sell..any bowe of ewe of the taxe called elke, aboue the price of iii. s. iiii. d. **1618** BOLTON *Florus* IV. xii. (1636) 331 Poyson..is commonly there scruzed out of tax-trees. **1651** G. HILL *On Cartwright's Incomparable Poems* in *C.'s Poems*, Their unbridled Muse [can] securely run Undaunted through the rage of Tax or Gun.

tax (tæks), *v.* Also 4-7 **taxe**. [app. a. OF. *taxe-r* (13th c. in Littré), ad. L. *taxāre* to censure, charge, tax with a fault; to rate, value, reckon, compute (at so much), make a valuation of; in med.L. also to impose a tax. The inherited form was OF. *tausser*, *taucer* (later, by assimilation, *tauxer*), It. *tassare*, Sp. *tasar*, Pg. *taxar*. Senses 1, 3, 6 are all in French.]

I. 1. To estimate or determine the amount of (a tallage, fine, penalty, damages, etc.); to assess; rarely, to impose, levy (a tax); also, to settle the price or value of. *Obs.* exc. in *Law*, to assess (costs). Const. †*to* (the amount).

[**680** K. CÆDUALLA *Grant* in Earle *Land-Charters* 281 Hanc libertatem sub estimatione LXX tributariorum taxauimus.] *c* **1290** *Beket* 397 in *S. Eng. Leg.* I. 118 A taillage þov taxt fram ȝer to ȝer þoruȝ-out al þi londe. [**1314-15** *Rolls of Parlt.* I. 290/2 La partie serra atteynt du trespas..& les damages taxes a la volunte son adversair.] **13..** *Cursor M.* 27321 (Cott.) [To] knau þe circumstances o þe plight, for to tax þe penance right. **1387** TREVISA *Higden* (Rolls) VIII. 271 Þe chirches of Engelond were i-taxed to þe verray value [orig. *secundum valorem taxatæ sunt*]. **1424** *Paston Lett.* I. 13 The damages..were taxed to cxx li. **1530-1** *Act 22 Hen. VIII*, c. 15 Fines and amerciamentes affiered, taxed, sette, extreted, or judged. **1551** in W. H. Turner *Select. Rec. Oxford* (1880) 207 Taxable..to suche taxe and tallenge as shall be uppon hym taxed and sessyd. **1552** HULOET, Taxe damages in sute, *æstimare litem*. **1592** *Acts Court Requests* 97 The costs to be taxed to the vttermost charge approved due. **1768** BLACKSTONE *Comm.* III. xxiv. 400 These costs on both sides are taxed and moderated by the..proper officer of the court. **1885** *Daily Tel.* 24 Dec. (Cassell), A returning officer, whose bill of costs has been taxed on the application of the candidates.

†**2.** To impose, ordain, prescribe (a thing) *to* a person; also, to order (a person) *to* or *to do* something. *Obs.*

c **1350** *Will. Palerne* 5124 Loke..þat neuer þe pore porayle be piled for þi sake, ne taxed to taliage. **1390** GOWER *Conf.* I. 147 To the knyht this lawe he taxeth, That he schal gon and come ayein [etc.]. *Ibid.* 287 Such a Statut thanne he sette, And in this wise his lawe taxeth. *c* **1450** *Songs, Carols*, etc. (E.E.T.S.) 79/249 [Fortune] as her-self liste ordre & devise, Doth euery man his parte devide & taxe. *c* **1500** *Melusine* 210 We taxe you to pay to this noble pucelle all such dommages that she hath had at your cause. **1814** SCOTT *Diary* 6 Aug. in *Lockhart*, The islanders retort, that a man can do no more than he can; that they are not used to be taxed to their work so severely.

†**b.** To settle, fix, determine the extent of. *Obs.*

1390 GOWER *Conf.* III. 223 Whan Salomon his bone hath taxed, The god of that which he hath axed Was riht wel paid.

3. To impose a tax upon; to subject to taxation. Also *fig.*

c **1330** R. BRUNNE *Chron.* (1810) 247 Þe dettes þat men þam auht, þer stedes & þer wonyng, Wer taxed & bitauht to þe eschete of þe kyng. *c* **1380** WYCLIF *Sel. Wks.* III. 342 For oon mai seie þat..he [the Pope] haþ power singuler to taxe gracis, as him likiþ. **1453** *Rolls of Parlt.* V. 233/1 Rightfully charged or taxed to the Dismes. **1560** DAUS tr. *Sleidane's Comm.* 360 It shalbe lawfull for euery Magistrate to taxe ye people for ye same cause. **1598** HAKLUYT *Voy.* I. 486 The people of the countrie..being taxed and pilled so often as he thinketh good. **1627** SIR E. COKE in Rushw. *Hist. Coll.* (1659) I. 501 The King cannot tax any by way of Loans. **1657** in Picton *L'pool Munic. Rec.* (1883) I. 214 The same Ley..being unduly taxed. **1776** ADAM SMITH *W.N.* v. ii. (1869) II. 420 In the Venetian territory all the arable lands which are given in lease to farmers are taxed at a tenth of the rent. **1857** BUCKLE *Civiliz.* I. vii. 351 It was in the same reign that there was settled the right of the people to be taxed entirely by their representatives.

b. *to tax into* or *out of* some state.

1891 SCRIVENER *Fields & Cities* 70 Proposals have been made..to tax the landlords out of existence.

4. *fig.* To burden; to make serious demands upon; to put a strain on.

1672 MARVELL *Rehearsal Transp.* I. 51 Some Critical People, who will..tax up an old-wife's fable to the punctuality of History. **1697** DRYDEN *Æneid* Ded., Ess. (ed. Ker) II. 232 What had become of me, if Virgil had taxed me with another book. **1772** MACKENZIE *Man World* II. v, I have no right to tax you with my sorrows. **1832** LYTTON *Eugene A.* I. x, We will not tax the patience of the reader. **1853** KANE *Grinnell Exp.* xxxvi, My ingenuity was often taxed for expedients. **1876** GEO. ELIOT *Dan. Der.* III. xxvi, Most men are afraid of being bored or taxed by a wife's family.

5. *U.S.* (esp. *New Engl.*) *colloq.* To price (a thing *at* so much); to charge (a person so much *for* a thing).

1846-7 MRS. WHITCHER *Widow Bedott Papers* 218 (Bartl.) In trading with the clergy [he] only taxed his goods at half price. **1860** BARTLETT *Dict. Amer.* s.v., 'What will you tax me a yard for this cloth?' **1888** FARMER *Americanisms* s.v., An everyday colloquialism is 'What will you tax me?'

II. 6. To censure; to reprove, blame (a person, his action, etc.); to accuse, charge; to take to task, call to account.

1569 LD. CECIL *Let.* in Strype *Ann. Ref.* (1709) I. liii. 532 To think of us as our evil willers are disposed..to tax us. **1589** PUTTENHAM *Eng. Poesie* I. xi. (Arb.) 41 Another kind of Poet, who intended to taxe the common abuses and vice of the people in rough and bitter speaches. *a* **1619** FLETCHER, etc. *Knt. Malta* I. iii, If any therefore can their manners tax ..Let 'em speak now. **1692** DRYDEN *Cleomenes* II. ii, I have been to blame; And you have justly taxed my long neglect. **1709** POPE *Ess. Crit.* 589 Fear most to tax an Honourable Fool Whose right it is, uncensur'd to be dull. **1768** H. WALPOLE *Hist. Doubts* 12 *note*, That Chronicle..which seems to tax the envy and rapaciousness of Clarence as the Causes of the dissention. *a* **1806** BP. HORSLEY *Serm.* (1816) II. xvi. 39 Eve..taxes the serpent as her seducer. **1873** TRISTRAM *Moab* v. 96, I was next taxed, and replied that [etc.].

b. Const. †*for*, *of* (now rare), *with* (now usual); †also inf. and obj. clause (*obs.*).

1548 PATTEN *Exped. Scotl.* E viij, Apertly to tax their goouernour w[t] y[e] note of dissimulacion. **1603** KNOLLES *Hist. Turks* (1621) 1375 All the world would taxe him to have violated the law of nations. **1615** BRATHWAIT *Strappado* (1878) 82 Thy lippes..so modest as nere taxt of sinne. **1624** CAPT. SMITH *Virginia* IV. 159, I know I shall bee taxed for writing so much of my selfe. **1651** *Life Father Sarpi* (1676) 11 Taxing him to be an Usurper and an unjust Tyrant. **1665** DRYDEN *Ind. Emperor* III. ii, None shall tax me with base Perjury. **1697** DRYDEN *Virg. Past.* Pref. (1721) I. 86 A celebrated French Writer taxes him for permitting Æneas to do nothing without the assistance of some God. **1703** *Rules Civility* 262 A Magistrate..has been taxed, that instead of Administring Justice fairly, he sells it to the highest Bidder. **1726** POPE *Odyss.* xx. 437 Tax not..Of rage, or folly, my prophetic mind. **1777** [see sense 7]. **1833** HT. MARTINEAU *Berkeley* I. iii, I do not mean to tax Rhoda with falsehood. **1871** R. ELLIS *Catullus* lxiv. 322 Chants which an after-time shall tax of vanity never.

†**c.** *absol.* To censure, find fault. *Obs.*

1589 PUTTENHAM *Eng. Poesie* I. xv. (Arb.) 48 In those days when the Poets first taxed by Satyre and Comedy, there was [etc.]. **1621** BURTON *Anat. Mel.* Democr. to Rdr. 4, I did sometime laugh and scoffe with Lucian, and Satyrically taxe with Menippus.

†**7.** To call in question; to challenge, dispute (a statement, etc.). *Obs.*

1614 SIR R. DUDLEY in *Fortesc. Papers* (Camden) 8 In all wherin my honour nor honestye may not be taxed. **1642** ROGERS *Naaman* 24 Prone to taxe Gods wisedom, and call him to our barre. **1777** PRIESTLEY *Matt. & Spir.* (1782) I. xvi. 191 If..any person will tax my opinion..I shall tax him with great stupidity.

III. †**8.** Used to render Gr. ἀπογράφειν, to enter in a list, to register, enroll, enter in a list or statement of property. *Obs. rare.*

1526 TINDALE *Luke* ii. 3 And every man went in to his awne shyre toune there to be taxed. *Ibid.* 5 And Joseph also ascended from Galile..in to a cite of David, which is called bethleem..to be taxed. **1534** (ed. 2) *Ibid.* ii. 1 Ther went oute a commaundment from Auguste the Emperour, that all the woorlde shulde be taxed [**1526** shulde be valued; *Vulg.* describeretur; WYCLIF schuld be discryued; *Geneva*, **1611** taxed; *Rheims*, **1881** (R.V.) enrolled].

taxable ('tæksəb(ə)l), *a.* (*sb.*) [a. AF. *taxable* (13th c. in Godef.), f. TAXER to tax + -ABLE.]

†**1.** Liable to be assessed (*to* a tax, impost, or charge); assessable. *Obs.*

1474 *Rolls of Parlt.* VI. 115/2 Which to the Dismes with the Possessions of the Clergie be not taxed nor taxable. **1551** in W. H. Turner *Select. Rec. Oxford* (O.H.S.) 207 The same to be taxable..to suche taxe and tallenge as shall be uppon hym taxed and sessyd. **1569** ABP. PARKER *Let. to Sir W. Cecil* 18 May, Benefices of xxx *li.* and upward taxable to the provision of armour.

2. Liable to be taxed; subject to a tax or duty.

In quot. 1685, liable to the *taille* in France, from which nobles were exempt.

1583 GOLDING *Calvin on Deut.* xcv. 587 Whereas there are some persons which are still taxable (as they terme it).. whether it be in their goods or in their persons. **1647** *Virginia Stat.* (1823) I. 341 A just and exact list of all taxable goods, land and tithable persons. **1683** *Apol. Prot. France* iii. 2 They ruine all the Protestants that are Taxable in France. **1685** COTTON tr. *Montaigne* (1711) I. xv. 68 Both himself and his Posterity [were] declared ignoble, taxable, and for ever incapable of bearing arms. **1762** tr. *Busching's Syst. Geog.* VI. 319 This structure is reckoned a taxable house. **1817-18** COBBETT *Resid. U.S.* (1822) 84 To learn..the taxable capacities of their farms. **1870** *Sat. Rev.* 2 Apr. 432 The consumers of taxable commodities had no reason to complain of Mr. Lowe's Budget. **1908** *Daily Chron.* 11 Jan. 4/3 He forgot that if taxation has increased, so also has what the politicians call 'taxable capacity'.

†**3.** Liable to a charge or accusation; chargeable (*with* some fault); censurable, blamable, reprehensible. *Obs.*

1610 HEALEY *St. Augustine's Citie of God*, To affect soueraignty..is taxable of indecency. **1617** HIERON *Wks.* II. 402 Men..worthily taxeable with this doctrine. **1654** H. L'ESTRANGE *Chas. I.* (1655) 266 Not taxable with any vice. **1690** NORRIS *Beatitudes* (1692) 10 Taxable for a too earthly and downward disposition of soul. **1792** W. ROBERTS *Looker-on* No. 2 (1794) I. 20 The old Bachelar was thought too taxable a shape to appear in.

4. *Law.* Of legal costs or fees: Liable to be taxed or reduced by the taxing-master.

1828-32 WEBSTER, *Taxable*..2. That may be legally charged by a court against the plaintif or defendant in a suit; as, taxable costs. **1885** *Law Times* 14 Feb. 286/2 The fees of a manor steward as such, though a solicitor, are not taxable.

B. *sb.* One who or that which is subject to taxation; *esp.* in *pl.* persons or things liable to a tax. Orig. *U.S.*

1662 in *Mag. Amer. Hist.* Jan. (1884) 39 (Act of Assembly, Maryland) That every householder and freeman..should take up ten shillings per poll..for every taxable under their charge and custody. **1701** *Maryland Laws* v. (1723) 17 To levy such Tax by the Poll on the Taxables of such Parishes. **1825** JEFFERSON *Autobiog.* Wks. 1859 I. 32 He..was for their voting..according to the number of taxables. **1861** J. G. SHEPPARD *Fall Rome* x. 565 Thus, the population was divided in the language into horsemen and taxables.

Hence **taxa'bility, 'taxableness**, the quality or condition of being taxable; liability to taxation; **'taxably** *adv.*, in a taxable manner; in quot. 1906, in relation to taxability.

1804 W. TAYLOR in *Ann. Rev.* II. 351 When one considers the easy taxability of the rent derived from all this shipping, and of that yielded by our lands, houses, [and] machines. **1847** WEBSTER, Taxableness, Taxably. **1865** MERIVALE *Rom. Emp.* VIII. lxvii. 289 The citizenship with its attendant taxability was bestowed on many. **1906** *Contemp. Rev.* Jan. 94 Its Lowland-Scots virtues of thrift and adhesiveness, which made the province taxably so capable.

taxaceous (tæk'seɪʃəs), *a. Bot.* [f. mod.L. *Taxace-æ* (f. *taxus* yew) + -OUS: see -ACEOUS.] Belonging to the N.O. *Taxaceæ* (often made a suborder of *Coniferæ*), including the yew. So **'taxad** ('tæksəd) [cf. ARAD], Lindley's name for a tree or shrub belonging to the *Taxaceæ*.

1846 LINDLEY *Veg. Kingd.* 230 Mr. Bennett..is of opinion that Taxads should not form a distinct Natural Order, but ought to be associated with Conifers. **1904** *Jrnl. R. Microsc. Soc.* Feb. 78 *Taxoxylon Philpii*..represents the first taxaceous fossil wood from Queensland.

†**'taxage.** *Obs. rare.* [f. TAX *v.* + -AGE: cf. med.L. *taxāgium* (1216 in Du Cange).] Taxation.

1483 *Cath. Angl.* 378/2 A Taxage, *taxacio.*

taxameter, -metric: see TAXIMETER, -RIC.

taxaspidean (tæksæ'spɪdiːən), *a. Ornith.* [f. mod.L. *Taxaspidea*, neut. pl. (f. Gr. τάξις arrangement + ἀσπίς shield) + -AN.] Belonging to the division *Taxaspidea* of passerine birds, having the metatarsus regularly scutellated behind.

1899 A. H. EVANS in *Cambr. Nat. Hist.* IX. 488 The taxaspidean metatarsus is moderate or short in the Thamnophilinæ, and remarkably long in the Grallariinæ.

taxation (tæk'seɪʃən). Forms: 4 **taxacioun**, 5-7 **-acion**, 6 **-atioun** (*Sc.* **taxtatioun**, 7 **taxtion, taction**), 6- **taxation**. [a. AF. *taxacioun* = OF. *taxation* (13th c. in Godef. *Compl.*), ad. L. *taxātiōn-em*, n. of action f. *taxāre* to TAX.]

1. The fixing of the sum of an impost, damages, price, etc.; assessment, valuation. *Obs.* exc. *Hist.*

[**1297** *Rolls of Parlt.* I. 239/2 E la taxacioun des Biens de ceaus des villes seit fete par autres loiaux gentz.] *c* **1325** *Poem Times Edw. II* 301 in *Pol. Songs* (Camden) 337 If the king in his lond maketh a taxacioun. **1387** TREVISA *Higden* (Rolls) VIII. 271 þe chirches of Engelond were i-taxed to the verray value, and seþþe voyded þe taxacioun of Norþwiche [L. *taxatio Norwycensis*] þat was made by þe fourþe Innocencius. **1543-4** *Act 35 Hen. VIII*, c. 10 Suche somes as..shal be taxed..for satisfaccion of any suche breakyng and defacyng..shal be paide..wᵗⁿ ten dayes next after the saide Taxacion. **1592** WEST *1st Pt. Symbol.* §24 Buying and selling is perfected, by the certein appointing of the thing to be sold, and the taxation of the price thereof, with the mutuall consent of the buyer and seller. **1601** SHAKS. *Twel. N.* I. v. 225, I bring no ouerture of warre, no taxation of homage; I hold the Olyffe in my hand. **1622** BACON *Hen. VII* 67 When the Commissioners entred into the Taxation of the subsidie in Yorkeshire,..the people vpon a sudaine grew into great mutinie. **1859** EYTON *Antiq. Shropshire* IX. 28 The Taxation of 1291 values the Church..at £10 per annum. **1895** RASHDALL *Univ. of Middle Ages* II. 399 The taxation of Halls by a joint board of burgesses and Masters is a custom which was established from the earliest times in all medieval Studia.

b. ***taxation of costs***, the allowing or disallowing, by certain officials of courts of law, of the charges made by solicitors or other persons (e.g. arbitrators) subject to the jurisdiction of the court.

1552 HULOET, Taxacion, or assessment of a taxe or subsidye, or of costes in iudgement, *taxacio.* **1760** FOOTE *Minor* I. Wks. 1799 I. 235 He is generous, and will discharge your bill without taxation. **1883** *Wharton's Law Lex.* s.v., As between party and party a taxation of costs is always had.

2. The imposition or levying of taxes (formerly including local rates); the action of taxing or the fact of being taxed; also *transf.* the revenue raised by taxes. With *a* and *pl.*, an instance of this.

1447-8 *Shillingford Lett.* (Camden) 79 Al other taxacions taliages and charges..to the Kyng owre soverayne lord graunted. *a* **1578** LINDESAY (Pitscottie) *Chron. Scot.* (S.T.S.) II. 260 Thair was gret taxtatiounis layd on thame befoir. **1593** SHAKS. *Rich. II*, II. i. 260 He hath not monie for these Irish warres: (His burthenous taxations notwithstanding). **1647** in Picton *L'pool Munic. Rec.* (1883) I. 143 Agreed that a Ley or Taxacion of xiiˡ be imposed upon the Towne. **1776** ADAM SMITH *W.N.* v. ii. (1869) II. 442 There are..two circumstances which render the interest of money a much less proper subject of direct taxation than the rent of land. **1781** GIBBON *Decl. & F.* xvii. II. 61 The policy of Constantine and his successors preferred a simple and direct mode of taxation, more congenial to the spirit of an arbitrary government. **1827** WHATELY *Logic* (1837) 318 Taxation—the revenue levied from the subject in return for the protection afforded by the Sovereign. **1838** THIRLWALL *Greece* V. xlii. 205 A new valuation of all private property had been made with a view to a more equable system of taxation. **1863** FAWCETT *Pol. Econ.* IV. i. (1876) 518 Taxation implies that the right to levy a tax is given by law.

attrib. **1886** CHAMBERLAIN in *Pall Mall G.* 22 Apr. 11/1 It is to deal with three-fourths of the taxation revenue of Ireland. **1905** *Daily Chron.* 26 Apr. 5/2 The railways..are not merely a transport agency, but are utilised as a machine for taxation purposes.

†**3.** A charging with a fault or offence; accusation; censure, reproof, blame. *Obs.*

1591 SYLVESTER *Du Bartas* I. iii. 6 Sharpe taxation Of Bribes, Ambition, Treason, Avarice. **1600** SHAKS. *A.Y.L.* I. ii. 91 You'l be whipt for taxation one of these daies. **1631** BP. WEBBE *Quietn.* (1657) 147 Some..there are who deserve this sharp taxation. *a* **1653** GOUGE *Comm. Heb.* (1655) 474 The Apostles taxation of the Hebrews non-proficiency.

†**4.** Enrolment, registration, census. Cf. TAX *v.* 8. *Obs. rare*⁻¹.

1686 PLOT *Staffordsh.* 324 The last taxation, numbering, or review of the Provinces, taken under the Cæsars Vespasians Father and Son, both Emperors and Censors.

Hence **ta'xational** *a.*, of or pertaining to taxation.

1879 R. H. ELLIOT *Written on Foreheads* I. 205 You will have no taxational draft on your captial till you have coffee to meet it.

taxative ('tæksətɪv), *a. rare.* [ad. med. or mod.L. *taxātīvus* (Alciatus *c* 1530), f. ppl. stem of *taxāre* to TAX: see -ATIVE. (Cf. F. *taxativement*, Littré *Suppl.*)]

†**1.** Of limiting or defining nature. *rare.*

1676 FOUNTAINHALL in M. P. Brown *Suppl. Decis.* (1826) III. 67 Where it allows them to work in such and such work, which fell not naturally and properly under the subject-matter of their own occupation, the same is so far from being taxative, that it is demonstrative and in their favours. **1726** [implied in TAXATIVELY].

2. Having the function of taxing; of or pertaining to taxation.

1862 R. H. PATTERSON *Ess. Hist. & Art* 174 A taxative system which..had been in operation for two thousand years. **1870** STUBBS *Sel. Charters* Introd. 50 This completed the taxative powers of parliament. **1902** *Cambr. Mod. Hist.* I. 301 Upholding the representative legislative and taxative body by frequent sessions of Parliament.

Hence **'taxatively** *adv.*, in a taxative manner.

1726 AYLIFFE *Parergon* 339 If these Ornaments or Furniture had been put Taxatively and by Way of Limitation, such a Thing bequeath'd as a Legacy shall not be paid, if it wants Ornaments or Furniture.

taxator (tæk'seɪtə(r)). Also 5-6 **-our**. [ad. med.L. *taxātor*, agent-n. from *taxāre* to TAX. So F. *taxateur* (16th c. in Hatz.-Darm.).]

1. One who assesses a subsidy, impost, or tax; an assessor; one who levies a tax. Now *Hist.*

1424 *Sc. Acts Jas. I* (1814) II. 5 þat ilk bischop in ilk denry of his diocise gar his officiall and his dene summonde all þe tenandis and frehaldaris befor him, and cheiss taxatouris. **1585-6** *Reg. Privy Council Scot.* IV. 47 Allegeing that the saidis taxatouris hes stentit thame..abone thair habilitie. **1848** *Fraser's Mag.* XXXVII. 129 The loan is under the *surveillance* of the Woods and Forests, and pinched by the long-clawed taxators.

2. In the mediæval universities: = TAXER 1 b. (In contemporary use as a Latin word.)

1831 SIR W. HAMILTON *Discuss.* (1852) 412 In the same year [1231] Taxators are established in both Universities. **1897** A. GORDON in *Dict. Nat. Biog.* LII. 182/2 In 1608 he [R. Sibbes] was appointed taxator [Camb.].

†**tax-cart.** *Obs.* = *taxed cart*: see next, 2 a.

1796 J. WOODFORDE *Diary* 31 Oct. (1929) IV. 316 They came in Mrs. Bodhams little Tax-Cart. **1806-7** J. BERESFORD *Miseries Hum. Life* xx. *Poet. Epist.* 29 While each tax-cart and shay To the Fair jolts away. **1837** HOWITT *Rur. Life* VI. x. (1862) 503 Away they go, in gigs and tax-carts, or on scampering horses. **1858** SIMMONDS *Dict. Trade, Tax-cart*, a spring-cart paying a low rate of duty. **1884** DOWELL *Taxation* III. III. iii. 231 Vehicles not over the value of 21 l., formerly termed 'taxed carts', and since their exemption from tax, usually called, in the provinces, tax carts.

taxed (tækst), *ppl. a.* [f. TAX *v.* + -ED¹.]

1. †**a.** Assessed, determined by authority. *Obs.* **b.** Subjected to a tax. Of a motor vehicle: having had excise duty paid for the current period.

1483 *Cath. Angl.* 378/2 Taxed, *taxatus.* **1552** HULOET, Taxed, *census. Ibid.*, Taxed by the pole,..*capite census.* **1689** BURNET *Tracts* I. 5 To buy of it at a taxed price. **1773** Taxed duty [see 2 c]. **1776** ADAM SMITH *W.N.* v. ii. (1828) III. 446 The rise in the price of the taxed commodities. **1842** W. C. TAYLOR *Anc. Hist.* xvii. §8 (ed. 3) 544 His payment of the tax, by buying the taxed article, seems to be voluntary. **1933** *Motor* 2 May (Suppl.) 99/3 (Advt.), Riley... 4-door coachbuilt sunshine saloon.., maroon, taxed. **1976** *Jrnl.* (Newcastle) 26 Nov., (Advt.), Volvo 144 Saloon 1974 N regn, orange, red striped upholstery, taxed Oct. '77.

2. In special collocations. **a. taxed cart**, a two-wheeled (orig. springless) open cart drawn by one horse, and used mainly for agricultural or trade purposes, on which was charged only a reduced duty (afterwards taken off entirely).

1795 *Act 35 Geo. III*, c. 109 §2 For and upon every Carriage with less than four Wheels,..which shall have the Words 'A taxed Cart', and also the Owner's Name and Place of Abode, there shall be charged and paid the yearly Sum of ten Shillings. **1801** W. FELTON *Carriages* Suppl. vi. 115 Taxed Carts. **1837** GEN. P. THOMPSON *Exerc.* (1842) IV. 279 The remission of taxation upon what by an odd perversion is called a taxed cart. **1859** GEO. ELIOT *A. Bede* xxxviii, The inn-keeper..offered to take him back to Oakbourne in his own 'taxed cart'.

b. taxed costs: see quot.

1858 SIMMONDS *Dict. Trade, Taxed-costs*, the allowed charges of a solicitor, which have been legally examined and assessed before a taxing-master.

c. taxed ward, formerly, in Scottish land tenure, a wardship in which a fixed annual sum was paid to the superior in lieu of the whole profits.

1603 *Reg. Privy Council Scot.* Ser. I. VI. 545 To grant the warde landis in taxt warde. **1710** FOUNTAINHALL in M. P. Brown *Suppl. Decis.* (1826) IV. 788 Part of the lands holding black or simple-ward, and part taxed-ward. **1773** ERSKINE *Instit.* II. v. §5 If the ward was taxed, the minor retained the possession, and the superior had nothing to demand but the yearly taxed duty.

‖**taxe de séjour** (taks də seʒur). [Fr., lit. 'tax of visit'.] A tax imposed on visitors to spas or tourist resorts in France and other countries.

1922 *Michelin Guide Gt. Brit.* 764 France... 'Taxe de Séjour.'—The following special taxes are payable. **1979** G. POTTINGER *Secretaries of State for Scotland 1926-76* xiv. 151 Another proposal that emerged from the Fraser exercise was to levy a *kurtax* [sic], or *taxe de séjour*, on the continental model, to find funds for tourist amenities.

taxeme ('tæksiːm). *Linguistics.* [f. Gr. τάξ-ις arrangement + -EME.] A unit of syntactic relationship, esp. one that cannot be further analysed or lacks meaning by itself, such as word order or stress. Hence **ta'xemic** *a.*; **ta'xemics** *sb. pl.* (const. as *sing.*), the study and description of language in terms of taxemes.

1933 L. BLOOMFIELD *Lang.* x. 166 A simple feature of grammatical arrangement is a grammatical feature or taxeme. A taxeme is in grammar what a phoneme is in the lexicon—namely, the smallest unit of form. **1943** [see TAGMEME 2]. **1947** Taxemics [see TAGMEMICS *sb. pl.*]. **1950** WEBSTER Add., Taxemic. **1967** M. SCHLAUCH *Language* vi. 127 A taxeme, taken by itself, may have no meaning; when one or more taken together do have meaning the combination is called a tagmeme (for instance, *duch + ess*). *Ibid.* 128 It would seem that the terminology of taxemics requires further study. **1970** G. C. LEPSCHY *Survey Structural Linguistics* v. 89 Taxemes occur in conventional grammatical arrangements.

taxeopodous (tæksiː'ɒpədəs), *a. Zool.* [irreg. f. Gr. τάξις (gen. τάξεως) arrangement + -ποδος -footed (f. πούς foot) + -OUS.] Having each one of the carpal or tarsal bones of one row articulated with one of the other row; opposed to *diplarthrous.* So **'taxeopod,** *a.* = *taxeopodous*; *sb.* a member of the division *Taxeopoda* of ungulate mammals (comprising the *Proboscidea* and the extinct *Condylarthra*), having this arrangement of the tarsal bones; **taxe'opody**, taxeopodous condition.

1887 E. D. COPE in *Amer. Nat.* XXI. 987 All ungulates in passing from the taxeopodous to the diplarthrous stages, traversed the amblyopodous. **1890** *Ibid.* May 471 In the equine line, after the development of diplarthry in the posterior foot, a tendency to revert to taxeopody appears. **1891** *Cent. Dict.*, Taxeopod, *a.* and *sb.* **1897** COPE in *Amer. Nat.* June 485 In this order of Ungulates the carpus is taxeopodous.

taxer, taxor ('tæksə(r), -ɔː(r)). Forms: 4 **taxour(e**, 6-9 **taxor**, 6- **taxer**. [a. AF. *taxour*, agent-n. from *taxer* to TAX; with suffix subseq. reduced: see -ER[2] 3.]

†**1.** One who determines the amount of a tax, fine, price, etc.; an assessor. *Obs.*

[**1297** *Rolls of Parlt.* I. 239 Qe en chescun Counte seient deus Chivaliers, Taxours e Quilleurs, ou un Chevalier & un Serjaunt.] **1377** LANGL. *P. Pl.* B. VI. 40 þowgh ȝe mowe amercy hem, late mercy be taxoure. **1552** HULOET, Taxer of prises, *agoranomus*. **1611** COTGR., *Tauxeur*, a rater, taxer, assessor, prisor, praisor. **1695** KENNETT *Par. Antiq.* ix. 312 In every Deanery new Taxers were commission'd.

b. *spec.* In the ancient universities, An officer (one of two) who fixed the rents of students' lodgings. At Cambridge, where the 'Taxors' also regulated the prices of commodities, kept the standard of weights and measures, and punished those who offended in these matters, the office and title (*taxor*) continued into the 19th c. Now *Hist.*

1532-3 *Act 24 Hen. VIII*, c. 1 §10 This Acte..shall not..bee prejudiciall..to the Chancellers Vychancellers Proctours Taxers & Scholers..of the Vnyversities. **1563** ABP. SANDYS in Strype *Ann. Ref.* (1709) I. xxxv. 359, I was scrutitor, I was taxer, I was proctor, and I was vicechancellor. *c* **1618** MORYSON *Itin.* IV. IV. i. (1903) 315 The vniversityes of Germany, haue no Taxers (or Clarkes of the Markett) for the price of vittles (as our vniversityes haue). *Ibid.* 429 [At Bologna] two Taxers are chosen to taxe the Students lodgings, and see that they pay not more then in former yeares. **1797** *Cambr. Univ. Calendar* 141 The taxatores, taxers or taxors in this university,..were first appointed to regulate the price of the lodgings of the students. **1841** G. PEACOCK *Stat. Cambr.* 25 The two taxors were regents appointed by the house of regents, who were empowered, in conjunction with two burgesses, to tax or fix the rent of hostels and houses occupied by students, in conformity with the letters patent of Henry III (1231). They also assisted the proctors in making the assize of bread and beer, and in other affairs relating to the regulation of the markets. **1895** RASHDALL *Universities in Middle Ages* II. 361 It is worthy of notice that the office of Taxor, which has only recently been abolished in the University of Cambridge, was the earliest University office at Oxford [*c* 1209].

2. One who levies a tax or taxes.

1603-4 BACON *Sp. touching Purveyors*, Instead of takers, they become taxers; instead of taking provision for your Majesty's service, they tax your people *ad redimendam vexationem*. **1820** LAMB *Elia* Ser. I. *Two Races Men*, He [the borrower] is the true taxer who 'calleth all the world up to be taxed'. **1884** DOWELL *Taxation* I. v. i. 96 The taxors and collectors and their clerks..were accused of acting in an arbitrary..manner.

†**3.** One who finds fault or censures. *Obs.*

1601 W. PARRY *Trav. Sir A. Sherley* 8 The Turks (our Taxers) told us. **1611** SPEED *Hist. Gr. Brit.* IX. viii. (1623) 559 [They] were also..his most bitter Taxers.

'tax-,gatherer. *arch.* A collector of taxes.

[**1552** HULOET, Taske gatherer, *exactor*.] **1693** DRYDEN *Disc. Orig. & Progr. Satire* in *Ess.* (ed. Ker) II. 77 Casaubon ..says that Horace, being the son of a tax-gatherer..smells everywhere of the meanness of his birth. **1771** GOLDSM. *Hist. Eng.* (1789) IV. 271 The oppressions of the tax-gatherers..were considered as so severe, that the army once more rose to vindicate their freedom. **1826** SYD. SMITH *Let. on Cath. Quest.* Wks. 1859 II. 232/1 The tax-gatherer is the most indulgent and liberal of human beings;..and is candidly and impartially oppressive to every description of the Christian world. **1904** *Expositor* Mar. 213 Christ.. certainly had a taxgatherer for one of his chief disciples.

taxi ('tæksɪ), *sb.* Also **taxy**. Pl. **taxis**, †**taxies**.

I. 1. a. Colloquial abbreviation, orig. of TAXIMETER, and hence, more usu., of TAXI-CAB.

1907 *Daily Chron.* 26 Mar. 6/7 Every journalist..has his idea of what the vehicle should be called. It has been described as the (1) taxi, (2) motor-cab, (3) taxi-cab, (4) taximo,..(7) taximeter-cab. **1908** *Ibid.* 4 Feb. 4/7 Within the past few months the 'taxi' has been the name given to the motor-cab. **1908** *Daily News* 30 Apr. 2 Many ladies..now take a 'taxy' regularly for the morning's shopping. There are about 350 horsed 'taxies' on the road. **1908** E. V. LUCAS *Over Bemertons* iv, He went away in a taxi. **1911** G. B. SHAW *Getting Married* 285 Me and the beadle have been all over the place in a couple of taxies, maam. **1914** —— *Pygmalion* (1916) III. 128 In future you shall have as many taxis as you want. **1923** A. BENNETT *Riceyman Steps* IV. v. 198 Even in the daytime taxies were few in King's Cross Road. **1925** F. SCOTT FITZGERALD *Great Gatsby* iii. 70 Forms leaned together in the taxis as they waited, and voices sang. **1979** *United States 1980/81* (Penguin Travel Guides) 150 Taxis cannot be hailed in the streets.

b. *colloq.* A (small) passenger aeroplane; also short for *taxiplane* (see sense 4 below).

1911 *Flight* 11 Nov. 986/1 Baldwin, Sabelli and Lieut. Esnie Chinnery were making straight flights on the taxi. **1918** *Atlantic Monthly* Aug. 260 Our hero is..helping his mechanic give the 'taxi' a final looking over. **1919** *N.Y. Times Mag.* 30 Mar. 4 An airplane was..usually [called] a boat, ship, bus, or taxi. **1922** *Daily Mail Year Bk. 1923* 74/2 The 100 miles-an-hour 'aerial taxi'. *Ibid.*, He kept his winged 'taxi' waiting while he transacted urgent business, and then flew on. **1923** *Daily Mail* 7 Aug. 8/2 Companies.. which send 'taxis', or aerial tramps, to anywhere between Plymouth and Stockholm. **1943** C. H. WARD-JACKSON *It's Piece of Cake* 60 *Taxi*, an aircraft for the conveyance of a small number of passengers.

2. [f. the vb.] An act or spell of taxiing.

1931 *Daily Mirror* 27 Aug. 2/2 The machine..was lost in clouds of spray as it ploughed its way in a graceful 'taxi'. **1965** 'J. LE CARRÉ' *Looking-Glass War* i. 9 The plane..began the long taxi to the reception point.

II. 3. *U.S. slang.* A prison sentence of between five and fifteen years.

1930 J. LAIT *Big House* i. 1 Five to fifteen years, the judge had decreed—a 'stretch' that the convicts call a 'taxi', because most New York cabs bear conspicuously their rates, and are known as 'fifteen-and-fives'. **1935** A. J. POLLOCK *Underworld Speaks* 119/2 *Taxi*, 5, 10 or 15 years prison sentence. **1962** 'D. SHANNON' *Extra Kill* viii. 127 Whalen had done a five-to-fifteen year stretch—that's a taxi.

III. 4. *attrib.* and *Comb.*, as (sense 1) ***taxi fare***, ***fleet***, ***-horn***, ***man***, ***queue***, ***rank*** [RANK *sb.*[1] 1 c], ***stand***, ***station***; ***taxi-driving*** vbl. sb. and ppl. adj.; (sense 2) ***taxi apron***, ***clearance***, ***work***; **taxi-boat**, a boat that may be hired like a taxi; **taxi-dance** orig. and chiefly *U.S.*, a dance at which taxi-dancers are available; so ***taxi-dance hall***; **taxi-dancer** orig. *U.S.*, a woman (or man) whose services as a dance-partner may be hired; a professional dance-partner; so **taxi-dance** *v. intr.*, **-dancing** *vbl. sb.*; **taxi-driver**, the driver of a taxi-cab; also *transf.*, esp. (*colloq.*) an aeroplane pilot; **taxi-girl**, a young female taxi-dancer; **taxiplane**, a piloted light aeroplane available for public hire; **taxi-ride**, a journey in a taxi; a short distance by car; also *transf.*; **taxi service**, a service providing transport in taxi-cabs (in quot. 1952, a shuttle service of aircraft); **taxi squad** *N. Amer. Football*, a group of players who take part in practices and can serve as reserves for the team; hence **taxi squadder**, a member of such a group; **taxi strip**, **track** = *taxiway* below; **taxi-truck** *Austral.*, a van, with a driver, for public hire; **taxiway** [after RUNWAY 2 b], a route along which aircraft can taxi on the way to or from a runway.

1978 T. L. SMITH *Money War* I. 136 Captain Imman eased the 727 forward on the taxi apron. **1949** *Newsweek* 26 Sept. 44/2 A taxiboat pilot told how, 'as soon as I pulled alongside, the passengers began plummeting down'. **1953** R. GODDEN *Kingfishers catch Fire* x. 117 Subhan's *shikara* had not cushions and curtains like a real taxi-boat. **1974** *Islander* (Victoria, B.C.) 8 Sept. 6/4 There was a 24-hour taxiboat service supplied. **1966** D. FRANCIS *Flying Finish* ii. 25, I filed my flight plan, checked with the control tower for taxy clearance. **1932** P. G. CRESSY (*title*) The taxi-dance hall. **1938** W. SMITTER *F.O.B. Detroit* 9 On it there was the name of a taxi-dance place over a store on Woodward Avenue. **1955** N. MARSH *Scales of Justice* ix. 205 [He] cohabited with a so-called Miss Kitty de Vere whom he.. met at a taxi-dance. **1972** J. WAMBAUGH *Blue Knight* (1973) i. 26 She was thirty-eight years old now..and taxi dancing part-time down the street at the ballroom. **1976** *New Yorker* 1 Mar. 80/2 He also played in a taxi-dance-hall band. **1930** *Variety* 12 Feb. 49/4 The Filipino is a much better spender than his white brother and a favorite with the gal taxi-dancers. **1979** P. DRISCOLL *Pangolin* iii. 36 He would simply pay Mama-san Julie..to take one of her taxi dancers home for the night. **1982** *Times* 8 Feb. 22/7 The ancient (well, 61-year-old) custom of taxi-dancing has returned in style to New York. **1907** *Daily Chron.* 27 Aug. 4/7 'Take me to the New Theatre', said the fare. 'Which one, sir?' respectfully asked the 'taxy' driver. **1924** J. BUCHAN *Three Hostages* vi. 84 It is an outlandish place to get to, but most taxi-drivers know it. **1937** PARTRIDGE *Dict. Slang* 868/1 *Taxi-driver*, an aeroplane pilot. **1955** W. FAULKNER *Fable* 110 Somebody owes something for that poor bloodstained taxi-driver [*sc.* an aeroplane pilot]. **1971** *Daily Tel.* 30 Jan. 3/3 For the first time separate experiments are being performed by the 'taxi driver', the lonely astronaut in the orbiting Command Module. **1975** J. MELDRUM *Semonov Impulse* x. 173 She leaned forward and gave the taxi driver Dörflinger's address. **1909** *Westm. Gaz.* 20 Sept. 5/4 To qualify for the taxi-driving 'profession'. **1951** KOESTLER *Age of Longing* II. iii. 234 But there were no grand dukes, taxi-driving generals, or princesses at the Kronstadt. **1932** H. CRANE *Let.* Feb. (1965) 401 I'm sure you wouldn't mind advancing the bus and taxi fare, would you? **1965** F. SARGESON *Memoirs of Peon* viii. 264 The taxi fleet was being doubled. **1963** J. KIRKUP *Tropic Temper* xv. 163 The professional dance-girls, or taxi-girls as they are sometimes called in Singapore and Hong Kong, sit in a long row in front of the band. **1974** E. BRAWLEY *Rap* (1975) I. xii. 166 Freddy paid a few piastres and danced with the taxi girls on the bandstand. **1943** G. GREENE *Ministry of Fear* I. iv. 54 Far away a taxi-horn cried through an empty world. **1909** *Daily News* 3 Mar. 6 You can safely leave the rest to the taximen. **1946** E. O'NEILL *Iceman Cometh* II. 111 Sneaking? Why, me and the taxi man made enough noise..to wake the dead. **1982** P. FITZGERALD *At Freddie's* vii. 54 They could all see him..cutting short whatever the taxi-man was saying. **1920** *Daily Tel.* 13 Apr. 1/7 Taxiplanes for any journey. Per mile, *2s. 6d.* **1926** *Bulletin* 6 Aug. 3/1 He made a dash to Constantinople with a taxiplane. **1982** G. HAMMOND *Game* v. 60, I whistled up the taxi-plane. **1969** G. LYALL *Venus with Pistol* xv. 98 Everybody else in the coach..charged out to get into the taxi queue. **1929** T. S. MOORE in *Yeats & Moore: Corr.* (1953) 155 There is a taxi-rank a few steps above the station. **1943** G. GREENE *Ministry of Fear* IV. i. 222 A taxi-rank with one cab left. **1917** KIPLING *Diversity of Creatures* 333 It demanded Work in the shape of many taxi-rides daily. **1941** B. SCHULBERG *What makes Sammy Run?* iii. 44 It was a five-dollar taxi ride from the Villa España. **1976** E. WARD *Hanged Man* x. 59 He was no good for the tricky stuff. Just taxi-rides. Light planes over flat country. **1952** *Times* 23 Aug. 4/6 British European Airways..are to make eight flights daily, mainly to Hanover, in addition to a new public 'taxi' service..to west Germany. **1962** L. DAVIDSON *Rose of Tibet* 316 The p.c. questioned the local taxi service. **1981** L. DEIGHTON *XPD* xxvi. 214 London... The parking problem was horrendous, the taxi service inadequate. **1966** ROTE & WINTER *Lang. Pro Football* III. 141 *Taxi squad*, group of players under contract who practice with team but are not included on official team roster and do not take part in league games. **1967** *N.Y. Times* 8 Dec. 64 The Atlanta Falcons of the National Football League..activated a cornerback.. from the taxi squad. **1976** *Globe & Mail* (Toronto) 19 July s9/2 This is the first season the CFL has allowed teams an official taxi squad. **1975** B. MEGGS *Matter of Paradise* v. iv. 154 These boys are first string, and a taxi squader like yourself..can get hurt. **1922** M. A. VON ARNIM *Enchanted April* ix. 135 A taxi stand was at the end of the road. **1982** T. ALLBEURY *Shadow of Shadows* xxii. 190 He had to walk almost to the bridge before he found a taxi stand. **1930** J. DOS PASSOS *42nd Parallel* v. 366 Instead she went out to the taxistation. **1943** *Yank* 12 Nov. 6/3 We rode up the taxi strips to our head stand where the crew stood around the ship. **1976** B. JACKSON *Flameout* (1977) xii. 209 The small jet began to lose height, and soon airport buildings, a runway, and taxi strips were in sight. **1945** *Tee Emm* (Air Ministry) V. 42 The unit did not use lighted tar barrels to mark taxi tracks. **1966** D. FRANCIS *Flying Finish* x. 127 Patrick moved down the taxy track and turned on to the apron. **1962** *Southerly* XXIII. 98 Taxi-truck. **1974** P. CAVE *Dirtiest Picture Postcard* ii. 13 He packed all his books and records into two large cardboard boxes and phoned a taxi-truck. **1933** C. K. STEWART *Speech Amer. Airman* (thesis, Univ. of Akron) 96 *Taxi-way*, a route along the field designated for planes to taxi upon. **1939** *Sun* (Baltimore) 17 Apr. 8/1 The remaining $70,000 would be used for roadways, aprons, taxiways and fences. **1982** I. JOHNSTON *Special Drug Squad* ii. 25 The taxiway..allows aircraft to be towed across the perimeter road to British Airways' maintenance hangars. **1945** *Ann. Reg. 1944* 23 A small land plane of 8,000 lb. to seat eight passengers and suitable for taxi work.

taxi ('tæksɪ), *v.* Also **taxy** (now only in pres. pple.). [f. the sb.] **1. a.** *intr.* Of an aeroplane, etc., or its pilot: to travel slowly along the ground or water under the machine's own power. Also *transf.* ***to taxi in***, to taxi from a runway to a terminal or hangar; similarly ***to taxi out***.

1911 [see REMOUS]. **1914** *Aeroplane* 5 Feb. 140/1 He taxied out to leeward,..turned,..opened out his engine. *Ibid.* 1 July 21/2 The de Bolotoff triplane was 'taxying', but showed no signs of lifting. **1915** [see COME *v.* 24 d]. **1918** H. BARBER *Aerobatics* I. 37 In a high wind don't taxy unless necessary. **1927** C. A. LINDBERGH *We* ii. 19, I..taxied back to the hangar. **1932** S. GIBBONS *Cold Comfort Farm* xxiii. 304 The aeroplane..was taxi-ing comfortably to a standstill. **1955** *Times* 24 Aug. 6/4 Crowds waited at London Airport, and the Canberra was greeted with cheers as it taxied in. **1959** D. A. BANNERMAN *Birds Brit. Isles* VIII. 280 When well out from the land both birds became silent and 'taxied' heavily over the water until air-borne. **1961** J. HELLER *Catch 22* (1962) v. 47 The planes lumbered around and nosed forward lamely..until they taxied into the line at the foot of the landing strip and took off swiftly. **1975** *Daily Tel.* (Colour Suppl.) 4 Apr. 16/2 The ton of fuel..would be burnt while taxiing out to the runway.

b. *trans.* To cause (an aeroplane, etc.) to taxi.

1915 H. ROSHER *In R.N.A.S.* (1916) 67, I was taxying my machine to the far end of the aerodrome, to start off into the wind. **1933** *Discovery* Mar. 79 A Moth fuselage is used to 'taxy' a 25 ft. model of a flying boat hull by means of a force-recording undercarriage. **1946** *Proc. IRE* XXXIV. 380/2 (*caption*) General Motors Bug being taxied by radio control from B-23 airplane at Muroc Lake, California. **1977** *R.A.F. Yearbk.* 29 Taxying the aircraft requires a little practice.

2. a. *intr.* To travel in a taxi.

1918 A. QUILLER-COUCH *Foe-Farrell* xxiv. 397 From Victoria that evening I taxi'd straight to Jermyn Street. **1942** E. PAUL *Narrow St.* iv. 33 Anne's father..used to taxi to the rue de la Huchette from the avenue de la Bourdonnais. **1971** L. BLACKWELL *Blackwell Remembers* xxii. 200 As we taxied down the Mall it was gaily set out with Union Jacks and the Finnish flag.

b. *trans.* To convey in a taxi. Also *transf.*

1973 J. THOMSON *Death Cap* ix. 134 I'll get where I want to on my own feet... I don't want no bloody police taxiing me around. **1977** G. MCDONALD *Confess, Fletch* xxxviii. 178 He taxies Ms. Fryer to her motel. Allows her time to change.

Hence **'taxiing** *vbl. sb.* and *ppl. a.*, in sense 1 a above; also *fig.*

1916 N. J. GILL *Flyer's Guide* iii. 32 If, however, the machine is subject to a sudden loss of forward way (i.e., taxying over rough ground) the planes then tend to go on. **1946** R. A. MCFARLAND *Human Factors in Air Transport Design* ix. 390 To permit good ground vision during taxiing. **1958** CASTLE & 'HAILEY' *Flight into Danger* vi. 76 One slowly taxi-ing aircraft came to a stop and cut its engines. **1968** J. ZIMAN *Public Knowledge* i. 10 Greek Science never finally took off from its brilliant taxying runs. **1972** *Guardian* 22 Dec. 4/1 An airliner ran into a taxi-ing plane while taking off. **1982** L. COOK *Under Etna* I. i. 11 The first jarring bounce of touchdown and..the gentle taxi-ing in.

taxiarch ('tæksɪɑːk). *Anc. Gr. Hist.* [ad. Gr. *ταξίαρχ-ος*, f. *τάξι-ς*, TAXIS + *ἀρχός*, f. *ἄρχειν* to rule.] The commander of a taxis: see TAXIS 3.

1808 MITFORD *Hist. Greece* I. v. iv. 287 The rank of the [Athenian] Taxiarch..was nearly that of our colonel. **1837** WHEELWRIGHT tr. *Aristophanes* II. 269 A taxiarch or general, to receive some share of honour. **1846** GROTE *Greece* II. viii. II. 607 The tribe appears to have been the only military classification known to Athens, and the taxiarch the only tribe-officer for infantry, as the phylarch was for cavalry, under the general-in-chief. **1875** JOWETT *Plato* (ed. 2) V. 83 The generals thus elected shall propose the taxiarchs or brigadiers.

taxi-cab, taxicab ('tæksɪkæb). [Short for TAXIMETER *cab*, and itself shortened to TAXI *sb.*] A cab for public hire, fitted with a taximeter; *esp.* an automobile or motor-cab so furnished.

1907 *Daily Chron.* 28 Mar. 2/5 The 'taxicab', as the new taximeter motor-cab is called, is fast becoming a familiar feature in the streets of London. **1907** *Ibid.* 3 May 8/3 London has taken kindly to the Taxicab. **1908** *Westm. Gaz.* 7 May 4/2 How much the taxi-cab has done..to educate the non-motoring public to the utility of the motor-car. **1916** G. B. SHAW *Pygmalion* I. 116 She gets in and pulls the door to with a slam as the taxicab starts. **1978** M. GILBERT *Empty House* xii. 102 An aged taxi-cab parked in the [station] forecourt. **1981** P. THEROUX *Mosquito Coast* xxxi. 392 The world..was glorious even here, in this old taxi-cab, with the radio playing.

attrib. and *Comb.* **1907** *Daily Chron.* 3 May 8/3 Any taxicab driver who demands payment for an extra passenger is breaking the law. **1909** *Ibid.* 12 Jan. 1/4 She made quickly for her taxicab door, which was held open by police.

Hence **'taxi-cabby**, a driver of a taxi-cab.

1910 'W. LAWTON' *Boy Aviators in Nicaragua* 19 The taxi-cabby, like most of his kind, was not averse to making a tip. **1918** G. FRANKAU *One of Them* xx. 155 Whether five-bob tip to taxi-cabby Presaged the sorting-bells of Hell Fire Abbey?

taxicorn ('tæksɪkɔːn), *a.* and *sb.* *Entom.* [a. mod.L. *Taxicornes* pl. (Latreille, 1817), app. f. Gr. τάξις order, arrangement, a row or series + L. *cornu* horn: perh. after Gr. ταξίφυλλος with leaves set in rows.] **a.** *adj.* Having perfoliate antennæ, as the beetles of the obsolete family *Taxicornes* (now mostly referred to *Tenebrionidæ*). **b.** *sb.* A beetle of this family. Also **taxi'cornate, taxi'cornous** *adjs.*

1842 BRANDE *Dict. Sc.*, etc., *Taxicorns*, [L.] *Taxicornes*.. The name of a family of Coleopterous insects, including those in which the antennæ gradually augment in size as they extend from the head, or terminate in an enlargement. **1860** MAYNE *Expos. Lex.*, Taxicornate.

taxidermal (tæksɪ'dɜːməl), *a.* [f. TAXIDERM-Y + -AL[1].] = next.

1877 COUES & ALLEN *N. Amer. Rod.* 20 At first, we thought this was a taxidermal or other accident, but all the specimens show the same thing. *Ibid.* 67. **1898** *Naturalist* 171 The material More turned out from his taxidermal or herbarial laboratories.

taxidermic (tæksɪ'dɜːmɪk), *a.* [f. as prec. + -IC.] Of or pertaining to taxidermy.

1847 in WEBSTER. **1860** in MAYNE *Expos. Lex.*

taxidermist ('tæksɪdɜːmɪst). [f. TAXIDERMY + -IST.] One skilled in taxidermy; a professional stuffer of animals for preservation. Also *attrib.*

1828 in WEBSTER. **1849** LONGF. *Kavanagh* xv, The taxidermist..was not there. **1851** MANTELL *Petrifact.* ii. §3. 108 *note*, The eminent taxidermist..to whom I entrusted the skins of Notornis, Apteryx, &c. to be stuffed and mounted. **1869** *Eng. Mech.* 31 Dec. 381/1 The glass eyes used by taxidermists are generally too spherical.

taxidermize ('tæksɪˌdɜːmaɪz), *v.* [f. as prec. + -IZE.] **a.** *trans.* To treat by taxidermy; to prepare, preserve, and set up (a skin, etc.). **b.** *absol.* or *intr.* To practise taxidermy (*Funk's Stand. Dict.* 1895). Hence **'taxiˌdermized** *ppl. a.*, prepared by taxidermy.

1889 *Pop. Sci. Monthly* Apr. 779 His [the buffalo's] head taxidermized..fetches as much as the robe or even more. **1890** LEFFINGWELL *Shooting* 307 Game pictures, taxidermised specimens, wood-paintings of birds.

taxidermy ('tæksɪˌdɜːmɪ). [mod. f. Gr. τάξι-ς arranging, arrangement + δέρμα skin: cf. Gr. παχυδερμία thickness of skin.] The art of preparing and preserving the skins of animals, and stuffing and mounting them so as to present the appearance, attitude, etc. of the living animal.

1820 (*title*) Taxidermy: or the Art of Collecting, Preparing, and Mounting Objects of Natural History. For the Use of Museums and Travellers. **1842** BRANDE *Dict. Sc.*, etc. s.v., The most popular treatise on taxidermy is Mr. Swainson's volume in Lardner's Cyclopedia. **1854** BADHAM *Halieut.* 112 The inhabitants of the sea cannot be preserved except as mummies; they are the opprobrium of taxidermy.

taxildar, variant of TAHSILDAR.

taximeter ('tæksɪmiːtə(r), formerly tæk'sɪmɪtə(r)). Also 9 **taxameter**. [ad. F. *taximètre*, f. *taxe* tariff + *-mètre* = -METER. The form *taxameter*, used a few years earlier, was from German: cf. med.L. *taxa* tax. (An earlier German name from *c* 1875 was *taxanom*.)]

a. An automatic contrivance fitted on a cab or other vehicle to indicate to the passenger at any point the distance traversed and the fare due. Also *ellipt.* for *taximeter cab* (*rare*).

The earliest forms of this indicator were simply distance-recorders, but it was soon made to comprise an automatic fare-reckoner and index.

α. [**1890** *German Patent Spec.* 56310 Taxameter-Fabrik Westendorp & Pieper in Hamburg.] **1894** *Times* 2 June 19/1, I have severally interviewed the proprietors of the 'taxameter', owners of cabs at Hamburg, and several of their *employés*. **1898** *Daily Chron.* 21 Mar., An illustration and description of the taxameter has been sent us. **1898** *Westm. Gaz.* 30 Apr. 7/3 Each vehicle will be provided with a taxameter—the little instrument for registering distance which has found such favour in Paris and Berlin.

β. **1898** *Daily News* 14 Apr. 7/2 One of the new Berlin taximeters, attached to a London hansom cab, on which it has been in operation for the past six months in an experimental way, was shown [etc.]. **1907** *Ibid.* 4 Feb. 7/5 The Committee's report..declared strongly in favour of the taximeter as a means of regulating fares. **1908** *Whitaker's Almanack* 434/1 The fare payable for the hiring of a Motor Hackney Carriage fitted with a Taximeter shall be..(a) Not exceeding one mile, or..ten minutes..8d. **1908** A. BENNETT *Buried Alive* iv. 102 He then hailed a taximeter from the stand opposite the Army and Navy Stores. **1909** *Westm. Gaz.* 22 June 7/3 A taxi-meter was tried on horse-cabs in London over half-a-century ago.

b. *attrib.* and *Comb.*, as ***taximeter cab, -cabriolet, -driver, hansom, -maker, scale, system, vehicle.***

α. **1899** *Westm. Gaz.* 23 Mar. 8/1 A report..from our Consul-General at Berlin on the subject of taxameter cabs in that city, and its nature should bid our Taxameter Syndicate, Limited, be of good cheer despite recent rebuffs. **1903** *Daily Chron.* 16 Nov. 4/5 Some years ago there was an attempt to introduce the taxameter system, which is the rule in all big German towns. The London cabman would have none of it. **1906** *Ibid.* 20 Feb. 4/1 A few minutes later a taxameter motor brougham drove up with the bride.

β. **1907** *Daily News* 18 Mar. 9 By the end of this week London may expect that about sixty taximeter motor cabs will be plying for hire in the streets. **1907** *Daily Chron.* 23 Sept. 3/4 A horse cab driver..was charged with assaulting [a] taximeter cab driver. **1959** P. BULL *I know the Face, But* ... xi. 200 Lambert kindly escorted me in a taximeter-cabriolet.

Hence **taximetered** *a.* (also **taxi'metric** *a.*), provided with a taximeter.

1907 *Daily Chron.* 18 Mar. 4/7 The competition of the *taximetered motor-cab will entitle the poor old four-wheeler more than ever to the name of 'growler'. **1908** *Even. Standard* 1 Feb. 1/3 Seventeen taximetered hansoms took the London streets to-day. **1906** *Westm. Gaz.* 15 Mar. 2/3, I have just returned from Paris, where most cabs are now '*taxametric'.

taxin ('tæksɪn). *Chem.* [f. L. *tax-us* yew + -IN[1].] 'A resinous substance obtained from the leaves of the yew-tree' (Watts *Dict. Chem.* (1868) V. 702). So **'taxine** (-aɪn) *sb.*, a poisonous alkaloid found in these leaves (*Syd. Soc. Lex.* 1899).

1907 *Daily News* 21 Dec. 9 A post-mortem examination showed that he had eaten a quantity of yew leaves, which.. contained taxine, a very active poison.

taxine ('tæksaɪn), *a. Bot.* [f. as prec. + -INE[1].] Pertaining to, connected with, or resembling the genus *Taxus*; yew-like.

1888 DAWSON *Geol. Hist. Plants* 22 The débris of fossil taxine woods, mineralised after long maceration in water.

'taxing, *vbl. sb.* [f. TAX *v.* + -ING[1].] The action of the verb TAX in various senses.

1413 *Pilgr. Sowle* (Caxton 1483) IV. xxxiv. 83 To these shyrreues belongeth to punysshe mysdoers by taxyng of money. **1526** TINDALE *Luke* ii. 2 This taxynge [WYCLIF discryuyng, *Rheims* enrolling, *R.V.* enrolment] was fyrst executed when Syrenus was leftenaunt in Siria. **1535** COVERDALE *1 Esdras* ii. 19 They shal not only refuse to geue trybutes and taxinges, but also rebell vtterly agaynst the kynge. **1676** DRYDEN *Aurengzebe* II. i, Impose; but use your power of Taxing well. **1737** WHISTON *Josephus, Antiq.* XVIII. ii. (1812) III. 60 The taxings were come to a conclusion. **1841** MYERS *Cath. Th.* III. §35. 128 This is an undue taxing of any man's faith. *a* **1859** MACAULAY *Hist. Eng.* xxiii. (1861) V. 56 The only power which..Washington and Franklin denied to the Imperial legislature was the power of taxing.

b. *attrib.* and *Comb.* **taxing district** (U.S.): see quot.; **taxing-master**, an officer in a court of law who examines and allows or disallows items in a solicitor's bill of costs when disputed.

1890 *Cent. Dict.* s.v. *District*, *Taxing district, in the United States, the territory or region into which (for the purpose of assessment merely) a State, county, town, or other political district is divided. *H. H. Emmons.* **1848** WHARTON *Law Lex.*, **Taxing masters*, officers of the courts, who examine and allow costs. **1882** H. C. MERIVALE *Faucit of B.* II. I. xvii. 22 That exquisite and rational product of British law, the taxing-master.

'taxing, *ppl. a.* [f. TAX *v.* + -ING[2].] That taxes, in various senses of the verb.

1798 *Anti-Jacobin* xix. (1852) 84 Again the taxing-man [Pitt] appear'd—No deadlier foe could be. **1813** SCOTT *Let. to Joanna Baillie* 10 Dec. in *Lockhart*, As to the taxing men, I must battle them as I can: they are worse than the great Emathian conqueror. **1859** DICKENS *T. Two Cities* II. ix, All the taxing authorities were armed.

taxinomy (tæk'sɪnəmɪ), a more etymological form of TAXONOMY. So **taxi'nomic** *a.* = TAXONOMIC; **ta'xinomist** = TAXONOMIST.

1865 BENDYSHE tr. *Blumenbach's Anthropol. Treat.* Pref. 11 Truths whose importance no one can dispute in anthropological taxinomy. **1866** *Reader* 15 Dec. 1066 Those sciences of life which modern teaching has, with inexact taxinomy, and worse Greek, termed Biology. **1899** *Nature* 21 Sept. 489/2 The position that all taxinomy (which form he prefers, on etymological grounds, to the more usual 'taxonomy') must conform to logical requirements. *Ibid.*, Labours of scientific taxinomists. *Ibid.* 490/1 All who engage in taxinomic work.

‖**taxis** ('tæksɪs). Pl. **taxes** (-iːz). [a. Gr. τάξις arrangement, order, n. of action from τάσσειν to arrange.]

1. *Surg.* A manipulative operation employed for replacing parts which have quitted their natural situation, reducing hernia, etc.

1758 J. S. *Le Dran's Observ. Surg.* (1771) 198 The Reduction was attempted in vain, by the Operation called the *Taxis*. **1800** *Med. Jrnl.* IV. 38 In about an hour after, the reduction was compleated, by again having recourse to the inverted position and the taxis. **1887** D. MAGUIRE *Massage* iii. (ed. 4) 43 The taxis which surgeons use on ruptures, is but..a methodical pressure used by the hand on a ruptured tumour for reducing it.

†**2.** *Arch.* Structural adaptation of elements; the adaptation of parts to the end for which a building is erected; ordonnance. *Obs.*

1727–41 CHAMBERS *Cycl.*, *Taxis*.., in the ancient architecture, signifies the same with Ordonnance in the new, and is described by Vitruvius to be that which gives every part of a building its just dimensions, with regard to its use.

3. *Anc. Gr. Hist.* A company of soldiers, esp. foot-soldiers; a division of troops varying in size in different military organizations, and accordingly answering to a modern company, battalion, regiment, or brigade; in Athens, the quota of foot-soldiers supplied by each of the ten local tribes or Phylæ.

1850 GROTE *Greece* II. lvi. VII. 108 Each taxis or company,..had its own taxiarch. **1856** *Ibid.* II. xcii. XII. 80 The Macedonian Phalanx... The largest division of it which we find mentioned..is called a Taxis. How many of these Taxeis there were in all, we do not know.

4. *Philol.* Order or arrangement of words.

1885 *Amer. Jrnl. Philol.* VI. 361 The double taxis (grammatical and logical) of the Latin.

5. *Nat. Hist.* Classification, taxonomy.

1891 in *Cent. Dict.*

6. *Biol.* The reaction of a free organism to external stimulus by movement in a particular direction. [Introduced in this sense in Ger. by F. Czapek 1898, in *Jahrb. für wissensch. Bot.* XXXII. 308.]

1899 *Jrnl. R. Microsc. Soc.* 180 The phenomena of this [irritability] reaction may be classed under the following heads:—(1) Taxis or movement ('geo-' or 'photo-taxis') [etc.]. **1904** *Science* 14 Oct. 487 The mechanical interpretations of the tropisms and taxes as held by Loeb, Bethe and Uexkull. **1908** DRIESCH *Sc. & Philos. Organism* II. 9 In the simple free directive movement or 'taxis' it is the typical relation between the direction of the stimulus and the direction of the effect, with regard to the main axis or the plane of symmetry of the organism, which separates this type of motion from others. *Ibid.* 13 'Taxis' signifies the specific orientation of a specific axis of the organism with regard to the direction of any directed agent of the medium. **1940**, **1955** [see KINESIS 2]. **1973** *Nature* 17 Aug. 468/1 Behaviourism as a general theory of animal behaviour was woefully inadequate—a fact of which anyone must be convinced who tries today to read Jacques Loeb on tropism, taxes and the like.

-taxis ('tæksɪs), the word TAXIS (sense 6) used as a suffix in *Biol.*, as in *geotaxis* s.v. GEO-, PHOTOTAXIS, etc.

taxless ('tækslɪs), *a.* [f. TAX *sb.*[1] + -LESS.] Free from taxes or taxation; untaxed.

1615 SYLVESTER *Job Triumphant* III. 555 If Tithe-lesse, Taxe-lesse, Wage-lesse, Right-lesse, I Have eat the Crop, or caused the Owners dye. **1845** LD. CAMPBELL *Chancellors* (1857) IV. lxxviii. 61 They depicted..the happy tranquil, taxless times which the more aged might still remember. **1909** *Daily Chron.* 3 Sept. 4/4 Compelled to fly the Channel, and seek some taxless shore.

Hence **'taxlessly** *adv.*, without taxation.

1894 J. S. MORTON in *Forum* (U.S.) June 389 The most efficacious remedy..is, to give the farmers of the United States the right to taxlessly buy in the markets of all the civilized world wherein they are compelled to sell.

taxman, obs. f. TACKSMAN; see also TAX *sb.*[1] 7.

†**taxment**. *Obs. rare*$^{-1}$. [f. TAX *v.* + -MENT: perh. a. AF. *taxement* (13–15th c. in Godef.), med.L. *taxāmentum*.] Assessment of a tax.

1612 in W. M. Williams *Ann. Founders' Co.* (1867) 226 Pd...to the Chamberlain of the Cytie of London for the laste payment of £35. for the taxments for Ireland ..£7. 10. 0.

taxo-, irreg. used as combining form of Gr. τάξις arrangement (of which the comb. form in Greek is ταξι-, *taxi-*): see TAXOLOGY, -ONOMY, etc.

taxocrinid (tæksəʊ'krɪnɪd). *Palæont.* [f. mod.L. *Taxocrinidæ*, f. *Taxocrinus*, name of the typical genus, f. Gr. τάξος yew + κρίνον lily: see -ID[3].] A member of the extinct family *Taxocrinidæ* of articulate crinoids. So **taxocrinoid** (-'krɪnɔɪd) *a.*, belonging to this family; *sb.* = taxocrinid.

‖**taxodium** (tæk'səʊdɪəm). *Bot.* [mod.L., f. Gr. τάξος, L. *taxus* yew: see -ODE[1].] An American genus of coniferous trees, comprising the bald cypress, *T. distichum*, of the United States, and the Mexican cypress, *T. mucronatum*.

1836 J. MITFORD *Lett. & Remin.* (1891) 82 You will outlive all the Ba-o-babs and taxodiums in the world.

taxodont ('tæksədɒnt), *a. Zool.* [f. Gr. τάξις arrangement + ὀδούς, ὀδοντ-, tooth.] Of a bivalve shell: Having the hinge formed by a long series of similar teeth and sockets, as in the group *Taxodonta*, containing the ark-shells and the genus *Leda*. Said also of the hinge, and of the arrangement.

1896 *Science* 27 Nov. 771 A series of vertical crenulations or taxodont denticles.

taxogen ('tæksədʒən). *Chem.* [f. TAXO- + -GEN.] The monomer in the chain of a telomer.

1948 [see TELOMER]. **1974** C. M. STARKS *Free Radical Telomerization* i. 2 The term *monomer* is normally employed instead of taxogen, except in the patent literature. **1980** *U.S. Patent 4,183,901* 2 The maleic acid telomers are lower molecular weight polymers formed by reacting a chain transfer agent, or telogen with an olefinic monomer of taxogen.

taxology (tæk'sɒlədʒɪ). *rare*$^{-0}$. [f. TAXO- + -LOGY.] The science of classification; the study of taxonomy.

1860 MAYNE *Expos. Lex.*, *Taxologia*,..applied by Devereux to all that relates to classification: taxology.

taxon ('tæksɒn). Pl. **taxa**. [a. G. *taxon* (A. Meyer *Logik der Morphologie* (1926) 127), f. *taxonomie* TAXONOMY.] A taxonomic group, as a genus or species. Also *fig.*

1929 *Scientific Monthly* Feb. 107/2 Such conceptions as the 'species', or 'taxon' in taxonomy. **1936** *Acta Biotheoretica* II. 180 Meyer's taxa (and phyla) are more valuable concepts in theory than in practice. **1948** *Minutes Utrecht Conf.* 14 June in *Chronica Botanica* (1950) XII. 12 Dr. Lam explained that in order to simplify the wording of the Rules, it is proposed to indicate a taxonomic group of any rank with the term taxon (plural taxa). **1951** [see ENDEMIC *a.* a]. **1953** *Proc. 7th Internat. Bot. Congr. 1950* 465/1 Taxon..was, however, a very convenient word, and after two years [*sc.* by 1950] 60% to 70% of botanists were using it. **1961** *Watsonia* V. 68 Many infraspecific taxa [of *Trifolium repens*] have been described for wild populations. **1971** J. Z. YOUNG *Introd. Study Man* xxviii. 400 There is no fixed typological criterion of an extinct species, genus, family, or other taxon. **1973** *Jrnl. Indo-European Studies* I. 405 A few words should be said about the main taxon in question; namely: Indo-Europeanist. **1976** *Sci. Amer.* Aug. 32/3 His work has revealed a surprisingly wide range of vertebrates: at least a dozen taxa of mammals, 22 of birds, three of fishes and one taxon of reptiles. **1980** *Dædalus* Spring 85 A Renaissance similitude (biblical giants) eventually converted into an Enlightenment taxon (species-giants).

taxonomic, *a.* [f. TAXONOMY + -IC.]

a. Pertaining or relating to taxonomy, classificatory.

1852 DANA *Crust.* I. 10 We deem it of so little taxonomic importance. **1894** NEWTON *Dict. Birds* 820 The taxonomic position of the *Palamedeidæ*..has been much debated.

b. *spec.* in *Linguistics*, involving or concerned with the identification and classification of the terms into which languages are analysed; esp. as ***taxonomic linguistics*** (the dominant methodology of the 1940s and 1950s), ***phonetics***, etc.

1962 N. CHOMSKY in *Internat. Preprints Papers 9th Internat. Congr. of Linguists* 556 In the case of perception of language,..the step-by-step analytic models of taxonomic linguistics are not in the least convincing. **1964** —— in *Proc. 9th Internat. Congr. Linguists* 951 Structural linguistics marks a departure from a more traditional point of view... Let us coin the term 'taxonomic phonemics' to refer to this body of doctrine, thus emphasizing its striking reliance..on procedures of segmentation and classification. **1968** P. M. POSTAL *Aspects Phonol. Theory* p. x, I shall refer..to the dominant conception of phonological structure as 'autonomous phonology' or 'autonomous phonemics', considering this terminology preferable to that of 'taxonomic phonemics' which has been used in the recent past. **1973** *Archivum Linguisticum* IV. 117 He goes on to claim a tacit dependence of transformational grammar on the findings of taxonomic analysis. **1976** *Canad. Jrnl. Linguistics* Spring 128 FBG present excellent discussions of taxonomic structural linguistics, how it is done, what it discovered about language (observing that many of the facts about language structure that taxonomic grammarians set out to capture are real), and the psycholinguistics of taxonomic grammar.

Hence **taxonomical** *a.*; **taxonomically** *adv.*

1875 C. C. BLAKE *Zool.* Pref., A sub-class which vindicates the value of its *taxonomical character by its numerical superiority. **1880** HUXLEY in *Times* 25 Dec. 4/1 The palæontological facts which have come to light..have completely broken down existing taxonomical conceptions. **1899** *Nature* 14 Sept. 460/1 To successfully handle *taxonomically groups so dissimilarly ordained as the Bony Fishes and Echinoderms.

taxonomy (tæk'sɒnəmɪ). [ad. F. *taxonomie* (De Candolle 1813), irreg. f. Gr. τάξις arrangement, order (see TAXIS) + -νομία distribution: see TAXO- and -NOMY. See also TAXINOMY.]

1. Classification, esp. in relation to its general laws or principles; that department of science, or of a particular science or subject, which consists in or relates to classification; *esp.* the systematic classification of living organisms.

[**1813** DE CANDOLLE *Theor. Elem. de la Botanique.*] **1828** in WEBSTER. **1832** *Encycl. Brit.* (ed. 7) V. 70/2 Taxonomy is that branch of botany which has for its object the combination of all our observations on plants, so as to form a system or classification. **1839** G. ROBERTS *Dict. Geol.*, *Taxonomy*, the classification or putting things in their proper order. **1852** DANA *Crust.* I. 59 The long posterior legs of certain Maioid species have been allowed to have the same value in Taxonomy. **1872** COUES *N. Amer. Birds* 49.

2. (With *a* and *pl.*) A classification *of* anything.

1960 *Times Lit. Suppl.* 29 Apr. 277/4 Professor Goldschmidt..has constructed what he calls a 'taxonomy' of human societies. **1971** *Nature* 10 Dec. 319/2 He complained of the taxonomy put forward by Sir Frederick Dainton's committee, with its concept of basic research, strategic research and technical research. **1972** *Sci. Amer.* Jan. 116/3 His taxonomy of bridge structures before the age of steel and concrete. **1979** *Dictionaries* I. 64 The prefatory notes to the volumes of the *DAE* offer taxonomies of American usages and Americanisms. **1983** *Sci. Amer.* Mar. 102/2 We can outline a taxonomy of chlorite oscillators, and we are beginning to see how they can be related to oscillators of the bromate and iodate families.

So **ta'xonomer**, a scientific classifier; **ta'xonomist** = *taxonomer*. (See also *taxinomic*, *taxinomist*, s.v. TAXINOMY.)

1885 *Athenæum* 1 Aug. 146/2 It is now generally admitted by *taxonomers that their affinities are..close. **1897** *Naturalist* 94 One instance wherein the author differs from most recent taxonomers. **1877** HUXLEY *Anat. Inv. Anim.* xii. 656 The views of *Taxonomists..are undergoing..incessant modifications. **1904** *Athenæum* 6 Aug. 175/3 Then the pendulum swung in the opposite direction:..field botanists were placed on a level with postage-stamp collectors, taxonomists were looked on as laborious triflers.

taxor, -our(e: see TAXER.

'tax,payer, tax-payer. **1.** One who pays a tax or the taxes generally; one who is liable to taxation; in U.S. including local rate-payers.

1816 J. KENNEDY in A. McKay *Hist. Kilmarnock* (1880) 229 Only 2,700 have a right of voting for members of Parliament;..197,300, although tax-payers, directly or indirectly, having no more right of voting than if they were an importation of slaves from Africa. **1853** *Inaug. Address Mayor of Boston (U.S.)*, [Of] interest to every water taker and tax payer in the City. **1855** MACAULAY *Hist. Eng.* xix. IV. 324 Some part..might, with advantage to the proprietor, to the taxpayer and to the State, be attracted into the Treasury. **1878** JEVONS *Prim. Pol. Econ.* xvi. 130 To demand a tax when the taxpayer is likely to be able to pay it.

2. *U.S. colloq.* A building just large enough to provide an income sufficient to meet the expenses it incurs; hence, any small building.

1921 B. MATTHEWS *Ess. on Eng.* vi. 134 A resplendent electric sign on top of a two-story tax-payer. **1950** *N.Y. Times* 28 Dec. (Late city ed.) 39/8 The three-story tax-payer at 288 Jackson Avenue in Jersey City, N.J...has been sold.

So **'tax,paying** *sb.*, the payment of taxes; *a.*, that pays taxes (or rates); subject to taxation.

1832 *Reg. Deb. Congress U.S.* 4 Apr. 2390 As a representative of the tax paying people of the South, I must ask..what becomes of the excessive heavy amount of revenue? **1849** J. S. MILL in *Westm. Rev.* LI. 44 A tax-paying or other property qualification. **1851** *Inaug. Address Mayor of Boston (U.S.)*, The sale would cause discontent..to a very large number of tax-paying citizens. **1882** T. HUGHES in *Macm. Mag.* XLV. 281 Doing his share of fighting, taxpaying, keeping the peace. **1894** *Pop. Sci. Monthly* XLV. 719 Formerly they were checked by the rage of the taxpaying classes.

taxt, obs. Sc. f. TAX *sb.*[1]; var. of TAXED.

'tax-,taker. One who takes or collects taxes; a levier or receiver of taxes.

1610 HEALEY *St. Aug. Citie of God* II. xix. 85 Even the very soldiers and taxe-takers themselves would heare and regard well. **1656** EARL MONM. tr. *Boccalini's Advts. fr. Parnass.* II. lxxxii. (1674) 234 Their grievances were encreased by the greedy Tax takers. **1832** HT. MARTINEAU *Each & All* iii. 43 We must reach the extreme..of having our whole produce in the hands of land-owners and tax-takers. **1860** DICKENS *Lett.* (1880) II. 117 The tax-taker was the authority for the wretched creature's impoverishment.

taxt ward: see TAXED 2 c.

‖**'taxus.** *Obs.* Mediæval Latin name of the badger: formerly sometimes used in English.

1535 COVERDALE *Ezek.* xvi. 10, I made the shues of Taxus lether. **1567** MAPLET *Gr. Forest* 104 b, Of Taxus or the Badger. **1577** tr. *Bullinger's Decades* III. v. (1592) 340 Three couerings more, the vppermost whereof was of Taxus leather, wel able in rain to keep water out. **1753** CHAMBERS *Cycl. Supp.*, *Taxus*, in zoology, the name of the badger.

taxwax ('tækswæks). Now *dial.* Also 9 **taxy waxy**. [Var. of PAXWAX.] The tendon of the neck: = PAXWAX.

1709 BLAIR in *Phil. Trans.* XXVII. 78 From above this Tax-Wax in the Neck, do arise two Muscles. **1713** DERHAM *Phys.-Theol.* VI. iii. 362 That strong tendinous and insensible Aponeurosis, or Ligament—Called the Whitleather, Packwax, Taxwax, and Fixfax. **1829** J. HUNTER *Hallamsh. Gloss.*, *Tax-wax*, the tendon of the neck. **1879** MISS JACKSON *Shropsh. Word-bk.* s.v., Gie the baby that piece o' taxy waxy, it's better than india-rubber.

taxy: see TAXI *sb.*

-taxy, comb. element, ad. Gr. -ταξια, f. τάξις arrangement, order; as in ATAXY, PHYLLOTAXY.

†**tay, tey.** *Obs.* Also 5 **teye**, 6 **taie**, 6–7 **taye**. [In 5 *teye*, a. obs. F. *teie*, in Palsgr. *taye* (in senses 2, 3):—L. *t(h)ēca*:—Gr. θήκη case, covering, sheath.]

1. A case, sheath, outer covering.

c **1440** *Promp. Parv.* 487/2 Teye, of a cofyr or forcer, *teca*, *thecarium*.

2. A web or cataract in the eye.

1547 RECORDE *Judic. Ur.* 59 b, It healeth creythys, and also the webbe and the tey in the eye. **1597** LOWE *Chirurg.* (1634) 31 Some cataract or taye which covereth the prunall called the windowe of the eye. *Ibid.* 166 The Cataract or tey.

3. The outer membrane of the brain. [Cf. F. *teie dure* = *dura mater*.] Also taken as 'skull', and 'brain'.

a **1568** '*My wofull Hairt*', etc. 44 in *Bannatyne Poems* (Hunter Cl.) 83 Vpoun my heid thay thrang a croun of thorn,.. The thorne pykis thay to my tay dang doun. *c* **1580** JEFFERIE *Bugbears* I. i. in *Archiv Stud. Neu. Spr.* (1897) XCVIII. 306 In stide of taies, he hathe bugbeares in his head.

tay, obs. or dial. f. TEA, THEE, TIE, TOE; obs. form of THEY after a dental.

tay, taye, variants of TAEL.

Tayacian (tə'jeɪʃən), *a.* *Archæol.* [ad. F. *Tayacien* (H. Breuil 1932, in *Préhistoire* I. 131), f. *Tayac* (see def.): see -IAN.] Of, pertaining to, or designating a palæolithic flake industry of which remains were first found at Tayac (Dordogne), SW France. Also *absol.*

1934 *Nature* 7 July 30/1 The Carmel cave series covers from Natufian (Mesolithic) to Tayacian, the recently recognised rough flake industry. **1946** F. E. ZEUNER *Dating the Past* ix. 288 The combination of Levalloisian, Acheulian and Tayacian or Clactonian elements which resulted in the Mousterian industry of Europe occurred during the Last Interglacial. **1974** *Encycl. Brit. Macropædia* VIII. 1050/1 The earlier flake tools at this site [*sc.* Fontéchevade] are termed Clactonian tools.., while the later are known as Tayacian tools. **1979** M. LEAKEY *Olduvai Gorge* ix. 87 The chopper-small-tool complex..is represented in Europe by the Clactonian..and the Tayacian.

‖**tayassu, tayaçu** (tɑːjə'suː). Also **tajacu, tajassu**. [Tupi *taya'çu* (Diaz *Dicc. Ling. Tupy* 1858), = tania-eater, f. *taña*, *taja*, TANIA + *çu* to eat.] The common or collared peccary, *Dicotyles torquatus* (*D. tajacu*).

[**1580** DE LERY *Voy. Brésil* 312 Taiasou, sanglier du pays. **1648** MARCGRAVE *Hist. Nat. Brasil.* VI. vii. 229 Tajaçu Brasiliensibus, porcus est silvestris.] **1698** TYSON in *Phil. Trans.* XX. 137 The Tajacu, or the Mexico Musk Hog. **1774** GOLDSM. *Nat. Hist.* III. 183 That animal which..most resembles an hog,..is called the Peccary, or Tajacu.

tayberry ('teɪbərɪ). Also **Tay-**. [f. *Tay*, the name of a river in Scotland + BERRY *sb.*[1]] A dark purple soft fruit produced by crossing the blackberry and the raspberry, introduced in Scotland in 1977; also, the plant bearing this fruit.

1977 *Ann. Rep. Scottish Hort. Res. Inst. 1976* 42 The new *Rubus* hybrid has been named 'Tayberry' and is being propagated for release. **1980** *Economist* 9 Aug. 63/2 To the strawberry, gooseberry, raspberry, blackcurrant and blackberry cycle is now added a new fruit—the tayberry. **1980** *Amateur Gardening* 8 Nov. 35 The tayberry is deep purple in colour, roughly $1\frac{1}{2}$ in. long and has a refreshing, not-too-sweet flavour. **1982** *Observer* 7 Feb. 43/4 (Advt.), Delicious soft fruits for autumn planting... The new virus-free Tayberry and all soft fruits.

taych, variant of TACHE *sb.*[3], sugar-pan.

tayel, tayewe, obs. ff. TAEL, TAU.

tayke, obs. form of TAKE *v.* and *sb.*

tayl(e, tayll(e, obs. ff. TAEL, TALE, TAIL, TEAL.

taylage, tayllage, obs. ff. TALLAGE *sb.*[1]

taylagier: see TALLAGER.

tayler, -or, -ur, etc., obs. ff. TAILOR.

Taylor ('teɪlə(r)). **1.** *Math.* [The name of Brook *Taylor* (1685–1731), English mathematician, who published the theorem in his *Methodus Incrementorum Directa et Inversa* (1715).] ***Taylor('s) series***, an infinite series of the form $f(a) + hf'(a) + h^2f''(a)/2! + \ldots + h^{n-1}f^{(n-1)}(a)/(n-1)! + \ldots$, where $f^{(i)}(a)$ is the value of the *i*th derivative of a function $f(x)$ at $x = a$; an analogous series for a function of more than one variable; ***Taylor's theorem***, the theorem that a function $f(x)$ can be approximated over any interval throughout which its first n derivatives exist by the first n terms of Taylor's series (with $h = x - a$) plus a remainder dependent on $f^{(n)}(a + \theta h)$ $(0 < \theta < 1)$.

1816 [see THEOREM *sb.* a]. **1842** *Penny Cycl.* XXIV. 126/2 Lagrange's paper in the Berlin Memoirs for 1772, in which he proposed to make Taylor's theorem the foundation of the Differential Calculus. *Ibid.*, D'Alembert..gave for the first time..a method of finding the remnant of Taylor's series after a certain number of terms have been taken. **1908** G. H. HARDY *Pure Math.* vii. 255 This expansion of f(a + h) is known as Taylor's series. *Ibid.* 287 (*heading*) Proof of Taylor's theorem by integration of parts. **1968** C. G. KUPER *Introd. Theory Superconductivity* ii. 24 Near the transition temperature, g may be expanded in a Taylor series: $g = g_0 + \alpha\zeta + \frac{1}{2}\beta\zeta^2 + \ldots$ **1972** A. W. F. EDWARDS *Likelihood* v. 72 An alternative method, which readily generalizes to the case of many parameters, is to obtain the Taylor's series approximation to the support curve in the region of the maximum. **1972** M. KLINE *Math. Thought* xx. 442 Taylor's theorem for $a = 0$ is now called Maclaurin's theorem. **1979** PAGE & WILSON *Introd. Computational Combinatorics* ii. 10 We write E = 1 + Δ and expand the polynomial f by Taylor's theorem.

2. The name of F. W. *Taylor* (1856–1915), U.S. engineer, used *attrib.* to designate the system of scientific management and work efficiency that he expounded.

1911 *Assoc. Machinists Circular* in C. B. Thompson *Scientific Managem.* (1914) 783 The latest danger..is the so-called Taylor system of shop management. **1926** WHITEMAN & MCBRIDE *Jazz* vii. 154 At their work, men and women are the victims of efficiency, the Taylor system, so that humanity itself is being made into machines. **1972** [see *scientific management* s.v. SCIENTIFIC *a.* 6].

3. Port wine shipped by the firm of *Taylor*, Fladgate, and Yeatman.

1940 M. HEALY *Stay me with Flagons* 212 We had some Taylor of the same year, and the connoisseurs usually accorded it a higher place. **1952** H. W. ALLEN *Sherry & Port* II. i. 126, I tasted some of these wines in the Oporto Lodges, notably Sandeman 1942 and 1945 and Taylor of the same years. **1968** 'J. WELCOME' *Hell is where you find It* x. 137 Benson brought in the decanter and put it beside me. 'It's the Taylor 47, sir,' he said.

Taylorian (teɪ'lɔːrɪən), *a.* and *sb.* [f. the name *Taylor* (see def.) + -IAN.] The familiar name (used as *adj.* and *sb.*) of the Taylor Institution of the University of Oxford, established for the teaching of modern languages from money left for the purpose by Sir Robert Taylor (1714–88), English architect.

1898 *Dict. Nat. Biogr.* LV. s.v. *Taylor, Sir Robert*, The lecture-rooms and library which compose the Taylorian buildings were built in 1841–5. **1913** H. E. SALTER *Oxford Deeds of Balliol College* 212 Ball's house was..on the site of the Taylorian. **1932** L. MAGNUS *Herbert Warren* v. 147 He took much interest as Vice-Chancellor in the Taylorian Institute. **1937** H. NICOLSON *Diary* 26 Nov. (1966) 313 Then to the Taylorian where I address a large and interested audience on the German colonies. **1965** DOUGHTY & WAHL *Lett. D. G. Rossetti* I. 47 There is a copy of this letter at Oxford, in the Taylorian.

Taylorism ('teɪlərɪz(ə)m). **1.** [f. the name of N. W. Taylor, of New Haven, Connecticut (1786–1858): see -ISM.] The theological system of N. W. Taylor, a modified form of Calvinism.

1882–3 *Schaff's Encycl. Relig. Knowl.* III. 2306 It was popularly termed 'The New Haven Theology'. Sometimes it was called 'Taylorism'. **1885** C. A. BRIGGS in *Encycl. Brit.* XIX. 700/1 Puritan theology had developed in New England into Edwardism and then into Hopkinsianism, Emmonism, and Taylorism.

2. [f. the name of F. W. *Taylor*: see TAYLOR 2.] The principles or practice of the Taylor system of management.

1928 *Times Lit. Suppl.* 11 Oct. 724/2 The second [essential] was the substitution of exact scientific investigation and knowledge for the old individual judgment or opinion. Mr. Meakin, who speaks somewhat slightingly of 'Taylorism', seems to be unacquainted with this passage. **1952** E. H. CARR *Bolshevik Rev.* II. xvi. 111 The Menshevik journal declared that the Bolsheviks..'are attempting to abolish the eight-hour day and introduce piece-rates and Taylorism'. **1983** *Futurist* June 25/1 Taylorism reduces work to machine-tending that requires little training and effort and that maximizes productivity.

taylorite ('teɪlərаɪt). *Min.* [f. the name of its discoverer, W. J. *Taylor* (1833–64), U.S. mineral chemist + -ITE[1].] A sulphate of potassium and ammonia found in Peruvian guano beds as yellowish white bitter-tasting orthorhombic crystals.

1868 J. D. DANA *Syst. Min.* (ed. 5) 614 Taylorite... In small compact lumps or concretions. **1968** I. KOSTOV *Mineralogy* 503 Arcanite and mascagnite are isostructural.. and form mixed crystals $(K,NH_4)_2SO_4$ termed taylorite. **1975** *Mineral. Abstr.* XXVI. 353/1 The annual mineral lists for newly recorded Western Australian minerals include.. taylorite.

Taylorize ('teɪləraɪz), *v.* Also taylorize. [f. TAYLOR + -IZE.] *trans.* To introduce the Taylor system into (see TAYLOR 2); to manage in accordance with this system. Chiefly as **'Taylorized, 'Taylorizing** *ppl. adjs.* Also **Taylori'zation**, the action of Taylorizing; Taylorism.

1929 A. HUXLEY *Holy Face* 64 Machinery, Taylorization ..had not yet begun to produce their dehumanizing effects. **1930** *N. & Q.* 26 Apr. 301/2 'Taylorize', then, means 'manage scientifically'. **1939** J. A. SCHUMPETER *Business Cycles* II. xiv. 783n. A major movement, which however resolves itself into an almost infinite number of small ones, is what may be called Taylorization. Its spread during our period is a typical consequence of the struggle for survival amidst the readjustments of down-grades. **1957** R. BURLINGAME *Henry Ford* v. 76 In the 'taylorized' industries the pay rise had been more gradual. *Ibid.*, A good many industrialists had repudiated 'taylorization' and called Taylor a crackpot. **1979** *Internat. Jrnl. Sociol. of Law* Feb. 112 Their Taylorizing bureaucracies are only matched by British amateurism..and American razmatazz.

taym(e, obs. or dial. f. TAME, TIME.

tayn, var. T'IEN.

tayn(e), obs. var. *tane, ta'en*, pa. pple. of TAKE.

taynt(e, taynter, obs. ff. TAINT, TENT, TENTER.

†**tayout**, obs. form of TALLY-HO.

1808 SCOTT in *Strutt's Queenhoo Hall* iv, Gregory.. followed, encouraging the hounds with a loud tayout.

‖**tayra** ('taɪrə). Also taira. [Tupi *taira*.] Native name in Brazil of a mammal of the weasel family, *Galera* (or *Galictis*) *barbara*.

1854 *Zoologist* XII. 4283 The Tayra is another American form, whose marten-like agility renders it always conspicuous. **1896** *List of Animals Zool. Soc.* 85 Galictis barbara (Linn.). Tayra..South America.

†**tays, teys.** *Obs.* ? Some material or accessory used for vestments.

1350–1 *Durham Acc. Rolls* (Surtees) 381 In ture, orfrays, teyses, frenges, filo. **1380–81** *Ibid.* 389 In ij peciis de tays empt. pro vestimentis, ij s. **1395–6** *Ibid.* 392 In freyns, tays, carde, et aliis diversis necessariis. xxx s. j. d. **1404** *Ibid.* 395 Item iiij pecie de tayses de cerico pro vestimentis.

Tay-Sachs (teɪ'sæks). *Path.* The names of Warren *Tay* (1843–1927), British ophthalmologist, and Bernard *Sachs* (1858–1944), American physician and neurologist, used *attrib.* and *absol.* with reference to a fatal inherited metabolic disorder in which an enzyme deficiency causes accumulation of a ganglioside in the brain and elsewhere, resulting in idiocy and death in childhood (described by them in 1881 and 1887 respectively). [Named in Ger. by H. Higier 1901, in *Neurologisches Centralblatt* XX. 851.]

1907 *Index Medicus* V. 841/1 Hereditary infantile cerebellar ataxy and the Tay-Sachs disease. **1937** [see AMAUROTIC *a.*]. **1974** *Sci. Amer.* Mar. 63/2 (Advt.), A Tay-Sachs child develops normally for his first six months. Then, as excessive fatty deposits accumulate in his brain cells, he regresses.. Usually before his fifth birthday, he dies. **1975** *Nature* 8 May 101/3 Israel's best known ethnic malady is Tay-Sachs Disease, a fatal genetic disorder limited almost entirely to infants whose forebears came here from certain parts of East Europe.

tayse, var. TEISE *sb.* and *v. Obs.*

tayt, var. TAIT *a. Obs.*, cheerful.

tayte, north. dial. f. TOTE *Obs.*, hill.

taythe, tayu, obs. ff. TITHE, TAU.

taz (tæz). *colloq.* = TASH.

1951 PARTRIDGE *Dict. Slang* (ed. 4) 1198/1 *Taz.* A beard: Cockneys': C. 20... 2. An immature moustache; youthful down, wherever growing: mostly Cockneys': since ca. 1920. **1969** M. DUFFY *Wounds* i. 19 He was proud of his little toothbrush taz and elegant white raincoat.

taz, tazel(l, -ill, tazle, obs. ff. TAWSE, TEASEL.

tazetta (tæ'zɛtə). Also Tazetta. [mod.L., specific epithet (Linnæus *Species Plantarum* (1753) I. 290), ad. It. *tazzetta* little cup, f. *tazza* (see TASS[2]): see -ET.] A fragrant white or yellow polyanthus narcissus, *Narcissus tazetta*, native to the Mediterranean, or any of the numerous varieties developed from it.

1847 *Jrnl. Hort. Soc.* II. 26 Sweet's Hermione Cypri are the produce of poeticus and a white-limbed Hermione, and N[arcissus] bifrons and compressus of Tazetta and jonquil. **1924** L. H. BAILEY *Man. Cultivated Plants* 187 They [*sc.* the Poetaz narcissi] are like large-flowered Tazetta. **1956** C. MACKENZIE *Thin Ice* iii. 36 The rising sun lighted a green plain covered with tazetta narcissus. **1977** *Chicago Tribune* 2 Oct. XI. 13/2 Midseason... Short-cupped daffodils; poeticus narcissus; jonquils; tazetta daffodils.

‖**tazia** (ta'zia). Also tazieh, taziyah, tazzia, etc. [ad. Arab. *ta'ziya* consolation, mourning.]

1. A representation of the tombs of Hasan and Husain (grandsons of Muhammad) carried in the Moharram procession.

1809 T. D. BROUGHTON *Let.* 26 Feb. (1813) 72 There were more than a hundred *Taziyas*, each followed by a long train of *Fuqeers*..beating their breasts. **1862** [see TABOOT[1]]. **1885** T. P. HUGHES *Dict. Islam* 410/2 Against the side of the Imambarrah, directed towards Mecca, is set the *tabut*—also called *tazia* (*ta'ziyah*), or model of the tombs at Kerbela. **1889** KIPLING *In Black & White* 94 Gilt and painted paper presentations of their tombs are borne with shouting and wailing..which fakements are called *tazias*. **1924** *Glasgow Herald* 26 Sept. 10 The procession was a long one, including a number of tazias, or many-storeyed turrets, and followed by 7000 Mussulmans. **1946** *Times of India* 6 Dec. 10/4 Richly decorated in customary Muslim fashion *tazias* looked resplendent.

2. A play commemorating the 'martyrdom' of Hasan and Husain, performed esp. on the anniversary of the event each year.

1893 E. G. BROWNE *Year amongst Persians* iv. 70 Many people were assembled to witness a *ta'ziya*, or representation of the sufferings of the Imáms Hasan and Huseyn. **1911** D. S. MARGOLIOUTH *Mohammedanism* iv. 127 The Indo-Germanic affinities of the Persians have led to the production of miracle-plays, called *ta'ziyah* (consolation), whereby the atrocities are more vividly brought home. **1951** G. E. VON GRUNEBAUM *Muhammadan Festivals* (1976) v. 89 At a comparatively recent date..the *ta'ziya*, or Passion play ..became the real climax of the Shî'ite Tenth of Muharram celebrations. **1972** *Times* 28 Sept. 9/3 In place of the traditional *ta'zieh* and *ruhozi* performances, a pair of new Iranian plays figured on the main bill. **1974** F. ROSENTHAL in Schacht & Bosworth *Legacy of Islam* (ed. 2) vii. 335 Numerous librettos for such *ta'ziya* plays have been preserved.

‖**tazza** ('tattsa). Pl. **tazze** ('tattse). [It. *tazza*: see TASS[2].] A shallow ornamental bowl or vase; properly, one supported on a foot.

1824 LADY BLESSINGTON *Jrnl.* May in E. Clay *Lady Blessington at Naples* (1979) 86 Antique vases and *tazze*, on which are sculptured bacchanalian orgies. **1841** *Civil Eng. & Arch. Jrnl.* IV. 141/1 The symmetrical forms of the many elegant vases and tazzas. **1877** *Times* 17 Feb. (Stanf.), Silver vases and tazze. **1877** MRS. M. GRANT *Sun-maid* viii, Beautiful tazzas of jasper, lapis-lazuli, and malachite.

attrib. and *Comb.* **1871** E. J. WORBOISE *Nobly Born* 404, I saw her take up her large tazza-glass, and dispose of its contents. **1878** NESBITT *Catal. Glass Vessels S. Kens. Mus.* 118 Tazza Bowl. Plain glass. **1895** *Daily News* 24 May 6/6 A fine green jade tazza-shaped dish.

Tazzie, Tazzy, varr. TASSIE[3].

T-bandage, -bar, -beard, etc.: see T 2, 3.

T-bone steak: see T 3 b.

tch, *int.* Also tchk, tcht. A representation of the dental click (freq. reduplicated) used to express vexation (cf. TCHICK *sb.*, TCK *int.*, TUT *int.* (*sb.*[3])). Hence **tch** *v. intr.*, to utter this exclamation; also as *sb.*, an utterance of this exclamation.

1898 G. B. SHAW *Mrs. Warren's Profession* I. 176 (Correcting him quickly in a loud whisper) Tch! Nonsense. **1906** N. MUNRO *Daft Days* ix. 74 'You'll find a curious fearless independence in her.' The twins held up their hands in amazement, 'tcht-tcht-tchting' simultaneously. '*What* a pity!' said Miss Jean, as if it were a physical affliction. **1910** —— in *Blackw. Mag.* Aug. 236/2 Aunt Amelia..tchk-tchked at such preposterous views. **1930** G. B. SHAW *Apple Cart* I. 21 Tch-tch-tch! Gently, Amanda, gently. **1971** *N.Z. Listener* 16 Aug. 50/3 The mind boggles. The dreadful deeds the little monkeys might perpetrate. Tch tch. **1977** *Daily Mirror* 31 Mar. 24 Tch! Of all the times to go down wi' flu! We've got a very important darts match tonight!

tch-, occas. used for CH- (tʃ), esp. in foreign words.

tcha, tchah (tʃɑː), *int.* An exclamation of impatience or contempt; = PSHAW.

1844 DICKENS *Mart. Chuz.* xxxvii, 'Tcha, Mr. Pinch!' cried Charity, with sharp impatience. **1887** FENN *Dick o' Fens* (1888) 22 Tchah! who cares? I don't.

Tchaikovskian (tʃaɪ'kɒfskɪən), *a.* and *sb.* Also Tchaikovskyan, Tschaikowskian. [f. the name of Peter Ilyich *Tchaikovsky* (1840–93), Russian composer + -IAN.] **A.** *adj.* Of, pertaining to, or characteristic of Tchaikovsky or his style. **B.** *sb.* One who favours or imitates the style of Tchaikovsky.

1937 *Observer* 15 Aug. 3/3 When the time comes for an appraisal..it will not be the Tschaikowskian.., or the Egdon Heath Sibelius..who seems nearest to being a composer of the very greatest rank. **1945** G. ABRAHAM *Tchaikovsky* VII. 138 The G minor andante portion of the.. penultimate scene stands out as truly Tchaikovskian. **1967** *Listener* 12 Jan. 73/3 It reminds one of what Tchaikovsky thought about Mozart, and incidentally of what Stravinsky —a Tchaikovskian to the hilt—thought about musical expression in general. **1973** *Gramophone* 29 June 15/3 The violin concerto is the least Finnish of Sibelius's major works, and its combination of Tchaikovskyan elements with a cosmopolitan concerto-style was emphasised by Pinchas Zukerman's suave, uncommitted manner. **1977** *Ibid.* Dec. 1097/2 The reprise of the Symphony's big tune at the end.. lacks the expansive richness that can give the Tchaikovskian a real *frisson* of pleasure. **1979** *Guardian* 23 Mar. 12/7 Tchaikovskian delicacy misses fire in this theatre.

tchaush, tchawoosh, varr. CHIAUS.

1819 T. HOPE *Anastasius* (1820) II. 377 A Tchawoosh.. walked in, and summoned me before the Soo-bashee. **1902** *Encycl. Brit.* XXVII. 213/2 The Sultan's guard consists of ..the 'Tufenkdjis'..the 'Tchaush', of whom there are between 50 and 60, and who are messengers as well as guards [etc.]. **1930** *Observer* 26 Jan. 11 In the last war a peasant's wife, Fatma Hanem, served in the Army as a tchaush, i.e. a sergeant.

tche, var. SE.

Tchehovian, var. CHEKHOVIAN *a.* and *sb.*

†**tcheir, tchyre**, obs. Sc. forms of CHAIR.

1535 LYNDESAY *Satyre* 1941 Heir sall the Carle clim vp and sit in the Kings tchyre. *Ibid.* 1953, I sall sit heir, into this tcheir.

Tcheka, var. CHEKA.

Tcheremiss, var. CHEREMIS(S.

tchernozem, var. CHERNOZEM.

tchervonetz, var. CHERVONETZ.

‖**tchetvert** ('tʃɛtvɛrt). Also chetvert. [Russian *tchetvert'* quarter, f. *tchetvero* four.] A Russian measure of capacity, = .68 of an imperial quarter.

1814 *The Commercial Secretary—Il Segretario di Commercio* (Leghorn) 290 Wheat. R 10 1f2 Stock expected to increase to nearly 15/m tschetwer, which embarasses the holders greatly. **1855** *Englishwoman in Russia* 184 The landowners in Russia..sent millions of tchetvas of corn out of the country, and left their own people in a state of absolute starvation. **1890** *Daily News* 5 Nov. 5/6 Of rye,..there were yielded 113 million tchetverts, the Russian quarter, as against 112, the average for the last five years.

tchibouk, variant spelling of CHIBOUK.

tchick (tʃɪk), *sb.* Also chick, tchek. A representation of the click made by pressing some part of the tongue against the palate and withdrawing it with suction. Properly, the unilateral palatal click, used to urge on a horse; in quot. 1849, the dental click used to express vexation (in this case also spelt *'ts*, or *tut*). So

tchick *v. intr.*, to utter this exclamation, or to make a sound resembling it.

1823 SCOTT *Quentin D.* xiv, Summing up the whole with a provoking wink and such an interjectional *tchick* as men quicken a dull horse with. **1824** —— *Redgauntlet* Let. vii, We heard Benjie gee-hupping, tchek-tcheking, and above all flogging, in great style. **1849** MRS. CARLYLE in *Lett.* (1883) II. 55 The young lady tchick-tchicked, and looked deprecatingly. **1887** *Harper's Mag.* Dec. 32/2 'That thar's moughty good string',.. Sterling could not refrain from observing, as the stout twine 'tchicked' in several pieces under a garden knife.

‖**tchin** (tʃin). [Russian *chin* rank.] Rank; person or persons of quality.

1861 R. CECIL in *Sat. Rev.* 2 Mar. 228/2 The Emperor is practically an absentee landlord, knowing nothing of his estate except what the tchin is pleased to tell him. **1885** *Contemp. Rev.* Jan. 105 The name of the father is also the same: the tchin (rank) likewise! **1904** *Daily Chron.* 29 July 4/4 M. Plehve.. well knew that the Tsar, the amiable youngster,.. was a tool in the hands of the omnipotent tchin.

Comb. **1904** *Contemp. Rev.* Aug. 165 The dismal tchin-ridden Russian villages.

‖**tchincou** (ˈtʃɪŋkuː). [Javanese.] A black-crested monkey of Java, *Semnopithecus melalophus.*

1891 in *Cent. Dict.*

tchinovnik, var. CHINOVNIK.

tchornozem, var. CHERNOZEM.

tchotchke: see TSATSKE.

tchu, tchuh (tʃʌ), *int.* An exclamation expressing impatience, dissent, or the like.

1859 GEO. ELIOT *A. Bede* ii, 'Tchu!' said Ben,.. 'what's folks's kin got to do wi't? Not a chip'. **1861** —— *Silas M.* vii, 'Tchuh!', said the farrier. And then he asked,.. 'How much money might there be in the bags, Master Marner?'

Tchuktchi, var. CHUKCHEE, CHUKCHI.

tchyre, obs. Sc. f. CHAIR: see TCHEIR.

tck, *int.* [Palatal click formed by suction.] An exclamation of surprise or vexation: cf. TCHICK.

1893 KIPLING *Many Invent.* 199 Tck! Tck! And thou art in charge.

te[1], **ti** (tiː). *Mus.* Also tee. Now the more usual name, in English-speaking countries, of SI. Cf. *tonic sol-fa* s.v. TONIC *a.* 3 b.

1839 S. A. GLOVER *Scheme for rendering Psalmody Congregational* (ed. 2) 41 *Te* is the *subsemitone* or leading half tone *below* the tonic. **1889** GROVE *Dict. Mus.* IV. 144/1 Tonic Sol-fa... The ancient sound-names do, re, mi, etc... are put before a class.. in the form of a printed picture of the scale, called a 'Modulator'. For simplicity's sake they are spelt English-wise, and *si* is called *te* to avoid having two names with the same initial letter. **1944** W. APPEL *Harvard Dict. Mus.* 690/1 The syllables mostly used today are: *do.., re, mi, fa, sol, la, si* (*ti*). **1969** *Listener* 31 July 162/2 Everything becomes dubious if you suddenly decide to make tee a new doh. **1980** C. HEADINGTON *Illustr. Dict. Mus. Terms* 134/1 Solmisation, a system of designating the notes of a diatonic scale by syllables.. *do, re, mi, fa, sol.., la, ti.*

‖**te**[2] (də). Also Te, teh, tih. [Chinese *dé* virtue.] **a.** In Taoism, the essence of Tao inherent in all beings. **b.** In Confucianism and in extended use, moral virtue.

1895 G. G. ALEXANDER *Lâo-Tsze: Great Thinker* 123 It is very puzzling to know when '*tih*' is to be treated as a Divine attribute, and when it is to be taken as a moral virtue. **1904** W. G. OLD tr. *Laotze's Bk. of Simple Way* li. 114 Tao brings forth, and Teh nourishes. **1912** [see LI[3]]. **1934** A. D. WALEY *Way & its Power* 32 Hence *tê* means a latent power, a 'virtue' inherent in something. **1955** E. HERBERT *Taoist Notebk.* 18 If allowed free play.. these gifts of *Tê* were ample to insure the orderly progression of 'heaven and earth', the disciplined march of 'the ten thousand creatures', all in their ranks and all in step with *Tao*. **1963** D. C. LAU *Lao Tzu* 42 *Te* means 'virtue', and seems to be related to its homophone meaning 'to get'. In its Taoist usage, *te* refers to the virtue of a thing (which is what it 'gets' from the *tao*). In other words, *te* is the nature of a thing, because it is in virtue of its *te* that a thing is what it is. **1975** C.-Y. CHANG *Tao* xxxviii. 107 The real meaning of *Tê* is thus the attainment of the self-cultivation of non-discrimination, non-differentiation, and above all, non-willing.

te, var. TEE *v.*[1] *Obs.*; obs. f. TO *prep.*

te, ME. assimilated form of THE, THEE, after dentals, etc.: see T 8.

te-, obs. or dial. variant of TO- *pref.*

tea (tiː), *sb.* Forms: 7 (9) **tay, tey,** 7 **té, thé, the,** 7–8 **tee, thea,** 7– **tea.** See also CHA, CHIA. [= F. *thé*, Sp. *te*, It. *tè*, Du. and Ger. *thee*, Da., Sw. *te*, mod.L. *thea*; ad. (perh. through Malay *te, teh*) Chinese, Amoy dialect *te*, in Fuchau *tiä* = Mandarin *ch'a* (in ancient Chinese prob. *kia*); whence Pg. and obs. Sp. *cha*, obs. It. *ciá*, Russian *chaĭ*, Pers., Urdu *chā* (10th c.), Arab. *shāy*, Turkish *chāy*. The Portuguese brought the form *cha* (which is Cantonese as well as Mandarin) from Macao. This form also passed overland into Russia. The form *te* (*thé*) was brought into Europe by the Dutch, prob. from the Malay at Bantam (if not from Formosa, where the Fuhkien or Amoy form was used). The original English pronunciation (teː), sometimes indicated by spelling *tay*, is found in rimes down to 1762, and remains in many dialects; but the current (tiː) is found already in the 17th c., shown in rimes and by the spelling *tee.*]

1. a. The leaves of the tea-plant (see 3), usually in a dried and prepared state for making the drink (see 2); first imported into Europe in the 17th century, and now extensively used in various parts of the world.

According to Meyer, *Konversations-Lexikon*, the first mention of it in Europe is due to the Portuguese in 1559 (under the name *cha*); *chia* is mentioned in Maffei's *Historia Indica* in 1588. Under the name *te, thee*, it was imported by the Dutch from Bantam (where brought by Chinese merchants from Amoy) *c* 1610; first known in Paris 1635, in Russia (by way of Tartary) 1638, in England about 1650–55.

[**1598** W. PHILLIP tr. *Linschoten* I. xxvi. 46/1 The aforesaid warme water is made with the powder of a certaine hearbe called Chaa.] **1655** tr. *Semedo's Hist. China* I. iii. 19 *Chá* is a leafe of a tree, about the bignesse of Mirtle; [*marg. note*] its called also Tay. *c* **1660** [T. GARWAY] (*title*) An Exact Description of the Growth, Quality, and Vertues of the Leaf Tee, alias Tay. *c* **1665** *Ibid.*, These are to give notice that the said Thomas Garway hath Tea to sell from sixteen to fifty shillings the pound. **1667** *Lond. Gaz.* No. 206/3 The most considerable Wares being Cinamon, Ebony, Thea, and Camphire. **1667–8** *E. Ind. Co.'s Let.* 24 Jan. (Letter Bks. IV. 137), Wee desire you to procure and send us by these ships 100[lb]. waight of the best Tey that you can gett. **1676** BEAL in *Phil. Trans.* XI. 586 The tops of red Sage in blossom,.. dried in the shade,.. did excel the famous Thea, the Chinois themselves being Judges. **1680** *Lond. Gaz.* No. 1573/4 A small parcel of most excellent tea.. to be sold,.. the lowest price is 30s. a pound. **1728** MRS. DELANY in *Life & Corr.* Ser. I. (1861) I. 172 The man at the Poultry has tea of all prices,—Bohea from thirteen to twenty shillings, and green from twelve to thirty. **1832** *Veg. Subst. Food* 375 Tea.. first imported into Europe by the Dutch East-India Company, in the.. seventeenth century. **1838** T. THOMSON *Chem. Org. Bodies* 858 Tea.. is composed of the dried leaves of the *thea bohea* and *thea viridis*.

b. With qualifying words, denoting various kinds, chiefly distinguished by the mode of preparation (also applied to the beverages made from these: see 2): the main classes being **black tea,** which is exposed to the air for some time, so as to produce fermentation, before roasting; and **green tea,** which is roasted almost immediately after gathering, and often also artificially coloured.

Black teas include BOHEA, CONGOU, OOLONG, PEKOE, SOUCHONG; green teas, GUNPOWDER (or PEARL), HYSON, etc. See also *brick-tea* (BRICK *sb.*[1] 10), †*cowslip tea* (COWSLIP 3).

1704 *Lond. Gaz.* No. 4059/4 Green and Bohee Tea. **1712** ADDISON *Spect.* No. 328 Green, Imperial, Peco, and Bohea-Tea. **1785** *Rolliad* 53 What tongue can tell the various kinds of Tea? Of Blacks and Greens, of Hyson and Bohea; With Singlo, Congou, Pekoe and Souchong, Couslip the fragrant, Gun-powder the Strong. **1795** ANDERSON *Brit. Embassy China* 186 The Imperial and gunpowder teas:.. the former .. collected from the first, and the other from the successive blossoms of that plant. **1832** *Veg. Subst. Food* 379 There are three kinds of green tea.. one called hyson, hayssuen, is composed of leaves.. carefully picked. **1888** J. PATON *Tea* in *Encycl. Brit.* XXIII. 97/2 Black and green tea are made indifferently from the leaves of the same plant.

c. Phrases. ***given away with a pound of tea***: see GIVE *v.* 54 a; ***not for all the tea in China*** (colloq., orig. Austral.): not at any price.

1937 PARTRIDGE *Dict. Slang* 148/1 *China!, not for all the tea in*, certainly not!; on no account: Australian coll.: from the 1890's. **1943** K. TENNANT *Ride on Stranger* ii. 19 I'm not going to stand in my girl's light for all the tea in China. **1958** J. CANNAN *And be Villain* vi. 137 She wouldn't get into a sidecar or on a pillion for all the tea in China. **1978** *Radio Times* 11–24 Mar. 25/5, I wouldn't change Newcastle for all the tea in China... It's a lovely place to live in.

2. a. A drink made by infusing these leaves in hot water, having a somewhat bitter and aromatic flavour, and acting as a moderate stimulant; largely used as a beverage.

[**1601–1625**: see CHIA. **1631** BONTIUS *Hist. Nat. et Med. Indiæ Orient.* I. vi. (1658) 12 *Dur.* Memineras de Chinensium *Thee* vocato Potu, quid tu de eo sentis? *Bont.* Herbula unde hoc The conficitur [etc.].] **1658** *Mercurius Politicus* 23 Sept. 887 *Advt.*, That excellent.. drink called by the Chineans Tcha, by other Nations Tay alias Tee. **1660** PEPYS *Diary* 25 Sept., I did send for a cup of tee (a China drink) of which I never had drunk before. **1663** DRYDEN *Wild Gallant* I. ii, I sent for three dishes of tea. **1679** LOCKE in Ld. King *Life* (ed. Bohn) 135 Foreign drinks to be found in England are.. coffé, thé and chocolate at coffee houses. **1694** CONGREVE *Double Dealer* I. i, They are at the end of the gallery, retired to their tea and scandal.. after dinner. **1711** ADDISON *Spect.* No. 10 ¶2 All well-regulated Families, that set apart an Hour in every Morning for Tea and Bread and Butter. **1711** POPE *Rape of Lock* III. 8 Here, thou, great Anna! whom three realms obey, Dost sometimes counsel take—and sometimes Tea. *c* **1720** PRIOR *To Yng. Gentl. in Love* 58 He thank'd her on his bended knee; Then drank a quart of milk and tea. **1762** *Gentl. Mag.* Apr. 187/2 No crowding sycophants from day to day, Came to admire the babe—but more the tea. **1834** LANG in *Tait's Mag.* I. 414/1 In the bush, or uncultivated country in New South Wales, tea is the universal beverage. **1858** LYTTON *What will he do* I. vi, Your tea will get quite cold.

b. ***cup of tea*** (colloq. phr.): see CUP *sb.* 12 b.

c. A cupful of tea.

1922 JOYCE *Ulysses* 729 We both ordered 2 teas and plain bread and butter. **1976** B. GIBSON *Birmingham Bombs* xii. 104 Three teas, two coffees, and a large steak and kidney pie.

d. ***one's tea***: what interests or suits one. *rare.* Cf. CUP *sb.* 12 b (ii).

1934 E. WAUGH *Handful of Dust* iii. 135 Are you *certain* Jenny will be Tony's tea?

e. ***tea and sympathy***: consolation offered to a distressed person. Also *attrib.*

1956 (*film title*) Tea and sympathy. **1958** *Listener* 2 Oct. 537/1 We leave Mrs. Newby enjoying tea and sympathy. **1970** Y. CARTER *Mr. Campion's Falcon* i. 7 He was a tea-and-sympathy man, full of tactful advice. **1978** J. HIGGINS *Day of Judgment* xii. 168 'There may be something I could do.' 'Tea and sympathy... No more than that.'

3. The plant from which tea is obtained, a shrub of the genus *Thea* (now often included in *Camellia*), N.O. *Ternstrœmiaceæ*, with white flowers, and oval pointed slightly toothed evergreen leaves; cultivated from ancient times in China, Japan, India, and adjacent countries. (Now chiefly in comb., as *tea-leaf, -plant*, etc.)

The plants yielding the tea of commerce are comprised in the species *T. chinensis* or *C. theifera* (including two varieties *T. Bohea* and *T. viridis*, sometimes reckoned as different species), of China and Japan, and *T.* (or *C.*) *assamica*, of Assam and India; the latter is found wild in Upper Assam, and is by some supposed to be the original type.

1663 BOYLE *Usef. Exp. Nat. Philos.* II. ii. 104 That Herb, which the French and we call *Thé*, or *Té*, which is much magnified here. **1685** J. CHAMBERLAYNE *Coffee, Tea & Choc.* 38 The most excellent leaves of Cha, or Tea, are found in the provinces of Kiangnon. **1745** P. THOMAS *Jrnl. Anson's Voy.* 193 Because warm Water is unpalatable.., they [the Chinese] bethought themselves of putting some Leaves of a Tree into it, to give it a better Taste. Those of Tea seemed to be the best.

4. a. A meal or social entertainment at which tea is served; *esp.* an ordinary afternoon or evening meal, at which the usual beverage is tea (but sometimes cocoa, chocolate, coffee, or other substitute). Now usu. a light meal in the late afternoon, but locally in the U.K. (esp. northern), and in Australia and N.Z., a cooked evening meal; in Jamaica, the first meal of the day.

high tea, meat tea: see HIGH *a.* 21, MEAT *sb.* 6. ***tea and turn-out***: see TURN-OUT.

1738 SWIFT *Pol. Conversat.* Introd. 2 Whether they meet ..at Meals, Tea, or Visits. **1778** MISS BURNEY *Evelina* (1791) I. xxvi. 144, I was relieved by a summons to tea. **1789** WESLEY *Wks.* (1872) IV. 453 At breakfast and at tea, on these two days, I met all the Society. **1833** HT. MARTINEAU *Loom & Lugger* I. iii, She asked Rebecca if she would come to tea at their house. **1882** FR. A. KEMBLE *Later Life* II. 187 My first introduction to 'afternoon tea' took place during this visit to Belvoir [in 1842]. I do not believe that the now universally-honoured institution of 'five o'clock tea' dates further back than this. **1897** MISS HARRADEN *H. Strafford, Remitt. Man* iii, A rattling good tea—hot rolls, fried potatoes, and quail. **1901** CLARK RUSSELL *Ship's Adv.* iv, Mrs. Brierly spread a liberal tea upon the table. **1914** G. B. SHAW *Misalliance* 80 He calls his lunch his dinner, and has his tea at half-past six. Havnt you, dear? *a* **1925** [see MARKET *sb.* 1 b]. **1938** N. MARSH *Artists in Crime* vi. 81 'We finished tea at half-past eight, about.' 'The gentleman is talking of the evening meal. They dine at noon in the Antipodes, I understand.' **1952** in Cassidy & Le Page *Dict. Jamaican English* (1967) 439/1 Tea—same as chaklata... Tea at 6:30 A.M. **1957** *N.Z. Listener* 22 Nov. 4/3 More than one New Zealander has been invited to 'tea' in England and arrived hours too late, the meal finished and the guests gone. **1968** *Southerly* XXVIII. 5 'What have you got for tea?' he asked. .. 'It's a coupla nice little bits of fillet Mr. Ballard let me have.'

b. ***to take tea with*** (colonial slang): to have dealings with, associate with; *esp.* to deal with in a hostile manner, engage with, encounter.

1888 'R. BOLDREWOOD' *Robbery under Arms* xxxvii, 'Maybe we'll take tay with the rest of 'em now'. They didn't know the man they were after, or they'd have just as soon have gone to 'take tea', as they called it, with a tiger. **1896** KIPLING *Seven Seas, Lost Legion* ii, Take tea with the giddy Masai. **1905** *Daily Chron.* 2 June 3/3 In polite circles genealogies are tabooed, the slightest trace of hybridity barring 'taking tea', as the local phrase has it.

c. ***to go*** (***out***) ***for one's tea*** (see quots.). *N. Ir. slang.*

1978 F. BURTON *Politics of Legitimacy* iii. 78 A Provo would scoff at the Officials' merely elocutionary skills while they were 'going out for their tea' (that is, going on military operations which might result in their death). **1979** *Courier-Mail* (Brisbane) 1 Mar. 5/1 'Going for your tea' in Belfast can be a painful experience—being dragged out by a terrorist punishment squad to get a bullet in the legs.

5. Used as a general name for infusions made in the same way as tea (sense 2), usually from the leaves, blossoms, or other parts of plants; mostly used medicinally, sometimes as ordinary drinks.

Commonly with defining words, as ***alehoof, balm, beef, camomile, camphor, coffee, cowslip, hartshorn, laurel, lemon, lemon-grass, poppy, rosemary, sage, saloop, sassafras, senna, tilleul, valerian, willow*** (etc.) ***tea***: see these words. So humorously ***limestone tea*** (quot. 1723).

1665–6 *Phil. Trans.* I. 250 They dry.. Sage-leaves.. and prepare them like The, and.. get for one pound of it, four times as much The. **1699** EVELYN *Acetaria* §27. 27 Some of them [flowers] are Pickl'd, and divers of them make also very pleasant and wholsome Theas, as do likewise the Wild Time, Bugloss, Mint, &c. **1723** STUKELEY *Let.* 22 July, in *Mem.* (Surtees) III. 249, I am just drinking your health in a swinger of limestone thea [Bath water]. **1724** WATTS *Logic* I. iv. §4 Tea, which was the proper name of one sort of Indian leaf, is now-a-days become a common name for many infusions of herbs, or plants, in water: as sage-tea, alehoof-tea, limon-tea, etc. **1727** A. HAMILTON *New Acc. E. Ind.* II. l. 222 He treated me with Tartarian Tea, which I took to be

Beans boyled in Milk, with some salt. **1731** *Gentl. Mag.* I. 314 Of some of these Ingredients [Marsh Mallow, &c.] so dried, make Tea, as you do common Tea, with boiling hot Water. **1778** R. JAMES *Diss. Fevers* 135 Any syrup, jelly of currants, barley-water, gruel, or any sort of tea. **1783** S. CHAPMAN in *Med. Commun.* I. 305 He was advised to leave off drinking foreign tea, and to drink valerian, or rosemary, tea. **1795** tr. *Thunberg's Trav.* I. 128 Of the leaves of the *barbonia cordata* the country people made tea. **1863** BATES *Nat. Amazon* iv. (1864) 92 The men had made a fire in the galley, to make tea of an acid herb called 'erva cidreira'. **1866** *Treas. Bot.* 1127 *Lemon-grass Tea*, an infusion of the leaves of *Andropogon Schœnanthus*, substituted for tea in many of the interior districts of India. *Ibid.*, *Tea..of heaven*, a Japanese name for the leaves of *Hydrangea Thunbergii.* **1881** *Trans. Obstet. Soc. Lond.* XXII. 32 The word 'tea' is by the natives of this island [Jamaica] applied to any infusion made from leaves of plants either fresh or dry. 'Cotton leaf tea' is made from the green leaves of one of the shrubs that produces the cotton of commerce. **1893** BARING-GOULD *Cheap Jack Z.* II. xvi. 41 It is given poppy tea, and that sends it to sleep.

6. With defining words, applied to various plants whose leaves, flowers, etc. are used in the same way as tea, either for beverages, or medicinally (also to the leaves, etc. themselves, or the drink infused from them). (See also TEA-PLANT, TEA-TREE.)

Abyssinian tea = *Arabian tea*, (*a*). **Algerian tea**, species of *Paronychia*, from whose flowers a medicinal tea is made. **Appalachian tea**, (*a*) *Viburnum cassinoides*; (*b*) *Ilex Cassine*, *I. vomitoria*, or *Prinos glaber*. **Arabian tea**, (*a*) *Catha edulis*, whose leaves furnish a stimulating beverage used in Arabia; (*b*) = *Algerian tea*. **Australian tea**, (*a*) 'several species of *Leptospermum* and *Melaleuca*' (*Treas. Bot.* 1866): see TEA-TREE 2; (*b*) = *Botany Bay tea* (Morris *Austral Eng.* 1898). **Barbary tea**, the box-thorn or Duke of Argyll's tea-tree, *Lycium barbarum*. **Bencoolen tea**, *Glaphyria nitida* (*Leptospermum nitidum*), of the Malayan islands. **Blue Mountain** or **golden rod tea**, *Solidago odora* of North America, from whose leaves and flowers a beverage is made. **Botany Bay tea**, an Australian species of sarsaparilla, *Smilax glycyphylla*, also called *sweet tea*. **Bourbon tea** = *Faham tea*. **Brazil** or **Brazilian tea**, *Stachytarpha jamaicensis*. **bush tea**, *Cyclopia genistoides* of S. Africa. **Canada tea** = TEA-BERRY: see CANADA. **Canary tea**, *Sida canariensis* (*S. rhombifolia*). **Carolina tea**, *Ilex vomitoria*: = *Appalachian tea*, (*b*). †**Ceylon tea**, *Elæodendron glaucum*: see TEA-TREE 3 (*obs.*). **faham tea**, a tropical orchid, *Angræcum fragrans*. †**false tea** = *Paraguay tea*. **Hottentot's tea**, *Helichrysum serpyllifolium* (see HOTTENTOT 3). **Jesuits' tea**, (*a*) *Psoralea glandulosa* (see JESUIT *sb.* 4 c; (*b*) = *Paraguay tea* (Cent. Dict.). **Kaffir tea**, *Helichrysum nudifolium* (see KAFFIR 4). **Labrador tea**, *Ledum latifolium* and *L. palustre* (see LABRADOR). **Malay tea**, (*a*) = *Bencoolen tea*; (*b*) *Eugenia variabilis*. **marsh tea**, *Ledum palustre* (Cent. Dict.). **Mexican tea**, (*a*) *Ambrina* (*Chenopodium*) *ambrosioides*; (*b*) = *Jesuits' tea*, (*a*): see MEXICAN A. b. **mountain tea** = TEA-BERRY: see MOUNTAIN 9 d. **New Jersey tea**, *Ceanothus americanus* (see quot. 1858). **New Zealand tea**, *Leptospermum scoparium*: see TEA-TREE 2. **Oswego tea**: see OSWEGO 2. **Paraguay tea**, *Ilex paraguayensis*, extensively used in S. America as a substitute for tea: see PARAGUAY 1. **St. Bartholomew's tea** = *Paraguay tea* (Cent. Dict.). **St. Helena tea**, *Beatsonia* (*Frankenia*) *portulacifolia*. **soldiers' tea** = MATICO. **South Sea tea** = *Paraguay tea*; also an erroneous name for Carolina tea. **Surinam tea**, 'various species of *Lantana*' (Miller *Plant-n.*). **sweet tea** = *Botany Bay tea*. **teamster's tea**, a N. American plant, *Ephedra antisyphilitica*, used as a remedy for venereal affections. **Theezan tea**, *Sageretia theezans*, a thorny rhamnaceous shrub of S. China, whose leaves are said to be used for tea by the poorer classes. **West Indian tea**, *Capraria biflora*, also called *goat-weed*. **wild tea**, a N. American leguminous shrub, *Amorpha canescens*, also called *lead-plant*.

1727–41 CHAMBERS *Cycl.*, South-Sea tea [see PARAGUAY 1]. **1760** J. LEE *Introd. Bot.* App. 321 Osweego Thea, *Monarda* [*didyma*]. *Ibid.* 329 False Tea, *Ilex*. *Ibid.*, New Jersey Tea, *Ceanothus*. *Ibid.*, Paraguay Tea, *Ilex*. *Ibid.*, South-sea Tea, *Ilex*. **1764** *Museum Rust.* II. xxxviii. 117 The South-Sea tea, which is thought to be the same plant as the Paraguay tea; but whether it is the same as the tea brought from China, is yet undetermined. **1788** D. CONSIDEN *Let. to Banks* in *Hist. Rec. N.S. Wales* (1892) I. II. 220, I have sent you some of the sweet tea of this country,.. it is a good anti-scorbutic. **1790** J. WHITE *Voy. N.S. Wales* 195 The sweet-tea is a creeping kind of vine..the taste is sweet, exactly like the liquorice root of the shops. **1814** ROXBURGH *Hort. Bengal.* 18 *Elæodendrum glaucum*, Ceylon Tea. **1857** HENFREY *Elem. Bot.* § 508. 336 [The leaves] of *Ilex Paraguayensis*, called Maté or Paraguay Tea, resemble Tea in property. **1858** HOGG *Veg. Kingd.* lxvi. 237 The leaves of *Ceanothus americanus* were used during the revolutionary war as a substitute for tea, and hence it is called New Jersey Tea. *Ibid.* cxv. 482 The leaves [of *Gaultheria procumbens*].. make an excellent substitute for tea,..and the plant is.. called Tea-berry and Mountain Tea. *Ibid.* cxix. 489 *Ilex vomitoria* has been erroneously called South Sea Tea, from the supposition that it was the same plant as *I. paraguensis*. **1866** *Treas. Bot.* 49 *Ambrina ambrosioides*, or Mexican Tea, ..long naturalised in the south of Europe, is used medicinally. *Ibid.* 369 The leaflets of [*Cyclopia genistoides*] are used at the Cape in infusion or decoction for promoting expectoration... It is called Bush Tea. [*Ibid.* 1005 *S*[*ageretia*] *theezans*, the Tia of the Chinese, is a thorny shrub, with..finely-toothed egg-shaped leaves..somewhat resembling those of the tea-shrub.] *Ibid.* 1090 [The] leaves [of *Stachytarpha jamaicensis*] are sometimes used to adulterate tea, and in Austria they are sold under the name of Brazilian tea. *Ibid.* 1127 Tea, Abyssinian,..Appalachian [etc.],..Arabian,..Australian [etc.]. **1904** *Dunglison's Dict. Med.* (ed. 23), *Matico*... the leaves of Piper angustifolium or soldiers' tea or herb.

7. *slang.* **a.** Spirituous or intoxicating liquor. †**b.** Urine (*obs.*).

1693 *Remonstr. Batchelors* in *Harl. Misc.* (ed. Park) IV. 505 Since their sex has been so familiar with brandy (blasphemed by the name of cold tea). **1716** GAY *Trivia* II. 176 The thoughtless Wits..Who 'gainst the Centry's Box discharge their Tea. **1887** HISSEY *Holiday on Road* 370 Tea or coffee were always at our command, Scotch tea also (i.e. whisky). **1902** *Times* 29 Oct. 5/6 It was all owing to the 'tea'. .. He understood that this was a slang term for drink.

c. Marijuana; *spec.* marijuana brewed in hot water to make a drink. orig. *U.S.*

1935 A. J. POLLOCK *Underworld Speaks* 119/2 *Tea*, mariahuana; hashish. **1940** [see JU-JU[2]]. **1950** *San Francisco Chron.* 22 Feb. 20/1 A couple of years ago she started blowing tea. **1957** [see CONNEXION 6 c]. **1967** *Boston Sunday Herald* 26 Mar. IV. 1/1 Marijuana..when brewed with hot water,..is called 'tea'. **1979** *High Times* Mar. 18/2 Consider the number of words that served for a time and then passed into embarrassed silence. 'Muggles' and 'tea'—words that sound right only in Raymond Chandler novels now.

8. Florists' abbreviation of TEA-ROSE.

1869 S. R. HOLE *Bk. Roses* vi. 77 The autumn leaves.., decayed to mould, are very advantageous to the Teas, Noisettes, and Bourbons. **1889** *Pall Mall G.* 6 July 3/2 At Cheshunt about 200,000 standard rose seedlings and 40,000 'teas' are sown every year. **1901** *Eliza. & German Gard.* 17, I wish now I had put teas there. *Ibid.* 18, I made my teas face a northern winter.

9. *attrib.* and *Comb.* **a.** *attrib.* Of, pertaining or relating to, dealing or connected with tea as a commodity, as ***tea act, bill, -broker, -dealer, -duty, -hong*** (see HONG), ***industry, merchant, -tax, trade, warehouse***; or as a beverage, as ***tea-breakfast, -dinner, -dregs, junketing, picnic, soirée, -supper, -visit***; containing or intended to contain tea, as ***tea-bowl, -hamper, -jar, -mug, -pail, -slop***; of or pertaining to the tea-plant or its cultivation, as ***tea crop, cultivation, culture, district, estate, -farming, -field, -hill, nursery, plantation, -seed, -tract***. **b.** Objective and obj. gen., as ***tea-blender, -grower, -packer, -producer, -sipper, -spiller, -strainer; tea-blending, -growing, -loving, -packing, -picking, -swilling*** sbs. and adjs.; instrumental and parasynthetic, as ***tea-bathed, -coated, -coloured, -covered, -drowned, -dunked, -inspired, -sodden*** adjs.; also similative, as ***tea-brown*** adj.

1746 LOCKMAN *To 1st Promoter Cambrick & Tea Bills* 13 *note*, Since the *Tea-Act pass'd last session, the revenue is increased 85,000*l.* per annum. **1922** JOYCE *Ulysses* 258 He smiled at bronze's *tea-bathed lips, at listening lips and eyes. **1904** *Westm. Gaz.* 15 Aug. 6/2 The big *tea-blenders naturally took advantage of this cheapness to push and extend their business. **1901** *Daily Chron.* 6 May 9/3 Man wanted for *tea blending warehouse. **1865** G. MEREDITH *Rhoda Fleming* xxxii, The squire..drank, defying ladies and the new-fangled subserviency to those flustering *tea-bodies. **1886** *Guide Galleries Brit. Mus.* 209 On the upper shelves are examples of..*tea-bowls. **1825** HONE *Every-day Bk.* I. 951, I..got up to a hot *tea-breakfast. **1770** *Chron.* in *Ann. Reg.* 154/2 A *tea-broker, charged with forging a warrant for the delivery of three chests of tea. **1922** JOYCE *Ulysses* 532 A nymph with hair unbound, lightly clad in *tea-brown art colours, descends from her grotto. **1902** *Westm. Gaz.* 31 Dec. 9/3 The *Tea Clearing House has succumbed to the attack of tea producers, importers, dealers, and brokers. **1953** DYLAN THOMAS *Under Milk Wood* (1954) 48 Willy Nilly the Postman's dark and sizzling damp *tea-coated misty pygmy kitchen. **1829** W. H. MAXWELL *Stories Waterloo* I. 194 Short tights of *tea-coloured leather. **1897** J. A. GRAHAM *Threshold Three Closed Lands* ii. 30 As our eye follows up one of the *tea-covered spurs it lights on the houses of Darjeeling. **1906** *Month* Feb. 177 Sides green with sprouting *tea crops. **1842** *Penny Cycl.* XXIV. 286/2 Papers respecting *tea cultivation in India. *Ibid.* 286/1 The *tea-culture in Assam. **1758** *Chron.* in *Ann. Reg.* I. 111/1 Four *tea dealers were tried before the commissioners of excise. **1886** C. E. PASCOE *London of To-day* xxii. (ed. 3) 216 The premises of one of the oldest firms in London—those of the Messrs. Twining, tea-dealers and bankers. **1862** R. C. MAYNE *Brit. Columbia* 121 We lunched with him, returning to the fort for a *tea-dinner. **1896** *Allbutt's Syst. Med.* I. 402 That customary but very unwholesome combination the tea-dinner is to be avoided. **1842** *Penny Cycl.* XXIV. 286/1 There are green tea and black *tea districts. **1882** W. D. HAY *Brighter Britain!* I. 161 What will be the future of these young *tea-drowned nations? **1973** M. AMIS *Rachel Papers* 68 A small middle-aged man (with unusually big brown ears, like *tea-dunked ginger-biscuits). **1842** *Penny Cycl.* XXIV. 291/1 The tariff of 1842 has made no alteration in the *tea-duty. **1886** *Pall Mall G.* 19 May 6/1 The new industry of *tea-farming.. promises to become a new source of wealth to Ceylon. **1895** CLIVE HOLLAND *Jap. Wife* 110 The cemeteries and *tea-fields stretched below us. **1888** J. PATON in *Encycl. Brit.* XXIII. 99/1 Comparatively few regions are suited for practical *tea-growing. *Ibid.* 99/1 The capacities of Assam as a tea-growing country. **1854** *Zoologist* XII. 4206 The *tea-hills in the province of Chekiang. **1885** *Cornh. Mag.* Mar. 281 [The tea-leaves are] fired under their own supervision in the great *tea-hongs. **1888** J. PATON in *Encycl. Brit.* XXIII. 102/1 Next to the United Kingdom, the greatest *tea-importing nation is the United States. *Ibid.* 99/1 The *tea industry has developed in Ceylon with marvellous rapidity. **1891** B. E. MARTIN *Footpr. Chas. Lamb* iii. 65 Hazlitt, with..his *tea-inspired turgidity. **1870** C. SCHREIBER *Jrnl.* (1911) I. 74 An old Staffordshire Ware *tea-jar. *Ibid.*, Our purchase of the George III tea-jar. **1983** J. SLIGO *Concert Masters* iv. 105 The Chinese tea jar on the mantelpiece. **1820** W. IRVING *Sketch Bk.* xxvi. (1859) 189 Little humdrum *tea junketings. **1883** *Cassell's Fam. Mag.* Aug. 529/1 The *tea-loving English public. **1888** J. PATON in *Encycl. Brit.* XXIII. 99/1 It is these tender shoots.. which alone are gathered for *tea manufacture. **1781** S. A. PETERS *Hist. Connecticut* 407 [To] exert themselves..in favour of the Bostonian *tea-merchants. **1842** *Penny Cycl.* XXIV. 291/2 The number of tea merchants who resort to Canton. **1955** T. H. PEAR *English Social Differences* viii. 186 There is said to be a class which considers the *tea-mug very *chic*. **1842** *Penny Cycl.* XXIV. 286/2 When the *tea nurseries were established in Assam. **1904** *Daily News* 13 Oct. 12 The dispute between the *tea-packers and the management of the Co-operative Wholesale Society. **1898** *Daily Chron.* 24 Sept. 10/6 Boy wanted..in *tea-packing warehouse. **1906** *Macm. Mag.* Apr. 457 Their..method is to stalk the Chinese of either sex when they are engaged in *tea-picking. **1842** *Penny Cycl.* XXIV. 286/2 The *tea plantations established in the Kumaon and Gurhwal districts. **1894** *Westm. Gaz.* 5 Jan. 6/3 The British have become..the greatest *tea-producers..in the world. **1888** J. PATON in *Encycl. Brit.* XXIII. 98/2 Till well into the 19th century..China and Japan were the only two *tea-producing countries. **1786** M. CUTLER in *Life*, etc. (1888) I. 190, I have no doubt the *tea seed..may be obtained from the East Indies in a vegetative state. **1756** HANWAY *Ess. Tea* viii. 245 Were they the sons of *tea-sippers, who won the fields of Cressy and Agincourt? **1906** JOYCE *Let.* 8 Dec. (1966) II. 201 Your friend..ought to get a running kick in the arse for writing his *tea-slop about it. **1967** E. A. GOLLSCHEWSKY in *Coast to Coast 1965–6* 94 Ettie surveyed the tea-table. It was still fairly orderly... No tea-slops in saucers. **1849** THACKERAY *Pendennis* xliv, A brilliant **tea soirée*. **1877** G. W. BALFOUR in *Encycl. Brit.* VII. 482/1 *Tea-sots are well known to be affected with palpitation and irregularity of the heart. **1837** W. PHILLIPS in C. Martyn *Life* (1890) 96 Certainly we sons of the *tea-spillers are a marvellously patient generation! [Cf. TEA-PARTY 2 a.] **1906** *Daily Colonist* (Victoria, B.C.) 26 Jan. 4/6 Kitchen utilities ..*Tea Strainers. **1970** *Kay's Catal.* *1970/71 Autumn/Winter* 895 A stainless steel tea strainer and a decorated ceramic tile are set into a Teak wood base in this contemporary Danish design. **1892** ZANGWILL *Childr. Ghetto* I. 198 The story-book which Moses read out after *tea-supper. **1888** J. PATON in *Encycl. Brit.* XXIII. 101/1 Dependent on China for its *tea supply. **1961** *Times* 2 Oct. 13/4 Arms akimbo, bridling, bristling, and scolding, the *tea-swilling Dame would at last be caught in the mangle. **1907** *Edin. Rev.* July 97 The *tea-tax strikes tea-drinkers only. **1842** *Penny Cycl.* XXIV. 286/2 At first only a few [indigenous] *tea-tracts were discovered [in Assam]. **1756** HANWAY *Ess. Tea* xii. 258 The *tea trade employs six hundred seamen..together with six ships, which we annually send to Canton. **1888** J. PATON in *Encycl. Brit.* XXIII. 102/2 The only other considerable *tea-using nation is Russia. **1765** J. BROWN *Chr. Jrnl.* (1814) 331 Yonder professors come from a *tea-visit. **1807–8** W. IRVING *Salmag.* i. (1824) 7 When ladies paid tea-visits at three in the afternoon. **1888** *Pall Mall G.* 9 May 10/1 Certain *tea warehousemen of the City of London.

c. Special Combs.: **tea-bag**, (*a*) *Canad.*, a bag for carrying provisions; (*b*) a small permeable bag of paper or cloth containing tea for infusion; **tea ball**, a ball of wire or perforated metal in which tea is placed for infusion; **tea bar**, a bar (BAR *sb.*[1] 28) at which tea is sold as a beverage; **tea basket**, a basket containing the requisites for afternoon tea in a railway train or the like; **tea-bell**, a bell rung to summon a household or company to tea; **tea-billy** (BILLY[3]), a tin can used by Australian bushmen as a tea-kettle or tea-pot; also used in New Zealand; **tea-boiler**, a vessel used for boiling tea; **tea-bottle**, a bottle containing tea (sense 2 a); also *slang*, an old maid; **tea-box**, (*a*) a box for containing tea; in quot. 1825 = TEA-CHEST 2; (*b*) *Canad.*, a box for carrying food and cooking utensils on an expedition; **tea-boy**, (*a*) a man-servant; (*b*) a youth (occas. a man) employed to serve tea to workers; **tea-bread**, a kind of light bread eaten at tea; **tea-break**, an interval, usu. between periods of work, when tea is drunk; **tea-brick**, a brick of compressed tea leaves (cf. *brick-tea* s.v. BRICK *sb.*[1] 10); **tea-broom**, New Zealand name for *Leptospermum scoparium* and *L. ericoides* (= MANUKA a, b, TEA-TREE 2); **tea-bug**, a destructive insect which infests tea-plants; **tea-bush** = *tea-shrub*; **tea-caddy**, a small box with divisions for holding tea (= CADDY *sb.* 1); **tea-cake**, a light kind of flat cake to be eaten at tea; in quot. 1892 *attrib.* resembling a tea-cake; **tea-can**, a metal can used for brewing or carrying tea; **tea-canister** = *tea-caddy*; also, *slang* for 'brandy-flask' (cf. 7 a); **tea cart** *U.S.*, a tea-trolley; **tea-case**, a case for holding a set of small articles, as spoons, etc. used at tea (*Cent. Dict.*); **tea ceremony**, in Japan, the preparation and consumption of green tea, according to strict rules of ceremony, as an expression of Zen Buddhist philosophy; **tea-china**, china tea-cups and saucers, etc.; **tea-chop** [CHOP *sb.*[5] 5], in China, a chop-boat or lighter for the transportation of tea; **tea-circle**, a group or society of persons who meet and take tea together; **tea-clam**, a name in U.S. for a very small clam (CLAM *sb.*[2] 1 d: see quot.); **tea-clipper**, a clipper or fast-sailing vessel formerly employed in the tea trade; **tea-cloth**, (*a*) a cloth used for wiping tea-things after washing them; (*b*) *afternoon t.*, a small table-cloth used at afternoon tea; **tea-coat**, a garment worn by women at the tea-table (cf. COAT *sb.* 2 b, and *tea-jacket*); †**tea-conversation** (see CONVERSATION 9, quot. 1787); **tea-cooper**, a workman at a dock who unloads tea and does any necessary repairs to the packing, etc.: cf. COOPER *sb.*[1] 1; **tea-cosy**, (*a*) a covering for a tea-pot to keep it hot (see COSY B. 2); (*b*) in full ***tea-cosy hat***, a round knitted woollen hat resembling a tea-cosy; **tea dance** = *thé dansant* s.v. DANSANT *a.*; also *Canad.*, 'a social gathering held by Indians, so called because in the early days the Hudson's Bay Company contributed tea, bannock, etc.' (*Dict. Canadianisms*, 1967); hence **tea-dance** *v. intr.*; **tea-dancer**; **tea-dancing** *vbl. sb.*; †**tea-dish**, old name for a tea-cup (cf. DISH *sb.* 1 b); **tea-drunkard**, one who habitually drinks tea to such excess as to suffer from its toxic effects; **tea-dust**, tea of inferior quality, often made from leaves broken in the course of production; *attrib.* [tr. Chinese *chá yè mò* tea-leaf dust], used to designate a dark green or brownish (often speckled) glaze on Chinese pottery (see quot. 1899), esp. used on decorative ware; †**tea-equipage** = *tea-service*, *tea-things*; †**tea-faced** *a.*, ? having a sallow or effeminate countenance like one addicted to tea-drinking; **tea-fight**, *colloq.* or *slang*, humorous name for a tea-party or tea-meeting; **tea-frock, tea-gown**, names for special fashions of garments worn by girls and women at tea; **tea-girl**, a girl who serves tea; **tea-glass**, a glass from which tea (esp. without milk) is drunk; **tea-green**, a shade of greyish green resembling the colour of tea; †**tea-grouter** (see quot.); **tea-head** *slang* (orig. *U.S.*), a habitual user of marijuana (cf. sense 7 c above and HEAD *sb.*[1] 7 e); **tea hostess**, a woman in charge of serving tea at a tea-party or other social occasion; **tea-hound** [HOUND *sb.*[1] 4 e] *U.S. slang* (now *rare*), a man given to frequenting tea-parties; also in extended use, a lady's man (see quot. 1921); **tea-hour**, the hour at which tea is taken, or the time occupied by it; **tea-house**, a refreshment-house where tea is served (esp. in China or Japan); **tea infuser** = *tea-maker* (*c*); **tea interval**, a break for afternoon tea or light refreshment (esp. during a cricket match); **tea-jacket**, a garment worn by women at tea (cf. *tea-coat*); †**tea-kitchen**, a tea-urn (cf. KITCHEN *sb.* 2 b); †**tea-ladle**, a ladle for serving tea; **tea-lady**, a woman who serves tea (esp. in an office); **tea-lead**, an alloy used for lining tea-chests (see quot.); **tea machine**, a machine which makes or dispenses tea; **tea-maker**, (*a*) a person who dries the leaves and prepares the tea of commerce; (*b*) one who makes or infuses tea; (*c*) a vessel or apparatus for infusing tea; (*d*) an apparatus incorporating a timer and designed to be kept at the bedside which can be pre-set to make tea automatically at any time (typically on awaking); so **tea-making** *sb.* and *a.*; **tea master**, an expert in the proper conduct of the tea ceremony; **tea-meeting**, a public social meeting (usually in connexion with a religious organization) at which tea is taken; **tea money**, money paid by employees for drinks of tea at work (in quot. 1906, money paid by an employer to employees to buy their own tea); also *transf.* (see quot. 1979); **tea-night**, an evening on which guests are entertained at tea; **tea oil**, (*a*) an oil resembling olive-oil, obtained from the seeds of species of *Camellia* (allied to the tea-plant), and used for various purposes in China and Japan; (*b*) a narcotic essential oil obtained from tea-leaves; **tea olive** [from the Chinese use of the flowers to add scent to tea] = *sweet olive* s.v. SWEET *a.* and *adv.* C. 1 b; **tea pad** *U.S. slang*, a place where one can purchase and smoke marijuana; †**tea-paper**, the ornamental paper used as a wrapper for tea (*obs.*); **tea place** = TEA-SHOP b; **tea plate**, a small shallow plate for use at tea-time; **tea-punch**, punch containing tea as an ingredient; **tea-roller**, a machine for rolling or curling tea-leaves for the market; so **tea-rolling**; **tea room**, (*a*) a room in which tea is served in a refreshment-house, etc.; notably, that of the British House of Commons, the scene of numerous informal meetings of members; (*b*) *U.S. slang*, a public lavatory used as a meeting-place by homosexuals; **tea-root**, the root of a tea-plant; **tea-sage**, a species or variety of sage used for making sage-tea; †**tea-saucer**, a saucer for supporting a tea-cup; **tea-scent**, 'a European fern, *Nephrodium montanum*' (*Cent. Dict.*); **tea-scented** *a.*, having a scent like that of tea: applied to a variety of rose (see TEA-ROSE); **tea-scrub**, a scrub or thicket of 'tea-trees' (in Australia, etc.): see TEA-TREE; **tea-seed oil** = *tea oil* (*a*); **tea-service, tea-set**, a set of articles used in serving tea at table; a set of tea-things; †**tea-shine**, *colloq.* a tea-party (cf. *tea-fight*); **tea-ship**, (*a*) a ship engaged in the tea-trade; (*b*) a tea-stand with two or more shelves or 'decks'; **tea-shrub**, the common tea-plant (see 3); **tea-sifter**, (*a*) a person engaged in sifting tea; (*b*) an apparatus for sifting tea; **tea-stall, tea-stand**, (*a*) a stand on which cups, saucers, plates, etc. are placed for use at tea; (*b*) a stall at which tea is sold; **tea-stick**, a stick cut from the Australian tea-tree; **tea-stone**: see quots.; **tea-tent**, a tent in which tea is served at an outdoor event; **tea-things** *sb. pl.*, the articles used for serving tea at table, as tea-pot, milk-jug, sugar-basin, cups, saucers, plates, etc., together forming a *tea-set* or *tea-service*; **tea-time**, (*a*) the time at which the meal called tea is taken (see sense 4); also *transf.*; (*b*) (*rare*), the time occupied by or allowed for taking tea; †**tea-tongs**, a former name for sugar-tongs; **tea-towel** = *tea-cloth* (*a*); **tea-treat**, (chiefly in Cornwall) a publicly provided out-door tea-party for children, esp. of a Sunday-school; also *attrib.*; **tea-trolley**, a trolley (sense 3 c) for conveying tea-things; **tea-urn**, an urn with a tap, placed upon a tea-table, to hold hot water for making tea; **tea-wagon**, †(*a*) an East Indiaman used to carry cargoes of tea (*obs.*); (*b*) = *tea-trolley* above; **tea-ware**, vessels, etc. for serving tea, tea-things; **tea-water**, (*a*) water for making tea; (*b*) *Sc.* the beverage tea (= sense 2); **tea-wine**, a fermented liquor made from tea (see quot.); **tea-wrap**, a wrap worn by women and girls at tea (*rare*); **tea yellows**, a deficiency disease of the tea-plant, esp. in Africa, caused by a lack of sulphur and indicated by small, chlorotic leaves, and the eventual death of the bush. See also TEA-BERRY, -BOARD, -CHEST, etc.

1898 F. RUSSELL *Explorations in Far North* 161 If a crooked knife, a *tea bag, or anything that is in the heap is needed, everything is tumbled about until it is found. **1936** K. CONIBEAR *Northland Footprints* p. xii, Give him a large piece of bannock from your tea-bag. **1940** R. CHANDLER *Farewell, my Lovely* xiii. 102 They put Dad in charge of the Bureau of Records and Identification, which in Bay City is about the size of a tea-bag. **1958** *Sunday Times* 30 Mar. 12/3 The sale of tea-bags is creeping up. **1977** *Lancashire Life* Feb. 19/1 Those who think that tea is grown in teabags will be pleasantly surprised to find the enormous number of teas blended and packaged in Britain. **1895** *Montgomery Ward Catal.* Spring & Summer 187/1 Pure Aluminium, *Tea Ball, total length, 7 in. Ball 1½ in. dia. **1929** *Nation* (N.Y.) 4 Dec. 666 The tea ball enables one to pull the tea out before it has given off its tannin. **1976** *National Observer* (U.S.) 16 Oct. 10/3 Peel and crush six cloves of garlic and tie them in a piece of cheesecloth or put them in a tea ball and add this to the warm liquid. **1952** *Times* 12 Nov. 3/2 *Tea bars are increasing. **1976** *Lancs. Evening Post* 7 Dec. 2/2 Mrs. Alice Durdle serves tea to the over 60s at the Lilian Wood Memorial Centre tea bar in Market Street, Preston. **1891** *Queen* 31 Oct. p. xxxvii (Advt.), Drews' Patent En Route 5 o'clock *Tea Basket. **1901** *Wide World Mag.* VIII. 135/1 There is a lump of sugar in the tea-basket. **1836** *Knickerbocker* VIII. 418 It was nearly time for the *tea-bell to ring. **1867** AUG. J. E. WILSON *Vashti* i, The sound of the tea-bell terminated her reverie, and she walked to the dining-room. **1894** H. NISBET *Bush Girl's Rom.* 133 A number of *tea-billies were ranged on the clay hobs, some with tea already brewed, and some with water only. **1939** J. MULGAN *Man Alone* 81 viii. 81 Around him were spread his belongings..clothes, boots, two black tea-billies..and a grey blanket. **1839** A. LANGTON *Jrnl. in Gentlewoman Upper Canada* (1950) 101 The pie plates, too, are very nice, and also the little *tea-boiler. **1909** J. R. WARE *Passing Eng.* 241/2 **Tea-bottle* (*Mid.-class*), and old maid—from the ordinary drink of spinsters. **1975** B. MEYRICK *Behind Light* xv. 198 He unwedged the sought-after tea bottle from its place behind the pipes. **1758** A. PITT *Let.* 10 Nov. in *Lett. Lady Suffolk* (1824) II. 252 So I design to send it [*sc.* a letter] with a *tea box my sister left and does not want. **1825** J. NICHOLSON *Operat. Mechanic* 632 The lead which lines the Chinese tea-boxes is reduced to a thinness which our plumbers cannot, it is said, approach. **1972** S. BURNFORD *One Woman's Arctic* vii. 154 In no time at all had the team hitched up, and his rifle and teabox abroad. **1848** THACKERAY *Van. Fair* xxvii, Major O'Dowd..was..as obedient to his wife as if he had been her *tay-boy. **1852** LD. GRANVILLE *Let.* 19 Jan. in E. Fitzmaurice *Life Ld. Granville* (1905) I. iii. 68 The teaboys of our own and our neighbour's establishments. **1954** *Atlantic Monthly* Aug. 35/1 The auction porters ate their dinners off thick white plates brought over by a cross-eyed teaboy from a café down the road. **1963** *Times* 31 May 12/6 Brutus..said that because of the banning order he was no longer able to work as a teacher and had had to take a job as a 'tea boy' with a research worker at the University of the Witwatersrand, for which he got £10 a month. **1977** *Time Out* 28 Jan.–3 Feb. 3/2 He certainly writes with all the flowing panache of a trainee teaboy. **1831** JANE PORTER *Sir E. Seaward's Narr.* I. 229 Some johnny cakes, a West Indian sort of *tea-bread. **1948** *Brit. Jrnl. Psychol.* Mar. 113 Many reasons were given for the almost universal appreciation of the *tea break. **1958** A. SILLITOE *Saturday Night & Sunday Morning* ii. 35 The light flashed: tea-break over. **1981** *Economist* 18 Nov. 17/2 Strikes during the contract period (like the present tea-break strike at BL) would bring heavy damages on the unions. **1962** L. DAVIDSON *Rose of Tibet* v. 87 He had bought *tea bricks.. and a large cake of yak butter. **1981** *Times* 7 July 12/7 A food shop in Covent Garden..has introduced.. tea-bricks, such as Chinese mandarins once used to pay their taxes. **1872** A. DOMETT *Ranolf* Notes 505 Mánuka... The settlers often call it '*tea-broom'. **1893** *Athenæum* 16 Dec. 853/3 Mr. Waterhouse..exhibited male and female specimens of a Helopeltis (the *tea-bug),..and stated that it had occurred only in Assam. **1908** *Dollar Mag.* Mar. 32 The *tea bushes were miserably poor just there. **1790** *Pennsylvania Packet* 7 Dec. 3/3 Joseph Anthony, Junior,..Has Imported..*Tea cadies, cannisters and salts. **1837** HOWITT *Rur. Life* VI. ix. (1862) 500 Tea-caddies, workboxes of rosewood and pearl. **1866** R. M. BALLANTYNE *Shift. Winds* xvii, [She] went to a cupboard..and took therefrom a tea-caddy, which she set on the table. **1832** L. M. CHILD *Amer. Frugal Housewife* 71 There is a kind of *tea cake still cheaper. **1844** DICKENS *Martin Chuzzlewit* xvii. 216 Tea and coffee arrived (with sweet preserves, and cunning tea-cakes in its train). **1892** *Daily News* 31 Dec. 2/1 The bonnet of the moment is set well back on the head, forming a sort of garland above the 'teacake' coiffure. **1897** R. HICHENS *Londoners* ix. 156 Mr. Bush..was closely engaged with a tea-cake. **1890** H. K. DANIELS *Me & Jim* 67 The new plumber he gave him no answer except to drink from his *tea-can and go on reading where he'd left off. **1951** J. FLEMING *Man who looked Back* x. 120 He picked up his tea-can. **1978** *Lancashire Life* Nov. 75/2 Erect, at Uncle Dan's immediate righthand, was a large, shining tea-can, its lid back in place. **1726** in *N. & Q.* (1942) 24 Jan. 46/1 Bowl & *tea canister. **1800** HELENA WELLS *Constantia Neville* (ed. 2) III. 121 The tea-canister contained only Congou of no very superior quality. **1859** F. FRANCIS *Newton Dogvane* (1888) 184 Pass us the tea-canister. **1934** WEBSTER, *Tea cart. **1958** P. DE VRIES *Mackerel Plaza* iv. 56 A teacart hove into view, laden with goodies. **1978** M. DELVING *No Sign of Life* i. 15 His wife came into the room followed by the maid pushing a tea-cart. **1886** E. S. MORSE *Jap. Homes* iii. 149 The party comes about by the host inviting a company of four to attend the *tea-ceremony, and in their presence making the tea in a bowl after certain prescribed forms, and offering it to the guests. **1935** *Burlington Mag.* Mar. 147/2 The tea ceremony, a rite so essentially Japanese that it might be said to epitomize Japanese culture. **1980** J. MELVILLE *Chrysanthemum Chain* 16 A classic four-and-a-half mat tea room with a blond foreigner in full formal Japanese dress performing the tea ceremony. **1790** J. WOODFORDE *Diary* 15 Dec. (1927) III. 235 My Maid Betty Dade breaking likewise the only *Tea China-Slop-Basin..made me more fretful. **1830** MISS MITFORD *Village* Ser. IV. 332 The dresser was.. adorned with the remains of a long preserved set of tea-china, of a light rambling pattern. **1876** F. W. H. SYMONDSON *Two Yrs. abaft Mast* vii. 136 A large '*tea chop' (a tea barge) came alongside. **1886** R. BROWN *Spunyarn & Spindrift* xxvii. 328 The river was so swollen by the rains that the tea-chops could not get through Foo-chow bridge. **1831** CARLYLE *Sart. Res.* III. ix, Thou..perhaps in many a literary *Tea-circle wilt open thy kind lips. **1883** G. B. GOODE *Fish. Indust. U.S.A.* 47 Some are taken so small that 2,000 are required to fill a barrel; these, when about one inch in diameter, are called '*tea-clams'. **1895** *Mem. Jas. Anderson* ii. 8 Mr. and Mrs. Anderson set sail from London in a *tea-clipper. **1770** C. CARROLL *Let.* 11 Oct. in *Maryland Hist. Mag.* (1918) XIII. 62 A Hierling..stole a napkin two Towels & a *Tea Cloath w^h we Recovered. **1881** C. C. HARRISON *Woman's Handiwork* I. 49 The beautiful tea-cloth linen, with its firm round thread, the warp and woof of equal thickness, so common in England. **1888** *Cassell's Encycl. Dict.*, *Tea-cloth*, a cloth used in washing up tea-things. **1891** *Cent. Dict.*, *Tea-cloth*, a cloth for a tea-table or a tea-tray. **1899** *Westm. Gaz.* 12 Aug. 2/1 She came into the room..in a black-and-blue sort of *tea-coat. **1887** *Pall Mall G.* 19 Sept. 2 Years ago the *tea-coopers, who are skilled workmen, had a union. **1871** 'M. LEGRAND' *Camb. Freshm.* 18 The elaborate worsted-work teapot cover—technically termed, I believe, a *tea-cosey. **1886** [see COSY B. 2]. **1966** Tea-cosy [see ENSEMBLE *v.*]. **1975** M. RUSSELL *Murder by Mile* x. 101 A scarlet tea-cosy hat perched on top of her hair. **1885** T. GOWANLOCK *Two Months Camp of Big Bear* 119 When the Indians held their *tea-dances or pow-wows in times of peace, the squaws and their children joined in and it was a very amusing sight to watch them. **1916** W. STEVENS *Let.* 23 Apr. (1967) 193 People are pretty much dependent on the same things as in New-York: band concerts, tea-dances and..coffee-parties. **1965** *News of North* (Yellowknife, N.W. Territories) 29 July 5/4 The ceremony was marked by a tea dance, in which everyone joined. **1978** *Lancashire Life* Nov. 129/2 For in a brave gesture of defiance in the punk era, the management has resurrected the Sunday Afternoon Tea Dance. It's all very Palm Court, even if the palms are plastic. **1980** *Radio Times* 29 Nov.–5 Dec. 87/4 So keen are the *Tea Dancers that they have picked up all these [dances]. **1946** *New Yorker* 2 Feb. 4 A Melba trio plays in the Café Pierre, where there is *tea dancing daily. **1962** A. BUCHWALD *How much is that in Dollars?* 128 Now you can see why the Patterson-Johansson fight didn't mean much to me. Those kids in the U.S. were just tea-dancing. **1964** *Camsell Arrow* (Edmonton, Alberta) Summer 60/4 High point of their four months in the north was the invitation to join the Indians 'tea dancing' Anne said. **1977** *New Yorker* 3 Oct. 95/1 Tea dancing at the Kempinski. This goes on every day. **1711** EUSDEN *Spect.* No. 87 ¶8, I saw a gentleman turn as pale as ashes, because an idol turned the sugar in a *tea-dish for his rival. **1716** LADY M. W. MONTAGU *Lett.* 10 Oct. (1887) I. 129 They showed me..a cup, about the size of a tea-dish, of one entire emerald. **1899** S. W. BUSHELL *Oriental Ceramic Art* xviii. 518 One of the best-known glazes..is the *Ch'a-yeh-mo*, or '*Tea-dust' glaze, produced by the insufflation of green enamel upon a yellowish-brown ground, which owes its color to iron. The combination produces a peculiarly soft tint of greenish tone, which was highly prized in the reign of *Ch'ien-lung*. **1909** *Cent. Dict.* Suppl., Tea-dust. **1922** JOYCE *Ulysses* 57 Through the open doorway the bar squirted out whiffs of ginger, teadust, biscuitmush. **1945** W. B. HONEY *Ceramic Art of China* 145 The 'iron-rust' and greenish 'tea-dust' glazes..are usually of Ch'ien Lung date. **1979** P. NIHALANI et al. *Indian & Brit. English* I. 175 Good quality tea packaged in the form of leaf and known as 'leaf tea', and an inferior variety, comparatively inexpensive, called tea-dust. **1980** *Catal. Fine Chinese Ceramics* (Sotheby, Hong Kong) 84 A massive tea-dust bowl..with a finely speckled deep olive-green glaze,..the base covered in an ochre-yellow glaze. **1709** MRS. MANLEY *Secret Mem.* (1720) II. 290 He cleans his *Tea-Equipage with his own Hands. **1833** T. HOOK *Parson's Dan.* I. ii, The tea equipage was on the table. **1728** RAMSAY *Archers diverting themselves* 26 When av'rice, luxury, and ease, A *tea-fac'd generation please. **1849** ALB. SMITH *Pottleton Leg.* xxxv, Their various small parties—'*tea-fights' as young Grant called them. **1901** *Scotsman* 5 Mar. 7/5 The good people..organise a splendid weekly tea-fight and concert for our behoof. **1903** *Westm. Gaz.* 27 Aug. 4/1 The *tea-frock—the form of the tea-gown nice for the younger folks. **1889** KIPLING *From Sea to Sea* (1900) I. 444

The *tea-girls giggled. **1976** *S. Wales Echo* 23 Nov. 6/9 Every employee.., from senior executives to tea girls, would be interviewed. **1898** A. Cahan *Imported Bridegroom* xi. 121 Jealousy..of the empty *tea-glasses.., of the whole excited crowd. **1979** D. Gurr *Troika* xxxiv. 260 Alexey grabbing at the rail, tea glass dropping from his fingers. **1878** *The World* in *Royal Exchange* 9 Nov., Ladies, who a few years ago would have considered the idea appalling, calmly array themselves in the glorified dressing robe known as a '*tea gown'. **1891** *Woman* 15 Jan. 4/1 The factor which has revolutionised the novelistic attire of to-day is the evolution of the tea-gown. **1956** W. Edwards in D. L. Linton *Sheffield* 16 East of the River Trent it [*sc.* the Rhaetic] overlies the '*Tea-Green Marls' at the top of the Keuper. **1967** *Vogue* 1 Mar. (International Collection) 161/1 She loves the colours. White, pink, blue, butterscotch, tea green, [etc.]. *a***1833** J. T. Smith *Bk. for Rainy Day* (1905) 76 A prognostication announced to my dear mother by an old star-gazer and *tea-grouter. *Note.* A fortune-teller by tea-leaves, the leaves being 'grouted', or turned over in the cup. **1953** W. Burroughs *Junkie* (1972) ii. 29 Perhaps weed does affect the brain with constant use, or maybe *teaheads are naturally silly. **1967** *Guardian* 8 July 6/2 Doctors, commissions, and plain tea-heads have been ready to go on record about the innocence of the weed cannabis sativa. **1970** Tea-head [see HEAD *sb.*[1] 7 e]. **1976** *Norwich Mercury* 19 Nov. 2/5 Mrs J. Bowhill acted as model for the evening dress... *Tea hostesses were Mrs Kedge and Mrs Williams. **1921** *Dialect Notes* V. 111 **Tea-hound*, a lady's man. **1925** *Scribner's Mag.* Oct. 353/2 He was a regular tea-hound, he was seen at so many teas. **1884** G. Allen *Philistia* I. 109 Monopolised the..visitor himself for almost the entire *tea-hour. **1689** *Lond. Gaz.* No. 2481/4 Catalogues are given at ..Mr. Mainwaring's *Tea-house. **1763** J. Bell *Travels from St. Petersburg* II. x. 54 From the temple we went to a publick tea-house, where we saw many people drinking tea [in Peking]. **1909** *Daily Chron.* 7 June 4/6 This revolution.. practically commenced when in 1657 Garraway opened his famous tea-house in Exchange-alley. **1959** L.-H. Liang tr. *Ting Yi's Short Hist. Mod. Chinese Lit.* x. 221 In the rear areas, there were other dramatic forms akin to the 'street play', such as the 'tea-house play', 'demonstration play' and the 'lantern play'. **1972** K. Lo *Chinese Food* i. 50 There are no pubs or bars and most of the informal leisurely drinking takes place in tea-houses. **1889** A. James *Diary* 5 Aug. (1965) 52 A note of farewell from Mr. Godkin with a *tea-infuser. **1907** *Yesterday's Shopping* (1969) 188/3 Travellers' Companion... For making tea when touring, boating, &c. .. Comprises kettle,..stand, spirit stove,..and muslin tea infuser. **1960** *Guardian* 4 Jan. 3/1 Collapsible tea infusers. **1923** E. P. Oppenheim *Inevitable Millionaires* xxix. 288 'I haven't done wrong in making the tea, have I?' she asked timidly... 'Of course not,' George Henry assured her. 'The *tea interval is an established custom.' **1976** Dexter & Makins *Testkill* 143 In the tea interval..I slipped into the pavilion. **1887** *Girl's Own Paper* 25 June 618/3 New *tea-jacket, or *après midi*, for indoor wear. **1896** *Daily News* 5 Dec. 6/4 The increasing neatness of the tea-gown is perhaps partly owing to the smartness of cut of its rival, the tea jacket. **1770** J. Wedgwood *Let.* 24-26 Dec. (1965) 100 Mr. Boulton..shewed me some bodys and necks made of Porcelaine coloured green to be mounted in Ormoleau for *Tea Kitchens. **1808** Jane Austen *Let.* 27 Dec. (1952) 243 A silver *tea-ladle is also added [to the list]. **1964** *Listener* 13 Feb. 287/1 'Filthy,' said a friend's *tea-lady the next morning. **1980** *Times* 13 Nov. 4/8 The tea trolley is being wheeled back... Two years ago, it seemed the ubiquitous tea lady was vanishing beneath a tide of vending machines. This year..automated services are in decline. **1815** J. Smith *Panorama Sc. & Art* I. 52 The metal with which tea-chests are lined, familiarly called *tea-lead, is an alloy principally composed of lead and tin. **1963** *Punch* 8 May 675/1, I..fetched the *tea machine into the house. **1972** J. Thomson *Not One of Us* xvii. 227, I kept..some paper cups. I used to nick them from the tea machine at the warehouse. **1814** Jane Austen *Mansfield Park* III. vii. 160 There was.. found a chair, and with some hasty washing of the young *tea-maker's, a cup and saucer. **1842** *Penny Cycl.* XXIV. 266/1 The process..as practised in Assam and Java by the Chinese tea-makers. **1868** Holme Lee *B. Godfrey* ii, The parson asked the tea-maker for another cup. **1900** *Daily News* 18 Sept. 6/3 It is put into a perforated receiver, suspended in the 'tea-maker', and boiling water poured over it. **1961** 'T. Hinde' *For Good of Company* xix. 214 Mary had switched on the bedside tea-maker. **1970** *Sunday Times* 20 Dec. 26/3 When the clock on the tea-maker began to go backwards its owners got their alarm call and a nice pot of tea at three a.m. **1826** (*title*) Tsiology; a discourse on Tea. Being an account of that exotic,..*Tea-making... By a Tea Dealer. **1833** T. Hook *Parson's Dau.* I. xii, The operation, which, at Cambridge, is not called by so gentle a term as tea-making. **1888** *Encycl. Brit.* XXIII. 100/1 In Chinese tea-making that juice is squeezed out of the leaves. **1894** Mrs. Dyan *All in a Man's K.* (1899) 207 Without a falter she performed the dainty little service of tea-making. **1914** Y. Noguchi *Through Torii* 2 It is the high art of the *tea-master to make you really taste the water beside the taste of the tea. **1974** *Times Lit. Suppl.* 25 Oct. 1190/3 In Kamakura for the first time a tea master did the tea ceremony for me. **1897** *St. James's Gaz.* 18 Feb. 11/1 The posting of bills for soirees and *tea-meetings. **1906** E. Dyson *Fact'ry 'Ands* xvii. 225 We're..puttin' down er mill that'll..never look fer *tea money. **1962** L. Deighton *Ipcress File* i. 11 The office tea money. **1979** *Rydge's* (Sydney) Apr. 68/2, I observed a case in Thailand, where payoffs are euphemistically called tea-money. **1824** Scott *St. Ronan's* xxxiv, To secure the necessary degree of crowd upon her *tea-nights, Lady Penelope was obliged to employ some coaxing. **1837** R. D. Thomson in *Brit. Ann.* 358 *Tea oil. **1838** T. Thomson *Chem. Org. Bodies* 439 Tea oil is expressed from the seeds of the Camellia oleifera. **1952** M. Steen *Phoenix Rising* vi. 117 An over-powering fragrance of *tea-olive rose from under her window. **1975** *Country Life* 2 Jan. 39/3 The grassy glade leading from river to house..heavy with the scent of tea olive..and banana tree. **1938** *New Yorker* 12 Mar. 47/1 All *tea pads, or marijuana joints, use the blue lamps and nickel machines to induce and sustain the hashish mood. **1963** *Lancet* 9 Nov. 989/2 For a few years the cult of the 'tea pad' ..threatened to be imported from the United States. **1814** F. Burney *Let.* 28 Oct. (1978) VII. 488 If this reaches you write to me again upon a scrap that can hardly arrive—I shall answer upon a bit of *Tea paper. **1884** *Birmingham Daily Post* 23 Feb. 3/4 Lithographic printers. Wanted, a man..well up in Tea-paper and Commercial Work. **1929** D. H. Lawrence *Let.* 11 Jan. (1932) 780 We were in Toulon yesterday..and went to the same *tea-place. **1978** P. Marsh et al. *Rules of Disorder* iii. 72 At the back there you can see down to the tea place underneath. **1862** M. D. Colt *Went to Kansas* iii. 48 Have arranged or them..our five tin plates, two tin cups, one tin tumbler, the nine *tea-plates. **1972** *Country Life* 9 Mar. 547/3 These plates were made by the Britannia China Company..between 1895 and 1906. Such plates were known as..tea plates. **1728** Chambers *Cycl.* s.v. *Punch*, Punch Royal. Milk-Punch. *Tea-Punch. **1890** *Pall Mall G.* 1 Oct. 2/3 The *tea-rolling machine represented in our view ..is the first *tea-roller which has been used on English soil. *c***1702** C. Fiennes *Journeys* (1947) iv. 359 Another little closet with the tea equipage and under that was such a little *tea roome within the drawing roome. *c***1748** Richardson *Let.* in *Corr.* (1804) III. 317 Miss Chudleigh is gone into the tea-room. **1796** Mme. D'Arblay *Camilla* I. 167 They were proceeding to the tea-room. **1884** *Pall Mall G.* 26 Sept. 2/2 Even a tea-room compromise [between political parties] would be welcome at the present moment. **1970** [see NELLY[2] 3]. **1976** *New Society* 29 Jan. 227/2 Sentences for what are known in America as 'tearoom' offences—homosexual sodomy or oral copulation—vary. **1690** Evelyn *Diary* 11 Mar., I much admired the contortions of the *Thea root, which was so perplexed, large, and intricate. **1727-41** Chambers *Cycl.* s.v. *Sage*, Kinds..used and cultivated by us are the *Tea-Sage, or Sage of Virtue [etc.]. **1761** Dunn in *Phil. Trans.* LII. 185 An artificial horizon of sweet oil in a *tea-saucer. **1845** *Florist's Jrnl.* 207 Coupe de Hebe (*tea-scented). **1849** *Florist* 318 Tea-scented Roses cannot be cultivated with success as border Roses, unless in the extreme south and west of England. **1852** Mundy *Our Antipodes* (1857) 13 Shady paths,..winding among the '*tea-scrub', or skirting the rocky shores [at Sydney]. **1884** *Encycl. Brit.* XVII. 746/2 *Tea-seed oil is a commercial product in China, where it is used for food, lighting, and soap-making. **1951** E. David *French Country Cooking* 220 Tea seed oil. Much lighter than olive oil and preferred by many for salads. **1809** A. Burr *Private Jrnl.* (1903) I. 253 A splendid *tea service of silver and two cups. **1838** J. Romilly *Diary* 26 Feb. (1967) 140 Treated myself with a new tea Service for the occasion (cost 5½ Gnas). **1858** Simmonds *Dict. Trade*, Tea-service, Tea-things. **1869** Trollope *He knew he was right* i, He gave silver cups when the girls were born, and now bestows tea-services as they get married. **1786** J. Wedgwood *Let.* 30 June (1965) 297 A single line of colour put on..while it is in the clay state.. upon our beer mugs, flower-pots, *tea and coffee sets.. constitutes *fayence*. **1849** Lytton *Caxtons* I. iv, I would rather the best tea-set were broken. **1838** Mrs. Carlyle *Lett.* (1883) I. 98 Two *tea-shines went off with *éclat*. **1859** *Harper's Mag.* Sept. 507/2 You might have seen their sing —ay, and their fine staunch *tea-ships too—any day you chose to stroll down South. **1876** Bancroft *Hist. U.S.* IV. I. 273 The Boston tea-ships had sailed. **1905** *Westm. Gaz.* 11 Nov. 3/1 The servant went out, and, returning with a three-decker tea-ship, asked whether anything else was required. **1704** Petiver *Gazophyl.* III. xxi, The *Thea Shrub is here Figured. **1798** *Monthly Mag.* July 30/1 The Arabs, to whom we stand indebted for the first accounts of the tea-shrub. **1871** *Windsor & Eton Express* 4 Nov., Two silver *tea-sifters having the Royal crest engraved upon them. **1889** Kipling *From Sea to Sea* (1900) I. 360 The lower stories were full of *tea-stalls and tea-drinkers. **1902** *Westm. Gaz.* 31 Jan. 2/1 The wheeled tea-stall which appears at about four o'clock in all large stations. **1962** R. Prawer Jhabvala *Get Ready for Battle* ii. 94 A tea-stall under a tree built on upturned kerosene tins. **1697** in *14th Rep. Hist. MSS. Comm.* App. II. (1894) 592 Your Lord who broke the *tea-stand. **1865** H. Kingsley *Hillyars & Burtons* lxii, You should have a *tea-stick, and take them [dogs] by the tail,..and lay on like old gooseberry. **1848** S. W. Williams *Middle Kingd.* xiii. II. 116 Spectacles are cut.. from..a variety of rose quartz resembling the cairngorm stone, which the Chinese call *cha-tsing*, or *tea-stone, from its color. **1860** J. Scarth *Twelve Yrs. China* 5 Shaded..by a huge pair of tea-stone spectacles. **1890** *Monthly Packet* Christmas 188 She..was not sorry to depart to the *tea-tent. **1934** 'E. M. Delafield' *Provincial Lady in Amer.* 6 Go with Robert..to..Agricultural Show... We..repair to tea-tent. .. I drink strong tea and eat chudleighs. **1977** *Oxf. Diocesan Mag.* Oct. 20/2 A tea-tent..apart from affecting the custom of the catering contractors, would give a false picture of the Church as a tea-making machine. **1747** H. Walpole *Lett.* (1846) II. 192 You will think I have removed my philosophy from Windsor with my *tea-things hither. **1869** Trollope *He knew he was Right* xxxi, Dorothy was seated behind the urn and tea-things at a large table. **1741** Richardson *Pamela* II. 223, I hope to join you there by your *Tea-time in the Afternoon. **1749** J. Cleland *Mem. Woman Pleasure* I. 47 He sat down..and all tea-time kept ogling me. **1756** *Pol. Ballads* (1860) II. 332 And now being tea-time..we put on the kettle. **1782** Miss Burney *Cecilia* VI. iii, Sometimes he appeared again at tea-time. **1889** J. S. Winter' *Mrs. Bob* (1891) 46, I shall be back before tea-time. **1936** *Punch* 19 Feb. 204/1 It's still tea-time, you know. **1963** *Times* 31 Jan. 3/3 In the evening of life—or at any rate the tea-time—it is occasionally pleasant to look back. **1738** Swift *Pol. Conversat.* iii. 200 Lady Smart mistakes the *Tea-tongs for the Spoon. **1797** *Nicholson's Jrnl. Nat. Philos.* I. 63 Bended up in the figure of a pair of tea-tongs. **1863** S. S. Jones *Northumberland* 116 The guid lady shakes her lap an' rubs an' scrapes at her gown wi' the *tea-towel. *c***1909** D. H. Lawrence *Collier's Friday Night* (1934) II. 55 *Beatrice*:..You want to wrap it in a damp cloth now. Have you got a cloth? *Ernest*: What?—a clean tea-towel? **1980** *Habitat Catal.* 1980/81 111/1 Honeycomb weave teatowel. Pure cotton. Excellent for easy drying up. *c***1748** Richardson *Let.* in *Corr.* (1804) III 317, I thought..you were of the party at the *tea-treats. **1898** C. P. Penberthy *Warp & Woof of Cornish Life* 153 Whas our lil tay-trait to a townser? *Ibid.* 168 Go long up tay-trait field. **1977** *West Briton* 25 Aug. 22/6 Mr. Ken Roberts..said 150 traditional tea-treat buns would be distributed free to children on the estate. **1937** A. Thirkell *Summer Half* x. 275 Mrs. Keith had then bought an excellent *tea-trolley with rubber wheels and ball bearings. **1958** J. Cannan *To be a Villain* i. 24 A tea-trolley now stood laden with sandwiches, cakes and buttered buns. **1980** *Times* 13 Nov. 4/8 The tea trolley is being wheeled back. **1786** Cowper *Let. to Lady Hesketh* 24 Dec., You may purchase..a *tea-urn. **1808** T. Macgill *Trav.* I. xviii. 231 The Russian tea-urns..are made of brass ..in place of an iron heater, they have long tubes, into which live charcoal is put. *a***1948** D. Welch *Voice through Cloud* (1950) i. 9 This noble room was spoilt by a counter with sizzling tea-urns. **1840** R. H. Dana *Two Yrs. before Mast* xxxiv. 428 Like a true English '*tea-wagon'. **1878** *Appleton's Jrnl.* Jan. 9/2 The good, heavy-bowed, square-countered 'tea-wagons', as the sailors call them, meant for cumbrous freight, heavy stowage, and long passages. **1921** *Daily Colonist* (Victoria, B.C.) 30 Mar. 18/2 A neat Tea Wagon, in walnut finish, fitted with a moveable glass tray top, and mounted on four rubber tired wheels. **1939** J. B. Priestley *Let People Sing* ii. 23 The magazine boy..called to the tea-wagon girl: 'Come and 'ave a look.' **1978** D. Bloodworth *Crosstalk* xv. 122 Don't tell me the tea wagon's come and gone already? **1766** J. Wedgwood *Let.* 15 Sept. (1965) 42 The *Teaware, vases, and all other pretty things I shall let alone until I have the pleasure of seeing you here. **1825** J. Nicholson *Operat. Mechanic* 483 The insides of tea-ware are well washed with a liquid which forms, when fired, a thin coating of glass. **1693** Southerne *Maid's last Prayer* III. iii, Betty, set on the *Tea-water. **1818** Scott *Hrt. Midl.* xxvi, Breakfast wi' us yoursell—ye ken how to manage thae porringers of tea-water. **1892** Walsh *Tea* (Philad.) 203 A pleasing drink is also prepared by treating the ordinary infusion with a little yeast and sugar, a *tea-wine being produced from it. **1909** H. G. Wells *Tono-Bungay* II. ii. 176 My aunt too, looking bright and pretty, in a blue-patterned tea-wrap. **1931** *Ann. Rep. Dept. Agric. Nyasaland 1930* 32 *Tea Yellows—Investigations into this disease have been carried out. **1958** T. Eden *Tea* ix. 91 Tea yellows, caused by sulphur deficiency, is less severe under shade trees than in open situations.

Hence (*nonce-wds.*) **'teaey** *a.*, having the characteristic properties of tea; **'teaish** *a.*, resembling or relating to tea; **'teaism**, addiction to tea.

1890 *Spectator* 3 May, We believe Indian tea has conquered because it is the most *tea-ey of teas. **1836** *Tait's Mag.* III. 572 The *teaish propensities of her inamorato. **1904** E. Nesbit *Phœnix & Carpet* vii. 134 The meal..was not exactly tea. Let us call it a tea-ish meal. **1904** G. S. Hall *Adolescence* ix. II. 14 Excessive *teaism, coffeeism, etc.,..to the prejudice of appetite for plain, wholesome nutritives,.. jeopard the highest maturation of powers.

tea, *v. colloq.* [f. prec. sb.]

1. *trans.* To supply or regale with tea; to entertain at tea; to give a tea to.

1812 Sir R. Wilson *Diary* (1861) I. 250 General Tormanssow fed us, and the duke tea'd; so the day passed well. **1844** J. T. Hewlett *Parsons & W.* xxxvi, I breakfast, tea, and sup my lodgers. **1888** Freeman in Stephens *Life & Lett.* (1895) II. 386 We *tea* the local body on Wednesday.

2. *intr.* To drink tea; *esp.* to take the meal called tea, to have one's tea.

1810 G. Betts *Diary* in K. F. Doughty *Betts of Wortham* (1912) xxix. 286 Mr. Lee..came and *tea-ed* here. **1823** in *Spirit Pub. Jrnls.* 551 'Twas moved to proceed To the hall of debate, where my Lady had 'tea'd!' **1863-5** J. Thomson *Sunday at Hampstead* IV. i, Eight of us promised to meet here And tea together at five. **1892** Furnivall *Hoccleve's Minor P.* Introd. 47 We dined on the bank opposite Hampton Court and teaed on Tatham's island.

Hence **'teaing** *vbl. sb.* and *ppl. a.*; also **'teaer**, one who takes tea, or attends a tea-meeting.

1845 *Ainsworth's Mag.* VII. 504 During my 'teaing' I was amused with the conversation of my companions. **1852** R. S. Surtees *Sponge's Sp. Tour* xx. (1893) 94 Staying guests have the advantage over mere dining or teaing ones, inasmuch as they cannot well be talked over..as those who go away are. **1874** Aldrich *Prud. Palfrey* xi, Picnics up the river..and innumerable teaings on shore. **1892** *Sat. Rev.* 30 July 141/2 But 270 Congregational teaers would surely require more than eight quarts of milk?

tea-act, -basket, etc.: see TEA *sb.* 9.

'tea-ˌberry. The American wintergreen, *Gaultheria procumbens*: see quot.; also called *Canada tea* or *mountain tea*. Also, the fruit of this.

1818 W. P. C. Barton *Compendium Floræ Philadelphicæ* I. 194 *Gaultheria..procumbens*... Mountain Tea. Tea-berry. Partridge-berry. Wintergreen. **1858** Hogg *Veg. Kingd.* cxv. 482 The leaves [of *Gaultheria procumbens*]..when..dried.. make an excellent substitute for tea,..and the plant is on that account called Tea-berry and Mountain Tea. **1884** *Cassell's Fam. Mag.* Mar. 239/1 Here [in Houston, Texas].. the tea-berry tree, and huge orange trees..made me forget for a moment that I was expecting something very different. **1895** *Outing* (U.S.) XXVII. 18/1 Tiny white capillaire tea-berries, with a flavor like some rare perfume.

'tea-board. Now *local.* A tea-tray, esp. a wooden one.

1748 Smollett *Rod. Rand.* lvii. (1760) II. 202 The coming of a servant with the tea-board prevented my presumption. **1771** Mrs. Haywood *New Present* 256 Tea-boards are cleaned by rubbing them well with an oily flannel. **1780** *Newgate Cal.* V. 270 They doubled a silver tea-board together..and carried it away. **1868** Holme Lee *B. Godfrey* vi, The teaboard at the top of the table.

Hence **'teaboardy** *a. nonce-wd*, like a tea-board.

1890 *Athenæum* 1 Mar. 283/1 The hardness, smoothness, and laboured polish of the surface, almost fit to be called 'teaboardy'.

tea-boiler to **-case**: see TEA *sb.* 9.

teach (tiːtʃ), *v.* Pa. t. and pa. pple. **taught** (tɔːt). Forms: see below. [OE. *tǽcan*, *tǽcean*, pa. t. *tǽhte*, pa. pple. *(*ʒe*)*tǽht*:—OTeut. **taikjan*, cognate with OE. *tácn*, Goth. *taikns*, OS. *têkan*, OHG. *zeihhan*, TOKEN, from an ablaut series *teik-*, *taik-*, *tik-* to show, pre-Teut. *dig-*, *deig-*, also *deik-*, in Skr. *diç-*, Gr. δεικ-νύναι, δεῖγμα. Not found elsewhere in Teutonic; Ger. *zeigen*, OHG. *zeigôn* to show, has the same root. The vowel of the OE. pa. t. and pple. *tǽht(e* was apparently shortened before the two consonants, giving the Early ME. *tahte, taȝte*, whence the later *taught*, which appears already *c* 1300 dialectally as *taut(e*. But in the pa. t. a form with the long vowel survived to *c* 1300 as *tǽhte, têhte, teihte, taihte, teite, taite*. A normalized form *teached* (cf. *reached*) has been in partial use since the 14th c., but is not now accepted in educated speech.]

A. Illustration of Forms.

1. *Infin.* 1 tǽc(e)an, 2–3 tachen, 3 teachen, (*Orm.*) tæchenn, 3–4 tache, (theche), 3–5 techen, 3–6 teche, 4–6 tech, teiche (4–5 teyche, 5 techyn, 6 teich, teache, teatch), 6– teach.

c **888** K. ÆLFRED *Boeth.* xxxviii. §3 Ic þe mæg ʒiet tæcan oðer þing. **971** *Blickl. Hom.* 109 Him tæcean lifes weʒ. *c* **1200** ORMIN 3468 To tæchenn hemm. *c* **1200** *Trin. Coll. Hom.* 17 Ic wile..tachen hit ew. *c* **1205** LAY. 2419 He..sculde..tuhlen him teachen. *c* **1325** *Spec. Gy Warw.* 141 Tweie þinges it wole þe teche. *c* **1330** R. BRUNNE *Chron.* (1810) 115 Of þe bisshop Thurston haf I comandment, þe clerkes forto tech. *c* **1375** *Cursor M.* 18710 (Fairf.) þe trauþ to teiche [*other MSS.* teche]. *Ibid.* 27391 þen agh þe leche Calde medicine þar to teyche. *c* **1375** Theching [see TEACHING *vbl. sb.* 2]. **1535** COVERDALE *2 Sam.* i. 18 To teach the children of Iuda the bow. **1536** WRIOTHESLEY *Chron.* (Camden) I. 55 The curates should..teatch their parishiones the 'Pater noster'. **1538** STARKEY *England* I. iv. 132 Schold prech..and tech the pepul. **1596** DALRYMPLE tr. *Leslie's Hist. Scot.* I. (S.T.S.) 125 Our prædecessours..appoyntet sik magistratis ..to teiche thame..to the people.

2. *Imper.* 1 tǽce, tǽc, 3 teke, 3–5 teche, tech, 4 teyche, 6 teache, 6– teach.

? *a* **1000** [see B. 6 c]. *c* **1000** ÆLFRIC *Hom.* I. 258 Leof, tæce us hu we maʒon us ʒebiddan. *a* **1240** *Ureisun* in *Cott. Hom.* 183 Ihesu teke þet tu art se softe and se swote. *a* **1272** *Luue Ron* 198 in *O.E. Misc.* 99 Tech hit oþer maydenes wel. **13..** *Cursor M.* 20795 (Cott.) Teche til him þat all might. *c* **1400** *Cato's Morals* 188 in *Cursor M.* p. 1671 Teyche þou þe vnwise. **1564–78** BULLEYN *Dial. agst. Pest.* (1888) 53 Teache me a Pomeander. **1573** TUSSER *Husb.* (1878) 137 Troth twise to thee teached, teach twentie times ten.

3. *Pres. Indic.* **a.** *1st pers. sing.* 1 tǽce, 3–5 teche, 6 teache, 6– teach.

c **1000** ÆLFRIC *Gram.* xxviii. (Z.) 173 Ic tæce sumum men his weʒ. *a* **1272** *Luue Ron* 83 in *O.E. Misc.* 95 Ich teche þe enne treowe king.

b. *2nd pers. sing.* 1 tǽcst, 4 teches, teychis, 4–5 techest, 6– teachest.

c **1000** ÆLFRIC *Exod.* xix. 12 þu tæcst Israhela folce ʒemæro. **13..** *Cursor M.* 20189 (Cott.) þat þou teches [*F.* teychis; *Tr.* techest] til oþer men.

c. *3rd pers. sing.* 1 tǽcþ, tǽhð, 2 tecð, 2–5 techeþ, 3 tekeðe, 4 tekþ, teychis, 4–6 techeth (5 -ith, 6 -yth), 6– teacheth (now *arch.*), teaches.

c **1000** ÆLFRIC *Gen.* Pref. 4 Se þe tæcþ of Ledene on Englisc. *c* **1000** —— *Hom.* I. 322 Se Halʒa Gast ðe tæhð rihtwisnysse. *a* **1225** *Ancr. R.* 50 þe blake cloð also tekeðe bitocnunge. *c* **1230** *Hali Meid.* 13, & techeð her on eorðe..þe liflade of heouene. **1340** *Ayenb.* 54 To huam þe holy gost tekþ to hyealde ordre. *Ibid.* 56 Alle uelþe he tekþ þer. *c* **1375** *Cursor M.* 12250 (Fairf.) Sum angel..teychis him alle atte he melis. **1377** LANGL. *P. Pl.* B. I. 13 As his worde techeth [*v.r.* thecheth]. **1388** WYCLIF *Prov.* xiii. 24 He that loueth him, techith bisili. **1538** STARKEY *England* I. ii. 38 Vertue hyt ys that techyth vs al.

d. *pl.* 1 tǽcað, 3–5 techen, 3–6 teche, 5–6 *Sc.* techis, 6 teache, (-en), *Sc.* teiche, 6– teach.

c **1400** *Rom. Rose* 5159 As ye me teche. *a* **1425** *Cursor M.* 12192 (Trin.) What þei teche her feres. **1456** SIR G. HAYE *Law Arms* (S.T.S.) 16 Quhilkis..techis othir symple folk.. errouris. *c* **1460** *Pol. Rel. & L. Poems* (1866) 198 Whanne þei þee techen. **1563** *Homilies* II. *Peril Idolatry* III. (1859) 242 As the Scriptures teachen. **1580** J. HAY *Demands* §40 in *Cath. Tractates* (S.T.S.) 44 As ye teiche.

4. *Past tense.* α. 1–3 tǽhte (1 ʒe-), 1 *north.* táhte, 2–4 tahte, tachte, (2 tahhte, tochte), 3–5 taȝte, tauhte, taute, 4 tawhte, tawghte, (taghtte), 4–5 taghte, tauȝte, taughte; 4–5 taȝt, tauht, taght, tauȝt, tawht, tawȝt, tawght, *Sc.* tacht, 5 taut, tawt, 5–6 *Sc.* taucht, tawcht, 5– taught; (5 toght, towght, 6 tought).

a **900** tr. *Bæda's Hist.* III. viii. [x.] (1890) 180 Him mon setl tæhte. *c* **950** *Lindisf. Gosp.* Mark xii. 38 And tæhte *vel* lærde ðæm *vel* him [*et docebat eis*]. [So **975** *Rushw. Gosp.*] *c* **1000** ÆLFRIC *Hom.* I. 68 Symle ðu tæhtest mildheortnysse. *c* **1050** *Byrhtferth's Handboc* in *Anglia* (1885) VIII. 304 An snotor wita me ʒetæhte þisne cræft. *a* **1200** *Vices & Virtues* 27 Ðis ne tahte ðe non eorðlic mann. *a* **1200** *Moral Ode* 268 Al þet þe laþe gast hechte to and tachte. *c* **1200** ORMIN 1071 Hiss boc himm tahhte. *c* **1205** LAY. 804 Brutus heom taute [*c* 1275 tehte]. *a* **1225** *Juliana* 62 þat te engel to þe tahten. *c* **1250** *Gen. & Ex.* 3392 God taȝte hem weie. *c* **1330** R. BRUNNE *Chron.* (1810) 196 God þat þam it tauht. **13..** *Cursor M.* 741 (Cott.) Graitli taght [*v.rr.* taȝt, tauȝte] hi him þe gin. *Ibid.* 17074 (Fairf.) Ther tawghtyst [*T.* tauȝtest] þou vs the way. **1375** BARBOUR *Bruce* II. 130 He taucht him siluer to dispend. *c* **1386** CHAUCER *Pard. T.* 36 As thilke hooly Iew oure eldres taughte [*v.rr.* taghte, tauȝt, tauȝte, tauht]. **1390** GOWER *Conf.* I. 285 Nature..tawht hem so. *c* **1400** *Apol. Loll.* 42 þus He tawt hem to do. *c* **1400** *Emare* 973 Emare thawȝte her sone ȝynge. **1447** BOKENHAM *Seyntys* (Roxb.) 12 And tawth hyr the feyth of Crist Jesu. **1451** CAPGRAVE *Life St. Gilbert* 87 He taute hem ferþermor oþir vertues. ? *a* **1500** *Kyng & Hermyt* 324 in Hazl. *E.P.P.* I. 25 And tauȝt hym priuely to a sted, To feche the hors corne and bred. **1568** GRAFTON *Chron.* I. 15 Those also he taught his invention.

β. 2–3 têhte; 3 teihte, taihte, taite, 3–4 teiȝte, teite.

c **1175** *Lamb. Hom.* 107 He us tehte. *c* **1200** *Trin. Coll. Hom.* 83 þe tehte..alle wise witeȝe here wisdom. *c* **1200** *Moral Ode* 272 *ibid.* 228 Al þat þe loðe gost hem tihte to and taihte. *a* **1225** *Ancr. R.* 158 He teihte us openliche. *a* **1275** *Prov. Ælfred* 634 in *O.E. Misc.* 136 Wel worþe þe wid, þad þe first taite. *c* **1290** *Christopher* 173 in *S. Eng. Leg.* I. 276 Cristofre heom teiȝte þe riȝte bi-leue. *c* **1300** *Harrow. Hell* 233 (Digby MS.) þou teitest me þene riȝte wey.

γ. 4–5 teched, -id, 5–6 *Sc.* techit, 6 *Sc.* teichit, -et, -ed, 6–7 (–9 *dial.*) teached.

13.. *Cursor M.* 12180 (Cott.) Maister leui, þat ald man, Teched [*Gött.* Techid] him a letter þan. **1456** SIR G. HAYE *Law Arms* (S.T.S.) 38 [He] techit the folk of that contree to mak housis. **1596** DALRYMPLE tr. *Leslie's Hist. Scot.* IV. (S.T.S.) 232 Godlie men..quha..teiched the Scotis. *Ibid.* 242 Sigenie, a Scotis Preist..teichet his peiple. **1608** WILLET *Hexapla Exod.* 714 They were taught, and teached not. **1890** W. A. WALLACE *Only a Sister* x. 75 Old Mary Morley teached me that when I was growed up.

5. *Past pple.* α. 1 *ʒetǽht, 2–4 taht, (tahht), 3–4 (i)taȝt, 4 itawt, 4–5 taght, tauht, taut, tauwȝt, (i)tauȝt, (y)tawȝt, itaught, tawht, tauwȝt, (y-tawȝtte), *Sc.* tawcht, 5–6 *Sc.* taucht, 5– taught; (5 toght, towght, 6 tought).

c **1200** ORMIN 18741 He þuss haffde uss tahht. *a* **1300** *Floriz & Bl.* 404 Floris hath iwroȝt As daris him haþ itaȝt [*v.r.* itawt]. **13..** *Cursor M.* 24243 (Edin.) Ik haf him taht [*v.rr.* tagh, taȝt, taght] to þi seruis. **1340–70** *Alex. & Dind.* 217 We weren tauht Of oure doctourus dere. **1362** LANGL. *P. Pl.* A. XI. 169, I grette..his wyf..And tolde hire þe tokenes þat me I-tauȝt were. **1377** *Ibid.* B. xx. 185 Euelytawȝte elde. *c* **1375** *Sc. Leg. Saints* ii. (*Paulus*) 201 To thre knychttis þane wes he tawcht. *c* **1380** WYCLIF *Wks.* (1880) 157 No man schulde here goddis lawe tauwȝt. *c* **1386** CHAUCER *Melib.* ¶300 Whiche of hem han..taught yow best conseil. **1390** GOWER *Conf.* I. 118 The king hath..His brother tawht. *c* **1400** *Destr. Troy* 881 The tokyn hym taght. *Ibid.* 9232 When he hade..toght hym to go. **14..** *Six Ballads* (Percy Soc. No. 50) 14, I wyll nowyse be towght. **14..** in *Babees Bk.* (1868) 357 The wyse man hath hys sone y-tawȝ tte. **1570** B. GOOGE *Pop. Kingd.* 6 That Christ himselfe had tought. **1573** *Satir. Poems Reform.* xlii. 20 His toung weill taucht. **1746** FRANCIS tr. *Hor., Sat.* II. vii. 125 But should not you with heavier Stripes be taught?

β. 4 techid, 4–5 -ed, 6 *Sc.* techit, teichit, 6–7 (–9 *dial.*) teached.

13.. *Cursor M.* 18760 (Cott.) Quen iesus had..teched þam al þat he wild. *Ibid.* 6450 (Gött.) Grete chargis..þat fell to gastlines, Suld techid be thoru moyses. **1544** *Suppl. to Hen. VIII* in *Four Supplic.* (1871) 34 He hathe enstructe and teached the people. **1560** ROLLAND *Seven Sages* 31 Is this ȝour sone..[That] hes bene teichit? **1560–78** *Bk. Discipl. Ch. Scot.* (1621) 38 Experience hath teached us what pestilence hath been ingendered in the Kirk.

B. Signification.

I. To show, etc. [OE. or early ME. (exc. 3 b).]

†1. *trans.* To show, present or offer to view.

a **900** tr. *Bæda's Hist.* IV. i. §2 (MS. T) Tæhte þa þam biscope..sumne ʒedefne munuc, þæs noma wæs Andreas.

†2. To show or point out (a thing, the way, a place, etc.) to a person. *Obs.*

a **900** tr. *Bæda's Hist.* III. viii. [x.], Him mon setl tæhte, and he sæt mid him æt þæm symble. *Ibid.* v. xvii. [xix.] §4. **971** *Blickl. Hom.* 109 þa men þe bearn habban..him tæcean lifes weʒ. *c* **1000** ÆLFRIC *Gram.* xxviii. (Z.) 173 Ic tæce sumum men his weʒ. *c* **1250** *Gen. & Ex.* 3392 God taȝte him weie, wis and pert. *c* **1400** *Destr. Troy* 7836 He..went with þo worthy, & þe way taght.

†3. a. To show (a person) the way; to direct, conduct, convoy, guide (*to*, *from* a place); to send away; also, to direct or refer (*to* something). *Obs.*

Orig. with dative of person and prep. (*to, into, over, from*), as if elliptical for *teach him (the way) to a place*.

c **893** K. ÆLFRED *Oros.* III. iii. §1 Ic ʒehwam wille þærto [= to þinum bocum] tæcan þe hiene his lyst ma to witanne. **925–35** *Laws of Athelstan* II. c. 22 Non mon ne tæce his ʒetihtledan mon from him. *c* **961** ÆTHELWOLD *Rule St. Benet* lviii. (1885) 97 Tæce him mon siððan to niʒcumenra manna huse. *a* **1000** *Cædmon's Gen.* 2900 (Gr.) On þære stowe þe him se stranga to, wærfest metod wordum tæhte. **13..** *K. Alis.* 5204 (Bodl. MS.) He shulde hem teche to sum Ryuere. *Ibid.* 5206 He hem tauȝtte ouer a wode. *c* **1386** CHAUCER *Nun's Pr. T.* 129, I shal my self to herbes techen yow That shul been for youre hele. *c* **1425** *Cast. Persev.* 553 in *Macro Plays* 93 þou art a nobyl knawe to techyn men fyrst fro goode! *a* **1440** *Sir Degrev.* 914 Damesel..Teche me to that ylke place. *c* **1450** *Merlin* xx. 316 Oo hym taught in-to a chamber wher thei were. ? *a* **1500** *Kyng & Hermit* 136 in Hazl. *E.P.P.* I. 18 Late thy knave go, To teche me a myle or two.

b. *Ship-building.* (*absol.*) Of a line: To point in a particular direction.

c **1850** *Rudim. Navig.* (Weale) 155 We say, 'let the line or mould *teach fair* to such a spot'. **1867** SMYTH *Sailor's Word-bk.*, To *Teach*, in marine architecture, is applied to the direction which any line or curve seems to point out.

†4. To show what is to be observed or done; to direct, appoint, prescribe, decree, enjoin. Const. as in II. *Obs.* or absorbed in II.

c **897** K. ÆLFRED *Gregory's Past. C.* xxi. 161 Eft he him tæhte to fultome ðæt he him ʒename ane iserne hearstepannan. *c* **1000** ÆLFRIC *Exod.* xix. 12 þu tæcst Israhela folce ʒemæro abutan þone munt. *a* **1023** WULFSTAN *Hom.* xxxiii. 165 þæt hy betan heora misdæda, swa swa bec tæcan. *c* **1175** *Lamb. Hom.* 107 Uten don elmessen swa he us tehte, gode to luue. *c* **1250** *Long Life* 23 in *O.E. Misc.* 156 Do ase he [Solomon] þe tahte [*v.r.* tauhte]. **1362** LANGL. *P. Pl.* A. II. 7, I lokede on þe luft half as þe ladi me tauhte. *c* **1380** WYCLIF *Sel. Wks.* III. 431 Cerimonyes of þe olde lawe..ben tauht to be left. *c* **1420** *Chron. Vilod.* 3838 þe whyche tauȝt hym euer to don amys. **1567** *Gude & Godlie B.* (S.T.S.) 45 Syne he did his Apostillis teiche Throw all the warld for to pas.

II. To show by way of information or instruction. (Now the leading sense.)

In this group the original construction had an accusative of the thing imparted, with dative of the person or recipient when expressed. The loss of the dative inflexion, or, as in the pronouns, its identification with the accusative, was sometimes replaced by the preposition *to*, but oftener left two objects, of which the indirect, denoting the recipient, became more and more viewed as the direct object, and as such was made the subject of the passive voice, not only when the original direct object was an infinitive, as *he was taught to dance*, but even when it was a sb., as *he was taught Latin*, in preference to *Latin was taught him*.

5. *to teach a thing*: To impart or convey the knowledge of; to give instruction or lessons in (a subject); †to make known, deliver (a message). With simple obj. or obj. clause.

971 *Blickl. Hom.* 43 þa mæsse-preostas..sceolan heora scrift-bec mid rihte tæcan and læran. ? *a* **1000** *K. Ælfred's Boeth.* xxxiv. §9 (MS. B.) þæt þu..ne forʒite þæt þæt ic ær tæhte. *c* **1000** ÆLFRIC *Hom.* I. 322 Se Halʒa Gast ðe tæhð rihtwisnysse. *a* **1175** *Cott. Hom.* 229 [Christ] tochte richwisnesse and soðfestnesse. **13..** *Gaw. & Gr. Knt.* 1485 þou hatz for-ȝeten ȝederly þat ȝisterday I taȝtte. **1340–70** *Alex. & Dind.* 1077 þis kariede sonde þat þus tiþinge tolde & tauhte þis wordus. *c* **1380** WYCLIF *Wks.* (1880) 235 Crist & his apostlis tauten neuere..siche profession. **1451** CAPGRAVE *Life St. Aug.* 12 He cam first hom..and þer taute he gramer. **1560** DAUS tr. *Sleidane's Comm.* 42 The Preachers shall teache the Gospell. **1563** WINȜET *Four Scoir Thre Quest.* xix. Wks. (S.T.S.) I. 85 Quhy tech ȝe that thai are all indifferentlie of ane efficacitie? **1653** WALTON *Angler* To Rdr. 4 To teach the Art of Fencing. **1790** PALEY *Horæ Paul.* xvi, He was convinced of the truth of what he taught. *Mod.* What subjects does he teach in the school?

6. *to teach a person a thing, a thing to a person* (or *agent*): **a.** To communicate something to a person, by way of instruction; †to inform.

c **888** K. ÆLFRED *Boeth.* xxxviii. § 3 Ic þe mæg ʒiet tæcan oðer þing. *a* **1050** in *Sax. Leechd.* III. 256 Eac ʒewisse dæʒmæl us swa tæcað. *c* **1200** *Trin. Coll. Hom.* 99 Ure helende sat ofte and tahte wisdom þan þe him folȝeden. **1297** R. GLOUC. (Rolls) 4827 ȝif ȝe nolle englissemen godes lawes teche. *a* **1300** *Cursor M.* 24306 (Edin.) To techen þaim quat tai sul don. **1426** LYDG. *De Guil. Pilgr.* 36 Thynges that I shal teche the. **1564–78** BULLEYN *Dial. agst. Pest.* (1888) 53, I praie you teache me one or twoo kinde of Pilles. **1715–20** POPE *Iliad* VI. 108 Thou Hector to the town retire, And teach our mother what the gods require. **1741–2** GRAY *Agrippina* 135 Wrinkled beldams Teach it their grandchildren. **1820** SCOTT *Monast.* xxxv, I see it is ill done to teach the cat the way to the kirn. **1857** BUCKLE *Civiliz.* I. xii. 667 It was English literature which taught the lessons of political liberty, first to France, and through France to the rest of Europe. **1874** GREEN *Short Hist.* vii. §1. 352 The sufferings of the Protestants had failed to teach them the worth of religious liberty.

b. The subject of the passive voice was originally the thing taught; it is now usually the person or indirect object.

a **1300** *Cursor M.* 16324 Qui askes þou? it es þe forthwit taght. **1390** GOWER *Conf.* II. 363 Upon the pointz, as we ben taught, Stant sacrilege. **1573** TUSSER *Husb.* (1878) 30 As huswiues are teached, in stead of a clock, How winter nights passeth, by crowing of cock. **1637** (*title*) Romvlvs and Tarqvin. First Written in Italian by the Marques Virgilio Malvezzi: And now taught [= translated into] English, by H. C[arey]. **1745** BUTLER *Serm.* Wks. 1874 II. 276 It is true ..children may be taught superstition, under the notion of religion. **1825** R. H. FROUDE *Rem.* (1838) I. 190, I am being taught French.

c. With the thing taught expressed by an infinitive (or sb. clause): To show or make known to a person (how to do something, etc.).

971 *Blickl. Hom.* 43 þa lareowas sceolan synnfullum mannum eadmodlice tæcan and læran þæt, hie [etc.]. ? *a* **1000** *K. Ælfred's Boethius* Final Prayer (MS. B.), Tæc me þinne willan to wyrcenne. *c* **1250** *O. Kentish Serm.* in *O.E. Misc.* 35 Ne apostle ne prechur..ne hem tachte hu [h]i solde [etc.]. *a* **1300** *Cursor M.* 15373, I sal yow teche him for to knau. *a* **1352** MINOT *Poems* (ed. Hall) ix. 3 þe north end of England teched him to daunce. **1470–85** MALORY *Arthur* VII. xvii. 238 His [the red knight's] wyly fyghtyng taughte syr Beaumayns to be wyse. **1542** UDALL *Erasm. Apoph.* II. 342 b, For which we saie in Englyshe to teache our dame to spynne. **1616** *Withal's Dict.* 575 You teach your good Maister: teach your grandam to grope her duck. **1750** GRAY *Elegy* 84 Many a holy text..that teach the rustic moralist to die. **1868** RUSKIN *Arrows of Chace* (1880) II. 178 Education..means teaching children to be clean, active, honest, and useful. *fig.* *c* **1400** *Rom. Rose* 3319 He tought it [my heart] so hym for to obey. **1625** BACON *Ess., Of Delayes* (Arb.) 525 To teach dangers to come on, by ouer early Buckling towards them, is another Extreme. **1633** P. FLETCHER *Purple Isl.* XI. iv, Thou..taught'st his heart to frame his Canto's best. **1715–20** POPE *Iliad* IX. 723 Is it for him these tears are taught to flow? **1825** T. HOOK *Sayings* Ser. II. *Sutherl.* (Colburn) 35 James's lank hair..was taught to curl gracefully *à la Brutus*.

d. Used by way of threat: To let one know the cost or penalty of something. Also without direct object.

1575 *Gamm. Gurton* III. iii. C iij b, And I get once on foote ..ile teach the what longs to it. *a* **1619** FLETCHER *Mad Lover* III. ii, I'll teach you to be treacherous! **1697** DRYDEN *Virg. Past.* III. 76 I'll teach you how to brag another time. **1778** MISS BURNEY *Evelina* (1791) I. xxxvi. 191 She will..teach you to know who she is. *c* **1863** T. TAYLOR *Ticket-of-Leave Man* II. 33 Sam! is it? Confound him! I'll teach him. **1889** A. LANG *Pr. Prigio* ii. 10 I'll teach you to be too clever, my lad.

e. *teach yourself* (a subject): vbl. phr. used *attrib.* to designate a textbook or manual intended for use without the assistance of a teacher.

The phr. is derived from the titles of books in the Teach Yourself series, published from 1938.

1938 M. THOMAS (*title*) Teach yourself embroidery. **1960** G. BUTLER *Death lives Next Door* He was..going through the Catalogue issued with the Teach Yourself Everything Series. **1961** *Guardian* 4 Feb. 14/6 As I was taught in a teach-yourself book. **1978** P. O'DONNELL *Dragon's Claw* ii. 29, I usually spend a few hours with the tape recorder and a Teach Yourself Russian course.

7. a. *to teach a person* or *agent* (with personal object only): To impart knowledge to, give instruction to; to inform, instruct, educate, train, school. *to teach (a) school*: see SCHOOL *sb.*[1] 1 d.

c **1000** *Eccl. Instit.* 20 in Thorpe *Ags. Laws* II. 414 Hiȝ sceolon swiðe lustlice his onfon, and him estlice tæcan. *c* **1250** *Hymn Virg.* 34 in *Trin. Coll. Hom.* 256 Maide dreiȝ & wel itaucht. *a* **1275** *Prov. Ælfred* 442 in *O.E. Misc.* 129 He sal banne þat wiȝt þat him first taȝte. *c* **1325** *Spec. Gy Warw.* 570 Houre swete lord..Hise deciples began to teche. **1393** LANGL. *P. Pl.* C. I. 120 ȝe sholde be here fadres and techen hem betere. **1484** CAXTON *Fables of Auian* iii, He whiche will teche and lerne some other, ought first to corryge & examyne hym self. **1558** *Peebles Burgh Rec.* (1872) 244 The haill inqueist ordanis Walter Haldane to teche thair Grammare Scoill. **1596** DALRYMPLE tr. *Leslie's Hist. Scot.* VIII. (S.T.S.) 110 A wyfe..weil taucht and brocht vp. **1667** MILTON *P.L.* XII. 446 All Nations they shall teach. **1722** in Picton *L'pool Munic. Rec.* (1886) II. 75 A charity school..for teaching and instructing poor children in. **1877–9** RUSKIN *St. Mark's Rest* ii. §18 There is nothing like a little work with the fingers for teaching the eyes. **1908** [MISS FOWLER] *Betw. Trent & Ancholme* 21 Master Teanby..taught him and others.

b. With prepositional extensions (*to teach of*, etc.). † *to teach to*: to train to, to accustom to the use or practice of (*obs.*).

1297 R. GLOUC. (Rolls) 2197 Men bet iteiȝt to ssofle & to spade. **1382** WYCLIF *Matt.* xxi. 17 There he dwelte, and tauȝte hem of the kyngdam of God. *c* **1450** *St. Cuthbert* (Surtees) 6659 A clerke..þat couthe teche his men to faythe. *a* **1553** UDALL *Royster D.* I. iii. (Arb.) 24, I haue not bene taught to kissing and licking. **1660** F. BROOKE tr. *Le Blanc's Trav.* 166 These Lions..are taught to it, when they are young.

8. *absol.* or *intr.* To communicate knowledge; to act as a teacher; to give instruction.

c **1000** ÆLFRIC *Hom.* I. 242 ȝif se lareow wel tæce..doð swa swa he tæcð. **1340–70** *Alex. & Dind.* 237 Folk þat fain is to teche. **1382** WYCLIF *Matt.* xi. 1 Jhesus..passide fro thennes for to preche and teche in the citees of hem. *c* **1440** *Gesta Rom.* xlv. 178 (Harl. MS.) The whiche prophesied and tawte aȝenst synne. **1552** HULOET, Teache in a schole, *didascolo.* **1651** HOBBES *Leviath.* II. xxvii. 158 One that teacheth by publique Authority. **1674** (Mar. 15) *Warrant for appreh. Bunyan*, One John Bunnyon..Tynker hath divers times within one month last past..preached or teached at a Conventicle meeting or assembly. **1878** R. W. DALE *Lect. Preach.* viii. 226 He must learn how to teach.

III. †**9. a.** To deliver, hand over, give; to give in trust, commit, entrust, commend to the keeping of some one. *Obs.*

In OE. usually expressed by *betæcan*, BETEACH; even quot. *c* 1000 below is difficult to separate from sense 4.

c **1000** ÆLFRIC *Hom.* I. 46 Ða ȝesetnysse ðe us Moyses tæhte [*Vulg.* tradidit nobis Moyses]. *c* **1205** LAY. 22599 Ich tache þe mine leofen sunen. *a* **1300** *Cursor M.* 15349 His bodi suld be taght His fas þat war felun. *Ibid.* 15411 In handes yur i sal him teche. *c* **1300** *Havelok* 2214 Hauelok his sone he him tauhte, And hise two douhtres, and al his auhte. *c* **1375** *Sc. Leg. Saints* xxii. (*Laurentius*) 84 To sancte Syxt þane tacht [he] It. **1375** BARBOUR *Bruce* x. 43 To the gud lorde of Douglas,..He taucht the archaris euirilkane. *c* **1420** *Anturs of Arth.* 605 Swylke a touche at þat tyme he taughte hym in tene. *c* **1475** *Rauf Coilȝear* 772 Ane Chalmer with Armour the King gart richt than Be taucht to ane Squyar.

†**b.** To commend or commit (a person) to God; to bid adieu to; to wish (good day) to: cf. BETEACH *v.* 4, 4 b. *Obs. rare.*

c **1400** *Rowland & O.* 1268 Charlles..Taughte hym to godde. *a* **1425** *Cursor M.* 8068 (Trin.) Þe kyng..tauȝte hem god & good day.

teach (tiːtʃ), *sb.* Colloq. abbrev. of TEACHER 2 a.

1958 F. NORMAN *Bang to Rights* III. 90 'Now now give him a chance,' said the teach. **1976** A. HILL *Summer's End* i. 6, 'I always suspected it, Hill,' Teach had called across the classroom. *Ibid.* 9 The Teach with the cardboard box stopped in front of each kid and gave him or her a paper bag.

teachable ('tiːtʃəb(ə)l), *a.* [f. TEACH *v.* + -ABLE.]

†**1.** Able or apt to teach. *Obs.*

1483 *Cath. Angl.* 378/2 Techeabylle, *docibilis, qui faciliter docet alios*; *docilis, qui faciliter docetur.* **1641**, **1695** [implied in TEACHABLENESS 2].

2. Capable of being taught (as a person); apt to receive instruction; docile; tractable.

1483 [see in 1]. **1583** GOLDING *Calvin on Deut.* ii. 7 And let such knowledge make us teachable. **1684** J. SCOTT *Chr. Life* (ed. 3) 160 To keep our Minds in a teachable temper. **1725** BERKELEY *Proposal*, etc. Wks. 1871 III. 226 They are..less conceited, and more teachable. **1855** KINGSLEY *Heroes* Pref. (1868) 12 These old Greeks were teachable, and learnt from all the nations round.

3. Capable of being taught (as a subject); that may be communicated or imparted by instruction.

1669 GALE *Crt. Gentiles* I. III. v. 63 He brings in Socrates refuting that opinion of the Stoics, That virtue was.. teachable. **1816** BENTHAM *Chrestom.* 17 The subject,—in so far as teachable by exhibition of figure, colour, and other sensible qualities,—will be taught. **1860** RUSKIN *Mod. Paint.* V. VIII. ii. §12. 174 To teach you..everything that is teachable.

Hence **teacha'bility** = next 1, 3.

1876 *Daily News* 4 Dec. 3/1 It requires an unusual modesty and teachability of disposition. **1882** *Pop. Sc. Monthly* XXI. 435 Carnivores..exhibit only moderate teachability. **1887** ST. G. STOCK *Plato's Meno* 26 The same diversity of opinion..with regard to the teachability of virtue.

'teachableness. [f. TEACHABLE + -NESS.] The quality or state of being teachable.

1. Aptness or capacity for being taught; readiness to receive instruction, docility.

1571 GOLDING *Calvin on Ps.* xxv. 9 This teachablenesse will nowhere bee founde, as long as the mynde [is] lifted up with pryde. **1651** BAXTER *Inf. Bapt.* 105 Not only Docible, but Exemplary, for their Teachableness. **1726** SWIFT *Gulliver* IV. iii, My teachableness, civility, and cleanliness, astonished him. **1863** HOLLAND *Lett. Joneses* xii. 172 The prominent characteristic of all really great men is teachableness. **1897** BP. CREIGHTON in *Life & Lett.* (1904) II. vii. 255 Humble submission and teachableness to a higher law.

†**2.** Capacity of teaching; instructiveness. *Obs.*

1641 MILTON *Animadv.* v. Wks. 1851 III. 224 Wherefore wee should not attribute a right Method to the teachableness of Scripture, there can bee no reason given. **1695** TRYON *Dreams & Vis.* iv. 57 There would be much teachableness in Dreams, as they are derived from, and demonstrate [etc.].

3. The quality of being communicable by instruction.

1871 JOWETT *Plato* I. 109 Protagoras began by asserting.. the teachableness of virtue.

'teachably, *adv.* [f. as prec. + -LY[2].] In a teachable manner; with docility.

1804 EUGENIA DE ACTON *Tale without Title* I. 143 If these superficial gentry would..be teachably humble. **1849** MACAULAY *Hist. Eng.* i. I. 47 The child who teachably and undoubtingly listens to the instructions of his elders.

teache, variant of TACHE *sb.*[3]

teached (tiːtʃt), *ppl. a. Obs.* or *dial.* = TAUGHT.

1639 LD. DIGBY, etc. *Lett. conc. Relig.* (1651) 96 By the frequent misapprehension of the teached,..either let slip or supplanted. **1644** G. PLATTES in *Hartlib's Legacy* (1655) 176 The Teachers and the Teached were nothing else but the blind leading of the blind.

teacher ('tiːtʃə(r)), *sb.* Forms: see TEACH *v.*; also 4 *Sc.* -ure, 5–6 -ar, *Sc.* -our. [f. TEACH *v.* + -ER[1].]

†**1.** That which shows or points out; an indicator; the index-finger. *Obs. rare.*

c **1290** *S. Eng. Leg.* I. 308/314 The feorþe finguer hatte 'techere', for þere-with men techez i-wis.

2. a. One who or that which teaches or instructs; an instructor; also *fig.*; *spec.* one whose function is to give instruction, esp. in a school.

13.. *K. Alis.* 17 (Bodl. MS.) For Caton seiþ, þe gode techer, Oþere mannes liif is oure shewer. *c* **1375** *Sc. Leg. Saints* xl. (*Ninian*) 98 Scorne it ware gret to se þe thechure suld vnkennand be. **1382** WYCLIF *Matt.* xxii. 35 Oon of hem, a techer of the lawe, axede Jhesus, temptynge hym. **1439** *Coventry Leet Bk.* 190 To sette hys chylde to skole to what techer off Gramer that he likyth. **1456** SIR G. HAYE *Law Arms* (S.T.S.) 16 Fals prechouris and techouris of errouris. **1538** STARKEY *England* I. iv. 136 For lake of gud techarys and instructarys. **1662** PLAYFORD *Skill Mus.* I. xi. (1674) 48 Experience is the Teacher of all things. **1799** *Med. Jrnl.* I. 302 The retirement of Dr. Matthew Baillie, as a teacher of anatomy. **1807** WORDSW. *Song Feast Brougham Castle* 162 His daily teachers had been woods and rills,.. The sleep that is among the lonely hills. **1870** *Act 33 & 34 Vict.* c. 75 §3 The term 'teacher' includes..every person who forms part of the educational staff of a school. **1884** H. COXWELL in *Contemp. Rev.* Oct. 533 The French are our acknowledged teachers in ballooning.

b. Formerly, in New England Congregational churches, One of several officers appointed to teach.

1834 BARNES *On Romans* xii. 7 The churches in New England had, at first, a class of men who were called teachers ..distinct from the pastor.

c. *teacher's node* (Path.), name given to a chronic inflammation of the vocal chords, characterized by minute whitish nodules on the upper surface of the chords. (Cf. NODE *sb.* 3 a.)

1897 *Allbutt's Syst. Med.* IV. 832 *Chorditis tuberosa*, or 'singer's nodule', or 'teacher's node', is a clinical variety of pachydermia.

3. *attrib.* and *Comb.*, as *teacher-factory*, *-habit*, *-student*, *-trainee*, *-trainer*, *-training*; *teacher-proof*, *-ridden* adjs.; appositive, as *teacher-librarian*; also pertaining to each element, as *teacher-pupil* adj. (cf. *pupil-teacher* s.v. PUPIL *sb.*[1] 3 b); **teacher edition**, an edition of a work prepared especially for the use of teachers; **teachers' aide**, an assistant employed to help the teaching staff of a school in a variety of duties (see quot. 1967).

1889 'MARK TWAIN' *Connecticut Yankee* x. 118, I had started a teacher-factory and a lot of Sunday-schools. **1900** STODDARD *Evol. Eng. Novel* 63 A picture of the soul-life of the struggling teacher-governess of Haworth. **1865** DICKENS *Mut. Fr.* II. i, Perhaps it scarcely required the teacher-habit to perceive that [etc.]. **1975** *Language for Life* (Dept. Educ. & Sci.) xxi. 304 Except for the Teacher-Librarians' Certificate there have been few opportunities for teachers to acquire help in how to organise and manage a library. **1979** *Jrnl. R. Soc. Arts* July 487/1 A simple handbook for those teacher-librarians in Commonwealth developing countries who are called on to undertake this duty without any previous experience. **1964** P. STREVENS *Papers in Lang.* (1965) ii. 32 It is sometimes necessary to prepare 'teacher-proof' materials, if it is known in advance that the proficiency of the teacher is not going to be up to the optimum required. **1965** M. MORSE *Unattached* iv. 131 Despite the teacher-pupil relationship the worker could in no way afford to make the girls feel inferior to herself. **1977** *New Yorker* 19 Sept. 44/1 He is a warm, compassionate man, outside the private teacher-pupil relationship in music. *a* **1704** T. BROWN *Two Oxford Scholars* Wks. 1730 I. 11 They have been Teacher-ridden for many Years. **1956** *Sun* (Baltimore) 17 Nov. 6/3 It is another thing when a teacher is also required to be clerk, accountant and nursemaid, as the Parent-Teacher Association of Howard Park Elementary School has recognized in its hiring of two teachers' aides. **1967** *Children & their Primary Schools* (Dept. Educ. & Sci.) I. VI. xxiv. 330 The type of help that is ..given by teachers' aides, who ought to have equal status with nursery assistants.., falls into three kinds: (a) Help that amounts to an extra pair of hands for the teacher... (b) help..from those with special skills. This could be available for needlework, art and craft, handicraft... (c) supervising children after school hours while they are waiting for their parents. **1894** *Westm. Gaz.* 28 Mar. 2/2 A certain number of teacher-students. **1959** *Listener* 12 Mar. 463/1 A graduate teacher-trainee. **1982** *Underground Grammarian* Nov. 6/2 He might actually decide to become a student of something rather than a teacher-trainee. **1964** *Economist* 22 Aug. 709/3 Sending teachers, and teacher-trainers, to the country in question. **1977** P. STREVENS *New Orientations Teaching Eng.* vi. 79 Many teacher-trainers regard statements of the kind 'We concentrate on practical teaching—none of this theoretical nonsense!' as if they were robust common sense. **1894** *Westm. Gaz.* 28 Mar. 2/2 Our only example of the teacher-training institution. **1949** M. MEAD *Male & Female* 456 Directed towards particular problems—adolescence, teacher-training, nutrition, housing. **1967** *Listener* 14 Sept. 351/2 You could go to a college of education—they used to be called teacher training colleges. **1975** *Language for Life* (Dept. Educ. & Sci.) xxiii. 331 Our Report emerges at a critical and uncertain time in the development of teacher training.

Hence †**'teacher** *v. Obs. rare*, *trans.*, to tutor, prompt, 'coach'; **'teacherdom**, the community of teachers; **'teacheress**, a female teacher.

1619 VISCT. DONCASTER in *Eng. & Germ.* (Camden) 164 Finding him as I thinke..*teachered by some higher directions (whether it be of Rome or Spayne or both in one). **1908** *Times, Lit. Supp.* 6 Aug. 252/1 She ruled her staff and spread her unconscious influence throughout *teacherdom. **1382** WYCLIF *Wisd.* viii. 4 Forsothe the *techeresse [Vulg. *doctrix*] it [wisdom] is of the discipline of God. **1657** J. SERGEANT *Schism Dispach't* 630 The word Mistress may signify..a Teacheress (as I may say) or one which instructs, and so is coincident with Magistra.

teacherage ('tiːtʃərɪdʒ). *N. Amer.* [f. TEACHER *sb.* + -AGE, after PARSONAGE (sense 2), VICARAGE (sense 3), etc.] A house or lodgings provided for a teacher by a school.

1916 *Boston Evening Transcript* 12 July XI. 3 Education officials of Monroe County are showing much interest in the new movement for establishing so-called teacherages—cottages for country school teachers—which is spreading rapidly in several Far-Western States. **1959** R. E. CAMPBELL *I would do it Again* vi. 22 There was a teacherage with all the necessaries. **1968** *Globe & Mail* (Toronto) 15 Jan. 26/6 (Advt.), Required immediately, qualified teacher for one-room school... Three-room teacherage available. **1976** T. WALKER *Spatsizi* ix. 81 Hungry dogs rushed out to bark, and this brought Lester Dorsey to the door of the teacherage.

teacherly ('tiːtʃəlɪ), *a.* [f. TEACHER *sb.* + LY[1].] Of, pertaining to, or characteristic of a teacher; schoolmasterly, schoolmistressy; pedagogic.

a **1683** J. HULL in *Archeologia Americana* (Amer. Antiquarian Soc.) (1857) III. 173 Mr. John Norton..who continued with us three years and upward..laboring in God's work, and joined in a teacherly office with us.

1934 WEBSTER, *Teacherly*,..teacherlike. **1979** *Washington Post* 21 Jan. G1/5 Hesse the German who became a Swiss, the teacherly Peter Pan who hankered after things Asian. **1980** E. BLISHEN *Nest of Teachers* II. xii. 124 He knew the teacherly value of conspiracy. **1982** *N. & Q.* Feb. 80/2 A symptom of the book's teacherly liveliness is its wit.

teachership ('tiːtʃəʃɪp). [f. TEACHER + -SHIP.] The office, function, or position of a teacher.

1846 THORPE *Ælfric's Hom.* II. 35 Stephen..is first in martyrdom, and first in teachership. **1868** M. PATTISON *Academ. Org.* vi. 253 The teacherships are filled by men of real knowledge. **1870** *Athenæum* 14 May 643 The most pressing wants of the University, in which they included.. a Demonstratorship of Chemistry and Teachership of Palæontology and Modern Languages. **1885** *Harper's Mag.* LXX. 210 If she had succeeded in getting the little town school teachership.

'tea-chest. [f. TEA *sb.* + CHEST *sb.*[1]]

†**1.** = *tea-caddy*: see TEA *sb.* 9 c. *Obs.*

1740 MRS. DELANY in *Life & Corr.* (1861) II. 97, I have got a very neat tea-chest for Mrs. Yate, which shall be filled with tea, and delivered to her. **1775** ASH, *Teachest*, a small kind of cabinet in which tea is brought to table. **1780** MME. D'ARBLAY *Diary* Apr., I was putting away the tea-chest. *c* **1850** [Remembered in use at Cambridge].

2. A large box or chest of cubical form, lined with sheet-lead, in which tea is packed for transport: cf. CHEST *sb.*[1] 6. Also *attrib.*

1801 HULME in *Phil. Trans.* XCI. 403 Flat lead, such as lines Chinese tea-chests. **1893** F. F. MOORE *I Forbid Banns* (1899) 100 The furniture had not the appearance of being made out of flour barrels and tea-chests. There was not much of the tea-chest look about the old oak dresser.

teachie, teachily, obs. ff. TETCHY, TETCHILY.

'teach-in, orig. *U.S.* [f. TEACH *v.* + -IN[3] (after *sit-in*, etc.).] An informal debate (often of some length) on a matter of public, usu. political, interest, orig. between the staff and students of a university. Hence, a conference attended by members of a profession on topics of common concern. Also *loosely*, a lecture or meeting held for the purpose of discussion or disseminating information.

1965 *N.Y. Times* 25 Mar. 9/1 Bomb scares marked the start tonight of a 12-hour series of rallies, speeches and seminars sponsored by some 200 University of Michigan faculty members to protest United States policy in Vietnam. .. Policemen evacuated.. the site of the protest gathering which the faculty members have named a 'teach-in'. **1965** *Economist* 24 Apr. 416/1 Universities all over the country [*sc.* USA] have conducted informal 'teach-ins' on Vietnam, running from eight in the evening to eight the following morning. **1965** *Times* 17 June 8/5 This free-for-all debate.. was called by the ugly new jargon name of 'teach-in'—a concept recently invented at Harvard, which has crossed the Atlantic. **1967** McLuhan & Fiore *Medium is Massage* 101 The dropout represents a rejection of nineteenth-century technology... The teach-in represents, a creative effort. **1969** *New Scientist* 30 Jan. 219/1 The great Edinburgh Teach-in.. on chemical and biological warfare. **1971** *Ibid.* 24 June 741/1 Engineers have run a series of 'teach-ins' to show designers how they wish to apply the new rules. **1973** R. Ludlum *Matlock Paper* iii. 21 Six days of riots on campus. Half a semester lost on teach-ins. **1975** D. Lodge *Changing Places* iv. 138 A two day teach-in on the constitution and scope of the proposed commission.

'teaching, *vbl. sb.* Forms: see the verb. [f. teach *v.* + -ing[1].] The action of the verb teach.

†**1.** Showing the way; direction, guidance. *Obs.*

13.. *Cursor M.* 11656 (Gött.) Forth þai went þar wai fra þan Widvten teching of ani man.

2. a. The imparting of instruction or knowledge; the occupation or function of a teacher.

c **1175** *Lamb. Hom.* 93 Alle þeo.. him ihersummede efter godes tecunge. *c* **1275** *Passion* 255 in *O.E. Misc.* 44 He hym axede of his techinge And of his disciples. *c* **1375** *Sc. Leg. Saints* xxvii. (*Machor*) 372 Thru theching of þe haly gast. **1456** Sir G. Haye *Law Arms* (S.T.S.) 68 The barnis.. wald nouther tak teching na chastisement of the fader. **1530** Palsgr. 279/2 Teching, lerning, *enseignement*. **1617** Hieron *Wks.* II. 189 It may bee for teaching-sake parted into two portions. **1656** tr. *Hobbes's Elem. Philos.* (1839) 80 Teaching is nothing but leading the mind of him we teach, to the knowledge of our inventions, in that track by which we attained the same. **1715** De Foe *Fam. Instruct.* I. i. (1841) I. 8, I can say that without teaching. **1862** Helps *Organization* 50 In teaching, he has not to display knowledge, but to impart it.

b. That which is taught; a thing taught, doctrine, instruction, precept.

a **1300** *Cursor M.* 2655 And if þou halds mi techeyng; O þe sal com bath prince and king. **1377** Langl. *P. Pl.* B. vii. 74 *Cui des, videto* is catounes techynge. **1482** *Monk of Evesham* (Arb.) 42 Whyche may be to alle the worlde a nobylle document and techyng. **1542–3** *Act 34 & 35 Hen. VIII*, c. 1 Suche bookes, writinges.. teachinges and instructions, as be pestiferous, and noysome. **1853** J. H. Newman *Hist. Sk.* (1873) II. i. iii. 139 In the middle of the fourteenth century, the teaching of Wickliffe gained ground in England. **1856** Stanley *Sinai & Pal.* xiii. 426 A character and teaching, human Hebrew, Syrian, in its outward form and colour, but in its inward spirit.. Divine.

†**3.** Delivering, handing over. *Obs. rare.*

c **1300** *Cursor M.* 15416 (Cott.) In handes yur i [Judas] sal him teche;.. And godder-hail þan sal þou se, For luue o þis techeing.

4. *attrib.* and *Comb.* as ***teaching aid, load, material, post, process***; **teaching hospital**, a hospital at which medical students are instructed; **teaching machine**, a mechanical device for giving instruction in the form of a teaching programme which allows a pupil to progress according to his response to questions of choice.

1966 *Rep. Comm. Inquiry Univ. Oxf.* II. 470 They might even be encouraged to use occasionally the odd teaching aid. **1980** *Underground Grammarian* Dec. 1/2 Think of the audio-visual devices and the teaching aids. **1617** Hieron *Wks.* II. 169 God.. hath put this teaching-businesse into their hands. **1963** in A. Heron *Towards Quaker View of Sex* 51 All the large teaching hospitals have psychiatric out-patient departments. **1980** *Brit. Med. Jrnl.* 29 Mar. 924/2 The London teaching hospitals, which for so long had served their local population, and which had now been set aside to serve the needs of education, began instead to bear the brunt of the specialised services. **1849** Rock *Ch. of Fathers* I. iv. 300 The Church is the teaching-house of holiness. **1958**, etc. Teaching load [see load *sb.* 4c]. **1958** *Science* 24 Oct. 971 (*caption*) Student at work on a teaching machine. **1969** J. Argenti *Managem. Techniques* 215 This method can be used.. with a teaching machine. These machines consist of a box like a television set in which there is a film strip. **1972** H. J. Eysenck *Psychol. is about People* iii. 147 Sidney L. Pressey in the mid-1920s designed the precursors of our modern automated teaching machines. **1960** *Tuscaloosa* (Alabama) *News* 20 Nov. 4/4 The student fits teaching material into the box and then uses them [*sic*] at his own speed. **1962** *Sunday Times* (Colour Suppl.) 10 June 4 There have been no sinecures or teaching posts for famous jazzmen. **1975** *Language for Life* (Dept. Educ. & Sci.) xvii. 254 We regard recording as an essential element in the actual teaching process. **1617** Hieron *Wks.* II. 283 Vnable to performe this teaching-seruice. **1881** *Nature* 17 Feb. 379/2 Preserving the soft tissues.. as teaching-specimens. **1879** P. Brooks *Influence of Jesus* i. 25 Jesus is coming home from one of his teaching-tours in Galilee.

'teaching, *ppl. a.* [f. as prec. + -ing[2].]

a. That teaches, or has the quality or function of teaching.

1853 J. Cumming *Foreshadows* vii. (1854) 188 The great typical and teaching disease. **1899** *Allbutt's Syst. Med.* VIII. 217 Differences of opinion between the teaching and the medical professions. **1899** *Daily News* 19 Apr. 3/5 What was needed was teaching sermons. *Mod.* To change the University of London from a merely examining into a teaching university.

b. Special collocations, as **teaching elder**: see elder *sb.*[3] 4; **teaching fellow** *U.S.*, a student at a graduate school who carries out teaching or laboratory duties in return for a stipend, free tuition, or other benefit.

1642 T. Lechford *Plain Dealing* 15 Some Churches have no ruling Elders, some but one, some but one teaching Elder, some have two ruling, and two teaching Elders. **1735** in C. Hazard *Thos. Hazard* (1893) 226 We the Subscribers, Teaching Elders or Pastors of the first gathered.. Church in Boston New England. **1936** S. E. Morison *Three Centuries of Harvard* i. 18 There were no funds to maintain more than two teaching fellows. **1979** C. MacLeod *Luck runs Out* (1981) xvii. 169 He'd come there as a teaching fellow... He taught the subject ably.

Hence **'teachingly** *adv. rare*, in a way that teaches, instructively.

1870 Spurgeon *Treas. David* Ps. xxx. 7 How touchingly and teachingly God corrected his servant's mistake.

teachless ('tiːtʃlɪs), *a. rare.* [f. teach *v.* + -less.] Without teaching, untaught.

1819 Shelley *Julian & Maddalo* 164 The religions and old saws.. Which break a teachless nature to the yoke.

†**'teachment.** *Sc. Obs.* [f. teach *v.* + -ment.] Teaching, instruction.

1562 Winȝet *Cert. Tractates* i. Wks. (S.T.S.) I. 5 Hes not mony throw inlak of techement in mad ignorance mys-knawin thair deuty? **1563** Davidson *Confut. Kennedy* in *Wodrow Soc. Misc.* (1844) 200 Without teachement and instructione of uthers. *a* **1578** Lindesay (Pitscottie) *Chron. Scot.* (S.T.S.) I. 147 To abolische and put away the rude maner of the teichment.

teachy, obs. form of tetchy.

tea-circle to **-crop**: see tea *sb.* 9.

'tea-cup. a. (*a*) A cup from which tea is drunk: usually of small or moderate size, with a handle.

1700 Congreve *Way of World* iv. xi, Let Mahometan Fools.. be damned over Tea-Cups and Coffee. **1714** Addison *Lover* No. 10 ¶4 The fashion of the teacup.. has run through a wonderful variety of colour, shape, and size. **1770** Goldsm. *Des. Vill.* 235 While broken tea-cups.. Ranged o'er the chimney, glistened in a row. **1884** H. P. Spofford in *Harper's Mag.* Nov. 889/1 In a sort of Oriental divination they always turned their tea-cups,.. after the tea-drinking which they loved. *Mod.* The subject has been mentioned 'over the tea-cups' [*i.e.* unofficially; speaking of the establishment of a public institution].

(*b*) With reference to fortune-telling by means of interpreting the arrangement of tea-leaves left in a cup. Cf. tea-leaf 1.

1883 C. S. Burne *Shropshire Folk-Lore* xxi. 277 The apparitions which.. nurses used to discover in their tea-cups when they had.. emptied the last remains of the tea in such a manner as to leave the dregs scattered well over the bottom and sides of the cup. **1921** C. Kent *Fortune-Telling by Tea-Leaves* ii. 24 A confused looking tea-cup, without any symbols.. is useless for the purpose of divination. **1954** M. Sharp *Gipsy in Parlour* xii. 127 Cook.. had an eye for tall dark strangers, who frequently appeared in her tea-cup. **1976** A. E. Lindop in *Winter's Crimes 8* 216 She can 'see' what's best for us... She'll look into our teacups.

b. As much as a tea-cup contains, a teacupful.

1757 Pulteney in *Phil. Trans.* L. 81 She took something more than a tea-cup of the infusion.

c. Phr. ***a storm in a tea-cup***: a great commotion in a circumscribed circle, or about a matter of small or only local importance: see storm. Similarly ***tea-cup storm***, etc.

1854 W. B. Bernard (*title*) A storm in a teacup. **1872** Black *Adv. Phaeton* xix, She has raised a storm in a tea-cup by her.. unwarranted assault. **1884** *Pall Mall G.* 19 Sept. 4/1 M. Renan's visit.. to his birthplace in Brittany has raised a storm in the clerical teacup. **1900** G. C. Brodrick *Mem. & Impr.* 360 Here the storm in the Oxford tea-cup raged as furiously as in the open sea. **1932** *Times Lit. Suppl.* 15 Sept. 639/1 Those old disputes were no teacup squalls. **1951** *Sport* 16–22 Mar. 14/3 Earlier this season a slight 'teacup storm' occurred in Yorkshire Rugby Union circles. **1981** W. Safire in *N.Y. Times Mag.* 15 Feb. 11/1 In the midst of this teacup contretemps came a clear message from John Radosta.

d. *attrib.* ***tea-cup-and-saucer comedy***, comedy of a mild and 'proper' character.

1830 Tennyson *Talking Oak* xvi, Beauties, that were born In teacup-times of hood and hoop, Or while the patch was worn. **1895** *Athenæum* 8 June 748/2 'Tea-cup-and-saucer comedy'.. was the invention of Thomas Purnell. **1898** *Westm. Gaz.* 30 Mar. 2/3 A little too much like.. the tea-cup business of Alice in Wonderland. **1902** *Daily Chron.* 23 Sept. 3/3 Young girls.. find a gentle interest in her mild heroics of tea-cup-and-saucer comedy.

Hence **'teacupful**, as much as a tea-cup will contain. (Pl. *teacupfuls*; erron. *tea-cups full.*)

1705 *Phil. Trans.* XXV. 1790 [I] took about a Tea-cupful. **1789** Pilkington *View Derby.* I. viii. 355 The dose 2 tea-cups full or more. **1838** *Q. Jrnl. Agric.* IX. 290 A salt-spoonful of salt and a tea-cupful of warm water.

tead, teade, var. tede *Obs.*, torch.

tea-dealer to **-dregs**: see tea *sb.* 9.

'tea-,drinker. One who drinks tea, *esp.* one who drinks it habitually or in large quantities.

1737 *London Mag.* Apr. 186/1 Considering the Number of Tea Drinkers, it [*sc.* tea-drinking] had done a great deal more Hurt than Dram-Drinking. **1756** Hanway *Ess. Tea* v. 225 The pernicious effects of tea.. as it is used by the bulk of tea-drinkers. **1888** J. Paton in *Encycl. Brit.* XXIII. 101/1 The quantity of theine consumed by even the most hardened tea-drinker is exceedingly minute.

So **'tea-,drinking**, (*a*) *vbl. sb.* the drinking of tea; †also, a social gathering at which tea is provided (*obs.*); also *attrib.*; (*b*) *ppl. a.* that drinks tea.*vbl. sb.*

1737 *London Mag.* Apr. 183/2 (*heading*) Of Diet in general, and the bad Effects of Tea-drinking. **1756** Hanway *Ess. Tea* viii. 243 (*heading*) The Prevalency of Example in Tea-drinking. **1781** A. Storer *Let.* 28 June in *15th Rep. R. Comm. Hist. MSS.* App. vi. 508 in *Parl. Papers 1897* (C.8551) LI. 1. Lady Craven gave a tea-drinking last night. **1793** W. B. Stevens *Jrnl.* 8 July (1965) 91 Walked with Mrs Cutts, etc... to Schobley Mill, a Tea-Drinking Place. **1799** Mar. Edgeworth *Lottery* i, She learned to love gossiping and tea-drinkings. **1813–14** T. Somerville *Life & Times* (1861) 280 The individuals who met at a tea-drinking party one afternoon. **1675** Wycherley *Country Wife* ii. i, Every raw, peevish, out-of-humoured, affected, dull, *tea-drinking, arithmetical fop, sets up for a wit. **1845** Agnes Strickland *Queens Eng.* VIII. 310 Catherine of Braganza was certainly the first tea-drinking queen of England.

tea-drunkard: see tea *sb.* 9.

teaed (tiːd), *a. U.S. slang.* Also **tea-d.** [f. tea *sb.* 7c + -ed[2].] In a state of euphoria induced by alcohol or marijuana. Usu. with *up*.

1928 L. E. Lawes *Life & Death in Sing Sing* iv. 53 'Didn't alcohol have something to do with your coming here?' 'Yes, sah, dey was bofe considerable teaed up.' **1944** *War Med.* VI. 383/2 Just those thoughts will drive me mad—thinking about my 'boys' all 'tea-d up', and here I am, sitting and thinking about it, and I can't get it. **1966** C. Himes *Heat's On* xvii. 157 The driver was teaed to the gills and on a livewire edge.

tea-equipage: see tea *sb.* 9.

teaer, teaey: see after tea *v.*, *sb.*

tea-faced to **-frock**: see tea *sb.* 9.

'tea-,garden.

1. A garden or open-air enclosure, connected with a house of entertainment, where tea and other refreshments are served.

1802 *Picture of London* 370 Shepherd and Shepherdess Tea Gardens, &c., City Road... Much frequented in the summer time by tea parties, &c. **1829** De Vega *Jrnl. Tour* ix. (1847) 81 A charge of three-pence is demanded on entering the delightful 'Tea Gardens'. **1900** *Daily News* 12 Nov. 6/3 Tea garden resorts.. have entirely vanished.

2. A plantation in which tea-plants are grown. (Cf. *hop-garden.*)

1882 Spons *Encycl. Manuf.* v. 1994 There is scarcely a tea-garden but what is mainly filled with hybrids.. between these two species [*Thea chinensis* and *T. assamica*]. **1888** J. Paton in *Encycl. Brit.* XXIII. 98/2 Undulating well-watered tracts.. are the most valuable for tea-gardens.

Hence **'tea-,gardened** *a.*, having a tea-garden; **'tea-,gardener**, the keeper of, or a worker in, a tea-garden; **'tea-,gardeny** *a.*, *colloq.* resembling, or having the style of, a tea-garden (sense 1).

1843 Thackeray *Irish Sk.-Bk.* vii, What a prim,.. green-railinged, tea-gardened, gravel-walked place would it have been. **1862** G. H. Kingsley *Sport & Trav.* (1900) 368 The public gardens, small and insignificant enough, indeed a little tea-gardeny. **1879** *Dickens's Dict. Thames* (1880) 120/2 There is little.. of the ancient abbey to be found among the present tea-gardeny ruins. **1903** *Daily Chron.* 16 Sept. 6/7 Miura, a [Japanese] tea gardener, assures his young and pretty wife Ohana that she is unsightly.

teagle ('tiːg(ə)l), *sb.* [A dial. var., chiefly northern, of tackle; cf. the forms *taikle, teakle, -kil*, s.v.] A hoisting apparatus: = tackle *sb.* 3; *esp.* one used for moving goods from floor to floor of a warehouse, etc. Also *attrib.*

1828 *Craven Gloss.*, *Teagle*, a crane. **1835** Ure *Philos. Manuf.* 45 This apparatus is called a hoist or teagle. **1887** *Manchester Courier* 21 May 7/2 The teagle did not hang over the street, but was in a recess. He saw no one guiding the teagle rope. **1901** *Act 1 Edw. VII*, c. 22 §10 Every hoist or teagle and every fly wheel.

b. *transf.* (See quot.)

1908 *Times, Lit. Supp.* 4 June 180/3 A detestable method of bird-catching.. specially-manufactured fish-hooks are baited and fastened to a string, known as a 'teagle', which is laid down in a place which the birds are likely to frequent. **1909** *Spectator* 21 Aug. 269/1 A law was passed making it illegal to catch any bird by means of the teagle.

Hence **'teagle** *v. trans.*, (*a*) to hoist or raise with or as with a teagle; = tackle *v.* 2; (*b*) to catch birds with a teagle (see b above). *dial.*

1841 R. W. Hamilton *Nugæ Lit.* 355 To *Teagle* is to raise any thing by pulley or wheel. **1892** M. C. F. Morris *Yorksh. Folk-Talk* 386 Wa mun start ti teeagle 'em up wi' t'hosses. **1910** *Sat. Rev.* 4 June 712/1 Sympathy with 'teagling', a barbarous but popular practice.

tea-gown to **-growing:** see TEA *sb.* 9.

Teague (teɪg, tiːg), **Taig** (teɪg). *colloq.* Also 7 teg, 8 teigue. [Anglicized spelling of the Irish name *Tadhg*, variously pronounced (teɪg, tiːg, taɪg), fancifully identified with *Thaddeus* and its familiar form *Thady*.]

†**1.** A nickname for an Irishman. *Obs.* or *arch.*

[**1583** in Dillwyn *Contrib. Hist. Swansea* (1840) 18 William Tege and Daniell John, Irishmen, made suet to be admytted Fremen.] **1661** *Merry Drollery* II. 143 Let not poor Teg and Shone Vencer from der houses. **1682** *New News fr. Bedlam* 3 Those Sham Intrigues, From French, from English, and from Irish Teagues. **1689** in *Harl. Misc.* (1746) VIII. 603/1 Irish Frize..to rig a whole Regiment of his new-raised Teagues. *c* **1720** PRIOR *On Person who wrote ill*, His case appears to me like honest Teague's, When he was run away with, by his legs. **1727** SWIFT *Market-hill Thorn* Wks. 1755 IV. I. 90 Pigs and fanaticks, cows and teagues..To tear thy hedges join in leagues. **1865** LOWELL *Pr. Wks.* (1890) II. 20 If we took warning by the example of Teague and Taffy. **1899** H. C. HART in *Phil. Soc. Trans.* 8 *Jeremiah* has Irish equivalent *Diarmid* or *Darby*; ..*Theophilus, Teddy; Thaddeus, Thady*... The last two are from Irish *Tadhg* or *Teig* or *Thady*, a poet, which gives rise also to *Teague*, a name not now in use, but formerly a sobriquet (like the modern Paddy) for an Irishman. **1900** S. J. WEYMAN *Sophia* i, A raw-boned, uncouth Teague.

2. Usu. in form Taig. In Northern Ireland, a Protestant term of contempt for a Roman Catholic.

1971 *Times* 13 May 2/6 Taig is Protestant slang for a Roman Catholic. **1973** *Spectator* 3 Mar. 263/2 The Prods are only having their shops blown up and suffering a few slight cases of murder; the Teagues are losing their souls. **1978** D. MURPHY *Place Apart* vii. 133 In times of stress Loyalist paramilitaries can easily rouse large mobs and lead them out of the ghettos on Taig-bashing expeditions. **1982** *Observer* 31 Oct. 8/3 This week a new slogan appeared along the Shankill Road, the backbone of Protestant West Belfast. It read: 'All Taigs are targets.'

Hence †ˈ**Teaguism**, the characteristics of a Teague or Irishman; †ˈ**Teagueland**, Ireland; †ˈ**Teaguelander**, an Irishman. *Obs.*

1689 *Answ. Lords & Commoners Sp.* 27 Not to mention those Teague Land Sparks put over them. *Ibid.* 28 The Teague-Landers and others like them. *a* **1700** B. E. *Dict. Cant. Crew, Teague-land*, Ireland. *Teague-landers*, Irishmen. **1710–11** SWIFT *Jrnl. to Stella* 30 Mar., Sir Thomas Mansel..saw Patrick, and swore he was a Teaguelander. **1732** SIR C. WOGAN *Let. to Swift* 27 Feb., The English writers take the hints from them [Irish]..and delight in gratifying the flattest nonsense..upon teigueism.

tea-hamper to **-junketing:** see TEA *sb.* 9.

teaish, teaism: see after TEA *sb.*

teak (tiːk). Forms: 7–8 teke, 8 teek, tecka, 8–9 teck, 9 tick, tæk, teake, 8– teak. [ad. Pg. *teca* (1602–1644 in Yule), ad. Malayāl. *tēkka*; in Tamil *tēkku*, Telugu *tēku*, Tulu *tekki*, Canarese *tēgu*, *tēga*, *tēngu*.]

1. a. A large East Indian tree (*Tectona grandis*, N.O. *Verbenaceæ*), with opposite egg-shaped leaves and panicles of white flowers; more usually, its timber, a dark, heavy, oily wood of great strength and durability, used largely in the construction of ships and railway carriages, and in India also for building houses, and for sleepers, furniture, etc.; distinctively called *Indian teak*.

1698 FRYER *Acc. E. India & P.* 142 The Sheds here were round, thatch'd, and lined with broad Leaves of Teke (the Timber Ships are built with). *Ibid.* 178 Teke..is the firmest Wood they have for Building. **1757** J. H. GROSE *Voy. E. Indies* 174 As to the wood, it is a sort, called teak, to the full as durable as oak. **1783** JUSTAMOND tr. *Raynal's Hist. Indies* II. 244 Their ships..of a very strong wood called Teck. **1793** HODGES *Trav. India* 87, I found the teek, a timber remarkable for its hardness and size. **1808** A. PARSONS *Trav.* x. 215 This timber and plank are peculiar to India only;..it is called tick. **1811** *Niebuhr's Trav. Arab.* cliv, That excellent wood called Tæk. **1853** WAYLAND *Mem. Judson* I. xi. 413 Large forests of teak have been discovered in the interior [of Burma]. **1883** *Chambers's Encycl.* IX. 325/1 Indian Teak (*Tectona grandis*).

b. A fashion shade resembling the colour of teak-wood, a rich reddish brown.

1934 in WEBSTER. **1971** [see MOLE *sb.*[2] 7].

2. Applied, usually with defining words, to other trees which produce strong or durable timber, or otherwise resemble the Indian teak; as

African teak, *Oldfieldia africana* (N.O. *Euphorbiaceæ*), or its wood, which is too heavy to be exclusively used in shipbuilding. **bastard teak**, an East Indian tree, *Pterocarpus Marsupium*, from which kino is obtained; yielding hard and durable timber. **ben teak**, *Lagerstræmia microcarpa*, of tropical Asia; also, a poor quality of teak. **teak of New South Wales**, a small tree, *Endiandra glauca*, N.O. *Leguminosæ*, the wood of which is fine-grained and dense (Miller *Plant-n.* 1884). **teak of New Zealand**, the PURIRI, *Vitex littoralis*. **white teak**, of Queensland, a species of *Flindersia*, N.O. *Meliaceæ*. In Australia also applied to *Dissilaria baloghioides*, N.O. *Euphorbiaceæ* (Morris *Austral Eng.*).

1842 BRANDE *Dict. Sc.*, etc. 1217/1 A species of timber called African teak is pretty largely imported..from the west coast of Africa... It is not teak. **1858** HOGG *Veg. Kingd.* 663 African Teak, or Oak, is the wood of *Oldfieldia africana*. **1866** *Treas. Bot.* 1128 Ben Teak, the wood of *Lagerströmia microcarpa*; also applied to inferior Teak. New South Wales Teak, *Endiandra glauca*. **1878** H. M. STANLEY *Dark Cont.* II. vi. 156 Many a village stood..embowered in the thick shade of tamarind and bombax, teak. **1883** *Chambers's Encycl.* IX. 325/1 The leaves of many different trees have been brought to botanists as those of the African teak. **1884** MILLER *Plant-n.*, *Vitex littoralis*, New Zealand Teak or Puriri-tree.

3. *attrib.* and *Comb.*, as ***teak forest, log, -oil, ship, timber, -tree, -wood***; ***teak-built*** (in quot. 1848 fig.), ***-lined, -panelled, -producing, -veneered*** adjs.; **teak-oak**, the teak (sense 1).

1727 A. HAMILTON *New Acc. E. Ind.* I. xv. 177 Gundavee .., where good Quantities of Teak Timber are cut. **1783** J. PRICE *Tracts* I. 191 (Y.) Ships..built in India of tekewood, and bound with iron spikes and bolts. **1783** RENNELL *Mem. Map Hindoostan* vi. 89 *note*, Teek ships of 40 years old and upwards, are no uncommon objects. **1800** *Misc. Tr.* in *Asiat. Ann. Reg.* 187 During the two last days I had occasionally observed the teak-tree. **1835** J. E. ALEXANDER *Sketches in Portugal* viii. 179 In May, the fleet of her Most Faithful Majesty consisted of the following ships:—..50, Don Pedro,..Very strong, teak-built. **1848** DICKENS *Dombey* xxxii, That teak-built and trim ballad. **1869** SIR E. J. REED *Iron-Clad Ships* ii. 26 In the 'Bellerophon', the armour-plating is 6 inches, and the teak backing 10 inches thick. **1884** MILLER *Eng. Plant-n.*, African Teak-tree, *Oldfieldia africana*. **1889** KIPLING *From Sea to Sea* (1899) I. iii. 220, I saw the elephants playing with the teak logs. **1896** *Daily News* 30 Dec. 6/3 The library at Groote Schuur is a cosy, teak-lined room. **1968** A. DIMONT *Bang Bang Birds* vi. 89 We stepped into a small, teak-panelled lift. **1968** J. ARNOLD *Shell Bk. Country Crafts* 198 For such articles as salad-bowls..teak-oil is used. **1970** *Interior Design* Dec. 753/3 Small teak-veneered tables. **1979** P. WAY *Sunrise* xv. 157 Two wrought-iron gates, massively reinforced by teak logs.

ˈ**tea-,kettle.** A kettle in which water is boiled for making tea. Phr. *ass* (= arse) ***over tea-kettle***, head over heels (cf. *arse over tip* s.v. ARSE *sb.* 1 b). *U.S. slang.*

1705 *Lond. Gaz.* No. 4063/4 A Tea Kettle, a gilt Tea-Pot. *a* **1774** TUCKER *Lt. Nat.* (1834) II. 397 He that snatches up the copper handle of a tea kettle, and burns his fingers. **1865** *Times* 23 Aug., Wiesbaden..is as close and hot in the summer as a steaming tea-kettle.

transf. **1857** DUFFERIN *Lett. High Lat.* iv. (ed. 3) 18 There was a great demand in Australia for small river steamers... The difficulty, however, was to get such fragile tea-kettles across the ocean.

attrib. **1746** MILES in *Phil. Trans.* XLIV. 55 The Spirits were such as we use for the Tea-kettle Lamp. **1837** DICKENS *Pickw.* vi, Crimson silk tea-kettle holders. **1896** *Peterson Mag.* Jan. 63/2 Martha dropped the tea-kettle cover with a bang.

phr. **1963** T. PYNCHON *V.* i. 23 Fast enough..only to send Profane, garbage can and lettuce leaves flying ass over teakettle in a great green shower. **1977** J. CROSBY *Company of Friends* vii. 51 Sascha's horse..stopped short... Sascha went ass over teakettle into the brambles.

teakil, -kle, obs. forms of TACKLE.

teal (tiːl). Forms: 4–6 tele, 5 teill, 5–6 teele, 6–7 teyle, teale, 7 teil, tayle, 8 teall, 7– teal. [ME. *tele*, exemplified early in 14th c., but pointing to an unrecorded OE. *tæle, téle*:—WGer. **taili*. Du. has a deriv. form *taling, teling* masc., in Kilian *teelingh*, MDu. *têling, teiling*, MLG. *têlink* masc., teal. (Connexion with Du. *teling* fem., generation, LG. *teling* fem., brood, from Du., and LG. *têlen* to breed, is improbable.)]

1. a. A small fresh-water fowl, *Querquedula* or *Anas crecca*, or other species of the genus, the smallest of the ducks, widely distributed in Europe, Asia, and America; also locally applied to other genera of the *Anatidæ*. Also as collective pl.

1314 in *Wardrobe Acc. Edw. II* 21, 2 teles 3[d]. *c* **1325** *Gloss. W. de Bibbesw.* in Wright *Voc.* 151 Turbe de cercels [*gl.* teles]. **14..** *Voc.* in Wr.-Wülcker 563/45 *Anacius*, a tele. *c* **1440** *Promp. Parv.* 487/2 Tele, bryd, *turcella, turbella*. **1486** *Bk. St. Albans* d j, I haue seen them made sum to sle the pie sum to sle the Tele vppon the Reuer. **1530** PALSGR. 279/2 Teele a byrde, *plignon*. *c* **1532** DU WES *Introd. Fr.* ibid. 912 The teyle, *le cercelle*. **1538** ELYOT, *Querquedula*, a waterfowle callyd a teale. **1575** TURBERV. *Falconrie* 191 Some water plashet or pitte where wylde fowle lye, as Teales or suche lyke. **1614** MARKHAM *Cheap Husb.* VII. xviii. (1668) 123 So you may nourish Teils, Widgens, Sheldrakes or green Plovers. **1661** LOVELL *Hist. Anim. & Min.* 183 Teales and Widgins... Commonly they are very fat and sweet of taste. **1773** G. WHITE *Selborne* xxxix. 99, I saw young teals taken alive in the ponds of Wolmer Forest. **1873** G. C. DAVIES *Mountain & Mere* ix. 70 A couple of teal came within shot. **1876** SMILES *Sc. Natur.* xiii. (ed. 4) 259 The Teal..and the Eider duck visit the loch occasionally in winter.

b. The flesh of this bird as food.

? *c* **1475** *Sqr. lowe Degre* 320 With deynty meates that were dere,..The tele, the ducke and the drake. **1620** VENNER *Via Recta* iii. 65 Teale..excelleth all other water-fowle. **1735** SHERIDAN in Swift *Let. to Mrs. Whiteway* 8 Nov., His teal was spoiled in the roasting.

c. A shade of dark greenish blue resembling the patches of this colour on the head and wings of the teal.

1923 *Daily Mail* 14 Feb. 10 (Advt.), Jersey frocks... Colours: Teal, Purple and Champ. **1978** *N.Y. Times* 29 Mar. A 14 (Advt.), Both in a delicious new shade of teal... we call it Prussian blue!

2. With distinctive prefixes, applied to various species of *Querquedula* and allied genera: as

American or **green-winged teal**, *Q. carolinensis*; **Baikal** or **Japanese teal**, *Q.* (*Eunetta*) *formosa*; **blue-winged teal** of N. and S. America, *Q. discors* or *cyanoptera*; **Brazilian teal**, *Q. brasiliensis*; **Chilean Teal**, *Q. flavirostris*; **cinnamon** or **redbreasted teal**, *Q. cyanoptera*; **falcated teal**, *Q. falcata*, of China; **summer, cricket** (see CRICKET *sb.*[1] 3), or **garganey teal**, the GARGANEY, *Q. circia*; also **Chinese Teal**, the mandarin duck, *Aix galericulata*; **goose teal**: see GOOSE *sb.* 8; **salt-water** or **brown diving teal**, the RUDDER-*duck* (G. Trumbull *Game Birds* 1888).

1678 RAY *Willughby's Ornith.* 378 Of the Summer-Teal, called by Gesner Ana circia. **1754** CATESBY *Carol.* I. 99 The Blue-Wing Teal. **1785** PENNANT *Arct. Zool.* II. 569 American Teal. **1785** LATHAM *Gen. Syn.* VI. 557 Baikal Teal. **1824** STEPHENS in *Shaw's Gen. Zool.* XII. II. 143 Garganey Teal. *Ibid.* 153 Mexican Teal. **1837** *Penny Cycl.* IX. 181/2 The beautiful *Anas* (*Boschas*) *formosa*, Sw., or Baikal Teal of methodists. *Ibid.* 182/1 Such a species is actually the blue-winged Teal of North America. **1896** *List Anim. Zool. Soc.* 447 [Seven species named]. **1896** NEWTON *Dict. Birds* 949 In ordinary talk 'Teal' stands for any Duck-like bird of small size. *Ibid.*, In the same loose sense the word is often applied to the two most beautiful of the Family *Anatidæ*, belonging to the genus *Æx*..—the Carolina or Wood-Duck of North America, *Æ. sponsa*.., and the Mandarin-Duck of China, *Æ. galericulata*.

3. *attrib.* and *Comb.*, as ***teal-catcher, -duck, -flapper*** (FLAPPER *sb.*[1] 3), ***-shooting, -springing***; **teal blue**, a shade of dark blue tinged with green (cf. sense 1 c above); **teal-house** = *tealery* (see below).

1668 WILKINS *Real Char.* II. v. §4. 156 To the Teal-kind should be reduced that other fowl..called Gargane. **1845** *Statist. Acc. Scot.* XIV. 122 Teal-duck..are found here. **1874** J. W. LONG *Amer. Wild-fowl* xv. 193 In no other branch of wild-fowling is a breech-loader of more advantage than in teal-shooting. **1888** 'R. BOLDREWOOD' *Robbery under Arms* iii. (1890) 16, I was off the old pony and into the water like a teal-flapper. **1902** T. W. WEBBER *Forests Upper India* xviii. 247 A..canoe..which belongs to the teal-catchers. *Ibid.*, Most bungalows in Gorakhpur have a teal house.. where teal are fattened. **1949** *Dict. Colours Interior Decoration* (Brit. Colour Council) III. 26/2 *Teal blue*, a descriptive colour name from the plumage of the small freshwater duck. **1963** *New Yorker* 1 June 75 Sandwich-board sheaths in teal-blue linen are piped down the sides with double rows of lime. **1980** M. H. CLARK *Cradle will Fall* iv. 24 Her teal-blue uniform.

Hence ˈ**tealery**, a place in which teal are kept and fattened.

1890 *Cornh. Mag.* July 17 Here are..the cow-house, and the tealery, and the quailery. **1894** E. BRADDON in *Blackw. Mag.* Sept. 387/2 The teal..kept and fattened in a tealery.

teal, tealer: see TELE, TIL, TILL, TILLER.

tealde, obs. f. *told*: see TELL *v.*

teale, dial. form of TALE.

ˈ**tea-leaf. 1.** The leaf of the tea-plant; *esp.* in *pl.* the leaves after being infused to make the beverage. Also with reference to fortune-telling. Cf. TEA-CUP a (*b*).

1756 HANWAY *Ess. Tea* vi. 237 You have also heard that your maids dry your tea-leaves, and sell them. **1798** *Monthly Mag.* July 30/1 Texeira, a Spaniard who visited the East Indies about the year 1600, saw the dried tea-leaves first in Malacca. **1851** MAYHEW *Lond. Labour* II. 133/1 An extensive trade..is carried on in tea-leaves..after their having been subjected, in the usual way, to decoction. *Ibid.* 133/2 The tea-leaves are often reserved..to be thrown on the carpets when swept, as a means of allaying the dust. *c* **1865** *Circ. Sc.* I. 351/2 The tea-leaves have..to be infused with boiling-water. **1883** C. S. BURNE *Shropshire Folk-Lore* xxi. 277 A stalk or long tea-leaf floating in the tea was called a 'chap'..was at once taken out and laid on the back of one hand, which was then struck sharply with the palm of the other, in order to see whether the 'chap' would come to the back door or the front. **1931** E. SACKVILLE-WEST *Simpson* I. 66 Tea-leaves, thought Amy, tell fortunes. **1941** [see RIDDLE *v.*[1] 2 c]. **1981** *Times* 21 Jan. 11/4 They..read marriage prospects in the tea leaves.

2. Rhyming slang for 'thief'. So ˈ**tea-leafing**, thieving.

1899 C. ROOK *Hooligan Nights* ii. 23 He could do more than his share at tea-leafing, which denotes the picking up of inconsidered trifles. **1903** C. BOOTH *Life & Labour of People in London* XVII. II. 139 'Tea-leaf' is for some inexplicable reason the name used by the police for pick-pockets. **1930** A. BENNETT *Imperial Palace* v. 20 The badinage..was more picturesque... 'You dirty old tea-leaf.' **1963** J. PRESCOT *Case for Hearing* ii. 36 Proper tea-leaves they looked, the pair of 'em. **1977** D. CLARK *Gimmel Flask* iv. 63 A tea-leaf wouldn't find the key on your person if he broke in.

So **tea-leaved** (ˈtiːliːvd) *a.*, having leaves like those of the tea-plant: specifically applied to a species of willow (*Salix phylicifolia*).

1806 GALPINE *Brit. Bot.* §409. **1861** MISS PRATT *Flower. Pl.* V. 106.

tealess (ˈtiːlɪs), *a.* [f. TEA *sb.* + -LESS.] Without or destitute of tea; not having had one's tea.

1821 *Blackw. Mag.* X. 562 Day pass'd, defrauded of its moistest meals, Breakfastless, milkless, tealess, soupless. **1849** THACKERAY *Pendennis* lxiv, He..sat..rapt in wonder, tealess, and bread-and-butterless. **1858** TROLLOPE *Dr. Thorne* xxx, There she waited till ten o'clock, tealess.

teallite (ˈtiːlaɪt). *Min.* [f. the name of Sir J. J. H. *Teall* (1849–1924), English geologist + -ITE[1].] An orthorhombic sulphide of lead and tin, $PbSnS_2$, found as soft, thin, dark grey crystals having a metallic lustre.

1904 G. T. PRIOR in *Mineral. Mag.* XIV. 21 (*heading*) On teallite, a new sulphostannite of lead from Bolivia. **1962** W. A. DEER et al. *Rock-Forming Minerals* V. 8. It [*sc.* cassiterite] ..has also been recorded from the weathering of teallite and stannite.

†**tealt**, *a.* *Obs.* [OE. *tealt* adj. (whence *tealtian*, *tealtrian*, to be unsteady, shake, totter); app. not represented in the cognate languages] Unsteady, insecure, shaky; *fig.* unreliable, precarious, uncertain. Hence †**tealte** *adv.*, insecurely.

a **1000** *Runic Poem* xxi. (Gr.), ȝif hi sculun neðan on nacan tealtum, and hi sæyða swiðe breȝað. *a* **1023** WULFSTAN *Hom.* xxx. (N.) 149 Swa tealte syndon eorðan welan. *Ibid.* l. 273 Hu læne and hu lyðre þis lif is, .. hu tealt. *c* **1315** SHOREHAM i. 231 For ȝef þat water his kende lest, þat cristning stant te tealte.

team (tiːm), *sb.* Forms: 1–4 **team, tem,** (2–7 **theam, theme**), 3–6 **teme,** 4 **teom(e, tyme,** (3–7 **them**), 4–7 **teeme, teem** (9 *dial.*), 6 **teyme,** 6–7 **teame,** 7 **taime,** *Sc.* **thame,** 7– **team.** [OE. *téam* = OFris. *tám*, WFris. *team*, bridle, also progeny, family, line of descendants; OS. *tôm*, MDu., Du. *toom* bridle, rein, Du. dial. *toom* brood, NFris. *toom* rope, LG. *toom* draught with the net; OHG., MHG. *zoum*, Ger. *zaum* bridle, rein, ON. *taumr* rein, bridle, rope, cord :—OTeut. **taumo*^{z}, prob. from **taugmo*^{z} the action of drawing, draught, from ablaut series *teuh-*, *tauh-*, *tuh-*, *tug-*, to draw, L. *dūcĕre* to lead: cf. TEE *v.*[1] The original literal sense is not found in OE., but perh. appears later in sense 9; our sense 1 is known also in OFris., and in Dutch dialects. The developed branches II and III are only in Eng. German has, in senses 1, 2, 8, 9, the cognate *zucht*:—OTeut. **tuhti*^{z}.]

I. †**1. a.** The bringing forth of children; childbearing. *Obs.* [Cf. MHG. *kint ziehen* to bring forth children, Ger. *viehzucht* cattle breeding.]

c **1000** ÆLFRIC *Hom.* in Assmann *Ags. Hom.* (1889) 20/159 þæt eald wif sceole ceorles brucan, þonne heo forwerod byð and teames ætealdod. *Ibid.* 38/339 His wif.. wearð mid.. Esau and Iacob, and heo ȝeswac ða teames. *c* **1200** *Trin. Coll. Hom.* 133 God ches two lif holi men him [Seint iohan baptiste] to fader and to moder, þe weren boðe teames ateald.

b. A family or brood of young animals; now *dial.* applied to a litter of pigs, a brood of ducks. In quot. *a* 1225 *fig.*

c **1000** ÆLFRIC *Hom.* II. 10 Beon: hi tymað heora team mid clænnysse. *a* **1225** *Ancr. R.* 336 Drauh togedere al þene team [of sins] under þe moder. **14..** *Voc.* in Wr.-Wülcker 579/39 *Educamen*, a teme of checonn. **1511** *MS. Acc. St. John's Hosp., Canterb.*, For a teme off ix pygys iiijs iijd. **1767** G. WHITE *Selborne* xi, We have a few teams of ducks, bred in the moors. **1887** *Kentish Gloss.*, *Team*, a litter of pigs or a brood of ducks.

†**2.** Offspring, progeny, issue, family, line of descendants; race, stock; cf. BAIRN-TEAM. *Obs.*

902 in Thorpe *Charters* (1865) 152 Ðreo witeþeowe men ..ða me salde bisceop & þa hiwan to ryhtre æhta & hire team. *c* **950** *Lindisf. Gosp.* Mark xii. 21 Ðe æfterra onfeng ða ilca & dead wæs & ne ðes forleort sed *vel* team [Vulg. *semen*]. *c* **1000** ÆLFRIC *Saints' Lives* (1885) I. 432 Eall his team wearð ȝewurðod þurh god. *c* **1000** —— *Gen.* v. 31 *Rubric*, Hu he Noe bearh and his wife and his teame æt þam miclan flode. *a* **1225** *Juliana* 60 Weox swa his team þat ne mahte hit namon tellen. **1297** R. GLOUC. (Rolls) 5241 Is foure gode sones woxe uaste ynou, Adelbold & adelbriȝt, adelred & alfred, þis was a stalwarde tem [*v.rr.* teme, tyme]. *c* **1330** R. BRUNNE *Chron. Wace* (Rolls) 4794 Cassibolan was Androcheus eem, Luddes broþer of þat teem. *c* **1330** —— *Chron.* (1810) 20 Ethelbert.. Adelwolfes broþer, of Egbrihtes team. *c* **1435** *Torr. Portugal* 2022 This child is come of gentille teme.

II. 3. a. A set of draught animals; two or more oxen, horses, dogs, or other animals harnessed to draw together. (Plural, after a numeral, *team*.)

[*c* **825** *Vesp. Hymns* v. 34 Mid feoðurtemum [L. *cum quadrigis*].] *c* **1000** ÆLFRIC *Voc.* in Wr.-Wülcker 120/32–3 *Imus*, oxa on þam forman teame. *Binus*, on þam æfteran teame. *a* **1250** *Owl & Night.* 776 An hors.. drahþ bi sweore [*v.r.* biuore] grete temes. *c* **1290** *St. Lucy* 129 in *E.E. Poems* (1862) I. 105 Stronge temes he let fecche: of Oxen menie on. **1362** LANGL. *P. Pl.* A. VII. 127 Bote Treuþe schal techen ow his Teome for to dryue. **1377** *Ibid.* B. IX. 257 Grace gaue Piers a teme [C. XXII. 262 teome] foure gret oxen. **1486** *Nottingham Rec.* III. 249 Drawyng þerof.. with a teme of oxen. **1590** SPENSER *F.Q.* III. iv. 33 A teme of Dolphins raunged in aray Drew the smooth charett of sad Cymoent. **1621** G. SANDYS *Ovid's Met.* xii, A log he tooke Which scarce two teeme could draw. **1633** G. HERBERT *Temple, Praise* III. iii, Not all the teams of Albion in a row Can hale or draw it out of doore. **1688** *Andros Tracts* III. 89 Greatly disappointed by this loss [of a horse] which was all the Teame he had. **1805** W. TAYLOR in *Ann. Rev.* III. 258 The cannons are.. dragged about with a team of eight horses. **1835** SIR J. ROSS *Narr. 2nd Voy.* xix. 292 Drawn by a team of six good dogs. **1840** THIRLWALL *Greece* VII. lviii. 298 A thousand team of cattle conveyed the timber to the coast. **1870** MORRIS *Earthly Par.* II. III. 283 With jingling bit and trace Came the grey team from field.

b. *transf.* The stock or 'lot' of horses (or other beasts) belonging to one owner or stable. *dial.*

1655 tr. *Com. Hist. Francion* VII. 6, I would have laid Pyebald against the best Mare in my Brother-in-Laws teem. **1876** *Surrey Gloss.* s.v., 'A good team of cows' is the general expression for a nice lot of cows.

4. a. *fig.* Applied to persons drawing together.

1614 B. JONSON *Barth. Fair* II. v, 'Twere like falling into a whole Shire of butter: they had need be a teeme of Dutchmen, should draw him out. **1668** BP. HOPKINS *Serm., Vanity* (1685) 123 They are so enslaved to the work of the devil, that he puts them into his team, makes them draw and strain for their iniquities. **1748** RICHARDSON *Clarissa* (1811) VII. x. 61, I will add a string of bells to it, to complete thee for the fore-horse of the idiot team. **1837** CARLYLE *Fr. Rev.* I. III. vi, When a team of Twenty-five Millions begins rearing, what is Loménie's whip?

b. *transf.* A number of persons associated in some joint action; now *esp.* a definite number of persons forming a side in a match, in any team sport; hence, a group collaborating in their professional work or in some enterprise or assignment.

In *Shoe-making*, etc., a company of workmen each of whom performs one operation in completing a process.

a **1529** ? SKELTON *Vox Populi* 204 All theise men goo to wracke, That are the body and the staye Of your graces realme allwaye... Thei must be.. Your streinghe and your teme, For to defende your realme. **1622** MASSINGER & DEKKER *Virg. Martyr* IV. ii, Hear me, my little team of villains, hear me. **1644–7** CLEVELAND *Char. Lond. Diurn.* 6 Beleeve him [Cromwell] as he whistles to his Cambridge Teeme of Committee-men. **1846** W. DENISON *Cricket: Sk. Players* 32 Hayward.. having become a resident at Cambridge, joined the 'team' of that distinguished Club. **1859** DICKENS *T. Two Cities* I. ii, The team had capitulated and returned to their duty. **1874** *Bell's Life in London* 14 Mar. 5/2 Although the game was won by Scotland.. the English team played splendidly. **1885** *Manch. Exam.* 10 July 5/1 The Northern [cricket] team, batting first, were disposed of for 192. **1888** *Daily News* 20 July 7/3 'A team' [in boot-making] here would consist of three men, while in America there would be six in 'a team'. **1902** *Westm. Gaz.* 28 Apr. 5/2 They were beaten by a [football] team superior to themselves. *Ibid.*, The two teams took up their positions. **1921** G. B. SHAW *Back to Methuselah* II. 53 You will find yourself at the head of a rabble of Socialists and anti-Socialists, of Jingo Imperialists and Little Englanders, .. of Syndicalists and Bureaucrats.. and the impossibility of keeping such a team together will force you to sell the pass again to the solid Conservative Opposition. **1923** *N.Y. Times* 15 July VI. 1/6 The method of the comedy team remains more or less unvaried. The team is composed, in the first place, of a comedian and a 'straight' man. **1947** *Ann. Reg. 1946* 314 To prevent further clashes General Marshall organised 'teams' composed of an American, a Nationalist, and a Communist member, to visit both parties and to try to create a better spirit [in China]. **1951** *Times* 26 Nov. 2/5 The report.. has been compiled by a team from the [metal-finishing] industry which visited the United States last year. **1965** M. SPARK *Mandelbaum Gate* iii. 66 Russeifa's one of the most conscientious men in the medical team. **1972** *N.Y. Law Jrnl.* 24 Oct. 15/9 Team I is assigned to preside on the circuit for the October 1972 Term. **1978** *Nagel's Encycl.-Guide: China* 272 The basic cells of agrarian collectivisation are the brigade and the team for the moment.

c. *spec.* A gang. *slang* (chiefly *Criminals'*).

1950 in Partridge *Dict. Underworld* Add. (1961) 814/1. **1955** D. W. MAURER in *Publ. Amer. Dialect Soc.* XXIV. 83 Sometimes a *team* [of pickpockets] is *two handed*, while a *troupe* is *three handed* or larger. **1959** *Observer* 1 Mar. 10/1 Mainly the older brothers in long-resident.. families, they are known and feared by other 'teams' (gangs) in North London as the Punchers. **1970** P. LAURIE *Scotland Yard* viii. 184 We had a whisper about a team going to do a certain pay van. **1973** 'J. PATRICK' *Glasgow Gang Observed* ii. 21 The boys themselves never used the word 'gang', always 'team'.

5. a. Two or more beasts, or a single beast, along with the vehicle which they draw; a horse and cart, or wagon with two horses (now *dial.*); also, *U.S. local*, a cart, wagon, or other vehicle of burden for one horse (***single team***) or two horses (***double team***).

1641 *Boston* (U.S.) *Town Records* 27 Sept., The Richer.. Inhabitants shall afford three dayes' worke of one man, except such as have Teames. **1675** *3 Inhumane Murthers* 2 He being out with his Father-in-Law's Teame.. to fetch Coals. **1688** R. HOLME *Armoury* III. 339/2 A Waine, or Oxe Taime, when drawn by Oxen, and hath a Waine Cop. **1787** (Mar. 1) *Massachusetts Statute* (Bridge-toll), Toll.. for each team drawn by more than one beast, nine pence. **1806** (Mar. 4) *Ibid.*, Toll.. for each cart, sled, sleigh, or other team of burthen, drawn by one beast, sixteen cents. **1798** *Sporting Mag.* XI. 48 He was returning from Cowley with a loaded team. **1898** *Boston Even. Transcript* 23 Feb. 16/3 To make the hill less perilous to the poor horses obliged to drag teams up or down it.

†**b.** A team-load. *Obs. rare.*

1789 *Trans. Soc. Arts* VII. 36 The quantity of manure was two teams of dung to each pit, value three pence per team.

c. *fig.* Usually ***a whole team***. *U.S. colloq.*

1832 *Polit. Examiner* (Shelbyville, Kentucky) 17 Nov. 4/2 'Whoop! Ain't I a horse?' 'A whole team, I should think,' said Rainsford. **1832** [see HALF *sb.* 7h]. **1843** 'J. SLICK' *High Life N.Y.* II. 193, I tell you what, he's a hull team, and a horse to let. **1854** *Knickerbocker* XLIV. 416 (Th.), Jump him up when you will, and you'll find him a 'full team' at anything. **1856** G. D. BREWERTON *War in Kansas* 270 Avow yourself ready to declare that.. a clear-grit Yankee woman quite equal, upon an emergency, to what, in vulgar parlance, is quaintly styled 'a whole team, and *a dog under the wagon*' to boot. **1922** *Dialect Notes* V. 180 *Whole team an(d) little dog under the waggin*', n. phr. Used facetiously to indicate one's self-importance, energy, etc. Alabama.

6. A flock of wild ducks or other birds flying in a line or string.

1688 R. HOLME *Armoury* II. xiii. 311/1 Team of ducks. **1697** DRYDEN *Æneid* VII. 965 Like a long team of snowy swans on high, Which clap their wings, and cleave the liquid sky. **1726** POPE *Odyss.* XIX. 627 A team of twenty geese (a snow-white train!). **1720** *Humourist* Ded. 5 [He] took a trip to your Dominions upon a Team of wild Geese. **1848** H. W. HERBERT *Field Sports* II. App. B. 334. **1871** 'STONEHENGE' *Brit. Sports* I. ix. §1 Wild-fowl Nomencl... A 'team' of ducks (when in the air).

7. Phrases. **a.** *Naval*: see quots.

1829 MARRYAT *F. Mildmay* viii, Nothing can be more dull and monotonous than a blockading cruize 'in the team', as we call it; that is, the ships of the line stationed to watch an enemy. **1867** SMYTH *Sailor's Word-bk.* s.v., Ships blockading a port, being generally formed in a line, are said to be 'in the team'.

†**b.** ***to lay in team***: to couple, join together.

13.. *E.E. Allit. P.* C. 37, I schall me poruay pacyence, & play me with boþe; For in þe tyxte, þere þyse two arn in teme layde, Hit arne fettled in on forme, þe forme and þe laste.

III. In Anglo-Saxon Law.

(In this sense recorded only in Eng.; but in MHG. the cognate vb. *ziehen* was used to express the bringing of an action, and the action is expressed by *zug* in *Gewährzug*.)

8. a. In a suit for the recovery of goods alleged to have been stolen, the action or procedure by which the holder transferred or referred it back to a third person (generally the party from whom he received the goods) to defend the title to them; vouching to warranty. *Obs.* exc. *Hist.*

In med. (Anglo) L. *advocatio ad warantum*; in Anglo-Fr. *revoche garaunt*; called by Liebermann *Gewährzug*, by Schmid *Gewährschaftszug* (*Gesetze* Glossar s.v.).

a **800** *Laws Hlothhære & Eadric* (*c* 685) c. 16 Þonne tæme he to wic to cyngæs sele to þam mæn þe him sealde, ȝif he þane wite and æt þam teame ȝebrengen mæȝe. **901–924** *Laws Eadweard* I. c. 1 §1 And ȝif hwa butan porte ceapiȝe, ðonne sy he cyninges oferhyrnesse scyldiȝ; and gange se team þeah forð, oð þæt man wite, hwær he oðstande. **946–*c* 961** *Laws Edgar* I. c. 4 Buton þara oðer hæbbe, nele him mon nænne team [*Lat. text* cenningam] ȝeþafian. **960–975** in Earle *Land Charters* 201 Ða tymde Wulfstan hine to Æðelstane æt Sunnanbyrȝ. Ða cende he tem, let ðone forberstan, forbeh ðone andaȝen. ? **997** *Laws Æthelred* III. c. 6 Ælc team and ælc ordal beo on þæs kyninges byriȝ. **1027–34** *Laws Cnut* II. c. 24 §1 And ȝyf.. he þyllice ȝewitnesse næbbe, ne beo þær nan team, ac aȝyfe man þam aȝenfriȝan his aȝen. **1130–35** *Laws Edw. Conf.* c. 22 §3 Team [*v.rr.* Theam, Them]: quod, si aliquis aliquid interciebatur [*v.r.* intertietur] super aliquem, et ipse non poterit warantum suum habere, erit foresfactura et iusticia; similiter de calumpniatore, si deficiebat. **12..** *Leges Burgorum* c. 12 in *Scot. Stat.* (1844) I. 335 Per legem burgi se defendet nisi sit de prodicione vel de them [*c* **1400** *transl.* thruch lauch of burgh he sall were hym bot gif it be of tresoun or of theme]. **1387** TREVISA *Higden* (Rolls) II. 95 [see also in c] *Theam*, Frensche, *reuoche garant* [**1432–50** tr. *Higden* ibid., *Thean*, that is, to lawde the auctor, in Frenche, *reuouche g*[*a*]*raunte*; orig. *Theam* [*v.r. them*], id est, laudare auctorem; Gallice, *reuoucher garaunt*]. **1628** COKE [see c]. **1900** A. LANG *Hist. Scotl.* I. vi. 148.

b. The right or prerogative of jurisdiction in a suit of *téam*, together with the fees and profits thence accruing; from the 11th c. usually included in charters granting land (in which it regularly followed *toll*, esp. in the formula ***with sac and soc, toll and team, infangthief***, etc.).

Saca and socne (without *toll and team*) is first found in a charter of 1020 or later (see INFANGTHIEF); *toll and team* (alone) is known first in a charter *a* 1023; the formula combining them appears just after the accession of Edward the Confessor, 1042, and occurs in numerous charters ascribed to him, mostly existing only in later copies. It occurs also in the Laws of Wm. I and Henry I. The meaning of *team* was still known when the 'Laws of Edw. the Confessor' were compiled *c* 1130–35 (see above). After the 12th c. it was an obsolete term, the meaning of which was largely a matter of conjecture, and was generally mistaken: see c.

1066 *Charter Edw. Conf.* in Thorpe *Charters* (1865) 405 Donavi.. abbati Eadwino.. consuetudinem que dicitur teames. *a* **1400** in *Scot. Stat.* (1844) I. 742 De Curia de theme. **1664** SPELMAN *Gloss.* 533 s.v. *Team* al. *Theam*, *Theam* significare videtur jurisdictionem cognoscendi in Curiâ suâ de advocationibus, sive intertiatis; hoc est.. *de vocatis ad Warrantiam.* **1895** POLLOCK & MAITLAND *Hist. Eng. Law* II. 157 *note*, The team of the Anglo-Norman charters seems to be the right to hold a court into which foreigners, i.e. persons not resident within the jurisdiction, may be vouched.

1017–23 *Charter of Ælfweard Abbot* (Earle *Land Charters* 236), And toll and team sy aȝifen into þam mynstre. **1046–60** *Charter of Ealdred Bishop* (Kemble No. 805), Ut habeant et possideant iure aecclesiastico perpetua haereditate, cum saca et socne, tolle et teame, reditibus et campis [etc.]. **1046–60** *Charter Edw. Conf.* (Kemble No. 829, later copy), And icc an heom eft alswa ðat hi habben ðarto sacc and socne, toll and team, infangeneðef and flemenesfermð [etc.]. *a* **1066** *Charter* (Kemble No. 843) [see INFANGTHIEF]. **1090–1135** *Laws of Wm. I*, c. 2 §3 E cil francs hom ki ad e sache e soche e toll e tem e infangentheof, se il est enplaidé [etc.]. **1114–18** *Laws Hen. I*, c. 20 §2 Archiepiscopi, episcopi, comites.. sacam et socnam habent, tol et theam et infongentheaf. **12..** *Reg. Maj.* I. ii. in *Scot. Stat.* (1844) I. App. i. 234 Qui habent et tenent terras suas cum soko et sako furca et fossa toll et them et infangandthefe et vtfangandthefe. [SKENE *tr.* Judges.. quha hes power to hald their courts, with sock, sack, gallous, and pit, toll, and thame, infang-thief, and outfang-thief.] **1657** SIR W. MURE *Hist. Rowallane* Wks. (S.T.S.) II. 241 The Mures.. being free Barones y^{r}of, holding in cheife of the crowne, infeft cum furca et fossa, sock et sack, thole et theam, infang theif et outfang theif. **1871** FREEMAN *Norm. Conq.* IV. xviii. 208 One among them, whether by seniority or by hereditary right, further enjoyed the profitable privileges of toll and team.

¶**c.** By the end of the 12th c., the process of *téam* being obsolete, the meaning of the word was to a great extent forgotten. Legal writers erroneously explained it from sense 2, as 'the property of the lord in the *team* or offspring and posterity of his serfs'.

This appears in a 12–13th c. Latin version of a charter of Edward the Confessor, whence it was regularly repeated by later writers, some of whom, as Higden, Rastall, Skene, and Coke, offer both explanations.

1200–25 *Latin version of Charter of Edw. Conf.* (Kemble No. 843) [..saca and socna, toll and team] cum priuilegio habendi totam suorum seruorum propaginem. *c* **1250**

Expositio Vocab. in *Placita de Quo Warranto* (1818) 275/2 *Them*, aver progeny de vos humes. *c* **1290** FLETA I. xlvii. §9 *Them*, acquietantiam amerciamentorum sequelæ propriorum suorum. **1387** TREVISA *Higden* (Rolls) II. 95 [see also in a] Somtyme *Theam* is i-cleped þe sewte of bonde men [orig. *Them*.. quandoque dicitur sequela nativorum]. **1579** *Expos. Terms Law* 177 b, *Them*, that is that you shall haue all yᵉ generations of your Villaines wyth ther suites & cattel wheresoeuer they shall bee found in England. **1597** SKENE *De Verb. Sign.*, *Theme*, is power to haue servandes and slaues, quhilk ar called *nativi*, *bondi*, *villani*, and all Barronnes infeft with Theme, hes the same power: For vnto them all their bond-men, their bairnes, gudes, and geare properly perteinis, swa that they may dispone thereupon at their pleasure. **1628** COKE *On Litt.* II. xi. §172. 116 *Theme* (sometime written Theame corruptly) is an old Saxon word, and signifieth *Potestatem habendi in nativos sive villanos cum eorum sequelis, terris, bonis & catallis*. But *Teame*, sometime corruptly written *Theam*, .. is also an old Saxon word and signifieth where a man cannot produce his Warrant of that which he bought according to his Voucher. **1895** POLLOCK & MAITLAND *Hist. Eng. Law* I. 566 Then [13th c.] *team* is taken to mean the brood, the offspring, the 'sequela' of one's villeins; but this we may be sure is a mistake.

¶ **d.** At other times *team* was app. taken as a mere complement to *toll*, and was evidently thought to be some kind of impost.

1456 SIR G. HAYE *Law Arms* (S.T.S.) 238 Pilgrymes.. suld nouthir pay toll na teme, aucht na custume, na payage, quhill thai ar on thair voyage.

IV. Later senses related to II.

(But sense 9 may represent an Anglicizing of ON. *taumr*. In that sense also, apparently sometimes associated with L. *tēmo* a beam, pole, tongue of a plough, sometimes carriage, cart, etc.)

9. Part of the gear by which oxen or horses were harnessed to a plough, harrow, or wain. In mod. dialect use, 'a chain to which oxen are yoked in lieu of a pole' (*Eng. Dial. Dict.*); 'in plough equipment, the main or leading chain, by which the whole of the oxen or horses drag the implement' (F. T. Elworthy). *foot-team*, the foot-chain of a plough.

c **1350** *Nominale Gall.-Angl.* 858 *Trecters et temons*, Plowestryngges and tem. *c* **1425** *Voc.* in Wr.-Wülcker 665/20 Nomina pertinencia ad carectariam... *Hoc plaustrum*, wayne. *Hec tema*, teme. *Hec torques*, wythe. **1483** *Cath. Angl.* 379/2 A Teme, *temo*. **1523** FITZHERB. *Husb.* §4 Yf he wyll haue his plough to go a narowe forowe.. he setteth his fote-teame in the nycke nexte to the ploughe-beame. *Ibid.* §15 An oxe-harowe.. the formes[t] slote must be bygger than the other, bycause the fote-teame shall be fastened to the same with a shakyll, or a withe to drawe by. **1530** PALSGR. 279/2 Teme of a plough or oxen, *atellee*. *c* **1540** *Inv. Monast. Lylleshull* in *Archæologia* XLIII. 209, iij waynes with themes and other thyngys necessary. **1570** LEVINS *Manip.* 208/17 A Teame cheane, *temo, onis*. **1575** *Richmond Wills* (Surtees) 255, ij yooks furnysshed viijᵈ, ij teymes, j horse draught, j buck shackill, j plewghryng, ij paire toggwethes, ij axill nayles iijᵈ. iiijᵈ. **1605–6** in *N. Riding Rec.* (1884) I. 27 Duos torques ferreos, Angl. Iron horse-teames. **1616** SURFL. & MARKH. *Country Farme* 533 When they draw two and two together in the bearegeares,.. then there is needfull the plow-cleuise, and teame [etc.]. **1788** W. MARSHALL *Yorksh.* Gloss., *Team*, an ox-chain, passing from yoke to yoke. **1889** *N.W. Linc. Gloss.*, *Team*,.. (2) harness for a draught of horses or oxen.

10. *dial.* A chain (generally).

1828 *Craven Gloss.*, *Team*, a strong iron chain. **1840** SPURDENS *Suppl. to Forby's Voc. E. Anglia* s.v., A string or chain of sausages is called 'a team of links'. **1904** *Eng. Dial. Dict.*, *Team*.. an iron chain usually with a ring at one end and hook at the other. Used for putting round stones to fasten the crane chain to when lifting. (W. Yorksh.)

V. 11. *attrib.* and *Comb.*, as, in sense 3, ***team-beast***, ***-driving***, ***-horse***, ***-labour***, ***leader***, ***-length***, ***-master***, ***-plough***; in sense 4 b, ***team-building***, ***-game***, ***manager***, ***-match***, ***-play***, ***player***, ***-race***, ***sport***, ***-system***, ***-training***; (in a team ministry; see below) ***team rector***, ***vicar***; also **team-band**, a fastening for securing the drawing-gear to the plough, etc.; **team-boat**, a boat drawn or propelled by horse-power; **team handball**, a game played by two teams of seven players each on a rectangular court using a ball directed only with the hands; **team honours**, honours awarded to a sporting team; †**team-land**, = PLOUGH-LAND; **team-man** (also **teamsman**, a teamster); (*b*) with preceding descriptive adj., a member of a sporting team who co-operates (well or badly) with his colleagues; **team-mate**, (*a*) = TEAMSTER (Webster 1934); (*b*) a fellow member of a team; **team ministry**, a group of clergy of incumbent status who minister jointly to several parishes under the leadership of the team rector (contrasted with *group ministry*, in which all members function as equals); the administration of a scheme for such an operation; **team policing**, community policing; **team race**, a race which is won by the team whose members finish on aggregate in higher positions than their opponents; **team-railway**, a railway system worked by horse-power (Ogilvie 1882); **team-shovel**: see quot.; **team spirit**, the spirit of subordination of personal interests to those of the team; **team-talk**, a talk addressed to a team, or a discussion amongst a team; **team-teach** *v. intr.* and *trans.*; **team-teaching** *vbl. sb.*, the teaching of students by a team of teachers working together; hence (as back-formation) †**team-ware**, (*a*) a team of horses, etc.; (*b*) = *team-land*; **team-work**, (*a*) work done with a team of beasts; (*b*) the combined action of a team of players, etc.; (*c*) work done by a team of operatives; (*d*) work done by persons working as a team, i.e. with concerted effort.

1808 VANCOUVER *Agric. Devon* 115 A swing-plough with a beam.. at the end of this beam is occasionally fastened a graduated iron to which the *team-band is affixed. **1847–78** HALLIWELL, *Team-bands*, the same as *Start-chains*. **1573–80** BARET *Alv.* T 96 A *Teame beast, euerie beast that draweth or beareth burdens. **1818** *Pict. New York* 222 A *team or horse boat sails.. to Brooklyn every quarter of an hour. **1820** *Boston* (U.S.) *Daily Advert.* 26 Apr. 2/4 A team-boat propelled by twenty-five horses. **1867** SMYTH *Sailor's Word-bk.*, *Team-boat*, a ferry-boat worked with horses by paddle-wheel propulsion. **1895** *Forum* (N.Y.) May 378 The 'team-boat', or ferry-boat propelled by horse power,.. ran for some time in competition with steam ferries. **1946** *Nature* 12 Oct. 497/1 These are essential conditions for successful *team-building and the inherent loyalty it implies. **1893** *Westm. Gaz.* 3 Feb. 10/3 As recently as last week he was.. able to give lessons in *team-driving. **1907** *Daily Chron.* 18 Jan. 9/5 The very essence of all *team games is unity of action. **1970** *Jrnl. Health, Phys. Educ. & Recreation* Mar. 46/1 To the uninformed spectator, the game of *team handball would look like a combination of football, basketball, and lacrosse... It is often confused with a popular squash-related sport also dubbed 'handball'. **1978** *Official Associated Press Sports Almanac* 764 The sport spread to gymnasiums throughout Germany and Eastern Europe and full recognition of team handball was achieved when it was included in the 1936 Berlin Olympics. **1928** *Daily Mail* 7 Aug. 15/5 Eagle Road Club secured *team honours. **1698** FRYER *Acc. E. India & P.* 58 Such Trappings as our finest *Team-Horses in England wear. **1778** [W. MARSHALL] *Minutes Agric., Digest* 18 Sheep are profitable.. because they save, considerably, the expence of *team-labour. **1387** TREVISA *Higden* (Rolls) VIII. 177 Iohn.. toke anon tribute of everiche *teme lond [orig. *hyda, id est carucata*] in Engelond þre schelynges. **1627** SPEED *England* xxviii. §3 In the Booke of Domesday *Caruca*—the Teame-land— was in quantitie of Acres proportioned to the qualitie of Soile. **1904** *N. & Q.* 10th Ser. I. 354/2 The extent of the plough or teamland. **1962** E. SNOW *Other Side of River* (1963) lviii. 440 They chose me as *team leader. **1977** *R.A.F. News* 11–24 May 8/4 Deputy team leader Chf Tech Mick Young. **1977** *Times* 9 Sept. 3/5 Team leaders, the preferred name for those formerly known as charge hands. **1387** TREVISA *Higden* (Rolls) VII. 225 I-leide þre *teme lengþe from þe stok. **1867** MORLEY *Burke* vi. 56 He would talk of.. the turnips, and the hay, with the *team-men and the farm-bailiff. **1954** A. G. MOYES *Austral. Batsmen* x. 151 A fighter who was an excellent team-man and therefore most valuable. **1976** J. SNOW *Cricket Rebel* 138 His brother Eric [Bedser].. was overheard to say that I was not a good team man. **1895** *Wales* Apr. 168/1 He was able to drive a furrow to the delight of even the most envious of surrounding *teamsmen. **1909** *Daily News* 1 Mar. 12 Their demands are for an increase of wages of teamsmen to 28s. **1926** E. HEMINGWAY *Sun also Rises* xix. 247, I had coffee out on the terrasse with the *team manager of one of the big bicycle manufacturers. He said it had been a very pleasant race. **1976** *Evening Post* (Nottingham) 15 Dec. 23/1 Team manager John Sherriff believes the side is now on the right track. **1894** *Westm. Gaz.* 13 Dec. 7/2 The Manhattan Chess Club has sent by mail to the British Chess Club a challenge for a *team match of five boards, to occupy one sitting, the moves being cabled. **1915** M. E. MCLOUGHLIN *Tennis as I play It* xi. 231 Service and the net position go together, the initial stroke giving the server the opportunity to reach the net where his *team-mate is already stationed. **1942** BERREY & VAN DEN BARK *Amer. Thes. Slang* §440/4 *Confederate or partner*.. team-mate. **1954** W. K. HANCOCK *Country & Calling* viii. 223 An orderly row of boxes into which to put the facts that he and his team-mates (for 'team work' is very much the fashion) are collecting. **1977** *Times* 15 July (Motor Racing Suppl.) p. vi/1 James Hunt.. was put out of the race by a crash... His German team-mate.. had retired three laps earlier. **1964** L. PAUL *Deployment & Payment of Clergy* xv. 142 One much-publicised remedy for manpower shortage is a group or *team ministry. Caution is necessary here... Group or team ministries in town may cut down 'the plant', or what a tradesman might call the points of service, but they ought eventually to increase the total urban ministry rather than decrease it. **1968** *Pastoral Measure* II. 13 in *Parl. Papers 1967–68* XVII. 843 A pastoral scheme may provide for the establishment of a team ministry for the area of any benefice, that is to say, for the sharing of the cure of souls in that area by a team of ministers consisting of —(*a*) the incumbent of the benefice which, if it is not or would not otherwise be a rectory, shall be a rectory; (*b*) one or more other ministers who shall have the title of vicar and a status equal to that of an incumbent of a benefice. **1980** *Oxf. Diocesan Mag.* May 15/2 The faint hearts in the Diocese who see team ministry as a threat. **1895** *Outing* (U.S.) XXVII. 247 Our game [Canadian football].. abounding in combined skill and *team play unknown to English experts. **1886** H. CHADWICK *Art of Batting* 7 The practical effect of all this is to destroy a batsman's ambition to excel as a '*team player' in batting. **1980** *Newsweek* 17 Nov. 13/3 Reagan wants 'team players' for his Administration—men and women loyal to him personally and to his philosophy generally, willing to argue over policy, but not fundamental ideology. **1805** DICKSON *Pract. Agric.* I. 346 The breast-spade or common *team-plough.. will be found preferable. **1977** J. WAMBAUGH *Black Marble* (1978) iv. 42 Every few years the brass had to come up with some new catchword to justify the budget. '*Team policing.' **1976** *Southern Even. Echo* (Southampton) 10 Nov. 21/7 Southampton were always in control in the *team race and were easy team winners from Portsmouth, through Tony Nixon 5th, Bryan Dawkins 8th, and Malcolm Beavis 10th. **1976** *Milton Keynes Express* 11 June 15/1 He will be assisting the Rev Christopher Drummond, *team rector from the Christ Church Centre at Stantonbury. **1877** KNIGHT *Dict. Mech.*, **Team-shovel*, an earth-scraper. A scoop drawn by horses or oxen. **1928** *Britain's Industrial Future* (Liberal Industrial Inquiry) III. xvi. 195 The 'fellowship-bonus' system.. evokes the *team-spirit. **1938** R. G. COLLINGWOOD *Princ. Art* iv. 74 These sports, we are told, inculcate a team-spirit. **1976** F. MUIR *Frank Muir Bk.* 96 The schools.. were sending forth.. superbly fit chaps, light on imagination but strong on team-spirit. **1964** G. MCDONALD *Running Scared* iii. 37 He had never gone out for any *team sport. **1895** *Daily News* 15 Apr. 2/3 The '*team system' [in boot-making] is also strongly resisted, as tantamount to a decline in the remuneration. **1947** A. P. GASKELL *Big Game* 12 And then of course, the *team-talk on Friday night. The coach would stand on the platform and start on his old game of building us up to fighting pitch. **1960** V. JENKINS *Lions Down Under* viii. 114 The post-mortem at a team-talk in Timaru was a searching one. **1976** *Science News* 28 Feb. 135 Two answers to this problem.. are to teach science ethics to college students by presenting them realistic case studies and to bring industrial scientists into the universities to *team-teach. **1979** *Maledicta* III. 144 Mary Salawuh Warren, a Yoruba, has team-taught Yoruba and other West African languages with her husband, D. M. Warren, at Iowa State University and in Peace Corps training programs. **1960** *Washington Post* 20 Dec. B2 Principal Harold Wilson.. tallied the benefits of *team teaching at his school. **1964** *Observer* 13 Sept. 11/8 Team teaching, in which a corps of teachers work with a very large group, already has a long history in the United States. **1976** *Church Times* 8 Oct. 17/5 **Team vicar* required for church of St. Martin, Southdene, to serve large neighbourhood unit and to work as a member of a large established team. **1981** *Ibid.* 10 July 17/4 (Advt.), Applications invited for team vicar to complete established team of three. Priest appointed will have particular pastoral responsibility for four attractively-situated villages. **1567** GOLDING *Ovid's Met.* v. (1593) 125 His sacred *teeme-ware through the aire to drive abroad agen. **1577** HARRISON *England* I. viii. in *Holinshed* I. 12/2, 600 families which are all one with Hidelandes, Plowghlandes, Carrucates, or Temewares. **1828** WEBSTER, **Team-work*, work done by a team, as distinguished from personal labor. *New England.* **1886** *S.W. Linc. Gloss.*, *Team-work*, work done with wagon and horses; a regular item in a way-warden's Account Book. **1887** MRS. H. CAMPBELL *Prisoners of Poverty* ii. 26 (Funk) What is known as 'team work', flaps [of shirts] being done by one, bosoms by another, and so on. **1909** *World To-day* (U.S.) Sept. 3 (*heading*) Team work in municipal progress. *a* **1911** *Mod. U.S.* The team-work of the [base-ball] nine is excellent. **1954** [see *team-mate* above]. **1977** *Lancet* 23 Apr. 899/2 We need hospitals, health visitors, and homes, but we must be sure that by effective communication and teamwork (and these do not cost money), the service we offer is of the highest.

team (tiːm), *v.* Also 6 **teem.** [f. TEAM *sb.* II.: cf. *to yoke*, *to harness*, etc. A late formation, the original derivative verb being TEEM *v.*¹]

1. a. *trans.* To harness (beasts) in a team; to yoke. Also *fig.*

1552 HULOET, Teame horses togyther, *dextero, as. Ibid.*, Teame oxen togither, *iugo, as.* **1597** MIDDLETON *Wisdom Solomon* xiv. 1 The shipman cannot team dame Tethys waves. **1733** TULL *Horse-Hoeing Husb.* xxiii. 172 Every Workman knows how to team the Limbers. **1875** *Encycl. Brit.* II. 663/1 The horses [in a horse-artillery battery] are teamed in pairs,—lead, centre, and wheel.

b. *intr.* Chiefly with *up*: to join together in or as in a team; to ally oneself or get together *with* someone. Occas. *trans.*

1932 W. FAULKNER *Light in August* iv. 86 Like man and wife for three years, until Brown and him teamed up. **1932** J. T. FLYNN *God's Gold* VII. x. 314 Whetmore was not Rockefeller's agent, but a lawyer and independent promoter who teamed up with the Merritts and worked with them. **1950** D. HYDE *I Believed* ii. 14 The war-wounded were everywhere... Blinded, they teamed up into bands. **1965** J. LAWLOR in J. Gibb *Light on C. S. Lewis* 73, I had thought of myself as God's gift to Lindsay's Balliol, with which Magdalen was teamed for scholarship purposes. **1967** M. CHANDLER *Ceramics in Mod. World* v. 157 In practice two or three refractories may have to be teamed up to do one exacting job. **1978** J. R. L. ANDERSON *Sprig of Sea Lavender* vi. 94 He seems to have teamed up with Trudi... He was a little in love with Sandra once.

c. *trans.* To use or wear in conjunction *with*. Also *intr.* for *pass.*

1948 M. LASKI in *New Statesman* 13 Nov. 417/1 *Team*, vb.: to wear one thing with another; e.g., team your palest grey dress with the subtle flattery of a brief scarlet bolero. **1954** C. L. B. HUBBARD *Compl. Dog Breeders' Man.* xx. 203 Well-pressed linen slacks.. can look really nice, especially if teamed up with a contrasting blouse, shirt or jumper. **1958** *House & Garden* Feb. 22 (Advt.), [The furniture] will team happily with the pieces you wish to retain. **1960** *Housewife* May 104/2 This sweater teams happily with pants or shorts. **1977** *Jersey Even. Post* 26 July 10/1 A long, tiered empire-line voile dress, made of a yellow and red floral patterned material with a white background. This was teamed with a white floppy hat.

2. a. To convey or transport by means of a team. **b.** *absol.* or *intr.* To drive a team, to do teamster's work. *N.Amer.* Cf. TEAMING.

1841 EMERSON *Ess.* Ser. I. ii. (1876) 66 A sturdy lad.., who teams it, farms it, peddles. **1852** WIGGINS *Embanking* 114 A portion was teamed 1½ mile. **1856** WHITTIER *Ranger* 126, I.. can hear him teaming Down the locust-shaded way. **1888** L. OLIPHANT *Sci. Relig.* iii. 60, I.. teamed as a common teamster through the rigours of a Canadian winter. **1951** K. M. WELLS *Owl Pen Reader* (1969) iii. 253 He took the road, teamin' hay er cordwood to town. **1968** E. RUSSENHOLT *Heart of Continent* III. ix. 162 A sudden freeze-up ends the navigation season, catching many vessels in the ice. Freight which cannot, now, be moved by steamboat, must be teamed.

3. *trans.* To get (work) done by a team or teams of workmen; to let (work) to a contractor who employs teams of workmen. *U.S.*

1877 [see TEAMING]. **1891** in *Cent. Dict.*

4. *Comb.* **team-up**, an instance of teaming up (sense 1 b above). *colloq.*

1945 *Richmond* (Va.) *Times-Dispatch* 21 Nov. 15 (Advt.), Santa's a 'good Joe' in their language when he delivers these team-ups [*sc.* a dressing-gown, pyjamas, and slippers]. **1960** *Farmer & Stockbreeder* 8 Mar. 74/1 (*heading*) Poor show but the team-up of American and French manufacturers will be a 'shot in the arm'.

Hence **teamed** *ppl. a.*, harnessed in a team.

1591 SPENSER *Virgil's Gnat* 314 By this the Night forth from the darksome bowre Of Herebus her teemed steedes gan call.

tea-maker, etc.: see TEA *sb.* 9 c.

teaman, tea-man ('tiːmən, -mæn).

1. A merchant who deals in tea; a tea-dealer.

1837 WHITTOCK, etc. *Bk. Trades* 441 Teaman. Such is the simple title assumed for their trade by many distinguished dealers in London—indeed, the most distinguished. They are generally those who deal in tea only. *Ibid.*, This system of tasting is what constitutes the acme of the great Teaman's trade. **1891** *Daily News* 16 May 5/4 The Chinese tea-men are reported to maintain a sort of incredulous nonchalance . . in the face of that almost complete capture of the English market by the Indian and Ceylon teas.

2. *Prison slang.* (See quot.)

1877 *5 Years' Penal Servitude* ii. 85 'Tea men' . . have the privilege . . of having one pint of tea every evening instead of gruel.

3. *U.S. Criminals' slang.* (See quot. 1950.)

1938 *Amer. Speech* XIII. 192/1 *Tea-man*, a reefer-man or marijuana addict. **1950** H. E. GOLDIN *Dict. Amer. Underworld Lingo* 220/2 *Tea-man*, a smoker or purveyor of marijuana. **1959** in J. E. Schmidt *Narcotics Lingo & Lore* 182.

teamer ('tiːmə(r)). [f. TEAM *sb.* or *v.* + -ER[1].]

1. One who drives a team; a teamster.

1778 E. PARKMAN *Diary* 26 Dec. (1899) 81 May God extend pity to ye miserable poor,—to Sailors, to Soldiers, to Teamers abroad. **1840** *Civil Eng. & Arch. Jrnl.* III. 391/2 These latter . . discharging their contents, and leaving none to be shovelled out by the teamers. **1879** *Daily News* 8 Apr. 3/7 A horse was instantaneously killed by a flying brickbat, but the teamer, who stood near, . . escaped uninjured. **1895** *Ibid.* 4 Dec. 3/7, I let my ten acres of glebe to an industrious fellow—once a 'teamer' or team man on a farm near by.

2. A member of a team; esp. a member of the first (or second, etc.) team in sport.

1934 R. MACAULAY *Going Abroad* ii. 32 Loyal teamers, they agreed that . . their team leader's should be the only Guidance sought. **1950** *Sport* 24–30 Mar. 10/1 Phil was in and out of the Liverpool senior side the following season, but was an established first-teamer by 1938–39. **1976** *Evening Post* (Nottingham) 15 Dec. 24/7 Nottingham first teamers Ken MacDonald and Graeme Fraser came back after injury to help Corsairs defeat Nottingham University 36–0 at Beeston last night.

'teaming, *vbl. sb.* [f. TEAM *v.* + -ING[1].] The action of the verb TEAM. Also *attrib.* and with *up* in senses 1 b and c of TEAM *v.*

1733 W. ELLIS *Chiltern & Vale Farm.* 317 A Teaming-pin of about eleven Inches long. **1829** *Glover's Hist. Derby* I. 182 The breeding of heavy, or teaming horses. **1852** WIGGINS *Embanking* 115 Cutting and filling 5*d.* per yard. Teaming ⅝ths of a mile 0¾*d.* per yard. **1877** KNIGHT *Dict. Mech.*, *Teaming* . . 2. The operation of transporting earth from the cutting to the embankment. 3. A certain mode of manufacturing work, which is given out to a boss, who hires a gang or team to do it, and is responsible to the owner of the stock. **1883** *Harper's Mag.* Aug. 390/2 All the teaming is done with one-horse carts. **1960** *Farmer & Stockbreeder* 8 Mar. 74/1 The teaming-up of some well-known French manufacturers with . . American companies is bound to act as a 'shot in the arm' to the French engineering industry. **1966** *Guardian* 25 Apr. 6/4 A Jaeger shop . . in Southport . . is making a strong feature of 'teaming up'—that is, exactly matching colours can be found in coats, suits, hats, skirts, slacks, blouses, and knitwear.

'teamless, *a. rare.* [f. TEAM *sb.* + -LESS.] Without a team: cf. TEAM *sb.* 5.

1894 *Columbus* (Ohio) *Dispatch* 5 Sept., The majority of the pioneers brought with them no personalty . . save their teams, . . some came even teamless.

teamster ('tiːmstə(r)). [f. TEAM *sb.* + -STER.]

1. The driver or owner of a team; a teamer.

1777 in *New Hampshire Hist. Soc. Coll.* (1863) VII. 88 The Committee delivered the Several Teamsters. **1779** *Boston* (*Mass.*) *Town Records* 19 Feb. *Ibid.* 17 Aug., Thomas Chase . . had agreed with a Number of Teamsters for the Publick service at the rate of eighteen Shillings a Mile. **1824** W. IRVING *T. Trav.* I. 219 Drovers and teamsters who travel that road. **1840** J. BUEL *Farmer's Comp.* 144 In using the harrow, the teamster should understand the object, and take care to accomplish it. **1901** *Census Schedule Instructions*, Agricultural labourers should be entered according to the particular work on which they are usually engaged, such as . . Teamster on farm.

2. *N. Amer.* A lorry-driver, a truck-driver; one who drives a truck as his occupation.

1907 J. LONDON *Iron Heel* (1908) x. 182 The teamsters' strike had been broken. **1957** *Economist* 28 Sept. 1024/1 The delegates who are packing their bags this week-end for the convention of the teamsters—as lorry drivers are still called—will also take with them the knowledge that this is likely to be the most momentous meeting in the history of organised labour. **1958** *Daily Express* 29 Aug. 4/2 This type of entertainment is as suspect as the Teamsters' Union. **1978** *New York* 3 Apr. 100/3 The 8,000 sanitationmen represented by a local of the teamsters, usually the most truculent of city unions, are still participating in the coalition talks.

Tean, var. TEIAN *a.*

teanel ('tiːnəl). Now *n.w. dial.* Forms: 1 tænil, -el, tenil; 5 tenel; 9 teanal(e, teanel, tennil. [OE. *tænil*, *-el* = MHG. *zeinel*, deriv. of OTeut. **tainjā*, in Goth. *tainjô* wicker basket, OHG. *zeinnâ*, *zeinâ*, MHG. *zeine* weak fem., ON. **teina*, pl. *teinur* basket, creel; deriv. of **tainoz*, ON. *teinn* (:—*teinr*), OE. *tán*, OHG. *zein* twig, osier-wand.] A basket.

a **700** *Epinal Gloss.* (O.E.T.) 403 *Fiscilla*, taenil. *a* **800** *Erfurt Gloss.* 403 *Fiscella*, tenil. *c* **1000** ÆLFRIC *Saints' Lives* (1890) II. 44 Him on hand ȝenam ænne lytelne tænel mid caricum ȝefylledne. *a* **1100** *Ags. Voc.* in Wr.-Wülcker 336/9 *Sportella*, tænel. *c* **1440** *Promp. Parv.* 489/1 Tenel, or crele, *cartallus*. *Ibid.*, Tenel, vessel, *tenella*. **1869** *Lonsdale Gloss.*, *Teanel*, an osier fish-basket. **1882** *Lancs. Gloss.*, *Tennil*, a large basket.

tea-night to **tea-pail**: see TEA *sb.* 9.

teany, var. TENNÉ, the heraldic tincture.

'tea-ˌparty.

1. A party assembled to take tea together; a social entertainment at which tea is taken.

1778 MISS BURNEY *Evelina* (1791) I. xvi. 61 The arched recesses that are appropriated for tea-parties [at Ranelagh]. **1843** THACKERAY *Men's Wives, Mr. & Mrs. Berry* ii, The Reverend Lemuel Whey is a tea-party man. **1851** D. JERROLD *St. Giles* xix. 196 As comfortable as any dowager at a tea-party.

2. *transf.* (*colloq.* or *slang.*) **a.** ***Boston tea-party***, a humorous name for the revolutionary proceeding in 1773, when the tea was thrown overboard from the ships in Boston harbour as a protest against the taxation of the American colonies by the British Government. **b.** A lively proceeding, a disturbance.

1864 WEBSTER *App.*, *Names Fiction*, Boston Tea-party. **1874** O. W. HOLMES *Ballad of Boston Tea-party* 28 The storm broke loose, but first of all The Boston teapot bubbled! **1903** *Westm. Gaz.* 20 Jan. 9/2 An electrician's 'tea-party' is brought about by a short circuit . . . In particularly bad cases . . explosions of the circuit breakers occur, and showers of molten copper, which often start fires, render the 'tea-party' of the liveliest description.

c. A gathering at which marijuana is smoked. *slang.*

1944 *War Med.* VI. 383/2 Have you ever been on a 'tea' party? No? You've missed a sensation of a lifetime. **1956** J. SYMONS *Paper Chase* vii. 32 Used to give tea parties—marihuana. **1972** 'J. QUARTERMAIN' *Rock of Diamond* i. 7 Jane hadn't taken tea. She . . gave no clue . . as to what an inhibited Englishman should do at a midtown Manhattan tea-party.

3. *attrib.* of attitudes, behaviour, etc., held to be typical of a tea-party; bland, insipid, trite, trivial.

1961 M. BEADLE *These Ruins are Inhabited* (1963) ii. 28, I think he expected the boys to have . . tea-party manners. **1962** [see PENGUIN 2 c]. **1973** C. MULLARD *Black Britain* ix. 105 Liberal do-gooders with a tea-party attitude towards race.

'tea-plant.

1. The plant from which tea is obtained, the tea-shrub: = TEA *sb.* 3.

1727–41 CHAMBERS *Cycl.* s.v. *Tea*, The Tea plant affects valleys, and the feet of mountains, and a stony soil. **1770** ELLIS in *Phil. Trans.* LX. 525 One of the first tea-plants that has been produced from seed in this kingdom. **1888** J. PATON in *Encycl. Brit.* XXIII. 97/2 The tea-plant is cultivated in China as an evergreen shrub.

2. Applied to various other plants: see TEA *sb.* 6.

1798 *Monthly Mag.* Mar. 211 The tea plant of St. Domingo; *Capraria biflora*, . . the leaves of which are employed . . for the same purpose as the tea of China and Japan. **1864** *Athenæum* 10 Dec. 788/2 Leptospermum, the tea-plant of Australia. **1866** *Treas. Bot.* 701 *L*[*ycium*] *barbarum* . . is commonly known as the Tea plant. **1884** [see TEA-TREE 3]. **1903** A. C. P. HAGGARD *Sporting Yarns* 136 (*Canada*) The long grass and Labrador tea-plants on the banks.

'tea-ˌplanter. One who makes it his business to cultivate tea-plants. So **'tea-ˌplanting.**

1887 KIPLING *Plain Tales* (1888) 112 A Subaltern, or a Tea-Planter's Assistant, or anybody who . . has no care for to-morrow. **1888** J. PATON in *Encycl. Brit.* XXIII. 99/1 Tea-planting has also been successfully established in Natal. **1897** *Daily News* 19 June 2/2 Japan must . . abandon her primitive methods of tea-planting in small patches. **1897** *Allbutt's Syst. Med.* III. 736 A case that I saw some years ago in a tea-planter. *Mod.* He is now a tea-planter in Assam.

'tea-pot, *sb.* **1. a.** A pot with a lid, spout, and handle, in which tea is made or brought to table.

[**1616** COCKS *Diary* (Hakl. Soc.) I. 215, I sent . . a silver *chaw* pot . . to Capt. China wife. **1662** J. DAVIES tr. *Mandelslo's Trav.* II. (1669) 156 There have been Tsia-pots, which had cost between six and seven thousand pound sterling.] **1705** *Lond. Gaz.* No. 4063/4 A Tea Kettle, a gilt Tea-Pot. **1784** COWPER *Task* IV. 776 There the pitcher stands A fragment, and the spoutless tea-pot there. **1867** TROLLOPE *Chron. Barset* II. lxix. 261 She sat behind her old teapot, with her hands clasped. **1874** [see TEA-PARTY 2].

b. Phr. ***tea-pot tempest***, ***tempest in a tea-pot*** (U.S.): = *storm in a tea-cup* (see TEA-CUP 4). Also in similar phrases.

1854 ANDREWS *Lat. Dict.* s.v. *Simpulum*, *Excitare fluctus in simpulo*, . . to raise a tempest in a teapot. Cic. Leg. 3. 16, 36. **1891** *Cent. Dict.* s.v. *Tempest*, *A tempest in a tea-pot*, a great disturbance over a small matter. **1896** *Peterson Mag.* Jan. 104/1 What a ridiculous tea-pot tempest! **1928** R. CAMPBELL *Wayzgoose* i. 16 Storms in a teapot often have occurred. **1942** T. DUBOIS *Body goes round & Round* xiii. 172 You have been indulging in your favourite occupation of stirring up a tempest in a teapot. **1973** *Times* 1 Aug. 6/5 Senator Ervin said the issue of whether the subpoenas were continuing was 'a difference in a teapot'.

2. *attrib.* and *Comb.*, as ***tea-pot stand.***

1895 *Montgomery Ward Catal.* Spring & Summer 439/1 Tea or Coffee Pot Stands. **1968** *Canad. Antiques Collector* June 12/2 A tea service at this period . . normally consisted of twelve saucers, twelve cups, twelve coffee cups, a tea pot and cover (occasionally a tea pot stand), a sucrier, [etc.].

Hence **tea-pot** *v.*, to present with a tea-pot (*Obs. rare*); **'teapotful**, as much as a tea-pot contains.

1842 J. PAGET *Let.* 25 July in *Mem. & Lett.* (1901) 117 My pupils have proposed to make a demonstration in my favour, and have asked me if they may open a subscription to 'tea-pot' or commit some similar dignity upon me. **1854** 'C. BEDE' *Verdant Green* II. v, Gentlemen who get upon their legs to return thanks for having been 'tea-potted'. **1881** V. LUSH *Jrnl.* 26 Oct. (1975) 247, I reminded him that for some time past I had been mulcted of my stipend and that to be 'tea-potted' under such circumstances seemed to me to be a case parallel to that of allowing a man to starve and when he is dead to give him an expensive funeral. **1895** W. WRIGHT *Palmyra & Zenobia* xxii. 255 The teapotful of dirty water.

Teapot Dome ('tiːpɒt dəʊm). The name of a naval oil reserve in Wyoming, irregularly leased by the U.S. Government in 1922, used *attrib.* and *absol.* to designate the resulting political scandal and, allusively, any similar later scandal.

1936 F. D. ROOSEVELT *Nothing to Fear* (1947) 64 In spite of all the demand for speed, the complexity of the problem and all the vast sums of money involved, we have had no Teapot Dome. **1973** *New Yorker* 28 Apr. 31/2 Senator Barry Goldwater made his statement: 'The Watergate. The Watergate. It's beginning to be like Teapot Dome.' **1977** *Time* 23 May 54/2 In an era of Teapot Dome and bathtub gin, he [*sc.* Lindbergh] seemed to Americans a cleaner, sharper version of themselves.

‖**teapoy** ('tiːpɔɪ). *Anglo-Ind.* Also **tepoy.** [f. Hindī *tīn*, in comb. *tir-* three + Pers. *pāë*, *pāī* foot. The legitimate Persian name is *sihpāya* or *sipāī*; the Hindī *tirpad* or *tripad* (Yule).]

A small three-legged table or stand, or any tripod; (by erron. association with *tea*), such a table with a receptacle for tea or a tea-caddy.

1828 MRS. SHERWOOD *Lady of Manor* VI. xxix. 246 A low *teapoy* of *sessoo* wood. **1844** [? SIR J. KAYE] *Peregrine Pultuney* I. v. 112 A tepoy or tinpoy is a thing with three feet, used in India to denote a little table. **1887** YAN PHOU LEE *When I was a Boy in China* 25 [The tables] were flanked by two rows of chairs . . with tea-poys between that served to hold the cups of guests.

1858 SIMMONDS *Dict. Trade*, *Tea-poy*, an ornamental pedestal table, with lifting top, enclosing caddies for holding tea. **1886** YULE & BURNELL *Hobson-Jobson*, *Teapoy*, . . often in England imagined to have some connexion with *tea*, and hence, in London shops for japanned ware and the like, a *teapoy* means a tea-chest fixed on legs. But this is quite erroneous.

tear (tɪə(r)), *sb.*[1] Forms: see below. [OE. *téar* = OFris. *târ*, ON. *tár* (Sw. *tår*, Da. *taar*, *taare*), contr. from earlier OE. **teahr*, **teaȝr*, *teaȝor*, ONorthumb. *tehr* = OHG. *zahar*, *zahhar* (MHG. *zaher*, *zâr*, Ger. *zähre*), Goth. *tagr*; cogn. with Gr. δάκρ-υ, OL. *dacrima* (L. *lacrima*, *-uma*), OPr. *dacr*, *dêr*, Welsh *dagr* tear. The medial *h* or *ȝ*, already lost in OE., is found as *ch* in 16th c. Sc.]

A. Illustration of Forms.

α. OE. **teaȝor**, ONorthumb. **teher, tæher, tehher, tehr**; 5–6 *Sc.* **techyr** (*pl.* **techrys**), **tichwr, teicher.**

a **1000** *Guthlac* (E.E.T.S.) 1340 Teaȝor yðum weol hate hleordropan. *a* **950** *Rituale Eccl. Dunelm.* (Surtees) 40 Folces tehhero eft bisih (*gloss on* populi lacrimas respice). *Ibid.* 192 Pund saltes, of ðon sindon salto tehero. *c* **950** *Lindisf. Gosp.* Mark ix. 24 Mið teherum he ȝecuæð ic ȝelefo. —— Luke vii. 38 Mið tæherum *vel* tearum. *Ibid.* 44 Mið tearum *vel* tehrum. **1513** DOUGLAS *Æneis* IV. xii. 5 With cheikis freklit, and all of tichwris [*ed.* 1553 teris] bysprent. *Ibid.* XIII. Prol. 26 At euery pilis point and cornis croppis The techrys [*ed.* **1553** teicheris] stude, as lemand beriall droppis.

β. 1–3 **téar (teor)**, 1–6 **ter**, 2 **tiar**, 3 **ti(e)r, tær**, 4 **tyar**, 4–5 **teer**, 4–6 **tere**, 5 **terre**, 5–6 **teere, tyer**, 5–8 *Sc.* **teir**, 6–7 **teare**, 6– **tear.**

c **888** K. ÆLFRED *Boeth.* x, Fulneah dead for tearum & for unrotnesse. *a* **900** tr. *Bæda's Eccl. Hist.* IV. xxix. [xxviii.] §2 Mæniȝe þara broðra . . tearas guton. *c* **975** *Rushw. Gosp.* Mark ix. 24 Mið teorum [*Lindisf.* teherum] he ȝicwæð ic ȝilefo. *c* **1000** *Sax. Leechd.* III. 292 Wiþ mist & wiþ ter. *a* **1175** *Cotton Hom.* 217 Al swa an huni tiar felle upe ȝiure hierte. *c* **1200** *Vices & Virt.* 57 Mid bitere teares. *c* **1200** ORMIN 13849 Þurrh beȝȝske & sallte tæress. *a* **1300** *K. Horn* 654 Wiþ tieres al birunne. *Ibid.* 960 Spak wiþ bidere tires. **13 . .** *Cursor M.* 25551 Wit tere [*Gött.* ter] of ei. **1340** *Ayenb.* 173 Y-kuegt . . be tyares of ssrifte. *c* **1380** WYCLIF *Serm.* Sel. Wks. II. 205 She þis haþ waished my feet wiþ teeris. **1422** tr. *Secreta Secret.*, *Priv. Priv.* 199, I haue . . Seyn thy terris. *c* **1440** *Promp. Parv.* 489/1 Teere, of wepynge, *lacrima*. *c* **1489** CAXTON *Blanchardyn* xxxiii. 123 He fonde him the terres at the eyes of hym. **1500–20** DUNBAR *Poems* ix. 15 With teiris of sorrow. **1563** WINȜET *Four Scoir Thre Quest.* §46 Wks. (S.T.S.) I. 107 Mourning and teris. **1584** POWEL *Lloyd's Cambria* 199 The women check their tears. **1593** SHAKS. *3 Hen. VI*, II. v. 76 Weepe wretched man: Ile ayde thee Teare for Teare. *a* **1600** MONTGOMERIE *Sonn.* iv. 5 With bendit brou, and tuinkling teirs, I trou. **1661** LOVELL *Hist. Anim. & Min.* 72 The teares found dry in the corners of the eyes.

B. Signification.

1. a. A drop of the limpid fluid secreted by the lachrymal gland appearing in or flowing from the eye; chiefly as the result of emotion, esp. grief, but also of physical irritation or nervous stimulus: usually in *pl.*

Beowulf 1872 Hruron him tearas blondenfeaxum. 971 *Blickl. Hom.* 189 þa wæron his eaȝan ȝefyllede mid tearum. c1175 *Lamb. Hom.* 159 þe ter þat Mon schet. c1300 *Havelok* 285 For hire was mani a ter igroten. 1377 Langl. *P. Pl.* B. xiii. 45 But if þei synge for þo soules and wepe salt teres. 1422, 1593, a1600 [see A. β]. 1737 [S. Berington] *G. di Lucca's Mem.* (1738) 62, I saw his [Eyes] swimming in Tears. 1782 Cowper *Let. to W. Unwin* 4 Nov., You tell me that John Gilpin made you laugh tears. 1808 Scott *Marm.* i. Introd. 186 Drop upon Fox's grave the tear, 'Twill trickle to his rival's bier. 1855 Bain *Senses & Int.* ii. iv. §22 (1864) 297 There are also tears of joy. 1866 Huxley *Phys.* (1869) ix. §25 Under certain circumstances..the secretion of the lachrymal gland exceeds the drainage power of the lachrymal duct, and the fluid, accumulating,..overflows in the form of tears.

b. As the visible feature of weeping: hence, put for this, or as the expression of grief or sorrow. ***in tears***, weeping, in sorrow or commiseration.

a1340 Hampole *Psalter* cxxv. 6 þa þat dos goed werkis in terys of penaunce. 1388 Wyclif *Ps.* cxxv[i]. 5 Thei that sowen in teeris; schulen repe in ful out ioiyng. 1435 Misyn *Fire of Love* 18 Is not þis þe vayle of teris & tribulacion? 1560 Daus tr. *Sleidane's Comm.* 18 The people..are all in teares and mournyng. 1637 Milton *Lycidas* 14 He must not flote upon his watry bear..Without the meed of som melodious tear. 1719 De Foe *Crusoe* (1840) II. i. 7, I was happy in listening to her tears. 1750 Gray *Elegy, Epitaph* ii, He gave to Mis'ry all he had, a tear. 1814 Wordsw. *Laodamia* 164 Yet tears to human suffering are due.

c. In colloq. phr. ***without tears***, without difficulty or distress (freq. used to describe a method whereby some discipline is easily mastered). Also ***without-tears*** attrib. phr.

1857 F. L. Mortimer (*title*) Reading without tears. 1877 —— (*title*) Latin without tears; or, One word a day. 1896 G. B. Shaw in *Sat. Rev.* 12 Dec. 623/2 (*heading*) Ibsen without tears. 1914 W. Owen *Let.* 1 June (1967) 257, I have a design in sending you this, viz. to keep you hungry to learn French I hope it won't be long before you read such works 'without tears'; at least without tears due to grammatical difficulties. 1932 A. Huxley *Brave New World* xvii. 280 Anybody can be virtuous now. You can carry at least half your morality about in a bottle. Christianity without tears—that's what *soma* is. 1937 T. M. Rattigan (*title*) French without tears. 1956 *New Statesman* 11 Feb. 143/1 The late 19th-century concept of progress without tears. 1962 *Times* 7 June 17/3 It is a without-tears book. 1974 J. I. M. Stewart *Gaudy* i. 19 Charles and Mary..were well-mannered young people, and docile at least to the extent of being resigned to Scrabble as a species of Philology without tears.

2. *transf.* and *fig.* **a.** A drop of any liquid; *spec.* a drop or bead of liquid spontaneously exuding.

(Sometimes with allusion to grief or lamentation: cf. 1 b.) a900 Cynewulf *Crist* 1174 Ða wearð beam moniȝ blodiȝum tearum birunnen. c1000 *Sax. Leechd.* II. 28 ȝenim cileþonian..& huniȝes teares. a1175 [see A. β]. a1240 *Ureisun* in *Cott. Hom.* 200 Swete iesu..min huni ter. 1594 Shaks. *Rich. III*, v. iii. 284, I would these dewy teares were from the ground. 1616 Surfl. & Markh. *Country Farme* 609 The vine sometimes poureth forth great store of teares, whereupon..it looseth his force altogether. a1626 Bacon *New Atl.* (1650) 29 The Teares or Woundings of Trees. 1697 Dryden *Virg. Georg* iii. 505 The pearly tears Of Morning Dews. 1820 L. Hunt *Indicator* No. 20 I. 156 The tears of the sky at least were dried up. 18.. B. Taylor *Manuela* Poems (1866) 316 With the tears of amber dropping. 1865 Dickens *Mut. Fr.* i. xiv, Hawse-holes long discoloured with the iron's rusty tears. 1883 *Century Mag.* Oct. 873/1 Carrying large candles, which drip their waxen tears along the road [at a funeral].

†**b.** *pl.* The Italian sweet wine known as Lachryma Christi. *Obs. rare*⁻¹.

1526 *Pilgr. Perf.* (1531) 53b, There groweth the myghty swete wynes, as malueseys, tyeres & muscadels.

3. *spec.* Applied to various gums that exude from plants in tear-shaped or globular beads, which then become solid or resinous.

a1000 Ælfric *Voc.* in Wr.-Wülcker 139/28 *Opobalsamum*, balsames tear. a1400-50 *Alexander* 4974 þar trekild doun of þa teres of iemmes, Boyland out of þe barke bawme & mirre. 1578 Lyte *Dodoens* iii. xvi. 308 Evphorbium is the gumme or teare of a certayne strange plante growing in Lybia. 1585 T. Washington tr. *Nicholay's Voy.* ii. vi. 36 The Mastic is the teare or droppings of the Lentiscus. 1604 E. G[rimstone] *D'Acosta's Hist. Indies* iv. xxviii. 286 One kinde..which they call Opobalsamum, which be the very teares that distil. 1686 W. Harris tr. *Lemery's Course Chym.* (ed. 2) 467 Opium is a Tear which distils of itself, or by Incision of the heads of Poppies. 1715 tr. *Pancirollus' Rerum Mem.* I. i. xii. 29 Myrrh, is a Drop or Tear, distill'd from a Tree in Arabia Felix. 1825 J. Nicholson *Operat. Mechanic* 573, ½ oz. mastic in tears. 1838 T. Thomson *Chem. Org. Bodies* 671 Gum arabic..is in small rounded drops or tears. 1895 *Daily News* 25 Nov. 7/1 Fine tears of frankincense, the gum resin produced by an Indian tree.

4. Anything resembling or suggesting a tear: see quots.; e.g. (*a*) a defect in glass caused by a small particle of vitrified clay: see quot. 1832; (*b*) a detonating bulb, or Prince Rupert's drop.

1832 G. R. Porter *Porcelain & Gl.* xi. 249 Tears are, perhaps, the greatest defect that can be found in glass. *Ibid.*, Wherever these tears exist, the material is brittle in a very high degree, so as frequently to crack, without any apparent cause. 1837 *Penny Cycl.* VII. 15/1 The smaller and rounder the eyes, the better the cheese is reckoned. They should contain a clear salt liquor, which is called the tears. 1839 Ure *Dict. Arts* 746 It [Plomb gomme] has been found only at Huelgoet, near Poullaouen, in Brittany, covering with its tears or small concretions the ores of white lead and galena. *Ibid.* 1250 The block of metal is heated till it becomes brittle, when..it is broken to pieces, and presents an agglomeration of elongated grains or tears; whence it is called grain tin. 1857 Livingstone *Trav.* xxxi. 650 It [iron] occurs generally in tears or rounded lumps. 1858 O. W. Holmes *Aut. Breakf.-t.* ii, A Prince-Rupert's-drop..is a tear of unannealed glass. 1877 Knight *Dict. Mech.*, *Tears*, the vitreous drops from the melting of the walls of a furnace.

5. With defining words, in special senses: as ***glass tear*** [F. *larme de verre*], (*a*) a detonating bulb (see detonating *ppl. a.*); (*b*) a pear-shaped glass-drop used for ornament (*Cent. Dict.* 1891); ***St. Lawrence's tears***, a popular name for the Perseids, the meteors occurring about St. Lawrence's day, Aug. 10; ***tears of St. Peter***, a West Indian plant, *Anthacanthus microphyllus* (*Treas. Bot.*); ***tears of strong wine***, drops of liquid forming on the inner sides of a glass partly filled with strong wine. Also crocodile *tears*, job's *tears*, juno's *tears*.

1899 R. H. Allen *Star Names* 335 In the later Middle Ages they were known as the *Larmes de Saint Laurent*, Saint Laurence's Tears, his martyrdom upon the red-hot gridiron having taken place on the 10th of August, 258.

6. *attrib.* and *Comb.*: **a.** attributive, as ***tear-bath***, ***-dripping***, ***-flood***, ***-fount***, ***-spring***, ***-tap***, ***-track***; **b.** objective and obj. gen., as ***tear-compeller***, ***tear-compelling***, ***-creative***, ***-distilling***, ***-falling*** (fall *v.* 49), ***-shedding***, ***-wiping*** adjs.; **c.** instrumental, as ***tear-baptized***, ***-bedabbled***, ***-bedewed***, ***-besprinkled***, ***-blinded***, ***-bound***, ***-commixed***, ***-composed***, ***-dabbled***, ***-dewed***, ***-dimmed***, ***-distained***, ***-dropped***, ***-drowned***, ***-filled***, ***-fraught***, ***-freshened***, ***-glistening***, ***-logged***, ***-shot*** (cf. *bloodshot*), ***-stained***, ***-streaked***, ***-strewn***, ***-stubbed***, ***-stuffed***, ***-swollen***, ***-tricked***, ***-washed***, ***-wet***, ***-worn***, ***-wrung*** adjs.; ***tear-nourish*** vb.; **d.** of other kinds, as ***tear-bright***, ***tear-like***, ***tear-shaped***, ***tear-thirsty*** (cf. *bloodthirsty*), ***-tight***, ***-trembling*** adjs.

1624 Quarles *Sion's Sonn.* Div. Poems (1717) 359 My *tears-baptized Love. c1600 in Farr. *S.P. Eliz.* (1845) II. 444 Thou let'st me wash thy feete in my *teare-bath. a1644 Quarles *Sol. Recant.* ch. xii. 5 (1645) 58 To meet Thy *tear-bedabled fun'rals in the Street. c1610 *God Hears*, etc. in Farr *S.P. Jas. I* (1848) 110 Thy *teares-bedewed praiers, And thy repentant sighes, shall haue accesse Before the throne of heaven. 1906 *United Free Ch. Mag.* Mar. 28/1 Crowds with tear-bedewed cheeks thronged the streets. 1809 Malkin *Gil Blas* ix. iv. (Rtldg.) 314 My *tear-besprinkled visage. 1813 Scott *Rokeby* v. xvi, *Tear-blinded to the Castle-hall Came as to bear her funeral pall. 1938 E. Bowen *Death of Heart* ii. i. 178 Her manner..had threatened the afternoon like a cloud that covers the sky but is almost certain never to break. Her eyelids looked rigid —*tear-bound, you would have said. 1874 M. Collins *Frances* II. 191 Her hazel eyes *tear-bright with glee. 1868 —— *Sweet Anne Page* I. 210 That *tear-compelling tragedy. a1618 Sylvester *Panthea* Author's Invoc. 5 In this *teare-composed terrene Globe. 1915 *Pearson's Mag.* Jan. 46/2 She raised a *tear dabbled countenance. 1944 W. de la Mare *Coll. Rhymes & Verses* 217 Tear-dabbled cheeks, wild eyes I see. a1600 J. Bryan in Farr *S.P. Eliz.* (1845) II. 333 Heare, heare with acceptation The *teare-dew'd words I speake. 1811 W. Bristow *Little Wanderer* ii, She cannot see my *tear-dim'd eye. 1593 Shaks. *Lucrece* 1586 About her *teare-distained eye Blew circles stream'd. 1893 F. Thompson *Hound of Heaven* in *Poems* 53 And now my heart is as a broken fount, Wherein *tear-drippings stagnate. 1776 Mickle tr. *Camoens' Lusiad* vii. 298 The *tear-dropt bough hangs weeping in the vale. 1598 Sylvester *Du Bartas* ii. i. ii. *Imposture* 406 His *tear-drown'd eyes, a night of Clouds bedims. 1594 Shaks. *Rich. III*, iv. ii. 66 *Teare-falling Pittie dwells not in this Eye. 1951 in M. McLuhan *Mech. Bride* (1967) 11/2 Miss Grable, with *tear-filled eyes, showed..a letter she'd received from a soldier's buddy. a1631 Donne *Valediction* ii, No *teare-floods, nor sigh-tempests move. 1916 R. Graves *Over the Brazier* 21 Till it seemed through a swift tear-flood That dead men blossomed in the garden-close. a1600 J. Bryan in Farr *S.P. Eliz.* (1845) II. 334 My long *teare-fraught eies Haue seene thy plagues redoble Vpon mine enemies. 1842 Faber *Styrian Lake*, etc. 261 White flowers, *tear-freshened, for pale sorrow's brow. 1811 W. Bristow *Stanzas written in —— church-yd.* iii, At widow'd Love's *tear-glistning shrine. 1567 Maplet *Gr. Forest* 32 This Tree..by and by droppeth and distilleth a certaine humor, in a manner *tearlike. 1931 R. Campbell *Georgiad* ii. 41 Holding our course among the *tear-logged wrecks. 1873 E. Brennan *Witch of Nemi*, etc. 70 For she *Tear-nourishes the bud her true love bare Unto her lord. 1632 Lithgow *Trav.* i. 5 *Teare-rent Sophyre, Synon-like betrayd What votall oathes, loues sterne fort, ne'er bewrayd. 1893 Hodges *Elem. Photogr.* (1907) 88 *Tear-shaped markings may be produced. 1598 Drayton *Heroic. Ep.*, *Matilda to K. John*, If all remorcelesse, no *teare-shedding eie, My selfe will moane my selfe. 1840 Browning *Sordello* iii. 744 Lashless eyes Inveterately *tear-shot. 1593 Shaks. *2 Hen. VI*, ii. iv. 16 Ile prepare My *teare-stayn'd eyes, to see her Miseries. 1868 Adah I. Menken *Infelicia* (1883) 120 Take my cold, tear-stained face up to yours. 1923 Galsworthy *Captures* 181 The girl's face, *tear-streaked, confusedly pretty, had come up before him. 1942 S. Smith *Mother, what is Man?* 76 My reverent reveries and fruitful plod Of *tear-strewn steps. 1593 Nashe *Christ's T.* Wks. (Grosart) IV. 12 That which my *Teare-stubbed penne..hath attempted. 1939 Dylan Thomas *Map of Love* 12 After the feast of *tear-stuffed time and thistles. 1768 C. Shaw *Monody* i, These *tear-swoln eyes beheld her fall. 1922 Joyce *Ulysses* 753 That was the last time she turned on the *teartap. 1579 Gosson *Sch. Abuse* (Arb.) 49 Calling [Mars] the bloody God, the angry God,..πολύδακρυς the *tearethirsty God. 1938 S. Beckett *Murphy* iv. 51 The human eyelid is not *teartight. 1965 S. Smith in *Listener* 2 Sept. 347/3 Those awful *tear-tracks on her cheeks, As if she had cried a lot! 1916 D. H. Lawrence *Amores* 74 *Tear-trembling stars of autumn. 1880 G. M. Hopkins *Poems* (1967) 88 In his hands he has flung His *tear-tricked cheeks of flame. 1755 J. Shebbeare *Lydia* (1769) II. 431 The *tear-washed eye surveyed the severe trials. 1916 H. G. Wells *Mr. Britling sees it Through* iii. i. 389 Her tear-washed mind became vaguely friendly. 1922 Joyce *Ulysses* 175 Davy Byrne, sated after his yawn, said with tearwashed eyes:—And is that a fact? c1630 Drumm. of Hawth. *Poems* Wks. (1711) 33 Her *tear-wet locks hang'd o'er her face. 1605 Sylvester *Du Bartas* ii. iii. i. *Vocation* 151 O contrite heart's restorer! *Tears-wiping tame-griefe! 1786 Burns *Lament* viii, My toil-beat nerves, and *tear-worn eye. 1823 Byron *Age of Bronze* xiv, They voted..*tear-wrung millions—why? for rent!

e. Special Combs.: **tear-bag**, (*a*) = *tear-pit*; (*b*) = *tear-gland*; **tear bomb**, a bomb containing tear gas; **tear-drop**, (*a*) = sense 1; (*b*) *transf.*, freq. *attrib.*, denoting something resembling a tear-drop in shape as: (i) an air cavity in glassware; (ii) a tear-shaped run in paintwork or ceramic glaze; (iii) a streamlined body or component of a vehicle, boat, etc.; (iv) *Surfing* = *pig board* s.v. pig *sb.*[1] 14; (v) a bead or jewel of tear-drop shape; **tear-duct**, (*a*) the lachrymal or nasal duct, which carries off tears from the eye to the nose; (*b*) the lachrymal canal, which supplies tears to the eyes; **tear-gas**, a lachrymatory gas used in warfare or riot control to disable opponents or make crowds disperse; hence as *v. trans.*, to attack with tear gas, to drive *out of* a place with tear gas; **tear-gland**, the lachrymal gland; **tear-jug** *rare* = tear-bottle; **tear-passage**, = *tear-duct*; **tear-pit**, the lachrymal or sub-orbital sinus found in many species of deer, a fold or cavity beneath the inner corner of the eye, containing a thin waxy secretion; = larmier 2; **tear-pump** (*slang*) [cf. pump *sb.*[1] d, *v.* 6], the source of tears shed effusively or in feigned emotion; **tear-punctum**: see punctum 4 b; **tear-sac**, = *tear-pit*; **tear-shell**, a shell (shell *sb.*[1] 21) containing tear-gas; **tear-smoke** = *tear gas* above. See also tear-bottle.

1893 Lydekker *Horns & Hoofs* 64 The lachrymal fossa —in which rests the gland termed the crumen, larmier, or '*tear-bag'. 1929 M. Lief *Hangover* xv. 238 I'm going to have Katie actually taken for a ride..and Rat-Face Walsh's yeggs following..with machine guns and *tear bombs. 1953 Wendt & Kogan *Big Bill of Chicago* xxiii. 271 Police squads cruising the city, machine-guns in their laps and tear bombs in their pockets. 1799 H. Gurney *Cupid & Psyche* 10 (Jod.) No *tear-drop fills his frozen eye. 1830 Tennyson *Talking Oak* xli, A teardrop trembled from its source, And down my surface crept. 1904 *Burlington Mag.* IV. 141/1 Immediately under the bowl at the top of the stem is an air cavity, known as a 'tear-drop'..a frequent form of decoration. 1922 [see curtain *sb.*[1] 1 e]. 1933 *Burlington Mag.* June 265/1 The presence of 'tear drops' in the glaze [of Chinese porcelain]. 1936 *Times* 29 Dec. 12/6 The new design will allow the manufacturer [of motor vehicles] to indulge in the 'tear-drop' streamlining which has often been discussed in recent years but never achieved. 1948 *Shell Aviation News* No. 115. 6/1 A 25-foot, streamlined, teardrop antenna will project below the fuselage... This will be the main broadcasting antenna. 1962 *Austral. Women's Weekly* Suppl. 24 Oct. 3/4 *Teardrop*, type of surfboard with wide back and pointed front. 1965 *Harper's Bazaar* June 24 Diamond teardrop, £500. 1980 D. Creed *Scarab* i. 9 A large and most marvellous pendant..suspending a teardrop pearl. 1917 W. Owen *Let.* 19 Jan. (1967) 429 It was only *tear-gas from a shell, and I got safely back (to the party) in my helmet. 1927 *New Republic* 12 Oct. 202/2 The troopers on the outskirts..hurled tear-gas bombs and charged. 1927 *Daily Express* 16 Dec. 15, I imagine him, first, tear-gassing a river bank and so reducing all the crocodiles to genuinely hopeless grief. 1934 R. Stout *Fer-de-Lance* ii. 25 A gangster had been tear-gassed out of a Brooklyn flat. 1978 R. Ludlum *Holcroft Covenant* xliii. 499 Tear gas and Mace were not unknown in Yakov's line of work. 1869 *Tear-jug [see Pisan *a.*]. 1892 *Pall Mall G.* 30 Mar. 4/3 The treatment of obstructions of the *tear passages. 1834 *Penny Cycl.* II. 69/1 The possession of lachrymal sinuses, or, as they are vernacularly called with reference to the stag and fallow-deer, *tear-pits,..distinguishes the greater number of the antelopes. 1903 Farmer *Slang Dict.* s.v., *To work the *tear-pump*,..to weep. 1878 T. Bryant *Pract. Surg.* I. 348 The *tear puncta..lie in contact with the ocular conjunctiva. 1916 *War Illustr.* 23 Dec. 451/3 Don't you know the scent of *tear-shells when you smell it? 1946 F. Burrows *Let.* 22 Aug. in Mansergh & Moon *Transfer of Power* (1979) VIII. 296 He added that the Police had used *tear-smoke on crowds frequently. 1949 Koestler *Promise & Fulfilment* i. xii. 136 The boarding party finally gained control of the vessel by using tear-smoke grenades..against them.

tear (tɛə(r)), *sb.*[2] [f. tear *v.*[1]]

1. An act of tearing or rending; the action of tearing; hence, damage caused by tearing (or similar violent action); usually in phr. ***tear and wear***, ***wear and tear***, including damage due both to accident and to ordinary wear: see wear; also used *fig.* in reference to body or mind.

1666 Pepys *Diary* 29 Sept., The wages, victuals, wear and tear..will come to above £3,000,000. 1705 R. Cromwell *Let.* in *Eng. Hist. Rev.* (1898) XIII. 123 A third for wages tare and wear, and upholding the stock. 1765 Foote *Commissary* i. Wks. 1799 II. 12 At that time of life, men can bustle and stir..; it is the only tear and wear season. 1767 A. Young *Farmer's Lett. to People* 282 With ease to the horses, and not half the tear of irons, &c. 1874 Blackie *Self-Cult.* 65 Plated work will never stand the tear and wear of life.

1901 *Scotsman* 6 Mar. 9/7 The tear and wear of the campaign is telling severely on the..Yeomanry.

2. *concr.* **a.** A torn part or place; a rent or fissure.

1611 COTGR., *Deschirure*, a teare, a rent. **1755** JOHNSON, *Tear*,..a rent, a fissure. **1824** MRS. CAMERON *Pink Tippet* II. 21 Mother has darned up the tears. **1891** *Amiel's Jrnl.* 195 Each darn and tear has its story. **190.** *Bookseller's Catal.*, This copy has the title cut round and mounted, a few slight tears in margins, in one case the tear extends to text.

b. The line along which a piece of cloth or the like naturally tears.

1857 H. MILLER *Test. Rocks* vi. 232 What a draper would term the *tear* of the one layer or fold.

3. An act of tearing, in senses 8 and 9 of the verb. **a.** A rushing gallop or pace; esp. in advb. phrase ***full tear***, full tilt, headlong. **b.** A spree (*U.S. slang*). **c.** A rage or passion; a violent flurry. **d.** Here may belong the Irish interjectional phr. ***tear and ages*** (? *aches*), ***wounds***, expressing astonishment.

a. 1838 DICKENS *O. Twist* xxxiii, He could have..galloped away, full tear, to the next stage. **1892** *Sat. Rev.* 2 Jan. 16/1 The rattling tear across country.

b. 1869 B. HARTE *How Santa Claus*, etc. Wks. (1872) 363 May be ye'd all like to come over to my house to-night and have a sort of tear round. **1895** *Outing* (U.S.) XXVII. 189/2 Then I should go on a tear—a regular one you know—and not come home for three whole days. **1896** *Harper's Mag.* XCII. 775/2 Got me off on a tear somehow, and by the time I was sober again the money was 'most all gone.

c. 1880 *W. Cornwall Gloss.* s.v. *Taer*, 'She got into a pretty taer'. **1890** *Anthony's Photogr. Bull.* III. 128 If you keep quiet you may see a way out of the difficulty that you most certainly would not if you got in a 'tare'.

d. 1841 LEVER *C. O'Malley* lxvii, Tear and ages! how sore my back is. **1842** S. LOVER *Handy Andy* iii, 'Tare an' ouns!' roared Murphy, 'how Andy runs'. **1893** BARING-GOULD *Cheap Jack Z.* I. i. 13 'Tear and ages!' sez I; 'that's a wonder of the world'.

4. Special Comb.: **tear-fault** *Geol.* = *strike-slip fault* s.v. STRIKE *sb.* 20.

1900 *Proc. Geologists' Assoc.* XVI. 465 It is this ['lag' fault] which gives one a clue as to the nature of some of the most striking 'tear' faults. **1924** J. G. A. SKERL tr. *Wegener's Orig. Continents & Oceans* 58 A lateral displacement of great dimensions, a so-called tear fault. **1957** [see SLICE *sb.*[1] 2 b]. **1977** A. HALLAM *Planet Earth* 60/1 Another common type of shear—which caused little trouble to miners and so was unrecognised for many years—is variously known as a strike-slip, wrench, tear or transcurrent fault.

tear (tɛə(r)), *a.* and *sb.*[3] Now *techn.* Forms: 5 ter, 5–6 tere, 5–7 teer(e, 6 teir, teyre, 7 teare, 7–8 tare, 7– tear. [Known *c* 1400; app. from Du. or LG.: cf. MDu., MFl., MLG., LG. *teer, têr*, contracted from *teeder, têder* fine, thin, delicate, tender: cf. OE. *tíedre, týdre, tydder* tender.]

†**A.** *adj.* Fine, delicate; of the best quality. (Said esp. of flour and hemp.) *Obs.*

c **1400** *Trevisa's Higden* (Rolls) III. 9 Salomon his mete was euery day pritty corues of clene [*v.rr.* teer, tere, ter] floure and foure score corues of mele. **1501** DOUGLAS *Pal. Hon.* I. 542 Damisflure, tere pyle, quhairon thair lyis Peirle, Orphany quhilk euerie stait renewis. **1532** *Test. Ebor.* (Surtees) VI. 34, ij pare of harden shettes, ij pare of hempe tere, and ij pare of lynan shettes. **1544** *Ibid.* 214 A pare of newe hempe tere shetes. **1541–2** in *Lanc. Wills* (1857) 80 A xj payre of teir hempen shetis.

B. *sb.* (The adj. used absol.) Something of the finest or best quality: †**a.** The finest wheaten flour. *Obs.* **b.** The finest fibre of flax or hemp.

a. *c* **1440** *Promp. Parv.* 489/1 Teere, of flowre, *amolum.* **1521** WHITINTON *Gram.* B vj, *Pollis vel pollen..est idem in tritico quod flos in siligine*, the tere of floure. **1521** *Coventry Leet Bk.* 669 But on haly-cake, and that they put no more theryn but the Teyre of thre stryke of whete.

b. 1541–2 in *Lanc. Wills* (1857) 81, xxv teir of hempe slippingis. **1601** HOLLAND *Pliny* XIX. i, As for the good Flax indeed, which is the teere or marrow as it were within of the Line. **1657** W. COLES *Adam in Eden* cclxxxi, The Summer Hemp affordeth most Teere as they call it. **1706** PHILLIPS (ed. 6), *Tare of Flax*, the finest dress'd part of it made ready for the Spinner. **1805** *Usef. Proj.* in *Ann. Reg.* 851/2 A machine for discharging a woolcomb or combs, by separating the tears from the noiles. **1837** WHITTOCK, etc. *Bk. Trades* (1842) 238 (Flax Dresser) The strike is to pass through a fine hackle, and the hurds coming from thence saved for middling cloth, and the tear itself for the best linen.

tear (tɛə(r)), *v.*[1] Pa. t. tore (tɔə(r)), *arch.* and *dial.* tare (tɛə(r)). Pa. pple. torn (tɔːn). Forms: see below. [OE. *ter-an*, pa. t. *tær*, pl. *tǽron*, pa. pple. *toren*, = OLG. **teran* (MD., MLG. *teren*, Du. *teren*, OHG. *zeran* (MHG. *zeren, zern*, Ger. *zehren*) to destroy, consume, Goth. *gataíran* to destroy. OTeut. **teran* (*tar*, '*târon*, '*toran-*) was cognate with Gr. δέρειν to flay, OSlav. *derą* to tear asunder, Skr. *dar-* to burst. The OE. pa. t. *tær* (:—*tar*) survived as *tare* to 17th c., when it gave place in standard Eng. to *tore*, with *o* from pa. pple. *toren, torn*: cf. *bore, swore*. A weak pa. t. and pple. *terede, tered*, found in 15th c., are still dialectal, along with a mixed form *tored, tord*.]

A. Illustration of Forms.

1. *Infin.* and *Pres. Stem.* 1 teran (teoran, tearan) (3 *pers. sing.* tirð, tyrþ), 2–5 teren, 3 teoren, 3–6 tere, 4 teere, 5 teer, 6– *Sc.* teir, 6–7 teare, 6– tear. *dial.* 7– tare, 9 teer, teear (tiːr, tɪə(r)).

a **850** *Lorica Gloss.* in *O.E.T.* 172/2 *Lacerandum*, to teorenne. *c* **888** K. ÆLFRED *Boeth.* xxii. §1 He þe tirð on ða þrotan. *c* **950** *Lindisf. Gosp.* Mark ix. 26 Suiðe ȝetearende hine. *c* **975** *Rushw. Gosp.* ibid., Moniȝe teorende hine. *a* **1000** *Riddles* xxii. 14 (Gr.) Fæst and forðweard feallеþ on sidan ðæt ic [a plough] toþum tere. *a* **1050** *Liber Scintill.* 105 Hit tyrþ ealswa snaca. *a* **1200** Tereð [see B. 2]. [*a* **1225** *Juliana* 12 Ichulle leoten deor to teoren ant to luken þe.] **1382** WYCLIF *Gen.* xl. 19 Fowlis shulen teere thi fleish. *c* **1430** *Hymns Virg.* 49 To teer him from þe top to þe toon. **1552** HULOET, Teare in pieces, *delacero. Ibid.*, Tear, *lacero.* **1567** *Satir. Poems Reform.* xi. 58 With glowing gunne that man to teir. **1662** *Rump Songs* (1874) I. 192 To tare the Rochet to such rags as these.

2. *Past Tense.* α. 1–2 tær, 3–5 tar, 4–5 taar, 4–7 tare; 6 *Sc.* (9 *dial.*) tor, 7– tore (9 *dial.* tar, Sc. tuir (tør)). *Pl.* 1–2 tǽron, 3 tiere, 3–4 tere(n, 4 tare(n, 4–5 ter, 5 terre; 5– same as sing.

α. *c* **1000** ÆLFRIC *Gen.* xxxvii. 29 Ða tær he his claðas [L. *scissis vestibus*]. *c* **1000** in Cockayne *Narrat.* (1861) 15 Hie mid þæm þa men wundodon and tæron. *c* **1275** LAY. 25850 [Ʒeo] tar hire bi þan ere. *Ibid.* 24843 Hii..tiere ȝam bi þan heere. **13..** *K. Alis.* 4642 Alisaunder his cloþes taar. *Ibid.* 6876 Heore heir heo taren. *c* **1330** Tar [see B. 4]. *c* **1400** MAUNDEV. (1839) ix. 81 And there weren Marie Cleophee and Marie Magdaleyne, and teren here heer. **14..** HOCCLEVE *Compl. Virgin* 239 A modir þat so soone hir cote taar Or rente. [**1513** DOUGLAS *Æneis* XII. x. 129 Hyr rosy chekis to-tor and scartis sche.] *c* **1530** *Hickscorner* A ij b, The knottes the skyn tare. **1611** BIBLE 2 *Sam.* xiii. 31 The king arose, and tare his garments. **1653–4** WHITELOCKE *Jrnl. Swed. Emb.* (1772) I. 378 Three Dutch men of war.., whom she tore, and killed many of their men. **1828** *Craven Gloss.* s.v. *Tar*, He tar his breeks to tatters.

β. 5 terede, terid, 6 teared, tearde, teard.

[*a* **1450** *Alexander* 4148 All þaire tents it to-terid.] **1578** BOWES *Let. to Burghley* in Tytler *Hist. Scot.* (1864) IV. 317 The king..teared his hairs. **1593** *Pass. Morrice* (1876) 78 Now tearde she her haire. **1599** M[OUFET] *Silkwormes* 73 Whilst herbage greene with vnseene teeth they teard.

3. *Pa. pple.* α. 1–7 toren, 5–8 torne, 5 toryn, 6– torn. β. 4 i-tore, 4–9 (now *dial.*) tore. γ. 5 teryd, 6 teard, 6–7 (9 *dial.*) teared, 9 *dial.* tored.

α. [*a* **1000** *Aldhelm Gloss.* 5386 in Napier *O.E. Glosses* 135/2 *Lacerari*, totoren.] *c* **1325** *Deus Caritas* 25 in *E.E.P.* (1862) 127 Crist was toren vche a lym. *c* **1489** CAXTON *Sonnes of Aymon* ii. 62 Many heres pulled and many gownes toren. **1499** *Promp. Parv.* 522/2 (Pynson) Weryd or worne or torne. **1619** S. ATKINSON *Gold Mynes Scotl.* (Bann. Cl.) 15 Forced and torn from his bedd. *a* **1631** DONNE *Hymn to Christ* 1 In what torne shipp soever I embark. **1658** WOOD *Life* May (O.H.S.) I. 253 Toren downe.

β. **1387** TREVISA *Higden* (Rolls) IV. 331 Whan þey were i-tore. *a* **1400** *Leg. Rood* (1871) 143 Til trie fruit weore tore and toyled. *c* **1422** HOCCLEVE *Min. Poems* (1892) 227 Hir clothes hath shee al to-rent & tore. **1730** A. GORDON *Maffei's Amphith.* 103 They were tore to pieces. **1777** *Horæ Subsecivæ* 427 (E.D.D.) Joan's pitcher is tore.

γ. *c* **1440** *Promp. Parv.* 522/2 Weryd, or teryd, or torvon. *a* **1529** SKELTON *Col. Cloute* 1203 To be teared thus and torne. **1558** PHAER *Æneid* II. D j b, By Grekes shall Troy not now be teard. *a* **1649** DRUMM. OF HAWTH. *Poems* Wks. (1711) 37/1 Kingdoms got by wrongs, by wrongs are tear'd. **1879** MISS JACKSON *Shropsh. Word-bk.* 432 I've tard my throck. **1897** E. PHILLPOTTS *Lying Proph.* I. vi, Just a rag tored off a petticoat.

B. Signification.

I. 1. a. *trans.* To pull asunder by force (a body or substance, now esp. one of thin and flexible consistence, as cloth or paper), usually so as to leave ragged or irregular edges; to rend. (Expressing either partial or complete separation of parts; in the latter case usually with adv. or advb. phr., as ***to tear up, to tear in*** (or ***to***) ***pieces***, etc.)

c **1000** [see A. 2]. **13..** *Seuyn Sag.* (W.) 782 The grehound wolde nowt sessed be, Til that adder ware toren of thre. *c* **1386** CHAUCER *Shipman's T.* 136 Though men me wolde al in to pieces tere. *a* **1440** *Sir Degrev.* 1688 Leve syre, where have ȝe bene, ȝoure clothus to tere. **1530** PALSGR. 754/2 He hath torne my gowne a foote and more. **1592** SHAKS. *Rom. & Jul.* v. iii. 35 By heauen I will teare thee ioynt by ioynt. **1649** BP. REYNOLDS *Serm. Hosea* i. 32 The Serpent can sting, but he cannot teare in pieces. **1709** M. PIERREPOINT *Let. to Mrs. Wortley* in *Lady M. W. Montagu's Lett.* lxiii. 104 She will..tear the letter, and never answer it. **1777** COOK *Voy. Pacific* II. vii. (1784) I. 291 They are always careful to join the small pieces lengthwise, which makes it impossible to tear the cloth in any direction but one. **1841** W. SPALDING *Italy & It. Isl.* III. 96 The unpopular minister of finance was torn in pieces by the mob. **1857** HUGHES *Tom Brown* I. vii, Engaged in tearing up old newspapers..into small pieces. **1902** BUCHAN *Watcher by Threshold* 268 The boy had torn his clothes.

b. *transf.* To make (a hole, etc.) by tearing.

1593 SHAKS. *Rich. II*, v. v. 20 How these vaine weake nailes May teare a passage through the Flinty ribbes Of this hard world. *Mod.* You've torn a hole in my coat.

c. To break (a hard solid body) by force or violent impact; to shatter, split, rive. Now *dial.*

1582 N. LICHEFIELD tr. *Castanheda's Conq. E. Ind.* I. lxxi. 145 b, Their Fregates..were torne in pieces and sunke. **1588** SIR W. WYNTER *Let. to J. Hawkyns* 28 Feb. (P.R.O.), This winters weather..hath..torn many of our blocks, pulleis and sheevers. *a* **1600** HOOKER *Answ. to Travers* §25 As water split or poured into a torn dish. *c* **1626** *Dick of Devon* I. ii. in Bullen *O. Pl.* (1883) II. 16 From the armed winds an hoast brake forth which tare their shipps and sav'd ours. **1746** FRANCIS tr. *Horace, Art of Poetry* 642 Like a baited Bear, If he hath Strength enough his Den to tear. **1828** *Wheeler's Mag.* Nov. 481 In this county [Hampshire] break is used for tear, and tear for break, as, I have torn my best decanter, or china dish; I have broke my cambric apron. **1888** ELWORTHY *W. Somerset Word-bk.* s.v., Mind you don't tear the pitcher. Who've a-bin an' a-tord the winder?

†**d.** Phr. ***to tear a*** (***the***) ***cat***: to play the part of a roistering hero; to rant and bluster: cf. *tear-cat* in TEAR- 2. *Obs.*

1590 SHAKS. *Mids. N.* I. ii. 31, I could play Ercles rarely, or a part to teare a Cat in, to make all split. **1610** *Histrio-m.* 8 Sirrha is this you, would rend and teare the cat upon a stage?

2. To wound or injure by rending; to lacerate.

a **1000** *Ecgbert's Confessional* §40 (Thorpe *Laws* II. 164) ȝif hy[swin] deade men terað [*laceraverint*]. *a* **1050** *Liber Scintill.* 78 Terende weleras his he ȝefremð yfel. *a* **1200** *Moral Ode* 274 (Lamb.) Þeor beð naddren and snaken..þa tereð and freteð þe uuele speken. **13..** *K. Alis.* 5969 (Bodl. MS.) Hij ne shulle hem wiþ tooþ tere. *c* **1440** *Pallad. on Husb.* VIII. 91 To tere her skynnes bothe. **1526** TINDALE *Mark* ix. 20 As sone as the sprete sawe him, he tare him. **1573–80** BARET *Alv.* T 297 All his bodie is rent, or torne ..*laceratus est toto corpore.* **1697** DRYDEN *Virg. Georg.* III. 678 Their defenceless Limbs the Brambles tear. **1743** FRANCIS tr. *Hor., Epod.* iv. 3 Thou Wretch, whose Back with flagrant Whips is torn. **1813** J. THOMSON *Lect. Inflam.* 207 In wounds, in which the divided surfaces are much torn or bruised. **1875** SIR T. SEATON *Fret Cutting* 96 To avoid tearing the wood when cutting against the grain.

absol. c **1000** ÆLFRIC *Hom.* II. 532 Ne sceal he teran ne bitan swa swa wulf. **1545** BRINKLOW *Compl.* 46 b, To teare lyke bearys, and to byte lyke cruel woluys.

3. a. In various *fig.* applications; *esp.*, in later use, to split into parties or factions.

c **1000** *St. Basil's Admonitio* v. (1849) 46 Ne ðu hine ne tæl ne ne ter mid wordum. **1560** DAUS tr. *Sleidane's Comm.* 122 The members of the churche tore a sondre. **1593** SHAKS. *Rich. II*, III. iii. 83 Though you thinke, that all, as you haue done, Haue torne their Soules. **1602** —— *Ham.* III. ii. 11 To see a robustious Pery-wig-pated Fellow, tear a Passion to tatters. **1609** *Ev. Woman in Hum.* D ij, A Rogue..so tearing the sence, I neuer met with. **1697** DRYDEN *Virg. Georg.* II. 707 Nor, when contending Kindred tear the Crown, Will set up one, or pull another down. **1779** *Mirror* No. 21 ⁋2 My sneezing..which, she said, tore her poor nerves in pieces. **1845** S. AUSTIN *Ranke's Hist. Ref.* III. 113 Christendom itself was torn with divisions. **1908** *Daily News* 24 Mar. 6 He, too, tears his finish, while he still has his old fault.

†**b.** ***to tear*** (***the name of***) ***God, the body of Christ***, etc.: to blaspheme; *esp.* to swear profanely by Christ's limbs, etc. *Obs.*

c **1325** *Song of Mercy* 150 in *E.E.P.* (1862) 123 We stunt noþer for schame ne drede To teren vr god from top to to. [*c* **1386** CHAUCER *Pard. T.* 146 It is grisly for to heere hem swere Oure blissed lordes body they to-tere.] **1539** [see TEARING *vbl. sb.*[1] 1]. **1557** F. SEAGER *Sch. Vertue* xi. C vij, What better art thou for this thy swearyng Blasfamouslye, the name of god tearyng? *a* **1624** BP. M. SMITH *Serm.* (1632) 126 Did not the Spaniards sweare, and curse, and teare God?

c. Used of the effect of sounds, esp. loud or 'piercing' noises, on the air, etc.: = REND *v.* 4 b.

1592 SHAKS. *Rom. & Jul.* II. ii. 162 Else would I teare the Caue where Eccho lies,..With repetition of my Romeo. **1607** —— *Cor.* v. iii. 151 To teare with Thunder the wide Cheekes a' th' Ayre. **1671** MILTON *Samson* 1472 What noise or shout was that? it tore the Skie. **1697** DRYDEN *Virg. Georg.* IV. 665 All her fellow Nymphs the Mountains tear With loud Laments. **1822** LAMB *Elia* Ser. I. *Praise Chimneysweepers*, A shout that tore the concave.

d. To harrow, wound, 'rend' (the heart, soul, feelings, etc.). Also with *apart, up*: to render distraught, upset (a person). In *pass.* with *up* (dial. *out*): to be distressed, upset. *N. Amer. colloq.*

1666 BUNYAN *Grace Ab.* §46 Now was I tore and rent in heavy case for many days together. **1718** POPE *Iliad* XXII. 526 Grief tears his heart. **1859** HELPS *Friends in C.* Ser. II. I. 28 That man torn by domestic affliction. **1872** BLACK *Adv. Phaeton* xi, The young man is torn asunder with doubts and fears. **1898** F. P. DUNNE *Mr. Dooley in Peace & War* 47 They say th' Spanyards is all tore up about it. **1950** R. MOORE *Candlemas Bay* 240 Jeb, poor lamb, he was so tore out about you that he never said nothing. **1956** B. HOLIDAY *Lady sings Blues* (1973) xiii. 117 The few I did see when they came back tore me apart. One night..a kid came in to see me... His hair had turned completely white. **1972** *Even. Telegram* (St. John's, Newfoundland) 24 June 9/1 Robert A. Power, who said he was tore up from work in his younger days and was 'no good now to trade and no good to sell.' **1974** K. MILLETT *Flying* (1975) III. 323 Pete is too delicate to pattern. Tears him up just to hear Winnie yell.

e. ***to be torn between***: to be distracted by (two equal but conflicting desires, emotions, or loyalties).

1871 L. W. M. LOCKHART *Fair to See* I. viii. 148 Torn between her desire to underrate Eila and to preserve her own dignity. **1888** MRS. H. WARD *Robert Elsmere* III. xxxv. 111 Agnes, torn between her interest in what was going on and her desire to get back to her mother, had at last hurriedly accepted this Mrs. Sherwood's offer. **1922** T. WOLFE *Lett.* (1956) ii. 31 The girl Laura, 'torn between' (as the saying goes) love for her beaten father and the blunt young apple grower. **1948** A. PATON *Cry, Beloved Country* II. viii. 172 Jarvis was torn between compassion and irritation, and he stood and watched uncomfortably. **1971** G. CHARLES *Destiny Waltz* iii. 104 As usual in such cases he was torn between both sides, angry with Dorn for his patronage of the couple, impatient with them for being what they were.

f. Colloq. phr. (chiefly in *pa. t.* and *perfect*) ***to tear it***: to spoil one's chances; to put an end to one's hopes, plans, etc.

1909 'I. HAY' *Man's Man* xvii. 320 'I've fairly torn it, this time!' he reflected morosely. *a* **1918** W. OWEN in *Poems* (1920) 22 First wave we are, first ruddy wave; that's tore it. **1924** KIPLING *Debits & Credits* (1926) 258, I expect I must 'ave kept carryin' on, till Headquarters give me that wire from Ma... That wire tore it. **1938** G. GREENE *Nineteen Stories* (1947) 77 'I *am* English,' Mr. Calloway said. Even that didn't tear it. **1954** M. Procter *Hell is City* vi. iii. 180 He looked at his watch. 'That's torn it,' he said. **1960** D. Lessing *In Pursuit of English* v. 185 Oh, my God, that tears it, if he's going to start. **1972** D. Delman *Sudden Death* (1973) iv. 110 'Ouch,' she said, grinning... 'Well, that tears that, doesn't it?'

g. In phrases with *up* and indefinite obj., descriptive of unrestrained excitement; esp. in Jazz. *U.S. slang.*

1932 J. Dos Passos *1919* 270 Bud had been tearing things up at the University and was on the edge of getting fired. **1955** Shapiro & Hentoff *Hear Me talkin' to Ya* 204 He had the first big colored band that hit the road and tore it up. **1963** *Listener* 14 Mar. 478/3 The trumpeter Wild Bill Davison, who 'tore it up' with admirable primitivity and sensuality. **1968** [see identify *v.* 1 b].

h. ***to tear down***: to punish; to criticize severely. *U.S. colloq.*

1938 M. K. Rawlings *Yearling* xxix. 381 I'll tear down all two of you. Now git down and pick up ever' one o' them peas and wash 'em off. **1978** I. B. Singer *Shosha* vii. 128 The insolence of a writer tearing down a piece before it's been performed!

i. ***to tear apart***, (*a*) to subject to criticism; (*b*) to search (a place) thoroughly.

1953 *Manch. Guardian Weekly* 1 Jan. 13/2 Carefully tear apart your editorial. **1977** 'C. Aird' *Parting Breath* xv. 176 Somebody was ready to tear the place apart. You should have seen Miss Moleyn's house.

4. ***to tear (out) the hair*** in a frenzy of grief or anger: now a hyperbolical expression.

c **1000** *Judith* 281 He þa..onȝan his feax teran hreoh on mode & his hræȝl somod. *c* **1330** *K. Tars* 100 He tar the her of hed and berd. *c* **1489** Caxton *Sonnes of Aymon* i. 34 He ..wrange his handes and pulled his berde and tare alle his heres. **1580** Lyly *Euphues* (Arb.) 374 He tare his haire, rent his clothes. **1700** Dryden *Pal. & Arc.* i. 523 He roared, he beat his breast, he tore his hair. **1848** Thackeray *Van. Fair* li, She might tear her long hair and cry her great eyes out. **1855** —— *Rose & Ring* ix, Bulbo began to cry bitterly, and tore quantities of hair out of his head.

5. a. To pull, wrench, or drag by main force from its attachment or fixed place. (With various advbs. or preps. according to sense.)

1297 R. Glouc. (Rolls) App. XX. 188 Hare fon come þere, Adoun of his hors henri hi tere Mid yrene crokes. *c* **1400** *Rom. Rose* 7315 That men ne may in no manere Teren the wolf out of his hide. *c* **1400** *Destr. Troy* 1966, I shuld tere out þi tunge and þi tethe euyn. *a* **1425** *Cursor M.* 9072 (Trin.) My kingis robe of me ȝe tere. *a* **1533** Ld. Berners *Huon* lv. 188 He..tare of helmes & strake out braynes. **1590** Spenser *F.Q.* ii. x. 36 The noble braunch from th' antique stock was torne Through discord. **1614** Raleigh *Hist. World* ii. (1634) 481 A great Earth-quake, which did teare downe halfe an Hill. **1667** Wood *Life* (O.H.S.) II. 121, I find many leaves..toren out. **1699** Dampier *Voy.* II. iii. vi. 67 By tearing up the Trees by the Roots. **1704** Swift *Batt. Bks.* Misc. (1711) 239 Who had tore off his Title-Page. **1705** Addison *Italy* 7 (tr. Lucan i.) Ships from their Anchors torn. **1821** Scott *Kenilw.* xl, I could tear out mine eyes for their blindness! **1849** Macaulay *Hist. Eng.* iii. I. 387 The porters..tore down the placards in which the scheme was announced. **1899** *Allbutt's Syst. Med.* VIII. 872 They [molluscan tumours] may be easily torn out of the skin when mature.

b. *fig.* To take away or remove by force or violence; to force; *refl.* to force oneself away.

1574 Hellowes *Gueuara's Fam. Ep.* (1577) 310 Despiteful wordes that..breake her hart, & teare ye teares out of her eyes. **1590** Shaks. *Mids. N.* iii. ii. 287 What, will you teare Impatient answers from my gentle tongue? **1647** May *Hist. Parl.* i. vii. 77 If a King will suffer men to be torne from him, he shall never have any good service done him. **1797** Mrs. Radcliffe *Italian* i, At length he tore himself away. **1829** Lytton *Devereux* iii. ii, I think I see her now, as she stood the moment after I had torn myself from her embrace. **1888** J. Payn *Myst. Mirbridge* (ed. Tauchn.) II. ii. 27 Before the gentlemen come in and tear you away from me.

c. Phrases. ***to tear off a strip, tear a strip off***: see strip *sb.*^{2} 1 i; ***to tear off a bit, piece*** slang (orig. *Austral.*): to copulate with a woman.

1941 Baker *Dict. Austral. Slang* 76 *Tear off a piece*, to coit with a woman. **1951** S. Longstreet *Pedlocks* iv. v. 222 Look, you come down and tear off a piece anytime. And the wine—*Asti Spumante*—she is ona me. I stand the wine. The girls, that is up to you. **1970** G. Greer *Female Eunuch* 265 The vocabulary of impersonal sex is peculiarly desolating. Who wants to 'tear off a piece of ass?' **1977** *Custom Car* Nov. 67/2 Italian wives must sit and suffer if the men tear off a bit on the sly.

6. *intr.* To perform the art of tearing; to make a tear or rent. ***to tear at***, to continue to pull at in order to rend or lacerate.

1526 *Pilgr. Perf.* (W. de W. 1531) 253b, Ye, and many moo sorowes dyd teare & thryll thorowe her herte. **1848** W. E. Burton *Waggeries*, etc. 25 (Farmer) They..kept on tearin at each other like a pack o' wolves. **1867** Aug. J. E. Wilson *Vashti* xxxi, His hands, partially confined, were tearing at the inflamed flesh.

7. *intr.* (for *refl.* and *pass.*) To become torn or rent; *dial.* to burst asunder, split, snap, break.

1526 *Pilgr. Perf.* (W. de W. 1531) 260b, His handes & fete dyd rent & teare for the weyght of his blessed body. **1703** Moxon *Mech. Exerc.* 149 The Boards will Tear or Shake, which is in vulgar English, Split or Crack. **1710** J. Clarke *Rohault's Nat. Phil.* (1729) I. 229 Cloths and other Stuffs of this Colour must tear and wear sooner than those of any other Colour. **1776** Withering *Brit. Plants* (1796) III. 352 Veil before the capsule swells, 4-sided; afterwards it tears into 2, 3, or 4 segments. **1838** Drummond in *Mag. Zool. & Bot.* II. 156 If attempted to be restored without..being first damped, the specimen tears through the middle. **1865** Kingsley *Herew.* vi, All of a sudden..the clouds rose, tore up into ribands, and..blew clean away.

II. 8. *intr.* †To rant and bluster as a roisterer (*obs.*); †to vociferate (*obs.*); to 'go on' violently, to rave in anger or excitement, to rage (*dial.*).

1601 B. Jonson *Poetaster* iii. iv, Hee will teach thee to teare and rand, Rascall, to him. **1672** Dryden *Marriage à-la-Mode* iii. i, Three tailors..who were tearing out as loud as ever they could sing. **1690** *Andros Tracts* I. 207 Towns.. which Rant and Tear at a great rate, because of a small Rate. **1736** Ainsworth *Lat. Dict.* (1783) s.v. *Tear*, To rant, or tear along, *tumultuor, debacchor, vociferationibus vias incessu implere.* **1853** Thackeray *Eng. Hum.* i. (1858) 33 He goes through life, tearing, like a man possessed with a devil. **1897** G. Bartram *People of Clepton* v. 132 She stamped and foamed, and swore and tore.

9. a. *intr.* To move with violence or impetuosity; to rush or 'burst' impetuously or violently. *colloq.*

Sometimes with the notion of a force that would tear its way through obstacles.

1599 Massinger, etc. *Old Law* v. i, The nimble fencer this, that made me tear And traverse 'bout the chamber? **1637** Suckling *Aglaura* v. i, (Stage direct.) Enter, tearing in, Pasithas. **1779** Mme. D'Arblay *Diary* Nov., I cannot bear to see Othello tearing about in that violent manner. **1786** tr. *Beckford's Vathek* 56, I thought I heard..the shrieks of a thousand bats, tearing from their crannies. **1842** Thackeray *Miss Tickletoby's Lect.* ix, Edward came tearing down to the borders on the news. **1877** A. B. Edwards *Up Nile* vi. 142 The boat tears on before the wind. **1894** Fenn *In Alpine Valley* I. 43 This river tore down the narrow valley with headlong violence. **1901** H. Furniss *Confess. Caricaturist* I. iii. 79 The animals snorted..and..tore off.. at a tremendous rate.

b. To make *one's way* violently or impetuously.

1853 C. Kingsley *Hypatia* II. xiv. 328 Furiously..he burst up as if from the ground..tearing his way toward his idol. **1888** Mrs. H. Ward *Robert Elsemere* I. x. 282 A little gully deep in bracken, up which the blast was tearing its tempestuous way.

c. ***to tear into***: (*a*) to make a vigorous start on (an activity, performance, or the like); (*b*) to attack vituperatively, reprimand.

(*a*) **1901** M. Franklin *My Brilliant Career* xxxvi. 301 'Syb, I want to speak to you.'.. 'Very well; "tear into it",' as Horace would say. **1929** W. Smyth *Girl from Mason Creek* xiii. 131 'Three notes a man if we win out!'.. 'Aw, make it five an' we'll tear into th' job.' **1949** R. Harvey *Curtain Time* 8 Then the lights went down, the baton rapped sharply, and the orchestra tore into the overture. **1961** J. B. Priestley *Saturn over Water* ii. 12, I tore into the business of getting visas.

(*b*) **1934** in Webster. **1945** F. Sargeson *That Summer* 93 You could still hear them tearing into each other. **1954** J. Masters *Bhowani Junction* ii. xi. 94 The sahib tore into me as if I was a little boy he'd caught making a mess on the carpet. **1984** *Miami Herald* 5 Apr. 10A/1 Jackson..tore into both candidates in past debates.

tear (tɪə(r)), *v.*^{2} Now *rare.* [f. tear *sb.*^{1}]

†**1. a.** *intr.* To shed tears, to weep. *Obs.* or *dial.*

c **950** *Lindisf. Gosp.* John xi. 35 Tæherende [*Rushw.* teherende] uæs se hælend. *c* **1430** *Pilgr. Lyf Manhode* ii. li. (1869) 95, I bigan to tere and to weepe and to sigh. **1599** T. M[oufet] *Silkwormes* 9 Its mother..Who absent blear'd and tear'd as much for him. *a* **1660** *Contemp. Hist. Irel.* (Ir. Archæol. Soc.) II. 60 Eneas himself..too often teared for the losse of Troye. **1719** Hamilton in *Christ. Instructor* (1832) 694 Some of them were so affected that they teared also. **1806** Cock *Simple Strains* (1810) I. 103 (E.D.D.), I fell in wi' Geordy Brown, And he, poor saul, was tearin'.

†**b.** *trans.* To pass (time) in weeping. *Obs.*

1575 Gascoigne *Fruite of Fetters* iii, I teare my time (ay me) in prison pent.

c. Of the eyes: To shed or emit tears. Now chiefly *N. Amer.*

c **1000**, **1527** [see *tearing* ppl. a. below]. **1650** in Ritchie *Ch. St. Baldred* (1880) 86 Putting sneishen in his eyes to mak them tear. **1879** [see *tearing* vbl sb. below]. **1971** E. Shorris *Death of Great Spirit* i. 16 When your eyes teared and your head fell, I was afraid you were dying. **1980** J. Ball *Then came Violence* (1981) vi. 47 When her eyes teared again, he pulled out his own clean handkerchief.

2. *trans.* To fill or sprinkle with or as with tears.

c **1620** Z. Boyd *Zion's Flowers* (1855) 112 Feare teares your eyes. **18..** *Century Mag.* XXXVII. 545 (Cent. Dict.) The lorn lily teared with dew.

Hence ˈ**tearing** *vbl. sb.* and *ppl. a.*

c **1000** *Sax. Leechd.* I. 72 Wiþ tyrende eaȝan, ȝenim þa ylcan wyrte betonican. **1527** Andrew *Brunswyke's Distyll. Waters* C iv b, The same is good put in the iyen agaynst tering iyen. *a* **1660** *Contemp. Hist. Irel.* (Ir. Archæol. Soc.) II. 135 The tearinge and fatherlie intercession of the saide religious persons. **1879** *St. George's Hosp. Rep.* IX. 778 A white spot formed on the cornea, along with much 'tearing' and 'fear of light'.

tear, obs. form of teer *v.*, to plaster, smear.

tear-, the stem of tear *v.*^{1} in comb.

1. With adv., forming sbs. or adjs., as **tear-away**, *adj.*, characterized by impetuous speed, tearing (cf. tear *v.*^{1} 9); *sb.*, one who or that which 'tears' or rushes away, or acts with great impetuosity; now usu. (written *tearaway*), an unruly young person, a hooligan, ruffian, or petty criminal (formerly applied *spec.* to a kind of thief: see quot. 1938); **tear-down**, the complete dismantling of a piece of machinery; **tear-off**, *adj.*, adapted to be torn off; *sb.*, a sheet or slip of paper so attached as to be easily torn off; **tear-out**, the action of pulling out the fitments, décor, etc., of a room; **tear-up** *sb.*, an uprooting; a violent removal (*Cent. Dict.* 1891); also (*slang*), the action or an instance of tearing up; a spell of wild, destructive behaviour; a mêlée; in *Jazz*, a lively, rousing performance (cf. tear *v.*^{1} 3 g).

1833 T. Hook *Parson's Dau.* iii. vii, To mount a great *tear-away chestnut horse. **1891** N. Gould *Double Event* 67 The tearaway [a horse] of that morning..had suddenly developed into a mild, affectionate creature. **1901** S. F. Bullock *Irish Past.* iv. 100 Now that lassie's a tear-away. **1903** *Windsor Mag.* Sept. 394/2 The substitutes also were tear-away bowlers, but they were not so fast as the first pair. **1938** F. D. Sharpe *Sharpe of Flying Squad* i. 15 A type of crime which has almost died out now was that carried out by thieves known as 'Tearaways' who used to hang about outside the theatres after the show and snatch costly brooches from women's dress fronts. **1950** *Observer* 2 Apr. 7/3 He..boasted of being a proper 'tearaway' (one who sticks at nothing). **1958** *Punch* 19 Feb. 263/2 You get some proper tearaways (quarrelsome fellows) at the dogs. **1962** *Observer* 18 Feb. 21/3 My grandfather was a pickpocket, my six uncles were all villains and tearaways, my brothers and friends were thieves. **1978** L. Davidson *Chelsea Murders* xxiii. 140 He had a bit of form..in younger days a tearaway, the odd charge of violence. **1976** *Lebende Sprachen* XXI. 152/2 After engine *teardown exercise special care to replace damaged carbon rubbing type seals. **1981** *Pop. Hot Rodding* Feb. 51/1 Installing new pistons means removing the engine, an almost complete tear-down, and then a re-installation job. **1889** *Pall Mall G.* 21 Dec. 3/1 Blotting pads, with a *tear-off engagement-sheet at the side. **1910** Tear-off [see block *sb.* 10 c]. **1945** J. Rhys-Williams *Stern Daughter* xxx. 207 The little calendar..was the tear-off kind, with quotations. **1961** 'B. Wells' *Day Earth caught Fire* i. 7 An alert..youngish man..was at his desk busily working on tear-offs with swift, practised strokes of his red pencil. **1980** T. Barling *Goodbye Piccadilly* ii. 50 A big tear-off calendar gave today's date. **1976** *Billings* (Montana) *Gaz.* 17 June 3-f/1 (Advt.), Custom Homes. Apartments. Remodeling... 'Specializing in *Tear-Out.' Every kind of concrete work. **1886** H. Baumann *Londinismen* 206/2 **Tear-up*.., feine(s) Geschäft. **1890** in Barrère & Leland *Dict. Slang* II. 339/2 'What is it this time?'.. 'Only a tear up.'.. Among the readers of the *St. James's Gazette* there may be some who are unacquainted with the accepted method of obtaining a fresh outfit among the casual poor. *Ibid.* 340/1 At his feet, in a heap on the floor, lay some filthy rags,..the remnants of what had recently been his garments... The heap was the result of the tear up. **1958** S. Race in P. Gammond *Decca Bk. Jazz* x. 125 Max Kaminsky ..and of course Bunny Berigan all took turns to roughen up that smooth ensemble.., with the historic Berigan tear-ups especially welcome. **1964** E. Parr *Grafters All* xiii. 151 He enters an orgy of crime, more commonly known as 'having a tear-up'. **1974** J. McVicar *McVicar* i. iii. 62, I decided to have a tear-up. **1982** *New Society* 9 Dec. 422/2 We've had a tear-up with the police. **1983** *Listener* 9 June 35/3 The music is not the tear-up associated with jazz at the Phil.

2. With sb. in objective relation, forming sbs. or adjs., as **tear-arse** *slang*, a very active busy person; hence as *v. intr.* (also *U.S.* **tear-ass**), to drive recklessly, rush *around* wildly and rowdily; †ˈ**tear-brain**: see quot.; **tear-brass** *a.*, rowdy, prodigal; **tear-bridge** *a.*, that tears or destroys bridges: used as epithet of a river; **tear-cat**, *adj.*, swaggering, ranting, bombastic (see tear *v.*^{1} 1 d); *sb.*, a bully, swaggerer, 'fire-eater'; †**tear-mouth**, an epithet applied to a ranting actor; †**tear-placket**, ? a cutpurse; †**tear-rogue**, ? a roistering disreputable fellow; **tear-sheet** chiefly *U.S.*, a sheet torn from a publication (or, later, separately printed and unbound) to be sent to an advertiser whose advertisement appears on it as proof of insertion; also one containing an article; more generally, a tear-off sheet from a teleprinter or calendar; †**tear-throat**, *adj.*, that 'tears' or irritates the throat; *sb.*, a ranting actor; **tear-thumb**, two species of *Polygonum* native to North America (and Asia), the halberd-leaved tear-thumb, *P. arifolium*, and the arrow-leaved, *P. sagittatum*; so called from the hooked prickles on the petioles and angles of the stems.

1923 J. Manchon *Le Slang* 308 *Tear-arse,..un qui s'échine (à travailler). **1942** Berry & Van den Bark *Amer. Thes. Slang* §53/8 *Tear-ass* &c. *around*,..to hasten or rush around. **1954** *Amer. Speech* XXIX. 103 *Tear ass*, v. phr., to drive fast or recklessly. **1968** J. Wainwright *Edge of Extinction* 34 We're the..killjoys. The miserable bastards who won't let 'em tear-arse around the town at sixty miles an hour. **1972** A. Draper *Death Penalty* xix. 119 Some lads were picked up after the cup match for tear-arsing around. **1976** J. Fraser *Who steals my Name?* ii. 17 You'll need to settle down. You can't be a teararse all your life. **1796** G. M. Woodward *Eccentric Excurs.* 80 Another curious liquor called *tear-brain, composed entirely of Rum and Brandy. **1880** T. Hardy *Trumpet-Major* ix, To..provide goods for his breaking, and house-room and drink for his *tear-brass set. **1598** Sylvester *Du Bartas* ii. ii. iii. *Colonies* 429 The di'pry verges Of *tear-bridge Tygris. **1606** Day *Ile of Guls* Prol. (1881) 6, I had rather heare two good baudie iests then a whole play of such *teare-cat thunderclaps. **1611** Middleton & Dekker *Roaring Girl* D.'s Wks. 1873 III. 215 *D.* What's thy name fellow souldier? *T.* I am cal'd by those who haue seen my valour, Tear-Cat. **1821** Scott *Kenilw.* xii, A man of mettle—one of those ruffling tear-cats, who maintain their master's quarrel with sword and buckler. **1601** B. Jonson *Poetaster* iii. iv, You grow rich, doe you? and purchase, you two-penny *teare-mouth? **1819** Scott *Let. to Southey* 4 Apr., in *Lockhart*, A copper-laced, twopenny tearmouth. *c* **1600** Day *Begg. Bednall Gr.* iv. i, I have spent many a gray groat of honest swaggerers and *tear-Plackets..that I never drunk for. **1685** *Depos. fr. Cast. York* (Surtees) 275 He was a Monmouth *teare-rogue, and ..had raysed men..for Monmouth's service. **1930** H. A. Groesbeck *Practical Photo-Engraving* ii. 4 The '*tear-sheet' of the newspaper advertisement, also the drawing from which it was made, have just been received. **1950** R. Chandler *Let.* 15 Feb. (1981) 210 Herewith the tear sheets from a *Pocket Atlantic* with..the article you desired. **1962** *Listener* 19 Apr. 672/1 One of the President's advisers came in with a tear-sheet from the news ticker. **1972** M. J. Bosse *Incident at Naha* i. 16 He was slowly flipping the tear sheets of the desk calendar. **1630** J. Taylor (Water P.) *Praise Hempseed* Wks. iii. 65 The *teare-throat cough and tisick, From which, to health men are restor'd by Physicke. **1654** Gayton *Pleas. Notes* i. vii. 24 The Poets of the Fortune and red Bull, had alwayes a mouth-measure for their Actors (who were terrible teare throats). **1866** *Treas. Bot.*, *Tear-thumb. **1926** *W. Virginia Legislature Hand Bk.* 488 Do you see among those [wild flowers] present, any exotics?.. Yes ..This bit of smart-weed or tear thumb. **1978** C. B. Dugdale *Mod. Amer. Herbal* II. 124 Tearthumb; Arrow-leaved Tearthumb... The small cluster of flowers varies in color from pinkish to whitish.

tearable ('tɛərəb(ə)l), *a.* [f. tear *v.*¹ + -able.] Capable of being torn.

1859 [implied in untearable]. **1895** *Daily News* 7 Jan. 3/3 Everything that was breakable was broken in fragments, and everything tearable torn in pieces.

tear-bottle ('tɪə,bɒt(ə)l). A bottle containing tears (cf. Ps. lvi. 8 'put my tears into thy bottle'); also *transf.*; *spec.* = lachrymatory B. 1, applied to small bottles or phials, such as are found in ancient tombs, supposed, with doubtful correctness, to have contained tears shed for the deceased.

1658 [see lachrymatory B. 1]. **1662** J. Bargrave *Pope Alex. VII* (1867) 122 Called *lachrymatorij*, or tear-bottles, because the friends and relations of the defunct were in ancient time accustomed at the funeral to carry each of them a *lachrymatorio* in his hand, to save his tears that he shed for his deceased friend, and then leave those bottles behind them with the immurall d corps. **1884** 'H. Collingwood' *Under Meteor Flag* 259 Stow away the tear-bottles, coil down all tender feeling out of sight.

attrib. **1904** Budge *3rd & 4th Egypt. Rooms Brit. Mus.* 35 Glass vessels..of the well-known *lacrimarium*, or 'tear-bottle' type, and belonging to the Roman period.

tearce, obs. form of terse, tierce.

teard, -e, obs. pa. t. and pa. pple. of tear *v.*¹

teare, obs. form of tear, tier.

tearer ('tɛərə(r)). [f. tear *v.*¹ + -er¹.]

1. a. One who or that which tears or rends.

In quot. 1828 applied to a (? canine) tooth; in quot. 1862, to a mechanical device for tearing something; in quot. 1886 to a 'tearing' cold.

1625 Massinger *New Way* v. i, I know you are a tearer. But I'll have first your fangs pared off, and then Come nearer to you. **1682** *Sec. Plea Nonconf.* 4 The Tearers of the Church have made at me,..but..have hurt their Nails and Fingers. **1719** D'Urfey *Pills* II. 81 To Wearers and Tearers Of Manteau and Gown. **1828** Fleming *Brit. Zool.* 9 In the lower jaw [of the badger], the bruiser is small, the chewer large, and there is an additional tearer. **1862** *Jrnl. Soc. Arts* X. 329/2 The doughy mass is put into an iron box, or tearer, in which an iron cylinder, with iron teeth, rapidly revolves, tearing it into shreds. **1886** C. Keene *Let.* in *Life* xi. (1892) 359, I suppose I've been boasting of my immunity from colds, for I've just had a tearer, so hoarse that I couldn't sound a note.

†**b.** *tearer of God*, a blasphemer or profane swearer (see tear *v.*¹ 3 b). *Obs.*

a **1550** *Hye Way to Spyttel H.* 851 in Hazl. *E.P.P.* IV. 61 These blasphemers and these God terers. **1570** Foxe *A. & M.* (ed. 2) 2303/1 Blasphemous and abominable swearers or rather tearers of God.

c. *tearer-downer* (U.S.), one who tears down, a carping critic (cf. tear *v.*¹ 3 h).

1942 Berrey & Van den Bark *Amer. Thes. Slag*, §421/1 Critic; opposer..tearer-downer. **1944** [see builder c]. **1955** J. D. Salinger in *New Yorker* 29 Jan. 28/1 I'm just so sick of pedants and conceited little tearer-downers I could scream.

2. A person who tears or rushes along or about; a ranter, roisterer, swaggerer, bully.

1625, **1682** [see sense 1]. **1664** Cotton *Scarron.* i. Poet Wks. (1717) 8 A huffing Jack, a plund'ring Tearer. **1693** Congreve *Old Bach.* iv. ix, Hist! hist! bully; dost thou see those tearers [Araminta and Belinda masked]? **1828** Webster, *Tearer*,..one that rages or raves with violence. **1862** M'Gilvray *Poems* (ed. 2) 56 (E.D.D.) For faith she is a tearer, She frights the very swine.

tearful ('tɪəfʊl), *a.* [f. tear *sb.*¹ + -ful.]

1. Full of tears; weeping; lachrymose.

a **1586** Sidney *Arcadia* iii. (1598) 372 My Pyrocles said she (with tearefull eyes and pittifull countenance). **1597** J. Payne *Royal Exch.* 28 Sory and fearefull, yea penitent and tearefull. **1726** Pope *Odyss.* xxi. 233 With tear full eyes o'er all their master gaz'd. **1855** Ht. Martineau *Autobiog.* ii. (1877) 30 The old folks and their daughters came out to meet us, all tearful and agitated. **1884** *Mem. Pr. Alice* 16 The parting was tearful, but full of hope.

2. Causing tears; mournful, melancholy. ? *Obs.*

c **1611** Chapman *Iliad* xix. 315 Then the warre, was tearefull to our foe, But now to me.

Hence '**tearfully** *adv.*, in a tearful manner, with tears; '**tearfulness**, the state of being tearful.

1820 L. Hunt *Indicator* No. 37 (1822) I. 296 A breathing tearfulness. **1835** Lytton *Rienzi* i. i, Anxiously and tearfully he looked..up the steep ascent of the Aventine. **1863** Monsell *Hymn*, '*O worship the Lord*' iv, Mornings of joy..for evenings of tearfulness.

tearing ('tɛərɪŋ), *vbl. sb.*¹ [f. tear *v.*¹ + -ing¹.]

1. The action of tear *v.*¹, in various senses.

14.. *Beryn* 644 The warrok..held hym right a square, by þat othir syde, As holsom was at that tyme, for tereing of his hyde. **1539** Tonstall *Serm. Palm Sund.* (1823) 80 The tearynge of goddis name, and particular mention of all the woundes and peynes that Christe suffered for vs. **1768** Tucker *Lt. Nat.* (1834) I. 640 Tearings of ravenous beasts, stings of venomous serpents. **1904** Benson *Challoners* ix, It ..cut like a blunt knife with sawing and tearing.

2. The result of this action: **a.** A wound made by tearing. **b.** A fragment torn off.

1607 Topsell *Four-f. Beasts* (1658) 346 Their flesh also being eaten, doth quickly cure and heal the bitings or tearings of a ravenous Dog. **1891** E. Arnold *Lt. of World* iv. 193 Truth, Lord! but crumbs fall, and the dogs may eat The children's tearings!

3. *attrib.* **tearing-machine**: see quot.

1877 Knight *Dict. Mech.*, *Tearing-machine*, a machine for disintegrating woven fabric to make fiber for reworking.

'**tearing**, *ppl. a.*¹ [f. tear *v.*¹ + -ing².] That tears, in various senses of the verb.

1. Generally (chiefly in *fig.* applications); *esp.* that wounds the feelings; severely distressing, harrowing; also, causing a sensation as of rending.

1606 Shaks. *Ant. & Cl.* iv. xiv. 31 She..Then in the midd'st a tearing grone did breake The name of Anthony. **1686** Burnet *Lett.* (1708) 235 The tearing Anxieties, that Want brings with it. **1736** Ainsworth *Lat. Dict.* (1783) s.v., A tearing, or very loud, voice, *vox stentora vincens.* **1839** Mrs. Carlyle *Lett., to Mrs. Aitken* 22 Nov. (1903) I. 86 One might think one's maid's tears could do little for a tearing headache; but they do comfort a little. **1898** *Allbutt's Syst. Med.* V. 11 The cough [in bronchitis is described] as 'tearing'.

2. Of a wind or storm: So violent as to tear things up or in pieces; raging.

1633 T. James *Voy.* 29 We had a tearing storme at North. **1889** Barrie *Window in Thrums* 201 A tearing gale had blown the upper part of the brae clear.

3. Moving with impetuous speed; rushing.

1765 Sterne *Tr. Shandy* VII. xix, You do get on at a tearing rate. **1876** *World* V. No. 106. 18 Soon afterwards the band began to play a tearing galop—the sign of the conclusion. **1887** T. A. Trollope *What I remember* II. iv. 66 Readers who are not in such a tearing hurry as the unhappy world is in these latter days. **1908** *Westm. Gaz.* 11 Aug. 10/3 To that [traffic] there has lately been added the tearing motor-'buses.

4. a. Violent or reckless in action or behaviour; full of excitement; headstrong, passionate; ranting, roistering; boisterous, rollicking, exuberant. *colloq.* or *slang.* (Now *rare.*)

1654 Gayton *Pleas. Notes* iv. xxi. 271 Some tearing Tragedy full of fights and skirmishes. **1667** Pepys *Diary* 7 Oct., There was so much tearing company in the house, that we could not see the landlady. **1673** S. C. *Art of Complaisance* 65 Like the two tearing fellows which the poet had designed for the characters of gentlemen. **1790** *Bystander* 343 Half a dozen young tearing rascals. **1823** Scott *Peveril* xxxviii, So in stole this termagant, tearing gallant. **1869** J. R. Green *Lett.* iii. (1901) 232, I am in such tearing spirits at the prospect of freedom.

b. Impressive, splendid, grand; 'ripping', 'rattling', 'stunning'. *colloq.* or *slang.* (Now *rare.*)

1693 *Humours Town* 100 That so she may make a notable Figure, and a taring show the next Sunday in the Village-Church. **1721** Amherst *Terræ Fil.* No. 33 (1754) 176 Persons..who cut a taring figure in silk-gowns, and bosh it about town in lace ruffles, and flaxon tye-wigs. **1850** Cumming *Hunter's Life S. Afr.* (1902) 29/1 A large bright comet, having a tearing, fiery tail. **1897** *Outing* (U.S.) XXX. 270/2 A mighty fine woman and a tearing beauty besides.

5. quasi-*adv.* Furiously. (Cf. *raving mad.*)

1692 R. L'Estrange *Fables* ccxlv. 213 This Bull..that ran Tearing Mad for the Pinching of a Mouse. **1867** A. Stock *Evidence against & for Walter Tricker* 4 Mrs Hitchins, at the Inquest, says 'It was not ordinary barking. They [*sc.* the dogs] were barking like tearing mad.' **1886** E. L. Dorsey *Midshipman Bob* ii. xi. 219 'Don't you get mad ever, eh?'.. 'Yes, I'm sorry to say I do—tearing mad sometimes.' **1906** [see jim]. **1942** Berrey & Van den Bark *Amer. Thes. Slang* §284/8 Angry..tearing, tearing angry or mad.

tearing, *vbl. sb.*² and *ppl. a.*²: see tear *v.*²

tear-jerker ('tɪə,dʒɜːkə(r)). *colloq.* (orig. *U.S.*). [f. tear *sb.*¹ + jerker¹; for the sense of *jerker*, cf. *soda-jerker* s.v. soda *sb.*¹ 9.] Something calculated to evoke sadness or sympathy, usu. a sentimental film, play, song, story, etc. Also applied to a person and, *rarely*, to an event.

1921 *Double Dealer* II. 143/2 But no one today, I believe, mistakes his [*sc.* James Whitcomb Riley's] productions for anything but somewhat shallow, fairly easy tear-jerkers. **1935** *Amer. Mercury* Aug. 400/1 A lawyer was imported from California, a magniloquent tear-jerker named Delphin Delmas. **1936** *New Yorker* 7 Mar. 32/2 'Love on the Dole' turns out to be far more than a conventional tear-jerker. **1940** *Manch. Guardian Weekly* 27 Sept. 212 The German description of the torpedoing of the evacuee ship as a 'tear-jerker' recalls Geobbels's clumsy attempt to deny the torpedoing of the Athenia at the beginning of the war. **1948** *Sunday Pictorial* 18 July 11/3 The cameos are linked with a quiet humour and smooth pathos which make the film an A-plus tear-jerker. **1953** 'P. Wentworth' *Watersplash* xix. 109 Three copies of the famous *East Lynne.* A notorious tear-jerker. **1958** B. Nichols *Sweet & Twenties* xiv. 187 This number, as sung by Al Jolson, became one of the most efficient tear-jerkers of all time. **1975** *Islander* (Victoria, B.C.) 9 Feb. 2/3 He concluded [his speech] with a real tear-jerker.

Hence (as back-formations) '**tear-jerk** *sb.*, a sentimental effusion; also as *v. trans.*; '**tear-jerking** *vbl. sb.* and *ppl. a.*

1940 S. Lewis *Bethel Merriday* xv. 127 You..made me understand how much that poor gutter pup longed for a chance to parade, and yet you didn't do much tear-jerking. **1941** E. Snow *Battle for Asia* iv. 88, I remember a tear-jerking letter from a correspondent appealing for people to boil their garbage and put it beside their ash cans for the hungry—*dogs.* **1953** *Times Lit. Suppl.* 31 July 490/5 The ex-Governor of Illinois does not disdain the obvious 'tear-jerk'. **1961** D. Holbrook *English for Maturity* i. iv. 55 The vague undefined tear-jerk of popular graveyard and funeral verses. **1962** 'K. Orvis' *Damned & Destroyed* xvi. 123 She tear-jerked it from a drugstore without a prescription. **1962** Auden *Dyer's Hand* (1963) 430 If Homer had tried reading the Iliad to the gods of Olympus, they would..possibly, even, reacting like ourselves to a tear-jerking movie, have poured pleasing tears. **1965** *Spectator* 5 Feb. 157/3 The prize for tear-jerking seemed..destined for..the *Daily Mail.* **1979** D. Meiring *Foreign Body* xii. 126 Even he [*sc.* God] had sometimes needed a hand, and Hussein had provided that brilliantly, in turn cajoling, tear-jerking, and threatening Americans of huge stature in the oil business. **1981** *Times* 14 Feb. 8/7 An idealized Shavian heroine..the armour-plated, tear-jerking martyr.

tearless ('tɪəlɪs), *a.* [f. tear *sb.*¹ + -less.] Void of tears; shedding no tears, not weeping.

1603 North *Plutarch* (1612) 1123 This dayes iourney was called for them the tearelesse battell. **1591** Sylvester *Du Bartas* i. ii. 879 Canst thou tear-lesse gaze..on that prodigious blaze, That hairy Comet? **1743** Shenstone *Elegies* xix, Ye saw with tearless eye When your fleet perish'd on the Punic wave. **1868** Lynch *Rivulet* cxxxii. v, A star, that..Shines..to point thy way On to the tearless country bright.

Hence '**tearlessly** *adv.*, in a tearless manner, without weeping; '**tearlessness**, the quality or condition of being tearless.

1853 C. Bronte *Villette* xxx, He watched tearlessly. **1894** *Westm. Gaz.* 1 Mar. 3/1 What could be more..tearlessly pathetic?

tearlet ('tɪəlɪt). [f. tear *sb.*¹ + -let.] A little or tiny tear.

1858 Bailey *The Age* 201 The sun's bright tearlets. **1964** V. Nabokov *Defence* x. 162 A warm tearlet would roll down her face.

tearm, tearn, obs. ff. term, tarn.

tea-roller, etc.: see tea *sb.* 9 c.

'**tea-'rose, tea rose.**

a. A variety (or group of varieties) of cultivated rose, derived from the species *Rosa indica*, var. *odorata*, having flowers of a pale yellow colour, with a delicate scent supposed to resemble that of tea. Originally, *tea-scented rose.*

1850 *Florist* Aug. 191 The delicate and odorous Tea Rose fated to be admired and to languish in the drawing-room. **1882** *Garden* 11 Mar., Tea Roses may be pruned in April.

b. The colour of this rose. Also *attrib.*

1872 *Young Englishwoman* Nov. 599/1 The rose colours are *rose frais*..; tea-rose, with yellow tints; and faded rose. **1884** *Chr. World Fam. Circle* 4 Nov. 260/4 Amongst the favourite colours are imperial yellow, Nile blue, tea rose and cardinal. **1900** *St. James' Gaz.* 21 Sept. 6/2 A bolero of tea-rose silk.

c. A perfume made from or named after this rose.

1897 *Sears, Roebuck Catal.* 19/2 Perfumes..Sweet Pea.. Tea Rose..Tuberose. **1926–7** *Army & Navy Stores Catal.* 486/2 Atkinsons' Perfumes..Sweet Pea, Tea Rose, Verbena. **1977** *New Yorker* 10 Oct. 35/3 She..ended with a commercial for her new fragrance, Tea Rose, samples of which her assistants passed around.

tearse, obs. f. tierce.

teart (tiːət), *a.* and *sb.* [Dial. var. of tart *a.*] **A.** *adj.* Sour; used of pastures containing an excess of molybdenum. **B.** *sb.* Teart quality in grass; the diarrhœa suffered by cattle grazing a teart pasture.

1850 Sir T. D. Acland in *Jrnl. Roy. Agric. Soc.* 755 There is a great deal of grass land on the borders of the lias hills, which scours cattle. It is said to be 'teart'; that is tart or sour. **1896** *Jrnl. Bath & West Soc.* VI. 207 The herbage possesses the peculiar purging quality known as 'teart'. **1903** *Lancet* 6 June 1590/1 This disease, known as parasitic enteritis, is found to be persistently associated with certain pastures (called 'teart' lands in the West of England) upon heavy moisture-retaining soils. **1939** *Nature* 23 Sept. 532/2 Teart, to which cattle in certain areas are subject, is found to be associated with an increased molybdenum content in the herbage. **1970** W. H. Parker *Health & Dis. in Farm Animals* xiv. 193 The teart pastures of Somerset are on the blue Lyas clay.

Hence '**teartness** *sb.* = teart *sb.*

1940 *Nature* 15 June 941/2 The cause of teartness is the presence in the herbage of molybdenum. **1979** *Jrnl. Compar. Pathol.* LXXXIX. 495 'Teartness' i.e. the scouring which occurs in cattle but not in horses on 'teart' pastures of high Mo content.

teart, obs. f. tart.

teartane, obs. f. TARTAN *sb.*[1]

teary ('tɪərɪ), *a.* [f. TEAR *sb.*[1] + -Y.]

1. Full of or suffused with tears; tearful. Now *colloq.* Also *transf.*

c **1374** CHAUCER *Troylus* IV. 793 (821) She gan for sorwe anon Hire tery face atwixe hire armes hyde. *a* **1541** WYATT *How Lover perisheth in his delight*, With my teary eyn, swolne, and vnstable. **1848** LOWELL *Biglow Pap.* Ser. I. *Courtin'* xxi, All kin' o' smily roun' the lips An' teary roun' the lashes. **1863** W. MILLAR in *Whistle Binkie* (1890) I. 473 My e'e grew dim and tearie. **1890** *Pall Mall G.* 18 Dec. 2/1 As we drop down the grey Thames we are a teary and a melancholy company. **1941** B. SCHULBERG *What makes Sammy Run?* iii. 45 Full of teary nostalgia for the glories of his youth. **1976** *Times Lit. Suppl.* 13 Aug. 1010/2 Paul delivers a long, teary monologue about his homosexuality. *Comb.* **1949** N. R. NASH *Young & Fair* I. i. 10 But *Patty* is unashamedly teary-eyed. **1960** R. ST. JOHN *Foreign Correspondent* iv. 64 We grew teary-eyed trying to fry a fish or a piece of meat over the brazier.

2. Of the nature of or consisting of tears. *rare.*

c **1420** LYDG. *Story of Thebes* III. Chaucer's Wks. (1560) 372/2 Whan the stormes, and the teary shoure Of her weping, was somwhat ouergon. **1594** CONSTABLE *Sonn.* v. viii, And on the shoare of that tearie sea. *a* **1600** MONTGOMERIE *Misc. Poems* xxxvii. 4 A tearie fluid does blind thir ees of myne. **1830** *Fraser's Mag.* I. 503 Did the God of Hell..weep..the iron sleet of teary shower?

teasable ('tiːzəb(ə)l), *a.* [f. TEASE *v.*[1] + -ABLE.] Capable of being teased.

1865 G. MACDONALD *A. Forbes* viii, Children..are ready to tease any child who simply looks teasable.

tea-sage to **tea-scrub**: see TEA *sb.* 9 c.

tease, *sb.* Also 7-9 teaze. [f. TEASE *v.*[1]]

1. a. The action of teasing. †***upon the tease***, uneasy from trifling irritation (*obs.*). *rare.*

1693 C. MATHER *Wond. Invis. World* (1862) 162 After she had undergone a deal of Teaze from the Annoyance of the Spectre. **1706** MRS. CENTLIVRE *Basset-Table* III. 34 There's One upon the Teaze already. **1707** —— *Platonick Lady* v. 61, I left her upon the Teaze. **1878-9** LANIER *Poems, Individuality* 10 No pitiless tease of risk or bottomry.

b. ***tease number***, a strip-tease act. *U.S.*

1927 *Variety* 13 July 35/5 The four feminine principals alternated in 'tease' numbers with the help of the chorus. **1930** *Ibid.* 3 Dec. 54 With a fair voice, a nice figure and lots of personality, Miss Almond clicked easily in her tease numbers.

2. a. A person addicted to teasing; one who irritates another in a trifling or sportive way. *colloq.*

1852 DICKENS *Bleak Ho.* xxx, What a teaze you are. **1899** MISS HARRADEN *Fowler* II. v. 190, I am a tease by nature.

b. *spec.* = *cock teaser* s.v. COCK *sb.*[1] 23 (but less coarse). Also *transf.*

1976 *New Yorker* 16 Feb. 107/2 It's easy to get laughs by ..showing women..as rich teases, like Mariangela Melato's role in 'Swept Away'. **1978** D. DEVINE *Sunk without Trace* xxii. 202 Sorry, Ken, but..it's not fair to encourage you to try. I will not be a *tease*. **1979** *Arizona Daily Star* 5 Aug. I. 1/2 Lulu is..a cruel tease to the lesbian countess Geschwitz.

tease (tiːz), *v.*[1] Forms: 1 tǽsan, 4-5 tese, 5 teese, 7 teise, 7-9 teize, teaze, 8 teez, teaz, 6- tease. [OE. *tǽsan* to tear or pull to pieces, tease (wool, etc.), wk. vb. = OLG. *têsan (MLG., LG. *têsen*, MDu. *têzen*, Du. *teezen* to draw, pull, scratch, NFris. *tiese*), OHG. *zeisan* str. vb., MHG. *zeisen* wk. vb., Ger. dial. (Bav.) *zaisen, zeisen* (Schade) to tease, pick wool:—OTeut. **taisjan* and **taisan*: cf. also TOASE *v.*]

1. a. *trans.* To separate or pull asunder the fibres of; to comb or card (wool, flax, etc.) in preparation for spinning; to open *out* by pulling asunder; to shred.

c **1000** *Sax. Leechd.* III. 112 Nim þanne wulle & tæs hy. ?*c* **1390** *Forme of Cury* in Warner *Antiq. Culin.* (1791) 17 Take the brawn, and tese it smal. **14..** *Noble Bk. Cookry* (Napier 1882) 102 Then teese the braun of capon or henn small. **1591** PERCIVALL *Sp. Dict.*, *Carmenar*, to picke wooll, to tease wooll, *carminare*. **1612** WOODALL *Surg. Mate* Wks. (1653) 344 Take Saffron..then tease it, I mean, pull the parts thereof asunder. **1634** MILTON *Comus* 751 To ply The sampler, and to teize the huswifes wool. **1683** MOXON *Mech. Exerc., Printing* xxiv. ¶ 19 [He] Teizes his Wooll, by opening all the..matted knots he finds in it. **1828** P. CUNNINGHAM *N.S. Wales* (ed. 3) II. 151 While teasing out the tobacco-leaf to charge his pipe. **1851** *Art Jrnl. Illustr. Catal.* p. iv**/2 The quick moving cards teaze out the fibres, and gradually, very gradually, disentangle them. **1875** HUXLEY & MARTIN *Elem. Biol.* xi. (1876) 122 Tease out a bit of the liver in water, and examine with ⅛ obj. **1893** A. N. PALMER *Hist. Wrexham* IV. 10 The flax dressers prepared the flax for the linen spinners and weavers by 'teasing' it.

b. To comb the surface of cloth, after weaving, with teasels, which draw all the free hairs or fibres in one direction, so as to form a nap.

1755 JOHNSON, *Tease*,..to scratch cloth in order to level the nap. **1829** J. L. KNAPP *Jrnl. Nat.* 48 Many of these [teasel] heads are fixed in a frame; and with this the surface of the cloth is teased, or brushed, until all the ends are drawn out. **1861** MISS PRATT *Flower. Pl.* III. 172 Blankets were made of goats'-wool, teased into a satiny surface by little Teazel-like brushes of bamboo.

†**c.** To tear in pieces. *Obs.*

a **1550** *Hye Way to Spyttel H.* 888 in Hazl. *E.P.P.* IV. 63 Lyke as wolues the shepe dooth take and tease.

d. *U.S. Hairdressing.* = *back-comb* vb. trans. s.v. BACK- B.

1957 *Amer. Hairdresser* Sept. 66 Pick up one inch of hair and with comb, tease the strand. This creates the lift so necessary to the style. **1962** E. FRANK *Best Hairdos* 7 Tease entire head gently for fullness. **1978** J. UPDIKE *Coup* (1979) iv. 171 Her hair bleached platinum and teased to a bouffant mass.

e. ***to tease out*** (*fig.*): to extract, get out, obtain, esp. by painstaking effort. Also ***to tease on to.***

1959 N. MAILER *Advts. for Myself* (1961) 17 There was a time when Pirandello could tease a comedy of pain out of six characters in search of an author. **1971** *Language* XLVII. 525 It is only by the most careful discrimination that we are able to tease out the critical referential features from the mass of inferential stuff that surrounds them in normal speech. **1974** J. A. MICHENER *Centennial* x. 580 He was struck with how easy life was in Pennsylvania and how brutally difficult in Colorado, where you had to dig a ditch twenty miles before you could tease a little water onto your land.

2. a. To worry or irritate by persistent action which vexes or annoys; now *esp.* in lighter sense, to disturb by persistent petty annoyance, out of mere mischief or sport; to bother or plague in a petty way.

1627 [see TEASED 2]. **1679** C. HATTON in *H. Corr.* (Camden) 210 After he had thus teised them for 2 or 3 houres he left them. **1686** tr. *Chardin's Trav. Persia* 162 Teizing me for two Hours together with a Thousand Impertinences. **1710** SWIFT *Lett.* (1767) III. 23 Lord Halifax is always teazing me to go down to his country house, which will cost me a guinea to his servants, and twelve shillings coach hire. **1774** PENNANT *Tour Scot. in 1772*, 283 The violent squalls of wind..teized us for an hour. **1774** GOLDSM. *Nat. Hist.* IV. 74 To avoid teizing the reader with a minute description. **1782** MME. D'ARBLAY *Diary* 8 Dec., [They] resisted reading the book till they were teased into it. **1827** D. JOHNSON *Ind. Field Sports* 208 A boy ..was teizing the animal to make it bite him. **1881** BESANT & RICE *Chapl. of Fleet* I. 14 Harry ceased to tease and torment them with little tricks and devices of mischief.

fig. **1774** GOLDSM. *Nat. Hist.* I. 54 The earth..constantly teized more to furnish..luxuries..than..necessities. **1856** MRS. BROWNING *Aur. Leigh* I. 1050, I..teased The patient needle till it split the thread. **1893** *Westm. Gaz.* 17 Feb. 3/1 It is all done with that flowing brush.., and there is nothing teased or overworked in the whole of it.

b. *absol.* or *intr.* (With first quot., cf. TOUSE *v.*)

1619 FLETCHER *M. Thomas* v. vii. What a coyle has this fellow kept i' th' Nunnery,..Pray Heavens he be not teasing. **1693** DRYDEN *Juvenal* vi. 377 Conscious of Crimes her self, she teizes first. **1751** JOHNSON *Rambler* No. 144 ¶6 To teize with feeble blows and impotent disturbance. *a* **1861** MRS. BROWNING *Little Mattie* vii, Love both ways, kiss and tease.

c. = *strip-tease* vb. intr. s.v. STRIP-TEASE *sb.* *U.S.*

1927 *Variety* 13 July 35/5 Where they cooch in New York they 'tease' here. **1953** BERREY & VAN DEN BARK *Amer. Thes. Slang* (1954) §593/22 'Do a striptease.'.. Strip, striptease, tease.

3. *slang.* To flog. ? *Obs.*

1812 J. H. VAUX *Flash Dict.*, *Teaze*, to flog or whip. **1865** [see TEASING *vbl. sb.*[1] 3].

tease, *v.*[2] *local.* Also teaze. [ad. mod.F. *tiser* (technical) 'to introduce fuel into a melting-furnace' (Littré); to fire a furnace; app. aphetic for *attiser* = It. *attizzare*, Sp., Prov. *atizar* to stir (the fire), f. *à*:—L. *ad* to + It. *tizzo*, Sp. *tizo*, L. *titio*, burning brand, fire-brand.] *trans.* To feed (a furnace fire) with fuel; to attend to (a fire or furnace).

1818 J. ADLEY *Coal Trade* (Northumb. Gloss.), You must have furnacemen to teaze and rouse the fire. **1894** [see TEASING *vbl. sb.*[2]].

teased (tiːzd), *ppl. a.* [f. TEASE *v.*[1] + -ED[1].]

1. a. Having the fibres pulled asunder: see TEASE *v.*[1] 1. In quot. 1620 *fig.* Also ***teased out.***

c **1430** *Two Cookery-bks.* 22 Caste þer-to tesyd brawn. **1620** BRINSLEY tr. *Virgil* 58 To sing a teased verse..a pastorall song.., drawne out small like wooll in spinning. **1851** *Art Jrnl. Illustr. Catal.* p. iv**/1 This cylinder is cleaned of the teazed cotton by means of brushes. **1875** HUXLEY & MARTIN *Elem. Biol.* (1877) 258 Treat a fresh bit of teased-out nerve with chloroform.

b. Of hair: fluffed out by back-combing. *U.S.*

1965 A. LURIE *Nowhere City* xiv. 147 A waitress appeared in the courtyard, shivering in a teased hair-do and a pink uniform. **1983** J. VALIN *Natural Causes* xxix. 200 A pretty nurse with teased brown hair.

2. a. Irritated or annoyed in a petty way.

1627 MAY *Lucan* III. 527 Vntill the townesmens teased valour broke..The fence. **1852-5** M. ARNOLD *Faded Leaves, River* v, This teased o'erlabour'd heart.

b. With *out.* Worn out, exhausted. *colloq. rare.*

1943 HUNT & PRINGLE *Service Slang* 65 *Teased out*, worn out or tired after a long spell of flying or other duty. **1961** D. MOORE *Highway of Fear* i. 9 What about you? Still with that teased-out shipping company?

'**tease-hole.** [f. TEASE *v.*[2] – HOLE *sb.*]

1858 SIMMONDS *Dict. Trade*, *Teaze-hole*, the opening in the furnace of a glass-work, through which coals are put in.

teasel, teazle ('tiːz(ə)l), *sb.* Forms: *α.* 1 tǽsl, tǽsel, 3-5 tesel, 5 tesell, -yl(l, tesle, 5-7 tessel, 6 tesill, teasell, teassell, teysyll, 6-7 tessele, teazell, tezel, -ill, 7-8 teasil, 7- teasel, teasle, teazel, teazle, 8 testle. *β.* 4-6 tasel, 4-7 -il, 5 -yl, -ylle, -ul, -elle, taysill, 5-7 tazel, 6 tasill, -yll, tassyll, 6-7 tasell, tasle, tazell, tassill, 7 tassel, tazill, tazle, 8 tassell. [OE. *tǽsel, tǽsl* = OHG. *zeisala, -ila*, str. fem., MHG. *zeisel*:—OTeut. **taisilā*, f. **taisan*, OE. *tǽsan* to tease, with instr. suffix *-lā*. Hence AF. *teizel*.]

1. A plant of the genus *Dipsacus*, comprising herbs with prickly leaves and flower-heads; *esp.* **fullers' teasel**, *D. fullonum*, the heads of which have hooked prickles between the flowers, and are used for teasing cloth (see 2); and **wild teasel**, *D. sylvestris*, held by some to be the original type, but having straight instead of hooked prickles.

[*c* **1000** *Sax. Leechd.* I. 282 Đeos wyrt þe man camelleon alba & oþrum naman wulfes tæsl [*MS. B.* tæsel] nemneþ.] *c* **1265** *Voc. Names Plants* in Wr.-Wülcker 559/7 *Virga pastoris*, wilde tesel. **1326** *Lett.-bk. Lond. E.* lf. 168 in Riley *Memorials* (1868) 150 [The thistles that in English are called] taseles. **1382** WYCLIF *Isa.* xxxiv. 13 Ther shul springe in his houses thornes and netles, and tasil in the strengthis of it. *a* **1387** *Sinon. Barthol.* (Anecd. Oxon.) 43/1 *Virga pastoris*, i. carduus agrestis, herba est quæ multum assimulatur carduo fullonum, an. wilde tasel. *c* **1440** *Pallad. on Husb.* IV. 128 The tasul now in donged lond is sowe. **14..** *Voc.* in Wr.-Wülcker 570/41 *Cardo*, a thystell, or a tesell. *c* **1450** *Godstow Reg.* 648 All tethe of tesyls that longyn to the office of fullers. **1598** STOW *Surv.* xviii. (1603) 167 There were Tasels planted for the use of Cloth workers. **1601** HOLLAND *Pliny* II. 280 The Tazill, called in Greeke Dipsacos, hath leaues much resembling Lectuce. **1626** A. SPEED *Adam out of Ed.* ix. (1659) 62 Tassels for Cloath-workers..will thrive..in England. **1630** DRAYTON *Muses' Elysium* Nymph. III. lv, By stinging Nettles, pricking Teasels Raysing blisters like the measels. **1725** *R. Bradley's Fam. Dict.* s.v., They sow their Lands in some Parts of Essex with Teasils, to dress their Bays and Cloth with. **1872** OLIVER *Elem. Bot.* II. 193 The connate leaves of Common Teasel..collect the rain and dew that trickle down the stem.

2. a. The dried prickly flower-head or bur of the fuller's teasel (see 1), used for teasing or dressing cloth so as to raise a nap on the surface.

1377 LANGL. *P. Pl.* B. xv. 446 Cloth..is nouȝt comly to were, Tyl it is fulled.., Wasshen wel with water, and with taseles [*v.rr.* taselles, taslis] cracched. **1463-4** *Rolls of Parlt.* V. 502/2 That every Fuller..use Tazels, and noo Cardes, in disseyvably hurtyng the same Cloth. **1545** *Rates of Customs* c vij, Tasels the kyue conteining v.c. viij.d. *Ibid.* c vij b, Tasels the pipe xl.s. Tasels the thousande iij.s. iiij.d. **1564** HAWKINS *Voy.* (Hakl. Soc.) 27 A kinde of corne called Maise,..the eare whereof is much like to a teasell. **1565-73** COOPER *Thesaurus, Gnaphos*, a tesill that tuckers vse to dresse cloth. **1611** COTGR. s.v. *Applanisseur*, The Cloathworker..with his cards of tazle. **1658** GURNALL *Chr. in Arm.* verse 14. III. iii. §5 (1669) 80/2 Afflictions Bernard compares to the Tezel, which though it be sharp and scratching, is to make the cloth more pure and fine. **1829** J. L. KNAPP *Jrnl. Nat.* 47 The use of the teazle is to draw out the ends of the wool from the manufactured cloth, so as to bring a regular pile or nap upon the surface. **1835** Teasels [see TEASEL *v.*]. **1870** YEATS *Nat. Hist. Comm.* 252 The best clothiers still prefer the teazel for finishing their cloth.

b. As a heraldic bearing.

1660 *Guillim's Heraldry* IV. vii. 289 Sable, a Cheuron Ermine, between two Habicks in chief, and a Tessell in base, proper. This is the bearing of the worshipfull Company of the Cloath-workers. **1864** BOUTELL *Her. Hist. & Pop.* xxi. §11 (ed. 3) 369 A tezel slipped in base or.

c. *fig.*

1630 J. TAYLOR (Water P.) *Water Cormorant's Compl.* Wks. III. 14/1 Though from terme to terme it be worne long, 'Tis drest still with the teazle of the tongue. **1863** COWDEN CLARKE *Shaks. Char.* viii. 200 She is never content except when plying the teazle upon one hapless pate or other.

3. *transf.* A mechanical substitute for the natural teasel in cloth-working.

1835 URE *Philos. Manuf.* 193 Many contrivances have.. been made for substituting metallic teasels..mounted in self-acting machines, for the thistle balls.

†**4.** Cf. TEASEL *v.* b. *Obs. rare.*

1688 R. HOLME *Armoury* III. 334/1 In good Tessel, [is] ground in good order for Plowing and Sowing.

5. *attrib.* and *Comb.*, as ***teasel crop, seed***; ***teasel-like*** adj.; **teasel-bur, teasel-head, teasel-top**, the dried flower-head of the teasel: (= sense 2); **teasel-frame**, a frame in which teasel-heads are fixed for dressing cloth (so **teasel-board, teasel-cylinder, teasel-rod**); **teaselwort**, in *pl.*, Lindley's name for plants of the N.O. *Dipsacaceæ.*

1835 URE *Philos. Manuf.* 195 Springs that shall support the *teasel-boards when mounted on the barrel. **1821** CLARE *Vill. Minstr.* II. 135 Lone spots..Where wildness rears her lings and *teazle-burs. **1877** KNIGHT *Dict. Mech.* s.v. *Teaseling-machine*, The teasel-burs..press..upon the whole width of the cloth which passes beneath them. **1766** *Museum Rust.* VI. 4 This crop is no injury to the *teasel crop the first year. **1835** URE *Philos. Manuf.* 196 Conduct the cloth over the *teasel-cylinder, and keep it smoothly distended. *Ibid.* 193 Two men,..seizing the *teasel-frame by the handles, scrubbed the face of the cloth. **1743** W. ELLIS *Mod. Husbandman* Aug. xvi. 55 One of these stalks has produced..an hundred *Teasel Heads. **1764** *Museum Rust.* III. 242 After cutting off the teazel heads, and tying them in bunches. **1844** G. DODD *Textile Manuf.* iii. 105 The use of teazle-heads is a remarkable feature in the process; for no combination of wires has yet been found that will effect the required object so efficiently as the little elastic prickles on the surface of these teazles. **1835** URE *Philos. Manuf.* 202 Cleaning the *teasel-rods and handles. **1721** MORTIMER *Husb.* (ed. 5) II. 202 The latter end of February or the beginning of March they sow the *Teasil-seed. **1902** CORNISH *Naturalist Thames* 91 The forest of tall *teazle-tops. **1846** LINDLEY *Veg. Kingd.* 699 Dipsacaceæ. *Teazelworts. **1866** *Treas. Bot.* 249.

'teasel, 'teazle, *v.* [f. prec. sb.] *trans.* To raise a smooth nap on (cloth) with or as with teasels; to tease. Also *transf.* Hence **'teaseling (teasling)** *vbl. sb.* (also *attrib.*).

[**1464** *Act 4 Edw. IV.* c. 1 Qe chescun fullour..en sa arte & occupacion de fuller & scalpier ou tezeiler de drap excercise & use teizels & nulls cardes.] **1543** *transl.* That euery fuller..in his crafte & occupacyon of fullynge rowynge or taseylynge of clothe, shall exercise tasels and no cardes. **1603** FLORIO *Montaigne* (1634) 393 He..led him in a fullers or cloth-workers shoppe, where with Cardes and Teazels..he made him to be carded, scraped, and teazled so long, untill he died of it. **1607** MARKHAM *Caval.* VI. (1617) 55 Dride sinewes of an Oxe, well tasled and mixt with well tempered glewe. **1733** P. LINDSAY *Interest Scot.* 109 We understand the picking of Cloth..but we are not so adroit at the tasselling it. **1835** URE *Philos. Manuf.* 192 The object..is to raise up the loose fibres of the woollen yarn into a nap..by scratching it either with thistle-heads called teasels, or with teasling-cards or brushes, made of wires. *Ibid.* 193 Moisture also softens their points and impairs their teasling powers. **1877** KNIGHT *Dict. Mech.*, *Teaseling-machine*,..in which woolen cloth is teaseled to raise a nap upon it.

†**b.** *transf.* ? To dress or improve the surface of (land). Cf. TEASEL *sb.* 4. *Obs. rare.*

1610 W. FOLKINGHAM *Art of Survey* I. x. 28 They teasil their perring wild sand with stall dung.

teaseler ('tiːz(ə)lə(r)). Also 5 tesel(l)er, 7 tasler, 8 teazeller. [f. TEASEL *sb.* + -ER[1]. AF. *teizeler.*]

1. One whose occupation is to teasel cloth.

14.. *Voc.* in Wr.-Wülcker 570/42 *Cardinarius*, a teselere. **1485** in *10th Rep. Hist. MSS. Comm.* App. v. 318 Frizers and tesellers dwellyng..within the citie. **1779** KELHAM *Dict. Norm. Lang.*, *Teizeler de draps*, a teazeller of cloth.

2. An implement for teaseling; in quot., a comb for thinning out a horse's mane, etc.

1607 MARKHAM *Caval.* v. (1617) 28 If your horses mayne be too thicke..you may with a tasler made of yron with three or foure teeth make it..as thinne as you please.

teasement ('tiːzmənt). [f. TEASE *v.*[1] + -MENT.] The action of teasing; petty annoyance.

1888 KIPLING *Wee Willie Winkie, Baa Baa, Black Sheep* ii, Beyond reach of..Harry and his teasements.

teaser[1] ('tiːzə(r)). Forms: 4 tezir, 5 teser, 6 teasor, 7 teyser, 7–9 teazer, 8 teizer, 8– teaser. [f. TEASE *v.*[1] + -ER[1].] One who or that which teases, in various senses.

1. a. One who teases wool, cotton, or the like.

1483 *Cath. Angl.* 380/2 A Teser, *carponarius.* **1591** PERCIVALL *Sp. Dict.*, *Carmenador*, a teasor, *carminator.* **1611** COTGR., *Tireur de laine*, a Teyser of wooll. **1824** GALT *Rothelan* II. IV. i. 99 The teasers and carders had started in alarm from their tasks. **1864** JANE CAMERON *Mem. Convict* I. 119 Among the female convicts there were oakum-pickers and teazers,..hair and cotton teazers.

b. An instrument or machine for teasing wool, etc.

1395 *Cartular. Abb. de Whiteby* (Surtees) 614 Item pro viii swewyls, viii.d. Item pro iiii tezirs, xiiii.d. **1852** DICKENS in *Househ. Words* 24 Apr. 118/2 The clay..is put into mills or teazers, and is sliced, and dug, and cut at. **1876** *Daily News* 17 June, The fire is thought to have originated with the 'teazer', a machine used for 'teazing' the wool in its rough state. **1879** *Cassell's Techn. Educ.* IV. 289/1 The teaser [for gutta-percha]..a drum containing a rotating cylinder armed with teeth.

Comb. **1882** W. GIBSON *Remin. Dollar* 152 The teazer-house with all its contents was burnt down.

2. a. One who teases or annoys: see TEASE *v.*[1] 2.

1659 *Commonwealth Ballads* (Percy Soc.) 200 Old Oliver was a teazer. **1712** STEELE *Spect.* No. 288 ¶3 One who would lessen the Number of Teazers of the Muses. **1844** DICKENS *Mart. Chuz.* xi, She's a regular teazer.

b. Local name of several birds which chase gulls and force them to disgorge their prey, as the skua. (Cf. *dung-teaser*, DUNG 5 c, *gull-teaser*, GULL[1] c.)

1833 *G. Montagu's Ornith. Dict.* 143 Teaser... A prov. name for Buffon's Skua, *Lestris Buffonii.* **1885** SWAINSON *Provinc. Names Birds* 210 Richardson's Skua. Gulls..when engaged in fishing, are pursued and harassed by these birds till they disgorge their prey... Hence the name Teaser.

c. An inferior stallion or ram used to excite mares or ewes.

1823 BEE *Dict. Turf* s.v. **1888** ELWORTHY *W. Somerset Word-bk.*, *Teaser*, a young ram which is allowed to run with the ewes, but is artificially prevented from copulation.

†**d.** A hound used in hunting: see TEISER. *Obs.*

e. In elephant-hunting: see quot.

1888 *Pall Mall G.* 30 May 6/1 When we find them, the teasers, who are the most courageous of the hunters, begin to tease the leaders of the herd. The bulls soon become angry and excited and give chase to the teasers.

f. A woman who arouses but evades amorous advances; a 'cock-teaser'. *colloq.*

1895 *Cornh. Mag.* Apr. 395 My Joan allus be a teäzer, zur, and when I's wanted to kiss zhe, zhe zes 'Noa, it ain't proper.' **1939** C. R. COOPER *Teen-Age Vice* (1959) iii. 54 The true B-girl is often nothing more than a professional teaser..selling drinks by fraudulent inferences. **1957** J. BRAINE *Room at Top* vi. 57 She leads young men on and then she turns prim... She's a born teaser. **1980** J. GARDNER *Garden of Weapons* I. xi. 111 Martha..sensual in a very obvious way. Herbert always suspected she was a teaser with men.

g. A strip-tease act; a strip-tease artist.

1929 [see RUNWAY 2 a]. **1930** *Variety* 1 Oct. 49 Miss Dix copped the show from the other femmes with her naughty numbers and teasers. **1931** C. BEATON *Diary* 13 Feb. in *Wandering Years* (1961) 217 There were lots of 'teaser' numbers... The leading lady..tantalisingly takes off one piece of clothing at a time.

3. a. Something that teases, or causes annoyance; something difficult to deal with, a 'poser'. *colloq.* In *Pugilistic slang*, an opponent difficult to tackle or overcome.

1759 FRANKLIN *Ess.* Wks. 1840 III. 380 He plyed them with another teaser. **1812** *Sporting Mag.* XL. 66 The writer cannot encourage the beaten man with hopes of ever being a teazer in the gymnastic line. **1844** DICKENS *Mart. Chuz.* l, It was a teaser to read. **1883** E. PENNELL-ELMHIRST *Cream Leicestersh.* 75 The next [fence] is indeed a teaser, where the best horse..might crack under the saddle.

b. *slang.* A flogging. ? *Obs.*

1832 *Examiner* 188/1 What they had done was 'not big enough for transportation, nor for a teaser' (a whipping).

c. In *Cricket*, a ball that is difficult to play. ? *Obs.*

1856 G. L. H. in V. Dayrell *Weeds from Isis* 69 Your cricketing boy, full of teasers and twisters. **1905** H. A. VACHELL *Hill* xii. 249 Fluff's brother bowled slows of a good length, with an awkward break from the off to the leg. 'Teasers,' said the caterpillar critically.

d. *Naut. slang.* A knotted rope's end.

1910 [see *blood-knot* s.v. BLOOD sb. 21]. **1953** J. MASEFIELD *Conway* (rev. ed.) IV. 217 The rope's end, or teaser, made one learn very quickly. **1962** W. GRANVILLE *Dict. Sailor's Slang* 118/2 *Teaser*, short length of rope with a 'hangman's knot' at the end, used for chastising *Conway* cadets in the 'tough old days'.

e. *U.S. Theatr.* (See quots.)

1916 A. E. KROWS *Play Production in Amer.* xii. 87 The first border (all the borders are numbered consecutively from front to back) is called the teaser. **1923** C. J. DE GOVEIA *Community Playhouse* vii. 80 Just inside the proscenium arch stand two strips of scenery, one on each side of the stage, and usually with a third piece, a border, stretched across the top. The two strips are called *Tormentors* and the particular border the *Teaser.* These pieces are movable. **1933** P. GODFREY *Back-Stage* iii. 34 The 'teaser' and the 'tormentor' are the respective names by which an overhead and side masking arrangement prevents the audience from looking into the wings and the flies.

f. A fisherman's device (orig. live bait) for attracting fish. orig. *U.S.*

1919 Z. GREY *Tales of Fishes* xi. 203 We had three of these flying-fish out as teasers, all close to the boat. **1924** —— *Tales Southern Rivers* 14 The use of teasers..was first used by Avalon boatmen in Marlin fishing. I tried it.., and pronounced it a failure because mackerel, barracuda, and other fish snapped off the cut-bait teasers as fast as they could be put out. **1937** E. HEMINGWAY *To have & have Not* I. i. 17 Eddy put the two big teasers out and the nigger had baits on three rods. **1939** H. MAJOR *Salt Water Fishing Tackle* ii. 69 The first artificial teasers of which I've heard were used by Zane Grey, and I believe he originated them. Most of them are made of wood or metal, brightly colored. **1960** A. UPFIELD *Myst. Swordfish Reef* vi. 56 To these lines were attached brightly painted cylinders of wood which, when tossed overboard..darted beneath and skimmed over the surface..Teasers, Wilton explained..'the bait-fish and the two teasers look to a shark or swordie just like a small shoal of fish.' **1967** [see PLUGGER d].

g. A kind of toy pipe with a coil (of paper, etc.) at the end which shoots out when one blows down the stem.

1935 A. J. CRONIN *Stars look Down* III. viii. 554 They had teasers, too, which blew out and hit you as you passed. **1977** D. JONES *My Friend Dylan Thomas* i. 6 Some of them were wearing paper hats..some..blew feather 'teasers' at each other.

4. *Electr. Engin.* †**a.** The shunt winding of a compound-wound dynamo or motor. *Obs.* **b.** The winding or transformer that is connected to the middle of the other transformer in a T-connection. Freq. *attrib.*

1878 C. BRUSH *Brit. Pat. 2003* 9 This device, which I have called a 'teaser', is used in connection with field magnets..for the purpose of..increasing the magnetic field. *Ibid.*, The teaser wire may be coarser than the principal magnet wire. **1884** S. P. THOMPSON *Dynamo-Electric Machinery* vi. 92 The shunt part of the circuit, originally called the 'teazer', was adopted at first in machines for electro-plating. **1886** *Ibid.* (ed. 2) x. 238 Brush made the important invention of exciting the field magnets with a compound winding; coarse wire coils being connected in series, with the addition of a so-called 'teazer' coil of finer wire to maintain the magnetism when the main circuit was opened. **1900** —— *Polyphase Electric Currents* (ed. 2) v. 143 The teazer winding is connected with one end to the middle of the main winding. **1937** J. B. GIBBS *Transformer Princ. & Pract.* xi. 82 One transformer, called the 'main transformer' is connected between two of the three-phase lines,..and the 'teaser transformer' is connected between the third line and the 50 per cent tap of the main transformer, using the 86.6 per cent tap of the teaser. **1981** G. MCPHERSON *Introd. Electr. Machines* iii. 221 In the T connection, one transformer has its primary connected directly across two lines. This is called the 'main transformer'. The second transformer is called the 'teaser'.

5. An introductory advertisement, *esp.* an excerpt or sample designed to stimulate interest or curiosity. orig. and chiefly *U.S.*

1934 WEBSTER, *Teaser*, an advertisement meant to arouse curiosity, sometimes by withholding part of the material information (*Trade Slang, U.S.*). **1940** *Chambers's Techn. Dict.* 835/2 *Teaser*, colloquialism for a *trailer* which is intended to advertise films for future exhibition in a cinema. **1960** M. T. WILLIAMS *Art of Jazz* 86 Old Town..was plastered with 'teaser' posters heralding the coming of the famous..Minstrels. **1962** *Daily Progress* (Charlottesville, Va.) 8 Nov. 38/1 A teaser is..a stimulating bit from the story to follow and opens a show. **1962** S. E. HYMAN *Tangled Bank* 378 At the end of a lecture, Freud will sometimes tack on a teaser for the next, such as: 'At the next lecture we shall see whether we can agree with the poets in their conception of the meaning of psychological errors.' **1977** 'J. LE CARRÉ' *Hon. Schoolboy* xii. 270 Our agent asked Ricardo for a teaser so's the information could be evaluated back home.

'teaser[2]. *local.* Also 8 **tisor.** [ad. mod.F. *tiseur* a fireman; cf. TEASE *v.*[2]] **a.** One who 'teases' or attends to a fire or furnace; a stoker, fireman.

1797 P. WAKEFIELD *Mental Improv.* (1801) I. 148 The tisors, or persons employed in heating the large furnaces. **1835** SIR J. ROSS *Narr. 2nd Voy.* xxvi. 377 Two mates, and one of the fire teasers. **1858** SIMMONDS *Dict. Trade*, *Teazer*, the stoker or fireman in a glass-work who attends the furnace. **1894** [see TEASING *vbl. sb.*[2]].

b. An instrument for 'teasing' a fire; a poker.

1839 URE *Dict. Arts* 63 The furnace and implements used for assaying in the Royal Mint and the Goldsmiths' Hall... Fig. 66, the teaser for cleaning the grate. Fig. 67, a larger teaser, which is introduced at the top of the furnace, for keeping a complete supply of charcoal around the muffle.

tea-service, etc.: see TEA *sb.* 9.

'tea-shop. [f. TEA *sb.* + SHOP *sb.*] **a.** A shop where tea (sense 1) is sold. **b.** A café where tea (sense 2 or 4) is served.

a **1745** SWIFT (J.), The mistress of the tea shop. **1856** A. M. LANG *Diary* (Meean Meer, Punjab) 17 Sept. (MS.), Went to Tea Shop and billiards..at Artillery Mess. **1860** J. R. EDKINS *Chinese Scenes* (1863) 153 Drinking tea with about forty nondescript Chinamen... I shall try to give you a little picture of the tea-shop. **1915** W. S. MAUGHAM *Of Human Bondage* lvi. 288 He thought of going to lunch at the tea-shop. **1933** DYLAN THOMAS *Let.* Oct. (1966) 43 Gower is a very beautiful peninsula,..and so far the Tea-Shop philistines have not spoilt the more beautiful of its bays. **1962** L. DAVIDSON *Rose of Tibet* ii. 48 There were a number of small teashops in the town [*sc.* Kalimpong]; ramshackle sheds with trestle tables containing tea urns and trays of sweetmeats.

c. In the affected spelling **tea-shoppe** [cf. SHOPPE] applied (freq. disparagingly) to a tea-shop with sham antique decoration.

Second element sometimes pronounced ('ʃɒpiː).

1925 *Amer. Speech* I. 153/1 These names are not intended to be 'quaint' like 'Betty Anne' of Massachusetts and her eternal 'Tea Shoppe'. **1933**, etc. [see SHOPPE]. **1959** *Times* 12 May 3/7 As artificial as a Tudor Tea Shoppe. **1973** WODEHOUSE *Bachelors Anonymous* v. 50 She had been planning a roll and butter and a cup of coffee at some wayside tea shoppe.

Hence **'tea-shoppy** *a.*, characteristic of or resembling a tea-shop (sense b or c).

1931 *Time & Tide* 22 Aug. 992 There are other debatable points, too, in this rather tea-shoppy story. **1959** *Good Food Guide* 52 Portions are ample and not tea-shoppy. **1975** *Times* 27 Dec. 7/3 A restaurant..in a tea-shoppy basement.

†**'teasicke,** obs. illit. f. PHTHISIC, consumption.

a **1585** MONTGOMERIE *Flyting* 321 The teasicke, the toothaike, the tittes and the tirles.

teasing ('tiːzɪŋ), *vbl. sb.*[1] [f. TEASE *v.*[1] + -ING[1].] The action of TEASE *v.*[1]

1. a. The pulling asunder of the fibres of wool, hair, animal tissue, etc.: see TEASE *v.*[1] 1. Also *attrib.*, as *teasing-needle.*

1591 PERCIVALL *Sp. Dict.*, *Carmenadura*, teasing, *carminatio.* **1851** *Art Jrnl. Illustr. Catal.* p. iv**/1 The web of cleaned cotton..is passed through a lapping machine, and..undergoes a further teazing. **1873** T. H. GREEN *Introd. Pathol.* (ed. 2) 118 The cells have been separated by teasing. **1891** *Cent. Dict.*, *Teasing-needle*, a needle for teasing, or tearing into minute shreds, a specimen for microscopic examination.

b. *U.S. Hairdressing.* Back-combing; also, a similar treatment given with a small brush.

1923 F. KORF *Art & Fundamentals of Hairdressing* II. ii. 31 The public seems to fear the back-combing, or as it is often called, teasing of the hair, perhaps with some justification. **1964** D. Z. HANLE *Hairdo Handbk.* vii. 71 Properly done, teasing can play an important part in finishing a hairstyle... Use a small..teasing brush. **1975** C. CALASIBETTA *Fairchild's Dict. Fashion* 260/1 *Bouffant*, hair exaggeratedly puffed out by means of teasing.

2. Petty irritation: see TEASE *v.*[1] 2.

1678 BUTLER *Hud.* III. II. 452 Not by the force of Carnal Reason, But indefatigable Teazing. **1731** SWIFT *On Pulteney* 1 Sir Robert weary'd by Will Pulteney's teazings. **1858** DORAN *Crt. Fools* 212 He was compelled to endure the teazing of the domestics.

3. *slang.* A flogging: see TEASE *v.*[1] 3. ? *Obs.*

1807 H. TUFTS in E. Pearson *Autobiogr. of Criminal* (1930) II. iv. 292 *Teasing*, whipping. **1821** P. EGAN *Life in London* I. 11 The innumerable teazings they had book'd. **1865** *Daily Tel.* 27 Oct. 5/2 'When I've had another teasing,' said a boy thief..alluding to the hangman and his cat, 'I shall be as good as Tommy So-and-So'.

'teasing, *vbl. sb.*[2] *local.* [f. TEASE *v.*[2] + -ING[1].] The keeping up of the fire in a furnace. In quot. *attrib.*

1894 *Northumbld. Gloss.* s.v. *Teaser*, The glass-house teasers wore broad-brimmed felt hats..to protect them from the scorching fires. They also wore 'hand-hats' of thick felt, to enable them to hold the long iron teasing pokers.

'teasing, *ppl. a.* [f. TEASE *v.*[1] + -ING[2].] That teases; pettily irritating, annoying, or vexatious.

1694 ADDISON *Ovid's Met.* II. *Coronis* 19 And by a thousand teizing questions drew The important secret from him. **1800** *Med. Jrnl.* IV. 311 She complains of a teazing cough. **1847** HELPS *Friends in C.* I. iii. 34 This is better than to be the sport of a teasing hope without reason.

Hence **'teasingly** *adv.*, in a teasing manner.

1754 RICHARDSON *Grandison* (1781) IV. xxviii. 206 You are disposed to be teazingly facetious. **1906** *Athenæum* 17 Mar. 321/3 He never becomes teasingly minute.

teasle, teassell, obs. variants of TEASEL.

Teasmade ('ti:zmeɪd). [perh. f. phr. *tea's made*.] The proprietary name of a brand of automatic tea-maker (see *tea-maker* (*d*) s.v. TEA *sb.* 9 c).

1938 *Trade Marks Jrnl.* 26 Jan. 93/2 *Goblin Teasmade*... Time controlled electric water heating and tea making apparatus. The British Vacuum Cleaner & Engineering Company Limited,.. Fulham, London, S.W.6; manufacturers. **1958** *Spectator* 6 June 754/2 The Goblin Vacuum Cleaner, Goblin Washing Machines and the Goblin Teasmades. **1980** A. N. WILSON *Healing Art* 271 The electric clock on the Teasmade in the bedroom. **1983** *Sunday Tel.* 31 July 8/7 He was wearing a watch—one of those that.. cannot be used as a calculator and do not double as a Teasmade. It merely gives the time.

tea-sodden, etc.: see TEA *sb.* 9.

'tea-spoon. a. A small spoon, usually of silver or silvered metal, of a size suitable for stirring tea or other beverage in a cup.

1686 *Lond. Gaz.* No. 2203/4 Three small gilt Tea Spoons. **1704** *Ibid.* No. 4055/4, 4 Spoons, and 5 Tea-Spoons. **1825** T. HOOK *Sayings* Ser. II. *Passion & Princ.* i, Mr. Welsted.. in his agitation knocked the tea-spoon out of his glass of negus. **1849** DICKENS *Dav. Copp.* lix, We have something in the shape of tea-spoons... But they're Britannia metal.

b. = TEASPOONFUL.

1791 J. WOODFORDE *Diary* 19 Apr. (1927) III. 266, I took half a very small Tea-Spoon of Ether in Water this Evening. **1935** M. MORPHY *Recipes of All Nations* 767 A teaspoon of the mixture is wrapped in.. a blanched vine leaf. **1963** R. CARRIER *Great Dishes of World* ii. 60/2, 1 level teaspoon dried mustard.

Hence **'teaspoonful**, as much as a tea-spoon will hold; in medical prescriptions taken as equal to 1 fluid-drachm.

1731 MORTIMER in *Phil. Trans.* XXXVII. 170 Not above a Tea Spoonful of Water. **1825** J. NEAL *Bro. Jonathan* II. 53 A tea-spoonful of the ashes. **1844** EMERSON *Lect., Yng. American* Wks. (Bohn) II. 301 Agricultural chemistry.. offering by means of a tea-spoonful of artificial guano, to turn a sandbank into corn. **1847** J. F. SOUTH *Housh. Surg.* (1880) 27 Adding a teaspoonful of laudanum. **1904** MARIE CORELLI *God's Gd. Man* viii, Two.. teaspoonfuls of cream.

teast, obs. or dial. f. TASTE *v.*

teast, teaster, teasty, etc., obs. ff. TEST, TESTER, TESTY, etc.

teasy ('ti:zɪ), *a. colloq.* and *dial.* [f. TEASE *v.*[1] + -Y.] **a.** Teasing, irritating.

1901 J. H. HARRIS *Luck of Wheal Veor* 164 A poor woman wethout a man, an' three gert stramming maids to keep, es like a cow wethout a tail when the flies is taisey. **1908** *19th Cent.* Jan. 188 It's a teasy job. **1938** E. POUND *Let.* 8 May (1971) 315, I forget what he and Domenik have to say, but teckon it's teasy.

b. Bad-tempered, irritable, tetchy.

1866 T. R. HIGHAM *Dial. between Two Cornish Miners* 5 My owld 'umman was.. so taisy that I cudden live in the house. **1907** A. QUILLER-COUCH *Major Vigoureux* xvii. 167 He'll be as teasy as fire when he hears about it. **1931** C. C. ROGERS *Gwendra Cove* 193 'E was a teasy oald bachelor, I reckon. **1976** J. C. TREWIN in D. V. Baker *Cornish Short Stories* 135 'Go 'long, you teasy toad!' shrilled Mrs Bosworthick.

Hence **'teasily** *adv.*

1928 A. BENNETT in *Daily Express* 1 Sept. 5/5 'And what will Mrs. Meadowes say to all this Red politics?' Alan demanded teasily.

teat (ti:t). Forms: α. 1 tit, titt, 3 titte, 3–5 tytte, 9 *dial.* tit (*dim.* tittie). See also TIT *sb.*[6] β. 3–6 tete, 4–5 teet(e, 4–7 teate, 6– teat. γ. 4–6 tette, 4–8 tet, 8 tett. δ. 4 tute. [OE. *tit(t* masc., cognate with MLG., MDu. *titte*, LG. *tit(t*, *titte* (Du. dial. *tet*), late MHG. *zitze* fem., Ger. *zitz* masc. str., *zitze* masc. and fem. wk. *Tit* (*tittie*), for long dialectal, has come into gen. use as TIT *sb.*[6] The γ-form *tette, tett, tet*, and perh. also the β-form *tête, teet(e, teate*, whence the current *teat*, appear to represent F. *tette*, in OF. *tete* (12–13th c.), *tette, taite*; but the form-history is not clear, and in ME. there was probably mixture of the OE. and OF. forms. The OF. as well as Sp. *teta*, It. *tetta* (and *zizza*) are themselves generally held to be of German origin, and point to an OLG. *titte* fem. Ulterior etymology unknown. (The ordinary OHG. word *tutta, tuta* fem., *tutto, tuto* masc., MHG. *tutte, tute* fem., was app. unconnected.)]

1. The small protuberance at the tip of each breast or udder in female mammalia (except monotremes), upon which the ducts of the mammary gland open, and from which the milk is sucked by the young; the nipple. Formerly also applied to the whole breast or udder. (In early use, and still *dial.*, of women; now usually of quadrupeds.)

α. *c* **950** *Lindisf. Gosp.* Luke xi. 27 Eadiᵹ womb *vel* hrif seðe ðec ᵹebær & ða titto *vel* ða breosto ða ðu ᵹediides [*c* **975** *Rushw.* ða tito *vel* ða breost ða ðu deðedes]. *c* **1000** *Sax. Leechd.* I. 112 Wið titta sar wifa þe beoð melce. *c* **1205** LAY. 5025 þu eært mi bærn deore. Loka her þa tittes þet þu suke mid þine lippes. *Ibid.* 11936 Ich heom wullen alle for-don & bi þan titten [*c* **1275** tyttes] an-hon. **1387** TREVISA *Higden* (Rolls) III. 43 A wolfesse.. fedde.. þe children, and made hem ofte souke of here owne tetes [*v.r.* tyttes]. *a* **1825** FORBY *Voc. E. Anglia, Titties, Tits*, s. pl. teats.

β. *c* **1290** *S. Eng. Leg.* I. 473/376 þanne may mi luytel sone to hire tete take. **1382** WYCLIF *Luke* xi. 27 Blessid be the teetis whiche thou hast sokun. *c* **1386** CHAUCER *Miller's T.* 518, I moorne as dooth a lamb after the tete. **1450–1530** *Myrr. our Ladye* 233 Blysse we.. the grete lorde, souckynge the maydenly teates of the moste meke vyrgyn. **1578** BANISTER *Hist. Man* I. 9 The fashion of Tetes in a Cowes vdder. **1662** GURNALL *Chr. in Arm.* verse 17. I. v. §1 (1669) 255/2 Here his soul sweetly sleeps, as the Child, with the Teat in its mouth. **1774** GOLDSM. *Nat. Hist.* (1776) II. 103 The teats of some, as in the ape and the elephant, are like those of men, being but two. **1844** STEPHENS *Bk. Farm* II. 700 Sometimes there are more pigs littered than the sow has teats to give to each.

γ. *a* **1325** Tettes [see b]. **13..** *S.E. Leg.* (MS. Bodl. 779) in Herrig *Archiv* LXXXII. 342/322 þis me lykeþ bet þan me dede in my ȝouþe mylk of any tet. **1565–73** COOPER *Thesaurus* s.v. *Admitto, Admittere pastum ad vbera*, to receiue to the tette. **1669** WORLIDGE *Syst. Agric.* (1681) 323 The Cows Dug by some is called the Tet. **1709** PRIOR *Callimachus' 1st Hymn to Jupiter* 55 Kind Amalthea reach'd her Tett, distent With Milk.

δ. *c* **1400** *R. Glouc.'s Chron.* (Rolls) App. G. 196 þeos tutes [*v.r.* tetys] þou soke ylome.

†**b.** In allusive expressions, as *at the teat*, (a suckling) at the breast; *from the teat(s*, from infancy.

a **1325** *Prose Psalter* xxi[i]. 8 þou art myn hope from þe tettes of my moder. *c* **1440** CAPGRAVE *St. Kath.* I. 242 Mercy fro þe tetys grew wyth hyr. **1588** SHAKS. *Tit. A.* II. iii. 145 Euen at thy Teat thou had'st thy Tyranny. **1602** *2nd Pt. Return fr. Parnass.* III. v. 1454 Vs our kinde Colledge from the teate did teare. *a* **1635** NAUNTON *Fragm. Reg.* (Arb.) 26 He left a plentiful Estate and such a Son, who, as the vulgar speaks it, could live without the teat.

†**c.** *fig.* A source of nourishment or supply. *Obs.*

c **1440** *Jacob's Well* 232 Putte fro þe þe tetys of ydylnes, þat þou souke no more þer-of for no delyȝt! **1569** *Irish Act 11 Eliz.* Stat. III. c. 1 *Preamb.*, That.. most detestable coyne and liverie, which was the very nurse and teat that gave suck and nutriment to all disobediences. *a* **1631** DONNE *Lett.* (1651) 102 The channels of God's mercies run through both fields, and they are sister teats of his graces. **1675** HOBBES *Odyssey* VII. (1686) 88 His Riches was a never-dying Teat.

2. *transf.* A structure, natural or artificial, resembling a teat; a nipple: see quots.

1587 MASCALL *Govt. Cattle, Oxen* (1627) 12 Such superfluous flesh on the tongue of cattel will hinder the beast oftentimes in eating his meate, being called of some husbandes the Barbes, Teates. **1774** GOLDSM. *Nat. Hist.* (1776) VII. 253 Nature has supplied this animal [spider] with.. five dugs or teats for spinning it into thread. **1835** KIRBY *Hab. & Inst. Anim.* xix. II. 284 These teats are connected with internal reservoirs, which yield the fluid matter forming the thread or web. **1864** WEBSTER, *Teat*.. 2. (*Mach.*) A small nozzle resembling a teat. **1877** KNIGHT *Dict. Mech.*, *Teat*, a small, rounded, perforated projection, otherwise called a *nipple*, as that of a gun. **1890** [see *teat drill* in 3].

3. *attrib.* and *Comb.*, as *teat-like* adj.; **teat-cup, teat drill** (see quots.); **teat-fish** (*Australia*), a sea-slug of the genus *Holothuria*, esp. *H. mammifera*, so called from its papillæ; †**teat-head**, the nipple; **teat-stud**, one of the metal studs, commonly called 'buttons', with which the front of a page's jacket is ornamented; **teat-worm**, the common thread-worm (*Oxyuris vermicularis*).

1862 *Morn. Star* 19 June, The cow-milker.. consisting of two diaphragm pumps.. to which four *teat-cups are attached for receiving the teats of the cow. **1895** *Westm. Gaz.* 8 Oct. 8/2 A glass lid.. enables the attendant to see when a cow is finished, and then by simply turning a stop-cock the teat-cups fall off. **1890** *Cent. Dict.* s.v. *Drill*, **Teat drill*, a square-faced cylindrical drill with a sharp, pyramidal projection or teat issuing from the center of the cutting face. **1894** B. THOMSON *S. Sea Yarns* 256 The reef swarmed with *teat-fish. **1601** HOLLAND *Pliny* I. 347 Such beasts as be very fruitful.. haue many nipples or *teat heads all along their belly. **1826** KIRBY & SP. *Entomol.* III. xxx. 149 A great number of Lepidopterous larvæ.. have between the under-lip and fore-legs a slender transverse opening, containing a *teat-like protuberance. **1910** J. PLATT Jun. *Let. to Editor*, **Teat-stud*, technical term, used by tailors for the tiny plated or gilt buttons which are sewn as closely together as possible down the front of a page's jacket. The teat-stud or tit-stud is quite unique in shape. **1899** CAGNEY *Jaksch's Clin. Diagn.* vi. (ed. 4) 226 Oxyuris vermicularis (common thread-worm or *teat worm).

teat, obs. form of TATE, tuft, etc.

'tea-,table, *sb.* [f. TEA *sb.* 4 + TABLE *sb.* 6.]

1. A table at which tea is taken, or on which tea-things are placed for a meal.

a. As a special piece of furniture, usually small and of a light and elegant make.

In quot. 1804, a table for the sale of tea and refreshments.

1703 *Lond. Gaz.* No. 3891/3 Lackered Tea-Tables. **1740** LADY HARTFORD *Corr.* (1806) II. 12 The Duchess of Dorset was presented with.. a tea-table with a gold tea-canister, kettle and lamp. **1804** *Naval Chron.* XII. 307, I fell foul of a.. woman's tea-table, at the corner of a street, and had like to have thrown the.. tea-things all about. **1898** G. B. SHAW *Plays* II. *You never can tell* 274 The bamboo tea table, with folding shelves.

b. A table spread for tea, or as the place of a social gathering for tea and conversation.

1688 SHADWELL *Sqr. Alsatia* Epil. 37 Here no Chit chat, here no Tea Tables are. **1700** CONGREVE *Way of World* IV. v, To the Dominion of the Tea-table I submit.. but.. I banish all Auxiliaries to the Tea-table, as Orange-brandy, all Aniseed [etc.]. **1792** A. MURPHY *Ess. Johnson* 88 During the whole time he presided at his tea-table. **1854** MRS. GASKELL *North & S.* x, She stood by the tea-table.. as if she was not attending to the conversation, but solely busy with the tea-cups.

2. *transf.* The company assembled at tea.

1712 ADDISON *Spect.* No. 536 ¶1 The.. publication of it would.. oblige.. a whole tea-table of my friends. **1856** KANE *Arct. Expl.* II. i. 19 Explaining to the tea-table this evening's outfit.

3. *attrib.* (chiefly in reference to social gatherings: see 1 b).

1700 CONGREVE *Way of World* IV. v, Restrain yourself to .. simple Tea-table Drinks, as Tea, Chocolate, and Coffee. As likewise to genuine and authorised Tea-table Talk—Such as mending of Fashions, spoiling Reputations, railing at absent Friends. **1724** RAMSAY (*title*) The Tea-table Miscellany. **1779** (*title*) Tea-Table Dialogues, between a Governess and Miss Sensible. **1852** H. SPENCER *Use & Beauty* in *Ess.* (1858) 387 While ghost-stories.. enliven tea-table conversation.

Hence (*humorous nonce-wds.*) †**teata'bellically** *adv.*, at the tea-table, in familiar conversation at tea; **tea-'tabular** *a.*, pertaining to the tea-table.

1768 TUCKER *Lt. Nat.* (1834) I. 475 The vast Pacific Ocean, commonly, yea, vulgarly, not to say, news-paperically, nor yet, teatabellically,.. called.. the South-sea. **1855** BAGEHOT *Lit. Stud.* (1895) I. 125 Torpid, indoor, tea-tabular felicity.

'tea-table, *v.* [f. the sb.] *trans.* In literature, to treat a dramatic event in a trivial or casual way. Hence **'tea-tabling** *vbl. sb.*

1938 C. ISHERWOOD *Lions & Shadows* iv. 175 The accident was to be in the best Forster tradition, 'tea-tabled', slightly absurd. *Ibid.* vi. 258 The murder was cut—'tea-tabled' down to an indecisive, undignified scuffle; and the ending was an apotheosis of the Tea-Table, a decrescendo of anti-climaxes. **1962** *Times Lit. Suppl.* 22 June 460/4 Certain critics have made far too much of Mr. Forster's 'tea-tabling' and of his casual sudden deaths. **1977** *Ibid.* 28 Jan. 97/2 Christina Rossetti's oblique treatment of detail is an early case of what Isherwood, discussing Forster in *Lions and Shadows*, calls 'tea-tabling', the novel's lyrical domestication of disaster.

tea-taster ('ti:,teɪstə(r)). One whose business is to test the quality of samples of tea by tasting them; a tea-expert. So **'tea-,tasting**, the occupation or business of a tea-taster.

1858 in SIMMONDS *Dict. Trade.* **1859** *All Year Round* No. 2. 38 The tea-tasters and clerks of the different English and American houses. **1888** J. PATON in *Encycl. Brit.* XXIII. 100/2 The qualities of a sample of tea and its commercial value can only with accuracy be determined by actual infusion and trial by a skilled tea-taster. **1907** *Gentl. Mag.* May 494 Tea-tasters use the weight of a new sixpence to three and a half ounces of water.

teated ('ti:tɪd), *a.* [f. TEAT + -ED[2].] Furnished with or having teats. Also in comb.

1661 LOVELL *Hist. Anim. & Min.* 90 The Lionesse is smooth and teated. **1769** *Aclome Inclos. Act* 2 A customary .. payment of three half-pence for every new teated cow. **1891** T. HARDY *Tess* xvii, The milkers formed quite a little battalion of men and maids, the men operating on the hard-teated animals.

teater, obs. f. TETTER.

teath, var. TATH(E; obs. f. TITHE.

teather, obs. f. TETHER.

tea-things, -time, etc.: see TEA *sb.* 9.

teathy, var. TEETHY.

teatish, teaty: see TETTISH, TEETY.

†**'teatling.** *Obs. rare*[−1]. [f. TEAT + -LING.] A young animal at the teat; a suckling.

1631 *Celestina* II. 130 The teatling lambe which suckes both her damm's teat, and that of another Ewe.

tea-total, etc.: see TEETOTAL.

'tea-tray. A tray on which tea-things are placed.

1773 *H. Clay's Pat.* in *Sixth Rep. Dep. Kpr.* App. II. 161 Of an invention of making, in paper.. Screens, Chimney Pieces, Tables, Tea Trays, and Waiters. **1831** WILLIAMS *Life & Corr. Sir T. Lawrence* I. 75 Painting sign-boards or tea-trays. **1862** MRS. H. WOOD *Mrs. Hallib.* I. i, Two candles.. stood on the table behind the tea-tray.

teatre, obs. form of THEATRE.

'tea-tree. 1. *properly*, The shrub or low tree, the dried leaves of which form the tea of commerce; = TEA *sb.* 3.

1760 J. LEE *Introd. Bot.* App. 329 Tea-tree, *Thea.* **1771** *Chron.* in *Ann. Reg.* 151/2 The Duke of Northumberland has at this time a tea-tree in full flower. It is the first that ever flowered in Europe. **1832** *Veg. Subst. Food* 377 The flowers of the tea-tree are white, and resemble the wild rose. **1888** J. PATON in *Encycl. Brit.* XXIII. 97/2 An indigenous tea-tree.. is found in Assam.

2. a. *transf.* Applied in Australia, Tasmania, and New Zealand to various shrubs or trees of the myrtle family, chiefly of the genera *Leptospermum* and *Melaleuca*, of which the leaves have been used as a substitute for tea.

(Often spelt *ti-tree*, occasionally *ti-tri*, as if a native name.) Also with qualifying words denoting different species.
1790 J. WHITE *Voy. N.S. Wales* 229 Tea Tree of New South Wales. *Melaleuca? Trinervia.* **1802** BARRINGTON *Hist. N.S. Wales* ix. 331 The roof was bark, resembling that of the Tea-tree at Port Jackson. **1858** HOGG *Veg. Kingd.* xc. 350 *Leptospermum scoparium*, or New Zealand Tea-tree... The leaves of this species were used by Captain Cook's crew as a substitute for tea. **1866** *Treas. Bot.* 674 *L[eptospermum] lanigerum*,..commonly called Tea tree on account of its leaves having been used by the early settlers..as a substitute for tea. **1885** MRS. PRAED *Australian Life* 112 The bottle-brush flowers of the ti-trees. **1891** *Coo-ee* (ed. Mrs. P. Martin) 282 The brown twisted branches of the ti-trees.. shook their scented bottle-brush blossoms in our faces. **1891** *Cent. Dict.* s.v., *Broad-leaved tea-tree*, a myrtaceous shrub or tree, *Callistemon salignus*, of Australia and Tasmania... *Prickly tea-tree*, same as *naambarr* [*Melaleuca styphelioides*, of N.S. Wales]. *Red Scrub tea-tree*, the Australian *Rhodamnia trinervia*, a myrtaceous shrub or tree. **1909** *Westm. Gaz.* 16 Aug. 4/1 A Winter Scene in Australia... Down by the sea the tea-tree is commencing to weave its veil of flowers.

b. *attrib.*, as ***tea-tree bark, bush, marsh, oil, scrub.***
1820 C. JEFFREYS *Van Dieman's Land* iii. 133 For tea they [the Bush Rangers] drink a decoction of the sassafras and other shrubs, particularly one which they call the tea-tree bush. **1828** P. CUNNINGHAM *N.S. Wales* (ed. 3) II. 13 Building comfortable huts of tea-tree bark. **1835** J. BATMAN in Cornwallis *New World* (1859) I. 406 A dense tea-tree scrub, which we knew to be the surest indication of good water in its neighbourhood. **1883** C. HARPUR *Poems* 78 Why roar the bull-frogs in the tea-tree marsh? **1933** *Bulletin* (Sydney) 12 July 19/2 The distillation of essential oil from *Melaleuca alternifolia* (tea-tree) has become an established N.S.W. industry... Some 40 tea-tree-oil preparations are on the market. **1954** *Econ. Bot.* VIII. 324/1 Tea-Tree Oil... Collection of leaf material differs from that in operation for eucalyptus leaves.

3. Applied to various other trees: see TEA *sb.* 6; in Great Britain esp. to the flowering shrub *Lycium barbarum* or *chinense* (N.O. *Solanaceæ*), a native of China, also called ***Duke of Argyll's tea-tree*** (see quot. 1838). **African tea-tree**, *Lycium afrum*; **Ceylon tea-tree**, etc.: see quots.
1777 G. FORSTER *Voy. round World* I. 130 The spruce and the tea-trees. **1812** *New Bot. Gard.* I. 113 Ceanothus Americanus, New Jersey Tea-tree. **1838** LOUDON *Trees & Shrubs Gt. Brit.* III. 1269 One species, *L[ycium] barbarum*, is commonly called the Duke of Argyll's tea tree from the circumstance of a tea plant, (*Thea viridis*), having been sent to the Duke of Argyll at the same time as this plant, and the labels having been accidentally changed. **1858** HOGG *Veg. Kingd.* lxiv. 231 *Elæodendron glaucum*, a native of Ceylon and Coromandel, has been introduced [into S. Africa] under the name of Ceylon Tea Tree. **1884** MILLER *Plant-n.*, Tea-plant, or Tea-tree,..African, *Lycium afrum*...—, Blue Mountain, or Golden-rod, *Solidago odora*...—, St. Helena, *Beatsonia portulacæfolia*...—, Surinam, various species of *Lantana*. **1909** *Westm. Gaz.* 24 Feb. 5/1 The plant commonly known as the Duke of Argyll's tea tree, belonging to the same natural order (*Solanaceæ*) as the potato and tomato.

tea-urn to **tea-wine**: see TEA *sb.* 9.

teave, var. TAVE.

teaw, -e, obs. forms of TEW.

teaz, app. earlier form of TEE *sb.*², *v.*³ (*Golf.*)

teaze, teazel: see TEASE, TEASEL.

teaze-tenon ('tiːz,tɛnən). *Carp.* ? *Obs.* Also **teazle-tenon.** (See quotations.)
1703 T. N. *City & C. Purchaser* 30 If it be a Timber Building, the Teazle Tennons of the Posts are Framed. Teazle Tennons are made at right Angles to those..on the Posts. **1823** P. NICHOLSON *Pract. Build.* Gloss., *Teaze-tenon.* **1842–76** GWILT *Archit.* Gloss., *Teaze Tenon*, a tenon on the top of a post, with a double shoulder and tenon from each for supporting two level pieces of timber at right angles to each other.

teazle, variant form of TEASEL.

Tebele (tə'biːliː). Also **Tabele.** [Native name.] A Niger-Congo language belonging to the South Eastern Bantu group. Cf. NDEBELE.
1883 R. N. CUST *Mod. Lang. Africa* II. xii. 300 Travellers write about..the Language of the Ma-tabéle, but there is reason to believe that it is Zulu... Syke, of the London Missionary Society, prepared School Books..: this gives the idea that Tabéle is a separate Language. **1897** W. A. ELLIOTT *Dict. Tebele & Shuna Lang.* p. v, The Tebele language is of course only a variety of the Zulu. *Ibid.* p. vi, Different types have been used for the two languages, clarendon for the Tebele, and small capitals for the Shuna. **1919** [see MATABELE 1]. **1977** C. F. & F. M. VOEGELIN *Classification & Index World's Lang.* 70 Ndebele = Tabele = Tebele.

Tebeth ('tɛbɛθ, 'tɛbɛt). Also **Tebet, Tevet** ('tɛvɛt). [Heb. *ṭēbēt*] The fourth month of the Jewish year (though placed tenth in the traditional list of months), corresponding to parts of December and January.
c **1382** BIBLE (Wycliffe) *Esther* ii. 16 And so she is lad to the priue chaumbre of king Assuer, the tenthe moneth, that is clepid Thebeth, that is, Januer. **1611** *Ibid.* (A.V.), So Esther was taken vnto king Ahasuerus..in the tenth moneth (which is the moneth Tebeth). **1973** *Jewish Chron.* 19 Jan. 22/5 The Fast of Tevet is mentioned in the Talmud and is therefore observed even on Friday.

Tebilized ('tiːbɪlaɪzd), *a.* Also **-ised** and with small initial. [f. the initials of *T*ootal *B*roadhurst *L*ee Company Ltd., the inventors of the process + -IZE + -ED¹.] A proprietary name for cotton and other fabrics which have been rendered crease-resistant by impregnation with a synthetic resin.
1937 *Official Gaz.* (U.S. Patent Office) 7 Dec. 36/1 Tootal Broadhurst Lee Company Limited. Manchester, England. Filed Oct. 16, 1937. Tebilized. For Piece Goods of Cotton, Linen, and Artificial Silk. Claims use since May 10, 1934. **1945** *Trade Marks Jrnl.* 28 Mar. 166/2 Tebilized. **1950** *Sun* (Baltimore) 8 May 10/4 This year with all the wonderful 'ized' things (tebilized and sanforized) that have happened to fabrics. **1955** *Times* 4 June 7 Irish linen for dresses or suits. Tebilized for crease-resistance. **1967** H. THOMPSON *Fibres & Fabrics of Today* 98 The name 'Tebilised' was adopted by Tootal Broadhurst Lee when they introduced this now universal finish.

tec (tɛk), *sb. slang.* †**teck.**
1. Abbreviation for DETECTIVE.
1879 *Sessions Papers* 25 July 238 Look out, there is a b—— *tec* from Chalk Farm watching. **1888** *Pall Mall G.* 11 Oct. 2/1 'Tecs and inspectors examine the place, make notes, and go away. **1888** *Daily News* 27 Dec. 7/2 Witness seized Wright and said 'I am a police officer'. Wright replied 'You are no 'tec; give me a chance', struggled violently, and got away. **1909** GALSWORTHY *Silver Box* II. i. 47 Drop it, I say, you blooming teck. *a* **1940** [see FINK *sb.*²]. **1977** *Daily Mirror* 30 Mar. 13/4 (*heading*) Porn tec admits bribe plot.
attrib. **1928** D. L. SAYERS *Unpleasantness at Bellona Club* viii. 90 He complained of being spied on..like the blighters in the 'tec stories. **1976** *Evening Times* (Glasgow) 1 Dec. 2/1 Softly, Softly: Task Force. Plodding 'tec series which has dragged on too long.

2. Ellipt. for *tec story*, a detective story.
1934 E. POUND *ABC of Reading* ii. 29 Only a very good 'tec' will stand re-reading. **1949** R. CHANDLER *Let.* 28 Dec. (1966) 76 The mystery and 'tec are on the wane. **1978** S. HODGES *Gollancz* ix. 194 Anthony Price, Nicholas Freeling and Helen McCloy are some of the writers whose 'tecs have been published by Gollancz.

Hence **tec** *v. trans.*, to watch as a detective.
1900 G. SWIFT *Somerley* 57 Let's watch the 'head'; he might be a kleptomaniac, or whatever they call it... I'd like to 'tec the 'head'.

tecal, tecat: see TICAL, TICKET.

‖**tecbir** ('tɛkbɪə(r)). Also **tekbir.** [Arab. *tekbīr* 'to magnify, proclaim the greatness of'; inf. of 2nd form of *kabura* to be great.] See quot. 1708.
1708 OCKLEY *Saracens* 111 The poor Christians, assoon as ever they heard the *Tecbîr*, (so the Arabs call the crying out *Allàh Acbar* ['God is greater']) were sensible that the City was lost. **1823** MRS. HEMANS *Siege Valencia* vi, The Moor is on his way! With the tambour-peal and the tecbir-shout. **1904** J. PARKINSON *Lays Love & War* 44 Shout the tekbir loud and long: On! swords of Islam.

tecch(e, techch(e, obs. ff. TACHE *sb.*¹

tecchy, obs. f. TETCHY.

tech (tɛk), *sb.*¹ *colloq.* (orig. *U.S.*). Also **tec.** Abbreviation for *Technical College, Technical School* (see TECHNICAL *a.* 3a), and *Institute of Technology.*
1906 *Dialect Notes* III. 161 *The Boston Tech., n. phr.* Massachusetts Institute of Technology. 'The best engineering school is Cornell; the next best is Michigan; and the next, Arkansas. *The Boston Tech.* aint in it.' **1911** H. QUICK *Yellowstone Nights* iii. 63 The insufferable breed of dubs—..who..called an Institute of Technology a 'Tech'. *Ibid.*, I shall have outlived the disgrace of my Tech. training. **1915** E. WALLACE *Man who bought London* viii. 79 'I'm off to the "Tec",' he said. *c* **1921** D. H. LAWRENCE *Mr. Noon* viii, in *Mod. Lover* (1934) 264 He vowed he'd go up to the Tech. with the book. **1947** *Book* (Christchurch, N.Z.) IX. 32, I told him no, I'd have to finish Tech, I wanted to get matric. **1969** D. COLLYER in R. Blythe *Akenfield* iv. 94 The young people..go to Ipswich Tec. or even to the university and they learn to talk about anything. **1974** *Sunday* (Charleston, S. Carolina) 7 Apr. 16-C/1 Texas Tech scientists will visit drought-stricken Africa to try to improve its resources and find a cure for famine and proverty. **1980** R. MCCRUM *In secret State* x. 86 Rosie's pride would not let her admit that she..had been to the local Tech.

tech (tɛk), *sb.*² Slang abbrev. of TECHNICIAN c.
1942 *Yank* 21 Oct. 15 They're the same kind of tech chevrons. **1953** *Mag. Fantasy & Sci. Fiction* Nov. 30 Let the techs worry about that. **1976** *Amer. Speech 1973* XLVIII. 194 They used to be called *orderlies.* Today, however, many of these assistants demand the title of *nursing tech* or *emergency room tech.* **1977** *R.A.F. News* 11–24 May 8/4 Chf Tech Mick Young..took part in a cycling expedition... Jnr Tech Rob Patrick..was a schoolboy.. cycling champion. **1980** A. SKINNER *Mind's Eye* xx. 258 He's got..a thing the other techs made him.

tech (tɛk), *sb.*³ [Abbrev. of TECHNOLOGY.]
1. high-tech = *high-technology* attrib. phr. s.v. TECHNOLOGY 1 d; *spec.* with reference to a style of architecture and interior design that imitates the functionalism of industrial technology. Also (unhyphened) as *sb. phr.* Similarly **low-tech** *attrib. phr.*
1972 *Last Whole Earth Catalog* (Portola Inst.) 247/1 It's the only high-tech home I've found at all lovable. **1978** KRON & SLESIN *High-Tech* 1 Some people call this phenomenon 'the industrial style', but we call it 'high-tech'. High-tech..is a term currently used in architectural circles to describe buildings incorporating prefabricated..building components. **1979** *Jrnl. R. Soc. Arts* Nov. 743/2 Late-Modernism takes the ideas and forms of the Modern Movement to an extreme, exaggerating the structure and technological image of the building beyond the point which the Modernists would have found acceptable, sometimes meriting the label 'High-Tech' as a result. **1980** *New Age* (U.S.) Oct. 36/2 A pocket calculator, a very high-tech gadget. **1981** *Farmstead Mag.* Winter 24/2 These solar greenhouses are often hi-tech. *Ibid.* 26/1 The low-tech greenhouse. **1983** *Times* 25 Jan. 26/7 Mrs Williams touched on such subjects as..the need for more 'high-tech'.

2. Chiefly *attrib.* = TECHNOLOGY 1 b. *rare.*
1982 *Times* 6 May 17/6 (*heading*) Whitehall backs new tech firms. **1983** *New Scientist* 16 June 769/3 (Advt.), Signaal, Philips space-tech company, has developed a meteorological ground station.

tech (tɛk), *a.* Colloq. (orig. *U.S.*) abbrev. of TECHNICAL *a.* ***techspeak*** [-SPEAK], technical jargon.
1956 [see LATENT *a.* j]. **1974** *Some Technical Terms & Slang* (Granada Television), *Tech run*, technical run. A rehearsal by the actors in the rehearsal room to which the technical staff who will be responsible for the programme in the studio are invited to sort out technical problems. **1974** *Globe & Mail* (Toronto) 20 Feb. 34/9 Will Genge aim at the championship aside from his duties as tech supervisor? **1982** *80 Microcomputing* Feb. 330/1 This is code, jargon, techspeak, whatever.

tech, var. TETCH, TACHE *Obs.*

teche, obs. f. TEACH; obs. f. *techy*: see TETCHY.

techie, techily, etc., obs. ff. TETCHY, etc.

technetium (tɛk'niːʃ(ɪ)əm). [mod.L., f. Gr. τεχνητ-ός artificial (f. τεχνᾶσθαι to make by art, f. τέχνη art, craft) + -IUM.] A dense, refractory, radioactive metallic element, chemically similar to rhenium, which occurs naturally only in trace amounts but is produced in reactors as a fission product of uranium and by neutron irradiation of molybdenum 98 and is used medically as a tracer in scintigraphy. Symbol Tc; atomic number 43. Formerly called MASURIUM.
1947 PERRIER & SEGRÈ in *Nature* 4 Jan. 24/1 We would like to propose the name of 'technetium', from the Greek τεχνητός, artificial, in recognition of the fact that technetium is the first artificially made element. The corresponding chemical symbol should be 'Tc'. **1960** J. KLEINBERG et al. *Inorg. Chem.* xxi. 535 The existence of the heptasulfides of technetium and rhenium and their mode of preparation emphasize the high degree of stability of these elements in the + 7 state. **1962** [see MASURIUM]. **1969** *New Scientist* 13 Mar. 564/1 Astrophysicists are puzzled to explain how the element technetium, which must be produced in the hot cores of stars, reaches the surface. **1974** *Encycl. Brit. Micropædia* IX. 859/2 Technetium metal looks like platinum but is usually obtained as a gray powder. **1977** *Lancet* 7 May 1012/1 Individual limbs were scanned 5–6 hr after administration of 10 mCi technetium-99m diphosphonate.

technetronic (,tɛknɪ'trɒnɪk), *a.* [ult. f. Gr. τέχνη art, craft + ELEC)TRONIC *a.*] Conditioned, determined, or shaped by advanced technology and electronic communications.
1967 Z. BRZEZINSKI in *New Republic* 23 Dec. 18/2 Our society..is entering a more self-conscious stage; ceasing to be an industrial society, it is being shaped to an ever-increasing extent by technology and electronics, and thus becoming the first *technetronic society.* **1970** D. GABOR *Innovations* i. 7 The 'modern industrial state' or the '*technetronic* society', as it has been variously called, is indeed above the head of the man in the street. **1977** *Time* 8 Aug. 10/2 The old order, based largely on military power and nationalism, is giving way to 'a technetronic age' in which there will be increasing emphasis on economic development and social justice.

technic ('tɛknɪk), *a.* and *sb.* [ad. L. *technic-us* (Quint.), a. Gr. τεχνικ-ός of or pertaining to art, f. τέχνη art, craft: see -IC. So F. *technique* (1721 in Hatz.-Darm.).]
A. *adj.* **1.** Pertaining to art, or to an art: = TECHNICAL. Now *rare.*
1612 STURTEVANT *Metallica* iii. 49 Define the Technick part. **1714** MANDEVILLE *Fab. Bees* (1729) II. vi. 347 All technick Words..and Terms of Art, belong to the respective Artists and Dealers, that primarily and literally make use of them in their Business. **1760** *Phil. Trans.* LI. 756 Terms..used in the strict technic sense. **1845** R. W. HAMILTON *Pop. Educ.* (ed. 2) viii. 187 The inhabitant of a manufacturing town has frequent proof of the intellectual difference between the rural, and the technic labourer. **1905** *Contemp. Rev.* Mar. 425 Our practical problem is now a technic and constructive one.

2. Skilfully made or constructed. [After Gr. τεχνικός (Hippocrates).] *rare*⁻¹.
1877 BLACKIE *Wise Men* 245 What a wealth of sounds Wends through the technic chambers of the ear.

B. *sb.* **1.** A technical term, expression, point, or detail; a technicality. Chiefly *U.S. rare.*
1826 T. FLINT *Recoll. Valley Mississippi* 86 A process, which, in the technics of the [Mississippi] boatmen is called *bush-whacking.* **1872** T. L. CUYLER *Heart Th.* 8 A right estimate of sin..is a vital point in the soul's salvation: it is more than a technic of theology. **1875** EMERSON *Lett. & Soc. Aims, Greatness* Wks. (Bohn) III. 272, I find it easy to translate all his [Napoleon's] technics into all of mine.

2. a. Technical details or methods collectively; the technical department of a subject; *esp.* the formal or mechanical part of an art (now chiefly *U.S.*; more commonly TECHNIQUE, q.v.).

[**1798** WILLICH *Adelung's Elem. Crit. Philos.* 181 Technic 1, in a proper sense, means art, causality according to ideas, purposes.] **1855** LEWES *Goethe* I. I. v. 49 His impatient susceptibility which..prevented his ever thoroughly mastering the technic of any one subject. **1867** M. ARNOLD *Celtic Lit.* 142 Icelandic poetry..shows a powerful and developed technic. **1887** LOWELL *Old Eng. Dram.* (1892) 56 In the technic of this art, perfection can be reached only by long training. **1908** *Arch. Internal Med.* II. 107 Cunningham's technic was crude. **1922** [see *encephalography* s.v. ENCEPHALO-]. **1931** [see PLASMODESMA]. **1943** H. L. MENCKEN *Heathen Days* vii. 93 The Fourth..went even worse than the Eroica, though it actually makes much less demand on technic. **1954** [see *immunohæmatology* s.v. IMMUNO-].

b. Collective pl. **technics** in same sense: also construed as a singular.

1850 LEITCH tr. *C. O. Müller's Anc. Art* §257 Antique vases..also, very grandly and beautifully designed, of the more perfect style of technics. **1871** MORLEY *Crit. Misc.* Ser. I. 256 Conformity to the accepted rules that constitute the technics of poetry. **1909** *Contemp. Rev.* Aug. 204 Literary technics, especially that of the novel, depends on reproducing experiments from life.

3. The science or study of art or arts, esp. of the mechanical or industrial arts: = TECHNOLOGY 1. Usually in pl. **technics**.

1864 in WEBSTER. **1865** S. H. HODGSON *Time & Space* II. ix. §68 Technic and Teleologic are the two branches of practical knowledge..and are both together, as Ethic, opposed to Theoretic. **1874** R. TYRWHITT *Sketch. Club* 87 You must study history, literature, and technics.

‖**technica** ('tɛknɪkə). [Latinized form of Gr. τεχνικά neuter pl. = technical matters, and of τεχνική fem. sing.] = TECHNIC B. 2, TECHNIQUE.

1782 [see CANCRIZANS *a.*]. **1796** BURNEY *Mem. Metastasio* III. 359 Definitions of the technica of ancient music. **1855** tr. *Labarte's Arts Mid. Ages* 2 Christian art, unable so immediately to create for itself a new technica, adopted the style of antiquity in its then degenerate state.

technical ('tɛknɪkəl), *a.* (*sb.*) [f. Gr. τεχνικ-ός (see TECHNIC) + -AL[1].]

A. *adj.* **1.** Of a person: Skilled in or practically conversant with some particular art or subject. Also *spec.* in the official designations of certain ranks in the armed forces of the U.K. and U.S.

1617 HALES *Serm. 2 Pet.* iii. 16. 19 Not to think themselues sufficiently provided vpon their acquaintance with some *Notitia*, or systeme of some technicall divine. **1817** JAS. MILL *Brit. India* III. ii. 81 The managers..not being technical men. **1917** 'CONTACT' *Airman's Outings* i. 6 As regards the mechanics, the quality of their skilled work is tempered by the technical sergeant-major, who knows most things about an aeroplane, and the quality of their behaviour by the disciplinary sergeant-major, usually an ex-regular with a lively talent for blasting. **1920** *Army & Navy Jrnl.* (U.S.) 26 June 1338/2 Enlisted men of the 'second grade' will be designated as Technical Sergeants or First Sergeants. **1926** *Brit. Gaz.* 12 May 3/2 At Basingstoke there is a supply of technical engineers available for work elsewhere. **1937** *Discovery* June 168/2 Behind the barge followed the baggage canoe, with two technical assistants and two polers. **1961** G. MILLERSON *Technique Television Production* 15 The technical director is in charge of the technical operational staff on the show. **1978** J. IRVING *World according to Garp* i. 15 Technical Sergeant Garp..served with the Eighth Air Force.

†**2.** Of a thing: Skilfully done or made: cf. TECHNIC *a.* 2. *Obs. rare*$^{-0}$.

1656 BLOUNT *Glossogr.*, *Technical* (*technicus*), artificial, cunning, done like a workman. [Perhaps never in Eng.]

3. a. Belonging or relating to an art or arts; appropriate or peculiar to, or characteristic of, a particular art, science, profession, or occupation; also, of or pertaining to the mechanical arts and applied sciences generally, as in ***technical education***, or ***technical college, school, university***.

technical difficulty, a difficulty arising in connexion with the method of procedure (esp. legal). ***technical fix*** (U.S.), a solution produced by technological means (sometimes used with an implication of superficiality). ***technical hitch***, an interruption or breakdown due to mechanical failure; *loosely*, an unexpected obstacle or snag. †***technical verse***, a verse intended to assist in memorizing something connected with a particular subject: cf. MEMORIA TECHNICA (*obs.*).

1727-41 CHAMBERS *Cycl.* s.v., Technical verses are commonly composed in Latin: they are generally wretched ones, and often barbarous; but..utility is all that is aimed at. **1739** *Works Learned* I. 139 He makes use of some Technical Lines or Verses. **1755** JOHNSON *Dict.* Pref., Of the terms of art I have received such as could be found either in books of science or technical dictionaries. **1855** MACAULAY *Hist. Eng.* xv. III. 714 Torrington had..been sent to the Tower... A technical difficulty had arisen about the mode of bringing him to trial. **1868** ROGERS *Pol. Econ.* xx. (1876) 265 Technical education, that is, the acquisition of scientific method and a knowledge of the principles and practice of the applied sciences. **1879** Technical university [see BUFF *sb.*[7] 1]. **1886** S. A. BARNETT in H. Barnett *Canon Barnett* (1918) II. xlv. 246 Relief must..provide training. It may be in technical schools in town. **1886** *Times* 20 May 5/5 Yesterday afternoon the foundation-stone of the Technical College, an extension of the existing Mechanics' Institute, was laid at Keighley. **1909** *Kelly's Directory of Oxf.* 128/2 The City of Oxford Municipal Technical Schools..are secondary and technical schools under the regulation of the Board of Education... They consist of chemical and physical laboratories and lecture rooms, workshops, art rooms, and class rooms. **1940** P. FLEMING *Flying Visit* v. 37 [Hitler] remained an equally great man to-day and (despite a technical hitch) equally capable of fulfilling his mission. **1958** 'R. CROMPTON' *William's Television Show* v. 148 Couldn't we say there's been a technical hitch? **1962** D. LESSING *Golden Notebk.* 528 It [*sc.* a film] was running slowly, because there was a technical hitch of some kind. **1971** *N.Y. Times* 8 Sept. 44/2 In recent centuries the scientific revolution has provided much warrant for the notion of the 'technical fix', the idea that scientists or technologists can find an appropriate solution for every problem. **1978** *Nagel's Encycl.-Guide: China* 318 The Technical Universities are in fact like polytechnic or engineering schools, and contain as many faculties as they do specialities. **1980** *Directory of Technical & Further Educ.* (ed. 18) p. xvi, *Technical colleges*, so-called, are usually fairly old-established, with a range of courses for full-time and part-time, day release or block release students, traditionally in engineering, at the levels of Ordinary and often Higher National Certificate..or Diploma. **1980** *New Age* (U.S.) Oct. 30/1 It greatly under-estimates the energy savings possible through technical fixes alone—that is, through well-known and presently economic technical measures that would have no significant effect on our lifestyles or economic output.

b. *spec.* said of words, terms, phrases, etc., or of their senses or acceptations; as, the ***technical terms*** of logic; the ***technical sense*** of 'subject' in logic.

[**1634** JACKSON *Creed* VII. xxviii. §3 'The mercy of the Lord' or of 'the word of God' is τὸ τεχνικὸν, that is a word or term whose full importance cannot be had from any ordinary lexicon, unless it be such as is proper unto divinity.] *a* **1652** [implied in TECHNICALLY *adv.*]. **1704** J. HARRIS *Lex. Techn.* I. s.v., The Terms of Art are commonly called *Technical Words*. **1739** LABELYE *Short Acc. Piers Westm. Bridge* p. iv, Avoiding as much as possible all technical Terms. **1778** JEFFERSON *Autobiog.* App., Wks. 1859 I. 146 Preserving..the very words of the established law, wherever their meaning had been..rendered technical by usage. **1809** SYD. SMITH *Charac. Fox* Wks. 1859 I. 153/1 In a science like law there must be technical phrases, known only to professional men. **1875** JOWETT *Plato* (ed. 2) IV. 420 No former philosopher had ever carried the use of technical terms to the same extent as Hegel.

c. *transf.* Of an author, a treatise, etc.: Using technical terms; treating a subject technically.

1779 *Mirror* No. 48 ¶ 1, I have since been endeavouring to make it a little less technical, in order to fit it more for general perusal. *a* **1832** MACKINTOSH *Rev. of 1688* Wks. 1846 II. 295 The Crown lawyers... Powis was feebly technical, and Williams was offensively violent. **1896** *N. & Q.* 8th Ser. IX. 160/2 [The book] is somewhat too technical for any one who is not a botanist.

d. Technically so called or regarded; that is such from the technical point of view. ***technical foul*** (Basketball), a foul which does not involve contact between opponents; also *ellipt.* as *sb.*; ***technical knockout*** (Boxing), the termination of a fight by the referee on the grounds of one boxer's inability to continue (though not counted out), his opponent being declared the winner; abbrev. *TKO*, *t.k.o.*: see T 6.

1860 MOTLEY *Netherl.* (1868) I. i. 20 Permission for soldiers to retreat with technical honour. **1868** [cf. TECHNICALLY]. **1921** *Daily Colonist* (Victoria, B.C.) 6 Apr. 10/3 Denial of a report from Saskatoon that in a boxing match in that city on March 24 Bill Barton, of Vancouver, had secured a technical knockout over Billy Mackenzie. **1934** WEBSTER s.v. Foul, *Technical foul*. **1958** F. C. AVIS *Boxing Ref. Dict.* 112 *Technical Knock Out*, the decision of the referee when stopping the contest in which one of the boxers, though not knocked out, is scarcely capable of proceeding. **1962** *Times* 2 Aug. 3/3 The ball went to hand off his bat on seven occasions. Most were only technical chances [of a catch], although both Taylor and Swallow..would have held their respective catches more often than not. **1974** *Spartanburg* (S. Carolina) *Herald-Jrnl.* 21 Apr. B1/3 Oscar Robertson sank a free throw on the technical, and Jon McGlocklin hit a long jumper after the Bucks put the ball in play. **1977** *Times* 21 June 10/1 Other technical chances escaped McCosker and O'Keeffe, both at slip, as the ball..moved about off the seam. **1981** *Washington Post* 17 Feb. D2/2 Before they sat down they had been assessed a technical foul... After Davis missed the first shot of the technical Skipper made the second.

e. So regarded according to a strict legal interpretation. Usu. in phr. ***technical assault***.

1911 *Encycl. Brit.* XX. 769/1 Finding himself non-suited in a court of law he commits a technical assault upon..some high legal functionary. **1914** A. HARRISON *Kaiser's War* 126 He [*sc.* an officer] may not accept an apology in the event of a technical assault. Thus a man who on leaving a café, for example, brushes against an officer, is technically liable to be cut down. **1920** WODEHOUSE *Damsel in Distress* vi. 84 'You ought to have had the scoundrel arrested,' he said vehemently. 'It was a technical assault.'

4. *Finance.* Of, pertaining to, or designating a market in which prices are determined chiefly by internal factors (see also quot. 1962).

1909 in WEBSTER. **1946** *Sun* (Baltimore) 17 July 14/1 A certain amount of support was attracted to individual favorites on the idea the list may have been oversold and was due for a technical comeback. **1962** S. STRAND *Marketing Dict.* 732 *Technical position*, a term applied to the various internal factors affecting the market; opposed to external forces such as earnings, dividends, political considerations and general economic conditions. Some internal factors considered in appraising the market's technical position include the size of the short interest, whether the market has had a sustained advance or decline without interruption, a sharp advance or decline on a small volume and the amount of credit in use in the market. **1981** *Times* 22 July 22/6 Most sections of the market staged a technical rally. **1983** *Times* 2 Apr. 10/5 The market remained technical, with positions being covered, and a marked reluctance shown to open new positions.

B. *sb.* In *pl.* Technical terms or points; technicalities.

1790 *Bystander* 352 Prone to..scold in technicals which they know not how to apply. **1825** *Eng. Life* II. 254 The cramped and barbarous technicals of law. **1863** D. G. MITCHELL *My Farm of Edgewood* 236 The latter has a wall about him of self-confidence, ignorance of technicals.

Hence '**technicalism**, technical style, method, or treatment; addiction to technicalities; '**technicalist**, one versed in or addicted to technicalities; '**technicalize** *v. trans.*, to make technical, give a technical meaning to; '**technicalness**, the quality of being technical, technicality.

1808 BENTHAM *Sc. Reform* 80 Such ingenuity is not wanting to English-bred *technicalism. **1857** TOULMIN SMITH *Parish* Pref. 111 Not frozen-up in dry technicalism, but dealing with the human reality attaching to an important Institution of free men. **1802-12** BENTHAM *Ration. Judic. Evid.* (1827) II. 415 Not altogether a secret to the *technicalists. **1884** *Times* 9 Feb., Every technicalist takes too narrow a view. **1852** LEWIS *Methods Obs. & Reason. Politics* I. 78 Words current in the language of ordinary life..were (if we may be allowed the expression) *technicalized. **1828-32** WEBSTER, **Technicalness*.

technicality (tɛknɪ'kælɪtɪ). [f. prec. + -ITY.]

1. Technical quality or character; the use of technical terms or methods.

1828-32 WEBSTER, *Technicalness*, *Technicality*, the quality or state of being technical or peculiar to the arts. *Forster*. **1857** TOULMIN SMITH *Parish* 266 The case is a very simple one, when divested of technicality. **1863** COWDEN CLARKE *Shaks. Char.* iii. 88 He dilates upon the weapons..with an accurate and professor-like technicality.

2. A technical point, detail, term, or expression; something peculiar or specially belonging to the art or subject referred to. Usually in *pl.*

1814 SCOTT *Wav.* lii, A sort of martinet attention to the minutiæ and technicalities of discipline. **1859** GULLICK & TIMBS *Paint.* 190 Various other technicalities and artistic appliances may also be explained. **1874** L. STEPHEN *Hours in Library* (1892) I. vii. 261 To translate the technicalities of Kant into plain English. **1885** S. COX *Expositions* I. xxxii. 372 This phrase, 'the Saviour of the world', has come to be little more than a technicality, which we use without much thought or emotion.

technically ('tɛknɪkəlɪ), *adv.* [f. as prec. + -LY[2].] In a technical manner; in relation to the arts and applied sciences, or to a particular art or subject; according to technical methods; in technical phraseology; in a technical sense.

a **1652** J. SMITH *Sel. Disc.* vi. 247 That part of divine inspiration, which was more technically and properly by the Jews called prophecy. **1774** WARTON *Hist. Eng. Poetry* lxii. (1840) III. 404 The first professed English satirist, to speak technically, is bishop Joseph Hall. **1834-5** J. PHILLIPS *Geol.* in *Encycl. Metrop.* VI. 535/1 Confined to what is technically called the Crust of the Earth. **1868** FREEMAN *Norm. Conq.* II. viii. 223 A family which, though perhaps not technically noble, was..eminent and honourable.

technician (tɛk'nɪʃən). [f. TECHNIC + -IAN.]

a. A person conversant with the technicalities of a particular subject. **b.** One skilled in the technique or mechanical part of an art, as music or painting.

1833 SARAH AUSTIN *Charac. Goethe* I. 216 Grammarians and technicians are bound..to acknowledge these his efforts. **1895** H. A. KENNEDY in *19th Cent.* Aug. 331 The mere technician can never interest; the literary man, even if inexpert in stage *technique*, may do so in a high degree. **1905** *Times* 20 May 8/3 The modern violinist is not necessarily a mere technician. **1909** *Athenæum* 7 Aug. 158/3 The book..not being sufficiently detailed for the technician.

c. *spec.* A person qualified in the practical application of one of the sciences or mechanical arts; now esp., a person whose job is to carry out practical work in a laboratory or to give assistance with technical equipment.

1939 W. A. RICHARDSON *Technical College* xxv. 476 There are certain high-grade technicians, e.g. chemists, physicists, mathematical engineers, who will be engaged in the more elaborate design problems, in industrial research and investigation. **1952**, etc. [see TECHNOLOGIST]. **1954** *Rep. Patent Cases* LXX. 150 The Defendants have a most elaborate system for bringing to the attention of their technicians all technical developments relevant to their work. **1968** *Ibid.* LXXXV. 104 Extracts from laboratory notebooks or other specific records pertaining to the particular strains employed by the laboratory technicians. **1972** *Daily Tel.* 9 Feb. 12 Note that word 'technician'. From today there are no more 'mechanics' at Ford Sure dealers. 'We have changed the name because we think it is time that we built up the image of the man in the workshop.' **1983** *N.Y. Times* 11 Aug. A10/6 French technicians scurry around at the military air base assembling machine guns and helicopters.

technicism ('tɛknɪsɪz(ə)m). [f. as prec. + -ISM: cf. mod.L. *technicismus*, Kant 1790.]

1. A technical term or expression, a technicality.

1799 ANNA SEWARD *Lett.* (1821) V. 263 Bewildered in a maze of scholastic technicisms.

2. Technical quality or character; a condition in which practical results or methods are stressed.

1932 tr. *Ortega y Gasset's Revolt of Masses* vi. 61 Three principals have made possible this new world: liberal democracy, scientific experiment, and industrialism. The two latter may be summed-up in one word: technicism. **1951** *Archit. Rev.* CX. 203/2 There is also research into aesthetic functions, and it is due only to this latter, if, instead of arriving at a dry technicism or mere utilitarianism, the modern movement has led to a true new style in architecture. **1977** *Times Educ. Suppl.* 21 Oct. 32/3 Even in the Bullock report.. one yet senses, ultimately, a dreary technicism of mind... The report is written in the language of death.

technicist ('tɛknɪsɪst). [f. as prec. + -IST.]

1. = TECHNICIAN; one who has technical knowledge.

1881 T. HARDY *Laodicean* III. xi, Somerset himself [an architect] as chief technicist working out his designs on the spot. **1906** *Academy* 20 June 617/1 Turner's greatest admirers are the painters, and Mr. Wyllie.. enjoys it [T.'s work] with the exquisite pleasure of the technicist.

2. *attrib.* or as *adj.* Of or pertaining to technicism (sense 2).

1932 tr. *Ortega y Gasset's Revolt of Masses* 151 We are told quite seriously that the essence of America is its practical and technicist conception of life. **1974** *Times* 16 Mar. 16 A technicist society indifferent to location and continuity will undermine itself by wrecking the structures of meaning on which any society must rest.

technicize ('tɛknɪsaɪz), *v. rare.* [f. TECHNIC *a.* + -IZE.] *trans.* To make technical; to subject to a high degree of technicality. Hence **technici'zation**; **'technicized** *ppl. a.*

1927 A. HUXLEY *Proper Studies* 137 The world will become even more completely technicized, even more elaborately regimented, than it is at present. **1959** —— *Let.* 6 May (1969) 869 It dealt with.. advancing technicization of everything. **1972** *Listener* 31 Aug. 270/3 The predominant effort.. to hang on to and 'technicise' the cult of the socialised warrior—ally the socialised warrior with technology, that is. **1975** J. DE BRES tr. *Mandel's Late Capitalism* vii. 243 A far more technicized division of labour now replaces the old factory hierarchy.

technico-, combining element from Gr. τεχνικός (see TECHNIC). **1.** Forming sbs., as **techni'cology**, = TECHNOLOGY (senses 1 and 2). **techni'cophilist**, *nonce-wd.* [Gr. -φιλος -loving], a lover of technicalities.

1849 SEARS *Regeneration* III. xii. (1859) 242 The barren *technicologies of schools and sects. **1880** W. SENIOR *Trav. & Trout in Antipodes* 80 Reading out the botanical technicology. **1884** *Manch. Exam.* 17 May 4/8 Schools and museums of technicology scattered over the Continent. **1861** *Zoologist* Ser. I. XIX. 7299 This word.. has the.. merit, always prized by *technicophilists, of being more difficult to pronounce.

2. Forming adjs., as ***technico-architectonic***, ***-diplomatic***, ***-economic***, etc.

1951 M. LOWRY *Let.* Feb. (1967) 233 Is this a technical technico-architechtonic [*sic*]term? **1970** *New Scientist* 30 July 219/1 Prime Minister Vorster.. scored a considerable technico-diplomatic success. **1970** E. SNOW *Red China Today* (new ed.) 36 The solution of technico-economic problems of social transformation. *Ibid.*, Centrally led priority programs for essential technico-scientific specialists. **1973** D. OSMOND-SMITH tr. *Bettetini's Lang. & Technique of Film* i. 45 However, a morphological study of the film, even if conducted on a syntactic level, cannot leave out of account considerations of a technico-grammatical nature.

Technicolor ('tɛknɪkʌlə(r)). Also **-our**.

1. A proprietary name for various processes of colour cinematography, esp. ones employing dye transfer and separation negatives. Freq. *attrib.*

1917 *U.S. Patent 1,231,710* Daniel F. Comstock... Assignor, by Mesne Assignments, to Technicolor Motion Picture Corporation, of Boston, Massachusetts. **1929** *Official Gaz.* (U.S. Patent Office) 3 Dec. 24/1 *Technicolor* for motion-picture films. **1930** *Punch* 2 Apr. 385 *Show of Shows* at the Tivoli, the latest and greatest of technicolour talkie reviews. **1932** *Discovery* Dec. 382/2 The subtractive process .. has been familiar to picture-goers in the many Technicolor films shown in this country. **1948** *Time* 22 Mar. 85/3 Herbert T. Kalmus,.. the co-inventor, developer, majority stockholder and president of Technicolor,.. is a graduate of Massachusetts Institute of Technology (after which Technicolor was named). **1950** *Trade Marks Jrnl.* 5 Apr. 314/2 *Technicolor*... Photographic apparatus, cinematographic apparatus, television apparatus, apparatus capable of transmitting and receiving pictures in colour, and talking machines. Technicolor Motion Picture Corporation... 4th August 1949. **1976** L.-A. BAWDEN *Oxf. Compan. Film* 681/1 A special projector with two apertures —one with a red filter, the other with a green filter—was needed to show early Technicolor films. *Ibid.* 682/1 Eastman Color, introduced in 1949, changed the whole nature of colour filming and from 1951 onwards Technicolor prints were made, still by dye transfer, almost exclusively from Eastman Color negative. **1978** *Amer. Poetry Rev.* Sept./Oct. 10/2 'On the Towpath' begins in black-and-white and quickly shifts to technicolor.

2. *transf.* and *fig.* (Also with small initial.) Vivid colour characteristic of colour cinematography. Chiefly *attrib.* and in phr. ***in glorious*** (***gorgeous***, etc.) ***Technicolor***.

a **1940** F. SCOTT FITZGERALD *Last Tycoon* (1941) v. 95 The theme.. would come in some such guise as the auto horns from the Technicolor boulevards below. **1946** J. B. PRIESTLEY *Bright Day* v. 130 She looked very beautiful, and in glorious technicolour. **1954** M. PROCTER *Hell is City* I. vi. 35 A natural blonde of Technicolor brilliance. **1960** M. STEWART *My Brother Michael* ii. 25 The heavy Technicolor prosperity of the plains. **1962** N. DEL MAR *Richard Strauss* iii. 85 The glorious technicolour of Strauss's orchestra. **1966** *Listener* 13 Jan. 71/2 Illustrations in black and white and gorgeous Technicolor. **1977** *New Yorker* 12 Sept. 32/3 A Technicolor-red leotard that matched her lips and her spike heels. **1979** *Church Times* 2 Nov. 9/1 Evelyn Waugh has described how some glamorise it [*sc.* death] in glorious technicolour.

Hence **'technicolored** *a.*

1947 E. F. RUSSELL in Aldiss & Harrison *Decade 1940s* (1975) 166 'Laura [*sc.* a macaw] loves nuts.' 'I know it, you technicoloured bully.' **1954** *Newsweek* 27 Dec. 60/2 The palpable business of this Technicolored and CinemaScope production lies in its physical trappings, its underwater photography, and its action. **1962** *Movie* Sept. 22/1 Setting the events of the previous summer on the Riviera as technicolored flashbacks from the black-and-white Parisian winter. **1982** *New Scientist* 21 Jan. 179/2 Our face fuzz makes a pretty poor showing when compared with that bird's [*sc.* the peacock's] exuberant sensuality: you'd think evolution would have provided us with something more spectacular and 'Technicolored'.

technics: see TECHNIC B.

‖**technicum** ('tɛknɪkəm). Also **tekhnikum**. Pl. **-s**, ‖**-y**. [ad. Russ. *tekhnikum*, f. mod.L. *technicum*, neut. sing. of *technicus* technical (see TECHNIC *a.* and *sb.*).] In the U.S.S.R., a technical college.

1932 M. DOBB *Soviet Russia & World* ii. 43 To-day there are 663 middle technical schools, or *technicums.* **1957** H. BOWER *Short Guide Soviet Life* xiii. 52 Technical Colleges (tekhnikumy) train specialist technicians for a wide range of industries and take pupils from 14 to 30. **1963** *Higher Educ.: Rep. Comm. under Ld. Robbins 1961–3* v. 43 in *Parl. Papers 1962–3* (Cmnd. 2154) XI. 639 In the Soviet Union, the output of *Technicums* is not included. **1974** T. P. WHITNEY tr. *Solzhenitsyn's Gulag Archipelago* I. I. ii. 72 In Leningrad .. the Latvian Technicum, and the Latvian and Estonian newspapers were all closed down.

technification (ˌtɛknɪfɪ'keɪʃən). [f. *techn-* as in TECHNICAL *a.*, etc. + -IFICATION.] The adoption or imposition of technical methods. Also **'technified** *ppl. a.*, **'technify** *v. intr.* (both *rare*).

1959 A. HUXLEY *Let.* 4 Jan. (1969) 859 In time, I suspect, all fully technified societies will adopt the Russian solution. **1959** *Ibid.* 5 Jan., It may be that the only satisfactory solution.. is to accept the inevitability of the technification of everything. **1962** *Spectator* 16 Feb. 199/2 The technification of conditioning minds by emotional images. **1970** J. COTLER in I. L. Horowitz *Masses in Lat. Amer.* xii. 429 Those who might have found employment in the exploitation of sugar and have been unable to do so due to technification, have had to remain in their miserable plots. **1972** *Listener* 18 May 640 This method is designed to be effective against other industrial and technified countries, whose organisation can be so disrupted that they simply can no longer function. **1973** *Harper's Mag.* Nov. 82 They internalized their intelligence activities with headlong speed. They technified senselessly—charts, graphs, bugs, concealed cameras.

technique (tɛk'niːk). [a. F. (*la*) *technique*, subst. use of *technique* adj., TECHNIC. Cf. Ger. *die technik.*]

a. Manner of artistic execution or performance in relation to formal or practical details (as distinct from general effect, expression, sentiment, etc.); the mechanical or formal part of an art, esp. of any of the fine arts; the manner of execution or performance in any discipline, profession, or sport; also, skill or ability in this department of one's art; mechanical skill in artistic or technical work (freq. used without article or qualifying word). *loosely*, a skilful or efficient means of achieving a purpose; a characteristic way of proceeding; a knack, a trick.

(At first used most commonly in reference to painting or musical performance.)

1817 COLERIDGE *Biog. Lit.* I. iv. 83 Illogical phrases.. which hold so distinguished a place in the *technique* of ordinary poetry. **1875** FORTNUM *Maiolica* xii. 122 Mr. Robinson speaks of this specimen as 'being of the most perfect technique of the master'. **1876** STEDMAN *Victorian Poets* 289 Their [poetic] work, however curious in technique, fails to permanently impress even the refined reader. **1884** GROVE *Dict. Mus.* IV. 66 A player may be perfect in technique, and yet have neither soul nor intelligence. **1885** *Spectator* 30 May 704/2 [Victor Hugo's] improvement of the technique of versification. **1886** *Mag. Art* Dec. 42/1 (Stanf.) His technique is somewhat sketchy, .. and his colours extremely light. **1900** *Jrnl. Sch. Geog.* (U.S.) June 213 The technique of raising cotton, or celery, or Indian corn. **1903** [see ASTROPHOTOGRAPHY]. **1920** OSWALD & PRYCE *Terra Sigillata* ii. 3 The technique of the green-glazed ware was also to a great extent similar to that of the red-glazed fabric; *e.g.* in the use of moulds with impressed designs.. and both techniques were obviously inspired by prototypes in beaten metal. **1932** A. HUXLEY *Brave New World* i. 15 If they could discover a technique for shortening the period of maturation what a triumph, what a benefaction to Society! **1940** K. MANNHEIM *Man & Society* v. i. 244 Any deliberate rebuilding of human groups in terms of more elastic organization represents another chapter in the development of social techniques. **1959** C. PORTER *Rowing to Win* ii. 40 The measure by which the appearance and technique of a Russian crew differs from that of an American crew is that of the difference in their styles... By style, then, I mean largely the technique of rowing. **1968** J. D. WATSON *Double Helix* (1970) x. 63 The witchcraft-like techniques of the biochemist. **1972** M. KLINE *Math. Thought* xiii. 282 The more complicated algebraic techniques.

(*b*) **1905** A. BENNETT *Sacred & Profane Love* I. ii. 23 A generation of pianists who had lifted technique to a plane of which neither Liszt nor Rubenstein dreamed. **1935** W. S. MAUGHAM *Don Fernando* x. 185 Technique is only the method by which the artist achieves his aim. **1960** P. GOODMAN *Growing Up Absurd* iv. 89 'The trainee,' says William H. Whyte, Jr., 'believes managing is an end in itself —technique is more vital than content.'

(*c*) **1936** J. A. LEE *Hunted* II. 49 When brought back they told the story of their venturings, so that northern runaways knew the technique of stealing a passage. **1941** *Punch* 31 Dec. 583/1 There is quite a technique to washing a blanket. **1944** E. S. GARDNER *Case of Black-eyed Blonde* ii. 22 Now then, you little son-of-a-bitch,.. that technique of planting the diamond pendant is something you used about three years ago on that maid your mother had. **1955** L. P. HARTLEY *Perfect Woman* xiii. 126 She'll want to know all about you—that's her technique. **1979** D. HALBERSTAM *Powers that Be* (1980) I. v. 273 In 1953 Barth wrote an editorial attacking the FBI's technique of gathering irrelevant information in its investigations and making the information a part of a person's dossier.

b. *spec.* Manner of performance or skill in sexual relations.

1921 M. ARLEN *Romantic Lady* 11 She was very close to me, smiling, intimate. Pure coquetry, of course—but what perfect *technique*! **1930** V. SACKVILLE-WEST *Edwardians* vi. 296 When he chose, his technique could be faultless... He was very gentle with Teresa. **1964** R. BRADDON *Year Angry Rabbit* ix. 80 The American servicemen appeared to retain an atavistic but irresistible technique with girls which outraged the local boys. **1974** V. GIELGUD *In Such a Night* viii. 71 Alec looks at every woman.. like that... He hasn't altered his technique.

technism ('tɛknɪz(ə)m). *rare*[−0]. [f. Gr. τέχνη art, or Eng. TECHN-IC + -ISM; cf. *mechanism.*] 'Technicality' (Webster 1864). So **'technist**, one who deals with a subject technically.

1885 *Nature* 5 Feb. 314/2 The light of that comet was of the kind familiarly known among technists as 'the candle-spectrum'.

techno- (tɛknəʊ), repr. Gr. τεχνο-, combining form of τέχνη art, occurring in TECHNOLOGY, etc.; ***techno-co'mmercial***, ***-eco'nomic*** adjs.; also in the following terms: **'technocomplex** *Archæol.* (see quot. 1968). **'technofear** = *technophobia* below. **'technofreak** [FREAK *sb.*[1] 4 c], an enthusiast for technology or for the technical complexities of a particular piece of equipment; hence **techno-'freakish** *a.* **techno'graphic** *a.* **techno-graphy** (-'ɒgrəfɪ) [-GRAPHY], the description of the arts, forming the preliminary stage of technology (TECHNOLOGY 1); hence **tech'nographer**, one versed in technography; **technographic** (-'græfɪk) *a.* **techno-'manager**, a person who is both a technologist and a manager; hence **ˌtechno-mana'gerial** *a.* **techno'mania**, a mania for technology; hence **techno'maniac**. **ˌtechno-me'chanic** *a.* (*nonce-wd.*), pertaining to mechanical art (in quot. absol. as *sb.*). **technonomy** (-'ɒnəmɪ) [-NOMY], the practical application of the principles of the arts, forming the final stage of technology; hence **technonomic** (-'nɒmɪk) *a.* (*Cent. Dict.* 1891). **'technophile**, one who favours technology. **techno'phobia**, fear of technology; so **'technophobe**, a person who fears technology. **tech'nopolis** [-POLIS], a society dominated by technology; hence **techno'politan** *a.* **'technosphere** [-SPHERE], the technological aspect of human activity. **'technostress** orig. *U.S.*, (psychosomatic illness caused by) stress arising from working in an environment dominated by (*esp.* computer) technology; hence **'technostressed** *a.*, affected by technostress. **'technostructure**, a group of technologists or technical experts that controls the workings of industry or government. **techno'tronic** *a.* = TECHNETRONIC *a.*

1937 *Discovery* Aug. 254/1 The history of this material [*sc.* synthetic rubber] from the early 'academic synthesis' period, through the 'techno-commercial' period, up to the present time. **1979** J. E. ROWLEY *Mechanised In-House Information Syst.* II. 107 Some units.. assign equal importance to scientific and technical information and techno-commercial material. **1968** D. L. CLARKE *Analytical Archaeol.* viii. 357 *Technocomplex*, a group of cultures characterized by assemblages sharing a polythetic range but differing specific types of the same general families of artefact-types, shared as a widely diffused and interlinked response to common factors in environment, economy and technology. **1976** *Sci. Amer.* Feb. 94/2 What game animals supported the hunters of the Tanged Point Techno-complex? **1980** *Cambr. Encycl. Archaeol.* 69/1 The long, stable period of the Oldowan technocomplex. **1960** Techno-economic [see FEED *v.* 8 e (ii)]. **1976** *Nature* 5 Feb. 355/2 A team.. will be responsible for investigations into the cost-benefit of research done by the BSC and for techno-economic analysis. **1980** *Times* 14 Mar. 20/3 The consumer is still suffering from what many dealers are beginning to call 'technofear'—fear of commitment to purchasing anything in case the technology changes. **1983** *Times* 28 Sept. 3/3 Techno-fear.. is defined as 'difficulties in accepting and using high-technology products in the home'. **1973** *Absolute Sound* I. II. 42 We have always known it [*sc.* the audio industry] was dominated by techno freaks with an unhealthy irreverence for the live sound. *Ibid.* III. 173 His prose is.. so technofreakish,.. so filled with demonstrations that the Great Expert is at work that it is incomprehensible to virtually every informed audiophile we know. **1983** *Austral. Personal Computer* June/July 62/1 A neat piece of technology that.. ought to interest any technofreak simply because it's such a good idea. **1900** *Amer. Anthropologist* Jan.–Mar. 164 The technographer pursues a single art over time and place until he knows it thoroughly. **1891** *Ann. Rep. Smithsonian Inst. 1889–90* I. 611 The Kunstgewerbe Museum contains much that is like the ethnographic collection, but the reigning concept is technographic. **1895** *Funk's Stand. Dict.*, *Technographic.* **1900** *Amer. Anthropologist* Jan.–Mar. 164 There are two ways of looking at human inventions, the one ethnographic, the other technographic. **1881** MASON in *Smithsonian Rep.* 501 Observing and descriptive stage... Technography. Inductive and classifying stage... Technology. Deductive and predictive stage... Technonomy. **1962** A. SAMPSON *Anat. Britain* xiii. 211 It was only after France and Germany had founded their *polytechniques* and *hochschule* [sic] for techno-managers that Britain gradually felt the need to adapt their universities to technical education. **1979** *Times of India* 17 Aug. 12 (Advt.), It has set up a full-fledged Consultancy & Promotional Cell with Indian and Foreign experts for providing technomanagerial Consultancy Services for improving the operational and managerial efficiency of consumer cooperatives. **1969** *Daily Tel.* 29 May 28/3 The days when almost any scientific team could wrest enormous sums from the taxpayer to finance big, glamorous and spectacular projects were coming to an end... 'The era of technomania is passing—and high time too,' Mr. Benn said. *Ibid.* 30 May 20/3 Shall I, who have hated technology all my life... Turn technomaniac myself? **1833** SARAH AUSTIN *Charac. Goethe* I. 187 Persuaded of the co-operation of the Techno-mechanic with the Dynamo-ideal, [I] had Seebeck's cross embroidered like damask, and could now see it in whatever light I chose, clear or dim, on an uniform surface. **1968** H. WEAVER tr. *Ellul's Critique of New Commonplaces* 236 This commonplace is really very common among technicians, technologists, technolasters, technophagi, technophiles, technocrats, [etc.] **1983** *Daily Tel.* 28 Nov. 12/1 Those technophiles disappointed by the absence of innovative features in IBM's newly announced P.C. Junior home computer have overlooked one splendid novelty. **1965** *New Statesman* 27 Aug. 286/1 Instead of leading us to the golden age, science is dragging us down into a servile, stable hell. Shades of Orwell! Technophobia has struck another good man down. *Ibid.*, The incipient technophobe will rage against the motor-murder of 20 people a day in Britain, without once considering that cars also carry 50 million people and their goods. **1965** H. C. COX *Secular City* 5 We shall make use of a somewhat contrived word, *technopolis*. It will be used here to signify the fusion of technological and political components into the base on which a new cultural style has appeared... it will call to mind the fact that the contemporary secular metropolis was not possible before modern technology. *Ibid.* iii. 63 To say that technopolitan man is pragmatic means that he is a kind of modern ascetic. He disciplines himself to give up certain things... Life for him is a set of problems, not an unfathomable mystery. **1969** HUXLEY & NICHOLSON in *Times* 7 Oct. 8/1 The most striking change which it has brought is to create out of a mass of economic, social and technical developments, an entire semi-autonomous new system, which we may call the technosphere, with its own structure and anatomy, its own programmed inputs and outputs, and its accidental or deliberate releases into the biosphere. **1983** *Washington Post* 15 June B5 A new exercise guide featuring an array of do-at-your-desk stretches designed to combat techno-stress. **1984** *Eastern Airlines Rev.* Sept. 27/2 Technostress is a modern disease of adaptation caused by an inability to cope with the new computer technologies in a healthy manner. **1986** *Datalink* 26 May 14/5 Technostress.. can be cured by greater involvement with people and less involvement with computers. **1984** C. BROD *Technostress* ii. 41 Mental fatigue becomes a familiar feeling for the technostressed individual. **1967** J. K. GALBRAITH *New Industrial State* vi. 71 Management.. includes.. only a small proportion of those who.. contribute information to group decisions. This.. group.. extends from the most senior officials of the corporation to.. blue collar workers... This.. is the guiding intelligence—the brain—of the enterprise... I propose to call this organization the Technostructure. **1978** *Nature* 9 Nov. 147/2 In discussing the origins of the Soviet technical intelligentsia (throughout inelegantly and inaccurately termed the 'technostructure'), Bailes draws on an impressive range of sources, both Soviet and Western. **1969** *Daily Tel.* 23 Apr. 16/3 The 'technotronic society', as the mass technical world is now sometimes labelled, creates its own problems.

technocracy (tɛk'nɒkrəsɪ). orig. *U.S.* [f. TECHNO- + -CRACY.] The control of society or industry by technical experts; a ruling body of such experts.

Technocracy has been the name of various groups advocating the technical control of society, esp. Technocracy, Inc., established in New York in 1932–3 by Howard Scott.

1919 W. H. SMYTH in *Industr. Management* Mar. 211/2 For this unique experiment in rationalized Industrial Democracy I have coined the term 'technocracy'. **1932** *N.Y. Herald-Tribune* 15 Dec. 11/1 Technocracy.. the name for a new system and philosophy of government, in which the nation's industrial resources should be organized and managed by technically competent persons for the good of everyone instead of being left to the management of private interests for their own advantage. **1945** C. S. LEWIS *That Hideous Strength* xii. 318 The effect of modern war is to eliminate retrogressive types, while sparing the technocracy and increasing its hold upon public affairs. **1947** *Mind* LVI. 164 Such notions as social and economic planning, technocracy,.. the denial of natural rights and individual liberties, etc., are due to them [*sc.* French Utopians, St. Simon, etc.] more than to Godwin or the Utilitarians. **1955** *Times* 23 May 3/4 On the unlikely day when England elects a benevolent technocracy to power a Bill will be passed forbidding more than one performance per year per town of such works as *The Messiah*, the *St. Matthew Passion*, [etc.]. **1975** *Political Studies* XXIII. 82 Nevertheless, if technocracy means rule not just by *individuals* who are members of a particular technocratic *élite*, but rule by a technocratic class as such, one has to show that the latter has either a common interest to defend or a common ideology to pursue.

Hence **'technocrat**, (*a*) an advocate of technocracy; (*b*) a member of a technocracy, a technologist exercising administrative power; **techno'cratic** *a.*; **tech'nocratism**.

1932 *Sun* (Baltimore) 12 Dec. 6/3 The Technocrats, thanks.. largely to a peculiarly fetching 'trade label' which embodies in one word two of the most far-reaching of current concepts, technology and democracy, are succeeding in a remarkable degree in breaking down the apathy. **1932** *N.Y. Herald-Tribune* 15 Dec. 11/2 The haunts of technocratic science were situated at numerous places about town, principally in cubbyhole restaurants in Greenwich village. **1933** *Times Lit. Suppl.* 26 Jan. 46/2 An age that was already substituting the technocrat for the monarch. **1945** C. S. LEWIS *That Hideous Strength* xii. 318 It was not the great technocrats of Koenigsberg or Moscow who supplied the casualties in the siege of Stalingrad. **1949** *Mind* LVIII. 416 Lersch denies the widely accepted thesis that man's uniqueness consists in his activities (activism, pragmatism, technocratism) since these are characteristic only of the Male's relation to the world. **1957** *London Mag.* Jan. 48 Sprawling in my revolving chair, behind a man-sized desk, I could imagine myself a brisk and efficient technocrat, a kind of highbrow tycoon. **1958** *Times Lit. Suppl.* 26 Dec. 751/1 Either tending towards reliance on a tradition which has been made obsolete.. or else attempting a technocratic rule for which no tradition exists. **1965** W. H. G. ARMYTAGE *Rise of Technocrats* v. 65 St. Simonians were the first technocrats: apostles of the religion of industry. **1974** J. WHITE tr. *Poulantzas's Fascism & Dictatorship* v. ii. 254 Imperialist ideology in effect represents a displacement of domination within bourgeois ideology itself, from the juridico-political region which was dominant in liberal-bourgeois ideology to economic technocratism. **1980** *Times* 11 Aug. 11/1 Dr Hoss was chosen after the Syrian-imposed end to the civil war in 1976 to head a 'technocratic', ie non-political, government.

technologic (tɛknəʊ'lɒdʒɪk), *a. rare*⁻⁰. [f. as TECHNOLOGY + -IC. Cf. mod.L. *terminus technologicus* (Alsted *Encycl.* 1630); F. *technologique* (1812 in Hatz.-Darm.).] = next.

1864 in WEBSTER. **1971** *Amer. N. & Q.* Dec. 61/2 The thread of technologic changes is woven throughout the text. **1979** *Bull. Amer. Acad. Arts & Sci.* Mar. 20 The early insights about the 'technologic misfit' and the need for social and technological 'congruence' have given way to more systematic analysis.

technological (tɛknəʊ'lɒdʒɪkəl), *a.* [f. as prec. + -ICAL.] Pertaining or relating to technology.

1. Belonging to technical phraseology or methods: esp. of terms, words, senses; = TECHNICAL 3 b. Now *rare.*

1627 in Capt. Smith *Seaman's Gram.* a iij, Each Science termes of Art hath wherewithall To expresse themselues, calld Technologicall. **1704** NORRIS *Ideal World* II. Pref. 20 The word λογος.. being a technological term well known among the Jews (probably from the writings of Philo). **1854** J. SCOFFERN in *Orr's Circ. Sc., Chem.* 432 This material, considered in a technological sense, may be described as an alkaline silicate.

2. Relating to or dealing with the study of the arts, esp. the industrial arts.

1800 *Monthly Mag.* June 458/2 A new work.. consecrated entirely to the arts and manufactures, in the way of annals or technological memoirs. **1864** DASENT *Jest & Earnest* (1873) II. 34 The dreary columns of a technological dictionary. **1868** *Rep. U.S. Commissioner Agric.* (1869) 59 The exposition of the industrial and the technological value of the mineral wealth of the country.

3. Pertaining to or characterized by technology; resulting from developments in technology (esp. ***technological unemployment***).

1930 *Econ. Jrnl.* XL. 55 (*title*) Rationalisation and Technological Unemployment. **1942** J. H. OLDHAM in *Christian News-Let.* 6 May 5/2 The question of the stability of our modern technological civilization. **1957** *Technology* Mar. 1/1 The Government is spending millions on the scientific and technological departments of universities and on the technical colleges. **1961** P. DRUCKER *Technology & Culture* II. 348 There is only one thing we do not know about the Technological Revolution—but it is essential: What happened to bring about the basic change.. which released it? **1968** *Economist* 6 July 54/2 Technological forecasting is an exercise in logical deduction rather than straight mathematical calculation... The biggest incentive to technological forecasting is commercial: as industry becomes bigger and more capital-intensive, the cost of mistakes rises. **1970** *Nature* 24 Oct. 387/2 The one dimensional 'technological fixes' that society has so far provided to solve its problems. **1983** *Wall St. Jrnl.* (European ed.) 14 Apr. 1 Computer yahoos who electronically invade other people's computers... 'I call it electronic vandalism or technological trespassing,' says.. a computer-security consultant.

technologically (tɛknəʊ'lɒdʒɪkəlɪ), *adv.* [TECHNOLOGICAL *a.* + -LY².] In a technological manner; from a technological point of view.

1862 H. MAYHEW *London Labour* Extra vol. 5/2 So that, technologically considered, there is no difference between them. **1951** R. FIRTH *Elements Soc. Organization* ii. 51 Technologically its culture is very undeveloped. **1976** *Gramophone* June 103/3 The inventiveness of the Japanese mind can operate with special freedom in such a technologically biased society.

techno'logico-'Benthamite, *a. nonce-wd.* [f. TECHNOLOGIC *a.* + -O + BENTHAMITE *a.*] Characterized by the implementation of Benthamite principles through the agency of technology.

1969 F. R. LEAVIS in *Times Lit. Suppl.* 29 May 569/1 The problem.. is one of cultural disinheritance and the meaninglessness of the technologico-Benthamite world. **1973** I. ROBINSON *Survival of English* 247 The principal target of our comment will be the disastrous unwisdom of the prevailing climate of our 'technologico-Benthamite' enlightenment which controls all three parties, the daily and weekly press, and all the television channels.

tech'nologism. *rare.* [f. TECHNOLOGY + -ISM.] Belief in the governance of society according to technological principles.

1969 B. BREWSTER tr. *Althusser's For Marx* iii. 108 There are names for these temptations in the history of Marxism: *economism* and even *technologism*. **1980** C. E. SCHORSKE *Fin-de-Siècle Vienna* p. xix, The trends in post-Nietzschean culture—irrationalism, subjectivism, abstractionism, anxiety, technologism.

technologist (tɛk'nɒlədʒɪst). [f. TECHNOLOGY + -IST.] One versed in technology; one who studies or treats of arts and manufactures. Also *U.S.* = TECHNICIAN c.

1859 R. F. BURTON *Centr. Afr.* in *Jrnl. Geog. Soc.* XXIX. 437 European technologists have.. vainly proposed theoretical methods for the.. operation. **1884** P. HIGGS *Magn. Dynamo-Electr. Mach.* vi. 140 In a book such as this, intended for the use of technologists, it will be necessary to discuss those theoretical principles. **1952** *Economist* 21 June 796/1 Technical colleges should be raised in status in order to produce technologists—as opposed to technicians. **1956** *Technical Educ.* 2 in *Parl. Papers* 1955–56 (Cmnd. 9703) XXXVI. 987 A technologist has the qualifications and experience required for membership of a professional institution... A technician is qualified by specialist technical education and practical training to work under the general direction of a technologist. **1966** *Amer. Jrnl. Clin. Path.* XLVI. 465/2, 3 tubes of blood were given to each of 2 technologists who worked in separate rooms; they were instructed to invert 1 tube until it clotted, then the second tube, and finally the third tube. **1977** *Chicago Tribune* 2 Oct. XII. 70/2 (Advt.), Our busy emergency room requires capable technologist to work weekends.

technologize (tɛk'nɒlədʒaɪz), *v.* [f. TECHNOLOGY + -IZE.] *trans.* To make technological. Also *intr.*, to use technical methods. So **tech'nologized** *ppl. a.*; **tech'nologizing** *vbl. sb.*

1960 *Mod. Lang. Rev.* Jan. 113 The tensions between liberty and equality in technologized society. **1960** *Punch* 27 Apr. 574/1 The arts are in self-defence compelled to technologize themselves, inventing new areas of study which require machinery and grants.. in order to maintain a foothold in the university premises. **1964** M. MCLUHAN *Understanding Media* (1967) II. xvi. 173 The West had to technologize more intensively than the ancient world. **1965** M. BRADBURY *Stepping Westward* vi. 298 Look at this vast urbanized and technologized mass-society. **1965** K. AMIS *James Bond Dossier* 147 Nothing could be more characteristic of science fiction than this strategy of technologizing the fairy tale. **1966** D. JENKINS *Educated Society* iv. 165 That technologizing of life which we have seen as constituting a major threat to personal freedom today. **1980** D. MORAES *Mrs Gandhi* iii. 40 The construction of an urban, technologised India.

technology (tɛk'nɒlədʒɪ). [ad. Gr. τεχνολογία systematic treatment (of grammar, etc.), f. τέχνη art, craft: see -LOGY. So F. *technologie* (1812 in Hatz.-Darm.).]

1. a. A discourse or treatise on an art or arts; the scientific study of the practical or industrial arts.

1615 BUCK *Third Univ. Eng.* xlviii, An apt close of this general Technologie. **1628** VENNER *Baths of Bathe* 9 Heere I cannot but lay open Baths Technologie. **1706** PHILLIPS (ed. Kersey), *Technology*, a Description of Arts, especially the Mechanical. **1802–12** BENTHAM *Ration. Judic. Evid.* (1827) I. 19 Questions in technology in all its branches. **1881** P. GEDDES in *Nature* 29 Sept. 524/2 Of economic physics, geology, botany, and zoology, of technology and the fine arts. **1882** *Mechanical World* 4 Mar. 130/1 The Department of Applied Science and Technology.

b. *transf.* Practical arts collectively.

1859 R. F. BURTON *Centr. Afr.* in *Jrnl. Geog. Soc.* XXIX. 437 Little valued in European technology it [the chakazi, or 'jackass' copal] is exported to Bombay, where it is converted into an inferior varnish. **1864** —— *Dahome* II. 202 His technology consists of weaving, cutting canoes, making rude weapons, and in some places practising a rude metallurgy. **1949** in W. A. Visser t' Hooft *First Assembly World Council of Churches* 75 There is no inescapable necessity for society to succumb to undirected developments of technology. **1958** J. K. GALBRAITH *Affluent Society* ix. 99 Improvements in technology.. are the result of investment in highly organized scientific and engineering knowledge and skills. **1971** *Daily Tel.* (Colour Suppl.) 10 Dec. 18/2 In the production of millions of children a year, it is not surprising that occasionally nature's complex technology should break down to produce an imbalance of hormones with masculinisation of the female foetus or feminisation of the male. **1975** *Ecologist* V. 120/1 Guiding technological development effectively is not a matter of being for or against technology, which is the form the discussion usually assumes.

c. With *a* and *pl.* A particular practical or industrial art.

1957 *Technology* Apr. 56/1 It [*sc.* Chemical Engineering] is now recognized as one of the four primary technologies, alongside civil, mechanical, and electrical engineering. **1960** *Electronic Engin.* Mar. 148/1 Electronic data-processing for business is a young technology. **1969** *Listener* 5 June 778/1 To compare one technology with another. **1979** *Computers in Shell* (Shell Internat. Petroleum Co.) 2 Highly complex problems involving the many technologies needed within the energy and associated industries.

d. high-technology applied *attrib.* to a firm, industry, etc., that produces or utilizes highly advanced and specialized technology, or to the products of such a firm. Also (unhyphened) as *sb. phr.* Similarly **low-technology**. Cf. *high tech* s.v. TECH³ 1.

1964 S. M. MILLER in I. L. Horowitz *New Sociology* 292 The youthful poor possess limited or outmoded skills and inadequate credentials in a high-technology, certificate-demanding economy. **1970** *Physics Bull.* Apr. 146/1 'High technology' industries demand huge capital and R and D investments. **1972** *Nature* 28 Jan. 183/2 In high technology ..errors in estimates of development cost are more serious in their effects. **1973** *Newsweek* 18 June 92/2 As their old, low-technology industries wilt under the pressure of mounting labor costs. **1981** *Times* 14 May 1/7 Export licences are required for a variety of high technology goods including computers, electronic equipment, chemicals, metals and building equipment.

2. The terminology of a particular art or subject; technical nomenclature.

1658 SIR T. BROWNE *Gard. Cyrus* v. 70 The mother of Life and Fountain of souls in Cabalisticall Technology is called Binah. **1793** W. TAYLOR in *Monthly Rev.* XI. 563 The port-customs, the technology, and the maritime laws, all wear marks of this original character. **1802–12** BENTHAM *Ration. Judic. Evid.* (1827) IV. 252 An engine, called, in the technology of that day, *fork*. **1862** *Morn. Star* 21 May, Aluminium, and its alloy with copper—which the manufacturers, with a slight laxity of technology, denominate bronze.

†**3.** = Gr. τεχνολογία: see etym. *Obs. rare*⁻¹.

1683 TWELLS *Exam. Gram.* Pref. 17 There were not any further Essays made in Technology, for above Fourscore years; but all men acquiesced in the Common Grammar.

4. Special Combs.: **technology assessment**, the assessment of the effects on society of new technology; **technology transfer**, the transfer of new technology or advanced technological information from the developed to the less developed countries of the world.

1966 *Inquiries, Legislation, Policy Stud. Subcomm. Sci., Res., & Devel.* (U.S. Congress: House: Comm. Sci. & Astronaut.) 27 We must be cognizant of what technology is doing to us—the bad as well as the good. Toward this end we would consider the exploration of legislation to establish a Technology Assessment Board—with the somewhat appropriate acronym TAB, since this would be its function. **1979** *Bull. Amer. Acad. Arts & Sci.* Mar. 21 Unanswered questions are threatening to leave technology assessment a mere intellectual pastime. **1969** *Listener* 24 July 106/3 This seems to show that Africa can use western techniques to her advantage, but only so long as the different cultural, intellectual and material contexts are kept firmly in mind when the technology-transfer is being planned. **1978** *Internat. Relations Dict.* (U.S. Dept. State Library) 40/2 *Technology transfer* has been defined as 'the transfer of knowledge generated and developed in one place to another, where it is used to achieve some practical end.'

† **techomahac**, obs. form of TACAMAHAC.

1693 *Phil. Trans.* XVII. 622 The Techomahac-Tree from Mexico.

techy, obs. and arch. variant of TETCHY.

Teck (tɛk). The title of Francis, Prince of *Teck* (1837–1900), applied *attrib.* and *absol.* to a kind of necktie fashionable in the late nineteenth century; = FOUR-IN-HAND 1 b.

1895 *Montgomery Ward Catal.* Spring & Summer 95/3 Pique fancy Teck Scarfs... Fine Lawn Flowing End Tecks. **1897** *Sears, Roebuck Catal.* 223/1 Our 35c All Silk Tecks... Men's Handsome Silk and Satin Fancy Teck Scarves.

teck, obs. form of TEAK.

teckel ('tɛkɪl). [a. Ger.] = DACHSHUND.

1877 F. E. KINGSLEY *C. Kingsley* II. xvi. 9 'Victor', a favourite Teckel, given to him by the Queen. **1922** [see (DOBERMANN]. **1952** C. L. B. HUBBARD *Pembrokeshire Corgi Handbk.* i. 8 The very short-legged Teckel or Dachshund types of central Europe. **1971** F. HAMILTON *World Encycl. Dogs* 337 The Dachshund, or Teckel as it is known in Germany, has been evolved from the oldest known breeds of dog.

† **'Teckelite.** *Obs.* [f. name of Count Teckely, a Hungarian Protestant leader who rose against the persecuting Austrian government, and allied himself with the Turks, whom he joined in the siege of Vienna in 1683.] In *Eng. Hist.*, A nickname given in 1683 to the Whigs, alleged to sympathize with Count Teckely in waging war against a Roman Catholic government.

1683 R. L'ESTRANGE *Observator* 29 Aug., Why where hast thou been Bury'd of late, that thou know'st Nothing of the Teckelites? There's Another Design afoot, for the Reconciling of the True-Protestants, and the Mahometans. **1684** DRYDEN *Epil. Constantine Gt.* 22 Besides all these, there were a sort of wights, (I think my author calls them Teckelites,) Such hearty rogues against the king and laws, They favoured even a foreign rebel's cause. **1688** *Lond. Gaz.* No. 2348/1 (*Addr. fr. Carlisle*) We likewise thank Your Majesty for Your Royal Army, which really is both the Honour and Safety of the Nation; Let the Teckelites think and say what they wiil.

teckle, obs. Sc. form of TACKLE: cf. *taikle*.

Tecla ('tɛklə). The proprietary name of a make of artificial pearl.

1908 *Trade Marks Jrnl.* 9 Sept. 1481 *Tecla*... Imitation or reconstructed pearls, imitation or reconstructed rubies, imitation emeralds, and imitation or reconstructed sapphires. Isaac Blumenthal,..Hendon, Middlesex; merchant and manufacturer. **1923** [see TITIAN]. **1930** E. WAUGH *Vile Bodies* vi. 113 Heirlooms of priceless value.. among Tecla pearls.

tecno- (also tekno-), repr. Gr. τεκνο-, combining form of τέκνον child (as in τεκνογόνος bearing children, etc.); used in Eng. in a few rare technical words. ‖**tecnoc'tonia** [Gr. -κτόνος murderer], child-murder, infanticide. ‖**tecno'gonia** [Gr. γονή generation], †(*a*) the age of a father at his eldest child's birth; (*b*) child-bearing, pregnancy. **tecnolater, tek-** (tɛk'nɒlətə(r)), one who worships or idolizes children; so **tec'nolatry** [-LATRY]; **tecnology** (tɛk'nɒlədʒɪ) [-LOGY], the scientific study of children; pædology. **tecnonymy**, now usu. **tek-** (tɛk'nɒnɪmɪ) [Gr. ὄνομα, ὄνυμα name], the practice among certain peoples of naming a parent from his or her child; so **tec'nonymous** (tɛk-) *a.*, practising tecnonymy.

1857 DUNGLISON *Med. Lex.*, *Tecnoctonia. *a* **1677** HALE *Prim. Orig. Man.* 178 Partly by adding 100 Years to that *Technogonia of the Patriarchs before Abraham, have made the Period larger by 884 Years. **1860** MAYNE *Expos. Lex.*, Tecnogonia. **1914** A. H. SIDGWICK *Promenade Ticket* 30 'Those who are called so [*sc.* happy]' (i.e. by Froebel, Wordsworth, and *teknolaters generally) 'are simply congratulated on account of their promise.' **1899** M. BEERBOHM *More* 174 A perfect example of our *tecnolatry, our delight in the undirected oddities of children. **1857** DUNGLISON *Med. Lex.*, **Tecnology*.., a treatise on children. **1899** *Syd. Soc. Lex.*, *Tecnology*, the study or scientific knowledge of childhood. **1888** E. B. TYLOR in *Jrnl. Anthrop. Inst.* (1889) Feb. 248 Another custom..is the practice of naming the parent from the child... There are above thirty peoples spread over the earth who thus name the father, and, though less often, the mother. They may be called, coining a name for them, **teknonymous* peoples. When beginning to notice the wide distribution of this custom of **teknonymy* [etc.]. **1888** *Athenæum* 1 Dec. 740/1 Another custom, here called teknonymy [by Dr. E. B. Tylor]..; as an example was mentioned the name of Ra-Mary, or Father of Mary, by which Moffat was generally known in Africa. **1937** R. H. LOWIE *Hist. Ethnological Theory* vii. 81 Teknonymy is no longer the inevitable effect of matrilocal residence or of an avoidance rule. **1951** R. FIRTH *Elem. Social Organization* i. 9 A child does not take its name from its parents; on the contrary, in the institution of teknonymy they are known as 'Father and Mother of So-and-so'.

‖**Tecoma** (tɪ'kəʊmə). *Bot.* [mod.L. (Jussieu 1789), from Aztec *tecomaxochitl*, mistakenly supposed by Jussieu to be the name of a species of the genus to which he gave this name (but really the native name of *Solandra guttata*, N.O. *Solanaceæ*).

The Aztec name is a compound of *tecomatl* + *xochitl* 'rose, flower'; the plant being named from the resemblance of its flower to that of the *tecomatl* or Calabash-tree (*Crescentia Cujete*, N.O. *Bignoniaceæ*), lit. 'pot-tree', f. *tecomatl* earthen vessel, pot.]

A large genus of *Bignoniaceæ*, mostly natives of warm climates, consisting chiefly of shrubs (erect, climbing, or twining), with leaves usually pinnate, and showy trumpet-shaped flowers of various colours (chiefly different shades of yellow and red), whence the name *trumpet-flower*; many are cultivated in greenhouses, etc. for their beauty.

Some shrubby species have sometimes been reckoned in separate genera *Tecomaria*, *Stenolobium*, *Campsis* (or *Campsidium*), and *Pandorea*; others (of which some are tall trees used for timber and in medicine) formerly included in *Tecoma*, but with digitate leaves, are now separated as *Tabebuia*. Several species are also often called *Bignonia*.

1846 *Penny Cycl.* Suppl. II. 614/1 Several..species of Tecoma have reputed medicinal virtues. **1884** *Mag. Art* Mar. 181/2 In the foreground the brilliant tecoma climbs a tall ailanthus tree. **1888** MRS. M'CANN *Poet. Wks.* 197 Its nest the lyre bird weaves with tecomas twining o'er it.

† **tecon.** *Obs. rare*⁻¹. A fish mentioned by Walton as a kind of salmon: see quots.

1653 WALTON *Angler* vi. 141 There is more then one sort of them [salmon], as namely, a Tecon, and another called in some places a Samlet, or by some, a Skegger: but these.. may be fish of another kind. **1760** HAWKINS *Note*, There is another small fish,..called the Gravel Last-Spring, found only in the rivers Wye and Severn... Perhaps this is what Walton calls the Tecon. **1853** 'EPHEMERA' *Note* ibid., All the fish named, except the gravel-last-spring, are salmon-fry of different ages, from three or four months to twelve. Walton's 'tecon' may be the parr.

† **tect**, *sb. Obs. rare*⁻¹. [ad. L. *tect-um* roof, prop. neut. of *tectus*, pa. pple. 'covered': see next.] A roof. In comb. **'tect-de'molished** *a.*, having the roof demolished, disroofed.

1632 LITHGOW *Trav.* x. 432 Tect-demolished Churches, vnpassable Bridges.

† **tect**, *ppl. a. Obs. rare.* [ad. L. *tect-us*, pa. pple. of *tegĕre* to cover.] Covered, hidden. (Const. as pa. pple. See also TECTLY.) So † **'tected**.

c **1440** *Pallad. on Husb.* VI. 180 With chaf or fern this boordis do be tecte. *Ibid.* VIII. 79 The tuppe is chosun fair of altitude, Ywombed side, and tecte in whitest wolle. *c* **1557** ABP. PARKER *Ps.* cxv. 332 Why els no doubt, the Heathen sect, Would say where is their God so tect? **1657** TOMLINSON *Renou's Disp.* 459 The shells wherewith they are tected.

tectal, *a.*: see TECTUM.

‖**tec-tec.** [? from its note.] A species of whinchat (*Pratincola sybilla*) found in some of the islands off the E. coast of Africa.

1886 H. A. WEBSTER in *Encycl. Brit.* XX. 492/2 (*Réunion*) Among the more familiar birds are the 'oiseau de la vierge' (*Muscipeta borbonica*), the tec-tec (*Pratincola sybilla*).

tectibranch ('tɛktɪbræŋk), *a.* and *sb. Zool.* [f. L. *tect-us* covered + *branchiæ* (Gr. βράγχια) gills.]

a. *adj.* Belonging to the order or sub-order *Tectibranchiata* of gastropod molluscs, comprising marine forms having the gills covered by the mantle, and small shells often concealed by the mantle. **b.** *sb.* A gastropod belonging to this division. So **tecti'branchian, tecti'branchiate** *adjs.* and *sbs.* in same senses.

1836–9 *Todd's Cycl. Anat.* II. 381/1 The internal or dermic shells are formed in many of the..tectibranchiate orders. **1839** *Penny Cycl.* XIV. 322/1 Gastropods are divided into the following orders..:—1. Nudibranchians... 2. Inferobranchians... 3. Tectibranchians [etc.]. **1851** WOODWARD *Mollusca* I. 34 The respiratory organs form tufts..protected by a fold of the mantle, as in the Inferobranchs and Tectibranchs of Cuvier. **1894** *Proc. Zool. Soc.* 20 Nov. 666 The posterior pallial lobes of various genera of Bulloid Tectibranchs.

tectiform ('tɛktɪfɔːm), *a. Zool.* [ad. mod.L. *tectiform-is*, f. *tect-um* roof: see -FORM.]

1. a. Roof-shaped; sloping downwards on each side from a central ridge. **b.** Serving as a covering or lid.

1834 MCMURTRIE *Cuvier's Anim. Kingd.* 414 Phryganea. .. The wings are..strongly tectiform. **1880** WATSON in *Jrnl. Linn. Soc.* XV. 95 Shell,—high, conical, tectiform. **1884** tr. *Claus' Zool.* I. x. 582 Of slender build and with large wings, which in repose are tectiform. **1895** *Funk's Stand. Dict.*, *Tectiform*, having the form of a roof; serving as a cover or lid: as, tectiform maxillaries.

2. *Archæol.* **a.** Applied to a roof-shaped design or symbol found in palæolithic cave-paintings and engravings. **b.** *sb.* A design or symbol of this type.

1921 R. A. S. MACALISTER *Text-bk. Europ. Archæol.* I. ix. 491 Tectiform devices are essentially shaped like a more or less isosceles triangle, with a vertical line running from apex to base. *Ibid.* 492 The resemblance between such huts and the tectiform devices is striking, but not wholly convincing. .. I have another suggestion to offer..namely, that they are intended to represent traps. **1921** M. C. BURKITT *Prehist.* 382 (*caption*) The painted tectiform from La Mouthe. **1962** S. GIEDION *Eternal Present* I. iii. 254 The tectiforms of Font-de-Gaume also belong to the class of symbols with more or less straight lines.

† **'tectly**, *adv. Obs. rare.* [f. TECT *ppl. a.* + -LY².] In a concealed manner, covertly.

1587 HOLINSHED *Chron. Irel.* II. 176/2 He laid verie close & tectlie a companie of his men in an old house fast by the castell. **1687** *Catholic Balance* 29 Opposing these Doctoral Principles either tectly or openly.

tecto- ('tɛktəʊ), comb. form of L. *tectum* roof, as in **'tecto,cuticle** *Ent.* (see quot. 1951); **'tecto,spinal** *a. Anat.*, applied to a group of nerve fibres which run from the tectum of the midbrain to the spinal cord.

1951 A. G. RICHARDS *Integument of Insects* xvi. 149 The term tectocuticle..is here proposed for any material poured onto the outer surface of the formed epicuticle and hardening there as a reasonably permanent component. **1974** R. H. HACKMAN in M. Rockstein *Physiol. Insecta* (ed. 2) VI. iii. 216 The cuticle is divided into..an inner relatively thick procuticle and a thin outer epicuticle... A cement layer or 'tectocuticle' may also be present. **1916** *Gray's Anat.* (ed. 19) 744 The tectospinal fasciculus originates in the superior colliculus..of the opposite side. **1974** D. & M. WEBSTER *Compar. Vertebr. Morphol.* xii. 290 Another prominent component of the extrapyramidal system is the tectospinal tract.

tectocephalic (tɛktəʊsɪ'fælɪk), *a. Path.* [f. L. *tect-um* roof + Gr. κεφαλή head + -IC: cf. CEPHALIC.] = SCAPHOCEPHALIC. So **tecto-cephaly** (-'sɛfəlɪ) = SCAPHOCEPHALY.

1888 CLEVINGER in *Amer. Nat.* July 614 The Esquimaux are tectocephalic (rafter-headed), with flat pyramidal, or lozenge-shaped faces, due to excessive zygoma projection, and narrow foreheads.

tectogenesis (tɛktə'dʒɛnɪsɪs). *Geol.* [ad. G. *tektogenese* (E. Haarman 1926, in *Zeitschr. f. Deutsch. Geol. Ges.* LXXVIII. B. 106), f. Gr. τέκτων, -ον- carpenter, builder: see -GENESIS.] The formation of the highly distorted rock structures characteristic of mountain ranges, as distinct from the formation of mountainous topography itself. Hence **tectoge'netic, tecto'genic** *adjs.*, of, pertaining to, or involving tectogenesis. Also **'tectogene** [ad. G. *tektogen* (E. Haarman 1926, loc. cit., 107): see -GEN 3], a long, narrow belt of downwarping in the earth's crust, said to be an underlying feature of mountain ranges and oceanic trenches.

1937 *Bull. Amer. Assoc. Petroleum Geologists* XXI. 1596 Orogenesis means 'mountain-making', but the term refers only to the production of mountain structure, not to that of mountain topography. Hence, it seems desirable to replace it by 'tectogenesis', as Haarman suggested. *Ibid.*, Tectogenic movements..are incongruent, making stuctures that vary in the different stories of the crust; and the deformation they produce is wholly irreversible. **1937** *Leidsche Geol. Med.* VIII. 204 (*caption*) Tectogene with root. **1965** *Phil. Trans. R. Soc.* A. CCLVIII. 65 The later Palaeozoic..tectogene stretched in a belt from the Appalachians, through southern Britain and central and southern Europe, to Suess's massive Altaids in the heart of Asia. *Ibid.* 68 Throughout the Caledonides (Spitzbergen, Greenland, Scandinavia and Britain) there seems little doubt that the main tectogenic phase was centred in Silurian time. *Ibid.* 74 Undisturbed marine successions do not necessarily rule out synchronous tectogenesis of a neighbouring region. **1975** *Nature* 24 Jan. 257/1 Sicilian data indicate a time span of only 3–4 Myr for a single 'tectogenetic cycle'. *Ibid.* 10 July 116/1 The radial pattern of transverse folds with respect to the arc..has been taken into account in tectogenetic models of the Alps.

tectology (tɛk'tɒlədʒɪ). *Biol.* [ad. Ger. *tektologie* (Haeckel), for **tektonologie*, f. Gr. τέκτων carpenter, builder (cf. ARCHITECT *sb.*): see -LOGY.] (See quot., and cf. PROMORPHOLOGY.) So **tecto'logical** *a.*, pertaining to tectology.

1883 P. GEDDES in *Encycl Brit.* XVI. 842/1 In 1866 appeared the *Generelle Morphologie* of Haeckel. Here pure morphology is distinguished into two sub-sciences,—the first purely structural, *tectology*, which regards the organism as composed of organic individuals of different orders; the second essentially stereometric, *promorphology*.

tectonic (tɛk'tɒnɪk), *a.* [ad. late L. *tectonicus*, a. Gr. τεκτονικός pertaining to building, f. τέκτων, -ον-, carpenter, builder.]

1. Of or pertaining to building, or construction in general; constructional, constructive: used esp. in reference to architecture and kindred arts.

1656 BLOUNT *Glossogr.*, *Tectonick* (*tectonicus*), of or belonging to a builder. **1864** *Daily Tel.* 1 Aug., That law of necessity and of demand which is at the foundation of all tectonic art. **1903** G. B. BROWN *Arts in Early Eng.* II. 178 A form produced..by the exigencies of construction—or, to use a convenient term familiar in Germany, a tectonic form.

2. *Geol.* Belonging to the actual structure of the earth's crust, or to general changes affecting it. Also with reference to other planets. Cf. also *plate-tectonic* adj. s.v. PLATE *sb.* 21.

1894 BOYD-DAWKINS in *Geol. Mag.* Oct. 459 The relation existing between the tectonic anticlines and synclines in the districts of South Wales, Gloucester, and the West of England. **1902** LD. AVEBURY *Scenery Eng.* 213 The primary configuration of the country's surface is no doubt due to tectonic causes. **1905** *Athenæum* 1 Apr. 404/3 Whilst the most powerful and destructive disturbances are of this tectonic character, many other earthquakes are no doubt connected with volcanic phenomena. **1962** F. I. ORDWAY et al. *Basic Astronautics* iii. 65 They [*sc.* the rills on the moon] are apparently the result of tectonic activity. **1976** *Science* 24 Dec. 1386/3 By 2·5 billion years ago the volcanic-tectonic circus on Mars had folded. **1982** *Nature* 28 Jan. 293/2 Additional mapping and analysis based on Voyager images should help resolve many remaining questions about the tectonic evolution of Ganymede.

Hence **tec'tonical** *a.*, in sense 2; **tec'tonically** *adv.*, as regards tectonism; by tectonic processes.

1925 J. JOLY *Surface-Hist. Earth* 191 *Laccolith*, and intrusive mass of igneous rock..generally associated tectonically with a mountain range. **1939** *Geogr. Jrnl.* XCIV. 499 There are also discussions of the tectonical..and general geological problems of Tanganyika Territory. **1972** *Rep. 24th Internat. Geol. Congr.* III. 3 Among the most important geological (tectonical) factors..are the concentrations of heat flow and juvenile matter ascending from the mantle..along steep, deep-seated tectonic zones. **1974** *Nature* 25 Jan. 194/1 Many investigators interpret ophiolites as slices of oceanic crust which have been tectonically emplaced in orogenic belts. **1976** J. KLECZEK *Universe* iv. 155 On the whole, the Moon is tectonically a very quiet body.

tectonician (tɛktə'nɪʃən). *Geol.* [f. TECTON(ICS + -ICIAN.] = TECTONIST 2.

1951 *Amer. Jrnl. Sci.* CCXLIX. 594 For the tectonician, the most useful definition of fold-axis is that given by Wegmann. **1965** *Phil. Trans. R. Soc.* A. CCLVIII. 56 Such tremendous crustal movements within the Alpine fold belt are of a much larger size than those required by the most nappist of tectonicians. **1975** *Nature* 6 Feb. 396/2 The Soviet tectonician Belousov has gone so far as to invoke extensive 'oceanisation' of continental crust to account for the ocean basins.

tectonics. [= Ger. *tektonik*]

1. A term for the constructive arts in general.

1850 LEITCH tr. *C. O. Müller's Anc. Art* §22 A series of arts which form and perfect vessels, implements, dwellings, and places of assembly... We call this class of artistic activities tectonics.

2. *Geol.* The structural arrangement of rocks in the earth's crust (or on another planet); the branch of geology concerned with the understanding of rock structures, esp. large-scale ones. Cf. *plate tectonics* s.v. PLATE *sb.* 21.

1899 *Q. Jrnl. Geol. Soc.* LV. 399 (*heading*) The tectonics of the district. **1914** J. PARK *Textbk. Geol.* xxxiv. 489 By a series of pressure experiments in 1888, Cadell obtained instructive imitations of the tectonics of mountain-building. **1935** [see AUTOCHTHONOUS *a.*]. **1976** *Daily Colonist* (Victoria, B.C.) 15 May 5/5 The science of tectonics—the study of the movement of these plates—shows that Africa and Europe are in collision. **1982** *Nature* 28 Jan. 290 (*heading*) The tectonics of Ganymede.

tectonism ('tɛktənɪz(ə)m). *Geol.* [f. TECTON(IC *a.* + ISM.] = DIASTROPHISM.

1949 F. J. PETTIJOHN *Sedimentary Rocks* vi. 193 The feldspar content [in sands] is primarily an index of crystal [*read* crustal] instability or tectonism. **1960** *Bull. Amer. Assoc. Petroleum Geologists* XLIV. 1924/2 The San Joaquin Valley was undergoing tremendous tectonism during the Middle Tertiary. **1972** *Gloss. Geol.* (Amer. Geol. Inst.) 726/2 *Tectonism*, a less preferred syn. of diastrophism. **1975** G. ANDERSON *Coring* i. 10 Two basic types of tectonism affect a rock's acceptability and transmissibility of fluids—shearing and flexure folding. **1982** *Nature* 28 Jan. 292/1 Further evidence for distinguishing the style of tectonism on Ganymede is provided by structural features.

'tectonist. [f. TECTONIC *a.* + -IST.]

†**1.** A constructor, a builder. *obs. nonce-wd.*

1634 W. WOOD *New Eng. Prosp.* II. xx. (1865) 106 As is their husbands occasion these poor tectonists [the squaws] are often troubled like snailes, to carrie their houses on their backs.

2. *Geol.* A specialist in tectonics. *rare.*

1933 *Amer. Jrnl. Sci.* CCXXV. 441 Becker's work has been to a large extent discarded by tectonists as being too highly theoretical to be of practical value in the interpretation of rock structure. **1935** [see HERCYNIAN *a.* 2 c].

tectonite ('tɛktənaɪt). *Petrol.* [ad. G. *tektonit* (B. Sander), f. Gr. τέκτων, -ον-, carpenter, builder: see -ITE[1].] A rock whose fabric shows evidence of differential movement during its formation.

1933 *Amer. Jrnl. Sci.* CCXXV. 433 Rocks that owe their present characters to..the integration of differential movements, he [*sc.* Sander] calls tectonites in distinction to non-tectonites, which are formed under conditions involving no differential movement. **1950** *Geol. Mag.* LXXXVII. 331 (*heading*) Note on two lineated tectonites. **1960** TURNER & VERHOOGEN *Igneous & Metamorphic Petrol.* (ed. 2) xxiii. 638, B-tectonites are tectonites in whose fabrics a linear parallelism of elements with reference to the *b* (= B) axis of the fabric is the outstanding structural feature.

tectonization (ˌtɛktənaɪ'zeɪʃən). *Geol.* [f. TECTON(IC *a.* + -IZATION.] Modification (of rocks, etc.) by tectonic processes.

1959 *Jrnl. Geol.* LXVII. 26/2 The last schistosity produced was also folded and now preserves the impress of the last phase of tectonization. **1971** *Nature* 2 July 21/1 Part of the central gap may be intermediate crust which has been incorporated, after tectonization, into the neocratons of the Greater Antilles. **1979** *Ibid.* 27 Sept. 267/1 Extensive mélange exists near the base of the Trondheim Nappe, indicating tectonisation of syndepositionally deformed chaotic deposits.

Hence (as a back-formation) **'tectonize** *v. trans.*, to alter by tectonic processes; **'tectonized** *ppl. a.*

1970 *Nature* 25 July 351/1 Sedimentary layers have been heavily tectonized. **1975** *Ibid.* 13 Feb. 521/2 Future work should also show whether the distribution of tectonised mantle inclusions in kimberlites is related to tectonic lineaments. **1977** A. HALLAM *Planet Earth* 204 In British Columbia the stratigraphy is less clear in the tectonized zone of the Rockies.

tectono- (tɛktɒnəʊ), comb. form of TECTONIC *a.*, TECTONICS, used in *Geol.*, as in **tecˌtono'physics**, a branch of geophysics concerned with the forces that cause movement and deformation in the Earth's crust; so **tecˌtono'physical** *a.*; **tecˌtono'physicist**, a specialist in tectonophysics; **tec'tonosphere** (see quot. 1926); **tecˌtono-strati'graphic** *a.*, of or pertaining to the correlation of rock formations with one another in terms of their connection with a tectonic event; **ˌtectono'thermal** *a.*, involving both tectonism and geothermal activity.

1960 *Bull. Geol. Soc. Amer.* LXXI. 1255 (*heading*) Tectonophysical investigations. **1979** *Nature* 8 Feb. 495/1 Recently I have been involved in tectonophysical research in the Witwatersrand collar sequence of the Vredefort dome. **1957** *Bull. Geol. Soc. Amer.* LXVIII. 642/1 The various tectonophysicists..have sought to explain the mechanism of the deep-focus earthquakes associated with island arcs. **1978** *Nature* 26 Oct. 733/1 The mechanism by which stress is released in intermediate and deep focus earthquakes is of particular interest to seismologists and tectonophysicists. **1959** *Geosci. Abstr.* July 5/1 The author..theoretically proves the possibility of using scale models in tectonophysics. **1960** *Bull. Geol. Soc. Amer.* LXXI. 1255/1 To Soviet specialists, tectonophysics is a scientific trend dealing with investigations into the physical mechanism of tectonic deformations. Investigators in other countries use the term in a broader, less definite sense. **1971** *Nature* 26 Nov. 185/2 Geophysics as a discipline covers everything from cosmic rays to seismology by way of..tectonophysics and geomagnetism. **1926** G. W. TYRRELL *Princ. Petrol.* i. 2 The inaccessible heavy interior [of the earth] is known as the barysphere. This is followed outwardly by the lithosphere, the thin, rocky crust of the earth... Other zones have been distinguished and named for special purposes... The zone in which crustal movements originate has been named the tectonosphere by certain continental geologists. **1949** R. W. VAN BEMMELEN *Geol. of Indonesia* IA. iv. 283/2 The tectonosphere comprises three shells: the sial-, salsima- and sima- layers. **1971** M. H. P. BOTT *Interior of Earth* vii. 220 It is a well-established facet of isostatic theory that the weak asthenosphere is overlain by a relatively strong lithosphere (or tectonosphere) about 50–100 km thick. **1971** *Nature* 24 Sept. 246/2 The geology of the Scotia Arc region can be simplified by emphasizing what seem to us to be the fundamental tectonostratigraphic units. **1976** *Ibid.* 9 Sept. 117/2 Taking..the tectonostratigraphic evidence into consideration..an alternative model [of the origin of the Himalaya], based on plate tectonics, involving microcontinents, is suggested here. **1971** I. G. GASS et al. *Understanding Earth* xxii. 323/2 It seems likely that the relative paucity of major deposits of these ores is due to the modifying and/or dissipating influences of younger tectonothermal activity. **1976** *Nature* 8 Apr. 516/2 It is significant that there is, as yet, no evidence for pre-Dalradian tectonothermal events affecting the Central Highland Granulites.

tectorial (tɛk'tɔərɪəl), *a.* *Anat.* [f. L. *tectōrium* covering, a cover (f. *tectōrius*: see next) + -AL[1].] Covering like a roof: applied to a membrane in the internal ear (see quot.).

1890 BILLINGS *Nat. Med. Dict.*, *Tectorial membrane*, a gelatinous structure covering [the] organ of Corti, stretching from upper part of the limbus spiralis over the outer hair-cells.

†**tec'torian,** *a.* *Obs. rare*[−0]. [f. L. *tectōrius* serving for covering walls, from *tegĕre* to cover.]

1656 BLOUNT *Glossogr.*, *Tectorian* (*tectorius*), of or belonging to covering, pargetting, washing or whitelyming.

tectosilicate ('tɛktəʊˌsɪlɪkət). *Min.* Also **tekto-**. [ad. G. *tektosilikat* (H. Strunz 1938, in *Zeitschr. f. ges. Naturwiss.* IV. 189), f. Gr. τεκτο-νεία workshops (or τεκτο-νία carpentry), taken as = framework + G. *silikat* SILICATE.] Any of the group of silicates in which the four oxygen atoms of each SiO_4 tetrahedron are shared with four neighbouring tetrahedra in a three-dimensional framework, with a ratio of silicon to oxygen of 1:2.

1947 [see PHYLLOSILICATE]. **1959** BERRY & MASON *Mineralogy* xv. 471 All the tektosilicates are colorless, white, or pale gray when free from inclusions. **1971** I. G. GASS et al. *Understanding Earth* i. 16/2 The feldspars and quartz are examples of tectosilicates (three-dimensional framework structures).

tectosphere ('tɛktəʊsfɪə(r)). *Geol.* [f. Gr. τέκτ-ων, -ον- carpenter, builder + -O + SPHERE *sb.*] That part of the earth which moves in coherent sections during plate-tectonic activity (see quot. 1979[1]). Hence **tecto'spheric** *a.*, of or pertaining to the tectosphere.

Tectosphere is sometimes confused in dicts. with TEKTOSPHERE.

1968 *Jrnl. Geophysical Res.* LXXIII. 1980/2 The required strength [to maintain rigidity] cannot be in the crust alone; the oceanic crust is too thin for this. We instead favor a strong tectosphere, perhaps 100 km thick, sliding over a weak asthenosphere. **1969** W. M. ELSASSER in S. K. Runcorn *Applic. Mod. Physics to Earth & Planetary Interiors* 223 Horizontal sliding of the top layer, here called the 'tectosphere', can be more easily achieved than circulation in the material underneath. **1979** *Sci. Amer.* Jan. 76/3 Under the oceans the tectosphere and the lithosphere are..identical in spatial extent... Under the continents, however,..the cratonic tectosphere extends below the lithosphere, perhaps to depths of 400 kilometers or more. *Ibid.*, Tectospheric thickness also correlates with crustal age.

‖**tectrix** ('tɛktrɪks). *Ornith.* Usually in pl. **tectrices** (tɛk'traɪsiːz). [mod.L. *tectrix* (fem. of L. *tector*), f. *tect-*, ppl. stem of *tegĕre* to cover: see -TRIX. So F. *tectrice*.] Each of the feathers that cover the base of the quill-feathers of the wing and tail in birds: = COVERT *sb.* 5.

[**1768** PENNANT *Zool.* I. *111 Lesser coverts of the wings. Tectrices primæ... Greater coverts. Tectrices secundæ. **1842** BRANDE *Dict. Sc.*, etc., *Tectrices*, *Coverts*, the name of the feathers which cover the quill feathers and other parts of the wing.] **1874** COUES *Birds N.W.* 693 Under parts, including the inferior alar tectrices, pure white. **1896** NEWTON *Dict. Birds* 950 Each tectrix being placed on the proximal side of its corresponding remex.

Hence **tectricial** (tɛk'trɪʃəl) *a.*, pertaining to the tectrices.

1891 in *Cent. Dict.*

tectum ('tɛktəm). *Anat.* [L., = roof.] **a.** More fully ***tectum mesencephali***. The roof of the midbrain, lying dorsal to the cerebral aqueduct.

1907 J. B. JOHNSTON *Nervous Syst. Vertebrates* xvi. 255 It must be remembered always that the tectum opticum is only a part of the tectum mesencephali. **1921** TILNEY & RILEY *Form & Functions Central Nervous Syst.* xxviii. 487 Like other suprasegmental parts of the nervous system, the tectum is capable of great expansion to meet the demands of adaptation. **1979** *Sci. Amer.* Sept. 82/1 The mesencephalon ..in mammals includes two pairs of structures that together form a region of four hills known as the lamina quadrigemina, the tectum mesencephali or simply the tectum.

b. More fully ***optic tectum*** (or ***tectum opticum***). That part of the tectum mesencephali concerned with the functioning of the visual system.

1907 J. B. JOHNSTON *Nervous Syst. Vertebrates* viii. 147 Structure of the tectum opticum.—In the lower fishes the tectum contains a large number of cells of several forms. **1926** *Jrnl. Compar. Neurol.* XL. 217 The optic tectum far surpasses the cortical areas of the reptilian hemispheres. **1982** *Sci. Amer.* Mar. 104/3 The optic tectum, also known in mammals as the superior colliculus, is one of the major visual centers of the brain.

Hence **'tectal** *a.*, of or pertaining to the tectum mesencephali or the optic tectum.

1926 *Jrnl. Compar. Neurol.* XL. 217 A group of nuclei which serve as way-stations between the tectal areas and other centers. **1974** *Sci. Amer.* Mar. 38/2 Recording from individual tectal neurons..tells one how the individual retinal ganglion cells that excite them are reacting. **1975** *Nature* 30 Oct. 738/1 In the vertebrates below mammals, the tectal and subtectal areas are the main centres of termination of sensory pathways.

†'**tecture.** *Obs.* [ad. L. *tectūra* a covering.] A covering (*lit.* or *fig.*); a canopy, a roof.

1624 F. White *Repl. Fisher* 579 Your..Blandishments are but Maskes and Tectures of latent perfidiousnesse. **1632** Lithgow *Trav.* x. 443 This palatiat cloyster is quadrangled foure stories high, the vppermost whereof, is window-set in the blew tecture. **1651** *Raleigh's Ghost* Pref., He may seem to shadow..his blasphemy under the tecture of some weak and feeble reasons. **1657** Tomlinson *Renou's Disp.* 471* Caves were their houses, the tectures of wood their cottages.

Hence †'**tectured** *a.*, canopied, roofed; formed with or as a roof.

1632 Lithgow *Trav.* viii. 366 The streetes being couered aboue,..haue large Lights cut through the tectur'd tops.

tecul, obs. form of tical.

ted (tɛd), *v.*[1] Forms: 5–6 **tedd**, 5–7 **tedde**, 6 **teede**, 7 **tede**, 6– **ted**. [Known from 15th c.; app. representing an OE. **teddan*, cognate with Icel. *tęðja*, pa. t. *tadda*, in special sense, to dung, manure, prob. to spread (manure) or spread (the ground) with manure: see tathe. The more general sense appears in OHG., MHG., and mod.HG. dial. *zetten* to spread out, scatter :—**zatjan*:—OTeut. **tadjan*. The non-appearance of this vb. in OE. and ME., and in LG. and Du., is notable.]

1. *trans.* To spread out, scatter, or strew abroad (new-mown grass) for drying. Also *absol.*

Sometimes including the turning of the grass when dried on one side: see quot. 1669; but *tedding* and *turning* are properly distinct processes: cf. quots. 1577, 1616, 1746.

14.. [implied in tedder]. **1481–90** [see tedding]. **1523** Fitzherb. *Husb.* §25 Whan thy medowes be mowed, they wolde be well tedded and layde euen vppon the grounde. **1530** Palsgr. 753/2, I teede hey, I tourne it afore it is made in cockes, *je fene*. **1577** B. Googe *Heresbach's Husb.* i. (1586) 45 b, The Grasse being cutte, must be well tedded and turned in the Sommer. **1616** Surfl. & Markh. *Country Farme* 500 After you haue mowed it, and tedded it, you shall turne it twice or thrice ere you cocke it. **1669** Worlidge *Syst. Agric.* (1681) 333 To *Ted*, to turn or spread new mown Grass. **1746** *Poor Robin* (Nares), Tedding, turning, cocking, raking, And such bus'ness in hay making. **1815** J. Smith *Panorama Sc. & Art* II. 624 In Middlesex,..all the grass mown on the first day, before nine o'clock in the morning, is tedded, that is, uniformly strewn over the field. *c* **1830** *Glouc. Farm Rep.* 14 in *Libr. Usef. Knowl.*, *Husb.* III, The hay-making machine is put to work in the field to ted or shake out every day's work.

2. *transf.* and *fig.* To scatter; to dissipate.

c **1560** A. Scott *Poems* (S.T.S.) xxi. 23 Thow held hir curage he on hoft, And ted my tendir hairt lyk toft. **1580** Lyly *Euphues* (Arb.) 228 Then fall they to al disorder that may be, tedding that with a forke in one yeare, which was not gathered together with a rake, in twentie. **1589** *Pappe w. Hatchet* Lyly's Wks. 1902 III. 412 What foole more couetous than he, that seekes to tedd abroad the Churches goods with a forke, and scratch it to himselfe with a rake. **1788** E. Picken *Poems* Gloss. 246 *Ted*, to scatter, to spread. **1813** —— *Misc. Poems* I. 120 (E.D.D.) Megg tedd the saut upo' the stool. **1870** J. Hamilton *Moses* xi. 188 A day-dreamer gets hold of a beautiful..thought, and teases and teds it, and tosses it out into a cloud fine and filmy.

3. *dial.* **a.** To spread out (cut corn or flax) on the ground to dry. **b.** To dress (flax). **c.** To arrange, tidy (the hair, a room, etc.).

1796 *Monthly Mag.* Apr. 223/2 When the mowers went afield The yellow corn to ted. **1811** Willan *W. Riding Gloss.* (E.D.S. B. 7), *Tedding*,..applied..also to the dressing of hair and flax. **1832** J. Bree *St. Herbert's Isle* 13 To mark the vale-hind ted the ripened shock. **1847–78** Halliwell, *Ted*, ..to turn flax when it has been laid on the ground to dry. *West.* **1858** R. S. Surtees *Ask Mamma* lxviii. 306 Producing a black..pocket-book, and tedding up a lot of characters, bills, etc. **1887** *Jamieson's Sc. Dict.*, *Supp.* s.v., Ted your hair, and tedd up the house: West of Sc.

ted, *v.*[2] *local techn.* [app. local var. of ME. *teth*, teethe.] *trans.* To give a finely-toothed or serrated edge to (a reaping-hook or sickle). Hence '**tedded** *ppl. a.*[2], '**tedder**[2], '**tedding** *vbl. sb.*[2]

1833 J. Holland *Manuf. Metal* II. 55 The next operation [in making sickles] is cutting or toothing, or *tedding* as it is technically called. *Ibid.* 56 There is..a peculiarity in the handling of his hammer and chisel by a sickle tedder, which it requires considerable practice to attain. **1888** *Sheffield Gloss.*, *Tedded*, serrated, indented. Sickles are tedded in order to make them cut better. [Cf. *c* **1440** *Promp. Parv.* 498/2 Tothyd, or tod wythe teethe, *dentatus*. **1781** Hutton *Tour Caves* Gloss., *Tod*, to tooth sickles.]

Ted (tɛd), *sb.*[1] *Services' slang.* [Abbrev. of tedesco *sb.*] A German soldier. *Disused.*

1947 D. M. Davin *Gorse blooms Pale* 193 D'you know what those bloody Teds have been up to? They've been bloody well shelling us.

Ted (tɛd), *sb.*[2] Also with small initial. Short for Teddy boy. Cf. Teddy 4.

1956 in I. & P. Opie *Lore & Lang. Schoolch.* (1959) vii. 119 Joined the Teds when he was only three, Coshed a cop when he was only four. **1956** *Time* 24 Sept. 28/1 The Ted's notion of sartorial splendor ranges from a caricature of Edwardian elegance to the zoot padding of a Harlem hepcat. **1959** C. MacInnes *Absolute Beginners* 44 Appearing in a telly programme on the Ted question. **1968** *New Scientist* 11 July 64/3 The gangs [of baboons] appeared to carry out his orders, roaming through the troupe like a bunch of leather-jacketed teds. **1977** *Daily Tel.* 19 July 15 A Metropolitan magistrate complained yesterday that he had inadequate power to deal with gangs of 'punk rockers' and 'Teds' who clashed in the King's Road, Chelsea. **1980** *Daily Mirror* 10 Apr. 12/2 The term Ted is a little less popular nowadays, and Rockabilly is Eighties style.

teddar, -er, -ir, obs. forms of tether.

tedded ('tɛdɪd), *ppl. a.*[1] [f. ted *v.*[1] + -ed[1].] Spread out for drying, as grass.

1667 Milton *P.L.* ix. 450 The smell of Grain, or tedded Grass, or Kine. **1844** Stephens *Bk. Farm* III. 970 The hay-rake..is employed to rake the tedded grass into a windrow.

tedded, *ppl. a.*[2]: see ted *v.*[2]

tedder[1] ('tɛdə(r)). [f. ted *v.*[1] + -er[1].] One who teds new-mown grass; also, a machine for doing this; a tedding-machine.

14.. *Voc.* in Wr.-Wülcker 578/44 *Disgerbigator*,..a Teddere. *Ibid.* 587/48 *Herbarius*,..a teddere. **1800** Hurdis *Fav. Village* 22 Thick swarms the field with tedders. **1877** Knight *Dict. Mech.*, *Tedder*,..a machine for stirring and spreading hay, to expedite its being dried. **1886** P. S. Robinson *Valley Teet. Trees* 141 The mowers and tedders, sitting in the shade with their bread and cheese.

tedder[2]: see ted *v.*[2]

tedding ('tɛdɪŋ), *vbl. sb.*[1] [f. ted *v.*[1] + -ing[1].] The action of spreading out or scattering (new-mown grass) to be dried by the sun and wind.

1481–90 *Howard Househ. Bks.* (Roxb.) 226 Item, to Baker for iiij. dayes teddynge of gresse iiij. d. **1523** Fitzherbert *Husb.* §25 Good teddynge is the chiefe poynte to make good hey. **1688** R. Holme *Armoury* iii. 72/2 Tedding is with a Pitchfork or Pikill throwing it abroad out of those rows in which the Sithe left it on the ground. **1844** Stephens *Bk. Farm* III. 966 The process for putting it into cocks after the tedding.

b. *attrib.*, as *tedding-machine*.

[**1826–44** Loudon *Encycl. Agric.* 420 The hay-tedding machine, invented about 1800, by Salmon of Woburn.] **1843** *Jrnl. Roy. Agric. Soc.* IV. ii. 482 Mr. Wedlake.. produced a spreading or tedding machine. **1847–78** Halliwell, *Tedding-pole*, the long stick used for turning or tedding flax. *West.* **1906** *Times* 25 June 14/3 The old custom of tedding either by hand or by tedding machine is avoided.

tedding, *vbl. sb.*[2]: see ted *v.*[2]

teddy. Also **Teddy.** [Pet-form of certain Christian names, as *Edward*, *Edmund*, *Theodore*.]

1. Short for teddy bear 1. Freq. as a proper name for a teddy bear.

1907 *New England Mag.* July 629/2 The Teddy-bear.. suggests to the imaginative owner whatever special being his fancy would have 'Teddy' personify. **1910** *Postcard caption* [to picture of a little girl scrubbing a teddy bear.] You dirty Teddy. **1924** A. A. Milne *When we were very Young* 90 Then said, 'Excuse me,' with an air, 'But is it Mr. Edward Bear?' And Teddy, bending very low, Replied politely, 'Even so!' **1934** E. Tietjens in *Child Life* May 214/2, I always find things I'd forgotten, An old brown Teddy stuffed with cotton. **1940** D. Wheatley *Faked Passports* xxii. 262 It seemed a rotten business to shoot that harmless Bruin which was so reminiscent of a large teddy in a children's toyshop. **1960** *Sunday Times* 3 Jan. 30/3 My aunt ..brought two brown teddies from Vienna in 1904, and in 1905 my mother bought me a white one in Ipswich. **1963** *Sunday Express* 10 Mar. 4/3 Look at teddy—he's got new fur. **1979** *Guardian* 14 June 12/3, I would rather fulfil my role as a mother than have a teddy act as a substitute.

2. [Perh. f. the name of *Theodore* Roosevelt.] (See quot. 1925.)

1917 E. Pound *Let.* 25 Aug. (1971) 118 The *Morning Chronicle* assures me my compatriots are called 'Teddies', which is one in the eye for Mr. Woodie Wilson. **1925** Fraser & Gibbons *Soldier & Sailor Words* 279 *Teddies, the*, one of the names for the U.S. troops on first landing in France; disliked by the Americans equally with 'Sammies', and soon dropped.

3. orig. and chiefly *N. Amer.* [perh. *transf.* use of sense 1.] A woman's undergarment combining chemise and panties. Also in pl. *teddies*.

1924 H. C. Witwer in *Cosmopolitan* May 122/2 She added..she'd personally get enough enjoyment out of standing before her mirror garbed in a sheer silk teddy to warrant any sacrifice. **1929** *Amer. Speech* IV. 422 There is an article of feminine wearing apparel, a sort of overall piece of underwear, I believe, which is known as a *teddy*. I would suppose that this was so-called from its real or fancied resemblance in general shape (or shapelessness) to the teddy-bear. **1934** J. T. Farrell *Young Manhood* (1936) xi. 298 Slug whispered to a big..blonde Polack in pink teddies. **1949** Gilbreth & Carey *Cheaper by Dozen* xvii. 206 Anne.. bought silk stockings, two short dresses and four flimsy pieces of underwear known as teddies. *Ibid.* 208 She doesn't even wear a teddy. **1977** *Hartford* (Conn.) *Courant* 6 June 24/4 Teddys are no longer synonymous with teddy bears alone. They also represent the sexiest lingerie around... The teddy is a camisole and tap pants set combined. The chemise bodice, often fashioned after a camisole, unbuttons either in the front or back... The all-in-one feature of teddys has made them more popular as sleepwear. **1978** *Chatelaine* Dec. 72/2 (*caption*) Left: A body-smoothing teddy with deep insets of lace by Emilio Pucci/Formfit Rogers, $30. **1983** *Daily Tel.* 17 Dec. 10/4 The silver satin 'teddy' we picture is one of this Christmas's best-sellers.

4. Short for Teddy boy.

[**1955** *Britannica Bk. of Year* 489/2 *Teddy-boy*, *Teddy-gang* and *Edwardian* were terms used half derisively to describe youths who affected an Edwardian style of dress and who sometimes formed themselves into hooligan or criminal gangs.] **1956** *Saturday Bk.* 213 Our modern 'teddies' are named after their Edwardian clothes—dress in the manner of the times of King Edward VII—popularly known as 'King Teddy'. **1958** *People* 4 May 12/3 'He'd treat you real good,' said this Teddy. **1960** N. Mitford *Don't tell Alfred* i. 8 His clothes had been distinctly on the Teddy side. **1963** J. Fowles *Collector* ii. 165 We saw a group of teddies standing round two middle-aged Indians... The teddies were shouting, chivvying and bullying them off the pavement on to the road. **1968** [see *chukka boot* s.v. chukka].

teddy bear ('tɛdɪˌbɛə(r)). **1.** A stuffed figure of a bear, made of rough plush, used as a toy or as a kind of mascot. ***teddy bears' picnic***, the title of a song (*c* 1932) by Jimmy Kennedy and J. W. Bratton, used allusively to denote an occasion of innocent enjoyment.

[The 'teddy bear' came into vogue about 1907, and was so called in humorous allusion to Theodore Roosevelt (President of U.S. 1901–1909). Theodore Roosevelt's bear-hunting expeditions occasioned a celebrated comic poem, accompanied by cartoons, in the *N.Y. Times* of 7 Jan. 1906, concerning the adventures of two bears named 'Teddy B' and 'Teddy G'; these names were transferred to two bears (also known as the 'Roosevelt bears') presented to Bronx Zoo in the same year; finally the fame of these bears was turned to advantage by toy dealers, whose toy 'Roosevelt bears', imported from Germany, became an instant fashion in the U.S.]

1906 *Amer. Stationer* 22 Sept. 18/2 Probably no novelty of recent years has been so popular as the Teddy Bears. **1907** *New England Mag.* July 629/1 The Teddy-bear has come, and one suspects that he has come to stay. **1907** *Daily Chron.* 13 Sept. 4/7 While Europe is sending aloft the..'diabolo', America is playing with bears... The sudden delight in these mere things of the toy-shop..is due to their name—'Teddy-bears'. **1907** *Motor Boat* 19 Sept. 190/1 The boat with a Teddy bear or golliwog on the bow. **1908** *Daily Chron.* 5 Nov. 7/1 The Teddy bear, popularly so-called because the retiring President of the United States has a reputation as a bear hunter. **1922**, etc. [see kewpie]. **1927** [see Bonzo]. **1948** *Parents' Mag.* Mar. 8/2 His gently gruff appearance is in best Teddy Bear tradition. **1959** D. Beaty *Cone of Silence* xvii. 188 'Judd and George in the same cockpit together—' Dallas grunted. 'Must have been a Teddy Bear's picnic!' **1962** A. Lurie *Love & Friendship* i. viii. 160 What do you think I am, a Teddy bear, first you pick me up and then you put me down, whenever you feel like it? **1968** *Listener* 11 July 44/3 Can we go on indefinitely enjoying the fun of a teddy bears' picnic? **1977** R. Barnard *Death on High C's* iv. 41 You stop her and you'll have an industrial dispute on your hands that will make Lord Harewood's troubles look like the Teddy-bears' picnic.

b. *transf.* A person who resembles a teddy bear in appearance or in being lovable.

1957 K. Mann (*song-title*) (Let me be your) teddy bear. **1961** J. le Carré *Call for Dead* i. 15 His débutante secretary..referred to him..as 'My darling teddy-bear'. **1972** *Radio Times* 1 Dec. 9/1 David Mercer..is a round, comfortable-looking man..a Teddy Bear with a..West Riding accent. **1979** P. Levi *Head in Soup* v. 93 He was an enormous teddy-bear of a man.

2. a. *U.S. slang.* A fur-lined high-altitude flying suit. Freq. *attrib.*

1917 *Let.* 24 Dec. in Hall & Nordhoff *Lafayette Flying Corps* (1920) II. 58 He has issued to him a fur-lined teddy-bear suit. **1920** E. Haslett *Luck on Wing* ix. 196, I immediately threw off my flying 'teddy bear' and hastily ran through my pockets. **1937** C. Codman *Contact* ii. 29 We issue forth..clad in fur-lined Teddy Bears and fleece-lined overshoes. **1968** J. J. Hudson *Hostile Skies* vii. 132 Lieutenant Horace Gilbert..received three bullets in his 'Teddy Bear' flying suit.

b. A heavy or furry coat; *spec.* one of natural-coloured alpaca-pile fabric. Usu. *attrib.*

1925 Fraser & Gibbons *Soldier & Sailor Words* 279 *Teddy bear*, the name given to the shaggy goatskin and fur coats issued for winter wear in the trenches in 1915. **1932** *Daily Tel.* 23 Sept. 13/2 [The Prince of Wales] was hatless and wore a heavy fawn 'Teddy Bear' overcoat. **1944** A. Thirkell *Headmistress* xii. 267 Mr. Adams, looking more thickset than ever in a thick Teddy Bear coat of orange-brown hue. **1965** P. Moyes *Johnny Under Ground* xviii. 210 He pulled his Teddy Bear greatcoat more closely round his plump form. **1979** 'P. O'Connor' *Into Strong City* i. xii. 35 A very tall man in a teddy-bear overcoat.

c. A furry fabric resembling plush. Usu. *attrib.*

1930 *Daily Express* 6 Oct. 5/1 (Advt.), Men's overcoats... Lined with a teddy bear plush, to give extra warmth. **1977** *New Yorker* 11 July 77/1 Others showed full-blown psychedelic-playtime styles: a mini in canary-colored Teddy-bear pile. **1982** *Times* 2 Apr. 10/3 Teddy bear fur over skinny suede skirts.

3. Austral. rhyming slang for lair *sb.*[4]

1953 S. J. Baker *Australia Speaks* v. 135 *Teddy bear*, a flashily-dressed, exhibitionistic person; by rhyme on *lair*. **1965** W. Grout *My Country's 'Keeper* 55 Umpire Col Egar was so furious at this amateurish attempt at time-wasting that he snapped to the Pakistani bowler: 'Get up you Teddy Bear' (an Australian expression not meant to be complimentary). **1974** K. Stackpole *Not just for Openers* 128 When Parfitt made the catch Greig jumped in the air, and, as he landed, thumped his fist into the pitch... I said to Greig as I walked past, 'You're nothing but a bloody Teddy Bear.' He returned the pleasantries.

4. = teddy 3.

1978 *Maledicta* 1977 I. 273 Priorly, she had begun to haul out of the hour-glass corset into teddy-bear and slip. **1979** *Amer. Speech* 1976 LI. 8 The new underwear was a convenient garment, a hip-length *chemise* with a narrow strap between the thighs which was secured by two small buttons or snaps. It was affectionately known first as a *teddy-bear*, then as a *teddy* or *shimmy*.

Hence **teddy-bearish** *a.*, resembling a teddy bear.

1973 *Guardian* 9 Mar. 17/1 Tall, dark, teddy-bearish, charming and persuasive. *a* **1976** A. CHRISTIE *Autobiogr.* (1977) IX. iii. 451 They took on board eight or ten darling little brown bears... Completely teddy-bearish.

Teddy boy ('tɛdɪ bɔɪ). *colloq.* [f. *Teddy*, pet-form of *Edward* (VII), with reference to the style of dress (cf. EDWARDIAN *sb.* 3) + BOY *sb.*[1]] A youth affecting a style of dress and appearance held to be characteristic of Edward VII's reign, typically a long velvet-collared jacket and 'drain-pipe' trousers (see *drape suit* s.v. DRAPE *sb.*[1] d) and sideburns; in extended use, any youthful street rowdy. Hence **'Teddy-boyish** *a.*, characteristic of a Teddy boy; **'Teddy-boyism**, the state or condition of being a Teddy boy; group behaviour of a kind associated with Teddy boys. Similarly **Teddy girl**, a girl who associates with or behaves like Teddy boys.

1954 A. HECKSTALL-SMITH *Eighteen Months* x. 118 Craig was just such a fellow. Ronald Coleman, the leader of the 'Edwardians' or the 'Teddy Boys', the gang of young hooligans who ran amok on Clapham Common, was another. **1955** in I. & P. Opie *Lore & Lang. Schoolch.* (1959) vii. 106 Slip-on shoes and a rainbow tie, Kissing his Teddy girl goodbye! **1955** *Times* 27 July 5/1 Young soldiers are now forbidden to 'walk out' when off duty in plain clothes of unorthodox pattern, particularly the so-called Edwardian or 'Teddy boy' style... The forbidden style is not specifically defined in the order but is understood to be that of the long, draped-fronted jacket with velvet collar, and tight trousers shortened to show white socks at the ankles. **1957** *Sunday Times* 17 Feb. 4/4 The girls who are an integral part of the gangs—the so-called Teddy-girls—are probably the worst influence of all. **1959** *Times* 9 Oct. 15/7 The growing tide of teddy-boyism, chiefly in the Athens-Piraeus area, forced the authorities to act. **1960** *Guardian* 7 May 6/6 Looking back with teddy-boyish anger. **1960** *News Chron.* 9 June 9/1 We should not consider them as Teddy boys or Teddy girls, but potential customers. **1962** [see SLIM JIM 3]. **1977** *Daily Tel.* 19 July 15/4 A group of about 40 'punk rockers' being chased by Teddy boys.

† **tede**, *sb. Obs.* Also tead(-e. [ad. L. *tæda*, *tēda* pine-torch.] A resinous piece of pine used as a torch; a wood-torch.

1562 TURNER *Herbal* II. 89 A tede is a fat and roseny pece of a pyne or pich tre, which hewen of, serueth for torches. **1591** SPENSER *Muiopotmos* 293 A burning Teade about his head did move. **1624** DARCIE *Birth of Heresies* xv. 61 A Lamp or high Taper, which ordinarily was of Tede or Pine. **1637** WHITING *Albino & Bellama* 27 Bellama's bridall tede is lighted now.

† **tede**, *a. Obs. rare*[−1]. ? Tied, joined together.

13.. *E.E. Allit. P.* B. 1634 Fyrst telle me þe tyxte of þe tede lettres, & syþen þe mater of þe mode, mene me þer-after.

tede, teder, obs. forms of TED *v.*, TETHER.

‖ **tedesco** (te'desko), *a.* (*sb.*) Pl. tedeschi (-ki). Also tedesque (-'ɛsk). [It. *tedesco* German; ad. med.L. *theodisc-us*: cf. Goth. *þiudisk*, OE. *þéodisc*, OHG. *diutisc*, MHG. *tiutsch*, *diutsch*, Ger. *deutsch*: see DUTCH.] The Italian word for German; esp. used to express Teutonic influence as shown in some spheres of Italian art.

1814 BYRON *Jrnl.* 20 Feb. in Moore *Life* (1830) I. 501 The Tedeschi dramatists. **1845** FORD *Handbk. Spain* I. 551/2 The *Coro Alto* was carved in a quaint tedesque style. **1874** T. G. APPLETON in *Longfellow's Life* (1891) III. 232 Achille denounced the *Tedesco* with the traditionary hatred of the Austrian. **1883** C. C. PERKINS *Ital. Sculpture* I. iv. 51 *note*, Minute works in the 'semi-tedesco' style, then in fashion.

Tedesco, var. TUDESCO.

‖ **Te Deum** ('tiː 'diːəm). [From the opening words of the Latin original, *Te Deum laudamus*, 'Thee, God, we praise'.] An ancient Latin hymn of praise in the form of a psalm, sung as a thanksgiving on special occasions, as after a victory or deliverance; also regularly at Matins in the R.C. Ch., and (in an English translation) at Morning Prayer in the Church of England.

c **961** ÆTHELWOLD *Rule St. Benet* xi. (1885) 35 Æfter þæm glorian þæs feorþan repses beginne se abbod þæne lofsang Te deum laudamus. [So in *c* **1200** *Winteney Rule St. Benet* xi. 47.] *c* **1386** CHAUCER *Sompn. T.* 158 Te deum was oure song and no thyng elles. *c* **1485** *Digby Myst.* III. 2140 Te Deum lavdamus lett vs syng. **1547–8** *Rec. St. Mary at Hill* 387 Item, for iiij songe bokes of te deum in Englisshe.. viij d. **1613** SHAKS. *Hen. VIII*, IV. i. 92 The Quire With all the choysest Musicke of the Kingdome Together sung Te Deum. **1822** BYRON *Werner* v. i. 94 'Te Deum' peal'd from nations. **1896** C. K. PAUL tr. *Huysman's En Route* viii. 107 Standing, he intoned the 'Te Deum'.

b. With *a* and in *pl.* **Te Deums**, in reference to a recital of this, or (allusively) to any public utterance of praise to God; also, a service of (public) thanksgiving marked by the singing of this hymn.

1679 SHADWELL *True Widow* I. 3 At home they are alwayes roaring out Te Deums for Stealing of some Town or other. **1711** *Lond. Gaz.* No. 4794/3 Letters from France begin to own that their *Te Deum* cost them extreamly dear. **1903** MORLEY *Gladstone* I. IV. x. 615 The archbishop ordered a *Te Deum*. Neither te-deums nor prayers melted the heart of the British cabinet.

c. A musical setting of this hymn.

1864 [Jackson's *Te Deum* regularly used in church services.] **1880** W. H. HUSK in *Grove's Dict. Mus.* I. 625/1 In addition to the before-named compositions, Greene produced a Te Deum in D major, with orchestral accompaniments.

d. *attrib.* and *Comb.*

1874 RUSKIN *Fors Clav.* xlv. (1896) II. 419 Te-Deum-singing Princes. **1896** *Daily News* 4 Aug. 3/7 A Te Deum mass in celebration of the birthday of the Empress Dowager of Russia took place yesterday at the Orthodox Church in the Rue Daru in Paris.

Hence **Te-'Deuming** (*nonce-wd.*), the singing of a Te Deum or Te Deums.

1862 CARLYLE *Fredk. Gt.* XIII. vii. (1873) V. 82 With much processioning, blaring and *te-deum*-ing. **1864** *Ibid.* xv. i. V. 270 *Te-deum*-ing on an extensive scale.

tedge (tɛdʒ). *rare*[−0]. [Etymology unknown.] = INGATE *sb.*[2]: see quots.

1858 SIMMONDS *Dict. Trade*, *Ingate*, an aperture in a mould for pouring in metal; technically called the tedge. **1877** KNIGHT *Dict. Mech.*, *Tedge*, the ingate or aperture in a mold through which the molten metal is poured.

† **tedi'ation.** *Obs. rare*[−1]. [n. of action f. late L. *tædiāre* to feel loathing: see -ATION. Perh. aphetic for *ated(y)acyon* (also in Caxton), a. OF.: see ATTEDIATION.] The action of wearying or condition of being wearied.

1485 CAXTON *Chas. Gt.* 112 Ye shall do Iustyce wyth lasse tedyacyon.

† **te'diferous**, *a. Obs. rare*[−0]. [f. L. *tædifer* (f. *tæda* torch + *-fer* bearing) + -OUS: see -FEROUS.] Bearing a torch.

1656 BLOUNT *Glossogr.*, *Tediferous* (*tedifer*), that beareth a torch or taper. **1658** in PHILLIPS. **1721** in BAILEY.

† **'tedify**, *v. nonce-wd.* [irreg. f. L. *tædium*, TEDIUM + -FY, after *edify*.] *trans.* To affect with tedium; to weary, bore. So † **tedifi'cation**.

1613 T. ADAMS *Sinner's Passing-bell* Wks. 1861 I. 348 An odious, tedious, endless inculcation of things doth often tire those with whom a soft and short reproof would find good impression. Such, whiles they would intend to edify, do in event tedify. **1616** —— *Divine Herbal* ibid. II. 442 Too often, till edification turn to tedification. **1633** —— *Exp. 2 Peter* iii. 4 To be all utterance, no materials, and so not to edify but tedify their hearers.

teding-penny, obs. f. TITHING-PENNY.

tedious ('tiːdɪəs), *a.* Forms: 5 ted(e)us, tedi-, tidiose, 5–7 tedy-, 6 tede-, tide-, tydy-, tyde-, *Sc.* tidi-, 6–7 teydi-, 7–8 teadi-, 8 tædi-, 5– tedious. (Also 6 tedy-, tiddius, *Sc.* tideus, -ews, 6–7 tedius.) [ad. late L. *tædiōs-us* irksome, f. *tædium*, TEDIUM: see -OUS; perh. partly ad. OF. *tedieus*, *-eux* (1387 in Godef.).]

1. 'Wearisome by continuance' (J.); long and tiresome: said of anything occupying time, as a task, or a journey; *esp.* of a speech or narrative, hence of a speaker or writer: prolix, so as to cause weariness.

1412–20 LYDG. *Chron. Troy* IV. xxxiii. Me liste no more of hir woo to endite Leste vn to 3ow that it were tedious. *c* **1475** *Babees Bk.* 75 Many wordes ben rihte Tedious. **1526** TINDALE *Acts* xxiv. 4 Lest I be tedeous vnto the. **1549** *Compl. Scot.* vi. 62, I pray the to decist fra that tideus melancolic orison. **1552** LYNDESAY *Monarche* 4065 Bot tiddius it wer to tell. **1552** HULOET, Tedious speaker, or patterer, *battologus*. **1592** SHAKS. *Rom. & Jul.* v. iii. 230, I will be briefe, for my short date of breath Is not so long as is a tedious tale. **1603** —— *Meas. for M.* II. i. 119 Come: you are a tedious foole: to the purpose. **1675** T. TULLY *Let. Baxter* 27 The tediousest taske I ever yet undertooke. **1709** STEELE & ADDISON *Tatler* No. 75 ¶8, I would not be tedious in this Discourse. **1756** C. LUCAS *Ess. Waters* I. Pref., A series of teadious and laborious experiments. **1819** SCOTT *Let. to Ld. Montagu* 4 Mar., in *Lockhart*, Tedious hours occur on board of ship. **1875** JOWETT *Plato* (ed. 2) V. 36 If I am to discuss all these matters, I cannot avoid being tedious.

† **b.** *humorously.* Long (in time or extent). *Obs.*

1601 SHAKS. *All's Well* II. iii. 33 Nay 'tis strange, 'tis very straunge, that is the breefe and the tedious of it. **1630** *R. Johnson's Kingd. & Commw.* 56 An old sheep-biter, with a nose too tedious for his face.

2. Wearisome in general; annoying, irksome, troublesome, disagreeable, painful. *Obs.* exc. *dial.*

1454 *Paston Lett.* I. 279 To arere a power to resyst the sayd riotts, which to hem on that holy tyme was tediose and heynous. **1526** TINDALE *Rom.* xii. 11 Let not that busynes which ye have in honde be tedious to you. *c* **1689** J. WHICKER in Arb. *Garner* VII. 375 A sort of flies.. drew blisters and bladders in our skin.. which were very tedious for our bodies too. *a* **1694** TILLOTSON *Serm.* (1742) III. 181, I may be tedious, but I will not be long. *c* **1845** in *J. Mitford's Lett. & Rem.* 143 Johnstone ain't a drinking man nor a wife-beater, but he makes her a tedious husband. **1868** ATKINSON *Cleveland Gloss.*, *Tedious*,..fidgetty, uneasy, requiring constant attention; of an infant or young child when teething, or poorly. **1871** R. ELLIS *Catullus* l. 17 Did I, a poem Write, my tedious anguish all revealing.

† **3.** Tired, wearied, exhausted; also, disgusted or annoyed, esp. by iteration or excess; bored.

1430–40 LYDG. *Bochas* VIII. viii. (MS. Bodl. 263) lf. 375 Galerius.. Throuh at [*sic*] thorient wex victorious Til he for age, gan wexen tedious. **1509** BARCLAY *Shyp of Folys* (1874) II. 148 So whan the Father is tedyous and old. **1540–1** ELYOT *Image Gov.* (1544) Bij, Being also tedious of his abhominations. *Ibid.* xxviii. Qiij b, Beinge tediouse of that beastely lycence.

4. Late, tardy, dilatory, slow. *Obs.* exc. *dial.*

c **1485** *Digby Myst.* IV. 1079, I was to tidiose, That holy sight to see. **1605** BACON *Adv. Learn.* I. ii. §7 The most active or busy man.. hath.. many vacant times of leisure.. except he be.. tedious and of no dispatch. **1698** CONGREVE *Semele* II. i, Though thou hadst on lightning rode, Still thou tedious art, and slow. **1728** MORGAN *Algiers* II. iii. 249 Barbarossa was not.. very tedious in gratifying their curiosity. **1833** T. HOOK *Parson's Dau.* II. i, 'I expect Lord Weybridge; we are not ready for dinner till his lordship comes.' 'What can make him so tedious?' said Maria-Jane. **1898** [see *Eng. Dial. Dict.*].

So **'tedisome, tediousome** *a.* (*Sc.*), tedious; **tedi'osity** (*rare*), † **tediouste** [= OF. *tedieusete*, 15th c.], tediousness.

? *a* **1412** LYDG. *Two Merch.* 900 Lest tediouste your erys did assayl. **1612** *Two Noble K.* III. v, What tediosity and disensanity Is here among ye! **1790** J. BYNG *Diary* 18 July (1935) II. 257 They are sad sluggards: Mrs. B. most idly breakfasts in bed; C[ec]y is tediocity. **1824** SCOTT *St. Ronan's* xxii, It was an unco pleasant show,.. only it was a pity it was sae tediousome. **1934** *Jrnl. Theol. Stud.* XXXV. 289 In spite of his tediosity, however, his books present some interesting and picturesque features.

tediously ('tiːdɪəslɪ), *adv.* [f. prec. + -LY[2].] In a tedious manner; at great and wearisome length; tiresomely; slowly, tardily.

a **1557** MRS. M. BASSET *More's Treat. Passion* M.'s Wks. 1376/1 Oftentimes tediousely without any nede thei were faine to repete twise euery worde they said in their praiour. **1583** HOLLYBAND *Campo di Fior* 323 Thou hast made me to forget it interrupting me so tediousely. **1599** SHAKS. *Hen. V*, IV. Chorus 22 The creeple-tardy-gated Night, Who like a foule and ougly Witch doth limpe So tediously away. **1653** WALTON *Angler* To Rdr. 2 Not to read dull, and tediously. **1779–81** JOHNSON *L.P.*, *Milton* Wks. II. 154 [Comus] a drama in the epick style, inelegantly splendid, and tediously instructive. **1837** HALLAM *Hist. Lit.* III. ii. §72 Hall.. dilates upon it sometimes more tediously, but more appositely.

tediousness ('tiːdɪəsnɪs). [f. as prec. + -NESS.] The quality or condition of being tedious.

1. Wearisomeness on account of long continuance; tiresome lengthiness, prolixity; also, wearisomeness in general; irksomeness, troublesomeness; trouble, annoyance (*obs.* or *dial.*).

1432–50 tr. *Higden* (Rolls) II. 229 Tubal exercisede firste musike to alleuiate the tediosenes pastoralle. *Ibid.* IV. 255 The vthe age of the worlde.. afflicte with moche tediousenesse [*orig.* crebris malis quassata]. **1553** T. WILSON *Rhet.* (1580) 139 Euen in this our tyme, some offende much in tediousnesse. **1599** DAVIES *Immort. Soul* cccix, She distastes them all, within a while; And in the sweetest, finds a tediousness. **1658** ROWLAND *Moufet's Theat. Ins.* 936 The bloud of beasts, which with great tediousnesse and pain he [the bee-fly] sucks out. **1798** S. & HT. LEE *Canterb. T.*, *Yng. Lady's T.* II. 434 He.. resolved rather to endure the tediousness of a passage by sea. **1881** *Times* 9 Apr. 11/3 Ecclesiastical litigation abuses the common legal privilege of tediousness.

† **2.** Weariness, ennui; disgust, distaste. *Obs.*

1482 *Monk of Evesham* (Arb.) 25 Vnto the tedusnes of some stondyng by, he thankyd owr lord and redemer.. for innumerabulle benefetis. *c* **1561** VERON *Free-will* 46 To engender in them a hatred and tediousnesse of vyce. **1576** FLEMING tr. *Caius' Eng. Dogs* (1880) 5 These Dogges.. applying to their pursuit, agilitie and nimblenesse, without tediousnesse. **1684** *Contempl. St. Man* II. v. (1699) 171 All there know God without Error... Love him without Tediousness.

3. Slowness, tardiness; dilatoriness. *Obs.* exc. *dial.*

1691 T. H[ALE] *Acc. New Invent.* 6 Its tediousness in bringing on and off. **1742** H. WALPOLE *Lett. to Mann* (1834) I. xlviii. 189 By the tediousness of the post and distance of place I am still receiving letters from you about the Secret Committee. **1900** [see *Eng. Dial. Dict.*].

tedium ('tiːdɪəm). Also 7–9 tædium. [a. L. *tædium* weariness, disgust, f. *tæd-ēre* to weary.] The state or quality of being tedious; wearisomeness, tediousness, ennui.

1662 PETTY *Taxes* ii. §37 Whereby the charge and tedium of travelling.. may be greatly lessened. **1663** J. SPENCER *Prodigies* (1665) 16 Stories of Prodigies may.. deceive the tædium of a winter night. **1779** J. MOORE *View Soc. Fr.* (1789) I. xviii. 141 A more infallible specific against tedium and fatigue. **1814** SCOTT *Wav.* xxv, When he remembered the tædium of his quarters. **1874** GREEN *Short Hist.* v. §1. 216 In some of the stories.. there is the tedium of the old romance.

Comb. **1827** CARLYLE *Germ. Lit.* Misc. Ess. 1872 I. 28 One or two sleek clerical tutors, with here and there a tedium-stricken 'squire.

tedure, -yr(e, obs. forms of TETHER.

tee (tiː), *sb.*[1] [The origin of senses 2 and 3 is obscure: possibly they do not belong here.]

I. 1. a. The name of the letter T; also applied to objects having the form of this (**T** or ⊢). See also T (the letter) 2.

1610 GUILLIM *Heraldry* IV. v. (1611) 199 He beareth Argent, a cheveron betweene three Text Tees, sable. **1877** KNIGHT *Dict. Mech.*, *Tee*, a T-shaped pipe-coupling. **1882** *Worc. Exhib. Catal.* iii. 5 Connections, elbows, tees, syphons. **1891** *Times* 28 Sept. 3/6 The demand for angles and tees is quiet, but bridge and roofing makers are taking fair lots.

b. Phr. *to a tee*: see T I. c.

II. 2. *Sc.* (See quot. 1882.)

1494–5 *Acc. Ld. High Treas. Scot.* I. 228 To mak knoppis and fassis to the harnysing of briddillis and teis, xxxij pirnis of gold. **1505** *Ibid.* III. 160 For ane courpale and tee..xs. **1675** CUNNINGHAM *Diary* 27 July (1887) 56 Sent to Glasgow for a new Curpell and Tee. **1776** R. FERGUSON in Whitelaw *Bk. Scot. Song* (1875) 100 With..hat, and a feather, And housing at curpen and tee. **1882** *Jamieson's Dict.*, *Tee.* Pl. *tees, teis*, iron holdfasts, in shape like the letter T, suspended from a horse's collar for attachment to the shafts of a vehicle, or for connecting the bit and bridle; also, the ropes by which a sailyard is suspended.

3. *Mining.* (See quot. 1851.)

1653 MANLOVE *Lead Mines* 266 Fell, Bous, and Knock-barke, Forstid-oar, and Tees. **1747** HOOSON *Miner's Dict.* S ij, After crossing of Pees, Tees, Braks, Jumbles, or what other disorder may happen that the Vein cannot be easily made out. **1851** TAPPING *Gloss. Lead-mining Terms*, *Tee*, or *Tye*, is where a cross vein approaches another vein at nearly right angles, whose side it joins without intersecting or breaking through it.

III. 4. *attrib.* Shaped like a **T**, having a cross-piece at the top or end, as ***tee-beam***, ***-frame***, ***-iron***, ***-joint***, ***-piece***, ***section***, ***slot***, ***-square***; also in other combs., as ***tee-headed***, ***-shaped*** adjs. See also T (the letter) 3.

1819 PECKSTON *Gas-Lighting* 300 Wrought-iron tee-pieces for branching off from the principal service-pipe in two directions. **1822** IMISON *Sc. & Art* II. 344 Tee-squares are rulers made in the form of the letter T. **1877** KNIGHT *Dict. Mech.*, *Tee-iron*, a rod with a cross-bar at the end, for withdrawing the lower valve-box of a pump. **1884** *Health Exhib. Catal.* p. liii/2 Fire and Thief-resisting Safes..solid tee frame, and solid flange lock case. **1887** D. A. LOW *Machine Draw.* (1892) 18 At (*c*) is shown a tee-headed bolt. **1888** *Lockwood's Dict. Mech. Engin.* 368 *Tee joint*, a welded joint employed for uniting pieces of bar iron standing at right angles with each other. *Ibid.*, *Tee shots*, slots or grooves cast in the tables of planing, shaping, slotting, and drilling machines for carrying the heads of tee-headed bolts. **1904** *Daily Chron.* 4 May 3/2 Tee-shaped and substantially built, the new pier..has a frontage of 650 ft. **1930** *Engineering* 9 May 591/1 (*title*) Simplified formulae for the design of reinforced concrete tee beams. **1963** JONES & SCHUBERT *Engin. Encycl.* 1278 *Tee section*, the standard structural section known as a tee has a T shape. **1964** S. CRAWFORD *Basic Engin. Processes* iii. 93 The down-hand fillet or tee joint is shown in Fig. 14 (a). *Ibid.* v. 116 A circular tee-slot machined in the top face of the centre-slide provides movement for the heads of the clamping bolts. **1965** R. HAMMOND *Dict. Civil Engin.* 228 *Tee-beam*, a rolled steel section..in the shape of the letter T, the flat top being the table.

tee (tiː), *sb.*[2] *Golf.* Orig. *Sc.* [app. a curtailed form of *teaz*, used in 17th c., the origin of which is not ascertained. For the formation cf. *pease*, *pea*.] The starting-place (formerly a little heap of earth or sand) from which the ball is driven in commencing to play each hole: now usu. a wooden or plastic peg with a concave top; also called ***tee-peg*** or ***peg-tee***.

1673 *Wedderburn's Vocab.* 37, 38 (Jam.) *Baculus*, *Pila clavaria*, a goulfe-ball. *Statumen*, the Teaz. **1721** RAMSAY *Ode to Ph*— ii, Driving their baws frae whins or tee. **1875** W. A. SMITH *Lewsiana* 147 Each [shell] is seated on a sandy 'tee', formed by the wind sweeping away the sand around it. **1879** *Encycl. Brit.* X. 765/1 In starting from the hole, the ball may be teed (i.e. placed where the player chooses, with a little pinch of sand under it called a tee). **1905** *Daily News* 7 Jan. 12 At two o'clock,..the golfing party were at the first tee. **1921** *Daily Colonist* (Victoria, B.C.) 9 Oct. 11/6 Golf clubs..bags, balls, tees, [etc.]. **1926** *Amer. Speech* I. 631/2 There are also tees of rubber, and recently wooden pegs on which balls may be teed have come into vogue. **1952** L. T. STANLEY *Woman Golfer* 53 Many players prefer to play iron shots to a short hole off a peg-tee. **1959** D. THOMAS *Instructions to Young Golfers* xix. 106 He takes a ball.., places it on a tee-peg..and..smites it a good fifty yards. **1962** *Times* 3 Jan. 3/6 The only indication of a satisfactory hit is the speed with which the striker bends down to recover his tee. **1975** *Oxf. Compan. Sports & Games* 422/2 It is usual for the first shot at each hole to be played off a wooden or plastic tee-peg... The tee-peg was invented in 1920 by Lowel of New Jersey.

attrib. **1862** R. CHAMBERS *Rambling Remarks* 14 The tee-shots are usually the furthest, long drivers being able to send a ball upwards of two hundred yards. **1901** *Daily Chron.* 7 June 8/3 Vardon was beaten in the tee shots.

tee (tiː), *sb.*[3] *Curling*, etc. Orig. *Sc.* [Origin uncertain: perh. orig. the same word as TEE *sb.*[1], from the use of such a mark to define an exact spot.

(A suggested derivation from ON. *tjá* to show, mark, note, is untenable.)]

The mark, a cross made on the ice and surrounded by circles, at which the stones are aimed; applied also to the 'jack' at bowls, and the 'hob' at quoits.

1789 D. DAVIDSON *Th. Seasons, Winter* 167 Clim o' the Cleugh..A slow shot drew, wi' muckle care, Which settled on the tee. **1812** *Sporting Mag.* XL. 51 A mark is made at each end [of the rink] called a *tee, toesee*, or *witter*. **1820** *Blackw. Mag.* VI. 572 Each player endeavouring to possess himself of a birth near the *Tee*. **1885** *New Bk. Sports* 100 (Curling) The players who open the game begin by playing short of the tee. **1888** W. BLACK *In Far Lochaber* ii. I. 66 A trimly kept bowling-green, in which the club-members practise the gentle art of reaching the tee.

b. *attrib.* and *Comb.*, as ***tee-shot***; ***tee-drawn*** adj.

1850 J. STRUTHERS *Winter Day* II. ix, Tee-drawn shots the smooth-lead fill, Or ports are wick'd with hair-breadth skill. **1853** W. WATSON *Poems* 64 (E.D.D.) [He] Sen's up a tee-shot to a hair.

‖**tee** (tiː), *sb.*[4] Also **htee**. [Burmese *h'ti* umbrella.] A metallic decoration, in the shape of an umbrella, usually gilded and hung with bells, surmounting the topes and pagodas of Burma and adjacent countries.

1800 M. SYMES *Embassy Ava* v. 188 The whole [building] is crowned by a *Tee*, or umbrella, of open iron-work, from which rises a rod with a gilded pennant. The tee or umbrella is to be seen on every sacred building that is of a spiral form. **1858** H. YULE *Mission to Ava* ii. 42 [The Gauda-palen Temple at Pagan] is cruciform in plan..crowned by a spire and *htee*. **1882** *Edin. Rev.* Oct. 360 On the summit of the tope was a square construction known among archæologists as the 'tee'.

†**tee**, *v.*[1] *Obs.* Forms: see below. [OE. *téon* (contr. from *téohan*), pa. t. *téah*, *tuᵹon*, pa. pple. *toᵹen*, a Com. Teutonic str. vb., cogn. with OSax. *tiohan*, *tôh*, *tugun*, *gitogan* (MLG. *tien*, *ten*, MDu. *tijen*, *tijghen*, LG. *teën*, EFris. *tîen*, *têjen*, *têen*), OFris. *tia* (WFris. *tjean*, Saterl. *tejen*, NFris. *tjin*), OHG. *ziohan*, *zôh*, *zugun*, *gizogan* (Ger. *ziehen*, *zog*, *gezogen*), ON. pa. pple. *toginn*, Goth. *tiuhan*, *táuh*, *tauhum*, *tauhans*, to draw, lead; = L. *dūc-ĕre* to lead, draw. A primitive Aryan vb., still important in German, but lost in Eng. by 1500. Derivatives of the same root survive in *taut*, *team*, *tie*, *tight*, *tough*, *tow*, *tug*.]

A. Illustration of Forms.

1. *Present stem.* **a.** *Inf.* 1 **téon**, 2–4 **teon**, 3–4 **tuen**, 3–5 **teen**, **ten**, **teo**, **tee**, **te**; 5 **tegh**.

971 *Blickl. Hom.* 241 ᵹif eow swa liciᵹe..hine teon þurh þisse ceastre lanan. *c* **1205** LAY. 791 Ich wille teo [*c* 1275 go] to-foren. *c* **1250** *Gen. & Ex.* 1344 To bersabe he gunne teen. *Ibid.* 1953 To-warde egipte he gunne ten. *c* **1290** *St. Eustace* 165 in Horstm. *Altengl. Leg.* (1881) 214 To londe he moste te. *c* **1300** *Harrow. Hell* 234 Alle..þat mine buen shule to blisse wiþ me tuen. *c* **1320** *Cast. Love* 821 Þorw on of þeos bayles he mot teon. *Ibid.* 877 Þorw þe faste ȝat he con in teo. *c* **1400** *Destr. Troy* 2541 Let hym tegh to þe tempull. *c* **1425** *Cast. Persev.* 1564 in *Macro Plays* 123 Þedyr raþely wyl I tee. *c* **1450** LOVELICH *Grail* xiii. 56 Owt of the castel of Come þat he wolde te.

b. *Pres. Indic.*, *Imper.* 1 **teoh**, **teo**, **tio**, 3–4 **tee**, **te**; 2 (*Subj.*) **tye**; *pl.* 1 **teon**, 3–4 **teen**, **ten**. *Imper.* 1 **teoh**, 3 **tih**.

c **897** [see B. 1 b]. *c* **1000** ÆLFRIC *Gram.* xxviii. (Z.) 176 *Traho*, ic teo,..*pertraho*, ic teo swyðe. *c* **1000** *Ags. Gosp.* John vi. 44 Buton se fæder..hyne teo [*c* **1160** *Hatton G.* hyne tye]. *Ibid.* Luke v. 4 Teoh hit on dypan. **1027–34** *Secular Laws Cnut* c. 70 Ne teo se hlaford na mare on his æhta. *c* **1205** LAY. 17416 Vther, tih þe aȝan. *c* **1220** *Bestiary* 353 Ðe hertes..If he fer fecchen fode, and he ouer water ten. **13..** *E.E. Allit. P.* B. 9 Thay teen vnto his temmple. *Ibid.* 1262 Er he to þe tempple tee. **13..** *Guy Warw.* (A.) 2018 Er þe sonne doun te.

c. *Pres. Indic.*, *2nd pers. sing.* 1 **tiehst**, **tyhst**, *3rd. pers. sing.* 1 **tiehþ**, **tyhþ**, **tihþ**, 2 **tið**, 3 **tiȝth**, **tihth**, **teð**, **teoð**, 4 **teȝt**.

c **897** K. ÆLFRED *Gregory's Past. C.* xxxv. 241 He tiehð his heafod in to him. *c* **1000** *Sax. Leechd.* II. 256 Læcedom se þæt yfel ut tihð of þam milte. *Ibid.* 262 Þonne þu..tyhst blod. *c* **1175** *Lamb. Hom.* 27 Hit hine tið to þan bittre deðe. *c* **1200** *Trin. Coll. Hom.* 37 Iefned to þe deore [h]wuas geres he forðteoð. *c* **1220** *Bestiary* 64 Up he teð, Til ðat he ðe heuene seð. *a* **1250** *Owl & Night.* 1435 An sum sot man hit tyhþ [*v.r.* tihþ] þar to. *c* **1315** SHOREHAM iii. 236 As he teȝt atte font-stone.

2. *Pa. t.* 1 **téah**, 2 **teah**, 2–3 **teh**, **teih**, **tæh**, **tah**, 3–4 **teȝ**, **teiȝ**, **tey**, **teye**, **teiȝe**, 4 **tyh**, 5 **teȝe**, **tegh**. *Pl.* 1 **tuᵹon**, 3 **tuȝen**, **tuhen**, **tuwen**, 5 **tyen**.

a **900** CYNEWULF *Judith* 99 [Heo] ᵹenam ða þone hæðenan mannan fæste be feaxe sinum, teah hyne. *c* **1175** *Lamb. Hom.* 129 Þurh hwam ure drihtan teh to him al moncun. *c* **1205** LAY. 640 He tah hine aȝein. *Ibid.* 805 He him seolf teih [*c* **1275** eode] bi-foren. *Ibid.* 1641 Tæh [see B. 1 b]. *Ibid.* 21616 Touwarde þæ hulle [he] tæh. *c* **1250** *Gen. & Ex.* 1135 Wið hise two dowtres ut he teȝ. *a* **1300** *Vox & Wolf* 279 in *Rel. Ant.* II. 278 The frere mid al his maine tey So longe, that [etc.]. *a* **1375** *Joseph Arim.* 57 Ioseph teiȝ to non hous bote euene to þe temple. **1390** GOWER *Conf.* II. 318 Unto his contre hom he tyh. *c* **1400** *Destr. Troy* 12907 He light into hauyn,..Tegh vnto Tuskan, & turnyt to londe.

c **1000** *Ags. Gosp.* Luke v. 11 And hiᵹ tuᵹon heora scypu to lande. *c* **1205** LAY. 1834 Heo tuȝen [*c* 1275 drowen] alle to gadere. *Ibid.* 2619 Him tuwen hired men to. *a* **1225** *St. Marher.* 22 Ant tuhen alle to hire bodi. *c* **1400** *Sege Jerus.* 843 His burnes Tyen to her tentis myd tene þat þey hadde.

3. *Pa. pple.* 1 (**ᵹe**)**toᵹen**, 3 **i-toȝen**, **i-tohen**, **i-towen**, **-un**, **toȝen**, 4–5 **towen**.

971 *Blickl. Hom.* 241 Se eadiᵹa Andreas wæs toᵹen. *c* **1205** LAY. 10099 Luces wes wel itoȝen. *a* **1225** *Ancr. R.* 108 Heo is a grucchild, & ful itowen [*v.r.* itohen]. *Ibid.* 204 Þe nome one muhte hurten alle wel itowune earen. *c* **1250** *Gen. & Ex.* 3647 Ðis folc is after softe toȝen. **13..** *Gaw. & Gr. Knt.* 1093 For ȝe haf trauayled, towen fro ferre.

B. Signification.

1. *trans.* To draw, pull, drag, tug.

a **900** tr. *Bæda's Hist.* v. xiii. [xii.] (1890) 428 Tuᵹon heo ða werᵹan gastas. *c* **1122** *O.E. Chron.* an. 1052, Godwine eorl ..teah þa up his seᵹl. *a* **1225** *Juliana* 8 Ant tuhen him ȝont te tun, from strete to strete. *a* **1225** *Ancr. R.* 324 Hwo is þet durste slepen þeo hwule þet his deadlich fo heolde on itowen sweord ouer his heaued? *c* **1275** LAY. 4995 Þane hem ȝeo vp teh [*c* **1205** i-tæh] to hire cneon wel neh. **13..** *K. Alis.* 7070 To shipp he may hem beren & teen. **1375** BARBOUR *Bruce* xv. 282 He gert men..Salys to the toppis te. *c* **1400** *Destr. Troy* 10382 To tegh as a traytor, and traile vpon þe erthe. **1446** LYDG. *Nightingale Poems* ii. 166 The Iewes my flessh asonder dide tee.

b. To draw to oneself, to take to or upon oneself.

c **897** K. ÆLFRED *Gregory's Past. C.* xvi. 99 Ðæt he tio [*v.r.* teo] on hine selfne oðerra monna scylda. **925–35** *Laws Athelstan* II. c. 9 Þæt he hit on folc ryht him to teo. *c* **1205** LAY. 1641 He..tæh hit to his aȝre hond. *c* **1315** SHOREHAM iii. 285 For al hys þefte þat man teȝt. *c* **1400** *St. Alexius* (Trin.) 449 Þat writ he drouȝ & ȝerne teiȝ. *a* **1500** *Sir Beues* (S.) 2319 His ryng he gan to him tee.

c. To lead, bring (an army, etc.). Only OE.

a **900** tr. *Bæda's Hist.* III. xiv. [xviii.] (1890) 208 Penda Mercna cyning teah here and fyrd wið Eastengle.

2. *fig.* To draw, lead, entice, allure; to bring into some condition. Const. *to*.

c **888** K. ÆLFRED *Boeth.* xxvi. § 1 Sio ᵹecynd eow tihð to ðæm andᵹite. [**971** *Blickl. Hom.* 37 Seo oferfyll þæs lichoman ᵹetyhþ þone mon to synnum.] *c* **1200** *Trin. Coll. Hom.* 139 And teh folc to him to heren his wise word. *a* **1250** [see A. 1 c].

3. To bring up, train, discipline, educate, teach.

c **1000** ÆLFRIC *Gram.* (Z.) 166 *Imbuo*, ic ty [*v.r.* ic teo] oððe ic lære; *imbui*, ic teah. *c* **1205**, *a* **1225** [see A. 3]. *a* **1250** *Owl & Night.* 1725 Heo wes itowen [*v.r.* itoȝen] among mankunne. *c* **1250** *Gen. & Ex.* 1913 He wulde ðat he sulde hem ten Ðat he wel-ðewed sulde ben.

4. To bring forth, produce. Only OE. (Cf. TEAM *sb.*, TEEM *v.*[1])

c **1000** ÆLFRIC *Gen.* i. 20 Teon nu þa wæteru forð swimmende cynn. *Ibid.* 21 Eall libbende fisccinn..þe þa wæteru tuᵹon forð on heora hiwum.

5. To draw out, protract, prolong.

c **1200** *Trin. Coll. Hom.* 149 Wumme..þat min biwist is teȝed here swo longe.

6. a. *refl.* To betake oneself; to withdraw. (Cf. DRAW *v.* 67.)

c **1205** LAY. 640 He tah hine aȝein ane þrowe. *c* **1275** *Ibid.* 20086 Þis i-seh Arthur..and teh hine [*c* 1205 thehte hine] a bacward.

b. *intr.* To proceed, go: = DRAW *v.* 68. (Cf. Ger. *ziehen*. The most usual sense in ME.)

c **888** K. ÆLFRED *Boeth.* xxxv. § 7 He..teah to wuda. *c* **1122** *O.E. Chron.* an. 1096, Fela..ham tuᵹon. *c* **1205** LAY. 18274 Þat folc ut of wude teh. **1297** R. GLOUC. (Rolls) 4370 So gret folc of romeins..þat sone wolleþ out te [*v.r.* teo]. *c* **1300** *Harrow. Hell* 8 Þat alle mosten to helle te. **13..** *Sir Beues* (A.) 501 Forþ þe kniȝtes gonne te, Til þat hii come to þe se. **13..** *E.E. Allit. P.* C. 87, I schal tee in-to Tarce, & tary þere a whyle. *c* **1450** LOVELICH *Grail* lii. 568 Aȝens that knyht ȝe scholen not Te. *c* **1450** *Cov. Myst.* iii. (1841) 33 As to my fadyr, lete us now tee.

†**tee**, *v.*[2] *Obs. rare.* [OE. *tíon*, *téon*, contr. from **tîhan*, = OS. *tîhan* in *aftîhan* to refuse, OHG. *zîhan*, MHG. *zîhen* to accuse, show to be guilty, inform against, ON. *tjá* from **tíha* to show, tell, relate, report, Goth. *ga-teihan* to show, make known. Orig. a strong vb. **tíhan* (*táh*, *tiᵹon*, *tiᵹen*), of ablaut series *tīh-*, *taih-*, *tih-*, cognate with Gr. δεικ-νύναι to show, L. *dīc-ĕre* to tell, Skr. *diç-* to show, point out. But already in OE. confused in inflexion with *téon* from **téohan* to draw, TEE *v.*[1], in consequence of the falling together of the contracted pres. stems *tío-*, *téo-*. Rare in ME. In quot. *c* 1440 *tyxste* app. = *tyhst*.] *trans.* To accuse. (In quot. *a* 1300, ? to show, make known; or ? to tell, relate.)

871–901 *Laws of Ælfred* c. 33 Gif hwa oðerne..tion [*v.r.* teon] wille, þæt he hwelcne ne ᵹelæste þara ða he him ᵹesealde [etc.]. *Ibid.* c. 36 § 1 Gif hine mon tio [*v.r.* teo] ᵹewealdes on ðære dæde, ᵹetriowe hine be þam wite. *c* **1000** ÆLFRIC *Gen.* xxxi. 31 Nu þu me stale tyhst. *Ibid.* xliv. 7 Hwi tihþ ure hlaford us swa micles falses? *a* **1300** *Beket* 1180 Holi churche he aboute dure [*v.r.* a-bouȝte deore] that me tiȝth on wide [*v.r.* tellez of wel wide]. *c* **1440** *York Myst.* xxxii. 287 *Kaiph.*.. Fye on the, traytoure attayntе, at þis tyde; Of treasoune þou tyxste hym, þat triste þe for trewe.

tee (tiː), *v.*[3] *Golf.* [f. TEE *sb.*[2], and like it app. a clipt form of the 17th c. *teaz*.]

1. a. *trans.* To place (a ball) on the tee. Also with *up*. Hence *intr.* with *up*: to place a ball on a tee; (*transf.*) to prepare to play. **b.** *intr.* with *off*: To play a ball from the tee. Also *transf.*, to begin a game or performance.

1673 *Wedderburn's Vocab.* 37, 38 (Jam.) *Statumina pilam arena*, Teaz your ball on the sand. **1737** [see *teed* below]. **1828** SCOTT *Jrnl.* 14 May, I can only tee the ball; he must strike the blow with the golf club himself. **1862** *Chambers' Encycl.* IV. 823/2 An attendant, called a caddy, who carries his clubs and 'tees' his balls. **1895** LINSKILL *Golf* ii. (ed. 3) 10 To tee a ball for driving, it is usual to place it on some small eminence on the surface of the turf... A ball is sometimes teed on a few short blades of stiff grass. **1895** *Westm. Gaz.* 19 June 7/2 Will any golfer send a shilling to open the subscription? Or, preferably, will the Royal and Ancient tee off? **1906** J. BRAID *Golf Guide* v. 34 It is not a good thing to tee up very near to the teeing-box. **1906** *Macm. Mag.* Aug. 773 The golfer proceeds to the tee-ing off spot, tees up his ball, mentally imagines that he is standing on a species of gridiron, and places his feet in the position [etc.]. **1960** *Times* 3 Feb. 15/7 [Rugby] As Pennington teed up, the Thomas's touch judge..was leaning against one of the uprights. **1961** A. BERKMAN *Singers' Gloss. Show Business Jargon* 86 *Tee off*, to open the show. **1974** *Spartanburg* (S. Carolina) *Herald* 18 Apr. c2/2 Coluccio teed off on a 3–1 offering from the reliever. **1975** *Daily Tel.* (Colour Suppl.) 12 Sept. 9/4 The players are allowed to tee up every shot, since the ball may land in a tree or a pile of rocks.

2. *fig.* **a.** Chiefly *trans.* with *up*: to make ready, to arrange. *colloq.*

1938 PARTRIDGE *World of Words* ix. 269 Modern sports have provided us with..few words but a very fair 'bag' of phrases..*tee up*..from golf. **1941** [see PROMOTE *v.* 8]. **1943** C. H. WARD-JACKSON *It's a Piece of Cake* 60 *Teed up*, all set to start. **1958** N. CULOTTA *They're a Weird Mob* iii. 34, I gotta go an' see about all that metal an' stuff, an' tee up the mixer. **1961** 'J. LE CARRÉ' *Call for Dead* vii. 78, I left the car out in the yard, full of petrol and teed up. **1973** *Times* 22 Jan. 19/1 Initially he will go to the capitals of the member states for talks with central governments and to tee up trips to problem areas.

b. [Prob. *euphem.* alteration of *peed off* (= *pissed off*: see PISS *v.* 3 b).] *trans.* with *off*: to anger, annoy, irritate. Hence **teed off** *ppl. a.*, angry, annoyed, disgruntled, indignant. *N. Amer. slang.*

1955 *Amer. Speech* XXX. 120 *Teed off*.., angry, indignant. **1961** *Lebende Sprachen* VI. 100/1 Don't tee him off,..raise his dander, get his Irish up. **1963** D. HUGHES *Expendable Man* i. 22 You're teed off at me, aren't you? **1969** C. F. BURKE *God is Beautiful, Man* (1970) 34 Well this makes old Pharaoh really teed off. So he gets his army and he says, 'Get 'em.' **1977** *New Yorker* 27 June 68/2 Frankly, it just tees me off. I consider them to be a god-damned curse. **1981** G. V. HIGGINS *Rat on Fire* xvii. 119 He is kind of teed off. .. I mean, this man is *angry*.

c. *intr.* with *off* (const. *on*): to hit out at, attack, reprimand, criticize severely. *U.S. slang.*

1955 H. KURNITZ *Invasion of Privacy* (1956) i. 10, I thought you were about to tee off on Ben... Let's both stop making cracks. **1976** *Billings* (Montana) *Gaz.* 4 July 2-E/1 Our country is not at war. Despite all the sabre rattling.., the nation is not about to tee off on another nation, large or small.

Hence **teed** (tiːd) *ppl. a.*, placed on or played from a tee; **teeing** ('tiːɪŋ) *vbl. sb.*; also *attrib.* as **teeing-ground**, a small patch of ground from which the ball is teed off.

1737 RAMSAY *Scot. Prov.* xxxiii. (1750) 89 That's a tee'd ba'. **1824** SCOTT *Redgauntlet* Let. xiii, All that is managed for ye like a tee'd ball. **1890** *John Bull* 5 Apr. 226/2 Two hundred yards..distance from the teeing-ground. **1893** STEVENSON *Catriona* xviii, They had taken a word from the golfing green, and called me the 'Tee'd Ball'. **1903** *Westm. Gaz.* 11 Sept. 4/2 Far better to recognise that placing is virtually teeing, and have done with it.

tee, *v.*[4] [f. TEE *sb.*[1]] *trans.* To connect or branch off by a tee-piece. (In quot. *absol.*)

1908 *Installation News* II. 83/1 Bring a ½-in. tube..to the light in the hall, teeing off to the switch on the wall and from thence to the living room lights.

tee, obs. f. TEA; obs. and dial. f. TIE.

teeack ('tiːək). *Ork. dial.* Also teaoo, teeock, teeoo. [Echoic: cf. TEWHIT, TEWIT.] = LAPWING.

1869 D. GORRIE *Summers & Winters in Orkneys* (ed. 2) v. 194 The plaint of teeacks..blended finely with the shrill pipings of shore-birds. **1884** D. W. YAIR in D. H. Edwards *Mod. Scot. Poets* VII. 248 Teeocks, bleatin', skimmed alang. **1909** *Old-Lore Misc.* II. i. 29 Like a doo or a teaoo. **1927** H. CAMPBELL *Jean's Garden* 26 The teeoos crying ower the brecks. **1969** G. M. BROWN *Orkney Tapestry* 97 That's a plover... There's a teeack.

teebee, var. TEPEE.

teeder, obs. form of TETHER.

teedle ('tiːd(ə)l), *v. Sc.* [? Echoic. Cf. *deedle* in *Eng. Dial. Dict.*; also *doodle, toodle, tootle.*] *trans.* To sing (a tune) without words; to hum.

?*a* **1800** *Sc. Song, Had awa frae me Donald* (Jam.), But rock your weeane in a scull And teedle Heelan sing, Matam. **1824** MACTAGGART *Gallovid. Encycl.* (1876) 444 *Teedling*, singing a tune without accompanying it with the words. **1827** SCOTT *Chron. Canongate* v, My little Highland landlady..stood at the door 'teedling' to herself a Highland song as she shook a table-napkin over the fore-stair.

tee-hee ('tiː'hiː), *int.* and *sb.* Forms: 4–8 ti-, 4–9 te-, 6–7 ty-, 6– tee-, 7 teh-, tih-, tigh-, 9 tie-; 4– -he, -hee, 6 -heegh, -hei, -hy, 7 -hi, 7–9 -hie: as one word, or as two, or hyphened.

A. *int.* A representation of the sound of a light laugh, usually derisive. In quots. usually in female use. Cf. HE *int.*[2]

c **1386** CHAUCER *Miller's T.* 554 Tehee [*v.rr.* Te hee; *Cambr.* Te he; *Corpus* Tehe; *Petw.* Ti he], quod she, and clapte the wyndow to. **1500–20** DUNBAR *Poems* lxxv. 22 'Tehe!' quod scho, and gaif ane gaufe. *c* **1550** *Peblis to the Play* xxi, Than all the wenschis Te he thai playit. **1588** N. YONGE *Mus. Transalpina* xli. Fj b, When I lament my case thou cryest..ty hy, and no no no. **1654** GAYTON *Pleas. Notes* To Rdr., Monsters where be yee? I'm Hercules, club too, Ti-hee, wi-hee. **1773** MASON *Heroic Ep. to Sir W. Chambers* 134 And all the Maids of Honour cry Te! He! **1944** A. HUXLEY *Let.* 24 Feb. (1969) 500 Tee hee, tee hee, oh sweet delight!

B. *sb.* A laugh of this kind; a titter, a giggle.

1593 G. HARVEY *Pierce's Super.* Wks. (Grosart) II. 273 The *Tutt* of Gentlemen, the *Tee-heegh* of Gentlewomen. **1600** E. BLOUNT *Hosp. Incur. Fooles* 116 As manie tigh-hees as euer came out of god Liber or Bacchus his mouth. **1753** A. MURPHY *Gray's-Inn Jrnl.* No. 58 (1756) II. 36 Tehees and Titters in the Women..totally destroy their Beauty. *a* **1754** FIELDING *Charac. Men* Wks. 1784 IX. 411 The various laughs, titters, tehes, &c. of the fair sex. **1837** CARLYLE *Fr. Rev.* I. II. v, Our poor young Prince gets his Opera plaudits changed into mocking tehees. **1858** —— *Fredk. Gt.* VI. vi. (1872) II. 199 Astonishment, *flebile ludibrium*, tragical tehee from gods and men, will come of the Duel!

C. *attrib.* or as *adj.* **tee-hee farm** (*nonce*), a mental hospital; cf. *funny farm* s.v. FUNNY *a.* 4.

1955 W. GADDIS *Recognitions* I. v. 172 Everybody knows about Rose, that they've sent her sister Rose back from the tee-hee farm and Esther has to take her in. **1971** *Publishers' Weekly* 1 Nov. 17/2 This accounts for *Newsweek's* rather snide coverage and the tee-hee reports in the press.

Hence **tee'hee** *v.*, *intr.* to utter *tehee* in laughing; to laugh affectedly or derisively; to titter, giggle; also as ***tee and hee*** (nonce). Hence **tee'heeing** *vbl. sb.* and *ppl. a.*

?*a* **1300** *Proverb. Verses* in *Rel. Ant.* II. 14 Liþer lok and tuinkling Tihing and tikeling. **1580** HARVEY *Lett. betw. Spenser & H.* Wks. (Grosart) I. 61 The Gentlewoomen.. tyhying betweene them selues. **1598** B. JONSON *Ev. Man in Hum.* I. iii, And the wenches they doe so geere, and ti-he at him. **1603** HOLLAND *Plutarch's Mor.* 96 They fell to teighing, and now they laugh you to skorne. **1622** MABBE tr. *Aleman's Guzman d'Alf.* I. 158 My money..began to laugh and tighie in my purse. **1721** D'URFEY *Ariadne* II. i, Oh! how she would Teehee, and simper, and sneer. **1886** STEVENSON *Kidnapped* xiv, What frightened me most of all, the new man tee-hee'd with laughter as he..looked at me. **1904** J. C. LINCOLN *Cap'n Eri* v. 81 'That's it, laff!' almost sobbed Captain Jerry. 'Set there and tee-hee like a Bedlamite.' **1928** V. WOOLF *Orlando* iv. 163 He teed and heed intolerably. **1935** 'G. ORWELL' in *New English Weekly* 14 Nov. 96/1 Life is full of misery when you believe that the grave really finishes you... Hence the tee-heeing brightness of *Punch*, hence Barrie and his bluebells, hence H. G. Wells and his Utopiæ infested by nude school-marms.

tee-hole ('tiːhəʊl). *dial.* The hole forming the entrance to a bee-hive.

1669 WORLIDGE *Syst. Agric.* ix. §3. 160 At the bottom of your little [bee-hive] doors..make an open square place just against the Tee-hole. **1891** DOYLE *White Comp.* vi. I. 110 As thick as bees at a tee-hole.

teek, obs. f. TEAK.

teel, dial. var. TILL *v.*

teel, teel-oil, teel-seed: see TIL, sesame.

teeld(e, obs. pa. t. and pple. of TELL *v.*; var. TELD *sb.* and *v. Obs.*, tent.

teele, obs. f. TEAL.

teem (tiːm), *v.*[1] Forms: 1 tíeman, týman, tíman, tæman, 1–2 teman, 3 timen, tæmenn (*Orm.*), teamen, tumen(*ü*), 3–5 temen, 3–6 teme, (4 tem, 5 temyn), 6–7 teeme, 7–8 team, 6– teem. [OE. *tieman*, etc.:—**taumjan*, f. OE. *téam*:—**taum*: see TEAM *sb.*]

I. Belonging to TEAM *sb.* I.

1. *trans.* To bring forth, produce, give birth to, bear (offspring). Also *fig. Obs.* or *arch.*

c **1000** ÆLFRIC *Hom.* I. 238 Hit bið þonne..þæt 'Nan wer ne wifað, ne wif ne ceorlað, ne team ne bið ȝetymed'. *Ibid.* II. 212 þæt folc tymde micelne team on ðam westene. *c* **1200** ORMIN 2415 Wurrþenn swa wiþþ childe & tæmenn hire tæm wiþþ himm Alls oþ re wimmenn tæmenn? *a* **1225** *Ancr. R.* 220 Two tentacions..þet temeþ alle þe oðre. *c* **1230** *Hali Meid.* 33, & cleopeð ham wunne & weolefulle þat teamen hare teames. **1599** SHAKS. *Hen. V*, v. ii. 51 The euen Meade ..Conceiues by idlenesse, and nothing teemes But hatefull Docks, rough Thistles, Keksyes, Burres. **1607** —— *Timon* IV. iii. 179 Common Mother, thou Whose wombe vnmeasureable, and infinite brest Teemes and feeds all. **1654** GAYTON *Pleas. Notes* III. viii. 126 My Mother,..whose very picture I am, when she teem'd of me under the Line. **1667** MILTON *P.L.* VII. 454 The Earth obey'd, and..teem'd at a Birth Innumerous living Creatures. **1675** PLUME *Life Hacket* (1865) 8 It was but a small lustre..that the place where any man was teemed could cast upon him. **1786** tr. *Swedenborg's True Chr. Relig.* x. §585 The earth..being their common mother..brings them forth, that is, teems them from her womb into the open day.

†**2.** *intr.* To bring forth young, bear or produce offspring; to be or become pregnant. *Obs.*

c **1000** ÆLFRIC *Gen.* vi. 4 Godes bearn tymdon wið manna dohtra and hiȝ cendon. *c* **1000** —— *Hom.* I. 250 Fuȝelas ne tymað swa swa oðre nytenu. *Ibid.* II. 10 Sindon þeah-hwæðere sume ȝesceafta þe tymað buton hæmede..; þæt sind beon. *a* **1023** WULFSTAN *Hom.* xiii. 81 Wa ðam wifum þe þonne tymað. *c* **1200** ORMIN 130 Forr þatt 3ho wass swa bifundenn wif þatt 3ho ne mihhte tæmenn. *a* **1225** *Ancr. R.* 308 Fares & Zaram ne temeð heo neuer. *c* **1250** *Gen. & Ex.* 982 An angel..seide ȝhe sulde sunen wel And timen, and clepen it Ismael. **1532** MORE *Confut. Tindale* Wks. 644/2 Lest it should feble hys fleshe..and hyndre hys harlot of teming. **1591** *Troub. Raigne K. John* (1611) 15 Thou saist she teemde sixe weekes before her time. **1604** SHAKS. *Oth.* IV. i. 256 If that the Earth could teeme with womans teares, Each drop she falls, would proue a Crocodile. **1607** —— *Timon* IV. iii. 190. **1636** JAMES *Felix's Octavius* 91 Except Jupiter be waxed old and Juno hath left off teeming.

3. *intr.* To be full, as if ready to give birth; to be prolific or fertile; to abound, swarm. Usually cont. *with.*

1593 [see TEEMING *ppl. a.*[1] 2]. *a* **1719** ADDISON (J.), A nation where there is scarce a single head that does not teem with politicks. **1746** SMOLLETT *Reproof* 28 Hallowed be the mouth That teems with moral zeal and dauntless truth! **1748** GRAY *Alliance* 6 The soil, tho' fertile, will not teem in vain. **1802** PALEY *Nat. Theol.* xxvi. (1819) 404 The air, the earth, the water, teem with delighted existence. **1838–9** HALLAM *Hist. Lit.* II. II. v. §8c. 234 Every canto of this book teems with the choicest beauties of imagination. **1840** DICKENS *Barn. Rudge* lxxvii, The house-tops teemed with people. **1868** E. EDWARDS *Ralegh* I. Introd. 33 A mind which..was still teeming with projects for a good time to come.

II. Belonging to TEAM *sb.* III.

†**4.** *trans.* In Anglo-Saxon law: To refer or trace (property), for evidence of ownership, *to* a third person representing the party from whom it was acquired; to vouch to warranty. Only OE.

a **700** *Laws Ine* c. 47 Gif mon forstolenne ceap befehð, ne mot hine mon tieman [*v.r.* tyman] to ðeowum men. *Ibid.* c. 75. *a* **800, 960–975** [see TEAM *sb.* 7].

†**5.** *intr.* To refer or appeal *to* for confirmation or testimony. *to God I teme*, I call God to witness. Also *trans.* To cite or call to witness (quot. *c* 1200).

c **1000** ÆLFRIC *Saints' Lives* (1881) I. 58 Benedictus.. tymde to þam reȝole þe Basilius ȝesette. *c* **1000** *St. Basil's Admonitio* Prol. (1849) 32 Benedictus..tymde swa ðeah to Basilies tæcinge for his trumnysse. *c* **1200** *Moral Ode* 108 (Trin. MS.) His oȝen werc and his þanc to witnesse he sal temen. *a* **1300** *Cursor M.* 5070 (Cott.) And al was for i tald a drem þat cummen es now, to godd i tem. *Ibid.* 12797. *Ibid.* 14791 þ e bok is wittnes for to tem.

†**6.** *intr.* To attach oneself (*to* any one) in fealty, dependence, trust, or love; to turn or draw *to. Obs.*

c **1205** LAY. 1265 He bi-heihte hire biheste & he hit wel laste þat to hire he wolde teman [*c* 1275 hire wolde he louie] & wrchen hire ane temple. *Ibid.* 16800 Al hit trukeð us an hond þæt we to temden. *Ibid.* 24816 ȝif þu i þissen twælf wiken temest to þan rihten and þu wult of Rome þolien æi dome. **1303** R. BRUNNE *Handl. Synne* 9546 Al þat euer to Cryst wyl teme, Behoueþ be baptysed yn watyr and creme. **13..** *St. Erkenwolde* 15 in Horstm. *Altengl. Leg.* (1881) 266 He turnyd temples þat tyme þat temyd to þe deuelle. **13..** *E.E. Allit. P.* C. 316 ȝet surely I hope, Efte to trede on þy temple & teme to þy seluen. *c* **1400** *Destr. Troy* 3306 Tho truly þat are takon and temyn to you, Shalbe plesit with plenty at þere playne wille.

†**7.** *trans.* To acclaim (as lord); to offer or dedicate (to God); to bring into a position or condition.

c **1205** LAY. 1956 He wes ihaten Brutus..þa Troinisce men þa temden hine to hærre [*c* 1275 makede hine louerd]. **13..** *Cursor M.* 6170 (Cott.) þe forbirth o þair barntem Fra þan þai suld to drightin tem. *c* **1384** CHAUCER *H. Fame* III. 654 But myghten temen vs opon bere.

†**8.** *intr.* or *refl.* To betake oneself, to repair, go, proceed *to*; *trans.* to repair to (q. *c* 1330). *Obs.*

c **1205** LAY. 1245 Albion hatte þat lond..þer to þu scalt teman [*c* 1275 wende] & ane neowe Troye þar makian. *Ibid.* 7174 He hehte Tenancius to Cornwale temen [*c* 1275 wende]. *Ibid.* 27919 Arður ȝæf him þene tun and he þer to tumde [*v.r.* tumbde]. *c* **1320** *Sir Tristr.* 431 For drede þai wald him slo, He temed him to þe king. *c* **1330** R. BRUNNE *Chron. Wace* (Rolls) 11177 Fot-folk þat come to & fro, Innes for to teme & take.

†**b.** *intr.* To lead *to* (an issue). *Obs.*

c **1205** LAY. 9135 Ic wolde iwite æt þe..to whan þis tocne wule ten, to wulche þinge temen.

teem (tiːm), *v.*[2] Chiefly *dial.* and *techn.* Forms: 4–6 teme, 5 *Sc.* teym, 6 *Sc.* teim, 7 teame, teeme, 7–9 team, 8 tem, 7– teem. [ME. *tēme-n*, a. ON. *tœma* (Sw. *tömma*, Da. *tömme*) to empty:—**tômjan*, f. *tómr* empty, TOOM.]

1. *trans.* **a.** To empty (a vessel, etc.); to discharge or remove the contents of; to empty (a wagon, etc.).

a **1300** *Cursor M.* 12020 Bath he ditted þe water lade, And temed lakes þat he made. *a* **1340** HAMPOLE *Psalter* lxvii. 27 Fayre saules, þat has temyd þaire fleyss, and driyd it of þe humor of syn. *c* **1375** *Sc. Leg. Saints* xxv. (*Julian*) 544 Scho ..temyt þe poyttis thre. *c* **1440** *Promp. Parv.* 488/1 Temyn or maken empty.., *vacuo, evacuo.* *c* **1470** HENRY *Wallace* VIII. 213 Saidlys thai teym off hors bot maistris thar. **1500–20** DUNBAR *Poems* xxxviii. 36 The fetteris lowsit and the dungeoun temit. **1596** DALRYMPLE tr. *Leslie's Hist. Scot.* IV. (S.T.S.) 204 Quhen he had teimed the hartes of mony of the foul puddil of errour and vice. **1650** H. MORE *Observ.* in *Enthus. Tri.*, etc. (1650) 92 Magicus will not stick to teem Urinals on your heads. **1789** BRAND *Hist. Newcastle* II. 684 *note*, Above ground..two banks-men..take off the corves at top, and empty, or, as the work-men call it, 'teem' them. **1854** MISS BAKER *Northampt. Gloss.*, *Teem*, to empty, to pour out. 'Teem the tub.'

b. To discharge (something out of or from a vessel, a cart, etc.); to empty out, pour out.

1482 *Burgh Rec. Edinb.* (1869) I. 45 Gudis ventit or temyt in the rade havin or toun of Leith. **1562** TURNER *Baths* 5 They teme or emptye out euel humores. **1648** HERRICK *Hesper.*, *To Primroses*, Just as the modest morne Teem'd her refreshing dew. **1729** SWIFT *Direct. Servants, Butler*, You immediately teem out the remainder of the ale into the tankard. **1812** J. J. HENRY *Camp. agst. Quebec* 96 The contents were teemed into a large bason. **1863** MRS. GASKELL *Sylvia's L.* II. xv. 13 Better help her t' teem t' milk. **1863** MRS. TOOGOOD *Yorks. Dial.*, Team the water out of the kettle. **1889** *Q. Rev.* July 138 Blister steel is..poured or 'teemed' into suitable ingot moulds.

c. *absol.*

1641 BEST *Farm. Bks.* (Surtees) 36 Wee have allwayes one man..whose office is to helpe to teame, that the waines be not hindered. **1855** J. R. LEIFCHILD *Cornwall Mines* 38 Six men were teaming from the bottom into the pump. **1896** *Warwickshire Gloss.*, This teapot don't teem well.

d. To drain the water off (boiled potatoes, etc.).

1890 in *Eng. Dial. Dict.* (1905) VI. s.v., sense 8. **1922** JOYCE *Ulysses* 751 Wouldnt even teem the potatoes for you of course shes right not to ruin her hands. **1982** P. MCGINLEY *Goosefoot* xiii. 210 'The potatoes are done.'.. 'When you've teemed them, we'll all guess the number in the pot.'

2. *intr.* Of water, etc.: To pour, flow in a stream, flow copiously; of rain: to pour.

No longer *dial.* when used with reference to rain. Perh. associated with TEEM *v.*[1] 3.

1828 *Craven Gloss.* s.v., It rains and teems. *a* **1846** G. DARLEY *Song*, '*Sweet in her green dell*' ii, Down from the high cliffs the rivulet is teeming. *a* **1880** *Jack & William* ii. in Child *Eng. & Sc. Pop. Ball.* (1884) I. 444/2 The blood was teeming down. **1880** *Leeds Mercury* 13 Sept. 8 The water then came teeming down the shafts. **1979** J. GRIMOND *Memoirs* vii. 105 The rain which seemed to teem down incessantly. **1981** G. BOYCOTT *In Fast Lane* v. 22 Not just a drop or a shower but three clammy inches in forty-eight hours, teeming out of a slate-grey sky.

Hence **teem** *sb. dial.*, a 'pour', a downpour of rain: see *Eng. Dial. Dict.*

†**teem**, *v.*[3] *Obs. rare*$^{-1}$. [app. either the simple root-verb of BETEEM *v.*[1], or perh. more prob. shortened from that vb.] *intr.* To think fit, vouchsafe.

1593 GIFFORD *Dial. Witches* B j b, Alas man, I could teeme it to goe, and some counsell me to goe to the man at T.B. and some to the woman at R.H.

teem, *a. dial.*, empty: see TOOM.

teem, -e, obs. or dial. ff. TEAM.

teeme, obs. f. THEME.

teemer[1] ('tiːmə(r)). *rare.* [f. TEEM *v.*[1] + -ER[1].] One who or that which teems or gives birth.

1646 H. P. *Medit. Seige* 69 But such hastie teemers many times bring forth blind whelpes.

teemer[2] ('tiːmə(r)). Now *dial.* and *techn.* Also *erron.* **teamer**. [f. TEEM *v.*[2] + -ER[1].] One who teems, empties, or unloads.

1667 ? MARVELL in *Roxb. Ball.* (1883) IV. 546 Weeping to see their sons degenerate: His Romans taking up the teemer's trade, The Britons jigging it in masquerade. **1866** J. E. BROGDEN *Provinc. Words Lincolnsh.* 204 *Teamer*, the man who empties the grain from a laden cart to the stack. **1891** *Labour Commission Gloss.*, *Teemers*, men employed at the top of the coal-shoots by means of which coal is tipped into the hold of the vessel. **1894** *Northumbld. Gloss.*, *Teemer*, the man at a coal shipping staith who lets the coal out of the waggons.

teemful ('tiːmfʊl), *a.*[1] [app. f. TEEM *v.*[1] + -FUL: cf. *forgetful*. OE. had *téamfull*, f. TEAM *sb.*, in the same sense.] Prolific, productive, fruitful, teeming. Hence '**teemfulness**, prolificness.

[*a* **1000** *Gloss.* in Wr.-Wülcker 238/3 *Fetose*, tudderfulle, teamfulle, *uel* tuddre. *c* **1000** *Lambeth Ps.* cxliii. 13 Sceap heora teamfulle & berende.] **1755** JOHNSON, *Teemful*, pregnant, prolifick. **1855** SINGLETON *Virgil* I. 34 As standing corn To teemful tilths,—so thou all grace to thine. *Ibid.* 47 But do thou, if teemfulness Our flock shall have recruited, be of gold. **1863** G. H. CALVERT *Gentlem.* vi. 79 Exhilarated by hope,—which is the teemful mother of the ideal.

teem-full, teemful ('tiːmfʊl), *a.*[2] *dial.* Also **team-**. [f. TEEM *v.*[2] + FULL *a.*] See quots.

1674 RAY *N.C. Words* 47 *Teamful*, Brim-ful, having as much as can be teemed in. **1727** BAILEY vol. II, *Teemful*, full up to the Top. **1787** in GROSE *Provinc. Gloss.* **1876** *Whitby Gloss.*, *Teeam-full*, brim-full; requiring to be poured out. *c* **1900** in most northern glossaries: see E.D.D.

teeming ('tiːmɪŋ), *vbl. sb.*[1] [f. TEEM *v.*[1] + -ING[1].] The action of TEEM *v.*[1]

†**1.** The production or bringing forth of offspring; breeding; child-bearing. Also *fig. Obs.*

c **1430** *Hymns Virg.* 4 Heil þat alle wommen on doon calle in temynge, whanne þei ben hard bistadde! **1540** HYRDE tr. *Vives' Instr. Chr. Wom.* II. ix. (1557) 104 To haue enui at other for their beautie, & their welfare, or plentous teming. **1549** COVERDALE, etc. *Erasm. Par. Rom.* 10 Thoughe hymself was feble, and his wyfe lykewyse passed temyng. **1607** MARKHAM *Caval.* I. (1617) 50 The onely time of danger is at the first conception, and at the time of teaming. **1672** MARVELL *Reh. Transp.* I. 148 Mr. Bayes in the Preface of his Defence to excuse his long teeming before it were brought forth. **1705** HICKERINGILL *Priest-cr.* III. Wks. 1716 III. 160 They were Twins .. and if old Eve had miscarried of them at her first Teeming, I think it had been no great loss.

†**b.** *concr.* Offspring, produce, progeny. *Obs.*

1654 WHITLOCK *Zootomia* 429 The Suns .. that shined with gladding Influences, on worthy Teemings of a fruitfull Brain.

2. Abundant productiveness, fecundity, fertility, fruitfulness.

1856 DOVE *Logic Chr. Faith* v. i. §2. 279 The prolific teeming of the everbearing World. **1879** *Times* 6 Sept., The rushing of water from the .. rills keeps pace with the teeming of the earth and with the ripening of its fruits.

3. *attrib.* and *Comb.*: †**teeming-date**, **teeming-time**, breeding-time, reproductive period.

1593 SHAKS. *Rich. II*, v. ii. 91 Is not my teeming date drunke vp with time? *a* **1700** *Roxb. Ball.* (1890) VII. 117 And Teeming-time we are loath to lose, and why should not Damsels go? **1737** FIELDING *Tumble-down Dick* Wks. (1766) 251/1 What shall I do to get another son, For now, alas! my teeming-time is done?

'**teeming**, *vbl. sb.*[2] Now *dial.* and *techn.* Also *erron.* **teaming**. [f. TEEM *v.*[2] + -ING[1].]

1. The action of emptying, pouring out, or unloading; *spec.* the pouring of the molten steel into the ingot-moulds in steel-manufacture. Also *attrib.*

1641 BEST *Farm. Bks.* (Surtees) 36 Wee usually leade to one place till such time as it beginne to bee troublesome teaminge, and then goe wee to another. **1840** *Civil Eng. & Arch. Jrnl.* III. 391/2 The wagons when teamed retaining a third of their contents plastered to the sides and bottom, and so requiring double the time for teaming. **1875** KNIGHT *Dict. Mech.* 1183/2 The operation of pouring the metal is called teaming. **1877** *Ibid.*, *Teeming-punch*, one for starting or driving a bolt out of a hole. A drift.

2. Phr. ***teeming and lading*** (lit. 'unloading and loading'): see quot. 1937. *slang.*

1937 PARTRIDGE *Dict. Slang* 869/2 *Teeming and lading*, accountants' slang. 'Using cash received to-day to make up cash embezzled yesterday.' **1957** J. BRAINE *Room at Top* v. 45 He'd made a dreadful mess of his Cash and Deposits book; such a mess that for a moment I suspected him of teeming and lading. **1979** *Financial Times* 18 May 8/5 Mr Jaggard had .. covered the theft by 'accelerating the banking of cheques received in a subsequent accounting period' and later falsifying records—a practice known among accountants as 'teeming and lading'.

'**teeming**, *ppl. a.*[1] [f. TEEM *v.*[1] + -ING[2].]

1. That bears or breeds offspring; pregnant, gravid, 'breeding'. *arch.* and *dial.*

1535 *Goodly Primer, Litany*, That teeming women may have joyful speed in their labour. **1593** DRAYTON *Eclogues* x. 46 Their teeming Eawes to helpe when they did yeane. **1676** GREW *Anat. Flowers* II. i. §3 As Teeming Women, gradually slaken their Laces. *a* **1719** ADDISON tr. *Ovid, Calisto* 99 A lovely boy the teeming rival bore. **1822** SCOTT *Pirate* iv, Mrs. Yellowley had a remarkable dream, as is the usual practice of teeming mothers previous to the birth of an illustrious offspring.

†**b.** Fructifying; germinating, sprouting. *Obs.*

1704 POPE *Windsor For.* 53 Kind seasons swell'd the teeming grain. **1835** URE *Phil. Manuf.* 231 The teeming seed is now covered with a sheet of paper pierced with holes.

2. Abundantly productive; fertile, prolific.

1593 SHAKS. *Rich. II*, II. i. 51 This blessed plot, this earth, this Realme, this England, This Nurse, this teeming wombe of Royall Kings. *c* **1600** —— *Sonn.* xcvii, The teeming Autumne big with ritch increase. **1768** BEATTIE *Minstr.* II. l, Where Nature loads the teeming plain With the full pomp of vegetable store. **1840** DICKENS *Barn. Rudge* xl, The plan .. which had suggested itself to the teeming brain of his .. commander.

b. *transf.* Abounding; swarming; crowded.

1715 *Pattern True Love* in Halliw. *Yorks. Anthol.* (1851) 13 Odd tales which heretofore Did so amuse the teeming throng. **1725** POPE *Odyss.* IV. 240 With teeming plenty to reward their toil. **1838** PRESCOTT *Ferd. & Is.* (1846) II. ix. 464 The teeming treasures of the Indies. **1869** TOZER *Highl. Turkey* II. 202 The teeming multitudes which must have crowded the cities. *a* **1873** DEUTSCH *Rem.* (1874) 136 It shews us the teeming streets of Jerusalem.

Hence '**teemingly** *adv.*, productively; '**teemingness**, productiveness, fecundity.

1674 N. FAIRFAX *Bulk & Selv.* 120 The hand giving a kind of teemingness to the spring. **1895** *Clarion* 2 Nov. 1/4 Our cause spreads teemingly.

'**teeming**, *ppl. a.*[2] [f. TEEM *v.*[2] + -ING[2].] That 'teems' or pours, pouring. Now *dial.* except with reference to rain.

1695 LD. PRESTON *Boeth.* I. 2 The weeping Muse .. whose teeming Eyes Keep time with her's. **1880** A. B. TODD *Poet. Wks.* (1907) 222 The streams, swoln by the teeming rain. **1955** *Times* 14 May 4/1 Teeming rain ushered in the evening session, but stopped before the arrival of the Queen, who drove round the ring on her arrival.

'**teemless**, *a. rare.* [f. TEEM *v.*[1] + -LESS.] Not bringing forth young or fruit; barren.

1687 DRYDEN *Hind & P.* I. 228 Such fiery tracks of dearth Their zeal has left, and such a teemless earth.

teen (tiːn), *sb.*[1] *arch.* Forms: 1–3 **téona**, (1 **téon**, **teane**), 1–5 **teone**, (3 **tuone**, **toune**, **tone**), 4 (*Ayenb.*) **tyene**, 3–6 **tene**, (4 **tean**), 4–5 **ten**, 4–5 (6 *Sc.*) **teyn(e**, 4–7 **teene**, (5 **tyune**, **tuene**), 6 *Sc.* **teine**, 6–9 *Sc.* **tein**, 6– **teen**. [OE. *téona* masc. hurt, trouble = OFris. *tiona*, *tiuna* injury, OS. *tiono* wrong, injury; also OE. *téon* neut. = ON. *tjón* neut. and fem. damage, loss. Cf. OFris. *tiona*, *tiuna* vb. to injure: see TEEN *v.*[1]]

†**1.** Harm inflicted or suffered; injury, hurt, mischief; damage. *Obs.*

971 *Blickl. Hom.* 51 Æt þæm ytmestan dæʒe eal hit him wyrþ to teonan. *c* **975** *Rushw. Gosp.* Matt. xx. 13 Freond, ne do ic ðe teane. *c* **1000** *Ags. Gosp.* ibid., Eala þu freond, ne do ic þe nænne teonan. *c* **1175** *Lamb. Hom.* 15 Ne do he þe neure swa muchelne teone. *c* **1205** LAY. 6013 While he dude us tuone [*c* **1275** teone]. *a* **1300** *Cursor M.* 7980 (Cott.) His fas philistiens, þat had don him mani tenis [*v.r.* -es]. *c* **1400** *Rule St. Benet* 978 It be-houes folk of religioun Suffer tenes & tribulacioun. **1590** SPENSER *F.Q.* I. xii. 18 Gainst that proud Paynim king that works her teene. **1609** HOLLAND *Amm. Marcell.* XXXI. i. 399 Working much teene and losse.

2. Irritation, vexation, annoyance; anger, wrath, rage; spite, ill-will, malice. *Obs.* exc. *Sc.*

c **1200** ORMIN 19606, & forrþi let he takenn himm To wrekenn hise tene. **1340** *Ayenb.* 66 Þe dyeuel beginþ þet uer of tyene and euel wyl uor to becleppe. **1362** LANGL. *P. Pl.* A. VIII. 100 Pers for puire teone pollede hit a-sonder. *c* **1386** CHAUCER *Knt.'s T.* 2248 Neuere was ther no word hem bitwene Of Ialousie or any oother tene. *c* **1400** *Destr. Troy* 1978 Lest the tyrand in his tene hade turnyt hym to sle. *c* **1500** *Lancelot* 3237 So hard o knycht he strykith in his ten. **1613–16** W. BROWNE *Brit. Past.* II. iv, Before a tempest's rough regardlesse teene. **1690** W. WALKER *Idiomat. Anglo-Lat.* 534, I will wreak my teen on them. **1719** RAMSAY *2nd Answ. to Hamilton* xi, Pegh, fry, and girn, wi' spite and teen. **1819** W. TENNANT *Papistry Storm'd* (1827) 37 He waxed wud wi' vera teen.

†**b.** *transf.* Something vexatious, a cause of annoyance; a trouble. *Obs.*

971 *Blickl. Hom.* 47 Þis weorc biþ deoflum se mæsta teona. *c* **1275** LAY. 10087 Ac he ne lifuede noht longe; þat was mochel teone [*c* 1205 þat wes his leodene hærm]. **13..** *Gaw. & Gr. Knt.* 1008 For to telle þerof hit me tene were. **1496** *Dives & Paup.* (W. de W.) IV. ix. 172 The fooll child is wrathe & tene of his fader, and sorowe of his moder.

3. Affliction, trouble, suffering, grief, woe. *arch.*

c **1290** *Beket* 1533 in *S. Eng. Leg.* I. 150 ȝwane a man is In mest soruwe and teone, þ anne is ore louerdes grace next. *a* **1300** *Cursor M.* 10472 Vp sco ras and yod a-wai, And went hir þeþen in tene and trei. **13..** in *Pol. Rel. & L. Poems* (1866) 224 Teone and trauail shal beo my lif. **1387–8** T. USK *Test. Love* I. i. (Skeat) l. 13 Mirth is chaunged in to tene. **1393** LANGL. *P. Pl.* C. XIV. 7 Abraam for al hus good hadde muche teene, In gret pouerte he was yput. *c* **1460** *Towneley Myst.* iii. 533 With tray and with teyn and dreed mekill wogh. **1556** LAUDER *Tractate* 488 Syne turne ȝour myrth and Ioye in teine. **1594** SHAKS. *Rich. III*, IV. i. 97 Each howres ioy wrackt with a weeke of teene. *c* **1620** *Verses Death R. W.* in Farr *S. P. Jas. I* (1848) 103 Such is the verse compos'd in mournefull teene. **1719** D'URFEY *Pills* (1872) IV. 268 And bloody Knife did end the Smart, Which she sustained in woful Teen. **1801** WORDSW. *Cuckoo & Night.* xxxviii, The God of Love afflict thee with all teen. **1885–94** R. BRIDGES *Eros & Psyche* Aug. xxi, The wan face spent with tears and teen.

b. Trouble or pains taken about something. *arch.*

1377 LANGL. *P. Pl.* B. VI. 135 Ȝe wasten þat men wynnen with trauaille and with tene. **1435** MISYN *Fire of Love* II. i. 70 Contemplacion in greet tynn & with greet labour is gettyn. **1600** TOURNEUR *Transf. Metamorph.* lxxvi, Much teen they bide in search for such an one. **1880** *Contemp. Rev.* Mar. 428 Art's high toil and teen.

†**c.** Pain, physical suffering. *Obs.*

c **1400** *Song Roland* 632 He shall tell in the town, who the tale heris, That it is correct, for tean of his eyres. *c* **1430** LYDG. *Min. Poems* (Percy Soc.) 133 For hunger I [Chichevache] feele so grete teene. ? *a* **1500** *Chester Pl.* (Shaks. Soc.) I. 224 Lazarre .. Lyeth sicke .. And suffereth moche teene.

†**4.** Name of a disease of hawks. *Obs.*

1486 *Bk. St. Albans* B vj b, A medicine for an hawke that hath the teyne. An hawke that hath the teyne .. will pante more for oon batyng then an other for iiii. **1678** PHILLIPS (ed. 4), *Teine*, a disease in Hawks that makes them pant, .. growing heavy, and losing her breath when she flies.

†**5.** Phr. ***to take teen***, ? to take heed.

Perhaps a different word. (But not an error for *tent*.)

? *a* **1500** *Chester Pl.* vi. 734 Her hand roted, as you have seene, Wherby you may take good teene, That unbeleefe is a foule synne.

teen (tiːn), *sb.*[2] Usually in pl. **teens** (tiːnz). [The element -TEEN in numerals treated as a separate word, usually in plural.]

1. a. *pl.* The years of the life of any person (*rarely*, of the age of anything) of which the numbers end in *-teen*, i.e. from thirteen to nineteen; chiefly in phrases ***in, out of one's teens***.

1673 WYCHERLEY *Gentl. Dancing Master* IV. i, Your poor young things, when they are once in the teens, think they shall never be married. **1693** *Humours Town* 98 A young Girl in the Teens. **1709** E. W. *Life Donna Rosina* 10 Her Daughter, who was by this time come into the Teens. **1763** CHURCHILL *Proph. Famine* 3 The stripling raw, just enter'd in his teens. **1809** MALKIN *Gil Blas* I. i. ¶ 1 A chamber-maid who was not exactly in her teens. **1818** KEATS *Let.* Wks. 1889 III. 101 Your friendship for me is now getting into its teens. **1883** *Fortn. Rev.* Feb. 296 The Republic, in the art of government .. is still in its teens.

β. sing. **1834** T. HAWKINS *Mem. Ichthyosauri* 30, I was too young .. and as inquisitive as a boy in his first 'teen' could possibly be.

attrib. **1886** RUSKIN *Præterita* I. viii. 252 It must have been about the beginning of the teen period.

b. *transf.* (With *sing.* and *pl.*) A young person in the teens. Now chiefly *N. Amer.* and apprehended as short for TEENAGER. Freq. *attrib.* and *Comb.*

1818 I. TAYLOR (*title*) Advice to the Teens; or, Practical Helps to the Formation of Character.

1951 *Deseret News* (Salt Lake City) 30 July F-1/1 Doing something fun like redecorating your room .. is really interesting biz for a teen who loves being busy. **1959** *Charlottesville* (Va.) *Daily Progress* 18 Aug. 11/2 Today's teens spend money carefully. **1971** *Daily Colonist* (Victoria, B.C.) 30 June 20/3 When a teen leaves home it almost never works out well to call the law and have the kid dragged home. **1978** *Chicago* June 179/1 If you're over 21, you can make a significant contribution by taking an abandoned teen, 16–20 years old, into your home.

attrib. and *Comb.* **1945** *Britannica Bk. of Year* 771/2 *Teen can, teen canteen, teen town*, recreation centre for teen-agers (1944). **1948** *Observer* 28 Mar. 1/7 (Advt.), Teen girls' frocks in a lovely crepe. **1957** *Sun* (Baltimore) 15 Feb. 29/3 The Baltimore Highlands School .. had been used .. for Friday night dances by a local teen-center. **1960** *Vogue Pattern Bk.* Early Autumn 64 Formula for teen chic. **1967** *Crescendo* Oct. 25 Bob Miller, who has successfully promoted his band in the 'teen-beat field. **1969** N. COHN *AWopBopaLooBop* (1970) xviii. 170 He chronicled teen lives better than anyone since Eddie Cochran. **1972** *Jazz & Blues* Sept. 12/2 The lyrics became more 'teen-orientated'. **1976** *National Observer* (U.S.) 17 Apr. 17/1 The small red mouth of an eager teen princess. **1977** *Sounds* 1 Jan. 2/4 The 32-year-old teen idol. **1977** *Time Out* 17–23 June 9/2 Irresistibly melodic teendream romance. **1979–80** *Verbatim* Winter 7/1 Teen-crammed schoolbuses. **1980** *Daily Tel.* 25 June 17/1 It takes little investigation of British teen magazines to see that there is a big gap in the market.

2. The numbers of which the names end in *-teen*. Also, years, temperatures, pay, etc., measured in quantities which end in *-teen*.

1885 *Blackw. Mag.* Apr. 548/1 We are to change the small hours of our afternoons into teens and twenties. **1932** *Times Lit. Suppl.* 7 July 493/1 Books of the 'teens and early twenties of the last century. **1958** *Listener* 4 Dec. 944/1 In the teens and twenties of this century. **1966** E. P. HAMP in Birnbaum & Puhvel *Ancient Indo-Europ. Dial.* 119 The syntax of the 'teens of the numerals. **1977** *Chicago Tribune* 2 Oct. XII. 59/9 (Advt.), This position may be of interest to you if your current salary is in the upper teens. **1981** *Northeast Woods & Waters* Jan. 11/1 With the mercury plunging into the teens for five nights, the entire river valley was iced-in.

Hence **'teener**, one in his or her teens (*U.S.*); **'teenhood**, the state of being in one's teens; **'teening** *a.*, in one's teens; **'teenish** *a.*, characteristic of persons in their teens, youthful.

1894 BLACKMORE *Perlycross* 242 This rigid man was wound round the finger of a female '*teener'—as the Americans beautifully express it. **1947** *Richmond* (Va.) *Times-Dispatch* 30 Aug. 7/8 (*heading*) Teener told married life is no game. **1956** *Sun* (Baltimore) 27 Oct. 7/6 Attention, teeners! Come meet these Young Jr. Board members. **1979–80** *Verbatim* Winter 7/1 I've heard things from teeners that widened my education considerably. **1893** *Scott. Leader* 14 Aug. 2 Whilst in her *teenhood she was placed with Mr. and Mrs. Charles Kean. **1818** *Religio Clerici* 169 *Teening misses, for a day-school prize, Transpose the types, and mar the prophecies. **1811** *Morn. Post* 20 Dec., Their *teenish tricks, at fifty-six, all wise folks should forego. **1818** *Blackw. Mag.* IV. 256 She's just of age! shall teenish frailties wrong her?

†**teen**, *a.* Chiefly *north. Eng.* and *Sc. Obs.* Forms: 4–5 **teyn(e**, 4–6 **tene**, 6 **teene**, 7 **teen**. [app. f. TEEN *sb.*[1]]

1. Angry, vexed, enraged.

13.. *E.E. Allit. P.* B. 1808 Entyses hym to be tene, telles [*MS.* telled] vp his wrake; Ande clannes is his comfort, and coyntyse he louyes. *c* **1375** *Sc. Leg. Saints* xxviii. (*Margaret*) 542 þane wes þe tyrand vondir tene Quhene he hard þis of þe maydine clene. *c* **1400** *Melayne* 710 Kyng Charls.. At the byschoppe was so tene. **1536** BELLENDEN *Cron. Scot.* (1821) I. 202 He wox sa tene, that he gart drown this woman. **1570** *Satir. Poems Reform.* xxi. 53 It suld 3ow mufe all to be tene. **1674** RAY *N.C. Words* 47 *Teen*, angry. **1828** *Craven Gloss.*, *Teen*, angry.

2. Vexatious; troublesome, distressing.

c **1470** *Golagros & Gaw.* 33 With outin beilding of blis, of bern or of byre; Bot torris and tene wais, teirfull quha tellis.

¶**3.** ? Corruption of *keen*. *rare*.

1579 LYLY *Euphues* (Arb.) 34 The freshest colours soonest fade, the teenest Rasor soonest tourneth his edge. **1580** *Ibid.* 249 Setting a teene edge, wher thou desirest to haue a sharp poynt. [*So edd.* **1580–1587**; *edd.* **1595–** keenest, keen.]

†**teen**, *v.*[1] *Obs.* or *dial.* Forms: α. 1 **téonian**, 3–4 **teone(n**, 3–6 **tene**, 4 **tyeny**, 4–6 **teyn** (*pa. t.* and *pple.* **teind**, **teynt**), 4–7 **teene**, (5 **tuene**, 6 *pa. t.* **teynd**, 7 *pa. pple.* **teend**). β. 1 ***tíenan**, **týnan**, 4 (*Ayenb.*) **tyenen**. [a. OE. *téonian*, f. *téon*:—**tiun-*, TEEN *sb.*[1] = OS. (*ge*)*tiunean*:—**tiunôjan*. β. OE. **tíenan*, *týnan*:—**tiunjan* = ON. *týna*, ODa., Sw. dial. *tyne* to injure, destroy, lose; see TINE; thence in 14th c. Kentish, *tyeny*.]

1. *trans.* **a.** To vex, irritate, annoy, anger, enrage.

α. *c* **1000** *Lambeth Ps.* cv. 16 Et irritaverunt *gl.* And hy teonedon *uel* hig gremedon. *a* **1225** *Ancr. R.* 118 Pellican is .. so wreðful þet hit sleað ofte uor grome his owune briddes, hwon heo teoneð him. **1362** LANGL. *P. Pl.* A. XI. 136 Bote Teologye haþ teened [B. x. 180 tened; C. XII. 129 teened] me ten score tymes; For þe more I muse þeron þe mistiloker hit semeþ. *c* **1440** *Promp. Parv.* 489/1 Tenyn, or wrethyn, or ertyn.., *irrito*. **1496** *Dives & Paup.* (W. de W.) VII. iv. 279 Ne tene, ne angre thou not the poore in his myscheue. **1522** *World & Child* in Hazl. *Dodsley* I. 251 There is no emperor so keen, That dare me lightly tene. *a* **1825** FORBY *Voc. E. Anglia*, *Teen*, *v.* to trouble; to vex.

β. **971** *Blickl. Hom.* 47 Ne ablinnan we.. þæt we Gode cwemon, & deofol tynan, dæges & nihtes. *c* **1000** *St. Basil's Admon.* iv. (1849) 44 Se wellwillenda man wyle.. forberan 3if hine man ahwær tynð. *c* **1000** *Laws of Ethelred* VI. c. 48 And þæt hy ælþeodige men.. ne tyrian ne ne tynan.

b. To inflict suffering upon; to afflict, harass; to injure, harm.

c **1275** *Orison of our Lord* 22 in *O.E. Misc.* 139 Wunderliche þurh wacche and fast þi swete lychome þu teonedest. **13..** *E.E. Allit. P.* B. 759 If þat twenty be trwe I tene hem no more. **1362** LANGL. *P. Pl.* A. VII. 40 Loke þou teone [**1377** B. VI. 39 tene; **1393** C. IX. 36 tene, *v.r.* tuene] no tenaunt bote treuþe wol assente. *c* **1400** *Destr. Troy* 8228 Then the grekes.. turnit to the Troiens, tenit hom full euill. *c* **1430** *Hymns Virg.* 62 Quod wrappe, 'loke þou bere þee bolde; What man þee teene, His heed þou breest'.

c. To cause (physical) pain or injury to; to hurt.

1399 LANGL. *Rich. Redeles* III. 79 þey bablid with her billis how þei bete were And tenyd with twiggis two and twenty 3eris. *c* **1460** J. RUSSELL *Bk. Nurture* 319 Hold alwey thy knyfe sure, þy self not to tene. *a* **1550** *Christis Kirke Gr.* x, That torment so him teynd. **1607** WALKINGTON *Opt. Glass* xi. 121 The body is teend and accloid with divers.. maladies.

2. To cause grief or sorrow to; to grieve, distress: in various const. **a.** *trans.*; also *absol.*

a **1300** *Cursor M.* 10470 þan was soruful son dame anna, Quen vtaine hir had tened [*v.r.* greuid] sua. *Ibid.* 15694 To wacken þam ne wald he noght, þat teind war wit trai. **1340** *Ayenb.* 142 Alle wordes him tyeneþ and greueþ, bote yef hi ne by to god, oþer of god, oþer uor god. *Ibid.* 161 And þus beginþ þis wordle to tyeny.. þe more þet tyeneþ þis lif, þe more me wylneþ þet oþer. *c* **1430** *Pilgr. Lyf Manhode* II. cxxix. (1869) 125 Ootheres ioye teeneth me; ootheres sorwe is my mete.

b. *impersonal* = grieves.

a **1300** *Cursor M.* 19119 (Cott.) At þair talking þam tenid sare [*Trin.* Hem tened sore]. **14..** *Tundale's Vis.* (Wagner) 2288 Fulle sore hym tened at hymself than.

c. *refl.* To be vexed, to be angry; to distress oneself, grieve, be grieved.

a **1300** *Cursor M.* 10462 (Cott.) Vtaine hir can wit þis to tene. **1340** *Ayenb.* 73 Nou loke eftzone a lyte, and ne tyene þe na3t, to þise þri þinges. *Ibid.* 99 þet non ne ssolde him tyeny hit uorto zigge. **1362** LANGL. *P. Pl.* A. II. 83 þen teonede him Teologye whon he þis tale herde. *c* **1400** *Destr. Troy* 4600 If ye tary ouer tyme þai tene hom þereat.

d. *intr.* (for *refl.*) = c.

13.. *Cursor M.* 10462 (Gött.) Vtayne wid þis word gan tene. *a* **1400–50** *Alexander* 2193 þen tened þe Thebees folke. *c* **1460** *Towneley Myst.* iii. 210 We women may wary all ill husbandis; I haue one, bi mary!.. If he teyn I must tary how so euer it standis. **1566** DRANT *Horace* A vij, [He] teenes if that his neyghbours goate a bygger bagge doth beare Then his. **1611** COTGR. s.v. *Dueil*, They tiple now as much as erst they teend.

Hence †**'teening** *vbl. sb.*, injuring, wrong-doing; affliction; sorrowing, grief.

a **1200** *Moral Ode* 253 þe lueeden tening and stale. *a* **1300** *Cursor M.* 24439 (Cott.), I sagh him dei, i sorud ai,.. Mi tening es sa togh.

teen, *v.*[2] dial. form (chiefly Kentish) of TINE (OE. *týnan*) to fence, hedge in, make a hedge with raddles: see TINE. Hence **'teenage** *sb.*[1], **'teenet**, **-it**, brushwood for fences and hedges; **'teener**, a man who teens or keeps in order a raddle fence; **teen-hedge**, a pleached or raddle hedge.

c **1700** KENNETT *MS. Lansd. 1033*, lf. 389 To **Teen* (Lanc. to *Tine*), to hedge or to enclose a field, in Kent the longer wood cut for the use of hedghing is calld **Teenage*. **1706** PHILLIPS (ed. Kersey), *Teenage*, (Country-word) Brushwood for Hedges or Fences. **1902** *Kentish Express* 29 Mar. 10/2 (*N. & Q.* 10th Ser. XI. 57/2) For sale, stakes, binders, *tenet, peasticks, good cheap, to clear. **1616** *MS. Acc. St. John's Hosp., Canterb.*, For bread and drink for the *teners and wood-makers. **1638** *Ibid.*, Payd.. for brishinge of the *teene-hedge downe js. vjd.

teen, obs. or dial. f. *tend*, TIND *v.* to kindle, TINE *v.* to lose; dial. f. TEIND.

-teen (tiːn), combining element. [OE. *-*tíene*, -*týne*, -*téne*, ME. -*tēne* = OFris. -*téna*, -*tíne*, OS. -*tein* (-*tian*), LG. -*tein*, Du. -*tien*, OHG. -*zehan* (-*zeheni*), Ger. -*zehn*.] An inflected form of TEN, added to the simple numerals from *three* to *nine*, to form the names of those from *thirteen* to *nineteen*.

Hence **-teenth** (-tiːnθ), forming ordinal numerals from the cardinals in *-teen*, from *thirteenth* to *nineteenth*. In ME. this took the place of earlier -*teþe*, OE. *téoþe*: cf. TENTH and -TH[1].

In early OE., as in the cognate langs., the simple numerals, from four upwards, had an inflected and an uninflected form, the latter commonly used before a sb., *seofon dagas*, the former in other positions, e.g. *swa ealle seofone*. The inflected forms were sbs. of the *-i* declension, with nominative pl. in *-e* (neut. *-u*, *-o*). Subsequently these forms were levelled, the numerals up to *twelve* retaining the uninflected form, those from thirteen to nineteen the inflected, as *teon, ten, fīftēne, fifteen*. In ME. the final *-e* of *-tēne*, *-teene* became mute; in mod. Eng. *-teen* it is no longer written, but the stem vowel remains long.

These compounds had originally the stress on the first element ('θɜːtiːn), as in '*dreizehn*, '*tredecim*, '*tredici*, δώδεκα, etc. In modern Eng. this is retained in counting: 'twelve, 'thirteen, 'fourteen, 'fifteen', etc. also before *hundred*, as "eighteen 'hundred and ninety'; but before a sb. there is a secondary stress on *-teen*, as "ˌeighˌteen 'men'. Otherwise the two elements have usually equal stress, '*thir*'*teen*, '*seven*'*teen*, '*eigh*'*teen*, which in the pause may become ˌ—' (not —'), as 'at the age of ˌthir'teen', 'sweet ˌseven'teen'. This stressing may have arisen to distinguish them clearly from the numerals in *-ty*: 'not ˌseven'teen but 'seventy'; 'the 'forty days have been reduced to ˌfour'teen'. The stressing of the ordinals in *-teenth* follows the same lines.

teenage ('tiːneɪdʒ), *a.* and *sb.*[2] orig. *N. Amer.* Also **teen-age**, **teen age**. [f. TEEN *sb.*[2] + AGE *sb.*]

A. *adj.* **1.** Designating someone in their teens.

1921 *Daily Colonist* (Victoria, B.C.) 11 Mar. 8/2 All 'teen age' girls of the city are cordially invited to attend the mass meeting to be held this evening. **1935** *Amer. Speech* X. 192/1 The dress is probably slinky and suitable for the teen-age group. **1948** *Evening Standard* 22 Mar. 6/4 The teen-age twins.. reject severe masculine fashions. **1957** *Time* 2 Sept. 62/2 Starting as a teen-age bank runner, he had become president of the Bank of Commerce. **1977** *Dædalus* Fall 83 Society may wish to eliminate teenage street corner gangs, but this does not lead sociologists to write articles on the optimal techniques for eliminating such gangs.

2. Pertaining to, suitable for, or characteristic of a young person in his or her teens.

1942 *Amer. Speech* XVII. 41 Teen age hats now on sale. Teenage apparel of all types. **1950** N. STREATFEILD *Mothering Sunday* 200 All those sweetly pretty teen-age frocks. **1967** M. ARGYLE *Psychol. Interpersonal Behaviour* viii. 140 They [*sc.* normal adolescents] too show a tremendous conformity to the group, for example in clothes, and in the use of teenage slang. **1979** L. MEYNELL *Hooky & Villainous Chauffeur* i. 14 The first time I ever saw Maude .. was at some teenage party.

B. *sb.*[2] (Usu. as two words.) The period of a person's life between the ages of thirteen and nineteen inclusive, the teens; an age falling between these limits.

1934 WEBSTER s.v. *Teen* adj., Boys of teen age. **1941** *Jrnl. Pediatrics* XIX. 392 The pediatrician's almost unrestricted field.. begins shortly after the birth of his patient and does not terminate until the 'teen' age is well advanced. **1973** M. AMIS *Rachel Papers* 8 Five hours of teenage to go... Then I wander into that noisome Brobdingnagian world the child sees as adulthood. **1973** *Sci. Amer.* Dec. 135/3 Readers of teen age and beyond will find in its plain language and concrete situations a smooth path to an ethical discussion as deepgoing as the dilemmas of life and death.

Hence **'teenaged** *a.*, of teen age; so **'teenagedness**.

1952 *Listener* 31 Jan. 183/1, I hope that modern youth enter 'teen-agedness' with a suitably elated conviction of its own self-importance. **1953** BERREY & VAN DEN BARK *Amer. Thes. Slang* (1954) §383/1 The teenaged set;.. a teenaged person. **1971** J. GRAY *Red Lights on Prairies* i. 10 In one two-roomed house there was a family of seven, including teen-aged boys and girls. **1981** *Times* 4 Mar. 6/5 A teenaged schoolboy ambulance driver.

teenage: see TEEN *v.*[2]

teenager ('tiːneɪdʒə(r)). orig. *U.S.* Also **teen-ager**. [f. prec. + -ER[1].] One who is in his or her teens; *loosely*, an adolescent.

1941 *Pop. Sci. Monthly* Apr. 223/2, I never knew teen-agers could be so serious. **1947** AUDEN *Age of Anxiety* (1948) i. 26 Tops in tests by teen-agers. **1952** M. STEEN *Phoenix Rising* ii. 38 Do we have to behave like a couple of hysterical 'teen-agers? **1960** K. AMIS *Take Girl like You* xxii. 260 Jenny thought to herself that here she was nearly twenty-one, and instead of having been a teenager all she had managed to do was spend a certain amount of time getting from the age of twelve to the age of twenty. **1962** *Guardian* 21 Sept. 11/7 He must be constantly new and different to be able to please the younger teenagers. And 'teenagers' start at the age of nine. **1980** *Times Lit. Suppl.* 15 Aug. 908/1 Teenagers, of course, had not been invented in the 1880s.

teend, obs. f. TEIND, tithe, *tend* TIND *v.* to kindle.

teener: see TEEN *sb.*[2], TEEN *v.*[2]

†**'teenful**, *a. Obs.* or *dial.* Forms: see TEEN *sb.*[1] [OE. *téonful*, ME. *teneful*, f. TEEN *sb.*[1] + -FUL.] Full of 'teen': see TEEN *sb.*[1]

1. Causing trouble or sorrow; vexatious, troublesome, painful, grievous, distressing.

c **1000** *Ags. Ps.* (Spelman) lxxvii. 10 Mægþ teonful, *generatio exasperans*. *a* **1023** WULFSTAN *Hom.* l. (1883) 273 Hu læne and hu lyðre þis lif is, hu sarlic and hu sorhful and hu 3eswincful and hu teonful. *a* **1300** *E.E. Psalter* lxxviii. 8 þat þai ne be als þar fadres fals, Getynge wik and tene-fulle als. **1340–70** *Alisaunder* 282 Hee made a uery uow auenged too beene Of þat teenefull tach þat hee tooke þere. *c* **1350** *Will. Palerne* 2666 3e grettli aren a-greued.. For þise tenful trauayles. *c* **1425** *Cast. Persev.* 1755 in *Macro Plays* 129 Teneful talys I may þee sey. *a* **1825** FORBY *Voc. E. Anglia*, *Teenful*, troublesome; vexatious.

b. Harmful, injurious.

(In first quot. perh. Lamentable, deplorable: cf. 1.)

1340–70 *Alex. & Dind.* 566 Many men vp-on molde made hue by slithe To haunte hure in hordom.. Of hure tenful tach 3e taken ensample. *a* **1400–50** *Alexander* 3907 Wild berys.. With ilka tenefull tothe as tyndis of harowis.

2. Angry, wrathful; malicious, spiteful.

c **1205** LAY. 4585 þer þreo & fifti scipen.. In þa teonfulle sæ torneden sæiles. *c* **1400** *Destr. Troy* 12252 þen Thelamon was tenfull, & turnyt into yre. **1570** *Sat. P. Ref.* xiii. 89 O Teinfull tratouris! **1572** *Ibid.* xxxii. 97 O tenefull Tyrane!

b. Feeling sorrow; sorrowful, grieved, sad.

1387–8 T. USK *Test. Love* II. v. (Skeat) l. 49 O bad and straite been thilke, that at their departyng, maketh men teneful and sorie. **14..** *Siege Jerus.* 213 Ac without tribute or trewes tenfulle wyes, þe kny3tes with þe kerchef comen ful blyue.

Hence †**'teenfully** *adv. Obs.*, sorrowfully, sadly, lamentably, grievously; harmfully, injuriously; angrily, wrathfully.

13.. *E.E. Allit. P.* B. 160 Greuing, and gretyng, and gryspyng harde Of teþe tenfully to geder. ? *a* **1400** *Morte Arth.* 272 He askyde me tyrauntly tribute of Rome, That tenefully tynt was in tyme of myne elders. *c* **1400** *Destr. Troy* 12233 Than Thelamon.. tenfully spake.. all in grym yre. *c* **1460** *Towneley Myst.* xvi. 56 Free men ar his thrall full teynfully torne.

teenhood, teening, teenish: see TEEN *sb.*[2]

†**'teenous**, *a. Sc. Obs. rare*—[0]. [f. TEEN *sb.*[1] + -OUS.] = TEENFUL. Hence †**'teenously** *adv.* = TEENFULLY.

a **1600** *Flodden F.* 88 in Furniv. *Percy Folio* I. 321 Our prince was moued theratt.. & returned him right teenouslye.

teensy ('tiːnzɪ), *a. colloq.* (orig. *U.S. dial.*). Also **teenzy**. [prob. f. TEENY *a.*[2] + -SY.] = TEENY *a.*[2] Also in Comb. or redupl. form **teensy-weensy**, **teensie-weensie**, etc. = *teeny-weeny* (see TEENY *a.*[2]).

1899 in H. Wentworth *Amer. Dial. Dict.* (1944) 626/1 Little teensy bit of a boy. **1902** W. N. HARBEN *Abner Daniel* 197 Then Jimmy's young wife come with her little teensy baby. **1906** in H. Wentworth *Amer. Dial. Dict.* (1944) 626/1 Teentsy-weentsy. **1933** O. NASH in *Sat. Even. Post* 2 Sept. 58/4 For the word was out, In palace and cot, Of the teensy, weensy, talented tot. **1951** 'J. TEY' *Daughter of Time* i. 12 Didn't you even try a little teensy taste? **1966** [see OFF *adv.* 1 g]. **1973** *Times* 21 Aug. 13/7 The statement as it stands is

..just a teensie-weensie bit unfair to my own firm. **1973** P. WHITE *Eye of Storm* xii. 592 He ordered himself another teenzy bottle of Scotch. **1981** S. STRUTT *On Edge of Love* vi. 116 'Would you like a drink?'.. 'Darling, that would be lovely. Perhaps just a teensy one!'

-teenth: see -TEEN.

'teenty, *a. U.S. colloq.* [From TEENY *a.*[2]] Very tiny, delicately small, 'wee'. Also **teenty-taunty, teenty-tointy** *adjs.*

1844 'J. SLICK' *High Life N.Y.* II. 227 A little teenty tointy handful of wood keeps 'em [*sc.* stoves] warm as blazes. *Ibid.* 230 Then she took up one teenty glove. **1863** A. D. WHITNEY *Faith Gartney's Girlhood* v. 46 She would open the window a 'teenty little crack'. **1863** *Harper's Mag.* Dec. 112/2 A pretty little teenty-taunty babe as ever you see. **1894** C. F. WOOLSON in *Harper's Mag.* Feb. 429 You were six months old—a little teenty baby. **1896** *Chicago Advance* 20 Feb. 260/2 Saving our teenty, dainty roses.

teeny ('tiːnɪ), *a.*[1] *Obs.* exc. *dial.* [f. TEEN *sb.*[1]] Characterized by 'teen'; malicious; peevish.

1594 CAREW *Tasso* (1881) 102 [He] growes so teasty, that by teeny spight, Past reasons bounds he is transported quite. **1825** J. NEAL *Bro. Jonathan* I. 342 A..teeny, mischievous, good for nothin'. **1847–78** HALLIWELL, *Teeny*..(2) Fretful; peevish; fractious. *Lanc.*

'teeny, *a.*[2] *dial.* and *colloq.* An emphasized form of TINY; orig. in childish use. Also as *sb.* and in comb. **teeny-tiny, teeny-weeny.**

1825 J. NEAL *Bro. Jonathan* I. 342 A leetle—teeny, mischievous, good for nothin'. **1847–78** HALLIWELL, *Teeny.* (1) Tiny; very small. *North.* **1867** *New Comical Nursery Rhymes* 157 With a teeny-tiny thump It broke her teeny nose. **1888** 'R. BOLDREWOOD' *Robbery under Arms* li, All the small, teeny bits of a man's life. **1889** 'LEWIS CARROLL' *Sylvie & Bruno* xvii, Such delicious *tiny* music it was! Such teeny-tiny music! **1894** BARING-GOULD *Queen of L.* I. 32, I am a teeny-weeny mite. **1905** ELINOR GLYN *Viciss. Evangeline* 85 He did look such a teeny shrimp, climbing after me! **1929** [see KERRY 2]. **1931** *Daily Express* 1 Sept. 5/1 But never cold ham and tongue for the tiny 'teenies'. **1931** E. V. LUCAS *Visibility Good* 18 Model tea-sets, and all the other teeny weenies. **1948** [see *bird-brain* s.v. BIRD *sb.* 9]. **1953** [see *fly-whisk* s.v. FLY *sb.*[1] 11]. **1957** [see ITSY-BITSY *a.*]. **1966** [see BRANDADE]. **1970** *Oxf. Mail* 27 Jan. 1/9 Today at Courreges in Paris we had teenie-weenie nappies knotted loosely on the loins. **1982** *New Yorker* 17 May 34/1 Their [videodisc] system has a teeny laser beam instead of a needle to get the images onto the TV screen.

teeny ('tiːnɪ), *sb. colloq.* Also **teeney.** [f. as, or abbrev. of, TEENY-BOPPER but infl. by TEENY *a.*[2]] A young teenager or pre-teenager, esp. one who is a fan of pop music; a teeny-bopper.

1969 *Oz* Apr. 40/1 A good part of that audience was composed of teeneys, nine to twelve year olds. **1976** *N.Y. Times* 29 July 26 He's [*sc.* 16-year-old Prince Andrew] the biggest thing for teenies since Bjorn Borg. **1977** *Daily Mirror* 21 Mar. 13/3 Teenies find hot line to hope... In 1976 at least 8,000 new callers were under fifteen.

teenybop ('tiːnɪbɒp), *a. colloq.* [Back-formation from next.] Of, pertaining to, or consisting of teeny-boppers.

[**1966** *Current Slang* (Univ. S. Dakota) Winter 3 Teeny-bop, teeny-bopper, high school student who carefully adheres to fads.] **1967** *Observer* 1 Oct. 3/3 We hope it will have more than a teeny-bop audience. **1969** N. COHN *AWopBopaLooBop* (1970) xxi. 201 They grew their hair long and dressed like teenybop tramps. **1979** *Fortune* 23 Apr. 65/1 The three British-born Bee Gee brothers, whose recent success has overshadowed the considerable fame they achieved as teenybop idols in the mid-Sixties.

teeny-bopper ('tiːnɪˌbɒpə(r)). *colloq.* Also as one word. [f. TEEN *sb.*[2] or TEEN(AGER + -Y[6] + BOPPER and infl. by TEENY *a.*[2]] A girl in her teens or younger, esp. one who is a fan of pop music and follows the latest fashions.

1966 *Telegraph* (Austral.) 12 Oct. 58/3 The teenybopper is aptly named because her two distinguishing features are her teeny size and her cool boppy with-it attitude to life. **1967** *Punch* 6 Dec. 847/1 To protest about long-haired commies or mini-skirted teenyboppers. **1969** FABIAN & BYRNE *Groupie* (1970) v. 35, I..suffered paranoid fantasies about him pulling lots of teeny-boppers and groupies when he was away on gigs. **1977** *Time* 18 Apr. 39/1 David Cassidy, 26, teeny-bopper heartthrob who sang his way to rock stardom. **1979** *Guardian* 4 Aug. 19/3 'I think we should be paid for going to school.' Thus my teenybopper daughter.

tee-off ('tiːɒf). [f. the vbl. phr. *to tee off*: see TEE *v.*[3] b.] The start of play in Golf; now also in other sports.

1952 *Sun* (Baltimore) 19 June (B ed.) 19/1 Boros.. dropped his bombshell an hour before his scheduled 1.52 P.M. teeoff. **1978** *Cornish Guardian* 27 Apr. 5/6 Tee-off on Sunday is at 10.30 when the two teams will play nine holes.

teepe, teepee, var. TEPEE, N. Amer. Indian hut.

Teepol ('tiːpɒl). [prob. f. TEE *sb.*[1] + *p* (repr. initial letters of the name of the orig. manufacturer) + -OL 3.] The proprietary name of an alkyl sulphate industrial detergent obtained by reacting olefins with sulphuric acid and neutralizing the products.

1942 *Progress Appl. Chem.* XXVII. 81 A synthetic detergent, Teepol..is being manufactured from a petroleum fraction. **1942** *Trade Marks Jrnl.* 9 Dec. 514/1 *Teepol*... Detergents. Technical Products Limited, 29, Great St. Helens, London, E.C.3. **1945** *Official Gaz.* (U.S. Patent Office) 10 July 171/2 Shell Union Oil Corporation, San Francisco... *Teepol* for detergent preparation for the cleaning of fabrics..and ceramics. **1976** *Nature* 3 June 406/1 The section [of rock] was first cleaned with 'Teepol' to remove all grease or immersion oil.

teer (tɪə(r)), *v.* Now *dial.* and *techn.* Also 5 **tere,** 7–9 **tear,** 8 **tire,** 9 **teere.** [ME. *teren, teeren*, app. a. OF. *terer, terrer* to cover or spread with earth, to plaster, to daub, f. *terre* earth.]

1. *trans.* To spread or cover with earth; to daub with clay, to construct (a wall, etc.) with clay or cob; to coat with plaster or the like, to plaster.

1382 WYCLIF *Amos* vii. 7 Loo! the Lord stondynge on a wall teerid [*v.rr.* plastrid, pargeted; *Vulg.* stans super murum litum], or morterd, and in the hond of hym a truel of masoun. [Cf. *Ezek.* xiii. 10 thei dawbeden, *gloss* or pargetiden, it [a wall] with fen with outen chaffis: *Vulg.* liniebant eum luto absque paleis: *French Bible*, 1543, ilz le terroient de mortier sans paille.] **14..** *Voc.* in Wr.-Wülcker 616/11 *Terro*, i. *terram alicui supponere*, to tere or daube. **1426–7** *Rec. St. Mary at Hill* 66 Also for ij lode lomb for teringe of þe chambre... Also for a lode lyme. *c* **1440** *Promp. Parv.* 489/2 Teryn, or hylle wythe erþe, *terriculo.* **1632** in *Fraser's Mag.* Oct. (1864) 518 P[d] for tearing of the house & chimney, 8. o. **1742** in Graham *Soc. Life Scotl. in 18th C.* (1901) I. viii. 55 *note*, For colouring and tearing the church doors and lettering them and colouring and tearing the wall opposite to your burial-place and lettering the same, 8 sh. **1847–78** HALLIWELL, *Teer*, (3) to daub with clay. Hence a clay wall is sometimes called a *teer-wall. Teere*, to plaster between rafters. *Lanc.*

b. To plaster or spread thickly (butter, etc.).

c **1850** *Northampt. Dial.*, You teer the butter all over the bread just as if it cost nothing. **1881** *Leicester Gloss.*, *Teer*, to smear; daub; spread... 'Teer the treacle', *i.e.* spread it on bread.

2. *Calico-printing.* (See quot. 1839.)

1839 URE *Dict. Arts* 226 The colour is teared [*ed.* **1875** teered].., or spread even, with a wooden scraper as broad as the canvass. **1899** WALLACE *Schoolmaster* ix. 354 *Teerer*, a boy or girl employed to teer..the colour-sieve stretched.. on a frame at printworks.

Hence **'teering** *vbl. sb.* (from sense 1), daubing or plastering with clay or cob; also, plastering or daubing generally; **'teering** *ppl. a.* that 'teers'; esp. in **teering-boy** (also **teer-boy, tire-boy**), in calico-printing, a boy whose work was to spread a fresh surface of colour on the printer's 'pad' each time he used it; also **'teerer** (see quots.); **'teery** *a. dial.*, sticky, smeary.

1426–7, 1632 Teering [see sense 1]. **1780** A. YOUNG *Tour Irel.* II. 36 Twelve printers. Twelve tire boys. Three print cutters. **1839** URE *Dict. Arts* 226 The instant before the printer daubs the block upon the canvass, the tearer [*ed.* **1875** teerer], boy or girl, runs the scraper across it to renew its surface. **1847–78** HALLIWELL, *Tiring-boy*, one who stirs the colour about in printing cloth, &c. *Lanc.* **1848** A. B. EVANS *Leicester Words* 96 *Teary*, pron. *Teery*, sticky. 'Handling the sugar will make your hands teary'... 'The ground's so very "teary" after the frost', i.e. heavy and clogging. **1895** *Oracle Encycl.* I. 585/2 For each [calico-] printer an attendant or 'teerer' was required—a boy whose duty was to spread evenly the colour on a prepared smooth cloth surface, on to which the printer dipped his block. **1904** in *Eng. Dial. Dict.* s.v., Tear-boys were very common in Lancashire.

teer, obs. f. TAR, TEAR, TIER *sb.*[1]

teercel, teerd, teerme, teers, obs. ff. TERCEL, TIRED, TERM, TIERCE.

teery-leery, etc.: see TIRRA-LIRRA.

teese, obs. f. TEASE; var. TEISE *v.*[2] *Obs.*

tee-shirt, tee-shirted: see T-SHIRT.

‖**teesoo** ('tiːsuː). *E. Ind.* Also **tesu, tesoo, teeso, tisso.** [Hindī, etc. *tēsū.*] The brilliant orange-red flowers of the DHAK or PALAS of India (*Butea frondosa* and *B. superba*), or the yellow dye obtained from these. Also *attrib.*, as ***teesoo-flower.***

1823 PLAYFAIR tr. *Tale of Shereef* 333 Tesoo. **1835** ROYLE *Bot. of Himalayas* 195 Teesoo, Keesoo. **1848** IRVINE *Mat. Medica Patna* 475 Tesu. **1855** J. F. ROYLE *Fibrous Plants India* 297 Useful from its large flowers, called *teesoo* and *keesoo*, yielding a beautiful dye. **1858** SIMMONDS *Dict. Trade*, *Teeso-flowers, Keeso-flowers*, the large flowers of *Butea frondosa.* **1862** BALFOUR *Timber Trees* 61 Tesu. **1871** —— in *Cycl. India* s.v. *Butea frondosa*, Tesu, Kisu [names of the flowers in Deccan].

tee-square: see TEE *sb.*[1] 4, and T (the letter) 3.

teest (tiːst). [Origin unascertained.] A small anvil which is set in a socket on the ordinary anvil or bench.

1877 KNIGHT *Dict. Mech.*, *Teest*, a stake or small anvil used by sheet-iron workers.

teest, teester, teestif, obs. ff. TEST, TESTER, TESTY.

Teeswater ('tiːzˌwɔːtə(r)). [f. the name of the *Teeswater* district in County Durham.] **1.** Used *attrib.* and *absol.* to designate a breed of long-wool sheep, originally developed in the Tees valley and recently revived; also, a sheep of this breed.

1786 G. CULLEY *Obs. Live Stock* 82 The Tees-water breed ..differs from the Lincolnshire, in their wool not being so long and heavy. **1837** W. YOUATT *Sheep* viii. 329 The wool of the Teeswater sheep was remarkably long and coarse. **1861** MRS. BEETON *Bk. Househ. Managem.* 323 The domesticated sheep..embracing..the Old Leicester, and the Teeswater, or New Leicester. **1951** A. FRASER *Sheep Husbandry* (ed. 2) ii. 67 A local breed, the Teeswater Mug, is coming into greater prominence. **1967** *Brit. Sheep Breeds* (Brit. Wool Marketing Board) 69/1 The Teeswater ram has been found to cross extremely well with hill breeds. **1979** *Country Life* 6 Dec. 2228/3 The Longwool breeds being farmed in Britain today—the Teeswater, Romney and Leicesters are among the other best-known names.

2. *attrib.* = SHORTHORN.

1810 J. BAILEY *Gen. View Agric. Co. Durham* xiv. 226 The short-horned kind..have for a great many years been known by the appellation of the Tees Water Breed. **1873** G. ARMATAGE *Cattle* i. 9 These fine animals appear to have descended from the Teeswater breed. **1919** K. J. J. MACKENZIE *Cattle* vii. 74 The bulk of the Teeswater or Holderness herds..were very famous for their milking qualities. **1950** G. T. BURROWS *Hist. Dairy Shorthorn Cattle* i. 11 Men..believed in the dual-purpose merits of their 'Teeswater' breed.

teet, -e, obs. forms of TEAT.

teetee ('tiːtiː). Also **ti-ti.** [Maori name.] A name in New Zealand for the Diving Petrel (*Pelecanoides* or *Halodroma urinatrix*), and for allied species.

1882 OGILVIE (Annandale), Tee-tee. **1891** *Australasian* 14 Nov. 963/1 (Morris) The petrels—there are nine kinds,.. the short-billed ti-ti, the long-billed ti-ti [etc.]. **1898** MORRIS *Austral Eng.*, *Ti-ti*, a Maori name for the sea-bird *Pelecanoides urinatrix.*

teetee, var. of TITI[2].

teeter ('tiːtə(r)), *sb. dial.* and *U.S.* Also **teater, teter.** [f. TEETER *v.*]

1. A see-saw; a see-sawing or swaying motion; the game of see-saw; also *fig.* hesitation between two alternatives, vacillation. Also *attrib.*, ***teeter-board*** (*spec.* in circus use.)

1855 *Knickerbocker* XLVI. 88 We were having a grand time with our 'teeter'-boards upon the highest fence. **1863** *Harper's Mag.* Aug. 343/2 Teeters to jump on, rings to swing by. **1867** LOWELL *Biglow P.* Ser. II. iii, I tell you you've gut to larn thet War ain't one long teeter Betwixt I wan' to an 'T wunt du. **1883** *U.S. Patent* No. 292254, In a teeter, the stands A, having inclined posts *a*, that are connected on top by the socketed pivot-castings *b*, substantially as and for the purpose set forth. **1887** HAVERGAL *Hereford Gloss.* 34 'All on the teater'. **1895** *N. Brit. Daily Mail* 15 Oct. 5 The 'teter' or undulating motion ..in the present cars is entirely got rid of. **1897** *Chicago Advance* 30 Sept. 437/2 We [in the U.S.] are not on a teeter-board and have no need to be incessantly concerned about the balance of power. **1965** *Sun* 26 Oct. 5/1 The Seven Halasi, a Hungarian family using teeter boards. **1979** *Times* 13 Dec. 7/6 The Kovatchevi troupe..will..bounce a performer from a teeter-board to the shoulders of the top performer.

2. The spotted sandpiper, *Actitis macularia*, found in eastern North America.

1842 J. E. DEKAY *Zool. N.Y.* I. 247 The Spotted Sand-Lark..is known..[as] Teeter and Tiltup, from its often repeated grotesque jerking motions. **1848** BARTLETT *Dict. Amer.*, *Peet-Weet*..the spotted Sandpiper.., better known ..by the name of..Teeter and Tilt-up or Tip-up, from its often repeated grotesque jerking motions. **1895** *Outing* XXXVII. 69/2 The 'teeter' is fat and well flavored.

teeter ('tiːtə(r)), *v.* Also **teter.** [var. of TITTER *v.* to totter, move unsteadily.]

1. *intr.* **a.** To see-saw. *dial.* and *U.S.*

1843 MRS. STOWE *Mayflower* 47 Then he was tetering [**1855** *ed.*: teetering] with her on a long board. **1846** WORCESTER, *Teeter*.., to seesaw on a balanced plank, as children, for amusement. (U.S.) **1847** WEBSTER, *Teeter*, *v.* (prov. Eng. *titter*, to tremble, to seesaw..), to seesaw. (U.S.)

b. To move like a see-saw; to sway from side to side; to move unsteadily; *esp.* of a person or animal, to walk with a swaying motion; to balance oneself unsteadily on alternate feet. So **teeter-totter, teter-totter.**

1844 'J. SLICK' *High Life N.Y.* II. 231, I teetered up tu her a tiptoe. *c* **1850** E. G. PAIGE *Serm.* I. 184 You tip and teeter about, thinking that you excite the admiration of all. **1854** THOREAU *Walden* ix. (1886) 184 The peetweets..'teter' along its stony shores all summer. **1888** J. W. RILEY in *Voice* (N.Y.) 21 June, Turn to the lane where we used to 'teeter-totter', Printing little foot-palms in the mellow mold. **1904** WINSTON CHURCHILL *Crossing* II. xiv. 422, I felt the ground teetering under my feet. **1904** in *Eng. Dial. Dict.* (Essex), A watch-maker said of a wheel of which the pivot was bent, 'It teeters'. **1943** C. MCCULLERS *Heart is Lonely Hunter* I. 29 They helped Blount to his feet. He teetered weakly. **1950** R. MACAULAY *World my Wilderness* vii. 66 The iron spokes swung teetering and creaking in the breeze. **1961** B. PYM *No Fond Return of Love* xii. 111 Marian left the house, teetering down the path to the bus stop on her stiletto heels. **1973** O. SACKS *Awakenings* 35 Miss D. would teeter forward in tiny rapid steps. **1982** T. BERGER *Reinhart's Women* ii. 35 'I'll teeter on the curb,' said Reinhart, 'and try not to fall into the gutter.'

c. Also *fig.*, esp. in phr. ***to teeter on the brink*** and varr.

1902 A. H. LEWIS *Wolfville Nights* xvii. 259 A quorum of the committee is away teeterin' about in their own affairs. **1930** *Punch* 26 Feb. 237/1, I really have not time to go into the whole story now... I will quit stalling lest I teeter. **1937**

'G. ORWELL' *Road to Wigan Pier* xiii. 261 Every bank clerk dreaming of the sack, every shopkeeper teetering on the brink of bankruptcy, is in essentially the same position. **1949** *Times* 29 Sept. 5/2 The Government..still tremble and teeter on the verge. **1958** *Daily Sketch* 2 June 13/7 He effectively suggested an officer teetering on the edge of sanity. **1979** C. JAMES *Pillars of Hercules* I. i. 25 He was teetering on the verge of declaring himself outright. **1980** D. ADAMS *Restaurant at End of Universe* iii. 25 Zaphod felt he was teetering on the edge of madness. **1983** *Brit. Med. Jrnl.* 23 July 279/2 Subsistence farming is widespread with nutrition teetering on the inadequate.

2. *trans.* To move (anything) with a see-saw motion; to tip up and down, to tilt. To see-saw. *dial.* and *U.S.*

1874 COUES *Birds N.W.* 30 All the while 'teetering' its body, and performing odd, nervous antics. **1906** *Daily Chron.* 14 Feb. 3/3 The author escaped the charge of a rhinoceros by the animal stepping on the same log on which Mr. Whitney was standing, and thus 'teetering' him aside. **1907** *Black Cat* June 36 As he teetered the fretting baby on his knee.

3. *Comb.* **teeter-tail**, the American sandpiper: = TEETER *sb.* 2.

1917 *Dialect Notes* IV. 424 The spotted sandpiper..also called swee-swee, teeter-tail. **1937** *National Geogr. Mag.* Aug. 201/2 Spotted Sandpiper... Nearly every pond, stream, or lake shore has its 'tip-up' or 'teeter-tail', as it is familiarly called.

Hence **'teetering** *vbl. sb.* and *ppl. a.*

1845 C. M. KIRKLAND *Western Clearings* 213, I laid a teterin' board over it, so that if you stepped on it, down you went. **1851** H. MELVILLE *Moby Dick* III. xxxviii. 218 The tetering ship loweringly pitched down her bowsprit. **1855** —— *Israel Potter* xiv. 147 Israel smote him over the taffrail into the sea, as if the man had fallen backwards over a teetering chair. **1878** MRS. STOWE *Poganuc P.* xxxv, Settled herself..on the back seat of the creaking, tetering old stage on the way to Poganuc. **1884** *Century Mag.* Jan. 359/1 The steady rolling and teetering of the ship. **1936** M. ALLINGHAM *Flowers for Judge* xiv. 202 He was lying on his face with a teetering, kicking thing trying to force him through the concrete floor. **1973** 'M. INNES' *Appleby's Answer* III. xv. 129 The tea-shop was..kept by teetering old ladies in the interest of their health. **1975** in W. Viereck *Lexikalische Ergebnisse des Lowman-Survey* I. iv. 141 Children also like to play on a..teetering pole.

teeter-totter ('tiːtəˌtɒtə(r)), *sb.* (and *a.*). *dial.* and *N. Amer.* [Reduplication from stem of TEETER *v.* or TOTTER *v.*; cf. TITTER-TOTTER *sb.* (*adv.*) and *teeter-totter* (vb.) s.v. TEETER *v.* 1 b.] A see-saw; formerly also, the game of see-saw. Also *attrib.* or as *adj.*

[**1895** W. RYE *Gloss. Words E. Anglia* 225 *Teeter-cum-tauter*, a see-saw.] **1905** *Dialect Notes* III. 66 *Teeter-totter*, *n.* or *v.* See-saw. 'We played teeter-totter.' **1933** *Sun* (Baltimore) 19 Aug. 2/6 Wallace explained the teeter-totter economics of hogs and corn made a solution more difficult, and said the Government had waited for the farmers themselves to produce a plan. **1959** *A. Hitchcock's Mystery Mag.* Feb. 70/2 Her body, which had bounced off a section of hedge onto the fulcrum of a teeter-totter. **1962** W. O. MITCHELL *Kite* xv. 197 Got to balance exactly..like two boys on a teeter-totter—same weight to the ounce. **1973** *Jrnl. Genetic Psychol.* June 289 A teeter-totter task and water-level apparatus. **1975** in W. Viereck *Lexikalische Ergebnisse des Lowman-Survey* I. iv. 141 Children also like to play on a...teeter-totter.

teetery ('tiːtərɪ), *a.* [f. TEETER *v.* + -Y[1].] Tottery, insecure; faint, unsteady.

1900 *N.Y. Jrnl.* 25 Nov. 59/2 An attendant was there to help you off if you feel teetery or uncertain. **1905** R. BEACH *Pardners* (1912) i. 34 The orchestra spieled some teetery music. **1935** H. DAVIS *Honey in Horn* ii. 17 Dogged if I didn't feel teetery to look at it. **1936** 'J. TEY' *Shilling for Candles* vii. 86 My shoes..I feel dreadful in them. Teetery. **1979** *Amer. Poetry Rev.* Mar.–Apr. 45/1 Above the stalks—whole islands teetery over the wasting pedestals, natural bulwarks lifting them free from heavy swells and pounding surf.

teeth, plural of TOOTH, q.v. for phrases, etc.

teeth, teethe, obs. ff. TITHE.

teethe (tiːð), *v.* Forms: 5 **teth**, 8–9 **teeth**, 9 **teethe**. [f. *teeth*, pl. of TOOTH: there might also have been an OE. **tēðan* from **tanþjan*; cf. BLEED, FEED.]

1. *intr.* To develop or 'cut' teeth. (Now only in pr. pple. and vbl. sb.: see TEETHING.)

c **1410** *Master of Game* (MS. Digby 182) vi. lf. 17 b, þei teth twyse in þe yere whan þei be wolfes [*v.r.* whelpes]. **1732** [see TEETHING *vbl. sb.* 1]. **1755** JOHNSON, *Teeth v. n.*, to breed teeth; to be at the time of dentition. **1865** PRINCESS ALICE *Mem.* 11 Mar. (1884) 90 Victoria is teething, which makes her pale and poorly.

2. *trans.* To furnish with teeth, to set teeth in. Chiefly *dial.*

1775 in ASH. **1794** BURNS *Song*, O merry hae I been teethin' a heckle, And merry hae I been shapin' a spoon. **1832** W. A. FOSTER in *Minstrelsy Merse* (1893) 153 Out through the mark the arrows flew, They teethed it like a harrow. **1865** E. BURRITT *Walk Land's End* 424 The cliffs that teeth the rift look as if they would shut into each other.

3. To 'point' (a wall, etc.) with lime or mortar.

1794 *St. Acc. Scot.* XI. 482 Stone walls teethed with lime.

Hence **'teething** *ppl. a.* (in sense 1).

1832 MARRYAT *N. Forster* xxiv, The teething infant. **1897** *Allbutt's Syst. Med.* III. 761 Looseness of the bowels..common in teething infants.

teethed (tiːθt), *a.* Chiefly *Sc.* and *dial.* [f. *teeth*, pl. of TOOTH *sb.* + -ED[2].] Furnished with or having teeth; toothed.

1775 ASH, *Teethed*, furnished with teeth. **1825** J. NICHOLSON *Operat. Mechanic* 659 Some persons imagine..that teethed wheels and rackwork would be necessary where the railway was not perfectly level. **1879** J. WHITE *Jottings* 49 (E.D.D.) The instrument used for reaping in our young days was the teethed sickle.

b. In parasynthetic compounds, as *pearly-teethed*.

1844 W. CROSS *Disruption* xxiii. (E.D.D.), A lang-teethed heckle.

teether ('tiːðə(r)). [f. TEETHE *v.* + -ER[1].] A small object for an infant to bite on while teething; a teething ring.

1949 M. MEAD *Male & Female* xiii. 272 Mother is there to put things—bottles, spoons, crackers, teethers—into your mouth. **1966** A. PRICE *Generous Man* (1967) ii. 177 She touched her breasts..and Milo said, 'They must have got a heap of exercise since then.'..'If acting as teethers for a middle-aged man with false teeth anyhow is your idea of exercise, they have.' **1974** *Daily Colonist* (Victoria, B.C.) 28 Sept. 21/5 Two of her bells were originally babies' rattles. They are rattle-shaped with tiny bells surrounding the metal body, a teether of either agate or coral as the handle.

teethful ('tiːθfʊl), *a.* [f. *teeth*, pl. of TOOTH *sb.* + -FUL.] Full of teeth: = TOOTHFUL *a.* 1.

1729 SAVAGE *Wanderer* v. 632 Fishers..With teethful tridents strike the scaly train.

† **teething** ('tiːθɪŋ), *sb. Obs. rare*[−1]. [f. *teeth*, pl. of TOOTH *sb.* + -ING[1].] Material on which to exercise the teeth; provisions, food.

1673 F. KIRKMAN *Unlucky Citizen* 210 By such time as he and his are fitted with Clothing, Teething and Tooling, his money is gone.

teething ('tiːðɪŋ), *vbl. sb.* [f. TEETHE *v.* + -ING[1].]

1. The action of the verb TEETHE; the process of developing teeth, dentition; usually applied to the cutting of the milk-teeth.

1732 ARBUTHNOT *Rules of Diet* iv. in *Aliments*, etc. (1736) 414 When the Symptoms of Teething appear, the Gums ought to be relax'd by softening Ointment. **1872** L. P. MEREDITH *Teeth* (1878) 31 Fatal diseases incident to early childhood..not caused by the irritation of teething.

2. The pointing of the interstices between stones in a wall, or slates on a roof, with lime or mortar.

1844 STEPHENS *Bk. Farm* I. 198 The putting them [slates] on, including dressing, holing, pins for the slates, and nails for the laths, cost only 15s., and with moss for bedding 1s., ..and lime for teething 5s., 22s. the rood.

3. *attrib.* and *Comb.*, as *teething fever*, *period*, *rash*, *stage* (fig.); **teething bannock**, **teething plaster**, an oatmeal cake given in Scotland to a child beginning to cut its teeth; **teething powder**, a medicinal powder given to children when teething; **teething ring**, a small ring or disc for an infant to bite on while teething; **teething troubles** *fig.*, problems arising in the early stages of an enterprise.

1861 W. F. COLLIER *Hist. Eng. Lit.* 400 A severe teething fever deprived him of the use of his right leg. **1866** W. GREGOR *Dial. Banffshire*, Teething-bannock. **1869** *Bradshaw's Railway Man.* XXI. App. 102 Pritchard's teething and fever powders, for..children cutting their teeth. **1872** 'MARK TWAIN' *Roughing It* xv. 125 Soothing-syrup! Teething-rings! **1881** W. GREGOR *Folk-lore* 9 The teethin bannock..was baked of oatmeal and butter or cream. **1899** *Allbutt's Syst. Med.* VIII. 586 'Red gum', 'teething rash', usually regarded as a sweat rash. **1937** *Jrnl. R. Aeronaut. Soc.* XLI. 917 The dynamometer had now been in use for eight or nine months. It was not quite free from small 'teething' troubles. **1954** 'N. SHUTE' *Slide Rule* iv. 92 These were the inevitable teething troubles of any very large aircraft. **1959** *Observer* 19 Apr. 5/3 They speculated on whether Britain should jump the 'teething' stage of supersonic airliners and concentrate on producing an adult machine in twenty years' time. **1967** *Guardian* 21 Sept. 3/4 It was highly likely that many 'corner shops' still contained stocks of teething powders containing mercury. **1980** 'J. BELL' *Question of Inheritance* i. 18 His favourite toy, the bone ring..a teething ring, with three little bells on it. **1980** *Bookseller* 21 June 2560/1 TBL Book Service was still involved in teething troubles and costs.

teethy ('tiːθɪ), *a.*[1] Now *Sc.* and *north. dial.* Forms: 5 **tethee**, 6 **tethy(e**, 9 **teathy**, **teethy**. [Etymology obscure: app. another form of TEETY, TETTY.] Touchy, testy, peevish, crabbed.

c **1460** *Towneley Myst.* iii. 136 She is full tethee, ffor litill oft angre, If any thyng wrang be, Soyne is she wroth. **1566** DRANT *Horace* v. H iv b, The testie, tethye, waspishe churle, with pratlynge is offended. **1825** BROCKETT *N.C. Words*, *Teethy*, cross, fretful, peevish; generally spoken of children. **1825** JAMIESON s.v., 'A teethy answer', a tart reply. **1828** *Craven Gloss.*, *Teathy*, peevish, cross. **1892** BOYD *25 Yrs. St. Andrews* II. 96 Nor did he fail to condemn wrong doing in a fashion which Scotch folk call teethy.

Hence **'teethily** *adv.*, testily.

1879 P. R. DRUMMOND *Perthshire in Bygone Days* xiv. 81 The Colonel pointed to a letter lying open on the table and said teethily [etc.].

teethy ('tiːθɪ), *a.*[2] [f. *teeth*, pl. of TOOTH *sb.* + -Y.] Well supplied with teeth.

1805 A. SCOTT *Poems* (1808) 160 (E.D.D.) At his expense our teethy faes are fed. **1835** D. WEBSTER *Scot. Rhymes* 136 (E.D.D.) With hero's heart and teethy jaw, Nane like him could badger draw. **1887** *Jamieson's Dict., Suppl.*, *Teethy*, *Toothy*, having many or large teeth.

† **teetotaciously** (tiːtəʊ'teɪʃəslɪ), *adv. U.S. dial. Obs.* Also **tetotaciously**. [Fanciful elaboration of TEETOTALLY *adv.*[1]: see -ACIOUS and cf. BODACIOUS *a.*] = TEETOTALLY *adv.*[1]

1833 J. K. PAULDING *Lion of West* (1954) II. ii. 54 I'm the best man—if I ain't, I wish I may be tetotaciously exflunctified! **1837** R. M. BIRD *Nick of Woods* I. xvi. 220 If that don't make me eat a niggur, may I be tetotaciously chawed up myself! **1859** T. DE QUINCEY *Coll. Works* X. 247 The slave in Terence, viz., Davus, though otherwise a clever fellow, when puzzled by a secret, or (as in America they say) *teetotaciously exfluncticated*, excuses himself by saying—'Davus sum, non Oedipus.'

teetotal (tiː'təʊtəl), *a.* (*sb.*) Also erron. **tea-**. [A kind of emphasizing reduplication or extension of the word TOTAL: see Note below.]

1. Of or pertaining to total abstinence from alcoholic drinks; pledged to, or devoted to the furtherance of, total abstinence.

1834 *Preston Temperance Advocate* Apr. 29/2 (Letter signed) A Lover of Sociality, and a 'Tee-Total' Abstainer. *Ibid.* 30/2 He..is now a tee-total abstinence member, and is an ornament to the Society. *Ibid.* May 38/2 The same man has since..signed the tee-total pledge. *Ibid.* Sept. 65/2 The tee-total system is a saving of time, a saving of money. **1837** *Ibid.* Apr. 29/1 A request, that a return should be made from all the tee-total societies in the kingdom. **1837** BARHAM *Let.* in *Life* (1871), And surely the captain Won't think of adapting His taste to these teetotal fancies. **1840** DR. W. PATTON in *Jrnl. Amer. Temp. Union* June 87 Total abstinence from all intoxicating drinks is a principle of English manufacture... So they adopted what they call the *teetotal* pledge (though I don't like the name); and they sent that back to us. **1885** RUNCIMAN *Skippers & Sh.* 14 You've made me be teetotal for three months. **1899** *Allbutt's Syst. Med.* VIII. 234 Much stress has been laid by teetotal advocates on the paramount influence of parental intemperance on the procreation of a mentally deficient progeny.

2. *dial.* Absolute, complete, perfect, entire. (More emphatic than *total*.) Cf. TEETOTALLY.

1840 MARRYAT *Olla Podr.*, *S.W. and by W. ¾ W*, A man in Bedlam is a very useless member of society, and a tee-total non-productive. **1849** J. O'CONNELL *Parl. Recoll.* II. 136 The Corn Law Abolitionists—the Teetotal men..of course saw through Sir Robert Peel's speech at once. **1884** *Lays & Leg. N. Irel.* 69 The Divil well knowin'..his teetotal want av contrition.

B. *sb.* (The adj. used *absol.*; now *rare* or *dial.*) **a.** The total abstinence principle or pledge; teetotalism; a society for the promotion of total abstinence. **b.** A total abstainer; a teetotaller. *rare.*

1834 *Preston Temp. Adv.* May 38/1 The number of members is about 196: the tee-totals about 30. *Ibid.* Nov. 85/1 Every system that does not go on the basis of tee-total is quackery. *Ibid.* Oct. 77/2 Mr. H. Snell..then came forward and signed the tee-total. *Ibid.* Nov. 83/2 There is no remedy for the sufferings of the working classes except joining the tee-total. **1845** DISRAELI *Sybil* II. x, Glass of water for the Secretary of the Mowbray Temperance and Teetotal. **1855** O. W. HOLMES *Poems* 200 Statesmen grow merry, lean attorneys laugh, And weak teetotals warm to half and half. **1857** J. STEWART *Sk. Scot. Charac.*, etc. 149 (E.D.D.), I maun join the Teetotal.

Hence **tee'total** *v.*, *intr.* to practise or advocate total abstinence; whence **tee'totalling** *ppl. a.*

1839 *Brit. Critic* No. 50. 267 The case of Timothy..is..made a text for 'tee-totalling' discourses. **1843** *Fraser's Mag.* XXVII. 408 The regular..religious and teetotalling artisan. **1883** *Cambridge Staircase* iii. 37 We all indulge in intoxicants..except Westbury, who teetotals.

[*Note.* The most specific account of this word is that it was first used (in sense 1) by a working-man, Richard Turner of Preston, about September, 1833, in a speech advocating total abstinence from intoxicating liquors, in preference to abstinence from ardent spirits only, as practised by some early temperance reformers. Among those present on the occasion was Mr. Joseph Livesey, one of the 'Seven men of Preston', who there formed the first Total Abstinence Society on 22 March 1832, and in whose *Autobiography* (1867–8), included in his *Life & Labours* by John Pearce (1885), particulars will be found. The *Preston Temperance Advocate*, a monthly magazine started by Mr. Livesey in Jan. 1834, shows the rapid advance of 'Dicky Turner's word' from a humorous or allusive to a fully adopted term (see quots. above). The issue for April 1836 has a full-page portrait of 'Dicky Turner, now celebrated as being the author of the word Tee-total'. This statement is also made on his tomb-stone at Preston, where he died 27 Oct. 1846. It has been suggested that Turner only used a word colloquially current in Lancashire in the general sense 2. But to this the whole tenor of contemporary evidence is opposed: and the examples of *tee-total* in sense 2 in the *Eng. Dialect Dictionary* are all of much later date. But there is proof that the adverb *tee-totally*, as an emphasized form of *totally*, was used in U.S. in 1832, and it has also been said to have been common in Ireland from a much earlier date. *Totally* is much more frequent in colloquial use than *total*, and it is quite possible that it was strengthened to *tee-totally* much earlier, and that *tee-total* in the specific sense arose independently, and without any knowledge of the adverb. It has also been asserted that, in the total abstinence sense, the word arose at Lansing, New York, in Jan. 1827, from the use on pledge cards of T. to indicate 'total', and the consequent collocation 'T.-total'. This is particularly stated in the *Century Dictionary* 1891, on the authority of the Rev. Joel Jewell, but without any contemporary evidence; while the correspondence in the *Life of Livesey* above mentioned (Pt. I. cviii–cxv) shows that the total abstinence movement in U.S., and with it the use of *teetotal*, followed and was greatly influenced by the Preston movement. By Worcester, 1846, *teetotal* is called 'a modern cant word', the letter T standing for *temperance*: 'that is *temperance-totalism*'; for it reference is made only to British periodicals. So to Webster 1847 *Teetotaler* was 'a cant word formed in England'. Cf. 1840 in sense 1.]

tee'totalish, *a.* [f. prec. + -ISH[1].] Inclined or tending to teetotalism.

1838 W. E. FORSTER in T. W. Reid *Life* (1888) I. iii. 96, I was teetotalish for my stomach's sake, before I left Norwich. **1847** B. BARTON *Select.* (1849) 32 A song of which the chorus was certainly not teetotalish.

tee'totalism. [See -ISM.] The principle or practice of total abstinence from alcoholic liquors.

1834 *Preston Temp. Adv.* Aug. 62/2 The flame of real teetotalism was communicated at this meeting. **1839** W. JAY in *Autobiog.* x. (1854) 104 The subject of Teetotallism I have examined physically, morally and Christianly. **1863** J. PAGET *Paradoxes & Puzzles, Ess. Art* iii. (1874) 456 Mr. Cruikshank has embraced the doctrines of teetotalism with the zeal natural to his genius. **1897** W. H. G. TEMPLE in *Chicago Advance* 18 Nov. 712/2 [On the] question of drink, there is but one safe, one reasonable stand—that of absolute teetotalism.

tee'totalist. Now *rare.* [f. as prec. + -IST.] = TEETOTALLER.

1840 *Fraser's Mag.* XXI. 154 It joins the Teetotalists, and avoids a thimbleful of alcohol. **1865** *Pall Mall G.* 25 Nov. 9 Is Mr. Wood the builder not a teetotalist, but a firm and sensible man?

So **tee'totalize** *v. trans.*, to convert to teetotalism; *intr.*, to practise teetotalism, to abstain; hence **tee'totalized** *ppl. a.*

1847-8 H. MILLER *First Impr.* v. (1857) 69 Alas for even teetotalized human nature, when placed in trying circumstances! **1898** G. B. SHAW *Let.* 18 Oct. (1972) II. 66 If I began to eat three beefsteaks a day, the ground would.. be shifted to the want of stimulants; but as it is,.. I am allowed to teetotallize [*sic*] in comparative peace.

tee'totaller, -aler. [f. as TEETOTALIST + -ER[1].] One who abstains (*esp.* one who pledges himself to abstain) from the use of any intoxicating liquor; a total abstainer.

1834 *Preston Temp. Adv.* Aug. 57/2 What is the whole matter in dispute betwixt the moderates and the teetotallers? **1835** E. C. DELAVAN *Let.* (Jan. 23) in *Life of J. Livesey* I. p. cxii, We [in U.S.] begin to feel the influence of your noble example. Our people by thousands are becoming *tee-totallers.* **1836** (*title*) Brief Sketch of the Life of Charles Watson, a Tee-Totaller in Liverpool. **1839** MARRYAT *Diary Amer.* Ser. I. III. 182 Massachusetts is now divided into two very strange political parties, to wit, the *topers* and the *teetotallers.* **1869** E. A. PARKES *Pract. Hygiene* (ed. 3) 268 The 84th Regiment.. numbered many teetotallers.

Hence **tee'totalleress** *nonce-wd.*, a female teetotaller.

1854 THACKERAY *J. Leech's Pict. Life & Char.* Wks. 1900 XIII. 484 And there was George [Cruikshank].. handing some teetotaleresses over a plank to the table where the pledge was being administered.

,tee'totally, *adv.*[1] *dial.* and *U.S.* [Reduplicated form of TOTALLY.] Totally, entirely, wholly.

1832 JUDGE JAS. HALL *Legends of W. Philadelphia* 38 [Kentucky backwoodsman says] These Mingoes.. ought to be essentially, and particularly, and tee-totally obflisticated off of the face of the whole yearth. **1836** HALIBURTON *Clockm.* xix. (1837) 195, I hope I may be tee-totally ruinated, if I'd take eight hundred dollars for him. **1839** DE QUINCEY *Casuistry Rom. Meals* Wks. 1854 III. 277 An ugly little parenthesis between two still uglier clauses of a teetotally ugly sentence. **1888** DR. TANNER *Sp. Ho. Com.* 20 July, The division, if it were taken now, would be taken entirely and tee-totally—(great laughter)—upon party lines. **1890** 'R. BOLDREWOOD' *Col. Reformer* (1891) 232 They weren't tee-totally lost.

b. With allusion to TEETOTAL 1.

1841 HOOD *Tale Trumpet* xxxviii, The man teetotally wean'd from liquor. **1850** *Tait's Mag.* XVII. 548/1 [Drink] a thing accursed, to be tee-totally abhorred and abandoned.

teetotally, *adv.*[2] *rare.* [f. TEETOTAL *a.* 1; see TEETOTALLY *adv.*[1] b.] In a teetotal manner, with total abstinence from alcoholic drinks.

1934 H. G. WELLS *Exper. Autobiogr.* II. viii. 533, I lived through my Bohemian days as sober as Shaw if not nearly so teetotally.

teetotum (tiː'təʊtəm), *sb.*[1] Forms: 8 **T totum**, 8–9 **te(-)totum, tee(-)totum,** 9 (erron.) **te-totum, tee-to-tum**; see also TOTUM. [Orig. *T totum*, formed by prefixing to L. *tōtum* 'all, the whole', its initial T, which stood for it on one of the four sides of the toy (itself in earlier use called simply a TOTUM, as in 17th c. French *totum*, now *toton*).]

1. a. A small four-sided disk or die having an initial letter inscribed on each of its sides, and a spindle passing down through it by which it could be twirled or spun with the fingers like a small top, the letter which lay uppermost, when it fell, deciding the fortune of the player; now, any light top (sometimes a circular disk pierced by a short peg), spun with the fingers, used as a toy.

The letters were originally the initials of Latin words, viz. T *totum*, A *aufer*, D *depone*, N *nihil*. Subsequently they were the initials of English words, T being interpreted as *take-all*: see quot. 1801. On the French *totum* or *toton*, the letters are T, A, D, R, meaning, according to Littré, *Totum*, tout, *Accipe*, prends, *Da*, donne, *Rien* (nothing).

1720 DE FOE *Life D. Campbell* (1841) 50 A very fine ivory T totum, as children call it. **1778** MISS BURNEY *Evelina* (1791) II. xxxvii. 245 And turn round like a tetotum. **1800** *Sporting Mag.* XV. 48 A man was lately convicted.. for selling a teetotum. **1801** STRUTT *Sports & Past* IV. iv. 341 When I was a boy the te-totum had only four sides, each of them marked with a letter; a T for take all; an H for half, that is, of the stake; an N for nothing; and a P for put down, that is, a stake equal to that you put down at first. **1818** MOORE *Fudge Fam. Paris* v. 23 Though, like a tee-totum, I'm all in a twirl, Yet even (as you wittily say) a tee-totum Between all its twirls gives a letter to note 'em. **1893** W. S. GILBERT *Utopia* 11, She'll waltz away like a teetotum.

b. *fig.* (*a*) *Sc.* and *Ir.* A very little person. (*b*) Something very unsteady.

1822 GALT *Sir A. Wylie* III. xxvi. 221, I didna think Miss Mary would ever tak sic a tee totum. **1860** THACKERAY *Round. Papers, Week's Holiday* 223 Who knows how long that dear teetotum happiness can be made to spin without toppling over? **1922** JOYCE *Ulysses* 759 Comical little teetotum always stuck up in some pub corner and her or her son waiting.

2. A game of chance played with this device.

1753 SMOLLETT *Ct. Fathom* (1784) 65/1 Continue to divert ourselves at all fours, brag, cribbidge, tetotum, &c. **1842** S. LOVER *Handy Andy* xiv, O'Grady gruffly broke in with 'You'd better ask him, does he love teetotum'.

3. *attrib.* and *Comb.*, whirling like the top.

1819 *Metropolis* II. 97 Mrs. S—m-r's tetotum-like turn, not without grace or activity, but with a sportive kind of oddity. **1863** COWDEN CLARKE *Shaks. Char.* x. 258 His own teetotum brain is upset.

Hence **tee'totum, tee'totumize** *vbs., intr.* to spin like a teetotum, to gyrate; **tee'totumism** (*nonce-wd.*), the condition of being 'in a whirl' like a teetotum; **tee'totumwise** *adv.*, in the manner of a teetotum.

1831 MOORE *Summer Fête* 556 No blither nymph *tee-totumed round To Collinet's immortal strain. **1897** MARY KINGSLEY *W. Africa* 199 If that wretch, the current.. did not grab hold of the nose of my canoe, and we teetotummed. **1841** T. NOEL *Rymes & Roundelays* 212 Brother bards.. Ye, who.. Set your brains *tetotum-izing. **1813** W. BULL in *Mem.* xvi. (1864) 350 The whirligigism of your situation, —I might have said the *teetotumism, for I think your brain must very much resemble a teetotum. **1881** *Daily News* 1 Feb. 5/4 The *Mevliveeyeh*, profanely called Dancing Dervishes, still revolve *teetotum-wise.

tee'totum, *sb.*[2] [A whimsical formation from TEETOTAL, app. after prec.] A teetotal or temperance restaurant.

1891 *Independent* 10 Apr. 233/3 There is little to distinguish 'the Teetotum' from the ordinary Coffee Tavern or Temperance Club except the peculiarity of being 'a tied house'. **1892** *Daily News* 24 June 2/8 His Royal Highness.. expressed satisfaction.. at the starting of 'tee-to-tums', or temperance restaurants. **1895** *Westm. Gaz.* 7 Jan. 7/1 A kind of cross between the Gothenburg system and the Tee-to-tum scheme.

teety, tetty, *a.* Now *dial.* Also 9 **teaty,** (**tedy**). [Of obscure origin: cf. TEETHY *a.*[1]] (See quots.)

1621 BURTON *Anat. Mel.* I. ii. III. xiii. (1651) 119 They are so cholerick and tetty that no man may speak with them. **1787** GROSE *Provinc. Gloss., Teety*, fretful, fractious. **1809** T. DONALDSON *Poems* 170 I'd be as tedy as a child. **1855** ROBINSON *Whitby Gloss., Teaty* or *Tutty*, easily offended, testy or touchy.

teevee (ˌtiː'viː). Also **Teevee, tee-vee.** [A rendering of the names of the letters *T* and *V*.] = TV.

1949 *N. Y. Mirror* 18 Apr. 10/2 Warners, unworried about teevee, showed a 1948 profit of 3 million. **1959** G. FREEMAN *Jack would be Gentleman* i. 7 It was wonderful what you learned from the tee-vee. **1963** *Guardian* 10 Jan. 6/6 Often .. viewers do not know which channel they have been watching, and.. will say 'Oh, it was the Tee-vee.' **1975** *Listener* 11 Sept. 350/3 In California, he achieves success as a low-budget teevee film-maker.

teewit, etc., var. TEWIT *dial.*, peewit, lapwing.

teez, obs. form of TEASE.

‖**teff** (tɛf). Also **tef, taff,** *erron.* **thaff, theff.** [a. Amharic *ṭēf, ṭiēf*, Tigré *ṭâf*, native names in Abyssinia.] The principal cereal of Abyssinia, *Poa* (*Eragrostis*) *abyssinica*, producing minute red or white grains from which bread is made; introduced elsewhere as a fodder plant. Also *attrib.*

1790 J. BRUCE *Trav. Source Nile* V. 77 Teff is used by all sorts of people from the king downwards, and there are kinds of it which are esteemed fully as much as wheat. **1797** *Encycl. Brit.* (ed. 3) XVIII. 333/2 There are three kinds of meal made from teff, of which the best.. is as white as flour, .. the second is of a browner colour; and the last.. is nearly black. **1858** HOGG *Veg. Kingd.* 823. **1887** *Kew Bulletin* Jan. 2-6. **1894** *Ibid.* Nov. 378 A slender annual grass, known in Abyssinia as 'Taff', 'Ttheff', or 'Thaff'.. cultivated for the sake of its grain all over Abyssinia... According to Richard there are green, white, red, and purple Teffs.

teffites, obs. Sc. form of TAFFETA.

‖**tefillin** (tiː'fɪliːn), *sb. pl.* Also **tephillim, -in.** [Rabb. Heb. *t'phillīm*, Aramaic *t'phillīn*, heteroclite pl. of *t'phillāh* prayer.] A name for Jewish phylacteries, or (quot. 1863) for the texts inscribed on them: see PHYLACTERY 1.

1613 PURCHAS *Pilgrimage* II. xv. 162 This peece of worke they call Tephillin, to put them in mind of often prayer. **1842** BONAR & M'CHEYNE *Miss. to Jews* 1 July (1843) 237 There were about thirty in the synagogue, all wearing the *Tallith* or shawl with fringes, and the *Tephillin* or phylacteries, because this was the hour of morning prayer. **1863** *Smith's Dict. Bible* III. 1167/2 (*Scribes*) Repeating their Tephillim, the texts inscribed on their phylacteries. **1865** *Chambers's Encycl.* VII. 519/2 Certain strips of parchment, inscribed with certain passages from the Scripture.., enclosed in small cases, and fastened to the forehead and the left arm (*Tefillin*).. in use with the Jews.. are.. called in the New Testament phylacteries. **1967** C. POTOK *Chosen* I. iii. 61, I got the tefillin and prayer book out of the drawer of the night table and began to put on the tefillin. *Ibid.*, When I finished praying, I took off the tefillin and put them and the prayer book back in the drawer. **1978** J. SACKS in P. Moore *Man, Woman & Priesthood* iii. 33 They [*sc.* women] are not obliged, as men are, to put on the phylacteries (*tefillin*) or the fringed garment (*tzitzit*).

Teflon ('tɛflɒn). Also **teflon.** [f. TE(TRA- + FL(UOR- + *-on*, arbitrary ending.]

a. A proprietary name for POLYTETRAFLUOROETHYLENE.

1945 *Official Gaz.* (U.S. Patent Office) 23 Oct. 531/1 E. I. du Pont de Nemours and Company... *Teflon* for synthetic resinous fluorine-containing polymers. **1951** *Jrnl. Amer. Chem. Soc.* LXXIII. 5195 (*heading*) Tracer studies of oxidation-reduction polymerization and molecular weight of 'Teflon' tetrafluoroethylene resin. **1954** *Trade Marks Jrnl.* 5 May 438/2 *Teflon*... Mouldable plastics in the form of powder, sheets, rods, tubes, tapes, filaments (non-textile) and shaped pieces. **1965** *New Scientist* 11 Mar. 618/2 One end of the blood-carrying teflon tube is joined to a side opening made in the wall of the pulmonary artery. **1970** *Nature* 25 July 382/2 Exudates were.. homogenized using a 'Teflon' grinder to rupture any cells present. **1979** A. L. LYDERSEN *Fluid Flow & Heat Transfer* vi. 150 The mesh is available in materials, such as, acid resistant steel, nickel, copper, aluminium, tantalum, hastelloy and Teflon.

b. *Comb.*

1965 *Family Circle* Oct. 92 Won't scratch, scar or mar Teflon coated cookware. **1972** M. CRICHTON *Terminal Man* II. i. 64 The team was now using Briggs stainless-steel Teflon-coated electrode arrays. **1979** A. L. LYDERSEN *Fluid Flow & Heat Transfer* iv. 80 They.. have Teflon-covered piston rings.

c. *transf.* and *joc.* Used *attrib.* or in comb., of politicians whose reputation remains undamaged by scandal or misjudgement, or who manage to deflect criticism on to others, so that nothing 'sticks' to them. orig. *U.S.*

Teflon* (*coated*) *President: introduced *spec.* as an epithet applied to U.S. President Reagan. Also ***Teflon Presidency.***

1983 P. SCHROEDER in *Congress Rec.* 2 Aug. H6216/1 After carefully watching Ronald Reagan he is attempting a great break-through in political technology—he has been perfecting the Teflon coated Presidency. He sees to it that nothing sticks to him. **1983** *N.Y. Times* 9 Aug. A18/4 (*heading*) The Teflon Presidency. **1985** *New Yorker* 28 Jan. 74/2 The Mayor is celebrated for.. distancing himself as far as possible from whatever may have gone wrong... The executive director of the largest local public-employees' union has called him 'the Teflon mayor'. **1985** *Times* 19 Sept. 12/1 His skill in ducking out of tricky situations.. has led to his being dubbed the Teflon Prime Minister, because nothing sticks. **1987** *Los Angeles Times* 15 Feb. v. 4/5 We have never had either a 'Teflon President' or a 'Great Communicator'.

[**teft** *a.*, in Peele *Tale of Troy* ed. 1589, apparently mispr. for *toft* = *toght*, TAUT, as in ed. 1604.]

teg (tɛg), **tag** (tæg). Forms: α. 6 **tegge**, 6–9 **tegg**, 7– **teg**; β. 6–7 **tagge**, 9 **tag.** [Of uncertain origin; perh. Scandinavian: cf. Sw. *tacka* a ewe.]

1. A sheep in its second year, or from the time it is weaned till its first shearing; a yearling sheep; = HOG *sb.*[1] 4, HOGGET 2. Formerly restricted to the female; now applied to both sexes (***ewe*** and ***wether tegs***). Also *attrib.* as ***teg sheep, wool*** (see b).

1537 in *Priory of Hexham* (Surtees) I. App. 130 One Stringor, that brought a tegg from Wresill. **1607** TOPSELL *Four-f. Beasts* (1658) 495 The first year, we call it.. a Lamb, .. the second year a Hog, Lam-hog, or Teg if it be a female. **1674** RAY *S. & E.C. Words* 77 *Tagge*, a sheep of the first year. *Suss.* **1688** *Lond. Gaz.* No. 2346/4, 20 Sheep.. whereof 15 were Wethers, and 5 Tegs. **1733** TULL *Horse-Hoeing Husb.* x. 104 Lambs of three Weeks old.. are called Tegs. **1789** *Trans. Soc. Arts* I. 141, I turned in my Tegs (or one year old sheep). **1844** STEPHENS *Bk. Farm* II. 39 In England.. sheep bear the name of *lamb* until 8 months old, after which they are called *ewe* and *wether teggs* until once clipped. **1866** [see HOG *sb.*[1] 4 b].

attrib. *a* **1722** LISLE *Husbandry* (1757) 388, I had a few teg or hog-sheep. **1889** *Daily News* 16 Dec. 3/5 With regard to teg sheep, weaned within a fortnight of each other.

b. ***teg wool***, also ellipt. *teg.* Cf. HOG *sb.*[1] 4 c.)

1854 MISS BAKER *Northampt. Gloss.* II. 223 The fleeces of the first shearing, amongst wool-dealers, are called indiscriminately *Tegs* or *Hogs*. *Ibid.* 331 Teg wool is the wool of the first shearing when the sheep is little more than a year old. **1879** *Cassell's Techn. Educ.* IV. 259. **1886** ELWORTHY *W. Somerset Word-bk., Teg*.. is not so often applied to the sheep as 'hog', but more frequently to the wool.

†**2.** A doe or female deer in its second year. *Obs.*

1530 PALSGR. 279/2 Tegge or pricket, *saillant.* **1568** *Hist. Jacob & Esau* I. i. A iij, If we haue lucke thys day to kill Hare, Teg, or Doe. **1636** *Althorp MS.* in Simpkinson *Washingtons* (1860) App. 78 A journey to Wormleighton with a bucke and a tegg. **1774** GOLDSM. *Nat. Hist.* (1862) I. II. v. 329 The female is called a *doe*; the first year, a *fawn*; and the second, a *tegg*.

†**3.** Applied contemptuously to a woman. *Obs.*

a **1529** SKELTON *El. Rummyng* 151 Full vntydy tegges, Lyke rotten egges. —— *Agst. Garnesche* I. 31 Your wynde schakyn shankkes, your longe lothy legges,.. Bryngges yow out of fauyr with alle femall teggys.

Teg, obs. var. TEAGUE, an Irishman.

Tegean (tɛ'dʒiːən, 'tɛdʒɪən), *sb.* and *a.* [f. Gr. *Τεγέα*, L. *Tegea* Tegea.] **A.** *sb.* A native or inhabitant of the ancient city of Tegea in Arcadia. **B.** *adj.* Of or pertaining to Tegea or its inhabitants. Also **Tegeate** *sb.* and *a.* [ad. L. *Tegeātēs*].

1584 B. RICH tr. *Herodotus' History* I. fol. 17 The Lacedæmonians, hauing escaped a scowring, were triumphant conquerous ouer ye Tegeates. **1709** I. LITTLEBURY tr. *Herodotus' History* II. IX. 377 Next to themselves, the Lacedemonians plac'd the Tegeans, consisting of fifteen hundred Men. **1767** A. STRAHAN tr. *Virgil's Æneid* I. v. 137 He from Arcarnania came, This from Arcadia of Tegæan blood. **1808** [see MANTINEAN *sb.* and *a.*]. **1858** G. RAWLINSON tr. *Herodotus' History* I. I. lxvi. 204 These persons.. measured the Tegean plain as they executed their labours. **1888** *Encycl. Brit.* XXIII. 110/1 At Plataea (479 B.C.) 3000 Tegeans fought the good fight of freedom. **1919** E. POUND *Quia pauper Amavi* 35 Tegean Pan. **1949** *Oxf. Classical Dict.* 881/1 C. 550 B.C. Sparta came to terms with Tegea after a long war; and for two centuries it followed the Spartan lead, though at times unwillingly, for the Tegeans were tough fighters. **1951** [see MANTINEAN *sb.* and *a.*]. **1952** C. DAY LEWIS tr. *Virgil's Aeneid* v. 101 After him, side by side, Salius and Patron, the one Acarnanian, the other Arcadian, of a Tegaean family.

tegestology (tɛdʒɛ'stɒlədʒɪ). [Irreg. f. L. *teges, -etis* covering, mat, f. *teg-ĕre* to cover + *-t* + -OLOGY.] The collecting of beer mats. So **tege'stologist**.

1960 *Ironmonger* 23 Jan. 123 Tegestologists (beer-mat secreters). **1960** [see PHILLUMENIST]. **1966** *Punch* 9 Feb. 202/2 'Here let tegestology exact its tribute from a royal embrace' (meaning, pinch a beer-mat from the *Queen's Arms*) is the sort of thing which any rallyist can work out in between emptying the ashtrays and giving the 'V' sign to a fellow competitor. **1977** *Titbits* 20–26 Jan. 17/5 The British tegestologists (a posh name for beermat collectors) are very upset to discover criminals who.. scoop up mats.. and decamp.

tegh: see TEE *v.*[1], TIE *v.*

teght, teȝt, pa. t. of TIGHT *v.*

tegir, obs. f. TIGER.

‖**tegmen** ('tɛgmɛn). Pl. 'tegmina. [L. *tegmen* (*tegimen, tegumen*) covering, f. *teg-ĕre* to cover; so F. *tegmen*.] A cover, covering, coating, integument. (Only in scientific use.) **a.** *gen.*

1807 HEADRICK *Arran* 61 The pitchstone assumes a greyish tegmen, or crust, by exposure to the air.

b. *Entom.* (*pl.*) The wing-covers, i.e. the fore wings when modified so as to serve as coverings for the hind wings; esp. those of orthopterous insects (corresponding to the *elytra* of beetles).

1817 KIRBY & SP. *Entomol.* xxiii. (1818) II. 350 Probably in the next order (*Orthoptera*), the *Tegmina*, or wing-covers .. assist them in flying. **1826** *Ibid.* xlvii. IV. 371 The horizontal portion of one tegmen lies longitudinally over that of the other. **1877** HUXLEY *Anat. Inv. Anim.* vii. 400 The female [cockroach] has moveable tegmina.

c. *Bot.* The thin inner coat of a seed, immediately enveloping the nucleus; the *endopleura*.

[**1832** LINDLEY *Introd. Bot.* 183 The internal integument, .. *endopleura* of De Candolle, *hilofère* and *tegmen* of Mirbel.] **1857** HENFREY *Bot.* §296 The inner integument, the tegmen or endopleura, is not generally distinguishable.

d. Anat. ***tegmen tympani***, a plate of bone forming the roof of the tympanum of the ear, being a part of the temporal bone. Also *ellipt.* as *tegmen*.

1890 in BILLINGS *Nat. Med. Dict.* **1902** D. J. CUNNINGHAM *Text-bk. Anat.* 704 The roof [of the tympanic cavity].. is formed by a thin plate of bone, the tegmen tympani. **1939** JOYCE *Finnegans Wake* 249 There lies her word, you reder!.. It vibroverberates upon the tegmen. **1977** *Proc. R. Soc. Med.* LXX. 821/2 In mandibulofacial dysostosis the attic and antrum are typically absent.. being replaced.. by descent of the tegmen. **1980** *Gray's Anat.* (ed. 36) 312/1 In a young skull the suture between the petrous and the squamous parts of the temporal bone may be visible at the lateral limit of the tegmen tympani.

e. *Ornith.* (*pl.*) = *tectrices*: see TECTRIX.

1891 in *Cent. Dict.*

tegment ('tɛgmənt). *rare.* [ad. L. *tegmentum*: see below.] A covering, integument. †**a.** *gen. Obs. rare*⁻⁰. **b.** = TEGMENTUM (1 and 2).

1656 BLOUNT *Glossogr.*, *Tegment* (*tegmentum*), a covering, a garment or cloathing. **1888** *Cassell's Encycl. Dict.*, *Tegment*... 1. *Anat.*: The upper part of the *crura cerebri*.. 2. *Bot.* (*Pl.*): The scales of a bud. **1899** *Allbutt's Syst. Med.* VI. 769 Cells, whose axis-cylinder processes pass as root fibres vertically through the tegment and pyramids.

Hence **tegmented** ('tɛgməntɪd) *ppl. a.*, covered as with a roof, roofed over.

1891 *Cent. Dict.* s.v. *Teiidæ*, A family of.. lacertilians,.. having supratemporal fossæ not tegmented or roofed over.

tegmental (tɛg'mɛntəl), *a.* [f. as prec. + -AL[1].] Of or pertaining to the tegmentum.

1890 in BILLINGS *Nat. Med. Dict.* **1899** *Allbutt's Syst. Med.* VII. 351 Lesions of the tegmental region are specially apt to affect the fifth, sixth, seventh, and eighth nerves.

‖**tegmentum** (tɛg'mɛntəm). Pl. -a. [L. collateral form of *tegumentum* TEGUMENT.]

1. *Bot.* Each of the scales forming the covering of a leaf-bud; a bud-scale.

1832 LINDLEY *Introd. Bot.* 51 Thus, in the Beech, the tegmenta are thin, smooth, and dry. **1842** BRANDE *Dict. Sc.* **1861** BENTLEY *Man. Bot.* (1870) 94 These external modified leaves,.. termed scales,.. have also received the name of tegmenta.

2. *Anat.* The upper and hinder portion of each of the *crura cerebri*.

1879 *St. George's Hosp. Rep.* IX. 670 Those on the opposite surface of the crus, which form the tegmentum. **1893** SIR W. R. GOWERS *Dis. Nerv. Syst.* II. 438 There may be hemianæsthesia from softening of the tegmentum of the crus.

tegminal ('tɛgmɪnəl), *a. rare*⁻⁰. [f. L. *tegmen, tegmin-*, TEGMEN + -AL[1].] Of the nature of a *tegmen*; covering, protecting.

1891 in *Cent. Dict.*

tegre, obs. form of TIGER.

tegu ('tɛguː). Abbrev. of TEGUEXIN.

1954 G. DURRELL *Three Singles to Adventure* i. 28 One of the tegus opened his eyes. **1974** D. & M. WEBSTER *Compar. Vertebr. Morphol.* viii. 164 (*caption*) Surface view of a freshly shed skin of a tegu lizard.

‖**teguexin** (tɛ'gwɛksɪn). *Zool.* [ad. Aztec *tecoixin, tecouixin* (tɛ'kwɪʃɪn) a lizard.] A large South American lizard of the genus *Tupinambis* or a similar member of the family Teiidæ.

[**1540** SAGAHUN *Historia de Nueva España* XI. iv. (1829) 202 Hay lagartos en esta tierra, y llamanlos *tecouixin*.] **1879** E. P. WRIGHT *Anim. Life* 376 The Teguexin (*Teius teguexin*) is not uncommon in Surinam and the Brazils. It attains a length of from three to four feet. **1892** W. H. HUDSON *Natur. La Plata* 74 The large teguexin lizard of the pampas, called iguana by the country people, is a notable snake-killer.

‖**tegula** ('tɛgjʊlə). *Entom.* Pl. -æ. [L., a tile, f. *teg-ĕre* to cover.]

1. a. A small scale-like structure covering the base of the fore-wing in hymenopterous and other insects. **b.** Each of a pair of membranous scales (PREHALTERES) in front of the halteres in dipterous insects.

1826 KIRBY & SP. *Entomol.* xxxiii. III. 377 *Tegulæ*.., small corneous concavo-convex scales, which in many Orders, particularly *Hymenoptera*, cover and defend the base of the Upper-Wings. *Ibid.* xlvii. IV. 381 The tegulæ, or base-covers.. cover and defend the base of their wings. **1893** A. E. SHIPLEY *Zool. Invertebrata* xix. 376 On the mesothorax [of Hymenoptera] are two small scales known as the tegulae, covering the base of the wings. **1972** M. S. GARDINER *Biol. Invertebrates* xiv. 573/1 Newly hatched wasps.. have been made to sting bees near their tegulae.

2. *Archæol.* and *Archit.* A flat roof-tile (see quot. 1964). Cf. IMBREX I. Also *fig.*

1871 R. BURN *Rome & Campagna* p. lxxv, The Roman tiles were of two kinds, flat tiles and smaller curved tiles. The flat tiles had raised rims at the sides... The small curved tiles were.. laid over the joined edges.. and formed a complete protection for the joint... Tegulæ and imbrices. **1938** in P. E. Thomas *Mod. Building Practice* III. 229 The Double Roman tile.. is a descendant of the Roman *tegula* and *imbrex*.., which the Romans used extensively for their villa roofs. **1956** 'H. MACDIARMID' *Stony Limits & Scots Unbound* 9 The gold edging of a bough at sunset, its pantile way Forming a double curve, tegula and imbrex in one. **1964** J. S. SCOTT *Dict. Building* 178 *Italian tiling*.., single-lap tiles which form a roof covering with two different sorts of tiles, the curved over-tile or imbrex and the flat, tray shaped under-tile or tegula. **1977** *Antiquaries Jrnl.* LVII. 264 Bricks and tegulae can frequently be seen in the debris.

tegular ('tɛgjʊlə(r)), *a.* [f. as prec. + -AR; cf. F. *tégulaire*.]

a. Pertaining to or of the nature of a tile; composed of or arranged like tiles. **b.** *Entom.* Pertaining to or of the nature of a *tegula* (*Cent. Dict.* 1891). Hence **tegularly** *adv.*, in the manner of tiles; so as to overlap like tiles. So '**tegulated** *a.*, (of armour) composed of overlapping plates.

1796 KIRWAN *Elem. Min.* (ed. 2) II. 162 In flat hexahædral masses tegularly accumulated or implicated. **1828** WEBSTER, *Tegular*, pertaining to a tile; resembling a tile; consisting of tiles. **1834** PLANCHÉ *Brit. Costume* 72 A suit of.. tegulated armour.. composed of small square plates of steel, lapping over each other like tiles. **1842** *Blackw. Mag.* LII. 171 In rastred, or ringed, or tegulated armour.

‖'**tegumen**. *rare*⁻⁰. [L., var. form of *tegimen*, TEGMEN.] = TEGMEN.

1882 OGILVIE, Tegmen, Tegumen.

tegument ('tɛgjʊmənt). [ad. L. *tegument-um* covering, f. *teg-ĕre* to cover: see -MENT. So OF. *tegument* (13th c. in Godef.).] Something that serves to cover; a covering, coating, envelope, investment, integument. **a.** *gen.* (natural or artificial).

c **1440** *Pallad. on Husb.* IV. 20 Ffor sunne and wynde hem make a tegument, Lest they in this be shake, in that to brent. **1658** SIR T. BROWNE *Hydriot.* iii. 32 Whatever was the solid Tegument, we finde the immediate covering to be a purple peece of silk. **1674** *Phil. Trans.* IX. 205 They have only a few teguments to cover themselves with in the night. **1713** DERHAM *Phys.-Theol.* III. i. 64 Beds.. lying under that upper Stratum, or Tegument of the Earth. *c* **1830** HOR. SMITH *Addr. Mummy* xiii, Why should this worthless tegument endure If its undying guest be lost for ever? **1888** A. S. WILSON *Lyric Hopeless Love* CVIII. 315 Beneath the tegument of clay.

b. *Nat. Hist.* and *Anat.* The natural covering of the body, or of some part or organ, of an animal or plant; a skin, coat, shell, husk, or the like; *spec.* = TEGMEN b (Brande *Dict. Sci.*, 1842). Now *rare* or *Obs.*; mostly replaced by INTEGUMENT.

1646 SIR T. BROWNE *Pseud. Ep.* II. vi. 97 A harder tegument or shell [in the nutmeg], which lyeth under the Mace. **1760** J. LEE *Introd. Bot.* I. ix. (1765) 19 Corolla and Calyx, are the Teguments or Covers of the Stamina and Pistillum. **1822** IMISON *Sc. & Art* I. 250 It [the eye] is composed of three coats, or teguments, one covering the other. **1864** MAX MÜLLER *Sc. Lang.* Ser. II. ii. (1868) 74 If we never find skins except as the teguments of animals.

tegumental (tɛgjʊ'mɛntəl), *a.* [f. prec. + -AL[1].] Of, pertaining to, or of the nature of a tegument; integumental: = next.

1822–34 *Good's Study Med.* (ed. 4) IV. 463 The order of the tegumental laminæ. **1888** HUXLEY & MARTIN *Elem. Biol.* iv. 276 Visual and tegumental sense organs.

tegumentary (tɛgjʊ'mɛntərɪ), *a.* [f. as prec. + -ARY[1]: cf. F. *tégumentaire*.] Constituting, or serving as, a tegument; pertaining to or occurring in the tegument; integumentary.

1828–32 WEBSTER, *Tegumentary*, pertaining to teguments, or consisting of teguments. **1831** R. KNOX *Cloquet's Anat.* 235 They communicate with the vessels of the tegumentary membranes. **1848** LINDLEY *Introd. Bot.* (ed. 4) II. 227 The nucleus has only one tegumentary membrane. **1853** H. WALTON *Dis. Eye* (1875) 138 Tegumentary mole is a congenital tumour, often spoken of as nævus.

†**te'guryon.** *Obs. rare*⁻¹. [ad. L. *tegurium*, also *tigurium, tugurium*, a hut, cottage, f. *teg-ĕre* to cover; in med.L. also *tegorium* a shrine (Du Cange).] A shrine, a canopy over a tomb.

1483 CAXTON *Gold. Leg.* 190/1 The hows of saynt denys.. the teguryon of marble whyche is vpon hym.

tehr, var. of TAHR.

Tehrani (tɛ'(h)rɑːnɪ), *sb.* and *a.* Also **Teherani**. [f. *Tehran*, name of a city in northern Iran + -I.]

A. *sb.* A native or inhabitant of Tehran, the capital of Iran. **B.** *adj.* Of, pertaining to, or characteristic of the city of Tehran, or of its inhabitants.

1939 W. V. EMANUEL *Wild Asses* xiii. 145 'Assassin's' appearance belied his name; he was a strikingly handsome young Teherani, with a Greek nose. **1941** L. P. ELWELL-SUTTON *Modern Iran* i. 11 The favourite summer resorts of the Tehranis are all along this coast. **1953** A. SMITH *Blind White Fish in Persia* vii. 130 The Tehranis cast soulful glances towards America. **1973** *Times* 22 May (Teheran Suppl.) p. i/1 Few Teheranis.. have ever seen a drop of domestically produced crude oil. **1975** P. SOMERVILLE-LARGE *Couch of Earth* x. 178 The Tehrāni police consider it unlikely that you killed Mr Otway. **1977** H. OSBORNE *White Poppy* xii. 96 He was a Tehrani.

tehsil, var. TAHSIL.

tehsildar: see TAHSILDAR.

Tê-hua (teɪhwɑː, ‖dehwa). Also (Pinyin) ‖**Dehua**. The name of a place in the province of Fujian in south-eastern China, used *attrib.* and *absol.* to designate porcelain made there, also known as BLANC DE CHINE.

1923 R. L. HOBSON *Wares Ming Dynasty* xiii. 173 The term Chien yao was now transferred to a ware.. made more than a hundred miles south at Tê-hua (Tehwa)... There are .. no lack of actual examples of the Tehwa porcelain. **1945** W. B. HONEY *Ceramic Art of China* II. 133 The whole body of Tê-hua wares, familiarly called Fukien porcelain,.. holds together in a remarkable.. manner. **1953** R. S. JENYNS *Ming Pott. & Porc.* x. 146 Decorated pieces of Têhua, whether painted in blue or enamelled.. are of poorer quality than the undecorated pieces. **1980** *Catal. Fine Chinese Ceramics* (Sotheby, Hong Kong) 102 A well modelled Dehua (Te Hua) Seal in the form of a *qilin* (*ch'i-lin*).., the fabulous beast with bushy tail and curly mane shown crouching with horned head sharply turned to one side.

tei, teiche, obs. Sc. forms of TIE *sb.*, TACHE *sb.*[1]

Teian ('tiːən), *a.* Also **Tean**. [f. Gr. *τήϊος* of or from *τέως Teos* + -IAN.] Of or relating to Teos, an ancient Ionian city on the western coast of Asia Minor north of Ephesus.

1646 J. HALL *Poems* 34 Who light'st Love's dying Torch with purer fire, And breath'st new life into the Teian lyre. **1787** J. NOTT *Select Odes from Hafez* p. ix, Whether Anacreon borrowed the gaiety of his Odes from the Persian *Gazel*, or whether Hafez enriched his native language by an imitation of the Teian bard, I will not venture to determine. **1821** BYRON *Don Juan* III. lxxxvi. 47 The Scian and the Teian muse, The hero's harp, the lover's lute, Have found the fame your shores refuse. **1858** [see ARGIVE *a.*]. **1902** E. R. BEVAN *House of Seleucus* II. xix. 47 Antiochus.. backed the envoys of the Teians in other places. **1941** M.

ROSTOVTZEFF *Social & Econ. Hist. Hellenistic World* III. 1348 The Tean decree..which may refer to the synoecism of Teos and Lebedos. **1983** R. E. ALLEN *Attalid Kingdom* iii. 50 Teian envoys had been sent to Antiochos.

teicher, Sc. and north. f. TEAR *sb.*[1] and *v.*[2]

teichoic (taɪ'kəʊɪk), *a. Biochem.* [f. Gr. τεῖχο-ς wall + -IC.] ***teichoic acid***: any of various polymers of ribitol or glycerol phosphate that are found in the walls of Gram-positive bacteria.

1958 J. J. ARMSTRONG et al. in *Jrnl. Chem. Soc.* 4346 The general name 'teichoic acid'..is suggested for these polymers of ribitol phosphate with or without other substituents. **1973** *Nature* 4 May 43/2 The wall teichoic acid is responsible for the ability of the cell walls of Gram-positive bacteria to bind divalent cations and the membrane teichoic acid mediates an interaction between magnesium ions..and the cytoplasmic membrane.

‖**teichopsia** (taɪ'kɒpsɪə). *Path.* [f. Gr. τεῖχος wall + ὄψις sight + -IA[1].] Temporary blindness sometimes accompanying ophthalmic headache.

1872 *Nature* 21 Mar. 416/1 On Teichopsia, a form of transient half-blindness. **1899** *Allbutt's Syst. Med.* VIII. 223 The so-called Teichopsia, the appearance as of ebullition in objects, and other curious optical illusions, are familiar precursors of migraine.

tei'choscopy. [ad. Gr. τειχοσκοπία, f. τεῖχος wall + -σκοπια, from -σκοπος -looking.] A looking from the walls; a descriptive title of the third book of Homer's Iliad.

1875 *Contemp. Rev.* XXVI. 263 He [Ulysses] is by far the most prominent person in this portrait gallery of the Teichoscopy.

teie, obs. f. TIE *v.*

teigh, teiȝ-e, pa. t. of TEE *v.*[1] *Obs.*; obs. f. TIE *v.*

teighing: see TEE-HEE *v.*

‖**Te igitur** (tiː'ɪdʒɪtə(r)). [L., = 'thee therefore', the opening words of the prayer.] The first prayer in the canon of the Mass in the Roman and some other Latin liturgies; hence extended to the liturgical book itself.

1819 SCOTT *Ivanhoe* xliii, Bring forward the crucifix and the *Te igitur* [*Gloss.* The service book on which oaths were sworn]. **1877** J. D. CHAMBERS *Div. Worship* IV. v. 349 The subsequent petitions are taken..from the 'Te Igitur' or first part of the Canon.

Teigue, -ism, obs. f. TEAGUE, Irishman, etc.

teil (tiːl). Now *rare* or *Obs.* Forms: 6 tilie, 6–7 teyle, 7 teile, tiel, 7–8 tile, teyl, 9 til, 7– teil. [Partly ad. L. *tilia* linden-tree; partly a. OF. *til* (12–14th c. in Godef.), *teil* (13–17th c., and mod.dial., Berry), masc. forms collateral with *tille, teille*, ad. L. *tilia*; cf. It. *tiglio*, †*tilio*, beside †*tilia* (Florio), Sp. *tilo, tila*, Pg. *til, tilia*. (Mod.F. has *tilleul*:—L. **tiliolus*, dim. of **tilius*.)] The lime or linden tree, *Tilia europæa*. Usually ***teil-tree***.

[**1398** TREVISA *Barth. De P.R.* XVII. cxcii. (MS. Bodl.) lf. 238 b/2 Þe tre tilia..bene hauntеþ þe floures þerof and gadreþ þerof swetnes of hony.] **1589** FLEMING *Virg. Georg.* I. 7 The light wood of the Tilie tree is cut downe for a yoke. **1613** PURCHAS *Pilgrimage* (1614) 395 Some of them practise diuination with the leaues of the Teil-tree which they fold and vnfold in their hands. **1617** MORYSON *Itin.* I. 26 A faire meadow,..wherein is a faire Lynden or teyle tree. **1646** J. HALL *Horæ Vac.* 87 Like the shade of a Tile tree, very pleasant though the tree be unfruitfull. **1658** ROWLAND *Moufet's Theat. Ins.* 1032 They live on softer leaves, especially on the Tiel-tree. **1694** ADDISON *Virg. Georg.* IV. 233 From purple violets and the teile they [bees] bring Their gather'd sweets, and rifle all the spring. **1721** *New Gen. Atlas* 120 There are stately Walks of Tile-trees on its North Bank. **1837** WHEELWRIGHT tr. *Aristoph.* I. 270 *note*, Boards of the teil or linden. **1866** *Treas. Bot.*, Til-tree, *Tilia europæa*.

attrib. **1731** J. MONCRIEFF in Graham *Soc. Life Scotl. in 18th C.* (1901) I. vii. 52 A little tile-tree water.

b. In the Bibles of 1568 and 1611, used in one place to render Heb. *ēlāh* (elsewhere rendered 'oak' and once 'elm').

1568 BIBLE (Bishops') *Isa.* vi. 13 As a Teyle tree [so **1611**; Vulg. *terebinthus*, WYCLIF terebynt, COVERD. terebyntes, CRANM. terebintes, *Geneva* elme, *Douay* and *R.V.* (1885) terebinth] and the Oke in the fall of their leaues haue yet the sappe remayning in them. **1647** TRAPP *Comm. Phil.* iv. 10 It had..withered, as an Oak in winter..and as a Teyl tree whose sap is in the root.

teil(l, obs. form of TAIL, TEAL, TILL *v.*

teild, var. TELD *v. Obs.*, to pitch a tent.

Teilhardian (teɪ'jɑːdɪən), *a.* and *sb.* [f. the name of Pierre *Teilhard* de Chardin (1881–1955), French scientist and theologian + -IAN.]

A. *adj.* Of or pertaining to Teilhard de Chardin or his writings, which are noted for their attempt to synthesize science and the Christian faith. **B.** *sb.* An adherent or follower of Teilhard de Chardin.

1967 *Sat. Rev.* (U.S.) 15 Apr. 18/3 Teilhard de Chardin..restores all the dynamic energies and heroism of Milton's Satan to the Teilhardian Christ. **1970** T. P. O'MALLEY in *Studia Patristica* X. 194 Even if Tertullian was not a Teilhardian, he nevertheless held for a very palpable world here and hereafter. **1971** *Time* 19 Apr. 34 From the Teilhardians, the confidence that God, whoever he is, has something to do with the future and may yet meet man there. **1977** P. JOHNSON *Enemies of Society* ix. 125 Teilhardian phenomenology is a system which enables the more leisured class to accommodate scientific knowledge in a religious setting but which makes no intolerable demands on either flesh or intellect. **1983** KING & SALMON *Teilhard & Unity of Knowledge* i. 1 Teilhardians had long known that May 1, 1981—the centennial of the birth of Pierre Teilhard de Chardin—had to be celebrated in a special way. Two Teilhardian Jesuits would be at Georgetown University on that date.

teim, tein, obs. Sc. ff. TEEM *v.*[2], TEEN.

teind (tiːnd), (*a.*) *sb. Sc.* and *north.* Forms: 3–5 **tende, tend, 4–6 teynde, 4–7 teinde, (5 tyende, teend), 5–7 teynd, (6 teand, 8–9 tiend), 4– teind.** (Also 5 tene, 6 teine, 9 teen, tein.) [Early ME. *tende*, adj. and sb., collateral form of TENTH, q.v.: cf. also TITHE.]

A. *adj.* See TENTH A. 1 γ, and 3.

B. *sb.* †**1.** The tenth part (of anything); a tenth.

a **1300** *Cursor M.* 968 (Cott.) O þi winning giue me þe tend [*v.r.* tende]; Of alkin fruit haf þou þe nine, For I wil þat þe tend [*Fairf.* teynde, *Trin.* tenþe] be mine. **13..** *Ibid.* 16968 (Gött.) All þe tunges of þis werld cuth noght tell þe tend [*Cott.* teind]. *c* **1330** R. BRUNNE *Chron.* (1810) 145 Þat burgh no Citez of taliage suld non telle, þe tende suld be nouht, no þe tuende non make. *c* **1375** BARBOUR *Troy-bk.* I. 475 That mene lest nocht þe teynde to here. *c* **1375** *Sc. Leg. Saints* xii. (*Mathias*) 265 Of thre hundir þe teynd leyly, þat cumys be raknyne to thretty. *c* **1475** *Rauf Coilȝear* 474 The teind of his iewellis to tell war full teir. *c* **1475** *Golagros & Gaw.* 1083 For ony trety may tyde, I tell the the teynd [*rimes*, schend, freynde, wende].

2. *spec.* A tenth part of the produce of land or labour paid (voluntarily, or by legal enactment) for the support of religion: = TITHE *sb.* 1; now, in Scotland, that portion of the estates of the laity which is liable to be assessed for the stipend of the clergy of the established church. Now chiefly in pl.

[*c* **1200** ORMIN 2715 To ȝifenn Godd te tende del Off all þin aȝhenn ahhte. —— 6125 Off all þatt god te birrþ þin Godd þe tende dale brinngenn.] *a* **1300** *Cursor M.* 1062 (Cott.) Rightwis he was, and godds freind, And leli gaf he him his tend [*v.r.* tende]. **13..** *Ibid.* 27249 Quar he tas til his teindis tent. *a* **1340** HAMPOLE *Psalter* lxxviii. 1 Þai gedire þaire tendis and offrandis, And reckis noght of þe saules þat þai sould kepe. *c* **1425** WYNTOUN *Cron.* V. ix. 1810 Teyndis or monay That wes gevin in offerand. *c* **1440** *Alphabet of Tales* 168 Go byd þe preste feche þis ton of wyne for his tend. *c* **1450** *St. Cuthbert* (Surtees) 5438 Þare was a monke þe teend ast. **1535** STEWART *Cron. Scot.* (Rolls) III. 94 For to the kirk no teyndis tha wald pa. **1588** *Wills & Inv. N.C.* (Surtees) II. 256 *note*, I geue vnto my wyff the holle teand of Foulburye. **1596** DALRYMPLE tr. *Leslie's Hist. Scot.* IV. (S.T.S.) 226 This escheit suld first, of the first ȝeirlie teines, be payet to the Preistes. **1637–50** ROW *Hist. Kirk* (Wodrow Soc.) 28 The teinds are the Kirk's patrimonie, whereby the ministrie and the poore ought to be intertained. **1799** J. ROBERTSON *Agric. Perth* 78 The livings of the ministers..are fixed by the supreme court of this country, acting as a court of teinds or tithes. **1844** W. CROSS *Disruption* xiii. (E.D.D.), Raizin a plea against the laird for sumthing they call the teens. **1889** *Chambers' Encycl.* III. 528/1 The Court or Commission of Teinds, in which questions relating to the law of teinds or church tithes were decided.

b. *transf.* The payment, institution or system of teinds.

c **1817** HOGG *Tales & Sk.* II. 150 A wearisome debate on the rights of teind. **1905** *Sat. Rev.* 4 Feb. 14/2 Dr. Brown considers that teind was felt as an 'iniquitous oppression'.

c. ***the teind to hell*** (*Folk-lore*), in reference to the reputed obligation of the fairies to furnish a victim to Satan every seventh year: see Scott *Minstrelsy* Introd. to *Young Tamlane.*

17.. *Young Tamlane* xxxvii. in Scott *Minstr. Scot. Border* (1869) 478 For aye, at every seven years, They pay the teind to hell. **1852** *Alice Learmont* ix. 124 There cam up that black road the Evil Ane,..He took back nae mortal, but an elf, as the teind to hell.

3. *attrib.* and *Comb.* **a.** *attrib.* Of or pertaining to teinds or tithes, as ***teind-barn, court, day, -lathe*** (= tithe-barn), ***law, -master, office***; paid as tithe, as ***teind calf, coal, corn, fish, grice, hay, lamb, sheaf, silver, skate, wheat.*** **b.** objective, etc., as ***teind-payer***; ***teind-free*** adj.

In some of these, *teind* may have been at first merely the adj. = tenth, as *teind sheaf* tenth sheaf or tithe sheaf.

1885 W. ROSS *Aberdour & Inchcolme* v. 145 Conveying the teind-sheaves..to the *teind-barns at Aberdour. *a* **1555** LYNDESAY *Tragedy* 300 Ȝe wyll not want teind cheif nor offrandis, Teinde woll, teind lambe, *teind calf, teind gryce and guse. **1475** in *Finchale Priory* (Surtees) 37 For *tende cole in Le wood. *Ibid.* 39 An accion..in the Consistory..for tyende cole of our coal minez. **1463** *Burgh Rec. Edin.* (1869) I. 21 The said fermoraris, sall gif..the *tene corne of all cornes of the said mylne. **1842** J. AITON *Domest. Econ.* (1857) 54 Another proof that the *Teind Court are set upon paring down the income of the clergy to a mere existence. **1825** SCOTT *Jrnl.* 7 Dec., *Teind day;—at home of course. **1547** *Reg. Privy Council Scot.* I. 69 As to the *teynd fische of the Kirk of Kynfawnyes. **1621** *Sc. Acts Jas. VI* (1816) IV. 612/2 Act declairing summes Grasse..to be *teyndfrie. **1507–8** *Acc. Ld. High Treas. Scot.* IV. 103 For tua ȝeris *teynd hay of ane medow that the Kingis hors eit. **1547** *Test. Ebor.* (Surtees) VI. 265 The teynde haye of the hall banke. **1586** *Reg. Privy Council Scot.* IV. 73 Ressaving his *teynd lambis. **1828** *Craven Gloss.*, **Teen lathe*, tithe-barn. **1801** *Farmer's Mag.* Aug. 283 Our Scots *teind laws are founded upon this principle. **1710** *Dict. Feudal Law*, **Teind-masters*, are these who have Right to Teinds. **1890** *Oliver & Boyd's Edin. Almanac* 91 The tables have been prepared from official documents in the *Teind Office. **1685** RENWICK *Serm.*, etc. (1776) 151 Then shall *teind-payers be paid home. **1446** *Rental Bk. Cupar-Angus* (1879) I. 125 Our landis..and the *tende schef of the sayd landis. **1876** A. LAING *Lindores Abbey* xiv. 133 Patrick Leslie granted a tack of the teind sheaves of the parish of Dudhope to James Scrymgeour. **1505** *Acc. Ld. High Treas. Scot.* III. 171 Payit..the *teynd silvir of the Kingis staggis in tua ȝeris..xvj *d.* **1819** W. TENNANT *Papistry Storm'd* (1827) 13 He'd sooner fling them back i' the sea Than gie ae *teind-skate to the bishop. **1837** LOCKHART *Scott* an. 1806 II. iii. 103 There is also another blank day every other week,—the *Teind Wednesday, as it is called, when the Judges are assembled for the hearing of tithe questions.

teind (tiːnd), *v. Sc.* and *north.* ?*Obs.* Forms: see TEIND *sb.* [f. TEIND *sb.*: cf. *to tithe*.]

1. *intr.* To pay teinds or tithes.

c **1375** *Creation* 490 in Horstm. *Altengl. Leg.* (1878) 130 Þerfore wel to tenden buþ lef [= be glad]. **13..** *Cursor M.* 29324 (Cott. Galba) Þam..Þat witandly with-haldes tendes Or falsly tendes. *c* **1460** *Towneley Myst.* ii. 294 If thou tend right thou gettis thi mede;..if thou teynd fals, thou bese alowed ther after als.

2. *trans.* To assess or take the tenth or tithe of.

1483 *Cath. Angl.* 379/2 To Tende, *decimare*. **1566** *Reg. Privy Council Scot.* I. 480 To pas and teynd the cornis of the saidis toun. **1567** *Gude & Godlie B.* (S.T.S.) 188 The hirdis teindit all the corne. **1641** BEST *Farm. Bks.* (Surtees) 26 As for the wooll, it may be teended and wayed that wee may knowe what is of it. *a* **1722** FOUNTAINHALL *Decis.* (1761) 391 Herrings taken on the coast of Fife, though teinded there, yet if brought to Dunbar, pay again.

Hence **'teinder**, one who pays or takes teind or tithe; **'teinding** *vbl. sb.*, tithing.

13.. *Cursor M.* 27267 [In scrift þe preist sal frain] Anentes til-men of enuie And o þair tending [*v.r.* teinding] namli. *c* **1440** *Gesta Rom.* vi. 17 (Harl. MS.) Þe lewde men most holde vp..men of holy church, thoroȝ almesse offryngys, and tendingys. **1627** in A. Allan *Hist. Channelkirk* (1900) 147 Quhen the ground is punishit, the heritour and teinder must nott be frie. **1655** *Records Baron Crt. Stitchill* (S.H.S.) 2 Until the first day of the teynding be past. **1884** J. TAIT in *United Presbyt. Mag.* Apr. 156 The arrangement of thirders and teinders described by Arthur Young. **1905** C. B. GUNN *Baron Crt. Stitchill* Introd. 15 The minister might delay teinding until the weather was breaking.

teind, obs. Sc. f. TEND, TIND *v.*

teindable ('tiːndəb(ə)l), *a. Sc.* [f. TEIND *v.* + -ABLE.] Tithable.

1705 W. FORBES *Treatise on Churchlands* 289 All other Teindable Subjects in Scotland. **1832** *Fife Herald* 14 June, The planted park is valued at £2 10s. sterling, but is found not to be Teindable. **1924** *Kelso Chronicle* 25 July 4 The mansion house, cottages, joiner's shop, smithy and yard..were not teindable.

teine, Sc. f. TEEN, TINE, *sb.*[1]; var. TEYNE *Obs.*

teineite ('teɪnəaɪt). *Min.* [See quot. 1939 and -ITE[1].] A hydrated sulphate and tellurite of copper, $Cu(Te)O_3{\cdot}2H_2O$, found as blue, prismatic orthorhombic crystals and as fine crusts.

1939 T. YOSIMURA in *Jrnl. Faculty Sci. Hokkaido Univ.: Ser. 4* IV. 465 Professor..Harada collected some..crystals of a blue mineral... The author proposes the name 'Teineite' from the Teine mine where this new mineral has first been found. **1977** *Mineral. Abstr.* XXVIII. 487/1 A copper-bearing quartz vein cutting phyllites shows..rare azure-blue teineite as single crystals ($\leq$ 1 mm) or crystalline patches ($\leq$ 2·5 mm).

teing, obs. f. *tying*: see TIE *v.*

teinland, erron. f. *thegenland*, THANELAND.

teinoscope ('taɪnəʊskəʊp). [f. Gr. τείνειν to stretch, extend + -SCOPE.] An optical instrument in which prisms are so arranged and combined as to increase or diminish the apparent linear dimensions of objects, while the chromatic aberration of the light is corrected.

1822 BREWSTER in *Edin. Phil. Jrnl.* Apr. 334 (*heading*) Description of a Teinoscope for altering the Lineal Proportions of Objects, with Observations on Professor Amici's Memoir on Telescopes without Lenses... The Instrument which I propose to describe..was invented and constructed in its simplest form about the beginning of the year 1812. **1832** *Nat. Philos.* II. *Optic. Instr.* xvi. §110. 55 (Usef. Knowl. Soc.) Amici's teinoscope consists of four right angular prisms, having their refractive angles different and connected by pairs.

teint, -e, obs. ff. TAINT, TENT, TINT.

teinter, obs. f. TENTER.

teir, obs. Sc. f. TEAR; Sc. f. TERE *Obs.*, difficult.

teirce, teirs, -e, obs. ff. TIERCE.

teis, obs. Sc. pl. of TIE *sb.*

†**teise, taise**, *sb. Obs.* Also 5 teis, teys, tayse, tese. [ME. a. OF. *teise* (11th c. in Godef. *Compl.*), mod.F. *toise*, = It. *tēsa*:—late L. *tensa* (sc. *brachia*) the outstretched arms.]

1. A lineal measure of six feet, a fathom; = TOISE.

13.. *Sir Beues* (A.) 1417 In me prisoun þow schelt abide Vnder þerþe twenti teise [*v.rr.* paise, pase]. *c* **1330** *Florice & Bl.* (1857) 241 A thousan[d] taisen be his heihe.. And an hundre[d] taises he is wid And imaked with mochel prid.

2. A superficial measure, a square toise.

1426-7 *Rec. St. Mary at Hill* 66 A pavier and his man to paue..v teys ijs xi d. **1477-9** *Ibid.* 89, For pavyng xj teis of pament for euery teis vij d—vj s v d. **1486** *Nottingham Rec.* III. 259 To þe pauer for workyng of vj. tayses in þe same gate..he takyng for a tayse vj d: summa iij s. **1492-3** *Rec. St. Mary at Hill* 190 Item, for pavyng of þe pamentt..for viij tese, pris þe tese, vij d.

†**teise, taise,** *v.*[1] *Obs.* Also 4 teyse, tese, 4-6 tayse, 5 tase, 6 tais. [a. OF. *teser*, 3rd sing. pres. *teise, toise* (13th c. in Godef.):—late L. type **tēsāre*:—*tensāre* to stretch, bend (a bow), f. *tensus* stretched, bent.] *trans.* To stretch, to bend (a bow); hence, to fit (an arrow or quarrel in a bow or arbalest) in order to shoot; to aim or direct (a shaft, etc.); to poise (a weapon) in taking aim. Also *absol.* or *intr.*

13.. *Seuyn Sag.* (W.) 1978 And in his hond an arblast heldand, And therinne a quarel taisand. *c* **1330** R. BRUNNE *Chron. Wace* (Rolls) 13699 He teysed his dint, Bokkes to smyte. **1375** BARBOUR *Bruce* v. 623 He tait the vyre and leit it fle, And hit the fader in the E. 13.. *Minor Poems fr. Vernon MS.* xliv. 43 So doþ þe ffisschere wiþ his hok: Hou he tesep on þe Banke A brodly breyd I þe Brok. **1382** WYCLIF *Wisd.* v. 22 As at the teising the bowe of cloudis bent. *c* **1400** *Laud Troy Bk.* 6938 Paris at him euel taysed. *c* **1412** HOCCLEVE *De Reg. Princ.* 5262 Sore in þe bowe of treccherye he teisyth. *c* **1450** *Merlin* 590 Kynge Ban.. spronge that wey with his swerde vp teysed to hym that hadde his knyght slayn. **1513** DOUGLAS *Æneis* x. viii. 102 A bustuus lance..That lang quhile taysit he in proper tene, Leit gird at Pallas. *Ibid.* vi. 106.

†**teise,** *v.*[2] *Obs.* Also 4 tayse, 5 teyse (6 teese), 7 tease, teaze. [Origin unascertained. The forms agree with those of TEISE *v.*[1], with which however the sense does not seem compatible. Both forms and sense separate it from TEASE *v.*, although in late use it may have been sometimes associated with the latter in its modern sense, and hence confounded in spelling with it.] *trans.* app. To drive (esp. a hunted beast); to chase; to urge on.

13.. *Gaw. & Gr. Knt.* 1169 Bi þay [the deer] were tened at þe hyȝe, & taysed to þe wattrez. *c* **1410** *Master of Game* (MS. Digby 182) xxxv, Who so be teysoures to þe kynge.. as ofte as any hert cometh oute, he shulde..blowe a moot and rechate and late renne after to teyse it forth. *c* **1475** *Partenay* 1295 Into see thay went, the sayl vp gan reise, To cipresse contre ther shippes gan teise. **1559** *Mirr. Mag.* (1562) B b ij, A shyppe vpon the stormy seas, Which.. From shore to shore the wynde and tide do teese. **1615** WITHER *Sheph. Hunt.* III. in *Juvenilia* (1633) 407 My eager Dogs.. Then I began with quicker speed to follow And teaz'd them on with a more cheerful hallow. **1819** KEATS *Isabella* xxviii, They..did tease Their horses homeward, with convulsed spur. [Cf. **1888** ELWORTHY *W. Som. Words, Tease* (tēz), to drive; to harass. The only way to get rid o' they rabbits is to keep on *tazin'* o'm.]

teise, obs. bad spelling of TEASE.

†**teiser.** *Obs.* Forms: 5 teysoure, 6 teiser, 6-7 teaser, teazer, 7 teizer. [Agent-n. from TEISE *v.*[2]] One who rouses the game; *spec.* one of the first brace or leash of deerhounds let slip. (In later use confused in spelling with TEASER.)

c **1410** *Master of Game* (MS. Digby 182) xxxv, Þe firste teysoure and þe resceyuour that draweth hym doune, shull parte þe skynne. *Ibid.* [see TEISE *v.*[2]]. **1575** TURBERV. *Venerie* 266 By this worde teasers is ment, the first grey-houndes or brase or lease of greyhoundes which is let slip. *c* **1590** GREENE *Fr. Bacon* i. 5 The loftie frolicke bucks, That scudded fore the teisers like the wind. **1616** SURFL. & MARKH. *Country Farme* 686 As neere the couert as you can conueniently, you shall place your Teasers, that is, the first brace of greyhounds for the course, which should be the lightest, nimblest, and swiftest dogges you haue. **1688** R. HOLME *Armoury* III. 189/1.

fig. **1642** FULLER *Holy & Prof. St.* II. v. 66 But these Teazers, rather to rouze then pinch the Game, onely made Whitaker find his spirits. **1647** CLARENDON *Hist. Reb.* v. §339 The Lord Paget likewise, who..had been one of their Teizers, to broach those bold, high Overtures. **1796** *Campaigns 1793-4* II. v. 21 Francis himself, the great Carmagnol teizer.

teistie, var. TYSTIE.

teisty, teize, obs. ff. TESTY, TEASE.

tej (tɛdʒ). Also † tedge, tedje; tedj. [Amharic.] A kind of mead that is the national drink of Ethiopia.

1853 M. PARKYNS *Life in Abyssinia* I. xvii. 210 Spirits are of an inferior kind, distilled..from the refuse of the wine or from honey... The grape is called 'wainy', the wine 'wain tedge'. **1877** E. A. DE COSSONS *Cradle of Blue Nile* I. vii. 100 As soon as the baskets of bread had been removed, bottles of tedge were served. **1901** A. B. WYLDE *Mod. Abyssinia* viii. 182 The tedj bearer always pouring out a little of the liquid into..his hand. *Ibid.* xvii. 377 The honey taken from the wanza flowers being greatly prized, as being of a white colour makes very clear tedj. **1925** H. C. MAYDON *Simen* ii. 24 Abdulla, the cook, was..too apt to celebrate with the local tej and marissa (mead and beer). **1936** E. WAUGH *Waugh in Abyssinia* i. 26 A weekly visit to the cinema, a preference for whisky over *tedj*..were the western innovations that these young men relished. *Ibid.* v. 169 They got very drunk in the *tedj* houses. **1952** [see POMBE]. **1974** *Country Life* 18 Apr. 938/3 *Tej*, a mead of honey, hops and water. **1981** E. NORTH *Dames* i. 12 It is known as *tedj*. .. A sort of honey-mead... Some call it *mies*.

‖**Tejano** (tə'hɑːnəʊ). [Amer. Sp., formerly written *Texano*, f. *Texas* TEXAS.] A native or inhabitant of Texas, esp. one of Mexican stock; a Texan.

1925 O. P. WHITE *Them was Days* 75 The fear of God, as represented by the wrath of the *Tejanos* (Texans). **1933** H. ALLEN *Anthony Adverse* III. IX. lxiv. 1175 The convoy, when it did start, consisted of about sixty unfortunate mestizos and Indians bound for the mines at Chihuahua as well as the captured Americans, or 'Tejanos', whose cases were to be disposed of by the Viceroy Calleja at Mexico. **1976** *Monitor* (McAllen, Texas) 26 Sept. 7E/2 *Tejanos* more than any other ethnic group in Texas have provided a bridge to Texas' past.

tek (tɛk), *v.* Also teck. Repr. U.S. Black and regional pronunc. of TAKE *v.*

1905 [see WE *pron.* 1 g]. **1924** M. W. BECKWITH in *Mem. Amer. Folklore Soc.* XVII. 76 Him couldn't get away from de woman until rain tek him in de yard. **1938** C. HIMES *Pork Chop Paradise* in *Black on Black* (1973) 165 W'en de panic cum an' de Lawd tek yo' food..den laff. **1981** *Westindian World* 2 Oct. 4/1 One of London's better known Radio London presenters tek time off te go compere beauty show.

tek, tekat, obs. forms of TICK *sb.*, TICKET.

tekbir: see TECBIR.

†**teke, teken,** *adv.* and *prep. Obs.* Forms: 1 to éacan, 1-4 to eke(n, 3 teken (tekenn), teke. [OE. *tó éacan*, f. *tó* to, for + *éaca* addition, EKE.]

a. *adv.* In addition, besides, moreover, eke. **b.** *prep.* In addition to, besides.

c **888-1200** [see EKE *sb.*[1] 4]. *c* **975** *Rushw. Gosp.* Matt. xxv. 20 Oþre fife ic to-eke gestrionde. *c* **1200** ORMIN 2886, & tekenn þatt he wass rihhtwis He was ædmod & milde. *a* **1225** *Ancr. R.* 78 Teke þet, he seið,..þet ine silence & ine hope schal beon vre strencðe. *Ibid.* 170 Let ter teken þet ȝe beon swifte ase þe sunne gleam. *c* **1230** *Hali Meid.* 25 Teke þe murhðe & te menske in heuene. 13.. *Guy Warw.* (A.) 1855 To eken þat þou art mi lordes nevou.

teke, obs. form of TEAK, TICK.

†'**tekelite.** *Obs. slang.* [? f. '*Tekel*: weighed in the balances, and found wanting' (Dan. v. 27) + -ITE[1].] (In the cant of the Debtors' Prison, Whitecross Street, London) A defaulter, a defaulting debtor.

1834 *New Monthly Mag.* XL. 328 This, though expressly denominated 'the defaulter's table', the only one to which the poor 'tekelite' has right of access, is invariably appropriated by the free and unexcepted knights to the washing of cups and platters.

teket, obs. Sc. f. TICKET.

tekhnikum, var. TECHNICUM.

tekke[1] ('tɛkeɪ). Also 7 teke; 9 takia, takiya(h; 9- tek(k)i(y)eh (tɛ'kiːjeɪ). [a. Turk. *tekke*, Ottoman *tekye* (whence Arab. *tak(k)īya*), ad. Pers. *takya* pillow, place of repose, abode of a fakir.] A monastery of dervishes, esp. in Ottoman Turkey.

1668 P. RYCAUT *Pres. State Ottoman Empire* II. xx. 150 Their poverty..as I have seen in some of their *Tekes* where I have been. **1842** C. MASSON *Baluchistan* II. 278 Many takías are interspersed amongst all the burial-places. **1855** R. F. BURTON *Personal Narr. Pilgrimage to El-Medinah* I. 124 A Takiya is a place where Dervishes have rooms, and perform their devotions. *Ibid.* II. 29 It is flanked on the left ..by the domes and minarets of a pretty Turkish building, a 'takiyah', erected by the late Mohammed Ali for the reception of Dervish travellers. **1856** LADY EASTHOPE tr. *Ubicini's Lett. on Turkey* I. 109 He had finished and issued forth from the precincts of the tekieh. **1868** J. P. BROWN *Derwishes* 103, I may here add that of the two hundred, or more, *Tekkiehs* in Constantinople, some fifty only are possessed of sufficient wealth for their support. **1875** *Encycl. Brit.* III. 233/1 The Tekiyeh, or shrine of the Bektash dervishes, on the western bank of the [Tigris] river. **1900** 'ODYSSEUS' *Turkey in Europe* v. 194 Monograms of his name [Ali] are a conspicuous feature in most dervish Tekkes. **1932** G. KAMPFFMEYER in H. A. R. Gibb *Whither Islam?* 167 The *tekkes* or monasteries of the religious orders and the *turbes* or the tombs of the saints are closed. **1977** H. KAPLAN *Damascus Cover* (1978) x. 90 Damascus is overflowing with exotic sights: the tomb of Saladin,..the Tekkiyeh of Suleiman. **1980** A. ALPERS *Life K. Mansfield* xxi. 376 Gurdjieff['s]..'study-house'..resembled..a Dervish tekke.

Tekke[2] ('tɛkeɪ). [Turkic.] The name of a Turkic people inhabiting the Turkmen Soviet Socialist Republic, used to designate a short-piled basically red carpet or rug made by members of this people. Also *Tekke Bokhara*.

1900 J. K. MUMFORD *Oriental Rugs* iv. 40 From the rest of it [*sc.* angora fleece] Kashmir shawls are made, and carpet-weaving is illustrated in the finer Tartar fabrics—Tekkes, Yomuds, and Bokhara prayer rugs. *Ibid.* xii. 227 Tekke rugs ..will continue to be sold as Bokharas. **1911** G. GRIFFIN LEWIS *Practical Bk. Oriental Rugs* I. x. 135 *Tekke Field Design.*—A repetition of a..Y-shaped design. Found only in the Tekke rugs, especially those of the prayer variety. *Ibid.* II. xvi. 276 *Tekke Bokhara.* Why so named.—Because they are made by the Tekke Turko-man tribes of Nomads. **1931** A. U. DILLEY *Oriental Rugs & Carpets* Pl. 57 (*caption*) Bokhara garden rug. Compare garden designs in Tekke and Saryk prayer rugs. **1967** *Times* 21 Feb. 21/4 (Advt.), A number of fine Turkomans: *Tekke Bokhara.* **1974** *Encycl. Brit. Micropædia* IX. 867/1 *Tekke carpets*... Primarily the rugs that were commonly on the market as Royal Bokharas a generation or two ago... The standard field pattern for the large rugs is a repeat in rows of a particoloured, multifoiled lozenge, a basic motif that serves as the symbol, or gul, of this tribe.

tekno-: see TECNO-.

tekoretin (tiːkəʊ'riːtɪn). *Chem.* Also tec-. [Named 1839 by Forchhammer, app. 'f. Gr. τήκειν to melt, dissolve + ῥητίνη resin, because separated by solution in hot alcohol' (Chester).] A resin similar to or identical with Fichtelite.

1858 T. E. CLARK in *Amer. Jrnl. Sc.* Ser. II. XXV. 167 Tekoretin, being less soluble than phylloretin, crystallized first. **1868** DANA *Min.* 736 Tecoretin was obtained from pine trees [*Pinus sylvestris*] in marshes near Holtegard in Denmark. The resin from the wood..was found to contain two substances... The tecoretin was the least soluble.

tektite ('tɛktaɪt). [ad. G. *tektit* (F. E. Suess 1900, in *Jahrb. d. K.-K. Geol. Reichsanstalt* L. 194), f. Gr. τηκτ-ός molten (f. τήκειν to make molten): see -ITE[1].] One of the small, roundish, glassy bodies of unknown origin that occur scattered over various parts of the earth.

1909 [see BILLITONITE]. **1935** *Times* 28 Jan. 15/4 'Tektites' from Bohemia and Moravia have for more than 150 years been cut as gem stones under the names 'obsidian', 'water chrysolite' and 'moldavite'. **1936** [see AUSTRALITE]. **1956** *Antiquity* XXX. 70 These stone implements, together with the fossil remains of the stegodon (an extinct elephant), rhinoceros and other mammals, were often found in association with tektites, a form of glass meteorite. **1963** [see OBSIDIANITE]. **1969** *Times* 29 Aug. 10/3 Tektites, glassy, button-shaped objects which are probably of extraterrestrial origin, have been found in the Libyan desert and dated by radioactive methods to 35 million years ago. **1971** *Sci. Amer.* Oct. 55/2 Well-preserved Australian tektites show clear evidence of aerodynamic shaping.

b. *attrib.*, as **tektite field** = STREWN FIELD.

1960 *Listener* 22 Dec. 1141/2 Some of the tektite fields are well away from either active or extinct volcanoes. **1968** R. A. LYTTLETON *Mysteries Solar Syst.* vi. 183 There are eight main areas in the world generally accepted to be genuine tektite-fields.

†**tektosphere** ('tɛktəʊsfɪə(r)). *Geol. Obs.* Also (in dicts.) tecto-. [f. as prec. + -O + -SPHERE.] = ASTHENOSPHERE.

1900 J. MURRAY in *Rep. Brit. Assoc. Adv. Sci. 1899* 796 Within [the earth] is situated the vast nucleus or centrosphere; surrounding this is what may be called the tektosphere, a shell of materials in a state bordering on fusion. **1913** [see *geosphere* s.v. GEO-].

†**tel.** *Obs.* [Shortened from OE. *ȝetæl*, *ȝetel*, early ME. *itel*: cf. TALE *sb.*] Number.

c **1000** ÆLFRIC *Hom.* I. 536 Heora tel bið swa menigfeald, þæt [etc.]. *a* **1225** *Ancr. R.* 372 Hundred is ful tel, & noteð perfectiun.

tel: see TELE *sb.*[1], TELL, TILL.

telacoustic: see TELE-.

‖**telæsthesia** (tɛlɪs-, tɛlɪs'θiːsɪə). *Psychics.* [mod.L. (Myers, 1882), f. Gr. τῆλε far off (see TELE-) + αἴσθησις perception + -IA[1].] 'Perception at a distance; direct sensation or perception of objects or conditions independently of the recognized channels of sense' (Myers *Human Personality*, Gloss.).

1882 MYERS in *Proc. Soc. Psychical Research* I. II. 147 We venture to introduce the words *Telæsthesia* and *Telepathy* to cover all cases of impression received at a distance without the normal operation of the recognised sense organs. **1903** —— *Human Personality* I. 136. **1908** *Nation* 26 Sept. 907/1 Telepathy, telaesthesia and the subliminal part of man's mental being play a vast part in all these curious psychical phenomena.

telæsthetic (tɛlɪs'θɛtɪk, -ɪs'θɛtɪk), *a.* [f. as prec. + ÆSTHETIC.]

1. Having physical perception of things at a distance.

1890 C. LL. MORGAN *Anim. Life & Intell.* (1891) 249 This temperature-sense, unlike the sense of touch, may make us aware of distant bodies. It is what we may term a *telæsthetic* sense in contradistinction to a contact sense... Sight like hearing is a telæsthetic sense. Through it we become aware of certain vibratory states of more or less distant objects.

2. *Psychics.* Of or belonging to telæsthesia.

1903 MYERS *Human Personality* I. p. xlv, This may be done through..telæsthetic dreams or visions. **1903** *Athenæum* 28 Feb. 277/1 Examples of apparently clairvoyant, or telepathic, or telæsthetic cases.

‖**Telamon** ('tɛləmən). *Arch.* Pl. Telamones (tɛlə'məʊniːz). [In pl. a. L. *telamōnes*, = Gr. τελαμῶνες, pl. of Τελαμών name of a hero in mythology.] A figure of a man used as a column to support an entablature or other structure: = ATLAS *sb.*[1] 1 b.

1706 PHILLIPS (ed. Kersey), *Telamones*,..the Images of Men that seem'd to bear up the Out-jettings of Cornishes in the Roman Buildings, which among the Greeks were call'd Atlantes. **1797** HOLCROFT *Stolberg's Trav.* (ed. 2) III. lxiv. 12 Male statues of this kind were called..*Telamones*. **1882** FENNELL tr. *Michaelis' Anc. Marb. Gt. Brit.* 594 A kneeling youth..serves as a *Telamon* or *Atlas*, bearing on his head and his fore-arms a large, low cup, which forms the top of the whole candelabrum.

telanemograph: see TELE-.

‖**telangiectasis** (tɪlændʒɪˈɛktəsɪs). *Path.* Pl. **-ses** (-siːz). Also †**teleang-**, **-ectasia** (pl. **-iæ**). [mod.L., f. Gr. τέλος end + ἀγγεῖον vessel + ἔκτασις extension, dilatation.] Dilatation of the small blood-vessels, producing small red or purple tumours in the skin; one of such tumours. Also **telangiˈectasy** [ad. mod.L. *telangiectasia*]. Hence **telangiectatic** (-ˈtætɪk) *a.*, pertaining to or resulting from telangiectasis.

1831 J. F. South *Otto's Path. Anat.* II. 342 In telangiectasy, there is a peculiar degeneration of the blood-vessels connected also with widening of the smaller veins. **1868** T. G. Thomas *Dis. Women* (1872) 486 Tumors thus affected have been styled telangiectatic tumors. **1873** T. H. Green *Introd. Pathol.* (ed. 2) 178 The various forms of nævi, and telangiectasis. **1876** Van Duyn & Seguin tr. *Wagner's Man. Gen. Path.* III. 390 Cavernous, or venous tumor. It exists rarely at birth,..and proceeds probably in many cases from teleangiectasia. **1887** T. M'C. Anderson *Treat. Dis. Skin* 436 (*heading*) Capillary nævus; mother's mark; port wine or strawberry mark; teleangiectasis. **1899** *Allbutt's Syst. Med.* VIII. 833 Telangiectatic warts. *Ibid.*, The telangiectases range themselves in little groups. **1948** J. Minckler in W. A. D. Anderson *Pathology* xlv. 1390 Telangectasia of cerebral vessels is a fairly common occurrence..and represents a malformation rather than a neoplasm. **1974** Passmore & Robson *Compan. Med. Stud.* III. xxxiv. 77/1 The disease usually presents in infancy with cerebellar ataxia. Telangiectasiae appear some years later and are distributed over the ears, nose and cheeks.

Telanthropus (tɛˈlænθrəpəs). [mod.L., f. Gr. τέλ-ος end, consummation + ἄνθρωπος man.] A type of hominid, *Telanthropus capensis*, represented by the fragmentary fossil remains found at Swartkrans near Johannesburg, S. Africa, in 1949.

More recent investigation has led some scholars to believe that Telanthropus properly belongs to the species *Homo erectus*.

[**1949** Broom & Robinson in *Nature* 20 Aug. 323/2 In the cave at Swartkrans..there was found by Mr. J. T. Robinson, on April 29, 1949, the lower jaw of what is fairly manifestly a new type of man... The new type of man represented by this fossil jaw we propose to call *Telanthropus capensis*. We regard him as somewhat allied to Heidelberg man, and intermediate between one of the ape-men and true man.] **1955** *Ann. Reg. 1954* 466 The artefacts were probably made by *Telanthropus* who was either a very advanced Australopithecine or a very primitive true man. **1959** J. D. Clark *Prehist. S. Afr.* iii. 63 In addition some rather fragmentary remains, considered to be essentially more human-like though still preserving Australopithecine features, have been described by Robinson under the generic name of *Telanthropus*. **1960** W. Howells *Mankind in Making* xii. 178 *Telanthropus*' teeth are smaller. **1977** A. Hallam *Planet Earth* 286 In addition to these is a jaw which represents another line, closer to modern Man. It has been named Telanthropus.

telapoi, telapoon: see TALAPOIN.

telar (ˈtiːlə(r)), *a. rare*⁻⁰. [f. L. *tēla* web + -AR¹.] Pertaining to or of the nature of a web. Hence **ˈtelarly** *adv.*, in the manner of a web. So **telarian** (tiːˈlɛərɪən) *a.*, that spins a web, as a spider; *sb.* a spider that spins a web; †**ˈtelary** *a.* = *telar, telarian* adj.

1646 Sir T. Browne *Pseud. Ep.* v. xix. 262 We will not dispute the pictures of Telary Spiders, and their position in the web. **1658** —— *Gard. Cyrus* iii. 58 Conformable to the Spiders web, and the Radii in like manner telarely interwoven. **1853** G. Johnston *Nat. Hist. E. Bord.* I. 126 Slender spokes..'telarly interwoven' somewhat after the fashion of the spider's web. **1891** *Cent. Dict.*, Telarian.

telar, -are, obs. forms of TILLER.

teˈlautogram. [f. next: after *telegram*.] A record produced by a telautograph.

1895 in *Funk's Stand. Dict.*

telautograph (tɛˈlɔːtəgrɑːf, -æ-). Also (less correctly) **teleautograph.** [f. Gr. τῆλε far off (see TELE-) + AUTOGRAPH, after *telegraph*.] A telegraphic apparatus by which writing or drawing done with a pen or pencil at the transmitting end is reproduced in facsimile at the receiving end, by means of an electric current conveyed along a wire, and (in the usual forms of the instrument) communicating movements to the receiving pen corresponding to those made with the transmitting pen or pencil. Hence **telautoˈgraphic** *a.*, pertaining to the telautograph; **telauˈtography**, the use of the telautograph.

1884 Knight *Dict. Mech.* Supp., *Telautograph*, an electrical device for transmitting autographs, or copying designs... The possibility of deception and the impossibility of automatic unquestionable record..are removed, it is said, by the employment of telautography. **1887** *Tribune* (Chicago) 25 June, Prof. Elisha Gray..is perfecting an invention with wonderful possibilities... The 'Telautograph' is the name by which the instrument will be known. **1888** *Daily News* 9 Aug. 5/7 What is known as the telautographic system, invented by Professor Elisha Gray. **1894** *Westm. Gaz.* 20 Dec. 7/1 The electricians..were shown numerous slips of paper covered with autograph writing traced by the telautograph receiver in Paris, in obedience to a person writing in London with the telautograph transmitter. **1905** *Daily Chron.* 10 Jan. 5/6 Some very successful experiments in telautography were made yesterday between the Paris Central Telephone Office and the Rouen Bourse Exchange.

Tel Avivian (tɛl əˈviːvɪən), *sb.* and *a.* [f. *Tel Aviv* (see below) + -IAN.] **A.** *sb.* A native or inhabitant of Tel Aviv, the largest city in the state of Israel. **B.** *adj.* Of or pertaining to Tel Aviv.

1939 *Palestine Post* 14 Aug. 2/2 (*heading*) New park benches for tired Tel Avivians. **1941** G. G. Scholem *Major Trends in Jewish Mysticism* 384 A Tel-Avivian scholar, Reuben Margulies, has begun to publish an annotated edition of the Zohar. **1949** Koestler *Promise & Fulfilment* II. v. 263 Most Tel Avivians agree that the black-out is logically unwarranted. **1983** *Economist* 30 July 39/3 No fewer than 10 construction companies are vying to provide land- and air-hungry Tel Avivians with a variety of lodgings.

telbent, obs. form of TURBAN.

†**teld,** *sb. Obs.* Forms: 1–5 teld, 1, 4–5 telde, (3 tȝeld), 4 tield, teeld, 4–5 tilde, 5 tild, tyld, -e, telte. [OE. *teld*, *ȝeteld* = OLG. **teld* (MDu. *telde*, *telte*, Kilian), MLG. *telt*, *telde*, LG. *telt*; OHG. *zelt* (mostly *gizelt*), MHG. *zelt* (usually *gezelt*), Ger. *zelt*; ON. *tjald* (:—**teld*), pl. *tjǫld*, Norw. *tjeld*, Sw. *tält*, dial. *tjäll*, Da. *telt*, tent, pavilion, app. a deriv. of *teld-an* str. vb. to cover (cf. OE. *beteldan*, *oferteldan*). The late form *telte* may have been influenced by continental forms: see also TILT.] A tent, pavilion, covering; hence, a tabernacle, dwelling.

a **900** tr. *Bæda's Hist.* III. ix. [xi.] §2 (Camb. MS.) Mon teld [*v.r.* ȝ eteld] þærofer abrædde. *c* **1000** Ælfric *Gen.* xviii. 9 On þam telde heo ys. **1037** in Thorpe *Charters* (1865) 566/32 And Alfric biscop I biqueðe mine teld and min bedreaf. *c* **1205** Lay. 17491 Niȝe þusend teldes. *Ibid.* 24436 Þer weore on uelden moni þusend telden. *c* **1330** R. Brunne *Chron. Wace* (Rolls) 12598 Þey come to þe Emperours telde. When þey were at his pauyloun..þey lyghte alle doun. **13..** *Childh. Jesus* 44 in Herrig's *Archiv* LXXIV. 327 That owtelawe tuke hire to his tilde [*rimes* wilde, childe, mylde]. **1387** Trevisa *Higden* (Rolls) I. 127 Þese men..woneþ in tabernacles and in teeldis. *a* **1400–50** *Alexander* 4581 How suld ȝe telle withouten toles or any tild rere? *c* **1400** *Laud Troy Bk.* 4656 Thei reysed vp bothe halle and tylde. *c* **1440** *Promp. Parv.* 488/1 Telte, or tente, *tentorium.* ? *a* **1500** *Chester Pl.* vii. 6 From stif stormes my sheepe to sheild.. Under Tildes them to hyde.

b. The tilt or awning of a boat or vessel: cf. TILT.

1307–8 *Acc. Exch. K. R.* Bd. 14 No. 14 (P.R.O.), Tieldes emptis..pro dicta Bargia. **1495** *Wills Doctors' Commons* (Camden) 3 The barge with bailles, tilde, and ores belonging to the same.

c. A cage for carrying hawks.

1391 *Earl Derby's Exp.* (Camden) 88 Pro tieldes per ipsum emptis ibidem ad cariandum les haukes, xiiij scot.

d. *Comb.*, as **teld-stede**, dwelling-place, 'tabernacle'; **teldwyrhta** (OE.), tent-wright, tentmaker.

c **1000** Ælfric *Hom.* I. 392 Paulus..seðe wæs on woruld-cræfte teld-wyrhta. *a* **1300** *E.E. Psalter* cxix. [cxx.] 5 Wa to me, for mi telde-stede swa Forth-ferred es me fra [1388 Wyclif *ibid.*, My dwelling in an alien lond is maad long].

†**teld, tild,** *v. Obs.* Forms: *Inf.* 1 *teld-ian, 2–3 teld-en, tild-en, 3–5 teld(e, tild, 5 tield. *Pa. t.* α. 1 teldede, -ode, 4–5 tilded(e, teildid. β. (3 tȝelt), 4 tilde, teilde, 4–5 teld, telt, tilld (tillede), tulde, tilte, 4–6 telde, 5–6 tild. *Pa. pple.* α. 1 *(ȝe)telded, 3 i-tælded, 3–4 i-telded, 4 telded, 4–5 -id, -it, 5 i-teldyde, 6 *Sc.* tyldit, -et. β. 4 y-telde, y-tielde, 4–5 ytelt (i-tilled), teld, -e, 4 teeld, -e, 5 y-teld, y-tilde, tild. [OE. *teldian* wk. vb., f. TELD *sb.*; = ON. *tjalda*. In ME. the *d* of the stem was often merged in that of the pa. t. and pa. pple. This brought the vb. into contact with TILL *v.*, pa. t. *tilde*.]

1. *trans.* To 'spread', set up, pitch (a tent); hence, to erect (a building of any kind), to build, raise. Also *fig.*

c **725** *Corpus Gloss.* (O.E.T.) 591 *Con[n]ectit*, teldat. *c* **1205** Lay. 17489 Weoren a þan walde teldes itælded. **13..** *K. Alis.* 3434 (Bodl. MS.) Pauylouns were alle wiþinne Strongelich ytelt [*Linc. Inn MS.* y-tielde] by gynne. *Ibid.* 3464 Þe kyng þer telt [*v.r.* teildid] his pauylouns. *Ibid.* 5885 There biside his pauylouns, Weren y-telde by dales and dovnes. **13..** *Gaw. & Gr. Knt.* 795 Towre telded bytwene trochet ful þik. **1362** Langl. *P. Pl.* A. II. 44 Ten þousend of Tentes I-tilled [*v.rr.* I-teldyde, teldit, teled] be-sydes. **1388** Wyclif *2 Sam.* xvi. 22 Therfor thei tildeden Absolon a tabernacle in the soler. *c* **1400** *Destr. Troy* 11664 Here he tild vp a temple of a trew godde. *a* **1400–50** *Alexander* 1159 A hiȝe tilde as a toure teldid on schippis. *Ibid.* 2174 (Dubl. MS.) To tergarontes he tiȝt þar telde was a mynster. *c* **1460** *Launfal* 263 A pavyloun yteld he sygh. **1515** *Scot. Field* 38 in *Chetham Misc.* (1856) II, Beside the towne of Tirwin, our tentes downe we telden.

2. *intr.* To pitch one's tent; to encamp; to take one's station or residence; in *pa. pple.* encamped, lodged, stationed.

c **1250** *Gen. & Ex.* 1840 Iacob fro ðeðen wente, ic wot, tȝelt on a stede, and cald it sochot. *c* **1330** R. Brunne *Chron. Wace* (Rolls) 12588 [On] þat playne..were þe Romayns telded. *c* **1330** —— *Chron.* (1810) 242 Biside a more a mod quayntly was he teld. **1393** Langl. *P. Pl.* C. xv. 150 Ryȝt as traianus, þe trewe knyght, tulde [*v.rr.* tillede, telde; B. XII. 210 tilde, tilte, dwelte] nat deep in helle. *a* **1400** *Pistill of Susan* 56 Þeos perlous prestes..turned fro his teching, þat teeld [*v.rr.* teelde, told] is in trone. *c* **1440** *York Myst.* x. 14 Wher I was telde vnder a tree.

3. *trans. Sc.* To cover with an awning or curtain.

1501 Douglas *Pal. Hon.* I. 432 Reparrellit was that god-like plesand wone Tyldit abone, and to the eirth adoun. **1825** Jamieson s.v. *Tyld*, A window is said to be *tyldit*, when it is covered in the inside with a cloth or curtain.

4. To spread (a net), set (a trap or snare). (See also TILL *v.*)

c **1000** *Ags. Ps.* (Thorpe) xxxiv. 8 Hi teldedon gryne and ða ȝehyddon. *c* **1175** *Lamb. Hom.* 53 Þenne þe mon wule tilden his musestoch he bindeð uppon þa swike chese. *c* **1200** *Trin. Coll. Hom.* 211 At pleȝe [þe deuel] teldeð þe grune of idelnesse. *a* **1225** *Ancr. R.* (Corpus MS.: Camden 334), Triste is þer me sit mid te greahunz forte kepe þe heare, oðer tildeð [so *Cleop.*, *Caius*; *Titus* tildes; *Nero* tillen; *Vern.* tilleþ] þe nettes aȝein him. **1413** *Pilgr. Sowle* (Caxton 1483) I. xviii. 14 Teldyng nettes, arrayng trappys and other engynes. *c* **1440** *Pallad. on Husb.* IV. 164 A green another hath for hem ytilde.

Hence †**telding** (**tildunge**) *vbl. sb.*, laying of snares.

a **1225** *Ancr. R.* 278 Seint Antonie þet iseih al þene world ful of þes deofles tildunge.

teld, -e, -en, obs. inflexions of TELL *v.*

†**tele, tel,** *sb.*¹ *Obs.* Forms: 1 tǽl, 4 tél, teyl, 5 tele. [OE. *tǽl* fem. (also *tál*: see TOLE *sb.*¹) = OHG. *zâla* danger, snare, trap, ON. *tál* bait, allurement. OTeut. **tǣlâ* str. fem., had app. some such general sense as 'hostile or malevolent attack, persecution', whence the specialized senses in the various langs. See also TELE *v.*]

1. Evil speaking, detraction, calumny, blame.

c **897** K. Ælfred *Gregory's Past. C.* xxxiii. 222 Ælc ðweora, & ælc ierre..& tæl sie anumen fram eow. *a* **1000** *Gloss.* in Wr.-Wülcker 196/16 *Blasphemia, uituperatio*, tæl. *Ibid.* 220/23. **1303** R. Brunne *Handl. Synne* 2042 But þogh a man sey neuer so weyl Vnto hys sawys men fynden teyl.

2. Deceit; enticement, allurement.

c **1300** *Havelok* 191 Þat he sholde yemen hire wel With-uten lac, with-uten tel Til þat she were tuelf winter hold. *a* **1450** Myrc *Par. Pr.* 368 So with cha[r]mes & wyth tele, He ys I-broȝte aȝeyn to hele.

tele (ˈtɛliː), *sb.*² Colloq. abbrev. of TELEVISION. Cf. TELLY. Also *attrib.* and *Comb.* (not sharply distinguishable from TELE- 2).

1936 *Billboard* 14 Nov. 3 (*heading*) RCA-NBC tele progress. **1944** R. E. Lee *Television* vi. 88 The motion picture is a novel; tele is a short-story, or a newspaper article. **1946** [see *lip-read* vb. s.v. LIP *sb.* 7]. **1956** A. Wilson *Anglo-Saxon Att.* I. iii. 47, I see him on the Tele. **1960** A. Kimmins *Lugs O'Leary* iii. 33 'Where were you?' 'In my room watching the tele.' **1961** A. Wilson *Old Men at Zoo* iii. 128 Oh, it was on the tele news in the pub I was in. **1964** *Punch* 3 June 833/1 Large sections of the tele-watching population. **1973** J. Wainwright *Devil you Don't* 5 Sprawling in front of a tele, watching one-day cricket. **1977** *Gay News* 7–20 Apr. 37/2 Hardly home-loving types, likely to be content with baked beans on toast and the tele.

tele (ˈtɛliː), *sb.*³ *Psychics.* [a. Gr. τῆλε afar, far off.] Psychic affinity between two (or more) people separated by time or space. Cf. *telepsychic* sb. s.v. TELE- 1.

1937 J. L. Moreno in *Sociometry* I. 16 Tele is defined as a feeling process projected into space and time in which one, two, or more persons may participate. It is an experience of some real factor in the other person and not a subjective fiction... The tele process is..the chief factor in determining the position of an individual in the group. **1952** W. Sprott *Social Psychol.* ii. 34 A 'monistic origin of life from a common unit' out of which existing networks of 'tele' have been differentiated. *Ibid.* 35 In Moreno's own convention a red line from A towards B represents 'positive tele'.

†**tele,** *v. Obs.* Forms: 1 tǽlan (télan), 2–3 tælen (3 (*Orm.*) tælenn, 3–5 tellen), 2–4 telen, 3–4 tele. [OE. (WSax.) *tǽlan* (Angl. *télan*) = ON. *tæla* to deceive, betray, entice:—OTeut. **tǣljan*, f. *tǣlâ*: see TELE *sb.*¹ Cf. OHG. *zâlôn* (:—*tǣlôjan*) to rob, pillage.]

1. *trans.* To speak evil of, or to; to revile, calumniate; to mock, scorn, deride.

c **888** K. Ælfred *Boeth.* xxxviii. §3 Ic wolde unðeawas tælan & goode herian. *c* **890** *Laws K. Ælfred* c. 37 Ne tæl ðu ðinne Dryhten. *a* **900** *Kentish Gloss.* in Wr.-Wülcker 55/19 *Et detraxerunt*, and his teldan. *Ibid.* 75/13 *Deridet*, teld. *Ibid.* 76/31 *Detrahent*, telað. *c* **950** *Lindisf. Gosp.* John xii. 48 Seðe mec teles [*c* **975** *Rushw.* teleð]. **10..** *Glosses* (Cott. Cleop.) in Wr.-Wülcker 373/26 *Carpere*, telan. *c* **1160** *Hatton Gosp.* Luke xiv. 29 Ealle þe hit ȝe-seoð aginned hine tælen [*Ags. Gosp.* tælan]. *c* **1200** Ormin 2039–40 3iff þatt tu willt tælenn me þe birrþ ec hire tælenn. *a* **1250** *Prov. Ælfred* 237 in *O.E. Misc.* 116 Byfore he þe meneþ, by-hynde he þe teleþ. *c* **1490** *Promp. Parv.* 488/1 (MS.K.) Tellynge, or grochynge, *murmuracio*.

2. To deceive, entrap [cf. ON. *tæla* to betray].

c **1325** *Metr. Hom.* (1862) 12 His [Christ's] godhed in fleis was felid Als hok in bait, quare thoru he telid The fend, that telid our fadir Adam. *Ibid.* 152 That he no haf miht us to tele With gastly dranc and wit darnele. **13..** *Metr. Hom.* (Vernon MS.) in Herrig's *Archiv* LVII. 276 But faste he fondeþ mon to tele. Vre lord vs schilde from his teolyng.

Hence †**teling** *vbl. sb.* (also 3 **teolunge**, 4 **-yng**, **teliinge**, 4–5 **telyng**, **teeling**), deception, sorcery, witchcraft.

a **1225** *Ancr. R.* 208 Sigaldren, & false teolunges, leuunge on ore & of swefnes & alle wichchecreftes. *c* **1315** SHOREHAM III. 178 By-lef þou in no wychecraft, Ne ine none teliinge. **13..** [see TELE *v.* 2]. **1387** TREVISA *Higden* (Rolls) III. 343 He triste on his endynge [*v.r.* enditynge] and tellynges [*v.rr.* teelingis, telyngs, tellyngys] as olde wifes useþ. *a* **1450** MYRC *Par. Pr.* 360 Wychecrafte and telynge. *c* **1490** [see TELE *v.* 1].

tele (ˈtɛliː), *a.* Abbrev. of TELEPHOTOGRAPHIC *a.*[2] Cf. TELEPHOTO *a.* and *tele-lens* s.v. TELE- 1.

1979 *SLR Camera* Jan. 42/3 We chose the FD 135 mm f2.5 SC and the FD 200 mm f2.8 SC as being representative of the popular tele range. **1981** *What Camera Weekly* 5 Dec. 3/2 (*heading*) Tele tactics: long lenses with focal lengths of 400 and 500 mm need careful handling.

tele, obs. f. TEAL, TELL *v.*, TILE *sb.*, TILL *v.*

tele- (ˈtɛlɪ). **1.** (Before a vowel properly **tel-**, but more often in the full form), repr. Gr. τηλε-, combining form of τῆλε afar, far off; used in numerous (chiefly recent) scientific and technical terms, mostly denoting or connected with special appliances or methods for operating over long distances; also in several terms connected with psychical research, denoting actions or impressions produced at a distance from the exciting cause, independently of the normal means of communication. (The second element is properly and usually from Greek, exceptionally from Latin or English.) The earlier and more important of these words will be found in their alphabetical places; others follow here.

telaˈcoustic *a.*, *Psychics* [ACOUSTIC], pertaining to or involving the perception of a sound beyond or apart from the possibility of ordinary hearing (cf. *teloptic* below). **ˌteleaˈnemograph**, 'an anemograph that records at a distance by means of electricity' (*Cent. Dict.* 1891). **ˈteleˌbanking**, a method of effecting banking transactions at a distance by electronic means. **teleˈbarograph**, 'a barograph that records at a distance by means of electricity' (*Cent. Dict.* 1891). **ˌtelebaˈrometer**, 'a barometer that registers its indications at a distance by means of electric apparatus' (*ibid.*). **ˈteleˌcamera**, (*a*) a telephotographic camera; (*b*) a television camera. **teleˈcentric** *a.*, *Optics*, applied to a lens system of which the aperture or stop is at the principal focus; also *absol.* as *sb.*, a telecentric lens. **teleˈchirograph** [Gr. χείρ hand], a form of TELAUTOGRAPH [cf. definition of TELAUTOGRAPH]. **teleˈcobalt**, radioactive cobalt used as a radiation source in teletherapy; usu. *attrib.* **ˌtelecoˈmmand**, the remote control of machines or the like by electronic means; freq. *attrib.* **telecoˈmmute** *v. intr.*, to work from home (esp. at a traditionally office job), communicating with one's place of employment, colleagues, etc., by telephone line or data link; hence **telecoˈmmuter**; **telecoˈmmuting** *vbl. sb.* and *ppl. a.* **ˈtele-coˈnnection** *Geol.* [tr. Sw. *fjärrkonnektion* (G. De Geer 1916, in *Geol. Fören. Förhandl.* XXXVIII. 18)], the correlation over long distances of varves or other deposits that can be used for dating purposes; also *transf.* **ˌteleconˈtrol** = *telecommand* above; freq. *attrib.* **teleconˈverter** *Photogr.*, a camera lens designed to be fitted in front of a standard lens to increase its effective focal length. **teleˈcryptograph**, a form of printing telegraph adopted for secret or private communication. **teˈlectrograph**, **teˈlectroscope**: see *telelectro-*. **ˌtelecurieˈtherapy** *Med.* [CURIE] = *teletherapy* below. **teˈlediphone** [*Ediphone*, name of a recording machine], a machine for recording speech from a telephone line or radio for subsequent transcription or broadcasting; hence **teˈlediphoned** *a.* **ˈteleflash** *U.S.*, (equipment for transmitting) telegraphic news of racing results, odds, etc. **ˌteleˈgenesis**, the technique of artificial insemination. **teˈlegnomy**, **teleˈgnosis** *Psychics*, psychic perception of events happening at a distant place; clairvoyance; hence **teleˈgnostic** *a.* **telehydrobaˈrometer** [Gr. ὕδωρ water: see BAROMETER], an instrument for recording electrically at a distance the pressure of a head of water or other liquid. **ˌteleiˈconograph** [Gr. εἰκών image: see -GRAPH], an apparatus consisting of a telescope combined with a camera lucida, by which images of distant objects may be cast upon paper and traced. **ˈtelekin** [mod., f. Gr. κιν-εῖν to move], a device for the electric control of machinery from a distance. **telekiˈnesis**, *Psychics* [mod.L., f. Gr. κίνησις motion], movement of or in a body alleged to occur at a distance from, and without material connexion with, the motive cause or agent; hence **telekiˈnetic** *a.*, belonging to telekinesis.: also *transf.* and *fig.*; **ˌtelekiˈneticist**, one who practises or has the power of telekinesis. **teleˈlectric** *a.*, producing mechanical motions or effects at a distance by electrical means. **teleˈlectrograph**, shortened **teˈlectrograph**: cf. ELECTROGRAPH, an apparatus for producing at the receiving end a copy of a photograph or print at the transmitting end, by means of electric telegraphy. **teleˈlectroscope**, shortened **teˈlectroscope** [cf. prec. and -SCOPE], an apparatus for reproducing at a distance a visual image, as that in a camera obscura, by means of electric telegraphy. **ˈtele-lens** *Photogr.*, a telephoto lens. **ˌtelemaˈnometer**, a manometer which registers at a distance by means of electricity. **telemeˈchanics**, the art of transmitting power to a distance, esp. by electromagnetic waves as in wireless telegraphy; so **teleˈmechanism**. **ˈteleˌmessage**, a form of telegram introduced in October 1981 to replace the inland telegram, and abolished one year later. **ˌtelemetaˈcarpal** *a.*, *Comp. Anat.*, having vestiges only of the distal portion of the first and fifth metacarpals, as in one group of the *Cervidæ*. **teleˈmeteorograph**, a meteorograph which records electrically at a distance; a combination of telethermograph, telebarograph, and teleanemograph; hence **teleˌmeteoroˈgraphic** *a.*, **teleˌmeteoˈrography**. **teleˈmicroscope**, an optical instrument combining the functions of a telescope and a microscope; e.g. in enlarging a telescopic image or in projecting a microscopic image to a distance (e.g. upon a screen). **ˈteleˌmotor**, an apparatus for transmitting motive power to a distance; *esp.* a device for steering a ship from some part distant from the tiller, by means of hydraulic or pneumatic pressure, etc. **tele-ˈnegative** *a.* in ***telenegative lens***, the negative element in a telephotographic lens: cf. TELEPHOTOGRAPHIC *a.*[2], quot. 1892[3]. **telengyscope** (-ˈɛndʒɪskəʊp), incorrectly **-engi-** [see ENGYSCOPE], an optical instrument combining the powers of a telescope and microscope (*Cent. Dict.* 1891). **ˌtele-obˈjective** *a.*, having an object-glass adapted to photographing distant objects; as a ***tele-objective camera***; *sb.* (see quot.). **ˈteleordering** *vbl. sb.*, the computerized ordering of books by book sellers from publishers. **teleˈphotogram**, a message in the form of a picture transmitted by radio or television. **ˌtelephoˈtometer**, an instrument for measuring the brightness of a distant light source. **teleplasm** *Psychics*, a hypothetical substance psychically materialized; ectoplasm; hence **teleˈplasmic** *a.* **teleˈplastic** *a.*, *Psychics* [PLASTIC; after *telepathy*, etc.]: see quot. 1890. **ˈTele-player** [PLAYER[1]], the proprietary name in the U.S. of a device for recording and playing back videotape. **ˌtelepoˈlariscope**, an optical instrument consisting of a telescope combined with a polariscope. **tele-ˈpositive** *a.*, *Optics*: see quot. **teleˈprocessing** *vbl. sb.*, data processing that involves terminals located at a distance from the processor. **teleˈpsychic** *sb.*, a medium whose psychical powers are exerted at a distance; *adj.*, pertaining to or involving the exertion of psychic powers at a distance. **ˈtelepuppet** *colloq.*, a telechiric device, esp. one used in space. **ˌteleradiˈography** *Med.*, radiography in which the X-ray tube is placed some distance from the plate in order to minimize distortion. **teleˈradiophone**, a radiophone producing sounds at a distance by means of an electric current as in telegraphy. **teleˈradium**, radium used as a radiation source in teletherapy. **teˈlergic** *a.*, pertaining to or involving telergy. **ˈtelergy**, *Psychics* [after *energy*], the supposed force operating in telepathy, regarded as correlated with the various forms of physical energy, or as directly affecting the brain or organism of the percipient; so **teˈlergically** *adv.*, by means of telergy. **ˌteleˌroentgeˈnography** (also **-röntgen-**) *Med.* (chiefly *U.S.*) = *teleradiography* above **teleseism** (ˈtɛlɪsaɪz(ə)m) [SEISM], a distant or remote earth-tremor as recorded on a seismograph; hence **teleˈseismic** *a.*; **teleˈseismically** *adv.* **ˈteleseme** (-siːm) [Gr. σῆμα sign], an electric signalling apparatus used in hotels, etc., fitted with an indicator which shows the article or service required. **ˈteleˌshopping**, a method of ordering goods from shops by electronic means. **teleˈsoftware** *Computers*, software transmitted by wire or broadcast for use by any number of independent receiving terminals. **ˌtelesoˈmatic** *a.*, *Psychics* [Gr. σῶμα body]: see ***teleplastic***, quot. 1890. **teleˈspectroscope**, a combination of a telescope and a spectroscope, for spectroscopic observations of the heavenly bodies. **teleˈstereoscope**, an instrument with two pairs of mirrors so arranged that distant objects viewed by means of it appear to stand out in relief, as in a stereoscope. **ˈtele-talkies**, cinematographic films broadcast by television (*disused*). **teleˈtherapy** *Med.*, radiotherapy using a source of radiation at a distance from the patient. **teleˈthermograph**, a thermograph which records electrically at a distance; a self-registering telethermometer; hence **teleˈthermogram**. **ˌtelethérˈmometer**, a thermometer which indicates the temperature measured elsewhere; hence **telethérˈmometry**, the use of a telethermometer. **ˌteletoˈpometer** [Gr. τόπος place: see -METER], name for a special form of telemeter (TELEMETER *sb.* 1). **ˌteletransporˈtation** = TELEPORTATION (*rare*); hence (as a back-formation) **teletransˈport** *v. trans.* **ˈteletype**, a type-printing telegraph; hence **teleˈtypic** *a.*; **teleˈtypograph**, a form of machine telegraph which records its message by perforating a tape that sets in motion a typesetting machine. **telewriter** (tɛlɪˈraɪtə(r)), an instrument which electrically reproduces in facsimile a written message; a form of TELAUTOGRAPH; hence **ˈtelewrite** *v.* (*nonce-wd.*), to send a message by a telewriter. **teˈloptic** *a.*, *Psychics* [OPTIC], pertaining to or involving the perception as if by sight of an object beyond or apart from the possibility of ordinary vision (cf. *telacoustic* above); so **teˈlosmic** *a.* [Gr. ὀσμή smell], involving the perception of a smell in a similar way.

1893 *Telacoustic [see *teleplastic*]. **1981** *Amer. Banker* 18 Feb. 12/3 Consider the things you will be able to do—telereservations, telegames, *telebanking, teleshopping. **1910** O. WHEELER *Mod. Telephotography* 68 Messrs. Zeiss also make a special *tele-camera. **1951** I. ASIMOV *Stars like Dust* xvii. 162 The movement of the tele-camera can be so adjusted as to counteract the motion of the ship in its orbit. **1960** *Harper's Bazaar* Oct. 82/2 It is not too late even now to bring in the tele-cameras. **1980** T. HOLME *Neapolitan Streak* 42 There were tele-camera teams from the RAI. **1902** MANN & MILLIKAN tr. *Drude's Theory of Optics* I. iv. 75 Certain positions of the iris can be chosen for which the entrance- or exit-pupils lie at infinity... To attain this it is necessary to place the iris behind S_1 at its principal focus... The system is then called *telecentric. **1921** *Glasgow Herald* 15 June 7 It was fitted with..a 12 in. Telecentric, and a variant of my 'Dodo' tele-lens. **1973** D. A. SPENCER *Focal Dict. Photogr. Technol.* 619 (*caption*) Telecentric optical system. **1903** *Electr. Wld. & Engineer* 20 June 1055 *Telechirograph. **1956** C. W. WILSON *Radium Therapy* (ed. 2) 286/1 (Index), *telecobalt therapy. **1959** [see *teleradium* below]. **1980** *Jrnl. R. Soc. Arts* Jan. 95/1 These telecobalt.. machines are now part of the routine equipment of most radiotherapy departments. **1972** *Sunday Tel.* 30 Apr. 34/4 He sees on a television screen the view he would have from the driver's seat of the car he is controlling remotely. These '*telecommand' cars are about to be used for complex.. handling tests. **1978** *Times* 3 Nov. 27/4 The Post Office itself has listed the main telecommunications services.. envisaged for the years 1985 and 2000... By 1985 there will be..view-data,..telemetry (the radio transmission of measurements), telecommand (remote control of machines). **1980** *Times* 15 Jan. 16 A low-power microcomputer system has been built..and a telecommand receiver has been completed. **1974** *Economist* 5 Jan. 14/1 As there is no logical reason why the cost of telecommunication should vary with distance, quite a lot of people by the late 1980s will *telecommute daily to their London offices while living on a Pacific island if they want to. **1975** *Ibid.* 25 Oct. 39/3 *telecommuting is coming. When production is properly automated even in service industries, probably 60% of American breadwinners will be brainworkers. *Ibid.* 43/3 *telecommuter terminals will stop social interaction at the workplace. **1976** *Ibid.* 25 Dec. 56/1 Small ones, employing various piecework-earning *telecommuting housewives in their own homes. **1981** *Ibid.* 5 Sept. 20/1 telecommuters are workers who do not have to travel to their office... They need only their terminal links of today, enhanced by new gadgetry, to make sure they never have to leave their villages. **1982** *N.Y. Times Mag.* 14 Nov. 133 A situation known as 'telecommuting' or, more cozily, the 'electronic cottage'. **1934** G. DE GEER in *Geografiska Annaler* XVI. 3 The general law that the annual amount of meltwater deposits along the ice-border varied congruently is.. definitely fixed. *teleconnections were thus, by a great number of close connections,..acting every year for..the whole of Fennoscandia. **1939** G. CLARK *Archæol. & Society* v. 141 Attempts to extend the sequence across the Baltic have not met with general acceptance any more than have the still more ambitious 'teleconnexions' between the Swedish varve-sequence and those in North and South America. **1970** S. THORARINSSON in R. Berger *Sci. Methods Medieval Archaeol.* 325 A young Swedish scientist..has realized my old dream of establishing tephrochronological teleconnection between Iceland and Scandinavia. **1979** *Harvard Mag.* May–June 14 Meterologists have coined the phrase 'teleconnections' to describe the apparent correlation between El Niño [*sc.* an erratically recurring ocean current in the Pacific] and disruptive weather patterns all around the earth. **1983** *Nature* 18 Aug. 583/3 Teleconnection with the

Bristlecone pine absolute scale..has already been achieved for Bronze Age varves in south Russia and for tree-rings in Turkey. **1933** *Sci. Abstr.* B. XXXVI. 225 A general survey of the subject of telemeasuring with a brief account of *telecontrol systems. **1959** *Times* 30 July 2/3 The installation and commissioning of telecontrol and telemetering systems [for an oil company]. **1974** *Sci. Amer.* Nov. 41/1 The control tasks described so far, including the gathering and presentation of information about the system .., can be realized in principle by analogue control circuits, ..telecontrol devices and the like. **1966** 'A. HALL' *9th Directive* ix. 83 A Pentax X-15 35 mm single reflex with a 135 mm lens that took a ×2 Auto *teleconverter. **1979** *SLR Camera* Mar. 36/3 A short cut to getting involved in tele photography, where your budget is tight, is to use a teleconverter. **1904** *Athenæum* 5 Nov. 628/3 The device for secret telegraphy or *telecryptograph of Messrs. Siemens and Halske also deserves notice. **1909** *Daily Mirror* 13 Aug. 14/2 The pictures were wired from Manchester to London last night in six minutes by the Thorne-Baker *telectrograph. **1884** KNIGHT *Dict. Mech.* Supp., **Telectroscope*, an apparatus for reproducing by telegraph the images obtained in the camera obscura..based on the property possessed by selenium of offering a variable and very sensitive electrical resistance according to the different gradations of light. **1939** E. LILJENKRANTZ *Cancer Handbk.* ii. 23 *telecurietherapy with 10 gm of radium (a quarter of a million dollars' worth) means usually treatment distance of 15 cm. **1954** *Arch. Otolaryngol.* LIX. 345 Advanced inoperable carcinoma is best treated by telecurietherapy. **1953** *Brit. Jrnl. Psychol.* XLIV. 117 The *telediphone records of the [television] programmes were broken up into what appeared to be the principal points contained in the programme. **1973** *Listener* 7 June 757/1 The BBC started making telediphone transcripts of what people actually did say, unscripted, on the air. **1957** *Oxford Mag.* 31 Oct. 70/2, I have before me the B.B.C.'s *telediphoned transcript of the discussion. **1937** *Sun* (Baltimore) 16 June 4/5 A '*teleflash' and racing slips taken by police in the tavern were not sufficient for a conviction. **1951** *Ibid.* 23 Mar. 28/1 Equipment of the 'teleflash' type which..was used for announcements of racing results and odds. **1935** *telegenesis [see EUTELEGENESIS]. **1958** *News Chron.* 4 Feb. 4/8 (*heading*) Telegenesis. **1911** W. F. BARRETT *Psychical Research* xi. 161 Dr. Heysinger..suggests the term *telegnosis, or knowing at a distance, instead of clairvoyance. **1932** J. BUCHAN *Gap in Curtain* i. 44 The instinct which had its seat in this cell specialised in time-perception... I had been reading lately about telegnosis. **1962** C. D. BROAD *Lect. on Psychical Res.* viii. 222 The distinction between explicitly referential and merely unwilling telegnosis. *Ibid.* 223 Experiences which are only unwittingly *telegnostic. **1906** *Pall Mall Gaz.* 24 Mar. 4 Mr. Grier possesses the faculty of '*telegnomy', which enables him..to perceive..events which are taking place on the other side of the Atlantic. **1891** *Cent. Dict.*, *Telehydrobarometer. **1877** KNIGHT *Dict. Mech.*, *Teleiconograph. **1905** *Sci. Amer., Suppl.* 6 May 24539 The inventor distinguishes between a simple *telekin, wherein only a single motion is considered, and a multiple telekin, which permits of a complexity of motions. **1890** MYERS in *Proc. Soc. Psych. Research* Dec. 668 *Extramediumistic* operations, as thought-transference, telepathy, *telekinesis (*Fernwirkung*), or movements of objects without contact. **1905** *Sat. Rev.* 19 Aug. 250 Of the other phenomena..that of telekinesis, or movement of objects without material contact. **1962** *Punch* 5 Dec. 805/3 Dusailly..has made a first step towards telekinesis by using the electrical cavity of the brain to operate a switch. **1983** J. MELVILLE *Hand of Glass* vi. 146, I *had* seen it move... If you didn't believe in telekinesis..then Merry must have practised some form of hypnotism on me. **1890** MYERS in *Proc. Soc. Psych. Research* Dec. 669 For the alleged movements without contact..M. Aksakof's new word '*telekinetic' seems to me the best attainable. *a* **1966** 'M. NA GOPALEEN' *Best of Myles* (1968) 94 An œuvre which would show his telekinetic treatment of over-tonality. **1972** *Countryman* Winter 83 Almost all contemporary investment in the countryside is a telekinetic expression of the distracted town. **1977** A. WILSON *Strange Ride R. Kipling* vi. 291 Trix accumulated clairvoyant, time-travelling, telekinetic and exorcistic powers. **1949** *Startling Stories* May 22/1 'Just what are his potentialities?' queried Shey. 'Is he a hypnotist? A *telekineticist?' **1965** J. KINGSTON in J. Carnell *New Writings in S-F* III. 68 Telekineticists..are people who can move things without touching them, change physical states at a distance. **1909** *Cent. Dict., Suppl.* s.v., An organ with a *telelectric attachment. **1898** *Daily News* 10 Mar. 6/3 It is called the '*Telelectroscope', because it renders objects visible in their natural colours at a distant place by means of electricity. *Ibid.*, If we had had the 'Telelectroscope' in operation some time ago, we might have gone into a theatre in London and witnessed the eclipse of the sun in India for ourselves. **1921** *Tele-lens [see *telecentric* adj. above]. **1979** *Amat. Photographer* Feb. 74/2 The modern telelens (and a tele can be as short as 100 mm) ..is the biggest boon since sliced bread. **1891** *Cent. Dict.*, *Telemanometer. **1909** *Athenæum* 6 Mar. 293/1 The researches now being made..into what is called *telemechanics, or the art of transmitting power to a distance by waves in the ether and without wires. **1907** *Ibid.* 29 June 798/3 The phenomena..of *tele-mechanism, or the operation of machines at a distance. **1981** *Times* 20 Oct. 28/4 A new, cheaper form of telegram called the *telemessage is to be introduced by British Telecom as an inland service next Monday. **1878** *Proc. Zool. Soc. Lond.* 887 Plesiometacarpal and *telemetacarpal limb—characters.. closely corresponding with the distribution of the Cervidæ. **1881** *Nature* 14 Apr. 564/2 On March 26.. There were repeated at the Brussels Observatory experiments with Van Rysselberghes' *telemeteorograph, which prove that the registration of the meteorological elements..may be made automatically at very great distances. *Ibid.*, The author explained to the Minister a plan of International *Telemeteorography. **1883** *Science* I. 88 The establishment of an international *telemeteorographic system. **1860** MAYNE *Expos. Lex.*, *Teleomicroscopium*,..an instrument for enlarging or increasing the forms of more remote or indistinct objects: a *teleomicroscope [*sic*]. **1895** *Arena* (Boston) App. 13 Prof. D. S. Holman, the celebrated microscopist... His lectures..are illustrated by the telemicroscope, which projects upon a screen nearly all conceivable experiments. **1897** *Tit-Bits* 11 Dec. 207/3 A 10 in. telescope can, by means of the new telemicroscope be made to magnify 25000 diameters. **1890** *Nature* 3 Apr. 516/2 The steering motor is placed directly on the quadrant of the tiller, and is actuated from the bridge by means of what the author describes as a *telemotor. **1897** *Daily News* 20 Sept. 3/1 A new steam steering engine has been added, having a telemotor on Messrs. Brown Bros.' system. **1905** *Tele-negative [see *tele-positive*]. **1902** MANN, etc. tr. *P. Drude's The. Optics* I. v. 94 A..*teleobjective, which consists of a combination of a convergent and a divergent system placed at a distance apart. **1977** *Bookseller* 14 May 2432/2 A *teleordering terminal for bookshops... The value of teleordering from the bookseller's point of view is partly to receive books a few days sooner from publishers. **1929** *Telegr. & Telephone Jrnl.* XVI. 49/1 The transmission of pictures by telegraphic means is coming to the front in the U.S.A... An enterprising firm in New York recently sent out 300 *telephotograms of the latest feminine fashions to all parts of the States. **1937** *Times* 30 Oct. 14/2 The London television station transmitted last night the first 'telephotogram' to a ship at sea—a visual message of greeting to the master of the Britannic. **1930** *Monthly Weather Rev.* Nov. 440/2 In the measurements over the sea..the *telephotometer..and the theodolite were set up on the point of the mole. **1949** *Proc. Inst. Electr. Engineers* XCVI. II. 456/2 It was possible to calibrate the telephotometer in daylight by reference to tungsten-filament standard lamps of 1-, 2- and 5-kW sizes over ranges varying from 1 500 to 5 000 ft. **1927** *Daily Express* 28 Sept. 9 *Teleplasm..was shown issuing from the face of the tranced woman. **1978** SMYTH & STEMMAN *Mysteries of Afterlife* 225 (*caption*) The teleplasm..is compared with a control sample of ordinary paper. **1930** *Times Lit. Suppl.* 28 Aug. 683/1 *Teleplasmic masses resembling arms and hands were seen. **1890** MYERS in *Proc. Soc. Psych. Research* Dec. 669 M. Aksakof uses the term 'telesomatic' for the phenomena of so-called 'materialisation'... It would be better, I think, to give the name **teleplastic* to all this class of alleged phenomena. **1893** *Chicago Advance* 31 Aug., Certain teleplastic, telacoustic, teloptic, and telosmic occurrences. **1968** *Daily Tel.* 12 Dec. 25/3 The *tele-player will cost about £200 and each tele-cartridge..£20. **1971** *Official Gaz.* (U.S. Patent Office) 23 Nov. TM206/1 *Teleplayer.* For television apparatus... First use Mar. 24 1970. **1878** LOCKYER *Stargazing* 441 The *Telepolariscope. **1905** *Sci. Amer., Suppl.* 30 Sept. 24861 This lens, called *tele-negative*, need not be connected permanently with the ordinary objective (which is called **tele-positive*), a loose connection by means of a removable short tube being quite sufficient. [**1961** *Official Gaz.* (U.S. Patent Office) 22 Aug. TM124 **Tele-processing*... For services in organizing, planning, developing, installing, maintaining and operating data processing systems [etc.].] **1962** *Engineering* 8 June 758/2 The development of 'remote computing' or 'teleprocessing' as it is sometimes called. **1970** *Computers & Humanities* IV. 323 Classrooms equipped with voice recorders; and with teletypewriters.. for creating perforated paper tape for batch teleprocessing. **1980** R. L. DUNCAN *Brimstone* x. 263 'How will the reprogramming take place?' 'Teleprocessing. Over the telephone lines.' **1914** A. L. TEIXEIRA DE MATTOS tr. *Maeterlinck's Unknown Guest* ii. 63 There are seers, so-called '*telepsychics', who are not psychometers. **1926** F. CAZZAMALLI in *Jrnl. Amer. Soc. Psychical Res.* XX. 1 (*title*) Telepsychic phenomena and cerebral radiations. **1960** *Sci. News Let.* 2 Jan. 4/2 The '*telepuppet', as he [*sc.* F. L. Whipple] called it, would have a little feedback on handling pressure to give the human operator a feel of the object the machine is working on. **1963** *Flight Internat.* LXXXIII. 244/2 It is foreseen that the adaptive machine or 'telepuppet', primitive versions of which are already used in handling radio-active materials, have a key role in space missions. **1973** C. SAGAN *Cosmic Connection* I. viii. 62 There may be telepuppets, devices landed on another planet but fully controlled by an individual human being in orbit. **1909** *Arch. Roentgen Ray* XIV. 38 (*heading*) An instantaneous shutter for *teleradiography. **1928** *Brit. Jrnl. Radiol.* I. 368 Arising out of these large milliampereages are the screening stands and radiographic appliances for teleradiography. **1974** *Biol. Abstr.* LVII. 6326/1 Teleradiography and tomography were used to investigate 57 able-bodied male patients. **1881** *Nature* 13 Oct. 576/2 Multiple inverse electric *teleradiophone, by M. Mercadier. **1937** *Nature* 25 Dec. 1109/1 *Teleradium has been practised by several centres in Great Britain over a period of years. **1959** R. W. RAVEN *Cancer* V. 157 Usually a single teleradium or telecobalt field is applied to the undersurface of the chin beneath the tumour. **1909** O. LODGE *Survival of Man* IV. xi. 163 This is the hypothesis of actual telepathic or *telergic influence from some outside intelligence. **1908** SIR O. LODGE in *Hibbert Jrnl.* Apr. 575 A foreign intelligence, acting either telepathically through the mind or *telergically by a more direct process straight on the brain. **1884** GURNEY & MYERS in *19th Cent.* May 814 Unless some such relation [of telepathy to space and to matter] can be demonstrated we cannot reasonably speak of a psychical *telergy—an action of mind on mind at a distance—as correlated with any energy which we have learnt to measure. **1903** MYERS *Hum. Personality* I. Gloss., Telergy. **1912** *Index-Catal. Libr. Surg.-General's Office, U.S. Army* XVII. 712 *Teleröntgenography. **1923** R. KNOX *Radiogr. & Radio-Therapy* I. 303 When it is possible to obtain full exposures of the thorax at a distance of 2 metres, then teleröntgenography of the thorax is of decided advantage. **1972** J. E. CULLINAN *Illustrated Guide to X-Ray Technics* i. 3/1 (*caption*) A 72 inch focus-film distance is used for teleroentgenography to minimize geometric enlargement and distortion. **1905** *Rep. Brit. Assoc. Adv. Sci. 1904* 47 [In Italy] there are fifteen first-class observatories provided with apparatus to record *teleseisms and local shocks. **1972** J. G. DENNIS *Struct. Geol.* xvi. 363 (*caption*) Teleseism (distant earthquake). **1905** *Rep. Brit. Assoc. Adv. Sci. 1904* 47 Japan has at least five stations for *teleseismic observations. **1969** *New Scientist* 25 Dec. 627/1 The so-called teleseismic data..have provided a rich new fund of research material for analysing the Earth's interior. **1974** *Nature* 23 Aug. 622/3 Nakamura and his colleagues have attempted to determine both P and S wave velocities throughout the lunar mantle from..high frequency teleseismic events and deep moonquakes. **1971** I. G. GASS et al. *Understanding Earth* xxiv. 336/2 A relatively narrow cone at the source can be seen *teleseismically. **1890** *Telesomatic [see *teleplastic* above]. **1891** *Cent. Dict.*, *Teleseme. **1899** *Westm. Gaz.* 8 June 10/2 The bedrooms are fitted with a model kind of call, the Teleseme—a dumb waiter. **1901** F. HARRISON in *19th Cent.* June 916 Life in the States is one perpetual whirl of telephones, telesemes, phonographs, electric bells, etc. **1981** *Teleshopping [see *telebanking* above]. **1983** *Times* 17 Aug. 3/6 The channel will also have the facility for shopping from the armchair at the touch of a switch, now termed 'teleshopping'. **1976** W. J. G. OVERINGTON in *Computing Europe* 4 Mar. 8/2, I have..been theoretically developing a computing system based on Ceefax/Oracle which I call *Telesoftware (*ie* software at a distance). **1977** *Wireless World* Sept. 50/2 Perhaps the most marketable use for Telesoftware might be in video games. **1979** *Guardian* 24 Sept. 21/5 Experiments are under way to use Prestel for exchanging software programs and 'telesoftware' is also available for teletext services. **1982** *Datalink* 18 Jan. 5/1 The programme forms only part of the project... There's telesoftware, which uses the BBC's Ceefax teletext service to broadcast software. **1871** tr. *Schellen's Spectr. Anal.* liii. 247 Young's *tele-spectroscope. **1882** YOUNG *Sun* iii. 77 The combined instrument is then often called a tele-spectroscope. **1864** WEBSTER, **Telestereoscope*, a stereoscope adapted to view distant natural objects or landscapes; a telescopic stereoscope. **1887** *Encycl. Brit.* XXII. 541/1 Von Helmholtz invented the Telestereoscope, an instrument which places as it were the point of view of both eyes wide apart. **1930** MOSELEY & CHAPPLE *Television* viii. 95 Since *tele-talkies are sent out in a manner very similar to the transmission of television, they can be received on the identical machine which receives television images. **1913** DORLAND *Med. Dict.* (ed. 7) 946/1 **Teletherapy*, absent treatment. **1929** *Brit. Med. Jrnl.* 11 May 845/1 In teletherapy proper the radium is employed at distances as great as 16 cm. **1945** C. W. WILSON *Radium Therapy* vii. 159 As the name implies, radium teletherapy.. is the therapeutic use of a quantity of radium at a distance from the patient. **1974** *Nature* 11 Oct. 521/2 Hyperthermia in conjunction with readily available radiation sources (such as cobalt teletherapy units..) might provide some of the same advantages as heavy particle therapy. **1891** *Cent. Dict.*, *Telethermograph..*Telethermometer..*Telethermometry. **1972** *Science* 5 May 532/3 A thermistor probe which recorded rectal temperatures was connected to a telethermometer. **1891** *Cent. Dict.*, **Teletopometer*, a telemeter in which two telescopes are used. **1905** *Daily Chron.* 9 Feb. 3/6 To the instrument, known as the teletopometer, a telescope is fixed, in which appear two pictures of the distant object. One picture is stationary, while the other moves and is brought to cover the first. A scale attached..indicates at once the distance of the object. **1968** *Punch* 2 Oct. 488/1 A Royal Martian Vole ..*teletransported herself to your planet in 1964. **1966** *New Scientist* 20 Jan. 169/3 Each contributing a special faculty such as telekinesis, *teletransportation, and so on. **1908** *Times* 5 Dec. 16/3 An apparatus called a '*telewriter' for electrically reproducing at a distance handwriting, drawings [etc.]. **1908** *Daily Chron.* 21 Dec., The Lord Mayor, '*telewriting' to the Lord Mayor of Manchester, tendered his cordial greetings to him and his fellow-citizens from the City of London and himself. **1909** *Ibid.* 13 Jan. 6/1 Telewriters with telephones attached will be put in in the case of a limited number of original subscribers without any rental charges or other initial expenses. **1893** *Teloptic, *Telosmic [see *teleplastic* above].

2. [f. TELE(VISION.] Used to form sbs. denoting activities, persons, things, etc., connected with television (not sharply distinguishable from an attrib. use of TELE *sb.*[2]) **a.** In a virtually limitless range of largely colloq., humorous, or journalistic formations, as ***telechair***, ***-course***, ***-drama***, ***-studio***, etc.

1940 *Chambers's Techn. Dict.* 837/2 *Telestudio*,..the enclosure, sound-proofed and treated acoustically, which is used for originating television or broadcasting programmes. **1942** O. E. DUNLAP *Future of Television* vi. 80 The excitement of watching an actual event in progress compensated for any blur or foggy effects, caused chiefly by the tele-eyes' lack of depth and focus. **1953** *Sat. Rev. Lit.* (U.S.) 3 Jan. 3/3 Mr. Sherwood's first tele-drama will be seen in the spring by an anticipating nation. **1953** *Sun* (Baltimore) 15 Dec. (B ed.) 10/2 Mr. Gould's teleplay was the better of the two, although by no means a masterpiece. **1954** *Ibid.* 5 Feb. (B ed.) 8/1 The tele-version..reflected both the assets and faults of the original. **1955** *House & Garden* Apr. 70/1 Yellow appears again on the back of the black-seated telechair. **1957** *Economist* 19 Oct. 226/1 'Tele-courses' [in the U.S.] have in some cases completely replaced conventional classes. **1957** *Cinema* 4 Sept. 3 (*heading*) Tele-movies start in U.S. **1957** P. WILDEBLOOD *Main Chance* 54 Ginny had..blossomed out into a quite new kind of star: the Telepersonality. **1958** *Spectator* 10 Jan. 37/2 The Duke [of Bedford] is so anxious to please the tele-masses that he has taken voice-production lessons. **1962** *Listener* 30 Aug. 327/1 Three of Mr Bowen's teleplays. **1967** *Daily Tel.* (Colour Suppl.) 22 Mar. 27/1 A few swinging teleclerics try vainly to up-date God's image. **1967** *Which?* Oct. 290/1 Telepundits donned ceremonial expressions of awe. **1970** *Times* 25 July 12 The director of telemedicine at the Massachusetts hospital..says that 60 per cent of the patients have found the automated consultations acceptable. **1972** *Observer* 30 Jan. 9/7 They became something that was to be crucial to the development of television—the first tele-journalists. **1978** *Ibid.* 29 Jan. 29/1, I say 'familiar' because teledrama modes are well established. **1983** *Times* 18 Aug. 7/6 We were hanging on the halting lips of all those returning officers..and marvelling at the sharpness and stamina of the telepundits who could divine at the drop of a percentage that the Tories were sweeping the seaside resorts. **1983** *Listener* 22 Sept. 28/3 This was also the week of *The Godfather*, in Coppola's long tele-version, played on BBC1 at 9.25 pm. every week-night but Wednesday.

b. Special Combs.: **'telefilm**, a cinematographic film shown on television, esp. one made for that purpose; also, the film medium itself; such films collectively; **ˌtele'politics**, political activity conducted through television; **teleroman** (telerɔmɑ̃) [Canad. Fr. *téléroman* (also used): see ROMAN *sb.*[4]], a French Canadian television soap opera;

'**telescreen**, a television screen; **tele'varsity** [VARSITY], a university that teaches its students by means of television, an open university (*disused*); **tele-vérité** (televerite) (also in Fr. form **télé-vérité**) [f. as CINÉMA-VÉRITÉ], television broadcasting that presents real life; documentary television; **televersity** [*uni*)*ver-sity*] = *televarsity* above (disused).

1939 *Los Angeles Extended Area Telephone Directory* 1003/1 Telefilm 16 mm Productions Co... 6039 Hollywood Blvd. **1950** *Electronic Engin.* XXII. 8/1 With the advent of television recording or 'telefilm' as it is called, a new tool has been placed in the hands of the television programme builders. **1958** *Times* 20 Nov. 3/4 Plans were announced for the largest Anglo-American co-production scheme yet envisaged in the field of the tele-film. **1975** *New Yorker* 19 May 88/2 It has been translated into telefilm with a greater concern for the Indian position than has been shown by most filmmakers in the past. **1959** *Observer* 4 Oct. 21/3 Lennox-Boyd looked a bit tense, but was certainly controlled. His exit line, to the effect that he had been doing the most wonderful work in the world, deserves a place for itself in the annals of telepolitics. **1975** *Listener* 9 Oct. 479/1 It is a pity telepolitics are so unlike the real thing. **1973** *Globe & Mail* (Toronto) 13 July 13/3 CBC President Laurent Picard's marked liking for the numerous serials seen on CBC French TV, called teleromans. **1942** O. E. DUNLAP *Future of Television* vi. 80 The clarity of the telescreen could not be compared to the sharpness of a newsreel. **1949** 'G. ORWELL' *Nineteen Eighty-Four* I. 6 The telescreen received and transmitted simultaneously. **1979** *Globe & Mail* (Toronto) 13 July 14/3 This wit pales towards the end, as Smith is systematically reduced through the clever interplay of video playbacks (read telescreen for life in Oceania) with O'Brien's stiff and triumphant martinet's voice. **1961** *Economist* 16 Dec. 1105/2 The daytime hours on this network, when the voluntary 'televarsity' students would be at their ordinary everyday work. **1964** *New Statesman* 14 Feb. 264/3 *Télé-verité* may have reached its apogee.. when a man was tortured to within a few minutes of death in front of the camera. **1976** *Listener* 11 Mar. 310/1 Selected by their daughter's boyfriend, a television producer, as the subject of his *tele-vérité* film. **1950** *Time* 21 Aug. 44/2 *Televersity*. For years, educators have been talking about television as an ideal teaching medium... [The University of] Michigan will start weekly Sunday afternoon telecasts.

3. [f. TELE(PHONE *sb.*] Prefixed to sbs. with reference to a service obtained by means of the telephone, as '**tele-ad**, an advertisement placed in a newspaper by telephone; '**telebus**, (a service offering) a bus that can be summoned by telephone; ˌ**telefac'simile** (see quot. 1967); '**telelecture** (see quot. 1969); '**telemarketing** *vbl. sb.* (orig. *U.S.*), the marketing of goods, services, etc., by means of (freq. unsolicited) telephone calls to prospective customers; hence (as back-formation) '**telemarket** *v. trans.*; also '**telemarketer**; '**telesale**, a sale effected by a salesperson who telephones prospective customers.

1976 *Southern Even. Echo* (Southampton) 3 Nov. 3/8 Tele-Ads from telephone subscribers within the 'Southern Evening Echo' circulation area only are accepted. **1977** *Financial Times* 23 Apr. 13/6 Journalists and tele-ad girls should have direct access to the terminals. **1969** Telebus [see DIAL *v.* 4 b]. **1972** *Daily Colonist* (Victoria, B.C.) 25 Feb. 8/1 The telebus service.. uses half-size buses that pick passengers up at their homes and drive them to the nearest regular bus route terminal. **1967** *Britannica Bk. of Year* 804/3 *Telefacsimile*, a system for the transmission and reproduction of fixed graphic matter (as printing) involving the use of signals transmitted over telephone wires (as between libraries). **1968** *Sat. Rev.* (U.S.) 17 Feb. 60 Colleges today are.. piping the specialist's voice and face in by telelecture and television. **1969** *Britannica Bk. of Year* 801/1 *Telelecture*, 1. A loudspeaker connected to a telephone line for amplifying voice communication. 2. A lecture delivered to an audience by telelecture. **1981** *Monitor* (McAllen, Texas) 1 Mar. 24/5 A series of telelectures entitled 'Good Health—the key to Happy Living' is continuing at Knapp Memorial Methodist Hospital. **1983** *Inc.* July 51/1 (*caption*) Al Felly.. had a great way to telemarket his flowers. **1985** *DM News* 1 Dec. 6/3 Each working day, an average of 200 selected companies are telemarketed. **1984** *Inc.* Apr. 111/2 He's got 25 telemarketers who phone high net worth individuals. **1987** *Business Week* 9 Feb. 85/3 It also compiles phone numbers of homeowners for telemarketers. **1980** *Advertising Age* 22 Sept. 66/1 A very fine balance—continued excellence in technological development combined with the targeted, personalized methods of telemarketing. **1981** *Harvard Business Rev.* July–Aug. 104/1 The newer tools include national account management, demonstration centers, telemarketing, and new improved forms of catalog selling. **1986** *E. Anglian Daily Times* 22 May 41/4 (Advt.), Part-time tele-marketing vacancy working from home. **1963** *Spectator* 12 Apr. 478/3 The advantages of 'telesales' over direct mail. **1981** *Event* 16 Oct. 99/3 (Advt.), Dynamic telesales personnel.

tele-ad: see TELE- 3.

teleangiectasis, -ia, varr. TELANGIECTASIS

telearch ('tɛlɪɑːk). *Gr. Hist.* [ad. Gr. τελέαρχος, f. τέλος office: see -ARCH.] The title of a magistrate in ancient Thebes.

1797 W. JOHNSTONE tr. *Beckmann's Invent.* II. 23 At Thebes the streets were under the inspection of the telearchs.

teleautograph: see TELAUTOGRAPH.

telebanking to **tele-camera**: see TELE- 1.

telecast ('tɛlɪkɑːst, -æ-), *sb.* orig. *U.S.* [f. TELE- + BROAD)CAST *sb.*] The action or an act of broadcasting by television; a television broadcast or programme.

1937 *Atlantic Monthly* CLIX. 531/2 He can be assured that any receiver he buys will give him the telecasts sent out by all the major systems of transmission. **1951** M. EHRLICH *Big Eye* i. 11 The Telecast Building way downtown. **1954** 'J. CHRISTOPHER' *22nd Cent.* 21 Within three hours of the Atomics telecast there were riotous assemblies in Canberra. **1961** G. MILLERSON *Technique Television Production* iii. 32 The forms of perspective-distortion introduced by narrow-angle lenses are a familiar feature in telecasts where the camera has to be positioned some way from the subject. **1978** J. IRVING *World according to Garp* xvi. 349 Except for the fact that there had been no nudity in the telecast, the event was an X-rated soap opera from start to finish. **1980** *Daily Tel.* 12 July 5/1 The Minister also said in a telecast that value-added tax would be applied to more products.

telecast ('tɛlɪkɑːst, -æ-), *v.* orig. *U.S.* [f. TELE- + BROAD)CAST *v.* 3: cf. prec.] *trans.* To broadcast by television.

1940 *Topeka* (Kansas) *Daily Capital* 25 Mar. 1/4 Easter Services.. were telecast today. **1949** R. GRAVES *Seven Days in New Crete* iv. 44 The garish, raucous, three-dimensioned cartoon-comedies telecast every hour in mid-air over the harbour. **1952** *Economist* 26 July 228/1 Old films.. are telecast over 49 stations. **1968** *Globe & Mail* (Toronto) 13 Jan. 26/3 In Saint Joan (telecast last month) I searched through myself for parts I could put into Joan. **1978** G. VIDAL *Kalki* viii. 182 Since the networks refused to telecast the Kalki-Arlene Wagstaff interview, Giles was obliged to buy thirty minutes of prime-time television.

So '**telecasting** *vbl. sb.* and *attrib.* or as *ppl. a.*; '**telecaster**, one who broadcasts on television.

1937 *Electronics* Sept. 13/1 (*caption*) 'Telecasting' in Great Britain. **1940** A. H. MORTON in Porterfield & Reynolds *We present Television* i. 47 Television standards in the United States must be uniformly adopted by all telecasters. **1945** F. BROWN *Angels & Spaceships* (1955) 90 Every major broadcasting and telecasting station in the world has gone off the air. *Ibid.* 92 With telecasting suspended there were no pictures on their screens. **1951** M. EHRLICH *Big Eye* i. 26 News of the world!.. Here is your telecaster—Arthur Morrow! **1957** *Observer* 25 Aug. 11/1 This was a commendable piece of telecasting, though a military exercise unopposed.. is always a bit of an anticlimax. **1974** *Times* 8 Jan. 13/7 The 10.30 shut-down has shortened the telecasting day.

telecentric: see TELE- 1.

telechiric (tɛlɪ'kaɪərɪk), *a.* and *sb.* [f. TELE- + Gr. χείρ hand + -IC.]

A. *adj.* Applied to a device which carries out manipulative operations under the control of a person who is not in the immediate vicinity, but who receives feedback from sensors in the device; also applied to a process or system involving such devices. **B.** *sb.* **a.** *pl.* The branch of technology concerned with telechiric devices. **b.** A telechiric device or system.

1963 J. W. CLARK in *Battelle Technical Rev.* Oct. 3/2 Since the system.. can be considered as an extension of man's manipulative and sensory capabilities, even to the use of hand tools, it is well described by the term 'telechirics'. The word is formed from two Greek words—'tele'.., meaning distant, and 'kheir or chir'.. which means hand. *Ibid.* 4/2 A well-designed telechiric system replaces man's eyes, hands, and feet with somewhat equivalent mechanical devices. **1968** *Sci. Jrnl.* Oct. 65/2 The commercial cost advantages of the telechiric will displace all competition for work duties undersea. **1970** *Physics Bull.* Oct. 450/1 The telechiric machine requires complete sensing devices, but it presents the sense information to a human as if he were receiving it directly. **1977** *Daily Mail* 11 July 24 (*heading*) Send the telechiric down the pits. *Ibid.* Professor Meredith Thring, Professor of Mechanical Engineering at Queen Mary College, London, is pressing for the development of telechiric mining in Britain. **1978** *Jrnl. R. Soc. Arts* CXXVI. 493/2, I am working on telechirics in mining. It means we shall be able to mine coal in the future without miners going underground, because miners can do their job remotely from the surface.

Hence **telechir** ('tɛlɪkiːə(r)) = TELECHIRIC *sb.* b.

1980 *New Scientist* 3 Jan. 5 A telechir is a mobile machine equipped with TV, sensor devices, mechanical arms and hands, and controlled by a skilled human operator situated at the surface.

telechirograph: see TELE- 1.

telecine (tɛlɪ'sɪnɪ). [f. TELE- 2 + CINE, or f. next.] The broadcasting of cinematographic film on television, or its conversion into television signals; also, apparatus or an organization involved in doing this. Freq. *attrib.*

1935 *Illustr. London News* 23 Feb. 306/1 In the Telecinė apparatus, ordinary standard sound-films may be used. **1937** *Electronics* Aug. 34/3 *Telecine transmission*, the process of transmitting motion-picture film subjects by television. **1938** *Ibid.* July 25/1 A succession of stationary images is projected upon the photoelectric cathode of the pick-up tube in the telecine camera. **1949** *Electronic Engin.* XXI. 194 Two sets of telecine equipment.. have just been installed at Alexandra Palace, where they are now being used for televising film programmes. **1959** *Viewpoint* July 32 The telecine operator's in now. Didn't you want to see that piece of film? **1960** D. WILSON *Flight of Dove* 223 Superimpose main title. End telecine (1). **1961** G. MILLERSON *Technique Television Production* vii. 124 Film televising equipment (Telecine) ranges in complexity from slightly adapted cinema projection apparatus, to electronic scanners. **1972** I. HAMILTON *Thrill Machine* xxxix. 187 Joe gave his cues to the men in telecine. **1978** *Gramophone* Aug. 391/3 They have even announced a telecine attachment to use the camera for transcribing home films to video tape. **1983** *New Scientist* 26 May 546/3 The film image is converted to video in the usual way with a 'telecine' machine, which combines a film projector with a video camera.

† **telecinema** (tɛlɪ'sɪnɪmə). *Obs.* exc. *Hist.* Also **telekinema** and with hyphen. [f. TELE- 2 + CINEMA, KINEMA.] **1.** = prec.

1930 MOSELEY & CHAPPLE *Television* viii. 93 An extraordinary situation in the fascinating history of television was the development of what is now called the tele-cinema.

2. (Also with capital initial.) The name of a building in the Festival of Britain of 1951 in which television programmes could be shown on a large screen as in a cinema; the system or process involved in producing this display.

1951 I. COX *South Bank Exhibition* 83 The Telecinema is the first cinema in the world to be specially designed and built for the showing of both films and television. **1952** *Times* 6 Feb. 4/7 The Minister had suggested that, except for the Telekinema and possibly, also, the Waterloo Road administration blocks, none of the festival buildings should be retained unless the council wished to take them over. **1953** A. K. C. OTTAWAY *Educ. & Society* v. 81 Many new means of mechanical amusement have been created. We have the telecinema; shall we even yet have the 'Feelies'. **1976** *Oxf. Compan. Film* 495/2 *National Film Theatre*, a club cinema established and run by the British Film Institute, took over and rebuilt the Telekinema. **1977** M. STRICKLAND *A. Thirkell* x. 157 Angela treated the events [of the Festival of Britain, 1951] with the greatest scorn, but she agreed nevertheless to be interviewed on the 'telecinema'.

telecobalt: see TELE- 1.

telecom ('tɛlɪkɒm). Colloq. abbrev. of TELECOMMUNICATION. Also (chiefly *attrib.*) in *pl.*

British Telecom, the popular name of British Telecommunications plc, a public corporation providing telecommunications and data processing services, separated from the Post Office on 1 October 1981.

1963 *Telecoms Topics* Aug. 1 This new publication, *Telecoms Topics*,.. will contain the latest information about ..*G.E.C. Telecommunications*. **1964** D. MACARTHUR *Reminiscences* IX. 331 By 'telecom' I was directed to use the Navy and the Air Force to assist South Korean defenses by whatever use I could make of these two arms. **1970** T. LILLEY *Projects Section* v. 45 That patrol.. was now accompanied by telecom and explosive experts. **1981** *Economist* 24 Jan. 100/1 Every big telecoms company is evaluating bubbles (or already buying them) for use in private branch exchanges.

telecommand: see TELE- 1.

telecommunication (ˌtɛlɪkəmjuːnɪ'keɪʃən). [f. TELE- + COMMUNICATION, after F. *télé-communication*.] Communication over long distances, esp. by electrical means such as by telegraphy, telephony, or broadcasting; (usu. in *pl.*) the branch of technology concerned with this. Also *concr.*, a means or channel of such communication. Freq. *attrib.*, esp. in *pl.*

The term *télécommunication* was adopted by the Convention Internationale des Télécommunications at Madrid in 1932 (the official language at the conference was French). The definition then accepted ('toute communication télégraphique ou téléphonique de signes, de signaux, d'écrits, d'images et de sons de toute nature, par fil, radio ou autres systèmes ou procédés de signalisation électriques ou visuels (sémaphore)'), in so far as it includes non-electrical means of communication, is no longer applicable.

1932 *Times* 18 Nov. 13/4 The new convention which is being drawn up by the International Telegraph and Radiotelegraph Conference.. will be called International Telecommunications Convention. **1942** *Electronic Engin.* Aug. 128/2 A telecommunication system where intelligence is communicated by means of a radio-frequency carrier. *Ibid.* Dec. 306/1 Rigid frequency control has become a necessity in radio broadcasting and indeed in all forms of telecommunication. **1944** *Times* 21 July 3/4 Resistance groups in Belgium have.. been engaged in the systematic destruction of railways, road bridges, telecommunications, [etc.]. **1953** *Science News* XXX. 70 One has only to consider the field of automatic telecommunication to accept the process [*sc.* electrical manipulation of information] as commonplace. **1957** *Technology* July 187/2 The possible applications of solar batteries in telecommunications. **1961** *Engineering* 6 Jan. 33/1 The plan.. to put a telecommunications satellite into orbit round the earth. **1971** F. J. M. LAVER in B. de Ferranti *Living with Computer* v. 44 The capture of data at its point of origin, its rapid transmission over telecommunication links, and its filtering and analysis by computers. *a* **1974** R. CROSSMAN *Diaries* (1977) III. 583 It was an impressive telecommunications feat, which is why Kennedy decided to do it. **1979** MILLER & CHYNOWETH (*title*) Optical fiber telecommunications.

telecon ('tɛlɪkɒn). *U.S. Mil.* [f. *teletype* s.v. TELE- + CON(FERENCE *sb.*: see next.] **1.** A device of the U.S. army which sends teletype messages over long distances by means of radio or underwater cable and which typically displays them on a screen; a conference held by this means.

1950 *N.Y. Times* 2 July 8E/1 This was the 'telecon' room, equipped with machines that enable officers in Washington to confer with headquarters overseas... The telecon, essentially, is just a teletype machine, but it has certain modifications which make it especially useful for military communications. **1951** *Sun* (Baltimore) 31 Oct. (B ed.) 7/2 Gen. Douglas MacArthur participated in four history-making telecons. **1969** D. ACHESON *Present at Creation* (1970) xliv. 412 A telecon is a secure device by which a typewriter operated at one end records both there and through a similar machine at the other end.

2. [orig. *trans.* from sense 1; later re-formed as shortening of next.] A long-distance conference held by means of teletype or telephone.

1951 *Sun* (Baltimore) 31 Oct. (B ed.) 7/2 The generals like to impress each other with 'sorry, can't see you then, have a telecon with Washington at that time'. **1981** *Aviation Week & Space Technol.* 15 June 128/3 Reference our telecon regarding the operation of company flights to Antarctica and return nonstop. **1982** *Legal Times* 10 May 14/2 A client.. may yelp about a 'six-minute telecon' on his bill that costs $10.

teleconference ('tɛlɪˌkɒnfərəns). [f. TELE- + CONFERENCE *sb.*] A conference held by people who, though separated physically, are linked by telecommunication devices (e.g. telephones, television screens, etc.). So **tele'conferencing**.

1953 *Language* XXIX. 71 A general at a teleconference writes out a message for transmission. **1973** *Times* 4 Oct. 35/5 The prospect of similar teleconference equipment in every main commercial or industrial building—just like the telephone on the business desk—is no longer a pipe dream. **1975** *Financial Times* 21 July 6/2 The psychological and travel-replacement aspects of teleconferencing were underlined in a paper by Quebec University. **1981** *Times* 9 Feb. 20/1 Teleconferencing brings together a number of people in different locations for a meeting by means of a tele-audio link.

teleconnection to **-converter**: see TELE- 1.

telecopier ('tɛlɪˌkɒpɪə(r)). Also (*U.S.*) Tele-. [f. TELE- 3 + COPIER.] A facsimile device which transmits and reproduces graphic material over telephone lines.

A proprietary term in the U.S.

1967 *Official Gaz.* (U.S. Patent Office) 24 Jan. TM 152/2 Telecopier. For transmitting and receiving equipment for producing facsimile copies of documents. First use June 13, 1966. **1972** M. GILBERT *Body of Girl* xviii. 160 A photograph.. was sent by tele-copier to the Isle of Wight. **1979** *Fortune* 21 May 123/2 He kept a telecopier in his bedroom to take messages and transmit urgent documents.

telecryptograph to **telecurietherapy**: see TELE- 1.

telediagnosis (ˌtɛlɪdaɪəg'nəʊsɪs). [f. TELE- + DIAGNOSIS.] The long-distance assessment of a patient's condition by a doctor using closed-circuit television.

1961 *New Scientist* 7 Dec. 604/1 The most recent use of television in medicine is in 'telediagnosis' now being used in Paris. **1972** D. V. TANSLEY *Radionics* 6 He then experimented with telediagnosis which utilized the overhead telephone wires to link him with the patient sample.

telediphone: see TELE- 1.

‖**teledu** ('tɛlədu:). Also †telagu. [Native name in Javanese.] A carnivorous animal of Java and Sumatra (*Mydaus javanensis*), allied to the skunk and of similar habits; also called *stinking badger* or *stinkard*.

1821 T. S. RAFFLES in *Trans. Linnean Soc.* XIII. 251 *Mephitis Javanensis* Desm. Telagu of the Malays. **1824** HORSFIELD *Zool. Res. Java*, *Tĕlĕdu*, in the language of Java, East of Cheribon. *Ibid.*, The covering of the Tĕlĕdu is adapted to the elevated and cold regions which it inhabits. *Ibid.*, The entire neighbourhood of a village is infected by the odour of an irritated Tĕlĕdu. **1906** E. INGERSOLL *Life of Animals: Mammals* 176 Two related animals of the East are the teledu, or stinking badger, a small nocturnal burrower of Java and Sumatra.. and the large, long-snouted, piglike sand badgers. **1965** D. MORRIS *Mammals* 292 The Teledu is well able to defend itself by means of the offensive secretions of its large anal glands.

teledynamic: see TELODYNAMIC.

telefacsimile: see TELE- 3.

teleferic (tɛlɪ'fɛrɪk). Also ‖teleferica, telepheric. [ad. It. *teleferica*, f. Gr. τῆλε TELE- + φέρειν to carry + -ικος -IC: see next.] A cableway.

1916 *Windsor Mag.* Oct. 498 We walk a little way and then go up by the teleferic. **1918** W. HUTCHINSON *Doctor in War* (1919) xviii. 262 The miniature cable-railway, or teleferica. **1931** R. H. BEADON *Royal Army Service Corps* II. xi. 336 It was found necessary.. to use what was known as the Teleferica, or wire rope carrying cradles, which was extensively used by the Italians. **1964** *Harper's Bazaar* Nov. 140/3 New teleferic extension of the Grandes Rousses lift at Alpe d'Huez. **1973** *Good Motoring* May 31/2 A telepheric takes visitors up part of the hill.

‖**téléférique, téléphérique** (teleferik). [Fr., f. as prec.] = prec.

1956 I. BROMIGE *Enchanted Garden* III. 150 We'll go up on the *téléphérique* after tea. **1958** *Times* 15 Nov. 11/5 At present there are no ski-lifts or téléfériques [in the Loetschental]. **1965** G. MCINNES *Road to Gundagai* vi. 97 We.. hoped emptily that.. a little téléférique would appear to carry us all up high in the clouds. **1977** *New Yorker* 26 Sept. 107/1 The Brévent, to be sure, could be reached in a few minutes by a system of *téléphériques*.

telefilm: see TELE- 2 b.

teleflash: see TELE- 1.

‖**telega** (tɛ'leɪgə). Also 6 telego, 9 telaga, telegga, teljĕga, (telegue). [a. Russ. *teljĕga*; whence also F. *télègue.*] A four-wheeled Russian cart, of rough construction, without springs.

1558 in Hakluyt *Voy.* (1599) 315 With these Telegoes they caried our stuffe from Vologhda vnto the Mosco. **1807** SIR R. WILSON *Jrnl.* 7 Sept., in *Life* (1862) II. viii. 365, I mounted my telaga and drove to Lord Gower's. **1833** R. PINKERTON *Russia* 21 Government couriers travel in telegas, or four-wheeled simply-constructed carts. **1877** MAR. M. GRANT *Sun-Maid* x, We travelled for weeks in a teljĕga, a sort of queer snow carriage. **1903** *19th Cent.* Mar. 421 A party of poor telega-drivers.

telegenesis: see TELE- 1.

telegenic (tɛlɪ'dʒɛnɪk), *a.* orig. *U.S.* [f. TELE- 2 + -GENIC b, after *photogenic.*] Of a person or thing: that shows to advantage on television; providing an interesting or attractive subject for a television broadcast.

1939 *Sun* (Baltimore) 16 Oct. 6/8 Judith Barrett, pretty and blonde actress, is the first Telegenic Girl to go on record. In other words she is the perfect type of beauty for television... She is slated for the first television motion picture. **1948** *Daily Tel.* 23 June 6/4 One word that is playing an important part at this gathering is 'telegenic'. With everything that happens.. being reproduced on thousands of television screens, the ability of any speaker to look as attractive as he sounds has become an important political asset. **1950** *New Yorker* 26 Aug. 18/3 Korman has spent many hours in the WOR Television studios, experimenting with telegenic properties of various weaves and colors of cloth and styles of suits. **1962** P. FERRIS *Church of England* ii. 35 The letters 'C.R.' after a man's name keep cropping up.. in the *TV Times*, television having discovered that the religious communities have some telegenic personalities. **1971** H. WILSON *Labour Govt.* (1974) xvi. 372 We had not yet reached the position where telegenic situations were planned in advance between a television authority and the demonstrators. **1980** *Times* 7 Nov. 12/2 Conscious that jazz by itself is not very telegenic, producers compensate by building shiny sets.

telegnomy: see TELE- 1.

telegony (tɪ'lɛgənɪ). *Biol.* [f. Gr. τῆλε, TELE- + -γονια begetting; cf. Gr. τηλέγονος 'born far from one's fatherland'.] The (hypothetical) influence of a previous sire seen in the progeny of a subsequent sire from the same mother.

1893 W. N. PARKER tr. *Weismann's Germ-Plasm* xii. 383 The phenomenon generally known as 'infection of the germ',—which, in case it really exists, I should prefer to speak of as *telegony*. **1899** *Daily News* 20 June 8/5 'The Penycuik Experiments',.. undertaken to try and throw some light upon reversion and the difficult problem of telegony. **1900** *Brit. Med. Jrnl.* No. 2046. 638 Telegony might prevail in the case of hereditary predisposition.

Hence **tele'gonic** *a.*, of or pertaining to telegony; **te'legonous** *a.*, 'of, pertaining to, or produced by telegony' (*Funk's Stand. Dict.* 1895).

1893 F. FINN in *Nat. Science* Dec. 436 Cases which seem difficult of explanation on any other than the Telegonic theory. **1897** *Ibid.* Feb. 80 Telegonic influence of the zebra will be looked for.

telegram ('tɛlɪgræm), *sb.* [f. Gr. τῆλε, TELE- + -GRAM; so F. *télégramme* (1867 in Littré), Ger. *telegramm* (1865 in Sanders).] A message sent by telegraph; a telegraphic dispatch or communication. Also *transf.* and *fig.*

(This term encountered at first much opposition from scholars, as not being formed on Greek analogies, which give, as in mod.Gr., τηλεγράφημα, TELEGRAPHEME; but its practical convenience led in a few years to its general adoption. In the *Panmure Papers* it takes the place of 'telegraphic despatch' from 11 Oct. 1855. Cf. also TELEGRAPH 3.)

1852 *Albany Even. Jrnl.* 6 Apr. (Bartlett), A friend desires us to give notice that he will ask leave.. to introduce a new word... It is *telegram*, instead of *telegraphic dispatch*, or *telegraphic communication*. **1855** LD. CLARENDON 31 May in *Panmure Papers* (1908) I. 218 A message should go forthwith by telegram. **1857** LADY CANNING *Let. fr. Calcutta* 16 Jan. in A. Hare *Two Noble Lives* (1893) II. 140 'A telegram'—a new Yankee word for a telegraphic despatch. **1857** [see TELEGRAPHEME]. **1857** MAJ. BIRCH *Let.* 21 Apr. in *Morn. Chron.* 23 Oct. 4/5 A telegram to the following effect has this day been transmitted to you [etc.]. **1858** *Chamb. Jrnl.* IX. 75/2 The Longmans have promised to include the word *telegram* in their forthcoming dictionary. **1859** LYTTON *What will he do* XII. xi, I sent a telegram (oh that I should live to see such a word introduced into the English language!). **1860** LYTTON ('O. Meredith') *Lucile* II. iv. §5 *note*, Ere a cable went under the hoary Atlantic, Or the word *telegram* drove grammarians frantic. **1873** F. HALL *Mod. Eng.* 158 *note*, There is, as against the exact, but surfeiting, *telegrapheme*, our lawless *telegram*. **1908** E. J. BANFIELD *Confessions of Beachcomber* II. i. 244 Telegrams along the line from the sucker [*sc.* a fish] give precise information. **1963** *Listener* 3 Jan. 14/1 A slim, solid brick tower, a kind of telegram about all the best and strongest things in Germany, stands a few feet away.

attrib. and *Comb.* **1875** G. AGER (*title*) The Telegram Code, for the Use of Bankers, Merchants, and Shipowners. **1881** *Blackw. Mag.* Apr. 470 The general telegram-sender. **1895** *Daily News* 3 Dec. 5/3 For some years past the Parisians have had the benefit of a system of 'telegram postcards' which are sent by pneumatic tubes. **1922** JOYCE *Ulysses* 117 A telegram boy stepped in nimbly, threw an envelope on the counter and stepped off posthaste.

Hence **'telegram** *v. intr.* to send a telegram, to telegraph (*rare*); *trans.* (*a*) to telegraph to; (*b*) to send (news, information, etc.) by telegraph; **'telegrammed** *ppl. a.*, that has been sent by telegraph; **'telegramming** *vbl. sb.* Also **ˌtelegra'mese** (*nonce-wd.*) = TELEGRAPHESE 1; **ˌtelegra'mmatic**, **tele'grammic** *adjs.*, of or pertaining to telegrams; concise or condensed like a telegram. All *rare*.

1864 SALA in *Daily Tel.* 27 July, Every patriotic man is bound to resent.. any insult offered to the flag of his country .. without being told or *telegrammed to shoot anybody. **1876** E. FITZGERALD *Let.* 2 Aug., I ought to have telegrammed back to you. **1952** M. TRIPP *Faith is Windsock* x. 149 In hospital with a broken leg. His mother has just telegrammed the news. **1969** R. MILLAR *Kut* vii. 154 A miserable Aylmer telegrammed Lake with a copy to Townshend. **1970** *Nature* 18 July 225/1 This information was simultaneously telegrammed to doctors. **1972** D. DOUGLASS *Pit Life in Co. Durham* (History Workshop Pamphlets No. 6) 53 The Executive Committee issued telegrammed instructions to the Lodge. **1973** A. BROINOWSKI *Take One Ambassador* ii. 16 The telephoning and telegramming was to begin once more. **1977** C. MCCULLOUGH *Thorn Birds* ix. 201 Mrs. Cleary telegrammed me, a.. courtesy I appreciated very much. **1981** *Washington Post* 26 May A15/1 Israeli Premier Menachem Begin's suggestion in telegramming his congratulations for Mitterand's election. **1894** *Pall Mall Mag.* Mar. 733 It [the telegram] was not written in *telegramese, and it cost more money than it ought. **1866** VISCT. STRANGFORD *Selection* (1869) II. 14 The *telegrammatic battle is no longer a simple duel between Athens and Constantinople. **1864** WEBSTER, **Telegrammic*, .. in the nature of a telegram; hence, laconic; concise; brief; succinct. **1866** *London Rev.* 25 Aug. 216/1 People insist that thought should be expressed with telegrammic brevity. **1891** G. MEREDITH *One of our Conq.* II. ix. 237 The letter was telegrammic in the essential point.

telegraph ('tɛlɪgrɑ:f, -æ-), *sb.* [a. F. *télégraphe* (Chappe 1792), f. Gr. τῆλε afar + -γραφ-ος that writes, writer: see TELE- and -GRAPH; so Ger. *telegraph*.

Miot de Mélito states in his *Mémoires* I. 38, that Chappe the inventor proposed to call his invention a *tachygraphe*, but was told by Miot that the name was bad, and ought to be *télégraphe*, which he at once adopted. (See Littré.)]

1. a. An apparatus for transmitting messages to a distance, usually by signs of some kind. Devices for this purpose have been in use from ancient times, but the name was first applied to that invented by Chappe in France in 1792, consisting of an upright post with movable arms, the signals being made by various positions of the arms according to a pre-arranged code. Hence applied to various other devices subsequently used, operating by movable disks, shutters, etc., flashes of light, movements in a column of liquid, sounds of bells, horns, etc., or other means. (Now *rare* in this sense, such contrivances being usually called *semaphores* or *signalling apparatus.*)

[**1794** *Europ. Mag.* Sept. 166/2 It was announced to them by the Telegraphe from Lisle.] **1794** *Hist.* in *Ann. Reg.* 394 The invention of the telegraph... A number of posts are erected at convenient distances; and on each.. is fixed a transverse beam with two moveable arms, the beam itself being also moveable. The different forms which the machine is capable of assuming is 16, and these represent the telegraphic alphabet. **1795** *Times* 30 Dec., in Ashton *Old Times* (1885) 127 A chain of Telegraphs is erected from Shuter's Hill to Dover. **1798** *Hull Advertiser* 14 Apr. 2/4 Orders were.. transmitted by the telegraph and by express to Portsmouth. **1805** in A. Duncan *Nelson* (1806) 297 Lord Nelson conveyed the following sentence by telegraph, to the fleet—'England expects every man will do his duty'. **1813** J. W. CROKER in *Cr. Papers* (1884) I. ii. 53 The Plymouth telegraph announces another complete victory of Lord W. over Soult on the 30th. **18..** MOORE *Fragm. Character* v, Scarcely a telegraph could wag Its wooden finger, but Ned knew it. **1823** PASLEY (*title*) Description of the Universal Telegraph for Day and Night Signals. **1834-47** J. S. MACAULAY *Field Fortif.* (1851) 256 A soldier makes an excellent telegraph.. varying the gestures to meet the various circumstances. **1863** W. LADD in *Rep. British Assoc.* 19 On an Acoustic Telegraph.

b. Applied retrospectively to ancient devices.

1794 *Times* 20 Sept., in Ashton *Old Times* (1885) 125 The invention of the Telegraphe is now traced back to 1655, and particularly mentioned in a little book.. by the Marquis of Worcester... He there gives it the name of Visual Correspondence, and calls it his own invention. **1808** J. MACDONALD *Telegraphic Commun.* 37 Julius Africanus minutely details a mode of spelling words by a Telegraph. It appears, that fires of various substances, were the means made use of. **1842** *Penny Cycl.* XXIV. 145/2 Bishop Wilkins,.. after describing this telegraph of Polybius, mentions another which requires only three lights or torches.

c. *fig.* See also *bush telegraph* s.v. BUSH *sb.*[1] 11.

1795 O'KEEFE *Irish Mimick* I. i, Love is a monstrous telegraph. **1817** COLERIDGE '*Blessed are ye*' 103 When princely capitals are often but the Telegraphs of distant calamity. **1866** *Tumut & Adelong* (N.S.W.) *Times* 1 Jan. 2/3 They approached to within one hundred yards of the camp unobserved, and then it was apparent that the 'telegraph' had done its work. **1891** 'OLD TIME' *Convict Hulk 'Success'* 20 The 'telegraph' was very extensively worked on board these hulks... The 'telegraph' was a system of speaking from one cell to another by means of tapping on the walls. **1964** D. MACARTHUR *Reminiscences* VI. 206 News of the first such shipment spread rapidly by the 'bamboo telegraph' through the Philippines. **1969** *New Yorker* 14 June 76/2 He would look down at his plate and find two steaks there. He knew what was happening. A message had come from the kitchen, on the Afro-American telegraph.

2. In full, ***electric*** (or ***magnetic***) ***telegraph***: An apparatus consisting of a transmitting instrument (*transmitter*), a receiving instrument (*receiver*), and a line or wire of any length connecting these, along which an electric current from a battery or other source passes, the circuit being made and broken by working the transmitter, so as to produce movements, as of a needle or pointer, in the receiver, which indicate letters, etc., either according to a code of signs, or by pointing to characters upon a dial; in some forms the receiver works so as to print or trace the message upon a prepared strip of paper.

Also, an apparatus for wireless telegraphy: see WIRELESS.

1797 *Monthly Mag.* Feb. 148 Dr. Don Francisco Salva had read, at the Royal Academy of Sciences, at Barcelona, a Memoir on the Application of Electricity to the Telegraph, and presented..an Electrical Telegraph of his own invention. **1823** RONALDS (*title*) Descriptions of an Electrical Telegraph. **1834** BREWSTER in *Encycl. Brit.* (ed. 7) VIII. 582/1 Mr. F. Ronalds..erected at Hammersmith an electrical telegraph, on which the inflections of the wire composed one continuous length of more than eight miles. *Ibid.* 662/2 Some German and American authors have proposed to construct galvanic telegraphs by the decomposition of water. **1840** *Monthly Chron.* I. 383/2 Electric Telegraph.—This extraordinary machine is now being worked on the great western rail-road [in Britain]. **1842** *Penny Cycl.* XXIV. 154/1 It is to the joint labours of Messrs. W. F. Cooke and Professor Wheatstone that electric telegraphs owe their practical application. *Ibid.* 155/1 The electro-magnetic telegraph... The longest continuous line yet completed is that from Paddington to West Drayton. *Ibid.*, It is reported (July, 1842) that an electric telegraph is about to be laid down along the South-Western Railway, from London to Gosport. **1845** COL. HAWKER *Diary* (1893) II. 264, I saw the magnetic telegraph at the railway station. **1854** G. B. RICHARDSON *Univ. Code* v. 7420 Have you received any communication by electric telegraph? **1858** LONGFELLOW in *Life* (1891) II. 361 Presently the clerk says, 'The Atlantic Telegraph is laid!' **1878** G. B. PRESCOTT *Sp. Telephone* (1879) 1 More than one hundred years ago Lesage established a telegraph in Geneva by the use of frictional electricity. **1881** W. M. SPRINGER in *N. Amer. Rev.* CXXXII. 369 In..thirty years the telegraphs of the world have grown to nearly half a million miles of line, and more than a million miles of wire.

fig. **1864** LOWELL *Fireside Trav.* 123 The magnetic telegraph of human sympathy flashes swift news from brain to brain.

†**3.** A message sent by telegraph; a telegram. *Obs.*

1821 G. GLEIG *Campaigns Brit. Army at Washington & New Orleans 1814–15* vii. 89 We had not proceeded many miles from the river's mouth, when a telegraph from the admiral gave orders for the troops to be in readiness to land. **1850** D. WEBSTER *Lett.* (1902) 392, I received your Telegraph last eve. **1857** LADY CANNING *Let. fr. Calcutta* 12 May in Hare *Two Noble Lives* (1893) II. 161 A telegraph had come telling of a violent outbreak of the 3rd cavalry at Meerut. *a* **1861** CLOUGH *Poems* (1869) II. 423 He..found a telegraph that bade him come Straight to the country. **1862** MISS YONGE *Stokesley Secret* x. 149 Suppose a telegraph should come!

4. In *Cricket*, A board upon which the numbers of runs obtained and wickets taken are exhibited during a match in large figures so as to be visible at a distance; a scoring-board. Also a similar device used in other athletic sports (see *telegraph-board*, quot. 1868, in 8).

1849 *Sussex Agricultural Express* 8 Sept. 6/4 At the close of the first innings the telegraph showed to the people a score of 61 runs. **1859** *All Year Round* No. 13. 305 There was a proper telegraph to show the 'runs got' and the 'wickets down'.

5. *slang.* **a.** A scout or spy.

1825 C. M. WESTMACOTT *Eng. Spy* I. 162 Dick's a trump and no telegraph. **1888** 'R. BOLDREWOOD' *Robbery under Arms* xxiii, Warrigal [was sent out] to meet one of our telegraphs..and to bring us any information he could pick up. **1890** —— *Miner's Right* xviii, These 'bush telegraphs', as the modern robber slang has dubbed them, are of all avocations and both sexes.

b. *spec.* One who warns bush-rangers about the movements of police and pursuing troopers. *Austral.*

1864 *Goulburn* (N.S.W.) *Herald* 17 Aug. 2/3 These young scoundrels have got their 'telegraphs' in town, and there is not a stir the police can make but it is known. **1867** *Ibid.* 12 Oct. 4/5 It would make me look a gamer man to the police and other people as has got a down on me for being a telegraph to you chaps. **1908** C. WHITE *John Vane, Bushranger* xv. 76 One of our 'telegraphs' rode up and told us that a party of three police had just gone along the road towards Carcoar.

†**6.** A fancy name for some kind of carriage. *Obs.*

1810 S. GREEN *Reformist* II. 130 The whimsical vehicle which conveys the man of high *ton*, be it either dog-cart, telegraph, or *barouchette*.

7. Used as individual name of a newspaper, a variety of plant, etc.

1794 COLERIDGE *Lett.* I. 122, I will accept of the reporter's place to the 'Telegraph' and live upon a guinea a week. **1882** *Garden* 14 Jan. 31/1 A few seeds of Telegraph [cucumbers] may now be sown in small pots.

8. *attrib.* and *Comb.*, as ***telegraph boy***, ***cable*** (CABLE *sb.* 3), ***clerk***, ***dial***, ***house***, ***instrument***, ***line*** (LINE *sb.*[2] 1 e), ***message***, ***office***, ***service***, ***signal***, ***station***, ***wire***; **telegraph blank** *U.S.* = *telegraph form*; **telegraph-block**, *Naut.* a number of small brass sheaves in a long narrow shell, with which several flags may be hoisted at the same time: used in making signals; **telegraph-board** = sense 4; **telegraph-carriage** (see quot.); **telegraph-clock**, a clock connected with another in a different room or building by means of a telegraph-wire conveying an electric current, so that the movements of the one are controlled by those of the other, and thus both indicate the same time; **telegraph coach** = *telegraph-carriage*; **telegraph-cock**, 'a compression-cock operated by a pivoted lever like the key of a telegraphic transmitter' (*Funk's Stand. Dict.*); **telegraph code** (see quot. 1971); **telegraph editor** *U.S.*, on the staff of a newspaper, one who edits news received by telegraph; **telegraph form**, a paper printed with spaces in which the words of a telegram are to be written for dispatch (FORM 12 b); **telegraph-key**, a small lever or other device in a telegraphic transmitter, worked by the hand, for making and breaking the circuit (KEY *sb.*[1] 12 a); **telegraph-plant**, an East Indian leguminous plant, *Desmodium gyrans*, remarkable for the spontaneous movements of its leaflets, suggesting signalling; also called *moving plant*; **telegraph pole, -post**, one of a series of poles upon which a telegraph wire or wires are carried above the ground; **telegraph-reel**, a reel on which is wound the strip of paper on which the messages are traced in a recording telegraph; **telegraph-register**, a telegraphic receiver, or part of one, which gives a permanent record of the messages received.

1893 S. MERRILL in M. Philips *Making of Newspaper* 99 He struck out the formal matter in the heading of the *telegraph blank. **1904** [see BLANK *sb.* 6]. **1928** F. N. HART *Bellamy Trial* i. 3 [He] had..a good-sized stack of telegraph blanks clasped to his heart. **1868** H. F. WILKINSON *Mod. Athletics* 17 *Telegraph Board... Before each race or heat, the numbers of the starters..should be posted on the board. **1897** 'TIVOLI' (H. W. Bleakley) *Short Innings* iii. 48 The hundred appeared on the telegraph board. Still the batsmen hit. **1860** *Illustr. Lond. News* 25 Feb. 187/1 The servant girl, and even the *telegraph boy stand staring. **1855** *Lardner's Museum Sci. & Art* III. IV. Index, *Telegraph-cables, durability of. **1877** KNIGHT *Dict. Mech.* 2507/1 The essential features of a submarine telegraph-cable are a wire or wires for conducting and a protecting compound. *Ibid.*, **Telegraph-carriage*, a vehicle provided with the apparatus necessary for opening temporary communication with a permanent line..used..where no line of telegraph is immediately at hand. **1858** SIMMONDS *Dict. Trade*, **Telegraph-clerk*, a subordinate officer in a telegraph-office. **1879** *Daily News* 1 Aug. (Ho. Comm.), Lord J. Manners.. stated that..the name of telegraph clerks had been changed to that of telegraphists. **1877** KNIGHT *Dict. Mech.*, *Telegraph-clock. **1812** A. CONSTABLE *Let.* 22 Nov. in J. Constable *Corr.* (1962) I. 85 To Mr. Farrington by last night's *Telegraph Coach, a brace of pheasants were forwarded. **1835** *N.Y. Commercial Advertiser* 23 July 4/2 Two Telegraph Coaches will leave Albany every day at half-past 10, A.M...and arrive at Rochester in 44 hours. **1885** *List of Subscribers, Classified* (United Telephone Co.) (ed. 6) 231 Universal Translations Institute,..Specialities:.. patent specifications, *telegraph codes. **1971** *Gloss. Electrotechnical, Power Terms* (*B.S.I.*) III. iii. 12 *Telegraph code*, a system of rules and conventions according to which the telegraph signals forming a message, or the data signal forming a block, should be formed, transmitted, received and processed. **1877** KNIGHT *Dict. Mech.*, *Telegraph-dial. **1875** C. F. WINGATE *Views & Interviews* 195 Have been continuously employed on the *Missouri Republican* [as] *telegraph editor. **1923** G. C. BASTIAN *Editing Day's News* 9 Inside the News Room..[we find the] Managing Editor.. City Editor..Telegraph Editor [etc.]. **1981** *N.Y. Times* 15 June A20/3 The telegraph editors of our [*sc.* the Associated Press's] member papers take our word for it and put it in print. **1895** *Telegraph form [see FORM *sb.* 12 b]. **1808** LD. DUNDONALD *Let.* 28 Sept. in *Autobiogr. Seaman* (1860) I. 288 The newly constructed semaphoric telegraphs..have been blown up and completely demolished, together with their *telegraph houses. **1823** in Cobbett *Rur. Rides* (1885) I. 268 For what reason this pretty name [Semaphore] is given to a sort of Telegraph house..I must leave the reader to guess. **1923** KIPLING *Land & Sea Tales* 239 My father is at the telegraph-house sending telegrams. **1877** KNIGHT *Dict. Mech.*, *Telegraph-instrument. **1897** FLANDRAU *Harvard Episodes* 111 [It] sounded like the clicking of a telegraph instrument. **1877** KNIGHT *Dict. Mech.*, *Telegraph-key. **1847** *Michigan Gen. Statutes* (1882) I. 944 The owner of any land through which said *telegraph line may pass..having first given consent. **1858** SIMMONDS *Dict. Trade*, Telegraph-line. **1860** TROLLOPE *Framley P.* xxxii, A *telegraph message makes such a fuss in the country, frightening people's wives. **1886** C. E. PASCOE *London of To-day* xxvi. (ed. 3) 242 Post-offices and railway stations opened for the receipt and dispatch of telegraph messages. **1858** J. B. NORTON *Topics* 69 On the night of the 24th, the *telegraph-office was burnt down. **1884** MILLER *Plant-n.*, *Telegraph-plant, *Desmodium gyrans*. **1851** THOREAU *Jrnl.* 12 Sept. in *Writings* (1906) VIII. 497, I instantly sat down on a stone at the foot of the *telegraph-pole, and attended to the communication. **1869** *Daily News* 20 Dec., She is now 83 years old, and erect as a telegraph pole. **1884** J. TAIT *Mind in Matter* (1892) 71 As callous as a telegraph pole. **1851** THOREAU *Jrnl.* 30 Sept. in *Writings* (1906) IX. 37 Methinks these *telegraph-posts should bear a great price with musical instrument makers. **1858** SIMMONDS *Dict. Trade*, Telegraph-post. **1877** KNIGHT *Dict. Mech.*, *Telegraph-reel. *Ibid.*, *Telegraph-register. **1817** *Salisbury & Winchester Jrnl.* 29 Sept., The church of Fromelles..was reduced to ashes by lightning... An individual..in the belfry, on the *telegraph service, perished in the flames. **1821** G. GLEIG *Campaigns Brit. Army at Washington & New Orleans 1814–15* xv. 206 The minds of all were set at ease, as to the place whither we were going, a *telegraph signal being made to steer for Jamaica. **1830** M. EDGEWORTH *Let.* 18 Oct. (1971) 419 They use Telegraph signals— flags white —red—and blue—for *all right—moderate speed—stop.* **1971** *Gloss. Electrotechnical, Power Terms* (*B.S.I.*) III. iii. 12 *Telegraph signal*,..the set of conventional elements established by the code to enable the transmission of a written character [etc.]. **1839** *Knickerbocker* XIV. 187 A recent excursion..from New-Brighton to the *telegraph station. **1973** P. BERTON *Drifting Home* vii. 101 We had stopped at one or more of these solitary telegraph stations whose operators were always fanatically overjoyed to see us. **1848** *Knickerbocker* XXXI. 455 The wrecks of hundreds of little urchins' high-soaring 'hopes'..[hang] on all the *telegraph-wires. **1869** *Bradshaw's Railway Man.* XXI. App. 114 Telegraph Wire, Plain or Galvanised, of any length. **1875** URE *Dict. Arts*, etc. II. 242 Telegraph wires are suspended to poles by insulators of earthenware, glass, or porcelain.

'telegraph, *v.* [f. prec. sb.; cf. F. *télégraphier*.]

1. a. *intr.* To signal or communicate by telegraph; to send a telegram.

1815 J. CAMPBELL *Trav. S. Afr.* xlii. 508 On the succeeding morning..the Carmarthen Indiaman, after hailing us, and finding we had no news, telegraphed, as follows: 'Peace with France!! Buonaparte dethroned!!!' **1831** TRELAWNY *Adv. Younger Son* I. 253 We saw the frigate hoist the recal signal.., and telegraph to her companion. **1858** DICKENS *Lett.* (1880) II. 79 We have telegraphed to know. **1870** MISS BRIDGMAN *Rob. Lynne* II. ix. 181, I should like Charles telegraphed for.

b. *trans.* To send, transmit, or announce (a message, news, etc.) by telegraph (with *simple obj.* or *obj. cl.*). In *Cricket*, etc., to exhibit (the score, etc.) on the telegraph-board (see prec. 4).

1805 CAPT. CRUMBY in *19th Cent.* Nov. (1899) 720 Seeing the Admiral telegraph to Captain Blackwood..'I rely on your keeping sight of the enemy through the night'. **1832** MARRYAT *N. Forster* xli, The reconnoitring ships telegraphing 'a French squadron'. **1842** DICKENS *Amer. Notes* ii. (1850) 15/2 Soon afterwards the Britannia steam-packet, from Liverpool, eighteen days out, was telegraphed at Boston. **1862** F. LILLYWHITE *Guide to Cricketers* 37 A model of a newly-built covered stand on rollers, with figures for telegraphing on each side. **1895** *Westm. Gaz.* 9 May 5/3 The play was again spirited, and in less than ten minutes 200 was telegraphed.

fig. **1885** RANNEY in *Harper's Mag.* Mar. 636/2 The eye.. telegraphs the outline..to the cells in the cortex.

c. To send a message to (a person, etc.) by telegraph; to summon by a telegram.

1810 CAPT. MAURICE in *Naval Chron.* XXV. 218 The.. gun-brig was telegraphed to send a boat. **1828** *Sporting Mag.* XXII. 130 The pointers were telegraphed, and so were his attending boys. **1891** F. W. ROBINSON *Her Love & His Life* VII. v, Felix has been telegraphed to town.

2. *fig.* **a.** *intr.* To make signs, signal (*to* a person). **b.** *trans.* To make (a signal); to convey or announce by signs. **c.** To signal to (a person). Now *rare.*

1818 'T. BROWN' *Brighton* I. 230 They nod and telegraph to their favourites. **1825** [see *telegraphing* below]. **1825** C. M. WESTMACOTT *Eng. Spy* I. 167 Never telegraph'd the big wigs. **1842** S. LOVER *Handy Andy* viii, Tom Durfy..began telegraphing Biddy, who..had shoved herself well before the door. **1844** ALB. SMITH *Adv. Mr. Ledbury* xiii, Emma telegraphed a nod of assent. **1848** THACKERAY *Bk. Snobs* l, They telegraphed each other with wondering eyes. **1888** BURGON *Lives 12 Gd. Men* II. v. 63 He telegraphed to me (I was in the area) to come up to him.

†**3.** *trans.* To send (*esp.* information about police movements) by bush telegraph. *Austral. colloq. Obs.*

1863 *Mudgee* (N.S.W.) *Liberal* 15 Oct. 2/4 The police might have scouts if they would; scouts which would be a match for any system of telegraphing among the bush-rangers. **1878** *Australasian Sketcher* 23 Nov. 135/2 The object of the expedition leaked out, and, no doubt, was rapidly telegraphed across the bush to Edward Kelly. **1880** *Victorian Rev.* I. 428 News of the movements of the troopers were 'telegraphed' to them by their confederates.

4. a. In Boxing and other sports: to initiate (a punch, throw, etc.) in such an obvious way as to reveal one's intention. Also in fig. contexts.

1925 J. J. CORBETT *Roar of Crowd* v. 77 Before I would start my right I would, as they say in boxing, 'telegraph' the blow, purposely. **1937** *Daily Mirror* 16 Mar. 30/4 Ford was also landing with some heavy left hooks to the body and although he had never telegraphed his right hand punches.. he was now finding Farr's face with such regularity [etc.]. **1945** E. NICHOLS *Hunky Johnny* 68 He telegraphs every curve he throws. **1959** *Charlottesville* (Va.) *Daily Progress* 18 Apr. 10/1 (*caption*), I thought you said he telegraphed his punches! All I saw he delivered personally. **1969** *Wall St. Jrnl.* 1 Dec. 14/1 For competitive reasons, the company won't disclose the nature of the new products now, Mr. Arneson said. 'We're not about to telegraph our punches.'

b. *gen.* To give a clumsily obvious hint or premature indication of (something to come).

1952 *N.Y. Times* 13 Aug. (Late City ed.) 29/5 Inevitably the pay-off gag was 'telegraphed' to the audience far in advance. **1959** *Wall St. Jrnl.* (Eastern ed.) 3 Mar. 12/6 One subplot involving Claudell's mother figures in the story but this development is telegraphed early and does nothing to broaden the book. **1968** *Punch* 16 Oct. 558/3 The exasperating way music [in a film] sometimes not only over-emphasizes but even telegraphs effects. **1977** *Time* 7 Nov. 14/2 Young was accurately telegraphing the Administration's view.

Hence **ˈtelegraphed** (-grɑːft, -æ-) *ppl. a.*, **ˈtelegraphing** *vbl. sb.* and *ppl. a.*; also **ˌtelegraˈphee**, the person to whom a telegram is sent.

1825 T. Hook *Sayings* Ser. II. *Sutherl.* (Colburn) 15 Nor was this telegraphing wholly unnoticed by George. *a* **1837** Warren *Diary Late Physic.* (1838) III. 275 A kind of telegraphing courtship was carried on between them daily. **1875** Kinglake *Crimea* V. vi. 91 *note*, Telegraphed signals. **1894** H. Drummond *Ascent Man* 234 More perfect forms of human intercourse than telegraphed or telephoned words. **1895** *Westm. Gaz.* 4 Nov. 2/3 A decision of Lord Coleridge's that there was no property in a special telegram, though it may have cost the telegraphee a thousand pounds to procure.

†**ˌtelegraˈpheme.** [ad. Gr. type τηλεγράφημα, f. *τηλεγραφεῖν to telegraph. (Both used in mod.Gr.)] A word suggested instead of telegram *sb.*, as being more correctly formed; but never generally adopted.

1857 R. Shilleto in *Times* 15 Oct. 7/5 May I suggest to such as are not contented with 'Telegraphic Despatch' the rightly constructed word 'telegrapheme'? I do not want it, but..I protest against such a barbarism as 'telegram'. **1867** *Routledge's Ev. Boy's Ann.* Jan. 53 The word telegram superseded telegrapheme. **1873** [see telegram *sb.*]. **1896** *Westm. Gaz.* 22 Feb. 8/2 The public..absolutely revolted against telegrapheme, and insisted on telegram, though..the famous Cambridge scholar Shilleto always talked about 'sending a telegrapheme'—never a telegram.

telegrapher (ˈtɛlɪgrɑːfə(r), -æ-). [f. telegraph *sb.* or *v.* + -er¹.]

1. a. One who works a telegraph. (Now chiefly U.S.: the technical term being *telegraphist.*) In first two quots., one who signals by means of a semaphore or other mechanical means (telegraph *sb.* 1).

1795 Edgeworth in *Trans. R. Irish Acad.* (1797) VI. 95 Flushed with victory the young telegrapher forgot his signal. **1842** *Penny Cycl.* XXIV. 151/2 Standing..with both discs held down and turned edgewise to the observer, the telegrapher indicated 'attention'. **1851** C. Cist *Sk. Cincinnati in 1851* 51 Telegraphers, 7. *c* **1865** J. Wylde in *Circ. Sc.* I. 262/1 Another..source of annoyance to telegraphers. **1910** J. Hart *Vigilante Girl* 376 This was the room of the man who filled the manifold offices of station-master, ticket-agent, express-agent,..and telegrapher. **1932** E. Wilson *Devil take Hindmost* xvii. 177 The telegrapher..telephoned ahead along the line to have the niggers taken off. **1955** H. Kurnitz *Invasion of Privacy* (1956) xii. 79 He shared Zorn's hatred of the teletype but..he sometimes operated it himself when the telegrapher was off duty. **1974** T. P. Whitney tr. *Solzhenitsyn's Gulag Archipelago* I. I. vi. 268 His White Guard father was just a rank-and-file, unpropertied telegrapher.

b. ***telegrapher's cramp*** or ***palsy***: = telegraphist's cramp: see telegraphist b.

1890 Billings *Nat. Med. Dict.*, *Telegraphers' cramp*, neurosis analogous to writers' cramp, affecting muscles of forearm of telegraph-operators.

2. One who telegraphs a message or news; the sender of a telegram.

1865 *Morn. Star* 2 Feb., The telegraphers take the liberty to assert [etc.]. **1890** *Spectator* 19 Apr., If he had been flustered by the noisy memorialists and telegraphers who did their best to disturb his judgment. **1901** *Westm. Gaz.* 17 Dec. 2/3 He has not succeeded enough to induce the telegrapher to desert the wiring mode for the wireless.

telegraphese (ˌtɛlɪgrɑːˈfiːz, -æ-). *colloq.* or *humorous.* [f. telegraph *sb.* + -ese.]

1. The concise and elliptical style in which telegrams are worded. Also *attrib.* or as *adj.*

1885 *Pall Mall G.* 26 Sept. 2/2 We shall gradually give up English in favour of Telegraphese, and Electric Telegraphese is as short and spare as Daily Telegraphese is longwinded and redundant. **1905** *Athenæum* 7 Oct. 469/2 We rather relish the leisurely semicolons and sentences of the eighteenth century after..the 'telegraphese' of many a modern stylist. **1951** R. Hoggart *Auden* i. 18 Auden's 'telegraphese' style..is distinguished by its omission of articles, relatives, connectives, personal, demonstrative and other pronouns, and auxiliary verbs. **1978** *Radio Times* 18–24 Mar. 15/1 The actor's opinion hardened into the following telegraphese note: 'Willy beyond question toughest director I've ever worked for.'

2. An elaborate or inflated style, such as was attributed to leading articles in the (London) *Daily Telegraph* newspaper.

1885 [see 1]. **1889** *Universal Rev.* Oct. 215 The man who writes for the *Telegraph* must write Telegraphese. **1892** *Leisure Hour* May 455/2 The elaborate, rounded, allusive style which has gone down to fame as Telegraphese. **1895** *Westm. Gaz.* 9 Dec. 3/1 Sala was not only the patentee of *Telegraphese.* He was also the first, and in some ways the best.

telegraphic (tɛlɪˈgræfɪk), *a.* [f. as prec. + -ic. Cf. F. *télégraphique.*]

1. Of, pertaining to, of the nature of, or connected with a telegraph; made, sent, or transmitted by telegraph. **a.** In reference to the earlier 'telegraphs' or signalling devices. Now *rare.*

1794 [see telegraph *sb.* 1]. **1794** *Gentl. Mag.* LXIV. II. 815/2 The new-invented telegraphic language of signals. **1794** *European Mag.* Sept. 166 By a new Telegraphic Machine, invented by Citizen Chapelle the news..has been received..in one hour. **1805** Capt. Crumby in *19th Cent.* Nov. (1899) 722 Lord Nelson made the telegraphic signal, 'England expects that every man will do his duty'. **1808** J. Macdonald *Telegraphic Commun.* 36 Homer is the first who mentions the Telegraphic art. **1829** Marryat *F. Mildmay* vi, Looking for the telegraphic signal-box. **1842** Alison *Hist. Europe* (1850) XIII. lxxii. §85. 569 On the morning of the 3d March, a telegraphic despatch from the prefect of Toulon announced the landing of Napoleon.

b. In reference to the electric telegraph. Also ***telegraphic address***, a brief style of address registered with the postal authorities and designed to reduce the number of words in a telegram.

[**1823** Ronalds *Descr. Electr. Tel.* 8 By the use of a telegraphic dictionary a word, or even a whole sentence could be conveyed by..three discharges.] **1839** *Ann. Electricity, Magnetism & Chemistry* III. 442 The telegraph as constructed by Chappe has met with a favourable reception, and since 1793, when the first telegraphic line was established in France, been very generally adopted. **1840** [see telephonic]. **1841** *Encycl. Brit.* (ed. 7) XXI. 689/2 Wheatstone's Electro-magnetic Telegraph..We are convinced..will not be confined to long telegraphic lines, but will also be extensively employed in public and private establishments. **1854** B'ness Bunsen in Hare *Life* (1879) II. iv. 168 We received yesterday the telegraphic announcement [etc.]. **1854** Gilfillan *Life R. Blair* B.'s Wks. 128 As if on telegraphic wires. **1857** Lady Canning in Hare *Two Noble Lives* (1893) II. 199 The wording of telegraphic messages requires the utmost care. **1877** W. Thomson *Voy. Challenger* I. i. 1 The wonderful project of establishing a telegraphic communication between the old world and the new. **1885** *List of Subscribers, Classified* (United Telephone Co.) (ed. 6) 4 Fraser & Fraser,.. Manufacturers of..Steam Boilers. *Telegraphic address,* 'Pressure, London.' **1910** *Nation* 9 Apr. 54/1 The necessity of being on the right side is self-evident; therefore, when in doubt, write or wire to Mr. Shaw. (Telegraphic address: 'Infallibility', London.) **1930** 'Hay' & Wodehouse *Baa, Baa, Black Sheep* I. i. 12 We'll go to the Grotto!..What-ho for the Grott-ho! Telegraphic address—Tighter London! **1963** *B.S.I. News* May 7/2 BSI's telegraphic addresses have been changed. Overseas cables should now be addressed to 'Standards London W 1' and inland telegrams should be addressed to 'Standards Audley London'.

2. *fig.* †**a.** Large and conspicuous, like the letters exhibited by some early forms of telegraph. *Obs.* **b.** Making signals (as by glance or gesture); conveyed by a sign or signal: cf. telegraph *v.* 2. ? *Obs.* **c.** Resembling an (electric) telegraph; conveying impulses or intelligence as by electricity. **d.** Abbreviated or concise like a telegram. *spec.* In *Linguistics*, in the context of language acquisition.

1809 Simeon *Let.* in Carus *Life* xi. (1847) 276 His attacks on me were frequent, with my name in telegraphic characters. **18..** T. Moore *Country Dance & Quad.* xxix, Watchful chaperons,..Who intercept all signal tones, And read all telegraphic faces. **1838** Buckstone *Shocking Events* (French's ed.) 9 Sir..I cannot allow any telegraphic dispatches with my female domestic—no winking here. **1871** Tyndall *Fragm. Sci.* (1879) I. iii. 95 Who..put the soul into this telegraphic body? **1896** 'Curtis Yorke' *Those Children* vi, [His] words..were few, and his speech as telegraphic as though each word were paid for. **1963** Brown & Fraser in C. N. Cofer *Verbal Behavior & Learning* 192 Young children speak a rather uniform telegraphic English. **1970** D. McNeill *Acquisition of Lang.* iii. 20 Telegraphic speech is the outcome of the process of language acquisition. **1973** R. Brown *First Lang.* I. 143 Telegraphic speech is speech entirely composed of contentive words..and entirely lacking functors or function words. **1978** *Sci. Amer.* Nov. 92/2 Early telegraphic speech is characterized by short, simple sentences made up primarily of content words: words that are rich in semantic content, usually nouns and verbs.

Hence **teleˈgraphical** *a.* (*rare*), telegraphic; **teleˈgraphically** *adv.* [see -ically], by means of a telegraph, by telegraph or telegram; in relation to a telegraph.

1808 J. Macdonald *Telegraphic Commun.* Pref. 34 Whenever a word is to be spelt, Telegraphically. **1846** Worcester, Telegraphic, Telegraphical. **1847** De Quincey in *Tait's Mag.* XIV. 668 Brought down telegraphically from some altitude inaccessible to himself. **1883** *Standard* 14 Feb. 5/4 He was summoned telegraphically. **1905** *Daily News* 17 Mar. 7 Queenstown is cut off telegraphically, all the poles having been blown down.

telegraphist (tɪ-, tɛˈlɛgrəfɪst, ˈtɛlɪgrɑːfɪst, -æ-). [f. as prec. + -ist. Cf. F. *télégraphiste.*] **a.** A person employed, or skilled, in working a telegraph; a telegraph-operator.

1847 *Brit. Patent 11,926* 10 Signals are..quickly received by the mind of the telegraphist. **1854** *Lardner's Museum Sci. & Art* IV. 60 Different telegraphists have very different powers as to celerity. *c* **1865** J. Wylde in *Circ. Sc.* I. 261/1 No one suddenly became an expert telegraphist. **1876** Preece & Sivewright *Telegraphy* 113 The amount of work ..will not justify the employment of a trained telegraphist. **1879** [see telegraph *clerk*]. **1908** *Daily Chron.* 3 June 1/4 A wireless telegraphist had a terrifying experience during a terrific thunderstorm.., where the wireless station was struck by lightning.

b. ***telegraphist's cramp***: a paralytic affection of the muscles of the fore-arm, to which telegraph-operators are liable: cf. cramp *sb.*¹

1899 *Allbutt's Syst. Med.* VI. 539 The so-called 'Professional hyperkineses' (writer's cramp, histrionic spasm, pianist's cramp, telegraphist's cramp, &c.) admit of a similar explanation. **1908** *Daily Chron.* 26 Nov. 6/2 The supplementary report..recommended that telegraphists' cramp should be added to the compensation list.

telegraphone (tɪ-, tɛˈlɛgrəfəʊn). [Short for *telegraphophone*, f. tele- + graphophone, after *telephone.*] A form of telephone in which the spoken message is recorded at the receiving end magnetically on an iron ribbon, so as to be capable of reproduction; invented by Poulsen of Copenhagen about 1900. (See also telephonograph.)

[**1890**: see below.] **1900** *Engineering Mag.* XIX. 757/1 The telegraphon, or magneto-telephonograph, an invention of the Danish engineer, Valdemar Poulsen, makes use of the fact of permanent magnetism to record..sounds..so that they can be reproduced whenever..desired. **1902** *Harper's Mag.* Feb. 496 This apparatus..has been variously designated as the 'telegraphone', the 'microphonograph', and the 'magnetophonograph' in Europe.

So **telegraphophone** (tɛlɪˈgræfəʊfəʊn): see quot.

[**1890** *Voice* (N.Y.) 13 Feb., A new instrument called the telegraphone.] **1891** *Cent. Dict.*, *Telegraphophone*, an apparatus for reproducing at a distance the sounds which produced a graphophonic record; also, an apparatus for producing a graphophonic record at a distance by means of a telephonic circuit.

telegraphy (tɪ-, tɛˈlɛgrəfɪ, ˈtɛlɪgrɑːfɪ, -æ-). [f. tele- + -graphy. Cf. Ger. *telegraphie* (Böckmann 1794), F. *télégraphie* (Mozin *Dict. franç.-allem.* 1812).] The art or science of constructing or using telegraphs; the working of a telegraph or telegraphs.

wireless telegraphy: see wireless.

1795 Edgeworth in *Trans. R. Irish Acad.* (1797) VI. 96 Tamerlane's telegraphy was not very refined... Whenever he laid siege to any town he used to employ three signals —the first day he set up a white flag [etc.]. *Ibid.* 111 The advantages which by means of Telegraphy would result to commerce must..be extensive. **1847** in Webster. **1858** *Times* 28 Aug. 10/6 The cause of telegraphy has too many demands upon the labours of..these practised cable layers, to permit them to be idle here. **1861** W. Fairbairn *Addr. to Brit. Assoc.*, In land telegraphy the chief difficulties have been surmounted, but in submarine telegraphy much remains to be accomplished. **1878** Huxley *Physiogr.* 101 In these days of electric telegraphy every one is familiar with the..galvanic or voltaic battery. **1901** *Westm. Gaz.* 7 Oct. 10/1 It was on July 25, 1837, that the first practical trial of telegraphy was made between Euston and Camden, on the London and North-Western Railway, by Cooke and Wheatstone.

fig. **1864** *Daily Tel.* 26 May, That kind of social telegraphy which seems to convey intelligence with a mystery and rapidity quite as wonderful as the electric wire. **1891** 'Mark Twain' in *Harper's Mag.* Christm. No., (*title*) Mental Telegraphy.

Telegu, var. Telugu, Teloogoo.

teleguide (ˈtɛlɪgaɪd), *v.* [f. F. *teleguider* (1947), Quemada (1980): see tele-, guide *v.*] *trans.* To control (a missile, etc.) at a distance or indirectly. So **ˈteleguided** *ppl. a.*, **ˈteleguiding** *vbl. sb.* Also ***teleˈguidance*** [F. *téléguidage*].

[**1954** *John o' London's Weekly* 12 Feb. 154/3 The French have shortened 'long distance radio control' to 'teleguidance'.] **1960** *Export Service Bull., Suppl.* 4 June 41 The Bell Aircraft Corporation announced that it had signed an agreement..for the production..of the two teleguided target missiles..produced by the French company. **1964** N. Freeling *Double-Barrel* IV. v. 128 'And the aeroplane?' 'Oh that. I built it. We've used it for various experiments; teleguiding and so on.' *Ibid.* 129 If these toys were that simple everyone could have teleguided missiles. **1969** *Africa Digest* June 51/2 An attempt at subversion teleguided from abroad. **1972** *Daily Tel.* 6 May 5/1 Among the new weapons is a teleguided anti-tank rocket fired from a helicopter, which has never previously been used in combat. **1977** *Dædalus* Fall 150 Jacquart does not celebrate the triumph of small familial agriculture, but rather its defeat by the offensive of the 'large enterprises' teleguided by the urban nobility and the Parisian *notables* of the classical age. **1977** N. Freeling *Gadget* v. 218 He's been thinking all day about teleguidance systems.

telehydrobarometer, -iconograph: see tele-.

teleianthous (tɛlaɪˈænθəs), *a.* *Bot. rare*⁻⁰. [f. Gr. τέλειος perfect + ἄνθος flower + -ous.]

1860 Mayne *Expos. Lex.*, *Teleianthus*,..applied by Wachsendorff to plants provided with stamens and pistils: teleianthous.

‖**teleiosis** (tɛlaɪˈəʊsɪs). *rare*⁻¹. [a. Gr. τελείωσις, f. τελειοῦν to perfect, to complete.] Perfection, completion, consummation. So †**teleiˈotical** *a.* *Obs. rare*⁻¹, making perfect, perfective.

1601 Bp. W. Barlow *Defence* 92 The teleioticall or finall cause eternall life. **1898** Gladstone in *Times* 5 Jan., Truth and beauty, truth the first, and beauty the handmaid or teleiosis of truth, are the divinely appointed sustenance of the human soul.

telekinesis to **tele-lens**: see tele-.

telelograph: see tellograph.

ˈtelelogue (-lɒg). [f. tele- + Gr. λόγος word.] A message transmitted by telephone, a telephonic message; = telepheme.

1881 I. W. Batten in *Times* 10 Nov. 8/3 The United Telephone Co...would..supply London with a penny Telelogue in..addition to the..sixpenny Telegram. **1884** *Pall Mall G.* 25 Apr. 5/2 They resolutely refuse to allow the United Telephone Company to give the public a penny telelogue. **1898** (*Heading of a book of forms for Mercantile use*) Confirmation of Telelogue.

teleman, obs. Sc. form of TILLMAN.

telemanometer, etc.: see TELE-.

telemark, Telemark (ˈtɛlmɑːk). *Skiing*. [f. *Telemark*, the name of an administrative district in southern Norway, where this originated.] A swing turn, now little used, with the leading ski considerably advanced and the knee bent, employed to change direction or stop short. Freq. *attrib.* Also as *v. intr.*

1904 E. C. RICHARDSON *Ski-Running* 59 The telemark swing..should be practised constantly. **1905** *Ibid.* (ed. 2) 78 We propose to deal with the 'Telemark' first. **1920** A. LUNN *Cross-Country Ski-ing* 88 In powder snow one can Telemark in various undefined ways. **1934** WEBSTER, Telemark turn. **1979** R. FIENNES *Hell on Ice* i. 13 Bending low, I began a curving telemark, leading with the left knee. **1981** *Nordic Skiing* Jan. 49/3 It specializes in teaching downhill technique and telemark turns on some of the finest powder in the Sierra Nevada.

telematics (tɛlɪˈmætɪks), *sb. pl.* [f. TELE(COMMUNICATION + INFOR)MATICS; cf. F. *télématique* adj.] (The science of) the long-distance transmission of computerized information. So **teleˈmatic** *a.*, of or pertaining to telematics.

1979 *Economist* 13 Oct. 52/3 The EEC commission is to launch a programme to help European telematics, the new vogue word for the high-growth industries of telecommunications, computers, microchips and databanks. *Ibid.*, Studies to set up a telematic network for the community institutions. **1981** *Jrnl. R. Soc. Arts* CXXIX. 401/2 This story illustrates the importance of possessing advanced telematic equipment. **1982** *Times* 1 Sept. 3/3 Advances in telematics will be far more significant than aircraft design over the next two decades.

telemessage: see TELE- 1.

telemeter (tɪ-, tɛˈlɛmɪtə(r), ˈtɛlɪˌmiːtə(r)), *sb.* Also telometer. [f. TELE-, TELO-² + -METER. Cf. F. *télémètre*, 1852 in *Cosmos* II. 222.]

1. An instrument for ascertaining the distances of objects: applied to instruments of various kinds used in surveying, and in military operations.

acoustic telemeter, one in which the distance is ascertained by observing the time occupied by sound in traversing it.

1860 G. RICHARDSON *Patent Specif.* No. 2102 This improved instrument (which in commerce I intend to call a telometer). **1869** *Pall Mall G.* 31 Aug. 4 Of two batteries coming into action, the one with and the other without a telemeter, a difference of about a minute in opening fire would make the difference between accurate shooting and shooting by guesswork. **1888** A. W. WHITE in *Encycl. Brit.* XXIII. 126/1 Telemeter, or Rangefinder... Telemeters have been made on three distinct principles, and classified as acoustic, optical, and trigonometrical respectively. *Ibid.* 126/2 The Nolan range finder..was the first telemeter used by the British artillery. **1900** H. M. WILSON *Topogr. Surv.* xiii. 274 The gradienter is used as a telemeter in measuring horizontal distances in two ways.

attrib. **1900** H. M. WILSON *Topogr. Surv.* 236 The stadia, telemeter, or subtend system [of measuring distances].

2. An apparatus for recording the readings of any physical instrument at a distance by means of an electric current; a general term including the *teleanemograph, telebarometer, telethermometer*, etc. (see TELE-). In mod. use, an instrument for measuring a quantity at a distance from the place where the result is displayed or recorded.

1891 in *Cent. Dict.* **1929** *Jrnl. Amer. Inst. Electr. Engineers* XLVIII. 183/1 In addition to surveying the field of application of 'telemetering'..the paper presents several innovations in the types of 'telemeters' available. **1941** T. J. RHODES *Industr. Instruments for Measurem. & Control* viii. 363 One advantage of this telemeter is that the measuring device requires very little power to move the condenser plate. **1947** *Sun* (Baltimore) 10 Nov. 9/2 Electronic gadgets called 'telemeters'..are installed in high-speed missiles and tuned to send back to the ground by radio whatever information the scientists need. **1975** D. G. FINK *Electronics Engineers' Handbk.* XXVI. 43 The passive implant telemeter may contain a resonant circuit in which the resonant frequency, made to vary with the body signal, can be detected with a grid dip meter.

3. (Usu. with capital initial.) A proprietary term for a system of pay-TV involving the use of a coin-box attached to the television set. *U.S.*

1953 *Wall St. Jrnl.* 27 Nov. 18/4 Another pay-as-you-look television set-up makes its debut here... It [*sc.* the International Telemeter Corp.] has installed 'Telemeters' in 78 local homes. **1955** *Amer. Speech* XXX. 232 For *Telemeter*, the subscriber pays for each program by dropping coins into a box which is attached to the receiver. **1961** *Spectator* 24 Mar. 394/3, 580c telemeter sets were installed [in Canada]. **1961** *Official Gaz.* (U.S. Patent Office) 17 Oct TM87/1 Telemeter. For pay-television systems including a television transmitter.., equipment at a receiver for processing subscription-television signals, and computer equipment for processing records made at each subscription-television subscriber receiver. First use during June 1951.

Hence **telemetric** (tɛlɪˈmɛtrɪk), **teleˈmetrical** *adjs.*, pertaining to, connected with, or serving as a telemeter; **teleˈmetrically** *adv.*, by means of telemetry; also **teleˈmetrograph**, an instrument for measuring and drawing plans of distant objects or areas (*Sci. Amer.* Supp., 1 Aug. 1885, 7975).

1877 KNIGHT *Dict. Mech.* 2513 Another form of telemetric marine-glass... The telemetrical telescope of Captain Gautier. **1900** H. M. WILSON *Topogr. Surv.* xiii. 282 The range-finder furnishes a..rough telemetric method of obtaining a fairly accurate measure of inaccessible distances. **1957** *Times* 11 Nov. 10/5 The radio transmitters ..and the telemetric apparatus on board have..ceased work. **1961** WEBSTER, Telemetrically. **1970** *Sci. Jrnl.* Aug. 7/1 A cosmonaut in the command module working the Vulcan welding equipment telemetrically by cable. **1971** *Nature* 2 July 65/2 The use of telemetric recording of physiological information from free swimming fish in their natural environment. **1974** W. GARNER *Big Enough Wreath* viii. 98 It's definitely a satellite. Multitone telemetric signals. **1977** *Offshore Engineer* May 75/2 Telemetrically operated valves are controlled by two systems in the experiment.

telemeter (ˈtɛlɪmiːtə(r), tɪˈlɛmɪtə(r)), *v.* [f. the sb.] *trans.* To measure (a quantity) and transmit the result to a distant point; to transmit (a measurement or observation). Freq. with *back*.

1929 *Jrnl. Amer. Inst. Electr. Engineers* XLVIII. 185/2 A carrier wave of constant frequency modulated by an audio frequency which varies with the magnitude of the quantity being telemetered. **1941** T. J. RHODES *Industr. Instruments for Measurem. & Control* viii. 356 The pressure or liquid-level indication is telemetered to the operating floor. **1953** A. C. CLARKE *Prelude to Space* xii. 64 'Alpha's' main instrument readings are telemetered back to Earth. **1965** W. L. DONN *Meteorology* i. 4 The radiosonde..telemeters the most complete information on the vertical distribution of temperature, pressure and humidity to radio receivers in the laboratory. **1969** *Times* 2 May 16/4 Spacecraft designed to telemeter photographs of the moon's surface back to the earth. **1971** G. G. LUCE *Body Time* v. 155 His heart rate was telemetered by a small radio capsule in his undershirt.

Hence **ˈtelemetered** *ppl. a.*, **ˈtelemetering** *vbl. sb.* and *ppl. a.*

1929 [see TELEMETER *sb.* 2]. **1929** *Jrnl. Amer. Inst. Electr. Engineers* XLVIII. 183/1 In the design of a telemetering equipment it is necessary to study the channel limitations. **1953** *Proc. Inst. Electr. Engineers* C. I. 44/2 The rate of change of a telemetered value can be obtained by means of a feedback amplifier. **1955** *Sci. News Let.* 21 May 324/3 Other methods currently used to track missiles are telemetering, in which the missile radios instrument readings to the ground, and radar. **1960** *Brit. Communications & Electronics* VII. 598/1 Telemetering from the digestive tract. **1976** *Offshore Platforms & Pipelining* 211/1 The operator has a complete telemetering system plus sonar and television. **1978** *Broadcast* 5 June 21/2 All the telemetered information is available on..wall mounted key and lamp panels.

telemetry (tɪ-, tɛˈlɛmɪtrɪ). [f. TELE- + -METRY.]

1. a. The process or practice of obtaining measurements in one place and relaying them for recording or display to a point at a distance; the transmission of measurements by the apparatus making them.

1885 *Electrician* 9 May 525/1 Telemetry has been practically applied in America..the temperature registrations being exceedingly accurate. **1957** *Economist* 12 Oct. 149 (Advt.), Mullard products are used in almost every electronic application—from radar to radio, from telemetry to television. **1967** *Technology Week* 20 Feb. 10/3 Orbital telemetry indicated that the capsule battery should have sufficient charge to operate the radio beacon and flashing light that serve as recovery aids. **1979** *Sunday Mail* (Brisbane) 7 Jan. 46/5 Occasionally pilots do become disorientated and so a system called air-to-ground telemetry was introduced... Data about the spinning aircraft is transmitted to the ground where another pilot can monitor information and advise the pilot flying how to recover.

b. Apparatus used for telemetry (sense a above).

1958 *Engineering* 28 Feb. 263/3 Instrumentation and telemetry in the satellite are designed to gather and transmit four types of information. **1962** S. CARPENTER in *Into Orbit* 160 Everyone keeps one eye on the telemetry to see how the capsule responds.

c. Telemetered information.

1962 *Flight Internat.* LXXXII. 239/2 These receiving stations have been set up..for receiving telemetry from future topside-sounder satellites. **1979** F. POHL *Jem* i. 8 He had made himself one of the..top experts in reading the telemetry from a tachyon-transmitter probe. **1982** *Daily Tel.* 26 Oct. 28/5 An American spy..gave the Russians details of an NSA satellite system 'rhyolite', which monitored the telemetry of Soviet missile tests.

2. *attrib.*

1953 [see DOWN-RANGE, DOWNRANGE *adv.*]. **1958** *Times* 10 Oct. 12/7 Telemetry codes provided from the third Russian satellite are expected to permit an analysis of tape recordings made of the sputnik's transmitters. **1962** S. CARPENTER in *Into Orbit* 53 Each time the capsule performs an important function it automatically sends a telemetry report to this effect down to earth. **1976** *Offshore Platforms & Pipelining* 214/2 The latest cable has 65 cores plus telemetry circuits. **1978** R. V. JONES *Most Secret War* xxxviii. 347 Dr. Steinhoff, Head of the Telemetry Department..escaped in his air-raid shelter.

telemicroscope, etc.: see TELE-.

telencephalon (ˌtɛlɛnˈsɛfəlɒn). *Anat.* [f. TEL(E- + ENCEPHALON.] The anterior of the two vesicles into which the prosencephalon or fore-brain divides in the embryo, or the two antero-lateral vesicles that it gives rise to; the corresponding part of the adult brain, comprising the cerebral hemispheres and the anterior parts of the hypothalamus and the third ventricle.

1897 C. L. DANA *Text-bk. Nerv. Dis.* (ed. 4) i. 3 The anterior vesicle develops two secondary vesicles: the anterior portion of these, including the corpora striata, olfactory lobes, and the cerebral hemispheres, forms the telencephalon. **1934** [see PALLIUM 3 d]. **1946** B. M. PATTEN *Human Embryol.* v. 111 By the sixth week of development.. the prosencephalon has divided to form the telencephalon and diencephalon. **1948** A. BRODAL *Neurol. Anat.* x. 323 In fishes and amphibians the telencephalon is dominated by afferent fibres carrying olfactory impulses to its pallial part. **1977** *Lancet* 9 July 64/1 There was no injury to the mesencephalon in 3 cases, while the telencephalon escaped injury in 2 cases.

Hence **ˌtelenceˈphalic** *a.*, of or pertaining to the telencephalon.

1911 *Jrnl. Compar. Neurol.* XXI. 2 The exact limits of the thalamic and telencephalic gray are discussed later. **1974** D. & M. WEBSTER *Compar. Vertebr. Morphol.* xi. 268 It is not definitely established whether..some of the more superficial avian striatal structures, which are actually large telencephalic nuclei, are homologically related to mammalian cortical structures.

teleo-¹ (ˈtɛliːəʊ), before a vowel tele-, repr. Gr. τελεο- (τελειο-), combining form of τέλεος, τέλειος perfect, complete, f. τέλος end: employed in Eng. in some scientific terms. **teleobranchiate** (-ˈbræŋkɪət), *Zool.* [Gr. βράγχια gills], *a.* belonging to the division *Teleobranchia* of gastropod molluscs, having the respiratory organs specially developed; *sb.* a gastropod of this division. **teleocephalous** (-ˈsɛfələs) *a.*, *Ichth.* [Gr. κεφαλή head], belonging to the order *Teleocephali* of teleostean fishes, having the full number of bones in the skull; so **teleoˈcephal**, a teleocephalous fish. **teleodesmacean** (-dɛsˈmeɪʃ(ɪ)ən), *Zool.* [Gr. δεσμός band], *a.* belonging to the group *Teleodesmacea* (*Amer. Jrnl. Sc.* Dec. 1889) of bivalve molluscs, having a specially developed hinge to the shell; *sb.* a mollusc of this group. **ˈteleodont** (-əʊdɒnt) *a.*, *Entom.* [Gr. ὀδούς, ὀδοντ- tooth], applied to that form of the mandibles in stag-beetles in which the projections or 'teeth' are most highly developed. **ˈteleophyte** (-faɪt), *Biol.* [Gr. φύτον plant], a plant of perfect or complete organization; one of the higher plants. **teleoptile** (-ˈɒptɪl, -aɪl), *Ornith.* [Gr. πτίλον down-feather], one of the later or mature feathers of a bird: opp. to NEOSSOPTILE. **ˈteleosaur** (-sɔː(r)), *Palæont.* [Gr. σαῦρος lizard], a crocodile of the extinct genus *Teleosaurus* or family *Teleosauridæ*; so **teleoˈsaurian** *a.*, belonging to this genus or family; *sb.* = *teleosaur*. **teleoˈtemporal**, *Anat.* and *Zool.* [TEMPORAL *a.*²], *a.* and *sb.*, a name for the bone called POSTCLAVICLE. ‖**teleozoon** (-ˈzəʊən), *Biol.* (pl. **-zoa**) [Gr. ζῷον animal], an animal of perfect or complete organization; one of the higher animals; hence **teleozoic** (-ˈzəʊɪk) *a.*, pertaining to the teleozoa. See also TELEOSTEAN, etc.

1890 *Amer. Nat.* May 481 *Tæniosomi.* *Teleocephals with the scapular arch subnormal, posttemporal undivided and closely applied to the back of the cranium. **1883** LEUTHNER in *Trans. Zool. Soc. Lond.* (1885) XI. 400 The gap between the mesodont and *tel[e]odont forms long remained unbridged. **1899** D. SHARP in *Camb. Nat. Hist.* VI. 193 The largest developments being called teleodont, the smallest priodont. **1863** H. SPENCER *Biol.* (1864) I. II. i. §43. 109 A tree is an assemblage of numerous united shoots. One of these great *teleophytes is thus an aggregate of aggregates of aggregates of units, which severally resemble protophytes in their sizes and structures. **1893** GADOW in Newton *Dict. Birds* 243 The first clothing of the newly-hatched bird consists of..soft feathers..possessing..characters which make it advisable to distinguish them, by the name of 'Neossoptiles' (νεοσσός, a chick), from those feathers which subsequently appear, and may be called '*Teleoptiles' (τέλεος, mature). [**1839** G. ROBERTS *Dict. Geol.*, **Teleosaurus*, perfect or complete lizard; a new genus of fossil saurian or lizard, established by M. Geoffroy St. Hilaire.] **1841** OWEN in *Rep. Brit. Assoc.* X. 76 The atlas in the Teleosaur corresponds essentially with that of the Crocodiles. *Ibid.* 70 They are longer in proportion to their breadth than most of the *Teleosaurian scutes. **1896** H. WOODWARD *Guide Fossil Reptiles Brit. Mus.* 6 Long and slender-jawed Teleosaurs and Steneosaurs. **1869** HUXLEY in *Q. Jrnl. Geol. Soc.* XXVI. 47 The ilium of a Teleosaurian. **1865** H. SPENCER *Biol.* (1867) II. IV. iv. §169. 77 Among the *Protozoa*..and from the minute anatomy of all creatures above these, up to the **Teleozoa.*

teleo-², before a vowel tele-, combining form repr. Gr. τέλος end (stem τελε-: cf. TELEARCH), as in TELEOLOGY and its derivatives, q.v.: also in **teleˈocracy**, an organization designed to fulfil a specific purpose; hence **ˈteleocrat**, **teleoˈcratic** *a.*; ‖**teleoˈphobia** [mod.L.: see -PHOBIA], an aversion or unwillingness to admit the existence of design or final causes in nature; **teleorˈganic** *a.*, serving the purposes of an organism; necessary to organic life (*Cent. Dict.*, 1891). (See also TELO-¹.)

1973 L. L. & J. M. CONSTANTINE *Group Marriage* xiii. 141 In a teleocratic system, leadership depends on the task at hand; teleocratic means 'purpose-centered'. **1975** *Times Lit.*

Suppl. 12 Sept. 1018/4 Two notions, both derived from the Roman law, 'societas' and 'universitas'... The latter applies to teleocratic organizations which are supposed to produce specified outcomes. *Ibid.* 1018/5 The full character of the modern state is a condition of unresolved tension between 'societas' and 'universitas'. Teleocracy has always been one of its aspects... He has permitted the teleocrats to impose their self-image upon him. **1976** F. A. HAYEK *Law, Legislation & Liberty* II. vii. 15, I understand that Professor Michael Oakeshott, in his oral teaching, has long used the terms *teleocratic* (and *teleocracy*) and *nomocratic*.. to bring out the same distinction [*sc.* as between an organization and a spontaneous order].

teleologic (tɛliːəʊˈlɒdʒɪk), *a.* and *sb.* [f. TELEOLOGY + -IC.] **A.** *adj.* = next.

1842 DE QUINCEY in *Blackw. Mag.* LII. 730/2 The peculiar beauty of a kitchen-garden, or of a machine, which must be derived from their tendency to certain ends or uses, is called teleologic beauty. **1848** MILL *Pol. Econ.* III. i. §2 (1876) 264 Value in use, or as Mr. De Quincey calls it, teleologic value, is the extreme limit of value in exchange.

B. *sb.* The science of final causes; that branch of knowledge which deals with ends or purposes.

1865 S. H. HODGSON *Time & Space* II. ix. §68. 566 Technic and Teleologic are the two branches of practical knowledge, founded respectively on conation and feeling.

teleological (tɛliːəˈlɒdʒɪkəl), *a.* [f. as prec. + -ICAL.] Of, pertaining to, or involving teleology; relating to ends or final causes; dealing with design or purpose, esp. in natural phenomena. *teleological ethics* (see quot. 1967).

1798 A. F. M. WILLICH *Elem. Critical Philos.* II. 112 (*heading*) Analysis of the teleological faculty of judging. **1809–10** COLERIDGE *Friend* (1818) III. 180 A teleological ground in physics and physiology. **1847** BUCH tr. *Hagenbach's Hist. Doctr.* I. 96 What is commonly called the physico-theological, or teleological proof—i.e. they infer the existence of a Creator from the works of creation. **1875** SIR W. TURNER in *Encycl. Brit.* I. 799/1 The special anatomy of an animal may be studied..(*c*) with reference to the function, use, or purpose performed by a part or structure .., termed Teleological or Physiological Anatomy. **1907** J. R. ILLINGWORTH *Doctr. Trin.* xii. 248 The great teleological question.. what is the end of man? what is the true purpose of life's voyage? **1930** C. D. BROAD *Five Types of Ethical Theory* vi. 206, I would first divide ethical theories into two classes, which I will call respectively *deontological* and *teleological*. **1966** F. COPLESTON *Hist. Philos.* VIII. ii. 34 Any form of teleological ethics which interprets the moral imperative as.. an assertoric hypothetical imperative. **1967** *Encycl. Philos.* VIII. 88/1 Teleological ethics.. is the subordination of the concept of duty, right conduct, or moral obligation to the concept of the good or the humanly desirable. **1973** S. F. COHEN *Bukharin* vii. 228 Rykov.. a perennial foe of grandiose economic projects and teleological planning.

Hence **teleoˈlogically** *adv.*, in a teleological manner; in relation to teleology.

1842 DE QUINCEY in *Blackw. Mag.* LII. 730/2 Teleologically, that is, considered as means to an end—diamonds have as undeniably a value in use as any other article. **1907** J. R. ILLINGWORTH *Doctr. Trin.* ix. 176 The context of a rational and teleologically ordered world.

teleologist (tɛliːˈɒlədʒɪst). [f. as prec. + -IST.] A believer in or maintainer of the doctrine of teleology; one versed in this.

1864 H. SPENCER *Princ. Biol.* I. II. vii. §79. 234 The explanation of the teleologist is untrue,.. things are not arranged thus or thus for the securing of special ends. **1881** G. J. ROMANES in *Nature* 5 May 2/1 The burden of proof lies with the teleologists to show that any special cases.. are to be regarded as inexplicable.

So **teleˈologism**, teleological theory or doctrine.

1889 *Pop. Sci. Monthly* June 278/1 In the course of his transition from strict teleologism to the full acceptance of the theory of evolution.

teleology (tɛliːˈɒlədʒɪ). [ad. mod.L. *teleologia* (Chr. Wolf, 1728); f. Gr. τέλος end (see TELEO-[2]) + -λογια (see -LOGY), whence also Ger. *teleologie*, F. *téléologie*.]

The doctrine or study of ends or final causes, esp. as related to the evidences of design or purpose in nature; also *transf.* such design as exhibited in natural objects or phenomena.

[**1728** WOLF *Logica* §85 Datur.. præter eas alia adhuc philosophiæ naturalis pars, quæ fines rerum explicat, nomine adhuc destituta, etsi amplissima sit et utilissima. Dici posset *Teleologia*.]

1740 ZOLLMAN (tr. fr. French) in *Phil. Trans.* XLI. 299 Teleology is one of those Parts of Philosophy, in which there has been but little Progress made. **1807** *Edin. Rev.* X. 151 The subject of Teleology, or the doctrine of final causes, was one which occupied the thoughts of Le Sage. **1868** F. BUCKLAND in Bompas *Life* x. (1885) 224 This is the doctrine of Teleology: i.e. the doctrine that every organ is adapted to a special use. **1881** G. J. ROMANES in *Nature* 27 Oct. 604/2 Teleology in this larger sense, or the doctrine that behind all the facts open to scientific enquiry.. there is 'Mind and Will' as the ultimate cause of all things.. does not fall within the scope of scientific method. **1893** H. DRUMMOND in Barrows *Parl. Relig.* II. 1322 Darwin has not written a chapter that is not full of teleology.

teleometer, erron. form for TELEMETER *sb.*

1891 in *Cent. Dict.*

teleonomy (tɛliːˈɒnəmɪ). *Biol.* [f. TELEO-[2] + -NOMY.] The property, common to all living systems, of being organized towards the attainment of ends (see quots.). Hence **teleoˈnomic** *a.*, of or pertaining to teleonomy.

1958 C. S. PITTENDRIGH in Roe & Simpson *Behavior & Evolution* xviii. 391 (*heading*) Adaptation: teleonomy versus teleology. *Ibid.* 394 It seems unfortunate that the term 'teleology' should be resurrected... The biologist's long-standing confusion would be more fully removed if all end-directed systems were described by some other term, like 'teleonomic', in order to emphasize that.. end-directedness does not carry a commitment to Aristotelian teleology. **1961** *Cold Spring Harbor Symp. Quantitative Biol.* XXVI. 1 (*heading*) The teleonomic significance of biosynthetic control mechanisms. **1976** *Ann. Rev. Microbiol.* XXX. 538 The hoped-for aim of this review is to promote more studies on the diverse glycerol systems in a teleonomic context. **1977** P. B. & J. S. MEDAWAR *Life Sci.* i. 11 Biologists prefer to use the genteelism teleonomy with merely descriptive connotations to signify the goal-directed or 'as-if-purposive' character of biological performances. **1978** J. Z. YOUNG *Programs of Brain* iii. 16 The conception of 'teleology' has been associated with that of a final aim of life, implying metaphysical or religious beliefs. To avoid this, recent authors have used the word 'teleonomy' to describe the directional character of living activities... But words of this sort confuse many people and one is enough, let us keep to 'teleology'.

teleophobia to **teleoptile**: see TELEO-[1], [2].

teleordering: see TELE- 1.

teleorganic, teleosaur, -saurian: see TELEO- [1,2].

teleostean (tɛlɪˈɒstiːən), *a.* and *sb.* *Ichth.* [f. mod.L. *teleosteus* (f. Gr. τέλεος, -ειος finished, complete, TELEO-[1] + ὀστέ-ον bone) + -AN.]

a. *adj.* Belonging to or characteristic of the order *Teleostei* (Joh. Müller 1844) or osseous fishes, having the skeleton (usually) completely ossified. **b.** *sb.* A fish of this order.

1859 DARWIN *Orig. Species* ix. 305 Some palæontologists believe that certain much older fishes.. are really teleostean. **1872** *Ibid.* x. (ed. 6) 285 If the teleosteans had really appeared suddenly.. at the commencement of the chalk formation. **1888** ROLLESTON & JACKSON *Anim. Life* 90 The Perch... Its skeleton is typically Teleostean. *Ibid.* 429.

So **ˈteleost** *sb.* and *a.*, also **teliost** (= F. *téléoste*), **teleˈosteous** *a.* = TELEOSTEAN.

1862 DANA *Man. Geol.* iii. 278 *note*, The skeleton is bony, as the name Teliost.. implies. **1880** GÜNTHER *Fishes* i. 22 The organisation of the Teleosteous fishes. **1891** *Cent. Dict.* 6216 (figure) Skull of Pike (*Esox lucius*), a teleost fish. **1895** B. DEAN *Fishes* vii. 139 'Teleost' must be used in a popular and convenient.. sense.. to denote.. the modern 'bony fish'. **1955** AUDEN *Shield of Achilles* i. 15 Had He picked a teleost Or an arthropod to inspire, Would our death also have come? **1979** C. E. BOND *Biol. Fishes* i. 6 Arranging the teleosts into lower, middle, and higher levels of organization may be a gross oversimplification.

teleostome (ˈtɛliːəstəʊm). *Ichth.* [ad. mod.L. *teleostom-us*, f. TELEO-[1] + Gr. στόμα mouth.] A fish of the division *Teleostomi* (Th. Gill 1872), including the teleosts and ganoids (i.e. all the higher fishes), characterized by well-developed maxillary, dentary, and membrane bones. So **teˈleostomate**, ˌ**teleostomatous** (-ˈstɒmətəs), **teleˈostomous** *adjs.*, belonging to or having the characters of the *Teleostomi*.

1896 H. WOODWARD *Guide Fossil Reptiles Brit. Mus.* 109 A break in the series of Teleostomatous fishes. **1900** *Nature* 20 Sept. 505/2 The Crossopterygii are a group of Teleostomous fishes. **1901** *Ibid.* 14 Nov. 38/1 The difference between the typically meroblastic egg of the shark and the holoblastic egg of such a teleostome as the sturgeon.

teleotemporal to **teleozoon**: see TELEO-[1].

telepathy (tɪ-, tɛˈlɛpəθɪ, ˈtɛlɪpæθɪ). *Psychics.* [f. TELE- + Gr. -πάθεια feeling, perception: see -PATHY.] 'The communication of impressions of any kind from one mind to another, independently of the recognised channels of sense' (Myers *Human Personality*, Gloss.).

1882 MYERS in *Proc. Soc. Psychical Research* I. ii. 147 [see TELÆSTHESIA]. **1888** *Athenæum* 18 Aug. 213/3 In.. after-dinner experiments.. telepathy, thought-reading, and hypnotism are trifled with as amusements. **1894** H. DRUMMOND *Ascent Man* 234 Telepathy is theoretically the next stage in the Evolution of Language.

So **telepath** (ˈtɛlɪpæθ) *sb.*, **teˈlepathist**, an adept in, subject of, or believer in telepathy; ˈ**telepath** *v.*, (*a*) *trans.* to convey or transmit by means of telepathy; (*b*) *intr.* to practise telepathy; **telepaˈthetic** (*rare*), **teleˈpathic** *adjs.*, pertaining to, of the nature of, or effected by telepathy; **teleˈpathically** *adv.*, in a telepathic manner, by means of telepathy; **telepathize** (ˈtɛlɪpəθaɪz, tɪˈlɛpəθaɪz) *v.*, (*a*) *trans.* to communicate with or affect (a person) by telepathy; (*b*) *intr.* to practise telepathy; (*c*) *trans.*, to discern by means of telepathy. *rare.*

1907 *Westm. Gaz.* 9 Feb. 3/2 There is a pleasant mystery about the origin of the 9-in. shell which startled Selsey the other day... It looks as though the *telepaths would have to be called in to account for its origin. **1886** *Sat. Rev.* 4 Dec. 751/1 Whether spooks are *telepathed about.. by promiscuous persons, or whether the Thibetan Adepts go spooking astrally through the world. **1891** *Review of Rev.* 15 Oct. 347/2 As soon as a man begins to speculate as to how he telepaths, he loses the power of telepathing. **1895** *Edin. Rev.* Jan. 93 It may be that these communications have really been 'telepathed' from some living mind. **1892** *Sat. Rev.* 6 Aug. 157/1 Was there, then, some 'communication' of a '*telepathetic' sort? **1949** KOESTLER *Insight & Outlook* ix. 119 The functional interactions of hypnotic and telepathetic rapports. **1884** GURNEY & MYERS in *19th Century* May 800 We hope to show that the lowest *telepathic manifestations may be used to explain and corroborate the highest. **1903** MYERS *Human Personality* II. p. xv, Telepathic intercourse, if carried far enough, corresponds to possession or to ecstasy. **1884** —— in *Proc. Soc. Psychical Research* VII. 219 Drawing a picture which he feels to be *telepathically presented to his mind's eye. **1886** GURNEY, etc. *Phantasms of Living* I. 111 His aspect.. is telepathically perceived. **1894** *Westm. Gaz.* 12 Sept. 3/3 Knowing myself now to be a *telepathist,.. I look with regret to the many opportunities I have missed. **1900** *Pall Mall G.* 31 Oct. 3 Mr. Andrew Lang discourses.. of three female professors of telepathy, concluding that Joan of Arc was a true telepathist. **1895** in *Funk's Stand. Dict.* **1919** E. H. JONES *Road to En-dor* xi. 115 He had put me on parole.. not to telepathize with the good folk of Yozgad. **1941** *Mind* L. 315 But this just is telepathy except that you have made the provision that it shall be done by having the same sensation as the person one telepathises. **1954** 'J. CHRISTOPHER' *22nd Cent.* 145 Did they telepathize our coming and retreat to some more civilized solar system? **1963** *Jrnl. Soc. for Psychical Res.* XLII. 33, I have examined a subject telepathized in this way and questioned him. **1980** C. FITZGIBBON *Rat Report* ii. 38 If the rat had telepathized once, then perhaps it would again.

telepheme (ˈtɛlɪfiːm). [f. TELE- + Gr. φήμη voice, report, message, etc.] Name for a message sent by telephone; a telephonic communication.

1882 W. BALESTIER in *Rochester* (N.Y.) *Post-Express* 5 Aug. (Cent.), We shall ask a dispensation to permit us to introduce a new word.. telepheme. The use of such phrases as 'telephonic communication', 'telephonic message', 'news by telephone', and the like seems a little clumsy. **1898** R. O. HESLOP *Let. to Editor*, Telepheme: a telephonic message. The term is occasionally met with in commercial correspondence.

telepherage: see TELPHERAGE.

telepheric, var. TELEFERIC.

telephonable (tɛlɪˈfəʊnəb(ə)l), *a.* [f. TELEPHONE *v.* + -ABLE.] Of a place or person: able to be reached or contacted by telephone.

1908 G. B. SHAW *Lett. to Granville Barker* (1956) 126 She is ill and not telephonable. **1932** *New Statesman* 23 Jan. 88/1 The advertising campaign which is so largely increasing the number of telephonable people. **1973** S. ALSOP *Stay of Execution* (1974) I. 20 Katmandu was not easily telephonable.

telephone (ˈtɛlɪfəʊn), *sb.* [f. Gr. τῆλε afar, TELE- + φωνή voice, sound, -φων-ος -voiced, -sounding (as in εὔφωνος sweet-voiced).]

1. An instrument, apparatus, or device for conveying sound to a distance. Now chiefly *Obs.*

†**a.** Name for a system of signalling by musical notes, devised by Sudré in 1828. †**b.** An instrument like a fog-horn, used on ships, railway trains, etc., for signalling by loud sounds or notes. †**c.** A tube or other device for conveying the sound of the voice to a distance, as a speaking-tube. **d.** ***lovers'*** or ***string telephone***, a toy consisting of two stretched membranes or metal disks connected by a tense cord which mechanically transmits sound-waves from the one to the other.

(The name has also been applied by writers to an apparatus invented by Wheatstone, called by him 'the Enchanted Lyre', consisting of a rod connected with a sound-board, by which sounds (e.g. of a musical instrument) were conveyed from one room to another.)

1835 *Musical Libr.* [implied in TELEPHONIC q.v.]. **1844** *Times* 19 July 6/5 Yesterday week was a levee day at the Admiralty, and amongst the numerous models.. was Captain J. N. Tayler's telephone instrument... The chief object of this powerful wind instrument is to convey signals during foggy weather. **1844** *Illustr. Lond. News* 24 Aug. 118/1 The Telephone; a Telegraphic Alarum. Amongst the many valuable inventions.. that of the 'Telephone, or Marine Alarum and Signal Trumpet', by Captain J. N. Taylor, R.N. **1849** *Chambers' Jrnl.* 30 June 408 Mr. Whishaw's inventions: among these are speaking-tubes,.. we are, it seems, to be able to speak to a distance without any connecting tube at all: across the inner quadrangle of a building, for instance, by means of large concave gutta-percha reflectors.. the portable telephone would be available where the telegraph.. does not admit of application. **1851** *Catal. Exhibition* I. 442 [F. Whishaw's] Gutta percha telephone. **1860** WHEATSTONE *Patent Specif.* No. 2462 Telephones in which musical pipes or free tongues are acted upon by wind. Compressed air or gas is admitted to the pipe by means of a valve acted upon by the magnetized needle of an electro-magnet. The alternation of long and short sounds may be grouped in a similar manner to the long and short lines in the alphabet of a Morse's telegraph. **1877** KNIGHT *Dict. Mech.*, *Telephone*, an instrument for conveying signals by sound... The term, until lately, has been particularly applied to a signal adapted for nautical or railroad use, in which a body of compressed air is released from a narrow orifice and divided upon a sharp edge, in the manner of a steam-whistle. **1879** tr. *Du Moncel, The Telephone* 2 One step more led to the membrane employed in string telephones.

2. An apparatus for reproducing sound, esp. that of the voice, at a great distance, by means of electricity; consisting, like the electric telegraph, of transmitting and receiving instruments connected by a line or wire which conveys the electric current.

a. Applied to an instrument devised by P. Reis in Dec. 1861, and called by him (in German) *Telephon*.

In this the sounds were received on thin vibrating membranes, whose motion was transmitted electrically to an electromagnetic receiver. This was never perfected as a practical means of communication.

1866 R. M. FERGUSON *Electricity* 257 The Telephone. 158. This is an instrument for telegraphing notes of the same pitch. Reis's Telephone (invented 1861) accomplishes this in the following way. **1883** S. P. THOMPSON *P. Reis* 49 We have now shown that Philipp Reis was the undisputed inventor [1861] of an instrument which he called the Telephone. **1889** PREECE & MAIER *Telephone* 3 Philipp Reis, of Friedrichsdorf, wrote [in German] in 1868:—I succeeded in inventing an apparatus..in which also one can produce tones of all kinds at any desired distance by means of the galvanic current, I named the instrument 'Telephon'.

b. Applied to the 'Electrical Speaking Telephone' of Alex. Graham Bell, introduced in 1876, and to its various modifications by Elisha Gray, Edison, Hunnings, etc.

In this the sounds of speech or music are received on and reproduced by thin vibrating disks or diaphragms. ***on the telephone***, (*a*) connected with a system of telephonic intercommunication; (*b*) making a telephone call, ringing up; using or by means of the telephone.

1876 (May 10) A. G. BELL in *Proc. Amer. Acad. Arts & Sc.*, I placed the membrane of the telephone near my mouth. **1876** (Dec. 9) —— *Patent Specif.* No. 4765. 8 The telephones being illustrated separately in figs. 19 and 20. **1878** EDISON in *N. Amer. Rev.* CXXVI. 534 The phonograph will perfect the telephone, and revolutionize present systems of telegraphy. **1879** *Cassell's Techn. Educ.* IV. 154/2 The telephone and microphone have far distanced any previous attempts to convey sounds from one place to another. **1879** tr. *Du Moncel, The Telephone* 8 Mr. Elisha Gray..arranged in fact about the 15th Jan. 1876, a system of speaking telephones. **1884** C. G. W. LOCK *Workshop Receipts* Ser. III. 189/2 The telephone proper differs from other instruments of a like class, in that it reproduces instead of merely conveying vibrations. **1885** *List of Subscribers, Classified* (United Telephone Co.) (ed. 6) 18 Other people have their own tradesmen, who are doubtless also on the telephone. **1900** C. H. CHAMBERS *Tyranny of Tears* I. 36 (*The telephone bell rings.*).. There's some one on the telephone—forgive me. (*Goes to telephone.*) **1905** F. YOUNG *Sands of Pleasure* II. iv, The hotel in the Rue de Calais was not on the telephone. **1906** *Westm. Gaz.* 29 Aug. 10/1 'It is the wonder of wonders' exclaimed Sir William Thomson (now Lord Kelvin) after he had tested the first telephone shown to the public at the Centennial Exhibition in Philadelphia in 1876. **1925** F. SCOTT FITZGERALD *Great Gatsby* ii. 35 Mrs. Wilson called up several people on the telephone. *Ibid.* vii. 138 That's Tom's girl on the telephone. *Ibid.* ix. 214 You threw me over on the telephone. **1934** G. B. SHAW *Village Wooing* 135 Oh, speak English: you're not on the telephone now. **1963** K. AMIS *One Fat Englishman* xi. 126 Hearing her voice on the telephone in the next room brought an unwelcome reminder of the small hours. **1965** J. H. ROBERTS '*Q' Document* iv. 101 Those moments when he was forced to abandon conversation with Cooper to talk on the telephone.

c. *transf.* and *fig.*

1878 MRQ. SALISBURY *Sp. Newsp. Press Fund* 19 May, He will see the telephone [i.e. the reporters] by which these arguments and facts are conveyed to persons still open to conviction. **1898** J. ARCH *Story of Life* xvi. 396 Now the agricultural labourer has his political telephone of his vote, his Board Schools, his County Council, his Parish Council.

d. *ellipt.* for *telephone call*, sense 3 below, esp. in *Indian English*. Cf. PHONE *sb.*² 1.

1935 F. W. CROFT *Crime at Guildford* xxi. 298 A telephone to the manager of the hotel produced the needed information. **1979** P. NIHALANI et al. *Indian & Brit. English* I. 176 'Your telephones have not been very clear.' 'He gave me a telephone.'..In BS..the phrase 'telephone call', or simply 'call', would be used.

3. *attrib.* and *Comb.*, as ***telephone bell, call, caller, cord, dial, drum*** (sense 1 b), ***extension, instrument, line, message, office, operator, -receiver, -stud, survey, table, transmitter, trumpet, -user, wire***; ***telephone-answering*** adj.; **telephone bill** = *phone bill* s.v. PHONE *sb.*² 3; **telephone book** = *telephone directory* below; **telephone booth, box** = *phone booth, box* s.v. PHONE *sb.*² 3; **telephone directory**, a book containing an alphabetical list of the names, addresses, and numbers of telephone subscribers; *spec.* (with def. article) such a list covering a particular locality and printed by a telephone company; **telephone exchange**, the office or central station of a local telephone system, where the various lines are brought to a central switchboard, and communication between subscribers is effected; sometimes applied to the switchboard itself, as in an 'automatic exchange'; **telephone girl**, a girl employed at the switchboard to connect the wires so as to put two persons into communication; **telephone kiosk** = *phone booth, box* s.v. PHONE *sb.*² 3; **telephone number** = *phone number* s.v. PHONE *sb.*² 3; *colloq.*, a large number (esp. with reference to a sum of money or a prison sentence); **telephone pad**, a writing pad for noting telephone messages, etc.; **telephone set**, the assembly of components including a telephone transmitter, receiver, etc., which make up a telephone (sense 2 b); **telephone tapping** *vbl. sb.*, the act of making a connection to a telephone wire so as to listen in on private telephone conversations; cf. TAPPING *vbl. sb.*¹ a; so **telephone tap**, an instance of telephone tapping; **telephone token**, a small counter designed to operate a public telephone and on sale in certain countries of Europe; cf. JETON 2.

1963 *Times* 5 Feb. 11/4 This is the *telephone-answering machine of the coke department... The machine will record your order or message... Please speak clearly... Please speak now. **1900** *Telephone bell [see sense 2 b (*b*) above]. **1907** H. WYNDHAM *Flare Footlights* xxviii, The warning tinkle of the telephone bell on the office wall. **1935** C. ISHERWOOD *Mr Norris Changes Trains* viii. 117 In the present state of Arthur's finances, it was hardly to be expected that he would have settled his *telephone bill. **1915** J. BUCHAN *39 Steps* viii. 201, I picked up the *telephone book and looked up the number of his house. **1975** D. LODGE *Changing Places* iii. 132, I got out the telephone book and began ringing round. **1895** *Funk's Stand. Dict.*, *Telephone-booth. *a* **1910** [see CALL *v.* 35 h]. **1982** T. HOLME *Devil of Dolce Vita* xxii. 178 There is [in Venice] a plethora of squares, some scarcely bigger than a telephone booth. **1904** *McClure's Mag.* Feb. 405 Golden could snatch only two opportunities to step into the *telephone box that morning. **1980** I. MURDOCH *Nuns & Soldiers* i. 44 I'm in a telephone box near Victoria Station. **1885** *List of Subscribers, Classified* (United Telephone Co.) (ed. 6) 9 *Telephone Call Rooms have just been opened at Clapham and Kilburn. **1910** 'O. HENRY' *Strictly Business* 13 She pointed out to him clearly how it [*sc.* a play] could be improved by introducing a messenger instead of a telephone call. **1980** I. MURDOCH *Nuns & Soldiers* iv. 243 The Count was sitting..in torment, waiting for her telephone call. **1948** 'J. TEY' *Franchise Affair* x 103 Your *telephone callers: were they male or female? **1855** (May 10) *Bill, Polytechnic Inst.*, Lecture by J. H. Pepper, Esq., on Professor Wheatstone's experiments.., illustrated by a *Telephone concert, in which sounds of various instruments pass inaudible through an intermediate hall, and are reproduced in the lecture room. **1878** EDISON in *N. Amer. Rev.* CXXVI. 535 Were..our *telephone-conversation automatically recorded. **1934** WEBSTER, *Telephone cord. **1966** 'A. HALL' *9th Directive* xv. 143, I..fiddled with the telephone cord. **1960** COOKE & MARKUS *Electronics & Nucleonics Dict.* 478/2 **Telephone dial*, a switch operated by a finger wheel, used to make and break a pair of contacts the required number of times for setting up a telephone circuit to the party being called. **1972** 'E. MCBAIN' *Sadie when she Died* viii. 81 There is still all day tomorrow to twirl those little holes in the telephone dial and ring up this or that hot number. **1907** *Yesterday's Shopping* (1969) 397/3 Private *Telephone Directory..Spanish roan, lettered in gold, 24 leaves, to stand or hang. **1913** W. P. EATON *Barn Doors & Byways* 81 We fail to find this sort of thing any more thrilling or 'literary' than the telephone directory. **1969** B. WEIL *Dossier IX* iii. 20 The *Service* are always up to date with their telephone directories. **1844** *Illustr. Lond. News* 24 Aug. 118/1 The Indicator..to be placed on the *Telephone Drum, to denote the signals made... The Telephone gamut notes are arranged for numbers either by the public or private key. **1879** *Print. Trades Jrnl.* XXVIII. 6 On Saturday the *Telephone Exchange commenced operations. **1945** C. MILBURN *Diary* 2 Jan. (1979) 261 The telephone handy men had arrived to instal a *telephone extension up into Alan's room. **1977** 'J. LE CARRÉ' *Hon. Schoolboy* II. xiv. 322 A telephone extension hung on the wall. **1893** *Chicago Tribune* 2 July 13/3 The *telephone girl sits on her high stool..as she produces alternate order and chaos at her switchboard. **1906** *Daily Chron.* 27 June 2/3 An installation which was going to do away with the telephone girl. **1931** G. B. SHAW *Fabian Ess.* p. viii, A couple of pennies to drop into the slot in a *telephone kiosk. **1974** M. BABSON *Stalking Lamb* II. xxiv. 178 George had entered the telephone kiosk and could be clearly seen inside the brightly lit box. **1882** T. D. LOCKWOOD *Pract. Information for Telephonists* 163 Now, to consider the possible disturbing influence that electric light wires may exercise upon *telephone lines. **1962** A. NISBETT *Technique Sound Studio* 261 *Music line*, broad-band circuit for carrying programme (including speech), as distinct from a telephone line. **1982** A. BROOKNER *Providence* ix. 109 Supposing there is a *telephone message waiting for me at the hotel? **1885** *List of Subscribers, Classified* (United Telephone Co.) (ed. 6) 3 Edwin Fox & Compy.. *Telephone No. 5,110. **1950** T. S. ELIOT *Cocktail Party* I. i. 17 You have the address, and the telephone number? **1963** L. DEIGHTON *Horse under Water* xliv. 171 It looked like he was going up the river for a telephone number. **1878** G. H. LEWES *Jrnl.* 21 Mar. in *Geo. Eliot. Lett.* (1956) VII. 16 We went to the *Telephone office to have the Telephone explained and demonstrated. **1894** *Life* 19 Apr. 256/1 One of the young lady *telephone operators might be listening to our talk and we don't want our telephone taken out. **1964** M. MCLUHAN *Understanding Media* xxiv. 243 Boors, who inundate defenseless telephone operators. **1923** *Sci. Amer.* Feb. 115/3 When this *telephone pad is not in use it rests out of sight beneath..the telephone. **1967** A. WILSON *No Laughing Matter* III. 386 Jack, seeing the telephone pad, did not want to break the mood by asking Marcus if he had rung Gladys. **1884** *List of Subscribers* (London & Globe Telephone Co.) 3 Any form of *telephone transmitter or receiver. **1906** *Blackw. Mag.* June 832/2 The tired clerk at the telephone-receiver rebuffed our advances. **1911** *Encycl. Brit.* XXV. 552/1 Each *telephone set was equipped with a special key. **1976** P. LOVESEY, *Swing, swing Together* xxx. 146 If anything develops here, you can use the telephone set to leave a message at the Yard. **1889** PREECE & MAIER *Telephone* 111 The object of the Button Telephone is to replace the press button of an ordinary electric bell by a *telephone-stud, which permits not only to ring up a person but to converse with him. **1976** *National Observer* (U.S.) 13 Mar. 1/6 The Knight-Ridder newspapers asked a similar question in a *telephone survey in January and found 81 per cent agreement. **1929** 'E. QUEEN' *Roman Hat Mystery* III. xvii. 251 They..shook out the pages of the telephone-book in the bedside *telephone-table. **1977** M. RUSSELL *Dial Death* II. i. 39 The figure slumped across the telephone table. **1958** 'E. MCBAIN' *Killer's Payoff* (1960) xv. 153 There was no intention of maintaining a **telephone tap* in the strictest sense of the word. **1958** *Listener* 12 June 971/1 Some of the evidence had been obtained by *telephone tapping. **1978** *Peace News* 25 Aug. 9/1 It is important to note that firstly, the Special Branch 'ambush' was only made possible by some combination of mail interception and telephone tapping. **1963** 'D. CORY' *Hammerhead* x. 127 He..asked for a glass of cognac and a *telephone token. **1884** *Telephone transmitter [see *telephone receiver* above]. **1937** *Discovery* Jan. 27/2 The use of this material for.. telephone transmitter diaphragms, is suggested. **1844** *Times* 19 July 6/5 *Telephone trumpet [see sense 1]. **1881** 'MARK TWAIN' *Let.* 31 Jan. in C. Clemens *Mark Twain* (1932) 36 In one place the *telephone wire running along six inches above the comb [of the roof] is covered. **1978** 'A. YORK' *Tallant for Disaster* xii. 172, I want a start made on getting the telephone wires back up again.

'telephone, *v.* [f. prec. sb.]

1. a. *intr.* To convey sound to a distance by or as by a telephone; *esp.* to send a message or communicate by speaking through a telephone.

1880 *Times* 22 Sept. 7/6 Mr. Bell..has succeeded in telegraphing, or rather 'telephoning', along a beam of light. **1881** *Chicago Times* 4 June, Mr. Smith..telephoned immediately to headquarters about the matter. **1899** *Westm. Gaz.* 25 July 4/2 Instruments by which telephoning without wires can be successfully accomplished.

b. *trans.* To convey or announce by telephone (in quot. 1879 by sound generally). Also *fig.*

1878 W. TEGG *Posts & Telegraphs* III. 305 It is said that the results of these experiments were 'telephoned' to the *Boston Guide*. **1879** CALDERWOOD *Mind & Br.* 139 He will interpret such signs as whistling, calling,..and..proceed to the execution of the fresh orders so 'telegraphed', perhaps I should say 'telephoned'. **1882** *Daily News* 25 Aug. 3/1 You may safely defer setting out..until No. 2 has been telephoned. **1888** *Encycl. Brit.* XXIII. 127/1 This [Wheatstone's 'magic lyre'] only answers for telephoning musical sounds to short distances. **1888** *Montreal Weekly Witness* 13 June 1/4 The news was at once telephoned to Mrs. Cleveland. **1908** KIPLING *Lett. to Family* vi. 47, I hear the hard trail telephone a far-off horse's feet. **1923** D. H. LAWRENCE *Birds, Beasts & Flowers* 44 Almond tree... What are you doing in the December rain?.. Do you telephone the roar of the water over the earth?

c. To speak to or summon by telephone.

1877 *Telegraphic Jrnl.* 1 Sept. 201/2, I [*sc.* Prof. Graham Bell] telephoned the leader of the band. **1889** WESTGARTH *Austral. Progress* 153 As he might be there, they would 'telephone' him. **1894** HOWELLS in *Harper's Mag.* Feb. 378 She telephoned you on the impulse of the moment.

2. To furnish with telephones; to establish a system of telephones in (a place).

1901 *Speaker* 14 Dec. 296/1 The London County Council prepared..estimates for telephoning London in 1898. **1904** *Daily News* 19 Apr. 2 If the United Kingdom were 'telephoned' in the same proportion there would be nearly 800,000 instruments on its various exchange systems, instead of some 250,000 only.

Hence **'telephoned** *ppl. a.*; **'telephoning** *vbl. sb.*; also **'telephoner**, one who telephones.

1884 *Whitaker's Almanack* 385/1 Remarkable trials of long distance telephoning. **1891** *Cent. Dict.*, Telephoner. **1894** Telephoned words [see TELEGRAPHED]. **1902** *Westm. Gaz.* 26 Aug. 1/3 When one has had actual experience of a thoroughly telephoned town. **1918** A. BENNETT *Pretty Lady* xviii. 116 The telephone-bell rang... The telephoner was Gilbert. **1932** *New Statesman* 23 Jan. 87/1, I have often watched one of these fanatical telephoners sitting opposite the telephone with his hand on the receiver. **1972** *New Yorker* 21 Oct. 31/3 We picked up a mimeographed sheet that tells the telephoners what to say.

ˌtelepho'netics, *sb. pl. nonce-wd.* [f. TELEPHONE *sb.*, after *phonetics*; or f. TELE- + PHONETICS.] The practice of using a telephone; also (quot. 1893) signalling by sounds.

1877 *Daily News* 30 Nov. 5/1 The general public..must apparently be content for the present to indulge in telephonetics only between..10 p.m. and 10 a.m. **1893** *Church Q. Rev.* Oct. 242 There was also what may be almost styled a code of telephonetics among the Benedictines, who understood what the Abbot meant when he jingled his spoons.

telephonic (tɛlɪ'fɒnɪk), *a.* [In earlier use, f. Gr. τῆλε (TELE-) + φωνή voice + -IC: in later use, f. TELEPHONE *sb.* + -IC.] Transmitting, or relating to the transmission of, sound to a distance.

†**a.** Applied to a system of signalling by musical sounds: cf. TELEPHONY 1. *Obs.* **b.** Of, pertaining to, of the nature of, or conveyed by a telephone.

1834 WILSON *New Dict. Mus.* 259 *Telephonic Sounds*, a musical language invented by M. Sudré..for the purposes of conversation,..the communication of military or naval orders [etc.] to any distance. **1835** *Musical Library* Aug. *Suppl.* 78 This Telephonic system is one of the most ingenious contrivances we ever witnessed. **1840** WHEATSTONE *Let.* in Cooke *Electr. Telegraph* (1857) I. 114 The most efficient..means of establishing a telegraphic (or rather a telephonic) communication between two remote points. **1877** *Daily News* 30 Nov. 5/1 We do not exactly anticipate that telephonic offices will have to be superadded by the Post Office to its existing arrangements. **1878** G. B. PRESCOTT *Sp. Telephone* (1879) 17 In the summer of 1876 Professor A. G. Bell..exhibited a telephonic apparatus. *Ibid.* 39 Mr. Edison has recently invented a telephonic repeater, which is designed to be used..for increasing the distance over which [the telephone] may be made available. **1892** *Montreal Weekly Gaz.* 21 July 8/7 The Public may now obtain telephonic communication over its long distance metallic circuit lines.

fig. **1884** J. TAIT *Mind in Matter* (1892) 99 Mind segregates itself..from the matter..on whose telephonic powers it depends for intercourse with the world.

Hence **tele'phonically** *adv.*, in the manner of or by means of a telephone.

1878 G. B. PRESCOTT *Speaking Telephone* vi. 226 Stations could exchange business telephonically. **1879** S. P. THOMPSON in *Nature* XXI. 180 Sounds transmitted telephonically. **1882** *Pall Mall G.* 1 May 4 It is connected telephonically with the hotel at Dalmally.

telephonist (tɪ-, tɛ'lɛfənɪst, formerly also 'tɛlɪfəʊnɪst). [f. TELEPHONE *sb.* + -IST.]

a. A person employed in transmitting messages by telephone; one who works a telephone. **b.** One versed in telephony (*rare*$^{-0}$).

1880 *Harper's Mag.* Oct. 723/1 Nor are the Chicago telephonists driven to such an access of rage. **1882** OGILVIE, *Telephonist*, a person versed in telephony, or who operates on the telephone. **1884** *Pall Mall G.* 9 May 4/2 The female voice is always clearer, and..a clear voice..is one of the chief requirements of a telephonist. **1898** *Daily News* 13 Sept. 6/5 Employed as season telephonist at the observatory on the summit of Ben Nevis.

c. = TELEPHONER. *rare.*

1956 [see CRADLE *v.* 5 b].

telephonitis (ˌtɛlɪfəʊ'naɪtɪs). *joc.* [f. TELEPHONE *sb.* or *v.* + -ITIS.] A compulsive desire to make telephone calls.

1935 *Even. Sun* (Baltimore) 24 Apr. 4/6 Garrison was suffering from 'telephonitis'. She [*sc.* his wife] has an injunction forbidding him from calling her on the telephone and..Garrison had violated the order because he 'couldn't help it'. **1962** *Punch* 3 Jan. 71 One of the tragedies of telephonitis is that sufferers are unable to help one another. **1979** *Washington Post* 14 Dec. B3/5 Ted [*sc.* Edward Kennedy] has telephonitis and he's on the phone every night.

telephonograph (tɛlɪ'fəʊnəgrɑːf, -æ-). [f. TELE- + PHONOGRAPH, or f. TELEPHONE + -GRAPH.] An instrument consisting of a combination of telephone and phonograph, by which telephone messages can be recorded and subsequently reproduced. Also applied (in U.S.) to Poulsen's TELEGRAPHONE. Hence **ˌtelephono'graphic** *a.*, pertaining to or of the nature of a telephonograph; **ˌtelepho'nography**, the working or use of a telephonograph.

1878 G. B. PRESCOTT *Sp. Telephone* (1879) 549 The phonograph and telephone, when combined, form an instrument known as the telephonograph. **1889** *Telegr. Jrnl. & Electr. Rev.* 10 May 523/2 Mr. J. Hanmer, the originator of the recent telephonographic experiments between New York and Philadelphia. **1889** *Ibid.* 17 May 558/2 After the recent improvements made in the phonograph..the problem of telephonography has naturally cropped up. **1902** *Harper's Mag.* Feb. 496 The Poulsen telephonograph in its ordinary form does not speak louder than an ordinary Bell telephone.

telephony (tɪ-, tɛ'lɛfənɪ, 'tɛlɪfəʊnɪ). [f. Gr. τῆλε afar, TELE- + -φωνία -sounding, forming abstr. sbs. from adjs. in -φωνος, -voiced, -sounding. So mod.Ger. *telephonie*, F. *téléphonie*.]

†**1.** Name for a system of signalling by means of musical sounds, and for the practice of other early forms of telephone. *Obs.*

1835 *Athenæum* July 531 M. Sudré, whose new system of telegraphic communication, or telephony (as he calls it) we mentioned some weeks ago. **1835** *Mech. Mag.* XXIII. 269 (*heading*) The Telephony, or Musical Telegraph.

2. The art or science of constructing telephones; the working of a telephone or telephones.

[**1861** (Dec.) P. REIS in *Jahres-Bericht, Frankfurt. Physik. Verein* (*title*) Ueber Telephonie durch den galvanischen Strom.] **1876** A. GRAHAM BELL in *Proc. Amer. Acad. Arts & Sc.* 10 May (*Title of Lecture*) Researches in Telephony. **1876** —— in *Boston Advertiser*..Oct., Telephony. Audible speech conveyed two miles by telegraph. Prof. A. Graham Bell's Discovery. **1878** G. B. PRESCOTT *Sp. Telephone* (1879) 53 When I commenced my researches in electric telephony. **1884** *St. James's Gaz.* 23 Oct. 5/1 The Belgians..have just started a system of public telephony. **1885** *Pall Mall G.* 18 Sept. 6/2 The solution of the problem of long distance telephony and along with it the much more important question of submarine telephony is said to be within sight. **1900** *Westm. Gaz.* 20 June 10/2 Some interesting experiments in wireless telephony are being conducted by the Post Office between the..Skerries Island and Anglesey.

telephotal (-'fəʊtəl), *a.* [f. as TELEPHOTE d, TELEPHOTO *sb.*^{1} + -AL^{1}.] = TELEPHOTOGRAPHIC *a.*^{2}

1905 *Westm. Gaz.* 29 Aug. 5/1 Several..observers will be taking photographs [of the sun at an eclipse] with small cameras—some with telephotal lenses.

telephote ('tɛlɪfəʊt), *sb.* Also **telephot**. [f. Gr. τῆλε afar, at a distance, TELE- + φῶς, φωτ-, light.] A name employed or proposed for various devices or apparatus used or projected:

a. A means of transmitting signals or messages from a distance by means of light, (*a*) by flashing beams of light by a mirror (cf. HELIOGRAPH); (*b*) by letting out flashes from a brilliant lamp by means of a moving shutter; (*c*) by using flashed beams to work a sensitive photo-electric receiving apparatus (cf. PHOTOPHONE). **b.** A device for the electric transmission of pictures, so that they are reproduced as pictures at a distance: cf. TELEPHOTOGRAPH^{1}, *telelectrograph* in TELE-. **c.** A projected or suggested device for the electrical transmission to a distance of visual images of things, persons, or actual scenes (cf. *telelectroscope* in TELE-): not yet practically realized. **d.** An apparatus for photographing at a great distance; a telephotographic lens or camera: see TELEPHOTOGRAPH^{2}.

1880 [implied in TELEPHOTE *v.*]. **1884** KNIGHT *Dict. Mech.* Supp., *Telephote*, an instrument or apparatus for conveying messages or images by transmission of light. **1889** *Scott. Leader* 26 July 7 M. Courtonne..has deposited under seal his description of a new apparatus called a telephote, which enables one to see at a distance as the telephone enables one to hear at a distance. **1896** *Current Hist.* (Buffalo, N.Y.) VI. 950 A 'telephot'..invented by Dr. Robert d'Unger, of Chicago, Ill. [for picture telegraphy]. **1903** *Sci. American* 27 June 486/1 (*heading*) The 'Telephot', a novel apparatus for photographing at great distances. *Ibid.* 486/2 The 'Téléphot' may, moreover, be, at a moment's notice, converted into a terrestrial or astronomical telescope.

Hence **'telephote** *v.*, to transmit an optical image to a distance by means of electricity. **telephotic** (-'fɒtɪk) *a.*, of or pertaining to a telephote (actual or conceived), or to TELEPHOTY.

1880 *Engineering* 7 May 361/2 Visual Telegraphy... An image of the object to be 'telephoted' is focussed on the mirror by means of a lens, and the resulting current started in each [selenium] square of the mirror by the portion of the image falling on it is transmitted by the corresponding wire to the distant station. **1889** tr. *Jules Verne* in *Tablet* 16 Feb. 249/1 Each reporter..has in front of him a set of commutators which enable him to communicate with any desired telephotic line. **1896** FLAMMARION in *N. Amer. Rev.* May 557 We need to be able to enter into telephotic communication with them [inhabitants of Mars].

tele'photo, *a.* and *sb.*^{1} [Abbrev. of TELEPHOTOGRAPHIC *a.*^{2}, etc.: cf. PHOTO 2.]

A. *adj.* = TELEPHOTOGRAPHIC *a.*^{2}

1898 *Westm. Gaz.* 26 Jan. 5/3 By means of a tele-photo lens..Mr. Lodge has secured many photographic records of great value to the ornithologist. **1900** H. M. WILSON *Topographic Surv.* xli. 869 An attachment called a *telephoto combination*, which consists in the addition of a negative or magnifying element in the rear of the combination proper. This produces larger images of distant objects. **1913** KIPLING *Diversity of Creatures* (1917) 290 J'ever see a bird's eye telephoto-survey of England for military purposes? **1920** H. E. IVES *Airplane Photography* xxxi. 383 The telephoto lenses used for spotting would be of long equivalent focus..but of handy size. **1947** A. RANSOME *Great Northern?* i. 17 He would have..a camera with a telephoto lens to take photographs of birds without having to come near enough to disturb them. **1964** M. MCLUHAN *Understanding Media* (1967) II. xxi. 230 The press is now not only a telephoto mosaic of the human community hour by hour, but its technology is also a mosaic of all the technologies of the community. **1977** J. HEDGECOE *Photographer's Handbk.* 119 Some telephoto converters are designed to fit between lens and camera.

B. *sb.* **1.** A telephoto lens or camera.

1904 L. W. BROWNELL *Photogr. for Sportsman Naturalist* v. 72 It is always well, in work with the telephoto, to presuppose that your negative is under-exposed. **1931** O. G. PIKE *Nature Photogr.* iii. 16 A telephoto lens is..a most important part of the nature photographer's equipment... A modern telephoto is a very great advance on those used thirty years ago. **1975** BYFIELD & TEDESCHI *Solemn High Murder* (1976) v. 86, I used a time exposure..with a 135 mm telephoto. They were long exposures.

2. = TELEPHOTOGRAPH *sb.*^{2} *rare.*

1974 J. IRVING *158-Pound Marriage* i. 11, I see the close-ups of the shelling of Reims. The telephoto is still unclear.

telephoto *sb.*^{2} Also *U.S.* **Tele-**. [Abbrev. of TELEPHOTOGRAPH *sb.*^{1} or one of its derivatives.] Name for a system of telephotographic transmission.

A proprietary term in the U.S.

1925 *Official Gaz.* (U.S. Patent Office) 3 Feb. 46/1 Telephoto... Photographs. *Ibid.* 7 Apr. 27/2 Telephoto... Machines and apparatus for distance transmission of photographs electrically. **1931** *Daily Express* 13 Oct. 1/6 Picture by telephoto. **1938** F. D. SHARPE *Sharpe of Flying Squad* xxvi. 264 Photographs of finger-prints are greatly reduced in size and are flashed across the sea by the telephoto process to European countries.

telephotogram: see TELE- 1.

telephotograph, *sb.*^{1} (tɛlɪ'fəʊtəgrɑːf, -æ-). [f. as TELEPHOTE *sb.* b, c + -GRAPH.] A picture or image electrically reproduced at a distance, a *telectrograph*; also, an apparatus for doing this. So **telephotographic** (ˌtɛlɪfəʊtəʊ'græfɪk) *a.*^{1}, applied to an apparatus (***telephotographic instrument***) for producing photographs at a distance by means of an electric current. **telephotography**^{1} (ˌtɛlɪfəʊ'tɒgrəfɪ), the reproduction of pictures or scenes at a distance by means of the electric current as in the telegraph and telephone; = TELEPHOTY, *phototelegraphy*.

(This application of *telephotograph* and its derivatives had priority of date over that of TELEPHOTOGRAPH^{2}, by which it has been almost superseded in current use.)

1881 S. BIDWELL in *Nature* 10 Feb. 344/1 (*heading*) Telephotography. *Ibid.* 345/1, I made a pair of 'telephotographic' instruments... They produced a 'telephotograph' of a gas-flame. *Ibid.* 563 Mr. Shelford Bidwell's telephotographic machine. **1881** *Standard* 30 Dec. 5/3 Mr. Shelford Bidwell's Telephotograph has gone far to prove that..the actual handwriting of the sender of a message, as well as drawings..may be transmitted by telegraph and reproduced at the other end. **1891** G. M. MINCHIN in *Philos. Mag.* Mar. 235 The second problem..is the electrical transmission of an image to any distance; in other words the construction of a telephotograph. **1895** *Current Hist.* (Buffalo, N.Y.) V. 962 The Telephotograph. This Swedish invention will reproduce to the eye pictures transmitted from a distance.

tele'photograph, *sb.*^{2} [f. Gr. τῆλε (see TELE-) + PHOTOGRAPH; a back formation from TELEPHOTOGRAPHIC *a.*^{2} (see note), or TELEPHOTOGRAPHY.] A photograph of a distant object taken with a telephotographic lens.

1900 *Army & Navy Jrnl.* 14 July 1097 Good telephotographs have been obtained at a distance of over forty miles, and those taken beyond artillery range (ten miles) are on a sufficiently large scale to be of practical use. **1904** *Times, Lit. Supp.* 8 Apr. 109/2 We must give the palm to the striking telephotograph, facing page 184. **1909** MARRIAGE *Sculptures Chartres Cathedral* Pref. 8 Those..illustrations, generally speaking, in which the detail is on the largest scale are telephotographs.

Hence **tele'photograph** *v.*, *trans.* to photograph with a telephotographic lens or apparatus; **ˌtelepho'tographer**, one who takes a telephotograph. So **ˌtelepho'tography**^{2}, the art or practice of taking photographs of distant objects by a camera with a telephotographic lens.

1900 *Westm. Gaz.* 27 Jan. 4/3 Owing to haze it was impossible to *telephotograph the Boers. **1899** *Pall Mall G.* 21 Dec. 3 The would-be *telephotographer was turned back. **1892** *Anthony's Photographic Bull.* XXIII. 168 A great deal of discussion is going on at present on the subject of *telephotography. **1899** DALLMEYER (*title*) Telephotography, an Elementary Treatise on the Construction and Application of the Telephotographic Lens. **1899** *Pall Mall G.* 21 Dec. 3 It is difficult to understand why the War Office has not taken advantage of telephotography.

telephotographic (ˌtɛlɪfəʊtəʊ'græfɪk), *a.*^{2} [f. Gr. τῆλε afar off + PHOTOGRAPHIC *a.*

This word is properly formed and clearly expresses its meaning; its use and that of its derived group (see prec.), has practically superseded that of TELEPHOTOGRAPH^{1} and its derivatives coinciding in form with these, which were differently composed, and of quite different application.]

Of, pertaining to, or used in the photographing of distant objects, within the field of sight but beyond the limits of distinct vision, esp. in ***telephotographic lens***, a lens or combination of lenses for this purpose. (Invented by Dallmeyer 1891.)

1892 T. R. DALLMEYER *Paper read to Camera Club* 10 Mar., A compound Telephotographic Lens. **1892** *Daily News* 26 Sept. 2/6 A remarkable view of Mont Blanc taken at a distance of 56 miles, with Dallmeyer's *telephotographic lens. **1892** *Nature* 15 Dec. 161/2 In the simple telephotographic lens the anterior element, which is of large aperture and short focus, is a positive lens, while the posterior is negative, and of a fractional part of the focal length of the former lens. **1904** *Archæol. Surv. Ceylon, Epigr. Zeylanica* I. p. iv, The new telephotographic apparatus should be used for inscriptions on which an ordinary camera cannot be brought to bear. **1906** *Athenæum* 3 Mar. 268/2 Khan Tengri from the south, the telephotographic view of the same peak from the north.

telephotometer: see TELE- 1.

telephoty ('tɛlɪfəʊtɪ). [f. as TELEPHOTE + -Y.] The art or practice of reproducing pictures or views at a distance by means of the electric current; the theory and practice of the telephote; = TELEPHOTOGRAPHY^{1}.

1908 *Westm. Gaz.* 30 Apr. 5/2 The problem of 'seeing electrically' really resolves itself into the problem of electrical reproduction, and many men have been more or less successful in solving it. The system of 'telephoty', which is gaining some attention just now, was well known amongst specialists twenty-five years or more ago, but hitherto all the men who have experimented with it have given up sooner or later.

teleplastic to **teleplayer**: see TELE-.

telepolitics: see TELE- 2 b.

teleportation (ˌtɛlɪpɔː'teɪʃən). *Psychics* and *Sci. Fiction.* [f. TELE- + TRANS)PORTATION.] The conveyance of persons (esp. of oneself) or things by psychic power; also in futuristic description, apparently instantaneous transportation of persons, etc., across space by advanced technological means. Cf. *telekinesis* s.v. TELE-, PSYCHOKINESIS 1.

1931 C. FORT *Lo!* I. iv. 42 Sometimes, in what I call 'teleportations', there seems to be 'agency' and sometimes not... Some other time I may be able more clearly to think out an expression upon flows of pigeons to their homes, and flows of migratory birds, as teleportative, or quasi-teleportative. **1945** N. COLLINS *London belongs to Me* IV. liv. 421 The weekly copy of *The Spirit World* lay on the occasional table... They were wonderful letters—full of glimpses through the veil, and teleportations and proofs of survival. **1951** 'J. WYNDHAM' in *Science-Fantasy* Winter 8 Suppose the Russians..could project things or people here by teleportation. **1960** *Analog Science Fact & Fiction* Nov. 14/1 It took a latent ability to learn teleportation, and some people had it while others didn't. *Ibid.* 36/1 Going from one place to another is teleportation. **1977** 'L. Egan' *Blind Search* i. 4 Telepathy, telekinesis, teleportation, apports, whatever the hell psychic forces.

Hence (as a back-formation) **'teleport** *v.* (*a*) *intr.*, to convey oneself by teleportation; (*b*) *trans.*, to convey by teleportation; also *absol.*; **'teleporting** *ppl. a.* and *vbl. sb.*; also **'teleport** *sb.*, one who practises teleportation; **tele'portage** *rare* = TELEPORTATION; **tele'portative** *a. rare*, pertaining to teleportation.

1931 Teleportative [see TELEPORTATION]. **1951** 'J. Wyndham' in *Science-Fantasy* Winter 5 If there could be teleportation, or teleportage, or whatever it is. *Ibid.* 6 This teleporting guy. **1953** 'T. Sturgeon' *More than Human* III. 204 Bonnie and Beanie can't carry so much as a toothpick with them when they teleport, let alone clothes. **1954–5** *Planet Stories* Winter 26 It might teleport him, too, if he attracted its attention. **1955** *Astounding Sci. Fiction* Feb. 11 The Martian was back in the chair again. 'It's not teleportation. We don't teleport.' **1960** *Analog Science Fact & Fiction* Nov. 41/2 After all, he'd found telepaths in insane asylums, and teleports among the juvenile delinquents of New York. **1965** *New Statesman* 5 Nov. 705/2 So we must adjust to instant teleporting from Raspail Métro to the Donnybrook tram by way of Strangeways Gaol. **1967** E. B. Nickerson *Kayaks to Arctic* ix. 79 It was a steep bushy bank but he [*sc.* a bear] made it as if teleported and did not rustle even a leaf. **1979** B. Shaw *Dagger of Mind* vii. 116 Albert can teleport people... Miss Connie..does it with objects. Psychokinesis.

teleprinter ('tɛlɪˌprɪntə(r)). [f. TELE- + PRINTER.] A telegraph instrument for transmitting telegraph messages as they are typed on a keyboard and printing incoming ones.

1929 *Telegr. & Teleph. Jrnl.* Dec. 42/1 The first Teleprinters to be tried in this country were produced by the Morkrum Corporation under the proprietary name of 'The Teletype'. **1932** *Times Educ. Suppl.* 6 Aug. p. i/4 A service of teleprinters will be opened in London on August 15. **1933** *Post Office Guide* 138 This service is afforded by.. the teleprinter, which is a special kind of telegraph instrument operated by a keyboard closely resembling that of an ordinary commercial typewriter, working over the telephone exchange system. **1939** *Daily Tel.* 18 Dec. 12/4 (Advt.), Applicants who are not trained teleprinter operators should possess a typing speed of at least 30 words per minute. **1942** *R.A.F. Jrnl.* 27 June 22 One tribe of Grand Gremlins lives behind typewriter and teleprinter keys. **1957** *Technology* Apr. 68/4 Pushing a button then causes the positions of film-holder and lens to be punched on teleprinter tape. **1959** *Times Rev. Industry* Sept. 34/1 The teleprinter is not a substitute for a telephone. **1964** M. McLuhan *Understanding Media* (1967) II. xxv. 263 The teleprinter and the wireless made it possible for orders from the highest levels to be given direct to the lowest levels. **1978** R. V. Jones *Most Secret War* xviii. 148 Grant's interpretation was circulated by teleprinter. *Ibid.* xviii. 150 The teleprinter room into which the messages came was immediately across the corridor from my own.

Hence (as a back-formation) **'teleprint** *v. trans.*, to send or print (a message, etc.) by teleprinter; **'teleprinted** *ppl. a.*

1971 H. Wilson *Labour Govt.* xxvi. 519 On Saturday, 30 March, I was told on the telephone that a very long telegram was coming in from Washington and would be teleprinted to me at Chequers. **1973** G. Talbot *Ten Seconds from Now* iv. 44 Sheets of teleprinted news 'tape' from the clattering machines. **1980** *Daily Tel.* 4 Aug. 3/3 Some piece of international news,..important enough to rate a teleprinted 'flash'. **1981** *Sci. Digest* Aug. 50/2 Blood samples and X-rays are taken, and the lab data is teleprinted to the team.

teleprocessing: see TELE- 1.

teleprompter ('tɛlɪprɒm(p)tə(r)). orig. *U.S.* [f. TELE- + PROMPTER.] An electronic device, placed out of range of the television or cinematographic camera, that slowly unrolls the speaker's script, in order to prompt or assist him.

Formerly a proprietary name in the U.S. The equivalent British proprietary name is AUTOCUE.

1951 *Life* 12 Mar. 131 Set at the eye level of performers, the Teleprompter unrolls a script whose inch-high letters, printed by special typewriter, can be read 25 feet away. **1953** *Official Gaz.* (U.S. Patent Office) 10 Feb. 232/1 *Teleprompter.* For electrically-operated apparatus for the cuing of speakers and actors by means of scripts advanced in conformity with the action and/or dialogue... Claims use since Sept. 1, 1950. **1958** *Daily Mail* 13 Dec. 8/8 Last night he [*sc.* Lord Montgomery] seemed to be using a teleprompter, so rapidly did the words rattle out. **1961** S. Price *Just for Record* ii. 18 That's what the boys in the backroom had written, and it was staring at him..from the teleprompter. **1978** G. Vidal *Kalki* i. 20 Although most of Arlene's professional career depended upon her ability to read Teleprompters and cue cards, she refused to wear glasses in public.

Hence (as a back-formation) **'teleprompt** *v. trans.*, to assist by means of a teleprompter. Also **'teleprompted** *ppl. a.*, assisted by or by means of a teleprompter.

1956 *Sun* (Baltimore) 29 Aug. (B ed.) 14/2 Two weeks of nominations,..commentaries, teleprompted oratory and gavel-thumping. **1958** *Spectator* 18 July 87/1 Does my conscience need tele-prompting? **1960** *Time* 16 Nov. (Extra ed.) 15/1 The 1960 campaign had been televised, teleguided, teleprompted and telephoned as no other had been before.

telepsychic, telepuppet: see TELE- 1.

† **'teler.** *Obs. rare*$^{-1}$. [app. a. AF. **teler* = OF. *telier*, *teilier*, F. *toilier*, = Pr. *telier*, Cat. *teler*:—late L. *tēlārius* (Du Cange), f. *tēla* web, cloth.] A maker or seller of cloth; a cloth-merchant.

c **1400** *Destr. Troy* 1586 Taliours, Telers, Turners of vesselles.

teler, obs. form of TILER, TILLER.

telerecording ('tɛlɪrɪkɔːdɪŋ), *vbl. sb.* [f. TELE- 2 + RECORDING *vbl. sb.*] A recording of a television programme made while it is being transmitted. Also *occas.*, the action of making such a recording.

1953 *Radio Times* 22 May 44/2 A telerecording of the Abbey Ceremonies and a special Coronation edition of Television Newsreel. **1957** *Times* 16 Nov. 8/4 After the Queen's Christmas Day broadcast, which is to be televised this year for the first time, telerecordings will be flown to Canada and Australia. **1959** *P.O. Telecomm. Jrnl.* Winter 10/1 The signals are..used to operate a slow-speed film telerecording equipment. **1970** A. Glyn *Blood of Britishman* xvi. 186 A telerecording of a Football Cup semi-final. **1975** *Gramophone* Jan. 1330/1 Next month the BBC will take its cameras to Covent Garden for a tele-recording.

Hence (as a back-formation) **'telerecord** *v. trans.*, to record (a television programme) during transmission. Also **'telerecorded** *ppl. a.*

1955 *Radio Times* 22 Apr. 15/2 Monday's telerecorded programme *The Secret Arts.* **1956** *Ann. Reg. 1955* 390 A.. television production of *Romeo and Juliet* was telerecorded and sent to the U.S.S.R. **1960** *News Chron.* 24 June 3/7 The programme was telerecorded this week. **1978** *Times* 4 Sept. 9/4 BBC 2's cameras will..telerecord the new production.

telergic to **teleroentgenography:** see TELE- 1.

teleroman, telesale: see TELE- 2 b, 3.

telescope ('tɛlɪskəʊp), *sb.* Also 7 **tellescope.** [ad. It. *telescopio* or mod.L. *telescopium*, the former used by Galilei, 1611, the latter by Porta in Italy and by Kepler, 1613, f. Gr. *τηλεσκόπ-ος* far-seeing, f. *τῆλε* afar off, at a distance + *σκοπ-εῖν* to look, *-σκοπ-ος* looker: see -SCOPE. The earliest English examples are in the L. and It. forms.

Telescopio is frequent in letters of Galilei from 1 Sept. 1611, but does not appear to have been invented by him; J. B. Porta, member of the Roman Academy of the Lincei (to which Galilei also belonged), in a letter assigned to 1613, appears to attribute the name to Prince Cesi, founder and head of the Academy: 'Telescopium multis ostendi (lubet hoc uti nomine a meo principe reperto)' (*Galilei Opere* (1901) XI. 611). Galilei had previously, in 1610–11, used *perspicillum*, Kepler in 1610 *perspicillum*, *conspicillum*, *specillum*, *penicillium*.]

1. a. An optical instrument for making distant objects appear nearer and larger, consisting of one or more tubes with an arrangement of lenses, or of one or more mirrors and lenses, by which the rays of light are collected and brought to a focus and the resulting image magnified. Also, an instrument or apparatus that serves the same purpose at other wavelengths of the electromagnetic spectrum.

Optical telescopes are of two kinds: *refracting*, in which the image is produced by a lens (the object-glass), and *reflecting*, in which it is produced by a mirror or *speculum*; being magnified in each case by a lens or combination of lenses (the EYE-PIECE, q.v.). Large telescopes of both these kinds are used by astronomers. The smaller hand-telescopes are always refracting, and consist of two or more tubes made to slide one within another for convenience of packing into a narrow compass and for adjusting the lenses as required for focusing the image; cf. TELESCOPE *v.* 1.

[**1619** Bainbridge *Descr. Late Comet* 19 For the more perspicuous distinction whereof I vsed the *Telescopium* or Trunke-spectacle.] **1648** Boyle *Seraph. Love* xi. (1663) 59 Galileo's optick Glasses,..one of which Telescopioes, that I remember I saw at Florence. **1657** W. Rand tr. *Gassendi's Life Peiresc* I. 143 Galilæus, by his newly invented Telescope had discovered certain great and wonderfull sights, concerning the Stars. *Ibid.*, The cause of the effects of the Telescope, or Perspective-Glasse. **1671** Milton *P.R.* IV. 42 By what strange Parallax or Optic skill Of vision multiplyed through air, or glass Of Telescope. **1774** Mackenzie *Maritime Surv.* I. iv. 27 Turn the Theodolite till, through the Telescope, you see the Pole A at the vertical Wire. **1837** Dickens *Pickw.* ii, Mr. Pickwick..with his telescope in his great-coat pocket. **1842** *Penny Cycl.* XXIV. 163/2 It is..manifest that reflecting telescopes, or optical instruments containing combinations of mirrors and lenses, were known in England before the end of the sixteenth century. **1855** Brewster *Newton* I. iii. 59 Sir William Herschel..completed in 1789 his gigantic telescope, forty feet in focal length, with a speculum forty-seven and a half inches in diameter! **1865** 'L. Carroll' *Alice in Wonderland* i, Oh, how I wish I could shut up like a telescope! **1870** Emerson *Soc. & Solit.*, *Art* Wks. (Bohn) III. 16 Dollond formed his achromatic telescope on the model of the human eye. **1875** R. Adamson in *Encycl. Brit.* III. 221/2 He [Roger Bacon] certainly describes a method of constructing a telescope. **1948**, etc. [see *radio telescope* s.v. RADIO *sb.* 7]. **1970** [see *light bucket* s.v. LIGHT *sb.* 16]. **1974** *Physics Bull.* May 208/4 A balloon-borne gamma ray telescope, sensitive to photons with energies greater than 50 MeV, has observed several regions of the sky. **1978** Pasachoff & Kutner *University Astron.* xi. 315 Telescopes in orbit that are sensitive to x-rays have detected a number of strong x-ray sources.

b. *fig.* and *allusively.*

1656 Owen *Mortification Sin* Wks. 1851 VI. 65 We see through a glass darkly... It is not a telescope that helps us to see things afar off. **1666** J. Fraser *Polichron.* (S.H.S.) 18 It [History] is indeed that telescope by which we see into distant ages. **1751** Johnson *Rambler* No. 176. ⁋11 Others are furnished by criticism with a telescope. **1885** J. K. Jerome *On the Stage* p. v, Now that..duty no longer demands that memory should use a telescope.

c. *Astron.* (Also in mod.L. form **Telescopium.**) Name (introduced by Lacaille in 1752) of a constellation south of Sagittarius.

2. *attrib.* and *Comb.*, as ***telescope-maker***, ***-making***, ***-stand***, ***-tube***; ***telescope-shaped*** adj.; also applied to various things consisting of or having parts which fit or slide one within another like the tubes of a hand-telescope (cf. TELESCOPIC 4), as ***telescope-bag***, ***-chimney*** (on a steamboat), ***-joint***, ***-rod***, ***-table***; also **telescope-carp**, a monstrous variety of goldfish, having protruding eyes; also called *scarlet-fish*; **telescope-driver**, a clockwork apparatus for driving an astronomical telescope so as to follow the apparent movements of the heavenly bodies and thus keep the same object continually in the field of view; so ***telescope-driving*** adj.; **telescope-eye**, an eye which can be protruded and retracted like a telescope-tube, as in gastropod molluscs; **telescope-fish** = *telescope-carp*; **telescope-fly**, a fly of the genus *Diopsis*, having the eyes on long stalks; **telescope-shell**, the long conical shell with numerous whorls of an Indian gastropod (*Telescopium fuscum*); **telescope-sight**, a small telescope mounted as a sight upon a firearm or surveying instrument, a telescopic sight; **telescope word** chiefly *U.S.*, a portmanteau word.

1885 J. Short *Diary* 10 Apr. in *Kingston* (Ontario) *Whig-Standard* (1973) 11 Apr. 29/3 *Telescope bags packed, in case we have to start for Calgary in a hurry. **1949** W. Faulkner *Knight's Gambit* (1951) 110 A tremendous old-fashioned telescope bag, strapped and bulging, sat on a chair. **1804** Shaw *Gen. Zool.* V. 211 *Telescope Carp... Scarlet-Carp, with protuberant eyes, all the fins half white. **1874** Sir E. Beckett *Clocks & Watches* 213 The following plan for a *telescope-driving clock... A still simpler *telescope-driver. **1875** *Zoologist* X. 4501 The so-called '*telescope fishes' are common gold-fishes with double tails and projecting eyes. **1882** Ogilvie, **Telescope-fly*, a dipterous insect of the genus *Diopsis.* **1858** Simmonds *Dict. Trade*, *Telescope-maker, Telescope-stand. **1881** T. Hardy *Let.* 13 Dec. (1978) I. 97 The *telescope-making in the catalogue is also useful. **1937** *Discovery* Nov. 360/1 Amateur telescope-making is a hobby that has found many more enthusiasts in the United States than in the British Isles. **1891** Const. MacEwen *3 Women in Boat* 73 We began to fish. We had three little common Japanese *telescope-rods. **1867** Latham *Black & White* 76 In the *telescope-shaped jacketed guns. **1753** Chambers *Cycl. Supp.* App., **Telescope-shell*, the English name of a species of *turbo*, of a conic figure, with plane, striated, and very numerous spires. **1715** tr. *Gregory's Astron.* (1726) I. 284 Instruments..furnished with *Telescope Sights. **1869** C. L. Eastlake *Hints on Househ. Taste* (ed. 2) iii. 67 What is commonly called a '*telescope' table, or one which can be pulled out to twice its usual length, and, by the addition of extra leaves in its middle, accommodates twice the usual number of diners. **1881** Young *Ev. Man his own Mechanic* §763 A telescope-table must be studied in all its parts and movements before any attempt can be made to mend or make one. **1909** *Cent. Dict.* Suppl., *Telescope-word. **1933** H. Wentworth *Blends in Eng.* 3 *Telescope word* has also been applied to one formed from the first syllables of words. **1977** *Lebende Sprachen* XXII. 9/1 A rather special form of collocation are the so-called blends or telescope words.

'telescope, *v.* [f. prec. sb.]

1. a. *trans.* To force or drive one into another (or into something else) after the manner of the sliding tubes of a hand-telescope: usually said in reference to railway carriages in a collision. Also *fig.* to combine, compress, or condense (a number of things) *into* a more compact or concise form; to combine or conflate (several things, or one thing *with* another); to shorten by compression.

1872 *Amer. R.R. Jrnl.* 20 Apr. 493 Telescoping..car raised up and sent through the advancing car, after the manner of a closing telescope. **1876** *World* V. No. 112. 14 No one has ever yet been killed in a Pullman, in which, says its inventor, you can never be 'telescoped'. **1879** *Times* 11 Oct. 5/6 A Pacific express train..ran into a locomotive, completely telescoping the baggage wagons of the express. **1890** Clark Russell *Ocean Trag.* II. xviii. 101 He closed the glass with a ringing of the tubes as he telescoped them.

fig. **1894** *Cornh. Mag.* Mar. 289 The stages which occupy the broom for the whole of its lifetime are telescoped, as it were, in the gorse into the first three weeks. **1909** *Expositor* July 57 It would then be just possible that St. John had to this slight extent 'telescoped' the two accounts together. **1911** Beerbohm *Zuleika Dobson* xvi. 243, I telescoped my toilet and came rushing round to you. **1953** *Essays in Criticism* III. 57 Shelley's mind..has telescoped the shattered autumn landscape with a stormy Heaven and Ocean. **1958** *Listener* 2 Jan. 13/2 Our own effort at telescoping education is a biological retrogressive step. **1961** *Amer. Speech* XXXVI. 162 Generalizing over all such cases, the linguist can telescope them into one single, economical rule of agreement as a formal requirement for well-formed English sentences. **1965** *Listener* 20 May 756/1 The complex is worked out in the book with poetry and psychological insight... The adaptation had to telescope something of this. **1978** *Jrnl. R. Soc. Arts* Dec. 29/2 And so, telescoping time, I now leap from 1909..to 6th October 1927.

b. *intr.* To slide, run, or be driven one into another (or into something else); to have its parts made to slide in this manner (see quot. 1882, s.v. *telescoping* below); to collapse so that its parts fall into one another (quot. 1905).

1877 KNIGHT *Dict. Mech.* 2524/2 Two screws.., one working within the other, and both sinking or telescoping within the base. **1877** O. W. HOLMES *How not to settle it* 92 They telescoped like cars in railroad smashes. **1881** *Metal World* No. 19. 295 The proposals to stop a train by applying the power on the locomotive, which..would cause the carriages to 'telescope'. **1905** BOND *Gothic Archit.* 594 Chichester central tower telescoped within the memory of man.

2. *trans.* To make into or use as a telescope.

1861 [see *telescoped* below]. **1889** *Macm. Mag.* Apr. 419/1 Telescoping my hand, [I] sent a long searching look into the length of the dingy shadow.

Hence **'telescoped** (-skəʊpt) *ppl. a.*; **'telescoping** *vbl. sb.* and *ppl. a.*

1861 THORNBURY *Turner* (1862) II. 170 *note*, Looking through his telescoped hand. **1867** *Commercial & Financial Chron.* V. 6/2 There are two principal dangers which have to be guarded against—the 'telescoping' of cars into each other in case of collision [etc.]. **1882** *Standard* 2 Aug. 3/5 [He] had a telescoping rod in his hand. **1890** *Nature* 11 Sept. 473/1 The telescoping of the limbs and other organs within the body of an insect larva. *Ibid.*, What may be termed the telescoping of ancestral stages one within another. **1898** *Westm. Gaz.* 3 June 3/2 The telescoped carriages and the injured men and women lying about. **1937** 'M. INNES' *Hamlet, Revenge!* I. ii. 42 Clay's picture of Pepys *as* Hamlet was..something extraordinary... He had..been examined both in Shakespeare's *Hamlet* and Pepys's *Diaries*. But this sudden telescoping was beyond him. **1951** M. MCLUHAN *Mech. Bridge* (1967) 85/2 The very name 'Wurlitzer', with its telescoping of 'waltz' and 'whirl', conveys the idea of vertigo. **1958** *Listener* 20 Feb. 341 The way in which this telescoping of development and recapitulation is achieved represents the greatest single master-stroke in the work. **1979** *Internat. Jrnl. Sociol. of Law* Feb. 123 Then there is the problem of what has curiously become known as 'telescoping'—the uncertainty and inaccuracy of respondents in identifying precisely the date on which a particular incident took place—which will inflate or deflate the researcher's estimates.

telescopic (tɛlɪ'skɒpɪk), *a.* (*sb.*) [f. TELESCOPE *sb.* + -IC.]

1. Of or pertaining to a telescope; of the nature of or consisting of a telescope, as ***telescopic sight*** = *telescope-sight* (TELESCOPE *sb.* 2); ***telescopic(-sighted) rifle***, a rifle with a telescopic sight; done by means of a telescope, as ***telescopic observations***.

1705 J. HODGSON in *Phil. Trans.* XXV. 1630 The Brass Quadrant..with Tellescopick Sights. **1855** BREWSTER *Newton* I. iii. 66 The limits of telescopic vision have not been reached. **1880** W. JAMES in *Atlantic Monthly* Oct. 447/2 An Ajax gets no fame in the day of telescopic-sighted rifles. **1907** J. R. ILLINGWORTH *Doctr. Trin.* vii. 138 Like the telescopic discovery of a star which mathematical calculations have already prophesied. **1918** E. A. MACKINTOSH *War, the Liberator* 114 With a telescopic rifle he is looking for a Hun. **1936** *Discovery* Aug. 237 His new giant nine-lens aerial camera. On the right is seen the Telescopic viewfinder. **1947** *E. African Ann.* 1946–7 35/2, I use a 12-inch fixed separation telescopic lens for most bird photographs. **1958** *Observer* 10 Aug. 10/2 The use of the Hasselblad long-distance telescopic camera from a concealed position. **1963** 'E. MCBAIN' *Ten plus One* ii. 30 Forrest's murderer must have used a telescopic sight, the distance..being something over a hundred and fifty yards. **1983** J. SLIGO *Concert Masters* v. 109 As Barbarossa pocketed the passports the telescopic lens of a camera focused from among the sand-dunes. *Ibid.* vi. 155 With a telescopic rifle and night sights, he will be a perfect target.

2. Seen by means of a telescope; *spec.* of a heavenly body, visible only through a telescope (cf. MICROSCOPIC 3). Ellipt. as *sb.* a telescopic star.

1714 DERHAM *Astro-Theol.* Pref. (1726) A vj b, It is not very easy to distinguish which are Satellites, and which are Telescopick Stars. **1784** HERSCHEL in *Phil. Trans.* LXXV. 83 About 1 degree n. of..the six telescopics. **1831** BREWSTER *Nat. Magic* vi. (1833) 143 The general telescopic appearance of the coast. **1893** SIR R. BALL *Sun* 18 These asteroids..are ..entirely telescopic.

3. Having the property of a telescope; having the power of distant vision, far-seeing; contemplating something distant. (*lit.* and *fig.*) In quot. 1886, admitting of distant vision.

1781 COWPER *Truth* 98 Turn eastward now, and fancy shall apply To your weak sight her telescopic eye. **1856** EMERSON *Eng. Traits, Ability*, These Saxons..have.. the telescopic appreciation of distant gain. **1886** BURROUGHS *Signs & Seasons, Sharp Lookout* 6 When the atmosphere is telescopic, and distant objects stand out unusually clear and sharp, a storm is near.

4. Consisting of parts made to slide one within another like the tubes of a hand-telescope, so as to be capable of being lengthened or shortened.

1846 *Penny Cycl.* 1st Suppl. II. 665/2 The commissioners express a very decided opinion against the safety of *telescopic axles*..by which the wheels..might be shifted at pleasure to suit different gauges. **1864** WEBSTER s.v., Constructed of concentric tubes, either stationary, as in the telescopic boiler, or movable, as in the telescopic chimney of a war-vessel. **1871** B. STEWART *Heat* §83 Water or gas pipes are fitted to each other by telescopic joints. **1931** [see *shock strut* s.v. SHOCK *sb.*[2] 7 a]. **1962** *Evening Standard* 2 Oct. 7/3 An umbrella, unless you have one of the portable telescopic kind, is best avoided if you have really a long walk ahead of you. **1973** 'A. HALL' *Tango Briefing* x. 124, I..pulled up the telescopic aerial.

tele'scopical, *a.* Now *rare.* [f. as prec.: see -ICAL.] **1.** = prec. 1.

1672 *Phil. Trans.* VII. 4004 Telescopical Tubes may be considerably shortned without prejudice to their magnifying effect. **1722** WOLLASTON *Relig. Nat.* v. 81 Surveyed..by the help of..telescopical glasses. **1793** SIR G. SHUCKBURGH in *Phil. Trans.* LXXXIII. 103 For telescopical observations of the planets. **1864–90** WEBSTER, *Telescopically*, in a telescopical manner.

2. = prec. 2.

1665–6 *Phil. Trans.* I. 150 By Telescopical Stars are understood such as are not seen, but by the help of a Telescope. **17..** BOLINGBROKE *Ess. Human Knowl.* iii, There are microscopical corpuscles in bodies, as there are telescopical stars in the heavens.

tele'scopically, *adv.* [f. TELESCOPIC, -AL: see -ICALLY.] In a telescopic manner.

1. By or as by means of a telescope; as, or as if, seen through a telescope.

1846 WORCESTER, *Telescopically*, by use of a telescope. **1867–77** G. CHAMBERS *Astron.* I. i. 7 When telescopically examined. **1879** NEWCOMB & HOLDEN *Astron.* 373 Telescopically..we might classify them with Mercury and Venus.

2. In the manner of the tubes of a hand-telescope; by the sliding of one part within another.

1894 BARING-GOULD *Queen of L.* I. vi. 67 It appeared as though the pole were collapsing telescopically. **1898** SEDGWICK *Text-bk. Zool.* I. viii. 299 The foot or pseudopodium [in *Rotifera*] may be jointed, and the joints are often telescopically retractile.

telescopiform (tɛlɪ'skɒpɪfɔːm), *a. Entom.* [f. TELESCOPE + -[I]FORM.] Having the form of a telescope; consisting of a series of joints or tubes retractile one within another.

1826 KIRBY & SP. *Entomol.* IV. xlvi. 352 Ovipositor.. Telescopiform. **1848** *Jrnl. R. Agric. Soc.* IX. I. 190 With her telescopiform oviduct she..pierces the cuticle.

telescopist (tɪ-, tɛ'lɛskəpɪst, 'tɛlɪskəʊpɪst). [f. TELESCOPE + -IST.] One skilled in using a telescope; one who makes telescopic observations.

1870 PROCTOR *Other Worlds* Pref. 6 One of the most surprising phenomena ever witnessed by the telescopist. **1878** NEWCOMB *Pop. Astron.* III. iii. 291 The earlier telescopists..scrutinized the planets very carefully.

telescopy (tɪ-, tɛ'lɛskəʊpɪ, 'tɛlɪskəʊpɪ). *rare*$^{-0}$. [f. as TELESCOPE + -Y, after Gr. words in -σκοπία. Cf. MICROSCOPY.] The art or practice of using the telescope, or of making telescopes.

1861 in COOLEY *Dict.* **1879** in WEBSTER *Supp.*

telescreen: see TELE- 2 b.

teleseismic to **teleshopping**: see TELE- 1.

† **te'lesia**, *sb. pl. Obs.* [mod.L., a. Gr. τελέσια, pl. neuter of τελέσι-ος finishing, completing, perfecting. In Fr. *télésie* (Haüy 1796).] A name for the precious stones composed of crystallized alumina, as the sapphire and its class.

1812 SIR H. DAVY *Chem. Philos.* 357 Alumina..in its crystallized form coloured by small quantities of iron,.. constitutes a beautiful class of gems, distinguished by the name Telesia, including the ruby, the sapphire, the oriental topaz. **1819** *Pantologia, Telesia*,..a name given by Hauy to the sapphire.

‖ **telesis** ('tɛlɪsɪs). [mod.L., a. Gr. type *τέλεσις (f. τελεῖν to finish, complete, f. τέλος end) implied in compounds, as τελεσίδρομος completing the course.] The intelligent direction of effort toward the achievement of an end.

1896 L. F. WARD in *Amer. Jrnl. Sociol.* II. 248 The only serious lack..is a similar antithetical term to be set over against *genesis*, to denote the distinctively social process which results from the application of the indirect, intellectual or telic method [of human evolution]. In order to supply such a term I propose to revive the Greek form *telesis*. **1898** L. F. WARD *Outl. Sociology* 181, 186–190. **1905** DEALEY & WARD *Text-bk. Sociology* IV. xvi. §280. 237 If we regard all the forces of nature..as so many means to the ends of man and society, telesis becomes the adjustment of means to ends, and all human effort is expended upon the means.

† **telesi'urgic**, *a.* (*sb.*) *Obs.* [ad. late Gr. τελεσιουργικός, f. τελεσιουργεῖν in its later sense (Pollux *c* 176 A.D.) 'to perform mystic or magical rites'.] Relating to the performance of mystic or magical rites; = TELESTIC. **b.** as *sb. pl.* **telesi'urgics**, telesiurgic matters or subjects.

1678 CUDWORTH *Intell. Syst.* I. iv. §16. 293 Julian a Chaldean and Theurgist..(who wrote concerning Dæmons and Telesiurgicks).

† **telesm** ('tɛlɪz(ə)m). *Obs.* Also 7 **telesme, -isme**. Also in Gr. form **telesma**, *pl.* **-mata**. [ad. late Gr. τέλεσμα completion, performance, religious rite (*a* 200 Clem. Alex.); later, a consecrated object endowed with a magic virtue to avert evil; f. τελεῖν to complete, fulfil, perform (rites), officiate (in the mysteries), consecrate; f. τέλος end, etc.] = TALISMAN[2] 1; *esp.* in Byzantine Greece, and in Asia, a statue set up, or an object buried under a pillar or the like to preserve the community, house, etc. from danger.

1646 J. GREGORY *Notes & Obs.* (1650) 33 The Claudi and the Cæci..were no other than those..Statuary Telesmes so much celebrated of old, which unless they kept the City, the watchman laboured but in vaine. *Ibid.* 38 Apollonius fetching a deep sigh, refused to make any further Telesmes against the Earthquakes. **1660** H. MORE *Myst. Godl.* VIII. xv. 432 Gaffarel tells us a very reverend story of a Telesme against Fire found under a bridge at Paris. **1693** W. FREKE *Sel. Ess.* iv. 32 Thus Telesmes, or Talismans also,—are a spawn of Astrology.

teles'matic, *a. rare.* [as next + -IC.] = next.

1877 SYMONDS *Renaiss. Italy* iii. 143 Telesmatic virtues were attributed to figures carved on temple-fronts and friezes.

† **teles'matical**, *a. Obs.* [f. Gr. τελέσματ-, stem of τέλεσμα, TELESM + -ICAL.] Of or pertaining to a telesm; talismanic; magical.

1646 J. GREGORY *Notes & Obs.* (1650) 41, I undertake not that the golden Mice were so ceremoniously consecrated, yet that they had a Telesmaticall way of preparation. **1658** ROBINSON *Endoxa* x. 52 The Rain bow hath a Telesmatical signification, for the preservation of the Universe from Inundation. **1693** J. EDWARDS *Author. O. & N. Test.* 145 The telesmatical figure of a stork.

Hence **teles'matically** *adv.*, magically.

1646 J. GREGORY *Notes & Obs.* (1650) 32 The Part of Fortune..was mysteriously included in a Statue of Brasse, Telesmatically prepared,..the Statue was called The Fortune of the City. *Ibid.* 33 Silver statues..Telesmatically consecrated..against the incursions of the Barbarians.

telesoftware to **telestereoscope**: see TELE- 1.

te'lestic, *a. rare.* [ad. Gr. τελεστικός, f. τελεστής hierophant in the mysteries, f. τελεῖν: see TELESM.] Of or pertaining to the mysteries, or to a hierophant; mystical.

1678 CUDWORTH *Intell. Syst.* 293 Julian, in the time of Marcus Antoninus..wrote the Theurgick and Telestick Oracles in Verse. *Ibid.* 792. **1788** T. TAYLOR *Proclus* I. 19 By the highest and most mystical step, he ascended to the greatest and most consummate or telestic virtues. **1822** —— *Apuleius* XI. 276 *note*, As the telestic art, through certain symbols and arcane signatures, assimilates statues to the Gods. **1981** *Times Lit. Suppl.* 23 Jan. 79/5 Plato's four types of mania (telestic, or ritual; mantic or divinatory; poetic; and erotic).

telestich (tɪ-, tɛ'lɛstɪk, 'tɛlɪstɪk). [irreg. f. Gr. τέλος, τελε- end + στίχος a row, line of verse, after ACROSTIC.] A short poem (or other composition) in which the final letters of the lines, taken in order, spell a word or words. (Cf. ACROSTIC.)

a **1637** B. JONSON *Underwoods* lxi. 39 Had I pump'd for.. Acrostichs, and telestichs. **1673** *S' too him Bayes* 44 The arrantest dunce that ever made acrostick, telestick, or anagram. **1862** H. B. WHEATLEY *Anagrams* 46 A very ingenious form of the double acrostic, called the Telestich, has been invented. **1883** H. KENNEDY tr. *Ten Brink's E. Eng. Lit.* 36 A predilection for other metrical diversions, especially the acrostic and telestich.

tele-talkies: see TELE- 1.

Teletex ('tɛlɪtɛks). [prob. blend of TELEX and TEXT *sb.*[1]] A proprietary name for a data processing and communication system using interconnected computer terminals.

1978 *Washington Post* 16 Dec. C11/2 It [*sc.* a low cost computer time-sharing network] is directly competitive with the British Viewdata and Teletex system. **1979** *Trade Marks Jrnl.* 16 May 820/1 *Teletex*... Apparatus for the input, output and recording of printed data; printed data storing apparatus and instruments, keyboards for data processing apparatus; [etc.]... Siemens Aktiengesellschaft.; Munich, Federal Republic of Germany; manufacturers and merchants. **1981** *Sci. Amer.* Oct. E5/1 (Advt.), Siemens, for example, is pioneering teletex which is a synthesis of the typewriter and teleprinter and is the first step towards full-scale electronic mail. **1982** *Nature* 27 May 257/1 The information technology community is calling the new service 'teletex'. It is, however, a far cry from teletext, the broadcast information service. Teletex is either a sophisticated form of telex or a standard that allows computer terminals to communicate with each other.

teletext ('tɛlɪtɛkst). [f. TELE- 2 + TEXT *sb.*[1]] A system in which a user's television set is adapted so as to be able to show alphanumeric information selected from displays transmitted using the spare capacity of existing television channels. Cf. ORACLE *sb.*[1] 10; contrast VIEWDATA.

1974 *Wireless World* Nov. 441/1 (*heading*) Teletext to go ahead. **1975** *Electronics & Power* 15 May 548/1 In March 1974, the British Radio Equipment Manufacturers' Association, BBC and IBA reached agreement on a unified standard system, known as TELETEXT, based largely on the CEEFAX system. **1975**, **1976** [see ORACLE *sb.* 10]. **1980** S. MONEY in K. G. Jackson *Bk. of Video* 89/2 By using the same page format and data coding, viewdata and teletext have been made compatible so that a large part of the decoder can be common for both systems.

teletherapy to **telethermometer**: see TELE- 1.

telethon ('tɛlɪθɒn). orig. and chiefly *U.S.* [f. TELE- 2 + -THON.] An especially prolonged television programme used to raise money for a charity or cause; also in extended use, a lengthy television programme for some other purpose.

1949 *Examiner* (San Francisco) 10 Apr. 22/5 'Telethon' nets $702,000. **1952** *Sun* (Baltimore) 23 June (B ed.) 1/6 Bing Crosby and Bob Hope, in a 14½-hour coast-to-coast telethon today raised more than $1,000,000 in contributions and pledges for the United States Olympic fund. **1960** *Daily Tel.* 8 Nov. 1/2 As the climax to his campaign, Mr. Nixon, Republican, answered telephoned questions for four hours in a nation-wide 'telethon'. **1968** *Courier-Mail* (Brisbane) 16 Sept. 6/5 The telethon, now a widely-used fund raising mechanism. **1973** G. W. HART *Right from Start* iv. 303 Metzenbaum proposed a series of state-wide telethons which would provide an opportunity for the Senator to appear on television hook-ups in the key states in a format in which he excels, answering individual citizens' questions. **1982** *Listener* 8 July 3/2 Perhaps we have all been corrupted by the telethons of Vietnam television reporting.

teletransport(ation: see TELE- 1.

Teletype ('tɛlɪtaɪp), *sb.* Also **teletype**. [f. TELE- + TYPE(WRITER.] **1. a.** A proprietary name for a make of teleprinter. Hence *loosely*, any teleprinter.

1904 *Sci. Amer.* 17 Sept. 193/3 At Brussels it is the telecryptograph of Engineer Malcotti, at Berlin the teletype and the Heljes apparatus. **1922** *Telegr. & Teleph. Jrnl.* VIII. 71/1 The latent innovation in the way of apparatus in the London C.T.O. [*sc.* Central Telegraph Office] is that of the Teletype. **1925** *Official Gaz.* (U.S. Patent Office) 26 May 815/1 Morkrum-Kleinschmidt Corporation, Chicago. .. *Teletype*... Printing-telegraph apparatus. **1933** *Jrnl. R. Aeronaut. Soc.* XXXVII. 12 America, where the teletype, or electrical distant-controlled typewriter, is such an important part of the weather reporting system. **1952** *Trade Marks Jrnl.* 17 Dec. 1167/2 *Teletype*... Printing telegraph apparatus. **1958** *Times Rev. Industry* July (Suppl.) p. ii/1 The bedrock of the work of most British information posts is the daily Press service sent to them by radio, Morse, Hellschreiber or teletype, from C.O.I.'s telecommunications room. **1968** J. SANGSTER *Touchfeather* xiv. 161 As security officer, he had no doubt put the details of my visit on the teletype to all branches of the.. Corporation. **1976** *Physics Bull.* July 298/2 Teletypes are rapidly being superseded by cathode ray display terminals.

b. A message received and printed by a teleprinter.

1961 in WEBSTER. **1966** 'D. SHANNON' *With a Vengeance* xiii. 184 'I'd sent a teletype off.'.. He reached into his breast pocket and brought out two folded pages of teletype. **1972** B. F. CONNERS *Don't embarrass Bureau* (1973) II. 104 He had read his Bureau mail, received a few teletypes from the Director. **1978** S. SHELDON *Bloodline* iii. 56 The messenger .. handed him an envelope. Inside was a teletype from Rhys Williams.

2. *attrib.*, as ***Teletype circuit, key, line, machine, message, network, operator, system, terminal.***

1933 *Sun* (Baltimore) 21 July 22/5 At noon .. police of all districts were notified on the department's teletype system to pick up Roft. **1934** W. SAROYAN *Daring Young Man* 76, I used to sit at a table all day, working a teletype machine, sending and receiving telegrams. **1937** *Sci. Abstr.* B. XL. 302 (*heading*) Teletype network in civil aviation. **1941** C. G. HALPINE *Pilot's Meteorol.* iii. 32 Radiosonde observations are made.. and the reports transmitted over the teletype circuits. **1950** *Times* 2 Mar. 7/6 The Austrians cannot instal new telephone or even teletype lines to other countries without Allied Council approval. **1962** *New Scientist* 1 Feb. 260/1 A transistorized microwave system for transmitting verbal data and teletype messages. **1971** *Ibid.* 18 Mar. 617/1 Fingers that itch to perform on the teletype keys. **1973** *Physics Bull.* Oct. 632/1 Since January 1973 a 'conversational' reference retrieval system has been available.., providing access to 10 000 references and abstracts through any teletype terminal or visual display unit. **1978** *N.Y. Times* 30 Mar. B-20/1 (Advt.), Shipping co needs expd teletype operator.

teletype ('tɛlɪtaɪp), *v.* [f. prec. sb.] **a.** *intr.* To operate a teleprinter; also, to put in a request *for* by means of a teleprinter. **b.** *trans.* To send by means of a teleprinter.

1924 *Daily News* 19 Dec. 5/4 We must teletype as well as teletalk. **1934** WEBSTER, Teletype *v.t. & i.* **1971** 'D. SHANNON' *Ringer* viii. 130 Palliser had teletyped an inquiry up to Lompoc... That wasn't a very big town. **1977** D. ANTHONY *Stud Game* xxvi. 175 Seems he has a record in Texas. We've teletyped for a full report.

So **'teletyped** *ppl. a.*, **'teletyping** *vbl. sb.*

1904 *Knowledge* Feb. 18/2 The Berlin Teletyping Central Station. *Ibid.* 19/2 Teletyping service. **1967** *New Scientist* 28 Dec. 766/2 Professor L. Goldberg and his colleagues.. control the course of their observations by daily teletyped instructions to NASA's Goddard Space Flight Center. **1971** *Nature* 25 June 482/3 A human telegraph operator reads the address on an incoming teletyped message, then retypes it in full to send it to its destination.

teletyper ('tɛlɪtaɪpə(r)). [f. as TELETYPE *sb.* + -ER[1].] A teleprinter.

1904 *Electr. Mag.* I. 64/2 The operation.. may.. be acquired by anybody in the shortest possible time, the teletyper being nothing else than a teletypewriter. **1948** A. BARON *From City, from Plough* 81 Somewhere in an office.. teletypers were clacking their frantic messages. **1965** *Punch* 20 Jan. 76/2 If you can make room between the telephones, dictating machines, office intercoms and teletypers. **1976** *National Observer* (U.S.) 10 Apr. 9/1 The equipment includes telephone-answering devices, burglar-alarm systems, automatic dialers, teletypers.

Teletypesetter (ˌtɛlɪ'taɪpsɛtə(r)). Also with small initial. [f. TELE- + *type-setter* s.v. TYPE *sb.*[1] 10.] The proprietary name of an apparatus for the automatic casting and setting of type in response to telegraphed signals recorded on perforated tape; also used loosely for any such apparatus. Hence ˌ**tele'typesetting** *vbl. sb.*, the action of a Teletypesetter.

1928 *N.Y. Times* 7 Dec. 1/2 Frank E. Gannett, head of the Gannett newspapers.. threw the switch which set in motion the new device known as the Teletypesetter. **1931** *Official Gaz.* (U.S. Patent Office) 17 Mar. 551/1 Teletypesetter. For electrically-controlled typesetting and typecasting apparatus. **1953** *Trade Marks Jrnl.* 22 Apr. 343/1 *Teletypesetter*... Apparatus using perforated tape for the control of type casting machines, and parts thereof included in Class 9. Teletypesetter Corporation.., Chicago 14, Illinois, United States of America; manufacturers. **1961** *Spectator* 14 Apr. 509 He referred to teletypesetting, the process by which the *Guardian* proposes to print in London as well as Manchester. **1965** *Economist* 22 May p. xii/3 The West Coast edition of the *Wall St. Journal*.. is being printed with much use of modern long-distance tele-typesetting. **1967** [see KEYBOARD *v.*].

tele'typewriter. [f. TELE- + TYPEWRITER.] = TELEPRINTER.

1904 *Knowledge* Feb 18/2 The apparatus.. is.. a tele-typewriter, any letters, figures, or signs of punctuation being printed by pressing down a key corresponding with the signal in question. **1922** *Glasgow Herald* 4 Sept. 11 Another great stride in the advance of civilization is demonstrated by the tele-typewriter. **1954** *Electronic Engin.* XXVI. 260 The effect of one form of telegraph distortion on the teleprinter (British) and teletypewriter (American) will be considered. **1968** *Economist* 21 Dec. 32/2 With time-sharing, he can communicate with a computer by means of a special teletypewriter by his desk. **1979** J. E. ROWLEY *Mechanised In-House Information Syst.* i. 59 Other devices, such as the tele-typewriter, the visual display unit and the graphical display unit may function both in input and output.

teleutosorus (təˌljuːtəʊ'sɔːrəs). *Bot.* [f. as TELEUTOSPORE + SORUS[1].] A pustule consisting of a group of teleutospores (teleutospores) and their supporting hyphæ.

1905 [see TELIUM]. **1922** H. GWYNNE-VAUGHAN *Fungi* viii. 205 Sooner or later the mycelium of binucleate cells gives rise to teleutospores; these are characteristically grouped together in teleutosori. **1970** J. WEBSTER *Introd. Fungi* II. iv. 377 *Gymnosporangium* forms teleutosori on *Juniperus*.

teleutospore (tɪ-, tɛ'ljuːtəspɔə(r)). *Bot.* [f. Gr. τελευτή completion, end (f. τέλος end) + SPORE.] A special form of spore, usually produced at the end of the period of fructification, in parasitic fungi of the family *Uredineæ*. Hence **teleutosporic** (-'spɒrɪk) *a.*, of or pertaining to a teleutospore. So **te'leuto-ˌform**, that form or stage of the fungus which produces teleutospores.

1874 COOKE *Fungi* 202 These spores.. may conveniently be called resting spores, or as De Bary calls them, teleutospores, being the last which are produced. **1882** VINES *Sachs' Bot.* 331. **1884** *Athenæum* 18 Oct. 499/3 The probability that the teleutospore of *Puccinia* is also analogous to an egg, the uredospore being 'probably a pupa state'. **1891** *Ibid.* 23 May 671/1 The extraordinary abundance.. of the teleutosporic stage as compared with the comparative scarcity of the æcidial stage. **1898** tr. *Strasburger's Bot.* 367 The genus *Cronartium*, with uredo- and teleuto-forms on *Vincetoxicum* and *Ribes*.

televangelist (tɛlɪ'vændʒəlɪst). orig. *U.S.* Also **tele-evangelist**. [Blend of TELEVISION and EVANGELIST.] An evangelical preacher who uses the mass media, and particularly television, to promote esp. fundamentalist doctrine. Cf. *television evangelist* s.v. TELEVISION 3c; *TV evangelist* s.v. TV b.

1973 *Time* 5 Mar 66/1 (*caption*) Televangelist Rex Humbard with map showing TV broadcast centers. **1981** *N.Y. Times* 26 July VII. 12/1 This fascinating book is a catalogue and primer of the 'televangelists'' theology. **1985** *Time* 18 Mar. 70/1 His syndicated Sunday morning TV service.. reaches an audience of almost 3 million, placing him among the nation's top-rated televangelists. **1986** *Washington Post* 5 Feb. C11/1 A study.. performed by the A. C. Nielson Co. found that 34 million people watched one of the top 10 tele-evangelists during the month studied. **1987** *Independent* 26 Mar. 9/3 With mutual hatreds now so vividly exposed, the 'televangelists' may find it difficult in future to retain the support of their flocks.

Hence **tele'vangelism**, the promulgation of such doctrine on television; **televan'gelical** *a.*, of or pertaining to televangelism; also as *sb.* = TELEVANGELIST.

1980 *Pantagraph* (Bloomington, Illinois) 4 Oct. 13/1 Televangelism has been around for years, but just now it's making more of an impact than it ever has. **1985** *Washington Post* 19 Aug. A7/6 Robertson lacks the hellfire and damnation style of such televangelicals as Jimmy Swaggart and James Robison. **1987** *San Diego Union* 26 Mar. B9/4 There is a great deal of unsettling news emerging these days from the underside of a phenomenon known as 'televangelism'. **1987** *Washington Post* 3 Nov. D4/4 The tour was announced seven months after Jim Bakker resigned as leader of the televangelical empire he and his wife had founded.

televarsity, tele-vérité, televersity: see TELE- 2b.

televiewer ('tɛlɪˌvjuːə(r)). [f. TELE- 2 + VIEWER.] One who watches television.

1935 *Discovery* Oct. 285/2 An excellent answer to the questions of the.. would-be 'televiewer'. **1937** *Daily Herald* 2 Feb. 3/4 Televiewers will not have to change over a switch on their sets each week to suit the alternate systems of transmission. **1950** *Sun* (Baltimore) 4 Jan. 18/2 Thirty-nine per cent of the entire television and radio broadcast audience during this period were Baltimore televiewers. **1957** E. HYAMS *Into Dream* I. v. 40 There was *Dentix*: a half-tone of a face well known to televiewers leered out of the page. **1971** L. KOPPETT *N.Y. Times Guide Spectator Sports* 3 Many televiewers.. had no prior intention to watch a football or basketball game. **1982** *Daily Tel.* 20 Sept. 15/7 Millions of televiewers around the world saw the moving spectacle of Prince Rainier's grief.

So **'teleview** *v. intr.*, to watch television (*rare*); **'televiewing** *vbl. sb.* and *ppl. a.*

1935 *Times* 15 May 13/2 The German Post Office yesterday opened the first public televiewing post outside Berlin.. at Potsdam. **1945** COOKE & MARKUS *Electronics Dict.* 382 *Teleview*, to watch a scene by means of a television system. **1956** *Encycl. Brit. Bk. of Year* 492/2 *Televiewing*, formerly used as a noun, now appearing as an adjective, as in the phrase 'televiewing families', meaning families habituated to watching television. **1959** *New Statesman* 4 July 10/1 People still like and are permitted to laugh, and occasionally break off from televiewing to have a go at the printed word. **1960** *Twentieth Cent.* Dec. 541 A considerable impression was made.. upon the televiewing public. **1976** *Listener* 23 Sept. 366/2 My own loss of televiewing had no effect on the number of times I hit anybody. **1982** *Economist* 5 June 25 By overestimating the numbers who would come, instead of televiewing, they left sellers of hot dogs and papal souvenirs bankrupt. **1982** *Nature* 9 Dec. 468/2 Channel 4.. seems to have won the allegiance of a mere four per cent of the British televiewing audience.

televisable ('tɛlɪ-, tɛlɪ'vaɪzəb(ə)l), *a.* [f. TELEVISE *v.* + -ABLE.] Capable of being televised, suitable for presentation on television. Similarly **televisible** (tɛlɪ'vɪzɪb(ə)l) [after *visible*] *nonce-wd.*

1974 *Times* 18 May 14/7 Unfortunately.. Mrs Fawcett [was] eminently less televisable than Mrs Pankhurst. **1975** A. POWELL *Hearing Secret Harmonies* ii. 38, I resign St John Clarke to the makers of all things televisible. **1979** *Economist* 3 Nov. 48/1 'Land people' who.. have been a deeper tragedy than the more televisable 'boat people'.

televise ('tɛlɪvaɪz), *v.* [Back-formation from TELEVISON on the model of verbs that end in -(*v*)*ise* and are related to nouns ending in -(*v*)*ision*, such as *revise*.] **1. a.** *trans.* To transmit (pictures, programmes, scenes, etc.) by television; formerly also, to transmit television pictures of (a person). Also *fig.*

1927 *Glasgow Herald* 14 Jan. 9/1 The distance over which pictures can be televised. **1928** *Television* Mar. 40/3 The subject who is being 'televised' had to face a powerful battery of blinding lights. **1931** *Daily Progress* (Charlottesville, Va.) 2 May 3/4 The first marriage ceremony to be 'televised', if that's the word—is a matter of history today. **1939** [see INTERVIEWER]. **1950** *Sport* 7-11 Apr. 22/2 The Final will definitely not be televised. **1975** *Observer* (Colour Suppl.) 6 Apr. 64 (Advt.), It [*sc.* a series of books on history] is a 'programme' which combines lively and informative reading with vivid illustrations, helpful maps and guides, in such a way that it televises the past for you and your children to understand and enjoy as never before. **1979** S. BRETT *Comedian Dies* ix. 95 This.. Awards lunch... Big do, being televised. **1983** *Economist* 23 July 24/1 The BBC's Panorama programme on blacks and the police, televised on July 18th.

b. *intr.* for *pass.* To be (well, etc.) suited for television presentation.

1930 *Times* 1 Apr. 28/3 Some faces appear to 'televise' better than others. **1961** G. MILLERSON *Techn. Telev. Production* 129 Where an iconoscope camera-tube is used as the pick-up device, film shots of dark scenes may televise better in negative form.

2. *intr.* To make a television broadcast.

1948 L. BIRCH *Something Done* (Central Office of Information) 15 Many performers who are under contract to the big music-halls are not allowed to televise. **1957** [implied at TELEVISING *ppl. a.*].

Hence **'televised** *ppl. a.*; **'televising** *vbl. sb.* and *ppl. a.*

1932 *Jrnl. Television Soc.* I. 107/1 The televising of 'The Man with the Flower in his Mouth', in July, 1930. **1934** *Jrnl. Inst. Electr. Engineers* LXXV. 86/2 The difference in detail between a good Baird televized picture and the cathode-ray picture. **1935** *Times* 1 Feb. 8/4 No doubt the televising of sporting and other public events will have a wide appeal. **1946** *Astounding Sci. Fiction* July 63/1 A man he had seen many times before in televised addresses. **1951** M. EHRLICH *Big Eye* i. 34 The blonde began to take off her robe in a kind of televised strip tease. **1957** D. J. ENRIGHT *Apoth. Shop* 221 True pleasure—our moralizing, politicizing and.. televising generation has thrown *that* overboard. **1958** *Times Lit. Suppl.* 21 Nov. p. xxix/2 Miss Edwards opens her story with the televising of Punchbowl Farm and the Thornton family. **1978** S. BRILL *Teamsters* iii. 80 Fumbling through televised testimony like this to protect Hoffa was worth it to Fitzsimmons.

television ('tɛlɪvɪʒən, tɛlɪ'vɪʒən). [f. TELE- + VISION *sb.*] **1. a.** A system for reproducing an actual or recorded scene at a distance on a screen by radio transmission, usu. with appropriate sounds; the vision of distant objects obtained thus.

The term normally refers to a system of general transmission over the air, but it also includes systems of restricted transmission to subscribers by wire, such as ***cable television***; see also *closed circuit* s.v. CLOSED *ppl. a.* 3.

[**1904** *Daily News* 3 June 7 Dr. Low talks very modestly of the 'televista' (the name he has given to his 'seeing by wire' invention).] **1907** *Sci. Amer. Suppl.* 15 June 26292/1 Now that the photo-telegraph invented by Prof. Korn is on the eve of being introduced into general practice, we are informed of some similar inventions in the same field, all of which tend to achieve some step toward the solution of the problem of television. **1909** *Athenæum* 25 Sept. 367/3 The efforts made by Prof. Rukmer of Berlin to realize 'television'. **1913** *Wireless World* Sept. 353/2 The television,.. being based upon the same principle as photo-telegraphy, is possible in itself. **1926** *Glasgow Herald* 20 Dec. 11/8 Mr. John L. Baird, a native of Helensburgh,..

recently invented an apparatus which makes television possible. **1930** J. BUCKINGHAM *Matter & Radiation* 122 We have heard so much about Television lately that we are apt to forget that no portion of the apparatus used is novel to scientists. **1942** T. S. ELIOT *Music of Poetry* 18 There are words which are ugly because of foreignness or ill-breeding (e.g. *televison*): but I do not believe that any word well-established in its own language is either beautiful or ugly. **1948** N. WIENER *Cybernetics* 10 Television was destined to be more useful to engineering by the introduction of such new techniques than as an independent industry. **1957** *Technology* Mar. 9/2 The solution of the major problems in colour television, the public introduction of which is now more a question of economics than of technical difficulty. **1970** *Toronto Daily Star* 24 Sept. 28/1 (Advt.), You can receive Channel 19 by..cable television. **1972** *Times* 21 Jan. 2/5 Cable televison was originally introduced in the area in 1962 to provide better reception because Shooters Hill in the south consistently interfered with Television pictures.

b. Organized television broadcasting; the television broadcasting service as a whole or (with defining word) a particular television service. Phr. ***on (the) television.***

1927 [see HEEBIE-JEEBIE(s)]. **1930** N. COWARD *Private Lives* II. 49 Aeroplanes..and Cosmic Atoms, and Television. **1938** *Observer* 26 June 12/6, I reviewed this film three weeks ago when I saw it on television. **1951** *N.Y. Herald-Tribune* 12 Dec. 27/3 Buster is an old playmate and I'm glad to see he..crashed television successfully. **1958**, etc. [see INDEPENDENT *a.* 5 e]. **1962** *Friend* 1 June 665/1, I have sometimes thought how different life might have been at Haworth if only they had had the television, and Tide, and a Morris Minor. **1965** M. DRABBLE *Millstone* 194 You could get a job on the television. **1968** *Globe & Mail* (Toronto) 17 Feb. 36 (Advt.), Private balconies, cable television, off street parking. **1976** *Jrnl. R. Soc. Arts* June 365/2 Are there any recent figures of the cost to every household in the country of the advertising on independent television? **1980** *Private Eye* 26 Sept. 13/1 That ghastly woman with the teeth who's always on the television. **1982** *Listener* 16 Dec. 17/1, I have mixed feelings about cable television's 'autumn of debate'.

c. Television entertainment; television broadcasting considered as a medium of communication or as an art form. Cf. GOOD *a.* 1 f.

1931 *Daily Progress* (Charlottesville, Va.) 2 May 3/4 The ceremony is television, but in every other way the wedding is absolutely regular. **1957** *Observer* 27 Oct. 17/4 It proved, as discussions on these emotive imponderabilia always do, highly absorbing television. **1977** *Times* 2 Sept. 7/3 Television, the art..that speaks daily to almost everybody. **1982** *Sunday Tel.* 3 Jan. 16/7 Attenborough's 'Life on Earth' was perfect television.

2. A television set.

1955 *Observer* 28 Aug. 7/4 The South London landlady was seeking 'a nice new television'. **1972** *Daily Express* 8 Jan. 12/4 We have never been able to afford a car but we do have a television. **1973** D. FRANCIS *Slay-Ride* viii. 96 Behind me on a wide shelf stood my portable television. **1982** *Sunday Sun-Times* (Chicago) 3 Oct. 72/1 Industry workers last year averaged $75 a month. They buy televisions and send money home to wives.

3. *attrib.* and *Comb.* **a.** In general uses, as ***television aerial, antenna, apparatus, box, channel, coverage, dealer, frequency, lounge, receiver, room, screen, service, set, signal, studio, supper, system, theatre, transmission, transmitter, van.***

1940 *Amateur Radio Handbk.* (ed. 2) 306/1 (Index), Television aerials. **1972** J. PORTER *Meddler & her Murderer* xi. 136 Rows of ugly little houses, their roofs buckling under a forest of television aerials. **1947** *Electronics* May 96/2 (*heading*) Television antennas for apartments. **1951** W. FAULKNER *Requiem for Nun* III. 246 Lonely farmhouses glittering and gleaming with automatic stoves and washing machines and television antennae. **1930** *Aberdeen Press & Jrnl.* 14 Apr. 6, I do not suppose that many Scottish listeners have yet adopted television apparatus. **1932** A. HUXLEY *Brave New World* xiv. 234 At the foot of every bed..was a television box. **1950** K. HENNEY *Radio Engin. Handbk.* (ed. 4) xix. 1024 Allocation of television channels. Figure 40 shows the allocation of twelve 6-Mc channels for television. **1981** *Ann. Reg. 1980* 427 Plans for the setting up of the fourth television channel..went ahead. **1966** *B.B.C. Handbk.* 51 Gaps of the existing BBC radio and television coverage. **1949** *Radio Times* 15 July 42/1 Your nearest Ultra Television dealer. **1955** *Ibid.* 22 Apr. 3/1 The present television frequencies..are in the V.H.F. band. **1970** K. GILES *Death in Church* v. 150 The ladies have arrived... In the television lounge. **1976** W. J. BURLEY *Wycliffe & Schoolgirls* ii. 42 The door of the television lounge was open and he could see several patients sitting round the set. **1927** Television receiver [see RECEIVER[1] 7 c]. **1980** *Whitaker's Almanack 1981* 816/1 About 3·8 million television receivers are in use [in the Argentine Republic]. **1959** 'O. MILLS' *Stairway to Murder* viii. 95 The Residents' Lounge and Television Room are both at your disposal. **1971** *Country Life* 23 Dec. (Suppl.) 3/2 (Advt.), Mansion. Ideally suitable for institutional purposes... 2 television rooms, chapel. **1927** *Pictorial Weekly* 5 Mar. 100/1 These sets will combine a Television screen and loud-speaker. **1973** D. MAY *Laughter in Djakarta* i. 13 Little figures mouthing words that did not reach him, like a television screen with no sound. **1935** *Times* 1 Feb. 7/4 These first steps being taken towards the establishment of a public television service. **1936** *Radio Times* 30 Oct. 5/3 Television programmes. The BBC Television Service from Alexandra Palace will be opened by the Postmaster-General on Monday. **1966** *B.B.C. Handbk.* 15 *The Northern Echo* [said]..'some parts of the television service are falling asleep'. **1931** *N.Y. Times* 31 May IX. 9/2 The Radio Corporation of America..is concentrating its efforts upon the primary technical developments to be completed before undertaking the manufacture and sale of television sets on a commercial basis. **1976** W. TREVOR *Children of Dynmouth* i. 25 Slowly he walked through Dynmouth again, examining the goods in the shop windows, watching golf being played on various television sets. **1927** *Bell System Technical Jrnl.* VI. 560 (*heading*) The production and utilization of television signals. **1935** *Illustr. London News* 23 Feb. 307 (*caption*) The Baird television studios at the Crystal Palace. **1981** S. BRETT *Situation Tragedy* iv. 43 He wished he knew a bit more about television studios and their sound systems. **1973** D. MILLER *Chinese Jade Affair* xi. 108 This was where the old lady had her television suppers. **1983** *Times* 1 Oct. 8/6 The art of conversation, of manners, of social interplay..cannot be acquired at the nursery table or when eating a solitary television supper with the baby-minder. **1931** *Proc. IRE* XXI. 1655 The experimental television system placed in operation by RCA Victor in..1931..was based on the use of a cathode ray tube as the image reproducing element. **1966** *B.B.C. Handbk.* 35 BBC Television..along with other Western television systems. *Ibid.* 33 There are in the London area six..production studios.., a television theatre, two news studios, and two remote control studios. **1929** *Radio Times* 8 Nov. 412/1, 11.00–11.30 (*London only.*) Experimental television transmission by the Baird Process. **1928** *N.Y. Times* 22 Aug. 1/2 Puppets being used because of the limitations of the television transmitter. **1939** *Electronics* Mar. 26 (*heading*) Television transmitters. **1956** R. ROBINSON *Landscape with Dead Dons* xiii. 117 'You refer to the television van?' 'The one you told me the little men come in.'

b. Connected with, participating in, or transmitted as part of organized television broadcasting, as ***television announcer, audience, broadcast, broadcasting, commercial, crew, critic, discussion, drama, dramatist, film, interview, journalist, magazine, news, personality, play, producer, programme, public, pundit, reporter, serial, series, show, spot, star, version, viewer.***

1938 *Radio Times* 23 Dec. 36/1 It would be nice to say that the television announcers will hang up their stockings. **1972** J. MOSEDALE *Football* xi. 148 Gifford, then a television announcer, talked briefly with the coach. **1937** *Discovery* Nov. 331/2 Building up a television audience. **1959** *Twentieth Cent.* Nov. 335 Because of its great size, the television audience now closely resembles the population as a whole. **1928** *N.Y. Times* 21 Aug. 26 Hourly television broadcasts over WRNY to aid amateurs and experimenters will begin tomorrow. **1935** *Times* 1 Feb. 8/3 There will be little, if any, scope for television broadcasts unaccompanied by sound. **1928** *Daily Mail* 3 Aug. 9/5 Mr. J. L. Baird, the inventor of television, stated yesterday that television broadcasting would begin in this country in the autumn. **1977** *Rep. Comm. Future of Broadcasting* (Cmnd. 6753) ii. 10 All sound and television broadcasting which uses radio waves for transmission is in the charge of two public Authorities, the British Broadcasting Corporation and the Independent Broadcasting Authority. **1957** Television commercial [see COMMERCIAL *sb.* 2]. **1975** R. RENDELL *Shake Hands for Ever* x. 95 Those children's toys which he had often seen on television commercials. **1964** J. MITFORD in *Making of Muckraker* (1979) 90 Our house..was transformed..by television crews filming interviews about the book. **1978** W. F. BUCKLEY *Stained Glass* xviii. 172 All Monday the television crews were at work. **1966** *B.B.C. Handbk.* 13 Television critic Peter Black..asked for a definition of this phrase. **1981** *Listener* 22 Oct. 465/3 He was the best partner I ever had in television discussions. **1949** *Radio Times* 15 July 41/2 A variegated week for television drama. **1973** *Listener* 5 July 27/1 Watergate makes television drama, which rests on an illusion of reality, look pretty thin. **1964** *Ibid.* 16 Apr. 624/2 'Television dramatists'..have the cheek to use television techniques in stage plays. **1951** R. CHANDLER *Let.* 5 Jan. (1981) 256, I have seen a number of the television films of your stories. **1967** M. ARGYLE *Psychol. Interpersonal Behaviour* x. 189 A television film is played back to the trainee after his performance. **1964** D. FRANCIS *Nerve* xiv. 192 That was just what I needed... A big race win and a television interview. **1974** *Listener* 29 Oct. 525/1 A bad, sad month for television journalists. **1955** *Radio Times* 22 Apr. 15/2 The fortnightly television magazine *Ulster Mirror*, broadcast since November. **1947** *Billboard* 1 Nov. 16 Television news borrows from the radio, it is related to the newsreel. **1977** D. L. ALTHEIDE in Douglas & Johnson *Existential Sociol.* iv. 147 Research on television news. **1958** *Times Lit. Suppl.* 4 Apr. 179/1 The man of letters is no longer a household figure—unless, by coincidence, he is also a television personality. **1978** *Times* 15 Aug. 13/7 Who does qualify for VIP lounges; presumably some television 'personalities' and some entertainers? **1946** *B.B.C. Year Book* 21 The old hand may in time come to ear-mark his evenings primarily for full-length television plays. **1968** Television play [see PREVIEW *v.* 2 a]. **1951** *Catal. Exhibits, South Bank Exhib., Festival of Britain* 176 *Television Producer* Malcolm Baker Smith. **1982** *Sunday Tel.* 3 Jan. 16/4 Television and film producers..go for their inspiration to the printed word. **1930** *Billboard* 20 Sept. 30/1 Television programs were being broadcast daily from two studios. **1935** *Radio Times* 27 Dec. 3/1 Television programmes from the new station at the Alexandra Palace start next year. **1981** *Ann. Reg. 1980* 428 By far the greatest impact made by a single television programme in 1980 resulted from the screening..of ATV's *Death of a Princess*. **1937** *Discovery* Nov. 332/2 A television public has not been developed at all. **1981** *Listener* 22 Oct. 465/3 Robert McKenzie..was the greatest of all television pundits on politics and elections. **1959** *Housewife* June 32 As a television reporter I've certainly got used to meeting a lot of unhappy people. **1957** M. SUMMERTON *Sunset Hour* x. 133 He hoped to clinch a contract for a part in a television serial. **1965** B. GLANVILLE *Second Home* xii. 301 He had to go up to Birmingham next day for some television series he was directing. **1982** *Sunday Tel.* 3 Jan. 16/7 The most successful television series..are not from books of the very first rank. **1950** R. CHANDLER *Let.* 22 Nov. (1981) 241 I'd like to have a television show. **1976** W. TREVOR *Children of Dynmouth* i. 25 He'd asked Timothy what he found interesting outside the Comprehensive and Timothy had said television shows. **1960** Television spot [see SPOT *sb.*[1] 8 d]. **1951** A. C. CLARKE *Sands of Mars* xiii. 163 A..caricature of a well-known television star. **1982** *Sunday Tel.* 3 Jan. 16/5 The experience of watching the television version [of *Brideshead Revisited*] differed very little from that of reading Evelyn Waugh's masterpiece. **1952** *Sun* (Baltimore) 17 Mar. 1/6 (*heading*) Television viewers are able to see operation in hospital. **1961** *Times* 11 Dec. 13/6 Here is a population consisting almost wholly of industrial workers..car owners, television-viewers.

c. Special Combs. **television camera**: see CAMERA 3 c; **television camera tube**, an electron tube of the kind used in television cameras for converting a visual image into an electrical signal; **television engineer**, one who designs and maintains the mechanical and electrical processes involved in the transmission and reception of television signals; a television repairman; **television evangelist** orig. *U.S.* = TELEVANGELIST; also **television evangelism**; **television image** = *television picture* below; **television licence**, a licence to use a television set, renewable annually on payment of a fee; **television mast**, (*a*) a tall mast, usu. set up on high ground, carrying a television transmitting aerial; (*b*) = *television aerial*, sense 3 a above; **television network**, a system of television broadcasting stations; a television broadcasting organization or channel; **television picture**, the visual image received on a television screen; **television region**, a region of the country receiving television broadcasts from a local as well as a national transmitting station; **television satellite**, a satellite put into orbit round the earth to reflect back television signals; **television station**, a television broadcasting station (see STATION *sb.* 13 f); **television tube**, (*a*) = *picture tube* s.v. PICTURE *sb.* 6 d; (*b*) = *television camera tube* above.

1940 D. G. FINK *Princ. Television Engin.* i. 17 (*caption*) A typical television camera tube, the type 1849 iconoscope, now widely used in television broadcasting. **1974** *Encycl. Brit. Macropædia* XVIII. 112/1 The image orthicon is the most highly developed of the television camera tubes. **1930** *Billboard* 20 Sept. 15/2 Equipment to be used will come from General Electric, under the supervision of Dr. E. F. W. Alexanderson, television engineer. **1978** F. KING *Action* x. 31 The failure of the television engineer to call to repair the set. **1977** *Washington Post* 25 July B1/6 The man his staff calls the 'Johnny Carson' of television evangelism..strolls onstage. **1987** *Los Angeles Times* 31 Mar. I. 20/2 Soon many of the biggest names in television evangelism were sniping or commenting. **1977** *Washington Post* 30 Apr. A21/2 The fund had had..assets in..race tracks, gambling casinos, nursing homes..and a cathedral for a television evangelist. **1987** *Financial Times* 9 Oct. 5/1 Mr Pat Robertson, the..former television evangelist, has conceded that he had lied..about the date of his marriage. **1933** *Proc. IRE* XXI. 1631 (*heading*) A study of television image characteristics. **1949** *Times* 17 Feb. 5/3 The first hundred thousand mark is about to be reached in..television licences..compared with the eleven million for sound. **1972** C. DRUMMOND *Death at Bar* ii. 52 Jarvis..abandoned the cinema the instant he had paid his first television licence fee. **1958** S. HYLAND *Who goes Hang?* I. vii. 39 They could see the enormous, meccano structure of the television mast on top of Sydenham Hill. **1968** M. ALLINGHAM *Cargo of Eagles* iv. 54 They drove.. through an area of open planned villas, writhing television masts, mini cars. **1947** *Billboard* 1 Nov. 16/2 Now that the Columbia Broadcasting System (CBS) has joined the routes of companies working toward a television network [etc.]. **1974** *B.B.C. Handbk. 1975* 19/1 One..fairly brief consequence of the energy crisis was the decision to close down all television networks at 10.30 pm. **1937** *Chron. & Echo* (Northampton) 8 May 6/1 (Advt.), Real television... Demonstration in advance of how Television pictures should appear when broadcast. **1977** J. FRASER *Heart's Ease in Death* i. 7 The wind shaking the aerial had distorted the television picture. **1974** Television region [see REGION 5 d]. **1960** *Aeroplane* XCVIII. 419/2 Nowhere will the successful launching of the U.S. television satellite be noted with more interest than in this country. **1976** I. LEVIN *Boys from Brazil* vi. 180 Speaking to the whole world at once..by television satellite. **1931** *Billboard* 1 Aug. 4/1 As soon as television stations increase in number so that they can't be fitted into low channel, high band will be used for them exclusively. **1980** *Whitaker's Almanack 1981* 816/1 In addition there are 65 television stations, of which 4 are in Buenos Aires. **1943** *Electronic Engin.* XV. 329/2 The modern television tube has many ancestors. We could start its history in 1897. **1975** D. G. FINK *Electronics Engineers' Handbk.* XI. 57 Antimony trisulfide vidicons, lead oxide vidicons, and image orthicons are the work-horse television tubes.

televisionary (ˌtɛlɪˈvɪʒənərɪ), *sb.* and *a.* *Humorous.* [Blend of TELEVISION + VISIONARY *a.* and *sb.*; in adj. use treated as compound with -ARY[1].] **A.** *sb.* **a.** An enthusiast for television. **b.** A television personality.

1928 *Observer* 12 Feb. 11/2 Many 'televisionaries' have spent fortunes in the quest. **1961** A. CLARKE *Later Poems* 94 The Pope forbade the clergy..to indulge in daily amusement. He warned them, too, of the danger of becoming televisionaries. **1962** *Listener* 24 May 924/2 With Dylan Thomas and Gilbert Harding gone, Gwyn Thomas has a great future as a televisionary. **1981** Q. CRISP *How to become a Virgin* 156 Impresarios are frequently asked by televisionaries when some scheme or other first occurred to them.

B. *adj.* Of, possessing, or induced by television.

1934 in WEBSTER s.v. *Television.* **1937** E. BLUNDEN *Elegy* 50 The televisionary world to come. **1958** *Times* 5 July 7/2 If, in a televisionary trance, we are induced to buy some commodity for which our waking self has no appetite [etc.]. **1966** *New Statesman* 16 Dec. 917/3 The longish orchestral interludes, which are enough to drive the average televisionary producer to despair. **1980** *Daily Tel.* 5 Sept. 12/1 Televisionary indoctrination in Luanda.

televisioner (tɛlɪˈvɪʒənə(r)). *rare.* [f. TELEVISION + -ER[1].] One who watches television.
1928 *Television* Mar. 12/1 (*caption*) Some new uses for television. For the toilet—enabling the televisioner to see the back of his head when brushing his hair.

televisionless (ˈtɛlɪ-, tɛlɪˈvɪʒənlɪs), *a.* [f. TELEVISION + -LESS.] Without a television set; that does not include watching television.
1962 *Guardian* 8 Jan. 2/3 Parents.. should provide a warm and undisturbed televisionless place for homework. **1981** *Times Lit. Suppl.* 8 May 516/3 Our customary, televisionless routine.

ˈtelevision-wise, *adv.* [-WISE.] In the manner of television; with regard to television.
1962 *Listener* 19 Apr. 702/1 Television-wise, his performance was more convincing. **1968** [see SCAN *v.* 6 c].

televisor (ˈtɛlɪvaɪzə(r)). Also Televisor. [f. as TELEVISE *v.*: see -OR.] **1.** An apparatus for transmitting or receiving television pictures; orig. the name of that designed and patented by John Logie Baird (1888–1946). Now only *Hist.*
1926 *Glasgow Herald* 11 Jan. 7 The Televisor. *Ibid.* 8 Oct. 9/1 The scene in front of the transmitting televisor is turned into electrical impulses. **1927** *Ibid.* 2 Feb. 9 The cost of televisor equipment for practical use. **1930** MOSELEY & CHAPPLE *Television* viii. 95 The audience can see on the screen of their 'televisors', and hear the person who is broadcasting from the studio. **1935** H. G. WELLS *Things to Come* xii. 98 There is a large televisor disk and telephone and other apparatus on the desk before Cabal. *Ibid.* xiii. 119 A man stands up and switches on a televisor and everybody listens. **1946** *Astounding Science Fiction* July 61/2 The televisor muttered at his elbow and he reached out to flip the toggle. **1984** *Financial Times* 13 June 17/6 A rare John Logie Baird televisor of around 1930 sold for £1,760.
2. A television broadcaster. *rare.*
1942 BERREY & VAN DEN BARK *Amer. Thes. Slang* §618/3 *Televisor*, the television transmitting apparatus; also a television artist or technician. **1966** *New Statesman* 30 Sept. 497/4 (Advt.), Heather Jenner, televisor, broadcaster and writer.

televisual (ˌtɛlɪˈvɪʒjuːəl, -ˈvɪzjuːəl), *a.* [f. TELEVISON, after VISUAL *a.*] Of, pertaining to, characteristic of, or appearing on television; suitable for or effective in the medium of television.
1934 in WEBSTER. **1956** *Observer* 15 Jan. 8/5 All day he lies in bed, while televisual phantoms flit across his ruffled cerebral screen. **1959** *Listener* 12 Feb. 303/1 Here was something that the theatre could not do, something essentially televisual. **1960** K. AMIS *New Maps of Hell* iii. 82 Televisual views of actual historical scenes. **1973** *Church Times* 16 Nov. 9 Filmic or televisual violence breeds or releases violence in the viewer. **1980** *Times Lit. Suppl.* 25 July 842/2 It is because he keeps in practice with televisual mannerisms that he is so successful a natural in a television-dominated world.
Hence **teleˈvisually** *adv.*, from the point of view of or as regards television, on or for television.
1957 *Observer* 29 Sept. 13/2 Televisually.. there was a surprising amount to be said in favour of this experiment so rich in every kind of producer's death-trap. **1967** *Listener* 9 Feb. 207/2 We had on this uncomfortable occasion not Shakespeare re-worked televisually.. but a kind of compromise with what had already been worked in an alien medium. **1979** *Ibid.* 3 May 602/2 A generation ago, we still lived in an age of innocence, televisually, and politicians were apt to come on the box as themselves. **1981** *Times* 27 June 6/2 Who better than Russell, with his televisually perfect mane of white hair?

telewriter: see TELE- 1.

telex, Telex (ˈtɛlɛks). [f. TELE(PRINTER + EX(CHANGE *sb.* 10 c.] **1.** A system of telegraphy in which printed messages are transmitted and received by teleprinters using the public telecommunication lines; the apparatus used in this process. Freq. *attrib.*, esp. in *telex service*.
Despite the frequent use of a capital initial, *telex* in the ordinary uses defined here is not a proprietary term. The names of some specific products (radio equipment, hearing aids, etc.) of the Telex Corporation are registered as trade marks, however.
1932 *Telegr. & Teleph. Jrnl.* Oct. 2/1 In August 1932, came the opening in London of 'Telex' service, otherwise 'teleprinter exchange service'. **1939** *Electrical Communication* Jan. 222/2 Strong grounds exist for the belief that.. a spontaneous and universal growth of Telex will follow. **1954** *Communications & Electronics* Nov. 40/1 Telex is an internationally agreed name for a subscriber-to-subscriber public teleprinter exchange service; it is for the printed word what the telephone exchange system is for the spoken word. **1958** *Times* 2 Sept. 5/2 Telex subscribers are linked to a system by which they can exchange typed messages by teleprinter. **1964** C. DENT *Quantity Surveying by Computer* vii. 101 Equipment can be obtained enabling these tapes to be input over the Telex system directly to the computer. **1968** R. V. BESTE *Repeat Instructions* xxii. 233 He .. was told to ring back at midnight when they should have the answer on the Telex. **1970** *New Scientist* 16 July (Suppl.) 2/1 It is estimated that by 1980 the total of telex and similar machine to machine (including computer) messages in the United States will be just over one billion. **1974** C. HAMPTON *Savages* (1976) xiii. 64 Installing a telex in the interests of business efficiency. **1981** *Sci. Amer.* Oct. E5/1 (Advt.), Transmission is at 2,400 bits/s and a page of 1500 characters can be sent in ten seconds—20–30 times faster than telex—and received on telexes, electronic typewriters, word processors or other compatible terminals.
2. A message so transmitted.
1978 *Globe & Mail* (Toronto) 12 Oct. 4/4 Here was the only apparent flaw in the Telexes. Mr. Lalonde wasn't elected to the House of Commons and appointed to Cabinet until the following year. **1980** *Daily Tel.* 9 July 16 The first I heard of it was when I got a telex of congratulation.
Hence **ˈtelex** *v.* (*a*) *trans.*, (i) to contact by telex; (ii) to send (a message) by telex; (*b*) *intr.*, to send a telex message; **ˈtelexed** *ppl. a.*
1960 *Guardian* 13 Dec. 8/6 In a telexed message to 18 cities and towns Mr. Bevins declared that direct dialling.. was planned to start in six months. **1968** *Aramco World Mag.* May–June 25/1 He.. waited while the story was telexed—at 60 words a minute—to a communications center in London. **1968** C. BURKE *Elephant across Border* ii. 74, I must telex Allard by eleven. **1972** *Daily Tel.* 8 Mar. 17 (Advt.), Write, telephone or telex for information now. **1979** *Courier-Mail* (Brisbane) 4 Oct. 3/6 The managing director of Hudson Conway Holdings Ltd... said yesterday he had telexed the Queensland Opposition offering to open his company's files to them. **1983** *Listener* 28 Apr. 24/2 One didn't know one's every word was being.. telexed direct to the Shah for his comment.

Telford (ˈtɛlfəd). Surname of a celebrated civil engineer, Thomas Telford (1757–1834), used to designate the kind of road constructed by him.
1896 J. O'DONNELL in *Voice* (N.Y.) 2 Jan. 3/1 This gutter track takes care of the water perfectly. It costs less than a macadam or telford road.

telharmonium (ˌtɛlhɑːˈməʊnɪəm). [f. TEL(E- + HARMONIUM.] An electrophonic instrument, invented by the American scientist Thaddeus Cahill (1867–1934) and designed to produce tones for transmission over telephone wires by means of rotating electro-magnetic generators.
1906 *Chambers's Jrnl.* June 495/1 In the telharmonium the qualifying ripples are ingeniously added to the waves of the fundamental note by a separate contrivance. **1934** *N.Y. Times* 13 Apr. 19/1 Thaddeus Cahill, who invented an electric typewriter and the device for producing music electrically, known as the telharmonium, died suddenly at 10 o'clock yesterday of a heart attack. **1978** P. GRIFFITHS *Conc. Hist. Mod. Music* viii. 111 The pioneer.. was Thaddeus Cahill, a Canadian scientist who demonstrated an extraordinarily bulky 'telharmonium' in 1906.

telic (ˈtɛlɪk), *a.* [ad. Gr. τελικ-ός final, f. τέλος end.]
1. *Gram.* Of a conjunction or clause: Expressing end or purpose.
1846 in WORCESTER (citing Prof. Stuart). **1856** ALFORD *Grk. Test.* III. 90 *note*/2 [In Eph. ii. 9 ἵνα μή τις καυχήσηται] ἵνα has in matter of fact its strictest telic sense. With God, results are all purposed. **1882** FARRAR *Early Chr.* II. 507 *note*, St. John's use of ἵνα is far wider than that of classical writers. It often loses its telic sense ('in order that') and becomes simply ekbatic or explanatory, as in Luke i. 43, John xv. 13. **1904** *Sat. Rev.* 9 Apr. 460/1 It expresses a purpose or intention, and is therefore telic.
2. Directed or tending to a definite end; purposive.
1889 MIVART *Truth* xxv. 438 The telic series of cyclical changes which are characteristic of all duly organized living bodies. **1903** L. F. WARD *Pure Sociology* II. v. 94 All causes are either efficient, conative, or telic. *Ibid.* II. vi. 97 The telic or final cause is not a force .. but it utilizes efficient causes in a manner wholly its own, and thus produces effects. **1906** DEALEY & WARD *Text-bk. Sociology* §280 Civilisation chiefly consists in the exercise of the telic faculty.

teliferous (tɪˈlɪfərəs), *a.* [f. L. *tēlifer dart-bearing, f. *tēlum* dart: see -FEROUS.]
†**1.** Bearing darts or missiles. *Obs. rare.*
1656 BLOUNT *Glossogr.*, *Teliferous*, .. which beareth darts, arrows or weapons. **1658** in PHILLIPS.
2. *Zool.* Armed with nematocysts or stinging cells, as the *Telifera*, a division of the Cœlenterata comprising all except the Sponges (*Porifera*).
1860 GOSSE *Hist. Brit. Sea-Anemones* Introd. 22 Teliferous System... The Actinaria are furnished with a system of armature of most extraordinary character... Their tissues contain excessively minute bodies, in the form of oblong or oval transparent vesicles, which have the power of shooting out a long thread of extensive tenuity.

teligraph, variant of TELLIGRAPH.

teling, *vbl. sb.*: See TELE *v.*

Telinga (təˈlɪŋgə), *sb.* and *a.* Also 8–9 Tellinga, 8 -ger, -gy, Telingee, Talinga. [Of uncertain origin: supposed by some to be the original form of the word *Telugu*, and held to be itself derived from Skr. *Trilinga* meaning 'the three lingams', according to an alleged tradition that the god Śiva descended in the form of a lingam upon three mountains said to mark the boundaries of the Telugu country. But Dravidian scholars are inclined to view this as a mere etymological figment, and even doubt whether Telugu and Telinga have any original connexion. It is certain however that 17th c. English writers called the language *Telinga*, and that in Hindūstānī a Telugu is called *Tilanga* and the Telugu country *Tilangānā*: cf. *Rājpūtāna*.]
1. The TELUGU language. (As *sb.* or *a.*)
1698 FRYER *Acc. E. India & P.* 33 Their Language they call generally *Gentu*... The peculiar Name of their Speech is *Telinga*. **1800** *Asiatic Ann. Reg.* 186/2, I had now entered on that part of India which bears the name of Tellingana, whose inhabitants are called Tellingies, who speak what is denominated the Tellingy language.
2. One of the Telugu people.
1800 [see 1]. **1840** MALCOM *Trav.* 19/1 This people, whose name is often written *Telinga*, or *Kalinga*, are generally called, by European writers, *Gentoos*.
†**b.** *spec.* A native Indian soldier disciplined and dressed in quasi-European fashion; a sepoy. *Obs.*
1760 in J. Long *Select. Unpubl. Records* (1869) 235 (Y.), 300 Telingees are run away, and entered into the Beerboom Rajah's service. **1761** *Ibid.* 258 Tellingers. **1766** GROSE *Voy. E. Ind.* (1772) I. Gloss. (Y.), Sepoys, sometimes called Tellingas. **1789** *Seir Mutaqherin* II. 92 (Y.) Hindu soldiers, armed and accoutred and disciplined in the European manner of fighting; I mean those soldiers that are become so famous under the name of Talingas. **1827** SCOTT *Surgeon's Dau.* xiii, I have been a Telinga.. in the Company's service, and have eaten their salt. **1883** *Sat. Rev.* 27 Jan. 120/1 The Oriental portions of Clive's army were known to the Bengalis of Nuddea as Telingas, because they came, or were supposed to have accompanied him, from Telingana or Madras.
3. (See quot.)
1858 SIMMONDS *Dict. Trade*, *Tellinga*, a dhoney or native coasting-vessel on the coast of Coromandel.
4. *attrib.* **telinga potato**, *Amorphophallus campanulatus*: see POTATO 4.

teliospore (ˈtiːlɪəʊspɔə(r)). *Bot.* [f. TELI(UM + -O + SPORE.] A spore of the rust fungi (Uredinales) which produces a basidium on germination, often after overwintering; a teleutospore.
1905 [see TELIUM]. **1970** J. WEBSTER *Introd. Fungi* II. iv. 369 The teliospores [of *Puccinia graminis*] represent the overwintering stage and only develop further after a period of maturation corresponding to winter dormancy. **1981** *Trans. Brit. Mycol. Soc.* LXXVII. 439/2 If in autumn a rusted rose leaf is shaken gently above a glass slide, many single teliospores fall on to it.

teliost, variant of TELEOST.

telisman, Sc. var. TILLSMAN *Obs.*

telium (ˈtiːlɪəm). *Bot.* Pl. telia. [mod.L., f. Gr. τέλ-ος end.] = TELEUTOSORUS.
1905 J. C. ARTHUR in *Bot. Gaz.* XXXIX. 222 For the sorus of the third spore-stage, usually.. called teleutosorus, I propose *telium*..; derivatives *telial*, *teliospore*, etc. **1937** *Nature* 8 May 800/2 (*heading*) Production of uredia and telia of *Puccinia graminis* on *Berberis vulgaris*. **1979** *Trans. Brit. Mycol. Soc.* LXXIII. 231/1 Only telia are present on the leaves.., but a few uredinoid spores are found in some telia of this specimen.
Hence **ˈtelial** *a.*
1905 [see above]. **1925** *Jrnl. Agric. Res.* XXXI. 643 [In *Gallowaya pinicola*] there is very little intermingling or intertwining of hyphae as a preliminary to the formation of the telial sorus. **1967** *Trans. Brit. Mycol. Soc.* L. 190 In taxonomic study of *Endophyllum* and *Kunkelia* there are two possibilities. Their sori can either be compared with aecia of other rusts or with telia of other rusts... I propose that they should properly be called 'telial aecia'.

tell (tɛl), *sb.*[1] Now *dial.* [f. TELL *v.*]
1. What one tells or has to tell; a tale, a statement, an account.
1742 H. WALPOLE *Lett. to Mann* 29 July, I am at the end of my tell. **1827** F. COOPER *Prairie* I. ii. 32 From his tell, it must be a considerable stream. **1899** WESTCOTT *David Harum* xxx, As near's I c'n make out f'm Dave's tell, he must 'a' ben red-headed.
2. A talk, conversation, gossip.
1864 MRS. LLOYD *Ladies Polc.* 101, I made so bould as to come to see if you'd plase to have a bit of a tell with me afore I goes. **1901** 'ZACK' *Tales Dunstable Weir* 99 Having a tongue she dearly liked a tell.

‖**tell** (tɛl), *sb.*[2] Also tel. [a. Arab. *tall* a hillock.] The Arab name for an artificial hillock or mound, usually one covering the ruins of an ancient city.
1864 W. F. AINSWORTH *Comm. Xenophon's Anabasis* 285 The hill.. appears to have been one of the numerous artificial mounds, topes, or tells, sometimes sepulchral, sometimes heaps of ruin, which abound on the plain of Babylonia. **1878** CONDER *Tentwork Pal.* (1879) II. 46 We may next notice the most remarkable of its antiquities, namely the Tellûl or Tells there found. **1878** MACLEAR *Bk. Joshua* xv. (1880) 149 The tell is very strong and it rises about 200 feet high. **1882** F. S. DE HASS *Buried Cities* III. v. 380 (Funk) Tells or conical hills.., many of them the craters of extinct volcanoes.

tell (tɛl), *v.* Pa. t. and pple. told (təʊld). Forms: see below. [OE. *tęllan*, pa. t. *tealde*, pa. pple. (*ʒe*)*teald*, cognate with OFris. *talja*, *tella*, OS. *tęlljan* (*talda*, *gitald*), senses as in OE.; MLG., MDu., LG., Du. *tellen* to count, reckon, etc., OHG. **zęlljan*, *zęllen* (*zalta*, *gizalt*), senses as in OE. (MHG. *zęln*, Ger. *zählen* to reckon, count), ON. *tęlja* to tell, relate, say, count, speak, Sw. *tälja*, Da. *tælle* to count, number, reckon; all:—OTeut. **taljan*, f. **talā*, OE. *talu*, TALE *sb.* OE. had also a pa. pple. *ʒetęled* (in poetry, Beda, Orosius, Lindisf. and Rushw. Gl.); Anglian had pres. t. *tęlest*, *tęleð*, and pa. t. and pple. *talde*, *ʒetald* (Vesp. Ps.), whence ME. *tāld*, and *tōld*. *Tealde* remained in Early ME. in southern dialects. The later dial. *telld*, *tell'd*, *telt* is a new formation from *tell*: cf. the forms of SELL *v.*]

A. Illustration of Inflexional Forms.

1. Present stem. *Inf.* OE. **tellan**, ME. **telle(n, tel** (4–7), Mod.E. **tell.**

c **888** K. ÆLFRED *Boeth.* vii. §3 Ute nu tellan. *Ibid.* xviii. §3 Tele nu þa lengu. *c* **1000** *Ags. Gosp.* Matt. xi. 16 Hwam telle ic. *a* **1090**, *c* **1175** Telle [see B. 2, 1]. *c* **1200** ORMIN 9500 Crist..wrohhte wundre miccle ma þann icc ȝuw maȝȝ nu tellenn. *c* **1250** *Kentish Serm.* in *O.E. Misc.* 27 þet us telþ þet holi godespel. **13..** *Cursor M.* 96 Inogh to tell. *Ibid.* 10913 (Cott.) Wat þou quat for soth i tell [*Gött.* talle]? *Ibid.* 11477 Cums again and tels me. *c* **1375** *Sc. Leg. Saints* x. (*Mathou*) 30, I thinke to tel here why [etc.]. *c* **1386**, *c* **1440** Telle [see B. 1]. **1513** DOUGLAS *Æneis* VIII. viii. *heading*, Evander telland Eneas thingis seir. *a* **1592** GREENE *Vision* Wks. (Grosart) XII. 200 Thus to tellen all the truth, He infected Romes youth. **1632** Tel [see B. 3 (*b*)].

2. *Pa. t.* α. 1–4 **tealde** (1 **telede**), 3 **tælde**, 4 **teelde.**

c **888**, *c* **1000** Tealde [see B. 1]. *a* **1000** *Andreas* 1105 (Gr.) Hi..hluton..teledon. *c* **1205** LAY. 13181 þet heo nane manne ne tælden. *c* **1315** Tealde [see B. 4].

β. 1, 3–5 **talde**, 4– 6 **tald**, 5–9 *Sc.* **tauld.**

a **900** CYNEWULF *Elene* 909 þone ic ær on firenum fæstne talde. *c* **1205** LAY. 1350 A steores-man ham talde. *Ibid.* 26884 Al heo talden [*c* 1275 tolde] þene wæi. **13..** *Cursor M.* 511 Als i tald [*Fairf.* talde] ar. **1375** BARBOUR *Bruce* I. 563 The Cwmyn raid to the king..& tald all this cass. **1567** Tauld [see B. 17]. **1816** SCOTT *Old Mort.* xxiv, Only he tauld me about it.

γ. 3–6 **tolde**, 4– **told.** (Also 5 **toold, tolled, tolded**, 6 **tould(e**, 8 *dial.* **towd.**)

c **1250** *Gen. & Ex.* 3449 Moyses tolde ðis israel. *c* **1340** He told [see B. 2]. *c* **1340** HAMPOLE *Medit. Passion* Wks. 1895 I. 93 þou toldist it him biforen. **1418** ABP. CHICHELE in Ellis *Orig. Lett.* Ser. I. I. 5, I..toold him owre comun avis. *c* **1449** PECOCK *Repr.* 353 Which appering Constantyn toold in greet secretnes to the same Eusebi. *c* **1450** LOVELICH *Grail* xliii. 225 ȝit tolded thow it Neuere to non Man. **1540** HYRDE tr. *Vives' Instr. Chr. Wom.* (1592) F viij, What hurt should come, Cato tolde before. **1582** N. LICHEFIELD tr. *Castanheda's Conq. E. Ind.* I. vi. 15 b, All which things the Generall tolde him. **1601** Told [see B. 5]. **1790** MRS. WHEELER *Westmld. Dial.* 90 He towd Sammy he wor baun et wed wie his Cusin Ann.

δ. 4 **tellde**, 4–5 **telde**, 4–6 **teld**, 5 **tellid**, 5–6 **-yd**, 5–6 (9 *dial.*) **telled**, 9 *dial.* **tell'd**, 6–9 *dial.* **telt.**

c **1330** R. BRUNNE *Chron.* (1810) 82 þer men him teld, who was his aduersere. **13..** *Cursor M.* 871 (Gött.), I teld [*Cott.* tald] þe. *c* **1380** WYCLIF *Serm.* Sel. Wks. I. 166 If God tellde him specialy. **1399** LANGL. *Rich. Redeles* II. 151 Trouthe..telde somme her sothes. **1453** AGNES PASTON in *P. Lett.* I. 255 Gurney tellyd hym he had byn at London. **1537** LATIMER *Let. to Cromwell* 14 Oct. in *Rem.* (Parker Soc.) 384, I telled him plainly my mind therein. **1554** *Cal. Anc. Rec. Dublin* (1889) 436 The sam telt to the wywes. **1596** SPENSER *F.Q.* VI. i. 44 Sir Calidore upcheard, and to her teld All this accord. **1790** MRS. WHEELER *Westmld. Dial.* 34, I telt Bet I wad drive tea it. **1825** BROCKETT *N.C. Words* s.v., Aw tell'd him on't. **1826** J. WILSON *Noct. Ambr.* Wks. 1856 I. 144 Mr. Scroope telt Sir Walter.

3. *Pa. pple.* α. 1–2 (**ȝe)teald**, 3 **teald**, 3–4 **i-teld**, 4 **teeld.**

c **1000** *Leg. Rood* (1871) 5 Ða þis þam mæran kasere constantine ȝeteald wæs. *c* **1200** *Trin. Coll. Hom.* 215 Swo ich iteld habbe. *c* **1380** WYCLIF *Serm.* Sel. Wks. I. 169 Crist haþ teeld þat þis hiȝe charite techiþ a man to putte his lyf for love of hise frendis.

β. 3 **i-tald**, 4 **y-tald, taald**, 4–8 **tald(e**, 5 *Sc.* **tallde**, 5–9 *Sc.* **tauld**, 6 **tawld.**

c **1205** LAY. 12092 Nes hit neowhær itald. *Ibid.* 22999 þar nas na cniht wel itald [*c* 1275 itold]. **13..** *Cursor M.* 3330 Til he þam had his errand tald. *Ibid.* 8765 þis tre i haf of forwit taald. **1340** Y-tald [see B. 1]. **1488** *Acc. Ld. High Treas. Scot.* I. 79 Tauld in presence of the Chancellare. **1588** A. KING tr. *Canisius' Catech.* 185 As I haue tauld in tymes past. **1725** RAMSAY *Gentle Sheph.* III. ii, Do you get them tald you in your sleep? **1816** SCOTT *Old Mort.* xxxviii, I wadna hae tauld ye.

γ. 3–5 **i-told(-e)**, 3– **told.** (Also 3–7 **tolde**, 4–5 **toold** (5 **y-tolte**), 6 **tould, towld, (tollyd).**)

c **1220** *Bestiary* 758 in *O.E. Misc.* 24 Ilk der..foleȝen him [the panther]..For ðe swetnesse ðe ic ȝu haue told. **1297** R. GLOUC. (Rolls) 1634 King aruirag of wan we abbeþ itold. *Ibid.* 7569 As me aþ er ytold. **1303** Tolde [see B. 1]. **1382** WYCLIF *2 Sam* iii. 23 So it is toold to Joab of tellers. **1387** TREVISA *Higden* (Rolls) VIII. 149 Rehersed how it was i-told. *c* **1400** *Destr. Troy* 12816 Tithinges hor tolde were. *c* **1420** *Chron. Vilod.* 1830 Hit was..To seynt Dunston ysende & by tokon to hym y-tolte. *c* **1430** *Hymns Virg.* 37/69 Theise .iij. þat y haue of toold. **1538** STARKEY *England* I. i. 22 A tale tollyd among deffe men. **1584** in *Cath. Rec. Soc. Publ.* V. 64 Yt was towld him by his cosine. **1586** HUNSDON in *Border Papers* (1894) I. 367, I toulde him of sondrie cawses.

δ. 4 **telld**, 4–6 **teld**, 5–6 (8–9 *dial.*) **telled**, 6–9 **telt**, 8–9 *dial.* **tell'd**, *Sc.* **tell't.**

13.. *Cursor M.* 4640 (Gött.) Nou has he Teld me. *Ibid.* 6752 (Cott.) It sal be slaghter telld o man. *c* **1489** CAXTON *Sonnes of Aymon* 174 Nowe have I telled you that that ye have asked me. **1560** PILKINGTON *Expos. Aggeus* (1562) 13 The thinge is true which is telled. **1596** SPENSER *F.Q.* VII. vi. 27 Witnesse, ye Heavens, the truth of all that I have teld. *a* **1818** in Scott *Hrt. Midl.* Introd., In a' thae wee bits o' ways I ha'e tell't ye. **1824** SCOTT *St. Ronan's* ii, I hae been tell'd by ane that suld ken. **1900** Telled [see B. 8 b].

B. Signification.

I. To mention in order, narrate, relate, make known, declare.

* *trans. to tell things or a thing.*

†**1.** To mention or name (a series of things) one after another in order; to recount, enumerate; to give a list of. *Obs.*

c **888** K. ÆLFRED *Boeth.* xxxvii. §2 Do ðæs lean to ðæm forsprecenan goodum þe ic þe ær tealde on þære þriddan bec. *c* **1000** ÆLFRIC *Hom.* (Th.) II. 428 Se sunder-halȝa..He..tealde his godan dæda. *c* **1175** *Lamb. Hom.* 9 Feole oðre..werke þe nu were long eou to telle. *c* **1200** *Trin. Coll. Hom.* 71 þere we shule tellen alle ure gultes. *c* **1250** *Gen. & Ex.* 497 Ic wile riȝt tellen, if ic can, Adam, Seth, Enos, Caynan, Malaleel, Iareth, Enoch. **1303** R. BRUNNE *Handl. Synne* 12624 ȝow to withholde Fro þe synnes þat byfore are tolde. **1340** *Ayenb.* 24 Alle þise guodes of kende þet ich habbe ssortiliche y-tald. *c* **1386** CHAUCER *Can. Yeom. Prol. & T.* 246 Arsenyk sal Armonyak and Brymstoon And herbes koude I telle eek many oon. *c* **1440** *Jacob's Well* 152 Out of euyll tunge springeth x. braunchys. þe v. I telde ȝou þe oþer day, þe oþere v. I schal telle ȝow now.

2. a. To give an account or narrative of (facts, actions, or events); to narrate, relate. (With simple obj. or obj. clause; sometimes with indirect obj. as in 3.) Also *to tell over.*

c **1000** *Leg. Rood* (1871) 5 Hi..tealdon him þa þrowunga þe ure hælend on þære rode ðrowode. *a* **1090** *O.E. Chron.* an. 1085, þeah ic hit lengre telle. *a* **1154** *Ibid.* an. 1137, I ne can ne i ne mai tellen alle þe wunder. *a* **1225** *Juliana* 40 þah ich þe talde al dei ne mahte ich þe tellen þe wundres. **1297** R. GLOUC. (Rolls) 7198 þo gan he to tellen þis [vision]. *a* **1300** *Cursor M.* 141 þar neist sal be sythen tald How þat ioseph was boght and sald. *c* **1340** *Ibid.* 1330 (Gött.) He..told him all þat he had sene. *c* **1380** WYCLIF *Sel. Wks.* II. 105 þis gospel telliþ furþere how þes Jewis pursueden Crist. **1470–85** MALORY *Arthur* II. xiii. 91 It telleth after in the sangraylle that syre Percyualis syster halpe that lady with her blood wherof she was dede. **1526** TINDALE *Acts* xv. 12 Barnabas and Paul..tolde what signes and wondres God had shewed. **1671** MILTON *P.R.* II. 306 Others of some note, As story tells, have trod this Wilderness. **1746** FRANCIS tr. *Hor. Sat.* II. vi. 163 A country mouse, as authors tell, Of old invited to his cell A city mouse. **1779** *Mirror* No. 23 ¶5 These [actions] were told to his honour. **1821** SCOTT *Kenilw.* xvi, Thou art..a tattling knave to tell over again his fooleries. **1833** CRUSE *Eusebius* VII. xi. 289 After these..he proceeds to tell what happened to him. *c* **1850** *Arab. Nts.* (Rtldg.) 552 She then went on with her narrative, and told him in what manner she had obtained an audience. *Mod.* What happened to him there has often been told.

b. With the narrative as obj. Now only with *tale* or *story*: see 17.

1576 GASCOIGNE *Philomene* (Arb.) 92 She by whom I meane To tell this woful Tragedie Was called Phylomene.

c. *intr.* for *pass.* To be related with a particular effect; to sound (well, etc.) when told.

1584 HUDSON *Du Bartas' Judith* in *Sylvester* (1621) 696 Then, fathers, choose your warres; for better tels To lose like Jewes, then winne like infidels. **1782** MISS BURNEY *Cecilia* VI. ii, I had as lieve the things were false as not, for they tell as well the one way as the other.

3. a. To make known by speech or writing; to communicate (information, facts, ideas, news, etc.); to state, announce, report, intimate. Usually const. with indirect obj. (*dat.*) or *to.*

(*a*) With the direct object a *sb.* or *pron.*

Examples of the direct passive are included here; for the indirect passive with the person as subj., see 8 b.

c **1122** [see (*b*)]. *c* **1200** *Trin. Coll. Hom.* 31 Gode tiðinge..us telleð..seinte lucas on þe holie godspelle. *c* **1290** *Beket* 1188 in *S. Eng. Leg.* I. 140 He..tolde hire al is þouȝt. **13..** *Cursor M.* 4624, I wat þou tells [*v.rr.* tellis, tellest] it me for noght. **1340–70** *Alex. & Dind.* 207 Tel me þe soþe. *c* **1380** WYCLIF *Wks.* (1880) 300 Poul telliþ here a rewele þat cristen men shulden holde. **1390** GOWER *Conf.* III. 368 Ech his oghne avis Hath told, on that, an other this. *c* **1400** *Brut* lxii. 57 Telle me þe enchesone wherefore I ame to ȝow brouȝt. **1474** CAXTON *Chesse* II. iv. (1883) 47 And they told hym the trouthe. **1513** DOUGLAS *Æneis* VIII. iv. *heading*, Evander tellis till Enee but baid, The verray caus. **1526** TINDALE *Luke* i. 45 Thoose thinges..which were tolde the from the lorde. —— *Acts* xxvii. 25, I beleve God that so it shalbe even as it was tolde me. **1611** BIBLE *Gen.* xxiv. 33, I will not eate, vntill I haue tolde mine errand. **1606** SHAKS. *Tr. & Cr.* I. iii. 284 This shall be told our Louers. **1673** *S'too him Bayes* 23 I'le tell you one piece of my mind. **1746** FRANCIS *Hor. Epist.* I. vi. 74 Let's buy a Slave to tell each Voter's Name. **1759** JOHNSON *Idler* No. 63 ¶6 The studious and ambitious contend..who shall tell their thoughts in the most pleasing manner. **1821** SCOTT *Kenilw.* xv, Tell us your mystery of multiplying. **1856** J. H. NEWMAN *Serm. Var. Occas.* (1881) i. 12 Nor, even though it be told to her, can she enter into it. **1896** *Standard* 15 Jan. 7/2 He said much, but told little, at to-day's meeting. *Mod.* Who told you that?

(*b*) With direct obj. a *clause*, with or without *that.*

In the direct passive the clause usually follows the vb., its place before the vb. being supplied by *it* (*it was told him that*, etc.). For the indirect passive, see 8 b.

c **1122** *O.E. Chron.* an. 1046, þa..Sweȝen..tealde þæt his sciperes woldon wændon fram him buton he þe raðor come. **1297** R. GLOUC. (Rolls) 5357 þou ssalt þi wille abide as ich þe abbe ytold here. *a* **1300** *Cursor M.* 4843 Tells me quat kin man yur fader be. *c* **1380** [see A. 3 α]. *c* **1440** *Jacob's Well* 203, I teld ȝou þat a schouyl hath iij. partys: a scho, an heued, & an handyl. **1535** LYNDESAY *Satyre* 1506 Now I will rin, but rest, And tell that all is ready. **1535** COVERDALE *1 Sam.* xxiii. 7 Then was it tolde Saul that Dauid was come to Cegila. **1560** DAUS tr. *Sleidane's Comm.* 90 b, He tolde to the other playnely that..he would take from him the ward-shyp of his nephewe. **1611** BIBLE *Acts* xxiii. 30 When it was tolde me, how that the Iewes laid waite for the man. **1632** SANDERSON *Serm.* 6 Yet Salomon tels us, the poore mans wisdome is despised. **1681–6** J. SCOTT *Chr. Life* (1747) III. 523 Our Saviour himself tells us, that the Father judgeth no Man. **1790** BURNS *Tam O'Shanter* 19 She tauld thee weel thou was a skellum. **1833** T. HOOK *Parson's Dau.* I. v, And I say, Charles, tell her we are coming to coffee forthwith. **1838** LONGFELLOW *Ps. Life*, Tell me not, in mournful numbers, Life is but an empty dream! **1908** R. BAGOT *A. Cuthbert* xxviii. 367 There had always been something mysterious about Anthony Cuthbert, the doctor told himself. *Mod.* It was told me that you had been inquiring about me.

b. To declare, state formally or publicly; to announce, proclaim, publish. Also *fig.*

tell it not in Gath (from *2 Sam.* i. 20), publish it not to the enemy, or to the Philistine, or to the world.

a **1300** *E.E. Psalter* xviii. [xix.] 1 Heuens telles goddis blisse. *a* **1325** *Prose Psalter* xlix. 7 [l. 6] þe heuens shul tellen his riȝtfulnes. *Ibid.* l. 16 [li. 15] My mouþe shall tellen þyn heryyng. **1382** WYCLIF *2 Sam.* i. 20 Woleth ȝe not telle in Geth, ne telle ȝe in..Aschalon. **1382** —— *Acts* xvii. 18 He [Paul] telde to hem Jhesu and aȝen rysing. **1535** COVERDALE *Ps.* xcv[i]. 10 Tell it out amonge the Heithen, that the Lorde is kynge. **1602** SHAKS. *Ham.* I. ii. 126 No iocond health that Denmarke drinkes to day But the great Cannon to the Clowds shall tell. **1656** EARL MONM. tr. *Boccalini's Advts. fr. Parnass.* II. xxxviii. (1674) 190 The Master of the Colledge, told in the name of the whole Senate, That [etc.]. **1751** S. RICHARDSON *Let.* 11 July (1964) 185 A wise man to be in love! Tell it not in Gath. *c* **1795** COWPER *Needless Alarm* 34 Ere yet with ruthless joy the happy hound Told hill and dale that Reynard's track was found. **1816** M. R. MITFORD *Let.* 20 Oct. (1925) 135 My favourite play ('tell it not in Gath!') is the first part of *King Henry the Fourth.* **1819** KEATS *Isabella* x. xix, Many a chapel bell the hour is telling. **1904** MARIE CORELLI *God's Gd. Man* xx, The fact is—but tell it not in Gath—I was happier without them!

c. *fig.* To make known or indicate as if by language; to bespeak.

1809 HEBER *Poems, Europe* 29 May those bleak summits tell The field of Anger where the mighty fell. **1827** CLARE *Sheph. Cal.* 148, I care not what this foolish trifling tells.

4. a. To utter (words); to say over, recite (a passage, composition, etc.); to say. Now *dial.*

c **1315** SHOREHAM iii. 120 Many man..hym ne douteþ of no breche Of godes hestes healde [= old]; Ac he not nefer wat hy beeþ, Ne neuer hy ne tealde. **1382** WYCLIF *Ps.* cxviii. [cxix.] 171 My lippis shuln tellen out an impne. **1390** GOWER *Conf.* I. 107 It semeth that a belle Lik to the wordes that men telle Answerth riht. **1567** *Gude & Godlie B.* (S.T.S.) 201 His [the Pope's] numerat Aueis, and Psalmes tauld. **1573–80** BARET *Alv.* T 105 To tell by heart, *recito.* *a* **1653** BINNING *Serm.* (1845) 445 You use to tell over some words in your prayers. **1841** HELPS *Ess., Self-Discipline* (1875) 21 To think that a man can find nothing better to do, in the presence of his Creator, than telling off so many words! **1880** *Cornwall Gloss.* s.v., Can you tell your lessons?

b. To utter, speak, say (things).

1377 LANGL. *P. Pl.* B. v. 408 ȝif I bidde any bedes..þat I telle with my tonge is two myle fro myne herte. **1535** COVERDALE *Ecclus.* xxi. 25 The lippes of the vnwyse wylbe tellynge foolish thinges. **1628** HOBBES *Thucyd.* (1822) 79 Many prophecies were told and many sung by the priests of the oracles. **1715–20** POPE *Iliad* IX. 412 Who dares think one thing, and another tell, My heart detests him as the gates of hell. **1787** BURNS *Birthday Ode* 47 Till all the frighted echoes tell The blood-notes of the chase! **1888** ELWORTHY *W. Som. Gloss.* s.v., Don't tell up such stuff.

c. To express in words (thoughts, things known).

c **1200** *Moral Ode* 285 Ne mai non heorte it þenche, ne no tunge ne can telle. *c* **1250** *Death* 57 in *O.E. Misc.* 172 Ne miȝte no tunge tellen þat euer wes iboren þe stronge pine of helle. *a* **1300** *Cursor M.* 96 (Cott.) Qua sa will of hyr fayrnes spell, Find he sal inogh to tell. *c* **1430** *Freemasonry* 664 The vertu therof no mon telle may. **1650** CROMWELL *Let.* 12 Sept., in *Carlyle*, Which speaking the instructed, the edified and comforted can best tell the energy and effect of. **1875** JOWETT *Plato* (ed. 2) I. 82 Let me tell you the pleasure which I feel in hearing of your fame.

d. *to tell out, away* (*dial.*): to drive away (pain, etc.) by uttering incantations.

1822 HIBBERT *Shetl. Isl.* (1891) 272 (E.D.D.) The religious charmer of Shetland would mutter some words over water,..and limbs were washed with it, for the purpose of telling out pains. **1869** REID *Art Rambles in Shetl.* 25 Papa Stourians believed that the beadle of the kirk had the power of 'telling' the sparrows away so as never to return. **1879** LOW *Tour Ork. & Shetl.* 203 When she was a child..she has heard from others that a pain or a stitch has been *telled out* in that manner.

5. a. To disclose or reveal (something secret or private); to divulge. Also in phr. *to tell all*, to reveal the whole truth, esp. in a sensational manner (freq. with ref. to the printed word); now usu. without indirect obj. *to tell tales*: see TALE *sb.* 3 c.

a **1400** *Pistill of Susan* 141 We schal telle trewely We toke þe wiþ a-voutri. **1445** tr. *Claudian* in *Anglia* XXVIII. 277 Thise goddis the telle þin enemyes sleightes, and lede to þe couchis of fraude. **1601** SHAKS. *Twel. N.* II. iv. 113 She neuer told her loue. **1615** G. SANDYS *Trav.* 72 Many there are that undertake to tell fortunes. **1819** KEATS *Isabella* v, I may not speak, And yet I will, and tell my love all plain. **1848** THACKERAY *Van. Fair* xviii, She told no more of her thoughts now than she had before. **1897** B. STOKER *Dracula* v. 57, I *do so* want to tell you all. **1936** *Mademoiselle* Aug. 16 (*heading*) Mrs Chester tells all. **1971** J. LOFLAND *Analyzing Social Settings* vi. 132 We delude ourselves if we expect very many field workers actually to 'tell all' in print.

†**b.** To reveal (something future); to foretell, predict.

1340–70 *Alex. & Dind.* 776 Tokne of þat turment tolde ȝoure eldren. **13..** *Cursor M.* 9265 (Fairf.) Crist was talde wiþ prophecy. *c* **1380** WYCLIF *Serm.* Sel. Wks. II. 2 þis Gospel of Mark bigynneþ how Crist was teld in þe olde lawe. *a* **1400–50** *Alexander* 200 Alle þe sawis of þaire Syre as Siraphis tald þare gan þai graithly þam graue. [**1884** tr. *Lotze's Logic* 303 No perception can tell us the future with the present.]

†**6.** To pray for, beg, ask. *Obs. rare.*

1393 LANGL. *P. Pl.* C. VIII. 298 Ich praye ȝow, peers, paraunter yf ȝe meteþ Treuthe, telleþ to hym þat ich be excused. **14..** *Trentalle St. Gregorii* in *Tundale's Vis.* (1843) 79 God moder my dere dame..Of Gode to tell mercy thou gine. **14..** *Lybeaus Disc.* 1755 To the castell he rod,..To Jhesu bad and tolde, To sende hym tydynge glad.

7. a. To discern so as to be able to say with knowledge or certainty; hence, to distinguish, recognize, decide, determine. Also with *apart*.

1687 A. LOVELL tr. *Thevenot's Trav.* II. 142 It is hard to tell whether it be a Horse or an Elephant. **1746** FRANCIS tr. *Hor. Sat.* II. iv. 58 None before me so sapient to engage To tell the various nature, or the age Of fish and fowl. **1840** R. H. DANA *Bef. Mast* xiii. 29 They can be told by their complexions, dress, manner, and also by their speech. **1883** GILMOUR *Mongols* xvi. 195 An ordinary man of common intelligence can tell a wall raised by..a competent builder from the attempted imitation of a bungling amateur. **1899** A. BIRRELL in *Daily News* 4 Nov. 3/2 Is it possible to tell a good book from a bad one? **1925** A. LOOS *Gentlemen prefer Blondes* (1982) iv. 86 How are we going to tell you gentlemen apart? **1958** K. AMIS *I like it Here* xiv. 178 Barbara had complained to him..that she couldn't tell people apart (he found as little difficulty here as he found in telling female film-stars apart). **1982** B. CHATWIN *On Black Hill* i. 10 As boys, only their mother could tell them apart.

b. Preceded by *can*: To be able to state; to know; to discern, perceive, make out, understand. Often in negative or interrogative sentences, as ***nobody can tell, who can tell?*** Cf. SAY *v.*[1] 6 b.

?**1370** *Robt. Cicyle* 244 Wher such cloþ was to selle, Ne ho hit made, couþe noman telle. *a* **1400–50** *Alexander* 248 Þai can swyth of a sweuyn all þe swepe tell. *c* **1449** PECOCK *Repr.* III. xii. 353 No man can telle who wroot it. **1526** TINDALE *John* xvi. 18 We cannot tell what he saith [Gr. οὐκ οἴδαμεν τί λαλεῖ: *R.V.* 1881 We know not what he saith]. **1553** T. WILSON *Rhet.* (1580) 160 Neither can he otherwise chuse but stumble: that gropyng in the darcke can not tell where he is. **1783** JOHNSON *Let. to Mrs. Thrale* 23 July, Whether this short rustication has done me any good I cannot tell. **1838** ARNOLD *Hist. Rome* (1848) I. 99 Nor can any one tell at what time they attained to their present shape. **1873** MRS. OLIPHANT *Innocent* II. 231 It was..a dog-cart.. he could tell as much by the sound. **1888** 'J. S. WINTER' *Bootle's Childr.* vi, Jane doesn't seem to like it—I can't tell why. **1920** F. SCOTT FITZGERALD *This Side of Paradise* I. ii. 56 He was.., as Amory could tell from his general appearance, without much conception of social competition. **1924** 'K. MANSFIELD' *Something Childish* 124 They're not respectable women—you can tell at a glance. **1936** 'G. ORWELL' *Diary* 11 Feb. in *Coll. Essays* (1968) I. 176 You can always tell a miner by the blue tattooing of coal dust on the bridge of his nose. **1963** J. FOWLES *Collector* I. 49, I always thought people could tell I lived on my own. **1966** S. HEANEY *Death of Naturalist* 15 You could tell the weather by frogs too.

*** *trans. to tell a person*** (the originally indirect or dative personal object becoming the direct).

Some uses, as 9, hover between * and **.

8. a. To inform (a person) of something; to make aware, apprise, acquaint; to instruct. Also *colloq.* and *dial.* To direct the attention of (a person) to a fault or the like by way of admonition. Const. *of*, *about*, and with direct speech as obj.

c **1205** LAY. 12946 Ic þe wulle tællen Of uncuðe spællen. **1297** R. GLOUC. (Rolls) 322 Of þe maumet hii tolde brut þat hii fonde þere. *Ibid.* 3510 Me tolde him of a gret duc þat het theldryk. *a* **1300** *Cursor M.* 11393 (Cott.) Vs telles alsua iohn ..Of a folk ferr and first vncuth. *c* **1440** *Jacob's Well* 152 The oþer day, I told ȝow of þe wose of glotonye. *c* **1470** HENRY *Wallace* I. 263 He tald his modyr of his sodane cas. **1573–80** BARET *Alv.* T 108 He shewed me, or tolde me of my fault. **1713** BERKELEY *Hylas & Phil* iii, Moses tells us of a creation. *a* **1911** *Mod.* Sit down and tell us about it. **1916** H. S. WALPOLE *Dark Forest* I. v. 135 'I can't marry you,' she told him, 'because I don't love you.' **1943** G. GREENE *Ministry of Fear* II. i. 135 'Mr Digby,' she told him, 'there's a visitor for you.' **1976** H. MACINNES *Agent in Place* xxii. 231 'The police—call the police.' 'It's done,' Tony told her.

(*b*) Const. *so* (representing *that*, or an object clause, and thus coming very near 3 a (*a*, *b*). *Phr.* ***I told you so***, used to remind the person addressed that he has previously been warned that his actions would incur misfortune. As *sb.*, a person who uses this expression or adopts this attitude; such an expression or attitude; used *attrib.* (as *I-told-you-so*) to denote such an attitude. Also used as a kind of quasi-vb.

c **1412** HOCCLEVE *De Reg. Princ.* 717, I tolde hyme so; & euer he seyde nay. **1609** B. JONSON *Sil. Wom.* IV. ii, I told you so, sir, and you would not beleeue me. **1823** BYRON *Don Juan* XIV. l. 3 Sadder than owl-songs or the midnight blast, Is that portentous phrase, 'I told you so'. **1898** We-told-you-so (*attrib.*) [see *poker-backed* s.v. POKER *sb.*[1] 9]. **1904** [see BOUQUET 1 b]. **1919** W. DE MORGAN *Old Madhouse* xxviii. 435 Perhaps I'm only I-told-you-soing. **1926** WHITEMAN & MCBRIDE *Jazz* iii. 49, I really did debate whether I hadn't better give up and let the I-told-you-so's, who said jazz would bring me to no good end, have it their own way. **1930** J. DOS PASSOS *42nd Parallel* IV. 299 Alice had an Itoldyouso manner. **1936** M. PLOWMAN *Faith called Pacifism* 81 Mr. Lloyd George, as the wild cat of the House of David, said: 'I told you so.' **1954** W. FAULKNER *Fable* (1955) 43 His I-told-you-so to the elders. **1959** A. LEJEUNE *Crowded & Dangerous* xi. 125 She'll..put on that disapproving I-told-you-so look.

b. The passive is not only used with the const. *of*, *about*, but is often substituted for that of sense 3 (*a*), as in *he was told the truth*, *we were not told the reason*; and now usually for that of 3 (*b*), as *I was told that you were coming*.

1600 SHAKS. *A.Y.L.* III. ii. 361, I haue bin told so of many. **1607** —— *Timon* IV. iii. 214 Thou wast told thus. **1611** —— *Wint. T.* II. ii. 31 He must be told on't, and he shall. **1781** COWPER *Expost.* 66 Pleasure is deaf when told of future pain. **1821** SCOTT *Kenilw.* xxxvi, Wherefore was I not told of all this? **1898** MRS. H. WARD *Helbeck* I. v. 101 He's that masterful he woan't be towd. **1900** H. SUTCLIFFE *Shameless Wayne* xiii. 170 He's getten a peffing cough.., but he willun't be telled. *Mod.* Has any one been told about it? **1599** SHAKS. *Hen. V*, III. vii. 113, I was told that, by one that knowes him. **1599** —— *Much Ado* v. iv. 96, I was told, you were in a consumption. **1863** KINGSLEY *Lett.* (1878) II. 149 When I am told that the Lancashire system is perfect. **1895** KAY in *Law Times Rep.* LXXIII. 623/1 He asked if his wife was there, and being told she was not, he..left the lodge.

c. Const. *on.* To act as informer to (a person) about (another). Cf. sense 16.

1901 M. FRANKLIN *My Brilliant Career* xiii. 107 Now, not a step do you go, my fine young blood, until you pick up every jolly lemon and put them away tidily, or I'll tell the missus on you. **1943** *Crisis* Mar. 78/3 If he told the Big God on them, no telling what would happen.

9. To assert positively to; to assure (a person). Often *parenthetically* in expressions of emphasis.

c **1440** *York Myst.* xxx. 452 This touches no tresoune, I telle you. **1526** TINDALE *Luke* xii. 59, I tell the thou departest not thence, tyll thou have made goode the vtmose farthynge. *a* **1596** *Sir T. More* I. i. 110 And he is in a good forwardnesse, I telle ye, if all hit right. **1712** STEELE *Spect.* No. 480 ⁋3 Give me leave to tell you, Sir, this is the reason. **1732** BERKELEY *Alciphr.* IV. §2 Let me tell you I am not to be persuaded by metaphysical arguments. **1817** T. L. PEACOCK *Melincourt* vii, Very orthodox old wine in the cellar, I can tell you. **1905** F. YOUNG *Sands Pleas.* I. iii, I tell you, it got on my nerves.

10. To order or direct (a person) *to do* something; to bid, to request authoritatively.

1599 B. JONSON *Cynthia's Rev.* II. i, Place your mirror in your hat, as I told you. [In *passive*, as you were told.] **1693** R. LYDE *Retaking Ship called Friend's Adventure* 10, I told him to knock down that Man at the Helm. **1879** T. L. CUYLER *Pointed Papers* 19 Christ nowhere tells sinners to wait for revivals. **1891** MISS DOWIE *Girl in Karp.* 19, I told the man to go on. [In *passive*, The man was told to go on.] **1899** KIPLING *Stalky* i. 15 Tell the Sergeant to keep his eye open.

†**11.** To direct (a person) to a place: cf. TEACH *v.* 3. *Obs. rare.*

1470–85 MALORY *Arthur* XVI. x. 678 Canst thow telle me vnto somme chappel where that I may burye this body?

*** *Intransitive uses.*

12. To give an account, description, or report. Const. *of*, *about.* (*intr.* of 1 and 2.)

a **1300** *Cursor M.* 2139 Begine we now to tell at sem And siþen of his bern-tem. *Ibid.* 4238 Leue we now iacob in þis care To tell of ioseph and his fare. *c* **1440** *Alphabet of Tales* 164 Seneca tellis of a philosophur þat hight Pictagoricus. **1590** SPENSER *F.Q.* I. v. 26 What art thou, that telst of Nephews kilt? **1738** GRAY *Propertius* III. 59 Sailors to tell of Winds and Seas delight **1812** CRABBE *Tales* II. 510 He told of bloody fights. **1830** SCOTT *Hrt. Midl.* vi. *note*, A near relation of the Author's used to tell of having been stopped by the rioters, and escorted home in the manner described.

†**13.** To make a statement, communication, or announcement; to speak, discourse. *Obs.* (*intr.* of 3.)

c **888** K. ÆLFRED *Boeth.* vii. §3 Ute nu tellan beforan swilcum deman swilce þu wille. **13..** *Seuyn Sag.* (W.) 1228 'Sei on dame!' and sche bigan To tellen als a fals wimman. **1382** WYCLIF *Isa.* vii. 2 And thei tolden to the hous of Dauid, seiende, Siria rested vp on Effraym. *c* **1450** *Merlin* i. 21, I pray the..tellith to Blesse my moders confessour. **1535** LYNDESAY *Satyre* 2154 Tell on. Ar ȝe content? **1558** PHAER *Æneid.* II. C iij b, They..fixt with eies ententiue did behold, Whan Lord Æneas..from his bench thus he told.

14. *fig.* To give evidence, be an indication *of.* (*intr.* of 3 c.)

1798 COLERIDGE *Anc. Mar.* VII. x, All was still, save that the hill Was telling of the sound. **1833** HT. MARTINEAU *Briery Creek* v, There was so little that told of delusion in the calm simplicity of the doctor's countenance. **1853** KINGSLEY *Hypatia* i, His hard hands and sinewy sunburnt limbs told of labour and endurance. **1873** TRISTRAM *Moab* vi. 111 Blocks of basalt..telling of a still more ancient Moabite city.

15. To speak, talk, converse, gossip. Cf. TALE *v.* 6. Now *dial.* (*intr.* of 4.)

a **1652** BROME *Damoiselle* I. i. Wks. 1873 I. 385 At his Inne in Holborne Telling a little with the Host. **1888** ELWORTHY *W. Somerset Gloss.* s.v., I zeed 'em tellin' together..the night avore. **1892** SARAH HEWETT *Peasant Sp. Devon* 21 'E's behind telling tu Mr. Baker.

16. To disclose something wished to be kept secret; to play the informer, inform, tell tales, blab. Const. *on*, *of* (a person). (*intr.* of 5.)

1539 BIBLE (Great) *1 Sam.* xxvii. 11 Dauid saued nether man nor woman alyue..for feare (sayeth he) leste they shuld telle on vs. **1818** SCOTT *Rob Roy* xi, I ask no questions—no man bound to tell on himsell. **1835** MARRYAT *Jac. Faithf.* xxxiii, I had resolved to tell, and did so, narrating distinctly the circumstances by which the money had been obtained. **1860** GEO. ELIOT *Mill on Fl.* I. v, He didn't want to 'tell' of Maggie. **1897** 'TIVOLI' (H. W. Bleakley) *Short Innings* xiv, Oh, I'll not tell if you don't want me to. **1897** C. M. CAMPBELL *Deilie Jock* i. 16 Bobe..used to get mair than his fair share o' the tawse as it was, without my tellin' on him. **1943** B. SMITH *Tree grows in Brooklyn* III. xxxv. 206 And I didn't tell on you either, the time you made a cigarette out of coffee grounds and when you smoked it the paper caught fire and fell on her blouse and burned a big hole in it. **1955** J. MASTERS *Coromandel!* 41 Do you think she'll tell on us? **1968** J. LOCK *Lady Policeman* xx. 162 They felt they ought not to 'tell on her' unless it was absolutely necessary. **1974** *Age* (Melbourne) 12 Oct. 12/1 Ooh Aah! I'm going to tell on you: I will inform the authorities.

**** *Phrases and locutions.*

17. a. ***to tell a tale***, to relate a story or narrative; ***to tell one's tale***, to relate one's story; also, to say what one has to tell, to deliver one's message: see TALE *sb.* 3; ***to tell the tale***, to relate a false or exaggerated story, esp. in order to evoke a sympathetic response.

c **1275** *Passion* 1 in *O.E. Misc.* 37 One lutele tale, þat ich eu wille telle. *c* **1386** CHAUCER *Prol.* 792 That ech of yow to shorte with oure weye In this viage shal telle tales tweye. *c* **1450** tr. *De Imitatione* I. xvii. 19 Þou art called to suffre & to labore, not to be idel & telle tales. *a* **1548** HALL *Chron., Edw. IV* 199 b, The erle had not halfe tolde his tale. **1549** *Compl. Scot.* vi. 63, I thynk it best that euyrie ane of vs tel ane gude tayl or fabil, to pas the tyme quhil euyn... Than the eldest scheiphird began, and al the laif follouit, ane be ane in ther auen place. **1567** *Satir. Poems Reform.* vii. 4 Eich of thame his taill in ordoure tauld. **1596** SHAKS. *Merch. V.* IV. i. 276 When the tale is told, bid her be iudge. **1601** WEEVER *Mirr. Mart.* iv, One tale is good, untill another's told. **1613** PURCHAS *Pilgrimage* (1614) 208 A great part of the day after they sit at Cardes, or telling of Tales. **1875** JOWETT *Plato* (ed. 2) V. 366 My tale is one which many a man would be afraid to tell. **1918** W. J. LOCKE *Rough Road* xi. 133 The temptation to 'tell the tale', to the new-comer was too strong. **1928** *Daily Express* 15 Dec. 7/4 Moneylender at Bow County Court. What did you tell me when you borrowed the money? Debtor: Oh, we all tell the tale when we want money. **1943** J. B. PRIESTLEY *Daylight on Saturday* ii. 9 The absentees tell the tale to the National Service Officer, and he tells the tale to Proscot, and nothing's done. **1968** 'J. LE CARRÉ' *Small Town in Germany* xiii. 204 He couldn't half tell the tale... He could tell you *any* bloody tale and you believed it. **1979** R. BLYTHE *View in Winter* iv. 175 I'm not tellin' the tale. We all went to the war.

In the passage **1632** MILTON *L'Allegro* 67 'And every Shepherd tells his tale Under the Hawthorn in the dale', *tells his tale* probably belongs here, though some modern editors refer it to sense 21, taking it as 'counts his number or sum (i.e. of sheep)'; but no instance has been found before the 19th c., of 'tell his (or a) tale' in a numerical sense: while the expression in its ordinary sense has been common since the 13th century. Cf. also quot. 1549 for the telling of tales by each shepherd in turn, and see the whole passage, also the context of quot. 1613 in sense 21, where 'underneath a hawthorn' appears as the place of the shepherds' recreation.

b. ***to tell tales***: see TALE *sb.* 3 c.

c. So ***to tell a story***: see STORY.

a **1225** *Ancr. R.* 154 Me schal..tellen ou þeos storie, uor hit were to long to writen ham here. **1590** SHAKS. *Com. Err.* I. i. 121 To tell sad stories of my owne mishaps. **1681** DRYDEN *Span. Friar* IV. ii, Before I tell my fatal story out. **1798** FERRIAR *Illustr. Sterne* ii. 45 Another of his speakers tells the following story. **1840** W. H. MILL *Observ.*, etc. I. 114 The experience and history of mankind tells, uniformly, a different story from this. **1841** LANE *Arab. Nts.* I. 97 This is not a time for telling stories, when I am in this prison.

d. ***to tell*** (someone) ***goodbye, hello***, etc., to say goodbye, hello, etc., (to someone). Chiefly *U.S.*

1859 BARTLETT *Dict. Amer.* (ed. 2) 475 To *tell* one good-bye, is the Southern phrase for to bid one good-bye. **1872** E. EGGLESTON *End of World* xviii. 128 You aren't going without telling me good-by? **1884** AUGUSTA J. E. WILSON *Vashti* vii. (*U.S.*), 'Did Ulpian tell you good-bye?' 'No, I have not seen him.' **1905** B. TARKINGTON *In Arena* 253 She told me to tell you good-bye. **1973** V. CANNING *Flight of Grey Goose* ii. 28 Tell Albert hello and love to you both. **1979** L. MEYNELL *Hooky & Villainous Chauffeur* viii. 111 Mr Furlong asked me to tell you goodbye.

18. ***to tell*** (***the***) ***truth*** (†***sooth***), to make a true statement; to state or report the fact or circumstance as it really is. Also used parenthetically (***to tell the truth, truth to tell***, etc.) to emphasize a statement: cf. SAY *v.*[1] B. 7. So ***to tell a lie*** (***a falsehood, an untruth***), to make a wilfully false statement or report. (See also the sbs. SOOTH, TRUTH, LIE, etc.)

c **1350** *Will. Palerne* 34 Soþ forto telle, al his cler colour comsed forto fade. *Ibid.* 160 But trewþe for to telle whan time come of daye [etc.]. *c* **1400** *Destr. Troy* 2338, I shall telle you the trewthe how me tyde euyn. **1536** CHEKE *Rem. Sedition* B ij, All thynges telle truthe but man. **1596** SHAKS. *1 Hen. IV*, III. i. 58 Tell truth, and shame the Deuill. **1596–** [see LIE *sb.*[1] 1]. **1764** GRAY *J. Twitcher* 27 The prophet of Bethel, we read, told a lie. **1848** THACKERAY *Van. Fair* lii, It was not the habit of this dear creature to tell falsehoods, except when necessity compelled. **1855** H. ROGERS *Ess.* II. vii. 323 Sooth to tell, the narrative of the achievements.. draws largely on our faith.

19. ***to hear tell*** (†***told***); usually const. *of*: see HEAR *v.* 3 c. Now chiefly *dial.* and *colloq.*

c **1220** Herd told, **1297** Hurde tell [see HEAR *v.* 3 c]. *c* **1330** R. BRUNNE *Chron.* (1810) 101, I haf herd told of þis duke Roberd. **1375** BARBOUR *Bruce* II. 46 That Ik herd neuir in Romanys tell. *c* **1400** *Melayne* 47 That Charls was thare he herde telle. **1545** ASCHAM *Toxoph.* I. (Arb.) 100 Was never sene nor hard tel on yet. **1589, 1603, 1861, 1892** [see HEAR *v.* 3 b]. **1886** STEVENSON *Kidnapped* ii. 9, I asked him if he had ever heard tell of a house they called the house of Shaws.

20. In various colloquial expressions:

never tell me, expressing incredulity or impatience; ***do tell!*** (U.S., New Engl.), an exclamation of surprise, = 'is it possible?', 'you don't say so!'; ***don't tell me***, expressing incredulity, impatience, or (with dependent clause) dismay; ***I'll tell you what*** = 'I'll tell you what it is', or 'I'll tell you something'; ***to tell any one his own***: to tell him frankly of his faults; ***to tell the world***, to announce openly; to assert emphatically; ***I tell*** (or ***I am telling***) ***a lie***, (in trivial use) I am mistaken (cf. LIAR 1 a); ***you're telling me***, there is no need to tell me; I know that only too well; ***to tell*** (someone) ***what to do with*** (something) or ***where to put*** (something), expressing emphatic rejection with impolite implications; ***to tell it like it is***, to relate the facts of a matter realistically or honestly, holding nothing back *colloq.* (orig. *U.S. Blacks*'). Also ***tell that to the marines***: see MARINE *sb.* 4 c; ***to tell*** (someone) ***where he gets*** (or ***to get***) ***off***: see GET *v.* 70 j.

1604 SHAKS. *Oth.* I. i. 1 Neuer tell me, I take it much vnkindly. **1842** J. S. BUCKINGHAM *Eastern & Western States Amer.* I. 177 When a person..has concluded his narrative, the hearer will reply, 'Oh! *do* tell.' **1860** BARTLETT *Dict. Amer.* s.v. *Do*, The dairy-maid after hearing the story through, exclaimed, *Do tell!* **1883** C. F. WILDER *Sister Ridnour's Sacrifice* 138 'Come fur?' 'About eighty miles.'

..'Du tell!' **1979** C. MacLeod *Luck runs Out* (1981) i. 17 Do tell. Did she leave any children? **1764** Foote *Patron* III. Wks. 1799 I. 356 Not to be spoke with! Don't tell me, Sir; he must, he shall. **1848** J. H. Newman *Loss & Gain* III. ix. (1904) 323 Error of judgment! don't tell me. I know how these things happen quite well. **1861** Geo. Eliot *Silas Marner* I. ix. 143 Not come to live in this house? Don't tell me. **1944** M. Laski *Love on Supertax* iv. 52 Who's your latest pick-up?..Not Sir Hubert Porkington! Don't tell me you've actually hooked him! **1952** H. Garner *Yellow Sweater* 15 'Don't tell me you're in trouble [*sc.* pregnant]?' he asked. **1973** *Farm & Country* 10 Apr. 11/4 'Don't tell me we've got to go through that again,' said one executive member in an audible groan. **1596** Shaks. *2 Hen. IV*, I. i. 51 My Lord: Ile tell you what, If my yong Lord your Sonne, haue not the day [etc.]. **1877** Tennyson *Harold* I. ii, I'll tell thee what, my child; Thou hast misread this merry dream of thine. **1897** Violet Hunt *Unkist, Unkind* ii, I tell you what, Janet, we must have a man down who doesn't shoot—to amuse us! **1519** Horman *Vulg.* 61, I shall tell hym his owne, in a lytell byll of myne owne hande. **1865** R. Hunt *Pop. Rom. W. Eng.* Ser. II. 182 Every one is humorously 'told their own', without offence being taken. **1781** Cowper *Table Talk* in *Poems* (1782) I. 38 And tell the world.. That he, who died below and reigns above, Inspires the song, and that his name is love. *a* **1871** T. Carlyle in *Coll. Lett. T. & J. W. Carlyle* (1981) IX. 318 This I *cd* tell the world, you have not had, for 100 years, any Book that came more direct and flamingly sincere from the heart of a living man. **1923** [see Jeez(e *int.*]. **1933** *Punch* 11 Jan. 29/3 Say, can he act orr can he act? Ah'll tell de woirrld. **1956** 'C. Blackstock' *Dewey Death* viii. 169 She persistently told the world about her fiancé, her marriage problems, her piano playing. **1925** S. O'Casey *Shadow of Gunman* II, in *Two Plays* 172 Adolphus ..after takin' his tea at six o'clock—no, I'm tellin' a lie—it was before six, for I remember the Angelus was ringin' out. **1956** 'A. Burgess' *Time for Tiger* i. 7 Those Japanese tattooists... I seen one fellow in Jerusalem, wait, I'm telling a lie, it was in Alex,..one fellow with a complete foxhunt on his back. **1968** L. Deighton *Only when I Larf* vii. 89 Six Centurion Mark Fives on that hillock... No tell a lie, one of them is a Mark Two. **1973** J. Mann *Only Security* xii. 172 Oh, it must have been fifteen years or so—..No, I tell a lie, I'm afraid,..can't have been more than five or six years that she was like that, poor lady. **1932** G. Kahn (*song-title*) You're telling me. **1938** M. Allingham *Fashion in Shrouds* xix. 338 'Things are bad enough as they are.' 'You're telling me.' **1954** *Times* 16 July 9/4 When he declares that 'overnutrition has its dangers'..the layman is inclined to reply 'You're telling me.' **1977** 'C. Aird' *Parting Breath* xvii. 194 'Forensic pathologists don't take chances.' 'You're telling me,' said Crosby with audible scorn. **1946** M. Shulman *Zebra Derby* (1947) xxi. 133 Green, an upholsterer, said that he was through with upholstering and had told his old boss what to do with his old job. **1958** M. Dickens *Man Overboard* xii. 176 He had been going to tell Glenn what he could do with his job. **1968** M. Bragg *Without City Wall* II. xxi. 207 You could tell the people at the hall what to do with that job of theirs. She'd had enough of being a servant. **1977** *Listener* 14 Apr. 483/2 Protestations that if the government did any such thing, the BBC would probably tell it where to stuff such an instruction. **1964** *Down Beat* 19 Nov. 8/2 (*heading*) Mann tells it like it is. **1965** *New Statesman* 1 Oct. 473/1 Although sometimes tardy, all his speeches make their intended points; as they say in Harlem, he tells it like it is. **1969** L. Lokos *House Divided* i. 58 The crowd responded fervently with 'Amen, amen,' and 'Tell it like it is.' **1973** *Field & Stream* Jan. 8/3 Keep this tell-it-like-it-is kind of article going. **1979** *Guardian* 14 Apr. 8/6 'Tell it like it is,' said Hemingway, but that was..before we all became ethnic-conscious.

II. To mention numerically, to count, reckon.

21. a. *trans.* To mention or name (the single members of a series or group) one by one, specifying them as *one, two, three*, etc.; hence, to ascertain from the number of the last how many there are in the whole series; to enumerate, reckon in; to reckon up, count, number. Also *absol.* Now *arch.* or *dial.*

c **1000** Ælfric (*Heptat.*) *Gen.* xv. 5 Telle þas steorran. —— *Num.* iii. 15, 16 Telle ælcne wepnedman.. Moises þa tealde. *c* **1175** *Lamb. Hom.* 87 Fram þan halie hester dei boð italde fifti daȝa to þisse deie. *c* **1200** Ormin 4550, & whase wile tellenn hemm Bi tale he findeþþ ehhte. *c* **1205** Lay. 24377 To tellen þat folc of Kairliun Ne mihte hit na mon idon. *a* **1300** *Cursor M.* 13302 (Cott.) Tuelue þai war to tell in tale. **1398** Trevisa *Barth. De P.R.* VIII. xxi. (Bodl. MS.), He knowithe how many þei bene þat nombreþ and telleþ þe sterres. **1483** Caxton *Gold. Leg.* 143/2 He tolde atte table syttyng xiii poure pylgryms. **1523** Fitzherb. *Husb.* §30 Let hym goo to the ende of his lande, and begynne and tell .ix. sheues, and let hym caste out the .x. shefe in the name of god. **1535** Coverdale *1 Sam.* xiv. 17 Tell and se which of vs is gone awaye. And whan they nombred, beholde, Ionathas & his wapen bearer was not there. **1613** W. Browne *Sheph. Pipe* v. i, Morne had got the start of night.. When the shepheards from the fold All their bleating charges told. **1657** J. Watts *Vind. Ch. Eng.* 43 Every countreyman can tell his Geese, and reckon right. **1719** De Foe *Crusoe* (1850) 236 He could not tell twenty in English, but he numbered them, by laying so many stones in a row, and pointing to me to tell them over. **1748** J. Mason *Elocut.* 24 A Comma stops the Voice while we may privately tell one, a Semi-colon two; a Colon three: and a Period four. **1821** Clare *Vill. Minstr.* II. 31 The shepherd had told all his sheep. **1869** [see telling *vbl. sb.* 3].

b. *spec.* To count (voters or votes). Also *absol.* *to tell noses*, to count heads: see nose *sb.* 6 d.

1511 in W. H. Turner *Select. Rec. Oxford* (1880) 4 Foster desyred off the mayre.. to tell the fremen.. for thalecc'on off a alderman;..they were men truly told. **1657**, *a* **1734** [see nose *sb.* 6 d]. **1669** Marvell *Corr.* Wks. (Grosart) II. 289 The tellers for the ayes chanced to be very ill reckoners, so that they were forced to tell severall times over. **1731** Swift *To Gay* 60 Nor think yourself secure in doing wrong By telling noses with a party strong. **1870** *Daily News* 7 May 2/1 After the division Mr. Dodson brought to the knowledge of the Committee the circumstance that he had appointed Sir H. B. a teller, but that that hon. baronet had refused to tell. **1899** *Jrnls. Ho. Comm.* 18 May, The House was told by Mr. Speaker, and, 24 members only being present, Mr. Speaker retired from the Chair until four of the clock, when the House was again told.

c. Phrases. (*a*) ***to tell one's beads*** (***rosary***): see bead *sb.* 2 b; so ***to tell one's prayers***. †Also allusively ***to tell tears***, to weep (quot. 1588).

1588 T. L. *To Ch. Rome* (1651) 18 Thow..canst not goe downe and sit, and tell tears with him. **1641**, **1759** [see bead *sb.* 2 b]. **1789** Mrs. Piozzi *Journ. France* I. 265, I..see nothing..but people telling their beads. **1819** Scott *Ivanhoe* xl, Richard..beheld the jovial Friar on his knees, telling his rosary. **1852** Rock *Ch. of Fathers* III. ix. 326 That noble Anglo-Saxon lady Godiva told her prayers on gems threaded together for that purpose. **1857** Emerson *Hermione* i, On a mound an Arab lay,..And told his amulets. **1871** L. Stephen *Playgr. Eur.* x. (1894) 250 The women..kneel reverently..whilst they diligently tell their beads.

†(*b*) ***to tell the clock***, to count the hours as shown by a clock; hence, to pass one's time idly; cf. *tell-clock* in tell-. *Obs.*

1678 Butler *Hud.* III. III. 577 An old dull Sot, who'd told the Clock For many years at Bridewel-dock. **1738** tr. *Guazzo's Art Conversation* 14 They are fit for nothing, unless it be to tell the Clock [*ed.* 1586 count the clock], which they always think goes too slowly.

(*c*) ***to tell*** (so many) ***years***: to have lived (so many) years; to be aged (so much). Cf. number *v.* 6. *Obs.* or *arch.*

1810 S. Green *Reformist* I. 103 The little girl had not quite told five years. **1818** Lamb *Elia* Ser. II. *Wedding*, [She at] nineteen was [married] by her..cousin..who told some few years older. **1835** Lytton *Rienzi* I. iv, Thou hadst told but thy tenth year.

(*d*) ***all told***: when all are counted; in all.

1850 Scoresby *Cheever's Whalem. Adv.* ii. (1858) 24 They are four hundred all told. **1858** J. S. Mansfield in *Merc. Marine Mag.* V. 19 The hands numbered 19 all told. **1885** Ld. Wolseley in *Times* 22 Jan. 5/4 Stewart's force was about 1,500 all told.

22. a. To count out (pieces of money) in payment; hence, to pay (money); now chiefly ***to tell down, out, into one's hand***, etc. *arch.* or *dial.*

c **1250** *Gen. & Ex.* 1993 So michel fe ðor is hem told, He hauen him [Joseph] boȝt, he hauen sold. *a* **1300** *Cursor M.* 4835 We..haue..Al redi penijs for to tell If we moght find her oght to .sel. *c* **1375** *Sc. Leg. Saints* xii. (*Mathias*) 270 He [h]is master to þame sald, For thretty pennys to hym talde. **1515** *Scot. Field* 40 They paid him tribute trulie: many told thousands, that the[y] might liue in their land. **1565–73** Cooper *Thesaurus* s.v. *Dinumero, Dinumerare pecuniam, pro Dissoluere, sæpissime accipitur*, to pay or tell out money. **1621** T. Williamson tr. *Goulart's Wise Vieillard* 84 His promise should passe for ready pay, and for money told on the nayle. **1645** Rutherford *Tryal & Tri. Faith* (1845) 34 Should any buy a field of land, and refuse to tell down the money. **1723** De Foe *Col. Jack* (1840) 37 He told the money into my hand. **1739** *Joe Miller's Jests* No. 200 The money'd Man fell to telling out the Sum in Shillings. **1819** Scott *Ivanhoe* xxxiii, Tell down with all speed an hundred crowns. **1893** W. Raymond *Gentl. Upcott* ii, Biddlecombe drew a bag from his pocket and told the money out in gold.

fig. **1637** Shirley *Gamester* IV. ii, Let her tell down Her virgin tears on Delamore's cold marble.

b. To reckon up or calculate the total amount or value of (money or other things); to count. Also ***to tell out, over***. *arch.*

c **1000** *Ags. Gosp.* Luke xiv. 28 Hu ne sytt he ærest & teleð [*Lindisf. G.* ȝetelles] þa andfengas þe him behefe synt. **1340–70** *Alex. & Dind.* 323 We mowe tellen our time whan þe time fallus. *c* **1380** Wyclif *Wks.* (1880) 46 þei wolen tell gold and money. **1475** *Bk. Noblesse* (Roxb.) 85 Forto numbre and telle the quantite and porcion of everie manis part that they broughte. **1526** *Pilgr. Perf.* (W. de W. 1531) 160 b, Yf I sholde tell money or carue, wryte, or sowe ony subtyll worke, whiche requireth synglar or specyall study. **1594** Greene & Lodge *Looking Gl.* Wks. (Rtldg.) 121/2 Come, sir, will you dispatch, and tell your money? **1653** Marvell *Corr.* Wks. (Grosart) II. 4 Those who weigh and tell over money. **1723** De Foe *Col. Jack* (1840) 78 What its cargo amounted to I knew not, for I never told it. **1827–35** Willis *Wife's Appeal* 99 As a miser tells his gold.

c. *intr.* with refl. or passive sense: To be counted; also ***to tell for***, (***up***) ***to***: to count as, count for, amount to. Now *rare*.

1362 Langl. *P. Pl.* A. v. 128 Putte hem in a pressour and pinnede hem þer-Inne Til ten ȝerdes oþer twelue tolden out þrettene. **1774** Burke *Corr.* (1844) I. 488 Lord Verney..has told in parliament, including himself, for four members. *c* **1794** Susanna Blamire *Poems, Meeting* ii, Our butter tells to fourteen pun'. **1825** Esther Hewlett *Cottage Comforts* vi. 45 Put it in the savings' bank, and it will tell up to something.

d. ***to be telling***: to be worth or as good as (so much) to; to be to the advantage or credit of (a person). *Sc.* and *north. dial.*

1629 *Orkney Witch Trial* in *County Folk-lore* (1903) III. 79 Haid [she] lettin yow abid with your brother it haid bene telling hir xl.£. **1822** *Corspatrick of Raymondsholm* II. 8 (Jam.) It wad hae been telling some that are now safe frae skaith gin it had never been blither. **1875** P. Ponder *Kirkcumdoon* 85 (E.D.D.) It wud be tellin' the pairish an' himsel' gin Josey gaed less aboot the Wallace Arms. **1889** H. Johnston *Chron. Glenbuckie* vii. 80 It would have been telling me a ten-pound note [if I had taken your advice]. *Mod. Sc.* It would be telling some people if they took a leaf out of his book.

23. With adverbs: **a.** ***tell out***: to separate or exclude by counting; to count out. *arch.* or *dial.*

1535 Coverdale *2 Chron.* ii. 2 Salomon..tolde out thre score and ten thousande men to beare burthens. **1812** *Sporting Mag.* XXXIX. 138 Burn..had been long told out of the London list as a cur.

b. ***tell off***: to count off from the whole number or company; to separate, detach, esp. so many men for a particular duty; hence *gen.* to appoint to a particular task, object, position, or the like.

1804 J. Whitehouse in Lewis & Clark *Orig. Jrnls. Lewis & Clark Exped.* (1905) VII. I. 70 The Cap^{tn}. form^d. his men On the S.W. Side of the river Missourie and told them off in Sections, from the right. **1827** Scott *Jrnl.* 29 Jan., How could the castes be distinguished or told off in a populous nation? **1837** Marryat *Dog-Fiend* l, The troops were told-off into the boats. **1858** Froude *Hist. Eng.* III. xiii. 173 Ten knights were then told off, and ten followers for every knight, to ride down to Doncaster. **1890** *Guardian* 23 July 1159/3 A constable had been told off to watch the defendant. **1893** Forbes-Mitchell *Remin. Gt. Mutiny* 84 The sentries were posted on the ramparts and regular reliefs told off.

c. ***tell off*** (*intr.* for *refl.*). *Mil.* Of a rank or troop of men: To number themselves in succession.

1833 *Regul. Instr. Cavalry* I. 86 The men are to be instructed to tell off by files and by threes.

d. *fig.* ***to tell*** (someone) ***off***, to scold or reprimand (someone). Cf. *tick off* s.v. tick *v.*[1] 3.

1919 *Cassell's New Eng. Dict.* s.v. *Tell, to tell off*, (colloq.) to scold. **1927** A. Christie *Big Four* xiv. 202 They don't like you to notice things—especially if it should seem you were telling them off about it. **1938** G. Arthur *Not Worth Reading* xiv. 216 'It required a very great man,' said F. E. when he emerged from his interview, 'to resist the temptation to tell me off.' **1941** G. Homes *Forty Whacks* ix. 90 The man had just been told off, and told off plenty. **1974** M. Birmingham *You can help Me* iv. 97 She's..telling off the police good and proper... She blames them for all the dirt.

III. To account, or estimate, qualitatively.

†**24. a.** To account, consider, reckon, estimate, esteem as being (something). With *compl.* or *for*. *Obs.*

c **897** K. Ælfred *Gregory's Past. C.* iii. 35 He fleah ðæt rice, & tealde hine selfne his suiðe unwierðne. *c* **1000** *Ags. Gosp.* Matt. xi. 16 Hwam telle ic þas cneorysse ȝelice? *c* **1230** *Hali Meid.* 43 Sone so þu telles te betere þen an oðer. *c* **1330** R. Brunne *Chron. Wace* (Rolls) 2789 ȝyf men dide hem any wo, Hit was teld for felonye. *Ibid.* 10555 He [a knight] was told of non honour Bot he had ben wyþ kyng Arthour. *c* **1374** Chaucer *Troylus* III. 765 (814) Wordly selynesse Which clerkes tellyn fals felicite. **1411** *Rolls of Parlt.* III. 651/1 They schall tellen hem well payed with favour and grace. *c* **1425** *Eng. Conq. Irel.* 1 Leynyster, that is I-told þe fifte parte of Irland. *c* **1430** *Syr Gener.* (Roxb.) 4132 Doo way, quod the king.., I tel hir myne.

†**b.** ***to tell scorn***: to count it scorn, to scorn (*to do* something). *Obs.*

1477 *Paston Lett.* III. 185 The fawcon Which is alofte, tellith scorne to loke a down.

†**25.** *intr.*, or *trans.* with cognate *obj.* (***to tell tale***): To make account *of*; to have a specified estimate or opinion *of*; to think (much or little) *of*; to set (much or little) store *by* (*to*). ***to tell*** (***more***, etc.) ***price***: see price *sb.* 8. *Obs.*

c **1175** *Lamb. Hom.* 147 An oðer is þet he telle swa lutel tale þerof. *a* **1225** *Leg. Kath.* 89 To..beon icleopet lefdi, þet feole telleð wel to. *a* **1250** *Owl & Night.* 793 Telstu bi me þe wrs for þan þat ic bute enne craft ne kan? *c* **1380** Wyclif *Wks.* (1880) 468 Whanne þey tellen more bi a cronycle of foly..þan þey tellen bi cristis lawe. *c* **1400** *Rom. Rose* 5053 For litel sholde a man telle Of hir, that wolle hir body selle. *c* **1400** *Laud Troy Bk.* 2178 Thei tolde right nauȝt of thyn awe. *c* **1450** Lovelich *Grail* xlv. 38 This peple, he seide ful Schortly, Nis non thing Forto tellen by. *c* **1475** *Partenay* 3029 Thys Geaunt noght told of hym in no degre.

26. a. *intr.* To count (for something); to be of account or weight; to have its effect, be effective, act or operate with effect; to make an impression.

Perh. orig. a pugilistic expression.

1783 *Public Advertiser* 7 Oct. 2/2 Yet strange to tell it, this Distinction, which as the Players call it, tells most forcibly, Garrick overlooked. **1797** *Monthly Mag.* III. 546 Every blow that they receive upon their projecting surface, tells. **1811** Lamb *Genius & Char. Hogarth* Wks. (1895) 277 Everything in the print, to use a vulgar expression, tells. **1812** *Sporting Mag.* XXXIX. 102 Several blows of consequence told. **1833** L. Ritchie *Wand. by Loire* 24 These peculiarities make the place tell well in an outside view. **1865** Kingsley *Herew.* iii, Martin Lightfoot saw that his appeal to the antipathies of race had told. **1887** Sir R. H. Roberts *In the Shires* ii. 32 Going..at a pace..that began to tell upon the horses.

b. To have weight or influence *in favour of* or *against*.

1799 Dundas in Owen *Wellesley's Desp.* (1877) 637 It is a transaction which tells in our favour. **1870** Freeman *Norm. Conq.* I. App. 648 It tells somewhat against his interpretation.

tell, telle, obs. ff. till *v.*, *prep.*, and *conj.*

tell-, the stem of tell *v.* in combination with a sb. (in objective or attributive relation), used as *sb.* or *adj.*: **tell-all** *a.* and *sb.*, (an account which is) revelatory, tending to disclose private information; cf. tell v. 5 a.; **tell-box, tell-card**, contrivances used by card-sharpers, to enable them to turn up a particular card; †**tell-cause**, *Rhet.*: see quot.; †**tell-clock**, one who 'tells the clock': see tell *v.* 21 c (*b*); an idler who merely marks time; **tell-fare** = tell-tale 2 f; †**tell-love**: see quot.; **tell-pie, tell-piet**, a tale-bearer: cf. *tale-piet*, tale *sb.* 10. See also tell-tale, tell-truth.

1959 J. Fingleton *Four Chukkas to Australia* (1960) i. 2 This position—in cricket and other sports—has been aggravated by the flood of '*tell-all' books. **1974** *Nat. Geogr. Mag.* Dec. 851/2 A tell-all historian of the time reported that the prince loved to drink and was notably fond of women. **1976** *Publishers Weekly* 7 June 68/1 This man's sometimes engrossing, frenetic, first-person tell-all. **1978** in K. Hudson *Jargon of Professions* iii. 64 A totally engrossing tell-all. Few autobiographies convey so intimately what is involved in creativity. **1865** *Athenæum* No. 1941. 13/1 This simple *tell-a-story style. **1894** MASKELYNE *Sharps & Flats* viii. 194 The contrivances..are known as '*tell-boxes'. *Ibid.*, Any card which lies immediately upon the smooth face of a '*tell-card' will slip easily. **1589** PUTTENHAM *Eng. Poesie* III. xix. (Arb.) 236 This assignation of cause the Greekes called *Etiologia*, which if we might without scorne of a new inuented terme call *Tell cause it were right according to the Greeke originall. **1609** ELLESMERE *Sp. on Post-nati* 17 They are called thither by the Kings Writ, not to sit as *Tell-clockes, or idle hearers. **1618** S. WARD *Jethro's Justice* (1627) 65 Is there no meane betweene busiebodies and tell-clocks, betweeen factotum and fay't neant? **1865** GASKELL (*title*) Patent Cab Indicator, or *Tell-Fare. **1640** *Erotomania* 176 Poppy..Theocritus cals this hearb τηλίφιλον..as if we should say, *Tel-loue. **1828** *Craven Gloss.*, **Tell-pye*, a tell-tale. **1897** SARAH GRAND *Beth Bk.* xii, If you tell secrets, you know, you're a tell-pie. *Ibid.* xv, Don't you be put upon by tell-pie-tits. **1855** ROBINSON *Whitby Gloss.*, **Tell-pyet* or *Telly-pie*, a tale-bearer, a tell-tale.

tellable ('tɛləb(ə)l), *a.* [f. TELL *v.* + -ABLE.] Capable of being told or narrated; fit to be told; worth telling.

1483 *Cath. Angl.* 379/1 Tellabylle, *vbi* spekabylle. **1818** MOORE *Mem.* (1853) II. 196 Practical jokes, not easily tellable. **1830** GREVILLE in *Mem.* (1875) I. vii. 272 The details of his life are not tellable.

tellar, var. TILLER *sb.*[3], a young tree.

tell-box, etc.: see TELL-.

Tell el-Amarna: see AMARNA.

tellen ('tɛlən). Also tellin. [ad. L. *tellīna*, a. Gr. τελλίνη a kind of shell-fish. So F. *telline*, It. *tellina*.] A bivalve of the genus *Tellina* or family *Tellinidæ*.

*c*1711 PETIVER *Gazophyl.* Dec. vii-viii. Tab. 78 Rib-welted Limington Tellen. **1833** *Penny Cycl.* I. 466/2 They are supposed to have long syphons, like the Tellens. **1854** WOODWARD *Mollusca* II. 310 The Tellens are found in all seas, chiefly in the littoral and laminarian zones. **1901** E. STEP *Shell Life* viii. 118 The members of the Tellin family ..are distinctly deep burrowers in sand or mud. **1971** S. P. DANCE *Seashells* 77 The right and left valves of many tellins are unequal in shape and size.

Comb. **1839** *Penny Cycl.* XIV. 319/1 Tellen-like Nymphidæ.

teller ('tɛlə(r)). Also 4 -ere, 6 -or. [f. TELL *v.* + -ER[1].] One who or that which tells, in various senses.

I. 1. a. One who relates, makes known, or announces.

13.. *K. Alis.* 1577 Teller of jeste is ofte myslike. **1382** WYCLIF *Acts* xvii. 18 He is seyn for to be a tellere of newe deuelis. **1547-64** BAULDWIN *Mor. Philos.* (Palfr.) 125 There is no difference betweene a great teller of tydings and a lyer. **1548** UDALL, etc. *Erasm. Par. Mark* xii. 76 We knowe ryght well that thou arte a teller of trouthe, and feareste no man. **1552** HULOET, Teller of fortune, *ominator, uel trix.* **1606** SHAKS. *Ant. & Cl.* I. ii. 99 The Nature of bad newes infects the Teller. **1825** LAMB *Elia* Ser. II. *Stage Illusion*, The teller of a mirthful tale has latitude allowed him. **1874** L. STEPHEN *Hours in Library* (1892) I. iv. 145 He had been a teller of stories before he was well in breeches.

b. A thing that makes known or announces.

1761 BLISS in *Phil. Trans.* LII. 176 Mr. Phelps lost the final contact, by mistaking the teller of the clock. **1877** *N. & Q.* 5th Ser. VII. 164/1 At Frisby and elsewhere these tolls [for the dead] are called 'tellers'. **1898** TYACK *Bk. about Bells* i. 8 The use of bells as tellers of the passing time. **1909** DEEDES & WALTERS *Ch. Bells Essex* 149 We now come to the uses of the tellers, for which the normal custom is 3 × 3 strokes for a man, 3 × 2 for a woman, including children, usually both beginning and end of tolling.

II. 2. a. One who counts or keeps tally; now *esp.* one who counts money; *spec.* an officer in a bank who receives or pays money over the counter.

1480 *Howard Househ. Bks.* (Roxb.) 9 John Fytzherberd, one of the tellers of the money. **1535** *Act 27 Hen. VIII*, c. 14 §2 Euery porte..where no tellers nor packers at this present time be. **1576** GASCOIGNE *Steele Gl.* (Arb.) 80 When Siluer sticks not on the Tellers fingers. **1601** J. KEYMER *Obs. Dutch Fish.* (1664) 7 Shee [the Herring-Buss] imployeth..at Land ..Packers, Tellers, Dressers. **1632** BROME *Court Begg.* I. i, To put you to some Tellers Clearke to teach you Ambo-dexterity in telling money. **1766** ENTICK *London* IV. 342 [At the mint] A weigher and teller,..blanchers, moniers, &c. **1843** *Civil Eng. & Arch. Jrnl.* VI. 278/2 The inconveniences to which the 'tellers' were subjected in weighing gold for the public. **1887** *Times* 26 Aug. 8/4 The bank, in which there were only the teller and a clerk.

b. One of four officers of the Exchequer formerly charged with the receipt and payment of moneys.

The office was abolished in 1834, the duties being subsequently performed by the Comptroller of the Exchequer.

1488 *Naval Acc. Hen. VII* (1896) 34 William Page oon o. the Tellers of the Kyngs said Receipt. **1583** in Feuillerat *Revels Q. Eliz.* (1908) 360-1 Table iii, One of the Tellors of the saide receipte. **1702** *Lond. Gaz.* No. 3782/3 One of the Four Tellers of His Majesty's Exchequer. **1812** WHITBREAD *Sp. Ho. Comm.* 7 May, The..emolument drawn by the late first Lord of the Admiralty as Teller of Exchequer. **1884** T. WALDEN in *Harper's Mag.* Aug. 424/2 At the entrance of the Hall..you passed the Exchequer. You may yet see over the doorway the grotesque effigies of the teller.

c. In a deliberative assembly (as the House of Commons), A person (usually one of two or more) who counts the votes on a division. Also *attrib.* in ***teller vote*** (U.S.), a vote taken by tellers as members file past them; *spec.* a category of vote in the House of Representatives, in which the tellers record the votes of members but not (until 1970) their names.

1669 [see TELL *v.* 21 b]. **1682** N. O. *Boileau's Lutrin* IV. 146 Let faithful tellers take the Poll, and note The Ay's and Noe's. **1775** BURKE *Corr.* (1844) II. 8 Rose Fuller was..one of the tellers on the division. **1857** TOULMIN SMITH *Parish* 62 The tellers must then give in to the Chairman the number found on each side, as agreed on between them. **1888** *Times* (weekly ed.) 29 June 10/1, 644 members, including the Speaker and tellers.

Comb. **1924** *Congressional Rec.* 11 Apr. 6142/1 Is not the teller vote the highest in the committee? **1935** *Sun* (Baltimore) 1 July 1/8 The House is working under a rule which precludes a direct roll-call vote..but a teller vote..is to be taken. **1972** W. WEAVER *Both Your Houses* vii. 99 If the outcome of a division is unsatisfactory to at least twenty members of the Committee of the Whole..they can demand a teller vote. **1974** *Encycl. Brit. Macropædia* XIV. 722/1 Voting procedures range from the formal procedure of the division or teller vote in the British House of Commons to the electric voting methods employed in the California legislature.

III. 3. *Pugil. slang.* A telling blow.

1814 *Sporting Mag.* XLIII. 70 He sometimes put in some good tellers on his opponent's body. **1834** H. AINSWORTH *Rookwood* IV. ii, A teller was planted..upon his smeller.

teller, dial. variant of TILLER, sapling.

Teller mine ('tɛlə maɪn). Also with hyphen and as one word. [Anglicization of G. *tellermine*, f. *teller* plate + *mine* MINE *sb.* 3.] A disc-shaped German anti-tank mine containing TNT, used in the war of 1939-45.

1943 *Hutchinson's Pict. Hist. War 4 Aug.-26 Oct.* 11 A huge collection of teller-mines, or disc mines, discovered by the allied forces near Roccalumba. **1945** *Finito! Po Valley Campaign* (15th Army Group) 41 The 10th Mountain Division pushed forward..across a valley studded with Teller mines. **1967** *Punch* 11 Jan. 40/1 We were..taking the fuses out of those wretched Tellermines.

tellership ('tɛləʃɪp). [f. TELLER + -SHIP.] The office or position of a teller.

1788 W. EDEN in G. Rose *Diaries* (1860) I. 77 Ought I to seek for my son the second reversion of a Tellership? **1807** W. TAYLOR in *Ann. Rev.* V. 565 Abolishing tellerships and auditorships of the exchequer. **1875** *Contemp. Rev.* XXVI. 454 The interesting history of the Exchequer, its sinecure tellerships,..its clerkships of the pells.

tell-fare: see TELL-.

'tellicherry bark. [f. *Tellicherry*, a town on the Malabar coast, north of Calicut.] The bark of *Wrightia dysenterica*; also called CONESSINE bark.

1822-34 *Good's Study of Med.* (ed. 4) I. 626.

'telligraph. *Hist.* [ad. med. (Anglo-) L. *telligraphum*, *-ium*, irreg. f. L. *tellus* land: see -GRAPH.] A description of the boundaries of land; a charter of lands in which the bounds are described: = TERRIER *sb.*[1]

[**816** in Haddan & Stubbs *Councils* (1871) III. 582 Tamen serventur libros primordiales cum aliis telligraffis, ne inposterum aliquod scrupulum contraditionis innitere conantur. **1783** REEVES *Hist. Eng. Law* I. i. 8 An Anglo-Saxon charter of land has also been called *Telligraphum*,.. but this appellation has been given to them most likely since the Conquest, as a translation of the word *Landboc*.] **1882** W. BEAMONT *Domesday Bk.* (ed. 2) Introd. 6 The witnesses would probably produce the telligraphs by which they held their lands. **1903** G. F. BROWNE *St. Aldhelm* 249 These land-books were sometimes called telligraphs, a word which sounds curiously modern.

tellina (tɛ'laɪnə). Also Tellina. [mod.L. (G. E. Rumphius *D'Amboinsche Rariteitkamer* (1705) II. 145), f. Gr. τελλίνη.] = TELLEN. Also *attrib.* Hence **'tellinoid** *a.*, resembling a bivalve of the genus *Tellina*.

1877 C. M. YONGE in C. Coleridge *C. M. Yonge* (1903) ii. 70 Waves from the Atlantic, bringing in..tellinas of a delicate pink. **1884** G. W. TRYON *Struct. & Syst. Conchol.* III. 170 The branchial apparatus..is..a departure from the Tellina type. **1900** *Proc. U.S. Nat. Mus.* XXIII. 287 The Tellinas are mostly inhabitants of moderate depths. *Ibid.* 291 Shell tellinoid, thin. **1936** A. H. VERRILL *Strange Sea Shells* xiv. 132 Why..is the tellina so beautifully colored within its shells.

†tellinet. *Obs.* [f. L. *tellīna* TELLEN + -ET[1].] A small shell of the genus *Tellina*.

1708 *Phil. Trans.* XXVI. 79 *Tellinites*, the Tellinet, or Lesser Muscle-shell.

telling ('tɛlɪŋ), *vbl. sb.* [f. TELL *v.* + -ING[1].] The action of the verb TELL.

1. a. The action of relating, making known, or saying; relation; communication, conversation (now *dial.*).

13.. *Cursor M.* 29163 (Cott. Galba) If þe prest..Be vnwise in his gifing, Or els þe synful in his telling. **1382** WYCLIF *2 Macc.* ii. 25 The tellyngis of stories. **1390** GOWER *Conf.* I. 296 So wolde I my wordes plie, That mihten Wraththe and Cheste avale With tellinge of my softe tale. **1546** J. HEYWOOD *Prov.* (1867) 57 A good tale yll tolde, in the tellyng is marde. **1700** DRYDEN *Pref. Fables* Wks. (Globe) 496 The form which he has given to the telling makes the tale his own. **1789** MRS. PIOZZI *Journ. France* I. 117 The theatres here are beautiful beyond all telling.

b. An account, description. Now *dial.* or *arch.*

1382 WYCLIF *1 John* i. 5 This is the tellyng, that we herden of him, and tellen to ȝou. **1904** *Blackw. Mag.* Dec. 811/2 The father was a terrible man by all tellings.

c. Phrase ***that's telling(s***, that would be to divulge something secret (*colloq.*); similarly ***that would be telling***; ***to lose nothing in the telling***, (of a story) to become embellished in the course of frequent narration.

1837 MARRYAT *Dog-Fiend* xiv, 'Where is this cargo to be seen, and when?'..'That's tellings', replied the man. **1878** E. JENKINS *Haverholme* 178 'How do you get your information?' 'That's tellings', said the Monsignor. **1897** 'S. GRAND' *Beth Bk.* xiii. 112 'May I ask..by whom you were informed?'..'Ah, that would be telling,' said Beth. **1921** S. KAYE-SMITH *Joanna Godden* III. 136 'What sort of surprise?' 'That's telling.' **1930** A. CHRISTIE *Murder at Vicarage* x. 78 'When was she talking of earning her own living?'..'That would be telling, wouldn't it?' **1973** G. MITCHELL *Murder of Busy Lizzie* xii. 144 'But what could you inform about?' 'That's telling, isn't it?' **1980** A. PRICE *Hour of Donkey* i. 23 'Are the Germans in Peronne, Dickie?'..'That would be telling!'

[**1721** J. KELLY *Scottish Proverbs* 55 A Tale never loses in the telling. The Fame or Report of a matter of Fact.. commonly receives an Addition as it goes from Hand to Hand.] **1906** *Athenæum* 13 Oct. 434 The narrative loses nothing in the telling. **1914** E. R. BURROUGHS *Tarzan of Apes* vi. 68 The story of the thunder-stick having lost nothing in the telling during these ten years. **1954** L. P. HARTLEY *White Wand* 15 No doubt Antonio was telling the story to his fellow-gondoliers at the traghetto, and it would lose nothing in the telling.

2. a. The action of counting or numbering.

1387-8 T. USK *Test. Love* II. i. (Skeat) l. 114, I can not passen the tellinge of thre as yet. *c*1440 *Promp. Parv.* 488/1 Tellynge, or nowmerynge, *numeracio.* **1589** [? LYLY] *Pappe w. Hatchet* E j b, I thinke them [sheep] woorth neither the tarring, nor the telling. **1594** PLAT *Jewell-ho.* III. 89 There must bee no time lost in the telling [of the money]. **1689** *Answ. Lords & Commoner's Sp.* 12 Notwithstanding the often telling of Noses. **1847** *Infantry Man.* (1854) 60 The telling off by threes. **1901** *Scotsman* 13 Mar. 9/4 This mixed telling did not mean mixed voting, for the division closely followed party lines.

†b. *transf.* Value, amount, force. *Obs. rare*[−1].

1636 RUTHERFORD *Lett.* (1862) I. 188 There is much telling in Christ's Kindness!

c. ***telling-off***, a scolding or reprimand. Cf. TELL *v.* 23 d. *colloq.*

1911 KIPLING *Diversity of Creatures* (1917) 121 The boys ..had had a wildish night..that ended with a telling-off from an artist. **1920** A. J. L. SCOTT *Hist. Sixty Squadron R.A.F.* 57 He got..a well-deserved and proper 'telling-off' from the Brigadier and Wing Commander. **1959** *Times* 22 July 7/4 Then there was and to some extent still is 'a telling off', sometimes met with in the degenerate form of 'ticking off'. **1974** W. FOLEY *Child in Forest* II. 231 Still smarting from my 'telling-off'..and in militant mood.

3. *Comb.*, as ***†telling-board***, ***-house***: see quots.

1552 HULOET, *Tellinge bourde or table for exchaunge to tell money. **1597** *Catal. Anc. Deeds* (1906) V. 485 In the *Telling howse usuallie appointed for receiptes and paimentes. **1869** BLACKMORE *Lorna D.* ii. *note*, The 'telling-houses' on the moor are rude cots where the shepherds meet, to tell their sheep at the end of the pasturing season.

'telling, *ppl. a.* [f. TELL *v.* + -ING[2].] That tells; effective, forcible, striking.

1851 H. MELVILLE *Moby Dick* I. xxv. 180 A staid, steadfast man, whose life for the most part was a telling pantomime of action. **1852** J. A. ROEBUCK *Hist. Whig Ministry* II. i. 129 This observation..was..what is called in debating language, a *telling* reply. **1859** DE QUINCEY *Wks.* XI. Pref. 18 Into this great *chef-d'œuvre* of Milton, it was no doubt Johnson's secret determination to send a telling shot at parting. **1870** STANHOPE *Hist. Reign Anne* (1872) I. i. 28 It was drawn up with telling force. **1903** *Times, Lit. Supp.* 8 May 143/1 He is master of a singularly lucid, nervous, and telling style.

Hence **'tellingly** *adv.*, effectively.

1860 THACKERAY *Round. Papers, Notes Week's Holiday*, How tellingly the cool lights and warm shadows are made to contrast. **1875** WHITNEY *Life Lang.* xiv. 299 A curious fact, and one tellingly illustrative.

tellinite ('tɛlɪnaɪt). *Palæont.* [ad. mod.L. *tellīnītēs*, f. *tellīna*: see TELLEN and -ITE[1].] A fossil shell of, or resembling, the genus *Tellina*; a fossil tellen.

1799 R. KIRWAN *Geol. Essays* 252 A number of shells, mostly tellinites, filled with striated shining hornblende. **1802-3** tr. *Pallas's Trav.* (1812) I. 515 Hard layers.. interspersed throughout with pectinites, tellinites, and oolites.

tellograph ('tɛləʊgrɑːf, -æ-). [Short for **telelogograph*, f. Gr. τῆλε (TELE-) + λόγος word + -GRAPH.] A form of 'telegraph' or signalling apparatus invented by R. L. Edgeworth, consisting of a number of posts, each carrying a pointer in the form of an isosceles triangle which could be turned into various positions so as to express different numbers, the combinations of which denoted letters or words according to a pre-arranged code.

1795 EDGEWORTH in *Trans. R. Irish Acad.* (1797) VI. 126 I shall, with a slight alteration, adopt it [the name telegraph] for the apparatus which I am going to describe. *Telegraph* is a proper name for a machine which describes at a distance. *Telelograph*, or contractedly *Tellograph*, is a proper name for a machine that describes *words* at a distance. **1796** *Let.* 17

Nov. in *13th Rep. Hist. MSS. Comm.* App. VIII. 288 Your plan for establishing a communication of intelligence between Cork and Dublin and between Dublin and Belfast ..by means of a tellograph of your invention.

Hence **tello'graphic** *a.*

1797 EDGEWORTH in *Trans. R. Irish Acad.* VI. 138 The means of Tellographic communication which I have invented.

tellor, obs. form of TELLER.

tell-tale ('tɛlteɪl), *sb.* (*a.*)

1. a. One who tells tales (TALE *sb.* 3 c); one who idly or maliciously discloses private or secret matters; a tale-bearer, a tattler. So, in nursery phrase, ***tell-tale-tit***.

a **1548** HALL *Chron., Hen. IV* 2 b, He..was very glad (as tell tales and scicophantes bee..) to declare to the kyng what he had heard. **1597** MIDDLETON *Wisd. Solomon* xvii. 18 Babbling Echo, tell-tale of each sound. *a* **1639** W. WHATELEY *Prototypes* III. xxxix. (1640) 4 Most men will hate such as complaine of them, and call them tel-tales. **1731** SWIFT *Strephon & Chloe* Wks. 1755 IV. I. 158 A tell-tale out of school Is of all wits the greatest fool. **1841** HOOD *Tale of Trumpet* iii, Falsehood, or folly, or tell-tale-tit. **1877** BLACK *Green Past.* xxxi, Peace, you chatterer, you tell-tale. **1906** *Times* 10 Oct. 5/1 Booksellers..who had failed to receive the library orders..played tell-tale-tit to the Publishers' Association.

b. *transf.* A thing that reveals or discloses something not intended to be made known. Also *spec.*, a small hidden object placed so as to reveal a secret intrusion by its disturbance (see quots.).

1754 RICHARDSON *Grandison* II. 295, I was very earnest to know, since my eyes had been such tell-tales, if their brother had any suspicion of my regard for him. **1778** (*title*) The Fashionable Tell-Tale; containing a Great Variety of Curious and Interesting Anecdotes of Kings [etc.]. **1829** SCOTT *Anne of G.* xv, This gown may be a tell-tale..help me to pull off my upper garment. **1849** M. ARNOLD *Memory Picture* 42 Paint those eyes, so blue, so kind, Eager tell-tales of her mind. **1953** *Sun* (Baltimore) 30 Mar. (B ed.) 26/7 A broken 'tell-tale', one of the little devices policemen set in doorways and fire escapes to help them check on burglars. **1968** 'H. HOWARD' *Eye of Hurricane* iii. 33 After I'd searched..I was well satisfied that nobody had planted tell-tales anywhere..no microphones, no built-in radio transmitters. **1975** B. GARFIELD *Death Sentence* (1976) vii. 44 His hands began to sweat: the familiar telltale. **1979** K. FOLLETT *Triple* viii. 184 There were dozens of ways of planting telltales. A hair lightly stuck across the crack of the door..; a lump of sugar under a thick carpet would be silently crushed by a footstep.

c. A name of species of Sandpiper (*spec.* in *U.S.*), from their loud cry: see quots.

1824 STEPHENS in Shaw *Gen. Zool.* XII. 154 Tell-Tale Sandpiper (*Totanus melanoleucus*). It is a noisy and clamorous species..; it is much dreaded by sportsmen.. upon the appearance of any one it immediately sounds the alarm, and totally frustrates his intentions. [**1876** BLACK *Madcap V.* xxii, That abominable wretch the curlew, for he is a screaming tell-tale.] **1882** in OGILVIE. **1896** NEWTON *Dict. Birds, Tell-tale*, the name long used in North America for *Totanus melanoleucus* and *T. flavipes*..from 'their faithful vigilance in alarming the ducks'.

2. *Mech.* A device for mechanically indicating or recording some fact or condition not otherwise apparent; an indicator, a gauge.

spec. **a.** A pointer or the like attached to an organ to show the state of the wind-supply. **b.** *Naut.* An indicator near the wheel which shows the position of the tiller; an automatic or patent log; a tell-tale compass: see 3 c. **c.** A turnstile which registers the number of persons who pass through it. **d.** A gauge which indicates the pressure of wind, or of steam or gas in a cylinder or the like; also, an apparatus attached to the meter at a gasworks which registers any irregularity in the production of gas. **e.** A row of cords or straps suspended over a tramway or railway in such a position as to give warning of one's approach to a bridge or other overhead obstruction (*Cent. Dict.* 1891). **f.** An indicator of distance travelled or fare due in a cab, etc.; also called *tell-fare*; a TAXIMETER. **g.** = *tell-tale clock*; see 3 c. **h.** *Building.* A piece of glass or clear plastic, often graduated, fixed over a crack in a building to reveal whether there is further movement in the fabric. **i.** A light on the dashboard of a motor vehicle which shows when the direction indicator or main-beam lights are in use.

1832 *Examiner* 801/2 A contrivance called the tell-tale, which denotes any error in the working of the machinery. **1881** *Chicago Times* 4 June, An ingenious machine, called the 'tell-tale', has been introduced recently on the Erie railroad. It registers the speed of trains, when and where they stop, and how long. **1884** C. G. W. LOCK *Workshop Receipts* Ser. III. 68/2 Electrical apparatus is eminently adapted for alarms, tell-tales, and time signals.

a. 1801 BUSBY *Dict. Mus., Tell-Tale*, a moveable piece of ivory or lead, suspended in the front of a chamber organ on one side of the keys, by a string, one end of which being attached to the bellows within, rises as they sink, and apprises the performer, in what degree the wind is exhausted.

b. 1815 BURNEY *Falconer's Dict. Marine, Tell-tale* (*axiometre*, Fr.), a small piece of wood, traversing in a groove across the front of the poop-deck, which, by communicating with a small barrel on the axis of the steering-wheel, indicates the situation of the helm. **1858** H. BURRIDGE in *Merc. Marine Mag.* V. 53 The steering-compass at the wheel, and a tell-tale in the Master's berth.

c. 1824 *Examiner* 552/1 He paid the toll, and went through the piece of machinery called a tell-tale.

d. 1877 KNIGHT *Dict. Mech., Telltale*,..4. Gas-making. A device attached to a station-meter to point out any irregularity in the production of gas.

f. 1863 GASKELL *Patent Specif.* No. 2989 Improvements in Telltales or Indicators for Cabs, &c.

g. 1832 BABBAGE *Econ. Manuf.* viii. (ed. 3) 55 The instrument, aptly called a *tell-tale*, informs the owner whether the man had missed any, and what hours during the night.

h. 1938 *Times* 16 Feb. 14/1 Of the many tell-tales planted by Mr. Harvey only a few are known to have broken. **1972** *Besselsleigh & Dry Sandford* (Berks.) *Parish Mag.* Oct., The church council has agreed to the architect's suggestion that a few glass tell-tales should be fixed in some of these cracks. **1976** *Daily Tel.* 25 Sept. 21/4 They will hold back on the job while they put up 'telltales' at strategic points.

i. 1962 *Autocar* Spring 62/2 When any driving lamps are on, a small green warning light appears, and this is supplemented by a blue tell-tale for the main beams. **1966** *Guardian* 17 Oct. 6/3 The winker tell-tale is..self-cancelling. **1970** K. BALL *Fiat 600, 600D Autobook* xi. 138/1 The high beam indicator is on the dashboard behind a blue screen lens, the parking light indicator behind a green and the direction indicator tell-tale behind another green lens.

3. *attrib.* or as *adj.* **a.** That tells tales, that is a tell-tale. Now *rare* or *Obs.* in *lit.* sense.

1594 SHAKS. *Rich. III*, IV. iv. 149 Let not the Heauens heare these Tell-tale women Raile. **1678** DRYDEN & LEE *Œdipus* III. i, This tell-tale ghost Perhaps will clear 'em both. **1824** [see 1 c].

b. Applied to a thing: That reveals or betrays something meant to be kept secret.

a **1577** GASCOIGNE *Adv. F. I.* Wks. (Roxb.) I. 416 This teltale paper. **1579** G. HARVEY *Letter-bk.* (Camden) 75 This wofull letter with the telltale obligation. **1628** E. SPENCER *Brittain's Ida* II. iii, The thicke-lockt bowes shut out the tell-tale Sunne. **1743** R. BLAIR *Grave* 508 The tell-tale echo, and the babbling stream. **1821** SCOTT *Kenilw.* xxxvi, These tell-tale articles must not remain here. **1862** MRS. H. WOOD *Mrs. Hallib. Troub.* I. iii, He might have accomplished it better, but for his tell-tale face.

c. That gives notice or warning of something. ***tell-tale clock***, a clock with an attachment of some kind requiring attention at certain intervals, by which the vigilance of a watchman may be checked; ***tell-tale compass***: see quot. 1877; ***tell-tale pipe***, a pipe from a tank or cistern which overflows when the contents reach the level at which it is fixed.

1867 SMYTH *Sailor's Word-bk., Tell-tale shake*, the shake [i.e. shaking] of a rope from aloft to denote that it wants letting go. **1877** KNIGHT *Dict. Mech., Tell-tale compass* (*Nautical*). A compass is suspended overhead in the cabin. The face of the card is downward, so that it is visible from below, and enables the captain to detect any error or irregularity in steering. **1879** *Nature* 12 June 145/2 A small 'tell-tale' pipe from the cistern.., designed to show when the cistern had been filled. **1890** *Times* 21 Jan. 9/3 There should be tell-tale clocks to afford evidence of the punctual discharge of their duties.

'tell-truth. ? *Obs.* Also 6 -troath, 7–8 -troth.

1. One who or that which tells the truth; a veracious or candid person or writing.

1558 *Cranmer's Confut. Unwritten Verities* Pref. B iv b, Which sermon & al other tel truthes, openinge the abuses and tirannye of the bishop of Rome, are now put to silence. **1580** H. GIFFORD *Gilloflowers* (1875) 147 Is not Tom teltroath euerywhere, A busie cockcombe deem[d]e? **1600** J. LANE *Tom Tel-troth* 5 That, like a tell-troth, it may boldly blaze. **1618** *Barnevelt's Apology* C, Are you, with whome lying is familiar and ordinary, a telle-truth? **1692** WASHINGTON tr. *Milton's Def. Pop.* v. M.'s Wks. 1851 VII. 139 But hear what follows, my honest Tell-troth. **1700** ASTRY tr. *Saavedra-Faxardo* I. 345 Would these Tell-truths be guided by Prudence..a Prince would more value Truth. **1809–10** COLERIDGE *Friend* vi. (1865) 27 Tell-truths in the service of falsehood we find everywhere.

2. The telling of the truth; candour. *rare.*

a **1734** NORTH *Lives* (1826) II. 419 He was very seldom guilty of offence to any except in the way of tell-truth, which he could scarce ever forbear.

'tellur-, te'lluri-, *Chem.*, used as combining forms of TELLURIUM in certain names of compounds; as **tellu'rethyl**, ethyl telluride, $(C_2H_5)_2Te$, also called ***tellurhydric ether*** or ***hydrotelluric ether***; **tellur'hydric** ***acid***, a synonym of hydrogen telluride; † **te'lluri-salt**, a salt of telluric or tellurous acid.

1857 MILLER *Elem. Chem.* III. 215 *Tellurethyl. **1864** WATTS *Dict. Chem.* II. 550 Tellurethyl is a deep yellowish-red liquid heavier than water... It appears to be very poisonous. **1873** —— *Fownes' Chem.* (ed. 11) 215 *Tellurhydric acid is a gas, resembling sulphuretted and seleniętted hydrogen. **1877** *Ibid.* (ed. 12) I. 228 Hydrogen telluride, H_2Te, Tellurhydric acid, Hydrotelluric acid, or Telluretted hydrogen. **1860** MAYNE *Expos. Lex., Tellurisal* ..term applied to a Class..resulting from the combination of tellurides with tellururets..: a *tellurisalt.

tellural (tɛ'l(j)ʊərəl, 'tɛl(j)ʊərəl), *a.* [f. L. *tellūr-em* the earth + -AL[1].] Of or pertaining to the earth; terrestrial.

1847 in WEBSTER; and in later Dicts.

†**'tellurane.** *Chem. Obs.* [f. TELLUR-IUM + -ANE 2 a.] Davy's name for tellurium chloride.

1812 SIR H. DAVY *Chem. Philos.* 410 When tellurium is burnt in chlorine an easily fusible substance is formed, which rises in vapour at a strong heat, and crystallizes... It appears this compound, or tellurane, consists of 2 in weight of metal to 1.83 of chlorine.

tellurate ('tɛl(j)ʊəreɪt). *Chem.* [f. TELLUR- + -ATE[1] 1 c.] A salt of telluric acid.

1826 HENRY *Chem.* II. 112 It not only unites as a base with acids, but also itself possesses the character of an acid, and forms a class of salts, which may be called tellurates. **1868** WATTS *Dict. Chem.* V. 716 *Tellurates.*—Telluric acid forms with the alkali-metals, neutral, acid, and hyperacid salts, represented by the formulæ, M_2TeO_4, $MHTeO_4$, and $MHTeO_4.H_2TeO_4$, respectively.

telluret ('tɛl(j)ʊərɛt). *Chem.* Now *rare.* Also †**te'llururet.** [f. TELLURIUM: see -URET.] A compound of tellurium with hydrogen or a metal, as ***telluret of sodium***, $TeNa_2$: now usually TELLURIDE.

1842 PARNELL *Chem. Anal.* (1845) 259 Tellurets. **1854** J. SCOFFERN in *Orr's Circ. Sc., Chem.* 476 Metallic bismuth is liberated, and sulphuret and telluret of sodium formed. **1860** MAYNE *Expos. Lex.* s.v. *Tellururetum*, Berzelius reserves this name for a combination of tellurium with an electro-positive metal, in which the atomic relations are the same as in the bases: a tellururet.

telluretted ('tɛl(j)ʊərɛtɪd), *a. Chem.* Now *rare.* [f. as prec. + -ED.] Combined with tellurium, as in ***tellure(t)ted hydrogen***, a gaseous compound of hydrogen and tellurium, TeH_2, formerly also called *hydrotelluric* or *tellurhydric acid*, and now *hydrogen telluride*.

1819 CHILDREN *Chem. Anal.* 49 Telluretted Hydrogen Gas. **1826** HENRY *Chem.* II. 502 Telluretted hydrogen is absorbed by liquid potassa, but not by acetate of lead. **1869** ROSCOE *Elem. Chem.* (1871) 146 With hydrogen tellurium forms a colourless gas, telluretted hydrogen, which cannot be distinguished by its smell from sulphuretted hydrogen.

tellurian (tɛ'l(j)ʊərɪən), *a.* and *sb.* [f. L. *tellūr-em* the earth + -IAN.] **A.** *adj.* Of or pertaining to the earth; earthly, terrestrial.

1846 DE QUINCEY *Syst. Heavens* Wks. 1854 III. 172 They absolutely hear the tellurian lungs wheezing, panting, crying. **1862** *Parthenon* 26 July 405 The stratified cemetery of the 'tellurian' crust. **1887** A. LANG *Myth, Ritual, & Relig.* II. 120 There were..solar, lunar...[and] tellurian.. methods of accounting for a myth.

B. *sb.* An inhabitant of the earth.

1847 DE QUINCEY *Joan of Arc* Wks. 1854 III. 237 If any distant worlds..are so far ahead of us Tellurians in optical resources. *c* **1851** —— *Ess. Finlay's Greece* Posth. Wks. 1893 II. 75 Our own case, the case of poor mediocre Tellurians.

telluric (tɛ'l(j)ʊərɪk), *a.*[1] *Chem.* and *Min.* [f. TELLURIUM + -IC.] Derived from or containing tellurium. Applied to compounds in which tellurium is present in a smaller proportion than in tellurous compounds, as ***telluric acid***, H_2TeO_4; ***telluric oxide*** = ***tellurium trioxide***, TeO_3, etc. Also in ***telluric gold***, ***silver***, ***bismuth***, the tellurides of these metals occurring as native alloys: see TELLURIDE. ***telluric ochre*** = TELLURITE 1.

1800 HENRY *Epit. Chem.* (1808) 253 Carbonated and pure alkalies precipitate the telluric oxide. **1842** BRANDE *Dict. Sc.*, etc. s.v. *Tellurium*, It forms a protoxide and a peroxide, often called tellurous and telluric acids. **1864** WEBSTER s.v., *Telluric silver*, a mineral consisting of tellurium and silver in combination. **1868** DANA *Min.* (ed. 5) 30 Telluric Bismuth. *Ibid.* 50 Telluric Silver. **1873** WATTS *Fownes' Chem.* (ed. 11) 214 Crystallised telluric acid is freely, although slowly, soluble in water. **1882** *Rep. to Ho. Repr. Prec. Met. U.S.* 607, I have only found, as yet, telluric gold in two mines in Nevada County.

telluric (tɛ'l(j)ʊərɪk), *a.*[2] [f. L. *tellūr-em* the earth + -IC.] Of or belonging to the earth, terrestrial; pertaining to the earth as a planet; also, of or arising from the earth or soil.

1836 I. TAYLOR *Phys. The. Another Life* ii. 24 The equal periods that are marked for us by the celestial and telluric revolutions. **1842** *United Service Mag.* I. 289 The great problem of telluric magnetism. **1849** SIR J. STEPHEN *Eccl. Biog.* (1850) II. 433 If my ideas had still obeyed those laws of association to which, in my telluric state, they had been subject. **1861** T. J. GRAHAM *Pract. Med.* 666 Epidemic influences..dependent in a great measure upon obscure atmospheric or telluric conditions. **1883** *St. James' Gaz.* 21 Dec. 5/1 The spectrum..exhibits great breadth in the telluric or atmospheric lines,..due to aqueous vapours..in ..the atmosphere. **1884** *19th Cent.* Feb. 320 A 'telluric poison' is generated in it [the Campagna] by the energy of the soil.

telluride ('tɛl(j)ʊəraɪd). *Chem.* [f. TELLUR-IUM + -IDE.] A combination of tellurium with an electro-positive element (e.g. hydrogen or a metal), or with a radical; as ***telluride of hydrogen***, ***hydrogen telluride***, the same as *telluretted hydrogen*, H_2Te; ***organic tellurides***, those of organic radicals, as ***ethyl telluride***.

telluride of bismuth, telluric bismuth, tetradymite, or bornite, perh. an isomorphous mixture of tellurium and bismuth, sometimes Bi_2Te_3. ***telluride of gold and silver*** = SYLVANITE. ***telluride of lead***, black telluride, PbTe, found native as NAGYAGITE. ***telluride of silver***, bitelluret of silver, Ag_2Te, found native as HESSITE and PETZITE.

1849 D. CAMPBELL *Inorg. Chem.* 307 Telluride of hydrogen..is colourless, and in odour resembles sulphide of hydrogen gas... It forms with metals tellurides, analogous to the sulphides. **1868** WATTS *Dict. Chem.* V. 707 The tellurides belong to the class of metallic alloys: those of bismuth, gold, lead, and silver are found native. *Ibid.* 708 Organic tellurides: Tellurides of amyl, ethyl, methyl. **1877** —— *Fownes' Chem.* (ed. 12) II. 141 *Ethyl Telluride*, Telluric Ethide, or Tellurethyl, $Te(C_2H_5)_2$..is a heavy, oily, yellowish-red liquid..having a most intolerable odour. **1897** *Daily News* 30 Apr. 2/7 The vein contains telluride of gold, good quality.

attrib. **1877** RAYMOND *Statist. Mines & Mining* 305 The prominent mines of the telluride belt. *Ibid.* 311 Small seams of the usual telluride ore.

tellurion (tɛ'l(j)ʊərɪən). Also tellurium. [f. L. *tellūs*, *tellūr-em* the earth.] An apparatus illustrating the effect of the earth's diurnal rotation and annual revolution and obliquity of axis in causing the alternations of day and night and the succession of the seasons; a simple kind of orrery.

1831 *Mechanics' Mag.* XIV. 370/2 When the tellurion [*pr.* -ian] is to be used, the sign Cancer must be set toward the north. **1842** Francis *Dict. Arts, Tellurion*, an instrument for showing the effect of the earth's motions and the obliquity of her axis. **1891** *Cath. News* 24 Jan. 4/4 Irreverent persons echoed the inquisitive auditor's query as to the uses of a tellurion. **1905** *Nature* 14 Sept. 493/2 The ordinary wire model or 'tellurium'.

tellurious, *a.*: see TELLUROUS.

tellurism ('tɛl(j)ʊərɪz(ə)m). [f. L. *tellūr-em* the earth + -ISM: in sense 1 = Ger. *tellurismus*, in sense 2 = F. *tellurisme*.]

1. A magnetic influence or principle supposed by some to pervade all nature and to produce the phenomena of animal magnetism; also the theory of animal magnetism based on this, propounded in 1822 by Kieser in Germany.

1843 Hartshorn tr. *Deleuze's Anim. Magn.* x. 209 There are in magnetism two different actions. One which depends upon a vital principle spread throughout nature, and circulating in all bodies;.. the first sort of magnetism, which he calls tellurism or siderism. **1849** S. R. Maitland *Illustr. Mesmerism* 63 They [the Ancients] did not write systems of Animal Magnetism, or Tellurism, or Geisterkunde.

2. Influence of the soil in producing disease.

1890 in Billings *Nat. Med. Dict.* **1899** in *Syd. Soc. Lex.*

tellurite ('tɛl(j)ʊəraɪt) [f. TELLUR-IUM + -ITE[1] 2 b, 4 b.]

1. *Min.* Native oxide of tellurium, found in minute whitish or yellow crystals; telluric ochre.

1799 *Monthly Rev.* XXX. 349 Among the metals, are overlooked the Tellurite, the Chromite, and Titanite. **1849** Nicol *Min.* 429. **1868** Dana *Min.* (ed. 5) 188.

2. *Chem.* A salt of tellurous acid.

1847 in Webster. **1868** Watts *Dict. Chem.* V. 714 *Tellurites.* Tellurous acid forms, with the alkali-metals, neutral and acid salts analogous to the sulphites and selenites. *Ibid.*, Tellurites are mostly fusible. **1869** Roscoe *Elem. Chem.* (1871) 146 When tellurium or a tellurite is fused with nitre, potassium tellurate is formed.

tellurium (tɛ'l(j)ʊərɪəm). *Chem.* [mod.L., f. L. *tellūs, tellūr-em* the earth + *-ium*, suffix of names of metals. So called by Klaproth, 1798, prob. in contrast to *uranium* (Gr. οὐρανός heaven), a metal which he had discovered in 1789.

Cf. Klaproth in Crell's *Chem. Annalen* 1798, pt. 1. 100, 'welchem ich hiermit den von der alten Muttererde entlehnten Namen Tellurium beylege'.]

One of the rarer elements, a tin-white shining brittle substance, formerly from its outward characters classed among the metals, but in its chemical properties and relations belonging to the same series as sulphur and selenium. It occurs native in rhombohedral crystals, isomorphous with those of antimony, arsenic, and bismuth. Symbol Te; atomic weight 128.

1800 tr. *Lagrange's Chem.* I. 447 With sulphur this metal forms a grey sulphuret of tellurium, of a radiated structure. **1801** Hatchett in *Phil. Trans.* XCII. 63 Other metals lately discovered, such as uranium, titanium, and tellurium. **1816** P. Cleaveland *Min.* 565 Native Tellurium is never perfectly pure. It always contains a greater or less quantity of gold, and sometimes embraces iron, silver, lead, copper, and sulphur. **1862** Miller *Elem. Chem.* (ed. 2) III. 52. **1866** Roscoe *Elem. Chem.* xiv. 124 Oxygen, sulphur, selenium, and tellurium form a natural group of elements, each uniting with two atoms of hydrogen to form a series of bodies possessing analogous properties. **1881** Lubbock in *Nature* 1 Sept. 409/2 In Aldebaran..we may infer the presence of hydrogen, sodium, magnesium, iron, calcium, tellurium, antimony, bismuth, and mercury; some of which are not yet known to occur in the sun.

b. With qualifying words, applied to minerals or ores containing a preponderance of tellurium, as ***bismuthic tellurium***; ***black tellurium***, ***foliated tellurium***, synonyms of NAGYAGITE; ***graphic tellurium***, ***yellow*** or ***white tellurium***, synonyms of SYLVANITE. (Dana *Min.* 1864.)

1849 D. Campbell *Inorg. Chem.* 304 The [ore] named bismuthic tellurium is that from which it is most easily obtained. **1864** [see c.].

c. *attrib.* and *Comb.* (*a*) *attrib.* = 'of tellurium', in names of chemical compounds, as ***tellurium bromide***, ***chloride***, ***dioxide***, ***salts***, ***nitrate***, ***sulphate***, etc.; in other uses, as ***tellurium acids***, ***alloys***, ***minerals***, ***ores***; (*b*) in obj. relation, as ***tellurium-bearing*** adj.; (*c*) **tellurium glance** *Min.*, nagyagite, or black telluride of lead.

1834 Prout *Chem.*, etc. I. ix. §3 (1855) 113 Sulphur acids, selenium acids, and tellurium acids. **1853** Ure *Dict. Arts* II. 200 They are celebrated for their tellurium ore. **1864** Dana (Webster), *Tellurium glance*, a blackish or lead-gray sectile mineral, of a splendent luster, consisting chiefly of tellurium, sulphur, lead, and gold;—called also *black tellurium.* **1866** Roscoe *Elem. Chem.* xiv. 124 When heated in the air it [tellurium] burns with a bluish-green flame, forming white fumes of tellurium dioxide. **1874** Raymond *Statist. Mines & Mining* 298 The belt of tellurium-bearing veins is found to extend from the Gray Eagle lode.., in a southerly direction. **1877** *Ibid.* 304 In all, the characteristic tellurium minerals have been found. **1877** Watts *Fownes' Chem.* (ed. 12) I. 227 Tellurium salts—sulphate, nitrate, oxalate, chloride. *Ibid.* 228 Tellurium sulphides..chlorides.

tellurometer (tɛl(j)ʊə'rɒmɪtə(r)). [f. L. *tellūr-em* the earth + -O + -METER.] An instrument that accurately measures distances on land by transmitting a microwave signal and timing the arrival of a return signal that it triggers at the distant point.

1957 T. L. Wadley in *Empire Survey Rev.* July 100 (*heading*) The tellurometer system of distance measurement. **1961** *Aeroplane* C. 63/2 Five of the parties were to do levelling, and the other two distance measuring with tellurometers. **1975** J. B. Harley *O.S. Maps* i. 7 The 'Tellurometer'..has been used to measure distances of 135 km between Great Britain and Ireland as part of the process of checking the triangulation.

tellurous ('tɛl(j)ʊərəs), *a.* *Chem.* Also 9 †**tellurious.** [f. TELLUR-IUM + -OUS; substituted for the more regularly-formed *tellurious.*] Characterized by or of the nature of tellurium; said of compounds containing a greater proportion of tellurium than those called *telluric*; as ***tellurous acid***, H_2TeO_3; also formerly applied to ***tellurous oxide*** (= tellurium dioxide), TeO_2.

1842 [see TELLURIC *a.*[1]]. **1849** D. Campbell *Inorg. Chem.* 307 It deposits anhydrous tellurous acid in octohedral crystals. Tellurous acid hydrated precipitates in white flocks, of a bitter metallic taste. **1854** J. Scoffern in *Orr's Circ. Sc., Chem.* 475 Two oxides of tellurium are known, tellurious acid Te O_2, and telluric acid Te O_3. **1869** Roscoe *Elem. Chem.* (1871) 146 With water the dioxide forms tellurous acid.

tellururet: see TELLURET.

‖**Tellus** ('tɛləs). [L. *tellūs.*] In Roman mythology, the goddess of the earth; hence, the earth personified; the planet Earth, the terrestrial globe.

c **1430** Lydg. *Min. Poems* (Percy Soc.) 24 Tellus and Ymo be dullid of theire chere. **1602** Shaks. *Ham.* III. ii. 166 Neptunes salt Wash and Tellus Orbed ground. **1608** —— *Per.* IV. i. 14, I will rob Tellus of her weede. **1681** Cotton *Wond. Peake* (ed. 4) 28 The Spring swell'd by some smoaking Shower, That teeming Clouds on Tellus surface poure. **1738** *Gentl. Mag.* VIII. 544/2 Reason, like Sol to Tellus kind, Ripens the products of the mind. **1818** Keats *Endymion* III. 71 Tellus feels her forehead's cumbrous load.

telly ('tɛlɪ). *colloq.* [Shortening of TELEVISION. Cf. TELE.] **1.** = TELEVISION 1. Phr. ***on (the) telly.***

[**1940** *Chambers's Techn. Dict.* 837/2 *Tellies*, colloquialism for cinematograph films with sound; also for television.] **1942** Berrey & Van den Bark *Amer. Thes. Slang* §618/3 Lookies, tellies, telly. **1957** *Observer* 3 Nov. 4/5 For all practical purposes, if it hasn't been on telly, it doesn't exist. **1957** *Economist* 7 Dec. 842/1 An evening when Sheffield Wednesday were playing Juventus of Milan at football on the telly. **1958** M. Spark *The Go-Away Bird* 152 He said, 'What do you do in the evenings, Lorna? Do you watch Telly?' I did take this as an insult, because we call it TV, and his remark made me out to be uneducated. **1967** E. Williams *Beyond Belief* III. xix. 204 Tonight, the eve of Christmas Eve,..they are watching telly, nice thriller. **1968** J. Arnold *Shell Bk. Country Crafts* 70 A growing tendency in domestic life of subordinating activities to the 'telly'. **1970** G. F. Newman *Sir, You Bastard* iv. 117 On the news, on the telly this evening. **1977** *New Yorker* 26 Sept. 37/1 His parents lived an isolated life, but now had the telly.

2. = TELEVISION 2.

1955 M. Allingham *Beckoning Lady* i. 5 He..walked back to the village and the telly. **1957** F. King *Man on Rock* i. 7, I can't even afford to pay the never-never on a wireless, let alone a telly. **1969** A. Glyn *Dragon Variation* vi. 176 An occasional bluish light behind chintz curtains betrayed the night-owls, those who were still glued to the telly, watching the news headlines, the weather forecast. **1978** K. Amis *Jake's Thing* iii. 30 Let's be absolute devils and have the heating on and huddle round the telly.

3. A television performance; a booking or session of filming for this. *Theatr.* and *Broadcasting.*

1963 E. Humphreys *Gift* 8 Every time I did a telly it was a lovely day, while I sweated my guts out under the artificial light. **1979** S. Brett *Comedian Dies* ii. 23 I've got you a telly. .. It's an *Alexander Hervey Show.*

4. *attrib.* and *Comb.*, as ***telly ad***, ***don***, ***mast***, ***-viewer***, etc.; **telly man**, a man who works professionally for a television service.

1958 *Times Lit. Suppl.* 15 Aug. p. xii/3 Turning their backs upon the 'telly' screen, they will strain their eyes in the semi-darkness of the living-room. **1960** C. MacInnes *Mr Love & Justice* 85 His part-time trade of mending radios and telly sets. **1963** *Spectator* 22 Feb. 230/3 The Third Programme..is becoming more and more a private club or experimental research establishment unwittingly financed by the telly-viewers. **1963** *Punch* 2 Oct. 475/1 Small vociferous pockets trying to attract tellymen. **1966** J. Betjeman *High & Low* 4 Slate cottages with sycamore between, Small fields and telly-masts and wires and poles. **1969** Fabian & Byrne *Groupie* (1970) i. 9, I even believe telly ads and things like that. **1971** *Author* LXXXII. 111 Many a paper fills its review columns with inoffensive, but basically uninteresting, books butchered to make a well-known telly don's holiday in the dead summer months. **1977** *Irish Democrat* Mar. 5/2 Surrounded by a regiment of security men, aides, advisers, journalists, tellymen and Unionists. **1977** *Irish Times* 8 June 11/5 But there might have been long telly-watching sessions behind locked doors.

telmatology (tɛlmə'tɒlədʒɪ). [f. Gr. τέλμα, τελματ- a bog + -OLOGY.] That department of physiography which deals with peat-bogs.

1903 Olsson-Seffer in *Amer. Nat.* XXXVII. 784 A name of a more international character, telmatology,..has been used by some authors (Klinge, J., for example, nearly twenty years ago), and seems acceptable.

telo-[1] ('tɛləʊ, 'tiːləʊ), combining form repr. Gr. τέλος, τέλε-ος end, occurring in a few scientific (biological, etc.) terms: see also TELEO-[2]. **'teloblast** [Gr. βλαστός germ], each of a number of proliferating cells at one end of the embryo in segmented animals, as insects and annelids; **telo'dendrion, -'dendron** (pl. **-dendria** is used for both forms) *Anat.* [Gr. δενδρίον, dim. of δένδρον tree], one of the terminal branches into which the axon of a nerve cell divides; **telolecithal** (-'lɛsɪθəl) *a.* [Gr. λέκιθος yolk], applied to an ovum having food-yolk collected at or near one end (opp. to *alecithal* and *centrolecithal*); **'telomere** *Cytology* [-MERE], the compound structure found at the end of a chromosome in eukaryotes, having only one spindle pole; **telo'mitic** *a. Cytology* [Gr. μίτ-ος thread] = TELOCENTRIC *a.*; **telo'peptide** *Biochem.*, a peptide which is at or near the end of a polypeptide molecule; **'telopore** [PORE *sb.*[1]], an opening at one end of an embryo, formed by invagination of the *teloblasts*; **telo'stomiate** *a.* [f. Gr. στόμι-ον dim. of στόμα mouth], having the mouth at one end of the main axis of the body; **telosy'napsis** *Cytology*, a supposed end-to-end pairing of chromosomes during the zygotene stage of meiosis; = *telosyndesis* below; hence **telosy'naptic** *a.*, **telosy'naptically** *adv.*; †**telosyn'desis** *Cytology* = *telosynapsis* above.

1890 Patten in *Q. Jrnl. Microsc. Sc.* Aug. 369 Three longitudinal sections, showing successive stages in the formation of a telopore by the invagination of *teloblasts. **1899** L. F. Barker *Nervous System* viii. 82 The ultimate terminals (*telodendrions) of the axones have been carefully and exactly studied. **1907** I. Hardesty in Morris & McMurrich *Morris's Treat. Human Anat.* (ed. 4) 751 The axone bearing the impulse on approaching its termination loses its sheath and breaks up into its numerous terminal twigs, the final of which are called telodendria. **1949** *New Gould Med. Dict.* 1030/2 *Telodendrion.* See *telodendron.* **1966** C. R. & T. S. Leeson *Histology* x. 178/2 In some cases, the telodendria are so numerous as to surround the neuron on which they terminate in a basket-like arrangement. **1880** Balfour *Comp. Embryol.* I. iii. 90 The ova in which the yolk is especially concentrated at one pole I should propose to call *telolecithal. **1888** E. R. Lankester in *Nature* 29 Mar. 507/1 The classification of animal eggs proposed by Balfour is adopted, viz. alecithal, telolecithal, and centrolecithal. **1940** H. J. Muller in *Jrnl. Genetics* XL. 2 The reconstructed chromosome cannot continue to be transported..unless it happens to be monocentric and—in *Drosophila* at least—ditelic, one centromere and two *telomeres being necessary and permanent organelles. **1960** L. Picken *Organization of Cells* vii. 261 Within the nucleus the chromosomes present their telomeres—'centromeres' connected to the chromosomes by terminal filaments—to the aspect of the nuclear membrane nearest to the spindle. **1983** *Nature* 13 Jan. 112/1 Telomeres are very stable as free ends, whereas ends of [DNA] molecules broken *in vivo* tend to stick together irreversibly. **1917** E. E. Carothers in *Jrnl. Morphology* XXVIII. 449 The unusual conditions of the chromosomes in this group have made advisable the introduction of..new terms... *Telomitic—a term used to indicate terminal fiber attachment. **1934** L. W. Sharp *Introd. Cytol.* (ed. 3) ix. 116 Supposedly telomitic chromosomes have been shown in some instances to have their attachment region slightly back from the end. **1964** F. O. Schmitt et al. in *Proc. Nat. Acad. Sci.* LI. 494 The term 'end-chains' with its terminal connotation has been replaced by the term '*telopeptides'. **1971** *Nature* 22 Jan. 242/1 Every third residue in the chain is glycine, except in short 'non-collagenous' telopeptides at the N-terminal ends of the chains. **1975** *Ibid.* 10 July 125/1 Rabbit anti-collagen serum is primarily directed to terminal (telopeptide) antigenic sites, and not to helical or central sites. **1890** Patten in *Q. Jrnl. Microsc. Sc.* Aug. 369 A forward continuation of the anterior wall of the terminal pore or *telopore. **1877** E. R. Lankester in *Q. Jrnl. Microsc. Sc.* Oct. 422 Radial and bilateral symmetry and *telostomiate and prostomiate conditions. *Ibid.* 423 A specialisation of the ciliated ectoderm at a time when the organism was telostomiate. **1909** *Telosynapsis [see *parasynapsis* s.v. PARA-[1] 1]. **1920** W. E. Agar *Cytology* ii. 43 Parasyndesis and Telosyndesis. [*Note*] Called parasynapsis and telosynapsis by cytologists, who employ the term synapsis in the sense in which syndesis is here used. **1945** M. J. D. White *Animal Cytol. & Evolution* v. 79 The old controversy between adherants of the theory of telosynapsis and those who believed in the alternative viewpoint..is only of historical interest, since 'parasynapsis'..is now known to be universal. **1912** *Jrnl. Exper. Zool.* XIII. 394 Attention may be called to the increasing tendency..to reject, or at least restrict, the theory of parasynapsis.., in favor of a *telosynaptic conception. **1929** *Jrnl. Genetics* XXI. 47 Digby's interpretation, so much quoted in support of the telosynaptic view.., is due to a misunderstanding of the essential features of meiosis. **1910** *Telosynaptically [see *parasynaptically* adv. s.v. PARA-[1]]. **1926** *Genetics* XI. 274 The third element is joined telosynaptically to the other two chromosomes. **1920** L. Doncaster *Introd. Study Cytol.* v. 68 The end-to-end union [of chromosomes] (formerly supposed to be frequent or universal) is *telosyndesis (or telosynapsis).

telo-[2], repr. Gr. τηλο-, combining form of τῆλε or τηλοῦ far off, occurring exceptionally instead of τηλε- (TELE-), as in τηλοπέτης far-flying. Rarely used in Eng. compounds, as in TELODYNAMIC, *telometer* (see TELEMETER *sb.*), TELOTYPE.

telocentric (tɛləʊ-, tiːləʊ'sɛntrɪk), *a.* (and *sb.*) *Cytology.* [f. TELO-[1] + -CENTRIC.] Of a chromosome: having the centromere at the end. Hence as *sb.* Cf. ACROCENTRIC, METACENTRIC *adjs.*

1939 C. D. DARLINGTON in *Jrnl. Genetics* XXXVII. 349 This does not mean that terminal centromeres or telocentric chromosomes work satisfactorily or survive permanently. *Ibid.* 352 The misdivided chromosomes..will give the functional telocentrics that I have already described at second anaphase. **1949** DARLINGTON & MATHER *Elem. Genetics* v. 103 Misdivision of the centromere and Formation of two telocentric chromosomes. **1964** *Hereditas* LII. 209 Most cytologists agree that the centromere in acrocentric chromosomes is less terminal than in telocentric chromosomes. **1971** [see METACENTRIC *sb.*]. **1976** *Nature* 12 Aug. 580/1 The X chromosome is telocentric (X^t) in F344 and AC1 strains.

telodynamic (ˌtɛləʊdɪ'næmɪk, -daɪ-), *a.* Also (more regularly) **teledynamic.** [f. TELO-[2] + DYNAMIC.] Term applied to a cable used for transmitting mechanical power to a distance.

1870 J. ANDERSON in *Eng. Mech.* 14 Jan. 427/1 A given pressure on the piston.., like the telodynamic cord, will transmit mechanical work in proportion. **1877** KNIGHT *Dict. Mech.*, *Telodynamic Cable*, a means for transmitting power, ..in which high speed is employed to give the momentive effect of great mass. **1889** E. MATHESON *Aid Bk. Engineer. Enterpr.* II. 466 The teledynamic cables—as the endless, transmitting ropes are called—are of comparatively recent introduction.

telogen ('tɛləʊdʒən). [f. TELO-[1] + -GEN.]

1. *Biol.* The stage in the life of a hair or hair follicle following cessation of growth of the hair.

1926 F. W. DRY in *Jrnl. Genetics* XVI. 297 For the present purpose it is convenient to divide the developmental history into the following three phases: (1) The Anagen phase... (2) The Catagen phase... (3) The Telogen phase, the hair having become a dub-hair and not growing further. **1955** *Proc. Soc. Exper. Biol. & Med.* LXXXVIII. 450/1 Telogen is the resting stage of a follicle and it is reached approximately 19 days after plucking. **1980** *Practitioner* Nov. 1161/1 Hair growth..is..phasic, there being a phase of growth (anagen) lasting approximately three to five years in normal scalp hair and a resting phase (telogen) lasting for around three months.

2. *Chem.* A simple compound that provides chain-terminating radicals in polymerization and limits the degree of polymerization.

1948 [see TELOMER]. **1974** C. M. STARKS *Free Radical Polymerization* i. 2 Chain transfer agents (telogens) are often added to polymerization recipes as molecular weight regulators. **1980** [see TAXOGEN].

telomer ('tɛləʊmə(r)). *Chem.* [f. TELO-[1] + -MER.] A low-molecular-weight polymer consisting of a chain of a limited number of units (taxogens) terminated at each end by a radical from a different compound (the telogen).

1948 HANFORD & JOYCE *U.S. Patent 2,440,800* 1 It has been found necessary to coin new terms to describe the reaction and the participants therein... 'Telomerization' is defined as the process of reacting..a molecule YZ which is called a 'telogen' with more than one unit of a polymerizable compound..called a 'taxogen' to form products called 'telomers' having the formula $Y(A)_nZ$. **1951** *Jrnl. Amer. Chem. Soc.* LXXIII. 5197/1 When it [*sc.* the polymerization] is conducted in the presence of any one of a wide variety of organic compounds, telomers containing 1–25 tetrafluoroethylene units combined with one molecule of the chain transfer compound are obtained. **1966** J. A. BRYDSON *Plastics Materials* xv. 295 With an ethylene-carbon tetrachloride ratio of about 4:1 about 60% of the telomers have 7, 9 or 11 carbon atoms in the molecule. **1980** [see TAXOGEN].

So ˌ**telomeri'zation**, polymerization that is limited by the action of a telogen; also '**telomerized** *ppl. a.*, '**telomerizing** *vbl. sb.*

1948 Telomerization [see TELOMER]. **1954** *Jrnl. Res. Nat. Bureau Standards* (U.S.) LIII. 122 $YZ + nCX_2 = CX_2 \rightarrow Y(CX_2CX_2)_nZ$... Such a reaction is called telomerization. **1967** *Gloss. Terms Plastics Industry* (*B.S.I.*) I. 7 *Telomerized polymer*, a polymer chain-stopped by a telomer. **1968** G. TRAPPE in P. D. Ritchie *Vinyl & Allied Polymers* xii. 265 Low molecular weight oils, greases, and waxes of polychlorotrifluoroethylene are made by polymerisation in the presence of telomerising agents such as carbon tetrachloride. **1974** H. I. BOLKER *Natural & Synthetic Polymers* iii. 136 About 0·5–1·0 mole % of acetic acid is added as a telomerization agent.., which limits the formation of chains of excessively high molecular weight.

telometer: see TELEMETER *sb.*

teloogoo: see TELUGU.

telophase ('tɛləʊfeɪz). *Cytology.* [a. G. *telophase* (M. Heidenhain 1894, in *Arch. f. mikr. Anat.* XLIII. 524): see TELO-[1] and PHASE.] The final phase of mitosis and meiosis, following anaphase and preceding interphase, at which the chromatids or chromosomes are at opposite poles of the cell; also, a cell at this stage.

1895 *Jrnl. R. Microsc. Soc.* 35 The fourth chapter discusses the final movements of mitosis (telophases, telokinesis). **1900** G. C. BOURNE *Comp. Anat.* iii. 115 The last stages of mitosis are known as the Telophase. *Ibid.* 116 The centrosomata..divide very precociously during the telophase. **1934** *Nature* 26 May 800/1 The anaphase and telophase chromosomes thus contain two spiral chromonemata... In late telophase the two threads are found to approximate very closely. **1971** J. Z. YOUNG *Introd. Study Man* xiv. 179 At the end of mitosis (telophase) these enzymes associate with the chromosomes. **1973** *Nature* 6 Apr. 403/2 The DNA determinations were carried out in metaphases and telophases of the original stained lung cultures.

Hence **telo'phasic** *a.*, of or pertaining to telophase.

1907 *Rep. Brit. Assoc. Adv. Sci. 1906* 757 It [*sc.* the nucleolus] lies in the centre of the telophasic figure. **1929** *Bot. Gaz.* LXXXVIII. 360 The foregoing investigators were correct in interpreting some (although not all) of the telophasic aspects they observed as chromosome doubleness. **1976** *Biol. Abstr.* LXII. 693/1 The telophasic plaque in the root meristem of *Triticum vulgare.*

teloptic: see TELE-.

‖**telos** ('tɛlɒs). [a. Gr. τέλος end.] End, purpose, ultimate object or aim.

1904 *Daily Chron.* 5 Aug. 3/2 The triple aim which had formed the telos of every development. **1905** F. HARRISON *Herbert Spencer Lecture*, The Telos of Philosophy is a constructive reorganization of all human knowledge in a synthesis, or correlation of parts. The Telos of human life is the practical and continuous amelioration of the material, social, and moral conditions of the Human Organism—the unity of the Brotherhood of Man on this planet.

telosmic: see TELE-.

telotaxis (tɛləʊ'tæksɪs). *Biol.* [mod.L., coined in Ger. (A. Kühn *Die Orientierung der Tiere im Raum* (1919) 60): see TELO-[1] and TAXIS 6.] Directional movement made by an animal in order to keep a particular source of stimulation acting on its sense receptor(s).

1934 *Jrnl. Exper. Biol.* XI. 129 Those movements in which the animal is truly orientated Kühn calls topotaxis, and these again fall into two main groups: tropotaxis and telotaxis. **1976** D. J. HORN *Biol. Insects* vi. 229 An example of telotaxis that has fascinated researchers is light-compass orientation.

telotroch ('tɛləʊtrɒk). *Zool.* [f. Gr. τέλος end (TELO-[1]) + τροχός wheel. Cf. mod.L. *Telotrocha* neut. pl., as name for larvæ having this structure.] A zone of cilia circling either, or each, end of the preoral (and perianal) segments of a free-swimming polychætous annelid larva. **b.** A larva of this kind. Hence **te'lotrochal, te'lotrochous** *adjs.*, possessing a telotroch or telotrochs; of the nature of a telotroch.

1877 E. R. LANKESTER in *Q. Jrnl. Microsc. Sc.* Oct. 426 The telotroch appears to be a metameric repetition of the architroch, or of its branchiotrochal moiety. **1877** HUXLEY *Anat. Inv. Anim.* 186 This larva exactly resembles those forms of polychætous Annelidan larvæ which are called Telotrocha. *Ibid.* 192 The free Rotifers present marked resemblances to the telotrochous larvæ of Annelids. **1878** BELL *Gegenbaur's Comp. Anat.* 137 By these the larvæ of the Chætopoda are divided into mesotrochal, telotrochal, and polytrochal forms.

telotype ('tɛləʊtaɪp). [f. TELO-[2] + TYPE.] An electric telegraph that automatically prints the messages as received; also, a telegram so printed.

1850 F. GALTON *Telotype* 3 In the Telotype (as our instrument may be termed), by merely touching a key on which any letter is marked that letter is to be printed, almost instantaneously, at the opposite end of the line. **1858** SIMMONDS *Dict. Trade Products*, *Telotype*, the name given to a printing electric telegraph. **1877** KNIGHT *Dict. Mech.*, *Telotype*, a printed telegram.

telpher ('tɛlfə(r)), *a.* and *sb.* [Syncopated from *telepher* or *telephore* (see quot. 1884 in TELPHERAGE), f. Gr. τῆλε, TELE- + -φορος bearing.] **a.** *adj.* or *attrib. sb.* Of or relating to a system of telpherage; ***telpher line, railway***, a light overhead line on which the haulage is worked by electric power; so ***telpher train.*** **b.** *sb.* Any travelling unit on a telpher line; also, the plant and rolling stock of a system of telpherage. **c.** *Comb.*, as ***telpherman.***

1884 (May 14) F. JENKIN in *Jrnl. Soc. Arts* XXXII. 648/2 Telpher lines are adapted for the conveyance of minerals and other goods at a slow pace, and at a cheap rate. *Ibid.* 655/2 We are enabled to start or stop any number of telpher trains without disturbing the running of others. **1884** *Sat. Rev.* 31 May 712/2 In hilly country, where roads are difficult to construct, the telpher line might be eminently useful. **1888** W. E. AYRTON in *Times* 10 Sept. 11/3 The first track on which electric trams were run in series was the experimental 'Telpher line' erected in Glynde in 1883..for the automatic electric transport of goods. **1901** *Munsey's Mag.* XXV. 363/1 The traveling unit is called a 'telpher'. The fixed cable serves as a rail.., and above it, in the same vertical plane, is a feed wire from which the telpher takes current. **1904** *Jrnl. Franklin Inst.* Oct. 266 With a machine and an assistant, a telpherman can convey 250 tons per day over a distance of 1,000 feet.

Hence '**telpher** *v. trans.*, to transport (goods, etc.) by means of telpherage.

1885 F. JENKIN in *Gd. Words* 132 We may possibly hereafter speak of telphering goods as we now speak of telegraphing messages. **1890** W. E. AYRTON in *Spectator* 19 Apr., To electrically propel may be aptly named to 'telepher', or, say 'telpher' as an abbreviation.

telpherage ('tɛlfərɪdʒ). [f. as TELPHER + -AGE.] Transport effected automatically by the aid of electricity; *spec.* a system adapted to the conveyance of minerals and other goods in vessels suspended from a cable, and moved by means of an electric motor supplied with current from an adjacent conductor. Also *attrib.*

1883 *Engineering* 23 Nov. 481/2 The transmission of vehicles to a distance by electricity, independently of any control exercised from the vehicle, is called 'Telpherage' by Professor Fleeming Jenkin. **1884** F. JENKIN in *Jrnl. Soc. Arts* XXXII. 648/2 The word [telpherage] is intended to designate all modes of transport effected automatically with the aid of electricity. According to strict rules of derivation, the word would be 'telephorage'; but in order to avoid confusion with 'telephone'..I have ventured..to substitute ..'telpher' for 'telephore'. **1888** W. H. PREECE in *Times* 7 Sept. 5/3 Goods, minerals, and fuel can be transmitted by telpherage.

‖**tel quel** (tɛl kɛl), *adj. phr.* Also in Fr. pl., **tels quels** (masc.), **telles quelles** (fem.). [Fr.] Just as it is; without improvement or modification.

1876 GEO. ELIOT *Let.* 3 Feb. (1956) VI. 220 Don't wear glasses *telles quelles* but consult about getting the right ones. **1903** W. JAMES *Let.* 5 June in R. B. Perry *Thought & Char. W. James* (1935) II. VI. lxxvi. 427 You spoke of publishing these lectures, but not, I hope, *tel quels* [*sic*]. **1967** *Listener* 16 Mar. 368/3 The culled facts have been presented *tel quel*, with inconsistencies noted but not resolved.

telson ('tɛlsən). *Zool.* [a. Gr. τέλσον a limit.] The last segment of the abdomen or its median axis in certain crustaceans and arachnidans, as the middle flipper of a lobster's tail-fin, the long sharp spine of the king-crab, or the sting of the scorpion.

1855 C. SPENCE BATE in *Brit. Assoc. Rep.* 28 The last [appendage of the abdomen], which for convenience we shall designate by the name of Telson,..is a rudimentary appendage, modified upon the type of the preceding three. **1872** NICHOLSON *Palæont.* 144 The last segment of the abdomen is known as the 'telson', and it is variously regarded as a somite without appendages, or as an unpaired appendage placed in the middle line of the body. **1880** HUXLEY *Crayfish* i. 19 The abdomen [has] a terminal flap which is called the *telson.*

Hence **tel'sonic** *a.*

1934 in WEBSTER. **1946** *Nature* 28 Dec. 935/2 The caudal segment was probably composed of the sixth abdominal segment with which the telson had become fused, and thus these appendages must be telsonic. **1981** *Israel Jrnl. Zool.* XXX. 115 The more primitive Hyssuridae have no telsonic statocysts.

Teltag ('tɛltæg). [?f. TELL- + TAG *sb.*[1]] A label attached to goods manufactured in the U.K. giving information about the size, weight, performance, etc., of the goods.

1965 *Observer* 23 May 9/4 A new label will appear on British goods next year. Called the 'teltag', it has been designed by the Government-backed Consumer Council to give shoppers clear information on the hidden characteristics of their purchases. **1967** *Spectator* 1 Dec. 682/1 So far isn't necessarily very far, since manufacturers are under no obligation to use, and pay for, Teltags. **1971** *Reader's Digest Family Guide to Law* 335/1 The Teltag scheme, devised by the now defunct Consumer Council, is still used to give details of composition, size, performance and use of appliances.

telthe, obs. form of TILTH.

‖**Telugu, Teloogoo** ('tɛluːguː), *sb.* and *a.* Also 8 Telougou, 9 Telug; 9– Telegu. [Native name of the language, and of a man of the race. Origin and derivation uncertain. The language is also called *Tenugu*, which native pundits treat as the original form, and explain as 'mellifluous', from *tēne* honey. The relationship of either of these names to TELINGA, formerly applied to the same language and people, is disputed. The Tamil name for the language is *Vaḍugu* or 'the Northern'; thence the old Portuguese name *Badages*, and the old German *Waruga.*]

1. The name of a Dravidian language, spoken on the Coromandel coast of India, north of Madras.

[**1731** T. S. BAYER *Let. to La Croze*, Hinc natione Tamulis, Tamulica; Warugis, Warrugica. **1748** J. F. FRITZ *Orient. u. Occident. Sprachm.* 87 Alphabethum Telugicum sive Warugicum.] **1813** *Q. Rev.* Oct. 257 Languages and Dialects... Sanscrit..Telug. **1850** S. HISLOP in G. Smith *Life* iii. (1889) 82 The Telugu began to be spoken even at that village. **1856** BP. CALDWELL *Dravid. Gram.* Introd. 5 The Telugu is spoken all along the eastern coast of the Peninsula, from the neighbourhood of Pulicat, where it supersedes the Tamil, to Chicacole, where it begins to yield to the Uriya; and inland it prevails as far as the eastern boundary of the Maratha country and Mysore. **1886** YULE & BURNELL *Hobson-Jobson*, *Teloogoo*, the first in point of diffusion, and the second in culture and copiousness, of the Dravidian languages of the Indian Peninsula. *Ibid.*, *Telugu* is the name given to the language by the people themselves, as the language of Telingāna. **1893** *Madras Manual of Administr.* III. s.v., Teloogoo is the softest of all Eastern languages..but Teloogoo is a very poor language in everything except outward appearance. **1937** W. H. SAUMAREZ SMITH *Let.* 31 Jan. in *Young Man's Country* (1977) ii. 54 Kanarese is the vernacular of Mysore, a language allied to Tamil and Telugu. **1957** *Encycl. Brit.* IV. 978/1 Great movements of people: the Telugu- and Tamil-speaking caste groups to the rubber plantations of Burma and

Malaya. **1978** 'M. M. KAYE' *Far Pavilions* I. i. 17 He picked up a number of tongues.. Tamil, Gujerati and Telegu from the southerners.

2. One of the Dravidian people or race who speak this language. (See also GENTOO.)

1789 *Seir Mutaqherin* II. 93 *note* (Y.), The first Sipahees that came in Bengal.. were all Talingas or Telougous born. **1893** *Madras Manual of Administr.* III. s.v., The pronunciation of Sanscrit among the Teloogoos corresponds with the purest pronunciation used at Benares. **1903** J. TORRANCE *Story Maratha Missions* viii. 65 A Telugu applied for baptism.

3. *attrib.* or *adj.* Of or pertaining to this language, people, or country.

1816 A. D. CAMPBELL (*title*) A grammar of the Teloogoo language. **1821** —— *Dict. Teloogoo Language*, Advt., The following Dictionary was commenced soon after the publication of the Author's Teloogoo Grammar. *Ibid.* Many of the most common Teloogoo words are arranged, absurdly enough, in the order of the *French*, and not of the Teloogoo, alphabet. **1888** G. SMITH *S. Hislop* iii. (1889) 83 The Hislops marched slowly south to Nellore, the Telugu station of his Church. **1891** C. R. DAY *Music of S. India* v. 61 They ..were probably composed by some Telegu pandit at the court of Mysore. **1909** E. THURSTON *Castes & Tribes S. India* VII. 13 The Telugu soldiers might come to be regarded as the Telugus.. *par excellence*. **1977** *Listener* 7 Apr. 447 Publishing Telegu books largely for Indians in the Midlands.

4. *Comb.* as ***Telugu-speaking*** adj.

1903 *United Free Ch. Scot. Mission. Record* Aug. 352/2 There are always in them Telugu-speaking girls.

†**telwe**, *v. Obs. rare.* [a. ON. *telgja* to cut to shape, cut with a knife: prob. introduced into late OE. as **telȝian*, or into Early ME. as **telȝen*: cf. OE. *folȝian*, ME. *folȝen*, *folwen*, to FOLLOW.] *trans.* To thwite, to whittle (a stick).

c **1440** *Promp. Parv.* 488/1 Telwyn, or thwytyn (*H.* twhytyn, *S.*, *P.* twytyn), *absecc*, *reseco*. *Ibid.*, Telwynge, or twhytynge (*K.* telwhynge or whytynge), *scissulatus*.

telyevie, telȝevie, var. TAILYEVEY *Sc. Obs.*

tem, phonetic var. of *þem*, THEM, after a dental.

temantale: see TENMANTALE.

temazepam (tə'meɪzɪpæm). *Pharm.* [f. *tem-* (of unknown origin) + AZ(O- + *-ep*(*ine* (see OXAZEPAM) + AM(IDE.] A tricyclic compound, $C_{16}H_{13}ClN_2O_2$, used as a tranquillizer and short-acting hypnotic.

1970 *Approved Names* (Brit. Pharmacopœia Comm.) 74 *Temazepam*. 7-Chloro-3-hydroxy-1-methyl-5-phenyl-1*H*-1,4-benzodiazepin-2(3*H*)-one. **1971** *Pharmacol. Res. Communications* III. 166 Besides the three known benzodiazepines.., in the present experiment a fourth one —temazepam, recently introduced in therapeutic use—was also studied. **1980** *Brit. Med. Jrnl.* 29 Mar. 910/1 Pharmacological differences between 'long'-acting benzodiazepines.. and the 'short'-acting rapidly cleared compounds, such as.. temazepam. **1984** *Daily Tel.* 11 Feb. 10/2 [He] chose temazepam, a hypnotic drug marketed.. for transient insomnia under the trade name of Normison.

‖**tembe** ('tɛmbeɪ). [Swahili.] In East Africa, a rectangular house with mud walls and a flat roof.

1887 W. H. G. KINGSTON *Trav. Dr. Livingstone* vii. 135 Sheikh Said Ben Salim invited him [*sc.* Stanley] to take up his quarters in his tembe, or house, a comfortable looking place for the Centre of Africa. **1896** B. K. GREGORY *Story of David Livingstone* xiii. 121 Then the two brave men retired into the doctor's *tembe*, and conversation began, but Stanley could not recollect what it was all about. **1947** *E. African Ann.* 1946–7 93/2 David Livingstone lived for some time in a *tembe* house on the outskirts of Tabora and the house is preserved as a memorial to his name. **1955** *Times* 25 July 5/1 A replica of the tembe (hut) occupied by Livingstone and Stanley, erected near Tabora some years ago and badly damaged by fire recently, is to be rebuilt this year. **1978** J. UPDIKE *Coup* (1979) iii. 111 The space between the square earth houses, the *tembes*, widens.

temblor (tɛm'blɔː(r)). *South-western U.S.* Pl. **temblores**. [a. Amer. Sp.] An earthquake.

1876 B. HARTE *Gabriel Conroy* v. xvii. 288 The temblor has swallowed him. **1896** *Land of Sunshine* July 72 One freshet of one Ohio river a dozen years ago took more lives than all the *temblores* in California in a century and a half have taken. **1932** F. L. WRIGHT *Autobiogr.* II. 147 One of the features of construction that insured the life of that building in the terrific temblor of 1922. **1950** *Los Angeles Times* 3 Jan. 1/6 The temblor was reported from both Ogden and Logan.

‖**tembo** ('tɛmbəʊ). Also **tembu**. [Swahili.] An alcoholic drink made in East Africa, usu. from the sap of the coconut palm; palm wine.

1860 J. KRAPF *Travels, Researches & Missionary Labours* I. ix. 149 One of the elders said that it was really true that God loved men, for He gave the Wanika rain, tembo, and clothes. **1937** K. BLIXEN *Out of Africa* III. i. 170, I sometimes asked the D.C.'s permission for my Squatters to make tembu, a deadly drink, fabricated from sugar cane. *Ibid.* v. v. 411 The old women took a keen interest in everything that was going on on the farm..; a joke, on a cup of tembu, would make their wrinkled toothless faces dissolve in laughter. **1964** R. M. GATHERU *Child of Two Worlds* vii. 101 Others would be drinking some stinking municipally brewed drink—'Tembo'—at Pumwani as an outlet for their handicapped life.

tembre, obs. form of TIMBER.

Tembu ('tɛmbuː), *sb.* and *a.* Forms: 9 **Tymba**, 9– **Tembu**; **Thembu**. [Xhosa.] **A.** *sb.* A member of a Xhosa-speaking people of the south-eastern part of South Africa; also, this people collectively. **B.** *adj.* Of, pertaining to, or designating this people. Cf. TAMBOUKI *sb.* and *a.*

1827 G. THOMPSON *Trav. & Adv. Southern Afr.* I. I. xvii. 349 A Tambookie Caffer is termed Tymba or Tembu, while the tribe collectively is called Amatymbae. **1874** *Cape Monthly Mag.* IX. 207 He then dilated upon the enormities of Gangelizwe, the Tambookie Chief, and the ability of the present Resident amongst the Tembus. **1912** WHITESIDE & AYLIFF *Hist. Abambo* i. 4 Madikana and his people, at a certain time, were feasting, when they were attacked by a combined force of the Tembus and Xosas. **1927** C. G. BOTHA in *Wreck of Grosvenor* (Van Riebeeck Soc.) p. iv, The expedition was obliged to turn back owing to the hostile attitude of the Tembu tribe of natives. **1941** C. W. DE KIEWIET *Hist. S. Afr.* 73 It was densest in Kafirland, where dwelt the Ama-Xosa the Tembu, the Pondo, the Xesibe, and the Ama-Baca. **1961** *Guardian* 27 May 6/3 Mr Mandela is.. the son of a Tembu chief. **1967** J. A. BROSTER *Red Blanket Valley* 4 Remember, the Thembu, one of the chief tribes of the Transkei, were never conquered: they asked the European traders to settle. **1971** *Daily Dispatch* (East London, Cape Province) 11 May 2 We have to honour and respect our national leaders such as Faku of the Pondos and Ngubengcuka of the Tembus. **1974** J. FLINT *Cecil Rhodes* (1976) ix. 205 The foundations [of peace] were laid by an African.. a Tembu man fluent in English and Ndebele. **1976** *Times* 4 Nov. 17/4 Chief Matanzima.. is a Thembu leader.

†**teme**, *v. Obs.* Forms: 1 **tęmman**, **tęmian**, **tymian**, 2–3 **temien**, 3 **temie**, 3–4 **teme**, 4 **tyme**. [OE. *tęmman*, *tęmian*, = OLG. **temmjan* (MLG., MDu. *temmen*, *temen*, Du., LG. *temmen*, LG. *tämen*), OHG. **zammjan*, *zęmman* (MHG. *zem*(*m*)*en*, Ger. *zähmen*), ON., Norw. *tęmja* (Sw. *tämja*, Da. *tæmme*), Goth. *tamjan*, f. OTeut. **tamo*-, TAME *a.* The OE. regular form *tęmman* was superseded by *tęmian* (Sievers *Ags. Gram.* §400 Anm. 2), whence ME. *temien*, *teme*, which was displaced in 15th c. by *tamen*, TAME *v.*, conformed to TAME *a.* (The forms *tymian*, *tymen*, are irregular.) The cognate langs. have preserved the umlauted form.]

1. *trans.* To bring (a wild animal, etc.) under the control of man; to reclaim from the wild state, to domesticate; = TAME *v.* 1.

c **1000** ÆLFRIC *Gram.* xxiv. (Z.) 138 Ic temiȝe, *domo*. *c* **1000** *Sax. Leechd.* III. 184 Nytenu tymian. *Ibid.* 200 Wilde deor temian. *c* **1290** *S. Eng. Leg.* I. 39/173 Þe Bollokes wilde were.. For huy ne scholden heom temie nouȝt. **1387** TREVISA *Higden* (Rolls) II. 357 Hercules.. temede þe world.

2. To bring (a person, passions, etc.) under control; to subdue, subjugate, curb; = TAME *v.* 2.

c **897** K. ÆLFRED *Gregory's Past. C.* lvi. 433 Mon temeþ nis unaliefde lustas mid ðæm wordum ðære halȝan lare. *c* **950** *Lindisf. Gosp.* Mark v. 4 Næniȝ monn mæhte hine temma. [So *c* **975** *Rushw. Gosp.*] *c* **1200** *Trin. Coll. Hom.* 63 To temien þe lichames erguil. **1306** *Pol. Songs* (Camden) 214 So hue [bishops and barons] were temed tho. *a* **1340** HAMPOLE *Psalter* lxvii. 27 Fayre saules, þat has temyd þaire fleyss. *c* **1394** *P. Pl. Crede* 742 Y miȝt tymen þo troiflardes to toilen wiþ þe erþe.

teme, obs. f. TEAM, TEEM, THEME.

‖**temenggong** (təmeŋ'gɒŋ). Forms: 8 **tamongoong**, 9 **tumângong**; **temenggong**. [Malay.] In traditional Malay states, a high-ranking official, usu. commanding the army and the police. Also, the title of the rulers of Johore, 1824–85.

1783 W. MARSDEN *Hist. Sumatra* 285 The *tamongoong*, or commander in the wars. **1859** L. OLIPHANT *Narr. Lord Elgin's Mission to China & Japan* ii. 23 We ascended to the comfortable bungalow of the Tumângong. **1907** F. SWETTENHAM *Brit. Malaya* iv. 67 A new treaty was made.. between Raffles on the one hand and the Sultan Husein and the Têmĕnggong on the other. **1964** M. TURNBULL in W. Gungwu *Malaysia* II. vii. 133 This political vacuum encouraged the bid for independence by the subordinate chiefs, the temenggong of Johore and the bendahara of Pahang. **1972** M. SHEPPARD *Taman Indera* 108 During the reign of Sultan Mahmud of Malacca (1488–1511), Tun Hassan, the Temenggong, who ranked second only to the chief minister, started a new fashion by wearing the sleeves of his tunic long and loose.

‖**temenos** ('tɛmənɒs). *Gr. Antiq.* [a. Gr. τέμενος, f. τεμ-, stem of τέμν-ειν to cut off, sever.] A piece of ground surrounding or adjacent to a temple; a sacred enclosure or precinct.

1820 T. S. HUGHES *Trav. Sicily* I. iv. 108 Tradition says, that this square formed in very early ages the temenos of a temple. **1885** *Times* 3 Jan. 12 Pious sons had set up.. a dedicatory inscription in a temenos, or sacred enclosure.

attrib. **1891** A. B. EDWARDS *Pharaohs, Fellahs & Expl.* 29 Close outside the temenos-wall of one of these temples.

temerack, obs. var. TAMARACK.

†'**teme,rare**, *a. Sc. Obs.* Also 6 **temerar**, **-air**. [a. F. *temeraire* (1461 in Godef. *Compl.*), ad. L. *temerārius*: cf. next and TEMERARY.] = next, 1.

1549 *Compl. Scot.* (1873) 6, I.. hes tane ane temerare consait to present to ȝour nobil grace ane tracteit of the fyrst laubir of my pen. *Ibid.* xvii. 153 Kyng cresus vas temerair in his questioun. **1581** *Sat. Poems Reform.* xliv. 333 Of haly Kirk ȝour temerar dispysing.

temerarious (tɛmə'rɛərɪəs), *a.* Now only *literary*. [f. L. *temerāri-us* fortuitous, rash (f. *temere* blindly, rashly (see TEMEROUS) + *-āri-us*; cf. *contr-ārius*, *extr-ārius*, *necess-ārius*) + -OUS.]

1. Characterized by temerity; unreasonably adventurous; reckless, heedless, rash.

1532 MORE *Confut. Tindale* Wks. 620/2 He is somwhat ouer temerarious & bold. *a* **1533** FRITH *Answ. More* (1548) E vj b, Because they shall not of temeraryous presumpcion reiect this olde father. **1611** SPEED *Hist. Gt. Brit.* IX. xvi. §37 The King was one of the first that entred [the breach], choosing rather to be thought temerarious than timorous. **1645** HAMMOND *View Infallib.* 38 Your resolves are temerarious and presumptuous. **1781** JOHNSON in *Boswell* (1887) IV. 130 Does it not suppose, that the former judgment was temerarious or negligent? **1890** J. R. LUNN in *Ch. Times* 21 Feb. 196/4, I do not think any one will be temerarious enough to maintain that.

†**2.** Acting or happening at random; fortuitous, casual, haphazard. *Obs.*

1660 STANLEY *Hist. Philos.* IX. (1701) 386/1 Now in heaven nothing is produced casually, nothing temerarious. **1682** NORRIS *Hierocles* 53 But we should ascribe nothing.. to a fortuitous and temerarious cause. **1775** HARRIS *Philos. Arrangem.* iii, These two principles are not merely casual and temerarious.

Hence **teme'rariousness**.

1711 in *10th Rep. Hist. MSS. Comm.* App. v. 133 He was overruled by the temerariousness of Orange. **1775** ASH, *Temerariousness*, rashness, temerity.

teme'rariously, *adv.* [f. prec. + -LY[2].]

1. With temerity; rashly.

1535 JOYE *Apol. Tindale* (Arb.) 24 Thus temerariously and abominably to write. **1638** SIR T. HERBERT *Trav.* (ed. 2) 310 They account them happiest, who out of a frantick zeale, temerariously throw their naked bodies in the way. *a* **1745** SWIFT *Disc. Antiq. Eng. Tongue* ad fin., I have ventured (perhaps too temerariously) to contribute my mite to the learned world. **1863** LYTTON *Caxtoniana* I. 50 To be.. corrected in any subsequent edition of the work in which such descriptions had been temerariously adventured.

†**2.** At random; fortuitously. *Obs.*

1669 *Address yng. Gentry Eng.* 86 As temerariously and blindly they [Gamesters] cast round about them these fire-brands. **1678** CUDWORTH *Intell. Syst.* I. iv. §7. 198 The Atheists make the Universe.. to be devoid of Counsel, and therefore.. to be carried on Temerariously and Fortuitously.

†**teme'rarity**. *Sc. Law. Obs.* [f. L. *temerāri-us*: see next and -ITY.] Reprehensible or culpable heedlessness or negligence.

1475 *Sc. Acts Jas. III* (1814) II. 112/1 Gif it be fundin þ[t] þe first assise acqwite þe trespassour be temerarite,.. sa mony as beis conuict of þ[t] temerarite to be punist eftir þe forme of þe auld law. **1499** *Reg. Privy Seal Scotl.* I. 62 Schir William Dowy.. of wilfull temerarite perseverand in his said baratry.

†'**temerary**, *a. Obs.* [ad. L. *temerārius* fortuitous, rash, f. *temere*: see TEMEROUS and -ARY[1]. Cf. TEMERARE.] Rash, reckless; = TEMERARIOUS 1.

c **1410** LOVE *Bonavent. Mirr.* xv. (1908) 93 A presumptuouse and temerarie demere of othere men. *c* **1425** tr. *Arderne's Surgery* (E.E.T.S.) 4 That he be noȝt y-founden temerarie or bosteful in his seyingis or in his dedes. *c* **1450** tr. *De Imitatione* I. Contents 1 Of eschuying of temerary iuggement. **1650** GENTILIS *Cons.* 176, I should be reputed rash and temerary.

b. *Civ.* and *Eccl. Law.* Reprehensibly heedless or careless; culpably negligent: cf. TEMERARITY.

1681 CONSETT *Pract. Spir. Crts.* I. iii. I. §2 If it.. appear there was.. Administration granted by any other Judge.. and that it is evident touching their temerary Administring. *Ibid.* VI. I. I. §18 In a Matrimonial Cause.. a Testamentary Cause, a Cause of Temerary Administration.

Hence †'**temerarily** *adv.*, rashly.

c **1450** tr. *De Imitatione* III. xxix. 98 Of oþir mennes dedes or seienges deme no þinge temerarily.

†'**temerat**, *a. Sc. Obs. rare*[−1]. [In form, ad. L. *temerāt-us*, pa. pple. of *temerāre*: see next.] Adventurous, headstrong, forward.

c **1560** A. SCOTT *Poems* (S.T.S.) xxx. 37 Thocht wemen self be temerat, Thay luve no man effeminat.

†'**temerate**, *v. Obs.* [f. L. *temerāt-*, ppl. stem of *temerāre*, f. *temere* rashly; as if to treat presumptuously or irreverently.] *trans.* To violate or break (a promise, bond, etc.); to profane.

1635 SIR S. D'EWES *Autobiog.* (1845) II. 131 They have temerated the oath they had taken. **1637** BASTWICK *Litany* II. 23 To say nothing of my owne experience, as I am a Physitian,.. because I will not in any thing temerate our function. **1654** H. L'ESTRANGE *Chas. I* (1655) 57 The French King returned answer that the Rochellers had first temerated and slighted their Faith with him.

†**teme'ration**. *Obs. rare.* [n. of action from prec.: see -ATION; cf. post-cl. L. *temerātio* a forging.] Violation, profanation.

1641 SIR S. D'EWES in Rushw. *Hist. Coll.* (1692) III. I. 314 After the reiterated temeration of his Faith and Promises. **16..** JER. TAYLOR *2nd Serm. Ministers' Duty* ¶6 Those Cryptick ways of institution by which the Ancients did hide a light, and keep it.. from the temeration of ruder handlings.

temeritous (tɪ'mɛrɪtəs), *a.* [f. TEMERIT-Y + -OUS; cf. *iniquitous*.] Full of temerity; rash.

1892 *Daily Chron.* 18 Feb. 3/2 And his book is dedicated to Professor Dowden. O temeritous Mr. Shorter! **1900**

Academy 21 July 51/1 The attempt to define is, we know, foolishly temeritous.

†**te'meritude.** *Obs. rare*—⁰. [ad. L. *temeritūdo.*] = next.

1623 COCKERAM II, Rashnesse.. *Temeritude.*

temerity (tɪ'mɛrɪtɪ). Forms: 5 **-yte**, 6 **-ite**, **-atie**, 6–7 **-itie**, 6– **-ity**, (6–7 **timeritie**, 7 **-ity**). [ad. L. *temeritās*, *-tātem*, rashness, f. *temere* adv. by chance, blindly: see -ITY. So F. *témérité* (15th c. in Godef. *Compl.*).]

1. Excessive boldness; rashness; foolhardiness, recklessness.

1432–50 tr. *Higden* (Rolls) III. 467 Infancy ioyethe in simplicite, yowthe in temeryte [*temeritate* [*gaudet*] *juventus*], age in debilite. **1551** BP. GARDINER *Explic. True Cath. Faith* 20 b, To auoyde the temerite of deniyng (as neuer) or affirmyng (as euer) which be extremities. **1598** BARCKLEY *Felic. Man* VI. (1603) 595 Fortitude referred to any other thing, then to godlinesse, falleth into temeritie or rashness. **1656** STANLEY *Hist. Philos.* VIII. (1701) 336/2 Affirming, that they have done wickedly, is not to be attributed to their timerity, but to Fate. **1750** JOHNSON *Rambler* No. 19 ¶9 Marlborough might have been made to repent his temerity at Blenheim. **1803** REPTON *Landscape Gard.* (1805) 33 There is..no more temerity in marking trees to be taken down than those to be planted. **1884** F. J. BRITTEN *Watch & Clockm.* 80 Mr. Denison's temerity was justified by his success.

b. with *a* and *pl.* An act or instance of rashness.

a **1677** BARROW *Serm. Titus iii 2* Wks. 1687 I. 237 Among all temerities this is one of the most noxious. **1847** LEWES *Hist. Philos.* Introd. (1857) 33 The unhesitating temerities of Plato and Plotinus.

†**2.** Chance, fortuity: cf. TEMERARIOUS 2. *Obs.*

1678 CUDWORTH *Intell. Syst.* i. iii. §23. 168 Although there be not the least appearance of fortuitousness or temerity in it. *Ibid.* iv. §24. 415 Of all things.. most opposite to Chance, Fortune, and Temerity.

temerity, -itie, var. TIMERITY *Obs.*, timidity.

temerosity, obs. f. TIMOROSITY, timidity.

temerous ('tɛmərəs), *a.* Now *rare.* [f. L. type **temerōsus* rash, f. *temere* adv., by chance, blindly, heedlessly: see -OUS.

(*Temere* is generally held to be the loc. sing. of a sb. **temos* = Skr. *támas* darkness, hence in darkness, blindly.)]

Rash, foolhardy; = TEMERARIOUS 1.

1461 [implied in TEMEROUSLY]. **1535** *Act 27 Hen. VIII*, c. 20 §1 Diuers.. dispise the.. decrees of the ecclesiastical courtes.. in more temerous and large maner than before this time hath ben sene. *a* **1562** G. CAVENDISH *Wolsey* Prol. (1893) 2 Thus may all men of wisdom and discretion understand the temerous madness of the rude commonalty. **1622** MISSELDEN *Free Trade* 88 Temerous, rash, and litigious suites of law. **1678** COLEMAN *Two Lett.* i. 3 Our Parliament.. by the temerous Counsels of our Ministers, who then Governed, could never be useful. **1888** *Atlantic Monthly* Feb. 281, I have not the temerous intention of disputing.. the correctness of the modern Latin pronunciation.

Hence **'temerously** *adv.*, with temerity; rashly, presumptuously; **'temerousness**, rashness, temerity.

1461 *Rolls of Parlt.* V. 463/2 Henry.. temerously ayenst rightwisnes.. rered were at Flynte in Wales. **1550** COVERDALE *Spir. Perle* xiii. (1588) 140 [They] attempt not any thing temerously and rashly. **1562** WINȜET *Last Blast* Wks. (S.T.S.) I. 40 Osias, quha temeruslie in his arrogance ingerit him self to make sacrifice at the altare of God. **1597** A. M. tr. *Guillemeau's Fr. Chirurg.* 42 b/1 Or els throughe temerousnes & timorousnes of the Chyrurgian. **1727** BAILEY Vol. II, *Temerousness*, Rashness, Unadvisedness.

temerous, obs. form of TIMOROUS.

‖**temia** ('teɪmɪə). *Ornith.* [The native Javanese name of the bird.] (See quots.)

1809 SHAW *Gen. Zool.* VII. 372 Temia Crow. *Corvus Temia*... Size of a Thrush, but longer bodied: bill and legs black. **1890** *Cent. Dict.* s.v. *Crypsirhina*, The temia or so-called variable crow of Java.

Temiar ('tɛmɪɑː(r)), *sb.* and *a.* [Native name.]

A. *sb.* An aboriginal people of the Malay Peninsula, also called Sakai; a member of this people. **B.** *adj.* Of or pertaining to this people or their language.

1933 *Jrnl. R. Asiatic Soc.* (Malayan Branch) XI. 291 The Temiars showed an extraordinary desire to sample European medicines. *Ibid.*, The most interesting feature in the Temiar life.. was their obvious happiness. **1958** J. SLIMMING *Temiar Jungle* iv. 54 A Temiar community lives on the centre tongue of land. **1958** *Listener* 13 Nov. 793/3 A Temiar who coveted his wife. **1965** R. MCKIE *Company of Animals* v. 91 The Temiar are animists who, living among jungle-covered mountains, are perfectly attuned to their environment. **1972** *Times* 6 Dec. (Europe & Third World Suppl.) p. vii/4 (*caption*) Temiar aborigines at the Gombak Aborigine Hospital, Malaysia, for treatment.

te-mine, var. TAMEIN.

temir, obs. Sc. var. *timmer*, TIMBER.

temize, Temmes, obs. ff. TEMSE, THAMES.

temmoku ('tɛməʊkuː). Also **tenmoku**. [Jap., ad. Chinese *tiān-mù* eye of heaven (see quot. 1923).] The Japanese name for a type of Chinese porcelain with lustrous black or brown glaze; also, the glaze so used.

1880 A. W. FRANKS *Jap. Pottery* 5 A tea bowl of porcelain or earthenware (*cha-wan*, or, when of large size, *temmoku*), simple in form, but remarkable for its antiquity or historical associations. **1915** R. L. HOBSON *Chinese Pott. & Porc.* I. 31 *Temmoku*.. glaze is sometimes flecked with tea green as well as with golden brown. *Ibid.* 131 The Japanese.. have always prized the Chien Yao bowls to which they gave the name *temmoku*. **1923** —— & HETHERINGTON *Art of Chinese Potter* 15 The name *temmoku* (*t'ien mu*, or Eye of Heaven) was first given to a bowl, probably of Fukien origin, brought to Japan during the Sung period by a Zen priest from the Zen temple of the *T'ien mu shan* (Eye of Heaven mountain) in the north-west of Chekiang. In later times the generic name of *temmoku* came to be applied to the whole category of wares of this type. **1924** *Trans. Oriental Ceramics Soc.* *1923–4* 26 (*title*) The chemistry of the Temmoku glazes. **1934** [see *hare's fur* s.v. HARE *sb.* 6]. **1940** B. LEACH *Potter's Bk.* viii. 231 Into the tenmoku I dipped several large jars and bowls. **1958** W. WILLETTS *Chinese Art* II. vi. 394 *Temmoku* bowls.. made to-day at P'êng-ch'êng.. and at T'ai-yüan.., which in many respects can hardly be told apart from their Sung models. **1971** S. JENYNS *Jap. Pottery* iii. 84 The glazes particularly associated with the Toshiros and their successors for tea ceremony wares are of this *tenmoku* variety: 'thick' and semi-transparent but coloured often to opacity by the presence of iron oxide. **1976** *Canadian Collector* Mar.–Apr. 43/1 In Japan this type of black-glazed ware became known as *temmoku*.

Temne ('tɛmniː), *sb.* and *a.* Forms: 8 **Timmany**; 9 **Timan(n)ee, Timmanah, -ee, -eh, -i**; 9– **Temne**; **Temnee, Timini, Timne, Timni.** [Native name; cf. quot. 1861.] **A.** *sb.* **a.** A people of Sierra Leone; also, a member of this people. **b.** A West Atlantic language spoken by this people. **B.** *adj.* Of, pertaining to, or designating this people or their language.

1791 A. M. FALCONBRIDGE *Let.* 8 June in *Narr. Two Voyages to Sierra Leone* (1802) 81 The Burees.. were conquered and drove away to other parts of the country by the Timmany's. **1792** —— *Let.* 10 Feb. in *Ibid.* 27 In every house I was accosted by whoever we found at home, in the Timmany language *Currea Yaa*, which signifies—How do you do, mother? **1803** T. WINTERBOTTOM *Acct. of Native Africans of Sierra Leone* I. iv. 65 The largest kind [of pepper] is distinguished.. in Timmanee, by kik bengbay pootoo; and in Soosoo, by foorootoo bengbay. *Ibid.* v. 80 Timanee towns.. have Ro *in general* prefixed to them, as Ro-mak-baynee, a town where they finish things. **1825** [see KORANKO]. **1841** *Penny Cycl.* XXI. 503/1 The Timannees occupy a country extending 90 miles from east to west, and 55 from north to south. **1850** T. E. POOLE *Life, Scenery & Customs in Sierra Leone* II. xvii. 274 He gave himself up to the most diligent study of the Timmanah language. **1861** C. F. SCHLENKER *Collect. Temne Traditions* p. iii, The signification of the term: Témne seems to be 'an old man himself'. They derive it.. from *o*-tem, 'an old man, an old gentleman', to which is affixed the reflexive suffix *-ne*, 'self'; because they believe that the Temne nation will ever exist. **1887** *Encycl. Brit.* XXII. 44/2 The following.. can be distinctly classified:—Mandingos, 1190; Timmanehs, 7443 [etc.]. **1903** J. J. CROOKS *Hist. Sierra Leone* ix. 121 Many Timini children were carefully brought up according to the Mohammedan creed. **1911** *Encycl. Brit.* XXV. 55/1 Sierra Leone is inhabited by various negro tribes, the chief being the Timni, the Sulima, the Susu and the Mendi. **1916** H. OSMAN NEWLAND *Sierra Leone* iii. 28 The name of the village is essentially a reminder of the old Temne domination when Kwaia.. country embraced all this territory. **1916** N. W. THOMAS *Anthropol. Rep. on Sierra Leone* I. i. 7 The remaining languages are Soudanese, and fall into two main groups, prefix and non-prefix tongues. To the former.. belong (a) Timne, (b) Limba, [etc.]. **1926** F. W. H. MIGEOD *View of Sierra Leone* I. iii. 18 The Temne influence is so great that practically all the Bullom north of Freetown speak Temne. **1955** [see MANDE *sb.* and *a.*]. **1957** M. BANTON *W. Afr. City* iii. 54 The Temne, conservative as he is in many matters, has a readiness to copy certain new ways. **1957** LD. HAILEY *African Survey 1956* iii. 104 In the Protectorate Mende is the language generally used in education, but Temne and the Kono dialect of Vai are used in mission schools. **1980** E. G. WILSON *John Clarkson* vi. 81 Alexander Falconbridge.. had been prevailed upon.. to return to Sierra Leone where his experience with the Temne people would pave the way for the immigrant fleet. *Ibid.* vi. 82 John Clarkson could soothe Falconbridge and win the confidence of the Temne as well.

temnospondylous (tɛmnəʊ'spɒndɪləs), *a.* *Comp. Anat.* [f. Gr. τέμν-ειν to cut + σπόνδυλ-ος vertebra + -OUS.] Having vertebræ composed of separately ossified parts.

1901 GADOW in *Camb. Nat. Hist.* VIII. viii. 286 The vertebræ are typically temnospondylous, consisting each of three pairs of separately ossified pieces.

temp. (tɛmp), abbrev. of L. *tempore* (also used) = in the time of.

1658 W. DUGDALE *Hist. St. Paul's Cathedral* 127 Of this, the first mention that I finde, is in that Grant of *Richard de Beaumeir* Bishop of London (*temp.* H.I.) concerning the School. **1767** A. C. DUCAREL *Tour through Normandy* 96 Leases of Crown-Lands in Kent, temp. Eliz. **1859** S. A. ALLIBONE *Dict. Eng. Lit.* I. 27 As we have frequently occasion to refer to the reigns of different English sovereigns without specifying dates,—*temp.* Edward II., *temp.* Henry II., &c. **1892** F. W. MAITLAND *Let.* 6 Sept. (1965) 105 Are you likely to write anything about the frequency of eyres temp. Hen. II? **1932** *N. & Q.* 16 Jan. 46/1 Old registers *tempore* mid-seventeenth century. **1955** *Times* 16 July 7/4 A flying machine, *tempore* Blériot, would almost certainly have crashed in the shrubbery. **1983** W. BLUNT *Married to Single Life* i. 2 My great-grandfather, John Blunt of Lindfield in Sussex (*temp.* James I).

temp (tɛmp), *sb.*[1] Colloq. abbrev. of TEMPERATURE 7.

1886 R. ROOSE *Let.* 15 Mar. in R. S. Churchill *Winston S. Churchill* (1967) I. Compan. I. iv. 117 As long as I can fight the temp and keep it under 105 I shall not feel anxious. **1916** G. BELL *Let.* 23 July (1927) I. xv. 383, I shan't be sorry when the temp. drops 20°. **1924** GALSWORTHY *Forest* II. ii. 48 Collie's temp.'s down. **1940** M. DICKENS *Mariana* v. 170, I wish I had a thermometer with me, I'd take your temp. **1972** J. MCCLURE *Caterpillar Cop* ii. 27 The body temp is above normal. **1977** *Hot Car* Oct. 89/3 The original CF radiator, cooled by a second-hand Kenlowe fan keeps the temps down, no sweat, even in that long hot summer of '76.

temp (tɛmp), *sb.*[2] *colloq.* [f. next or as abbrev. of TEMPORARY *sb.* 4.] A temporary employee; esp., a temporary secretary (see TEMPORARY *sb.* 4).

1932 *Amer. Speech* VII. 278 *A temp*, a part-timer [i.e. a part-time non-civil service employee of the U.S. Post Office]. **1967** *Economist* 22 Apr. 374/1 Overstaffing is not solely the result of the unwillingness to use temps. **1970** R. HILL *Clubbable Woman* viii. 238 One of his women, a temp, only comes in at weekends [at a public house]. **1975** *Sunday Sun* (Brisbane) 23 Nov. 51/1 A year ago she sold cattle. Now she sells Temps.

temp (tɛmp), *a.* Colloq. abbrev. of TEMPORARY *a.* 1 a.

1909 in WEBSTER. **1964** in Hamblett & Deverson *Generation X* 173 Between school and university I had several temp. jobs ranging from accounts clerk to van driver. **1968** D. E. KNUTH *Art of Computer Programming* I. 632 *Temp storage*, part of memory used to hold a value for a comparatively short time while other values occupy the registers. **1972** *Homes & Gardens* Dec. 22/2 'You do realise it's only temp, dear?' said the Lady Supervisor when I arrived to begin my duties as part-time untrained telephonist. **1977** 'D. CORY' *Bennett* iv. 121 Detective-Inspector (temp.) Eric Hunter.

temp (tɛmp), *v. colloq.* [f. TEMP *sb.*[2]] *intr.* To work as a temp (see TEMP *sb.*[2]). So **'temping** *vbl. sb.*

1973 *Times* 15 Mar. 30/5 (Advt.), Bored with temping? We specialise in short term assignments.. in the artistic and creative fields. **1974** *Harpers & Queen* Sept. 180/1 You meet such civilized people when temping for Bernardette. **1978** *Times* 2 Oct. (Business Efficiency Suppl.) p. iii/3 Most of the students had given as their explanation for deciding to temp: 'To gain office experience before taking up a permanent job.' **1979** A. PRICE *Tomorrow's Ghost* i. 9 I'm a bit cheesed off with this temping—I think it's time to dig in somewhere comfy.

temp, Sc. form of TEMPT.

Tempe ('tɛmpiː). [a. L. *Tempē*, a. Gr. Τέμπη.] The proper name of a charming valley in Thessaly, watered by the Peneus, between Mounts Olympus and Ossa; used (already by the Roman writers) as a general name for a beautiful valley; hence for any delightful rural spot.

1594 NASHE *Terrors of Night* Wks. (Grosart) III. 264 Farre vnworthie am I to spend the least breath of commendation in the extolling so delightfull and pleasant a Tempe. **1612** DRAYTON *Poly-olb.* To Rdr., Refusing to walke forth into the *Tempe* and Feelds of the Muses. **1616** SURFL. & MARKH. *Country Farme* To Rdr., Seeing that the whole earth was once a Tempe, an Eden (that is, a place of all pleasures and delights). **1770** H. WALPOLE *Let. to G. Montagu* 17 July, The gay solitude of my own little Tempe.

Hence **Tempean** (tɛm'piːən) *a.*, of or pertaining to Tempe; resembling Tempe in natural beauty.

1864 in WEBSTER; hence in mod. Dicts.

tempeh ('tɛmpeɪ). Also **tempe**. [ad. Indonesian *tempe.*] An Indonesian foodstuff made by fermenting soya beans with Rhizopus and deep-frying them in fat.

1966 *N.Y. Times* 17 Apr. IV. 11/4 A cake of food material.. somewhat comparable to Indonesian fermented food called tempeh. **1977** *Daily Colonist* (Victoria, B.C.) 9 Jan. 28/5 Sixty-nine persons died and 265 others in East Java were in hospital for food poisoning after eating tempe, a local dish made from soy beans. **1980** *San Francisco Bay Guardian* 16–23 Oct. 13 (Advt.), Delicious Natural Foods to Eat: Soy Ice Cream, Sushi, Tofu, Tempeh, Mochi, Fresh Juices, Organic Burritos.

temper ('tɛmpə(r)), *sb.* Forms: 4–6 **tempre**, 5 **tempere, -yr, -our, -ure, tymper**, 6– **temper**. [f. TEMPER *v.* Cf. rare OF. *tempre* proportion, etc. (12th c. in Godef. *Compl.*), later and mod.F. *trempe* (15th c.) tempering, temper of steel, physical constitution of man.]

I. †**1.** The due or proportionate mixture or combination of elements or qualities; the condition or state resulting from such combination; proper or fit condition; ***in temper, out of temper***, in, out of proper condition, etc. Now *rare* or *Obs.*

1387 TREVISA *Higden* (Rolls) I. 75 þere is helþe, for þe aier is in tempre, noþer to hote noþer to colde. **1422** tr. *Secreta Secret., Priv. Priv.* 246 Als longe as the natural hette duryth in ryght tempure by euenesse of the foure humores. **1548** UDALL *Erasm. Par. Luke* ix. 86 b, The delectable swetenesse of the glorie should be brought to a tempre with the mencion of death. **1573** *Treas. Hid. Secrets* (1633) xviii, Keepe your water in a temper; and, when it is very hot, let it out, and put it in cold water. **1579** LYLY *Euphues* (Arb.) 138 For the curing and keeping in temper of the body. **1607** HIERON *Wks.* I. 191 It shall be wisedome for vs.. to sing of mercy and iudgment too; both together will make an excellent temper. **1622** *Rel. Eng. Plant. in Plymouth N. Eng.* in Arber *Pilgr. Fathers* (1897) 448 To make our pieces and furniture ready, which by the moisture and rain were out of temper. **1651** T. STANLEY *Poems* 106 As soon as the cup was brought tempered with water, they call on Jupiter..the author of temper and commixtion. **1655** MOUFET & BENNET *Health's Impr.* (1746) 389 Health itself is but a kind of Temper gotten and preserved by a convenient Mixture of Contrarieties. **1734** tr. *Rollin's Anc. Hist.* (1827) I. 82 To keep their limbs pliable and in a right temper. **1743** *Lond. & Country Brew.* II. (ed. 2) 120 The London Brewer..lets in a parcel of cold Water directly and thereby brings all his Liquor into a Temper at once. [**1879** GEO. ELIOT *Theo. Such* 117 What is temper? Its primary meaning, 'the proportion and mode in which qualities are mingled', is much neglected in popular speech.]

2. Proportionate arrangement of parts; regulation, adjustment; hence, mean or medium, a middle course; a compromise; a settlement. *arch.*

1523 FITZHERB. *Husb.* § 4 Their most speciall temper is at the bolster, where as the plough beame lyeth. [Cf. TEMPER *v.* 17.] **1597** HOOKER *Eccl. Pol.* v. lxxvi. §5 A moderate, indifferent temper, betweene fulnesse of bread, and emptinesse. **1647** JER. TAYLOR *Lib. Proph.* Ep. Ded. 24 Therefore they made Decrees of Toleration, and appointed tempers and expedients. **1692** BURNET *Past. Care* viii. 95 So strongly does the World love Extreams, and avoid a Temper. **1757** BURKE *Abridgm. Eng. Hist.* III. iv, The king ..compiled a new body of laws, in order to find a temper between both. **1855** MACAULAY *Hist. Eng.* xiii. III. 260 He would probably have preferred a temper between the two rival systems, a hierarchy in which the chief spiritual functionaries should have been something more than moderators and something less than prelates.

3. Mental balance or composure, esp. under provocation of any kind; moderation in or command over the emotions, esp. anger; calmness, equanimity: now usually in the phrases ***to keep*** or ***lose*** (***one's***) ***temper***, ***to be out of temper***.

1603 SHAKS. *Meas. for M.* II. ii. 185 Neuer could the Strumpet..Once stir my temper. **1611** B. JONSON *Catiline* IV. ii, Restore your selves unto your temper, fathers, And, without perturbation, hear me speak. **1659** HAMMOND *On Ps.* civ. 9. Paraphr. 511 It observes..a temper in its madness. **1694** CONGREVE *Double Dealer* v. iv, Let your wild fury have a vent; and when you have temper, tell me. **1697** COLLIER *Immor. Stage* iii. (1698) 120 Creon keeps himself within Temper, and gives no ill Language. **1703** ROWE *Ulyss.* Ded., The Temper which you have restor'd to our Councils. **1711** STEELE *Spect.* No. 140 ¶11, I keep my Temper, and win their Money. **1743** J. MORRIS *Serm.* vii. 191 The good man was out of temper. **1782** V. KNOX *Ess.* (1819) II. lxxxvi. 148 Public affairs are seldom treated with temper either in writing or conversation. **1838** THIRLWALL *Greece* V. xxxvii. 20 Teleutias entirely lost his temper. **1840** DICKENS *Barn. Rudge* xxxii, It would put me out of temper, which is a state of mind I can't endure. **1871** SMILES *Charac.* i. (1876) 9 A weakness..was his want of temper; his genius was sacrificed to his irritability. **1878** S. WALPOLE *Hist. Eng.* II. 458 Sir Joseph Yorke told him that he would lose his place if he did not keep his temper.

II. †4. a. The constitution, character, or quality of a substance or body (orig. supposed to depend upon the 'temper' or combination of the elements); = TEMPERAMENT 3. *Obs.*

c **1400** *Lanfranc's Cirurgie* 332 Coold mater..ne schal not be putt awei wiþ repercussiuis, but wiþ medicyns þat ben hoot and drie in tempere. **1483** *Cath. Angl.* 379/2 A Tempyr ..*temperacio rerum.* **1604** E. G[RIMSTONE] *D'Acosta's Hist. Indies* IV. iii. 209 In the highest mountains and inaccessible rockes of a rough temper. **1625** N. CARPENTER *Geog. Del.* I. iii. (1635) 45 [He] found the causes of most magneticall motions hid in the magneticall temper and constitution of the Earth. **1703** MOXON *Mech. Exerc.* 67 Examine the Temper of your Stuff, by easy Trials, how the Plane will work upon it. **1707** MORTIMER *Husb.* (1721) I. 60 In sowing of Land great regard ought to be had to the Weather, and the Temper of the Land you design to sow. **1759** J. MILLS *Duhamel's Husb.* I. ix. (1762) 52, I come now to your lands of a light temper.

†b. Of things immaterial: Character, quality.

1598 B. YOUNG tr. *Montemayor's Diana* 109 His strength and courage was not of such a temper, that mortall wounds could daunt his minde. **1602** *Life T. Cromwell* II. i. 86 Now, sir, your heart is fram'd of milder temper. **1635** PAGITT *Christianogr.* I. iii. (1636) 125 The Georgians have.. a peculiar language of a middle temper, which well agreeth with the position of their country, betweene the Tartarians and the Armenians. **1651** BACON *Disc. Govt. Eng.* II. lxii. 194 Treason was anciently used only as a crime of breach of trust or fealty..; now it grows into a sadder temper, and is made all one with that of *Laesa Majestas.*

5. The particular degree of hardness and elasticity or resiliency imparted to steel by tempering: see TEMPER *v.* 14.

c **1470** HENRY *Wallace* II. 189 O wareide suerd, of tempyr neuir trew. **1590** SIR J. SMYTH *Disc. Weapons* 4 Rapier blades..made of a verie hard temper to fight in priuat fraies. **1591** SHAKS. *1 Hen. VI*, II. iv. 13 Between two blades, which beares the better temper. **1611** CORYAT *Crudities* 340 Milanese Cutlers..are accounted very excellent workmen for making of kniues, targets and swordes of a singular temper. **1703** MOXON *Mech. Exerc.* 61 The blew Colour gives the Temper to Springs in general. **1881** *Metal World* 8 Oct. 338 The temper of steel is due to the chemical union of the iron with the carbon.

fig. **1601** B. JONSON *Ev. Man in Hum.* (Qo.) II. ii. 73 Not caring how the temper of your spirits [*Fol.* metal of your minds] Is eaten with the rust of idlenesse. **1784** COWPER *Task* v. 664 Harden'd his heart's temper in the forge Of lust, and on the anvil of despair. **1866** J. MARTINEAU *Ess.* I. 41 Intellectual implements of more ethereal temper.

†6. The condition of the atmosphere with regard to heat and cold, dryness and humidity; the prevailing condition of the weather at a place; = CLIMATE *sb.* 3, TEMPERAMENT 4. *Obs.*

1483 *Cath. Angl.* 379/2 A Tempyr,..*temperies Aeris est.* **1525** LD. BERNERS *Froiss.* II. clxvi. [clxvii.] 500 The wether was fayre and clere, and the ayre in good temper. **1604** E. G[RIMSTONE] *D'Acosta's Hist. Indies* I. ix. 33 It is a land of an excellent temper, being in the midst of two extremes. **1622** *Rel. Eng. Plant. in Plymouth N. Eng.* in Arber *Pilgr. Fathers* (1897) 490 For the temper of the air here, it agreeth well with that in England. **1697** DRYDEN *Virg. Georg.* I. 565 With the changeful Temper of the Skies, As Rains condense, and Sunshine rarifies. **1705** ADDISON *Italy* 208 The Temper of their Climate..relaxes the Fibers of their Bodies.

†7. The relative condition of a body in respect of warmth or coldness; = TEMPERATURE 7. *Obs.*

1562 TURNER *Baths* 16 Let therefore your both meat and drinke be in such temper, that they be not cold but warme. **1626** BACON *Sylva* §326 This will be performed partly by the Temper of the Fire. **1657** R. LIGON *Barbadoes* 27 The other foure months it is not so hot, but is neer the temper of the aire in England. **1677** YARRANTON *Eng. Improv.* 109 The Cloth is always kept in a constant heat and temper. **1693** E. HALLEY in *Phil. Trans.* XVII. 655 The Thermometers..in use are of Two sorts; the one shewing the differing Temper of Heat and Cold by the Expansion of Spirit of Wine, the other by the Air. **1733** MILLER *Gard. Dict.* s.v. *Tan*, The Bark will begin to heat, and when it is found of a due Temper, the Plants may be removed into it. **1884** F. J. BRITTEN *Watch & Clockm.* 75 Sufficient heat will pass along the wire to lower the temper of the hole.

†8. Bodily habit, constitution, or condition. *Obs.*

Sometimes attributed to the various proportions in which the four humours are combined; sometimes to the combination of physical qualities: see TEMPERAMENT 3, 6.

1599 B. JONSON *Cynthia's Rev.* II. i, A creature of a most perfect and divine temper: one, in whom the humours and elements are peaceably met..he is neither too..melancholy, too..phlegmatic [etc.]. **1615** CROOKE *Body of Man* 272 The Temper of the whole body is to be esteemed according to the Temper of the principall parts, especially of the heart and the Liuer. **1634** W. WOOD *New Eng. Prosp.* I. ii, Agreeing well with the temper of our English bodies. **1650** [see EXQUISITENESS d]. **1653** H. MORE *Antid. Ath.* II. x. §7 (1712) 71 The Hare, whose temper and frame of body are plainly fitted on purpose for her Condition. **1661** LOVELL *Hist. Anim. & Min.* Introd. As for their [serpents'] temper, some are cold, and others hot. **1707** FLOYER *Physic. Pulse-Watch* 300 All the Climates above 45 towards the Æquator have exceeding Pulses, and Choleric thin Tempers and Habits.

9. Mental constitution; habitual disposition; = TEMPERAMENT 7.

1595 SHAKS. *John* V. ii. 40 A noble temper dost thou shew in this. **1611** —— *Wint. T.* IV. iv. 478 You know my Fathers temper: at this time He will allow no speech. **1669** STILLINGFL. *Serm. Whitsunday* ¶14 Did the being Christians alter their natural temper? **1720** HEARNE *Collect.* (O.H.S.) VII. 111 A Lady of a sweet Temper, strict Virtue. **1754** EDWARDS *Freed. Will* I. ii. 10 The particular Temper which the Mind has by Nature, or that has been introduced and established by Education, Example, Custom or some other Means. **1777** H. BLAIR *Serm.* (1780) II. 70 Temper is the disposition which remains after these emotions are past; and which forms the habitual propensity of the soul. **1842** BORROW *Bible in Spain* xlviii, He..had been educated for the Church, which not suiting his temper, he had abandoned. **1874** GREEN *Short Hist.* viii. §2. 466 The temper of the Puritan was eminently a temper of law.

10. a. Actual state or attitude of the mind or feelings; frame of mind; inclination, humour.

a **1628** PRESTON *New Covt.* (1634) 118 If thy heart continue in that temper, it is impossible. **1680** BURNET *Rochester* (1692) 62 Thereby to nourish a devout temper in us. **1719** DE FOE *Crusoe* I. 320 He brought me an Account of the Temper he found them in. **1777** BURKE *Let. Sheriffs Bristol* Wks. III. 162 A conciliatory temper must precede and prepare every plan of reconciliation. **1838** LYTTON *Leila* IV. vii, The excitement, the wrath of the troops, produced the temper most fit for action. **1855** MACAULAY *Hist. Eng.* xv. III. 501 The Commons were in no temper to listen to such excuses. **1875** JOWETT *Plato* (ed. 2) IV. 317, I would recommend you..not to encourage yourself in this polemical and controversial temper.

b. In ***good-temper***, ***ill-temper***, ***bad temper*** (the latter leading to sense 11).

1768 [implied in GOOD-TEMPERED]. **1792** A. YOUNG *Trav. France* 69 A feature of that good temper which appears to me so visible every where in France. **1793** BURKE *Cond. Minority* Wks. VII. 267 He would not be able to get the better of the ill temper, and the ill doctrines, he has been the means of exciting. **1828** WEBSTER s.v., Disposition of mind; the constitution of the mind, particularly with regard to the passions and affections; as, a calm temper; a hasty temper; a fretful temper. This is applicable to beasts as well as to man. *a* **1832** BENTHAM *Deontology* (1834) I. 26 *note*, The tranquillity and good temper of a disputant. **1855** Bad temper [see BAD *a.* 6]. **1884** J. HALL *Chr. Home* 159 Servants ..sometimes suffer from the ill-temper of their employers.

11. = *ill-temper*: Heat of mind or passion, showing itself by outbursts of irritation or anger upon slight provocation; explosive ill-humour.

1828 WEBSTER, *Temper*..5. Heat of mind or passion; irritation. The boy showed a great deal of temper when I reproved him. So we say, a man of violent temper, when we speak of his irritability. (This use of the word is common, though a deviation from its original and genuine meaning.) **1836** SMART, *Temper*,..from the original sense, calmness, moderation; by a special application of the latter derivative senses, heat, irritation. *a* **1846** J. W. CROKER (Worc.), Johnson, when the first ebullition of temper had subsided, felt that he had been unreasonably violent. **1880** CHURCH *Cathedral & Univ. Serm.* (1892) 197 What we all understand when we speak of a man 'showing temper'. **1900** ELEANOR GLYN *Visits Elizabeth* (1906) 21, I can't tell you, Mamma, what a temper I was in.

III. 12. Concrete senses, in technical use.

†a. Applied to mortar or plaster. *Obs. rare*$^{-1}$.

1594 PLAT *Jewell-ho.* I. 18 An olde wall whose temper was made of Lime and Sand.

b. *Sugar-making.* A solution containing lime or some other alkaline substance serving to neutralize the acid in the raw cane-juice and clarify it.

1657 R. LIGON *Barbadoes* 90 A liquor made of water and Withs which they call Temper. **1797** *Encycl. Brit.* (ed. 3) XVIII. 59/1 When the clarifier is filled, a fire is lighted, and a quantity of Bristol quicklime in powder..called temper, is poured into the vessel. **1839** URE *Dict. Arts* 1202 If an excess of temper be used, the gluten is taken up again by the strong affinity which..exist[s] between sugar and lime.

c. An alloy of tin and copper.

1875 KNIGHT *Dict. Mech.*, *Pewterer's Temper*, an alloy of 2 parts tin and 1 copper. **1885** *Encycl. Brit.* XVIII. 725/1 The finest pewter (sometimes called 'tin and temper') is simply tin hardened by the addition of a trifle of copper.

d. (See quot. 1975.)

1925 C. E. GUTHE *Pueblo Pottery Making* 20 The mixing ..consists of the addition of temper. **1936** K. M. CHAPMAN *Pottery of Santo Domingo Pueblo* 11 The clay and temper are moistened and kneaded together. **1955** BUSHNELL & DIGBY *Anc. Amer. Pottery* iv. 32 The temper is normally rather coarse, but in at least one of the three examples..it is very fine. **1975** R. L. BEALS *Peasant Marketing System of Oaxaca, Mexico* ii. 18 Temper used in pottery making is a coarse material such as sand or decomposed rock to make the clay more ductile and prevent cracking of the shaped vessel during drying.

IV. 13. *attrib.* and *Comb.*, as ***temper-fit***, ***-flaw***, ***tantrum***; ***temper-spoiling***, ***-wearing*** adjs.

1788 COWPER *Poet's N.-Y. Gift* ii, To wish thee fairer is no need,..Or more ingenious, or more freed From temper-flaws unsightly. **1884** W. JAMES in *Mind* IX. 199 In injuries to the brain..we have tears, laughter, and temper-fits, on the most insignificant provocation. **1893** *Outing* (U.S.) XXII. 121/2 Fly-fishing is pretty, but it is a futile and temper-spoiling art on a narrow, crooked, bush-grown brook. **1895** KIPLING in *Daily Chron.* 3 July 3/7 The mass of profitless, temper-wearing detail that attaches itself to any extended market-work. **1930** G. C. MYERS *Mod. Parent* x. 168 There are vague symptoms of temper tantrum at the age of several weeks when [an infant's] accustomed satisfactions are withheld. **1951** AUDEN *Nones* (1952) 11 Unable To conceive a god whose temper-tantrums are moral. **1980** *Jrnl. R. Soc. Med.* LXXIII. 217 The affected children themselves are liable to behavioural problems such as temper tantrums.

14. Special Comb. (perh. from stem of TEMPER *v.*): **temper-brittleness** *Metallurgy*, notch-brittleness produced in certain types of steel when it is held in or cooled slowly through a certain temperature range; hence **temper-brittle** *a.*; **temper-pot**: see quots.; **temper-screw**, a set-screw for adjustment; *esp.* in boring, a screw-connexion for automatically adjusting the drill as the boring proceeds. See also TEMPER-PIN.

1918 *Proc. Inst. Automobile Engin.* XII. 349 If an absolutely unnotched bar is taken and tested under impact conditions, it is frequently found that even if that bar happens to show the peculiar '*temper brittleness' it will bend over without any sign of brittleness in the unnotched state... There is..no difference..between the micro-structure of the 'temper-brittle' steel and the micro-structure of the same steel giving the good impact value. **1930** *Engineering* 24 Oct. 525/3 The metal had been rendered 'temper brittle' by being cooled too slowly in the tempering process. **1967** A. H. COTTRELL *Introd. Metallurgy* xx. 384 This temper-brittleness..is associated with fracture along grain boundaries. **1875** URE *Dict. Arts* III. 67 When ..the ladle becomes chilled, it is dipped into a small vessel containing lead of a higher temperature than that which is being worked, and known by the name of a *temper-pot. **1884** C. G. W. LOCK *Workshop Receipts* Ser. III. 361/2 The temper-pots hold about a ton of metal each. *a* **1864** GESNER *Coal, Petrol.*, etc. (1865) 28 The *Temper Screw is attached to a rope which connects with the end of the walking-beam, and serves to regulate the descent of the drill, without the inconvenience of lengthening the rope at short intervals. **1877** KNIGHT *Dict. Mech.*, *Temper-screw*,..one which brings its point against a bearing or an object. **1883** *Century Mag.* July 330/1 Then there is the 'temper-screw' which lowers the drilling apparatus inch by inch as it goes down.

temper ('tɛmpə(r)), *v.* Forms: 1 **temprian**, 3 **temprien**, (*Orm.*) **temmprenn**, 3–4 **tempren**, 3–6 **tempre**, (4–5 **tempire**, 4–6 **-ere**, **-ir**, **-or**, 5 **-yr**, **-ore**, 5–6 **-ier**), 4– **temper**. See also TAMPER *v.*^{1} [OE. *temprian* (so also in OS. *temperon*), ad. L. *temperāre* to divide or proportion duly, to mingle in due proportion, to combine properly; to qualify, temper; to arrange or keep in due measure or proportion, to keep within limits, to regulate, rule. Thence OF. *temprer* (12th c.), later (*trempren*) *tremper*, 13th c. in Godef. (whence TRAMP *v.*^{2} to soak); also *tempérer* (learned form after L.) to moderate by some mixture. The sense-development of the Eng. verb. was prob. influenced by the French. A differentiated form is TAMPER *v.*^{1}

L. *temperāre* is generally held to be a deriv. of *tempus*, *tempor-* a time or season, the proper time or season; but the sense history of both words is prehistoric and obscure: see Walde *Lat. Etymol.*]

I. 1. *trans.* To bring (anything) to a proper or suitable condition, state, or quality, by mingling with something else; to qualify, alloy, or dilute by such mixture or combination. Also *fig.* *arch.*

a **1000** *Blickl. Glosses* Ps. ci. 10 Potum meum cum fletu temperabam, *glossed* ic temprede. **13..** *K. Alis.* 7850

Venym he tok, and tempred hit with wyn. **1382** WYCLIF *1 Cor.* xii. 24 But god tempride the bodi [Vulg. *Deus temperavit corpus*], ȝyuynge more worschipe to it, to whom it failide. *c* **1425** tr. *Arderne's Surgery* (E.E.T.S.) 72 Þe ȝolk of a raw ey tempered with bole armoniac to sich þikknes þat it may by a clistery be ȝette into þe lure. **1486** *Bk. St. Albans* b vj b, Take Oyle of spayne and tempere it with clere wyne. **1544** PHAER *Pestilence* (1553) Mv, In a hote season it is good to temper ye said wine with a litle rose-water. *a* **1591** H. SMITH *Serm.* (1637) 134 As wine is tempered with water, so let discretion temper zeale. **1660** BURNEY *Κέρδ. Δῶρον* (1661) 110 To compound an absolute one (*Temperamentum ad pondus*) of the other 3 forms of Government [Spartan, Athenian, Roman], as the ingredients, and..tampering with Monarchy. **1711** ADDISON *Spect.* No. 106 ¶3 The good old Knight..tempered the Inquiries after his own Affairs with several kind Questions relating to themselves. **1756** NUGENT *Montesquieu's Spir. Laws* (1758) I. iv. viii. 55 There was a necessity for tempering them with others that might soften their manners.

2. a. To modify (some unsuitable or excessive state or quality, or some thing or person in respect of such), esp. by admixture of some other quality, etc.; to reduce to the suitable or desirable (middle) degree or condition free from excess in either direction; to moderate, mitigate, assuage, tone down.

c **1000** ÆLFRIC *Hom.* II. 46 And eft ȝetemprie seo bile-witnys þæt fyr, þæt hit to reðe ne sy. *a* **1050** *Liber Scintill.* x. 52 Bryne lichamena mid ealdrum estum to temprigenne ys [L. *temperandus est*]. *c* **1200** ORMIN 2893 Forr aȝȝ birrþ rihhtwisnesse ben þurrh mildheorrtnesse temmpredd. *a* **1340** HAMPOLE *Psalter* cvi. 29 þe persecuciouns he tempird and made þaim suffrabil. **1552** HULOET, Temper sorow with mirth. **1596** SPENSER *State Irel.* Pref. 2 We may wish that in some passages it had bin tempered with more moderation. **1596** BACON *Max. & Use Com. Law* Ep. Ded. (1636) 3 Kings which..do temper their magnanimity with justice. **1768** STERNE *Sent. Journ.* (1778) II. 176 (*Maria*) God tempers the wind, said Maria, to the shorn lamb. **1781** J. MOORE *View Soc. It.* (1790) I. xxxix. 420 Our admiration of the Romans is tempered with horror. **1834** MRS. SOMERVILLE *Connex. Phys. Sc.* xxvi. (1849) 291 The cold currents from the poles tempering the intense heat of the equatorial regions. **1871** MACDUFF *Mem. Patmos* x. 132 He ..who tempers judgment with mercy. **1878** HUXLEY *Physiogr.* 80 In tempering the activity of the oxygen with which it is associated.

b. *intr.* (for *pass.*)

1860 DICKENS *Uncomm. Trav.* ix, A flavour of damaged oranges, which, a little further down towards the river, tempered into herrings, and gradually toned into a cosmopolitan blast of fish.

3. To mix, mingle, blend (ingredients) *together*, or (one ingredient) *with* another, in proper proportions. Also *fig. arch.*

c **1386** CHAUCER *Can. Yeom. Prol. & T.* 348 Er þat the pot be on the fir ydo Of metals with a certeyn quantitee My lord hem tempreth and no man but he. *c* **1440** *Promp. Parv.* 488/1 Temperyn, or menge to-gedur, *commisceo, misceo.* **1530** PALSGR. 754/1 Whan metalles be well tempered togyther they wyll be all as one. **1671** J. WEBSTER *Metallogr.* v. 88 They are said to grow of sulphur and argent vive mixt and tempered together. **1759** J. MILLS *Duhamel's Husb.* I. viii. (1762) 21 To fling and temper amongst it ashes or chalk. **1876** BLACKIE *Songs Relig. & Life* 195 If wisely you temper, and skilfully blend The hard-headed Scot with the quick-witted Grecian.

4. To prepare by mingling; to make by due mixture or combination; to concoct, compound, compose, make up, devise. *lit.* and *fig. Obs.* or *arch.*

1390 GOWER *Conf.* III. 10 In cold I brenne and frese in hete: And thanne I drinke a biter swete With dreie lippe and yhen wete. Lo, thus I tempre mi diete. **1542** UDALL *Erasm. Apoph.* 195 He wrote..to Pausanias his physician that he should..tempre drynkes and medecines for hym. *a* **1569** KINGESMYLL *Man's Est.* ix. (1580) 44 But there is a strong medicine a temperyng. **1600** HOLLAND *Livy* VIII. xviii. 294 That certain dames of Rome..boiled and tempered ranke poisons (to kill their husbands). **1650** BULWER *Anthropomet.* 155 Sometimes they will temper a certaine Colour, with Hens dung and Saffron.

†**5.** To restore the proper 'temper' or 'temperament' to; to bring into a good or desirable state of body or health; to cure, heal, refresh.

c **1000** ÆLFRIC *Hom.* I. 474 Se ðe wile mid soðum læce-cræfte his lichaman ȝetemprian, swa swa dyde se witeȝa Isaias. *c* **1430** LYDG. *Min. Poems* (Percy Soc.) 196 Ayer of nature yevith inspiracioun..To tempre the spiritis by vertu vegetatiff. **1486** *Bk. St. Albans* b ij b, Bot it tempur yowre hawke, that is to say ensayme yowre hawke with in .iiij. days, I meruell. **1561** HOLLYBUSH *Hom. Apoth.* 44 b, He may drinke a litle wyne vpon it, to tempere hys mouth of the bitternesse. **1613** PURCHAS *Pilgrimage* III. xvii. 284 Gallus, a riuer..the waters whereof, temperatly drunken, did exceedingly temper the braine, and take away madnes.

6. To bring into a suitable or desirable frame of mind; to dispose favourably, to persuade; also, to appease, mollify, pacify. *Obs.* or *arch.*

1525 LD. BERNERS *Froiss.* II. xci. [lxxxvii.] 271 If he be nat reasonable, the duke of Berrey and the duke of Burgoyne wyll so temper hym, that ye shal be frendes and cosyn to the kynge. **1546** *St. Papers Hen. VIII*, XI. 44 How moch the Emperour hath doone soo to tempre the French King, it appered in his last bargayn with Fraunce. **1588** SHAKS. *Tit. A.* IV. iv. 109 Now will I to that old Andronicus, And temper him with all the Art I haue, To plucke proud Lucius from the warlike Gothes. **1678** TEMPLE *Let. to Sir L. Jenkins* Wks. 1731 II. 470, I found both the King and the Duke growing so angry upon it, that I thought it my part to temper them as far as I could. **1710** STEELE *Tatler* No. 194 ¶7 The Lady so well tempered and reconciled them both, that She forced them to join Hands. **1874** BUSHNELL *Forgiven. & Law* 59 Is it true that God must be gained or tempered transactionally ..in order to the letting forth of grace upon his enemies?

II. 7. To keep, conduct, or manage in just measure; to regulate; to control, direct, guide, rule, govern, overrule. *Obs.* exc. *dial.*

c **1000** *Sax. Leechd.* III. 250 Ac heo [seo sunne] temprað ða eorðlican wæstmas æȝðer ȝe on wæstme ȝe on ripunge. **13..** *Coer de L.* 659 Kyng Rychard the fyre bet, Thomas to the spytte hym set, Fouk Doyly tempryd the wood. *a* **1340** HAMPOLE *Pr. Consc.* 7616 Þai [the heavens] tempre þe streng[t]he of alle þe elementes. *c* **1400** GOWER *Praise of Peace* 160 Though thou the werres darst wel undirtake, Aftir reson yit tempre thi corage. *c* **1440** *Promp. Parv.* 488/1 Temporyn, or sette yn mesure, *tempero.* **1528** TINDALE *Obed. Chr. Man* 148 b, All the Apostles chose two..and cast lottes desyringe God to temper them that the lotte myght fall on the most ablest. **1576** GOSSON *Spec. Hum.* vi. in *Sch. Abuse* (Arb.) 77 Thou God..that..turnes the spheares, and tempers all on hie. **1591** SPENSER *M. Hubberd* 1294 His snakie wand, With which the damned ghosts he governeth, And furies rules and Tartare tempereth. **1659** LEAK *Waterwks.* 32 There is a Pipe with a Cock..which serves to temper the course of the Water. **1725** POPE *Odyss.* IV. 326 Supremest Jove Tempers the fates of human race above. **1835** D. WEBSTER *Orig. Scot. Rhymes* 152 (E.D.D.) This birkie bodie can wi' speed Temper yer ilka thrum and thread.

8. a. To restrain within due limits, or within the bounds of moderation; in later use often simply, to restrain, check, curb.

a **1050** *Liber Scintill.* xxviii. (1889) 107 Forþi hi na tempredon [L. *non temperauerunt*] ȝefernysse hætan. **1297** R. GLOUC. (Rolls) 1624 He dude hom ssame ynou & temprede hom vol wel & made hom sone milde ynou þo hii were rebel. **13..** *E.E. Allit. P.* B. 775 ȝif þou tynez þat toun, tempre þyn yre. *c* **1394** *P. Pl. Crede* 743 To toilen wiþ þe erþe, Tylen & trewliche lyven & her flech tempren. *c* **1400** *Brut* 31 Lud his sone..gouernede wel þe lande, and miche honourrede gode folc, and temprede and amendit wickede folc. **1538** STARKEY *England* I. iv. 120 Yf we coude fynd a way to tempur and refrayne thayr malyce. **1599** *Warn. Faire Wom.* II. 737 Learne to temper your excessive griefe. **1777** ROBERTSON *Hist. Amer.* II. v. 81 Cortes..was more solicitous to temper than to inflame their ardour. **1821** BYRON *Sardan.* I. ii. 347 Since they are tumultuous, Let them be temper'd, yet not roughly.

†**b.** *refl.* To control or restrain oneself. *Obs.*

c **1000** ÆLFRIC *Hom.* I. 360 An is, þæt ȝehwa hine sylfne ȝetempriȝe mid ȝemete on æte and on wæte. **13..** *Cursor M.* 17244 (Cott.) For-sak þi serc o silk and line, And temper þe wit[h] alle and wine. **1531** ELYOT *Gov.* III. xxiv. (1883) 379 He coulde nat tempre him selfe in redyng Greke bokes whyles the Senate was syttyng. **1600** HOLLAND *Livy* v. xlv. 209 So as they could scarcely temper themselves and forbeare, but presently set upon them. **1651** HOBBES *Govt. & Soc.* vii. §4. 114, I wish that not onely Kings, but all other Persons..would so temper themselves as to commit no wrong.

†**c.** *refl.* To restrain oneself or refrain *from* (†*of*).

1560 DAUS tr. *Sleidane's Comm.* 100 b, Warnyng men to tempre themselues from entryng in to wycked warres. **1561** T. NORTON *Calvin's Inst.* I. 42 If the readers will temper them of curiositie, and not more gredily than mete is, seke for combersome and entangled disputations. **1658** W. BURTON *Itin. Anton.* 180, I could not temper my self..from causing his discourse to be transcribed hither.

9. To regulate suitably to need or requirement; to fit, adapt, conform, accommodate, make suitable. Const. *to.* Now *rare* or *Obs.*

1450–1530 *Myrr. our Ladye* 86 The sufferaunce of god, whyche temperyth all thynges to hys seruauntes, as they may bere to theyr mooste profyt. **1573–80** BARET *Alv.* T 113 To Temper his talke to the fantasie and pleasure. **1649** MILTON *Eikon.* i. 5 They were indeed not temper'd to his temper. **1662** STILLINGFL. *Orig. Sacr.* II. v. §8 God tempered the Ceremoniall Law much according to the condition and capacity of the persons it was prescribed to. **1665** MANLEY *Grotius' Low C. Warres* 243 If the one King ..had tempered himself and his Laws, according to the strength and prevalence of parties.

III. Various technical uses.

10. To bring (clay, mortar, etc.) to a proper consistence for use by mixing and working it up *with* water, etc. Also *fig.*

13.. *Cursor M.* 22940 (Fairf.) Þe potter..al new he tempris his clay. **1387** TREVISA *Higden* (Rolls) I. 271 Whan þat stoon is i-tempred wiþ water and torned to playstre. *c* **1400** *Brut* 57 Wille ȝe slee me for my blode forto temper wiþ ȝoure morter? **1535** COVERDALE *Ecclus.* xxxviii. 30 He fashioneth the claye with his arme, and with his fete he tempereth it. **1617** MORYSON *Itin.* I. 32 Lime tempered, not with water, but with wine, incredibly durable. **1719** YOUNG *Busiris* v. i, Yes, I will..temper all my cement with their blood. **1884** C. T. DAVIS *Manuf. Bricks*, etc. v. (1889) 130 The object of tempering the clay is to thoroughly mix it, and prepare the material for the use of the moulder.

†**11. a.** To moisten (a substance, usually medicinal or culinary ingredients in a comminuted state) so as to form a paste or mixture; to mix to a paste.

c **1400** MAUNDEV. (Roxb.) xxi. 94 Take þe lefes..and stampe þam and tempre þam with water and drink it. *c* **1400** *Rom. Rose* 4180 A plastre dolorous..Which is not tempred with vynegre, But with poverte & indigence. *c* **1440** *Anc. Cookery* in *Househ. Ord.* (1790) 426 Take soden porke and grynde hit smal, and tempur hit with rawe yolkes of eyren. **1563** T. GALE *Antidot.* II. 15 The herbes must be mixed and tempered with Axungia. **1668** CULPEPPER & COLE *Barthol. Anat.* I. ix. 22 Some moisture to temper the meat and make it liquid. **1674** RAY *Collect. Words, Smelting Silver* 115 With water tempered into a past to a due quality.

b. *spec.* in *Painting*: To prepare (colours) for use by mixing them with oil, etc.

1531 ELYOT *Gov.* III. xix. (1883) 318 In temperynge his colours, he lacked good size, wherwith they shulde have ben bounden, and made to endure. **1691** RAY *Creation* I. (1692) 97 The most skilful Painter cannot so mingle and temper his Colours. **1837** SIR F. PALGRAVE *Merch. & Friar* (1844) 9 The metallic or body colours are to be tempered or mixed with oil. **1859** SALA *Gaslight & D.* ii. 25 Colours..ground in water, and subsequently tempered with size.

†**12.** To steep or dissolve (a substance) in a liquid (cf. TRAMP *v.*[2]); *fig.* to drench, suffuse. *Obs.*

c **1489** CAXTON *Blanchardyn* 147 Wyth eyen all tempred wyth teerys. **1530** PALSGR. 754/1, I temper, I laye breed or other thynges in stepe... You muste temper your breed in vynayger. **1600** HOLLAND *Livy* XXX. xv. 750 Which [poison] hee commaunded him to temper in a goblet of wine, and to carie it to Sophonisba. **1669** STURMY *Mariner's Mag.* VII. xxxiv. 50 Take blew Smalts, temper it in Water, and rub the Picture with it.

†**13.** *trans.* To soften (iron, wax, etc.) by heating; to melt. Also *intr.* for *pass. Obs.*

1535 COVERDALE *Isa.* xliv. 12 The smyth taketh yron, and tempreth it with hote coles, and fashioneth it with hammers. **1590** SIR J. SMYTH *Disc. Weapons* 19 b, The Archers did vse to temper with fire a conuenient quantitie of waxe, rosen, and fine tallowe together. **1597** SHAKS. *2 Hen. IV*, IV. iii. 140, I haue him alreadie tempering betweene my finger and my thombe, and shortly will I seale with him.

14. a. To bring (steel) to a suitable degree of hardness and elasticity or resiliency by heating it to the required temperature and immersing it, while hot, in some liquid, usually cold water; applied also to the hardening of copper, etc. Also *fig.*

c **1381** CHAUCER *Parl. Foules* 214, I say Cupide..hise arwis forge & file..And wel his doughtyr temperede al this whyle The heuedis in the welle. **14..** *Tundale's Vis.* 1059 As men shulde temper irne or stele. **1530** PALSGR. 754/1 They have a great advauntage in Spayne, to temper their blades well, bycause of the nature of their ryvers. **1603** HOLLAND *Plutarch's Mor.* 115 We must doe as the Smithes who temper yron: For when they have given it a fire, and made it by that meanes soft, loose and pliable, they drench and dip it in cold water, whereby it becommeth compact and hard, taking thereby the due temperature of stiffe steele. **1758** REID tr. *Macquer's Chym.* I. 64 The hardness of Steel may be considerably augmented by tempering it; that is, by making it red-hot, and suddenly quenching it in some cold liquor. **1881** *Metal World* No. 8. 121 This they converted into the purest steel, and tempered to the hardest and yet the most elastic pitch.

b. *intr.* (for *pass.*).

1881 RAYMOND *Mining Gloss.* s.v., A metallic compound in which these qualities [hardness and elasticity] can thus be produced is said to temper, or to take temper. **1884** W. H. GREENWOOD *Steel & Iron* xvii. §669 Mild steel containing from 0·05 to 0·20 per cent. of carbon will weld, but does not temper.

c. *trans.* To reduce the brittleness in (hardened steel) by reheating it to a certain temperature and allowing it to cool. Cf. ANNEAL *v.* 4.

1925 *Jrnl. Iron & Steel Inst.* CXI. 334 Careful observations made on specimens which had been tempered just below 200°C. **1967** A. H. COTTRELL *Introd. Metallurgy* xx. 384 If plain carbon or low-alloy steels are tempered below about 250°C they usually remain somewhat brittle.

†**15. a.** To tune, adjust the pitch of (a musical instrument). *Obs.* exc. as in b.

c **1300** *Prov. Hending* x. in *Salomon & Sat.*, etc. (1848) 272 He nul no gle bygynne er he haue tempred is pype. **1390** GOWER *Conf.* III. 301 He takth the Harpe and in his wise He tempreth, and of such assise Singende he harpeth forth withal. **1575** LANEHAM *Let.* (1871) 41 For fyling his napkin, temperd a string or too with his wreast. **1593** *Bacchus Bountie* in *Harl. Misc.* (Malh.) II. 274 Whereupon M. Barlycap tempered up his fiddle, and began.

b. *spec.* To tune (a note or instrument) according to some temperament: see TEMPERAMENT 10. See also TEMPERED 1 e.

1727–41 CHAMBERS *Cycl.* s.v. *Temperament*, To mend these imperfect concords, the musicians have bethought themselves to temper, i.e. give them part of the agreeableness of perfect ones... All such divisions of the octave are called tempered, or temperative systems. **1788** CAVALLO in *Phil. Trans.* LXXVIII. 250 All the fifths, all the thirds, and in short all the chords of the same denomination, are equally tempered throughout. **1875** A. J. ELLIS tr. *Helmholtz' Sensat. Tone* III. xvi. 509 It is clearly not necessary to temper the instruments to which the singer practises.

16. To bring into harmony, attune. Const. *to. Obs.* or *arch.*

c **1374** CHAUCER *Boeth.* III. met. xii. 84 (Camb. MS.) And there he [Orpheus] temprede hise blaundysshynge soonges by resownynge strenges. **1637** MILTON *Lycidas* 33 Mean while the Rural ditties were not mute, Temper'd to th' Oaten Flute. **1754** GRAY *Progr. Poesy* 26 Thee the voice, the dance, obey, Temper'd to thy warbled lay. **1860** WARTER *Sea-board* II. 367 If we make melody in our hearts, and if our souls are tempered to harmony, then is the Divinity enlarged within us.

17. To set or adjust the share and other parts of (a plough) in the proper position for making the furrow of the required depth and width. ?*Obs.*

1523 FITZHERB. *Husb.* §4 It is necessarye for an housbande to knowe howe these plowes shulde be tempered, to plowe and turne clene, and to make no reste balkes. *Ibid.*, All these maner of plowes shulde haue all lyke one maner of temperyng in the yrens. **1844** STEPHENS *Bk. Farm* I. 33 The ploughman will be able to afford him ocular proof how he places (*tempers*) all the irons of the plough in relation to the state of the land. *Ibid.* 404 To 'temper a plough' is the great aim of the good ploughman.

†**18.** To regulate (a clock). *Sc. Obs.*

1538 *Aberdeen Regr.* (1844) I. 157 For his gud seruice to be done in keiping and temporing of thair knok within the tolbuth, for his fee. **1592–3** in *Spottiswoode Misc.* (1845) II. 269 Wnderstanding the great pains and travels of Archibald Stedman in tempering the knock.

19. To increase the pliability of straw for corn-dolly making by dampening it with water.

1963 M. LAMBETH *Golden Dolly* 11 When plaiting out of season it is necessary to temper the straw. **1976** S. J. REID *Art of Weaving Corn Dollies* 9 After a period of storage.., straw dries out... To restore it to a supple condition it is necessary to temper (or dampen) the straw.

temper, obs. var. TAMPER *v.*; obs. f. TEMPTER; var. TEMPRE *a. Obs.*

‖**tempera** ('tɛmpərə). Also 9 **tempra**. [It. *tempera*, in phr. *pingere a tempera* to paint in distemper.] The method of painting in distemper: see DISTEMPER *sb.*[2] 1.

1832 GELL *Pompeiana* I. viii. 148 A beautiful Venus painted in tempra. **1888** *Encycl. Brit.* XXIII. 157/2 Tempera is called in Italy 'fresco a secco' as distinguished from 'fresco buono', or true fresco, painted on freshly laid patches of stucco. *a* **1890** W. B. SCOTT *Autobiogr. Notes* I. 168 The best preserved early pictures there [Italy] are tempera, not fresco.

b. *Comb.*, as ***tempera-painting***, ***-picture***.

1862 THORNBURY *Turner* I. 142 Passages of transparent colour, either upon white grounds, or introduced to enrich tempera pictures. **1898** HUEFFER in *Contemp. Rev.* Aug. 185 In the same year, he again attempted tempera-painting.

temperable ('tɛmpərəb(ə)l), *a.* Now *rare.* [prob. ad. med.L. *temperābil-is*; but perh. f. TEMPER *sb.* and *v.* + -ABLE: cf. *agreeable*, *customable*, *peaceable.*] †**a.** Of weather or climate: = TEMPERATE *a.* 3. †**b.** Of a person: = TEMPERATE *a.* 1.

c **1400** *Lanfranc's Cirurg.* 16 In somer he muste haue temperable eir. *c* **1450** LOVELICH *Grail* xxxvi. 496 That he myhte beste herberwed to be, Into Most temperable place Abowtes þe see. **1570** LEVINS *Manip.* 4/18 Temperable, *temperabilis.* **1618** BOLTON *Florus* I. viii. 30 That the fierce people might bee made temperable, through the feare of the Gods. **1629** MAXWELL tr. *Herodian* (1635) 31 Yet for a while, was the Prince more temperable, out of respect to his Fathers memory, and his Counsellours gravitie.

c. That may be tempered or made plastic.

1841 EMERSON *Ess., Hist.* ¶44 The fusible, hard, and temperable texture of metals.

Hence **tempera'bility** (*Funk's Stand. Dict.* 1895).

†**tempe'rade.** *Obs.* (See quot.)

a **1700** B. E. *Dict. Cant. Crew*, *Temperade*, an East-Indian-dish, now in use in England, being a Fowl Fricasied, with high Sauce, Blancht Almonds and Rice.

'**temperal**, *a. nonce-wd.* [f. TEMPER *sb.* + -AL[1].] Of, pertaining to, or resulting from tempering.

1816 ACCUM *Chem. Tests* (1818) 206 Other articles of steel ..either bend or lose their shape in the hardening..or resist the tool, when wrought in the temperal state.

temperal(l, -alite, -alte, obs. ff. TEMPORAL, -ALITY, -ALTY.

†**temperality.** *Obs.* Humorously misused for TEMPER or TEMPERATURE.

1597 SHAKS. *2 Hen. IV*, II. iv. 25 Me thinkes now you are in an excellent good temperalitie.

temperament ('tɛmpərəmənt), *sb.* Also 5 **temperment**. [ad. L. *temperāmentum* due mixture, f. *temperāre* to TEMPER: see -MENT. So Fr. *tempérament* (16th c. in Godef. *Compl.*).]

I. †**1.** A moderate and proportionable mixture of elements in a compound; the condition in which elements are combined in their due proportions.

? *a* **1412** LYDG. *Two Merch.* 303 Yiff..heete or blood passe his temperament, In to a fevere anoon a man it leedith. **1576** NEWTON *Lemnie's Complex.* (1633) 50 Crasis or Temperament..is an agreement, and conveniency of the first qualities and Elements among themselves: Or, an equall mixture or proportion of the qualities of the Elements, wherein no excesse blame-worthy or faulty is to be found. **1658** PHILLIPS, *Temperament*, a moderate and proportionable mixture of any thing, but more peculiarly of the four humours of the body. **1684** tr. *Bonet's Merc. Compit.* IV. 124 The cure of a wasting Flux..consists in the restitution of the temperament. **1684** J. P. tr. *Frambresar. Art Physick* i. 18 A Temperament is a proportion of the four chief Elementary Qualities proper for the true exercise of the Natural Functions.

†**2.** State or condition with respect to the proportion of ingredients or manner of mixing; consistence, composition; mixture. *Obs.*

1471 RIPLEY *Comp. Alch.* IV. xiv. in Ashm. *Theat. Chem. Brit.* (1652) 147 A temperament not so thyk as the Body ys, Nother so thyn as Water. **1610** BARROUGH *Meth. Physick* VIII. (1639) 469 Boyle it again until it come to the temperament of an ointment. **1641** MILTON *Reform.* II. Wks. 1851 III. 57 The best founded Commonwealths.. have aym'd at a certaine mixture and temperament, partaking the severall vertues of each other State. **1660** N. INGELO *Bentiv. & Ur.* II. (1682) 203 That the Soul is not a Temperament of Corporeal Humours is manifest. *a* **1673** J. CARYL in Spurgeon *Treas. Dav.* Ps. lxvi. 12 A due temperament of heat and cold, of dryness and moistness.

II. †**3.** In the natural philosophy of the Middle Ages: The combination of supposed qualities (*hot* or *cold*, *moist* or *dry*) in a certain proportion, determining the nature of a plant or other body (= COMPLEXION *sb.* 1); characteristic nature; known *spec.* as ***universal temperament*** (cf. 6). *Obs.*

1471 RIPLEY *Comp. Alch.* I. xviii. in Ashm. *Theat. Chem. Brit.* (1652) 133 For soe to temperment ys brought our Stone, And Natures contraryose, fower be made one. **1578** LYTE *Dodoens* I. lxvi. 97 Some men write of this herbe [Water Plantayne], that it is of temperament colde and dry. **1612** WOODALL *Surg. Mate* Wks. (1653) 209 Let no man attribute to all salts one temperament. **1665** G. HAVERS *P. della Valle's Trav. E. India* 70 Of temperament, 'tis held to be hot, and good to promote digestion. *a* **1677** HALE *Prim. Orig. Man.* II. iv. 153 The experience of various temperaments and operations of those Herbs.

4. The condition of the weather or climate as resulting from the different combinations of the qualities, heat or cold, dryness or humidity; climate. *Obs.* or *arch.*

1610 BARROUGH *Meth. Physick* IV. xiii. (1639) 245 Of all temperaments of the aire, the worst is that which is hot and moist. **1684** R. WALLER *Nat. Exper.* 10 Not onely from the season of the Year, and temperament of the Air, but from the Nature of the Soils and Countries themselves. **1713** DERHAM *Phys.-Theol.* I. ii. 17 The Cause assigned to malignant, epidemical Diseases;—and that is, an hot and moist Temperament of the Air. **1822–34** *Good's Study Med.* (ed. 4) I. 459 Change of air..where the difference of temperament, or even of temperature, can be rendered very considerable. **1875** JOWETT *Plato* (ed. 2) I. 492 The temperament of their seasons is such that they have no disease.

†**5.** Condition with regard to warmth or coldness; = TEMPERATURE 7. *Obs.*

1658 A. FOX *Würtz' Surg.* IV. i. 304 Wound Unguents and wound Plaisters should alwaies stand in one temperament. *a* **1704** LOCKE *Elem. Nat. Phil.* xi. (1754) 51 Bodies are denominated hot and cold in proportion to the present temperament of that part of our body to which they are applied. **1741** *Compl. Fam.-Piece* II. iii. 352 To keep up your Heat to the same Temperament. **1799** *Phil. Mag.* III. 419 A given quantity of cold water, or water of any given temperament.

6. In mediæval physiology: The combination of the four cardinal humours (see HUMOUR *sb.* 2b) of the body, by the relative proportion of which the physical and mental constitution were held to be determined; known *spec.* as ***animal temperament***; also, The bodily habit attributed to this, as ***a sanguine, choleric, phlegmatic***, or ***melancholic temperament*** (see the adjs.). See TEMPER *sb.* 8.

In modern use the term *temperament* and the names of the four temperaments continue, without any theory of combination of humours.

1628 FELTHAM *Resolves* II [I.] xxx. 95 Though the soule be not caused by the body; yet in the generall it followes the temperament of it. **1652** BP. HALL *Invisible World* II. §1 Galen was not a better Physician than an ill Divine, while he determines the soul to be the complexion and temperament of the prime qualities. **1657** TOMLINSON *Renou's Disp.* 10 That [Medicament]..which..doth work a manifest mutation on our bodies,..either in temperament, in matter or form. **1676** DRYDEN *Aurengzebe* Ded., Our Minds are perpetually wrought on by the Temperaments of our Bodies. **1727–41** CHAMBERS *Cycl.* s.v., The ancient physicians brought these animal temperaments to correspond with the universal temperament..: the sanguine temperament was supposed to coincide with hot and moist, the phlegmatic with cold and moist [etc.]. **1818** T. L. PEACOCK *Nightmare Abb.* i, This gentleman was naturally of an atrabilarious temperament. **1836** A. WALKER *Beauty in Wom.* 202 The ancients classed individuals in one or other of four temperaments, founded on the hypothesis of four humours,..the red part [of the blood], phlegm, yellow, and black bile... Hence were derived the names of the sanguine, the phlegmatic, the choleric, and the melancholic temperaments. **1843** R. J. GRAVES *Syst. Clin. Med.* xxxi. 421 Edward Fitzgerald, labourer... temperament sanguineous.

7. Constitution or habit of mind, esp. as depending upon or connected with physical constitution; natural disposition; = TEMPER *sb.* 9.

1821 BYRON *Juan* III. liii, He was a man of a strange temperament. **1842** MRS. BROWNING *Grk. Chr. Poets* 135 The poetic temperament. **1843** LYTTON *Last Bar.* III. v, Despite this general smoothness of mien, his temperament was naturally irritable [and] quick. **1856** EMERSON *Eng. Traits, Truth* Wks. (Bohn) II. 55 A slow temperament makes them less rapid and ready than other countrymen. **1868** MISS BRADDON *Dead Sea Fr.* III. v. 64 Visions..such ..as the man of sanguine temperament can always evolve. **1873** HAMERTON *Intell. Life* I. iv. (1875) 25 The active temperament likes physical action for its own sake. **1891** *Speaker* 2 May 534/1 The unbiassed temperament which is essential to the true historian. **1894** W. B. CARPENTER *Son of Man amg. Sons of Men* v, Temperament is a convenient phrase to describe those qualities and dispositions which belong to him from birth.

III. The action or fact of tempering.

8. Moderating, moderation; lightening, alleviation, mitigation; due regulation. *Obs.* or *arch.*

1475 *Rolls of Parlt.* VI. 144/2 That a dewe moderation and temperament be observed. **1576** NEWTON *Lemnie's Complex.* (1633) 2 Unlesse he have the knowledge of his owne body, and be ripe and skilfull in the temperament thereof. **1697** BP. PATRICK *Comm. Exod.* xxii. 11 But there were some Temperaments of this Law; for every Man was not admitted to purge himself by an Oath. **1861** *Temple Bar Mag.* IV. 54 That a certain temperament of speed was ensured.

9. The action of duly combining or adjusting different principles, claims, etc.; adjustment, compromise. *Obs.* or *arch.*

1660 *Trial Regic.* 12 There is that excellent Temperament in our laws, that..the King cannot rule, but by His Laws. **1678** SIR G. MACKENZIE *Crim. Laws Scot.* II. xxiv. §6 (1699) 261 By this just Temperament, the Interest of the Commonwealth, and the Imbicility of Minors are both salved. **1686** F. SPENCE tr. *Varillas' Ho. Medicis* 52 The friends of Piero ..propounded a temperament which equally fitted the king of Naples and duke of Milan's turn. **1790** BURKE *Fr. Rev.* 86 These admit no temperament and no compromise. **1794** —— *Corr.* (1844) IV. 253 There is no medium,—there is no temperament, there is no compromise with Jacobinism. **1818** HALLAM *Mid. Ages* (1872) II. iv. 43 As a fortunate temperament of law and justice with the royal authority.

b. A middle course or state between extremes of any kind; a medium, mean. *Obs.* or *arch.*

1604 R. CAWDREY *Table Alph.*, *Temperament*, temperatenesse, meane, or due proportion. **1656** BLOUNT *Glossogr.*, *Temperament*,..a moderation, mean or measure. **1697** tr. *C'tess D'Aunoy's Trav.* (1706) 45 Wearied and tired, roasted by the heat of the Sun, or frozen by the Snows (for there is seldom any Temperament between these Two Extreams). **1741** MIDDLETON *Cicero* II. xi. 476 Rewards and punishments; in which..as in every thing else, a certain medium and temperament is to be observed. **1823** BENTHAM *Not Paul* 249 The causes..of this temperament—this *mezzo termino*—this middle course. **1827** HALLAM *Const. Hist.* (1876) I. ii. §4. 88 A judicious temperament, which the reformers would have done well to adopt in some other points.

10. *Mus.* The adjustment of the intervals of the scale (in the tuning of instruments of fixed intonation, as keyboard instruments), so as to adapt them to the purposes of practical harmony: consisting in slight variations of the pitch of the notes from true or 'just' intonation in order to make them available in different keys; a particular system of doing this. (Sometimes extended to any system of tuning, including that of just intonation.)

The chief temperaments that have been practically used are ***mean-tone temperament*** (see MEAN TONE); and ***equal temperament*** (now almost universal), in which the octave is divided into twelve (theoretically) equal semitones, so that the variations of pitch are evenly distributed throughout all keys.

1727–41 CHAMBERS *Cycl.*, *Temperament*,..in music, denotes a rectifying or mending the false or imperfect concords, by transferring to them part of the beauty of the perfect ones. **1788** CAVALLO in *Phil. Trans.* LXXVIII. 242 This alteration of the just lengths of strings, necessary for adapting them to several key-notes, is called the temperament. **1881** BROADHOUSE *Mus. Acoustics* 354 Mean tone temperament was perfected by Salinas, A.D. 1577. *Ibid.* 356 The principle usually adopted at the present day for all keyed instruments is that called 'Equal Temperament', which professes to divide the octave into twelve exactly equal parts, though it does not actually so divide it. **1898** STAINER & BARRETT *Dict. Mus. Terms* 437/1 The question of melodic progressions, as affecting the excellence of temperaments, is too extensive for our limits.

'**temperament**, *v. rare.* [f. prec. sb.] *trans.* To endow with a temperament; in '**tempera-mented**, '**temperamenting** *ppl. adjs.*

1855 EMERSON *Woman* Misc. (1884) 349 Men are not to the same degree temperamented. **1870** —— *Soc. & Solit.*, *Work & Days* Wks. (Bohn) III. 70 The earth with its foods; the intellectual temperamenting air;..are given immeasurably to all.

temperamental (tɛmpərə'mɛntəl), *a.* [f. TEMPERAMENT *sb.* + -AL[1].]

1. Of or relating to the temperament (chiefly in sense 7); constitutional.

1646 SIR T. BROWNE *Pseud. Ep.* 18 By a temperamentall inactivity we are unready to put in execution the suggestions or dictates of reason. **1650** CHARLETON *Paradoxes* 139 The constitution or temperamentall disposition of the organ. **1812** COLERIDGE in *Lit. Rem.* (1836) I. 381 These temperamental *pro*-virtues will too often fail. **1824** *New Monthly Mag.* XI. 321 In spite of her temperamental gaiety ..she had moments of intense melancholy. **1907** H. WALES *The Yoke* i, People there are who appear to have been given a special temperamental adaptation for an ascetic and abstinent life.

2. Of a person: liable to peculiar moods, having or giving way to an erratic or neurotic temperament. Hence, of a thing: behaving erratically or unpredictably.

1907 *Amer. Mag.* LXIII. 355/2 The Celtic race is above all things temperamental. **1923** E. WALLACE *Clue of New Pin* xxix. 255 Tab decided that she was a little temperamental, and loved her for it. **1939** F. THOMPSON *Lark Rise* iii. 42 A temperamental person was said to be 'one o' them as is either up on the roof or down the well'. **1962** *Amer. N. & Q.* I. 31/1 The horse was particularly suitable in northern Europe where the temperamental climate often made rapid ploughing and planting important. **1965** *Wireless World* Sept. 436/1 He [*sc.* Dr. W. H. Eccles] also started a study of the coherer, the only detector of the period, which led to a better understanding of the action of that temperamental device. **1977** M. DRABBLE *Ice Age* i. 79 The central heating worked, and he had boosted it with an electric fire, albeit a temperamental electric fire, which needed the occasional kick.

Hence ˌ**tempera'mentalist**, a temperamental person. *rare.*

1924 *Blackw. Mag.* June 786/1, I was what you might call a temperamentalist, and very easily hypnotised.

tempera'mentally, *adv.* [f. prec. + -LY².] By temperament; constitutionally.

1861 *Romance Dull Life* xxviii. 204 They were both temperamentally incapacitated for catching a prevalent emotion. **1908** *Times, Lit. Supp.* 17 Dec. 479/1 Persons who are temperamentally faddists.

temperance ('tɛmpərəns). Also 4-5 **temperans**, 4-6 **-aunce**, 6 **-anse**; (5-6 **temporaunce**, 7 **-ance**). [a. AF. *temperaunce* (R. Grosseteste *a* 1250), ad. L. *temperāntia* moderation, f. *temperānt-em*, pr. pple. of *temperāre* to TEMPER. As to previous history, see Note below.]

I. 1. The practice or habit of restraining oneself in provocation, passion, desire, etc.; rational self-restraint. (One of the four cardinal virtues.)

a. Self-restraint and moderation in action of any kind, in the expression of opinion, etc.; suppression of any tendency to passionate action; in early use, esp. self-control, restraint, or forbearance, when provoked to anger or impatience.

[*a* **1250** R. GROSSETESTE (in Godef. *Compl.*), C'est force et temperaunce.]

a **1340** HAMPOLE *Psalter* xxxiii. 2 Debonere men þat has temperaunce in all thynge. **1382** WYCLIF *Col.* iii. 12 Therfore clothe ȝou..[with] the entrailis of mercy, benygnite, and mekenesse, temperaunce [Gr. πραότητα, L. *modestiam*, TINDALE to *R.V.* meekness], and pacience. *c* **1386** CHAUCER *Frankl. T.* 57 On euery wrong a man may nat be wreken, After the tyme moste be temperaunce. **14..** in *Tundale's Vis.* (1843) 135 Hys hart dawnt so by temperance To voyde rancour and plante in sufferaunce. **14..** in *Wars Eng. in France* (1864) II. 521 The iiij. cardinalle vertuse, named Justice, Prudence, Force, and Temperaunce. **1511** COLET *Serm. Conf. & Ref.* B vij b, The lawes that commaunde sobernes..and temperance in adournynge of the body. **1552** HULOET, Temperaunce..is a moderate gouernaunce of reason, and also as one of the car[di]nall vertues. **1590** SPENSER *F.Q.* I. viii. 34 He..calmd his wrath with goodly temperance. **1654** WHITELOCKE *Jrnl. Swed. Emb.* (1772) II. 421 Yett it pleased God to give me much patience and temperance to beare this..ingratitude. **1781** GIBBON *Decl. & F.* xxvii. III. 9 The choice of a venerable old man..announced to the court of Constantinople the gravity and temperance of the British usurper. **1851** HUSSEY *Papal Power* iii. 162 The moral force of the testimony..is weakened by the manifest defects of the case, and some want of temperance in the mode of conducting it.

b. Self-restraint in the indulgence of any natural affection or appetency; moderation in the pursuit of a gratification, in the exercise of a feeling, or in the use of anything; in early use often = chastity.

1340 *Ayenb.* 124 Temperance [lokeþ þane man] þet he ne by be none kuede loue amerd. **1526** TINDALE *Acts* xxiv. 25 As he preached of Iustice, temperaunce [*Vulg.* castitate, WYCLIF, COVERD. chastite, *Rhem.* chastitie], and Iudgement to come, Felix trembled. **1535** COVERDALE *Gal.* v. 23 The frute of the sprete is loue, ioye, peace,..goodnesse, faithfulnes, mekenesse, temperaunce. **1576** FLEMING *Panopl. Epist.* 270 She forgetteth temperance, and waxeth incontinent. **1603** HOLLAND *Plutarch's Mor.* 65 When it ruleth and ordereth our lust or concupiscense, limiting out a certaine measure, and lawfull proportion of time unto pleasures, it is called Temperance. **1656** STANLEY *Hist. Philos.* v. (1701) 164 Temperance, the Principle of subduing Desires, and yielding to no Pleasures, but living Moderately. **1846** TRENCH *Mirac.* i. (1862) 112 The secret of temperance lies not in the scanty supply, but in the strong self-restraint. **1875** MANNING *Mission H. Ghost* x. 266 Temperance is the excellence of the will in controlling the passion for pleasure.

2. a. *spec.* The avoidance of excess in eating and drinking; *esp.*, in later use, moderation in regard to intoxicants, sobriety. Now often applied to the practice or principle of total abstinence from alcoholic drink; teetotalism.

[**1509** FISHER *Funeral Serm. C'tess of Richmond* Wks. (1876) 293 Her sobre temperaunce in metes & drynkes was knowen to al them that were conuersaunt with her.] **1542** BOORDE *Dyetary* ix. (1870) 251 Surfetes do kyll many men, and temporaunce doth prolonge the lyfe. **1697** DAMPIER *Voy.* (1729) I. 69 Having..agreed upon some particular Rules, especially of Temperance and Sobriety. *a* **1718** PENN *Tracts* Wks. 1726 I. 909 Temperance,..Properly and strictly speaking it refers to Diet. **1727** BAILEY vol. II, *Temperance*..the two Species of it are *Sobriety*, which moderates our eating and drinking, and *Chastity*. **1727-46** THOMSON *Summer* 1609 Sound Temperance, Healthful in heart and look. **1775** ASH, *Temperance*, Moderation, the opposite to gluttony and drunkenness. **1826** (*title*) American Society for the Promotion of Temperance. **1849** COBDEN in Morley *Life* xviii. (1902) 69/1 With a delicate frame..I have been enabled, by temperance, to do the work of a strong man. **1887** MISS BRADDON *Like & Unlike* i, Where I can enjoy a stiff glass of grog with my feet on the hobs, and with nobody to preach temperance. **1890** BESANT *Demoniac* i, Not the least breath of suspicion had ever rested upon him in the matter of temperance.

b. *attrib.* usually, Pertaining to, practising, or advocating total abstinence, as ***temperance address, association, badge, drink, lecture, man, meeting, movement, reformation, ship, society, work***; **temperance hall**, a building used for public meetings or entertainments at which no intoxicants are sold or provided; **temperance hotel, inn**, one where no intoxicants are sold or provided; **temperance house** = *temperance hotel*; **temperance pledge**: see PLEDGE *sb.* 5 b.

1831 (*title*) Report of the American Temperance Society. **1833** E. T. COKE *Subaltern's Furlough* ii, in *Waldie's Sel. Circulating Library* 24 Sept. 380/3 Many hotels have 'temperance house' inscribed in large gilded letters over the door or sign. **1833** C. F. HOFFMAN *Let.* 26 Dec. in *Winter in West* (1835) I. 211 The most devout temperance man could see no harm in that! **1834** J. J. STRANG *Diary* 1 July in M. M. Quaife *Kingdom of St. James* (1930) 219, I shall soon have to make the temperance address. **1836** J. HUME *Sp. Ho. Com.* 24 Mar., There were perhaps many present, who were advocates of Temperance Societies. **1837** DICKENS *Pickw.* xxxiii, The Brick Lane Branch of the United Grand Junction Ebenezer Temperance Association. **1837** W. JENKINS *Ohio Gaz.* 69 Barnesville..has..2 taverns, and 1 temperance hotel. **1840** R. H. DANA *Two Years before Mast* (1841) xxxi. 118/2 This was a 'temperance ship'; and like too many such ships, the temperance was all in the forecastle... The captain..can drink as much as he chooses. **1841** *Cultivator* VIII. 163, I witnessed..a very large temperance meeting at which I saw 'female influence' fully exerted in a most glorious cause. **1843** Temperance hall [see PERAMBULATORY *sb.* a]. **1850** E. ELLIOTT *More Verse & Prose, Beware Dogmas* 9 James..keeps, abjuring rum and gin, A Temperance inn. **1855** *Zoologist* XIII. 4681 Assisting Father Mathew in the temperance-movement. **1862** G. BORROW *Wild Wales* II. xiv. 154, I drew nigh..and read: 'tea made here, the draught which cheers but not inebriates.' I was before what is generally termed a temperance house. **1869** J. H. BROWNE *Great Metropolis* 327 A large number remain open, pretending to sell nothing but 'temperance drinks'. **1881** I. M. RITTENHOUSE *Maud* (1939) 17 Went to the Temperance Meeting last night with Emma and Mabel. **1886** C. E. PASCOE *London of Today* iii. (ed. 3) 55 One of the best 'temperance' dining-places in London. **1890** BESANT *Demoniac* v, Captain and crew must be all temperance men: there is not to be one single drop of drink..put on board. **1890** DAWSON BURNS (*title*) Temperance History. **1902** O. WISTER *Virginian* 454 Once I had to sleep in a room next a ladies' temperance meetin'. **1922** JOYCE *Ulysses* 476 Bloom's bodyguard distribute..loaves and fishes, temperance badges, expensive Henry Clay cigars. **1933** E. O'NEILL *Ah, Wilderness!* IV. iii. 153 I'm not going to read you any temperance lecture. **1978** P. BAILEY *Leisure & Class in Victorian Eng.* iv. 82 Bolton... A vast new town hall, opened in 1873, looked down upon the Free Library..a Second Temperance Hall. **1978** *Times* 5 Apr. (Tourism in Britain Suppl.) 4/9 For those seeking an unusual experience Birmingham..has a famous temperance hotel.

c. Used as *predic. adj.* Practising or advocating total abstinence.

1907 J. MASEFIELD *Tarpaulin Muster* xiii. 138 They're temperance down at the Point in these times. **1977** H. FAST *Immigrants* III. 193 You're not temperance, are you?

II. †3. a. The action or fact of tempering; mingling or combining in due proportion, adjusting, moderating, modification, toning down, bringing into a temperate or moderate state (see TEMPER *v.* 1-5): = TEMPERAMENT 8, 9.

1398 TREVISA *Barth. De P.R.* v. xli. (Bodl. MS.), For temperans and keling of þe lifte side. *c* **1440** *Alphabet of Tales* 280 Be temperans of a mervalos evynhed, ather of þaim loste ane ee. **1530** PALSGR. 279/2 Temperaunce, *atrempance, attemperance.* **1531** ELYOT *Gov.* III. xxiv, By the whiche mutuall coniunction and iust temperaunce of those two studyes he attayned to suche a fourme in all his gouernaunce. **1552** HULOET, Temperaunce or temperynge, or moderation of mynglyng thynges togither, *temperatura.* **1596** DALRYMPLE tr. *Leslie's Hist. Scot.* I. (S.T.S.) 111 A forme of commoune weil, quhair the people haue the hail authoritie,..bot wᵗ sik temperance, that cheif vpon thair king, and counsel..the Repub. does depend.

†b. A tempered or properly proportioned consistence, constitution, or state; temperate condition, moderateness: = TEMPERAMENT 1, 2. *Obs.*

1471 RIPLEY *Comp. Alch.* IV. iv. in Ashm. *Theat. Chem. Brit.* (1652) 145 And so promotyd unto most perfyt temperance. **1533** ELYOT *Cast. Helthe* (1539) 1 b, Fyre..is the clarifier of other elementes, if they be vyciate or out of their naturall temperaunce. *Ibid.* 17 They be in the highest degree of heate and drithe, aboue the iuste temperaunce of mannes body. **1595** SPENSER *Col. Clout* 553 Through the myld temperance of her goodly raies. **1607** TOPSELL *Four-f. Beasts* (1658) 345 Boiled until they come unto a soft temperance. **1638** COWLEY *Love's Riddle* III. i, But were all Men of my Temperance, and Wisdom too, You should woo us.

†c. The keeping of time in music. *Obs.*

1549 *Compl. Scotl.* vi. 39 Ther syndry soundis hed nothir temperance nor tune.

†4. Moderate temperature; freedom from the extremes of heat and cold; mildness of weather or climate; temperateness; cf. TEMPERAMENT 4, 5, TEMPERATURE 6, 7. *Obs.*

1432-50 tr. *Higden* (Rolls) I. 75 Hit ioyethe in temperaunce, felenge neither coldenesse ne heete. *c* **1440** *Alphabet of Tales* 96 Whar þer was temperans of þe ayr & sownd of watir rynyng, & syngyng of burdis, and gude smell of flowris. **1542** BOORDE *Dyetary* viii. (1870) 247 In your beed lye not to hote nor to colde, but in a temporaunce. **1596** DALRYMPLE tr. *Leslie's Hist. Scot.* (S.T.S.) I. 5 Sa grett clemencie and temperance of the wathir. **1610** SHAKS. *Temp.* II. i. 42 It [the island] must needs be of subtle, tender, and delicate temperance.

[*Note.* L. *temperantia* (whence F. and Eng. *temperance*) was used by Cicero to render Plato's σωφροσύνη 'soundmindedness, prudence, moderation, sobriety, self-control', in Plato and in the Stoics, one of the original four (cardinal) virtues, φρόνησις, δικαιοσύνη, ανδρεία, σωφροσύνη, rendered in L. by Jerome and Augustine *prudentia, iustitia, fortitudo, temperantia*; also in Albertus Magnus, Aquinas, and the mediæval writers generally, and in the med.L. version of Aristotle's Nicom. Ethics. Thence the use of *temperaunce* by Grosseteste, and the earlier Eng. use. But *temperantia* was not orig. a Christian word: it occurs nowhere in the Vulgate or the Antiqua; it is not one of the 'fruits of the Spirit', even in the expanded list in the Vulgate, in Galat. v. 23 By Wyclif, however, *temperaunce* was used to render L. *modestia* 'moderation' from Tindale onward, in the Rhemish, *modestie.* In the Eng. versions from Tindale onward, *temperance* or *temperancie*, renders Gr. ἐγκράτεια 'self-mastery or restraint, esp. of certain sensual impulses', in L. commonly *continentia.* In Acts xxiv. 25 Tindale, Cranmer, Geneva, 1611, and Revised have *temperance*, where Vulgate has *castitate*, Wyclif, Coverdale, Rhemish *chastite, -tie.* In 2 Peter i. 6 (bis) T. and Cov. have *temperancy*, Cr., Gen. etc., *temperaunce, -ance*; V. *abstinentia*, W. and Rhem. *absty-, abstinence.* In Gal. v. 22, T., Cr., Gen., have *temperancy(e, -ie*, Cov., 1611, Rev., *tempera(u)nce*; Vulg. (which interpolates 3 additional 'fruits of the spirit'), *continentia*, Wycl. and Rhem., *contynaunce, continencie.* Of the Engl. senses above, 1 a. corresponds to the L. *temperantia*, Gr. σωφροσύνη; 1 b. in general to Gr. ἐγκράτεια, of which sense 2 may be considered a specialized use.]

†'**temperancy.** *Obs.* Also 6 -ie. [ad. L. *temperāntia*: see prec. and -ANCY.] = prec., as a quality or state, in senses 1, 2, 3 b; *esp.* moderation. Common in 16th c.; rare after 1630.

As to use in N.T. translations, see note to prec.

1526 TINDALE *Gal.* v. 23 The frute off the sprete is love, ioye, peace, longe sufferynge,..meknes, temperancy [so CRANMER]. —— *2 Pet.* i. 6 In vertue knowledge, and in knowledge temperancy [so COVERDALE], and in temperancy pacience. **1545** RAYNOLD *Byrth Mankynde* IV. iii. (1634) 190 If the matrix be distempered..then must ye reduce it againe to temperancie, by such remedies. **1577** tr. *Bullinger's Decades* (1592) 237 Some..will haue temperancie to extend farther than continencie. **1594** T. B. *La Primaud. Fr. Acad.* II. 232 According to the temperancie or intemperancie that is in vs, the affections of the soule also will be more moderate or immoderate. **1620** VENNER *Via Recta* IX. (1650) 263 Variety..of meats may offend with immoderation, never with temperancy. **1635** A. STAFFORD *Fem. Glory* (1869) 21 She knew Temperancy to be Gods, and Natures Favorite.

†**temperant**, *a.* (*sb.*) *Obs.* Also 5 -aunt(e. [ad. L. *temperānt-em*, pr. pple. of *temperāre* to observe moderation: see TEMPER *v.* So F. *tempérant* (16th c. in Godef. *Compl.*).]

1. Of persons: Observing temperance or moderation; sober, temperate.

1382 WYCLIF *1 Tim.* iii. 3 Not ȝouun moche to wyn, not smyter, but temperaunt [*v.r.* and 1388 temperat]. **1382** —— *Tit.* iii. 2 Amoneste hem..for to be not litygious but temperaunt [*gloss* or pacient; *v.r.* and 1388 temperat] schewinge al myldenesse to alle men. *a* **1400** HYLTON *Scala Perf.* (W. de W. 1494) II. xxxix, Sleeth lustes of glotenye & makyth the soule sobre & temperaunte. **1594** T. B. *La Primaud. Fr. Acad.* II. 235 If the body be not temperant, hardly wil the soule be; and if the soule be intemperate, the body desireth not to be temperant.

2. Of climate: Temperate, mild, equable.

c **1440** *Pallad. on Husb.* I. 121 Northwarde in places hote, in places colde Southwarde, and temporaunt in Est and West.

B. *sb.* (*pl.*) Medicines that correct sharp humours; palliatives: = med.L. *temperantia.*

1661 LOVELL *Hist. Anim. & Min.* 418 The catarrhe, cough, and difficulty of respiration..are..cured by temperants and impedients.

temperate ('tɛmpərət), *a.* Forms: 4-7 **temperat**, (4-6 **-orat(e)**, 6-7 **temprate**, 5- **temperate.** [ad. L. *temperāt-us* tempered, regulated, restrained, pa. pple. of *temperāre* to TEMPER.]

1. Of persons, their conduct, practices, etc.: Keeping due measure, self-restrained, moderate.

a. (*a*) in earlier use *esp.* = L. *modestus*, Gr. ἐπιεικής, Not swayed by passion, gentle, mild, forbearing; in later use *esp.* not extreme, violent, or strongly partisan; moderate, dispassionate.

c **1380** WYCLIF *Wks.* (1880) 305 Clene religioun..is chast, pesible, temperat, tretable. **1382-8** [see TEMPERANT 1]. **1538** ELYOT, *Moderatus*, moderate, temperate. *Modestus*, temperate, well aduised. **1546** J. HEYWOOD *Prov.* (1867) 61 Without any temprate protestacion, Thus he began. **1560** DAUS tr. *Sleidane's Comm.* 378 He waxed hote..and rayled moste bitterly on them both, being a Germain,..both the Spaniardes and Italians were a great deale more temperate. **1595** SHAKS. *John* II. i. 195 Peace Lady, pause, or be more temperate. **1797** MRS. RADCLIFFE *Italian* xvii, Their conduct was more temperate. **1840** MILL *Diss. & Disc.* (1875) I. 407 This is a temperate statement. **1849** MACAULAY *Hist. Eng.* iv. I. 490 He belonged to the mildest and most temperate section of the Puritan body. **1888** BRYCE *Amer. Commw.* (1889) II. lxxxv. 337 A majority is tyrannical when it..suppresses fair and temperate criticism.

(*b*) Of a horse: Not over-excitable or impetuous.

1890 'R. BOLDREWOOD' *Col. Reformer* (1891) 150 The filly ..proving after trial high-couraged and temperate.

b. Moderate and self-controlled as regards the indulgence of appetites or desires; abstemious, sober; continent; in late use *spec.* moderate or abstemious in the use of alcoholic drinks.

c **1430** LYDG. *Min. Poems* (Percy Soc.) 66 Temperat dyete, temperat travaile. **1531** ELYOT *Gov.* III. xx, He that is temperate fleeth pleasures voluptuous, and with the absence of them is nat discontented. **1573-80** BARET *Alv.* T 116 A moderate and temperate supper. **1598** BARCKLEY *Felic. Man* (1631) 503 A temperate man that is contented with little. **1678** tr. *Lessius*, etc. (title) The Temperate Man, or the right way of Preserving Life and Health. **1799** S. & HT. LEE *Canterb. T., Old Wom.* (ed. 2) I. 367 [His] temperate habits made him look on luxury with disgust. **1836** J. HUME *Sp. Ho. Com.* 24 Mar., I would wish to bring the people round to temperate habits by giving them cheaper wines. **1875** JOWETT *Plato* (ed. 2) V. 76 The temperate life has gentle pains and pleasures. **1890** BESANT *Demoniac* ii, That a young man of strictly temperate habits should thus suddenly become a drunkard.

2. Of things, actions, qualities, conditions, etc.: Tempered, not excessive in degree; moderate.

1398 TREVISA *Barth. De P.R.* v. xxiii. (Bodl. MS.), He makeþ þe voice smeþe & euen & temperatte. *Ibid.* x. viii. (1495) 379 By temperate blaste of wynde sparkles ben kyndlyd, and quenchyd by stronge blaste. **1471** RIPLEY *Comp. Alch.* v. xviii. in *Ashm.* (1652) 152 Make thy fyre so temperat. *Ibid.* x. xi [see QUINARITY]. **1551** TURNER *Herbal* I. Fij, Thys herbe semeth to be of a temporate warmnes. **1610** HOLLAND *Camden's Brit.* (1637) 689 Yorkeshire..is thought to be in a temperate measure fruitfull. **1625** BACON *Ess., Plantations* (Arb.) 533 Let not the Gouernment.. depend vpon too many Counsellours,..but vpon a temperate Number. **1687** A. LOVELL tr. *Thevenot's Trav.* I. 144 They put their Eggs in Ovens, which they heat with so temperate a warmth,..that chickens are..hatched in them. **1844** H. H. WILSON *Brit. India* I. I. viii. 561 With respect to extending Christianity..it must proceed from temperate and gradual proceedings. **1855** PRESCOTT *Philip II*, I. I. iv. 51 At the temperate hour of nine, the bridal festivities closed.

3. *spec.* **a.** Of the weather, season, climate, etc.: Moderate in respect of warmth: neither too hot nor too cold; of mild and equable temperature.

1432-50 tr. *Higden* (Rolls) II. 239 That tyme was as the temperate tyme of yer. **1484** CAXTON *Fables of Æsop* v. viii, This yere shalle be the most temperate and the moost fertyle ..that euer thou sawest. **1587** *Mirr. Mag., Albanact* xliv, So cleare the ayre, so temperate the clime. **1625** N. CARPENTER *Geog. Del.* II. ii. (1635) 22 Who findes not by experience one Countrey hot, another cold, a third temperate? **1698** FRYER *Acc. E. India & P.* 186 It enjoys a Temperater Air than would be allowed by the Poet under the Fifth Zone. **1781** GIBBON *Decl. & F.* xvii. (1869) I. 437 The climate was healthy and temperate. **1830** LYELL *Princ. Geol.* I. 107 Mild winters and less temperate summers.

b. *temperate zone*: Each of the two zones or belts of the earth's surface lying between the torrid and frigid zones; i.e. the ***north temperate zone*** between the tropic of Cancer and the arctic circle, and the ***south temperate zone*** between the tropic of Capricorn and the antarctic circle.

1551 RECORDE *Cast. Knowl.* (1556) 64 Betweene those Frozen zones, and the Burning zone, they appointed two Temperat zones. **1625** N. CARPENTER *Geog. Del.* I. ix. (1635) 206 The Temperate Zone is the space contained betwixt the Tropicke and the Polar circle. **1880** HAUGHTON *Phys. Geog.* iii. 125 The temperate zones owe very little of their heat to the latent heat of vapour formed in the torrid zone.

c. Of food: produced in, or suitable for production in, a moderate climate.

1960 *Economist* 8 Oct. 125/3 The New Zealanders..have recognised that reconciling their highly competitive exports of temperate farm products with a common European agricultural policy will be an extremely difficult task. **1962** *Listener* 27 Sept. 462/1 The so-called temperate foodstuffs —that's to say corn and meat and dairy produce. **1980** *Nature* 7 Feb. 514/3 In many parts of the Third World people eat temperate vegetables: cauliflower, onions, carrots, potatoes, cucumber, tomatoes.

4. Of monarchy or sovereignty, hence also of the sovereign: Restricted in extent of authority; not absolute; limited; constitutional. *Obs.* or *arch.*

1560 DAUS tr. *Sleidane's Comm.* 307 Themperour hath done herein the duty of a temperate Prince. **1604** E. G[RIMSTONE] *D'Acosta's Hist. Indies* VII. x. 525 These Barbarians, of temperate Kings became tyrants. **1621** BURTON *Anat. Mel.* II. iii. III. (1651) 325 Whether Monarchies should be mixt, temperate, or absolute. **1852** TENNYSON *Ode on Wellington* vii, That sober freedom out of which there springs Our loyal passion for our temperate Kings.

†**5.** Of clay or earth: = TEMPERED 1 d. *Obs.*

1574 HYLL *Planting* 85 Close it with good temperate earth about the graffe.

6. *Music.* = TEMPERED 1 e.

1876 tr. *Blaserna's Sound* vii. 137 The fruit of these manifold attempts..is the temperate scale, which reached its full development in the middle of the last century, especially by means of the works of Sebastian Bach.

†**7.** = *tempered*, pa. pple. of TEMPER *v. Obs.*

1398 TREVISA *Barth. De P.R.* III. xix. (1495) d vj b/1 By the drawynge of the ayre the brayne is temperat & comforted. **1634** HOLLAND *Pliny* XX. xiv. II. 61 [Nep] mixed with a third part of bread, and so temperat [*ed.* **1601** tempered] and incorporat with vinegre to the form of a liniment.

8. *Microbiology.* Of a phage: not necessarily causing lysis of the host cell, but able to exist as a prophage for a number of generations; giving rise to lysogenic bacteria. [tr. F. *tempéré* (F. Jacob et al. 1953, in *Ann. de l'Inst. Pasteur* LXXXIV. 223).]

1953 *Cold Spring Harbor Symp. Quantitative Biol.* XVIII. 65/1 It has been proposed..to call temperate (as opposed to virulent) those phages which are able to establish the lysogenic condition in their host cells. **1961** M. HYNES *Med. Bacteriol.* (ed. 7) xxvi. 401 The virulent phages are often termed lytic, since they disrupt the bacteria they infect; the symbiotic phages are usually termed temperate. Cultures infected with a temperate phage are confusingly termed lysogenic. **1979** ARMS & CAMP *Biology* xvi. 244 A virulent, lytic bacteriophage..can only replicate and cause cell lysis. Other phages, known as temperate phages, may either replicate and lyse the cell they invade, or may instead enter a dormant phase in which the phage DNA is joined to that of the host cell..and replicated with it over many cell generations.

†**'temperate,** *v. Obs.* [f. ppl. stem of L. *temperāre* to TEMPER. (Occurs earlier as pa. pple. = L. *temperātus*: see prec. 7: cf. -ATE[3] 3-5.)] = TEMPER *v.*

1. *trans.* To mix suitably; to moderate, qualify, mitigate, allay; = TEMPER *v.* 1, 2; to bring into a proper state or condition; = TEMPER *v.* 5.

a **1540** BARNES *Wks.* (1573) 217/1 For mollifying, and temperatyng of those thinges, that seemed to bee somewhat hardly spoken. **1549** *Compl. Scot.* vi. 53 The verteous heyt of it [the sun] temperatis al the sternis of the firmament. **1597** A. M. tr. *Guillemeau's Fr. Chirurg.* *iv, I endevoured to temperate the rigoure of the first Chyrurgians. **1607** TOPSELL *Four-f. Beasts* (1658) 431 The same..doth temperate and confirm the brains of any man. **1615** G. SANDYS *Trav.* 228 A clime..exceeding hote;..yet sometimes temperated by the comfortable winds. **1698** CROWNE *Caligula* IV. Dram. Wks. 1874 IV. 407 If I were wise I'd temp'rate love with art. **1750** JOHNSON *Rambler* 17 ¶10 Nor is fear..less to be temperated by this universal medicine of the mind.

2. To rule; to curb, restrain; = TEMPER *v.* 7, 8.

a **1568** ASCHAM *Scholem.* (Arb.) 112 This fulnes as it is not to be misliked in a yong man, so in farder aige..it is to be temperated, or else discretion and iudgement shall seeme to be wanting in him. **1642** H. MORE *Song of Soul* II. i. II. xliii, She temperates Her starrie orb, makes her bright forms to wend Even as she list. **1648** LIGHTFOOT *Horæ Hebraicæ* (1684) II. 572 Let him..learn from you to temperate his passions.

Hence **'temperated** *ppl. a.*, tempered, moderated; **'temperating** *vbl. sb.* and *ppl. a.*

a **1540** Temperatyng [see sense 1]. **1643** PRYNNE *Sov. Power Parl.* App. 77 Placing the power in such sort in the King, that the temperating of it should be in the middle Iudge. **1737** BOYSE *The Olive* xviii, Hence the mild Sweets of tempered Sway. **1753** N. TORRIANO *Gangr. Sore Throat* 22 Broths mixt with Juice of aperitive and temperating Herbs. **1788** *Misc.* in *Ann. Reg.* 134/2 The moon was darting her temperated rays through the shade. **1831** J. DAVIES *Manual Mat. Med.* 5 Acids, when weak or diluted, act..as refrigerant and temperating medicines.

temperately ('tɛmpərətlɪ), *adv.* [f. TEMPERATE *a.* + -LY[2].] In a temperate manner or degree; moderately; in or with moderation, without excess.

1398 TREVISA *Barth. De P.R.* v. xxv. (Bodl. MS.), If þe heed is temperatlich greete and þe nolle of þe nekke sommedele greet. **1528** PAYNELL *Salerne's Regim.* a iv b, Blud..is temperatlye hotte and moyste. **1542** BOORDE *Dyetary* xi. (1870) 262 Breade..must be temporatly salted. **1594** BLUNDEVIL *Exerc.* IV. xix. (1636) 474 Venus is temperatly cold and moyst. **1670** EACHARD *Cont. Clergy* 91 Oh, how prettily and temperately may half a score children be maintained with almost twenty pounds per annum! **1870** J. BRUCE *Life Gideon* xvii. 316 The Lord's own quiet and kindly admonition would excite temperately the fears of Gideon.

b. With self-restraint; without violence or passion; dispassionately; chastely.

1525 LD. BERNERS *Froiss.* II. xli. 127 [He] determyned in hymselfe to answere temporatly. **1556** J. HEYWOOD *Spider & F.* v. 31, I temprately must temper mine inuension, To pleade my right in reason not in rage. **1613** FLETCHER, etc. *Hon. Man's Fort.* I. iii, When our affections had their liberty, Our kisses met as temperatelie as The hands of sisters, or of brothers. **1796** BURKE *Regic. Peace* iv. Wks. IX. 32 It must be pardoned by those, who are very regularly and temperately in the wrong. **1818** A. THOMSON in Landreth *Life & Min.* iv. (1869) 168, I and other dissenting ministers firmly but temperately remonstrated against this. **1869** H. AINSWORTH *Hilary St. Ives* II. xxiii, When you speak more temperately,..I will answer you.

c. With moderation in eating and drinking; soberly, abstemiously.

c **1400** MAUNDEV. (Roxb.) xxxii. 144 Þai liffe so temperately and so soberly in mete and drink. **1617** MORYSON *Itin.* III. 87 He could not..use it temperately, but either would allow us no wine at all, or at one meale drinke off a whole great bottell. **1741** MIDDLETON *Cicero* I. vi. 449 The more temperately they would use it. *Mod.* A hot climate is not dangerous to those who live temperately.

'temperateness. [f. as prec. + -NESS.] The quality of being temperate.

1. Moderateness, moderation; freedom from excess; temperance.

1398 TREVISA *Barth. De P.R.* v. xxvii. (Bodl. MS.), Þe spirites þat comeþ fro þe senewes and veynes ben isaued by temperatnes and ynorsched. *Ibid.* VIII. iii, It was nede þat þere were wateres to bringe þat heuenlich heete to temperattnes. **1592** WYRLEY *Armorie, Ld. Chandos* 56, I.. would not spare But liberall be, fraught with temperatenesse. **1651** *Life of Bucer* in *Fuller's Abel Rediv.* (1867) I. 186 He was much admired..for his temperateness in his diet. **1746** R. JAMES *Health's Impr.* Introd. 56 All Heat beyond Temperateness..must necessarily be pernicious in all Distempers, where there is a Tendency to an alcaline Putrefaction.

b. Self-restraint; freedom from passion or mental heat; mildness, calmness.

1595 DANIEL *Civ. Wars* (1609) I. xxv, Langley; whose mild temperatenesse Did tend unto a calmer quietnesse. **1865** *Sat. Rev.* 18 Feb. 184/2 The peculiar temperateness of assertion,..for which extremely young men are so notorious. **1871** *Athenæum* 15 July 84 The same temperateness and fairness is displayed; while the author maintains what is commonly called orthodoxy.

2. *spec.* Of climatic conditions: Freedom from extremes of heat and cold or atmospheric disturbance; equability and mildness of climate.

1525 LD. BERNERS *Froiss.* II. clxxi. [clxvii.] 506 By reason of this hayle the ayre was brought into a good temperatenesse. **1563** GOLDING *Cæsar* Pref. (1565) 7 The fertility of the soile, the temperatenesse of the aire. **1603** KNOLLES *Hist. Turks* (1638) 265 Where the temperatenesse of the aire, and liuely springs, with the fruitfulnesse of the soile, doth euery where yeeld plenty. **1610** HOLLAND *Camden's Brit.* I. 2 The temperatenesse..of this Iland. **1828** WEBSTER s.v., The temperateness of the weather or of a climate.

†**tempe'ration.** *Obs. rare*[−1]. [ad. L. *temperātiōn-em*, n. of action from *temperāre* to TEMPER.] The action of tempering; qualification.

1615 CROOKE *Body of Man* 408 The end also is the same, to wit, nutrition, temperation or qualification, and expurgation.

temperative, *a.* Now *rare* or *Obs.* [ad. late L. *temperātīv-us*, f. *temperāre*: see TEMPER *v.* and -IVE.] Having the quality of tempering; alleviative, mitigating; tending to temperateness.

c **1430** LYDG. *Min. Poems* (Percy Soc.) 196 Ayer of nature yevith inspiracioun, To mannys herte thyng moost temperatiff. **1621** T. GRANGER *On Eccles.* 15 The ayr drawne in, and sent forth by the breath, which is temperatiue of the hearts heate. **1825** J. WEDDELL *Voy.* 95 This climate appears to be in general much more temperative now than it was forty years ago.

b. *Mus.* Having the purpose of tempering or producing temperament: see TEMPERAMENT 10.

1727-41 [see TEMPER *v.* 15 b].

†**'temperator.** *Obs. rare.* In 6 -our. [ad. L. *temperātor.*] One who tempers, rules, or directs.

1591 SPARRY tr. *Cattan's Geomancie* 25 They called ♄ [Saturn] the Father of the gods, and temperatour of times.

temperature ('tɛmpərətjʊə(r)). [ad. L. *temperātūra* the process or result of tempering, due measure and proportion, f. ppl. stem of *temperāre*: see -URE. Cf. F. *température* (1539 in Godef.).]

†**1. a.** The action or process of tempering, in various senses of the verb; mixing or combination (of elements). *Obs.*

1550 LATIMER *Serm. at Stamford* Serm. (1562) 100 We should learne *viam dei*, Goddes waye, and that truly, withoute mixture, temperature, blaunching, powderyng. **1569** J. SANFORD tr. *Agrippa's Van. Artes* 159 Plinie declareth that, in the time of Tiberius..the temperature of glasse was invented. **1600** HOLLAND *Livy* IX. xlvi. 350 Upon this good temperature of degrees, he purchased the surname of Maximus. **16..** HOLLAND (Webster, 1864), Made a temperature of brass and iron together. **1677** *Cleveland's Poems* Life, He was Judge Advocate..and, by an excellent temperature of both, was a just and prudent Judge for the King, and a faithful Advocate for the Countrey.

†**b.** *concr.* That which tempers. *Obs. rare.*

1609 BIBLE (Douay) *Ezek.* xiii. *Comm.*, A wal of clay or morter without straw or other temperature, is washed away with rayne.

†**2.** The fact or state of being tempered or mixed, mixture; also, the condition resulting from the mixture or combination in various proportions of ingredients or elements; the composition, consistence, or complexion, so produced. *Obs.*

1533 ELYOT *Cast. Helthe* (1541) 8 By the increase or diminution of any of them [the four humours] in quantitie or qualytie, ouer or vnder their natural assignement, inequall temperature commeth into the body. **1538** —— *Dict.* Addit., *Crasis*, a greke worde, sygnyfieth complexion, temperature, or myxture of naturall humours. **1562** TURNER *Herbal* II. 28 b, There is in it a small temperature of the principales of the ayer and fyre. **1601** HOLLAND *Pliny* XXIV. ix. II. 505 The last temperature is that, which in Latine they call Ollaria, as one would say, the pot-brasse, for it taketh the name of that vessell whereto it is most emploied; and this is by tempering with every hundred pound weight of brasse, three or four pound weight of argentine lead or tin. **1602** *How Man may Chuse Gd. Wife* IV. iii, Hath he not..Upon that crimson temperature of your cheeks, Laid a lead colour with his boist'rous blows? **1605** TIMME *Quersit.* I. ix. 36 Ashes have not exactly one temperature. **1675** *Art Contentm.* IV. xii, In all the concerns [of human life]..there is such a temperature and mixture, that the good do's more than equal the ill. *a* **1768** SECKER *Serm.* (1770) III. i. 6 The first of these, and the Foundation of all the rest, is a proper Temperature of Fear and Love. **1786-7** BONNYCASTLE *Astron.* xxi. 374 It is not credible that beings of our make and temperature could live upon them. **1826** R. HALL *Wks.* (1832) VI. 53 Such a temperature of light and shade as that which distinguishes all his discoveries of himself.

†**3. a.** Due measure and proportion in action, speech, thought, etc.; freedom from excess or violence; moderation. *Obs.*

1536 CROMWELL in Merriman *Life & Lett.* (1902) II. 3 To haue the same vsed and setfurthe in suche a temperature, as by your wisedome ye shall thinke may conduce to thadvauncement of his affayres there. **1539** *Ibid.* 172 Vsing ..in the proposicion therof & answers to be geven that sobernes and temperature as he may perceive is to be vsed. **1609** HOLLAND *Amm. Marcell.* XXVI. ii. 286 As I hope, Fortune..will give the same unto me, seeking diligently.. after a temperature and moderation. **1659** C. NOBLE *Mod. Answ. Immod. Queries* 14 If he would but say and do with that moderation and temperature as the late Protector..has said and done.

†**b.** A middle condition or position, a mean between opposites; a middle course, a compromise.

1594 *Mirr. Policie* (1599) D iij, A vertuous temperature betweene two vicious extremities. **1601** HOLLAND *Pliny* (1634) I. 37 In the midst of the earth there is an wholesome mixture from both sides:..the habit of mens bodies of a mean and indifferent constitution, the colour also shewing a great temperature. **1652** NEEDHAM tr. *Selden's Mare Cl.* 37 To finde..some kinde of temperature, whereby the Republick might receive the Rights belonging thereunto from the Austrian subjects sailing those Seas. **1712** ? HUGHES *Spect.* No. 467 ¶9 His Constitution is a just Temperature between Indolence on one hand and Violence on the other.

†**4.** The character or nature of a substance as supposed to be determined by the proportions of the four qualities (*hot* or *cold*, and *dry* or *moist*); = TEMPERAMENT 3. *Obs.*

1533 ELYOT *Cast. Helthe* (1539) 17 Of the temperature of meates to be receyued. *Ibid.* 34 b, Drythe..happeneth in the substance of the body, either by to moche labour, or by the proper temperature of age. **1578** LYTE *Dodoens* lxiv. 95 Hartes Horne is colde and dry in temperature much like Plantayne. **1601** HOLLAND *Pliny* XVII. xxii. I. 529 If the ground be of a middle temperature, there ought to bee a space of fiue foot distance betweene every vine. **1610** GUILLIM *Heraldry* III. xii. (1611) 120 The general received opinion is that the life of all things doth consist in calido and humido which is the temperature of blood. **1616** SURFL. & MARKH. *Country Farme* 589 As concerning the temperature of beere there is no doubt but that it is hot. [**1771** LUCKOMBE *Hist. Print.* 366 An unproper temperature of the Tympan.. is, when it is dry in one place and moist in another.]

†**5. a.** The combination of 'humours' in the body; also, the bodily habit or constitution attributed to this; = TEMPERAMENT 6. *Obs.*

1561 HOLLYBUSH *Hom. Apoth.* 15 b, To know by what complexion or temperatur yᵉ diseases are caused. *a* **1577** SIR T. SMITH *Commw. Eng.* (1609) 5 In a mans body foure complexions or temperatures, as cholericke, sanguine, flegmatique & melancholique. **1600** HAKLUYT *Voy.* (1810) III. 340 The victuall of the countrey..might have been thought to have altered our temperatures. *a* **1618** RALEIGH *Rem.* (1644) 134 It is evident also, that men differ very much in the temperature of their bodies. **1750** JOHNSON *Rambler* No. 43 ¶1 There is no temperature so exactly regulated but that some humour is fatally predominant. **1837** T. JONES *Chr. Warrior* IV. vi. 97 He [Satan] observes the temperature and complexion of such a man. If he be sanguine..he tempts him to incontinency.

†**b.** Constitutional bent of mind; disposition; = TEMPERAMENT 7. *Obs.*

1594 SPENSER *Amoretti* xiii, In that proud port..Most goodly temperature ye may descry; Myld humblesse, mixt with awfull majesty. **1605** BACON *Adv. Learn.* I. iii. §4 As touching the manners of learned men..no doubt there be amongst them, as in other professions, of all temperatures. **1610** BARROUGH *Meth. Physick* I. xxviii. (1639) 45 It..is chiefly engendred of melancholy occupying the mind, and changing the temperature of it. **1768** STERNE *Sent. Journ.* (1778) I. 167 Any one may do a casual act of good-nature, but a continuation of them shews it is a part of the temperature.

†**6.** A tempered or temperate condition of the weather or climate; also, a (qualified or specified) condition of these. *Obs.*

1531 ELYOT *Gov.* III. xxvi, The temperature or distemperature of the regions. **1578** T. N. tr. *Conq. W. India* 217 Desiring of Him by Prayers to give raine and temperature, that the Earth may bring foorth Corne, Fruite, Hearbes,..and all other necessaries. **1585** T. WASHINGTON tr. *Nicholay's Voy.* IV. xxiv. 139 Thracia..[is] of an yll temperature, the ayre being vnwholesome, & not healthfull. **1624** CAPT. SMITH *Virginia* II. 21 The temperature of this Country doth agree well with English constitutions. **1697** DAMPIER *Voy.* I. xix. 529, I look upon this latitude [the Cape of Good Hope] to be one of the mildest and sweetest for its temperature, of any whatsoever. **1727** SWIFT *State Irel.* ¶35 A country so favoured by nature..both in fruitfulness of soil, and temperature of climate.

7. a. The state of a substance or body with regard to sensible warmth or coldness, referred to some standard of comparison; *spec.* that quality or condition of a body which in degree varies directly with the amount of heat contained in the body, and inversely with its heat-capacity; commonly manifested by its imparting heat to, or receiving it from, contiguous bodies, and usually measured by means of a thermometer or similar instrument. (Now the ordinary sense.)

1670 BOYLE (*title*) Of the Temperature of the Submarine Regions as to Heat and Cold. *Ibid.* iii, This person I diligently examined..as to the temperature of the lower parts of the sea (the knowledge of which is that alone that concerns us in this place); he several times complained to me of the coldness of the deep water. **1710** STEELE *Tatler* No. 179 ¶7 A moderate Expence of Fire,..serves to keep this large Room in a due Temperature. *a* **1743** G. MARTINE *Ess. & Obs. Thermometers* (1772) 46 There is a Thermometer in frequent use in England, wherein they conceive the middle temperature of the air as neither hot nor cold, which..they mark Gr. 0, and number both above and below. **1791** tr. *Pictet's Ess. Fire* 11 The thermometer will show, by the degree observed on its scale, the temperature of the liquid. **1815** J. SMITH *Panorama Sc. & Art* II. 47 The cause of them is, the difference in temperature between the air over the land and that over the water. **1820** W. SCORESBY *Acc. Arctic Reg.* I. 48, I have determined the mean temperature of the month of May. **1860** TYNDALL *Glac.* I. xvi. 113 To record the lowest winter temperatures at the summit of the mountain. **1876** BRISTOWE *The. & Pract. Med.* (1878) 99 The normal temperature of the body has been variously estimated; but, on the average, seems, in the adult, to range between 98·4° and 99·5°. **1878** HUXLEY *Physiogr.* 72 A comparison of the temperatures shown by the two thermometers. **1888** MISS BRADDON *Fatal Three* I. v, I took their temperatures this morning before I went to church.

fig. **1862** STANLEY *Jew. Ch.* (1877) I. xiv. 272 The temperature of the zeal of the different portions of the nation.

b. (*colloq.*) ***to have a temperature***, i.e. one higher than the normal, as in fever.

1898 P. WHITE *Millionaire's Dau.* (ed. Tauchn.) 88 Do you think I have a temperature? **1904** E. F. BENSON *Challoners* (ed. Tauchn.) 318 He has..had a temperature for nearly a week.

†**8.** The temper of steel; = TEMPER *sb.* 5. *Obs.*

1580 FRAMPTON *Iron & Steele* in *Joyf. News* (1596) 145 Iron so harde..that being wrought, it serueth for Steele, chiefly with a temperature that is giuen to it. **1601** HOLLAND *Pliny* XXXIV. xiv. II. 514 All our steele is of a more soft and gentle temperature than that of the Levant. **1603** [see TEMPER *v.* 14]. **1630** *R. Johnson's Kingd. & Commw.* 249 Giving them the Iron Mines of Biskay..with the temperature of Baion, Bilbo, Toledo, and Calataiut.

†**9.** *Music.* = TEMPERAMENT *sb.* 10. *Obs. rare*⁻¹.

1592 LYLY *Gallathea* III. iii, An Organist to tune your temperatures.

10. *attrib.* and *Comb.*, as ***temperature-compensator, control, correction, -dependence, -dependency, -independence, log, sense; temperature-controlled, -dependent, -independent, -regulating, -sensitive*** adjs.; **temperature-alarm**: see quot. 1877; **temperature-chart**, (*a*) a chart or card containing a *temperature-curve* or its equivalent; (*b*) a chart of a region indicating temperatures at different points, as by isotherms; **temperature coefficient** *Physics*, a coefficient expressing the relation between a change in a physical property and the change in temperature that causes it; **temperature-curve**, a curve showing variations of temperature, usually in relation to equal periods of time, *esp.* in clinical use; **temperature gradient**, a gradient (sense 2) of temperature; **temperature inversion** *Meteorol.*, the phenomenon of an increase of temperature with height above the ground; **temperature-regulation** *Biol.* = THERMOREGULATION; **temperature-salinity** *adj. phr.*, relating to the temperature and salinity of water; *spec.* applied to a diagram in which both are plotted as a function of depth.

1877 KNIGHT *Dict. Mech.*, *Temperature alarm*, a device which automatically makes a signal when the temperature of the place where it is exceeds or falls below a determinate point. **1888** H. MORTEN *Hospital Life* 29, I admire her neat temperature chart, and then pass on to Nurse Lorna. **1902** *Encycl. Brit.* XXVIII. 8/1 The quantity *a* is then called the temperature-coefficient, and its reciprocal is the temperature at which the resistivity would become zero. **1962** *Newnes Conc. Encycl. Nucl. Energy* 791/2 For the practical operation of a reactor the temperature coefficient of reactivity should be small so that a steady power can be maintained by moving control rods at a moderate speed. **1901** *Daily News* 12 Jan. 6/2 All the levers,..connecting rods, carriers, supporting rods, bell cranks, temperature compensators. **1923** GLAZEBROOK *Dict. Appl. Physics* III. 582/1 (*heading*) Temperature control. **1959** E. T. HALL *Silent Language* iii. 79 Clothes and houses are extensions of man's biological temperature-control mechanisms. **1935** *Discovery* Nov. 322/1 The centres are passed by an automatic feeding attachment through a curtain of temperature-controlled chocolate. **1970** *Jrnl. General Psychol.* Oct. 163 They were housed in individual cages in a temperature-controlled laboratory. **1899** *Allbutt's Syst. Med.* VII. 639 A high temperature, marked fluctuations in the temperature curve, a rapid pulse. **1946** *Nature* 7 Sept. 333/1 Experiments on the temperature-dependence of the breakdown strength F. **1974** J. W. DRAKE in Carlile & Skehol *Evolution in Microbial World* 53 The temperature-dependencies of the *Neurospora* and T4 rates differed markedly. **1962** SIMPSON & RICHARDS *Physical Princ. Junction Transistors* ix. 200 The most important temperature-dependent property of transistors is the collector cutoff current. **1882, 1962** Temperature gradient [see GRADIENT *sb.* 2]. **1978** *Jrnl. R. Soc. Arts* CXXVI. 683/1 Structures of supersonic aircraft are subject to thermal stresses due to temperature gradients. **1965** *Math. in Biol. & Med.* (Med. Res. Council) VI. 256 The same difficulty arose with the temperature-independence of temporal rhythms. **1946** *Nature* 7 Sept. 333/1 The latter is temperature-independent but increases with the concentration of foreign atoms. **1945** E. BOLLAY in F. A. Berry et al. *Handbk. Meteorol.* x. 758 (*caption*) Characteristic properties of nonfrontal temperature inversions. **1977** I. M. CAMPBELL *Energy & Atmosphere* viii. 252 A further circumstance of temperature inversion occurs where there is an enclosed valley in which cold air..tends to collect. **1911** J. A. THOMSON *Biol. Seasons* IV. 338 It represents an interesting reminiscence of a more primitive physiological state when the temperature-regulating mechanism was not yet well established in the ancestral mammals. **1957** J. S. HUXLEY *Relig. without Revelation* (rev. ed.) ix. 216 The temperature-regulating mechanism of higher mammals. **1927** HALDANE & HUXLEY *Animal Biol.* xi. 240 The mammals..possess proper temperature-regulation. **1930** *Rep. 'Michael Sars' N. Atlantic Deep-Sea Exped. 1910* I. I. 19 The 'normal' temperature-salinity curve is reproduced ..in such a way that the corresponding values of temperature and salinity can easily be read off. **1942** H. U. SVERDRUP et al. *Oceans* IV. 141 Water masses can be classified on the basis of their temperature-salinity characteristics. **1959** H. BARNES *Oceanogr. & Marine Biol.* 157 As one passes across the Gulf Stream there is a fairly sharp temperature-salinity boundary between Gulf Stream water and the so-called Slope water lying over the Continental Shelf. **1893** A. S. ECCLES *Sciatica* 59 It appears to be possible, by close attention to the distribution of hyperæsthesia, temperature-sense for heat, and loss of cutaneous temperature, to localize in a measure the extent to which the nerve-trunk or its branches is involved. **1962** *Science Survey* XX. 308 The surface of the body contains a number of temperature-sensitive patches which produce patterns of nerve impulses related to the ambient temperature. **1871** W. SQUIRE (*title*) Temperature Variations in the Diseases of Children.

Hence **'temperatured** *a.*, in comb., having temperature of a stated kind.

1892 *Temple Bar Mag.* Nov. 444 The inner door shuts her ..into this pleasant-temperatured privacy.

tempere, var. TEMPRE *a. Obs.*

tempered ('tɛmpəd), *a.* [f. TEMPER *v.* and *sb.* + -ED.]

†**1.** Brought to or having a proper or desired temper, quality, or consistence (usually by mixture of elements or mingling of qualities); hence, of an intermediate or moderate quality free from either extreme; temperate. *Obs.* except as below.

c **1375** *Sc. Leg. Saints* xliv. (*Lucy*) 288 þat [pyk & brynstan] grewit hyre nomare Na It a temptyt bath ware. **1422** tr. *Secreta Secret., Priv. Priv.* 222 The fryste tokyn of good complexcion Is temperid flesshe betwene nesshe and harde, and namely be-twen lene and fatte. *a* **1450** *Knt. de la Tour* (1906) 9 It is good to serue God..and lyue tempered and moderat lyff. **1577** HANMER *Anc. Eccl. Hist.* (1619) 422 Leaving in the midst a court, open to the tempered aire.

b. with adverbial qualification.

1638 JUNIUS *Paint. Ancients* 284 To worke in us the impression of an excellently tempered complexion. **1726** LEONI *Alberti's Archit.* I. 101/2 Wine..kept in a dry cool place, always equally tempered. **1875** JOWETT *Plato* (ed. 2) III. 692 In the heaven above an excellently tempered climate.

c. That has been brought to the required degree of hardness and elasticity, as steel; also said vaguely or poetically of other metals.

1655 MRQ. WORCESTER *Cent. Inv.* §85 Such..bolts.. being made of tempered Steel. **1697** DRYDEN *Æneid* VIII. 699 The temper'd metals clash, and yield a silver sound. **1727** GAY *Fables* xii. 6 Some..head the darts with tempered gold. **1789** R. HOLE *Arthur* v, No temper'd mail resists Fiacha's might. **1884** C. G. W. LOCK *Workshop Receipts* Ser. III. 271/1 The word 'tempered' (as applied to steel) should properly apply to all degrees of hardness denotable by colour in the colour test.

d. Mixed or compounded in due proportion; worked up to a suitable consistency.

1697 DRYDEN *Virg. Georg.* I. 259 Delve of convenient Depth your thrashing Floor; With temper'd Clay then fill and face it o'er. **1707** MORTIMER *Husb.* (1721) II. 255 Cover the Head of the Stock with temper'd Clay, or with soft Wax. **1778** BP. LOWTH *Transl. Isaiah* Notes 158 Bricks, made with tempered clay and chopped straw.

e. *Mus.* That has been tuned or adjusted in pitch according to some TEMPERAMENT (sense 10).

1727-41 [see TEMPER *v.* 15 b]. **1788** CAVALLO in *Phil. Trans.* LXXVIII. 250 One may easily perceive, how small is the difference between the perfect fifths of the latter, and the tempered ones of the former. **1829-32** GEN. P. THOMPSON *Exerc.* (1842) II. 139 Nobody denies that the different keys on tempered instruments have different qualities. **1875** ELLIS tr. *Helmholtz' Sensat. Tone* III. xvi. 510 We cannot.. fail to recognise the influence of tempered intonation upon the style of composition. **1879** C. H. H. PARRY in Grove *Dict. Mus.* II. 11/2 The larger intervals contained in the tempered octave are all to a certain extent out of tune.

2. Constituted or endowed with a specified temper or disposition (in various senses of *temper*). **a.** Qualified by an adv.

1390 GOWER *Conf.* I. 266 For his corage is tempred so, That thogh he mihte himself relieve, Yit wolde he noght an other grieve. **1456** SIR G. HAYE *Law Arms* (S.T.S.) 119 He that is vertuous in the vertu of that force, is ay temperit that he excedis nocht. **1529** MORE *Dyaloge* I. Wks. 162/2 It is so meruaylously tempered that a mouse may wade therin, and an Olyphaunt be drowned therin. **1615** BRATHWAIT *Strappado* (1878) 143 Perseus (one better tempered, Then to behold a Virgine slaughtered, Without assayd reuenge). *a* **1628** F. GREVIL *Sidney* (1907) 13 A quiet and equally tempered people. **1760-72** H. BROOKE *Fool of Qual.* (1809) III. 119 Children, sweetly tempered like their mother. **1839** THIRLWALL *Greece* VI. xlv. 15 Indications that its form of government was not unhappily tempered.

b. Qualified by an adj., so as to become a parasynthetic deriv. of TEMPER *sb.*: Having a temper of such a kind (*mild-tempered* = of mild temper).

(The 18th c. quots. show the gradual change from a.)

1680 MOXON *Mech. Exerc.* x. 178 Heavy unequal tempered Stuff. **1747** tr. *Astruc's Fevers* 169 A cold mild-tempered easy patient. **1747** RICHARDSON *Clarissa* I. ii. 11 She aimed to be worse-tempered than ordinary. **1768** [see GOOD-TEMPERED]. **1788** MRS. HUGHES *Henry & Isabella* I. 80 Lamented that so mild a tempered, pretty kind of woman, should be subject to his tyranny. **1796** CHARLOTTE SMITH *Marchmont* III. 146 So unhappy a tempered woman. **1868** FARRAR *Seekers* III. i. (1875) 267 Controlled, modest, faithful, and even-tempered. **1901** *Wide World Mag.* VIII. 149/2 Hard at bargaining..and cross-tempered withal.

3. Modified by the admixture or influence of some other element; seasoned; moderated, mitigated, allayed, toned-down; limited.

1654 JER. TAYLOR *Real Pres.* 298 In a moderated proportion..wine is mingled with water, as the Spirit with a man. And he receivs in the Feast..tempered wine unto faith. **1763** J. BROWN *Poetry & Mus.* v. 85 Sophocles appeared next; of a more sedate and tempered Majesty. **1791** BURKE *App. Whigs* Wks. VI. 135 No man can be a friend to a tempered monarchy who bears a decided hatred to monarchy itself. **1794** MRS. RADCLIFFE *Myst. Udolpho* xliv, They proceeded to a third room with a more tempered step. **1828** D'ISRAELI *Chas. I*, I. vi. 157 At this crisis, the tempered wisdom of the Queen saved the nation. **1893** *Westm. Gaz.* 23 Mar. 2/3 He..listened to his tempered speech—it was a much milder note than on Tuesday.

temperel, obs. form of TEMPORAL.

temperer ('tɛmpərə(r)). [f. TEMPER *v.* + -ER[1].] One who or that which tempers.

1. †One who mixes (*obs.*); one who prepares (clay, mortar, etc.); one who tempers (steel).

a **1617** HIERON *Wks.* II. 2 Still there will be..some temperers of leaven with the sweet lumpe of Gods sacred truth. *a* **1619** FOTHERBY *Atheom.* (1622) Pref. 6 Temperers of Lyme and Mortar. **1629** in Cochran-Patrick *Rec. Coinage Scotl.* (1876) II. 19 The Wardane Counterwardane Sinker and Temperer of the yrnes. **1839** URE *Dict. Arts* 883 The needles are now ready for the tempering..they..are carried in boxes to the temperer. **1896** *Chambers's Jrnl.* XIII. 22/2 The temperer requires a supply of water for the sufficient moistening of the clay.

†**2.** One who or that which allays or mitigates.

1630 *R. Johnson's Kingd. & Commw.* 6 Whereas cold can without doors receiue no temperer; heat on the contrarie is capable of very many. **1638** RIDER *Hor. Odes* I. (1644) 32 O thou my labour's sweetest temperer [L. *lenimen*].

3. One who uses or advocates temperament in music: see TEMPERAMENT 10.

1829–32 GEN. P. THOMPSON *Exerc.* (1842) II. 140 Do the temperers maintain..that it is possible to mend this passage by any alteration in the intonation?

†**4.** = CRATER *sb.* 1, mixing vessel. *Obs.*

1675 HOBBES *Odyssey* 32 Then Nestor bids one fill the temperer With wine that aged was eleven year. **1676** —— *Iliad* I. 452 Filled with sweet wine the Temp'rers stood.

tempering ('tɛmpərɪŋ), *vbl. sb.* [f. TEMPER *v.* + -ING[1].] **a.** The action of the verb TEMPER, in various senses; an instance of this.

1382 WYCLIF *Prov.* xii. 11 Who is sweete, liueth in tempringis [**1388** temperaunces]. —— *Ezek.* xiii. 14 [see TEMPERURE 1]. *c* **1440** *Promp. Parv.* 488/2 Temperynge, or mesurynge of sundry thyngys to-gedyr. **1486** *Nottingham Rec.* III. 241 To a warkman for temperyng of morter. **1523** FITZHERB. *Husb.* §4 The temperynge [of the plough] to go brode and narowe is in the settyng of the culture. **1538** [see TEMPER *v.* 18]. **1592** SHAKS. *Ven. & Ad.* 565 What waxe so frozen but dissolues with tempering? **1600** HOLLAND *Livy* XLI. xxv. 1113 Proxenus..dranke a cup of poison of his wives tempering, whereof he died. **1655** MOUFET & BENNET *Health's Improv.* (1746) 90 Concerning the tempering of the Air in our Houses. **1661** BOYLE *Unsucceeding Exper.* Wks. 1772 I. 341 The tempering of steel. **1726** LEONI tr. *Alberti's Archit.* I. 42/1 The Workman's..Manner of Building depends partly upon..his Stone, and partly upon the tempering of his Mortar. **1839** [see TEMPERER 1]. **1848** R. I. WILBERFORCE *Doctr. Incarnation* xiv. (1852) 409 Through the happy tempering of His natural qualities. **1875** OUSELEY *Harmony* v. 67 This interval..in tuning a keyed instrument, will require a much greater alteration, or tempering. **1881** *Encycl. Brit.* XIII. 352/2 The generic phrase 'tempering' is usually applied to mean a combination of the hardening and annealing processes..hardening [the steel] to a red heat and suddenly cooling, and then heating up again to a somewhat lower temperature and allowing to cool slowly. **1941** JONES & SCHUBERT *Engineering Encycl* II. 1274 The object of tempering, or 'drawing', is to reduce the brittleness in hardened steel.

b. *attrib.* and *Comb.*, as *tempering-bar*, *-bath*, *-furnace*, *-machine*, *-screw*, *temperature*, *-wheel*: see quots.

1823 J. BADCOCK *Dom. Amusem.* 138 The fusion is to be raised to the tempering height. **1825** J. NICHOLSON *Operat. Mechanic* 668 The tempering screw..is..added to keep the waggon in its proper situation, in whatever way the spring of the weighing machine may be acted upon by the friction. **1864** WEBSTER, *Tempering color*, the shade of color that indicates the degree of temper in tempering steel. **1877** KNIGHT *Dict. Mech.*, *Tempering-furnace*,..one specially contrived for imparting an equal heat to the articles to be tempered. *Ibid.*, *Tempering-machine*, one for handling heavy steel plates during the operations in tempering. *Ibid.*, *Tempering-wheel*, a device for..tempering clay for making brick, etc. **1891** *Cent. Dict.*, *Tempering-oven*, in glass-manuf., an annealing-oven used after the melting-oven. **1910** *Encycl. Brit.* XIV. 808/1 The higher the tempering-temperature, *i.e.* that to which the hardened steel is.. reheated, the more is the molecular rigidity relaxed. **1967** A. H. COTTRELL *Introd. Metallurgy* xx. 384 Higher tempering temperatures may be used, thereby improving the toughness of the steel.

'**tempering**, *ppl. a.* [f. as prec. + -ING[2].] That tempers; softening, mitigating.

1612 SELDEN *Drayton's Poly-olb.* vi. Notes 97 Those that sing the tempering and mollifying Pæans to Apollo. **1817** BYRON *Lam. of Tasso* viii, Like steel in tempering fire. **1846** MCCULLOCH *Acc. Brit. Emp.* (1854) I. 91 The tempering influence of the ocean.

temperish ('tɛmpərɪʃ), *a.* [f. TEMPER *sb.* 11 + -ISH[1].] Inclined to or exhibiting bad temper.

1925 *Chambers's Jrnl.* Nov. 764/1 From these temperish folk arise strange quarrels. **1929** *Times* 16 Jan. 13/5 His [*sc.* Lord Haig's] reply was more than emphatic; it was almost temperish. **1935** [see *riding-blanket* s.v. RIDING *vbl. sb.* 5 a].

'**temperless**, *a. rare.* [f. TEMPER *sb.* + -LESS.] Having no moderation of temper.

a **1618** SYLVESTER *Panaretus* 1374 So swelling proud; so surly-browd the while; So temper-lesse.

temperment: see TEMPERAMENT 3, quot. 1471.

temperour, variant of TEMPERURE *Obs.*

temper-pin. *Sc.* [f. TEMPER *sb.* + PIN *sb.*]

1. The wooden screw used in regulating the tightness of the band of a spinning-wheel; *fig.* temper, disposition.

17.. in Ritson *Sc. Songs* (1794) I. 175 My spinning-wheel is auld and stiff,..To keep the temper pin in tiff, Employs aft my hand, sir. *a* **1796** BURNS *There was a Lass* i, Ay she shook the temper-pin. **1864** LATTO *Tam. Bodkin* iii, A hole in her chackit apron claught haud o' the temper pin, whan doon gaed Bessie an' the wheel. *Ibid.* x, Mr. G.'s temper pin was nae wise improved by the..catastrophe.

†**2.** A tuning-screw or peg of a violin, etc. *Obs.*

1786 BURNS *Ep. Maj. Logan* iv, Heaven send your heart-strings aye in tune, And screw your temper-pins aboon. **1788** SHIRREFS *Poems* (1790) 339 Gin the temper-pin ye'll screw, And gi'es a sang.

temper-pot, -screw: see TEMPER *sb.* 14.

tempersome ('tɛmpəsəm), *a.* orig. *dial.* [f. TEMPER *sb.* + -SOME[1].] Quick-tempered. Also pseudo-*arch.* [after TEMPER *sb.* 6], displaying extreme conditions of weather. Hence '**tempersomeness**.

1875 W. D. PARISH *Dict. Sussex Dial.* 119 *Tempersome*, hasty-tempered. **1879–81** G. F. JACKSON *Shropshire Word-bk.* 434 *Tempersome*, adj., hot-tempered; passionate. **1906** W. DE MORGAN *Joseph Vance* xliii. 392 He was very tempersome about it. **1909** —— *It never can happen Again* I. xxv. 370 Marianne, for all her tempersomeness and jealousy, loved and reverenced Challis. **1946** M. PEAKE *Titus Groan* 234 And now that it is so tempersome and cold you are always going out into the nastiness and getting wet or frozen.

†**temperure.** *Obs.* Also 4–5 temprure, temperour(e. [a. OF. *temprēure* (12th c. in Godef.):—L. *temperātūra*: see TEMPERATURE.]

1. Tempering; *concr.* tempering liquid, etc.

1388 WYCLIF *Ezek.* xiii. 14, Y schal distrie the wal, which ȝe pargetiden with out temperure [**1382** temperynge; *Vulg.* absque temperamento]. *c* **1400** *Rom. Rose* 4177 The temprure of the mortere Was maad of licour wonder dere. **1426** LYDG. *De Guil. Pilgr.* 23524 Of their morter the temprure, Founded vppoun charyte, Of concord and fraternyte.

2. Adjustment of pitch, tuning; tunefulness.

1390 GOWER *Conf.* I. 39 Arion, Which hadde an harpe of such temprure, And therto of so good mesure [etc.]. *Ibid.* III. 303 Of hire Harpe the temprure He tawhte hire ek.

3. Condition of the weather or climate; *esp.* temperate or good condition; = TEMPERATURE 6.

1387 TREVISA *Higden* (Rolls) I. 179 Good corn contray, where þere is good temperure of heuene and of wedir [*coeli temperies*]. *Ibid.* II. 291 Þe temperure þat comeþ of hiȝnesse and lownesse of sterres and planetes, comeþ aȝen to temperure at þe fifteþe ȝere. *a* **1485** FORTESCUE *Wks.* (1869) 477 Temperour of the ayre, clerenes of the sea.

4. = TEMPER *sb.* 5 (of steel, etc.), TEMPERATURE 8.

c **1407** LYDG. *Reson & Sens.* 1191 A bryght helme..of swych temprure, That pollex swerde ne noon armure May do therto no violence. *c* **1440** *Partonope* 1943 Hawbrek..of goode mesure Mighty and strong and of good temperure.

5. Temperance, self-control, moderation.

c **1380** WYCLIF *Sel. Wks.* III. 256 Þe þridde vertue..is temperoure in oure dede. *c* **1440** *Jacob's Well* 142 Glotonye is, whan þou hast a talent, wyth-outyn temperure & mesure, to mete or drynke.

tempery ('tɛmpərɪ), *a. dial.* [f. TEMPER *sb.* + -Y[1].] Short-tempered.

1905 *Eng. Dial. Dict.* VI. 60/1 Yorks... 'She was a tempery body.' **1951** H. GILES *Harbin's Ridge* xiii. 116 She had tempery ways..and sometimes I felt like I was in a pot of water with it boiling. **1954** *Landfall* VIII. 266, I cursed on like a tempery child deprived Of what he'd loved.

tempest ('tɛmpɪst), *sb.* Forms: 3– **tempest**; also 3–6 **tempeste**, 4–5 **tempast**, **-e**. [a. OF. *tempeste*, fem. (11th c. in *Roland*) = It., Prov. *tempesta*:—pop. L. **tempesta-m*, for cl. L. *tempestās*, *-ātem* season, weather, storm, f. *tempus* a time, a season; also a. OF. *tempest* masc. (13th c. in Godef.) = Prov. *tempest*:—L. **tempestum*. OF. had also **tempeste*, acc. sing. *tempesté*, pl. *tempestez* (12th c.) = Sp. *tempestád*, Pg. *tempestade*, It. *-ate*, *-ade*,:—L. *tem'pestās*, *tempestā-t-em*.]

1. a. A violent storm of wind, usually accompanied by a downfall of rain, hail, or snow, or by thunder.

c **1250** *Old Kentish Serm.* in *O.E. Misc.* 32 So hi were in þo ssipe so a-ros a great tempeste of winde. **1297** R. GLOUC. (Rolls) 1151 Hor folc hii lore in þe se þoru tempest [*v.r.* tempeste] moni on. *a* **1300** *Cursor M.* 6027 (Cott.) Israel for þis tempest [*Gött.* tempast] Was noþer harmed, man ne beist. **13..** *K. Alis.* 5810 (Bodl. MS.) Þe wederes stronge and tempestes þat hem duden grete molestes. *c* **1386** CHAUCER *Manciple's T.* 197 Euere crie agayn tempest and rayn. **1390** GOWER *Conf.* III. 203 A cruel king lich the tempeste, The whom no Pite myhte areste. *c* **1400** *Destr. Troy* 12467 Trees thurgh tempestes, tynde hade þere leues. **1535** COVERDALE *2 Kings* ii. 1 When the Lorde was mynded to take vp Elias in the tempest. **1665** SIR T. HERBERT *Trav.* (1677) 389 Seven whole dayes and nights this tempest lasted. **1697** DRYDEN *Virg. Georg.* IV. 608 A Station safe for Ships, when Tempests roar. **1815** J. SMITH *Panorama Sc. & Art* II. 46 In some places the time of change is attended with calms, in others..with violent tempests. **1856** STANLEY *Sinai & Pal.* i. §3. 68 The whole air filled..with a tempest of sand driving in your face like sleet.

b. A thunder-storm. *U.K. dial.* and *North-eastern N. Amer.*

c **1532** DU WES *Introd. Fr.* in *Palsgr.* 946/1 To be killed with tempest, *fouldroier*. **1712** HEARNE *Collect.* 30 June (O.H.S.) III. 408 We were forc'd by a tempest to stop at Yarnton. **1839** G. BIRD *Nat. Phil.* 212 Several instances have occurred of the fatal effects of a tempest..at a considerable distance from the spot..where the violence of the lightning appeared to have been chiefly exerted. *c* **1860** *Northamp. Dial.*, It's very still and black. I think we shall have a tempest to-night. **1877** R. T. COOKE in *Harper's Mag.* Jan. 297/1 Ominous flashes of tempest began to play about the far horizon. **1883** *Hampsh. Gloss.*, *Tempest*, a thunder-storm. **1892** *Dialect Notes* I. 211 *Tempest*, a thunder-shower. [Plymouth, Massachusetts.] **1951** *Amer. Speech* XXVI. 251 Such localized terms as..the southeastern New England tempest (thunderstorm)... Tempest was recorded from a Schuylerville (Saratoga Co.) informant, definitely conscious of his ultimate Nantucket ancestry. **1965** E. RICHARDSON *Living Island* 171 August is also the month of tempests (for here [in Nova Scotia] electrical storms keep the name used by Shakespeare).

2. *transf.* and *fig.* **a.** A violent commotion or disturbance; a tumult, rush; agitation, perturbation. *tempest in a tea-pot*: see TEA-POT *sb.*

c **1315** SHOREHAM vii. 642 Þat best..þat hyt hedde ine hym y-nome Soche a tempeste. **13..** *Guy Warw.* (A.) 273 Now is Gij in gret tempest, Sorwe he makeþ wiþ þe mest. **1472** *Coventry Leet Bk.* 373 The gret tempestes diuisions & troubles that in late daies haue be in this our Reaume. **1588** SHAKS. *Tit. A.* I. i. 458 Cheere the heart, That dies in tempest of thy angry frowne. **1606** S. GARDINER *Bk. Angling* 12 Waues of tribulation, tempests of tentations. **1770** BURKE *Corr.* (1844) I. 243 In the midst of all this tempest the ministers..seem much at their ease. **1894** H. NISBET *Bush Girl's Rom.* 61 Helen Craven was very pale and very silent during this parental tempest. **1909** *Daily Chron.* 3 Dec. 1/2 This fine passage..drew a tempest of cheering.

†**b.** Calamity, misfortune, trouble. *Obs.*

c **1330** R. BRUNNE *Chron. Wace* (Rolls) 16541 Moryne & hunger..had reft..al þe folk wyþ tempest vnkynde. *c* **1470** HENRY *Wallace* VII. 394 For sleuth nor sleip sall nayne remayne in me, Off this tempest till I a wengeance se.

3. a. A confused or tumultuous throng; †a crowded assembly: cf. HURRICANE 2 b (*obs.*); a rushing or tearing crowd.

1746 SMOLLETT *Advice* 30 *note*, Not unaptly styled a drum, from the noise and emptiness of the entertainment. There are also drum-major, rout, tempest, and hurricane, differing only in degrees of multitude and uproar. **1755** J. SHEBBEARE *Lydia* (1769) II. 309 How to spend their hours in London more agreeably than in routs, drums, huricanes, and tempests. **1866** CARLYLE in *Morning Star* 5 Apr. 5/5 It turned out to be a tempest of wild horses, managed by young lads who had a turn for hunting with their grooms.

b. A person of stormy temper.

1852 MRS. STOWE *Uncle Tom's C.* xxiii, Henrique is a regular little tempest—his mother and I have given him up long ago.

†**4.** A time; a period, an occasion. (A verbalism of translation.) *Obs.*

1382 WYCLIF *2 Chron.* xxviii. 9 In that tempest [Vulg. *ea tempestate*] was ther a prophete of the Lord. **1387** TREVISA *Higden* (Rolls) II. 337 In þat tempest [*sub ea tempestate*] went out þat man þat heet Liber pater.

5. *attrib.* and *Comb.* **a.** simple attrib., as *tempest-anger*, *-cloud*, *-pitch*, *-rack* (RACK *sb.*[1] 3), *-shock*, *-speed*, *-spirit*, *-time*; **b.** instrumental, etc., as *tempest-beaten*, *-blown*, *-born*, *-charged*, *-driven*, *-flung*, *-harrowed*, *-haunted*, *-rent*, *-rocked*, *-shaken*, *-shattered*, *-smitten*, *-swept*, *-throttled*, *-torn*, *-troubled*, *-winged*, *-worn* adjs.; also TEMPEST-TOSSED; **c.** objective, etc., as *tempest-bearing*, *-clear*, *-cleaving*, *-loving*, *-proof*, *-scoffing*, *-walking* adjs.; also *tempest-raiser*.

1898 W. WATSON *Poems*, *Tomb of Burns*, Byron's *tempest-anger, tempest-mirth. **1747** DUNKIN in *Francis's* tr. *Horace*, *Ep.* II. ii. 307 Nor yet expos'd to *Tempest-bearing Strife. **1591** SYLVESTER *Du Bartas* I. v. 433 The *tempest-beaten Vessel's stern. **1759** JOHNSON *Rasselas* xxi, I rejoiced like a tempest-beaten sailor at his entrance into the harbour. **1865** BARING-GOULD *Werewolves* x. 177 To leave the summer cirrus and turn to the *tempest-born rain-cloud. **1826** J. G. WHITTIER *Vale of Merrimac* in *Free Press* (Newburyport, Mass.) 29 June 4/1 And the *tempest-charg'd vapor their tall tops embraces. **1868** M. COLLINS *Sweet Anne Page* I. 149 Always the white sky should be *tempest-clear. **1818** SHELLEY *Rosalind & Helen* (1819) 77 That a *tempest-cleaving swan Of the songs of Albion.. Found a nest in Thee. **1849** tr. *De la Motte Fouqué's Sir Elidoc* 166 His *tempest-driven heart. **1776** MICKLE tr. *Camoens' Lusiad* 80 On many a *tempest-harrowed ocean tost. **1880** LONGFELLOW *Ultima Thule* 7 Are not these The *tempest-haunted Hebrides, Where sea-gulls scream? **1727–46** THOMSON *Summer* 1123 The *tempest-loving raven scarce Dares wing the dubious dusk. **1660** BOND *Scut. Reg.* 403 Like one Ship..*tempest-proof upon a troubled Sea. **1844** LOWELL *Legend of Brittany* II. xi, Before its eyes the sullen *tempest-rack Would fade. **1877** tr. *Lacroix's Sc. & Lit. Mid. Ages* (1878) 225 A special class of sorcerers called *tempest-raisers. **1822** T. MITCHELL *Aristoph.* I. 186 Must I be thus *tempest-rent? *c* **1820** S. ROGERS *Italy*, *Camp. Florence* 176 Now *tempest-rocked, now whirling round and round. **1817** SHELLEY *Laon* I. 23 The *tempest-shaken wood, The waves, the fountains, and the hush of night. **1845** LONGFELLOW *Seaweed* vii, in *Poems* 99 From the wreck of Hopes far-scattered, *Tempest-shattered, Floating waste and desolate. **1837** *Spirit of the Woods* 84 Mid sorrow's *tempest-shock. **1844** J. G. WHITTIER *Bridal of Pennacook* in *United States Mag.* Sept. 239 Sometimes The *tempest-smitten tree receives From one small root the sap which climbs Its topmost spray and crowning leaves. **1854**

J. S. C. ABBOTT *Napoleon* (1855) II. iv. 79 Struggling along the drifted and *tempest-swept defile. **1633** FORD *Broken H.* IV. ii, Like *tempest-threaten'd trees unfirmly rooted. **1930** R. CAMPBELL *Adamastor* 51 Doomed vessels.. Reared to the stars their *tempest-throttled cry. **1598** DRAYTON *Heroic Ep., Brandon to Q. Mary* 77 After long trauaile, *tempest-torne and wrack'd. **1918** W. S. CHURCHILL in M. Gilbert *Winston S. Churchill* (1977) IV. Compan. I. 418 Prompt and clear must be those great decisions which assign definite limits to the increasing confusion and miseries of the vanquished and above the tempest-torn waters light again the beacons of mankind. **1939** R. CAMPBELL *Flowering Rifle* II. 64 The wide-winged and wounded Albatross The tempest-torn that rides (and bears) the strife. **1825** RICHARDSON *Sonnets* 141, I marked the *tempest-troubled wave. **1952** R. CAMPBELL tr. *Baudelaire's Poems* 183 She sought, with tempest-troubled gaze, the skies Of her first innocence. **1820** SHELLEY *Prometh. Unb.* I. 35 These are Jove's *tempest-walking hounds. **1727–46** THOMSON *Summer* 344 Till, *tempest-wing'd, Fierce Winter sweeps them from the face of day.

tempest (ˈtɛmpɪst, †tɛmˈpɛst), *v.* [ad. OF. *tempeste-r* (12th c.), f. *tempeste*: see prec.]

1. *trans.* To affect by or as by a tempest; to throw into violent commotion, to agitate violently.

1390 GOWER *Conf.* II. 167 And whan hir list the Sky tempeste, The reinbowe is hir Messager. *c* **1430** *Pilgr. Lyf Manhode* IV. i. (1869) 174 Tempested it was gretliche, of gret tempestes and of wyind. **1480** CAXTON *Ovid's Met.* XI. xix, The wyndes.. renne so radely, that nothing may lette them to tempeste alle the see. **1638** *Penit. Conf.* (1657) 346 Rooted most when most tempested. **1667** MILTON *P.L.* VII. 412 Fish.. part huge of bulk Wallowing unweildie, enormous in thir Gate, Tempest the Ocean. **1715–20** POPE *Iliad* XXI. 30 The huge dolphin tempesting the main. **1830** H. N. COLERIDGE *Grk. Poets* (1834) 129 As when two winds —the north and west.. suddenly tempest the sea. **1857** H. MILLER *Test. Rocks* iii. 137 Its wonderful whales.. of the reptilian class.. must have tempested the deep.

2. *fig.* To disturb violently (a person, the mind).

c **1374** CHAUCER *Boeth.* II. pr. iv. 28 (Camb. MS.), I haue som what conforted the so þat thow tempest the nat thus with al thi fortune. *a* **1415** LYDGATE *Temple of Glas* 1157 For no turment, þat þe fallen shal, Tempest þe not. **1521** FISHER *Serm. Luther* Wks. (1876) 312 Ioannes wiccliff with other moo which sore tempested the chyrche. **1621** T. WILLIAMSON tr. *Goulart's Wise Vieillard* 25 Tempested with disordered thoughts and vnruly passions. **1762** GOLDSM. *Cit. W.* xlvii, A mind.. tempested up by a thousand various passions. **1819** CAMPBELL *Spec. Brit. Poets* I. 164 A man.. has hardly tied the fatal knot when his house is tempested by female eloquence.

3. *intr.* Of the wind, weather, etc., and *impers.*: To be tempestuous, to blow tempestuously; to rage, storm. Also *fig. dial.* or *arch.*

c **1477** CAXTON *Jason* 56 Sone after the winde began to rise and tempest horrible and impetuouse. **1530** PALSGR. 754/1 Herde you nat howe it tempested to nyght? **1601** B. JONSON *Poetaster* v. i, Other Princes.. Thunder, and tempest, on those learned heads, Whom Caesar with such honour doth aduance. **1615** G. SANDYS *Trav.* 207 (tr. *Ovid's Met.* XI. 521) Blind night in darkness tempests. **1875** W. D. PARISH *Dict. Sussex Dial.* 119 It tempestes so as we're troubled to pitch the hay upon to the stack anyhows in the wurreld. *a* **1907** F. THOMPSON *Works* (1913) I. 120 Flew spurned the pebbled stars: those splendours then Had tempested on earth, star upon star.

Hence ˈ**tempested** *ppl. a.*, tossed or afflicted by a tempest; ˈ**tempesting** *vbl. sb.*

a **1631** DONNE *Serm.* xxxvii. (1640) 366 No repentance [can] stay his tempested and weather-beaten conscience. **1811** SHELLEY *St. Irvyne* ix. Pr. Wks. 1888 I. 196 And the moon dimly gleam'd through the tempested air. **1846** TRENCH *Miracles* iv, The Church of Christ has evermore resembled this tempested bark. **1882** MYERS *Renewal of Youth* 288 Rocked by strange blast and stormy tempestings.

†**tempeˈstarian.** *Obs. rare*$^{-1}$. In 8 (erron.) tempestrian. [f. med.L. *tempestāri-us* (8th c. in Du Cange) + -AN.] (See quot.)

1708–22 BINGHAM *Antiq.* XVI. v. §6 (1840) VI. 68 The capitulars of Charles the Great, where decrees were made against calculators, enchanters, and 'tempestrians', as they are called, that is raisers of storms and tempests.

†**tempestative**, *a. Obs. rare*$^{-1}$. [a. obs. F. *tempestatif, -ive* (15th c. in Godef.): see TEMPEST *sb.* and -ATIVE.] That raises a tempest.

1694 MOTTEUX *Rabelais* IV. xx, If I come near thee.. and chastise thee like any Tempestative Devil.

tempesteous, -ious: see TEMPESTUOUS.

tempestive (tɛmˈpɛstɪv), *a. arch.* [ad. L. *tempestīvus* timely: see TEMPEST and -IVE.]

1. Timely, seasonable.

1611 SPEED *Hist. Gt. Brit.* IX. ix. §60 That prouidence which the King of Scotland.. vsed, was, as more tempestiue, so more commendable. **1620** VENNER *Via Recta* vii. 107 The moderate and tempestiue vse of them may be very good and profitable. **1635** HEYWOOD *Hierarch.* VIII. Comm. 532 The chearefull and tempestiue showres. **1852** *Fraser's Mag.* XLV. 172 After the tempestive banquet at two o'clock.

¶**2.** *erron.* = TEMPESTUOUS 2.

1848 *Tait's Mag.* XV. 118 Every reader will.. point out living examples amid brawling and tempestive politicians.

temˈpestively, *adv. arch.* [f. prec. + -LY².] Seasonably, opportunely.

1621 BURTON *Anat. Mel.* III. ii. III. iv. (1676) 305/2 Dancing is a pleasant recreation of body and mind.. if tempestively used. **1654** H. L'ESTRANGE *Chas. I* (1655) 131 The severall processes.. will more tempestively occurre in the ensuing series of this narration. **1702** BAYNARD in Sir J. Floyer *Hot & Cold Bath.* II. (1706) 367 Hot and Cold Baths.. tempestively, cautiously, and wisely prescrib'd.

†**tempeˈstivious**, *a. Obs. rare*$^{-1}$. [Erron. for *tempestivous, f. as prec. + -OUS.] Seasonable; = TEMPESTIVE 1.

1574 NEWTON *Health Mag.* 6 Exercise fittest to be vsed.. in seasonable and tempestiuious times of the yeare.

†**tempeˈstivity.** *Obs.* [ad. L. *tempestīvitās*, f. *tempestīv-us* TEMPESTIVE: see -ITY.]

1. Seasonableness, timeliness.

1576 NEWTON *Lemnie's Complex.* (1633) 124 Appointing to each function his proper turne, and tempestiuity. **1646** SIR T. BROWNE *Pseud. Ep.* 287 Since their [Jews'] dispersion and habitation in Countries, whose constitutions admit not such tempestivity of harvests. **1656** BLOUNT *Glossogr.*, *Tempestivity*,.. fitnesse of time, seasonablenesse.

2. A season, a time of a particular character.

1569 NEWTON *Cicero's Olde Age* 21 b, To euery part of a mans life and age, are geeuen hys conuenyente tymes and propre tempestiuytyes. **1642** S. ASHE *Best Refuge* 19 Times. The word signifies the tempestivity, the season of time. The Septuagint renders it right, Ἐν εὐκαιρίαις. **1683** E. HOOKER *Pref. Pordage's M. Div.* 20 In these last Daies there wil hang over us.. periculous tempestivities, hard seasons.

†ˈ**tempestous**, *a. Obs.* [a. AF. *tempestous*, OF. *-eus*, ad. L. type *tempestōs-us, for L. *tempestuōsus*; in It. *tempestoso*, Prov. *tempestos* and *tempestuos* (Littré).] = TEMPESTUOUS 1, 2.

c **1374** CHAUCER *Troylus* II. Proem 5 This see clepe I þe tempestous matere Of desper þat Troylus was Inne. *c* **1500** *Three Kings Sons* 131 If bifore dyner he were hote and tempestous, now is he colde and sobre. **1508** FISHER 7 *Penit. Ps.* xxxviii. I. Wks. (1876) 69 The tempestous trybulacyons wherwith the herte of synners is troubled & vexed.

tempestrian: see TEMPESTARIAN.

ˈ**tempest-ˌtossed, -ˌtost** (-tɒst, *poet.* -ˌtɒsɪd; also -tɔː-), *a.* Tossed by or as by a tempest. Hence ˈ**tempest-ˌtoss** *v. trans.* and *intr.*, to toss or pitch about as a tempest or a tempestuous sea; to agitate or be agitated violently; ˈ**tempest-ˌtossing**, violent agitation by or as by a tempest, etc.

1592 SHAKS. *Rom. & Jul.* III. v. 138 The windes thy sighes.. will ouer set Thy tempest tossed body. **1605** —— *Macb.* I. iii. 25 Though his Barke cannot be lost, Yet it shall be Tempest-tost. **1681** *Roxb. Ball.* (1886) VI. 77 Where peevish coyness and disdain Do tempest-toss the mind. **1747** FRANCIS tr. *Horace, Ep.* I. xi. 19 Though by strong Winds your Bark were Tempest-tost. **1817** SHELLEY *Prince Athanase* in *Posthumous Poems* (1824) II. ii. 251 Thus had his age, dark, cold and tempest-tost, shone truth upon Zonoras. **1867** H. MACMILLAN *Bible Teach.* xii. (1870) 233 Those very afflictions and tempest-tossings which the Church bewails. *a* **1887** E. LAZARUS *New Colossus* in *Poems* (1889) I. 203 Send these, the homeless, tempest-tost to me, I lift my lamp beside the golden door! **1955** E. POUND *Classic Anthol.* I. 8 My heart is no more tempest-toss'd. **1984** *Times* 10 Mar. 17/1 People wrangle and row as though they were part of a tempest-tossed drama by John Cassavetes.

†**temˈpestuate**, *v. Obs. rare*$^{-1}$. [f. L. *tempestu-*, stem of next: see -ATE³ 7.] = TEMPEST *v.*

1702 C. MATHER *Magn. Chr.* VII. vi. (1852) 577 Those parts of New England.. were thus tempestuated by a terrible war.

tempestuous (tɛmˈpɛstjuːəs), *a.* Forms: α. 5 tempesteuous (? = -evous), 6 -eous, -yous, 6–8 -ious; β. 6 -uouse, -uus, 6– tempestuous. [In the β. form, ad. L. *tempestuōs-us*: cf. *tempestu-s*, collateral form of *tempestās* TEMPEST; so obs. F. *tempestueus, -uos* (14th c.), mod.F. *tempêtueux* = Pr. *tempestuos*, Sp., Pg. *tempestuoso*. The α. forms appear to be analogical, after other adjs. in *-eous, -ious*, of various etymology.]

1. Of, pertaining to, involving, or resembling a tempest; subject to or characterized by tempests; stormy, very rough or violent.

α. **1509** HAWES *Past. Pleas.* xxxvii. (Percy Soc.) 194 It thondred loude wyth clappes tempestious. *a* **1548** HALL *Chron., Hen. IV* 18 b, A great tempesteous rage and furious storme. **1592** MORYSON *Let.* in *Itin.* I. (1617) 37 The weather was very tempestious, and not likely to change.

β. **1538** STARKEY *England* I. ii. 61 The trowblus and tempestuus see. **1538** ELYOT, *Tempestuosum*, tempestuous or stormy. **1610** HOLLAND *Camden's Brit.* (1637) 501 A turbulent and tempestuous storme arose. **1639–40** LAUD *Diary* 25 Jan., A very blustering and a tempestuous day. **1799** HT. LEE *Canterb. T., Old Wom.* (ed. 2) I. 348 The weather grew lowering and tempestuous. **1878** BOSWORTH SMITH *Carthage* 121 The dangerous storms to which the south of Sicily was exposed after the rising of the tempestuous Orion.

2. *transf.* and *fig.* Characterized by violent agitation or commotion; turbulent, tumultuous; impetuous, passionate; agitated as by a tempest.

α. **1447** [implied in *tempesteuously*: see next]. **1509** HAWES *Past. Pleas.* xxvii. (Percy Soc.) 120 O Mars! me succoure in tyme tempestyous. *Ibid.* xxxiv. 177 So shall you swage the tempesteous floode Of their stormy myndes. *a* **1586** SIDNEY *Ps.* XXXI. xi, In that tempestious hast, I said, that I from out thy sight was cast. **1710** *Brit. Apollo* III. No. 25. 3/1 Tempestious Ills, in wild Confusion hurl'd.

β. **1509** HAWES *Past. Pleas.* xxxiii. (Percy Soc.) 169 To the last ende of my matter troublous, With waves enclosed so tempestuous. **1648** HERRICK *Hesper., Delight in Disorder*, A winning wave (deserving note) In the tempestuous petticote. **1653** R. SANDERS *Physiogn., Moles* 21 The tempestuous persecutions of her own kindred. **1663** DAVENANT *Siege of Rhodes* Wks. (1672) 2 The Shriller Trumpet and Tempestuous Drum. **1782** MISS BURNEY *Cecilia* VIII. iv, Cecilia was still in this tempestuous state. **1865** SWINBURNE *Atalanta* 1016 Fill the dance up with tempestuous feet.

temˈpestuously, *adv.* [f. prec. + -LY².] In a tempestuous manner.

1447 BOKENHAM *Seyntys* (Roxb.) 73 Trowblyd in hym selph tempesteuously. **1596** WARNER *Alb. Eng.* XI. lxiii. (1612) 272 Tempestiously Arzinaas Rhode receiued Sir Hugh at last. **1642** MILTON *Apol. Smect.* Pref., Wks. 1851 III. 276 Signe, that he meant ere long to be most tempestuously bold, and shamelesse? **1721** R. KEITH tr. *T. à Kempis' Solil. Soul* xvi. 230 The Air may of a sudden be tempestuously stirred. **1876** F. HARRISON *Choice Bks.* (1886) 138 The evils of which you tempestuously complain.

temˈpestuousness. [f. as prec. + -NESS.] The state or quality of being tempestuous or stormy; storminess, turbulence.

1648 HEXHAM *Dutch Dict.* II, *De stuerigheyt der Zee*, the tempestuousnesse, or the storminesse of the Sea. *a* **1652** J. SMITH *Sel. Disc.* x. iv. (1673) 461 That impetuous violence and tempestuousness with which men are acted in pretensions of Religion. **1798** *Hist.* in *Ann. Reg.* 154/2 The tempestuousness of the times appeared favourable to such an attempt. **1877** DOWDEN *Shaks. Prim.* vi. 117 There is no tempestuousness of passion and no artistic mystery.

‖**tempête** (tɑ̃pɛt). [Fr., lit. 'tempest'.] An English country-dance (and tune) of the late-nineteenth century.

1873 L. TROUBRIDGE *Life amongst Troubridges* (1966) viii. 72 We had a *Tempête*, the Boulanger and 'Wiss'. **1879** *Manners & Tone of Good Society* viii. 139 Country dances, such as the 'Tempête', 'Sir Roger de Coverley', etc., are usually danced at private balls when given in the country. **1923** G. ARTHUR *Further Lett. from Man of no Importance* (1932) 155 Yes, the Tempête was the popular dance at children's and semi-grown-up dances of our young days, and even later at country balls; fancy its being danced again in Paris.

‖**tempietto** (temˈpjɛtto). Pl. **tempietti.** [It., lit. 'little temple': cf. TEMPLET⁴.] A colonnaded building, freq. of circular form, surmounted by a dome.

1896 W. J. ANDERSON *Archit. Renaissance in Italy* iv. 77 Bramante's *Tempietto* in the Cloisters of San Pietro in Montorio (1502). **1901** M. CARMICHAEL *In Tuscany* 158 Civitali was.. a fine and practical architect. He is thought to have built the Palazzo Pretorio, and to him belongs the honour of having built the dome-like chapel (*Tempietto*) in which is preserved the sacrosanct and venerable Volto Santo. **1922** G. GROMORT *Italian Renaissance Archit.* iv. 80 Palladio himself, half a century later, made a drawing of Bramante's Tempietto. **1960** E. BOWEN *Time in Rome* ii. 47 A *tempietto* in a moist northern garden. **1962** *Listener* 1 Feb. 228/1 The ancient Romans had filled their gardens with statuary as well as with *tempietti*, colonnades, covered galleries, apses, and pavilions. **1971** *Country Life* 7 Oct. 887/1 The Hafeziye [in Shiraz, Iran] is much more than the pleasant municipal garden one might expect, the formal approach, open colonnade and delightful tempietto beyond achieving a simple grandeur that is very memorable.

temping, *vbl. sb.*: see TEMP *v.*

tempir(e, obs. forms of TEMPER *v.*

Templar (ˈtɛmplə(r)), *sb.* Forms: 3–7 templer, 4–5 -ere, (5 templeer), 5– templar. [a. AF. *templer*, OF. *templier* (*c* 1200 in Godef.), = med.L. *templārius* (Du Cange), f. *templum*, TEMPLE *sb.*¹: see -ER² 2; also *templārēs*, pl. of cl. L. *templāris*, in papal document of 1157 in Muratori *Antiq., Diss.* XI. (1774) II. 329. For later spelling see -AR².]

1. A member of a military and religious order, consisting of knights (***Knights Templars***, *Knights* or *Poor Soldiers of the Temple*), chaplains, and men-at-arms, founded *c* 1118, chiefly for the protection of the Holy Sepulchre and of Christian pilgrims visiting the Holy Land: so called from their occupation of a building on or contiguous to the site of the Temple of Solomon at Jerusalem. They were suppressed in 1312.

c **1290** *Beket* 2264 in *S. Eng. Leg.* I. 171 He [K. Hen. II, as part of his penance] scholde finde to hundret knyȝtes to fiȝte Al ane ȝer with þe templers for holi churche riȝte. **13..** *Coer de L.* 3920 Hys.. Templeres and hys Hospytalers. *c* **1330** R. BRUNNE *Chron.* (1810) 305 A templer of pris, Sir Brian þe geay, Maister templere he was on þis half þe se. **1387** TREVISA *Higden* (Rolls) VIII. 293 Þe fifte Clement was pope.. he dampned þe ordre of Frere Templers. **14..** *Nom.* in Wr.-Wülcker 681/23 *Hic templarius*, a templer. **1598** HAKLUYT *Voy.* I. 146 The Templars which were therein returned home out of Fraunce. **1603** KNOLLES *Hist. Turks* (1638) 29 Hugh Paganus first Master of the Templers.. returned with a great number of zealous Christians, ready to lay down their liues for defence of the Christian faith and religion. **1610** HOLLAND *Camden's Brit.* (1637) 427 A church for Knights Templars, which they had newly built according to the forme of the Temple neere unto the Sepulchre of Our Lord at Hierusalem. **1700** TYRRELL *Hist. Eng.* II. 745 One Durand a Knight-Templar. **1839** KEIGHTLEY *Hist. Eng.* I. 266 It was in the reign of Edward II that the potent and wealthy order of Knights Templars was suppressed throughout Europe. **1910** C. PERKINS in *Eng. Hist. Rev.* Apr. 224 There do not appear to have been over fifteen or twenty knights in the total of 144 Templars in the British Isles.

b. Phrase.
1653 URQUHART *Rabelais* I. v. 26, I drink no more then a spunge, I drink like a Templer Knight [*orig.* je boy comme ung Templier]. 1819 SCOTT *Ivanhoe* xxxv, Now, to drink like a Templar is the boast of each jolly boon companion!

2. A barrister or other person who occupies chambers in the Inner or Middle Temple (see TEMPLE *sb.*^{1} 5).
1588 *Marprel. Epist.* (Arb.) 26 Let the Templars haue M. Trauers their preacher restored againe vnto them. 1628 in *Crt. & Times Chas. I* (1848) I. 311 On Saturday last, the Templars chose one Mr. Palmes..their lord of misrule. 1683 TRYON *Way to Health* 481 But very few Inns of Court Gentlemen or Templers. 1687 MONTAGUE & PRIOR *Hind & P. Transv.* 22 Many a young Templer will save his shilling by this Stratagem of my Mice. *a*1760 H. BROWNE *Pipe Tobacco, Imit.* v, Blest leaf! whose aromatic gales dispense To Templars modesty, to Parsons sense. 1815 LAMB *Let. to Southey* 6 May, I am a Christian, Englishman, Londoner, Templar. 1818 SCOTT *Hrt. Midl.* i, The part which is common to the higher classes of the law at Edinburgh, and which nearly resembles that of the young Templars in the days of Steele and Addison. 1902 J. HUTCHINSON (*title*) A Catalogue of Notable Middle Templars.

3. a. A member of an order of Freemasons calling themselves Knights Templars, extensively established in the United States.
1859 (*title*) A Service for the Encampments of Knights Templars together with a Sketch of the History of the Order. *Ibid.* 30 [see TEMPLARY *sb.* 3]. 1878 [see ENCAMPMENT 3]. 1904 *Westm. Gaz.* 2 Aug. 2/3 The Royal Arch degree, the possession of which in these later times has been held essential to a Knight Templar.

b. Short for GOOD TEMPLAR, q.v.
1874- [see GOOD TEMPLAR]. 1885 *Daily Chron.* 3 Sept. (Cassell) He had often feared lest any of..their juvenile templars should be decoyed away on their journey to or from the meetings. 1905 *Daily News* 30 Oct. 8 The Baron..being by no means a templar according to the jargon of today—'templar' or 'teetotaler', whatever the phrase may be.

4. An official of the Jewish temple. *nonce-use.*
1884 H. W. BEECHER in *Chr. World Pulpit* XXV. 11/3 It was this [the raising of Lazarus]..that brought..the determination of the templars that He should perish.

5. *attrib.*, as ***Templar Knight, order***, etc.
*c*1440 *Alphabet of Tales* 233 Cesarius tellis how some tyme þer was a preste of þe Templer ordur. 1537 *Orig. & Sprynge Sectes* 15 Templare Lordes. *Ibid.* 16 Templare Knyghtes. 1819 SCOTT *Ivanhoe* xxxviii, A huge volume, which contained the proceedings of the Templar Knights.

Hence **'Templardom**, the community or body of Templars; †**Tem'plarian** *a. Obs.*, of or pertaining to the Templars; **'Templarism**, the principles of Templars (in any of the senses, e.g. = *Good Templarism*); **'Templarlike** *adv.*, like a Templar.
1877 G. H. KINGSLEY *Sport & Trav.* (1900) 345 The most temperate races of the world are apt to burst out..to the utter confusion of all 'Good *Templardom'. 1600 W. WATSON *Decacordon* (1602) 19 Seditious *Templarian Iesuiticall sectaries. 1612 T. JAMES *Jesuits' Downf.* 48 For as they liue iust Templarlike in all things, so there will be a right Templarian downefall. 1888 J. SHALLOW *Templars Trials* 69 M. Loiseleur dilates..on the difference between Gnosticism and *Templarism. 1893 *Voice* (N.Y.) 15 June, He spoke of the drink question as affecting native races, and the spread of Templarism in India, Africa and Australasia.

templar ('tɛmplə(r)), *a.* [ad. late L. *templār-is*, f. *templum*, TEMPLE *sb.*^{1}: see -AR^{1}.] Of, pertaining to, or characteristic of a (or the Jewish) temple.
1728 R. MORRIS *Ess. Anc. Archit.* 3 The Example of..Solomon in Templar and Domal Architecture. 1812-29 COLERIDGE in *Lit. Rem.* (1838) III. 112 It would be better to regard solitary, family, and templar devotion as distinctions in sort, rather than differences in degree. 1840 MILMAN *Hist. Chr.* II. 415 In the East, where the churches retained probably more of the templar form. 1845 J. MARTINEAU *Misc.* (1852) 118 They have no templar and sacerdotal duties, can offer no sacrifice, absolve from no sin.

Templary ('tɛmplərɪ), *sb.* Also 5 *pl.* -arijs. [ad. med.L. *templāri-us*, TEMPLAR *sb.*: see -ARY^{1}.]
†**1.** = TEMPLAR *sb.* 1. *Obs.*
1432-50 tr. *Higden* (Rolls) VIII. 293 þis pope..dampned the ordre of Templaryes [*ordinem Templariorum*]. 1460 CAPGRAVE *Chron.* (Rolls) 177 He procured the distruccion of Templaries. *c*1460 tr. *Oseney Regr.* 108 þe templarijs. 1599 HAKLUYT *Voy.* II. I. 35 (an. 1249) The [holy] land..might soone be woon to Christendome, were it not for rebellious Templaries, with the Hospitalaries, and their followers. 1616 BULLOKAR *Eng. Expos.*, *Templaries*, certaine Christian souldiours dwelling about the Temple at Hierusalem, whose office was to entertain Christian strangers that came hither for deuotion. 1656 BLOUNT *Glossogr.*, *Templaries*, Knights of the Temple.
†**2.** An estate or benefice belonging to the Knights Templars. *Obs. rare*$^{-1}$.
1592 *Sc. Acts Jas. VI* (1814) III. 564/1 þe rentaillis of all bischoiprikis, abbacies, priorijs, provestries,..chaiplanries, templaries, and vtheris benefices.
3. Templars collectively; *Hist.* the system or organization of the Templars; in 19th c., the Masonic and Temperance societies so called.
*a*1661 FULLER *Worthies, Oxford.* (1662) II. 329 The Holy Land, where thorough the Treachery of Templary, cowardize of the Greeks, diversity of the Climate, distance of the place, and differences betwixt Christian Princes, much time was spent,..many lives lost,..but little profit produced. 1859 *Service for Encampments of Knights Templars* 30 Any attempt..to make Masonry perfect without Templary, or on the other hand, to perpetuate an order of Templars independent of Freemasonry must only shew ignorance of the real history of both Societies. 1874, 1897 [see GOOD TEMPLAR]. 1904 *Westm. Gaz.* 2 Aug. 2/3 At Louisville [in 1901]..a colossal pageant descriptive of the history of Knight Templary from the time of the Crusades.

†'**templary**, *a. Obs. rare.* [ad. late L. *templāris* pertaining to a temple: see -ARY^{2}.]
1. Of or pertaining to a temple: = TEMPLAR *a.*
1607 *Schol. Disc. agst Antichr.* I. i. 55 We scorne papistes that pretende a ciuill worshippe in templarie bowing.
2. Of, pertaining to, or named from the Temple at Jerusalem; ***Templary Knights*** = Knights Templars: see TEMPLAR *sb.* 1.
1617 MORYSON *Itin.* I. 84 In the Priory of St. Iohn, belonging of old to the Templary Knights, and now to the Knights of Rhodes or Malta. *Ibid.* 190 (*Paris*) On the left hand as you come in, is the house of the Templary Knights.

template ('tɛmpleɪt). Also 7- **templet** ('tɛmplɪt). [Of uncertain origin.
L. *templum* 'temple' had also the sense 'rafter'; *templet* in sense 1 here (but hardly in sense 2) might possibly be a dim. from this. F. *templet* is given by Littré only as a synonym and presumably a derivative of *temple* fem., a weaver's stretcher, TEMPLE *sb.*^{3} The spelling *template*, with its spelling-pronunciation, is evidently pseudo-etymological after *plate*.]
1. a. *Building.* A horizontal piece of timber in a wall, or spanning a window or doorway, to take and distribute the pressure of a girder, or of joists or rafters; a plate.
1677 MOXON *Mech. Exerc.* (ed. 2) 26 When you lay any timber on brickwork as lintels over windows, or templets under girders, lay them in loom. 1802 *Trans. Soc. Arts* XX. 216 The templets or wall-plates on which the Girder rests. 1819 P. NICHOLSON *Archit. Dict.*, *Templet.* 1855 *Act 18 & 19 Vict.* c. 122 §15 Every bressummer bearing upon any party wall must be borne by a templet, or corbel of stone or iron, tailed through at least half the thickness of such wall, and of the full breadth of the bressummer. 1879 *Cassell's Techn. Educ.* III. 195 The purpose of templates is similar to that of wall-plates. 1901 *J. Black's Carp. & Build., Scaffolding* 53 The templets must..be bedded in good strong portland cement mortar before being wedged up tightly.
b. *Shipbuilding.* One of the wedges for a block under the keel.
1877 in KNIGHT *Dict. Mech.*
2. a. An instrument used as a gauge or guide in bringing any piece of work to the desired shape; usually a flat piece of wood or metal having one edge shaped to correspond to the outline of the finished work; also used as a tool in moulding, and as a guide in forming moulds for castings or pottery, in an automatic lathe, etc.
1819 P. NICHOLSON *Archit. Dict.*, *Templet*, a mould used in masonry and brickwork for the purpose of cutting or setting the work. 1823 —— *Pract. Build.* 359 It will be necessary to have one templet made convex, to try the faces of bricks to. 1825 J. NICHOLSON *Operat. Mechanic* 586 Form a templet or cradle to the surface intended. 1844 *Civil Engin. & Arch. Jrnl.* VII. 187/1 The propeller was of cast iron, and was moulded in loam without a model, by means of iron templates cut to the required curve. 1863 SMILES *Indust. Biog.* 271 His [R. Roberts's] system of templets and gauges, by means of which every part of an engine or tender corresponded with that of every other engine or tender of the same class. 1879 *Cassell's Techn. Educ.* I. 3/2. 1929 D. S. STEWART *Pract. Design Simple Steel Struct.* I. iii. 24 Templates may be either..the bars which are to be used in the structure or..made from some light and easily worked material. 1942 *Sun* (Baltimore) 25 Nov. 6/4 A ship starts being a ship in the mold loft, where skilled hands make wooden patterns, called templates, from the designer's blueprints. 1967 E. SHORT *Embroidery & Fabric Collage* iii. 71 The main lines of the design can be chalked in or tacked on to the top fabric, details being put in freely or drawn round a template. 1977 *Early Music* July 443/3 (Advt.), Set of three, fully-explanatory A2 drawings, two templates, [etc.].
b. A flat plate or strip perforated with holes used as a guide in marking out holes for riveting or drilling. Also *attrib.*
Also, a wooden frame corresponding to the base of any piece of machinery that requires to be fixed by bolts, having holes by means of which the permanent holding-down bolts can be previously fixed in concrete in the exact position to pass through the bolt-holes in the base in question.
1874 THEARLE *Naval Archit.* 98 Templates are used for taking account of the rivet holes in the inside strakes corresponding to those in the frames, when the plates are too heavy to be held in place, and there marked. 1877 KNIGHT *Dict. Mech.* 2529/2 Perforated templets are used by boiler-makers and others to lay out the holes for punching. 1895 A. J. EVANS in *Jrnl. Hellenic Stud.* XIV. 320 The symbol might have been a simple kind of stencilling plate known as a 'template', such as is still in use among decorators. *Ibid.* 323 The template symbol.
c. *Oil Industry.* A frame anchored to the sea-floor to which an offshore platform may be attached.
1975 *Petroleum Rev.* XXIX 142/1 The system is mounted on a tubular steel frame called a template, which is 124 ft wide and 42 ft high. 1976 *Offshore Platforms & Pipelining* 19/1 The riser..is anchored to a template on the sea floor.
3. Chiefly *Biol.* A molecule or molecular pattern that determines the sequence in which other molecules are assembled into a macromolecule; *spec.* a molecule of nucleic acid that acts thus in the synthesis of nucleic acids or proteins.
[1904 *Proc. R. Soc.* LXXIII. 542 The protoplasmic complex may be regarded as built up of a series of associated templates which serve as patterns to determine change in the various directions necessary for the maintenance of vital processes and of growth.] 1949 *Q. Rev. Biol.* XXIV. 98/1 If we accept the view that the normal cellular proteins are formed as negative replicas of a positive cellular template, we are confronted with a serious dilemma. 1953 WATSON & CRICK in *Nature* 30 May 966/1 Previous discussions of self-duplication have usually involved the concept of a template, or mould... Our model for deoxyribonucleic acid is, in effect, a *pair* of templates. 1961 *Ann. Reg. 1960* 402 This theory differed from the older 'instructive' theory in which any cell was able to produce antibody to any pattern using the antigen itself as a template. 1964 *Proc. Nat. Acad. Sci.* LI. 801 (*heading*) A complex of enzymatically synthesised RNA and template DNA. 1970 *Nature* 5 Sept. 1012/2 RNA tumour viruses can act as templates for the synthesis of DNA. 1977 *N.Y. Rev. Bks.* 27 Oct. 17/1 Segments of DNA, selected because they are templates for valuable products such as hormones, antigens or antibodies, might be produced in bulk by multiplying them in culture of *E. coli.* 1980 N. K. MATHUR et al. *Polymers as Aids in Org. Chem.* iii. 161 The polymer was prepared with functional groups juxtaposed in an exact, predetermined steric relationship by polymerizing monomers around an optically active template —either D-glyceric acid or [etc.].
4. *transf.* and *fig.*
1965 *Science & Psychoanalysis* VIII. 64 What is established is rather a probabilistic system of implicit or 'unconscious' schemas..which serve as some kind of abstract templates for comparison. 1973 *Computers & Humanities* VII. 159 Each English text to be translated goes through a fragmentation and reordering that allows it to match a template form... The translation into French is then made from the template and the original text. 1976 NICHOLS & ARMSTRONG *Workers Divided* II. 143 Their usual point of reference is the old/Northern/real working class. This forms the template against which they judge the modern/militant..generation. 1983 *Microcomputer Printout* Sept. 57/1 Some companies market ready-written models, sometimes called templates on a disk, for standard functions such as a Profit and Loss statement.

temple ('tɛmp(ə)l), *sb.*^{1} Forms: 1-2 templ, tempel, (3 *Orm.* temmple), 3- temple. Also 4 tempel, -ele, -ile, -ille, (templee), 4-6 tempil(l, -yll, 5 -yl(e, -ul, 5-6 -ull(e, 6 -ell. [OE. *templ*, *tempel*, ad. L. *templum*; reinforced in ME. by F. *temple* (10th c. in Godef. *Compl.*) = Pr. *temple*, Sp., Pg. *templo*, It. *tempio*:—L. *templum*.]
I. 1. An edifice or place regarded primarily as the dwelling-place or 'house' of a deity or deities; hence, an edifice devoted to divine worship.
a. In a general sense. (Often, as in quot. *c*825, going back to a specific use.)
cave- or ***cavern-temple***, a natural cave used as a temple.
*c*825 *Vesp. Psalter* xlvii. 10 We onfengun god mildheortnisse ðine in midle temples ðines. *Ibid.* lxxviii. 1 Tempel haliȝ ðin. 13.. *E.E. Allit. P.* A. 1061 Chapel ne temple þat euer watz set. 14.. *Voc.* in Wr.-Wülcker 626/2 Tempulle, *templum.* 1526 TINDALE *Acts* vii. 48 But he that is hyest of all dweleth not in temples made with hondes. 1529 MORE *Dyaloge* I, God is as myghtye in the stable as in the temple. 1610 SHAKS. *Temp.* IV. i. 153 The Clowd-capt Towres, the gorgeous Pallaces, the solemn Temples, the great Globe it selfe..shall dissolue. 1642 FULLER *Holy & Prof. St.* III. xxiv. 219 Take Temple for a covered standing structure, and the Jews had none till the time of Solomon. 1832 DISRAELI *Cont. Flem.* V. iv, There is not a more beautiful and solemn temple in the world, than the great Cathedral of Seville. 1837 PRICHARD *Phys. Hist. Man.* (ed. 3) II. 243 The great cavern-temple of Tulzis. *a*1845 SYD. SMITH in Lady Holland *Mem.* (1855) I. iii. 55 The true Christian..loves the good, under whatever temple, at whatever altar he may find them. 1850 LEITCH tr. *C. O. Müller's Anc. Art* §52. 26 The simplest temples (σηκοί) of the primitive ages were merely hollow trees in which images were placed.
b. Historically applied to the sacred buildings of the Egyptians, Greeks, Romans, and other ancient nations; now, to those of Hinduism, Buddhism, Confucianism, Taoism, Shintoism, and the ethnic religions generally.
971 *Blickl. Hom.* 221 He maniȝ templ & deofolgyld ȝebræc & ȝefylde. *c*1000 ÆLFRIC *Hom.* II. 574 [Hi] ðam fela templa arærdon. *c*1205 LAY. 10178 Alle þa templen [*c*1275 temples] þe þa heðene hafden itimbrid. 1297 R. GLOUC. (Rolls) 318 A temple hii vovnde vair inou & a maumet amidde. *c*1375 *Sc. Leg. Saints* v. (Johannes) 293 þe tempil of dyane. *c*1400 *Destr. Troy* 1358 All tight to þe tempull of þere tore goddes. 1596 DALRYMPLE tr. *Leslie's Hist. Scot.* II. (S.T.S.) 135 *margin*, Tempilis & places of sacrifice to prophane Godis. 1634 SIR T. HERBERT *Trav.* 205 The Citie [Meaco in Japan] has seuenty Temples, in one of which are set three thousand three hundred thirty three gilded Idols. 1667 MILTON *P.L.* I. 402 The wisest heart Of Solomon he [Moloch] led by fraud to build His Temple right against the Temple of God. 1756-7 tr. *Keysler's Trav.* (1760) II. 441 The temple of the Sibylla Tiburtina spoken of by Lactantius. 1860 GARDNER *Faiths World* II. 588/2 Pagoda..In Hindustan, Burmah, and China..implies a temple in which idols are worshipped. *Ibid.* 894/1 Their [Taoists] priests live in the temples, and are supported by the produce of the grounds attached to the establishment.
c. *spec.* The sacred edifice (or any one of the successive edifices) at Jerusalem, the 'House of the Lord', and seat of the Jewish worship of Jehovah.
*c*897 K. ÆLFRED *Gregory's Past. C.* xxxvi. 252 þa stanas on ðæm mæran temple Salomonnes wæron ær swæ wel ȝefeȝede. 971 *Blickl. Hom.* 27 He hine asette ofer þæs temples scylf. *c*1000 *Ags. Gosp.* Matt. iv. 5 Ða ȝebrohte se deofol hine..and asette hine ofer þæs temples heahnesse. *c*1200 ORMIN 11880 Te deofell brohhte Crist Uppo þatt hallȝhe temmple. *c*1325 *Metr. Hom.* 75 In the temple fand thai than Seynt Symeon. 1382 WYCLIF *Matt.* xxi. 12 Jhesus entride in to the temple of God. *a*1425 *Cursor M.* 10946 (Laud) Zakarie to tempille yede. *Ibid.* 13745 (Trin.) Ihesu

..say noon in þe tempul leued. **1533** GAU *Richt Vay* (S.T.S.) 23 The rewlers of the tempil and the cheif prestis. **1611** BIBLE *John* viii. 2 Earely in the morning hee came againe into the Temple. **1877** C. GEIKIE *Christ* lvii. (1879) 692 The Temple was built of white stones of great size, the length of each about 37½ ft., some even 45 ft.

d. *transf.* and *fig.*

c **1607** DONNE *Lett., to Sir H. Goodere* 14 Aug. (1651) 116 That time [for the outward service] to me towards you is Tuesday, and my Temple, the Rose in Smith-field. **1771** *Junius Lett.* lix. (1820) 311 The temple of fame is the shortest passage to riches and preferment. **1860** TYNDALL *Glac.* I. ii. 19 A temple of science now in ruins. **1877** C. GEIKIE *Christ* xxxi. (1879) 370 The true worship has its temple in the inmost soul. **1879** STAINER *Music of Bible* 5 Whose temple of worship was the canopy of heaven.

e. A Jewish synagogue; now *spec.* the place of worship of Reform (and some Conservative) Jews. Now chiefly *U.S.*

1598 J. STOW *Survey of London* 277 But that this house hath beene a Temple or Jewish Sinagogue..I allow not. **1830** *Monthly Intelligence* May 75/2 There is at Frankfort.. a considerable body of Jews, belonging to what is called the 'New Temple'... Mr. Moritz mentions having visited their Temple. **1850** G. AGUILAR *Vale of Cedars* v. 27 The little temple was erected..and the solemn rites of their peculiar faith adhered to. **1914** I. COHEN *Jewish Life in Modern Times* xi. 287 So occidentalized has the Reform temple become that a visitor at first sight can hardly distinguish whether he is in a synagogue or a chapel. **1942** C. ROTH in *Menorah Jrnl.* Winter 4 Their place of worship (no longer a homely *Schul* but, with unhappy retrogression, a Temple). **1978** H. KEMELMAN *Thursday the Rabbi walked Out* (1979) ii. 14 It's the place of women in the temple service I want to talk about, Rabbi. *Ibid.* vii. 45 The synagogue, or as we call it, the temple. **1981** G. V. HIGGINS *Rat on Fire* vii. 56 Saturdays everybody dressed up and went to temple.

2. *transf.* **a.** A building dedicated to public Christian worship; a church: esp. applied to a large or grand edifice.

1399 LANGL. *Rich. Redeles* Prol. 3 A temple of þe trinite [in Bristol]..That cristis chirche is cleped. **1538** STARKEY *England* II. i. 176 Magnyfycal and gudly housys, fayr tempullys and churchys. **1560** DAUS tr. *Sleidane's Comm.* 367 Whan the last of them are come to the church, the Souldiours by and by discharge their pieces: and..about the Temple kepe warde till the counsell breake vp. **1849** MACAULAY *Hist. Eng.* iv. I. 471 The king determined to hear mass with the same pomp with which his predecessors had been surrounded when they repaired to the temples of the established religion. **1867** D. DUNCAN *Disc.* 120 By some classes of professing Christians, their places of worship are called temples..and are reverenced as sacred or holy. **1876** *Haydn's Dict. Dates* 706/2 The 'City Temple', a dissenters' chapel..was opened 19 May, 1874.

b. *spec.* In France and some French-speaking countries, a Protestant as distinguished from a Roman Catholic place of worship (the term 'church' (*église*) being usually confined to the latter).

1566 CLOUGH in Burgon *Life Gresham* (1839) II. 154 *note*, They have laid and begun the foundation of four new tempells [in Antwerp], besides the great barne at St. Mychell's, which ys very handsomely trymmed for a preaching place. [**1843** *Murray's France* 465/2 There are 12,000 Protestants at Nismes, who have 2 churches (*temples*).] **1879** STEVENSON *Trav. Cevennes* (1886) 150 One of the first things I encountered in Pont de Montvert was.. the Protestant temple.

c. The central place of worship of the Mormons.

1858 *Encycl. Brit.* (ed. 8) XV. 591/1 This great undertaking of Nauvoo was the building of the Mormon temple. **1874** J. H. BLUNT *Dict. Sects* 347/2 A revelation of great length..gave directions for the building of a splendid temple, the first stone of which was laid with great pomp on April 6th, 1841. *Ibid.* 354/1 The tithes are supposed to be devoted to the building of the temple.

3. *fig.* Any place regarded as occupied by the divine presence; *spec.* the person or body of a Christian.

c **975** *Rushw. Gosp.* John ii. 19 Un-duað ðone tempel ðis & on ðrim daȝum ic awecco ðæt. *Ibid.* 21 He wutudlice ȝicwæð of temple lichoma his. *c* **1000** ÆLFRIC *Hom.* II. 580 Nyte ȝe þæt eowere lima syndon þæs Halȝan Gastes tempel, seðe on eow is? *c* **1200** ORMIN 15843 Crisstene follc iss Cristess hus & Cristess hallȝhe temmple. *c* **1290** *St. Kath.* 21 in *S. Eng. Leg.* I. 92 ȝwy ne bi-holde ȝe þe heiȝe temple..Of þe heie heuene þat geth a-boute a-bouen eov niȝt and dai. **1388** WYCLIF *1 Cor.* iii. 16 Witen ȝe not, that ȝe ben the temple of God, and the spirit of God dwellith in ȝou? *c* **1400** *Destr. Troy* 11781 Couetous men comynly are cald aftur right, A temple to the tyrand, þat tises to syn. *c* **1450** *Godstow Reg.* 5 Iff we make clene oure tempil with-ynne. *a* **1515** DUNBAR *Poems* lxxxvi. 19 Tryumphand tempill of the Trinite.. Princes of peiss..O mater Jhesu, salue Maria! **1605** SHAKS. *Macb.* II. iii. 73 Most sacrilegious Murther hath broke ope The Lords anoynted Temple, and stole thence The Life o'th'Building. **1681-6** J. SCOTT *Chr. Life* (1747) III. 55 How could his Spirit's dwelling in us constitute us Temples of God, unless he himself were God? *a* **1700** DRYDEN tr. *Hymn, Veni, Creator Spiritus* 6 From sin and sorrow set us free, And make thy temples worthy thee. **1839-52** BAILEY *Festus* (ed. 5) 464 My favoured temple is an humble heart. **1875** MANNING *Mission H. Ghost* i. 21 Yet they have been made temples of the Holy Ghost.

II. †**4.** The head-quarters of the Knights Templars, on or contiguous to the site of the temple at Jerusalem; hence, the order or organization of the Templars. *Obs.*

a **1131** *O.E. Chron.* an. 1128 Ðes ilces ȝeares com fram Ierusalem Hugo of þe temple. *c* **1400** MAUNDEV. (1839) x. 88 Towardes the south right nygh, is the temple of Salomon... And in þat temple duellen the knyghtes of the temple, that weren wont to be clept Templeres, & þat was the fundacioun of here ordre. *c* **1400** *Brut* 148 Amonge þe castelles he made an house of þe temple. **1656** BLOUNT *Glossogr., Templaries*, or Knights of the Temple.

5. *spec.* **a.** Name of two of the Inns of Court (see INN *sb.* 5 c) in London, known as the ***Inner*** and the ***Middle Temple*** (see quot. 1727-41), which stand on the site of the buildings once occupied by the Templars (of which the church alone remains).

c **1386** CHAUCER *C.T.* Prol. 567 A gentil Maunciple was ther of a temple. **1462** J. PASTON in *P. Lett.* II. 92 To myn ryth reverent..fader, John Paston, beyng in the Inder Temple. **1556** *Chron. Gr. Friars* (Camden) 97 The xviij day of August [1556] the mayer dynned at the rederes denner at the Tempulle. **1591** SHAKS. *1 Hen. VI*, II. v. 19 We sent vnto the Temple, vnto his Chamber. **1656** BLOUNT *Glossogr.* s.v. *Templaries*, These Templars first founded and built the Temples or Templars Inne in Fleetstreet. **1709** STEELE *Tatler* No. 60 ¶ 1 A Student of the Inner Temple. **1727-41** CHAMBERS *Cycl., Temples*,.. two inns of court, thus called, because anciently the dwelling-house of the knights-templars..They are called the inner and middle temple, in relation to Essex-house, which was also a part of the house of the templars, and called the outer temple, because situate without Temple-Bar. **1905** C. T. MARTIN (*title*) Minutes of Parliament of the Middle Temple.

b. Name of the place in Paris which formed the head-quarters of the Templars in Europe.

1617 MORYSON *Itin.* I. 190 (Paris) The second gate towards the East, is the gate of the Temple. **1735** [see *temple diamond* in 6]. **1888** T. A. ARCHER in *Encycl. Brit.* XXIII. 160/2 Louis VII..gave them a piece of marsh land outside Paris, which in later times became known as the Temple, and was the headquarters of the order in Europe.

III. 6. *attrib.* and *Comb.* **a.** Simple attrib., in senses 1-3, as ***temple-book***, ***-building***, ***-captain***, ***-chamber***, ***-chief***, ***-companion***, ***-court***, ***-door***, ***-end***, ***-fellow***, ***-festival***, ***-fronton***, ***-gate***, ***-gift***, ***-guard***, ***-hill***, ***-hospital***, ***-land***, ***-master***, ***-ministrant***, ***-mount***, ***-music***, ***-musician***, ***-pavement***, ***-pediment***, ***-porch***, ***-priest***, ***-priesthood***, ***-prophet***, ***-revenue***, ***-roof***, ***-ruin***, ***-sanctuary***, ***-sculpture***, ***-service***, ***-shrine***, ***-singer***, ***-staff***, ***-stair***, ***-stead***, ***-system***, ***-tax***, ***-treasury***, ***-union***, ***-veil***, ***-vision***, ***-wall***, ***-warden***, ***-wardenship***, ***-worship***, ***-yard***; in sense 5, as ***temple-exchange***, ***-garden***, ***-hall***, etc.; appositive, as ***temple-house***, ***-palace***, ***-pyramid***, ***-tomb***, ***-tower***. **b.** Obj. and obj. gen., as ***temple-keeper***, ***-robber***, ***-sweeper***, ***-visiting***; ***temple-haunting*** adj.; instrumental, similative, etc., as ***temple-crowned***, ***-like***, ***-sacred***, ***-treated*** adjs. **c.** Special combs.: **temple block**, a percussion instrument of oriental origin consisting of a hollow block of wood which is struck with a drum-stick; also known as a WOOD BLOCK; usu. in *pl.*; **temple children**, children in the service of temples in India; **Temple church**: see 5; †**temple diamond** (see quot.); **temple-foundling**, ? a foundling deposited at the Temple (sense 5); **Temple parliament**, = PARLIAMENT *sb.*[1] 5 b; †**temple-pickling** (*obs. slang*): see quot.; **temple prostitute**, a woman maintained by a temple, who performs rituals of a sexual nature (cf. DEVADASI); also *fig.*; hence **temple prostitution**; **temple-ring** (see quot.); **temple-state**: in antiquity, a city-state centred on a temple or similar sacred edifice; **temple-title**, the name under which a deceased Chinese emperor is worshipped; **temple-trotter** (see quot.). Also TEMPLE-BAR.

1929 *Melody Maker* Mar. 295/2 The same remark applies to the *Temple blocks, and even the tambourine can easily be played too loudly. **1964** J. CARTER in Norton & Spacey *Drums & Drumming Today* 40 How I yearn for the days of temple blocks and saucepan lids. **1448-9** METHAM *Amoryus & Cleopes* 28 Ther othe thei toke, Sweryng vpon the *tempyl-boke. **1857** J. HAMILTON *Lessons fr. Gt. Biog.* (1859) 219 The occupants of these *temple-chambers. **1727-41** CHAMBERS *Cycl.* s.v., The chief officer was the master of the temple... And from him the chief minister of the *temple-church is still called the master of the temple. **1846** GROTE *Greece* I. xi. 263 Pindar,..Euripidês and Apollodôrus, name Erichthonius..as the being who was thus adopted and made the *temple-companion of Athênê. **1820** SHELLEY *Witch of Atlas* in *Posthumous Poems* (1824) 50 And round each *temple-court In dormitories ranged..She saw the priests asleep. **1930** R. GRAVES *Ten Poems More* 13 In every temple-court, for all to see Flourishes one example of each tree In tricunx. **1884** R. BRIDGES *Prometheus* 758 The *temple-crowned heights. **1735** *Dict. Polygraph.* I. S vij, The factitious diamonds..call'd *temple Diamonds, because the best of them are made in the temple at Paris, are vastly short of the genuine ones. *c* **1386** CHAUCER *Knight's Tale* (1875, Harl. MS. 7334) 2422 The rynges on þe *tempul dore þat hange. **1729** SWIFT *Directions for Birth-day Song* in *Poems* (1958) 462 What tho for fifteen years and more, Janus hath lock'd his Temple-door? **1921** G. B. SHAW *Back to Methuselah* IV. 178 The temple door is in the middle of the portico. **1760** FOOTE *Minor* I. Wks. 1799 I. 239 He sits.. every evening, from five till eight, under the clock, at the *Temple-exchange. **1614** SELDEN *Titles Hon.* Pref. Cj, Honor and deseruing Vertue..were *Temple-fellowes in old Rome. **1905** *Athenæum* 29 July 146/1 The last of the *Temple foundlings, Mary Ann Littlefield, survived as late as 1865, and was supposed to have been the original of Miss Flite in Dickens's 'Bleak House'. **1591** SHAKS. *1 Hen. VI*, II. iv. 125 This brawle to day, Growne to this faction in the *Temple Garden, Shall send betweene the Red-Rose and the White, A thousand Soules to Death and deadly Night. **1595** SPENSER *Epithal.* xii, Open the *temple gates unto my love, Open them wide that she may enter in. **1605** SHAKS. *Macb.* I. vi. 4 This Guest of Summer, The *Temple-haunting Martlet. ? **13..** *All Saints* 41 in Herrig's *Archiv* LXXIX. 435 Thus was ordeynd þis *temple-hous [the Pantheon] Off all deuyllus, to haue þer cours. *a* **1670** SPALDING *Troub. Chas. I* (1829) 63 He gave them the superiorities of the haill *temple-lands within their burrow. **1663** GERBIER *Counsel* e iij, Representing Solomons *Temple-like Foundations of a State. **1860** PUSEY *Min. Proph.* 398 Habakkuk must have been entitled to take part in the *temple-music, and so must have been a Levite. **1891** CHEYNE *Psalter* ii. 69 It [Ps. 37] is evidently the work of a *temple-musician. **1851** *Buried City East Nineveh* vii. 105 The architecture of the Assyrians, as illustrated in its only relics, the great *Temple-palaces. **1641** W. MOUNTAGU in *Buccleuch MSS.* (Hist. MSS. Comm.) I. 285 Friday is the day of *Temple parliament. **1905** *Daily News* 15 July 4 The transactions of the Middle Temple 'Parliaments', beginning from the year 1501. *a* **1700** B. E. *Dict. Cant. Crew*, **Temple-pickling*, the Pumping of Bailives, Bumms, Setters, Pick-pockets, &c. *a* **1711** KEN *Hymnotheo* Poet. Wks. 1721 III. 77 The *Temple-Porch two arched Cloysters flank'd. *a* **1911** *Temple-priest in *N.E.D.* **1941** J. MASEFIELD *Gautama* 31 Like a temple-priest intoning. **1711** HICKES *Two Treat. Chr. Priesth.* (1847) II. 251 A dissolution of the *temple-priesthood. **1890** A. B. ELLIS *Ewe-Speaking Peoples of Slave Coast of W. Afr.* ix. 141 Girls dedicated to a god do not necessarily serve him during the whole of their lives... In Dahomi there seems to be a marked distinction between those who actually minister to the service of the temple, and those who are merely *temple prostitutes. **1951** AUDEN *Nones* (1952) 28 Private rites of magic send The temple prostitutes to sleep. **1980** S. T. HAYMON *Death & Pregnant Virgin* xi. 84 Poor old Charlie! Thought he'd recruited a vestal virgin when what he'd got was a temple prostitute! **1912** J. N. FARQUHAR *Primer of Hinduism* xvi. 194 We are now in a position to realise how it has been possible for the Hindu to admit such things as..cruel torture, *temple prostitution. **1961** L. MUMFORD *City in History* iv. 106 The custom of temple prostitution has not merely been preserved down to our own day.., but the temples of the goddesses of love..were traditionally the favored places of assignation for lovers. **1948** *Nat. Geogr. Mag.* Jan. 127 (*caption*) High and steep were the *temple pyramids of the Maya. **1966** M. D. COE *Maya* v. 94 Towering above all are the mighty temple-pyramids built from limestone blocks over a rubble core. **1905** D. SMITH *Days His Flesh* vii. 59 Every adult Israelite..had to pay an annual tax of half a shekel to the *Temple-revenue. **1877** W. JONES *Finger-ring* 298 Another betrothal ring..called '*temple' or 'tower', from the figure of the sacred temple placed on their summit. **1637** NABBES *Microcosm.* in Dodsley *O. Pl.* IX. 163 The *temple-robber..to the altar flies. *a* **1661** HOLYDAY *Juvenal* (1673) 249 Temple-robbers..stealing away plates of gold from the statues of the gods. **1857** J. HAMILTON *Lessons fr. Gt. Biog.* (1859) 86 He heard from the *temple-roof a whisper in his ear. **1860** PUSEY *Min. Proph.* 24 The condition..in which there should be none of the special *Temple-service. *a* **1711** KEN *Hymnotheo* Poet. Wks. 1721 III. 78 Hymnotheo..Kiss'd the Saints' feet, who trod the *Temple-Stairs. **1920** H. G. WELLS *Outl. Hist.* 150/2 There is no *temple-state stage, no stage of priest Kings, in the Greek record. **1931** *Times Lit. Suppl.* 1 Jan. 3/2 The Pope's temporal domain..is not a city-state but a temple-state. **1870** MORRIS *Earthly Par.* III. 299 Now fain I would unto the *temple-stead. **1904** R. J. FARRER *Garden Asia* 118 The great *temple-tomb is in high festival for the Birthday of the Saviour [Buddha]. **1863** *W. Smith's Dict. Bible* 158/2 s.v. *Babel*, An ancient Babylonian *temple-tower. **1873** BROWNING *Red Cott. Nt.-cap* 680 A quaint device, Pillared and *temple-treated Belvedere. **1861** *Sat. Rev.* 30 Nov. 560 An extremely low lawyer's clerk, of the genus which in old professional slang was called '*Temple-trotter'. *c* **1340** *Cursor M.* 16762 + 85 (Cott.) þe *temple vayl clef in twoo. **1609** BIBLE (Douay) *Zeph.* i. 4 The names of the *templewardens with the priests. **1904** W. M. RAMSAY *Lett. to Seven Ch.* xvii. 232 The fourth *Temple-Wardenship seems to be of Artemis. **1680** ALLEN *Peace & Unity* 102 The corrupt estate of the Jewish church..both in *Temple-worship and in Synagogue-worship. **1714** R. FIDDES *Pract. Disc.* II. 138 The ceremonial ordinances which chiefly gave directions about the temple-worship.

Hence '**templeful**, as many or as much as fills a temple; '**templeward** *adv.*, towards the temple.

1868 WHITTIER *Meeting* 21 Nor ritual-bound nor templeward Walks the free spirit of the Lord! **1909** *Expositor* Oct. 316 A whole templeful of men whose consciences kept them from casting a stone.

temple ('tɛmp(ə)l), *sb.*[2] Also 4-5 **tempil**, 5 **-elle**, **-ylle**, 6 *Sc.* **tympille**. [a. OF. *temple* fem. (11th c. in *Roland*), = Prov. *templa*, It. *tempia*:—pop. L. type **tempula*, **templa*, app. for cl.L. *tempora*, pl. of *tempus* 'temple of the head' (taken later as fem. sing.: cf. BIBLE). OF. *temple* (still in Dict. Acad. 1694-1740) is represented in mod.F. by *tempe* (already in Palsgr., 1530).]

1. The flattened region on each side of the (human) forehead. (Chiefly in *pl.*)

c **1310** *St. Margaret* 219 in Horstm. *Altengl. Leg.* (1881) 231 Sche toke him bi þe temples [*earlier version* bi þe toppe]; about sche him swong. *a* **1340** HAMPOLE *Psalter* cxxxi. 5 þe tempils of þi heued waxis heuy. *a* **1400** *Poem on Blood-letting* in *Rel. Ant.* I. 189 Two [places] at the templys thay mot blede. **14..** *Voc.* in Wr.-Wülcker 631/2 Tempelle, *tempora*. **1535** COVERDALE *Judg.* iv. 21 Then Iael..smote the nale in thorow the temples of his heade, so y^{t} he sancke to ye earth. **1643** SIR T. BROWNE *Relig. Med.* II. §12 Let no dreames my head infest, But such as Jacobs temples blest. **1703** POPE *Vertumnus* 34 And wreaths of hay his sun-burnt temples shade. **1813** SCOTT *Rokeby* I. viii, A scorching clime, And toil, had..Roughened the brow, the temples bared. **1814** CARY *Dante, Paradise* xxv. 11, I..shall claim the wreath Due to the poet's temples.

b. *transf.* A corresponding part in lower animals.

1769 E. BANCROFT *Guiana* 181 The temples, rump and belly are of a violet colour. **1826** KIRBY & SP. *Entomol.* III. 365 External anatomy of insects... *Tempora* (the Temples). Those parts which lie on the outside of the posterior half of the eyes. **1850** R. G. CUMMING *Hunter's Life S. Afr.* (1902) 87/1 My dinner consisted of a piece of flesh from the temple of the elephant. **1860** MAYNE *Expos. Lex.*, *Temple*,.. *Ornithol.*, *Zool.* Applied to the lateral region of the head comprised between the eyes and ears.

†**2.** *pl.* Ornaments of jewellery or needlework formerly worn by ladies on the sides of the forehead. *Obs.*

c **1430** LYDG. *Min. Poems* (Percy Soc.) 56 A fowle visage with gay temples of atyre. **1439** *E.E. Wills* (1882) 116 (C'tess Warwick) That my grete templys with the Baleys be sold to the vtmest pryse. [**1656** DUGDALE *Antiq. Warwick.* 330/1 [marg. note on quot. 1439] Jewels hanging on womens foreheads by Bodkins thrust into their hair.]

3. Each of the side-members or limbs of a pair of spectacles, which clasp the sides of the head of the wearer. *U.S.*

1877 KNIGHT *Dict. Mech.*, *Temple*.. one of the bars on the outer ends of the spectacle bows [i.e. rims of the lenses] by which the spectacles are made to clasp the head of the wearer. [Hence in later Dicts.]

4. *attrib.* and *Comb.*, as ***temple-bone***, ***-pulse***, ***-shot***; **temple-spectacles**, spectacles having jointed sidelimbs that grasp the temples.

1615 CROOKE *Body of Man* 583 Where it yssueth out of the *Temple-bone it is broader and thicker. **1793** HOLCROFT *Lavater's Physiogn.* xiv. 75 The temple-bones.. are slow in coming to perfection. **1891** *Daily News* 28 Oct. 7/2 The witness was feeling the *temple pulse while administering. **1899** F. V. KIRBY *Sport E.C. Africa* xxi. 232, I ran in and killed him with a *temple shot from my Metford. **1762** GOLDSM. *Cit. W.* lv, He had more powder in his hair,.. a pair of *temple spectacles, and his hat under his arm.

temple ('tɛmp(ə)l), *sb.*³ [a. F. *temple* fem. (also *templet*, *temploir*, *templu*), Littré: perh. orig. the same word as *temple*, *tempe*, TEMPLE *sb.*²]

1. A contrivance for keeping cloth stretched to its proper width in the loom during the process of weaving. Usually *pl.*

In the hand-loom, a pair of flat rods, having toothed ends which caught the selvedge on each side; in the power-loom, various rotary devices are used.

1483 *Cath. Angl.* 379/2 A Tempylle of a wefere, *virgula*. **1688** R. HOLME *Armoury* III. viii. 348/1 *Temples*,.. two Staves with broad ends set with sharp Pins,.. by the pins putting into the selvage of the Cloth it is kept open while it is in Weaving. **1733** P. LINDSAY *Interest Scotl.* 169 The Sum that is now given for the Encouragement of that Branch [Weaving], exclusive of the Reeds, Harness, Shuttles, and Temples. **1863** J. WATSON *Art Weaving* 150 The Breast Beam is the rail in front of the loom... It is on this rail that the self acting temples are fixed. **1888** ELWORTHY *West Somerset Word-bk.*, *Temples*, a wooden stretcher of adjustable length, having points at either end, used by weavers to keep the cloth as woven of the proper width in the loom... Often called a 'pair o' temples'. **1898** *Leeds Mercury Suppl.* 10 Dec. (E.D.D.), The temples on looms to-day.. consist of wheels on either side of the woven piece, having projecting pins all round their circumferences.

2. = TEMPLATE¹ 2. Also *attrib.*

1688 R. HOLME *Armoury* III. ix. 394/2 Temple Moulds.. are Boards cut in that for[m] as the Stone is to be cut. **1847–78** HALLIWELL, *Temple-mold*, a pattern, or mould used by masons in fashioning their work.

temple ('tɛmp(ə)l), *v.* [f. TEMPLE *sb.*¹]

1. *trans.* To enclose in or as in a temple, to enshrine; to honour with a temple or temples, to build a temple to or for. Also *fig.*

1593 SOUTHWELL *St. Peters Compl.* 27 Christ, as my God, was templed in my thought. **1628** FELTHAM *Resolves* II. [I] lxxxiv. 242 The Heathen (in many places) Templed and adored this drunken god. **1838** S. BELLAMY *Betrayal* 57 Templed, and taught, and rited as thou art. **1839** BAILEY *Festus* xxxi. (1852) 514 Immured.. In.. her holy home, With many a lovely handmaiden around In starry palace templed. **1936** A. CLARKE *Coll. Poems* 98 We saw again How Brigid, while her women slept Around her, temple'd by the flame, Sat in a carven chair.

2. To make or fashion into a temple.

1839–49 [implied in TEMPLED *ppl. a.* 2].

†**3.** *intr.* To reside or dwell as in a temple. *Obs.*

a **1711** KEN *Hymns Evang.* Poet. Wks. 1721 I. 62 Bless'd Jesu! deign to Temple in my Mind. —— *Sion* ibid. IV. 412 O Jesu,.. I feel thee templing in my Heart.

Hence **'templing** *vbl. sb.*

a **1638** MEDE *Wks.* (1672) 641 The Deifying and invocating of Saints and Angels,.. the adoring and templing of Reliques. **1677** GALE *Crt. Gentiles* II. III. 105 In the Demon-worship they had many other rites, as worshipping of Columnes, Templing of Reliques.

,Temple-'bar. [f. TEMPLE *sb.*¹ 5 (because of its position close to the Temple buildings) + BAR *sb.*¹ 13.] The name of the barrier or gateway closing the entrance into the City of London from the Strand; removed in 1878.

[**1314–15** *Rolls of Parlt.* I. 302/2 Le pavement du chemyn par entre la Barre du Novel Temple de Lundres.] **1354** *Ibid.* II. 262/1 Qe l'Estaple de Westmr. comence sa bounde a Temple-barre. *c* **1400** *Brut* 238 Seynt Clementis cherche wiþout Temple-Barr. **1467–8** *Rolls of Parlt.* V. 579/2 A Tenement withoute the Temple Barres of London. **1598** STOW *Surv.* (1908) I. 193 The Queenes Maiestie.. entered the citie by Temple Barre, through Fleetstreete, Cheape [etc.]. **1727–41** [see TEMPLE *sb.*¹ 5]. **1773** JOHNSON 30 Apr. in Boswell *Life* (1887) II. 238 When we got to Temple-bar he [Goldsmith] stopped me, pointed to the [rebels'] heads upon it, and slily whispered me 'Forsitan et nostrum nomen miscebitur istis'. **1851** *London as it is To-day* i. (1855) 9 At [the] extremity [of Fleet St.], separating the cities of London and Westminster, stands Temple Bar, the only one of the city boundaries now remaining. **1864** *Chambers' Bk. Days* II. 233/2 The heads of these two [Jacobites executed in 1746] were.. stuck over Temple Bar, where they remained till 1772.

templed ('tɛmp(ə)ld), *ppl. a.* [f. TEMPLE *v.* or *sb.*¹ + -ED.]

1. Enshrined in a temple.

1610 G. FLETCHER *Christ's Vict.* I. xx, Gods of wood, Of stocks, and stones, with crowns of laurell stood Templed. **1854** S. DOBELL *Balder* iii. 15 The seat of templed Power.

2. Made into or like a temple.

1839 BAILEY *Festus* i. (1852) 3 O'er which ye rise in templed majesty. **1849** QUINTON *Heaven's Antid. Curse Labour* 42 Canticles of praise will resound through the templed cottage. **1935** T. S. ELIOT *Murder in Cathedral* i. 27 Power obtained grows to glory,.. a permanent possession, A templed tomb. **1951** L. MACNEICE tr. *Goethe's Faust* 217 Does not your templed home persist!

3. Furnished or adorned with a temple or temples.

1822 SHELLEY *Charles the First* in *Posthumous Poems* (1824) ii. 245 Innocent sleep of templed cities and the smiling fields. **1852** *Meanderings of Mem.* I. 114 We.. Rambled such river sides and templed lands. **1878** H. RICE *Sel. Poems* 35 Go tread the templed hills of Orient clime.

templeless ('tɛmp(ə)llɪs), *a.* [f. TEMPLE *sb.*¹ + -LESS.] Having no temple, destitute of a temple.

c **1460** *Towneley Myst.* xxiii. 493 He shuld make vs tempylles, And gar it cleyn downe fall. **1642** FULLER *Holy & Prof. St.* III. xxiv. 221 And yet that the Persians were wholly Temple-lesse will hardly be believed. **1848** LYTTON *Caxtons* IV. ii, Druidism, passing from its earliest templeless belief into the later corruptions.

Templer, -ere, obs. forms of TEMPLAR.

templet¹, **-ette.** [In sense 1, a. F. *templette*, dim. of *temple* fem. (in mod.F. *tempe*), TEMPLE *sb.*² Sense 2 may be a different word.]

†**1.** An ornament worn by women on the head; = TEMPLE *sb.*² 2. *Obs.*

1530 PALSGR. 279/2 Templet a thynge made of latyn, *templete*. *c* **1532** DU WES *Introd. Fr.* in *Palsgr.* 907 (Names of womens rementes) The templettes, *les templettes*.

2. Each of the four-sided facets which surround and 'support' the table of a brilliant.

1889 *Cent. Dict.*, *Bezel*.. 2, the oblique side or face of a gem; *spec.* one of four similarly situated four-sided facets on the top or crown of a brilliant, which are sometimes called templets.

templet². *Weaving.* [dim. of TEMPLE *sb.*³: as mod.F. *templet* (which may be the source).] = TEMPLE *sb.*³ 1.

1831 G. R. PORTER *Silk Manuf.* 223 The woven silk is kept at its proper degree of extension by small hooks, called templets. **1877** KNIGHT *Dict. Mech.* 2529/2 The templet of the horsehair-loom is a pair of jaws for each selvedge.

templet³ ('tɛmplɪt). Also -ette. [f. TEMPLE *sb.*¹ + -ET¹.] A small or miniature temple.

a **1843** in Southey *Comm.-pl. Bk.* III. 657/1 *Fagutal*, a beechen temple or templet under Jupiter Fagutalis. **1848** J. G. WILKINSON *Dalmatia*, etc. I. 183 A little round templet, or open lantern on columns, in style and name worthy of a tea-garden. **1892** *Harper's Mag.* Aug. 355/1 This temple —it is so small that they might call it a templette.

templet, var. TEMPLATE.

'templify, *v. rare.* [f. L. *templ-um*, TEMPLE *sb.*¹ + -FY.] *trans.* To make into a temple.

1615 BP. ANDREWES *Serm.*, *John* ii. 19 (1841) II. 361 If we can take order that while we be here, before we go hence, our bodies, we get them templified as I may say. **1690** C. NESSE *O. & N. Test.* I. 101 The body must be a stately structure which is thus templify'd by the Holy Ghost.

'templin-,oil. [= Ger. *Templinöl*, Pharmaceut. L. *oleum templinum*, said by Flückiger (*Mittheil. naturf. Gesellsch. Bern*, 1855, 139) to have been used by Haller, 1755: origin unascertained.] (See quots.)

[**1860** MAYNE *Expos. Lex.*, *Templinum oleum*,.. oil obtained from the cones or nuts of the pine-tree. Germ. syn. *Tannenzapfenöl*.] **1868** WATTS *Dict. Chem.* V. 719 *Templin-oil, oil of Pine-cones*.. isomeric with, and very similar to, oil of turpentine, obtained by distillation of the cones of *Pinus Pumilio*.., and in some parts of Switzerland from the cones of the silver-fir (*Abies Picea*).

†**'templize,** *v. Obs. nonce-wd.* [f. TEMPLE *sb.*¹ + -IZE.] *intr.* To assume the form or character of a temple.

1650 FULLER *Pisgah* IV. iv. 72 The Rabbins conceive that during the abode thereof at Shiloh, the Tabernacle began to templize, getting walls.. round about it, chiefly because about that time it is thrice termed a Temple.

tempo ('tɛmpəʊ). Pl. **tempi** ('tɛmpiː), **tempos.** [It.,:—L. *tempus* time.]

1. a. *Mus.* Relative speed or rate of movement; pace; time; *spec.* the proper or characteristic speed and rhythm of a dance or other tune (in phr. ‖ ***tempo di gavotta***, ***tempo di marcia***, ***tempo di minuetto***, etc.).

tempo giusto ('dʒuːstəʊ), strict time; the proper speed that a style of music demands. *tempo primo*, first or former time; a direction to resume the original speed after an alteration of it. *tempo rubato*, 'robbed or stolen time; time occasionally slackened or hastened for the purposes of expression' (Stainer & Barrett).

1724 *Short Explic. For. Wds. in Mus. Bks.*, *Tempo*, Time. Thus, *Tempo Di Gavotta*, is Gavot Time, or the Time or Movement observed in playing a Gavot. *Tempo Di Minuetto*,.. *Tempo Di Sarabanda*. **1740** GRASSINEAU *Mus. Dict.* 283 *Tempo*, or *Tempo giusto*, is often met with after Recitatives, and intimates that the Time be beat equal, which during that recitative was managed otherwise. **1773** C. BURNEY *Present State of Mus. in Germany* II. 175 It was from her that Quantz first heard what professors call *tempo rubato*. **1810** D. CORRI *Singers Preceptor* I. 6 Tempo rubato is a detraction of part of the time from one note, and restoring it by increasing the length of another. **1839** LONGF. *Hyperion* IV. iv, In his hurry he got the *tempo* about twice too slow. **1866** ENGEL *Nat. Mus.* ii. 63 They sing in a more subdued tone; the *tempo* is slower. **1884** F. TAYLOR in Grove *Dict. Mus.* IV. 82 Verbal directions as to tempo are generally written in Italian. **1886** G. M. HOPKINS *Let.* 11 Dec. (1935) I. 246 This sonnet shd. be almost sung: it is most carefully timed in *tempo rubato*. **1888** *Athenæum* 17 Mar. 349/1 The composer has reconsidered the *tempi* of some portions..; he also indulged.. in the *tempo rubato*. **1931** M. D. CALVOCORESSI tr. *Bartok's Hungarian Folk Music* 23 A few tunes in *tempo giusto*. *Ibid.* 80 In fairly old tunes.. a liking for variable *tempo giusto* rhythm is evinced. **1934** WEBSTER, *Tempo*, n.; pl. *tempi*.., *tempos*. **1956** R. C. MARSH *Toscanini* ii. 83 The earlier performance being somewhat more relaxed and containing some *tempo rubato* that the version of thirty years later lacks. **1967** A. L. LLOYD *Folk Song in England* iv. 312 The group refrains.. were always sung plain and in a strict *tempo giusto*. **1980** *Times* 13 May 15/3 Tempos were excellently chosen, most of all perhaps, for the Minuet.

b. *transf.* and *fig.* The rate of motion or activity (*of* someone or something).

1898 G. B. SHAW *You never can Tell* II. 249 *Again changing his tempo to say to Valentine*.. If youll allow me, sir? **1901** *Cassell's Mag.* Sept. 388/2 His *tempo*, to use the expression of our acrobats, is perfect—that is to say, he yields at the proper time and at the proper rate to the descending ball. **1918** A. GRAY tr. *Grelling's Crime* II. 239 He describes their readiness 'to retard the tempo of the construction of our warships'. **1925** C. FOX *Educ. Psychol.* 271 Each person is possessed of a vital tempo. **1930** W. K. HANCOCK *Australia* vii. 139 The State might not have achieved as much if it had been content.. to quicken the *tempo* of the economic harmonies—by taxing, by disseminating knowledge, by mobilising credit. **1940** W. FAULKNER *Hamlet* 219 But when he stood in the door again, save for the slightly increased rasp and tempo of his breathing, he might never have left it. **1961** A. CHRISTIE *Pale Horse* xviii. 198 It's a changing world, Easterbrook... Now the changes come more rapidly. The tempo has quickened. **1974** I. MURDOCH *Sacred & Profane Love Machine* 202 The partner who created the confidence and set the tempo was Luca.

†**2.** A term in fencing: see quot. *Obs. rare.*

1688 R. HOLME *Armoury* III. xix. (Roxb.) 159/2 A Tempo, is to take heed neuer to make a thrust or blow at aduersarie, without thou hast a faire opportunity to hit, or within measure, that he be within thy reach.

tempor, -e, obs. forms of TEMPER *v.*

temporad ('tɛmpəræd), *adv. Physiol.* [f. TEMPOR-AL *a.*² + *-ad*, as in DEXTRAD, etc.] Towards the temples.

1808 BARCLAY *Muscular Motions* 470 Rotatory motions Mesiad, and Temporad. *Ibid.* 471 In such motions the *coronal rectus* is made to turn the pupil coronad;.. the *temporal*, temporad.

temporal ('tɛmpərəl), *a.*¹ and *sb.*¹ Also 4–7 -er-; 4–5 -el, -ell(e, -ale, 4–6 -alle, 4–7 -all. [ad. L. *temporāl-is*, f. *tempus*, *tempor-*, a space or point of time, time; in B. 2, ad. eccl. L. *temporāle*.]

A. *adj.* **1.** Lasting or existing only for a time; passing, temporary. Now *rare* or merged in 2.

1382 WYCLIF *Matt.* xiii. 21 He hath nat roote in hym self, but it is temporal; that is, it lastith bot a litil tyme. **1382** —— *2 Cor.* iv. 18 Sothli tho thingis that ben seyn, ben temperal, or duryng by short tyme. **1598** SYLVESTER *Du Bartas* II. ii. I. *Ark* 500 [Rainbow] A temporall beauty of the lampfull skies. **1762** tr. *Busching's Syst. Geog.* I. 49 Others begin to run in spring,.. and cease again towards autumn, and are called temporal Springs. **1879** STEVENSON *Trav. Cevennes* (1886) 127 What seems a kind of temporal death to people choked between walls.. is only a.. living slumber to the man who sleeps a-field.

2. Of or pertaining to time as the sphere of human life; terrestrial as opposed to heavenly; of man's present life as distinguished from a future existence; concerning or involving merely the material interests of this world; worldly, earthly. (Opp. to *eternal* or *spiritual*.)

c **1375** *Sc. Leg. Saints* vi. (*Thomas*) 315 þat þai.. ȝarnis til hafe na temporale gud, outane anerly clath & fud. *c* **1380** WYCLIF *Wks.* (1880) 5 Temperal almes. *c* **1400** *Rom. Rose* 7066 So that the tour were stuffed wel With alle richesse temporel. *c* **1532** DU WES *Introd. Fr.* in *Palsgr.* 1036 The lytell goodes temporals that it hath pleased to God to sende me. **1685** BAXTER *Paraphr. N.T.* Mark ii. 15 He would not set up a temporal Kingdom. **1772** PRIESTLEY *Inst. Relig.* (1782) I. 306 The Jews.. expected.. a temporal prince. **1832** HT. MARTINEAU *Life in Wilds* vii. 91 Fear for the temporal prosperity of the whole race.

3. Secular as opposed to sacred; lay as distinguished from clerical. Of law: civil or common as distinguished from canon. Of rule, authority, or government: civil as distinguished from ecclesiastical. ***Lords Temporal***: see LORD *sb.* 9. (Opp. to *spiritual*.)

c **1340** HAMPOLE *Prose Tr.* 24 Itt longith to som temporalle men the which han soueraynte. *c* **1400** MAUNDEV. (1839) v. 43 He was Lord Spirituelle & Temporelle. *c* **1440** *Brut* 468 þe King..borowed a somme of gold þurghout þe Reame, of temporall peple, þat amounted a c. M[l] marc of money, to sende his peple ouer the see. **1451** CAPGRAVE *Life St. Aug.* 27 Ambrose had..mad neuly many ympnys, for all þe temperal ympnys ar ny of his making, as primo dierum omnium, & þoo þat folow. **1578** *Knaresborough Wills* (Surtees) I. 130 And after come to practice as a temporall Lawyer. **1596** SHAKS. *Merch. V.* IV. i. 190 His Scepter shewes the force of temporall power, The attribute to awe and Maiestie. **1672** PETTY *Pol. Anat.* (1691) 36 The Government of Ireland is by the King, 21 Bishops..and the Temporal Peers. **1774** PENNANT *Tour Scot. in 1772* 149 A charter erecting the lands belonging to the abbacy into a temporal lordship. **1898** C. H. BOWDEN *Dict. Cath.*, *Temporal Power of the Pope.*—1. His right to possess and govern the Patrimony of St. Peter and other States of the Church; 2. His rights as Vicar of Christ in relation to other sovereigns and states.

†**4.** Applied to 'artificial hours', i.e. twelfths of an 'artificial day': see ARTIFICIAL 5. *Obs. rare.*

1594 BLUNDEVIL *Exerc.* III. I. lii. (1636) 370 Note also that the unequall houres are called sometime artificiall, and sometime temporall houres.

5. a. *Gram.* and *Pros.* Relating to or depending on the quantity of syllables (i.e. the time taken in pronouncing them). ***temporal augment*** (Gr. Gram.): see AUGMENT *sb.* 2.

1678 PHILLIPS (ed. 4), *Temporal Augment*, an Augmentation which is made in a Greek Verb, by increasing in several Tenses, the quantity of the first Vowel or Dipthong, as ἄγω ἦγον. **1860** MARSH *Lect. Eng. Lang.* 540 The ancient temporal metres were inexhaustible, because the permutations and combinations of the prosodical feet were infinite. **1867** tr. *Curtius's Gr. Gram.* (ed. 2) §235 The Temporal Augment is used in all verbs which begin with a vowel.

b. *Gram.* Of or pertaining to the tenses of a verb; of tense; also, expressing or denoting time, as an adverb, a clause, etc.

1786 H. TOOKE *Purley* II. viii. (1798) 650 Our language has made but small progress, compared either with the Greek or with the Latin..even in this Modal and Temporal abbreviation. **1886** W. G. HALE in *Amer. Jrnl. Philol.* VII. 459 The tenseless phrase *in order to*, used alike for present and past purposes in English, fails to convey the temporal ideas conveyed by the Latin present and imperfect subjunctive. **1889** *Ibid.* X. 334 In Latin all the uses of the ablative absolute sprang from the temporal use of the ablative.

6. In general sense: Of, pertaining, or relating to time, the present time, or a particular time.

1877 MALLOCK *New Republic* II. III. ii. 15 Merely temporal people, who are just as narrow-minded and dull as ..merely local people—the natives of a neighbourhood. **1886** A. WEIR *Hist. Basis Mod. Europe* (1889) 481 A vast quantity of temporal and spatial experience. **1906** D. W. FORREST *Authority Christ* VI. i. 309 In speaking of the last day we are using a temporal expression for an unspeakable and timeless reality.

B. *sb.* **1. a.** That which is temporal: esp. in *pl.* Temporal things or matters.

1390 GOWER *Conf.* I. 32 Noght only of the temporal But of the spirital also. *Ibid.* 276 To day is venym schad In holi cherche of temporal, Which medleth with the spirital. **1471** FORTESCUE *Wks.* (1869) 534 In his persone and his kingdome, which bothe be temporales onely. **1625** BURGES *Pers. Tithes* 16 Hee that partakes of Gods blessing in Temporals. **1755** YOUNG *Centaur* iv, Joy from temporals, is a terrestrial joy, And, like all things terrestrial, has a dreg in it. **1897** H. DRUMMOND *Ideal Life* 140 Trying by some other way than through these homely temporals, to learn the spiritual life.

b. Temporal power, possession, or estate; TEMPORALITY; chiefly in *pl.* = temporalities.

c **1450** HOLLAND *Howlat* 277 That sen it nechit Natur, thar alleris mastriss, Thai couth nocht trete but entent of the Temperale. **1545** BRINKLOW *Compl.* xxii. (1874) 51 Of their temporals, let .viij. or .x. pound and not aboue of euery hundreth be granted to the Kyng. **1594** R. ASHLEY tr. *Loys le Roy* 54 b, The Pope commaundeth ouer the temporall of the Church called S. Peters patrimonie, as King. **1795** ABBE BARRUEL *Hist. Clergy during Fr. Rev.* 99 They did not reject the new French constitution, or the laws concerning temporals. **1863** BLYTH *Hist. Fincham* 39 The temporals were such lands or other property as may have accrued to the church by gift or purchase, and belonged chiefly to the regular or monastic clergy. **1880** BROWNING *Dram. Idylls* Ser. II. *Pietro* 362 I'll to Rome, before Rome's feet the temporal-supreme lay prostrate!

2. (Also in L. form **temporale** (tɛmpɒˈreɪliː, -ɑːleɪ).) That part of the breviary and missal which contains the daily offices in the order of the ecclesiastical year, as distinct from those proper for Saints' days: cf. SANCTORALE.

14.. *Table Lessons*, etc. in *Wyclif's Bible* IV. 690 Here endith the Temperal, and here bigynneth the Propre Sanctorum. *c* **1475** *Pict. Voc.* in Wr.-Wülcker 755/21 *Hoc temperalium*, a temperal. **1483** CAXTON *Gold. Leg.* 63/2 This is the Rewle of the temporal thurgh the yere. **1517** in *Archæologia* LXI. 83 Item a legend hoole of the temporall. .. Item a legend hoole of the Sanctorum. **1872** Temporale [see SANCTORALE].

temporal (ˈtɛmpərəl), *a.*[2] and *sb.*[2] *Anat.* Also 6 tymporall. [ad. L. *temporāl-is*, f. *tempora* the temples: see TEMPLE *sb.*[2]] Of, belonging to, or situated in the temples: esp. in names of structures, as ***temporal artery***, ***bone***, ***muscle***, ***vein***, etc.

temporal canals, small passages for vessels and nerves through the malar bone to the temporal surface; ***temporal lobe***, the lowest lobe of the brain lying below the Sylvian fissure; ***temporal fossa***, that in which the temporal muscle originates.

1597 A. M. tr. *Guillemeau's Fr. Chirurg.* 11/2 We should not hurte the temporalle muscle. *Ibid.* 29 b/1 The thirde is called the temporall, or vayne of the temples, which in divers branches ascendeth in the temples of the heade. **1732** ARBUTHNOT *Rules of Diet* in *Aliments*, etc. 327 Copious Bleeding by opening the temporal Arteries. **1842** E. WILSON *Anat. Vade M.* (ed. 2) 23 The Temporal Bone is..divisible into a squamous, mastoid, and petrous portion. **1854** H. SPENCER *Personal Beauty* Ess. 1891 II. 390 The chief agents in closing the jaws are the temporal muscles.

B. *sb.* Elliptical for *temporal artery*, *bone*, *muscle*, etc.

1541 R. COPLAND *Guydon's Quest. Chirurg.* Fj, Those [muscles] are called tymporalles, and are ryght noble and very sensyble, & therfore theyr hurt is very peryllous. **1758** J. S. *Le Dran's Observ. Surg.* 8 The Temporal became ossified. **1899** *Allbutt's Syst. Med.* VII. 228 The muscles of mastication—the masseters, temporals, and pterygoids. **1900** J. HUTCHINSON in *Arch. Surg.* XI. No. 41. 23 The old woman's temporals were scarcely, if at all, enlarged.

temporale (tɛmpəˈrɑːl). Also ‖**temporal.** [ad. Sp. *temporal* storm, spell of rainy weather.] A weather condition of the Pacific coast of Central America consisting of strong south-west winds bringing heavy rain.

1853 tr. *F. Gerstaecker's Narr. Journey round World* I. ix. 145 A temporale, however, might happen at any moment. *Ibid.* ix. 160 All the threatened dangers of the cordilleras, of snow-drifts and temporales, were past. **1923** J. HERGESHEIMER *Bright Shawl* 141 The April temporale lay in an even heat over the city. **1936** L. J. HALLE *Transcaribbean* ii. 32 Twice or more in the season there will be 'temporals', when it will rain interminably for a week. **1982** *N.Y. Times* 4 Apr. x. 18/4 There is scarcely one temporale, that sudden downpour of sheet-rain bringing with it a fine red tufa dust.

‖**temporale:** see TEMPORAL *sb.*[1] 2.

temporalis (tɛmpəˈreɪlɪs). *Anat.* [L.: see TEMPORAL *a.*[2] and *sb.*[2]] Also ***temporalis muscle.*** A fan-shaped muscle which closes the lower jaw and which arises from the temporal fossa, passes through the gap between the zygomatic arch and the side of the skull, and is attached to the coronoid process and the anterior border of the ramus of the mandible.

1676 W. MOLINS *Μυοτομια or Anat. Admin. of Muscles Humane Body* 17 If you throw this Muscle either from his origination or insertion, *Temporalis* will appear in his insertion. **1713** W. CHESELDEN *Anat. Human Body* II. ii. 55 Temporalis, arises from the Os Frontis, Parietale, Sphænoides, and Temporis, and..is inserted externally into the Processus Corone of the Lower Jaw which it pulls upwards. **1873** G. FLEMING tr. *Chauveau's Compar. Anat.* I. §3. ii. 223 To dissect the temporalis, excise the external pterygoideus from its inferior border. **1910** *Bull. Amer. Museum Nat. Hist.* XXVIII. 302 The *temporalis* is the most powerful jaw muscle in *Carnivora*. **1938** H. L. WIEMAN *Gen. Zool.* (ed. 3) iv. 78 A portion of the *temporalis* muscle can be seen between the orbit and the tympanum. **1978** *Sci. Amer.* Apr. 64/2 In 1944 a German surgeon..tried attaching a flap of muscle (the temporalis) from the side of the head to the surface of the brain, hoping that the muscle's blood vessels would join the cerebral arteries and supply them.

temporalism (ˈtɛmpərəlɪz(ə)m). [f. TEMPORAL *a.*[1] + -ISM.]

1. The spirit of 'the world' (as opposed to a religious spirit); secularism; addiction to temporal or mundane interests.

1872 *Dublin Rev.* Jan. 10 Exhibition of the evil spirit which we have called 'temporalism', in that hatred of restraint and subordination. **1897** *N. York Voice* 16 Sept. 3/1 He..takes leave of animalism, temporalism, provincialism, and becomes consciously a son of God.

2. The principle of the temporal power of the Pope.

1899 *Spectator* 7 Jan. 15 This war, which is not the warfare, nor in the interest, of the Roman Catholic Church, but of temporalism, is carried into every field where intolerant Catholicism has any power.

So ˈ**temporalist**, one who maintains or supports the temporal power of the Pope.

1901 *Mission. Record U.F. Ch. Scot.* June 272/1 The next Pope will be a strong Temporalist.

temporality (tɛmpəˈrælɪtɪ). Also 5 **-er-**; 4–6 **-ite**, 5 **-yte**, **-itee**, **-ytee**, 5–6 **-itie**, (6 **temporallytie**). [ad. late L. *temporālitās* (Tertullian), f. *temporāl-is*, TEMPORAL: see -ITY. Substituted in 14–15th c. for *temperalté*, TEMPORALTY, q.v.]

†**1.** Temporal power, jurisdiction, affairs, property, etc.: *esp.* the temporal property of the clergy; = TEMPORALTY 1. *Obs.*

1393 LANGL. *P. Pl.* C. XXIII. 128 Prelates thei maden, To holde with Antecrist here temporalite to saue. **1497** *Acc. Ld. High Treas. Scot.* I. 314 Resauit fra Maister Johne Fresel, elect of Ros, for the compositioun of his admissioune to the temporalitee of Ros. **1501** *Reg. Privy Seal Scotl.* I. 93/1 A Precept of Admission made to Jane Forman, Prioress of Eklis, to the temporalite of al landis, rentis, and possessionis of the sammyn. **1613** SHERLEY *Trav. Persia* 3 The lesser Princes of Italy being not likely to endure the Churches so great encrease of Temporality. **1818** SCOTT *Hrt. Midl.* xlii[i], That the said incumbent might lawfully enjoy the spirituality and temporality of the cure of souls at Knocktarlitie.

b. *pl.* Temporal or material possessions (esp. of the church or clergy).

c **1475** *Harl. Contn. Higden* (Rolls) VIII. 546 The comons putte up a bylle in the parlement to the kynge as for the temporalytees beynge in the handes of the spirituelte. *a* **1552** LELAND *Itin.* VI. 1 The Kynge had reteynid the Temporallyties of the Byshoprike for a tyme. **1593** in Row *Hist. Kirk* (Wodrow Soc.) 150 To considder what great prejudice the Kirk sustains by the erecting of the tithes of diverss prelacies into temporalities, so that these kirks cannot be planted. **1660** R. COKE *Power & Subj.* 204 The Pope..gave to the said Nicholas the said Abby, with all the said Spiritualities, and Temporalities. **1726** AYLIFFE *Parergon* 129 After all which, the Bishop is introduced into the King's Presence to do his Homage for his Temporalities or Barony. **1854** H. MILLER *Sch. & Schm.* xxv. (1857) 546 The Church..might, I believed, have to forfeit the temporalities, if her decision differed from that of the law courts.

2. The body or class of temporal persons; = TEMPORALTY 2.

1456 SIR G. HAYE *Law Arms* (S.T.S.) 24 The Emperour ..to be lord and juge..of the temporalitee. *c* **1470** HENRY *Wallace* x. 1002 The byschoprykis inclynyt till his croune, Bathe temperalite and all the religioune. **1543** HEN. VIII *Sp. Parl.* 24 Dec., in *Coll. Poems* 165 You of the Temporality be not clean and unspotted of Malice and Envy. **1679** BURNET *Hist. Ref.* I. 582 Here both the temporality and spirituality gave great subsidies to the king.

3. The quality or condition of being temporal or temporary; temporariness; relation to time.

1634 RAINBOW *Labour* (1635) 11 Though in the act of our labours..we place temporality, yet ought we alwayes before our intentions to set æternity. **1659** H. L'ESTRANGE *Alliance Div. Off.* v. 158 As the Western Church observed this very day [All Saints day], so did also the Eastern, or at least some other, in temporality and point of time very near it. **1678** T. JONES *Heart & its Right Sov.* 587 What can any mortal excellency, that has..perishing temporality stamp'd upon it signifie to Christians, who are not of this world? **1909** *Westm. Gaz.* 15 May 4/1 Gaining thereby the attributes of eternity, without losing its own qualities of temporality.

ˈ**temporalize,** *v. rare.* [f. TEMPORAL *a.*[1] + -IZE.] *trans.* To make temporal in character.

a. To secularize; **b.** to limit in time.

1828 PUSEY *Hist. Enq.* I. 146 They led to the ultimate temporalizing and annihilation of everything peculiarly Christian in the system. **1890** *Spectator* 5 July, Many who turned from a worship which seemed to localise and temporalise the Divine.

ˈ**temporally,** *adv.* [f. as prec. + -LY[2].]

1. For a time, temporarily. *rare.*

1450–1530 *Myrr. our Ladye* 185 The maker of all thynges rested temperally in the,..thow vyrgyn.

2. In regard to temporal matters; in, or with respect to, this world; in the present life.

c **1380** *Antecrist* in Todd *3 Treat. Wyclif* 119 Antecrist havyng glorie of þe world temporally. **1456** SIR G. HAYE *Law Arms* (S.T.S.) 20 As evill bitter wateris gerris mony folk dee temporaly, sa dois..heresy and lollardry the saule dee spiritualy. **1552** ABP. HAMILTON *Catech.* (1884) 39 Punitions quhilk God sendis to synnaris temporallie. **1679** WHITEBREAD in *Speeches Jesuits* 2, I pray God bless His Majesty both Temporally and Eternally. *a* **1716** SOUTH *Serm.* (J.), Sinners who are in such a temporally happy condition, owe it not to their sins, but wholly to their luck.

3. With regard to time.

1961 in WEBSTER. **1971** *Nature* 21 May 172/1 Temporally varying deviations between 40° and 60° were found. **1974** *Sci. Amer.* June 31/2 The pulse, which contains only about 10^{-3} joule of laser energy, is shaped spatially (and also temporally, if desired) prior to amplification. **1982** *Ibid.* Feb. 129/2 Temporally coherent light would show at the sampling point a continuous variation between crest and trough.

ˈ**temporalness.** *rare.* [f. as prec. + -NESS.] The quality of being temporal.

1611 COTGR., *Secularité*,..worldlinesse, temporallnesse.

temporalty (ˈtɛmpərəltɪ). *Obs.* or *arch.* Also 4–6 **temper-**; 4–5 **-el-**; 4–6 **-te**, **-tee**, 4–7 **-tie**, 5–6 **-tye**, (6 **temporalltie**). [app. a. AF. **temporelté* = F. *temporalité* (13th c.), f. OF. *temporel*, TEMPORAL: see -TY. Cf. *commonalty*, *cruelty*, *loyalty*, etc. In 14–15th c. assimilated to the L. form, as *temper-*, *temporalité*; now TEMPORALITY.]

1. Temporal or secular things, affairs, business; temporal authority. ? *Obs.*

1396–7 in *Eng. Hist. Rev.* (1907) XXII. 299 Temporelte and spirituelte ben to partys of holi chirche. *c* **1400** MAUNDEV. (Roxb.) iii. 10 He es þare lorde bathe of temperaltee and of spiritualtee. *c* **1483** CAXTON *Dialogues* 45 *Cest grand folye De donner le eternalite Pour le temporalite*, it is grete folye For to gyve the eternalite For the temporalte. *c* **1511** *1st Eng. Bk. Amer.* (Arb.) Introd. 30/2 In ye temperalte haue they one Emperour. **1621** BURTON *Anat. Mel.* III. i. I. ii. (1651) 415 The mutability of all temporalties. **1651** *Life Father Sarpi* (1676) 47 Lands that in the temporalty are subject to the state of Venice, and in the spirituality are under the Arch-Bishop of Milan. **1700** ASTRY tr. *Saavedra-Faxardo* I. 183 The Spiritualty and Temporalty are two distinct Jurisdictions.

b. Chiefly *pl.* Temporal possessions; esp. those of an ecclesiastical person or body: = TEMPORALITY 1 b. ? *Obs.*

[**1306** *Rolls of Parlt.* I. 220/1 Ont donez terres, tenementz, & avoesons, & tieles autres temporautez, as Prelatz de seinte Eglise.] **1377** LANGL. *P. Pl.* B. xx. 127 Prelates þei hem maden, To holden with antecryste her temperaltes to saue. *c* **1380** WYCLIF *Wks.* (1880) 103 Subsidies & dymes for here temperalties. **1449** *Rolls of Parlt.* V. 157/2 Prouffitez of the temperaltees of Bisshuprichez. **1570–6** LAMBARDE *Peramb. Kent* (1826) 229 A stately Monasterie (the temporalties whereof did amount to a hundreth fiftie and five poundes). **1607** COWELL *Interpr.*, *Temporalties of Bishops* (*Temporalia Episcoporum*) be such reuenewes, lands, and tenements, as Bishops haue had laid to their Sees by the Kings and other great personages of this land from time to time. *a* **1715**

BURNET *Own Time* I. IV. (1724) 760 The Cardinal was chosen by the Chapter Vicar, or Guardian of the temporalties.

2. The body of temporal persons or laymen, the laity; the temporal estate or estates of the realm, i.e. the temporal peers and the commons.

1387 TREVISA *Higden* (Rolls) VII. 335 Kyng William was sterne..and rulede boþe temperalte and spiritualte at his owne wille. **1480** CAXTON *Chron. Eng.* ccxliv. 301 Ther was graunted vnto the kyng..bothe of spirituelte and of temporalte an hole taxe and a disme. *a* **1529** SKELTON *Col. Cloute* 61 For the temporalte Accuseth the spiritualte. **1621** ELSING *Debates Ho. Lords* (Camden) App. 129 The subsidies of the Temporalty and the Clergie brought into the House from the King. *a* **1715** BURNET *Own Time* an. 1663 (1823) I. II. 340 The convocation gave..four subsidies, which proved as heavy on them, as they were light on the temporalty. **1874** S. WILBERFORCE *Ess.* II. 191 The old compact between the spirituality and the temporalty.

†**b.** The condition or estate of a layman. *Obs.*

c **1440** *Bone Flor.* 1032 Ther was no man in that town ..That was of temporalte. **1482** *Monk of Evesham* (Arb.) 38 Sothely some flowryd in prosperite in the spyrytualte. Some in the temporalte and some in relygyon.

'temporal,ward, *adv. rare.* [f. TEMPORAL *a.*² + -WARD.] Towards the temples or temporal region; = TEMPORAD.

1904 TITCHENER tr. *Wundt's Physiol. Psychol.* I. 236 Retinal points that lie temporalward.

‖**tempora mutantur** ('tɛmpərə mjuː'tæntə(r)), *Latin phr.* [L., in full *tempora mutantur nos et* (or *et nos*) *mutamur in illis* (also used), times change and we change with them.] A statement emphasizing the inevitability of change in human affairs and customs.

A similar saying *Omnia mutentur, nos et mutamur in illis* is found in *Delitiæ Poetarum Germanorum* (1612) I. 685, where it is ascribed to the Emperor Lothair I by the author (who may be Matthias Borbonius), but there is no evidence that it has a medieval origin. The phrase *tempora mutantur*, however, occurs earlier in other contexts: see quot. *c* 1440.

[*c* **1440** *Gesta Romanorum* (Harl. MS.) x. 28 And þei founde þis y-wreten, Tempora mutantur; Homines deteriorantur;..this is to sey, 'tymys ben chaungid; and men ben hyndred, or turnyd, or I-made worse.'] **1577** W. HARRISON *Descr. Britayne* III. iii. 99 in Holinshed *Chron.* I, Oft in one age, diuers iudgementes doe passe upon one maner of casse, wherby the saying of the poet *Tempora mutantur, & nos mutamur in illis.* [**1666** G. TORRIANO *Piazza Universale di Proverbi Italiani* 281 Times change, and we with them... [*Note*, 292] The Latin says the same, *Tempora mutantur, et nos mutamur in illis.*] **1855** W. CHAPPELL *Popular Music* I. 309 However unobjectionable this song may have been in Queen Mary's time, the three remaining stanzas would not be very courteously received in Queen Victoria's. *Tempora mutantur.* **1934** BLUNDEN *Mind's Eye* 154 He could not repress an exclamatory *Tempora mutantur.* **1961** *Times* 7 Apr. 20/7 The Rugby-watching public can in no way afford to be smug. *Tempora mutantur* indeed, and..not so many years ago a boo would have caused apoplexy in older Rugby followers. **1978** J. I. M. STEWART *Full Term* iv. 56 'Giles has my old rooms..on the floor above this.' 'More *tempora mutantur* stuff.' **1980** *Times* 7 May 18/2 Charlie Chan was always successful... This was '*because*' he was Chinese... *Tempora mutantur, nos et mutamur in illis*, particularly the progeny of a nasty modern breed of censors... working up a protest against the revival of Charlie Chan.

temporance, obs. form of TEMPERANCE.

†**tempo'raneal**, *a. Obs. rare*⁻¹. [f. as next + -AL¹.] = next (in quot. in sense 2).

1625 JACKSON *Creed* v. xviii. §2 As if the temporaneal coexistence of these two effects had sufficiently argued the one's causal dependence upon the other.

temporaneous (tɛmpə'reɪnɪəs), *a.* Now *rare* or *Obs.* [f. L. *temporāne-us* timely, opportune (f. *tempus, tempor-* time) + -OUS.]

†**1.** Lasting only for a time, temporary. *Obs.*

1656 [see 2]. **1681** HALLYWELL *Melampr.* 68 (T.) Those things may cause a temporaneous disunion. **1782** A. MONRO *Compar. Anat.* 120 The temporaneous grinders are placed ..upon the internal set. **1806** W. TAYLOR in *Ann. Rev.* IV. 244 This book is so driftless, so useless, so temporaneous. **1818** [implied in *temporaneously, -ness*: see below].

2. Pertaining or relating to time, temporal.

1656 BLOUNT *Glossogr.*, *Temporaneous*, done suddenly, at a certaine time, pertaining to time; variable for the time. **1694** *Phil. Trans.* XVIII. 67 A Temporaneous progressive motion of the parts of the Air at the rate of 276 Paces in a second Minute of time. **1878** F. FERGUSON *Pop. Life Christ* x. 40 He uses only the connective particle 'and' and not the temporaneous 'then'.

Hence **tempo'raneously** *adv.*, for the time; **tempo'raneousness**, temporary character.

1727 BAILEY vol. II, Temporaneousness. **1818** G. S. FABER *Horæ Mosaicæ* I. 328 His title to the perpetually entailed, though temporaneously alienated, inheritance of his forefathers. *Ibid.* II. 208 The testimony which it bears respecting its own temporaneousness.

temporarily ('tɛmpərərɪlɪ), *adv.* [f. TEMPORARY *a.* + -LY².] In a temporary manner.

1. For a time (only); during a limited time.

c **1694** in Somers *Tracts* (1748) I. 193 Derogatory to the King's Prerogative, relative to Parliaments, and temporarily changing the very Constitution thereof. **1803** GODWIN *Life Chaucer* III. 189 (Jod.) An oligarchical council temporarily administering the affairs of the nation. **1873** *Act 36 & 37 Vict.* c. 88 §7 The vacancy shall be temporarily filled.

2. In relation to time, temporally. *rare.*

1877 E. CAIRD *Philos. Kant* II. xi. 447 All spatially or temporarily determined phenomena.

temporariness ('tɛmpərərɪnɪs). [f. next + -NESS.] The quality or state of being temporary.

1695 J. SAGE *Article* etc. Wks. 1844 I. 197 The perpetuity or temporariness of it doth not affect its nature. **1876** W. BATHGATE *Deep Things of God* ii. 36 The..suddenness and temporariness of the physical process of breathing.

temporary ('tɛmpərərɪ), *a.* (*sb.*) [ad. L. *temporāri-us*, f. *tempus, tempor-* time: see -ARY.]

A. *adj.* **1. a.** Lasting for a limited time; existing or valid for a time (only); not permanent; transient; made to supply a passing need.

1547–64 BAULDWIN *Mor. Philos.* (Palfr.) 60 The authority of princes & gouernors..is truely to be called temporarie, that is, but for a time. *a* **1628** PRESTON *New Covt.* (1634) 45 The creature is temporary, whereas the soul is immortall. **1651** HOBBES *Leviath.* II. xix. 99 For their perpetuall, and not temporary security. **1777** COOK *Voy. Pacific* II. vii. (1784) I. 292 A large space had been cleared, before the temporary hut of this Chief. **1817** JAS. MILL *Brit. India* II. IV. ix. 293 The adaptation of temporary expedients to temporary exigencies. **1858** J. H. NEWMAN *Hist. Sk.* (1873) III. v. i. 434 Inconveniences which they felt to be only temporary.

b. *temporary hardness*, hardness of water that can be removed by boiling, because it is due to bicarbonates which are thereby precipitated; *temporary star* (*Astron.*), a star which appears suddenly, shines for a time, and then almost or entirely disappears; *temporary tooth*, a deciduous tooth, milk-tooth.

1802 *Med. Jrnl.* VIII. 559 The first teeth, or those of childhood, the author calls temporary, the set which succeeds them he terms permanent. **1833** HERSCHEL *Astron.* xii. 383 The phænomena we allude to are those of temporary stars. **1842** E. WILSON *Anat. Vade M.* (ed. 2) 51 The Temporary teeth are 20 in number, 8 incisors, 4 canine, and 8 molars. **1895** H. COLLET *Water Softening & Purification* i. 2 The temporary hardness is that due to the bicarbonates of lime and magnesia. **1969** Temporary hardness [see *permanent hardness* s.v. FERMANENT *a.* (*sb.*) 1 d].

†**c.** Belonging or relating to the particular time; of the period; hence, of passing interest, ephemeral. ? *Obs.* (or merged in 1).

1777 BURKE *Corr.* (1844) II. 164, I send you a trifling temporary production, made for the occasion of the day, and to perish with it. **1778** MUSGRAVE 25 Apr., in Boswell *Johnson*, A temporary poem always entertains us. **1805** W. COOKE *S. Foote* I. 152 Though it ['Devil upon Two Sticks'] admits of some temporary strokes, such as the ridicule on the college of physicians,..&c., [it] exhibits them worked up in so brilliant and general a manner, as to be always new.

d. Designating one who is commissioned for the duration of a war (esp. that of 1914–18), as *temporary captain, officer*, etc. Also *temporary gent*(*leman*) (in colloq. or pejorative Services' use); abbrev. *T.G.* s.v. T 6 a.

1918 BARRIE *Echoes of War* 68 Socially he had fallen..; even..in his uniform the hasty might say something clever about 'temporary gentlemen'. **1925** W. DEEPING *Sorrell & Son* ii. 21 'My name is Sorrell, Captain Sorrell.' 'You will have to drop the 'captain'. Temporary, I suppose?' **1938** S. BECKETT *Murphy* x. 234 He withheld his hand, the little temporary gent and pure in heart. **1958** S. RAVEN in H. Thomas *Establishment* 72 Temporary Captain C.C. had been in the very first intake at Sandhurst. **1976** *N.Y. Rev. Bks.* 5 Feb. 20/3 The lower-middle-class officer..who in the First World War would have been called a 'temporary gentleman'. **1983** T. POCOCK *1945: Dawn came up like Thunder* v. 151 There were two officers' messes—'A' and 'B'; the former primarily for staff officers..the latter, mostly made up of temporary officers.

†**2.** Belonging to the present life or this world: = TEMPORAL *a.*¹ 2. *Obs.*

(In quot. 1603, of a person: 'not a meddler with temporal or secular affairs'.)

1603 SHAKS. *Meas. for M.* v. i. 145 *Duke.* Know you that Frier Lodowick that she speakes of? *Peter.* I know him for a man diuine and holy, Not scuruy, nor a temporary medler, As he's reported by this Gentleman. **1668** HOWE *Bless. Righteous* (1825) 63 In our temporary state, while we are under the measure of time. **1674** OWEN *Holy Spirit* (1693) 207 Spiritual and Eternal things are more excellent than things Carnal and Temporary. **1751** JOHNSON *Rambler* No. 153 ¶13 The wise use of temporary riches.

†**3.** *Metaph.* Occurring or existing in time (not from eternity). *Obs.* (Cf. TEMPORAL *a.*¹ 6.)

a **1677** HALE *Prim. Orig. Man.* I. ii. 69 Collectively they make up a good moral evidence touching a temporary inception of the humane Nature. **1678** CUDWORTH *Intell. Syst.* I. i. §31. 39 They who conceived the World to have had a Temporary Beginning or Creation, held the Coevity of all Souls with it. **1701** NORRIS *Ideal World* 327 These truths are temporary, because those relations could not begin to exist before those created beings were produced.

†**4.** = TEMPORAL *a.*¹ 4. *Obs. rare.*

a **1656** USSHER *Ann.* To Rdr. ¶10 That from the evening ushering in the first day of the World, to that midnight which began the first day of the Christian æra, there was 4003 years, seventy dayes, and six temporarie howers.

B. *sb.*

†**1.** *pl.* Things belonging to this life, temporal goods. Cf. TEMPORALITY 1 b. *Obs.*

1596 H. CLAPHAM *Briefe Bible* II. 218 Wee haue taken Bread and other temporaries without begging them at thy hands. **1665** SIR T. HERBERT *Trav.* (1677) 172 A large Castle, which now by age or war (the canker-worms of all temporaries) is moth-eaten

†**2.** A person whose religious life or devotion endures only for a time. (In allusion to Matt. xiii. 21, etc.) *Obs.* (In quot. 1903 used (? by misunderstanding) for: a time-server, temporizer.)

1619 W. SCLATER *Exp. 1 Thess.* (1630) 59 Our Temporaries, or rather Temporizers..are carried full saile to the profession of Faith; whom yet the least note of reproach..makes ready to deny and abiure the Truth. **1647** TRAPP *Comm. 2 Cor.* xiii. 8 A temporary may so fall away as to persecute the truth that he once professed. [**1903** A. SMELLIE *Men of Covt.* xxiii. (1904) 253 A Temporary,—one who tries year in and year out to 'carry his dish level', and adjusts his sails to catch the changing winds.]

†**3.** A contemporary. *Obs.*

1649 *Alcoran* 6 We left this punishment, as an advertisement to their temporaries and posteritie.

4. A person employed or holding a post temporarily; a 'casual'; *spec.* a secretary or clerical worker supplied by an agency to cover absences or vacancies for a short period.

1848 DICKENS *Dombey* iii, Being only a permanency I couldn't be expected to show it like a temporary. **1892** *Pall Mall G.* 7 Oct. 7/1 The 'permanent temporaries' are liable to dismissal at any time, but are practically fixed, some having been in the service from eight to ten years. **1907** *Westm. Gaz.* 1 July 7/2 Servants who are merely casuals (i.e., temporaries) in purely private families. **1956** C. BLACKSTOCK *Dewey Death* vii. 159 Temporaries came, and temporaries went..and the work produced [was] shocking beyond belief. **1957** R. HART-DAVIS *Let.* 7 July in *Lyttelton-Hart-Davis Lett.* (1979) II. 123 This might have been possible if my secretary hadn't been on holiday. Instead I was burdened with a pudding-faced 'temporary'. **1970** *New Yorker* 17 Oct. 148/1 (*caption*) But Mr. Clark! I'm just a temporary.

temporat(e, -aunce: see TEMPERATE, -ANCE.

tempore: see TEMP. (abbrev.).

temporicide ('tɛmpərɪsaɪd). *nonce-wd.* [f. L. *tempus, tempor-* time + -CIDE.]

1. The 'killing' of time.

1851 *Chambers' Papers for People* IX. No. 72. 9 Short romantic stories, adaptable for purposes of temporicide. **1856** GRINDON *Life* xxiv. (1875) 305 Pleasure..such as will outweigh whole nights of the mere temporicide popularly esteemed the *beau idéal* of pastime.

2. One who 'kills' time.

a **1876** M. COLLINS *Th. in Gard.* (1880) II. 208 D., who would catch the tide, G., with his notions wide, Each is temporicide—Time's reckless murderer.

†**'temporist.** *Obs.* [f. as prec. + -IST: cf. TEMPORIZE *v.*] A temporizer, a time-server.

1596 NASHE *Saffron-Walden* Wks. (Grosart) III. 123 Heilding Dicke..is a temporist that hath faith inough for all Religions. **1607** MARSTON *What you will* II. i, Why, turne a temporist, row with the tide, Pursew the cut, the fashion of the age. **1650–66** WHARTON *Poems* Wks. (1683) 333 Touch me not, Traytor!.. I am no Temporist.

temporization (tɛmpəraɪ'zeɪʃən). [f. next + -ATION.] The action of temporizing.

1. Time-serving, 'trimming'; compromise.

1763 JOHNSON *Misc. Lives, Ascham* Wks. IV. 631 Charges of temporization and compliance had somewhat sullied his reputation. **1839** *Fraser's Mag.* XX. 97 Her policy is one of temporisation. **1851** *Ibid.* XLIII. 139 A union..was consequently thought of, as the best means of temporization.

2. Procrastination, delay; gaining of time.

1888 *Times* 19 Oct. 5/1 The inevitable reaction against the policy of adjournment and temporization.

temporize ('tɛmpəraɪz), *v.* [a. F. *temporiser* (14–15th c. in Hatz.-Darm.) to pass one's time, wait one's time, = med.L. *temporizāre* = *temporāre* to put off the time, delay (Du Cange), It. *temporeggiare* to observe, obey, or follow times (Florio), f. L. *tempus, tempor-* time: see -IZE.]

1. *intr.* To adopt some course for the time or occasion; hence, to adapt oneself or conform to the time and circumstances; to 'trim'.

[**1555–63**: cf. TEMPORIZER 1.] **1579** G. HARVEY *Letter-bk.* (Camden) 69, I pray the spare the world And give men leave to temporize. **1617** MORYSON *Itin.* II. 51 Most part of the rest temporised with the State, openly professing obedience ..but secretly relieuing the rebels. **1752** FIELDING *Amelia* IX. ix, How do you expect to rise in the church, if you cannot temporise, and give in to the opinion of your supporters? **1849** MACAULAY *Hist. Eng.* viii. II. 298 Penn, therefore, exhorted the fellows.. to submit, or at least to temporise. **1877** FROUDE *Short Stud.* (1883) IV. I. iii. 38 The pope..had privately advised Becket to avoid a quarrel with the king and to temporise.

†**b.** *trans. Obs. rare.*

1600 [see TEMPORIZED below].

†**2.** *intr.* To let time pass, spend time, 'mark time'; to procrastinate; to delay or wait for a more favourable moment. Also with *it. Obs.* exc. as in 3.

1579–80 NORTH *Plutarch* (1676) 358 Charging them they should not stir, and only to temporize and forbear, untill the Enemies came within a stones cast of them. **1600** HOLLAND *Livy* XXIV. xiii. 517 So Anniball contrariwise temporised, being not so readie now to credite the Nolanes. **1633** T. STAFFORD *Pac. Hib.* I. xiii. (1821) 147 Having temporized all this while. **1694** MOTTEUX *Rabelais* v. xviii. (1737) 76 We lay by and run adrift, that is, in a Landlopers Phrase, we temporis'd it. **1696** PHILLIPS (ed. 5), *Temporize*..also, to delay, to take time to consider.

3. *intr.* To act, negotiate, parley, treat, deal (*with* a person, etc.), so as to gain time.

1586 J. HOOKER *Hist. Irel.* in *Holinshed* II. 118/1 They did yet so temporise with them, as they gained time, till further order might be taken. **1586** DAY *Eng. Secretary* I. (1625) A iij b, My prouision is too small to perfect on a sudden so spacious a ground-worke, I will temporize with those duties which..by time may be in me supported. **1871** FREEMAN *Norm. Conq.* IV. xviii. 133 William was still temporizing with Stigand; the time for his degradation was not yet come.

4. To negotiate, to discuss terms; to arrange or make terms, to effect a compromise (*with* a person, etc., *between* persons or parties).

1579 FENTON *Guicciard.* I. (1599) 4 Knowing discreetely howe to temporise betweene Princes confederate. **1586** J. HOOKER *Hist. Irel.* in *Holinshed* II. 142/1 His lordship granted hir request, and temporised with the earle. **1636** E. DACRES tr. *Machiavel's Disc. Livy* I. 137 The safer course is, to temporise with it, then strive forthwith to extinguish it. **1823** SCOTT *Peveril* xxxvi, I have behaved like a fool..; I ought to have temporised with this singular being, learned the motives of its interference, and availed myself of its succour. **1863** KINGLAKE *Crimea* I. iii. 48 This calm Mahometan..strove to temporise as well as he could betwixt the angry Churches.

†**b.** *trans.* ? To negotiate, manage, accomplish (a result). *Obs. rare.*

1596 WARNER *Alb. Eng.* x. lvii. (1612) 251 Of ancient Peeres, of valiant Men, great Lords, and Wise men all, By forced Warre, or fraudfull peace to temporize the fall.

¶ **5.** *trans.* To provide for the time, improvise, extemporize. (*Erroneous use.*)

1880 J. NICOL *Poems & Songs* 41 No fire nor firing, goblet, pan, nor pot Nor wherewithal to temporize a bed.

Hence **'temporized** *ppl. a.*; †**'temporizement** (*obs. nonce-wd.*), = TEMPORIZATION 1.

1600 W. WATSON *Decacordon* (1602) 20 Whether then all religious zeale, being turned into temporized platformes, to cast *omnia pro tempore, nihil pro veritate*. *Ibid.* 33 [The Jesuits] were vnworthy the name of temporized statists..if they should not denie all and change their opinions, agreeing to time, person and place. **1647** M. HUDSON *Div. Right Govt.* Ep. Ded. 5, I hope..[to] vindicate the innocency of my thoughts from all such unworthy Sycophancy and Temporizement.

temporizer ('tɛmpəraɪzə(r)). Also 6 **-our**, *Sc.* **-ar**, 7 **-or.** [Agent-noun f. prec.: cf. F. *temporiseur* (*a* 1600 in Littré).] One who temporizes.

1. One who complies for the time, or yields to the time; a time-server, a 'trimmer'.

1555 R. P[OWNOLL] tr. *Musculus* (title) The Temporisour (that is to say, the Observer of Tyme) translated into Inglishe. **1563** WINȜET *Four Scoir Thre Quest.* To Rdr., Wks. (S.T.S.) I. 53 Werray finȝeit hypocritis, and temperizaris with the tyme contrare thair conscience. **1563–87** FOXE *A. & M.* (1596) 1885/1 One by iudgement reformed, is more worth then a thousand transformed temporizers. **1611** SHAKS. *Wint. T.* I. ii. 302 A mindlesse Slaue, Or else a houering Temporizer. **1617** MORYSON *Itin.* II. 290 They would neuer be dissembling temporisors. **1710** NORRIS *Chr. Prud.* ii. 101 The Policy of Temporizers, men that steer their course by the compass of Worldly Interests. **1812** SHELLEY *Address* Prose Wks. 1888 I. 258 The dangers which lie beneath the footsteps of the hypocrite or temporizer.

2. One who seeks to gain time; a procrastinator, delayer; one who waits for a favourable time.

1609 HOLLAND *Amm. Marcell.* 370 Like unto that auncient and warie temporizer [Q. Fabius Maximus]. **1636** FEATLY *Clavis Myst.* xxix. 383 Doth Satan play the temporizer and time all his suggestions? **1736** *Gentl. Mag.* VI. 469/1 The famous Advice..which ought to be observed by all Temporizers; viz. Time was; Time is: but take Care to lay hold on the Opportunity before the Time is past.

temporizing ('tɛmpəraɪzɪŋ), *vbl. sb.* [f. as prec. + -ING[1].] The action of the verb TEMPORIZE.

1. Temporary compliance, etc.; time-serving, 'trimming'; parleying: see TEMPORIZE 1.

1590 J. SMYTHE in *Lett. Lit. Men* (Camden) 64 By your Majesties bearinge and temporizinge with the woonderfull disorders and abuses. *c* **1618** MORYSON *Itin.* (1903) 287 Our Ministers could not safely liue [in Ireland] without some temporising, and applying himselfe to thaire humours. **1707** NORRIS *Treat. Humility* iii. 98 By temporizing or time-serving, I mean, when a man conforms his principles or practices to the times,..so as to be ready to take up new principles,..whenever a new turn of the times..shall make it for his advantage so to do. **1757** BURKE *Abridgm. Eng. Hist.* viii, John, deserted by all, had no resource but in temporizing and submission. **1816** SCOTT *Old Mort.* xxxviii, This..is no time for temporising with our duty.

2. Putting off, delaying, procrastination; negotiation so as to gain time: see TEMPORIZE 2, 3.

1586 J. HOOKER *Hist. Irel.* in *Holinshed* II. 113/2 By temporising and gaining of time all matters were pacified. **1653** H. COGAN tr. *Pinto's Trav.* xlvii. 270 Without further temporising, he passed over the very same day to the other side of the river. **1685** *Gracian's Courtiers Orac.* 49 A rational temporizing ripens secrets and resolutions.

'temporizing, *ppl. a.* [f. as prec. + -ING[2].] That temporizes: see the verb.

1. Time-serving, 'trimming'.

1600 E. BLOUNT *Hosp. Incur. Fooles* a ij, Another puts on the Foxe with temporizing humilitie. **1680** C. NESSE *Church Hist.* 210 That temporizing parasitical priest. **1693** DRYDEN *Juvenal* Ded. (1697) 65 A Temporizing Poet, a Well-manner'd Court-Slave, and a Man who is often afraid of Laughing in the right place. **1796** BURKE *Regic. Peace* i. Wks. VIII. 87 They..consider a temporizing meanness as the only source of safety. **1828** J. W. CROKER *Diary* 12 July, I thought a timid or temporising course would create great dissatisfaction.

2. Designed to gain time.

1800 *Misc. Tr.* in *Asiat. Ann. Reg.* 140/1 My people became so clamorous that temporizing measures were no longer to be pursued. **1843** R. J. GRAVES *Syst. Clin. Med.* xvi. 191 His treatment was purely expectant and temporising. **1903** J. GAIRDNER in *Camb. Mod. Hist.* II. xiii. 447 Henry wrote a temporising reply.

Hence **'temporizingly** *adv.*, in a temporizing way, in a way designed to gain time.

1847 in WEBSTER. **1894** *Temple Bar Mag.* CII. 136 He..talked temporizingly, with suggestions of possible arrangements.

temporo- ('tɛmpərəʊ), before a vowel sometimes **tempor-**, used in *Anat.* as combining form of L. *tempora* temples (of the head), forming adjectives in the sense 'pertaining to the temple or temples and (some other part)', as ***temporo-alar*** belonging to the temporal region and the wing: noting a muscle in birds, ***-auricular, -facial, -hyoid, -malar, -mandibular, -mastoid, -maxillary, -occipital*** (also ***temporoccipital***), ***-parietal, -sphenoid, -sphenoidal, -zygomatic.***

1842 E. WILSON *Anat. Vade M.* (ed. 2) 400 The *Temporo-facial gives off a number of branches which are distributed over the temple and upper half of the face. **1899** *Allbutt's Syst. Med.* VIII. 168 The distribution of the *temporo-malar or any other sensory nerve. **1889** A. MACALISTER *Text-bk. Human Anat.* 243 The *temporo-mandibular joint forms a double condylarthrosis. **1974** *Nature* 8 Mar. 165/2 An asymmetrical functional activity of both temporomandibular joint mechanisms must compensate during chewing and non-chewing activities. **1842** E. WILSON *Anat. Vade M.* (ed. 2) 337 The *Temporo-maxillary vein formed by the union of the temporal and internal maxillary. **1890** BILLINGS *Nat. Med. Dict.*, **Temporo-occipital artery*... **Temporo-parietal suture*, that between temporal and parietal bones. **1879** *St. George's Hosp. Rep.* IX. 341 Between the frontal and *temporo-sphenoid lobes. **1890** BILLINGS *Nat. Med. Dict.*, **Temporo-zygomatic surface*, external surface of great wing of sphenoid.

tempour, tempra, obs. ff. TEMPER, TEMPERA.

temprate, obs. variant of TEMPERATE.

†**'tempre,** *a. Obs.* Also 4–5 **temper(e,** 5 **tempur(e.** [a. AF., OF. *tempré* (12th c. in Godef.), pa. pple. of *temprer* to TEMPER. The final *-e*, originally pronounced, became at length mute: cf. ASSIGN, COSTIVE.] Tempered; temperate.

a **1340** HAMPOLE *Psalter* l. 1 It is a tempre kynd of praiynge. *Ibid.* cxxxvii. 5 All tempre men, þat gouernes þair flesch in mesure. *c* **1385** CHAUCER *L.G.W.* Prol. 128 Now hadde the tempre sonne al that releuyd. *c* **1400** *Laud Troy Bk.* 130 Large of ȝifftes and ryght ffre, Wondur fair and ryght tempere. **1422** tr. *Secreta Secret., Priv. Priv.* 247 Slepe..vpon a nessh Bedde and in a place tempure.

tempre, -en, obs. forms of TEMPER *v.*

†**temprely,** *adv. Obs.* Also 4 **temperel(l)y.** [f. TEMPRE *a.* + -LY[2].] In moderation, temperately.

c **1386** CHAUCER *Shipm. T.* 262 (Harl. MS.) Gouerneth ȝow also of ȝour diete Al temperelly [*v.rr.* temperally [?-atly], atemprely] and namely in þis hete. **1422** tr. *Secreta Secret., Priv. Priv.* 237 Men whych kepyth reysonabill diette and lywen temprely, bene more hole of body. *Ibid.* 242 Drynke a lytill and colde temprely.

So †**'tempreness (tempurnes), temperateness.**

1486 *Bk. St. Albans, Her.* a ij, That other theirde parte of the worlde which shall be calde affrica, that is to say the contre of tempurnes.

temprure, variant of TEMPERURE *Obs.*

‖**temps** (tɑ̃). *Ballet.* [Fr., lit. = time.] A term used in the names of various ballet movements in which there is no transfer of weight from one foot to the other (see quots.).

1890 G. B. SHAW in *Star* 21 Feb. 2/4, I do not know..which particular *temps* is a *battement* and which a *ronde de jambe*. **1922** BEAUMONT & IDZIKOWSKI *Man. Classical Theatr. Dancing* V. 195 Ballonné à trois temps. *Ibid.* 196 Temps de cuisse.. Temps levé. *Ibid.* 200 Temps d'Allegre. **1930** CRASKE & BEAUMONT *Theory & Pract. Allegro in Classical Ballet* (1960) 9 In a *pas d'élévation*, such as a *Temps de Poisson*, the arms are raised *en attitude*. **1947** N. NICOLAEVA-LEGAT *Ballet Educ.* IV. 72 *Temps lié* is a set combination of steps and arm movements executed to the count of 4 or $\frac{3}{4}$. **1948** *Ballet Ann.* II. 66, I set to work on recording a number of *temps d'allegro* and enchaînements. **1957** G. B. L. WILSON *Dict. Ballet* 265 *Temps*..is variously used to describe a movement in which there is no transfer of weight (e.g. temps levé) or the division of a step into a number of movements (e.g. ballonné à trois temps). *c* **1973** J. CHOLERTON *Theory of Acrobatics* (Assoc. Amer. Dancing) (ed. 12) 9 *Q. What is a Temps lévé?* A. A hop.

temps, tempse, obs. ff. TENSE, TEMSE.

‖**temps perdu** (tɑ̃ pɛrdy). [Fr., 'time lost'; used with allusion to Proust: see RECHERCHE DU TEMPS PERDU.] The past, contemplated with nostalgia and a sense of irretrievability.

1932 S. O'FAOLÁIN *Midsummer Night Madness* 75 Life is too pitiful in these recapturings of the *temps perdu*, these brief intervals of reality. **1942** PARTRIDGE *Usage & Abusage* 95/2 One may question whether peace and prosperity will return with or without this word.. the 'Sesame' of *le temps perdu*. **1962** *John o' London's* 20 Sept. 287/3 A nostalgic atmosphere, an old-timers' *temps perdu*. **1969** *Listener* 22 May 734/2 The wizened wordsmith..was on the scent of *temps perdu*: in particular those heady years of the early Thirties. **1975** A. PRICE *Our Man in Camelot* vi. 111 It's a natural human feeling to yearn for the good old days, *le temps perdu*.

tempt (tɛm(p)t), *v.* Forms: 3– **tempt,** 3–7 **temt,** 4–6 (*Sc.* -9) **temp.** [a. OF. and AF. *tempte-r* (12–14th c.), learned form, beside the popular form *tenter, tanter*:—L. *temptāre, temtāre* to handle, touch, feel, try the strength of, put to the test, try, attempt: cf. Pr. *temptar*, Cat., Sp., Pg. *tentar*, It. *tentare*. The Eng. form has always followed L. *tem(p)tare*, the form *tent* being very rare (see TENT *v.*[2]); but the sb. *temptation* had from 13th c. the collateral form *tentation*, which during the 16th and 17th c. was much used by theological writers.

In inscriptions and early MSS., the Latin vb. is always *tempt-* or *temtāre*; this became in due course *tentāre* in Romanic (see above, and cf. *promptus, pronto*, etc.); about the 13th c. scribes began to introduce this spelling in Latin MSS., whence it came into printed books and Latin Dicts., being supported by an assumed etymology as freq. of *tendĕre, tentum* to stretch, strive, aim, endeavour, try (meeting at length with sense 3 below); but this is now rejected in favour of a root *tem-, temp-*: see Walde *Lat. Etym. Wörterbuch* s.v. *tempto*.

Sense 4, a later development in L., common in the Vulgate and Christian use, is the earliest recorded in Eng.]

I. To test, put to the test, try.

†**1.** To try, make trial of, put to the test or proof; to try the quality, worth, or truth of. *Obs.* exc. as in 2.

a **1300** *Cursor M.* 5030 Lauerd..þat..tempted abraham þi dere Of his aun sun offrand to mak. **1382** WYCLIF *Gen.* xxii. 1 Aftyr that thes thingis weren doon, God temptide [**1388** assaiede] Abraham [**1535** COVERD. *ibid.*, After these actes God tempted Abraham; **1611** BIBLE *ibid.*, It came to pass after these things, that God did tempt [**1885** (*R.V.*) prove] Abraham]. **1382** —— *Dan.* i. 12 Tempte [*gloss* or assaie; **1535** COVERD. Proue with; **1611, 1885** Prove] vs thi seruauntis ten days, and be potage ȝouen to vs for to ete. *c* **1386** CHAUCER *Clerk's T.* 402 He hadde assayed hire ynogh bifore..what neded it Hire for to tempte and alwey moore and moore? **1390** GOWER *Conf.* III. 45 With questions echon of tho He tempteth ofte. **1483** CAXTON *Gold. Leg.* 73/1 The quene of Saba cam fro fer contreys to see hym & to tempte hym in demaundes and questyons. **1538** STARKEY *England* II. i. 176 To haue some [sick persons] to go aboute ..to proue and tempt theyr louyng charyte. **16..** SIR W. MURE *Sonn.* iii. 6 To try my treuth and temp my loyall loue. *a* **1644** QUARLES *Hieroglyph.* xiii. Wks. 1881 III. 195 Tempt not your Salt beyond her power.

†**b.** *transf.* To act upon as a 'trial' or severe test; to try with afflictions; to afflict sorely, distress. Cf. ATTEMPT *v.* 4. *Obs. rare.*

13.. *E.E. Allit. P.* B. 283 Felle temptande tene towched his hert. **1483** CAXTON *Gold. Leg.* 152 b/2 And thise xvii first yere I was moche tempted by the brennyng of the sonne moche asprely.

2. To make trial of, put to the proof, or test, in a way that involves risk or peril.

a. *to tempt God*: to put to the test, or experiment presumptuously upon, His power, forbearance, etc.; to try how far one can go with Him; hence sometimes passing into 'to provoke, defy'. So ***to tempt providence***, etc.

a **1340** HAMPOLE *Psalter* lxxvii. 21 þai tempte god þat puttis þaim selfe in any perill forto fande if god will delyuer þaim. **1382** WYCLIF *Deut.* vi. 16 Thow shalt not tempte the Lord thi God, as thow hast temptid in the place of temptynge. **1390** GOWER *Conf.* III. 43 He tempteth hevene and erthe and helle. **1533** GAU *Richt Vay* (S.T.S.) 12 Thay sine alsua aganis this command that tempis god. **1552** HULOET, Tempt or prouoke, *pellitio, tento, temto, verso.* **1611** BIBLE *Acts* v. 9 How is it that yee have agreed together, to tempt the Spirit of the Lord? **1714** SWIFT *Pres. St. Affairs* ¶22 Religion teacheth us, that providence ought not to be tempted. **1715–20** POPE *Iliad* v. 44 Nor tempt the wrath of Heav'ns avenging Sire.

b. In ***to tempt fate, fortune***, etc., the sense approaches a.

1603 KNOLLES *Hist. Turks* (1621) 119 Who thus overthrowne, resolved no more to tempt fortune. **1693** CREECH in *Dryden's Juvenal* xiii. (1697) 339 Thy Perjur'd Friend will quickly tempt his Fate. **1746** FRANCIS tr. *Hor., Epist.* I. i. 9 Wisely resolv'd to tempt his Fate no more.

c. ***to tempt*** (***the storm, flood, sea***, etc.): to adventure oneself in or upon; to risk the perils of. (Cf. ATTEMPT *v.* 2.) Chiefly *poet.* Also ***to tempt the worst, tempt reprisals***, etc.

1667 MILTON *P.L.* II. 404 Who shall tempt with wandring feet The dark unbottom'd infinite Abyss? **1697** DRYDEN *Virg. Georg.* III. 123 The first to lead the Way, to tempt the Flood. *Ibid.* 581 Nor tempt th' inclemency of Heav'n abroad. **1703** ROWE *Ulyss.* IV. i, Know'st thou what 'tis to tempt a Rage like mine? **1704** POPE *Windsor For.* 389 Tempt icy seas, where scarce the waters roll. **1797** MRS. RADCLIFFE *Italian* i, I will tempt the worst at once. **1835** J. P. KENNEDY *Horse Shoe R.* lii, [They] preferred to tempt the rigors of the mountain rather than remain in their own dwellings.

†**3.** To try, endeavour, essay: with *inf.* (*to do* something), or equiv. clause; = ATTEMPT *v.* 1.

Sometimes aphetic for ATTEMPT.

c **1375** *Sc. Leg. Saints* xxii. (*Laurentius*) 697 þe feynd, þat ay wil besy be to tempt þat þame twa had Inwy. **1382** WYCLIF *2 Macc.* ii. 24 So we temptiden, or assayeden, for to abregge in to oo boke, thingus comprehendid..in fyue bookis. —— *Acts* xvi. 7 Whanne thei camen into Misye, thei temptiden [COVERD. proved, **1611** assayed] for to go into Bithinie. **1494** FABYAN *Chron.* v. cxiv. 88 Whan Chilperich had temptyd by many sondrye meanes to haue theym out of the sayde preuylege. **1538** STARKEY *England* I. i. 21 Yet in some tyme and certayn place hyt ys not to be temptyd of wyse men [to meddyl wyth materys perteynyng to the wele of hys hole cuntrey].

b. *with simple object.* To attempt, to try.

1697 DRYDEN *Æneid* VI. 214 Ere leave be giv'n to tempt the nether skies. [**1730** SWIFT *Panegyrick on Dean* 324 In vain I 'tempt too high a flight.]

†**c.** To make an attempt upon, to try to obtain; to assail. (Aphetic for ATTEMPT.) *Obs.*

a **1721** PRIOR *Henry & Emma* 518 O wretched maid! Whose roving fancy would resolve the same With him, who next should tempt her easy fame. **1746** FRANCIS tr. *Hor., Epist.* I. xviii. 127 Be not by foolish Love betray'd To tempt your Patron's favourite Maid.

II. To try to attract, allure, incite, induce.

4. *trans.* To try to attract, to entice (a person) to do evil; to present attractions to the passions or frailties of; to allure or incite to evil with the prospect of some pleasure or advantage. Const. *to* something, *to do* something. Also *absol.* (The earliest use in Eng.)

a **1225** *Ancr. R.* 60 Tauh ne rouhte heo neuer þauh he þouhte toward hire, & were of hire itempted [*MS. Cott.* ifondet]. *Ibid.* 226 Strongliche was he itemted er he so ueolle. *a* **1300** *Cursor M.* 15654 (Cott.) Rises vp, and wakes wel, Ar yee tempted [*Gött.* tempid] be. *a* **1340** HAMPOLE *Psalter* lv. 1 þe deuel, þat neuyre styntis to temp þi seruauntis. *c* **1380** WYCLIF *Sel. Wks.* III. 107 To praye þat we be nouȝt ytempted of þe fende. *c* **1440** *Alphabet of Tales* 127 Ane vnwyse confessur began to tempe hur vnto syn. *c* **1450** *Cov. Myst.* xxv. (Shaks. Soc.) 240 Thryes I tempte hym..Aftyr he fast fourty dayes. **1500–20** DUNBAR *Poems* xxxiv. 2 Me thocht the Devill wes tempand fast The peple. **1530** PALSGR. 754/1 He hath tempted me..to go a thevynge with hym. **1548** UDALL *Erasm. Par. Luke* iii. 48 b, Adam also was tempted, and ouercomed: Christe beeyng tempted, ouercame the temptour. **1606** SHAKS. *Tr. & Cr.* IV. iv. 93. **1665** MANLEY *Grotius' Low C. Warres* 317 Then they tempted the Fidelity of Caspar Ensem the Governour, both by Rewards and Terrour, but he was resolv'd against both. **1667** MILTON *P.L.* IX. 296 For hee who tempts, though in vain, at least asperses The tempted with dishonour foul. **1706** PHILLIPS (ed. Kersey), To *Tempt*, to allure or entice, to egg on or set a-gog, to induce to Evil. **1852** MRS. STOWE *Uncle Tom's C.* xix, Only when I've been very much tempted. **1869** SPURGEON *J. Ploughm. Talk* 9 Idle men tempt the devil to tempt them.

b. To try to draw (a person) to contradict, confute, or commit himself. *arch.*

(In N.T. versions, repr. Vulg. *tem(p)tare*, Gr. πειράζειν.)

1382 WYCLIF *Matt.* xxii. 35 Oon of hem, a techer of the lawe, axede Jhesus, temptynge hym, Maistre, whiche is a greet maundement in the lawe? —— *John* viii. 6 Sothli thei seiden this thing temptinge him, that thei myȝten accuse him. —— *Mark* xii. 15 What tempten ȝe me? brynge ȝe to me a peny, that I se. **1526** TINDALE *ibid.*, Why tempte ye me? Brynge me a peny, that I maye se yt. [So **1611** and *R.V.* **1881**.]

5. To attract or incite *to* some action or *to do* something; to allure, entice, invite, attract; to dispose, incline. Sometimes, contextually, To induce, persuade.

1340–70 *Alex. & Dind.* 98 þat i ne am temted ful tid to turne me þennus. *a* **1548** HALL *Chron., Edw. IV* 226 b, The vsing of such gentill fashions toward them,..so tempted theim that they could none otherwise do. *a* **1674** CLARENDON *Surv. Leviath.* (1676) 15 Which might temt him to undervalue. **1716** GAY *Trivia* I. 164 The rowing crew, To tempt a fare, clothe all their tilts in blue. **1742** W. COLLINS *Pers. Ecl.* IV. 31 Unhappy land! whose blessings tempt the sword. **1825** SCOTT *Betrothed* xix, He was tempted to think that he had been something hasty in listening to the arguments of the Archbishop. **1875** JOWETT *Plato* (ed. 2) V. 42 The sick are tempted by pleasant meats and drinks. *Mod.* One is tempted to think that it had been pre-arranged. The fine morning had tempted many out.

Hence **'tempted** *ppl. a.* (also *absol.*).

c **1340** HAMPOLE *Prose Tr.* 5 Sothely I haue na wondyr if þe temptid fall. **1591** SHAKS. *Two Gent.* II. vi. 8 If thou hast sin'd, Teach me (thy tempted subiect) to excuse it. **1603** [see TEMPTER 1]. *c* **1611** CHAPMAN *Iliad* x. 436 Lest from their tempted rest Some other God should stir the foe. **1667** [see 4]. **1839** BAILEY *Festus* xxix. (1852) 484 May God forbear, To judge the tempted purpose of my heart! **1844** MRS. BROWNING *Brown Rosary* xiv, The Tempted is sinning.

†**tempt,** *sb. Obs. rare.* [app. aphetic f. ATTEMPT *sb.*] = ATTEMPT *sb.*

1597 HOOKER *Eccl. Pol.* V. lxxvi. §6 By the issues of all tempts they found no certaine conclusion but this. **1652** BENLOWES *Theoph.* VIII. xxxvii, Because Gods Æqual, Serpents tempts are quell'd. *a* **1668** LASSELS *Voy. Italy* (1670) I. 114 Which [Castle] staveth off all tempts of strangers.

temptable ('tɛm(p)təb(ə)l), *a.* Also 9 -ible. [f. TEMPT *v.* + -ABLE.] That may be tempted; liable or open to temptation.

1628 FELTHAM *Resolves* II. [I.] lxvi. 188 There is sometimes a selfe-constancie, that is not temptable. **1678** CUDWORTH *Intell. Syst.* I. iv. §15. 268 Whether or no a Philosopher be temptable by it, or illaqueable into it. **1724** SWIFT *Drapier's Lett.* iv. ¶21 If the parliament of Ireland were as temptable as any other assembly within a mile of Christendom. **1819** COLERIDGE in *Lit. Rem.* (1836) II. 239 Macbeth's mind, rendered temptible by previous dalliance ..with ambitious thoughts. **1883** J. PARKER *Apost. Life* II. 319 In all points temptable though invulnerable.

Hence **tempta'bility, 'temptableness,** accessibility to temptation.

1682 H. MORE *Annot. Glanvill's Lux O.* 78 What can this freedom of Will consist in so much as in a temptableness by other Objects that are of an inferiour nature? **1825** COLERIDGE *Aids Refl.* (1848) I. 223 A soul surrounded with temptation, and having the worst temptation within itself in its own temptability.

temptation (tɛm(p)'teɪʃən). Forms: α. 4– tempt-, 5–7 temt-; β. 3–7 (9 *arch.*) tent-. [a. OF. *temptaciun, -tation* (12th c.), *tentation* (13th c. in Godef. *Compl.*), ad. L. *tempt, tentātiōn-em*, n. of action from *temptāre, tentāre* to TEMPT, q.v.]

1. The action of tempting or fact of being tempted, esp. to evil; enticement, allurement, attraction.

(Sometimes with more or less approach to senses 2 and 3.) *the temptation* (in *Christian Theol.* and *Art*), that of Jesus in the wilderness (Matt. iv, etc.). Also used of those of mediæval saints by evil spirits, e.g. 'The Temptation of St. Anthony'.

α. **1340** *Ayenb.* 158 Huanne he [the devil] comþ ine gyse of angle..þanne is þe temptacion mest strang. *Ibid.* 228 Temptaciun. **13..** *Matt.* vi. 13 in Paues *14th C. Eng. Bibl. Version*, And ne lede us not in temptacyon. *c* **1450** *Mankind* 219 in *Macro Plays* 9 The temtacyon of þe flesch, ȝe must resyst lyke a man. **1526** TINDALE *Matt.* xxvi. 41 Watche and praye that ye fall not into temptacion. **1667** MILTON *P.L.* VIII. 643 And all temptation to transgress repel. *Ibid.* IX. 364 Seek not temptation then, which to avoide Were better. **1837** DICKENS *Pickw.* ii, The temptation to take the stranger with him was equally great. **1846** TRENCH *Mirac.* i. (1862) 112 But man is to be perfected, not by exemption from temptation, but rather by victory in temptation. **1877** MOZLEY *Univ. Serm.* xvi. 271 Old-established rank has the temptation to luxurious indolence and pride. **1887** CLARA BELL tr. *Woltmann & Woermann's Hist. Paint.* II. III. II. i. 109 [Martin Schongauer's] well-known plate of the Temptation of S. Antony.

β. **1447** BOKENHAM *Seyntys* (Roxb.) 9 As for the cardiacle that tentacyoun Betoknyth..Of oure gostly enmye. **1534** MORE *Comf. agst. Trib.* II. Wks. 1177/2 The first might we cal tentation, the second persecucion... So is tentacion tribulacion to a good man. **1563** WINȜET *Four Scoir Thre Quest.* Wks. (S.T.S.) I. 120 The guid in the battell throw tentatioun may fall. **1650** BULWER *Anthropomet.* 58 To suffer this tentation from evil spirits. **1650** (*Scottish*) *Psalms in Metre* xcv. 8 Then harden not your hearts, as in the provocation, As in the desert, on the day of the tentation. **1678** SIR G. MACKENZIE *Crim. Laws Scot.* I. xvii. §6 (1699) 89 He is more guilty, seing he wants the natural tentation of the Adulterer.

b. With *a* and *pl.* An instance of this.

α. *a* **1225** *Ancr. R.* 32 þeo þet beoð ine stronge temptaciuns. *a* **1340** HAMPOLE *Psalter* xxvi. 6 If temptacyons wax ageynes me. *c* **1491** *Chast. Goddes Chyld.* 2 The more knoweng a man hathe the stronger ben his temptacyons. **1848** MAURICE *Lord's Prayer* vii. 91 We shall gain little..by changing that word for 'trials', as if every 'trial' did not of necessity involve a temptation.

β. *a* **1225** *Ancr. R.* 246 Al so a muchel tentaciun, þet is þes feondes bles. *a* **1568** COVERDALE *Hope Faithf.* xvii. (1574) 136 Bodely fraile lustes and tentations. **1625** DONNE *Serm.* iii. (1640) 22 Such a measure of grace as shall make me discerne a tentation and resist a tentation. **1693** *Apol. Clergy Scot.* 43 The many Incumbrances, Tentations, Weaknesses, that we daily encounter. **1818** SCOTT *Hrt. Midl.* xliii, When ye are pressed wi' ensnaring trials and tentations and heart-plagues.

c. Tempting quality, enticingness. *rare.* ? *Obs.*

c **1430** LYDG. *Min. Poems* (Percy Soc.) 108 Lordes and laymen and spryttualle her gave chase, For her fayer beawté grette temtacyon she hase. **1760–72** H. BROOKE *Fool of Qual.* (1809) III. 5 The..trees reached forth fruits of irresistible temptation.

d. *transf.* A thing that tempts; a cause or source of temptation.

1596 SHAKS. *Merch. V.* I. ii. 106 Set a deepe glasse of Reinish-wine on the contrary Casket, for if the diuel be within, and that temptation without, I know he will choose it. **1676** DRYDEN *Aureng-z.* v. ii, Dare to be great, without a guilty crown; View it, and lay the bright temptation down. **1786** BURNS *Address to Unco Guid* vi, Ye're aiblins nae temptation. **1856** FROUDE *Hist. Eng.* (1858) I. i. 17 The command of a permanent military force was a temptation to ambition.

2. The action or process of testing or proving; trial, test. *Obs.* or *arch.*

1382 WYCLIF *1 Macc.* ii. 52 Wher [**1388** Whether] Abraham in temptation was not founden feithful. **1535** COVERDALE *Ecclus.* xxvii. 5 The ouen proueth the potters vessell, so doth tentacion of trouble trye righteous men. **1552** ABP. HAMILTON *Catech.* (1884) 21 Thair is temptatioun quhairby man temptis God. **1677** GILPIN *Demonol.* (1867) 58 Temptations are distinguished into trials merely, and seducements. **1885** BIBLE (R.V.) *Deut.* iv. 34 To..take him a nation from the midst of another nation by temptations [so all versions from Wyclif: *marg.* Or, trials; or, evidences], by signs, and by wonders.

†**3.** A severe or painful trial or experience; an affliction, a trial. *Obs.*

c **1595** CAPT. WYATT *R. Dudley's Voy. W. Ind.* (Hakl. Soc.) 43 Theire victuall spent and fresh water consumed, they susteyned a great temptacion. *c* **1610** *Women Saints* 198 Troubles and tentations which I endured by being..driuen out of my contrie. **1652** CROMWELL *Let. to Ld. Wharton* 30 June in *Carlyle*, [They] may be too great a tentation to her spirit.

4. *Comb.*, as *temptation-proof*, adj., etc.

a **1631** DONNE *Serm.* lx. (1640) 603 To bring me to thinke myselfe tentation-proofe, above tentation. **1691** NORRIS *Pract. Disc.* 197 The Greatness of the happiness there..will make him Temptation-Proof against any present good or evil. **1889** C. C. R. *Up for Season* 101, I leave without reluctance your temptation-guarded fold. **1908** *Westm. Gaz.* 30 Oct. 13/3 The champion temptation-resisters.

Hence **temp'tational** *a.*, of the nature of temptation; **temp'tationless** *a.*, without temptation, to which there is no temptation.

1643 HAMMOND *Serm. John xviii. 40* Wks. 1683 IV. 513 An empty, profitless, temptationless sin. **1882** J. CALDWELL in *Homiletic Q. Mag.* VI. 106/2 The two verbs used here to describe the temptational agency of Lust.

temptatious (tɛm(p)'teɪʃəs), *a.* Also 8 tent-. [f. prec.: see -OUS.] Full of temptation; tempting, seductive, alluring.

1601 CHETTLE & MUNDAY *Death Robt. Earl of Huntingdon* II. ii. Fj, I my Liege, I: O! that temptatious tongue Had no where to be plac't but in your head. **1702** C. MATHER *Magn. Chr.* III. I. iv. (1852) 329 His removal..was clogged with many temptatious difficulties. **1724** R. WELTON *Chr. Faith & Pract.* 210 Those that in this tentatious world deny their religion. **1889** *Harper's Mag.* Mar. 665/2 There was something..winning and temptatious in it.

†**'temptative,** *a. Obs. rare*$^{-1}$. [f. TEMPT *v.* + -ATIVE; or ad. med.L. *temptātīv-us* 'seducens, fallax' (1377 in Du Cange).] = prec.

c **1449** PECOCK *Repr.* (Rolls) 105 The natural temptatyue wrecchidnessis which other men haue.

†**temp'tator.** *Obs.* [a. L. *temptātor, tentātor*, agent-n. from *temptāre* to tempt. Cf. F. *temptateur* (14th c. in Godef.), mod.F. *tentateur*.] = TEMPTER.

1491 CAXTON *Vitas Patr.* (W. de W. 1495) I. xlvii. 85 b/2 Whanne we haue good hope, we ouercome the deuyll our temptatour. **1632** LITHGOW *Trav.* x. 438 First they be Imitators; next, Mutators; thirdly, Temptators.

'temptatory, *a. rare.* [f. ppl. stem of L. *temptāre* to tempt + -ORY[2]; cf. F. *tentatoire* tempting (Palsgr. 279/2).] Of tempting nature; temptatious.

1900 G. SWIFT *Somerley* 88 We were jolly ready to spend an hour or so with the temptatory damsel.

tempter ('tɛm(p)tə(r)). Also 4–6 -our. [ME. *temptour* = obs. F. *tempteur* (14th c.), *tenteur* (16th c.), OF. **tempteor*, in nom. *temptere, -teire* (13–14th c. in Godef.):—L. *temptātōr-em*, agent-n. from *temptāre* to tempt.]

1. One who or that which tempts or entices to evil; *the tempter*, (*spec.*) the devil.

a **1380** *St. Bernard* 717 in Horstm. *Altengl. Leg.* (1878) 53 To þe temptour softeliche He seide þeos wordus. **1382** WYCLIF *Matt.* iv. 3 And the tempter cummynge niȝ, saide to hym, ȝif thou be Goddis sone, say that these stoons be maad looues. **1533** GAU *Richt Vay* (S.T.S.) 95 We haiff iii tempers (and we ar tempit be iii vayis) quhilk is of ye body of the dewil and of ye vardil. **1548** Temptour [see TEMPT *v.* 4]. **1603** SHAKS. *Meas. for M.* II. ii. 163 The Tempter, or the Tempted, who sins most? **1673** O. WALKER *Educ.* 60 That the Temter may find no bait to cover his poyson. **1788** WESLEY *Wks.* (1872) VI. 377 Because he is continually inciting men to evil, he is emphatically called 'the Tempter'. **1907** SANDAY *Life Christ in rec. Res.* I. i. 28 There are three scenes in which the Son of God is assailed by the Tempter.

†**2.** One who tests; a taster of ale or bread. *Obs.*

c **1450** *Godstow Reg.* 101 That they shold have ben tempters or tapsters of brede and ale in the said towne.

'tempting, *vbl. sb.* [f. TEMPT *v.* + -ING[1].] The action of the verb TEMPT; temptation; †trying (*obs.*).

1303 R. BRUNNE *Handl. Synne* 7506 Ihesu..sagh weyl hys grete temptyng. *c* **1450** *Mirour Saluacioun* 4054 The temptyngs of the werld ere many. **1613** SHAKS. *Hen. VIII*, I. ii. 55, I am much too venturous In tempting of your patience. **1628** WITHER *Brit. Rememb.* I. 709 He having meanes to doe His pleasure, and perhaps, strong temptings too. **1903** W. H. GRAY *Div. Sheph.* iv. 71 If others tempt us let us not yield to their temptings.

attrib. **1814** BYRON *Lara* I. xviii, And this same impulse would, in tempting time, Mislead his spirit equally to crime.

'tempting, *ppl. a.* [f. as prec. + -ING[2].] That tempts.

1. That entices to evil, or with evil design.

1546 BALE *Eng. Votaries* Pref. A iij, The more part of their temptynge spretes they haue made she deuyls. **1644** MILTON *Jdgm. Bucer* xliii. Wks. 1851 IV. 336 Let us see what our Lord answer'd to the tempting Pharisees about Divorce, and second Marriage. **1850** MRS. JAMESON *Leg. Monast. Ord.* (1863) 329 A tempting demon.

2. Seductive, attractive, alluring, inviting.

1596 SHAKS. *Tam. Shr.* Induct. i. 118 With kinde embracements, tempting kisses. **1680** OTWAY *Orphan* v. i, If a tempting Fair you find That's very lovely, very kind. **1818** SIR T. LAWRENCE 23 May in Williams *Life & Corr.* (1831) II. iii. 173 'Tis such a tempting offer. **1855** MACAULAY *Hist. Eng.* xviii. IV. 135 The profits of the Indian trade were so tempting.

†**3.** Afflicting, distressing, 'trying'. *Obs.*

13.. *E.E. Allit. P.* B. 283 Felle temptande tene towched his hert.

4. *Comb.*, as *tempting-looking*.

1875 J. P. HOPPS *Princ. Relig.* xv. (1878) 47 If you are told not to eat this or that tempting-looking berry, and you disobey and get poisoned.

Hence **'temptingly** *adv.*, **'temptingness.**

1593 NASHE *Christ's T.* 2 b, They erred most temptingly and contemptuously. **1802** BENTHAM *Mem. & Corr.* Wks. 1843 X. 396 My first act of mendicancy, and that extorted from me by the mere temptingness of the opportunity. **1877** LADY BRASSEY *Voy. Sunbeam* xiv. (1878) 246 Articles of apparel are temptingly displayed. **1976** *Conc. Oxf. Dict.* (ed. 6) s.v. *Seduce*, Persuade by temptingness or attractiveness.

temptive ('tɛm(p)tɪv), *a. rare.* [f. TEMPT *v.* + -IVE.] Tending to tempt, tempting.

1886 J. M. LUDLOW in *Homilet. Rev.* (U.S.) Sept. 260 While..every man 'is tempted by his own lusts', we are unwise to overlook the temptive occasions.

temptress ('tɛm(p)trɪs). [f. TEMPTER + -ESS.] A female tempter.

1594 NASHE *Unfort. Trav.* Wks. (Grosart) V. 80 The place ..was a pernicious curtizans house named Tabitha the Temptresses. **1633** FORD *Broken H.* v. ii, Be not jealous, Euphranea; I shall scarcely prove a temptress. **1826** SCOTT *Woodst.* ii, That the daughter..would, like the wicked wife of Job, become a temptress to her father in the hour of affliction. **1883** G. H. BOUGHTON in *Harper's Mag.* Jan. 179/1 St. Anthony and his undraped temptress.

'temptsome, *a. rare.* [f. TEMPT *v.* + -SOME.] Apt to tempt, tempting.

1849 *Tait's Mag.* XVI. 629 Temptsome bargains catch her eager gaze.

tempur(e, -nes, var. TEMPRE, -NESS, *Obs.*

‖**tempura** ('tɛmpʊrə). [Jap., prob. ad. Pg. *tempêro* seasoning.] A Japanese dish consisting of prawn, shrimp, or white fish, and often vegetables, coated in batter and deep-fried. Also *attrib.*, esp. in ***tempura bar, restaurant.***

1920 *Japan Advertiser* 22 Aug. 5 Tempura means a certain way of cooking,—namely, dipping in thin wheat-flour batter and frying in deep oil... The food which forms the base is some kind of fish. **1936** K. TEZUKA *Jap. Food* 71 *Tempura* is a characteristic dish of Japan made by dipping fish or shrimps or shell-fish in batter and frying in deep gingelly oil or torreya oil. **1958** *Japan* (Unesco) (1964) 724/1 *Tempura* was adopted from a recipe in Spain and Portugal. **1967** D. & E. T. RIESMAN *Conversations in Japan* 223 Donald joined us for lunch at a *tempura* restaurant nearby. **1969** *Sat. Rev.* (U.S.) 13 Sept. 62/3 Some of the most popular eateries are *tempura* bars. **1979** *United States 1980/81* (Penguin Travel Guides) 73 This thoughtfully designed Japanese restaurant has separate dining rooms for teppan-yaki, sukiyaki, and tempura.

temse (tɛms, tɛmz), *sb.* Now *dial.* Forms: 1 temes-, 4 temys, 5 temeze, tymze, 5–7 temze, tem(m)es, tempse (9 *dial.*), 7 temize, 7–9 tems, 5– temse; 9 *dial.* temmis, timse, teems. [OE. **tęmes* (in *tęmes-pile, tęmesian*), app. Common WGer.; cf. MLG. *tēmes(e, temse*, LG. *têms* (*tams*); MDu. *têms(e, teems(e*, Du. *teems*; EFris. *têms(e, täms(e*, NFris. *tems*; HG. dial. *zims*; all fem., meaning 'sieve'; the cognate OHG. *zemisa* renders 'furfures', i.e. bran, siftings. These forms point to a Common WGer. **tamis(j)ô-*, coinciding with the Romanic stem *tamisio-* of F. *tamis*, It. *tamigio* (Florio), med.L. *tamisium* (Du Cange), by many thought to be from WGer. A Celtic source has been conjectured, but Thurneysen finds no satisfactory Celtic root.]

1. A sieve, esp. one used for bolting meal; a searce, a strainer. In mod. local use *esp.* a sieve used in brewing.

[*a* **1050** *Gerefa* c. 17 in Liebermann *Gesetze* 455 Man sceal habban syfa..hriddel, hersyfe, tæmespilan (= temsing-staff), fanna.] ? **1362** *Durham Acc. Rolls* (Surtees) 566 Pro duabus temys emptis pro pistrina, ij s. *c* **1425** *Voc.* in Wr.-Wülcker 633/4 *Hoc taratantarum*, temse. *c* **1440** *Promp. Parv.* 488/2 Temze, sive (*K.,P.* temse, syue, *S.* temeze), *setarium*. *c* **1483** CAXTON *Dialogues* 38/22 Ghyselin the mande maker Hath sold..his temmesis to clense with [F. *a vendu..ses tammis*]. **1483** *Cath. Angl.* 379/2 A Tempse (A. *taratantorium*). **1557** in *Wills & Inv. N.C.* (Surtees) I. 159 A borde wᵗʰ ij trestes & ij temeses ijˢ viijᵈ. **1612** CAPT. SMITH *Map Virginia* 17 They use a small basket for their Temmes. **1616** SURFL. & MARKH. *Country Farme* 577 The boulter which is for this purpose must bee a course searse or a fine temze. **1674** RAY *N.C. Words* 47 A *Temse*, a fine sierce, a small sieve..whence comes our Temse bread. **1725** [see *temms-maker* in 2]. **1904** *Eng. Dial. Dict.*, *Tems(e*, teems, temes, temis, tempse, temz, timse [in various dialects, Roxb. to Lancash., Notts., Lincoln]... 3. A sieve used in brewing. W. Yks. Still common. Used when speaking of the strainer used in brewing to separate the hops, etc., from the ale.

¶A suggested substitution of *temse* for *Thames* in 'to set the Thames on fire' has no historical basis: see THAMES.

2. *attrib.* and *Comb.*, as ***temse-maker, -sieve***; **temse-bread, -loaf**, bread or a loaf made of finely sifted flour, temsed bread.

1600 CHETTLE & DAY *Blind Begg.* II. (1902) 24 Good Beef, Norfolk *temes bread, and Country home bred drink. **1611** COTGR., *Miche*,..the countrey people of France call so also, a loafe of boulted bread, or Tems bread. **1674** [see 1]. **1552** *Will of Leppingwell* (Comm. Crt. Lond.), A *Temes loffe. **1573** TUSSER *Husb.* (1878) 39 Temmes lofe on his table to haue for to eate. **1725** *Lond. Gaz.* No. 6432/6 Hosea Emmott, late of Bridgehouses.., *Temms-maker.

temse (tɛms, tɛmz), *v.* Now *dial.* Forms: see prec. [OE. *tęm(e)sian*, f. *tęmese* (see prec.): cf. MLG. *temesen*, MDu., Du. *temsen, teemsen* to sift.] *trans.* To sift or bolt (flour, etc.) with a temse.

c **950** *Lindisf. Gosp.* Mark ii. 26 Huu inn-eode hus godes ..& hlafo fore-ȝeȝearwad *vel* temised ȝebréc. *c* **1440** *Promp. Parv.* 488/2 Temzyn wythe a tymze (*S.* temsyn with a tenze),.. *attamino, setario*. **1483** *Cath. Angl.* 379/2 To Tempse, *taratantarizare*. **1600** SURFLET *Countrie Farme* v. xx. 714 Barley bread must be made..of that..which hath beene temzed and cleansed from his grosse bran. **1641** BEST *Farm. Bks.* (Surtees) 103 To measure the meale..afore it be temsed. **1809** T. DONALDSON *Poems* 73 Sifting meal..Or timsing flour. **1828** *Craven Gloss.*, *Tems*, to sift. **1904** *Eng. Dial. Dict.* s.v., Fifty years ago flour was not very common with cottagers esp., and when they wanted some they would temse some rough meal.

Hence **temsed** *ppl. a.*; ***temsed bread*** = *temse-bread* (see prec. 2); **'temsing** *vbl. sb.*, chiefly in comb. as ***temsing bread, -chamber, -staff, -trough.*** Also **'temser, 'temzer** = TEMSE *sb.* 1.

1641 BEST *Farm. Bks.* (Surtees) 104 Our own *tempsed-breade. *Ibid.*, An upheaped bushell of tempsed meale. **1777** *Horæ Subsecivæ* 428 (E.D.D.) Tems'd or temmas bread, white [bread] made of flour finely sifted. **1696–7** in Kennett *MS. Lansd. 1033* lf. 4 **Temzer*, a range or coarse searche. *c* **1450** *Medulla* in *Promp. Parv.* 488 *note*, *Cervida*, lignum quod portat cribrum, a *temsynge staffe. [Cf. **1904** *Eng. Dial. Dict.*, *Timse-sticks*, the small frame supporting two laths or sticks on which the 'timse' slides.] **1599** *Wills & Inv. N.C.* (Surtees) II. 287 In the bowltinge house. One temsinge troughe. *a* **1800** PEGGE *Suppl. Grose*, *Temsing-chamber*, the sifting-room. **1828** *Craven Gl.*, *Temsin-breead*.

temulence ('tɛmjʊləns). *rare.* [f. as next: see -ENCE.] = next.

1803 D. H. URQUHART *Comm. Class. Learn.* iv. *Euripides* 149 An eulogium on wine and temulence. **1860** MAYNE *Expos. Lex.*, *Temulentia*,..temulence.

temulency ('tɛmjʊlənsɪ). Now *rare.* [ad. post-cl. L. *tēmulentia* drunkenness, f. *tēmulent-us*: see next and -ENCY.] Drunkenness, inebriety.

1623 COCKERAM, *Temulencie*, drunkennesse. *a* **1640** JACKSON *Creed* x. vii, Without impeachment to his sobriety, or censure of temulency. **1732** ARBUTHNOT *Rules of Diet* in *Aliments*, etc. 260 Used in great Quantities it will produce Temulency or Drunkenness. **1853** BADHAM *Halieut.* (1854) 525 The vigorous lines in which Crabbe depicts the progress of temulency amongst a club of topers.

temulent ('tɛmjʊlənt), *a.* Now *rare.* [ad. L. *tēmulent-us*, from root *tēm-* in *tēmētum* intoxicating drink, after *vinolentus* from *vinum* wine.] Drunken, intoxicated; given to, characterized by, or proceeding from drunkenness; intoxicating.

1628 JACKSON *Creed* VI. xiii. §1 Clytus, whom he had newly slain in his temulent rage. **1668** G. C. in H. More *Div. Dial.* Pref. i. (1713) 14 Such tipsie and temulent Raptures. *a* **1770** CHATTERTON in *Europ. Mag.* (1804) XLV. 85 Sooner ..Than I, to frenzy temulent, with love, False to its palpitating precepts prove. **1822–34** *Good's Study Med.* (ed. 4) III. 494 Sometimes it produces a temulent effect.

Hence **'temulently** *adv.*, **'temulentness**; also, †**temu'lentious**, †**temu'lentive** *adjs.*, drunken.

1652 URQUHART *Jewel* Wks. (1834) 210 The Spaniards are proud: The French inconstant:..the Dutch *temulencious. **1628** FELTHAM *Resolves* II. [I.] lxxxiv. 241 A swimming Eye; a Face both roast and sod; a *temulentiue Tongue. **1623** COCKERAM II, Drunkenly done, **temulently*. **1727** BAILEY vol. II, *Temulently*, after a drunken Manner. **Temulentness*, Drunkenness.

temura(h (təmuːˈrɑː). *Jewish Lit.* Also **Themurah.** [Heb. *tĕmūrāh* exchange.] In cabalistic phraseology, a systematic replacement of the letters of a word with other letters in order to find the hidden meaning of events, laws, etc., in the Torah.

1902 A. E. WAITE *Doctrine & Lit. of Kabalah* I. iv. 27 Very curious results were sometimes obtained by these solemn follies which appear so childish and ridiculous at the present day. They comprise: *a. Gematria..b. Notaricon..c. Themurah*, that is the transposition of letters in a given word or sentence. **1911** 'SEPHARIAL' *Kabala of Numbers* I. iii. 31 The *Temurah*, in which the letters of a word were replaced by others after a definite method. **1974** C. PONCÉ *Kabbalah* ii. 172 Turning now to Jeremiah xxv. 26,..we discover that Sheshak is none other than Babel. How did the writer of this Biblical passage arrive at Sheshak as another name for Babel? Through the method of *temura*.

temys, Temze, obs. ff. TEMSE, THAMES.

ten (tɛn), *a.*, *sb.* (*adv.*) Forms: α. *uninflected*: 1 tíen, tén, later týn, (*north.* téa), 2 tyen, teon, 4–6 tenn, 4–7 tenne, 6 tien; 1– ten. β. *inflected*: 1 tíene, týne, 1–5 téne. [OE. *tíen, -e*, Anglian *tén, -e*, Comm. Teut., = OLG. **tehan*, OFris. *tîan, tîen*, OS. *tehan* (*tîan, tein*), (MDu., Du. *tien*, MLG. *tein*, LG. *tein, tien*, EFris. *tein, tian, tien*); OHG. *zehan* (MHG. *zehen, zên*, Ger. *zehn*); Goth. *taihun*; ON. *tíu, tío* (Norw. *tie, tio*, Sw. *tio*, Da. *ti*):—OTeut. **teχan*, beside **teχun* = pre-Teut. *'*dekm*, L. *decem*, Gr. δέκα, OSl. *desja*(*tʲ*), Skr. *daça*(*n*-. As final -*n* regularly fell away in OTeut., the normal form for OE. would have been **teha, téa* (as found in ONorthumbrian); but the actual form, as in OFris., OS., and OHG., had final -*n*, app. taken from the inflected form, whence also the umlaut in *tíen, týn, tén*. The inflected form, a plural *i*-stem (:—*teχanīᶻ*), in OE. *tíene*, etc. (neut. -*u*, -*o*, gen. -*a*, dat. -*um*), ME. *tēne*, was used when the numeral stood absolutely (sense 2); the uninflected was used with a sb., and at length, in ME., in all positions. (But see -TEEN, from -*tēne*.)]

The cardinal numeral next higher than nine; the number of the digits on both hands or feet, and hence the basis of the ordinary or decimal numeration.

Expressed by the figures 10, or symbol X, x.

A. *adj.* **1. a.** In concord with a sb. expressed.

c **888** K. ÆLFRED *Boeth.* xxxviii. §1 Þa wæron hi sume ten ȝear on þam ȝewinne. *c* **897** —— *Gregory's Past. C.* xvii. 124 Þa stænenan bredu þe sio æw wæs on awriten mid tien bebodum. *a* **900** tr. *Bæda's Hist.* I. xiii. [xxiii.] §1 Þreotteno ȝer & syx monað & tyn daȝas. *c* **1050** *Charter of Eadwine* in Kemble *Cod. Dipl.* IV. 259 Ic an ðat lond..buten ten acres ic ȝiue ðer into ðere kirke. *a* **1175** *Cott. Hom.* 219 He ȝescop tyen engle werod. *a* **1300** *Cursor M.* 7015 Tene [*v.r.* ten] yeir had [Manigath] þe folk in yeme. **1382** WYCLIF *Matt.* xxv. 1 The kyngdam of heuenes shal be lic to ten virgynys. *a* **1400** *R. Glouc. Chron.* (MS. B) (1724) 430 Hys doȝter was a ten ȝer old. *a* **1400–50** *Alexander* 649 Ten ȝere of age. **1502** ARNOLDE *Chron.* (1811) 189 The rood of reynysh wyne of Dordreight is x. awames. **1513** MORE *Rich. III* (1641) 299 Which rage of water lasted tenne dayes. **1571** *Act 13 Eliz.* c. 8 The rate of tenne pound for the lone of one hundred pound for a yeare. **1653** HOLCROFT *Procopius, Pers. Wars* I. 4 A narrow passage, for ten Horse abreast. **1805** SCOTT *Last Minstr.* I. v, Ten squires, ten yeomen, mail-clad men, Waited the beck of the warders ten. *Mod.* I shall be with you in ten minutes.

b. As multiple of another higher cardinal number, as in ***ten hundred, ten thousand***, etc.; also in the ordinals of these, as ***ten thousandth.***

c **950** *Lindisf. Gosp.* Matt. xviii. 24 Tea ðusendo cræftas. *c* **975** *Rushw. Gosp.* ibid., Ten þusende. *c* **1000** *Ags. Gosp.* ibid., Tyn þusend punda. *c* **1160** *Hatton Gosp.* ibid., Teon þusend punde. *c* **1400** *Apol. Loll.* 107 Sunnar is þe prayor hard of o buxum man, þan tenþowzand of a dispicer. **1560** DAUS tr. *Sleidane's Comm.* 257 b, The footemen were teen thousande. **1685** BOYLE *Enq. Notion Nat.* iii. 53 The cælestial part of the universe, in comparison of which the sublunary is not perhaps the ten thousandth part. **1709** CHANDLER *Effort agst. Popery* 20 'Tis Ten Thousand Pities that a Difference in Opinion and Practice herein should cause such Distances and Withdrawings. **1782** PRIESTLEY *Corrupt. Chr.* I. I. 5 The subject [is] considered by thousands and ten thousands. **1893** GOW *Comp. Sch. Classics* xxxiii. (ed. 3) 303 The ten-thousandth part of each grain must make a proportionate part of noise. **1905** *Westm. Gaz.* 23 Mar. 2/2 The guarantee for the ten-million loan.

c. Used vaguely or hyperbolically, esp. in ***ten times, tenfold***, and the like. Cf. HUNDRED, THOUSAND.

For hyperbolical use of *ten thousand* see THOUSAND.

1388 WYCLIF *Baruch* iv. 28 Ȝe..schulen seke hym ten sithis so myche. **1508** DUNBAR *Flyting* 87 Suppois thy heid war armit tymis ten. **1593** SHAKS. *Rich. II*, I. i. 180 A Iewell in a ten times barr'd vp Chest. **1883** D. C. MURRAY *Hearts* II. 162 His easy cynicism made him ten times more believable than any moral profession could have done.

†**d.** Occasionally used in the sense of the ordinal TENTH. *Obs.*

(But in 10 Jan., 10 Vict., etc., usually read *tenth.*)

14.. in Todd *Three Treat. Wyclif* p. xxvii, Siþ þe ten part [*v.r.* tenþe part] of þe fruyt sufficide for alle þes clerkis. **1567** in *Cath. Record Soc. Publ.* I. 49 Commytyd the x. day of June 1562. **1582** L. KIRBY in Allen *Martyrd. Campion* (1908) 77 This morning, the x of Januarie, he was committed to the dongeon. **1586** W. WEBBE *Eng. Poetrie* (Arb.) 62 Make short either the two, foure, sixe, eight, tenne, twelue sillable, and it will..fall out very absurdly. **1597** J. PAYNE *Royal Exch.* 24 Let vs solace our selves with these words in the tenn of the Hebr.

e. In special applications.

† ***ten bones***, the ten fingers: ***by these ten bones*** (ellipt. ***these ten***), also ***ten ends of flesh and blood***, an oath (*obs.*). ***Ten Commandments*** (also † ***bebode, bodewords, hests***, etc.), the Mosaic decalogue; *slang*, the ten fingers; see also COMMANDMENT 2, 3. † ***ten groats***, formerly a lawyer's fee, or that paid to the priest for reading the marriage service (*obs.*). ***ten tribes***, the lost tribes of Israel; *humorously*, the Jews, as money-lenders.

c **1485** *Digby Myst.* (1882) I. 20 By thes bonys ten thei be to you vntrue. *c* **1537** *Thersites* in Hazl. *Dodsley* I. 429 By this ten bones, She served me once A touch for the nonce. **1562–3** *Jack Juggler* ibid. II. 125, I am a servant of this house, by these ten bones. **1601** CHETTLE & MUNDAY *Death Robt. Earl of Huntington* v. i. ibid. VIII. 305 By these ten ends of flesh and blood I swear. **1621** B. JONSON *Masque Gipsies* vi. Wks. (Rtldg.) 621/2, I swear by these ten, You shall have it agen.

971 *Blickl. Hom.* 35 We sceolan þa ten bebodu healdan. *c* **1200** ORMIN 4377 Þa tene bodewordess. **1362** LANGL. *P. Pl.* A. VIII. 170 To Breke þe ten hestes. *c* **1375** *Sc. Leg. Saints* xxxiv. (*Pelagia*) 213 Þe commaundmentis tene, þat god mad for to teche men. *c* **1540** J. HEYWOOD *Four P's* in Hazl. *Dodsley* I. 381 [That] thy wife's ten commandments may search thy five wits. **1902** SNAITH *Wayfarers* vi, She's not seen you use your ten commandments, young man.

1601 SHAKS. *All's Well* II. ii. 22 As fit as ten groats is for the hand of an Atturney. *a* **1625** FLETCHER *Woman's Prize* I. iii, I'll take Petruchio In's shirt, with one ten groats, to pay the priest, Before the best man living.

1889 DOYLE *Micah Clarke* 118 The ten tribes have been upon me, and I have been harried..and despoiled.

2. a. Absolutely or with ellipsis of sb. (which may usually be supplied from the context).

Often short for *ten years* of age; also (now *Hist.*) for *ten shillings*, in *ten and six(pence*, or other number of pence, *ten-and-sixpenny*. In OE. and Early ME. inflected, nom. -*e*, neut. -*o*, -*u*; gen. -*a*, dat. -*um*.

Beowulf 2847 Ða hild-latan..tyne æt-somne. *c* **950** *Lindisf. Gosp.* Mark x. 41, & ȝe-herdon ða teno. *c* **975** *Rushw. Gosp.* ibid., & ȝiherdun ða tenu. *c* **1000** *Ags. Gosp.* ibid., þa ȝe-bulȝon þa tyne hi. *c* **1160** *Hatton Gosp.* ibid., þa ȝe-bulȝe þa teone hyo. *a* **1000** *Ags. Gloss.* in Wr.-Wülcker 217/21 *Decanus*,..tyna aldor. *c* **1205** LAY. 3388 Do we awai þane twenti, a tene [*c* **1275** ten] beoð inohȝe. *Ibid.* 31930 Bi sixe bi seouene, bi tene bi eolleue, bi twelue bi twenti. *a* **1300** *Cursor M.* 4848 Elleuen breþer es we liuand, An at ham, ten in þis land. *c* **1375** *Sc. Leg. Saints* xviii. (*Egipciane*) 514 Sone I fand Of ȝongmen tenne in a place stanand. **1377** LANGL. *P. Pl.* B. XIII. 270 In þe date of owre dryȝte..A þousande and thre hondreth tweis thretty & ten. ?*a* **1500** *Chester Pl.* xxii. 143 But of the Tenne the first three sone wear consumed away. **1548–9** (Mar.) *Bk. Com. Prayer, Catechism, Q.* Tell me how many [commandments] there bee. *A.* Tenne. **1726** DE FOE *Hist. Devil* I. x. (1840) 169 Ten of the twelve tribes. **1814** SCOTT *Wav.* xv, When I was a girl about ten, there was a skirmish fought. **1823** BYRON *Juan* x. xxxiii, Thermometers sunk down to ten, Or five, or one, or zero. **1837** DICKENS *Let.* 10 Feb. (1965) I. 235, I made it five pounds instead of two pounds ten. **1872** RUSKIN *Munera Pulveris* p. ix, Worth as many ten-and-sixpences as the impressions which might be taken from the lithographic stones. **1874** T. HARDY *Far fr. Madding Crowd* xxvi, Am I any worse for breaking the third of that Terrible Ten than you for breaking the ninth? **1891** C. JAMES *Rom. Rigmarole* 25 Two girls of, perhaps, eight and ten. **1908** *Installation News* II. 30/2 Witness our first attempt of a ten-and-six-penny kettle.

b. *esp.* of the hour of the day: orig. ***ten hours***, ***ten of the clock***: see CLOCK *sb.*[1] 3. Also with ellipsis of 'minutes' in phr. ***ten past*** or ***to*** or (*U.S.*) ***till***, ten minutes after or before the hour; ***to take ten*** (*U.S.*): see TAKE *v.* 52c.

c **1386** CHAUCER *Pars. Prol.* 5 Ten of the clokke it was tho as I gesse. [**1427** [see HOUR 1 b]. **1582–8** *Hist. Jas. VI* (1804) 116 At ten hor in the morning.] **1681** T. WHITE in *12th Rep. Hist. MSS. Comm.* App. v. 55 Yesterday about tenne in the morning. **1712–13** SWIFT *Jrnl. to Stella* 27 Jan., He went away at ten. **1753** HANWAY *Trav.* (1762) II. I. v. 25 There is admittance till ten, for a toll of one stiver each person. **1795** tr. *Moritz's Trav. Eng.* ii. (1886) 17 It might be about ten or eleven o'clock. **1810** SCOTT *Let. to Miss J. Baillie* 30 Jan. in *Lockhart*, The play..lasting till half-past ten. **1843** BORROW *Bible in Spain* xxxix. (Pelh. Libr.) 268 About ten at night, Maria Diaz..arrived with her son. **1852** [see TO *prep.* 6 b]. **1897** *Daily News* 18 Nov. 8/5 'You are the ten o'clock man', meaning that he came on duty at that time. **1937** 'P. WENTWORTH' *Case is Closed* ix. 95 Then it couldn't have been later than ten past eight when you heard that shot? **1960** S. BARSTOW *Kind of Loving* I. ii. 53 Nobody ever arranges to meet somebody at ten to and so she must either be late or not coming. **1963** [see TILL *prep.* 5 d]. **1979** 'J. LE CARRÉ' *Smiley's People* xxiii. 265 The time was ten to eleven.

c. In phrases and specific uses.

† ***ten in the hundred***, a rate of interest on loans formerly current; hence usury; also *transf.* a usurer. ***ten to one***, ten chances to one; odds of ten times the amount offered in a bet; hence, an expression of very strong probability. ***ten out of ten***, ten marks or points out of ten; hence *transf.* = *full marks* s.v. MARK *sb.*[1] 11 g. [The phrase is much older but printed evidence is lacking.] ***card of ten***: see CARD *sb.*[2] 2. ***to count ten***: see COUNT *v.* 1; *spec.*, to do this in order to check oneself from speaking impetuously; also ***to count up to ten***. ***hart of ten***: see HART 1 b. ***upper ten*** (= ***upper ten thousand***): see UPPER *a.*

1594 *Death of Usury* 10 He that puts forth money dare not exceede the rate of 10. in the 100. **1618** *Epitaph J. Combe* in Brathwait *Rem. after Death* (ad fin.), Ten in the hundred must lie in his graue, But a hundred to ten whether God will him haue. **1589** *Hay any Work* 30 Ten to one [I haue bin] among some of these puritans. **1650** W. BROUGH *Sacr. Princ.* (1659) 481 Is it not ten to one odds if ever thou be called? **1782** MISS BURNEY *Cecilia* VI. vii, Ten to one but that happens to be the very thing I want. **1889** J. K. JEROME *Three Men in Boat* 248 Bet us ten to one we didn't. **1981** P. O'DONNELL *Xanadu Talisman* iv. 69, I can't claim ten out of ten... I was a bit indecisive. **1981** *Listener* 22 Oct. 481/2 For beating down Whitehall opposition, Mr Sproat gets ten out of ten. **1817** T. JEFFERSON *Let.* 12 July in *Writings* (1899) X. 93 When angry count 10. before you speak. **1939** F. THOMPSON *Lark Rise* xi. 205 Copper-plate maxims..; 'Count ten before you speak', and so on. **1953** E. SIMON *Past Masters* II. 122 Don't say anything. Hold it. Count ten. **1976** R. PERRY *One Good Death deserves Another* vii. 116 He counted up to ten before he answered me. *c* **1410** *Master of Game* (MS. Digby 182) xxii, An hynde commonlyche hathe ..more openn þe clee before þen an herte of tenn. **1486** *Bk. St. Albans* E j b, Then shall ye call hym forchyd an hert of tenne. **1637** B. JONSON *Sad Sheph.* I. ii, A hart of ten, I trow he be.

d. ***the Ten***, †(*a*) the Decemvirs; (*b*) the Council of Ten: see COUNCIL *sb.* 9.

1636 E. DACRES tr. *Machiavel's Disc. Livy* I. 231 As it appear'd in the example of Manlius, and in that of the tenne. **1820** BYRON *Mar. Fal.* III. ii. 193 A sceptic of all measures which had not The sanction of 'the Ten'. **1878** VILLARI *Life & Times Machiavelli* (1898) I. IV. iv. 205 The old Magistracy of the Ten for war affairs was preserved. *Ibid.* II. iii. 41 The Ten brought swift and exemplary justice to bear.

(*c*) the group of countries comprising the European Economic Community after January 1981 when Greece joined the existing group of nine countries (the expectation expressed in quot. 1971, but not fulfilled, was that Norway would become a member in 1973 together with Denmark, the Republic of Ireland, and the United Kingdom) (cf. SIX *a.* 2 j).

1971 *Guardian* 20 Dec. 10/2 The objective for the Six (and the prospective Ten) should be to bring down the trade barriers. **1981** *Times* 24 Dec. 1/2 The EEC denounced 'the grave violation of the human and civil rights of the Polish people'..and said these were causing 'growing concern' among the people and governments of the Ten.

B. *sb.* (With plural *tens*; and (less usually) possessive *ten's*.)

1. a. The abstract number; also, a symbol or the figures representing this.

c **950** *Lindisf. Gosp.* Matt., Prol. (1887) 4 Oðer..tal..ðe to tenum wið fore-cyme. *c* **1000** *Sax. Leechd.* III. 228 Tele þu ..oð þæt þu cume to þrittiga foh eft on þone niwan oð tyne. *c* **1200** ORMIN 4312 Þe firrste staff iss nemmnedd I, & tacneþþ tale off tene. **1398** TREVISA *Barth. De P.R.* XIX. cxxiii. (1495) 923 The nombre of ten passyth nyne by one. *c* **1440** *Promp. Parv.* 488/2 Tenne, nowmyr, *decem.* **1530** PALSGR. 367 *Dix*, tenne, x. **1594** BLUNDEVIL *Exerc.* I. (1636) 84, 12 tens, which do make 2 sixties. **1837** WHEWELL *Hist. Induct. Sc.* (1857) I. 52 Ten is a perfect number. *Mod.* Five tens are fifty.

b. In a number expressed in decimal notation, the digit expressing the number of tens, e.g. in 1837 the figure 3.

1542 RECORDE *Gr. Artes* 116 b, Then come I to the articles of tennes, where in the fyrste summe I fynde 90, and in the seconde summe but only 40. **1806** HUTTON *Course Math.* I. 9 Set..the numbers under each other,..that is, units under units, tens under tens, hundreds under hundreds, &c... Add up the figures in the column or row of units, and find how many tens are contained in that sum.

c. A thing or person distinguished by the number ten, usually as the tenth of a series; ***10 A*** (see quot. 1907). ***number ten***, also ***No. 10***: see NUMBER *sb.* 5 e.

1888 H. MORTEN *Sk. Hosp. Life* 70, I say, tell Ten I am so sorry for him. I wish I could go to the ward! **1906** H. MÜLLER *Reminiscences* 43 Giovanni endured the punishment that is the Austrian equivalent for '10 A'. **1907** *Cassell's Mag.* Feb. 295/1 For fourteen [days] he was put on '10 A', which is short for no grog, no tobacco. *a* **1911** *Mod.* Number ten, it is your turn to play. **1927** P. RILEY *Memories* 74 The drastic punishment, known as '10.A' was introduced into the Service at the same time [*sc.* Jan. 1875].

2. A set of ten things or persons.

ten of rupees, a unit of account in Indian money.

c **961** ÆTHELWOLD *Rule St. Benet* xxii. (1885) 47 Tynum and twentigum on anum inne ætgædere restan mid heora ealdrum. **1539** BIBLE (Great) *Gen.* xviii. 32, I wil not destroye them for tens sake [**1885** BIBLE (*R.V.*) for the ten's sake]. **1611** BIBLE *Deut.* i. 15, I..made them..captaines ouer tennes. **1894** *Field* 9 June 839/1 They came forth in their tens, for thirty-eight members turned out on the occasion of the first meet. **1895** *Westm Gaz.* 4 Sept. 5/1 The revenue was better by 74,000 tens of rupees. **1897** FLANDRAU *Harvard Episodes* 94 One never said of Wolcott, as is said of some fellows, 'He made the first ten of the Dicky'.

3. *Coal-mining.* A measure of coal, locally varying between 48 and 50 tons, being the unit of calculation on which the lessor's rent or royalty is based. (See quot. 1894.) *north. dial.*

1590 *Wills & Inv. N.C.* (Surtees) II. 181 At the grannde lease pitts, ccclxxxviij tenns of coolls, the twelfth parte is xxxij tenns, and the thirde parte of a tenn, praised worthe 2[l] per tenn is 64[l] 13[s]–4[d]. **1789** BRAND *Hist. Newcastle* II. 279 In the year 1622 there were vended by the society of hostmen of Newcastle 14,420 tens of coals. **1851** GREENWELL *Coal-trade Terms Northumb. & Durh.* 54 Ten, the measure of coals upon which the landlord's rent is paid. It usually consists of 440 bolls of 8 pecks, but varies much under different landlords, generally, however, within the range of from 418 to 440 bolls. **1894** *Northumbld. Gloss.*, *Ten*, a measure of coals upon which the lessor's rent or royalty is paid. In the seventeenth century the term meant ten score bolls, barrows, or corves of coal.

4. A playing-card marked with ten pips. ***catch the ten***, a card-game played in Scotland in which the ten of trumps may be taken by any honour-card, and counts ten points, the game being a hundred. ***long ten***, the ten of trumps in this game: cf. *long trump* (LONG *a.*[1] 5 b). See also quot. 1870.

1593 SHAKS. *3 Hen. VI*, v. i. 43 But whiles he thought to steale the single Ten, The King was slyly finger'd from the Deck. **1680** COTTON *Compl. Gamester* xv. (ed. 2) 94 The rest follow in preheminence thus; the King, the Queen, the Knave, the Ten. *Ibid.* xvi. 97 You are not to play a ten first. **1816** SCOTT *Old Mort.* xli, These were Claver'se's lads a while syne, and wad be again, maybe, if he had the lang ten in his hand. **1870** *Modern Hoyle, Cribbage* 77 The court-cards and the ten of each suit count ten, and they are all indiscriminately spoken of as 'tens' during the game. **1887** P. M'NEILL *Blawearie* 146 They are playing at 'catch the ten', the stake being a few pence a-head.

5. Short for (*a*) a ten-oared boat; (*b*) a ten-pound note; (*c*) a ten-dollar note; (*d*) a ten-horse-power car.

1875 BLAKE-HUMFREY *Eton Boating Bk.* p. ix, The first eight had a strong picked crew, whilst the ten had several 'courtesy' oars... Mr. Canning was sitter in the ten. *c* **1863** T. TAYLOR *Ticket-of-Leave Man* III. 54 Here are notes—two hundreds—a ten—and two fives. **1894** A. ROBERTSON *Nuggets*, etc. 190 To their intense disgust they only got about £200 in notes (chiefly tens). **1829** *Vancouver Herald* (Fredericksburg) 18 Apr. 3/3 The public are cautioned against receiving spurious 5's 10's and 20 dollar bills, purporting to be on the Bank of Virginia. **1907** 'O. HENRY' *Trimmed Lamp* 171 He drew out his 'roll' and slapped five tens upon the bar. **1977** J. CROSBY *Company of Friends* xxvi. 161 Roger tipped the waiter a ten. **1931** *Daily Express* 16 Oct. 11/2 Cheap 'Tens'. There was a big demand also for cars just above the 'baby' class, the numerous 10's that are cheap to buy. **1942** *R.A.F. Jrnl.* 3 Oct. 24 He would soon be driving around in a family eight or ten. **1968** *Compl. Encycl. Motorcars* 59/1 In 1910 a 1·6 litre 4-cylinder [Austin] Ten was made for export only. *Ibid.* 399/1 That year [*sc.* 1933] Morris's sv 1·3-litre Ten-Four came out as an answer to Austin's Ten and Hillman's Minx.

6. a. Short for *tenpenny nail* (i.e. costing 10*d.* a hundred); ***double ten***, a nail costing the double of the tenpenny (i.e. 20*d.* a hundred). **b.** A tallow candle weighing ten to a pound.

1572 in Feuillerat *Revels Q. Eliz.* (1908) 175 Nayles v[c] of single tenns—iiij s. ij d. c Dubble tens—xviij d. **1629** *MS. Acc. St. John's Hosp., Canterb.*, Itm halfe a hundred of double tennes xd. **1665** J. WEBB *Stone-Heng* (1725) 124 An huge old Nail, in Shape somewhat like those which we call commonly double Tens, or Spikes, such as are used in Scaffolding. **1717** [see DOUBLE A. 6]. **1802** *Sporting Mag.* XX. 15 Some have gone so far as to illuminate our discussions with tens instead of long-sixes.

†**C.** *quasi*-adv. Ten times, tenfold. *Obs.*

c **1330** *King of Tars* (Ritson) 336 Thaugh heo weore ten so briht. *c* **1385** CHAUCER *L.G.W.* 736 (*Thisbe*) Forbede a loue & it is ten so wod. **1387** TREVISA *Higden* (Rolls) II. 177 Þe lengþe of a manis body..be..ten so moche as þe depnesse þat is from þe rugge to þe wombe. **1399** LANGL. *Rich. Redeles* III. 168 Þei ffor þe pesinge paieth pens ten duble That þe cloþe costened. *c* **1400** *Siege of Troy* 396 in *Archiv neu. Spr.* LXXII. 21 Ector is ten so strong as þou [*older version*, ten siþe streyngor þen þow]. *c* **1420** *Sir Amadas* (Weber) 746 Yette was Y ten so glad When that thou gaffe all that thou had.

D. Combinations.

Comb. **1. a.** Adjectives, formed by *ten* with a sb., meaning consisting of, containing, measuring, or costing ten of the things named (also occasionally *ellipt.* as sb.), as ***ten-acre***, ***-bell***, ***-cell***, ***-cent***, ***-course***, ***-day***, ***-dollar***, ***-drachm***, ***-figure***, ***-grain***, ***-guinea***, ***-horse***, ***-hour***, ***-inch***, ***-league***, ***-mile***, ***-minute***, ***-month***, ***-point***, ***-second***, ***-shilling***, ***-stone***, ***-syllable***, ***-toe***, ***-ton***, etc.; also, phrases thus formed prefixed to a simple adjective, forming a compound adj., as ***ten-mile-long***, ***ten-inch-thick***, etc. See also 2, and TENPENNY. **b.** Parasynthetic adjs., formed on such phrases as those in a, as ***ten-acred***, ***-armed***, ***-barrelled***, ***-coupled***, ***-cylindered***, ***-fingered***, ***-footed***, ***-headed***, ***-horned***, ***-jointed***, ***-keyed***, ***-oared***, ***-parted***, ***-peaked***, ***-rayed***, ***-ribbed***, ***-roomed***, ***-spined***, ***-stringed***, ***-syllabled***, ***-talented***, ***-tongued***, ***-toothed***, (also ***-teethed***), ***-wheeled***, etc. **c.** Parasynthetic sbs. (see -ER[1] 1), as ***ten-bedder***, ***-knotter***, ***-seater***, ***-tonner***, ***-wheeler***; see also *ten-pointer* in 2, TENPOUNDER. **d.** Compounds of *ten* sb., as ***ten bed*** (= bed No. 10), ***ten-bore***, ***ten-team*** (team of ten); also ***ten-shaped*** adj. (= X-shaped); ***tentale*** [TALE *sb.* 6], used *attrib.* in phr. ***tentale rent***: see quots.

1826 MISS MITFORD *Village* Ser. II. 55 (*Copse*) On inquiring my destination, and hearing that I was bent to the *ten-acre copse. **1871** KINGSLEY *At Last* ii, Having a considerable quantity of land in each parish allotted to ten-acre men (i.e. white yeomen). **1807** VANCOUVER *Agric. Devon* (1813) 377 A *ten-acred enclosure might be as.. proper a size as any other. **1881** *Times* 15 Jan. 5/6 The short *ten-barrelled Gatling was brought to the front. **1888** H. MORTEN *Sk. Hosp. Life* 69 [He] operated on that boy in *Ten bed; but, I fear, unsuccessfully. **1899** KIPLING *Stalky* iii. 79 She's busy in the middle of King's big upper *ten-bedder. **1905** *Daily News* 24 Apr. 2 In 1817 a *ten-bell record of 12,312 changes of Grandsire Caters was rung on these bells. **1892** GREENER *Breech Loader* 127 The *10-bore duck-gun full-choked, weighing 8½ lbs. and over. **1876** PREECE & SIVEWRIGHT *Telegraphy* 28 A *ten-cell Leclanché [battery]. **1846** D. CORCORAN *Pickings* 26, I gave him a $2 bill, and he only gave me thirteen of these (*ten cent pieces) in change. **1873** E. EGGLESTON *Myst. Metrop.* xviii. 158 The joyful keys and the cheerful ten-cent coins lay in his pocket. **1901** H. ROBERTSON *Inlander* 118 The sleepers in the grass-grown churchyard..had been removed elsewhere to make room for the thriving innovation known as the 'Ten Cent Store'. **1962** E. SNOW *Other Side of River* (1963) xxxix. 283 Ten-cent prints are also sold of Italian Renaissance painters and a few French impressionists. **1903** J. K. JEROME *Tea Table Talk* (ed. Tauchn.) 31 The *ten-course banquet. **1883** 'MARK TWAIN' *Life on Mississippi* lx. 582 A *ten-day trip by steamer. **1898** *Westm. Gaz.* 1 Nov. 10/1 The ten-day fog of 1880, credited with such heavy mortality. **1807** *Deb. Congr. U.S.* 19 Aug. (1852) 429, I got two of the notes changed, and one, a *ten dollar note, was returned on my hands. **1825** J. NEAL *Bro. Jonathan* I. 221 For a 'ten-dollar bill'..Peters would have set fire to it. **1891** H. HERMAN *His Angel* 138 Underwood took three ten-dollar bills from his wallet. **1886** *Guide Exhib. Galleries Brit. Mus.* 145 A *ten-drachm piece of Athens. **1842** *Penny Cycl.* XXIII. 498/1 Nathaniel Roe, 'Tabulæ Logarithmicæ', London. Seven-figure numbers to 100 thousand, *ten-figure sines, &c. to hundredths of degrees. **1922** *Biometrika* XIV. 160 It was necessary to calculate τ_1 to eight places, which was done with the help of Vega's ten-figure logarithms. **1861** *Photogr. News Alm.* in *Circ. Sc.* (1865) I. 160/2 A *ten-grain silver solution. **1752** FOOTE *Taste* I. Wks. 1799 I. 8 A poor *ten-guinea job. **1678** BUTLER *Hud.* III. II. 1117 And turn'd the Men to *Ten-Horn'd Cattel, Because they came not out to Battel. **1837** P. KEITH *Bot. Lex.* 107 It is as if there was a certain ponderable mass which the application of a *ten-horse power was utterly incapable of moving. **1905** *Westm. Gaz.* 7 Mar. 5/2 The new scale is calculated on a *ten-hour basis. **1903** *Ibid.* 18 June 5/1 The shell which was being filled was a *ten-inch shell. **1839** *Penny Cycl.* XV. 84/1 In the genus Melolontha the antennæ are *ten-jointed. **1843** BORROW *Bible in Spain* xxxi. (Pelh. Libr.) 228 After the *ten-league journey of the preceding day. **1876** 'OUIDA' *Winter City* ix, A *ten-mile stretch across the open country. **1806** LAMB *Let. to Manning* 5 Dec., They all had their *ten-minute speeches. **1711** SHAFTESB. *Charac.* (1737) III. 265 To find a plain defect in these *ten-monosyllable heroicks. **1886** C. SCOTT *Sheep-Farming* 64 *Ten months old lambs. **1800** *Hull Advertiser* 16 Aug. 1/4 A *ten-oared cutter..with twelve volunteers. **1874** GARROD & BAXTER *Mat. Med.* (1880) 297 Capsule ovoid, inflated, *ten-ribbed. **1882** MISS BRADDON *Mt. Royal* II. ix. 180 The shabby little *ten-roomed house in South Belgravia. **1898** *Westm. Gaz.* 30 Nov. 5/3 Doubt..whether the Oriten '*ten-seater' machine exhibited at the Stanley Show could be ridden. **1907** *Daily Chron.* 30 Nov. 4/6 More technically known as the 'crux decussata'—the '*ten-shaped cross', because its form is identical with that of the Latin numeral X. **1745** M. FOLKES *Eng. Gold Coins* 9 Double-crowns or *ten shilling pieces. **1959** A. CHRISTIE *Cat among Pigeons* iv. 51 She accepted the ten shilling note her mother handed to her. *a* **1974** R. CROSSMAN *Diaries* (1976) II. 279 Then there came fifteen speakers of whom the ten well-informed were all passionately for the ten-shilling unit. **1900** *Daily News* 4 Dec. 6/1 A *ten-stone man, who has to ride, is of more use than a twelve-stone man. *a* **1300** *E.E. Psalter* cxliii[i]. 9 To þe sal I sing in *ten-strenged sautre.

1535 COVERDALE *ibid.*, That I maye .. synge prayses vnto the vpon a tenstrynged lute. **1881** H. MORLEY *Eng. Lit. Q. Vict.* iii. (ed. Tauchn.) 89 The all pervading couplets of *ten-syllabled lines. **1883** GRESLEY *Coal Mining Gloss.*, **Tentail rent*, a rent or royalty paid by a lessee upon every ten of coals which are worked in excess of a minimum or certain rent. **1888** NICHOLSON *Coal Trade Gloss.* s.v. *Rent* (E.D.D.), A surplus or tentale rent payable for the coal worked .. above the certain quantity. **1901** *Daily Chron.* 17 July 5/2 One *ten-team of one N.C. officer of any rank and nine lance-corporals or privates from any regiment, battalion, or depot. **1883** *Harper's Mag.* Aug. 442/2 Some of the rated *ten-tonners were .. over twenty-two tons in displacement. **1844** STEPHENS *Bk. Farm* II. 536 The wheels .. are *ten-toothed. **1867** EMERSON *May-Day* 86 Speaking by the tongues of flowers, By the *ten-tongued laurel speaking. **1904** *Westm. Gaz.* 28 Dec. 3/2 Powerful *ten-wheeled tank engines. **1904** *Ibid.* 29 Jan. 5/1 This mammoth *ten-wheeler cost £5,000.

2. Special combinations and collocations: **ten-code**, a code of signals (all beginning with the number ten) originally used in radio communication by police in the U.S. and later adopted by Citizens' Band radio operators; **ten-eighty** (more commonly **1080**) [see quot. 1945], a formation of sodium fluoroacetate used as a poison against predatory animals; **ten-finger**, a species of star-fish: cf. FIVE-FINGER 2; **ten-foot** *a.*, measuring, or having, ten feet; fig. phr. ***ten feet tall*** used contextually to convey extreme self-assurance or pride; ***ten-foot coal***, a thick seam in Yorkshire; ***ten-foot rod***, a levelling-pole; **ten-four, 10-4** *int.*, in the ten-code (see above), the code phrase for 'message received'; used *loosely* as an expression of affirmation; also as *v. intr.*; **ten-gallon** *a.*, that can contain ten gallons; **ten-gallon hat, sombrero**, a high-crowned, wide-brimmed hat of a kind esp. worn in the south-western U.S. (cf. STETSON); **ten-gauge** *a.*, having a calibre such that ten balls of matching size weigh one pound; also *ellipt.* for *ten-gauge shotgun*; **ten-hours act**, a law limiting the hours of work in factories; *spec.* the popular name of the Act 10 & 11 Vict., c. 29; so, in U.S.A., **ten-hour law** (*Cent. Dict.* 1891); **ten-inch** *a.*, measuring ten inches; *spec.* designating a 78 r.p.m. coarse-groove gramophone record having this diameter; also *ellipt.* = *seventy-eight* s.v. SEVENTY *a.* 2 b; **ten-minute rule** (also **ten minutes rule**), a standing order of the House of Commons allowing brief discussion of a motion for leave to introduce a bill, each speech being limited to ten minutes' duration; **ten o'clock**, (*a*) an American name for *Ornithogalum umbellatum*, the flowers of which open late in the morning (*Cent. Dict.* 1891); (*b*) a name for *Portulaca grandiflora*, a subtropical annual herb whose flowers open late in the morning; (*c*) a light meal taken at ten o'clock; **ten per center** *U.S. Theatr. slang*, a theatrical agent (so called from the ten per cent commission that an agent takes); **ten-pointer**, a stag having antlers with ten points; a 'hart of ten'; **ten-pound** *a.*, of or involving the amount or value of ten pounds; also, weighing ten pounds; spec. ***ten-pound land*** (*Sc.*), land of the annual value of ten pounds; ***ten-pound householder***, = TEN-POUNDER 2 b; **ten signal** *U.S.*, any of the signals that form part of the ten-code (see above); **ten-speed**, a multiple-speed set of gears on a vehicle, esp. a bicycle; freq. *attrib.*; **ten-spot** *a.*, having ten spots, as 'ten-spot ladybird', *Coccinella decem-punctata*; *sb.* (*U.S.*), a ten-dollar 'bill'; also, a playing-card, = TEN *sb.* 4; **ten-strike**, in the game of ten-pins, a throw which bowls over all the pins; hence *fig.*, *spec.* a success, esp. in phr. ***to make a ten-strike***, to score a success (*U.S. colloq.*); **ten tenth(s)** *attrib.* (orig. *Meteorol.*), complete, one hundred per cent; **ten-to-two**, a position of the hands or feet resembling that of the hands of a clock at ten minutes to two, *esp.* a position of the hands on the steering-wheel of a car; freq. *attrib.*; **ten-week stock**, *Matthiola annua*, said to continue ten weeks in flower; **ten-yard coal**, a very thick seam of coal near Dudley; **ten-year** *a.*, of ten years' duration or standing, as *ten-year-old*, also as *sb.*; spec. ***ten-year-man***, at Cambridge University: see quot. 1903. See also TENPENNY, TEN-PINS, etc.

1969 T. E. DRABNEK *Lab. Simulation Police Communications Syst. under Stress* 135 Above code corresponds to the '*Ten-Code System' used by many police agencies. **1976** *CB Mag.* June 67/2 Well, it really grabbed me, all this 'good buddy' stuff, the ten-code. **1977** *Rolling Stone* 13 Jan. 45/3 Get a CB and take on a persona, use the 10 code and all the language, and be anybody you want to be. **1945** *Science* 31 Aug. 232 (*heading*) '*Ten-eighty', a war-produced rodenticide. *Ibid.*, One, commonly referred to under its laboratory serial number, '1080', .. has been subjected to sufficiently adequate field-testing to warrant the assertion that a promising new rodenticide has been discovered. **1961** *New Scientist* 13 Apr. 17/1 About one and a half grains of 'ten-eighty' are dissolved in a little water and injected into 100 lb of meat. **1971** W. HILLEN *Blackwater River* xii. 117 Then Compound 1080 (ten-eighty) .. reached British Columbia and created a 'predator control' bureaucracy more difficult to eliminate than wolves. **1701** MOXON *Math. Instr.* 19 **Ten foot Rods*, See Station-staffs. **1793** ANNA SEWARD *Lett.* (1811) III. 322 The iambic accent, unmixed with the trochaic, especially in the ten-feet couplet. **1834–5** J. PHILLIPS *Man. Geol.* (1855) 190 The thickest coal in the district, .. that called the thick or ten-foot coal in Yorkshire. [**1955** (*television film title*) The man is *10 feet tall.] **1962** M. HASTINGS *Yes, & After* II. i. 72 You must always be ten feet tall imagining yourself doing this or doing that. **1964** D. FRANCIS *Nerve* xvii. 237 It made me feel warm inside... I felt ten feet tall. **1970** A. DRAPER *Swansong for Rare Bird* i. 11, I must say I felt 10 feet tall and there was a soppy grin on my face. **1962** *Amer. Speech* XXXVII. 272 **Ten-four* (verb), to understand a message. From the radio code *10-4*, meaning 'I receive you clearly'. **1976** *National Observer* (U.S.) 30 Oct. 5/1 Judge Floyd Smith, a CB operator himself, went by the 'handle' of 'Marryin' Sam', the bride was 'Little Lulu', and the groom was 'Stanley Steamer'. They didn't say 'I do'; they said '10-4'. And the judge didn't pronounce them man and wife; he said, 'Put the hammer down.' **1978** *N.Y. Times Mag.* 23 July 23/2 The CB'ers have a language that's 10-4 with them. **1841** C. GRAY *Lays & Lyrics* 241 This song was written on the presentation of a *Ten-Gallon China Punch-Bowl ... to the Club. **1922** JOYCE *Ulysses* 303 Hard by the block stood the grim figure of the executioner, his visage being concealed in a tengallon pot with two circular perforated apertures. **1928** *Daily Express* 7 Oct. 3/7 She instinctively recognized that he was a cowboy, even though he did not wear a ten-gallon hat and a jacket embroidered with Mexican dollars. **1929** T. WOLFE *Look homeward, Angel* (1930) xxvii. 374 He removed from his head the ten-gallon grey sombrero. **1939** *Amer. Speech* XIV. 201/1 In the nomenclature of the South-western cowboy, *sombrero* is used interchangeably for hat, but the qualifying phrase of 'ten gallon' has been arrived at by a mistaken translation of a Spanish word. The word 'gallon' .. served to describe the braid with which a vaquero's hat was trimmed .. it should have been 'galloon'. **1977** C. MCCULLOUGH *Thorn Birds* xiv. 331 Only the handful of half-caste aborigines .. aped the cowboys of the American West, in high-heeled fancy boots and ten-gallon Stetsons. **1894** *Outing* (U.S.) XXIV. 443/1 A couple of *ten-gauge breech-loaders. **1936** J. STEINBECK *In Dubious Battle* v. 70 'Shot-guns,' he said... 'Soon's somebody sounds off with a ten-gauge, they go for the brush like rabbits.' **1940** W. FAULKNER *Hamlet* III. 194 Looking .. into the face which with his own was wedded and twinned forever now by the explosion of that ten-gauge shell. **1908** *Sears, Roebuck Catal.* 201/2 Disc Record Cases... No. 2 holds 50 *10-inch disc records. **1959** *Manch. Guardian* 11 Aug. 5/7 Beecham (whose reading has just reappeared on a Fontana ten-inch, KFR 4003). **1979** *Listener* 4 Oct. 461/3 Nearly all the 23 Gillespie tracks .. were originally marketed on ten-inch, 78 rpm discs. **1908** A. E. STEINTHAL tr. *J. Redlich's Procedure House of Commons* III. II. x. i. 86 Under a standing order passed in 1888, popularly known as the '*ten minutes rule' (Standing Order 11) an abbreviated mode of procedure is authorised for the introduction of bills. **1971** HINDELL & SIMMS *Abortion Law Reformed* xi. 232 Ten minute rule bills can be brought before the House with a short speech each Tuesday and Wednesday after question time, but if the House agrees to the introduction of such a bill *all* further progress to a second reading and beyond depends, in practice, on the Government .. giving it parliamentary time. **1826** W. DARLINGTON *Flora Cestrica* 40 *Ornithogalum .. umbellatum*... *Ten o'clock. Twelve o'clock. Star of Bethlehem. **1838** HOWITT *Rur. Life* I. II. iii. 161 Betty mean-time has put up their 'luncheons' or '*ten-o'clocks'. **1953** *Caribbean Q.* III. I. 10 Ten o'clock is a kind of portulaca which blooms in mid morning. **1926** *Variety* 29 Dec. XI. 5/4 Broadway chatter is full of theatrical cracks such as .. '*ten per center'. **1962** *Punch* 26 Dec. 920/1 A condition of the licence being granted is that the applicant advertises for two weeks in The Stage, stating his intention of joining the ten-percenters. **1883** E. L. PEEL in *Longm. Mag.* Nov. 72 We had .. stalked and slain a fine *ten-pointer upon the Caenlochan marches. **1673** *S'too him Bayes* 5 You .. would have lost your *ten pound wager. **1845** DISRAELI *Sybil* II. vi, It is a great thing in these ten-pound [franchise] days to win your first contest. **1855** J. R. LEIFCHILD *Cornwall Mines* 263 Send the author a ten-pound-note for his advice—good in either event! **1863** H. COX *Instit.* I. viii. 106 A new uniform qualification [to vote] .. frequently designated that of the 'ten-pounds householders'. **1890** *Cent. Dict.* s.v. *Pound*, *Ten-pound Act*, a statute of the colony of New York (1769) giving to justices of the peace and other local magistrates jurisdiction of civil cases involving not more than the sum named. **1951** *Directory Nat. Police Communications Network* (ed. 6) 19 The '*10' signals were developed by A.P.C.O... and the system has been widely adopted. **1970** V. A. LEONARD *Police Communications Syst.* ii. 34 APCO's Project Series Foundation has produced four nationally recognized projects: .. the publication of the APCO Ten Signal Cards. **1971** M. TAK *Truck Talk* 165 **Ten-speed*, a ten-speed Roadranger transmission. **1977** C. MCFADDEN *Serial* (1978) i. 8/2 They spent it rapidly on .. twin Motobecane ten-speeds. **1977** *New Yorker* 9 May 34/1 The owner of a ten-speed model asked her why. **1844** 'J. SLICK' *High Life N.Y.* II. 215 'Jest so,' sez I, a flingin' down the *ten-spot o' clubs. **1848** 'N. BUNTLINE' *Mysteries & Miseries N.Y.* IV. iii. 27 Be quick, and I'll give you a *ten spot!* **1888** *Boston* (Mass.) *Jrnl.* 6 Nov. 2/3 The point was seen at once, and the 'ten spot' was forthcoming. *c* **1895** *Thompson St. Poker Club* 65 The Rev. Mr. Smith dealt Mr. Williams two cards, .. helped himself to the last ten-spot remaining in the pack. **1936** E. CULBERTSON *Contract Bridge Complete* 21 Any six-card suit, even without a ten-spot, is a biddable suit. **1971** B. MALAMUD *Tenants* 153 Hi, sugar, I took a ten-spot out of your loose change. **1840** *Spirit of Times* 11 July 228/1 [This] he says is an extra touch—a *ten strike and two spare balls. **1850** HAWTHORNE in Bridge *Pers. Recollect.* (1893) 111, I may calculate on what bowlers call a ten-strike. **1887** *Scribner's Mag.* May 624/1 But I have got the family to consider, and I am in a position now where I can make a ten-strike for it. **1889** FARMER *Dict. Amer.*, *Ten-strike*, where .. all the men are bowled over at one throw... Hence .. a fortunate occurrence: a thoroughly well done and complete work. **1900** G. ADE *Fables in Slang* 72 He could tell by the Scared Look of the People in Front that he had made a Ten-Strike. **1949** E. POUND *Pisan Cantos* lxxxiii. 124 It comes over me that Mr. Walls must be a ten-strike With the signorinas. [**1945** *Meteorol. Office Air Obs. Handbk.* 34 In estimating the amount of cloud the observer should aim to give the fraction (in tenths) of sky covered by cloud.] **1948** *Daily Tel.* 23 Apr. 6/6 There was *ten-tenth cloud at the time. **1973** 'A. HALL' *Tango Briefing* ix. 114 There was a ten-tenths flap on in London so they'd have alerted the whole network. **1977** C. FORBES *Avalanche Express* xviii. 186 One moment he had ten-tenths vision, the next second he was blind. **1979** D. BRIERLEY *Cold War* vii. 57 There was ten-tenths cloud cover, the clouds coming from the north-east .. like billowing poison gas. **1961** C. H. D. TODD *Pop. Whippet* iv. 68 It stands with its feet at '*ten to two'. **1962** *Which? Car Suppl.* Apr. 55/2 The steering wheel was .. rather high. This made a 'ten-to-two' hand position uncomfortable after a time. **1974** *Drive* Autumn 26/2 We found the square wheel made it difficult for drivers to hold the rim in the ten-to-two position they are taught to adopt. **1785** MARTYN *Rousseau's Bot.* xxiii. (1794) 323 The Annual or *Ten-week Stock differs in having an herbaceous stalk. **1909** *Daily Chron.* 20 Mar. 7/6 A well-grown aster or ten-week stock is a beautiful object in itself. **1834–5** J. PHILLIPS *Geol.* in *Encycl. Metrop.* VI. 594/2 The upper part of the *ten-yard coal separates from the rest of the beds. **1839** URE *Dict. Arts* 980 The very remarkable seam near the town of Dudley, known by the name of the ten-yard coal, about 7 miles long, and 4 broad. **1693** G. STEPNEY in *Dryden's Juvenal* viii. (1697) 216 Courage to sustain a *Ten Years War. **1813** *Gentl. Mag.* LXXXIII. II. 530. **1816** *Ibid.* LXXXVI. I. 200/1 A query respecting the Ten-Year-Men at Cambridge. **1838** DICKENS *Nich. Nick.* xxx, Ever since he had first played the *ten-year-old imps in the Christmas pantomimes. **1868** *Rep. U.S. Commissioner Agric.* (1869) 443 The average yield for a three-year old vine is one peck; .. full grown, ten-year old vine, twenty-five bushels. **1895** *Westm. Gaz.* 17 July 8/1 What terrible tyrants these ten-year-olds are! **1900** *Ibid.* 7 Mar. 7/1 What the terms of the new war loan for thirty millions in ten-year bonds will be, or ought to be. **1903** *Daily Chron.* 4 Feb. 5/1 The Ten Year man .. being over twenty-four years of age, was admitted, and after keeping his name on the boards of a college for ten years was allowed to proceed B.D. on payment of certain fees. **1906** *Ibid.* 18 Aug. 4/4 An average of 11.4 in the previous ten-year period.

ten, obs. form of TEE *v.*[1], TEEN *sb.*[1]

†**ten**, obs. variant of TENNÉ, *Her.*

1677 PLOT *Oxfordsh.* To Rdr. b ij b, If ever hereafter I shall meet with any bearing Purpure, Ten, or Sanguine; .. Ten [shall be represented] with lines salter-ways, mixt of Vert and Purpure.

tena'bility. [f. next: see -ITY.] = TENABLENESS.

1845 S. WILBERFORCE in Ashwell *Life* (1879) I. viii. 303 Only to maintain in the abstract, the tenability of a certain position. **1865** MASSON *Rec. Brit. Philos.* 201 When one looked again at his own position .. one could not see its superior tenability in the new conditions of the campaign. **1875** RUSKIN *Fors Clav.* li. 67 *note*, Discussing the relative tenability of insects between the fingers.

tenable ('tɛnəb(ə)l, †'tiːn-), *a.* Also 7 **teneable.** [a. F. *tenable* (12th c. in Godef.), f. *ten-ir* to hold + -ABLE: see -BLE, and cf. TENIBLE.]

1. Capable of being held (in various senses of HOLD *v.*); that may be kept, kept in, kept back, retained, restrained, or held in control. Now *rare.*

1602 SHAKS. *Ham.* I. ii. 248 (Qo.) If you have hitherto concealed this sight Let it be tenable [*Fol.*[1] treble] in your silence still. **1649** HEYLIN *Relat. & Observ.* II. 1 That Party .. being .. tenable by no Oaths, Principles Promises, Declarations. **1856** RUSKIN *Mod. Paint.* IV. v. xii. §14 Others tottering and crumbling away from time to time, until the cliff had got in some degree settled into a tenable form.

2. Capable of being held against attack; that may be successfully defended.

1579 FENTON *Guicciard.* xv. (1599) 693 The City being not tenable .. it yeelded. **1673** *S'too him Bayes* 105 Except you .. thrust your self in at every place that is not tenable. **1793** GOUV. MORRIS in Sparks *Life & Writ.* (1832) II. 297, I do not think the position taken at Louvain is tenable. **1855** PRESCOTT *Philip II*, I. IV. iii. 421 They might retire from a post that was no longer tenable.

b. *fig.* Of statements, opinions, etc.: Capable of being maintained or defended against attack or objection.

1711 ADDISON *Spect.* No. 186 ¶5 The Atheist has not found his Post tenable, and is therefore retired into Deism. **1796** BURKE *Regic. Peace* iv. Wks. IX. 67 The Tartarian doctrine is the most tenable opinion. **1837** WHEWELL *Hist. Induct. Sc.* (1857) I. 286 The letter of their theories is no longer tenable.

3. Capable of being held, occupied, possessed, or enjoyed.

1840 THIRLWALL *Greece* VII. lvi. 142 The office was tenable for four years. **1883** *L'pool Courier* 5 Oct. 4/9 The scholarships .. are tenable for three years.

tenable, -s, corruption of TENEBRES.

tenableness ('tɛnəb(ə)lnɪs). [f. TENABLE + -NESS.] The quality of being tenable.

1647 SPRIGGE *Anglia Rediv.* IV. vii. (1854) 266 Distrusting their own strength, or the garrison's tenableness. **1849** J. H. NEWMAN *Disc. Mixed Congregat.* Ded., A doubt .. of the tenableness of the theological theory.

tenace ('tɛnəs). *Whist* and *Bridge*. [ad. Sp. *tenaza*, lit. 'pincers, tongs', used in card-playing as here. Cf. also F. *demeurer tenace* (*Dict. de Trevoux*, 17..) 'to have the tenace'.] A name given to the combination of two cards of any suit, consisting of the next higher and the next lower in value than a card (in *Whist*, the highest card) held by the other side, esp. when this combination is held by the fourth player: see quot. 1746. Used esp. in phr. ***to have the tenace***, formerly ***tenaces***.

1655 J. COTGRAVE *Wits Interpr.* (1662) 356 If you have Tenaces in your hand, that is two cards which, if you have the Leading, you are sure to lose one of them; if the Player lead to you, you are sure to win them both. **1710** SWIFT *Lett.* (1767) III. 17 Then in that game of spades, you blundered when you had ten-ace. **1746** HOYLE *Whist* (ed. 6) 70 Having the Tenace in any Suit supposes the having the first and third best Cards, and being the last Player, and consequently you catch the Adversary when that Suit is play'd. **1870** *Modern Hoyle* 12 Tenaces... 1st major tenace —ace, queen. 2nd major tenace—king, knave. 3rd major tenace—queen, ten... 1st minor tenace—four, two. 2nd minor tenace—five, three. 3rd minor tenace—six, four. *Ibid.* 19 Tenaces are always most valuable, because most certain, to the fourth player. **1905** 'CUT-CAVENDISH' *Compl. Bridge Player* 11 *Tenace*, the best and the third best cards of any suit, ace and queen if the king has not been played. **1936** [see *end-play* s.v. END *sb.* 25]. **1959** *Listener* 10 Sept. 414/1 The K J 8 will still constitute a tenace over the 10 9 x. **1984** *Guardian* 6 Oct. 17/2 The ten of diamonds now end-played West to return a club into declarer's tenace.

tenacious (tɪˈneɪʃəs), *a.* Also 7 -atious, -aceous. [f. L. *tenāx*, *tenāci-* holding fast (f. *ten-ēre* to hold) + -OUS: see -ACIOUS.]

1. a. Holding together, cohesive; tough; not easily pulled in pieces or broken.

1607 TOPSELL *Four-f. Beasts* (1658) 152 The bones of Fishes are more tenacious. **1750** tr. *Leonardus' Mirr. Stones* 71 Amiaton is..like feathered alumn, but more tenacious. **1834** *Brit. Husb.* I. xiii. 310 It acts as manure physically, or substantially, through the effect of the clay in rendering soils tenacious. **1869** ROSCOE *Elem. Chem.* (1871) 185 Gun-metal, or bronze, is a hard and tenacious alloy.

b. Adhesive; viscous, glutinous; sticky.

1641 WILKINS *Math. Magick* II. xii. (1648) 251 Provided, that this oyl..bee supposed of so close and tenacious substance, that may slowly evaporate. **1697** DRYDEN *Virg. Georg.* IV. 58 Not Birdlime, or Idean Pitch, produce A more tenacious Mass of clammy Juice. **1784** COWPER *Task* I. 216 Female feet, Too weak to struggle with tenacious clay. **1868** CARPENTER in *Sci. Opinion* 6 Jan. (1869) 174/2 The bottom consisted of a bluish-white tenacious mud.

2. Holding fast or inclined to hold fast; grasping hard; clinging tightly.

1656 BLOUNT *Glossogr.*, *Tenacious*, that holds fast,..good and sure. **1681** tr. *Willis' Rem. Med. Wks.* Vocab., *Tenacious*, holding or cleaving fast. **1800–24** CAMPBELL *Poems, Chaucer & Windsor* 4 Old oaks..Whose gnarled roots, tenacious and profound. **1869** TOZER *Highl. Turkey* I. 232 The palluria..is covered all over with tenacious hooked prickles.

3. Keeping a firm hold, retentive *of* something.

c **1645** HOWELL *Lett.* (1650) II. ii. 2 The Badger..is said to be so tenacious of his bite, that he will not give over his hold, till hee feels his teeth meet. **1726** LEONI *Alberti's Archit.* I. 27/1 The Fir..is..very dry, and very tenacious of the Glue. **1758** R. BROWN *Compl. Farmer* II. (1760) 23 All.. are very tenacious of water on the surface.

4. *fig.* Strongly retaining or inclined to retain, persist in, preserve, or maintain (a principle, method, secret, etc.); holding persistently; of memory, retentive. Const. *of*.

1640–1 LD. J. DIGBY *Sp. in Ho. Com.* 9 Feb. 13 A man tenatious of the liberty..of the subject. **1656** EARL MONM. tr. *Boccalini's Advts. fr. Parnass.*, The tenacious memory of benefits received. **1657** JER. TAYLOR *Disc. Friendship* ¶ 13 Free of his money and tenacious of a secret. **1708** ROWE *Royal Convert* I. i, Tenacious of his Purpose once resolv'd. **1800** MAVOR *Nat. Hist.* (1811) 230 The frog is remarkably tenacious of life. **1877** FROUDE *Short Stud.* (1883) IV. I. xii. 145 He had read largely, and his memory was extremely tenacious. **1898** J. T. FOWLER *Durham Cath.* 62 So tenacious are boys of traditional terms.

5. Persistently continuing; persistent; resolute; perseveringly firm; obstinate, stubborn, pertinacious.

1656 BLOUNT *Glossogr.*, *Tenacious*,..also hard to be moved, stiff necked. **1661** LOVELL *Hist. Anim. & Min.* Introd., The life is more tenacious in them, than in the sanguineous. **1750** JOHNSON *Rambler* No. 14 ¶ 14 He is hot and dogmatical, quick in opposition and tenacious in defence. **1861** STANLEY *East. Ch.* vi. (1869) 193 Tenacious adherence to the ancient God of Light.

†6. *spec.* Unwilling to part with or spend money or the like; close-fisted, niggardly. Also *transf.*

1676 DRYDEN *Aurengzebe* V. i. 82 True love's a Miser; so tenacious grown, He weighs to the least grain of what's his own. **1681–6** J. SCOTT *Chr. Life* (1747) III. 79 Give me a covetous, a niggardly and tenacious Man; I will return him to thee liberal.

†7. Persistently chary of or averse to any action. (*erroneous use.*) *Obs.*

1766 *Compl. Farmer* s.v. *Tuberose*, Mons. Le Cour, of Leyden..for many years was so tenacious of parting with any of the roots..that he caused them to be cut in pieces, that he might have the vanity to boast of being the only person in Europe who was possessed of this flower. **1802** MARIAN MOORE *Lascelles* I. 142 Since the adventure..Mrs. Carisbrooke had been very tenacious of being late on the road. **1811** *R. Cecil's Wks.* I. 69 Mr. Cecil..was tenacious of being interrupted in his pursuits.

tenaciously (tɪˈneɪʃəslɪ), *adv.* [f. prec. + -LY².] In a tenacious manner; with a strong hold; persistently, steadfastly, stubbornly.

a **1667** JER. TAYLOR *Serm. for Year* III. i. (1841) 352/2 To resent an error deeply,..to remember it tenaciously, to repeat it frequently. *a* **1677** HALE *Prim. Orig. Man.* 250 Ocellus Lucanus..tenaciously asserted the Eternity of the World. **1777** ROBERTSON *Hist. Amer.* I. II. 111 Columbus adhered tenaciously to his original opinion. **1808** SCOTT in *Lockhart* (1837) I. i. 37 My memory..seldom failed to preserve most tenaciously a favourite passage of poetry. **1882** A. W. WARD *Dickens* i. 16 It is not surprising that..the name should have clung to him so tenaciously.

tenaciousness (tɪˈneɪʃəsnɪs). [f. as prec. + -NESS.] The quality of being tenacious; tenacity.

1. = TENACITY 1.

1658 ROWLAND *Moufet's Theat. Ins.* 1069 Clammy stuffe that drawes like Bird-lime, which loseth not its tenaciousnesse by drinesse nor by moysture. **1794** SULLIVAN *View Nat.* II. 44 The tenaciousness of their cohesion.. seem[s] to prove them to consist of viscous parts.

2. = TENACITY 2.

1642 ROGERS *Naaman* 128 Fourthly and lastly, the Tenaciousnesse of their selfe: I meane when she is put hard to it. **1669** W. SIMPSON *Hydrol. Chym.* 122 Solidity of judgement, and tenaciousness of memory. **1786** JEFFERSON *Writ.* (1859) II. 78 What I learn of the temper of my countrymen and their tenaciousness of money. **1860** *All Year Round* No. 43. 389 Extraordinary examples of tenaciousness of life.

tenacity (tɪˈnæsɪtɪ). [ad. rare L. *tenācitās*, f. *tenāx*, *tenāci-* tenacious: see -ACITY. So F. *tenacité* (14th c. in Godef. *Compl.*).] The quality or property of being tenacious.

1. Cohesiveness, toughness; viscosity, clamminess (of a liquid); also, adhesive quality, stickiness.

1555 EDEN *Decades* 145 A certeyne..iuise, whose substaunce is of suche tenacitie and clamminesse, that it wyll neuer weare awaye. **1660** BOYLE *New Exp. Phys. Mech.* ii. 41 Water, to which Some has given a Tenacity. **1718** QUINCY *Compl. Disp.* 3 For the same reason..many light Substances have such strong Cohesions or Tenacities. **1805–17** R. JAMESON *Char. Min.* (ed. 3) 261 By tenacity is understood..the different degrees of cohesion of the particles of minerals. **1866** ROGERS *Agric. & Prices* I. xxi. 538 No doubt the bigness of the [plough-]shoe varied..with the lightness or tenacity of the soil.

2. The quality of retaining what is held, physically or mentally; firmness of hold or attachment; firmness of purpose, persistence, obstinacy.

1526 *Pilgr. Perf.* (W. de W. 1531) 175 Some whose tenacite & hardnes is reproued in this peticyon. **1682** SIR T. BROWNE *Chr. Mor.* II. §5 The tenacity of Prejudice and Prescription. **1794** PALEY *Evid.* I. i. (1817) 21 They clung to this hope..with more tenacity as their dangers or calamities increased. **1823** *Spirit Pub. Jrnls.* (1824) 492 They..began tugging him towards the door, he..clinging to every hold he made with astonishing tenacity. **1830** J. W. CROKER in *C. Papers* 14 May, That tenacity of life which his family have constitutionally. **1878** LECKY *Eng. in 18th C.* I. iv. 552 The tenacity of the English bull-dog.

b. Retentiveness (of memory).

1814 SCOTT *Wav.* iii, A memory of uncommon tenacity. **1871** BLACKIE *Four Phases* I. 93 What animal when it has learned anything can retain the lesson with equal tenacity?

†3. Tendency to keep fast hold of money; miserliness, niggardliness, parsimony. *Obs.*

1586 DAY *Eng. Secretary* I. (1625) 32 Vnbridled lust, couetous tenacitie, prodigality, or detestable excesse. **1651** HOBBES *Leviath.* II. xxix. 173 The passage of mony to the publique Treasure obstructed, by the tenacity of the people. **1656** BLOUNT *Glossogr.*, *Tenacity*, fast-keeping, sure holding, niggardlinesse, misery. **1706** in PHILLIPS.

tenacle (ˈtɛnək(ə)l). Now *rare*. [ad. L. *tenāculum* holder: see below.]

†1. *pl.* Forceps, pincers, nippers; cf. next, 1. *Obs.*

c **1400** *Lanfranc's Cirurg.* 308 þou schalt take vp þe skyn wiþ tenaclis, and putt in þin hoot iren þoruȝ þe hole of þe tenaclis, & brenne þe skyn. **1597** A. M. tr. *Guillemeau's Fr. Chirurg.* 15 b/2 Rounde pinsers or tenacles, to take away the trepanede percelle of bone.

2. That by which a plant, a fruit, etc. is upheld or supported: †a stalk, peduncle, or petiole (*obs.*); in *pl.* the organs by which some climbing plants attach themselves.

c **1500** BOLLARD tr. *Godfredi on Pallad.* 157 The furste [kind of cherry] hath shorte tenacles v. stalkys. **1658** SIR T. BROWNE *Gard. Cyrus* iv, Ivy, divided from the root, we have observed to live some years, by the cirrous parts commonly conceived but as tenacles and holdfasts unto it. **1860** TRENCH *Serm. Westm. Abb.* xxvi. 305 We all know how the ivy..casts out innumerable little arms and tenacles by which it attaches and fastens itself.

†3. ? A holster or the like in which to hold the staff of a standard or flag when borne. *Obs.*

1556 *Chron. Gr. Fr.* (Camd.) 50 A generalle processione from Powlles unto sent Peters in Cornehylle with alle the chelderne of Powlles scole, & a crosse of every parishe churche with a banner and one to ber it in a tenacle [*MS.* tenache].

tenacull, obs. form of TUNICLE.

‖**tenaculum** (tɪˈnækjʊləm). Pl. -ula. [mod. uses of L. *tenāculum* a holder, f. *ten-ēre* to hold.]

1. *Surg.* A species of forceps: see quots.

1693 tr. *Blancard's Phys. Dict.* (ed. 2), *Tenaculum*, the same with *Forceps*. **1726** QUINCY *Lex. Physico-Med.*, *Tenacula*,..a chirurgical Instrument, not much differing from the Forceps. **1857** DUNGLISON *Med. Lex.*, *Tenaculum, Assalini's*,..consists of a forceps, or double tenaculum. **1899** *Syd. Soc. Lex.*, *Tenaculum*, a variety of artery forceps for arresting hæmorrhage.

b. See quot. 1842.

1842 BRANDE *Dict. Sc.* etc., *Tenaculum*, a surgical instrument, consisting of a fine sharp-pointed hook, by which the mouths of bleeding arteries are drawn out, so that in operations they may be secured by ligaments. **1860** J. M. CARNOCHAN *Operat. Surg.* 62 (Cent.) These [arterial branches] are difficult to tie, even when picked up by the tenaculum.

2. *Entom.* The abdominal process by which the springing organ is retained in the *Poduridæ* or spring-tails.

1878 PACKARD *Guide Stud. Insects* 622 The Collembola [are characterized] by their spring (*elater*), its holder (*tenaculum*) [etc.].

‖**tenaille** (tɪˈneɪl). Forms: 6–8 tenaile, 7 tenal, 8–9 tenail, 7– tenaille. [F. *tenaille* (tənɑj) forceps (12th c. in Godef. *Compl.*), also in Fortification as in sense 2 (16th c. in Littré) = Pr. *tenalhia*, It. *tanaglia*:—L. *tenācula*, pl. of *tenāculum* holder: see prec.]

†1. *pl.* Pincers, forceps: cf. prec., 1. *Obs.*

1597 LOWE *Chirurg.* (1634) 98 To doe that operation, thou shalt be meetest, and with smallest paine to be done, with Tenals incisiues. **1727** *Bradley's Fam. Dict.* s.v. *Cray-fish*, They have forked Claws, in the Form of black Tenails, or Pincers.

2. In *Fortification*, A small low work, consisting of one or two re-entering angles (***single*** or ***double tenaille***), placed before the curtain between two bastions. ***tenaille of the place***, the face of a fortress: see FACE *sb.* 17.

1589 IVE *Fortif.* 33 The defences in so small Forts as these proceede chiefly, either of bulwarks, halfe bulwarks, and tenailes [etc.]. **1677** R. BOYLE *Treat. Art War* 81 All sort of Works by which the Camp is invironed, and shut up, as Redoubts, Bastions, Ravelins, Forts, Tennailes, Hornworks [etc.]. **1708** *Brit. Apollo* No. 63. 4/2 They will fill up the Ditch, in order to storm the Tenaile. **1886** N. L. WALFORD *Parl. Generals Grt. Civ. War* 214 A second party of forty or fifty men..attacked a tenaille which by its fire flanked one of the breaches.

‖**tenaillon** (tɪˈnæljən). *Fortif.* [F. *tenaillon* (tənɑjɔ̃) in same sense, f. *tenaille* (see prec.).] A work sometimes placed before each of the faces of a ravelin, leaving the salient angle exposed.

1842 BRANDE *Dict. Sc.* etc., *Tenaillon*... Seldom adopted. **1845** STOCQUELER *Handbk. Brit. India* (1854) 287 On the north side where Lally attacked, the bastion and demi-bastion are detached and the works near the sea covered by a tenaillon. **1859** F. A. GRIFFITHS *Artill. Man.* (1862) 262 *Lunettes* and *Tenaillons* are works (consisting of two faces) constructed on each side of ravelins.

‖**tena koe** (tɛˈnɑː kweɪ, ˈtɛnɑː ˈkɔe), *int. New Zealand.* Also 9 teneako, tenáqui; (with dual and pl. forms of the pronoun) **tena korua**, **tena koutou**. [Maori, lit. = 'there you are'.] A Maori greeting. Also **tenaˈkoeing** *vbl. sb.* (nonce-wd.).

a **1842** H. WEEKES in Rutherford & Skinner *Establishment of New Plymouth Settlement in N.Z.* (1940) I. 92 The period of *teneāko*-ing, handshaking, etc. *a* **1847** —— in *Ibid.* 119 Came towards me with extended hand and a friendly *Tenáqui*. **1901** A. A. GRACE *Tales of Dying Race* 190 'Aaaaah! *tena koutou*,' wailed she, seizing them by the hands. '*Tena koe! tena koe! Katahi te koa!*' she cried, as she rubbed noses with them one by one. **1905** W. BAUCKE *Where White Man Treads* 170 When I neared the fence I cried the old-time greeting, 'Tena koutou'. **1947** A. P. GASKELL *Big Game* 90 They smiled up at her. 'Tenakoe'. 'A lovely day Miss Brown,' said Mrs. Terari. **1949** P. BUCK *Coming of Maori* (rev. ed.) I. vi. 79 The usual Maori greeting of *Tena koe* applies to one person, *Tena korua* applies to two, and *Tena koutou* to more than two. **1960** N. HILLIARD *Maori Girl* II. 92 She could not catch what he said but..she guessed it was 'Tenakoe!'

‖**teˈnalia**, *sb. pl. Obs. rare.* [med.L. *tenālia* forceps (Du Cange), latinized from F. *tenaille(s*, It. *tanaglia*.]

1. Pincers, forceps: = TENAILLE 1.

In quot. for tearing the flesh.

1603 KNOLLES *Hist. Turks* (1621) 1119 Some they roasted, and some they put unto the Tenalia.

2. *Fortif.* = TENAILLE 2.

1649 CROMWELL *Let.* 16 Sept., in *Carlyle*, Colonel Brandly did with forty or fifty of his men very gallantly storm the *Tenalia*; for which he deserves the thanks of the State. *Ibid.* 17 Sept., There was a *Tenalia* to flanker the south wall of the Town, between Duleek Gate, and the corner Tower.

tenancy (ˈtɛnənsɪ). [f. TENANT: see -ANCY; representing med.L. *tenentia* (1116 in Muratori *Antiquitates* IX. (1776) 430), also *tenantia* (*c* 1200 in Du Cange). Cf. OF. *tenance* (12th c. in Godef.).] The state or position of being a tenant; the holding or occupation of lands, etc.; tenure.

1. *Law.* A holding or possession of lands or tenements, by any title of ownership.

1590 SWINBURNE *Testaments* 72 Besides this men married lost their tenanc[i]es by the curtesie, women their dowries; finally the prince himselfe lost the profits of the landes of persons attainted. **1598** KITCHIN *Courts Leet* (1675) 484 The other pleads several Tenancy. **1614** SELDEN *Titles Hon.* 266 By the substance, I mean their being immediat Tenancies of the Crown, or as we say in chief. **1766** BLACKSTONE *Comm.* II. xii. 194 As to the incidents attending a tenancy in common. **1818** CRUISE *Digest* (ed. 2) I. 51 The practice of creating manors or tenancies in gross was effectually prevented by the statute *Quia Emptores*. *Ibid.* VI. 418 The Court at first held this to be a tenancy in common; but afterwards upon good consideration it was adjudged to be a joint tenancy, for so it was implied.

b. Occupancy of lands or tenements under a lease. (The ordinary current sense.) Also (contextually) the duration of a tenure; the period during which a tenement is held.

1598 MARSTON *Sco. Villanie* I. ii, Tis all one, for life to be a beast, A slaue, as haue a short term'd tenancie. **1817** W. SELWYN *Law Nisi Prius* (ed. 4) II. 673 A notice to quit at the expiration of the current year of the tenancy. **1834** HT. MARTINEAU *Moral* II. 75 Partnership tenantcies affect the security of property by rendering one tenant answerable for the obligations of all his partners. **1858** LD. ST. LEONARDS *Handy Bk. Prop. Law* xv. 99 Such a lease..creates a tenancy from year to year, and terminable by half a year's notice. **1875** *Report* in Woodfall *Law Landl. & Ten.* (1877) 719 Some counties pay for no guano used in the last year but one of the tenancy. **1876** DIGBY *Real Prop.* v. §1. 208 A tenancy at will is where the land is held by the tenant so long as lessor and lessee please that the tenancy should continue.

attrib. **1906** *Westm. Gaz.* 30 July 5/2 Conspiring by false pretences to acquire several valuable tenancy agreements in various parts of London.

2. Occupation or enjoyment of, or residence in, any place, position, or condition.

1597–8 BP. HALL *Sat.* IV. ii. 124 Thine heyr, thine heyres heyre, and his heire againe,..Shall climbe up to the chancell pewes on high, And rule and raigne in their rich tenancie. **1856** FROUDE *Hist. Eng.* I. v. 425 The queen was at Ampthill,..having entered on her sad tenancy..as soon as the place had been evacuated by the gaudy hunting party.

attrib. **1903** *Westm. Gaz.* 2 June 2/1 The district contract system was expanded into a district tenancy system, wherein the whole of the business was conducted by the contractor.

†**3.** That which is held by a tenant. **a.** A holding, a TENEMENT. **b.** A post or office; occupation, employment. *Obs. rare.*

1579 J. STUBBES *Gaping Gulf* D iij, The greatest castelles, honors, and manors are but mesnalties or rather very messuages and tenancyes paraual. **1580–1** *Act 23 Eliz.* c. 4 Parte of the same Habytacions, Tenauncyes and Farmes have byn reduced rather to pasturing of Cattell then to the Mayntenaunce of Men of Service. *Ibid.*, What Tenauncyes and Howses of Habitacions be..ruyned and decayed. **1597–8** *Proc. Star Chamb.* in Ribton-Turner *Vagrants & Vagr.* (1887) 123 The said John Scripe had..divided a Tenement in Shordich, into, or about seventeene Tenancies or dwellings,..inhabited by divers persons. **1670** BLOUNT *Law Dict.*, *Tenancies*, (23 Eliz. c. 4) are Houses for Habitation, Tenements, or places to live in, held of another.

tenant ('tɛnənt), *sb.* Forms: α. 4–6 **tenaunt**, **-aunte**, **-ante**, *Sc.* **-ente** (4 *pl.* **-auns**), 5 **ten(e)awnte**, **-awunt**, *pl.* **-aunce**, 5–6 **tennaunte**, 6–7 **-ant**, **-ent(e**, 7 **-ent**, 7–8 **tenent**, 4– **tenant**. β. *Sc.* and *n. dial.* 4– 6 **tenand(e**, 5 **tennend**, 5–6 **-and**, 6 **tenaind**. [a. F. *tenant* sb. (12th c. in Godef.), orig. pr. pple. of *tenir*:—L. *tenēre* to hold.]

1. *Law.* **a.** One who holds or possesses lands or tenements by any kind of title. (In English Law implying a *lord*, of whom the tenant holds.)

[**1292** BRITTON I. i. §13 En counteez et hundrez et en Court de chescun fraunc tenaunt.] *c* **1330** R. BRUNNE *Chron.* (1810) 19 Adelwolf of Westsex, after his fadere dede, At Chestre sette his parlement, his tenantz þerto bede. *c* **1375** *Lay Folks Mass Bk.* (MS. B.) 369 Oure frendes, tenandes, & seruandes. *c* **1380** WYCLIF *Serm.* Sel. Wks. I. 22 Oþir tenauntis of þe lord shal receyve me into þere housis. *c* **1450** HOLLAND *Howlat* 609 An ilk scheld in that place Thar tennend or man was. *c* **1460** FORTESCUE *Abs. & Lim. Mon.* x. (1885) 134 By escheittes þer mey not so muche lande fall to any man as to þe kyng, by cause þat no man hath so many tenantes as he. **1563** *Homilies* II. *Rogation Week* IV. (1859) 496 Whereby the lord's records, (which be the tenant's evidences,) be perverted..sometime to the disheriting of the right owner. **1594** SHAKS. *Rich. III*, IV. iv. 481 Where be thy Tenants, and thy followers? **1607** COWELL *Interpr.* (1672), *Tenant* or *Tenent*,..one that holds or possesses Lands or Tenements by any kind of Right, be it in Fee, for Life, Years, or at Will. **1766** BLACKSTONE *Comm.* II. v. 59 The thing holden is therefore styled a tenement, the possessors thereof tenants, and the manner of their possession a tenure. **1827** HALLAM *Const. Hist.* (1876) II. ix. 129 The military tenants were frequently called upon in expeditions against Scotland, and last of all in that of 1640. **1845** POLSON *Eng. Law* in *Encycl. Metrop.* II. 828/1 He is called *tenant* [*in fee simple*] in virtue of the doctrine..which treats the king as the universal landlord—a doctrine so far recognised by our law, that in corporeal inheritances..the tenant in fee simple is formally styled as being seised in *his demesne as of fee*.

b. With qualifications indicating the species of tenure, the relation between lord and tenant, etc., as ***customary***, ***kindly***, ***mesne***, ***several***, ***sole***, ***very tenant***: see the adjs. Also JOINT-TENANT; ***tenant in burgage***, ***in capite***, ***in chief***, ***in common***, ***by courtesy***, ***in dower***, ***paravail***, etc.: see these words, and quots. here. ***tenant through law of England*** = tenant by courtesy; ***tenant to the præcipe***, a tenant against whom the writ præcipe was brought, being one to whom an entailed estate had been granted by the owner in order that it might be alienated by a recovery; see RECOVERY 4. See also TENANT AT WILL.

a **1325** *MS. Rawl. B. 520* lf. 17 b, þat is i-seid for women holdinde in dowere, ant tenauns þoru lawe of yngelonde. **1461** *Rolls of Parlt.* V. 485/2 The same halfendele..enjoye to hym, for terme of his lyf, as Tenaunt by the Curtesie. **1475** *Ibid.* VI. 149/1 That the said Maude have..actions by Writts of Dower,..ayenst all persones Tenaunt or Tenauntes of the Frehold. **1495** *Ibid.* 508/2 Discontinuances made by Tenauntes in Dower. [**1602** COKE *Reports* III. *Case of Fines* 88 Entant qu'il ne fuit tenant al Precipe.] **1607** COWELL *Interpr.* (1672), *Tenant per Statute-Merchant*, that holds Land by vertue of a Statute forfeited to him... *Tenant in Frank-marriage*.., he that holds Lands or Tenements by vertue of a Gift thereof made to him upon Marriage between him and his Wife... *Tenant by Elegit*, that holds by vertue of the Writ called an Elegit. *Tenant in Mortgage*, that holds by means of a Mortgage. *Tenant by the Verge* in ancient Demesne.., is he that is admitted by the Rod in a Court of ancient Demesne. *Tenant by Copy of Court-Roll*, is one admitted Tenant of any Lands, &c. within a Mannor, which time out of mind have been demisable, according to the Custome of the Mannor... *Tenant by Charter*, is he that holdeth by Feoffment in Writing, or other Deed... *Tenant in Chief*, that holdeth of the King in Right of his Crown... *Very Tenant*, that holds immediately of his Lord... For if there be Lord, Mesne and Tenant, the Tenant is very Tenant of the Mesne, but not to the Lord above... There are also *Joynt-tenants*, that have equal Right in Lands..by vertue of one Title... *Tenants in Common*, that have equal Right, but hold by divers Titles... *Sole tenant*.., he that hath no other joyned with him. *Several tenant* is opposite to Joynt-tenant, or Tenants in Common. *Tenant al Præcipe* is he against whom the Writ *Præcipe* is to be brought... *Tenant in Demesne*.., is he that holdeth the Demeans of a Mannor for a Rent without Service. *Tenant in Service*.., is he that holdeth by Service... *Tenant by Execution*.., that holds Land by vertue of an Execution upon any Statute, Recognisance, &c. **1818** CRUISE *Digest* (ed. 2) V. 333 So that he could make a good tenant to the *præcipe*. **1827** JARMAN *Powell's Devises* (ed. 3) II. 113 It was held that the reversion in the settled lands passed, although the wife was tenant for life, and the daughter tenant in tail, in those lands under the settlement. **1844** SIR J. STEPHEN *Eccl. Biog.* (1850) I. 26 And held them [their crowns and mitres]..immediately, as tenants *in capite*, from the one legitimate representative of the great postle. **1863** H. COX *Instit.* I. iii. 11 The right of all tenants-in-chief of the Crown ..to be summoned to a common council of the realm.

2. One who holds a piece of land, a house, etc., by lease for a term of years or a set time. (The ordinary current sense. Correlative of *landlord*.)

1377 LANGL. *P. Pl.* B. xv. 305 To take of her tenauntz more þan treuth wolde. *c* **1380** WYCLIF *Sel. Wks.* III. 414 He begges not þis rent of þo lordis tenaunte. **1479–81** *Rec. St. Mary at Hill* 110 Yevyn to ther tenauntes at the Receyvyng of the Rentes, and in potacions amonge them.. xs. vd. **1523** FITZHERB. *Husb.* §123 Than shall his farme be twyse so good in profyte to the tenaunt as it was before. **1526** TINDALE *Mark* xii. 2 When tyme was come he sentt to the tennauntes a servaunt that he myght of the tenauntes receave of the frute of the vyneyarde. **1639** HORN & ROB. *Gate Lang. Unl.* xxxii. § 386 He is a tenant, to whom house and grounds, and hired farms are, for a certain rent, let out to farm for a set time. **1770** *Junius Lett.* xxxvi. (1820) 179 Like broken tenants, who have had warning to quit the premises. **1838** DICKENS *Nich. Nick.* xvi, Of this chamber, Nicholas became the tenant; and having..paid the first week's hire in advance [etc.]. *Mod.* (*Title*) The Law of Landlord and Tenant.

3. *transf.* and *fig.* One who or that which inhabits or occupies any place; a denizen, inhabitant, occupant, dweller.

1388 WYCLIF *Job* xix. 15 The tenauntis of myn hows, and myn handmaydis hadden me as a straunger. **1602** SHAKS. *Ham.* v. i. 50 That Frame [the gallows] outliues a thousand Tenants. **1728–46** THOMSON *Spring* 788 While thus the gentle tenants of the shade Indulge their purer loves. **1764** GOLDSM. *Trav.* 65 The shudd'ring tenant of the frigid zone. **1774** —— *Nat. Hist.* (1824) II. 327 One of the most splendid tenants of the Mexican forests. **1799** CAMPBELL *Pleas. Hope* I. 268 The dim-eyed tenant of the dungeon gloom. **1827** SCOTT *Highl. Widow* v, As if sorrow, or even deep thought, should as short a while as possible be the tenant of the soldier's bosom. **1879** *Daily News* 27 Sept. 6/3 Tenants of our British waters. **1882** *Daily Tel.* 19 May, Mr. Bettesworth was the incoming tenant [i.e. batsman], and, after some slow play, the 50 went up.

4. *attrib.* and *Comb.* Simple attrib., as ***tenant-holding*** (HOLDING *vbl. sb.* 3), ***-risk***, ***-system***; appositive, as ***tenant-cultivator***, ***-farmer*** (hence ***tenant-farming*** sb. and adj., and as back-formation, ***tenant-farm*** vb. trans., ***tenant farm*** sb.), ***tenant-occupier***, ***-purchaser***, ***-soul***; also **tenant-sted** *a. Sc.*, occupied by a tenant. See also TENANT-RIGHT.

1949 *Time* 27 June 84/2 The 1,600 acres he *tenant-farms. **1979** P. THEROUX *Old Patagonian Express* xvii. 263 These are tenant farms..these people own nothing but the clothes on their backs. **1748** RICHARDSON *Clarissa* V. 208 Attended by Susan Morrison, a *tenant-farmer's daughter. **1860** *All Year Round* No. 71. 485 Those down-trodden vassals, the tenant farmers. **1861** *Trans. Illinois Agric. Soc.* IV. 203 On the greater part of this farm are the usual indices of *tenant farming. **1887** *Edin. Rev.* Oct. 301 In Rhône..tenant-farming is unprofitable. **1891** *Daily News* 11 Dec. 6/4 He came of a tenant farming race. **1591** in A. McKay *Hist. Kilmarnock* (1880) 359 We give and grant all the *tenant-holdings, free holdings [etc.]. **1906** *Westm. Gaz.* 7 Nov. 9/2 Entitled to be on the list as the *tenant-occupier of a dwelling-house, being part of a house, and such part being separately occupied. **1895** J. E. REDMOND in *19th Cent.* Dec. 913 The *tenant-purchasers have been remarkably punctual in their payments. **1880** A. ARNOLD *Free Land* 68 *Tenant-risk and the absence of tenant-right have contributed to drive capital away from agriculture. **1710** LD. FOUNTAINHALL *Decis.* (1761) II. 568 The rest of the rooms were lying waste, and this was only *tenant-sted. **1906** *Daily Chron.* 13 Sept. 5/7 The canteen is run on the *tenant system.

tenant ('tɛnənt), *v.* [f. prec. sb.]

1. *trans.* To hold as tenant, to be the tenant of (land, a house, etc.); *esp.* to occupy, inhabit.

1634 HABINGTON *Castara* (Arb.) 125 To the cold humble hermitage Not tenanted but by discoloured age. **1667** PRIMATT *City & C. Build.* 34 Houses..without Tenants, decay sooner than those which are Tenanted. **1711** STEELE *Spect.* No. 107 ¶5 The greatest Part of Sir Roger's Estate is tenanted by Persons who have served himself or his Ancestors. **1795** SOUTHEY *Vis. Maid of Orleans* I. 96 Damsel, look here! survey this house of death; O soon to tenant it. **1830** LYELL *Princ. Geol.* (1872) I. I. xiv. 300 Birds, quadrupeds, and reptiles, which tenanted the fertile region. **1855** TENNYSON *Brook* 222 We bought the farm we tenanted before.

b. *fig.* To occupy, fill, take up (a space, etc.).

1670 J. NEWBURGH *Observ. Cider* in Evelyn *Pomona* 54 A Barrel newly tenanted by small Beer. **1806–7** J. BERESFORD *Miseries Hum. Life* (1826) VI. x, A pair of boundless slippers that have been tenanted by a thousand feet. **1873** MISS BROUGHTON *Nancy* II. 183 Alternate clouds and sunshine tenant the sky.

2. *intr.* To reside, dwell, live *in*. *rare.*

1650 WELDON *Crt. Jas. I* 133 Surely never so many brave parts, and so base and abject a spirit tenanted together in any one earthen Cottage. **1851** S. WARREN *Lily & Bee* II. 190 A sparrow..In yonder tree he tenanteth alone.

†**3.** *trans.* To let *out* to a tenant or tenants. *rare.*

1721 STRYPE *Eccl. Mem.* I. xvi. 123 Three acres more he converted into a highway..; and the rest he tenanted out. **1776** ADAM SMITH *W.N.* v. iii. (1869) II. 536 The lands in America and the West Indies, indeed, are in general not tenanted nor leased out to farmers.

Hence '**tenanted** *ppl. a.*, held by a tenant or tenants, occupied; '**tenanting** *vbl. sb.* and *ppl. a.* So '**tenanter**, one who tenants, an occupant.

1798 J. HUCKS *Poems* 43 The little family of hope, The young-ey'd tenanters of happiness. **1886** *Pall Mall G.* 22 Apr. 8/2 The immediate landlord of any tenanted estate. **1903** MORLEY *Gladstone* I. ii. 38 An eager pilgrimage to the newly tenanted grave of his hero.

tenant, obs. form of TENENT, TENON[1].

tenantable ('tɛnəntəb(ə)l), *a.* [f. TENANT *v.* and *sb.* + -ABLE.]

1. Capable of being tenanted or inhabited; fit for occupation. Also *fig.*

1542 *Richmond Wills* (Surtees) 32 Ye same howse so to be mayde tenandhable. **1576** in W. H. Turner *Select. Rec. Oxford* (1880) 382 To leve yt repayred and tenaunteable. **1633** FORD *Love's Sacr.* IV. ii, A good tenantable and fertile womb. **1753** HERVEY *Theron & Asp.* (1757) I. xii. 472 It [the body] is kept in tenantable condition for the soul. **1849** DE QUINCEY *Eng. Mail Coach* Wks. 1862 IV. 292 The only room tenantable by gentlemen. **1852** BEARN in *Jrnl. R. Agric. Soc. Eng.* XIII. I. 90 He therefore cannot keep the property in tenantable repair.

2. [f. the sb.] Befitting a tenant. *rare.*

1856 H. BROOME *Comm. Common Law* 15 A tenant..is bound to use a farm in a good and tenantable manner, and according to the rules of good husbandry.

Hence '**tenantableness**, tenantable condition.

1727 in BAILEY vol. II.

'**tenant at 'will.** *Law.* A tenant who holds at the will or pleasure of the lessor. Also *fig.*

c **1500** *Lichfield Gild Ord.* (E.E.T.S.) 14 It is ordenyd that ..no tenaind at wyll shall make a tenand. **1598** *Child-Marriages* 164 Acceptans of the said Robert Fletcher to be his tenaunte at will of the said shop. **1628** COKE *On Litt.* 55 The lessee is called Tenant at will, because hee hath no certain nor sure estate, for the lessor may put him out at what time it pleaseth him. **1746–7** HERVEY *Medit.* (1818) 27 Let us look upon ourselves only as 'tenants at will'; and hold ourselves in perpetual readiness to depart at a moment's warning. **1878** JEVONS *Prim. Pol. Econ.* x. 92 Tenants at will have no inducement to improve their farms.

tenantcy, erron. form of TENANCY.

tenanting: see TENANT *v.*, TENONING.

'**tenantism.** *nonce-wd.* [f. TENANT *sb.* + -ISM, after *landlordism*.] The principles and practice of tenants; tenantry; the tenant interest collectively.

1880 *Daily News* 3 Nov. 5/6 Exacting 'landlordism' and recalcitrant 'tenantism' seem..to have said their last word.

tenantless ('tɛnəntlɪs), *a.* [f. as prec. + -LESS.] Without a tenant or tenants; untenanted, unoccupied, empty. *lit.* and *fig.*

1591 SHAKS. *Two Gent.* v. iv. 8 Leaue not the Mansion so longe Tenant-lesse, Lest growing ruinous, the building fall. **1814** CARY *Dante, Inf.* xx. 85 Plying her arts, remain'd, and lived, and left Her body tenantless. **1826** DISRAELI *Viv. Grey* II. ix, Is it true that all the houses..are tenantless? **1871** R. ELLIS *Catullus* lxiv. 181 Also a desert lies this region, a tenantless island.

b. Const. *of*: Untenanted by.

1613–16 W. BROWNE *Brit. Past.* II. ii. 46 Or haue the Parcæ..Left some friends body tenantlesse of life? **1868** *Rep. U.S. Commissioner Agric.* (1869) 346 Streams heretofore tenantless of fish are now well stocked artificially.

'**tenant-right.** [f. TENANT *sb.* + RIGHT *sb.*] In general sense, The right that a person has as a tenant (of any kind). With special applications varying in time and place, as **a.** the right of a customary tenant: see quot. 1886; **b.** the right of a tenant at will or for a term of years to compensation for unexhausted improvements; **c.** the right of a tenant at will to sell his interest and goodwill to the incoming tenant. ***Ulster tenant-right***: see quot. 1878.

1542 *Richmond Wills* (Surtees) 27 Item I gyve and bewheth mye hole tityll and tenandright off my howse and farmehold.., aftere my decesse, unto Thomas Borowe. **1596** *Calr. Border Pap.* II. 134 The said tenantes hould the seuerall landes and tenementes aforesaid by a custumary estate, which they call and claime to be, Tennant right. **1665** MANLEY *Grotius' Low C. Warres* 906 There is extant a Charter..which grants to the Earl of Holland, to possess as his own Free-hold, what before he enjoy'd but by a kind of Tenant-Right. *a* **1734** NORTH *Lives* (1826) I. 289 In Cumberland the people had joined in.., pretending a tenant-right; which, there, is a customary estate, not unlike our copyholds. **1778** *Phil. Surv. S. Irel.* 315 So it is with us, where the present occupier is supposed to have a tenant-right. **1851** SIR F. PALGRAVE *Norm. & Eng.* I. 519 The tenant right of the beneficiary or feudal vassals. **1868** T. HUGHES *Sp. Ho. Com.* in *Morn. Star* 13 Mar., Tenant right was really an immemorial custom prevailing in a great portion of Ireland, but unrecognised yet in courts of law, or statute books, under which the ordinary tenant at will has acquired the right of selling the succession to his holding. **1874** STUBBS *Const. Hist.* (1875) I. iii. 52 The practice of careful husbandry demanded for the cultivator a tenant-right in his allotment. **1878** JEVONS *Prim. Pol. Econ.* x. 93 Tenant right, which consists in giving the tenant a right to claim the value of any unexhausted improvements, which he may have made in his farm, if he be turned out of it. *Ibid.*, Tenant right..has existed for a long time in the north of Ireland, where it is called the Ulster tenant right. A new tenant there pays the old tenant a considerable sum of money for the privilege of getting a good farm with various improvements. **1880** LD. DUFFERIN in *Times* 4 Jan. (1881) 4/4 Under the Act of 1870, if the landlord buys up the tenant-right of a farm, it is declared to be extinguished for ever. **1886** H. HALL *Soc. Eliz. Age* App. i. 154 The customary tenants enjoy [in 1583] the ancient custom called tenant-right: namely, 'To have their messuages and tenements to them during their lives, and after their deceases to the eldest issues of their bodies lawfully begotten.

attrib. **1713** *Act 12 Anne* Stat. I. c. 2 §49 Copies of Admittances to Custom-Right, or Tenant-Right Estates, not being Copyhold, which pass by Deed, Surrender, and Admittance.

Hence **'tenant-'righter** (*colloq.*), an advocate or supporter of tenant-right.

1865 *Morn. Star* 13 Mar., Mr. Greer, you are aware, is a great tenant-righter, and in the palmy days of the League he occupied a prominent place in that body. **1886** *Pall Mall G.* 4 Oct. 8/1 Recognized as a prominent representative of his class in the North and as a strong tenant-righter.

tenantry ('tɛnəntrɪ). Forms: 4 *Sc.* teneindri, 4–6 *Sc.* ten(n)andry, -endry, 5–6 tenentry, 5– tenantry. [f. TENANT *sb.* + -RY.]

1. The state or condition of being a tenant; occupancy as a tenant; tenancy; tenantship.

1391 in Fraser *Lennox* (1874) II. 43 Murthow..sal indow hir in the barony of the Redehall with the apportenantis in tenandry and in demayn. **1597** SKENE *De Verb. Sign.* s.v. *Manus*, The King may be thereby prejudged in his tenendrie, dewtie and service. **1606** WARNER *Alb. Eng.* XVI. ciii. 406 To take the foyson Lords haue skill, On Tainters setting Tenentries, oft for Expences ill. **1846** J. BAXTER *Libr. Pract. Agric.* (ed. 4) I. p. xxi, It was only by the tenantry of the peaceful monks that the land was even tolerably tilled. **1889** *Cornh. Mag.* Dec. 563 The Miss Tremenheeres had almost come to an end of their tenantry at Elm Place.

2. Land held of a superior; land let out to tenants; also, the profits of such land.

1385 in *3rd Rep. Hist. MSS. Comm.* 410/1 Somonde at the chef plaz of the teneindri of Lytilton. **1438** *St. Andrews Regr.* (Bann. Cl.) 430 Ovirmalgask is fundin a tenandry in yhour awyn court of þe fornemmyt lordschip. *c* **1460** *Oseney Regr.* 20 With all churchis and chapells londis rentis tenauntries and tithes possessions and other thynges to þe saide church of seynte George perteynyng. **1584** *Reg. Privy Council Scot.* III. 673 Thair saidis tennendreis salbe annext to the Kingis Majesteis propirtie as his propir rent. **1597** SKENE *De Verb. Sign.* s.v. *Recognition*, Lands..annalied, and sauld be them heritably, to be halden of themselues and their aires, ceasis to be propertie to them, and becomes tennendry immediately halden of them and their aires.

†**b.** The holding of a tenant; a piece of land, a dwelling-house, or the like, held by a tenant under the landlord. Also *transf.* *Obs.*

c **1450** *Godstow Regr.* 149 To lete to oony man the foresayde tenantry ne no perte of hit with-owte speciall licence of þe foresayde abbesse. **1465** MARG. PASTON in *P. Lett.* II. 176 Ther be dyvers of your tenantrys at Mauteby that had gret ned for to be repayred. **1521** *MS. Acc. St. John's Hosp., Canterb.*, The wyndowes of the tenauntry in Doklane. **1528** TINDALE *Obed. Chr. Man* 50 b, Let Christen londlordes be contente with their rent and olde customes not ..lettinge ij. or iij. tenauntryes vnto one man. **1547** *Act 1 Edw. VI*, c. 3 §9 Tenauntries cotages or other convenient howses to be lodged in. **1613–14** *Taxt Roll* 20 Jan. in *Glasgow Daily Herald* (1864) 24 Sept., Cruixsfie propertie and tennandrie, 100 lib.

c. A set of houses owned by tenants collectively.

1905 *Westm. Gaz.* 23 Aug. 8/3 It is here sought to prove as a sound economical principle..the collective ownership of a house with individual responsibility. No one tenant owns any distinct house in any 'tenantry', but the profits that accrue from that particular 'tenantry', after the deduction of interest on the money, cost of repairs, &c., are shared amongst the tenants.

3. *spec.* That part of a manor or estate under common or open-field husbandry (Tusser's 'champion countrie', *Husb.* lxiii.) occupied by tenants, as distinct from the lord's demesne (as in Domesday Survey, 'terra *in dominio*' and 'terra *in villenagio*'). Hence, locally applied to the condition or system of tenancy under open-field husbandry. See also *tenantry acre, field, flock, land*, in 5.

1794 T. DAVIS *Agric. Wilts.* 14 The abolition of common-field husbandry (or as it is called in Wiltshire 'Tenantry'). *Ibid.*, Modern improvements..cannot be adopted to any extent, in lands lying in a state of tenantry. *Ibid.*, Tenantry yard-lands (or customary tenements)..are still subject to the rights of common. **1844** LITTLE in *Jrnl. R. Agric. Soc. Eng.* V. I. 178 Most of these commons are now enclosed;.. some still remain in pasture, and the common field husbandry, or 'tenantry', as it is called, is abolished.

4. The body of tenants on an estate or estates. (Now the most usual sense.)

1628 WITHER *Brit. Rememb.* VII. 752 That they have begger'd halfe their Tenantry. **1781** COWPER *Hope* 252 Kind souls! to teach their tenantry to prize What they themselves, without remorse, despise. **1868** MILL *Eng. & Irel.* 37 Those landlords who are the least useful in Ireland, and on the worst terms with their tenantry. **1875** MRS. RANDOLPH *W. Hyacinth* I. 46, I shall introduce you to the tenantry as their future mistress.

b. *transf.* A set of occupants or inhabitants.

1798 H. MELVILLE in Spurgeon *Treas. Dav.* Ps. cxix. 18 The tiny tenantry [of a drop of water] are carrying on their usual concerns. **1880** E. KIRKE *Garfield* 44 Under the sway of terrestrial laws, winds blow, waters flow, and all the tenantries of the planet live and move.

5. *attrib.* and *Comb.*, as, in sense 3, ***tenantry acre, down, field, flock, land, road*****; tenantry dinner**, a dinner given to the tenants on an estate.

1794 T. DAVIS *Agric. Wilts.* 61 In the common fields..the usual rule is, to allow one thousand sheep to fold what they call a *tenantry acre [about three-fourths of a statute acre] per night. **1903** *Westm. Gaz.* 9 Jan. 7/2 The *tenantry dinner. **1794** T. DAVIS *Agric. Wilts.* 58 The old custom of the *tenantry fields of Wiltshire was..to give a year's fallow previous to wheat. **1813** *Ibid.* Gloss., *Tenantry Fields and Downs*, fields and downs in a state of commonage on the ancient feudal system of copyhold tenancy. **1793** A. YOUNG *Agric. Sussex* 69 A *tenantry flock [of sheep] (the joint property of several people) belonging to the parish of Denton. **1853** W. D. COOPER *Sussex Gloss.* 65 *note*, The proportion between the tenantry and the statute acre is very uncertain. The *tenantry land was divided first into laines, of several acres in extent, with good roads..between them; at right angles with these were formed..*tenantry roads,.. dividing the laines into furlongs.

tenantship ('tɛnəntʃɪp). [f. TENANT *sb.* + -SHIP.] The condition or position of a tenant; tenancy, occupancy.

1883 A. WILDER in Max Müller *India* ii. 67 The tenure and law of inheritance varies with the different native races, but tenantship for a specific period seems to be the most common. **1889** T. GIFT *Not for Night-time* 127 He handed me the key in token of my new tenantship. **1892** *Daily News* 25 Mar. 4/8 To aim at the extension of tenantships as well as that of peasant proprietorships.

†**'tenanty.** *Obs.* [? erroneous form, or mispr.] = TENANCY 3 a.

1612 DAVIES *Why Irel.*, etc. 168 By the Irish Custome of Gauellkinde, the inferiour Tennanties were partible amongst all the Males of the Sept. [**1875** So quoted in MAINE *Hist. Inst.* vii. 185.]

tenar, obs. variant of THENAR.

tenas ('tɛnæs), *a.* (and *sb.*) [Chinook Jargon, ad. Nootka *t'an'as* child.] Small. Also as *sb.*, and in **tenas man** [cf. KLOOCHMAN], a child.

1870 *Mainland Guardian* (New Westminster, B.C.) 16 Apr. 3/3 There trip about a few Tenass-men, some with the remains of an old coat and beaver hat, and some [in] almost naked savagedom. **1904** *Wide World Mag.* Sept. 541/2 Klootchmen, tenasses, old bucks, and young hunters..were crowded on the schooner's deck. **1935** H. DAVIS *Honey in Horn* xxii. 371 Nobody but this *tenas* buck [*i.e.* small Indian] here. **1969** *Islander* (Victoria, B.C.) 19 Oct. 3/2 They were very insolent..laughing at the *tenass* warship for wasting her powder and shot.

tenasm(e, -asmus, obs. forms of TENESMUS.

†**te'nasmon.** *Obs. rare.* [a. obs. F. *tenasmon* (15th c. in Godef.), f. med.L. *tenasmus*, TENESMUS, q.v.] = TENESMUS.

c **1425** tr. *Arderne's Treat. Fistula*, etc. 39 He shal fele.. akyng, stirryng, and prikkyng, and tenasmon; þat is, appetite of egestion. *Ibid.* 71 Tenasmon is a sekenez within þe lure þat makeþ þe pacient for to desire purgyng of his womb byneþ-forþ.

tenaunt(e, obs. form of TENANT, TENON[1].

tenax ('tɛnæks, 'tiːnæks), *a.* and *sb.* [a. L. *tenax* tough: see TENACIOUS.]

†**A.** *adj.* Tough, tenacious. *Obs. rare*⁻¹.

1605 TIMME *Quersit.* III. 144 The substance of sulphur.. is tenax & retentiue.

B. *sb.* A trade name of fine carded oakum used as a surgical dressing (Billings).

1889 *Athenæum* 31 Aug. 283/1 She..made a pillow for the back out of a piece of pink cambric stuffed with tenax [at Ladysmith]. **1891** *Scenes Life Nurse* 20 Some tenax (a kind of oakum) was lying with some other dressings on the side table.

Tenby ('tɛnbɪ). The name of a town on the coast of Wales, used *attrib.* in **Tenby daffodil** to designate *Narcissus obvallaris*, a small yellow daffodil sometimes found as a wild flower in the region.

[**1830** A. H. HAWORTH in *Phil. Mag.* VIII. 130 Truby [*sic*] 6-lobed Daffodil.] **1884** J. D. HOOKER *Student's Flora Brit. Isles* (ed. 3) 399 The Tenby Daffodil..scarcely differs. **1894** W. ROBINSON *Wild Garden* (ed. 4) ii. 19 The little Tenby Daffodil is very sturdy and pretty. **1966** J. BERRISFORD *Wild Garden* iii. 35 The early-blooming *Narcissus obvallaris*, the small 'Tenby Daffodil'. **1981** W. CONDRY *Nat. Hist. Wales* vi. 171 The Tenby daffodil..has long puzzled the world.

tence, obs. form of TENSE.

tench[1] (tɛnʃ). Also 4–6 **tenche**, 5 **tenych**, 6 **teyns(h)e**. Pl. **tenches**, collect. **tench.** [a. OF. *tenche* (in Cotgr.; cf. Picard *tenke* in Godef. *Compl.*), mod.F. *tanche* (13th c. in Littré):—late L. *tinca*.]

1. A thick-bodied freshwater fish, *Tinca vulgaris*, allied to the carp, inhabiting still and deep waters; also, the flesh of this fish as food.

1390 *Earl Derby's Exp.* (Camden) 73 Pro tenches et roches .., iiij scot. xij d. **1392** *Ibid.* 155 Pro xij tench et xij anguillis grossis, iij s. vj d. *c* **1425** *Voc.* in Wr.-Wülcker 614/24 *Suctus*, a tenche. *Ibid.* 615/43 *Tengiagio*, a tenche. *c* **1440** *Promp. Parv.* 488/2 Tenche, fysche, *tencha*. **1485** *Nottingham Rec.* III. 240, ij grete eles and a grete tenche. *a* **1552** LELAND *Itin.* V. 73 A preati Poole wherin be good Luces and Tenchis. **1653** WALTON *Angler* ix. 175–6. **1787** BEST *Angling* (ed. 2) 49 The tench the fishes physician (so called because his slime is said to be very healing to wounded fishes). **1802** BINGLEY *Anim. Biog.* (1813) III. 80 Tench are partial to foul and weedy waters. **1867** F. FRANCIS *Angling* iii. (1880) 86 The tench is a very curious fish in his habits.

2. *attrib.* and *Comb.*, as ***tench-broth, -fishing*****; tench-weed**, a local name of pondweed.

1598 *Epulario* I j, Halfe a pint of Pike or *Tench broth. **1888** GOODE *Amer. Fishes* 419 The season for *Tench fishing in Germany is from July to October. *a* **1825** FORBY *Voc. E. Anglia*, **Tench-weed*, a sort of pond-weed, having a slime or mucilage about it... It is *Potamogeton natans*.

†**tench**[2]. *Sc. Obs. rare.* [a. Picard *tenche*, OF. *tence* dispute (12th c. in Godef.), f. *tencier*, *tencer* to contend:—pop. L. type **tentiāre*, f. *tentus*, pa. pple. of *tendĕre* to stretch, strive, etc.] (?) A taunt, reproach.

1513 DOUGLAS *Æneis* IX. Prol. 23 The ryall style, clepyt heroycall,..Suld be compilit but tenchis or voyd word.

tench[3] (tɛnʃ). *slang.* Abbreviation of *detention, penitentiary*.

1850 *Broad Arrow* ii. 32 (Farmer) Prisoners' barracks, sir —us calls it Tench [Hobart Town Penitentiary]. **1887** HORSLEY *Jottings fr. Jail* i. 12, 'I..got remanded to the Tench' (House of Detention). **1897** P. WARUNG *Tales Old Regime* 143 We were all sent to a place called a tench and there we were signed off to Defferent masters.

†**tencion** ('tɛnʃən). *Obs.* Also **-chon, -cyon.** [ad. OF. *tençon, tenchon, tenson* (12th c.) a contest, a quarrel = Pr. *tenso*, It. *tenzone*, ad. L. *tensiōn-em*, f. *tend-ĕre* to stretch, strive, contend.] A contention, dispute, quarrel.

1471 CAXTON *Recuyell* (Sommer) 521 A grete strif or tenchon [F. *une tençon et debat*] that is fallen betwene them. **1474** —— *Chesse* III. vi. (1883) 129 Hit happeth ofte tymes that ther cometh of glotonye tencyons stryfs ryottes [etc.]. *c* **1477** —— *Jason* 8 That the wyn had surmounted hem in wordes and tencions.

†**'ten-city.** *Obs. rare*⁻¹. Literal translation of Gr. *Δεκάπολις Decapolis*, a district of Roman Palestine comprising ten cities.

c **1550** CHEKE *Matt.* iv. 25 A greet nomber from galilee, yᵉ tencitee,..and places beiond Jordan.

tend, *sb. rare.* [f. TEND *v.*[1]] The action or fact of tending; aim, tendency.

1655 MRQ. WORCESTER *Cent. Inv.* Ded. ii. (1663) A vij, The taking off such Taxes or Burthens..which, I dare say, is the continual Tend of all your indefatigable pains. **1937** V. WOOLF *Let.* 30 Apr. (1980) VI. 122 I'm very glad you saw that the tend of the book, its slope to one quarter of the compass and not another, was different from the tend in my other books.

tend (tɛnd), *v.*[1] Also 4–7 **tende**, (5 **tenne**). Pa. t. and pple. **tended** (5 **tende**). [Aphetic form of ATTEND *v.*, ENTEND *v.*, INTEND *v.*, F. *attendre*, *entendre*, which largely ran together in sense in OF. and ME.]

†**1.** To turn one's ear, give auditory attention, listen, hearken; = ATTEND *v.* I.

a. *intr.* *Obs.*

13.. *Cursor M.* 2542 (Gött.) Abram..all bad till him tendand [*Cott.* tentand] be. **1340–70** *Alisaunder* 7 Tend yee tytely to mee & take goode heede. *c* **1430** *Hymns Virg.* 99 To þe ten heestis y haue not tende þoruȝ slouþe, wraþþe, & glotenie. *a* **1550** *Friar & Boy* 6 in Hazl. *E.P.P.* III. 60 God ..gyue them good lyfe and longe That lysteneth to my songe, Or tendeth to my tale. **1610** SHAKS. *Temp.* I. i. 8 Take in the toppe-sale: Tend to th' Masters whistle. **1816** G. MUIR *Clydesdale Minstr.* 61 'Tend to my plaint, ye bonny lasses.

†**b.** *trans.* To turn one's ear to, listen to. *Obs.*

1340–70 *Alisaunder* 997 Whan þis tale was tolde & tended of all. **1340–70** *Alex. & Dind.* 365 Tale tende we non þat turneþ to harme.

2. To turn the mind, attention, or energies; to apply oneself. **a.** *intr.* with *to, unto*: to attend to, look after (a thing, business, etc.); = ATTEND *v.* 2, 4. Now only *dial.* and *U.S.*

13.. *Cursor M.* 255 (Gött.) Sum quat to þat thing to tende [*C.* tent] þat þai þair mede may wid amende. *c* **1330** R. BRUNNE *Chron. Wace* (Rolls) 655 þat scheo tende to no þynge elles. *c* **1380** *Sir Ferumb.* 5122 þe Amyral..ne miȝt noȝt tendy þer-to. *c* **1460** *Play Sacram.* 195 Ye owe tenderli to tende me tylle. **1523–4** *Rec. St. Mary at Hill* 323 For blowyng the Orgons and tendyng to the chirch euery sonday, to haue ij d. **1880** 'MARK TWAIN' *Tramp Abroad* 39, I got to 'tend to business. **1901** *Cornh. Mag.* Nov. 678 Some folks..cassn't be satisfite wi' 'tendin' to their own [business]. **1901** J. PRIOR *Forest Folk* ii. 14 To let me tend to the commoners first. **1917** G. B. McCutcheon *Green Fancy* 68 They..paid their bills regular, 'tended to their own business, and that's all. **1930** W. Faulkner *As I lay Dying* (1935) 155 You got to wait a little while. Then I'll tend to you. **1936** M. Mitchell *Gone with Wind* x. 197 If anybody dares say one little word about you, I'll tend to them. **1975** A. Davis *Autobiogr.* v. 309 The men's linens and jail clothes were sent elsewhere for laundering; the women were expected to tend to their own.

†**b.** with *inf.* To turn one's attention, apply oneself *to do* something; = attend *v.* 4d, intend *v.* 9.

c **1330** R. Brunne *Chron. Wace* (Rolls) 14100 þey tenden nought hem self to fende. **1340–70** *Alex. & Dind.* 846 ȝe tende nauht to tulye þe erþe. **1623** Whitbourne *Newfoundland* 82 Three men may fetch a-land salt, and tend to wash fish, and dry the same. **1682** Bunyan *Greatness Soul* Wks. 1853 I. 136 He could tend to do nothing but to find out how to be clothed in purple and fine-linen. *a* **1688** —— *Accept. Sacrif.* ibid. 691 There is none else that either understand or that can tend to hearken to Him... But now the broken in heart can tend it.

c. *trans.* To attend to, mind (a thing); = attend *v.* 4, intend *v.* 12. Now *rare.*

1549 Chaloner *Erasm. on Folly* O ij, How many princes ..dooe..onely tende theyr owne pleasure. **1594** Barnfield *Affect. Sheph.* ii. lvi, Speake ill of no man, tend thine owne affaires. **1650** Jer. Taylor *Holy Living* iv. §6 (1727) 224 We rest also that we may tend holy duties. **1741–2** Gray *Agrippina* 7 To tend Her household cares, a woman's best employment. **1847** Helps *Friends in C.* I. i. 11 Your business..will be best tended in this way. **1866** Jul. Kavanagh *Sybil's Second Love* i, Tending the fire.

3. a. *trans.* To apply oneself to the care and service of (a person); now *esp.* to watch over and wait upon, to minister to (the sick or helpless); = attend *v.* 6, intend *v.* 11b.

c **1489** Caxton *Sonnes of Aymon* xxv. 539, I..praye you that ye tende well my children. **1697** Dampier *Voy.* I. xviii. 520 Jeoly..had been sick for 3 months: in all which time I tended him as carefully, as if he had been my Brother. **1712–14** Pope *Rape Lock* ii. 91 Our humbler province is to tend the Fair. **1722** De Foe *Plague* (1840) 84 Nurses to tend those that were sick. **1805** Scott *Last Minstr.* i. Introd. ii, That they should tend the old man well.

b. To have the care and oversight of; to take charge of, look after (a flock, herd, etc.); = attend *v.* 5. Said also (now *dial.* and *U.S.*) of a shop, toll-gate, bridge, etc., and (*U.S.*) in phr. *to tend bar* (cf. bartender). Also *absol.*

1515 Barclay *Egloges* iv. (1570) C iv, Nedes must a Shepheard bestowe his whole labour In tending his flockes. **1593** Shaks. *3 Hen. VI*, ii. v. 31 So many Houres, must I tend my Flocke. **1602** Rowlands *Tis Merrie* 16 My Husband's forth, our Shoppe must needes be tended. **1702** Pope *Sappho* 100 Bid Endymion nightly tend his sheep. **1809** A. Putnam in *Danvers Hist. Soc. Coll.* (1918) VI. 15 My brother has hired Asa Fletcher a young fellow of my age, who has been tending for Mr. Marcy. **1843** Carlyle *Past & Pr.* iv. i, Gurth could only tend pigs. **1855** Macaulay *Hist. Eng.* xii. III. 359 The horses had been ill fed and ill tended among the Grampians. **1870** 'Mark Twain' in *Galaxy* Nov. 726/2 Tending bar, and reporting for the newspapers. **1889** Farmer *Dict. Amer.* s.v., Shops, stores, and businesses of every description are in America *tended* and not kept. **1959** *Washington Post* 9 Dec. A7/3 Nixon is staying in Washington to help tend the store while the President is away on his 3-week tour. **1978** *Detroit Free Press* 2 Apr. 4C/3, In 1976, he tended bar and sold swimming pools and encyclopedias.

c. To bestow attention upon, attend to; *esp.* to foster, cultivate (a plant, etc.); to work or mind (a pump, a machine, etc.).

1631 Gouge *God's Arrows* iii. §95. 367 By peace.. gardens, vineyards, and other like fruitfull places [are] tended. **1667** Milton *P.L.* ix. 206 Well may we labour still to dress This Garden, still to tend Plant, Herb, and Flour. **1703** *Lond. Gaz.* No. 3915/3 The Men..not being able to tend the Pumps, she sunk. **1838** Arnold *Hist. Rome* I. xi. 203 This Lucius Quinctius let his hair grow, and tended it carefully. **1865** Kingsley *Herew.* x, He..tended the graves hewn in the living stone. **1885** S. Cox *Expositions* xxix. 386 Always seeking to multiply the seed they sow and tend.

4. a. To wait upon as attendant or servant; to attend on; to escort, follow, or accompany for the purpose of rendering service or giving assistance; = attend *v.* 7. Now *dial.*

a **1400–50** *Alexander* 4534 Appollo with a quite swan is paid him to tende. ?*c* **1500** in *Eng. Gilds* (1870) 418 It is ordered..that the new Mayor tenne the old Mayor at his owne house and goe home with the sword before him. **1594** Shaks. *Rich. III*, iv. i. 93 Go thou to Richard, and good Angels tend thee. *a* **1625** Fletcher, etc. *Fair Maid Inn* ii. ii, By your leave, Sir, I'll tend my master, and instantly be with you. **1719** De Foe *Crusoe* (1840) II. xii. 248 The man that tended the carpenter had a great iron ladle in his hand. **1888** Elworthy *W. Somerset Word-bk.* s.v., A mason's labourer always describes his work 'I do tend masons'.

b. *intr.* To attend *on* or *upon*; *spec.* to wait at table; = attend *v.* 7b, c. Also *fig.*

1593 Shaks. *2 Hen. VI*, iii. ii. 304 Three-fold Vengeance tend vpon your steps. **1641** Best *Farm. Bks.* (Surtees) 117 The bridegroome and the brides brothers or freinds tende att dinner. **1642** Rogers *Naaman* 41 Not [to] expect till Elisha tend upon him. **1722** De Foe *Plague* (1840) 106, I tend on them, to fetch things for them. **1818** Mrs. Shelley *Frankenst.* i. (1865) 35, I loved to tend on her. **1859** Tennyson *Enid* 1772 And Enid tended on him there.

5. *trans.* To give one's presence at (a meeting, ceremony, etc.); = attend *v.* 12. Now *dial.* and *U.S.* Also *intr.* with †*of* (*obs.*), *on* (*dial.*).

1460 *Rolls of Parlt.* V. 375/1 So that the seid Waulter may tende daily of this youre Parlement, as his dute is to doo. **1579–80** North *Plutarch* (1676) 290 Cato said that Scipio.. tended Plays, Comedies, and Wrestlings. **1801** H. Macneill *Poet. Wks.* (1856) 220 (E.D.D.) Our lads are doing little but tending the drill. **18..** *Maj. Jones's Trav.* (Bartlett), Most of the passengers..had been up to Augusta to tend the convention. **1890** *Dialect Notes* I. i. 22 *U.S.* One 'tends out on' church, 'tends out on' the public library. **1901** El. G. Hayden *Trav. Round our Vill.* x. 168, I 'tends church reg'lar!

6. a. *trans.* †To wait for, await; to look out for expectantly; = attend *v.* 13; also, to watch, observe (*obs.*); in *dial.* use, to watch for and scare away (birds), = tent *v.*[1] 6.

1604 T. Wright *Passions* v. §3. 182 Then tend thy turne, when neighbors housen burne. **1669** Sturmy *Mariner's Mag.* ii. xiv. 85 Tending the Sun until he be upon the Meridian. **1675** Bunyan *Light in Darkn.* 178 Now the Soul can tend to look about it, and thus consider with it self. **1818** Keats *Endymion* ii. 185 By all the stars That tend thy bidding. **1875** *Sussex Gloss.* s.v., He goos to work rook-tending, and he comes home of nights that hoarse that you can't hardly hear him speak.

†**b.** *absol.* or *intr.* To wait in expectation or readiness; = attend *v.* 16. *Obs.*

1602 Shaks. *Ham.* i. iii. 83 The time inuites you, goe, your seruants tend. *Ibid.* iv. iii. 47 The Barke is readie, and the winde at helpe, Th' Associates tend.

7. To have it in the mind as a purpose *to do* something; = intend *v.* 18. (Cf. attend *v.* IV.) *Obs.* exc. *dial.* (After 1500 chiefly *Sc.*)

1340–70 *Alex. & Dind.* 1128 Now tende we to touche more of þis tale. *c* **1500** *Melusine* 128 We tende & purpose to gyue bataylle to the Sawdan. **1525** *Sc. Acts Jas. V* (1814) II. 293/2, I neuir as ȝit did hir grace ony harme..nor neuer tendis to do. **1580** *Reg. Privy Council Scot.* III. 291 Tending ..to be fugitive fra the law. *a* **1615** *Cron. Erlis of Ross* (1850) 6 The sepulture of his fathers, quhair he tendit to be buryed. **1897** R. M. Gilchrist *Peakland Faggot* 95 I'm tendin' to do well for them. **1900** N. Lloyd *Chronic Loafer* i. 13 [U.S.], I didn't 'tend to open it.

†**8.** *trans.* To understand or apprehend (a matter, a word, etc.); = intend *v.* IV, ME. *entende*, F. *entendre*. *Obs.*

c **1375** *Cursor M.* 21803 (Fairf.) Qua-sim þis tale can beter tende [*Cott.* a-tend] For cristis loue he hit amende. *c* **1450** Holland *Howlat* 434 The siluer in the samyn half, trewly to tend, Is cleir corage in armes.

Hence ˈ**tending** *vbl. sb.*[1] and *ppl. a.*; **tending-string**, a leading-string; **tending boy**, a boy employed to 'tend' or scare birds.

1605 Shaks. *Macb.* i. v. 38 One of my fellowes..almost dead for breath..Giue him tending, He brings great newes. **1816** T. Chalmers in Hanna *Mem.* (1849) II. iv. 81 The shrubbery, in absence of the tending hand, had become a tangled wilderness. **1821** Clare *Vill. Minstr.* II. 73 The cowboy..Leading tam'd cattle in their tending-strings. **1865** Dickens *Mut. Fr.* iii. viii, In its tending of the sick. **1898** *Agric. Gaz.* 7 Mar. 276/3, I am dressing the seed with tar, otherwise tending boys would be at a premium. **1909** *Lady's Realm* Feb. 466/1 The large log-house..and the tending slaves.

tend (tɛnd), *v.*[2] Forms: 6–7 **tende**, 6 *Sc.* **teind**, 4– **tend**. See also tent *v.*[5] [In branch I, a. F. *tendre* (11th c.):—L. *tendĕre* to stretch, stretch out, extend, also intr. for *tendere cursum*, *gressum*, *passus*, to direct one's course, one's steps, to proceed in any direction. The main sense-development took place in L. and F., and the Eng. sense-groups II and III have been taken in at different times, and not in logical order.]

I. To have a motion or disposition to move towards, and derived senses. [= OF. *tendre* (11th c.), L. *tendĕre* intr.]

1. *intr.* To direct one's course, make one's way, move or proceed towards something.

a. *lit.* of persons or things in motion. *Obs.* or *arch.*

c **1350** *Will. Palerne* 1781 To me tended þei nouȝt, but tok forþ here wey wilfulli to sum wildernesse. **1426** Lydg. *De Guil. Pilgr.* 10797 Wheder that euery goode Pylgryme Tendyth in his pylgrymage. **1500–20** Dunbar *Poems* lxix. 29 Tending to ane uther place, A journay going everie day. **1667** Milton *P.L.* i. 183 Thither let us tend From off the tossing of these fiery waves. **1745** *Paraphr. Sc. Ch.* xxvii. xi, As the Rains from Heaven distil Nor thither tend again.

b. Of a road, course, journey, series of things.

1574 *Calr. Scott. Papers* V. 9 Leith wes his port quhair-unto his course teindit. **1703** Moxon *Mech. Exerc.* 256 Arches..whose Joints tend to the Center. **1863** Hawthorne *Our Old Home* (1879) 64 A green lane..tended towards a square, gray tower. **1873** Black *Pr. Thule* xxv, Understanding that their voyage should tend in that direction.

c. *intr.* To have a natural inclination to move (in some direction). (Cf. 2, 3.)

1641 Wilkins *Math. Magick* i. ii. (1648) 12 Whereby condensed bodies do of themselves tend downwards. **1711** Pope *Temp. Fame* 429 As weighty bodies to the centre tend. **1776** Adam Smith *W.N.* iv. vii. (1869) II. 217 That part of the capital..which..tended and inclined, if I may say so, towards the East India trade. **1828** Hutton *Course Math.* II. 140 The power or force in moving bodies, by which they continually tend from their present places. **1834** Mrs. Somerville *Connex. Phys. Sc.* xxxvii. (1849) 432 Though the stars in every region of the sky tend towards a point in Hercules.

2. *fig.* **a.** *intr.* To have a disposition to advance, go on, come finally, or attain *to* (*unto*, *towards*) some point in time, degree, quality, state, or other non-material category; to be drawn *to* or *towards* in affection.

c **1374** Chaucer *Boeth.* i. pr. vi. 17 (Camb. MS.) Remembres thow..whider þat the entensy[o]n of alle kynde tendeth? *c* **1440** *Gesta Rom.* lv. 238 (Harl. MS.) Whenne I saide þat oþer was thi childe, þou tendeist al to him, and dispisidist þat oþere. **1538** Elyot, *Specto*.., to behold,..to tende to some conclusion. **1581** Pettie *Guazzo's Civ. Conv.* iii. (1586) 127b, Nature alwaies tendeth to the best. **1659** Pearson *Creed* (1839) 110 Towards the setting of the sun, when the light of the world was tending unto a night of darkness. **1776** Burke *Corr.* (1844) II. 96 It is to this point all their speeches, writings, and intrigues of all sorts, tend. **1818** Cruise *Digest* (ed. 2) VI. 517 The trust being expressly limited for life, the same did not tend to a perpetuity. **1893** J. A. Hodges *Elem. Photogr.* (1907) 157 Their use.. certainly tends in the direction of uniformity.

b. *tending to*, approaching (in quality, colour, etc.); having a tendency to.

1600 Hakluyt *Voy.* III. 51 A temperate aire rather tending to cold. **1615** W. Lawson *Country Housew. Gard.* (1626) 18 A faire and broad leafe, in colour tending to a greenish yellow.

3. a. *intr.* To have a specified result, if allowed to act; to lead or conduce *to* some state or condition. Const. *to*, rarely *against*.

1560 Bible (Genev.) *Prov.* x. 16 The labour of the righteous tendeth to life. **1615** G. Sandys *Trav.* 289 The place doth not greatly tend vnto tranquillity. **1729** Law *Serious C.* xxii. (1732) 441 [Not to] do anything to us, but what certainly tended to our benefit. **1818** Cruise *Digest* (ed. 2) IV. 558 The register acts would tend much more to the security of purchasers and mortgagees..if it were established [etc.]. **1847** Helps *Friends in C.* i. iii. 34 To indulge in despair as a habit..manifestly tends against nature. **1868** Farrar *Silence & V.* ii. (1875) 35 We know that righteousness tendeth to life.

b. To lead or conduce to some action.

(*a*) Const. *to* with noun of action.

1565 *Reg. Privy Council Scot.* I. 36 Tending to the furthsetting of thair Majesteis autoritie. **1651** Hobbes *Leviath.* ii. xxiii. 126 Other acts tending to the conservation of the Peace. **1765** Blackstone *Comm.* I. xv. 422 Such declaration cannot now tend to the reformation of the parties. **1849** Macaulay *Hist. Eng.* iv. I. 484 None of them said anything tending to his vindication. **1874** Green *Short Hist.* ii. §5. 82 The King's reforms tended directly to the increase of the royal power.

(*b*) Const. *to* with *inf.* Now usu. in weakened sense: To have a tendency, to be apt or inclined.

1604 Bacon *Apol.* Wks. 1879 I. 436 A sonnet directly tending and alluding to draw on her Majesty's reconcilement to my lord. **1662** Stillingfl. *Orig. Sacr.* iii. iv. §10 It may further tend to clear the truth of the Scriptures. **1710** *Lond. Gaz.* No. 4688/2 All the..Warlike Preparations..tended only to amuse the King of Sweden. **1800** *Med. Jrnl.* IV. 337 If they tend in the least to diminish the sufferings of the child. **1851** Carpenter *Man. Phys.* (ed. 2) 378 It tends to undergo a rapid and complete degeneration. **1879** M. Arnold *Mixed Ess., Democr.* 10 To live in a society of equals tends..to make a man's spirits expand. **1936** J. Cary *African Witch* ii. 38 Obstinacy and stupidity are things that tend to annoy quick-minded and intelligent people. **1956** H. L. Mencken *Minority Report* 251 Unfortunately, the machine thus devised to halt heresy also tends to halt progress. **1976** M. Machlin *Pipeline* xxxiii. 372 After the initial uproar over the Wainwright raid, the papers tended to ignore it. **1981** *Daily Tel.* 26 Aug. 11/2 She went to Oxford to read English. 'I didn't really want to, but I tended to do what my parents advised then.'

4. *Naut.* **a.** Of a ship at anchor: To swing round with the turn of the tide or wind.

1770 Cook *Voy. round World* iii. ix. (1773) III. 651 In the mean time, as the ship tended, I weighed anchor. **1776, 1867** [see *tending* below]. **1794** *Rigging & Seamanship* II. 299 The ship begins to tend to leeward. **1828** Webster, *Tend*..to swing round an anchor, as a ship.

b. *trans.* (app. a causal use of prec.; in quot. 1867, erroneously associated with tend *v.*[1] 6).

1794 *Rigging & Seamanship* II. 300 To tend a ship for a weather tide. The simplest way of tending a ship, is to keep each tide to leeward of her anchor. **1815** Burney *Falconer's Dict. Marine* 553/1 To *Tend*..is to turn or swing a ship round when at single anchor, or moored by the head in a tide-way, at the beginning of the flood or ebb. *Ibid.*, To Tend a Ship with the Wind a few points across the Tide. **1867** Smyth *Sailor's Word-bk.*, *Tend*, to watch a vessel at anchor on the turn of a tide, and cast her by the helm, and some sail if necessary, so as to keep the cable clear of the anchor or turns out of her cables when moored.

II. [= F. *tendre.*]

†**5. a.** *trans.* To offer, proffer; *spec.* in *Law* = tender *v.*[1] 1. *Obs.*

1475 *Rolls of Parlt.* VI. 148/1 Uppon the same Travers tended, or title shewed. **1483–4** *Act 1 Rich. III*, c. 6 §1 The seid defendaunt..may..tende an issue [F. *de tendre issue*], that the same contract..was not..made within the feire tyme. **1529** *Act 21 Hen. VIII*, c. 5 §1 Suche testament beyng laufully tended or offred to them to be proved.

b. To furnish, provide, supply; to reach or hand (a thing) to some one. *Obs.* exc. *dial.*

1579 Lyly *Euphues* (Arb.) 130 Dilligent in tending and prouiding all things necessary. **1882** Jago *Cornwall Gloss.* s.v., One boy tended the stones as the other threw them at the apples.

†**6.** *intr.* To extend, stretch, or reach (*to* a point, or in a particular direction). Also *fig.* *Obs.*

1604 E. G[rimstone] *D'Acosta's Hist. Indies* vi. vi. 444 All the knowledge of the Chinois, tendes only to reade and write, and no farther. **1630** *R. Johnson's Kingd. & Commw.* 223 That huge tract of Land, which tendeth from Cape Aguer, to Cape Guardafu. **1725** De Foe *Voy. round World* (1840) 145 The land tending to the west.

III. [Later senses from F. *tendre* and L. *tendĕre*.]

†**7.** *trans.* To stretch, make tense or taut; to set (a trap, snare, etc.). *Obs.*

1646 H. LAWRENCE *Comm. Angells* 45 Their nets are alwayes spread; they tende their snares alwayes. **1677** PLOT *Oxfordsh.* 289 The longer, or less tended, any string is, the farther it moves. **1799**, **1834** [see TENDED *ppl. a.*[2]].

†**8.** To bend or direct (one's steps): cf. L. *tendere gressum, passus. Obs.*

1611 RICH *Honest. Age* (Percy Soc.) 17 Whether will you tend your steppes. *a* **1644** QUARLES *Sol. Recant.* ch. III. xx, Both tend Their paces to the self-same Journies end.

†**9.** To relate or refer to; to concern. (*trans.*, or *intr.* with *to.*) *Obs.*

1571 SIR R. LANE in *Euccleuch MSS.* (Hist. MSS. Comm.) I. 224, I have received your letter with a packet... The matter which they do tend indeed requireth speed. **1576** FLEMING *Panopl. Epist.* 156 My taulke tendeth to matters of such moment and weight. **1647** N. BACON *Disc. Govt. Eng.* I. lxxi. (1739) 196 The rule foregoing tended only to Freemen and their Lands. **1654** MARVELL *Corr.* Wks. (Grosart) II. 11 Which I attributed to our dispatch, and some other businesse tendinge thereto.

Hence **'tending** *vbl. sb.*[2]

1587 GOLDING *De Mornay* ii. (1592) 18 The whole worlde and all things contayned therein, do by their tending vnto vs, teach vs to tend vnto one alone. **1846** D. KING *Lord's Supper* vi. 175 It is all outward in its tendings.

b. *Naut.* **1776** FALCONER *Dict. Marine, Tending*, the movement by which a ship turns or swings round her anchor in a tide-way, at the beginning of the flood or ebb. **1867** SMYTH *Sailor's Word-bk., Tending*, the movement by which a ship turns or swings round when at single anchor, or moored by the head, at every change of tide or wind.

tend, obs. f. TEIND *sb.* and *v.*, tithe; earlier form of TIND *v. Obs.*, to kindle.

†**'tendable**, *a. Obs.* [f. TEND *v.*[1] + -ABLE: cf. *suitable.*] Ready to give attention; attentive.

c **1450** [implied in TENDABLY]. **1509** HAWES *Joyf. Medit.* xxvii, Vnto our souerayne be meke and tendable. **1530** PALSGR. 327/1 Tendable, as one that dothe wayte well ..*ententif.* **1533** MORE *Debell. Salem* Wks. 943/2 Good sad honeste vertuous wydowes, that wolde be tendable & tender to sicke folke. **1547** BOORDE *Brev. of Health* Pref. 5 Let euery person be tendable aboute theym [physicians] and do as they shall commaunde them. **1654** GAYTON *Pleas. Notes* IV. ii. 180 Wherein shee is very tendable, and handy.

So †**'tendably** *adv.*, attentively, with care.

c **1450** in Aungier *Syon* (184c) 312 Eche of them schal enforme suche as be assygned to them..charitably and tendably.

Tendai ('tɛndaɪ). [a. Jap., ad. Chinese *T'ient'ai*, the name of the mountain in S.E. China where the doctrines were formulated.] A Buddhist sect introduced into Japan from China by the monk Saichō (767–822), founded by Zhi Yi (515–97) and characterized by elaborate ritual, moral idealism, and philosophical eclecticism.

1727 J. G. SCHEUCHZER tr. *Kæmpfer's Hist. Japan* I. I. viii. 106 Not far from this hot Bath is a Monastery of the sect of *Tendai.* **1833** *Chinese Repository* (1834) Nov. II. 323 There are now in Japan the following sects which are tolerated by government. 1. Zen... 2. Zyoodo .. 4. Tendai. **1880** E. J. REED *Japan* I. iv. 91 The Tendai, founded by the priest Saicho, under Kuwammu. **1894** *Trans. Asiatic Soc. Japan* XXII. 382 This comprehensiveness ensured the success of the Tendai Sect. **1938** D. T. SUZUKI *Zen Buddhism & its Influence on Japanese Culture* I. ii. 23 The philosophy of Tendai is too abstract and abstruse to be understood by the masses. **1973** *Times Lit. Suppl.* 2 Mar. 237/4 Something of the awe Tendai ritual inspired can still be felt by the visitor to the Komponchudo on Hiei-san.

tendance ('tɛndəns). Also 8–9 (*improperly*) **tendence**. [Aphetic form of ATTENDANCE, or sometimes f. TEND *v.*[1] + -ANCE.]

1. The attending to, or looking after, anything; tending, attention, care.

1573 TUSSER *Husb.* (1878) 128 Hops dried in loft, aske tendance oft. **1667** MILTON *P.L.* VIII 47 They at her coming sprung And toucht by her fair tendance gladlier grew. **1790** H. BOYD *Ruins of Athens*, What cautious care The propagation, tendence, nutriment Of this ethereal seminary claim. **1835** TRENCH *Justin Martyr*, etc. (1862) 17 That by careful watering And earnest tendance we might bring The bud, the blossom and the fruit. **1897** *Scotsman* 10 Nov. 8/4 The working and tendence of every machine..should be reserved for its members.

b. The object of care or attention. *rare*[−1].

1645 MILTON *Tetrach.* I. Wks. 1851 IV. 153 Whether it [loneliness] be a thing, or the want of somthing, I labour not; let it be their tendance, who have the art to be industriously idle.

2. The bestowal of personal attention and care; ministration to the sick or weak.

1578 *Chr. Prayers* in *Priv. Prayers* (Parker Soc.) 544 That I may not have need of so great strength, tendance, and cunning. **1683** KENNETT tr. *Erasm. on Folly* 42 How troublesome our tendance in the cradle. **1760–72** H. BROOKE *Fool of Qual.* (1809) IV. 39 My..affectionate tendance shall.. compensate for my want of address. **1876** GEO. ELIOT *Dan. Der.* lxvi, His daughter's dutiful tendance.

b. Attendants collectively; train or retinue.

1607 SHAKS. *Timon* I. i. 80 All those.. Follow his strides, his Lobbies fill with tendance. **1814** SCOTT *Ld. of Isles* III. vii, Now torch and menial tendance led Chieftain and knight to bower and bed. **1868** GEO. ELIOT *Sp. Gipsy* I. 113, I shall send tendance as I pass, to bear This casket to your chamber.

†**3.** Waiting in expectation. *Obs.*

1591 SPENSER *M. Hubberd* 908 Unhappie wight.. That doth his life in so long tendance spend.

tendance, obs. form of TENDENCE.

†**'tendancy.** *Obs. rare*[−1]. In 8 (*improp.*) -ency. [f. TEND *v.*[1] + -ANCY.] Attention, care.

a **1774** TUCKER *Lt. Nat.* (1834) II. 86 Man..may, indeed, contrive machines that shall go a little way in performing his works;..but then they require correcting, repairing, and continual tendency.

'tendant, *a.* and *sb. arch.* Also 4 -aunt, 7 (*improp.*) -ent. [Aphetic f. ATTENDANT.]

A. *adj.* Attending, giving attention or service, waiting (upon).

13.. *Cursor M.* 15034 (Gött.) Thre hundreth men and wiuis, þat desseli bath late and are þar tendant to þe apostlisware. **1387** TREVISA *Higden* (Rolls) III. 279 Socrates, þat was alway tendaunt to a spirit þat was i-cleped demon. **1592** WARNER *Alb. Eng.* VIII. xliii. (1612) 206 Henry the second vpon whom the Scotch-King tendant was. **1824** WIFFEN *Tasso* II. lvii, Tendant on each knight Rode many a page and armour-bearer bold.

B. *sb.* An attendant.

1586 DAY *Eng. Secretary* II. (1625) 111 A farre other end and purpose, then of euery ordinary tendant is commonly required. **1614** T. ADAMS *Devil's Banquet* 24 Great men are vnmercifull to their Tenants, that they may be ouermercifull to their Tencents; that stretch them as fast as they retch the others. **1632** VICARS *Æneid* IV. 114 Her tendants saw her fal'n upon her sword.

tendant, obs. f. TENDENT *a.*, tending.

tende, obs. f. TEIND; var. TIND *v. Obs.*, to kindle, TINE *v.*[1], to enclose.

'tended, *ppl. a.*[1] [f. TEND *v.*[1] + -ED[1].] Attended to, looked after, cared for.

1667 MILTON *P.L.* V. 22 Mark how spring Our tended Plants. **1866** NEALE *Sequences & Hymns* 82 Year by year, the steeple-music O'er the tended graves shall pour.

†**'tended**, *ppl. a.*[2] *Obs.* [f. TEND *v.*[2] 7 + ED[1].] Stretched; taut, tense.

1799 YOUNG in *Phil. Trans.* XC. 134 It may be proved, that every impulse is communicated along a tended chord with an uniform velocity. **1834** MRS. SOMERVILLE *Connex. Phys. Sc.* xvii. (1849) 164 A body vibrating near insulated tended strings.

tendence ('tɛndəns). Now *rare* and *literary*. Also 7–8 -ance. [ad. med.L. *tendentia* (Bonaventura *a* 1274, Duns Scotus *a* 1308), f. L. *tendentem*, pr. pple. of *tendĕre*: see TEND *v.*[2] and -ENCE: cf. F. *tendance* (12th c. in Godef. *Compl.*).] = next.

1. = TENDENCY I.

1627 SANDERSON *Serm.* I. 259 There shall appear..a direct tendance to the advancement of Gods glory. **1669** GALE *Crt. Gentiles* I. I. i. 7 The scope and tendence of this Discourse is to Demonstrate, that [etc.]. **1714** R. FIDDES *Pract. Disc.* II. 219 Afflictions have..a tendence to promote our spiritual good. **1833** SARAH AUSTIN *Charac. Goethe* II. 331 A melancholy proof of the modern realistic tendence.

†**2.** = TENDENCY I b. Also *fig. Obs.*

1644 DIGBY *Nat. Bodies* xi. (1658) 116 These atoms..are forced from the complete effect of their tendance, by the violence of the current. **1645** OWEN *Two Catech.* xii. Wks. 1855 I. 482 *note*, The death that Christ underwent was eternal in its own nature and tendence. **1698** TYSON in *Phil. Trans.* XX. 118 The Tendence or Direction of the Muscular Fibres of this Pair.

b. *attrib.*: **tendence-writing**, a writing with a purpose (Ger. *tendenz-schrift*). Cf. TENDENCY 3.

1875 M. ARNOLD in *Contemp. Rev.* XXV. 968 Our Gospels are more or less *Tendenz-Schriften*, tendence-writings,—writings to serve an aim or bent of their several authors.

tendence, -ency, obs. ff. TENDANCE, -ANCY.

tendencious, variant of TENDENTIOUS.

tendency ('tɛndənsɪ). [f. as TENDENCE: see -ENCY.]

1. a. The fact or quality of tending to something; a constant disposition to move or act in some direction or toward some point, end, or purpose; leaning, inclination, bias, or bent toward some object, effect, or result.

1628 T. SPENCER *Logick* 53 If any inquire how tendency.. can haue an actuall exercise vnto doing. **1671** FLAVEL *Fount. Life* vii, He did not..do an Act..but it had some Tendency to promote the great Design of our Salvation. **1679** C. NESSE *Antid. agst. Popery* Ded. 6 Gods prevalent actings, in tendency to our deliverance. *c* **1680** BUTLER *Rem.* (1759) II. 185 He seldom converses but with Men of his own Tendency. **1710** J. CLARKE *Rohault's Nat. Phil.* (1729) I. 80 A Body in Motion has always a Tendency to describe that Line, which it would describe if it were at liberty. **1778** [W. MARSHALL] *Minutes Agric.* 13 Sept. an. 1774, Placed..with their points tending forward, the line of their tendency making an angle with the horizon of about 45°. **1806** A. HUNTER *Culina* (ed. 3) 104 Where there is a gouty tendency, this dish must seldom be indulged in. **1870** JEVONS *Elem. Logic* xxxi. 267 A tendency..is a cause which may or may not be counteracted. **1870** J. H. NEWMAN *Gram. Assent* II. viii. 313 A regular polygon, inscribed [in a circle], its sides being continually diminished, tends to become that circle, as its limit; but..its tendency to be the circle, though ever nearer fulfilment, never in fact gets beyond a tendency.

†**b.** Movement or advance in the direction of something; a making toward something. *Obs.*

1654 Z. COKE *Logick* A ij, As if the Donations of Heaven were opposed, subordinated in mans tendency to Bliss and Glory. **1661** BLOUNT *Glossogr.* (ed. 2), *Tendency*..a going forward, a making toward. **1721** BRADLEY *Philos. Acc. Wks. Nat.* 1 Which time of their Tendency to Perfection I shall.. call the Time of their Growth.

c. Drift, trend, or aim of a discourse; in recent use, conscious or designed purpose of a story, novel, or the like. (= Ger. *tendenz.*)

1732 BERKELEY *Alciphr.* II. §21 Upon hearing this, and other lectures of the same tendency. **1751** JOHNSON *Rambler* No. 153 ¶2 My narrative has no other tendency than to illustrate and corroborate your own observations. **1791** BURKE *App. Whigs* Wks. VI. 132 Neither can they shew any thing in the general tendency and spirit of the whole work unfavourable to a rational and generous spirit of liberty. **1832** HT. MARTINEAU *Demerara* i. 12 The tendency of all he said was to prove his own merits.

d. *pl.* in pregnant use, tendencies towards homosexuality. *colloq.*

1938 J. BETJEMAN *Oxf. Univ. Chest* ii. 42 Someone who has 'tendencies' as an undergraduate, will in ten years time be settled down to married life. **1958** L. DURRELL *Balthazar* ii. 32 Now the Egyptians, they don't give a damn about a man if he has Tendencies.

e. *Pol.* [Infl. by F. *tendance.*] A political association within a larger party or movement, esp. a left-wing group within a socialist party.

1974 J. WHITE tr. *Poulantzas's Fascism & Dictatorship* IV. ii. 171 The communists of the Ruhr, a left tendency, went into combat in isolation in April. **1977** *Politics of Militant* 1 The tendency grouped around the weekly paper 'Militant' has grown considerably in recent years. It absolutely dominates the Labour Party Young Socialists. **1980** *Times* 14 Jan. 1/4 The 'Militant Tendency', a clandestine Trotskyist organization, with its own full-time staff, whose aims are to penetrate the Labour Party. **1981** *Daily Tel.* 10 Dec. 32/5 The arguments of the tendency and other Marxist, Leninist, Stalinist and Trotskyist groups.

†**2.** A relation *to*, or bearing upon something.

1651 BAXTER *Inf. Bapt.* 195 They will say that all their obedience hath no other tendency to their salvation and finall Absolution, but as meer signs.

3. *attrib.* and *Comb.* ***tendency drama, novel, story***, one composed with an unexpressed but definite purpose [after Ger. *tendenz-drama, -roman*, etc.]; ***tendency wit*** [after Ger. *tendenzwitz*].

1838 DE MORGAN *Ess. Probab.* 23 They may all be referred either to that [assertion] just made, or to a tendency argument of the same character. **1889** JACOBS *Æsop* 206 The Fable..is a Moral Tendency-Beast-Droll. **1909** *Cent. Dict.* Suppl., *Tendency theory*..the theory of the Tübingen school that the books of the New Testament..were put together for the purpose of upholding current opinions, and that they thus have a 'tendency'. **1916** A. A. BRILL tr. *Freud's Wit & its Relation to Unconscious* iii. 138 By virtue of its purpose, the tendency-wit has at its disposal sources of pleasure to which harmless wit has no access. **1954** D. RIESMAN *Individualism Reconsidered* (1955) xxii. 349 The id expresses its criticism by what Freud called tendency-wit, but then turns to its masters with a smile, saying, 'After all, ..it's only a joke.' **1964** M. WOHLGELERNTER *Israel Zangwill* vi. 87 A determination to self-criticism that Freud called 'tendency-wit'.

tendent ('tɛndənt), *a.* Now *rare*. Also 4–7 -ant, 6 -aunt. [a. OF. *tendant*, pr. pple. of *tendre* to stretch, to proceed: see TEND *v.*[2]] Tending, having a tendency (*to* or *towards* some end). *Obs.* before 18th c.; revived late in 19th.

a **1340** HAMPOLE *Psalter* iv. 9 It is tendant in til lastandnes and vnchaungeable ioy. **1512** *Helyas* in Thoms *Prose Rom.* (1828) III. 92 Tendaunt to the ende to take and holde in his hande the said duchy. **1657** *Divine Lover* 14 Wee..shal remayne vnable as not tendant towards our foresaid end. **1900** STODDARD *Evol. Eng. Novel* 103 The historical novel is magnetized history in which every fact is quiveringly tendent toward some focal pole of unity.

tendent, obs. var. TENDANT.

tendential (tɛn'dɛnʃəl), *a.* [f. as next + -AL[1].] Of the nature of, or characterized by having, a tendency; *spec.* = next.

1847 J. D. MORELL *Hist. Philos.* (ed. 2) II. vii. 396 He [*sc.* Buchez] has brought to his aid the notion of progress, the logical development of ideas, and the tendential movements of society. **1889** J. M. ROBERTSON *Ess. Crit. Method* Pref. 3 A division of thinking men into tendential parties, in each of which there is a substantial agreement, resulting in different degrees from bias, prejudice, and reasoning towards consistency. **1904** *Amer. Jrnl. Relig.*, etc. May 75 (Cent. D., Supp.) Deliverance..from the power of those other tendential ideas against which he has been struggling.

tendentious (tɛn'dɛnʃəs), *a.* Also -cious. [as if f. med.L. *tendenti-a* TENDENCY + -OUS, after G. *tendenziös.*] Having a purposed tendency; composed or written with such a tendency or aim.

1900 T. DAVIDSON *Hist. Educ.* I. iv. 70 Xenophon's *Cyropædia*..is a mere edifying, tendentious romance, intended to recommend to the Athenians the Spartan type of education. **1905** *Times, Lit. Suppl.* 28 July 239/2 He [Zimmer, in 'Die Keltische Kirche'] thinks that the legend of St. Patrick was tendencious, springing up to support a special ecclesiastical thesis. **1909** C. LOWE in *Contemp. Rev.* July 42 A false and tendencious account of what had taken place.

tendentiously (tɛn'dɛnʃəslɪ), *adv.* [f. TENDENTIOUS *a.* + -LY[2].] In a tendentious manner; with a purposed tendency or aim. So **ten'dentiousness**.

1920 *Glasgow Herald* 9 Apr. 8 This was not due to any tendenciousness on the part of official reports. **1924** *History* Oct. 215 If we could..speak with our enemies in the gate, we should doubtless teach geography.. tendenciously. **1946** *Law. Rep.* 2 Mar. 265 One may perhaps describe the two sides, as little tendentiously as possible, [etc.]. **1966** *Listener* 17 Nov. 745/1 Confessions on the telephone,..and witnesses complaining they were not allowed to say what they wanted to say at the trial. As an exercise in tendentiousness it would be hard to beat. **1983** *Washington Post* 2 Oct. C1/4 The result is a book of findings, tendentiously presented. *Ibid.* 11 Oct. C3/3 The tendentiousness of 'The Final Option' may come as a perversely amusing shock.

‖**tendenz** (tɛn'dɛnts). [Ger., ad. Eng. TENDENCE or F. *tendance*.] = TENDENCY 1 c.

1896 A. W. SMALL *Let.* 22 May in *Social Forces* (1935) Mar. 337/2 Its connotations are to my mind necessarily with some 'Tendenz' which is exploited. **1951** A. L. ROWSE *England of Eliz.* ix. 379 One sees the *tendenz* of this... Coke's view was extremely tendencious, but the *tendenz* was good: it was all in favour of the supremacy of law in the State and of the liberty of the subject. **1967** G. STEINER *Lang. & Silence* 336 He argues that the type of *Tendenz*..which Engels would find acceptable is..'identical with that "Party element" which materialism..encloses in itself'.

Also **ten'denzro,man** [G. *roman* novel] = *tendency novel* s.v. TENDENCY 3, *roman à thèse* s.v. ROMAN *sb.*[4]; similarly, with partial translation, **tendenz novel**.

1855 GEO. ELIOT in *Westm. Rev.* July 294 'Constance Herbert' is a *Tendenz-roman*; the characters and incidents are selected with a view to the enforcement of a principle. **1896** J. JACOBS *Jewish Ideals & Other Essays* p. xii, George Eliot's novels..were to us *Tendenz-Romane*, and we studied them as much for the *Tendenz* as for the *Roman*. *a* **1896** G. DU MAURIER *Martian* (1897) ix. 396 The elderly..virgins who knew nothing of life but what they had read..in 'Tendenz' novels. **1917** A. WAUGH *Loom of Youth* ii, I was surprised to find that my young friend..had harnessed his views..to the philosophic poem and the *tendenz* novel of the latest phase of fictional evolution. **1975** *Listener* 18 Dec. 819/2 *Oliver Twist*..has suffered more than some of the others... Humphrey House, the eminent Dickens critic, said that it was the closest thing to a *tendenzroman* that Dickens ever wrote, and yet..very little of that political quality survives.

tender ('tɛndə(r)), *sb.*[1] Also 5 **-our**. [f. TEND *v.*[1] + -ER[1], or aphetic form of ATTENDER.]

1. †One who tends, or waits upon, another; an attendant, nurse, ministrant (*obs.*); a waiter; an assistant to a builder or other skilled workman (*dial.*).

c **1470** HENRYSON *Orpheus & Eur.* 20 The anseane and sad wyse men of Age Wer tendouris to ȝung and Insolent, To mak þame in all vertewis excellent. **1601** R. JOHNSON *Kingd. & Commw.* 139 Two hundred horsemen in Moscouie, require three hundred packehorses, and so many tenders, who must all be fedde. **1637** BRIAN *Pisse-Proph.* iii. (1679) 25 Some nurse or tender of sick persons. **1683** TRYON *Way to Health* 285 As Waiters, Tenders or Servitors to execute and obey the Commands of the Spirit of the Lord. *a* **1825** FORBY *Voc. E. Anglia, Tender*, a waiter at a public table, or place of entertainment. *c* **1830** *Glouc. Farm Rep.* 11 in *Libr. Usef. Knowl., Husb.* III, On the other rick there are one or two builders, with a sufficiency of tenders to carry on the work with expedition and efficiency. **1880** *W. Cornw. Gloss., Tendar*, a waiter at an inn; the guard of a train.

2. One who attends to, or has charge of, a machine, a business, etc., as ***bar-tender*** (a barman), ***bridge-tender, machine-tender***; now esp. *U.S.*

1825 J. NICHOLSON *Operat. Mechanic* 671 That the engine tender may not be at a loss when to throw his machinery into geer. **1856** EMERSON *Eng. Traits* vi. 107 The machines.. prove too much for their tenders. **1883** *Daily News* 16 Oct 6/2 The bar tender [in U.S.]..demanded payment. **1897** RHOSCOMYL *White Rose Arno* 94 'Show thy brass then', said the bridge-tender. **1910** *Times* 18 May 10/2 Dissatisfaction among the power-loom tenders at their scale of pay... The wages of the tenders..were increased to 35*s*.

3. A ship or boat employed to attend a larger one in various capacities. **a.** Originally, A vessel commissioned to attend men-of-war, chiefly for supplying provisions and munitions of war, also for conveying intelligence, dispatches, etc. Subsequently, in the British Royal Navy, A vessel commissioned to act (in any capacity) under the orders of another vessel, her officers and crew being borne on the ship's books of the latter (called the parent ship).

'In current use the term includes torpedo-boats and torpedo-boat destroyers. All the 'destroyers' of a flotilla are technically tenders of the depôt-ship, although this exists merely in order to carry stores for them, and the necessary staff for doing their clerical work' N.E.D.

1675 *Lond. Gaz.* No. 1054/2 Here are arrived five Dutch Men of War, and four Tenders. **1710** *Ibid.* No. 4677/3 Yesterday..came down hither her Majesty's Ship the Lyme, with the Star-Bomb and her Tender. **1732** LEDIARD *Sethos* II. IX. 291 The greater seem'd only to be the retinue or tenders upon the less. **1772** *Hist. Rochester* 18 A tender in the river..employed in pressing seamen. **1812** SHELLEY *Let. to Miss Hitchener* 10 Mar., A Magistrate..gave him the alternative of the tender or of military servitude. **1898** *Whitaker's Almanack* 223/1 Cockchafer, 2nd cl. gunboat.. tender to *Rodney* [1st cl. battle-ship, used as coastguard] Queensferry N.B. **1906** *King's Regul. & Admiralty Instr.* Art. 1802 §2 The Officer in charge of stores in the parent ship is to be responsible, and is to account for stores supplied to the tender. **1910** *Naval & Mil. Rec.* 21 Sept., The Wear, destroyer,..recommissioned..for service in the third (Nore) Destroyer flotilla as tender to the St. George.

b. In general use, A small ship used to carry passengers, luggage, mails, goods, stores, etc., to or from a larger vessel (usually a liner), esp. when not otherwise accessible from shore. Also, in U.S., a boat or ship attending on fishing or whaling ships, to carry supplies to them, and to bring the fish, oil, or whalebone, to the ports or landing-places.

1853 KANE *Grinnell Exp.* xxi. (1856) 162 It was wisely determined by..old Sir John that he would leave the Mary, his tender of twelve tons. **1868** *Daily News* 20 July, As the tender was puffing out to us in Queenstown Harbour. **1887** J. BALL *Nat. in S. Amer.* 28 To go on board a small tender that lay alongside of a half-ruined wharf. **1910** AGNES WESTON *Life among Bluejackets* 54 We waited at the Royal Hotel, Plymouth, for the signal that the tender would shortly put off.

c. *fig.*

1700 CONGREVE *Way of World* II. v, Here she comes, i' faith, full sail, with..a shoal of fools for tenders. **1865** *Even. Standard* 6 June, [A weekly newspaper] a tender to this peculating concern..conducted upon the same principle, or with the same lack of principle. **1889** *Daily News* 27 Dec. 2/3 They are jolly tars and..have a couple of smart-looking tenders [sweethearts] in tow.

4. A carriage specially constructed to carry fuel and water for a locomotive engine, to the rear of which it is attached.

1825 MACLAREN *Railways* 32 *note*, A small waggon bearing water and coals follows close behind the engine, and is called the Tender, i.e. the 'Attender'. **1878** F. S. WILLIAMS *Midl. Railw.* 662 The tender will hold 2320 gallons of water, it has a coal space for 4 tons.

attrib. **1838** *Civil Eng. & Arch. Jrnl.* I. 134/1 The same apparatus may be attached to the tender axles. **1894** *Westm. Gaz.* 6 Feb. 7/2 In the outrush of water from the tender tank. **1897** *Daily News* 1 Sept. 2/2 He applied the vacuum brake and the fireman the tender brake, but could not stop the engine.

5. In specific technical uses: see quots.

1877 KNIGHT *Dict. Mech., Tender*..a small reservoir attached to a mop, scrubber, or similar utensil. **1894** *Northumbld. Gloss., Tender*, in a pit, the former name for a small rapper or signal rope.

tender ('tɛndə(r)), *sb.*[2] Also 6 **tendre, tendour**. [f. TENDER *v.*[1]] An act of tendering.

1. *Law.* **a.** A formal offer duly made by one party to another.

tender of amends, an offer of compensation by the delinquent party. ***tender of issue***, a plea which in effect invites the adverse party to join issue upon it.

1562–3 *Act 5 Eliz.* c. 1 §17 All suche persons shalbee compellable to take the Othe upon the seconde Tender or Offer of the same. **1647** HAMMOND *Power of Keys* iv. 60 This magisteriall affirmation having no tender or offer of proof annext to it. **1768** BLACKSTONE *Comm.* III. i. 15 If tender of amends is made before any action is brought. **1848** WHARTON *Law Lex.* s.v., A tender of satisfaction is allowed to be made in most actions for money demands,..and a tender to one of several joint creditors is sufficient. **1872** *Ibid.* s.v. *Amends, Tender of Amends*, is by particular statutes made a defence in an action for a wrong.

b. *spec.* An offer of money, or the like, in discharge of a debt or liability, *esp.* an offer which thus fulfils the terms of the law and of the liability.

plea of tender, a plea advanced by a defendant that he has always been ready to pay and has tendered to the plaintiff the amount due, which he now produces in court.

1542–3 *Act 34 & 35 Hen. VIII*, c. 2 §2 The same Collectour..as shall so make tendre of all suche money. **1544** tr. *Littleton's Tenures* (1574) 70 Where such lawefull tender of the money is made. **1817** W. SELWYN *Law Nisi Prius* (ed. 4) II. 966 The defendant pleaded non-assumpsit as to all except 3*l.*, and as to that a tender. **1863** A. J. HORWOOD *Yearbks. 30 & 31 Edw. I*, Pref. 26 *note*, The reason for the tender of the demy-mark in a writ of right. **1883** *Wharton's Law Lex.* s.v., By the Coinage Act, 1870.., it is provided that a tender of payment of money, if made in coins legally issued by the Mint..shall be a legal tender.

2. *gen.* An offer of anything for acceptance.

1577 HARRISON *England* Pref., I dare presume to make tendour of the protection thereof vnto your Lordships hands. **1602** SHAKS. *Ham.* I. iii. 100 O. He hath my Lord of late made many tenders Of his affection to me. *P.*.. Doe you beleeue his tenders, as you call them? **1761–2** HUME *Hist. Eng.* (1806) V. lxxi. 286 [He] made a tender of his sword and purse to the prince of Orange. **1855** MACAULAY *Hist. Eng.* xiii. III. 287 They had not yet been put into possession of the royal authority by a formal tender and a formal acceptance. **1871** R. ELLIS tr. *Catullus* l. 6 Tenders jocular o'er the merry wine-cup.

3. *Comm.* **a.** An offer made in writing by one party to another (usually to a public body) to execute, at an exclusive price or uniform rate, an order for the supply or purchase of goods, or for the execution of work, the details of which have been submitted, often through the public press, by the second party.

1666 PEPYS *Diary* 14 July, The business of Captain Cocke's tender of hempe. **1691** *Lond. Gaz.* No. 2636/3 The Principal Officers and Commissioners of Their Majesties Navy,..will..be ready to receive any Tenders.., and to Treat and Contract with the Tenderers thereof. **1851** MAYHEW *Lond. Labour* I. 291/2 The privilege..is disposed of by tender. **1868** ROGERS *Pol. Econ.* xxiii. (1876) 312 The Government..may fix the sum and invite tenders for the lowest amount of interest at which borrowers will be willing to make the loan. **1882** *Statist* X. 485 The lowest tender was accepted.

b. ***tender offer*** (*U.S.*) (see quot. 1979), usu. for the purpose of obtaining effective control.

1964 J. LOW *Investor's Dict.* 198 In general when an outside interest makes a tender offer the market price rises close to the tender price. **1979** *Yale Law Jrnl.* LXXXVIII. 510 A tender offer is conventionally defined as a public solicitation of the shareholders of a corporation to tender their shares to the offeror at a specified price.

4. (esp. ***legal, lawful***, or ***common tender.***) Money or other things that may be legally tendered or offered in payment; currency prescribed by law as that in which payment may be made.

In the United Kingdom, Bank of England notes are legal tender up to any amount throughout the country; fifty-pence coins are legal tender for sums not exceeding £10; other current cupro-nickel coins for sums not exceeding £5; and current bronze coins for sums not exceeding twenty pence (1988).

1740 W. DOUGLASS *Disc. Curr. Brit. Plant. Amer.* 20 France never made their State Bills a common Tender. **1765** T. HUTCHINSON *Hist. Mass.* I. i. 27 Indian corn..was made a tender in discharge of all debt. **1777** *Jrnls. Amer. Congress* 14 June, Recommended..to pass laws to make the bills of credit, issued by the Congress, a lawful tender, in payments of public and private debts. **1838–42** ARNOLD *Hist. Rome* II. xxvii. 73 Land and cattle became legal tender at a certain fixed rate of value. **1866** CRUMP *Banking* iv. 95 A cheque is not a legal tender, and for that reason may be objected to. **1883** GILMOUR *Mongols* xxxii. 369 In Urga, brick tea and silver are the common tenders.

tender ('tɛndə(r)), *a.* (*adv.*) and *sb.*[3] Forms: 3–6 **tendre**, 4– **tender**; also 4 **teyndir**, 4–5 **tendyr, -ere**, 4–6 (chiefly *Sc.*) **-ir**, 5 **-ire, -ur(e**. [a. F. *tendre* (11th c.) = Pr. *tenre, tendre*, Sp. *tierno*, Pg. *tenro*, It. *tenero*:—L. *tener-um* (nom. *tener*) tender, delicate.]

A. *adj.* **I.** Literal and physical senses.

1. a. Soft or delicate in texture or consistence; yielding easily to force or pressure; fragile; easily broken, divided, compressed, or injured; of food, easily masticated, succulent. †***tender bread***, newly baked bread (*obs.*).

Formerly (and still *dial.*) used in wide sense as a synonym of *soft* (e.g. of stone or coal).

a **1225** *Ancr. R.* 114 Vor his fleschs was al cwic ase is þe tendre eien. *a* **1300** *Cursor M.* 18844 (Cott.) Forked fair þe chin he bare And tender berd wit mikel hare. **13..** *E.E. Allit. P.* B. 630 A calf..þat watz tender & not toȝe. **13..** *Coer de L.* 3413 Eet theroff..As it wer a tendyr chycke. *c* **1400** MAUNDEV. xxxiii. 150 þe tendre erthe was removed fra his place and þare become a valay, and þe hard erthe habade still. **1422** tr. *Secreta Secret., Priv. Priv.* 247 Tendyr brede makyd of the floure of Whete. *a* **1500** *Sir Beues* 2529 (Pynson) Beuys..hyt the dragon vnder the wynge,..There was he tender wythout skale. **1596** DALRYMPLE tr. *Leslie's Hist. Scot.* (S.T.S.) I. 26 The Skout..being sodin,..is maist tendir. **1650** BULWER *Anthropomet.* 186 Their bones being yet tender, soft, and cartilaginious. **1697** DRYDEN *Virg. Georg.* III. 501 The tender Grass, and budding Flower. **1787** BEST *Angling* (ed. 2) 39 He bites very freely, but is often lost when struck, his mouth being very tender. **1793** SMEATON *Edystone L.* §272 Moorstone..being a tender kind of stone in respect to the union of its component parts. **1832** LYELL *Princ. Geol.* II. 281 Many tender and fragile shells. **1881** BINNS *Guide Worc. Porcelain Wks.* (1883) 24 The ware up to this point..is most tender, and can only be handled with the greatest care.

fig. *c* **1386** CHAUCER *Merch. T.* 946, I haue..a soule for to kepe..and also myn honour And of my wyfhod, thilke tendre flour. **1709** STEELE & SWIFT *Tatler* No. 67 ¶12 There is Nothing of so tender a Nature as the Reputation and Conduct of Ladies.

b. Of the ground: Soft with moisture; easily giving way beneath the feet; 'rotten'. *dial.*

1727 D. EATON *Let.* 25 Mar. (1971) 105 He has carted at a very unseasonable time when the ground was tender. **1789** *Trans. Soc. Arts* VII. 68 Some of the lands are so tender, that a board or patten..is fixed to each foot of every horse. **1904** *Eng. Dial. Dict.* s.v. (Warwick), Behand Spetchley the roads was very tender.

c. ***tender porcelain***: soft porcelain; see quots.

1839 URE *Dict. Arts* 1021 There are two species of porcelain..; the one is called hard, and the other tender. *Ibid.* 1022 Tender porcelain, styled also vitreous porcelain ..always consists of a vitreous frit, rendered opaque and less fusible by the addition of a calcareous and marly clay. **1884** KNIGHT *Dict. Mech.* Suppl., *Tender porcelain*, a soft body porcelain made in Europe.

†**2.** Frail, thin, fine, slender. *Obs. rare.*

1390 GOWER *Conf.* III. 52 The happes over mannes hed Ben honged with a tendre thred. **1703** MOXON *Mech. Exerc.* 208 That..it draw not the thin and tender Blade of the Hook into it.

II. Transferred from I.

3. a. Of weak or delicate constitution; not strong, hardy, or robust; unable or unaccustomed to endure hardship, fatigue, or the like; delicately reared, effeminate.

a **1225** *Ancr. R.* 112 Godes fleschs..þet was inumen of þe tendre meldene. **1297** R. GLOUC. (Rolls) 6441 Non byleued nere, Bote is tueye ȝonge sones, þat so feble & tendre were. **1340** *Ayenb.* 31 þou ne miȝt naȝt do þe greate penonces. þou art to tendre. **1382** WYCLIF *Deut.* xxviii. 56 A tendre womman and a delicate. **1484** CAXTON *Fables of Æsop* v. x, I shalle not ete the, For thow sholdest hurte my tendre stomak. **1535** COVERDALE *Susanna* 31 Now Susanna was a tender person, and maruelous fayre of face. **1552** HULOET, Tender man not able to indure hardnes, *effæminatus*. *a* **1627** MIDDLETON *More Dissemblers* III. i, A tender, puling, nice, chitty-fac'd squal 'tis. **1859** TENNYSON *Enid* 395 To stoop and kiss the tender little thumb, That crost the trencher as she laid it down.

b. Of animals or plants: Delicate, easily injured by severe weather or unfavourable conditions; not hardy; needing protection. ***tender annual***, an annual plant needing the protection of a greenhouse all through its life; cf.

hardy annual s.v. HARDY *a.* 4 b; ***tender plant*** (*fig.*), something needing careful nurture if it is to survive and develop.

1614 MARKHAM *Cheap Husb.* VII. xvii. (1668) 121 Turkies when they are young are very tender to bring up. **1657** AUSTEN *Fruit Trees* I. 56 The May-Cherries are tender, the Trees must be set in a warm place. **1769** RUTTER & CARTER *Mod. Eden* II. iv. 218 (*heading*) Of raising tender annuals on hot-beds. **1791** E. DARWIN *Bot. Gard.* I. Note xiv. 27 The bulbs..are found in the perennial herbaceous plants which are too tender to bear the cold of the winter. **1796** C. MARSHALL *Garden.* xii. (1813) 161 Fig trees will mostly survive hard winters, when in standards,..though shoots trained to a wall are tenderer. **1822** J. C. LOUDON *Encycl. Gardening* 1070 The green-house is now filled with tender annuals. **1867** T. BRIDGEMAN *Amer. Gardener's Assistant* III. 21 Varieties from warm climates..may with great propriety be treated as tender annuals, by sowing the seed every spring. **1933** *Discovery* Mar. 76/2 The runner bean..of Mexican parentage or origin is here grown as a tender annual. **1969** *Times* 10 Mar. 10/7 These capital sources are conditioned by..the confidence felt in the future profitability of agriculture. That confidence is, at present, rather a tender plant. **1974** J. WARREN *Macself's Amat. Greenhouse* (ed. 5) viii. 238 The tender annuals of all kinds should be sown in spring rather than autumn. **1978** *U.S. News & World Rep.* 12 June 56/1 Academic and cultural freedom is a very tender plant, which this country has nurtured very effectively.

c. *dial.* In delicate health, weakly, frail.

1645 R. BAILLIE *Let. to G. Young* 8 July, Mr. Henderson is much tenderer than he wont. **1747** WESLEY *Prim. Physic* (1762) p. xviii, Tender People should have those..who are much about them sound and healthy. **1818** SCOTT *Hrt. Midl.* v, I had been tender a' the simmer, and scarce ower the door o' my room for twal weeks. **1864** LD. HOUGHTON *Let.* in *Life* (1891) II. 124 It keeps me rather 'tender' and nervous.

4. Having the weakness and delicacy of youth; not strengthened by age or experience; youthful, immature. Chiefly in phrases ***tender age, years*** (also †***tender of age***).

c **1330** R. BRUNNE *Chron.* (1810) 252 He was tendre & ȝing. **13..** *E.E. Allit. P.* A. 412, I watz ful ȝong & tender of age. **1454** *Rolls of Parlt.* V. 242/1 An Acte made in the tendre age of the Kyng. **1539** BIBLE (Great) *Gen.* xxxiii. 13 My Lorde, Thou knowest, that the chyldren are tendre. **1563** *Homilies* II. *Sacrament* II. (1859) 449 The true Christians in the tender time of Christ's Church called this Supper Love. **1586** *Let. Earle Leycester* 8 Infected with Poperie from her tender youth. **1610** HOLLAND *Camden's Brit.* (1637) 250 He departed this life in his tender yeares. **1732** BERKELEY *Alciphr.* I. §5 Early instruction instilled into our tender minds. **1844** LD. BROUGHAM *Brit. Const.* xix. §3 (1862) 332 The great evil of imprisoning boys and girls of a tender age.

5. In reference to colour or light (rarely, sound): Of fine or delicate quality or nature; soft, subdued; not deep, strong, or glaring.

1503 DUNBAR *Thistle & Rose* 50 The purpour sone, with tendir bemys reid. *c* **1694** PRIOR *Celia to Damon* 67 The tender accents of a woman's cry Will pass unheard. **1754** GRAY *Pleasure* 8 April..Scatters his freshest, tenderest green. **1812** J. WILSON *Isle of Palms* I. 19 A zone of dim and tender light. **1894** FENN *In Alpine Valley* I. 42 The tender green of the young ferns.

6. Of things immaterial, subjects, topics, etc.: Easy to be injured by tactless treatment; needing cautious or delicate handling; delicate, ticklish.

1625 BACON *Ess., Cunning* (Arb.) 437 In Things, that are tender and vnpleasing, it is good to breake the Ice, by some whose Words are of lesse weight. **1647** N. BACON *Disc. Govt. Eng.* I. vi. (1739) 14 The times were too tender to endure them to be declarative on either part. **1725** DE FOE *Voy. round World* (1840) 325 They considered not..upon what tender and ticklish terms their navigation stood. **1821** SCOTT *Kenilw.* xi, Fearful of touching upon a topic too tender to be tampered with.

III. Tender toward or in regard to others.

7. a. Of an action or instrument: Not forcible or rough; gentle, soft; acting or touching gently.

1340-70 *Alex. & Dind.* 952 In tendere touchinge of þing & tastinge of swete. **1592** SHAKS. *Ven. & Ad.* 353 Her other tender hand his faire cheeke feeles: His tendrer cheeke, receiues her soft hands print. **1602** MARSTON *Antonio's Rev.* III. i, I presse you softly with a tender foote. *a* **1628** PRESTON *Breastpl. Faith* (1630) 128 The smoking Flax, he did blow with a tender breath to kindle it more, hee dealt not roughly with it. **1833** COLERIDGE *Table-t.* 30 Aug., The more exquisite and delicate a flower of joy, the tenderer must be the hand that plucks it.

†**b.** Easy; not 'hard' or difficult. *Obs. rare*$^{-1}$.

13.. *Gaw. & Gr. Knt.* 2436 How tender hit is to entyse teches of fylþe.

8. a. Of persons, their feelings, or the expression of these: Characterized by, exhibiting, or expressing delicacy of feeling or susceptibility to the gentle emotions; kind, loving, gentle, mild, affectionate.

tender loving care (*colloq.*), especially solicitous care such as is given by nurses; also *transf.*; ***tender mercies*** (occas. ***tender mercy***) a Biblical phrase usu. used *ironically* (perh. with spec. allusion to quot. 1611) of attention, care, or treatment thought unlikely to be in the best interests of its object; ***the tender passion*** or ***sentiment***, sexual love.

a **1300** *Cursor M.* 24245 (Cott.) Mi suet moder, tender of hert. *c* **1375** *Sc. Leg. Saints* vi. (*Thomas*) 444 Synciane, þat wes vorthy, & tendir frende to mygdony. *c* **1420** *Brut* 346 He kept þat office but iiij wokis, because he was so tendir and gentill vn-to þe cetezens of London. **1534** MORE *Treat. Passion* Wks. 1273/1 The wily wrech perceiued..the tender mynde that the man had to hys make. **1535** COVERDALE *Ps.* xxiv. [xxv.] 6 Call to remembrance, O Lorde, thy tender mercies & thy louing kindnesses. **1576** in Feuillerat *Revels Q. Eliz.* (1908) 416 In tendre consideracion wherof may yt please your honour. **1611** BIBLE *Prov.* xii. 10 A righteous man regardeth the life of his beast: but the tender mercies of the wicked are cruell. **1691** T. H[ALE] *Acc. New Invent.* p. cxxiii, Seamen..are entituled to a more tender Protection from the Crown than other Subjects are. **1775** SHERIDAN *Duenna* I. iii, I delight in the tender passions. **1848** THACKERAY *Van. Fair* xxxvii, His little sisters, in whose welfare she still took the tenderest interest. **1867** *Athenæum* 20 July 77/2 The rivalry of the class-room is unfavourable to the tender sentiment. **1893** [see MERCY *sb.* 5 c]. **1906** CONRAD *Mirror of Sea* xxxiii. 182 A ship anchored..is not abandoned by her own men to the tender mercies of shore people. **1925** GALSWORTHY *Caravan* 575 His feelings revolted against handing 'that poor little beggar' over to the tender mercy of his country's law. **1960**, etc. [see *TLC* s.v. T 6 a]. **1965** *Listener* 17 June 892/2 Smaller..traders and manufacturers..left to the tender mercies of the open property market. **1973** *Computers & Humanities* VII. 166 The Bernard Quemada *Concordance* to *Les Fleurs du Mal*, which was perhaps prepared with more tender loving care, corrected such mechanical deficiencies. **1977** *Listener* 12 May 605/3 It is in a nurse's nature and in her tradition to give the sick what is well called 'TLC', 'tender loving care', some constant little service to the sick.

†**b.** *transf.* That is the object of tender feeling; tenderly loved; dear, beloved, precious. *Obs.*

c **1450** HOLLAND *Howlat* 439 As his tenderest and deir In his maist misteir. **1485** *Sc. Acts Jas. III* (1814) II. 171/1 His hienes has diuers tymez..maid supplicacioun..for þe promocioun of his tendir clerk & consalour. **1591** SHAKS. *Two Gent.* v. iv. 37 How I loue Valentine, Whose life's as tender to me as my soule. **1611** BIBLE *Prov.* iv. 3 Tender and onely belouved in the sight of my mother [COVERD. tenderly beloved of my mother].

†**c.** *Sc.* Nearly related, akin; esp. in phrase ***tender of blood***. *Obs.*

1508 DUNBAR *Poems* vii. 15 Welcum our tendir blude of hie parage. **1565** Q. MARY in Keith *Hist.* (1734) App. 103 Lady Margaret Countes of Lennox, being alswa sa tendir of Blude to hir Majestie. **1630-56** SIR R. GORDON *Hist. Earls Sutherland* (1813) 125 One who wes so tender of kinred and blood to him.

9. a. ***tender of*** (***for, on behalf of***, etc.): Careful of the welfare of; careful to preserve from harm or injury; considerate of, thoughtful for; fond of.

c **1305** *St. Kenelm* 136 in *E.E.P.* (1862) 51 His norice.. Tendre was of þis child, for heo him hadde deorest iboȝt. **1340** HAMPOLE *Pr. Consc.* 905 Whar-to þan es man..Swa tendre of his vile body? *a* **1400-50** *Alexander* 3317 Be tendire of my kniȝtis. **1551** T. WILSON *Logike* (1580) 33 Then should all Capitaines..be tender ouer their poore warriours and base Souldiours. **1605** BACON *Adv. Learn.* I. iii. §10 Some person, tender on the behalf of philosophy, reproved Aristippus. **1642** *Declar. Lords & Com.* in Rushw. *Hist. Coll.* (1721) V. 45 The Priviledges of Parliament, which the Contrivers..seem to be so tender of. **1709** SWIFT *Vind. Bickerstaff* ¶ 1, I am too tender of his reputation to publish them. **1783** BURKE *Affairs India* Wks. XI. 334 Mr. Barwell..ought to have been tender for his honour. **1868** ROGERS *Pol. Econ.* xvii. (1876) 240 So tender is the legislature of his interest.

b. Solicitous or careful to avoid or prevent something; chary *of*; scrupulous, cautious, circumspect; reluctant, loth. Const. *of, in.*

1651 N. BACON *Disc. Govt. Eng.* II. xxvii. (1739) 120 He was tender of the least diminution of his Honour. **1656** FINETT *For. Ambass.* 41, I was tender in taking any course without his Lordship's directions. **1667** PEPYS *Diary* 28 Oct., I confess, I am sorry to find him so tender of appearing. **1729** LAW *Serious C.* xxiii. (1732) 478 Very tender in censuring and condemning other people. **1840** LADY C. BURY *Hist. Flirt* xix, Her heart should be tender of ridiculing their suffering.

IV. Easily affected, sensitive.

10. Sensitive to, or easily affected by, external physical forces or impressions; *spec.* †**a.** Having a delicate or finely sensitive perception of smell.

c **1410, 1700** [see *tender-nosed* in C.]. **1445** tr. *Claudian* in *Anglia* XXVIII. 277 As blode houndys with her tendir nose tel thingis or thei appiere. **1593** SHAKS. *Lucr.* 695 Looke as the full-fed Hound, or gorged Hawke, Vnapt for tender smell, or speedie flight.

b. Sensitive in relation to bodily feeling or touch.

c **1600** SHAKS. *Sonn.* cxli. 6, I doe not loue thee with mine eyes... Nor are mine eares with thy toungs tune delighted, Nor tender feeling to base touches prone. **1715** DESAGULIERS *Fires Impr.* 43 The difference between the Action of Cold Air upon animate and tender, or inanimate and insensible Bodies.

c. *spec.* Acutely sensitive to pain; painful when touched; easily hurt.

[**1613** SHAKS. *Hen. VIII*, II. ii. 142 But Conscience, Conscience; O 'tis a tender place, and I must leaue her.] **1709** [implied in TENDERNESS 3]. **1799** *Med. Jrnl.* I. 159 The tumor being hard, and very tender. **1898** *Allbutt's Syst. Med.* V. 749 The skin over the pericardium was tender and sensitive.

†**d.** Of scales for weighing: Delicate, sensitive.

1665-6 *Phil. Trans.* I. 232 If I had had..tender Scales.

e. Of a ship: Leaning over too easily under sail-pressure; crank, not 'stiff'.

1722 DE FOE *Col. Jack* (1840) 190 The ship..was leaky and tender. **1726** SHELVOCKE *Voy. round World* 5, I told them, 'if the ship was tender, it was caus'd by her being pester'd so much aloft'. **1823** SCORESBY *Jrnl. Whale Fish.* 293 We found the ship so tender (yielding greatly to the influence of the wind), that we could scarcely carry sail. **1899** F. T. BULLEN *Log Sea-waif* 201 We..slid gently down the coast under easy sail, the vessel being 'tender' from scanty allowance of ballast.

f. Of a horse: ***to go tender***, to go as if lame or sore-footed and unable to put down his foot freely.

1849 LEVER *R. Cashel* II. 269, I defy any one to know whether a horse goes tender, while galloping in deep ground.

11. a. Susceptible to moral or spiritual influence; impressionable, sympathetic; sensitive to pious emotions. Now chiefly in phrase 'tender conscience'; formerly also of persons.

c **1586** BRYSKETT *Mourn. Muse Thestylis* 55 Your teares a hart of flint Might tender make. [**1613**: see sense 10 c.] **1655** FULLER *Ch. Hist.* II. vi. §21 The sight of him made all tender Beholders Cripples by Sympathie. **1660** CHAS. II *Declar. fr. Breda*, We do declare a Liberty to tender Consciences. **1672** G. FOX *Jrnl.*, The people being generally tender and open. **1685** EVELYN *Mrs. Godolphin* 46, I found her..all in feares, for never was Creature more devout and tender. **1728** P. WALKER *Peden* Pref. (1827) 23 Which have made so many tender Christians to scruple and scunner to take the Food of their Souls out of their unclean Hands. **1788** WESLEY *Wks.* (1872) VII. 191 One of a tender conscience is exact in observing any deviation from the word of God, whether in thought, or word, or work. **1844** LD. BROUGHAM *Brit. Const.* xvi. (1862) 250 The form of words used, out of regard to tender consciences.

†**b.** as *adv.* Tenderly, impressionably. *Obs.*

1424 *Coventry Leet Bk.* 96 That causyd the people the more & tenderer to her his prechyng.

12. Sensitive to injury; ready to take offence; 'touchy'. *Obs.* exc. as *fig.* from 10 c.

a **1635** NAUNTON *Fragm. Reg.* (Arb.) 46 On such trespasses she was quick and tender, and would not spare any whatsoever. **1645** FULLER *Good Th. in Bad T.* (1841) 3, I am choleric by my nature and tender by my temper. **1749** CHESTERF. *Lett.* (1792) II. 300 Men are in this respect tender too, and will sooner forgive an injury than an insult. **1857** BUCKLE *Civiliz.* I. x. 613 The nobles, however, who felt that they had been aggrieved in their most tender point, were not yet satisfied.

†**13.** *transf.* Sensitively felt; that touches sensitive feelings or emotions. *Obs.*

1705 STANHOPE *Paraphr.* I. 115 Which cannot but..make the Sense of present Sufferings more tender and afflicting. **1779** *Mirror* No. 1 (1787) I. 5 A misfortune of the tenderest kind threw me, for some time, into retirement.

B. *sb.* [absolute use of the adj.]

†**1.** Tender state or condition. *Obs.*

c **1400** *Brut* 254 þat þe Kyng, for tendre of his age, shulde be gouernede be tuelf grete Lordes of Engeland. *a* **1691** BOYLE *Hist. Air* xx. (1692) 196 Not only to blast the Fruit, but the very Leaves of such Trees..just in the Tender,..*i.e.* when they are newly expanded out of the Buds.

†**2.** Tender feeling, tenderness. (Cf. TENDRE.) *Obs.*

1668 DRYDEN *Evening's Love* v. i, To disengage my heart from this furious tender, which I have for him. **1710** MRS. CENTLIVRE *Man's Bewitched* Pref., 'Tis Natural to have a kind of a Tender for our own Productions. *Ibid.* v. *ad fin.*, I had a kind of a Tender for Dolly; but since she's dispos'd of, I'll stand as I do. **1742** RICHARDSON *Pamela* IV. 113 Let the Musick express, as I may say, Love and the Tender, ever so much.

†**3.** Tender consideration; care, regard, concern. (Cf. TENDER *v.*^{2} 3.) *Obs. rare.*

1596 SHAKS. *1 Hen. IV*, v. iv. 49 Thou hast..shew'd thou mak'st some tender of my life In this faire rescue thou hast brought to mee. **1605** —— *Lear* I. iv. 230 The redresses.. Which in the tender of a wholesome weale, Might in their working do you that offence.

C. Combinations; chiefly parasynthetic adjs., as ***tender-bearded, -bladed, -bodied, -bowelled, -faced, -handed, -hoofed, -hued, -natured, -personed, -skinned, -slanted, -souled, -spirited, -tempered, -witted***, etc. Also, = tenderly, in ***tender-domestic, -imped, -looking, -taken*** adjs. Special Combs.: **tender-dying** *a.*, dying young; **tender-eared** *a.*, having tender ears; (*fig.*), sensitive to blame or criticism; **tender-eyed** *a.*, (*a*) having tender or sore eyes; †(*b*) fond, doting, partial; **tender-floss** [FLOSS^{3}]: see quot.; **tender-foreheaded** *a.*, modest, ready to blush; †**tender-hefted** *a.*, set in a delicate 'haft' or bodily frame; hence, womanly, gentle; **tender-mouthed** *a.*, (*a*) of a horse: having a tender mouth, answering readily to the rein; †(*b*) fastidious, dainty, choice; (*c*) gentle in speaking, not harsh; †**tender-nosed** *a.*, (*a*) keen-scented; (*b*) timid, timorous; **tender-sided** *a.* [? after *crank-sided*], = sense 10 e (*Cent. Dict.* 1891); **tenderpad** [f. after TENDERFOOT 2: see PAD *sb.*^{3} 7], a recruit to the Cub Scout movement who has passed the tenderpad test; †**tender-skull**, a variety of walnut; †**tender-tinder**, ? readily inflammable material (in quot. *fig.*). See also TENDER-CONSCIENCED, TENDERFOOT, etc.

1591 SYLVESTER *Du Bartas* I. iii. 296 A Tree, whose *tender-bearded Root being spred In dryest sand. **1804** tr. *Ovid's Remedy of Love* I. 102 (Jod.) The *tender-bladed grain, Shot up to stalk. **1607** SHAKS. *Cor.* I. iii. 6 When yet hee was but *tender-bodied. **1650** JER. TAYLOR *Holy Living* (1727) 162 Be *tender-bowelled, pitiful, and gentle. **1849** CLOUGH *Amours de Voy.* I. 116 One of those natures Which have their perfect delight in the general *tender-domestic. **1591** SHAKS. *1 Hen. VI*, III. iii. 48 As lookes the Mother on her lowly Babe, When Death doth close his *tender-dying Eyes. **1529** MORE *Dyaloge* IV. Wks. 248/1 The bad themself be not so *tendereared, that for the only talking of their faultes they would banish the bokes that were good in other thinges besyde. **1683** KENNETT tr. *Erasm. on Folly* Pref. (1709) 8 Which makes me wonder at the tender-eared humour of this age. **1911** J. MASEFIELD *Everlasting Mercy* (1912) 88 Two hares..Wide-eyed and tender-eared. **1535** COVERDALE *Gen.* xxix. 17 Lea was *tender eyed [WYCLIF, with blerid eyen]. **1591** PERCIVALL *Sp. Dict.*, *Pitaňoso*, bleare eied, tender eied. *a* **1619** FLETCHER *Wit without M.* III. i, You must not think your sister, so tender eyed as not to see your follies. **1823** W. TAYLOR in *Mirror* 12 July, He [Thomson] was so *tender-faced..and so devilish difficult to shave. **1839** URE *Dict. Arts* 712 If its fracture be contorted, and contains a great many empty spaces or air-cells, the metal [cast iron] takes the name of cavernous-floss, or *tender-floss. **1659** *Tender-foreheaded [see FOREHEADED 1]. **1825** COLERIDGE *Aids Refl.* Aph. xvii. 67 What need that Christians should be so tender-foreheaded as to be put out of countenance. *a* **1750** A. HILL *Wks.* (1753) IV. 120 *Tender-handed stroke a nettle, And it stings you for your pains. **1605** SHAKS. *Lear* II. iv. 176 Thy *tender-hefted [Q^os hested] Nature shall not giue Thee o're to harshnesse. **1624** MIDDLETON *Game at Chess* III. i, Thy conscience is so *tender-hoof'd of late, Every nail pricks it. **1598** SYLVESTER *Du Bartas* II. Ded. 12 Observe a while our *tender-imped Lark. **1620** VENNER *Via Recta* iv. 72 Some (That are very *tender mouthed) deeme this fish not so pleasant in taste. **1708** *Yorkshire-Racers* 3 He's tender-mouthed, manag'd with easy bit. **1656** DUCHESS NEWCASTLE *True Relation* in *Life* (1886) 313 Also I am *tender natured, for it troubles my conscience to kill a fly. *c* **1410** *Master of Game* (MS. Digby 182) xxxiii, þe redyer and moste *tendrenosed hounde. **1700** R. CROMWELL *Let.* in *Eng. Hist. Rev.* XIII. 120 The other tow tender nosed gentlemen would not come. **1916** R. BADEN-POWELL *Wolf Cub's Handbk.* I. ii. 25 A boy Wolf Cub is called a 'Recruit' till he has learnt the Cub laws and secret signs, and then he is admitted to be a '*Tender-pad', and to wear the uniform of the Wolf Cubs. **1965** G. MCINNES *Road to Gundagai* x. 158, I received a cap, but no badge ('Not till you pass yer tenderpad test.'). **1819** KEATS *Lamia* II. 238 The *tender-personed Lamia. **1679** EVELYN *Kal. Hort.* (ed. 5) 38 Wallnuts, the Early nut: the *Tender-Scull, the Hard shell. *a* **1868** G. M. HOPKINS *Poems* (1967) 175 Crisp lips, straight nose, and *tender-slanted cheek. **1872** SYMONDS *Introd. Stud. Dante* 248 Most *tender-souled of feudal heroes. **1853** MRS. GASKELL *Cranford* xv. 230 Martha was so tearful and *tender-spirited, and unlike her usual self, that I said as little as possible about myself. *a* **1821** KEATS *Last Sonnet*, Still, still to hear her *tender-taken breath, And so live ever—or else swoon to death. **1882** F. M. CRAWFORD *Mr. Isaacs* ii, Arab stallions,..sure-footed as a mule, and *tender-tempered as a baby. **1615** BRATHWAIT *Strappado* (1878) 94 *Tender-tinder of Affection, If I harbour thee againe, I will doe it by direction Of some graue experienc't swaine. **1560** BECON *New Catech.* Wks. I. 542 b, The children, whiche eyther are tender, or *tender witted, or fearefull, or easye to be reclaymed: the Scholemaster ought gently to entreat.

tender ('tɛndə(r)), *v.*[1] Also 6–8 **tendre.** [a. F. *tendre* to hold out, offer (11th c. in Godef. *Compl.*):—L. *tendĕre* to stretch, hold forth. (The retention of the ending of the French infinitive is unusual, but cf. RENDER *v.*)]

To offer or present formally for acceptance.

1. *trans. Law.* To offer or advance (a plea, issue, averment; evidence, etc.) in due and formal terms; *spec.* to offer (money, etc.) in discharge of a debt or liability, esp. in exact fulfilment of the requirements of the law and of the obligation.

1542–3 *Act 34 & 35 Hen. VIII*, c. 2 §2 If..the saide Collectoures..tendre paiement of all suche money..within the saide three monethes. **1544** tr. *Littleton's Tenures* (1574) 22 b, The Lorde maye tender a conuenient mariage wythout disparagyng of such an heire female. **1607** COWELL *Interpr.* s.v., To tender his law of *non Summons*..is to offer himselfe ready to make his law, whereby to prooue that he was not summoned. *c* **1611** CHAPMAN *Iliad* XXII. 302 If ten or twenty times so much, as friends would rate thy price, Were tendered here. **1621** ELSING *Debates Ho. Lords* (Camden) 97 Sr John Bennett was ready to tender his appearaunce. **1730–6** BAILEY (folio), To *Tender an Averment* (in Law), to offer a Proof or Evidence in Court. *a* **1774** TUCKER *Lt. Nat.* (1834) II. 120 In all courts of judgment the burden of the proof lies upon him who tenders the issue. **1848** WHARTON *Law Lex.* s.v., No copper coin can be tendered when the debt is such an amount that it can be paid in silver or gold. **1885** *Law Times Rep.* LIII. 51/2 Evidence was..tendered on behalf of the appellant to prove the construction of the furnace.

†**b.** *tender down*: to lay down (money) in payment: cf. *pay down.* Also *transf. Obs. rare.*

1602 HEYWOOD *Wom. Kilde* Wks. 1874 II. 108 Sir I accept it [money],..Come gentlemen, and see it tendred downe. **1603** SHAKS. *Meas. for M.* II. iv. 180 Had he twentie heads to tender downe On twentie bloodie blockes, hee'ld yeeld them vp. **1607** —— *Timon* I. i. 54 You see how all Conditions ..tender downe Their seruices to Lord Timon.

2. *gen.* To present (anything) for approval and acceptance; to offer, proffer.

1587 HARRISON *England* II. xxii. (1877) I. 340 Then doo they tender licences, and offer large dispensations vnto him. **1593** SHAKS. *Rich. II*, II. iii. 41 My gracious Lord, I tender you my seruice. **1607** DEKKER & WEBSTER *Hist. Sir T. Wyatt* Wks. 1873 III. 110 Who was it yonder, that tendered vp his life To natures death? **1635** A. STAFFORD *Fem. Glory* (1869) 149 All tendred their respects. **1713** ADDISON *Ct. Tariff* ¶21 As he tendered his ears. **1786** tr. *Beckford's Vathek* (1868) 45 The governor..tendered every kind of refreshment. **1849** MACAULAY *Hist. Eng.* vi. II. 101 Several Aldermen, who.. loved neither Popery nor martial law, tendered their resignations. **1853** C. BRONTË *Villette* xii, She tendered not even a remonstrance. **1871** R. ELLIS *Catullus* lxv. 15 Yet mid such desolation a verse I tender.

fig. **1588** SHAKS. *L.L.L.* II. i. 244 As Iewels in Christall.. tendring their own worth from whence they were glast.

b. *to tender an oath*, to offer or present an oath *to* a person, that he may take it; to put it *to* anyone to take an oath. (*Rarely* to take the oath: quot. 1838.)

1562 *Act 5 Eliz.* c. 1 §6 To tender or minister the Othe aforesayd, to every..Ecclesiasticall person. **1710** HEARNE *Collect.* (O.H.S.) II. 355 The Oaths are also order'd to be tender'd to them. **1838** PRESCOTT *Ferd. & Is.* (1846) I. v. 222 The principal grandees..soon presented themselves from all quarters, in order to tender the customary oaths of allegiance. **1871** MORLEY *Crit. Misc.* Ser. I. *J. De Maistre* (1878) 107 The authorities vainly tendered him the oath.

†**c.** To offer *to do* something. *Obs. rare*[−1].

a **1618** RALEIGH *Maxims St.* (1651) 31 Especially if it tender to take from them their commodities.

3. [from TENDER *sb.*[2] 3.] *intr.* To offer by tender *for* a proposed contract, or the like.

1865 *Pall Mall G.* 12 Oct. 5 Cases..in which the grocery supply..is regulated by friendship [with] some particular grocer—a condition under which open tendering becomes altogether a farce. **1910** *Times* 9 Feb. 4 Seven firms tendered in competition.., the tenderers all sat at a table.

Hence **'tendered** (-əd) *ppl. a.*[1]; **'tendering** *vbl. sb.*[1]

1613 T. GODWIN *Rom. Antiq.* (1658) 112 A certain ticket or token..at the tendring whereof..certain doles and measures of corn were given. *a* **1677** BARROW *Wks.* (1686) III. xxxvi. 404 His tendering upon so fair and easie terms an endless life in perfect joy and bliss. **1883** *Pall Mall G.* 12 May 4/1 Mdlle. Jeanne receives the tendered homage with the condescension of well-acknowledged desert. **1955** *Times* 17 June 9/3 The President of the Board of Trade..proposed to send to the Commission a second general reference covering 'common prices and level tendering'. **1972** G. L. REES *Britain's Commodity Markets* vii. 165 For this purpose granaries ('tendering points') have been nominated by the Association.

tender ('tɛndə(r)), *v.*[2] *arch.* or *dial.* [f. TENDER *a.*: cf. OF. *tendr-ir.*]

†**1.** *intr.* To become tender; to be affected with pity; to grow soft, soften. *Obs.*

1390 GOWER *Conf.* I. 270 The wo the children made, Wherof that al his herte tendreth. *c* **1400** *Laud Troy Bk.* 17447 The kynges herte full sore tendres. *c* **1489** CAXTON *Sonnes of Aymon* xix. 430 Whan Reynawde herde his brother Rycharde speke so to hym, his herte tendred with all ryght sore. **1553** *Respublica* III. iv. 753, I on youe soo tendre.

2. *trans.* To make tender (in various senses).

a. To render gentle, compassionate, or contrite; to soften. ? *Obs.* exc. among Quakers.

1390 GOWER *Conf.* I. 115 Al naked bot of smok and scherte, To tendre with the kynges herte. **1483** CAXTON *Gold. Leg.* 14 b/2 He added therto wepyng..to tendre our hertis. **1678** R. BARCLAY *Apol. Quakers* v. xvi. 147 It works powerfully upon the Soul, mightily tenders it, and breaks it. **16..** PENN *To J. H.*, etc. (Cent.), I pray God forgive you, open your eyes, tender your hearts. *a* **1718** —— *Life* Wks. 1726 I. 61 We were all sweetly tender'd and broken together. **1797** LAMB *To Chas. Lloyd* 15 Deal with me, Omniscient Father! as thou judgest best And in thy season tender thou my heart. **1812** MRS. FRY in Clay *Prison Chaplain* (1861) 81, I heard weeping, and I thought they [female convicts] appeared much tendered.

†**b.** To make less stringent or strict; to mitigate. *Obs. rare.*

a **1656** BP. HALL *Specialties Life* Rem. Wks. (1660) 10, I ..þesought him to tender that hard condition.

c. To make tender or delicate. Now *dial.*

1725 CHEYNE *Ess. Health* vii. §7 Much and heavy Cloaths ..tender and debilitate the Habit, and weaken the Strength. **1805** R. W. DICKSON *Pract. Agric.* II. 1042 Manure.. blanching and tendering the grass plants in the spots where it remains. **1886** *S.W. Linc. Gloss.*, *Tender*, to make tender: as 'It'll tender him for the winter'.

d. To make (physically) tender, soft, or weak; to soften, weaken. Now *dial.* and *techn.*

1764 *Museum Rust.* II. lxxvi. 261 The band seldom breaks there, unless it be made of too small a quantity, or of corn much tendered. **1806** A. HUNTER *Culina* (ed. 3) 182 Stew it till quite tender... When sufficiently tendered, take out the bones. **1874** W. CROOKES *Dyeing & Calico-print.* II. vii. 517 If too strongly acid or alkaline it [the mordant] will have a corrosive action, and the goods, as it is technically called, will be 'tendered'. **1880** *Antrim & Down Gloss* s.v., The fibre (of flax) tendered by excess of moisture.

3. To feel or act tenderly towards; to regard or treat with tenderness: with various shades of meaning. **a.** To have a tender regard for, to hold dear; to be concerned for or solicitous about; to treat with consideration; to regard, care for, value, esteem. *arch.* See also f.

1439 *Rolls of Parlt.* V. 8/2 þeir worshipp which þei tendre most of any ertly thing. **1469** *Paston Lett.* II. 352 Be my trowthe ther is no gentylwoman on lyve that my herte tendreth more then it dothe her. **1524** [see f.]. **1579** GOSSON *Sch. Abuse* (Arb.) 30 Dion..forbiddeth..gentlewomen that tender their name and honor, to come to Theaters. **1633** BP. HALL *Hard Texts, N.T.* 87 It must needs be more cause of joy to all that tender the glory of God. *a* **1677** BARROW *Wks.* (1687) I. viii. 98 By our charity and benignity to those whose good he tenders. **1786** *Francis the Philanthropist* III. 72 He advised me, as I tendered my own safety, to keep aloof from his house. **1828** SOUTHEY in *Q. Rev.* XXXVIII. 569 As we tender the safety of the Royal Oak. **1857** [see f].

†**b.** To regard or receive favourably; to attend to or comply with (a request) graciously. *Obs.*

c **1430** *Life St. Kath.* (1884) 9 Besechynge ȝowre hyȝe excellence to tendre our desyr and to graunte vs..a gracīouse answer. **1523** SKELTON *Garl. Laurel* 56 My supplycacyon to thee I arrecte, Whereof I beseche you to tender the effecte. **1593** SHAKS. *Lucr.* 534 Then for thy husband and thy childrens sake, Tender my suite.

†**c.** To regard or treat with pity; to take pity on, have mercy on; to feel or show compassion for.

1442 HEN. VI in Ellis *Orig. Lett.* Ser. III. I. 78 That ye soo tendryng thees oure necessitees wol lene vnto vs for the socours and relief of oure seid Duchie [etc.]. **1523** LD. BERNERS *Froiss.* I. ccxxxi. 311 To knowe yf he wolde receyue you..and for pytie somwhat to tendre your nede and necessyte. **1581** T. HOWELL *Deuises* (1879) 183 The Lyon doth tender the beast that doth yeelde. **1649** ROBERTS *Clavis Bibl.* 25 Seeing he so tenders them in affliction.

d. To treat with affectionate care; to cherish, foster; to take care of, look after. *Obs.* or *dial.*

1449 *Rolls of Parlt.* V. 152/2 Fadres of the Church, that shuld most specially tendir þe dere bought monnys soule. **1556** J. HEYWOOD *Spider & F.* lxvii. 15 He tenderlie tendreth his childerne and wife. **1611** SPEED *Hist. Gt. Brit.* IX. ix. (1623) 617 He rather ought to haue tendred him as a Father. *a* **1711** KEN *Hymns Festiv.* Poet. Wks. 1721 I. 386 You in their Infant-age, To tender them engage. **1844** MRS. SHERWOOD *Hist. J. Marten* xxv, [Irish lad says] I was obliged to lead him about,..and tender him, and help him, as if he had been a girl.

†**e.** To have regard or respect to as something to be dreaded and avoided. *Obs.*

1615, 1625 [see f]. **1633** T. STAFFORD *Pac. Hib.* I. viii. (1821) 113 Beseeching your Lordship..not to faile, as you tender the overthrow of our Action. **1672–1901** [see f].

f. *Phrases.* Royal Proclamations formerly ended with the phrase 'as they [you, etc.] tender our pleasure' (in sense a above), which was used as late as 1701, but in the 17th c. was largely supplanted by 'as they tender our displeasure' (see sense e), which occurs as early as 1615, and remained in use in proclamations for continuing persons in office, issued on the accession of a sovereign, down to the accession of Edward VII, after which the Demise of the Crown Act (of July 1901) rendered such proclamations unnecessary. Proclamations for general fasts or thanksgivings have from 1641 ended with the phrase 'as they tender the favour of Almighty God'.

1490 *Warrant* in *Coventry Leet Bk.* 539 Fayle ye not herof ..as ye & every of yowe tendre our singler pleasir and woll eshewe þe contrarie. **1524** HEN. VIII in *Buccleuch MSS.* (Hist. MSS. Comm.) I. 220 We..commaunde you..to.. suffre hym so to do, without any your let, chalenge, or contradiccion, as ye tender our pleasur. **1618** (July 6) *Procl. 16 Jas. I*, (Inhibiting all persons, etc.) as they tender Our pleasure and will avoid Our indignation and displeasure. **1619** (Nov. 10) *Procl. 17 Jas. I*, As they tender Our pleasure, and will avoide the contrary. **1669** (June 23) *Procl. 21 Chas. II.* **1701** (Mar. 9) *Procl. 1 Anne* (Continuing Persons in Office) as they and every of them tender Her Majesty's pleasure.

1615 (Dec. 9) *Procl. 13 Jas. I* (Requiring the Residencie of Noblemen, etc.) as they tender Our indignation and displeasure. **1625** (May 26) *Procl. 1 Chas. I* (For reforming disorders in His Majesty's Household) as they will give account to Us thereof and tender Our high displeasure for neglect of this service. **1672** DK. NEWCASTLE in *12th Rep. Hist. MSS. Comm.* App. v. 24 His Majesty..hath required me to prohibit your further proceeding therein as you tender His Majesty's displeasure. **1688** (Feb. 19) *Procl. 1 Wm. & Mary* (Continuing Officers in Plantations) as they and every of them tender Our Displeasure. **1701** (Mar. 8) *Procl. 1 Anne* (Continuing Persons in Offices) as they and every of them tender Her Majesty's utmost displeasure. **1704** N. N. tr. *Boccalini's Advts. fr. Parnass.* III. 156 But above all things, as he tender'd his Majesty's Displeasure, he should take particular Care never to part with any of 'em. **1727** (June 16) *Procl. 1 Geo. II*, As they and every of them tender Our utmost Displeasure. **1901** (Jan. 23) *Procl. 1 Edw. VII*, [same words].

1625 (July 3) *Procl. 1 Chas. I* (For a public generall and solemn Fast) as they tender their duties to Almighty God, and to their Prince and Countrey. **1641** (Jan. 8) *Procl. 17 Chas. I* (For a general Fast) as they tender the favour of Almighty God. **1805** (Nov. 7) *Procl. 46 Geo. III* (For a General Thanksgiving) [same words]. **1857** (Sept. 24) *Procl. 21 Vict.* (For a day of solemn Fast) [same words].

Hence **'tendered** *ppl. a.*[2]; **'tendering** *vbl. sb.*[2], a making or becoming tender; **'tendering** *ppl. a.*, that produces tenderness; affecting. *arch.*

1635 J. HAYWARD tr. *Biondi's Banish'd Virg.* 66 Parting from her deerely-*tendred girle. **1577** B. GOOGE *Heresbach's Husb.* II. (1586) 92 b, Diligent in the *tendering of the tree. **1640** BP. REYNOLDS *Passions* xxvii, Out of a tendering of its own safety. **1684** O. HEYWOOD *Diaries* (1885) IV. 104, I.. poured out my soul to god for him, and now at last see some tenderings. **1762** J. WOOLMAN *Jrnl.* viii. (1840) 115 Pure gospel love was felt to the tendering of some of our hearts. *c* **1694** PENN in Janney *Life* xxvii. (1856) 388 In a *tendering and living power she broke out.., 'Let us all prepare [etc.].' **1760** J. RUTTY *Spir. Diary* (ed. 2) 154 A sweet humbling, tendering time. **1824** *Summary View of Amer.* x. 137 He kissed one, took another in his arms, and proved himself so affectionate a father, that it was a tendering sight.

'tender, *v.*[3] [f. TENDER *sb.*[1]] *trans.* To ship (mails, luggage, etc.) on board a tender.

1905 *Westm. Gaz.* 4 Dec. 12/1 The work of 'tendering' and stowing the bags accomplished, the usual special train run on occasions of the kind left Plymouth Docks at 6.43 p.m...and arrived at Paddington at 10.53 p.m.—247 miles in 250 minutes.

tenderable ('tɛndərəb(ə)l), *a. Comm.* [f. TENDER *v.*[1] + -ABLE.] That may be tendered; available for delivery in fulfilment of contract.

1868 *Harper's Mag.* Dec. 89/1 The view of Judge Denio that the word 'money' implies the creation of what is tenderable for debts is a much more reasonable.. interpretation of the Constitution. **1882** *Manch. Guard.* 29 Oct. 4 The supply of 'tenderable' American [cotton] in Liverpool, that is to say of qualities suitable to be accepted in fulfilment of contracts for future delivery. **1884** *Pall Mall G.* 13 Dec. 5/2 By the existing rules of the Petroleum Association the oil tenderable in fulfilment of a contract must be American. **1891** *Standard* 7 Feb. 6/2 The rapid rise has naturally made a large volume of tea tenderable.

†'**tenderance**. *Obs. rare.* [f. TENDER *v.*[2] + -ANCE.] Tender treatment or regard.

1454 *Rolls of Parlt.* V. 257/2 For the grete tenderaunce, trust and love, that the seid James..hade. *c* **1500** MEDWALL *Nature* (Brandl) 296 Of great tenderaunce and spyrytuall loue that god oweth to mankynde. *Ibid.* 606 To accept hym to your fauour and tendraunce.

tender-conscienced ('tɛndə'kɒnʃənst), *a.* [Parasynthetic f. *tender conscience* (TENDER *a.* 11) + -ED[2].] Having a tender conscience; scrupulous.

a **1617** HIERON *Wks.* II. 246 As if you were so tender conscienced that you would not keepe ought from him that were his. **1710** *Let. to New Member Parlt.* in *Harl. Misc.* (1810) XI. 156 Those tender-conscienced people, our moderate dissenters. **1880** SWINBURNE *Stud. Shaks.* 169 The high-hearted and tender-conscienced Hamlet.

tende'ree. [f. as next + -EE[1].] The person to whom a tender is made.

1883 JUDGE T. MILLER in *New York Reports* XCI. 536 Where a tender is made, for the purpose of obtaining property..sold and in the hands of the tenderee claiming to own the same.

tenderer[1] ('tɛndərə(r)). [f. TENDER *v.*[1] + -ER[1].] One who tenders or makes a formal offer; *spec.* one who tenders for a proposed contract.

1650 J. MUSGRAVE *Pressures & Grievances N.C.* 21 Mr Chambers at Allhallowes, tenderer of oath for the Lord Newcastle. **1691** [see TENDER *sb.*[2] 3]. **1865** *Pall Mall G.* 1 Nov. 4 We announced that the workhouse contracts must in future be given to the lowest tenderer.

tenderer[2] ('tɛndərə(r)). [f. TENDER *v.*[2] + -ER[1].]

1. One who tenders or treats with pity.

1584 LODGE *Alarum* (Shaks. Soc.) 72 Fatherly, and prudent tenderers of gentry grown into povertie.

2. One who or that which makes something tender.

1890 *Sci. Amer.* 8 Mar. 158/1 Inventions... Steak tenderer.

tenderfoot ('tɛndəfʊt). Pl. -foots, -feet. [f. *tender foot*: for sense 1, see quot. 1887[1].]

1. *U.S.* and *Colonial.* **a.** A name given, originally in the ranching and mining regions of the western U.S., to a newly arrived immigrant, unused to the hardships of pioneer life; a greenhorn; hence, a raw, inexperienced person.

1881 L. P. BROCKETT *West. Empire* I. vii. (1882) 72 (Funk) Slang expressions of this mining dialect... New-comers are 'Tender-feet'. **1887** L. SWINBURNE in *Scribner's Mag.* II. 508 'Pilgrim' and 'tenderfoot' were formerly applied almost exclusively to newly imported cattle. **1887** *Q. Rev.* July 49 British 'tenderfeet' were induced to invest a great deal of cattle in the business. **1891** *Pall Mall G.* 4 Jan. 2/1 Wailings of inexperienced men and 'tender foots'.

b. *attrib.* or as *adj.*

1888 *San Francisco Wkly. Bulletin* (Farmer *Dict. Amer.*), The boys were of the tenderfoot kind. **1897** *Daily News* 30 July 7/1 Most of the best claims have already been secured by tenderfoot prospectors. **1900** O. WISTER *Virginian* ii, In my tenderfoot innocence I was looking indoors for the washing arrangements.

2. In the Scout and Guide movements, a recruit who has passed the enrolment tests (the ***tenderfoot tests***); also ***tenderfoot badge***, and *ellipt.* = tenderfoot badge, tests.

1908 R. S. S. BADEN-POWELL *Scouting for Boys* iii. 36 *A Tenderfoot* is a boy who is not yet a scout. **1911** *Boy Scout Tests* (Boy Scouts Assoc.) 1 It should be noted that a tenderfoot may not wear the button-hole badge until he has passed the Tenderfoot Tests. **1918** R. S. S. BADEN-POWELL *Girl Guiding* II. i. 64 At first you rank as a Recruit until you pass your Tenderfoot tests. Then you can go on and rise to the following ranks:—Recruit. Tenderfoot. Second-Class Guide. **1920** *Girl Guide Badges* (Girl Guide Assoc.) 6 No Guider or Guide is entitled to wear the Tenderfoot Badge unless she has been enrolled, and has passed the following tests. **1965** G. MCINNES *Road to Gundagai* x. 160 He..saw that loads were properly distributed..between..strong scouts and not so strong tenderfeet. **1982** *Times* 19 Jan. 18/5 Mr Bass, who is 6ft. 3ins., resigned after passing his Tenderfoot because he did not like wearing short trousers.

'**tender-'footed,** *a.* [f. as prec. + -ED[2].] Having tender feet; hence, moving with or as with tender feet; also *fig.* cautious, timid. Hence '**tender'footedness**.

1682 *Lond. Gaz.* No. 1694/4 Stolen.., an Iron Grey Gelding,..a little tender-footed on the Stones. **1690** *Ibid.* No. 2535/4 A white Stone-horse..tender-footed before. **1854** J. W. GRIMES in *N. Amer. Rev.* CXXIII. 189 My friends were tender-footed, and did not wish me to denounce the Nebraska infamy. **1891** *Cent. Dict.*, Tenderfootedness.

'**tenderful,** *a. Obs.* or *dial.* [f. TENDER *a.* + -FUL.] Full of tenderness; affectionate, tenderly kind or attentive. Hence '**tenderfully** *adv.*

1640 O. SEDGWICK *Christ's Counsell* 25 Oh how cheerfully, how tenderfully, how much more fully and fruitfully is thy soule inabled after those duties rightly performed. **1901** 'ZACK' *Tales Dunstable Weir* 136 Tenderful for others.

'**tender-'hearted,** *a.* [Parasynthetic f. *tender heart* + -ED[2].] Having a tender heart; easily moved by †fear, pity, sorrow, or love; †timid; pitiful, compassionate; loving; impressionable.

1539 BIBLE (Great) *2 Chron.* xiii. 7 Whan Rehoboam was young & tender hearted. **1560** —— (Genev.) *Eph.* iv. 32 Be ye courteous one to another, & tender hearted [1539 mercyfull], forgiuing one another. **1652** KIRKMAN *Clerio & Lozia* 69 Tenderhearted mothers bewail the loss of their dear children. **1888** 'J. S. WINTER' *Bootle's Childr.* vii, Terry was very tender-hearted when women and children were concerned.

Hence '**tender-'heartedness**.

1607 HIERON *Wks.* I. 186 Few men haue that tender-heartednesse, to account themselues..parties in the calamities of other Christians. **1798** SOUTHEY *Grandmother's T.* Poet. Wks. 1838 III. 12 She little thought This tender-heartedness would cause her death! **1876** L. STEPHEN *Eng. Th. in 18th C.* II. XII. vii. 444 They lay a new stress upon the advantage of tender-heartedness and sympathy.

So '**tender-heart**, a tender-hearted person.

1904 *Blackw. Mag.* Oct. 513/1 Cheer up, little tender-heart.

'**tenderish,** *a.* [f. TENDER *a.* + -ISH[1].] Somewhat tender, rather tender.

1796 C. MARSHALL *Garden.* xix. (1813) 354 The variegated [snapdragon] (as all stripes are) is tenderish. **1922** JOYCE *Ulysses* 436 With a sour tenderish smile.

tenderize ('tɛndəraɪz), *v.* [f. as prec. + -IZE.] *trans.* To make tender: = TENDER *v.*[2] 1. *spec.* (orig. *U.S.*) to make (food, esp. meat) tender. Also *absol.* Hence '**tenderized** *ppl. a.*; '**tenderizing** *vbl. sb.* and *ppl. a.*

1733 M. L. KILLIGREW in *Jrnl. Roy. Inst. Cornw.* (1887) Dec., At his going away, his behaviour had tenderised me. **1772** *Test Filial Duty* II. 182 This pastoral life has tenderized you prodigiously. **1934** WEBSTER, Tenderize, v.t. **1935** A. P. HERBERT in *Punch* 8 May 548/1 He has seen some prunes commended as being 'tenderized by a special process.'.. If enough prune-purveyors go on saying 'tenderize' it will be in the next edition of all the dictionaries! **1936** *Amer. Speech* XI. 374/2 Sunsweet Tenderized Prunes, refreshed and pasteurized. **1939** *Sun* (Baltimore) 22 Mar. 3/1 A process of 'tenderizing' meat through the use of ultra violet rays. **1950** [see PRESSURE COOKER a]. **1958** *House & Garden* Feb. 77/2 Wine has a slightly tenderizing effect, so when it is used the meat will cook a little more quickly. **1960** *Times* 24 Sept. 6/6 The new method..ensures that tenderizing liquid gets into the innermost tissues. **1961** *Harper's Bazaar* June 84/2 Diced cubes [of avocado] which have been 'tenderized' and flavoured by the marinade. **1968** L. DURRELL *Tunc* v. 235 She's as sweet as a tenderised steak. **1977** *Time* 19 Sept. 61/2 (Advt.), Touchmatic Control Panel—enables you to slow cook, simmer, tenderize and blend flavours.

tenderizer ('tɛndə,raɪzə(r)). [f. TENDERIZE *v.* + -ER[1].] Something used to make meat tender, either (*a*) the enzyme papain, or (*b*) a steak hammer.

1958 *Catal. County Stores, Taunton* June 12 Papaya Juice (meat tenderiser)—a bot 2/-. **1959** *Housewife* June 75 Steak tenderisers in sycamore. **1969**, **1970** [see *meat tenderizer* s.v. MEAT *sb.* 5b]. **1975** A. AYCKBOURN *Round & Round the Garden* in *Norman Conquests* 18, I line up the dishes and smash them—slowly—with the steak tenderizer.

tenderling ('tɛndəlɪŋ). [See -LING[1].]

1. A delicate person or creature; *contemptuously*, an effeminate person. Now *rare.*

1541 COVERDALE tr. *Chr. State Matrimonye* (1543) 86b, The more gorgiouse tenderlynges they be, the better shall they please theyr heade the deuell. **1556** OLDE *Antichrist* 9 As for the talkes of some fyne fyngred tendrelinges, they are not worth the hearing. **1649** W. SCLATER *Comm. Malachy* (1650) 123 Those tenderlings unused to hardship, how doth a little affright them? **1802** BEDDOES *Hygëia* v. 29 Persons, accustomed to be buffetted by storms..much exceed the inactive fireside tenderling.

2. A person of tender years; a young child.

1587 HOLINSHED *Chron.* III. 628/1 The verie tenderlings who might appeare to be toward and teachable. **1606** WARNER *Alb. Eng.* XIV. lxxxiii. 348 His Highness then a Tenderling. **18..** G. MASSEY *Babe Christabel*, Poems (ed. 1889) 13 They [angels] snatched our little tenderling, So shyly opening into view.

†**3.** *pl.* The soft tops of a deer's horns when they are coming through. *Obs.*

1575 TURBERV. *Venerie* 129 The Noombles, handes and tenderlings, which are the soft toppes of his hornes when they are in bloude, doe pertayne to the Prime or chiefe personage. **1688** R. HOLME *Armoury* III. 189/1.

'**tenderloin.** *U.S.* [f. TENDER *a.* + LOIN *sb.*]

1. The tenderest or most juicy part of the loin of beef, pork, etc., lying under the short ribs in the hind quarter, and consisting of the psoas muscle; the fillet or 'undercut' of a sirloin. Also *attrib.*, esp. as ***tenderloin steak***.

1828 in WEBSTER. **1864** *Daily Tel.* 27 Sept. 5/2 The 'tenderloin', the 'porterhouse' steak of America, are infinitely superior to our much-vaunted rump steak. **1869** T. W. HIGGINSON *Army Life* (1870) 37 Is it customary to help to tenderloin with one's fingers? **1875** *Scribner's Monthly* July 274/2 A tenderloin steak,..potatoes, bread and butter, and a cup of coffee will cost fifty cents. **1884** G. P. KEESE in *Harper's Mag.* July 299/1 The division is made into the various pieces here named,..viz., loins, ribs,.. hams, shoulders, tenderloins, striploins, sirloins, butts, rump butts, strips, rounds, and canning beef. **1906** *Breakfast Menu, S.Y. Argonaut* 10 July, Tenderloin Beefsteaks. **1954** [see ALASKA b]. **1975** *Times* 19 Mar. 16/3 A tenderloin steak made from textured soy protein..sells for 89 cents a pound—as against two dollars for the real thing.

2. *slang.* In full ***tenderloin district***: applied to the police district of New York which includes the great mass of theatres, hotels, and places of amusement; thence extended to similar districts of other American cities.

Understood to have reference to the large amount of 'graft' said to be got by the police for protecting illegitimate houses in this district, which rendered it the 'juicy part' of the service.

1887 *Harper's Mag.* Mar. 500/2 His precinct is known as the 'Tenderloin', because of its social characteristics. **1898** *N. York Voice* 6 Jan. 4/3 If laws generally suitable to a city do not suit some Slavic, Polish, or other quarter, or some 'tenderloin' district, the local police must pass upon those laws. **1907** *Amer. Trial* in *Daily Chron.* 9 Feb. 5/3 This loose tattle of the Tenderloin. **1908** H. TRAIN *True Stories Crime* xi. 317 Apart from a handsome weekly stipend to his sister, Hummel's money all went into the Tenderloin or the race-track.

tenderly ('tɛndəlɪ), *adv.* [f. TENDER *a.* + -LY[2].] In a tender manner; with tenderness.

1. With delicacy or softness of touch, action, or treatment; softly, gently.

c **1385** CHAUCER *L.G.W.* Prol. 171 And Zepherus and flora gentilly Yaf to the floures softe and tenderly. *c* **1440** *York Myst.* xxx. 135 Tendirly me touche. **1604** SHAKS. *Oth.* I. iii. 407 The Moore..will as tenderly be led by'th' Nose As Asses are. **1712** STEELE *Spect.* No. 526 ⁋3, I should be glad to have them handled a little tenderly. **1885** *Athenæum* 23 May 669/1 *Sous Bois*..is another tenderly painted, broad, and expressive piece.

†**b.** So as to be tender or soft. †**c.** In a slight or fragile manner. *Obs.*

1604 E. GRIMSTONE *Hist. Siege Ostend* 220 Old shooes tenderly sodden. **1721** BRADLEY *Philos. Acc. Wks. Nat.* 142 The Body of the Bee is divided into three Parts, very tenderly join'd together.

2. With tender feeling. **a.** With affection or compassion; lovingly, dearly, kindly; pityingly, mercifully, leniently.

13.. *Cursor M.* 17288 + 281 Oute-taken his moder þat loued him tenderly. **1465** *Paston Lett.* II. 200, I pray yow that ye will tenderly understond this letter. **1593** SHAKS. *Rich. II*, III. iii. 48 The which..My stooping dutie tenderly shall shew. **1663** BUTLER *Hud.* I. I. 226 Rather than fail, they will defy That which they love most tenderly. **1826** PENN in *Pa. Hist. Soc. Mem.* I. 204 Thy remembrance..I tenderly received. **1849** MACAULAY *Hist. Eng.* v. I. 640 He will generally connive at it, or punish it very tenderly. **1891** E. PEACOCK *N. Brendon* I. 230 She looked at Basil tenderly. **1900** *Westm. Gaz.* 30 July 7/2 A tenderly-worded message of condolence.

†**b.** With kind or friendly consideration or attention; indulgently. (Cf. TENDER *v.*[2] 3.) *Obs.*

c **1380** WYCLIF *Wks.* (1880) 371 þerfore lordis schulden take hede fulle tendirly to þis voyce of criste. **1571** in Feuillerat *Revels Q. Eliz.* (1908) 408 All which I beseech your honour tenderly to consider. **1594** WEST *2nd Pt. Symbol., Chancerie* §98 The premisses tenderly considered.

c. With tender emotion; with acute sensibility or sensitiveness.

a **1300** *Cursor M.* 14308 Tenderli he wep, and said, 'And quar haf yee his bode laid?' *c* **1400** MAUNDEV. (Roxb.) xi. 46 Petre grette full tenderly, when he had forsaken Criste. **1609** DANIEL *Civ. Wars* VIII. lxxxii, The Lady Bona takes most tenderly To be so mockt. *a* **1674** CLARENDON *Life* (1759) I. 163 [This] the Chancellor took very heavily, and the Lord Falkland out of his Friendship to him, more tenderly. **1796** H. HUNTER tr. *St.-Pierre's Stud. Nat.* (1799) II. 320 Greece alone, you tell me, presents scenes and points of view so tenderly affecting.

3. With delicate nurture; softly, indulgently; effeminately; also, with the tenderness of youth.

c **1386** CHAUCER *Man of Law's T.* 171 Sent..Fro freendes þat so tendrely hire kepte. *c* **1440** *Jacob's Well* 104 þou hast be norysched tenderly. **1552** HULOET, Tenderlye, *molliter, muliebriter.* **1638** JUNIUS *Paint. Ancients* 182 Polycletus made Diadumenon tenderly youthfull. **1848** MRS. JAMESON *Sacr. & Leg. Art* (1850) 369 Such works..as tenderly-nurtured women shrink from.

4. Timidly, charily, cautiously. (Cf. 1.)

a **1628** PRESTON *Breastpl. Love* (1631) 149 When a man hath no ground to set his foote on, he will doe it tenderly and warily. **1822** LAMB *Elia* Ser. II. *Detached Th. on Bks.*, The poor gentry..venturing tenderly, page after page.

†'**tenderly,** *a. Sc. Obs. rare.* [f. as prec. + -LY[1].] Of a tender sort.

1567 *Sc. Acts Jas. VI* (1814) III. 13/2 Experience of the naturall affectioun and tenderly lufe he hes in all tymes borne.

tender-minded, *a.* (and *sb.*). [Parasynthetic, f. *tender mind* (TENDER *a.* 8): see -ED[2].] Having a tender mind; sensitive and idealistic (in W. James opp. TOUGH-MINDED *a.*). Also *absol.* as *sb.* Hence ,**tender-'mindedness**.

1605 SHAKS. *Lear* v. iii. 31 To be tender minded Do's not become a Sword. **1907** W. JAMES *Pragmatism* i. 12 You will ..recognize the two types of mental make-up that I mean if I head the columns..*The Tender-Minded*: Rationalistic, Intellectualistic, Idealistic, Optimistic, Religious, Free-Willist, Monistic, Dogmatic. *Ibid.* viii. 295 May not the claims of tender-mindedness go too far? May not the notion of a world already saved *in toto* anyhow, be too saccharine to stand? **1924** T. S. ELIOT *Homage to Dryden* iii. 45 It is not cynicism, though it has a kind of toughness which may be confused with cynicism by the tender-minded. **1952** H. J. EYSENCK in Mace & Vernon *Current Trends Brit. Psychol.* xvii. 210 Idealistic..tender-minded attitudes, such as those approving of church-going and religion, pacifism. **1965** *Listener* 28 Jan. 153/1 According to James, the tender-minded were those who could not endure the violation of a general law... Mathematics, he said, was the typical study of the tender-minded. **1972** H. J. EYSENCK *Psychol. is about People* v. 202, I did in fact discover some evidence in favour of the notion that tender-mindedness and tough-mindedness were correlated with personality as hypothesized.

tenderness ('tɛndənɪs). [f. TENDER *a.* + -NESS.] The quality or state of being tender.

1. Physical softness or delicacy; fragility; inability to stand rough usage; weakness, frailty; †youthfulness (*obs.*); effeminacy, womanishness.

13.. *Cursor M.* 25337 (Cott.) Thoru tendernes of vr flexs. **1387** TREVISA *Higden* (Rolls) VI. 301 þou doost riȝtfulliche ..þat confortest þe tendernesse [= newness] of my professioun. *c* **1430** LYDG. *Min. Poems* (Percy Soc.) 220 How myght I the woo endure, In tendrenesse of wommanheede? **1596** DALRYMPLE tr. *Leslie's Hist. Scot.* (S.T.S.) I. 19 In tendirnes of thair flesh thay [sheep] are lyke the cattel. **1623–33** FLETCHER & SHIRLEY *Night-Walker* I. iii, Alas poor gentlewoman, Must she become a nurse now in her tenderness? **1708** J. C. *Compl. Collier* (1845) 35 According to the tenderness or hardness of the Coal. **1774** PENNANT *Tour Scotl. in 1772* 258 Through the age and tenderness of the parchment, little could be read. **1856** RUSKIN *Mod. Paint.* IV. v. xx. §4 [Such a person] can hardly be said to know what tenderness in colour means at all.

b. quasi-*concr.* Tender substance.

1382 WYCLIF *Jer.* li. 34 He fulfilde his wombe with my tendernesse. **14..** *Metr. Voc.* in Wr.-Wülcker 627/7 Thye, *crus*, hepe, *femur*, the tendurnesse of þe thye, *famen*. **1548** THOMAS *Ital. Dict.* (1567), *Lanugine*, the tendernesse or downe of a yonge bearde.

2. The quality of being tender in regard or treatment of others; gentleness, kindness, compassion, love; considerateness, mercy, leniency.

a **1300** *Cursor M.* 9994 (Cott.) Takening..O tendernes and truth stedfast. *c* **1450** *Merlin* i. 2 Grete loue he hadde to man and gret tendirnesse. **1526** *Pilgr. Perf.* (W. de W. 1531) 58 b, So longe as suche tenderness is to the no distraccion from goostlynes. **1668** OWEN *Expos. Ps.* cxxx. Wks. 1851 VI. 415 What love and tenderness there is in God to receive us. **1751** JOHNSON *Rambler* No. 179 ⁋3 Deformity itself is regarded with tenderness rather than aversion. **1844** LD. BROUGHAM *Brit. Const.* xix. §5 (1862) 343 Who visited their offences with tenderness.

b. with *a* and *pl.* An instance of this.

1660 F. BROOKE tr. *Le Blanc's Trav.* 284 Then there was amongst us such a tyde of tendernesses. **1850** LYNCH *Theo. Trin.* ix. 154 Hypocritical exhibitors of prettynesses and tendernesses.

3. Sensitiveness to impression; impressionableness, soft-heartedness; sensibility to pain, esp. when touched; crankness (of a ship).

c **1440** *Partonope* 2713 Som wept for tendyrnesse of hert. **1594** CAREW *Huarte's Exam. Wits* vi. (1596) 78 Memory is nothing els but a tendernesse of the braine, disposed..to receiue & preserue that which the imaginatiue apprehendeth. **1709** STANHOPE *Paraphr.* IV. 176 Till the Patient be awaken'd into Tenderness and Smart, there is no Hope of a Cure. *a* **1716** SOUTH *Serm.* (J.), True tenderness of conscience is nothing else but an awful and exact sense of the rule which should direct it. **1781** GIBSON *Decl. & F.* xxix. III. 113 The disgrace of his daughter..wounded the tenderness, or, at least, the pride, of Rufinus. **1843** R. J. GRAVES *Syst. Clin. Med.* xviii. 210 Judging from the extreme epigastric and abdominal tenderness during life. **1854** BREWSTER *More Worlds* xvi. 231 Such a tenderness of retina, that he could, in a dark night, see and distinguish plainly colours of ribands. **1887** *Daily Tel.* 10 Sept. 2/5 She stood up well under her canvas. She showed no signs of tenderness.

tenderometer (tɛndə'rɒmɪtə(r)). [f. TENDER *a.* + -O + -METER.] An instrument for testing the tenderness of raw peas for picking, processing, etc.

1938 *Encycl. Brit. Bk. of Year* 137/2 The 'Tenderometer' intended to determine the tenderness of raw peas used for canning. **1947** *N.Y. Herald Tribune* 18 May II. 10 The tenderometer shown when green peas reach their scientific peak of ripeness by registering the amount of pressure it takes for the gadget to shear through a sample pod. **1960** *Farmer & Stockbreeder* 16 Feb. 97/1 The tenderometer readings of the placement peas were 10 better than the broadcast averages. **1971** *Power Farming* Mar. 12/4 Peas can be valued on a tenderometer reading. **1981** *Southern Horticulture* (N.Z.) Spring 36/1 As soon as the tenderometer reading is at its optimum the whole paddock must be cleared within hours.

†'**tendership.** *Obs.* *rare*$^{-1}$. [f. as TENDER *a.* + -SHIP.] Tenderness; tender regard or esteem.

c **1460** *Wisdom* 634 in *Macro Plays* 56, I serue myghty lordeschyppe, Ande am in grett tendurschyppe.

†'**tendful,** *a.* *Obs.* *rare*$^{-1}$. [f. TEND *v.*[1] + -FUL I.] Assiduous in tending; attentive.

a **1697** AUBREY *Brief Lives* (1898) II. 209 A good woman ..who was very carefull and tendfull of him.

†'**tendicle.** *Obs.* *rare*$^{-0}$. [ad. L. *tendicula* snare: see next.]

1727 BAILEY vol. II, *Tendicle* (*tendicula*, L.), a Gin or Snare to take Birds or Beasts, &c. **1780** in SHERIDAN.

†'**tendicule.** *Surg.* *Obs.* *rare.* [ad. L. *tendicula*, f. *tendĕre* to stretch: see -CULE.] Name of an instrument for dilating an opening; a dilator.

c **1425** tr. *Arderne's Treat. Fistula*, etc. 24 þan take þe tendicule and putte þe snowte of þe nedle in þe hole of þe fistule in puttyng it strongly.

‖**tendido** (ten'diðo). [Sp., pa. pple. of *tender* to stretch.] An open tier of seats above the barrera at a bull-fight.

1838 *Q. Rev.* LVII. 407 Those whose poverty..consents, sit in the 'tendido', and brave the sun's perpendicular height. **1967** MCCORMICK & MASCAREÑAS *Compl. Aficionado* ii. 59 The toro lopes off from the horse to the sunny side, where it seems to have spotted a man in a blue shirt in the lower *tendido*.

tendinal ('tɛndɪnəl), *a.* *rare*$^{-1}$. [ad. mod.L. type **tendināl-is*, f. mod.L. *tendo*, *-din-em*: see TENDON and -AL[1].] = TENDINOUS. So **tendineal** (tɛn'dɪniːəl) *a.* *rare*$^{-1}$.

1887 *Science* 24 June 624/2 A tendinal slip is shown cut short,..which evidently belongs to this muscle. *Ibid.* 5 Aug. 71/2 [The propatagial slip] also raises the elongated neck-feathers, while special development of its tendineal portion aids in strengthening the *tensor propatagii*.

tending *vbl. sb.*[1] and [2]: see TEND *v.*[1] and [2].

tendinitis (tɛndɪ'naɪtɪs). *Path.* Also **tendonitis.** [f. med.L. *tendin-em*, *tendōn-em* TENDON + -ITIS.] Inflammation of a tendon.

1900 in DORLAND *Med. Dict.* **1940** B. I. COMROE *Arthritis* xxx. 368 Classified according to location, fibrositis is known as:..Tendinitis—involvement of the fibrous tissue of tendons. **1948** *Nomencl. Disease* (R. Coll. Physicians) (ed. 7) v. 99/1 Calcareous tendonitis. **1972** *Time* 18 Sept. 35/1 Tendinitis of the knees. **1975** *Daily Colonist* (Victoria, B.C.) 9 Jan. 2/2 Tendonitis is a fairly common occurence, especially in the shoulder or elbow or heel. In tendonitis (tennis elbow is an example of it) the joint has been injured or irritated in some way.

tendinous ('tɛndɪnəs), *a.* [ad. F. *tendineux* (Paré, 16th c.), f. med. or mod.L. *tendo*, *tendin-em* TENDON.] Of the nature of a tendon; consisting of tendons.

1658 ROWLAND *Moufet's Theat. Ins.* 931 His head is full of sinewes, his body soft, his tail tendinous. **1715** CHEYNE *Philos. Princ. Relig.* I. 110 The Elasticity of Tendinous Bodies. **1822** J. PARKINSON *Outl. Oryctol.* 194 A bivalve shell adherent to marine bodies..by a tendinous cord. **1875** HUXLEY & MARTIN *Elem. Biol.* (1883) 200 The pectoral region; part..only covered by tendinous tissue.

†**tendite** = *to endite*: see T' and INDITE *v.*

c **1384** CHAUCER *H. Fame* I. 381 To longe tendyte. *c* **1385** —— *L.G.W.* 1345 (*Dido*) So gret a reuthe I haue for tendite.

†'**tendle.** *Obs.* or ? *dial.* Also 9 **tennle, tennel.** [A deriv. of OE. *tend-an*, TIND *v.* to kindle, light: perh. a variant of TANDLE *sb.* Cf. also TINDLE.]

a. In 15th c. Exact sense uncertain: perh. (as suggested by editors of *Destr. of Troy*) 'a splint of resinous wood used as a candle'; but perh. rather = TANDLE, a beacon-fire or bonfire. **b.** In later use: see quot. 1887.

c **1400** *Destr. Troy* 6038 Brode firis & brem beccyn in þe ost, Torchis and tendlis the tenttes to light. *Ibid.* 7353 Tore fyres in the tenttes, tendlis olofte! **1887** DONALDSON *Suppl. to Jamieson*, *Tendle*, *Tennle*, *Tennel*, lit. Firewood; dried twigs, furze, scrub, &c., gathered for fuel. [No authority or locality given.]

†'**tendment.** *Obs.* *rare.* [Aphetic f. ATTENDMENT. Cf. TEND *v.*[1] and OF. *tendement* intention.]

1. Meaning, significance. [Cf. F. *entendement*.]

1519 HORMAN *Vulg.* 77 That worde may haue double tendement.

2. Care, attention.

1597–8 BP. HALL *Sat.* II. iv. 21 Whether ill tendment, or recurelesse paine Procure his death.

‖**tendo** ('tɛndəʊ). *Anat.* [med. or mod.L.: see next.] = TENDON: frequent in ***tendo Achillis*** (see next), and in comb. as **tendo calcaneus** (also as one word) [L. *calcāneus*, *-um* heel] = *tendon of Achilles* s.v. TENDON a.; **tendo-synovitis,** inflammation of the synovial membrane of a tendon.

[**1693** tr. *Blancard's Phys. Dict.* (ed. 2), *Tendo*, a Tendon, a similar nervous part annexed to Muscles and Bones.] **1874** CARPENTER *Ment. Phys.* I. ii. §30 (1879) 30 Pulling upwards the heel by means of the great Tendo Achillis. **1899** *Allbutt's Syst. Med.* VI. 528 Hence the terms 'elbow-jerk', 'wrist-jerk', 'tendo-Achillis-jerk'. *Ibid.* 598 Tendo-synovitis of the flexor tendons of this finger. **1900** DORLAND *Med. Dict.* 674 Tendo calcaneus. **1909** *Gray's Anat.* (ed. 17) 582 The tendo Achillis (tendo calcaneus)..is the thickest and strongest tendon in the body. **1937** J. C. B. GRANT *Method Anat.* iv. 302/2 The bellies end at the middle of the leg in a broad aponeurosis that blends with the aponeurosis of the Soleus to form the tendo calcaneus or tendo Achillis. **1967** G. M. WYBURN et al. *Conc. Anat.* vi. 171/1 The muscle groups of the leg are the extensors in front.., the peroneal muscles on the lateral side..and posteriorly the muscles of the calf forming the tendocalcaneus and more deeply the flexors. **1977** *Bone & Joint Diseases* (B.M.A.) 118 At this stage it is essential to elongate the tendocalcaneus through a transverse incision over the heel.

tendon ('tɛndən). Also β. 6 **tenaunt, tennon,** 7 **tenon, tendant,** 8 **tendent.** *Pl.* 6–7 (perh. Lat.) **tendones.** [ad. med.L. *tendo*, *tendōn-em* and *tendin-em*, app. ad. Gr. τένων, τενοντ- sinew, tendon, influenced by L. *tend-ĕre* to stretch; so F. *tendon* (16th c.), also It. *tendone*, *tendine*, Sp. *tendon*.

To Celsus, A.D. 50, τένων was still a Greek word. In Cælius Aurelianus, *c* 400–420, it retains Gr. inflexions, e.g. acc. pl. *tenontas*; but in Theod. Priscianus has L. abl. pl. *tenontibus*. In med.L. it became *tendon* or *tendo*: the latter in Theod. Gaza, tr. Aristotle's *Hist. Anim.*, 1476. The pl. occurs as *tendones* in the tr. of Galen by Nicolaus Calaber of Reggio *a* 1350, and there is later evidence that the *o* was long, *tendōnes*. Another pl. *tendines* (after *ordines*, etc.) was used in 16th c. and later. (I. Bywater.) The β-forms *tenon*, *tenaunt* perh. preserve traces of the Gr. forms, confused with other words.]

a. A band or cord of dense fibrous tissue forming the termination of a muscle, by which it is attached to a bone or other part; a sinew: usually applied to such when rounded or cord-like, broad flat tendons being called *fasciæ* and *aponeuroses*.

tendon of Achilles (L. *tendo Achillis*), the tendon of the heel; the tendon by which the muscles of the calf of the leg are attached to the heel, being the principal extensor of the foot. So named from the mythological account that when the infant Achilles was dipped by his mother Thetis in the Styx, to render him invulnerable, he was held by the heel, which thereby escaped dipping and remained vulnerable.

1543 TRAHERON *Vigo's Chirurg.* 1 b/1 Chordes or tendones. **1563** T. GALE *Enchirid.* 41 b (Stanf.) Nerues, tendons, ligamentes. **1578** BANISTER *Hist. Man* III. 44 b, A tendon is the white part in the Muscle beyng hard, thicke, and shynnyng. **1610** HEALEY *St. Aug. Citie of God* XIV. xxiv. (1620) 498 Small sinews and *Tendones*. **1726** GAY in *Swift's Lett.* (1766) II. 59 The surgeon..told him, that his fingers were safe, that there were two nerves cut, but no tendon. **1872** MIVART *Anat.* 149 The radius,..its posterior surface is grooved for the passage of tendons.

β. **1541** R. COPLAND *Guydon's Quest. Chirurg.* F iv, The tenauntes moeuyng the heade and the necke, whiche are .xx. in nombre. *Ibid.*, The tenaunt muscles and the strynges.. that maketh the heade bowe. **1598** FLORIO, *Tendini*, as *Tendoni*, the tennons. **1607** MARKHAM *Caval.* VII. (1617) 7 There is one maine tendant or sinewe. **1630** J. TAYLOR (Water P.) *Praise Cleane Linnen* Ded., Wks. II. 166 The Legge..ennamel'd with Sinewes, interwoven with Membranes, intermixt with Tenons, embost with Ankles. **1708** *Lond. Gaz.* No. 4484/1 Convulsive Motions of the Tendents.

b. *Entom.* (See quot.)

1826 KIRBY & SP. *Entomol.* III. 381 *Tendo* (the *Tendon*), a strong bristle, or bristles observable at the base underneath in the under-wings of many *Lepidoptera*, which plays in the *Hamus* of the upper-wings.

c. *Engin.* A steel rod or wire that is stretched while in liquid concrete so as to prestress it as it sets.

1958 F. S. MERRITT *Building Construction Handbk.* v. 56 After the concrete has attained sufficient strength, the steel is secured to the anchor plates and the jacks are removed. The tendons will tend to shorten and therefore will put compression in the concrete. **1974** [see PRESTRESSING *vbl. sb.*]. **1975** [see PRE-TENSIONING *vbl. sb.*]. **1981** *Sci. Amer.* June 45/3 The prestressed-concrete reactor vessel..is kept in compression at all times by a network of redundant, tensioned steel tendons that can be monitored and retensioned or even replaced if necessary.

d. *attrib.* and *Comb.*, as ***tendon cell***, ***corpuscle*** (see quot.), ***jerk*** (JERK *sb.*[1] 2 b), ***muscle***, ***reaction***, ***reflex*** (REFLEX *sb.* 6), ***sheath***, ***thread***; **tendon organ, spindle** = SPINDLE *sb.* 4 e.

1890 BILLINGS *Nat. Med. Dict.*, **T*[*endon*] *cells* or *corpuscles*, connective tissue cells found in tendons and ligaments, arranged in rows following the course of the fibres. **1899** *Allbutt's Syst. Med.* VII. 62 The increased activity of the *tendon-jerks is manifested by an excessive jaw-jerk. **1541** *Tenaunt muscles [see β above]. **1923** V. H. MOTTRAM *Man. Histol.* vii. 225 Similar apparatus is seen in the Golgi *tendon organ. **1974** D. & M. WEBSTER *Compar. Vertebr. Morphol.* x. 202 Both the tendon organ and the muscle spindle fire in response to stretch. **1878** *Med. Times* 2 Feb. 107 [Erb] applied to it the name '*tendon-reflex'. **1899** *Allbutt's Syst. Med.* VI. 519 The knee-jerk is sometimes spoken of as a 'tendon reflex'. **1897** *Ibid.* III. 67 Effusion into the *tendon sheaths. **1896** *Tendon-spindle [see SPINDLE *sb.* 4 e]. **1930** MAXIMOW & BLOOM *Text-bk. Histol.* xiv. 276 Not infrequently, of two branches of the same sensory fiber one supplies a muscle spindle, the other a tendon spindle. **1977** D. P. WINSTANLEY tr. *Leonhardt's Human Histol.* 249 Tendon spindles are situated in the tendon close to its junction with the muscle. **1906** SIR F. TREVES in *Daily Chron.* 3 Aug. 3/4 Skins sewn together with a bone needle and a *tendon thread.

tendonitis, var. TENDINITIS.

tendonous ('tɛndənəs), *a.* [f. TENDON + -OUS.] = TENDINOUS. Hence '**tendonousness,** *rare*$^{-1}$ (in quot. 1597 = tendinous part).

1597 A. M. tr. *Guillemeau's Fr. Chirurg.* 20/2 We must avoyde the synnuishe tendonousnes of the right muscle. **1660** BOYLE *New Exp. Phys. Mech., Digress.* 341 Having stabb'd himself, and pierced the Diaphragme in the thinner or tendonous part. **1753** HERVEY *Theron & Asp.* (1757) I. xii. 450 An assemblage of fine tendonous fibres. **1877** ROSENTHAL *Muscles & Nerves* xi. 199 The natural ends of the muscle-fibres while still closed with the tendonous substance.

tendoor, -our, var. of TANDOUR, Persian stove.

'**tendotome.** *Surg.* An improper form of TENOTOME, assimilated to *tendon*.

1882 in OGILVIE (Annandale).

tendour, obs. form of TENDER *sb.*[1], [2].

tendrac, variant of TANREC.

‖**tendre** (tɑ̃dr). [F. *tendre* sb., from *tendre*, TENDER *a.*] **a.** A tender feeling or regard; a fondness, an affection; a tenderness.

1673 DRYDEN *Marr. à la Mode* III. i, I have such a *tendre* for the court, that I love it even from the drawing-room to the lobby. **1695** CONGREVE *Love for L.* I. xv, I will, because I have a *tendre* for your ladyship. **1748** SMOLLETT *Rod. Rand.* xlii, A pretty maid, who had a *tendre* for me. **1833** T. HOOK *Parson's Dau.* II. ii, I am quite relieved.. since you tell me there had been no *tendre* between her and Mr. Harvey. **1848** THACKERAY *Van. Fair* xv, You poor friendless creatures are always having some foolish *tendre*. **1887** E. SIMCOX in K. A. McKenzie *Edith Simcox & George Eliot* (1961) 7 Having towards.. Garibaldi.. perhaps the same sort of *tendre* as that professed by Charlotte Bronte for the Duke of Wellington. **1921** D. H. LAWRENCE *Sea & Sardinia* vii. 298 She.. was relieved to escape the new attachment, though she had a great *tendre* for him. **1980** G. M. FRASER *Mr American* xxii. 439 The cunning old gentleman's reading of her character, and of her supposed *tendre* for Mr Franklin.

†**b.** An expression of tenderness. *Obs. rare.*

1705 VANBRUGH *Confed.* IV. i, O Pox!.. I desire none of your *Tendres*.

tendre, obs. form of TENDER, TINDER.

tendren, obs. form of TENDRON.

‖**tendresse.** *Obs.* exc. as Fr. [F. *tendresse* (tɑ̃drɛs), 14th c. in Godef., f. *tendre*, TENDER *a.*] = TENDERNESS.

1390 GOWER *Conf.* I. 195 For Moderhed and for tendresse. **1399** *Rolls of Parlt.* III. 451/2 To have rewarde to tendresse of her age. *a* **1766** MRS. F. SHERIDAN *Sidney Bidulph* IV. 64 But have not you at the same time a small tendresse for her fortune? **1850** W. IRVING in *Life & Lett.* (1864) IV. 76 The fair Truffi, for whom I still cherish a certain degree of *tendresse*. **1885** *Athenæum* 17 Oct. 503/2 The.. sister who conceals her *tendresse* for the hero in maidenly fashion.

tendril (ˈtɛndrɪl), *sb.* Also 6 -yll, -elle, 6–8 -el, 7 -ell, 8 -ill. [Origin uncertain; app. from L. *tendĕre*, F. *tendre* to stretch; in its actual form and sense only in Eng. See Note below.]

1. a. A slender thread-like organ or appendage of a plant (consisting of a modified stem, branch, flower-stalk, leaf, or part of a leaf), often growing in a spiral form, which stretches out and attaches itself to or twines round some other body so as to support the plant. (Distinguished from a *twining stem* by not bearing leaves.)

1538 ELYOT, *Capreolus*,.. the tendrell of a vyne, whiche wyndeth diuers ways, called also Pampinus. **1578** LYTE *Dodoens* III. lxxxviii. 441 Litle claspers or tendrelles, wherewithal it taketh holdefast vpon hedges, trees, poles, and rayles. **1611** COTGR., *Tendron*.. a tendrell, or the tender branch, or sprig of a plant. **1667** MILTON *P.L.* IV. 307 Her.. tresses.. in wanton ringlets wav'd As the Vine curles her tendrils. **1768** STERNE *Sent. Journ.* (1778) II. 175 (*Maria*) A couple of vine leaves, tied round with a tendril. **1807** J. E. SMITH *Phys. Bot.* 224 *Cirrus*. Tendrils or claspers when young are usually put forth in a straight direction; but they presently become spiral. **1858** CARPENTER *Veg. Phys.* §538 Nearly all the plants of the group are climbers, and most of them support themselves by tendrils.

b. *transf.* Something resembling a tendril of a plant: as, a slender branch of a vein; a curl or ringlet of hair. (Cf. also *tendril-footed* in 3 b.)

1615 CROOKE *Body of Man* 79 Sometime also seueral tendrils are communicated vnto it from the spermatical veines. **1814** BYRON *Lara* II. xxi, The glossy tendrils of his raven hair. **1859** GEO. ELIOT *A. Bede* xliii, The dark tendrils of hair,.. the rounded cheek and the pouting lips.

c. *fig.*, esp. in reference to a 'clinging' affection or attachment.

1841 EMERSON *Lect.*, *Man the Reformer* Wks. (Bohn) II. 238 Inextricable seem to be the twinings and tendrils of this evil. **1852** MRS. STOWE *Uncle Tom's C.* xxii, Her own earnest nature threw out its tendrils, and wound itself around the majestic book. **1891** T. HARDY *Tess* II. xiv, Her foolish soul sent back tendrils of yearning towards it [her father's house].

†**2.** Used to render F. *tendron* bud (see TENDRON) in fig. sense 'young girl'. *Obs.*

1603 FLORIO *Montaigne* III. ix. (1632) 554 Continually stored with young tendrels or lasses, to keepe his old-frozen limbs warme a nights. **1639** S. DU VERGER tr. *Camus' Admir. Events* 313 Hee sends this tendrell to schoole againe.

3. *attrib.* and *Comb.* **a.** *attrib.* Having or bearing tendrils, as ***tendril brier, hop, vine***; of or belonging to a tendril, resembling or consisting of a tendril, as ***tendril career, finger, hand, -hold, -ring, -talon***. **b.** objective, instrumental, parasynthetic, etc., as ***tendril-bearer, -climber***; ***tendril-footed, -like*** adjs.

1872 DARWIN *Orig. Spec.* vii. (ed. 6) 196 Gradations.. between simple twiners and *tendril-bearers. *c* **1711** PETIVER *Gazophyl.* VI. Tab. lviii, Triangular *Tendril Bryar... A very odd Anomalous Plant. **1957** C. DAY LEWIS *Pegasus* 45 Or too much reason chill the air For your *tendril career. **1875** BENNETT & DYER *Sachs' Bot.* 197 A distinction is drawn between *Tendril-climbers (as *Vitis*) and Stem-climbers (as *Phaseolus, Humulus, Convolvulus*, &c.). **1929** *Oxford Poetry* 5 The *tendril fingers groping for the bright Eternal beauty. **1843** CARPENTER *Anim. Phys.* 94 The class *Cirrhipoda*, or *tendril-footed animals. **1939** DYLAN THOMAS *Map of Love* 14 Shall she receive a bellyful of weeds And bear those *tendril hands I touch across The agonized, two seas. **1967** J. STALLWORTHY *Almond Tree* 11, I am called to the cot to see your focus shift, take *tendril-hold on a shaft of sun. **1757** DYER *Fleece* I. 62 The curling growth Of *tendril hops, that flaunt upon their poles. **1836–9** *Todd's Cycl. Anat.* II. 146/2 The *tendril-like branches of the arteria profunda. **1791** E. DARWIN *Bot. Gard.* II. 150 Long horrent thorns his mossy legs surround, And *tendril-talons root him to the ground. **1743** FRANCIS tr. *Hor.*, *Epod.* xv. 3 When round my Neck as curls the *Tendril-Vine—(Loose are its Curlings, if compar'd to thine). **1896** *Westm. Gaz.* 20 Oct. 10/2 Framed in Romanesque *tendril work.

Hence **ˈtendril** *v.* (*nonce-wd.*) *intr.* to curl like a tendril; **ˈtendrilled, -iled** (-ɪld) *a.*, having a tendril or tendrils (in quot. 1839 *transf.* curly); **tendriˈliferous** *a.* [-FEROUS], bearing tendrils; **ˈtendrilly, ˈtendrilous** *adjs.*, full of tendrils; resembling a tendril.

1894 CROCKETT *Lilac Sunbonnet* 18 Fair hair, crisping and *tendrilling over her brow. **1806** GALPINE *Brit. Bot.* §319 Fumaria.. stem climbing: petioles *tendrilled. **1822** *Hortus Angl.* II. 126 *A*[*ntirrhinum*] *Cirrhosa*. Tendriled Toad Flax. **1839** BAILEY *Festus* xx (1852) 375 Some young thing with tiny hands, And rosy cheeks, and flossy tendrilled locks. **1900** W. WALLACE in *Ann. Bot.* Dec. 639 A *tendriliferous liane. **1863** HOLME LEE *Annie Warleigh* III. 25 A Virginian creeper twined its thousands of *tendrilly sprays up the rustic pillars. **1857** WOOD *Com. Objects Sea Shore* 58 The long, curling, *tendrilous appendages.. affix themselves to sea-weeds.. and.. anchor the egg firmly.

[*Note.* With *tendril*, cf. F. *tendrillon* bud, tender sprout or shoot, dim. of *tendron* in same sense, also fig. a 'bud', a young girl; also cartilage; which Hatz.-Darm. refer to *tendre* adj. tender. But Paré (16th c.) took *tendron* as synonymous with *capréole* tendril, clasper ('La vigne par ses tendrons ou capréoles tortues embrasse toutes choses'), and L. *capreolus* (rendered by Elyot 1538 'tendrell') was by R. Estienne, 1536, glossed by *tendon*, a deriv. of L. *tendĕre*, F. *tendre* to stretch. There was thus in 16th c. F. some confusion between *tendon* and *tendron*, which appears to have influenced the Eng. use of *tendril* and associated it with *tendre* to stretch rather than with *tendre* tender. See also Weekley in *Trans. Philol. Soc.* 1909.]

tendron (ˈtɛndrən). Also 5 tenderon, tendrone, 5–6 -ren, -ringe, 7 -ering, 8 -ring, 9 -erone. [a. F. *tendron* bud, young sprout or shoot; also cartilage; f. *tendre*, TENDER *a.*: but see prec.]

1. A young tender shoot or sprout of a plant; a bud. Now *rare.*

14.. *Stockh. Med. MS.* I. 340 in *Anglia* XVIII. 303 Take þe lewys of þe reed docke, þe tendronys in þe mydward awey do knocke. *c* **1420** *Liber Cocorum* (1862) 34 Take tenderons of sauge.. And stop one [cofyn] fulle up to þo ryng. *c* **1440** *Promp. Parv.* 488/2 Tendrone, of a vyne.., *botrio*. **1601** HOLLAND *Pliny* (1634) II. 28 So soon as new buds and tendrons appeare aboue ground from the root. *Ibid.* 196 The juice drawne and pressed out of the tendrons or yong sprouts of brambles. **1707** MORTIMER *Husb.* (1721) II. 152 Cut off all the Blossoms that are likely to bear no Fruit, also the small tendrings, the barren Branches. **1895** W. RAYMOND *Tryphena in Love* 5 The inconstant shade of leafy tendrons quivering in the wind.

†**b.** *transf.* A small branch, as of a vein. *Obs.*

1578 BANISTER *Hist. Man* I. 7 The little Tendringes or Spriggie braunches of veines.

2. (*pl.*) The cartilages of the ribs (*esp.* in *Cookery*, of a deer or calf).

1398 TREVISA *Barth. De P.R.* v. i. (1495) f vij/2 The tendrenes of the ribbes defende the lyuer. **15..** *Wyll Burke his Test.* (Halliw.) 54 Bake dowcetts and tendrens and the liver rostid. **1768** *Chron* in *Ann. Reg.* 170/2 The bill of fare Venison, Tendrons, Quails. **1806** J. SIMPSON *Cookery* (1816) 43 (Stanf.) The tenderones are the gristle bone of the breast of veal cut into thin slices. **1845** BREGION & MILLER *Pract. Cook* 43 Tendrons (Veal), are found near the extremity of the ribs.

†**tendry.** *Obs.* [f. TENDER *v.*[1], F. *tendre*: cf. OF. *tend(e)rie* (14th c.) the act of stretching, etc., f. *tendre* to stretch; cf. RENDRY.]

1. An act of tendering or offering; a tender, offer, proffer; a formal offer.

1624 BP. MOUNTAGU *Immed. Addr.* 18, I suppose it a tendry of Kindness rather, a Gentle Inuitation, to come and Call. **1656** HEYLIN *Surv. France* 322 The Tenants made no tendry of this Champart, and so it lay amongst concealments. *a* **1667** JER. TAYLOR *Reverence due to Altar* Wks. 1849 V. 319 A tendry of our service. **1681–6** J. SCOTT *Chr. Life* II. vii. §5 God.. had as undoubted a Right to exchange them with Christ's for his Life, upon the free Tendry which he made of it.

2. *spec.* The tendering or delivering of something to be mentally accepted or considered; hence, a doctrine delivered or presented for acceptance, a deliverance; *pl.* articles of belief, tenets.

1624 BP. MOUNTAGU *Immed. Addr.* 146 In Gods Precepts and Tendries of beleefe, I will subiect.. my enquiring into plaine beleefe. **1636** HEYLIN *Sabbath* I. Pref. A v, You would not shut your eyes, against the tendrie of those truths. **1652–62** —— *Cosmogr.* I. (1677) 209/1 Arianism: not ejurated till the year 583, when that whole Nation did submit to more Catholick tendries. *a* **1662** —— *Laud* (1668) 261 The general Tendries of the Protestant, Lutheran, and Calvinian Writers beyond the Seas. **1675** V. ALSOP *Anti-Sozzo* 467 Religion must appear before the Tribunal of Reason; and if it does not acquit itself well, and give a Rational and Satisfactory account of its Tendries, it must be bored through the Tongue with a red hot Iron for an Heretic.

[**tendsome**, *a.* Explained as: Requiring much attendance. Known only in the following Dict. entries.

1847 WEBSTER, *Tendsome*, requiring much attendance; as, a *tendsome* child... *Tensome*, see Tendsome. So **1850** OGILVIE, adding (*Obs.* or *fam.*). **1864** WEBSTER, adding (Written also *tensome*). **1891** *Century Dict.*]

‖**tendu** (tɑ̃dy), *a. Ballet.* [Fr., pa. pple. of *tendre* to stretch.] Stretched out or held tautly, esp. in *battement tendu* (see BATTEMENT).

1922 BEAUMONT & IDZIKOWSKI *Man. Classical Theatr. Dancing* I. 34 *Battements Tendus* serve to stretch and strengthen the muscles. **1950** *Ballet Ann.* IV. 129/2 The return, with the Russian masters of 1925–30, of the traditional French style, strictly *tendu*. **1952** [see BATTEMENT].

†**tendure** = *to endure*: see T'.

1480 CAXTON *Descr. Brit.*, *Irel.* 27 These swyne may not be kept.. for tendure in likenes of swyne ouer thre dayes.

tendy, obs. inf. of TEND *v.*[1]

tene, obs. f. TEEN; var. TIND *v. Obs.*, to kindle.

-tene (tiːn), f. Gr. ταινία band, ribbon, used in *Cytology* as a formative element of terms denoting stages of the first meiotic division (in nomenclature due to H. von Winiwarter 1900, in *Arch. de Biol.* XVII).

teneble, -blus: see TENEBRES.

‖**Tenebræ** (ˈtɛnɪbriː, -breɪ). *R.C. Ch.* See also TENEBRES. [L. *tenebræ* darkness; in med.L. in the eccles. sense: see Du Cange.] The name given to the office of matins and lauds of the following day, usually sung in the afternoon or evening of Wednesday, Thursday, and Friday in Holy Week, at which the candles lighted at the beginning of the service are extinguished one by one after each psalm, in memory of the darkness at the time of the crucifixion. Also *attrib.*

1651 in Morris *Troubles Cath. Foref.* I. vi. (1872) 304 We were forced to read our Office and even the Tenebræ Matins in the work chamber. **1656** BLOUNT *Glossogr.* s.v., The service or mattins used in the Roman Church.. cal'd *tenebræ* (thence *tenebræ wednesday, thursday, &c.*). **1708** OZELL *Boileau's Lutrin* IV. (1730) 192 Others more sad and phlegmatick than he Guess'd it the Toning of the Tenebrae. **1753** CHALLONER *Cath. Chr. Instr.* 219 Called the Tenebræ Office. **1864** J. H. NEWMAN *Apol.* i. (1904) 21/1 We attended the Tenebræ, at the Sestine, for the sake of the Miserere.

†**ˈtenebrate**, *ppl. a. Obs. rare.* [ad. L. *tenebrāt-us*, pa. pple. of *tenebrāre* to darken, f. *tenebræ* darkness.] Darkened, dark. So **teneˈbration**, *rare*$^{-0}$ [ad. L. *tenebrātiōn-em*: see -ATION], darkening, obscuration.

1492 RYMAN *Poems* lxxxv. 3 in Herrig's *Archiv* LXXXIX. 255 The orient Phebus And the tenebrat nyght In nature be full different. **1862** A. J. COOLEY *Dict.*, Tenebration.

†**ˈtenebres.** *Obs.* Forms: *α.* 5–9 tenebres; in sing. form 5 tenebre, 6 teneber, tenabur. *β.* 5 teneblus, 5–6 tenables; in sing. 6 teneble, -byll, tenable. [a. F. *tenèbres* (11th c., in sense 1), ad. L. *tenebræ, -ās*, darkness. The *β*-forms were corruptions, confusing the word with *tenable*.]

1. Darkness, obscurity.

α. **1413** *Pilgr. Sowle* (Caxton 1483) III. iii. 51 Enuy is the doughter of the grete tenebre. **1483** CAXTON *Gold. Leg.* 420 b/1 Thou shalte deye here in tenebres or derknesse. **1483** —— *G. de la Tour* I vj b, For grete pyte.. to see them goo and falle in the tenebres of helle. **1490** —— *Eneydos* ii. 14 Under the tenebres and derkenes, departed Eneas. **1656** BLOUNT *Glossogr.*, *Tenebres*.., darkness, obscurity.

β. **1530** PALSGR. 184 *Les tenebres*.. a sodayne darkenesse or tenables,.. or want of lyght in the night season.

2. = TENEBRÆ.

1539 *Bk. Ceremonies* in Strype *Eccl. Mem.* (1721) I. App. cix. 292 The same service is called tenebres. **1658** PHILLIPS, *Tenebres*. **1703** in *Cath. Rec. Soc. Publ.* VII. 146 Mr Nelson.. was wth him at ye Tenebres at St Thos. **1801** *Lusignan* IV. 138 [He] arrived there at the hour of the tenebres.

β. *a* **1450** MYRC *Festial* 117 Hyt ys called wyth you teneblus; but holy chyrch callyþe hit tenebras, þat is to say, derkenes.

b. *attrib.* in sing. form **tenebre, teneber** (but the former may be the L. *tenebræ*), as ***tenebre candle, lesson, matins, service, Tenebre Wednesday***.

1477–9 *Rec. St. Mary at Hill* 91 Paid to Roger Middilton, wex Chaundeler, for.. tapris, prickettes and tenebre candill, for euery lb, ob—xj s. ix d. **1525** in Nichols *Churchw. Acc.* (1797) 273 For makyng of the paskall, w^t^ the tenabur candell. **1529** MORE *Dyaloge* I. xviii. Wks. 143/2 In the tenebre lessons leueth her candel burning styll. **1530** PALSGR. 811/2 On Tenebre wednysdaye, *le mercredy des Tenebres*. *a* **1548** HALL *Chron.*, *Hen. VIII* 199 b, Which Richard.. was boyled in Smythfelde the Teneber wednisday followyng.

β. **1530** PALSGR. 280/1 Teneble wednisday,.. *mercredy saint*. **1554** *Rec. St. Mary at Hill* 397 Lyghtes that was burned of tenebyll weddyns day. **15..** in *Brand's Pop. Antiq.* (1849) I. 48 Tenable candylls for the Judas. **1588** PARKE tr. *Mendoza's Hist. China* 151 [He] ariued at the mouth of the riuer Pagansinan vpon tenable wednesday.

tenebrescence (tɛnɪˈbrɛsəns). *Physics.* [ad. L. *tenebrescens*, pr. pple. of *tenebrescere* to grow dark, f. *tenebræ* darkness.] The property of reversibly darkening and bleaching in response to radiation of different wavelengths (orig. restricted to the property of darkening only).

Hence **tene'brescent** *a.*; **tene'bresce** *v. intr.*, to darken or bleach thus.

1946 H. W. Leverenz in *RCA Rev.* VII. 199 (*heading*) Luminescence and tenebrescence as applied in radar. [*Note*] The terms 'tenebrescence' and 'scotophor' are derived.. to correspond to the terms 'luminescence' and 'phosphor'... Tenebrescence is any absorption of light not intrinsic to the materials involved;.. a scotophor is a tenebrescent material .. which may be made to tenebresce reversibly, i.e., visibly darken and bleach (irrespective of chromaticity), under suitable irradiations. **1953** *Amer. Mineralogist* XXXVIII. 919 (*heading*) Composition, tenebrescence and luminescence of spodumene minerals. *Ibid.*, Only non-chromian spodumene is luminescent and tenebrescent. **1970** Dorion & Weibe *Photochromism* i. 9 Tenebrescent and scotophoric materials are crystals that may be colored by radiation such as electron bombardment, X-rays, or light, and that are bleached by other radiation.

te'nebricose, *a. rare.* [ad. L. *tenebricōs-us*, f. *tenebric-us* dark, gloomy: see -ose.] Full of darkness; dark, obscure; gloomy.

1730–6 in Bailey (folio). **1817** T. L. Peacock *Melincourt* xxxi, He.. has taken a very opaque and tenebricose view of how much of the spheroidical perception belongs to the object.

tenebrific (tɛnɪˈbrɪfɪk), *a.* [f. (? mod.L. *tenebrific-us*, f.) L. *tenebræ* darkness: see -fic.] Causing or producing darkness; obscuring. (In quot. 1785 loosely for 'dark, gloomy'.)

tenebrific stars or ***constellations***: see tenebrificous.

1785 Burns *Ep. to Davie* x, It lightens, it brightens, The tenebrific scene. **1825** Carlyle *Schiller* iii. (1873) 99 Its interpreters with us have been like 'tenebrific stars'. **1827** —— *Misc. Ess., St. Germ. Lit.* (1840) I. 92 These are its 'tenebrific constellation', from which it 'doth ray out darkness' over the earth. **1848** Lowell *Biglow P.* Poems 1890 II. 113 Grammar, a topic rendered only more tenebrific by the labors of his successors. **1858** Carlyle *Fredk. Gt.* iv. i. I. 383 Books done by pedants and tenebrific persons under the name of men. **1868** Browning *Ring & Bk.* iii. 789 Now begins The tenebrific passage of the tale.

So **tene'brificate** *v. rare*, *trans.* to darken, obfuscate; † **tene'brificous** *a. Obs.*, tenebrific.

c **1743** in *Mem. Eliz. Carter* (1808) II. 147 The complete science of circumlocution, and the whole art of confounding, perplexing, puzzling, and *tenebrificating a subject. **16..** 'W. Ramsey' (quoted in *Spectator*: see next quot.), There are *tenebrificous and dark stars, by whose influence night is brought on, and which do ray out darkness and obscurity upon the earth as the sun does light. **1714** *Spect.* No. 582 ¶5, I could mention several Authors who are tenebrificous Stars of the first Magnitude. **1852** K. H. Digby *Compitum* VI. 8.

‖**tenebrio** (tɪˈnɛbrɪəʊ). Also 7 tenebrion. [L. *tenebrio* one who lurks in the dark, f. *tenebræ* darkness; F. *ténébrion* (Rabelais, 16th c.).]

†**1.** One who lurks in the dark; a night-prowler; also, a night-spirit, a nocturnal visitant. *Obs. rare.*

1656 Blount *Glossogr.*, *Tenebrion*, one that will not be seen by day, a lurker, a night-thief; also a night-spirit, a hobgoblin. *a* **1693** *Urquhart's Rabelais* iii. xxiv, The approach of the Suns radiant Beams expelleth Goblins, Bugbears,.. Night-walking Spirits, and Tenebrions. *a* **1734** North *Exam.* i. i. §7 (1740), The very rankest of [the Hackney Libellers], which.. came forth, like Nocturnal Tenebrios, from the dark and dirty Recesses of the Party.

2. *Entom.* The typical genus of the family *Tenebrionidæ* of heteromerous beetles, which live in dark places on decaying matter and excrement (hence known as stinking beetles). It includes the two meal-worms, *Tenebrio molitor* and *T. obscurus*, and numerous species that live in decayed trees.

1753 Chambers *Cycl. Supp.* App., *Tenebrio*... Mouffet has called it the *blatta fœtida*. **1811** Pinkerton *Voy.* X. 190 The women of Arabia and Turkey make use of another tenebrio, which is found among the filth of gardens. **1833** A. Crichton *Hist. Arabia* II. ix. 462.

tenebrionid (tɪˌnɛbrɪˈɒnɪd), *sb.* (and *a.*) [a. mod.L. family name *Tenebrionidæ*, f. tenebrio 2, adopted as a generic name by Linnæus (*Fauna suecica* (1746) 189): see -id³.] A dark-coloured beetle of the family Tenebrionidæ, which is widely distributed, esp. in dry regions. Also as *adj.*, of or designating a beetle of this kind. Cf. *meal-worm* s.v. meal *sb.*¹ 3 b.

1921 C. A. Ealand *Insect Life* vi. 204 One of the commonest of our sand-loving Tenebrionids is *Heliopathes gibbus*. **1925** A. D. Imms *Gen. Textbk. Ent.* iii. 498 For a bibliography of Tenebrionid larvae vide Graveley. **1942** C. Barrett *On Wallaby* v. 96 Many kinds of Desert beetles are black, notably the large and active Tenebrionids. **1966** [see carabid *a.*]. **1979** *Jrnl. Arid Environments* II. 265 Such an aposematic function is admirably demonstrated.. in a Müllerian complex of American desert tenebrionids.

tenebrious (tɪˈnɛbrɪəs), *a.* [app. altered form of tenebrous: not on L. analogies.] Of or pertaining to darkness; of dark nature; = tenebrous.

1594 *Selimus* A iv b, The caue tenebrious, and damned spirits holt. **1624** Heywood *Gunaik.* ix. 459 A place so palpably tenebrious, into which the eyes of Heauen cannot pierce and see me. **1742** Young *Nt. Th.* ix. 963 Were Moon, and Stars, for Villains only made? To guide, yet screen them, with tenebrious Light? **1820** Foster *Ess. Evils Pop. Ignorance* 216 All this therefore passes before him with a tenebrious glimmer, and is gone. **1907** *Speaker* 19 Jan. 471/1 Thoughts tenebrious and impassioned.

Hence **te'nebriously** *adv.*, darkly.

1861 J. Thomson *Ladies of Death* xv, Thy lidless eyes tenebriously bright.

tenebrity (tɪˈnɛbrɪtɪ). [f. as next + -ity.] The quality of being dark; darkness, material or mental.

1792 A. Young *Trav. France* 147 With all these shades of darkness, these clouds of tenebrity, this universal mass of ignorance. **1973** E. P. Maten tr. *Budhasvāmin's Bṛhatkathāślokasaṃgraha* i. 32 Light.. soiled.. by a dense tenebrity.

†'**tenebrize**, *v. Obs.* [f. L. *tenebræ* darkness + -ize.] *intr.* To pass one's time in darkness.

a **1657** R. Loveday *Lett.* (1663) 68 So long as I tenebrize it here in this blind corner; where I almost live like a flye in winter.

tenebrose (ˈtɛnɪbrəʊs), *a.* [ad. L. *tenebrōsus* dark, f. *tenebræ* darkness: see -ose.] Dark.

1490 Caxton *Eneydos* xv. 53 The sprynge of the daye.. hadde putte awaye the nyghte tenebrose. **1801** *Lusignan* IV. 215 The tenebrose gloom of the place. **1830** W. Phillips *Mt. Sinai* ii. 274 At night's meridian tenebrose.

b. *fig.* Mentally or morally dark; gloomy; obscure in meaning.

1677 Gale *Crt. Gentiles* II. iii. 208 Those times were very tenebrose. **1825** *New Monthly Mag.* XIII. 450 All this was wormwood in the teeth of the tenebrose Visigoth of the middle ages. **1839** *Blackw. Mag.* XLV. 533 That most tenebrose of all poets, Fulke Greville, Lord Brooke.

tenebrosity (tɛnɪˈbrɒsɪtɪ). [a. F. *ténébrosité* (14th c. in Godef.), f. L. *tenebrōs-us*: see prec. and -ity.] Darkness, obscurity.

1490 Caxton *Eneydos* i. 13 The thicke tenebrosite of the blacke smoke. **1603** Holland *Plutarch's Mor.* 1080 That tenebrosity or darknesse is directly opposite unto light and cleerenesse. **1656** in Blount *Glossogr.* **1815** J. Gilchrist *Labyrinth Demolished* 19 But sure it must be the very essence of tenebrosity to suppose that the hand changes its nature or the name of it its meaning with change of purpose, and application or use. **1922** Joyce *Ulysses* 387 This tenebrosity of the interior.. hath not been illumined by the wit of the septuagint. **1924** *Times* 8 Apr. 14/1 Mr. Baldwin was joined by Mr. Asquith in his condemnation of the tenebrosity of the Government statements.

‖**tenebroso** (teneˈbroso), *sb.* and *a.* Also *pl.* (as *sb.*) tenebrosi. [It. *tenebroso* dark: see tenebrous *a.* (*sb.*).] **A.** *sb.* One of a group of early seventeenth-century Italian painters influenced by Caravaggio, whose work is characterized by dramatic contrasts of light and shade. **B.** *adj.* Designating the style of this group of painters.

1886 W. M. Rossetti in *Encycl. Brit.* XX. 532/1 The naturalist school, called also the school of the Tenebrosi, or shadow painters. *Ibid.*, Ribera.. had by this time acquired so much mastery over the tenebroso style that his performances were barely distinguishable from Caravaggio's own. **1938** *Burlington Mag.* Feb. 63/1 *The Last Supper*.. introduces us to a *tenebroso* effect. **1982** C. Whitfield in Whitfield & Martineau *Painting in Naples* (Catal. of R. Acad. Exhibition) 165/2 Artemisia Gentileschi trained with her father Orazio in the early Seicento, when his style was at its most *tenebroso*.

Hence '**tenebrist** = tenebroso *sb.*; '**tenebrism**, the style of the *tenebrosi*.

1923 F. J. Mather *Hist. Italian Painting* ix. 454 Both at Rome and Naples swaggering Caravaggio had enormous success... He boasted himself the greatest painter of all time, and he was often believed. From his swarthy tones his entire school took the name, the Tenebrists. **1958** *Archit. Rev.* CXXIV. 56/3 As a belated tenebrist, he [*sc.* Wright of Derby] handles artificial light intelligently without making any visual discoveries of his own. **1959** *Penguin Dict. Art* 313 Tenebrism.. is the name given to painting in a very low key, specifically to the works of those early 17th c. painters who were much influenced by Caravaggio. **1978** *Times Lit. Suppl.* 17 Feb. 213/3 Elsheimer's.. tenebrism sprang from the same source.

tenebrous (ˈtɛnɪbrəs), *a.* (*sb.*) [a. OF. *tenebrus* (11th c.), mod.F. *ténébreux*, Pr. *tenebros*, Sp., It. *tenebroso*, ad. L. *tenebrōs-us* tenebrose.]

1. Full of darkness, dark.

c **1420** ? Lydg. *Assembly of Gods* 1169 Tyll Cerberus Had hem beshut withyn hys gates tenebrus. *c* **1489** Caxton *Blanchardyn* xxxii. 121 A tenebrouse & derke dongeon. *c* **1530** Ld. Berners *Arth. Lyt. Bryt.* (1814) 204 The aduentures of the Tenebrous, or Darke Tower. **1608** R. Johnson *Seven Champions* ii. T iv, Therewith drewe on the darke and tenebrous night. **1725** *Bradley's Fam. Dict.* s.v. *Vertigo*, The other they call Scotomia, or Tenebrous Vertigo, when the Eyes are darkned and, as it were, cover'd with a Cloud. **1847** Longf. *Ev.* ii. ii. 29 Over their heads the towering and tenebrous boughs of the cypress Met in a dusky arch.

b. *fig.* Obscure, gloomy.

1599 Nashe *Lenten Stuffe* Wks. (Grosart) V. 220 To.. run astray.. raking out of the dust-heape or charnell house of tenebrous eld, the rottenest relique of the monuments. *a* **1693** *Urquhart's Rabelais* iii. xvii. 137 Heraclitus, the grand Scotist, and tenebrous darksome Philosopher. **1823** *New Monthly Mag.* VIII. 13 The most tenebrous holes and corners of their author's obscurity. **1849** *Blackw. Mag.* LXV. 307 Even in that tenebrous philosophy which he has imported.. he is very much at fault.

†**2.** as *sb.* Darkness. *Obs. rare*⁻¹.

c **1450** Lovelich *Grail* lvi. 418 At ȝoure Castel there is Swich tenebrowse, that No man there Other May se.

Hence '**tenebrousness** (*rare*⁻⁰), darkness.

1727 in Bailey vol. II.

†**tenedish.** *Obs.* See quot.

1688 R. Holme *Armoury* iii. 152/2 A Tenedish, which is a piece of Lead made like a Muscle shell, in which the black (called Painter) is kept moist to work withal. [? Some error: *Tin-dish* and *teint-dish* have been conjectured. See *N. & Q.* 11th Ser. II. 394.]

tenel, obs. f. teanel, a basket.

[**tenel, -ing**, in *E.E. Allit. P.*, etc.: see tevel.]

†**te'nellous**, *a. Obs. rare*⁻¹. [f. L. *tenell-us*, dim. of *tener* tender + -ous.] Somewhat tender.

1651 Biggs *New Disp.* §285 How much of more tenellous meats is swallowed in a surfet.

tenement (ˈtɛnɪmənt). Also 5 tenne-, 6 tennand-, tena-. [a. AF., = OF. *tenement* (12th c. in Godef.), ad. med.L. *tenement-um* (1081 in Muratori *Antiquitates* IX. (1776) 660), also *teni-*, *tena-*, *teneamentum* (12th c. in Du Cange), f. L. *tenēre* to hold + *-mentum*, -ment.]

†**1.** The fact of holding as a possession; tenure. ***free tenement*** = frank-tenement, freehold.

As by the theory of English Law all land is held immediately or ultimately of the sovereign, 'tenement' embraced all forms of proprietorship or occupation of real property.

a **1325** *MS. Rawl. B. 520* lf. 41 þoru suuche dede sokage is ibore out in to fre tenement. *c* **1330** R. Brunne *Chron.* (1810) 34 To do doun Edwy at a parlement, & tille his broþer Edgare gyf þe tenement. *Ibid.* 83 William passid þe se, þer of he mad þe skrite, Of France to hold þat fe of oþer tenement alle quite. *Ibid.* 225 Depriued þei our kyng of alle þe tenement Of londes of Gascoyn. **1651** G. W. tr. *Cowel's Inst.* 79 Free Tenement or free-hold is, where Lands and Tenements are held only for life of the Tenant.

2. a. Land or real property which is held of another by any tenure; a holding.

tenement at will, a tenement held at the will of the superior; also *fig.*

[**1315** *Rolls of Parlt.* I. 349/2 Johan de Eston demaunda ces Tenementz,.. come son dreit.] *c* **1330** R. Brunne *Chron.* (1810) 48 If he saued to his heyers oiþer lond or tenement. *c* **1460** Fortescue *Abs. & Lim. Mon.* iii. (1885) 114 Somme of thaim þat were wont to pay to his lorde for his tenement, wich he hiryth by the yere, a scute. *c* **1489** Caxton *Blanchardyn* xvi. 52, I shal.. make hym pryuated from all his tenementes that he holdeth of me. **1593** Shaks. *Rich. II*, ii. i. 60 This deere-deere Land,.. Is now Leas'd out.. Like to a Tenement or pelting Farme. **1700** Tyrrell *Hist. Eng.* II. 812 The Tenement (i.e. the Real Estate) of the Deceased. **1766** Blackstone *Comm.* II. ii. 16 *Tenement* is a word of still greater extent [than land], and though in it's vulgar acceptation it is only applied to houses and other buildings, yet in it's original, proper, and legal sense, it signifies every thing that may be *holden*, provided it be of a permanent nature; whether it be of a substantial and sensible, or of an unsubstantial ideal kind. **1822** Wordsw. *Scenery of Lakes* ii. (1823) 44 The multitude of tenements (I.. mean.. small divisions of land, which belonged formerly each to a several proprietor, and for which separate fines are paid to the manorial lord at this day).

b. *pl.* 'The technical expression for freehold interests in things immovable considered as subjects of property, they being not "owned" but "holden"' (Digby *Real Property* ii. §2); *esp.* in ***lands and tenements***, i.e. lands and all other freehold interests.

In the common modern usage of English lawyers leaseholds are included, though some authorities think this incorrect, for the reason that, being (in England) *personal property*, they are not the subject of tenure in the strict sense.

[**1292** Britton i. xix. §4 Et ausi des terres et des tenementz alienez par felouns.] *a* **1325** *MS. Rawl. B. 520* lf. 29 b, No religious or ani oþer ani londes ore tenemens buche ne sulle.. on ani maner.. ware þoru thulke londes or tenemens in ani manere miȝtte comen in to dede hond. **1387** Trevisa *Higden* (Rolls) VIII. 265 Kyng Edward and þe lordes made a statute aȝenst maynmort, so þat after þat tyme no man schulde ȝeve.. ne by oþere title assigne londes, tenementis ne oþer rentes to men of religioun wiþouten þe kynges leve. **1494** Fabyan *Chron.* vii. 390 Statutes made to refourme suche persones as mysused the landes and tenementes, commynge to theym by reason of the dower, or landes of theyr wyues. **1529** Cromwell *Will* in Merriman *Life & Lett.* (1902) I. 56, I will myn executours undernamed .. shall purchase londes tenementes and hereditamentes to the clere yerelye value of xxxiij^li vj^s viij^d. **1530** Palsgr. 280/1 Tenementes, *reuenues*. **1542** *Richmond Wills* (Surtees) 33 The one halff off all the saide lands, tennandments, rents and all other servyces, with reversions and appertenawnces belonging ye same. **1568** Grafton *Chron.* II. 142 The Shirifes of London at those dayes might lawfully enter into the towne of Westminster, and all other Tenementes, that the Abbot had within Middlesex. **1580** Lupton *Sivqila* 141 All deedes and writings of any lands, tenements, houses, woods, or such like, that are solde. **1622** Callis *Stat. Sewers* (1647) 108 The word *Tenements* is of larger extent then Lands; for it containeth all which the word *Lands* doth, and all things else which lyeth in Tenure. **1691** Wood *Ath. Oxon.* I. 322 He [was] then possessed of several lands and tenements in Taunton. **1818** Cruise *Digest* (ed. 2) VI. 219 The words lands, tenements, and hereditaments, will pass every species of property. **1848** Williams *Law Personal Property* (1870) 1 In ancient times property was divided into *lands, tenements and hereditaments* on the one hand, and *goods and chattels* on the other. **1876** Digby *Real Prop.* ii. §2. 72 *note.*

3. a. *gen.* A building or house to dwell in; a dwelling-place, a habitation, residence, abode.

c **1425** *Brut* 367 So was he brouȝt to þe Whit-Freris yn Flet-strete; and þere was do and made a ryal & solempne tenement for hym. **1477–9** *Rec. St. Mary at Hill* 84 For ij ml tiles spent in reparacion of the tenement of William Blase and of othir tenementes, x s viij d. **1513** Douglas *Æneis* xiii. x. 9 Syne Troianis foundis tenementis for thame self. **1588**

Knaresborough Wills (Surtees) I. 159 The lease..in the tenement where I now dwell. **1607** NORDEN *Surv. Dial.* III. 106 Whether are there within this Mannor, any new erected Tenements or Cotages, barnes, Walls. **1779** FORREST *Voy. N. Guinea* 95 The tenement contains many families, who live in cabins on each side of a wide common hall, that goes through the middle of it. **1833** HT. MARTINEAU *Briery Creek* iii, The resources which they wasted would have..turned their habitation of logs into a respectable brick tenement. **1844** WILLIAMS *Real Prop.* (1875) 13 The word *tenement* is often used in law, as in ordinary language, to signify a house. **1848** DICKENS *Dombey* vii, The dingy tenement inhabited by Miss Tox was her own.

b. *transf.* and *fig.* An abode; a dwelling-place, esp. applied to the body as the abode of the soul; also, the abode of any animal.

1592 G. HARVEY *Four Lett.* iii. Wks. (Grosart) I. 195 The poore tennement of his Purse..hath bene the Diuels Dauncing schoole, anie time this halfe yeare. **1604** T. WRIGHT *Passions* IV. ii. 136 Doubt not but selfe-loue and vanitie possesse the best tenement of his heart. **1635** QUARLES *Embl.* III. i. 40 My weary soul, that long hath been An inmate in this tenement of sin. *a* **1639** T. CAREW *Epit. Lady M. Villiers* 2 The purest Soule that e'er was sent Into a clayie tenemente. *a* **1668** DAVENANT *Jeffereidos* II. Wks. (1673) 226 Snaile..with all his Tenement on 's back. **1774** GOLDSM. *Nat. Hist.* (1776) III. 371 Their nest is generally the original tenement of the squirrel. **1847** C. BRONTE *J. Eyre* xxi, That spirit—now struggling to quit its material tenement.

4. *spec.* **a.** In England, A portion of a house, tenanted as a separate dwelling; a flat; a suite of apartments, or even a single room so let or occupied.

'In modern Eng. practice, a *tenement* is anything that can be separately held, including therefore a flat, etc.' (Sir F. Pollock).

1593 NASHE *Christ's T.* 53 b, Almes-houses..let out in Tenements. **1625** (May 2) *Procl. 1 Chas. I* (Concerning Buildings), That no person..within the City of London.. doe diuide any dwelling House..into or for any more Tenements or dwellings, then are at this present..vsed within the same. **1817** (April) D. WEBSTER *Speech in Goodrich Case* U.S. (Cent. Dict.), The two tenements, it was true, were under the same roof; but they were not on that acount the same tenements. **1898** *Daily News* 14 Nov. 5/1 The Council never have any unlet, except a few four-room tenements for which there is less demand than for those with only two or three rooms. **1905** *Ibid.* 28 Sept. 9 Mr. J. Keir Hardie, M.P., claimed as occupier of a tenement at Nevill's-court.

b. In Scotland, more particularly applied to a large house (i.e. edifice under one roof) constructed or adapted to be let in portions to a number of tenants, each portion so separately occupied being considered and called a 'house'. Called also *tenement of houses*, *land of houses* (= *tenement house* in 5).

Thus a 'house' in England may form one 'tenement', or contain a number of 'tenements' (and is then a 'tenement house': see 5); in Scotland, a 'tenement' may form one 'house', or contain a number of 'houses' or dwellings.

1693 STAIR *Inst. Law Scot.* II. vii. §6 When divers Owners have parts of the same Tenement, it cannot be said to be a perfect division, because the Roof remaineth Roof to both, and the ground supporteth both. **1808** JAMIESON, *Tenement* ..often denoting a building which includes several separate dwellings; as *a tenement of houses*. **1825** R. CHAMBERS *Tradit. Edinb.* 172 How the great of the land could live in the fourth and fifth flats of wooden tenements, the various apartments of which, as occupied at present by humble mechanics, seem confined and inconvenient to the last degree. **1841** in Rankine *Treat. Ownership Lands Scot.* xxxiii. (1879) 509 Houses so often found in Scotland, called technically 'lands', or 'tenements of land'—terms which have been defined as applicable to 'a single or individual building, although containing several dwelling-houses, with, it may be, separate means of access, but under the same roof and enclosed by the same gables or walls'. **1910** *Scotsman* 8 Oct. 3/3 For Sale by Public Roup..(1) Six self-contained Dwelling Houses... (2) House, No. 27 St. Bernard's Crescent... (3) Tenement, No. 12 St. Bernard's Crescent.

c. The offset at the back of a house. (Devon and Cornw.); cf. OUTSHOT 1, quots. 1817, 1820.

5. *attrib.* and *Comb.*: **tenement house** (orig. U.S.), a house or edifice let out in flats or sets of apartments for separate tenants; **tenement householder**, a tenant in a tenement house; †**tenement man**, an owner of tenements, a landlord.

1858 W. A. BUTLER *Two Millions* 47 The *Tenement House, o'er which no friendly movement Has waved the Enchanter's wand of 'Modern Improvement'. **1879** H. GEORGE *Progr. & Pov.* IX. iii. (1881) 405 To substitute for the tenement house, homes surrounded by gardens. **1884** *Q. Rev.* Jan. 150 Tenement-houses, *i.e.* houses let to more than one family, are placed under still stricter conditions. **1894** *Daily News* 7 June 7/3 Mr. Gibb led the way in placing all lodgers who lived in a house in which no landlord resided, on the householders' list... *Tenement householders have ever since been regarded not as lodgers but as householders. *c* **1500** *Merch. & Son* 7 in Hazl. *E.P.P.* I. 133 He was a grete *tenement man, and ryche of londe and lede.

tene'mental, *a.* [f. med.L. *tenement-um* TENEMENT + -AL[1].] Of, pertaining to, or of the nature of a tenement; let out to tenants.

1766 BLACKSTONE *Comm.* II. vi. 90 The other, or tenemental, lands they distributed among their tenants. **1875** MAINE *Hist. Inst.* v. 130 The Manor with its Tenemental lands held by the free tenants of the Lord. **1887** *Edin. Rev.* Jan. 10 In the fifteenth century the land was divided into the private demesne of the lord of the manor and the tenemental land of the association.

tene'mentary, *a.* [f. as prec. + -ARY[1]: cf. med.L. *tenementāri-us.*] **a.** Leased to tenants. **b.** Consisting of tenements or dwelling-houses. See also FRANK-TENEMENTARY.

a **1641** SPELMAN *Feuds & Tenures* vii, Such were the Ceorls among the Saxons; but of two sorts, one that hired the Lord's Outland or Tenementary Land (called also the Folcland) like our Farmers. **1701** *Cowell's Interpr.* s.v., The Saxon Thanes who possess'd Bocland, or Hereditary free Estates, divided them into..Inland and Outland... The Outland was granted out to Tenants under Arbitrary Rents and Services, and therefore call'd Tenementary Land, the Tenants Land, or the Tenancy. **1872** *B'ham Daily Post* 28 Feb. 7/2 Assisting her mother who was the owner of some small tenementary property at Saltley. **1905** *Daily Chron.* 31 Jan. 3/5 By doing this he [a landlord who removes from one of his tenement houses to another] converts the lodgers into tenementary occupiers and the tenementary occupiers into lodgers, the result being that all of them lose their votes.. through no fault of their own.

'tenemented, *ppl a.* [f. TENEMENT + -ED[1].] Let in tenements or separate dwellings: said of a building, house, or house property.

1883 *Pall Mall G.* 17 Feb. 4/1 They have..crowded into tenemented property in the immediate neighbourhood. **1888** *Ibid.* 24 Nov. 5 Most of the population of Glasgow living in the rooms of tenemented buildings. **1890** *Daily News* 18 July 2/4 The Chancellor of the Exchequer..stated that tenemented houses of less than 20*l.* per annum were exempt from house duty whether they had two front doors or not, so long as they were intended to be dwelling-houses within seven and sixpence per week.

'tenementer. [f. as prec. + -ER[1]. Cf. med.L. *tenementātor* (1214 in Du Cange).] The holder of a tenement; a lease-holder or tenant. ***frank-tenementer*** = FREEHOLDER.

1574 *Reg. Privy Council Scot.* II. 353 Alexander Dunbar frank tenementar of Cumnok. **1588** in *Scott. N. & Q.* Mar. (1890) 184 Robert Erskine, Elder, Frank tenementer of Dun, my grandschir. **1875** A. SMITH *Hist. Aberdeen.* II. 724 The holders of the Rawes appear to have been only tenementers.

‖**tenendas** (tɪ'nɛndæs). *Sc. Law.* [L. acc. pl. fem. of gerundive of *tenēre* to hold = '(the lands) to be held'.] See quot. 1710.

1681 STAIR *Inst. Law Scot* xiii. §15. 236 In all Charters, both by King and Subjects, the Clause *Tenendas* useth to be insert. **1710** *Dict. Feudal Law*, *Tenendas*, is that Clause of a Charter, which expresses what way and manner the Lands are to be holden of the Superior. **1765–8** ERSKINE *Inst. Law Scot.* II. iii. §24 The next clause in a charter is the *Tenendas*, so called from the first words, *Tenend. prædictas terras.* **1815** R. BELL *Treat. Conveyance* ii. 16 The charter, as an original right, necessarily contains the *tenendas*, by which the nature of the holding is expressed.

‖**tenendum** (tɪ'nɛndəm). *Eng. Law.* [L., = 'to be held', neut. gerundive of *tenēre* to hold.] That part of a deed which defines the tenure by which the things granted are to be held (cf. HABENDUM).

1628 COKE *On Litt.* 6 There haue beene eight formall or orderly parts of a deede of feoffment, viz. 1. the premisses of the deed implied by Littleton. 2. the habendum... 3. the tenendum... 4. the Reddendum. 5. the clause of warrantie [etc.]. **1766** BLACKSTONE *Comm.* II. xx. 298 Next come the *habendum* and *tenendum*... The *tenendum* 'and to hold', is now of very little use, and is only kept in by custom. It was sometimes formerly used to signify the tenure by which the estate granted was to be holden. **1787** C. BUTLER *Coke on Litt.* 108 a *note*, Those grants from the crown which in the *tenendum* are expressed to be *ut de honore et non in capite.* **1862** WASHBURN *Amer. Law Real Prop.* (1864) II. 612 (Funk) The *tenendum*, limiting and defining the tenure by which the lands are to be held, and once an important clause in the deed, is useless in this country. **1884** ELPHINSTONE *Conveyancing* 100 The tenendum was of use before the passing of the Statute of *Quia Emptores* to state whether the purchaser was to hold of the vendor or of his lord; but it is now useless.

†**tenent,** *sb. Obs.* Also 7 tenant. [a. L. *tenent* 'they hold', 3rd pers. pl. pres. indic. of *tenēre* to hold.] = TENET.

Etymologically a *tenet* ought to be the opinion of one, what *he holds*, a *tenent* the opinion of a number, what *they hold*; but this distinction, if ever observed in using the words as English, was soon lost. *Tenent* was apparently more used in the 17th c. than *tenet*, but became obs. *c* 1725.

1551 ABP. BROWNE (of Armagh) *Serm.* in *Phenix* (1721) I. 134 They shall be your greatest enemies, speaking against the Tenents of Rome, and yet be set on by Rome. **1618** HALES *Gold. Rem.* II. (1673) 59 Episcopius..required that it might be lawful for them to set down their own Tenents. **1621** BURTON *Anat. Mel.* II. ii III. (1651) 254 But..to grant this their tenent of the earths motion. **1643** FULLER *Serm.* 27 Mar. 18 Being so fickle in their Tenents. **1646** SIR T. BROWNE (*title*) Pseudodoxia Epicemica, or Enquiries into very many received tenents and commonly presumed Truths. **1722** WOLLASTON *Relig. Nat.* v. 111 People of differing religions judge and condemn each other by their own tenents.

tenent ('tɛnənt), *a. rare*[−1]. [ad. L. *tenēnt-em* holding, pr. pple. of *tenēre* to hold.] Holding.

1861 T. WEST in *Trans. Linn. Soc.* (1862) XXIII. 408 That these [hair-like appendages] are the immediate agents in holding is now admitted by almost all; it will be convenient to term them 'tenent hairs', in allusion to their office.

tenent, -ry, obs. ff. TENON[1], TENANTRY.

‖**tenente** (te'nɛnte). [It., Pg.] A lieutenant.

1929 E. HEMINGWAY *Farewell to Arms* iv. 15 'Do they ever shell that battery?'.. 'No, Signor Tenente.' **1969** M. GILBERT *Etruscan Net* III. i. 215 He sat down, and motioned the Tenente to be seated also. **1970** F. C. WEFFORT in I. L. Horowitz *Masses in Lat. Amer.* xi. 388 Their [*sc.* the Brazilian middle class's] most radical acts, generally undertaken by young military men—the *tentes.*

tener, obs. f. TEENER, TENNER, TENOR, TENURE.

teneral ('tɛnərəl), *a. Entom.* [f. L. *tener* tender + -AL[1].] Said of the imperfect imago of a neuropterous insect, when it has just emerged from the pupa state, and is still soft. Also *fig.*

1891 in *Cent. Dict.* **1900** W. J. LUCAS *Brit. Dragonflies* vi. 66 (*heading*) Immature colour. [*Note*] Also called 'teneral'. **1902** *Sat. Rev.* 1 Mar. 256 The Liberal League has now emerged in triumph, though at present perhaps in a teneral state, not yet endowed with its full brilliancy of colour. **1921** G. H. CARPENTER *Insect Transformation* ii. 52 For some time after it has acquired the power of flying the dragon-fly has not yet asssumed the deep colours and developed pattern that characterize its species; such a relatively newly-emerged insect is defined as teneral. **1957** *Jrnl. Exper. Biol.* XXXIV. 189 The word 'teneral' has been used to describe alate insects at about this time [between emergence and the first flight], although its usage varies between different orders. **1975** *Nature* 15 May 226/1 This [*sc.* a reduction in probing behaviour] was easier to demonstrate in teneral flies (newly emerged flies before their first meal) than in post-teneral flies.

Teneriffe (tɛnə'riːf). [The name of one of the Canary Islands.] **1.** A white wine produced on Teneriffe.

1791 J. WOODFORDE *Diary* 11 Nov. (1927) III. 312 Claret, Teneriffe, and Port Wines to drink. **1833** C. REDDING *Mod. Wines* vi. 194 What is called Vidonia is properly the dry Canary wine, best known as Teneriffe. **1855** E. ACTON *Mod. Cookery* (rev. ed.) xxxii. 611 A couple of wineglassesful of Madeira (Sherry or Teneriffe will do).

2. Used *attrib.* to designate a kind of lace made in the Canary Islands.

1907 *Yesterday's Shopping* (1969) 3520/2 Teneriffe D'Oyley. **1920** 'K. MANSFIELD' *Bliss* 137 Now my best little Teneriffe-work teacloth is simply in ribbons. **1969** R. T. WILCOX *Dict. Costume* 342/2 *Teneriffe lace*, a lace of circles and wheels similar to Paraguay lace, made chiefly in the Canary islands.

†**te'neritude.** *Obs. rare*[−1]. [ad. L. *teneritūdo*, f. *tener* tender.] Tenderness, softness. So †**te'nerity** *Obs.* [ad. L. *teneritās*], in same sense; †**'tenerous** *a. Obs.* [f. L. *tener* + -OUS], tender.

c **1440** *Pallad. on Husb.* VI. 157 So wol their fatnesse and *teneritude With hem be stille. **1623** COCKERAM, **Teneritie*, softnesse, tendernesse. **1642** H. MORE *Song of Soul* II. iii. III. lviii, Faithfulnesse, heart-struck teneritie; These be the lovely playmates of pure veritie. **1706** PHILLIPS (ed. Kersey), *Tenerity*, a Philosophical Word for Tenderness; as 'The tenerity of Young Plants'. **1597** A. M. tr. *Guillemeau's Fr. Chirurg.* 34/1 Engendring a *tenerouse fleshe, which by little and little, hardeneth.

‖**tenesmus** (tɪ'nɛzməs). *Path.* Also 6–8 **tenasmus**; *β.* (from Fr.) 6–7 **tenasm(e**, 7 **tinesm.** [med.L. *tēnesmus*, *tēnasmus* (Du Cange), = L. *tēnesmos* (Pliny), a. Gr. τεινεσμός, τηνεσμός straining, f. τείνειν to stretch, strain. So F. *ténesme* (16th c.).] A continual inclination to void the contents of the bowels or bladder, accompanied by straining, but with little or no discharge.

1527 ANDREW *Brunswyke's Distyll. Waters* D ij b, Payne of the gutte of the fondament named tenasmus, that is whan a man thynketh that he wolde go to stole, but he can do nothyng. **1578** LYTE *Dodoens* II. xxviii. 182 Good for them that haue the laske, the blouddie flixe and Tenasme. **1601** HOLLAND *Pliny* (1634) II. 443 The broth of fish.. dispatcheth those sharp and fretting humors which are the cause of the Tinesm. **1732** ARBUTHNOT *Rules of Diet* in *Aliments*, etc. 423 Attended with a Tenesmus. **1748** *Anson's Voy.* I. iv. 39 Afflicted with fluxes and tenasmus's. **1754–64** SMELLIE *Midwif.* I. 120 Something like a tenesmus at the *os uteri.* **1876** BRISTOWE *The. & Pract. Med.* (1878) 684.
fig. **1642** MILTON *Apol. Smect.* vi. Wks. 1851 III. 294 This tetter of Pedagoguisme that bespreads him with such a tenasmus of originating. **1669** *Address Hopeful Yng. Gentry Eng.* 48 That exulcerate feebleness of reason which by an impotent tenesmus betrays the infirmities of those we almost idoliz'd to scorn and hatred.

Hence **te'nesmic** *a.*, of, pertaining to, or of the nature of tenesmus.

1891 in *Cent. Dict.*

tenet ('tɛnɪt, †'tiːnɪt). [a. L. *tenet* 'he holds', 3 sing. of *tenēre* to hold. See also TENENT *sb.*

Prob. adopted from mod.Latin writings, in which it introduced the opinion or doctrine that a person, church, or sect holds. Cf. similar use of *habitat*, *incipit*, *explicit*.]

A doctrine, dogma, principle, or opinion, in religion, philosophy, politics, or the like, held by a school, sect, party, or person.

a **1619** FOTHERBY *Atheom.* II. iv. §3 (1622) 230 And this.. is not onely his owne particular opinion..; but the generall Tenet, of all the Philosophers. *a* **1641** BP. MOUNTAGU *Acts & Mon.* (1642) Summary 3/2 The Church of Englands Tenet, that no salvation, but by Christ alone. **1706** PHILLIPS (ed. Kersey), *Tenet*, or *Tenent*, a Doctrine, or Opinion. **1791** BURKE *App. Whigs* Wks. VI. 210 The practical consequences of any political tenet go a great way in deciding upon its value. **1858** BUCKLE *Civiliz.* (1869) II. i. 51

The liberality of every sect depends, not at all on its avowed tenets but on the circumstances in which it is placed.

b. More trivially: Any opinion held.

1630 BRATHWAIT *Eng. Gentlem.* (1641) 288 My tenet is, 'one cannot truely love, and not be wise'. **1656** EARL MONM. tr. *Boccalini's Advts. fr. Parnass.* I. lxxvii. (1674) 102 You have infinitely verified the Tenet which all the Literati have of you. **1742** *Lond. & Country Brew.* I. (ed. 4) 42 Vouching it to be a true Tenet, that, if Hops are boiled above thirty Minutes, the Wort will have some or more of their worser Quality. *c* **1765** GRAY *Satire* 28 The Master of Benet Is of the like tenet.

tenetz, teneys, obs. forms of TENNIS.

teneur, obs. form of TENOR.

tenfold ('tɛnfəʊld), *a.*, *adv.* [OE. *tíenfeald.*]

A. *adj.* **1.** Ten times as great or as much; ten times increased or intensified; also *indefinitely*, many times as great.

c **1200** *Trin. Coll. Hom.* 135 His michelnesse was unhiled on ten fold wise and mo. **1557** RECORDE *Whetst.* B ij, *Decupla* ..10 to 1: 20 to 2... Tennefolde. **1588** SHAKS. *Tit. A.* III. ii. 6 Thy Neece and I..cannot passionate our tenfold griefe, With foulded Armes. **1625** N. CARPENTER *Geog. Del.* II. ix. (1635) 149 The Aire..being by a Tenne-fold proportion thinner then the Water. **1849** MACAULAY *Hist. Eng.* iii. I. 412 His mind reacted with tenfold force on the spirit of the age.

b. As predicate, passing into substantive use; cf. HUNDREDFOLD C.

1769 HOME *Fatal Discov.* IV, Euran! whate'er the lavish Pict has promis'd To tempt thee to betray thy master's house, Tenfold I'll give thee to preserve thy faith. **1832** SOUTHEY *Hist. Penins. War* III. xxxvii. 219 But the loss had been tenfold of what was there stated.

2. Ranged in ten folds, or ten deep. *nonce-use.*

1807 J. BARLOW *Columb.* I. 316 Stretch'd o'er the broad-back'd hills, in long array, The tenfold Alleganies meet the day.

B. *adv.* Ten times (in amount or degree).

1538 ELYOT, *Decuplo*..if it be an aduerbe, it sygnifyeth tenne times, or tenne fold. *Decuplum*, like wyse. **1606** SHAKS. *Ant. & Cl.* IV. vii. 15, I will reward thee Once for thy sprightly comfort, and ten-fold For thy good valour. **1667** MILTON *P.L.* II. 705 The grieslie terrour..So speaking and so threatning, grew ten fold More dreadful and deform. **1827** SYD. SMITH *Wks.* (1850) 485 Is not the Church of England tenfold more rich and more strong than when the separation took place? **1884** TENNYSON *Becket* I. iii, False to himself, but ten-fold false to me!

Hence **'tenfoldness**, the condition or quality of being tenfold.

1891 J. E. H. THOMSON *Books which influenced our Lord* III. i. 382 There is no explanation of the tenfoldness exhibited in the symbols.

'tenfold, *v.* [f. prec.] *trans.* To increase ten times; *loosely*, to multiply indefinitely.

1858 BUSHNELL *Nat. & Supernat.* xiii. (1864) 420 Transforming the world, tenfolding its forces and uses, and all that constitutes its value. **1858** —— *Serm. New Life* viii. (1869) 102 The capacity of religion..may be fivefolded, tenfolded, indefinitely increased. **1902** KROPOTKIN *Mut. Aid* vi. (1904) 208 It tenfolded their forces.

tenful, variant of TEENFUL *Obs.*

tenger, var. TANGER.

tengerite ('tɛŋəraɪt). *Min.* [Named after a Swede, C. Tenger, who examined it: see -ITE[1].] According to Svanberg and Tenger, a carbonate of yttrium, found as a whitish coating on gadolite.

1868 DANA *Min.* (ed. 5) 710. **1889** *Nature* 19 Dec. 163/1 Many more [minerals], such as cyrtolite, molybdite, allanite, tengerite..have been found.

tengku, var. TUNKU.

tenia, tenioid, var. TÆNIA, TÆNIOID.

tenible ('tɛnɪb(ə)l), *a. rare.* [f. L. type **tenibilis*, f. *ten-ēre* to hold: cf. *docible*.]

†**1.** Capable of being held; = TENABLE 2. *Obs.*

1633 T. STAFFORD *Pac. Hib.* II. viii. (1821) 320 Corke was a weake towne and not tenible against a powerfull enemy.

2. Able to retain or hold in (i.e. in quot., the saliva). *rare.*

1871 R. ELLIS *Catullus* xliii. 3 A nose among the larger, Feet not dainty,..Mouth scarce tenible [L. *nec ore sicco*], hands not wholly faultless.

‖**teniente** (te'njente). [Sp.] A lieutenant.

1798 in *Lett. from Paraguay* (1805) 248 Every thing..is known to the tenientes. **1906** *Soldier Slang* in C. McGovern *Sarjint Larry an' Frinds, Teniente*, Spanish for 'Lieutenant'. **1938** *New Statesman* 1 Oct. 488 Aren't we going to eat today, teniente? **1979** A. MELVILLE-ROSS *Two Faces of Nemesis* xxii. 157 *Teniente* Descola had done his job well enough to be *Capitan* Descola by evening.

tenii-, var. TAENII-

tenis, tenise, obs. forms of TENNIS.

tenker, obs. form of TINKER.

‖**tenko** ('tɛŋkəʊ). [Jap.] In Japanese prison camps in the war of 1939–45: a muster parade or roll-call of prisoners.

1947 J. BERTRAM *Shadow of a War* VI. iii. 190 They drilled us by the hour..and firmly broke us in to the sacred mysteries of '*tenko*'—the morning and evening muster parade..that was routine in all prison camps in Japan... In time even *tenko* lost its terrors. **1961** R. BRADDON *Naked Island* in *Plays of Year, 1960* I. iii. 153, I got him a bashing on tenko tonight.

tenmanland. *Obs.* exc. *Hist.* A local name in East Anglia, in 12th and 13th c., for an aggregate of ten holdings; containing 120 acres, and so = CARUCATE. So, in same sense, **tenmanlot (-loth).**

c **1225** *Ely Inqu.* in *MS. Claudius C. xi* lf. 193 (Vinogr.) *De militibus et libere tenentibus*... Jacobus le franceis et Thomas de Northwaude tenent dimidium tenmanland, scilicet lx acras terre... *De Consuetudinariis et censuariis*, Alanus et Matheus..et eorum participes tenent unam tenmanland, scilicet sexies viginti acras terre. **1892** VINOGRADOFF *Villainage in Eng.* II. i. 255 In the Norfolk lands of Ely Minster we find tenmanlands of 120 acres in the possession of several copartitioners, *participes*. **1908** —— *Eng. Soc. in 11th c.* II. §1. ii, In the north [west] corner of Norfolk, in a fen-district bordering on Lincolnshire, we find in the local custom of the manor of Walpole, a division of the land according to tenmanlands or tenman-lots.

c **1200** *Inqu. of Walepole* in *MS. Cott. Tib. B. ii* lf. 167b, Willelmus Franceis et Thomas de Nordwolde tenent dimidium tenmanloth, scilicet sexaginta acras... *De Consuetudinariis*. Galfridus de Cattestone et participes tenent unam tenmanloth, scilicet sexcies uiginti acras pro decem solidis. ? *a* **1244** *Anc. Deed A.* 7435 (P.R.O.), Confirmauimus thome filio Alani de Walepol..sextam partem vnius tinmanlot in villa de Walepol.

'tenmantale, tenmentale. *Obs.* exc. *Hist.* Forms: 2 **tien, tyen, ten manna tale, tenmanne tale; the(n)manetale, temantale; tenemen-, teneman-, 7 te(n)men-, 8- te(n)man-tale.** [OE. type **tíen manna talu* 'numerum decem hominum', a number (tale, or reckoning) of ten men.]

1. According to the 'Laws of Edward the Confessor', the contemporary Yorkshire (or ? general Danelaw) name of the Anglo-Saxon TITHING, and also of the *friþborh* or FRANK-PLEDGE by which the members of a tithing were made sureties for each other.

(The only known ancient authority for this is the 'Laws of Edward the Confessor', compiled *c* 1130–35. The alleged addition to the *Treaty of Ælfred and Guðrum*, from which the term is quoted by Spelman and Du Cange, is found in no MS., and is apparently of later authorship.)

1130–35 *Laws Edw. Conf.* c. 20 Alia est pax..scilicet sub fideiussionis stabilitate, quam Angli uocant fri[th]borgas, preter Eboracenses, qui uocant eam tyen [*v.rr.* ten, tien] manna tale, hoc est numerum x hominum. *a* **1200** HOVEDEN *Chron.* (Rolls) II. 228 (quoting prec.) Quod sit Frithborg, quod Eboracenses vocant tenementale, id este, sermo decem hominum. **1664** SPELMAN *Gloss.*, Temental, *vel* Tenmentale, Sax. tienmantale, *Decuria, Tithinga.* **1872** E. W. ROBERTSON *Hist. Ess.* 118 A Tything, or Tenmantale, of the Hundred, in which a Decanus, annually chosen in the Hundred-court, presided in the petty court in the place of the Tungreve [*tun-ȝerefa*].

2. In parts of England under Danish influence, a name in 12th and 13th c. for the land tax levied on a carucate; the carucage.

In this sense the name was perh. connected with the *tenmanland* or *tenmanlot*, and *tale* may have had the sense 'sum, account, reckoning'.

c **1135** *Charter of Wm. Paganellus to Drax* (Charter Roll 4 Edw. II m. 4), Quam.. defendemus contra omnes homines de murdre de Danegelde, de The[n]mantale. *a* **1154** *Cartular. Abb. de Rievalle* (Surtees) 142 Et ii solidi de Danegeld, id est The[n]manetale, quoquo anno eveniebant super illas ix carrucatas. **1166–76** *Calr. Charter Rolls* (1908) III. 342 Tenementa predicta [at Lessness, Kent] habeant et teneant libera et quieta ab omnibus geldis et danegeldis et scutagiis et murdro et latrocinio..et clausuris et hidagiis et scotagiis et querelis et s[c]yris et hundredis et tethingis et tenemannetale. **1194** HOVEDEN *Chron.* (Rolls) III. 242 Rex constituit sibi dari de unaquaque carucata terræ totius Angliæ duos solidos, quod ab antiquis nominatur Temantale. *a* **1200** *Whitby Cartul.* (Surtees) I. 196 Quod Monasterium michi..duos solidos annuatim persolvent, et Themantel, pro omnibus serviciis. **1747** CARTE *Hist. Eng.* I. 760 An impost, called by some writers Carucage, and Temantale, but in the Pipe-rolls termed Hidage.

tenmoku, var. TEMMOKU.

tennand, -ant, obs. ff. TENANT, TENON[1].

tennandment, obs. corrupt f. TENEMENT.

tennantite ('tɛnəntaɪt). *Min.* [Named, 1819, in honour of Smithson Tennant: see -ITE[1].] A sulph-arsenide of copper and iron, closely related to tetrahedrite (Chester).

1839 DE LA BECHE *Rep. Geol. Cornwall*, etc. xv. 590 From among them tennantite has been separated by Phillips. **1851** MANTELL *Petrifact.* ii. §1. 78 In this case are specimens of..variegated copper ore; Tennantite. **1900** L. FLETCHER in *Brit. Mus. Return* 156 A crystallographic and chemical research.., the result of which has been to establish the specific identity of Binnite and Tennantite.

tenné, tenny ('tɛnɪ), *a.* and *sb. Her.* Also 7, 9- **tenney,** 9 **teany.** [a. obs. F. *tenné* (16th c.), var. of *tanné*, TAWNY; cf. *tennet*, var. of *tannet* tawny cloth (14th c. in Godef.).] 'Tawny' as a heraldic colour: variously described as 'orange-brown' or 'bright chestnut'; in engraving represented by diagonal lines from sinister to dexter, crossed by others, according to some authors, vertically, according to others, horizontally.

1562 LEIGH *Armorie* 19 Now to the sixth coloure, whiche we calle Tawney, and is blazed by thys woorde, Tenne. It is a worshipfull colour, and is of some Herhaughtes called Bruske,..it is made of two bright colours which is Redde and Yellowe. **1575** LANEHAM *Let.* (1871) 39 The Fess Tenny, which iz a cooler betokening dout & suspition. **1704** J. HARRIS *Lex. Techn.* I, *Tenny*, or *Tawney*,..is expressed in Engraving by thwart Strokes or Hatches. **1882** CUSSANS *Heraldry* 51 Tenné (bright chestnut). **1922** JOYCE *Ulysses* 47 On a field tenney a buck, trippant, proper unattired.

tennement, tennendrie, obs. ff. TENEMENT, TENANTRY.

tennent, obs. form of TENANT, TENON[1].

tenner ('tɛnə(r)). *colloq.* [f. TEN + -ER[1].] A term applied to a number or amount of ten; *spec.* **a.** A ten-pound note; in U.S. a ten-dollar bill.

1845 *Ainsworth's Mag.* VIII. 121 The races..he went to as a matter of course, though..he never betted at them beyond a 'tenner'. **1848** *Sessions Papers* 7 Mar. 847 'I was concerned in that affair of Covill's, for which I had a *tenner* out.'.. 'Oh, did they give you 10*l*?'.. I understood by a *tenner*, a 10*l*.-note. **1861** HUGHES *Tom Brown at Oxf.* xix,'No money?' 'Not much; perhaps a tenner.' **1884** G. ALLEN *Philistia* III. 218, I had in my purse..five tenners—Bank of England ten-pound notes, you know. **1887** BLACK *Sabina Zembra* xxi. 208 You might make the fiver a tenner. **1893** SALTUS *Madam Sapphira* xvi, At the rate of eight dollars a column and a tenner for the 'beat'.

b. A period of ten years.

1866 *Morn. Star* 19 Dec., I will tell the truth, or else I shall get a 'tenner' (ten years' penal servitude). **1904** *Daily News* 7 Nov. 9 [He] has been chief magistrate..for the past nine years uninterruptedly, and..the Corporation has just asked him to extend it and make a 'tenner' of it.

tenner, obs. form of TENOR; var. TANDOUR.

tennes, -ice, obs. ff. TENNIS.

Tennessean (tɛnə'siːən), *sb.* and *a.* Also **Tennesseean.** [f. next + -AN.] **A.** *sb.* A native or inhabitant of Tennessee. **B.** *adj.* Of, pertaining to, or characteristic of Tennessee.

1815 *Niles' Reg.* VII. 373/1 Glory to..the hardy and gallant Tennesseeans, Kentuckians and Louisianians. **1834** [see HUNT *v.* 3 b]. **1853** J. L. MCCONNEL *Western Characters* 269 Its dye a favorite 'Tennessean' brownish-yellow. **1872** 'MARK TWAIN' *Sketches* 135 The fervent spirit of Tennesseean journalism. **1945** H. F. WOODS *Amer. Sayings* 274 A Tennessean-born pioneer, he was in the tradition of Daniel Boone and other border heroes of his time. **1959** C. OGBURN *Marauders* (1960) ii. 49 Lieutenant Caldwell..was an angular young Tennessean. **1978** *Times* 24 Oct. 8/6 Her own campaign slogan..[claims] that she 'has not lost touch' with Tennesseans.

Tennessee (tɛnə'siː). The name of one of the United States of America, used *attrib.* in **Tennessee marble**, a kind of marble found in Tennessee and freq. used in building and sculpture; **Tennessee walker, walking horse**, a lightly built horse belonging to a breed developed in the region and distinguished by an easy natural gait.

1875 T. YELVERTON *Teresina in Amer.* II. xiv. 177 It is a lofty, domed structure, the dome supported upon pillars of the red Tennessee marble. **1947** J. C. RICH *Materials & Methods of Sculpture* viii. 226 *Tennessee* is the largest producer of marble in the United States... Many sculptors compare Tennessee marble to granite... Tennessee marble is an excellent sculptural stone. **1968** *N.Y. City* (Michelin Tire Corp.) 74 Pierpont Morgan Library..in pink Tennessee marble. **1960** J. W. PATTEN *Light Horse Breeds* 147 The breed is variously referred to as Tennessee Walkers, Tennessee Plantation Horses, Tennessee Walking Horses. **1979** *Arizona Daily Star* 1 Apr. (Advt. Section) 10/10 Tennessee walker 7 years old, well trained. **1938** *Reg. Tennessee Walking Horse Breeders' Assoc.* I. 5 The Tennessee Walking Horse Breeders' Association of America held its first meeting at Lewisburg, Tenn., April 27, 1935. **1950** *Congress. Rec.* XCVI. App. A 740/3, I [*sc.* Pat Sutton] am delighted today to advise the House that the United States Department of Agriculture in a letter to me dated February 1, 1950, has recognized the Tennessee walking horse as a distinct and standard breed. **1952** J. SHERMAN *Real Bk. about Horses* iii. 69 The Tennessee walking horse is noted for his three natural gaits—the flat-footed walk, the running walk and the canter. **1976** *Billings* (Montana) *Gaz.* 2 July 11-c/6 (Advt.), Registered Tennessee Walking horse mares, yearlings, and colts.

tennet, dial. variant of TINNET.

tenney, obs. f. TENNÉ.

tennies ('tɛnɪz), *sb. pl. U.S. colloq.* [f. *tenn(is shoe* + *ies* (repr. -Y[6] + *pl. suff.*).] Tennis shoes.

1969 *Rolling Stone* 28 June 19/3 Electric guitarist James Burton, replete in white turtleneck and matching 'tennies', puts together a lead. **1976** T. GIFFORD *Cavanaugh Quest* (1977) i. 17 Margaret, one of the cleaning ladies, got out in her green smock and blue shorts... Her costume was completed with blue tennies. **1980** *Outdoor Life* (U.S.) (Northeast ed.) Oct. 63/3 This is good-boot country, so leave your tennies home.

tennikill, obs. Sc. form of TUNICLE.

tennil, var. TEANEL *dial.*, basket.

tennis ('tɛnɪs), *sb.* Forms: *α.* 4–5 **te'netz,** 5 **teneys,** 6 **ten(n)es;** *β.* 5 **tenyce, tenyys,** 5–6 **tenys,**

-yse, tennys, -yse, 6 tenice, tennysse, (tinnis), 6–7 tenis, -ise, tennise, -ice, (7 *Sc.* tinneis), 6– tennis. [Known *c* 1400 in form *te'netz*, later *te'nnes, te'neys, -ys, -yce, te'nise*; in It. mentioned in the *Cronica di Firenze* of Donato Velluti (who died in 1370) as *tenes*, and said to have been introduced into Florence by French knights early in the year 1325. For ulterior history and etymology see Note below.]

1. A game in which a ball is struck with a racket and driven to and fro by two players in an enclosed oblong court, specially constructed for the purpose, and (in the developed form of the game) having an enclosed corridor on one of the long sides roofed over by a penthouse. Now usu. known as *real tennis* (see REAL *a.*[2] 2e) to distinguish the game from the more popular *lawn tennis* (see 2).

The game had originally a much simpler form, the ball being struck with the palm of the hand (hence F. *la paume*). It was also played in the open air, as still in some places in France, and down to about 1800 in England under the name *field-tennis*, of which *lawn-tennis* may be considered a greatly modified revival.

c **1400** GOWER *In Praise of Peace* 295 Of the Tenetz [*ed.* **1532** tennes] to winne or lese a chace, Mai no lif wite er that the bal be ronne. *c* **1440** *Promp. Parv.* 488/2 Teneys, pley, *teniludus* (P. *manupilatus, tenisia*). **1441** *Court Roll Pershore, Worc.* (Westminster Ch. Munim.), Nullus eorum.. frequentabit ludum qui vocatur the tenyse playng in communi via domini Regis nec in aliquo loco privato ibidem. *c* **1460** *Towneley Myst.* xiii. 736, I bryng the bot a balle: Haue and play the with alle, And go to the tenys [*rime* pennys]. **1463** *Mann. & Househ. Exp.* (Roxb.) 221 Pleyynd at the tennys. *a* **1470** TIPTOFT *Tulle on Friendsh.* (Caxton 1481) C iv, Lyke corage & disposicion to pleyeng atte tenyce. **1525** LD. BERNERS *Froiss.* II. xxvi. 74 Gascone and his brother yuan fell out toguyder, playeng at tennes. **1535** *Act 27 Hen. VIII*, c. 25 §8 Any open..place for commen bowling, dysyng, carding, closhe, tenys, or other unlawfull games. **1540** MORYSINE *Vives' Introd. Wysd.* C j b, Oft tymes he commeth vp a pase, that can playe well at tennysse. **1550** CROWLEY *Last Trumpet* 562 To play tenise, or tosse the ball. **1565–73** COOPER *Thesaurus* s.v. *Bonus*, Good at tennice. **1601** HOLLAND *Pliny* (1634) I. 190 Pythus was the first plaier at tennise. **1602** SHAKS. *Ham.* II. i. 59. **1617** MINSHEU *Ductor, Tennis play*..aut à *tenez* Gal: i. *hould*, which word the Frenchmen, the onely tennis players, vse to speake when they strike the ball, at tennis. **1634** ROWLEY *Noble Souldier* II. ii, I ha been at Tennis, Madam, with the King. I gave him 15 and all his faults. **1679** C. HATTON in *H. Corr.* (Camden) 189 Last Wednesday his Ma[ty] play'd at tenis. **1789** MRS. PIOZZI *Journ. France* II. 26 He invited them to..play a great match at tennis. **1793** *Sporting Mag.* 29 Sept. 371 Field-tennis threatens ere long to bowl out cricket. **1865** MERIVALE *Rom. Emp.* VIII. lxiv. 116 Then he uses strong exercise for a considerable space at tennis. **1878** JULIAN MARSHALL (*title*) The Annals of Tennis.

fig. **1611** TOURNEUR *Ath. Trag.* II. iv, Drop out Mine eye-bals and let enuious Fortune pla At tennis with 'em. **1654** WHITLOCK *Zootomia* 463 In the Tennis of Fortune. **1899** S. K. HOCKING in *Daily News* 2 Sept. 6/3 He had a decided objection to 'playing tennis with the seventh commandment'.

2. a. Short for LAWN-TENNIS (q.v.), a game played with a ball and rackets on an unenclosed rectangular space on a smooth grass lawn or a floor of hard gravel, cement, asphalt, etc., called a court. (This is now the usual sense.)

Introduced about 1874 (see LAWN-TENNIS); reduced to its present form in 1877. *Tennis* has replaced *lawn tennis* as the official international name of the sport.

1878 GEO. ELIOT *Let.* 8 Aug. (1956) VII. 54 My little man ..fights resolutely against these ills..having mild games of tennis. **1888** *St. James' Gaz.* Aug., It is melancholy to see a word which has held its own for centuries gradually losing its connotation. Such a word is 'tennis', by which nine persons out of ten to-day would understand the game of recent invention played on an unconfined court. **1895** SCULLY *Kafir Stories* 80 The tennis-ground was overgrown with grass—his predecessor's family evidently had not cared about tennis.

b. *anyone for tennis?, who's for tennis?*, etc., a typical entrance or exit line given to a young man in a superficial drawing-room comedy, used *attrib.* of (someone or something reminiscent of) this kind of comedy. Also in extended uses.

1953 J. VAN DRUTEN *Playwright at Work* viii. 99 There is no average Mr. and Mrs. Blank at all. An attempt to draw one..will lead you into the pit of emptiness, and you will emerge with something as unreal as the juveniles in plays who come in impertinently swinging tennis rackets, and when the time for their exit arrives, make it with the remark: 'Tennis, anyone?' **1965** *Listener* 17 June 911/3 One of the panel spoke of 'Who's-for-tennis' comedy,..now a too-familiar pejorative. **1973** *Times* 16 Jan. 11/1 The most unlikely men around London are now dressing as though they might say 'Anyone for tennis?' at any moment. **1974** N. FREELING *Dressing of Diamond* 34 She had seen him..spring up to answer the telephone with an Anyone-for-tennis voice that filled her with pity. **1978** H. MACINNES *Prelude to Terror* ii. 20 He walked over to the small group of staff members...'Who's for tennis?' he asked, and raised a smile.

c. See *table-tennis* s.v. TABLE *sb.* 22.

3. *attrib.* and *Comb.* **a.** Of, belonging to, or used in playing real tennis, as *tennis coat, tennis game*; see also TENNIS-BALL, -PLAY, etc.

1516 *Harl. MS. 2284* lf. 21 Blew velwete for *Tenes Cote for the king. **1552** HULOET, *Tennyse game, or playinge at tennyse, *sphæromachia*.

b. Of, pertaining to, used or worn in lawn-tennis, as ***tennis apron, -bag, dress, frock, -game, -ground, -hat, -jacket, -lawn, match*** (also *fig.*), ***netting, partner, party, -racket, shirt, shorts, sock, -suit, tournament***; **tennis arm, -elbow, -knee**, an arm, elbow, or knee sprained in playing lawn-tennis; **tennis club**: see CLUB *sb.* 14; **tennis flannels** (see FLANNEL *sb.* 2b); **tennis-ground**, a piece of ground laid or marked out for the game of lawn-tennis; a lawn-tennis court or set of courts; **tennis net**, a net stretched across the centre of a tennis-court, over which the players strike the ball; **tennis-pro(fessional**, a tennis player who is paid to act as an instructor and a player at a tennis club, holiday resort, etc.; **tennis shoe**, a light canvas soft-soled shoe suitable for tennis or general casual wear; **tennis stringer** *U.S.*, a person who strings tennis rackets; **tennis whites** (see WHITE *sb.* 9b). See also TENNIS-BALL, -COURT, -PLAYER.

1880 L. HIGGIN *Handbk. Needlework* ii. 11 *Kirriemuir Twill*..is good for *tennis aprons, dresses, curtains, &c. **1977** *New Yorker* 10 Oct. 123/3 It now sells not only tennis balls, racquets, and apparel but all sorts of knick-knacks—..telephone books, tennis aprons, [etc.]. **1887** *Epoch* 19 Aug. 26/2 The 'base-ball pitcher's arm' as well as the '*tennis arm' are recognized in the medical profession as special diseases. **1897** *Outing* (U.S.) XXX. 466/1 Each with a flannel *tennis-bag in her hand. **1908** R. W. CHAMBERS *Younger Set* viii, Eileen..strolled houseward across the lawn, switching the shaven sod with her *tennis bat. **1894** *Harper's Mag.* June 156/1 The champion player in our *tennis club. **1914** L. S. WOOLF *Wise Virgins* ii. 41 May was describing the tennis club dance. **1979** K. CONLON *Move in Game* I. i. 14 Why don't you take her with you to the tennis club? **1885** C. M. YONGE *Nuttie's Father* I. xi. 123 Nuttie was very much pleased with her own pretty *tennis dress. **1977** J. DIDION *Bk. Common Prayer* v. xvii. 258, I never saw her in a tennis dress. **1883** *Pall Mall G.* 30 May 3/1 If *tennis elbow becomes anything like as usual an ailment as tennis playing is an accomplishment. **1899** KIPLING *From Sea to Sea* I. xx. 404 Member of the Clapham Athletic Club in *tennis flannels. **1934** [see *gravel court* s.v. GRAVEL *sb.* 9]. **1981** J. JOHNSTON *Christmas Tree* 33 There was a green stain on his tennis flannels, just below the knee. **1934** A. THIRKELL *Wild Strawberries* ix. 191 Ursule, in a short silk *tennis frock, looked quite presentable. **1891** 'J. S. WINTER' *Lumley* v, He was sitting on the garden seat near the *tennis-ground. **1890** *Army & Navy Stores Catal.* Mar. 1180 *Tennis Hats various colours from 1/o. **1888** BARRIE *When a Man's Single* xiv, A man in a *tennis jacket, carrying a pail. **1901** *Brit. Med. Jrnl.* No. 2097. 562 The country doctor called it a '*tennis-knee', which might mean anything. **1882** *Wheelman* (Boston) I. 55 A *tennis-lawn..is seldom far removed from the smoke of the town. **1899** E. J. CHAPMAN *Drama Two Lives* 13 The tennis-lawns and pathways all Are bright with beauty. **1981** T. THOMPSON *Edwardian Childhoods* v. 130 My grandparents had a big house with a tennis lawn. **1895** E. F. BENSON *Dodo* II. xv. 314 A series of *tennis matches which he had taken part in a few years ago. **1961** *Listener* 28 Sept. 483/2 A brilliant 'tennis match' between God and Satan. **1979** REESE & FLINT *Trick 13* 134, I had a date to play in a tennis match. **1900** C. M. YONGE *Modern Broods* x. 94 Placing *tennis nets, arranging croquet hoops. **1977** *Listener* 7 Apr. 450/1 Table tennis..smashing or retrieving a small celluloid sphere over a miniature tennis net. **1915** KIPLING *Let.* 22 Aug. in C. Carrington *Rudyard Kipling* (1955) xvii. 436 Don't forget the beauty of rabbit netting overhead against hand-grenades. Even *tennis netting is better than nothing. **1934** P. BOTTOME *Private Worlds* iii. 26 The girl was going to be married to her *tennis partner. **1974** E. AMBLER *Dr Frigo* II. 133 My tennis partner at the army communication centre must have been busy. **1887** KIPLING *Plain Tales from Hills* (1888) 256 There are garden-parties, and *tennis-parties and picnics. **1981** *Times* 24 Mar. 4/4 Sir Roger Hollis..met an MI5 officer at a tennis party and was finally recommended for recruitment. **1942** A. CHRISTIE *Body in Library* iii. 31, I do a couple of exhibition dances every evening with Raymond..he's the *tennis and dancing pro. **1977** I. SHAW *Beggarman, Thief* III. vi. 257 A Belgian businessman..had offered him a contract for a year as a tennis pro. **1938** D. DU MAURIER *Rebecca* v. 52 The *tennis professional had complained, the manager has sent a note. **1979** K. CONLON *Move in Game* I. iii. 32 The bronzed tennis professional, who had all the ladies of the club in a lather of longing. **1892** F. M. CRAWFORD *Three Fates* II iv. 95 Her first *tennis-racket, now battered and half-unstrung. **1897** ANNE PAGE *Afternoon Ride* 7 A..girl with a tennis-racket in her hand. **1889** *Tennis shirt [see CELLULAR *a.* (and *sb.*) 2b]. **1978** *Country Life* 22 June 1841/1 Cotton tennis dress..navy and white tennis shirt..tennis shoes. **1887** KIPLING *Plain Tales* (1888) 222 Miss Hollis..was..five foot seven in her *tennis-shoes. **1908** R. W. CHAMBERS *Younger Set* viii, Yes, I've plenty of tennis-shoes. Help yourself. **1928** E. WALLACE *Flying Squad* xiii. 122 They walked noiselessly, for Mr. Tiser had obligingly supplied them with..tennis shoes. **1975** *Time* (Canada ed.) 22 Dec. 12/3 [He] once flew out to settle a strike at the Vancouver *Sun* wearing tennis shoes and carrying clothes in a Loblaws shopping bag. **1963** D. B. HUGHES *Expendable Man* (1964) iv. 122 She was in *tennis shorts and a white blouse. **1932** D. C. MINTER *Modern Needlecraft* 253/1 *Tennis Socks.. 3-ply fingering. **1976** *Washington Post* 19 Apr. C15/4 (Advt.), *Tennis stringer. Experience preferred but not necessary. **1897** MRS. RAYNER *Type-writer Girl* i, A baronet in a *tennis suit. **1892** C. M. YONGE *Cross Roads* xii. 127 Miss Clara caught a chill while driving home after a *tennis tournament. **1976** *Wymondham & Attleborough Express* 10 Dec. 21/6 Sue Rich..has made great progress in tennis tournaments in several parts of England this year. **1974** M. EHRLICH *Reincarnation* (1975) xxiii. 203 She was in *tennis whites now and volleying with the pro.

Hence **'tennisdom**, the world or realm of real- or lawn-tennis players; **'tennisy** *a.*, *colloq.* addicted to lawn-tennis.

1890 *Blackw. Mag.* Feb. 256/2 As with horsy women, ..*tennis-y* girls..become intolerable nuisances to their neighbours. **1897** *Outing* (U.S.) XXX. 464/2 The reputation of the Bentley brothers had gone forth into tennisdom with a very high brand on it.

[*Note.* The introduction of some form of tennis into Florence by the French knights in 1325, and the use of the name *tenes*, appear not to be recorded elsewhere than in Velluti's *Cronica*, nor does either game or name appear to have been long retained; the name was manifestly foreign, and opposed to Italian word-formation. But its use in Florence at least 30 and perhaps 70 years before the earliest known English example, implies either that the Eng. name came from Italy, or that both had a common source. The latter is the more likely; it was French knights who introduced the game at Florence, and the Eng. *te'netz, te'neys*, with their final stress, imply French origin. The difficulty is that the game has app. never borne any such name in Fr., where, from 1350 or earlier, it has been called *la paulme, la paume*. The only Fr. word akin in form is *tenez* (AF. *tenetz*), 2 pers. pl. pres. indic. and imper. of *tenir* 'to hold', also 'to take, receive what is offered'. Hence the suggestion made by Minsheu 1617, and favoured by Skeat, Jusserand, and others, that the name originated in the Fr. imperative *tenez* 'take, receive', called by the server to his opponent. There is of course the difficulty that no mention of this call has yet been found in French, where it must have been used if thence taken into It. and Eng. But in the Colloquies of Cordier and Erasmus, the server's call is latinized as *accipe* and *excipe*, and in the *Carmen de ludo pilæ reticulo* of R. Fressart, Paris, 1641, 'excipe', 'pilam excipe', 'mitto pilam in tectum, excipe', with other uses of *excipere* and *accipere*, occur eight times in the portion printed by Julian Marshall *Annals of Tennis* 27–29. These Latin words witness to the use of *tenez* or some equivalent call in French, and favour the conclusion that this call gave rise to the 14th c. It. and Eng. name.]

'tennis, *v.* Also 6 -esse. [f. prec. sb.]

†**1.** *trans.* To toss to and fro like a ball at real tennis. Also *absol. Obs.*

1565 W. ALLEN in Fulke *Confut. Purg.* (1577) 145 How fast they will tennesse one to an other in these shiftes. **1596** SPENSER *State Irel.* Wks. (Globe) 652/2 These fowre garrisons issuing foorthe..will so drive him [the enemy] from one side to another, and tennis him amongest them, that he shall finde no where safe.

2. †**a.** *intr.* To play real tennis. Hence †**'tennising** *vbl. sb.*, tennis-playing; also †**'tenniser**, a tennis-player. *Obs.*

a **1475** *Myrc's Par. Pr.* 11 *note*, Danseyng, cotteyng, bollyng, tenessyng, handball, fott ball, stoil ball & all manner other games. **1579** RICE *Invective agst. Vices* E iv b, Bowlyng, Dicyng, Cardyng, Tennesyng, with such like actes and deedes of the fleshe. *Ibid.* F j, Dicers, Bowlers, Carders,..Tenessers.

b. To play lawn-tennis. Also with quasi-*obj. rare.*

1895 KIPLING in *Cent. Mag.* Dec. 276/1 They picnicked and they tennised. **1979** *United States 1980/81* (Penguin Travel Guides) 493 Whether you tennis-it at a camp or a clinic, you're guaranteed a certain number of hours of court time every day. **1983** *Washington Post* 15 Aug. c8/6 They'd rather be golfing, or snorkeling, or tennising.

tennis-ball. [f. TENNIS *sb.* + BALL *sb.*[1] 4.] The small ball used in real tennis or lawn-tennis.

c **1450** *Brut* ccxliv. 374 Yn scorne & despite he [the Dauphin] sent to hym [King Henry V] a tonne fulle of teneys-ballis, be-cause he schulde haue sumwhat to play with-alle. **1561** T. NORTON *Calvin's Inst.* I. 60 As if God did to make himself pastime to tosse men like tennise balles. **1599** SHAKS. *Hen. V*, I. ii. 258. **1726** SWIFT *Gulliver* II. v, Such cruel bangs..as if I had been pelted with tennis-balls. **1805** SCOTT *Last Minstr.* II. xxxi, Like tennis-ball by raquet tossed.

attrib. **1786** ABERCROMBIE *Arr.* in *Gard. Assist.* p. vii, Tennis-ball cabbage lettuce.

b. *fig.*; *esp.* a thing or person that is tossed or bandied about like a tennis-ball.

1589 WARNER *Alb. Eng.* VI. xxx. 151 Vulcan, Venus,.. Daphne turnd to Tree..tennis balles to euery tongue of euery Deitee. **1610** HOLLAND *Camden's Brit.* (1637) 570 The very tennisse-ball, in some sort, of fortune. **1642** H. MORE *Song of Soul* II. App. lxxxviii, A cluster of them makes not half a Moon, What should such tennis-balls do in the skie? **1890** DAKYNS *Xenophon* I. p. xciv, We find this great Athenian captain playing the ignoble part of tennis-ball to rival Spartan harmosts.

'tennis-court. [f. TENNIS *sb.* + COURT *sb.* 4.]

1. The enclosed quadrangular area, or building, in which the game of real tennis is played. Also *fig.* and *Comb.* esp. ***tennis-court oath***, the pledge given on June 20, 1789, by members of the States General of France that they would not separate before a constitution was granted (see quot. 1911).

1564 in Willis & Clark *Cambridge* (1886) I. 143 Boards to make a tennyse court £1. o. o. **1611** COTGR., *Blouse*, a close Tennis court, or a Tennis court in a hall, hauing a house on either side to serue on. **1630** in *Proc. Soc. Antiq. Scot.* (1896) XXX. 57 The tinneis courtis thairof and all utheris houses. **1763** *Brit. Mag.* IV. 55 It was agreed to build a new theatre, where the Tennis-court then stood, in Lincoln's-inn-fields. **1791** MACKINTOSH *Vind. Gallicæ* Wks. 1846 III. 24 They were summoned by their President to a Tennis-Court, where they were reduced to hold their assembly. **1878** JULIAN MARSHALL *Annals of Tennis* 114 One of the greatest obstacles to the spreading of the love of Tennis has always been the scarcity of Tennis-courts. [*Ibid.* 113 Their number [in England] at the present moment is twenty-one.]

fig. **1605** EARL STIRLING *Alexand. Trag.* v. i, I thinke the world is but a Tennis-court where Fortune doth play States, tosse men for Balls. **1738** G. LILLO *Marina* I. ii, Winds and waters, In their vast tennis-court, have, as a ball, Used me to make them sport.

Comb. **1597** SHAKS. *2 Hen. IV*, II. ii. 21 But that the Tennis-Court-keeper knowes better than I. *a* **1637** B. JONSON *Eng. Gram.* viii. *note, Sæpè tria coagmentantur nomina, ut*, a foot-ball-player, a tennis-court-keeper. **1893** L. CREIGHTON *First Hist. France* xxvi. 231 The Tennis-Court Oath.—Under his [*sc.* Mirabeau's] guidance the Third estate now declared themselves the National Assembly. **1911** H. A. GUERBER *Story Mod. France* x. 55 The Third Estate met tumultuously in the Versailles Tennis Court, where..they bound themselves, by the famous 'Tennis Court Oath'. **1959** *Listener* 31 Dec. 1151/1 The integrity of Anatolia was the tennis-court oath of the Kemalist revolution. **1977** *Socialist Press* 2 Mar. 6/3 Faced with procedural fencing on the part of the King's ministers and the Court, they declare themselves a 'National Assembly' and vow (the 'tennis-court oath', June 20th) not to depart until a constitution is drawn up.

2. The plot of ground prepared and marked out for lawn-tennis.

1881 'RITA' *My Lady Coquette* i, I wanted to see the tennis-courts made.

'tennis-play. [f. TENNIS *sb.* + PLAY *sb.*]

1. The game of TENNIS (sense 1); playing at tennis.

c **1440** *Promp. Parv.* 68/1 Chace of tenys pley, or oþyr lyke, *sistencia.* **1530** PALSGR. 280/1 Tennysplay, *jeu de la paulme.* **1594** NASHE *Christ's T.* To Rdr., Prouided it bee not a Tennice-play of Pots and Cups, like the Centaurs feast. **1651** HOBBES *Leviath.* II. xxv. (1839) 249 He that useth able seconds at tennis play, placed in their proper stations. **1918** G. FRANKAU *One of Them* in *Poet. Wks.* (1923) II. xxiv. 143 Who in all Albion on that fateful day..Left not his office-work, his tennis-play, To read black Montmorency's slander-red lines?

†2. = TENNIS-COURT 1. *Obs.*

1507-8 *Court of Frank-pledge, Oxford*, Four men presented for keeping tenysplayes, an illegal sport. **1577-87** HOLINSHED *Chron.* III. 1223/1 In Wisbich was a garden, a tennise plaie, & a bowling allie walled about with bricke.

Comb. **1530** in *Vicary's Anat.* (1888) App. ii. 101 Item, for Anthony Annesley, tenesplay-keper vj s viij d.

'tennis-ˌplayer. [f. as prec.] One who plays at lawn-tennis or (formerly) real tennis.

c **1440** *Promp. Parv.* 488/2 Teneys pleyare, *teniludius.* **1635** STAFFORD *Fem. Glory* (1869) 106 The best Tennis-player living cannot shew his cunning. **1674** TEMPLE *Let. to Sir J. Temple* Wks. 1731 II. 297 We were both together young Travellers and Tennis Players in France. **1801** STRUTT *Sports & Past.* II. iii. (1876) 161 We have.. authority to prove that Henry VII was a tennis player. **1884** *Harper's Mag.* Jan. 304/2 The champion tennis-players.

So **'tennis-playing**, playing at tennis.

1441 [see TENNIS 1]. **1495** *Act 11 Hen. VII*, c. 2 §5 Where ..tenys pleiyng bowles Clossh or any other unlawfull game ..shalbe used. **1583** STUBBES *Anat. Abus.* II. (1882) 33 They spend it in dicing, carding, bowling, tennise plaieng.

tennis-playing, *ppl. a.* [f. as TENNIS-PLAYER.] That plays (lawn-)tennis.

1956 H. GOLD *Man who was not with It* (1965) vi. 58 The long, tennis-playing, suburban legs. **1965** M. SPARK *Mandelbaum Gate* ii. 27 Her energetic tennis-playing grandmother..sat on the arm of a chair. **1979** D. EDEN *Storrington Papers* iv. 47 'The new governess..arrived this afternoon.' 'Promising?'.. 'No more tennis-playing amazons.'

tennon, tennor, -our, tenny, tennys, -yse, obs. ff. TENON[1], TENOR, TENNÉ, TENNIS.

Tennysonian (tɛnɪ'səʊnɪən), *a.* and *sb.* [f. the name of the poet Alfred (Lord) *Tennyson* (1809–1892) + -IAN.]

A. *adj.* Of or pertaining to Tennyson, his works, or his style.

1846 LYTTON *New Timon* II. 51 Where all the airs of patchwork-pastoral chime To drowsy ears in Tennysonian rhyme! **1853** LONGF. in *Life* (1891) II. 249 [M. Arnold's poems] Very clever; with a little of the Tennysonian leaven in them. **1861** *Times* 10 Oct., His success exceeds that of his predecessors who have attempted the rendering of this Tennysonian classic [*Catullus*]. **1876** STEDMAN *Vict. Poets* vi. (1887) 227 These effects, which the Laureate employs with such variation and continuance that the resultant style is known as Tennysonian, were Dorian first of all.

B. *sb.* An admirer, imitator, disciple, or student of Tennyson.

1850 J. BROWN *Let.* Dec. (1912) 116, I am not a Tennysonian, as many are. **1864** H. SIDGWICK *Let.* May in A. & E. M. Sidgwick *Henry Sidgwick* (1906) ii. 108 The compressed *inhaltsvoll* classic style of Tennyson and Tennysonians. **1883** *Harper's Mag.* Feb. 469/1 By all the Tennysonians of this generation it will be deeply regretted. **1970** T. HILTON *Pre-Raphaelites* vi. 161 William Morris.. like all reading men, was a Tennysonian.

Hence **Tennysoni'ana** [-IANA], matters connected with Tennyson; **Tenny'sonianism, 'Tennysonism**, a characteristic trait or mannerism of Tennyson's style; an imitation of that style; **Tenny'sonianized** *ppl. a.*, rendered in the manner of Tennyson; **Tenny'sonianly** *adv.*; **Tenny'sonianness** = TENNYSONIANISM, TENNYSONISM; **Tenny'sonize** *v. trans.*, to render in the style of Tennyson.

1843 MRS. BROWNING *Let. to C. Mathews* 14 Mar. (in *Davey's Catal.* (1895) 15), I had been pleased with the poetical sense of his [Lowell's] book, which he sent me long ago,—notwithstanding the Tennysonianisms of it. *a* **1849** POE *Channing* Wks. 1864 III. 234 The affectations—the Tennysonisms of Mr. Channing. **1866** R. H. SHEPHERD (*title*) Tennysoniana. **1910** A. D. GODLEY *Lectures Eng. Lit.* ii, in *Reliquiae* (1926) II. 288 Tennyson is full of reminiscences of the great classics, thoughts and phrases not slavishly copied but Tennysonised—passed through the medium of an art which added beauty to everything it touched. **1915** E. POUND *Let.* Jan. (1971) 49 [In poetry] there must be..no straddled adjectives (as 'addled mosses dank'), no Tennysonianness of speech. **1916** *Ibid.* ? 20 July (1971) 87 Virgil is a second-rater, a Tennysonianized version of Homer. **1932** L. MAGNUS *Herbert Warren* viii. 215 His own annotated copy of the one-volume edition of the *Memoir* is a veritable treasure of Tennysoniana. **1964** *English Studies* XLV. 73 'Lycidas' once read 'under the glimmering eyelids of the morne', most Tennysonianly. **1975** *Listener* 20 Nov. 685/1 Superintendent Dalziel, on unwanted holiday in sodden fens, meets a Tennysonianly aqueous funeral cortège.

teno-, combining element, arbitrarily formed from Gr. τένων, TENDON: cf. TENONTO-. **tenography** (tɛ'nɒgrəfɪ) [-GRAPHY], description of tendons. **te'nology** [-LOGY], that part of anatomy which relates to the tendons. **te'norrhaphy** [Gr. ῥαφή a seam], suture of a tendon. **'tenoˌsuture** [L. *sūtūra* a seam], = *tenorrhaphy*. **ˌteno-syno'vitis** [see SYNOVIA and -ITIS], inflammation of a tendon and its sheath. See also TENOTOMY.

1890 BILLINGS *Nat. Med. Dict.*, *Tenography, *Tenology, *Tenorrhaphy. **1899** *Syd. Soc. Lex.*, **Tenosuture*, the sewing together of the divided ends of a tendon. **1890** BILLINGS *Nat. Med. Dict.*, *Tenosynovitis. **1896** *Allbutt's Syst. Med.* I. 379 The results [of massage] in sprains, tenosynovitis and the like, are sometimes amazing.

tenon ('tɛnən), *sb.*[1] Forms: α. 5 tenown, 5- tenon, (6-8 tennon); β. 6 tenaunt, -e, 6-7 (9 *dial.*) **tenant**, 7 -ent, 7-8 **tennant**, -ent. [a. F. *tenon* (15th c. in Godef. *Compl.*), f. *tenir* to hold + suffix *-on* (= L. *-ōnem*). The β-forms show assimilation to the word TENANT, and to L. *tenent-em* pr. pple., holding: cf. *talon, talent*, and see -ANT[3].]

1. a. A projection fashioned on the end or side of a piece of wood or other material, to fit into a corresponding cavity or MORTISE in another piece, so as to form a close and secure joint.

α. **14..** *Voc.* in Wr.-Wülcker 616/1 *Tentum*, a tenon, *quod ponitur in commissura.* *c* **1440** *Promp. Parv.* 489/1 Tenown, knyttynge of a balke or oþer lyke yn tymbyr (*S.* tenowre), ..*tenaculum, gumfus.* **1545** ELYOT, *Cardo*.. it is also the tenon, whiche is put into the mortayse. **1577** tr. *Bullinger's Decades* (1592) 339 Euery boorde had two tenons like pikes, whereby they were stucke into the sockets. *a* **1661** FULLER *Worthies* (1662) III. *Stafford.* 38 There is a fair House on London Bridge, commonly called None-such, which is reported to be made without either Nailes or Pins, with crooked Tennons fastened with wedges and other (as I may term them) circumferential devices. **1852** WRIGHT *Celt, Rom. & Sax.* ii. 59 Each of the upright stones [at Stonehenge] had two tenons or projections on the top. **1889** *Work* 29 June 227/1 In cutting dovetails and tenons.

β. **1551** RECORDE *Cast. Knowl.* (1556) 51 Then must you make lyke morteyses..to receaue those tenauntes. *a* **1677** HALE *Prim. Orig. Man.* IV. iv. 330 If Chance could make a Beam.., and..Tenents at either end, yet it is not possible to conceive that Chance could..fit the Mortises of other pieces of Timber to those Tenents. **1703** MOXON *Mech. Exerc.* 116 *Tennant*..a square end fitted into a Mortess. **1778** *Eng. Gazetteer* (ed. 2) s.v. *Yardley*, The spire..for want of tennents being pinned down, was blown off.

b. *tenon and mortise* (also *mortise and tenon*: see MORTISE *sb.* 1 b), the combination of these.

1610 HOLLAND *Camden's Brit.* 251 With a small tenents and mortescis. **1611** SPEED *Hist. Gt. Brit.* VII. xii. §3. 267 Fastned with tenons and mortaises, the one into the other. **1688** R. HOLME *Armoury* III. xviii. (Roxb.) 139/1 Fastned in them with a Mortais and Tenent. **1856** EMERSON *Eng. Traits, Stonehenge* Wks. (Bohn) II. 124 The good beasts must have known how to cut a well-wrought tenon and mortise.

†c. The lower part of a graft which is cut thin so as to be inserted into the stock. *Obs.*

1523 FITZHERB. *Husb.* §139 Take thy graffe and cut it in the ioynt to the myddes, & make the tenaunt therof half an inche longe or a lytell more al on the one syde. **1641** in Maidment *Bk. Scott. Pasquils* 131 Whose tennons small, if they be left in ground, Like ill weeds soon will waxe.

†d. *fig.* That which firmly connects or unites two things. *Obs. rare*[−1].

1617 HIERON *Wks.* II. 145 There are then two things concurre in the producing of man... This I thinke to bee the surest tenon.

2. *attrib.* and *Comb.*, as *tenon-helve, -joint, piece*; **tenon-auger**, a hollow auger for forming tenons on the ends of spokes, chair-legs, etc.; **tenon-saw**, a fine saw for making tenons, etc., having a thin blade, a thick back, and small teeth very slightly 'set'.

1881 RAYMOND *Mining Gloss.*, **Tenant-helve*, see *Frontal-hammer.* **1865** *Reader* No. 133. 73/3 Mortice and *tenon joints. **1901** *J. Black's Carp. & Build., Home Handicr.* 14 A pin of hard wood..driven in through the *tenon piece and the mortise. **1549** *Privy Council Acts* (1890) II. 351 *Tenant sawes, iiij. **1703** MOXON *Mech. Exerc.* 103 The Tennant-Saw, being thin, hath a Back to keep it from bending. **1823** P. NICHOLSON *Pract. Build.* 251 The Tenon-saw derives its name from being used for forming the shoulders of tenons. **1898** *Monthly South Dakotan* I. 57 This operation was successfully performed by Dr. Phillips with no further implements at hand than a large butcher's knife and a small tenon-saw. **1979** A. B. EMARY *Woodworking* xxix. 125 Saw (a hand saw and a tenon saw) can be stored in the lid.

Tenon ('tɛnən), *sb.*[2] *Anat.* The name of J. R. *Tenon* (1724–1816), French anatomist, used in the possessive as **Tenon's capsule**, a delicate band of fascia with involuntary muscle fibres disposed round the eyeball (*Syd. Soc. Lex.*); **Tenon's space**, the episcleral space between Tenon's capsule and the sclera.

1868 HACKLEY & ROOSA tr. *C. Stellwag von Carion's Treat. Dis. Eye* I. xi. 434 This anterior part of the sheath of the eye-ball..is also described as Tenon's capsule. **1892** A. DUANE tr. *Fuchs's Text-bk. Ophthalm.* II. xv. 285 Exudation into Tenon's space also occurs after it has been laid open by injuries. **1950** *Sci. News* XV. 25 The eye does not form part of a ball-and-socket joint, like the hip joint, but resembles a ball in a sling, the latter..being composed of a thin sheet of fibrous and smooth muscle tissue, called Tenon's Capsule. **1979** G. W. CIBIS tr. *Hollwich's Ophthalm.* xvi. 238 The inflammation involves Tenon's capsule in either a serous or a purulent form. As a rule it remains restricted to Tenon's space.

Also **Tenonian** (tə'nəʊnɪən) *a.*: discovered or described by Tenon, as in ***Tenonian fascia*** or ***capsule*** = *Tenon's capsule*; **teno'nitis**, inflammation of Tenon's capsule.

1890 BILLINGS *Nat. Med. Dict.*, Tenon's capsule. *Ibid.*, Tenonitis. **1891** *Cent. Dict.*, The Tenonian fascia or capsule. **1901** *Brit. Med. Jrnl.* No. 2097. 575 The symptoms of tenonitis.

tenon ('tɛnən), *v.* Also 7-8 **tenant, tennant**, 8 **tenent, tenont.** [f. prec. sb.]

1. a. *trans.* To fix together with tenon and mortise.

1649 BLITHE *Eng. Improv. Impr.* (1653) 203 The beam.. runs down into the plough-head, and is there tenanted and pinned into the head. **1665** J. WEBB *Stone-Heng* (1725) 91 If mortised and tenanted. **1711** W. SUTHERLAND *Shipbuild. Assist.* 25 Tenant [in *Errata* corr. to *Tenon*] the Post into the Keel. **1769** FALCONER *Dict. Marine* (1789) C iv b, The stern-post..is tenented into the keel. **1844** STEPHENS *Bk. Farm* II. 289 The whole of the posts are likewise tenoned into the sill. **1949** H. M. CAUTLEY *Norfolk Churches* 37 A massive sill, frequently unbroken at the entrance to chancel, into which the muntins are tenoned. **1980** *Early Music* Jan. 62/2 At the other end, the neck is tenoned into the post and pegged.

b. *fig.* To join or fix firmly and securely.

1596 BP. ANDREWES *Serm., Luke xvi. 25* (1841) II. 86 We tenon both these together, as antecedent and consequent. **1659** O. WALKER *Instruct. Oratory* 18 The several pieces of Invention..must next be sowed and tenanted together. **1856** WHITMAN in *Scott. Rev.* (1883) 285 My foothold is tenon'd and mortis'd in granite.

2. a. To furnish or fit with a tenon.

1771 LUCKOMBE *Hist. Print.* 302 These two Rails are each of them tenoned at each end. **1793** SMEATON *Edystone L.* §174 Cramping the stones together, as well as tenoning the ends. **1873** J. RICHARDS *Wood-w. Factories* 156 For this we have the remedy of tenoning both ends at the same time.

b. *intr.* To engage or fit in by or as by a tenon. Also *fig.*

1797 *Encycl. Brit.* (ed. 3) XVII. 404/1 The two beams.. should be placed conformable to the two uprights, so that they may tenon in them. **1842** *Civil Eng. & Arch. Jrnl.* V. 361/2 They tenon between the strings *e* and *n.* **1935** 'E. QUEEN' *Spanish Cape Mystery* iv. 103 There are a few facts floating about which don't precisely tenon with the psychopathic theory. **1981** *Rescue News* Mar. 8/1 The oak timbers..tenoned and pegged into sole-plates lying on the bottom of the moat.

Hence **'tenoned** *ppl. a.*, furnished or made with a tenon; **'tenoner**, a machine for forming tenons.

1771 LUCKOMBE *Hist. Print.* 323 [He] besmears the whole tenoned ends and tenons well with soap. **1875** *Carpentry & Join.* 49 The tenoned and mortised ends of the pieces. **1891** *Cent. Dict.*, Tenoner. **1944** J. C. JONES in N. W. Kay *Practical Carpenter & Joiner* x. 227/1 The rails are first fed into the tenoner edgeways up for the machining of the haunchings. **1971** *Cabinet Maker & Retail Furnisher* 24 Sept. 532 Mr Taylor has retained in use with the new line a Schwabedissen double end tenoner with overhead beam.

tenon, obs. and dial. form of TENDON.

tenonian: see TENON *sb.*[2]

'tenoning, *vbl. sb.* [f. TENON *v.* or *sb.* + -ING[1].] a. The process of jointing or joining together with tenon and mortise. b. Furnishing with tenons. So **'tenoning** *ppl. a.*, that tenons or furnishes with a tenon.

1678 *Lond. Gaz.* No. 1327/4 As in Plaining,..Mortessing and Tennanting, Moldings, &c. **1769** FALCONER *Dict. Marine* (1789), *Assembler*, to unite the several pieces of a ship, as by ..scarfing, scoring, tenenting, &c. **1847** SMEATON *Builder's Man.* 112 Little need be said..as to morticing and tenoning, or dovetailing.

c. *attrib.* and *Comb.* (of the *vbl. sb.* or *ppl. a.*), as **tenoning attachment**, a mechanical fitting for converting a moulding machine into a tenon-cutter; **tenoning chisel**, a double-blade chisel which makes two cuts, leaving a middle piece which forms a tenon (Knight *Dict. Mech.*); **tenoning cutter, tenoning machine**, a machine for cutting timber with a tenon.

1895 *Daily Chron.* 6 Dec. 1/5 Moulding Machine (4-cutter) with *tenoning attachment, band-saw, vertical spindle. **1870** *Eng. Mech.* 4 Feb. 498/1 For tenoning, the planing cutters..are replaced by *tenoning cutters. **1873** J. RICHARDS *Wood-working Factories* 157 To move them backward and forward is the main labour in operating a *tenoning machine. **1881** YOUNG *Ev. Man his own Mechanic* §216 Tenoning and trenching machines.

tenonitis: see TENON *sb.*[2]

tenonto-. [f. Gr. τένων, τενοντ- tendon.] A formative of technical terms relating to the tendons: cf. TENO-. **tenontography** (tɛnən'tɒgrəfɪ), = TENOGRAPHY. **tenon'tology**, = TENOLOGY. **tenontophyme** (tə'nɒntəʊfaɪm) [Gr. φῦμα growth], **te'nontophyte** [Gr. φυτόν plant], a tumour or morbid growth on a tendon. **te'nontostome** [*ostoma*, OSTEOMA], an osseous tumour in a tendon.

1860 MAYNE *Expos. Lex.*, *Tenontographia*..tenontography... *Tenontologia*..tenontology... *Tenontophyma*..tenontophyme... *Tenontophytum*..tenontophyte... *Tenontostoma*..tenontostome. **1899** *Syd. Soc. Lex.*, Tenontophyte.

tenor ('tɛnə(r)), *sb.*[1] (*a.*) Also 4 tenur, 4-6 -oure, 4-9 -our, 5 -owre, -eur, 6 -ore, -er, tennour, (teanor), 6-7 tennor, 7 tenner. β. 4-8 tenure (5 teneure). [a. OF. *tenor*, *-our*, 13th c. (also *tenoire*, *-eure*, *-ure*, 13-14th c.), mod.F. *teneur* fem., substance, import of a document, etc.:—L. *tenōr-em* course, import (of a law, etc.), f. *tenēre* to hold. The musical term was in 14-15th c. F. *tenor* masc. and fem., 'a tenor part, voice, or singer', mod.F. *ténor* masc., after It. *tenore* and med.L. *tenor*, to which also the English word in all senses has been conformed. Confusion with TENURE prevailed from 13th to 18th c.: see β.]

A. *sb.* **I. 1. a.** The course of meaning which holds on or continues through something written or spoken; the general sense or meaning of a document, speech, etc.; substance, purport, import, effect, drift.

In technical legal use (as in Fr.) implying the actual wording of a document, or a transcript thereof (distinguished from *effect*): cf. b. *proving of the tenor* (Sc. Law): see quot. 1838.

a **1300** *Cursor M.* 17614 Þai did þan for to write a writt, þis þan was þe tenur of hit. **13..** *K. Alis.* 2977 Anothir lettre he sent heom tho, And of a more bitter tenour. **1387** TREVISA *Higden* (Rolls) III. 35 Þe tenor of his laws was suche. **1413-22** MARG. OF ANJOU *Lett.* (Camden) 22 Youre gracieux letters of prive seal, the teneur of the which we have wel understand. **1526** TINDALE *Acts* viii. 32 The tener off the scripture which he redde was this. **1535** STEWART *Cron. Scot.* (Rolls) II. 355 This wes the tennour that tyme of thair band. **1603** SHAKS. *Meas. for M.* IV. ii. 216 Hee..receiues letters of strange tenor. **1664** H. MORE *Myst. Iniq.* 112 This is the tenour of the New Covenant. **1703** *Lond. Gaz.* No. 3953/1 (Scotl.) Act for proving the Tenor in Favours of Anna Cockburn. **1825** JEFFERSON *Autobiog.* Wks. 1859 I. 10 The tenor of these propositions being generally known. **1838** W. BELL *Dict. Law Scot.* s.v. *Proving*, The terms of a deed which has been lost or destroyed may be proved in an action peculiar to the Court of Session, called an action of proving the tenor. **1870** L'ESTRANGE *Miss Mitford* I. i. 20 Such was the general tenour of Mrs. Mitford's letters.

β. [**1292** BRITTON VI. iv. §9 Solom la tenure del Pone (*tr.* according to the tenor of the Pone).] **13..** *K. Alis.* 1707 (Bodl. MS.), A letter par amoure Of whiche swiche was þe tenure. **1427** *Rolls of Parlt.* IV. 332/2 Ayeins the teneure and forme of the saide Statutes. **1512** *Act 4 Hen. VIII*, c. 11 Certen Indentures wherof the tenure hereafter ensuyth. **1596** SHAKS. *Merch. V.* IV. i. 235 Bid me teare the bond. *Iew.* When it is paid according to the tenure. **1682** *Lond. Gaz.* No. 1733/4 According to the Tenure of his Majesties Letters Patents.

b. *concr.* An exact copy of a document, a transcript. (In quot. 1523, a written statement.) Now *techn.*: see prec. sense.

c **1450** *Godstow Reg.* 366 Even as hit apperith of submyssions of the same parties, Tenouris of the which folow bynethe. **1523** LD. BERNERS *Froiss.* I. ccxii. 257 Than he shall delyuer to vs a tenour of that he ought to do. **1588** LAMBARDE *Eiren.* IV. xviii. 591 Sometimes they are to certifie and send vp onely a Tenor (or Transcript) as I sayd, of the Record. **1842** S. GREENLEAF *Evidence* (1844) I. §502. 575 In such cases, nothing is returned but the tenor, that is, a literal transcript of the record, under the seal of the Court.

c. The value of a bank note or bill as stated on it: in phr. *old tenor*, *middle tenor*, *new tenor*, referring to the successive issues of paper currency in the colonies of Massachusetts and Rhode Island in the 18th c. *Hist.*

1740 W. DOUGLASS *Disc. Curr. Brit. Plant. Amer.* 40 All bills of the old Tenor when brought into their Treasury, to issue out no more. **1811** J. ADAMS *Wks.* (1854) IX. 638 It is worse than old tenor, continental currency, or any other paper money. **1878** F. A. WALKER *Money* xv. 319 In 1741 the Assembly made 6s. 9d. of the new-tenor equal to 27 shillings of the old. *Ibid.* 320 By act of 1770, the old-tenor notes were to be exchanged at this rate.

d. The underlying idea or subject to which a metaphor refers, as distinct from the literal meaning of the words used. Cf. VEHICLE *sb.* 3 d.

1936 I. A. RICHARDS *Philos. Rhet.* v. 96 A first step is to introduce two technical terms to assist us in distinguishing ..what Dr. Johnson called the two ideas that any metaphor, at its simplest, gives us. Let me call them the tenor and the vehicle. The tenor, as I am calling it—[is] the underlying idea or principal subject which the vehicle or figure means. *Ibid.* 100 The tenor may become almost a mere excuse for the introduction of the vehicle, and so no longer be 'the principal subject'. **1949** *Poetry* (Chicago) Feb. 304 The tenor is the *new* meaning, the vehicle the *old* meaning on which the new meaning is conveyed. **1962** S. ULLMANN *Semantics* viii. 213 An important factor in the effectiveness of a metaphor is the distance between tenor and vehicle. **1973** A. RODWAY in R. Fowler *Dict. Mod. Crit. Terms* 112 In the phrase 'Now is the winter of our discontent'.. discontentedness is the tenor, and an aspect of winter..the vehicle. **1980** G. B. CAIRD *Lang. & Imagery of Bible* viii. 152 In a living metaphor, although both speaker and hearer are aware that vehicle and tenor are distinct entities, they are not grasped as two but as one.

2. †**a.** The action or fact of holding on or continuing; continuance, duration. *Obs.*

1398 TREVISA *Barth. De P.R.* VI. i. (Bodl. MS.), Þe age is of a man noȝt elles is but tenour and during of kinde vertues. **1502** *Ord. Crysten Men* v. iv. (1506) 393 The melodye of the glorye of the blessyd shall not haue tenoure yf the paynes of the dampned were not eternall. **1621** BURTON *Anat. Mel.* I. i. I. v. (1651) 12 'Tis most absurd..for any mortal man to look for a perpetual tenor of happiness in his life. *a* **1694** TILLOTSON *Serm.* (1742) IV. 539 Let not a perpetual tenor of health and pleasure soften and dissolve your spirits.

b. Continuous progress, course, movement (*of* action, etc.); way of proceeding, procedure.

1398 TREVISA *Barth. De P.R.* VIII. ii. (Tollem. MS.), Heuen with his roundnesse and cerclis forsakeþ nouȝt, noþer leueþ þe sadde tenor of his ordre. **1596** SPENSER *F.Q.* IV. vii. 47 Ne ought mote make him change his wonted tenor. **1676** HALE *Contempl.* I. 400 The constant tenour of a just, virtuous, and pious life. **1750** GRAY *Elegy* 76 Along the cool sequester'd vale of life They kept the noiseless tenour of their way. **1784** JOHNSON *Let. to Mrs. Thrale* 26 June, Of doing good a continual tenour of distress allowed him few opportunities. **1814** CARY *Dante's Inf.* x. 133 She of thy life The future tenour will to thee unfold. **1865** SEELEY *Ecce Homo* iv. (ed. 8) 29 The contrast between Christ's pretensions and the homely tenour of his life.

β. **1720** W. GIBSON *Dict. Horses* xii. (1731) 185 A continued easy Motion, and constant Tenure in Feeding.

c. The length of time that a bill is drawn to run before presentation for payment.

1866 CRUMP *Banking* v. 100 The tenor [of foreign bills].. depends upon a variety of circumstances, and may be extended to almost any period, provided the parties thereto are agreed. *Ibid.* 101 The term 'usance'..denotes the customary tenor at which bills are drawn.

3. Quality, character, nature; condition, state. †**a.** in physical sense; in early use *esp.* quality of tone (cf. 4). *Obs.*

1530 PALSGR. 47 The redar shall sounde them all under one tenour, and never rest upon them nor lyft up his voice. **1595** SPENSER *Epithal.* 9 Your string could soone to sadder tenor turne. **1618** BP. HALL *Serm.* v. 103 There can be no harmony, where all the strings or voices are of one tenor. **1725** *Bradley's Fam. Dict.* s.v. *Elm*, The Tenor of the Grain makes it also fit for all Kinds of Carved-Work. **1729** SHELVOCKE *Artillery* II. 90 The Air in them must be of the same Tenor with the circumambient Air.

b. in non-physical sense: the way in which a thing continues; *esp.* habitual condition of mind. Now *rare* or merged in 2 b.

1589 PUTTENHAM *Eng. Poesie* III. v. (Arb.) 163 No fault or blemish, to confound the tennors of the stiles for that cause. **1697** DRYDEN *Æneid* XII. 305 Nor shake the steadfast tenour of my Mind. **1756** BURKE *Subl. & B.* II. viii, The senses, strongly affected in some one manner, cannot quickly change their tenour. **1831** CARLYLE *Misc.* (1857) II. 190 Spiritual, of calm tenour.

II. 4. *Mus.* **a.** The adult male voice intermediate between the bass and the counter-tenor or alto, usually ranging from the octave below middle C to the A above it; also, the part sung by such a voice, being the next above the bass in vocal part-music.

So called app. because the melody or *canto fermo* was formerly alloted to this part.

1388 [see COUNTER-TENOR 1 b]. *c* **1430** LYDG. *Minor Poems* (Percy Soc.) 54 Treble meene and tenor discordyng as I gesse. *c* **1460** *Wisdom* 620 in *Macro Plays* 55 *Mynde.* A tenowur to yow bothe I brynge;..*Wyll.* And, but a trebull I owt wrynge, The deuell hym spede, þat myrthe exyled! **1530** PALSGR. 280/1 Tenour a parte in pricke songe, *teneur.* **1597** MORLEY *Introd. Mus.* II. 100 You haue your plainsong changed from parte to part, firste in the treble, next in the tenor, lastlie in the base. **1638-56** COWLEY *Davideis* I. Wks. (1669) 13 Water and Air he for the Tenor chose, Earth made the Base, the Treble Flame arose. *a* **1791** WESLEY *Wks.* (1872) VIII. 319 When they [singers] would teach a tune to the congregation, they must sing only the tenor. **1873** HALE *In His Name* vi. 49 The voice was a perfectly clear and pure tenor.

b. A singer with a tenor voice; one who sings the tenor part; a tenor singer.

?*c* **1475** *Sqr. lowe Degre* 782 Than shall ye go to your euensong, With tenours and trebles a mong. **1552** HULOET, Tenor, or he that singeth a tenor, *succentor.* **1616** *Cheque Bk. Chapel Royal* (Camden) 9 The next place that shall..fall voyd by the deathe of any tenor. **1821** BYRON *Juan* IV. lxxxvii, The tenor's voice is spoilt by affectation. **1884** F. M. CRAWFORD *Rom. Singer* i, He asked me if I would not let him educate that young tenor.

c. = *tenor bell*: see B. 1. *second tenor* (quot. 1541), the next bell to the tenor. Also (quot. 1562) applied to a string of tenor pitch in an instrument, as a harp.

1541 *Ludlow Churchw. Acc.* (Camden) 7 Payde..for mendynge the whele of ye secounde tenor..ij d. **1562** J. HEYWOOD *Prov. & Epigr.* (1867) 186 Which string.. wouldst thou..harpe on. Not the base..Nor the standyng tennor... Nor the counter tennor. *a* **1627** MIDDLETON *Mayor Queenb.* v. i, Let the Bells ring... 'Las the Tenor's broken, ring out the Treble. **1909** *Daily Chron.* 1 Oct. 7/2 The present 'tenor', as the deepest bell of a peal is always called, was cast here in 1738.

d. A name for the tenor violin or VIOLA.

1785 *Daily Universal Register* 1 Jan. 3/2 (Advt.), Mr. Giardini's capital old Violins, Tenors, and Violoncellos for sale. **1833** [see ALTO *sb.*[2] 5]. **1836** DUBOURG *Violin* i. (1878) 11 The tenor, or *viol da braccia*, was larger than the modern tenor, or *viola.* **1883** H. R. HAWEIS in *Gentl. Mag.* July 48 He learns the violon-cello or tenor. **1884** *Girl's Own Paper* Nov. 21/2 The viola is sometimes called the tenor, but the former is the preferable name.

e. *ellipt.* for *tenor saxophone*, sense B. 1 below.

1876 [see ALTO *sb.*[2] 6]. **1927** *Melody Maker* Aug. 738 (Advt.), The manufacturers..have been hailed as the saviours of Tenor Saxophonists through their innovation of the astounding B♭ tenor with the extra automatic octave note. **1952** [see BARITONE]. **1975** [see SAXIST].

B. *attrib.* or *adj.*, and *Comb.* (in sense 4 above).

1. *attrib.* or *adj.* Applied to a voice, part, instrument, string, etc. of the pitch described in sense 4 above, or intermediate between bass and alto. *tenor banjo*: see BANJO 1; *tenor bell*, the largest bell of a peal or set; *tenor C*, the note an octave below middle C, being the lowest note of a tenor voice; *tenor clarinet*, an alto clarinet pitched in F; also, one who plays this instrument; *tenor clef*, the C clef when placed upon the fourth line of the stave; *tenor cor*: see COR[3]; *tenor drum*: see DRUM *sb.*[1] 1 b; *tenor horn* = ALTHORN; *tenor sax*, *saxophone*, a member of the saxophone family intermediate between the alto and the baritone, usu. pitched in B flat; also, one who plays this instrument; hence *tenor saxist*, *sax-man*, *saxophonist*; *tenor violin* (†*viol*), the viola.

1522 *MS. Acc. St. John's Hosp., Canterb.*, For a bawdryk to the tenoure bell. **1597** MORLEY *Introd. Mus.* I. 21 In the Tenor part of the Gloria of his Masse *Aue Maris stella.* **1609** B. JONSON *Masque Queenes* Wks. (1616) 964 That most excellent tenor voyce. **1662** PLAYFORD *Skill Mus.* (1674) 99 The Tenor-Viol is an excellent inward Part. *a* **1670** HACKET *Abp. Williams* II. §33 (1693) 30 The Bishop himself bearing the Tenour part among them often. **1802** Tenor violin [see ALTO- 1]. **1806** CALLCOTT *Mus. Gram.* ii. 10 The Tenor Clef is used for the middle voices of men. **1838-9** FR. A. KEMBLE *Resid. Georgia* (1863) 127 Their voices seem oftener tenor than any other quality. **1859**, etc. Tenor horn [see ALTHORN]. **1865** C. MANDEL *Mandel's Syst. Mus.* xvi. 68 There are various kinds of Saxophones. The smallest, or Soprano Saxophone, is in B flat... The..Tenor Saxophone is an octave lower than the Soprano Saxophone. **1879** GROVE *Dict. Mus.* I. 362/2 In F we have the tenor clarinet. **1926** WHITEMAN & MCBRIDE *Jazz* ix. 193 We have computed..that one tenor saxophone equals eight violas. **1927** Tenor saxophonist [see sense 4 e]. **1934** S. R. NELSON *All about Jazz* vi. 127 A brilliant tenor sax was unmistakable. **1938** D. BAKER *Young Man with Horn* I. iv. 28 There were five men in Jeff's band—a tenor clarinet, a trombone, a trumpet, traps, and a piano. **1954** *Grove's Dict. Mus.* (ed. 5) II. 326/2 The higher-pitched of the two [alto clarinets] was long known as the 'tenor clarinet' in England. *Ibid.* VIII. 809/1 The true Tenor Violin was the alto of the *viola da braccio* family... The gradual suppression of this instrument in the 18th century was a disaster: neither the lower register of the viola nor the upper register of the violoncello can give its effect. **1954**, etc. Tenor saxophone [see SAXOPHONE sb. 1]. **1955** KEEPNEWS & GRAUER *Pict. Hist. Jazz* x. 110 Key members included tenor sax Andy Brown. **1955** Tenor saxist [see BASSIST 2]. **1955** Tenor sax-man [see *sax-man* s.v. SAX *sb.*[2] 3]. **1958** T. HALL in P. Gammond *Decca Bk. Jazz* xix. 229 He was mainly featured on an E-flat tenor-horn, which produced a mellophone-like sound. **1963** *Listener* 7 Feb. 264/1 Two virtuoso tenor sax players. **1972** *Guardian* 4 Feb. 10/5 No one strove harder than the tenor saxist John Coltrane. **1979** *Country Life* 12 July 95/2 A.. solo by tenor saxophonist Steve Marcus. **1979** *Listener* 4 Oct. 461/3 Charlie Parker..plays tenor-sax on the Miles Davis set.

2. *Comb.*, as (sense 4 d) *tenor-maker*, (4 e) *-man*, *player*, *solo*, *soloist*, *style*, (4 c) *-wheel*.

1648-9 in Swayne *Sarum Churchw. Acc.* (1896) 219 Mending yͤ Tenor Wheele—1 s. **1836** DUBOURG *Violin* ix. (1878) 266 Martin Hoffman and Hunger, both of Leipsic, were excellent tenor-makers. **1928** *Melody Maker* Feb. 201/2 Quite a few successful tenor players. **1935** *Vanity Fair* (N.Y.) Nov. 38/2 Tenor-men like Hawkins or Fletcher Henderson, are stars in the hot sky. **1943** P. E. MILLER *Yearbk. Popular Music* 8/2 He borrowed a tenor from a fellow musician, sat in on a jam session, and from that point forward became a hot tenorman. **1958** R. HORRICKS in P. Gammond *Decca Bk. Jazz* ix. 118 The prominent tenor soloists outshone even those of the New York scene. **1959** 'F. NEWTON' *Jazz Scene* ii. 35 A fine tenor player in the Parker tradition. **1962** *Melody Maker* 21 July 7/3 The perfect tenor style for Dixieland jazz. **1966** *Crescendo* Dec. 9/2 Good clarinet, trumpet and tenor solos. **1977** J. WAINWRIGHT *Do Nothin'* viii. 125 Tenor men are not *that* hard to find.

Hence **tenor** *v.*[1] *intr.* (with *it*), to sing tenor; **'tenoring** *ppl. a.*; also **'tenorless** *a.*, having no tenor or purport.

1893 *Scribner's Mag.* XIV. 61 A tame cornet tenored it throatily Of beer-pots and spittoons. **1810** BENTHAM *Packing* (1821) 265 The purely conjectural, tenorless, uncognoscible, and impostrous state of unwritten, alias common law. **1905** H. G. WELLS *Mod. Utopia* iv. 127 It is not only such gross and palpable cases as our blond and tenoring friend. **1930** —— *Autocr. Mr. Parham* II. iii. 119 'But,' said Mr. Mountain in tenoring remonstrance to Sir Bussy, 'doesn't this evening satisfy you, sir?' **1934** —— *Exper. Autobiogr.* II. viii. 602 Bland was a thick-set, broad-faced aggressive man..with a tenoring voice.

tenor, *sb.*[2] Now *dial.* Also 5 tenowre, 8-9 tenner. Corrupted form of TENON *sb.*[1] **tenor-saw** = *tenon-saw.* Hence **tenor** *v.*[2] = TENON *v.*

a **1485** *Promp. Parv.* MS. S. (1908) 476 Tenowre, knytting of a balk or odyre lyk tymbre, *cenaculum.* **1747** HOOSON *Miner's Dict.* Q iij, Instead of a Collar made on the Forks, we make Tenners, so that the Forks are Tennered at both ends, and the Sliders are Slotted at both Ends to receive the Forks. **1851** W. ANDERSON *Rhymes* (1867) 116 (E.D.D.) You're just as rough's a tenor saw. **1877** *N.W. Linc. Gloss.*, *Tenner*, a tenon.

tenor, obs. form of TENURE.

† **tenoral**, *a. Obs. rare.* [f. TENOR *sb.*[1] + -AL[1].] Of or pertaining to the tenor or ordinary course.
1606 BIRNIE *Kirk-Buriall* xvi. (1833) Ej, Buriall exemple, in all the which there is a tenorall processe so equally and vnchangeably..obserued.

‖ **tenore** (te'nore). [It.; cf. TENOR *sb.*[1] (*a.*).] = TENOR *sb.*[1] 4 a and b. Usu. with qualifying adj. or phrase, as ***tenore di grazia***, a light or lyric tenor; ***tenore robusto*** (see quot. 1876), a dramatic tenor.
1740 GRASSINEAU *Mus. Dict.* 272 *Tenore*, the first mean or middle part: or that which is the ordinary pitch of the voice, when neither raised to a treble, or lowered to a bass. **1876** STAINER & BARRETT *Dict. Mus. Terms* 432/1 *Tenore robusto*, a tenor singer with a full, strong, sonorous voice. **1889** GROVE *Dict. Mus.* IV. 87/1 Hence we have *tenore robusto* (which used to be of about the compass of a modern high baritone), *tenore di forza, tenore di mezzo carattere, tenore di grazia*, and *tenore leggiero*, one type of which is sometimes called *tenore contraltino*. **1894** G. DU MAURIER *Trilby* I. i. 25 A voice so rich and deep and full as almost to suggest an incipient *tenore robusto*. **1925** *New Yorker* 19 Sept. 20/2 He is the first *tenore robusto* to emerge since Caruso. **1938** J. JOYCE *Let.* 8 Sept. (1966) III. 427 It needs a deep strong voice, not my *tenore di grazia*. **1960** *Times* 4 Mar. 4/1 Mr. Kenneth Macdonald, who has an enviable affinity for *tenore di grazie* singing. **1979** *Times* 19 Nov. 7/5 The..refinements of phrasing and nuance which are hall-marks of a *tenore di grazia*.

tenorino (teno'rino). Pl. -ini. [a. It., dim. of *tenore* tenor.] A high tenor; *spec.* a castrato alto.
1867 *Cornh. Mag.* Jan. 32 At present the signor is the pearl of tenorini, and no other artist can match his delivery of the embroidered melodies of the *Cenerentola*, or the *Italiana in Algieri*. **1898** *Harper's Mag.* XCVI. 512, I was..to be the tenor, or rather the *tenorino*. **1980** *New Grove Dict. Mus.* XVIII. 690/2 Another type of light tenor voice was known in the 19th century as the 'tenorino'; such singers were often amateurs who made a speciality of performing love-songs to salon audiences.

tenorist ('tɛnərɪst). [= F. *tenoriste* (15–16th c. in Godef.), It. *tenorista*, f. *tenore*, TENOR *sb.*[1] 4: see -IST.] **a.** *gen.* (See quot., e.g., 1898.) **b.** *spec.* One who plays the tenor saxophone.
[**1724** *Short Explic. For. Wds. in Mus. Bks.*, *Tenorista*, one that has a Voice proper for a Tenor.] **1865** tr. *Spohr's Autobiog.* II. 155 We were so successful as to engage..the tenorist Cornet of Hamburg. **1898** STAINER & BARRETT *Dict. Mus. Terms*, *Tenorist*, one who sings the tenor part, or plays the tenor violin. **1958** K. GOODWIN in P. Gammond *Decca Bk. Jazz* xiii. 154 Vinegar was also featured..when the tenorist opened a short season at Zardi's. **1962** *Melody Maker* 7 July 9 It is quite remarkable..that so popular a tenorist..has not had a broadcast or TV appearance for more than three years. **1972** *Blues & Jazz* Sept. 11/2 The backing on 'The Fat Man' was provided by the Bartholomew band, including tenorists Herb Hardesty and Red Tyler. **1977** *Listener* 1 Dec. 729/4 Roy Plomley has marooned tenorist Ronnie Scott..on his desert island.

tenorite ('tɛnəraɪt). *Min.* [Named, 1841, after Prof. G. Tenore, President of Naples Academy: see -ITE[1].] Black oxide of copper, found in thin iron-black scales on lava at Vesuvius: see quot.
1865 MASKELYNE in *Athenæum* No. 1980. 472/3 Crystallised Melaconite and Tenorite. **1868** DANA *Min.* 804 As the names tenorite and melaconite were given the same year, and tenorite was made non-isometric (hexagonal) by its describer, it appears to be right that tenorite should be sustained for the above mineral, and melaconite be left for the isometric kind, if any such proves to be a native species.

tenoroon (tɛnə'ruːn). [f. TENOR + *-oon* in *bassoon*, or short for *tenor bassoon*.] **a.** A wooden reed-instrument intermediate in pitch between the oboe and the bassoon; also called *tenor oboe* or *tenor bassoon*. Also *attrib.*, as ***tenoroon oboe***. Until recently *Hist.*, but now revived in performances of baroque music. **b.** A reed-stop in an organ, resembling the oboe stop, but not extending below tenor C. Also applied to any stop not extending below tenor C; also *attrib.*, as ***tenoroon diapason***.
1849 *Chambers' Inform. People* II. 766/2 The tenoroon, a wood instrument played with a reed, is seldom employed. **1879** STAINER *Music of Bible* 79 The tenor oboe or tenoroon. **1881** C. A. EDWARDS *Organs* xxii. 155 When it ceases at tenor C this stop [double open diapason] is named the Tenoroon. **1884** W. H. STONE in Grove *Dict. Mus.* IV. 88 *Tenoroon*, a name..given to the Tenor Bassoon or Alto Fagotto in F... It has entirely gone out of use. **1898** STAINER & BARRETT *Dict. Mus. Terms*, *Tenoroon*..(2) A word affixed to an organ stop to denote that it does not proceed below tenor C, as *tenoroon hautboy*. A *tenoroon diapason* is a double diapason which does not extend below tenor C. **1980** *Early Music Gaz.* Jan. 9/2 William Waterhouse..performed music by Selma, Böddecker..on racket, two original 18th-century bassoons (Handel period 4-key and Mozart period 7-key, tenoroon and modern Heckel).

tenorrhaphy, etc.: see TENO-.

† '**tenory.** *Obs. rare*[−1]. [Alteration of TENOR *sb.*[1] or It. *tenor*: cf. 13th c. F. *tenoire*, as if:—L. **tenoria*.] = TENOR *sb.* 4.
c **1460** *Towneley Myst.* xiii. 186 *Primus pastor.* Lett me syng the tenory. *Ijus pastor.* And I the tryble so hye.

tenotomy (tə'nɒtəmɪ). *Surg.* [ad. F. *tenotomie*: see TENO- and -TOMY.] Cutting or division of a tendon; also *attrib.*, as ***tenotomy knife***. So '**tenotome** ('tɛnətəʊm), a surgeon's slender knife for (subcutaneous) division of tendons; **te'notomist**, a surgeon who performs tenotomy; **te'notomize** *v. trans.*, to perform tenotomy upon.
1842 *Lancet* 31 Dec. 509/1 Discussions in the Académie Royale de la Médicine on the subject of Tenotomy, or the section of the muscular tendons for the relief of club-foot and other..deformities. *Ibid.*, There are two classes of tenotomists, the scientific and able.., and the empirical, or ignorant operators. **1846** BRITTAN tr. *Malgaigne's Man. Oper. Surg.* 7 Subcutaneous Incisions..may be made with the common straight bistoury, with the tenotome or tendon-knife, or any other special instrument. **1872** T. G. THOMAS *Dis. Women* (ed. 3) 123 Performed subcutaneously by an ordinary tenotomy knife. **1891** *Cent. Dict.*, Tenotomize. **1901** A. H. TUBBY in *Lancet* 12 Jan. 91/2 The tendons on the radial side were tenotomised.

tenoun, -own, tenour(e, -owr(e, obs. ff. TENON[1], TENOR, TENURE.

tenpence ('tɛnpəns). [TEN *a.* + PENCE.] A sum of money equal to ten pennies; sometimes used contemptuously, as ***only tenpence in the shilling***, etc. because the amount is incomplete: cf. next.; since 1971 in the *U.K.*, a coin worth ten (new) pence superseding the earlier two-shilling piece or florin; often as two words with pronunc. (tɛn pɛns). Also *attrib.* as ***tenpence coin, piece***, a decimal coin worth ten pence. † So *transf.*, a foreign coin of roughly equivalent value, a franc, a lira.
c **1592** MARLOWE *Jew of Malta* IV. iv, Gentleman! he flouts me: What gentry can be in a poor Turk of tenpence? **1749** FIELDING *Tom Jones* XIV. iii, As sure as ten-pence, this is the very young gentleman. **1860** HOTTEN *Dict. Slang* (ed. 2) 235 *Tenpence to the shilling*, a vulgar phrase denoting a deficiency in intellect. **18..** RUSKIN in *B'ham Inst. Mag.* Dec. (1896) 71, I never pass a begging friar without giving him sixpence, or the equivalent fivepence of foreign coin, extending the charity even occasionally as far as tenpence, if no fivepenny bit chance to be in my purse. **1903** FARMER & HENLEY *Slang* s.v., *Only tenpence in the shilling*, a description of weak intellect. **1922** J. BUCHAN *Huntingtower* vii. 142 There's a certain old lady, an aunt of Mr. Quentin and his sisters, who has always been about tenpence in the shilling. **1936** W. HOLTBY *South Riding* 9 'Mental?' 'Tenpence halfpenny in the shilling.' **1971** P. PURSER *Holy Father's Navy* xxiv. 114, I gave her a ten pence piece and hurried away. **1974** A. FOWLES *Pastime* xii. 98 Awkward, that had been, in a phone box. He'd used up two ten pences. **1976** G. SEYMOUR *Glory Boys* xi. 144 He put down two tenpence coins.

Hence '**tenpenceworth**, the amount of anything to be bought for tenpence; used contemptuously.
1896 G. B. SHAW *Let.* 16 Nov. in *Ellen Terry & Bernard Shaw* (1931) 124, I have been to Paris, and seen Peer Gynt done in the sentimentallest French style with tenpenceworth of scenery.

tenpenny ('tɛnpənɪ), *a.* (*sb.*)

A. *adj.* **1. a.** Valued at, costing, or amounting to ten pence; sold at tenpence the piece, dozen, hundred, pound, quart, gallon, yard, or other customary unit (see also b); also in contempt: cf. *twopenny*. ***tenpenny piece*** = B. 1.; also in the U.K., a decimal coin worth ten (new) pence. ***tenpenny-worth***, the amount of anything to be bought for tenpence.
1592 *Arden of Feversham* V. i, All the tenpenny ale-houses would stand euery morning with a quart pot in their hand, saying, 'will it please your worship drinke?' **1607** DEKKER & WEBSTER *Westw. Hoe* IV. ii. Wks. 1873 II. 339 If all the great Turks Concubins were but like thee, the ten-penny-infidell should neuer neede [etc.]. *c* **1645** HOWELL *Lett.* (1650) I. v. vii. 141 Lieutenant Felton..made a thrust with a common tenpeny knife..at the Duke. *a* **1668** DAVENANT *News fr. Plymouth* Wks. (1673) 2 A cloth Of Network edg'd with a Ten-penny-Lace. **1724** SWIFT *Drapier's Lett.* i. ¶ 36 A yard of ten-penny stuff. **1821** SCOTT *Kenilw.* ii, A tenpenny-worth of cord. **1842** S. LOVER *Handy Andy* xxi, She had given him a tenpenny-piece. **1875–7** RUSKIN *Morn. in Florence* Pref., I have done more work than you will ever know of, to make them good ten-pennyworths to you. **1968** *Guardian* 24 Apr. 3/3, I handed the woman a new tenpenny piece worth 2s. **1971** I. MURDOCH *Accidental Man* 305 The room was unheated except for a weak one-bar electric fire which had to be continually fed with tenpenny pieces. **1973** J. PORTER *It's Murder with Dover* xiii. 130 MacGregor watched his tenpenny pieces disappearing down the greedy slot of the one-armed bandit.

b. ***tenpenny nail***: originally, a nail sold at tenpence a hundred: see PENNY 10. Now, vaguely, a nail of large size; in U.S. *spec.* a three-inch nail.
1426–8 [see PENNY 10]. **1486** *Naval Acc. Hen. VII* (1896) 16 Xpeny nailes. *c* **1555** HARPSFIELD *Divorce Hen. VIII* (Camden) 172 To make the whole matter fast and sure, as it were with a tenpenny nail. **1666** W. BOGHURST *Loimographia* (1894) 66 Stomacks like Ostriches able to digest a tenpenny nail. **1826** SCOTT *Woodst.* xii, Were his nails tenpenny nails, and his teeth as long as those of a harrow. **1890** WEBSTER, *Penny*.., denoting pound weight for one thousand;—used in combination, with respect to nails; as, tenpenny nails, nails of which one thousand weigh ten pounds. **1906** *Dialect Notes* III. 146 *Mad enough to bite a tenpenny nail in two, adj. phr.*, very angry. **1909** WEBSTER, *Penny* is used in combination with prefixed numerals..to form adjectives denoting price or value. As applied to nails these adjectives now denote certain arbitrary sizes, though originally, in the 15th century, they designated the price per hundred; as, a *tenpenny* nail, one then costing tenpence per hundred. **1967** *Countryman* Autumn 29 My American companion said: 'I guess we should get some tenpenny nails.' Then he looked at me: 'I suppose you don't know what they are.' I did not. Next day, when we asked for them by that name at the hardware store, we got what we wanted—three-inch nails.

B. *sb.* **1.** A piece of money: = TENPENCE. **a.** The token of the Bank of Ireland for 10*d.*, issued in 1805, 1806, and 1813. **b.** A franc or lira.
1822 D. O'CONNELL *Let.* 13 Apr. (1972) II. 379, I will hug every tenpenny as a link in the chain that is to draw back my Mary to me. **1824** A. THOMSON in *Life & Min.* iv. (1869) 217 A gentleman..sent me seven ten-pennies—5*s.* 10*d.* Irish. **1825** *Hist. Little Pat* in *Houlston Tracts* I. No. 11. 12 Having received a present of a tenpenny from a gentleman. **1904** *Eng. Dial. Dict.* s.v. *Ten*, (Guernsey) When I get a bad tenpenny I put it in my purse and pass it.

2. a. A tenpenny nail. **b.** A child's school-book (originally) costing tenpence: formerly the third book used in teaching to read. *Sc.*
1820 J. H. REYNOLDS *Fancy* (1906) 22 We've driven a hundred tenpennies already. **1893** CROCKETT *Stickit Minister* iii. 35 They stammered like a boy new into the tenpenny.

ten-pins ('tɛnpɪnz), *sb. pl.* **a.** A game in which ten pins (see PIN *sb.*[1] 8) or 'men' are set up to be bowled at; cf. NINEPINS; *spec.* (orig. *U.S.*) a game so played, also called in England 'American bowls'. Also, the pins with which this game is played; in *sing.* ***tenpin***, one of these.
[**1600** ROWLANDS *Lett. Humours Blood* iv. 64 To play at loggets, nine holes, or ten pinnes.] **1807** CRABBE *Par. Reg.* III. 106 When justice winked on every jovial crew, And tenpins tumbled in the parson's view. **1842** DICKENS *Amer. Notes* vi, Tin-Pins being a game of mingled chance and skill, invented when the legislature passed an act forbidding Nine-Pins. **1884** H. C. BUNNER in *Harper's Mag.* Jan. 298/2 Base-ball and ten-pins are in no great favor. **1893** *Nation* (N.Y.) 20 July 54/2 Even a ten-pin must be set up before it is knocked down.

b. *attrib.* and *Comb.*, as ***ten-pin alley, ball, bowling***.
1835 P. H. NICKLIN *Lett. Descr. Va. Springs* 23 The means of amusement at the Warm Springs, consist of a bagatelle table..a tin-pin alley [etc.]. **1842** [see *bowling saloon* s.v. BOWLING *vbl. sb.* 3]. **1852** C. A. BRISTED *Upper Ten Thousand* v. 117 Perhaps we shall find him at the ten-pin alley. **1868** M. H. SMITH *Sunshine & Shadow N. York* 218 The click of the billiard ball, and the booming of the ten-pin alley, are distinctly heard. **1870** O. LOGAN *Before Footlights* 120 Finely cut bits of paper, for fatal snowstorms; ten-pin balls, for the distant muttering of the storm. **1895** *Outing* (U.S.) XXVI. 444/1 You rush to the bottom like a ten-pin ball sent spinning down its alley. **1934** *A.B.C. Bulletin* 25 Oct. 11/1 (*heading*) Tenpin Bowling—'The Sport of Kings'. **1960** *Observer* 17 Jan. 3/3 Ten-pin bowling, as its sponsors call it, went to America with the planters and the pilgrims. .. The game that is being re-imported is hedged about with expensive equipment and social ballyhoo, but is simple enough in itself. **1975** *Oxf. Compan. Sports & Games* 90/1 Tenpin bowling has reached a stage where it can claim to be the largest participant sport in the world.

ten-pounder (ˌtɛn'paʊndə(r)). [Parasynthetically f. *ten pound(s* + -ER[1].]

1. a. A thing (e.g. a ball, a fish) weighing ten pounds; *spec.* a fish, *Elops saurus*, about three feet long, inhabiting the warmer parts of the Pacific and Atlantic Oceans; also called Big-eyed Herring. **b.** A cannon throwing a ten-pound shot.
1695 *Lond. Gaz.* No. 3112/3, 69 Pieces of Cannon,..viz. .. 9 ten Pounders. **1699** DAMPIER *Voy.* II. II. 71 Tenpounders are shaped like Mullets, but are so full of very small stiff Bones..that you can hardly eat them. **1888** GOODE *Amer. Fishes* 407 The 'Big-eyed Herring' or 'Ten-pounder', *Elops saurus*.

2. Something of the value of, or rated at, ten pounds. **a.** A ten-pound note. **b.** A voter in a borough who was enfranchised in virtue of occupying property of the annual value of ten pounds.
a. 1755 JOHNSON s.v. *Pounder*, A note or bill is called a twenty pounder or ten pounder. **1829** MARRYAT *F. Mildmay* iv, I pocketed the little donation—it was a ten-pounder. **1844** *Ainsworth's Mag.* VI. 354, I feared I should very soon be obliged to change..my ten-pounder. **1888** C. M. YONGE *Our New Mistress* xii. 109 He took it from me as if I were paying him his wages, and..said..a crisp ten-pounder was a handier thing to drag about than a puling woman.
b. 1833 R. SOUTHEY *Let.* 13 Jan. in J. Aitken *Eng. Lett. of XIX Century* (1946) 147 The ten-pounders have sent just such members as might have been expected to *Parldemonium* from the great manufacturing towns. **1834** *Oxford Univ. Mag.* I. 46 No candidate would venture to present himself before a body of ten-pounders. **1880** DISRAELI *Endym.* xvii, There were several old boroughs where the freemen still outnumbered the ten-pounders.

Hence **ten-'poundery** *nonce-wd.*, the body of ten-pound householders.
1840 *Fraser's Mag.* XXI. 237 He was hanged to oblige the tenpoundery of the day.

tenrec: see TANREC.

tense (tɛns), *sb.* Also 4–6 **tens, temps**, 6 **tence**. [a. OF. *tens*, 11–13th c. (also *tans*, 11–16th c.); mod.F. *temps* from 13th c. = Pr. *temps*, Sp. *tiempo*, Pg., It. *tempo*:—L. *tempus* time.]

1. Time. *Obs.* or *arch.* (exc. in allusion to 2).

c **1315** SHOREHAM *Poems* i. 1061 And foluelle þat remenaunt Ine purgatoryes tense Eft-sone. *c* **1380** WYCLIF *Serm.* Sel. Wks. I. 377 Þe Gospel of Maudelen Dai is red on Fridai in Quarter Tense in Septembre among Ferials. [*Editor's note.* 'Quatuor Tempora', or, as it is called in Ireland, Quarter Tense; for the gospel read on St. Mary Magdalen's day (July 22) is the same as that for Ember Friday in September.] *c* **1386** CHAUCER *Can. Yeom. Prol. & T.* 322 It is to seken..That future temps hath maad men disseuere, In trust ther-of, from al þat euere they hadde. **1509** HAWES *Past. Pleas.* xliv. (Percy Soc.) 214 For onely of hym it is especiall,..in finall, The future tence to knowe directly. [**1843** CARLYLE *Past & Pr.* II. v, There are three Tenses, *Tempora*, or Times; and there is one Eternity.] **1922** JOYCE *Ulysses* 604 To fast and abstain on the days commanded, it being quarter tense or, if not, ember days or something like that.

2. a. *Gram.* Any one of the different forms or modifications (or word-groups) in the conjugation of a verb which indicate the different times (*past*, *present*, or *future*) at which the action or state denoted by it is viewed as happening or existing, and also (by extension) the different nature of such action or state, as continuing (*imperfect*) or completed (*perfect*); also *abstr.* that quality of a verb which depends on the expression of such differences.

1388 WYCLIF *Prol.* xv. 57 A participl of a present tens.. may be resoluid into a verbe of the same tens, and a coniunccion copulatif. **1530** PALSGR. Introd. 31 These thre accidentes, mode, tens and declination parsonall. **1571** GOLDING *Calvin on Ps.* vii. 2 The tenses or tymes of verbes are oftentymes chaunged among the Hebrewes. **1580**—— in Baret *Alv.* To Rdr. viii, The Coniugation, Number, Person, Tence, And Moode of Verbes. **1580** FULKE *Martiall Confut.* iv. 169 Findeth fault with him for giuing the aoristes the signification of the present temps. **1599** MASSINGER, etc. *Old Law* IV. i, Thou præterpluperfect tense of a woman. **1643** SIR T. BROWNE *Relig. Med.* I. §11 In Eternity there is no distinction of Tenses. **1751** HARRIS *Hermes* I. vii. Wks. (1841) 152 The tenses are used to mark present, past, and future time. **1871** ROBY *Lat. Gram.* II. xvi. §549 [In Latin there are] Six tenses... Three, denoting incomplete action. .. Three, denoting completed action. **1876** MASON *Eng. Gram.* (ed. 21) §212 The tenses of the English verb are made partly by inflection, partly by the use of auxiliary verbs.

b. *fig.* or *allusively*, in conjunction with *mood*: see MOOD *sb.*[2] 2 b.

3. *attrib.* and *Comb.*, as (in sense 2) ***tense-aspect***, ***-form***, ***-making***, ***marker***, ***stem***, ***system***; ***tense-expressing***, ***marking***, ***-modal*** adjs.

1892 H. SWEET *New Eng. Gram.* I. 101 By tense-aspect we understand distinctions of time independent of any reference to past, present, or future. **1980** *English World-Wide* I. I. 113 It seems as though the tense-aspect system of English has been restructured. **1886** *Amer. Jrnl. Philol.* Dec. 448 That the present subjunctives of *posse* and *videri*..can ..become tense-expressing. **1871** ROBY *Lat. Gram.* II. xvi. §550 All verbs in the passive have in the Indicative only three simple tense-forms. **1875** WHITNEY *Life Lang.* vii. 123 A case or two of verbal tense-making. **1971** E. JONES in J. Spencer *Eng. Lang. W. Afr.* 83 Krio is equipped with a range of tense markers, as may be seen from the following set. **1978** *Language* LIV. 84 The advocates of abstract remote structures posit auxiliaries including negative and tense markers as main verbs. **1962** C. L. BARBER in F. Behre *Contrib. Eng. Syntax* 27 Any combination of four tense-markings. **1921** E. SAPIR *Language* v. 96 Had the statement been made on another's authority, a totally different 'tense-modal' suffix would have had to be used. **1965** *Language* XLI. 173, 1200 adverbial suffixes, partly tense-modal. **1935** T. HUDSON-WILLIAMS *Short Introd. Study Compar. Gram.* xiii. 72 The endings were added to each tense-stem. **1971** *Archivum Linguisticum* II. 100 The subjunctive is originally independent from the so-called tense stems, as is evident in Celtic and Tocharian and also in Latin. **1951** W. K. MATTHEWS *Lang. U.S.S.R.* iv. 75 The tense system is complicated by being carried into the non-finite grammatical categories, including the gerund. **1963** J. LYONS *Structural Semantics* vi. 112 The 'tense-system' may be set out in terms of the two dimensions of time and aspect.

tense (tɛns), *a.* [ad. L. *tens-us*, pa. pple. of *tendĕre* to stretch.]

1. a. Drawn tight, stretched taut; strained to stiffness; tight, rigid: chiefly said of cords, fibres, or membranes. Opposed to *lax*, *flaccid*. Also *transf.* of a sensation, the breathing, the pulse.

1670 *Phil. Trans.* V. 2059 Whether the Mercury..be sustain'd by the external Air, or by a Tense matter within. **1676** WISEMAN *Surg.* (R.), The skin was tense, also rimpled and blistered. **1728** RUTTY in *Phil. Trans.* XXXV. 563 She complain'd..now and then of a tense Pain and a Difficulty in Respiration. **1756** C. LUCAS *Ess. Waters* I. 75 Fiddle-strings are..much more tense in wet weather than in dry. **1802** *Med. Jrnl.* VIII. 518 A small spasmodic and very tense pulse of 120, which as the pain increased, resembled the vibration of a musical string. **1834** J. FORBES *Laennec's Dis. Chest* (ed. 4) 529 The artery remains full and tense, and resists strongly the compressing finger. **1879** TOURGEE *Fool's Err.* xxxvi. 254 With every muscle as tense as those of the tiger waiting for his leap.

b. *Entom.* Applied to the abdomen when not divided or transversely folded, as in spiders.

1826 KIRBY & SP. *Entomol.* IV. 350 [Abdomen] *Tense*.. when it is not folded. Ex. Most *Araneidæ*.

c. *spec.* in *Phonetics*, applied to (the articulation of) a speech-sound pronounced with enhanced tension in the muscles of the speech organs. Cf. LAX *a.* 5 c, SLACK *a.* 7 e.

1909, etc. [see LAX *a.* 5 c]. **1909** [see SLACK *a.* 7 e]. **1918** D. JONES *Outl. Eng. Phonetics* 21 When pronouncing the.. tense vowel..the throat feels considerably tenser and is somewhat pushed forward. **1933** L. BLOOMFIELD *Language* vii. 109 In German the tense vowels are longer than the loose; this difference of length is more striking than that of tenseness. **1968** W. S. ALLEN *Vox Graeca* v. 103 The usually tenser articulation of voiceless plosives might also tend to emphasize the crescendo. **1978** *Canad. Jrnl. Linguistics* 1977 XXII. 211 *Rêve* and *âge* have inherited, underlying tense vowels.

2. *fig.* In a state of nervous or mental strain or tension; strained; highly strung; 'on the stretch'; excited, or excitable; keenly sensitive.

1821 COLERIDGE in *Blackw. Mag.* X. 254 These distinctive faculties being in a tense and active state. **1845–6** DE QUINCEY *Notes Gilfillan's Lit. Portr.* Wks. 1859 XII. 281 This collapse of a tense excitement. **1860** HOLLAND *Miss Gilbert* ix, Her sensibilities, kept tense through the long winter,..refused to respond. **1876** GEO. ELIOT *Dan. Der.* III. xxi, Gwendolen..looked at her with tense expectancy, but was silent. **1902** R. HICHENS *Londoners* 161 The house-party were now tense with excitement.

3. *Comb.*, as ***tense-drawn***, ***tense-fibred***, etc.

1761 PULTENEY in *Phil. Trans.* LII. 353 Robust and tense fibred. **1891** KIPLING *Light that Failed* vii. 134 The Americans, whose rasping voices..strain tense-drawn nerves to breaking-point. **1908** *Westm. Gaz.* 15 May 2/1 The haggard, tense-eyed men, the expensively attired, withered, yet beautiful women.

tense, *v.* [f. TENSE *a.*; perh. at first in pa. pple. *tensed*, repr. L. *tensus* stretched, strained.]

a. *trans.* To make tense; to stretch tight; *spec.* of vowel sounds (cf. TENSE *a.* 1 c). Also *refl.* and with *up*.

1676 [implied at TENSED *ppl. a.*]. **1884** *Mind* Jan. 109 A maximal effort of tensing the extensor instead of the flexor muscles. **1929** P. GIBBS *Hidden City* I Rage causes an increase of adrenal secretion, tensing up the nerve cells. **1942** G. CASEY *It's Harder for Girls* 130 When his turn came he tensed himself to go through with it. **1951** C. S. FORESTER *Randall & River of Time* xviii. 263 The constable was tensing himself, ready to restrain him if he should do anything violent. **1978** *Canad. Jrnl. Linguistics* 1977 XXII. 211 Historically, /ɛ/ and /ɛ̃/, although lengthening preceding vowels, did not automatically tense them.

b. *intr.* To become tense. Also const. *up*.

1946 *Sunday Express* 31 Mar. 8/2 The court tensed as Ribbentrop gave inside glimpses of events which shaped the war. **1959** *Encounter* Feb. 31, I was tensing for the death-blow. **1973** *Houston* (Texas) *Chron. Texas Mag.* 14 Oct. 2/3 They..feared the kids would tense up if they knew a reporter was in their midst. **1975** I. MCEWAN *First Love, Last Rites* 42 There was such a sudden ferocity in her silence that I found myself tensing like a sprinter on the starting line.

Hence **'tensing** *vbl. sb.* (also with *up*).

1921 L. R. FREEMAN *In Tracks of Trades* 85 There was a sharp tensing of the powerful frame. **1977** *Washington Post* 23 Nov. B2/3 It is the isometric tensing of muscles opposite ones that have been over-developed. **1983** *N.Y. Times* 9 Oct. VI. 56/2 More like a tensing-up that begged for relief.

tensed, *ppl. a.* [f. TENSE *v.* + -ED[1].] Stretched tight, tense. Freq. const. *up* and in *predic.* use. Also *fig.* (cf. TENSE *a.* 2).

1676 H. MORE *Remarks* 141 In his supposed tensed and rarefied bodies. *Ibid.* 156 The contraction or restitution of the tensed matter. **1911** J. LONDON *Adventure* i. 11 The tensed body relaxed. **1934** E. O'NEILL *Days without End* I. 29 His eyes fixed before him.., his body tensed defensively. **1952** G. THOMAS *Now lead us Home* 191 All tensed up in wait for the hand that will draw some heavenly melody out of them. **1971** S. HILL *Strange Meeting* i. 41 There would be no more anxieties..about how he could bear to sit in the sour-smelling room with the Major, tensed with dread of the night to come. **1980** 'R. B. DOMINIC' *Attending Physician* xxii. 198 Ben sounds pretty tensed-up to me.

tensed (tɛnst), *a.* [f. TENSE *sb.* + -ED[2].] Having a grammatical tense or tenses.

1972 *Language* XLVIII. 314 The situation of [examples] 34 and 35 is particularly interesting: we do not, in general, find this type of stress in tensed (i.e. non-infinitival) relative clauses. **1978** *Ibid.* LIV. 289 It is also common to most of these proposals to assume that deverbatives are derived from clauses which contain tensed verb forms or their equivalents. **1982** BAKER & HACKER in *Language & Communication* II. III. 240 Animals have immediate purposes and intentions, but long term goals, projects and intentions are available only to creatures who have forms of expression for such things, viz. a tensed language.

tensegrity (tɛn'sɛgrɪtɪ). [f. *tens(ional int)egrity*.] A stable three-dimensional structure consisting of members under tension that are contiguous and members under compression that are not; the characteristic property of such a structure; also *fig.* Freq. *attrib.*

1959 *Art News* Oct. 29 Of all the ways out of the blind alley in which so much of modern architecture luxuriously relaxes, R. Buckminster Fuller's 'tensegrity' structures seem the most inventive and promising. **1963** R. B. FULLER *Ideas & Integrities* viii. 170 We have in the Geodesic Tensegrity (my name for the discontinuous-compression, continuous-tension structures) the ability to assemble unprecedentedly large, clear-span structures. **1972** *Last Whole Earth Catalog* (Portola Inst.) 4/3 The Universe is a tensegrity. **1976** A. PUGH *Introd. Tensegrity* ii. 11 One of the most impressive Tensegrity figures has six struts which do not touch one another and twenty-four tendons. **1976** H. KENNER *Geodesic Math* p. viii, No useful structures exploiting pure Tensegrity—tension wholly separated from compression—have been built. **1976** *Sci. Amer.* Dec. 144/1 The Kenner book..derives the very nature of a geodesic dome..as the limiting case of a more complex skin of simple tensegrities.

'tenseless, *a.* [f. TENSE *sb.* + -LESS.] Having no tenses or distinctions of tense (*loosely*, not having the ordinary function of a tense, i.e. not expressing time). Hence **'tenselessness**.

1886 Tenseless [see TEMPORAL *a.*[1] 5 b]. **1887** W. G. HALE in *Amer. Jrnl. Philol.* Apr. 59 A sweeping doctrine like that of the tenselessness of all dependent subjunctives. **1889** *Classical Rev.* Feb. 9 Maintaining that the tenses of the subjunctive are not tenseless.., but have each their proper temporal significance.

tenselle, obs. form of TINSEL, loss.

tensely ('tɛnslɪ), *adv.* [f. TENSE *a.* + -LY[2].] In a tense manner. **1.** Tightly.

1782 A. MONRO *Compar. Anat.* (ed. 3) 16 The cellular part of the peritoneum..is tensely stretched over them. **1839** LONGF. *Beatrice* xiv, Even as a cross-bow breaks, when 'tis discharged, Too tensely drawn the bow-string and the bow. **1846** HAWTHORNE *Mosses* I. v, And girdled tensely by her virgin zone. **1860** O. W. HOLMES *Elsie V.* xxiii, To keep the thong tensely stretched between his neck and the peak of the saddle.

2. *fig.* With intellectual, mental, or nervous strain or tension; intensely.

1778 [W. MARSHALL] *Minutes Agric.*, *Digest* 2 Mathematics (..perhaps this, in preference to every other science, teaches and habituates Mankind to think systematically and tensely). **1849** *Tait's Mag.* XVI. 220 We left,..deeply moved, and with nerves more tensely strung. **1893** *Nat. Observ.* 23 Dec. 127/2 There are dozens most tensely anxious for the restitution.

tensen, variant of TINSEN *Obs.*

tenseness ('tɛnsnɪs). [f. TENSE *a.* + -NESS.] The state or condition of being tense (*lit.* or *fig.*); *spec.* of vowel sounds (cf. TENSE *a.* 1 c).

1707 FLOYER *Physic. Pulse-Watch* 29 The Tenseness makes the Distention less. **1776** SAUNDERS in T. Percival *Ess.* (1776) III. App. 307 According to the uniformity there is between the tenseness of the fibres of the several bodies, and the tone of the different pipes. **1904** W. M. RAMSAY *Lett. to 7 Ch.* xix. 261 [Grace] strains the city like a lyre into tenseness harmonious with itself. **1918** D. JONES *Outl. Eng. Phonetics* 20 The 'tenseness' or 'laxness' of a vowel may be observed mechanically in the case of some vowels by placing the finger on the throat. **1933** [see TENSE *a.* 1 c]. **1958** A. S. C. ROSS *Etym.* ii. 125 OE *e o* became opened to *ę ǫ* soon after 1200... This loss of tenseness is of great consequence in the development of new diphthongs. **1978** *Canad. Jrnl. Linguistics* 1977 XXII. 211 There appears to have been a recent tendency to attribute tenseness to all lengthened vowels.

tenser, -or ('tɛnsə(r)). *Obs.* exc. *Hist.* Also 5 -ur, -ure, 6 tenssar. [a. OF. **tensier* = med.L. **tensārius*, f. OF. *tense*, *tence* defence, protection (= med.L. **tensa*), f. OF. *tenser* = med.L. *tensāre* to defend, protect: cf. OF. *tense-*, *tencement*, med.L. *tensāmentum*, defence, protection, also a payment to a lord for his protection and defence; also OF. *tenserie*: see next. Ulterior etymology uncertain.] An inhabitant of a city or borough who was not a citizen or freeman, but paid a rate for permission to reside and trade; a denizen.

1444 *Rolls of Parlt.* V. 125/2 Yef eny Burgeys or Tenser of the seid Toun [Shrewsbury] be attached for eny accion personell, or for suerte of the pees within the seid Toun. **1467** in *Eng. Gilds* (1870) 383 [Ordinances of Worcester] That no maner citezen, tensur, nor inhabitaunt wᵗyn the seid cite..put out eny wolle in hurting of the seid cite. *Ibid.* 394 That euery tensure that hath ben wᵗyn the cyte a yere or more dwellynge,..be warned to be made citezen,..and yf he refuse that, that he shalle yerly pay to the comyn cofre xl.*d.* **15..** *Early Chron. Shrewsb.* in *Trans. Shropsh. Archæol. Soc.* (1880) III. 246 This yeare [1449–50] the burgesses and tenssars in Shrewsbury dyd varye. **1519** *Corpor. Accts.* in T. Phillips *Hist. Shrewsb.* (1779) 168 Ordered that Tensors selling ale should pay 6d. quarterly. **1779** T. PHILLIPS *Hist. Shrewsb.* 161 Tensors fines, to be levied before the feast of St. Catharine. **1891** F. A. HIBBERT *Eng. Gilds* 156 There could no longer be any invidious distinction between freemen and non-freemen..gildsmen and tensers.

So †**'tenserie** *Obs.* [corresp. to OF. *tenserie* protection, = med.L. *tenseria*, **tensāria* payment for protection, tallage (Du Cange): see above], a tallage or tax exacted by lords from their vassals or tenants, in name of a payment for protection and defence; **tensership**, the status of a tenser, or rate paid for this privilege.

[**1151** *Concilium Londin.* i. (Du Cange), Ut ecclesiæ et possessiones ecclesiasticæ ab..exactionibus, quas vulgo tenserias sive tallagias vocant, omnino liberæ permaneant.] **1154** *O.E. Chron.* (Laud MS.) an. 1137, Hi læiden gæildes o þe tunes..& clepeden it tenserie. [**1176** *Pipe Roll 22 Hen. II* (1904) 75 Baldwinus Spinc reddit compotum de .xx.s. pro tenseria [C.R. tensaria] quam accepit de Brantona]. **1700** GOUGH *Hist. of Myddle* 128 This Richard Muckleston.. commenced a suite against the Towne of Shrewsbury for exacting an imposition upon him which they call tensorship. **1747** *Poll for Borough of Shrewsb.* 29–30 June in *Trans. Shropsh. Archæol. Soc.* III. 234 This Tensership is a ffine or acknowledgment commonly paid by persons following trade in the town that are no Burgesses.

tensible ('tɛnsɪb(ə)l), *a.* [ad. mod.L. **tensibil-is* that may be stretched, f. *tens-*, ppl. stem of *tendĕre* to stretch.] Capable of being stretched; = TENSILE 1. Hence **tensi'bility**.

1626 BACON *Sylva* §327 Gold..is the Closest..of Metals: And is likewise the most Flexible, and Tensible. **1861** FAIRBAIRN *Iron* 191 Direct tensible strength, compressive strength. **1676** *Phil. Trans.* XI. 707 What is the matter, structure, tenacity, tensibility,.. and various use of Fibres?

tensify ('tɛnsɪfaɪ), *v. rare.* [f. L. *tens-us*, TENSE *a.* + -(I)FY.] *trans.* To make tense.

1869 BUSHNELL *Wom. Suffrage* iii. 50 Fibred, tensified and toned for action. **1932** V. WOOLF *Common Reader* 2nd Ser. 145 That strain of.. passion did.. not tensify the quiet of the country morning.

tensile ('tɛnsɪl, -aɪl), *a.* Also 7 **tensil.** [ad. mod.L. *tensil-is* capable of stretching, f. *tens-*, ppl. stem of *tendĕre* to stretch: see -IL, -ILE.]

1. Capable of being stretched; susceptible of extension; ductile.

1626 BACON *Sylva* §845 All bodies ductile, and tensile, that will be drawn into wires. **1666** J. SMITH *Old Age* (1676) 173 The dry, solid, tensile, hard, and crusty parts of the body. **1794** MRS. PIOZZI *Synon.* I. 175, I have omitted *tensile* on the list,.. only because 'tis out of use in talk. **1874** TAIT *Rec. Adv. Phys. Sc.* xiii. (1876) 313 It [a soap-bubble] has two tensile surfaces with a layer of water between them.

2. Of, of the nature of, or pertaining to tension; exercising or sustaining tension. *spec.* as ***tensile test*** (*Engin.*), a test for determining the tensile strength of a sample of material (usu. metal); so ***tensile testing*** (also *attrib.*).

1841 *Civil Engin. & Arch. Jrnl.* IV. 31/2 Cast iron.. will bear a very considerable tensile strain. **1857** WHEWELL *Hist. Induct. Sci.* (ed. 3) II. 444 Wrought iron yields to compressive somewhat more easily than to tensile force. **1868** JOYNSON *Metals* 90 It possesses a tensile strength double that of good malleable iron. *a* **1877** KNIGHT *Dict. Mech.* III. 2539/1 In the hydraulic tensile testing-machine .. the specimen is held by the two clips. **1883** *Jrnl. Iron & Steel Inst.* 98 (*heading*) Results of tensile tests made at University College, London. **1898** *Allbutt's Syst. Med.* V. 936 This tensile strain is due to the stress of the hypertrophied left ventricle. **1923** GLAZEBROOK *Dict. Appl. Physics* V. 53/1 Two types of testing machine are in use for the tensile testing of fabric specimens. **1953** D. J. O. BRANDT *Manuf. Iron & Steel* 362 Fig. 203 shows a tensile testing machine and the method of setting up the test piece. **1973** J. G. TWEEDDALE *Materials Technol.* I. iv. 78 (*caption*) A tensile test piece.

3. Of a musical instrument: Producing sounds from stretched strings. *rare*$^{-0}$.

In recent Dicts.

Hence **'tensiled** *a.* (*rare*$^{-0}$), 'made tensile; rendered capable of tension' (Webster 1864); **'tensilely** *adv.*, in relation to tension; **ten'sility**, tensile condition or quality.

1871 *Standard* 28 Jan., Small forgings are generally tensilely stronger proportionately than large ones. **1659** H. MORE *Immort. Soul* II. x. (1662) 102 The libration or reciprocation of the spirits in the tensility of the muscles. **1910** *Daily News* 14 Apr. 6 A tensility which almost doubles when the metal is wrought and drawn.

tensimeter (tɛn'sɪmɪtə(r)). [f. TENSI(ON *sb.* + -METER.] An instrument for measuring vapour pressure.

1907 *Jrnl. Amer. Chem. Soc.* XXIX. 1055 The hygrometer used above may conveniently serve the purpose of a tensimeter. **1946** J. R. PARTINGTON *Gen. & Inorg. Chem.* iii. 54 The dissociation pressure of a salt hydrate is measured in a tensimeter.

tensiometer (tɛnsɪ'ɒmɪtə(r)). [f. TENSI(ON *sb.* + -OMETER.] **1. a.** An instrument for measuring the surface tension of a liquid. **b.** One for measuring the tension of soil water.

1922 *Jrnl. Exper. Med.* XXXV. 576 The tensiometer was used with an accurately calibrated platinum-iridium ring.. and is reliable to ±0·1 dyne. **1936** RICHARDS & GARDNER in *Jrnl. Amer. Soc. Agronomy* XXVIII. 352 Rogers.., lacking a more suitable name, has called the combination a soil moisture meter. In the interest of brevity and unambiguity, the name tensiometer is here used. **1973** *McGraw-Hill Yearbk. Sci. & Technol.* 382/1 Tensiometers placed in the active root zone and near the bottom of the root zone.. provide information that permits control of deep percolation [in irrigated soil]. **1975** YONG & WARKENTIN *Soil Properties & Behaviour* iv. 129 Tensiometers are widely used to indicate when irrigation is required.

2. An instrument for measuring the tension in yarn, a rope, etc.

1947 *Textile Research Jrnl.* Jan. 27/1 The thread then passes to a tensiometer,.. which instrument feeds voltage proportional to the thread tension into a.. chart recorder. **1952** *Electronic Engin.* XXIV. 531 The most common instrument for measuring yarn tension is the pocket-size dial tensiometer. **1978** A. WELCH *Bk. of Airsports* vi. 98/2 The tensiometer is important, so that the canopy will never be overloaded by the car being driven too fast in strong winds.

Hence **tensio'metric** *a.*, **tensi'ometry**.

1965 *New Scientist* 18 Nov. 497/1 The rocks are simulated by microscopic glass balls and polymers... They claim that these models enable reliable forecasts of what will happen to the springs if this or that method of mining is adopted. Tensiometry.. and ultrasound measurements play an important role in this work. **1968** *McGraw-Hill Yearbk. Sci. & Technol.* 351/1 A tensiometric method utilizes a porous cup filled with water connected by a tube to a vacuum indicator. This approach measures the capillary potential or suction of soil water. **1979** *Acta Protozoologica* XVIII. 64 Two radial measurements by tensiometry.

tension ('tɛnʃən), *sb.* Also 7-8 **tention.** [prob. a. F. *tension* (*a* 1530 in Godef. *Compl.*), ad. late L. *tensiōn-em*, n. of action f. *tendĕre* to stretch (pa. pple. *tens-us, tent-us*). But the Eng. word may have been direct from 16th c. medical Latin.

With *tension* agree *distension, extension, pretension*; the variant *tention* agrees with *attention, contention, intention.*]

The action of stretching or condition of being stretched: in various senses.

1. a. *Physiol.* and *Path.* The condition, in any part of the body, of being stretched or strained; a sensation indicating or suggesting this; a feeling of tightness. (The earliest use in English.)

1533 ELYOT *Cast. Helthe* (1541) 59 b, There is felt within the bulke of a man.. a weyghtynesse with tension, or thrustyng outwarde. **1603** HOLLAND *Plutarch's Mor.* 656 The veines.. upon the tention and commotion whereof.. drunkennesse doth proceed. **1615** CROOKE *Body of Man* 739 The first is a streatching or Tention not without strife or contention. **1704** F. FULLER *Med. Gymn.* (1705) 30 What I mean by this Tension or Tone of the Parts. **1725** *Bradley's Fam. Dict.* s.v. *Vomiting*, The tention of the Hypocondria and confus'd Sight. **1756** BURKE *Subl. & B.* IV. iii, An unnatural tension of the nerves. **1855** H. SPENCER *Princ. Psychol.* II. xi. §55. 213 A correspondingly strong sensation of muscular tension.

b. *Bot.* Applied to a strain or pressure in the cells or tissues of plants arising from changes taking place in the course of growth.

1875 BENNETT & DYER *Sachs' Bot.* 708 Causes of the condition of Tension in Plants. The elasticity of the organised parts of plants results in tension chiefly from the operation of three causes. *Ibid.* 713 In a turgid cell, the cell-wall is.. in a state of negative, the contents in a state of positive tension. *Ibid.* 720 It is only when the epidermis is becoming cuticularised and the walls of the bast-cells are beginning to thicken that the tensions become perceptible.

2. *fig.* A straining, or strained condition, of the mind, feelings, or nerves. **a.** Straining of the mental powers or faculties; severe or strenuous intellectual effort; intense application.

a **1763** SHENSTONE *Economy* I. 151 When fancy's vivid spark impels the soul To scorn quotidian scenes,.. what nostrum shall compose Its fatal tension? **1826** W. GIFFORD *Let.* in Smiles *Mem. J. Murray* (1891) II. xxv. 172 It is a fearful thing to break down the mind by unremitted tension. **1875** JOWETT *Plato* (ed. 2) IV. 12 The mind cannot be always in a state of intellectual tension.

b. Nervous or emotional strain; intense suppressed excitement; a strained condition of feeling or mutual relations which is for the time outwardly calm, but is likely to result in a sudden collapse, or in an outburst of anger or violent action of some kind.

1847 DISRAELI *Tancred* IV. vi, The expression.. of extreme tension.. had disappeared. **1852** MRS. STOWE *Uncle Tom's C.* vii, As the danger decreased with the distance, the supernatural tension of the nervous system lessened. **1878** LECKY *Eng. in 18th C.* II. vii. 311 Society cannot permanently exist in a condition of extreme tension. **1885** *L'pool Daily Post* 11 Apr. 64/7 A tension of feeling which has had no parallel since the outbreak of the Crimean war.

c. Esp. in *Psychol.* A condition of strain produced by anxiety, need, or by a sense of mental, emotional, or physical disequilibrium; also *attrib.* or as *adj.*

1884 W. JAMES in *Mind* IX. 12 The states of tension.. have as positive an influence as the discharges in determining the total condition, and consequently in deciding what the *psychosis* shall be to which the complex *neurosis* corresponds. **1925** H. M. & E. R. GUTHRIE tr. *Janet's Princ. Psychotherapy* iv. 234 Psychic tension [is] characterized by the degree of activation and the hierarchical degree of acts. **1930** J. RIVIERE tr. *Freud's Civilization & its Discontents* 127 The sense of guilt.. is.. the ego's appreciation of the tension between its strivings and the standards of the super-ego; and the anxiety that lies behind. **1935** ADAMS & ZENER tr. *Lewin's Dynamic Theory of Personality* ii. 59 A tendency may readily be observed toward immediate discharge of tension (to a state of equilibrium at the lowest possible state of tension). **1958** H. A. MURRAY in G. Lindzey *Assessment of Human Motives* vii. 194 The concept of human nature.. is a concept of perpetually recurrent drives, or tensions.

d. The conflict created by interplay of the constituent elements of a work of art. Used esp. of poetry. (See also quot. 1941.)

1941 A. TATE *Reason in Madness* 72, I proposed.. the term *tension*.. using the term not as a general metaphor, but as a special one, derived from lopping the prefixes off the logical terms *ex*tension and *in*tension... The meaning of poetry is its 'tension', the full organized body of all the extension and intension that we can find in it. **1949** *Poetry* Feb. 305 *Tension*,.. the resultant effectual unity of the poem derived from the operation of such conflict-structures as wit, paradox and irony, slackness being the result of a failure in tension. **1957** N. FRYE *Anat. Crit.* 256 It is more likely to be the harsh, rugged, dissonant poem.. that will show in poetry the tension and the driving accented impetus of music. **1975** *Language* LI. 583 Metrical tension can be construed as the degree of difference between underlying and derived metrical patterns.

3. a. *Physics.* A constrained condition of the particles of a body when subjected to forces acting in opposite directions away from each other (usually along the body's greatest length), thus tending to draw them apart, balanced by forces of cohesion holding them together; the force or combination of forces acting in this way, esp. as a measurable quantity. (The opposite of *compression* or *pressure.*)

1685 BOYLE *Effects of Mot.* viii. 92 If you cut the string of a bent bow asunder, the.. extreams will fly from one another suddenly and forcibly enough to manifest that they were before in a violent state of Tension. **1782** V. KNOX *Ess.* xxi. I. 101 The string which is constantly kept in a state of tension will vibrate on the slightest impulse. **1825** J. NICHOLSON *Operat. Mechanic* 570 The strain occasioned by pulling timber in the direction of its length is called *tension.* **1853** KANE *Grinnell Exp.* xxviii. (1856) 232 The tension of the great field of ice over which we passed must have been enormous. It had a sensible curvature. **1881** *Metal World* No. 18. 277 A weight being placed on a beam or girder (.. resting on the support at each end..), the top is.. thrown into compression and the bottom into tension.

b. *Biol.* and *Med.* (also *Physics*) = PRESSURE 2 a.

1678 CUDWORTH *Intell. Syst.* I. v. 851 A pressure upon the optick nerve, by reason of a tension of the intermedious air, or æther. **1826** FARADAY *Exp. Res.* xxxiii. 200 The air.. has a certain degree of elasticity, or tension. **1844** *Civil Engin. & Arch. Jrnl.* VII. 155/1 The steam.. is retained between the boiler and the plate until by its 'tension' or elasticity it is forced downwards and underneath the edge of the plate. **1863** TYNDALL *Heat* i. §9 (1870) 8 He wishes to apply the force of his steam, or of the furnace which gives tension to his steam, to this particular purpose. **1906** W. MARRIOTT *Hints to Meteorol. Observers* (ed. 6) 69/1 Tension of vapour. **1907** J. H. PARSONS *Dis. Eye* ii. 18 The pressure inside the eye is called the intraocular pressure, or the tension of the eye. **1940** *Jrnl. Bacteriol.* XXXIX. 307 (*heading*) The effect of oxygen tension on the oxygen uptake of lake bacteria. **1971** *Brit. Med. Bull.* XXVII. 55/2 The oxygen tension in the arterial blood may be somewhat lowered. **1972** A. H. HALASA *Basic Aspects of Glaucomas* xi. 97 Low tension glaucoma refers to a condition characterized by a normal intraocular pressure associated with.. glaucomatous visual field defects.

c. *transf.* The degree of tightness or looseness of the stitches in machine sewing or in knitting. Hence (also ***tension-device***), a device in a sewing-machine for regulating the tightness of the stitch.

1877 KNIGHT *Dict. Mech.* s.v., By adjustment of the pressure at the tension device, the required tightness of stitch is obtained... There are many.. kinds of tensions, in different machines. Fig. 6309 shows the.. automatic tension... The automatic tension-device.. is placed in the standard of the machine. **1932** D. C. MINTER *Mod. Needlecraft* 199/2 Learn how to regulate machine stitch and tension. **1933** TILLOTSON & MINTER *Compl. Knitting Bk.* ii. 21 The knitted loops, for a correct tension, should just cling lightly and closely to the reader. **1950** J. NORBURY *Knitter's Craft* i. 10 A loose tension will produce a flabby, ill-fitting garment. **1973** *Tucson* (Arizona) *Daily Citizen* 22 Aug. 3 (Advt.), Brother sewing machine Lightweight zig zag.. fingertip touch tension. **1980** C. FREMLIN *With no Crying* x. 61 Alison was concentrating on those first vital rows of her knitting, making sure that she was getting the tension right.

4. *Electr.* The stress along lines of force in a dielectric. Formerly applied also to surface density of electric charge, and until about 1882 used vaguely as a synonym for potential, electromotive force, and mechanical force exerted by electricity: still so applied, in industrial and commercial use, in *high* and *low tension*: see sense 5.

1785 G. ADAMS *Essay on Electricity* (ed. 2) x. 208 The whole energy of electricity depends on its tension, or the force with which it endeavours to fly off from the electrified body. **1802** *Nicholson's Jrnl. Nat. Phil.* I. 137 (tr. Volta) In the one case, as well as in the other, the electric tension [*la tensione elettrica*] rises, during the contact, to the same point. **1833** FARADAY *Exp. Res.* (1855) I. 97 The attractions and repulsions due to the tension of ordinary electricity. **1837** BREWSTER *Magnet.* 159 The sun heating and illuminating the earth, and producing a magnetic tension. **1839** G. BIRD *Nat. Phil.* 218 On their separation they are found to possess .. a certain quantity of free electricity of low tension. **1841** W. FRANCIS (tr. Ohm 1827) in *Taylor's Sci. Mem.* II. 416 (*Ohm's Law*) The force of the current in a galvanic circuit is directly as the sum of all the tensions [*die Summe aller Spannungen*], and inversely as the entire reduced length of the circuit. **1849** NOAD *Electricity* (ed. 3) 135 *Tension*, Mr. Harris applies to the actual force of a charge to break down any non-conducting or dielectric medium between two terminating electrified planes. **1866** R. M. FERGUSON *Electr.* (1870) 64 Tension is the power to polarise and effect discharge. **1871** TYNDALL *Fragm. Sc.* (1879) II. xvi. 439 Such machines deliver a large quantity of electricity of low tension. **1873** MAXWELL *Electr. & Magn.* (1881) I. 59 Finding the phrase *electric tension* used in several vague senses, I have attempted to confine it to.. the state of stress in the dielectric medium which causes motion of the electrified bodies, and leads, when continually augmented, to disruptive discharge. **1881** S. P. THOMPSON *Electr. & Magn.* 203 *note*, The word *tension*.. is so often misapplied in text-books... The term would be invaluable if we might adopt it to denote only the mechanical stress across a dielectric, due to accumulated charges. **1882** *Nature* 12 Oct. 570/2 M. Gariel breaks free from servitude to the consecrated term 'tension', so often misused as a synonym for potential, electro-motive force, and we know not what.

fig. **1859** KINGSLEY *Misc.* (1860) II. 75 Everything.. has exasperated, not calmed, the electric tension of the European atmosphere.

5. high tension: a high degree of tension (of any kind); **a.** *esp.* in *Electr.*, a term for a high degree of electromotive force or difference of potential: now chiefly used by makers of motor-cars, and of magnetic and induction coils. So **low tension.** (See sense 4.) Chiefly *attrib.* as in ***high*** or ***low tension system*** (of electric lighting, etc.); also ***h. t.*** or ***l. t. charge, contact, current, fuse***, etc.

1833 FARADAY in *Phil. Trans. R. Soc.* CXXIII. 516, I was anxious.. to obtain some idea of the conducting power of ice and solid salts by electricity of high tension. **1877** *Telegr. Jrnl.* V. 289/2 (*heading*) On the effects produced by electric currents of high tension. **1889** *Daily News* 7 Oct. 3/1 Mr. Crompton does not say that the high tension system will not succeed. He says both will succeed; but that the low tension system is safer and cheaper. **1891** *Cent. Dict.* s.v. *Tension*, A body is said to have a high-tension charge, or a charge of high-tension electricity, and a conductor to carry a high-tension current, when the stress in the medium surrounding the body or the conductor is high. **1900** *Engineering Mag.* XIX. 715 When required for high-tension fuses, the armature of this exploder is wound with very fine wire; when for low-tension, with coarse wire. **1903** *Motor. Ann.* 221 The low tension system is one which will undoubtedly come to the fore. In this the actual current from the battery, or magneto machine, is interrupted inside the cylinder, thus causing a spark. **1906** *Westm. Gaz.* 13 Nov. 4/2 High-tension magneto, it is noted, is gaining in popularity—the low-tension system being confined almost exclusively to the very high-priced cars. **1907** *Ibid.* 5 Dec. 4/2 The low-tension make and break is made on platinum points by means of a cam, whilst the high-tension contact is made through metal contacts by a revolving carbon brush.

b. Of the pulse: cf. TENSE *a.* 1 (quot. 1802).

1898 *Allbutt's Syst. Med.* V. 983 The low-tension pulse presents marked fluctuations of the base line. *Ibid.* 1024 Sir W. Broadbent considers that this modified high tension pulse is almost constant in mitral stenosis.

c. *transf.* and *fig.*

1898 G. B. SHAW *Candida* III. 148 Eugene, strung to the highest tension, does not move a muscle. **1906** J. M. SYNGE *Let.* ? 6 Nov. (1971) 47, I am working now at very high tension. **1959** D. COOKE *Lang. Music* iv. 183 The high-tension 'current' of Beethoven's emotion, we may say, had to be converted into a high-tension rhythmic energy.

6. *attrib.* and *Comb.*, as ***tension area, device*** (see 3 c), ***thrill***; *spec.* applied to parts of a structure subjected to tensile stress, as ***tension-member, -rod***; (in sense 2) ***tension state, system***; ***tension-relieving*** adj.; **tension bar**, (*a*) (see quot. 1879); (*b*) a metal bar used to apply pressure or exert tension; **tension-bridge**, a bridge in which there is tensile stress between parts of the structure, as a bowstring-bridge (see BOWSTRING 3, and quot. below); **tension-fuse**, a form of electric fuse which is fired by a spark at a break in a circuit; **tension magnet** (see quot.); **tension-pulley, -roller**, a free pulley or roller over which a belt, etc. passes to keep it stretched tight; a tightening-pulley; **tension-rail**, a rail for stretching cloth during the process of printing; **tension-spicule**, in sponges (see quot.); **tension spring**, (*a*) a spring for carriages, etc. composed of inner and outer leaves, connected at the ends, but free in the middle, so as to elongate independently under strain; (*b*) a spring used to maintain a required degree of tautness; **tension wood** = *reaction wood* s.v. REACTION 5.

1871 TYNDALL *Fragm. Sc.* I. i. 20 At the beginning the *vis viva* was zero and the *tension area was a maximum. **1879** *Car-Builder's Dict.* 163/1 **Tension bar*, a bar which is subjected to a strain of tension. **1963** R. A. HIGHAM *Handbk. Papermaking* viii. 212 Tension bars are usually found on calendars, especially when treating light-weight papers, and in action these serve to keep the sheet flat and taut across the working width. **1977** 'E. MCBAIN' *Long Time no See* xiii. 215 The telephone was as vital a tool to policemen as was a tension bar to a burglar. **1877** KNIGHT *Dict. Mech.*, **Tension-bridge*, a bridge constructed on the principle of the bow, the arch supporting the track by means of tension-rods, and the string acting as a tie. **1890** *Cent. Dict.* s.v. *Fuse*, **Tension-fuse*, an electric fuse in which the conducting circuit is not complete, the firing being accomplished by the passage of a spark. **1891** *Ibid.* s.v., An electromagnet surrounded by a coil of many turns and high electrical resistance was called by Henry a **tension magnet*. **1844** STEPHENS *Bk. Farm* II. 303 For the purpose of keeping a due degree of tension on the chain, a small movable *tension pulley is applied. **1890** W. J. GORDON *Foundry* 169 To.. draw in the apparently endless plain white calico, zigzagging it over *tension rails, and running it on, giving it an extra colour at every turn. **1949** KOESTLER *Insight & Outlook* 421 Neglect of the emotional dynamics of laughter, of its *tension-relieving aspect. **1974** M. C. GERALD *Pharmacol.* xi. 201 *Quiet World* contains 'special calming and tension-relieving ingredients'. **1838** *Civil Eng. & Arch. Jrnl.* I. 126/1 Each pair of rafters is tied by means of a *tension rod. *Ibid.* 381/1 The platform, or roadway, was laid upon cast iron beams, suspended from the main chains by perpendicular iron bars or tension rods, about five feet apart. **1835** URE *Philos. Manuf.* 196 The *tension or stretching-roller has its axle mounted in the segment-racks as usual. **1886** VON LENDENFELD in *Proc. Zool. Soc.* 21 Dec. 564 Called Flesh-spicules or Microsclera (**Tension-spicules* of Bowerbank). **1877** KNIGHT *Dict. Mech.*, **Tension-spring*, a spring for wagons, railway-carriages, etc... The outer leaves.. impart a tensile strain to the inner ones. **1966** J. S. COX *Illustr. Dict. Hairdressing & Wigmaking* 148/1 *Tension spring*, a spirally wound and flattened wire spring which, when stretched returns to its original length... The tension spring is sometimes replaced by elastic. **1970** *Which?* Aug. 238/2 A faulty tension spring on the bobbin case stopped the tensioning adjustment from working properly. **1946** *Mind* LV. 149 We have, therefore, to discover these responses that are the most successful in resolving the personal *tension state of which political argument is the expression. **1977** J. D. DOUGLAS in Douglas & Johnson *Existential Sociol.* i. 43 Anomie appears to be a tension state that is produced in the individual by an inability to achieve success by legitimate means. **1936** *Mind* XLV. 248 The technique which seeks to make an undesired goal palatable or a desired goal unpalatable, by linking them up somehow with the 'natural' *tension-systems of the child. **1953** M. HORWITZ in Cartwright & Zander *Group Dynamics* xx. 371 Individuals develop tension systems coordinated to reaching their own goals. **1893** T. E. BROWN *Old John*, etc. 111 To him the sorrows are the *tension-thrills Of that serene endeavour. **1924** W. S. JONES *Timbers* iv. 27 '*Tension' or 'white' wood differs from 'red' wood in that the cell walls of the tracheids show a well-developed, strongly-lignified, tertiary layer. **1951** MCLEAN & IVIMEY-COOK *Textbk. Theoret. Bot.* I. xxi. 907 In conifers the lower wood is reddish, the upper white ..the upper wood being called tension-wood. **1972** *Gloss. Terms Timber (B.S.I.)* 15 Tension wood. Abnormal wood.. formed typically on the upper sides of branches and of leaning or crooked trunks of hardwood trees.

Hence **'tension** *v. trans.*, to subject to tension, tighten, make taut (hence **'tensioned** *ppl. a.*, **'tensioning** *vbl. sb.*); **'tensional** *a.*, of, pertaining to, of the nature of, or affected with tension; **'tensionally** *adv.*, by means of tension, as a result of tension; **'tensionless** *a.*, without tension, unstrained.

1891 *Engineer* LXXI. 120/2 [List of patents.] *Tensioning saddles of velocipedes, F. A. Matthews, London. **1950** *Jrnl. R. Aeronaut. Soc.* LIV. 631/1 The 'floating stud'..is a slotted template stud contained in a metal ring, and tensioned by three or four springs. **1975** KONG & EVANS *Reinforced & Prestressed Concrete* ix. 196 When the concrete has hardened sufficiently, the tendons are tensioned by jacking against one or both ends of the member. **1872** *Daily News* 28 Feb., The whole nation was hanging in a *tensioned spasm of fear. *a* **1879** TYNDALL (Webster Supp.), A highly tensioned string. **1893** DE LONG in *Chicago Advance* 28 Sept., How tensioned are our nerves! **1898** *Cycling* 48 Upon the correct *tensioning of the spokes [of a bicycle] depends the 'truth' of the wheel. **1906** *Cycl. Tour. Club Gaz.* Aug. 311 The tensioning is done by turning the three screws at the back of the saddle upwards from the right to left, so as to withdraw them. Most riders make the mistake when tensioning the saddle of turning the screws the wrong way. **1862** *Catal. Internat. Exhib.* II. x. 6 The *tensional parts of a pair of rigid trusses. **1881** *Athenæum* 2 July 16/3 The total energy of vibrations as being made up of two parts, one statical or tensional, and the other kinetic. **1960** R. W. MARKS *Dymaxion World of B. Fuller* 195 Magnesium ball-jointed tripods..were *tensionally opened by piston-elevated masts. **1975** *New Yorker* 12 May 41/1 Tensionally cohered universe here today and gone tomorrow. **1905** *Dundee Advertiser* 22 Dec. 9/2 A lecture on the subject of 'The *Tensionless Drive'. The lecturer treated of the efficacy of belts as a means of transmitting power.

tensioner ('tɛnʃənə(r)). *Mech.* [f. TENSION *sb.* + -ER[1].] A device for applying tension to cables, pipelines, etc.

1950 *Engineering* 5 May 489/3 Heavy spring tensioners are fitted to the front sprockets. **1972** L. M. HARRIS *Introd. Deepwater Floating Drilling Operations* xiii. 140 Marine-riser tensioning can be provided either by a dead-weight system or by the use of pneumatic tensioner cylinders. **1977** *Austral. Sailing* Jan. 54/1 The luff tensioner..is the most subtle control.

tensity ('tɛnsɪtɪ). [f. L. *tens-us* TENSE *a.* + -ITY: cf. *intensity*.] The quality or condition of being tense; a state of tension.

a. *lit.* (chiefly *Physiol.* and *Path.*).

1658 PHILLIPS, *Tensity*, stiffnesse, or a being stretched out hard. **1676** COLE in *Phil. Trans.* XI. 604 There could be, in that supposition of a Continuity of fibre, tensity enough in the Intestins to carry on such a motion. **1717** J. KEILL *Anim. Oecon.* (1738) 261 That robust Tensity of the Fibres, which makes strong People the less liable to accidents.

b. *fig.*

1862 CARLYLE *Fredk. Gt.* XI. vii. (1872) IV. 95 It braced him into such a tensity of spirit. **1884** W. COLLINS *I say No* I. ix, The first change of expression which relaxed the iron tensity of the housekeeper's face showed itself.

tensive ('tɛnsɪv), *a.* [a. F. *tensif, -ive* (Paré 16th c.), f. L. *tens-*, ppl. stem of *tendĕre* (see TENSE *a.* and -IVE). Cf. *intensive*.] Having the quality of stretching or straining; causing tension; in *Path.* applied to a sensation of tension or tightness in any part of the body.

1702 J. PURCELL *Cholick* (1714) 95 After violent Exercises we always feel a Tensive Pain in the Left side. **1897** *Allbutt's Syst. Med.* IV. 149 The pain is usually dull and tensive.

tensome ('tɛnsəm), *a.* (*sb.*) *Sc.* [f. TEN + -SOME.] Ten together, consisting of a company or set of ten. Also as *sb.* A set or cluster of ten.

1563 WINȜET tr. *Vincent. Lirinensis* Wks. (S.T.S.) II. 75 Al in the haly number of that table of ten-sum at Ephesus. *a* **1584** MONTGOMERIE *Cherrie & Slae* 453 Maire honor is to vanquisch ane, Nor feicht with tensum and be tane. **1898** J. PATON *Castlebraes* ix. 284 The glee o' Tensome an' Twalsome Faimilies.

tensometer (tɛn'sɒmɪtə(r)). [f. TENS(ION *sb.* + -OMETER.] **1.** An apparatus for measuring the tensile strength of a material.

1937 *Nature* 1 May 765/2 The Griffin Gale testing machine enables tensile..tests to be carried out on small samples of metals... In the same class is the Hounsfield tensometer. **1950** *Chem. Abstr.* XLIV. 7 (*heading*) Mechanical tensometer for measurements of deformations on temperature charge. **1971** *Nature* 2 Apr. 323/1 The specimens were strained at a rate of 1mm min^{-1}; the tensometer and electrometer head amplifier were enclosed in an earthed brass gauze to screen out extraneous electrical fields.

2. = TENSIOMETER 1 a.

1941 *Abstr. Sci. & Technical Press* No. 91. 178 The author has designed an interfacial tensometer... In this instrument the force exerted by the interfacial layer on a platinum ring is measured by means of a torsion balance.

3. = TENSIOMETER 2.

1953 K. H. INDERFURTH *Nylon Technol.* vii. 159 It is essential that the yarn tension be frequently checked with a tensometer.

‖**tenson** ('tɛnsən, tɑ̃sɔ̃). Also 9 tenzon. [F. *tenson* = Pr. *tenso*, a poetical contest; in OF. contention, contest: see TENCION.] A contest in verse between rival troubadours; a piece of verse or song composed for or sung in such a contest.

1840 BROWNING *Sordello* II. 686 While, out of dream, his day's work went To tune a crazy tenzon or sirvent. **1883** A. H. WODEHOUSE in Grove *Dict. Mus.* III. 585/1 The *tensons*, or contentions, were metrical dialogues of lively repartee on some disputed point of gallantry. **1895** H. GAELYN *To Elise*, Would I could write for my Elise Trim triolets and tensons tender!

tensor ('tɛnsə(r)). [a. mod.L. *tensor*, agent-n. from *tendĕre* to stretch.]

1. *Anat.* Also ***tensor muscle***. A muscle that stretches or tightens some part. Opp. to *laxator*.

In mod. use, distinguished from an *extensor* by not altering the direction of the part.

1704 J. HARRIS *Lex. Techn.* I, *Tensors*, or *Extensors*, are those common Muscles that serve to extend the Toes, and have their Tendons inserted into all the lesser Toes. **1799** HOME in *Phil. Trans.* XC. 10 The combined action of the tensor and laxator muscles varying the degree of its [the membrana tympani] tension. **1808** BARCLAY *Muscular Motions* 384 The biceps..being a flexor and supinator of the fore-arm, and at the same time a tensor of its fascia. **1879** *St. George's Hosp. Rep.* IX. 591 The functions of the adductors and tensors are more delicate.

2. *Math.* **a.** In Quaternions, a quantity expressing the ratio in which the length of a vector is increased.

1846 W. R. HAMILTON in *Phil. Mag.* XXIX. 27 Since the square of a scalar is always positive, while the square of a vector is always negative, the algebraical excess of the former over the latter square is always a positive number; if then we make $(TQ)^2 = (SQ)^2 - (VQ)^2$, and if we suppose TQ to be always a real and positive or absolute number, which we may call the tensor of the quaternion Q, we shall not thereby diminish the generality of that quaternion. This tensor is what was called in former articles the modulus. **1853** —— *Elem. Quaternions* II. i. (1866) 108 The former element of the complex relation..between..two lines or vectors [*viz.* their relative length], is..represented by a simple ratio.., or by a number expressing that ratio. *Note*, This number, which we shall..call the *tensor* of the quotient,..may always be equated..to a positive scalar. **1886** W. S. ALDIS *Solid Geom.* xiv. (ed. 4) 235 Since the operation denoted by a quarternion consists of two parts, one of rotating OA into the position OB and the other of extending OA into the length OB, a quaternion may be.. represented as the product of two factors,..the versor..and ..the tensor of the quaternion.

b. An abstract entity represented by an array of components that are functions of co-ordinates such that, under a transformation of co-ordinates, the new components are related to the transformation and to the original components in a definite way. [This sense is due to W. Voigt (*Die Fund. Physik. Eigenschaften der Krystalle* (1898) p. vi).]

1916 *Monthly Notices R. Astron. Soc.* LXXVI. 701 In the four-dimensional time-space we consider tensors of different orders. The tensor of order zero is a pure number (scalar), the tensor of the first order is a vector, which has 4 components, the tensor of the second order has 16 components, and so on. *Ibid.* 702 If once we have expressed the laws of nature in the form of linear relations between tensors, they will be invariant for all transformations. Thus with the aid of the calculus of tensors Einstein has succeeded in satisfying the postulate of general relativity. **1934** *Nature* 20 Oct. 612 The theory of tensors, so important in physics and geometry on account of their property of vanishing in every co-ordinate system if they vanish in one, was created by Ricci (1887) and his pupil Levi-Civita, although the name *tensor* was not introduced by them. **1943** *Jrnl. London Math. Soc.* XVIII. 109 The study of the particular class of invariants known as tensors goes back to the work of Riemann and Christoffel on quadratic differential forms. **1953** C.-T. WANG *Applied Elasticity* i. 1 Stress is called a tensor, because in addition to its magnitude, direction, and sense, which define a vector, it depends on another vector, which represents the surface upon which it acts. **1970** G. K. WOODGATE *Elem. Atomic Struct.* iii. 50 The operator in eqn. (3.95) is a component of a second-rank tensor, the atomic electric quadrupole moment. **1974** G. REECE tr. *Hund's Hist. Quantum Theory* xv. 211 ψ and χ were scalars, spinors, vectors or tensors.

c. *attrib.* and *Comb.*, as ***tensor algebra, analysis, calculus, product***; **tensor field**, a field for which a tensor is defined at each point; **tensor force**, a force between two bodies that has to be expressed as a tensor rather than a vector, *esp.* a non-central force between sub-atomic particles; **tensor-twist**, in Clifford's biquaternions, a twist multiplied by a tensor.

1922 Tensor algebra [see *tensor analysis* below]. **1936** *Electr. Engin.* LV. 1214/1 The object of this paper is to apply tensor algebra to the solution of the circuits of multi-winding transformers. **1971** C. W. CURTIS in Powell & Higman *Finite Simple Groups* iii. 142 Form a vector space M with basis X, and let $\mathscr{F}_X$ be the tensor algebra over M. **1922** H. L. BROSE tr. *Weyl's Space-Time-Matter* i. 58 Tensor analysis tells us how, by differentiating with respect to the space co-ordinates, a new tensor can be derived from the old one in a manner entirely independent of the co-ordinate system. This method, like tensor algebra, is of extreme simplicity. **1939** G. KRON *Tensor Analysis of Networks* p. xvi, Tensor analysis may be considered as an extension and generalization of vector analysis from three- to n-dimensional spaces and from Euclidean to non-Euclidean spaces. **1976** *Sci. Amer.* Aug. 98/2 Einstein's ideas were cast in a language very different from even non-Euclidean geometry, called the absolute differential calculus... Einstein used it and changed its name to tensor analysis. **1977** D. Bagley *Enemy* xxxiii. 266 This joker is using Hamiltonian quaternions!.. No one..has used Hamiltonian quaternions since 1915 when tensor analysis was invented. **1922** H. L. Brose tr. *Weyl's Space-Time-Matter* i. 53 The study of tensor-calculus is, without doubt, attended by conceptual difficulties—over and above the apprehension inspired by indices. **1944** G. B. Shaw *Everybody's Political What's What?* ii. 22 Experts in the tensor calculus. **1981** *Sci. Amer.* July 95/1 Tensor calculus..was essential to Einstein's formulation of his general theory of relativity. **1922** H. L. Brose tr. *Weyl's Space-Time-Matter* i. 61 An important example of a tensor field is offered by the stresses occurring in an elastic body. **1934** R. C. Tolman *Relativity, Thermodynamics, & Cosmol.* 36 Tensor fields may..be constructed, in which a value of the field tensor is associated with each point in the continuum. **1948** *Physical Rev.* LXXII. 987/1 The result of the present calculation and that of the proton-neutron scattering, which includes the tensor forces, show that the difference among the three potentials is quite pronounced at these high energies. **1972** *Physics Bull.* June 349/2 The noncentral force causing the anomalies mentioned above is called the tensor force, and it results from a neutron-protonspin-spin interaction. **1964** A. P. & W. Robertson *Topological Vector Spaces* vii. 141 It is essential to form the completion of the tensor product under the correct topology. **1971** E. C. Dade in Powell & Higman *Finite Simple Groups* viii. 252 The tensor product..is again a finite-dimensional vector space over *F*.

Hence **ten'sorial** *a.*

1934 [see anti-^{1} 2 d]. **1968** C. G. Kuper *Introd. Theory Superconductivity* iv. 58 Since..Pippard's experimental data..do not support the idea of a tensorial anisotropy, these equations have not proved useful.

tensor, tensur, -ure, var. ff. tenser *Obs.*

†**tensue** = *to ensue*: see T' and ensue *v.*

1513 Bradshaw *St. Werburge, 2nd Balade* 16 The for tensue, that art theyr lode-sterre.

†'**tensure.** *Obs.* [ad. mod.L. *tensūra* stretching, f. *tendĕre* to stretch: see -ure.] Stretching, strain; = tension.

1611 Barrey *Ram Alley* Epil. in Hazl. *Dodsley* X. 380 But he..Submits the tensures of his pains To those, whose wit and nimble brains Are able best to judge. **1626** Bacon *Sylva* §12 This Motion upon Pressure, and the Reciprocall thereof, which is Motion upon Tensure; we use to call (by one common Name) Motion of Liberty. **1653** R. G. tr. *Bacon's Hist. Winds* 318 As for the freeing from tensure or stretching. **1672** Wallis in *Phil. Trans.* VII. 5165 Its Spring being of a like tensure with that of the outward Air.

tensyn, variant of tinsen *Obs.*

tent (tent), *sb.*^{1} Forms: 3-6 **tente**, (5 **teinte**, **teynte**, 5-6 **tentt(e**, 6 **tenthe**), 4- **tent**. [a. OF. *tente* (12th c. in Godef. *Compl.*):—L. *tenta*, pl. of *tentum*, pa. pple. of *tendĕre* to stretch; = med.L. *tenta*, *tentum* tent (in Du Cange); cf. also It., Pr. *tenda*, Sp. *tienda*, med.L. *tenda* (13th c. in Du Cange), assimilated to *tendĕre*.]

1. a. A portable shelter or dwelling of canvas (formerly of skins or cloth), supported by means of a pole or poles, and usually extended and secured by ropes fastened to pegs which are driven into the ground; used by travellers, soldiers, nomads, and others; a pavilion; also, a similar shelter erected on a travelling boat or wagon.

1297 R. Glouc. (Rolls) 4156 Hii come to barbesflet & piȝte þer bi syde Hor tentes & hor pauilons. *a* **1300** *Cursor M.* 7709 He sett his tentes in a dale. *Ibid.* 7714 Þai went, Vn-to þe kings aun tent. *c* **1330** R. Brunne *Chron.* (1810) 67 Þar loges & þare tentis vp þei gan bigge. **1387** Trevisa *Higden* (Rolls) III. 125 Antecrist schal be slawe in his owne tent in þe mount Olyuete. *c* **1400** *Destr. Troy* 10190 The troiens..Takyn þere tenttes, turnyt hom vnder. *c* **1450** *Merlin* iii. 46 How he wolde come be nyght hym-self to his teynte. **1535** Coverdale *1 Kings* xii. 16 Get the to thy tentes [Wyclif, Turne aȝen into thi tabernaclis] O Israel [*Geneva*, **1611**, To your tents, O Israel]. **1552** Huloet, Tent or bouthe in a fayre or market. *a* **1570** in Feuillerat *Revels Q. Eliz.* (1908) 407 Comptroller of her graces Revelles tenthes & pavillions. **1594** Shaks. *Rich. III*, v. iii. 7 Vp with my Tent, heere wil I lye to night, But where to morrow? **1617** Moryson *Itin.* ii. 82 The weather grew so extreme, as it blew downe all our Tents, and tore them in pieces. **1717** Lady M. W. Montagu *Let. to Abbé Conti* 17 May, The Sultan is already gone to his tents, and all his Court. **1719** De Foe *Crusoe* i. 285 Friday and I, in about two Hours Time, made a very handsome Tent, cover'd with old Sails. **1844** Longf. *Day is done* 43 The cares, that infest the day, Shall fold their tents, like the Arabs, And as silently steal away. **1844** [see pitch *v.*^{1} 4].

†**b.** A sheet or screen of canvas or the like.

1572 in Feuillerat *Revels Q. Eliz.* (1908) 179 Hanging up Tentes to keepe away the wynde & snow from dryving into the hall.

2. *transf.* **a.** Something likened to or resembling a tent; *spec.* **b.** in *Photogr.*, a curtained box serving as a portable dark-room; **c.** the silken web of a tent-caterpillar.

1599 Davies *Immort. Soul* iv. xxi, Heav'ns wide-spreading Tent. **1862** B. Taylor *Poet's Jrnl.* iii. *Myst. Summer* 52 Its little bell expands, for me, A tent of silver lily fair. **1923** T. S. Eliot *Waste Land* iii. 14 The river's tent is broken: the last fingers of leaf Clutch and sink into the wet bank. **1929** *Oxford Poetry* 13 Here in this harbour where straw glows..and overhead The unbroken tent of heaven covers.

d. The name given to a local 'lodge' or 'habitation' of the Rechabites; also of the Zionists.

[From the tents in which the ancient Rechabites dwelt, Jer. xxxv. 7, and those in which Israel dwelt in the wilderness.]

1886 *Rechabite Mag.* July 151 (Cassell) The sick funds in the possession of the various tents. **1897** E. Reich in *19th Cent.* Aug. 261 At the head of religious Zionism are the numerous 'Tents' of the 'Lovers of Zion'. *Ibid.* Oct. 633 The English Association, known as the Chovevi Zion..has 35 established 'Tents', spread through the length and breadth of the United Kingdom.

e. Applied to a hut.

a **1873** Deutsch *Rem.* (1874) 178 The people dwelling during their lifetime in tents of mud. **1887** Hall Caine *Deemster* xxxvii. 247 A little disjointed gipsy encampment of mud-built tents pitched on the bare moor.

f. A plastic or fabric enclosure that can be placed round a patient in bed so that the air he or she breathes can be modified and controlled. Cf. *oxygen tent* s.v. oxygen 3 b.

1892 J. Carmichael *Dis. Children* xvii. 235 The room should be well ventilated, and the temperature of the tent kept between 65° and 70°. **1941** M. Davidson *Pract. Man. Dis. Chest* (ed. 2) xxxv. 559 Many varieties of tent have been constructed, all of which..demand considerable supervision. **1971** S. M. Bates *Pract. Pediatric Nursing* xii. 237 Both tents are designed to achieve cool super-saturation of the contained air with minimal wetting. **1979** Whaley & Wong *Nursing Care Infants & Children* xxxii. 1201/1 For continuous aerosol therapy a misting device is attached to or incorporated in the mist tent.

3. *fig.* An abode, residence, habitation, dwelling-place; esp. in phrases ***to have, pitch one's tent(s***.

c **1366** Chaucer *A.B.C.* 9 Bountee so fix hath in þin herte his tente. **1535** Coverdale *Ps.* lxxxiii[i]. 10 To dwell in the tentes of the vngodly [**1611** tents of wickednesse]. **1624** Davies *Psalm xv*, Lord! who shall dwell in thy bright tent with Thee? **1700** Dryden *Theodore & Hon.* 59 To Chassis' pleasing plains he took his way, There pitched his tents, and there resolved to stay. **1827** *Edin. Weekly Jrnl.* 28 Feb., They..spoke of the theatre as of the tents of sin. **1887** Hall Caine *Coleridge* iv, Roscoe invited him to pitch his tent in Liverpool.

4. *Sc.* A portable pulpit set up in the open air for the preacher on sacramental or other occasions when the worshippers are too numerous to be accommodated in the church.

1678 Lady Methven *Let.* in *Ladies of Covt.* (1853) Introd. 34 They had their tent set up upon your ground. **1689** in *Faithful Contendings* (1780) 381 A tent being set up before, Mr. Shields continued in his lecture. **1785** Burns *Holy Fair* xiv, But, hark! the tent has chang'd its voice. **1837** Lockhart *Scott* May an. 1819, Every kirk in the neighbourhood being left empty when it was known he was to mount the tent at any country sacrament. **1885** Edgar *Old Ch. Life Scot.* 177 Besides a church, every parish required a tent. This..was not a tabernacle of canvas for sheltering the worshippers, but a moveable pulpit made of wood for the preacher to stand in.

5. *attrib.* and *Comb.* **a.** Simple attrib. 'of, consisting of, belonging to, used in, dwelling in, a tent or tents', as ***tent accommodation, -cloth, -curtain, -fashion, -fellow, -flap, -frame, -hand, -house*** (also *fig.*), ***-life, -mate, -picket, -pole, -post, -roof, -rope, -sail*** (sail *sb.*^{1} 7), ***-school, -skirt, -staff, -table, -talk, -tomb, -wagon***; objective and obj. genitive, as ***tent-holder, -keeper, -owner, -pitcher, -pitching***; instrumental, etc., as ***tent-clad, -dotted, -dwelling, -like*** adjs.; also, in sense 4, ***tent-meeting, -preacher, -preaching, -reader, -sermon***.

?**1780** W. Carter *Disbanded Subaltern* 22 Close at the bottom of this *tent-clad hill. **1552** Huloet, *Tente clothes, wherwith tentes are couered. **1836** *Uncle Philip's Convers. Whale Fishery* 13 The sinews..they use in sewing their coats and tent cloths. **1835** N. P. Willis *Pencillings by Way* II. xviii. 199 Most of the officers lay asleep on low ottomans, with their *tent curtains undrawn. **1926** T. E. Lawrence *Seven Pillars* (1935) viii. xcvi. 532 He crawled back through the tent-curtain. **1648** Owen *Serm. Hab. iii. 1-9* Wks. 1851 VIII. 98 The *tent-dwelling Arabians. **1856** Kane *Arct. Expl.* II. xvi. 176 Their neat canvas housing rigged *tent-fashion. **1904** *Expositor* Apr. 311 Men from all parts of Greece were *tent fellows and messmates. **1920** *Blackw. Mag.* Sept. 319/2 He paused with his shaking hand on the *tent-flap. **1980** D. Hart-Davis *Heights of Rimring* vii. 67 He unrolled the tent-flaps and let them hang down. *Ibid.* vi. 65 The porters..began to fit *tent-frames together. **1938** N. Streatfeild *Circus is Coming* v. 57 The man finished fixing a seat. 'I'm a *tent hand.' **1965** H. Gold *Man who was not with It* xiv. 115 A couple of tenthands are taking their flannel shirts off a line. **1905** *Daily Chron.* 22 Aug. 6/5 At a largely-attended meeting of *tent-holders at Southend..it was pointed out that, according to legal advice, the tent-owners were in the position of trespassers. **1625** *Balcarres Proclam.* No. 1431 *Tent-keeper. **1688** R. Holme *Armoury* iii. xix. (Roxb.) 164/1 Dayly pay..Pioneers each 1s. Tent Keepers each 18d. **1858** G. Rhodes (*title*) Tents and *Tent-Life, from the Earliest Ages to the Present Time. **1864** Trevelyan *Compet. Wallah* (1866) 114 Tent-life in the winter months is very enjoyable. **1840** Longf. *Spanish Stud.* iii. v, Behold, how beautiful she stands Under the *tent-like trees! **1695** tr. *Colbatch's New Lt. Chirurg. put out* 48 Seeing some of his *Tent-mates, I asked them if he was distracted? **1972** J. Minifie *Homesteader* xviii. 158, I used the Army-issue straight blade [razor] myself, to the intense admiration of my tent-mates. **1950** *Reader's Digest* Jan. 85/2 Frakes joined the Methodist Church at an evangelistic *tent meeting. **1875** Sir T. Seaton *Fret Cutting* 77 Tell your *tent-pitcher to give me two long tent-pins and two short ones. **1913** S. O'Casey *Let.* 7 June (1975) I. 28 There will be exhibitions of drill, *tent-pitching, [etc.]. **1925** G. Bell *Let.* 28 Jan. (1927) II. xxv. 721 The ordinary Scout exercises and tent pitchings—which they did extremely well. **1706** *Lond. Gaz.* No. 4189/4 Out of the Albion Frigat,..Pictures, *Tent Poles. **1864** G. M. Hopkins *Poems* (1967) 14 Your hands have borne the tent-poles. **1974** R. Adams *Shardik* xviii. 134 His ugly, unmarriageable tent-pole of a daughter. **1979** *Guardian* 12 June 2/4 These..facts..were..'the fixed and rigid tentpoles' of the whole edifice of the prosecution case. **1855** Milman *Lat. Chr.* V. 13 The Mamelukes..tied him to a *tent-post with his hands behind his back. **1966** *Punch* 9 Mar. 362/2 A *tent-preacher and healer tells a diabetic woman she is cured. **1977** *Time* 26 Dec. 41/1 The latter include everything from Episcopalians to nearly a million Roman Catholics, to oddball healers and assorted tent preachers. *c* **1795** *Stat. Acct. Scotland 1791-9* XV. 537 At the celebration of..the Sacrament of the Supper, there is no field or *tent preaching..so derogatory from the solemnity of this institution. **1825** Jamieson s.v., Scottish Presbyterians..still feel some degree of partiality to tent-preaching. *a* **1722** Pennecuik *Wks.* (1815) 345 (E.D.D.) He was *tent-reader of our service book. **1424** *Mem. Ripon* (Surtees) III. 151 Pro ij wellrapis, ij *tente-rapis, et j veylrape cum j corda..5*s.* **1828-40** Tytler *Hist. Scot.* (1864) I. 152 Douglas..penetrated to the royal tent, [and] cut the tent-ropes. **1892** Rider Haggard *Nada* 2 The shivering natives..took refuge on the second waggon, drawing a *tent-sail over them. **1909** *Jrnl. Educ.* Apr. 294/2 South Australia... A new plan for the education of children in remote parts of the State... The first *tent school has already been established and is to be found in the Hundred of Shannon, or Eyre Peninsula. **1805** J. Ramsay *Scot. & Scotsm. in 18th C.* (1888) II. i. 25 *Tent-sermons were retained by general consent. **1896** 'M. Field' *Attila* iv. 106 At last they caught the *tent-skirt in their hands And entered one by one. **1864** Boutell *Her. Hist. & Pop.* xxi. §11 (ed. 3) 369 The *tent-staff and pennon all or. **1932** Auden *Orators* iii. 108 The *tent-talk pauses a little till a veteran answers 'Go to sleep, Sonny!' **1819** *Acct. Colony Cape of Good Hope* iii. 118 A light *tent waggon, drawn by six or eight horses, constitutes the carriage of the wine boor. **1893** *Month* Apr. 523, I live in a tent-wagon.

b. Special Combs.: **tent-barge**, a barge having a tent-like canvas awning; **tent-bottom**, a board floor fitted to a tent; **tent caterpillar**, the gregarious larva of a North American moth of the genus *Malacosoma* of the family Lasiocampidæ, which spins a tent-like web; **tent city**, a very large collection of tents; **tent club**: in India, a club organized for the sport of pig-sticking; **tent coat**, a coat resembling a tent in shape, being narrow at the shoulders and very wide at the hem; **tent-fly**: see fly *sb.*^{2} 4 b; also, an exterior sheet stretched over the ridge-pole so as to cover the ordinary tent-roof with an air-space between; **tent-man**, (*a*) a tent-dweller; (*b*) one who has charge of a tent; **tent-master**: see quot. 1660; **tent-pin** = tent-peg; **tent ring** *Canad.*, a ring of stones used to hold down a tent, teepee, etc.; **tent-sack** (see quot. 1940); **tent show**, a show (such as a circus) given in a tent; **tent-stake** *U.S.* = tent-peg; also in fig. phr. to ***pull up tent-stakes***: to close down a business etc.; cf. stake *sb.*^{1} 1 e; **tent town**, a temporary settlement (as of gold-miners or the like); **tent-trailer** orig. and chiefly *U.S.*, a kind of trailer consisting of a wheeled frame with a collapsible tent cover attached; **tent-tree**, a species of screw-pine: see quot.; **tent village**, a small encampment; *spec.* = douar, dowar. See also tent-bed, tent-door, etc.

1796 Stedman *Surinam* II. xix. 71 A decent *tent-barge with six oars. **1902** *Fortn. Rev.* June 988 The wooden *tent-bottoms are placed outside the tents and thoroughly scrubbed three times a week. **1854** E. Emmons *Agric. N.Y.* V. 236 To eradicate completely the *tent caterpillar, it will be necessary to give attention to the wild cherry trees. **1884** Roe *Nat. Ser. Story* iv, A colony of jays would soon destroy all the tent-caterpillars. **1901** *Board Agric. Leaflet* No. 69. 1 Two species of so-called 'Tent Caterpillars' are frequently found on various fruit trees. **1977** Richards & Davies *Imms's Gen. Textbk. Entomol.* (ed. 10) II. iii. 1135 The larvae of *M. americana*..are commonly known as 'tent-caterpillars', their webs measuring 2 feet or more in length. **1934** M. F. K. Fisher in *As they Were* (1983) 64 A *tent city, many umbrella and hot-dog concessions. **1980** J. Domatilla *Last Crime* 5 A tent city of tourists on a similar pilgrimage. **1889** R. S. S. Baden-Powell *Pigsticking or Hoghunting* xvii. 152 Every station near which pig are to be found has its *Tent Club. This is an association of the sportsmen of the place for carrying out the preservation of the pig, and successful hunting. **1895** Kipling in *Cent. Mag.* Dec. 271/1 He became a member of the local Tent Club, and chased the mighty boar on horseback. **1920** *Blackw. Mag.* Jan. 105/1 A Tent Club corresponds to a Hunt; the Hon. Secretary to the Master. **1961** *Guardian* 1 Feb. 7/5 A vast *tent coat..over an elegant little sheath dress. **1971** *Vogue* 15 Sept. 51 Short tent coat with cape yoke. **1849** T. T. Johnson *Sights Gold Region* 169 The *tent-fly is a second roof usually erected over the tent. **1897** H. Porter in *Cent. Mag.* Apr. 831 A hospital tent-fly was stretched in front of the office tent so as to make a shaded space. **1880** L. Wallace *Ben-Hur* 231 Drink, for this is the fear-naught of the *tentmen. **1945** *Sun* (Baltimore) 22 Feb. 7/2 Circus men sentenced... Chief tentman, two to seven years in State prison. **1961** *Times* 28 Mar. 12/6 The sweating 'tentman'..will be clown, drummer, lion-tamer rolled into one. **1978** *Illustr. London News* Nov. 32/3 As a kid..I used to take my waddie bottle..full of tea to the tentmen, they were travelling labourers, really. **1660** Hexham, *Een Tenten-meester*, a *Tent-master, or a Marshall of a Campe. **1864** Tent master [see tenter *sb.*^{2} 2]. **1938** N. Streatfeild *Circus is Coming* v. 57 You'll have the tent master after me.

1763 J. Bell *Trav. from St. Petersburg* I. 323 Our European tents are of little use, as there is no earth in which the *tent-pins can be fastened. **1807** Wilkinson in Pike *Sources Mississ.* II. (1810) App. 24 We found..many tent-pins made of wood. **1875** [see *tent pitcher* in a]. **1945** *Beaver* Mar. 39/2 When a tent is struck.., the ring of stones which held it down lies there for years to come, and these *tent rings are found today scattered ever more widely..than the old igloos. **1958** *Even. Telegram* (St. John's, Newfoundland) 29 Apr. 13/3 My large tent needed more rocks to hold it down firmly than the usual tent ring supplied. **1940** F. Smythe *Adventures of Mountaineer* vii. 89 There was little else we could do save..unpack our *tent-sack... It was simply a large sack of jaconet waterproof and windproof material intended to shelter climbers in an emergency. **1972** D. Haston *In High Places* iv. 52 As we were sitting comfortably in our tent sacks there was suddenly a loud explosion and a great hissing all around. **1878** M. Long *Life Mason Long* iv. 60, I made the acquaintance of a man named McCoole, who was travelling with a small *tent show. **1935** [see shill *sb.*]. **1973** *Times Lit. Suppl.* 28 Dec. 1593/4 Her life of the tent show, the Black touring company, race labels and buffet flats. **1862** *Rebellion Record* V. II. 156 The desolated, hard-trodden ground, and a few *tent-stakes, remain to tell the story. **1923** H. Crane *Let.* 15 Feb. (1965) 123 *Broom*..has busted; N.Y. office closed last Saturday; March issue, the last, to be distributed from Berlin while the tent-stakes are being pulled up. **1956** H. Gold *Man who was not with It* (1965) i. 7 The Popcorn Man was throwing canvas over his machine and had it almost covered when a rube heaved a tent-stake. **1878** J. H. Beadle *Western Wilds* 103 Along the track west of it had sprung up five *tent-towns. **1923** H. Steele *Spirit of Iron* 108 He came in touch with all the vice, wretchedness and stark tragedy abounding in the tent-towns and construction camps. **1965** *Globe & Mail* (Toronto) 26 May 3/2 Near this town..there is a tent-town of marginal people and transients. **1963** *Better Camping* Mar.-Apr. 32/2 It is only in the last six years or so that the *tent trailer has grown from modest beginnings—little more than a bed on a trailer and just canvas cover enough to turn around in—to fold-out apartment-size dwellings. **1970** *Daily Tel.* 14 Nov. 9 Midway between tent and caravan..come the tent-trailers. **1884** Miller *Plant-n.*, **Tent-tree*, of Lord Howe's Island, *Pandanus Forsteri*. **1899** A. E. W. Mason *Miranda of Balcony* x. 139 The Arab..belonged to a douar, a *tent village. **1977** *N.Z. Herald* 8 Jan. 1-3/6 They also called for reinforcements for their tent village.

Hence **'tentful**, as many as fill a tent; **'tentwards** *adv.*, towards a tent; **'tentwise** *adv.*[1], in the manner or shape of a tent.

1897 *Daily News* 24 May 6/5 The whole *tentful of people rose and the gentlemen reverently uncovered. **1893** *Westm. Gaz.* 7 Oct. 2/1 Four weird figures tramping *tentwards after a long day abroad. **1530** Tindale *Exodus* Table Expound. Words, *Tabernacle*, an house made *tentwise, or as a pauelion. **1846** Mrs. Gore *Sk. Eng. Char.* (1852) 39 A genteel youth..whose straight, yellow hair is combed up, tent-wise, on the top of his head.

tent (tɛnt), *sb.*[2] Now *Sc.* and *north. dial.* Also 4-5 **tente**, (5 **teynt**). [Aphetic for attent and *entent*, intent: cf. tend *v.*[1], of which *tent* is practically a deriv., as *attent* of *attend*, *intent* of *intend*.]

1. Attention, heed, care; nearly always in the phrases †*give tent*, to give heed, pay attention (*obs.*), and *take tent*, to take heed, take care; with *to*, to pay attention to, take heed to; = attent *sb.* 1, 2, intent *sb.* 2.

a **1300** *Cursor M.* 661 Lok for-þi, þat ȝee tak tent þat ȝee ne brek mi commament. *Ibid.* 19464 A child hight saulus.. Tok tent to-quils to þair wede. *Ibid.* 19514 þar þe folk wit full assent Til his wordes gaf þair tent. *c* **1325** *Song of Mercy* 8 in *E.E.P.* (1862) 118 Of whuche, to on i toke gode tent. *c* **1330** R. Brunne *Chron. Wace* (Rolls) 7025 Þe kyng til hym gaf no tent. **1382** Wyclif *Ps.* lxxvii. 1 Taketh tente, my puple, to my lawe. —— *1 Tim.* iv. 1 In the laste tymes summen schulen departe fro the feith, ȝyuynge tent to spiritis of errour. **1388** —— *Ps.* xxxix. [xl.] 1 He ȝaf tent to me. *c* **1400** *Laud Troy Bk.* 4333 To theire schippis hadde thei no teynt. **1533** Gau *Richt Vay* (S.T.S.) 65 Tak tent that thow sine na mair. *a* **1637** B. Jonson *Underwoods, Eupheme* I. viii, The high parliament Of Heaven; where Seraphim take tent Of ordering all. **1728** Ramsay *Last Sp. Miser* xvii, I took good tent, That double pawns..Lay in my hands. **1816** Scott *Old Mort.* xliii, 'This is the way', said the little girl; 'follow me, gin ye please, sir, but tak tent to your feet'. **1855** Robinson *Whitby Gloss.* s.v., Mind and tak tent on 'em.

†**2.** Intent, purpose; = intent *sb.* 1, attent *sb.* 3. *Obs.*

a **1300** *Cursor M.* 14288 Bot mari was in a-noþer tent [*v.r.* entent] Wit hir lauerd to speke sco went. **1399** Langl. *Rich. Redeles* II. 97 Trouthe haþe determyned þe tente to þe ende. **14..** *Beryn* 126 For ethir-is þouȝt & tent was, othir to begile. *c* **1450** *St. Cuthbert* (Surtees) 18 þe autours of his tente he tellys.

tent (tɛnt), *sb.*[3] *Surg.* Also 4-7 **tente**, 6 **teynte**, 6-8 **taint**, 7 **taynt**. [a. F. *tente* (12th c. in Godef. *Compl.*), sb. f. *tenter*:—L. *temptāre*, *tentāre*; see tent *v.*[2]: cf. It. *tenta*, Sp. *tienta* a probe.]

†**1.** A probe. Also *fig.* *Obs.*

c **1375** *Cursor M.* 26638 (Fairf.) A tent þe wers to hit will reche Quen hit rotis for defaute of leche. **1606** Shaks. *Tr. & Cr.* II. ii. 16 Modest Doubt is cal'd..the tent that searches To' th' bottome of the worst. **1693** tr. *Blancard's Phys. Dict.* (ed. 2) s.v. *Tenta*, A Chyrurgeons Instrument, called Specillum, the vulgar call it *Tenta*, a Tent, from trying.

2. A roll or pledget, usually of soft absorbent material, often medicated, or sometimes of a medicinal substance, formerly much used to search and cleanse a wound, or to keep open or distend a wound, sore, or natural orifice.

c **1400** *Lanfranc's Cirurg.* 34, I heeld þe wounde open aldai wiþ a litil smal tent & a schort. *c* **1425** tr. *Arderne's Treat. Fistula* 34, I putte in tuo tentes or þre..in þe larger holes. **1547** Boorde *Brev. Health* Pref. 4 Let them be sure in serchynge of the depnes of woundes and fystules, and accordyng to the depnes to make the tentes. **1610** Markham *Masterp.* II. cxiii. 407 Hauing cleansed the soare by tying a taint of flaxe or fine linnen cloth. **1639** T. de Gray *Compl. Horsem.* 292 A linnen clowt rowled up in the fashion of a great taynt. **1753** Chambers *Cycl. Supp.*, *Tent*[*s*] in surgery ..are of service [1.] to convey medicines to the most inner recesses..of the wound 2. To prevent the Lips of the wound from uniting before it is healed at the bottom... Tents whose office is to enlarge..the mouth of any wound, or ulcer..are usually called sponge-tents. **1867** Harris *Dict. Med. Terminol.*, *Sponge Tent*, a tent made of prepared sponge. **1872** T. G. Thomas *Dis. Women* 78 Preparation of sea-tangle tents.

fig. *a* **1548** Hall *Chron.*, *Hen. V* 35 b, Now to finde a remedy for a mischief and a tent to stop a wounde, the Clergy..agreed to offre..a greate some of money. **1672** T. Jordan *Lond. Triumphant* 15 But yet our wounds have neither tent nor balm, We freeze in Fire, drown in a Calm.

†**3.** *transf.* (from the shape or appearance.) *Obs.*

1578 Lyte *Dodoens* VI. lvi. 730 After these tentes or catkens the leaues begin to showe.

†**4.** A paste which sets hard, used in setting precious stones: see quot. 1656. *Obs.*

[This may be a different word.]

1594 Plat *Jewell-ho.* III. 62 An excellent tent for a Diamond. Byrne Iuorie in a crusible..into a blacke powder, then take a little..thereof, and mingle it with a few drops of ..Oyle of Masticke, and in the setting of the stone you must haue care that it touch not the tent. **1647** R. Stapylton *Juvenal* Ep. Ded., Just as a pigmey should throw away a diamond bigger then himself, only because the tent it stood upon was black. **1656** Blount *Glossogr.* s.v., Jewellers call that Tent which they put under Table Diamonds when they set them in work, and is made of mastick and turpentine.

Hence **tentwise** *adv.*[2], in the way of a surgical tent or plug.

1639 T. de Gray *Compl. Horsem.* 272 A salve..which must be applyed eyther plaister-wise or taint-wise.

tent (tɛnt), *sb.*[4] Forms: 6 **tynt**, **tente**, **teyne**, 7 **tint**, 7- **tent**. [ad. Sp. *tinto* dark-coloured:—L. *tinctus*, pa. pple. of *tingĕre* to dye: see tinct, tinge. Cf. Sp. '*vino Tinto*, a blackish wine in Spaine' (Minsheu 1599).] A Spanish wine of a deep red colour, and of low alcoholic content. Also *tent wine*. (Often used as a sacramental wine.)

1542 Boorde *Dyetary* x. (1870) 255 Also these hote wynes, as..caprycke, tynt. **1580** Frampton *Dial. Yron & Steele* 159 Casting wine called Tente vpon burning yron. **1612** in *Halyburton's Ledger* (1867) 335 Sackes Canareis Malagas Maderais..Teyns and Allacants. *c* **1645** Howell *Lett.* (1650) II. lv. 74 The Vinteners make Tent (which is a Name for all Wines in Spain except white) to supply the place of it. **1748** *Anson's Voy.* II. x 246 Spanish wines, such as tent and sherry. **1881** *Med. Temp. Jrnl.* XLVIII. 199 Tent..is the least objectionable of intoxicating wines.

tent, *sb.*[5] ? *Obs.* [f. tent *v.*[3]; or shortened from tenter *sb.*[1]] A frame on which embroidery or tapestry is kept stretched while making; a stretching frame for various purposes.

1548 Elyot, *Tendicula*..a nette or snare to take byrdes or beastes in, also a teynter, and a tent that brotherers woorke on. **1688** R. Holme *Armoury* III. xxi. (Roxb.) 251/2 A long square of wood, made after the maner of an Embrautherers tent to slip up and down. *a* **1704** *Compl. Servant-Maid* (ed. 7) 62 To wash and starch Points. Take your Points and put them into a Tent, then lay your Tent upon a Table. **1741** Lady Pomfret *Lett.* (1805) III. 113 The working of the tapestry, which is done in a different manner.., the tent being set edgewise.

†**tent**, *a.* *Sc. Obs. rare.* [Aphetic f. attent or intent *a.*] Attent, watchful; intent.

1789 Davidson *Seasons* 77 Up cam Tam Tell an' Sutor Sam..As tent upo' the aftergame, As hounds loos'd frae a kennel. *Ibid.* 90 Up started Rosy Dougan, As tent as if she had been a puss.

tent, *v.*[1] Now *Sc.* and *north. dial.* [Closely related to, and app. formed from, tent *sb.*[2]: perh. short for *take tent*; but cf. also tend *v.*[1]]

†**1.** *intr.* To give or pay attention, to 'take tent'; to attend, give heed, take notice. Const. *to*, *unto*, *till*; = tend *v.*[1] 1, 2. *Obs.*

a **1300** *Cursor M.* 16910 Armed knightes þar þai left þat to þe tumb suld tent. *Ibid.* 19034 þai..desseli bath late and are War tentand to þe apostels lare. *c* **1330** R. Brunne *Chron.* (1810) 91 þe Kyng was in affray, he might not tent þerto. *c* **1380** Wyclif *Serm.* Sel. Wks. II. 294 þei tenten neiþer to bodi ne to soule. *a* **1425** *Cursor M.* 3619 (Trin.) His modir tent [*Cott. & Gött.* tok tent] to ysaac And herde þo wordis þat he spac. *c* **1475** *Golagros & Gaw.* 342, I rede ye tent treuly to my teching. **1530** Palsgr. 754/2, I tente to my busynesse, I take hede to the thinges I have in hande. **1572** *Satir. Poems Reform.* xxxviii. 99 Tent to ȝoursellis.

†**b.** Const. *to* with *inf.* *Obs.*

a **1300** *Cursor M.* 21167 Symon zelote..His lauerd al to serue he tent. **1357** *Lay Folks Catech.* (MS. T.) 194 Noght than for to tent to tary with the world, Ne lyue in lykyng ne lust. *c* **1410** Love *Bonavent. Mirr.* xxxvi. (1908) 159 Onely tentinge to plese god.

c. *trans.* To give or pay mental attention to; to attend to, give heed to, take notice of (a person, his words, a matter); cf. tend *v.*[1] 1 b.

c **1330** R. Brunne *Chron. Wace* (Rolls) 13630 þey ne roughte where þey ȝede Ne nought rewarded how [*v.r.* no tentid not] þey were in drede. **13..** *E.E. Allit. P.* B. 935 þay token his as-tyt & tented hit lyttel. *Ibid.* C. 59 Wyl ȝe tary a lyttel tyme & tent me a whyle. *c* **1400** *Destr. Troy* 10237 He blamyt full bitturly þan his blithe qwene, þat euer he tentit hir tale. **1724** Ramsay *Gentle Sheph.*, *To Burchet* viii, Yet, tent a poet's zealous prayer. **1785** Burns *Death & Dr. Hornbook* ix, Ye're maybe come to stap my breath; But tent me, billie; I red ye weel, tak care o' skaith, See, there's a gully [= big knife]!

2. To attend to the safety and needs of, to take or have charge and care of; to look after, see to, mind, attend to, tend (a person, flock, plant, machine, etc.). Now *dial.* esp. *Sc.*

13.. *E.E. Allit. P.* B. 676 þis ilke wyȝ þat wendez with oure lorde, For to tent hym with tale & teche hym þe gate. *c* **1430** *Syr Gener.* 2832 Felows he had the toure to tent Which were redie at his comaundment. *c* **1450** *Bk. Curtasye* 430 in *Babees Bk.* 312 The lordys chambur, tho wadrop to, þo vssher of chambur schalle tent þo two. **1557** in Sharp *Cov. Myst.* (1825) 73 Payd for tyntyng the yerthe-quake, iiij d. **1641** Best *Farm. Bks.* (Surtees) 120 After that [he] setteth a boy or girle to tente them. **1686** G. Stuart *Joco-Ser. Disc.* 64 When Foxes preach tent weel your Geese. **1728** Ramsay *Tea-t. Misc.*, *There's my Thumb* iii, Tenting my flocks lest they should wander. **1789** Burns *Capt. Grose* i, If there's a hole in a' your coats, I rede you tent it. **1844** G. Dodd *Textile Manuf.* iv. 125 This 'plucker' is generally attended or 'tented', to use a factory phrase, by a boy. **1859** *Autobiog. Beggar Boy* 51, I soon got engaged to tent a herd of oxen for the day.

3. To take (ocular) notice of, observe, watch. *Sc.*

1721 Ramsay *Prospect of Plenty* 3 Tent how the Calidonians, lang supine, Begin, mair wise, to open baith their een. **1875** W. Walsh *Poet. & Pr. Wks.* 1 When young you heedless tent the sky. **1888** A. Reid *Sangs Heatherland* (1894) 86 Tent her when she hides her face.

4. To be careful, to beware (with clause). *Sc.*

1737 Ramsay *Scots Prov.* xxxiv. §88 Tent wha ye take by the hand. **1789** *Sheph. Wedding* (ed. 2) 15 (E.D.D.) Tent what you say!

5. To take care to prevent or hinder (a person) *from* doing something. *north. dial.*

1781 Hutton *Tour Caves* (ed. 2) Gloss., *Tent*, to watch or guard from doing a thing. **1863** Mrs. Toogood *Yorks. Dial.* s.v., He was going into toon but his father tented him. **1868** *Accrington Times* 16 May (E.D.D.) Tent 'em fro' breyking aot o' th' ranks. **1874** *Sheffield Indep.* (ibid.), He thinks to come here, but I'll tent him [i.e. take care that he does not].

6. To watch for and scare away (birds); also, to guard (corn, seed, etc.) from birds. *north. dial.*

1858 Bailey *Age* 73 I'd give you the congenial occupation Of scaring crows, and 'tenting' vegetation. **1877** *N.W. Linc. Gloss.*, *Tent*...to scare birds from corn. **1889** *Ibid.* (ed. 2), Tent is used either of the things watched over, or the things guarded against. 'Oor Bill's tentin' to'nup-seäd e' th' Beck-boddoms. When I was a lad I spent moäst o' my time tentin' craws an' stock-duvs.'

Hence **'tented** *ppl. a.*, **'tenting** *vbl. sb.*[2] and *ppl. a.*; **tenting-lad** *dial.*, a lad or boy employed to watch the crops and scare birds. Also combinations of the verb-stem, as **tent-boy** = *tenting-lad*.

c **1645** T. Tully *Siege of Carlisle* (1840) 14 Daily skirmishes..aboute yᵉ fetching in of Cattell, or yᵉ tenting yᵐ in their places of pastures. **1721** Ramsay *Prospect of Plenty* 37 The tempting bait, and tented string, Beguile the cod, the sea-cat, tusk, and ling. **1877** *N.W. Linc. Gloss.*, *Tenter*, *Tenting-lad*, a boy who scares birds from corn. **1888** L. Wilson in J. Brown *Lit. Laureat.* (1890) 63 Here seated in his rustic grace, The 'tent' boy blew his horn.

†**tent**, *v.*[2] *Obs.* [a. F. *tent-er* = Sp. *tentar*, It. *tentare*:—L. *temptāre* to tempt, in med.L. (after Romanic langs.) *tentāre*.] A variant of tempt, occasional down to 16th c. Hence †**tenting** *vbl. sb.*[3]

a **1225** *Ancr. R.* 228 Nu an oðer elne ouh muchel urouren ou, hwon ȝe beoð itented... God..is treowe: nul he neuer þolien þet te deouel tempti us ouer þet he isihð wel þet we muwen iðolien. *Ibid.* 230 Ure Louerd, hwon he iðoleð þet we beoð itented, he plaieð mid us. *c* **1440** *York Myst.* xxviii. 243 Euelle spiritis is neghand full nere, That will ȝou tarie at þis tyme with his tentyng. *a* **1555** Bp. Gardiner in Foxe *A. & M.* (1563) 738, I know your Grace only tenteth me with such reasones.

†**tent**, *v.*[3] *Obs.* Also 5 **tente**, **teynt**. [Connected with L. *tendĕre*, *tent-um*, F. *tendre* to stretch; also with tent *sb.*[5], tenter *sb.*[1]; but exact history not evidenced.] Hence †**tenting** *vbl. sb.*[4]

1. *trans.* To stretch (cloth) on tenters: = tenter *v.* 1.

1377 Langl. *P. Pl.* B. xv. 447 Cloth..is nouȝt comly to were Tyl it is fulled vnder fote..Ytouked, and ytented [*v.r.* y-teynted] & vnder tailloures hande. *c* **1440** *Promp. Parv.* 489/1 Tente clothe, *extendo*, *lacinio*. **1463-4** *Rolls of Parlt.* V. 501/1 Brode clote..after almanere rakkyng streynyng or teyntyng therof.

2. (?) To embroider in a tent or frame.

1507 *Acc. Ld. High Treas. Scot.* IV. 79 Payit to the broudstar for half ane hank gold threid for tenting, and gret papir for the Kingis doublat.

tent (tɛnt), *v.*[4] *arch.* [app. f. tent *sb.*[3]; but cf. F. *tenter* in obs. sense (= *sonder*) to try the depth of, to sound; = med.L. *tentāre* to try.]

†**a.** *trans.* To probe (*obs.*). **b.** To treat by means of a tent; to apply a tent to (a wound, etc., also to a person); to distend or plug with a tent. Also *fig.* Hence **'tenting** *vbl. sb.*[5]

1597 A. M. tr. *Guillemeau's Fr. Chirurg.* 51/2 Ether in tenting of the wounde, by incisione, by cauterisation. **1612** Webster *White Devil* v. ii, Search my wound deeper; tent it with the steel That made it. **1639** Shirley *Maid's Rev.* III. vi, I have a sword dares tent a wound as far As any. **1685**

CROWNE *Sir C. Nice* IV. Dram. Wks. 1874 III. 328 Yes, if you 'noint it presently with a good dish o' jelly-broth, and tent it with a bone o' roast beef. **1695** tr. *Colbatch's New Lt. Chirurg. Put out* 32 Stitched them up.. for fear they should have been kept open by tenting. **1828** SCOTT *F.M. Perth* vii, Methinks I can tent this wound, and treat it with emollients.

†**tent**, *v.*⁵ *Obs. rare.* [var. form of TEND *v.*², perh. on analogy of TEND *v.*¹ and TENT *v.*¹]

1. *trans. Law.* To offer, proffer: = TEND *v.*² 5, TENDER *v.*¹ 1.

1459 *Rolls of Parlt.* V. 371/1 An enquest takyn aforne his Eschetour.. the which Offices John Fastolf Knyght, and othir, tentid to traverse, and by that meane hadd the said Manere. **1512** *Act 4 Hen. VIII*, c. 18 §24 All Traverses peticions monstrance de droit.. to be tentyd or sued by eny persone or persones.

2. *intr.* To direct itself, be directed (*to* some end); = TEND *v.*² 2.

1551 UDALL, etc. *Erasm. Par. Mark* xii. 184 This deceiptful propheme tented [*ed.* 1548 tended] to this end, that if he had geuen sentence for the phariseis, then should he haue bene accused of the Herodians for an authour of rebellion, or insurreccion agaynst the Emperour.

tent (tɛnt), *v.*⁶ [f. TENT *sb.*¹: a number of unconnected uses.]

1. a. *intr.* To abide or live in a tent; to encamp; *spec.* of travelling circus folk. Also ***to tent it.***

1856 KANE *2nd Grinnell Exp.* I. xxvii. 357 We will be gone for some days probably, tenting it in the open air. **1867** LADY HERBERT *Cradle L.* 154 Our travellers tented on a small level sward just outside the Convent-gates. **1875** T. FROST *Circus Life* xvii. 292 During the summer months they 'tented', and in the winter erected temporary wooden buildings in populous towns. **1881** MRS. HOLMAN-HUNT *Childr. Jerus.* 189 Do you think we shall ever go tenting again, mother? **1893** *Scribner's Mag.* June 703/2 The river crew is tenting out and clearing the stream. **1931** S. MCKECHNIE *Pop. Entertainments* viii. 209 The circus.. was purchased by Frederick and Edward, who tented in the summer and spent the winter in.. towns. **1952** N. STREATFEILD *Aunt Clara* 111 They had been tenting with their mother.

b. *fig.* To dwell temporarily; to sojourn, to tabernacle; to have one's abode; of a thing: to have its seat, 'reside'.

1607 SHAKS. *Cor.* III. ii. 116 The smiles of Knaues Tent in my cheekes, and Schoole-boyes Teares take vp The Glasses of my sight. **1751** R. SHIRRA in *Rem.* (1850) 52 He tented or tabernacled in flesh among us. **1871** MACDUFF *Mem. Patmos* xxii. 305 The Word came and dwelt (or lit. 'tented') among us. **1893** E. G. HIRSCH in Barrows *Parl. Relig.* II. 1304 Wherever man may tent, there also will curve upward the burning incense of his sacrifice.

2. *trans.* To cover or canopy as with a tent.

1838 MRS. BROWNING *Seraphim* II. 604 The heavy darkness which doth tent the sky Floats backward as by a sudden wind. **1883** LD. R. GOWER *My Remin.* I. xx. 410 A garden flanked by colonnades and covered passages had been tented in.

3. To accommodate, put up, or lodge in tents. Also *fig.*

1863 LD. LYTTON *Ring Amasis* II. 81 Powers we can neither summon nor dismiss, are camped upon the brain and tented in the veins of men. **1869** E. A. PARKES *Pract. Hygiene* (ed. 3) 481 The men should be tented, the tents should be well ventilated. **1882** ARMSTRONG *Garland fr. Greece, Orithyia* 8, I have tented the nymphs of the rills in pavilions of frozen spray. **1898** *Daily News* 9 Mar. 3/2 All officers are tented in the same manner as the men.

†**4.** To pitch or spread (a tent); to put up, fix up, stretch, as a tent or its canvas. *Obs.*

1553 *Douglas's Æneis* VIII. x. 23 That from the top of the hillys hyght The army all thai mycht se at a sight With tentis tentit [*ed. Small*, stentit] strekand to the plane. **1634** W. WOOD *New Eng. Prosp.* I. ii. (1865) 7 By good fires they sleepe as well and quietly (having their mayne sayle tented at their backes, to shelter them from the winde) as if they were at home.

5. To arrange in a shape suggesting a tent; *esp.*, with the fingers as obj., = STEEPLE *v.* 4.

1966 D. BAGLEY *Wyatt's Hurricane* ii. 60 He tented his fingers and regarded Wyatt closely. **1977** 'E. MCBAIN' *Long Time no See* xi. 182 She herself sat on the sofa.. pulling her legs up under her Indian-fashion, the caftan tented over her knees. **1980** *TWA Ambassador* Oct. 57/2 Gatmun tented the fat sausages of his fingers.

tent, obs. and dial. form of TENTH.

tentability (tɛntəˈbɪlɪtɪ). *rare.* [f. Lat. type **tentābil-is*, OF. *tentable* liable to be tempted (*c* 1340 in Godef.), or from Eng. **tentable* for TEMPTABLE: see -BILITY.] = TEMPTABILITY.

1844 W. H. MILL *Serm. Tempt. Christ* ii. 39 The tentability of the Incarnate Lord. **1860** ELLICOTT *Life our Lord* iii. 112 *note*, In estimating the nature of our Lord's tentability. **1863** A. BARRY in *Smith's Dict. Bible* III. 1148/2 It is this tentability of man, even in his original nature, which is represented in Scripture as giving scope to the evil action of Satan.

tentable (ˈtɛntəb(ə)l), *a.* [f. med.L. *tentāre* for *temptāre* to try, or f. TENT *v.*⁴ to probe, etc. + -ABLE.] Liable to be probed, 'picked', or 'tried': cf. TENTATION 2 a.

1862 *Catal. Internat. Exhib.* II. XXXI. 10 Locks with crypted guards, not tentable by instrument or true key.

tentacle (ˈtɛntək(ə)l). [ad. mod.L. TENTACULUM.] **a.** *Zool.* A slender flexible process in animals, esp. invertebrates, serving as an organ of touch or feeling; = FEELER 3, PALP.

1762 DU PONT in *Phil. Trans.* LIII. 58 The fingers, or tentacles, end in a deep blue. **1835** KIRBY *Hab. & Inst. Anim.* I. v. 181 An infinity of cells.. from which the tentacles issue to collect their food. **1857** WOOD *Com. Obj. Seashore* v. 53 On the arms, legs, feet, or tentacles of the cuttles, are arranged rows of suckers. **1866** TATE *Brit. Mollusks* iii. 47 The head [of a snail or slug] bears two long slender tentacles or horns. **1868** OWEN *Vertebr. Anim.* I. v. 411 Tentacles depend from the rostral prolongation of the Sturgeon, and the mandibular symphysis of the Cod.

b. *Bot.* Applied to a sensitive filament, as the viscous gland-tipped leaf-hairs of the Sundew.

1875 DARWIN *Insectiv. Pl.* i. 5 A tentacle consists of a thin, straight, hair-like pedicel carrying a gland on the summit. **1879** LUBBOCK *Sci. Lect.* i. 4 In our Common Sundew.. the rounded leaves are covered with glutinous glandular hairs or tentacles.

c. *fig.* = FEELER 2 b.

1847 DE QUINCEY *Secret Societies* Wks. VI. 235 This plot .. stretched its horrid fangs, and threw out its forerunning feelers and *tentacles*, into many nations. **1883** H. DRUMMOND *Nat. Law in Spir. W.* viii. (ed. 2) 300 The soul .., waving its tentacles piteously in the empty air, feeling after God if so be that it may find Him. **1895** MAHAFFY *Empire Ptolemies* x, Prepared to fall easily into the tentacles of the all-devouring Republic [Rome]. **1901** *Scotsman* 7 Mar. 7/5 One of De Wet's tentacles had been stretched out to obscure the approach of Nesbitt's horse.

d. *attrib.* and *Comb.*, as ***tentacle-like*** adj.; **tentacle-feeder**, an invertebrate animal possessing tentacles to trap its food; **tentacle-sheath**, the sheath-like structure surrounding the base of the tentacles of many molluscs.

1835–6 *Todd's Cycl. Anat.* I. 683/2 Their tentacle-like arms [i.e. of Cirripeds] resemble the antennae of lobsters. **1953** J. S. HUXLEY *Evolution in Action* iii. 73 Tentacle-feeders may either float free in the water or be attached to the bottom. **1963** R. P. DALES *Annelids* 15 The more familiar tentacle-feeders include the terebellids, which have a mass of extensile tentacles.

Hence **tentacled** (ˈtɛntək(ə)ld) *a.*, furnished with or having tentacles.

1857 GOSSE *Omphalos* 119 Every individual cell,.. inhabited by its tentacled Hydra, has.. budded out from a branch.

tentacular (tɛnˈtækjʊlə(r)), *a.* [f. mod.L. TENTACULUM + -AR¹.] Of, pertaining to, or of the nature of a tentacle or tentacles.

1828 STARK *Elem. Nat. Hist.* II. 117 With two conical perforated and tentacular papillæ at its upper extremity. **1870** ROLLESTON *Anim. Life* Introd. 84 The mouth is surrounded by a cartilaginous ring, carrying anteriorly tentacular outgrowths.

tentaculate (tɛnˈtækjʊlət), *a.* (*sb.*) *Zool.* [f. as prec. + -ATE².]

1. Furnished with tentacles or tentaculiform appendages; rarely = TENTACULIFORM.

1846 DANA *Zooph.* (1848) 320 Polyps obsolescently tentaculate. **1877** HUXLEY *Anat. Inv. Anim.* ii. 109 In the Acinetae, the tentaculate stage is the more permanent, the ciliated stage transitory.

2. Of or pertaining to the *Tentaculata*, or stalked Echinoderms. **b.** *sb.* A member of the Tentaculata; a pelmatozoan.

tentaculated (tɛnˈtækjʊleɪtɪd), *a. Zool.* [f. as prec. + -ED¹.] = prec. 1.

1804 SHAW *Gen. Zool.* V. II. 359 *Tentaculated Shark*... Shark with serrated snout tentaculated on each side. **1880** BASTIAN *Brain* iii. 58 Sedentary forms of life, like the Hydra, the Sea-anemone, or some of the tentaculated worms.

tentacule (ˈtɛntəkjuːl). *Zool.* [a. F. *tentacule*, ad. mod.L. TENTACULUM: see -CULE.] = TENTACLE. Also in *Comb.* as ***tentacule-like*** adj.

1835–6 *Todd's Cycl. Anat.* I. 37/1 Very extensile tentacule-like cirri. **1851** RICHARDSON *Geol.* viii. (1855) 216 The mouth.. is surrounded with numerous filaments or tentacules.. furnished with vibratile cilia. **1870** P. M. DUNCAN *Transform. Insects* (1882) 77 It suddenly pokes out a spotted tentacule.

tentaculi- (tɛnˈtækjʊlɪ). Combining form of mod.L. TENTACULUM, used in zoological terms. **tenˌtaculiˈbranchiate** [L. *branchiæ* gills], *a.* of or pertaining to the *Tentaculibranchia*, i.e. the *Bryozoa* or *Polyzoa*, regarded (by Lankester 1877) as a class of the branch *Lipocephala* of the phylum *Mollusca*; *sb.* a member of this class. **tenˈtaculiˌcyst** = TENTACULOCYST; hence **tenˌtaculiˈcystic** *a.* **tenˈtaculiform** *a.*, having the form or appearance of a tentacle. **tentacuˈligerous** *a.* [-GEROUS], = next.

1902 *Cassell's Encycl. Dict., Suppl.*, *Tentaculibranchiate. **1891** *Cent. Dict.*, *Tentaculicyst. **1837** *Penny Cycl.* IX. 258/1 It.. gives exit to *tentaculiform cirrhi. **1880** W. S. KENT *Infusoria* I. 396 A prolonged tentaculiform appendage. **1877** HUXLEY *Anat. Inv. Anim.* iii. 174, m. *tentaculigerous canal.

tenˌtacuˈliferous, *a.* [f. mod.L. TENTACULUM + -(I)FEROUS.] Bearing tentacles: said of an animal or organ; *spec.* of or pertaining to the *Tentaculifera* or *Acinetaria*, a division of the Plegepod Protozoa; sometimes, pertaining to the *Tentaculifera* or *Glossophora*, among Mollusca.

1830 J. E. GRAY in *Encycl. Metrop.* (1845) XXI. 592/1 Its edge divided into four or eight diverging, tentaculiferous lobes. **1835** KIRBY *Hab. & Inst Anim.* I. v. 167 The tentaculiferous mouths of the polypes. **1880** W. S. KENT (*title*) A Manual of the Infusoria: including a Description of all known Flagellate, Ciliate, and Tentaculiferous Protozoa. **1883** —— in *Nature* 8 Mar. 433/1 In other tentaculiferous animals, such as a sea-anemone, tubiculous annelid, or cuttlefish. **1885** E. R. LANKESTER in *Encycl. Brit.* XIX. 431/2 The tentaculiferous 'arms' of the Brachiopoda.

tentaculite (tɛnˈtækjʊlaɪt). *Palæont.* [ad. mod.L. *Tentăculītēs*: see TENTACULUM and -ITE¹ 2 a.] A fossil mollusc of the genus *Tentaculites* or family *Tentaculitidæ* (thought by some to be allied to the Pteropods) of which the conical usually ringed shells abound in the Middle Devonian strata.

tentaculite beds, strata of the Ilfracombe group of Middle Devonian age, characterized by the abundance of *Tentaculites scalaris.* ***tentaculite limestone***, in the New York Geological Survey, a subdivision of the Water-lime group of Upper Silurian strata, similarly characterized.

1839 MURCHISON *Silur. Syst.* I. 628. **1863** DANA *Man. Geol.* 252.

tentaculocyst (tɛnˈtækjʊləʊˌsɪst). *Zool.* [f. TENTACULUM + Gr. κύστ-ις bladder, CYST.] One of the vesicular or cystic tentacles of a hydrozoan, representing a reduced and modified tentacle: see quots. Also TENTACULICYST.

1880 E. R. LANKESTER in *Nature* 4 Mar. 414/1 What I have elsewhere termed 'tentaculocysts', modified tentacles which act as auditory organs and have often eye-spots on them as well. **1881** —— in *Encycl. Brit.* XII. 555/2 Combined visual and auditory organs in the form of modified tentacles (tentaculocysts).

tentaculoid (tɛnˈtækjʊlɔɪd). *Biol.* [f. next + -OID.] A tentaculiform process in some diatoms.

1892 T. H. BUFFHAM in *Jrnl. Quekett Micr. Club* July 28 From the extremities of the minor axis there are mammiform protuberances through which pass long processes of the same substance [investing periglœa]: these we might call *tentaculoids*.

‖**tentaculum** (tɛnˈtækjʊləm). Pl. **-a.** [mod. L. *tentăcul-um*, f. *tentā-re* = *temptāre* to feel, try; cf. TENTACLE, TENTACULE, and see -CULE.] A feeler; = TENTACLE.

1752 J. HILL *Hist. Anim.* 100 The upper lip is prominent beyond the rest of the mouth, and has two tentacula. **1804** SHAW *Gen. Zool.* V. II. 360 From each side springs a long and flexible tentaculum or feeler, of a flattened shape. **1880** BASTIAN *Brain* iv. 71 This ganglion receives branches from the tentacula guarding the orifice of the oral funnel.

fig. **1867** BAGEHOT *Eng. Constit.* ix. (1882) 275 The political characteristic of the early Greeks, and of the early Romans, too, is that out of the *tentacula* of a monarchy they developed the organs of a republic. **1893** MCCARTHY *Dictator* xxiv, He had seen only too clearly which way her love was stretching its tentacula.

tentage (ˈtɛntɪdʒ). [f. TENT *sb.*¹ + -AGE.] Equipment of tents, tent accommodation.

1603 DRAYTON *Bar. Wars* II. xv, Upon the Mount the King his Tentage fixt. **1870** *Daily News* 27 July 5 Each mess was complete for all purposes of camping and tentage. **1905** 'L. HOPE' *Indian Love* 20 No more the rugged road of Khorasan, The scanty food and tentage of the past! **1948** *Sporting Mirror* 21 May 13/3 (Advt.), Every type of Marquee, tentage and camping equipment. **1978** *B.S.I. News* July 6/1 It is considered unreasonable to deal with the flammability of tentage in isolation from other important features such as resistance to water penetration.

‖**tentamen** (tɛnˈteɪmən). Pl. **tentamina** (-ˈæmɪnə). [L. *tentāmen*, f. *tentāre* = *temptāre* to try: see TEMPT.] An attempt, trial, experiment.

1673 MARVELL *Reh. Transp.* II. 284 After this Tentamen of your veracity you tax me for saying, ''Tis demonstrable [etc.]'. **1736** CHESTERF. in *Fog's Jrnl.* No. 376 An essay or tentamen to some greater design. **1863** N. W. SENIOR *Biog. Sk.* 387 [Bacon's Essays] were intended,.. as the word *essay* in its original acceptation expresses, to be *tentamina*; not finished treatises, but sketches, to be filled up by the reader.

tentar, obs. form of TENTER *sb.*¹

tentation (tɛnˈteɪʃən). [ad. L. *tentātiōn-em*, late form (after Romanic) of *temptātiōn-em*, n. of action from *temptāre* (*tentāre*) to try, TEMPT.]

1. Obsolete form of TEMPTATION, q.v.: sometimes specially expressing experimental trial, as distinct from enticement to evil.

2. *techn.* A mode of working or adjusting by trial or experiment.

a. '(*Locksmithing.*) A mode of picking locks in which the bolt is pressed backward constantly, and the tumblers released one by one from the stud.'

b. '(*Compass-adjusting.*) Professor Airy's mode of adjusting compasses in iron ships, in which boxes of iron chain and magnets are experimentally placed and shifted.. until the disturbing influence of the iron hull is neutralized' (Knight *Dict. Mech.* 1877 s.v.).

tentative (ˈtɛntətɪv), *a.* and *sb.* [ad. med.L. *tentātīvus* adj. (*tentātīva* sb. in Schol.L.), f. *tentāt-*, ppl. stem of *tentāre* for *temptāre* to try: see TEMPT *v.* and -IVE. So F. *tentative* sb. (16th

c. in Godef. *Compl.*), examination, attempt; also as adj., experimental (*obs.*).]

A. *adj.* Of the nature of an experiment, trial, or attempt; made or done provisionally as an experiment; experimental.

1588 [implied in TENTATIVELY]. **1626** BP. HALL *Contempl., O.T.* XX. iii, Falshood, though it be but tentative, is neither needed nor approved by the God of truth. **1768** JOHNSON *Pref. to Shaks.* Wks. IX. 240 Works tentative and experimental must be estimated by their proportion to the general and collective ability of man. **1851** D. WILSON *Preh. Ann.* (1863) II. IV. ii. 241 The interpretations must therefore be regarded as tentative. **1874** GREEN *Short Hist.* vii. §3. 364 A policy of this limited, practical, tentative order was.. best suited to the England of her day.

B. *sb.* Something done as an experiment or trial; an essay, an attempt; †a hostile attempt (*obs.*).

1632 J. HAYWARD tr. *Biondi's Eromena* 175 They had no time to get out.. any tentative of theirs serving them to no purpose, for that the citie was walled round about. **1687** RYCAUT *Hist. Turks* II. 321 He was going to make a tentative upon Palotta, a place of good strength. **1692** TEMPLE *Mem.* Wks. 1731 I. 431 They tried some little Tentatives upon us, whether we would be content to leave out all Mention of his Majesty's Mediation, as well as that of the Pope's? **1898** *Pop. Sci. Monthly* Sept. 609 Tentatives were made in both directions.

b. Trying, experimenting; experimentation.

1865 GROTE *Plato* I. xvii. 293 A process, more or less tedious, of tentative and groping.

tentatively ('tɛntətɪvlɪ), *adv.* [f. TENTATIVE *a.* + -LY².] In a tentative manner; by way of trial or experiment; experimentally.

1588 J. HARVEY *Disc. Probl.* 7 But to put the case, and.. to proceede tentatiuely, and discoursiuely, as the foresaid schoolemen vse to call it. **1637** JACKSON *3rd Serm. Jer. xxvi. 19* Wks. 1844 VI. 95 He said it solemnly and publicly, not tentatively or by way of trial only. **1874** GREEN *Short Hist.* iv. §2. 170 It was only slowly and tentatively that this principle was applied.

'tentativeness. [f. as prec. + -NESS.] The quality of being tentative; experimental character.

1861 DR. WOODHAM WEBB in *Med. Times* 18 May 526/1 In Hospital work especially, we want the steadying influence of age.. as well as the impetuous tentativeness of youth. **1894** *Athenæum* 6 Jan. 11/2 It only produces an appearance of uncertainty and tentativeness.

†**'tentatory,** *a. Obs. rare*⁻¹. [f. L. *tentāt-*, ppl. stem of *tentāre* = *temptāre* to try: see TEMPT *v.* and -ORY².] = TENTATIVE *a.*

a **1624** BP. M. SMITH *Serm.* (1632) 27 The question is tentatory, (will you also go away?) I haue deserued better of you.

'tent-'bed. [f. TENT *sb.*¹ + BED *sb.*] **a.** A small and low bed used in a tent; a camp bed. **b.** A bed having an arched canopy and covered sides. Hence **tent-bedstead.**

1752 H. WALPOLE *Lett.* (1846) II. 432 Offered her a tent-bed, for fear of bugs in the inns. **1802** ANNA SEWARD *Lett.* (1811) VI. 9 His daughter could be constantly with him, and sleep in a tent-bed in his apartment. **1815** SCOTT *Guy M.* xliv, One of the bed-posts of a sort of tent-bed was broken down. **1827** ROBERTS *Voy. Centr. Amer.* 231 [I found him lying] in an English tent-bed. **1838** DICKENS *Nich. Nick.* xi, In the other stood an old tent bed-stead.

†**'tentbob,** erron. form of ***taint-bob**: see TAINT *sb.* C. 3. *Obs.*

1696 AUBREY *Misc.* (1857) 138 The little red spider, called a tentbob (not so big as a great pins head).

tent-boy: see TENT *v.*¹

tent-door ('tɛnt'dɔə(r)). The entrance or opening of a tent.

1535 COVERDALE *Gen.* xviii. 1 He sat in his tent dore in the heate of yᵉ daie. **1725** DE FOE *Voy. round World* (1840) 336 Looking out at their tent-door. **1816** KEATINGE *Trav.* (1817) I. 205 [They] seat themselves cross-legged,.. before the Bassa's tent-door. **1867** LADY HERBERT *Cradle L.* v. 152 There are still women.. preparing the fatted kid at the open tent-door.

tented ('tɛntɪd), *a.* [f. TENT *sb.*¹ and *v.*⁶]

1. a. Of a place: Covered with or full of tents.

1604 SHAKS. *Oth.* I. iii. 85 These Armes of mine.. haue vs'd Their deerest action, in the Tented Field. **1725** POPE *Odyss.* IV. 584 Fast by the deep, Along the tented shore. **1773** WHEELER in *Gentl. Mag.* XLIII. 343/1 On Poictou's tented plains by valour won. **1832** LONGF. *Coplas de Manrique* lx, In tented field and bloody fray.

b. Of an encampment: consisting of tents.

1872 *Rep. Indian Affairs 1871* (U.S.) 261 Urah.. had collected some of the chiefs and headmen of the tribe to receive me in their tented camp. **1955** *Times* 25 May 13/5 The cost of their fares.. and their five months' stay in a tented camp in Cyprus will be about £300 each. **1982** *Listener* 23 and 30 Dec. 4/1 On a gentle rise.. there is the tented city for the RAF Phantom and Harrier squadrons.

2. a. Formed or shaped like a tent or pavilion; made into a tent-like structure.

1747 COLLINS *Ode on Poet. Charac.* 26 He, who call'd with thought to birth Yon tented sky, this laughing earth. **1825** SCOTT *Talism.* vi, Weapons.. were scattered about the tented apartment, or disposed upon the pillars which supported it. **1839** BAILEY *Festus* xix. (1852) 296 High as the tented mountains of the earth.

b. Having the wings when at rest meeting in a ridge over the back.

1849 HELPS *Friends in C.* II. 187 The tented moth said suddenly to me with a clear crisp voice.

3. a. Of persons: Lodged in, or furnished with, a tent or tents. Also *fig.*

1811 WORDSW. *Epist. to Sir G. H. Beaumont* 100 Wastes where now the tented Arabs dwell. **1902** SIR E. ARNOLD *Nativity* in *Delineator* Dec. 575 Grander than stricken fields and tented armies.

b. Of activities, etc.: held in or taking place in a tent or tents.

1898 N. E. JONES *Squirrel Hunters of Ohio* 131 Protracted, tented, or camp-meetings increased,.. becoming very popular with preachers and people. **1971** *Morning Star* 22 June 2/5 The percentage of people taking tented holidays in Britain has gone up by 50 per cent since 1965. **1976** J. WAINWRIGHT *Bastard* iii. 48 A circus was visiting a neighbouring town. One of the hand-to-mouth, tented circuses. **1976** *Time* 20 Dec. 31/1 Circus Vargas, billed as the world's largest tented show.

tenter ('tɛntə(r)), *sb.*¹ Forms: 4–5 teyntur, 5 tayntour, tentowre, 5–6 tentour, 5–7 taynter, teynter, tenture, 5–8 tentor, 6 teynto(u)r, -tree, tentar, 6–7 tainter, teinter, -or, 6– tenter. [The varieties of the suffix make the exact origin somewhat obscure: the forms in *-ur, -our, -or, -er, -ar,* point to an AF. or OF. **tentour*, L. **tentōr-em* stretcher, agent-n. from *tend-ĕre* to stretch, which suits the sense; but neither the OF. nor the L. word is known in the sense 'tenter'.

The rare form *tenture* is equated by Promp. Parv. with L. *tentūra*, but this ought to mean the process of stretching or its product: cf. F. *tenture* action of stretching, also tapestry hangings; which does not agree with the sense of 'stretching instrument or apparatus'. On the other hand, if the word were merely an Eng. agent-n. from TENT *v.*³, it would be difficult to account for the various forms of the ending. The forms in *teynt-, taynt-, teint-, taint-* also offer difficulty, suggesting some association with F. *teint* dye.]

1. A wooden framework on which cloth is stretched after being milled, so that it may set or dry evenly and without shrinking. Also † *a pair of tenters* (obs. rare) and in pl. form *tenters.*

Formerly tenters of the length of a web of cloth stood in rows in the open air in *tenter-fields* or *grounds*, and were a prominent feature in cloth-manufacturing districts; but the process of drying and stretching is now generally done much more rapidly in *tenter-houses* by *tenter-* or *tentering-machines.*

13.. *Charter Holy Ghost* (Vernon MS.) in *Hampole's Wks.* I. 361 Whon þe Iewes hedden þus nayled Criston þe cros as men doþ cloþ on a tey[n]tur [*v.rr.* streynour, rakke]. **1408** *Nottingham Rec.* II. 60 Johannes London occupat unum croftum cum taynters. **1435** *Coventry Leet Bk.* 172 No walker off the Cite of Couentre.. Shall Rakke no Clothe on the Tey[n]tur that schall be solde ffor wette-clothe. *c* **1440** *Promp. Parv.* 489/1 Tenture, for clothe (*S.* tentowre), .. Ug. V. in V. *tentura* (P. *constrictorium*). **1483** *Act 1 Rich. III*, c. 8 §1 Many of the seid Clothes.. ben sett uppon Tayntours and drawen out in leyngth and brede. **1495** *Nottingham Rec.* III. 284 Accyon off trespas for takynge vp teynters. **1530** PALSGR. 280/1 Tentar for clothe, *tend, tende.* *a* **1535** FISHER *Wks.* I. 394 Neuer anye Parchement skynne was more strayghtlye stratched by strength vpon the tentors. **1548** *Nottingham Rec.* IV. 94 For a gardeyn and a peyre of teyntors at the Bridgende. *a* **1552** LELAND *Itin.* I. 93 A great Numbre of Tainters for Wollen Clothes. **1592** GREENE *Upst. Courtier* in *Harl. Misc.* (Malh.) II. 242 That he drawe his cloth and pull it passing hard when he sets it vpon the tenters. **1642** in *J. Lister's Autobiog.* (1842) 78 The cannon.. beat down the barrs of a tenter. **1646** SIR J. TEMPLE *Irish Rebell.* 95 [He] led the boy to his Fathers tentors, and there hanged him. **1657** C. BECK *Univ. Charac.* Lvj, A tenture or tenter to stretch cloth in. **1727–41** CHAMBERS *Cycl.*, *Tenter, Tryer,* or *Prover*,.. in the cloth manufactory.. is usually about four feet and a half high, and for length exceeds that of the longest piece of cloth. **1791** HAMILTON *Berthollet's Dyeing* II. II. II. v. 108 It is dried on the tenters in the open air. **1849** C. BRONTE *Shirley* ii, The cloth was torn from his tenters and left in shreds in the field.

fig. **1602** DEKKER *Satirom.* Wks. 1873 I. 247 O Night.. That like a cloth of cloudes dost stretch thy limbes; Vpon the windy Tenters of the Ayre. **1611** SPEED *Hist. Gt. Brit.* IX. xvii. §4 Albeit his Words intended no Treason.. yet.. the tenture of the Law made them his death. **1674** N. FAIRFAX *Bulk & Selv.* To Rdr., As the one had wrackt and limm'd my thoughts, with endless tenters and boundless retchings out.

†**2.** = TENTERHOOK 1. *Obs.*

1598 SYLVESTER *Du Bartas* II. i. III. *Furies* 708 Then Avarice all-arm'd in hooking Tenters. **1678** *Massacre in Ireland* 3 Two Boys [were] wounded and hung upon Butchers Tenters. **1743** *Phil. Trans.* XLII. 425 The little Papillæ.. on the Surface of the Arms assist them like so many Hooks or Tenters to hold their Worms barely by touching them. **1795** WOLCOTT (P. Pindar) *Liberty's last Squeak* Wks. 1812 III. 422 And hang their Hearts, like Butcher's Meat, on tenters. **1810** CRABBE *Borough* I. 130 Fences.. (With tenters tipp'd) a strong repulsive bound.

fig. **1635** QUARLES *Embl.* I. v. 17 Abused Statutes had no tenters, And men could deal secure without indentures. **1849** J. STERLING in *Fraser's Mag.* XXXIX. 416 Slight Folly's pen, not Passion's burning tenter, Tears up our roots.

†**b.** *transf.* A hooked organ or part. *Obs.*

1613–16 W. BROWNE *Brit. Past.* II. i, Thornes and tangling bushes Whose tenters sticking in her garments sought.. to help her. **1817** KIRBY & SP. *Entomol.* (1818) II. xxiii. 323 Palms, pattens, or soles [of flies' feet].. beset underneath with small bristles or tenters.

†**3.** *fig.* esp. in phrases: **a.** *to put, set, stretch,* etc. *on (the) tenter(s,* = *to set on tenterhooks*; to rack: see TENTERHOOK 2, 2 b. *Obs.*

a **1533** LD. BERNERS *Gold. Bk. M. Aurel.* (1546) C c ij b, Ye haue strayned it on the tentours, and drawen it on the perche. *a* **1556** CRANMER *Wks.* (Parker Soc.) I. 60 But the papists have set Christ's words upon the tenters, and stretched them out so far, that they make his words to signify as pleaseth them, not as he meant. **1583** STUBBES *Anat. Abus.* II. (1882) 33 They inhance the rents, and set their fines on tenter. **1656** *Artif. Handsom.* 133 Nor ought the conscience in these to be set upon the rack and tainter. **1742** RICHARDSON *Pamela* III. 341, I have pity'd him many a time, when I have seen him stretched on the Tenters to keep thee in Countenance.

b. *to be on (the) tenter(s,* i.e. in a position of strain, difficulty, or uneasiness; to be in a state of anxious suspense. Now *rare* or *Obs.*, superseded by *on tenterhooks*: see TENTERHOOK 2 c.

1633 FORD *Broken H.* I. iii, My very heart-strings Are on the tenters. **1726** *Adv. Capt. R. Boyle* (1768) 27, I was upon the Tenters to know the Reason of my Confinement. **1796** SCOTT *Let. to Miss C. Rutherford* 5 June, Your curiosity will be upon the tenters to hear the wonderful events. **1806** FESSENDEN *Democr.* I. 39 Stretch'd on the tenters of anxiety By blunder, crime, or impropriety.

†**4.** A stretching implement: ? = TENT *sb.*³ *Obs.*

1607 TOPSELL *Four-f. Beasts* (1658) 147 Put in the Opponax, and of both together make like taynters or splints, and thrust them into the wound. *Ibid.* 808 This applied to the bitten place in a linnen cloth, and tentures twice a day, did perfectly recover her health within a month. **1681** GREW *Musæum* IV. i. 360 A Box of Anatomick Instruments; sc. Saws, Steel and Ivory Knives,.. a Tenter.

5. *attrib.* and *Comb.*, as ***tenter-stretched*** adj.; **tenter-balk (-bauk), -bar**: see quots.; **tenter-field, -place,** = TENTER-GROUND; **tenter-frame** = sense 1; **tenter-house, -machine**: see sense 1 (note); **tenter-timber,** timber for making tenters. See also TENTER-GROUND, -HOOK, -YARD.

1876 *Whitby Gloss.*, **Tenter-bauks*, the beams to which the butcher's meat-hooks are fastened. **1877** KNIGHT *Dict. Mech.*, **Tenter-bar*, a device for stretching cloth. **1844** G. DODD *Textile Manuf.* iii. 104 The cloth is stretched out and hung up to dry. This used to be done in the *tenter-fields. **1835** URE *Philos. Manuf.* 192 When the fulling is finished, the cloth is stretched once more on the *tenter-frame, and left in the open air till it is dry. **1861** C. C. ROBINSON *Leeds Gloss.* s.v. *Tenters*, The tenter-frames are upright bars placed at a short distance from each other and connected by other horizontal ones, top and bottom, having an array of hooks at equal distances on which the cloth is fastened by the listing of both sides. **1457** in Arnolde *Chron.* (1811) 72 All thoo in the said cite or subbarbis that ocupye.. *teynter placys for fullers. **1641** SIR B. RUDYARD in Rushw. *Hist. Coll.* III. (1692) I. 167 Not to press such *Tenter-stretched Arguments. **1562** *Richmond Wills* (Surtees) 152 Stees, stanggs, peatts, old *tenture tymber, xs.

tenter ('tɛntə(r)), *sb.*² [f. TENT *v.*⁶ + -ER¹.]

1. One who lives or lodges in a tent.

1846 *Indiana Hist. Mag.* XXIII. 409 The eating hours were the same as those of the tenters. **1888** *Harper's Mag.* Oct. 801/1 The pretty girl of our civilization, who pushes into the canvas home of the tenters. **1907** *Daily News* 27 Nov. 3/2 Originally intended for the benefit of gipsies, the evangelism.. has attracted adherents from all classes, now proud to style themselves 'tenters'.

2. One whose job is to erect and strike tents.

1864 'P. PATERSON' *Glimpses of Real Life* xiii. 123 There must be a tent-master and tenters, besides the agent in advance, the members of the brass band, [etc.]. **1979** *Daily Tel.* 23 Apr. 14/8 The slow building and dismantling of the marquee on stage was.. a documentary about tenters and their jobs.

tenter ('tɛntə(r)), *sb.*³ *dial.* [f. TENT *v.*¹ + -ER¹.]

1. One who minds, or has charge of, anything requiring attention, as a machine, a flock, etc.

1828 *Craven Gloss.*, *Tenters*, watchers, moor-tenters. **1863** MRS. TOOGOOD *Yorks. Dial.*, I will hire that boy as a tenter for my sheep. **1870** *Inquiry Yorks. Deaf & Dumb* 59 Simeon Smith, cropping-machine tenter. **1885** *Manch. Exam.* 20 Feb. 5/3 The engine tenter.. found the doors of the mill unlocked.

b. Applied to a watch-dog.

1844 S. BAMFORD *Walks S. Lancs.* 47 (E.D.D.) Will he do for a tenter? will he bark at night?

2. An attendant on a skilled workman, who gives him unskilled help, supplies materials, etc.

1894 *Labour Commission Gloss.*, *Tenters*, assistants to the weaver, generally children, who have gone through a short process of probation.

tenter ('tɛntə(r)), *v.* [f. TENTER *sb.*¹]

1. *trans.* To stretch (cloth) on a tenter or tenters.

1437 *Coventry Leet Bk.* 187 Yeff so be that hit wol-not bere the seyde lengeth than that the walker Teynter hym out to the lengethe off xv yerdes. **1473** in Arnolde *Chron.* (1811) 78 The vntrouth falshed and desept.. now daily vsed in the fullyng teynteryng or settyng and sheryng of wullen cloth. **1583** STUBBES *Anat. Abus.* II. (1882) 24 After they haue bought their cloth, they cause it to be tentered, racked, and so drawne out, as it shall be both broader and longer than it was. **1626** BACON *Sylva* §12 As when.. Leather or Cloth tentured spring back. **1673** O. HEYWOOD *Diaries*, etc. (1882) I. 354 Having some land.. where his cloth is tentered. **1789** BRAND *Hist. Newcastle* II. 320 The ordinary of this society, called anciently walkers,.. enacted that no brother should.. tentor cloth on a Sunday. **1876** CUDWORTH *Bradford* vii. 466 Returning home.., the cloth was 'tentered'—that is, if weather permitted.

†**b.** *transf.* To hang or stretch as on a tenter or tenters. *Obs.*

1615 CROOKE *Body of Man* 244 If the heart needed any tension, it might better haue beene tentered, and with shorter stringes to the spine of the back. **1648** BP. HALL *Easter at Higham* Rem. Wks. (1660) 194 Do the cruel tormentors tenter out his pretious limmes? *a* **1677** Barrow *Expos. Creed* Wks. 1716 I. 430 We may easily imagine what acerbity of pain must be endured in his limbs being stretched forth, racked and tentured.

† **2.** *fig.* To set on the tenter, or on tenterhooks: see tenter *sb.*¹ 3, tenterhook 2 b. Also, to injure or pain as by stretching; to rack, torture (the feelings, etc.). *Obs.*

1612 R. Fenton *Usury* 38 Verily if vsurie were not, men would tenter their wits, either in trading themselues or imploying others. **1622** Fletcher *Beggar's Bush* II. iii, He does stretch, Tenter his credit so. **1652** J. Wright tr. *Camus' Nat. Paradox* III. 49 It might be done without tentering his Conscience. *a* **1734** North *Exam.* II. iv. §32 (1740) 247 It is plain..that Pepys, being once tentered, should have come off *secundum artem*.

† **3.** *intr.* Of cloth: To admit of being stretched on the tenter; to bear tentering. *Obs. rare*⁻¹.

1626 Bacon *Sylva* §841 Parchment or leather will stretch, paper will not; woollen cloth will tenter, linen scarcely.

† **'tenter,belly.** *Obs.* [f. tenter *v.* + belly *sb.*] One who distends his belly; a glutton.

1621 Burton *Anat. Mel.* III. ii. vi. i. (1651) 546 Not with sweet wine..as many of those Tenterbellies do. **1630** J. Taylor (Water P.) *Gt. Eater Kent* 10 A cheating bable, in comparison of this Nicolaitan, Kentish tenterbelly.

tentered ('tɛntəd), *ppl. a.* [f. tenter *v.* and *sb.*¹ + -ed.]

1. Stretched on or as on a tenter; racked.

1652 Benlowes *Theoph.* VII. xxxvii, As my tenter'd Minde its Spirits still Strains forth. **1835** Ure *Philos. Manuf.* 203 In order to dry the tentered cloth within it.

2. Stuck or studded with tenter-hooks.

1768 Tucker *Lt. Nat.* (1834) I. 222 Another person.. might still expect uneasiness in the tentered cask, nevertheless, might choose it as the lesser evil. **1795** Southey *Joan of Arc* IV. 111 How Maximin,..In such deep fury bade the tenter'd wheel Rend her life piecemeal.

† **'tenter-ground.** *Obs.* [f. tenter *sb.*¹ + ground *sb.*] Ground occupied by tenters for stretching cloth, etc.

1714 *Lond. Gaz.* No. 5266/8 In the Tentor Ground by the Dog house in Bunhill fields. **1769** Gray *Let. to Wharton* 18 Oct., I entered Kendal almost in the dark, and could distinguish only a shadow of the castle on a hill, and tenter-grounds spread far and wide round the town. **1887** Lecky *Eng. in 18th C.* VI. xxiii. 247 To steal woollen cloth from a tenter-ground.

tenterhook ('tɛntəhʊk). Forms: see tenter *sb.*¹; also with hyphen, and 5 **tayntyr-, tentyr-,** 6 **tentur-,** 7 **tentry-.** [f. tenter *sb.*¹ + hook *sb.*¹]

1. One of the hooks or bent nails set in a close row along the upper and lower bar of a tenter, by which the edges of the cloth are firmly held; a hooked or right-angled nail or spike; *dial.* a metal hook upon which anything is hung.

1480 *Wardr. Acc. Edw. IV* (1830) 139 Tentourhokes, cc. **1492–3** *Rec. St. Mary at Hill* 186 Item, for tayntyrhokes and ffor wachyng of the sepulture, xij d. *a* **1518** Skelton *Magnyf.* 1002 Her naylys sharpe as tenter hokys! **1579** in Feuillerat *Revels Q. Eliz.* (1908) 324 Tainter Hookes at viii^d the c. *a* **1683** Sidney *Disc. Govt.* III. xxxii. (1704) 369 The King of Marocco may stab his Subjects, throw them to the Lions, or hang them upon tenterhooks. **1688** R. Holme *Armoury* III. 348/1 The *Tentry Hook* is a Nail with a crooked Head, yet sharp pointed, that it may strike into any thing hung upon it. **1777** Howard *Prisons Eng.* (1780) 404 The partition between this and the garden..strong palisades with tenter-hooks. **1825** Waterton *Wand. S. Amer.* III. iii. 254 On examining his teeth I found that they were all bent like tenter-hooks, pointing down his throat. **1888** *Sheffield Gloss., Tenter-hooks*, the hooks upon which the valances of a bed are hung. **1889** *N.W. Linc. Gloss.* (ed. 2), *Tenter-hooks*, strong iron hooks put in ceilings and..joists.., on which bacon and other such things are hung.

b. *transf.* = tenter *sb.*¹ 2 b.

1665 Hooke *Microgr.* xxxv. 164 It was arm'd likewise with the like Tenterhooks or claws with those of the sheath. **1713** Derham *Phys.-Theol.* To Rdr. 6 The Beards (or Tenter-hooks [of a bee's sting] as Dr. Hook calls them) lie only on one side of each Spear, not all round them. **1816** Kirby & Sp. *Entomol.* xxiii. (1818) II. 323 These tenter-hooks in the suckers of flies..are mere fancies.

2. *fig.* That on which something is stretched or strained; something that causes suffering or painful suspense. Cf. tenter *sb.*¹ 3.

1532 More *Confut. Barnes* VIII. Wks. 797/1 The churche ..is stretched out in the stretcher or tenter hookes of the crosse, as a churche well washed and cleansed. **1601** Chester *Love's Mart.* (1878) 138 Ract on the tenter-hookes of foule disgrace. **1823** Byron *Juan* XIV. xcvii, [It] keeps the atrocious reader in suspense; The surest way for ladies and for books To bait their tender or their tender-hooks.

b. esp. in phrases ***to put, set, strain, stretch on the tenterhooks***: to strain, distort the sense of (words) (? *obs.*); to strain (conscience, truth, authority, credit, etc.) beyond the proper, normal, or natural extent, limit, or scope; to put a strain on (a faculty, power, or capacity). Now *rare*.

1583 Stubbes *Anat. Abus.* II. (1882) 29 He racketh it, straineth it, and as it were so setteth it on the tenter hookes. **1603** H. Crosse *Vertues Commw.* (1878) 58 By setting the conscience on the tainter-hookes, to rise vp by his fall. **1630** *R. Johnson's Kingd. & Commw.* 134 Nor doe I here stretch my discourse on the tenter-hookes of partiality. **1700** W. King *Transactioneer* 57 The poor People have set their Wits, as if it were on the Tenter-hooks, to make Turnep-Bread in Essex. **1841** D'Israeli *Amen. Lit.* (1867) 213 (*Invent. Printing*) Honest men..sometimes strain truth on the tenter-hooks of fiction.

c. ***to be on (the) tenterhooks***: i.e. in a state of painful suspense or impatience: cf. tenter *sb.*¹ 3 b.

1748 Smollett *Rod. Rand.* xlv, I left him upon the tenter-hooks of impatient uncertainty. **1812** Sir R. Wilson *Pr. Diary* (1861) I. 127 Until I reach the imperial headquarters I shall be on tenter-hooks. **1897** *Sat. Rev.* 25 Dec. 754/1 The author keeps..the reader..on tenterhooks.

3. *attrib.*

1576 Fleming tr. *Caius' Dogs* (1880) 37 This dogge..is violent in fighting, & wheresoeuer he setteth his tenterhooke teeth, he taketh such sure & fast holde, that a man may sooner teare and rende him in sunder, then lose him and seperate his chappes. **1907** *Westm. Gaz.* 12 Sept. 2/1 What may be called 'tenterhook living' or existence on the crust of a volcano. **1980** P. Van Greenaway *Dissident* ii. 41 Alex had listened with tenterhook attention.

Hence † **'tenter-,hooking** *a.*, laying hold with tenterhooks (in quot. *fig.*).

1615 Brathwait *Strappado* (1878) 197 Avoid such tenter-hooking men.

tentering ('tɛntərɪŋ), *vbl. sb.* [f. tenter *v.* + -ing¹.] The action of the verb tenter; the stretching (of cloth) on tenters or by means of other mechanical devices.

1483–4 *Act 1 Rich. III*, c. 8 §7 No maner persone..set nor drawe..any maner of Wollen Cloth..by the meane of teynteryng or otherwise. **1597–8** *Act 39 Eliz.* c. 20 (*title*) An Acte aginst the deceitfull stretching and taintering of Northerne Cloth. **1677** Jordan *Lond. Tri.* 20 The Tentering I wot Must not be forgot. **1706** A. Boyer *Ann. Q. Anne* IV. 28 The tentring or stretching of any the aforesaid draperies. **1858** Simmonds *Dict. Trade, Tentering*, a technical term for stretching woven goods to dry, after being stiffened or dyed.

b. *attrib.*, as ***tentering-house, -machine, -room.***

1877 Knight *Dict. Mech., Tentering-machine*, a machine for stretching fabrics. **1881** *Daily News* 21 Jan. 5/6 Her body was found in the ruins of the tentering house. *c* **1890** W. H. Casmey *Ventilation* 19 These fans are supplied with warm air from the finishing and tentering rooms adjoining.

† **'tenter-yard.** *Obs.* [f. tenter *sb.*¹ + yard *sb.*] A yard or enclosure with tenters for stretching cloth, etc.

1481–90 *Howard Househ. Bks.* (Roxb.) 303 He to have his howse that he dwellyth in, and the teynter yerd. **1545** *Act 37 Hen. VIII*, c. 12 §10 Any mansion house with a..tymber yarde, teyntree yarde, or gardeyne bilonginge to the same. **1598** Stow *Surv.* (1908) I. 127 The fields on either side be turned into Garden plottes, teynter yardes, Bowling Allyes, and such like.

tentful, *sb.*: see tent *sb.*¹

'tentful, *a.* Now *dial.* [f. tent *sb.*² + -ful.] Careful; full of attention.

c **1450** Holland *Howlat* 420 And vthir signess, forsuth syndry I gess, Off metallis and colouris in tentfull atyr. **1870** Lady Verney *L. Lisle* vi. 77 He's a very 'tentful man.

tenth (tɛnθ), *a.* and *sb.* Forms: see below in A. 1. [Various formations from the cardinal numeral ten, at earlier and later stages of its history. The early forms represent Indo-Eur. **dekmtos* (Gr. δέκατος, Lith. *deszim̃tas*, OSlav. *desjätyĭ*) simply, or with assimilation to the form of the cardinal; the later are new formations on *ten*, with the suffix *-th*, *-d*, *-t*, ablaut forms of pre-Teut. *-tos*. Like the other ordinals, only of the weak declension: in OE. with sing. masc. *-a*, fem. and neut. *-e*, pl. *-an*. The form-groups are: α. OE. (Anglian) **teoȝoða*, *-eða*, *-ða* (Northumb. *teiȝ(e)ða*, *teiða*), corresp. to OFris. *tegotha*, *-atho*, *-etha*, OS. *tegotho*, *-atho* (MLG. *tegede*, *teigede*, LG. *tegede*, *tegde*), going back through **teȝuþo*, to OTeut. **teȝunþo-*. Its mod. repr. is tithe. β. The ordinary OE. (WSax.) *téoða* (early ME. *tēþe*), app. from **teoh(e)ða*, going back through **tehuþo*, to **tehunþo-*, with *h* in place of *ȝ* under the influence of the cardinal **tehun*. This form is found only in Eng.; it survived dialectally to the 16th c. as *tēthe*. γ. Early ME. *tēnde* (later *tend*, *teind*), appearing in Ormin *c* 1200, but probably existing earlier, also in Kentish in the Ayenbite 1340. It corresponds in consonants to OFris. *tianda*, *tienda* (Du. *tiende*), OS. *tehando*, OHG. *zehanto*; Goth. *taihunda*, Norse *tíonde*, *tíunde*. δ. Early ME. *tenðe* (*tyenðe*, *teonðe*), *tenþe*, now tenth, a new formation from *ten* with suffix -th¹. ε. ME. *tent*, also from *ten*, with suffix *-t*. Now *dial.*, chiefly northern and north midl. See *Note* below.]

The ordinal numeral corresponding to the cardinal number ten; that which comes next to the ninth.

A. *adj.* **1.** In concord with a substantive expressed or understood.

α. 1 *Anglian.* **teoȝoða** (in *teoȝoðian* tithe *v.*), **teoȝeða, teoȝða;** *Northumb.* (**teȝða:** in *teȝðiȝan* tithe *v.*), **teiȝða, teiða,** 2–3 **tiȝeðe,** 3 **tiȝðe,** 4–5 **tiþe, tyþe** [4–9 **tithe, tythe,** etc.: see tithe *sb.*].

a **900** tr. *Bæda's Hist.* v. xxii[i]. §1 Ðy teoȝeþan [*v.r.* teoðan] dæȝe Iunius monþes. *c* **950** *O.E. Martyrol.* (1900) 80 On þone teoȝðan [*MS. C.* teoðan] dæȝ þæs monðes. *Ibid.* 116 On ðone teoȝeþan [*MS. C.* teoðan] dæȝ þæs monðes. *c* **950** *Lindisf. Gosp.* John i. 39 Tid uæs suelce ðio teiȝða [*Ags. G.* teoðe tid]. *Ibid.* Matt. *Prolog. X Canon.* Skeat 3, l. 18 In regula ða teiða. *c* **1250** Tiȝðe [see A. 3]. **1297** R. Glouc. (Rolls) 8935 Het was ido in þe teþe [*v.rr.* teoþe, tenþe] ȝer of þe kinges kinedom, & enleue hondred & þe tiþe, þat vr louerd an-erþe com. *c* **1375** Tyþe [see A. 3].

β. 1 **téoða, téða,** 2 **tioðe, tieðe,** 3–4 **teoþe, teothe, teþe.**

c **900** tr. *Bæda's Hist.* v. xxii[i]. §1 þy teoðan [*Ca.* teoȝeþan] dæȝe Iunius monþes. *Ibid.* Teðan [see A. 3]. *c* **955** *O.E. Chron.* an. 955 He ricsade teoþe healf ȝear. *c* **1000** Ælfric *Gen.* viii. 5 And þa wætera..wanedon oþ þæne teoþan monþ. *a* **1175** *Cott. Hom.* 219 Swa fele þe me mihte þat tioðe hape fulfellen. *c* **1200** *Trin. Coll. Hom.* 137 þe tieðe [wise] is þat michele hereword þat ure helend him gaf. *c* **1290** *S. Eng. Leg.* I. 76/205 In þe teoþe ȝere also. *a* **1300** *Fall & Passion* 15 in *E.E.P.* (1862) 13 For þe prude of lucifer þe teþe angle fille in to helle. *c* **1315** Shoreham III. 329 þe teþe hest þe for-bet Wyl tou oþer manne þynge. **1387** Teþe [see A. 2].

γ. 2–5 **tende,** 4 **teinde, teynde,** 4–5 **tend, teind,** 5–6 **teynd** [8 **tiend,** etc.: see teind].

c **1200** Ormin 4518 þe tende bodeword wass sett þurrh Godd forr þine nede. *Ibid.* 12745 Summ itt off þatt daȝȝ þe tende time wære. *c* **1250** *Gen. & Ex.* 3141 Ðe tende dai it sulde ben laȝt, And ho(l)den in ðe tende naȝt. **1340** Hampole *Pr. Consc.* 3990 þe tend [token] es of þe grete dome final. **1340** *Ayenb.* 2 þe tende godes heste. *Ibid.* 13 þe tende article is þellich. **13..** Teind [see ε]. **1375** Barbour *Bruce* IV. 460 On the tend day..the king..Arivit. *c* **1460** *Towneley Myst.* i. 144 Thou art fallen, that was the teynd, ffrom an angell to a feynd.

δ. 2 **tenðe (tyenðe),** 2–4 **teonðe,** 4 **tenþe (tentþe, tennyth),** 4–6 **tenthe,** 4–5 **tienthe,** 5– **tenth.**

a **1150** *MS.* (in *Anglia* XI. 370), On þan tenðen dæiȝe. *a* **1175** *Cott. Hom.* 219 þat teonðe werod abreað. *Ibid.*, þa wes þes tyenðes [*ed.* tyendes] hapes alder swiþe feir isceapen. *c* **1175** *Lamb. Hom.* 117 þe teonðe [*ed.* teouðe] unþeau is þet biscop beo ȝemeles. *c* **1380** Wyclif *Wks.* (1880) 354 þe tentþe [*ed.* tenteþ] propirte þat suiþ. **1382** —— *John* i. 39 The our was as the tenthe. **1398** Trevisa *Barth. De P.R.* IX. xxxiii. (Bodl. MS.), In the moneþ of September..on tenþe dai of þat moneþ. **1480** Caxton Tienthe [see quot. 1387 in A. 2]. **1495** *Trevisa's Barth. De P.R.* IX. xxxiii. 369 The tenth daye of Septembre. **1526** Tindale *John* i. 39 It was about the tenthe [**1539** tenth] houre. **1530** Palsgr. 372/1 *Dixiesme*, tenthe. **1599** Shaks. *Hen. V*, I. ii. 77 King Lewes the Tenth. **1828** Scott *F.M. Perth* xiii, Not a man claiming in the tenth degree of kindred but must repair to the brattach of his tribe.

ε. 4– **tent** (*Sc.* 5–6 **teynt).**

13.. *Cursor M.* 515 (Cott.) þe tent [*v.rr.* tende, teind] ordir for to fullfill. *c* **1400** *Destr. Troy* 4480 To saile somyn vnto Troy..And the tent yere truly..þere worship to wyn. **1513** Douglas *Æneis* XI. vi. 156 The Grekis conquest.. prolongit was quhill the tent ȝeir. **1562** Winȝet *Cert. Tractates* ii. Wks. (S.T.S.) I. 18 The tent day of Marche, 1561. **1657** Sir W. Mure *Hist. Rowallane* Wks. (S.T.S.) II. 251, 1415, the tent year of his governale. **1905** [*Tent* is now the local form in Scotland, most of England down to Shropsh., Worcester, Leicester, Lincolnsh., and parts of Ulster. See Wright, *Eng. Dial. Gram.* 269.]

2. a. The last of each row or series of ten; each or every tenth individual or part.

c **890–901** *Laws K. Ælfred* Introd. c. 38 þine teoðan sceattas & þine frumripan..aȝif þu Gode. *a* **1000** *Cædmon's Gen.* 2122 (Gr.) Ðæs hereteames ealles teoðan sceat Abraham sealde Godes biscope. **1297** R. Glouc. (Rolls) 6713, & tolde of hom þe teþe out, & þe nine slou. **1387** Trevisa *Higden* (Rolls) I. 395 Al þe teþe [Caxton (**1480**) tienthe] londe, þat þe kyng hadde assigned him. **1535** Stewart *Cron. Scot.* (Rolls) III. 384 Confermit wes with the paip of the new..That king Dauid the tent penny suld haif. **1551** Crowley *Pleas. & Pain* 343 The tenth increase by sea and lande. **1617** Moryson *Itin.* II. 37 Disarming the souldiers and executing the tenth man. **1759** *Hist.* in *Ann. Reg.* 55 *note*, The French court have stopt the payment of.. the rents created on the two sols per pound of the tenth penny. **1844** Ld. Brougham *Brit. Const.* xi, In 1205 a Parliament..ordered every tenth knight to be raised and mounted at the charge of the other nine.

b. ***tenth wave***: every tenth wave was formerly held to be larger than the nine preceding waves; hence allusively. (Cf. decuman I.)

1585 Higins *Junius' Nomencl.* 400/1 *Fluctus decumanus*, the tenth waue, that is a mighty, huge, violent and great waue or surge. **1628** Le Grys tr. *Barclay's Argenis* 297 This tenth waue will either put an end to the storme or sinke my beaten barke. **1752** Young *Brothers* IV. i, This, Fate, is thy tenth wave, and quite o'erwhelms me. **1884** *Harper's Mag.* Aug. 472/1 A mighty tenth wave of cheers and cries.

3. ***tenth part*** (†*deal*, †*dole*), any one of the ten equal parts into which a whole may be divided.

854 *Charter of Æthelwolf* in Birch *Cart. Sax.* II. 80 Ða ða he teoðode ȝynd eall his cyne rice ðone teoðan dæl ealra his landa. *a* **900** tr. *Bæda's Hist.* IV. xxx. [xxix.] §4 Ealra wæstma & æppla & hræȝla ðone teoðan [*Ca.* teðan] dæl for Gode to ælmessum ðearfum sealde. **971** *Blickl. Hom.* 35 We sceolan ..syllan þone teoþan dæl ure worldspeda. *c* **1200** Ormin 6125 Off all þatt god te birrþ þin Godd þe tende dale brinngenn. *c* **1250** *Gen. & Ex.* 895 Habram ȝaf him ðe tiȝðe del Of alle [h]is biȝete. *a* **1300** *Cursor M.* 20026 A thusand yeir moght i noght reke..Til tend [*v.rr.* tende, tenþe] part of hir louing. *c* **1350** *Will. Palerne* 4715 What wise i miȝte quite þe tenþedel. *c* **1375** *E.E. Allit. P.* B. 216 Bot þer he tynt þe tyþe dool of his tour ryche. *c* **1400** Maundev. (Roxb.) xix. 87 Vnnethes will any Cristen man suffer half so mykill, ne þe tende parte. *c* **1460** *Towneley Myst.* i. 257 The ten [*v.r.* teynd] parte felle downe with me. *Ibid.* xx. 277 Of the tresure that to vs fell, the tent parte euer with me went. **1606** Shaks. *Tr. & Cr.* III. ii. 95 Discharging lesse then the tenth part of one. *Mod.* Not a tenth part of his income.

B. *absol.* and *sb.* [Orig. the adj. used elliptically or absolutely, and declined as adj., pl. *þa teoðan*; but from *c* 1200, treated as sb. with pl. (*tiȝeþes*, *tithes, tethes, tendes, tenthes) tenths.* In sense 1 b, form *α* was retained in standard Eng., and form *γ* in Scotland and north. Eng., giving TITHE and TEIND, q.v. for these differentiated uses.]

1. a. A tenth part (A. 3) *of* anything; any one of ten equal parts into which a whole may be divided.

submerged tenth (i.e. of the population): see SUBMERGED.

a **1300–***c* **1475** [see TEIND]. **1600** W. WATSON *Decacordon* (1602) 139 Neither all, nor halfe, nor third, nor tenths of all shall be saued. **1692** LOCKE *Lower. Interest* 52 Money now is $\frac{9}{10}$ less worth than it was the former year. **1707** MORTIMER *Husb.* (1721) II. 97, 1 Foot 5 Inches and 2 tenths of an Inch. **1873** LELAND *Egypt. Sketch Bk.* 291 Englishmen of culture, who have not seen one-tenth of the great cathedrals of their own country. **1909** *Daily Chron.* 14 July 4/7 There are things in the world that you can get for a tenth of a penny.

b. *spec.* A tenth part of produce or profits, or of the estimated value of personal property, appropriated as a religious or ecclesiastical due, a royal subsidy, etc.

In the ecclesiastical use, † (*a*) *orig.* = TITHE, TEIND. (*b*) *spec.* The tenth part of the annual profit of every living in the kingdom, originally paid to the pope, but by Act 26 Hen. VIII, c. 3 (1534) transferred to the crown, and afterwards made a part of the fund known as Queen Anne's Bounty (BOUNTY 5 a). As a royal subsidy or aid formerly levied, see quot. 1765, and cf. FIFTEENTH B. 1.

[*a* **1100** *Laws of Athelstan* I. 102 2 Ic ðe wille ȝesyllan mine teoþan. *Ibid.* §3 ȝif we ure teoðan ȝesyllan nyllaþ, us ða nyȝon dælas biþ ætbrædene, & se teoþa an us biþ to laf. *c* **1200** Tiȝeþes: see TITHE B. 1. *c* **1250** Tiȝeþes: see *ibid.* *a* **1300–***c* **1450**: see TEIND.] **1474** CAXTON *Chesse* III. i. (1883) 77 That they rendre and gyue to god the tienthes of her goodes. **1496–7** [see FIFTEENTH B. 1]. **1535–6** *Act 27 Hen. VIII*, c. 42 The said firste frutes and tenthe. **1560** DAUS tr. *Sleidane's Comm.* 39 b, The fyrst fruictes, & the tenthes. **1587** HARRISON *England* II. i. (1877) I. 24 To returne to our tenths, a paiement first as deuised by the pope. **1587** FLEMING *Contn. Holinshed* III. 1378/1 An vniuersall taxation was made in nature of a tenth and fifteenth ouer all the countrie of Kent. **1611** SPEED *Hist. Gt. Brit.* IX. ix. (1623) 628 The Tenths of the Clergie..should haue been receyued. **1686** tr. *Chardin's Coronat. Solyman* 147 They pay both Tribute and Tenths. **1765** BLACKSTONE *Comm.* I. viii. 308 Tenths and fifteenths were temporary aids issuing out of personal property, and were formerly the real tenth or fifteenth part of all the movables belonging to the subject. Originally the amount was uncertain, but was reduced to a certainty in the eighth year of Edward III., when new taxations were made of every township, borough, and city in the kingdom, and recorded in the Exchequer. **1792** A. YOUNG *Trav. France* 537 No such thing was known in any part of France..as a tenth: it was always a twelfth, or a thirteenth, or even a twentieth of the produce. **1855** MACAULAY *Hist. Eng.* xv. III. 557 The hereditary revenue.. was derived from the rents of the royal domains,..from the first fruits and tenths of benefices [etc.].

†**2.** Every tenth number (below a hundred) in the natural series of numbers; *pl.* the multiples of ten, the 'tens'. *Obs.*

1543 RECORDE *Ground of Artes* 136 These be all the nombers from 1 to 10, and then all the tenthes within 100. *Ibid.* 136 b, Loke how you did expresse single vnities and tenthes in the lefte hande, so must you expresse vnities and tenthes of hundredes, in the ryghte hande. *Ibid.*, So the fourme of euery tenthe in the lefte hande serueth [in the ryghte hand] to expresse lyke nomber of thousandes, so y[e] fourme of 40 standeth for 4000.

3. *Mus.* A note ten diatonic degrees above or below a given note (both notes being counted); the interval between, or consonance of, two notes ten diatonic degrees apart.

1597 MORLEY *Introd. Mus.* 71 *Phi.* Which distances do make vnperfect consonants? *Ma.* A third, a sixt, and their eightes: a tenth, a thirteenth [etc.]. **1694** HOLDER *Harmony* iv. (1731) 40 A Tenth ascending is an Octave above the Third. **1869** OUSELEY *Counterp.* xvi. 122 Double counterpoint at the tenth is that in which either of the parts is transposed a tenth, the other remaining unmoved. **1880** C. H. H. PARRY in Grove *Dict. Mus.* I. 670/1 The use of tenths in this example [of 'Diaphony' of the 10th century] is remarkable, and evidently unusual, for Guido of Arezzo,.. a full century later, speaks of the 'symphonia vocum' in his Antiphonarium, and mentions only fourths, fifths, and octaves.

4. The tenth day of the month.

1580 in H. Foley *Jesuits in Conflict* (1873) 105 The tenth of September, 1580. **1868** E. S. P. WARD in *Atlantic Monthly* Mar. 345 (*heading*) The tenth of January. **1951** W. FAULKNER *Requiem for a Nun* I. 36 It was barely the tenth of July. *Ibid.* III. 250 On the morning after June tenth.

C. *Comb.*: **tenthmetre**, a metre divided by the tenth power of ten (= one ten-millionth of a millimetre); **tenth-rate** *a.*, of the tenth rate or relative quality, very inferior; so **tenth-remove** *a.*; **tenth-value** *a.*, designating a thickness of material that reduces the intensity of radiation passing through it by a factor of 10.

1876 G. F. CHAMBERS *Astron.* x. iii. 848 The wave-lengths of the principal Fraunhofer lines expressed in *tenthmetres, a tenthmetre being the $1 \cdot 10^{10}$ of a metre. **1834** *Tait's Mag.* I. 440/1 He tears himself away from the smiles of a *tenth-rate figurante of the *Academie Royale.* **1889** *Spectator* 9 Nov. 626/2 A people seeking nothing but material prosperity of the tenth-rate kind. **1905** *Westm. Gaz.* 28 Mar. 4/1 Constable is too remote and difficult, but a *tenth-remove derivative, properly browned, will serve their turn. **1955** *Gloss. Terms Radiology* (*B.S.I.*) 17 *Tenth-value thickness. **1957** *Effects Nucl. Weapons* (U.S. Defense Atomic Support Agency) viii. 378 For concrete, the tenth-value thickness is ..about 48 cm.

[*Note.* The etymological history of some of the prec. forms (as in other numerals) presents points of which the explanations are more or less conjectural. The direct OTeut. repr. of Indo-Eur. **dekm̥'tos* was by Verner's Law **teȝundos*; with this the Gothic *taihunda*, OS. *tehando*, OHG. *zehanto*, agree except in having *h* for *g*, apparently under the influence of the cardinal **tehun, -an.* The OTeut. **teȝunþo-*, whence OS. and OFris. *tegotho, -a*, OAnglian *te(o)ȝoþa*, implies a pre-Teut. *'*dekm̥tos*, with shifted stress (implied also in some other ordinals). Assimilation of this form also to the cardinal would give **tehunþo-*, whence **tehūþa*, *teoh(o)ða*, *tēoða*. The history of *tēnde* is more uncertain: the four ordinals, *sefende, eȝtende, neȝende, tēnde*, in ME., Northern and Kentish, form a group of which only the first is known in OE., repr. by *siofunda, seofonða*, in the Lindisf. and Rushw. glosses. *Siofunda*, like Goth. **sibunda*, OS. *sibundo*, OHG. *sibunto*, represents an OTeut. **sibundo-*, Indo-Eur. *sep(t)m'tos*. OE. *niȝenda* (*a* 1066), OS. *nigundo*, OHG. *niunto*, Goth. *niunda*, had prob. a parallel history. The ME. *ehtende* appears to have been conformed in its ending to *sefende*; and *tende*, from its late appearance, was prob. formed from *tēn* on the same model. *Ten-th* has the suffix which in OE. appears in *feorða, seofoða, eahtoða, niȝoða, teoȝeða*, and which has now been extended to all the ordinals from *fourth* onward. On the other hand, *ten-t* has the form of the suffix which was regular in OE. *fifta* (OS. and OFris. *fifto, -ta*, OHG. *fimfto*, Goth. *fimfta*, OTeut. **fimfto-*), and *sixta* (OS. and OHG. *sehsto*, Goth. *saihsta*, OTeut. *seȝsto-*), which in OE. was also used in *enlefta* (*ellefta*) and *twelfta*, and in North. and North-Midl. dialects has since been extended to all the ordinals from *fourt* to *hundert*.]

tenth, *v. rare.* [f. TENTH *sb.*] *trans.* To decimate, to tithe.

1598 BARRET *Theor. Warres* I. ii. 9 As did Iulius Cæsar ..*Dezimare* or tenth the ninth Legion by sound of the horne. **1647** TRAPP *Comm. Ep., Heb.* vii. 6 371 Received tithes of Abraham. Gr. Tithed or tenthed Abraham. **1878** HOOKER & BALL *Marocco* 470 At last came the holiday *l'ashora*, or the day of the Sultan's tenthing.

tenthe, obs. form of TENT *sb.*[1]

tenthly ('tɛnθlɪ), *adv.* [f. TENTH *a.* + -LY[2].] In the tenth place.

1623 in *Fasti Aberd.* (1854) 282 Tentlie, that [etc.]... Tuellftlie, that [etc.]. **1648** D. JENKINS *Wks.* 38 Tenthly, wee maintaine that [etc.]. **1727** BAILEY vol. II, *Tenthly*, in the tenth Place or Order.

†**'tent-hook.** *Obs. rare.* In 5–6 taynt-. [f. TENT *sb.*[5] + HOOK *sb.*[1]] A tenterhook.

1491 *Churchw. Acc. St. Dunstan's, Canterb.*, Payde for threde and taynt hookes j d. **1533** *MS. Acc. St. John's Hosp., Canterb.*, For taynt hokys j d.

‖**Tenthredo** (tɛn'θriːdəʊ). *Entom.* [Latinized form of Gr. τενθρηδών, -δον-, a kind of wasp; the stem being taken erroneously as *tenthredin-*.] A saw-fly: in early use vaguely applied; in modern scientific use, after Linnæus 1748, and as restricted by Leach 1819, a genus of hymenopterous insects, typical of the family *Tenthredinidæ*, comprising the large saw-flies called hornet-flies.

1658 ROWLAND *Moufet's Theat. Ins.* 929 Now let us proceed to the Insect called Tenthredo. **1706** PHILLIPS (ed. Kersey), *Tenthredo*,..the lesser Hornet, or Bastard Hornet; an Insect. **1752** J. HILL *Hist. Anim.* 81 The black Tenthredo, with clavated antennæ. **1753** CHAMBERS *Cycl. Supp.*, *Tenthredo*, in natural history, the name of a fly of the stinging kind. [**1874** LUBBOCK *Orig. & Met. Ins.* ii. 33 Although Tenthredinidæ and Siricidæ are caterpillars, more or less closely resembling those of Lepidoptera.]

Hence **ten'thredinid**, *a.* belonging to the *Tenthredinidæ*; *sb.* a member of this family.

1890 *Insect Life* III. 157 Tenthredinid larva on black birch. **1913** *Oxf. Univ. Gaz.* 4 June 954/1 The Tenthredinid *Allantus arcuatus* together with a ♂ humble bee.., a much larger insect. **1970** G. ORDISH tr. *Chauvin's World of Ants* i. 61 The biologist Lange put some Tenthredinid larvae.. near an ant track.

†**'tentible,** *a. Obs. rare.* [f. TENT *v.*[1] to attend + -IBLE.] Apt to attend, attentive.

1603 H. CROSSE *Vertues Commw.* (1878) 29 If these see but a small moate amisse, a wrinkle awry, how tentible they be to mend it. *Ibid.* 120 The minde is nothing so tentible at a good instruction..as at a vaine and sportiue foolerie.

†**'tenticle.** *Obs.* [f. TENT *sb.*[1] as if after a L. type **tenticula*: see -CULE.] A small tent.

1548 PATTEN *Exped. Scotl.* K iv, These whyte ridges.. wear the tenticles or rather cabayns and couches of theyr souldiours. **1587** FLEMING *Contn. Holinshed* III. 988/2 Foure miles on this side Edenburgh, occupied in largenesse with diuerse tents and tenticles.

tentie, variant of TENTY *a.*

†**tentiginous** (tɛn'tɪdʒɪnəs), *a. Obs.* [f. L. *tentīgo, -in-em* (see next) + -OUS.]

1. Excited to lust; itching, lecherous.

1616 B. JONSON *Devil an Ass* II. iii, Were you tentiginous? ha? Would you be acting of the Incubus?

2. Provocative of lust; lascivious.

1684 tr. *Bonet's Merc. Compit.* XVI. 569 What he here orders to be given is heating and therefore tentiginous. **1704** SWIFT *Mech. Operat. Spirit* ii. Misc. (1711) 308 Nothing affects the Head so much as a tentiginous Humour, repel'd and elated to the upper Region.

‖**tentigo** (tɛn'taɪgəʊ). *Obs.* [L. *tentīgo* tenseness, lust.] An attack of priapism, an erection; lecherousness, lust.

a **1603** in Nichols *Progr. Q. Eliz.* (1823) III. 336 If any be trobled with the tentigo. **1827** D. JOHNSON *Ind. Field Sports* 228 Tentigo also attends. **1860** MAYNE *Expos. Lex.*, *Tentigo*, ..old term for Priapism.

†**'tentik,** *a. Obs. rare*$^{-1}$. Aphetic form of *attentik*, AUTHENTIC, duly qualified, trustworthy.

1534 *St. Papers Hen. VIII*, IV. 666 Yat ȝe sall speyk with Master Adem Oterbowrn, or cawis sowm tentyk man to speyk with hym.

‖**ten'tillum.** *Zool.* [mod.L., f. L. *tempt-, tent-*, stem of *temptāre, tentāre* to feel + dim. suffix: cf. *tentacle*.] One of the unbranched twigs which stud the retractile tentacles of some Siphonophora.

1898 SEDGWICK *Text-bk. Zool.* I. iv. 140 These aggregations of thread-cells are especially found upon the tentilla, where they give rise to..the cnidosacs or batteries.

tentily ('tɛntɪlɪ), *adv. Sc. rare.* [As if f. TENTY *a.* + -LY[2]; but perh. a worn-down form of TENTIVELY (see -IVE), TENTY not being found until much later.] With care and attention; carefully.

? *a* **1400** *Morte Arth.* 3618 Tolowris tentyly takelle they ryghttene. **1721** RAMSAY *Cupid Thrown* v, He tentily Myrtilla sought. **1768** ROSS *Helenore* I. 9 Back with the halesome girss in haste she hy'd, An' tentyly unto the sair apply'd.

'tenting, *ppl. a.* [f. TENT *sb.*[1] + -ING[2].]

1. Resembling a tent; converging as the sides of a tent.

1818 KEATS *Endym.* II. 400 Coverlids..Not hiding up an Apollonian curve Of neck and shoulder, nor the tenting swerve Of knee from knee, nor ankles pointing light. **1932** S. O'FAOLÁIN *Midsummer Night Madness* 26 The tenting chestnuts filled the lanes with darkness.

2. Of a circus: that tents (TENT *v.*[6] 1 a).

1875 T. FROST *Circus Life* iii. 67 The tenting circuses of those days were on a more limited scale than those of the present time, and were met with chiefly at fairs. **1931** S. MCKECHNIE *Popular Entertainments* viii. 206 The early tenting circuses were unpretentious concerns. **1981** P. O'DONNELL *Xanadu Talisman* i. 18 He..owned half a small tenting circus.

tenting ('tɛntɪŋ), *vbl. sb.*[1] and *sb.* [f. TENT *v.*[6] + -ING[1].]

A. *vbl. sb.* Lodging in or as in tents; encamping; sojourning. Also (with reference to a touring circus or the like) camping and performing in a tent. Chiefly *attrib.*

1858 MACDUFF *Bow in Cloud* (1870) 32 Tenting-time here —resting-time yonder. **1861** *All Year Round* 16 Nov. 186/1 The tenting system is now so well organised, that everything connected with it is conducted with effect and punctuality. **1870** *Standard* 14 Dec., They were in excellent marching trim, carryed neither knapsack nor tenting equipage. **1873** TRISTRAM *Moab* xiii. 234 A little plain.., a lovely tenting spot. **1878** L. M. ALCOTT *Under Lilacs* iv. 40 Father..went off sudden..just before the tentin' season was over. **1883** 'ANNIE THOMAS' *Mod. Housewife* 81 That a house in the country, a short distance from London, was a more expensive form of tenting than an equally highly-rented one in the heart of the great metropolis. **1931** S. MCKECHNIE *Pop. Entertainments* viii. 222 Bertram W. Mills' Circus and Menagerie..only in its second tenting season..has already revolutionised the status of the circus. **1952** N. STREATFEILD *Aunt Clara* 114 We have a little time when tenting is finished. **1971** *Esquire* July 88/2 The Hartford Circus fire of 1944..caused the big show to forswear tenting in 1956 and resolve to play only arena engagements indoors.

B. *sb.* [f. TENT *sb.*[1]; cf. *bedding, sacking.*] Material for tents.

1887 *Pall Mall G.* 4 June 8/2 The rain, instead of running off as it should have done on first-class tenting material, dripped through persistently, until the tents were perfectly uninhabitable. **1936** *Discovery* Dec. 381/1 The second assistant had been carried down the rapids on the tenting.

tenting, *vbl. sb.*[2–5]: see TENT *v.*[1–4].

†**tention**[1]. *Obs. rare.* Short for INTENTION.

1587 FLEMING *Contn. Holinshed* III. 1417/1 To further our tention and honorable and iust actions at that time in such sort. **1653** SCLATER *Fun. Serm.* 25 Sept. (1654) 13 In the will, perfect fruition of the Divine glory, tention, and (for the measure of the Creature) Comprehension.

†**tention**[2]. *Obs. rare.* Short for CONTENTION.

1602 FULBECKE *2nd Pt. Parallel* Introd. 6 My neyghbours are full of sension and tention, and so cunninge, that they will make you beleeue, that all is gold, which glistereth.

tention[3] **('tention)** Also ten-shun (cf. 'SHUN). Short for ATTENTION (5).

1908 M. BEERBOHM in *Sat. Rev.* 26 Sept. 390/1 He..stood at 'tention to be tapped on the chest by the hero. **1922** JOYCE *Ulysses* 417 Get a spurt on. Tention. **1978** J. BLACKBURN *Dead Man's Handle* viii. 91 He..bellowed an order. 'Ten-shun, Sarn't-Major.'

tention, obs. form of TENSION.

'tentive, *a. Obs.* exc. *dial.* Also 4–5 -if(e, -yf, 6 -yue. [a. OF. *tentif* (14th c. in Godef.), aphetic form of F. *atentif*; or aphetic form of INTENTIVE and (in later use) ATTENTIVE.] = ATTENTIVE.

c **1386** CHAUCER *Melib.* ¶ 149 (Harl. MS.) As to warisching of ȝoure douȝter..we schullen do so tentyf [*v.r.* ententif] besynes fro day to night þat..sche schal be hool. ? *a* **1400** *Cato's Mor.* 337 in *Cursor M.* p. 1673 Loke þou be tentife, if þou haue lered alle þi life. **1570** *Satir. Poems Reform.* xxiii. 66 With tentyue eir vnto my taill attend. **1582** STANYHURST *Æneis* II. (Arb.) 43 Wyth tentiue lystning eeche wight was setled in harckning. **1791** J. LEARMONT *Poems* 329 (E.D.D.) Nouther party's tentive how to please. **1902** R. M.

GILCHRIST *Natives of Milton* 97 Yo're as 'tentive an' as capable as onyone could be.

So **'tentively** *adv.* = ATTENTIVELY; **'tentiveness** = ATTENTIVENESS.

c **1350** *Will. Palerne* 2258 ȝif ȝe *tentifly take kepe & trewe be to-gadere. *Ibid.* 5124 But tentyfli þow help, þat al þis lond be lad in lawe as it ouȝt. **1438** *Rolls of Parlt.* V. 439/1 Thei put tentifiye their hole labours and diligences for his worship. **1876** *Whitby Gloss.*, *Tentifly*,.. with attention. **1382** WYCLIF *Wisd.* xii. 20 If forsothe the enemys of thi seruauns,.. with so myche *tentifnesse, thou tormentedist, and delieveredest. **1610** J. MELVILL *Diary* (Wodrow) 556 Want of skill, tentivnes, faithfulness and guid effectioune.

tentless ('tɛntlɪs), *a.*[1] *Sc.* [f. TENT *sb.*[2] + -LESS.] Heedless, careless, inattentive. Hence **'tentlessness**.

a **1584** MONTGOMERIE *Cherrie & Slae* 1290 Aftymes a tentless merchand tynes, For bying geir be gess. **1785** BURNS *To J. Smith* x, I'll wander on, wi' tentless heed How never-halting moments speed. **1836** J. STRUTHERS *Dychmont* Poet. Wks. 1850 II. 49, I With tentless step was wont to roam. **1883** D. R. SELLARS in *Mod. Scot. Poets* vi. 157 His tentlessness he rues In calmer mood.

tentless ('tɛntlɪs), *a.*[2] [f. TENT *sb.*[1] + -LESS.] Without a tent or tents; having no tent.

1814 BYRON *Lara* II. xi, The tentless rest beneath the humid sky. **1820** MILMAN *Fall Jerus.* (1821) 39 The wind That sweeps the tentless desert. **1901** KIPLING *Kim* xiii, They lay out somewhere below him, chartless, foodless, tentless.

tentlet ('tɛntlɪt). [f. TENT *sb.*[1] + -LET.] A miniature tent.

1879 STEVENSON *Trav. Cevennes* 7 In case of heavy rain I proposed to make myself a little tent, or tentlet.

†**'tently**, *adv. Obs.* [f. TENT *a.* + -LY[2].] Attently, attentively.

? *a* **1400** *Cato's Mor.* 303 in *Cursor M.* p. 1673 þe mare þou art of prise, And gracious to office, Serue þou mare tentli, þat þou ne be calde vn-wise.

'tent-ˌmaker. **1.** One who makes tents.

1565 T. STAPLETON *Fortr. Faith* 107 b, He that weareth the crowne on his head, besecheth the teintmaker [St. Paul], and the fisher both dead to be his protectours. **1582** N.T. (Rhem.) *Acts* xviii. 3 They were tentmakers by their craft [TINDALE, Their crafte was to make tentes; 1388 WYCLIF, of roop-makeris crafte]. **1884** J. HALL *Chr. Home* 87 Paul was a tent-maker, and he was not ashamed of it.

2. (See quot., and cf. TENT *sb.*[1] 2 c.)

1863 L. L. CLARKE in *Intell. Observer* IV. 1 Micro-lepidoptera. (Coleophora, or Tent-makers.)

So **'tent-ˌmaking**, the business of making tents.

1641 'SMECTYMNUUS' *Vind. Answ.* xii. 113 We pardon his .. comparison betweene S. Pauls Tent-making .. & the State imployment of our Bishops.

tent-man: see TENT *sb.*[1] 5 b.

tentor, obs. form of TENTER.

ten'torial, *a. Anat.* [f. L. *tentōri-um* (see below) + -AL[1].] Of or pertaining to the tentorium.

1863 HUXLEY *Man's Place Nat.* iii. 149 Longitudinal and vertical sections of the skulls of a Beaver .. and a Baboon .., the tentorial plane. **1881** MIVART *Cat* 69 The ossified tentorial plate. **1899** *Syd. Soc. Lex.*, *Tentorial angle*, angle formed by the intersection of the basio-cranial axis with plane of tentorium.

So †**ten'torian** *a. Obs. rare*⁻⁰.

1656 BLOUNT *Glossogr.*, *Tentorian*, belonging to a tent or pavilion.

‖**tentorium** (tɛn'təʊrɪəm). [L. *tentōrium* tent, f. *tend-ĕre*, *tent-* to stretch: see -ORIUM.]

†**1.** A tent-like covering; an awning; a canopy.

1661 EVELYN *Fumifug.* Misc. Writ. (1805) I. 230 If there were a solid tentorium, or canopy over London.

2. *Anat.* A membranous (sometimes ossified) partition between the cerebrum and cerebellum.

1800 *Phil. Trans.* XC. 435 There is a very uncommon peculiarity in it, which is, that there is a bony falx of some breadth, but no bony tentorium. **1801** HOME *ibid.* XCII. 78 The tentorium is entirely membranous. **1854** OWEN *Skel. & Teeth* in *Orr's Circ. Sc.* I. *Org. Nat.* 232 The parts of the dura mater or outer membrane of the brain, called 'tentorium',.. are ossified. **1863** HUXLEY *Man's Place Nat.* ii. 99 What is termed the *tentorium*—a sort of parchment-like shelf or partition which .. is interposed between the cerebrum and cerebellum. **1878** BELL *Gegenbaur's Comp. Anat.* 512 In many Mammalia the tentorium is ossified.

†**'tentory.** *Obs.* [ad. L. *tentōri-um* tent: see -ORY[1].] A tent; the awning of a tent.

1412-20 LYDG. *Chron. Troy* II. 7109 Wher þe kyng sat in his tentorie. *Ibid.* IV. 2515 For lak of socour þe Grekis wern eche in his tentorie Of Troylus slayn. **1664** EVELYN *Sylva* IV. viii. (1775) 615 The women .. who are said [2 Kings xxiii. 7] to weave hangings and curtains for the grove, were no other then makers of tentories, to spread from tree to tree.

†**tentour.** *Obs. rare*⁻¹. [In quot., rendering L. *tentōria* tents: cf. -OR 3.] A tent.

a **1325** *Prose Psalter, Hab.* iii. 7 Y seȝe þe tentours [Vulg. *tentoria*; LXX. σκηνώματα] of Ethiop for her wickednes, & þe skynnes [Vulg. *pelles*; LXX. σκηναί] of þe londe of Madian shul ben trubled.

tentour, -owre, obs. forms of TENTER.

'tent-peg. One of the (usually wooden) pegs, with a notch at the upper end, to which when stuck in the ground the ropes of a tent are fastened. Hence **'tent-ˌpegging**, an Indian cavalry sport, in which the player, riding at full speed, tries to transfix and carry off, on the point of his lance, a tent-peg fixed in the ground. Also *attrib.* So **'tent-ˌpegger**, one who takes part in this exercise.

1869 E. A. PARKES *Pract. Hygiene* (ed. 3) 326 Between the tent-pegs of every tent. **1878** *N. Amer. Rev.* CXXVII. 155 'Tent-pegging' is a very favorite amusement of the sowar. **1900** *Daily News* 26 June 3/1 The tugs-of-war, tent-peggings, V.C. races, etc., were well contested. **1901** *Daily Chron.* 31 May 6/2 'Bobs' .. was himself the champion tent-pegger against all comers.

tentral, erron. form of TRENTAL.

†**tentretene** = *to entertain*: see T'.

1481 CAXTON *Godeffroy* iii. 21 This puissaunt kynge .. assigned grete reuenues therto for tentretene it [the temple].

'tent-stitch. Also ten-. [First element uncertain. One conjecture would refer it to TENT *sb.*[5]] A kind of embroidery or worsted-work popular in the 17–18th c., in which the pattern is worked in series of parallel stitches arranged diagonally across the intersections of the threads. Also called *petit point*. Also *attrib.* So **tent-work**[2], needlework done in tent-stitch.

1639 MAYNE *City Match* IV. i, Let me never more Be thought fit to instruct young Gentlewomen, Or deale in Tent-stitch. **1669** MRS. THORNTON *Autobiog.* (Surtees) 12 Blacke velvett, imbroidered with flowrs of silke worke in ten stich. *c* **1710** CELIA FIENNES *Diary* (1888) 296 Many fine pictures under Glasses, of tentstitch, sattin stitch, .. and Strawwork. **1798** EDGEWORTH *Pract. Educ.* xx. II. 530 Our great grandmothers distinguished themselves by substantial tent work [*ed.* **1811** ten-stitch] chairs and carpets. **1800** MRS. HERVEY *Mourtray Fam.* III. 199 During the interesting scene, by the tent stitch frame. **1882** CAULFEILD & SAWARD *Dict. Needlewk.*, *Tent Stitch*, a stitch employed in Tapestry Work and in fine Embroideries,.. produced by crossing over one strand of canvas in a diagonal direction, sloped from right to left, and resembles the first half taken in Cross Stitch. **1908** *Westm. Gaz.* 1 July 2/1 An oval fire-screen in tent-stitch, of quaint pattern and beautiful execution.

†**tent-taker.** *Obs.* [TENT *sb.*[2] 1.] One who 'takes tent' or gives heed.

c **1430** in *Pol. Rel. & L. Poems* (1866) 187 To triflis y haue be a greet tent taker.

tenture ('tɛntjʊə(r)). *rare.* [a. F. *tenture* tapestry hangings, ad. L. type **tentūra* stretching, f. *tendĕre*, *tent-* to stretch.] Hangings for a wall; wall-paper.

1858 SIMMONDS *Dict. Trade.* **1877** KNIGHT *Dict. Mech.*

tenture, obs. form of TENTER.

tentwise, *adv.*[1], [2]: see TENT *sb.*[1], [3].

'tent-work[1]. [f. TENT *sb.*[1] + WORK *sb.*] **a.** The work of tent-making. **b.** A work of the nature or form of a tent. **c.** Work done or carried out in tents or under canvas.

1645 BP. HALL *Remedy Discontents* 92 There we find the most glorious Apostle .. stitching of skins for his Tent-work. **1866** H. COLLINS *Cistercian Order* 53 They erected a tent-work with some pieces of blanketing. **1878** CONDER (*title*) Tent-Work in Palestine.

tent-work[2]: see TENT-STITCH.

tentwort ('tɛntwɜːt). Also 6 **teynt-**. [? f. TAINT *sb.*: see quot. 1727.] An old name for a small fern, the Wall Rue, *Asplenium Ruta-muraria*.

c **1550** LLOYD *Treas. Health* Y ij, Agaynst the Tertian of yellowe choler .. take yᵉ rotes of fennel, parcely, teynt wort, mayden heare, endyue [etc.]. **1666** MERRETT *Pinax Brit.* 2 *Adianthum album*, sive Ruta muraria, sive Salvia Vitæ, Wall rue, and Tentwort. **1727** THRELKELD *Syn. Stirpes Hibern.* A ij, Our ancestors gave it [the Ruta muraria] the name of *Tent-wort*, deeming it a sovereign remedy against the .. *Taint*, doubling of the Joints, and in a more general word, Rickets. **1860** MAYNE *Expos. Lex.*, Tent-wort. **1866** *Treas. Bot.*, Tentwort.

tenty ('tɛntɪ), *a. Sc.* Also **tentie**. [Later form of *tentif*, TENTIVE, with *-if* reduced to *-ie*, *-y*: see -IVE.] Watchful, attentive, observant, cautious.

c **1555** MAITLAND in Pinkerton *Anc. Scot. Poems* (1786) 276 Be wyse, and tentie, in thy governing. **1728** RAMSAY *Tea-t. Misc.*, *Bonny Scot* iii, Fair winds and tenty boat-man. **1785** BURNS *Halloween* viii, Jean slips in twa wi' tentie e'e; Wha 'twas, she wadna tell. **1886** STEVENSON *Kidnapped* xii. 112 Never a gun or a sword left .. but what tenty folk have hidden in their thatch.

†**'tenuate**, *v. Obs. rare.* [f. L. *tenuāt-*, ppl. stem of *tenuāre* to make thin, f. *tenuis* thin.] *trans.* To make thin or slender; to attenuate.

1656 BLOUNT *Glossogr.*, *Tenuate*,.. to make small, thin or slender. **1657** TOMLINSON *Renou's Disp.* 505 To tenuate and prepare humours.

‖**tenue** (təny). [Fr. *tenue* deportment, sb. use of fem. pa. pple. of *tenir* to hold, keep; = Pr. *tenguda*, Sp., It. *tenuta*.] Carriage, bearing, deportment; also, costume, 'rig'. Also *transf.*

1828 LADY GRANVILLE *Let.* 30 Aug. in B. Askwith *Piety & Wit* (1982) x. 154 The tenue, the neatness, the training up of flowers and fruit trees .. are what in no other country is dreamt of. **1865** CROWN PRINCESS OF PRUSSIA *Let.* 12 Dec. in R. Fulford *Your Dear Letter* (1971) 46 She went through it all [*sc.* the marriage] .. with the most perfect *tenue*. **1892** *Q. Rev.* Apr. 380 To the end that he might appear in proper tenue at any place of fashionable resort. **1901** *Ibid.* Apr. 325 The Queen had an extreme respect for *tenue* in all its forms. **1929** R. FRY *Let.* 4 Sept. (1972) II. 641 The building has a certain Florentine *tenue*, very refreshing after the rather sloppy magnificence .. of the Venetians. **1956** S. BEDFORD *Legacy* I. i. 17 A tall, cool .. woman, .. who had complete *tenu* [sic] and a great deal of character. **1971** A. FREMANTLE *Three-Cornered Heart* vi. 97 We had quite as many 'love affairs' as girls have now, though we were more reticent about them and carried on our flirtations with a certain amount of *tenue*.

tenues, pl. of TENUIS.

tenui- (tɛnjuːɪ). Combining form of L. *tenuis* 'thin, narrow, slender', in scientific use in adjectives, as **ˌtenui'costate** [L. *costa* rib], having slender ribs; so **ˌtenui'fasciate** [L. *fascia* band], **ˌtenui'florous** [L. *flōs*, *flōrem* flower], **ˌtenui'folious** [L. *folium* leaf], having narrow or thin leaves, **'tenuipede** [L. *pēs*, *ped-em* foot], **ˌtenui'striate** [L. *stria* groove], having slender striæ.

1860 MAYNE *Expos. Lex.*, *Tenuicostatus*,.. *tenuicostate. *Ibid.*, *Tenuiflorus*,.. *tenuiflorous. **1657** *Physical Dict.*, **Tenuifolious*, thin leav'd. **1658** SIR T. BROWNE *Gard. Cyrus* iv, Why Coniferous trees are tenuifolious or narrow-leaved? **1860** MAYNE *Expos. Lex.*, *Tenuifolius*, .. tenuifolious. *Ibid.*, *Tenuipes*,.. having the feet small and compressed: *tenuipede. *Ibid.*, *Tenuistriatus*,.. *tenuistriate.

†**'tenuine**, *a. Obs. rare*⁻¹. [f. L. *tenu-is* thin, app. after *genuine*.] Attenuated; weak; weakened.

a **1660** *Contemp. Hist. Irel.* (Ir. Archæol. Soc.) II. 79 To continue .. in such tenuine condition as he was at present.

te'nuious, *a.* Now *rare.* [f. L. *tenui-s* thin + -OUS (cf. *lugubri-ous*).] Thin, attenuated.

1. = TENUOUS 1.

1495 *Trevisa's Barth. De P.R.* v. lxiv. I viij b/1 The skynne of the vysage is more tenurus [? tenuius; *orig.* aliis tenuior] & thynne. **1656** BLOUNT *Glossogr.*, *Tenuious*, *Tenuous*,.. slender, thin [etc.]. **1659** STANLEY *Hist. Philos.* XIII. (1701) 563/1 A natural Philosopher, who conceived that all things are generated of tenuious little Bodies. **1698** KEILL *Exam. Th. Earth* (1734) 185 Not huge lumps of solid matter, but little tenuious particles or small dust.

2. = TENUOUS 2.

1634 T. JOHNSON *Parey's Chirurg.* XI. (1678) 274 The Aqua vitæ .. is of so tenuious a substance, that it presently vanisheth into the air. **1696** WHISTON *Th. Earth* IV. (1722) 317 The Atmosphere would .. become in a greater degree tenuious. **1757** WALKER in *Phil. Trans.* L. 130, I observed a tenuious blueish vapour rising. **1760-72** tr. *Juan & Ulloa's Voy.* (ed. 3) II. 73 These mists are so tenuious.

3. *fig.* = TENUOUS 3.

1656 STANLEY *Hist. Philos.* I. v. 148 The tenuious, loose, remisse phantasy. **1885** G. MEREDITH *Diana* xii, Emma went through a sphere of tenuious reflections in a flash.

tenuiroster (ˌtɛnjuːɪ'rɒstə(r)). *Ornith.* [ad. F. *tenuirostre*, ad. mod.L. *tenuirostris*, f. *tenui-s* thin + *rostrum* beak, bill.] A member of the *Tenuirostres*, passerine or insessorial birds with slender bills; a slender-billed bird. So **ˌtenui'rostral** *a.*, of or pertaining to the *Tenuirostres*; also = next. **ˌtenui'rostrate** *a.*, slender-billed.

1837 SWAINSON *Nat. Hist. & Classif. Birds* III. iii. II. 13 This we think is the tenuirostral type of the circle. **1837** *Penny Cycl.* VIII. 146/2 According to Mr. Vigors, the Certhiadæ on one side lead the way to the Tenuirostral group. **1842** BRANDE *Dict. Sci.*, Tenuirosters. **1860** MAYNE *Expos. Lex.*, Tenuirostrate. **1874** WOOD *Nat. Hist.* 305 The large group of birds which are termed Tenuirostral, or Slender-billed.

‖**tenuis** ('tɛn(j)uːɪs). *Gram.* and *Phonology.* Pl. **tenues** ('tɛn(j)uːiːz). [L., = thin, slender, fine: used in Craston's Latin version of Lascaris's Greek Grammar 1480, and in other early Greek grammars, to translate Gr. ψιλόν 'bare, smooth', applied by Aristotle to the consonants κ, τ, π (for which Priscian's term was *lēvis* smooth), as opposed to the *aspiratæ* or aspirates (in Gr. δασέα, pl. of δασύ rough, thick).]

One of the Greek letters κ, τ, π, or the corresponding *k*, *t*, *p* of Latin, English, and other languages; esp. the sounds represented by these; also called *surds*, *hard mutes*, and by Bell *breath stops*.

[**1480** CRASTON *Lascaris Erotemata* a iij, Mutæ .. quarum tenues quidem tres, cappa, pi, taf.]

1650 E. REEVE *Introd. Gk. Tongue* 38 The Tenuis consonant .. is changed into his aspirate: as, ἀφ' ἡμῶν for ἀπὸ ἡμῶν. **1841** [see MEDIA 1]. **1842** *Proc. Philol. Soc.* I. 7 When the final letter of the verb was one of the tenues .. *t* was substituted. **1887** MAX MÜLLER in *Fortn. Rev.* May 705 The tenuis becomes aspirate in Low-German.

tenuity (tə'njuːɪtɪ). [ad. L. *tenuitās* thinness, f. *tenuis* thin: see -ITY. So F. *ténuité* (15th c.).]

1. Thinness of form or size; slenderness.

1578 BANISTER *Hist. Man* IV. 47 The other [muscle] .. sustayneth his sinewie tenuitie to the hard tunicle of the eye. *a* **1677** HALE *Prim. Orig. Man.* 8 If we consider .. the many parts thereof, that either in respect of their tenuity or distance escape the reach of our Senses. **1777** JOHNSON 22

Sept. in *Boswell*, He is not well-shaped; for there is not the quick transition from the thickness of the forepart, to the tenuity—the thin part—behind, which a bull-dog ought to have. **1802** PALEY *Nat. Theol.* ix. (ed. 2) 150 The tenuity of these muscles [in the iris of the eye and the drum of the ear] is astonishing. **1860** TYNDALL *Glac.* I. i. 3 Mica..is sufficiently tough to furnish films of extreme tenuity. **1882** *Nature* 12 Oct. 587/1 Platinum has been rolled into sheets which..reach the surprising tenuity of less than one twenty-five-thousandth of an English inch.

2. Thinness of consistence; dilute or rarified condition; rarity.

1603 HOLLAND *Plutarch's Mor.* 740 By reason of this tenuitie and continuitie when oile doth froth or fome, it suffereth no winde or spirit to enter in. **1658** R. WHITE tr. *Digby's Powd. Symp.* (1660) 23 It becomes part of the aire, which in regard of its tenuity is invisible unto us. **1759** JOHNSON *Rasselas* vi, Precipices..so high as to produce great tenuity of air. **1802** PLAYFAIR *Illustr. Hutton. Th.* 415 The tenuity and fineness of the mud. **1860** MAURY *Phys. Geog. Sea* (Low) i. §27 Air may be expanded to an indefinite degree of tenuity.

1794 G. ADAMS *Nat. & Exp. Philos.* IV. xliv. 206 The great distance of the planet Saturn, and the tenuity of its light. **1832** L. HUNT *Sir R. Esher* 123 He ran into high tenuities of voice. **1858** HAWTHORNE *Fr. & It. Note-Bks.* II. 10 A shrill, yet sweet, tenuity of voice.

3. *fig.* Meagreness; slightness, slenderness, weakness, poverty.

1535-6 *Act 27 Hen. VIII*, c. 42 §1 By reason of the tenuytie of lyvyng. **1648** *Eikon Bas.* xvii. 178 The tenuity and contempt of Clergy-men will soon let them see, what a poore carcasse they are, when parted from the influence of that Head, to whose Supremacy they have been sworn. *a* **1734** NORTH *Lives* (1826) I. Pref. 14 My tenuity of style and language. **1867** BURTON *Hist. Scot.* (1873) I. x. 343 The tenuity of the evidence. **1895** *Pop. Sci. Monthly* July 386 Any cause which makes for intellectual tenuity.

¶ **4.** 'Simplicity, or plainness. (*Obs.*)', Webster 1864: hence in later Dicts. App. an error.

tenuous ('tɛnju:əs), *a.* [A syncopated formation from L. *tenuis* thin + -OUS; the etymologically regular form, preserving the L. stem *tenui-*, being TENUIOUS, now obs. or rare.]

1. Thin or slender in form; of small transverse measure or calibre; slim.

1656 [see TENUIOUS 1]. **1664** POWER *Exp. Philos.* II. 134 The uppermost surface of the Quicksilver..is dilated into a tenuous Column, or Funicle. **1666** J. SMITH *Old Age* (1752) 77 A most tenuous vestment for the humours. **1822** *Blackw. Mag.* XII. 411 The spider..touches his tenuous line.

2. Thin in physical consistency; sparse; rare, rarified, subtile; unsubstantial.

1597 LOWE *Chirurg.* (1634) 147 When the vaines are repleat with a tenous blood. **1635** J. SWAN *Spec. M.* v. §2 (1643) 171 Their [wind and air] substances being too tenuous to be perceived. **1794** SULLIVAN *View Nat.* I. xvi. 192 Air..is too subtile, too tenuous a substance. **1864** SIR F. PALGRAVE *Norm. & Eng.* IV. 456 Just as a tenuous film of breath, imperceptible to our senses, prevents the globules of mercury from coalescing. **1892** *Leisure Hour* Aug. 706/1 A very tenuous medium called the ether exists everywhere. **1909** *Eng. Rev.* Apr. 70 Your dress brushed the shrubs: it was grey and tenuous.

3. *fig.* Slender, of slight importance or significance; meagre, weak; flimsy, vague, unsubstantial.

a **1817** T. DWIGHT *Theol.* (1830) I. xv. 254 A subject perhaps as tenuous, and difficult to be fastened upon. **1858** BUSHNELL *Serm. New Life* 312 The tenuous and fickle impulse. **1881** *Standard* 7 May, A more tenuous or unsatisfactory claim could hardly exist. **1903** *Speaker* 9 May 145/1 The poems of the three somewhat tenuous singers. **1905** *Athenæum* 5 Aug. 166/1 [They] are sure to live as letters apart from..the tenuous story in which they are set.

Hence **'tenuously** *adv.*, thinly, sparsely; **'tenuousness**, thinness, tenuity.

1892 ZANGWILL *Bow Mystery* i, When King Fog masses his molecules of carbon in serried squadrons in the City, while he scatters them tenuously in the suburbs. **1901** *Yorksh. Post.* 28 Nov. 6/6 The bubble..is better pricked than left to burst of its own tenuousness.

tenur, obs. form of TANDOUR, TENOR, TENURE.

tenurable ('tɛnjʊərəb(ə)l), *a.* Chiefly *U.S.* [f. next + -ABLE.] Of an academic post: subject to tenure (sense 1 c). Of an applicant for such a post: fit to be granted tenure.

1977 *Science* 4 Feb. 440/3 What is their effect on the bright ..young scholar-teacher who has not, unfortunately, been productive enough to be undebatably tenurable? **1977** *Nature* 10 Nov. p. xlvi/2 (Advt.), Applications are invited for a full-time, tenurable appointment in the Division of Pharmacy and Pharmaceutics.

tenure ('tɛnjʊə(r)). Forms: α. 5- **tenure**, (5 **tenur**, 7 **tenuer**); β. 6 **tener**, **ten(n)or**, 6-7 **tenour**. [a. AF., OF. *tenure* (13th c. in Godef.):—earlier OF. *teneüre* (11-15th c.), in med.L. *tenitūra*, *tenetūra* (*c* 1200 in Du Cange), f. *tenē-re* to hold: see -URE. Med.L. had also (from OF.) *teneura*, *tenura* (11th c. in Du Cange). OF. had in same sense *tenor*, *-our*, *teneur*, app. by some confusion with TENOR *sb.*, whence the β-forms in ME., etc.

A further result of this use of *tenor* in sense of *tenure* in OF. and ME. was that *tenure* was also used for TENOR: see the latter.]

1. a. The action or fact of holding a tenement (esp. in *Eng. Law*): see TENEMENT 1.

α. [**1292** BRITTON I. xix. §7 En les queus dreitz nul ne se deit eyder par excepcioun de lounge tenure (*tr.* to aid himself by exception of long tenure).] **1442** *Surtees Misc.* (1888) 18 We..serched a tenement,..in þe tenur of John Wetelay. **1546** *Mem. Ripon* (Surtees) III. 16, xv acres of arable lande..in tholdinge of Richard Carlell xvs. one tenemente in Northstanley in the tenure of John Hyrde vs. **1614** SELDEN *Titles Hon.* 31 Those inferior Kings are like in some proportion to those of Man, who haue had it alwayes by a tenure from their soueraigns, the Kings of England. **1614** RALEIGH *Hist. World* III. (1634) 113 Some land there was in the tenure of the Locrians. **1651** BAXTER *Inf. Bapt.* 100 Is not the Law of the Land..the cause of..every mans right in the Tenure of His Estate? **1874** STUBBS *Const. Hist.* I. ii. 34 We have not the mark system, but we have the principle of common tenure. **1878** SIMPSON *Sch. Shaks.* I. 53 Hooker wrote to Carew..that the Barony of Odrone was in the tenure of a sect called the Cavanaghs.

β. *c* **1505** *Plumpton Corr.* (Camden) 200 A certayne land in Rybstone, of long tyme in the tennor of one John Ampleforthe. **1589** *Wills & Inv. N.C.* (Surtees) II. 166 My glebe land in Learmouth, now in the tenor of Johne Moore, for xxj yeares. **1612-13** in *N. Riding Rec.* (1884) II. 11 A parcell of meadow called the Wraie in the tenour of Rich. Michell. **1658** *Knaresb. Wills* (Surtees) II. 237 A messuage with land..now in tenor of William Wilkenson.

b. *gen.* and *fig.* The action or fact of holding anything material or non-material; hold upon something; maintaining a hold; occupation.

1599 B. JONSON *Cynthia's Rev.* v. iv, Lady, vouchsafe the tenure of this ensigne. **1638** ROUSE *Heav. Univ.* (1702) Pref., A Christians tenure of religion is far more excellent and assured than that of the Pagan. **1738** *Gentl. Mag.* VIII. 411/1 They were more One than either Espousals, or a Joint-Tenure of the Throne, could make them. **1810** WELLINGTON in Gurw. *Desp.* (1838) V. 497 Their existence in safety at Seville depends upon the tenure of the pass of Monasterio. **1844** LD. BROUGHAM *Brit. Const.* App. ii. (1862) 414 Their salary cannot be altered during their tenure of office. **1855** BREWSTER *Newton* II. xxvi. 378 Warned of his slight tenure of life. **1875** JOWETT *Plato* (ed. 2) V. 330 The tenure of the priesthood should always be for a year and no longer.

c. *spec.* (orig. *U.S.*) Guaranteed tenure of office, as a right granted to the holder of a position (usu. in a university or school) after a probationary period and protecting him against dismissal under most circumstances.

1957 V. NABOKOV *Pnin* vi. 139 Pnin, who had no life tenure at Waindell, would be forced to leave—unless some other literature-and-language Department agreed to adopt him. *Ibid.* 167 'Naturally, I am expecting that I will get tenure at last,' said Pnin rather slyly. 'I am now Assistant Professor nine years.' **1975** *National Observer* (U.S.) 31 July 8/2 Idaho tried to abolish tenure a year ago, but the teachers' lobby was so strong the bill was defeated. **1981** *Listener* 5 Feb. 166/3 Can universities in a time of declining resources still preserve tenure in all its old form?

2. a. The condition of service, etc., under which a tenement is held of the superior; the title by which the property is held; the relations, rights, and duties of the tenant to the landlord. *tenure at will*: cf. TENANT AT WILL.

1436 *Rolls of Parlt.* IV. 501/2 Y^e^ Five Portes and tenure of Gavelkynde. **1523** FITZHERB. *Surv.* 12 All these tenauntes maye holde their landes by dyuers tenures, customes, and seruyces: as by homage, fealtie, escuage, socage..burgage tenures, and tenure in vyllenage. *Ibid.*, Also it is to be enquered..who holdeth by charter and who nat, and who by the olde tenure. **1554** *Act 1 & 2 Phil. & Mary*, c. 8 §54 The Donor..maye reserve to him and his heires for ever a Tenure in Franck Almoigne. **1605** CAMDEN *Rem.* (1637) 132 As he that held Land by tenure to say a certaine number of Pater nosters for the soules of the Kings of England. **1607** COWELL s.v., Tenure is the manner, whereby tenements are houlden of their Lords. **1628** COKE *On Litt.* 85 b, Tenure in Socage, is where the Tenant holdeth of his Lord the tenancie by certaine seruice for all manner of seruices, so that the seruice be not Knights seruice. **1641** CAPT. MERVIN in Rushw. *Hist. Coll.* III. (1692) I. 214 The abortive Judgment of the Tenure *in Capite*, where no Tenure was exprest. **1765** BLACKSTONE *Comm.* I. Introd. iii. 73 A very extensive comment upon a little excellent treatise of tenures, compiled by judge Littleton in the reign of Edward the fourth. *Ibid.* xiii. 398 Those, who by their military tenures were bound to perform forty days service in the field. **1774** PENNANT *Tour Scot. in 1772*, 45 The right of voting is vested by burgess tenure, in certain houses. **1818** CRUISE *Digest* (ed. 2) I. 7 The circumstance of annexing a condition of military service to a grant of lands does not imply that they are held by a feudal tenure. *Ibid.* 27 Where lands held by an allodial tenure were voluntarily converted into feuds. *Ibid.* 381 Enfranchisement, by which the tenure is changed from base to free. **1844** H. H. WILSON *Brit. India* II. xii. II. 549 Involving a complicated texture of rights and tenures, which almost defied unravelling. **1875** J. CURTIS *Hist. Eng.* 396 The statute 12 Car. II, c. 24, which abolished the military tenures, converting them into freehold. **1892** *Pall Mall G.* 17 Mar. 7/1 The new and purely tenure-at-will system gradually gaining ground. **1908** *Fenland N. & Q.* Apr. 177 Keyhold Tenure at Crowland... That house was his because he built it, and because he held the key which admitted him to it and enabled him to keep other people out of it.

β. ? **1510** PYNSON (*title*) Leteltun teners newe correcte. **1535** (ed. 1562) *Act 27 Hen. VIII*, c. 26 §2 After the english tenour without diuision or parcion. **1633** T. STAFFORD *Pac. Hib.* I. ii. (1821) 38, I hold my Lordships and Lands..by very ancient Tenour, which Service and Tenour none may dispence withall. **1649** G. DANIEL *Trinarch., Rich. II*, lxi, And some (who were in law more Conversant), Demand release of Tenors.

b. *transf.* Terms of holding; title; authority; hold over a person or thing; control.

1871 FREEMAN *Hist. Ess.* Ser. I. vii. 184 Few Englishmen understand the difference between the English tenure of Bourdeaux and the English tenure of Calais. *a* **1879** in Drysdale *Philemon* Introd. 2 To understand the tenure of Philemon over Onesimus, we should keep in mind the stringency of Phrygian bondage.

c. *fig.* (Cf. 1 b.)

1659 HAMMOND *On Ps.* xxxiv. 8 Paraphr. 181 There is no such assured tenure in or title to all the felicity in the world. **1726** SWIFT *Gulliver* III. iii, The office of a favourite hath a very uncertain tenure. **1790** BURKE *Fr. Rev.* 42 Rendering their government feeble in its operations, and precarious in its tenure. **1840** ALISON *Hist. Europe* (1847) XI. xlix. §7. 54 The mutable tenure of popular applause. **1863** W. PHILLIPS *Sp.* iii. 53 Republics exist only on the tenure of being constantly agitated.

β. **1682** H. MORE *Annot. Glanvill's Lux O.* 117 Whether Regeneration be not a stronger tenour for enduring Happiness.

3. *concr.* A holding; = TENEMENT 2. Now *rare*.

1439 *Rolls of Parlt.* V. 16/2 The saide Tennauntz dare nat abide in thaire Tenures and Places, ne no laboure there do. **1461** *Ibid.* 476/1 All Tenures within the same Lordship been Chartre land, and Free land. **1766** ENTICK *London* IV. 443 Greenwich-park..is still a royal tenure.

4. *attrib.* and *Comb.*, as ***tenure land***, ***roll***.

1859 EYTON *Antiq. Shropshire* IX. 39 The Tenure-Roll of 1285 brings up another Ralph de Clotley. **1891** *Pall Mall G.* 22 Sept. 7/2 Property, consisting of a mansion and several miles of tenure land (twenty-one villages)..in North Jutland.

b. In sense 1 c above, as ***tenure decision***, ***member***, ***system***; ***tenure-heavy*** adj.; **tenure track** *U.S.*, an employment structure whereby the holder of a post is guaranteed consideration for eventual tenure, usu. within a stated number of years.

1978 *Chron. Higher Educ.* 2 Oct. 8/3 Some 1,000 complaints of unfair tenure decisions his organization handles each year. **1979** *Yale Alumni Mag.* Apr. 13/1 Faculties are becoming increasingly tenure-heavy. **1960** J. J. CORSON *Governance of Colleges & Universities* v. 101 In some institutions only the tenure members of the faculty will be privileged to participate in the school faculty. **1971** *Nature* 31 Dec. 502/2 The tenure system simply allows dead wood to remain in the university. **1979** *Ibid.* 4 Oct. p. xix/1 (Advt.), Two-year appointment with the possibility of tenure track. **1981** *Washington Post* 2 Jan. B16/4 People get into the feeling that they are on a tenure track and that they are unshakeable.

Hence †**'tenurage**, *Obs.*, what belongs to a tenure or tenures; general conditions of tenure; †**'tenurer**, *Obs.* = TENANT; †**'tenurist**, *Obs.*, one who deals with or treats of tenures.

1610 W. FOLKINGHAM *Art of Survey* III. ii. 68 Tenant in the first signification sometimes imports duety of *Tenurage: as Tenant by Knight-seruice, Socage, Tenant in Villenage, Burgage. *Ibid.* IV. Concl. 88 Inroll all the Feudataries & Suiters to the Court with their Fees, Tenurage, Rents, and Seruices. **1660** WATERHOUSE *Arms & Arm.* 106 Nor could they be chargable with what should disable the *Tenurer to do his service. **1588** FRAUNCE *Lawiers Log.* Ded. ¶ij, It cannot bee, sayde one great *Tenurist, that a good scholler should euer prooue good Lawyer. *a* **1628** DODERIDGE *Eng. Lawyer* (1631) 53 Defiled by the Feudary Tenurist writers of the middle age.

tenured ('tɛnjʊəd), *a.* Chiefly *U.S.* [f. prec. + -ED².] Of an official position, usu. one in a university or school: carrying a guarantee of permanent employment until retirement. Of a teacher, lecturer, etc.: having guaranteed tenure of office.

1969 *Guardian* 24 May 1/6 Left-wing professors, whose only protection is tenured appointment. **1970** 'A. CROSS' *Poetic Justice* I. iv. 62 What does she look like?..I thought I knew all the tenured English faculty. **1975** *Nature* 25 Dec. 653/2 A growing number of French scientists have found themselves having to work on short-term contracts, as tenured posts have dried up. **1976** *Maclean's Mag.* 27 Dec. 46/1 A board's right to fire any teacher, probationary or tenured, who violates the moral principles [etc.].

Hence (as a back-formation) **'tenure** *v. trans.*, to provide (someone) with a tenured post.

1975 *Times Lit. Suppl.* 13 June 639/1 How you propose to recruit, train, tenure and retire faculty [*sc.* in an American university]. **1983** *N.Y. Times* 23 Oct. I. 35/1 We have 22 women who were tenured by this department as a result of evaluations that said they could do the job.

tenurial (tɛ'njʊərɪəl), *a.* [f. med.L. *tenūra* TENURE + -IAL.] Of, pertaining to, or of the nature of the tenure of land. Hence **te'nurially** *adv.*, in respect of tenure.

1896 F. W. MAITLAND in *Eng. Hist. Rev.* Jan. 18 The borough court is not founded on a tenurial or feudal principle. *Ibid.*, The burgesses were a tenurially heterogeneous group. **1898** —— *Township & Borough* 69 The tenurial rent paid by tenant to lord becomes practically indistinguishable from the mere rent charge which implies no tenure. *Ibid.* 72 Because feudally, tenurially, the borough is patch-work. **1908** *Spectator* 20 June 978/1 All land-holding having become tenurial, the lord's consent was necessary to each alienation.

‖**tenuto** (te'nuto), *a.*, *adv.* and *sb. Mus.* [It., = held.] **A.** *adj.* and *adv.* Held, sustained: a direction to a performer to sustain a note its full length. Usually abbreviated *ten.* Also *transf.*

1762 STERNE *Tr. Shandy* VI. xi. 50 What *Yorick* could mean by the words *lentamente*,—*tenutè* [sic],—*grave*,—and sometimes *adagio*,—as applied to theological compositions ..I dare not venture to guess. **1801** BUSBY *Dict. Mus.*, *Tenuto*, or *Ten.* (Ital.), a word signifying that the notes are to be sustained, or held on. **1931** D. F. TOVEY in Tovey & Craxton *Beethoven Pianoforte Sonatas* (Associated Board of Royal Schools of Music) III. 69/2 *Bars* 1-4.—The *forte* is a matter of string-tone and cantabile... Express the *tenuto* marks without hard accent, and see that in bar 3 the *piano* does not come too soon. **1975** *Gramophone* Nov. 839/1 In the *Meistersinger* piece I..like lots of notes played more *tenuto*.

B. *sb.* Pl. *tenutos.* A note or chord played *tenuto.*

1966 in *Random House Dict.* **1976** *Gramophone* Feb. 1349/3, I should have preferred him not to linger with so pronounced a tenuto on each bar in the bassoon solo. **1977** *Ibid.* Feb. 1279/2 He allows himself few of the momentary tenutos which have become a natural part of phrasing Franck melodies. **1982** *Guardian Weekly* 25 Apr. 20 Variations (with many tenutos Elgar never dreamed of).

tenys, -yse, obs. forms of TENNIS.

tenzon, variant of TENSON.

‖**teocalli** (tiːəʊˈkælɪ). Also 7 teucalli. [Mexican *teocallí*, f. *teotl* god + *callí* house.] A structure for purposes of worship among the ancient Mexicans and Central Americans, usually consisting of a four-sided truncated pyramid built terrace-wise, and surmounted by a temple.

1613 PURCHAS *Pilgrimage* VIII. xii. 670 Gomara saith, that this and other their Temples were called *Teucalli*, which signifieth Gods house. **1843** PRESCOTT *Mexico* II. viii. (1850) I. 304 The floor and walls of the *teocalli* were then cleansed, by command of Cortés, from their foul impurities. **1844** LONGF. *Arsenal at Springfield* v, And Aztec priests upon their teocallis [*rime* palace] Beat the wild war-drums. **1852** TH. ROSS *Humboldt's Trav.* Introd. 17 A description of the *teocalli*, or Mexican pyramids.

Teochew, Teo-chew (ˌtiːəʊ ˈtʃjuː). Also Teochieu, Teochiu, Tiuchiu. [A place-name in Swatow Chinese, = Putonghua *Cháozhoū*.] (A member of) a people of the Swatow district of Kwangtung in southern China; the dialect spoken by this people. Also *attrib.*

1893 J. D. BALL *Things Chinese* (ed. 2) 229 By..1891 there were 43,791 Teo Chews in the Straits Settlements: Teo Chews is the term applied generally to them in that part of the country, while Hoklo is the name by which they are generally known by the Cantonese speakers in China; the former name being derived from the Departmental city Ch'ao Chao fú (in the local dialect Tíú Chíú fú, or Teo Chew fu). **1927** in R. J. H. Sidney *In Brit. Malaya To-Day* xii. 144 Trouble had been brewing between Hok-kiens and the Teo-chews for some time. **1962** *B.B.C. Handbk.* 109 Adaptations ..in the following languages: Chibemba,..Teochew. **1966** M. FREEDMAN *Chinese Lineage & Society* iii. 95 People will assume for all Hakka or Hokkien or Cantonese or Tiuchiu that [etc.]. **1970** M. PEREIRA *Pigeon's Blood* xv. 164 He was speaking in the Teo-chieu dialect. **1979** *China Now* Jan.–Feb. 10/2 The Teochiu group from one district in Guangdong (Kwangtung) province.

teology, teom(e, teon(e, obs. ff. THEOLOGY, TEAM, TEEN, TUNE.

teonanacatl (ˌtiːənɑːnəˈkæt(ə)l). [a. Nahuatl, f. *teotl* god + *nancatl* mushroom.] Any of several hallucinogenic fungi, esp. *Psilocybe mexicana*, found in Central America. Also *attrib.*

1875 H. H. BANCROFT *Native Races Pacific States* II. 360 Among the ingredients used to make their drinks more intoxicating the most powerful was the *teonanacatl*, 'flesh of God', a kind of mushroom which excited the passions. **1915** *Jrnl. Heredity* VII. 294/2 The writer has sought diligently for a fungus having the properties attributed to the *teonanacatl.* **1940** *Amer. Anthropologist* XLII. 439 The identity of teonanacatl was unknown for three centuries. **1953** J. RAMSBOTTOM *Mushrooms & Toadstools* vi. 49 The Aztecs and Chichimecas were the earliest recorders of this teonanacatl. **1966** *Listener* 14 July 47/1 Another Mexican fantasy-producing drug that is used in religious ceremonial comes from the teonanacatl mushroom. **1975** [see PSILOCIN].

‖**ˈteopan.** [Shortened from Mex. *teo-*, *teupantlí* temple, f. *teotl* god + *pantlí* wall.] A Mexican temple, a teocalli.

1891 in *Cent. Dict.*

‖**teosinte** (tiːəʊˈsɪntiː). [In F. *téosinté* (*Bull. Soc. d'Acclim.* 1871, 38), ad. Mex. *teocintli* 'seu spica Maizii montana' (Hernandez *Op.* 1790, II. 120), app. f. *teotl* god + *cintli*, *centli* dry ear or cob of maize. In Ramirez *Sinon. Plant. Mex.* 67 *teoxintli*.] An annual grass of Central America, *Euchlæna luxurians*, of large size, allied to maize; now widely cultivated as a valuable fodder plant, sometimes also as a cereal.

1877 *Gardener's Chron.* 55 Teosinta. **1878** *Kew Report* 13 Téosinté. **1880** SCHOMBURGK (S. Australia) in *Kew Bulletin* (1894) 380, I have now cultivated Teosinte for three years, and it is one of the most prolific fodder plants. **1894** *Ibid.* Nov. 375 A very valuable fodder grass belonging to this group is the Teosinte (*Euchlæna luxurians*). *Ibid.* 381 The great value of Teosinte as a food plant has been established in many parts of India. **189.** *Experiment Station Recd.* IX. 346 Analyses were made of samples of corn-stover and teosinte from the inside and outside of the shocks.

teothe, teothinge, obs. ff. TITHE *v.*, TITHING.

tep, early form of TAP *v.*², to strike.

tepa (ˈtiːpə). *Chem.* Also TEPA. [f. *tri*ethylene *p*hosphor*a*mide.] An organophosphorus compound, $PO(N(CH_2)_2)_3$, used as an insect sterilant and formerly in the treatment of cancer.

1953 *Cancer* VI. 140/2 These observations justify the continuation of studies of the action of TEPA in advanced cancer. **1963** *New Scientist* 13 June 603/2 More than 3¼ million flies..had been sexually sterilised by dipping their pupae in a 5 per cent solution of tepa. **1973** J. J. MCKELVEY *Man against Tsetse* iii. 196 [Experimenters] tried to eradicate tsetse from an area in Rhodesia by sterilizing male flies with..tepa.

‖**tepache** (teˈpatʃe). [Mexican Sp., ad. Nahuatl *tepiatl*.] Any of several Mexican drinks of varying degrees of fermentation, typically made with pineapple, water, and brown sugar.

1926 D. H. LAWRENCE *Mornings in Mexico* (1927) 42 *Tepache* is a fermented drink of pineapple rinds and brown sugar. **1930** R. MACAULAY *Staying with Relations* xix. 273, I tried for a drink of Mexicali and only got tepache. **1983** M. GORMAN *Cooking with Fruit* III. 188 Tepache..is an old Mexican household fruit drink... It is a simple mixture that uses 1 pineapple.

tepal (ˈtɛpəl, ˈtiːpəl). *Bot.* [ad. F. *tépale* (A. P. de Candolle *Organographie Végétale* (1827) I. III. ii. 503): see quot. 1840.] A segment of a perianth which is not divided into a corolla and a calyx.

1840 B. KINGDON tr. *A. P. de Candolle's Veget. Organogr.* II. ii. 90 It is well to retain for these doubtful cases of a single envelope a particular name... Following the analogy of the terms sepals and petals, I propose..the name of Tepals. **1866** *Treas. Bot.*, *Tepal*, another name for petal. Also the pieces of a perianth, being of an ambiguous nature, between calyx and corolla. **1939** *Rep. Bot. Soc. Brit. Isles* XII. 120 It is proposed to refer to them [*sc.* the perianth segments of *Rumex*] as Inner and Outer Perianth Segments, or Tepals. **1951** G. H. M. LAWRENCE *Taxon. Vascular Plants* II. 413 Perianth..generally undifferentiated into corolla and calyx, and when so the segments termed tepals. **1968** A. CRONQUIST *Evol. & Classification Flowering Plants* iii. 87 The tepals of the more primitive angiosperm families are modified leaves. **1972** *Jrnl. R. Hort. Soc.* XCVII. 336 Because magnolia flowers usually have no distinction between petals and sepals the term tepal has been generally accepted for these floral parts.

tepary (ˈtɛpərɪ). Also tepari. [Origin unknown.] In full, ***tepary bean***. An annual legume, *Phaseolus acutifolius*, native to southwestern North America, or a cultivated plant belonging to a variety developed from it and resistant to drought; also, the seed of a plant of this kind.

1912 G. F. FREEMAN *Southwestern Beans* 582 The name tepary or tepari (Spanish) originated from the Papago. **1912** K. S. LUMHOLTZ *New Trails in Mexico* 318 He had cooked bones of mountain-sheep with tépari beans for us. **1925** K. BRYAN *Papago Country* 354 The beans known as tépari..are said to be so resistant to drought that the plants may wither three successive times and then, if enough rain comes, mature a crop. **1942** CASTETTER & BELL *Pima & Papago Indian Agric.* 92 The cultivated tepary bean antedates the coming of the white man in the southwest. *Ibid.* 191 The Papago made only one planting of teparies. **1972** Y. LOVELOCK *Vegetable Bk.* I. 56 The Texas or tepary bean.. grows wild and is much cultivated in Mexico and the adjoining states of the U.S.

tepat(e, tepet, obs. forms of TIPPET.

tepee (ˈtiːpiː, tiːˈpiː). Also †teebee, teepee, tepe, tepie, teepe, ti pee; tipi (sometimes preferred). [Sioux or Dakota Indian *ˈtīpī* tent, house, dwelling, abode (Rigg, *Dakota-Eng. Dict.* 1890).] **1.** A tent or wigwam of the American Indians, formed of bark, mats, skins, or canvas stretched over a frame of poles converging to and fastened together at the top. In extended uses, applied to a similar structure used by peoples of other parts of the world, as a child's toy, or for camping. Also *attrib.*

1743 J. ISHAM in *Publ. Hudson's Bay Record Soc.* (1949) XII. 45 A tent Build ti pee. **1847** G. W. FEATHERSTONHAUGH *Canoe Voyage* I. xxx. 338 Here, also, were their spring teebees, which they inhabit at that season. **1849** M. H. EASTMAN *Dahcotah* p. xxii, The messenger enters the wigwam (or *teepee*, as the houses of the Sioux are called) of the juggler. **1872** W. F. BUTLER *Gt. Lone Land* ix. 125 One has to travel far..before the smoke of your wigwam or of your tepie blurs the evening air. **1877** BLACK *Green Past.* xlv, At length we descried..three teepees—tall, narrow, conical tents with the tips of the poles on which the canvas is stretched appearing at the top. **1899** STUTFIELD in *Blackw. Mag.* Mar. 546 That evening we dispensed with the teepee and camped in the open air. **1910** *Encycl. Brit.* XIV. 469/1 The skin tents or tipis of many of the Plains peoples. **1959** A. MOOREHEAD *No Room in Ark* ix. 211 I liked the Dinka villages... They looked like Red Indian encampments of a century or two ago: tall teepees made of grass and arranged in a rough circle on the bank. **1960** D. JENNESS *Indians of Canada* (ed. 5) vii. 90 The plains' area was the home of the tipi, a tent of buffalo hide stretched around a conical framework formed by fourteen to eighteen long poles, whose points radiated like a funnel above the peak. **1970** *New Yorker* 12 Dec. 138/2 A six-and-a-half-foot tepee costs $25 [in a toy-shop]. **1974** N. GORDIMER *Conservationist* 42 The newly-ploughed field, where the mealie stalks are piled into tepees. **1976** *Billings* (Montana) *Gaz.* 2 July 8-A/1 (Advt.), You'll love the weekend activities in store for you at four nearby KOA Kampgrounds. All you need to take is your family or friends, sleeping bags and food. The Tepee or Tent will be waiting for you to move right in and there's a grill for cooking.

2. *attrib.* and *Comb.*, as ***tepee cloth***, ***cover***, ***pole***, ***trail***; ***tepee-like*** adj.; **tepee ring** (see quot.).

1877 *Rep. Indian Affairs* (U.S.) 50 Tepee cloth should be discontinued, and..log or frame houses should be substituted. **1890** E. CUSTER *Following Guidon* 6 The hides were dressed for robes or tepee covers. **1925** *Blackw. Mag.* May 658/1 There were three large tepee-like tents. **1897** J. W. TYRRELL *Across Sub-Arctics of Canada* 68 Instead of Indians, [we] found only old forsaken 'tepee' poles and blackened fire-places. **1899** STUTFIELD in *Blackw. Mag.* Mar. 542 Now and then we saw the teepee poles of old Indian camping-grounds. **1956** D. LEECHMAN *Native Tribes of Canada* 10 We find..on the prairies, tipi rings, circles of stones that once were used to hold down the edges of the skin tents. **1869** *Amer. Naturalist* II. 648 [We] follow upon the dim road or the tepe trail over the broad prairie.

tepefaction (tɛpɪˈfækʃən). *rare*⁻⁰. [n. of action f. L. *tepefacĕre*: see next and -FACTION.]

1658 PHILLIPS, *Tepefaction*,..a making lukewarm.

tepefy (ˈtɛpɪfaɪ), *v.* Also tepify. [f. L. *tepefacĕre* to make tepid, f. *tepē-re* to be lukewarm: see -FY.] **a.** *trans.* To make tepid or moderately warm; to warm. **b.** *intr.* To become tepid.

1656 BLOUNT *Glossogr.*, *Tepefie*.., to make warme. **1745** COOPER *Power Harm.* I. 17 The flood of life, Loos'd at its source by tepefying strains. **1774** GOLDSM. *Nat. Hist.* (1862) II. III. ii. 323 Except..the shallows at the edges of the stream become tepified by the..rays of the sun. **1847** WEBSTER, *Tepefy*, v. i. To become moderately warm. **1866** J. B. ROSE *Virg. Ecl. & Georg.* 129 As vital humours tepify.

tephigram (ˈtɛfɪgræm). *Meteorol.* [f. TE(E *sb.*¹ (*T* being a symbol for temperature) + PHI (ϕ being a symbol for entropy) + -GRAM.]

A diagram in which one axis represents temperature and another potential temperature (as a measure of entropy), used to represent the thermodynamic state of the atmosphere at different heights.

[*c* **1925** N. SHAW *Sel. Meteorol. Papers* (1955) 226/2, I have found the representation known to engineers as a θ, ϕ (temperature-entropy) diagram (or, as I shall call it here, a t ϕ diagram) has the advantage of being..more expressive than the direct pressure-temperature diagram.] **1929** W. J. HUMPHREYS *Physics of Air* (ed. 2) xv. 259 Tephigram... It is convenient, as developed by Sir Napier Shaw and his colleagues, to plot values on a temperature-entropy diagram. *Ibid.* 261 Figure 77 is a tephigram..of a balloon sounding. **1938** *Nature* 29 Oct. 804/1 Daily tephigrams based on aeroplane soundings constitute the most valuable items in forecasting..clearing or persistence of cloud. **1969** *Ibid.* 11 Oct. 170/1 The uniformity of weather conditions over the region in question justified our taking these tephigrams as representative of the state of the atmosphere over the area.

tephillim, -in, varr. TEFILLIN.

tephra (ˈtɛfrə). *Geol.* [ad. Sw. *tefra* (S. Thórarinsson 1944, in *Geografiska Annaler* XXVI. 114), f. Gr. τέφρα ash.] Dust and rock fragments that have been ejected into the air by a volcanic eruption. Freq. *attrib.*

1944 *Geografiska Annaler* XXVI. 210 The author suggests (*volcanic*) *ash* or (better) *tephra* as a collective term for all clastic ejectamenta. **1970** *Nature* 25 July 335/1 The maximum thickness of the tephra layer was 7 cm at 15 km from the volcano. **1972** *Nat. Geographic* CXLI. 718/2 Commercial interests are removing this layer—known as tephra—since it makes a highly cohesive and waterproof mortar, serves as an insulating material, and constitutes an important component of cement. **1973** *Nature* 9 Feb. 372/2 Because of its close vicinity to the eruption the town was threatened by tephra fall. **1979** *Sci. Amer.* Dec. 134/2 The cloud of tephra and gas rises high above the volcano, and particles in it are carried downwind, producing a rain of tephra that forms a deposit called a tephra mantle.

tephrite (ˈtɛfraɪt). *Min.* [f. Gr. τεφρός ash-coloured (f. τέφρα ashes) + -ITE¹. Cf. L. *tephrītis* (Pliny) an ash-coloured precious stone.] Name given to a class of volcanic rocks related to the basalts. Hence **tephritic** (-ˈrɪtɪk) *a.*, pertaining to or consisting of tephrite; **ˈtephritoid**, a variety of tephrite containing no nepheline.

1879 RUTLEY *Stud. Rocks* xiii. 253 The tephrites, or those rocks which are characterised by the presence of nepheline or leucite in conjunction with plagioclase. **1889** *Amer. Nat.* Apr. 259 According to the predominance of one or other of the constituents they are divided into basaltic, doleritic and tephritic varieties.

tephrochronology (ˌtɛfrəʊkrəʊˈnɒlədʒɪ). Also tephra-. [ad. Sw. *tefrokronologi* (S. Thórarinsson 1944, in *Geografiska Annaler* XXVI. 6), f. as TEPHRA: see CHRONOLOGY.] The dating of volcanic eruptions and other events by studying layers of tephra. Hence **ˌtephrochronoˈlogical** *a.*

1944 S. THÓRARINSSON in *Geografiska Annaler* XXVI. 204 As an international term to designate a geological chronology based on the measuring, interconnecting, and dating of volcanic ash layers in soil profiles the author suggests the term *Tephrochronology*. *Ibid.* (*heading*) Tephrochronological studies in Iceland. **1976** P. FRANCIS *Volcanoes* v. 178 The use of successive pumice or ash deposits in building up a history of the eruptive activity in an area is known as tephrachronology. **1979** *Nature* 25 Oct. 642/1 The tephrochronology of these ashes is well documented, but volcanological interpretations have seldom been attempted. **1979** *Sci. Amer.* Dec. 132/1 A volcano produces successive showers of tephra that fall throughout the surrounding countryside, forming layers that constitute a tephrochronological record of the volcano's activity.

tephroite (ˈtɛfrəʊaɪt). *Min.* [ad. Ger. *tephroit* (Breithaupt, 1823), irreg. f. Gr. τεφρός: see TEPHRITE and -ITE¹.] A silicate of manganese, occurring in crystalline masses of an ashy grey or reddish colour.

1868 DANA *Min.* 259.

tephromancy ('tɛfrəʊmænsɪ). Also erron. **tephra-**. [f. Gr. τέφρα ashes + -MANCY.] Divination by means of ashes: see quots.

1652 GAULE *Magastrom.* xix. 165 *Tephramancy* [*pr.* Tu-], by ashes; *Capnomancy*, by smoak. **1661** BLOUNT *Glossogr.* (ed. 2), *Tephramantie*..divination by ashes, blown or cast up in the air. *a* **1693** *Urquhart's Rabelais* III. xxv, Have you a mind..to have the truth..more fully..disclosed..by tephromancy: thou wilt see the ashes thus aloft dispersed, exhibiting thy wife in a fine posture. **1846** WORCESTER, *Tephramancy*, divination by the ashes of a sacrifice.

tepid ('tɛpɪd), *a.* Also 5 **teped**, 6 **tepit**. [ad. L. *tepid-us* lukewarm, f. *tepēre* to be warm. So obs. or dial. F. *tépide* (16th c. in Godef.).] Moderately or slightly warm; lukewarm.

a. *lit.* (Usually in reference to liquids.)

c **1400** *Lanfranc's Cirurgie* 157 He worchiþ riȝtfulliche þat vsiþ teped oilis. **1626** BACON *Sylva* §346 For as a great heat keepeth bodies from putrefaction, but a tepid heat inclineth them to putrefaction. **1664** EVELYN *Kal. Hort.* (1729) 201 Let the Water stand in the Sun till it grow tepid. **1744** BERKELEY *Siris* §78 A blister on the spot, and plenty of tepid tar-water. **1884** F. M. CRAWFORD *Rom. Singer* ii, A cold sirocco, bringing showers of tepid rain from the south.

b. *fig.* = LUKEWARM 2.

1513 DOUGLAS *Æneis* XI. Prol. 60 Gyf Crystis faithfull knychtis lyst ws be,..Than man we..Nowder be abasit, tepit, nor ȝit blunt. **1641** GAUDEN *Love of Truth* 30 A tepid and Laodicean love. **1740** CHEYNE *Regimen* 333 Of the two Evils, Infidelity and Tepidity is..the worst..in regard of the Infidels and Tepid themselves. **1873** H. SPENCER *Stud. Sociol.* viii. (1874) 179 Remind them of certain precepts..in the creed they profess, and the most you get is a tepid assent. **1926** *Scribner's Mag.* Sept. 259/2 Her smile said that pastels were thin things for tepid people. **1941** A. CHRISTIE *Evil under Sun* x. 197 Some tepid little man, vain and sensitive—the kind of man who broods.

Hence **'tepidly** *adv.*, in a tepid or lukewarm manner; **'tepidness** = TEPIDITY. So † **'tepidous** *a.*, tepid, lukewarm (*obs.*).

1696 PHILLIPS (ed. 5), **Tepidly*, lukewarm. **1873** H. SPENCER *Stud. Sociol.* viii. (1874) 179 The precepts tepidly assented to. **1821** BYRON *Diary* Poet. Wks. (1846) 510/2 Some **tepid*-ness on the part of Kean, or warmth on that of the author. **1903** LD. ROSEBERY in *Westm. Gaz.* 13 Oct. 8/2 This may explain a slight tepidness on the part of Australia. **1607** J. CARPENTER *Plaine Mans Plough* 186 Those Angells ..which were sometime *tepicous and backeward.

‖**tepidarium** (tɛpɪ'dɛərɪəm). Pl. **-ia**. Also 6 in anglicized form **tepidarie**. [L., f. *tepidus* TEPID: see -ARIUM.] The warm room in an ancient Roman bath, situated between the *frigidarium* and the *caldarium*. Hence also applied to a similar room in a Turkish bath.

1585 T. WASHINGTON tr. *Nicholay's Voy.* II. xxi. 58b, [Bathers] doe first goe in to the Tepidarie too make themselues sweate. **1818** E. BLAQUIERE tr. *Pananti* 223 He successively passes through the *frigidarium*, and *tepidarium*, until he reaches the *calidarium* of the Romans. **1834** LYTTON *Pompeii* I. vii, The more luxurious departed by another door to the *tepidarium*. **1969** J. WAINWRIGHT *Take-Over Men* ii. 27, I followed him..into the warm room (the *Tepidarium*).. into the hot room (the *Calidarium*); and finally..into the *Laconicum*. **1975** *Daily Colonist* (Victoria, B.C.) 5 Oct. 4/3 When you are gleaming horribly [with sweat], you go into the tepidarium.

tepidity (tɪ'pɪdɪtɪ). [ad. late or med.L. *tepiditās* (631 in *Gallia Christiana* II. 186), f. *tepidus* TEPID. So F. *tépidité* (14th c. in Godef. *Compl.*).] The quality or condition of being tepid; moderate or slight warmth; lukewarmness.

a. *lit.*

1656 BLOUNT *Glossogr.*, *Tepidity*, lukewarmnesse. **1676** in *Phil. Trans.* XI. 601 Any perceptible degree of tepidity. **1750** JOHNSON *Rambler* No. 80 ⁋3 The body, chilled with the weather, is gradually recovering its natural tepidity.

b. *fig.*

a **1631** DONNE *Select.* (1840) 220 This heat may ouercome my former frigidity and coldness, and..my succeeding tepidity and lukewarmness. **1740** [see TEPID b]. **1819** *Metropolis* I. 48 The mawkish tepidity of his manner. **1884** *Fortn. Rev.* Jan. 138 Tepidity of political belief.

tepit, obs. form of TAPET *sb.*, TEPID.

† **tepor.** *Obs.* Also 7 **-our**. [a. L. *tepor*, f. *tepēre* to be lukewarm. So obs. F. *tepeur* (14th c.).] Moderate or slight warmth; tepidity. Also *fig.*

[**1608** BP. ANDREWES *Serm.*, *Mark xvi. 1-7* (1629) 404 An hower of *fervor*, more worth then a month of *tepor*.] **1657** TOMLINSON *Renou's Disp.* 389 They will not grow..unless they find tepour. *a* **1735** ARBUTHNOT (J.), The small pox.. grew more favorable by the tepor and moisture in April.

So † **'teporous** *a.* (*Obs. rare*), tepid.

1821 SIR J. D. PAUL *Rouge et Noir* 29 The spirit must be tame, indeed, and teporous That's frightened by a scarecrow dress'd in dudds.

teporingo (tɛpɒ'rɪŋgəʊ). [a. Amer. Sp.] = *volcano rabbit* s.v. VOLCANO *sb.* 3.

1969 J. FISHER et al. *Red Bk.* 54/2 The *teporingo*..exists only on the middle slopes of Popocatépetl and Ixtacihuatl and some of the nearby ridges. **1972** [see *park ranger* s.v. PARK *sb.* 7]. **1980** *Listener* 17 July 90/3 The teporingo appears to be a kind of Mexican rabbit. There aren't many left.

tepoy, variant of TEAPOY.

‖**teppan-yaki** (ˌtepan'jaki). [Jap.] A Japanese dish consisting of meat, fish, (or both) fried with vegetables on a hot steel plate which forms the centre of the table at which the diners are seated.

1970 P. & J. MARTIN *Japanese Cooking* 83 (*heading*) Teppan-yaki steak. *Ibid.*, Teppan-yaki means literally 'iron plate grilling'. This type of cooking, too, is usually done in front of guests on a large, rectangular griddle. *Ibid.* 81 Teppan-yaki duck. **1972** *Mainichi Daily News* (Japan) 6 Nov. 11/6 (Advt.), A variety of foods including Teppan-yaki (meats roasted before your eyes on hot steel plates). **1979** *United States 1980/81* (Penguin Travel Guides) 73 This thoughtfully designed Japanese restaurant has separate dining rooms for teppan-yaki, sukiyaki, and tempura.

tequila (teɪ'kiːlə). Also **tequela**, **tequilla**. [a. Mexican Sp., f. the name of a town which is one of the centres of its production.] **a.** A gin-like Mexican spirit made by distilling the fermented sap of a maguey, *Agave tequilana*; cf. MESCAL.

1849 J. GREGG *Diary & Lett.* (1944) II. 317 So celebrated has this place become, for the manufacture of superior *mezcal*, that that taken from here is known by the name of *Tequila*. **1894** *Harper's Mag.* Feb. 351/2 Between various cigarettes, the last drink of tequela, and the drying of our clothes, we passed the time. **1926** [see MESCAL 1]. **1941** B. SCHULBERG *What makes Sammy Run?* vii. 110 Burning my stomach with *enchillada* and my brain with more *tequilla*. **1953** W. BURROUGHS *Junkie* (1972) xiii. 129 Every morning when I woke up, I washed down benzedrine, sanicin, and a piece of hop with black coffee and a shot of tequila. **1958** P. HIGHSMITH *Game for Living* (1959) ii. 22 Theodore heard.. liquor being poured into a glass, and he knew it would be Lelia's yellowish tequila. **1969** J. MANDER *Static Society* vii. 196 Fuentes had been initiating me into the art of drinking Mexican *tequila* (with salt and lemon). **1977** *Playgirl* May 124/1 For the woman whose liquor larder extends beyond beer and wine, tequila is now a necessity.

b. *attrib.* and *Comb.*, as *tequila sour*; *tequila-based* adj.; **tequila plant**, the maguey from the sap of which tequila is made; **tequila sunrise**, a name given to cocktails containing tequila and grenadine.

1977 T. HEALD *Just Desserts* vii. 156 He was drinking a tequila-based cocktail. **1979** P. THEROUX *Old Patagonian Express* iii. 52, I saw a field of upright swords. It might have been sisal, but more likely was the tequila plant. **1966** T. PYNCHON *Crying of Lot 49* iii. 59 'Who's your client?' asked Metzger, holding out a tequila sour. **1965** O. A. MENDELSOHN *Dict. Drink & Drinking* 336 *Tequila Sunrise*, mixed drink of tequila, lemon juice, grenadine and cinnamon liqueur. **1976** *Daily Tel.* (Colour Suppl.) 11 June 42/3 A Tequila Sunrise has become the 'in' drink at many ski resorts and single bars. It is tequila and orange juice, with half an ounce of grenadine poured on top to filter dramatically down through the drink.

Tequistlatec (teɪ'kɪstlətɛk). Also **Tequistla'teca**, **Tequistla'teco**. [Native name.] (A member of) an Indian people of south-east Oaxaca, Mexico; also, the language of this people. Hence **Tequistla'tecan**, the Tequistlatec language or (later) the linguistic family of which it is the principal member; also *attrib.*

1891 D. G. BRINTON *American Race* 112 Quite to the south, in the mountains of Oaxaco and Guerrero, the Tequistlatecas, usually known by the meaningless term, Chontales, belong to this stem. *Ibid.* 148 The only specimen of their idiom which I have obtained is a vocabulary of 23 words... Provisionally, however, I give it the name of *Tequistlatecan*, from the principal village of the tribe. **1902** *Encycl. Brit.* XXV. 374/1 [Linguistic families of Middle America] Tehuantepecan, Isthmus; Tequistlatecan, Oax. **1915** A. L. KROEBER in *Univ. Calif. Publ. Amer. Archaeol. & Ethnol.* XI. 279 (*title*) Serian, Tequistlatecan, and Hokan. **1929** E. SAPIR in *Encycl. Brit.* V. 140/2 *Hokan* proper, which includes Seri (coast of Sonora), Yuman (in Lower California) and Tequistlateco or Chontal (coast of Oaxaca). **1965** *Language* XLI. 305 Seri and Tequistlatec, both separate branches of Hokan. *Ibid.*, The Tequistlatecan form seems at least as similar to the Proto-Palaihnihan as the Proto-Shastan. **1974** *Encycl. Brit. Micropædia* IX. 894/1 Tequistlatec, Hokan-speaking Middle American Indians of the Sierra Madre del Sur of Oaxaca, Mex.

ter (tə), repr. vulg. and dial. pronunc. of TO *prep.*, *conj.*, *adv.* Cf. OUGHTA, OUGHTER; USETER.

1867 *Harper's New Monthly Mag.* Feb. 274/2 This yere is Colonel N——, who wants ter know yer. **1895** W. J. LOCKE *At Gate of Samaria* v. 49 She's bloomin' well got ter. **1926** J. K. STRECKER in J. F. Dobie *Rainbow in Morning* (1965) 61 Ef he sting yo, yo sho gwine ter die. **1934** [see *quarter-turn* s.v. QUARTER *sb.* 31]. **1944** E. THOMPSON *Robert Bridges* i. 7 One he used in print..that of the cockney who saw on his medicine chart the words *ter die*, and fled in terror to escape his scheduled destruction. **1952** [see KIN (var. CAN *v.*[1])]. **1976** *Southern Even. Echo* (Southampton) 13 Nov. 2/7 You gence wan' anyfing ter drink?

ter, obs. f. TAR, TARE, TEAR; var. TOR *a.* *Obs.*

ter- (tɜː(r)), the L. adv. *ter* 'thrice', in comb.

1. a. Prefixed to *adjs.*, in sense 'thrice, three times', as **ter-'trinal**, consisting of three sets of three; also expressing a high degree, as **ter-'sacred** [L. *ter sacer*], thrice sacred.

1600 W. WATSON *Decacordon* (1602) Pref. A vj b, The tersacred Apostolicall Romane Church. *Ibid.* 7 Directing his hand to that tender tersacred and euer blessed heart. **1876** DOUSE *Grimm's L.* §25. 53 It is certain that the symmetrical ter-trinal trinity constituted by all these three systems together cannot have existed from all time.

b. Prefixed to *adjs.* and *sbs.*: expressing threefold recurrence or continuance; as **ter-di'urnal** *a.*, occurring or done thrice a day; **ter-'millenary** [after *tercentenary*], a three-thousandth anniversary.

1892 LD. KELVIN *Presid. Addr. R. Soc.* 30 Nov., The largeness of the solar semi-diurnal, ter-diurnal, and quarter-diurnal constituents found by the harmonic analysis. **1864** *Realm* 15 June 6 The festivities held there by so many millions of our dusky fellow-subjects in honour of the ter-millenary of that sweet swan of Nerbudda.

c. See also TERCENTENARY, TERGEMINATE, etc.

2. *Chem.* **a.** With the names of classes of compounds, as *acetate*, *bromide*, *chloride*, *chromate*, *fluoride*, *iodate*, *nitrate*, *oxide*, *sulphate*, *tannate*, etc., expressing the presence of three atoms, molecules, or combining equivalents of the element or radical indicated by the rest of the word, as ***nitrogen terchloride***, NCl_3, ***potassium terchromate***, $K_2O.3CrO_3$, or $K_2Cr_3O_{10}$, ***ternitrate of bismuth***, $Bi(NO_3)_3$, etc. Now mostly superseded by TRI-.

1836 BRANDE *Chem.* (ed. 4) 773 Terchloride of Chromium. ($Chr+O_3C$.) **1838** T. THOMSON *Chem. Org. Bodies* 258 It is..a tertannate. **1849** D. CAMPBELL *Inorg. Chem.* 111 Besides this iodate of potash, there are other two, namely, a biniodate and a teriodate. **1853** W. GREGORY *Inorg. Chem.* (ed. 3) 240 Antimony... This valuable metal is chiefly found in the mineral called antimony, which is a tersulphuret, SbS_3. **1853** URE *Dict. Arts* I. 1058 The explosive compound, the teriodide of nitrogen. **1856** MILLER *Elem. Chem.* II. 914 Terfluoride of chromium forms deep red fumes of chromic acid. **1869** ROSCOE *Elem. Chem.* 230 A third salt, termed ter-chromate [*ed.* 1882 trichromate], $K_2Cr_3O_{10}$, crystallizes out. **1883** *Hardwich's Photogr. Chem.* (ed. Taylor) 55 There are two Chlorides of Gold—viz., the Protochloride and the Terchloride. The latter is the one used in Photography.

b. In other compounds, as † **ter-a'tomic** *a.*, of three atoms, TRIATOMIC; **ter-e'quivalent** *a.* = TRIVALENT; **termo'lecular** *a.*, involving three molecules; **ter'polymer**, a polymer whose molecule is composed of three different monomers; hence **terˌpolymeri'zation**, polymerization in which three different monomers go to form a terpolymer; **'tervalence** = TRIVALENCE; **'tervalent** *a.* = TRIVALENT.

1860 FRANKLAND in *Q. Jrnl. Chem. Soc.* XIII. 192 Organo-metallic compounds..are uniatomic, biatomic, teratomic, or quadratomic, according to the number of molecules requisite to complete their saturation. **1866** MACADAM *G. Wilson's Inorg. Chem.* §1109 The Triatomic, Trihydric, or Terequivalent (Terivalent) elements. **1901** *Jrnl. Chem. Soc.* LXXIX. I. 229 Even in darkness the action is termolecular. **1931** MAASS & STEACIE *Introd. Princ. Physical Chem.* xii. 199 The reaction between nitric oxide and chlorine is an example of a termolecular reaction. **1974** *Nature* 19 Apr. 666/2 The dimer must be formed by a termolecular collision. **1961** WEBSTER, Terpolymer. **1967** *New Scientist* 18 May 423/3 Terpolymers (e.g. ABS plastics) are in use already. **1975** *Sci. Amer.* Oct. 54/3 The three products that proved to be most broadly successful are generically classified as a urethane, a dimethyl silicone and a styrene acrylonitrile terpolymer. **1964** *Jrnl. Polymer Sci.* A. II. 2740 Penultimate effects in copolymerization can be determined more precisely from composition studies in terpolymerization experiments than in binary polymerizations. **1976** H. SAWADA *Thermodynamics of Polymerization* ix. 262 (*caption*) Heat of terpolymerization for the acrylonitrile-methyl methacrylate-styrene system. **1869** *Eng. Mech.* 12 Nov. 198/3 The elements are classified as..triatomic or tervalent, with three attractions, as nitrogen. **1903** *Athenæum* 3 Jan. 22/2 We wish that the translator had avoided the use of such hybrid words as monovalent, divalent, trivalent, tetravalent, and pentavalent when he had to hand the equally expressive and less mongrel words univalent, bivalent, tervalent, quadrivalent and quinquevalent.

tera- ('tɛrə), *prefix.* [f. Gr. τέρας monster.] Prefixed to the names of units to form the names of units 10^{12} (one millon million) times larger (symbol T), as ***terabit*** [BIT *sb.*[4]], ***-electron-volt***, ***-hertz***, ***-pascal***, ***-second***, ***-volt***, ***-watt*** (hence ***-watt-hour***, ***-year***).

[**1947** *Compt. Rend. de la 14ème Conf.* (Union Internat. de Chimie) 115 The following prefixes to abbreviations for the names of units should be used to indicate the specified multiples or sub-multiples of these units: T tira- 10^{12} ×.] **1951** *Symbols, Signs & Abbreviations* (R. Soc.) 15 Tera (× 10^{12}) T. **1971** *New Scientist* 8 July 80/2 A bigger machine.. which will be available next year, will have a 50-terabit memory with only slightly slower cycle time of 100 nanoseconds. **1974** *Sci. Amer.* Feb. 82/2 An energy of 1,000 GeV (one teraelectron-volt, or TeV) does not seem an impossible goal. **1970** *McGraw-Hill Yearbk. Sci. & Technol.* 233/1 M. A. Duguay and coworkers..tuned a mode-locked He-Ne laser..from −45 to +45 GHz, about the central optical frequency of 473·61 terahertz. **1980** *Nature* 21 Feb. 715/1 In relatively simple experiments laser-driven shock waves can be used to study the propagation of shocks in solids for shock pressures up to terapascals (1 TPa = 10^7 bar = 10^{13} dyne cm^{-2}). **1969** *Proc. Geol. Soc.* Aug. 142 Alternatively the second of time may prove to be a more convenient unit as recommended by S.I., thus 1 million years (m.y.) = 31·557 tera seconds (Ts). **1975** *Sci. Amer.* Feb. 40/2 A development program looking toward the creation of a proton beam of about 1,000 GeV, or one teravolt (TeV). **1970** *Britannica Bk. of Year* 322/2 It had an output of 4 trillion watts (4 terawatts). **1972** *Physics Bull.* Mar. 175/2 The terawatt carbon dioxide laser may not be far away. **1979** *Internat. Atomic Energy Agency Bull.* Jan. 7 Let us consider two scenarios which would lead to a total primary energy consumption rate of 50 terawatts (50 000 000 MW) at the end of the next century. **1979** *Times* 11 Dec. 18 The American Department of Energy, Dr Musgrove says,..could economically produce 500 tera-watt-hours (500 million mega-watt-hours) of electricity. **1980** *Sci. Amer.* Sept. 111/1 From the base year of the IIASA study (1975) to 2030 the total primary-energy consumption rate is projected to rise from 8.2 terawatt-years per year to 36 terawatt-years per year in the high-growth scenario and to 22 terawatt-years per year in the low-growth one.

terabracioun, terafyn, terage, obs. forms of TEREBRATION, TERAPHIM, TERRAGE.

teraglin ('tɛrəglɪn). [Aboriginal name.] A fish of New South Wales, *Otolithus atelodus*, sometimes called Silver Jew-fish.

1880 *Rep. Royal Comm. Fisheries N.S. Wales* 20 One of our species, the Teraglin. **1883** E. P. RAMSAY *Food-Fishes N.S.W.* 17 (Fish. Exhib. Publ.) The Teraglin..is in many respects very like the Jew-fish..but does not grow to such a large size, and the flesh is of a finer grain. **1895** *Chambers' Jrnl.* XII. 645/1 The deep waters..teem with..gurnard, flathead, whiting, trevally, teraglin, and other eatable species.

‖**terai** (tə'raɪ). Also tarai. [From *Terai* (Hindī *tarāī* moist (land), f. *tar* moist, damp: see sense 1.] **1.** The name of a belt of unhealthy marshy and jungly land, lying between the lower foothills of the Himalayas and the plains. Also *attrib.*

1852 T. SMITH *Narr. Five Years' Residence Nepaul* I. ii. 56 The Terai, or Turay, or Turyanee, is a long strip or belt of low level-land. **1860** W. H. RUSSELL *My Diary in India* II. ii. 31 This gentleman was one of the unhappy refugees who was sheltered in the terai..and, although he saved his life, he was struck down by terai fever. **1911** *Encycl. Brit.* XIX. 379/1 The low alluvial land of the tarai is well adapted for cultivation, and is, so to speak, the granary of Nepal. **1918** W. BEEBE *Jungle Peace* (1919) xi. 268 The *terai* jungles of Garhwal, the tree-ferns of Pahang, and the mighty *moras*.. will stand in silvery silence. **1954** O. H. K. SPATE *India & Pakistan* xviii. 496 Originally the terai covered a zone perhaps 50–60 miles wide... Much of this has been so altered by settlement that the true terai is now confined to a relatively narrow strip. **1981** V. POWELL *Flora Annie Steel* xii. 104 To soothe her fever—terai fever as it was then called—she was given hashish.

2. *transf.* A wide-brimmed felt hat with double crown and special ventilation, worn in sub-tropical regions where the heat is not so intense as to necessitate the use of the *sola topee* or pith sun-helmet. More fully ***terai hat.***

1888 KIPLING *Under Deodars* 43 Mrs. Boulte put on a big terai hat. *Ibid.* 73 She was wearing an unclean Terai with the elastic under her chin. **1894** *County Gentlemen's Catal.* 155/2 Soft drab terai double felt hats. **1899** F. V. KIRBY *Sport E.C. Africa* xix. 207 Nothing beats a broad-brimmed terai, with double crown, well-ventilated with holes at the sides. **1899** WARNER *Capt. of Locusts* 188 Replacing on his head a 'Terai' hat. **1904** D. SLADEN *Lovers in Japan* xi, Silk puggarees folded to a hair round their broad-brimmed grey *terai* hats.

terakihi, var. TARAKIHI.

‖**terakoya** (tera'ko:ja). *Japanese Hist.* [Jap., = temple school, f. *tera* temple + *ko* child(ren) + *ya* place.] In the Japanese feudal period, a private elementary school of a kind established orig. in the Buddhist temples.

1909 D. KIKUCHI *Japanese Education* ii. 33 The name *Terakoya*, or 'House for the Children of the Temple', given to elementary schools up to the beginning of the present era. **1911** *Encycl. Brit.* XV. 220/1 They [*sc.* Buddhist priests] organized schools at the temples.., and at these *tera-koya*.. lessons in ethics, calligraphy, reading and etiquette were given to the sons of samurai and even to youths of the mercantile and manufacturing classes. **1938** D. T. SUZUKI *Zen Buddhism & its Influence on Japanese Culture* I. v. 106 The *Terakoya* system was the only popular educational institution during the feudal ages of Japan. **1965** W. SWAAN *Jap. Lantern* xii. 143 The *terakoya*, or 'temple schools' attached to the monasteries, provide the only institution of popular education. **1974** *Encycl. Brit. Macropædia* VI. 342/2 As time passed, some *terakoya* used parts of the houses of commoners as classrooms.

terand, -ane, terandry, obs. ff. TYRANT, -RY.

terap (tə'ræp). Also tarap. [a. Malay.] An evergreen tree, *Artocarpus elasticus*, of the family Moraceæ, native to Malaysia and closely related to the bread-fruit tree, also, the large edible fruit of this tree or its fibrous bark, which is used to make string or cloth. Also *attrib.*

1839 T. J. NEWBOLD *Straits of Malacca* II. ix. 119 The cloth that encircles their loins is made from the fibrous bark of the Terap tree. **1900** W. W. SKEAT *Malay Magic* v. 225 A string of *tĕrap* bark to tie up the rice that is cut first. **1913** L. W. W. GUDGEON *Brit. N. Borneo* x. 69 The fruit falls in all directions. If it is 'durian' or 'tarap', the size and weight of which are considerable, the Dusuns stand clear. **1935** I. H. BURKILL *Dict. Econ. Products Malay Penin.* I. 248 Every one knows the name 'tĕrap' which is applied to *A[rtocarpus] elastica* by Malays and Sakai. **1940** E. J. H. CORNER *Wayside Trees of Malaya* I. 654 The *Terap* is, undoubtedly, the commonest and best known of our wild species of Artocarpus. **1964** M. E. D. POORE in Wang Gungwu *Malaysia* I. ii. 48 Such occur in..many species of terap or breadfruit (*Artocarpus*).

terap-: see THERAP-.

teraphim ('tɛrəfɪm). Forms: α. *pl.* 4 **theraphym, -yn, teraphyn, -fyn,** 4–6 **theraphim, -in,** 6– **teraphim** (7 **-in**); also const. as sing., whence 7– *pl.* **teraphims.** β. 9 *sing.* **teraph,** *pl.* **teraphs.** [a. eccl. L. *theraphim* (Vulg.), Gr. θεραφίν (LXX), ad. Heb. *tʰᵉrāphīm*, or Aram. *-in*.

A Heb. word of doubtful origin and meaning, plural in form, but often (as a pl. of majesty) sing. in use. Occurs 15 times (on 8 occasions) in O.T., in all of which it is retained in the Revised Version, 1885, but only 6 times (2 occasions) in that of 1611; in other places rendered *images*[5], *image*[2], *idols*[1], *idolatry*[1]. The LXX have θεραφίν[6] (τὸ[2], τὰ[1]), εἴδωλα[3], κενοτάφια[2], and other renderings; Vulgate *theraphim*[4], *idola*[6], also *statuam, simulacrum, -acra, idolatria, figuras idolarum*, once each. In Genesis xxxi. 30, Laban the Aramæan calls them *eth ĕlōhāi* 'my gods'.]

A kind of idols or images, or an idol or image; app. *esp.* household gods; an object of reverence and means of divination among the ancient Hebrews and kindred peoples.

a. Plural or indefinite.

1382 WYCLIF *Judg.* xvii. 5 Mychee..made a coope [1388 ephod], and theraphyn [**1388** theraphym, *v.r.* a theraphym], *gloss* that is, the prestis clooth, and mawmettis [1388 ydols]. **1382** —— *Hos.* iii. 4 The sonys of Yrael shuln sitte..with out teraphyn. **1388** *Ibid.*, With out terafyn [*gloss* that is, ymagis]. **1539** BIBLE (Great) *Judg.* xvii. 5 And the man Micah had a temple of goddes, and made an Ephod and Theraphin, (That is to saye, a garment for the prest, and Idolles). [**1560** (Geneva) Teraphim.] **1641** MILTON *Prel. Episc.* ad fin., If any shall strive to set up his ephod and teraphim of antiquity against the brightness and perfection of the gospel. **1707** M. HENRY *Serm.* Wks. 1853 II. 596/1 Some think Laban's teraphim were the effigies of his ancestors. **1860** PUSEY *Min. Proph.* 563 The *teraphim* were used as instruments of divination. **1862** STANLEY *Jew. Ch.* (1877) I. iii. 52 Rachel stole the *teraphim*, the household gods of her family.

b. as sing. with *a*; pl. *teraphims.*

1388 [see a]. **1624** T. GODWIN *Moses & Aaron* ix. (1641) 170 Michal tooke an Image, (a Teraphim) and laid it in the bed. *a* **1631** DONNE *Select.* (1840) 198 Without an ephod, and without a teraphim. *a* **1641** BP. MOUNTAGU *Acts & Mon.* vii. (1642) 382 Commonly they had Teraphims, Altars, Groves in high places. **1845** FORD *Handbk. Spain* II. 671/1 The silversmiths..by whom many workmen are employed in making little graven images, teraphims and lares. **1856** STANLEY *Sinai & Pal.* (1875) 396 A teraphim, and a graven image, and a priesthood of irregular creation.

c. sing. *teraph*; pl. *teraphs.*

1801 SOUTHEY *Thalaba* II. ix, Khawla to the Teraph turn'd, 'Tell me where the Prophet's hand Hides our destined enemy?' **1850** KITTO *Bible Illustr.* xxxiii. §6 (1881) 240 Michal has a teraph. **1886** FARRAR *Hist. Interpr.* vii. 366 Scripture was declared to be a sort of oracular teraph.

d. *Comb.*

1848 KINGSLEY *Saint's Trag.* v. ii, My magic teraph-bust, full packed, and labelled. **1905** J. ORR *Probl. O. Test.* v. 134 Teraphim-worship, human sacrifices and the like were prominent features of the religion.

terapin(e, obs. form of TERRAPIN.

teraplene, obs. form of TERREPLEIN.

terassed, obs. f. *terraced*: see TERRACE *v.*

‖**terata** ('tɛrətə), *sb. pl. Biol.* and *Path.* [mod.L., = Gr. τέρατα, pl. of τέρας a marvel, prodigy, monster.] Monstrous formations or births.

1902 *Brit. Med. Jrnl.* 5 Apr. 850 The..type of double terata known as pygopagous twins. **1904** *Ibid.* 17 Dec. 1643 In describing the embryonic terata.

teratical (tə'rætɪkəl), *a. rare.* [f. Gr. τέρας, τερατ- (see TERATA) + -IC + -AL[1].] Relating to marvels or prodigies. So **teratism** ('tɛrətɪz(ə)m), (*a*) love of the marvellous or prodigious; (*b*) 'monstrosity' (*Cent. Dict.* Supp.).

1722 WOLLASTON *Relig. Nat.* iii. §16 (1738) 56 Herodotus, possibly delighting in teratical stories. **1901** *Folk-Lore* Mar. 20 That attitude of mind for which Mr. Marett has invented the term Teratism.

terato-, comb. form repr. Gr. τέρας, τερατ-monster: ,**teratocarci'noma** *Path.*, a malignant teratoma containing carcinomatous elements, occurring chiefly in the testis.

1946 FRIEDMAN & MOORE in *Military Surgeon* XCIX. 573 A new term, 'teratocarcinoma', is proposed for the large group of pleomorphic tumours in which both differentiated teratoid structures and histologically malignant elements were present. **1958** *Jrnl. Amer. Med. Assoc.* 28 June 1066/2 A testicular teratocarcinoma occurring in a 35-year-old man was treated initially by surgery. **1975** [see TERATOMA]. **1979** *Sci. Amer.* Apr. 87/1 As long as the tumors contain embryonal carcinoma cells they continue to grow; such tumors are malignant and are referred to as teratocarcinomas.

teratogen (tɛ'rætədʒən, 'tɛrətɒdʒən). *Med.* [f. TERATO- + -GEN.] An agent or factor which causes malformation of the developing embryo.

1959 *Jrnl. Chronic Dis.* X. 125 Present knowledge of the mechanisms of teratogenic action is meager... The ultimate action of all teratogens seems to be to produce either cell death or an alteration in the rate of cell growth. **1970** G. LEACH *Biocrats* vi. 141 Animals are rarely good models for men when it comes to testing the effects of drugs and other teratogens on the foetus. **1978** *Jrnl. R. Soc. Med.* LXXI. 668 The patient should be seen earlier in pregnancy to help her avoid potential teratogens.

‖**teratogenesis** (,tɛrətəʊ'dʒɛnɪsɪs). *Biol.* and *Path.* [mod.L., f. Gr. τέρας, τερατ- (see TERATA) + γένεσις -GENESIS.] The production of monsters or misshapen organisms. So **tera'togeny,** in same sense; ,**teratoge'nicity,** teratogenic property; **teratogenetic** (-dʒɪ'nɛtɪk), **teratogenic** (-'dʒɛnɪk) *adjs.*, pertaining to teratogenesis; producing monsters.

1857 DUNGLISON *Med. Lex.*, *Teratogeny*, the formation of monsters. **1879** tr. *De Quatrefages' Hum. Spec.* 112 Among microcephali a teratogenic cause..acted on part of the organism. **1901** *Nature* 11 Apr. 579/1 On the comparative value of saline and sugar solutions in experimental teratogenesis. **1902** *Cassell's Encycl. Dict.*, *Supp.*, Teratogenetic. **1904** *Brit. Med. Jrnl.* 17 Dec. 1643 A very able historical account of the theories of teratogenesis. **1959** *Jrnl. Chronic Dis.* X. 117 More than 20 closely related azo dyes have been tested for teratogenicity in my laboratory. **1964** *Listener* 20 Feb. 311/1 It is apparent that many of the tests that can, in our present state of knowledge, be applied to new drugs to attempt to produce teratogenicity, are neither meaningful nor justifiable. **1981** *Internat. Jrnl. Environmental Stud.* XVII. 10/2 The weak teratogenicity and growth retardative propensity of such a ubiquitous drug as aspirin.

teratoid ('tɛrətɔɪd), *a. Biol.* and *Path.* [f. Gr. τέρας, τερατ- (see TERATA) + -OID.] Having the appearance or character of a monster or monstrous formation; ***teratoid tumour*** = TERATOMA.

1876 BRISTOWE *The. & Pract. Med.* (1878) 51 Tumours originating in proliferation, which he subdivides into histioid tumours,..organoid, and teratoid, or those comprising a combination of organs. **1890** BILLINGS *Nat. Med. Dict.*, *Teratoid tumour*, congenital tumour due to inclusion in one fœtus of portions of another.

teratolite ('tɛrətəʊlaɪt). *Min.* Also erron. terratolite (*Cent. Dict.*). [ad. Ger. *teratolith* (Glocker, 1839), f. Gr. τέρας, τερατ- marvel, prodigy + λίθος stone (see -LITE), in allusion to the earlier names *Saxonische wundererde* and *terra miraculosa Saxoniæ* (C. Richter, 1732), due to its supposed sovereign virtues.] An impure clay-like hydrous silicate of aluminium, allied to pholerite.

1868 DANA *Min.* 473 A. Knop holds (Jahrb. Min. 1859, 546) that the teratolite is an impure lithomarge-like pholerite.

teratological (,tɛrətəʊ'lɒdʒɪkəl), *a.* [f. TERATOLOGY + -IC + -AL[1].] Of or pertaining to teratology; treating of monstrosities or abnormal formations in animals or plants; involving monstrosity, monstrous. Also **terato'logic** *a.* (*rare*).

1857 E. C. OTTÉ tr. *De Quatrefages' Rambles Nat.* I. 346 *note*, A normal, and not a teratological or abnormal state. **1878** *N. Amer. Rev.* CXXVII. 507 Teratological researches. **1894** *Naturalist* 56 Singular from the teratologic view-point. **1898** *Allbutt's Syst. Med.* V. 708 Works on Teratological Anatomy. **1909** J. W. JENKINSON *Exper. Embryol.* 155 Experiments..of the highest interest from a general teratological point of view.

teratologist (tɛrə'tɒlədʒɪst). [f. next + -IST.] **a.** One who deals in stories of marvels or prodigies. *rare.* **b.** One versed in teratology (sense 2).

1844 *London & Edin. Monthly Jrnl. Med. Sci.* IV. 484 Teratologists are now agreed in referring a considerable number of malformations by defect to the occurrence of an interruption..of natural fœtal development. **1882** in OGILVIE. **1908** *Jrnl. Morphol.* XIX. 51 Teratologists are inclined to read these facts in favor of the germinal origin of monsters, which may even be hereditary. **1973** *Daily Tel.* 13 Jan. 16 Many distinguished obstetricians, pathologists, paediatricians, teratologists and editors were reluctant to accept my hypothesis that thalidomide did cause abnormalities.

teratology (tɛrə'tɒlədʒɪ). [f. Gr. τέρας, τερατ- a marvel, prodigy, monster + -LOGY. So F. *tératologie* (Littré).]

1. A discourse or narrative concerning prodigies; a marvellous tale, or collection of such tales.

1678 PHILLIPS (ed. 4), *Teratology*, a discourse of prodigies and wonders. **1727** BAILEY Vol. II, *Teratology*..is when bold Writers, fond of the sublime, intermix something great and prodigious in every Thing they write, whether there be Foundation for it in Reason or not, and this is what is call'd Bombast. [Hence **1755** JOHNSON, *Teratology*, bombast, affectation of false sublimity.] **1856** C. J. ELLICOTT in *Cambr. Ess.* 158 The aimless fables and teratologies of Thomas the Israelite or the Gospels of the Infancy. **1884** BLACKMORE *Tommy Upm.* II. 104 Big enough to exhaust even his teratology.

2. *Biol.* The study of monstrosities or abnormal formations in animals or plants.

1842 in BRANDE *Dict. Sc.*, etc. **1860** MAYNE *Expos. Lex.*, *Teratology*..name given by M. J. Geoffroy de St. Hilaire, to the study or consideration of monsters, or anomalies of organization. **1869** M. T. MASTERS (*title*) Vegetable Teratology. **1904** *Brit. Med. Jrnl.* 17 Dec. 1643 Almost the whole of embryonic pathology is..included within the limits of teratology.

‖**teratoma** (tɛrə'təʊmə). *Path.* Pl. teratomata (-'tɒmətə). [mod.L., f. Gr. τέρας, τερατ- (see TERATA), after *sarcoma*, etc.] A tumour, esp. of the gonads, characteristically formed of numerous distinct tissues and believed usually to arise from germ cells or their precursors.

1879 *Amer. Jrnl. Med. Sci.* LXXVII. 91 (*heading*) Extirpation of teratoma; or, teratoid tumor. *Ibid.* 93 To such tumors Virchow has applied the term teratoma. **1890** BILLINGS *Nat. Med. Dict.*, *Teratoma*, a tumor composed of various tissues or systems of tissue, as bone, teeth, etc., which do not normally exist at the place where the tumor grows. **1899** *Allbutt's Syst. Med.* VI. 100 Teratoma or dermoid cyst is another variety of dermoid tumour... It is affirmed that a teratoma never originates in the lung. **1906** [see LANGHANS]. **1948** R. A. WILLIS *Path. of Tumours* lxi. 940 A teratoma is a true tumour or neoplasm composed of multiple tissues of kinds foreign to the part in which it arises. **1975** *Nature* 6 Nov. 12/1 Teratomas and teratocarcinomas are rare tumours which arise in the gonads, and contain a whole variety of differentiated tissues of ectodermal, mesodermal and endodermal origin (such as skin, nerve, muscle, cartilage, gut and lung), mixed together in a disorganised mass. **1979** *Sci. Amer.* Apr. 87/1 When all the embryonal cells differentiate into various kinds of normal tissue, the tumors stop growing: they are benign and are usually referred to simply as teratomas.

Hence **tera'tomatous** *a.*, of the nature of a teratoma.

1891 in *Cent. Dict.* **1893** *Index-Catal. Library Surgeon-General's Office, U.S. Army* XIV. 896/1 (*heading*) Tumors (teratomatous). **1948** MARTIN & HYNES *Clinical Endocrinol.* ix. 193 A few arrhenoblastomata have been teratomatous, containing cartilage and other tissues. **1962** *Punch* 7 Nov. 658/2 A teratomatous growth of mixed tissues, probably of only low malignancy.

teratoscopy (tɛrə'tɒskəpɪ). *rare.* [f. Gr. *τέρας, τερατ-* marvel, prodigy – *-σκοπια* observation.] Observation of or augury from prodigies.

1663 J. SPENCER *Prodigies* (1665) Pref., When the Sunshine of the Gospel hath discovered the transparency of all those thin and curious Arts,..why should their contemporary, Teratoscopy, survive them all? *Ibid.* 298 Teratoscopy..was anciently only a rational attendance to those..signs with which the Providence of Nature..was noted to preface her works of greater note.

terawndry, **terawnte**, obs. ff. TYRANTRY, TYRANT.

terbentine, -yne, early forms of TURPENTINE.

terbium ('tɜːbɪəm). *Chem.* [mod.L., from the last two syllables of the name of *Ytterby* in Sweden: cf. ERBIUM.] One of the rare metallic elements found (together with yttrium and erbium) in gadolinite and other minerals. So **'terbia** [after ERBIA], the earth or oxide of terbium.

1843 MOSANDER in *L., E., & D. Philos. Mag.* XXIII. 251 What chemists have hitherto considered as yttria, does not consist of one oxide only, but is..to be regarded as a mixture of at least three... If the name of yttria be reserved for the strongest of these bases, and the next in order receive the name of oxide of terbium, while the weakest be called oxide of erbium, we find [etc.]. **1907** ROSCOE & SCHORLEMMER *Chemistry* II. 783 Terbium Tb = 158 (H = 1)... The existence of the earth originally called erbia by Mosander was denied by Berlin (1860), and by Bahr and Bunsen (1866), but was confirmed by Delafontaine (1878) and by Marignac. It then received the name of terbia... Pure terbium compounds were first obtained by Urbain [1905, 1906].

terce (tɜːs). Also 5 **teirs**, **tairs**, 7 **tearce**. [A variant of TIERCE, now used in a special sense.]

1. Obsolete, archaic, or variant form of TIERCE, q.v. in various senses.

2. *spec.* in *Sc. Law*, A life-rent competent by law to a widow (unless she has accepted some other special provision) of the third of the heritable subjects in which her husband dies infeft, provided that the marriage has endured for a year and a day, or has produced a living child. Cf. DOWER *sb.*[2] 1.

1473 in *Laing Charters* (1899) 43 The quhilk our teirs extendis ȝerly till viij markis. *Ibid.*, Tairs. **1476** *Acta Auditorum* 19 July, Hir brefe of terce anent ye land of Lethbert. **1568** *Reg. Privy Council Scot.* I. 619 Thair subwassellis, ladiis of terce, conjunct fearis, and lyverentaris. **1597** SKENE *De Verb. Sign.* s.v. *Breve*, The brieue of Terce. **1665** J. FRASER *Polichronicon* (S.H.S.) 197 Shee, haveing a tearce of the lordship, was well furnished.. with all manner of provision. **1681** *Sc. Acts Chas. II* (1820) VIII. 247/2 (*title*) Act concerning wives Terces. **1752** J. LOUTHIAN *Form of Process* (ed. 2) 286 That Services of Relicts to their Terce pay one Half of special Services. **1868** *Act 31 & 32 Vict.* c. 101 §118 All rights of courtesy and terce competent to the husband or wife of any such creditor.

b. *attrib.* **terce land**, the land of which the rent is assigned to a widow's terce (usu. in *pl.*).

1552 *Reg. Privy Council Scot.* I. 129 Spirituall menis landis, togidder with all waird landis, terce and conjunct fie landis. **1565** in J. Fraser *Polichronicon* (S.H.S.) 152 Item upon her terce lands of Lovat five oxen. **1581** *Reg. Privy Council Scot.* III. 409 Hir haill fermes of hir terce landis of Westraw.

Hence **'tercer** (†**tiercear**), a widow who has terce.

c **1575** *Balfour's Practicks* (1754) 336 A Lady tiercear, or conjunct-fear, havand ane tierce or conjunct-fie of ward landis, or blanche landis. **1773** ERSKINE *Instit. Laws Scot.* II. ix. §44 The widow [is hence styled] the tercer. **1808–25** JAMIESON, *Tercer, tiercer*..a term still commonly used in our courts of law.

terce, var. TARSE *Obs.*; obs. f. TERSE.

tercel, tiercel ('tɜːs(ə)l, 'tɪəs(ə)l). Forms: α. 5 **tercelle, -sell(e**, 5–7 **-cell, -sel**, 6–8 **-sal** (7 **terssell**), 4– **tercel**. β. 5–7 **tarcel(l, -sell**, 6 **-sall**, 7–8 **-sel**, 8 **-cel**. γ. 5–7 **tassell**, 6–9 **tassel** (7 **-il(l**, 6 **tossell**). δ. 6 **tyercelle**, 7 **-cell**, 7– **tiercel**. [a. OF. *tercel* (*a* 1200 in Godef.), beside *terçuel* (12–13th c.), also *tresuel*, *tercieul*, = Pr. *tersol*, *tresol*, Sp. *terzuelo*, It. *terz(u)olo*:—pop. L. *tertiolus* (13th c. in Du Cange), dim. from L. *tertius* third: cf. L. *fīlius*, dim. *fīliolus*, It. *figliuolo*, F. *filleul*. With the *tar*-forms, cf. *bark*, *barn*, *clerk*, etc.; the γ-forms confuse *tarsel* and *tassel*; the δ-forms are influenced by mod.F.]

The male of any kind of hawk; in Falconry esp. of the peregrine falcon (TERCEL-GENTLE) and the goshawk. ***tercel jerkin*** [JERKIN[2]]: see quot. 1623.

Said by some to have been so called as being one-third smaller than the female bird, by others because a third egg in a nest was believed to be smaller and to produce a male bird: cf. quot. s.v. TERCELLENE.

α. *c* **1381** (MSS. 1430–) CHAUCER *Parl. Foules* 405 And therwithal the tersel [*v.rr.* tarsell, tercel, tersell] gan she calle. **14..** *Nom.* in Wr.-Wülcker 701/28 *Hic tercellus*, a tercelle. **1486** *Bk. St. Albans* A iij, If she be a Goshawke or Tercell that shall be reclaymed euer fede hym with washe meete at the drawyng. **1615** BOYLE in *Lismore Papers* (1886) I. 78, I sent a Tercell of a goshawk to my cozen. **1623** COCKERAM III. s.v. *Hawks*, A Gerfalcon, the male is called the Tercell Ierkin thereof. **1834** R. MUDIE *Brit. Birds* (1841) I. 86 The falcon always means the female, and the male is called the tercel. **1842** BROWNING *Count Gismond* xxi, And have you brought my tercel back?

†β. **14..** *Voc.* in Wr.-Wülcker 615/24 *Tardarius*, a tarcel. *a* **1500** *Chaucer's Parl. Foules* 415 (MS. R. 3. 19, Trin. C.C.) Thys Royall Tarcell spake and taryed nought. **1500–20** DUNBAR *Poems* xxxiii. 81 The tarsall gaif him tug for tug. *c* **1640** J. SMYTH *Lives Berkeleys* (1883) I. 303 The falcons, tarsells, and other hawkes. *c* **1704** PRIOR *Henry & Emma* 110 When Emma hawks: With her of tarsels and of lures he talks. **1774** GOLDSM. *Nat. Hist.* (1862) II. II. i. 30 The male is called by falconers a *tarcel*; that is, a tierce or third less than the other [the female].

†γ. **1495** *Act 11 Hen. VII*, c. 17 §3 Any Hawke of the brede of Englond callid Nyesse, gossehauke, tassell,..or fawcon. **1545** *Rates of Customs* b iv, Goshaukes the pece xiii.*s.* iiii.*d.* The tassell vi.*s.* viii.*d.* **1635** SWAN *Spec. M.* (1670) 355 The Tassel of the Saker is called a Hobbie, or Mongrel Hawk. **1727** *Bradley's Fam. Dict.* s.v. *Hawk*, The Male of an Eyess, is an Eyess-Tassel,..and of a Haggard, the Haggard-Tassel.

δ. **1575** TURBERV. *Faulconrie* 3 All these kynde of hawkes haue their Tyercelles, whiche are the male byrdes and cockes. **1658** PHILLIPS, *Tiercel*,..the same as *Tassel* [**1678** adds] and *Tercel*. **1688** R. HOLME *Armoury* II. 236/1 A Tyerclet, or Tyercell of a Goshawk. **1865** *Cornh. Mag.* May 625 Tiercels are better than falcons for magpie-hawking, as they are unquestionably quicker amongst hedgerows, and can turn in a smaller compass.

b. *fig.* Applied to a person.

a **1585** MONTGOMERIE *Flyting* 90 Foule..tersell of a taide! **1611** CHAPMAN *May Day* Plays 1873 II. 355 Whose foole are you? are not you the tassell of a Gander? **1856** BOKER *Leonor de Guzman* I. ii, The ragged tercel that takes all our wealth.

tercelet, tiercelet ('tɜːslɪt, 'tɪəslɪt). Forms: 4–5 **ters-**, **terce-**, **terse-**, **tarse-**, 4–6 **tarce-**, 6 **tierse-**, **-let** (**-lett**); 4– **tercelet**, 6– **tiercelet**. [a. AF. *tercelet*, = F. *tiercelet* (dim. of OF. *tercel*, TERCEL), whence later Eng.] = prec.

[**1363** *Rolls of Parlt.* II. 282/2 Quiconque persone qui troeve Faukoun, Tercelet,..ou autre Faucoun.] *c* **1381** CHAUCER *Parl. Foules* 529 Foulis of rauyne Han chosyn.. The terselet of the facoun. **1580** HOLLYBAND *Treas. Fr. Tong*, *Vn Sacret*, the tiercelet of a Saker. **1616** SURFL. & MARKH. *Country Farme* 711 The Faulcon, as all other birds of prey, hath her Tiercelet, and they are called of the Latines *Pomiliones*. **1720** MRS. MANLEY *Power of Love* (1741) 249 He made bold to present his Lordship with a very excellent Tercelet of a Faulcon. **1813** SCOTT *Rokeby* VI. ii, Perched on his wonted eyrie high, Sleep sealed the tercelet's wearied eye. **1852** R. F. BURTON *Falconry Valley Indus* ii. 13 The tiercelet or male, is, as usual, much smaller than the female.

tercel-'gentle. [f. TERCEL (q.v. for Forms), after FALCON-GENTLE.] The male of the falcon.

1486 *Bk. St. Albans* D iij b, Ther is a Fawken gentill, and a Tercell gentill, and theys be for a prynce. **1546** *Will of Brinckley* (Somerset Ho.), Unto the vicar of Boston my tossell gentle. **1590** SPENSER *F.Q.* III. iv. 49 A Tassell gent, Which after her [a dove] his nimble winges doth straine. **1673** HICKERINGILL *Greg. F. Greyb.* 203 The tassil-gentle, once upon the wing..makes a stoop at a jack-daw. **1839** LONGF. *Hyperion* IV. i, Thou art not less a woman, because thou dost not sit aloft in a tower, with a tassel-gentle on thy wrist.

b. in *fig.* and allusive use.

1592 SHAKS. *Rom. & Jul.* II. ii. 160 Hist Romeo hist, o for a falkners voyce, To lure this Tassel gentle back againe. **1630** J. TAYLOR (Water P.) *Wks.* II. 95/2 So She..by casting out the Lure, makes the Tassell Gentle come to her fist. *a* **1700** B. E. *Dict. Cant. Crew*, *Tercel-gentle*, a Knight or Gentleman of a good Estate; also any rich Man. **1820** SCOTT *Abbot* iv, Marry, out upon thee, foul kite, that would fain be a tercel gentle!

†**tercellene.** *Obs.* *rare*$^{-1}$. [deriv. of TERCEL.] = TERCELET, TERCEL.

a **1682** SIR T. BROWNE *Tracts* v. (1683) 119 When they [hawks] lay three Eggs,..the first produceth a Female and large Hawk, the second of a midler sort, and the third a smaller Bird, Tercellene or Tassel of the Male Sex.

tercentenary (tɜː'sɛntɪnərɪ, -sɛn'tiːnərɪ), *a.* and *sb.* [f. TER- + CENTENARY, after L. *ter centēni* three hundred each. For the special use in reference to years cf. CENTENARY.]

A. *adj.* Of or belonging to the number of three hundred; usually, of or pertaining to a completed period of 300 years; tercentennial.

1844 S. R. MAITLAND *Dark Ages* xiii. 221, I mean no offence to the gentleman from whose tercentenary sermon it purports to be an extract. **1882–3** *Schaff's Encycl. Relig. Knowl.* III. 2421/1 Bishop Francis David..died in 1579,—an event which received in 1879 its tercentenary celebration in the land of his martyrdom [Transylvania].

B. *sb.* A duration of three hundred years; the three-hundredth anniversary of an event, or a celebration of it.

1855 W. G. CLARK in *Cambr. Ess.* 283 The grammar-schools, which have for the most part celebrated their tercentenary. **1879** *Sat. Rev.* 4 Oct. 412/1 Duo-centenaries, ter-centenaries, and quin-centenaries have all lately taken place. **1884** *Nonconf. & Indep.* 17 July 698/2 The tercentenary of the death of William of Nassau..has been celebrated this week at Delft.

Hence **tercente'narian** *a.*, that has lasted three centuries; three hundred years old (cf. *centenarian*); **tercen'tenarize** *v. trans. nonce-wd.*, to celebrate the tercentenary of.

1881 *Sat. Rev.* 23 July 116/2 The wholesale excommunication of a tercentenarian Established Church. **1866** *Pall Mall G.* 14 Nov. 10 How Shakespeare was lately tercentenarized everybody knows.

tercentennial (tɜːsɛn'tɛnɪəl), *a.* and *sb.* [f. TER- + CENTENNIAL.] **a.** *adj.* Of or belonging to a period of three hundred years; of three hundred years' standing; of or relating to the three-hundredth anniversary. **b.** *sb.* The three-hundredth anniversary *of* an event; a tercentenary.

1882–3 *Schaff's Encycl. Relig. Knowl.* III. 2007 The third tercentennial jubilee of the Reformation (1817) marks a return to the doctrines and principles of the Reformers. **1884** *Lit. World* (U.S.) 23 Feb. 58/2 The forthcoming celebration of the ter-centennial of the University of Edinburgh.

terceroon (tɜːsə'ruːn). *rare.* Also 8–9 **terceron**, 9 **tierceroon**. [a. Sp. **terceron*, f. *tercero* a third person, f. *tercio* third: cf. *cuarteron*, *quinteron*.] The offspring of a white person and a mulatto, being third in descent from a Negro; = QUADROON 1 a: see note there. (Distinguished from QUADROON 1 b.)

1760–72 tr. *Juan & Ulloa's Voy.* (ed. 3) I. 29 The Tercerones, produced from a White and a Mulatto, with some approximation to the former, but not so near as to obliterate their origin. **1819** W. LAWRENCE *Lect. Physiol.* etc. 296 Europeans and Mulattos produce Tercerons (sometimes also called Quarterons, Moriscos, and Mestizos)... Europeans and Tercerons produce Quarterons or Quadroons. **1878** BARTLEY tr. *Topinard's Anthropol.* II. vii. 374 The mixed breeds of negroes and Europeans have various names... The first are called mulatoes, the second, tierceroons.

tercet ('tɜːsɪt). Forms: 6–7 **terset**, 7 **tercett**, (**terzetta**), 7–9 **terzet**, 8 **-ett**, (9 **terzette**), 7–9 **tiercet**, 9 **tercet**. [ad. It. *terzetto*, dim. f. *terzo* (:—L. *tertius*) third + *-etto*, -ET[1]. Thence also obs. F. *tiercet* (*c* 1500 in Jean Le Maire) and mod.F. *tercet* (17th c. in Boileau), whence the later Eng. forms.]

1. *Pros.* A set or group of three lines riming together, or bound by double or triple rime with the adjacent triplet or triplets; *spec.* **a.** each of the triplets of the Italian TERZA RIMA; **b.** each of the two triplets usually forming the last six lines of a sonnet.

1598 FLORIO, *Terzetto*, a terset of rymes, rymes that ryme three and three. **1656** EARL MONM. tr. *Boccalini's Advts. fr. Parnass.* I. lxxvi. (1674) 93 The..Princes..were proof against every pungent Terzetta. *Ibid.* II. xiv. 154 The pleasant Tersets. **1755** JOHNSON, *Tiercet*..a triplet; three lines. **1838–9** HALLAM *Hist. Lit.* II. II. v. §44. 208 The first lines or quartets of the sonnet excite a soft expectation, which is harmoniously fulfilled by the tercets or last six lines. **1885** A. J. BUTLER *Dante, Paradise* XIX. 257 *note*, Observe the structure of this and the following tercets.

2. *Mus.* **a.** A third. (? An error.) **b.** A triplet (*Cent. Dict.* 1891).

1706 PHILLIPS (ed. Kersey), *Tercet*, a Third in Musick. [So **1721** BAILEY, **1775** ASH, and many 19th c. Dicts.]

tercia: see TERTIA.

tercian, -ane, etc., **terciar**, obs. ff. TERTIAN, TERTIAR.

tercine ('tɜːsɪn). *Bot.* [= F. *tercine* (Mirbel 1828), f. F. *tiers*, *tierce*, or L. *tertius* third: see -INE[1].] A third integument supposed by some to occur in certain ovules: cf. PRIMINE.

1832 *Encycl. Brit.* (ed. 7) V. 52 *note*, The extensible side of the secundine, and even of the tercine or nucleus, soon ceases to increase. **1861** BENTLEY *Man. Bot.* (1870) 322 The embryo-sac is surrounded by a thin layer of cells, which has received the name of tercine.

tercio, tertio ('tɜːsɪəʊ, 'tɜːʃɪəʊ). See also TERTIA. [a. Sp. *tercio* (Minsheu), obs. It. *tertio* (Florio), mod.It. *terzo*, Pg. *terço* a regiment:—L. *tertium* a third.]

1. *orig.* A regiment of the Spanish infantry of the 16–17th c.; applied also to the Italian forces of that period; hence, a body of foot forming a main division of an army. Subsequently used of Spanish units in mod. times.

1583 STOCKER *Civ. Warres Lowe C.* II. 65 Hee..sent thether Sardigne his Regiment or Tertio, with the Maister of his Campe, and three Ensignes of the Regiment or Tertio of Lombardes. **1590** SIR J. SMYTH *Disc. Weapons* 10 b, A Tercio is not to bee holden for compleate of anie smaller number than of 3000. soldiers. **1598** BARRET *Theor. Warres* 15 The Campe is deuided into sundry Tertios or Regiments. **1622** F. MARKHAM *Bk. War* v. i. 161 The Colonell of a Foot-Regiment..amongst the old Romans..commanded a Tertio or Regiment. **1904** *Edin. Rev.* July 116 The deep formation in solid squares—that of the renowned tercios—was still dominant. **1938** C. S. FORESTER *Ship of Line* xvii. 236, I am Colonel Juan Claros, of the third tercio of Catalan migueletes... That is to say a thousand men. **1957** P. KEMP *Mine were of Trouble* ii. 19 A Tercio in the sixteenth century was a Regiment of Spanish infantry. The Spanish Foreign Legion is also called *El Tercio*... But the Requetés in the Civil War also organized their fighting units into *tercios*, each approximately of battalion strength. **1965** C. D. EBY *Siege of Alcázar* i. 14 The crack Tercios of the Foreign Legion.

2. *Bull-fighting.* **a.** One of the three parts of a bullfight. **b.** Each of the three concentric circles into which a bullring is technically divided.

1932 E. HEMINGWAY *Death in Afternoon* 331 The bullfight is divided into three parts, the *tercio de varas*, that of the pic, *tercio de banderillas*, and *tercio del muerte* or third of death. **1932** R. CAMPBELL *Taurine Provence* iii. 68 The arena is divided into three areas—tablas, tercios, and medios. It is in the tercios, which extend from a third of the way to the centre until quite near the central area, that the bull is the best to deal with. **1962** J. STEWART tr. *J. Cousseau's Death of Miss Cunningham* 136 The final *tercio* was about to be sounded. **1967** MCCORMICK & MASCAREÑAS *Compl. Aficionado* i. 20 The luring of the bull,..and the ritual staining of the garments of the bridegroom with the bull's blood..aid us in comprehending both the origin of the tercio of the banderillas, and our response to that tercio.

Tercom (ˈtɜːkɒm). [Abbrev. f. initial letters of ter*rain* *co*ntour *m*atching.] A computerized system for controlling the flight path of a cruise missile which enables it to stay close to the ground.

1975 *Bull. Atomic Sci.* Apr. 13/2 Tercom—Terrain matching device—a system which enables a missile to hug the ground and follow a programmed path. **1980** R. L. DUNCAN *Brimstone* x. 261 The cruise missile would be guided by TERCOM—terrain contour matching.

tercyary, obs. form of TERTIARY.

terdle, obs. f. TREDDLE, dung of sheep, etc.

terdye, obs. form of TARDY.

†**tere, teir**, *a. Sc.* and *north. dial. Obs.* [Origin obscure. From the variant readings in *Wars of Alexander* 1404 and elsewhere, it would seem to have been an alteration of *tore*, TOR *a.*, in the same sense, under the influence of *tere* vb. to TIRE; or to have arisen out of *tere* vb. by change of syntax and identification of the resulting adj. with *tore*.] Difficult, tedious, tiresome, toilsome.

a **1400–50** *Alexander* 1404 (MS. A.) It ware tere [*MS. D.* It wald tere] any tonge to of his turnes rekyn. *Ibid.* 4918 It ware to tere me to tell þe tirement to-gedire. *a* **1400** *Anturs of Arth.* 121 To telle þe todes þereone my tonge were fulle tere [*v.r.* were to tere]. *a* **1440** *Sir Degrev.* 1409 To tell here metus was tere, That was served at here sopere. *c* **1450** HOLLAND *Howlat* 578 The order of thar armis, it war to tell teir. **1456** SIR G. HAYE *Law Arms* (S.T.S.) 27 Mony otheris that tere is to tell. **1513** DOUGLAS *Æneis* XI. Prol. 197 For sa schort renovne [thay] warryn so bald To sustene weir and panis teir ontald.

So †**ˈterefull** (5 **teirfull, tyrefull**) *a. Sc. Obs.*

c **1450** HOLLAND *Howlat* 421 It war tyrefull to tell, dyte or address. *c* **1475** *Golagros & Gaw.* 760 It war teirfull to tell treuly the tend Of thair strife sa strang. *Ibid.* 33, 42.

tere, obs. form of TAR, TEAR, TEER.

terebate: see under TEREBIC.

‖**Terebella** (tɛrɪˈbɛlə). Pl. **-æ**. [mod.L., dim. of *terebra* a borer.]

1. *Zool.* A genus of worms, typical of the *Terebellidæ*, a family of marine tubicolous polychætous annelids; a member of this genus.

1826 GOOD *Bk. Nat.* (1834) II. 11 Another genus of molluscous worms is the terebella. **1857** WOOD *Com. Obj. Sea-shore* viii. 95 Sometimes the terebella becomes ambitious, and..affixes a stone of some size to his tube. **1874** CARPENTER *Ment. Phys.* I. ii. §43 (1879) 43 A Terebella (a marine Worm that cases its body in a sandy tube).

†**2.** *Surg.* = TEREBELLUM 1. *Obs.*

1860 MAYNE *Expos. Lex.*, *Terebella*... *Med.*, *Surg.* Old name of an instrument with which bones were pierced;..it was the trepan or trephine.

3. *Entom.* The ovipositor of a saw-fly.

1826 KIRBY & SP. *Entomol.* III. 391 *Terebellæ*, instruments by which the insect saws or bores a passage for its eggs.

‖**terebellum** (tɛrɪˈbɛləm). Pl. **-a**. [mod.L. dim. of *terebrum*, collateral f. *terebra*: see prec.]

†**1.** *Surg.* A trepan or trephine. ? *Obs.*

1678 PHILLIPS (ed. 4), *Terebellum*, a Chyrurgions instrument. **1688** R. HOLME *Armoury* III. 420/2 The Terebellum..an Instrument to take up broken or bruised Skulls.

2. *Zool.* Lamarck's name for the genus Seraphs of bivalve molluscs.

1851 WOODWARD *Mollusca* 106 The animal of *terebellum* has an operculum like *strombus*.

terebene (ˈtɛrɪbiːn). *Chem.* [f. TEREB(INTH) + -ENE.]

†**1.** A name given by Soubeiran and Capitaine 1839 (*Comptes Rendus* IX. 654) to a liquid obtained by decomposing artificial camphor, $C_{10}H_{16}HCl$, with lime. *Obs.* **b.** Used by Deville 1840 (*Ann. Chimie* LXXV. 38) for a liquid obtained by the action of sulphuric acid on pinene, now known to be a mixture of terpenes together with cymene: one of the drugs of the British Pharmacopœia; hence *attrib.*, **terebene soap**, etc.

1898 *Brit. Pharmac.* 334 Terebenum. Terebene, a mixture of dipentene and other hydrocarbons, obtained by agitating oil of turpentine with successive quantities of sulphuric acid [etc.]. **1898** *Allbutt's Syst. Med.* V. 37 The inhalation of steam medicated with terebene. **1900** *C.S.S.A. Price List, Index*, Terebene hair-wash, lozenges, soap.

†**2.** Sometimes a synonym of TERPENE. *Obs.*

1857 MILLER *Elem. Chem.* III. vii. §1. 437 These isomeric bodies may be subdivided into two metameric classes; in one of which the molecule is represented by $C_{20}H_{16}$;..the members of which are termed *terebenes* or *camphogens*. **1871** ROSCOE *Elem. Chem.* 426 Oxidation products of the terebenes.

Hence **tereˈbenic** *a.*, in ***terebenic acid***, synonym of TEREBIC *acid*: see quot. 1868 s.v.

terebenthene (tɛrɪˈbɛnθiːn). *Chem.* [a. F. *térébenthène*, f. F. *térébenth-ine*, ad. L. *terebinthina* (*rēsina*): see TEREBINTHINE, TURPENTINE; with suffix -ENE as in BENZENE.] Name given by Berthelot to the TERPENE which forms the chief constituent of French turpentine-oil, obtained from *Pinus Pinaster* (*P. maritima*).

Terebenthene is the lævorotary form of pinene, and is now usually called *lævopinene*, as distinguished from *dextropinene*, the chief constituent of American turpentine oil (that most used in England), obtained from *Pinus australis*, whence formerly called *Austroterebenthene* and *Australene*.

1857 MILLER *Elem. Chem.* III. 439 According to Berthelot, if the ordinary Bordeaux turpentine be distilled *in vacuo*, after saturating the acids which it contains, a homogeneous hydrocarbon, *terebenthene*,..is obtained. **1873** ROSCOE *Elem. Chem.* 426 The best known natural varieties are *terebenthene* from *Pinus maritima*..possessing a left-handed rotation of $-42°\ 3'$, and *Austroterebenthene* from *Pinus australis*.

tereˈbentic, *a. Chem.* [f. L. *ter(e)bent-inus* (see TEREBINTHINE) + -IC.] Of the nature of turpentine; in ***terebentic acid***, $C_9H_{14}O_5$, a crystalline substance obtained by digesting oil of turpentine with oxide of lead.

1894 MORLEY & MUIR *Watts' Dict. Chem.* IV. 657.

terebentine, -tyne, early forms of TURPENTINE. Cf. TEREBINTHINA, TEREBINTHINE B. 2.

terebic (təˈrɛbɪk), *a. Chem.* [f. TEREB(INTH) + -IC.] Of, belonging to, or derived from turpentine, as in ***terebic acid***, $C_7H_{10}O_4$, a dibasic acid, a product of the action of nitric acid on turpentine-oil, also called *turpentinic*, *terebenic*, and *terebilic acid*. So ***terebic ether***, an acid ether of terebic acid. Hence **ˈterebate**, a salt of terebic acid.

1857 MILLER *Elem. Chem.* III. vii. §1. 502 The compound ..deposits when left to itself for some weeks small four-sided prisms with an oblique terminal face. This substance is named *terebic acid*. **1868** WATTS *Dict. Chem.* V. 723 *Terebic acid*..discovered by Bromeis.., who called it *turpentinic acid*; further examined by Rabourdin.., who designated it as *terebilic* or *terebenic acid*. *Ibid.* 724 Terebic acid is dibasic... The neutral terebates all contain water of crystallisation.

†**terebilene** (ˈtɛrɪbɪliːn). *Chem. Obs.* [Arbitrary from TEREBENE.] Name given 1839 by Soubeiran and Capitaine (*Comptes Rendus* IX. 654) to a liquid now regarded as a mixture of terpenes.

1857 MILLER *Elem. Chem.* III. vii. §1. 440 **1868** WATTS *Dict. Chem.* V. 925 Terebilene is a hydrocarbon obtained by distilling the liquid monohydrochlorate of turpentine-oil with quicklime or with potassium... It smells like terebene, and is optically inactive.

Hence **terebiˈlenic** *a.*, in ***terebilenic acid***, $C_7H_8O_4$, crystallizing in small prisms or needles, or in trimetric forms. So **tereˈbilic** *a.*, synonym of TEREBIC: see quot. 1868 s.v.

1894 MORLEY & MUIR *Watts' Dict. Chem.* IV. 657/2 Terebilenic Acid.

terebin, obs. form of TERRAPIN.

terebinth (ˈtɛrɪbɪnθ). Forms: 4 **theribynte, terebynt**, 5–6 **therebinthe**, 6 **terebynte, -bint, -binthe, teribinth**, 6– **terebinth**. [= OF. *therebint(e* (13th c. in Hatz.-Darm.), *-binthe*, *-bin*, *terebinte* (Godefroy *Compl.*), = Sp., It. *terebinto*; ad. L. *terebinth-us* (Pliny), a. Gr. τερέβινθος, earlier τέρβινθος and τέρμινθος, prob. a foreign word.]

1. A tree of moderate size, *Pistacia Terebinthus*, N.O. *Anacardiaceæ*, a native of Southern Europe, Northern Africa, and Western Asia, the source of Chian turpentine, and a common object of veneration; also called *turpentine tree*, and *Algerine* or *Barbary mastic-tree*.

1382 WYCLIF *Gen.* xxxv. 4 [Jacob] indeluede hem vndur an theribynte, that is bihynde the cite of Sichem. **1382** —— *Ecclus.* xxiv. 22, I as terebynt streiȝte out my braunchis. **1535** COVERDALE *Isa.* vi. 13 As the Terebyntes and Oketrees bringe forth their frutes. **1578** BIBLE (Genev.) *Ecclus.* xxiv. 18 *margin*, Terebinth is a hard tree..whereout runneth yᵉ gumme called a pure turpentine. **1579** SPENSER *Sheph. Cal.* July 86 Here growes Melampode..And Teribinth, good for Gotes. **1601** HOLLAND *Pliny* I. 389 In Syria grows the Terebinth or Terpentine tree... This fruit of the Terebinth ripeneth with grapes. **1609** BIBLE (Douay) *1 Kings* xiii. 14 He..found him sitting under a terebinth. **1860** TRISTRAM *Gt. Sahara* vii. 112 The terebinth is a fine oak-like tree, with a close-grained hard black wood..standing usually in solitary dignity. **1863** W. A. WRIGHT in *Smith's Dict. Bible* I. 858/1 (*Idolatry*) The terebinth at Mamre, beneath which Abraham built an altar. **1885** BIBLE (R.V.) *Isa.* vi. 13 As a terebinth, and as an oak.

b. Also *terebinth tree*.

1572 BOSSEWELL *Armorie* III. 23 b, The fielde is of the Moone, a Therebinthe tree, Saturne, floured and leafed, Veneris. **1861** MISS E. A. BEAUFORT *Egypt. Sepul.*, etc. II. xvi. 36 All about Kedesh there is still a remarkable number of lofty terebinth trees.

†**2.** The resin of this tree; = TURPENTINE. *Obs.*

1483 CAXTON *Gold. Leg.* 51 b/1 Presente to that man yeftes, a lytyl reysyns and hony..therebinthe and dates. **1585** T. WASHINGTON tr. *Nicholay's Voy.* III. xv. 99 b, To make [their hair] grow..they vse by continuall artifice Terebinthe and vernish. **1672–3** GREW *Anat. Roots* I. iii. §21 The Root of Common Wormwood bleeds..a true Terebinth, or a Balsame with all the defining properties of a Terebinth.

Hence †**tereˈbinthen** (in 5 **terebynten**) *a.*, of terebinth; †**tereˈbinthial, -ian** *adjs.*, of or belonging to the terebinth, or to turpentine; terebinthine.

c **1440** *Pallad. on Husb.* III. 1018 Putte in euery hole a wegge or pyn, A birchen here, a terebynten there. **1747** *Gentl. Mag.* Mar. 146/2 The Irish prelate's Terebinthian draughts Dilute all Antitrinitarian thoughts. **1750** G. HUGHES *Barbadoes* 158 These and every other Part of this Tree have so much of a terebinthial Quality in it, that it will ..burn like a candle.

terebinthaceous (tɛrɪbɪnˈθeɪʃəs), *a. Bot.* Also **-taceous**. [f. mod.L. *Terebinthāceæ*, f. L. *terebinthus*: see prec. and -ACEOUS.] Belonging to the N.O. *Terebinthaceæ*, in some classifications a synonym of *Anacardiaceæ*, or including both that and *Burseraceæ*.

1830 LINDLEY *Nat. Syst. Bot.* 126 From Anacardiaceæ and other terebintaceous orders they [*Connaraceæ*] are at once known by the total want of resinous juice. **1852** TH. ROSS *Humboldt's Trav.* I. vi. 213 *note*, Among terebinthaceous plants, the Rhus glabrum.

‖**tereˈbinthina.** [med.L. *terebinthina* sb., short for *terebinthina rēsina* terebinthine resin: see TEREBINTHINE B. 2.] The pharmacopœial name of turpentine.

1693 tr. *Blancard's Phys. Dict.* (ed. 2), *Terebinthina*, is twofold, vulgar and Venetian. **1859** GULLICK & TIMBS *Paint.* 209 By Turpentine and Terebinthina is understood the generally light-coloured resinous liquid which flows from many kinds of trees. **1899** *Syd. Soc. Lex* s.v., *Terebinthina* (Ph. U.S.) is the concrete oleo-resin..; also the juice of *Pinus australis* and other species of *Pinus*.

terebinthinate (tɛrɪˈbɪnθɪnət), *a.* and *sb.* [ad. med.L. *terebinthināt-us*, f. *terebinthina* turpentine: see -ATE[1], [2].]

A. *adj.* Impregnated with turpentine; having the nature or quality of turpentine; terebinthine.

1680 BOYLE *Produc. Chem. Princ.* III. 123 The Terebinthinate Oyle. **1702** H. VAUGHAN in *Phil. Trans.* XXIII. 1244, I ordered him a Terebinthinate Clyster. **1821** W. P. C. BARTON *Flora N. Amer.* I. 103 Emitting a terebinthinate odour. **1874** GARROD & BAXTER *Mat. Med.* (1880) 246 Copaiva acts as a stimulant like other terebinthinate drugs.

B. *sb.* A terebinthine product; a medicinal preparation of turpentine.

17.. FLOYER (J.), Salt serum may be evacuated by urine, by terebinthinates; as tops of pine in all our ale. **1822–34** *Good's Study Med.* (ed. 4) I. 248 The balsam of copaiba..is ..a terebinthinate of another kind. **1844** COPLAND *Dict. Pract. Med.* (1858) II. 130/1 The terebinthinates..are the most efficacious means of arresting the discharge.

So **tereˈbinthinate** *v. trans.*, to impregnate with turpentine; hence **tereˈbinthinated** *ppl. a.*

1651 FRENCH *Distill.* iv. 91 Take Spirit of Wine terebinthinated ten ounces. **1898** *Allbutt's Syst. Med.* V. 88 The inhalation of an oxygenated and terebinthinated atmosphere.

terebinthine (tɛrɪˈbɪnθɪn), *a.* and *sb.* Also 6 **terebynthine, -bintine, -thin**, 7 **teribinthine**. [ad. L. *terebinthinus*, *ter(e)bentinus*, f. Gr. type *τερεβίνθινος, f. τερέβινθ-ος terebinth: see -INE[1]. Cf. F. *térébenthine* turpentine.]

A. *adj.* **1.** Of, pertaining to, of the nature of, or allied to the terebinth.

c **1550** LLOYD *Treas. Health* Ciij, Make a coife or cappe of waxe terebintine..and put it vpon the head. **1555** W. WATREMAN *Fardle Facions* II. vii. 159 The fruicte of the Terebinthine tree. **1658** PHILLIPS, *Terebinthine*,..

belonging to the Terebinth, i. the Turpentine tree. **1838** JACKSON *Krummacher's Elisha* i. 2 Under the shade of the terebinthine groves of Mamre. **1846** KEIGHTLEY *Notes Virg., Flora* 393 It appears that it [a tree] was of the terebinthine, and not of the coniferous family.

2. Of, pertaining to, or consisting of turpentine; turpentinic, turpentiny.

1656 BLOUNT *Glossogr.*, *Terebinthine*, of or belonging to turpentine, or the tree out of which it issues. **1664** EVELYN *Sylva* 55 These knots.. are well impregnated with that Terebinthine and Resinous matter, which.. preserves them so long from putrifaction. **1710** T. FULLER *Pharm. Extemp.* 291 Copayba.. hath a bitter, hot, Terebinthine Taste. **1796** MORSE *Amer. Geog.* I. 191 Its knots and roots being full of the terebenthine oil. **1880** *Scribner's Mag.* Feb. 505 Pine rails.. spicing the air with their terebinthine perfume.

B. *sb.* (elliptical uses of the adj.)

†**1.** (= *terebinthine tree*.) The terebinth. *Obs.*

[*c* **1000** *Sax. Leechd.* II. 226 Nim ða wyrt þe hatte on suþerne terebintina, swa micel swa ele berge.] **1513** DOUGLAS *Æneis* x. iii. 39 Mair semely.. than amyd the blak terebynthine Growis by Orycia, and as the geit dois schyne.

†**2.** (= *terebinthine resin*: cf. TEREBINTHINA.) Turpentine. *Obs.*

1578 LYTE *Dodoens* VI. xcii. 776 The Rosen [of the larch] is called.. in Douche.. Termenthiin, or Terbenthiin, that is to say, Terebinthin, or Turpentyn. **1605** TIMME *Quersit.* I. xiii. 64 Out of teribinthine.. a mercuriall spirit.. may bee.. extracted. **1725** SLOANE *Jamaica* II. 90 Triangular berries.. smelling like terebinthine.

So **tere'binthinous**, †**tere'binthious** *adjs.*

1718 J. CHAMBERLAYNE *Relig. Philos.* (1730) II. xxiii. §29 The wonderful Particulars of Flowers, such as.. their Store-Houses of slimy and terebinthious Matters. **1840** F. D. BENNETT *Whaling Voy.* II. 352 Every part of the tree has.. a terebinthinous odour. **1869** *Eng. Mech.* 24 Dec. 354/2 Produced by a.. species of *Aphis* on a terebinthinous plant.

‖**terebra** ('tɛrɪbrə). Also 7–8 **terebrum**. [L. *terebra*, *terebrum* a borer.]

†**1.** An instrument for boring; in *Surgery*, a trephine, or the boring part of it; also, a miner's drill. *Obs.*

1611 COTGR., *Tirefond de Chirurgien*, a Surgeons Terebra, or Piercer; an Instrument which he puts vnto diuers vses. **1704** RAY *Disc.* II. v. (1713) 224 This ends at the Place which the Workmen pierce with their *Terebra*... The *Terebra* sometimes finds great Trees. **1706** PHILLIPS (ed. Kersey), *Terebra*, or *Terebrum*,.. also an Instrument to engrave on Stones. **1750** *Mem. Roy. Acad. Surg. Paris* I. 162 Instruments hitherto used to raise the bones of the cranium depressed on the dura mater are.. the Terebra. **1787** C. B. TRYE in *Med. Commun.* II. 149, I made several perforations in the cranium with the terebra of the trephine.

2. *Ent.* The modified ovipositor of certain female insects, esp. terebrant Hymenoptera, with which they puncture leaves, fruit, etc., in order to insert their eggs.

[**1691** RAY *Creation* II. (1692) 78 The hollow Instrument (*terebra* he [Malpighi] calls it, and we may English it *piercer*) wherewith many Flies are provided.] **1713** DERHAM *Phys.-Theol.* VIII. vi. 429 The.. Oak-Ball Ichneumon strikes its Terebra into an Oak-Apple.

terebral ('tɛrɪbrəl), *a.* [f. prec. + -AL[1].] Of or pertaining to, or of the nature of a terebra.

1836–9 *Todd's Cycl. Anat.* II. 868/2 The serrated terebral ovipositor.

terebrant ('tɛrɪbrənt), *a.* (*sb.*) [ad. L. *terebrānt-em*, pr. pple. of *terebrāre* to bore. So F. *térébrant*.] Boring, or having the function of boring; belonging to the division *Terebrantia* of hymenopterous insects, having a boring ovipositor.

1826 KIRBY & SP. *Entomol.* IV. xlvii. 373 Tail of the female without a terebrant, or pungent multivalve ovipositor. **1860** in MAYNE *Expos. Lex.*

B. *sb.* = BORE *sb.*[2] 3. *humorous nonce-use.*

1890 O. W. HOLMES *Over the Teacups* iv, Many a terebrant I have known who—'was great nor knew how great he was'.

terebrate ('tɛrɪbrət), *a. Ent.* [f. L. *terebra* borer + -ATE[2] 2.] Furnished with, or formed as, a terebra (TEREBRA 2).

1902 in *Cassell's Encycl. Dict.* Supp.

terebrate ('tɛrɪbreɪt), *v.* Now *rare*. [f. ppl. stem of L. *terebrāre* to bore.] *trans.* To bore, pierce, perforate; to penetrate by boring. Also *absol.* In quot. 1774, to form by boring. In quots. 1855, 1869 *humorously* for BORE *v.*[2]

1623 COCKERAM, *Terebrate*, to pierce with a Wimble. **1646** SIR T. BROWNE *Pseud. Ep.* II. vi. 100 If wee consider the threefold effect of Jupiters Trisulke, to burne, discusse and terebrate. **1683–4** ROBINSON in *Phil. Trans.* XXIX. 475 The Insects suck and terebrate the Tree. **1758** J. CLUBBE *Misc. Tracts* (1770) 100 An incrustated surface.. too hard for my finer sort of gimblets to terebrate. **1774** G. WHITE *Selborne* 26 Feb., The bank-martin terebrates a round and regular hole in the sand or earth. **1855** O. W. HOLMES *Poems* 250 O for a world where.. blunted dulness terebrates in vain! **1869** *Sat. Rev.* 14 May 582 They [women] succeed by dint of perseverance; their terebrating powers are, in the long run, irresistible.

terebration (tɛrɪ'breɪʃən). Now *rare* or *Obs.* Also 5 **terabracioun**. [ad. late L. *terebrātiōn-em*, n. of action f. *terebrāre* to bore; cf. F. *térébration* (15th c.).] The action of boring or perforating.

a. *Surg.* The operation of trephining.

c **1400** *Lanfranc's Cirurg.* 140 In almaner hurtynge of þe heed to vsen terabracioun eiþer remeuynge of þe boon wiþ handliche instrument is. **1676** WISEMAN *Surg.* V. ix. 389, I.. made a circular Incision, and raised up that part of the Hairy scalp in order to Terebration. **1767** GOOCH *Treat. Wounds* I. 261 Making terebrations to the Diploë. **1860** MAYNE *Expos. Lex.*, *Terebratio*,.. old term for the operation of applying the trephine: terebration.

b. *gen.* The action of boring, as with an auger; perforation (esp. of fruit-trees).

1623 COCKERAM, *Terebration*, a wimbling. **1626** BACON *Sylva* §463 It hath been touched before, that Terebration of Trees doth make them prosper better. **1725** *Bradley's Fam. Dict.* s.v. *Juice*, Another Way of getting these Juices is by Terebration, that is by piercing the Body of the Tree with an Augar. **1745** tr. *Columella's Husb.* IV. xxix, In that which is performed by terebration you must first mark out the fruitfullest vine in the neighbourhood.

‖**Terebratula** (tɛrɪ'brætjʊlə). *Zool.* and *Palæont.* Pl. **-æ** also **-as**. Also (after F.) **tere'bratule**. [mod.L. (Lhwyd, 1699), quasi-dim. of L. *terebrātus*, fem. *-a*, pa. pple. of *terebrāre* to bore. So F. *térébratule*.] A genus of brachiopods, mostly extinct: so called from the perforated beak of the ventral valve. Formerly used more widely to include any (esp. fossil) members of the *Terebratulidæ* and related families; the lamp-shells.

1822 J. FLINT *Lett. Amer.* 102 Limestone.. is literally conglomerated with organic remains. Amongst these, the most remarkable is a species of terebratula. **1822** J. PARKINSON *Outl. Oryctol.* 250 Some of the multilocular univalves, and of the terebratulas. **1851** WOODWARD *Mollusca* I. 12 Deepest of all, the *terebratulæ* are found, commonly at fifty.. and sometimes at one hundred fathoms, even in Polar seas. **1853** TH. ROSS *Humboldt's Trav.* III. xxix. 165 Petrifactions of pecten, cardites, terebratules, and madrepores.

Hence **tere'bratular** *a.*, of or pertaining to a terebratula; **tere'bratuliform** *a.*, having the form of a terebratula; **tere'bratuline** *a.*, belonging to or having the character of the *Terebratulidæ*; **tere'bratulite**, a fossil *Terebratula* or lamp-shell; **tere'bratuloid**, *a.* resembling or related to the genus *Terebratula*; *sb.* a species or congener of this genus.

1822 J. PARKINSON *Outl. Oryctol.* 334 In the masses of mountain limestone.. are immense accumulations of crinoideal and *terebratular remains. **1864** WEBSTER, **Terebratuliform*, having the general form of terebratula shell. **1891** *Cent. Dict.*, *Terebratuline. **1830** LYELL *Princ. Geol.* I. 127 A great calcareous formation,.. in which are included coral-lines, productæ, *terebratulites, &c. **1853** TH. ROSS *Humboldt's Trav.* III. xxix. 166 *note*, The 'Roche à ravets' of Martinique and Hayti.. is.. filled with terebratulites, and other vestiges of sea-shells. **1895** F. R. C. REED *Brachiopods* (*Fossils*) in *Camb. Nat. Hist.* III. 512 The *Terebratuloids can be traced back to the primitive type *Renssoellaria*.

terebrum: see TEREBRA.

terebynt(e, obs. form of TEREBINTH.

‖**Teredo** (tə'riːdəʊ). Pl. **teredines** (tə'riːdɪniːz), **teredos** (tə'riːdəʊz). [L. *terēdo*, ad. Gr. τερηδών a wood-gnawing worm, f. τερ-, root of τείρειν to rub hard, wear away, bore.]

1. *Zool.* A genus of lamellibranch boring molluscs; *esp.* the ship-worm, *T. navalis*, well known for its destruction of submerged timbers in ships, piers, sea-dikes, etc. by boring into the wood.

In accordance with the etymology, the name was formerly applied vaguely to any species of worm or larva that wears its way into wood; the ship-worm was at first supposed to be a worm, and was only in 1733 recognized as a mollusc.

1398 TREVISA *Barth. De P.R.* XVII. xxiii. (Bodl. MS.), Cedre.. is neuer destroied wiþ mowʒte noþer wiþ terredo þat is þe tree worme. *Ibid.* XVIII. cvi, Þe worme teredo is a litel worme of a tree,.. and freteþ & gnaweþ moche hard treen. **1616** T. ADAMS *Soul's Sickness* Wks. 1861 I. 505 The body's infirmities.. are few and scant, if compared to the soul's, which being a better piece of timber, hath the more teredines breeding in it. **1654** TRAPP *Comm. Jonah* iv, There is a worm lies couchant in every gourd to smite it, a teredo to waste it. **1707** MORTIMER *Husb.* (1721) II. 77 The Teredo.. and other Worms lying between the Body and the Bark. **1791** E. DARWIN *Bot. Gard.* I. 123 Meets fell Teredo, as he mines the keel With beaked head. **1839** G. ROBERTS *Dict. Geol.* s.v., The shield of the Teredo furnished Mr. Brunel with the idea for the shield used in the Thames Tunnel. **1850** MISS PRATT *Comm. Things Sea-side* iii. 202 The teredo works with astonishing rapidity, and will completely riddle a hard and sound piece of wood, in the space of five or six weeks. **1879** A. R. WALLACE *Australas.* x. 209 The jarrah.., an almost indestructible timber, which is free from the attacks of teredo and termites. **1879** E. P. WRIGHT *Anim. Life* 562 The teredo was first recognised as a bivalve mollusc by Sellius, who wrote an elaborate treatise on the subject in 1733.

fig. **1823** SIR D. BREWSTER in *Home Life* (1869) viii, If some teredo of an engineer cut out a tunnel beneath. **1861** W. H. RUSSELL in *Times* 23 Sept., Others of his colleagues.. are the teredos of every plank in the Ship of State.

2. *transf.* 'Any disease in plants produced by the boring of insects' (*Treas. Bot.*, 1866).

tereen, obs. form of TUREEN.

‖**Terek** ('tɛrɪk). [From the name of the river *Terek*.] More fully, ***Terek sandpiper***. A species of Sandpiper, *Xenus cinereus*, with a slightly recurved bill, found near the Caspian Sea, esp. about the mouth of the river Terek. Also called ***Terek avocet***, ***T. snipe***, ***T. godwit***.

1785 LATHAM *Gen. Syn. Birds* V. 155 Terek Sn[ipe]. **1785** PENNANT *Arct. Zool.* II. 502 American and Terek Avoset... Terek. *Scolopax cinerea*. **1824** STEPHENS in Shaw *Gen. Zool.* XII. I. 83 Terek Godwit... This curious species is probably referable to a distinct genus, as its beak materially differs in form from that of the true Godwits. **1879** *Ibis* XXI. 152 The Terek Sandpiper arrived at our quarters [in Siberia] on the 8th of June. **1915** *Brit. Birds* IX. 69 Three Terek Sandpipers.. were shot at Rye in the month of May, 1915. **1956** *Ibis* XCVIII. 161 The Terek Sandpiper thus becomes *Tringa terek* (Latham), the name *Tringa cinerea* being pre-occupied. **1982** *Times* 23 Mar. 10/5 Leicester Museum spent.. £400 on a family of [stuffed] Terek sandpipers.

terella, obs. form of TERRELLA.

‖**terem** ('tɛrəm). *Russ. Hist.* [Russ., lit. 'tower'.] Secluded separate quarters for women.

1898 G. B. SHAW in *Sat. Rev.* 8 Jan. 42/2 The seclusion of Russian women in the Terem was one of the sacred institutions of his [*sc.* Peter the Great's] country. **1908** *Cambr. Mod. Hist.* V. xvii. 519 The boy soon felt cramped and stifled in the dim and close semi-religious atmosphere of Natalia's *terem*. **1929** S. RUNCIMAN *Emperor Romanus Lecapenus* i. 28 It has been customary to regard the gynaecum as a prison from which Byzantine women never emerged—an exact equivalent of the Russian terem, which most historians say derived from it, forgetting Russia's two and a half centuries of Mongol rule. **1943** E. M. ALMEDINGEN *Frossia* iv. 169 The maiden lived in her *terem*, its windows strictly latticed.

Terena (tɛ'reɪnə). Also Ter(r)eno. (A member of) an Arawak group of South American Indians of the southern Mato Grosso in Brazil; the language of this group. Also *attrib.*

1891 D. G. BRINTON *American Race* 244 The Terenos.. are members of the Guaycuru stock of the Chaco. **1928** A. R. HAY *Indians of S. Amer. & Gospel* vi. 101 In the Terena tribe we have a typical group of forest Indians who are fast adopting civilized ways. **1932** P. RADIN *Indians of S. Amer.* xi. 204 No evidence exists for its presence [*sc.* class division] in any other of the continental Arawak tribes except the *Terreno*. **1946** *Internat. Jrnl. Amer. Linguistics* XII. 60/1 The basic unit of structure in Terena phonology is the syllable. **1952** E. FISCHER-JØRGENSEN in E. Hamp et al. *Readings in Linguistics II* (1966) 315 It is not at all rare to find particularly nasals entering into the category of phonemes never adjoining the vowel in clusters..; this is the case e.g. in Terena. **1960** *Word* XVI. 349 A phonemic analysis of Tereno establishes as full phonemes a bilabial nasal and an alveolar nasal. **1974** *Encycl. Brit. Macropædia* XVII. 125/1 The Terena.. work on cattle breeding farms.

terene, obs. form of TERRENE, TUREEN.

terenite ('tɛrɪnaɪt). *Min.* [Named by Emmons, 1837, f. Gr. τέρην tender + -ITE[1], from its brittleness.] 'An altered scapolite, of greenish or yellowish color, near algerite' (Chester).

1846 in WORCESTER. **1868** DANA *Min.* 323.

Terentian (tə'rɛnʃən), *a.* [ad. L. *Terentiān-us*, f. *Terenti-us* Terence.] Pertaining to, or in the style of, the ancient Roman dramatic poet Terence.

1599 B. JONSON *Ev. Man out of Hum.* Induct., According to the Terentian manner. **1902** BOND in *Lyly's Wks.* III. 168 A new departure, an essay in Terentian comedy.

terephthalic (tɛrəf'θælɪk), *a. Chem.* [f. TERE-BIC + PHTHALIC.] Derived from or containing terebic and phthalic acids, as in ***terephthalic acid*** (also called *insolinic acid*), $C_8H_6O_4 = C_6H_4(CO_2H)_2$, a dibasic acid produced as a white tasteless crystalline powder, nearly insoluble in water, alcohol, and ether.

1857 MILLER *Elem. Chem.* III. vii. §1. 443 The second is isomeric with phthalic acid, and is hence termed terephthalic acid. **1868** WATTS *Dict. Chem.* V. 725. **1964** N. G. CLARK *Mod. Org. Chem.* xxiii. 491 Terephthalic acid, after conversion to the dimethyl ester, is an important intermediate in the manufacture of 'Terylene'. **1971** D. POTTER *Brit. Eliz. Stamps* ii. 27 Lettalite B.3 or tere-phthalic acid became known as violet phosphor. **1973** *Materials & Technol.* VI. iv. 326 The starting materials for the manufacture of polyethylene terephthalate are ethylene glycol and terephthalic acid, both obtained from petroleum sources.

Hence **tere'phthalamide**, an amide of terephthalic acid: see quot. 1868; **tere'phthalate** (also *te're-*), a salt of this acid.

1868 WATTS *Dict. Chem.* V. 726 Terephthalate of Ammonium.. crystallises, by slow evaporation, in small crystals having a strong lustre. *Ibid.*, Terephthalic amides. 1. Terephthalamide, $C_8H_8N_2O_2 = N_2H_4.(C_8H_4O_2)''$, produced by the action of ammonia on terephthalic chloride, is a white amorphous body, not dissolved by any solution. **1946**, etc. [see *polyethylene terephthalate* s.v. POLYETHYLENE a]. **1958** *Times Rev. Industry* Aug. 57/3 Mylar polyester film.. is a polyester terephthalate film. **1973** *Materials & Technol.* VI. iv. 280 While other fibre-forming polyesters were prepared, none proved to be as satisfactory as the polyethylene terephthalate developed by Whinfield, and this has continued to dominate the commercial fibre-forming polyester field.

terepoile: see TERPOILE.

teres ('tɛriːz), *a.* and *sb. Anat.* [L.: see TERETE *a.*] **A.** *adj.* In *pronator teres*: a pronating muscle of the forearm that arises from the humerus and ulna, near the elbow, and is inserted into the radius. **B.** *sb.* [sc. *musculus*.] Either of two muscles arising from the shoulder blade and inserted into the upper part of the humerus: the *teres major* draws the humerus towards the body and rotates it inwards; the *teres minor* rotates it outwards and helps steady its head.
1713 W. CHESELDEN *Anat. Human Body* (ed. 3) II. iii. 59 Teres minor, is a small Muscle arising below the former [*sc.* infraspinatus] from the inferior Costa Scapulæ. *Ibid.*, Teres major, arises from the lower Angle of the Scapula. *Ibid.* 66 Pronator Teres, arises from the inner Apophysis of the Os Humeri, and upper and forepart of the Ulna. **1889** J. LEIDY *Elem. Treat. Human Anat.* (ed. 2) v. 295 The greater teres.. contributes with the latissimus to form the posterior border of the axilla. **1979** *Sci. Amer.* Dec. 99/3 This feature seems to reflect the strong development in Neanderthals of the teres minor muscle. **1980** *Gray's Anat.* (ed. 36) v. 574/1 The pronator teres rotates the radius upon the ulna, turning the palm of the hand backwards.

† **te'resa.** *Obs.* Also **the'rese.** [prob. from the name of the Empress Maria Theresa (1717–1780).] An article of female attire in the 18th c.: see quot. 1846.
1770 FOOTE *Lame Lover* III, Throwing her Teresa aside —upon my soul she is prodigious fine. **1846** FAIRHOLT *Costume in Eng.* (1860) Gloss., *Therese*, a light gauze kerchief worn over the ladies' head-dress about 1786.

Teresian, Theresian (tə'riːsɪən), *sb.* and *a.* Also 9 **Teresan.** [f. the name of St. Teresa (a Spanish Carmelite nun, 1515–1582) + -IAN.]
a. *sb.* A member of a reformed order of Carmelite nuns and friars founded by St. Teresa in the 16th c. **b.** *adj.* Belonging to this order.
1629 WADSWORTH *Pilgr.* vii. 73 There is..a monastery of the English poore Teresians at Antwerpe. **1767** S. PATERSON *Another Trav.* I. 352 That [sisterhood] of the Theresians is reckoned the poorest and most pitiable. **1882–3** *Schaff's Encycl. Relig. Knowl.* III. 2348 [St. Theresa] founded at Avila a convent for the Barefooted Carmelites, also called the Theresians. **1897** J. P. RUSHE (*title*) Carmel in Ireland: ..the Irish Province of Teresian, or Discalced Carmelites.

terester, terestr-: see TERR-.

terete (tə'riːt), *a.* Also 7 **teret** (9 *erron.* **terate**). [ad. L. *teres, teret-em* rounded (off).] Rounded, smooth and round; now almost always in *Nat. Hist.*, having a cylindrical or slightly tapering form, circular in cross-section, and a surface free from furrows or ridges.
a **1619** FOTHERBY *Atheom.* II. xi. §6 (1622) 326 Round and teret, like a globe. [**1760** J. LEE *Introd. Bot.* III. v. (1765) 184 Leaves are, *Teretes*, round like a Pillar; when they are for the most Part cylindric.] **1821** W. P. C. BARTON *Flora N. Amer.* I. 18 Stem about two feet high, terete. **1845** LINDLEY *Sch. Bot.* v. (1858) 68 *b*, Fruit terete, obovate, covered with scales or tubercles. **1877** COUES *Fur Anim.* iv. 98 Tail long, terete, uniformly bushy or very slender and close-haired, with a terminal pencil.
b. *Comb.*, as *terete-elliptical*, *-linear* adjs.
1847 W. E. STEELE *Field Bot.* 177 Sep[als] and pet[als] ovate-lanceolate, as long as the terate-elliptical, mucronate caps[ule]. *Ibid.* 108 Pods terate-linear.
Hence **te'retish** *a.*, somewhat terete. Also † **te'retial**, † **'teretous** *adjs.*, terete (*obs.*).
1658 SIR T. BROWNE *Gard. Cyrus* iv. 176 Why..there are so few [plants] with teretous or long round leaves? **18..** OWEN cited in *Cent. Dict.* for *teretial*. **190.** R. TUCKERMAN *N. Amer. Lichens* i. 22 (Cass. Supp.) Either narrowed and somewhat channelled, with teretish tips, or dilated.

tereted: see TERRIT.

teretenaunt, obs. form of TERRE-TENANT.

tereti- ('tɛrɪtɪ), combining form of L. *teres, teret-*, TERETE; used in a few scientific terms. **ˌtereti'caudate** *a.* [L. *cauda* tail], having a rounded tail, round-tailed (*Cent. Dict.*). **ˌtereti'folious** *a.* [L. *folium* leaf], having terete leaves. **ˌteretipro'nator**, the round pronating muscle of the forearm (*pronator radii teres*). ‖**ˌtereti'scapular** [SCAPULA], the greater round muscle (*teres major*) of the shoulder-blade.
1657 TOMLINSON *Renou's Disp.* 351 This setum..rather ..than any other..teretifolious esculent. **1890** BILLINGS *Med. Dict.* cites COUES for *tereti-pronator* and *tereti-scapularis*.

† **'teretism.** *Obs. rare*⁻¹. [ad. Gr. τερέτισμα twittering.] Twittering; *fig.* unmelodious writing.
1597–8 BP. HALL *Sat.* IV. i. 3 Rough-hewne Teretismes, writ in th' antique vain.

'tereto-, irregular combining form of L. *teres* (see TERETI-). **ˌtereto-se'taceous** *a.* [L. *sēta* bristle], having smooth round bristles. **ˌtereto-'subulate** *a.* [L. *subula* awl], terete and awl-shaped.
1846 DANA *Zooph.* (1848) 593 A stony axis,..tereto-subulate and truncate. *Ibid.* 663 Branches erect, tereto-setaceous.

tereu (tiː'ruː). Chiefly *poet.* A feigned note of the nightingale.
Tēreu vocative of Gr.-L. *Tēreus*, name in mythology of the husband of Philomela's sister Progne, and father of Itys; all, according to Ovid *Met.* VI. viii, transformed to birds; the nightingale's note being still a piteous cry to Tereus.
1576 GASCOIGNE *Compl. Philomene* in *Steele Gl.*, etc. (Arb.) 110 And for hir foremost note, Tereu Tereu doth sing. **1598** BARNFIELD *Ode* Poems (Arb.) 120 The Nightingale..(poore Bird)..sung the dolefulst Ditty, That to heare it was great Pitty. Fie, fie, fie, now would she cry Teru Teru, by and by. *a* **1627** MIDDLETON *Father Hubbard's T.* Wks. (Dyce) V. 603 Away she flew, Crying Tereu! **1657** THORNLEY tr. *Longus' Daphnis & Chloe* 124 The Nightingales began to jug and warble their Tereus and Ity's again. **1923** T. S. ELIOT *Waste Land* iii. 15 Twit twit twit Jug jug jug jug jug So rudely forc'd. Tereu. **1936** R. CAMPBELL *Mithraic Emblems* 125 Hear how it whistles 'jug, puff-puff, tereu' Better than any nightingale could do.

terf, obs. form of TURF.

tergal ('tɜːgəl), *a.*[1] *Zool.* [f. L. *terg-um* the back + -AL[1].] Belonging to the tergum; dorsal.
1860 MAYNE *Expos. Lex.*, *Tergalis*..tergal. **1870** NICHOLSON *Man. Zool.* I. xxxiv. 192 The tergal elements of the thoracic rings. **1870** ROLLESTON *Anim. Life* 91 The eyes and antennae do not really belong to the tergal aspect of the ..segment. **1880** HUXLEY *Crayfish* ii. 71 When the dorsal or tergal wall of the thorax is taken away.

Tergal ('tɜːgəl), *a.*[2] and *sb.* Also **tergal.** [a. F. *Tergal*, f. *tér-éphthalique* TEREPHTHALIC *a.* + *gal-lique* GALLIC *a.*[1]] A proprietary name for polyester fibre and fabrics. Cf. TERITAL.
1954 *Trade Marks Jrnl.* 22 Dec. 1301/2 *Tergal*... Textile piece goods; bed and table covers, curtains; and household textile articles... Societe Rhodiaceta.., Paris VIIIe, France; manufacturers. **1955** *Official Gaz.* (U.S. Patent Office) 26 Apr. TM 192/1 *Tergal*... For..textile fabrics..of synthetic fibers, table cloths and napkins, bed sheets, blankets, and quilts. **1959** *Guardian* 16 Oct. 7/3 Loden or tergal or plaid lined. **1967** *Jane's Surface Skimmer Systems 1967–68* 7/1 The airflow is ducted to ten individual neoprene-coated tergal skirts. **1968** *Economist* 15 June 72/2 Rhone Poulenc had a French monopoly of nylon and terylene (tergal). **1973** 'D. RUTHERFORD' *Kick Start* i. 12 My dark blue Tergal trousers.

tergant ('tɜːgənt), **tergiant** ('tɜːdʒɪənt), *a. Her. rare*⁻⁰. [f. L. *tergum* the back, after *rampant*, *passant*, etc.] Showing the back; having the back turned towards the spectator: said of an animal borne as a charge. (Cf. RECURSANT.)
c **1828** BERRY *Encycl. Her.* I. Gloss., *Tergant*, or *Tergiant*, showing the back part..; by some termed *invertant*, or *recursant*... *Tergiant, volant*, flying, showing the back part. *Tergiant, displayed*, an eagle, displayed, showing the back. *Tergiant, surgant*, or *surgiant*, as an eagle, &c. rising, with the back to sight. **1894** *Parker's Gloss. Her.*, *Tergiant*, of a Tortoise, &c., having the back turned towards the spectator.

tergat, terge, obs. forms of TARGET, TARGE.

tergeminate (tɜː'dʒɛmɪnət), *a. Bot.* [f. as next + -ATE[2].] (See quots.)
1793 MARTYN *Lang. Bot.*, *Tergeminum folium*, a Tergeminate or thrice-double leaf. **1832** LINDLEY *Introd. Bot.* IV. i. 391 *Tergeminate*.., when each of two secondary petioles bears towards its summit one pair of leaflets, and the common petiole bears a third pair at the origin of the two secondary petioles.

ter'geminous, *a. rare.* [f. L. *tergemin-us* (poet. for *trigeminus*, f. *tri-* three + *geminus* born together) triple: see -OUS.] (See quot. 1656.)
1656 BLOUNT *Glossogr.*, *Tergeminous*..threefold, triple; one of, or the three borne at, the same time. **1851** *Poems on Hawick Auld Brig* 4 The arch tergeminous which spanned the stream.

tergett, tergiant, var. TARGET, TERGANT.

tergiferous (tɜː'dʒɪfərəs), *a. Bot. rare*⁻⁰. [f. L. *terg-um* the back: see -FEROUS.] Bearing the fructification on the back of the frond, as a fern: = DORSIFEROUS 1. Also † **tergi'fetous** *a.* [FŒTUS] in same sense.
1704 J. HARRIS *Lex. Techn.* I, *Tergefœtous Plants*, such Herbs..as bear their Seeds on the backsides of their Leaves. **1847** WEBSTER s.v., Tergiferous plants.

† **'tergiment.** *Obs. rare*⁻⁰. [ad. med.L. *tergiment-um*, f. *tergere* to wipe, to correct.] (See quot.)
1656 BLOUNT *Glossogr.*, *Tergiment*, that which is put into the scales to make weight.

tergite ('tɜːdʒaɪt). *Zool.* [f. L. *terg-um* back + -ITE[1] 3.] A back-plate, formed by the fusion of a pair of serial plates of one of the somites or segments of an arthropod or other articulated animal.
1885 *Athenæum* 5 Dec. 736/2 On the opposite interior surface of the last tergite are chitinous points. **1899** G. H. CARPENTER *Insects* i. 21 The *pronotum*..is larger than the two succeeding tergites (*mesonotum* and *metanotum*).
Hence **tergitic** (tə'dʒɪtɪk) *a.*, of or pertaining to a tergite.
1891 in *Cent. Dict.*

tergiversant ('tɜːdʒɪˌvɜːsənt), *a.* and *sb.* [ad. L. *tergiversānt-em*, pres. pple. of *tergiversārī*: see next.] **a.** *adj.* Tergiversating, shuffling, evasive, shifty. **b.** *sb.* One who tergiversates; a turncoat, renegade.
1710 *Brit. Apollo* III. No. 17. 2/1 A Future Bride, but yet under her First Courtship, and at First Opposite, Recusant and Tergiversant. **1833** MOZLEY *Let.* 4 July in *Ess.* (1878) I. Introd. 20, I expect the tergiversants will be a considerable party.

tergiversate ('tɜːdʒɪvəseɪt, -ˌvɜːseɪt), *v.* [f. L. *tergiversāt-*, ppl. stem. of *tergiversārī* to turn one's back, shuffle, practise evasion, f. *terg-um* the back + *vers-*, ppl. stem of *vertĕre* to turn (cf. *versārī* to move about).]
1. *intr.* To practise tergiversation; to desert one's party, turn renegade, apostatize; to shift, shuffle, use subterfuge or evasion; †to refuse to obey, act the recusant. Hence **'tergiversated** *ppl. a.*, renegade, apostate; **'tergiversating** *vbl. sb.*, tergiversation, evasion; *ppl. a.*, apostatizing, renegade; †recusant; evasive, shifty.
1654 GAYTON *Pleas. Notes* II. vi. 61 That tergiversating and back-sliding Lady. **1678** CUDWORTH *Intell. Syst.* I. iv. §36. 569 Plotinus..as if he were conscious that this *assumentum* to the Platonick Theology, were not so defensible a thing, doth himself sometime as it were tergiversate and decline it by equivocating in the word *Henades.* **1831** J. WILSON in *Blackw. Mag.* XXIX. 725, 'I am liberal in my politics', says some twenty-times tergiversated turn-coat. **1852** MISS YONGE *Cameos* (1877) IV. xviii. 203 Wyatt was examined again and again, and wavered and tergiversated a good deal. **1862** WRAXALL *Hugo's Misérables* v. xvii, Tergiversation is useless, for what side of himself does a man show in tergiversating?
2. *lit.* To turn the back (for flight or retreat).
1875 POSTE *Gaius* IV. Comm. (ed. 2) 509 If the defendant on being summoned to appear before the magistrate tergiversates or attempts to flee.

tergiversation (ˌtɜːdʒɪvə'seɪʃən). [ad. L. *tergiversātiōn-em*, n. of action f. *tergiversārī*: see prec. and -ATION.]
1. The action of 'turning one's back on', i.e. forsaking, something in which one was previously engaged, interested, or concerned; desertion or abandonment of a cause, party, etc.; apostasy, renegation. Also with *a* and *pl.*, an instance of this; an act of desertion or apostasy.
1583 STUBBES *Anat. Abus.* II. (1882) 96 Their tergiuersation and backsliding from their duties. **1618** MYNSHUL *Ess. Prison* Ep. Ded., I haue now put my name to my Book (without tergiuersation or turne coating the letters). *a* **1631** DONNE *Serm.* (ed. Alford) V. 16 No tergiversation, nor abandoning the noble work he had begun. **1721** AMHERST *Terræ Fil.* Pref. (1754) 16 It will be very unreasonable for them to..charge their own fickleness upon those, who..will not join with them in their new counsels and tergiversations. **1878** STUBBS *Const. Hist.* III. xviii. 187 If betrayal or tergiversation is to be imputed to any.
† **b.** Refusal to obey; recusance. *Obs. rare.*
1676 OWEN *Worship of God* 114 All tergiversation and backwardness in persons duly qualified and called. *a* **1740** WATERLAND *Serm. Matt. xxvi. 41* Wks. 1823 IX. 126 Jonas the Prophet discovered the like tergiversation and backwardness as to the errand he was sent upon to the Ninevites.
2. Turning in a dishonourable manner from straightforward action or statement; shifting, shuffling, equivocation, prevarication. Also with *a* and *pl.*, an instance of this; an evasion, a subterfuge.
1570 FOXE *A. & M.* (ed. 2) 1505/1 For all hys crafty cauteles and tergiuersations alledged out of the lawe. **1660** H. MORE *Myst. Godl.* VII. vii. 304 For the preventing of all Cavils and Tergiversations. **1760** JORTIN *Erasmus* II. 265 Here is a little tergiversation, and Erasmus seems to retract what he had advanced in many places. **1821** SCOTT *Kenilw.* xxxv, The duplicity and tergiversation of which he had been guilty. **1871** G. MEREDITH *H. Richmond* xxxviii, Applying to friends to fortify him in his shifts and tergiversations.
3. † **a.** The literal turning of the back. *rare.*
1660 F. BROOKE tr. *Le Blanc's Trav.* 200 He holds a stately gravity, allowing audience to none but on the knee, nor tergiversation in retiring.
b. The turning of the back for flight; flight, retreat (*lit.* and *fig.*). ? *Obs.*
a **1652** J. SMITH *Sel. Disc.* x. iii. (1856) 475 Wicked men.. seek to avoid the dreadful sentence of their own consciences by a tergiversation and flying from themselves. **1654** H. L'ESTRANGE *Chas. I* (1655) 17 The Captain Governour of the Castle viewing the tergiversation and flight of his party. **1660** BURNEY *Κέρδ. Δῶρον* (1661) 129 The fear of the Lord is to hate evil. Evil has a tergiversation from holy fear.

tergiversator (ˌtɜːdʒɪvə'seɪtə (r)). [agent-n. f. TERGIVERSATE: see -OR; cf. late L. *tergiversātor* boggler, laggard.] One who tergiversates; a renegade; a shuffler.
1716 M. DAVIES *Athen. Brit.* II. 225 The same learned Arian Tergiversator. **1829** SOUTHEY *Lett.* (1856) IV. 129 [To] deliver King and country from a set of tergiversators. **1855** J. STRANG *Glasgow & Clubs* (1856) 485 Nothing better than a political recreant and tergiversator.
So **tergi'versatory** *a.*, shuffling, shifty.
1891 *Sat. Rev.* 12 Sept. 295/2 The tergiversatory performances of Mr. —— and Mr. ——.

tergiverse ('tɜːdʒɪvɜːs), *a. rare.* [f. L. *tergum* back + *versus* turned, pa. pple. of *vertĕre* to turn.] That has turned his back or practised tergiversation; renegade; shifty.

1852 ROEBUCK *Hist. Whig Min. of 1830* I. 290 *note* The tergiverse administration discovered, when too late, that they had broken the staff of their strength.

tergiverse (ˈtɜːdʒɪvɜːs), *v. rare.* [ad. L. *tergiversārī* to TERGIVERSATE; so F. *tergiverser.*]

† **1.** *trans.* To turn backwards, to reverse. (In quot. in *ppl. adj.* ˈ**tergiversed.**) *Obs.*

1600 W. WATSON *Decacordon* (1602) 23 A stay made of the planets course and heauens motion, by reason that *primum mobile*, in a tergiuersed violence of opposite race to the rest, runs a course against the haire.

2. *intr.* = TERGIVERSATE. Hence ˈ**tergiversing** *vbl. sb.*, tergiversation.

1675 (*title*) Quakerism Canvassed: Robin Barclay. found guilty of blasphemy, treason, lying, shifting, quibling, tergiversing, &c. **1688** J. GRUBB *St. George for England* 46 The Briton never tergivers'd, But was for adverse drubbing. **1718** *Entertainer* No. 36. 243 If they don't intirely tergiverse, and become Deserters. **1896** H. REID *Cameronian Apostle* vii. 109 The arbitrary dissolution of one Assembly, . . the 'tergiversing' of the Moderator and Clerk.

tergo- (tɜːgəʊ), combining form repr. L. *tergum* the back, used instead of the regular *tergi-* in a few rare scientific terms. **tergoˈlateral** *a. Zool.*, pertaining to the tergum and the lateral plates of the shell in cirripeds. **tergoˈrhabdite**, *Entom.*, one of the pieces forming the tergum or upper surface of the abdomen in an insect, *esp.* when modified to form part of the ovi-positor (cf. RHABDITE 2).

1851 DARWIN *Cirripedia* Introd. (Palæont. Soc.) 10 In Pollicipes the margin of the Scutum adjoining the Tergum and Upper Latus, is not divided . . into two distinct lines, as in Scalpellum, and is therefore called the tergolateral margin.

terguette, obs. form of TARGET.

‖ **tergum** (ˈtɜːgəm). Pl. **terga**. The Latin word for 'back' (synon. with DORSUM): in special scientific uses. **a.** The back, or upper surface or portion, of an arthropod or other articulated animal; more usually, the upper plate of each somite or segment of such an animal (= TERGITE): opp. to *sternum*. **b.** Each of the two upper plates of the shell in cirripeds.

1826 KIRBY & SP. *Entomol.* III. 387 *Tergum*, the upper or supine surface of the abdomen. **1851** DARWIN *Cirripedia* Introd. (Palæont. Soc.) 2 In almost all the Lepadidæ the Terga (*i.e.* the upper or posterior lateral valves) are not characteristic. **1880** HUXLEY *Crayfish* iii. 96 Each ring [of the abdomen] consists of a dorsal, arched portion, called the *tergum* [etc.].

-teria (ˈtɪərɪə), *suffix.* orig. and chiefly *U.S.* Also **-eteria.** [Derived from CAFETERIA by analysis of its components as *café* + *-teria.*] A suffix used commercially to form the names of self-service retail or catering establishments.

1923 *Mod. Lang. Notes* XXXVIII. 188 Every one knows by this time that a cafeteria is a 'help-yourself' restaurant. Apparently in the popular mind the ending *-teria* or *-eteria* has come to indicate just such a process. **1929** *Amer. Speech* IV. 334 To the vast and growing progeny of 'cafeteria' may be added the name given to 'Maxwell's Vegetarian Healthateria', 35 West Van Buren Street, Chicago. **1941** [see BURGER]. **1959** *Times* 27 Oct. 13/5 To the collection of *-teria* and *-toria* add 'Valeteria' and 'Washeteria'—in Cambridge, Massachusetts. **1965** *Listener* 2 Sept. 339/1 An Italian café-owner . . has . . switched his sign from Pizzeria to Pie-teria.

teribinth, etc., obs. form of TEREBINTH, etc.

terif, obs. form of TARIFF.

† ˈ**terin.** *Obs.* [ad. OF. *tarin*, *terin* (14th c.), F. *tarin*, of unknown origin.] The siskin.

? *a* **1366** CHAUCER *Rom. Rose* 665 Thrustles, terins, and mavys.

Terital (ˈtɛrɪtəl). Also **terital.** [a. It. *Terital*, f. *ter-eftalico* TEREPHTHALIC *a.* + *ital-iano* ITALIAN *a.*] A trade name for natural and synthetic (chiefly polyester) fibre, fabrics, and floor-coverings. Cf. TERGAL.

A proprietary name in the U.S.

1960 *Guardian* 28 Sept. 8/6 Lilion, helion, terital and viscose are blended with wool in textiles by the high fashion houses. **1963** *Official Gaz.* (U.S. Patent Office) 4 June TM 31/2 Società Rhodiatoce S.p.A., Milan. . . *Terital*. . . For fabrics (obtained from natural or synthetic fibers). **1963** *Times* 11 June 19/1 Output of 'Rhodia' and 'Albene' yarns was maintained at the 1961 level, while production of 'Nailon' and 'Terital' increased considerably. **1972** *Guardian* 22 Aug. 9/1 See-through blouse . . made in terital which is non-crushable and drip-dry.

‖ **teriyaki** (tɛrɪˈjɑːkɪ). [Jap., f. *teri* gloss, lustre + *yaki* roast.] A Japanese dish consisting of fish or meat marinated in soy sauce and broiled.

1962 M. DOI *Art of Japanese Cookery* 72 In *Teri-yaki*, rich sauce which gives a sheen to ingredients is used as seasoning. **1963** H. TANAKA *Pleasures of Japanese Cooking* iv. 76 Almost as popular as *yakitori* is *teriyaki*, usually fish marinated in a *shoyu* sauce, arranged on long skewers, and then broiled over charcoal. *Teriyaki* means 'glaze broiled'. **1972** A. FOWLES *Double Feature* i. 20 The predictable teriyaki dinner, more edible . . than its infra-red mini-grilled BOAC counterpart. **1978** *Amer. Speech* 1975 L. 304 The recipe, one of a number for Japanese dishes, calls for chicken livers marinated in teriyaki sauce, wrapped in bacon, and broiled.

‖ **terjiman.** *Obs.* [ad. Arab. *tarjamān*: see DRAGOMAN, TRUCHMAN.] Interpreter, dragoman.

1682 in Magens *Insurances* (1755) II. 691 The English Consul . . at Algiers . . shall be permitted to chuse his own Terjiman (Interpreter) and Broker.

terleis, terlyst, obs. Sc. form of TRELLIS, -ED.

† **terlerie, -lery.** *Obs.* [? Related to OF. *tirelire*, a kind of rhythmical utterance or refrain in singing or dancing.] In the following combinations applied to jinking or whisking about, or performing rapid circumvolutions, with the accompaniment of rhythmical meaningless words. Cf. TIRRA-LIRRA.

[Cf. ? *c* **1500** *Cov. Corpus Christi Plays* 31 They sange terli terlow; So mereli the sheppards ther pipes can blow.] **1599** NASHE *Lenten Stuffe* 25 So many heades so many whirlegigs; and if all these haue terlery-ginckt it so friuolously of they reckt not what, I may [etc.]. **1611** BEAUM. & FL. *Knt. Burning Pestle* v. iii, With hey tricksy terlerie-whiskie, The world it runs on wheels.

† **terlether**, obs. Sc. form of TARLEATHER[1].

c **1500** *Colkelbie Sow* 349 (Bann. MS.) A flekkit sowis skyn faw, With terletheris tyit hy.

† **terling.** *Obs. rare.* [a. MLG. *terlink* (Schiller & Lubben), name of a pack (app. of cloth) of a definite size or quantity, dim. of *tere*, name of a pack or bale twice the size. Derivation uncertain. It is not clear whether the Du. *teerling* (Kilian *teerlinck*) 'cube, die', is connected. The quots. refer to rates at Antwerp.]

a **1500** in *Arnolde's Chron.* (1811) 197 Item for a grete packe, the tolle ijs. g^t. Item for a myddel packe, the tolle xviii gret. Item for a terlyng, the tolle xij. g^t. Item for a fardel, the tolle vi g^t. *Ibid.*, Item for a terling in y^e krane iiij. g^t.

terlinguaite (tɜːˈlɪŋgwəaɪt). *Min.* [f. *Terlingua*, name of the village in Texas where it was found + -ITE[1].] An oxychloride of mercury, Hg_2OCl, found as transparent or translucent yellow or greenish yellow monoclinic crystals (see also quot. 1900).

1900 H. W. TURNER in *Mining & Sci. Press* (San Francisco) 21 July 64/1 In addition to cinnabar, mercury occurs in the native form . . and as yellow-green crystals. Prof. S. L. Penfield has identified the white coating as calomel or mercury chloride (Hg_2Cl_2), and the greenish crystals as an oxychloride of mercury, forming a new mineral species, for which I have suggested the name terlinguaite. **1903** A. J. MOSES in *Amer. Jrnl. Sci.* CLXVI. 259 Of the three possibly different substances to which the name terlinguaite has hitherto been applied we have . . 1st. The mineral here described. 2d. The undetermined rough yellow crystals mentioned in No. 5. 3d. The pulverulent yellow masses. *Ibid.*, Terlinguaite.—This name should be limited to the yellow monoclinic oxychloride of mercury here described. **1932** [see MONTROYDITE]. **1964** *Mineral. Abstr.* XVI. 619/1 The ore deposit is in Upper Cretaceous liparites and tuffs [in Kamchatka, U.S.S.R.]. Brief descriptions . . are given for native mercury, calomel, eglestonite, terlinguaite, and mosesite.

terli terlow: see TERLERIE.

term (tɜːm), *sb.* Forms: 3–7 **terme**, (4–5 **teerme**, 5 **tierme**), 5–7 **tearme**, 6–7 **tearm**, 4– **term**. [a. F. *terme* (in *Roland*, 11th c.) limit (of time or place):—**termne*:—L. *terminum* limit, boundary; = Pr. *terme*, It., Sp., Pg. *termino*.]

I. A limit in space, duration, etc.

1. a. That which limits the extent of anything; a limit, extremity, boundary, bound (e.g. of a territory, region, or space). Usually in *pl.* Limits, bounds, borders, confines. Now *rare* or *arch.*

13.. *E.E. Allit. P.* C. 61 Hit bitydde sum-tyme in þe termes of Iude. **1432–50** tr. *Higden* (Rolls) II. 51 That water of Seuerne . . was somme tyme a terme of Englonde and of Wales. **1483** CAXTON *Gold. Leg.* 53 b/1 Fro the laste termes of egipte vnto the vtterist endes of the same. **1570** BILLINGSLEY *Euclid* I. def. iii. 2 Pointes . . are . . only the termes and endes of quantitie. *Ibid.* xiii. 3 A limite or terme, is the ende of euery thing. **1626** BACON *Sylva* §328 Corruption is a Reciprocall to Generation: and they two, are as Natures two Terms or Boundaries. **1656** STANLEY *Hist. Philos.* VIII. (1701) 326/2 A Superficies is the term of a Body. . . A Line is the term of a Superficies. . . A Point is the term of a Line. **1855** BAIN *Senses & Int.* II. ii. §12 (1864) 202 The power of movement without contact or resistance, except at the extreme terms.

b. Utmost or extreme limit, end; *esp.* end of duration or existence, final cessation, close, conclusion, termination. Now *rare* or *arch.*

a **1300** *Cursor M.* 11287 (Cott.) At þe terme of fourti dais . . þai bar þe child . . vn-to þe temple. **1481** CAXTON *Myrr.* III. xxi. 182 No goodes what someuer they be shal neuer haue terme ne ende [in heaven]. **1579** SPENSER *Sheph. Cal.* Dec. 127 So now my yeare drawes to his latter terme. **1631** MILTON *On University Carrier* II. 14 Too long vacation hastned on his term. **1781** GIBBON *Decl. & F.* xxiv. (1869) I. 695 He had now reached the term of his prosperity. **1881** JOWETT *Thucyd.* I. 123 That the term of their happiness is likewise the term of their life.

c. That to which movement or action is directed or tends, as its object, end, or goal; (less commonly) that from which it begins or proceeds, starting-point, origin. Now *rare* or *Obs.*

c **1425** *Found. St. Bartholomew's* 39 We become for oure synnys to the butte and terme or marke of vniuersall kynde of man. **1551** BP. GARDINER *Explic. Cath. Faith* 108 b, Wherin eche chaunge hath his special ende and terme, (whervnto). *a* **1628** PRESTON *New Covt.* (1634) 184 There must be a place, a terme to which you walke, some whither. *a* **1769** R. RICCALTOUN *Notes Galatians* (1772) 33 The term from which they removed, was the Gospel which Paul preached. **1800** *Hist. Ind.* in *Asiat. Ann. Reg.* 2/2 The island of Ceylon . . was the usual term of their navigation. **1849** M. ARNOLD *Sonn. to Dk. Wellington* 12 Vehement actions without scope or term.

2. *Astrol.* A certain portion of each sign of the zodiac, assigned to a particular planet: see quots.

c **1386** CHAUCER *Frankl. T.* 560 He . . knew the arisyng of his moone weel, And in whos face, and terme, and euerydeel. *c* **1450** *Treat. Astrol.* (MS. Ashm. 337) lf. 7 b, Termys of planettes bene certen nombris of greis in euery signe in which degreis a planet makith gret impression. **1652** GAULE *Magastrom.* 263 There was Venus in termes, and in the house of Saturne. **1819** J. WILSON *Compl. Dict. Astrol.* 27 Essential Dignities are only five, viz. House, Exaltation, Triplicity, Term, and Face. *Ibid.* 382 Terms are certain degrees in a sign, supposed to possess the power of altering the nature of a planet to that of the planet in the term of which it is posited.

II. A limit in time; a space of time.

3. a. A definite point of time at which something is to be done, or which is the beginning or end of a period; a set or appointed time or date, esp. for payment of money due. *Obs.* or *arch.* exc. in specific uses.

a **1225** *Ancr. R.* 208 Etholden oðres hure, ouer his rihte terme, nis hit strong reflac? **1297** R. GLOUC. (Rolls) 5777 Þe welisse king . . sende him þes wolues fram ȝere to ȝere, þre þousend at certein terme. **13..** *Cursor M.* 5939 Sett vs term wen We sal for þe prai. *c* **1450** *Merlin* iii. 41 Vortiger . . somowned his peple a-geyn the tierme that Merlyn hadde seide. **1479** *Bury Wills* (Camden) 51, x marcs at too termes of the yeer. **1597** HOOKER *Eccl. Pol.* v. lxix. §1 They all haue . . their set . . termes, before which they had no being at all. **1662** STILLINGFL. *Orig. Sacr.* I. vi. §3 There was no certainty in the ancient Græcian history, because they had no certain term . . from whence to deduce their accounts. **1793** *Amer. State Papers* (1833) I. 143 State securities . . reimbursable on a given term. **1827** SCOTT *Chron. Canongate* ii, Fortune is apt to circumduce the term upon us.

b. *spec.* Each of the days in the year fixed for payment of rent, wages, and other dues, beginning and end of tenancy, etc.; = TERM-DAY, QUARTER-DAY. Chiefly *Sc.* (Cf. F. *terme* in same sense.)

The quarterly terms in Scotland, fixed by Acts of 1690 and 1693, were Candlemas Feb. 2, Whitsunday May 15, Lammas Aug. 1, Martinmas Nov. 11. At the change of style in 1752, Old Style was observed in most parts of Scotland for the terms, making the dates practically in use eleven days later. By an Act of 1886, the 'Removal terms', for change of houses, etc., were fixed as May 28 and Nov. 28, the dates fixed 1690–93 remaining for purposes of rent, interest, etc.

1426 *Coldstream Chartul.* (1879) 42 Payand till ws ȝerli xl s . . at thua vsuel termes of ye ȝher yat is to say Quvitsonday and Martimes. *c* **1450** *Godstow Reg.* 104, xij. d. of rente yerely . . to be resceived of Raf Marchaunte and his heires at ij. termes of the yere, that is to sey, vj. d. at the fest of oure lady in Marche and vj. d. at the fest of seynt Michell. **1584** *Exch. Rolls Scot.* XXI. 600 Sa far as thay ar detbound of the said Witsounday terme. **1670** *Moral State Eng.* 30 By the next Term [he] is presented with an Execution, from his Taylor, or Landlord. **1837** LOCKHART *Scott* xxvi, The term of Martinmas, always a critical one in Scotland, had passed before this letter reached Edinburgh. **1843** MRS. MATHESON *Mem. G. Ewing* v. (1847) 219 The usual term in Scotland for entering on possession of a dwelling house.

4. *transf.* **a.** A portion of time having definite limits; a period, *esp.* a set or appointed period; the space of time through which something lasts or is intended to last; duration, length of time.

a **1300** *Floriz & Bl.* 432 Bituene þis and þe þridde day . . Þulke terme him þuȝ te long. **13..** *Seuyn Sag.* (W.) 64 That dar I vndertak . . Within the terme of seuyn yere. **1444** *Rolls of Parlt.* V. 112/1 Departyng of Servauntz . . atte ende of theire termes. **1483** CAXTON *Cato* E iv, The prophete demaunded terme and space for to answere . . and the kynge gafe hym terme of thre dayes. **1579** FENTON *Guicciard.* (1618) 360 For that the tearme was expired. **1610** R. JONES *Muses Gard. Delights* XIV. ii, Full many lovely tearms Did passe in merrie glee. **1691** CONSETT *Pract. Eccl. Courts* (1700) 107 A Term-Probatory is said to be that time or delay, which was given to the Plaintiff, wherein he might prove what he Pleads or Sueth for. **1781** *Scot. Paraphr.* xv. i, As long as life its term extends, Hope's blest dominion never ends. **1823** BYRON *Juan* x. lxvi, Seven years (the usual term of transportation). **1868** M. E. G. DUFF *Pol. Surv.* 164 Presidents elected for a term of years.

b. *esp.* in phrase *for* (†*to*) *term of* (*one's*) *life*: formerly often without *for* or *to*: chiefly in legal use.

1340–70 *Alisaunder* 16 Amyntas . . Maister of Macedoine, þe marches hee aught, . . Trie toures, & tounes, terme of his life. *c* **1386** CHAUCER *Knt.'s T.* 171 And ther he lyueth in ioye and in honour Terme of lyue. **1544** tr. *Littleton's Tenures* (1574) 7 The husbande hath Estate in the speciall tayle, and the wife but for terme of lyfe. **1610** HOLLAND *Camden's Brit.* (1637) 725 That Henry the Sixth should enjoy the right of the Kingdome for terme of life only. **1788** V. KNOX *Winter Even.* I. iii. 34 What men draw from their education generally sticks by them for term of life.

c. ***long-term, short-term*** adjs.: see as main entries.

5. *spec.* Each of the periods (usually three or four in the year) appointed for the sitting of certain courts of law, or for instruction and study in a university or school. Opposed to *vacation*.

Commonly used without article, as ***in term*** = during the term. ***to keep terms***: see KEEP *v.* 13.

1454 *Rolls of Parlt.* V. 239/2 An action by Bille in Michell' terme last past. **1600** SHAKS. *A.Y.L.* III. ii. 350 *Orl.* Who staies it [time] stil withal? *Ros.* With Lawiers in the vacation: for they sleepe betweene Terme and Terme. **1610** HOLLAND *Camden's Brit.* (1637) 431 At certaine set times (wee call them Tearmes) yearely causes are heard and tryed. **1678** PHILLIPS (ed. 4) s.v., The first is called Hilary Term... The second is called Easter Term... The third.. Trinity Term... The fourth and last.. Michaelmas Term. **1705** HEARNE *Collect.* 4 Dec. (O.H.S.) I. 114 He might be admitted to the Degree of Master of Arts, without.. keeping Terms. **1842** ARNOLD in *Life & Corr.* (1844) II. x. 323, I am obliged to give up.. the hope of coming to Oxford this term. **1867** MRS. H. WOOD *Orville College* xiii, The explanation which he had deemed it well to defer until the [school] term should be over. **1883** *Wharton's Law Lex.* (ed. 7), *Terms*, the periods during which the superior courts at Westminster were open. *Ibid.* s.v. *Sittings*, By the Judicature Act, 1873, s. 26, the division of the legal year into terms is abolished, and sittings are substituted for it.

†**b.** *transf.* The session of a law-court during such a period; the court in session. *Obs.*

1525 LD. BERNERS *Froiss.* II. cciv. 629 Than Mychelmas came, and the generall counsayle began, suche as englysshemen call the terme. *a* **1548** HALL *Chron., Hen. VIII* 64 In the beginnyng of this yere, Trinite terme was begon at Oxenford, where it continued but one day, and was again adjourned to Westminster. **1591** GREENE *Disc. Coosnage* Pref. 2 The poore man, that commeth to the Terme to trie his right. **1648** D. JENKINS *Wks.* 45 At Yorke the Tearmes were kept for seven yeares, in Edward the first's time.

c. In *pl.* in phrases (esp. ***to keep terms***) indicating that a person has attended the required number of lectures at a university, has been in residence for the period of time laid down in the statutes, and has satisfied the authorities in other statutory respects. *N.Z. colloq.*

1959 G. SLATTER *Gun in my Hand* 37 The Old Prof.. gave me 'terms' out of the kindness of his heart, but it was no use. **1962** M. K. JOSEPH *Pound of Saffron* ii. 38 You know the way he barks at you like a sergeant-major and then sees you don't miss terms.

6. *Law.* An estate or interest in land, etc. for a certain period; in full, ***term of*** or ***for years***.

outstanding term, satisfied term: an estate for a long term of years was given, usually to the trustees of a strict settlement, to secure to beneficiaries under the settlement the payments due to them periodically from the tenant of the settled land. If these payments were not made, the trustees could take possession of the land for the term, and sell or mortgage it, to raise the money needed to make them. When the purposes for which the estate was created were fulfilled (e.g. by the death of all the beneficiaries) it was called a *satisfied term*; but unless express provision had been made that it should then cease, or unless it was conveyed to the tenant of the freehold so that it was destroyed by merger in the freehold, it continued to exist for the period for which it was created. It was then known as an *outstanding term*, or an ***attendant term***, i.e. a term accompanying the inheritance. By Act 8 & 9 Vict. c. 112 provision was made for the cessation of satisfied terms.

1424 R. FLORE in *E.E. Wills* (1882) 58, I wul þat.. my sone haue my termes þat I haf of Westminster in þe personage of Okeham. **1592** WEST *1st Pt. Symbol.* §41. B iv b, A Particuler estate which is but onely a terme, is an estate determinable by limitation of time. **1766** BLACKSTONE *Comm.* II. ix. 143 Every estate which must expire at a period certain and prefixed,.. is an estate for years. And therefore this estate is frequently called a term. **1818** CRUISE *Digest* (ed. 2) I. 502 Where a satisfied term is assigned to a trustee, upon an express trust to attend the inheritance, the owner of such inheritance acquires a right to the term, by the declaration of the parties. **1870** *Woodfall's Law Landl. & Tenant* (ed. 11) 42 A man possessed of a term of years in right of his wife.. has power to grant and convey the same.

7. a. The completion of the period of pregnancy; the (normal) time of childbirth.

1844 LOUISA S. COSTELLO *Bearn & Pyrenees* II. 62 The Princess of Navarre, being near her term. **1889** J. M. DUNCAN *Clin. Lect. Dis. Wom.* vi. (ed. 4) 32 The dangers attendant upon delivery of a child at or near term. **1899** *Allbutt's Syst. Med.* VII. 729 Children who.. are born at full term.

†**b.** *pl.* The menstrual periods; *transf.* the menstrual discharge, catamenia, menses, courses. *Obs.*

1545 RAYNOLD *Byrth Mankynde* (1564) 26 Termes be called in Latin *Menstrua*... In Englyshe they be named Termes, because they returne eftsoones at certayne seasons, tymes, and termes. *a* **1648** DIGBY *Chym. Secr.* II. (1682) 259 It provokes the Terms. **1714** JONTEL *Jrnl.*, etc. 143 When the Women have their Terms, they leave the Company of their Husbands.

III. Limiting conditions.

8. a. *pl.* Conditions or stipulations limiting what is proposed to be granted or done. Rarely in *sing.*; in quot. 1771, that which is so required or demanded, a condition or prerequisite *of* something.

c **1315** SHOREHAM *Poems* v. 165 Þo þat he scholde y-offred by In þe *templo domini*, Ase laȝe ȝef þe termes. *c* **1400** *Laud Troy Bk.* 79 How fele termes and trewes Were [*MS.* Where] take be-twene Troyens and Gruwes. **1599** SHAKS. *Hen. V*, v. ii. 357 Wee haue consented to all tearmes of reason. **1667** MILTON *P.L.* x. 751 Unable to performe Thy terms too hard, by which I was to hold The good I sought not. **1718** HICKES & NELSON *J. Kettlewell* III. lxvi. 353 The Church doth.. prescribe her Terms of Communion. **1754** HUME *Hist. Eng.* (1761) I. ix. 200 He was obliged.. to offer terms of peace. **1771** WESLEY *Wks.* (1872) V. 61 This faith is the term or condition of justification. **1861** MRS. H. WOOD *East Lynne* I. xiii, They acceded to all his terms.

b. Phr. ***in terms***: (*a*) (pred.) engaged in making or arranging conditions, in treaty, negotiating; † (*b*) (advb.) = *on terms* (*a*). ***on*** or ***upon terms***: (*a*) (advb.) on (such and such) conditions; also (without qualification) on certain conditions, conditionally; (*b*) (pred.) = *in terms* (*a*). ***terms of reference***: the points referred to an individual or body of persons for decision or report; that which defines the scope of an inquiry. ***to come to terms***: to agree upon conditions; to come to an agreement about something to be done; also *fig.* (const. *with*), to reconcile oneself to, to become reconciled with; so ***to bring to terms***. ***to keep terms***: to keep up negotiations, to have or continue to have dealings *with*; to deal *with* or treat in a particular way; also *fig.* to 'have to do *with*', be connected *with*. ***to make terms***: to agree upon conditions, come to a settlement (= *come to terms*). †***to stand on*** or ***upon terms***: to insist upon conditions; to stand upon one's rights or dignity.

1619 DRAYTON in *Drumm. of Hawth.'s Fam. Ep.* Wks. (1711) 153, I have done twelve books more,.. but it lyeth by me, for the booksellers and I are in terms. **1736** *Gentl. Mag.* VI. 730/2 No Sum of Money.. is to be.. given.. except in the Terms prescribed by this Bill. **1748** SMOLLETT *Rod. Rand.* (1812) I. 451 He was already engaged or at least in terms with Mr. Vaudal.

1611 J. MORE in *Buccleuch MSS.* (Hist. MSS. Comm.) I. 101 He hath not as yet taken a lease himself, but is upon terms to make up his four years to come 31 years. **1629** MASSINGER *Picture* III. vi, I left a letter in my chamber-window Which I would not have seen on any terms. **1647** CLARENDON *Hist. Reb.* I. § 146 A Peace was made with both, upon better terms, and conditions. **1693** DRYDEN *Persius' Sat.* vi. 124 Well; on my Terms thou wilt not be my Heir? **1708** *Lond. Gaz.* No. 4468/1 The Fortress.. had surrender'd upon Terms. **1795** T. PEAKE *Cases Nisi Prius* 56 *marg.*, If goods are delivered on the terms of sale or return. **1825** CARLYLE *Schiller* III. (1845) 241 The copyright.. for which he was on terms with Cotta of Tübingen. **1869** J. MARTINEAU *Ess.* II. 94 It offers initiation.. on the easiest terms. **1884** *Manch. Exam.* 11 June 5/1 To.. call in the help of the other Powers on their own terms.

1892 *Daily Graphic* (Suppl.) 30 Dec. 3/1 On the 14th October the constitution of the Commission and the exact terms of reference were made known. **1913** *Rep. Brit. Assoc. Adv. Sci. 1912* 549 The nature of the Inquiry of the Industrial Council is explained in the following 'terms of reference'. **1927** [see REFER *v.* 8 a]. **1967** G. F. FIENNES *I tried to run Railway* vii. 88 We wrote ourselves new terms of reference in that sense. *a* **1974** R. CROSSMAN *Diaries* (1976) II. 661, I had to point out this was not excluded by the Committee's terms of reference, which had been drafted after consultation with the Foreign Office.

a **1729** CONGREVE *Impossible Thing* Wks. 1730 III. 363 He to no Terms can bring One Twirl of that reluctant Thing. *a* **1734** NORTH *Lives* (1826) II. 231 The creditors.. rather than to contest accounts, came to terms, and agreed to take shares. **1855** PRESCOTT *Philip II*, I. vi. (1857) 103 He had no choice but to come to terms with the enemy at once. **1923** J. B. PRIESTLEY *I for One* 235 The few [pictures] that it has do not seem so bright, so ideal, but seem to have come to terms with sad reality, showing us the pudding as it is and not as it ought to be. **1934** R. MACAULAY *Milton* vii. 109 He had here come to terms with life, or bravely pretended to have done so. **1965** *Listener* 30 Dec. 1067/1 Kipling, I think characteristically, came to terms with his tormentor. **1970** L. DEIGHTON *Bomber* i. 12 Each of the airmen guests was already coming to terms with the return to duty.

c **1483** in *Chron. White Rose* (1845) 231 Seeing the evil terms the the King hath kept (with) him, and cast him out of the Realm. **1748** RICHARDSON *Clarissa* (1811) VI. i. 2 What terms wouldst thou have me to keep with such a sweet corruptress? **1806** R. CUMBERLAND *Memoirs* (1807) I. 184 A profusion of finery, that kept no terms with simplicity. **1856** MERIVALE *Rom. Emp.* (1871) V. xlii. 141 The chief of the state need keep terms no longer with the popular assemblies.

1856 FROUDE *Hist. Eng.* I. i. 58 Capital supported by force may make its own terms with labour. **1884** *Times* (weekly ed.) 17 Oct. 14/1 The Amarars have made terms with the Hadendowas, giving them a number of cattle.

1586 DAY *Eng. Secretary* I. (1625) 88 Before that time, I stood on some tearmes doubting the malicious dealings of the aduerse parties against me. **1611** COTGR., *Accrester*.. to strout it, or stand vpon high tearms. **1716** ATTERBURY *Serm., Matt. xvi. 20* (1734) I. viii. 224 One of those Great and Philosophical Minds, who stand upon their Terms with God.

c. *spec.* Stipulations for payment in return for goods or services; conditions with regard to price or wages; payment offered, or charges made. ***terms of trade***, the ratio between the prices paid for imports and those received for exports.

1670 R. COKE *Disc. Trade* 50 The Dutch have Pitch, Tar, Hemp.. in greater quantities, and for less terms than the English can, out of Norway. **1751** JOHNSON *Rambler* No. 132 ¶6 The terms offered were such as I should willingly have accepted. **1844** LD. BROUGHAM *A. Lunel* II. ii. 23, I was not very nice as to terms and agreed for my board and fifty louis a year. **1856** W. COLLINS *Rogue's Life* iii, To a member of the family, I suppose your terms will be moderate. **1923** A. MARSHALL *Money, Credit, & Commerce* III. vi. 161 Illustration of the demands of each of two countries which trade together, for the goods of the other: and the general dependence of the terms of trade on the relative volumes and intensities of those demands. **1942** J. R. HICKS *Social Framework* xvi. 174 *Terms of Trade*, the amount of other countries' products which the nation gets in exchange for a unit of its own products. **1957** A. C. L. DAY *Outl. Monetary Econ.* xxxi. 399 Home terms of trade. [*Note*] An index of the home price of exports divided by the home price of imports. **1976** *Economist* 16 Oct. 22/3 Until exports expand enough, and/or imports fall enough, to offset the terms of trade deterioration, a devaluation makes the balance of payments worse before better.

9. *pl.* Standing, footing, mutual relation between two persons or parties: in phrases †***in, on, upon terms***: **a.** with various qualifying words, as ***on*** (†***in, upon***) ***equal terms***, ***good terms***, ***speaking terms***, ***visiting terms***, ***terms of intimacy***, etc.

1543 SEYMOUR *Let.* in Maclean *Life Sir P. Carew* (1857) 142 Fforasmuche as we doo stande in verye doubtefull tearmes with ffraunce, and yet there is no playne warre. **1605** SHAKS. *Lear* I. ii. 171 Parted you in good termes? Found you no displeasure in him? **1653** H. COGAN tr. *Pinto's Trav.* xiii. 42 Though we stood in the terms of good friends with them. *a* **1660** *Cont. Hist. Irel.* (Ir. Arch. Soc.) I. 139 When they were in tearmes of greatest defiance.

1596 SHAKS. *1 Hen. IV*, v. i. 10 'Tis not well That you and I should meet vpon such tearmes, As now we meet. **1669** R. MONTAGU in *Buccleuch MSS.* (Hist. MSS. Comm.) I. 422, I was the willinger to put you upon good terms with her. **1670** DRYDEN *2nd Pt. Conq. Granada* III. i, The Brave own Faults when good Success is giv'n; For then they come on equal Terms to Heav'n. **1748** *Anson's Voy.* I. ix. 92 At war, or at least on ill terms with their Spanish neighbours. **1758** L. TEMPLE *Sketches* (ed. 2) 64, I could live upon good Terms even with a Deist; provided he keeps within the Bounds of Decency. **1796** *Hist.* in *Ann. Reg.* 115 Spain was.. on friendly terms with France. **1877** FREEMAN *Norm. Conq.* (ed. 3) II. vii. 97 On the closest terms of friendship. **1881** R. BUCHANAN *God & Man* I. 211 There never was a time when our folk were on speaking terms with these yeomen. **1885** SIR J. HANNEN in *Law Rep. 10 P.D.* 91 They had previously been on the most affectionate terms.

b. without qualification: ***on terms***, on friendly terms, friendly, sociable; in sporting slang, on terms of equality, on an equal footing (*with*); also in reference to the score at cricket.

1864 TROLLOPE *Small House at Allington* xvii. The earl and Lord Porlock were not on terms. **1887** SIR R. H. ROBERTS *In the Shires* ii. 27 So quickly did the hounds get on terms with their fox. **1897** *Daily News* 23 July 4/5 In the end Yorkshire got on terms and ran their total to within four of the southern county.

†**10.** *pl.* Condition, state, situation, position, circumstances; (in Shaks.) vaguely or redundantly: relation, respect (rarely in *sing.*). *Obs.*

1382 WYCLIF *Matt.* vi. 16 Ypocritis.. putten her facis out of kyndly termys [Vulg. *exterminant facies suas*], that thei seme fastynge to men. —— *Ecclus.* xxi. 21 As an hous set out of termes, so a wisdam to a fool. **1579–80** NORTH *Plutarch* (1676) 5 He found the Common-wealth turmoiled with seditions.. and.. the house of Ægeus in very ill termes also. **1596** SHAKS. *Merch. V.* II. i. 13 In tearmes of choise I am not solie led By nice direction of a maidens eies. **1602** —— *Ham.* IV. vii. 26 A Sister driuen into desperate tearmes. **1604** —— *Oth.* I. i. 39 Be iudge.. Whether I in any iust terme am Affin'd To loue the Moore? **1642** ROGERS *Naaman* Ep. Ded. 2 They liued at poore termes. **1656** EARL MONM. tr. *Boccalini's Advts. fr. Parnass.* II. xcii. (1674) 245 [He] shewed.. him in his naked tearms of devillish hypocrisie.

IV. Uses leading up to the sense 'expression'.

See *Note* at end of article.

11. *Math.* (*a*) Each of the two quantities composing a ratio (antecedent and consequent), or a fraction (numerator and denominator). †Also formerly, each of two quantities multiplied together (*obs.*; now called *factors*). (*b*) Each of the quantities (of any number) forming a series or progression. (*c*) Each of (two or more) quantities connected by the signs of addition (+) or subtraction (−) in an algebraical expression or equation.

absolute term, that term in an equation which does not involve the variable or unknown quantity. ***lowest*** (†***least***) ***terms*** (in phrases ***to reduce to its lowest terms***, ***in its lowest terms***): *Math.* the form of a fraction when the numerator and denominator are the least possible, i.e. have no common factor; hence *fig.* the simplest condition of anything.

1542 RECORDE *Gr. Artes* (1575) 356 You call the Numeratour and Denominatour, the Termes of the Fraction. **1570** BILLINGSLEY *Euclid* v. def. iii. 127 *marg.*, In proportions two quantities required, which are called termes. **1669** STURMY *Mariner's Mag.* I. ii. 34 As 16 to 7: So is 8 to what? Here.. the second Term is less than the first. **1706** PHILLIPS (ed. Kersey), *Diapente* (in *Musick*), the second of the Concords, whose Terms are as Three to Two. *Ibid.*, *Term of a Progression*,.. is every Member of the Progression, whether it be Arithmetical, or Geometrical. **1806** HUTTON *Course Math.* I. 13 Both the multiplier and multiplicand, are, in general, named the Terms or Factors. *Ibid.* 191 Divide both the terms of the fraction by the common measure thus found, and it will reduce it to its lowest terms. **1859** BARN. SMITH *Arith. & Algebra* (ed. 6) 194 When several quantities are connected together by the signs + and −, or either of them, each of these quantities is called a Term. **1881** BURNSIDE & PANTON *The. Equations* Introd. (1886) 2 The term p_n, which does not contain x, is called the absolute term.

b. ***in terms of***: (*Math.*) said of a series or expression stated in terms involving some particular quantity; hence *gen.*, by means of or in reference to (some particular set of symbols, ideas, etc.); in the modes of expression or thought belonging to (some particular subject or category): often associated with sense 14, as if =

in the phraseology of; also, ***in*** (..) ***terms***: in terms of what is designated by (..); ***to think in terms of*** (*colloq.*): to make (a particular consideration) the basis of one's attention, enquiries, plans, etc.

1743 EMERSON *Fluxions* 38 If a Series be required to be express'd in Terms of that Quantity whose 2d, 3d Fluxion, &c. is in the Equation. **1862** H. SPENCER *First Princ.* II. v. §58 (1875) 188 The continuity of Motion..is really known to us in terms of Force. **1866** HERSCHEL *Fam. Lect. Sc.* 102 The nearest distance of the orbits of Venus and the earth was concluded in terms of the earth's diameter. **1890** W. JAMES *Princ. Psychol.* xviii. II. 63 Most persons, on being asked in what sort of terms they imagine words, will say 'in terms of hearing'. **1947** MULGAN & DAVIN *Introd. Eng. Lit.* xiii. 164 The impact of Ibsen..did much to revitalize the degenerate English theatre and force it to think in terms of living ideas and contemporary realities. **1959** D. W. BROGAN in F. M. Joseph *As Others see Us* 4 I was predisposed to see American problems in European terms. **1973** 'E. MCBAIN' *Hail to Chief* iii. 39 Carella..had suspected the ditch murders were related to organized crime... As it turned out, the cops had been thinking correctly in terms of gang warfare. **1978** *Listener* 26 Jan. 119/1 The hour's delay—a mere hiccup in cricketing terms—was caused by politics.

c. *transf.* A member or item of any series; each of the things constituting a series. Also more vaguely, an element of any complex whole.

1841 MYERS *Cath. Th.* III. iii. 8 The Bible contains a series [of revelations] of which the earliest terms are the least. **1857** MILLER *Elem. Chem.* III. i. §2 (1862) 48 A series in which hydrogen forms the lowest term. **1863** LYELL *Antiq. Man* xxi. 419 Certain genera of plants..consist of a continuous series of varieties, between the terms of which no intermediate forms can be intercalated. **1881** WILLIAMSON in *Nature* 1 Sept. 416/1 The lower terms of the series are distinguished from one another by differences of boiling points approximately proportional to the number of atoms of carbon and hydrogen by which they differ from one another; whilst the higher terms..are distinguished..by differences of melting points.

d. *Physics.* Each of a set of numbers such that lines in the spectrum of an atom have wave numbers given by the differences between two numbers in the set; an atomic state corresponding to one of these numbers, the number being proportional to the binding energy of a valence electron; a symbol representing such a state. Freq. as ***spectral term.***

1909 *Sci. Abstr.* A. XII. 20 In any combination formula each of the terms represents the influence of one pole. **1915** *Astrophysical Jrnl.* XLI. 324 The difference in 'wave-number'..between the limit of the series and each member is called the 'term'... The limit itself is commonly a 'term' of some other series. **1922** A. D. UDDEN tr. *Bohr's Theory of Spectra* II. ii. 30 The arrangement of the states in horizontal rows corresponds to the ordinary arrangement of the 'spectral terms' in the spectroscopic tables. **1925** [see LEVEL *sb.* 3 e]. **1935** [see STATE *sb.* 4 b]. **1935** W. M. HICKS *Structure of Spectral Terms* i. 1 Any given term in a neutral spectrum is expressible in the form $R/(m + \phi)^2$, where R is a constant ..*m* is an ordinal integer and ϕ a fraction which depends on *m*. **1938** *Nature* 22 Oct. 735/1 Dr. Dobbie has extended the number of classified lines to some 1,700 and has identified 73 terms involving 218 levels. **1967** [see LYMAN]. **1970** G. K. WOODGATE *Elem. Atomic Struct.* vii. 110 For calcium..the ^{3}P and ^{1}P terms of the configuration *4s4p* are separated by about 8,000 cm^{-1}.

12. *Logic*, etc. Each of the two things or notions which are compared, or between which some relation is apprehended or stated, in an act of thought, or (more commonly) each of the words or phrases denoting these in a verbal statement; *spec.* in relation to a proposition, each of the two elements, viz. subject and predicate, which are connected by the copula; in relation to a syllogism, the subject or predicate of any of the propositions composing it, forming one of its three elements (***major term, minor term, middle term***), each of which occurs twice (see MAJOR *a.* 2, MINOR *a.* 4, MIDDLE *a.* 6).

1551 T. WILSON *Logike* (1580) 25 [*Medius terminus*, called the double repeate (whiche is a word rehearsed in bothe Propositions) must not enter into the conclusion, because the other twoo partes called *Termini*, bee proued by this]. *Ibid.* 25 b, There ought not to be mo termes in an argumentation [= syllogism] then three, for otherwise there is no good argument. **1628** T. SPENCER *Logick* 258 If the middle terme be both affirmed and denyed of both the extreames: then it is the second figure. **1690** LOCKE *Hum. Und.* IV. vi. §16 General Propositions..are then only capable of Certainty, when the Terms used in them stand for such Ideas, whose agreement or disagreement..is capable to be discovered by us. **1725** WATTS *Logic* III. i, The matter of which a syllogism is made up, is three propositions; and these three propositions are made up of three ideas, or terms, variously joined. **1771** *Junius Lett.* liv. (1820) 282 He changes the terms of the proposition. **1827** WHATELY *Logic* ii. I. §2 (ed. 2) 57 Each proposition containing two terms; of these terms, that which is spoken of is called the subject; that which is said of it, the predicate; and these two are called the terms (or extremes) because, logically, the Subject is placed first, and the Predicate last: and, in the middle, the Copula, which indicates the act of judgment. **1837–8** SIR W. HAMILTON *Logic* xvi. (1866) I. 298 The word term is applied to the ultimate constituents both of propositions and of syllogisms. **1843** MILL *Logic* I. ii. §5 (1856) I. 31 A non-connotative term is one which signifies a subject only, or an attribute only. A connotative term is one which denotes a subject, and implies an attribute. **1866** FOWLER *Deductive Logic* I. i, A Term (so called from *terminus*, a boundary, because the terms are the two extremes or boundaries of the proposition) is a word or combination of words which may stand by itself as the subject or predicate of a Proposition.

13. a. A word or phrase used in a definite or precise sense in some particular subject, as a science or art; a technical expression (more fully ***term of art***).

1377 LANGL. *P. Pl.* B XII. 237 Ac of briddes and of bestes men by olde tyme Ensamples token and termes. *c* **1386** CHAUCER *Prol.* 639 Than wolde he speke no word but latyn. A fewe termes hadde he, two or thre, That he had lerned out of som decree. —— *Frankl. T.* 538, I ne kan no termes of Astrologye. —— *Can. Yeom. Prol. & T.* 199 We semen wonder wyse, Oure termes [of alchemy] been so clergial and so queynte. —— *Pard. Prol.* 25 (Harl. MS.) Sayde I wel can I not speke in terme? **1486** *Bk. St. Albans* D ij, Som folke mysuse this terme 'draw', and say that thayr hauke will draw to the Ryuer. **1590** SIR J. SMYTH *Disc. Weapons* 2 b, To vse our ancient termes belonging to matters of warre. **1695** W. *W. Colbatch's New Lt. Chir. Put out* p. xi, Why he hath used so few Terms of Art, is, because he designs Plainness. **1703** MOXON *Mech. Exerc.* 109 An Explanation of Terms used among Joiners. **1748** SMOLLETT *Rod. Rand.* (1812) I. 376 The barrister who..had recollected himself and talked in terms. **1862** GROVE *Corr. Phys. Forces* (ed. 4) 96 The idea involved in the term latent heat. **1876** TAIT *Rec. Adv. Phys. Sc.* i. (ed. 2) 1 Explanation of new scientific terms. **1881** WILLIAMSON in *Nature* 1 Sept. 419/1 A chain of evidence involving the use of chemical terms.

b. In wider application: Any word or group of words expressing a notion or conception, or denoting an object of thought; an expression (*for* something). Generally with qualifying adj. or phrase (as an abstract term, a term of reproach).

contradiction in terms: see CONTRADICTION 5 b.

c **1477** CAXTON *Jason* 21 A trew louer vseth neuer suche termes as ye speke of. **1490** —— *Eneydos* Prol. 2 Some gentylmen..desired me to vse olde and homely termes in my translacyons. **1530** PALSGR. 518/1, I disconsolate... This terme is nat yet [= no longer] comenly used. **1586** DAY *Eng. Secretary* I. (1625) 2 Aptnesse of worde and sentences, consisteth in choice of good tearmes. **1605** *Play of Stucley* in Simpson *Sch. Shaks.* (1878) I. 258 Can there issue from your lips a term So base and beggarly as that of flight? **1653** HOLCROFT *Procopius* I 2 The Archers in Homer's time (whose Profession grew to be a tearm of reproach). **1791** D'ISRAELI *Cur. Lit.* (1858) III. 70 In politics, what evils have resulted from abstract terms to which no ideas are affixed. *a* **1860** WHATELY *Commpl. Bk.* (1864) 265 A term of reproach is one that denotes something which is denied and thought wrong by the person to whom it is applied. **1883** H. DRUMMOND *Nat. Law in Spir. W.* vii. (1884) 235 The apostles..accepted the term in its simple literal sense.

14. a. Only in *pl.* Words or expressions collectively or generally (usually of a specified kind); manner of expressing oneself, way of speaking, language. (Most commonly preceded by *in*.)

c **1386** CHAUCER *Reeve's Prol.* 63 Right in his cherles termes wol I speke. *c* **1470** HENRY *Wallace* II. 92 The stwart ..thocht Wallace chargyt him in termys rude. **1489** CAXTON *Faytes of A.* II. xx. 133 Thys present werke hathe spoken in general termes. **1590** SHAKS. *Mids. N.* IV. i. 63 She in milde termes beg'd my patience. **1600** —— *A.Y.L.* II. vii. 16 Who laid him downe..And rail'd on Lady Fortune in good termes, In good set termes, and yet a motley foole. **1651** HOBBES *Leviath.* III. xxxiii. 205 Which question is also propounded sometimes in other terms. **1759** ROBERTSON *Hist. Scot.* v. Wks. 1813 I. 374 The accusation..was conceived in the strongest terms. **1849** MACAULAY *Hist. Eng.* vii. II. 194 William..replied, in general terms, that he took a great interest in English affairs. **1885** *Athenæum* 23 May 660 Of the dialogue we can speak in terms of the very highest praise.

†**b.** ***in terms***: in express words, expressly, plainly, 'in so many words' (also ***by terms***). *Obs.*

13.. *E.E. Allit. P.* A. 1052 Alle þe apparaylmente..As Iohan þe apostel in termez ty3te. *c* **1380** WYCLIF *Wks.* (1880) 384 So oure clerkis..whan þai will speke in termis of her religion. *c* **1450** HOLLAND *Howlat* 253 All this trety has he tald be termess in test. **1613** PURCHAS *Pilgrimage* IV. iv. 305 Deuouring in hope, and threatening in tearmes all those Asian Prouinces. **1667** PEPYS *Diary* 29 July, He says in terms that the match..hath undone the nation.

V. 15. *Arch.* A statue or bust like those of the god TERMINUS, representing the upper part of the body, sometimes without the arms, and terminating below in a pillar or pedestal out of which it appears to spring; a terminal figure. Also the pillar or pedestal bearing such a figure. (Cf. HERMA.)

1604 DEKKER *King's Entertainm.* Wks. 1873 I. 278 On either side of the Gate, stood a great French *Terme*, of stone. **1630** B. JONSON *Chloridia* Wks. (Rtldg.) 656/2 An arbour.. the ornament of which was born up with termes of satyrs. **1688** R. HOLME *Armoury* IV. xiii. (Roxb.) 519/1 Their effigies..raised higher with a Terme or Pedestall or foot.. of a pillar. **1712** J. JAMES tr. *Le Blond's Gardening* 76 Busts, Terms, Half-length Figures. **1753** SPENCE in *Phil. Trans.* XLVIII. 486 Another brass bust, on a term, of a youth. **1891** T. HARDY *Tess* xii, She..lifted her face to his, and remained like a marble term while he imprinted a kiss upon her cheek.

16. *Ship-building.* (See quot.)

c **1850** *Rudim. Navig.* (Weale) 155 *Terms* or *term-pieces*, pieces of carved-work placed under each end of the taffrail, upon the side stern-timber, and reaching as low down as the foot-rail of the balcony.

VI. 17. *attrib.* and *Comb.*, as ***term-end, -keeping*** (see sense 5 and KEEP *v.* 13); **term-catalogue**, a catalogue of the books and other publications during a term or quarter; †**term-driver**, ? = *term-trotter* (*a*); **term-fee** (see quot.); **term-figure** = sense 15; **term paper** *U.S. Educ.*, an essay or dissertation representative of the work done during a single term; **term-piece** = sense 16; **term-policy**, an insurance policy issued for a definite term or period; †**term-suitor**, a suitor (during term) at the law-courts; **term symbol** *Physics*, a symbol of the type ^{3}P, denoting the values of *L* and *S* for a spectral term; †**term-trotter**, (*a*) one who comes up to the law-courts for the term; (*b*) see quot. 1782; **termwise** *adv.* and *a. Math.*, (carried out) term by term, treating each term separately. See also TERM-DAY, TERM-TIME.

a **1704** T. BROWN *Dial. Dead, Reas. Oaths* Wks. 1711 IV. 84 One of 'em preaches against Oppression and Covetousness once a Month at least, and perhaps has appear'd in a *Term-Catalogue upon that Subject. **1906** E. ARBER (*title*) The Term Catalogues 1668–1709 A.D. A Contemporary Bibliography of English Literature in the reigns of Chas. II, Jas. II, Wm. and Mary, and Anne. **1625** MASSINGER *New Way* II. ii, This *term-driver, Marrall, This snip of an attorney. **1828** WEBSTER, **Term-fee*, among lawyers, a fee or certain sum charged to a suitor for each term his cause is in court. **1880** WARREN *Book-plates* iii. 23 Male and female *term-figures, busts of fairies. **1887** RUSKIN *Præterita* II. 143 Some formal *term-keeping at Oxford. **1931** *High School Jrnl.* Jan. 17 A long *term paper that will incorporate the results of a semester's reading. **1962** A. LURIE *Love & Friendship* xiv. 281 Students plagiarizing their term papers. **1975** M. BRADBURY *History Man* x. 164 Students..discuss..term-papers, union politics, theses. **1896** *Allbutt's Syst. Med.* I. 476 *Term policies are issued for short or long periods. **1602** CAREW *Cornwall* I. 89 The *Terme-suiters may best speed their businesse. **1932** BACHER & GOUDSMIT *Atomic Energy States* i. 9 Each of the doublets occurs twice, and it is necessary to distinguish them in the *term symbols. **1977** I. M. CAMPBELL *Energy & Atmosphere* viii. 220 The first electronically excited state of the oxygen atom would have in principle the two unpaired electrons of the ground state with opposite spins, producing a singlet state. In fact more detailed quantum mechanical treatment shows that there are two such states, designated by term symbols ^{1}D and ^{1}S, with the former the lower in energy of the two. **1607** MIDDLETON *Phœnix* I. iv, I have been a *term-trotter myself any time this five and forty years. **1782** V. KNOX *Ess.* I. 336 The majority are what are called *term-trotters*, that is, persons who only keep the terms for form-sake..to qualify them for degrees. **1912** J. PIERPONT *Lect. Theory of Functions Real Variable* II. v. 180 In this case we can obviously integrate *termwise, although the convergence is not uniform. **1930** T. FORT *Infinite Series* vii. 74 Termwise multiplication of series. **1979** *Proc. London Math. Soc.* XXXVIII. 390 We then integrate termwise.

[*Note* to branch IV. Gr. ὅρος denoted 'boundary mark' and thence 'a boundary', as in Euclid (see 1570 in sense 1). Hence in Arithmetic, applied to each of the terms in a ratio, e.g. 2:4; also in a proportion, and in any related series of numbers; in the statement of a mean between two numbers, as 6:9:12, 6 and 12 were the ἄκροι ὅροι 'extreme terms', and, by extension 9 was called μέσος ὅρος 'the mean term'. In Logic, ὅρος was applied to the terms in an analogy, e.g. 'as A is to B, so is C to D', where A, B, C, and D were ὅροι; also to the terms (subject and predicate) in a proposition; hence to the terms in a syllogism, the major, minor, and middle (the last being analogous to the 'mean term' in Arithmetic). By late Latin philosophical writers, ὅρος in the geometrical, arithmetical, and logical senses was rendered by *terminus* (constantly used by Boethius *a* 524). The application of ὅρος and *terminus* to the definition or limitation of a word appears in Petrus Hispanus, and led finally to the application of *terminus* to any word used in a definite or limited sense (as in sense 13 above). In Aquinas (13th c.) *terminus* is synonymous with *dictio, locutio, nomen* (see the Thomas Lexicon s.v.).]

term, *v.* [In sense 1 prob. a. OF. *termer* (14th c. in Godef.) to bring to an end; to limit, fix; in sense 2, f. TERM *sb.*]

†**1.** *trans.* To bring to an end or conclusion; to terminate. *Obs.* (Cf. AF. OYER *et terminer*.)

c **1410** [see *terming* below]. *c* **1450** *Godstow Reg.* 89 They shold here the cause, and..terme hit with a dew ende. **1570** LEVINS *Manip.* 210/43 To Tearme, *terminare*.

2. To express or denote by a term or terms. †**a.** To express in particular terms, or in a specified form of words; to phrase. (Usually with *as*.) *Obs.*

a **1557** tr. *More's Treat. Passion* Wks. 1376/2 Now doth this man..two ways..continue his pilgrimage, that is to witte as maister Gersonne in the Latin tong termeth it,..in a naturall continuance, and in a moral continuance. **1557** RECORDE *Whetst.* N iij b, *Scholar*. This rule is very obscure in woordes. *Master*. Then will I terme it thus [etc.]. **1584** in *10th Rep. Hist. MSS. Comm.* App. v. 433 No merchant.. should transporte..any goodes that apertayned to unfreemen (as it is termed).

b. To give a particular or specified name to; to name, call, denominate, designate. Now only with *compl.* (for which *as* is substituted in a relative clause); formerly with other constructions.

1560 DAUS tr. *Sleidane's Comm.* 2 Master of the holy palace (as they terme it). **1579** W. WILKINSON *Confut. Familye of Loue, Brief Descr.*, The Heresie termed, The Familie of Loue. **1632** LITHGOW *Trav.* To Rdr., Good Bookes may be tearmed wise guides. **1643** SIR T. BROWNE *Relig. Med.* I. §36 The brain, which we tearme the seat of reason. **1726** SHELVOCKE *Voy. round World* 27 Incensing the people against..Officers, whom he term'd Blood-suckers. **1872** MIVART *Elem. Anat.* 282 Such muscles are termed rotators.

†**c.** With *obj.* and *inf.*: To state, affirm.

1577–87 HOLINSHED *Chron.* III. 1212/1 His enimies (whome he termed to be sir Oswold Ulstrop, and maister Vaughan) were about the parke. **1590** SIR J. SMYTH *Disc.*

Weapons Ded. 7 Terming those to be best soldiers that could liue without pay. **1632** LITHGOW *Trav.* III. 107 Tearming vs ..to haue monstrous backes, against the execution of Iustice.

†**3.** To spend or pass (time) as in term. *Obs.*

1654 WHITLOCK *Zootomia* 4 They Terme away their Dayes in Obsequious services of others, not allowing Themselves a Dayes vacation.

Hence ˈ**terming** *vbl. sb.*; also *attrib.*

c **1410** *Master of Game* (MS. Digby 182) Prol., Men wote well that the grettest termynge [*Bodl. MS.* termynynge] of sekenes þat may be is swote. **1549** COVERDALE, etc. *Erasm. Par. Eph.* Prol., To seke the edification of the playne vnlearned by playne termyng of wordes. **1591** SPARRY tr. *Cattan's Geomancie* 176 The place, house, or fygure is.. all one thing..yet there is some difference in the tearming. **1643** TRAPP *Comm. Gen.* xxiii. 2 We read in the Gospel of minstrels and people making a noise at the terming-house, as they call it.

termagant (ˈtɜːməgənt), *sb.* (*a.*) Forms: α. 3 teruagant, 3–5 -aunt. β. 4–7 termagaunt, 6 turmagant, *Sc.* tarmegant, termygant, 7 tarmagant, -gon, 7–8 termegant, 8 termigant, 6– termagant. [In early ME. *Tervagant*, OF. *Tervagan* (in La Fontaine 17th c. *Tarvagant*), proper name in *Chanson de Roland a* 1100, as in sense 1 here. So It. *Trivigante* (Ariosto, *a* 1516). For ulterior history cf. Skeat *Etymol. Dict.* s.v.]

1. (with capital T.) Name of an imaginary deity held in mediæval Christendom to be worshipped by Muslims: in the mystery plays represented as a violent overbearing personage. (Cf. MAHOUND 1.) *Obs.* or *arch.*

In Lay. applied to gods of the Romans and heathen Saxons.

c **1205** LAY. 5353 For ȝif hit wulled Teruagant þe us [is] oure god of þisse lond [Rome]. *Ibid.* 16427 þe heðene.. cleopeden 'Ure godd Teruagant! whi trukest þu us an hond?' *c* **1290** *S. Eng. Leg.* I. 468/205 Ne bilieuez nouȝht opon Mahun, ne on teruagaunt, [h]is fere. **1303** R. BRUNNE *Handl. Synne* 197 þe sarysyne to hys god ȝede, And askede cunseyl... þan answered hys termagaunt. *a* **1400** *Octouian* 919 The Sowdan, that left [= believed] yn Teruagaunt. **1570** FOXE *A. & M.* (ed. 2) 680/2 If he had made hym [Ld. Cobham] some Termagant or Mahounde out of Babilonia. **1597** BP. HALL *Sat.* I. i. 4 Nor fright the Reader with the Pagan vaunt Of mightie Mahound, and great Termagaunt. **1602** SHAKS. *Ham.* III. ii. 15, I could haue such a Fellow whipt for o'redoing Termagant: it out-Herod's Herod. **1637** HEYWOOD *Royall King* II. ii, I'le march where my Captaine leads, wer't into the Presence of the great Termagaunt. **1825** SCOTT *Talism.* iii, Down with Mahound, Termagaunt, and all their adherents.

In form **tryvigant** (from Italian).

1591 HARINGTON *Orl. Fur.* XII. xliv, Blaspheming Tryuigant and Mahomet [*Ariosto*: Bestemmiando Macone et Trivigante], And all the Gods adord in Turks profession.

2. A savage, violent, boisterous, overbearing, or quarrelsome person (or thing personified); a blusterer, bully. Now *rare* exc. as in b.

1500–20 DUNBAR *Poems* xxvi. 115 Thae tarmegantis [Erschemen], with tag and tatter, Ffull lowd in Ersche begowth to clatter. **1542** BALE *Yet a Course*, etc. 39 b, Thys terryble termagaunt, thys Neroth, thys Pharao. **1593** G. HARVEY *Pierce's Super.* 12 Oh, but Agrippa was an vrcheon ..Sigonius a toy, Cuiacius a bable to this Termagant. **1618** T. ADAMS *God's Bounty* ii. Wks. 1861 I. 149 Wealth may do us good service, but if it get the mastery of our trust, it will turn tyrant, termagant. **1824** SCOTT *St. Ronan's* xxi, The.. consequences that might follow from the displeasure of this Highland termagant [Captain MacTurk]. **1884** SIR S. ST. JOHN *Hayti* vii. 269 Bazin, the military termagant who led the prosecution..browbeat the witnesses, bullied the jury.

b. *spec.* A violent, overbearing, turbulent, brawling, quarrelsome woman; a virago, shrew, vixen. (Now the ordinary sense.)

1659 *Lady Alimony* I. iv. B ij, And just so must all our Tavern Tarmagons be us'd. **1732** GAY *Achilles* II. Wks. (1772) 239 This girl is..such an arrant termigant, that I could as soon fall in love with a tygress. **1861** THACKERAY *Four Georges* iii, Yonder is Sarah Marlborough's palace, just as it stood when that termagant occupied it. **1896** 'IAN MACLAREN' *Kate Carnegie* v. 77 A vulgar termagant..who would call her husband an idiot aloud before a dinner-table.

3. *attrib.* or *adj.* Having the character of a termagant; savage, violent, overbearing, turbulent, brawling, quarrelsome. **a.** Generally. Now *rare.*

1596 SHAKS. *1 Hen. IV*, v. iv. 114 'Twas time to counterfet, or that hotte Termagant Scot had paid me scot and lot too. **1596** NASHE *Saffron Walden* 49 Termagant inkhorne tearmes. **1695** *Remarks some late Serm.* (ed. 2) 3 Consider the fine Knack these Gentlemen have got at Representation and Character; which you will find so luscious and termagant, as would shame even the Modesty of the Stage. **1711** 'J. DISTAFF' *Char. Don Sacheverellio* 5 A Man of great Brawn and Muscle, Large, Tall and Termagant. **1869** J. MARTINEAU *Ess.* II. 213 His dialectic assumes a termagant character.

b. *spec.* Of a woman (or her attributes).

1667–8 DRYDEN & DK. NEWCASTLE *Sir Martin Mar-all* I. i, His wife, who is a termagant lady. **1678** DRYDEN *Limberham* I. i, But this Lady is so Termagant an Empress! **1761** MRS. F. SHERIDAN *Sidney Bidulph* II. 66 The most termagant spirit that ever animated a female breast. **1818** SCOTT *Hrt. Midl.* xviii, 'I tell ye', raising her termagant voice, 'I want my bairn!' **1868** FREEMAN *Norm. Conq.* II. viii. 275 The plans of his own termagant niece Queen Constance.

Hence **termagancy** (ˈtɜːməgənsɪ) [after nouns in -ANCY from adjs. in -ANT[1]], termagant quality, violence of temper or disposition; ˈ**termagantish** *a.*, resembling, or partaking of the character of, a termagant; ˈ**termagantly** *adv.*, like a termagant, with violence of temper, outrageously.

1709 MRS. MANLEY *Secret Mem.* (1720) III. 198 The good Emperor, mortifyed by the *Termagancy of his Mother. **1716** M. DAVIES *Athen. Brit.* II. 318 Exasperated by the sawcy Termigancy of some few insolent Dissenting Preachers. **1753** MISS COLLIER *Art Torment.* II. ii. 115 By a violent termagancy of temper, she may never suffer him to have a moment's peace. **1823** in *Spirit Pub. Jrnls.* 408 Mrs. Scarsfield had something so very *termagantish in her appearance. **1707** *Reflex. Ridicule* II. 375 To see..how *termagantly they treat their Husbands.

termagant, obs. erron. form of PTARMIGAN.

termage (ˈtɜːmɪdʒ). [f. TERM *sb.* + -AGE.]

†**1.** Name for the winnings in some form of gambling or cheating. *Obs. slang.*

1591 GREENE *Conny-Catching* II. Wks. (Grosart) X. 87 In Vincents Law..He that is coosened, the Vincent. Gaines gotten, Termage.

2. attrib. *termage fee* = term-fee (see quot.).

1834 *Regula Generalis* Michaelmas, in Bingham *New Cases* I. 411 Every attorney ought to pay to the clerk of the warrants..his termage fees, being eight pence in every term.

termashaw, erron. spelling of TAMASHA.

1842 DE QUINCEY *Philos. Herodotus* Wks. 1862 VIII. 181.

termatic (təˈmætɪk), *a.* (*sb.*) *Anat.* [f. Gr. τέρμα (τερματ-) end, limit + -IC.] Belonging to the *terma* or *lamina terminalis* of the brain, a thin layer of grey matter in front of the third ventricle. Also as *sb.*, ellipt. for *termatic artery.*

1885 WILDER in *New York Med. Jrnl.* 21 Mar. 325 The termatic artery, a small vessel arising from the junction of the precerebral arteries. **1890** BILLINGS *Nat. Med. Dict.*, *Termatic artery*, branch from anterior cerebral or anterior communicating arteries to region of lamina terminalis.

ˈ**term-day.** A day set as a term (TERM *sb.* 3); a day appointed for doing something, esp. for payment of money due. (In quot. *c* 1375, a final or concluding day; †*but terme day*, without end, for ever.) ? *Obs.* exc. as in b, c.

a **1300** *Cursor M.* 14040 Quen it com to þe term dai, þai had noght quar-of for to pai. *c* **1369** CHAUCER *Dethe Blaunche* 730 He had broke his terme day To come to hir. *c* **1375** *Sc. Leg. Saints* xxxiii. (*George*) 842 To duel with hyme but terme day. **1470–85** MALORY *Arthur* IV. xxviii. 158 Whan it drewe nygh the terme day that syr gawayn syr Marhaus and syre Vwayne shold mete.

b. *spec.* Each of the Scottish quarter-days, esp. Whitsunday and Martinmas day, at which houses are taken, and servants engaged for the summer or winter half-year: see TERM *sb.* 3 b.

1818 SCOTT *Hrt. Midl.* viii, On the very term-day when their ejection should have taken place. **1893** *Westm. Gaz.* 5 Apr. 6/3 The understanding..was that the bank which has now stopped might hold out till the 15th of May, which is the Scotch 'term' day. **1906** *Scot. Rev.* 1 Feb. 123/1 Candlemas Day is known to business men in Scotland as one of the quarterly term days.

c. Each of a series of days appointed for taking systematic scientific observations, e.g. of meteorological phenomena. In quots. *attrib.*

1843 *Proc. Amer. Phil. Soc.* II. 247 To keep up the term-day observations. **1856** KANE *Arct. Expl.* I. xiv. 153 *note*, Who bore the brunt of the term-day observations.

†**terment.** *Obs.* Forms: 4–6 **terement**, 5 **tyrrement**, 5–6 **tyr(e)ment**, **terment**, 6 **terrement**. [Aphetic form of INTERMENT.] Burial, funeral: = INTERMENT; also, a funeral service.

1389 in *Eng. Gilds* (1870) 92 þe skeueyns shullen don seyn þo messes wyhtinne vj. day after þe terement. **1402** *E.E. Wills* (1882) 11 Atte day of my terment. *c* **1440** *Promp. Parv.* 494/2 Tyrrement, or intyrrement, *funerale*. **1568** GRAFTON *Chron.* II. 578 King Henry caused a solempne obite and terrement to be kept within Paules Church of London, for Sigismond the Emperor.

termenteyne, obs. corrupt f. TURPENTINE.

termer (ˈtɜːmə(r)). Also 6–7 **tearmer.** [f. TERM *sb.* + -ER[1].]

1. One who resorted to London in term, either for business at a court of law, or for amusements, intrigues, or dishonest practices. Common *c* 1550–1675; now only *Hist.*

1556 J. HEYWOOD *Spider & F.* xiv. 11 In westminster hall I..may be a termer all tymes and howrs. **1602** ROWLANDS *Greene's Ghost* (1860) 22 There be a band of more needy mates called Termers, who trauell all the yeere from faire to faire, and haue great doings in Westminster Hall. *Ibid.* 48 A Countrey Gentleman..walking in Poules, as tearmers are wont that wait for their lawyers. **1607** MIDDLETON *Michaelmas Term* I. i, He was here three days before the Exchequer gaped Rearage Fie, such an early termer? **1646** SUCKLING *Goblins* III. Wks. (1694) 274 Country Ladies twelve. Tearmers all. *a* **1668** DAVENANT *Epilogue* Wks. (1673) 300 To cry Plays down Is half the business Termers have in Town. **1834** MEDWIN *Angler in Wales* I. 221 Being noted 'termers', they met at the Goat and Tun. **1875** A. W. WARD *Hist. Eng. Dram. Lit.* (1899) II. vi. 516 *note*, 'Termers' was a name of opprobrium applied to persons who came up to town to make their harvest in term-time.

†**2.** *gen.* or *allusively.* One who is bound to a particular time for doing something; one who holds office only for a term or limited period. *Obs.*

1634 R. CLERKE in Spurgeon *Treas. Dav.* Ps. cxxxvi. 1 Salvation is no termer; grace ties not itself to times. *a* **1641** BP. MOUNTAGU *Acts & Mon.* ii. (1642) 107 The High Priests being the ordinary standing Rulers of that people..and those of Iudah but Termers.

†**3.** Obs. form of TERMOR, q.v.

‖**termes** (ˈtɜːmiːz). Pl. **termites** (ˈtɜːmɪtiːz). [mod.L. (Linnæus 1748), a. late L. *termes* (Isidore) a wood-worm, earlier also *tarmes*, f. root of L. *terere*, Gr. τείρ-ειν to rub, bore.] = TERMITE.

[**1706** PHILLIPS (ed. Kersey), *Termes*, (Lat.)..also a little Worm commonly call'd a Death-watch; a Maggot, or Gentle.] **1781** Termites [see TERMITE]. **1800** *Asiat. Ann. Reg.* 5/2 The *termes*, or what is called the white ant, infests this island. **1834** PRINGLE *Afr. Sk.* viii. 287 The termes of South Africa is not the destructive species.

termigame, -gant, obs ff. PTARMIGAN, TERMAGANT.

termin, var. TERMINE *sb. Obs.*

terminable (ˈtɜːmɪnəb(ə)l), *a.* (*sb.*) [f. TERMINE *v.* + -ABLE. Cf. OF. *terminable* that comes to an end, not eternal (13th c. in Godef.).]

A. *adj.* †**1.** That may be or is to be terminated, determined, or finally decided. *Obs.*

1424 *Acts Privy Counc.* III. 149 Alle the billes that comprehende materes terminable at the commune lawe..be remitted there to be determined. *c* **1450** *Cov. Myst.* xxv. (1841) 246 *Cayphas*... Of the lawe of Moyses I have a chef governawns, To severe ryth and wrong in me is termynable. *Ibid.* xxix. 291 My sovereyn Lord, heyest of excillens, In ȝou alle jewgement is termynabyle.

2. Capable of being or liable to be terminated; that may come or be brought to an end (usually, in time); limitable, finite; not lasting or perpetual.

terminable annuity, an annuity which comes to an end after a definite term: see ANNUITY 3; ***terminable annuitant***, one who holds a terminable annuity. ***minimum terminable unit*** (see quot. 1975); abbrev. *T-unit* s.v. T 7.

1581 HANMER *Jesuites Banner* K iv b, Although the offence be infinite, and the satisfaction finite, or terminable. **1656** tr. *Hobbes' Elem. Philos.* (1839) 99 Space or time is said to be finite in power, or terminable, when there may be assigned a number of finite spaces or times, as of paces or hours. **1820** G. G. CAREY *Funds* 79 To find the cost..of a terminable annuity. **1858** W. M. CAMPION in *Cambr. Ess.* 199 Treated as a mere terminable annuitant. **1874** MOTLEY *Barneveld* II. xv. 185 Terminable at pleasure of any one. **1965** [see *T-unit* s.v. T 7]. **1975** *Language for Life* (Dept. Educ. & Sci.) iii. 39 The minimum terminable unit, or T-unit, is 'roughly any sentence or part of a sentence that is an independent clause, possibly containing, however, one or more dependent clauses'.

†**B.** *sb.* in phr. ***in terminables***: ? in definite terms, definitely (cf. *in terms*, TERM *sb.* 14 b). *Obs. rare*$^{-1}$.

a **1568** '*For Helth of Body*', etc. 70 in *Bannatyne Poems* (Hunter, Cl.) 198 Woyd all drinking with lymmaris and lechouris, And this I say in terminablis, I gess, Off dyce playeris and commoun hasardouris.

Hence **termina'bility**, ˈ**terminableness**, the quality of being terminable; ˈ**terminably** *adv.*, in the way of being terminable; in quot. 1584, within definite limits of space.

1584 R. SCOT *Discov. Witchcr.* (1886) 470 The holie spirit is [not] in us as a bodie placed in a place terminablie. **1846** WORCESTER, Terminableness. **1850** D. THOMAS *Crisis Being* iii. 51 Hell, its existence or non-existence, its terminableness or eternity. **1858** GOLDW. SMITH in *Oxford Ess.* 279 The choice between holding the fellowship perpetually as a resident, or terminably with leave of non-residence. **1884** *Q. Rev.* Jan. 9 He relies..on the terminability of the office. **1887** SAINTSBURY *Hist. Elizab. Lit.* ix. (1890) 344 An exception to the general rule of the terminableness of copyright.

terminal (ˈtɜːmɪnəl), *a.* and *sb.* [ad. L. *terminālis*, f. *termin-us* end, boundary: see -AL[1]. Cf. F. *terminal* (16th c. in Godef.).]

A. *adj.* †**1.** *Her.* (See quots.) *Obs.*

1486 *Bk. St. Albans, Her.* B j b, Ther be .ix. dyuisionis of cotarmures .v. perfite & .iiii. vnperfite. The .v. perfite be theys Termynall Collaterall Abstrakte Fixall and Bastard. *Ibid.*, Termynall is calde in armys all the bretheren of right lyne hethir by fadre or by modre may bere the right heyris cotarmure with a differens calde Enbordyng. **1586** FERNE *Blaz. Gentrie* 155 All these coates were called *Terminall* because that they were terminated or limited within their embordinges, as afore sayd.

2. a. Belonging to or placed at the boundary of a region, as a landmark; in quot. 1744, presiding over boundaries (cf. TERMINUS 2).

1744 PATERSON *Comm. on Milton's P.L.* 218 The emblem of his being the terminal god, defending the borders of that nation. **1847** GROTE *Greece* II. xvi. III. 283 A terminal pillar set up by Crœsus at Kydrara.

b. Applied to a statue, bust, or figure terminating in and apparently springing from a pillar or pedestal; also to the pillar or pedestal itself; and often inexactly to a pedestal which narrows towards the base. See TERM *sb.* 15, TERMINUS 3.

1857 BIRCH *Anc. Pottery* (1858) II. 283 Sometimes only his bust is seen, or he appears as a terminal statue. **1858** HAWTHORNE *Fr. & It. Note-Bks.* I. 177 Great urns and vases, terminal figures, temples.

3. a. Situated at or forming the end or extremity of something: chiefly in scientific use; *spec.* in *Cryst.* applied to the faces, edges, or angles of a crystal at the extremities of its longest axis; in *Zool.* and *Anat.* situated at or forming the (outer) end of a part or series of parts; in *Bot.* growing at the end of a stem, branch, or other part, as a bud, flower, or inflorescence, a style, etc. (opp. to *lateral* and *axillary*). ***terminal moraine*** (*Geol.*), a moraine at the lower end of a glacier: see MORAINE.

1805–17 R. JAMESON *Char. Min.* (ed. 3) 104 Terminal edges are formed by the junction of lateral and terminal planes. **1826** KIRBY & SP. *Entomol.* IV. 308 Mouth... Terminal.. When the mouth terminates the head. **1827** STEUART *Planter's G.* (1828) 448 Plantations.. pruned.. by the removal of Terminal Shoots, and Terminal Buds. **1833** J. DUNCAN *Beetles* (Nat. Libr.) 217 Terminal lobe of the maxillæ ending in a tuft of fine hair. **1847** W. E. STEELE *Field Bot.* 132 The uppermost whorl terminal and capitate. **1860** TYNDALL *Glac.* II. viii. 264 The rocks and débris carried down by the glacier are finally deposited at the lower extremity, forming there a terminal moraine. **1869** PHILLIPS *Vesuv.* x. 274 A prism with a six-sided terminal pyramid. **1876** PREECE & SIVEWRIGHT *Telegraphy* 160 By a terminal pole is meant not only the last pole at each end of the line to which the wires are terminated, but also any pole at which the wires form an angle approaching to 90°. **1884** HULME *Wild Fl.* p. vi, Inflorescence terminal and axillary.

b. Situated at the end of a line of railway; forming, or belonging to, a railway terminus.

1869 *Bradshaw's Railway Man.* XXI. 87 This line.. terminates in the city, at a great terminal station in Liverpool Street. **1878** F. S. WILLIAMS *Midl. Railw.* 68 The cost including two terminal stations and rolling stock, averaging £24,000 a mile. **1881** *Times* 13 July 6/3 In regard to terminal services the respondent [railway] company allowed a rebate. **1907** *Daily Chron.* 10 Sept. 4/6 When the Canadian Pacific Railway Company selected the spot for their western terminal port on the shores of the Pacific.

4. a. Occurring at the end of something (in time, or generally); forming the last member of a series or succession; closing, concluding, final, ultimate.

1831 *For. Q. Rev.* VII. 378 Alliterative metre is formed without.. dependence upon the aid of terminal rhyme. **1873** H. SPENCER *Stud. Sociol.* xiv. 336 The human being is at once the terminal problem of Biology and the initial factor of Sociology. **1877** DOWDEN *Shaks. Prim.* iv. 41 These may be found as terminal words in the blank verse of Milton and of Wordsworth. **1885** *Act 48 & 49 Vict.* c. 58 §2 The sums charged.. shall.. cover the costs of delivery.. within.. one mile of the terminal telegraphic office.

b. *Path.* (*a*) Applied to a morbid condition forming the final stage of a fatal disease; (*b*) applied to a patient suffering from such a disease; (*c*) applied to an institution or ward in which such patients are nursed.

(*a*) **1891** *Cent. Dict.*, *Terminal dementia*, dementia forming the final and permanent stage of many cases of acute insanity. **1898** *Allbutt's Syst. Med.* V. 422 In the moribund a 'terminal' leucocytosis is frequently observed. **1958** A. HUXLEY *Let.* 2 Feb. (1969) 845 The administration of LSD to terminal cancer cases, in the hope that it would make dying a more spiritual, less strictly physiological process. **1961** *Lancet* 2 Sept. 549/1 It is they who have the closest contact with people who are going through 'terminal illnesses'. **1976** *Church Times* 23 July 11/1, I now have several progressive illnesses; one is terminal. **1980** D. LODGE *How Far can you Go?* vi. 160 What would it be like to be told you had a terminal illness, he wondered.
(*b*) **1961** *Amer. Speech* XXXVI. 145 *Terminal* adj., approaching death, moribund. 'The patient looks terminal to me.' **1965** E. M. K. PILLERS in J. S. Mitchell *Treatment of Cancer* 91 Response to this has been disappointing and the patient is now terminal. **1969** *Guardian* 19 Aug. 2/2 We started off with patients who were going to die anyway—terminal patients.
(*c*) **1961** *Lancet* 2 Sept. 548/2 Excellent care of these patients has been carried out not only at St. Joseph's but also in other terminal homes and hospitals. **1974** F. WARNER *Meeting Ends* I. ii. 13 The old lady was taken into the terminal ward, inarticulate, jabbering away.

c. *colloq.* In various *transf.* and *fig.* uses of sense 4 b (freq. *joc.* or *trivial*).

1973 *Black Panther* 11 Aug. 8/2 The country was plunged into shock and the President faced a terminal crisis. **1975** D. LODGE *Changing Places* iii. 112, I continue to hope that our marital problems are not terminal. **1981** *Daily Tel.* 21 Dec. 2/1 Another contest for Labour's deputy leadership next year could prove 'terminal' for the party, Mr Neil Kinnock ..said. **1983** *Times* 23 Sept. 6/4 One commentator said yesterday that his insensitivity was terminal. *Ibid.* 26 Sept. 9/5 A bad case of terminal tiredness had lowered my resistance to every loitering bug.

5. Belonging to or lasting for a term or definite period; *esp.* pertaining to a university or law term; occurring every term or at fixed terms; termly.

1827 *Q. Rev.* XXXVI. 259 Strict terminal examinations, on the topics of the college lectures, have been generally introduced. **1875** STUBBS *Const. Hist.* II. xv. 260 This council sitting in terminal courts assisted the king in hearing suits. **1885** SIR N. LINDLEY in *Law Rep.* 29 *Ch. Div.* 593 This terminal rent-charge is an incumbrance on the inheritance. **1885** *Law Times* LXXX. 5/1 A set of rooms in college.. at a yearly rent payable by three terminal payments. **1885** M. PATTISON *Mem.* 87 A share in the terminal examinations called 'Collections'.

6. *Logic.* Pertaining to a term (TERM *sb.* 12).

1872 in LATHAM. **1891** *Cent. Dict.*, *Terminal quantity*, the quantity of a term, as universal or particular.

7. Special collocations: **terminal ballistics**, that branch of ballistics which deals with the impact of the projectile on the target; **terminal guidance** *Aeronaut.* (see quot. 1955); **terminal juncture** *Linguistics*, a juncture (sense 2 c) that occurs at the end of a syntactic unit; **terminal market** *Comm.*, a market that deals in futures; **terminal nose-dive** *Aeronaut.*, a nose-dive during which an aircraft reaches its terminal velocity; **terminal string** *Transformational Gram.*, a string consisting wholly of terminal symbols; **terminal symbol** *Transformational Gram.*, a symbol that denotes a lexical class and cannot be further rewritten; **terminal velocity**, the constant speed of fall that any particular object, given time will eventually attain, at which the air resistance is equal to its weight.

1947 L. E. SIMON *German Research World War II* vii. 109 Terminal ballistics is concerned with the motion of the projectile, its fragments, and gases in the neighbourhood of the target. **1974** *Encycl. Brit. Macropædia* II. 659/2 A theoretical structure for terminal ballistics is a relatively current development. **1955** A. S. LOCKE *Guidance* i. 19 Terminal guidance is the guidance applied to the missile between the end of the midcourse guidance and contact with or detonation in close proximity to the target. **1979** *Jrnl. R. Soc. Arts* CXXVII. 555/1 Long-range, sea-skimming missiles with terminal guidance. **1956** *Language* XXXII. 653 This set of phonemic phenomena we assign to the terminal juncture. **1975** *Ibid.* LI. 57 The final element, *hacer*, accompanied by terminal juncture, is associated with zero following elements, signals absolute completion, and receives maximum contrast. **1895** *Daily News* 14 Dec. 9/4 The terminal market, though dull, has been steadier, prices marking a recovery of 3d. to 6d. on the week. **1952** *Economist* 22 Nov. 567/1 There is little hope of restoration of a terminal market until the domestic allocation of sugar is freed from rationing. **1962** H. O. BEECHENO *Introd. Business Stud.* xi. 94 Future or terminal markets where goods can be bought and sold in advance. **1933** *Gloss. Aeronaut. Terms (B.S.I.)* 9 *Terminal nose-dive*, a dive at terminal velocity. **1956** N. CHOMSKY *Logical Struct. Linguistic Theory* (1975) vii. 274 The mapping in question may rearrange the order of elements of terminal strings and may specify their morphemic shape in various ways. **1967** D. G. HAYS *Introd. Computational Linguistics* vi. 118 A terminal string is composed of a certain number, say n, of terminal symbols. **1964** E. BACH *Introd. Transformational Gram.* ii. 14 Among the symbols of the grammar.. there are some which never appear to the left of the arrow in a rule as symbols to be replaced. These are called *terminal symbols*. **1967** D. G. HAYS *Introd. Computational Linguistics* vi. 119 In terms of dependency theory, let the level of a structure be one greater than the number of links from its origin to the terminal symbol furthest removed. **1832** BABBAGE *Econ. Manuf.* (ed. 3) 52 Bodies, in falling through a resisting medium, after a certain time acquire a uniform velocity, which is called their terminal velocity, with which they continue to descend. **1910** [see STOKES[1] c]. **1914** *Aeronaut. Jrnl.* XVIII. 50 He had dived, and had reached a speed so high that he thought it wise to straighten out without waiting to reach the terminal velocity. **1946** T. C. OHART *Elements Ammunition* IV. viii. 199 This theoretical maximum velocity for a given size and shape of bomb is called the terminal velocity; it is really a function of a given design, depending upon the aerodynamic characteristics of a bomb.

B. *sb.* † **1.** *pl.* Rendering L. *Terminālia*, name of an ancient Roman festival held annually in honour of the god Terminus: see TERMINUS 2, and cf. *Saturnals*, SATURNAL B. 2. *Obs. rare*$^{-0}$.

1656 BLOUNT *Glossogr.*, *Terminals* (*terminalia*), feasts.. kept in February at the eighth calends of March.

2. A terminal part or structure, i.e. one situated at or forming the end, or an end, of something; *spec.* **a.** in *Electr.* each of the free ends of an open circuit (by connecting which the circuit is closed), or any structure forming such an end, as the carbons in an arc light, or the clamping-screws in a voltaic battery by which it is connected with the wire that completes the circuit; **b.** *Physiol.* the end or end-structure of a nerve fibre or neuron; **c.** a carving or other ornament at the end of something, as a finial.

1838 W. STURGEON in *Ann. Electr., Magn., & Chem.* II. 11 That [part] which is connected with the positive pole of the exciting apparatus.. may very conveniently be called the 'salient terminal metal', or occasionally the 'salient terminal' only. **1850** GROVE *Corr. Phys. Forces* (ed. 2) 82 If the two platinum terminals of a voltaic battery be immersed in water, oxygen will be evolved at one and hydrogen at the other terminal. **1865** *Morn. Star* 27 Feb., Seats.. panelled with oak, the elbow rails having carved terminals. **1869** MRS. SOMERVILLE *Molec. Sc.* I. i. ii. 52 When the copper conducting wires are fitted with charcoal terminals and brought near to one another, the dazzling lights combine in one blaze. **1874** CARPENTER *Ment. Phys.* I. ii. §89 (1879) 99 The terminals of the sensory tract of the axial cord. **1899** *Allbutt's Syst. Med.* VIII. 325 The ultimate naked fibrils (collaterals and terminals). **1904** WINDLE *Rem. Prehist. Age Brit.* 100 Chapes or terminals to scabbards which may have belonged to daggers or to swords.

d. A device for feeding data into a computer or receiving its output; *esp.* one that can be used by a person as a means of two-way communication with a computer.

1954 *Trans. IRE Prof. Group Electronic Computers* Mar. 2/1 Since the two machines employ the same digital language, this attachment can easily be made through their regular input-output terminals. **1958** *Oxf. Mag.* 29 May 470/1 The 'terminal' equipment, consisting of punched paper tape and a teleprinter, is relatively slow. **1965** *Jrnl. Assoc. Computing Machinery* XII. 350 (*heading*) On a problem concerning a central storage device served by multiple terminals. **1970** O. DOPPING *Computers & Data Processing* ix. 131 An 'impersonal' terminal with card reader, line printer, etc. can be started automatically at the end of the waiting time, but in case of a 'personal' terminal, the computer may send a message to the terminal indicating that the conversation may begin. **1971** *Daily Tel.* (Colour Suppl.) 19 Feb. 5/3 The national police computer with 700 terminals throughout the country opens this year. **1973** *Nature* 12 Oct. p. xxviii/3 (Advt.), There are good in-house computing facilities and a terminal to an IBM 360/195. **1977** *Hongkong Standard* 12 Apr. (Business Suppl.) 5/1 Terminal operators have been responding actively to the encouraging scene. **1979** *Computers in Shell* (Shell Internat. Petroleum Co.) (*recto rear cover*), Types of terminals include card readers, printers, video screens and teletypes. **1981** *Sci. Amer.* Dec. 112/3 The computer executes the operation, simplifies the resulting expression and prints it or displays it on a video terminal.

3. A final syllable, letter, or word; a termination.

1831 *Westm. Rev.* Jan. 61 The derivation of one word from another.., or rather the different states in which a root presents itself with terminals added. **1866** *Sat. Rev.* 21 Apr. 474 Madlle. Orgeni (German in spite of her patronymic terminal) comes directly from Berlin. **1904** *Athenæum* 21 May 646/2 Mr. Coleridge transposes the rhyming terminals 'healthy' and 'wealthy'.

4. *pl.* Charges made by a railway company for the use of a terminus or other station, and for services rendered in loading or unloading goods, etc., there: see quot. 1887.

1878 F. S. WILLIAMS *Midl. Railw.* 188 There was a sum of £5000 or £6000 for 'terminals'. **1884** *Pall Mall G.* 27 May 3/1 To charge a reasonable sum for station terminals. **1887** *Contemp. Rev.* Jan. 82 The cost of collection, loading, covering, unloading, and delivering,.. are the chief items included under the denomination of 'terminals'.

5. a. A terminal station or premises on a railway, a terminus; a terminal point of a railway, a place or town at which it has a terminus (orig. and chiefly *U.S.*). Hence, in extended use, applied to the terminal point of an airline (= *air terminal* (a) s.v. AIR *sb.*[1] III. 1), a bus service (= *bus terminal* s.v. BUS *sb.*[2] 3), or occas. some other transportation service.

1888 *Boston* (Mass.) *Jrnl.* 7 Aug. 3/2 The Canadian Pacific ..company has purchased extensive dock property and terminals at Windsor, opposite Detroit. **1900** *Jrnl. Sch. Geog.* (U.S.) Apr. 135 The seaboard terminal is New York, with its three million of people. **1904** KITTREDGE *Old Farmer* 279 In 1801, King's Tavern, Boston, was the 'terminal' for the stages for Albany, New York, &c. **1921** *Flight* 16 June 401 (*caption*) Two London-Paris terminals. —The lower photograph shows Cricklewood aerodrome.. the upper picture shows the Paris air port. **1922** JOYCE *Ulysses* 699 When citybound frequent connection by train or tram from their respective intermediate station or terminal. **1924** *London Guide No. 3* 152 At all the principal traffic centres and at the route terminals are uniformed 'General' Inspectors [of buses]. **1937** *New Statesman* 25 Dec. 1094/1 A rail-cum-steamer terminal on the Firth of Clyde. **1958** 'N. SHUTE' *Rainbow & Rose* vi. 270 Walking from the hostel to the terminal [of an airline]. **1958** *Times* 1 Mar. 7/4 Each city or town would adopt the type of terminal [for helicopters] best suited to its own locality. **1969** *Jane's Freight Containers 1968–69* 113/3 Scheduled national services: door-to-door and terminal-to-terminal. **1975** N. LUARD *Robespierre Serial* xvii. 153 All he could do was head for the bus terminal... The terminal was only twenty minutes by taxi from the hotel. **1980** R. MCCRUM *In Secret State* xiii. 122 Quitman took the Piccadilly line to Heathrow. .. Soon he was standing on the travolator, riding up towards Terminal Three. **1981** M. MOORCOCK *Byzantium Endures* ii. 50 We eventually arrived at Glavnaya Station, the main terminal of Odessa situated in the heart of the city.

b. An installation where oil is stored, situated at the end of a pipeline or at a port of call for oil tankers.

[**1940** *Petroleum Press Service* 19 Apr. 182 This has included laying down a 100-mile 16 inch pipe-line to the coast and constructing ocean terminal facilities at Puerto La Cruz.] **1947** L. M. FANNING *Amer. Oil Operations Abroad* xi. (*caption*) Oil-loading dock, Puerto La Cruz Terminal. **1948** *Economist* 14 Aug. 259/2 It is obviously difficult to pump oil from an Arab source in Iraq to a terminal in a Jewish-held town. **1976** M. MACHLIN *Pipeline* vi. 70 The 707 could then descend to a relatively low level and follow the route of the pipeline to its terminal.

6. A terminal figure: = TERM *sb.* 15, TERMINUS 3.

1876 GWILT *Archit.* Gloss., *Term* or *Terminal*. *Ibid.*, *Vagina*, the lower part of a terminal in which a statue is apparently inserted.

7. One suffering from a terminal illness.

1960 J. G. BALLARD in *New Worlds* Oct. 95 The terminals sleeping in the adjacent dormitory block attracted hordes of would-be sightseers. **1976** *Church Times* 23 July 11/2 Mr. Rice recently paid a third visit to the nun—who is bedridden and a terminal—and questioned her again, mainly about prayer and intercession. **1982** P. VAN GREENAWAY *Lazarus Lie* vi. 61 'You have maybe a couple of thousand patients.' .. 'How many terminals?' 'Terminals?' 'Inoperables, end of the liners.'

8. Special Combs.: **terminal building**, a building housing the main facilities for air passengers; **terminal screw** *Electr.*, a screw for fastening an electric wire to the object with the screw hole.

1933 *Jrnl. R. Aeronaut. Soc.* XXXVII. 10 A terminal building will house traffic control and airport administration. **1977** G. SCOTT *Hot Pursuit* iv. 38 At the airport.. I got out of the terminal building and on to the bus. **1931** S. R. ROGET *Dict. Electr. Terms* (ed. 2) 349/2 Terminal screw. **1978** *N.Y. Times* 30 Mar. C-4/1 Aluminum wire is stiffer than copper wire and does not bend as easily when wrapped around small terminal screws on switches and outlets.

terminalia (tɜːmɪˈneɪlɪə). [mod.L. (Linnæus *Mantissa Plantarum* (1767) I. 21), f. L. *terminālis* TERMINAL *a.* + -IA[2].] An evergreen tree of the large genus of this name, belonging to the family Combretaceæ, native to tropical or sub-tropical regions, having leaves clustered at the end of branches, and often producing a valuable timber. Also *attrib.*

1830 *Curtis's Bot. Mag.* LVII. 3004 (*heading*) Broad Downy-leaved Terminalia. **1926** *Chambers's Jrnl.* June 411/2 He halted the elephant under one of the Terminalia trees. **1964** C. WILLOCK *Enormous Zoo* iii. 39 The elephants had taken a liking to *terminalia* bark. **1973** *Times* 20 Sept. 8/3 David Dibnah,..convicted of wilfully destroying a flowering terminalia tree, has been ordered by a magistrate to plant another.

terminalization (ˌtɜːmɪnəlaɪˈzeɪʃə n). *Cytology.* [f. TERMINAL *a.* and *sb.* + -IZATION.] The movement of a chiasma or chiasmata towards the end of a separating bivalent.

1929 C. D. DARLINGTON in *Jrnl. Genetics* XXI. 266 The post-diplotene stages in this species are characterised by a regular movement of chiasmata towards the attachment constriction. The opposite movement, which I will call 'terminalisation', affords a sufficient and indeed the only explanation of the exceptional metaphase configurations found in *Tradescantia*. **1932** *Amer. Naturalist* LXVI. 32 Related species differ in the degree of terminalization of chiasmata. **1979** *Nature* 22 Mar. 349/2 The issue of terminalisation is relevant both theoretically (assessment of chiasma and crossover frequency) and practically (alleged factor in maternal-age-dependent non-disjunction in mammals).

Hence **ˈterminalized** *ppl. a.*, (of a chiasma) having moved to, or situated at, the end of a separating bivalent.

1932 C. D. DARLINGTON *Rec. Adv. Cytol.* iv. 103 However many chiasmata are terminalised, the chromosomes remain associated by terminal chiasmata. *Ibid.* 104 (*caption*) Completely terminalised chiasmata. **1959** *Genetics* XLIV. 711 Incompletely terminalized chiasmata were observed in these configurations. **1979** *Nature* 22 Mar. 349/2 Our data do not indicate whether or not chiasmata are terminalised in the mouse.

terminally (ˈtɜːmɪnəlɪ), *adv.* [f. TERMINAL *a.* + -LY[2].]

†**1.** In relation to, or within, a term or limited period. *Obs.*

1657 GAULE *Sapientia Justif.* 89 That Death which reigned from Adam to Moses,..if you take the time of Deaths reigning to be betwixt them two, terminally and exclusively.

2. a. At the end or extremity.

1854 OWEN *Skel. & Teeth* in *Orr's Circ. Sc.* I. *Org. Nat.* 182 The..terminally confluent parapophyses. **1875** BENNETT & DYER *Sachs' Bot.* 460 Female flowers.. consisting of a naked axis..bearing the erect ovules terminally or laterally.

b. *Comb.* with an adj. in sense 4 b of TERMINAL *a.*

1973 *Sci. Amer.* Sept. 56/1 One of the terminally sick patients has been given a change of scene by moving his bed to the garden. **1976** M. MILLAR *Ask for me Tomorrow* (1977) iv. 37 This was Aragon's first time in the presence of a terminally ill person.

3. Every term, once a term.

1868 *Times* 26 Sept. 3/5 No house [at Oxford] can be licensed until it has been inspected by the delegates, and lodgings must be visited by them terminally. **1885** *Law Times* LXXIX. 366/2 An annual rent is paid by the undergraduate..in some cases quarterly, triennially, or terminally. **1896** *Oxford Univ. Gaz.* 10 Nov. 110/1 The Scholarship is of the annual value of £45, payable terminally and tenable for two years.

terminant (ˈtɜːmɪnənt), *a.* (*sb.*) Now *rare* or *Obs.* [ad. L. *termināntem*, pr. pple. of *termināre* to TERMINATE.]

1. Terminating, concluding, final. Also as *sb.* A final syllable, termination, terminal.

1589 PUTTENHAM *Eng. Poesie* II. viii. (Arb.) 94 If one should rime to this word (*Restore*) he may not match him with (*Doore*) or (*Poore*) for neither of both are of like terminant, either by good orthography or in naturall sound. *Ibid.* 95 Gower..to make vp his rime would..write his terminant sillable with false orthographie. *Ibid.* III. xvi. 185 Your clauses in prose should neither finish with the same nor with the like terminants.

†**2.** Determining, defining. *Obs.*

1603 HOLLAND *Plutarch's Mor.* 1044 The terminant and defining power loveth the universall and indivisible. *a* **1610** HEALEY *Theophrastus* (1636) To Rdr., There being certaine properties almost in every language, which cannot, word for word, in terms terminant be expressed in another.

†**terminary** (ˈtɜːmɪnərɪ). *rare.* [ad. med.L. *terminārius* (in Du Cange) pertaining to the end or boundary, f. *termin-us* end: see -ARY. So F. *terminaire.*] A building or structure placed at the end of a walk or vista to terminate a view.

1790 W. WRIGHTE *Grotesque Archit.* Title-p., Hermitages, Terminaries, Chinese, Gothic, and Natural Grottos.

terminate (ˈtɜːmɪnət), *ppl. a.* [ad. L. *terminātus*, pa. pple. of *termināre*: see next.] Terminated, in various senses: see the verb.

1. a. Limited, bounded; ended, brought to an end; having a definite limit or limits; of determinate form or magnitude. (In early quots. const. as *pa. pple.*) Now *rare* or *Obs.*

1432–50 tr. *Higden* (Rolls) I. 79 Inde is terminate from the este with the rysenge of the sonne, of the sowthe with the occean [etc.]. **1639** G. DANIEL *Ecclus.* xli. 38 What if the vncertaine Date Of Mortalls in ten years be Terminate. **1645** DIGBY *Nat. Bodies* xxviii. § 1. 301 A terminate [*ed.* 1644 determinate] quantity or multitude of parts. **1750** tr. *Leonardus' Mirr. Stones* 35 Colour is the extremity of the perspicuous in a terminate body.

b. *Math.* Capable of being expressed in a finite number of terms; *esp.* of a decimal, not recurring or infinite; opp. to INTERMINATE 1 b. *rare.*

1882 OGILVIE, *Terminate*, a., capable of coming to an end; limited; bounded; as, a *terminate* decimal.

c. *Gram.* = TERMINATIVE *a.* 4 b. Also as *sb.* Restricted to the writings of G. O. Curme and a few others.

1931 G. O. CURME *Syntax* xix. 385 A large number of simple and compound verbs indicate an action *as a whole*. Such verbs are called terminates. *Ibid.* 386 The terminate aspect has relations also to the durative aspect. **1935** —— *Gram. Eng. Lang.* II. 206 The expanded form often represents the act as a whole, hence it has terminate force: 'I am sorry you doubt my statement. I *am telling* you the truth.' *Ibid.* 237 In terminates it [*sc.* the present participle] represents the act as a whole, as a fact. **1946** [see PROGRESSIVE *a.* 3 h]. **1972** M. L. SAMUELS *Linguistic Evol.* 161 If a terminate or point-action meaning was required for a majority of its occurrences in the preterite, the short vowel was preferred.

†**2.** Determined, decided. *Obs. rare.* (as *pa. pple.*)

1432–50 tr. *Higden* (Rolls) VII. 275 The pope decrete that mater to be terminate afore the kynge of Ynglonde and bischoppes.

†**3. a.** Directed to a specified object. *Obs. rare.*

1624 F. WHITE *Repl. Fisher* 283 Their worship is terminate in the verie Image.

†**b.** ? Directed to some point; having a definite direction in space. *Obs. rare.*

1676 H. MORE *Remarks* xxiii. 37, I demand, if the mobility of water upwards be not as intrinsick to it as downwards..? for where the water is rightly placed, it has no terminate motion at all.

terminate (ˈtɜːmɪneɪt), *v.* [f. L. *termindruāt-*, ppl. stem of *termināre* to limit, end, f. *termin-us* end, boundary.] **I.** Transitive senses.

†**1.** To determine; to state definitely. *Obs. rare.*

1589 NASHE *Anat. Absurd.* 18 Who made them so priuie to the secrets of the Almightie, that they should foretell the tokens of his wrath, or terminate the time of his vengeaunce. **1706** PHILLIPS, To *Terminate*,..to determine, or decide.

†**2.** To express in terms or words, to denominate. *Obs. rare*[−1].

1589 NASHE *Pref. Greene's Menaphon* (Arb.) 13 Which strange language of the firmament..makes vs that are not vsed to terminate heauens moueings in the accents of any voice, esteeme of their triobulare interpreter, as of some Thrasionical huffe snuffe.

3. a. To direct (an action) to something as object or end (cf. TERM *sb.* 1 c). Const. *in, to, upon.* In quot. 1599, To destine to a place. ? *Obs.* (Cf. sense 8.)

1599 NASHE *Lenten Stuffe* (1871) 73 Leander..they terminated to the unquiet, cold coast of Iceland. **1645** RUTHERFORD *Tryal & Tri. Faith* Ded. 12 The first opening of the eye-lids of God is terminated upon the breast of Christ. **1652** GAULE *Magastrom.* 127 Idolatrous worship came..to be terminated upon other inferior creatures. **1724** R. WELTON *Chr. Faith & Pract.* 188 When they terminate their thoughts upon secondary instruments. **1746–7** HERVEY *Medit.* (1818) 147 The niggardly wretch whose aims are all turned inward, and meanly terminated upon himself.

†**b.** Of a thing: To be the object of (an action).

1656 JEANES *Mixt. Schol. Div.* 81 This union..is wrought by the whole three persons, terminated unto the second person onely; that alone terminates suppositall, or personall dependance of the manhood. **1662** STILLINGFL. *Orig. Sacr.* III. i. § 3 An Idea..is nothing else but the objective being of a thing as it terminates the understanding. **1704** NORRIS *Ideal World* II. iii. 108 The ideas that terminate our thoughts (and which therefore are the only true objects of them).

4. a. To bring to an end, put an end to, cause to cease; to end (an action, condition, etc.).

1615 CHAPMAN *Odyss.* xx. 92 Her eyes Opened with teares, in care of her estate, Which now, her friends resolu'd to terminate To more delaies; and make her marry one. **1623** COCKERAM, *Terminate*, to end. **1732** ARBUTHNOT *Rules of Diet* in *Aliments*, etc. 304 [It] will sooner terminate the cold Fit. **1796** MME. D'ARBLAY *Camilla* IV. 277 She had every hope that this..would terminate every perplexity. **1855** MILMAN *Lat. Chr.* VIII. ix, They had assisted in terminating a disastrous schism which had distracted Christendom.

b. To come at the end of, form the conclusion of.

1798 SOPHIA LEE *Canterb. T.*, *Yng. Lady's T.* II. 497 Cold thanks for her civilities..terminated the visit. **1799** *Monthly Rev.* XXX. 345 We cannot also but approve the choice of passages..which terminate this publication.

c. In pregnant use: (*a*) to dismiss from employment; (*b*) to assassinate; ***to terminate with extreme prejudice***: see PREJUDICE *sb.* 1 c. *N. Amer. colloq.*

(*a*) **1973** *N.Y. Law Jrnl.* 25 July 13/1 The complainant had been discharged because of an unauthorized absence.. and..there was no probable cause to believe that he had been terminated in retaliation for having filed previous complaints against petitioners. **1976** M. MACHLIN *Pipeline* xviii. 228 If the boss didn't care for you very much in the first place, you could be terminated without having any appeal to the union. **1980** R. L. DUNCAN *Brimstone* ii. 36 Adamson's putting pressure on me to terminate you.

(*b*) **1975** N. LUARD *Robespierre Serial* iv. 27 A free-lance agent who'd been given a contract to terminate an individual the Service had declared hostile. **1981** T. BARLING *Bikini Red North* ii. 51 Haddad was terminated by persons unknown.

†**5.** To bring (something) to a stop, so that it extends no further; to put a limit or limits to; to restrict, confine *to* (*in*). *Obs.*

a **1628** PRESTON *New Covt.* (1634) 157 When a man will so enjoy these things that he can terminate his comfort in them. **1660** R. COKE *Power & Subj.* 80 Where it is not slavery, there the Masters powers is terminated to years, moneths, weeks, daies, or houres. **1674** HICKMAN *Hist. Quinquart.* (ed. 2) 118 Both creation and generation are terminated to substances.

6. To bound or limit spatially; to form the material extremity of; to be situated at the end of.

1634 SIR T. HERBERT *Trav.* 42 The South [of Guzerat] is terminated by the Sea. **1713** POPE *Guardian* No. 173 ¶ 5 (Odyss. VII. 168) Beds of all various herbs, for ever green, In beauteous order terminate the scene. **1746–7** HERVEY *Medit.* (1818) 103 On another side, the great deep terminates the view. **1797** *Encycl. Brit.* (ed. 3) XVII. 404/2 That which comes under the foremost beam of the gun-deck may terminate the fore part of the orlop. **1828** STARK *Elem. Nat. Hist.* II. 391 Abdomen..elongated, conical, terminated in the female by a long perforator. **1840** LARDNER *Geom.* 264 Two such semi-diameters..will be terminated at points holding corresponding positions in the elliptical quadrants.

7. †**a.** To give a definite border or outline to, render distinct, define (visual objects). *Obs. rare.*

1756 FRANKLIN in *Phil. Trans.* LV. 190 Distant objects appear distinct, their figures sharply terminated. **1762** MASKELYNE *ibid.* LII. 610 M. de la Caille had a refracting telescope..which..did not terminate objects distinctly.

b. To finish, complete. *rare.*

1825 CHALMERS in Hanna *Mem.* (1851) III. iv. 56 Our science is a rudimental and not a terminating one. **1857** J. S. HARFORD *Michael Angelo* I. xi. 245 During this interval of calm and prosperity, he [Michael Angelo] terminated two figures of slaves..in an incomparable style of art.

II. Intransitive senses (corresponding to *refl.* or *pass.* uses of those in I.).

8. To be directed to something as object or end.

1699 BURNET *39 Art.* xxii. (1700) 240 In the Presence of the King, all Respects terminate in his Person. **1856** DOVE *Logic Chr. Faith* Introd. § 6. 23 The other [says] 'My thoughts all terminate in God'. **1909** SIR O. LODGE *Ether of Space* App. III. 153 The free portion [of ether]..is not amenable to either mechanical or electric forces. They are transmitted by it, but never terminate upon it.

9. a. To come to an end (in space); *esp.* to have its end or extremity at a specified place, or of a specified form; to end *at, in,* or *with* something.

1644 EVELYN *Diary* 27 Feb., A spacious gravel walke terminating in a grotto. **1675** OGILBY *Brit.* Pref. 3 Ascending till it terminate at the Top of the..Scroll. **1769** COOK *Voy. round World* 24 Apr. I. x. (1773) II. 99 These hills..continued for about three miles more, and then terminated in a large plain. **1796** MORSE *Amer. Geog.* I. 227 Their tails terminate with a hard horny spur. **1862** STANLEY *Jew. Ch.* (1877) I. v. 107 The spot where the present gulf terminates. **1868** OWEN *Vertebr. Anim.* III. 414 The left extremity of the stomach is bifid, and terminates in two round cul-de-sacs.

b. Of a word: To end *in* (a letter or sound).

1824 L. MURRAY *Eng. Gram.* (ed. 5) I. iii. 84 Sometimes also, when the singular terminates in *ss*, the apostrophic *s* is not added: as, 'For goodness' sake'. **1865** *Pall Mall G.* 25 July 4/1 Greek compounds terminating in 'on' are very fashionable, and have a truly learned smack.

10. To come to an end, so as to extend no further; to have its end or terminus *in* something; †also, to be confined or restricted within specified limits.

1613 JACKSON *Creed* I. xxiv. § 5 The like fearful earthquakes..fell out in Trajan's time at Antioch; but the harms [did] not terminate within her territories or the cities about her. **1646** SIR T. BROWNE *Pseud. Ep.* 130 The testimonies of ancient Writers..are but derivative, and terminate all in one Aristeus. *a* **1677** HALE *Prim. Orig. Man.* 19 My Understanding doth truly conclude that all this vicissitude of things must terminate in a first cause of things. *a* **1784** JOHNSON in *Boswell* (1816) I. 23 The rod produces an effect which terminates in itself.

11. a. To come to an end (in time); to end, cease, conclude, close.

1789 J. WOODFORDE *Diary* 24 Mar. (1927) III. 91 His case is a violent Stranguary and if some remedy or other does not soon, very soon do good, it will terminate fatally to him. **1815** WORDSW. *Sonn.*, '*The fairest brightest hues*' 2 The sweetest notes must terminate and die. **1849** MACAULAY *Hist. Eng.* ix. II. 519 At length the repast terminated. **1872** YEATS *Techn. Hist. Comm.* 375 The Middle Ages may be said to terminate with the invention of printing.

b. To issue, result (*in* something): = END *v.*[1] 5 b.

1710 LUTTRELL *Brief Rel.* (1857) VI. 620 There has been a 2d battle in Spain, which terminated in favour of King Charles. **1775** J. BRYANT *Mythol.* II. 308 The fate of Semiramis terminated in her being turned into a pigeon. **1867** H. MACMILLAN *Bible Teach.* x. (1870) 204 A career of worldliness and sin terminates in impenitence and despair.

Hence **'terminating** *vbl. sb.* and *ppl. a.*
1656 tr. *Hobbes' Elem. Philos.* (1839) 179 Within the same terminating lines there can be no more than one plane superficies. **1776** WITHERING *Brit. Plants* (1796) II. 187 Lateral and terminating fruit stalks. **1807** HUTTON *Course Math.* II. 75 At 954, the end of the first line, the o denotes its terminating in the hedge. **1837** G. PHILLIPS *Syriac Gram.* 4 The addition of a terminating consonant.

termination (tɜːmɪˈneɪʃən). [ad. L. *terminātiōn-em*, n. of action f. *termināre* to TERMINATE; in some senses perh. a. OF. *termination* (13–14th c.).]

I. The action of terminating or fact of being determined (in various senses).

†**1.** The action of determining; determination, decision. *Obs.*
c **1450** in Aungier *Syon* (1840) 359 The abbes..schal make al the terminacions in the chirche. **1455-6** *Cal. Anc. Rec. Dublin* (1889) 290 Wythoute eny contradiccyon aftyr the termynacyon aforesayd. *a* **1625** FLETCHER *Love's Pilgr.* II. i, You can consider The want in others of these terminations, And how unfurnish'd they appear. **1660** R. COKE *Justice Vind.* Pref. 13 If I could not ultimately resolve the dictates of my reason..into plain places of Scripture, so well as any Geometrician would any proposition of Geometry into the principles of Euclid's elements; I would be content to let them wander for ever without any termination.

†**2.** Alleged name of some operation of alchemy.
1584 R. SCOT *Discov. Witchcr.* XIV. i, Their..amalgaming ..terminations, mollifications and indurations of bodies.

3. The action of ending. †**a.** Bounding, limiting, separation by spatial limits (*obs.*). **b.** Putting an end to; bringing to a close.
1604 R. CAWDREY *Table Alph.*, *Termination*, an ending,.. finishing or bounding. **1646** SIR T. BROWNE *Pseud. Ep.* 55 The water entring the body, begets a division of parts, and a termination of Atoms united before unto continuity. **1658** PHILLIPS, *Termination*,..a limiting, ending, or bounding. **1910** *Expositor* Oct. 290 Adultery alone justifies the termination of a marriage union.

c. *Chem.* and *Biochem.* The cessation of the building up of a polymer molecule. Freq. *attrib.*
1951 *Jrnl. Amer. Chem. Soc.* LXXIII. 5197/1 It is assumed in the case of tetrafluoroethylene polymerization initiated by inorganic free radicals that chain termination occurs by combination of a polymer radical with either another polymer radical or an initiator radical. **1967** MARGERISON & EAST *Introd. Polymer Chem.* v. 246 Termination may be brought about by many types of reagent. **1968** A. WHITE et al. *Princ. Biochem.* (ed. 4) xxix. 678 The mechanism by which these three codons accomplish chain termination and polypeptide release is not understood. **1978** HAYES & GEORGE in C. E. Carraher et al. *Organometallic Polymers* 16 In vinylferrocene polymerizations, the termination step is monomolecular. **1981** *Sci. Amer.* Aug. 63/2 Two proteins called termination factors are involved, and it appears that UAG, UAA and UGA all serve as termination codons: triplets on the mRNA that cause the ribosome to release the messenger and the newly synthesized protein.

d. The ending of a person's employment; dismissal. Chiefly *N. Amer.*
1961 *Wall St. Jrnl.* 23 Jan. 2/3 They qualify for termination payments and most are eligible for deferred pensions. **1982** *Chicago Sun-Times* 3 Dec. 89 He and fellow workers were informed of the terminations at 10:30 a.m. Wednesday and told to 'pack up and leave immediately'. **1983** M. EDWARDES *Back from Brink* iv. 56 In most cases we allowed the manager to 'resign' but in truth most of these people were dismissed, and were paid termination payments.

e. The ending of pregnancy before term by artificial means; an induced abortion.
1969 *Times* 3 July 7/6 Women denied a legal abortion commonly seek termination elsewhere. **1973** *Times* 26 Nov. 6/1 The pregnant women walking about the hospital ward were all in for abortions. Or terminations, as they called them— a much nicer word. **1978** F. WELDON *Praxis* xxiv. 256 You can't possibly go through with the pregnancy... If you don't have a termination, you're finished.

f. Assassination (*spec.* of an intelligence agent).
1975 N. LUARD *Robespierre Serial* v. 28 The escort role.. was one Carswell had carried out..before, although this was the first occasion where it involved a termination mission. **1980** [see PREJUDICE *sb.* 1 c]. **1983** G. MARKSTEIN *Ferret* 164 Terminations are no longer as fashionable as they were. Unless the top says so.

†**4.** Direction to something as an object or end; purpose: cf. END *sb.* 14. *Obs.*
?**16..** WHITE (J), It is not an idol *ratione termini*, in respect of termination; for the religious observation thereof is referred..to the honour of God and Christ.

II. The point or part in which anything ends.

5. a. End (in time), cessation, close, conclusion.
c **1500** *Melusine* xxiii. 156 Ermyne said she wold see first the termynacion of her faders syknes or she shuld procide ony ferther. **1658** SIR T. BROWNE *Hydriot.* iv. (1736) 31 Christians have handsomely glossed the Deformity of Death, by..civil Rites, which take off brutal Terminations. **1755** JOHNSON, *Termination*..3. End; conclusion. **1848** THACKERAY *Van. Fair* xliii, She abruptly put a termination to a flirtation which Lieutenant Stubble..had commenced. **1853** J. H. NEWMAN *Hist. Sk.* (1873) II. I. iv. 160 All human power has its termination sooner or later.

b. Outcome, issue, result: = END *sb.* 13.
1806 V. KNOX *Serm. Isa. xxviii. 16* Wks. 1824 VI. 393 A good commencement has ever been found..auspicious to a good progress and a happy termination. **1824** SCOTT *St. Ronan's* xxix, If they do not indeed drive her to suicide, which I think the most likely termination. **1884** *Manch. Exam.* 3 May 5/1 Dissensions which could hardly have other than a hostile termination.

6. The ending of a word; the final syllable, letter, or group of letters; *spec.* in *Gram.* a final element affixed to a word or stem to express some relation or modification of sense; an (inflexional or derivative) ending, a suffix.
1530 PALSGR. Introd. 27 In these syxe termynations endeth no masculyne adjectyve syngular. **1588** FRAUNCE *Lawiers Log.* I. xii. 50 b, The diuers fallinges and terminations of woords. **1614** SELDEN *Titles Hon.* Pref., Lar is but the Turkish termination plurall. *a* **1677** HALE *Prim. Orig. Man.* 165 Many times the *Literati* and *Scholares* coyn new Words, and sometimes..give Terminations and Idiotisms sutable to their Native Language, unto Words newly invented..out of other Languages. **1788** GIBBON *Decl. & F.* l. (1790) IX. 227 [Mecca] was known to the Greeks under the name of Macoraba;..the termination of the word is expressive of its greatness. **1845** STODDART in *Encycl. Metrop.* (1847) I. 108/1 The addition of an adverbial particle, like our prefix *a*, or termination, *ly*.

7. a. A limit, bound; an end, extremity (of a material object, or of a portion of space).
1755 JOHNSON, *Termination*..2. Bound; limit. **1828** WEBSTER s.v., The termination of a line. **1830** BOOTH *L'pool & Manch. Railw.* 42 To improve the termination of the line at the Liverpool end. **1860** TYNDALL *Glac.* I. xvii. 120 To trace the glacier to its termination. **1870** F. R. WILSON *Ch. Lindisf.* 101 At the west end is a bell-cot, with a pyramidal termination.

b. *pl.* Used for 'trousers' or 'breeches'.
1863 R. F. BURTON *Wand. W. Africa* I. 32 The men are in shirts, and long terminations, or femoralia.

†**8.** ? A term, word, expression. *Obs. rare.*
1599 SHAKS. *Much Ado* II. i. 255 Shee speakes poynyards, and euery word stabbes: if her breath were as terrible as [her] terminations, there were no liuing neere her.

termi'national, *a.* Chiefly *Gram.* [f. prec. + -AL[1].] Of, pertaining to, or forming a termination or terminations; closing, final (quot. 1874).
1824 L. MURRAY *Eng. Gram.* (ed. 5) I. 347 We seem to have the three great principles of accentuation; namely, the radical, the terminational, and the distinctive. **1861** CRAIK *Hist. Eng. Lit.* I. 33 It expressed the relations of nouns and verbs..by terminational or other modifications. **1862** W. P. DICKSON tr. *Mommsen's Hist. Rome* (1875) I. 12 The richer terminational system of the Greeks. **1874** T. HARDY *Far fr. Madding Crowd* vi, His superiority was marked enough to lead several ruddy peasants..to speak to him inquiringly,.. and to use 'Sir' as a terminational word.

terminative (ˈtɜːmɪneɪtɪv, -ətɪv), *a.* [ad. L. type **terminātīvus*: see TERMINATE *v.* and -ATIVE. Cf. F. *terminatif*.] Having the function of terminating (in various senses).

1. Forming a boundary or limit, bounding (? *obs.*); forming the termination or extremity of something.
1432-50 tr. *Higden* (Rolls) II. 51 The water of Thammyse ..was somme tyme as a cause terminative of men of Kente, of Este Saxones, West Saxones, and of men of the Marches. *Ibid.* 109 Mersee in Englische sowndethe as a see terminatiue [Higd. *terminans mare*], for hit disterminate[d] oon realme from an other. **1750** tr. *Leonardus' Mirr. Stones* 36 Some colour, which should be the terminative colour of the perspicuous and opaque.

†**2. a.** Constituting an end, final, ultimate; *esp.* constituting the ultimate object or end of some action (nearly = OBJECTIVE *a.* 1). *Obs.*
1624 F. WHITE *Repl. Fisher* 224 Neither is the Picture or Image..the terminatiue object of Loue..or Worship. **1681** FLAVEL *Meth. Grace* ix. 195 No duties or ordinances (which are but the wayes or means by which we come to Christ) are or ought to be central and terminative to the soul. **1694** R. BURTHOGGE *Reason & Nat. Spirits* 244 That the Soul is but a Mediate Subject while it is in the Body, and not a Terminative. **1701** NORRIS *Ideal World* I. v. 235 There can be no act of the Divine understanding above them [the Divine Ideas], but what must of necessity suppose them as the terminative forms of it.

†**b.** Directed to something as ultimate object.
1660 JER. TAYLOR *Duct Dubit.* II. ii. VI. §27 To take off this trifle of worship Relative and worship Terminative. **1679** C. NESSE *Antid. agst. Popery* 38 Their worship being not..terminative in the creature.

3. Bringing or coming to an end; finishing, concluding; conclusive; in *Path.* = TERMINAL *a.* 4 b.
a **1680** CHARNOCK *Sinfulness & Cure Th.* Sel. Wks. (1849) 109 Thoughts are inchoative in the fancy, consummative in the understanding, terminative in all the other faculties. **1813-21** BENTHAM *Ontology* ii. §9 Terminating or terminative motions. **1887** T. HARDY *Woodlanders* i, The interior, as seen through the window, caused him to draw up with a terminative air and watch. **1899** *Allbutt's Syst. Med.* VIII. 417 Cases of..old standing terminative dementia.

4. *Gram.* **a.** Denoting destination or direction towards.
1860 *Trans. Philol. Soc. 1857* 34 The declension of the personal pronouns [in the Tushi language] is as follows.. Nominative..Genitive..Comitative..Terminative. **1903** *Amer. Anthropologist* Jan.–Mar. 13 Besides a general locative some of the most frequently occurring [suffixes] are inessive, superessive, introessive, ablative, and terminative.

b. Applied to an aspect of a verb which denotes a completed action, or its completion.
1911 KRUISINGA & ERADES *Eng. Gram.* (1953) I. II. vii. 257 Verbs of a terminative character, that is such as express the final stage of an activity. **1924** O. JESPERSEN *Philos. Gram.* xx. 273 Lindroth for the first class uses the term 'successive' (with the subdivisions 'terminative' and 'resultative'.) **1930** B. TRNKA *Syntax Eng. Verb* 32 A differentiation between two series of aspects, the *ingressive*, *continuative* and *terminative* (resultative) on the one hand, and the *imperfective* and *perfective*, on the other... The former, common to both Slavonic and Germanic languages, express the ingressive, continuative and terminative stages of the verbal action. **1963** F. T. VISSER *Hist. Syntax Eng. Lang.* III. ii. 1372 There are three kinds [of verbs of aspect]: (1) of egressive or terminative aspect. **1984** *Eng. World-Wide* IV. 208 The *terminative* markers *gaan* and *kom*, which occur only with motion verbs in this *perfective* function, follow the main verb.

'terminatively, *adv.* [f. prec. + -LY[2].] In a terminative manner.

1. So as to terminate or form the end or extremity; in the way of a boundary or limit.
1570 DEE *Math. Pref.* *j, Though a Poynt be no Magnitude, yet Terminatiuely we recken it a thing Mathematicall..by reason it is..the end and bound of a line.

†**2.** In the way of direction to something as ultimate object; in relation to, or as, the object (nearly = OBJECTIVELY 1); ultimately. *Obs.*
1627 BP. HALL *Best Bargaine* Wks. 515 This truth, being the thing it selfe subiectiuely, in words expressiuely, in the minde of man terminatiuely. **1661** H. D. *Disc. Liturgies* 45 Some..Pagans..might terminatively worship the Sun and Moon, as thinking those noble Creatures were the very first movers and principles. **1664** JER. TAYLOR *Dissuas. Popery* I. ii. §11 (1686) 197 It [the worship] is terminatively to Christ or God, but relatively to the image. **1720-1** *Lett. fr. Mist's Jrnl.* (1722) II. 55 After which that eminent Person is neither terminatively, or relatively mentioned.

3. So as to terminate, i.e. come or bring to an end; finally; conclusively.
1891 T. HARDY *Tess* xvii, 'O—ay, as a lad I knowed your part o' the country very well', he said terminatively.

terminator (ˈtɜːmɪneɪtə(r)). [a. late L. *terminātor*, agent-n. f. *termināre* to TERMINATE.]

1. One who or that which terminates.
1846 WORCESTER, *Terminator*, he or that which terminates or bounds. **1890** *Illustr. Lond. News* 27 Dec. 810/2 The terminator of delights,..the desolator of abodes.

2. *Astron.* The line of separation between the illuminated and unilluminated parts of the disk of the moon or a planet.
1770 HORSLEY in *Phil. Trans.* LX. 435 *note*, A great circle passing through the poles of the terminator. **1868** LOCKYER *Elem. Astron.* III. xvi. (1879) 92 The terminator—the name given to the boundary between the lit-up and shaded portions [of the Moon]. **1876** G. F. CHAMBERS *Astron.* 69 Schröter found the terminator [of Venus] slightly concave.

3. *Biochem.* A sequence of polynucleotides that causes transcription to end and results in the release of the newly synthesized nucleic acid from the template molecule. Freq. *attrib.*
1969 *Biochemistry* VIII. 4897/1 Would chains bearing such a chain-growth terminator be susceptible to the hydrolytic and pyrophosphorolytic reactions? **1977** *World Bk. Sci. Ann. 1978* 249 To get the gene to work..certain controlling base sequences had to be added at each end. One end had to have a 'promoter' sequence so transcription could start; the other end had to have a 'terminator' sequence to stop transcription. **1978** *Nature* 30 Mar. 398/1 Analysis of several ρ-independent terminators has revealed that in every case termination occurs distal to a GC-rich region within a run of uridine residues.

'terminatory, *a. rare.* [See prec. and -ORY[2].] Forming the end or extremity; terminal.
1756 J. HILL *Hist. Plants* 156 (Jod.) The blite with spicated terminatory heads. **1775** J. JENKINSON *Descr. Brit. Pl.* Gloss. s.v., By a terminatory flower is meant the end flower. **1853** TH. ROSS *Humboldt's Trav.* III. xxx. 219 The terminatory point of the group of little mountains.

†**termine**, *sb. Obs.* Also termin. [ad. L. *terminus* boundary. Cf. OE. *termen*, OF. *termine* (12–14th c. in Godef.).] = TERM *sb.* in various senses: boundary, limit; end, extremity; limited time or period (in quot. 1609); in quot *a* 1625 = TERM *sb.* 2.
[*c* **1000** *Sax. Leechd.* III. 228 On þam teoðan stent se termen þæt ȝemære si hwylc hit si.]
1570 LEVINS *Manip.* 133/31 A Termin, bound, *terminus.* **1609** HEYWOOD *Brit. Troy* VI. xlix, Our great Englands Ihoue..Hath at their suite granted a termine Truce. **1616** [see TERMININE]. *a* **1625** FLETCHER *Bloody Brother* IV. ii, [The sun] hath his Termin In the degrees where she [the moon] is, and enjoys By that six dignities.

†**'termine**, *v. Obs.* Also 4–5 -yne, -yn, -ene. [a. F. *termine-r* (in Wace, 12th c.), ad. L. *termināre* to TERMINATE.]

1. *trans.* To determine, decide, settle. (With simple obj. or obj. cl.; also *absol.*)
a **1325** *MS. Rawl. B.* 520 lf. 30 b, þat alle þe quo warantes ben..iplaited ant itermined in Eyre of Iustises. **1382** WYCLIF *1 Sam.* xx. 33 Jonathas vnderstood, that it was fulli termyned of his fader, that Dauyd shulde be slayn. *a* **1400-50** *Alexander* 3979 Lat vs twa termyn þe taite be-twene vs alane. **1423** *Rolls of Parlt.* IV. 256 May inquere, here, and termine all the defautes. **1496** *Dives & Paup.* (W. de W.) IV. xxvii. 194/2 They wyll entermete them of euery cause..& termine euery cause by ther wytt. **1628** T. SPENCER *Logick* 47 By the forme the essence is termined vnto some speciall kinde. **1705** W. WALL *Hist. Inf. Bapt.* (1845) I. 464, I have not termined anything by definitive authority as if I would be the author of any dogma.

2. To state finally or definitely; to declare, affirm. (Const. as in 1.)
c **1420** LYDG. *Thebes* III. in *Chaucer's Wks.* (1561) 370/2 Thus selde is sen, the trouthe to termine That age and youth drawe by O line. **1426** —— *De Guil. Pilgr.* 22599 And off my ffyle to termyne, It is I-called Dyscyplyne. **1429** *Pol. Poems*

(Rolls) II. 144 Folwe discrecioun Of thy fader, . . plainly to termyne, Late hym by thy myrrour and thy guyde. *c* **1475** *Harl. Contin. Higden* (Rolls) VIII. 521 The fifthe Henry, of knyȝhtehode the lodesterre, Wyse and fulle manly, pleynly to termyne.

3. *trans.* To cause to end *in* or *at* something; *intr.* to end *in* or *at* something: = TERMINATE *v.* 3, 8.

1634 Bp. Hall *Contempl., N.T.* iv. v, How absurd had these guests been, if they had termined the thanks in the servitors; and had said, 'We have it from you; whence ye had it, is no part of our care'. **1639** N. N. tr. *Du Bosq's Compl. Woman* i. 18 The other goodly qualities . . all termine in Conversation, as in their Center. *Ibid.* ii. 38 All their travell termines at voluptuousnesse. **1668** Culpepper & Cole *Barthol. Anat.* i. 26 Arising from the Cæcum, is termined in the Rectum.

4. *trans.* To set bounds to, bound; to define, outline; usually in *pass.* to be bounded, have its limit or end: = TERMINATE *v.* 6.

1398 Trevisa *Barth. De P.R.* xix. ii. (1495) 862 Clere thynge well termined [*Bodley MS.* lf. 291/1 ytermyned] is the matere of colour. **1555** Eden *Decades* 269 Towarde the west & north it is termined with an vnknowen ende of landes & seas. **1625** N. Carpenter *Geog. Del.* i. v. (1635) 99 An imaginary point, conceiued in a magnitude deuoyde of all quantity, yet bounding and termining all Magnitudes.

b. To confine or enclose within something.

1477 Norton *Ord. Alch.* v. in Ashm. *Theat. Chem. Brit.* (1652) 66 The shining of Gould is caused . . Of pure and subtile Water termined full well. *Ibid.*, For of a Mirrour the cause none other is, But moisture termined, as all Clerks gesse. **1631** J. Done *Polydoron* 51, I find in the most centrall and Terrestriall (that is) the Metalline bodies their life is termined, shut, imprisoned within themselues.

5. To bring to an end; to end, finish, conclude: = TERMINATE *v.* 4.

1390 Gower *Conf.* I. 168 Which to mi ladi stant enclined, And hath his love noght termined. *c* **1400** *Laud Troy Bk.* 9629 The trewes is passed and alle termened, And alle ben redy. *c* **1460** *Towneley Myst.* xxviii. 207 When he had termynd that fight he skypt outt of his wede. *c* **1500** *Melusine* xxii. 149 Before my dayes be termyned. *a* **1618** Sylvester *New Hierusalem* 75 For, Death is dead, Time termined, Corruption conquer'd clean.

b. To form the end or termination of: cf. TERMINATE *v.* 4 b.

c **1532** Du Wes *Introd. Fr.* in *Palsgr.* 933 They [verbs] be all termined with the above sayd termination. **1552** Huloet, Poynte terminynge a sentence, *comma*.

Hence †ˈ**termining** *vbl. sb.*

c **1430** *Pilgr. Lyf Manhode* iv. lxiii. (1869) 206 Deth . . which is þe ende of alle eerthliche thinges, and þe termininge.

terminer[1], in *oyer and terminer*: see OYER.

†ˈ**terminer**[2]. *Obs.* Also 5 termynour. [a. AF. *terminour* = F. *termineur* (13th c. in Godef.), agent-n. from *terminer* to TERMINE.] **a.** One who or that which terminates, ends, or limits. **b.** One who or that which determines or decides.

[*a* **1400** Langl. *P. Pl.* C. iv. 109 [see TERMISON quot.].] **1496** *Dives & Paup.* (W. de W.) vii. xv. 301/2 Consuetude or custome in lawe posytyue . . is expostour & termynour of the lawe. **1675** Woodhead, etc. *Paraphr. St. Paul* 38 The terminer and bound; the scope and aim; the perfection and accomplisher.

†ˈ**terminine.** *Obs. rare*$^{-1}$. ? Error for *termining*, or extended form of TERMINE *sb.*

c **1590** Marlowe *Faust.* vi. 42 One axletree, Whose terminine [*ed.* 1616 termine] is termd the worlds wide pole.

terminism (ˈtɜːmɪnɪz(ə)m). [mod. f. L. *terminus* end, limit + -ISM. So F. *terminisme*, G. *terminismus*.] **a.** *Philos.* The doctrine that universals are mere terms or names: = NOMINALISM b. **b.** *Theol.* The doctrine (maintained by Reichenberg at Leipzig in the 17th c.) that God has appointed a definite term or limit in the life of each individual, after which the opportunity for salvation is lost. So ˈ**terminist** (cf. med.L. *terminista*), one who holds or maintains terminism (in either sense); hence **termiˈnistic** *a.*

1727–41 Chambers *Cycl.*, *Terminists, Terministæ*, a sect or party among the Calvinists. **1758** Jortin *Erasmus* I. 335 *note*, The Terminists were Sectaries in the high Schools. . . They oppose the Thomists, the Scotists, and the Albertists: they are also called Occamists. **1764** Maclaine tr. *Mosheim's Eccl. Hist.* xv. ii. i. §7 The Realists maintained a manifest superiority over the Nominalists, to whom they also gave the appellation of Terminists. **1860** Gardner *Faiths of World*, *Terministic controversy*, a dispute which arose towards the end of the seventeenth century on the question, Whether God has fixed a *terminus gratiæ*, or determinate period in the life of an individual, within which he may repent. . . Those who agreed with Reichenberg received the name of *Terminists*. **1878** S. H. Hodgson *Philos. Reflection* I. i. 66 Nominalism . . in its later shape, in which it is opposed to Conceptualism and is then more properly to be called *Terminism*. **1882–3** *Schaff's Encycl. Relig. Knowl.* III. 2317 (heading) Terminism and the terministic controversy.

terminize (ˈtɜːmɪnaɪz), *v. rare.* [f. L. *terminus* TERM + -IZE.] *trans.* To supply with terms; to furnish a nomenclature for.

1899 *Army & Navy Jrnl.* 19 Aug. 1221 (Cent. Supp.) The adoption [in French] of so many English words, a condition that is paralleled in the terminizing of sports, such as football and bicycling, which crossed the Channel southward.

terminology (tɜːmɪˈnɒlədʒɪ). [mod. f. L. *termin-us*, in its med.L. sense 'term' + -LOGY: used in Ger. 1786 by Prof. C. G. Schütz of Jena: see *Kant's Briefwechsel* (1900) I. 446; so *terminologisch* 1788.] Etymologically, The doctrine or scientific study of terms; in use almost always, The system of terms belonging to any science or subject; technical terms collectively; nomenclature.

1801 *Med. Jrnl.* V. 587 Mr. Nemnich, of Hamburg, will shortly publish a complete Nosological Dictionary. . . It is to consist of two parts, in the first of which the Latin terminology will be given, and in the second, the dictionary of the above languages, relating to diseases, with a Latin explanation. **1815** Kirby & Sp. *Entomol.* (1843) I. Pref. 11 In the terminology or what, to avoid the barbarism of a word compounded of Latin and Greek, they would beg to call the orismology of the science. **1837** Whewell *Hist. Induct. Sc.* (1857) III. 258, I designate as Terminology the system of terms employed in the description of objects of natural history. **1847** Lewes *Hist. Philos.* (1867) II. 452 Kant, who . . gave old ideas a novelty by giving them a new terminology. **1854** S. Thomson *Wild Fl.* iii. (1861) 146 Some knowledge . . of botanical terms—Terminology—is requisite. **1880** Huxley *Crayfish* 14 Every calling has its technical terminology.

Hence ˌ**terminoˈlogical** *a.*, pertaining to terminology; ***terminological inexactitude***, a humorous expression for a falsehood; ˌ**terminoˈlogically** *adv.*; **termiˈnologist**, one versed in terminology.

1861 F. Winslow *Obsc. Dis. Brain & Mind* iii. (ed. 2) 36 Who can only distinguish terminologically and locally the coarser wheels of this piece of intellectual clockwork. **1894** *Pall Mall G.* 1 Nov. 3/1 A winding road ankle deep in mud . . called Orchard-street. Why an orchard was so persistently associated with this God-forsaken region is a question a terminologist only can answer. **1906** W. Churchill *Sp. Ho. Com.* 22 Feb., It could not . . be classified as slavery . . in the extreme acceptance of the word, without some risk of terminological inexactitude. **1907** *Month* July 57 Lynx-eyed censors, keenly on the look out for the least hint of terminological inexactitude. **1926** Fowler *Mod. Eng. Usage* 444/1 *Polysyllabic humour*. . . Of the long as distinguished from the abstruse, *terminological inexactitude* for lie or falsehood is a favourable example, but much less amusing at the hundredth than at the first time of hearing. **1940** C. Milburn *Diary* 19 July (1979) 49, I can't think . . why he [*sc.* Hitler] does not choke himself with his 'terminological inexactitudes'! **1976** A. Price *War Game* i. viii. 159 It all adds up to a little terminological inexactitude——he was lying through his goddamn teeth.

terminus (ˈtɜːmɪnəs). Pl. termini (-aɪ). [L., = end, limit, boundary; also as in sense 2.]

†**1.** *Math.* = TERM *sb.* 11. *Obs. rare.*

1571 Digges *Pantom.* ii. xx. Q iv, When anye proportion is geuen, there are two Numbers wherewithall it is expressed, and they are called *Termini*.

2. *Anc. Rom. Myth.* (With initial capital.) The deity who presided over boundaries or landmarks.

1600 Holland *Livy* i. lv. 38 The seat and house of Terminus was not stirred, and he the god alone that was not displaced and called forth of the limits to him consecrated. **1638** Sir T. Herbert *Trav.* (ed. 2) 15 This land is the furthest part of the old knowne world, god Terminus here especially triumphing.

3. A statue or bust of, or resembling those of, the god Terminus; also, the pedestal of such a statue: see TERM *sb.* 15. Sometimes, a boundary post or stone.

1645 Evelyn *Diary* 1 Mar., Statues and antiquities . . amongst which is . . a Terminus that formerly stood in the Appian Way. **1754** *Phil. Trans.* XLVIII. 822 At the several angles of the square was a terminus of marble. **1758** J. Kennedy *Curios. Wilton House* (1786) 3 Such Termini were set at their Doors without, as the Limits and Boundaries of their houses. **1842–76** Gwilt *Archit.* iii. i. §2686 What is called a *terminus*, which is, in fact, nothing more than a portion of an inverted obelisk.

4. a. The point to which motion or action tends, goal, end, finishing-point; sometimes that from which it starts; starting-point. = TERM *sb.* 1 c.

a **1617** Bayne *On Eph.* (1658) 42 This condition belongeth not to the chusing but to the terminus to life. **1651** tr. *Life Father Sarpi* (1676) 86 That perfection . . is the very Terminus whereunto the Church, and every faithful man ought to pretend. **1668** Wilkins *Real Char.* iii. iii. 310 Some of these are Absolutely determined, either to Motion, or to Rest, or the Terminus of motion. **1868** Lever *Bramleighs of Bp.'s Folly* I. xviii. 271, I go straight to my terminus, wherever it is.

b. *esp.* in phr. ***terminus a quo*** (= 'term from which'); also used *spec.* in dating to indicate the starting-point of a period; also ***terminus ad quem*** (= 'term to which'); similarly ***terminus ante quem***, ***terminus post quem*** (= 'term before which', 'term after which') used to indicate the finishing- or starting-point of a period; also *ellipt.*, as ***terminus ante***, ***terminus post***.

[*terminus a quo, ad quem* are phrases originating in Scholastic L.: *a* 1250 in Albertus Magnus, *Phys.* 5. 2. 2; also in Aquinas, Roger Bacon, Duns Scotus, etc.]

a **1555** Cranmer *Lord's Supper* (Parker Soc.) 272 In nutrition *terminus a quo* is the hunger and thirst of the man; and *terminus ad quem* is the feeding and satisfying of his hunger and thirst. **1618** T. Adams *Vict. Patience* Wks. 1861 I. 96 So there is *terminus à quo*, from whence we are freed; and *terminus ad quem*, to which we are exalted. **1905** J. R. Harris *Guiding Hand of God* vii. 107, I do not regard death . . as a terminus, but more and more as a starting-point. . . It is a *terminus a quo* and not a *terminus ad quem*. **1906** *Hibbert Jrnl.* Jan. 270 The *terminus ad quem*, or the end whither the theological movement of our age tends. **1930** A. H. Krappe *Sci. Folklore* i. 14 Generally speaking . . a *terminus ante quem* is furnished by the oldest European historical variant. **1936** *Burlington Mag.* Aug. 75/1 The dress the king is wearing did not become fashionable before 1796, a fact which indicates a *terminus post quem*. **1939** *Ibid.* May 218/1 The *termini post* and *ante* of the glass, thus given by the birth of Charles (1500) and the death of Philip (1506). **1953** R. J. C. Atkinson *Field Archæol.* vi. 166 It must be clearly understood that these *termini post* and *ante quem* are the closest that the archæologist can get (at least with present methods of research) to an absolute date. **1968** *English Studies* XLIX. 455 The chapter . . provides a good survey of the evidence . . that seems to point to a date around 1200 as the most probable date of composition. However, the *terminus a quo* (1193) that is suggested . . on p. 19, seems quite unwarranted. **1973** *Nature* 9 Nov. 77/1 These dates . . merely provide, however, a *terminus post quem* for the valley deepening and widening during which cavern opening occurred. **1974** *Bodleian Library Rec.* Dec. 174 Such evidence clearly establishes for the annotations a *terminus a quo* of 1602. **1978** *Maledicta* II. 243, I must now propose 1888 as a conservative *terminus ante quem* for that species, and the evidence at that date points back considerably farther.

5. A boundary, limit. *rare.*

1673 Ray *Journ. Low C.* 122 These Sutures I found . . to be the *Termini* or boundings of certain Diaphragms or partitions, which seemed to divide the Cavity of the Shell into a multitude of . . Cells. **1818** Hallam *Mid. Ages* (1872) II. vii. ii. 233 The retrocession of the Roman terminus under Adrian.

6. a. The end of a line of railway; also, the station at the end; the place at which a tramline, bus route, etc. ends. (The common current sense.)

1836 *Mech. Mag.* XXV. 317 Perhaps it would be well to substitute the plain English *termination* for the Latin *terminus*. **1837** R. Alderson in *Papers Corps Engineers* II. 94 Both lines commence from the same terminus. **1841** *Penny Cycl.* XX. 272/1 A class of buildings that have sprung up of late years, namely railway termini. **1848** Longf. in *Life* (1891) II. 137 Long walk . . to the railway terminus on the sea-shore. **1877** *Tramways Intelligence* 17 The lines of the company have their London termini at Westminster Bridge-road, Blackfriars-road. **1878** F. S. Williams *Midl. Railw.* 226 The . . competition that arises from the working of two independent routes between the same termini. **1886** C. E. Pascoe *London of To-day* xix. (ed. 3) 192 Hand-bills and time-tables to be easily had at any terminus or railway booking-office in London. **1936** J. B. Priestley *They walk in City* iii. 39 The tram was full, but they pushed their way in. . . By the time they had arrived at the terminus in Gladstone Lane . . a few drops [of rain] were falling. *Ibid.* iv. 85 Taking a bus as far as the edge of the moors, walking over to some place where he could get tea, then walking back to the terminus again. **1975** R. L. Beals *Peasant Marketing System of Oaxaca* i. 9. Around the peripheries of the district are the termini of most of the bus lines.

attrib. **1908** *Westm. Gaz.* 12 Mar. 10/2 With the coming of railways . . came terminus hotels, many of which were now palatial.

b. *transf.* or *gen.* An end, extremity; the point at which something comes to an end.

1855 Bain *Senses & Int.* i. ii. §8 (1864) 30 The grey matter [of the brain] is a terminus; to it the fibrous collections tend, or from it commence. **1860** Tyndall *Glac.* i. xxiii. 160 The . . glacier pushes its huge terminus right across the valley. **1888** Goode *Amer. Fish* 36 It is frequently found far above the terminus of the tide. **1891** *Cent. Dict.*, *Terminus*. . . 6. The point to which a vector carries a given or assumed point. **1906** *Blackw. Mag.* May 461/2 The rugged terminus of England seems to possess a charm of its own.

†**termison.** *Obs. rare*$^{-1}$. In 5 -yson, -isoun. [app. an imperfect adaptation of F. *terminaison*, TERMINATION.] = TERMINATION 6.

1393 Langl. *P. Pl.* C. iv. 409 An adjectif Of þre trewe termysons [*MS. M.* terminours].

termite (ˈtɜːmaɪt). [ad. L. *termes, termit-em*: see TERMES. So F. *termite* (Dict. Acad. 1835).

In early use always in pl. *termites*, orig. the L. plural, in 3 syllables, of *termēs*, but at length treated as Eng. and Fr. pl. in 2 syllables, whence singular *termite*: cf. -ITE 2.]

1. A pseudoneuropterous social insect of the genus *Termes* or family *Termitidæ*, chiefly tropical, and very destructive to timber; also called *white ant*.

1781 Smeathman in *Phil. Trans.* LXXI. 160 These turret nests, built by two different species of Termites. **1815** Kirby & Sp. *Entomol.* ix. (1818) I. 261 None of them do their business so expeditiously or effectually as the Termites. **1859** R. F. Burton *Centr. Afr.* in *Jrnl. Geog. Soc.* XXIX. 178 They [ant-hills] are generally built by the termite under some shady tree, which prevents too rapid drying. **1880** *Even. Standard* 3 Apr. 4/3 The whole village is said to be infested with the termite, which in the head resembles greatly the ant. . . It attacks woodwork, which it eats away.

2. *transf.* (with reference to the destructiveness of the insect).

1943 in S. J. Baker *Austral. Lang.* (1945) 245 The secretary of the party said 'We can't say too much; there are termites about.' **1949** Koestler *Promise & Fulfilment* ii. v. 282 One delegation would immediately settle down to silent termite work. **1951** *Economist* 8 Dec. 1402/2 'Any man who betrays the people's trust in a public office is a public enemy . .' declared the new chairman . . calling on his fellow members to punish the 'termites' relentlessly. **1961** A. Maund *Worthy Termites* ii. 22 'So you want me to police Great Port for woodpiles which might have somebody besides nigras under them,' Ed said. 'Yes. Look for the *termites*.'

3. *attrib.* and *Comb.*, as ***termite ant***; ***termite-proof*** adj.; **termite heap, mound** = *termite hill*; **termite-hill**, a conical mound constructed as a nest by termites.

1849 *Sk. Nat. Hist., Mammalia* IV. 208 The Great Ant-eater, or Ant-bear... The limbs are..furnished with huge hook-like claws well adapted for making forcible entrance into the solid dwellings of the termite ants. **1910** *Dundee Advertiser* 25 Nov. 6 The athletes had to..jump from a small termite heap. **1920** *Blackw. Mag.* Feb. 205/1 Several enormous termite heaps. **1871** TYLOR *Prim. Cult.* II. xv. 187 Rivers, lakes, and springs,..termite-hills, trees. **1977** 'J. McVEAN' *Bloodspoor* x. 96 Haston was lying by a termite mound. **1934** WEBSTER, Termite-proof. **1937** *Discovery* Feb. 63/1 Care must be taken to ensure that the timber work is termite-proof. **1971** *Guardian* 18 Nov. 15/1 The immediate problem is to make sure such a building is termite proof.

Hence **termitary** ('tɜːmɪtərɪ) [-ARY[1] B. 2], a termites' nest; also fig. and in mod.L. form **termi'tarium** [-ARIUM]; **termitic** (tə'mɪtɪk) *a.*, of, pertaining to, or formed by termites; **termitid** ('tɜːmɪtɪd), **termitine** ('tɜːmɪtaɪn) *a.*, belonging to the *Termitidæ*; *sb.* an insect of this family, a termite; **termitophagous** (-'ɒfəgəs) *a.* [Gr. -φαγος eating], feeding upon or devouring termites; **termitophilous** (-'ɒfɪləs) *a.* [Gr. φίλος loving], inhabiting the nests of termites, as certain beetles; so **'termitophile**, a termitophilous insect.

1863 BATES *Nat. Amazon* II. i. 63 The endless ramified galleries of which a *Termitarium is composed. **1934** *Discovery* Nov. 308/2 A big termitarium..must contain a population of seven million, or even more. **1971** *World Archaeology* III. 124 The large refuse filled pit near the adult burials is at the site of a termitarium dug cut for building material. **1981** *Atlantic Monthly* July 49 The nearest thing to a termitarium that I can think of in human behavior is the making of a language, which we do by keeping at each other all our lives,..changing the structure by some sort of instinct. **1826** KIRBY & SP. *Entomol.* IV. xlix. 478 The formicary, the *termitary, the vespiary, and the bee-hive send forth their thousands. **1901** *Jrnl. R. Microsc. Soc.* 32 The Cicindelids select the termitaries as sunny places well suited for play and for hunting. **1935** *Times* 11 Feb. 14/2 Man as a personality is destined to be a free citizen in a free world, not an ant in some human termitary. **1937** *Discovery* Sept. 292/2 One must consider a termitary as a single animal. **1955** J. B. PRIESTLEY in Priestley & Hawkes *Journey down Rainbow* xii. 177 I'd rather stand on the pavement and eat a sandwich than lunch in that underground termitary. **1961** L. MUMFORD *City in History* i. 6 The social functions of the beehive, the termitary, and the ant-hill..have indeed..many resemblances to those of the city. **1977** *Time* 10 Oct. 51/2 But they linger on paper as the dream architecture of the 20th century. Because these termitaries were never built, they could not be destroyed. **1881** PINTO *How I crossed Africa* I. v. 121 A soil..of *termitic formation. **1898** E. P. EVANS *Evol. Ethics* vi. 211 An advanced state of termitic civilization. **1899** *Camb. Nat. Hist.* VI. 171 One member of this genus [Leptogenys] is of *Termitophagous habits. **1922** *Termitophile [see PHYSOGASTRISM]. **1971** E. O. WILSON *Insect Societies* vi. 111/2 Termitophiles, often species-specific and highly modified. **1886** SCHWARZ in *Proc. Entom. Soc. Washington* I. 160 In North America only a few *termitophilous species have hitherto been observed.

termitologist (ˌtɜːmaɪ'tɒlədʒɪst). [f. TERMITE + -OLOGIST.] One who studies termites.

1936 *Times* 9 June 10/3 Dr. Noyes, of California—a celebrated termitologist—writes doubtfully of *Zootermopsis*. **1971** E. O. WILSON *Insect Societies* vi. 106/2 Termitologists had long looked to the Mesozoic or beyond for traces of a truly archaic termite fauna.

termless ('tɜːmlɪs), *a.* [f. TERM *sb.* + -LESS.]

1. Having no term or limit; boundless, endless.

c **1586** C'TESS PEMBROKE *Ps.* LXXXIX. xii, In tearmlesse turnes, my tearmlesse truth assuring. **1596** SPENSER *Hymn Heavenly Love* 75 Ne hath their day, ne hath their blisse, an end, But there their termelesse time in pleasure spend. **1652** BENLOWES *Theoph.* IV. xl, That pen was dipt i'ith Standish of thy Blood Which wrot th' Indenture of our termlesse Good! **1851** RUSKIN *Mod. Paint.* I. II. IV. iii. §14 The same ..laws which require perfect simplicity of mass, require infinite and termless complication of detail.

2. Incapable of being expressed by terms; inexpressible, indescribable. *poet.* (Cf. PHRASELESS.)

1597 SHAKS. *Lover's Compl.* 94 His phenix downe began but to appeare Like vnshorne veluet, on that termlesse skin.

3. Not dependent on or limited by any terms or conditions; unconditional.

1902 *Westm. Gaz.* 14 Oct. 1/3 Not a peace by interruption of hostilities; but the simple, unconditioned, termless peace supplied by a 'fight to the finish'.

termly ('tɜːmlɪ), *a.* [f. TERM *sb.* + -LY[1]; cf. *daily*, *weekly*, *monthly*.] Occurring every term or at fixed terms; periodical; *esp.* paid or due every recurrent term or at fixed terms. Now freq., occurring every academic term.

1598 LAMBARDE *Alienations* in *Bacon's Wks.* (1879) I. 595/1 The clerks are partly rewarded by that mean also [petty fees] for their..writings, besides that termly fee which they are allowed. **1695** *Sc. Acts Will. III*, c. 64 (1822) IX. 459/2 Men..who..earn their living by daily wages or by termly hire. **1829** SCOTT *Rob Roy* Introd., Chapel Errock, where the tenants of the Duke were summoned to appear with their termly rents. **1852** HANNA *Mem. Chalmers* IV. xvii. 329 Termly subscriptions for the support of the ministers..were obtained. **1969** T. FAWTHROP in Cockburn & Blackburn *Student Power* 101 There should be a variety of means by which assessment is arrived at: from termly work standards to dissertations. **1970** M. JONES *Ducal Brittany* vi. 166 The termly sums demanded from individual parishes were always the same. **1983** *Bull. Univ. Coll. London* May 8/2 A termly whole-day inter-disciplinary seminar is proposed.

'termly, *adv.* [f. as prec. + -LY[2].] Term by term; every term, or at fixed terms; periodically.

1484 *Exch. Rolls Scotl.* IX. 284 *note*, To be pait therof yerely and termely at the termes foresaidiis. **1598** LAMBARDE *Alienations* in *Bacon's Wks.* (1879) I. 595/1 The fees, or allowances, that are termly given to these deputies, receiver, and clerks, for recompence of these their pains. **1685** *Act of Supply* (Edin.) in *Lond. Gaz.* No. 2036/3 Payable at two Terms, viz. Whitsonday and Mertimas each year, beginning at Whitsonday next..and soforth termly. **1818** SCOTT *Rob Roy* ii, I would..put it in order for you termly, or weekly, or daily.

termon ('tɜːmən) *Irish Hist.* [a. OIrish *termonn* (*Annals of Ulster*, 810, 830), mod.Ir. *tearmann*, 'church-territory or -liberties, privilege, sanctuary, protection', ancient adaptation of L. *terminus* 'limit, bound'; cf. the use of Ir. *crich* 'finis, terminus', in the sense 'territory', L. *fines*.] Anciently in Ireland, Land belonging to, or forming the precinct or liberties of a religious house, which was free and exempt from all secular charges or imposts; church land. Hence **termon-land**, church land; **'termoner, termon-man** (Ir. *tearmannach*), a tenant of church land.

1533 *St. Papers Hen. VIII*, II. 164 That no Inglish lorde ..make any bande or covenaunte with any Irishman to have right ought of him, or bering of men of warre, or termons, to his awne use. **1537** *Calr. Carew MSS.* 116 Termoners. **1607** DAVIES *1st Let. to Earl Salisbury* Tracts (1787) 233 The rest of the spiritual lands, which the Irish call *Termons*, they were granted to sundry servitors. *Ibid.* 247 Termon doth signify, in the Irish tongue, a liberty, or freedom, and..all Church-lands whatsoever are called Termon-lands by the Irish. *Ibid.* 248 Glebe-lands, the tenants..whereof were called Termon men, and had privilege of clergy. **1764** W. HARRIS tr. *Ware's Antiq. Ireland* II. I. xxxv. 233 To him [the Erenach or Herenach] also and to his Family were antiently appropriated Lands called *Termon-Lands*, as being Lands freed and discharged from all Secular Impositions, but which were liable to certain Pensions and refections, payable yearly to the Bishop. **1848** O'DONOVAN tr. *Ann. Irel.* 1229 All the termoners of the province. **1890** J. HEALY *Insula Sanct.* 275 He plundered Clonmacnoise and its termon lands three times.

termor ('tɜːmə(r)). *Law.* Also 4 -ur, 6–7 -our, -er. [a. AF. *termer*, f. *terme*, TERM: see -ER[2]. In med.L. *terminārius* (Du C.).] One who hold lands or tenements for a term of years, or for life; one who has a term (TERM *sb.* 6).

[**1292** BRITTON II. xxxii. §4 Sicum en cas ou le chief seignur engette termers.] *a* **1325** *MS. Rawl. B.* 520 lf. 72 þe prou þerof were þe termurres. **1529** *Act 13 Hen. VIII*, c. 15 §1 The same Leasors..have..put the same Termers from their said Terms. **1598** KITCHIN *Courts Leet*, etc. (1675) 89 Glass fixt by the Termor, the Lessor cannot distrain for his Rent. *a* **1631** DONNE *To R. Woodward* xi, Wee are but termers of our selues, yet may, If we can stocke our selues, and thriue, uplay Much, much deare treasure for the great rent day. **1818** CRUISE *Digest* (ed. 2) I. 500 When terms for years became fully established, and the interest of the termor was secured against the effect of fictitious recoveries, long terms for years were frequently created.

termorrer (tə'mɒrə(r)), repr. vulgar or dial. pronunc. of TOMORROW *adv.* and *sb.* Cf. TER.

1898 J. D. BRAYSHAW *Slum Silhouettes* 118 That's ninepence I owes Newsy: must pay that or there won't be no papers to start wiv ter-morrer. **1932** S. GIBBONS *Cold Comfort Farm* xii. 178 Ter-day's dinner... Ter-morrer's too, for all I know. **1974** P. CAVE *Mama* (new ed.) iv. 28 Adolph slipped the merchandise into his pocket. 'I'll do it termorrer,' he vowed.

'term-time. The time of term.

a. The period during which the law-courts are in session; the period of study at a univeristy or school: see TERM *sb.* 5.

1426 *Rolls of Parlt.* V. 408/2 That oute of Terme tyme, nothyng be spedd in the Counsaille. **1435** *Ibid.* I. 491/1 All the high Courtes..been sette and holden..duryng all the four terme tymes of the yere. **1562–3** *Act 5 Eliz.* c. 23 §2 One Writ of Capias..returneable in the same Courte, in the Terme tyme. **1600–12** ROWLANDS *Four Knaves* (Percy Soc.) 6 A country blew-coate serving man, In tearme-time sent to towne. **1721** AMHERST *Terræ Fil.* No. 47 (1754) 251 The heads of colleges and halls..are obliged to assemble..every monday throughout the year, in vacation-time as well as in term-time. **1849** THACKERAY *Pendennis* xxix, In term-time Mr. Pen showed a most praise-worthy regularity in..eating his dinners in Hall.

b. In Scotland, the time or season of either term, Whitsuntide or Martinmas.

Mod. The rent payable at term-time.

tern (tɜːn), *sb.*[1] Also 7 terne. [Of Norse origin: cf. Da. *terne*, Sw. *tärna*, Norw. and Færo. *terna*:—ON. *þerna*, the tern or sea swallow.

Some consider *tern* to be related to *stearn*, *stern*, which occurs in OE. as a bird-name, and, in the form *starn*, is a name in E. Anglia of the Common and the Black Tern; it is mentioned by W. Turner *Avium præcipuarum historia*, 1544, as 'nostrati lingua *sterna* appellata', whence Linnæus took *Sterna* as a generic name.]

The common name of a group of sea-birds of the genus *Sterna*, or sub-family *Sterninæ*, akin to the gulls, but having generally a more slender body, long pointed wings, and a forked tail; a sea swallow.

Of the species, which are widely diffused from Arctic to extreme southern coasts, the British Museum Catalogue reckons more than 50, of which 33 are placed in the genus *Sterna*, and about 18 distributed in ten other genera. Of these, six are considered indigenous to the British coasts, and many more to those of N. America. The Common Tern of Britain and N. America is *Sterna hirundo* (or *fluviatilis*); the Sandwich T., the largest British species, now scarce, is *S. cantiaca*; the Arctic T., *S. macrura*; the Roseate T., *S. dougalli*; the Little T., *S. minuta*; the Black Tern, *Hydrochelidon* (formerly *Sterna*) *nigra*.

1678 RAY *Willughby's Ornith.* 352 This [Black Tern, *Sterna nigra*] is also the brown Tern of Mr. Johnson. *Ibid.* 353 In the Northern parts they call them Terns, whence Turner calls them in Latine, *Sternæ*. **1785** LATHAM *Gen. Syn.* III. II. 356 Sandwich Tern... This species is pretty common on the coasts of Kent. **1832** HT. MARTINEAU *Ella of Gar.* iii, The terns and gulls screaming. **1888** NEWTON in *Encycl. Brit.* XXIII. 189/1 The Sandwich Tern, *S. sandvicensis* or *S. cantiaca*..is the largest of the British species.

tern (tɜːn), *a.* and *sb.*[2] [As adj., ad. L. *ternī* three each. As sb., app. a. F. *terne* (15th c.).]

†**A.** *adj. Bot.* Arranged in threes; ternate.

1760 J. LEE *Introd. Bot.* III. xxii. (1788) 242 The Peduncle ..is said to be..*Tern*, or *three* from the same Axilla. *Ibid.* xxiii. 252 In respect to Opposition, opposite Leaves will sometimes become tern, quatern, or quine, growing by Threes, Fours, or Fives. **1828** in WEBSTER.

B. *sb.* **1.** A set of three; a trio, triplet. *spec.* †**a.** *pl.* [F. *un terne*, formerly *ternes*:—L. *ternās*.] A double three in dice playing. (In quot. *fig.*) *Obs.* **b.** In a lottery, three winning numbers drawn together; a prize gained by such a drawing. **c.** A group of three stanzas.

13.. *Coer de L.* 2009 King Richard held a tronchon true ..Ternes and quernes he gave him there. **1856** MRS. BROWNING *Aur. Leigh* VII. 1247 She'd win a tern in Thursday's lottery. **1869** BROWNING *Ring & Bk.* XII. 158 But that he forbid The Lottery, why, Twelve were Tern Quatern! **1879** FURNIVALL *Chaucer's Min. P.* 419 This late Poem [*Envoy to Scogan*] composed of two Terns and an Envoy.

2. *Math.* A system of three pairs of conjugate triads of planes which together contain the twenty-seven straight lines lying in a cubic surface (i.e. one represented by an equation of the third degree).

1891 in *Cent. Dict.*

3. A three-masted schooner; a three-master. (Local, New Eng.) (*Cent. Dict.* 1891.)

†**tern**, *v. Obs.* Also 5 teern. [ad. med.L. *ternāre* ? to treble: cf. F. *terner* 'to throw a tre[y] or three' (Cotgr. 1611).] ? To throw a tern or terns in dice playing. Hence †**terned** *ppl. a.*, †**'terning** *vbl. sb.*

c **1440** *Promp. Parv.* 489/2 Ternyd, in pley or oþer thyngys (*S.* teernyt in pley or other lyk), *ternatus*. Ternyn, yn gamys pleyynge, *terno*. Ternynge, *ternatus*, *ternacio*.

tern: see TERNE *a.*[1]; obs. var. TURN *v.* and *sb.*

terna ('tɜːnə). [a. L. *terna* (*nomina*) three (names) at once.] In *R.C. Ch.* A list of three names submitted to the Pope or other authority to choose from.

1885 W. J. WALSH *Let.* 7 Mar. in P. J. Walsh *William J. Walsh* (1928) vii. 163 Then I would, as a matter of course, vote for your Grace, which would put you on the *terna*. **1895** *Tablet* 28 Dec. 1030 A terna has been received at Propaganda for the appointment of a Coadjutor to the Bishop of Southwark. **1903** *Daily Chron.* 20 July 5/3 While Abbot —— is prominent on the terna, I am assured that the Bishop of ——'s name..does not appear.

ternado, obs. form of TORNADO.

ternal ('tɜːnəl), *a. rare.* [ad. med.L. *ternāl-is*, f. *tern-ī* distrib. numeral, 'three by three', f. *ter* thrice: see -AL[1]. So OF. *ternal* (15th c. in Godef.).]

1. Consisting of three; threefold, triple.

1599 A. M. tr. *Gabelhouer's Bk. Physicke* 193/1 Madefye therin a ternall reduplicated cloth [explained by 'trebled' in 'The Expositione of such wordes as are in this Booke derived of the Latines']. **1657** TOMLINSON *Renou's Disp.* 652 The Oyl..by its ternal maceration..acquires more vertue. *a* **1680** CHARNOCK in Spurgeon *Treas. Dav.* Ps. xcix. 3 A ternal repetition of his holiness.

2. Third (of each group of three); = TERNARY 3.

1804 SOUTHEY in *Ann. Rev.* II. 526 [Of *Lybeaus Desconus*] The four ternal lines rhyming..and also the two first couplets. [The stanzas rime: aad, aad, bbd, ccd.]

ternar, terner ('tɜːnə(r)). *Obs.* exc. *Hist.* [ad. late L. *ternāri-us*: see TERNARY.] A student of the third or lowest rank at St. Andrews, and app. in other of the Scottish Universities.

1698 (July) *Minute, St. Leonard's Coll., St. Andrews*, Many are of opinion that the distinctions of Primar, Secondar, and Ternar, ought to be taken away. **1807** GRIERSON *St. Andrews* 160 The Terners had gowns of an inferior sort of cloth, without trimming, and paid one guinea and a half of fees. Seconders and Terners are the only distinctions now in use. **1827** *Evid. Commissioners Scot. Univ.* (1837) III. 35 (St. Andrews) The Primars are the sons of Noblemen; the Secondars are what they call Gentlemen Commoners in England; and the Ternars are those of the common ranks of life. They pay different fees according to the rank they hold. **1907** LANG *Hist. Scotl.* IV. xiii. 407 Men who could afford to pay a Secondar's fee often entered themselves as Ternars.

ternariant (tə'nɛərɪənt). *Math.* [f. TERNARY + the ending of INVARIANT, etc.] (See quots.)

1882 SYLVESTER in *Amer. Jrnl. Math.* V. 81 *note,* I am inclined to substitute the word binariant for subinvariants, and to speak of simple, double, treble or multiple binariants. The functions similarly related to ternary forms will then be styled simple or multiple ternariants. **1890** FORSYTH *ibid.* XII. 1 *note,* It has proved convenient to use the word 'ternariants' as a generic term for concomitants of ternary quantics, instead of giving it the signification which Prof. Sylvester.. proposed,.. viz. the leading coefficients of those concomitants.

ternary ('tɜːnərɪ), *a.* and *sb.* [ad. late L. *ternārius* consisting of three, f. *tern-ī*: see TERNAL and -ARY[1]. Cf. F. *ternaire* (15th c.).]

A. *adj.* **1. a.** Pertaining to, consisting of, compounded of, or characterized by a set (or sets) of three; threefold, triple. ***ternary system*** (of classification), one in which each division is into three parts.

c **1430** *Art Nombryng* 19 Some vsen forto distingue the nombre by threes, and ay begynne forto wirche vndre the first of the last ternary other uncomplete nombre. **1596** BELL *Surv. Popery* II. II. vi. 169 The ternarie number doth not determine the apparitions in themselues. **1603** HOLLAND *Plutarch's Mor.* 1302 This ternary or threefold number. **1659** OWEN *Div. Orig. Script.* Wks. 1853 XVI. 340 The Trinity.. is a trinity in unity, or the ternary number of persons in the same essence. **1715** CHEYNE *Philos. Princ. Relig.* II. 129 The Profane and Ignorant may make a Jest of this Ternary Chain. **1724** WATERLAND *Further Vind. Christ's Div.* iv. §10 The equality is mentioned as belonging to the ternary number, here considered as a figure of the Trinity. **1881** WESTCOTT & HORT *Grk. N.T.* Introd. §152 Ternary variations in which each of the three groups approximately attests a different variant. **1909** *Cent. Dict. Suppl.* s.v. *Symmetry,* If [the angle is] 120°, or the crystal repeats itself three times, the symmetry is threefold or ternary and the axis is a triad axis.

b. *Mus.* ***ternary measure*** or ***time***: triple time (? *obs.*). ***ternary form***: the form of a movement which consists of three main divisions, *spec.* one in which the first subject recurs after a contrasting subject; also *absol.* as *ternary.*

[**1597** MORLEY *Introd. Mus.* Annot., The last of the two minimes is marked with a pricke.. for perfections sake, that the ternary number may be obserued.] **1727–41** CHAMBERS *Cycl.* s.v. *Measure,* Ternary, or triple measure, is.. where two minims are played during a fall, and but one in a rise. **1875** F. A. G. OUSELEY *Treat. Mus. Form & Gen. Composition* vi. 41 (*heading*) Of the ternary form. *Ibid.* vii. 44 If the minuet form is adopted for a complete and isolated composition, it should be lengthened considerably, and then both the minuet and trio may be written in the ternary form. **1896** W. H. HADOW *Sonata Form* iv. 29 In its use for purposes of the Folk-song the most primitive Ternary form consists of a melody in three clauses: one of assertion.. one of contrast.. one of re-assertion. **1898** STAINER & BARRETT *Dict. Mus. Terms, Ternary form,* rondo form. *Ternary measure,* triple time. **1908** *Athenæum* 18 July 78/1 Another interesting instance of modification is that of binary form, which by expansion became ternary. **1931** D. F. TOVEY *Compan. Beethoven's Pianoforte Sonatas* 2 The vital distinction between 'binary' and 'ternary' is that between an aggregate whose members are inseparable and an aggregate containing one or more things already complete. **1938** *Oxf. Compan. Mus.* 334/2 Properly, any composition in which the ear seizes two clear divisions is binary, and any in which it seizes three is ternary... 'Sonata Form'.. is often called 'Compound Binary'... Certain text-books.. speak of it as 'Ternary'. *Ibid.* 335/1 *Rondo Form.* This may be looked upon as an extension of simple ternary form. **1944** W. APEL *Harvard Dict. Mus.* 88/1 The principle of ternary structure appeared first in the French chansons of the 16th century... The idea of a contrasting middle section is quite clearly expressed in the shepherd's solo of Monteverdi's *Orfeo*... Ternary form became clearly established in the da-capo aria, *c.* 1700. **1980** *New Grove Dict. Mus.* XVIII. 694/1 Tripartite musical form designated symbolically as *ABA*. The two elements *A* and *B* are often thematically independent and each is generally a 'closed' structure tonally, so that the interdependence of the two sections characteristic of binary form is not necessarily evident in ternary.

c. *Chem.* and *Min.* Compounded or consisting of three elements or constituents; (of an alloy), composed of three principal metals; (of a mixture) containing three independent components; of or pertaining to such an alloy or mixture.

†By Dalton used in the sense 'consisting of three atoms'.

1808 HENRY in *Phil. Trans.* XCVIII. 283 Oxygen, hydrogen, and carbon, united in the form of a ternary compound. **1808** DALTON *Chem. Philos.* I. 213 If there are two bodies, A and B,.. 1 atom of A + 2 atoms of B = 1 atom of D, ternary. **1846** J. BAXTER *Libr. Pract. Agric.* (ed. 4) I. 22 These ternary compounds, such as starch, gum, sugar,.. are non-nitrogenized. **1851** RICHARDSON *Geol.* 464 *Perfect granite* is a ternary compound of quartz, felspar, and di-axial mica, universally diffused. **1864** H. SPENCER *Biol.* I. 11 In chemical stability these ternary compounds.. are in a marked degree below the binary ones. **1889** *Proc. R. Soc.* XLV. 481 Ternary alloys obtained by adding tin to the immiscible pairs of metals, zinc and bismuth, aluminium and lead. **1897** W. D. BANCROFT *Phase Rule* xi. 156 The change of isotherms with the temperature for a ternary system which permits of no compounds and no second solution phase. **1923** GLAZEBROOK *Dict. Appl. Physics* V. 251/2 (*heading*) Methods of representing ternary equilibria. **1969** BENNISON & WRIGHT *Geol. Hist. Brit. Isles* xi. 261 The theoretical succession of deposition of minerals produced by the evaporation of sea-water is supported to a large extent by experimental work... However, the detailed course of crystallization, which varies considerably with different temperatures, can only be adequately represented by ternary diagrams. **1978** P. W. ATKINS *Physical Chem.* x. 305 Consider a ternary solution of composition a_1. This is unsaturated, and is a single phase. **1979** *Sci. Amer.* Nov. 73/3 The new ternary alloys consist of between 68 and 80 percent copper.

d. *Bot.* Arranged in threes around a common axis: usually in reference to the parts of a flower.

1830 LINDLEY *Nat. Syst. Bot.* 251 The ternary division of the flower of Monocotyledons is often departed from..; many Dicotyledons have also ternary floral envelopes. **1866** *Treas. Bot., Ternary, ternate,* when three things are in opposition round a common axis. **1870** HOOKER *Stud. Flora* 12 Berberideæ.. analogy.. in the 3-nary floral whorls with Monocotyledons.

e. *Math.* Constructed on the number three as a base, as ***ternary logarithm***, ***ternary scale*** (of notation); involving three variables, as ***ternary quantic***.

1860 CAYLEY *Math. Papers* IV. 604 The number of variables (the function being homogeneous) is denoted by the words *binary, ternary,* &c. **1898** *Ibid.* XIV. Index, Ternary Quadratics... Ternary Quadrics... Ternary Quantics.

f. *Astron.* ***ternary system***, a system of three stars which revolve under mutual attraction, or round a common centre.

g. *Nucl. Physics.* ***ternary fission***, fission of an atomic nucleus into three parts.

1955 *Physical Rev.* XCVII. 748/2 There is some uncertainty regarding the occurrence in ternary fission of a light fragment having a mass and charge greater than an alpha particle. **1979** *Nature* 12 Apr. 615/2 Uranium and plutonium decay by ternary fission with only very low probability.

†**2.** ***ternary part***, one of three equal parts; a third part. *Obs. rare*[−1].

1599 A. M. tr. *Gabelhouer's Bk. Physicke* 108/2 Which poulder we must diuide into 3 æquall portions, then take therof a ternary parte.

3. Last of each successive group of three; third.

1690 LEYBOURN *Curs. Math.* 339 [In extracting roots] Squares.. are to be marked with Points.. over every Binary or second Figure. Cubes over every Ternary Figure.

4. Third in subordination, rank, or order.

1826 KIRBY & SP. *Entomol.* xlviii. IV. 443 This system.. in its ternary groups, equivalent to the Orders of Linné [etc.]. **1829** GEN. P. THOMPSON *Exerc.* (1842) I. 135 The only wonder is, that when they went to the secondary sense, they did not go to the ternary. **1831** CARLYLE *Misc.* (1857) II. 263 In a secondary and even a ternary reflex.

B. *sb.* †**1. a.** A set or group of three; a ternion, a trio. *Obs.*

1460 CAPGRAVE *Chron.* Ded. (Rolls) 3 Make in ȝoure soule to [= two] ternaries, on [= one] in feith anothir in love: beleve in God—Fadir, and Son, and Holy Gost: love God in al ȝoure hert, al ȝoure soule, and al ȝoure mynde. **1542** RECORDE *Gr. Artes* (1575) 48 Put a pricke ouer the fourthe Figure,.. ouer the vij... and so forthe, still leauing two figures betweene eche two pricks. And those two roomes betweene the prickes, are called Ternaries. **1654** WHITLOCK *Zootomia* 377, I conclude this Ternary of Worthies with Cato. **1686** tr. *Livy* I. I. xxiv. 15 There happened to be.. three Brothers in each Army... The two Kings treated with these two ternaries of Brethren. **1779–81** JOHNSON *L.P., Gray* ¶28 The second ternary of stanzas [in *The Progress of Poetry*].

†**b.** The Holy Trinity. [So OF. *ternaire.*] *Obs.*

1570 DEE *Math. Pref.* *j b, By the infinite goodness of the Almighty Ternarie. **1662** SPARROW tr. *Behme's Rem. Wks., 1st Apol. to B. Tylcken* 79 There was Joy in Heaven *in Ternario Sancto,* in the Holy Ternary.

†**2.** A number which is a multiple of three. *rare*[−1].

1557 RECORDE *Whetst.* (1558) O iv b, Thei muste all waies bee ternaries, as 3. 6. 9. or 12. &c.

Hence †**'ternariness** *Obs. rare,* ternary condition. So †**ter'narian,** †**ter'narious** *adjs.,* = TERNARY *a.*

1656 BLOUNT *Glossogr., Ternary, Ternarious,* of or belonging to three. **1662** J. CHANDLER *Van Helmont's Oriat.* 266 So the likeness of ternariness shall cease, & such an image shall badly square with the Type, whose image it is believed to be. **1715–20** POPE *Iliad* III. 214 The ternarian number.

ternate ('tɜːnət), *a.* [ad. mod.L. *ternāt-us* (in Linnæus 1750), in form pa. pple. of med.L. *ternāre* (*Promp. Parv.*) to treble or make threefold. Cf. F. *terné* (1783 in Hatz.-Darm.).] Produced or arranged in threes; *spec. Bot.* applied to a compound leaf composed of three leaflets, or to leaves arranged in whorls of three; also to leaflets borne on secondary or tertiary similarly arranged petioles (*biternate, triternate*).

1760 J. LEE *Introd. Bot.* III. vi. (1765) 188 *Biternate,* or *Duplicato-Ternate,* when there are three Folioles on a Petiole, and each Foliole is Ternate. **1785** MARTYN *Rousseau's Bot.* xvi. (1794) 177 The species is distinguished by its ternate leaves. **1812** *New Bot. Gard.* I. 28 The leaf [of *Anemone nemorosa*] is doubly ternate. **1861** MISS PRATT *Flower. Pl.* I. 4 A ternate leaf consists of three leaflets on a common stalk, as in the Clover.

So †**'ternated** *a. Obs. rare*[−1].

1753 CHAMBERS *Cycl. Supp.* s.v. *Leaf,* Ternated Leaf, a compound one,.. of three leaves on a common petiole.

ternately ('tɜːnətlɪ), *adv.* [f. TERNATE *a.* + -LY[2].] In a ternate manner; in threes.

1860 in WORCESTER citing GRAY. **1870** HOOKER *Stud. Flora* 167 Angelica... Leaves ternately 2-pinnate. **1897** A. DRUCKER tr. *Ihering's Evol. Aryan* 120 According to their duodecimal system, the Babylonians must have calculated their time for work and rest ternately: three sets or relays of working periods, each of three hours.

ternatisect (tə'neɪtɪsɛkt), *a. Bot.* [f. mod.L. *ternāt-us* TERNATE + *sect-us* cut.] Cut into three lobes, the divisions extending to the midrib.

1870 HOOKER *Stud. Flora* 8 Ranunculus bulbosus.. leaves 3-foliolate or ternatisect.

ternato-pinnate (təˌneɪtəʊ'pɪnət), *a. Bot.* [f. mod.L. *ternāt-us* TERNATE (after Greek combining forms in -*o*) + PINNATE.] Applied to a compound leaf having three pinnate divisions proceeding from a common petiole.

1857 HENFREY *Bot.* 60 What are called biternate and triternate compound leaves are in most cases pinnate leaves with unijugate and terminal leaflets. Such leaves should perhaps be called *ternato-pinnate* or *bi-ternato-pinnate,* &c.

terne, *a.*[1] (*sb.*[1]) *Obs.* exc. as F. (tɛrn). Also 6 tern. [a. F. *terne* dull, tarnished (15th c. in Godef.); of doubtful origin: see TARNISH *v.*]

†**1.** Gloomy; fierce. *Sc. Obs.* Also †**terned** *a.*

1508 DUNBAR *Tua Mariit Wemen* 261 Thought ȝe as tygris be terne, be tretable in luf. *a* **1568** *O wicket Wemen,* etc. 15 in *Bannatyne Poems* (Hunter. Cl.) 769 Als terne as tygir, of tung vntollerable, O thow violent virago vennemous. **1638** R. BAILLIE *Lett. & Jrnls.* (1841) I. 160 The Moderator a most grave and wise man yet naturally somewhat terned took me up a little accurtlie.

†**b.** as *sb.* Gloom. *Sc. Obs. rare*[−1].

1500–20 DUNBAR *Poems* lxxxv. (*Ballat of Our Lady*) 7 Our tern inferne for to dispern, Helpe rialest rosyne.

‖**2.** (as Fr.) Dull, lacking brilliancy of colouring.

1901 *Daily News* 5 Feb. 6/5 In the large sketch from Tintoret's 'Adoration',.. the colour is dull and terne.

terne (tɜːn), *a.*[2] and *sb.*[2] [The first element in *terne-plate* as a separate word.] **a.** *adj.* Of or pertaining to terne-plate. **b.** *sb.* = TERNE-PLATE.

1891 *Pall Mall G.* 9 Sept. 6/3 The terne mixture does not adhere to the sheets of iron, but runs off like quicksilver from certain parts of the sheet. **1904** *Daily Chron.* 15 Dec. 5/5 To the end of November he thought they would have shipped more tin, terne, and galvanised sheets than during any year in the history of Great Britain.

terne, obs. f. TARN.

terned: see TERNE *a.*[1] 1.

terne-plate ('tɜːnpleɪt). Also **tern-.** [prob. f. TERNE *a.*[1], dull, lacking brilliancy, in reference to the dullness of terne-plate, in comparison with tin-plate.] Thin sheet-iron coated with an alloy of lead and tin; an inferior kind of tin-plate; a sheet or plate of this. Also *attrib.*

1858 SIMMONDS *Dict. Trade, Terne-plates,* thin sheet-iron coated with an amalgam of tin and lead. **1880** *Echo* 15 Oct. 2/4 Some unscrupulous packers are using terne plates instead of tin plates. **1892** *Pall Mall G.* 10 Dec. 7/1 Inferior plates, known as tern-plates and mostly used for roofing, contain a great deal of lead. **1894** [see TAGGER[1] 4]. **1907** G. E. DUCKERING *Parl. Rep. Tinning Metals* 8 No evidence of lead absorption is to be found among terne-plate workers.

terner: see TERNAR.

ternery ('tɜːnərɪ). [f. TERN *sb.*[1] + -ERY.] A place where terns congregate to breed.

1891 in *Cent. Dict.* **1905** E. SELOUS *Bird Watcher in Shetlands* xxiii. 180, I have mentioned the case of a dog making regular daily expeditions to a ternery, in order to feast upon the eggs. **1932** *Times Lit. Suppl.* 15 Sept. 637/2 The sanctuary at Dungeness, established presumably for the protection of the interesting ternery. **1943** HAGGARD & WILLIAMSON *Norfolk Life* i. 12 There is the azure tide inflowing past the Ternery on the point. **1979** *Woman & Home* June 154/3 The ternery, no longer out of bounds, was uncannily silent.

ternion ('tɜːnɪən). [ad. L. *terniōn-em* a company of three, a triad.]

1. A set of three (things or persons); a triad.

1587 HOLINSHED *Chron.* III. 207/2 A quadrangle in geometrie compriseth in it a triangle, and a quaternion in arithmetike conteineth a ternion. **1600** HOLLAND *Livy* XXV. v. 548 The Senate.. agreed that there should bee chosen two Ternions of Triumvirs. **1652** BP. HALL *Invis. World* I. §7 Disposing them [angels] into Ternions of three general Hierarchies. *a* **1661** FULLER *Worthies, Surrey* (1662) III. 83 That happy Ternion of Brothers, whereof two eminent Prelats, the third, Lord Mayor of London. **1820** SOUTHEY *Wesley* I. 56 When I have such a Ternion to prosecute that war.

2. A quire of three sheets, each folded in two.

1609 *Skene's Reg. Maj.* H h iij b *note,* All the letters.. are Ternions, or thrie sheetes in one, except *H h* in the last Alphabet. **1886** *Amer. Jrnl. Philol.* Apr. 27 They say that a given manuscript is composed of quaternions and of ternions.

ternity, ternyte, obs. forms of TRINITY.

ternstrœmiaceous (tɜːnstreɪmɪ'eɪʃəs), *a. Bot.* [f. mod.L. *Ternstrœmiāceæ* (f. *Ternstrœmia,* a genus named after Ternström, a Swedish naturalist) + -OUS.] Belonging to the *Ternstrœmiaceæ*, an order of tropical trees and shrubs, with showy white (sometimes pink or red) flowers, generally borne in racemes; it includes the tea-plant and the camellia, and many plants valued as flowering shrubs.

1885 H. O. FORBES *Nat. Wand. E. Archip.* 400 Through dense forest, full of Ternstrœmiaceous trees.

† **te'rogatores**, obs. aphetic f. *interrogatories*: see INTERROGATORY *sb.*

1511–12 *Rec. St. Mary at Hill* 279 Costes of þe spirituall courte . . paid for wryting of the terogatores, iij s. iiij d.

terotechnology (ˌtɪərəʊ-, ˌterəʊtek'nɒlədʒɪ). [f. Gr. τηρεῖν to watch over, take care of + -O + TECHNOLOGY.] The branch of technology and engineering concerned with the installation, maintenance, and replacement of industrial plant and equipment and with related subjects and practices.

1970 H. P. JOST *Let.* 2 Feb. (in files of *Suppl. to O.E.D.*), Last Saturday a Mintech Steering Committee, which I chaired, took some decisions on a proposed 'Committee on Terotechnology'. We felt that Terotechnology was preferable to Teromechanics, particularly as a good deal of electronics were involved. **1970** *Hansard Commons: Written Answers* 29 Apr. 338 The scope of the subject . . includes . . installation, commissioning and replacement of plant, machinery and equipment, feedback to designers, and management techniques. . . It was considered advisable to utilise a name reflecting the wider concept now envisaged. The word Terotechnology has therefore been adopted. **1975** *Daily Tel.* 9 Dec. 11/6 British Leyland has won the award of 'Conservationist of the Year' for its work in saving materials, plant and manpower. The firm estimated that it saved £321,182 on terotechnology—economy in materials, plant and manpower. **1977** *Engin. Synopses* Jan.–Feb. 20 (Advt.), With the continual increase in size and complexity of industrial undertakings terotechnology has emerged as a discipline in its own right. **1980** *Sunday Times* 9 Nov. 19/4 The science of maintenance, or terotechnology if you want to sound knowledgeable about it, is beginning to attract serious interest in industry and universities.

Hence ˌ**terotechno'logical** *a.*, ˌ**terotech'nologist**.

1970 *Chartered Mech. Engineer* June 243/1 According to Mintech, this new high-status role will be filled by none other than the Terotechnologist. *Ibid.*, A Committee of Terotechnology . . will advise . . on how to introduce appropriate measures to effect terotechnological progress. **1973** *New Scientist* 12 Apr. 95 Terotechnologists quote the case of breakdowns of waste heat boilers for 300 tonne oxygen steelmaking vessels. **1977** *Engin. Synopses* Jan.–Feb. 20 (Advt.), The terotechnologist must be able to call upon a wide variety of other skills and specialisms.

terp[1] (tɜːp). Pl. ‖**terpen** (also *erron.* used as sing.) and **terps** (in *Archæol.* contexts). [WFris. *terp* village mound, pl. *terpen*, = EFris. *terp* (Saterland), NFris. *têrp* (Sylt), *sarp* (Amrum) village:—OFris. *therp*, umlaut variant of OFris. *thorp* village: cf. THORP.] An artificial mound or hillock, the site of a prehistoric village, and still in many cases occupied by a village or church, in parts of Friesland below sea-level or liable to inundation. Also applied to similar mounds outside Friesland itself. Also *attrib.*

These *terpen*, like the Italian *terremare* or terramares, have in modern times been excavated for the sake of the fertilizing soil which they yield, and more recently for the prehistoric remains found in them; the name has thus passed into archæological use.

[**1838** *Penny Cycl.* X. 481/1 The whole land is flat . . nor is there an eminence throughout it excepting some mounds, here called 'terpen', on which the antient Frisians were accustomed to take refuge in seasons of marine inundations.] **1866** *Jrnl. R. Agric. Soc. Eng.* II. I. 153 On the seaside little hillocks, 13 feet to 19½ feet high, may be observed at short distances: they are called *Terpens.* These hillocks were formed by the hand of man; and when opened, their contents prove that they belong to an ante-historical epoch. **1889** *Scott. Leader* 15 Jan. 7/1 An account of a visit to a terp mound at Aalzum in North Friesland . . by Dr. Robert Munro. *Ibid.*, The general character of the antiquities found is that of the Iron Age. In the museum at Leewarden there are two rooms devoted exclusively to the antiquities from the terpen mounds. **1899** MUNRO *Prehist. Scotl.* x. 401 Double-edged combs like those from the Terp-mounds in Holland. *Ibid.* xi. 436 The terpen are largely excavated on account of their rich ammoniacal deposits. **1939** G. CLARK *Archæol. & Society* iv. 105 '*Terps.*' Settlement mounds or tells are a commonplace feature of Greek and Middle Danubian prehistory. **1969** G. C. DICKINSON *Maps & Air Photographs* xiv. 217 (*caption*) The villages are built on or (now) around man-made mounds (*terps*) erected as a defence against flooding by the sea.

terp[2] (tɜːp). *Theatr. slang.* [Abbrev. of TERPSICHORE(AN *a.*).] A stage dancer, esp. a chorus-girl; also, a ballroom dancer. Also *attrib.* and *pl.*, dancing. Hence **terp** *v. intr.*, to dance; '**terping** *vbl. sb.*

1937 *Amer. Speech* XII. 317/2 *Terp*, a dancer. **1937** *Variety* 10 Nov. 58/3 Philly Orch on Thursday (11) night will preem composition of 23-year-old Omaha college soph. Cleffer, titled 'Mystic Pool'. . . 'Pool' originally composed for his terp. orch. **1942** BERREY & VAN DEN BARK *Amer. Thes. Slang* §594/1 *Stage dancing*, . . terping, terp stuff, toesmithing. **1945** MENCKEN *Amer. Lang.* Suppl. I. v. 338 It [sc. *Variety*] makes verbs of nouns, *e.g.* . . . *to preem* and *to terp.* **1951** GREEN & LAURIE *Show Biz* 571/2 *Terps*, dancing. *Ibid.* 572/1 *Terp team*, ballroom dance team. **1952** GRANVILLE *Dict. Theatr. Terms* 183 *Terp*, a stage dancer. **1974** *Spartanburg* (S. Carolina) *Herald* 18 Apr. A6/1 Donna McKechnie is the best dancer in the musical comedy theater (one dance critic tripped over his typewriter when he suggested Donna can't terp).

terpane ('tɜːpeɪn). *Chem.* [ad. G. *terpan* (A. Baeyer 1894, in *Ber. d. Deut. Chem. Ges.* XXVII. 436), f. *terpen* TERPENE: see -ANE.] Any of a class of saturated hydrocarbons related to the terpenes and possessing their carbon skeleton; *spec.* 4-methylprop-2-ylcyclohexane, $CH_3C_6H_{10}CH(CH_3)_2$, a monocyclic liquid.

1902 F. J. POND tr. *Heusler's Chem. Terpenes* 23 Baeyer has . . advanced the proposition to designate hexahydrocymene as *terpane.* **1965** *Proc. Nat. Acad. Sci.* LIV. 1412 Peaks [in the mass spectrum] at m/e 191, 203, and 231 probably arise from small amounts of terpane impurities. **1981** *Jrnl. Chromatogr. Sci.* XIX. 156/1 Terpanes and steranes are well-known biological marker hydrocarbons.

terpene ('tɜːpiːn). *Chem.* [f. *terp-* in *terp-entin*, obs. f. TURPENTINE, with suffix -ENE, used in forming the names of hydrocarbons related to BENZENE. Formerly called TEREBENE.] A general name of hydrocarbons having the formula $C_{10}H_{16}$, many of which occur in the volatile oils of plants, chiefly of the coniferous and aurantiaceous orders. The commonest is PINENE, the chief constituent of turpentine-oil.

Sometimes used to include hydrocarbons of formula C_5H_8, and its polymers $C_{10}H_{16}$, $C_{15}H_{24}$, $C_{20}H_{32}$, etc.

[**1866** KEKULÉ *Lehrb. Organ. Chemie* II. 437.] **1873** WATTS *Fownes' Chem.* (ed. 11) 778 Terpenes are volatile oils, existing in plants. **1885** REMSEN *Org. Chem.* (1888) 311 Artificial camphor . . when heated alone, or with bases, . . gives off hydrochloric acid, and a terpene different from the oil of turpentine is formed. **1902** POND tr. *Heusler's Chem. Terpenes* 17 Those hydrocarbons which have the empirical constitution C_5H_8 are termed terpenes. Four main classes are recognised: *Hemiterpenes*, C_5H_8, *Terpenes proper*, $C_{10}H_{16}$, *Sesquiterpenes*, $C_{15}H_{24}$, *Polyterpenes*, $(C_5H_8)x$.

Hence '**terpeneless** *a.*, rendered free of terpenes; **terpe'nylic** [f. TERPENE + -YL + -IC], in ***terpenylic acid***, a white crystalline compound, $C_8H_{12}O_4$, obtained by oxidizing a terpene, as turpentine-oil, with chromic acid.

1881 WATTS *Dict. Chem.* VIII. 1907 Terpenylic acid . . is obtained at first in the form of a syrup resembling glycerol. . . Terpenylic acid is monobasic. **1921** *Jrnl. R. Naval Med. Service* VII. 89 Terpeneless and sesquiterpeneless oils. **1972** *Materials & Technol.* V. i. 17 'Terpeneless bergamot oil' is used in high-class perfumes.

terpenoid ('tɜːpənɔɪd), *sb.* (and *a.*) *Chem.* [a. G. *terpenoid* (Vogel & Stohl 1933, in *Ber. d. Deut. Chem. Ges.* LXVI. B. 1066): see TERPENE and -OID.] A terpene in the broadest sense: used when *terpene* itself is restricted to compounds with the formula $C_{10}H_{16}$. Also *attrib.* and as *adj.*

1933 *Chem. Abstr.* XXVII. 4807 The name *terpenoids* is suggested for the resin alcs., resin acids, sterols and xanthophylls, including carotene. **1956** I. L. FINAR *Organic Chem.* II. viii. 250 There is . . a tendency to call the whole group terpenoids instead of terpenes, and to restrict the name terpene to the compounds $C_{10}H_{16}$. **1972** *Science* 5 May 512/2 Some species of caterpillars . . possess oxidases in their gut that are capable of metabolizing the repellent terpenoids such as pyrethrin from chrysanthemums. **1975** *Nature* 31 Jan. 365/2 Both substances are terpenoid, derived from the essential oils absinthol and cannabinol.

terpentin, early form of TURPENTINE.

terpiche, i.e. *tar-pitch*: see TAR *sb.*[1] 4.

terpin ('tɜːpɪn). *Chem.* Also -ine. [f. as TERPENE + -IN[1].] A derivative of pinene and other terpenes, $C_{10}H_{18}(OH)_2$, of which two modifications are known, *cisterpin*, melting at 103° C., and *transterpin*, at 156° C. **terpin-hydrate**, a crystalline compound obtained by shaking turpentine-oil with alcohol acidified with sulphuric or nitric acid.

1848 *Chem. Gaz.* 1 Aug. 296 On the so-called Hydrate of Oil of Turpentine. . . Its name had consequently to be altered, and the author [Dr. C. List] adopts that of *terpine*, proposed for it by Berzelius. **1868** WATTS *Dict. Chem.* V. 923 Terpin-hydrate usually crystallises in large rhombic prisms. **1894** MORLEY & MUIR *Watts' Dict. Chem.* IV. 665/2 Terpin is best known in the form of its hydrate, . . a beautifully crystalline compound which on heating to 100° loses water and leaves terpin as a vitreous mass.

Hence '**terpinene**, a terpene occurring in oil of cardamom; **ter'pineol**, formerly (and still in Pharmacy) '**terpinol**: see quots.; **ter'pinolene**, a terpene obtained by Wallach in 1885.

1848 *Chem. Gaz.* 1 Aug. 297 Terpinole is a colourless, very liquid oil, with the agreeable odour of hyacinths. *Ibid.* 298 When terpine is heated with concentrated hydriodic acid, it is converted into terpinole. **1857** MILLER *Elem. Chem.* III. vii. §1. 442 Terpinol. **1894** MORLEY & MUIR *Watts' Dict. Chem.* IV 665/1 Terpineol . . is a viscous liquid, having an odour of white lilac. **1902** POND tr. *Heusler's Chem. Terpenes* 105 Terpinolene is obtained by boiling terpine hydrate, terpineol, or cineole with dilute sulphuric acid. *Ibid.* 112 Terpinene escaped the notice of the earlier investigators because they assumed that it was identical with dipentene. Wallach recognized it as a definite terpene. *Ibid.* 254 The name terpineol was formerly used to designate a substance which to-day is recognized as a mixture of isomeric alcohols, $C_{10}H_{17}OH$.

† **ter'podion.** *Obs.* [app. f. Gr. τέρπ-ειν to delight + ᾠδή song: cf. *melodion*, etc.] Name given to a musical instrument, invented in 1816 and improved in 1832, but never actually in use.

1834 *Mus. Libr.* Suppl., Sept. 69 A concert has been given here by Prof. Buschmann and his son, both playing on the terpodion invented by the father. **1842** *Mech. Mag.* XXXVII. 563 Nearly allied to the instrument consisting of tuning forks is the terpodion [*pr.* -ian], but the vibrating springs instead of being in the form of forks are cylindrical rods of metal. **1898** STAINER & BARRETT *Dict. Mus. Terms, Terpodion*, an instrument . . resembling in appearance the pianoforte, but the tone was produced from blocks of wood struck with hammers.

† **terpoile**, *a. Sc. Obs.* Also 6 tere pyle. [a. OF. *a treis poils* three-pile.] Of patterned velvet, etc.: Three-pile; pile upon pile.

1489 *Acc. Ld. High Treas. Scot.* I. 135, v elne and a half of terpoile veluus for a halff lang gowne to the King. **1501** DOUGLAS *Pal. Hon.* 542 Satine figures . . , Damesflure, tere pyle, quhairon thair lyis Peirle.

‖**Terpsichore** (ˌtɜːp'sɪkərɪː). [a. Gr. Τερψιχόρη 'dance-enjoying', name of the Muse of dancing and of the dramatic chorus, f. τέρπειν to delight + χορός dance, CHORUS.] The Muse of dancing; hence, a female dancer; dancing as an art.

1711 SHAFTESB. *Charac.* (1737) I. 317 The Thalia's, the Polyhymnia's, the Terpsychore's, the Euterpe's willingly join their parts. **1756–7** tr. *Keysler's Trav.* (1760) III. 427 Stranger, approach, behold this homely chair, Which e'en Terpsichore herself might chuse. **1906** *19th Cent.* Mar. 457 We should lament the death of Terpsichore.

Hence **terpsichorean** (ˌtɜːpsɪkə'riːən) *a.*, of, pertaining to, or of the nature of dancing; saltatory. So **terpsicho'real** *a.* (*rare*) in same sense; hence **terpsicho'really** *adv.*, by means of dancing.

1869 *Daily News* 19 May, The loving couples . . hold themselves aloof from the busy hum, or mix in it for *terpsichoreal or restorative purposes only. **1900** *Ibid.* 12 Mar. 8/4 A poem, 'Voltigia', which poem the 'Tenth Muse' condescends to interpret *terpsichoreally. **1825** T. HOOK *Sayings* Ser. II. *Sutherl.* (Colburn) 26 She had seen their *Terpsichorean evolutions. **1865** DICKENS *Mut. Fr.* I. xi, An entirely new view of the Terpsichorean art. **1899** *Allbutt's Syst. Med.* VIII. 98 Sometimes a series of co-ordinated gestures and movements [in hysterical persons] constitute a regular terpsichorean display.

terpy'lonic, *a. Chem.* [f. as TERP-ENE + -YL + -ONE + -IC.] In ***terpylonic acid***, $C_9H_{14}O_6$, a product of the oxidation of turpentine by mixture with chromic acid.

1894 MORLEY & MUIR *Watts' Dict. Chem.* IV. 672/2.

terr (tɜː(r)). *Rhodesian slang.* [abbrev. of TERRORIST.] In Rhodesia (now Zimbabwe) prior to independence, a guerrilla fighting to overthrow the White minority government. Usu. in *pl.*

1976 *Verbatim* Sept. 14/2 Rhodesians, according to a recent news dispatch, now have one [*sc.* a 'clipping'] they could do without, namely *the Terrs* (general for 'the terrorists'). **1976** *Listener* 23/30 Dec. 835/3 It may help . . to know the kind of slang that they [*sc.* Rhodesian Whites] are going to be using. 'Terrs' is short for 'terrorists'. . . To 'rev' is to shoot somebody. **1980** *Times* 18 Jan. 19/2 Infiltration over the Zambesi River by 'terrs'—or terrorists/freedom fighters, depending on your politics.

terr, obs. form of TAR.

terr., abbrev. for TERRACE, TERRITORY (*U.S.*).

‖**terra** ('tɛrə). [L. (and It.) *terra* earth.]

1. Used, with qualifying adjectives, to form the names of medicinal and other earths, boles, and the like, as **terra alba**, (*a*) pipe-clay; (*b*) pulverized gypsum used industrially; **terra cariosa**, tripoli or rotten-stone; **terra chia**, also *chia terra*, Chian earth, an astringent and cosmetic bole formerly obtained from the island of Chios; see also quot. 1615; **terra foliata (tartari)**, = *foliated earth of tartar*, potassium acetate; **terra merita** = TURMERIC; **terra nera** [Ital. 'black earth'], see quot.; **terra nobilis**, an old name for the diamond (Ogilvie, Annandale, 1882); **terra ponderosa**, barium sulphate, heavy spar. Also used similarly in some general expressions, as **terra cognita** [as opp. to TERRA INCOGNITA], *fig.*, familiar territory; **terra ignota** = TERRA INCOGNITA; **terra irredenta** = IRREDENTA. See also TERRA FIRMA, TERRA JAPONICA, etc.

1871 NAPHEYS *Prev. & Cure Dis.* I. ii. 79 The insoluble white clay known in commerce as **terra alba.* **1905** H. RIES *Econ. Geol.* vii. 143 Gypsum is also used . . under the name of 'Terra Alba', as an adulterant of foods and medicinal preparations. **1917** J. SHELTON in G. Martin *Industr. & Manuf. Chem.* I. XXXI. 545 Under trade names, such as 'terra alba' . . , a certain amount of the purer forms of gypsum is employed by paint manufacturers for admixture with pigments. **1947** J. C. RICH *Materials & Methods of Sculpture* iv. 65 Terra Alba, a finely pulverized raw gypsum powder may be used [as an accelerator in casting plaster of Paris.] **1963** R. R. A. HIGHAM *Handbk. Papermaking* iv. 93 The form containing no water of crystallization . . is prepared by calcining the natural gypsum ($CaSO_4,2H_2O$), often referred to as terra alba. **1823** CRABB *Technol. Dict.*,

Terra cariosa*..rotten stone; a species of non effervescent chalk, of a brown colour. **1615 G. SANDYS *Trav.* 12 It [Chios] hath..a certaine greene earth like the rust of brasse, which the Turkes call *Terra Chia: but not that so reputed of by the ancient Physitions. **1753** CHAMBERS *Cycl. Supp.* s.v., *Chia Terra*, in the materia medica of the antients, an earth of the marle-kind, found in the island of Chio. **1962** E. SNOW *Other Side of River* (1963) xxxiii. 253 My last remark had put them back on *terra cognita and it would have been an appropriate moment to leave. **1975** *Publishers Weekly* 21 July 66/3 But it's all the same old *terra cognita* to those who have read Gerold Frank, Anne Edwards et al. **1753** CHAMBERS *Cycl. Supp.* s.v., **Terra foliata tartari.* **1758** REID tr. *Macquer's Chym.* I. 122 This solution being evaporated to dryness leaves a matter in the form of leaves lying on each other; on which account it hath obtained the name of *Terra Foliata*. *a* **1925** LD. CURZON *Leaves from Viceroy's Notebook* (1926) vi. 231 The whole country of Annam seems to be almost a **terra ignota* to our countrymen. **1977** *Times* 12 Oct. 9/5 These records [at Greenwich Museum] are largely terra ignota to the outside world. **1934** WEBSTER, *Terra irredenta. **1936** *International Affairs* XV. 39 *A terra irredenta*—that is to say, a territory, at present under foreign sovereignty, which, in the claimants' views, ought to be transferred to the sovereignty of his own State and to be incorporated (or re-incorporated) into his own national domain. **1965** *Listener* 20 May 735/1 French Somaliland,.. Ethiopian Somaliland, and..a strip of northern Kenya. These represent the Somalis' '*terra irredenta*'. **1753** CHAMBERS *Cycl. Supp.*, **Terra merita*,..a name given by some..to the curcuma, or turmeric-root. **1882** OGILVIE, **Terra nera*..a native, unctuous pigment, used by the ancient artists in fresco, oil, and tempera painting. **1794** SULLIVAN *View Nat.* I. 250 *Terra ponderosa.

2. *Science Fiction.* (With capital initial.) The Earth.

1947 E. F. RUSSELL in Aldiss & Harrison *Decade 1940s* (1975) 157 This world..was ten times the size of Terra. But his weight didn't seem abnormal. **1952** P. J. FARMER in —— *Decade 1950s* (1976) 215 It follows the moon around Terra ..a much smaller and unseen satellite.

‖**terra a terra**. *Obs.* Also 7 terra terra, (territerr). [It. *terra terra* level with the ground, influenced by corresp. F. *terre à terre*, Sp. *tierra á tierra*: see also TERRE-À-TERRE.]

1. An artificial gait formerly taught to horses, resembling a low curvet.

[**1611** COTGR., *Manege de terre à terre*, a manage more low, and more quicke then the ordinarie gallop, or curuet.] **1614** MARKHAM *Cheap Husb.* (1623) 29 In this practise you teach him [the horse] perfectly three lessons together, that is the turne Terra Terra, the Incavalare, and the Chambetta. *a* **1648** LD. HERBERT *Life* (1886) 74 The most useful *aer*, as the Frenchmen term it, is territerr. **1730** BAILEY (folio), *Terra a terra*..is a Series of low Leaps made by the Horse forward, bearing Sideways, and working upon two Treads.

2. = TERRE-À-TERRE.

1727–41 CHAMBERS *Cycl.*, *Terra a terra*..applied by the French to dancers, who cut no capers, nor scarce quit the ground. And hence it is also figuratively applied to authors, whose style and diction is low and creeping.

terrabill, terrable, obs. ff. TERRIBLE.

terrace ('tɛrəs), *sb.* Forms: α. 6 terries, 6–7 terrasse, (6 terres, 6–7 terris, 7 -ice), 7–9 terrass, -as, (8 -ase), 6– terrace. β. 6–7 tarrass(e, (tarris, -es), 6–8 taras, -ace, 7 tarasse, (tarrase, taras), taris, tarries. [a. F. *terrace* (12th c.), also *terrasse*, *tarrasse* (15th c.), rubble, a platform, a terrace, = It. *terraccia*, *-azza* bad earth or soil, 'filthie earth' (Florio), also a terrace, later †*terraccio*, now *terrazzo*, Sp. *terrazo*, Pg. *terraço* terrace, med.L. *terrācea*, *-ācia* an earthen mound, a raised terrace, a flat roof, *terrācium* useless earth (Du Cange):—L. **terrācea* fem. of **terrāceus* adj., earthen, of the nature of earth, earthy, f. *terra* earth: cf. -ACEOUS. This suffix was in the Romanic langs. used to form sbs., similative, augmentative, or pejorative; hence the primary sense, useless earth, heap of earth or rubbish, whence earthen mound made for a purpose. See also TARRAS (formerly *terras*, *terrace*), a differentiated form of the same word in the sense 'rubbish', 'rubble', as in It. and OFr.]

1. a. A raised level place for walking, with a vertical or sloping front or sides faced with masonry, turf, or the like, and sometimes having a balustrade; *esp.* a raised walk in a garden, or a level surface formed in front of a house on naturally sloping ground, or on the bank of a river, as 'The Terrace' at the Palace of Westminster.

α. **1575** LANEHAM *Let.* (1871) 48 Hard all along the Castl wall iz reared a pleazaunt Terres of a ten foot hy & a twelue brode. **1611** BIBLE *2 Chron.* ix. 11 And the king made.. terrises to the house of the Lord. **1669** WORLIDGE *Syst. Agric.* (1681) 333 *Terrasse*, a walk on a Bank or Bulwark. **1693** EVELYN *De la Quint. Compl. Gard.* I. 47 It might be allow'd twelve [foot] or more, it being a Terras,..since the Terrasses adjoyning to a House can hardly ever be too broad. **1712** LADY M. W. MONTAGU *Let. to W. Montagu* 9 or 11 Dec., The terrace is my place consecrated to meditation. **1739** GRAY *Let. to West* 21 Nov., Gardens and marble terrases full of orange and cypress trees. **1786** MRS. BARBAULD in *Mem. 70 Y.* vi. (1883) 62 A kind of terrass.. commands a most extensive view. **1814** SCOTT *Wav.* ix, The garden..was laid out in terraces, which descended rank by rank from the western wall to a large brook. **1866** GEO. ELIOT *F. Holt* ii, The glass door open towards the terrace.

β. **1579–80** NORTH *Plutarch* (1595) 570 Lucullus selfe would also many times be amongst them, in those tarrasses and pleasant walkes. **1587** CHURCHYARD *Worth. Wales* (1876) 104 Like tarres trim, to take the open ayre. **1599** B. JONSON *Ev. Man out of Hum.* II. i, Stand by close under this tarras. **1632** BURTON *Anat. Mel.* II. ii. IV. (ed. 4) 269 Euery Citty..hath his peculiar walkes, Cloysters, Tarraces. **1653** GREAVES *Seraglio* 14 Two men may walk a breast upon the Tarrase.

b. *transf.* and *fig.*

1605 BACON *Adv. Learn.* I. v. § 11 A tarrasse for a wandring and variable minde, to walke vp and downe. **1655** M. CARTER *Hon. Rediv.* (1660) 193 A Gennet of gold enamelled black and red, upon a terrasse or bank of flowers. **1758** REID tr. *Macquer's Chym.* I. 399 These rows of aludels are supported from end to end by a terrass, which runs from the body of the building, wherein the furnaces are erected. **1896** *Daily News* 10 Nov. 2/2 The living terraces of cripple children..added..their shrill plaudits to the general welcome.

†**c.** *Mil.* An earthwork thrown up by a besieging force; see also quot. 1816. *Obs.*

1579 FENTON *Guicciard.* XI. (1599) 510 Certaine of the Spanish footemen got vp to the terrasse or heape of Earth, and began to assaile the breach. **1600** HOLLAND *Livy* V. v. 182 What should I speake of the tarraces, torteises, rams, and all other engins of assault and batterie? **1816** JAMES *Milit. Dict.* (ed. 4) s.v., A terrace likewise signified..a sort of cavalier, which was carried to a great height, in order to overlook and command the walls of a town.

d. *Archæol.* = *cultivation terrace* s.v. CULTIVATION 1 a.

1796, etc. [see LYNCHET 2 b]. *a* **1964** G. UNDERWOOD *Pattern of Past* (1968) viii. 82 *Terraces*..are found on steep hillsides, and..mark places where a number of geodetic lines run parallel, with wide spaces between them... It seems reasonable to assume that they formed processional ways.

e. At an Association Football or other sports ground, a range of steps or tiers providing accommodation for standing spectators; one of these steps or tiers (usually in *pl.*) Also *attrib.* in *sing.* Cf. TERRACING *vbl. sb.* 1 b.

1950 *Sport* 7–11 Apr. 2/1 The terrace regulars are..the backbone of many present day clubs. **1959** *Listener* 19 Feb. 332/2 As I saw them from the terraces, I learnt that on top of everything else..they often had to play against their own supporters. **1971** [see FRIENDLY *a.* 3 c]. **1977** *Times* 6 May 2/5 [The] Minister of State for Sport..imposed his ban on the sale of terrace tickets to Chelsea supporters at away games. **1980** *Observer* 7 Sept. 11/6 It was more like a football terrace than Lord's.

2. A natural formation of this character; **a.** a table-land; **b.** *spec.* in *Geol.*, a horizontal shelf or bench on the side of a hill, or sloping ground.

The latter is usually of soft material, formed by the action of water, and exposed by the upheaval of the sea-margin, by the deepening of a river channel, or by the diminution in volume of a lake or river.

1674 JOSSELYN *Voy. New Eng.* 202 The white mountains, ..the highest Terrasse in New-England. **1753** HANWAY *Trav.* (1762) I. VII. xcvi. 446 Some of the steepest hills are supported by many terrasses. **1832** DE LA BECHE *Geol. Man.* 159 Captain Vetch describes six or seven terraces or lines of beach on the Isle of Jura.., which appear to have been successively raised above the present level of the ocean. **1878** HUXLEY *Physiogr.* xvii. 278 It is not uncommon to find successive terraces of gravel. **1882** GEIKIE *Text-bk. Geol.* VI. v. 901 Regular terraces, corresponding to former water-levels of the lake, run for miles along the shores at heights of 120, 150 and 200 ft.

†**c.** The ground on which anything stands. *rare.*

1735 MAHON tr. *L'Abbat's Fencing* Pref., By turning it too much it [the foot] would have no hold of the terrace.

3. † Orig., a gallery, open on one or both sides; a colonnade, a portico; a balcony on the outside of a building (*obs.*); also (formerly *obs.*, now revived), a raised platform or balcony in a theatre or the like (see quot. 1961). (The earliest sense in Eng.)

1515 *Will J. Fowler* (Somerset Ho.), To be buried w[t] in the Terres of the church of the Monastery of Syon. **1588** in Willis & Clark *Cambridge* (1886) II. 692 For paving the Inner court and the tarris without it. **1596** BP. W. BARLOW *Three Serm.* i. 17 Wee haue dyned abroad in our Tarrises and open Galleries for the great heat. **1617** MORYSON *Itin.* I. 145 This yard is compassed with a building all of Marble, which lies open like a Cloyster (we call it a terras). *Ibid.* III. 206 This place of Iudgement is commonly in a Porch or Terras under the Senate-house, hauing one side all open towards the market place. **1690** *The Gt. Scanderbeg* 131 A little Terrass, which rendred my Apartment very pleasant. **1703** T. N. *City & C. Purchaser* 258 *Tarrace*, or *Tarras*, an open Walk, or Gallary. **1961** *Ann. Rep. Lincoln Center for Performing Arts* (N.Y.) 10/1 The auditorium's shallow terraces—only six rows deep at the back and two to four seats wide at the sides—surround the orchestra level and flow towards the orchestra platform [in the Philharmonic Hall at the Lincoln Center, N.Y.]. **1963** *Guardian* 5 Mar. 7/3 The music sounds better in the top terrace..than in the lower terraces and orchestra.

†**4.** The flat roof of a house, resorted to for coolness in warm climates. *Obs.*

1572 ABP. PARKER *Let. to Ld. Burghley* 13 Dec., This shop is but little and lowe and leaded flatt,..and is made like the terris..fitt for men to stande vppon in any triumphe or shewe. **1582** N. LICHEFIELD tr. *Castanheda's Conq. E. Ind.* I. x. 27 Many faire houses of lime and stone, builded with many lofts, with their windowes and tarrisis made of Lime and earth. [**1613** PURCHAS *Pilgrimage* (1614) 268 To vnderprop the *Terratza*, or roofe.] **1687** A. LOVELL tr. *Thevenot's Trav.* I. 10 All the Houses of it are built with a terrass, or flat Roof, and one may go from one street to another upon the terrasses of the houses. **1764** HARMER *Observ.* III. iii. 93 This sleeping on the terraces of their houses is only in summer-time. **1892** E. REEVES *Homeward Bound* 203 On these roofs are 'terraces', guarded by high parapets, where the inmates sit in the cool of the evening.

5. A row of houses on a level above the general surface, or on the face of a rising ground; *loosely*, a row of houses of uniform style, on a site slightly, if at all, raised above the level of the roadway.

(Common in street nomenclature; *Adelphi Terrace* (formerly Royal Terrace), London, is one of the earliest examples.)

1769 (23 June) *Lease* (in *Mortgage* 20 Aug. 1782), A parcel of Ground..[which] adjoineth towards the north on vaults situate under the houses built on The Royal Taras [Adelphi, London]. **1796** *New Plan of London* [has] 'Lambeth Terrace, behind Lambeth Palace'. **1839** *Penny Cycl.* XIV. 113/2 The terraces in the Regent's Park, Hyde Park Terrace near Bayswater, and that in St. James's Park. **1850** KINGSLEY *Alt. Locke* i, My earliest recollections are of a suburban street: of its jumble of little shops and little terraces.

6. A soft spot in marble, which is cleaned out and the cavity filled up with a paste. Cf. TERRACY *a.*

1877 KNIGHT *Dict. Mech.*, *Terrases* (Masonry), hollow defects in marble or fissures filled with nodules of other substances. The hole, being cleared out, is filled with marble dust and mastic of the same color.

7. *attrib.* and *Comb.* **a.** Of or pertaining to, having, forming, or consisting of a terrace or terraces, as ***terrace-bank***, ***-bower***, ***cottage***, ***-garden***, ***-parapet***, ***-region***, ***-roof***, ***-stair***, ***-step***, ***-walk***, ***-wall***, ***-work***; obj. and obj. genitive, as ***terrace-keeper***, ***-maker***; ***terrace-like***, ***terrace-mantling*** adjs.; **terrace-cultivation**, the cultivation of hill-sides in terraces; so **terrace-culture**; **terrace-epoch** (*Geol.*), see quot. 1885; **terrace house**, one of a row of usu. similar houses joined by party-walls.

1834 L. RITCHIE *Wand. by Seine* 94 The *terrace-banks of the Seine. **1823** *Joanna Baillie's Collect. Poems* 119 Each whisper'd sigh Of the soft night-breeze through her *terrace-bowers Bore softer tones. **1973** A. HUNTER *Gently French* iv. 34 Adjacent to the Barge-House were three sad *terrace cottages. **1978** *Spectator* 13 May 12/2 Neat little freshly painted two-storey terrace cottages with gardens nearby—already a century old. **1860** PUSEY *Min. Proph.* 144 The *terrace-cultivation,..clothing with fertility the mountain-sides. **1903** *Bradford Antiquary* July 346 Signs of terrace-cultivation are to be met with in different parts of the county. **1863** FAWCETT *Pol. Econ.* II. vii. (1876) 212 The establishment of *terrace culture on the hills. **1862** DANA *Man. Geol.* 554 The time when they were raised.. corresponds to the *Terrace epoch; and during the process other parallel terraces were formed. **1885** GEIKIE *Text-bk. Geol.* III. II. ii. § 3. 369 In North America, the river-terraces exist on so grand a scale that the geologists of that country have named one of the later periods of geological history, during which those deposits were formed, the Terrace Epoch. **1705** ADDISON *Italy* 59, I went to see the *Terrace-Garden of Verona, that Travellers generally mention. **1861** QUEEN VICTORIA *Jrnl.* 20 Sept. (1980) 99 The Castle of Auch Mill, which..has traces of a terrace garden remaining. **1931** A. U. DILLEY *Oriental Rugs & Carpets* iii. 58 Many 'tree' and 'landscape' rugs are terrace-garden rugs. **1817** JANE AUSTEN *Sanditon* (1954) x. 413 They were in one of the *Terrace Houses. **1922** JOYCE *Ulysses* 697 A terracehouse or semidetached villa. **1958** *Listener* 5 June 947/1 Look at the new hospital-block in Guildford Street, Bloomsbury, and see how well it goes with the old terrace-houses. **1972** *Guardian* 6 Nov. 15/3 The rank and file knew that the real Ulster crisis was happening inside the terrace houses. **1880** 'MARK TWAIN' *Tramp Abr.* xxxv. 397 This pile of stone.. comes down out of the clouds in a succession of rounded, colossal, *terrace-like projections. **1963** *Times* 18 May 5/2 One of the finest things was his terrace-like build-up of the beginning of the allegretto from the Seventh Symphony. **1974** C. TAYLOR *Fieldwork in Medieval Archaeol.* iii. 28 These terrace-like features [*sc.* strip lynchets] on hillsides are the remains of medieval strip cultivation. **1824** CAMPBELL *Theodric* 37 Clustering trees and *terrace-mantling vines. **1854** DICKENS *Hard Times* II. vii. 207 Tom sat down on a *terrace-parapet, plucking buds. **1834** *Penny Cycl.* II. 472/2 Ten or twelve intermediate formations, constituting the *terrace-regions. **1802** GOUV. MORRIS in Sparks *Life & Writ.* (1832) III. 161, I have a *terrace roof. **1842** FRANCIS *Dict. Arts*, *Terrace Roof*, those which are flat like terraces. *a* **1668** DAVENANT *Man's the Master* IV. i, Pass through the gall'ry up the *tarras-stairs into my closet. **1865** J. H. INGRAHAM *Pillar of Fire* (1872) 218 We soon landed at the grand *terrace-steps of the quay. **1637** SUCKLING *Aglaura* III. i, Eleven; under the *Tarras walke; I will not faile you there. **1693** LUTTRELL *Brief Rel.* (1857) III. 174 The queens tarras walk at Whitehall, facing the Thames, is now finished. **1707** Terrace walk [see *side-wing* s.v. SIDE *sb.*[1] 27]. **1775** J. WOODFORDE *Diary* 14 Apr. (1924) I. 151 Round it is a fine Terrass Walk which commands the whole City. **1858** M. TUCKETT *Diary* 16 Sept. (*c* 1975) 5 A broad terrace walk goes along the front of the new part of the house. **1712** J. JAMES tr. *Le Blond's Gardening* 25 A low *Terrass-Wall, from whence you have a View of the Country round about. **1853** KANE *Grinnell Exp.* xv. (1856) 108 Its edges..were abrupt precipices, resembling the *terrace-work of trap-rock.

b. Used to designate a style of women's and girls' clothing suitable for wearing at an informal party.

1963 *Guardian* 2 Feb. 5/2 A series of terrace (ex-casino) dresses. **1965** *Sunday Mail* (Brisbane) 24 Oct. 24 (*caption*) Terrace skirt combines bright red, white, and blue in a lively outfit for girls who want to look graceful at casual parties. **1971** *Rand Daily Mail* (Johannesburg) 4 Dec. 3/8 (Advt.), A fabulous collection of the popular terrace gowns. **1972** *Times* 19 Dec. 11/3, I do not like the idea of little girls in low-cut evening dresses..but I do think that the pale blue terrace two-piece..is a delight.

Hence **'terracer**, one who stands or walks on a terrace: cf. TERRACING 2; **'terrace-wards** *adv.*, towards the terrace; **'terrace-wise** *adv.*, in the manner of a terrace.

1786 MME. D'ARBLAY *Diary* 7 Aug., All the *terracers stand up against the walls, to make a clear passage for the Royal Family. **1909** *Daily Chron.* 20 July 1/1 Pilgrims who arrived on the Westminster Bridge and bent their gaze *terrace-wards. **1638** SIR T. HERBERT *Trav.* (ed. 2) 156 Each shop.. archt above and.. atop *tarraswise framed, and with plaister.. cemented. **1898** *Daily News* 19 May 7/1 St. Pierre, Martinique,.. nestles terrace-wise against and amid a perfect paradise of greenery.

terrace, obs. form of TARRAS.

'terrace, *v.* Forms: see the sb.; also 7 *pa. pple.* terassed. [f. TERRACE *sb.*, or a. F. *terrasser* (16th c. in Godef. *Compl.*).]

1. *trans.* To form into a terrace or raised bank; to fashion or arrange in terraces. Also ***to terrace up.*** (Chiefly in *passive* until 19th c.; cf. next.)

1650 FULLER *Pisgah* III. ii. §5 The ascent.. was.. terrased on both sides with Pillasters made of.. Almuggin trees. **1682** WHELER *Journ. Greece* I. 13 The Walls also being well Terrassed. **1827** KEBLE *Chr. Y.* 3rd Sund. Advent, Mountains terrass'd high with mossy stone. **1848** MILL *Pol. Econ.* II. viii. §3 The plots, terrassed up one above another, are often not above four feet wide. **1880** MISS BIRD *Japan* I. 85 Fields formed by terracing sloping ground. **1895** *Westm. Gaz.* 7 Oct. 2/2 The Kusi River in Bengal.. brings down enormous quantities of silt,.. making fertile plains, terracing the land, changing its bed, destroying forests.

†**2.** To furnish with a 'terrace' or balcony; to provide (a house) with a loggia or terrace-roof. (Chiefly in *passive*: cf. next.) *Obs.*

1615 G. SANDYS *Trav.* I. 31 [Minarets] tarrast aloft on the out side like the maine top of a ship. **1624** WOTTON *Archit.* in *Reliq.* (1651) 260 Which [light] we must now supply.. by Tarrasing any Story which is in danger of darknesse. **1631** HEYWOOD *London's Jus. Hon.* Wks. 1874 IV. 276 A faire and curious structure archt and Tarrest aboue. **1634** SIR T. HERBERT *Trav.* 49 The houses.. are flat and tarrased atop.

3. *intr.* (*nonce-use.*) To rise in terraces (in quot., used of ranges of houses).

1900 *Speaker* 29 Dec. 342/1 Pink and white and blue tenements.. terrace recklessly above each other from the river to the sky-line.

terraced ('tɛrəst), *ppl. a.* [f. TERRACE *sb.* or *v.* + -ED.] Formed into or furnished with a terrace or terraces; arranged or constructed in terrace form. Of a house: cf. *terrace house* s.v. TERRACE *sb.* 7.

In quot. 1644, Furnished with a colonnade or covered ambulatory.

1644 EVELYN *Diary* 4 Nov., The court is square and tarrass'd. **1727-46** THOMSON *Summer* 1429 To Clermont's terrass'd height, and Esher's groves. **1797** MRS. RADCLIFFE *Ital.* i, Its terraced roofs crowded with spectators. **1869** TOZER *Highl. Turkey* I. 108 The dwellings.. are.. niched.. in the terraced cliffs. **1880** C. R. MARKHAM *Peruv. Bark* 365 The space between being sown with rice in terraced fields. **1904** J. T. FOWLER *Durh. Univ.* 63 The rebuilt keep conspicuous on a terraced mound. **1958** *Daily Express* 3 Apr. 7/7 Their tiny terraced home in the back streets of Horden, Durham. **1976** *Milton Keynes Express* 28 May 1/3 She has no intention of leaving her terraced home. **1979** *Guardian* 19 June 4/2 The old-fashioned terraced house.. is on the way back.

terra'centric, *a. nonce-wd.* [f. TERRA + CENTRIC *a.*] Having, or taking, the earth as centre; = GEOCENTRIC *a.* 2.

1932 G. B. SHAW *Adventures Black Girl* 66 As to Bible science.. its astronomy is terracentric.

terraceous (tɛ'reɪʃəs), *a. rare.* [f. L. type *terrāce-us (see TERRACE) + -OUS: cf. -ACEOUS.] Of earthy nature or composition.

1863 MOUAT *Adv. Andaman Island.* 151 The progress that we made through the terraceous compost was necessarily slow.

terracette (tɛrə'sɛt). *Geomorphol.* [f. TERRACE *sb.* + -ETTE.] A small (natural) terrace; *spec.* one of a parallel series on a steep hillside.

1922 H. ODUM in *Dan. Geol. Undersøg.* IV. I. 27 The phenomenon.. occurs on hill-slopes with a steep inclination, and consists in the surface being covered with a number of small terracettes or low ledges, all running parallel, horizontal and at about an equal distance from each other. **1959** G. H. DURY *Face of Earth* ii. 13 On very many steep slopes a kind of ribbed pattern appears on the surface of the creeping waste, with little steps a foot or two in height running horizontally. These steps are called terracettes. An alternative name is sheep-tracks, but this title is grossly misleading. Terracettes can be found where no sheep have ever been. **1971** I. G. GASS et al. *Understanding Earth* xiii. 182/2 Tiny terracettes can be cut into the sides of the ripples [on a beach]. **1974** C. TAYLOR *Fieldwork in Medieval Archaeol.* iv. 85 Terracettes are another form of natural feature likely to be misinterpreted.

terraciform (tɛ'ræsɪfɔːm), *a. rare.* [f. TERRACE *sb.* (or med.L. *terrāci-a*) + -FORM.] Having the form of a terrace.

1890 *Smithsonian Inst. Rep.* 72 The formation is sometimes fashioned into terraces; and some of its best developments in the District of Columbia.. are terraciform.

terracing ('tɛrəsɪŋ), *vbl. sb.* [f. TERRACE *v.* or *sb.* + -ING[1].]

1. a. The formation of terraces. **b.** *concr.* A terraced structure or formation; a series or range of terraces; a platform or stand with rows of seats rising in tiers behind each other; *spec.* = TERRACE *sb.* 1 e.

1826 CHALMERS in Hanna *Mem.* (1851) III. viii. 128 [We] enjoyed.. the noble terracing, and orange house. **1862** DANA *Man. Geol.* 558 The terracing of the borders of the lakes and rivers. **1864** CARLYLE *Fredk. Gt.* XVI. i. IV. 245 The diggings and terracings of the Hill-side. **1885** SIR R. BALL *Story of Heavens* iii. (1890) 67 The terracing shown in its interior [of the extinct lunar volcano Copernicus] is mainly due to the repeated alternate rise, partial congelation, and subsequent retreat of a vast sea of lava. **1902** *Daily Chron.* 8 Apr. 5/1 The terracing which collapsed with such disastrous results during the football match at Ibrox Park on Saturday. **1942** *R.A.F. Jrnl.* 30 May 33 It was like the empty terracings of Wembley or Hampden Park after an international. **1976** J. SNOW *Cricket Rebel* 63 The occasional fires on the terracing which are part and parcel of cricket matches in Pakistan. **1978** P. MARSH et al. *Rules of Disorder* iii. 58 Young supporters at every football league ground.. have defined sections of the terracing as their own territory.

2. Walking or promenading on a terrace. *rare.*

1786 MME. D'ARBLAY *Diary* 24 July, Here we have coffee till the Terracing is over. This is about eight o'clock.

‖**terra-cotta** (ˌtɛrə'kɒtə). [It., lit. baked (cooked) earth:—L. *terra cocta.* So F. *terre cuite.*]

1. A hard unglazed pottery of a fine quality, of which decorative tiles and bricks, architectural decorations, statuary, vases, and the like are made.

1722 J. RICHARDSON *Statues, etc. Italy* 177 A Model in Terra Cotta as fine as ever was done. **1752** HOLLIS in *Lett. Lit. Men* (Camden) 390 Many things in glass, many in terra cotta. **1842-76** GWILT *Archit.* §624 The west front of the church of Sta. Maria in Strada, a most elaborate work in brick and terra-cotta. **1867** W. W. SMYTH *Coal & Coal-mining* 190 The Romans have left us numerous examples in bronze and *terra cotta.*

b. With *a* and *pl.*: An object of art, as a statuette or figurine, made of this substance.

1810 T. COMBE (*title*) A Description of the Collection of Ancient Terracottas in the British Museum. **1842** *Smith's Dict. Grk. & Rom. Antiq.* s.v. *Fictile,* They reckoned some of their consecrated terra-cottas.. among the safe-guards of their imperial city. **1865** *Athenæum* 28 Jan. 127/3 The terra-cottas include some very remarkable coloured statuettes or *figurine* of Greek production.

2. The colour of this pottery, a brownish red of various shades.

1882 *Daily News* 3 June 3/1 That colour which the uninitiated would call golden brown, but which milliners call terra-cotta. **1890** *Pall Mall G.* 25 June 2/1 The splendid terra-cottas of the rocks and the bright greens of the trees. **1900** *Westm. Gaz.* 23 Apr. 3/2 An underdress of pale blue brocade over which is arranged a tunic of terra-cotta.

3. *attrib.* and *Comb.* **a.** Of or pertaining to terra-cotta, as ***terra-cotta works.*** **b.** Made of terra-cotta, as ***terra-cotta bust, figure, vase***; **c.** Of the colour of terra-cotta, as ***terra-cotta feather, paper, velvet***; also ***terra-cotta tinted*** adj.

1859 R. HUNT *Guide Mus. Pract. Geol.* (ed. 2) 96 Figures.. manufactured at the Mill Wall terra cotta works. **1868** *Pall Mall G.* 2 Dec. 8 Seventy-four terra cotta busts of the Roman Emperors and their families. **1877** W. S. W. VAUX *Grk. Cities Asia Minor* iv. 162 In 1853, Mr. Newton obtained many *terra-cotta* vases of a very archaic type. **1888** *Lady* 25 Oct. 378/1 Trimmings of terra-cotta faced cloth. **1891** *Truth* 10 Dec. 1242 All the doorways were draped with terra-cotta silk. **1899** *Westm. Gaz.* 19 July 3/1 Roofs.. terra-cotta tinted.

'terra,culture. *rare*⁻⁰. [irreg. f. L. *terra* earth + CULTURE: cf. *agriculture.*] = AGRICULTURE. Hence **terra'cultural** *a.* = AGRICULTURAL.

1847 in WEBSTER; whence in later Dicts.

terracy ('tɛrəsɪ), *a.* [f. TERRACE *sb.* 6 + -Y.] Of marble: Containing terraces or soft spots.

1727-41 CHAMBERS *Cycl.* s.v. *Marble,* Terracy Marble, that with soft places in it, which must be filled up with cement, as that of Languedoc.

Terra da (de, di) Sienna, varr. TERRA SIENNA.

‖**'terra dam'nata.** *Alchemy. Obs.* [L., = condemned or finally rejected earth.] = CAPUT MORTUUM 2: see quot. 1704.

1633 B. JONSON *Tale Tub* I. iii, She's such a vessel of fæces: all dried earth, Terra damnata! **1704** J. HARRIS *Lex. Techn.* I. s.v. *Earth,* Earth, which the Chymists call *Terra Damnata* and *Caput Mortuum,* is the last of the five Chymical Principles, and is that which remains after all the other Principles are extracted by Distilation, Calcination, &c. **1710** T. FULLER *Pharm. Extemp.* 146 (Stanf.) Calcin'd Harts-horn being a meer *Terra Damnata.*

†**,terræ'filial**, *a. Obs. rare.* [f. next, with *filial* from *filius.*] Earthly, worldly, sordid. So **,terræ'filian** *a.*, of or pertaining to a *terræ filius.*

1742 YOUNG *Nt. Th.* VIII. 277 Men of the world, the terræ-filial breed, Welcome the modest stranger to their sphere. **1783** BURNS *Let. to J. Murdoch* 15 Jan., Can he descend to mind the paltry concerns about which the terræfilial race fret, and fume..? **1887** SAINTSBURY *Hist. Elizab. Lit.* x. (1894) 364 His merits as well as his faults have a singular unpersonal, and, if I may so say, *terræfilian* connotation.

‖**terræ filius** ('tɛriː 'fɪlɪəs). Pl. terræ filii. [L. *terræ filius,* a son of the earth, a man of unknown origin.]

1. A person of obscure parentage.

[*c* **1590** GREENE *Fr. Bacon* ix. 51 Those geomantic spirits, That Hermes calleth *terræ filii.*] **1621** BURTON *Anat. Mel.* II. iii. II. (1676) 199/2 Let no *terræ filius,* or upstart, insult at this which I have said, no worthy Gentleman take offence. **1622** MABBE tr. *Aleman's Guzman d'Alf.* I. III. i. 186 As if my father had beene *terræ filius.* **1679** NESSE *Antichrist* 7 This is the Terræfilius, the base-born beast that springs out of the earth. **1883** *Sat. Rev.* 2 June 688/2 Abdel-Kader himself was very far from being *terræ filius.*

2. Formerly, at the University of Oxford: An orator privileged to make humorous and satirical strictures in a speech at the public 'act'. (In quot. 1882, applied to a similar orator at Dublin University.) Cf. PREVARICATOR 4.

1651-93 WOOD *Life* [passim: see ed. Clark (1900) V. 151/2]. **1656** BLOUNT *Glossogr., Terræ-filius*.. the foole in the Acts at Oxford. **1674** *Ibid.* (ed. 4), *Terræ-filius,*.. we may call him the *bon drol* in the Acts at Oxford.. who must be a Master of Arts, to qualifie him for this Office, and is commonly chosen out of the best Wits of the Univeristy. **1669** EVELYN *Diary* 10 July, The *Terræ filius* (the Universitie Buffoone) entertain'd the auditorie with a.. sarcastical rhapsodie. **1670** EACHARD *Cont. Clergy* 37 Wits.. who never.. were at all inspir'd from a Tripus's, Terræ-filius's, or Prævarecator's speech. **1713** STEELE *Guard.* No. 72 ¶2 In my time.. the Terræ-filius contented himself with being bitter upon the Pope, or chastising the Turk. **1721** AMHERST *Terræ Fil.* Ded., It is very uncertain when *Terræ-Filius* will be able to regain his antient privileges in the Sheldonian theatre. *Ibid.* No. 5. 23 All men are not *Terræ-Filius's.* **1882** *Q. Rev.* Apr. 389 A scurrilous harangue.. for the delivery of which, in the character of Terræ Filius, one of his [Swift's] College acquaintances narrowly escaped expulsion.

‖**terra firma** (ˌtɛrə 'fɜːmə). [L., = 'firm land', used in med. or mod.L. in special senses = It. *terra ferma,* F. *terre ferme*; cf. G. *festland.* In 17th c. partly a. It. *terra ferma.*]

†**1.** A mainland or continent, as distinct from portions of land partly or wholly isolated by water.

1665 SIR T. HERBERT *Trav.* (1677) 31 He [Ptolemy] draws his *Terra firma* only to 10 degrees South from the Æquator. **1706** PHILLIPS (ed. Kersey), *Terra firma,* the Continent, or main Land; so call'd by Geographers. **1725** DE FOE *Voy. round World* (1840) 164 Our men.. said that about three leagues off to the southward, there seemed to be a Terra Firma, or continent of land. **1727-41** CHAMBERS *Cycl., Terra firma*.. is sometimes used for a continent, in contradistinction to islands.

†**2.** *spec.* **a.** The territories on the Italian mainland which were subject to the state of Venice. *Obs.*

1605 B. JONSON *Volpone* II. i, Gentlemen of your City; strangers of the *terra-firma*; worshipful merchants; ay, and senators too. **1645** EVELYN *Diary* June (1819) I. 192 We went to Padua... The first *terra firma* we landed at was Fusina, being onely an inn, where we changed our barge. **1832** tr. *Sismondi's Ital. Rep.* xiv. 308 The two monarchs agreed to divide between them all the *terra firma* of the Venetians.

†**b.** The northern coast-land of South America (Colombia), as distinguished from the West India Islands; also, in narrower sense, the Isthmus of Panama. *Obs.*

1760-72 tr. *Juan & Ulloa's Voy.* (ed. 3) I. p. vii, Geographical desciptions.. of the country about Carthagena,.. the *Terra Firma.* **1827** ROBERTS *Voy. Centr. Amer.* 71 A race of people.. more civilized than most of the other tribes, inhabiting this part of *Terra Firma.*

3. The land as distinguished from the sea; dry or firm land; in quot. 1785, the earth. Also *fig.*

1693 RAY *Disc.* I. iii. 24 The whole *terra firma,* or dry Land. **1707** NORRIS *Treat. Humility* iii. 111 Here we have some *terra firma* to fix and stay our footing on. **1779** *Hist. Mod. Europe* II. l. 65 They again got footing on terra firma. **1785** BURNS *Ep. to W. Simpson* 105 While terra firma, on her axis, Diurnal turns. **1820** T. MITCHELL *Aristoph., Com.* I. 72 That their feet find no resting-place on sea Or terra-firma. **1887** MISS BRADDON *Like & Unlike* xxxiv, I was not often upon *terra firma* after I left Marseilles.

†**4.** *humor.* and *colloq.* Landed estate; land.

1698 FARQUHAR *Love & Bottle* III. ii, I have five thousand acres of as good fighting ground as any in England, good *terra firma,* sir. *a* **1700** B. E. *Dict. Cant. Crew* s.v. *Dipt, He has dipt his Terra firma,* he has mortgaged his dirty Acres. *Ibid., Terra-firma,* an Estate in Land. **1728** FIELDING *Love in Sev. Masques* v. vi, Does your estate lie in *terra firma,* or in the stocks?

†**'terrage.** *Obs.* Also 5 terage. [a. OF. *terage* (13th c. in Godef.):—pop. L. *terrāticum* (869 in Du Cange), f. L. *terra* earth: see -AGE. Hence med.L. *terrāgium* (1030 in Du Cange).]

1. Land; a territory, district.

c **1400** *Destr. Troy* 1072 þai comen to the cost.. of the terage of Troy. *Ibid.* 13631 þat Pirrus schuld haue þe terrage of tessayle and þe tryed corone. *c* **1440** *Promp. Parv.* 489/1 Terage, erthe, *humus, solum, terragium.*

2. *Old Law.* Some kind of payment or duty. (Actual meaning uncertain; see quots.)

The statements of the 17th c. law dicts. are guesses. Gross takes it as = PICKAGE. But, as some charters have *terrage* besides *stallage* and *pickage,* the meaning may be payment for the ground or 'stance' occupied at a fair or market without breaking the ground.

[**1301** *Lincoln Charter* in *Cal. Charter Rolls* III. 9. **1349** in W. Hardy *Lancaster Charters* (1845) 6 Quod.. sint quieti de pavagio, passagio, paagio, lastagio, stallagio, tallagio, cariagio, pesagio, piccagio, et terragio.] **1691** BLOUNT *Law Dict.*, *Terrage* (*Terragium*) [quotes the prec. patent, and says] which seems to be an exemption *á Præcariis*, viz. Boons of Plowing, Reaping, &c. and perhaps from Money paid for digging or breaking the Earth in Fairs and Markets. **1749** in Pote *Hist. Windsor* 120 (Transl. of a Charter) That the said Custos or Canons and their tenants should for ever be free from payment of Toll, Picage, Paviage, .. Terrage [etc.]. [**1890** GROSS *Gild Merchant* II. 420 *Terragium*. The same as *Picagium* (413), Duty paid by a stranger on markets and fairs to break the ground and erect a stall.]

3. ? A toll or duty paid for landing; landing dues.

[**1318** *Grimsby Charter* in *Cal. Charter Rolls* III. 411 [*tr.* quit of toll .. hansage, anchorage, terrage, quayage, passage, and pedage].] **1664** HALE *Treat.* II. iv. in Hargrave *Coll. Tracts* (1787) I. 57 The defendants .. shewed usage to have had certain customs called land-leave, terrage, &c. *Ibid.* vi. 76 *Terrage*, for the necessary unlading of goods before they come up to the common key.

‖**terraglia** (tɛr'raʎʎa). *Ceramics.* [It., = earthenware, china, f. L. *terra* earth.] An (Italian) cream-coloured earthenware, esp. that manufactured from 1728 at Nove, near Bassano, Italy, by G. B. Antonibon and his descendants.

1850 J. MARRYAT *Coll. Hist. Pott. & Porc.* 290 *Terraglia*, the Italian term for fine pottery of hard paste. **1870** W. CHAFFERS *Marks & Monogr. Pott. & Porc.* (ed. 3) 118 Pasqual [Antonibon] .. carried on .. the manufacture of *maioliche fine* or fayence, and *terraglia* or terre de pipe. **1877** C. SCHREIBER *Jrnl.* 20 June (1911) II. 28 A very fine Terraglia dish (red ground with figures in white ..) .. of old Paduan manufacture. **1960** R. G. HAGGAR *Conc. Encycl. Continental Pott. & Porc.* 471/1 *Terraglia*, cream-coloured earthenware.

‖**te'rraignol.** *Obs. rare*$^{-0}$. [obs. F. *terraignol* (Cotgr.), ad. It. *terrāgnolo* 'drooping, downe looking, dull, heauy, as some heauy-going horses' (Florio); f. OIt. *terragno* (Dante = *terreno*):—med.L. *terrāneus* of the earth + *-olo*, L. *-olus* dim.] A heavy-going horse: see quot.

1727 BAILEY vol. II, *Terraignol*, .. is a Horse who cleaves to the Ground [etc.] .. in general, one whose Motions are all short, and too near the Ground.

terrain (tɛ'reɪn), *sb.* (*a.*) Also 8–9 **terrein** (9 **terrane**, in sense 3). [a. F. *terrain* (also *terrein*), OF. *terain* (Wace 12th c.):—pop.L. **terrānum* = cl. L. *terrēnum* TERRENE.]

A. *sb.* **1.** †**a.** (See quot. 1727.) *Obs.* **b.** Standing-ground, position.

1727 BAILEY vol. II, *Terrain*, .. is the Manage-Ground upon which the Horse makes his Pist or Tread. **1753** in CHAMBERS *Cycl. Supp.* **1816** in JAMES *Milit. Dict.* **1832** LISTER *Arlington* II. vii. 117 Viewed in the same light, and from the same *terrain* from which they view it themselves.

2. a. A tract of country considered with regard to its natural features, configuration, etc.; in military use esp. as affecting its tactical advantages, fitness for manœuvring, etc.; also, an extent of ground, region, district, territory.

1766 W. DIGBY *Let. to G. Selwyn* 12 Apr., in Jesse *S. & Contemp.* (1843) II. 13 We rode to reconnoitre the *terrein*. **1816** JAMES *Milit. Dict.*, *Terrain*, .. generally any space or extent of ground. **1879** *Cassell's Techn. Educ.* IV. 95/1 Without reference .. to the physical irregularities of the terrain. **1889** BADEN-POWELL *Pigsticking* 9 Taking in at a glance the peculiarities of the terrain.

b. *fig.*

1860 PRINCESS ROYAL *Let.* 3 Dec. in R. Fulford *Dearest Child* (1964) 288 She will .. not [have] such a difficult 'terrain' to work upon as God knows I have here. **1979** *Amer. Poetry Rev.* Mar./Apr. 19/4 He found authors in that terrain of brotherhood and contact the reader calls for and which they, the writers I've named and so many others, gave and go on giving by the courses and the conduct which touch their responsibility as Latin Americans.

3. *Geol.* (Usually spelt **terrane**.) A name for a connected series, group, or system of rocks or formations; a stratigraphical subdivision.

1823 tr. *Humboldt's Geognost. Ess.* Introd. 2 The union of several formations constitutes a geological series or a district (*terrain*); but the terms rocks, formations, and *terrains*, are used as synonymous in many works on geognosy. **1864** DANA *Man. Geol.* 81 (Cent.) Terrane .. is used for any single rock or continuous series of rocks of a region, whether the formation be stratified or not. **1889** in *Q. Jrnl. Geol. Soc.* XLV. 63 The word *terrane* proposed by Prof. Gilbert to be used for a stratigraphical subdivision of any magnitude. **1895** *Pop. Sci. Monthly* Sept. 694 The slates of the Cambrian terrane.

4. *attrib.* and *Comb.*, as **terrain-following radar** *Aeronaut.*, a radar system which enables an aircraft or missile to fly at high speed close to the ground by automatically adjusting its altitude in relation to the surface over which it is flying; so **terrain follower**.

1961 *Daily Tel.* 4 Oct. 17/1 A device known as the 'terrain follower', which keeps the plane automatically at a predetermined height above the ground. **1970** *Times* 4 Sept. (Aviation Suppl.) p. ix/8 Advanced avionics technology for the European multirole combat aircraft will be shown, with strike and terrain-following radar. **1980** *Guardian Weekly* 13 July 1/2 Terrain-following radar for low-level penetration of enemy defences.

B. *adj.* Of the earth, terrene, terrestrial. **a.** *terrain tide*, a (supposed) rise and fall in the earth's crust, caused by the attraction of the sun or moon. **b.** *terrain cure*: see quot.

1882 MILNE in *Nature* 8 June 125/2 To determine the existence of a terrain tide, a gravitimeter might be established... If terrain tides exist, and they are sufficiently great from a geological point of view. **1897** *Allbutt's Syst. Med.* IV. 621 Regulated exercises, such as the gentle climbing, especially in mountain districts, known as the terrain cure.

‖**terra incognita** (ˌtɛrə ɪn'kɒgnɪtə). *Pl.* **terræ incognitæ** (*erron.* **terras incognitas**). [L., = 'unknown land'.] An unknown or unexplored region. Often *fig.*

1616 CAPT. SMITH *Descr. New Eng.* 6 The Spaniards know .. not so much as the true circumference of *Terra Incognita*, whose large dominions may equalize the greatnesse and goodnes of America. **1630** J. TAYLOR (Water P.) *Gt. Eater Kent* Wks. I. 143/2 The place of his birth, and names of his parents are to me a meere *Terra incognita*. **1756** LADY M. W. MONTAGU *Let. to C'tess of Bute* 1 Apr., Your provinces of politics, gallantry, and literature, all [are] *terra incognita*. **1821** ANNA M. PORTER *Village of Mariendorpt* II. 121 His friend and the field-marshall were nearly terras incognitas to each other. **1901** *Scotsman* 11 Mar. 6/4 The country within a day's ride .. is almost a terra incognita.

terraine, obs. form of TERRENE.

‖**terrain vague** (tɛrɛ̃ vag). [Fr. colloq., lit. 'waste ground'.] Wasteland, no man's land (*transf.* and *fig.*).

1920 R. FRY *Let.* 12 Oct. (1972) II. 493 I'm .. painting up on Montmartre in a *terrain vague* with the hideous white tower of the Sacré Coeur dominating a jumble of modern houses. **1934** C. LAMBERT *Music Ho!* III. 207 The same rapprochement between highbrow and lowbrow—both meeting in an emotional *terrain vague*—can be seen in literature. **1957** L. DURRELL *Bitter Lemons* 48 His desk was in the far corner against the wall, and to reach it one traversed a *terrain vague* which resembled the basement of Maple's, so crowded was it with armchairs, desks, prams .. and all the impedimenta of gracious living. **1984** *Sunday Times* 26 Aug. 38/8 Alastair Reid occupies a *terrain vague* between reportage and *belles lettres*.

‖**Terra Japonica** (ˌtɛrə dʒə'pɒnɪkə). [mod.L., = 'Japanese earth': see note s.v. CATECHU. So F. *terre du Japon*.] = CATECHU, formerly also known as *Japonic earth*.

[**1654, 1679**,] **1683** [see CATECHU]. **1693** tr. *Blancard's Phys. Dict.* (ed. 2), *Catechu*, improperly called *Terra Japonica*. **1725** *Lond. Gaz.* No. 6366/1 Half a Ton of Terra Japannica. **1845** *Encycl. Metrop.* XXII. 474/1 The exports from Népál are rice, ginger, terra Japonica (*i.e.* the gum, or inspissated juice of the *Mimosa catechu*).

‖**terral** (te'ral). [Sp., f. L. *terra* land; so F. *terral*.] The land-breeze off the coast of Spain or South America.

1863 H. W. BATES *Naturalist on River Amazons* II. ii. 144 Canoes, in descending, only travel at night, when the terral, or light land-breeze, blows off the eastern shore. **1884** H. COLLINGWOOD *Under Meteor Flag* 299 Obliged to take to our sweeps to get across the calm belt between the terral and the trade-wind. **1928** *Bryologist* XXXI. 125 The weather was very cold. We had been feeling the intense icy blasts of the *Terral* wind from the North [of Spain]. **1953** W. G. KENDREW *Climates of Continents* (ed. 4) xxxix. 481 The sea-breeze (virazon) and land-breeze (terral) are regular and prominent; the sea-breeze is often so strong on summer afternoons at Valparaiso .. that boat-work is stopped. **1961** L. D. STAMP *Gloss. Geogr. Terms* 448/2 *Terral*, the land breeze along the coasts of western Peru.

‖**Terra Lemnia.** [med. or mod.L., = 'Lemnian earth', f. *Lemnos*, an island in the Ægean sea. So F. *terre de Lemnos* (Littré), It. *terra lenia* (Florio), G. *lemnische erde*.] = TERRA SIGILLATA; known also as *Lemnian earth*.

1613 HARCOURT *Voy. Guiana* in *Harl. Misc.* (Malh.) III. 192 The earth yieldeth bole-armoniack and terra-lemnia. **1632** [see TERRA SIGILLATA 1]. **1797** *Encycl. Brit.* (ed. 3) IX. 784/2 Lemnian Earth, *Terra Lemnia*, a medicinal, astringent sort of earth, of a fatty consistence and reddish colour.

terralla, erron. form of TERRELLA.

terramare (tɛrə'mɑː(r), -'mɛə(r)). Pl. **-ares.** Also *β.* in It. form **terra'mara**, pl. **terre'mare** (sometimes used as an invariable form). [a. F. *terramare* (1867 *Rev. des Deux-Mondes*, 653, in Littré), ad. dial. It. *terramara* (used in Emilia, about Bologna), for *terra-marna* (Bellini), f. *terra* earth + *marna* (dial. *mara*) MARL.

Introduced into anthropological use by Strobel and Pigarini, 1862.]

An ammoniacal earth found in the valley of the Po, in Italy, and collected as a fertilizer; it occurs in flat mounds, identified as the sites of dwellings of a people of the later neolithic period. Hence *transf.* (*pl.*) The prehistoric settlements themselves. Also *attrib.*

α. **1866–8** BARING-GOULD *Curious Myths Mid. Ages*, *Leg. Cross* (1877) 365 These quarries go by the name of *terramares*. They are vast accumulations of cinders, charcoal, bones, fragments of pottery. **1871** TYLOR *Prim. Cult.* I. ii. 55 Relics discovered in gravel-beds, caves, shell-mounds, terramares, lake-dwellings.

β. **1890** HUXLEY in *19th Cent.* Nov. 761 The pre-historic people of the terremare. **1899** R. MUNRO *Prehist. Scot.* vi. 205 Combs of bronze have been found both in the Swiss lake-dwellings and in the Terremare. *Ibid.* xi. 434 There is .. in the eastern part of the Po Valley another class of ancient habitations known as *terremare*, .. they may be regarded as land palafittes. **1928** C. DAWSON *Age of Gods* xiv. 330 With the Bronze Age there appears in North Italy the new and highly distinctive type of culture known as the Terremare. It receives its name from the peculiar pile settlements which form its characteristic feature. Unlike the lake villages the Terremare were built on dry land and surrounded by an artificial moat and rampart. **1939** *Antiquity* XIII. 490 A terramara is defined by Säflund as 'a station containing the typical bronze-age culture of central and western Emilia'. **1961** L. MUMFORD *City in Hist.* viii. 206 It is doubtful if there is any direct connexion between the *terremare* settlements and the Roman towns.

Terramycin (tɛrə'maɪsɪn). *Pharm.* Also **terramycin.** [f. L. *terra* earth + -MYCIN.] A proprietary name for OXYTETRACYCLINE.

1950 A. C. FINLAY et al. in *Science* 27 Jan. 85/1 From both cultures of this organism, a crystalline antibiotic was isolated; the name Terramycin has been assigned to this compound. **1953** *Official Gaz.* (U.S. Patent Office) 5 May 22/1 Chas. Pfizer & Co., Inc. .. *Terramycin* for antibiotic preparation containing oxytetracycline or a derivative thereof. **1954** *Trade Marks Jrnl.* 11 May 479/1 *Terramycin*. .. Oxytetracycline and derivatives thereof, and substances containing oxytetracycline or derivatives thereof, all prepared for use as antibiotics. Chas. Pfizer & Co., Inc. **1956** A. HUXLEY *Let.* 25 Dec. (1969) 814, I was put on to acromycin, after terramycin had failed to do much good. **1960** *Spectator* 2 Sept. 353 As compensation for the loss of his farmyard freedom he gets a dose of aureomycin, terramycin or penicillin. **1976** *Daily Times* (Lagos) 5 Aug. 14/1 (Advt.), Terramycin eye ointment.

Terran ('tɛrən), *a.* and *sb.* *Science Fiction.* [f. L. *terra* earth + -AN.] **A.** *adj.* Of or pertaining to the planet Earth or its inhabitants. **B.** *sb.* An inhabitant of the planet Earth.

[**1881** W. D. HAY *Three Hundred Years Hence* xi. 267 I am speaking of the Terrane Exodus and the Cities of the Sea.] **1953** *Cosmos Sci. Fiction & Fantasy Mag.* Nov. 83 A chant rose to assail his ears, and the steady beat of a drum thundered in the Terran night. *Ibid.* 78 They set about the tremendous task of educating Martians and Terrans. **1960** K. AMIS *New Maps of Hell* (1961) ii. 63 Any Martian survey team would be well advised to read a sample of the stuff before reporting on Terran civilisation. **1962** E. F. RUSSELL *Great Explosion* i. 13 We shall face them and defeat them as Terrans always have done. **1969** *New Scientist* 23 Jan. 191/3 Like our planet, we Terrans tend to be fat and slow or thin and quick.

terrandry, -anye: see TYRANTRY, TYRANNY.

terrane: see TERRAIN.

terranean (tɛ'reɪniːən), *a.* and *sb.* [f. as next + -AN.] **A.** *adj.* Pertaining to, or proceeding from, the earth.

1653 W. RAMESEY *Astrol. Restored* 107 It is a terranean and earthy Angle. **18..** *Electr. Rev.* (U.S.) XVIII. I. 9 (Cent.) The great strain on the trolley wire .. would be a necessary incident of terranean supply. **1939** JOYCE *Finnegans Wake* 120 Of an early muddy terranean origin.

B. *sb.* Also **terranian.** An inhabitant of the planet Earth. *Science Fiction. rare.*

1913 'SEPHARIAL' *Kabala of Numbers* II. xi. 175 Red is an irritant to all but Martians, and to them green probably means the same thing as does red to us Terranians. **1965** *Punch* 27 Jan. 141/3 When one of the anemone-harnessers .. tells a couple of captive 'terraneans', i.e., grown-ups, 'You must be destroyed!' I could sense a tremble of joy in children everywhere.

terraneous (tɛ'reɪniːəs), *a.* *rare.* [f. L. **terrāneus* (cf. *subterrāneus*), f. *terra* earth: see -OUS.] Of or pertaining to the earth; terrestrial.

a **1711** KEN *Edmund* Poet. Wks. 1721 II. 210 As long as this terraneous Globe endur'd. **1725** *Brice's Weekly Jrnl.* 26 Nov. 1 There may be some Sea-Shells dug at Land containing Terraneous Insects.

b. *Bot.* Growing upon land.

1882 in OGILVIE (Annandale).

terrapin[1] ('tɛrəpɪn). Forms: 7 (**torope**), **tarapine**, 7–9 **terrapine**, 8 **torrepine**, **terebin**, 8–9 **tarapin**, 9 **terrapene**, **terapin**, **tarrapin**, 8– **terrapin**. [Of Algonquin origin; *torope* represented the Abenaki *turepé* (also *tourepé*) in Rasles *Abenaki Dict.* rendered 'tortue', in Delaware *tulpe*. The origin of the final *-in*, *-ine* is obscure.]

a. A name originally given to one or more species of North American turtles; thence extended to many allied species of the turtle and tortoise family, *Testudineæ*, widely distributed over North, Central, and South America, the East Indies, China, N. Africa, and other countries. In N. America, *spec.* the Diamond-backed or Saltmarsh terrapin, *Malaclemmys palustris*, famous for its delicate flesh.

Among other well-known American species are the red-bellied terrapin, *Pseudemys rugosa*, the alligator terrapin or snapping-turtle, *Chelydra serpentina*, and the pine-barren terrapin, Box-turtle, or Gopher, *Cistudo carolina*. The Catalogue of Animals in the London Zoological Gardens, 1896, contains thirty-three species of Terrapin, with distinctive appellations, as ***Caspian, Ceylonese, Floridan, Spanish, annulated, black-headed, ocellated, painted, roofed, speckled, wrinkled, Bennett's, Blanding's, Maw's, Oldham's, Spengler's terrapin***. These are distributed in fifteen genera.

1613 A. WHITAKER *Gd. Newes fr. Virginia* 42, I have caught with mine angle pike, carpe, eele, .. creafish, and the torope or little turtle. **1672** JOSSELYN *New Eng. Rarities* 34 The Turtle that lives in Lakes and is called in Virginia a Terrapine. **1672** J. LEDERER *Discov.* 4 Every Nation gives his particular ensigne or arms, the Sasquesahanaugh a tarapine or small tortoise. **1678** PHILLIPS (ed. 4), *Terrapine*, a word used among the Virginians for that which we commonly call a Tortoise, and many call a Turtle, .. the Lake Turtle which lives in Lakes, .. is that most properly called the *Terrapine*. **1714** J. LAWSON *Hist. Carolina* 133 Of terebins there are divers sorts, all which .. we will comprehend under the distinction of land and water terebins. **1722** BEVERLEY *Virginia* III. iv. §15. 151 A small kind of Turtle, or Tarapins (as we call them). *Ibid.* IV. xix. §80. 265 Snakes, Terrapins, and such like Vermine. **1764** SMOLLETT *Trav.* xix. (1766) I. 302 The land-turtle, or terrapin, is much better known at Nice, as being a native of this country. **1844** *P. Parley's Ann.* V. 115 The growth of the terrapene is very slow. **1854** OWEN *Skel. & Teeth* in *Orr's Circ. Sc.* I. *Org. Nat.* 217 The Australian long-necked terrapene (*Hydraspis longicollis*). **1862** TROLLOPE *N. Amer.* I. 467 The terrapin is a small turtle, found on the shores of Maryland and Virginia, out of which a very rich soup is made. **1908** *Times* 22 Feb. 13/3 Three-keeled terrapin .. from Guatemala.

b. The flesh of this animal as food.

1867 DIXON *New Amer.* (ed. 6) II. 335 Gentlemen sitting at table sipping soup, picking terapin. **1892** F. M. CRAWFORD *Three Fates* II. 139 He had eaten terrapin and canvas back off old Saxon China.

c. *attrib.* and *Comb.*, as ***terrapin meat, shell, soup***; **terrapin-farm**, a place where diamond-back terrapins are reared for the market; **terrapin paws**, a name, in Chesapeake Bay, for tongs used in capturing terrapins; **Terrapin State**, a colloquial name for the State of Maryland.

1775 ADAIR *Amer. Ind.* 110 Torrepine-shells containing pebbles. **1845** J. COULTER *Adv. in Pacific* ix. 110, I put to it some terrapin meat. **1862** RUSSELL *Diary North & S.* (1863) 340 The Terrapin soup excellent, though not comparable .. to the best turtle. **1901** H. GADOW in *Camb. Nat. Hist.* VIII. ix. 360 Enterprising men have established terrapin-farms or 'crawls' for the keeping and breeding of terrapins. **1937** G. E. SHANKLE *Amer. Nicknames* 338/1 Maryland is nicknamed *The Terrapin State* because of the extensive diamondback terrapin farms. **1949** B. A. BOTKIN *Treas. S. Folklore* I. ii. 35 Maryland has had half a dozen or more nicknames since colonial times, but only *Old Line State* and *Terrapin State* have any remaining vitality today.

Terrapin[2] ('tɛrəpɪn). Also **terrapin**. The proprietary name of a make of prefabricated building, usu. having one storey and designed for temporary use.

1949 *Trade Marks Jrnl.* 21 Sept. 841/2 *Terrapin*... Portable buildings. Harry Collett Bolt, 21, Kings Gardens, West End Lane, Hampstead, London, N.W... Manufacturer and Merchant. **1962** *Ibid.* 25 July 958/2 Terrapin Minihouses... All goods included in Class 19. Terrapin Limited, Haddon House, 2–4, Fitzroy Street, London, W.1; Manufacturers. **1972** *Guardian* 5 Dec. 17/6 The main concerns of [school] governors tend to be .. asking the Works Department for an extra radiator in an exposed 'terrapin'. **1976** T. SHARPE *Wilt* vi. 56 He looked round the car park at the terrapin huts and the main building.

terraplain, etc.: see TERREPLEIN.

te'rraquean, *a. rare*⁻¹. = next.

1861 *Macm. Mag.* Apr. 471/2 All the places on this terraquean globe.

terraqueous (tɛ'reɪkwiːəs), *a.* [f. L. *terra* earth + AQUEOUS. Cf. F. *terraqué(e* (Voltaire *Memnon* 1747) from Eng.; so Sp. (*el globo*) *terrácueo*.]

1. Consisting of, or formed of, land and water; nearly always in ***terraqueous globe***.

1658 PHILLIPS, *Terraqueous*, composed of earth and water together. **1664** POWER *Exp. Philos.* II. 99 The halituous Effluxions and Aporrhœa's of this terraqueous Globe below. **1678** CUDWORTH *Intell. Syst.* I. iii. §37. 171 The whole terrestrial (or terraqueous) Globe. **1742** YOUNG *Nt. Th.* I. 286 A part how small of the terraqueous globe Is tenanted by man! **1781** COWPER *Charity* 122 Providence enjoins to every soul An union with the vast terraqueous whole. **1834–5** J. PHILLIPS *Geol.* in *Encycl. Metrop.* VI. 701/1 *margin*, Relation of terraqueous agencies in ancient and modern eras. **1876** PAGE *Adv. Text-bk. Geol.* iii. 72 The maintenance of a habitable terraqueous surface.

2. Living in land and water, as a plant; extending over land and water, as a journey.

1694 WESTMACOTT *Script. Herb.* 164 These Reeds belong to the terraqueous plants. **1844** JEFFREY in Ld. Cockburn *Life* (1852) II. Let. clxxiv, We drove down to the pier and resumed our terraqueous promenade.

terrar, terrer. *Obs.* exc. *Hist.* Also 6 tarrer, 9 *erron.* terrarer. [ad. med.L. *terrārius* in same sense, f. *terrārius* adj., pertaining to land or lands (f. *terra* earth, land), whence also *terrāria, -ārium*, a piece of land, landed property, pl. *terrāria* possessions, lands, *terrārius* a tenant or holder of land, *terrārius liber*, also *terrarium, terrerium* a register of lands, rents, etc. (TERRIER *sb.*¹).] An officer of a religious house, who was originally bursar for the farms and manors belonging to the house, receiving rents and making disbursements on account of these; but whose office by the 16th c. at Durham was mainly connected with the entertainment of strangers.

1401 *Rotuli Terrariorum* in *Durham Acc. Rolls* (Surtees) 299 Compotus fratris Willelmi Barry Terrarii Dunelm. **1593** *Rites of Durham* (Surtees 1903) 99 Dane Roger Watson the Terrer of yᵉ house. The Tarrers checker was as yea goe into yᵉ geste Haule... His office was to se that all yᵉ geste chambers to be cleanly keapt [etc.] .. and he provyded provender for there horses [etc.]. **1864** RAINE *Priory of Hexham* I. p. cxxxiv, The Terrarer, the cellarer, the chamberlain and the bursar acted by his advice. **1901** J. T. FOWLER in *Durh. Acc. Rolls* Introd. 31 The Terrar had three copies of each roll written out. *Ibid.*, Expenses of the Terrar riding to Auckland . and other places.

terrar, obs. form of TERRIER.

terrarium (tɛ'rɛərɪəm). Pl. **-a** or (now more usually) **-iums**. [mod. f. L. *terra* earth, after *aquarium*. Also in Fr. (1873 in Littré *Suppl.*) and Ger. (Meyer *Conv. Lex.*).] **1.** A vivarium for land animals; *esp.* a glass case, or the like, in which small land animals are kept under scientific observation.

1890 *Science* 10 Jan. 24/2 [He] describes the ways of a snake, .. which he kept in his terrarium in Zurich. **1895** *Proc. Zool. Soc. Lond.* 160 Usually after they have lived for some time in the terrarium they get dark spots, especially on the sides of the body. **1952** M. K. WILSON tr. *Lorenz's King Solomon's Ring* vii. 67 On the table .. stands the nucleus of my golden hamster stud, a simple little terrarium. **1976** N. COLEMAN *Shell Collecting in Australia* ix. 149 The larger the terrarium and the smaller the number of snails, the less work will be involved in keeping it sanitary. **1977** *Sci. Amer.* Dec. 36/1 Spiders and scorpions in neat terrariums.

2. A sealed transparent globe or similar container in which plants are grown, usu. for decoration. Cf. WARDIAN CASE. orig. *U.S.*

1931 *St. Nicholas* Oct. 846/1 Have you ever tried making a terrarium? .. It means a little garden under glass—not a conservatory or a cold frame, but a real little landscape. **1942** *Amer. Speech* XVII. 284/1 He also saw on his rambles a *Terrarium*—a covered glass globe or fish-tank containing flowers and plants to be grown indoors during the winter. **1974** *Evening Herald* (Rock Hill, S. Carolina) 19 Apr. 6/5 (Advt.), Globe shaped terrarium kit... A unique way to display foliage. **1979** *Sunday Mail* (Brisbane) 6 May 5/1 (Advt.), Terrariums add life to any room. In long lasting plastic; each containing an African violet plus three other selected plants. **1982** *N.Y. Times* 11 Apr. II. 33/4 Partridgeberry .. is often used in terrariums for its evergreen foliage and red berries

terra rosa ('tɛrə 'rəʊzə). *Painting.* [a. It., lit. = rose-coloured earth.] A light red colour of paint similar to Venetian red.

1897 *Sears, Roebuck Catal.* 360/3 Colors for Artists .. Gold Ochre, .. Terra Rosa, Terre Verte. **1935** *Winsor & Newton's Sales Man.* 56 Colours which may be regarded .. inflexible under all conditions of Oil Painting .. Terra Rosa. **1973** F. TAUBES *Painter's Dict. Materials & Methods* 224 *Terra rosa* is a very light Iron Oxide Red of relatively slight Tinting Strength. For all practical purposes, this color is interchangeable with *Terra di Pozzuoli*.

terra rossa ('tɛrə 'rɒsə). [a. It., = red earth.] A reddish soil occurring on limestone in Mediterranean climates (see also quot. 1938).

1882 A. GEIKIE *Text-bk. Geol.* 458 Fuchs believes that the 'terra rossa' is only present in dry climates where the amount of humus is small. **1938** *U.S. Dept. Agric. Yearbk.* 991 Many writers have preferred to limit Terra Rossa to soils developed on limestones, while some would have it include any red soil in a Mediterranean climate... At present its only distinction lies in its color. **1956** *Proc. Prehist. Soc.* XXI. 53 Most brown-earths are characteristic of deciduous forests, chernozems of steppe, and terra rossas of Mediterranean forests on limestone. **1975** *Nature* 14 Aug. 566/1 Further evidence for the role of climate is provided by the fact that the limestone soils from Apulia, the Orbetello region and the southern Apennines, which are mainly of the red Mediterranean type (that is, terra rossa) exhibit higher percentage conversions than those from the Central Apennines which are mainly rendzinas.

‖**terra roxa** ('tɛrə 'rɒʃə). [Pg., = reddish-purple soil.] A deep, humus-rich soil of a dark reddish-purple colour on the Paraná Plateau in southern Brazil.

1870 C. F. HARTT *Thayer Exped.: Sci. Results Journey Brazil: Geol. & Physical Geogr.* xvii. 514 The terra roxa of Campinas Paulo is .. the continuation of the drift-paste of the higher lands and seaward slope of the serra. **1977** *Econ. Geogr.* LIII. 78/2 Areas with larger concentrations of *terra roxas*, the soil of exceptional fertility for coffee, are usually associated with higher levels of production.

terras, -ass(e, obs. ff. TARRAS, TERRACE.

‖**'Terra Si'enna.** Also Terra di (de) Sienna. [ad. It. *terra di Siena*, in F. *terre de Sienne*, lit. 'earth of Sienna'.] = SIENA. Also *attrib.*

1760 SHENSTONE *Wks. & Lett.* (1777) III. 309 A terra-sienna or very rich reddish brown. **1794** A. THOMAS *Newfoundland Jrnl.* (1968) ii. 29 The shores of the Scilly Islands abound with rare and very curious Shells. Some are highly polish'd, of the colour of Terra de Sina [*sic*] .., others are striped. *a* **1817** T. DWIGHT *Trav. New Eng.* (1821) I. 35 A beautiful yellow earth .. which yields a handsome colour than the Terra de Sienna. It is called Terra Columbiana. **1823** P. NICHOLSON *Pract. Build.* 413 Terra di Sienna is a native ochre, and is brought from Italy, where it is generally found. **1844** J. T. HEWLETT *Parsons & W.* xxviii, That light terra sienna tint which may be seen in many of our cathedrals. **1869** *Bradshaw's Railway Manual* XXI. 460/3 (Advt.), Browns. Vandyke Brown .. Terra de Sienna. **1885** *Encycl. Brit.* XIX. 87/1 The well-known ochre Terra da Sienna which in its raw state is a dull-coloured ochre, becomes when burnt a fine warm mahogany brown hue highly valued for artistic purposes.

‖**terra sigillata** ('tɛrə sɪdʒɪ'leɪtə). Also 5–6 terre sigillate, 6 terra sygyllata. [med.L., = 'sealed earth': so F. *terre seellée* (Cotgr.), *terre sigillée* (Littré), It. *terra sigillata* (Florio), G. *siegelerde*. For the reason of the name, see quot. 1802.]

1. An astringent bole, of fatty consistence and reddish colour, obtained from Lemnos; formerly esteemed as a medicine and antidote; sphragide; known also as †*sealed earth* (SEALED *ppl. a.* 1 d), *sigillate earth*, *Lemnian earth*, TERRA LEMNIA. Also applied to similar earths found elsewhere.

1398 TREVISA *Barth. De P.R.* XVI. xcvii. (Bodl. MS.), A Certeyn veyne of erþe is icleped *Terra sigillata*, and is singulerliche colde and druy. *c* **1400** *Lanfranc's Cirurg.* 61 Take þe pouder of crabbis brent vj. parties, gencian .iij parties, terre sigillate oon partie, make poudre. *c* **1550** LLOYD *Treas. Health* H ij, Take one parte of Terrasygyllata, and an other of the gumme called Sarasenicum. **1632** LITHGOW *Trav.* III. 97 The soueraigne minerall against infections, called Terra Lemnia, or Sigillata. **1756** NUGENT *Gr. Tour* II. 59 Germany is famous for that sort of earth, seldom found any where else, called *Terra sigillata*. **1802** *Brookes' Gazetteer* (ed. 12) s.v. *Lemnos*, This earth [of Lemnos] .. is called Terra Sigillata, being formed into small loaves sealed with the grand signior's seal, and thus dispersed over various parts of Europe.

†**2.** Red pigment; ruddle. *Obs.*

1563 WARDE tr. *Alexis' Secr.* II. 27 b, Terrasigillata or ruddle. **1608** CAPT. SMITH *True Relat.* 35 Two Indians, each with a cudgell, and all newly painted with Terra-sigillata, came circling about me as though they would have clubed me like a hare.

3. *Archæol.* [Cf. W. Dorow *Opferstätte und Grabhügel der Germanen und Römer am Rhein* (1821) II. 32, etc.] A type of fine Roman pottery made from the first century B.C. to the third century A.D. in Gaul (also Italy and Germany), usu. red in colour and sometimes decorated with stamped figures or patterns. Not the preferred term in English: see ARRETINE *a.*, SAMIAN *a.* and *sb.*

H. Brunsting, in *Overdruk uit Westerheem* (1972) XXI. 252–68, provides a detailed glossary of references to the ware in English and Continental sources. Quot. 1845 below is often mistaken for the first English use of the term: it relates in fact to the medicinal tablet or pastille (sense 1).

[**1845** E. B. PRICE in *Gentl. Mag.* Feb. 142/1 It is termed 'Terra Samia sigillata', of circular form, about ⅞ of an inch diameter... It is of a pale dull red colour, and has apparently been made into a paste and dried in a mould.] **1903** *Amer. Jrnl. Archaeol.* VII. 485 J. Déchelette publishes the results of a study of the *terra sigillata* .. in the territory of the Ruteni near Millau. **1920** OSWALD & PRYCE *Introd. Stud. Terra Sigillata* i. 1 Next to datable inscriptions, there is, perhaps, no relic of Roman occupation which yields such valuable chronological evidence as *Terra Sigillata*. **1936** *Oxoniensia* I. 50 In and immediately below this layer much pottery was found including Terra Sigillata of the second century. **1959** *Chambers's Encycl.* XI. 761/2 Italian *terra sigillata*, or Arretine ware, was chiefly manufactured at Arretium. **1978** M. GILBERT *Empty House* xi. 94 The stuff we call Samian, or Terra Sigillata, which was manufactured in Central Gaul.

'terrasphere. *rare.* [f. L. *terra* earth + SPHERE: cf. *planisphere*.] = TELLURION.

1891– in American dictionaries.

‖**terrasse** (tɛras). [Fr.: see TERRACE *sb.*] In France, etc.: a flat, paved area outside a building, esp. a café, where people sit to take refreshments.

1918 A. BENNETT *Roll-Call* I. ix. 197 They sat down on the *terrasse* of a large café near the Place des Ternes. **1930** —— *Imperial Palace* II. lvii. 433 Evelyn, in his big overcoat, was sitting on the *terrasse* of a large café. **1967** R. PETRIE *Foreign Bodies* i. 8 On the *terrasse* Nassim Yussif was turning between his hands a small white envelope. **1979** P. WAY *Sunrise* II. xii. 127 On the hotel *terrasse*, Olsen tipped his chair back and regarded Marriott.

terra verd(e, vert, etc., variants of TERRE-VERTE.

terrazzo (tə'rɑːtsəʊ). [a. It., = terrace, balcony.] A flooring material made of chips of marble or granite set in concrete and polished to give a smooth surface.

1902 *Encycl. Brit.* XXIX. 340/1 Wood has been superseded by terrazzo... Cracks may be seen in terrazzo floors introduced into several of the recently erected modern hospitals. **1925** *Glasgow Herald* 27 Feb. 7 Terazzo-faced concrete blocks. *Ibid.*, The outer walls being of the terrazzo block. **1958** *House & Garden* Mar. 69/1 The Esse-Dura stove sits on a terrazzo hearth in the living room. **1973** [see RAILED *ppl. a.* 1]. **1983** *Listener* 19 May 16/1 Italians were brought from Italy to lay terrazzo in a new building in West Africa.

†**terre**, *sb. Obs. rare*⁻¹. [a. F. *terre*:—L. *terra* earth.] Land; *pl.* lands, possessions.

1526 in Dillon *Customs of Pale* (1892) 83 Also he shall forfet to the kinge all his terres and tenements.

†**terre**, *v. Obs. rare.* [a. F. *terrer* (*a* 1200 in Godef.) f. *terre* earth.] *trans.* **a.** To cover with earth; = TEER *v.* 1. **b.** To throw on the ground.

c **1440** *Promp. Parv.* 489/2 Teryn, or hylle wythe erþe, *terriculo*. **1586** WARNER *Alb. Eng.* III. xvi. 72 Lo heer my gage! (he terr'd his gloue) thou knowst the victors meed.

terre, obs. f. TAR, TARE, TEAR *sb.*[1]; obs. pa. t. pl. of TEAR *v.*[1]

† **'terreal**, *a. Obs. rare*$^{-1}$. [f. L. *terre-us* earthy, earthly + -AL[1].] Of or pertaining to the earth; earthly, terrestrial, mundane.

1598 GALLOWAY *Let.* in *Napier's Mem.* (1834) 295 The knowledge of sens, as most confused and terreall, is the lowest.

† **'terrean**, *a. Obs. rare*$^{-1}$. [f. as prec. + -AN.] Of the earth; of earth.

1704 HEARNE *Duct. Hist.* (1714) I. 184 Dr. Burnet supposes his Terrean Crust which had for 1500 Years held in the Waters of the Abyss was by the heat of the Sun so parch'd and crack'd, that at last it broke.

‖ **terre-à-terre** (tɛr a tɛr), *adj.* (and *adv.*) *phr.* [Fr.: see TERRA A TERRA.] In *Ballet*, applied to a step or manner of dancing in which the feet remain on or close to the ground. In *transf.* use: without elevation of style; down-to-earth, realistic, matter-of-fact; pedestrian, unimaginative. Also as *adv. phr.*

(Fr. *terre à terre* 'pas de danse qui s'exécute sans sauter' Roquefort 1829.)

1727–41: see TERRA A TERRA. **1797** *Encycl. Brit.* (ed. 3) V. 668/1 The grander sort of dancing, and *terre à terre*, is the best adapted to such dancers. **1830** [see ELEVATION 1 e]. **1884** W. JAMES *Ess. Radical Empiricism* (1912) xii. 266 No seeker of truth can fail to rejoice at the terre-à-terre sort of discussion of the issues between Empiricism and Transcendentalism.. that seems to have begun in *Mind*. **1888** *Athenæum* 6 Oct. 443/3 His very matter-of-factness, his *terre-à-terre* fidelity to his authorities. **1898** *Daily News* 25 Oct. 2/3 It is so 'true', and yet just removed from that terre-à-terre fact which distinguishes so much portraiture. **1907** W. JAMES *Pragmatism* vii. 268 Shutting out all wider metaphysical views and condemning us to the most *terre-à-terre* naturalism. **1915** M. E. PERUGINI *Art of Ballet* iii. 33 To dance, '*terre-à-terre*', that is, with the feet, or one foot at least, on or close to the ground. **1920** *Athenæum* 5 Nov. 617/2 The author of 'Les Baisers' always elegantly *terre-à-terre*, formulates his more concrete desires. **1930** *Time & Tide* 18 Apr. 500/2 He was too frank not to admit that his friend and chief was, intellectually, very *terre-à-terre*. **1941** *Burlington Mag.* Aug. 37/2 The romanticism of this portrait is not the sophisticated, rarefied one..: it is definitely more terre-à-terre. **1961** *Times* 27 May 6/2 He regrets that the Bolshoi ballet seemed to pay so little attention to *terre à terre* dancing. **1981** *Listener* 26 Feb. 284/3 She..was 'a credible girl who suffered from menstrual cramps'... You can't get more *terre à terre* than that. **1983** M. KEYNES *Lydia Lopokova* 59 During the next year, 1912, Lydia..danced an extremely difficult terre-à-terre 'toe dance'.

‖ **terre bleue**. *Obs. rare*$^{-1}$. [F., = blue earth.] An earthy form of the blue mineral Azurite (a hydrated basic copper carbonate); as a pigment, known as *Lambert's Blue*.

1728 WOODWARD *Meth. Fossils* 3 *note*, Terre bleue..is..a light, loose, friable Kind of Lapis Armenus.

‖ **terre cuite** (tɛr kɥit). [Fr., lit. 'baked (cooked) earth'.] = TERRA-COTTA 1.

1869 C. SCHREIBER *Jrnl.* 14 Oct. (1911) I. 53 We were charmed with four ancient costume pictures of fêtes..and five terre cuites portraits by J. R. Nini. **1870** *Ibid.* 26 Feb. 76 One of the dealers..took us to her private house to show us some terre cuites. **1882** 'OUIDA' *Bimbi* 55 The *terres cuites* of Blasius date from 1560. **1926** R. FIRBANK *Concerning Eccentricities of Cardinal Pirelli* v. 57 A voluptuous small *terre cuite*, depicting a pair of hermaphrodites amusing themselves. **1951** N. MITFORD *Blessing* I. xi. 113 Once you fall into Louis XV you are immediately in the domain of restored terre cuite and broken china.

terreer, obs. form of TERRIER *sb.*[1]

terrein, obs. f. TERRAIN, TERRENE.

† **te'rreity**. *Obs. rare.* [ad. med.L. *terreitās* (*c* 1250 in Vincent of Beauvais, *Spec. Doctr.* XII. 109): see -ITY. So obs. It. *terreità* (Florio 1598).] The essential quality of earth; earthiness.

1610 B. JONSON *Alch.* II. v, The Aqueitie, Terreitie and Sulphureitie Shall runne together againe, and all be annull'd. **1757** tr. *Henckel's Pyritol.* 114 Such a body as returns not to its universal terreity, but is arrived to a more heightened degree of metalleity.

† **terrell**. *Obs. rare*$^{-1}$. [Anglicized form of next.] = next, sense 1.

1619 BAINBRIDGE *Descr. late Comet* 13 The rest intermediating in their motion, according to their distance from this little terrell, for whose vse especially those vast planetarie globes were created.

‖ **te'rrella**. [mod.L. dim. of *terra* earth: cf. L. *terrula*, and see -EL[2].]

1. A little Earth; a small orb or planet. Now *rare* or as *nonce-use*.

1657–83 EVELYN *Hist. Relig.* (1850) I. 162 Only signifying His making greater worlds, and not these microcosm terrellas. **1682** H. MORE *Annot. Glanvill's Lux O.* 141, I should rather suspect..that the Fire will more and more decay till it turn at last to a kind of Terrella, like that observed within the Ring of Saturn. *Ibid.* 142 To let its Central Fire to incrustate it self into a Terrella. **1959** *Daily Tel.* 23 Feb. 11/8 Col. Steinkamp used the word 'terrella'—a little world or earth—in the context of space flight.

†**2.** A spherical magnet, having like the earth two magnetic poles; sometimes, for experimental purposes, marked with lines representing the earth's equator, meridians, parallels, etc.: used to illustrate the dipping of the needle, and other phenomena of terrestrial magnetism. Also, a small artificial globe having a magnet within it, which behaves in the same way, and serves the same purposes. *Obs.*

1613 M. RIDLEY *Magn. Bodies* 4 The first form of the Magnet..is a large one in fashion of a round ball, boule or globe, and we do call it a *Terrella*. **1646** SIR T. BROWNE *Pseud. Ep.* 62 The Terrella or sphericall magnet geographically set out with circles of the Globe. **1773** LORIMER in *Phil. Trans.* LXV. 79 Whenever any one meets with a terrella, or spherical loadstone, the first thing he does is to find out its poles. **1822** IMISON *Sc. & Art* I. 405 A small globe, having a magnet enclosed within it, which..is called a *terrella*. **1837** BREWSTER *Magnetism* 304 Shape it..so as to give it any form.., whether of a terrella,..or any other.

† **'terremote**. *Obs.* [a. OF. *terremote* (12th c. in Godef.), ad. L. *terræ mōtus* earthquake. In It. and Sp. *terremoto*.] An earthquake.

1390 GOWER *Conf.* III. 75 Wherof that al the halle quok, As it a terremote were. *c* **1450** *Mirour Saluacioun* 4681 Terremote and of graves notable apercionne.

terremotive (ˌtɛrɪ'məʊtɪv), *a. rare.* [f. L. *terræ mōtus* earthquake + -IVE, after *motive*.] Of or pertaining to an earthquake; seismic.

1837 WHEWELL *Hist. Induct. Sc.* (1857) III. 459 The frequent sympathy of volcanic and terremotive action. **1840** —— *Philos. Induct. Sc.* x. iii. §4 II. 128 The greatest known paroxysms of volcanic and terremotive agency.

† **te'rrenal**, *a. Obs.* [f. L. *terrēn-us* TERRENE + -AL[1]; cf. OF. *terrenal* (13th c. in Godef.).] Of or pertaining to the earth; terrestrial; earthly; = TERRENE *a.* 1.

a **1555** PHILPOT *Exam. & Writ.* (Parker Soc.) 359 They looked for a terrenal kingdom. **1581** MARBECK *Bk. Notes* 934 That the Sacrament is made of two natures, of an heauenly nature, and of a terrenall and earthly nature. **1588** PARKE tr. *Mendoza's Hist. China* 397 The riuer Ganges, one of the foure that comme foorth of paradice terrenall.

terrene (tə'riːn), *a.* Forms: α. 4– terrene (6–8 terene, 7 terrhene). β. 5 terreyn, 6 -ein, -aine. γ. 6–7 terren. [ult. ad. L. *terrēn-us*, f. *terra* earth; an Anglo-Fr. *terrene* occurs in Wright *Lyric Poetry* (Percy) 4. Stressed '*terrene*, and sometimes spelt *terren*, down to *c* 1700; but *te'rrene* is instanced as early as 1635; '*terrene* in 1797 and 1865. (The 15–16th c. spellings in *-ein*, *-eyn*, *-aine*, suggest F. origin, and may have been influenced by F. *terrain*, or *terrien*.)]

1. Belonging to the earth or to this world; earthly; worldly, secular, temporal, material, human (as opposed to heavenly, eternal, spiritual, divine): = TERRESTRIAL 1.

α. **13..** *K. Alis.* 5685 Paradys terrene is riȝth in þe Est. **1509** BARCLAY *Shyp Folys* (1570) 192 From terrene lucre that day withdrawe thy minde. **1548** UDALL *Erasm. Par. Luke* i. 17 All terrene or yearthly Kyngdomes. **1563** *Homilies* II. *Sacrament* I. (1859) 443 Not as especially regarding the terene and earthly creatures which remain. **1606** SHAKS. *Ant. & Cl.* III. xiii. 153 Alacke our Terrene Moone is now Eclipst. **1630** J. TAYLOR (Water P.) *Urania* xxxii, To keepe their Queene secure from terrene treason. **1635** QUARLES *Embl.* IV. i. (1718) 190 The common period of terrene conceit. **1638** SIR T. HERBERT *Trav.* (ed. 2) 301 They are in apparition terrhene Idolls. *a* **1711** KEN *Wks.* (1721) IV. 80 With zeal wash your own spirit clean From all concupiscence terrene. **1844** MRS. BROWNING *Catarina to Camoens* xix, Whatsoever eyes terrene Be the sweetest his have seen. **1865** SWINBURNE *Atalanta* 525 Nearer than their life of terrene days.

β. *a* **1450** *Knt. de la Tour* (1906) 4 And yeuithe longe lyff and stont in this terreyn and wordly thing [F. *choses mondaines et terriennes*] like as hym lust. **1546** LANGLEY *Pol. Verg. De Invent.* IV. v. 89 To declare that thei oughte to reiect terrein and yearthly substaunce. **1576** R. HILL in Farr *S.P. Eliz.* (1845) II. 305 You worldly wights, that haue your fancies fixt On slipper ioy of terraine pleasures here.

γ. **1579** W. WILKINSON *Confut. Familye of Loue* 17 b, Our earthly and terren nature. **1620** J. WILKINSON *Of Courts Leet* 140 True faith and loialtie you shal beare of life, member, and terren honour. **1637** HEYWOOD *Dial.* v. Wks. 1874 VI. 200 Bury the thoughts of all such terren drosse.

2. Of the nature of earth (the substance); earthy.

1601 HOLLAND *Pliny* II. c. I. 44 Because ouermuch of the drie terrene element is mingled in it. **1756** P. BROWNE *Jamaica* 11 Here the soil is generally terrene or earthy. **1807** VANCOUVER *Agric. Devon* (1813) 301 Combined with the finest particles of terrene matter the tidal waters could hold in suspension. **1863** J. G. MURPHY *Comm. Gen.* i. 2 The..aerial, aqueous, and terrene materials of the preëxistent earth.

3. Occurring on or inhabiting the land as opposed to water: = TERRESTRIAL 5.

1661 LOVELL *Hist. Anim. & Min.* Introd., Members common with the terrene quadrupeds. **1774** GOLDSM. *Nat. Hist.* I. 20 These [shells]..are considered as substances entirely terrene. **1854** BREWSTER *More Worlds* iv. 86 In any terrene vertebrate.

4. Of or pertaining to the earth (as a planet): = TERRESTRIAL 2.

1635 SWAN *Spec. M.* (1670) 81 That the nature of the place above the Moon doth sufficiently deny the ascent of any terrene Exhalation. **1709–29** V. MANDEY *Syst. Math., Geogr.* 595 Of the Dimension of the Terrene Globe.

5. *absol.* or as *sb.* **a.** The earth, the world. **b.** A land or territory; also *fig.*

1667 MILTON *P.L.* VI. 78 Many a Province wide Tenfold the length of this terrene. **1735** SOMERVILLE *Chase* IV. 16 The teeming rav'nous Brutes Might fill the scanty Space of this Terrene. **1830** W. PHILLIPS *Mt. Sinai* II. 474 The vast terrene, Hereby deep shaken to its extremest bounds. **1863** COWDEN CLARKE *Shaks. Char.* ix. 215 That rich terrene of anthology, the pages of Shakespeare. **1894** R. J. HINTON in *Voice* (N.Y.) 18 Oct. 3/5 The conservation..of our..whole terrene—may yet be found through irrigation.

terrene, var. TERRINE, early f. TUREEN.

terrenely (tə'riːnlɪ), *adv.* [f. TERRENE + -LY[2].]

†**1.** As regards landed estate; territorially. *Obs.*

c **1475** *Partenay* 5014, I Hym make my proper enheritour, For yut shall he be wurthy terrenly.

2. In a terrene manner; mundanely.

a **1638** MEDE *Wks.* (1672) 290 Opposed..to an offering earthly and terrenely sanctified, as were the Typical Sacrifices of the Law by Fire and Bloud. **1747** RICHARDSON *Clarissa* (1810) I. xxxi. 213 Those confounded poets, with their terrenely celestial descriptions. **1906** *Westm. Gaz.* 9 Apr. 4/1 Let not thy plaited eyes be cast Terrenely on the pansied past.

te'rreneness. *rare.* Also 7 terreness. [f. as prec. + -NESS.] Terrene quality; earthiness.

1652 FRENCH *Yorksh. Spa* xiv. 106 He saith, that all kinds of tasts arise from a kind of terreness more or less adust. **1670** W. SIMPSON *Hydrol. Ess.* 90 The vapours of the burning bitumen and adust terreness therewith. **1727** BAILEY vol. II, *Terreneness*, Earthiness.

te'rrenity. Now *rare* or as *nonce-wd.* [f. as prec. + -ITY; cf. med.L. *terrēnitās* (Du Cange).] The quality or condition of being earthy; *concr.* earthy matter.

1627–77 FELTHAM *Resolves* 74 (L.) [It] debases all the spirits to a dull and low terrenity. **1650** CHARLETON *Paradoxes* Prol. 23 The Acid Spirit, immersed in an excessive quantity of Terrenity, becomes..languid. **1973** T. PYNCHON *Gravity's Rainbow* IV. 733 Trees creak in sorrow for the engineered wound through their terrain, their terrenity or earthhood.

‖ **terreno** (ter'reno). [= It. (*piano*) *terreno*:—L. *terrēnum* TERRENE.] A ground-floor; also, a parlour.

1740 H. WALPOLE *Let. to H. S. Conway* 9 July, I have a terreno all to myself. **1750** —— *Let. to Mann* 11 Mar., I am already planning a *terreno* for Strawberry Hill. **1787** BECKFORD *Lett. Italy* xvi. (1805) I. 156 The terreno, or ground-floor, where they live chiefly in summer, is excellent.

† **'terreous**, *a. Obs.* [f. L. *terre-us* earthen, earthy (f. *terra* earth) + -OUS.] Earthy, of earthy nature; pertaining to earth or ordinary soil.

1646 SIR T. BROWNE *Pseud. Ep.* II. v. 87 There remaines a grosse and terreous portion at the bottome. **1650** *Ibid.* VII. xiii. 312 According to the temper of the terreous parts at the bottome. **1794** SULLIVAN *View Nat.* I. xxix. 421 By the concretion of terreous and other particles, which..make either adamants, pebbles, or free-stone.

‖ **terre pisée** (tɛr pize). [Fr., lit. 'beaten earth'.] = PISÉ a. Cf. COB *sb.*[2] a.

1936 V. G. CHILDE *Man makes Himself* vi. 124 Soon houses built of mud or *terre pisée* were being erected. **1949** W. F. ALBRIGHT *Archaeol. of Palestine* v. 86 A concomitant of the introduction of chariotry into warfare was the spread of the art of building great fortifications of beaten earth (*terre pisée*), usually rectangular in plan. **1972** Y. YADIN *Hazor* 203 As for the claim that the earthen ramparts and *terre pisée* defences were first built in the MB IIA, only little has to be added here.

terreplein ('tɛəpleɪn, ‖ tɛrplɛ̃). *Fortif.* Forms: α. 6–7 terraplene, 7 -plana, -plane, teraplene, 8–9 terraplain. β. 6 terreplaine, 8–9 -plain, 9 -pleine, 8– terreplein. [In α. ad. It. *terrapieno*, in Sp. *terrapleno*, in same sense; cf. It. *terrapienare*, Sp. *terraplenar*, to fill up with earth, f. *terra* earth + *pieno* (:—L. *plēnus*) full; in β. a. corresponding French *terreplein*. Both in F. and Eng., the second element was sometimes erroneously taken as It. *piano*, F. *plain* plane, flat, level (so in Littré), whence the former spellings *-plain*, *-plane*: cf. sense 2. A form *terrapin* app. from It. *terrapieno* appears in F. in 1567 (Godefroy *Compl.*); cf. TERREPLEIN *v.* below.]

1. Originally, The talus or sloping bank of earth behind a wall or rampart; hence, the surface of a rampart behind the parapet; and strictly, the level space on which the guns are mounted, between the banquette and the inner talus.

α. **1598** BARRET *Theor. Warres* 130 Vpon these Terraplenes should trees be planted. *Ibid.* Gloss. 253 *Terraplene*, an Italian word,..the earth that is rampired and filled vp vnto the inside of any wall or bulwarke. **1688** R. HOLME *Armoury* III. xvi. (Roxb.) 100/1 The Terraplane or walk of the Rampire. **1689** G. WALKER *Siege of Derry* 9 The outside Wall of Stone, or Battlements above the Terra-plene is not more than two Foot in thickness. **1712** J. JAMES tr. *Le Blond's Gardening* 118 The Platform sustained by the Walls or Banks of the Terrasses..in Fortification, is call'd the Terra-plain. **1829** *Sun* 17 Sept. 1/5 The insignificance of their batteries and the smallness of their terraplains, which prevent cannons of large calibre being placed there. **1859** F. A. GRIFFITHS *Artil. Man.* (1862) 260 The Terraplein is the upper part of the rampart, which remains after having constructed the parapet.

β. **1591** *Garrard's Art Warre* 317 (Stanf.) If..you cannot make Trauerses vppon the Terreplaine, for that the Enemy doth hinder it. **1704** J. HARRIS *Lex. Techn.* I, *Terre-Plain*, in Fortification, is the Platform or Horizontal Surface of the Rampart. **1830** E. S. N. CAMPBELL *Dict. Mil. Sc.* 88 The Banquette is placed behind this parapet, and the clear space left on the rampart, called its terrepleine, has been limited to about eighteen or twenty toises, terminated towards the town by a slope of 45°. **1879** *Cassell's Techn. Educ.* IV. 138/1 Bastions are termed 'full' when the interior is level with the terre-plein of the rampart on either side of it.

transf. **1848** *Blackw. Mag.* July 99/2, I went out to the narrow terre-plain over the craig.

2. The level base (above, on, or below the natural surface of the ground) on which a battery is placed in field fortifications; sometimes, the natural surface of the ground (quots. 1669, 1756, 1853).

[This latter use is manifestly connected with the mistaken derivation from *plana, plaine* plain.]

1669 STAYNRED *Fortification* 8 The Height of the Rampire ..ought to be..18 Foot above the Terra Plana. **1756** *Dict. Arts*, etc. s.v. *Foundery of Bells*, They first dig a hole of a sufficient depth to contain the mould of the bell, together with the ear or cannon under ground, and six inches lower than the terreplain where the work is done. **1828** J. M. SPEARMAN *Brit. Gunner* (ed. 2) 37 Breaching batteries.. must be sunk to such a depth that the terreplein of the covered-way may coincide with the soles of the embrazures. **1853** STOCQUELER *Milit. Encycl.*, *Terre-plein*, in field fortification, the plane of site or level country around a work. **1884** *Mil. Engineering* (ed. 3) I. II. 64 Batteries may be classed as follows, viz.: 'Sunken batteries', in which the terreplein is sunk below the surface of the ground. 'Elevated batteries', in which the terreplein is on or above the natural surface of the ground.

Hence †**'terreplein** (corruptly **terrapin**) *v. Obs. rare*, to furnish with a terreplein.

1672 in *Fort St. George* (Madras) *Recds.*, Whither the Curtains of the Christian Town to bee strengthened and Terrapined.

†**terrer.** *Obs. rare.* [f. *terre*, TAR *v.*[2] + -ER[1].] A provoker, vexer: cf. *teryare* s.v. TARY *v.*

1382 WYCLIF *Ezek.* xxiv. 3 Thou shalt saye bi prouerbe a parable to the hous, terrer to wraththe [Vulg. *ad domum irritatricem*]. **1388** *Ibid.* ii. 7–8 Thei ben terreris to wraththe [1382 wraththers]..Nyle thou be a terrere to wraththe, as the hows of Israel is a terrere to wraththe.

terrer, variant of TERRAR.

terrer(e, terres, obs. ff. TERRIER, TERRACE.

terre sigillate, obs. f. TERRA SIGILLATA.

[**teresity**, mispr. in Arb. *Garner* II. 114 for *terrestritie* (see TERRESTRITY, quot. 1568), whence in dictionaries; in some assumed to be for **terrosity*.]

terresterity, erron. form of TERRESTRITY.

†**te'rrestre**, *a. Obs.* Also 4–6 terestre, 4–7 -er. [a. F. *terrestre* (12th c. in Godef. *Compl.*), ad. L. *terrestr-is* earthly, f. *terra* earth.] = TERRESTRIAL; chiefly in phr. ***paradise terrestre*** [OF. *paraïs, paradis terrestre* (12–13th c.), mod.Fr. *paradis t.*] earthly paradise, the Garden of Eden.

1340 *Ayenb.* 50 Ase he did to euen [= Eve] and to Adam in paradys terestre. *c* **1386** CHAUCER *Merch. T.* 88 Wyf is mannes helpe and his confort, His Paradys terrestre and his disport. *c* **1400** MAUNDEV. (1839) v. 44 The Ryvere of Gyson ..cometh out of Paradys terrestre. **1484** CAXTON *Chivalry* 1 In gouernynge and ordeynynge the bodyes terrestre and erthely. **1550** J. COKE *Eng. & Fr. Heralds* § 133 (1877) 97 A marvelous puissaunce and..army marytayne and terrestre. **1663** GERBIER *Counsel* a vj b, After his Building up of Terester Seats.

terrestreity: see TERRESTRITY.

†**terrestrene**, *a. Obs. rare*[−1]. [f. TERRESTRE, after TERRENE.] Terrestrial, earthly.

1599 A. M. tr. *Gabelhouer's Bk. Physicke* 235/1 It will helpe her, if any terrestrene thing will helpe her.

terrestrial (tə'rɛstrɪəl), *a.* and *sb.* Also 5 -yall(e, 5–7 -iall(e, 7 tere-. Also 5–8 **terrestial**(l after *celestial*. [f. L. *terrestri-s* (f. *terra* earth) + -AL[1]. Cf. obs. F. *terrestriel* (16th c. in Godef.).]

A. *adj.* **1.** Of or pertaining to this world, or to earth as opposed to heaven; earthly; worldly; mundane.

1432–50 tr. *Higden* (Rolls) II. 183 The hieste powere intellectiue..separate somme tyme from substaunces terrestrialle. *c* **1460** in *Pol. Rel. & L. Poems* (1866) 82 Graunt to man the blysse eternalle When he passith thys lyfe terrestryalle. *c* **1470** ASHBY *Active Policy* 592 What man is he that is terrestrial But of hym thus sadly wol speke & telle? **1526** TINDALE *1 Cor.* xv. 40 There are celestiall bodyes, and there are bodyes terrestriall. *a* **1548** HALL *Chron., Hen. VI* 182 b, Depriued of his terrestrial Croune, to be recompensed with an heauenly garland. **1593** NASHE *Christ's T.* T iij b, Their eyes are dazeled with terrestiall delights. **1750** JOHNSON *Rambler* No. 67 ¶ 2 The happiest lot of terrestrial existence. **1868** LAW *Beacons of Bible* (1869) 47 The guilty have then no terrestrial refuge.

2. a. Of, pertaining, or referring to the earth; often in ***terrestrial ball, globe, sphere***, the earth.

1593 SHAKS. *Rich. II*, III. ii. 41 From vnder this Terrestriall Ball. **1638** SIR T. HERBERT *Trav.* (ed. 2) 6 Extended to the plaine of the terrestriall Horizon. **1645** EVELYN *Diary* 21 Feb., The celestial, terrestrial, and subterranean deities. **1669** STURMY *Mariner's Mag.* v. v. 19 The Sphericality of this Terrestial [*ed.* **1684** -trial] Globe. **1796** H. HUNTER tr. *St.-Pierre's Stud. Nat.* I. 563 The two terrestrial Hemispheres are not projected in the same manner. **1837** WHEWELL *Hist. Induct. Sc.* (1857) III. 38 The subject of terrestrial magnetism.

†**b.** Proceeding from, or belonging to, the solid earth or its soil; not atmospheric. *Obs.*

1658 J. ROWLAND *Moufet's Theat. Ins.* 908 Terrestrial or earthy Honey we call that, because the dew going away, it is suckt out of the very sweat of the earth. **1660** BOYLE *New Exp. Phys.-Mech.* xviii. 139 The Terrestrial Steam may.. considerably alter the gravity or pressure of the Atmosphere.

c. Consisting of earth or soil. (*humorous.*)

1844 O. W. HOLMES *Lines Berksh. Jubilee* 48 No soil upon earth is so dear to our eyes As the soil we first stirred in terrestrial pies!

d. *spec.* ***terrestrial globe***, a globe with a map of the earth on its surface: see GLOBE *sb.* 3; †***terrestrial line*** (*obs.*): see quot. 1704; ***terrestrial telescope***, one used for observing terrestrial objects.

1559 [see GLOBE *sb.* 3]. **1617** MORYSON *Itin.* I. 31 In the Clocke [of Strassburg Cathedral]..there is a terrestrial globe. **1704** J. HARRIS *Lex. Techn.* I, *Terrestrial Line... Line Terrestrial*, in Perspective, is a Right Line, wherein the Geometrical Plane, and that of the Picture or Draught intersect one another. **1815** J. SMITH *Panorama Sc. & Art* I. 487 The Terrestrial Telescope, or Perspective Glass. **1837** GORING & PRITCHARD *Microgr.* 153 Terrestrial telescopes will not have received their finishing touch,.. until their secondary image is just as perfect as their first. **1869** TYNDALL in *Fortn. Rev.* 1 Feb. 245 The poles, equator, and parallel of latitude of an ordinary terrestrial globe.

e. *Astr.* Designating planets which are similar in size or composition to the Earth.

1888 C. A. YOUNG *Textbk. Gen. Astron.* xiv. 322 The terrestrial planets are Mercury, Venus, the earth, and Mars. They are bodies of the same order of magnitude.., not very different in density.., and are probably roughly alike in physical constitution. **1926** E. A. FATH *Elem. Astron.* xi. 135 The eight planets fall into two groups, the first usually being termed the terrestrial planets. **1973** *Nature* 17 Aug. 424/2 The terrestrial planets..are solid bodies. **1980** *Sci. Amer.* Jan. 68/2 Io..and Callisto belong to the family of objects designated terrestrial.

†**3.** Of the nature or character of earth, esp. as being dry and solid or pulverulent; possessing earth-like properties or qualities; earthy. *Obs.*

1594 PLAT *Jewell-ho.* I. 21 [Quick lime] whose moisture is altogether exhaled, so as there remaineth therein nothing else, but the terrestrial parts replenished with a fiery vertue. **1668** CULPEPPER & COLE *Barthol. Anat.* I. xviii. 49 The thick and terrestrial Excrements of the Kidneys. **1684–5** BOYLE *Min. Waters* 29 Of the division of the Cap. Mort. into saline and terrestrial and other parts not dissoluble in Water. **1756** *Phil. Trans.* XLIX. 903 Acids..do dissolve animal calculi, by acting upon their terrestrial parts.

4. Of, or pertaining to, the land of the world, as distinct from the waters.

1628 HOBBES *Thucyd.* (1822) 20 We offer you a naval not a terrestrial league. **1644** EVELYN *Diary* 7 Nov., The terrestrial and naval battailes here graven. **1839** ALISON *Hist. Europe* (1849–50) VII. xlii. § 55. 136 While England was..extending her naval dominion,..Napoleon was.. advancing in his career of terrestrial empire.

5. *Nat. Hist.* Occurring on, or inhabiting, land: **a.** *Zool.* Living on the land as distinguished from the waters, or on the ground as distinct from the air; applied *spec.* to birds of the order *Terrestres*, and to air-breathing molluscs and crustaceans.

1638 RAWLEY tr. *Bacon's Life & Death* (1650) 54 Fishes need lesse Refrigeration than Terrestriall Creatures. **1727–41** CHAMBERS *Cycl.* s.v. *Bird*, Birds are usually divided into terrestrial, and aquatic. **1830** LYELL *Princ. Geol.* I. 479 The subserviency of our planet to the support of terrestrial as well as aquatic species. **1859** DARWIN *Orig. Spec.* xii. (1873) 341 The distribution of terrestrial animals. **1888** ROLLESTON & JACKSON *Anim. Life* 455 A few *Gastropoda* are terrestrial and air-breathers.

b. *Bot.* Growing in the soil; distinguished from *aquatic, marine, parasitic*, or *epiphytic*.

1831 J. DAVIES *Manual Mat. Med.* 424 *Fungi.* Terrestrial or parasitical plants of very variable consistence, but never of a green colour. **1849** LYELL *2nd Visit U.S.* (1850) II. 305 Land covered with a luxuriant vegetation of terrestrial plants. **1875** BENNETT & DYER *Sachs' Bot.* 660 The autumn crocus, tulip, crown imperial, terrestrial orchids.

B. *sb.* (The adj. used absol.) **a.** A terrestrial being; *esp.* a human being, a mortal; in quot. 1598, a man of secular estate, a layman. **b.** The terrestrial world, the earth (*rare*). **c.** *pl.* Terrestrial animals, orders, or families: see quot. 1842.

a. 1598 SHAKS. *Merry W.* III. i. 108 (Qo. 1) Giue me thy hand, terestiall..Giue me thy hand, celestiall. **1725** POPE *Odyss.* XIX. 691 Heav'n that knows what all terrestrials need, Repose to night, and toil to day decreed. **1873** PROCTOR *Expanse Heav.* (1877) 235 Varieties of effect altogether unfamiliar to us terrestrials.

b. 1742 YOUNG *Nt. Th.* ix. 598 Thou,..Whose little heart, is moor'd within a nook Of this obscure terrestrial.

c. 1842 BRANDE & COX *Dict. Sc.*, etc., *Terrestrials*,..the name of a section of the class *Aves*, corresponding to the orders *Rasores* and *Cursores*; also of a family of Pulmonated Gastropods, and of a division of Isopodous Crustaceans.

Hence **te'rrestrialism**, worldliness (as a way of life), secularity; **te'rrestrialize** *v.*, *trans.*, to make terrestrial or earthly.

1856 GRINDON *Life* xxii. (1875) 297 Falling neither into fanaticism nor terrestrialism. **1829** WILSON in *Blackw. Mag.* XXV. 389 Every breath of air we draw is terrestrialized or etherealized by imagination. **1901** *Edin. Rev.* Apr. 357 Once terrestrialised, life..is 'not a dream but may become one'.

te'rrestrially, *adv.* [f. prec. + -LY[2].]

1. In a terrestrial manner; after the manner of earthly or worldly things.

1604 DRAYTON *Moses* II. 366 These plagues seem yet but nourished beneath, And even with man terrestrially to move. **1664** H. MORE *Exp. 7 Epist.* vii. 112 [They] grosly and carnally erre touching the nature of the Resurrection-Body,..phansying it as terrestrially modify'd. **1821** *Examiner* 220/2 Our own terrestrially transient duration.

2. As regards the ground or soil.

1857 T. MOORE *Handbk. Brit. Ferns* (ed. 3) 19 Indication that the locality is moist, either atmospherically or terrestrially, or both.

So **te'rrestrialness** *rare* (Bailey vol. II, 1727).

†**te'rrestrian**, *a. Obs. rare*[−1]. [f. L. *terrestri-s* terrestrial + -AN.] = TERRESTRIAL 5 a.

1608 TOPSELL *Serpents* (1658) 635 The signes of such as are hurt by the Chalidonian or Chersæan Asp, and the Terrestrian are all one, or of very little difference.

terrestriety: see TERRESTRITY.

†**te'rrestrify**, *v. Obs. rare.* [f. as next + -FY.] *trans.* To make terrestrial.

1646 SIR T. BROWNE *Pseud. Ep.* IV. xiii. 231 Though we should affirm..that heaven were but earth celestified, and earth but heaven terrestrified. **1656** BLOUNT *Glossogr.*, *Ter[r]estrify*, to make earthly or like earth.

†**te'rrestrious**, *a. Obs.* [f. L. *terrestri-s* terrestrial + -OUS: cf. *illustrious*.]

1. Having the nature of earth; earthy.

1600 SURFLET *Countrie Farme* III. xlix. 539 [The] terrestrious and earthie temperature which all sorts of peares doe much consist of. **1646** SIR T. BROWNE *Pseud. Ep.* 322 Beside the fixed and terrestrious Salt, there is in naturall bodies a *Sal niter* referring unto Sulphur. **1741** MONRO *Anat. Nerves* (ed. 3) 25 Saline and terrestrious Particles.

2. Of or consisting of the land surface of the earth.

1646 SIR T. BROWNE *Pseud. Ep.* II. ii. (1650) 49 This variation proceedeth not only from terrestrious eminencies, and magnetical veins of earth laterally respecting the needle. **1862** MARSH *Lect. Eng. Lang.* 24 The geographical centre of the terrestrious portion of the globe.

3. Of, pertaining to, or inhabiting the land; = TERRESTRIAL 5.

1646 SIR T. BROWNE *Pseud. Ep.* III. xxiv. 169 Some [animals] in the Sea..hold those shapes which terrestrious formes approach not. *Ibid.* 170 That nomenclature of Adam, which unto terrestrious animalls assigned a name appropriate unto their natures.

†**te'rrestrity, terre'streity.** *Obs.* [ad. med.L. *terrestritās* (*a* 1330 in Du Cange), f. *terrestri-s* earthly: see -TY, -ITY. Hence F. *terrestrité, -eté*, Eng. *terrestrity*. In 16th c. the L. form was altered to *terrestreitās* (1533 in Du Cange), app. after words properly in *-eitās*, from adjs. in *-eus*, as *terreitās, paneitās, vineitās*, etc., and this was imitated by It. *terrestreità* (Florio), F. *terrestréité* (Roquefort), Eng. *terrestreity*. *Terrestriety* is an individual error.] The quality or condition of being earthy, or of containing earthy matter; usually *concr.* earthy matter; applied esp. to gross or residual substances.

a. 1568 TURNER *Of Wines* B viij, Rhennish wyne..hath fewer dregges and lesse terrestritie [mispr. in Arb. *Garner* II. 114 teresity] or grosse earthlynesse than the Clared wine hath. **1603** HOLLAND *Plutarch's Mor.* 658 Referring all to the terrestrity of the sea: for that in sea water there is mingled much earthlie substance. **1605** TIMME *Quersit.* II. ii. 107 Salt peeter pure and seperated from all terrestritie and heterogeneal..substance.

β. **1605** TIMME *Quersit.* III. 153 The spirit of vitriol, seperated from all terrestreitie. **1662** MERRETT tr. *Neri's Art of Glass* iii. 12 The salt yields no more terrestriety, or dregs. **1681** *Phil. Collect.* XII. 105 That all the terrestreity thereof comes to be separated. **1683** SALMON *Doron Med.* II. 392 Freed from all its terrestreity [*mispr.* -terity]. **1750** tr. *Leonardus' Mirr. Stones* 42 From their own terrest[r]eity [orig. (1533) *suæ terrestreitatis*] they will sink in water.

terret, -it ('tɛrɪt). Forms: 5–8 **tyret, teret(t, tyrret, 6 tyrette, 7 tirret, terriet, 9 terret, -it.** See also TORRET. [In 15th c. *teret, tyret*, collateral form of *toret*, a. OF. *toret, touret*, dim. of OF. *tor* (12th c.), *tour* a round, circuit, circumference: see TOUR. The phonetic change from *toret, turet* to *teret, tyret* is unusual.] General sense: A round or circular loop or ring, esp. one turning on a swivel, by which a string, ribbon, or chain is attached to anything.

a. A ring on a dog's collar, by which a string can be attached, etc.

[**1376–7** *Durham Acc. Rolls* (Surtees) 387 In uno lese et uno pare de turetteis pro domino de Hilton. *c* **1386**: see TORRET]. **1530** PALSGR. 281/2 Tyrettes for a grayhoundes coller, *boucclettes*. **1688** R. HOLME *Armoury* II. 186/2 The Grey-hound, hath his Collar, and the Spaniel hath his Terriet.

b. Each of the two rings by which the leash is attached to the jesses of a hawk.

1486 *Bk. St. Albans, Hawking* b v b, The lewnes shulde be fastened to theym [jesses] with a payre of tyrettis [*ed.* **1496** tyrrettys] wich tyrettis shuld rest vppon the lewnes, and not vppon the gesses, for hyngyng and fastynyng vppon trees when she flyeth... The terettys serue to kepe hir from wyndyng whan she backes. [**1801** STRUTT *Sports & Past.* I. ii. §9 [from *Bk. St. Albans*] The lunes, or small thongs of leather, might be fastened to them [the jesses] with two tyrrits, or rings.]

c. A ring or the like by which any object can be attached to a chain; = TORRET c.

1515 in Carte *Life of Ormonde* (1736) I. Introd. 43 A white horn of ivory, garnished at both the ends with gold and corse thereunto of white silk barred with barres of gold and a tyret of gold thereupon. **1570–80** *Fabric Rolls York Minster* (Surtees) 118 For making a tyrret and a rynge of yron to the masons well buckett, 10*d.* [**1586–7** *Ibid.* 119 For a lowpe for the mason well buckett, 4*d.*] [**1900** J. T. FOWLER *Let. to Editor*, The ring by which the chain is attached to a watch is now called the 'torret' or 'turret', but the word is going out, and they call it the 'bow'.]

d. In horse-harness, One of the two (brass) rings fixed upright on the pad, or saddle, and on the hames, through which the driving reins pass. Also, any ring attached elsewhere to the harness for a similar purpose, as a ***head-terret***: see quot. 1794.

[**1429**: see TORRET.] **1724** BAILEY, *Tyrets*, Ornaments for Horse-Harness. **1794** FELTON *Carriages* (1801) II. 144 The Territs are what screws in the saddle, or housing, for the reins to run through... A short territ is often fixed at the top of a bridle, called a head-territ, for the leading-reins to go through. **1840** *New Monthly Mag.* LX. 173, I saw a leader's rein break halfway between the head-terret of the wheeler and the pad-terret of the leader. **1851** MAYHEW *Lond. Labour* I. 358/2, 'I..found I could make my pad territs' (the round loops of the harness pad, through which the reins are passed), 'my hooks, my buckles, my ornaments.., as well as any man.'

Hence **'terreted** (†**'tereted, tirr-, tyrr-**) *a.*, provided or fitted with a terret.

1572 BOSSEWELL *Armorie* II. 55b, Three Greyhoundes cursante, of the Moone, with colours Rubie, studded and tereted, Solis. **1610** GUILLIM *Heraldry* IV. xi. (1611) 218 Three greyhounds collars argent edged studded and tyrretted or. **1688** R. HOLME *Armoury* III. xvi. (Roxb.) 76/2 A dog collar,..edged, studded and Tirretted.

terret, obs. form of TURRET.

terre-tenant ('tɛə,tɛnənt). *Law.* Also 5–6 **tere-**, 6–7 **terr-**, 6–8 **ter-**. [a. AF. *terre tenaunt* 'holding land', f. *terre* land + *tenaunt* TENANT.] One who has the actual possession of land; the occupant of land.

[**1308–9** *Rolls of Parlt.* I. 275/2 Les heirs, & les terres tennauntz Gregorie de Rokesleye.] **1439** *Ibid.* V. 9/1 The said Feoffes, her Heirs, Executours and Teretenauntz. **1511–12** *Act 3 Hen. VIII*, c. 23 *Preamble*, Processe made.. ayenst theim..their heires executours or teretenauntes. **1601–2** FULBECKE *1st Pt. Parall.* 14 All the terre tenants of the village haue caried away their corn & hay except one man onely. **1607** in COWELL *Interpr.* **1702** *Lett. fr. Soldier to Ho. Com.* 19 They chusing rather to rely on the Oaths of the Tertenants and a View of the Lands. **1766** BLACKSTONE *Comm.* II. vi. 91 These mesne or middle lords, who were the immediate superiors of the *terre-tenant*, or him who occupied the land. **1818** HALLAM *Mid. Ages* (1841) I. ii. 151 The terre tenants in villenage, who occur in our old books, were not villeins.

terretour: see TERRITOIRE.

‖**terre-verte** (tɛrvɛrt). Also 7–8 **terra-vert**, 8 **terraverd**, 9 **terre verta**, 20 **terra verde, vert(e)**. [F. *terre verte* (De Lisle 1783), *terre verde* (Cotgr.), It. *terra verde* 'green earth'; cf. G. *grünerde*.] A soft green earth of varying composition used as a pigment; esp. that obtained from Italy (Verona), Cyprus, and France; = CELADONITE or *green earth*, a variety of glauconite.

1658 W. SANDERSON *Graphice* 82 Earth colours are best, as all Okers..Terre-vert. **1688** R. HOLME *Armoury* II. 313/2 Terra-vert colour, a kind of a dusky green,..is an earthy Clay Painters use. **1711** *Brit. Apollo* III. No. 141. 2/2 The smallest Body'd Terravert, Lake and the Pinks. **1730** GORDON *Maffei's Amphith.* 9 Crisocolla or Terraverd. **1748** J. HILL *Fossils* 31 Blueish green indurated Clay, called by the painters Terre Verte,..one of the best and most lasting greens they have. **1884** J. C. STAPLES in *Girl's Own Mag.* 8 Mar. 354/1 Emerald green and terre vert among the greens. **1897** *Sears, Roebuck Catal.* 361/1 Colors for Artists... King's Yellow, Lamp Black, Terra Verta. **1907** *Yesterday's Shopping* (1969) 471/2 Water Colours... Sunny green.. Terra vert..Turner brown. **1919** R. FRY *Let.* 27 Oct. (1972) II. 463, I use..burnt umber, indian red and terra verte. Terra verte pure is too bright for the sky. **1944** *Burlington Mag.* Apr. 92/2 According to the literary tradition this fresco was painted in *terra verde*. **1973** *Times Lit. Suppl.* 8 June 634/5 Florence,..where Uccello's fresco of him, in terra-verde, adorns a wall of the Duomo.

terreyn, terrhene, obs. ff. TERRENE.

terrial. ? Error for some term in hawking; ? for TERRET b.

1602 HEYWOOD *Wom. Killed w. Kindness* Wks. 1874 II. 99 Mine [hawk]..seisd a Fowle Within her talents; and you saw her pawes Full of the Feathers: both her petty singles [toes], And her long singles, grip'd her more then other; The Terrials of her legges were stain'd with blood. **1886** CORBETT *Fall of Asgard* II. 25 That we may strike..with claws and bill of steel, and soak our terrials with his blood.

terriar, obs. form of TERRIER *sb.*[2]

‖**terribilità** (teribili'ta). Also **terribiltà**. [It.]

a. In an artist or work of art: awesomeness of conception and execution, orig. as a quality attributed to Michelangelo by his contemporaries (e.g. by S. del Piombo in a letter of 9 Nov. 1520: see G. Milanesi *Les Correspondants de Michel-Ange* (1890) 24).

1883 *Encycl. Brit.* XVI. 230/2 In it the qualities afterwards proverbially associated with Michelangelo—his *furia*, his *terribilità*, the tempest and hurricane of the spirit which accompanied his unequalled technical mastery and knowledge—first found expression. **1923** A. HUXLEY *Antic Hay* xviii. 253 All this *folie de grandeur*, all this hankering after *terribiltà*..it's led so many people astray. **1948** *Penguin New Writing* XXXIV. 47 The Edwardian Mannerist arcade ..with its stork and swiss-roll terribiltà. **1961** *Daily Tel.* 5 Dec. 13/4 In these [*sc.* Piranesi's engravings of prisons] he conveys a degree of terribilità no one else has conferred upon architecture. **1970** *Oxf. Compan. Art* 720/1 That emotional intensity which Michelangelo's contemporaries recognized as his *terribilità* and which earned him the veneration of his juniors.

b. In general use: terrifying or awesome quality.

1957 J. RAYMOND in *New Statesman* 28 Sept. 386/2 Half the horror of Rolfe's life—and its accompanying virtue, his pathetic and gallant attempt to live up to a self-taught conception of honour, *terribilità*, and esteem..—sprang from the fact that he was a *déraciné* and a homosexual. **1959** *Times* 1 Apr. 11/4 The terribilità has long been drained from air travel. **1975** *New Yorker* 12 May 42/2 Fathers have voices, and each voice has a *terribilità* of its own.

terribility (tɛrɪ'bɪlɪtɪ). *rare.* Also 5 **terryblete**. [a. obs. F. *terribleté*, also later *terribilité* (15th c. in Godef.), ad. L. *terribilitās*, f. *terribilis*: see next and -ITY, -TY.] = TERRIBLENESS.

1471 CAXTON *Recuyell* (Sommer) 41 And the terryblete of the tyrant lichaon is not to be redoubtyd whan hit bleuyth vnpunysshid. **1593** G. HARVEY *Pierce's Super.* 58 Their valour and terribility in warre. **1823** G. DARLEY in *Lond. Mag.* Dec. 648/2 The energy, passion, terribility, and sublime eloquence of the stage. **1922** JOYCE *Ulysses* 686 The terribility of her..propinquity.

terrible ('tɛrɪb(ə)l), *a.* (*sb.*) Also 5–6 **terry-**, 6 **terra-, terre-, tirre.** [a. F. *terrible* (12th c.), ad. L. *terribilis*, f. *terrēre* to frighten: see -BLE.]

A. *adj.* **1.** Exciting or fitted to excite terror; such as to inspire great fear or dread; frightful, dreadful.

c **1430** LYDG. *Min. Poems* (Percy Soc.) 142 Ther roos up oon out of his sepulture, Terrible of face. *c* **1450** HOLLAND *Howlat* 620 That terrible felloun my spreit affrayd. **1508** DUNBAR *Tua Mariit Wemen* 266 With a terrebill tail.. stangand as edderis. **1565** in Sir J. Picton *L'pool Munic. Rec.* (1883) I. 108 The marvelloussest and terriblest storm. **1612** BRINSLEY *Lud. Lit.* xxvii. (1627) 277 In very many schooles ..the whole gouernment maintained only by continuall and terrible whipping. **1721** STRYPE *Eccl. Mem.* II. I. v. 36 Punished..to the terrible example of all others. **1791** COWPER *Iliad* IV. 515 The Greeks..With martial order terrible advanced. **1860** TYNDALL *Glac.* I. vii. 50 A foe more terrible than the avalanches. **1870** SWINBURNE *Ess. & Stud.* (1875) 311 Superb instances of terrible beauty undeformed by horrible detail.

2. a. Exciting some feeling akin to dread or awe; very violent, severe, painful, or bad; hence *colloq.* as a mere intensive: Very great, excessive. (Cf. the similar use of *tremendous, awful, frightful*, etc.)

1596 DALRYMPLE tr. *Leslie's Hist. Scot.* (S.T.S.) I. 128 Thair constant amitie..to thair nychtbouris the Britanis brocht a terrabill feir. **1628** EARLE *Microcosm.* (Arb.) 49 He is a terrible fastner on a piece of Beefe. **1670** MARVELL *Corr.* Wks. (Grosart) II. 315 The terrible Bill against Conventicles. **1737** L. CLARKE *Hist. Bible* IV. (1740) 227 The terriblest blow of all. **1779** *Mirror* No. 41 ¶6, I was told it was a great way off, and over terrible mountains. **1829** LYTTON *Devereux* I. ii, He was a terrible caviller at the holy mysteries of Catholicism. **1844** DICKENS *Mart. Chuz.* xi, She's a terrible one to laugh. **1853** KANE *Grinnell Exp.* xxxiv. (1856) 301 Even you, terrible worker as you are, could not study in the Arctic regions. **1884** QUEEN VICTORIA *Let.* 27 Feb. in R. Fulford *Beloved Mama* (1981) 161 The amount of writing is as they say at Balmoral 'just terrible'. **1924** 'K. MANSFIELD' in *Collier's* 5 Jan. 37/2 She leaned against him and looked into his eyes. 'Hasn't it been terrible, all to-day?' said Edna. 'I knew what was the matter.' **1939** G. B. SHAW *In Good King Charles's Golden Days* I. 7 Just as I have my terrible weakness for figures Mr. Rowley has a very similar weakness for women. **1945** [see SHOW *v.* 25 d]. **1965** E. J. HOWARD *After Julius* vii. 100 Her mother had made his life so terrible—not worth living.

b. Applied to a person who behaves in a shocking or outrageous manner; ***terrible child*** or ***infant*** = ENFANT TERRIBLE; ***terrible twins***, applied *joc.* to a pair of associates whose behaviour is troublesome or outrageous.

1859 C. READE *Love me Little, love me Long* I. i. 6 Poor Reginald was not analytical,..like certain pedanticules, who figure in story as children. He was a terrible infant, not a horrible one. **1926** A. HUXLEY *Two or Three Graces* 25 Peddley was not the man to be put out by even the most terrible of terrible infants. **1958** B. BEHAN *Borstal Boy* I. 77 When I was a child, my father used to get the *News of the World*... I used to wonder..why my mother said, half-laughing in spite of herself, that he was a terrible man, because it was banned at home. **1964** in Hamblett & Deverson *Generation X* 47, I used to be terrible. I couldn't stand my girls looking at other men, but I'm different now. **1965** M. SPARK *Mandelbaum Gate* vii. 207 An English female voice..said, 'Oh, look at that terrible man—,' obviously referring to Freddy. **1970** C. HAMPTON *Philanthropist* v. 69 All the men I fall in love with turn out to be such terrible people. **1976** *Evening Advertiser* (Swindon) 31 Dec. 8/1 The 'Terrible Twins' of yesteryear, Mr Jack Jones, general secretary of the Transport and General Workers, and Mr. Hugh Scanlon, president of the Engineering Workers, have mellowed. **1978** CADOGAN & CRAIG *Women & Children First* x. 222 Violet Elizabeth, the terrible child of the William books. **1982** *Financial Times* 10 May 10/3 Since the 'terrible twins', as they were dubbed, were both powerful figures, and did not always see eye-to-eye on matters, this rivalry was reflected down the line.

c. As a hyperbolic term of depreciation: of shockingly poor performance or quality; incompetent; defective.

1925 F. SCOTT FITZGERALD *Great Gatsby* ii. 35, I..read a chapter of 'Simon Called Peter'—either it was terrible stuff or the whiskey distorted things, because it didn't make any sense to me. **1946** 'E. CRISPIN' *Moving Toyshop* i. 8 Three books..about me (all terrible, but never mind that). **1948** C. FRY *Thor with Angels* 20 As far as he can remember, Though he has a terrible memory for names, His name is Merlin. **1964** in Hamblett & Deverson *Generation X* 88 He was hopeless—you follow me?—terrible in bed. That's why his missus left him..to himself. **1972** [see LINE *sb.*[2] I. e]. **1979** 'J. LE CARRÉ' *Smiley's People* (1980) xxi. 257 Grigorieva got herself a driving license two months ago... She's a terrible driver, George. And I mean terrible. **1983** R. RENDELL *Speaker of Mandarin* xvi. 190, I got this Hollywood offer and I went to Hollywood and made that terrible *Mind over Matter*.

3. quasi-*adv.* = TERRIBLY. (Esp. in sense 2.) Now chiefly *dial.* and *U.S.*

c **1489** CAXTON *Sonnes of Aymon* i. 42 The duke..spored hys horse terryble. **1606** S. GARDINER *Bk. Angling* 13 The world is a Sea..terrible salt thorough sin. **1634** SIR T. HERBERT *Trav.* 5 The weather being terrible hot. **1796** JANE AUSTEN *Lett.* (1884) I. 126 We were so terrible good as to take James in our carriage. **1877** FREEMAN in *Life & Lett.* (1895) II. viii. 158, I was in a terrible bad way. **1901** M. FRANKLIN *My Brilliant Career* (1966) xxxi. 197 The old yeos [ewes] looks terrible skinny. **1926** E. O'NEILL *Great God Brown* Prol. 16 My mother used to believe the full of the moon was the time to sow. She was terrible old-fashioned. **1959** L. HUGHES *Sel. Poems* 144 He mistreated her terrible.

4. *Comb.*, as ***terrible-browed, -looking***.

1876 GEO. ELIOT *Dan. Der.* liv, He seemed to her a terrible-browed angel. **1906** *Westm. Gaz.* 21 Apr. 4/1 There was only one burglar, by no means a terrible-looking fellow.

B. *sb.* A terrible thing or being; something that causes terror or dread. Usually in *pl.*

a **1619** FOTHERBY *Atheom.* I. xii. §5 (1622) 133 Which maketh the cogitation of death, of all other terribles, to seeme the most terrible. **1682** FLAVELL *Fear* ii. 9 Job calls it the king of terrors..or the most terrible of terribles. **1850** J. STRUTHERS *Poet. Wks.* II. 149 One has, between Grecian and Gothic story, generated a new race of terribles.

terribleness ('tɛrɪb(ə)lnɪs). [f. prec. + -NESS.] The quality of being terrible; frightfulness, dreadfulness, awfulness.

a **1533** LD. BERNERS *Gold. Bk. M. Aurel.* (1546) T vij, The most terrible, and the laste terrible of all terriblenes. **1535** COVERDALE *Deut.* xxvi. 8 The Lorde..brought vs out of Egipte..with greate terryblenesse thorow tokens and wonders. **1651** FULLER *Abel Rediv.* (1867) I. 257 He did not only bear the terribleness of imprisonment. **1710** ABP. SHARP *Serm. Acts xvii. 31* Wks. 1754 VI. 188 The..majesty, and terribleness of his appearance. **1887** SMILES *Life & Labour* 431 The sadness and terribleness of some of the aspects of life.

†**'terriblize**, *v. Obs. nonce-wd.* [f. TERRIBLE + -IZE.] *trans.* To make or render terrible.

1605 SYLVESTER *Du Bartas* II. iii. I. *Vocation* 271 Both Camps approach, their bloudy rage doth rise, And even the face of Cowards terriblize.

terribly ('tɛrɪblɪ), *adv.* [f. as prec. + -LY[2].] In a terrible manner.

1. So as to excite terror or dread; dreadfully.

1526 *Pilgr. Perf.* (W. de W. 1531) 245b, Impenitent synners..drawen downe to hell moost terribly or feerfully. **1610** SHAKS. *Temp.* II. i. 313 We heard a hollow burst of bellowing Like Buls, or rather Lyons,..It strooke mine eare most terribly. **1718** PRIOR *Solomon* I. 639 This ample azure sky, Terribly large, and wonderfully bright. *a* **1848** R. W. HAMILTON *Rew. & Punishm.* viii. (1853) 362 It is at death that the consequences of guilt are often most terribly revealed.

2. a. Very severely, painfully, or badly; passing colloquially into a general intensive: Exceedingly, extremely, excessively, very greatly.

1604 E. G[RIMSTONE] *D'Acosta's Hist. Indies* III. xx. 184 It raines and snowes terribly. **1707** *Curios. in Husb. & Gard.* 274 Tulips are charming to the Sight, but terribly offensive to the Smell. **1774** GOLDSM. *Nat. Hist.* (1776) VI. 101 Relying on its courage, and the strength of its bill, with which it [the puffin] bites most terribly. **1833** DICKENS *Let.* ? Oct. (1965) I. 31, I am terribly out of spirits this morning. **1867** TROLLOPE *Chron. Barset* II. lviii. 147 You must be terribly in want of your dinner. **1871** JOWETT *Plato* I. 49 Why then are they so terribly anxious to prevent you from being happy? *Mod.* I am at present terribly busy.

b. Extraordinarily badly; incompetently, feebly. Cf. sense 2 c of the adj. *colloq.*

1930 *Publishers' Weekly* 29 Mar. 1741 (Advt.), About 1,000,000 [bridge players] now play Contract, almost all of them terribly. **1964** J. MITCHELL *White Father* iii. 54 You can sing terribly and get away with it if only you have the right backing.

†**'terric.** *Obs. rare*[−1]. [f. L. *terr-a* earth + -IC.] (See quot.)

1612 STURTEVANT *Metallica* II. v. 59 Terrica is an Ignick Inuention, for the cheaper making of all kinds of Burnt-earths,..wherevpon the Materialls made by this Art, are called Terricks.

terrice, obs. form of TERRACE.

terricole ('tɛrɪkəʊl), *a.* (*sb.*) [ad. L. *terricola* earth-dweller, f. *terra* earth + *col-ĕre* to inhabit.]

A. *adj.* **1.** *Bot.* Growing on the ground, as some lichens.

1882 J. M. CROMBIE in *Encycl. Brit.* XIV. 562/1 With respect to terricole species [of lichens], some prefer peaty soil.., others calcareous soil.

2. *Zool.* Living on the ground or in the earth.

1899 *Proc. Zool. Soc.* 6 June 715 Some living specimens of the 'Harmut', *Clarias lazera*.., from Damietta..This curious Siluroid Fish..Mr. Boulenger was not able to confirm..the account of its terricole habits.

B. *sb.* An animal living on the ground, or burrowing in the earth; *spec.* a member of the *Terricolæ*, a group of annelids containing the common earthworm.

1896 *Naturalist* 78 The head-pore of aquatic species is wanting in adult terricoles.

terricoline (tɛ'rɪkəlaɪn), *a. Zool.* [f. as prec. + -INE[2].] = next.

1895 in *Funk's Standard Dict.* **1902** in WEBSTER *Suppl.*

terricolous (tɛ'rɪkələs), *a. Zool.* [f. as prec. + -OUS.] **1.** Inhabiting the ground, not aquatic or aerial; living in the earth; *spec.* of or belonging to the *Terricolæ* or earthworms; = TERRICOLE 2.

1835-6 *Todd's Cycl. Anat.* I. 167/1 In the terricolous annelida there are no cirri. **1860** MAYNE *Expos. Lex.*, *Terricolus*,..living on or in the earth, as the *Harpalus terricola*. Applied by Latreille and Macquart to a group.. of the *Tipularia* which deposit their eggs in the earth..: terricolous. **1877** HUXLEY *Anat. Inv. Anim.* v. 220 In the terricolous forms (Lumbricus) the vasa deferentia are continuous with the testes. **1881** DARWIN *Veg. Mould* 247 In the same manner as gallinaceous and struthious birds swallow stones to aid in the trituration of their food, so it appears to be with terricolous worms.

2. = TERRICOLE *a.* 1.

1921 A. L. SMITH *Handbk. Brit. Lichens* 142/1 Terricolous, living on soil. **1959** U. K. DUNCAN *Guide to Study of Lichens* p. xiv, Sand-dunes and heaths are usually rich in terricolous species.

† **te'rricrepant**, *a. Obs. rare*[−0]. [f. L. *terricrep-us*, f. stem of *terr-ēre* to frighten + *crep-āre* to rattle, make a noise; cf. *crepānt-em* pr. pple.]

1656 BLOUNT *Glossogr.*, *Terricrepant*..that rebuketh terribly or bitterly.

† **te'rriculament**, *sb. Obs.* Also 7 in L. form **-mentum**, pl. **-ta**. [ad. L. *terriculāment-um* (Apuleius) a bugbear, f. *terriculum* something that excites terror, f. *terrēre* to frighten: see -MENT.] A source or object of dread, esp. of needless dread; a bugbear.

1548 W. PATTEN *Exped. Scotl.* Pref. ciiij, His vaine terriculaments and rattelbladders. **1567-8** ABP. PARKER *Corr.* (Parker Soc.) 315 Afeared or dismayed with such vain terriculaments of the world. **1621** BURTON *Anat. Mel.* III. iv. II. vi. (1651) 720 Such terriculaments may proceed from natural causes. *a* **1661** FULLER *Worthies, Warwick* (1811) II. 404 Those who are not *Terriculamenta*, but *Terrores*, no fancy-formed Bugbears, but such as carry fear and fright to others about them. **1674** JOSSELYN *Voy. New Eng.* 182 Such like bugbears and Terriculamentaes.

Hence † **te'rriculament** *v. Obs.*, to inspire with groundless fear.

1644 J. GOODWIN *Innoc. & Truth Triumph.* (1645) 14 The man to whom the shadowes of the mountaines seemed men, was very prudent and advised in his feare, in respect of him that is terriculamented with such apocryphall pretences of feare as these.

‖**terridam, terrindam.** [Native Indian name.] (See quot.)

1727-41 CHAMBERS *Cycl.* s.v. *Muslin*, There are various kinds of muslins brought from the East-Indies; chiefly Bengall; betelles, tarnatans, mulmuls, tanjeebs, terrindams, doreas, &c. **1891** *Cent. Dict.*, Terridam.

† **terrie, terry.** *Obs. rare*[−1]. [app. a. OF. *terry*, *terri* (16th c. in Godef.), dial. forms of *terris* bank, mound, trodden ground.] A trodden path, sometimes a balk or ridge of earth separating fields or allotments.

1563 *Homilies* II. *Rogation Week* IV. (1859) 496 They do wickedly which do turn up the ancient terries of the fields, that old men beforetime with great pains did tread out.

† **'terrien**, *a. Obs.* Also 5 **-yen.** [a. OF. *ter(r)ien* terrestrial, seigniorial (12th c. in Godef. *Compl.*) f. *terre* land + *-ien*, -IAN: corresp. to a L. type **terriānus*.] Earthly, worldly; territorial.

[**1292** BRITTON III. iv. §21 Fey a noster Seignur le Roi..de vie et de membre, de cors et de chateaus et de terrien honour.] *c* **1450** *Merlin* xx. 334 The kynge Arthur, that is oure lorde terrien. **1484** CAXTON *Chivalry* 24 Thoffyce of a knyght is to mayntene and deffende his lord worldly or terryen. **1489** —— *Faytes of A.* I. i. 5 Emperours, kynges, dukes & other lordes terryens.

terrier ('tɛrɪə(r)), *sb.*[1] Now in limited use. Forms: 5 terrere, 5-9 terrar, 6 tarrar, terrour, -ore, 7 terreer, 7-8 terrer, 6- terrier. [a. OF. *terrier* (13-15th c. in Godef. *Compl.*) rent-roll, subst. use of *terrier* adj. (cf. F. *registre terrier* (15th c.) = med.L. *terrārius liber*):—med.L. *terrārius*, f. *terra* land. Thence med.L. *terrērium* rent-roll (Du Cange).] A register of landed property, formerly including lists of vassals and tenants, with particulars of their holdings, services, and rents; a rent-roll; in later use, a book in which the lands of a private person, or of a corporation civil or ecclesiastical, are described by their site, boundaries, acreage, etc. Also, in extended application, an inventory of property or goods.

1477 *Paston Lett.* III. 206 Increse the rente, and make a new terrar and rentall. **1492** *Bury Wills* (Camden) 78, I wyll that..the terrere wyth that oon partye of thys indentur be putte and kepte in the hutche of the Gyldehalle. **1527** *Luton Trin. Guild* (1906) 192 A terrore of y[e] land y[t] was Thomas Colemakers. **1569** *Nottingham Rec.* IV. 136 A tarrar of alle the landes and medowes..belongeng to the towne. **1584** *N. Riding Rec.* (1894) 231 An auncient and true terrour.. declaringe the limits [etc.]. **1594** WEST *2nd Pt. Symbol.*, *Chancerie* §87 The deedes, evidences, muniments, terriers. **1655** FULLER *Ch. Hist.* III. viii. §17 Some Dioceses in this Terreer were exactly done, and remain fairly legible at this day. **1670** BLOUNT *Law Dict.*, *Terrar*..is a Book, Survey, or Land-Roll, wherein the several Lands..are described; containing the quantity of Acres, boundaries, Tenants names, and such like. *a* **1695** WOOD *Life* (O.H.S.) I. 398 That there was no terrier taken of the goods he had, which were bought at the college charg. **1707** E. CHAMBERLAYNE *Pres. St. Eng.* II. ix. (ed. 22) 129 The Churchwardens, whose Office is to see..that there be an exact Terrier of the Glebe-Land. **1879** *Times* 22 Sept., The dimensions of each plot by number are preserved in the official parish terrier.

b. *transf.* and *fig.*

a **1640** JACKSON *Creed* XI. xxii. §5 Some..give a more particular terrar or distinct map of this heavenly life or kingdom. **1646** OWEN *Country Ess.* Wks. 1851 VIII. 55 What bounds, what terriers are to be assigned to the one or to the other. *a* **1649** R. HOLDSWORTH in Spurgeon *Treas. Dav.* Ps. cxix. 111 The holy terrier of the Celestial Canaan.

terrier ('tɛrɪə(r)), *sb.*[2] Forms: 5 terrere, terryare, 6 terryer, taryer, terrour, 7 terriar, terrar, tarier, tarriar, tarryer, 7-8 (9 *vulgar*) tarrier, 6- terrier. [a. F. (*chien*) *terrier*, also as subst. *terrier* 'a hunting-dog used to start badgers, etc., from their earth or burrow' (cf. TERRIER *sb.*[3]) = med.L. *terrārius*, f. *terra* earth (see prec.).]

1. a. A small, active, intelligent variety of dog, which pursues its quarry (the fox, badger, etc.) into its burrow or earth; the numerous breeds are distinguished into two classes, the *short-* or *smooth-haired*, as the fox-terrier, black and tan terrier, etc., and the *long-* or *rough-haired*, as the Scotch terrier, Skye terrier, etc. (See also BULL-TERRIER, TOY *terrier*, etc.) Formerly also ***terrier dog***.

c **1440** *Promp. Parv.* 489/1 Terrere, hownde (*v.r.* terryare), *terrarius*. **1530** PALSGR. 279/2 Taryer a dogge. *Ibid.* 280/1 Terryer a dogge, *chien terrier*. **1576** A. FLEMING tr. *Caius' Dogs* I. (1880) 4 Of the Dogge called Terrar, in Latine *Terrarius*. Another sorte..which hunteth the Foxe and the Badger or Greye onely, whome we call Terrars, because they..creepe into the grounde. **1602** *2nd Pt. Return fr. Parnass.* II. v. 871 An open table for all kinde of dogges ..He hath your..Terriers, Butchers dogs, Bloud-hounds. **1644-7** CLEVELAND *Char. Lond. Diurn.* 3 Who fitter to unkennell the Fox, then the Tarryer, that is a part of him. **1648** *Hunting of Fox* 25 Like so many Tarriars we must fasten upon them with tooth and nail. **1774** GOLDSM. *Nat. Hist.* II. 166 The terrier is a small kind of hound with rough hair. **1815** SCOTT *Guy M.* xxii, A rough terrier dog.. scampered at large. **1852** HUXLEY *Lect. Wkg. Men* 110 It is a physiological peculiarity..that impels the terrier to its rat-hunting propensity. **1863** H. KINGSLEY *A. Elliot* v, Rough long-legged English fox terriers, which ran on three legs, like Scotch terriers, and held their heads on one side knowingly.

b. *fig.*

1532 MORE *Confut. Tindale* Wks. 695/1 We shall..set in such terryers to him, that we shall..eyther course him abrode or make him euyll rest within. *c* **1622** FORD, etc. *Witch Edmonton* I. ii, Bonds and bills are but tarriers to catch fools. **1779-81** JOHNSON *L.P.*, *Otway* Wks. II. 220 Hunted ..by the terriers of the law. **1818** SCOTT *Hrt. Midl.* xxxiii, The opening quest of a well-scented terrier of the law drove me from the vicinity of Edinburgh.

†**2.** A name given to certain beavers said to burrow instead of building. *Obs.*

1733 MORTIMER in *Phil. Trans.* XXXVIII. 177 He [Sarrasin in *Mem. Acad. Sci.*, Paris, 1704, p. 64] says there are some Beavers called Terriers [*Castors terriers*], which burrow in the Earth. **1781** PENNANT *Hist. Quad.* II. 384 They [Beavers] are met with dispersed, or in the state of Terriers, in the wooded parts of independent Tartary. **1784** —— *Arct. Zool.* I. 103.

3. A punning appellation for a territorial: see TERRITORIAL 4 b. (Cf. TERRY *sb.*[2])

1908 *Daily Chron.* 31 Mar. 5/3 It may..be argued that 'Territorial' is not very much longer than 'Volunteer', but it is just the little that makes all the difference... [Of three suggestions, 'Terror', 'Terrier', 'Torral', it was] yesterday rather thought that 'Terrier' would carry the day. *Ibid.* 18 June 3/4 Next year, which will be the jubilee of the force now known as the 'Terriers', to distinguish them from the 'Tommies'. **1908** *Daily News* 5 Aug. 4 The admirable spirit in which his [Mr. Haldane's] 'Terriers', as the wit of London has nicknamed our Home Army, have met the [etc.]. **1915** [see DO *sb.*[1] 2 b]. **1935** *Economist* 7 Sept. 464/1 This change-over of responsibilities inside the War Office places the 'Terriers' within the same organisation as the 'Regulars'. **1980** *Times* 12 Mar. 12/4 More Terriers. The strength of the Territorial Army on December 31 last year was just under 62,000.

4. *attrib.* That is a terrier; of or like a terrier (for *terrier dog* see 1). Also *Comb.*, as ***terrier-like*** adj.; **terrier-man** *Hunting*, a man employed to head the terriers.

1809 SCOTT *Let. to G. Ellis* 8 July, in *Lockhart*, A terrier puppy of the old shaggy Celtic breed. **1858** LEWIS in Youatt *Dog* (N.Y.) v. 169 The imaginary beauty of a terrier crop consists in the foxy appearance of the ears. **1894** BLACKMORE *Perlycross* 292 Endowed with the terrier nose of suspicion. **1895** SCULLY *Kafir Stories* 133 He had a wiry and terrier-like appearance. **1930** C. FREDERICK et al. *Foxhunting* x. 130 If the bag is suspended..by strong pieces of india-rubber..it is more comfortable for the terrier and the terrier man. **1983** *Times* 19 Sept. 4/6 The terrierman..had slashed a fox's paw with a knife before releasing it for young hounds to chase.

† **terrier**, *sb.*[3] *Obs.* In 5 **terryer.** [a. F. *terrier* (14th c. in Littré):—late L. *terrārium* mound of earth, hillock, burrow, f. *terre* earth: see prec. sbs.] The earth or burrow of a badger or fox.

1484 CAXTON *Fables of Æsop* v. ix, The foxe..was within a terryer nyghe to the lodgys of the lyon.

terrier ('tɛrɪə(r)), *v. rare.* [f. TERRIER *sb.*[2]] *intr.* To burrow in the manner of a terrier; to make *one's way* like a terrier.

1959 R. COLLIER *City that wouldn't Die* ix. 155 Working with hand-shovels and even bare hands, Marotta and his crew began to terrier away. **1965** 'J. CHRISTOPHER' *Wrinkle in Skin* iii. 26 He began to terrier his way into the mound.

terrier, terriet, obs. ff. TARRIER[2], TERRET.

terrif, obs. form of TARIFF.

terrific (tə'rɪfɪk), *a.* (*sb.*) [ad. L. *terrific-us* terrifying, f. stem of *terrēre* to frighten: see -FIC. So obs. F. *terrifique* (15th c. in Godef.).]

A. *adj.* **1.** Causing terror, terrifying; fitted to terrify; dreadful, terrible, frightful.

1667 MILTON *P.L.* VII. 497 The Serpent..with brazen Eyes And hairie Main terrific. **1718** POPE *Iliad* x. 300 In arms terrific their huge limbs they dress'd. **1796** MORSE *Amer. Geog.* I. 345 Even Canonicus..the terrific Sachem of the Narragansetts, sued for peace. **1821** CRAIG *Lect. Drawing* iv. 214, I cannot..advise you to attempt any species of the terrific in painting. **1899** WARD *Hist. Dram. Lit.* (ed. 2) I. 307 A terrific woodcut depicts the most sensational situation in the story.

2. a. Applied intensively to anything very severe or excessive. *colloq.* (Cf. *awful*, *terrible*, *tremendous*.)

1809 J. W. CROKER in *Croker Papers* 12 Oct., I am..up to my eyes in business, the extent of which is quite terrific. **1855** MRS. CARLYLE *Lett.* (1883) II. 262 The crowd was immense, and the applause terrific. **1899** J. HUTCHINSON in *Arch. Surg.* X. No. 38. 177 The sensation of tingling burning pain remaining the same, while the itching is 'terrific'.

b. As an enthusiastic term of commendation: superlatively good, 'marvellous', 'great'. Also *Comb. colloq.*

1930 D. MACKAIL *Young Livingstones* xi. 271 'Thanks awfully,' said Rex. 'That'll be ripping.' 'Fine!' said Derek Yardley. 'Great! Terrific!' **1940** *Chatelaine* Dec. 10/3 But think what it means that they want to come to you. Your bedside manner must be terrific. **1944** *Sun* (Baltimore) 20 Dec. 1/7 Lee McCardell [a reporter] is terrific—first into Metz, first into St. Avold, first into Saarlautern. **1951** 'A. GARVE' *Murder in Moscow* iii. 47 Perdita..looked terrific in midnight-blue velvet. **1951** J. D. SALINGER *Catcher in Rye* xii. 103 This..guy had a terrific-looking girl with him. Boy, she was good-looking. **1971** *Farmer & Stockbreeder* 23 Feb. 39/1 He believes the soil is 'terrific' for potatoes and wheat. **1981** *Daily Mail* 14 October 15/1, 'I feel great, really terrific,' said the former Wings guitarist.

B. *sb.* in *pl.* Terrific things.

1798 ANNA SEWARD *Lett.* (1811) V. 174 To exhibit, among his mock-terrifics, some pictures that have the genuine grandeur of horror.

Hence **te'rrificly** *adv.* = TERRIFICALLY; **te'rrificness**, the quality of being terrific.

1727 BAILEY vol. II, *Terrifickness*, Terribleness. **1894** *Outing* (U.S.) XXIV. 360/1 A low mountain..over which a terrificly steep path led. **1904** *Adv. Elizabeth in Ruegen* 101 Her family wept and..told her the terrificness of marrying a widower with seven children.

te'rrifical, *a. rare.* [f. as prec. + -AL[1].] = TERRIFIC.

1831 FR. A. KEMBLE *Jrnl.* in *Recoll. Girlhood* (1878) III. 47 In the evening we had terrifical ghost stories. **1855** MISS MANNING *Old Chelsea Bun-Ho.* xvii. 286 Abundantly more terrifical.

te'rrifically, *adv.* [f. as prec. + -LY[2]: see -ICALLY.] In a terrific or terrifying manner; frightfully, dreadfully, shockingly.

1814 C. CLAIRMONT in Dowden *Shelley* (1887) I. 452 *note*, A most terrifically dirty inn. **1817** J. SCOTT *Paris Revisit.* (ed. 4) 79 The reports of the distant war sound terrifically in the ear. **1846** MRS. SHERWOOD in *P. Parley's Ann.* VII. 228 Arches of rock, which hung terrifically over my head. **1904** HICHENS *Gard. Allah* Prel. vi, Terrifically greater, more overpowering than man.

b. *colloq.* in intensive use: Alarmingly, excessively, extremely. (Cf. *awfully*, *dreadfully*.)

1859 DARWIN in *Life & Lett.* (1887) II. 160 My corrections are terrifically heavy. **1883** J. PARKER *Apost. Life* II. 188 Always be terrifically hard upon yourself. **1885** G. MEREDITH *Diana Crossways* ii, Terrifically precocious, he thought her.

terrification (ˌtɛrɪfɪˈkeɪʃən). Chiefly *Sc.* [ad. L. *terrificātiōn-em*, n. of action from *terrificāre* to TERRIFY.] The action of terrifying; the fact or condition of being terrified; consternation, extreme alarm, terror, fright.

1612 in W. James *Deeds East Lothian* (1899) 29 For ane exemplar terrificatioun to all Godles harlottis to flie and abhorre the lyk. **1797** EARL MALMESBURY *Diaries & Corr.* III. 504 Now and then he tried terrification, by letting out some strong Jacobin phrases. **1833** GALT in *Fraser's Mag.* VIII. 657 He was in an awful terrification.

b. *transf.* A source of alarm or dismay; a terror.

a **1806** MRS. GRANT *Lett. fr. Mount.* (1806) III. 180 She was a terrification to me.

terrify (ˈtɛrɪfaɪ), *v.* [ad. L. *terrificāre* to frighten, f. *terrificus* TERRIFIC: see -FY. Cf. F. *terrifier* (Littré).]

1. *trans.* To make much afraid, to fill with terror, to frighten or alarm greatly. Also *absol.*

1578 *Chr. Prayers* in *Priv. Prayers* (Parker Soc.) 501 Thou terrifiest none but such as most horribly are afraid of thee. **1638** *Penit. Conf.* ii. (1657) 15 No Conscience to accuse, no Devil to terrifie. **1667** MILTON *P.L.* x. 338 Terrifi'd Hee fled, not hoping to escape, but shun The present. **1774** GOLDSM. *Nat. Hist.* (1776) V. 215 The fowler then discovers himself, and terrifies the quail, who..entangles himself the more in the net, and is taken. **1868** MORRIS *Earthly Par.* I. *Son of Crœsus* xxiii, Girls, sent their water-jars to fill, Would come back pale, too terrified to cry.

b. To drive *from, out of, into*, etc. by terrifying; to deter *from*; to frighten *out of, into*, etc.

1575 tr. *Luther's Comm. Gal.* iii. 3. 100 b, To exhort the Galathians, and to terrifie them from a double daunger. **1690** NESSE *Hist. & Myst. O. & N.T.* I. 53 Those very angels which terrified them both from the tree. **1824** SCOTT *St. Ronan's* xxxvii, It may terrify her to death in the present weak state of her nerves. **1867** SMILES *Huguenots Eng.* iv. (1880) 55 The people who remained were at length terrified into orthodoxy.

2. To irritate, torment, worry, harass, annoy, tease. Now only *dial.*

1641 MILTON *Ch. Govt.* II. iii, Working only by terrifying Plaisters upon the rind and orifice of the Sore. *a* **1825** FORBY *Voc. E. Anglia, Terrify*, to teize; irritate; annoy. A blister or a caustic is said to terrify a patient. **1876** *N. & Q.* 5th Ser. VI. 56/1 He has been terrified all night by those insects. **1898** J. A. GIBBS *Cotswold Vill.* viii. 164 'Terrify him, sir; keep on terrifying of him'. This does not mean that you are to frighten the fish; on the contrary, he is urging you to stick to him till he gets tired of being harassed.

†**3.** To make terrible. *Obs. rare*[−1].

1643 MILTON *Divorce* II. iii, If the law, instead of aggravating and terrifying sin, shall give out licence, it foils itself.

Hence **ˈterrified** (-faɪd) *ppl. a.* (whence **ˈterrifiedly** *adv.*); **ˈterrifying** *vbl. sb.* and *ppl. a.* (whence **ˈterrifyingly** *adv.*); also **ˈterrifier** (-faɪə(r)), one who or that which terrifies.

1821 SCOTT *Kenilw.* xxxiv, Elizabeth..hastened..along the principal alley of the Pleasance, dragging with her the *terrified Countess. **1865** DICKENS *Mut. Fr.* I. i, Her terrified expostulation stopped him. **1890** *Temple Bar Mag.* Nov. 313 She is still *terrifiedly clutching his hand. **1617** COLLINS *Def. Bp. Ely* Suppl. 548 In stead of a *terrifier, he hath brought him about now, to be a praiser. **1870** R. C. JEBB *Sophocles' Electra* (ed. 2) 72/1 The terrifier of horses. **1617** J. WOODFORD in *Buccleuch MSS.* (Hist. MSS. Comm.) I. 199 A gibbet having been set up..for the *terrifying of the people. *c* **1586** C'TESS PEMBROKE *Ps.* LXXXVIII. xi, Thou dost me fill..With *terrifying feares. **1746–7** HERVEY *Medit.* (1818) 269 At the least terrifying appearance, they start from their seats. **1849** STOVEL *Introd. Canne's Necess.* 71 Exhibitions of terrifying depravity. **1805** SURR *Winter in Lond.* (1806) I. 271 If your honour had not been so *terrifyingly flurried, I should have given you the message before. **1908** H. G. WELLS *War in Air* vi. 194 It had crept in upon his mind, chillingly terrifyingly, that these illuminated black masses were great offices afire. **1944** D. WELCH *In Youth is Pleasure* v. 89 He grinned, and then began to make the flesh round his eyes terrifyingly inflamed.

terrifyingness (ˈtɛrɪfaɪɪŋnɪs). *rare.* [f. TERRIFYING *ppl. a.* + -NESS.] Frightening quality.

1940 *Scrutiny* IX. 294 It is not the terrifyingness of great poetry because it is too exclusively personal.

†**teˈrrigenal**, *a. Obs. rare*[−1]. [f. L. *terrigenus* earth-born + -AL[1].] = TERRIGENOUS 1.

a **1734** NORTH *Lives* (1826) III. 347 Even his terrigenal men would be void of ambition, or knowledge of wants.

†**teˈrrigenist.** *Obs. rare.* [f. as prec. + -IST.] One born of the earth.

1631 R. H. *Arraignm. Whole Creature* xiv. §2. 248 The men of this world, those Brutigenists, or Terrigenists, as they are called, Earth-bred wormes. *Ibid.* xvi. 286.

terrigenous (tɛˈrɪdʒɪnəs), *a.* Also *erron.* terrigeneous. [f. as prec. + -OUS.]

1. Produced or sprung from the earth; earth-born. *rare.*

1684 T. BURNET *Th. Earth* I. 189 Our terrigenous animals must have been wean'd as soon as they were born. **1830** LYELL *Princ. Geol.* I. I. iii. 31 Either these were terrigenous, or..the animals they so exactly represent have become extinct.

†**2.** *Chem.* A term for those metals of which the oxides are called earths. (Cf. CALCIGENOUS.) *Obs. rare.*

1854 J. SCOFFERN in *Orr's Circ. Sc., Chem.* 433 Silicates, either of the terrigenous or the calcigenous class. *c* **1865** J. WYLDE in *Circ. Sc.* I. 394 Tests for the terrigeneous earths.

3. *Geol.* Land-derived: applied esp. to marine deposits derived from the neighbouring land.

1882 GEIKIE *Text Bk. Geol.* III. II. ii. §6. 437 Mechanical deposits of the sea..Land-derived or Terrigenous. **1884** *Nature* 22 May 84/2 Terrigenous deposits in deep water near land. **1884**, etc. [see PELAGIC *a.* c]. **1957** G. E. HUTCHINSON *Treat. Limnol.* I. viii. 550 Most of the calcium in atmospheric precipitation is of terrigenous origin. **1973** *Nature* 27 July 202/1 Deformed early Cainozoic, terrigenous and carbonate sediments form the highest parts of the island.

terrine (təˈriːn). [Original form of TUREEN.]

1. Orig. = TUREEN (*arch.* exc. as French). Now, an earthenware or similar fireproof cooking vessel, esp. one in which a terrine (sense 2) is cooked.

1706, etc. [see TUREEN a]. **1888** TRAILL in *Eng. Illustr. Mag.* Apr. 508/2 A part of South America where the earth's crust seems to be so absurdly thin that you can almost see the internal contents of the telluric pie—or *terrine*, as it may perhaps be appropriately called. **1901** *Speaker* 19 Oct. 66/2 In a few moments the Republican had set before him..a terrine of Pâté de Foie Gras. **1905** A KENNEY-HERBERT *Common-Sense Cookery* (ed. 2) xxii. 358 Uncooked meats with forcemeat lining..arranged as within a paste-lined mould, can be baked and finished in a *terrine*. **1914** F. B. JACKS *Cookery for Every Household* 304/2 Compote of Game... Put the joints [of roasted birds] into a fireproof terrine or casserole with the mushrooms and cherries..and leave these until the sauce is prepared. **1960** E. DAVID *French Provincial Cooking* 69 A pâté *en terrine* indicates that the pâté concerned has been cooked and is served in the terrine rather than in a crust. **1979** *Homes & Gardens* June 135/2 The sheets of fat removed from the roast should be thinly sliced and used for lining terrines when making pâté.

2. *Cookery.* Orig. (see quots. 1706, 1736). In modern use, a kind of pâté cooked in a terrine (sense 1).

1706 PHILLIPS (ed. Kersey), *Terrine*,..in Cookery, a Mess made of a Breast of Mutton, cut into pieces, with Quails, Pigeons, and Chickens, cover'd with slices of Bacon..and stew'd in a Pan between two gentle Fires. **1736** BAILEY *Househ. Dict.* 565 *Terrine*, is a French dish, so call'd from *Terrine*, which signifies an earthen pan; it is made of half a dozen of quails, four young pigeons and a couple of chickens, and a breast of mutton cut to pieces; bake or stew them in an earthen pan between two gentle fires [etc.]. **1906** A. FILIPPINI *Internat. Cook Bk.* 631 (*heading*) Terrine of duckling. **1914** F. B. JACKS *Cookery for Every Household* 297/2 A terrine like this will keep good for two or three months in cold weather. **1968** D. BRIGGS *Entertaining Single-Handed* iv. 81 *Terrine Andrew.* A terrine is made from the same kind of bits and pieces as a pâté, but..the texture is rougher and it is cooked in a pie-dish or, indeed, a terrine. **1979** REESE & FLINT *Trick 13* 159, I bought an appetizing selection of rough terrine.

terring, provocation: see TAR, TARRE *v.*[2]

terris, obs. form of TERRACE.

†**teˈrrisonant**, *a. Obs. rare*[−0]. [f. L. *terrison-us*, f. stem of *terr-ēre* to frighten + *sonāre* to sound; cf. *sonānt-em* pr. pple.] (See quot.) So †**teˈrrisonous** *a. Obs. rare*[−0].

1656 BLOUNT *Glossogr.*, *Terrisonant*, that sounds bitterly [*ed.* 1674 terribly]. **1658** PHILLIPS, *Terrisonant*, sounding terribly. **1721** BAILEY, *Terrisonous*, that soundeth terribly.

territ, variant of TERRET.

†**territoire, -tor, -tour.** *Obs.* Also terre-. [ad. F. *territoire*.] = TERRITORY[1]; land.

1456 SIR G. HAYE *Law Arms* (S.T.S.) 115 That it be nocht our [= over] hye set,..or in our harde dry territoire, or our myry erde. **1547** *Aberdeen Regr.* (1844) I. 250 The terretour of the est part of the said burgh. **1589** FLEMING *Virg. Georg.* II. 24 Cæsar Who..Doost turne away th' vnwarlike Inde from territors of Rome. **1606** HOLLAND *Sueton.* Annot. 21 The Inhabitants of it, and the territour there about.

territoire, variant of TERRITORY[2].

territorial (tɛrɪˈtɔərɪəl), *a.* (*sb.*) [ad. late L. *territōriāl-is*, f. *territōri-um* TERRITORY[1]. Cf. F. *territorial* (18th c. in Hatz.-Darm.).]

1. a. Of, belonging or relating to territory or land, or to the territory of any state, sovereign, or ruler.

1768 R. WOOD *Ess. Homer* (1769) 22 Three other litigated cases with regard to territorial property and dominion. **1798** WASHINGTON *Let.* Writ. 1893 XIV. 20 An actual Invasion of our territorial rights. **1845** S. AUSTIN *Ranke's Hist. Ref.* III. iv. II. 135 Freeing themselves from the territorial jurisdiction of the temporal and spiritual princes. **1906** *Daily News* 28 May 9/1 The Jewish Territorial Organization, whose aim is to secure an autonomous home for the Jews in territory under the British flag.

b. Of or pertaining to landed property.

1773 *Gentl. Mag.* XLIII. 199 It will be more beneficial to the public and the East India Company, to let the territorial acquisitions remain in the possession of the Company for a limited time. **1800** *Proc. Parl.* in *Asiat. Ann. Reg.* 49/2 That the dead stock and territorial revenue of India were enlarged very much, he was ready to allow. **1844** H. H. WILSON *Brit. India* III. 492 A plan..for keeping the territorial and commercial accounts distinct in future. **1855** DELAMER *Kitch. Gard.* (1861) 1 Territorial possessions are too highly prized in England for men lightly to yield even a fraction of such property at a fair value.

c. Possessed of land, owning or having an estate in land; landed.

1832 SIR F. PALGRAVE *Rise Eng. Commw.* I. i. 15 The territorial aristocracy. **1867** R. CONGREVE *Ess.* (1874) 173 The territorial and moneyed aristocracy..is being brought daily into more direct..opposition to the people which it has governed. **1884** *Manch. Exam.* 25 Mar. 5/1 The preservation of that ascendency which the territorial class now enjoys.

d. ***territorial water(s)***, ***territorial sea***: the area of sea adjoining the shores of a state and under its jurisdiction (traditionally reckoned as three miles from low water mark, but recently extended by many states). Also ***territorial limits***, the limits of such water. Cf. WATER *sb.* 6 d.

1841 J. DODSON in Ld. McNair *Internat. Law Opinions* (1956) I. x. 334 A free permission to Foreign Fishing Vessels so to use the Ports and Territorial waters of our Coasts, would seem likely to lead to constant evasions and violations of the stipulation which prohibits them from fishing within the Limits. **1870** *Act 33 & 34 Vict.* c. 90 §2 This Act shall extend to all the dominions of Her Majesty, including the adjacent territorial waters. **1875** BEDFORD *Sailor's Pocket Bk.* vi. (ed. 2) 231 'Territorial water', in its essence means any water over which, or over the entrance to which, the Power possessing the coast can throw shot. Custom has given an arbitrary range of three miles. **1939** *Daily Tel.* 18 Dec. 1/1 Just beyond the three-mile limit of Uruguayan territorial waters, an unidentified British warship and an Argentine patrol boat had earlier been seen. **1955** *Times* 2 July 6/4 Passage is innocent as long as the vessel does not use the territorial sea for committing acts prejudicial to the security of the coastal State. **1962** *Britannia Bk. of Year* 207/2 Many states had declared, unilaterally, the right to exclusive fishing beyond the territorial limits claimed; *e.g.* Argentina, 3 mi. territorial limits (1869) and 10 mi. exclusive fisheries rights (1907); Thailand, 6 mi. (1958) and 12 mi. (1958). **1976** in R. Crossman *Diaries* II. 71 Since March 1964 pirate radio stations had been transmitting pop music and advertisements, usually from ships anchored outside territorial waters.

e. *Zool.* Of or pertaining to an area defended by an animal or a group of animals against others of the same species; also designating an animal or species that defends its territory in this way; ***territorial imperative***, the need to claim and defend a territory.

1920 E. HOWARD *Territory in Bird Life* vi. 228 Do these battles..contribute towards the attainment of the end for which the whole territorial system has been evolved? **1940** *Misc. Publ. Mus. Zool. Univ. Michigan* XLV (*title*) Territorial behavior and populations of some small mammals in southern Michigan. **1961** *Science* 10 Mar. 698/1 The well-defined pattern of year-around territorial behavior of the Uganda kob was discovered in March 1957. **1966** R. ARDREY (*title*) The territorial imperative. *Ibid.* iii. 101 That man is a territorial species has been the conclusion of many a scientist. **1968** K. LORENZ in *Harper's Mag.* May 74 The 'territorial imperative' does much to explain the causes of war, such as the Arab-Israeli dispute, which I consider almost purely territorial. **1971** *Nature* 4 June 295/2 A territorial bull establishes himself as supremely dominant within the confines of his territory. **1980** C. AIRD *Passing Strange* iv. 47 If any one single instinct came to the fore in Superintendent Leeyes it was the territorial imperative. **1981** *Oxf. Compan. Animal Behaviour* 551/1 One benefit of territorial defence is food acquisition.

2. a. Of or pertaining to a particular territory, district, or locality; local.

1625 BP. MOUNTAGU *App. Cæsar* i. 8 Each particular.. Church, for speciall and particular and territoriall questions & quærees. **1772** PRIESTLEY *Inst. Relig.* (1782) II. 131 The gods..were local and territorial divinities. **1857** TOULMIN SMITH *Parish* 4 'The Parish', whether as a mere territorial division or an active Institution, is not ecclesiastical either in origin or in purpose. **1868** GLADSTONE *Juv. Mundi* iv. (1869) 111 Phthie itself is..the only territorial name [etc.]..which we find in the Greece of Homer.

b. *Sc. Law.* Of jurisdiction: Extending over and restricted to a defined territory: see TERRITORY[1] 1 c.

1765–8 ERSKINE *Inst. Law Scot.* I. ii. §11 Because this kind of jurisdiction was incident to, and followed the lands or territory to which it was annexed,..it got the name of territorial. **1838** W. BELL *Dict. Law Scot.* s.v., *Territorial Jurisdiction* was at one time universal; but, becoming formidable, was repeatedly discouraged by different acts,.. and by 20 Geo. II. c. 43, all heritable jurisdictions..were abolished or annexed to the Crown, with the exception [etc.].

c. *Sc.* Of or pertaining to an ecclesiastical district, not a parish. ***territorial church***, one organized to serve a particular district, esp. a poor and thickly populated one, without regard to the existing parish boundaries. So ***territorial minister***. Now little used. (Introduced by Dr. Chalmers.)

1822 CHALMERS *Sp. Gen. Assembly* 24 May, Notes 52 The assignation of a territorial district to each chapel. **1863** A. H. CHARTERIS *J. Robertson* viii. 231 A territorial church furnishes the best of all means for leavening the people. **1863** W. G. BLAIKIE *Better Days for Working People* v. (1864) 119 They are the heart-breaks of the city missionary, the territorial minister and the district visitor. **1873** T. COCHRANE *Home Mission Work* vi. (1885) 144 A humble labourer in the territorial field.

3. Of or belonging to one of the 'territories' of the United States or of Canada: see TERRITORY[1] 4.

1802 A. GALLATIN *Let.* 13 Feb. in *Deb. Congr. U.S.* 30 Mar. (1851) 1101 If..it is..the interest of the United States to obtain some further security against an injurious sale, under the Territorial or State laws, of lands sold by them to individuals. **1812** BRACKENRIDGE *Views Louisiana* (1814) 99 The territorial governor [of Missouri] acts as well in the capacity of a general agent for the United States, as in that of civil magistrate. *Ibid.* 142 In 1805, it was erected into a territorial government..by the name of the Territory of Louisiana. **1888** BRYCE *Amer. Commw.* I. I. xiii. 167 There are also eight Territorial delegates, one from each of the Territories..not yet formed into States. **1935** *Chambers's Encycl.* II. 703/1 Yukon has a 'Gold Commissioner' and an elected territorial council. **1953** R. MOON *This is Saskatchewan* 18 That day [*sc.* 18 Dec. 1901] the Territorial Grain Growers' Association was formed.

4. *Mil.* **a.** ***Territorial Regiments***, the regiments of infantry of the line of the British Army, under the scheme of Army reorganization of 1881, by which each regiment is associated in name, depot, etc., with a particular county or locality.

1881 *Queen's Regul.* 1 Precedence of Corps... The Territorial Regiments. **1885** *Whitaker's Alm.* 158 Territorial Regiments of the Line... Arranged alphabetically by the titles directed to be used in official correspondence.

b. ***Territorial Army*** or ***Force***, the British Army of Home Defence orig. instituted (on a territorial or local basis) in 1908. *Territorial* as *sb.*: a member of the Territorial Army; esp. in *pl.* = *Territorial Army*. In other collocations: of or pertaining to the Territorial Army.

The Territorial and Army Volunteer Reserve was a civilian defence force created in 1967 by merging the Territorial Army and the Army Emergency Reserve and was itself renamed the Territorial Army in 1979.

1907 *Outlook* 30 Nov. 706/2 There is no evident reason why any old Volunteer should hesitate about joining the Territorial Army. *Ibid.*, There is nothing to deter the ex-Volunteer from becoming a Territorial. **1908** *Westm. Gaz.* 23 Mar. 7/3 So soon as the Reserves of the Regular Army were called out, the Territorial Force, the second line, should be mobilised to go into war training. **1908** *Daily Chron.* 1 Apr. 7/4 Yesterday the existence of the Volunteers as such terminated, and to-day the Territorial Army comes into being. **1910** KIPLING *Divers. Creatures* (1917) 315 That was when we found the Territorial battalion undressin' in slow time. It lay on the left flank o' the Blue Army. **1914** G. B. SHAW *Misalliance* 65 *Tarleton*: Why not join the Territorials? *The man*: Because I shouldnt be let. **1938** W. S. CHURCHILL *Into Battle* (1941) 31 Why..are the Guards drilling with flags instead of machine-guns? Why is it that our small Territorial Army is in such a rudimentary condition? **1940** GRAVES & HODGE *Long Week-end* xxvi. 441 Hore-Belisha..called in the Attorney-General, asking him to warn Sandys, who was a Territorial officer,..that he had rendered himself liable to a court martial..for being in possession of confidential data. **1940** J. F. KENNEDY *Why England Slept* vii. 158 From this time on, it was also established that the Territorial Army, which corresponded somewhat to our National Guard, had 'a claim on the same sources and standards of instruction as the Regular Army'. **1962** M. & M. HARDWICK *Sherlock Holmes Companion* 231 He [*sc.* Conan Doyle] campaigned incessantly for the better training of Territorial reservists. **1970** *Daily Tel.* 14 Jan. 16 Trying to get a snappy recruiting message home to the public is a testing business for the TAVR Council now that they have been saddled with the ponderous legal name 'Territorial Army Volunteer Reserve'. *a* **1974** R. CROSSMAN *Diaries* (1976) II. 664 The proposal to disband the Territorials would now naturally be discussed with the Territorial Association.

territorialism (tɛrɪˈtɔərɪəlɪz(ə)m). [f. prec. + -ISM.] A territorial system.

1. A system which gives predominance to the landed class; landlordism.

1881 PARNELL in *Philad. Record* No. 3357. 1 Appealing to the great masses of England and Scotland against the territorialism and shopocracy which dominates Parliament. **1882** KAY in *Macm. Mag.* XLVI. 150 The anomalies consequent on the various reigns of feudalism and territorialism. **1884** *Manch. Exam.* 19 June 5/1 The old flag of Tory territorialism or the new ensign of Tory democracy.

2. Rendering German *Territorialsystem*, applied to a theory of church government which places the supreme authority in the civil power. Cf. COLLEGIALISM.

1882–3 *Schaff's Encycl. Relig. Knowl.* III. 1821 [Pfaff] defended the collegial system against the reigning territorialism. **1888** SCHAFF *Hist. Chr. Ch.* VI. I. viii. 25 Territorialism, whose motto is *Cujus regio, ejus religio*.

3. *Sc.* The organization of church work on territorial lines; the extension of the parochial system to smaller areas: see TERRITORIAL 2 c.

1873 T. COCHRANE *Home Mission Work* vi. (1885) 133 The grand practical work of Territorialism. **1904** J. WELLS *J. H. Wilson* vi. 51 Territorialism is the parochial system in its perfection, adjusted to the needs of a great city.

4. The organization of the Army on a territorial or local basis: see TERRITORIAL 4.

1903 *Sat. Rev.* 24 Oct. 503/2 Territorialism may often be good as a recruiting principle, but seldom as a limit to a regiment's definition.

5. *Zool.* = TERRITORIALITY 2.

1933 M. M. NICE in *Fifty Years' Progress Amer. Ornithol.* (Amer. Ornithologists' Union) 89 (*title*) The theory of territorialism and its development. **1969** A. WHEELER *Fishes Brit. Isles & N.-W. Europe* 410 Strong territorialism is shown [in gobies], the males defending a suitable nesting site.

terriˈtorialist. [f. as prec. + -IST.]

1. A member or representative of the class of land-owners: cf. TERRITORIAL 1 c.

1865 *Pall Mall G.* 22 July 10/2 [The candidate] has no land in the county, and very little influence over the territorialists. **1867** B. CRACROFT in Brodrick *Ess. Reform* 164 If we add 246 to 256 we get 502 as the ascertained number of the territorialists in the House of Commons. **1901** *Daily Record & Mail* 21 Dec. 4 A compulsory disposal of the land from territorialists to settlers.

2. A member of a Jewish organization, whose aim was to secure a separate territory for the Jews: cf. quot. 1906 s.v. TERRITORIAL 1. *Hist.*

1905 *Daily Chron.* 31 July 5/3 The territorialists..were bent on forcing [the Zionist] congress to accept the Gnas Ngishu plateau as a counsel of despair. **1909** *Ibid.* 9 Sept. 3/4 The..'Territorialists'..maintain that the true aim of the Jews ought to be to obtain an autonomous settlement anywhere—Uganda, for instance, or even Argentina.

territoriˈality. [f. as prec. + -ITY.]

1. Territorial quality, condition, position, or status.

1894 E. P. EVANS in *Pop. Sc. Monthly* XLIV. 305 The consciousness of what might be called common territoriality tends..to bind together. **1906** *Daily Chron.* 17 Nov. 4/4 Lord Rosebery urged that territoriality was of the essence of good recruiting. **1907** *Sat. Rev.* 10 Aug. 163/2 Times have changed, and ability, common-sense and general knowledge must be added to territoriality.

2. *Zool.* A pattern of behaviour in which an animal or a group of animals defends an area against others of the same species. Cf. TERRITORIALISM.

1941 M. M. NICE in *Amer. Midland Naturalist* XXVI. 441 (*title*) The role of territoriality in bird life. **1943** *Jrnl. Mammalogy* XXIV. 346 The more we study the detailed behavior of animals, the larger is the list of kinds known to display some sort of territoriality. **1955** *Sci. Amer.* Oct. 92/3 No room was left for doubting..the territoriality of the owls. **1979** *Nature* 20–27 Dec. 885/1 Territoriality seems to be rare in bees and wasps, with the exception perhaps of males and their mate search behaviour.

territorialize (tɛrɪˈtɔərɪəlaɪz), *v.* [f. as prec. + -IZE.] *trans.* To make territorial; to place upon a territorial basis; to associate with or restrict to a particular territory or district. Hence **terriˌtorialiˈzation**.

1818 COLERIDGE in *Lit. Rem.* (1836) I. 158 The Pope had recently territorialized his authority to a great extent. **1897** MAITLAND *Domesday & Beyond* 157 It is not probable that the territorializing process will stop here. *Ibid.* 165 In the territorialization of military service. **1899** *Educat. Rev.* Nov. 379 What is called by students of railway questions the 'territorialization' of railways has been wellnigh accomplished. **1901** *Scotsman* 11 Mar. 6/3 His plan.. demanded the territorialisation of the army.

terriˈtorially, *adv.* [f. as prec. + -LY[2].] In relation to or in respect of territory.

1828 in WEBSTER citing E. EVERETT. **1885** J. FISKE in *Harper's Mag.* Feb. 408/2 The formation of the tribe, territorially regarded. **1899** F. V. KIRBY *Sport E.C. Africa* ix. 98 British Chinde was 'territorially' smaller than on my last visit. **1900** G. C. BRODRICK *Mem. & Impr.* 148 This little borough [Woodstock]..belonged politically as well as territorially to the Marlborough family.

Terriˈtorian. [f. L. *territōri-um* TERRITORY[1] + -AN.] An inhabitant of the Northern Territory of Australia.

1887 MRS. D. DALY *Digging*, etc. *S. Austral.* Introd. 4 The magnificent harbour of which all Territorians are so proud [i.e. those of the Northern Territory of S. Australia]. **1941** C. BARRETT *Coast of Adventure* 121 Old Territorians, over..a pannikin of tea by the campfire, will tell yarns as long as you'll listen. **1961** J. DANVERS *Living come First* vii. 121 All the people mixed up in the case are far more Territorians than South Australians. **1971** *Southerly* XXXI. 137 I'm a Territorian, Kenny Buckman's my name, n you gohher be good t'survive out there in the desert, I tell you.

ˈterritoried, *a. rare.* [f. TERRITORY[1] + -ED[2].] Possessing a territory. (Usually in comb.)

a **1654** SELDEN *Eng. Epir.* ii. Wks. 1726 III. 11 Their plurality of narrow-territoried princes.

‖**territorium** (tɛrɪˈtɔərɪəm). *Rom. Hist.* Pl. territoria. [L.] The area of land surrounding and within the boundaries of a Roman city, *municipium*, etc., and under its jurisdiction. Also *transf.* of States having dealings with Rome.

1918 [see CENTURIATE *v.* 2]. **1926** ABBOTT & JOHNSON *Municipal Admin. Roman Empire* ix. 134 The chief revenues of cities in other parts of the empire came from their *territoria*. **1949** *Oxf. Classical Dict.* 623/2 In Roman territory before 89 B.C. the chief *oppida* were those of the ex-Latin incorporated States. In them was centred the local administration of their former *territorium*. **1962** D. HARDEN *Phoenicians* v. 74 Carthage's fleet was burnt, her domain was henceforth to be confined to her *territorium* in eastern Tunisia.

territory[1] (ˈtɛrɪtərɪ). Also 5 teri-, tery-. [ad. L. *territōri-um* the land round a town, a domain, district, territory. Etymology unsettled: usually taken as a deriv. of *terra* earth, land (to which it was certainly referred in popular L. when altered to *terrātōrium*); but the original form has suggested derivation from *terrēre* to frighten, whence **territor* frightener, *territōrium* '? a place from which people are warned off' (Roby *Lat. Gr.* §943). So F. *territoire* (1278 in Godef. *Compl.*): see also TERROIR.]

1. † **a.** The land or district lying round a city or town and under its jurisdiction. Chiefly as a rendering of L. *territōrium*. *Obs.*

1432–50 tr. *Higden* (Rolls) V. 321 Boecius..was throtelede in the territory Mediolanense. *c* **1460** *Oseney Reg.* 99, ij. acres of Arable londe In þe territorye of grownde of Cudelynton. **1483** *Rolls of Parlt.* VI. 256/2 Persons havyng Lands and Tenements in the seid Netheracastre, and within the territory of the same. **1538** ELYOT, *Territorium*, the fyeldes or countraye lyenge within the iurisdiction and boundes of a citie, a territorie. **1598** MANWOOD *Lawes Forest* i. §3 (1615) 19 This word [*Territorie*] is most properly a circuit of ground, contayning a libertie within it selfe, wherein diuers men hauing land within it, and yet the Territorie it selfe doth lie open and not inclosed. **1651** HOBBES *Leviath.* II. xxii. 118 As they governed the City of Rome, and Territories adjacent.

b. The land or country belonging to or under the dominion of a ruler or state. Often applied contextually to the land or country itself of a state, as ***French territory*** (= France, the land of France).

1494 FABYAN *Chron.* VII. 304 A cytie or towne, called Menne or Meune, within the londe or territorye of y[e] emperour. **1548** UDALL, etc. *Erasm. Par. Acts* xxviii. 86 We came to Rhegium, a citie in ye borders of Italy situate and lyinge within the territory that belongeth to the Brutians. **1591** SHAKS. *1 Hen. VI*, v. iii. 146 Welcome braue Earle into our Territories. *a* **1687** PETTY *Pol. Arith.* x. (1691) 114 Not being above a sixth or seventh of the whole Territory of England. **1765** BLACKSTONE *Comm.* I. Introd. iv. 93 The kingdom of England, over which our municipal laws have jurisdiction, includes not, by the common law, either Wales, Scotland, or Ireland, or any other part..except the territory of England only. **1789** *Constitution U.S.* IV. §3 Rules and regulations respecting the territory or other property of the United States. **1799** HT. LEE *Canterb. T.*, *Old Wom. T.* (ed. 2) I. 359 A small port, still within the Neapolitan territories. **1835** THIRLWALL *Greece* I. i. 3 The original Hellas was included in the territory of a little tribe in the south of Thessaly. **1908** *Athenæum* 12 Dec. 754/1 The rearrangement of frontiers and territories by Napoleon.

c. *Sc. Law.* (See quots.)

1765–8 ERSKINE *Inst. Law Scot.* I. ii. §16. 27 Since no judge can pronounce sentence on persons or subjects without his territory, civil jurisdiction cannot be founded, unless the defender either, first, reside within the judge's territory, or, 2dly, be possessed of some estate or subject within it. **1838** W. BELL *Dict. Law Scot.*, *Territory of a Judge* is the district over which his jurisdiction extends in causes and in judicial acts proper to him, and beyond which he has no judicial authority.

d. *transf.* Each half of a football ground considered as belonging to one of the teams: so in hockey, baseball, etc.

1896 *Field* 4 Jan. 22/2 A moment later, the visitors.. invaded the home territory. Here Jones got smartly away.. and..scored a..try.

e. *Zool.* An area chosen by an animal or a group of animals and defended against others of the same species.

1774 O. GOLDSMITH *Hist. Earth* V. 301 All these small birds mark out a territory to themselves, which they will permit none of their own species to remain in. **1914** J. S. HUXLEY in *Proc. Zool. Soc.* 521 There may be hostility between members of one pair and members of another... The only reason I can discover for it is the trespassing of one or both birds of a strange pair upon the 'territory' of another. **1920** E. HOWARD *Territory in Bird Life* i. 3 Securing a territory is then part of a process which has for its goal the successful rearing of offspring. **1933** *Brit. Birds* XXVII. 20 A certain area of land or territory..extends around the nesting site. **1949** W. C. ALLEE et al. *Princ. Animal Ecol.* xxiii. 412/2 Territories tend to be larger when population pressure is low. **1953** N. TINBERGEN *Herring Gull's World* ix. 82 A Herring Gull returns to the same colony, and often even to the same territory. **1981** *Oxf. Compan. Animal Behaviour* 550/2 Territories range in size from the few millimetres that separate barnacles..on a rock to the distances of several kilometres that separate neighbouring herds of African buffalo.

f. The geographical area within which a firm or salesman operates. orig. *U.S.*

1900 *Cent. Mag.* Feb. 644/1 We've got to begin small. Our territory is Ohio. **1907** F. H. BURNETT *Shuttle* xxxviii. 379 Nick Baumgarten, who having for some time 'beaten' certain streets as assistant salesman.., had recently been elevated to a 'territory' of his own. **1925** *Daily Tel.* 13 May 20/7 Traveller Wanted... Live men can earn £10 a week. Territory given. **1931** *Economist* 26 Dec. 1235/2 A convenient pocket tabulation of the financial results of oil companies, which shows also the area of their territory, the number of wells. **1977** *Evening Gaz.* (Middlesbrough) 11 Jan. 9/1 (Advt.), A career in sales... Local territories available.

2. A tract of land, or district of undefined boundaries; a region.

1610 HOLLAND *Camden's Brit.* (1637) 112 The most fertile territories of Anjou. **1834** L. RITCHIE *Wand. by Seine* 5 It was necessary to wrest a territory from the sea itself for [Havre's] foundation. **1870** YEATS *Nat. Hist. Comm.* 89 The central territory is covered with forests. **1890** 'R. BOLDREWOOD' *Col. Reformer* xvii. 201 Fascinating territories of limitless mulga-downs.

3. *fig.* **a.** The domain, space, or region of fact, action, meaning, etc. belonging to or included in a science, art, class, word, etc.; sphere, province. Also in various vague figurative contexts.

1640 BP. REYNOLDS *Passions* xxxviii. 485 [Going] beyond their owne bounds, into the Territories (as I may so speake) of another Science. **1852** H. ROGERS *Ecl. Faith* (1864) 271 The whole field of historic investigation seems more or less the territory of scepticism. **1867** J. MARTINEAU *Ess.* II. 2 Psychology..has been allowed its title, but not its territory. **1875** WHITNEY *Life Lang.* vii. 110 It is the customary office of a word to cover, not a point, but a territory, and a territory that is irregular, heterogeneous, and variable. **1927** *Daily Express* 30 Nov. 3/1, I think it is a fine plan to refuse, if possible, to be affected by an opponent's play... But I am sure I took in entirely too much territory when I said that his work should be ignored. **1971** N. Chomsky *Probl. Knowledge & Freedom* (1972) i. 34 To illustrate further, I would like to turn to some still unexplored territory. **1977** J. I. M. Stewart *Madonna of Astrolabe* v. 93 She was frowning now, aware of having got on territory she hadn't designed to tread.

b. *Anat.* A tract or region of the body pertaining to a particular organ or structure.

1897 *Allbutt's Syst. Med.* IV. 125 The supply of blood to the corresponding hepatic territory is cut off. **1899** *Ibid.* VI. 716 The symptoms may be confined to the territory of a plexus. *Ibid.* VIII. 493 A vaso-motor..disturbance, confined to the territory of the vessels concerned.

4. A region administered by a federal or external government, esp. formerly in the United States, one of certain regions in the West belonging to and under the government of the American Republic, and having some degree of self-government, but not yet admitted as a State into the Union. Also, a part of Canada (now only North-west Territories and Yukon Territory) or Australia (Northern Territory) not organized as a province or state.

1799 J. Adams *Wks.* (1854) IX. 41 The organization of the government of the Mississippi territory..should perhaps be mentioned to Congress. **1806** Pike *Sources Mississ.* (1810) 90 A certificate that he had paid the tax required by a law of the Indian territory, on all retailers of merchandize. **1862** J. E. Cairnes *Rev. Amer.* 22 A 'territory'..is a portion of the domain of the Union which is not yet a 'state'. **1888** Schaff *Hist. Chr. Ch.* VI. I. xi. 84 The law of the United States is supreme in the Territories. **1897** C. R. Tuttle *Golden North* 119 Two new provisional districts or territories have been erected in the far northwest by the Canadian government. The first is that called Mackenzie, lying to the north of Athabasca... The second is called Yukon. **1935** *Chambers's Encycl.* II. 699/1 In 1871, after confederation, the population of Canada (including seven provinces and the territories) was 3,689,257. **1936** I. L. Idriess *Cattle King* xii. 106 It dribbles south close to the Territory border all in the sand-hill country, until here it crosses the South Australian border. **1957** *Encycl. Brit.* XVII. 12/1 The Territory of Papua in the south-east [of New Guinea], formerly a British protectorate, is administered by Australia under a governor. *Ibid.*, It [*sc.* Norfolk Island] is a dependency of the Commonwealth of Australia, known officially as the Territory of Norfolk Island. **1969** *Northern Territory News* (Darwin) 11 July 3/2 It also has mining interests in the Territory and Queensland. **1979** G. Woodcock *Canadians* II. x. 222 Even in Yellowknife, the capital of the [Northwest] Territories, I encountered an astonishing collection of people.

5. *attrib.* and *Comb.*

1898 *Westm. Gaz.* 28 Oct. 7/2 There can be no compromise..about the territory rights. **1901** *Ibid.* 21 Mar. 7/2 The Powers have been territory-hunting. **1929** E. M. Nicholson *How Birds Live* iii. 31 The solitary territory-holder can only deal with single intruders. **1953** N. Tinbergen *Herring Gull's World* vi. 55 A territory-holder stretches its neck as soon as a stranger alights in its neighbourhood. *Ibid.* 58 This [fight] happens..when a territory-holding bird makes a surprise attack. **1962** *Science Survey* XV. 238 A 'territory-holding' male robin will attack a bundle of red feathers.

† **territory**[2], **territoire.** *Obs.* Erroneously used by Caxton to render F. *tertre*, a rising ground, hill, or eminence.

c **1477** Caxton *Jason* 70 b, We shal enhabite with peple the lowe montaignes & the territoires. **1481** —— *Godeffroy* xxi. 53 They..began to reassemble, and gadred them to gydre on a territorie. *Ibid.* clviii. 233 Archys is a Cyte of the lande of Fenyce, and standeth atte foote of a montayne named Lybane, in a tereitorye moche stronge.

territour: see territoire.

terr-oceanic (ˌtɛrəʊʃiːˈænɪk), *a. rare*⁻¹. [f. L. *terra* earth + oceanic.] Of or belonging to both land and ocean: ***terr-oceanic basin***, a basin or hollow consisting of a sea-basin with the surrounding land within its watershed.

c **1860** R. Mallet in *Q. Rev.* Apr. (1909) 495 The lines of elevation which mark and divide the great oceanic or terr-oceanic basins..of the earth's surface.

terro-ceˈment. [f. *terro-*, taken as combining form of L. *terra* earth.] Cement of earthy nature.

1838 *Civil Eng. & Arch. Jrnl.* I. 373/2 Every one is aware that mortars and terro-cement, like other earthy matters, are non-conductors of heat.

† **terroir.** *Obs. rare.* [a. F. *terroir*, OF. *terëoir* (12th c. in Godef. *Compl.*), *terrouer* (13th c.):—med.L. *terrātōrium* (Du Cange: in Pr. *terrador*) = L. *territōrium* territory[1], q.v.]

a. = territory[1]. **b.** Soil.

1483 Caxton *Gold. Leg.* 18/2 For to berye it in the terroir of the cyte of Losane. **1660** *Charac. Italy* 83 Italy is the Garden of Europe, the *Terroir* being gentle and copious.

terror (ˈtɛrə(r)), *sb.* Also 4–6 -oure, 6–9 -our. [ME. *terrour*, a. F. *terreur* (14th c.):—L. *terrōrem*, nom. *terror*, f. *terrēre* to frighten: see -or I.]

1. The state of being terrified or greatly frightened; intense fear, fright, or dread. Also, with *a* and *pl.*, an instance of this.

c **1375** *Sc. Leg. Saints* xxxiii. (*George*) 701 He..but rednes ore terroure Of goddis son wes confessoure. **1500–20** Dunbar *Ballat of Passion* 137 For grit terrour of Chrystis deid, The erde did trymmil quhar I lay. **1560** Bible (Genev.) *Ps.* lv. 4 The terrors [**1611** feare] of death are fallen vpon me. **1605** Shaks. *Lear* IV. ii. 12 It is the Cowish terror of his spirit That dares not vndertake. **1615** G. Sandys *Trav.* 20 By little and little [they] descended as their terrors forsooke them. **1657** Thornley tr. *Longus' Daphnis & Chloe* 46 Pan sends a Terrour upon the Methymnæans. **1711** Addison *Spect.* No. 7 ⁋3 This Remark struck a pannick Terror into several who were present. *a* **1763** Shenstone *Ess.* xiii. Wks. 1765 II. 51 The gloom of night.. was productive of terrour. **1794** Godwin *Cal. Williams* 236 The terrors with which I was seized..were extreme. **1837** Whewell *Hist. Induct. Sc.* (1857) I. 227 Showed hesitation, alarm, increasing terrour. **1871** R. Ellis *Catullus* lxiv. 338 You shall a son see born that knows not terror, Achilles.

2. *transf.* **a.** The action or quality of causing dread; terrific quality, terribleness; *spec.* this action or quality in fiction, esp. in ***novel*** (or ***tale***) ***of terror***; also *concr.* a thing or person that excites terror; something terrifying.

1528 Roy *Rede me* (Arb.) 41 Threatnynge with fearfull terroure. **1560** Daus tr. *Sleidane's Comm.* 209 He vseth hys name sometime, only for a clooke and a terrour. **1667** Milton *P.L.* II. 704 So spake the grieslie terrour. **1712** Addison *Spect.* No. 333 ⁋22 The Messiah appears cloathed with so much Terrour and Majesty. **1788** Gibbon *Decl. & F.* l. (1846) V. 16 The ferocious Bedoweens, the terror of the desert. **1814** Scott *Ld. of Isles* VI. xvi, Clearing war's terrors from his eye. *a* **1832** G. Crabbe *Posthumous Tales* xv, in *Poet. Wks.* (1834) VIII. 205 Yet tales of terror are her dear delight, All in the wintry storm to read at night. **1841** Emerson *Ess., Prudence* Wks. (Bohn) I. 100 The terrors of the storm. **1864** Burton *Scot Abr.* I. ii. 61 He became..the terror of all the well-disposed within the district. **1917** D. Scarborough *Supernatural in Mod. Eng. Fiction* i. 6 And so the Gothic novel came into being. *Gothic* is here used to designate the eighteenth-century novel of terror dealing with mediaeval materials. **1921** E. Birkhead (*title*) The tale of terror: a study of the Gothic romance. **1977** M. Ashley *Who's who in Horror & Fantasy Fiction* 103 His masterpiece of terror was *The Castle of Ehrenstein* (1854), a superb portrayal of a ghost-ridden castle.

b. *Trivially.* A person (occas., a thing) fancied to excite terror; esp. a troublesome child; ***holy terror***: see holy *a.* 4 c.

1883, etc. [see holy *a.* 4 c]. **1889** *Harper's Mag.* May 933/1 That bright boy..who was a terror six months ago. **1892** Lady R. Churchill *Let.* 10 Jan. in R. S. Churchill *Winston S. Churchill* (1967) I. Compan. I. v. 305 Papa is very well & in good spirits but his beard is a 'terror'. **1900** G. Swift *Somerley* 14 There we kept up the reputation of 'little terrors' that we had earned with Miss Graten. **1908** G. Sanger *70 Yrs. a Showman* xvii. 58 Brumley..was a bit of a terror in his way, being a drunken bully. **1925** S. Lewis *Martin Arrowsmith* vi. 63 She's an old terror. If she found a child like you wandering around here she'd drag you out by the ear. **1953** K. Tennant *Joyful Condemned* xxxii. 311 It wasn't your fault. René was always a terror. You did what you could. **1979** A. McCowen *Young Gemini* 25 At school I was known as a terror and went looking for fights.

3. ***king of terrors***, Death personified.

1611 Bible *Job* xviii. 14 His confidence..shall bring him to the king of terrours [1560 King of feare; Coverd. very fearfulnesse shall brynge him to the kynge]. **1682** Flavell *Fear* 9 Job calls it the king of terrors..or the most terrible of terribles. **1794** Godwin *Cal. Williams* xxiv, It surely is not worse to encounter the king of terrors in health,..than to encounter him already half subdued by sickness and suffering. **1827–47** Hare *Guesses* (1874) 88 It is the only voice which can triumph over Death, and turn the King of terrours into an angel of light.

4. ***reign of terror***, a state of things in which the general community live in dread of death or outrage; esp. (with capital initials) *French Hist.* the period of the First Revolution from about March 1793 to July 1794, called also ***the Terror***, ***the Red Terror***, when the ruling faction remorselessly shed the blood of persons of both sexes and of all ages and conditions whom they regarded as obnoxious. Hence, without article or pl., the use of organized intimidation, terrorism.

Hence also ***White Terror***, applied to the counter-revolution that followed the *Red Terror*, and to other periods of remorseless repression in various countries; *the terror* is also used simply for a similar period of repression. See also *Red* and *White Terror* at the first element.

1801 Hel. M. Williams *Sk. Fr. Rep.* I. xviii. 231 This superb monument had suffered most from the reign of terror. **1831** *Wexford Herald* 11 June 2/3 The reign of terror —of Terryaltism. **1848** Geo. Eliot *Let.* 8 Mar. (1954) I. 255 The Glasgow riots are more serious, but one cannot believe in a Scotch Reign of Terror in these days. *c* **1870** *Miniature* xi. in *The Sibyl* 1 Apr. (1893), When the Terror, with hungry throat Ravished the homes of the wide Touraine. **1877** Morley *Crit. Misc.* Ser. II. 132 A White Terror succeeded the Red Terror. **1883** *Fortn. Rev.* 1 Nov. 701 The red terror of the French Jacobins is insignificant by the side of the white terror of Ferdinand VII. **1891** Ld. Rosebery *Pitt* xi. 186 On the one side there were murders, roastings, plunder of arms, and a reign of terror [in Ireland in 1797]. **1893** *Tablet* 9 Dec. 934 A little Terror reigned over the provincial commune. **1920** *Glasgow Herald* 7 May 9 It was admitted that outrages were committed against the Socialists [in Hungary], but it was denied that a 'terror' existed. **1937** Koestler *Spanish Testament* vi. 132 They had neither the inclination nor the need to terrorise the population, to make warning examples, to safeguard the territory behind the lines by the application of methods of Terror. **1951** H. Arendt *Burden of Our Time* I. i. 6 Terror as we know it today strikes without any preliminary provocation. **1966** G. Greene *Comedians* iii. 100 The Trianon soufflé au Grand Marnier was famous for a time, until the terror started [in Haiti] and the American Mission left. **1970** G. Jackson *Let.* 4 Apr. in *Soledad Brother* (1971) 212 All times of the day or night our cells were being invaded by the goon squad: you wake up, take your licks, get skin-searched... This treatment, fear therapy, was not accorded to all however... Mostly it came down on us. Rehabilitational terror. **1977** P. Johnson *Enemies of Society* xviii. 241 Thanks to their use of terror, they [*sc.* the Assassins] often controlled local authorities, and forced governments into compliance or impotence. **1978** *Encounter* July 15/1 Anyone who cannot see and appreciate the true difference between Russia today and Russia at the height of the Stalinist terror has a very poor idea of one or other of these phenomena.

5. *Comb.* **a.** attributive, as ***terror-drop***, ***-fit***, ***-gleam***, ***-novel***, ***-romance***; (in sense 4) ***terror act***, ***group***, ***organization***, ***régime***, ***tactics***. **b.** objective (with pr. pples.), as ***terror-breathing***, ***-causing***, ***-giving***, ***-inspiring***, ***-preaching***, ***-stirring***, ***-striking***, etc., adjs.; **c.** instrumental (with pa. pples.), as ***terror-crazed***, ***-fraught***, ***-haunted***, ***-mingled***, ***-ridden***, ***-riven***, ***-shaken***, ***-smitten***, ***-stiffened***, ***-stricken***, ***-struck***, etc., adjs.; so ***terror-strike*** vb. **d.** Special Combs. **terror-bombing**, intensive and indiscriminate bombing designed to frighten a country into surrender; **terror raid**, a bombing raid of this nature.

1946 Koestler *Thieves in Night* 243 While the usual *terror acts continued, the Jewish representative bodies issued their usual protests. **1941** *Reader's Digest* June 58/2 It must be remembered that this government today is Hitler, Göring, Goebbels, Himmler and a few others—men who.. ordered the *terror bombing of Rotterdam last summer and of London last winter. **1945** *Time* 26 Feb. 32/1 Terror bombing of German cities was deliberate military policy. **1959** R. Collier *City that wouldn't Die* ii. 27 To Sperrle the primary consideration was always that the pilot should see his target;..a Nuremberg tribunal absolved him of terror bombing. **1598** Drayton *Heroic Ep., Mortimer to Q. Isabel* 114 Curses..Through the sterne throte of *terror-breathing warre. **1922** Joyce *Ulysses* 384 The *terrorcausing shrieking of shrill women in their labour. **1873** W. Carleton *Burning of Chicago* viii, The panic-struck, *terror-crazed city. **1897** P. Warung *Tales Old Regime* 184 [Convicts] who sweated *terror-drops beneath their stamped blankets. **1868** Ld. Houghton *Select. fr. Wks.* 199 At doubt and *terror-fit he only laughed. **1868** Farrar *Seekers* I. vii. (1875) 98 All this *terror-fraught interspace between heaven and earth. *a* **1743** Savage *Public Spirit* 127 Instant we catch her *terror-giving cares. **1977** P. Johnson *Enemies of Society* xviii. 242 The diabolism of Stavrogin, who preaches the doctrine that the *terror-group can only be united by fear and moral depravity. **1844** Longfellow *Norman Baron* vii, The lays they chanted Reached the chamber *terror-haunted. **1839** Poe *William Wilson* in *Gift* 235 In a remote and *terror-inspiring angle was a square enclosure. **1854** Grace Greenwood *Haps & Mishaps* 91 Enrolment in this honourable terror-inspiring, omnipresent corps. **1799** Campbell *Pleas. Hope* II. 255 Nature hears, with *terror-mingled trust, The shock that hurls her fabric in the dust. **1917** D. Scarborough *Supernatural in Mod. Eng. Fiction* i. 6 The *terror novel proper is generally conceded to begin with his [*sc.* Horace Walpole's] Romantic curiosity, *The Castle of Otranto.* **1972** P. Haining *Gt. Brit. Tales of Terror* I. 117 William Beckford, author of the great Oriental terror-novel, *Vathek.* **1977** *Belfast Tel.* 22 Feb. 5/7 Growing police and Army success against the *terror organisations. **1630** Drayton *Noah* 225 This good man, this *terror-preaching Noy. **1945** *Ann. Reg. 1944* 3 Lord Cranborne..pointed out that the Royal Air Force had never indulged in purely *terror raids like those perpetrated by the Luftwaffe. **1977** J. Wainwright *Pool of Tears* 208 Dresden..That was a terror raid... A town turned into a blow-torch. **1952** Koestler *Arrow in Blue* viii. 68 Admiral Horthy established the first semi-Fascist *terror régime in post-war Europe. **1931** R. L. Mégroz *Conrad's Mind & Method* x. 237 The 'Gothic' *terror-romance of the eighteenth century. **1972** P. Haining *Gt. Brit. Tales of Terror* I. 477 From the later work comes the following grim story which contains much of that chilling atmosphere which made the Gothic terror-romance so widely popular in its time. **1887** Kipling *Departmental Ditties* (1888) 21 Felt the brute's proboscis fingering my *terror-stiffened hair. *c* **1611** Chapman *Iliad* XXII. 320 Then all the Greekes..admir'd his *terror-stirring lim. **1831** Poe *Poems* (ed. 2) 75 There the..clouds do fly..Through the *terror-stricken sky. **1845** Hirst *Com. Mammoth* 16 Our terror-stricken warriors quailed. **1871** Macduff *Mem. Patmos* iii. 35 He cowers like a terror-stricken child. **1611** Barksted *Hiren* (1876) 74 So her beames did *terror-strike his sight. **1598** Drayton *Heroic Ep., Owen Tudor to Q. Kath.* 23 His dreadfull *terror-striking name. **1799** Ht. Lee *Canterb. T., Frenchm. T.* (ed. 2) I. 270 She found herself alone,..*terror-struck, bewildered. **1974** *Encycl. Brit. Micropædia* V. 427/2 A 'provisional' wing [of the IRA].. comprising the younger, militant majority committed to the use of *terror tactics. **1824** Lamb *Elia* Ser. II. *Blakesmoor in H—shire*, A sneaking curiosity, *terror-tainted.

Hence **ˈterrorful**, **ˈterrorsome** *adjs.*, full of or fraught with terror, terrifying.

1870 *Contemp. Rev.* XIV. 491 The points..show themselves..with that dark jaggedness and terrorful meaning which [etc.]. **1890** *Leeds Merc.* 3 Feb. 5/1 A writer ..makes it terrorsome by the following anecdote.

ˈterror, *v. Obs.* or *arch.* [f. prec. sb.] *trans.* To strike with terror, to terrify. Also *absol.*

1635 Heywood *Hierarch.* VIII. 515 They, terror'd with these words, demand his name. **1655** Fuller *Ch. Hist.* IV. ii. Ded., A Law..as all other penal Statutes intended but to terrour. **1878** P. W. Wyatt *Hardrada* 3 The terror'd heart of Tostig.

terrorism (ˈtɛrərɪz(ə)m). [a. F. *terrorisme* (1798 in *Dict. Acad., Suppl.*), f. L. *terror* dread, terror: see -ism.] A system of terror.

1. Government by intimidation as directed and carried out by the party in power in France during the Revolution of 1789–94; the system of the 'Terror' (1793–4): see terror *sb.* 4.

1795 *Hist.* in *Ann. Reg.* 112/2 It would..renew the reign of terrorism. **1817** Lady Morgan *France* VIII. (1818) II. 357 He was obliged to remain abroad during the whole reign of terrorism. **1861** GOLDW. SMITH *Irish Hist.* 85 Like..the terrorism of the Jacobins..it was a moral epidemic.

2. *gen.* A policy intended to strike with terror those against whom it is adopted; the employment of methods of intimidation; the fact of terrorizing or condition of being terrorized. Also *transf.* Cf. TERRORIST 1 b.

1798 MATHIAS *Purs. Lit.* (ed. 7) 132 The causes of rebellion, insurrection,..terrorism, massacres, and revolutionary murders. **1847** GROTE *Greece* II. xxx. IV. 155 He could not but be sensible that this system of terrorism was full of peril to himself. **1863** FAWCETT *Pol. Econ.* II. ix. (1876) 248 If anyone should disobey the decision of the meeting, he would subject himself..to a social terrorism. **1936** W. H. S. SMITH *Let.* 27 July in *Young Man's Country* (1977) ii. 19 The Constitutional League [of India], whose main purpose is to rouse public opinion against terrorism. **1957** L. DURRELL *Bitter Lemons* 243 Though his complicity in EOKA was obvious, nevertheless he [*sc.* Makarios] was the only brake to terrorism and the only person who could curb it. **1958** B. BEHAN *Borstal Boy* III. 271 He said it was the fault of the British boss class that the Irish were forced always into terrorism to get their demands. **1963** *Ann. Reg. 1962* 236 The first half of the year was dominated by the difficulties of obtaining an Algerian settlement and, in particular, by the challenge to the authority of State presented by O.A.S. terrorism. **1973** *Cape Times* 27 Oct. 12 The Minister cannot expect journalists to do violence to the English language..by describing guerilla warfare as terrorism at all times and in all circumstances. **1977** *New Yorker* 24 Oct. 35/1 Last week's manifestations of political terrorism were crowded off the front pages..by more upbeat occurrences.

terrorist ('tɛrərɪst). [a. F. *terroriste*, f. L. *terror* TERROR: see -IST.]

1. As a political term: **a.** Applied to the Jacobins and their agents and partisans in the French Revolution, esp. to those connected with the Revolutionary tribunals during the 'Reign of Terror'.

1795 *Hist.* in *Ann. Reg.* 169 The terrorists, as they were justly denominated, from the cruel and impolitic maxim of keeping the people in implicit subjection by a merciless severity. **1795** BURKE *Regic. Peace* iv. Wks. IX. 75 Thousands of those Hell-hounds called Terrorists..are let loose on the people. **1818** HERVE *Beauties of Paris* II. 296 (Jod.) He assisted La Fayette in endeavouring to defend the king from the terrorists. **1877** MORLEY *Crit. Misc.* Ser. II. 83 That pithy chapter in Machiavelli's 'Prince' which treats of cruelty and clemency..anticipates the defence of the Terrorists.

b. Any one who attempts to further his views by a system of coercive intimidation.

In early use also applied *spec.* to members of one of the extreme revolutionary societies in Russia. The term now usually refers to a member of a clandestine or expatriate organization aiming to coerce an established government by acts of violence against it or its subjects.

1866 FITZPATRICK *Sham Sqr.* 180 Miss G——, the daughter of a Wexford terrorist, directed many of the tortures which were so extensively practised. **1883** *Harper's Mag.* Jan. 315/2 To [Russian] Terrorists it guarantees..security on condition of a .pledge to abandon.. the revolutionary party. **1905** *Westm. Gaz.* 20 Sept. 2/1 Several notables are believed to be more or less implicated in the actions of the Terrorists. **1947** *Ann. Reg. 1946* 60 The latest and worst of the outrages committed by the Jewish terrorists in Palestine—the blowing up of the King David Hotel in Jerusalem. **1956** H. NICOLSON *Diary* 29 Oct. (1968) 311 When people rise against foreign oppression, they are hailed as patriots and heroes; but the Greeks whom we are shooting and hanging in Cyprus are dismissed as terrorists. What cant! **1969** E. J. HOBSBAWM *Bandits* viii. 101 The war between police and terrorists is one of nerves as well as of guns. Whoever is more frightened has lost the initiative. **1977** P. JOHNSON *Enemies of Society* xviii. 240 The Baader-Meinhof gang of ultra-Left terrorists. **1979** *Spectator* 20 Oct. 20/1 (Advt.), In this enthralling autobiography the author of *Maquis*..retravels the course of his life from his childhood to his war-time exploits as a terrorist in the Resistance.

2. Dyslogistically: One who entertains, professes, or tries to awaken or spread a feeling of terror or alarm; an alarmist, a scaremonger.

1803 SYD. SMITH *Wks.* (1859) I. 26/1 The terrorists of this country are so extremely alarmed at the power of Bonaparte. **1805** W. TAYLOR in *Monthly Mag.* XIX. 570 Some book of the religious terrorists, which tended to infuse the alarm of foul perdition. **1861** GEN. P. THOMPSON *Audi Alt. Part.* III. clxxv. 209 What becomes of the pretended terrorists at home who affect to be alarmed for the condition of every white female in the Antilles?

3. *attrib.*

1801 HEL. M. WILLIAMS *Fr. Rep.* I. xi. 113 The defeat of the terrorist-party. *Ibid.* xvi. 194 Under the terrorist government of France. **1856** GOLDW. SMITH in *Oxford Ess.* 295 An advanced and slightly terrorist school of philanthropists. **1884** in *Pall Mall G.* 11 Sept. 7/2 In the struggle we are engaged in with the terrorist and autocratic Governments of Europe, and especially with that of Russia. **1937** KOESTLER *Spanish Testament* vi. 132 The civilian population..whose sympathies they could but alienate by terrorist acts. **1955** *Britannia Bk. of Year* 263/2, 756 Africans executed..incl. 219 for Mau Mau murders and 508 for other terrorist crimes. **1979** R. PERRY *Bishop's Pawn* viii. 130 We weren't dealing with ordinary kidnappers. We were faced by a relatively sophisticated terrorist organization. **1983** *Listener* 19 May 8/1 Terrorist theory..says that the brigades should be subdivided into tight terrorist cells.

Hence **terro'ristic, -'ristical** *adjs.*, characterized by or practising terrorism; also **terro'ristically.**

1850 *Bentley's Miscell.* XXVIII. 407 This was the Government styled 'terroristical' by the Austrians! **1875** POSTE *Gaius* I. Comm. (ed. 2) 81 This terroristic law..was not abrogated till the time of Justinian. **1884** STEPNIAK in *Contemp. Rev.* Mar. 327 The gradual progress of the terroristic tendency under the influence of Government repression. **1887** *Century Mag.* Nov. 54 The leaders of the 'terroristic' or extreme revolutionary party. **1919** M. BEER *Hist. Brit. Socialism* I. II. ii. 103 The terroristic acts and wars into which that social earthquake had degenerated. **1945** R. HARGREAVES *Enemy at Gate* 308 The terroristic procedure associated in these days with Nazism, Fascism and Bolshevism. **1951** MCWHINEY & SIMKINS in A. Dundes *Mother Wit* (1973) 590/2 The klansmen used the methods of violence as extensively as any of the other white terroristic organizations. **1972** *Econ. & Polit. Weekly* 1 Apr. 692/1 Consisting almost exclusively of guerilla squads, they [*sc.* the Naxals] moved secretively and acted terroristically. **1977** *Time* 26 Sept. 9/1 The background of terroristic acts is connected with a deep hatred of bourgeois society.

terrorize ('tɛrəraɪz), *v.* [f. TERROR + -IZE.]

1. *trans.* To fill or inspire with terror, reduce to a state of terror; *esp.* to coerce or deter by terror.

1823 *Douglas, or, Field of Otterburn* II. iii. 33 This was, alas! no crafty scheme to terrorize my mind. **1874** H. R. REYNOLDS *John Bapt.* IV. v. 260 He bade them [soldiers] to terrorize no one. **1885** CLODD *Myths & Dr.* I. ii. 18 Superstitions which yet more or less..terrorise the ignorant.

2. *intr.* To rule, or maintain power, by terrorism; to practise intimidation. (After *tyrannize.*)

1856 LEVER *Martins of Cro' M.* xxxvii, It is one of Kate's fancies to terrorise thus over weak minds. **1870** *Daily News* 9 Sept. 6 Count Bismarck..openly..terrorized over the Prussian Chamber by relying upon the support of the army.

Hence **'terrorized** *ppl. a.*; **'terrorizing** *vbl. sb.* and *ppl. a.*; also **terrori'zation**, the action of terrorizing; **'terrorizer**, one who terrorizes.

1889 *Columbus* (Ohio) *Dispatch* 26 Jan., The White Caps ..began their cowardly and brutal work of *terrorization in the great state of Ohio. **1903** *Contemp. Rev.* Oct. 586 The Powers can do much by terrorisation. **1865** *Sat. Rev.* 22 Apr. 470/2 The whimpering and *terrorized suppliants against High Church domination. **1892** *Ibid.* 19 Mar. 330/1 Night gangs of masked *terrorizers. **1880** MCCARTHY *Own Times* IV. liv. 153 It began to be common talk that among the trades-associations there was systematic *terrorising of the worst kind. **1865** *Sat. Rev.* 12 Aug. 194/2 A *terrorizing collection of ghastly models and pseudo-medical specimens.

terrorless ('tɛrəlɪs), *a.* [f. TERROR + -LESS.] Devoid of terror; exciting no dread.

1813 SHELLEY *Q. Mab* VI. 61 How terrorless the triumph of the grave! **1886** RUSKIN *Præterita* I. viii. 248 Like a cloudless and terrorless Arctic sea.

[**terrosity:** see TERRESITY.]

terrour, obs. form of TERRIER, TERROR.

†**'terrulent**, *a. Obs. rare*⁻⁰. [ad. L. *terrulentus*, f. *terra* earth: see -ULENT.] (See quots.) Hence †**'terrulentness.** So †**'terrulency** *Obs. rare*⁻⁰.

1656 BLOUNT *Glossogr.*, *Terrulent*..earthy or earthly, made of earth. **1721** BAILEY, *Terrulency*, an Earthiness, a fulness of Earth. *Ibid.*, *Terrulent*, full of Earth. **1727** —— vol. II, *Terrulentness*, Earthiness, earthy Nature or Quality.

terry ('tɛrɪ), *sb.*¹, *a.* [Origin uncertain: it is not clear whether the word was orig. sb. or adj.

If adj., it may have been a corruption of F. *tiré* drawn; cf. Ger. *gezogener Sammet* 'drawn velvet'.]

A. *sb.* **1.** The loop raised in pile-weaving (PILE *sb.*⁵ 3) left uncut; also short for *terry fabric*, *terry-velvet*, etc., see B. In later use = *terry cloth*, *terry towelling* (see B below).

1784 J. BENNETT *Patent Specif.* No. 1437 The Prince's everlasting union pearl or terry. *Ibid.*, The silk and mohair, pearl or terry, or wove, to float as a sattin. **1853** URE *Dict. Arts* I. 380 (Carpet weaving) Inserting a tag or wire to form the rib or terry. **1861** *Abridgm. Spec. Patents, Weaving* Index 1093, Terries raised on weft. **1879** WEBSTER *Suppl.*, *Terry*, 1. A kind of heavy silk and worsted material used in upholstery. 2. Heavy red poplin for ladies' dresses. **1888** HOWELLS *Annie Kilburn* xi, The furniture was in green terry. **1895** *Montgomery Ward Catal.* Spring & Summer 24/1 White Turkish Towelling or Terry. The following Terry or Turkish Towelling is for children's cloaking, roller towels, etc. **1972** *New Yorker* 22 July 74/1 Our new multicolor stripe combines red, navy, gold and sky-blue on white terry. **1981** *Guardian* 19 Oct. 14/5 Having immersed the terries in a steriliser, I give them a short cold water rinse. .. This regime means that washing terry nappies is no longer a great chore.

2. In rope-making, An open reel.

1877 in KNIGHT *Dict. Mech.* (Perh. not the same word.)

B. *adj.* Of pile-fabrics: Looped, having the loops that form the pile left uncut, as ***terry pile***, ***terry velvet*** (in F. *velours épinglé*). Also, Of or pertaining to such a fabric. Now esp. of or pertaining to ***terry towelling***, an absorbent cotton or linen cloth used for making towels, beachwear, babies' napkins, etc.; in the U.S. called ***terry cloth*** (freq. *attrib.*).

1835 *Ladies' Cabinet* Jan. 64 The new ones [hats] are composed of..plain velvet, and Terry velvet. *Ibid.* Feb. 202 A *toque* of pink terry velvet. **1851** *Mech. Mag.* 5 Apr. 278/2 Joseph Burch... For improvements in printing terry and pile carpets [etc.]... Patent dated September 28, 1850. **1853** URE *Dict. Arts* I. 380 The fabric produced will be plain or unornamented, with a looped or terry pile. **1878** BARLOW *Hist. Weaving* 210 Both cut and terry velvets are now woven in power looms. **1897** H. NEVILLE *Students' Handbk. Pract. Fabric Structure* xii. 136 Beginning with terry-towelling, as the simplest form of looped pile work. **1906** H. NISBET *Gram. Textile Design* vii. 163 Terry fabrics produced by means of terry motions are exemplified in so-called Turkish towels... The majority of these goods are produced entirely from cotton, although terry towels are sometimes produced either entirely or in part from linen. **1917** *Harrods Catal.* 1440/1 Terry Dusters or Paint Cloths. **1921** *Daily Colonist* (Victoria, B.C.) 15 Mar. 4/5 (Advt.), 36-Inch New Terry Cloth $1.69 a Yard. **1937** *Night & Day* 8 July 22/1 Terry towelling is responsible for a great many irresistible beach affairs. **1944** R. CHANDLER *Lady in Lake* iii. 18 A big guy in bathing trunks..and a white terrycloth bathrobe. **1959** *Harrods News* Summer 9 Terry towel for bath or beach. **1961** A. MILLER *Misfits* iv. 44 He turns and sees Roslyn in a terry-cloth robe emerging from the bedroom doorway. **1961** *Listener* 12 Oct. 558/1 An artificial mother constructed of wire and terry towelling. **1975** *Guardian* 27 Jan. 15/2 A completely new type of tufting machine which is directed specifically at the terry trade... [It] makes a cloth with one face of terry material. **1980** L. BIRNBACH et al. *Official Preppy Handbk.* 155/1 Need a pair of frog-print slacks or a terry cloth halter jumpsuit? **1981** [see sense A. 1 above].

C. *Comb.*, as ***terry-ribbed*** adj., ***terry-weaving***.

1885 *Girl's Own Paper* Jan. 202/1 The majority are made of terry-ribbed silk. **1907** *Macm. Mag.* Jan., Notes 19/2 New sections on terry weaving, the automatic supply of weft to looms, and warp stop motions, have been added.

terry ('tɛrɪ), *sb.*² A colloquial abbreviation of TERRITORIAL, applied to members of the Territorial Army; = TERRIER *sb.*² 3.

1907 *Daily Chron.* 31 Dec. 3/4 The 'Terries' will be made to feel that there is little or no difference between them and the Tommies. *Ibid.* 4/7 Obviously some kind of a nick-name must be found for the new Territorial Army... Upon another page Mr. Charles Lowe boldly calls our soldiers of the future 'The Terries'.

terry, *sb.*³: see TODDY.

terry, var. TARY *v. Obs.*, to provoke.

Terry Alt, Terryalt ('tɛrɪ ɔːlt). *Irish Hist.* Also *ellipt.* **Terry.** [According to a MS. diary of 1831 quoted in *Times Lit. Suppl.* (1932) 29 Sept. 691/4, *Terry Alts* was the name of an innocent bystander suspected of an outrage on a man.] A member of a secret agrarian association active in western Ireland in the 1830s. Also *attrib.*

1831 D. O'CONNELL *Let.* 15 May (1888) I. 263 It is probable that, without the aid of the 'Terry Alt' system, he could not poll one hundred votes by all his other exertions. **1931** *Dublin Even. Post* 31 May 3/3 Michael Connelly, a chief leader of the Terry Alts. **1832** *Courier* 17 Feb. 2/5 The Terries in the County of Galway are levying contributions. **1861** W. J. FITZPATRICK *Life Dr. Doyle* II. xxxix. 334 He urged the 'Shanavests', the 'Caravats', the 'Terryalts', and the 'Rockites', to abandon their deeds of blood; he implored of the Ribbonmen to cast their evil combinations to the winds. **1898** *Westm. Gaz.* 14 Nov. 4/2 The man was suspected of being a 'Terry Alt', or a member of a local agrarian conspiracy.

terryare, -yer, obs. ff. TERRIER *sb.*¹, *sb.*²

†**'terrye.** *Obs.* Short (or error) for TERRIER *sb.*²

1608 SYLVESTER *Du Bartas* II. iv. *Decay* 939 The eager Dogs are cheer'd with claps and cryes,..And all the Earth rings with the Terryes yearning.

terryen, var. TERRIEN *Obs.*, earthly.

†**'tersail.** *Sc. Obs.* In 6 tersaill. [app. ad. OF. *tercel*, *tiercel*, 'a measure of wine' (Godef.), deriv. of *tiers* third, TIERCE.] = TIERCE (of wine).

15.. *Aberdeen Regr.* (Jam.), Tersaill of wyne. [**1825** JAMIESON, *Tersaill*,..the third part of a pipe, a tierce.]

tersal, tersan, obs. ff. TERCEL, TERTIAN.

‖**Ter-sanctus** (ˌtɜː'sæŋktəs). [L. *ter* thrice + *sanctus* holy.] See quots., and SANCTUS, TRISAGION.

1832 W. PALMER *Orig. Liturg.* I. 39 After this follows the hymn *Tersanctus.* **1842** HOOK *Ch. Dict.*, *Tersanctus*, the Latin title of the hymn in the Liturgy beginning 'With Angels and Archangels', &c... In the Liturgy of Milan it has been used from time immemorial, under the name of *Trisagium.* **1892** C. WHITAKER *Stud. Aid Prayer Bk.* 81 The Triumphal or Seraphic Hymn. This hymn is sometimes called Ter-Sanctus (Thrice holy). It is indeed a Biblical Ter-Sanctus, but it is *not* the 'Liturgical Trisagion'.

terse (tɜːs), *a.* Also 7 terce, tearce, teirce. [ad. L. *ters-us*, pa. pple. of *tergēre*, *-ĕre* to wipe.]

†**1.** Wiped, brushed; smoothed; clean-cut, sharp-cut; polished, burnished; neat, trim, spruce.

1601 B. JONSON *Poetaster* III. i, I am enamour'd of this street..'tis so polite and terse. **1607** DEKKER & WEBSTER *Northw. Hoe* II. i, Ist neate, is it terse! am I hansome? ha! **1615** CROOKE *Body of Man* 20 This Man..so laboured vpon it, that he left it smooth and terce. **1623** COCKERAM, *Teirce*, fine, neat, spruce. **1640** WILKINS *New Planet* IX. (1707) 256 The concave Superficies of that Sphere [the Moon] is usually supposed to be exactly terse and smooth. **1824** MISS MITFORD *Village* Ser. I. 39 (*Mod. Antiq.*) Mrs. Frances' features..were rather terse and sharp.

†**2.** *fig.* Polite, polished, refined, cultured: esp. in reference to language. *Obs.* (passing into 3).

1621 BURTON *Anat. Mel.* I. ii. III. xv. (1628) 132 A polite and terse Academicke. **1631** MASSINGER *Emperor East* I. ii, Your polite and terser gallants. **1695** J. EDWARDS *Perfect. Script.* 6 Castellio hath turned the whole Bible into pure, terse, elegant Latin. **1774** WARTON *Hist. Eng. Poetry* Diss. ii. (1840) I. p. cxviii, Henry of Huntingdon..was likewise a terse and polite Latin poet of this period. *Ibid.* II. xxvii. 365 A terse conciseness of sentences.

3. *spec.* Freed from verbal redundancy; neatly concise; compact and pithy in style or language. (The current use.)

1777 W. WHITEHEAD *Goat's Beard* 1 In eight terse lines has Phædrus told..A tale of goats. **1849** MACAULAY *Hist. Eng.* vi. II. 16 *note*, An eminently clear, terse, and spirited summary. **1866** FELTON *Anc. & Mod. Gr.* I. II. i. 286 The tersest simplicity and most pregnant brevity of speech. **1868** FREEMAN *Norm. Conq.* II. x. 475 *note*, The Peterborough Chronicler is almost startling in his terse brevity.

†4. Applied to claret; also *absol.* as *sb. Obs.*

(Perh. not the same word. Some suggest *Thiers*, name of a wine-producing place in Puy-de-Dôme.)

1671 SHADWELL *Humourists* IV. Wks. 1720 I. 179 Must I stay 'till by the strength of terse claret you have wet yourself into courage. **1687** SEDLEY *Bellamira* II. i, I am so full I should spill terse at every jolt. *Ibid.*, He grudg'd his money for honest terse.

terse, var. TARSE *Obs.*; obs. f. TIERCE.

tersel, -ell(e, -elet, obs. ff. TERCEL, -CELET.

tersele, variant of TARSEL *Obs.*

tersely ('tɜːslɪ), *adv.* [f. TERSE + -LY².] In a terse manner or style. †**a.** In a refined or elegant manner; elegantly, politely. *Obs.*

1599 B. JONSON *Ev. Man out of Hum.* Dram. Pers., Fastidious Brisk..swears tersely, and with variety. **1648** HERRICK *Hesper., Country Life* 27 Thus thou canst tearcely live to satisfie The belly chiefly; not the eye. *a* **1661** FULLER *Worthies* (1662) II. *Lincoln*. 165 That one living in so ignorant and superstitious a generation could write so tercely.

b. In relation to language: Neatly, concisely.

1874 GREEN *Short Hist.* ix. §10. 704 The cry of the York mob..expressed tersely the creed of the English trader. **1903** *Times* 1 Apr. 9/5 The Judge has tersely summed this up.

terseness ('tɜːsnɪs). [f. TERSE *a.* + -NESS.] The quality of being terse: †**a.** of being clean-cut; sharpness or smoothness of outline. *Obs.*

1802 PALEY *Nat. Theol.* xv. (ed. 2) 294 The compactness of its form, arising from the terseness of its limbs. **1828** MISS MITFORD *Village* Ser. III. 183 (*Hay-carrying*) A well-made little man..with considerable terseness of feature.

b. Polish, elegance, or neatness of style; in mod. use, Neat and forcible conciseness.

1782 J. WARTON *Ess. Pope* II. 314 Gay..wrote with neatness, and terseness. **1808** HAN. MORE *Cœlebs* I. ii. 21 For giving a terseness and a polish to conversation..nothing is equal to the miscellaneous society of London. **1864** *Sat. Rev.* 31 Dec. 801/2 Landor had a..terseness and force of expression, which arrested the attention and won the admiration of his immediate contemporaries.

terset, tersia, obs. ff. TERCET, TARSIA.

†**tersion** ('tɜːʃən). *Obs. rare.* [ad. L. type *tersiōn-em, n. of action from *tergēre* (-*ĕre*), *ters-* to wipe: see -ION¹.] The action of wiping.

1676 BOYLE *Mech. Origin of Electr.* Wks. 1772 IV. 347 Another observation..about these bodies, is, that they require tersion as well as attrition;..weaker electricks require to be as well wiped as chafed. **1704** J. HARRIS *Lex. Techn.* I, *Tersion*, is Wiping or Cleansing the outside of any Body. [**1878** *Encycl. Brit.* VIII. 3/2 He [Boyle] found also that heat and *tersion* (or the cleaning or wiping of any body) increased its susceptibility of [electric] excitation.]

†'**tersive**, *a. Obs.* [f. L. *ters-*, ppl. stem of *tergēre*, -*ĕre* (see prec.) + -IVE.] Having power to cleanse as by wiping; detersive; detergent.

1665-6 *Phil. Trans.* I. 359 For the Eye-waters, I conceived them more strongly tersive, and clearing the Eyes. **1677** PLOT *Oxfordsh.* 49 Such a pleasant titillation, as invites the Patient to rub on the tersive water.

terslet, tertane, tertenant, obs. ff. TERCELET, TARTAN, TERRETENANT.

terter, var. TERTRE.

†**ter-terrify**, *v. Obs. nonce-wd..* [See TER-.] *trans.* To terrify threefold; to frighten extremely.

a **1618** SYLVESTER *Mysterie* Wks. (Grosart) II. 317/1 Destroyeth, Buildeth,..Confounds, Confirmes; Ter-terrifies, Sweet Consolation sings.

'**tertia.** Now *Hist.* Also 7 **tercia.** [app. an altered form of TERCIO, TERTIO, due to obscurity of final vowel.] A division of infantry: see quot. 1870; a TERCIO; a regiment; also *transf.*

1630 B. JONSON *New Inn* III. i, 'Twill be desired Only, the expressions were a little more Spanish;..To call them tertias—tertia of the kitchen, Tertia of the cellar, tertia of the chamber, And tertia of the stables. **1644** R. SYMONDS *Diary Civ. War* (Camden) 159 When the King's army was in Cornwall, the infantry was divided into three Tertias, and every tertia should consist of three brigades. *Ibid.* 167 Lord Astleys Tertia of foot made the approaches. **1670** DRYDEN *2nd Pt. Conq. Granada* I. i, That tertia of Italians did you guide. **1819** SCOTT *Leg. Montrose* ii. **1870** C. R. MARKHAM *Life Ld. Fairfax* vii. 61 A foot regiment was..formed in solid square battalions ten deep, called *tertias*, the pikes in the centre, and the musketeers on either flank.

tertial ('tɜːʃəl), *a.* and *sb. Ornith.* [f. L. *terti-us* third + -AL¹.] **a.** *adj.* Of or pertaining to the third rank or row of quill- or flight-feathers in the wing of a bird. **b.** *sb.* A flight-feather of the third row; sometimes erroneously applied to secondaries on the elbow-joint. See TERTIARY B. 3.

1836 SWAINSON *Nat. Hist. Birds* I. I. iii. 81 They [Quills]..form three divisions, distinguished as the primaries, the secondaries, and the tertials... The tertials..have their origin from the humerus. **1842** BRANDE *Dict. Sc.*, etc., *Tertials*. **1874** COUES *Birds N.W.* 665 The color of the mantle extends..to the tips of the tertials.

tertian ('tɜːʃən), *a.* and *sb.* Forms: 4 **tertiane,** 4–6 **-cian(e, -cyan,** 6 **-cyen, -san, (tarcian),** 8 **tercion,** 6– **tertian.** [ME. in *fever terciane*, or *terciane*, ad. L. *febris tertiāna*, also *tertiāna* sb., f. *tertius* third: see -AN. Cf. OF. *tierçain(e* adj. (13th c. in Godef.), *tierçaine* sb. a fever (12th c.).]

A. *adj.* **1.** *Path.* Of a fever or ague: Characterized by the occurrence of a paroxysm every third (i.e. every alternate) day.

In early use following the sb. as in F.; cf. QUOTIDIAN.

c **1386** CHAUCER *Nun's Pr. T.* 139 Ye shul haue a ffeuere terciane Or an Agu. **1398** TREVISA *Barth. De P.R.* VII. xxxix. (Bodl. MS.), A Feuere Terciane..greueþ fro þe þrid daye to the þrid and namelich aboute þe þrid houre. **1625** HART *Anat. Ur.* I. v. 48 During her husbands sicknesse, being a long and tedious, first Tertian, then double Tertian feauer. **1712** tr. *Pomet's Hist. Drugs* I. 37 To cure Quotidian, Tertian and Quartan Agues. **1834** J. FORBES *Laennec's Dis. Chest* (ed. 4) 318 Sometimes it is attended at the beginning by chills, which return with the tertian, double tertian, or quotidian type.

†**2.** Third in order. *Obs.*

1592 WYRLEY *Armorie, Capitall de Buz* 123 They made three battels and a reregard, The first had Glesquine,..The Earle of Aucer ruld the second ward, Th'archpriest did their tertian battell hold.

3. *Mus.* Applied to the mean-tone temperament (in which the major thirds are perfectly in tune).

1875 A. J. ELLIS *Helmholtz's Sensat. Tone* 649 Mean-tone, Mesotonic or Tertian Temperament.

4. ***Tertian Father***: in the Society of Jesus, a member of the order who is passing through the last of the three stages of probation, which prepares him for admission to the final vows.

1855 [implied in TERTIANSHIP]. **1876** J. MORRIS in J. H. Pollen *Life* vii. (1896) 181 Three different communities under one Rector—the novices, scholastics, and Tertian Fathers.

B. *sb.* **1.** Short for *tertian ague* or *fever*.

double tertian, one in which there are two sets of paroxysms, each recurring every third (i.e. alternate) day.

1362 LANGL. *P. Pl.* A. XII. 80 Mi name is feuere, on þe ferþe day I am a-þrest euere;..men haue I tweyne, þat on is called cotidian.., Tercian þat oþer, trewe drinkeres boþe! **1460** CAPGRAVE *Chron.* (Rolls) 291 He fel in a tercian, that continued many dayes. **1565** BLUNDEVIL *Horsemanship* IV. v. (1580) 4 Manie other speciall kinds, as Quotidians, Tertians, Quartanes. **1651** WITTIE *Primrose's Pop. Err.* III. 151 Lying sick of a Tertian. **1844** LEVER *T. Burke* lxxiii, The tertian of Egypt, so fatal among the French troops, now numbered him among its victims.

†**2.** An obsolete liquid measure for wine, oil, etc., the third of a tun, i.e. 84 wine gallons (= 70 imperial gallons); also, a large cask of this capacity; a puncheon. See also quot. 1542. *Obs.*

1423 *Rolls of Parlt.* IV. 256/1 The Terciane iiiixx iiii galons. **1531-2** *Act 23 Hen. VIII*, c. 7 Euery butt of Malmesey shuld conteyne cxxvi galons,..euery tarcian or poncheon lxxxiiii galons. **1542** RECORDE *Gr. Artes* (1575) 206 Of wine and oyle the Tertian holdeth 84 Gallons... But ..there bee other kindes of Tertians: for there be Tertians (yt is to saye) Thirdles of Pypes, of Hoggesheaddes, and Barrels. **1749** *Phil. Trans.* XLVI. 55 It is declared that the Tun of Wine, Oil, and Honey, should contain..252 Gallons; the Pipe or Butt 126; the Tertian 84.

3. In Scottish Universities (latterly only at Aberdeen), a student in his third year. Also *attrib.*

1857 CLERK MAXWELL in *Life* x. (1882) 296 Where Tertian and Semi are hot in dispute And the voice of the Magistrand never is mute. **1894** W. L. LOW *D. Thomson* iv. 83 During my Tertian year we were examined by him only once. **1895** ANNA M. STODDART *J. S. Blackie* I. 228 He followed the Natural Philosophy and Moral Philosophy courses as a tertian and a magistrand.

4. A mixture stop on an organ, consisting of a tierce and larigot combined.

1876 HILES *Catech. Organ* x. (1878) 77. **1898** STAINER & BARRETT *Dict. Mus. Terms, Tertian*, an organ stop composed of two ranks of pipes, sounding a major third and fifth of the foundation pipes, in the third octave above; a *Tierce* and *Larigot* on one slider.

5. *Geom.* A curve of the third order, a cubic. *rare.*

1891 in *Cent. Dict.*

6. Short for *Tertian Father*: see A. 4.

Hence '**tertianship** (*R.C. Ch.*), the position of being a Tertian Father (see A. 4).

1855 R. BOYLE *B. v. Wiseman* 56 After he has been associated with the Society [of Jesus] for fifteen or twenty years, he is required to retire into, what is technically called, a tertianship, or a third year's probation. **1892** J. H. POLLEN *Acts Eng. Martyrs* 358 He was Minister of the Tertianship at Ghent and then Prefect and Confessor at St. Omers.

†**tertiar**, *v. Obs. rare.* Also 6 **terciar.** [ad. It. *tertiare* 'to thirde the pike' (Florio 1598), or ad. Sp. *terciar* (*la pica*) 'to shake or brandish a pike, to come to push of pike with the enemy' (Minsheu 1599).] (See quots.)

1598 BARRET *Theor. Warres* 17 He ought, being a pike-man, to tertiar or charge his pike. *Ibid.* III. ii. 47 The pikes being Terciard or charged ouer hand. [*Ibid.* Gloss., *Tertiare*, a Spanish word, and is to third the pike, either to beare the same vpon his shoulder, or to charge the same ouer hand.]

tertiary ('tɜːʃ(ɪ)ərɪ), *a.* and *sb.* Also 6 **tercyary.** [f. L. *tertiāri-us* of the third part or rank, f. *tertius* third: see -ARY¹. So F. *tertiaire*.]

A. *adj.* **1. a.** Of, in, or belonging to the third order, rank, degree, class, or category; third.

1656 BLOUNT *Glossogr.*, *Tertiary*,..of, or belonging to the third, or third sort, tertian. **1831** BREWSTER *Optics* ix. 84 When one prism of a different angle is thus made to correct the dispersion of another prism, a tertiary spectrum is produced. **1860** MAYNE *Expos. Lex.* s.v., A tertiary peduncle is the second degree of ramification of a compound peduncle, or a bough of the branch which gives off the peduncle. **1865** RUSKIN *Sesame* i. §5, I venture to assume that you will admit duty as at least a secondary or tertiary motive. **1871** EARLE *Philol. Eng. Tongue* §428 The adverb is the tertiary or third presentive word.

b. *Chem.* (i) Applied to compounds regarded as being derived from ammonia by replacement of three hydrogen atoms by organic radicals, and to derivatives of such compounds; also extended to analogous derivatives of other elements, esp. phosphorus. [The sense is due to Gerhardt & Chiozza, who used F. *tertiaire* (*Compt. Rend.* (1853) XXXVII. 88).]

1854 *Q. Jrnl. Chem. Soc.* VI. 195 With regard to the tertiary amides,..their preparation is generally easier than that of the secondary amides. **1888**, etc. [see PRIMARY *a.* 6 f(i)]. **1964** N. G. CLARK *Mod. Org. Chem.* xii. 232 The tertiary amines,..with no available hydrogen, are the nitrogen counterparts of the ethers.

(ii) Applied to organic compounds other than amines, etc. (see sense (i)) in which the characteristic functional group is located on a saturated carbon atom which is itself bonded to three other carbon atoms. [Applied orig. to alcohols by H. Kolbe, who used G. *tertiär* (*Ann. der Chem. und Pharm.* (1864) CXXXII. 104).]

1872 *Jrnl. Chem. Soc.* XXV. 295 The oxidation of tertiary alcohols takes place according to a law similar to that which rules the oxidation of ketones. **1932** I. D. GARARD *Introd. Org. Chem.* iii. 34 This formation of a ketone having fewer carbon atoms than the alcohol is characteristic of the oxidation of tertiary alcohols. **1964** N. G. CLARK *Mod. Org. Chem.* xi. 222 The use of acyl chlorides in the above manner produces hydrogen chloride, which may have a deleterious effect on the compound undergoing acylation, e.g. tertiary alcohols readily give the alkyl chlorides. **1981** WINGROVE & CARET *Org. Chem.* x. 435 Under basic conditions, tertiary alcohols do not undergo oxidation.

(iii) Applied to a saturated carbon atom which is bonded to three other carbon atoms; also, bonded to or involving a tertiary carbon atom. Of an ion or a free radical: having (respectively) the electric charge or the unpaired electron located on a tertiary carbon atom.

1903, etc. [see SECONDARY *a.* 3 i(iii)]. **1972** [see PRIMARY *a.* 6 f(iii)].

c. *Surveying.* Designating triangulation derived by subdivision from secondary triangulation (which in turn results from subdivision of primary triangulation) or points, bench-marks, etc., established by this.

1851 C. DAVIES *Elementary Surveying* (rev. ed.) IV. i. 181 When the *secondary* and *tertiary* triangles have been considerably multiplied, the compass is taken in hand. **1883** J. R. OLIVER *Pract. Astron. for Surveyors* ii. ii. 121 The sides of the secondary triangles are from about 5 to 20 miles, and those of the tertiary triangles five or less. **1920** W. N. THOMAS *Surveying* xiii. 382 A further sub-division resulted in the 'Tertiary' triangulation. **1965** BANNISTER & RAYMOND *Surveying* (ed. 2) ix. 293 The fourth order points give closer spacing in towns—tertiary and higher order points cover almost the whole country at a density of 0·05 trig point per km², with a density of about 0·1 per km² in towns. **1975** [see SECONDARY *a.* 3 a].

d. *Physics.* Produced by the impact of secondary particles with matter.

1938 R. W. LAWSON tr. *Hevesy & Paneth's Man. Radioactivity* (ed. 2) v. 61 On the average 2 or 3 tertiary electrons result from each secondary electron, when the primary β-radiation has a velocity 33 per cent. that of light. **1961** G. R. CHOPPIN *Exper. Nuclear Chem.* iii. 35 Tertiary electrons may be produced by photoemission resulting from the photons of the secondary ionization process.

e. Designating the part of the economy or work-force concerned with services of all kinds, rather than with the production of foodstuffs or raw materials, or with manufacturing.

1940 *Economist* 21 Sept. 363/1 There is a steady tendency for labour to move out of primary production into secondary production (manufacture) and from secondary to tertiary production (all forms of services). **1961**, etc. [see QUATERNARY *a.* 3 a]. **1974** B. PEARCE tr. *Amin's Accumulation on World Scale* I. 16 The sectors of the tertiary part of the economy—transport, trade, financial services—..are grafted upon the foreign economy. **1975** *Guardian* 20 Jan. 16/4 Tertiary industries are also being introduced..plants for the preparation of prefabricated houses and timber for construction.

f. ***tertiary structure*** (Biochem.): the way the helix of a polynucleotide or polypeptide molecule is folded in three dimensions and bound to other helices.

1952, etc. [see PRIMARY *a.* 5v]. **1964** G. H. HAGGIS et al. *Introd. Molecular Biol.* iii. 59 The run of the peptide chain through the molecule..is known as the tertiary structure of a protein. **1978** *Nature* 5 Jan. 15/2 Studies on pancreatic trypsin inhibitor and hen egg white lysozyme suggest that at most there are only a limited number of folding pathways to the tertiary structure.

g. ***tertiary road*** (orig. *U.S.*), a Class III road.

1960 BAKER & STEBBINS *Dict. Highway Traffic* 114 *Land-service road*, a road which is used primarily to give access to land. Sometimes called: tertiary road. **1971** J. DRUMMOND *Farewell Party* xxx. 149 We were out on a tertiary road, and more or less alone. **1975** M. KENYON *Mr. Big* xxii. 224 The secondary road became a tertiary road of muddy craters.

h. ***tertiary education***, that which follows secondary education and precedes, includes, or replaces university or professional training; so ***tertiary level***; ***tertiary college***, one at which such education is provided.

1961 *Mind* LXX. 105 The spread of secondary and latterly of tertiary education has created a large population of people..educated far beyond their capacity to undertake analytical thought. **1969** *Guardian* 26 Aug. 16/4 A 'tertiary college'..in Exeter where sixth forms are to be merged in the College of Further Education. **1971** *New Scientist* 27 May 513/1 Whenever Britons wrote or talked about tertiary education, they generally meant university education. **1974** *Bookseller* 18 May 2402/1 (Advt.), Can you sell our tertiary-level academic titles to booksellers in Scotland and North-East England? **1981** *New Society* 29 Jan. 192/1 Tertiary colleges—providing everything from A level Russian to pre-nursing courses and apprenticeship courses in motor engineering—are the colleges of the future..A *sixth form college* is for the more traditional sixth form intake. A *tertiary college* provides for all over-16s whatever their needs.

i. ***tertiary recovery***, the recovery of oil by advanced methods after conventional artificial means have ceased to be productive. Cf. *secondary recovery* s.v. SECONDARY *a.* 5k.

1975 *Petroleum Economist* Aug. 292/2 Oil produced by tertiary recovery methods, from above the Arctic circle,..could sell at US $8·50 a barrel. **1976** *National Observer* (U.S.) 10 July 13/3 Given that profits hold, what is next for the oilmen? They answer, almost in unison: 'tertiary recovery'.

2. *Geol.* Forming a third series in point of origin or age. †**a.** Applied by early geologists to mountains of the most recent formation. **b.** In modern geology, Of or pertaining to the third series of stratified formations: formerly including all those above the chalk; now restricted to the strata from the Eocene to the Pliocene, both inclusive. Also called CAINOZOIC.

[G. ARDUINO *Lett.* in *Nuova Raccolta d'opusc. scient.* VI. 159 (1760) Monti..primitivi o primari..secondari..e terziari, li monti e colli del terzo ordine, che sta a ridosso del secondo e talvolta anche del primo.] **1794** SULLIVAN *View Nat.* I. x. 78 He [Pallas] maintained, that in addition to these primordial mountains, there were others of a more recent origin. These he called secondary and tertiary. [**18..** CUVIER & BRONGN. *Descr. Geol. Env. Paris* (1822) 9 Terrains tertiaires.] *a* **1812** KIRWAN (Webster 1828), Tertiary mountains are such as result from the ruins of other mountains promiscuously heaped together. **1822** CONYBEARE & PHILLIPS *Geol. Eng. & W.* 1 Tertiary Rocks. Comprising the Formations above the Chalk. **1824-5** D. OLMSTED *Geol. N. Carolina* (Webster), Tertiary formation, a series of horizontal strata, more recent than chalk beds... It comprehends the alluvial formation..and the diluvial formation. **1830** LYELL *Princ. Geol.* I. 49 Arduino, in his memoirs on the mountains of Padua, Vicenza, and Verona, first recognized the distinction between primary, secondary, and tertiary rocks. **1833** *Ibid.* III. p. vii, A large collection of tertiary shells. **1862** MCOSH *Supernatural* II. ii. §2. 183 Nor does Man descend from the mammals which preceded him in the tertiary age. **1863** LYELL *Antiq. Man* i. 3 Previously to the year 1833,..the strata called Tertiary had been divided by geologists into Lower, Middle, and Upper.

3. *Painting.* Applied to a colour formed by the mixture of two secondary colours.

1848 WORNUM in *Lect. Paint.* 2:1 *note*, Although there are but three primitive colours, painters have nine. These are—yellow, red, blue;..orange, purple, green, which are secondary;..russet, olive, citrine, which are tertiary, being compounds of the secondaries. **1967** E. SHORT *Embroidery & Fabric Collage* i. 11 A mixture of all three primary colours results in tertiary colours. These are the subtle colours such as khaki, various browns, etc.

4. *Path.* Of or belonging to the third or last stage of syphilis.

1875 H. C. WOOD *Therap.* (1879) 404 In *tertiary syphilis*, including in the term all cases of syphilitic bone, visceral, or nervous disease, the remedy is really of inestimable value. **1899** *Allbutt's Syst. Med.* VII. 668 It has..been considered inappropriate in this article to introduce the terms 'secondary' and 'tertiary' as applicable to the incidence of the phenomena of cerebral syphilis.

5. *R.C. Ch.* Of or belonging to the Third Order in certain religious fraternities: see B. 1.

A *Third Order*, of lay members not subject to the strict rule of the regulars, but retaining the secular life, was originated by St. Francis of Assisi, and is an established institution among the Franciscans, Dominicans, and others. (See *Catholic Dict.*)

1891 R. H. BUSK in *N. & Q.* 7th Ser. XI. 289/2 The Franciscans, who loved [Dante], and in whose tertiary habit he was shrouded in the supreme hour. **1899** *Westm. Gaz.* 1 Sept. 2/3 The Tertiary Sister was discharged yesterday. **1902** *Daily Chron.* 2 Sept. 5/6 The murderer was a tertiary lay brother of the Dominican order.

6. *Ornith.* Applied to certain feathers of the wing: see B. 3. Cf. TERTIAL.

1858 J. WILSON in *Encycl. Brit.* (ed. 8) XVI. 735/1 The tertials or tertiary feathers are derived from the humerus or arm-bone.

B. *sb.* **1.** *R.C. Ch.* A member of the Third Order of certain religious fraternities: see A. 5.

a **1550** *Image Ipocr.* IV. 213 in *Skelton's Wks.* (1843) II. 441/2 Some be Tercyaris, And some be of St. Marys. **1820** SOUTHEY *Wesley* II. 565 It may..deserve to be recognized as an auxiliary institution, its ministers being analogous to the regulars, and its members to the tertiaries and various confraternities of the Romish Church. **1909** *Westm. Gaz.* 15 July 3/3 The late Marquis [of Ripon], besides being a fervent Tertiary of St. Francis, was a friend in need to the Franciscan Order.

2. *Geol.* A stratum or formation belonging to the Tertiary system: see A. 2.

1851 WOODWARD *Mollusca* I. 45 In the miocene tertiaries of Asia Minor. **1885** *Lyell's Elem. Geol.* ix. (ed. 4) 110 The whole of the Tertiaries were at first confounded with the superficial alluviums of Europe.

3. *Ornith.* (*pl.*) The quill- or flight-feathers that grow upon the humerus in the wing of a bird.

1834 MUDIE *Feathered Tribes Brit. Isles* (1841) I. 10 The tertiaries or third quills of the wings. **1872** COUES *N. Amer. Birds* 36 The Tertiaries..are, properly, the remiges that grow upon the upper arm. [Cf. TERTIAL.]

4. *Path.* (*pl.*) Tertiary syphilitic symptoms: see A. 4.

1897 J. HUTCHINSON in *Arch. Surg.* VIII. 218 Those who remain well and never present tertiaries.

5. *Painting.* A tertiary colour: see A. 3.

1854 FAIRHOLT *Dict. Terms Art* s.v. *Secondary Colours*, When two secondaries are mixed together..they cannot neutralise each other, but only form half-tones or tertiaries. **1897** *Daily News* 20 May 7/4 Mr. Rhead is fortunate in handling effectively the most brilliant of positive colours as well as the quieter tertiaries.

6. *Gram.* In Jespersen's terminology, a word or group of words of tertiary rank or importance in a phrase or sentence; = SUBJUNCT. Cf. quote 1871, sense A. 1 a.

1924, **1940** [see SECONDARY *sb.* 12]. **1959** M. SCHLAUCH *Eng. Lang. in Mod. Times* viii. 221 In this system [of Otto Jespersen's]..the modifier of a modifier (e.g., an adverb) is a tertiary.

†**tertiate** ('tɜːʃɪeɪt), *v.* *Obs.* [f. ppl. stem of late L. *tertiāre*, f. *tertius* third.]

1. *trans.* To do (anything) for the third time: in quot. 1628, to introduce for the third time or support as third spokesman.

1623 COCKERAM, *Tertiate*, to doe a thing three times. **1628** WOTTON in *Reliq.* (1672) 559 The Personage that should first, or second or tertiate your business with the King. **1656** BLOUNT *Glossogr.*, *Tertiate*..to Till ground, or do any thing the third time [*ed.* 1674 *adds* to tri-fallow].

2. *Mil.* To poise (a lance or pike): cf. TERTIAR.

a **1691** BOYLE *Hist. Air* xix. (1692) 183 They tertiate their Lance,..that is, they poise it in their Hand.

3. *Mil.* To ascertain the strength of a cannon by measuring its thickness by means of caliper compasses, in three places: see quot. 1704.

1672 J. ROBERTS *Compl. Canonier* 35 To tertiate a Piece of Ordnance. **1704** J. HARRIS *Lex. Techn.* I. s.v., To Tertiate a Great Gun, is to know the thickness of the Metal at the Touch-hole, the Trunnions, and at the Muzzle. **1828** J. M. SPEARMAN *Brit. Gunner* (ed. 2) 393 To tertiate a piece of ordnance, is to examine whether it has the due thickness of metal at the vent, &c.

So †**terti'ation.**

1658 PHILLIPS, *Tertiation*,..a dividing into three, also a doing anything the third time.

tertio, variant of TERCIO *Obs.*, a regiment, etc.

'tertio-,geniture. *nonce-wd.* [f. *tertio-*, fr. L. *terti-us* third, after *primogeniture*.] Right of succession or inheritance belonging to the third-born.

1855 M. BRIDGES *Pop. Mod. Hist.* 420 Austria had a prospect..of ultimately succeeding to the beautiful dominions of Este, as a tertio-geniture for her family.

‖**tertium comparationis** ('tɜːʃɪəm kɒmpæreɪʃɪ'əʊnɪs, kɒmpærɑːtɪ'əʊnɪs). [L., = the third element in comparison.] The factor which links or is the common ground between two elements in comparison.

1922 J. RIVIERE tr. *Freud's Introd. Lectures Psycho-Anal.* x. 128 In one set of symbols the underlying comparison may be easily apparent, but there are others in which we have to look about for the common factor, the *tertium comparationis* contained in the supposed comparison. **1945** *Mind* LIV. 209 A comparison without a *tertium comparationis*. **1956** J. H. GREENBERG in Saporta & Bastian *Psycholinguistics* (1961) 470/1 With what cultural or other facts would one connect a contrast between aspirated and nonaspirated consonants in a given language? Where is the *tertium comparationis*?

‖**tertium non datur** ('tɜːʃɪəm nɒn 'deɪtə(r)), *Lat. phr.* No third possibility exists. Also as *sb. phr.* Cf. *excluded middle*, *third* s.v. EXCLUDED *ppl. a.* b.

1887 S. H. HODGSON *Let.* 8 Apr. in R. B. Perry *Tht. & Char. of W. James* (1935) I. 642 You are neither empiricist nor transcendentalist; and *tertium non datur*. **1932** tr. *Ortega y Gasset's Revolt of Masses* xiv. 190 The nation is always either in the making, or in the unmaking. *Tertium non datur*. **1948** H. REICHENBACH *Elem. Symb. Logic* vi. 227 An example of such a substitution is given by the various forms of the *tertium non datur* for higher functions. **1977** *Language* LIII. 319 After all, a pronoun must be either prefixed or infixed; tertium non datur.

‖**tertium quid** ('tɜːʃɪəm 'kwɪd). [L., app. rendering Gr. τρίτον τι, 'some third thing'.] Something (indefinite or left undefined) related in some way to two (definite or known) things, but distinct from both.

(Gr. τρίτον τι occurs in Plato *Sophist* 250. The Latin form is in Irenæus *Adv. Her.* 2. I. 3 (*c* 196), where it doubtless represents τρίτον τι of the lost Greek original; also, in Tertullian *Adv. Praxean* 27 (*a* 220), and *tertium nescio quid* in Hilary *Synod.* 73 (*c* 358). The passage in Tertullian mentions *electrum* as an example of a body produced by the mixture of gold and silver; and app. *tertium quid* was used by the alchemists of a third substance different from its two constituents: see quot. from Bailey, and cf. next. Examples of the phrase in English context are late.)

[**1613** *Theatrum Chemicum*, Index, Tertium quid. 1101, 1085.] **1724** BAILEY, *Tertium Quid*, (among Chymists) the Result of the Mixture of some two Things, which forms something very different from both. *L*[*atin*]. [**1809-10** COLERIDGE *Friend* (1818) I. 157 The baleful product or *tertium Aliquid*, of this union retarded the civilization of Europe for Centuries.] **1826** *Edin. Rev.* Sept. 255 Balancing the opinions of Gall against those of Spurzheim, or compounding out of them a *tertium quid*. **1881** R. ADAMSON *Fichte* v. 110 While..we appear to assert that the two orders of facts make up all that is, we have in reality placed alongside of them..the thinking subject or mind, a *tertium quid* which certainly stands in need of some explanation. **1902** MENZIES *Demonic Possess. N.T.* vi. 187 The achievement was either devilish or divine. There was no tertium quid.

‖**tertium sal** ('tɜːʃɪəm 'sæl). *Chem. Obs.* [med.L., = 'third salt'.] See quot.

1753 CHAMBERS *Cycl. Supp.*, *Tertium Sal, a third salt*, a term used in chemistry to express a salt resulting from the mixture of an acid and an alkali, which partakes so of the nature of both, as to be itself neither acid nor alkali, but neutral. **1860** in MAYNE *Expos. Lex.*

‖**tertius** ('tɜːʃɪəs). [L. *tertius* third.] Esp. in some public schools, appended to a surname to designate the youngest (in age or standing) of three persons, esp. pupils, of that name. Cf. MAJOR A. 7c, MINOR A. 7b, PRIMUS A. 2, SECUNDUS.

1818 *Blackw. Mag.* II. 424/2 Nicol Jarvie, tertius, M.D. **1870** (At Mill Hill School this year there were) Smith Major, Minor, and Tertius. **1899** KIPLING *Stalky* vi. 175 The Head called them over, too—majors, minors, and tertiuses.

‖**tertius gaudens** ('tɜːʃɪəs 'gaʊdɛnz). [L., f. *tertius* third + *gaudens*, pres. ppl. of *gaudere* to rejoice.] A third party that benefits by the conflict or estrangement of two others.

1892 tr. Bismarck in *Ann. Reg. 1891* 284, I should like to interfere in such cases, like a parish beadle bringing peace, and prove that the *tertius gaudens* is the worst enemy. **1933** G. ARTHUR *Septuagenarian's Scrap Bk.* 39 Having ascertained from M. Bompard..that France would flatly refuse..to be a *tertius gaudens* with Germany and Russia. **1957** R. K. MERTON *Social Theory* (rev. ed.) II. ix. 376 The occupant of the status..can become cast in the role of the *tertius gaudens*. **1974** 'M. INNES' *Mysterious Commission* xix. 170 He saw himself as a kind of third force—or even as what the learned would call a *tertius gaudens*, meaning a chap who nips in and does both contending sides down. **1980** D. NEWSOME *On Edge of Paradise* v. 160 It would be better for them both to withdraw to allow the election of a *tertius gaudens*.

†**tertre.** *Obs.* Also terter. [a. F. *tertre* a hillock (*Roland* 11th c.).] A little hill; a rising ground; an eminence. Cf. TERRITORY[2].

1480 CAXTON *Ovid's Met.* x. iv, He sat vpon a tertre in a playn felde. **1481** —— *Godeffroy* cxxii. 185 The barons acorded that they wold close this litil terter and waye.

tertschite ('tɜːtʃaɪt). *Min.* [ad. G. *tertschit* (H. Meixner 1953, in *Fortschritte der Mineral.*, etc. XXXI. 41), f. the name of H. *Tertsch* (1880–1962), Austrian mineralogist: see -ITE[1].] A hydrated calcium borate found as white, fibrous, probably monoclinic crystals.

1953 *Chem. Abstr.* XLVII. 10413 New borate deposits were discovered in 1951... The following types were distinguished:..tertschite, about $Ca_4B_{10}O_{19}.20H_2O$. **1978** *Mercian Geol.* VI. 261 Tertschite is found only in one locality in the Bigadiç deposits... It is white, contains very fine fibres, shines like silk... Its rare occurrence makes this mineral unique among the borate minerals.

‖**tertulia** (ter'tulja). Also 8 **tertulla**, 8–9 **tertullia**. [Sp. *tertulia* a conference, an evening party, soirée.] An evening party in Spain.

1785 BECKFORD *Italy, Spain* [etc.] (1834) II. 305 Of goings to balls, theatres, and tertullias. **1828** W. IRVING in *Life & Lett.* (1864) II. 273, I have become one of the most dissipated men upon town; continually at *soirées* and *tertullias*. **1845** FORD *Handbk. Spain* I. ii. 161 They meet in church, on the Alameda, and at their tertulias.

ter,tullia'nade. [f. as next + -ADE.] A tirade or invective after the manner of Tertullian.

1819 W. TAYLOR in *Monthly Rev.* XC. 182 A Philippic, or, rather, a Tertullianade, against theatricals.

Tertullianism (tə'tʌlɪənɪz(ə)m). *Eccl.* [f. proper name *Tertullian*, ad. L. *Tertulliān-us*.] The doctrine of Tertullian, a famous Christian writer of the late 2nd and early 3rd c., a modification of Montanism, or the rigid ascetic discipline connected with this. So **Ter'tullianist**, one of a sect who followed this doctrine and discipline.

1702 C. MATHER *Magn. Chr.* III. I. i. §14. 19/1 He [Mr. Cotton] practically appeared in opposition to Tertullianism, by proceeding unto a Second Marriage. **1710** *Brit. Apollo* II. No. 84. 2/1 He.. gave name to a Sect call'd Tertullianists about the Year 245. **1831-3** E. BURTON *Eccl. Hist.* xxii. (1845) 463 A sect of Tertullianists.. continued at Carthage till the end of the fourth century.

teru, teruagaunt, obs. ff. TEREU, TERMAGANT.

teruggite (tə'ruːdʒaɪt). *Min.* [f. the name of M. E. *Teruggi*, 20th-c. Argentinian geologist + -ITE[1].] A hydrated arsenate and borate of calcium and magnesium, $Ca_4MgB_{12}O_{20}(AsO_4)_2.18H_2O$, found as colourless or white monoclinic crystals.

1968 ARISTARAIN & HURLBUT in *Amer. Mineralogist* LIII. 1815 Teruggite, a new borate mineral, was collected in June, 1967, during a field study of Argentine borates. **1973** *Amer. Mineralogist* LVIII. 1034/2 No chemical analysis was made for the teruggite sample used in the present study. The crystal structure determination confirms the chemical composition reported by Aristarain and Hurlbut (1968) except for the water content which consists of twenty molecules instead of eighteen. **1978** *Mercian Geol.* VI. 264 Teruggite is rare, occurring sporadically at one horizon in the southern basin of the Emet deposits [in Turkey], as very pure white, powdery potato-shaped nodules containing countless minute white euhedral crystals.

‖**teru-tero** ('tɛruː'tɛrəʊ). Also tero-tero, teru-teru. [From its noisy cry.]

The Cayenne lapwing or spur-winged plover, *Vanellus cayennensis*.

1839 DARWIN *Voy. Nat.* vi. (1873) 114 The teru-tero.. is another bird, which often disturbs the stillness of the night. **1884** W. B. BARROWS in *The Auk* July 278 (Funk) Tero-tero .. is the bane of all water-fowl shooting in the marshes.

terve, variant of TIRVE *v. Obs.*, to turn.

Tervueren (tə'vʊərən). Also Tervuren. [a. Flemish *Tervueren*, Fr. *Tervuren*, the name of a small town in Belgium, some ten miles east of Brussels.] A fawn, rough-coated, Belgian sheepdog, with dark pricked ears and a black muzzle. Also *attrib.*

1947 C. L. B. HUBBARD *Working Dogs of World* II. 138 The Tervueren is the third main type among the sheep-dogs of Belgium. **1964** [see GROENENDAEL]. **1978** *Detroit Free Press* 2 Apr. 16F/3 Belgian Tervuren Pups, ex show-obedience-guard.

tery, terytory, obs. ff. TARRY *v.*, TERRITORY.

Terylene ('tɛrɪliːn). Also terylene. [f. *polyeth)ylene ter(ephthalate* s.v. POLYETHYLENE a, by inversion.] **a.** A proprietary name for polyethylene terephthalate used as a textile fibre.

1946 [see *fibre-forming* adj. s.v. FIBRE *sb.* 8]. **1946** [see *polyethylene terephthalate* s.v. POLYETHYLENE a]. **1947** *Trade Marks Jrnl.* 23 Apr. 233/1 *Terylene*... All goods in Class 23. Imperial Chemical Industries Limited. **1949** *Official Gaz.* (U.S. Patent Office) 27 Sept. 951/2 Imperial Chemical Industries, Limited... *Terylene*... For synthetic yarns and thread. **1951** *Economist* 22 Sept. 686/1 Dacron,.. known in Britain as Terylene and made under licence in the United States, replaces light-weight worsted for summer suits. **1958** *Sunday Times* 27 Apr. 7/5 New materials, nylon, Terylene and so on bring a certain spick-and-spanness within the reach of all. **1961** *Times* 30 May (I.C.I. Suppl.) p. vi, A conveyor belt made with 'Terylene' will out-work, out-last, out-wear any other belt. **1976** P. CAVE *High Flying Birds* i. 9 The sails are usually made of terylene.

b. *attrib.*

1951 *Catal. of Exhibits, South Bank Exhib., Festival of Britain* 109/1 Terylene lace, rope, silk, blanket, etc. **1958** *New Statesman* 28 June 831/1 The men who had nylon shirts and terylene suits before those fabrics got into Marks and Spencer's where the rest of us buy our clothes. **1967** E. SHORT *Embroidery & Fabric Collage* iii. 70 A synthetic interlining such as terylene wadding makes the quilt easy to launder. **1977** B. PYM *Quartet in Autumn* xi. 97 A crisp-looking terylene surplice was suspended from a hook.

‖**terza** ('tɛrtsa), *a.* and *sb. Mus.* Also (masc.) terzo. [It. *terza*, fem. of *terzo* third:—L. *tertia*.] **a.** *adj.* The third, as in ***opera terza***, the third work; ***violino terzo***, third violin. **b.** *sb.* A third; also ***in terza***, in three parts; ***terzo*** = TRIO.

1724 *Short Explic. For. Wds. in Mus. Bks.*, *Terza*, a Third. .. *Opera Terza*,.. *Violina Terza*. *Ibid.*, *In Terza*,.. Songs or Tunes in Three Parts, the same as *Trio* below.

terzain (tɜː'zeɪn). *rare*[−1]. [app. ad. It. *terzina*, after *quatrain*.] A stanza or set of three lines.

1855 MILMAN *Lat. Chr.* XI. ix, The sublime terzains of Dante.

‖**terza rima** ('tɛrtsa 'rima). [It., = 'third rime'.] An Italian form of iambic verse, consisting of sets of three lines, the middle line of each set riming with the first and last of the succeeding (*a b a*, *b c b*, *c d c*, etc.).

1819 BYRON *Proph. Dante* Pref., The measure adopted is the terza rima of Dante. **1869** TOZER *Highl. Turkey* II. 252 Italian in Dante's time rendered more manageable the intricacies of the terza rima.

terzet, -zetta, -zette, variants of TERCET.

‖**terzetto** (ter'tsɛtto). *Mus.* Pl. -i (-i). [It. *terzetto*: see TERCET.] A (small) trio, esp. vocal.

1724 *Short Explic. For. Wds. in Mus. Bks.*, *Terzetto*, little Airs in Three Parts. **1816** T. L. PEACOCK *Headlong Hall* xiii, Mr. Chromatic,.. with the assistance of his two.. daughters, regaled the ears of the company with the following terzetto. **1833** C. MACFARLANE *Banditti & Robbers* (1837) 187 (Stanf.) At the conclusion of the duetto they begged for the grace of a terzetto.

‖**terzina** (ter'tsina). [It. *terzina* a triplet.] A stanza or set of three lines; = TERCET.

1836 *Pop. Encycl.* II. 592/1 The terzina first reached its perfection in the time of Dante. **1893** *Nation* (N.Y.) 16 Feb. 129/1 Dante arranges his poem in stanzas of three lines each, and rarely overruns from *terzina* to *terzina*.

'tes, var. 'TIS.

tescare, -caria: see TEZKERE.

teschemacherite ('tɛʃɪˌmækəraɪt). *Min.* [f. the name of E. F. *Teschemacher* (1791-1863), English chemist, who first described it: see -ITE[1].] Ammonium bicarbonate, $(NH_4)HCO_3$, occurring as transparent white to yellowish orthorhombic crystals.

1868 J. D. DANA *Syst. Min.* (ed. 5) 705 (*heading*) Teschemacherite. **1968** [see KALICINE]. **1972** *Amer. Mineralogist* LVII. 1305 Teschemacherite, ammonium bicarbonate, was deposited inside the wellhead of the Broadlands [New Zealand] geothermal drillhole BR9 after the bore had been shut for several weeks... Teschemacherite has not been reported from other geothermal fields but occurs in some guano deposits.

teschenite ('tɛʃɪnaɪt). *Geol.* Also **teschinite**. [f. *Teschen* (see def.) + -ITE[1] 1 b.] A name given to certain eruptive rocks, occurring at Teschen in Silesia and elsewhere, intercalated and intrusive in the Cretaceous formation.

Used by different geologists with very varying extension.

1866 LAWRENCE *Cotta's Rocks Class.* (1878) 140 Teschinite is the name given.. to a rock whose mass is chiefly felsitic, and in which hypersthene forms long black needles. **1888** RUTLEY *Rock-Forming Min.* 115 A constant constituent of the rocks termed Teschenites.

tese, obs. f. TEASE; var. TEISE *sb.* and *v.*[1] *Obs.*

†**teseke**, obs. form of PHTHISIC.

c **1460** *Play Sacram.* 538 in *Non-Cycle Myst. Plays* (1909) 74 þe poose, þe sneke, or þe teseke.

tesel, tesill, tesle, obs. forms of TEASEL.

†**tesh(e.** *Obs.* Of uncertain origin and meaning.

If the meaning is 'task', cf. F. *tâche*, OF. *tasche*.

1596 HARINGTON *Apology* Bb vij b, I haue good authorityes, for my teshe. **1596** —— *Metam. Ajax* D v, I must still keep me to my tesh. **1596** —— *Ulysses upon Ajax* D v b, But return we to Misacmos' teshe, I long to hear his conclusion. **1625** BRATHWAIT *Five Senses* 309 The more numerous and odious they were; when they came to the Tesh.

Teshoo Lama, Teshu Lama, varr. TASHI LAMA.

teskari, teskere, etc.: see TEZKERE.

Tesla ('tɛzlə). [The name of Nicola *Tesla* (1856-1943), Croatian-born American electrical physicist.] **1.** ***Tesla coil***, a type of induction coil invented by Tesla, employing a spark gap in place of an interruptor and capable of producing an intense high-frequency discharge.

1896 *Amer. Jrnl. Sci.* CLI. 245 By changing the size of the spark gap in the primary circuit of the Tesla coil one has a great range of electrical energy at command. **1930** *Proc. R. Soc.* A. CXXIX. 479 If it is desired simply to obtain the highest possible potentials with the minimum of trouble then the Tesla coil is obviously the ideal solution. **1975** *Bio Systems* VII. 6/2 Thus far, energy has only been fed in by sparking electrodes kept at roughly controlled voltage level with Tesla coils.

2. *Physics.* (Usu. with small initial.) Pl. **tesla**, **teslas**. The SI unit of magnetic flux density, equal to one weber (WEBER) per square metre; 10,000 gauss. Symbol T.

1960 in COOKE & MARKUS *Electronics & Nucleonics Dict.* 482/2. **1961** *Symbols, Units & Nomencl. Physics* (Internat. Union Pure & Appl. Physics) 18 The following units of the MKSA system have special names and symbols, which have been approved by the General Conference on Weights and Measures:... tesla (Wb/m^2). **1969** *Sci. Jrnl.* June 36/3 The oscillating magnetic field in the radio pulse itself as it leaves the pulsar is probably greater than 10 teslas (10^5 gauss). **1971** *New Scientist* 24 June 737/2 Superconductors cannot yet sustain fields greater than 12 Tesla. **1980** J. F. O'HANLON *User's Guide Vacuum Technol.* ix. 216 Modern [sputter-ion] pumps are constructed.. with external permanent magnets of 0·1 to 0·2 Tesla strength.

teslet, -lot, obs. forms of TASLET.

tesmoingnal, -monage: see TESTIMONIAL, -MONAGE.

Teso ('tɛsəʊ). [Native name.] **a.** (Also *Iteso*.) A Nilo-Hamitic people of central Uganda and western Kenya; a member of this people. **b.** (Also *Ateso*.) The Nilo-Hamitic language of this people. Also *attrib.*

1910 *Bible in World* Nov. 323/2 Teso is the speech of one of the Nilotic tribes who are found in the north of the Uganda Protectorate. *Ibid.* 324/1 The Teso language belongs to a group which also includes the dialects spoken by the famous Masai.. and the Karamojo tribes. *Ibid.*, Kitching.. gave a most encouraging account of his successful work among the Teso. **1915** A. L. KITCHING *Handbk. Ateso Lang.* p. v, The Teso are a cheerful, industrious people, amenable to control.. yet the name of this tribe does not appear.. in any of the works on the peoples of the Uganda Protectorate... The Ateso dialect is spoken by a tribe of some 300,000 people living between Lake Kioga and Mt. Ehgon in.. the Ugandan Protectorate. **1935**, etc. [see SEBEI]. **1966** [see KARAMOJO]. **1973** *Sunday Tel.* 4 Mar. 8/2 The taller and more gaunt appearance of the Nilotic tribes—the Lango, the Acholi and the Iteso.

tessara- ('tɛsərə), also tessera-, a. Gr. τέσσαρα, -ερα, neuter pl. and comb. form of τέσσαρες, -ερες four, used in Greek compounds, and forming the first element in a few English words adopted from or formed on Greek. **ˌtessara-'decad** [DECAD], a group of fourteen. **tessaradeca'syllabon** [DECASYLLABON], a line of fourteen syllables. **'tessaraˌglot** *a.*, in, of, or pertaining to four languages; = TETRAGLOT. **'tessaraˌkost** [ad. Gr. τεσσαρακοστή a fortieth]: see quot. **tessa'raphthong** [after DIPHTHONG], a group of four vowels. **ˌtessera'tomic** *a.* [after *dichotomic*], involving division into four parts.

1855 W. H. MILL *Applic. Panth. Princ.* (1861) 152 In the text of St. Matthew, dividing the *tessarodecads at the captivity. **1874** FARRAR *Christ* 8 The symmetrical arrangement into tesseradecads. *c* **1610** BOLTON *Hypercritica* iv. §3 Chapman's Iliads, those I mean which are translated into *Tessara-decasyllabons, or lines of fourteen Syllables. **1716** M. DAVIES *Athen. Brit.* III. 73 Whose *Tessaraglott Bible [Complutensian Polyglot] was finish'd about 1517. **1851** BORROW *Lavengro* xiv. I. 191 A tessara-glot grammar.. of the French, Italian, Low Dutch, and English tongues. **1850** GROTE *Greece* II. lxiii. VIII. 138 Receiving.. three *tessarakosts (a Chian coin of unknown value) for each man among his seamen. **1887** *Sat. Rev.* 17 Dec. 818 What Mr. Gladstone would call the trichotomic, or rather the *tesseratomic, division of parties.

†**'tessel.** *Obs. rare.* [ad. L. or It. *tessella*. So F. *tesselle* (Littré).] = TESSELLA.

1657 TOMLINSON *Renou's Disp.* 132 Matter formed into Pils.. or planed into Tessels.

So †**'tesseled** *a.* [perh. ad. It. *tessellato*, pa. pple. of *tessellare* 'to make or worke checker-worke or inlaid worke' (Florio), f. *tessella* a small tessera: cf. F. *tessellé* (Littré)], tessellated.

1603 KNOLLES *Hist. Turks* (1621) 543 Yea all the house was paved with checker and tesseled worke.

tessel, -e, obs. forms of TEASEL.

‖**tessella** (tɛ'sɛlə). Pl. **-æ**; rarely **-as**. Also 8 **-ela**. [L., dim. of TESSERA.] A small tessera.

1693 tr. *Blancard's Phys. Dict.* (ed. 2), *Tessellæ*, the same with *Rotulæ* or *Tabellæ*. **1727-41** [see TESSELLATED 1]. **1753** CHAMBERS *Cycl. Supp.*, *Tesselæ*, a word used in pharmacy to express lozenges cut into regular figures. **1885** *Athenæum* 29 Aug. 278/3 No endeavour is made to fasten loose tessellæ into their sockets.

tessellar ('tɛsələ(r)), *a.* [f. prec. + -AR.] Of the nature or form of tessellæ.

1847 in WEBSTER. **1859** *Todd's Cycl. Anat.* V. 253/2 It [Lunaria Vulgaris] consists originally of a single layer of tessellar cells.

tessellate ('tɛsələt), *a.* (*sb.*) Also **-elate**. [ad. late L. *tessellāt-us*: see next.] = TESSELLATED.

1826 KIRBY & SP. *Entomol.* IV. xlvi. 289 *Tessellate*,.. painted in checquer-work. **1872** LONGF. *Wayside Inn* III. *Azrael* 2 King Solomon.. on the pavement tesselate Was walking. **1876** J. ELLIS *Caesar in Egypt* 30 Along the floor, Chromatic, tesselate with marbles rare.

B. *sb.* in ***variegated tessellate***, an American butterfly, *Hesperia montivagus*, found in Florida, Mexico, and the Rocky Mountains.

1909 in *Cent. Dict., Suppl.*

tessellate ('tɛsəleɪt), *v.* Also 8-9 **tesselate**. [f. ppl. stem of late or med.L. *tessellāre* (pa. pple. *tessellāt-us*: cf. also It. *tessellare* in Florio), f. L. *tessella* TESSELLA. The pa. pple. *tessellated* occurs earlier than the finite vb.: see next.]

1. *trans.* To make into a mosaic; to form a mosaic upon, adorn with mosaics; to construct (esp. a pavement) by combining variously coloured blocks so as to form a pattern.

1791 E. DARWIN *Bot. Gard.* I. 95 And dull Galena tessellates the floor. **1826** P. POUNDEN *France & It.* 27 The floor is tesselated with great elegance. **1862** RAWLINSON *Anc. Mon.* I. v. 125 Pieces of marble used for tesselating.

b. *transf.* and *fig.*

1817 COLERIDGE *Satyrane's Lett.* iii. in *Biog. Lit.*, etc. (1882) 264 The wood-work.. in old houses among us.. being painted red and green, it cuts and tesselates the buildings very gaily. **1858** E. FITZGERALD *Lett.* (1889) I. 269 It is most ingeniously tesselated into a sort of Epicurean Eclogue in a Persian Garden. **1869** LECKY *Europ. Mor.* I. ii. 335 The affectation of some to tesselate their conversation with antiquated and obsolete words.

2. To combine so as to form a mosaic; to fit into its place in a mosaic. In quots. *fig.*

1838–9 [implied in TESSELLATED 2]. **1861** J. PYCROFT *Ways & Words* 17 The sentences [of Sir J. Mackintosh] are rather tessellated than constructed; each word fitting admirably into its own place, but defying all transposition. **1879** FARRAR *St. Paul* II. 189 Many writers have maintained that this meaning is vague and general, .. impossible to tesselate into any formal scheme of salvation.

tessellated ('tɛsəleɪtɪd), *ppl. a.* [f. L. *tessellāt-us* or It. *tessellato* in same sense, with Eng. suffix. Used earlier than TESSELLATE *v.*, of which it subseq. became the pa. pple.]

1. Composed of small blocks of variously coloured material arranged to form a pattern; formed of or ornamented with mosaic work.

1712 HEARNE *Collect.* (O.H.S.) III. 311 The tessellated Pavement at Stansfield. **1727–41** CHAMBERS *Cycl.*, *Tessellated pavement, pavimentum Tessellatum*, a rich pavement of mosaic work, made of curious small square marbles, bricks or tyles, called *tesselæ*, from the form of dies. **1877** C. GEIKIE *Christ* lxii. (1879) 758 The old golden seat of Archelaus, was set down in the tessellated floor of the tribunal.

fig. **1828** MACAULAY *Misc. Writ.* (1860) I. 224 Laborious and tesselated imitations of Mason and Gray. **1864** *Sat. Rev.* 31 Dec. 789 The fall of a dovetailed and tesselated Cabinet. **1868** GLADSTONE *Juv. Mundi* xiv. §1 (1869) 490 The several squares of that tesselated nation, each with its local patriotism and limited traditions.

2. Combined or arranged so as to form a mosaic.

1838–9 HALLAM *Hist. Lit.* IV. IV. v. §51. 253 The mind is pleased to recognise the tesselated fragments of Ovid and Tibullus. **1853** C. L. BRACE *Home Life Germany* 116 The floors are .. of the most minutely tesselated marble.

3. *transf.* Consisting of or arranged in small cubes or squares; in *Bot.* and *Zool.* having colours or surface-divisions in regularly arranged squares or patches; chequered, reticulated.

tessellated cells, cells arranged in layers. ***tessellated epithelium***, pavement epithelium (PAVEMENT *sb.* 4). ***tessellated pyrites***, iron pyrites, crystallizing in cubes.

1695 WOODWARD *Nat. Hist. Earth* IV. (1723) 198 Crystallized Ores, and Minerals, e.g... the tessellated *Pyritæ*, or *Ludus Paracelsi*. **1777** WATSON in *Phil. Trans.* LXVIII. 866 A very pure specimen of tessellated lead ore. **1828** MISS MITFORD *Village* Ser. III. 60 (*Quiet Gentlew.*) A bit of white mosaic, a tessellated quilt. **1829** LOUDON *Encycl. Pl.* (1836) 113 Fruit .. a fleshy tesselated berry. **1839** DARWIN *Voy. Nat.* v. 97 The apar [armadillo] .. having only three moveable bands; the rest of its tesselated covering being nearly inflexible. **1854** *Pereira's Pol. Light* 237 What Dr. Brewster has termed tesselated or composite crystals .. consist of several crystals .. united so as to form a compound crystal. **1875** SIR W. TURNER in *Encycl. Brit.* I. 847/1 Tessellated .. or squamous epithelium is situated on the free surface of the mucous lining of the mouth.

tessellation (tɛsə'leɪʃən). [n. of action f. TESSELLATE *v.*: see -ATION.]

1. The action or art of tessellating; tessellated condition; *concr.* a piece of tessellated work.

1813 J. FORSYTH *Italy* 111 The work is not mosaic, for there is no tessellation. **1862** MERIVALE *Rom. Emp.* VII. lxvii. 540 Like the several pieces of a variegated tessellation. *a***1878** SIR G. G. SCOTT *Lect. Archit.* (1879) II. 253 Wide-spreading floors, rich with marble tesselation.

fig. **1840** H. ROGERS *Ess.* (1874) II. v. 250 Numberless passages of Jeremy Taylor .. are a little better than a curious tesselation of English, Greek, and Latin. **1863** LE FANU *Ho. by Chyd.* (ed. 2) III. 307 The writings of the Apostolic Fathers are, in a great measure, a tesselation of holy writ.

2. An arrangement or close fitting together of minute parts or distinct colours: cf. TESSELLATED 3.

1660 SHARROCK *Vegetables* 144 Yet they, instead of those elegant Tessellations, are beautified otherwise in their site with as great curiosity. **1822–34** *Good's Study Med.* (ed. 4) IV. 500 The whole surface of the body .. having exhibited a sordid tesselation of crusts. **1905** J. ORR *Probl. O. Test.* vii. 201 The newer criticism with its multiplication of documents .. and its minute tesselation of texts.

tessellite ('tɛsɪlaɪt). *Min.* Also tesselite. [f. TESSELLA + -ITE[1].] A variety of Apophyllite, exhibiting in polarized light a tessellated structure.

1819 BREWSTER in *Edin. Phil. Jrnl.* June 5 The tessellated structure .. is a property so singular and so distinctive, that I would propose to mark it by the name of Tesselite. **1868** DANA *Min.* (ed. 5) 416 Tesselite, from Faröe, is a cubical variety, exhibiting a tesselated structure in polarized light.

‖**tessera** ('tɛsərə). Pl. tesseræ. [L., f. Ionic Gr. τέσσερες, -ρα, = Attic τέσσαρες, -ρα four.]

1. *Anc. Hist.* A small quadrilateral tablet of wood, bone, ivory, or the like, used for various purposes, as a token, tally, ticket, label, etc.

tessera of hospitality (= L. *tessera hospitalis*), a die broken between host and guest, and kept as a means of recognition.

1656 BLOUNT *Glossogr.*, *Tessera*, a thing in every part square as a dye; also a watchword, or signal, a note, mark or token, &c. **1846** KEIGHTLEY *Notes Virg.*, *Georg.* II. 508 In the ancient theatres .. each spectator's *tessera* designated the *cuneus* and row in which he was to sit. **1850** LEITCH tr. *C. O. Müller's Anc. Art* §412 (ed. 2) 569 One brings him a tessera of hospitality from Sisyphus. **1886** *Guide Exhib. Galleries Brit. Mus.* 186 Objects in bone and ivory, such as caskets, gladiatorial *tesseræ*, tickets for the theatre, dice.

b. *fig.* A distinguishing sign or token; a watchword, a password. (The earliest use in English.)

1647 JER. TAYLOR *Lib. Proph.* i. 17 That Creed made so explicite as a tessera of a Christian. **1656** [see prec.]. **1662** OWEN *Animadv. Fiat Lux* ii. Wks. 1855 XIV. 29 Making subjection to the pope in all things the tessera and rule of all church communion. **1795** in Calderwood *Dying Testimonies* (1806) 460 Exacts it from them as a tessera of their loyalty. **1890** HATCH *Hibbert Lect.* xii. 344 It was, so to speak, a tessera or password.

2. *spec.* Each of the small square (usually cubical) pieces of marble, glass, tile, etc., of which a mosaic pavement or the like is composed. Usually in pl.

1797 S. LYSONS *Rom. Antiq. Woodchester* 4 The tesseræ of which this [mosaic] pavement is composed, are, for the most part, nearly cubes of half an inch... Many are triangular, and of various other shapes. **1843** *Civil Eng. & Arch. Jrnl.* VI. 125/1 The next point to be observed with reference to the Roman tesseræ, is the want of uniformity in their size and shape. **1894** *Times* 5 Mar. 14/1 The workmen had to learn to set the tesseræ, one by one and each in its proper place, into the cement on the wall.

b. *transf.* Any one of the quadrilateral divisions into which a surface is divided by intersecting lines; e.g. by the lines of latitude and longitude.

1873 MAXWELL *Electr. & Magn.* (1881) I. 198 So that the spherical surface is divided into quadrilaterals or tesseræ .. bounded by meridian circles and parallels of latitude.

c. *Zool.* Each of the plates of which the carapace of an armadillo is composed.

1909 in *Cent. Dict.*, *Suppl.*

†**3.** (See quots.) *Obs.*

1815 J. SMITH *Panorama Sc. & Art* I. 257 John's *tessera* is perhaps the best of those artificial compositions which are designed for roofing. **1842–76** GWILT *Archit.* Gloss., *Tessera* .. this name was .. applied to a composition used some years ago for covering flat roofs, but now .. quite abandoned.

tessera-: see TESSARA-.

tesseract ('tɛsərækt). *Math.* Also tessaract. [f. TESSARA- + Gr. ἀκτ-ίς ray.] A four-dimensional hypercube. Also *fig.* Hence **tesse'ractic** *a.*

1888 C. H. HINTON *New Era of Thought* II. iii. 118 We call the figure it [*sc.* a cube] traces a Tessaract. *Ibid.* vii. 161 The whole of the 81 cubes make one single tessaractic set extending three inches in each of the four directions. **1919** R. T. BROWNE *Mystery of Space* v. 134 The hyper-cube or tesseract is described by moving the generating cube in the direction in which the fourth dimension extends. **1960** *Electronic Engin.* XXXII. 347/1 Fig. 8 .. shows a four-dimensional 'tessaract' (the four-dimensional analogue of a cube). **1968** *Listener* 15 Feb. 201 He likes to see A gulping of tesseracts and Gondals in Our crazed search. **1974** S. SHELDON *Other Side of Midnight* xviii. 332 For Catherine time had lost its circadian rhythm; she had fallen into a tesseract of time, and day and night blended into one.

†**tesseraic** (tɛsə'reɪɪk), *a. Obs. rare.* [f. TESSERA + -IC, after *mosaic*.] Of, pertaining to, or composed of tesseræ; mosaic, tessellated.

*a***1711** SIR R. ATKYNS *Hist. Gloucester* (1712) 778/1 Stidcot .. where some of the Tesseraick Work of the Romans has lately been dug up. **1778** *Eng. Gazetteer* (ed. 2) s.v. *Woodchester*, There is a tesseraick pavement of painted beasts and flowers in its church-yard.

tesseral ('tɛsərəl), *a.* [f. TESSERA + -AL[1].]

1. Of, pertaining to, or resembling a tessera or tesseræ; composed of tesseræ.

1846 WORCESTER cites *Edinb. Rev.*

2. *Cryst.* = ISOMETRIC 3, CUBIC *a.* 1 c.

1854 *Pereira's Pol. Light* 191 The cubic or octohedral system. Synonymes.—The regular, the tessular, the tesseral, or the isometric system. **1878** GURNEY *Crystallogr.* 37 Crystals possessing this highest possible degree of symmetry are said to belong to the Cubic or Tesseral System.

3. *Math.* Relating to the tesseræ of a spherical surface (see TESSERA 2 b), as in ***tesseral harmonic***, a spherical surface harmonic which is the product of two factors depending respectively on latitude and longitude.

1873 MAXWELL *Electr. & Magn.* (1881) I. 196 We may now write the expressions for the two tesseral harmonics. *Ibid.* 198 To find the surface integral of the square of any tesseral harmonic taken over the sphere. **1887** HOBSON in *Trans. Camb. Philos. Soc.* (1889) XIV. 211 The zonal and tesseral harmonics .. are exhibited as series.

†**tesse'rarian**, *a. Obs. rare.* [f. L. *tesserārius* pertaining to tesseræ or dice + -AN.] Of or pertaining to dice or to gaming. ***tesserarian art*** [L. *ars tesseraria*], the art of dice-playing. So †**tesse'rarious** *a. Obs. rare*[−0], in same sense.

1656 BLOUNT *Glossogr.*, *Tesserarious* .. of, or belonging to a die, or to *tessera*. **1781** GIBBON *Decl. & F.* xxxi. III. 209 A superior degree of skill in the Tesserarian art (.. the game of dice and tables). **1797** *Sporting Mag.* X. 44.

tesserate ('tɛsərət), *a. rare*[−1]. [f. TESSERA + -ATE[2]. Cf. obs. F. *tesseré* (Cotgr.).] = TESSELLATED. So '**tesserated** *a. rare.* ? *Obs.*

1717 TABOR in *Phil. Trans.* XXX. 549 A Description of the tesserated Pavement at East Bourne, near Pevensey. **1812** HOBHOUSE *Journ.* I. (1813) 969 The tesserated mosaic [in S. Sophia's] with which the concave above the windows and the dome are encrusted. **1897** F. THOMPSON *New Poems* 139 With the gold-tesserate floors of Jove.

tesseratomic: see TESSARA-.

‖**tessi'tura.** *Mus.* [It.] The part of the total compass of a melody or voice-part in which most of its tones lie. Also *transf.*

1884 GROVE *Dict. Mus.* IV. 94/1 A term .. used by the Italians to indicate how the music of a piece 'lies'; .. what is the prevailing or average position of its notes in relation to the compass of the voice or instrument for which it is written... 'Range' does not at all give the idea, as the range may be extended, and the general *tessitura* limited; while the range may be high and the *tessitura* low or medium. **1891** in *Cent. Dict.* **1948** *Penguin Music Mag.* Feb. 76 One can hardly blame him, for the *tessitura* is sometimes cruelly high —so many Italian baritone parts seem to have been written for tenors in reduced circumstances. **1956** AUDEN & KALLMAN *Magic Flute* (1957) 116 You won't hear a word in Our high tessitura. **1978** *Early Music* Apr. 197/2 He chose singers for whom the resulting tessituras did not mean any strain. **1982** *English World-Wide* II. 136 Tessitura (or the characteristic range of notes, or compass, within which the pitch fluctuation falls) was felt to be generally wider in Br[itish] E[nglish] than in S[ingapore] E[nglish].

‖**tesson** ('tɛsən, ‖ tɛsɔ̃). [F. *tesson* piece of broken glass or earthenware (13th c.), deriv. of OF. *test* pot.] A fragment of glass or pottery.

1858 BIRCH *Anc. Pottery* II. 238 The tessons used for Mosaic pavements were made of marbles, glass, and of a red brick.

tessular ('tɛsjʊlə(r)), *a. Cryst.* [f. mod.L. **tessula*, irreg. dim. of TESSERA + -AR.] = TESSERAL 2.

1796 KIRWAN *Elem. Min.* (ed. 2) I. 139 In nodules, or in half rounded masses, or tessular. **1805–17** R. JAMESON *Char. Min.* (ed. 3) 132 Where there are many crystals together, but merely simply aggregated; and these are either, 1. On one another; .. [this] occurs principally in tessular crystals, as in galena or lead-glance, and calcareous-spar. **1854** *Pereira's Pol. Light* 165 The equiaxed crystals constitute one system, called the cubic, octohedral or tessular system. **1869** PHILLIPS *Vesuv.* x. 294 The crystallization is on the tessular pattern.

test (tɛst), *sb.*[1] Forms: 4–5 *pl.* testes, -is, 6 teste, taest, 7 tast, teast, 6– test. [a. OF. *test* masc., a pot (12th c.), mod.F. *têt* a cupel, etc.:—L. *testum, testu* neut., collateral form of *testa* a tile, earthen vessel, pot. In OF. *test* and *teste* (L. *testa*) were sometimes confused, and *teste* sometimes occurs in 15–16th c. Eng. In modern use, treated mainly as noun of action from TEST *v.*[2]]

1. *orig.* The cupel used in treating gold or silver alloys or ore; now *esp.* the cupel, with the iron frame or basket which contains it, forming the movable hearth of a reverberatory furnace: see CUPEL *sb.* 1.

*c***1386** CHAUCER *Can. Yeom. Prol. & T.* 265 Of oure siluer citrinacion .. Oure yngottes testes and many mo. **1552** in P. H. Hore *Wexford* (1901) II. 237 Of 1031 lbs. weight of lead they had from the taest 14 lbs. weight of silver. **1555** EDEN *Decades W. Ind.* VI. 339 Meltynge it [gold] in a fornace in a bayne or teste of leade. **1594** PLAT *Jewell-ho.* III. 36 Get a large panne, such as they make their testes of bone ashes in. **1622** MALYNES *Anc. Law-Merch.* 281 The Copple or Teast doth drinke in some two penny weight of Siluer with the Lead. **1674** RAY *Collect. Wds.*, *Smelting Silver* (E.D.S.) 9 The test is of an oval figure, and occupies all the bottom of the furnace. **1758** REID tr. *Macquer's Chym.* I. 315 Put one half of this Lead into a test, and spread it equally thereon. **1853** URE *Dict. Arts* II. 657 The bed or bottom of the furnace, when in operation, is formed by a shallow elliptical vessel, called a test or test-bottom. **1877** KNIGHT *Dict. Mech.* 2535/2 The test is fixed as a cupeling-hearth in the reverberatory furnace.

2. a. That by which the existence, quality, or genuineness of anything is or may be determined; 'means of trial' (J.); hence, in phrases ***to bring*** or ***put to the test***, ***to bear*** or ***stand the test***, the testing or trial of the quality of anything; examination, trial, proof.

(Cf. **1651** FRENCH *Distill.* v. 138 Prove this tree at the test, and it yeeldeth good gold. **1661** BLOUNT *Glossogr.* (ed. 2) s.v., A broad instrument .. on which Refiners do fine, refine and part gold and silver from other Mettals, or (as we use to say) *put them to the Test.*)

1594 NASHE *Unfort. Trav.* 40 A delicate wench .. which I would faine haue had to the grand test, whether she were cunning in Alcumie or no. **1602** SHAKS. *Ham.* III. iv. 142 It is not madnesse That I haue vttered; bring me to the Test. **1610** —— *Temp.* IV. i. 7 Thou Hast strangely stood the test. **1754** CHATHAM *Lett. Nephew* iv. 25 The noblest sentiment of the human breast is here brought to the test. **1813** SIR H. DAVY *Agric. Chem.* (1814) 11 Simple tests of the relative nourishing powers of the different species of food. **1820** W. IRVING *Sketch Bk.* II. 148 Invaluable maxims which have borne the test of time. **1838** JAMES *Robber* iv, I will not put them to the test. **1873** SYMONDS *Grk. Poets* iii. 89 Time, says Theognis, and experience and calamity are the true tests of friendship. **1904** NICHOLSON *Keltic Researches* Pref. 4 Even as between the Irishman and the Welshman, the language-test is not a race-test.

†**b.** A proof, sample, specimen. *Obs. rare.*

1769 COOK *Voy. round World* II. iii. (1773) II. 328 Rather satisfied with having given a test of their courage by twice insulting a vessel so much superior to their own, than intimidated by the shot.

c. *Cricket* and *Rugby Football.* Short for *test-match*: see 7 b. In *S. Afr.*, an international match in any of a wide range of games and sports, including Rugby.

1908 *Westm. Gaz.* 16 Jan. 7/1 England is now a game to the bad, and there are only two more 'Tests' to play. **1909** *Ibid.* 6 Sept. 10/4 We are to play sixteen matches in all, including five Tests. **1933** M. Nicholls in I. D. Difford *Hist. S. Afr. Rugby Football* xxiv. 336 In the first Test we won 16 scrums to their 36. **1934** [see Buckley's]. **1954** R. T. Gabe in Wooller & Owen *Fifty Years of All Blacks* i. 14 We travelled over land and a rough sea..to play a Test in Wellington..to lose by 9 points to 3. **1955** [see deputize *v.* 2]. **1971** *Rand Daily Mail* 4 Sept. 24/7 A series of diving Tests have been arranged against Rhodesia. **1972** *Daily Tel.* 14 Dec. 35/5 A week off before an international, or Test as we call them, is preferable to a mid-week match [New Zealander *loq.*].

3. That by which beliefs or opinions, esp. in religion, are tested or tried; *spec.* the oaths or declarations prescribed by the Test Act of 1673; esp. in phrase *to take the test*; also, either of the test acts.

1665 *Sp. Speaker Ho. Comm. to King* 31 Oct. in *Lords Jrnls.* XI. 700/1 We have prepared a Shiboleth a Test to distinguish amongst them, who..give Hopes of future Conformity, and who of..evil Disposition remain obdurate. **1672-3** (Mar. 12) in *Grey's Deb. Ho. Comm.* II. 97 [Mr. Harwood] Tendered a proviso for renouncing the doctrine of transubstantiation for a farther test. **1675** (May 10) *Calr. St. Papers, Dom., Chas. II* 112 The Test as now agreed on:—I, A. B., do declare [etc.]. **1682** in *Scott. Antiq.* July (1901) 4 One of the late regentis..having demurred to take the test apoynted by act of parliament. *a* **1715** Burnet *Own Time* an. 1685 iv. (1724) I. 654 The King..had declared that he would be served by none but those who would vote for the repeal of the Tests. **1789** *Constitution U.S.* Art. vi, No religious test shall ever be required as a qualification to any office. **1797** Hey *Lect. Div.* II. iii. xiv. §15. 155 A Man is deemed a Member of the Church of England, who takes the Sacrament according to the usage of the Church of England, and declares against Transubstantiation; from whence the Tests are called sacramental tests. **1889** *Pall Mall G.* 3 July 2/2 The Government promised last night to abolish tests in the case of the 'lay chairs' in the Scotch universities. **1906** H. Paul in *19th Cent.* May 717 The belief in tests ought to be dead as the belief in witches.

4. a. *Chem.* The action or process of examining a substance under known conditions in order to determine its identity or that of one of its constituents; also, a substance by means of which this may be done.

1800 Henry *Epit. Chem.* (1808) 322 The readiest method of judging of the contents of natural waters, is by applying what are termed tests, or re-agents. **1812** [see reagent 1]. **1854** J. Scoffern in *Orr's Circ. Sc., Chem.* 479 Arseniuretted hydrogen..employed, as a means of removing and discovering arsenic, is called *Marsh's test.* **1900** Briggs & Stewart *Inorg. Chem.* Gen. Direct., The student is advised to learn the tests for each metal and acid. **1900** Shenstone *Elem. Inorg. Chem.* xxv. §396 A solution of baryta affords us a most delicate test for carbon dioxide.

b. *Mechanics*, etc. The action by which the physical properties of substances, materials, machines, etc. are tested, in order to determine their ability to satisfy particular requirements.

Among these are ***bending test, compressive t., drop t., tensile t., transverse t.***, etc.; also with sb. in objective relation, as ***boiler, brake, engine test***; also road test.

1877 Knight *Dict. Mech.* 2539 Observations are made at short intervals..until the test is closed by rapid heating..and excessive increase of friction. **1884** *Ibid., Suppl.* 888 The machine requires but little change for making tests in compression. **1894** Lineham *Mech. Engin.* 376 The straining cylinder, having water admitted beneath its piston for tensile, and above it for compressive tests. **1904** *Kent's Mech. Engin. Pocket Bk.* (1910) 282 In Transverse tests the strength of bars of rectangular section is found to vary directly as the breadth of the specimen tested, as the square of its depth, and inversely as its length. *Ibid.* 864 Competitive tests were made of fourteen boilers. **1956** [see nuclear *a.* 3 c]. **1958** *Economist* 8 Nov. 481/2 Russia is trying to make the West agree to a ban on tests. **1968** [see *M.O.T.* s.v. M 5]. **1976** *Star* (Sheffield) 30 Nov. 12/6 Up to £50 paid for scrap and test failure cars and vans.

c. The process or an instance of testing the academic, mental, physiological, or other qualities and conditions of a human subject; in academic and similar contexts usu. implying a simpler, less formal procedure than an examination; freq. as the second element in a collocation or combination denoting a particular kind of test, or used contextually to imply one of these.

A number of other collocations and combinations will be found under the first element, as *aptitude, blood, breath, intelligence, means, mental, performance, pregnancy, screen, skin, spot test.*

1910, etc. [see Binet-Simon]. **1918** [see *proficiency test* s.v. proficiency 3]. **1927** [see *personality test* s.v. personality 7]. **1928** *Sunday Dispatch* 22 July 4/2 He had had a film test, at the conclusion of which he was told that he filmed remarkably well. **1933** [see driving *vbl. sb.* 3 a]. *a* **1935** [see fitness]. **1941** B. Schulberg *What makes Sammy Run?* xi. 198 I'm getting fed up with these floosies you're always promising..a day's work or a test [i.e. a screen test]. **1955** E. H. Clements *Discord in Air* xi. 149 Mummy always drives. I haven't taken my test yet. **1959** [see pass-fail *a.*]. **1960** [see breathalyser]. **1968** [see *I.Q.* s.v. I. III].

d. *Austral.* and *N.Z.* a test for the proportion of butter fat in milk.

1928 *Bulletin* (Sydney) 14 Mar. 32/1 'You should be proud of her,' said I... 'My oath I am!' he made reply—'She gives an eight-five test!' **1950** *N.Z. Jrnl. Agric.* Mar. 270/2 Several [milk] cans can be filled at the same time so that the tests of all cans are, as far as practicable, identical. **1966** G. W. Turner *Eng. Lang. Austral. & N.Z.* iii. 45 A cow with 'a good test', that is, milk rich in butter-fat, may be more valuable than another cow that gives more milk.

5. *Microsc.* A test object: see 7 b.

1832 Goring in Pritchard *Microsc. Cabinet* xviii. 175 A *test* is an object which serves to render sensible both the perfection and imperfection of an instrument, as to defining and penetrating power. **1837** Goring & Pritchard *Microgr.* 160 A..representation of an excellent and very beautiful test, a feather from the wing of Morpho Menelaüs, (being the first object in which I observed the very remarkable property of the lines as tests).

6. An apparatus for determining the flash-point of hydrocarbon oils.

1877 Knight *Dict. Mech., Test*,..4. An apparatus for proving petroleum and similar hydrocarbon oils by ascertaining the temperature at which they evolve explosive vapours.

7. *attrib.* and *Comb.* **a.** General combs.: 'of or pertaining to a test', 'taken, done, or made as a test'; as, in sense 2 a, ***test-bar, -ground, -log*** (log *sb.*[1] 7), ***-plaster, question, -room, -run, -sentence, symptom, -tree, -valve, -work***; in sense 2 c, ***test batsman, captain, cricket, cricketer, team, trial***; in sense 3, ***test-formula, -law, -man, -monger, -oath***; also ***test-free, -ridden*** adjs.; in sense 4, ***test-anxiety, bottle, certificate, -liquid, -liquor, performance, -phial, -solution, -spoon, -stirrer***.

1972 *Jrnl. Social Psychol.* LXXXVII. 155 Few studies have examined the relationship of birth order to *test anxiety. **1976** Dexter & Makins *Testkill* 139 The *Test batsman, even after net practice, is still forced to use the first few overs in the middle as a warm-up. **1839** Ure *Dict. Arts* 71 We pour into the *test bottle 2 thousandths of the *decime* solution of silver. **1975** *Cricketer* May 8/1 Ian Michael Chappell, the activist of *Test captains, has led Australia in 26 Tests in four countries. **1976** *Alyn & Deeside Observer* 10 Dec. 10/2 He did not have an excise licence, a driving licence or a *test certificate. **1931** J. Hobbs (*title*) Playing for England! My *test-cricket story. **1959** M. Gilbert *Blood & Judgement* iii. 36 In September a *test cricketer was still news. **1890** *Tablet* 5 July 14 A *test-ground for the historian. **1687** *Reasons to Move Protest. Dissenters* 3 You cannot say it is a Divine Law that requir'd the Parliament to make this *Test-Law... To abolish the Test-Laws therefore is Lawful. **1862** *Catal. Internat. Exhib.* II. xiii. 12 Apparatus for centigrade testing,..preparation of the *test liquors. **1904** *Electr. World & Engin.* 9 Jan. 90 (Cent. Suppl.) A typical *test-log upon a 550-hp engine. **1693** Shadwell *Volunteers* iii. i, A furious agitator and *test-man. **1687** *Reasons for Repeal of Tests* 4 In the Year 1675 the same Test was set on Foot in Parliament, by the *Test-Mongers, with design to have made it more Extensive. **1715-16** in J. O. Payne *Eng. Cath. Nonjurors of 1715* (1885) 9, I cannot take the *Test and Abjuration Oaths enjoined by Acts of Parliament. **1863** H. Cox *Instit.* iii. viii. 718 In consequence of his inability to take the test-oath. **1942** *Mind* LI. 175 A factor which improves certain *test-performances when it is not merely absent, but actually negative. **1909** *Service for the King* May 103 The heat is gauged by the potters..who place in the oven test-pieces of pottery, which can be drawn out. **1897** *Daily News* 19 Jan. 3/6 Continued movement of the front is manifested by the cracking of *test plaster put in the fractured groining..six months ago. **1867** Furniv. & Hales *Percy Folio* I. 247 The *test question put to the page before the assignation is disclosed. **1889** *Pall Mall G.* 3 July 2/2 This is why..English *test-ridden Theology lags so much behind German. **1905** *Westm. Gaz.* 20 Sept. 8/1 The methods of the *test-room are being applied..to the degree of moisture quicker methods involve. **1877** Raymond *Statist. Mines & Mining* 302 A *test-run made upon about three tons showed it to contain 51 ounces of silver and 41 per cent. of lead per ton. **1901** Kipling *Kim* x. 262 Kim repeated the *test-sentence. **1977** *Word 1972* XXVIII. 104 There were 15 test sentences in the battery in which the English strongly suggested the use of a diminutive ending in Gaelic. **1871** Garrod *Mat. Med.* (ed. 3) 428 The volumetric solutions of nitrate of silver and of iodine are also made use of as *test-solutions for qualitative analysis. **1955** *Radio Times* 22 Apr. 31/2 The *Test Team arrived in this country at the beginning of the week. **1883** G. M. Hopkins *Let.* 25 Oct. (1956) 323 This was the sin of Adam and Eve, who, both in different ways, eat of the '*Test-tree'. **1977** *Test trial [see pencil *v.* 2 c]. **1910** *Westm. Gaz.* 19 Jan. 4/2 She wanted to test the gas at the purifier..but found the *test-valve choked. **1895** *Daily News* 19 Feb. 9/2 Service in relieving distress..by means of carefully-planned *test-work.

b. Special Combs.: **test ban**, a ban on the testing of nuclear weapons; **test bed**, a piece of equipment for testing machines, esp. aircraft engines, before their acceptance for general use; also *attrib.* and *fig.*; **test board** (*Electr.*): see quot.; **test-body** *Physics*, the imaginary object on which a thought-experiment is carried out; **test-boiler**, a boiler for testing fuel or steam-apparatus, or supplying steam-pressure for testing other boilers (*Cent. Dict., Suppl.* 1909); **test-bottom**, = sense 1; also, the cake of gold or silver formed in the bottom of a cupel; **test-box** (*Telegr.*), a box fitted with terminals through which the wires are led, for convenience in testing; **test card**, (*a*) *Ophthalm.*, a large card printed with rows of letters of decreasing size for use in testing visual acuity (cf. Snellen); (*b*) *Television*, a diagrammatic still picture transmitted outside normal programme hours and designed for use in judging the quality and position of the image on any particular screen; **test-case** (*Law*), a case, the decision of which is taken as determining that of a number of others in which the same question of law is involved; also *transf.* and *attrib.*; **test chart** *Ophthalm.* = *test card* (a) above; **test-cock**, (*a*) a valved cock for clearing a steam engine cylinder of water; (*b*) a tap through which a sample of fluid may be drawn for examination; (*c*) a tap by means of which the level of water in a boiler or the like may be ascertained; **test-drive** *v. trans.* (orig. *U.S.*), to drive (a motor vehicle) in order to determine its qualities with a view to its regular use; **test-fire** orig. *U.S.*, to fire (a gun or missile) experimentally; **test flight**, a flight during which the performance of an aircraft is tested; **test-fly** *v. trans.*, to test the performance of (an aircraft) in flight; hence **test-flying** *vbl. sb.*; **test-frame**, the iron frame or basket in which a cupel is placed: see sense 1; **test-furnace**, a reverberatory refining furnace in which silver-bearing alloys are treated; also *fig.*; **test-glass**, a small cylindrical glass vessel for holding liquids while being tested; **test-hole**, (*a*) a tap-hole in a furnace; (*b*) = *test well* below; **test-lead**, pure granulated lead used in silver assays (*C.D., Suppl.* 1909); **test letter**, (*a*) a letter sent as a test of the honesty of the messenger; (*b*) see *test-type* (*C.D., Suppl.* 1909); **test-lines**, the lines on a test-plate (*Cassell's Encycl. Dict.* 1888); **test-market** *v. trans.* (and *intr.*) (orig. *U.S.*), to put (a new product) on to the market, usu. in a limited area, in order to determine consumers' response to it; also *transf.*; also as *sb.*, an area in which a product is test-marketed; hence **test-marketing** *vbl. sb.*; **test match** (*Cricket*), one of a series of matches played as a test which is the better of two bodies of players (e.g. of England and Australia); also in *Rugby Football* (orig. *S. Afr.*), one of a series of matches between a touring team and teams representing the country of the tour; an international; **test-meal**, a meal of specified quantity and composition, given as a test of digestive power; **test-meter**, (*a*) a meter for testing the consumption of gas by burners; (*b*) a meter used as a standard by which others are tried (*Funk's Stand. Dict.* 1895); **test-mixer**: see quot.; **test object**, (*a*) a minute object used as a test of the power of a microscope; (*b*) an object upon which a testing experiment is tried; **test-paper**, (*a*) a paper impregnated with a chemical solution which changes colour in contact with certain other chemicals, and thus becomes a test of the presence of the latter; (*b*) *U.S.* a document produced in court in determining a question of handwriting (Webster, 1847); (*c*) a paper set beforehand to try whether a student is fit and ready for an examination; **test-piece**, (*a*) a piece of anything used for testing; = *test-specimen*; (*b*) a piece performed by each of the competitors in a musical contest to determine which is the best; **test pilot**, one who test-flies an aircraft; also (with hyphen) as *v. trans.*; hence **test-piloting** *vbl. sb.*; **test-pit** *Archæol.*, a pit dug to gain an idea of the contents of a site; also *fig.*; **test-plate**, (*a*) a glass plate ruled with very fine lines, used in testing the power of microscope objectives (Knight *Dict. Mech.* 1877); (*b*) a piece of pottery on which colours are tried before being used on the pieces to be decorated (*Cent. Dict.* 1891); (*c*) a slip of glass used in mixing test-solutions (Knight); **test-pump**, a force-pump used in testing pipes, cylinders, and the like; **test range**, a range (range *sb.*[1] 11 c) where missiles are tested; **test-retest** *a. Psychol.*, of or designating a method by which a test is given to a subject on two occasions separated by a lapse of time; **test rig** *Engin.*, an apparatus used for assessing the performance of a piece of mechanical or electrical equipment; **test-ring**, (*a*) see quot.; (*b*) a ring-shaped piece of iron, etc., taken as a sample of the metal of which it is made (*Cent. Dict., Suppl.* 1909); **test-roll**, (*a*) a roll signed by those who have complied with a test or tests as prescribed by the various test acts; (*b*) the roll signed by a member of the House of Lords or Commons after having taken the oath or made the declaration required of him as such; **test signal**, a sequence of electrical impulses used for testing purposes in television broadcasting; **test specimen**, a piece of metal, etc. prepared for a mechanical test; **test strip**, (*a*) *Cinemat.* (see quot. 1940); (*b*) *Photogr.* (see quot. 1973); **test-type**, letters of graduated sizes used by opticians in testing sight; **test well** *Oil Industry*, a well made in testing a site for oil; **test-word**, (*a*) *Psychol.*, a word used in a test; (*b*) *Onomastics*, a word used to determine the presence of a particular linguistic form or influence. Also TEST ACT, TEST-TUBE.

1958 *New Statesman* 27 Dec. 898/1 More progress was registered at Geneva last week, when the *test-ban conference approved a British draft of Article Four of the treaty. **1971** H. TREVELYAN *Worlds Apart* xvi. 177 As we saw it, there were two elements in Soviet thinking about a test-ban. **1979** G. F. NEWMAN *List* vi. 55 Kennedy sees the test ban treaty as a step toward peace. **1914** *Flight* 21 Mar. 312/1 The 120 h.p. engine entered by the Green Engine Co. for the Military Aeroplane Engine Competition is mounted on a tilting *test bed. **1924** S. R. ROGET *Dict. Electr. Terms* 260 *Test bed*, a base plate or foundation upon which machines may readily be mounted for testing purposes. **1937** *Times* 13 Apr. (Brit. Motor Number) p. xv/4 The car engines undergo a long and thorough trial on the test-bed. **1961** *Aeroplane* CI. 791/1 Two VTOL test-bed aircraft using the G.E. J85-5 fan-lift engine. **1963** *Listener* 28 Mar. 542/2 The Russian leaders.. have spent the last fifteen years on the test-bed of world strategy, feeling the fearful and complex stresses and strains that that involves. **1978** *Sci. Amer.* July 30/1 On test beds turbine-inlet temperatures of well over 1,650 degrees C. have been achieved for at least a decade. **1902** T. O'C. SLOANE *Stand. Electr. Dict.* App., **Test Board*, a board provided with switches or spring-jacks connected to separate lines, so that testing instruments may be readily connected to any particular line. **1920** A. S. EDDINGTON *Space, Time & Gravitation* iv. 64 A massive body, such as the earth, seems to be surrounded by a field of latent force, ready, if another body enters the field, to become active, and transmit motion. One usually thinks of this influence as existing in the space round the earth even when there is no *test-body to be affected. **1955** L. ROSENFELD in W. Pauli *Niels Bohr* 71 This meant that in studying the measurability of field components we must use as test-bodies finite distributions of charge and current, and not point charges. **1853** *Test-bottom [see sense 1]. **1869** *Proc. Amer. Phil. Soc.* XI. 92 A cake or test-bottom [of silver]... Its weight was 4343 ounces Troy. **1876** PREECE & SIVEW. *Telegraphy* 273 The wire is.. put to earth at the *test-box there. **1892** A. DUANE tr. *Fuchs's Text-bk. Opthalm.* III. ii. 609 When the visual acuity has become so reduced that the largest letters of Snellen's *test-card can no longer be recognized at 6 metres, the patient must go up nearer it. **1935** *Popular Wireless* 16 Mar. 14/2 The 'test cards' radiated recently by the B.B.C. have.. been the cause of a lot of correspondence. **1949** H. C. WESTON *Sight, Light & Efficiency* vii. 245 External light sources must be relied upon for illuminating the test-cards. **1962** *Which?* Mar. 70/2 To measure the resolution, we used the BS test-slide which has blocks of parallel lines of various thicknesses and spacings, similar to the test card shown to television viewers so that they can adjust their sets for a clear, sharp picture. **1978** S. WILSON *Dealer's Move* III. vi. 103 A buzzing in my head to match the buzzing of the test card on the screen. **1894** W. ARCHER in *World* 31 Jan. 25/2 Mr. Gattie is of opinion that the insanity of one of the parties to a marriage should be.. a compulsory ground for divorce... He indicts the law by making his hero break it, and showing.. that his crime is a law-made crime. .. He is.. bent upon getting up a good '*test case'. **1906** *Daily News* 25 Apr. 9/1 Important charges of street betting, which were regarded by the police as test cases. **1911** M. CORELLI *Life Everlasting* ix. 205 Because he had seen in me the possibility of a 'test case', Santoris had tried his power upon me. **1959** B. & R. NORTH tr. *M. Duverger's Pol. Parties* (ed. 2) I. ii. 112 Such counts.. presuppose that the leaders of a number of test-case branches.. would make a very careful check of attendances over a period of time. **1910** H. C. PARKER *Handbk. Dis. Eye* v. 62 (*caption*) *Test chart for illiterates. **1978** J. PARR *Introd. Ophthalm.* II. 64 If a subject's visual acuity is less than 6/60 the distance from the test chart can be progressively reduced down to 1m. **1877** KNIGHT *Dict. Mech.*, **Test-cock* (Steam-engine), a small cock fitted to the top or bottom of a cylinder for clearing it of water. **1954** *Sun* (Baltimore) 1 Nov. (B ed.) 9/1 Shaw and his companions were returning from Detroit, where he had *test driven a 1955 Chrysler. **1971** *Guardian* 30 Oct. 20/1 Mrs Joy Johnson.. demolished a 'No Entry' sign while test-driving a double-deck bus. **1947** *Birmingham* (Alabama) *News* 27 Oct. 1/2 He stole the automatic pistol from an automobile and *test-fired it twice before calling for the cab. **1952** *N.Y. Times* 27 Apr. IV. E5/2 The atomic gun-fired shell .. will probably be test-fired in the course of the next year or so. **1960** *Daily Tel.* 8 Jan. 1/3 Russia is to test-fire new heavy rockets, intended for use on inter-planetary flights. **1980** N. FREELING *Castang's City* xxix. 202 We'll have it test-fired tomorrow and the cartridge marks compared. **1912** *Flight* 3 Feb. 106/2 No flying on Friday beyond a *test flight by Pizey on the Bristol. **1927** C. A. LINDBERGH *We* iv. 59, I took off for a test flight before taking the lady over Pensacola. **1976** *Derbyshire Times* (Peak ed.) 3 Sept. 28/1 The twin-engined Beechcraft monoplane.. was on a test flight at the time. **1936** *Meccano Mag.* Aug. 433/2, I hope it will fall to my lot to *test fly these great super-clippers. **1942** W. SIMPSON *One of our Pilots is Safe* ii. 40 During the day each aircraft received a special check-up and was test-flown by its pilot and crew. **1978** J. A. MICHENER *Chesapeake* 739 When the time came to test-fly the contraption,.. an aviator from Washington.. studied the seaplane. **1928** N. MACMILLAN *Art of Flying* 7 Immediately after the War, he took up *test-flying with considerable success. **1961** Test-flying [see *flight-testing* vbl. sb. s.v. FLIGHT *sb.*[1] 15]. **1839** URE *Dict. Arts* 1131 In forming the cupel, several layers of a mixture of moistened bone ashes, and fern ashes,.. are put into the *test-frame. **1877** KNIGHT *Dict. Mech.*, **Test-furnace*, one form of refining furnace for treating argentiferous alloy. **1896** *Godey's Mag.* Feb. 186/2, I don't believe that the immortal Sara Bernhardt could have gone through the fierce test-furnace of this rôle more superbly. **1827** FARADAY *Chem. Manip.* §619. 285 On the top of a *test-glass. **1909** *Chambers's Jrnl.* Mar. 160/1 He [*sc.* the prospector] digs here and there, making *test-holes. **1971** *Sunday Australian* 8 Aug. 17/2 The new test hole is sited about 100 miles south-west of Fitzroy Crossing, W.A. **1869** *Trans. 4th & 5th Ann. Meeting Amer. Ophthalm. Soc.* 68 (*heading*) On a new series of *test-letters for determining the acuteness of vision. **1897** *Daily News* 14 Apr. 7/5 The prisoner [a postman] was suspected. A test letter was sent, and it was not delivered. **1970** A. H. KEENEY *Ocular Examination* ii. 18/2 Snellen's real contribution was to standardize the size and form of test letters with relation to the distance from the observer. **1958** *Wall St. Jrnl.* 6 Nov. 23/5 A new line of cookingware which is now being *test-marketed in three cities of the United States. **1964** *Listener* 12 Mar. 422/1 Many products are produced and tried out in test-markets (usually medium-sized cities or commercial-television areas) for a year or more. *Ibid.*, Decisions about *test-marketing.. are the cause of severe anxiety. **1972** J. MELVILLE' *Ironwood* ix. 154 She had come to me seeking recipes for a new sort of cooking chocolate she was helping test-market in this area. **1862** W. J. HAMMERSLEY *Victorian Cricketer's Guide 1861–2* 159 Of the thirteen matches, five only can be termed '*test matches'; the three played at Melbourne, and the two played at Sydney. **1889** *Wisden's Cricketers' Almanack* 162 There was a considerable amount of anxiety as to the result of the first of the three great test matches. **1899** *Westm. Gaz.* 27 June 5/1 Not far below his big test-match average. *Ibid.* 15 Aug. 5/3 Two test-match records were broken during the day. **1905** *Westm. Gaz.* 19 Aug. 2/3 Until the year 1894 no one had ever heard of a 'Test' match, but.. since that time we have been accustomed thus to speak of an England v. Australia match. **1924** *Times* 15 Aug. 5/4 The British team for the first Rugby Football Test Match on Saturday will be selected [in S. Africa]. **1933** M. NICHOLLS in I. D. Difford *Hist. S. Afr. Rugby Football* xxiv. 335 We won this fourth Test match by 13 points to 5, and squared the rubber. **1974** *Encycl. Brit. Micropædia* IX. 458/2 Rugby League football. .. The three principal Test-match series stand as follows. **1891** *Cent. Dict.*, **Test-meal.* **1897** *Allbutt's Syst. Med.* III. 409 When the contents of the stomach are examined after a test-meal, the total acidity is found to be diminished. **1877** KNIGHT *Dict. Mech.*, **Test-mixer*, a tall cylindrical bottle.. graduated into.. equal parts.., and.. used in preparing test-alkalies, test-acids, and similar solutions. **1830** GORING *Microscopical Illustr.* 2 The difficulty of demonstrating many *test objects satisfactorily is very considerable. **1904** tr. *Hueppe's Ætiology Infectious Diseases* iii. 27 Guinea-pigs are so susceptible that we use them as the best test-object of tuberculosis. **1827** FARADAY *Chem. Manip.* §584. 270 *Test papers are far more advantageous for use than liquids: two of them in general application.. are litmus and turmeric papers. **1871** GARROD *Mat. Med.* (ed. 3) 68 The solution is neutral or slightly alkaline to test-paper. **1926** KIPLING *Debits & Credits* 273 To prepare for the Form a General Knowledge test-paper. **1876** PREECE & SIVEWRIGHT *Telegraphy* 179 The electrical resistance of the wire.. and the resistance of each *test-piece. **1877** KNIGHT *Dict. Mech.* 2537/2 The angle through which the test-piece yielded before its fracture became complete. **1927** *Melody Maker* Aug. 792/1 Some bandsmen tell you that after playing a test-piece for perhaps a hundred times they feel they are only just beginning to appreciate it. **1960** *Times* 23 May 16/6 It would make a good test-piece for an international Eisteddfod. **1917** W. L. WADE *Flying Bk.* 193/1 Now with Parnell and Sons, of Bristol, as chief *test pilot. **1927** C. A. LINDBERGH *We* iv. 61 The service parachute.. gave the test pilot a safe means of escape in most cases when all else had failed. **1947** *Sat. Even. Post* 6 Dec. 78/2 They reminded him of the fiery trail left by the high-altitude jet plane he had test-piloted in the last week of the war. **1978** J. A. MICHENER *Chesapeake* 740 The trial run was without incident, the test pilot pronouncing the craft airworthy. **1958** *Times Lit. Suppl.* 16 May 274/3 The beauty and immensity of the skies have always been a spiritual bonus added to the satisfactions of *test-piloting work well done. **1896** MARY H. FOOTE in *Atlantic Monthly* May 606/2 Sinking *test-pits through layers of crusted consciousness into depths of fiery nature. **1905** D. MACKENZIE *Let.* Sept. in *Observer* (1962) 11 Feb. 11/4 The examination of the later test-pits was reserved for a future time at your own express desire. **1952** V. G. CHILDE *New Light Most Anc. East* vii. 123 How far other innovations.. coincide with the change in pottery cannot be decided from the limited material furnished by a narrow test pit. **1973** *Lebende Sprachen* XVIII. 72/2 On 5th May.. Ariel 3 was successfully launched by a scout rocket from the western *test range.. at Vandenburg Air Force base, California. **1945** L. GUTTMAN in *Psychometrika* X. 255 (*heading*) A basis for analyzing *test-retest reliability. *Ibid.* 266 That the universe of trials be indefinitely large seems part of the *definition* of the problem of test-retest reliability. **1960** F. LAND *Lang. Math.* xiv. 253 The 'test re-test' method.. involves giving the test and then, after some lapse of time, giving it again to the same group of people... A correlation less than 0·9 between the two performances of the same test would indicate that its reliability was below the acceptable level. **1957** *Technology* Sept. 244/3 The.. mechanical engineering research laboratory.. developed a new *test rig for.. fittings for oil hydraulic circuits. **1978** R. V. JONES *Most Secret War* xlv. 435 If only we had complete photographic cover of the Blizna area we could have found the launching site or test rig. **1881** RAYMOND *Mining Gloss.*, **Test-ring*, an oval iron frame holding a test or movable cupelling-hearth. **1879** T. E. MAY *Parl. Practice* (ed. 8) 204 So soon as a member has been sworn, he subscribes the oath which he has taken, in a book, at the table, commonly called the '*test-roll'; and is then introduced to the Speaker by the clerk of the house. **1884** *Ninth Rep. Hist. MSS. Comm.* App. 68/2 Certificate.. Produced this day [17 Nov. 1675] on his taking the oaths and signing the Test Roll. **1945** *Daily Herald* 31 Aug. 4/4 The B.B.C. is already sending out *test signals on the sound channel. **1975** D. G. FINK *Electronics Engineers' Handbk.* XXI. 29 The use of test signals must not result in significant degradation of the program transmissions. **1894** LINEHAM *Mech. Engin.* 378 Shackles for *Test Specimens should be carefully designed. **1940** *Chambers's Techn. Dict.*, **Test strip* (*Cinema.*), the specially exposed unmodulated sound-track which is made to ascertain the current in the exciter lamp of a recording machine which gives the requisite density on the negative, after normal development. **1958** T. L. J. BENTLEY in *Newnes Compl. Amat. Photogr.* iv. 78 By giving a series of test strips different periods of development and measuring the resulting gammas and plotting them against development times, a curve is produced. **1973** D. A. SPENCER *Focal Dict. Photogr. Technol.* 623 *Test strip*, a piece of the sensitised material on which exposure is to be made which is exposed in sections, each receiving a different exposure to enable the correct exposure to be judged by the appearance of the developed strip. Each successive section typically receives twice the exposure of the previous section. **1864** W. D. MOORE tr. *Donders' Anomalies of Accommodation & Refraction* ii. 99 We give him small print—I to IV of Snellen's *test-types to read. **1907**, **1962** Test-type [see JAEGER[2]]. **1877** *Sci. Amer.* 22 Dec. 387/3 A large number of 'wildcats', or *test wells, have gone down off the eastern edge of the defined line, but with very few exceptions they have proved dusters. **1925** A. B. THOMPSON *Oil-Field Explor.* I. v. 208 The selection of sites for test wells is one of the most responsible duties that devolves on pioneers. **1975** *Offshore* Sept. 91/1 A total of 12 deep onshore test wells have been drilled, all of which have been dry holes. **1905** A. MEYER in *Psychol. Bull.* 15 July 242 The time was measured with a stop-watch from the chief syllable of the *test-word to the reaction. **1924** E. EKWALL in Mawer & Stenton *Introd. Survey Eng. Place-Names* iv. 60 Norwegian test-words are *breck, buth* (ON *búð*), *gill, scale, slack.* **1965** G. KRISTENSSON in *English Studies* Apr. 142 This surname [*sc.* Ladyman] is.. too unreliable to be used as a test-word for the appearance of OE *(ge)lād*.

test (tɛst), *sb.*[2] [ad. L. *testa* a piece of burned clay, a brick, tile, a piece of baked earthenware or pottery, an earthen pot or vessel, a potsherd, a shell of a mollusc or tortoise, a shell or covering of anything. Cf. also TEST *sb.*[1], and TESTA.]

†**1.** A piece of earthenware, an earthenware vessel; a broken piece of pottery, a potsherd. *Obs.*

1545 JOYE *Exp. Dan.* iv. D iij, Then was yᵉ test or pot-sherd, the brasse, gold & sylver redacte into duste. [Cf. *Vulg.* Dan. ii. 45 testam et ferrum et æs.] **1600** SURFLET *Country Farm* I. xii. 76 It is good.. to haue a dish of the plane tree or a test of earth.

2. a. *Zool.* The shell of certain invertebrates.

1842 *Penny Cycl.* XXII. 371/1 This external covering or *test*, extremely delicate and fragile towards the umbones of the valves. **1854** WOODWARD *Mollusca* II. 214 The vascular processes by which, in many ascidians, the 'tunic' adheres to the 'test'. **1872** NICHOLSON *Palæont.* 60 Rhizopoda in which the body is protected by a shell or 'test'. **1888** [see TESTACEA 2].

†**b.** *Bot.* The skin of a seed: = TESTA 1. *rare.*

1846 SMART Suppl., *Test* (or *Testa*..), the skin of a seed.

test (tɛst), *sb.*[3] *Obs.* exc. *dial.* Also 6–7 teste. [In sense 1, app. ad. L. *test-is* witness. In senses 2 and 3, perh. aphetic for *atest*, ATTEST *sb.*]

†**1.** A witness. Cf. TESTIS[1]. *Obs. rare.*

(Quot. 1528 may belong to TESTIS[1].)

1528 ROY *Rede me* II. (Arb.) 109 To prove it shall nede no testes. **1614** W. B. *Philosopher's Banquet* (ed. 2) 197 The faithful teste or witnesse. *a* **1626** BP. ANDREWES *Serm.*, *Holy Ghost* (1661) 488 A Witnesse is requisite. There is no matter of weight with us, if it be sped authentically.. but it is with a Teste.

†**2.** Evidence, witness borne. Cf. ATTEST *sb.* 1.

[*c* **1450** HOLLAND *Howlat* 253 All this trety has he tald be termess in test.] **1604** SHAKS. *Oth.* I. iii. 107 To vouch this, is no proofe, Without more wider, and more ouer Test. [Cf. **1606** —— *Tr. & Cr.* v. ii. 122 That test [*Qo.* th' attest] of eyes and eares.] **1658** SIR T. BROWNE *Hydriot.* ii. (1736) 21 The lasting Tests of old Boundaries.

†**3.** = TESTE[2]. Cf. ATTEST *sb.* 2. *Obs.*

1709 STRYPE *Ann. Ref.* I. xxvi. 277 In the term next after the test of the said writ. **1752** J. LOUTHIAN *Form of Process* (ed. 2) 174 The Court shall issue another Writ.. of the same Test, Return and Import with the former.

4. A will: = TESTAMENT *sb.* 1. *Sc.*

1890 J. SERVICE *Thir Notandums* iii. 13 By ane eik to his test, he left to Peter Scartle the soom of five shillings.

test (tɛst), *v.*[1] [orig. a. OF. *tester* to bequeath, ad. L. *testārī* to bear witness, give evidence, attest, make one's will, f. *testis* witness; but in 3 app. from TESTE *sb.*[2] 2, and in 4 perh. aphetic from ATTEST.]

I. †**1.** *trans.* To leave by will or testament, to bequeath. *Sc. Obs. rare*[−1].

1491 *Acta Dom. Conc.* (1839) 208/1 He allegeit It wes testit gudis, & he Intromettit þarwᵗ as executour.

2. *intr.* To make a will, execute a testament. (See also TESTING *vbl. sb.*[1] 1.) *Obs.* exc. *Sc.*

1582 N. T. (Rhem.) *Heb.* ix. 17 For a testament.. is yet of no value, whiles he that tested, liueth. **1681** STAIR *Inst. Law Scot.* xxx. §18 Persons.. condemned of Infamy could not test. **1822** SCOTT *Pirate* vi, I will test upon it [*Note*, i.e. leave it in my will] at my death, and keep it for a purse-penny till that day comes. **1838** W. BELL *Dict. Law Scot.* s.v. *Testament*, A wife has power to test without the consent of her husband. **1880** MUIRHEAD *Ulpian* xxiii. §10 [In Roman Law] Soldiers are allowed to test in any way they like.

II. 3. *trans. Eng. Law.* To date and sign the teste of a writ, etc. (see TESTE *sb.*[2] 2).

(The pa. pple. appears in Blackstone as *teste*'d, as if formed immediately on *teste*, but it is usually written and pronounced *tested*.)

1727 ASGILL *Metam. Man* 249 His title.. is tested and dated from the Death and Resurrection of Christ, as the Cause of it. **1745** *Col. Rec. Pennsylv.* IV. 775 A Commission Tested by me under the Great Seal of the Province. **1769** BLACKSTONE *Comm.* IV. xxi. 288 A warrant from the chief, or other, justice of the court of king's bench extends all over the kingdom: and is *teste*'d, or dated, England. **1883** *Wharton's Law Lex.* s.v., All writs.. were formerly tested in the name of the Lord Chancellor if issuing from the Court of Chancery, or of the Lord Chief Justice if issuing from the Queen's Bench, etc.

4. *Sc. Law.* To authenticate a deed or written instrument by a testing clause (TESTING *vbl. sb.*[1] 2) duly drawn up in statutory form and signed by witnesses.

1838 W. BELL *Dict. Law Scot.* s.v. *Testament*, A testament .. must be properly tested and signed before witnesses; but if it be in the testator's own handwriting, witnesses are not required. **1911** T. HUNTER *Let. to Editor*, The Scottish law requires writings (except those *in re mercatoria*) to be either holograph or tested.

test (tɛst), *v.*[2] [f. TEST *sb.*[1]
(Before 1800 chiefly in pa. pple.; the simple vb. was considered by Southey as an Americanism.)]

1. *trans.* To subject (gold or silver) to a process of separation and refining in a test or cupel; to assay.

1603 [see *tested* below]. [**1661**: ? implied in TESTER[4].] **1828** WEBSTER, *Test*, *v.*, 3. In *Metallurgy*, To refine gold or silver by means of lead, in a test, by the destruction, vitrification or scorification of all extraneous matter. **1871** [see *tested* below]. **1872** RAYMOND *Statist. Mines & Mining* 120 The ore tested yielded $25 per ton. *Ibid.* 335 These lodes have not been tested by the repeated and continuous milling of the ore raised from them. **1873** SYMONDS *Grk. Poets* iii. 89 You may test gold and silver, but there are no means of getting at the thoughts of men.

2. To subject to a test of any kind; to try, put to the proof; to ascertain the existence, genuineness, or quality of. ***to test out***, to put (a theory, etc.) to a practical test. Phrases: ***to test*** (something) ***to failure*** or ***destruction***; ***to test the water*** (fig.: cf. quot. 1888).

1748 [see *tested* below]. **1760–72** H. BROOKE *Fool of Qual.* (1809) I. 48 You have been sufficiently tested. *a* **1799** WASHINGTON *Address* (Webster 1828), Experience is the surest standard by which to test the real tendency of the existing constitution. **1815** JEFFERSON *Writ.* (1830) IV. 260 Materials which test the truth it contains. **1820** *Blackw. Mag.* Sept. 591/1 They have not the means of testing the statements. **1834–43** SOUTHEY *Doctor* cxlv. (1862) 397 But I will test (as an American would say..) I will test Mr. Campbell's assertion. **1837** J. H. NEWMAN *Proph. Office Ch.* 324 The Church is bound ever to test and verify her doctrine. **1838** GLADSTONE *State in Rel. Ch.* (1839) 186 This theory however has not been tested experimentally. **1888** MISS BRADDON *Fatal Three* I. v, I have tested the water in all the wells. **1926** *Publishers' Weekly* 29 May 1794/2 To test out the value of radio publicity. **1962** F. I. ORDWAY et al. *Basic Astronautics* vii. 325 We first select 100 units and test them to failure. **1972** D. RAMSAY *Little Murder Music* 62 'If you're attempting to establish a motive—' 'I'm just testing the water,' Meredith said. **1974** *Howard Jrnl.* XIV. 104 Legal philosophers could back up these efforts by testing out some of their theories with research projects. **1978** A. PRICE *'44 Vintage* xviii. 203 Sergeant Winston tested the statement to destruction. **1980** J. KRANTZ *Princess Daisy* xxv. 443 'I guess it's just..lucky..that Supracorp's such a big business,' Kiki said, testing the waters.

b. To subject (a person) to a test of a particular kind.

1939 *Brit. Jrnl. Psychol.* July 1 The range of chronological age of persons tested was so wide that a special enquiry had to be undertaken. **1957** C. N. PARKINSON *Parkinson's Law* (1958) 23 So much time has been spent in studying the art of being tested that the candidate has rarely had time for anything else. **1978** *Washington Post* 20 Jan. D 1 Hepburn had played bit or supporting roles in several European movies..before William Wyler tested her and cast her as the runaway princess in 'Roman Holiday'.

†**3.** To require or compel to fulfil the conditions of the Test Act as a necessary qualification for holding a public office. *Obs.*

1687 *Reason of Toleration* 36 There is no reason they should be so cruelly Tested for Doctrines that are but either obscurely reveal'd, or not necessarily enjoyn'd. [**1687**, **1689**: see TESTING *vbl. sb.*[2], *tested* below. **1697**: see TESTER[4].]

4. *Chem.* To subject to a chemical test.

1839 URE *Dict. Arts* 71 (Assay) The testing of the normal liquor..is..less tedious than might be supposed. **1842** PARNELL *Chem. Anal.* (1845) 35 Oxide of silver is most conveniently applied, in liquid testing, in the form of nitrate of silver. **1846** G. E. DAY tr. *Simon's Anim. Chem.* II. 135 The urine..must be tested with litmus paper. **1864** in WEBSTER.

5. *intr.* **a.** To undergo a test. *U.S.*

1934 in WEBSTER. **1961** in WEBSTER, Actors..best suited to the roles for which they tested. *Ibid.*, The great turboprop ..was still testing. **1981** *Times* 29 Apr. 12/3, I tested with Jack Nicholson for his own film *Goin' South*. It came down to a choice between myself and Mary Steenburger and she got the part.

b. With phrasal compl. To achieve a rating of (so much) as the result of a test. *U.S.*

1934 WEBSTER, s.v. A compound that tests ten per cent. *a* **1961** R. BENEDICT in Webster, The eyesight of different peoples may test the same. **1971** 'L. EGAN' *Malicious Mischief* viii. 135 They could guess that he might test dull-normal. He was seventeen, not very big and not very bright. **1976** M. MACHLIN *Pipeline* ii. 32 It tests over two thousand barrels a day.

6. *absol.* or *intr.* To apply or carry out a test.

1961 WEBSTER, s.v., Use the scratch technique in testing for allergies. **1978** T. SHARPE *Throwback* ix. 87 Then say 'Testing. Testing. Testing.' into that little transmitter.

Hence **'tested** *ppl. a.* (in senses 1 and 2); in quot. 1689, having taken the test-oaths.

1603 SHAKS. *Meas. for M.* II. ii. 149 Not with fond Sickles of the tested-gold, Or Stones, whose rate are either rich, or poore. **1689** *Let.* in *N. Brit. Daily Mail* 27 Dec. (1894), If we have a Convention chosen by our present tested magistrates we may expect little good from their hands. **1748** RICHARDSON *Clarissa* (1811) III. xxxi. 187 She cannot break through a well-tested modesty. **1871** TENNYSON *Last Tourn.* 284, I..heard it ring as true as tested gold.

test, obs. Sc. form of TASTE.

‖**testa** ('tɛstə). [L. *testa* a tile, earthen pot, shard, shell, etc.: see TEST *sb.*[2]]

1. *Bot.* The skin or coating of a seed.

1796 DE SERRA in *Phil. Trans.* LXXXVI. 500 (*Fruct. of Algæ*), Their very viscous albumen answers..all the purposes the testa accomplishes in other eggs. **1807** J. E. SMITH *Phys. Bot.* 294 *Testa*, the Skin, contains all the parts of a seed above described. **1877** HUXLEY & MARTIN *Elem. Biol.* 86 Carefully peel off the outer coat (*testa*) of the seed.

†**2.** *Zool.* The shell of certain invertebrates: = TEST *sb.*[2] 2 a. *Obs. rare.*

1847 in WEBSTER.

testability (tɛstə'bɪlɪtɪ). [f. TESTABLE *a.*[2] + -ITY.] The quality or state of being testable (see TESTABLE *a.*[2]).

1936 R. CARNAP in *Philos. of Sci.* III. 421 An attempt will be made to formulate the principle of empiricism in a more exact way, by stating a requirement of confirmability or testability as a criterion of meaning. **1945** [see CONFIRMABILITY]. **1952** C. G. HEMPEL *Fund. of Concept Formation in Empirical Sci.* 43 Just another formulation of the empiricist requirements of testability. **1968** K. R. POPPER *Conjectures & Refutations* (ed. 3) i. 37 The criterion of the scientific status of a theory is its falsifiability, or refutability, or testability. **1981** *Word 1980* XXXI. 151 It is only in this way that the model can attain a high degree of testability.

†**testable** ('tɛstəb(ə)l), *a.*[1] *Obs.* [ad. late L. *testābilis* that has a right to bear testimony (Gellius), f. *testārī*: see TESTATE *a.*[1] and *sb.* and -ABLE; cf. obs. F. *testable* capable of making a will (1514 in Godef.) from the same source.]

1. a. Legally qualified to bear witness. **b.** Legally able to make a will.

1611 COTGR., *Testable*, testable; that can make a Will; that may be deuised by Will. **1676** R. DIXON *Two Test.* 25 A Deed solemnly testified by the Testimony..of Seven Testable Persons that are..worthy to be believed. **1721** BAILEY, *Testable*.., that by the Law may bear witness.

2. Devisable by will.

1693 STAIR *Inst. Law Scot.* IV. xlii. §21 A power of legating ..the Deads part of Movables, which is..most ordinarily the third of Testable Movables. **1766** BLACKSTONE *Comm.* II. xxxii. 494 Such of his goods as were testable.

testable ('tɛstəb(ə)l), *a.*[2] [f. TEST *v.*[2] + -ABLE.] That may be tested or tried; *spec.* in *Philos. of Science*, of a theory: capable of being empirically tested. (In quot. 1647 app. 'That on being put to the test prove to be'.)

1647 TRAPP *Comm. Matt.* xii. 30 So are all testable indifferents, out of God's book of remembrance. Mal. iii. 17. **1922** *Glasgow Herald* 14 Apr. 8 Japanese history does not become a record of testable facts until the fifth or sixth century A.D. **1945** [see DISCONFIRM *v.*]. **1959** K. R. POPPER *Logic of Sci. Discovery* vi. 112 Theories may be more, or less, severely testable; that is to say, more, or less, easily falsifiable. The degree of their testability is of significance for the selection of theories. **1968** P. A. P. MORAN *Introd. Probability Theory* i. 57 The two laws differ in their empirical nature in that the first is empirically testable whilst the second is not. **1973** B. MAGEE *Popper* ii. 22 Scientific laws are testable in spite of being unprovable: they can be tested by systematic tests to refute them.

‖**testacea** (tɛ'steɪʃ(ɪ)ə), *sb. pl.* [L., neut. pl. of *testāce-us* adj., consisting of *testæ*, i.e. tiles, shells, etc.; also, covered with a shell: see -ACEA.]

†**1.** Testaceous substances, as limestone, chalk. Cf. TESTACYE. *Obs. rare*[−1].

1743 *Lond. & Country Brew.* III. (ed. 2) 241 Chalk and other Testacea will answer the same, but not so well.

2. *Zool.* A name for various groups of invertebrate animals having shells (excluding Crustacea). *spec.* †**a.** (*a*) used by Linnæus to designate his third order of *Vermes*, comprising the shell-bearing molluscs; (*b*) by Cuvier applied to the shell-bearing molluscs of his class *Acephala*. (*Obs.*) **b.** In present use, (*a*) A suborder of pteropod molluscs including all having calcareous shells, otherwise called *Thecosomata*; (*b*) an order of Protozoa having shells, with apertures through which the pseudopodia are protrusible.

1828 STARK *Elem. Nat. Hist.* II. 4 In the last edition of his *Systema Naturæ*, Linnæus,..in the third and fourth divisions of his third order, *Testacea*, places those possessed of shells. **1830** LYELL *Princ. Geol.* I. 52 Soldani..explained that microscopic testacea and zoophytes inhabited the depths of the Mediterranean. **1860** HARTWIG *Sea & Wond.* i. 11 Pholades and Lithodomas are marine testacea, that have the power of burying themselves in stone. **1888** ROLLESTON & JACKSON *Anim. Life* 905 The *Amœbina* may be classified as..: 1. *Nuda* s. *Gymnamœbæ*: devoid of a test... 2. *Testacea* s. *Lepamœbæ*: a test either chitinoid..or composed of chitinoid or siliceous plates cemented together.

testacean (tɛ'steɪʃ(ɪ)ən), *a.* and *sb.* *Zool.* [f. prec.: see -ACEAN.]

A. *adj.* Of or pertaining to the TESTACEA; shell-bearing; chiefly applied to molluscs.

1846 in WORCESTER, citing LYELL. **1871** LYELL *Elem. Geol.* ix. 119 Value of testacean fossils in classification.

B. *sb.* A member of the testacea; a shell-bearing invertebrate, *esp.* a mollusc.

1842 BRANDE *Dict. Sc.* etc., *Testaceans*. Testacea. **1847** WEBSTER, *Testaceans* (*Zool.*), marine animals covered with shells, especially mollusks; shell-fish.

Testacel, -elle ('tɛstəsəl, -ˌɛl). *Zool.* [ad. mod.L. testacella (also in Eng. use), dim. of *testācea*, fem. of *testāce-us* adj.: see TESTACEA.] A genus of carnivorous land-slugs, typical of the family *Testacellidæ*, having a small oval shield-like shell, which covers only a small part of the back. They live upon earthworms, and inhabit Southern Europe; one species is sometimes found in England.

1846 SMART Suppl., *Testacel*, a little shell; applied as the general name of a slug which is furnished with a diminutive shell that forms a shield to the heart. **1851** WOODWARD *Mollusca* I. 13 The testacelle..preys on the common earth-worm, following it in its burrow, and wearing a buckler, which protects it in the rear. **1910** *Daily News* 9 May 4 The slug which 'by good fortune we may catch sight of eating a worm', is testacella.

Hence **testa'cellid, testa'cellidan** *adjs.*, of or pertaining to the family *Testacellidæ*; *sbs.* a member of this family; **testa'celloid** *a.*, resembling the *Testacella* or *Testacellidæ*.

1895 *Funk's Stand. Dict.*, Testacellid..Testacelloid. **1895** *Cambridge Nat. Hist.* III. 440 Jaw present, radula Testacellidan, central tooth present.

testaceo- (tɛ'steɪʃiːəʊ), combining form of L. *testāceus*, used **a.** as in **testace'ography**, descriptive testaceology (Webster, 1828); **testace'ology**, the zoology of the testaceous animals; hence **testaceo'logical** *a. rare*; **testaceo-theology**, natural theology as illustrated by the study of testaceous animals. **b.** in sense 'of brick-red colour', as in **testaceo-fuscous, testaceo-piceous**, etc. *adjs.*: see the second elements.

1803 MATON in *Trans. Linn. Soc.* VII. 119 (*heading*) An Historical Account of Testaceological Writers. *Ibid.* 121 Aristotle..seems to have been also the first writer, and the inventor of method, in Testaceology. **1755** tr. *Pontoppidan's Nat. Hist. Norway* Pref. 7 That circumstantial examination of every part which hath been undertaken and..executed by Fabricius, in his pyro- and hydro-theology,..Lesser, in his litho- and testaceo-theology.
b. **1847** J. HARDY in *Proc. Berw. Nat. Club* II. v. 247 Legs testaceo-fuscous. *Ibid.* 256 The first joint testaceous, the rest testaceo-piceous.

testaceous (tɛ'steɪʃəs), *a.* [f. L. *testāce-us* consisting of tiles, shells, etc.; brick-coloured; covered with a shell: see TEST *sb.*[2] and -ACEOUS.]

†**1.** Made of baked clay; pertaining to or of the nature of earthenware or a potsherd. *Obs. rare.*

1658 SIR T. BROWNE *Hydriot.* iii. 22 In many Bricks, Tiles, Pots, and testaceous works. **1674** J. B[RIAN] *Harvest Home* ii. 6 Testaceous Vessels; obnoxious To casualties, that are most various. **1675** EVELYN *Terra* (1729) 15 Exotic Plants..confined..to their Wooden Cases and Testaceous prisons.

2. Having a shell, esp. a hard, calcareous, unarticulated shell. †*testaceous fish* = shell-fish.

1646 SIR T. BROWNE *Pseud. Ep.* 203 All [fishes] that are testaceous, as Oysters, Cocles, Wilks, Schollops, Muscles, are excluded. **1759** STILLINGFL. tr. *Biberg's Econ. Nat.* Misc. Tracts (1762) 57 Testaceous worms..eat away the hardest rocks. **1809** W. IRVING *Knickerb.* IV. iii, The testaceous marine animal, known commonly by the vulgar name of Oyster. **1875** C. C. BLAKE *Zool.* 232 When the shell is so much enlarged that the contracted animal finds shelter beneath or within it, the animal is said to be testaceous.

3. Of the nature or substance of shells; shelly; consisting of a shell or shelly material.

1668 WILKINS *Real Char.* 122 Exanguious Animals.. whose bones are on their outside..testaceous; of a more hard and brittle substance. **1676** GREW *Exper. Luctation* i. §21 Millipedes, Egg-shells, or any other testaceous Bodies of the same strength. **1794** SULLIVAN *View Nat.* I. 89 The testaceous matter of marine shells. **1881** WATSON in *Jrnl. Linn. Soc.* XV. 265 Operculum testaceous.

†**b.** *Pharmacy.* Of a medicinal powder: Prepared from the shells of animals. *Obs.*

1710 T. FULLER *Pharm. Extemp.* 392, I think testaceous Powders exert their Virtues much easier and sooner when fine. **1789** W. BUCHAN *Dom. Med.* (1790) 549 To give the pearl-julep, chalk, crabs eyes, and other testaceous powders. **1853** DUNGLISON *Med. Lex.*, *Testaceous*,..a powder, consisting of burnt shells.

4. Of the colour of a tile, a flower-pot, unglazed pottery, etc.; dull red; in *Zool.* and *Bot.* applied to shades of brownish red, brownish yellow, and reddish brown.

1688 R. HOLME *Armoury* II. 275/2 The upper part of the Body is testaceous, or potsheard colour. **1783** LATHAM *Gen. Synopsis* IV. 393 Testaceous Lark. Bill black: upper parts of the body testaceous. **1887** W. PHILLIPS *Brit. Discomycetes* 136 Cup..testaceous yellow. *Ibid.* 420 *Testaceous*, brick-coloured,..not so bright as *lateritious*.

Hence **te'staceousness** (*rare*[−0]).

1727 BAILEY vol. II, *Testaceousness*, shelly Nature or Quality.

'Test Act. [See TEST *sb.*[1] 3.] The name given in English History to various acts directed against Roman Catholics and Protestant Nonconformists; particularly, the act of 1673 (25 Chas. II. c. 2) by which the provisions of the Corporation Act of 1661 (see CORPORATION 7) were extended to include all persons holding office under the Crown, and a declaration against transubstantiation was introduced. It was repealed 9 May, 1828.

Also sometimes applied to (*a*) an act of Elizabeth, 1563, imposing the oath of allegiance, and abjuration of the temporal authority of Rome, on all office-holders except peers; (*b*) the Corporation Act of 1661; (*c*) a Scotch act of 1681, exacting a declaration of conformity to the Episcopal Church of all holders of municipal and government offices.

1708 *Lett. Gent. Scotl. agst. Sacr. Test* 5 This Test Act requires an End in the Receiving of the Sacrament, that must consequently prophane it. *a* **1715** BURNET *Own Time* an. 1673 (1823) II. 13 A sure law against popery,..all that continued in office after the time lapsed, they not taking the sacrament, and not renouncing transubstantiation (which came to be called the test, and the act from it the test act) were rendered incapable of holding any office: all the acts they did in it were declared invalid and illegal, besides a fine of five hundred pounds to the discoverer. **1738** NEAL *Hist. Purit.* IV. 458 This is commonly called the *Test Act*, and was levelled against the Duke of York and the present Ministry, who were chiefly of his persuasion. **1769** BLACKSTONE *Comm.* IV. iv. 57 To secure the established church against perils from non-conformists of all denominations, infidels, turks, jews, hereticks, papists, and sectaries, there are however two bulwarks erected; called the *corporation* and *test* acts. **1874** GREEN *Short Hist.* vii. §6. 400 But the Test Act [of 1563] placed the magistracy in Protestant hands. **1886** A. FERGUSON *Laird of Lag* iii. 36 The famous Test Act was passed by the Scots Parliament at one sitting on the 30 August 1681.

testacy (ˈtɛstəsɪ). *Law.* [f. TESTATE *a.*[1] and *sb.*, after INTESTACY.] The state of being testate; the condition of leaving a valid will at death.

1864 in WEBSTER. **1875** POSTE *Gaius* II. Comm. (ed. 2) 229 Contra-tabular possession was sometimes equivalent to intestacy, sometimes to partial testacy. **1880** GLADSTONE *Sp. Ho. Comm.* 15 Mar., The Chancellor of the Exchequer..has treated testacies and intestacies, as if they were something like equal. **1885** *Law Rep.* 29 *Ch. D.* 278 The suit settles as regards him the question of testacy or intestacy.

†**ˈtestacye.** *Obs. rare*$^{-1}$. [ad. L. *testāceum*: see TESTACEOUS.] Name for a kind of cement.

c **1440** *Pallad. on Husb.* VI. 192 Now yote on that scyment clept testacye Sex fynger thicke.

testament (ˈtɛstəmənt), *sb.* Also 5 **testement**, 5–6 **testment**. [ad. L. *testāment-um* a will; also, in early Christian Latin, used to render Gr. διαθήκη covenant (see II.), f. *testārī* to be a witness, attest, make a will, etc.: see -MENT. With the form *teste-*, *testment*, cf. OF. *testement*, beside the more usual *testament*.]

I. In original sense of L. *testāmentum*.

This is app. later in Eng. than branch II.

1. *Law.* A formal declaration, usually in writing, of a person's wishes as to the disposal of his property after his death; a will. Formerly, properly applied to a disposition of personal as distinct from real property (cf. c). Now *rare* (chiefly in phrase ***last will and testament***).

[**1306** *Rolls of Parlt.* I. 220/1 Les executors de tieux testaments.] *c* **1330** R. BRUNNE *Chron.* (1810) 20 þre þousand marke he gaf with testament fulle right. **13..** *Cursor M.* 28322 Ic seketur made of testament, Ne folud noght..þe testament for to fulfill. **1362** LANGL. *P. Pl.* A. VII. 78, I wole, ar I Wende write my Testament. **1463** *Bury Wills* (Camden) 36, I..calle vpon hym to do his part in alle thinges longyng to my testement and wille. **1464** *Rolls of Parlt.* V. 549/2 Ayenst the Testament and the last Wille of your seid noble Progenitour. **1590** SWINBURNE *Testaments* 3 A testament properly vnderstoode, is one kinde of last will, euen that wherein Executor is named. **1637** PRYNNE in *Documents agst. P.* (Camden) 99 Whom I make sole executors of this my last will and testament, revoking all former wills. **1766** BLACKSTONE *Comm.* II. i. 12 The right of disposing one's property, or a part of it, by testament. **1818** HALLAM *Mid. Ages* (1819) II. vii. 311 The ecclesiastical tribunals..took the execution of testaments into their hands, on account of the legacies to pious uses, which testators were advised to bequeath. **1880** MUIRHEAD *Ulpian* xx. §1 A testament is the testification of our will, in the form prescribed by law, made solemnly, on purpose that it may be effectual after our death.

b. *transf.* and *fig.* (Cf. *legacy.*)

?*a* **1400** *Morte Arth.* 668 Take here my testament of tresoure fulle huge, As I trayste appone the, be traye thowe me never! *c* **1532** DU WES *Introd. Fr.* in *Palsgr.* 1064 The masse is the testament the which our Lorde made before his deth & passyon. **1599** SHAKS. *Hen. V*, IV. vi. 27 And so espous'd to death, with blood he seal'd A Testament of Noble-ending-loue. **1667** JER. TAYLOR *Dissuas. Popery* II. I. iii. 110 The Gospels are Christ's Testament; and the Epistles are the Codicils annex'd. **1831–3** E. BURTON *Eccl. Hist.* xix. (1845) 403 The Testaments of the Twelve Patriarchs..professes to contain prophecies and exhortations delivered by the sons of Jacob shortly before their death.

†**c.** *transf.* Testamentary estate; personal as distinct from real property. *Obs.*

1424 *E.E. Wills* (1882) 56, I..declare my last will.., als well of my testament as of my land þat standez in feffez handes.

2. *Sc. Law.* The writing by which a person nominates an executor to administer his personal or movable estate after his decease. This writing is styled, in the decree of the Court granting confirmation (i.e. probate), a **testament-testamentar** (or **-ary**), and the executor is an *executor-nominate*. When no executor has been nominated, an *executor-dative* is appointed by the Court, and the decree appointing him is styled a **testament-dative**. (The latter answers to Letters of Administration in English Law.)

1526 *Sc. Acts Jas. V* (1814) II. 306/2 Quhar ony sic persouns deis wᵗin age may noᵗ mak þar testamentis. **1564** *Acts of Sederunt* 13 Apr. (1790) 6 To the collectoris and ressaveris of the quotts, for confirmation of the testamentis of the personis decessand within oure realm. **1666** *Ibid.* 28 Feb. 99 If there be no nomination or testament made by the defunct, or if the testament testamentar shall not be desired to be confirmed. *Ibid.* 101 Of all testaments, both great and small, which shall be confirmed, as well of testaments dative, as others. **1681** STAIR *Inst. Law Scot.* xxx. §33. 170 The Nomination of Executors, is properly called a Testament. **1768–73** ERSKINE *Inst. Sc. Law* III. ix. §7 Though nuncupative testaments are not effectual..to support the nomination of executors, yet nuncupative or verbal legacies are valid to the extent of L. 100 Scots. *Ibid.* §27 Where an executor named by the deceased is authorised by the Judge, it is called the confirmation of a testament-testamentary; and when the Judge confers the office of executor upon a person of his own nomination, it is styled the confirmation of a testament-dative. **1838** in W. BELL *Dict. Law Scot.*

¶**3.** *erroneously.* = TESTIMONY; witness.

1456 SIR G. HAYE *Law Arms* (S.T.S.) 8 The pape convertit sanct Tiburce, [and] sanct Valere be his testament. *c* **1533** *Disc. Antechrist* in Strype *Eccl. Mem.* (1721) I. App. xlv. 125 And when he shal end his testament the beast shal come from the bottomles pit..and shal slay them. **1904** in *Daily Chron.* 21 Oct. 5/7 There is first-hand testament to my statements.

II. In Christian Latin use of *testāmentum*.

Orig. a misuse of the word, arising from the fact that Gr. διαθήκη, 'disposition, arrangement', was applied both to a covenant (*pactum*, *fœdus*) between parties, and to a testament or will (*testamentum*). Prob. largely due to the use of διαθήκη (in the sense 'covenant') in the account of the Last Supper immediately before Christ's death, and its consequent association with the notion of a last will or testament. See also historical note s.v. COVENANT *sb.* 7.

4. *Script.* A covenant between God and man: = COVENANT *sb.* 7. *Obs.* or *arch.*

a **1300** *Cursor M.* 12778 Quen drightin gan to sprad his grace..þe testament bigan he neu. *Ibid.* 12886 þe ald testament hir-wit nu slakes, And sua þe neu begining takes. *c* **1315** SHOREHAM i. 541 þys hys þe chalis of my blode Of testament newe. *a* **1340** HAMPOLE *Psalter* cxxxi. 12 If þi sunnys hafe kepid my testament. **1382** WYCLIF *Baruch* ii. 35 And Y shal sette to them an other testament euere durende. —— *Acts* vii. 8 He 3af to him the testament of circumcisioun. —— *1 Cor.* xi. 25 This cuppe is the newe testament in my blood. *c* **1430** LYDG. *Letabundus* 248 in *Min. Poems*, In Reioysshyng of Crystes glad comynge; Two testamentys that day wer maad bothe Oon. **1509** HAWES *Past. Pleas.* xliv. (Percy Soc.) 216 His elect mother and arke of testament, Of holy chyrche the blessed lumynary. **1611** BIBLE *2 Cor.* iii. 6 Able ministers of the New Testament [Gr. διακόνους καινῆς διαθήκης: WYCLIF, able mynistris of the newe testament, 1881 *R.V.* ministers of a new covenant]. *Ibid.* 14 In the reading of the old testament [*R.V.* at the reading of the old covenant].

5. Hence, through the application of παλαιὰ and καινὴ διαθήκη, in the Itala and Vulgate *vetus* and *novum testamentum*, to the Mosaic and Christian 'covenants' or 'dispensations' (cf. 2 Cor. iii. 6, 14 cited in 4), the term passed in early Christian Latin (and thence in the languages of the West) to the books or records of the old and new covenants.

(This transition of sense took place many centuries before the adoption of the word in English, where the name was simply taken over from L. or Fr. in this transferred use.)

a. Each of the two main divisions of the Sacred Scriptures or Bible, the ***Old*** and the ***New Testament***, consisting of the books of the old or Mosaic and the new or Christian covenant or dispensation respectively.

a **1300** *Cursor M.* 120, I sal yow schew wit myn entent Brefli of aiþere testament. *a* **1340** HAMPOLE *Psalter* Prol., þe lare of þe ald testament & of þe new. **1387** TREVISA *Higden* (Rolls) II. 293 In þe olde testament me redeþ... In þe newe testament. **1447** BOKENHAM *Seyntys* (Roxb.) Introd. 3 As the old testament beryth witnesse. **1532** ELYOT *Let. to Dk. Norfolk* in *Gov.* (1880) Life 79 Thei..doo peruse euery daye one chapitre of the New Testament. *c* **1710** CELIA FIENNES *Diary* (1888) 235 A Large window full of fine paintings—the history of the testaments. **1711** ADDISON *Spect.* No. 160 ¶4 In the Old Testament we find several Passages more elevated and sublime than any in Homer. **1859** DICKENS *T. Two Cities* I. ii, The coachman could..have taken his oath on the two Testaments.

b. The New Testament as distinct from the Old; a copy of the New Testament; a volume containing this. Common in ***Greek Testament***.

1500–20 DUNBAR *Poems* xiv. 14 So quhene the Psalme and Testament to reid Within this land was nevir hard nor sene. **1831** R. SHENNAN *Tales*, etc. 53 (E.D.D.) The Testament was his school-book. **1834** *Encycl. Brit.* (ed. 7) IX. 355 He [Erasmus] had for some time been..employed in preparing an edition of the Greek Testament. **1842** BORROW *Bible in Spain* viii. 49, I had brought with me a certain quantity of Testaments. **1869** MCLENNAN *Peas. Life* I. xvii. (E.D.D.), The Testament, and next 'the Bible', are regular class-books. **1888** MRS. WARD *R. Elsmere* 118 Her little well-worn Testament open on her knee.

6. *attrib.* and *Comb.*, as (sense 1) ***testament-maker***, ***-making***, (sense 4) ***testament-book***; **testament-man**, a disciple of the New Testament.

1573 *New Custom* III. i. in Hazl. *Dodsley* III. 50 Here, take at my hands this *Testament-book. **1533** TINDALE *Supper of Lord* B vj, Where so euer is a testament, there muste the death of the *testament maker go betwene. **1880** MUIRHEAD *Gaius* II. §113 A female acquires the right of *testament-making on reaching twelve. **1819** W. TENNANT *Papistry Storm'd* III. (1827) 103 That mad ill-gainshon'd byke O' *Test'ment-men that doth us fyke.

Hence **ˈtestament** *v.*, *intr.* to make a will; *trans.* to leave by will, bequeath; whence **ˈtestamenting** *vbl. sb.*; **ˈtestamented** *a. nonce-wd.*, included in the Old or New Testament Scriptures.

1586 FERNE *Blaz. Gentrie* 117 In diuers cases in the matter of testamenting a knight is priuiledged. *a* **1878** H. AINSLIE *Pilgr. Land Burns* (1892) 198 What's cross'd the craig Can ne'er be testamented. **1907** C. GREGORY *Canon & Text N.T.* 220 He [Clement] makes short comments on all the testamented Scripture.

†**testaˈmentaire**, *a. Sc. Obs. rare*$^{-1}$. [a. F. *testamentaire* testamentary.] Of or belonging to a testament; ***Old Testamentaire***, of or pertaining to the Old Testament or Mosaic Covenant.

a **1671** in R. MacWard *True Nonconf.* i. 19 The resistance of the Maccabees was Old Testamentaire, and now antiquate.

testamental (tɛstəˈmɛntəl), *a.* Now *rare.* [ad. late or med.L. *testāmentāl-is*, f. L. *testāment-um* TESTAMENT: see -AL[1].] Of, pertaining to, or of the nature of a testament.

1606 *True & Perfect Relat.* Cc iij, And asked Garnet what interpretation hee made of this testamentall protestation. **1621** AINSWORTH *Annot. Pentat.*, *Gen.* vi. 18 Diathekee, that is, a Testament or Disposition..may be named a testamentall covenant, or a covenanting testament. *a* **1647** HABINGTON *Surv. Worc.* in *Worc. Hist. Soc. Proc.* III. 436, I omytt the Testamentall tombestone of William Edden of Darlingscott with his..last will. **1825** J. MONTGOMERY *Hymn 'According to thy gracious word'* ii, Thy testamental cup I take, And thus remember thee.

Hence **testaˈmentally** *adv.*, in a testamental manner, by way of a testament or will; **testaˈmentalness**, testamental quality or nature.

1774 T. WEST *Antiq. Furness* vi. 133 As well amongst the living, as testamentally. **1669** BP. PATRICK *Friendly Debate* 35 A fourth tells them there is a special Mystery in looking at the Testamentalness of Christ's Sufferings.

testaˈmentar, *a. Sc. Law.* [ad. F. *testamentaire* (16th c.), or L. *testamentār-ius*: see TESTAMENTARY and -AR[2].] = TESTAMENTARY 1, 2. ***testament-testamentar***: see TESTAMENT 2.

1546 *Reg. Privy Council Scot.* I. 50 Tutrix testamentar to hir barnes and said umquhile Hew. **1661** *Charters rel. Glasgow* (1906) II. 41 Mary..tutrix testamentar of Esmy duke of Lennox. **1681** STAIR *Instit.* I. vi. §5 There be three kinds of Tutors... The first is, Tutor Testamentar, or nominate.

testamentarily (tɛstəˈmɛntərɪlɪ), *adv. rare.* [f. TESTAMENTARY *a.* + -LY[2]. Cf. obs. F. *testamentairement* by will (1517 in Godef.).] In a testamentary manner, by will.

1774 T. WEST *Antiq. Furness* ii. 35 By these presents, I will, command, and testamentarily confirm. **1880** MUIRHEAD *Gaius* Digest 601 The manumitter was entitled to deal with it testamentarily as part of his own estate.

†**testamenˈtarious**, *a. Obs. rare*$^{-0}$. [f. L. *testāmentāri-us* (see next) + -OUS.]

1656 BLOUNT *Glossogr.*, *Testamentarious*, of, or belonging to a Testament or last Will. Hence in PHILLIPS, BAILEY, ASH.

testamentary (tɛstəˈmɛntərɪ), *a.* Also 6 *erron.* **-ory.** [ad. L. *testāmentāri-us*, f. *testāment-um* TESTAMENT; see -ARY[1]. Cf. TESTAMENTAR.]

1. Of, pertaining to, or having relation to a testament or will; of the nature of a will.

testamentary capacity, capacity to make a will. ***testamentary estate***, estate subject to disposal by will.

1456 *Paston Lett.* I. 373 My Lord Chaunceller..is.. souverain juge and ordinarie principalle under the Pope in a cause testamentarie. **1596** BACON *Max. & Use Com. Law* II. (1635) 24 Its not an estate testamentory. **1759** ROBERTSON *Hist. Scot.* II. Wks. 1813 I. 113 No matrimonial or testamentary cause could be tried but in the spiritual courts. *a* **1827** in Jarman *Powell's Devises* (ed. 3) II. 169 All the residue of his 'goods and chattels, rights, credits, personal and testamentary estate whatsoever'. **1885** *Manch. Exam.* 3 Feb. 5/1 Mrs. B. was not of testamentary capacity.

2. Made or done by will; appointed by will.

1547 *Bk. Marchauntes* e j b, To haue some aniuersari foundacion, or other testamentary gift. **1659** *Gentl. Calling* v. §24 Some testamentary charities. *a* **1794** FEARNE *Posth. Wks.* (1797) 435 In regard to testamentary dispositions of land. **1838** W. BELL *Dict. Law Scot.* 1016 A tutor-nominate or testamentary, is he whom the father..has nominated, either in a testament, or in some other writing. **1869** FREEMAN *Norm. Conq.* III. xii. 218 The groundwork of William's claim as testamentary successor to Eadward.

b. Expressed or contained in a will.

1762 STERNE *Tr. Shandy* V. x, This testamentary proof he gave of his affection to his master. **1851** HAWTHORNE *Ho. Sev. Gables* xviii, In compliance with his testamentary directions. **1910** *Daily News* 20 July 4/2 It has carried out the testamentary request.

3. Of or pertaining to the Old or New Testament.

1849 W. FITZGERALD tr. *Whitaker's Disput.* 28 These books..are comprised in the old and new Testaments, and are therefore styled Testamentary. **1905** J. ORR *Probl. O.T.* viii. (1906) 272 Delitzsch postulates written 'testamentary discourses' and laws of Moses.

†**testamenˈtation.** *Obs. rare*$^{-1}$. [n. of action f. med.L. *testāmentāre* to give by testament, whence some dictionaries have as Eng. *testaˈmentate v.*] The making of a testament; the disposing of one's property by will; = TESTATION 2.

c **1765** BURKE *Tracts on Popery Laws* Wks. XIII. 328 By this Law the right of testamentation is taken away, which the inferiour tenures had always enjoyed.

†**testamen'tiferous**, *a. Obs. nonce-wd.* [f. L. *testāment-um* + -FEROUS.] Bearing the covenant: applied to the Jewish 'ark of the covenant'.

1772 NUGENT tr. *Hist. Fr. Gerund* II. 92 And whither went wandering this concave testamentiferous ark?

†**testa'mentive**, *a. Obs. rare*$^{-1}$. [irreg. f. L. *testāment-um* TESTAMENT + -IVE.] Of the nature of or pertaining to a testament or will.

1622 MABBE tr. *Aleman's d'Alf.* II. 242 Other writings, processiue,.. testamentiue,.. and infinite other the like.

†**'testamentize**, *v. Obs. rare.* [f. TESTAMENT + -IZE.] *intr.* To make one's will.

a **1661** FULLER *Worthies, Denbigh.* (1662) IV. 34 Whether it was.. because Welsh Bishops in that age might not Testamentize without Royal assent.

‖**testamur** (tɛ'steɪmə(r)). [From the L. word *testāmur* 'we testify', used in the document, from *testārī* to testify.] In University use: A certificate from the examiners that a candidate has satisfied them. Also, A certificate generally.

1840 J. T. HEWLETT *P. Priggins* xvii, Balamson and Drinkwater.. though it certainly was a 'shave', got their testamurs. **1860** J. BATEMAN *D. Wilson* I. vii. 115 The result was a refusal to grant the required testamur. **1863** DOWDING *Life & Corr. G. Calixtus* xxvii. 269 A formal testamur from the leading Lutherans at the Congress. **1897** ESCOTT *Soc. Transf. Vict. Age* xiv. 182 In the place of the 'Smalls' testamur.. the special student was tested closely.

testate ('tɛstət), *a.*^{1} and *sb.* [ad. L. *testāt-us*, pa. pple. of *testārī* (also *testāre*) to bear witness, attest, make one's will, etc.]

A. *adj.* **1.** That has left a valid will at death.

1475 *Rolls of Parlt.* VI. 139/1 Persones diyng Testate and Intestate. **1589** WARNER *Alb. Eng.* v. xxvii. (1612) 136 Nor all die testate. **1726** AYLIFFE *Parergon* 132 The lawful Distribution of the Goods of Persons dying both Testate and Intestate. **1906** *Times* 27 July 3/6 He clearly desired when he died to die testate and not intestate.

2. *transf.* Disposed of or settled by will. *testate duty*, succession duty on an estate passing by will.

1792 J. BELKNAP *Hist. New Hampsh.* III. 273 All matters relative to the settlement and descent of estates, testate and intestate. **1875** POSTE *Gaius* II. Comm. (ed. 2) 229 His succession was partly intestate, partly testate. **1880** GLADSTONE *Sp. Ho. Comm.* 15 Mar., Between 1,000*l.* and 1,500*l.* the old testate duty was 30*l.*; the new.. is to be 31*l.*

B. *sb.* †**1.** One who has given testimony; a witness; also (app.) testimony, evidence. *Obs.*

1619 BRATHWAIT *New Spring* C ij b, When thousand Testates shall produced be, For to disclose their close hypocrisie. **1624** HEYWOOD *Captives* III. ii. in Bullen *O. Pl.* IV. 162 Is thy hart sear'd.. Against just testates and apparent truthes? **1635** —— *Hierarch.* VI. 357 The Stoicks Testates were to that Conviction. **1652** J. WRIGHT tr. *Camus' Nat. Paradox* a j, Reader, this Testate is just.

†**2.** The final protocol of a royal writ; = TESTE^2 2.

a **1604** HANMER *Chron. Irel.* (1809) 345 He granted a Charter to the towne of Kilkenny.. with the testate of Thomas Fitz Antony. **1641** EARL MONM. tr. *Biondi's Civil Warres* I. 3 Such gifts being of no validity without a testate of the great Seale.

3. One who at death has left a valid will.

1864 in WEBSTER. **1871** *Daily News* 21 Apr. 2 To place all personal property, whether of testates or intestates, on the same scale.. of a 2 per cent. duty.

testate ('tɛsteɪt), *a.*^{2} [f. as TESTACEAN *a.*: see -ATE^2.] = TESTACEAN *a.*, TESTACEOUS *a.* 2.

1947 *Ann. Rev. Microbiol.* I. 4 In the testate *Pontigulasia vas*, a hypothetical layer of endosomal granules or plaques disappears during the anaphase and reappears during the telophase. **1978** *Bio Systems* X. 79/2 The Foraminifera appear to have had an origin in organisms similar to the testate amoebae.

testate ('tɛsteɪt), *v. rare.* [f. ppl. stem of L. *testārī* (or *-āre*): see TESTATE *a.*^{1} and *sb.* and -ATE^3 5.]

1. *intr.* To bear witness, to testify, to attest.

1624 HEYWOOD *Gunaik.* I. 2 As Epiphanius testates of him. *Ibid.* 15 In Bauron.. she was likewise honoured, and as Lucan testates, in Taurus, a mountaine in Sicilie. **1908** *Westm. Gaz.* 22 July 9/4 Prisoner was also charged with.. forging the handwriting of the testating witness to the same deed.

2. To make one's will.

1892 *Pall Mall G.* 21 June 2/1 As good Mdme. Dubrai remarked whilst testating, with tears in her eyes, 'He [a cat] has all his life been accustomed to his little luxuries'.

testation (tɛ'steɪʃən). [ad. L. *testātiōn-em*, n. of action f. *testārī* (*-āre*): see TESTATE *a.*^{1} and *sb.* Cf. obs. F. *testacion* (14–16th c. in Godef.).]

†**1.** Attestation, testimony. *Obs.*

1642 H. MORE *Song of Soul* II. iii. II. xxix, A true testation Of the souls utter independency On this poor crasie Corse. *a* **1656** BP. HALL *Satan's Fiery Darts quenched* (R.), How clear a testation have the inspired prophets of God given of old to this truth? **1656** in BLOUNT *Glossogr.*

2. The disposal of property by will.

1832 GEN. P. THOMPSON in *Westm. Rev.* Apr. 298 That the right of testation.. is, *primâ facie*, nothing but an extension of the simple right of disposition, to the doing in a convenient way what must otherwise be done in an inconvenient one. **1861** MAINE *Anc. Law* vi. 196 It is doubtful whether a true power of testation was known to any original society except the Roman. **1876** DIGBY *Real Prop.* viii. 343.

testator (tɛ'steɪtə(r)). [In sense 1, a. AF. *testatour* = F. *-teur* (13th c. in Godef. *Compl.*), ad. late L. *testatōr-em*, agent-n. from *testārī* to witness, make a will. In sense 2 direct from L.]

1. One who makes a will; *esp.* one who has died leaving a will.

[**1306** *Rolls of Parlt.* I. 220/1 La volunte de chescun testatour.] **1447** *Ibid.* V. 129/2 Ther remayneth due to the saide Executours, for their saide Testatour,.. the sum of VII or VIII m. marcs. **1535** tr. *Littleton's Nat. Brev.* 29 b, The executours.. brought a wrytte of Erroure of vtlawry pronounced agaynst the testatoure in hys lyfe. **1664** *Protests Lords* (1875) I. 30 Provision made by the testator to pay honest debts. **1766** BLACKSTONE *Comm.* II. xxiii. 376 That all devises of lands and tenements shall not only be in writing, but signed by the testator. **1856** EMERSON *Eng. Traits, Cockayne* Wks. (Bohn) II. 64 A testator endows a dog or a rookery, and Europe cannot interfere with his absurdity.

†**2.** One who or that which testifies; a witness.

1600 W. WATSON *Decacordon* (1602) 350 Come false witnes, come true testator. **1632** LITHGOW *Trav.* x. 435 To all which, and much more haue I beene an occular Testator. **1698** in *Col. Rec. Pennsylv.* I. 549, I am a perfect Testator, by report of David Evans acquittance.

Hence **te'statorship**, the position or office of a testator; **'testatory** *a.*, pertaining to or of the nature of evidence.

1624 BP. ANDREWES *Serm., Heb. xiii. 20–21* (1629) 584 Both, in His [Christ's] Pastor-ship, and in His Testator-ship. **1907** *Daily News* 23 May 6 Whether anything would be gained by giving it a judicial position instead of a testatory we must be allowed to doubt.

testatrix (tɛ'steɪtrɪks). [a. late L. *testātrix*, fem. of *testātor*: see prec.] A female testator.

1591 *Knaresborough Wills* (Surtees) I. 175 This testatrix and her heires. **1751** SMOLLETT *Per. Pic.* (1779) I. vii. 57 Mr. H... who was generously remembered by the testatrix. **1880** J. W. SHERER *Conjuror's Daughter*, etc. 279 The Testatrix desired to mark her high sense of [his] merits and services.. by leaving the property unreservedly to him.

‖**testatum** (tɛ'steɪtəm). *Law.* [L., neut. pa. pple. of *testārī* (*-āre*) to attest, etc.]

†**1.** A writ formerly issued when a writ of capias was returned, the sheriff to whom it was first addressed testifying that the defendant was not to be found within his jurisdiction: see quots. *Obs.*

1607 COWELL *Interpr.* s.v., If the Shyreeue return (*nihil habet in balliva mea*),.. another writ shall be sent out into any other Countie.. which is termed a *Testatum*, because the Shyreeue hath formerly testified, that he found nothing in his Bayliweeke to serue the turne. **1672** T. CORY *Course & Pract. Comm.-Pl.* 27 Untill.. there be an Execution in the Proper County entred upon the Roll, and a *Testatum* awarded. **1848** WHARTON *Law Lex.*, *Testatum writ*, a process of execution which is issued into a different county than that in which the venue was laid in the declaration.

2. The witnessing-clause of a deed.

1844 WILLIAMS *Real Prop.* (1875) 193 The *testatum*, or witnessing part, 'Now this Indenture witnesseth'.

‖**te'statur.** [L., 'he testifies', from *testārī* to bear witness, etc.] An attestation.

1702 *Rouse's Heav. Univ.* Advert. 3 To which he prefixed his most solemn Vidit and Testatur.

'test-cross, *sb.* and *v. Genetics.* [f. TEST *sb.*^{1} + CROSS *sb.*] **A.** *sb.* A cross between an individual whose genotype for a certain trait is unknown and one that is homozygous recessive for that trait, so that the unknown genotype may be determined from that of the offspring.

1934 C. B. BRIDGES in *Jrnl. Heredity* XXV. 18 The type of cross designated.. as the 'backcross' is here to stay... Because of this characteristic we may employ the term 'testcross' wherever 'backcross' has been used in the special meaning. **1979** ARMS & CAMP *Biology* xiii. 198 If the red-flowered plant of unknown genotype were actually heterozygous (Rr), half the offspring of the test cross would be expected to be white-flowered and half red-flowered.

B. *v. trans.* To make the subject of such a cross.

1950 E. W. SINNOTT et al. *Princ. Genetics* (ed. 4) iii. 68 The trihybrid with round and yellow seeds and colored flowers.., when test-crossed to plants with wrinkled, green seeds and white flowers.. will produce 8 combinations. **1978** *Nature* 27 July 317/1 A proportion of the males from a wild population in Texas showed low levels of recombination when heterozygous males were test-crossed to homozygous marked females.

†**teste**^{1}. *Obs. rare.* [a. OF. *teste* (11th c.), mod.F. *tête* head:—L. *testa* an earthen pot, in late L. a skull, in pop.L. head.] The head.

13.. *K. Alis.* 7112 (Bodl. MS.) For Cades was a ferly beste þries shett teeþ weren in his teste. *c* **1450** *Two Cookery-bks.* 112 *Teste de cure.*—Nym rys.. & bray hem al to doust: tempre it vp with almand mylk, cast therto poudur and safron & sugur [etc.].

teste^2 ('tɛstiː). Also 6 **testey**, **-ty**, 7 **-tee**. [a. L. *teste*, abl. of *testis* witness.]

1. The L. word *teste* in ablative absolute constr. with a pronoun (e.g. *meipso* myself) or name of a person, as used in the authenticating clause of a writ, etc.: see sense 2; hence, in same construction, in non-legal use, before the name of a person cited as witness or authority, = (So and so) being witness, on the authority or evidence of (So and so); ***teste meipso, seipso***, on my or his own testimony or authority; also as *sb.* one's own evidence.

[*c* **1194**: see Note to sense 2.] **1607** COWELL *Interpr.*, *Teste*, is.. so called, because the very conclusion of euery writ wherein the date is contained, beginneth with these words (*teste meipso*, etc.).

1654 GAYTON *Pleas. Notes* IV. xxiii. 277 This proofe a *Teste seipso*, is not so current as the other. **1686** SOUTH *Serm.* (1727) II. 340 Presently the Sot.. vouched also by a *Teste Meipso*,.. steps forth an exact Politician. **1842** BARHAM *Ingol. Leg.* Ser. II. *Blasphemer's Warn.*, Many.. commanders 'Swore terribly (*teste* T. Shandy) in Flanders'. **1848** LOWELL *Biglow P.* Ser. I. ii, The Devil, *teste* Cotton Mather, is unversed in certain of the Indian dialects. **1916** G. SAINTSBURY *Peace of Augustans* iii. 130 Lamb (*teste* Hazlitt..) was inclined to agree with Scott. **1968** *Listener* 6 June 737/2 He tells us, *teste* Evelyn Waugh, of a Sitwellian habit of leaving Sitwell press cuttings (surely not *all* their press cuttings?) in bowls on the drawing-room table.

2. a. The final clause in a royal writ naming the person who authorizes the affixing of the king's seal.

Where (as in letters close and patent) the king himself authenticates the sealing, the clause has, since Rich. I, begun *teste meipso* 'witness I myself'. Where a high official authenticates (as in judicial and exchequer writs, and during the king's absence), his name and (usually) office are stated. As such a clause generally stated place and date of sealing, the term became practically = DATE *sb.*^{2}

1423 in *Letter-bk. I Lond.* (1909) 298 The teste of the which maundement ys the xx day of Feverer, the second yeer of his regne. **1467–8** *Rolls of Parlt.* V. 603/2 Oure said Letters Patentes, wherof the Teste is at Westm' the xixth day of Juyn. **1542–3** *Act 34 & 35 Hen. VIII*, c. 26 §14 The teste of euerye bill and judiciall proces that shall passe undre the saide judiciall Seall, shalbe undre the name of suche of the saide Justices.. in lyke maner and forme as it is used in the Common Place in Englande. **1577–87** HOLINSHED *Chron.* III. 1245/1 It was doone by the son in the fathers name, and vnder the teste of the son, the father yet being king in shew. **1588** LAMBARDE *Eiren.* II. ii. 106 Which.. may bee in the name of the Queene, and vnder the Teste of the Iustice of the Peace, thus.. Witnesse the said G. M. **1653** *Acts & Ordin. Parl.* (1658) 275 From and after the six and twentieth day of December, 1653, the Name, Style, Title and Teste of the 'Lord Protector.. of the Commonwealth of England, Scotland, and Ireland, and the Dominions thereto belonging', shall be used, and no other. **1658** *Practick Part of Law* 6 This Writ may bear Teste out of the Term. **1672** CORY *Course & Pract. Comm.-Pl.* 23 Of the Teste's and Retorns of Writs in all Actions real and personal. **1765** BLACKSTONE *Comm.* I. ii. 172 No candidate shall, after the date (usually called the *teste*) of the writs.. give any money or entertainment. **1792** *Act Congr.* in *Bouvier's Law Dict.* (1898) s.v., All writs and process issuing from the supreme or a circuit court shall bear teste of the chief justice of the supreme court. **1818** CRUISE *Digest* (ed. 2) V. 396 It appeared the *teste* of the warrant of attorney was after appearance.

b. Hence, more generally, a clause stating the name of a witness (as to a charter in writ-form).

1611 SPEED *Hist. Gt. Brit.* VII. xliv. §45. 380 His name is continually set downe, as a Witnesse in the testees of his fathers Charters. *c* **1617** in Hardy *Rot. Chart.* (1837) Introd. 30 There was some question about the marshalling of these testes in there due place. *Ibid.*, Whether the Duke.. should take his place in the teste as Earle of Richmond or Duke of Lenneux.

†**c.** Evidence, proof. *Obs.*

1567 FENTON *Trag. Disc.* 214 Whyche kynde of courtyng thamarus Luchyn forgatt not too prefer as a testey of hys seruice and a furtherer of his sut. *c* **1585** *Faire Em* II. i. 100 Whose glauncing eyes.. Giues testies of their Maisters amorous hart.

teste, obs. form of TEST *sb.*^{1}, ^{3}.

tested, teste'd, *ppl. a.*: see under TEST *v.*

†**te'stee**^{1}. *Obs. rare.* [Irreg. formation from L. *testis* witness, perh. with ending -EE as in *trustee*, etc.] A witness. Cf. TESTE^2.

1654 VILVAIN *Epit. Ess.* VI. lxxvi, No Murdrer be: Whorster: Theef: fals Testee [*rime* thee]. **1682** R. WARE *Foxes & Firebr.* II. 23 Three Testees were to wait on these Houses weekly, to take out what summs there were thrown in.

testee^2 (tɛ'stiː). [f. TEST *v.*^{2} + -EE^1.] One who is subjected to a test of his or her health, intelligence, knowledge, etc.

1932 W. S. DUKE-ELDER *Text-bk. Ophthalm.* I. xxv. 986 The fact that picking skeins of wool does not appeal to the average workman, while the reading of pseudochromatic diagrams requires a considerable amount of intelligence, has popularized the adoption of lantern tests wherein coloured glasses are illuminated and the testee is asked to name the colour and (sometimes) to match it with wools or some other coloured material. **1947** *Sci. News* IV. 19 The main difficulty with such tests was that the tester was usually as intoxicated as the testee, and often forgot to press the spindle of his stopwatch, or to take proper notes. **1952** C. P. BLACKER *Eugenics: Galton & After* 190 These gaps.. make it all the more surprising that so little account was taken of the testee's subsequent services and achievements. **1964** M. CRITCHLEY *Developmental Dyslexia* vii. 50 The testee is required to detect which of the simple figures lies concealed or incorporated within the complex design. **1976** K. S. BOWERS *Hypnosis for Seriously Curious* iii. 43 Even on the subset of questions for which the testee subjectively feels he is simply guessing, the likelihood is high that he will get more than 25% correct answers. **1983** *Daily Tel.* 22 Sept. 18 Gascoigne.. said of his testees [on a quiz programme]: 'They were far more argumentative in the 60s and 70s.'

tester[1] ('tɛstə(r)). Forms: α. 4- tester; 5 -ere, -our, -ir, -ur(e, testre, *Sc.* tyster, -yr, 5-6 teester, 6 (9) testor, 6-7 -ar, teaster (9 *dial.*), 7 taister. β. 6 test-, teasterne, testorne, 7 -arn, -ern. [prob. from OF.: cf. *testre* fem. (15th c., one example in Godef.) the vertical part of a bed behind the head; also OF. *testière*, mod.F. *têtière* a covering for the head, etc., It. *testiera*, Sp. *testera*, med.L. *testera*, *-eria* (see TESTER[2]); also med.L. *testerium*, *testrum*, *testūra*, also *testāle*, all, according to Du Cange, = 'the upper part, top, or upper covering of a bed', derivatives of L. *testa*, in late pop.L. and Comm. Romanic 'head'.

The historical relations of these words are not quite clear, but app. med.L. *testerium*, *-eria*, It. *testiera*, Sp. *testera*, OF. *testière*, and ME. *testere*, go together in form, as do med.L. *testrum*, OF. and ME. *testre*, and perh. also med.L. *testura* and ME. *testur*; though the senses are specialized in different langs. The other Eng. forms appear to have been assimilated to various endings in *-er*, *-ar*, *-or*, *-our*, and (erratically) *-ern*, *-orn*.]

1. A canopy over a bed, supported on the posts of the bedstead or suspended from the ceiling; formerly (esp. in phrase ***tester and celure***), the vertical part at the head of the bed which ascends to and sometimes supports the canopy, or (as some think) the wooden or metal framework supporting the canopy and curtains.

α. *c* **1380** WYCLIF *Wks.* (1880) 434 In aparel of chaumbre, as in proud beddis, testeris & curteyns. **14..** *Voc.* in Wr.-Wülcker 615/17 *Tapisterium*, an[ce] a Testour. *a* **1440** *Sir Degrev.* 1474 Hur bede was off azure, With testur and celure. *Ibid.* 1485 Ther was at hur testere The kyngus owne banere. *c* **1440** *Promp. Parv.* 489/2 Teester, or tethtere of a bed, *capitellum*. **1449** *Test. Ebor.* (Surtees) II. 156 Testur. **1454** *E.E. Wills* (1882) 133 My bed..wiþ the testour & Canape ther-to. **1530** PALSGR. 280/1 Testar for a bedde, *dossier*. **1548** in Strype *Eccl. Mem.* (1721) II. xvi. 129 A bedstead gilt, with a testor and counterpoint, with curtains belonging to the same. **1556** WITHALS *Dict.* (1568) 51/1 A teaster ouer the bedde, *canopus*. **1670** F. SANDFORD *Order Funeral Dk. Albemarle* (1722) 5 A Bed of State of black Velvet..with black Plumes at the four Corners of the Tester. **1801** tr. *Gabrielli's Myst. Husb.* III. 4 The tester of a bed..was suspended by cords to the lofty ceiling. **1899** *Q. Rev.* Apr. 394 The tester, carved and panelled, is surrounded by a cornice, inlaid with lighter wood, from which a crimson silk valance and curtains hang.

β. **1546** in Willis & Clark *Cambridge* (1886) III. 351 A bedstok with cortins of dornix, and testerne of the same. **1565-73** COOPER *Thesaurus*, *Conopeum*..a Canapie... Some haue vsed it for a testorne to hang ouer a bed. **1599** *Nottingham Rec.* IV. 252 One olde thinne silke teasterne for a bedd. **1655** tr. *Com. Hist. Francion* IV. 11 He took a Base Vioil from the testern of his Bed.

2. *transf.* and *fig.* Something that covers or overhangs; a shrine; a canopy carried over a dignitary; the soundboard of a pulpit, etc.

c **1425** WYNTOUN *Cron.* VI. x. 773 (Cott. MS.) He mad a tystyr [*v.r.* textuere] in þat qwhile, Qwhar in was cloyssit þe Ewangile, Platit oure withe siluir bricht. **1598** FLORIO, *Baldacchino*,..a testerne carried cuer Princes. **1611** COTGR., *Surciel*, the tester of a cloth of State. **1830** GALT *Lawrie T.* IV. iv, A night under the starry tester of the heavens. **1846-75** PARKER *Gloss. Archit.* s.v., The canopy over Queen Eleanor's tomb at Westminster is called a tester in old documents. **1908** *Athenæum* 1 Aug. 119/3 The remarkably fine pulpit and tester of the church of Bishop's Waltham.

3. *attrib.* and *Comb.*, as ***tester-bed***, ***-bedstead***, ***cloth***, ***-rail***; ***tester-covering*** adj.

1622 DRAYTON *Poly-olb.* xxvi. 85 The rich and sumptuous Beds, with Tester-couering plumes. **1730** SOUTHALL *Bugs* 35 Oak-Bedsteds, and plain Wainscot Head-Boards, and Tester-Rails of that Wood. **1776** in J. S. Moore *Goods & Chattels of our Forefathers* (1976) 270 Bedstead, Green Curtains, Vallens and Head and Tester Cloths etc. **1843** BORROW *Bible in Spain* xxiii. (Pelh. Libr.) 160, I was stretched on the tester bed. **1853** *Heal & Sons Catal.: Bedsteads* 59 Half-Tester Bedstead..Chintz Furniture.. fringed and fluted head and tester cloth. **1873** *Sat. Rev.* 29 Nov. 707/1 The mother of St. John the Baptist is supported by cushions in a tester bedstead.

Hence **testered** ('tɛstəd) *a.*, having a tester.

1790 MRS. A. M. JOHNSON *Monmouth* I. 70 The lofty testered bed..was in a ruinous state.

† **'tester**[2]. *Obs.* Also 5 te'stere, tee'steer, testor, ‖testiere. [a. OF. *testière* (12th c. in Godef. *Compl.*) 'any kind of head-peece, particularly a scull, sallet, or steele cap, also the crowne of a hat' (Cotgr.), mod.F. *têtière* covering of the top of the head, coif, headstall of a horse, = It. *testiera* 'head piece, a caske or helmet, testerne or head of any thing, head-stall of a bridle' (Florio), Sp. *testera* 'armour for the forehead of a horse' (Minsheu), Pg. *testeira* 'anything to cover the front', med.L. *testera*, *testeria* (Du Cange), f. *testa*, OF. *teste* head.]

A piece of armour for the head; a head-piece, a casque; also, a piece of armour for the head of a horse; a kind of mask or visor with holes for the eyes, apertures for the ears, etc.

c **1386** CHAUCER *Knt.'s T.* 1641 The sheeldes brighte, testeres [*v.rr.* testers, teesteers], and trappures, Gold hewen helmes, hauberkes. **1465** *Mann. & Househ. Exp. Eng.* (Roxb.) 285 The man that maketh his testor of mayle. **1484** CAXTON *Chivalry* 67 To his hors is gyuen in his hede a testiere to signefye that a knyȝt ought to do none armes without reason.

tester[3] ('tɛstə(r)). *arch.* Forms: α. 6 testourn, teastern, 6-7 testern, -erne, -orn, -orne; β. 6-7 testor, 7 -ar, teaster, 6- tester. [app. the result of a series of corruptions or perversions of TESTON.] A name for the TESTON of Henry VIII, esp. as debased and depreciated; subsequently a colloquial or slang term for a sixpence.

α. **1546** WRIOTHESLEY *Chron.* (Camden) I. 176 Condemned for treason for counterfeiting testornes. **1560** in *Buccleuch MSS.* (Hist. MSS. Comm.) I. 223 Knowledge of the better testornes from the worse. **1579** G. HARVEY *Letter-bk.* (Camden) 72 Eloquence..were more worth then a crackd testerne in his purse. **1614** J. COOKE *Greene's Tu Quoque* D iij b, A testerne or a shilling to a seruant that brings you a glasse of beere, bindes his hands to his lippes.

β. **1567-8** in *11th Rep. Dep. Kpr. Irel.* 180 With not more than two testors a day each. **1597** SHAKS. *2 Hen. IV*, III. ii. 296 Hold, there is a Tester for thee. **1608** DAY *Law Trickes* III. i, Prethee giue the Fidler a testar and send him packing. **1613** TAPP *Pathw. Knowl.* 53 There is also the Tester or halfe shilling which is 6d. **1765** FOOTE *Commissary* I. Wks. 1799 II. 8, I hope you'll tip me the tester to drink. **1822** LAMB *Elia* Ser. I. *Praise Chimneysweepers*, If it be starving weather..the demand on thy humanity will surely rise to a tester. *a* **1839** PRAED *Poems* (1864) I. 94 Well! it was worth a silver tester, To see how she frowned when the Abbess blessed her.

tester[4] ('tɛstə(r)). [Agent-n. f. TEST *v.*[2] or *sb.*[1]: see -ER[1].] **a.** One who tests or proves, or whose business is to test the quality or condition of anything; a device for testing. In quot. 1697, (?) a supporter of religious or political tests.

1661 BOYLE *Style of Script.* (1675) 128 Those wary testers, that like not to be cheated. **1697** ISABEL WRIGHT in *Collect. Dying Test.* (1806) 42 Testers, Banders, Bloodshedders, Consenters to Blood. **1702** *Lond. Gaz.* No. 3818/4 The Queen has been pleased to appoint..Hopton Hains Esq., Weigher and Tester of the Mint. **1882** OGILVIE (Annandale), *Tester*, one who tests [etc.]; as, a good tester. **1884** KNIGHT *Dict. Mech.*, *Suppl.*, *Steam Gage Tester*, an instrument to test the accuracy of the steam gage. **1899** *Westm. Gaz.* 14 Jan. 8/1 A train..stops; a tester is going round with his hammer striking the wheels. **1910** *Ibid.* 8 Mar. 5/2 A device which commends itself to..owners of motor-cars generally is the Acer brake horse-power tester.

b. *Biol.* A stock or strain of organism used to investigate some genetic characteristic of another strain.

1925 *Genetics* X. 421 Two other stocks were needed as 'testers'. **1969** A. M. CAMPBELL *Episomes* iii. 37 Operationally, a bacterial culture is termed F$^+$ if it will mate with an F$^-$ tester strain.

† **testern**, *v.* *Obs.* *nonce-wd.* [See TESTER[3].] *trans.* To present with a tester; to 'tip'.

1591 SHAKS. *Two Gent.* I. i. 153 To testifie your bounty, I thank you, you haue testern'd me.

testern(e, obs. form of TESTER[1], [3].

testes, pl. of TESTIS.

testey, obs. f. TESTE[2].

testibiopalladite (tɛ,stɪbɪəʊ'pælədaɪt). *Min.* [f. TE(LLURIUM + STIBI(UM (or STI(BIUM + BI(SMUTH) + -O + PALLAD)IUM[2] + -ITE[1].] A mineral, Pd(Sb,Bi)Te, found as minute whitish or grey cubic crystals having a metallic lustre.

1974 *Ti Ch'iu Hua Hsueh* (*Geochimica*) III. 181 Sixteen new minerals..were found from two nickelsulfide deposits in China. The three well studied are: Testibiopalladite, Pd(Sb,Bi)Te. **1978** *Canad. Mineralogist* XVI. 126/1 The first occurrence of testibiopalladite outside China is reported from Kambalda, Western Australia, where it occurs as cores to zoned inclusions of michenerite-testibiopalladite in altaite.

testibrachial (,tɛstɪ'breɪkɪəl), *a.* *Anat.* [f. mod.L. *testibrachi-um* (f. *testis* TESTIS + *brachium* arm) + -AL[1].] Of or pertaining to the *testibrachium* or prepeduncle of the cerebellum, being the process from the cerebellum to the testis of the brain.

1891 in *Cent. Dict.*

‖ **testicardines** (,tɛstɪ'kɑːdɪniːz), *sb. pl.* *Zool.* [mod.L., f. *testa* shell + *cardo* (*cardin-*) hinge.] A primary division of brachiopods, having hinged shells; opposed to *Ecardines*. Hence **testi'cardine** *a. rare*, **testi'cardinate** *a.*, having a hinged shell.

1878 BELL *Gegenbaur's Comp. Anat.* 308 In the Testicardines it is short and largely chitinised. **1888** ROLLESTON & JACKSON *Anim. Life* 693 In the hinged Brachiopoda or *Testicardines* the dorsal valve is furnished with a projecting cardinal process to which are attached the divaricator muscles. **1895** *Camb. Nat. Hist.* III. xvii. 467 On the inner surface of the shell of the Testicardinate Brachiopoda..are two lateral teeth.

testicle ('tɛstɪk(ə)l). Also 5 testicule. [ad. L. *testiculus*, dim. f. *testis* TESTIS[2]: see -CULE. Cf. F. *testicule*, Sp., Pg. *testiculo*, It. *testicolo*.] Each of the two ellipsoid glandular bodies, constituting the sperm-secreting organs in male mammals, and usually enclosed in a scrotum; = TESTIS[2] 1 a.

c **1425** tr. *Arderne's Treat. Fistula* 14 His testicules war bolned out of mesure. **1597** A. M. tr. *Guillemeau's Fr. Chirurg.* 21 b/1 This swellinge..of the testicles. **1646** SIR T. BROWNE *Pseud. Ep.* III. iv. 112 That a Bever to escape the Hunter, bites off his testicles or stones, is a tenent very ancient. **1783** JUSTAMOND tr. *Raynal's Hist. Indies* I. 307 It is very certain, and has often been observed that the Hottentot men have but one testicle. **1876** BRISTOWE *The. & Pract. Med.* (1878) 171 (Small-pox) Inflammation of the ovary or testicle is occasionally observed.

b. Rarely applied to the corresponding organs in non-mammals: see TESTIS[2] 1 b.

[**1634** R. H. *Salerne's Regiment* 36 Testicles or Stones, and especially stones of fatte Cockes..be very good and great nourishers.] **1713** WARDER *True Amazons* 10 [The Drone has] a large pair of Testicles, as big as great Pins Heads. **1841-71** T. R. JONES *Anim. Kingd.* (ed. 4) 282 Both the ovary and testicle are evidently temporary organs. **1877** HUXLEY *Anat. Inv. Anim.* vii. 389 The testicle is an elongated sac which lies on the ventral aspect of the intestine.

†**c.** *transf.* The ovary in females. *Obs.*

1545 RAYNOLD *Byrth Mankynde* I. (1634) 69 The right stone or testicle in a Woman. **1684** tr. *Bonet's Merc. Compit.* x. 364 The Womb with its Ligaments and the Testicles may hurt the Loins. **1691** RAY *Creation* II. (1692) 66 Membranes ..capable of a prodigious extension, as we see in the Hydatides of the female Testicles or Ovaries.

†**d.** *pl.* An old name for an orchid, from the form of the tubers: in quot. app. applied to *Spiranthes autumnalis*. *Obs.*

1597 GERARDE *Herbal* I. cii. 169 The first is called..in English sweete smelling Testicles or Stones.

e. *attrib.* and *Comb.*

1880 GÜNTHER *Fishes* 157 In the European species of Serranus a testicle-like body is attached to the lower part of the ovary. **1899** CAGNEY tr. *Jaksch's Clin. Diagn.* ix. (ed. 4) 424 Finely granular testicle-cells.

testicond ('tɛstɪkɒnd), *a.* *Zool.* [f. L. *testis*, TESTIS[2] + *cond-ĕre* to conceal.] Having the testes contained within the body, as the *Cetacea*.

1864 DANA cited in WEBSTER.

testicular (tɛ'stɪkjʊlə(r)), *a.* [f. L. *testiculus* TESTICLE: see -AR[1]; cf. F. *testiculaire*.]

1. a. Of or pertaining to, containing, or having the nature or function of a testicle or testicles.

1656 BLOUNT *Glossogr.*, *Testicular*,..belonging to the stones of man or beast. **1775** in ASH. **1841-71** T. R. JONES *Anim. Kingd.* (ed. 4) 255 The fifth segment [of the earthworm], from behind, is again testicular,..so that the first and the last segments in this region are testicular, the three intermediate ones being ovarian. **1899** CAGNEY tr. *Jaksch's Clin. Diagn.* ix, The spermatic or testicular secretion.

b. ***testicular feminization*** (or ***feminizing***): a familial condition produced in genetically male persons by the failure of tissue to respond to male sex hormones, resulting in a normal female appearance (including external genitalia) but with testes in place of ovaries; usu. *attrib.*

1953 J. M. MORRIS in *Amer. Jrnl. Obstetr. & Gynecol.* LXV. 1192 Actually these patients present a fairly typical clinical picture. For this reason they have been singled out from the other forms of intersexuality, and we have called the clinical syndrome 'testicular feminization'. **1959**, **1970** [see FEMINIZATION 2]. **1974** PASSMORE & ROBSON *Compan. Med. Stud.* III. xxix. 2/2 One other specific condition is the testicular feminizing syndrome in which XY individuals with testes nevertheless develop female external genitalia and female secondary development at puberty. **1978** *Price's Textbk. Practice of Med.* (ed. 12) v. 550/2 In the testicular feminization syndrome a different approach is indicated because..'she' may already be married and having satisfactory sexual intercourse.

2. Resembling a testicle in form; testiculate.

1769 E. BANCROFT *Guiana* 73 Berries of a reddish yellow colour, and testicular form. **1821** W. P. C. BARTON *Flora N. Amer.* I. 53 The genus orchis..derives its name from the testicular shape of the roots in many species.

testiculate (tɛ'stɪkjʊlət), *a.* [ad. late L. *testiculātus*: see TESTICLE and -ATE[2].] Formed like a testicle (= prec. 2); also, applied to the twin tubers of certain species of Orchis.

1760 J. LEE *Introd. Bot.* III. xxii. (1765) 220 In Orchis, where the Species are known by the Roots being fibrose, round or testiculate. **1828** in WEBSTER.

So **te'sticulated** *a.* [-ED[1] 2] in same sense.

1725 SLOANE *Jamaica* II. 95 Berries,..two always sticking close or being join'd together, as if testiculated. **1727** BAILEY vol. II, *Testiculated Root*..consists of two Knobs, resembling a Pair of Testicles. **1751** WATSON in *Phil. Trans.* XLVII. 178 From this testiculated appearance they called these plants males. **1775** in ASH.

† **te'sticulatory**, *a.* *Obs.* *rare*$^{-1}$. [f. as prec. + -ORY[2].] Generative.

a **1693** *Urquhart's Rabelais* III. xxvii. 224 Testiculatory Ability.

testicule, obs. form of TESTICLE.

† **testiculose**, *a.* *Obs.* *rare*$^{-0}$. [f. L. *testicul-us* TESTICLE + -OSE[1].] So † **testiculous** *a.*

1721 BAILEY, *Testiculous*, that hath great Cods. **1727** —— vol. II, *Testiculose*,..that hath large Cods. **1775** in ASH.

testie, dial. var. TEISTIE, Black Guillemot.

‖ **testiere**: see TESTER[2].

testif, -yf, obs. forms of TESTY.

† **testificate**. Chiefly *Sc.* *Obs.* [ad. L. *testificāt-um* (that which is) testified, subst. use of neut. pa. pple. of *testificārī* to TESTIFY.] A writing

wherein a fact is attested; a certificate; *spec.* in *Sc. Law*: see quot. 1838.

1610 in Row *Hist. Kirk* (Wodrow Soc.) 277 To requyre.. a testificat of his conversation past, abilitie, and qualification for the function. **1620** SHELTON *Quix.* (1746) IV. xxxiii. 258 Which Testificate he desired. **1676** W. ROW *Contn. Blair's Autobiog.* xi. (1848) 366 Three testificates were sent over to the Committee. *a* **1722** FOUNTAINHALL *Decis.* (1761) II. 394 A testificate being returned that there was no such thing to be found in their books. **1838** W. BELL *Dict. Law Scot.*, *Testificate*, was a solemn written assertion, not on oath, used in judicial procedure... The term is now obsolete.

b. *fig.* Evidence, indication.

1590 GREENE *Never too late* (1600) 98 The wenches eyes are a testificate. **1637** RUTHERFORD *Lett.* (1862) I. 349 Take Christ's testificate with you out of this life—'Well done, good and faithful servant!' **1833** GALT in *Fraser's Mag.* VIII. 65 He gave a deep sigh, which was a testificate to me that the leaven of unrighteousness was still within him.

testification (ˌtɛstɪfɪˈkeɪʃən). Now *rare.* [a. obs. F. *testificacion* (1400 in Godef.), or ad. L. *testificātiōn-em*, n. of action f. *testificārī* to TESTIFY.] The action or an act of testifying; the testimony borne; a fact or object (as a document, etc.) serving as evidence or proof.

c **1450** *Cov. Myst.* vii. (1841) 69 Wyttnessynge here, be trew testyficacion, That maydenys childe xal be prince of pes. **1593** ABP. BANCROFT *Daung. Posit.* I. iii. 10 A testification was made of their intentes. **1633** SANDERSON *Serm.* (1681) II. 30 Honour..is an acknowledgment or a testification of some excellency or other in the person honoured, by some reverence or observance answerable thereunto. **1640–1** *Kirkcudbr. War-Comm. Min. Bk.* (1855) 42 That he shall bring..Margaret Sampell's testification that he is her hired servant. **1671** FLAVEL *Fount. Life* xi, Thankofferings, in Testification of Homage, Duty and Service. **1718** HICKES & NELSON *J. Kettlewell* II. xxxii. 139 For the perpetual Testification whereof there was an Instrument drawn up. **1865** G. MEREDITH *Rhoda Fleming* ix, The thin blue-and-pink paper, and the foreign postmarks—testifications to Dahlia's journey.

testificator (tɛˈstɪfɪkeɪtə(r)). *rare.* [Agent-n. in Latin form f. L. *testificārī* to TESTIFY: see -OR.] One who testifies or attests; a testifier.

1730 in BAILEY (folio). **1755** in JOHNSON. **1854** W. WATERWORTH *Orig. Anglicanism* 10 There has been..from the Apostolic days, an uninterrupted body of testificators.

testificatory (tɛstɪfɪˈkeɪtərɪ, tɛˈstɪfɪkətərɪ), *a.* [See prec. and -ORY[2]; cf. OF. *testificatoire* (1387).] Of such a kind as to testify, or serve as evidence.

1593 NASHE *Christ's T.* (1613) 24 They shall haue..not one stone of thy Temple or Sanctuarie testificatory against them. **1821** CARLYLE in Froude *Life* (1882) I. xxii. 417 This morning came a decent testificatory letter from Buller. **1834** *Fraser's Mag.* IX. 169 A Fanatic..conceives the workings of his own mind..to be testificatory of the truth of opinion.

testified (ˈtɛstɪfaɪd), *ppl. a.* [f. TESTIFY *v.* + -ED[1].] Attested; made known, declared.

1552 HULOET, Testified or knowen of all men, *testatus.* **1648** MILTON *Tenure Kings* (1650) 4 Justice..is the Sword of God..in whose hand soever..his testified will is to put it.

testifier (ˈtɛstɪfaɪə(r)). [f. TESTIFY *v.* + -ER[1].] One who testifies; a witness.

1611 COTGR., *Tesmoing*, a witnesse, testis, testifier. **1659** PEARSON *Creed* i. (1662) 4 The strength and validity of every Testimony must bear proportion with the Authority of the Testifier. **1752** J. GILL *Trinity* i. 13 Though the Father, Word, and Spirit are one, yet not one person; because if so, they could not be three testifiers. **1854** E. G. HOLLAND *Mem. J. Badger* xi. 209 Testifiers to the same fact.

testify (ˈtɛstɪfaɪ), *v.* Also 5–6 testy-, 5–7 teste-; 4 -fiȝe, 4–6 -fye, 4–8 -fie, 6 (*Sc.*) -fei. [ad. late or med.L. *testificāre*, cl. L. *testificārī* to bear witness, proclaim, f. *testi-s* witness + *fic-us* making: see -FY. So obs. F. *testifier* (16th c.).]

1. *trans.* To bear witness to, or give proof of (a fact); to assert or affirm the truth of (a statement); to attest.

1393 LANGL. *P. Pl.* C. XIII. 172 Meny prouerbis ich myghte haue of meny holy seyntes, To testifie [*v.rr.* testefie, testefiȝe] for treuthe þe tale þat ich shewe. *c* **1420** ? LYDG. *Assembly of Gods* 452 That can Dame Nature well testyfy. **1495** *Act 11 Hen. VII*, c. 10 §2, ij witnesses or moo that woll witnesse and testefie the seid payment. **1526** TINDALE *John* iii. 11 We speake that we knowe, and testify that we have sene. **1560** DAUS tr. *Sleidane's Comm.* 55 b, A signe wherby he maye testifie, that he careth for vs. **16..** *Rolls of Parlt.* II. 438/1 It is testified by the said Earle..that the said Arnold was taken. **1820** JEFFERSON *Writ.* (1830) IV. 325 The superlative wisdom of Socrates is testified by all antiquity.

b. *intr.* (usually with *of*) and *absol.*

1377 LANGL. *P. Pl.* B. XIII. 93 þanne shal he testifye of a trinitee and take his felawe to witnesse. **1513** BRADSHAW *St. Werburge* I. 2448 That they shulde testyfy with hym in this case. **1526** TINDALE *John* ii. 25 Jesus..neded nott that eny man shulde testify off man. For he knewe what was in man. **1579** W. WILKINSON *Confut. Familye of Loue* To Rdr. *iv b, Those which take in hand to testifie of any matter whatsoever. **1746–7** HERVEY *Medit.* (1818) 192 Drop down, ye Showers, and testify as you fall, testify of His grace. **1884** J. QUINCY *Figures of Past* 228 [He] testified to me of the affection with which he was regarded by his slaves.

2. *transf.* of things: **a.** *trans.* To serve as evidence of; to constitute proof or testimony of. **b.** *intr.* and *absol.*

1445 in *Anglia* XXVIII. 271 Also thi writyng testifieth thi yiftes be not streyned. **1593** SHAKS. *2 Hen. VI*, IV. ii. 158 The brickes are aliue at this day to testifie it. **1644** EVELYN *Diary* 12 Nov., Dioclesian's Bathes, whose ruines testifie the vastness of the original foundation. **1794** SULLIVAN *View Nat.* II. 132 Do not these shells testify a present, or a former communication between these contending elements of fire and water? **1849** HANNA *Mem. Chalmers* I. ii. 42 The manuscript volumes..still remain to testify his diligence. **1879** HUXLEY *Hume* vi. 116 The proposition..must mean.. that the fact is testified by my present consciousness.

1596 SHAKS. *Tam. Shr.* IV. iii. 131 Why heere is the note of the fashion to testify... Reade it. **1879** M. PATTISON *Milton* iii. 37 His three Latin epigrams addressed to this lady ..testify to the enthusiasm she excited in the musical soul of Milton.

3. *trans.* To profess and openly acknowledge (a fact, belief, object of faith or devotion, etc.); to proclaim as something that one knows or believes. Chiefly *biblical.* **b.** *intr.* To bear testimony.

1526 TINDALE *Acts* xx. 24 The ministracion which I have receaved of the lorde Jesu to testify the gospell of the grace of god. **1535** COVERDALE *2 Esdras* ii. 36, I testifie my sauioure openly. *a* **1631** DONNE *Serm.* vii. (1640) 72 To testifie our fall in Adam, the Church appoints us to fall upon our knees. **1841** LANE *Arab. Nts.* I. ii. 112 He..stood upon his feet,.. and exclaimed, I testify that there is no deity but God. **1867** VISCT. STRANGFORD *Select.* (1869) II. 73 They testify their faith therein openly and aloud.

1784 COWPER *Task* v. 856 In vain thy creatures testify of thee, Till thou proclaim thyself. **1818** SCOTT *Hrt. Midl.* xii, Them that witnessed, and testified, and fought, and endured pit, prison-house, and transportation. **1853** KINGSLEY *Hypatia* xxx, They had no mind to be martyrs, for they had nothing for which to testify.

4. *intr.* and *trans.* To declare solemnly; = PROTEST *v.* 1. *Obs.* exc. in biblical use.

1526 TINDALE *John* xiii. 21 Jesus..was troubled in his sprete and testified sayinge: verely verely I saye vnto you, that won off you shall betraye me. —— *Gal.* v. 3, I testifie agayne to every man..that he is bounde to kepe the whole lawe. —— *2 Tim.* iv. 1, I testifie therfore before god, and before the lorde Jesu Christ..preache the worde, be fervent, be it in season or out of season. **1535** COVERDALE *1 Sam.* viii. 9 Testifye vnto them, and shewe them the lawe of the kynge that shall raigne ouer them. —— *Ps.* xlix. 7 Let me testifie amonge you, o Israel: I am God euen thy God. **1582** N. T. (Rhem.) *Acts* xx. 21 Testifying [Gr. διαμαρτυρόμενος; Vulg. *testificans*; *earlier vv.* witnessing] to Iewes and Gentils penance toward God and faith in our Lord Iesus Christ. **1667** MILTON *P.L.* XI. 721 At length a Reverend Sire among them came,..And testifi'd against thir wayes.

5. *trans.* To give evidence of, display, manifest, express (desire, emotion, etc.). *Obs.* or *arch.*

1560 DAUS tr. *Sleidane's Comm.* 120 b, An oration.. testifying the inward sorow, which he had conceaued. **1678** *Trans. Crt. Spain* 32 The people of Madrid testified a great desire of seeing our young Prince. **1701** W. WOTTON *Hist. Rome* vi. 107 Nothing was too much to testify the Peoples Joy. **1749** FIELDING *Tom Jones* XVIII. iv, He was the only person..who testified any real concern. **1855** PRESCOTT *Philip II*, I. II. viii. 228 She begs her brother..to testify his own satisfaction by the most gracious letters..that he can write. **1858** CARLYLE *Fredk. Gt.* X. viii. (1872) III. 292 The grimly sympathetic Generals testified assent.

Hence **ˈtestifying** *vbl. sb.* and *ppl. a.*

1575–85 ABP. SANDYS *Serm.* (Parker Soc.) 87 A testifying of our godliness towards him. **1596** NASHE *Saffron Walden* Wks. (Grosart) III. 19 For a testifying incouragement how much I wish thy encrease in those languages. **1651** BAXTER *Inf. Bapt.* 222 A seal is an engaging or obliging sign, or at least a testifying. **1818** SCOTT *Hrt. Midl.* xix, A man, exercised in the testimonies of that testifying period. **1901** C. G. MCCRIE *Ch. Scotl.* II. i. 151 It reveals no advance upon the testifyings of New Light Burghers.

†**ˈtestify,** *sb.* *Obs. rare*[−1]. In 6 *Sc.* pl. testefeis. [f. prec.] A certificate or testimony.

1600 *Sc. Acts Jas. VI* (1816) IV. 246/2 That..they may.. produce sic testefeis of thair antiquiteis as may informe the saidis commissionaris.

testily (ˈtɛstɪlɪ), *adv.* [f. TESTY + -LY[2].] In a testy manner; irritably.

1755 in JOHNSON. **1838** DICKENS *Nich. Nick.* xxxiv, 'What does the idiot mean?' cried Ralph, testily. **1885** *Manch. Exam.* 9 Jan. 5/4 The Lord Mayor rather testily..cut short his rhodomontade.

†**testimonage.** *Obs. rare.* In 5 testy-, 6 tesmonage. [ad. OF. *tesmonage* (f. *tesmoigner* :—med.L. *testimōniāre* to testify), with assimilation to the L. form.] = TESTIMONY *sb.* 1.

1483 CAXTON *Gold. Leg.* 436/2 Thys same epystle may also gyue vs testymonage that our lord wyl descende [etc.]. **1490** —— *Eneydos* xv. 53 She made it to couertely and close, wythoute testymonage and wythoute the knowleche of Iubyter. **1510–20** *Compl. too late Maryed* (1862) 14 Adam bereth wytnesse and Tesmonage.

†**testimoner.** *Obs. rare*[−1]. [app. f. TESTIMON(Y *v.* + -ER[1]. Cf. OF. *tesmoigneur.*] One who or that which bears testimony; a witness.

1607 R. C[AREW] tr. *Estienne's World of Wonders* 214 Sure and certen testimoners of sinnes.

testimonial (tɛstɪˈməʊnɪəl), *a.* and *sb.* Also 5 tesmoingnal; 5–6 testy-; 5 -mone-, 5–6 -mony-; 5 -ell, 5–7 -all(e. [a. OF. *tesmoignal* and *testimonial*, in phr. *lettres tes(ti)moniaulx* (13th c. in Godef. *Compl.*), ad. late L. *testimōniālis*, (*litteræ*) *testimōniālēs* credentials; f. OF. *tesmoin*, L. *testimōni-um* TESTIMONY: see -AL[1]]

A. *adj.* **a.** (now *arch.* or *technical.*) Of, pertaining to, or of the nature of testimony; serving as evidence; conducive to proof. ***testimonial proof***, proof by the testimony of a witness; parole evidence. (Quot. *c* 1430 may belong to the sb.)

c **1430** LYDG. *Min. Poems* (Percy Soc.) 254 To have memory upon thy passioun, Testimonial of my redempcioun. **1570** LEVINS *Manip.* 15/25 Testimoniall, *testimonialis.* **1588** J. HARVEY *Disc. Probl.* 111 Which argument how artificiall it is, being barely testimoniall, or how [etc.]. **1646** SIR T. BROWNE *Pseud. Ep.* I. vii. 25 We become emancipated from testimoniall engagements. **1680** J. C. *Vind. Oaths & Swearing* (ed. 2) 6 An Oath in matters Testimonial and pertaining to Witness-bearing is the highest proof and confirmation that can be. **1802–12** BENTHAM *Ration. Judic. Evid.* (1827) I. 69 Evidence which, though not properly testimonial, may..be called personal. **1883** *Wharton's Law Lex.*, *Testimonial proof*, parol evidence. *Civ. Law.*

†**b. letter testimonial**, rarely **testimonial letter** (usually pl. ***letters testimonial(s)***: a letter testifying to the bona fides of the bearer; credentials; = B. 3. *Obs.*

[**1421** *Rolls of Parlt.* IV. 158/1 Havynge lettres testimonyalx sufficeantz of on of those degrees of the Universite.] **1425** *Ibid.* 289/2 That the same Marchant.. brynge Lettres Tesmoingnals..under seel..of Maieur. **1439** *Ibid.* V. 33/2 Who so..come without Letters Testimoniall of the Chifteyn. **1597** HOOKER *Eccl. Pol.* v. lxxvii. §10 Is it the bringing of testimoniall letters wherein so great obliquitie consisteth? **1678** W. DILLINGHAM *Serm. Funeral Lady Alston* 26 St. Paul..hath recourse unto his own Conscience for his Letters Testimonial. **1751** LAVINGTON *Enthus. Meth. & Papists* III. (1754) 134 She was furnished with Letters Testimonial to obtain Provisions on the Road.

B. *sb.* [Cf. obs. F. *testimoniale* sb. (Cotgr.).]

†**1.** Verbal or documentary evidence; = TESTIMONY *sb.* 1. *Obs.*

1432–50 tr. *Higden* (Rolls) III. 251 Permenides, after the testimonialle of Boice,..laborede and founde the arte of logike. **1533** BELLENDEN *Livy* II. xxii. (S.T.S.) I. 222 Als Virginius..stude in testimoniall of his meritis and loving. **1621** ELSING *Debates Ho. Lords* (Camden) 35 Fowles being brought to the barre agayne, desyred that the testimonyall of theis dyers may not be used against him. **1707** (*title*) A Cry from the Desert, or Testimonials of Several Miraculous Things lately come to pass in the Cevennes.

†**2.** Something serving as proof or evidence; a token, record, manifestation. *Obs.*

1495 in S. P. H. Statham *Dover Charters* (1902) 278 Onlesse.. yᵉ said..purcer shew under auctentik, sufficient, or evident testimonialle yᵗ yᵉʳ is founde sufficient..surete in othir places. **1549** *Compl. Scot.* xiv. 113 Annibal send to cartage thre muis of gold ryngis..for ane testimonial of his grit victorie. *a* **1647** HABINGTON *Surv. Worc.* in *Worc. Hist. Soc. Proc.* III. 436 Without Armes or Inscription, as a testimonialle of her priveleadge. *a* **1716** SOUTH *Serm.* (1744) XI. 126 When he required a testimonial of Peter's affection. **1803** *Med. Jrnl.* IX. 182 In this second part numerous testimonials of the truth of this doctrine are given.

†**3. a.** A written attestation by some authorized or responsible person or persons, testifying to the truth of something; an affidavit, acknowledgement; a certificate; *spec.* an official warrant; a passport (as given to vagrants, labourers, discharged soldiers or sailors, etc.); a diploma; a credential or other authenticating document. *Obs.*

1461 *Paston Lett.* II. 22, I sent to yow a testymonyall, which is made by a greet assent of greet multitude of comons, to send to the Kyng. **1526** TINDALE *Matt.* v. 31 Hit ys sayd, whosoever put awaye his wyfe, let hym geve her a testymonyall of her devorcement. **1545** *Aberdeen Regr.* (1844) I. 223 Quhen ony strangear cumis with testimoniale, to cum and aduerteis the baiȝe that sic an strangear is at the port with testimoniale. **1560** DAUS tr. *Sleidane's Comm.* 143 b, After whan he had exhibited the testimoniall of his Ambassade, he procedeth. **1563** *Reg. Privy Council Scot.* I. 249 To direct out commissionis under the testimoniall of the greit seill. **1597–8** *Act 39 Eliz.* c. 17 §2 Euery..wandring Soldyer or Marryner..shall..haue a Testymonyall vnder the Hand of some one Justice of the Peace. **1622** MABBE tr. *Aleman's Guzman d'Alf.* II. 332 Giuing euery one of vs a Testimoniall of his sentence, wee were all chained one to another. **1698–9** *Act 11 Will. III*, c. 18 §1 Such Vagabonds or Beggers..very frequently forge or counterfeite Passes Testimonialls or Characters. **1702** W. J. *Bruyn's Voy. Levant* v. 12 Nor brought along with them Testimonials of their being in Health. **1796** JEFFERSON *Writ.* (1859) IV. 140, I will forward the testimonial of the death of Mrs. Mazzei. *a* **1806** C. J. FOX *Reign Jas. II* (1808) 119 The severity with which he had enforced the test, obtained him a testimonial from the Bishops of his affection to their Protestant Church.

†**b.** (? *erron.*) A will, testament. *Obs. rare*[−1].

1616 R. C. *Times' Whistle* 135 To dispossesse His children of his goodes & give her all By his last dying testimoniall.

4. A writing testifying to one's qualifications and character, written usually by a present or former employer, or by some responsible person who is competent to judge; a letter of recommendation of a person or thing. (The current sense.)

In quots. 1571, 1727–41, = TESTIMONIUM 1.

1571 *Act 13 Eliz.* c. 12 §4 None shalbe made Mynister.. under thage of foure and twenty yeres, nor unles he fyrst bring to the Bisshop..a Testimoniall..of his honest lyfe [etc.]. **1609** *Sc. Acts Jas. VI* (1816) IV. 406/2 A sufficient testimoniall of the bischop of the dyocie..Testifeing and approveing the said pedagog to be godlie and of good religioun. **1727–41** CHAMBERS *Cycl.*, *Testimonial*, a kind of certificate..required before holy orders are conferred. **1776** J. ADAMS in *Fam. Lett.* (1876) 144 The testimonials in his favor I shall inclose to you. **1798** M. CUTLER in *Life*, etc. (1888) II. 7 We have full testimonials that Mr. Perkins is a young man of an unblemished character. **1836** SIR H. TAYLOR *Statesman* xxix. 220 He is to make small account of testimonials and recommendations, unless subjected to severe scrutiny and supported by proved facts. **1868** M. PATTISON *Academ. Org.* v. 216 Testimonials seem in theory an unexceptionable mode of obtaining information.

5. A gift presented to some one by a number of persons as an expression of appreciation or acknowledgement of services or merit, or of admiration, esteem, or respect.

1838 LD. COCKBURN *Jrnl.* I. 211 The growth of the modern things called testimonials is very curious... It has come of late to denote..a sort of homage always as a donation, and generally in a permanent form, to supposed public virtue. **1856** W. COLLINS *After Dark* ii. Prol. (1862) 148 The portrait was intended as a testimonial, 'expressive ..of the eminent services of Mr. Boxsious in promoting and securing the prosperity of the town'. **1859** THACKERAY *Virgin.* xxxv, The late lamented O'Connell,..over whom a grateful country has raised such a magnificent testimonial.

6. *attrib.* and *Comb.*, as ***testimonial craze, -writer***; (sense 5) = serving as a testimonial or token of esteem, esp. in ***testimonial dinner, game, match.*** †**testimonial-man**, a person having a testimonial (sense 3) or passport.

1725 *Lond. Gaz.* No. 6396/4 Robert Mair, late of Liverpool, Testimonial-Man. **1851** 'BAT' *Cricketer's Man.* (ed. 5) 94 On the 26th July, 1847, the Committee at Lord's got up a testimonial match between Kent and England [for Mynn's benefit]. **1895** *Pall Mall G.* 27 Sept. 1/3 The testimonial craze is becoming quite a nuisance, and is highly inconvenient to people of moderate means. **1895** *Funk's Stand. Dict.* s.v., A testimonial certificate, benefit, or banquet. **1905** *Academy* 6 May 489/1 A good many other professional and unprofessional testimonial-writers. **1931** *Daily Express* 21 Sept. 11/5 A testimonial dinner was given to..the millionaire American capitalist. **1972** G. GREEN *Great Moments in Sport: Soccer* iii. 46 The Russians went to the unusual lengths of giving him [Yashin] a testimonial match at Lenin Stadium. **1977** in *Fremdsprachen* XXIII. (1979) 209/1 The long-serving defender, who collected £35,000 from a testimonial game on Friday, was due to retire. **1979** *Tucson (Arizona) Citizen* (Weekender Mag.) 28 Apr. 18/1 Sol Stein..was decorating a dais with his presence at a testimonial dinner for a minor television personality.

testimonialize (tɛstɪˈməʊnɪəlaɪz), *v.* [f. prec. + -IZE.] *trans.* To furnish with a letter of recommendation; also, to present with a public testimonial: see TESTIMONIAL *sb.* 4 and 5. (In quot. 1899 *Improperly*, To ask for testimonials.)

1852 *Tait's Mag.* XIX. 344 Hanging is going out of fashion, and testimonialising is coming in. **1855** THACKERAY *Newcomes* lxiii, People were testimonialising his wife. **1886** *West. Morn. News* 27 Apr. 4/6 Sir E—— H—— is to be testimonialised. **1899** C. SCOTT *Drama of Yesterday* I. xii. 417, I resolved..to testimonialise the influential friends of my father.

Hence **testiˈmonialized** *ppl. a.*; **testiˈmonializing** *vbl. sb.* and *ppl. a.*; also **testiˌmonialiˈzation**, celebration by means of testimonials; **testiˈmonializer**, one who furnishes, or contributes to, a testimonial.

1898 G. B. SHAW in *Daily Chron.* 13 Oct. 4/4 The celebration and *testimonialisation of remarkable events and eminent men will always be cherished in England as a means of procuring notoriety for noisy nobodies. **1893** *Chamb. Jrnl.* 11 Mar. 145/1 A much *testimonialised medicine. **1854** *Tait's Mag.* XXI. 386 The *testimonialisers threw themselves into the business with a truly heroical enthusiasm. **1891** E. KINGLAKE *Australian at H.* 53 *Testimonialising has been rather overdone of late.

‖**testimonium** (tɛstɪˈməʊnɪəm). [L., f. *testi-s* a witness + *-mōnium*: see -MONY.]

1. A letter of recommendation given to a candidate for holy orders testifying to his piety and learning; also, a certificate of proficiency given by a university, college, professor, etc.: = TESTAMUR.

1692 SWIFT in Earl Orrery *Remarks* (1752) 11, I am still to thank you for your care in my Testimonium. **1705** HEARNE *Collect.* 21 Aug. (O.H.S.) I. 32 Dr. Mill sent to me a Testimonium to be sign'd for Cyprian & Paul Appia, Vaudois, that they may be admitted into H. Orders. **1721** AMHERST *Terræ Fil.* No. 13. (1754) 66 Punishing undergraduates, or disposing of fellowships, degrees, and testimoniums. **1799** C. WINTER in Jay *Mem. & Lett.* (1843) 49 Mr. Whitefield desired me to procure him a testimonium of myself from different places whither I had gone. **1903** *Times* 24 Oct. 10/1 In 1860, a year after he became B.A., he obtained his testimonium in the divinity school.

2. *Law.* That concluding part of a document, usually commencing with the words 'In witness whereof', which states the manner of its execution; also ***testimonium clause.*** Cf. TESTATUM, TESTE[2].

1852 *Act 15 & 16 Vict.* c. 24 §1 The words of the testimonium clause or of the clause of attestation. **1905** *Law Soc. Gaz.* Dec. 16 Blanks had been left in the testimonium for the day and the month.

testimony (ˈtɛstɪmənɪ), *sb.* [ad. L. *testimōnium*: see prec. Cf. ONF. *testimonie*, OF. *testi-, testemoine* (11th c. in Godef.), learned forms from Latin; the inherited OF. word being *tesmoigne*, now *témoin*, whence also *tésmoignie* and *tesmoignage*, now *témoignage*: see TESTIMONAGE.]

1. a. Personal or documentary evidence or attestation in support of a fact or statement; hence, any form of evidence or proof.

1432-50 tr. *Higden* (Rolls) II. 423 Hit hathe somme testimony and wittenesse. *Ibid.* V. 393. **1526** TINDALE *John* viii. 17 Itt ys also writtẹn in youre lawe, that the testimony of two men ys true. **1553** EDEN *Treat. Newe Ind.* (Arb.) 9 Plinie rehearseth the testimonie of Cornelius Nepos. **1577-87** HOLINSHED *Chron.* I. 121/2 None of the cleargie.. comming from anie other place should be admitted, except he brought letters of testimonie with him. **1651** HOBBES *Leviath.* I. xiv. 70 Where a mans Testimony is not to be credited, he is not bound to give it. **1719** DE FOE *Crusoe* I. 303 He shewed all the Testimony of his Gratitude that he was able. **1805** FOSTER *Ess.* III. iii. 58 Determined by the testimony of facts. **1838** SIR W. HAMILTON *Logic* xxxiii. (1866) II. 177 Testimony, in the strictest sense of the term, therefore, is the communication of an experience or..the report of an observed phænomenon, made to those whose own experience or observation has not reached so far. **1843** R. R. MADDEN *United Irish.* Ser. II. II. xvii. 367 The Battalion of Testimony..a set of hired spies, informers, and witnesses, kept in the pay of the [Dublin] Castle.

b. Any object or act serving as proof or evidence.

1597 HOOKER *Eccl. Pol.* v. lxxix. §2 [Offerings] are Testimonies of our affection towardes God. **1601** SIR W. CORNWALLIS *Ess.* II. xxvi., To smell of sweat, the testimony of labour.

†**2.** A written certificate, a testimonial. *Obs.*

a **1589** *Jenkinson's Voy. & Trav.* (Hakl. Soc.) II. 375 When any man or woman dyeth..they..put a testimony in his right hand, which the priest giueth him, to testifie vnto S. Nicholas that he dyed a Christian. **1617** MORYSON *Itin.* I. 252 They that goe by land in Italy, must bring a Testimonie of Health called *Boletino*, before they can passe or conuerse. **1657** J. WATTS *Vind. Ch. Eng.* 97 The Arch-Deacon, having before examined us in private, and seen our publike Testimonies, presented us all to the Bishop.

†**3.** A sponsor. *Obs. rare.*

1547 HOOPER *Answ. Bp. Winchester* E iij, The testimonijs of the infant to be Christeynid ar examynid in the be halfe of the chyld.

4. In Scriptural language (chiefly in O.T.). **a.** *sing.* The Mosaic law or decalogue as inscribed on the two tables of stone, as in ***the two tables of testimony*** (Ex. xxxi. 18); ***ark of (the) testimony*** = ***ark of the covenant***, the chest containing the tables of the law and other sacred memorials; sometimes called simply ***the testimony***; ***tabernacle*** or ***tent of (the) testimony***, the tabernacle containing the ark with its contents.

[A literalism of translation, repr. Vulg. *testimonium*, LXX. τὸ μαρτύριον, rarely ἡ μαρτυρία, Heb. sing. *ʿēdūth*, pl. *ʿēdwōth*.]

1382 WYCLIF *Exod.* xxx. 6 The veyle, that hongith before the arke of testymonye. *Ibid.* xxxii. 15 Moyses..berynge in hoond two tablis of testymonye wrytun on eithir side. **1560** BIBLE (Genev.) *Exod.* xxv 16 Thou shalt put in the Arke the Testimonie which I shal giue thee. *Ibid.* xxxii. 15 Moses.. went downe from the mountaine with the Two Tables of the Testimonie [1539 wytnesse] in his hand. —— *Num.* x. 11 The cloude was taken vp from the Tabernacle of the Testimonie [1539 of witnesse]. **1611** BIBLE *Num.* i. 50 Thou shalt appoint the Leuites ouer the Tabernacle of [*R.V.* the] Testimonie. *Ibid.* ix. 15 The Tabernacle, namely the Tent of the Testimony. *Ibid.* xvii. 4 Thou shalt lay them vp in the Tabernacle..before the Testimony. —— *Transl. Pref.* 3 The forme [of Scripture being] Gods word, Gods testimonie, Gods oracles. **1667** MILTON *P.L.* XII. 251 Therein An Ark, and in the Ark his Testimony, The Records of his Cov'nant.

b. *pl.* The precepts (of God), the divine law. Rarely in *sing.*

1535 COVERDALE *Ps.* xviii. [xix.] 7 The testimony of yᵉ Lorde is true, & geueth wisdome euen vnto babes. *Ibid.* cxviii. [cxix.] 88 So shall I kepe the testimonies of thy mouth. **1560** BIBLE (Genev.) *2 Kings* xxiii. 3 That they shulde walke after the Lord, and kepe his commandements, and his testimonies, and his statutes. **1611** BIBLE *Deut.* vi. 17 You shall diligently keepe the Commandements of the Lord your God, and his Testimonies, and his Statutes.

5. a. Open attestation or acknowledgement; confession, profession. *Obs.* or *arch.* except in Evangelical circles. Phr. ***to give one's testimony*** = TESTIFY *v.* 3 b.

to seal one's testimony with one's blood, to die as a martyr for one's religious profession.

1550 (*title*) The Image of both Chvrches... Compyled by Iohn Bale an exyle also in this lyfe, for the faithfull testimony of Iesu. **1582** N. T. (Rhem.) *Rev.* i. 9, I..was in ..Patmos, for the word of God and the testimonie of Iesvs. **1597** HOOKER *Eccl. Pol.* v. lx. §5 To seale the testimonie thereof with death. **1667** MILTON *P.L.* VI. 33 Thou..for the testimonie of Truth hast born Universal reproach. **1687** A. SHIELDS (*title*) A Hind let loose; or an Historical Representation of the Testimonies of the Church of Scotland. *a* **1720** SEWEL *Hist. Quakers* v. (1722) 226 The two first [Quakers in New England] that sealed their Testimony with their Blood were William Robinson..and Marmaduke Stevenson. **1877** *Independent* 29 Mar. 12/1 A fine-looking young man gave a clear, decided testimony for Christ. **1885** C. T. STUDD *Let.* in N. P. Grubb *C. T. Studd* (1933) vi. 53 Now he is just as active for the Lord Jesus as he was formerly for the devil. He has three times publicly given his testimony. **1935** N. L. MCCLUNG *Clearing in West* iii. 21 So when an old man who stuttered, was giving his testimony and holding back the meeting with everyone getting impatient, I kept my one eye on the minister and the other one shut. **1966** H. ROSEVEARE *Give me this Mountain* ii. 31 Our leader opened the meeting for testimonies. I didn't know what she meant by a 'testimony' so I waited... She made another attempt to get us talking by pointing out what a blessing it could be to testify to others... 'Well, hasn't anyone anything to tell of what God has done for her during the week?'

b. *spec.* An expression or declaration of disapproval or condemnation of error; a protestation.

1582 N. T. (Rhem.) *Mark* vi. 11 Shake of the dust from your feete for a testimonie to them. **1818** SCOTT *Hrt. Midl.* ix, Mony an afternoon he wad sit and take up his testimony again the Paip. **1850** WHITTIER *Old Portr.*, *T. Ellwood* Wks. 1889 VI. 38 Plain, earnest men and women..having withal a strong testimony to bear against carnal wit and outside show and ornament. **1863** MRS. GASKELL *Sylvia's L.* xxxix, Alice Rose was not one to tolerate the coarse, careless talk.. without uplifting her voice in many a testimony against it. **1876** C. M. DAVIES *Unorth. Lond.* 90 A 'testimony' was.. circulated some years ago to the bishops and clergy of the Church of England.

†**ˈtestimony**, *v. Obs.* Also 4 testimon. [ME. ad. ONF. *testimoin-er* (11th c. in Littré), *testimonier, -moi(g)ner, testemogner* (12th c. in Godef. *Compl.*), learned forms ad. med.L. *testimōniāre* (8th c. in Du Cange), f. *testimōnium* TESTIMONY. (The inherited popular Fr. form of the L. is *tesmoi(g)ner*, mod.F. *témoigner*). In later use f. prec. sb.]

1. *trans.* and *intr.* To bear witness, testify (to).

c **1330** R. BRUNNE *Chron.* (1810) 8 Henry of Huntyngton testimons þis title. *c* **1400** *Emare* 1029 A grette feste þer was holde..As testymonyeth þys story. *c* **1450** *Cov. Myst.* xxv. (1841) 251 To se and recorde and testymonye. **1611** TOURNEUR *Ath. Trag.* I. ii, I salute you both..and will testimonie to the integritie——. **1642** EARL CLANRICARDE in Carte *Ormonde* (1735) III. 82 My Lord President will testimony with me in what a dangerous condition..the whole Province was in at that time.

2. *trans.* To test or prove by evidence.

1603 SHAKS. *Meas. for M.* III. ii. 153 Let him be but testimonied in his owne bringings forth, and hee shall appeare to the enuious, a Scholler, a Statesman, and a Soldier.

testiness (ˈtɛstɪnɪs). [f. TESTY + -NESS.] The quality or condition of being testy; petulance.

1526 *Pilgr. Perf.* (W. de W. 1531) 93 b, Testinesse or impacyency is a frayle & hasty disposycyon, or rather accustomed & vsed vyce of angre. **1574** HELLOWES *Gueuara's Fam. Ep.* (1584) 114 Ire groweth of an occasion, and testinesse of euil condition. **1593** G. HARVEY *Pierce's Super.* 196, I haue knowen few..so contrary to frowardnesse, or testiuenesse. *a* **1641** BP. MOUNTAGU *Acts & Mon.* iv. (1642) 304 Extreame choler, wrath and testivenesse had cleane spent him. **1690** LOCKE *Hum. Underst.* II. xxii. §10 Testiness is a Disposition or Aptness to be angry. **1838** DICKENS *Nich. Nick.* v, 'Mighty fine, certainly', said Ralph, with great testiness.

testing (ˈtɛstɪŋ), *vbl. sb.*[1] [f. TEST *v.*[1] + -ING[1].] The action of TEST *v.*[1]

1. The making of a will; the disposing of property by will.

1681 STAIR *Inst. Law Scot.* xxx. §37 The power of Testing is competent to all Persons, who have the use of Reason. **1788** PRIESTLEY *Lect. Hist.* v. xlviii. 362 The power of testing was first introduced by Solon. **1880** BLACKIE in *Contemp. Rev.* Jan. 44 The freedom of testing, which we derive from the law of the Twelve Tables. **1889** STEVENSON *Master of B.* 176 If I had been put to my oath, I must have declared he was incapable of testing.

2. *Sc. Law.* ***testing clause***: see quot. 1838.

(Here *testing* may be *ppl. a.*)

1765-8 ERSKINE *Inst. Law Scot.* II. iii. §33 That all precepts..should be ingrossed in the charter, towards the end of it; that is, immediately before the testing clause. **1838** W. BELL *Dict. Law Scot.* s.v., The testing clause is the technical name given to the clause whereby a formal written deed or instrument is authenticated. **1888** *Law Rep. 13 App. Cas.* XIII. 376 The testing clause was..'In witness whereof I and my said wife have subscribed these presents'.

ˈtesting, *vbl. sb.*[2] [f. TEST *v.*[2] + -ING[1].]

a. The action of TEST *v.*[2]; putting to the test, trying, proving; in quot. 1687, subjecting to the Test Act.

1687 *Good Advice* 61 The end of Testing and Persecuting. **1827** COLERIDGE in *Lit. Rem.* (1839) IV. 317 A philosophy, which has for its object the trial and testing of the weights and measures themselves. **1839, 1842** [see TEST *v.*[2] 4]. **1860** *Merc. Marine Mag.* VII. 141 The application of a severe strain in testing has an injurious effect on a cable.

b. *attrib.* and *Comb.* Pertaining to or used for testing, as ***testing-box, -machine, -office, station***, etc. **testing-ground**, an area used for demonstration and experiment; also *fig.*

1872 *Gentl. Mag.* Jan. 71 Since the battle field is the only thorough testing ground for weapons and military schemes. **1876** PREECE & SIVEWRIGHT *Telegraphy* 272 At certain stations along the line the wires are led into testing-boxes for the purpose of affording facilities for crossing, disconnecting, and putting them to earth... The testing station is always the most important station on the circuit. **1877** KNIGHT *Dict. Mech.* 2538/2 In Fairbanks's testing-machine, the crushing, breaking, or deflecting force is applied..by a cross-head. **1890** W. J. GORDON *Foundry* 111 In the same range as the roller shop is the laboratory, and further on is the testing-office. **1905** *Daily Chron.* 22 Apr. 6/4 A six-cylinder racing car with a testing body passed at a speed that was not less than forty-five miles an hour. **1919** H. S. WALPOLE *Secret City* II. vii. 213, I turned and devoted myself to Uncle Ivan, who was always delighted to make me a testing-ground for his English. **1943** in R. V. Jones *Most Secret War* (1978) xxxvii. 322 The new weapon is in the form of a rocket which has been seen fired from the testing ground.

'testing, *ppl. a.* [f. TEST *v.*[2] + -ING[2].] That tests or puts to the test or proof.

1847-8 H. MILLER *First Impr.* viii. (1857) 123 His writings ..had stood their testing century but indifferently well. **1878** GLADSTONE *Glean.* (1879) I. 179, I will add another and a very testing question. **1884** *Pall Mall G.* 13 Nov. 1/1 It is a testing crisis for English democracy. **1885** BEDDOE *Races Brit.* 271 An edifice of wood and stubble, which may..be consumed by the testing fire.

‖**'testis**[1]. *Obs.* Pl. testes ('tɛsti:z). The Latin word for 'witness': from its legal use (cf. TESTE[2]), occasional in English context.

In quot. *a* 1483 in Latin construction = *cum testibus* 'with the witnesses'.

a **1483** in *Househ. Ord.* (1790) 67 The Soveraynes here may send it with the testibus under theyre seales into the Chauncerie. **1525** LD. BERNERS *Froiss.* II. cci. [cxcvii.] 616 The charter..named in the ende many wytnesses of prelates and great lordes of Englande, who were for the more suretie testes of that dede. **1563-87** FOXE *A. & M.* (1596) 532/2 As the saide Edward Hall, your great maister and testis, was about the compiling of his storie. **1611** [see TESTIFIER].

‖**testis**[2] ('tɛstɪs). *Anat.* Chiefly in pl. testes ('tɛsti:z). [L.: etymology uncertain.

An assumed identity with *testis* witness (quasi 'the witness or evidence of virility') is rejected by Walde, who suggests connexion with *testa*, pot, shell, etc. In 16th c. Fr., however, *tesmoing* 'witness' appears in this sense: see Godef. s.v.]

1. = TESTICLE. **a.** in man and mammals.

[**1693** tr. *Blancard's Phys. Dict.* (ed. 2), *Testes viriles*, Mens Testicles.] **1704** J. HARRIS *Lex. Techn.* I, *Testes*, the Testicles of a Male. *c* **1720** GIBSON *Farrier's Guide* I. ii. (1738) 16 Next to the Yard, the Testes, or Stones properly take place. **1807-26** S. COOPER *First Lines Surg.* (ed. 5) 495 The formation of such adhesions between the bowels and testis before birth, may also sometimes prevent..its descent. **1881** MIVART *Cat* 241 Two glandular structures, the testes.

b. in other animals.

1841-71 T. R. JONES *Anim. Kingd.* (ed. 4) 445 In Crabs, the mass of the testis is exceedingly large. **1870** ROLLESTON *Anim. Life* Introd. 54 [In Birds] The testes are always retained within the abdomen anteriorly to the kidneys. **1877** HUXLEY *Anat. Inv. Anim.* iv. 179 The testes and vasa deferentia generally have the form of two long tubes. **1888** ROLLESTON & JACKSON *Anim. Life* 680 The testis [in Nematoda] is single; very rarely paired.

†**c.** *transf.* The ovary in females. *Obs.*

[**1693** tr. *Blancard's Phys. Dict.* (ed. 2), *Testes Muliebres*.] **1706** PHILLIPS (ed. Kersey), *Testes*,..the Organs of Seed in Men and Women. **1841** RAMSBOTHAM *Obstetr. Med.* (1855) 43 Previously to the time of Steno, who first asserted that they were analogous to true ovaria, they were called the female testes.

2. *transf. pl.* **a.** The posterior pair of the optic lobes or *corpora quadrigemina*, at the base of the brain in mammals.

1681 tr. *Willis' Rem. Med. Wks.* Vocab., *Testes*, certain tubercles in the brain of a man and beasts, so called because like to the stones of a man. **1704** J. HARRIS *Lex. Techn.* I, *Testes Cerebri*, are the two lower and lesser Protuberances of the Brain. **1899** *Allbutt's Syst. Med.* VII. 345 The posterior tubercles or testes are connected by the posterior brachia with the corpora geniculata interna.

†**b.** The tonsils. *Obs.*

1776 J. COLLIER *Mus. Trav.* 44 (Stanf.) There are other superfluities besides the *testes* and glands of the throat which obstruct the free course of the voice.

testive, -nesse, obs. ff. TESTY *a.*, TESTINESS.

‖**testo** ('tɛsto). *Mus.* [It. *testo*:—L. *textu-m* TEXT.] **a.** The text or words of a song; the libretto of an opera. **b.** The text, theme, or subject of a composition.

1724 *Short Explic. For. Wds. in Mus. Bks.*, *Testo*, the Text or Words of a Song. **1801** BUSBY *Dict. Mus.*, *Testo*,..the text, subject, or theme, of any composition... When the words are well written, the song is said to have a good *testo*. **1891** in *Cent. Dict.* **1898** in STAINER & BARRETT.

c. The narrator in an oratorio or similar piece of music.

1947 A. EINSTEIN *Music in Romantic Era* xiii. 177 Through the gradual elimination of the *testo* or narrator, oratorio had approached opera to such a degree as to be confused with it. **1980** *New Grove Dict. Mus.* XVIII. 706/2 The *testo* part as normally set as recitative with continuo accompaniment and sung either by one or more soloists... In secular music the term was occasionally used for the narrator in dramatic dialogues and similar works.

teston, testoon ('tɛstən, tɛ'stu:n). *Obs.* exc. *Hist.* Also 6 **testoune, -yon,** 6-7 **-one,** (*Sc.* **-an, -ane**), 7 **-oone.** [a. obs. F. *teston* (in Godef. *Compl.*) = obs. It. *testone*, augmentative of *testa* head: see -OON. See also TESTER[3].]

1. *orig.* The French name of a silver coin struck at Milan by Galeazzo Maria Sforza (1468-76), bearing a portrait or head of the duke, and called in Italian *testone*; then of the similar coin struck by Louis XII after his conquest of Milan, for currency in Italy, and by Francis I (1515-47) for use in France. Both in Italy and France, the name was soon applied to equivalent silver coins without a portrait; but always to pieces heavier than the *gros*.

1545 *Reg. Privy Council Scot.* I. 2 All smaller peces sik as halff testanys and halff soussis be taken efter the quantite of the prices forsaidis. **1547** BOORDE *Introd. Knowl.* xxvii. (1870) 191 In syluer they [the French] haue testons, which be worth halfe a Frenche crowne; it is worth .ii. s. .iiii. d. sterlyng. **1579** J. STUBBES *Gaping Gulf* C vij, He [Monsieur] is not able to dropp halfe testons for king Phillip's pistelas. **1617** MORYSON *Itin.* I. 185, I payed [in France] two testoones and a halfe for a paire of shooes. *Ibid.* 288 Those of Solothurn..coyne a peece of mony, which the Sweitzers call *Dickenpfenning*, and the French call *Testoone*, but it is lesse worth by the tenth part then the Testoone of France. **1686** tr. *Chardin's Trav. Persia* 7 This Money of theirs [the Dutch]..chiefly consists of Crowns, Half-Crowns, Testons or Eighteen-penny pieces, and pieces of Fifteen Sous. **1901** tr. *Hugo's Notre Dame* xxvii. 275 To gain a few testons in his turn [he] was parading round the circle.

2. In England, A name applied first to the shilling of Henry VII, being the first English coin with a true portrait; also to those of Henry VIII, and early pieces of Edward VI. It was declared in 1543 to be equal to 12 pence, but being of debased metal it sank successively to 10*d.*, 9*d.*, and 6*d.*, and was recalled in 1548. Subsequently those still in circulation were rated even lower: see quotations 1560 and 1635.

There appear also to have been counterfeit testons, difficult to distinguish from the debased coinage of Henry VIII, and valued in 1560 at $4\frac{1}{2}$*d.* and $2\frac{1}{4}$*d.* Quot. 1562 refers to the red or 'brazen' colour of the debased testons.

1543 *Mint Indenture* (P.R.O. Exch[r]. Accts. Bundle 306, No. 2), Shall make sixe maner of monys of sylver That is to saye oone piece of theym called a Teston running for xij*d.* of lawfull monye of Englande and there shalbe xlviij suche pieces of theym in the pownde weight of troye. **1548** *Roy. Proclam. for calling in of Testons*, The falsyng of his highnes coyne, nowe current, specially of the peces of xii.*d.* commonly named Testons. **1549** LATIMER *3rd Serm. bef. Edw. VI* (Arb.) 85 Thy syluer is turned into, what? into testyons? *Scoriam*, into drosse. **1560** *Roy. Proclam.* in *Arch. Bodl. F.* c. 11 lf. 30 For discernyng and knowyng of the basest Testons of two pence farthing, from thother Teston of foure pence halfpeny. **1562** J. HEYWOOD *Prov. & Epigr.* (1867) 189 Of Testons. Testons be gone to Oxforde, god be their speede: To studie in Brazennose, there to proceede. Of redde Testons. These Testons looke redde:..they blushe for shame. **1577-87** HOLINSHED *Chron.* III. 1066/2 In the moneth of Iulie [1551]..he abased the peece of twelue pence, commonlie called a teston vnto nine pence. **1592** *Sc. Acts Jas. VI* (1814) III. 527/1 Ordanis the inglis testane to haue cours heireftir w[t]in this realme vpoun the pryce of viii s. [Scotch]. **1635** N. R. *Camden's Hist. Eliz.* I. 36 Reducing the Teston of sixpence to foure pence, another Teston to two pence farthing, for more silver there was not in them. **1752** CARTE *Hist. Eng.* III. XVI. 229 This gentleman [Sir W. Sharington, an. 1549] had coined a vast quantity of testons, of a base alloy and under standard.

†**b.** A name for the sixpenny piece; = TESTER[3].

1577 HARRISON *England* II. xxv. (1877) I. 362 Six pence vsuallie named the testone. **1598** B. JONSON *Ev. Man in Hum.* IV. i, You cannot giue him lesse then a shilling,..for the booke..cost him a teston, at least.

†**c.** Proposed name for a suggested new coin of the value of 1*s.* 3*d.* *Obs.*

1691 LOCKE *Lower. Interest* Wks. 1727 II. 90 The present Shilling and new Testoon, going for fifteen Pence. **1695** LOWNDES *Ess. Amend. Silver Coins* 63 One other Piece which may be called the Testoon, or Fifteen Peny Piece.

3. Name of a Scottish silver coin bearing a portrait of Mary Stuart, issued in 1553, and weighing about 76 grains; also applied to coins of the same weight, without the portrait, struck in 1555.

1566 *Reg. Privy Council Scot.* I. 441 He sall..pay for his absence ane testane. **1577** *Ibid.* II. 616 His Hienes awin silver money of testanis and xxx, xx, and ten schilling pecis. **1583-4** *Burgh Rec. Edinb.* (1882) IV. 322 The payment of ane thowsand pund in Scottis fyue schilling testanes. **1621** *Compt Bk. D. Wedderburne* (S.H.S.) 171 Promisit him a mark for ilk testane he advances thairon.

4. The Portuguese *testão* or *tostão*, a silver coin first coined by Manoel I, *c* 1500, and weighing 122 grains; in 1911 = 100 reis, weighing 51.6 grains, and worth about $2\frac{1}{2}$*d.* Also an obsolete Italian coin.

1598 W. PHILLIP *Linschoten* (Hakl. Soc.) I. I. xxxv. 241 Pardaus Xeraphiins..which is as much as three Testones, or three hundred Reijs Portingall money. **1603** FLORIO *Montaigne* I. xlviii. (1632) 160, I saw the Prince of Sulmona at Naples..shew all manner of horsemanship: to hold testons or reals under his knees. **1676** W. B. *Man. Goldsm.* 114 Portugal Teston. **1706** PHILLIPS (ed. Kersey) s.v., The Testoon of Portugal is worth 1*s.* 3*d.* Of Spain and Navarre 1*s.* 8*d.* Of Switzerland 1*s.* 4*d.* Of Italy 1*s.* 4*d.* **1717** BERKELEY *Tour Italy* Wks. 1871 IV. 524 The owner of the horse gave him a testoon. **1740** H. WALPOLE *Let. to R. West* 16 Apr., What the chief princes [in Italy] allow for their own eating is a testoon a day.

†**'testor.** *Obs. rare.* [f. TEST *v.*[1] + -OR 2 d.] One who testifies; a witness.

1570 LEVINS *Manip.* 170/37 A Testor, *testator, -oris.* **1621** BURTON *Anat. Mel.* III. iv. II. iii, Conscience..a continual testor to give in evidence, to empanel a jury to examine us, to..cry guilty.

testor, -orne, -ourn, obs. forms of TESTER[3].

testosterone (tɛ'stɒstərəʊn). *Biol.* [a. G. *testosteron* (K. David et al. 1935, in *Zeitschr. f. physiol. Chem.* CCXXXIII. 281): see TESTIS[2] and -STERONE.] **a.** A steroid hormone that stimulates the development of male secondary sexual characteristics and which is produced in the testes, and, in very much smaller quantities, in the ovaries and adrenal cortex.

1935 *Chem. Abstr.* XXIX. 5165 *(heading)* Crystalline male hormone from testes (testosterone), more active than androsterone prepared from urine or cholesterol. **1939** A. HUXLEY *After Many a Summer* II. vi. 234 With a course of thiamin chloride and some testosterone I could have made him as happy as a sand-boy. **1947** *Nature* 4 Jan. 15/1 Many mammary cancers would regress when the influence of the female sex hormone was lessened by removal of the ovaries or by injections of testosterone. **1961** *New Scientist* 9 Nov. 340/1 Naturally occurring steroid sex hormones can inhibit ovulation... Testosterone, progesterone and the oestrogens fall into this group. **1969** *Nature* 6 Dec. 945/1 Celibacy apparently has no effect on the androgens, for most of the monks excreted as much testosterone—the most potent naturally occurring androgen—as normal sexually active males. **1976** *Maclean's Mag.* 3 May 60/3 Among women virilized in the womb from an excess of testosterone (the male sex hormone), 60% registered IQs over 110.

b. testosterone propionate, the propionic acid ester of testosterone, given parenterally as a longer-lasting alternative to testosterone.

1937 *Proc. R. Soc.* B. CXXIV. 363 Six normally cyclic rats ..were injected daily for 10 days with 0·2 mg. of testosterone propionate. **1941** [see PREMENOPAUSE]. **1970** PASSMORE & ROBSON *Compan. Med. Stud.* II. xii. 11/2 Testosterone propionate, given intramuscularly in oily solution, is active over a period of 1-3 days.

†**'testril.** *Obs.* [A dim. alteration, or corruption of TESTER[3].] A sixpence.

1601 SHAKS. *Twel. N.* II. iii. 34 *To.* Come on, there is sixe pence for you. Let's haue a song. *An.* There's a testrill of me too. [**1905** *Athenæum* 25 Mar. 366/3 Plenty of readers.. ready to expend their testril on such an attractive booklet.]

'test-tube. [f. TEST *sb.*[1] + TUBE.] **a.** A cylinder of thin transparent glass closed at one end, used to hold liquids under test. Also *transf.*

1846 G. E. DAY tr. *Simon's Anim. Chem.* II. 176 The sediment must then be placed in a test-tube..and gradually raised to the boiling point. **1860** F. WINSLOW *Obscure Dis. Brain & Mind* viii. (L.), There is no possibility of the medical expert placing the diseased mental element..in a psychological crucible or test-tube. **1888** RUTLEY *Rock-Forming Min.* 6 The test-tube..is plunged into cold water.

b. *attrib.*, as ***test-tube experiment***; **test-tube baby,** (*a*) a baby conceived by artificial insemination; (*b*) a baby that has developed from an ovum fertilized outside the mother's body; also *fig.* and in similar Combs., as ***test-tube child, pregnancy***; **test-tube cultivation, culture,** the raising of bacteria in a nutrient medium contained in a test-tube.

1886 H. M. BIGGS tr. *Hueppe's Bacteriol. Invest.* 142 In order to do this, test-tube cultures are employed, in which.. many peculiarities of growth can be better noted. **1899** CAGNEY *Jaksch's Clin. Diagn.* vi. (ed. 4) 212 The bactericidal power of such serum has been established by numerous test-tube-experiments. *Ibid.* x. 444 It is usually expedient to make plate and test-tube..cultivations together. **1935** E. NOVAK *Woman asks Doctor* xii. 155 There has been..a good deal of unfortunate newspaper discussion on the subject of artificial insemination and 'test-tube babies'. **1945** *Daily Herald* 20 Apr. 3/8 Warning on test tube babies. Artificial insemination of women is being performed on a small scale in this country. **1958** *Times* 18 Jan. 7/2 A 'test-tube' child cannot grow up knowing about his true origin. **1965** *New Scientist* 11 Nov. 392/3 The idea of 'test-tube babies' is no longer something to be woven into the plot of a science fiction novel. Serious-minded scientists are not only thinking about cultivating human embryos on the laboratory bench—they are developing the techniques which will make this a practical possibility. **1978** *Times* 26 July 1/1 The world's first test-tube baby, a girl, was born by caesarian section just before midnight at Oldham and District General Hospital, Greater Manchester... The embryo was implanted in Mrs Brown's womb after being fertilized in Mr Steptoe's laboratories. **1982** *New Scientist* 4 Feb. 290 Since the birth of the first 'test-tube baby' three and a half years ago it has become increasingly obvious that fertilising human eggs in the laboratory is not simply a clinical technique for relieving infertility.

testudinal (tɛ'stju:dɪnəl), *a.* [f. as next + -AL[1].] Pertaining to a tortoise; shaped like a testudo; vaulted, arched.

1823 P. NICHOLSON *Pract. Build.* 594 Testudinal Ceilings; those formed like the back of a tortoise. **1828** in WEBSTER.

testudinarious (tɛstju:dɪ'nɛərɪəs), *a.* [f. L. *testūdo, testūdin-em* (see TESTUDO) + -ARIOUS.] Having the character of a tortoise; marked or coloured like tortoise-shell.

1826 KIRBY & SP. *Entomol.* IV. xlvi. 288 *Testudinarious*.., painted with red, black, and yellow, like tortoise-shell. **1864** in WEBSTER.

testudinate (tɛ'stju:dɪnət), *a.* (*sb.*) [ad. late L. *testūdināt-us*, f. as prec.: see -ATE[2] 2.]

1. Formed like a testudo; arched, vaulted.

1847 in WEBSTER.

2. Of or pertaining to tortoises.

1850 BRODERIP *Leaves Note-bk. Nat.* (1852) 264 The various modifications of testudinate life.

B. *sb.* A tortoise.

1880 *Libr. Univ. Knowl.* (N.Y.) IV. 454 Cope.. enumerates.. 13 sea-saurians, 48 testudinates, and 50 sea serpents.

So **te'studinated** *ppl. a.* = sense 1 above.

1727 BAILEY vol. II, *Testudinated*,..vaulted, made like the Shell of a Tortoise. **1822** MRS. E. NATHAN *Langreath* II. 267 Smoky ceiling, testudinated with cobwebs.

testudineal (tɛstju:'dɪni:əl), *a. rare.* [f. as next + -AL[1].] Pertaining to or resembling a tortoise.

1891 in *Cent. Dict.*

testudineous (tɛstjuːˈdɪniːəs), *a.* [f. L. *testūdine-us*, f. TESTUDO, *testūdin-em*: see -EOUS.]

1. Resembling the shell of a tortoise, or a testudo.

1656 BLOUNT *Glossogr.*, *Testudineous*,..belonging to, or bowing like the shell of a tortoise, vaulted. Also pertaining to that ancient war-engine called *Testudo*. Hence in BAILEY, JOHNSON, and later Dicts.

2. Slow, dilatory, like the pace of a tortoise.

*a***1652** BROME *Love-sick Crt.* III. iii, With a countenance dejected, And testudineous pace. **1860** O. W. HOLMES *Prof. Breakf.-t.* ii, I don't think there is one of our boarders quite so testudineous as I am.

testudinian (tɛstjuːˈdɪnɪən), *a.* and *sb. Zool.* [f. L. *testūdin-em* tortoise + -IAN.] **a.** *adj.* Of or pertaining to tortoises. **b.** *sb.* A member of the tortoise family.

1854 OWEN *Skel. & T.* in *Orr's Circ. Sc.* I. *Org. Nat.* 213 Side-walls..are added in the..land-tortoises (testudinians).

teˈstudinous, *a. rare*$^{-0}$. [f. as prec. + -OUS.] = TESTUDINEOUS.

1692 COLES, *Testudinous*, belonging to or like a Testudo.

testudo (tɛˈstjuːdəʊ). Also 7 (in anglicized form) testude. [a. L. *testūdo* tortoise, etc., f. *testa* a pot, shell, etc.: see TEST *sb.*[2]]

1. *Path.* = TALPA 2: see quots.

*c***1400** *Lanfranc's Cirurg.* 215 Testudines..ben engendrid of hard fleume. **1693** tr. *Blancard's Phys. Dict.* (ed. 2), *Testudo*, a soft, large Swelling, or not very hard, in the Head, broad, in form of an Arch or Tortoise. **1727–41** CHAMBERS *Cycl.*, *Testudo*. **1857** DUNGLISON *Dict. Med. Sc.*, *Testudo*,..an encysted tumour, which has been supposed to resemble the shell of a turtle..Talpa.

2. *Zool.* The typical genus of the tortoise family, *Testudinidæ*; a member of this genus.

*c***1520** L. ANDREWE *Noble Lyfe* xcv, Testudo is a fysshe in a shelle & is in the se of Inde & his shelle is very great & like a muskle. **1706** PHILLIPS, *Testudo*,..the Tortoise, or Shell-crab. **1752** J. HILL *Hist. Anim.* 112 The Testudo has four legs, and its body is covered with a firm shell.

3. *Roman Antiq.* **a.** An engine of war used by besiegers, consisting of a screen or shelter, with a strong and usually fire-proof arched roof; it was wheeled up to the walls, which could then be attacked in safety. Also applied to similar contrivances in more recent times.

1609 HOLLAND *Amm. Marcell.* XXIII. iv. 222 There is a mightie Testudo or frame made, strengthened with very long pieces of timber. **1622** PEACHAM *Compl. Gent.* ix. 73 All engines of warre..Sambukes, Catapultes, Testudo's, Scorpions. **1632** J. HAYWARD tr. *Biondi's Eromena* 150 A Ram-engine..which, together with its testude, they setled on its wheels. **1644** *Lanc. Tracts* (Chetham Soc.) 187 A kind of testudo, a wooden engine running on wheeles, rooft towards the house with thick planks.

b. A shelter formed by a body of troops locking their shields together above their heads.

*a***1680** BUTLER *Rem.* (1759) II. 174 He will join as many Shields together as would make a Roman testudo. **1706** PHILLIPS (ed. Kersey), *Testudo*,..a Target-Fence. **1801** RANKEN *Hist. France* I. 65 A testudo preceded the main body; and two detachments..were ready..to rush out on the enemy's wings. **1827** ROBINSON *Archæol. Græca* IV. ix. (ed. 2) 372 The military testudo,..was when the soldiers were drawn up close to each other, and the rear ranks, bowing themselves, placed their targets above their heads.

c. *transf.* and *fig.* (See quots.)

1877 KNIGHT *Dict. Mech.*, *Testudo*,..is now applied to objects..employed as defenses for miners, etc. when working in ground or rock which is liable to cave in. **1903** *Daily Chron.* 30 Mar. 6/4 The stands were crowded, and a vast 'testudo' of gleaming umbrellas showed during those wild two hours how much the wretched dared.

4. *Anc. Music.* (See quots.)

1702 SIR T. MOLYNEUX in *Phil. Trans.* XXIII. 1270 Who ..could compose such sweet Harmony upon the Guilded Lyre or Testudo. **1727–41** CHAMBERS *Cycl.*, *Testudo*, in antiquity, was particularly used among the poets, &c. for the ancient lyre; by reason it was originally made, by its inventor Mercury of the..shell of a..sea tortoise. **1776** BURNEY *Hist. Mus.* (1789) I. i. 294 It is disputed whether this lyre is the same as the cithara or testudo.

5. *Comb.*, as ***testudo-shaped*** adj.

1875 POLLEN *Anc. & Mod. Furn.* 19 Occasionally they were covered in wholly with a testudo-shaped roof.

ˈtestule. *Bot.* [ad. L. *testula*, dim. of *testa* shell.] The silicified crust or shell of a diatom: more usually called FRUSTULE.

1891 in *Cent. Dict.*

testy (ˈtɛstɪ), *a.* Forms: α. 4–5 testif, -yf, 5 teestif, 6–7 testive. β. 5 testi, 6–7 -ie, 6– testy. γ. 6–7 teastie, 6– 7 (9 *dial.*) teasty (7 teisty). [a. AF. *testif*, *-ive* (cf. OF. *testu* heady, headstrong, obstinate, mod.F. *têtu*), f. *teste* head. For the reduction to *-ie*, *-y* see -IVE, par. 3.]

†**1.** Of headstrong courage; impetuous; precipitate, rash; in later use (passing into the next sense), Aggressive, contentious. *Obs.*

*c***1374** CHAUCER *Troylus* v. 802 This Diomede..Was..Hardy, testyf, strong and cheualrous. *c***1386** —— *Reeve's T.* 84 Clerkes two..Testif [*v. rr.* testyf, teestif] they were and lusty for to pleye. **1412–20** LYDG. *Chron. Troy* II. 4613 Hasty, testif, to smyte rek[e]les. **1489** CAXTON *Faytes of A.* I. vii. 17 That he be not testyf, hastyf, hoot, ne angry. *c***1510** BARCLAY *Mirr. Gd. Manners* (1570) G iij, If any testie foes..Assayle thee. **1611** COTGR., *Testu*,..testie, headie, head-strong, wilfull, obstinate. **1658** PHILLIPS, *Testif* (old word) wild-brained, furious.

2. Prone to be irritated by small checks and annoyances; impatient of being thwarted; resentful of contradiction or opposition; irascible, short-tempered, peevish, tetchy, 'crusty'.

1526 *Pilgr. Perf.* (W. de W. 1531) 106b, Whiche wyll suffre his pacyent though he be neuer so testy or angry. **1530** PALSGR. 327/1 Testy angrye..*ireux..testu*. *Ibid.* 777/2, I waxe testy, *Ie deuiens testyf*, or *testu*. **1549** CHALONER *Erasm. on Folly* K j, Some men there be so waywarde of nature, and so testiue. **1600** HOLLAND *Livy* XXXIX. v. 1025 A chollericke and testie Consull. *a***1713** ELLWOOD *Autobiog.* (1714) 70 This made the Warden hot and testy, and put him almost out of all Patience. **1822** W. IRVING *Braceb. Hall* ii, A testy old huntsman as hot as a pepper-corn. **1887** *Spectator* 27 Aug. 1147 Folks less intractable and testy than such prejudiced disputants.

b. Of words, actions, personal qualities, etc.

1538 CROMWELL in Merriman *Life & Lett.* (1902) II. 128 How can your testie wordes..delite me? **1601** SHAKS. *Jul. C.* IV. iii. 46 Must I stand and crouch Vnder your Testie Humour? **1637** HEYWOOD *Dial.* Wks. 1874 VI. 329 We a mistresse feare, And from her teasty fingers blowes oft beare. **1806** SIR C. BELL *Anat. & Phil. Expression* (1872) 172 The testy, pettish, peevish countenance. **1858** LYTTON *What will he do* I. viii, He resumed his pipe with a prolonged and testy whiff.

†**c.** Of a stream, current, etc.: 'Angry'. *Obs.*

1610 HOLLAND *Camden's Brit.* I. 697 It is made more fell and teasty with a number of stones lying in his chanell. **1833** HT. MARTINEAU *Charmed Sea* i, You will not cross the testy sea to-night.

testy, obs. f. TESTE[5].

testy-: see TESTI-.

testyon, obs. form of TESTON.

†**tesyk(e,** obs. form of PHTHISIC.

*a***1400–50** *Stockh. Med. MS.* 23 Tesyk. *c***1483** CAXTON *Dialogues* 41/40 Tesyque..Tesyke.

tesyl(l, obs. forms of TEASEL.

†**tet** = *thee't*, *thee it*: see T 8 and THET. *Obs.*

*c***1200** ORMIN 5264 Forr ȝiff þu lufesst Godd, tet birrþ Wiþþ gode dedess shæwenn. *Ibid.* 18279, & tet maȝȝ ille likenn.

‖**Tet** (tɛt). [Vietnamese.] **a.** The Vietnamese lunar New Year. Also *attrib.*

1885 J. G. SCOTT *France & Tongking* v. 104 The especial great season for every one, rich and poor, is the new year, the Têt, the Annamese new year..which corresponds with the Chinese and falls about the beginning of February. *Ibid.* 105 At a season such as the Têt, the evil spirits are particularly active and spiteful on account of the general rejoicing. **1931** H. NORDEN *Wanderer in Indo-China* iii. 55 Tet is the month-long New Year's festival which begins a month later than the Occidental new year. During Tet all work is suspended. **1968** *Times* 30 Jan. 4/1 The United States and South Vietnam authorities announced today that they would not observe the 36-hour Tet (Lunar New Year) truce. **1973** *Times* 28 Dec. 5/1 More than 4,000 civilian and military prisoners still held by the South Vietnamese and the communists are to be released before the Tet (Buddhist new year) celebrations on January 23. **1974** P. GORE-BOOTH *With Great Truth & Respect* 359 The truce agreed on for the traditional *Tet* (New Year) holiday in Vietnam would start on Wednesday 8 February, and finish on Sunday afternoon, 12 February.

b. Tet offensive, in the war in Vietnam, an offensive launched by North Vietnamese and Viet Cong forces on 30 January 1968.

1968 *Times* 17 Feb. 4/4 The Vietcong Tet new year offensive was evidence of the correctness of the United States analysis. *Ibid.* 19 Feb. 1/5 The Vietcong are expected to follow up their Tet offensive. **1977** J. CROSBY *Company of Friends* xiv. 95 The CIA had missed the Tet offensive.

tet, obs. f. TEAT.

‖**tetampan** (teˈtampan). [Malay.] In Western Malaysia, an ornate shoulder cloth worn by those serving royalty.

1821 J. LEYDEN tr. *Malay Annals* 342 Tun Sura di Raja..brought the creese from the raja..and covered it with a tetampan. **1909** R. O. WINSTEDT *Life & Customs* (Papers on Malay Subjects) II. 90 *Kain tĕtampan*, a shoulder-cloth of yellow silk, embroidered, and with gold or silver fringe, worn by court attendants when waiting on Rajas. **1972** M. SHEPPARD *Taman Indera* 26 Shoulder cloths of the first grade are called *Tetampan*. They are made of velvet and are usually embroidered with the royal emblem or cypher in gold thread. *Ibid.* 84 A short shoulder cloth of yellow velvet, embroidered with silver thread, called *Tetampan*.

tetan(e: see TETANUS.

tetanic (tɪˈtænɪk), *a.* (*sb.*) [ad. L. *tetanic-us*, a. Gr. τετανικός.] Of, pertaining to, or of the nature of tetanus; characterized by tetanus.

1727 BAILEY vol. II, *Tetanick*, having a Crick in the Neck or Cramp in it, that holdeth it so stiff that it cannot bow. **1805** *Med. Jrnl.* XIV. 304 In the warm climates, where tetanic affections very often follow the great operations. **1822–34** *Good's Study Med.* (ed. 4) III. 495 Clonic agitation instead of a tetanic spasm. **1869** E. A. PARKES *Pract. Hygiene* (ed. 3) 102 Convulsive and tetanic symptoms.

b. as *sb.* (See quot.)

1857 DUNGLISON *Dict. Med. Sc.*, *Tetanic*,..a remedy, which acts on the nerves, and, through them, on the muscles, occasioning, in large doses, convulsions.

So † **teˈtanical** *a.*, tetanic. *Obs. rare*$^{-0}$. Hence **teˈtanically** [see -ICALLY] *adv.*, by, or as by tetanus; spasmodically.

1656 BLOUNT *Glossogr.*, *Tetanical*,..that hath the crick in the neck [etc.]. **1877** ROSENTHAL *Muscles & Nerves* 36 The muscle..contracts tetanically.

tetaniform (ˈtɛtənɪfɔːm), *a.* [f. TETAN-US + -FORM.] = TETANOID.

1887 A. M. BROWN *Anim. Alkaloids* 153 In the common and ordinary form the dominant nervous factor is the delirium; in the cerebrospinal it is the tetaniform. **1899** *Allbutt's Syst. Med.* VII. 531 Tetaniform tonic convulsions.

tetanigenous (tɛtəˈnɪdʒɪnəs), *a. rare.* [f. TETAN-US + *-genous*: cf. -GEN and -OUS.] Producing tetanus.

1891 in *Cent. Dict.*

‖**tetanilla** (tɛtəˈnɪlə). [mod.L., irreg. dim. of TETANUS.] = TETANY.

1890 BILLINGS *Nat. Med. Dict.*, *Tetanilla*,..tetany. **1899** *Allbutt's Syst. Med.* VIII. 47 Tetanilla; Remittent Tetanus.

tetanine (ˈtɛtənaɪn). *Chem.* [f. TETANUS + -INE[5].] †**a.** An old name for strychnine. **b.** A ptomaine, $C_{13}H_{30}N_2O_4$, obtained from meat extract containing Rosenbach's microbe, the tetanus bacillus; occurring also in decaying corpses.

1857 DUNGLISON *Dict. Med. Sc.*, *Tetanine*, Strychnia. **1888** BRIEGER in *Jrnl. Chem. Soc.* LIV. 1317 Tetanine and Mytilotoxine..the hydrochlorides of these bases decompose gradually and lose their toxic properties. **1899** CAGNEY *Jaksch's Clin. Diagn.* i. (ed. 4) 55 From cultivations of the [tetanus] bacillus, Brieger has isolated several ptomaines—tetanin, tetanotoxin, and spasmotoxin.

†**ˈtetanism.** *Obs. rare.* [f. TETAN-US + -ISM.] The action of tetanus.

1681 tr. *Willis' Rem. Med. Wks.* Vocab., *Tetanism*, a kind of cramp that so stretcheth forth the member, that it cannot bow or bend any way.

tetanizant (ˈtɛtənaɪzənt). [a. F. *tétanisant*, pr. pple. of *tétaniser* to TETANIZE: see -ANT.] An agent or substance that causes tetanus.

1875 H. C. WOOD *Therap.* (1879) 357 One a tetanizant, the other a paralyzant.

tetanization (tɛtənaɪˈzeɪʃən). [n. of action f. TETANIZE: cf. F. *tétanisation.*] The production of tetanus or tetanic contraction in a muscle.

1881 TYNDALL *Floating Matter of Air* ii. 102 He found the rapidity of putrefaction to correspond with the violence of the tetanization. **1887** G. T. LADD *Physiol. Psychol.* iii. §4. 106 The application of rapidly repeated shocks to the nerve, such as would produce 'tetanic contraction' of the muscle, may be called the 'tetanization of a nerve'.

tetanize (ˈtɛtənaɪz), *v.* [f. TETAN-US + -IZE: so F. *tétaniser.*] *trans.* To produce tetanus or tetanic spasms in. Hence **ˈtetanized** *ppl. a.*, **ˈtetanizing** *vbl. sb.* and *ppl. a.*

1849 NOAD *Electricity* (ed. 3) 473 They then assume the tetanized condition, during which their limbs become completely stiffened. **1855** *Fraser's Mag.* LI. 544 The common crab,..finding itself a prisoner, draws in its legs rigid, as if tetanized by the touch. **1874** GARROD & BAXTER *Mat. Med.* (1880) 200 As a tetanising agent, it is inferior to strychnia and brucia. **1897** *Allbutt's Syst. Med.* IV. 819 A double electrode being applied to the posterior wall of the larynx so as to tetanise the interarytenoid.

tetano- (tɛtənəʊ), combining form of Gr. τέτανος TETANUS, as first element in some scientific terms. **ˌtetano-ˈcannabine** *Chem.* [Gr. κάνναβις hemp], an alkaloid causing tetanic spasms, obtained in colourless needle-like crystals from Indian hemp, *Cannabis indica*. **tetaˈnolysin** [Gr. λύσις a loosening], a toxin produced by the tetanus bacillus, to which the hæmolytic action of tetanus poison is due. **ˌtetanoˈmotor**: see quots. **ˌtetanoˈspasmin** [SPASM], a poison produced by the tetanus bacillus, to which tetanic convulsions are due (*Cent. Dict. Suppl.* 1909). **ˌtetanoˈtoxin**: see quot.

1883 HAY in *Pharm. Jrnl. & Trans.* XIII. 999 To this alkaloid I propose to give the name *tetano-cannabine, as indicative of its action. **1902** *Brit. Med. Jrnl.* 12 Apr. 920 Ehrlich and Madsen have studied *tetanolysin. **1904** *Ibid.* 10 Sept. 569 Expressed by a curve quite like the tetanolysin curve. **1860** *New Syd. Soc. Year-bk.* 35 A mechanical *Tetanomoter. **1890** BILLINGS *Nat. Med. Dict.*, *Tetanomotor*,..electro-magnetic instrument for producing muscular tetanus by repeated shocks. **1899** *Syd. Soc. Lex.*, *Tetanomotor*, Heidenhain's instrument for producing rapid direct mechanical stimulation by an ivory hammer attached to the vibrating spring of an induction machine. **1890** BILLINGS *Nat. Med. Dict.*, *Tetanotoxine, $C_5H_{11}N$, a base obtained from beef-broth cultures of the tetanus bacillus. It produces spasm and paralysis. **1899** [see TETANINE].

tetanoid (ˈtɛtənɔɪd), *a.* (*sb.*) [f. TETAN-US + -OID.] Of the nature of, or resembling tetanus. **b.** *sb.* A tetanoid spasm or attack.

1856 KANE *Arct. Expl.* I. xix. 231 Obscure tetanoid symptoms..disclosed themselves. *Ibid.* xxxii. 447 If one of these tetanoids should attack them on the road.

‖**tetanothrum** (-ˈəʊθrəm). *Obs.* Pl. **-othra.** Also 6 **tetanother.** [L. *tetanōthrum* (Pliny), a. Gr. τετάνωθρον, f. τετανοῦν to stretch, strain, f. τετανός stretched, smooth.] A cosmetic for removing wrinkles.

1519 HORMAN *Vulg.* 169 b, They fylle vp theyr frekyllys: and stretche abrode theyr skyn with tetanother. **1755** YOUNG *Centaur* v. Wks. 1757 IV. 214, I fear they would prefer a tetanothrum to an apotheosis. **1823** CRABB *Technol. Dict.*, Tetanothra.

‖**tetanus** (ˈtɛtənəs). Forms: α. 5–7 **tetane,** 7 **tetan.** β. 5 **tethanus,** 7–8 **tetanos, -on,** 7– **-us.** [L. *tetanus* (Pliny), a. Gr. τέτανος muscular spasm, f. τείν-ειν to stretch. Formerly anglicized *tetan(e.*]

1. A disease characterized by tonic spasm and rigidity of some or all of the voluntary muscles, usually occasioned by a wound or other injury. (Cf. LOCKJAW.)

α. *c* **1400** *Lanfranc's Cirurg.* 104 If þat a man haue a crampe or ellis a tetane þat is a sijknes þat halt þe membre lich streit on boþe sidis. *c* **1608** DONNE *Let.* in Gosse *Life* (1899) I. 195 [My sickness] hath so much of a tetane, that it withdraws and pulls the mouth. *a* **1614** —— *Βιαθανατος* (1644) 171 In Tetans, which are rigors..in the Muscles.

β. **1398** TREVISA *Barth. De P.R.* VII. xiii. (Bodl. MS.), This ..Crampe..haþ þre manere kinde..þe þrid hatte Tethanus, and is whanne þe for þer senewes and þe hinder schrinkeþ. **1576** NEWTON *Lemnie's Complex.* (1633) 24 In the Apoplexie, Palsey, Tetanus, and many diseases moe. **1753** N. TORRIANO *Non-naturals* 66 In Epilepsies and Distractions, swooning Fits, Tetanus's and Catalepsis. **1846** *J. Baxter's Libr. Pract. Agric.* (ed. 4) I. 430 Tetanus is one of the most formidable and fatal diseases to which the horse is liable. **1846** TRENCH *Mirac.* xi. (1862) 232 Paralysis with contraction of the joints..when united, as it much oftener is in the hot climates..than among us, with tetanus.

2. *Physiol.* A condition of prolonged contraction produced by rapidly repeated stimuli.

1877 ROSENTHAL *Muscles & Nerves* 34 Enduring contraction of this sort is called tetanus of the muscle to distinguish it from a series of distinct pulsations. **1877** FOSTER *Phys.* III. v. § 1 (1878) 471 The changes in which may be compared to the changes in a motor nerve during tetanus.

3. *attrib.* and *Comb.*, as ***tetanus antitoxin, bacillus, culture, poison; tetanus-afflicted, -like*** adjs.

1857 DUFFERIN *Lett. High Lat.* vii. (ed. 3) 92 Our dinner went off merrily; the tetanus-afflicted salmon proved excellent. **1896** *Allbutt's Syst. Med.* I. 237 The diphtheria and tetanus antitoxins act directly on the toxins. **1899** *Ibid.* VI. 541 In some cases..there are tetanus-like seizures. **1904** *Brit. Med. Jrnl.* No. 2280. 568 Tetanolysin, the hæmolytic substance of tetanus poison. **1908** J. RITCHIE in *Carnegie Trust Rep.* 25 The action of tetanus toxin on the central nervous system.

tetany (ˈtɛtənɪ). [ad. F. *tétanie* intermittent tetanus, f. prec.] A tetanoid affection characterized by intermittent muscular spasms. Also *attrib.*

1890 BILLINGS *Nat. Med. Dict.*, *Tetany*,..a succession of tonic muscular spasms, mostly symmetrical, following one another at irregular intervals. **1899** *Allbutt's Syst. Med.* VIII. 47 Tetany is an affection characterised by tonic muscular spasms involving especially the distal portion of the limbs. *Ibid.* 48 The tetany spasms ceased the day after a tape-worm had been expelled.

tetar, obs. form of TETTER.

tetarteron (tɪˈtɑːtərən). *Numism.* [a. Gr. τεταρτηρόν, lit. 'measure of capacity', f. τέταρτος fourth.] A Byzantine gold coin of the 10th–11th cent., a copper coin replacing the old follis from the late 11th cent. (see quot. 1969).

1908 W. WROTH *Catal. Imperial Byzantine Coins in Brit. Mus.* [I. p.l, This..coin is stated to have been called ..τεταρτερόν. This was probably..its popular nickname.] *Ibid.* II. 659/1 'Tetarteron', l. **1959** E. POUND *Thrones* xcvi. 12 Here, surely, is a refinement of language. ἢ καὶ νομίσματα ξέει Wd/ appear to be tetarteron tokens not affecting the aureus. **1969** M. S. HENDY *Coinage & Money in Byzantine Empire 1081–1261* vi. 28 The tetarteron nomisma.. originally a gold coin,..was first struck by Nicephorus II, and continued until early in the reign of Alexius I. At some point after this, the name was appropriated to describe a copper coin of similar small, thick fabric, first struck by Alexius as an element of his reformed coinage. This change had taken place by 1097. **1973** P. D. WHITTING *Byzantine Coins* iii. 40 A *new* gold coin lighter than the solidus was introduced... The new and lighter coin was called the nomisma tetarteron. These tetartera cannot be distinguished by eye until the later part of Basil II's reign. .. The name means 'a fourth part', *i.e.* a piece of standard weight diminished by a quarter of a tremissis equivalent to ½ of the whole.

tetarto- (tɪˈtɑːtəʊ), combining form of Gr. τέταρτος fourth (cf. TETRA-), in scientific terms belonging chiefly to crystallography. **teˌtartoˈhedral** *a.* [Gr. ἕδρα base], having one fourth of the number of faces required by the highest or holohedral degree of symmetry belonging to its system; hence **teˌtartoˈhedrally** *adv.*, in a tetartohedral manner. **teˌtartoˈhedric, -ˈhedrical** *adjs.*, = *tetartohedral.* **teˌtartoˈhedrism**, the property or quality of crystallizing in tetartohedral forms; the condition in which a crystal symmetrically develops only one fourth of the number of planes demanded by holohedral symmetry. **teˌtartoˈhedron**, a tetartohedral crystal. **teˌtartoˈhedry**, = *tetartohedrism.* **teˌtartoheˈxagonal** *a.*, having one quarter of the number of normals belonging to the hexagonal system. **teˌtartoprisˈmatic** *a.*, **teˌtartoˈpyramid**: see quots. **teˌtartosyˈmmetric, -syˈmmetrical** *adjs.*: see quot. **teˌtartoˈsymmetry**, a variety of merosymmetry, in which only one fourth of the faces of the holosymmetrical form are retained. **teˌtartosysteˈmatic** *a.*, said of a form in which only one fourth of the origin-planes are extant.

1858 DANA *Min.* (ed. 4) 49 They are *tetartohedral forms, or contain only one-fourth the number of planes occurring under complete symmetry. **1864** WATTS *Dict. Chem.* II. 144 Quartz likewise exhibits other forms of tetartohedral development. **1888** RUTLEY *Rock-Forming Min.* 64 The development of certain plagihedral, or tetartohedral, faces. **1864** WEBSTER, **Tetartohedrally.* **1854** *Pereira's Pol. Light* 234 Doubly oblique prismatic system..or the *tetartohedric-rhombic system. **1860** MAYNE *Expos. Lex.*, *Tetartohedrical. **1858** DANA *Min.* (ed. 4) 49 A form of this kind..is found in Titanic Iron, and is called rhombohedral *tetartohedrism. **1895** STORY-MASKELYNE *Crystallogr.* 160 The ambiguity in which the terms hemihedrism, tetartohedrism, etc. are involved. *Ibid.* 231 There can only be a single kind of *tetartohedron in the Cubic system. **1864** WATTS *Dict. Chem.* II. 144 **Tetartohedry.* Quartz affords a remarkable example of a combination in which only one-fourth of the possible faces are present. **1895** STORY-MASKELYNE *Crystallogr.* 284 Six faces corresponding to three normals: *tetarto-hexagonal diplohedral forms. Three faces corresponding to three normals: tetarto-hexagonal haplohedral forms. **1847** WEBSTER, **Tetartoprismatic*,..one fourth prismatic, applied to oblique rhombic prisms.— Mohs. **1851** *Richardson's Geol.* v. (1855) 98 Classification of Mohs..V. The Tetarto-Prismatic is composed of the oblique rhomboidal prism. **1891** *Cent. Dict.*, **Tetartopyramid*,..a quarter-pyramid: said of the pyramidal planes of the triclinic system, which appear in sets of two (that is, one fourth the number required by a complete pyramid). **1895** STORY-MASKELYNE *Crystallogr.* 159 Mero-symmetrical forms may be hemi-symmetrical ..*tetarto-symmetrical, presenting one-quarter only of the faces of the holo-symmetrical form. *Ibid.* 160 *Tetarto-symmetry, where the form is (i) hemi-systematic and haplohedral, (ii) *tetarto-systematic and diplohedral. *Ibid.* 308 Tetarto-systematic haplohedral forms.

b. *Path.* ‖**tetartoˈphyia** [Gr. φυή growth], a remitting quartan fever.

1857 DUNGLISON *Dict. Med. Sc.*, *Tetartophia*,..a quartan, in which the intermission is inordinately short or imperfect. **1895** *Funk's Stand. Dict.*, *Tetartophyia.*

tetaug, var. TAUTOG, N. American fish.

tetch (tɛtʃ). Now only *dial.* Also 7 **tech.** [Origin uncertain: see TETCHY.] A fit of petulance or anger; a tantrum.

1642 ROGERS *Naaman* 98, I mean not that such a tech as Naaman took here, may do it. *Ibid.* 143 An offer..which thou biddest faire for and forsookest at last in a tech. *Ibid.* 379 Meer tetches and pritches, very toyes and conceits, can alienate their love. *a* **1734** NORTH *Lives, Ld. Guilford* (1826) II. 218 But this frantic fellow took tetch at somewhat, and ran away into Ireland. **1876** J. RICHARDSON *Cummerland Talk* Ser. II. 73 Nater began to tak t' tetch wid him, an' wadden't be mead ghem on enny langer.

¶**1623** COCKERAM, *Tetch*, thriftinesse. (App. a mistake.)

tetch(e, obs. forms of TACHE *sb.*[1], [3].

tetched (tɛtʃt), *pa. pple.* and *ppl. a.* U.S. dial. and colloq. var. of *touched* (see TOUCH *v.* 23 b); mentally deranged to a slight degree; somewhat mad, crazy, or 'cracked'.

1930–41 in H. Wentworth *Amer. Dial. Dict.* (1944) 657/1. **1983** C. MCCARRY *Last Supper* III. vi. 333 These people are tetched in the head. **1984** S. BELLOW *Him with his Foot in his Mouth* 39 If she had been a little tetched before, melodramatic, in her fifties she seemed to become crazed.

tetchous (ˈtɛtʃəs), *a.* *U.S. dial.* Also **tetchious, tetchus.** [f. TETCHY *a.*: see -OUS.] = TETCHY, TECHY *a.* 1.

1890 *Dialect Notes* I. 66 *Tetchus*,..tetchy. **1893** H. A. SHANDS *Some Peculiarities of Speech in Mississippi* 62 *Tetchous*..., common among negroes and illiterate whites for *tetchy.* Used also in Kentucky. **1913** H. KEPHART *Our Southern Highlanders* xiii. 294 A choleric or fretful person is tetchious. **1948** A. LOMAX in A. Dundes *Mother Wit* (1973) 484/1 That's what makes the Negro so *tetchious* till today. **1959** W. FAULKNER *Mansion* iii. 58 A respectability that delicate and tetchous that wouldn't nothing else suit.

tetchy, techy (ˈtɛtʃɪ), *a.* Forms: α. 6–9 **techy,** 7 **techie, teachy, -ie,** 9 *dial.* **teachy, teechy.** β. 6– **tetchy;** also 7 **tetchie, tecchy, titchie, tichy,** 9 *dial.* **titchy, tertchy.** γ. *dial.* 8–9 **tatchy,** 9 **tachy.** [In form, a deriv. of TETCH, but that word being both less common and app. of later appearance, may be a back-formation from this. Derivation from TATCH *sb.*[1] (in ME. *tecche*, 16th c. *tetche*) has been suggested; but there are difficulties both of form and sense.]

1. Easily irritated or made angry; quick to take offence; short-tempered; peevish, irritable; testy. (Cf. TOUCHY, which has been associated with this from early in the 17th c.) **a.** Of persons.

α. **1592** SHAKS. *Rom. & Jul.* I. iii. 32 (Qos.) Pretty foole, to see it teachie, and fall out with the Dugge. **1639** W. PERKINS in *Lismore Papers* Ser. II. (1888) IV. 55 Hee is as teachy as any wasp. **1642** ROGERS *Naaman* 99 A techie toy, that is, his prejudicate and forestalled heart. **1674** RAY *S. & E.C. Words* (1691) 117 *Techy*, i.e. *Touchy*, peevish, cross, apt to be angry. **1817** J. GILCHRIST *Intell. Patrimony* 109 This pure and honourable body was very techy and ticklish on the point of privilege. **1853** W. IRVING in *Life & Lett.* (1864) IV. 159, I was a little techy under your bantering.

β. **1596** HARINGTON *Ulysses upon Ajax* E vj b, For which cause you are waxt so tetchie. **1611** COTGR., *Se piquer*, to be titchie, soone offended, quickly moued. *Ibid.* s.v. *Poincte*, *Chatouilleux à la poincte*..that readily answers the spurre; hence also, titchie, that will not indure to be touched. **1641** in 'Smectymnuus' *Vind. Answ.* § 2. 29 We are sullen.., tecchy and quarrelsome men. **1642** ROGERS *Naaman* 267 Jonas..was wondrous tetchy. **1733** SWIFT *Let. to D'chess Queensberry* 20 Mar., You are grown very tetchy since I lost the dear friend who was my supporter. **1851** TRENCH *St. Aug. on Serm. on Mt.* Introd. v. 69 *note*, Jerome..whom none can deny..to have been somewhat tetchy and prompt to take offence.

γ. **1746** *Exmoor Scolding* (E.D.S.) 21 Ya purting, tatchy,.. mincing Theng. **1892** HEWETT *Peas. Sp. Devon* 132, I niver zeed zich a tatchy, ill-contrived little twoad.

b. Of qualities, actions, etc.: Characterized by or proceeding from irritability.

1592 *Nobody & Someb.* in Simpson *Sch. Shaks.* (1878) I. 279 Nay, now youle fall into your techy humour. **1610** GUILLIM *Heraldry* III. vii. (1660) 134 The Nettle is of so tetchie and froward a nature. **1652** *Mod. Policies* III. (1653) Colasterion, King-killing,..I know it a techy subject. **1841** LEVER *C. O'Malley* xxx, Gradually increased to a sore and techy subject. **1864–5** WOOD *Homes without H.* xxiii. (1868) 425 A mere stinging creature with a tetchy temper.

2. *fig.* Of land: see quots. *dial.*

1847–78 HALLIWELL, *Tetchy*...applied to land that is difficult to work or to manage. **1904** in *Eng. Dial. Dict.*, If yer plough or roll when 'tis wet yer dew more harm nor good; that land's wonnerful tetchy, I can tell yer.

Hence **ˈtetchily** *adv.*; **ˈtetchiness.**

1647 TRAPP *Comm. Ep.* 664 As any man is more industrious and ingenious, so he teacheth more *teachily and painfully. **1755** JOHNSON, *Techily.* **1862** F. W. ROBINSON *Owen* IV. vi, 'I'll not touch bit or sup to-day', she cried, tetchily; 'you can't do better than leave me to myself'. **1623** BP. HALL *Contempl.*, *O.T.* XIX. viii, Not the unjust fury and *techiness of the patient shall cross the cure. **1793** ANNA SEWARD *Lett.* (1811) III. 246 The froward tetchiness; the unprincipled malice;..which generally darkened..the man's brain. **1905** *Times* 5 Mar. 10/3 Were it not for M. K——'s tetchiness..I should feel inclined to..issue..a classic excuse.

‖**tête** (‖tɛt, teɪt). *Obs.* exc. *Hist.* [F. *tête* head.] A woman's head of hair, or wig, dressed high and elaborately ornamented, in the fashion of the second half of the 18th c.

1756 C. SMART tr. *Horace, Sat.* I. viii. (1826) II. 71 Sagana's towering tête of false hair. **1772** R. GRAVES *Spir. Quixote* (1820) I. 140, I sell as many wigs or tetes as any barber in town. **1813** *Sk. Charac.* (ed. 2) I. 81 By way of Grecian têtes, they had large cockades of hair stuck at the back of their heads. **1816** SCOTT *Antiq.* vi, This unparalleled *tête*, which her brother was wont to say was fitter for a turban for Mahound or Termagant, than a head-gear for a.. Christian gentlewoman. **1884** *Pall Mall G.* 7 May 6/1 She [a lady of time of Geo. III] wears what is called a *tête*, the monstrous head-dress that was fashionable in her time.

b. *Comb.*, as ***tête-maker.***

1789 WOLCOTT (P. Pindar) *Subj. for Paint.* To Rdr., Wks. 1816 II. 121 Têtemakers, perfumers,..parliament speech-makers.

tete, obs. form of TEAT.

‖**tête-à-tête** (ˈteɪtəˈteɪt, ‖tɛtatɛt), *adv.*, *sb.*, and *a.* Also 7 **tate a tate.** [F. *tête à tête* adv. and sb., lit. 'head to head' (17th c. in Molière); cf. *teste à teste* together (in single combat), 16th c. in Godef. *Compl.*]

A. *adv.* Together without the presence of a third person; in private (of two persons); face to face.

1700 CONGREVE *Way of World* I. ix, Ay, tête-à-tête, but not in public. **1713** SWIFT *Hor. Sat.* II. vi. 106 My lord and he are grown so great, Always together *tête-à-tête*. **1790** SCOTT *Let. to W. Clerk* 3 Sept., I dined two days ago *tête à tête* with Lord Buchan. **1848** THACKERAY *Van. Fair* xxix, The General and I were moping together *tête-à-tête*.

B. *sb.* (pl. *tête-à-têtes.*)

1. A private conversation or interview between two persons; also *concr.* a party of two.

1697 VANBRUGH *Relapse* IV. iii, I..have pretended Letters to write, to give my Friends a Tate a Tate. **1738** *Gentl. Mag.* VIII. 31/1 The Morning Moments, which I take to be the *Mollia Tempora*, so propitious to *Tete a Tetes*. **1768** MME. D'ARBLAY *Early Diary* 16 Nov., I had the pleasure of a delightful Tête à Tête with him. **1880** MRS. FORRESTER *Roy & V.* I. 55 Seated together on a low couch made expressly for such a tête-à-tête.

2. The name of some special types of sofa, settee, etc., made of such a shape as to enable two persons to converse more or less face to face.

1864 WEBSTER, *Tête-à-tête*,..a form of sofa for two persons, so curved that they are brought face to face while sitting on different sides of the sofa. **1877** KNIGHT *Dict. Mech.*, *Tete-a-tete*, two chairs with seats attached and facing in opposite directions, the arms and backs forming an S-shape. **1889** MISS C. F. WOOLSON *Jupiter Lights* xiii. 126 The sofa of this set was of the pattern named tête-à-tête, very hard and slippery.

C. *adj.* (*attrib.* use of the sb.) Of or pertaining to a *tête-à-tête*; consisting of or attended by two persons; ***tête-à-tête set***, a tea-set for two.

1728 VANBRUGH & CIB. *Prov. Husb.* II. i, A pretty cheerful *tête-à-tête* dinner. **1779** JOHNSON 26 Mar. in *Boswell*, You must not indulge your delicacy too much; or you will be a *tête-à-tête* man all your life. **1847** C. BRONTË *J. Eyre* xxiv, I was determined not to spend the whole time in a *tête-à-tête* conversation. **1870** L. M. ALCOTT *Old-Fashioned Girl* viii. 163 Such a cunning teakettle and saucepan, and a tête-à-tête set.

Hence as *v. intr.*, to engage in private conversation (together or *with* another).

1861 MRS. GASKELL *Let.* 10 June (1966) 657 The reason why she & I were tête à têteing in this way was that Mr Gaskell was gone to Liverpool. **1943** *Two Masques* Nov. 4/2 Maureen O'Hara, Patricia Morison and Martha O'Driscoll are the ladies with whom Garfield goes 'tete-a-tete'ing. **1979** G. SWARTHOUT *Skeletons* 48 I'll tête-à-tête with him, too.

tête-bêche (tɛtbɛʃ), *sb.* (*a.*) *Philately.* [a. Fr., lit. '(sleeping) head to foot', f. *tête* head + *bêche*, reduced from *béchevet*, lit. 'double bedhead'.] (A stamp) printed upside down relative to the next stamp in the same row or column (see quot. 1913). Freq. *attrib.* in phr. ***tête-bêche pair.*** Also as *adv.*

1874 *Stamp-Collector's Mag.* XII. 10 The Marquis de L—— has kindly forwarded for notice a reversed 4 centime laureated French empire stamp; technically termed a *tête-bêche*. **1882** E. B. EVANS *Catal. Collectors Postage Stamps* 56 One or more stamps upside down,..forming the varieties termed *têtes-bêches*. *Ibid.*, Varieties 2 and 3 are the result of stamps placed *tête-bêche*. **1891** *S. Gibbons' Monthly Jrnl.* 30 Jan. 153/2 The sheets are composed of four horizontal rows of five stamps,..each row is placed *tête-bêche* to the one below it. **1913** E. B. EVANS *Stamps & Stamp Collecting* (ed. 4) 103 *Tête-bêche*. A term applied in French to stamps printed upside down in reference to one another. One such stamp may appear in a sheet, through one of the dies forming the plate being accidentally set the wrong way; this stamp will be *tête-bêche* as regards those surrounding it. Some of the stamps of Grenada were printed with alternate rows reversed, so that the stamps in one row were *tête-bêche* with reference to those in the next. Such varieties must of course be shown in pairs, as the stamps when separated exhibit no peculiarity. **1921** F. A. BELLAMY *Oxf. & Cambr. Coll. Messenger Postage Stamps* 14 Balliol, a number of impressions were made one way, then the paper strip was turned round; so a tête bêche pair can be found on each strip. **1971** *Daily Tel.* 16 July 7/6 The 2 annas is known in a tête bêche pair (one stamp upside down in relation to the other).

‖**tête de bœuf** (tɛt də bœf). *Embroidery.* [Fr., lit. 'ox's head'.] Used *attrib.* to designate an embroidery stitch (see quots.).

1882 CAULFEILD & SAWARD *Dict. Needlework* 195/1 *Tête de Bœuf Stitch.* The name of this stitch is derived from its shape, the two upper stitches having the appearance of horns, and the lower ones of an animal's head... The needle is inserted and brought out for the two slanting stitches that commence the next Tête de Bœuf. **1923** *Daily Mail* 19 Jan. 15 *Tete de bœuf stitch...* Two slanting stitches which meet in the form of a V are made, and from the inside of this, at the bottom, is taken a chain-stitch which is caught down with a short over-stitch. **1934** M. THOMAS *Dict. Embroidery Stitches* 198 Tête-de-bœuf filling stitch. Single daisy stitches set between two right-angled straight stitches make up this pretty filling.

‖**tête de cuvée** (tɛt də kyve). [Fr., lit. 'head of the vatful'.] A vineyard producing the best wine in a village area; wine from such a vineyard.

[**1833** C. REDDING *Hist. & Descr. Mod. Wines* v. 100 The best Burgundies, called *les têtes de cuves*, are from the choicest vines..grown on the best spots in the vineyard, having the finest aspect.] **1908** E. & A. VIZETELLY *Wines of France* 122 The finer Volnay, what is called the *tête-de-cuvée* wine, has a most refreshing flavour. **1952** W. STEVENS *Let.* 29 Sept. (1967) 761, I sat at lunch with a little Corton (1929, tete de cuvée). **1965** A. SICHEL *Penguin Bk. Wines* III. 147 The above listed vineyards are all *têtes de cuvées*, that is the highest class in their village area... It must not be assumed that the *têtes de cuvées* of different villages are equal in quality. Many names of the next category—the *premier cru* or *cuvée*..may be better.

‖**tête de mouton.** *Obs.* [Fr., lit 'sheep's head'.] A head-dress of close frizzly curls formerly worn by women.

1737 in *Lady Suffolk's Lett.* (1824) II. 159, I beg she will not leave off her *tête de mouton* and her *pannier*. **1758** *Humble Rem.*, etc. in *Ann. Reg.* I. 374/1 It may..become a French *friseur*, to acquaint the public that he makes a *tete de mouton*, or simply a *tete*.

‖**tête de nègre** (tɛːt də nɛːgr). [Fr., lit. 'Negro's head'.] A dark brown colour approaching black. Usu. *attrib.* Cf. *nigger brown* s.v. NIGGER *sb.* 2 d.

1916 in G. Howell *In Vogue* (1975) 20/1 (Advt.), Tête de Negre.. Hat, gold embroidery. **1923** *Daily Mail* 5 Mar. 15/3 A striking gown..is worn over a slip of tete de negre silk. **1973** *Country Life* 22 Feb. 455/1 Design of baskets of spring flowers..on a *tete de nègre* (that is a not dead black) ground.

‖**tête de pont** (tɛt də pɔ̃). Pl. têtes de pont. [Fr., lit. 'bridge head'.] A fortification defending the approach to a bridge; a bridge-head.

1794 *Amer. St. Papers, Mil. Affairs* (1832) I. 89 There ought to be..close to the chain, a small *tete de pont*. **1812** *Examiner* 31 Aug. 549/2 One bridge upon the Beresina, with double *tetes-de-pont*. **1829** SCOTT *Anne of G.* ix, They were not long of discovering the *tête-du-pont* on which the drawbridge, when lowered, had formerly rested. **1853** H. J. STOCQUELER *Milit. Encycl.* 283/2 In order to add to the defence of *Têtes de Pont*, reduits have been constructed within them. **1918** E. S. FARROW *Dict. Milit. Terms* 613 *Tête-de-pont*, a work thrown up at the end of a bridge to cover communication across a river; a bridgehead. **1926** FOWLER *Mod. Eng. Usage* 329/1 The strong tête-de-pont fortifications were rushed by our troops, & a battalion crossed the bridge.

‖**tête exaltée** (tɛːt ɛgzalte), *adv. phr.* [Fr., lit. 'with head elated'.] In an elated or euphoric manner. Also as *sb.*, someone behaving thus.

1841 C. FOX *Jrnl.* 6 June in *Memories of Old Friends* (1882) vii. 128 Carlyle..said, 'Give my love to your dear interesting nephew and nieces!'.. I walked *tête-exaltée* the rest of the day. **1856** C. M. YONGE *Daisy Chain* I. xxii. 232 Flora thought of the words '*tête exaltée*', and considered herself alone to have sober sense enough to see things in a true light. **1873** —— *Pillars of House* III. xxviii. 128 A pious utterance that only a *tête exaltée* takes literally.

tetel ('teɪtəl, 'tɛtəl). Also tetl. [Local name.] = TORA.

1867 S. W. BAKER *Nile Trib.* 308 We had hardly ridden half a mile, when I perceived a fine bull tétel..standing near a bush. **1894** SCLATER & THOMAS *Bk. Antelopes* I. 16 The Tora or Tétel was confounded by von Heaglin and Sir Samuel Baker, its first discoverers, with the Bubal. **1920** *Blackw. Mag.* Nov. 672/2 A great herd of tetl—big animals the size of a mule—sprang up.

‖**tête montée** (tɛːt mɔ̃te), *adj. phr.* Also *erron.* tête monté. [Fr., lit. 'excited head'.] Over-excited, agitated, worked up. Also as *sb.*, this state of mind.

1825 H. WILSON *Memoirs* I. 12, I had suffered severely from wounded pride, and, in fact, I was very much tête monté. **1836** E. GROSVENOR *Let.* in G. Huxley *Lady Elizabeth & Grosvenors* (1965) vii. 160 The tête montée state of the young *Brutus's* and patriots..in France. **1859** TROLLOPE *Bertrams* I. viii. 155 But in truth George was somewhat afflicted by a *tête montée* in this matter. **1882** E. W. HAMILTON *Diary* 29 Aug. (1972) I. 328 She regards Davitt as the incarnation of vanity and Dillon as a *tête montée*. **1936** J. M. KEYNES *Gen. Theory Employment* vi. 64 It might be, of course, that individuals were so *tête montée* in their decisions as to how much they themselves would save and invest respectively, that there would be no point of price equilibrium at which transactions could take place. **1960** L. COOPER *Certain Compass* 118 Adrian was *tête monté*.., in that slightly exalted state.

teter: see TEETER, TETTER.

teterrimous (tɪ'tɛrɪməs), *a. rare.* [f. L. *tēterrimus* most foul, superl. of *tæter* (*tēter*) foul + -OUS.] In phrase ***teterrimous cause***, after L. *teterrima belli causa* 'the most foul cause of war', i.e. woman (Horace *Sat.* I. iii. 107).

[**1704** SWIFT *T. Tub* ix. **1823** BYRON *Juan* IX. lv, Oh thou 'teterrima causa' of all 'belli'. **1845** FORD *Handbk. Spain* I. iii. 362 A Christian woman now was the *teterrima causa* of the Moslem downfall.] **1864** *Daily Tel.* 24 Aug., I pronounce Orangeism the teterrimous cause of the war that has been waged for two weeks past in the heart of the town.

teth, obs. form of TEETH, TEETHE.

tethanus, obs. form of TETANUS.

tethe, tething, obs. ff. TITHE *v.*, TITHING.

tethee, obs. form of TEETHY, testy.

tether ('tɛðə(r)), *sb.* Forms: *α.* 4 tethir, (thether), 6 teyther, 6–8 teather, 7 tither, teither, 6– tether. *β.* 4–5 tedyr, 5 -yre, 5–7 teder, 6 teddir, tedure, teeder, 6–8 (9 *dial.*) tedder, 7 teddar (tedir). [At first a northern word: app. a. ON. *tjóðr* 'tether' (Icel. and Fær. *tjóður*, Sw. *tjuder*); corresp. to 15th c. WFris. *tyader, tieder*; MLG., MDu. *tûder, tudder*, LG. *tüder, tüdder, töder, tider, tier, tir*, Du. *tuier*, all in sense 'tether'. Cf. also OHG. **ziotar, zeotar*, MHG. *zieter* (still in Bav. dial., Hess. *zetter*) in sense 'fore-pole or team'. A corresponding OE. **téoðor* has not been found.

The word points to an OTeut. **teudra-*, pre-Teut. **deutro-*, from a vb.-stem **deu-* to fasten, with instr. suffix *-tro.*]

1. A rope, cord, or other fastening by which a horse, cow, or other beast is tied to a stake or the like, so as to confine it to the spot.

1376–7 *Durham Acc. Rolls* (Surtees) 386 In duobus thethers et j feterlok pro equis. **1394–5** *Ibid.* 599 In iij Tethirs cum paribus de langalds. **1396–7** *Ibid.* 214, j tedyr. **14..** *Nominale* in Wr.-Wülcker 728/1 *Hoc ligatorium*, a tedyre. **1523** FITZHERB. *Husb.* §148 But make thy hors to longe a tedure. **1562** *Wills & Inv. N.C.* (Surtees) I. 207, ij wayne roopes, j haire teder xij^{d}. **1589** GREENE *Menaphon* (Arb.) 38 Who coueteth to tie the Lambe and the Lion in one tedder maketh a brawle. **1641** BEST *Farm. Bks.* (Surtees) 145 A peece of an olde broken teather. **1669** *Caldwell Papers* (Maitl. Cl.) I. 133 Ane hair tedir o. 13. 4. **1688** *Lond. Gaz.* No. 2368/4 Stolen out of the Tether.., a dark brown Gelding. **1782** BURNS *Death of Mailie* 2 As Mailie, an her lambs thegither, Were ae day nibbling on the tether. *a* **1854** H. REED *Lect. Brit. Poets* (1857) II. 70 A delicate colt at the end of each tether.

2. Applied to a rope used for other purposes. †**a.** A boat's painter; a tow-rope. *Obs.*

1503 HAWES *Examp. Virt.* ii. 1 Wher was a boote tyed with a teeder. **1818** W. MUIR *Poems* 12 (E.D.D.), I saw her in a tether Draw twa sloops after ane anither.

b. A rope for hanging malefactors; a halter.

1508 DUNBAR *Flyting* 176 Lyke to ane stark theif glowrand in ane tedder. *a* **1578** LINDESAY (Pitscottie) *Chron. Scot.* (S.T.S.) I. 175 They tuik ane hardin tedder and hangit him ower the brige of Lawder. **17..** *Sheriff-Muir* xvii. in *Sel. Coll. Sc. Ballads* (1790) II. 65 Then in a tether He'll swing from a ladder. **1819** W. TENNANT *Papistry Storm'd* (1827) 11 Weems cried out, 'Hang it in a tether'.

3. *fig.* The cause or measure of one's limitation; the radius of one's field of action; scope, limit.

1579 TOMSON *Calvin's Serm. Tim.* 18/1 Men must not passe their tedder. **1651** N. BACON *Disc. Govt. Eng.* II. xxx. (1739) 137 A large Teather, and greater privilege than ever the Crown had. **1706** BAYNARD in Sir J. Floyer *Hot & Cold Bath.* II. (1709) 272 The length of his short Tedder of Understanding. **1734** POPE *Let. to Swift* 19 Dec., We soon find the shortness of our tether. **1865** G. MACDONALD *A. Forbes* 51 Gin his mither has been jist raither saft wi' him, and gi'en him ower lang a tether.

b. A bond or fetter.

1609 F. GREVIL *Mustapha* Chorus ii, We scorne those Arts of Peace, that ciuile Tether, Which, in one bond, tie Craft and force together. **1817** BYRON *Beppo* xviii, When weary of the matrimonial tether. **1878** BROWNING *La Saisiaz* 413 Why should we expect new hindrance, novel tether?

4. Phrases: † ***within*** (*obs.*), ***beyond one's tether,*** within, beyond the limits of one's ability, position, or reasonable action; ***the end*** (†***extent, length***) ***of one's tether***, the extreme limit of one's resources.

1523 FITZHERB. *Husb.* §148 As longe as thou etest within Tedure. **1549** *Latimer's 2nd Serm. bef. Edw. VI*, To Rdr. (Arb.) 51 Learne to eat within thy teather. **1627** SANDERSON *Serm.* I. 276 He shall not be able to go an inch beyond his tedder. **1690** LOCKE *Hum. Underst.* I. i. §4 To prevail with the busy Mind..to stop, when it is at the utmost Extent of its Tether. *a* **1734** NORTH *Exam.* III. viii. §57 (1740) 627 As to the last Order..which properly belongs to the next Reign and so beyond my Tedder. **1809** MALKIN *Gil Blas* x. ii. ¶8 At length she got to the end of her tether, and I began. **1860–70** STUBBS *Lect. Europ. Hist.* (1904) I. ii. 23 They had got to the length of their tether.

5. *attrib.* and *Comb.*, as ***tether-end, -length, -rope, -string***; **tether-ball,** a ball fastened to or suspended from a pole by a string; the game played with this (Webster *Suppl.* 1902); **tether-peg, -stake, -stick, -stone,** a pin or stake of wood or iron, or a stone, fixed in the ground, to which an animal is tethered.

1725 RAMSAY *Gentle Sheph.* I. ii, He'll look upon you as his tether-stake. **1782** BURNS *Death of Mailie* 52 Gude keep thee frae a tether string. *a* **1800** *Kempy Kaye* in Child *Ballads* I. 302/1 His teeth they were like tether-sticks. **1859** CORNWALLIS *Panorama New World* I. 144 They took my tether rope, and commenced making me fast to a tree. **1884** *Lays & Leg. N. Irel.* 13 Put a tether-stone up on the face av the hill. **1900** *Queen* 29 Sept. (Advt.), Parlour tether ball... This..game consists of a perpendicular pole, to the top of which an india-rubber ball is attached by a cord... Each player is provided with a bat, with which to strike the ball. **1925** T. DREISER *Amer. Tragedy* I. II. xxxviii. 425 His own mental tether-length having been strained to the breaking point. **1937** J. BANCROFT *Games* 632 Tetherball... This is one of the most delightful and vigorous games that is adapted to small playing space. **1973** E. S. SHNEIDMAN *Deaths of Man* ix. 95 A..bachelor was found hanging from a tetherball pole.

tether ('tɛðə(r)), *v.* [f. prec. sb.]

1. *trans.* To make fast or confine with a tether.

1483 *Cath. Angl.* 379/1 To Tedyr, *restringere, retentare.* **1523** FITZHERB. *Surv.* xli. (1539) 58 To tye or tedder theyr horses and mares vpon. **1577** *Nottingham Rec.* IV. 170 No man shall not teyther [his beasts] amongs the hey vnto it be gone of the ground. **1719** DE FOE *Crusoe* I. 174, I tether'd the three Kids in the best part. **1800** WORDSW. *Pet Lamb* 6 The lamb was all alone, And by a slender cord was tethered to a stone. **1882** E. O'DONOVAN *Merv Oasis* I. 396 Hundreds of horses were tethered in every direction.

2. To fasten, make fast generally.

1563 WINȜET *Four Scoir Thre Quest.* §35 Wks. (S.T.S.) I. 100 *margin*, Heir Ioh. Knox be his awin sentence against wtheris, is fast tedderit in the girn. **1674** GREW *Anat. Trunks* II. vi. §4 The said Roots tethering it, as it trails along, to the ground. **1832** HT. MARTINEAU *Hill & Vall.* i, A gate,..too well tethered to be quickly opened. **1898** *Allbutt's Syst. Med.* V. 744 The heart is tethered to the bottom of the pericardium.

3. *fig.* To fasten or bind by conditions or circumstances; to bind so as to detain.

c **1470** HENRYSON *Orpheus & Eur.* 456 Suld our desyre be soucht wp in þe speris, Quhene It Is tedderit on þis warldis breris. **1624** BP. HALL *Contempl., N.T.* II. iii, He, that bounded thy power, tether'd thee shorter. **1790** BURNS *Tam O'Shanter* 67 Nae man can tether time or tide, The hour approaches Tam maun ride. **1879** H. JAMES *R. Hudson* I. 65 She would fain see me all my life tethered to the law.

Hence '**tethered** *ppl. a.*, fastened with a tether; limited, confined, 'tied'; '**tethering** *vbl. sb.* and *ppl. a.*, fastening with a tether or the like.

1573 TUSSER *Husb.* (1878) 42 Get home with thy brakes, er an sommer be gon, for *teddered cattle to sit there vpon. *a* **1680** CHARNOCK *Attrib. God* (1834) I. 237 Our contracted and tethered capacities. **1845** R. W. HAMILTON *Pop. Educ.* iii. (ed. 2) 43 All this may be preferable; but it is a tethered freedom still. **1890** DOYLE *White Company* 185 A dozen tethered horses and mules grazed around the encampment. **1671** GREW *Anat. Plants* iii. App. §9 By the Linking of their Claspers, and..by the *Tethering of their Trunk-Roots, being couched together. **1862** HISLOP *Prov. Scot.* 35 Better hands loose than in an ill tethering. **1863** WHYTE MELVILLE *Gladiators* 367 Not a vestige remained of halter or tethering ropes.

tethery ('tɛðərɪ), *a. rare.* [f. TETHER *sb.* + -Y.] Apt to become tangled or ravelled: said of long-stapled wool, the fibres of which cling together.

1894 C. VICKERMAN *Woollen Spinning* IX. 167 It is very obvious..that a long tethery wool would be extremely difficult to divide from the lap, either by the Bolette or Martin machine.

tethinge(s, var. *tithing(s*, TIDING(S.

†**tethy**, *a. Obs. rare.* Also 5 **tithy, thethy**. Of uncertain origin and meaning.

The sense of TEETHY *a.*[1] seems unsuitable. Can it be a corruption, or rather a series of errors, for TIDY *a.*, which occurs in this poem (and elsewhere) as an epithet of approval or praise, = good, excellent, worthy, apt, brave, doughty? But such an alteration of vowel and consonant in *tidy* is unknown elsewhere, and is phonetically unwarranted.

a **1400–50** *Alexander* 2198 ȝe of Tebet ere tried, þe tethiest [*D.* thethiest] on erth. *Ibid.* 2784 Of our wale princes Twa of þe tethiest [*D.* tithiest] ere tint, & termynd of lyue.

(Cf. *Ibid.* 2367 Ware noȝt þe tulkis out of Tire þe tidiest [*D.* triest] on erth. *Ibid.* 2371 Was noȝt þe Thebes þar-to þe th[r]eyᵉest [? theþeest; *D.* tithiest] of othire.)

Tethys ('tɛθɪs). *Geol.* [L. *Tēthys*, Gr. *Τηθύς*, a sea-goddess: see quot. 1893.] The name of a large sea that formerly lay between Eurasia and Africa. Hence '**Tethyan** *a.*

1893 E. SUESS in *Nat. Sci.* II. 183 Modern geology permits us to follow the first outlines of the history of a great ocean which once stretched across part of Eurasia. The folded and crumpled deposits of this ocean stand forth to heaven in Thibet, Himalaya, and the Alps. This ocean we designate by the name 'Tethys', after the sister and consort of Oceanus. *Ibid.* 184 The later Tethyan history .. forms certainly one of the most attractive chapters of historical geography. **1931** [see LAURASIA]. **1947** AUDEN *Age of Anxiety* vi. 133 The Laurentian Landshield was ruthlessly gerrymandered, And there was a terrible tussle over the Tethys Ocean. **1970** R. M. BLACK *Elements Palaeont.* vi. 52 The rudists occur mainly in the deposits of Tethys. **1971** *Nature* 29 Jan. 311/1 Old ocean floor was subducted into the Tethyan trench. **1972** *Sci. Amer.* June 61/3 In late Paleozoic times a wide tropical seaway, the Tethys, almost circled the globe. The only barrier to the Tethys Sea was formed by the combined land masses of North America and western Europe, which were then connected.

tetle, obs. f. TITLE.

Teton ('tiːtən). *U.S.* [ad. Dakota *tʰí* + *ʰuwą*, dwellers on the prairie.] **a.** (A member of) a Western division of the Dakota or Sioux Indian people. Also *attrib.*

1806 *Message from President of U.S., communicating Discoveries made in exploring the Missouri by Captains Lewis & Clark* 32 This trade, as small as it may appear, has been sufficient to render the Tetones independent of the trade of the Missouri. **1840** *N.Y. Mirror* 4 July 12/3 His household was the whole tribe of the Teton Dahcotas. **1873** *Forest & Stream* 9 Oct. 133/1 For several hours we followed on the trail of the Tetons. **1937** R. H. LOWIE *Hist. Ethnol. Theory* ix. 133 Boas has trained Miss Ella Delovia to take down Teton stories among her people. **1975** J. A. HANSON *Metal Weapons, Tools, & Ornaments of Teton Dakota Indians* i. 3 The Tetons, who spoke Lakota, took their name from the term *Titonwan*, 'Dwellers of the Prairie'.

b. The dialect spoken by this people.

1911 F. BOAS *Handbk. Amer. Indian Lang.* (U.S. Bureau Amer. Ethnol. Bull. No. 40) 880 We give here the description of the Teton as obtained by Dr. Swanton. **1933** [see DAKOTA *sb.* 2]. **1976** W. L. CHAFE in T. A. Sebeok *Native Lang. Americas* I. 542 There are usually said to be four major Dakota dialects: Santee (Dakota proper), Teton (Lakota), and Yankton and Assiniboine.

tetotaciously, var. TEETOTACIOUSLY *adv.*

tetotum, var. TEETOTUM.

tetra- (tɛtrə), before a vowel **tetr-**, a. Gr. τετρα-, combining form of the numeral τέτταρες, τέτταρα four, forming the first element of many words adapted from existing Greek compounds, and thence used in new analogous formations, mainly scientific and technical.

1. As a general etymological element.

‖**Tetrabelodon** (-'bɛlədɒn) [Gr. βέλος a dart, ὀδούς, ὀδοντ- tooth], a genus of extinct elephantine beasts; **tetra'blastic** *a.*, *Biol.* [Gr. βλαστός germ], having four blastodermic membranes or germinal layers, as animals having a true cœlome or body-cavity; **te'trabolo** [f. DI)ABOLO by deliberately false analogy (see quot. 1961)], a polyabolo composed of four triangles; **'tetrabrach** (-bræk), *Anc. Pros.* (also **tetrabrachys**) [Gr. τετράβραχ-υς in same sense], a word or foot of four short syllables, as *facinora, hominibus*; as a foot usually called *proceleusmatic*; ‖**tetrabrachius** (-'brækɪəs), pl. **-ii** [Gr. βραχίων arm], a monster having four arms (Billings *Nat. Med. Dict.* 1890); **tetra'camarous** *a.*, *Bot.* [Gr. καμάρα vault], having four closed carpels; **tetra'canthous** *a.* [Gr. ἄκανθα thorn], having four spines, as a fish, etc., or thorns in groups of four, as a plant (Mayne *Exp. L.* 1860); **tetra'carpellary** *a.*, *Bot.* of a compound fruit: having four carpels; **tetracerous** (tɪ'træsərəs), also †**tetra'ceratous**, *adjs.*, *Zool.* [Gr. τετράκερως four-horned], having four 'horns' or tentacles; belonging to the *Tetracera*, a family of four-horned gastropods; ‖**tetrachænium** (-ə'kiːnɪəm), *Bot.*, pl. **-ia** [see ACHENE], a fruit formed of four adherent achenes. **tetrachætous** (-'kiːtəs) *a.*, *Entom.* [Gr. χαίτη mane, hair], pertaining to the *Tetrachætæ*, a division of the brachycerous *Diptera*, comprising those in which the proboscis is composed of four pieces; ‖**tetrachirus** (-'kaɪərəs) [L., ad. Gr. τετράχειρ], a monster with four hands (Billings 1890); **tetrachro'matic** *a.*, of, pertaining to, having, or distinguishing four colours; **tetrachromic** (-'krəʊmɪk) *a.*, of four colours; capable of distinguishing (only) four colours of the spectrum; **'tetrachromist**, one who holds a theory of four colours; cf. POLYCHROMIST; **tetrachronous** (tɪ'trækrənəs) *a.*, *Anc. Pros.* [Gr. τετράχρονος containing four times], = *tetrasemic*; **'tetraclone** (-kləʊn) [Gr. κλών twig, spray], a four-rayed sponge-spicule with branched ends (*Cent. Dict. Suppl.* 1909); **tetracoccous** (-'kɒkəs) *a.*, *Bot.* [Gr. κόκκος berry], having four cocci or carpels; also, applied to bacteria when in four segments (Jackson *Gloss. Bot. T.* 1900); **tetra'coccus** (pl. **-cocci**) *Biol.* [COCCUS] (see quot. 1968); **tetra'coral**, one of the *Tetracoralla*, a division of corals (= *Rugosa*) in which the septa are in multiples of four; so **tetra'coralline** *a.*, of or pertaining to the *Tetracoralla*; **tetracotylean** (-kɒtɪ'liːən) *a.*, *Biol.* [Gr. κοτύλη cup], having four rounded pit-like suckers on the head or scolex, as a tapeworm; **tetracrepid** (-'kriːpɪd) *a.* [Gr. κρηπίς, κρηπιδ- boot, groundwork], a desmic sponge-spicule formed on a tetract nucleus; **te'tracron**, *Geom.*, pl. **-a, -ons** [Gr. ἄκρον summit], a solid having four vertices or solid angles, a tetrahedron; cf. POLYACRON; **tetra'denous** *a.*, *Bot.* [Gr. ἀδήν gland], having four glands (Mayne 1860); **tetra'ëterid**, also ‖**-is** [Gr. τετραετηρίς, -ιδ-, f. ἔτος year], a space of four years, a quadrennium; †**tetra'foliate**, †**tetra'folious** *adjs.*, *Bot.*, four-leaved; = *tetraphyllous*; bijugate (Mayne); **tetragamelian** (-gə'miːlɪən) [Gr. γαμήλιος bridal], *a.* belonging to the *Tetragamelia*, a division of discomedusans (*Hydrozoa Acraspeda*) having four subgenital pits; *sb.* a member of this division; **tetragamy** (tɪ'trægəmɪ) [Byz. Gr. τετραγαμία], a fourth marriage; also, marriage with four women simultaneously; **tetragenous** (tɪ'trædʒɪnəs) *a.*, *Bacteriol.* [-GEN[1] and -OUS], forming square groups of four, as certain micrococci; **te'tragnath** [Gr. τετράγναθ-ος], *a.* having four jaws; *sb.* a kind of spider with four jaws; so †**tetra'gnathian** *a.*; ‖**tetrago'nidium**, *Bot.*, = TETRASPORE; **tetraleioclone** (-'laɪəʊkləʊn) [Gr. λεῖ-ος smooth: see *tetraclone*], a four-rayed sponge-spicule with smooth arms (*Cent. Dict. Suppl.* 1909); **tetra'lemma**, *Logic* [cf. DILEMMA], a position presenting four alternatives; **tetra'lophodont** *a.* [Gr. λόφ-ος ridge + ὀδούς, ὀδοντ- tooth], having molars with four transverse ridges, as the sub-genus *Tetralophodon* of mastodons; **tetra'masthous** *a.* [Gr. μασθός breast], having four breasts; **tetra'mastigate** *a.* [Gr. μάστιξ, μαστιγ- whip], having four flagella (*Cent. Dict.* 1891); **tetramyrmeclone** (-'mɜːmɪkləʊn) [Gr. μυρμηκιά wart: see *tetraclone*], a four-rayed sponge-spicule, the arms covered with tubercles (*Cent. Dict. Suppl.* 1909); **tetranephric** (-'nɛfrɪk) *a.* [Gr. νεφρός kidney], having four uriniferous or Malpighian tubes; **tetra'nomial** *a.*, *Math.* [after BINOMIAL], consisting of four (algebraic) terms; quadrinomial; **tetrapa'rental** *a. Biol.*, (of an organism) produced by the fusion of two embryos; also as *sb.*, a tetraparental individual; **tetrapa'resis** *Path.* [PARESIS], muscular weakness of all four limbs; hence **tetrapa'retic** *a.*; **tetrapha'langeate** *a.*, *Comp. Anat.*, having four phalanges; ‖**tetra'pharmacon** (also in L. form **-pharmacum**) [Gr. τετραφάρμακον], a medicine or ointment consisting of four ingredients; hence **tetra'pharmacal** *a.*, compounded of four ingredients; **tetra'phonic** [Gr. φωνή voice, sound], applied to certain forms of quadraphonic recording and reproduction (see quots.); **te'traphony** [Gr. φωνή voice], in early mediæval music, diaphony for four voices; **tetraphy'letic** *a.* [Gr. φυλετικ-ός, f. φυλέτης tribesman, φυλή tribe]: see quot.; **tetra'phyllous** *a. Bot.* [Gr. φύλλον leaf], having or consisting of four leaves; abbreviated **4-phyllous**; **tetraplo'caulous** *a.*, *Bot.* [Gr. τετραπλοῦς fourfold + καυλό-ς stem]: see quot.; **tetrapneu'monian**, *Zool.*, *a.* of or pertaining to the *Tetrapneumones*, a division of spiders with two pairs of lung-sacs (*Cent. Dict.* 1891); *sb.* a spider of this division; **tetra'pneumonous** *a.*, *Zool.*, having four lungs or respiratory organs; applied to the *Tetrapneumones* (see prec.) and to the *Tetrapneumona*, a group of holothurians (sea-cucumbers); **tetra'polar** *a.*, *Biol.*, having four (instead of only two) poles or centres of radiation: said of a karyokinetic figure; **'tetrapous** *a.* [Gr. πούς foot], four-footed; **tetraprio'nidian** *a.* [Gr. πρίων a saw: cf. *Diprionidian*], applied to graptolites having four rows of thecæ showing four serrated edges; **tetraprostyle** (-'prɒstaɪl) *a.* [Gr. πρόστυλ-ος having pillars in front], of an ancient temple: having a portico with four pillars in front; †**te'traptative**, *a. rare* [see APTATE *v.*], that combines four things. **'tetraptote**, *Gram.* [Gr. τετράπτωτ-ος], a noun with (only) four cases; **te'traptych** (-ptɪk), *rare* [Gr. πτυχ- fold], a folding picture or the like in four compartments; cf. *triptych*; **tetra'pylon** [ad. Gr. τετράπυλον], a building or structure with four gates; **tetra'pyramid**, *Cryst.*, in the triclinic system, that form in which each of the two faces intercepts the three crystallographic axes; †**tetrapy'renous** *a.*, *Bot.* [Gr. πυρήν fruit-stone], having four stones, as a fruit; **tetra'quetrous** *a.*, *Bot.* [mod.L. *tetraquetr-us* four-angled], having four sharp angles; **tetrascele**: see *tetraskele*; ‖**tetrascelus** (tɪ'træsɪləs) [Gr. τετρασκελ-ής four-legged], a monster in which the legs are duplicated (Billings 1890); **tetraschistic** (-'skɪstɪk) *a.*, *Biol.* [Gr. σχιστός cloven], dividing into four by fission; **tetrase'lenodont** *a.* [SELENODONT], having four crescentic ridges, as a molar tooth; also said of a ruminant that has such teeth; **'tetraseme**, *Pros.* [Gr. τετράσημ-ος adj.], *sb.* a foot consisting of or equal to four short syllables; *a.* = *tetrasemic*; **tetra'semic** *a.*, *Pros.*, equivalent to four moræ or short syllables; **tetra'sepalous** *a.*, *Bot.*, having four sepals; **'tetraskele**, also **'tetrascele** (-siːl) and **tetra'skelion** [see *tetrascelus*], a figure consisting of four limbs radiating from a centre; *spec.* the FYLFOT (*C.D. Suppl.* 1909); ‖**tetra'spaston** [Gr. -σπαστος, -ον, drawn]: see quot.; **tetra'spermous** *a.*, *Bot.* [Gr. σπέρμα seed], having four seeds, or seeds in fours; so **tetra'spermal**, **tetra'spermatous** *adjs.*; **tetra'spheric**, **tetra'spherical** *adjs.*, *Math.*, of or pertaining to four spheres; **tetra'symmetry**, *Biol.*, symmetry characterized by division into four similar parts; †**tetra'syncrasy** [Gr. σύγκρασις: see CRASIS], a mixture of four elements; **'tetrateuch** *nonce-wd.*, a name for the first four books of the PENTATEUCH; **tetra'thecal** *a.*, *Bot.* [Gr. θήκη case, cell], four-celled, as an ovary; **'tetratheism**, the doctrine of four persons in the Godhead; **'tetratheite**, a believer in tetratheism; **'tetratone**, *Mus.*, also in form **te'tratonon** [ad. Gr. τετράτον-ον], an interval containing four whole tones; an augmented fifth; **'tetratop** [Gr. τόπ-ος place], 'the four-dimensional angular space inclosed between four straight lines drawn from a point not in the same three-dimensional space' (*Cent. Dict.* 1891); **tetra'wickmanite** *Min.*, a tetragonal polymorph of wickmanite, $MnSn(OH)_6$, found as yellow crystals; **te'traxial** *a.*, having four axes, as some sponge-spicules; so **te'traxile** *a.* in same sense; **te'traxon** [Gr. ἄξων axis], *sb.* a sponge-spicule with four axes radiating from a centre; *adj.* having four axes of growth; hence **tetra'xonian** *a.* = *tetraxon* adj.; **tetra'zomal** *a.* (*sb.*) *Geom.* [Gr. ζῶμα girdle], applied to a curve having an equation of the form $\sqrt{U} + \sqrt{V} + \sqrt{W} + \sqrt{T} = 0$, in relation to which the four curves $\sqrt{U} = 0$, $\sqrt{V} = 0$, etc. have properties of the nature of girdling: cf. POLYZOME; **tetra'zooid**, *Biol.*, any one of the four ascidiozooids developed from the germinal disk in the ascidian genus *Pyrosoma* (*Cent. Dict. Suppl.* 1909).

1904 *Athenæum* 4 Aug. 133/3 Prof. Lankester gave a curious theory of his own as to the derivation of the elephant's trunk from the soft upper jaw and nasal area of the extinct *Tetrabelodon. **1891** *Cent. Dict.*, *Tetrablastic. **1961** *New Scientist* 21 Dec. 752/3 Mr. S. J. Collins .. has experimented with the various plane shapes that can be formed by edgewise joins of four isosceles right-angled triangles; for these he most ingeniously suggests the name '*tetraboloes'. His excuse is that a 'diabolo' has two such triangles in its cross-section (joined pointwise, not edgewise: but no matter!). **1967** Tetrabolo [see *polyabolo* s.v. POLY- 1]. [**1860** MAYNE *Expos. Lex.*, **Tetracamarus*, .. applied by Mirbel to the etairium which is composed of four *camaræ*.] **1891** *Cent. Dict.*, Tetracamarous. **1900** B. D. JACKSON *Gloss. Bot. Terms.* **1860** MAYNE *Expos. Lex.*, *Tetraceratus*, .. *tetraceratous. **1891** *Cent. Dict.*, *Tetracerous. **1856** HENSLOW *Dict. Bot. Terms*, **Tetrachænium* .., a fruit formed by the separating of a single ovary into four nuts; as in the Labiatæ. **1902** BALDWIN *Dict. Philos. & Psychol.* II. 793 Ordinary vision, which is *tetrachromatic, .. was called, under the dominance of the colour-triangle, trichromatic. **1902** *19th Cent.* Apr. 605 The vision of the second eye was *tetrachromic. **1903** *Nature* 19 Nov. 71/2 The second class of the colour-blind see five, four, three, two, or one colour, according to the degree of their defect, and are called pentachromic, tetrachromic, etc. **1842** WORNUM in *Smith's Dict. Grk. & Rom. Antiq.* s.v. *Painting* §3 Ancient *tetrachromists or polychromists. **1891** *Cent. Dict.*, *Tetrachronous. *a* **1864** A. GRAY cited in WEBSTER for *Tetracoccous. **1893** W. R. DAWSON tr. *Schenk's Man. Bacteriol.* i. 2 Cocci are..found either singly or united in groups... If the elements are joined in pairs and fours we distinguish respectively, according to the number, diplococci and *tetracocci. **1907** *Practitioner* Apr. 488 Two diplococci are frequently seen together, giving a tetracoccus form. **1968** M. HYNES *Med. Bacteriol.* (ed. 9) i. 1 Cocci which divide regularly in two planes at right angles to one another result in collections of four organisms, and are known as tetrads or tetracocci. [**1888** ROLLESTON & JACKSON *Anim. Life* 743 The Palæozoic Corals are for the most part classified as *Rugosa* s. **Tetracoralla*... The septa are arranged in four systems, which are either disposed in a bilaterally symmetrical manner..or else are regularly radiate.] **1909** *Cent. Dict. Suppl.*, *Tetracotylean. **1888** SOLLAS in *Challenger Rep.* XXV. p. lix, It..is in some cases difficult to say, in the absence of a visible crepis, whether a desma is rhabdocrepid or *tetracrepid. *Ibid.* p. lx, Tetracrepid Desma. **1678** PHILLIPS *New World Wds.* (ed. 4), **Tetraeterid*,..the space of four years, a word used by Astronomers, and Astrologers. *a* **1727** NEWTON *Chronol. Amended* i. (1728) 75 [The Greeks] omitted an intercalary month once in eight years, which made their Octaeteris, one half of which was their Tetraeteris. **1881** LANKESTER in *Encycl. Brit.* XII. 557/1 In the *Tetragamelian *Rhizostomæ* these pits remain distinct from one another.., but in the Monogamelian *Rhizostomæ* they unite to form one continuous sub-genital cavity. **1862** J. C. ROBERTSON *Hist. Christ. Ch.* IV. v. II. 402 *note*, He [Symeon Magister] says that the lawfulness of '*tetragamy' was believed to have been revealed to Euthymius. **1907** W. DE MORGAN *Alice-for-Short* xviii. 203 Charles had said to his friend, jokingly, that if he had fifty sisters, single ones, Johnson was welcome to make offers to them all round.—'But then, my dear Paracelsus, that was to be *if* I *had* fifty. That would leave me forty-nine—or in case of bigamy, forty-eight; or quadrogamy—tetragamy—whatever it ought to be—forty-six. **1918** R. A. KNOX *Spiritual Aeneid* x. 166 We could always split the difference between monogamy and tetragamy by having two wives all round. **1888** *Science* 15 June 283/2 The constituents of the colony turned out to be a *tetragenous microbe quite distinct from the plain atmospheric micrococcus. **1608** TOPSELL *Serpents* (1658) 771 Nicander..confesseth, that the Ash-coloured *Tetragnath, doth not by his biting infuse any venom or like hurt. *Ibid.*, If a man be wounded of the *Tetragnathian Spider, the place waxeth whitish, with an intolerable, vehement, and continual pain in it. **1835** KIRBY *Hab. & Inst. Anim.* II. xvi. 85 Those Phalangians which are denominated *Tetragnatha*, or having four jaws. **1882** VINES *Sachs' Bot.* 289 The asexual organs of reproduction are gonidia: since four are usually formed in a mother-cell, they are termed **Tetragonidia*... When the thallus consists of rows of cells, the tetragonidia are produced in the apical cell of lateral branches. *a* **1856** W. HAMILTON *Lect. Metaphysics & Logic* (1860) III. xviii. 352 If it [*sc.* the syllogism] has three, four, or five members, it is called *trilemma* (*tricornis*), **tetralemma* (*quadricornis*), *pentalemma* (*quinquecornis*). **1867** ATWATER *Logic* 151 The names Trilemma, Tetralemma, Polylemma have been sometimes given to this sort of Syllogism according to the number of members or horns. **1889** NICHOLSON & LYDEKKER *Palæont.* (ed. 3) II. 1398 In the *Tetralophodont group the number of ridges in the cheek-teeth is greater than in the former group. **1860** MAYNE *Expos. Lex.*, *Tetramasthous. **1890** BILLINGS *Nat. Med. Dict.*, *Tetramasthous*, having four breasts. **1898** A. S. PACKARD *Text-bk. Entomol.* 355 In at least one case (Melolontha), the *tetranephric is ontogenetically derived from the hexanephric condition by the suppression of one pair of tubules. **1817** H. T. COLEBROOKE *Algebra*, etc. 280 Put the binomial root for first term;..then put the trinomial, and afterwards the *tetranomial, for first radical term; until the proposed number be exhausted. **1970** *Nature* 31 Jan. 462/2 *Tetraparental mice are produced by fusing two eight-cell stage embryos. *Ibid.*, Allelic differences between the strains produce mosaic patterns in the adult tetraparental which make possible inferences about development. **1971** *New Scientist* 8 Apr. 72/1 One of the most fascinating tools employed in studying these processes [of tissue differentiation]..is provided by 'tetra-parental' mice. **1979** *Nature* 11 Oct. 425/1 B. Mintz (Institute for Cancer Research, Philadelphia)..pioneered the use of allophenic mice (formed by aggregating cells from two 8-cell embryos from two different pregnant mice, hence tetraparental). **1972** *New Gould Med. Dict.* (ed. 3), **Tetraparesis*, weakness of all four extremities. **1980** *Brit. Med. Jrnl.* 29 Mar. 902/2 She was anarthric and bedridden with spastic tetraparesis and twitching tremors. **1978** *Jrnl. R. Soc. Med.* LXXI. 449 A woman..who was *tetraparetic following operation for a cerebral tumour. **1898** *Nature* 3 Feb. 319/1 In the full-grown fœtus of a *Vespertilio* the fourth digit of the manus is *tetraphalangeate. **1657** TOMLINSON *Renou's Disp.* 143 The *Tetrapharmacal unguent, which consists..of Wax, Rosine, Pitch and Bulls fat. **1727–41** CHAMBERS *Cycl.*, **Tetrapharmacum*,..denotes any remedy consisting of four ingredients. **1842** BRANDE *Dict. Sc.*, etc., *Tetrapharmacon*, an ointment composed of four remedies; namely wax, resin, lard, and pitch. **1969** *db Mag.* Dec. 23/2 Microphones are placed so channels 1 and 3, and 2 and 4 will operate as pairs to give three walls of sound... In addition, channels 3 and 4 operate as a stereo pair to sharpen the directionality of the reflected sound... When we discovered this..we called it *Tetraphonic Sound. **1974** *Wireless World* July 236/2 Gerzon's assertion that 'the optimum characteristic is not known' in regard to a particular tetraphonic technique could be equally well applied to any quadraphonic system. **1977** *Daily Tel.* 4 May 18 'Tetraphonic' has already been given the technical meaning of a set of signals giving complete first-order directional information including height. **1900** B. D. JACKSON *Gloss. Bot. Terms*, **Tetraphyletic*, applied to hybrids with four strains in their descent. **1731** BAILEY vol. II, **Tetraphyllous*. **1775** J. JENKINSON *Descr. Brit. Pl.* 158 The cup [of Charnock] is tetraphyllous and erect. **1900** B. D. JACKSON *Gloss. Bot. Terms*, **Tetraplocaulous*, having quaternary axes. **1842** BRANDE *Dict. Sc.*, etc., **Tetrapneumonians*, *Tetrapneumones*,..a section of spiders..comprehending those which have four pulmonary sacs. **1902** D. J. HAMILTON in *Encycl. Brit.* XXXI. 514/1 (Description of Plate) D. *Tetrapolar karyokinesis. E. Another form of tetrapolar division. [**1890** BILLINGS *Nat. Med. Dict.*, *Tetrapus*, having four feet.] **1899** *Syd. Soc. Lex.*, *Tetrapous. **1888** *Cassell's Encycl. Dict.*, *Tetraprionidian. **1891** *Cent. Dict.*, *Tetraprostyle. **1471** RIPLEY *Comp. Alch.* IV. viii. in Ashm. *Theat. Chem. Brit.* (1652) 146 The thyrd manner and also the last of all, Fowre Elements together whych joynyth to abyde, *Tetraptative certainely Phylosophers doth hyt call. **1656** BLOUNT *Glossogr.*, **Tetraptote*, declined in four cases. **1704** J. HARRIS *Lex. Techn.* I, *Tetraptotes*,..such defective Nouns, as have only four Cases; as *Plus*, which wants the Dative and Vocative Singular. **1904** H. C. BUTLER *Archit. & Other Arts* xii. 393 Conjectured to have been vaulted *tetrapylons at the crossing of the thoroughfares. [**1727** BAILEY vol. II, **Tetrapyrenos*, which has four Seeds or Kernels, as Agrifolium, Holly, &c.] **1882** MAW in *Jrnl. Bot.* XI. 88 The Scape..is either *tetraquetrous or triquetrous. **1885** LANKESTER in *Encycl. Brit.* XIX. 834/2 They [chlorophyll corpuscles] multiply by fission, usually *tetraschistic, independently of the general protoplasm. **1890** *Amer. Nat.* May 471 To sustain the view that the *tetraselenodont forms are the descendants of the pentaselenodont Artiodactyla. **1895** GILDERSLEEVE *Lat. Gram.* (ed. 3) 459 *Tetraseme long. **1891** *Cent. Dict.*, *Tetrasemic. **1829** LOUDON *Encycl. Pl.* (1836) 1069 A *tetrasepalous tetrapetalous flower. **1842** BRANDE *Dict. Sc.*, etc., **Tetraspaston*, in Mechanics, a machine in which four pulleys all act together. **1860** MAYNE *Expos. Lex.*, *Tetraspermatus*,..four-seeded: *tetraspermal: *tetraspermatous. **1760** J. LEE *Introd. Bot.* II. viii. (1765) 89 Monopetalous *Tetraspermous. **1889** F. A. BATHER in *Q. Jrnl. Geol. Soc.* XLV. II. 162 The structure above described for *Eugeniacrinus* is..also found..with the necessary modifications due to *tetrasymmetry, in *Tetracrinus*. **1651** BIGGS *New Disp.* §246 If they will have the pus to be made out of a *Tetrasyncrasy or commixture of the humors. **1906** *Rev. of Theol. & Philos.* Jan. 457 An elaborate work on the Pentateuch (or rather the *Tetrateuch, since Deuteronomy is lightly passed over). **1849** BALFOUR *Man. Bot.* §405 A quadrilocular..or *tetrathecal..anther. **1899** *Syd. Soc. Lex.*, *Tetrathecal, Biol.*, applied to a four-chambered ovary. **1874** J. H. BLUNT *Dict. Sects & Heresies* s.v. *Damianists*, Their theory led to the conclusion that there are four Gods, the three separate and subordinate Hypostases and the one superior Αὐτόθεος, hence they were also named *Tetratheites. **1740** J. GRASSINEAU *Mus. Dict.* 276 *Tetratonon; the superfluous fifth may be thus called, as containing four tones. **1775** ASH, *Tetratonon*, the superfluous fifth. **1801** in BUSBY *Dict. Mus.* **1973** WHITE & NELEN in *Mineral. Rec.* IV. 24/1 The mineral..was not wickmanite, but its tetragonal dimorph! To emphasize this dimorphic relationship the mineral has been named *tetrawickmanite. **1978** *Ibid.* IX. 41/2 The Langban tetrawickmanite occurs as bright yellow euhedra implanted on magnetite. **1888** ROLLESTON & JACKSON *Anim. Life* 810 Tetractina: spicules to a great extent *tetraxile. **1886** *Proc. Zool. Soc.* 21 Dec. 581 Spicules more or less clearly *tetraxon, often branched. **1887** SOLLAS in *Encycl. Brit.* XXII. 416/2 (*Sponges*) Tetraxon Quadriradiate Type (Calthrops).—Growth from a centre in four directions inclined at about 110° to each other. **1867** CAYLEY *Math. Papers* VI. 485 On the Trizomal Curve and the *Tetrazomal Curve. *Ibid.* 486 The tetrazomals are each of them a curve of the order 4*r*, and they intersect therefore in only $16r^2$ points.

2. In *Chemical* nomenclature, in the names of compounds and derivatives with the general sense of 'four-', 'four times'. **a.** In substantives: (*a*) Prefixed to names of binary compounds of elements or radicals, names of salts, etc., to signify four atoms, groups, or equivalents of the element or radical in question; as *tetrachloride*, (see below); so ***tetrasulphide***, ***tetriodide***, TETROXIDE, ***tetrahydroxide***, ***tetramethide***, ***tetracetate***, ***tetraphosphate***, etc. (*b*) Prefixed to names of elements or radicals (or the combining forms, as *bromo-*, *nitro-*, *oxy-*, *phospho-*, *azo-*) entering into the name of a compound, to signify that four atoms or groups of the element or radical are substituted in the substance designated by the rest of the name, as ***tetrabromobenzene***, $C_6H_2Br_4$, in which four of the hydrogen atoms of benzene, C_6H_6, are replaced by four bromine atoms; so ***tetramethylbenzene***, $C_6H_2(CH_3)_4$. (*c*) In some words used irregularly, as ***tetrasalicylide***, $C_{28}H_{18}O_9$: see quot. 1875[2].

,tetraalkyl'lead [ALKYL], any compound in which the molecule consists of four alkyl radicals bonded to an atom of lead; **tetra'benazine** *Pharm.* [f. *benzo(a)quinolizin-2-one*, f. BENZ(ENE + *-izine*, denoting two fused rings with a nitrogen atom common to both], a tricyclic compound, $C_{19}H_{27}NO_3$, used in the treatment of chorea; **tetrachloride**, a compound of four atoms of chlorine with some other element or radical; ***carbon tetrachloride***, a dense, colourless liquid, CCl_4, used chiefly in the manufacture of refrigerants and aerosols and in fire extinguishers, and also as a solvent; **tetra,chlorodi,benzo(para)di'oxin**, (in strict technical use written with italic *-p-* in place of *para*), a polychlorinated tricyclic hydrocarbon, $C_{12}H_4O_2Cl_4$, that is carcinogenic and teratogenic in animals and is formed in the manufacture of chlorinated phenols; also called *dioxin*; abbrev. *TCDD* (see T 6a); **,tetrachlor(o)'ethane**, either of two isomeric compounds, $C_2H_2Cl_4$, that are dense colourless liquids; *spec.* the symmetrical isomer, which is used chiefly in the manufacture of solvents and is toxic; **,tetradeca'peptide**, a polypeptide having fourteen amino-acid residues in the molecule; **,tetra,ethyla'mmonium** *Chem.* (also †**te,trethyl-**), the quaternary ion $(C_2H_5)_4N^+$, which is a ganglion-blocking agent and has been used (in the form of its chloride or bromide salt) in the treatment of hypertension; **tetraethyl lead**, a poisonous oily liquid, $Pb(C_2H_5)_4$, which is added to petrol as an anti-knock agent making possible higher compression ratios; = *lead tetraethyl* s.v. LEAD *sb.*[1] 12b; **tetra,ethylpyro'phosphate**, a colourless, hygroscopic liquid, $(C_2H_5)_4P_2O_7$, that is a cholinesterase inhibitor and is used as a garden insecticide and formerly to relieve the symptoms of myasthenia gravis; **tetra'hydrate**, a hydrate containing four molecules of water; **,tetra,hydro'cannabinol**, a hydrogenated derivative of cannabinol that is the active principle in cannabis and hashish; **,tetrahydro'furan**, a colourless liquid, C_4H_8O, used as a solvent for plastics and other polymers and as an intermediate in the manufacture of organic chemicals; **,tetra,hydro'furfuryl**, the monovalent radical $C_4H_7O.CH_2-$; **,tetra,hydro'naphthalene**, any compound derived from naphthalene by the addition of four hydrogen atoms; *spec.* ***1,2,3,4-tetrahydronaphthalene***, a colourless liquid used as a solvent for hydrocarbons, esp. varnishes, lacquers, etc.; = TETRALIN; **,tetraiodo'thyronine** *Biochem.* [THYRONINE] = THYROXINE; **tetra'methylene**, the gaseous alicyclic compound $(CH_2)_4$; also, (a compound containing) the bivalent straight-chain radical $-CH_2(CH_2)_2CH_2-$; **te'tramisole** *Pharm.* [f. I)MI(DE + *thia)zole* s.v. THIO- 1, with alteration of *z*], an anthelminthic drug used in man and animals, usu. as the hydrochloride, 2,3,5,6-tetrahydro-6-phenylimidazo[2,1-*b*]thiazole, $C_{11}H_{12}N_2S$; **tetra'peptide** *Biochem.* [ad. G. *tetrapeptid* (see PEPTIDE)], an oligopeptide in which there are four amino-acid residues in the molecule; **tetra'pyrrole** [PYRROL], any compound containing four pyrrole nuclei, esp. when in the form of a ring (cf. PORPHIN); hence **tetrapy'rrolic** *a.*

1923 *Jrnl. Amer. Chem. Soc.* July 1821 The method used by Krause..always yields a *tetra-alkyl lead compound when an alkyl halide is used. **1978** *Nature* 26 Oct. 738/1 Particulate lead and tetraalkyllead in the atmosphere are due principally to emissions from vehicles fuelled by leaded petrol. **1958** *Federation Proc.* XVII. 404/1 (*heading*) Inhibition of reserpine tranquilizing effects by *tetrabenazine, a synthetic tranquilizing agent. **1974** *Lancet* 26 Jan. 107/1 Tetrabenazine is the drug of first choice for the suppression of chorea in patients with Huntington's chorea. **1880** *Athenæum* 11 Dec. 781/3 The Formation of Carbon *Tetrabromide in the Manufacture of Bromine. **1888** MORLEY & MUIR *Watts' Dict. Chem.* I. 555 *Tetrabromobenzene, $C_6H_2Br_4$; from *p*-nitro-benzoic acid and Br at 280°. **1900** *Jrnl. Soc. Dyers* XVI. 7 The solutions of the *tetracetate in chloroform. **1866** ODLING *Anim. Chem.* 59 CCl_4, Carbon *tetrachloride. **1930** *Engineering* 26 Dec. 814/2 The use of chemical cleaners, such as..carbon tetrachloride,..is more effective. **1947** J. C. RICH *Materials & Methods of Sculpture* v. 94 The wax is placed in the carbon tetrachloride and set aside for about two days to dissolve, after which it can be used. **1972** *Materials & Technol.* IV. vi. 201 Carbon tetrachloride was originally made from coke and chlorine, carbon disulphide being used as an intermediate, but is now mainly produced by the chlorination of methane, or the chlorinolysis of higher hydrocarbons. **1959** *Jrnl. Pharm. Soc. Japan* LXXIX. 188 (*caption*) 2,3,7,8-*Tetrachlorodibenzo-*p*-dioxin. **1970** *Kirk-Othmer Encycl. Chem. Technol.* (ed. 2) XXII. 180 Dioxins, including 2,3,7,8-tetrachlorodibenzo-*p*-dioxin, have been detected as contaminants in samples of 2,4,5-T. **1976** *Daily Tel.* 2 Aug. 11/8 He is to attempt to clean an experimental patch of land 100 yards square by the introduction of healthy micro-organisms of yeast and mould, which he hopes will 'seed' upon the poisonous substance, breaking down the molecules of TCDD (Tetrachlorodibenzo-dioxine). **1977** *New Yorker* 25 July 30/1 The samples of the chemical used in the experiments had contained uncharacteristically high levels of a toxic contaminant, 2,3,7,8 tetrachlorodibenzo-*p*-dioxin—commonly referred to as TCDD, or, by chemists familiar with the subject, either as tetra dioxin or simply as dioxin. **1978** *Price's Textbk. Pract. Med.* (ed. 12) III. 284/2 Under conditions of high reaction temperatures in the manufacture of 2,4,5-T there has been formed tetrachlorodibenzoparadioxine (dioxine) which has produced chloracne in laboratory workers. **1980** *National Geographic* Aug. 181 TCDD—shorthand for 2,3,7,8-tetrachlorodibenzoparadioxin, frequently simply called dioxin—is the inevitable by-product of the manufacture of the herbicides 2,4,5-T and silvex. **1871** *Jrnl. Chem. Soc.* XXIV. 1191 The former has the composition of *tetra-chlorethane, $C_2H_2Cl_4$, and is formed, according to the usual reaction of phosphorus pentachloride on aldehydes, by the substitution of 2 at. Cl. for 1 at. O in dichloraldehyde. **1922** *Encycl. Brit.* XXX. 35/1 Tetrachlorethane was tried with success, but it proved dangerous to the operatives applying it in enclosed places. Moreover, sun-light decomposed tetrachlorethane. **1933** *Jrnl. R. Hort. Soc.* LVIII. 282 Tetrachlorethane as a Greenhouse Fumigant. **1934** H. Hiler *Notes on Technique of Painting* iii. 235 Dissolve hard copal resin in tetra-chlorethan [*sic*]. **1963** A. J. Hall *Textile Sci.* vii. 307 Dry cleaning involves the extraction of dirt, and grease, oil, fat and wax stains from all kinds of textile materials by treatment with a hot organic solvent such as.. tetrachloroethane. **1974** *Encycl. Brit. Micropædia* IX. 910/3 The other isomer, 1,1,1,2-tetrachloroethane,..has no commercial application. **1973** *Science* 5 Jan. 79/1 The linear *tetra-decapeptide was synthesized by solid-phase methodology. **1979** *Nature* 8 Nov. 208/2 A tetradecapeptide originally isolated from amphibian skin. **1852** A. W. Hofmann in *Q. Jrnl. Chem. Soc.* IV. 306 For this [organic] metal I propose..the name *Tetrethylammonium..which implies that it is built up by the intimate union of nitrogen with four equivalents of the hypothetical hydrocarbon called ethyl. **1940** *Thorpe's Dict. Appl. Chem.* (ed. 4) IV. 355/2 Tetraethylammonium hydroxide, $NEt_4 \cdot OH$, known only in solution or as solid hydrates. **1962** J. H. Burn *Drugs, Med. & Man* vi. 65 Two American workers attempted to use..tetraethylammonium to reduce blood pressure in patients in 1946, and then two workers in England introduced hexamethonium which was much more powerful and acted for a much longer time. **1923** *Jrnl. Amer. Chem. Soc.* July 1821 *Tetra-ethyl lead was prepared by P. Pfeiffer by the action of lead chloride on ethyl-magnesium iodide. **1940** *Economist* 30 Mar. 586/2 The 87-octane spirit is generally obtained by the addition of small quantities of tetra-ethyl lead to good-quality 'straight-run' petrol. **1970** *Nature* 14 Mar. 990/1 Lead, in the form which it is added to petrols—tetraethyl lead, $Pb(C_2H_5)_4$—is undoubtedly poisonous. **1947** *Ibid.* 29 Nov. 760/1 During the War, the Germans introduced as insecticides a series of phosphate esters, including *tetraethylpyrophosphate and hexaethyltetraphosphate. **1952** H. Beckman *Pharmacol. in Clin. Pract.* 568 Prostigmin may usually be discontinued at this point and tetraethylpyrophosphate cautiously increased ..until there is maximal relief of symptoms without toxic effects. **1974** *Encycl. Brit. Micropædia* IX. 911/3 Tetraethyl pyro-phosphate is extremely poisonous to humans, the toxic effects being similar to those of parathion. **1869** Roscoe *Elem. Chem.* xi. 121 Fluorine forms, with the silicon contained in the glass, a volatile compound called Silicon *tetrafluoride. **1886** *Jrnl. Chem. Soc.* XLIX. 418 The thermal reaction..is made up of two distinct quantities—(1) the decomposition of the trihydrate, (2) the formation of the *tetrahydrate. **1951** [see *hexahydrate* s.v. hexa-]. **1963** *Acta Crystallogr.* XVI. 376 (*heading*) Refinement of the structure of potassium pentaborate tetrahydrate. **1940** *Jrnl. Chem. Soc.* 1121 The compounds prepared include 6″-hydroxy-2:2:5′-trimethyl-4″-*n*-amyl-3′:4′:5′:6′-tetrahydrodibenzopyran.., which may be a *tetrahydrocannabinol. **1967** *New Scientist* 31 Aug. 436/1 The classical analysis of hashish..yielded three types of related compound as the characteristic components of the drug. These were cannabidiol, cannabinol and tetrahydrocannabinol. **1980** *Daily Tel.* 19 Sept. 11/2 If the female is pollinated, it uses some of its resinous tetrahydrocannabinol [*printed* -cannibol]—the stimulant in marijuana—to produce seeds. **1908** *Jrnl. Chem. Soc.* XCIV. 1. 280 When furan is hydrogenated at 170° by Sabatier and Senderens' method, the principal product consists of *tetrahydrofuran. **1956** *Nature* 21 Jan. 128/2 Both the nylon 6:6-cyclic monomer..and the cyclic dimer from caprolactam..were reduced by lithium aluminium hydride in boiling tetrahydrofuran without difficulty. **1978** *Further Perspectives Organic Chem.* (CIBA) 23 Why should the gas phase be a better model for enzymic reactions than a solvent which is more protein-like than, say, water..or tetrahydrofuran? **1928** *Jrnl. Amer. Chem. Soc.* L. 1821 α-*Tetrahydrofurfuryl alcohol will shortly be available on a commercial scale from the catalytic reduction of furfural. **1951** Kirk & Othmer *Encycl. Chem. Technol.* VI. 1004 In the United Kingdom, tetrahydrofurfuryl acetate has been used as a lipstick ingredient, based on the high solubility of eosin in it. *Ibid.*, Tetrahydrofurfuryl alcohol is used in the preparation of esters, especially tetrahydrofurfuryl oleate, which is almost colourless and has excellent light and heat stability. **1887** *Abstr. Proc. Chem. Soc.* III. 88 At the next meeting..the following Papers will be read... 'Derivatives of Hydrindonaphthene and *Tetrahydronaphthalene'. By W. H. Perkin, jun. **1904** [see decahydronaphthalene]. **1935** *Industr. & Engin. Chem.* (*News Ed.*) 20 Aug. 332/1 The merit of tetrahydronaphthalene for town gas mains lies in the fact that, being a close chemical relative of naphthalene it has the power of absorbing larger quantities of naphthalene than any of the other solvents in present use. **1964** N. G. Clark *Mod. Organic Chem.* xix. 391 Naphthalene quite readily undergoes addition reactions. For example at 200° catalytic hydrogenation over nickel yields tetrahydronaphthalene ('tetralin'). **1969** N. A. J. Rogers in S. Coffey *Rodd's Chem. Carbon Compounds* (ed. 2) IIc. x. 71, 1,4,5,8-Tetrahydronaphthalene, 'isotetralin'.., m.p. 58°, may be prepared by the reduction of 1,4-dihydronaphthalene by the 'metal in ammonia' method. **1880** Roscoe & Schorlemmer *Treat. Chem.* II. ii. 434 Rhodium *tetrahydroxide $Rh(OH)_4$..this compound separates out as a green powder. **1928** *Tetraiodothyronine [see thyronine]. **1974** D. & M. Webster *Compar. Vertebr. Morphol.* xiii. 310 The two hormones, triiodothyronine and tetraiodothyronine (thyroxine), are iodinated amino acids. **1899** Smith *Richter's Org. Chem.* I. 187 Lead *tetramethide, $Pb(CH_3)_4$, boils at 110°. **1885** W. H. Perkin in *Jrnl. Chem. Soc.* XLVII. 806 It was thought that the simplest method would be to regard the saturated hydrocarbons themselves as multiples of methylene, CH_2, and thus name them di-, tri-, tetra-, penta-, &c., methylene, as is easiest seen from the following table:—..*Tetra-methylene. **1898** J. Wade *Introd. Study Org. Chem.* xxxv. 219 The tetramethylene compound..is formed by the reduction of ethylene cyanide with sodium amalgam in alcoholic solution. **1909** [see *pentamethylene* s.v. penta-]. **1944** S. J. Smith *Princ. Org. Chem.* x. 197 Both their methods of preparation and their parachors..show them to be cyclic compounds containing no unsaturated linkage:..Cyclobutane tetramethylene. **1966** [see ethylene 2]. **1971** N. L. Allinger et al. *Org. Chem.* iv. 63 Frequently occurring hydrocarbon groupings that have more than one site for the attachment of substituents are also given common or trivial names.. $ICH_2CH_2CH_2CH_2I$ 1,4-Diiodobutane (Tetra-methylene iodide). **1966** D. Thienpont et al. in *Nature* 12 Mar. 1084/1 This article reports the discovery of *tetra-misole.., a new, potent broad spectrum anthelmintic. **1978** *Ibid.* 22 June 629/1 Tetramisole and/or its levorotatory isomer levamisole is used in many countries against a broad range of nematodal infections in birds, pigs, ruminants and man. **1906** *Jrnl. Chem. Soc.* XC. 1. 810 Triglycylglycine methyl ester, prepared by esterifying the *tetra-peptide with methyl alcohol and hydrogen chloride, crystallises in microscopic, glistening needles. **1927** P. A. Levene *Chem. Relationships of Sugars* 2 in *Contemp. Devel. in Chem.*, A tetrapeptide composed of naturally occurring amino acids is hydrolyzed by trypsin. **1970** R. W. McGilvery *Biochem.* iv. 51 Peptide subunits join to make the tetrapeptide because of interactions between side chains of residues exposed at the meshing surfaces. **1875** Watts *Dict. Chem.* VII. 1032 When the barium salt [of pyromucic acid] mixed with soda-lime is heated, a compound called *tetraphenol, C_4H_4O, distils over. **1917** *Chem. Abstr.* XI. 452 Baeyer's method..gives the cryst[alline] substance $C_{28}H_{36}N_4$..which may be named *tetrapyrroletetracetone. **1968** [see prodigiosin]. **1976** *Ann. Rev. Microbiol.* XXX. 410 Relatively general metabolic criteria, such as..tetra-pyrrole biosynthesis.. have proven useful in defining taxonomic relationships. **1944** *Ann. Reg. 1943* 358 Vitamins operate as coenzymes in plant respiration, which is catalysed by the same types of *tetrapyrrolic compounds as are present in animal tissues. **1975** *Nature* 22 May 357/2 The Hans Fischer school which then dominated tetrapyrrolic chemistry. **1875** Watts *Dict. Chem.* VII. 1067 Schiff..prepares salicylide, $C_7H_4O_2$, and *tetrasalicylide, $C_{28}H_{18}O_9$, by the action of phosphorous oxychloride on salicylic acid.

b. Prefixed to adjectives, in the names of acids, alcohols, aldehydes, ethers, salts, etc.; as ***tetrasodic***, containing four sodium atoms; so ***tetraboric***, etc.; ***tetrethylic***, containing four ethyl groups; so ***tetramylic***, etc.

1868 Watts *Dict. Chem.* V. 730 Tetraphosphamic acids.. are amic acids derived from tetraphosphoric acid. **1868** *Fownes' Chem.* (ed. 10) 347 Tetrasodic Phosphate or Sodium Pyrophosphate is prepared by strongly heating common disodic orthophosphate..and re-crystallising. **1888** Morley & Muir *Watts' Dict. Chem.* I. 528 Pyroboric (or tetraboric) acid, $2B_2O_3 \cdot H_2O$ (= $H_2B_4O_7$).

c. In verbs and their pples. derived from sbs. as in a., as ***tetrabrominated***, ***-chlorinated***, ***-hydrated*** (containing 4 molecules of water).

1857 Miller *Elem. Chem.* III. 46 Tetrachlorinated Hydrochloric Ether, $C_4HCl.Cl_4$. **1873** Watts *Fownes' Chem.* (ed. 11) 767 Propyl-benzene..forms with excess of bromine a viscid tetrabrominated compound.

tetraalkyllead: see tetra- 2 a.

tetrabasic (tɛtrəˈbeɪsɪk), *a. Chem.* [f. tetra- + basic.] Of an acid: Containing four atoms of hydrogen replaceable by more electropositive elements or radicals. Of a salt: Derived from such an acid.

1863–72 Watts *Dict. Chem.* I. 459 Modes of distinguishing between monobasic, dibasic, tribasic, and tetrabasic acids. **1869** Roscoe *Elem. Chem.* xv. 154 Pyrophosphoric Acid..$H_4P_2O_7$... This acid is tetrabasic, the four atoms of hydrogen being replaceable, either all or in part, by metals.

tetrabelodon to **-brachius**: see tetra-.

tetrabranch (ˈtɛtrəbræŋk), *sb.* and *a. Zool.* [f. tetra- + Gr. βράγχια gills.] **a.** *sb.* A four-gilled cephalopod: see next. **b.** *adj.* = tetrabranchiate *a.* (*Cent. Dict.* 1891).

1851 Woodward *Mollusca* i. 82 The Tetrabranchs could undoubtedly swim, by their respiratory jets. **1877** Le Conte *Elem. Geol.* ii. (1879) 305 If we divide all known Cephalopods into Dibranchs (two-gilled) and Tetrabranchs (four-gilled).

tetrabranchiate (tɛtrəˈbræŋkɪət), *a.* and *sb. Zool.* [ad. mod.L. *tetrabranchiāt-um*: see prec. and -ate² 2.] **a.** *adj.* Belonging to the *Tetrabranchiata*, an order of cephalopods (mostly extinct) having four branchiæ or gills. **b.** *sb.* A cephalopod belonging to this order; a tetrabranch.

1835–6 *Todd's Cycl. Anat.* I. 557/1 The Sepia..manifests ..a near affinity to the Tetrabranchiate order. **1851** Woodward *Mollusca* i. 78 The shell of the tetrabranchiate cephalopods is an extremely elongated cone. **1872** Nicholson *Palæont.* 189 The Tetrabranchiate forms, with chambered shells, attained their maximum in the..Silurian period.

tetracaine (ˈtɛtrəkeɪn). *U.S. Pharm.* [f. tetra- + co)caine.] A compound related to procaine that is used, as a solution of the hydrochloride, as a local anæsthetic, esp. for surface application; amethocaine, $C_4H_9NHC_6H_4COOCH_2CH_2N(CH_3)_2$.

1943 *Dispensatory U.S.A.* (ed. 23) 1121/1 Tetracaine Hydrochloride occurs as a fine, white, crystalline, odorless powder. **1974** [see *spinal anæsthesia* s.v. spinal *a.* 7]. **1979** Shnider & Levinson *Anesthesia for Obstetrics* ix. 110/2 Although tetracaine remains one of the most effective and popular drugs for subarachnoid block, it is a poor choice in epidural analgesia.

tetracamarous to **-carpellary**: see tetra-.

‖**Tetracaulodon** (-ˈkɔːlədɒn). [mod.L., f. tetra- + Gr. καυλό-ς stem + ὀδούς, ὀδοντ- tooth.] An extinct elephantine genus having four tusks.

1833 *Baltimore Med. & Surg. Jrnl.* Oct. (Mayne). **1839** G. Roberts *Dict. Geol.*, *Tetracaulodon*, a fossil extinct animal.. allied to the mastodon;..having four projecting teeth. **1859** Page *Handbk. Geol. Terms* (1865) s.v., Professor Owen and others regard the *tetracaulodon* of Dr. Godman as the immature state of the *Mastodon Giganteus*.

tetrachloro-: see tetra- 2 a.

tetrachloroethylene (ˌtɛtraklɔərəʊˈɛθɪliːn). *Chem.* Also **-chlorethylene**. [f. tetra- + chloro-² + ethyl + -ene.] = perchloroethylene. Also called ˌ**tetrachloroˈethene**.

1911 *Chem. Abstr.* V. 2815 In this way the author has obtained..tetrachloroethylene. **1930** A. F. Holleman *Text-bk. Org. Chem.* (ed. 7) i. 197 In contact with water tetrachloroethene reacts with chlorine under the influence of sunlight to form trichloroacetic acid. **1948** J. H. Burn *Lect. Notes Pharmacol.* 99 Hook worms..live in the duodenum. The infestation is treated by carbon tetrachloride and tetrachlorethylene. **1968** A. A. Baker *Unsaturation in Org. Chem.* iii. 27 Faraday..heated the perchloride of carbon to dull redness, finding that chlorine was liberated, and a new compound, which he called protochloride of carbon was formed..known today as tetrachloroethene (C_2Cl_4). **1969** *Times* 20 Feb. 17/5 Some 100,000 gallons of the cleaning fluid tetrachloroethylene were buried in a gold mine, so as to avoid contamination with cosmic rays, and left in place for nearly four months.

tetrachord (ˈtɛtrəkɔːd). [ad. Gr. τετράχορδον (*sc.* ὄργανον), a Greek musical instrument, f. τετρα-, tetra- + χορδή string.]

1. An ancient musical instrument with four strings.

1603 Holland *Plutarch* Explan. Words, *Tetrachord*, an instrument in old time of foure strings. **1814** *Mann. & Cust.* in *Ann. Reg.* 490/1 Most of the Greek women sing in a pleasing manner, accompanying themselves with a tetrachord, the tones of which are an excellent support to the voice. **1849** Donaldson *Theat. Greeks* (ed. 6) i. ii. 15 Terpander..substituted the seven-stringed cithara for the old tetrachord.

2. *Mus.* A scale-series of four notes, being the half of an octave. †**b.** The interval between the first and last notes of this series; a perfect fourth.

1603 Holland *Plutarch's Mor.* 1254 It was not for ignorance that in the Dorian tunes they forbare this Tetrachord. **1694** W. Holder *Harmony* iv. (1731) 66 (Table of Intervals), 4th, Diatessaron, Tetrachord. **1704** J. Harris *Lex. Techn.* I, *Tetrachord*, in Musick, is a Concord or Interval of 3 Tones. The Tetrachord of the Ancients was a rank of four Strings. **1847** Grote *Greece* ii. xvi. III. 285 Such were the three modes or scales, each including only a tetrachord, upon which the earliest Greek masters worked. **1890** *Athenæum* 4 Jan. 24/3 The tetrachord [on an Arab lute] thus comprised c, d, e flat, e, and f.

c. *transf.* A stanza of four lines. *rare.*

1817 N. Drake *Shakspeare* I. 54 The Octant, of two tetrachords of disjunct alternate rhime. *Ibid.* 55 Three tetrachords in alternate rhime.

Hence **tetraˈchordal** *a.*, of or pertaining to a tetrachord or tetrachords. Also ‖**tetrachordon** (-ˈkɔːdɒn) [see quot. 1876], an instrument like a cottage pianoforte in form, in which the strings are pressed against a revolving cylinder to produce the tone.

1740 J. Grassineau *Mus. Dict.* 274 Tetrachordon. See Tetrachord. ?**1850** Sarah A. Glover (*title*) Manual, containing a development of the tetrachordal System. **1876** Stainer & Barrett *Dict. Mus. Terms* s.v. *Tonic Sol-fa*, Miss Sarah A. Glover, of Norwich, about thirty years ago projected and taught..a system which she called the tetrachordal system, which was the Tonic Sol-fa notation in its original form. *Ibid.*, *Tetrachordon*..[so] called..from an idea that its sounds are similar to those produced by a string quartet.

tetrachoric (tɛtrəˈkɒərɪk), *a. Statistics.* [f. Gr. τετράχωρ-ος divided into four (f. χῶρος place: see tetra-) + -ic 1.] Applied to a table in which data are divided into two according to each of two criteria, and so having four subdivisions; of or pertaining to such a table; applied *esp.* to an estimate of the product-moment coefficient derived from such a table, and to concepts used in obtaining such an estimate.

1910 P. F. Everitt in *Biometrika* VII. 438 In the present tables the values of the first six τ functions, henceforth to be termed tetrachoric functions, have been computed for values of $\frac{1}{2}(1 - \alpha)$ from ·001 to ·500 by successive increments of ·001. **1918** *Ibid.* XII. 95 In the ordinary scheme for a tetrachoric table, the quadrants are denoted by *a*, *b*, *c*, *d*. **1943** M. G. Kendall *Adv. Theory Statistics* I. xiv. 354 Tetrachoric *r* and biserial η. Both these coefficients are, in effect, estimates of a putative product-moment correlation for data which are not specified with the detail of an ordinary bivariate table. **1956** J. Whatmough *Language* 241 The statistical method of the so-called 'tetrachoric R'..is valuable in revealing the degree of correlation..between languages which may be suspected of being historically akin. **1964** [see polychoric *a.*].

tetrachotomous (tɛtrəˈkɒtəməs), *a. Zool.* and *Bot.* [f. Gr. τέτραχα in four parts + -τομος cut +

-OUS.] Ramifying into four branches or divisions; doubly dichotomous.

1829 LOUDON *Encycl. Pl.* (1836) 403 *note*, Peduncles [of *Euphorbia*]..often dichotomous, trichotomous, or even tetrachotomous.

tetra'chotomy, *sb.* [f. as prec. + -TOMY.] **a.** Division into four branches. **b.** *Logic.* A division having four members.

a **1856** W. HAMILTON *Lect. Metaphysics & Logic* (1860) IV. xxv. 23 If a division has only two members, it is called a dichotomy;..if four, a tetrachotomy. **1858** C. J. ELLICOTT *Destiny Creature* Notes 172 Bull's theory is, in fact, really a "tetrachotomy"—body, soul, spirit, and Holy Spirit.

tetrachromatic to **-chronous**: see TETRA-.

tetraclade ('tɛtrəkleɪd), *a. Zool.* [f. TETRA- + Gr. κλάδ-ος shoot, sprout.] Branching in four; having four arms or rays. So **tetracladine** (-'kleɪdaɪn) *a.*, of or pertaining to the *Tetraclādina*, a suborder of lithistid sponges having spicules branching into four or more processes; also **tetracladose** (-'kleɪdəʊs) *a.* in same sense.

1881 P. M. DUNCAN in *Jrnl. Linn. Soc.* XV. No. 86. 324 The quadrifid or tetraclade spicula. **1887** SOLLAS in *Encycl. Brit.* XXII. 417/1 (*Sponges*) Some or all of the rays of the primitive calthrops..may bifurcate once or twice and finally terminate by subdividing into numerous variously shaped processes; such a tetracladine desma characterizes one division of the Lithistid sponges. *Ibid.* 422/1 A distinct passage can be traced from the Tetracladose to the Rhabdocrepid group. *Ibid.*, The scleroblast..in the Tetracladine Lithistids lies in an angle between the arms.

tetraclone to **tetracoccus**: see TETRA-.

‖**tetracolon** (tɛtrə'kəʊlɒn). *Gr. Pros.* Pl. -cola. [a. Gr. τετράκωλον, adj. neut., having four members: see TETRA- and COLON².] A metrical period consisting of four cola or members.

1706 PHILLIPS (ed. Kersey), *Tetracolon*,..a Stanza, or Division in Lyrick Poetry, consisting of four Verses or Lines. **1902** *Daily Chron.* 18 Dec. 3/1 The verses from the pen of Joseph and Eugenius, with their diversity and intricacy of metre (including a tetracolon heptastichon).

Hence **tetracolic** (-'kəʊlɪk) *a.*, of or pertaining to a tetracolon; consisting of four cola.

1891 in *Cent. Dict.*

tetracosactrin (ˌtɛtrəkɒ'sæktrɪn). *Pharm.* [f. TETRA- + I)COS- + A(DRENO)C(ORTICO) TR(OPH)IN.] A synthetic polypeptide (see quot. 1967) which resembles corticotrophin in its action and uses but lacks its antigenic property, and is given (as the acetate) by injection in the long-term treatment of inflammatory and degenerative disorders.

1967 *Brit. Med. Jrnl.* 18 Nov. 391/1 Tetracosactrin (β^{1-24} corticotrophin, Synacthen) is a synthetic poly-peptide containing the first 24 amino-acids found in naturally occurring corticotrophin (A.C.T.H.). **1972** *Ibid.* 11 Mar. 680/1 The pathognomic finding is their failure [*sc.* that of urinary and plasma corticosteroids] to show a rise after the administration of ACTH or tetracosactrin. **1979** *Jrnl. R. Soc. Med.* LXXII. 530 A tetracosactrin (Synacthen) stimulation test.

tetract ('tɛtrækt), *a.* and *sb. Zool.* [f. TETRA- + Gr. ἀκτ-ίς, ἀκτῖν- ray.] **a.** *adj.* Having four rays or branches; quadriradiate. **b.** *sb.* A four-rayed sponge-spicule. So **te'tractinal** *a.*, **te'tractine** *a.* and *sb.*, **te'tractinose** *a.*

1886 *Proc. Zool. Soc.* 21 Dec. 581 The chief spicules are tetract. **1887** SOLLAS in *Encycl. Brit.* XXII. 416 (Fig. 12) *d.* calthrops (tetraxon tetractine). **1888** —— in *Challenger Rep.* XXV. p. lix, *Tetractine*.—When all four actines of a tetraxon are present it is..a tetractine, but as the full designation of this required to distinguish it from a tetractinose triaxon is tetractine tetraxon, we shall substitute for it the equivalent "calthrops". **1891** *Cent. Dict.*, Tetractinal.

tetractinellid (tɪˌtræktɪ'nɛlɪd), *a.* and *sb. Zool.* [ad. mod.L. *Tetractinellidæ* (f. Gr. τετρα-, TETRA- + ἀκτίς (ἀκτῖν-) ray + L. dim. *-ella*): see -ID.] **a.** *adj.* Belonging to the *Tetractinellidæ* (also called *Tetractina*), a sub-order of siliceous sponges with four-rayed spicules. **b.** *sb.* A sponge of this order. So **tetracti'nellidan** *a.* and *sb.*, **tetracti'nelline** *a.*

1891 *Cent. Dict.*, Tetractinellidan, Tetractinelline. **1892** *Nat. Sc.* Mar. 20 Tetractinellid spicules..occur..in the shallower regions. **1892** *Athenæum* 13 Feb. 218/2 The sponge remains..belong largely to the Monactinellidæ though tetractinellid, lithistid, and hexactinellid spicules are also present.

‖**tetractys** (tɪ'træktɪs). Also 8 **tetrachty(s**, 9 **tetraktys**. [a. Gr. τετρακτύς.] A set of four; the number four; *esp.* the Pythagorean name for the sum of the first four numbers (1 + 2 + 3 + 4 = 10) regarded as the source of all things.

1603 HOLLAND *Plutarch's Mor.* 1317 That famous quaternarie of theirs, named Tetractys, which consisteth of foure nines, and amounteth to thirtie sixe, was their greatest oth. **1653** H. MORE *Conject. Cabbal.* Pref. (1713) 4 The Pythagoreans Oath, swearing by him that taught them the mystery of the Tetractys, or the number Four. *a* **1774** TUCKER *Lt. Nat.* (1834) II. 415 Pythagoras had his tetrachty, his mystic numbers, his symbols. **1865** GROTE *Plato* I. i. 12 *note*, The tetraktys (consecrated as the sum total of the first four numbers 1 + 2 + 3 + 4 = 10).

Hence **te'tractysm**, the Pythagorean doctrine of the tetractys.

1846 T. W. JENKYN *Baxter's Wks.* Pref. 50 Those who understand..what Tetractysm was to the Pythagoreans will ....comprehend what Triadism was to Baxter.

tetracyclic (tɛtrə'saɪklɪk, -'sɪklɪk), *a.* [f. TETRA- + CYCLIC *a.*] **1.** Having four cycles or circles; *spec.* in *Bot.*, having four whorls of floral organs.

1878 MACNAB *Botany* ix. (1883) 161 *Dicotyledones*... Flowers typically tetracyclic pentamerous.

2. *Chem.* Of a compound: containing four fused hydrocarbon rings in the molecule.

1928 *Chem. Abstr.* XXII. 2748 (*heading*) Synthesis of tetracyclic compounds and of pyrene. **1977** J. L. HARPER *Population Biol. of Plants* xiii. 414 Plants that are only lightly predated contained three or four isomers of lupanine and closely related tetracyclic compounds.

tetracycline (tɛtrə'saɪkliːn). *Pharm.* [f. TETRACYCL(IC *a.* + -INE⁵.] **a.** A tetracyclic compound, $C_{22}H_{24}N_2O_8$, which is a broad-spectrum antibiotic (usu. administered as the hydrochloride). **b.** Any of a number of antibiotics structurally related to this compound.

1952 C. R. STEPHENS et al. in *Jrnl. Amer. Chem. Soc.* LXXIV. 4977/1 Common to both Terramycin and aureomycin is the structure A for which we propose the name tetracycline. **1956** *Nature* 3 Mar. 433/2 (*heading*) Avidity of the tetracyclines for the cations of metals. *Ibid.*, This investigation is now extended to the parent substance, tetracycline...[and] also includes some new values for the substituted tetracyclines. **1966** I. JEFFERIES *House-Surgeon* vi. 115 Start her on one of the tetracyclines. **1974** M. C. GERALD *Pharmacol.* xxvi. 457 Tetracyclines are believed to inhibit protein synthesis by blocking the binding of the amino acid-transfer RNA complex to ribosomes. **1978** *Time* 3 July 43/2 Like almost all U.S. farmers, the cattleman is aggrieved... The costs of everything he buys—gasoline, fertilizer, tetracycline for ailing heifers..—have climbed like corn in August.

tetrad ('tɛtrəd). [ad. Gr. τετράς (τετραδ-) a group of four, the number four.]

1. A sum, group, or set of four; four (things, etc.) regarded as a single object of thought.

1653 H. MORE *Conject. Cabbal.* (1713) 82 It was a solemn Oath..to swear by him that delivered to them the mystery of the Tetractys, Tetrad, or number Four. *Ibid.* [see TETRACTYS]. **1832** COLERIDGE *Table Talk* 24 Apr., The adorable tetractys, or tetrad, is the formula of God. **1895** *Athenæum* 2 Feb. 151/1 The great tetrad of senior wranglers of 1840 to 1843.

2. In *spec.* uses. **a.** *Chem.* An element, compound, or radical having a combining power of four units, i.e. of four atoms of hydrogen; a tetravalent element, etc.

1865 *Reader* 1 Apr. 372/3 A tetratomic atom or tetrad. **1866** ROSCOE *Elem. Chem.* xxvii. 242 As in mineral chemistry we have radicals some of which are monads, and some dyads, triads, or tetrads. **1868** *Fownes' Chem.* (ed. 10) 259 Silicium and titanium are tetrads.

b. *Biol.* (*a*) A group of four cells, e.g. spores, pollen-grains. (*b*) A group of four chromosomes formed by the division of a single chromosome. (*c*) A quaternary unit of organization differentiated from a triad.

1876 tr. *Schützenberger's Ferment.* 52 In the tetrads arranged in the form of a cross, we observe, also, two plane surfaces at right angles. **1882** VINES *Sachs' Bot.* 456 The cavity of the sporangium becomes filled with a granular plasma in which lie the mother-cells and the tetrads of spores... All the spores of the sixteen tetrads formed in the microsporangia reach maturity. **1883** [see 3]. **1895** OLIVER tr. *Kerner's Nat. Hist. Plants* II. 101 In *Rhododendron hirsutum* all the pollen-tetrads of an anther-cavity are held together by a mass of sticky viscin. *a* **1909** (in sense *b*) WILSON (cited in C.D. Suppl.) **1909** J. W. JENKINSON *Exper. Embryol.* 108 Granules of chromatin took the place of the tetrads and were unequally distributed to the spindle poles.

c. *Mus.* A chord of four notes (after TRIAD).

1881 BROADHOUSE *Mus. Acoustics* 332 The great majority of major tetrads in Palestrina's Stabat Mater are in the positions 1, 10, 8, 5, 3, 2, 4, 9.

d. In ancient systems of arithmetical notation: A group or series of four characters corresponding to successive powers of ten.

1883 SIR E. C. BAYLEY *Geneal. Mod. Numerals* II. 90 They [[the Greeks] had however a system of 'octads' and 'tetrads' for expressing numbers of very high value.

e. *Math.* (See quot.)

1889 CAYLEY *Math. Papers* XII. 590 The term 'tetrad' is used in two distinct..senses, viz. a tetrad denotes any four points; and it also denotes the four vertices of a self-conjugate tetrahedron in regard to a quadric surface... Two or more tetrads, in regard to one and the same quadric surface, are called similar tetrads.

f. *Ecol.* (See quot. 1976.)

1963 HAWKES & READETT in P. J. Wanstall *Local Floras* 37 We soon realized that it would be impossible to record from every basic square in the county and we modified the method by considering the squares in blocks of four ('tetrads') and selecting one square at random from each tetrad for surveying. **1968** *Watsonia* VI. 351 This involved the detailed survey of 1 km squares as the unit of recording, one square at random being selected from each block of four or 'tetrad'. **1976** J. G. DONY *Bedfordshire Plant Atlas* 10/1 It has become usual in the survey of areas as small as Bedfordshire to divide the ten-kilometre grid squares into 25 smaller squares each 2 km. × 2 km. known as tetrads. Each tetrad has an area of four square kilometres. **1983** *Natural World* Spring 18 Distributional maps based on 2 × 2 kilometre squares, or tetrads.

3. *attrib.*, as ***tetrad metal***, ***term***; **tetrad-deme** *Biol.*, an aggregation of tetrads: see 2 b (*b*) and DEME² 2.

1866 ODLING *Anim. Chem.* 17 The fourth or tetrad term of our series of typical hydrides. **1868** *Fownes' Chem.* (ed. 10) 445 Tin is a tetrad metal. **1883** P. GEDDES in *Encycl. Brit.* XVI. 843/2 Starting from the unit of the first order, the plastid or *monad*, and terming any undifferentiated aggregate a *deme*, we have a *monad-deme* integrating into a secondary unit or *dyad*, this rising through *dyad-demes* into a *triad*, this forming *triad-demes*, and these when differentiated becoming *tetrads*, the Botryllus-colony with which the evolution of compound individuality terminates being a *tetrad-deme*.

tetradactyl (tɛtrə'dæktɪl), *a.* and *sb.* Also -dactyle. [ad. Gr. τετραδάκτυλ-ος having four digits, f. τετρα-, TETRA- + δάκτυλος finger.] **a.** *adj.* Having four fingers or toes. **b.** *sb.* A four-toed animal (esp. a vertebrate). Hence **tetradac'tylity**, **tetra'dactyly**, the condition of having four digits; also **tetra'dactylous** *a.* = a.

1835 KIRBY *Hab. & Inst. Anim.* xvii. II. 194 The foot of birds is most commonly *tetradactyle, with one toe or thumb at the heel and the other three in front. **1847** WEBSTER, *Tetradactyl*, an animal having four toes. **1891** *Nature* 5 Feb. 329/2 If..a man has a finger amputated, his **tetradactylity is a somatogenic property. **1828** WEBSTER, *Tetradactylous. **1851** MANTELL *Petrifact.* i. §3. 70 Narrow-toed tridactylous or tetradactylous species [of birds]. **1869** GILLMORE tr. *Figuier's Rept. & Birds* v. 421 The feet tetradactylous, and furnished with long and strong claws. **1904** *Amer. Nat.* XXXVIII. 3 From the ancestral canid Cynodictis of the Oligocene and lower Miocene,..to Lycaon in which structural *tetradactyly prevails.

tetradarchy ('tɛtrədɑːkɪ). [ad. Gr. τετραδαρχία, f. τετράς TETRAD + -αρχία rule.] = TETRARCHY.

1839 THIRLWALL *Greece* VI. xlv. 14 Philip revived the distinction of the tetradarchies. **1842** *Smith's Dict. Grk. & Rom. Antiq.* s.v. *Tagus*, The four divisions of the country, tetrarchies or tetradarchies, which he re-established.

'tetrade,cane. *Chem.* [f. Gr. τετρα- four + δέκα ten + -ANE 2 b.] The saturated hydrocarbon or paraffin of the 14-carbon series, $C_{14}H_{30}$, = tetradecyl hydride; a waxy solid.

1877 WATTS *Fownes' Chem.* (ed. 12) II. 50 The boiling points and specific gravities of the higher paraffins of unknown structure..are as follows:..Tetradecane $C_{14}H_{30}$. Boiling point 236–240°.

So **tetradecene** = *tetradecylene*. **tetra'decenyl**, the radical $C_{14}H_{27}$, as in ***tetradecenyl alcohol***, $C_{14}H_{27}.OH$, ***t. aldehyde***, etc. **tetradece'noic** *a.* in ***tetradecenoic acid***, $C_{14}H_{26}O_2$, a liquid boiling in vacuo at 275° to 280° C.; ***t. aldehyde***, $C_{14}H_{26}O$, an oil not solid at −20° C. **tetra'decinene** $C_{14}H_{26}$ = $CMe{:}C.C_{14}H_{23}$. **tetrade'coic** *a.*, in ***t. acid***, $C_{14}H_{28}O_2$ = $C_5H_{11}.CH(C_7H_{15}).CO_2H$, a liquid (not solid at −10° C.), got by the action of moist argentic oxide, Ag_2O, on the aldehyde; ***tetradecoic aldehyde***, $C_{14}H_{28}O$, obtained in tables very soluble in alcohol, a product of the action of sodium on an ethereal solution of œnanthol. **tetra'decyl** or **tetra'decatyl**, the monatomic alcohol radical, $C_{14}H_{29}$, of this series; also *attrib.* = *tetradecylic*, as in ***tetradecyl alcohol***. Hence **tetrade'cylic** *a.*, of or pertaining to this radical; so **tetra'decylene**, the olefine of this series, $C_{14}H_{28}$ = $CH_2{:}CH.C_{12}H_{25}$, a liquid substance; also *attrib.* as in ***tetradecylene glycol***.

1868 WATTS *Dict. Chem.* V. 728 *Tetradecyl*, or *Tetradecatyl*..also called *Myristyl*. The fourteenth term of the series of alcohol-radicles, C_nH_{2n+1}. *Tetradecylic hydride*, $C_{14}H_{30}$, is one of the constituents of American petroleum... *Tetradecylic* or *Myristic Alcohol*, or *Methal*, $C_{14}H_{30}O$, is one of the constituents of spermaceti.

tetradecapeptide: see TETRA- 2 a.

tetradecapod (tɛtrə'dɛkəpɒd), *a.* and *sb. Zool.* [ad. mod.L. *Tetradecapoda*, f. TETRA- + DECA-ten: cf. DECAPODA.] **a.** *adj.* Having fourteen feet; belonging to the *Tetradecapoda*, an order of Crustaceans. **b.** *sb.* A crustacean of this order. So (in same senses) **tetrade'capodan** *a.* and *sb.*; **tetrade'capodous** *a.*

1852 DANA *Crust.* II. 1528 The two types, the Decapodan and Tetradecapodan. *Ibid.* 1576 Among the Tetradecapods there is the Chilian genus *Amphoroidea*. **1854** *Chamb. Jrnl.* I. 26/1 Attached to each of them was a small, pale, tetradecapodous animal. **1862** DANA *Man. Geol., Crust.* 153 Fourteen-footed species or Tetradecapods.

†**tetradia'pason.** *Mus. Obs.* [f. TETRA- + DIAPASON.] An interval of four octaves.

1704 J. HARRIS *Lex. Techn.* I, *Tetradiapason*, a Quadruple Diapason,..otherwise called a Quadruple Eighth, or Nine and Twentieth. **1801** in BUSBY *Dict. Mus.*

tetradic (tɪ'trædɪk), *a.* [f. TETRAD + -IC. Cf. F. *tétradique* (in Cotgr.).] **a.** Of, pertaining to, or of the nature of a tetrad.

1788 T. Taylor *Proclus* (1792) I. 179 The tetradic ternary, and the triadic quaternary. *a*1914 C. S. Peirce *Coll. Papers* (1935) VI. 222 A tetradic, pentadic, etc. relationship is of no higher nature than a triadic relationship. 1921 [see monadic *a.* 1 b].

b. *Chem.* That is a tetrad; tetravalent.

1868 *Fownes' Chem.* (ed. 10) 257. 1872 Watts *Dict. Chem.* VI. 237 Carbon, which combines with 4 atoms of hydrogen, is tetratomic, tetradic, or quadrivalent. 1877 —— *Fownes' Chem.* (ed. 12) I. 267 With silver.. it [oxygen] forms the two oxides, Ag_2O and Ag_4O, in the latter of which it is tetradic.

c. *Anc. Pros.* (*a*) Containing four different metres or rhythms. (*b*) Composed of groups of systems, each of which contains four unlike systems.

1891 in *Cent. Dict.*

Tetradite ('tɛtrədaɪt). *Ch. Hist.* [ad. late Gr. τετραδίτης, pl. -αι, f. τετράς, -αδ- tetrad: see -ite 1.] (See quots.)

1727-41 Chambers *Cycl.*, *Tetraditæ, Tetradites*, in antiquity, a name given to several different sects of heretics, out of some particular respect they bore to the number four. 1842 Brande *Dict. Sc.* etc., *Tetradites*,.. the Manichees and others, who believed the Godhead to consist of four instead of three persons, bore this name. 1882-3 *Schaff's Encycl. Relig. Knowl.* I. 601 Their adversaries called them Tetradites, Τετραδῖται, because they had four gods,—the Father, the Son, the Holy Spirit, and the Divine Being—in which those three were united.

tetradon: see Tetrodon.

tetradrachm ('tɛtrədræm). *Gr. Antiq.* Also in L. and Gr. forms 6-9 **tetradrachma**, 7-8 **-drachmon**. [ad. Gr. τετράδραχμον: see tetra- and drachm.] A silver coin of ancient Greece, of the value of four drachms: see drachm 1.

1579-80 North *Plutarch* (1595) 313 Foure Tetradrachmas a day. 1770 Swinton in *Phil. Trans.* LXI. 92 A fine Punic tetradrachm. 1807 Robinson *Archæol. Græca* v. xxvi. 567 The less ancient tetradrachms were current during four or five centuries. 1879 H. Phillips *Notes Coins* 6 The cistophori are tetradrachms bearing as their generic type a wreath and berries of ivy, surrounding a chest whence issue serpents.

Hence **tetradrachmal** (-'drækməl) *a.*, of or pertaining to a tetradrachm.

1770 Swinton in *Phil. Trans.* LXI. 98 The medal.. is of the tetradrachmal form. 1771 Raper *ibid.* 533 Had the first Denarius been Didrachmal or Tetradrachmal, so well-informed a writer must have known it.

tetradymite (tɪ'trædɪmaɪt). *Min.* [a. Ger. *tetradymit* (W. Haidinger, 1831), f. Gr. τετράδυμος fourfold + -ite[1].] Telluride of bismuth, found in pale steel-grey laminæ with a bright metallic lustre.

(The name has also been applied to wehrlite.)

1850 Ansted *Elem. Geol.* §491 Tetradymite, Tellurium, and bismuth. 1859 Page *Handbk. Geol. Terms* (1865), *Tetradymite*.., sulphotelluride of bismuth.. from the quadruple macles in which its crystals usually appear. 1874 *Proc. Amer. Phil. Soc.* XIV. 224 The sulphurous variety of tetradymite has been observed at several new localities.

tetradymous (tɪ'trædɪməs), *a.* *Bot.* [f. Gr. τετράδυμ-ος (see prec.) + -ous.] Said of an agaric having each perfect lamella or gill separated from the next by four equal short lamellæ and three longer ones alternately placed; see also quots.

[1856 Henslow *Dict. Bot. Terms*, *Tetradymus*, where every alternate lamella of an Agaric is shorter than the two contiguous to it, and one complete lamella terminates a set of every four pairs of short and long... Also, where four cells or cases are combined.] 1866 *Treas. Bot.*, *Tetradymous*, having four cells or cases.

‖**Tetradynamia** (ˌtɛtrədɪ'neɪmɪə). *Bot.* [mod.L. (Linnæus, 1735), f. Gr. τετρα-, tetra- + δύναμ-ις power, strength + -ia[1]: cf. Didynamia.] The fifteenth class in the Linnæan Sexual System, comprising plants which bear hermaphrodite flowers with six stamens in pairs, four of which are longer than the others; corresponding to the N.O. *Cruciferæ*. Hence **tetrady'namian** *a.*, = *Tetradynamous*; *sb.*, a plant of the class *Tetradynamia*; **tetrady'namious, tetra'dynamous** *adjs.*, of or pertaining to this class; having four longer and two shorter stamens.

1760 J. Lee *Introd. Bot.* ii. ii. (1765) 74 *Tetradynamia*... There are in the Flowers of this Class six Stamina, four of which are longer than the rest. 1785 Martyn *Rousseau's Bot.* ix. (1794) 92 *Tetradynamia* is.. one of your first acquaintance under the gentler appellation of cruciform flowers. 1828 Webster, *Tetradynamian*. 1830 Lindley *Nat. Syst. Bot.* 20 The stamens are occasionally tetradynamous. 1860 Mayne *Expos. Lex.*, Tetradynamious, or tetradynamous.

tetraëdral, etc.: see tetrahedral, etc.

tetraëterid to **-ethyl(-)**: see tetra-.

ˌtetraˌfluoro'ethylene (-ˌfluːərəʊ'ɛθ-). *Chem.* Also **-fluorethylene**. [f. tetra- + fluoro- + ethylene.] A dense, colourless gas, $F_2C{:}CF_2$, which is polymerized to make plastics. Cf. polytetrafluoroethylene.

1933 *Jrnl. Amer. Chem. Soc.* LV. 3177 There is good evidence that tetrafluoroethylene is produced in small quantities. 1946 *Sci. News* IV. 63 Polymerisation of tetrafluorethylene.. yields heat-resistant, chemically inert solids, which can be moulded into any desired shape. 1958 *Times Rev. Industry* Feb. 81/2 A rather typical example of what can be achieved with fluorocarbons is the polymerization of tetrafluoroethylene to yield a commercial plastic. 1973 *Materials & Technol.* VI. 544 The monomer tetrafluoroethylene is obtained by pyrolysis from $CHFCl_2$ (.. that is, the refrigerants Freon-22 and Genetron-141).

tetragamy: see tetra- 1.

tetraglot ('tɛtrəglɒt), *a.* [ad. Gr. type *τετραγλωττ-ος, f. τετρα-, tetra- + γλῶττα tongue: cf. polyglot.] Speaking four languages; written or composed in four languages. So †**tetra'glottic**, †**tetra'glottical** *adjs.* *Obs.* in same sense.

1580 Fleming in *Baret's Alv.* Aaaaj, This Quadruple Dictionarie, or Lexicon tetraglottical. 1682 Wheler *Journ. Greece* i. 32 He hath printed a Dictionary Tetraglot, Ancient and Vulgar Greek, Latin, and Italian. 1721 Bailey, *Tetraglottick*. 1881 *N. & Q.* 6th Ser. III. 456/2 A tetraglot dictionary, a century older still.

tetragon ('tɛtrəgɒn), *sb.* (*a.*). Also 7 **-gone**. [ad. Gr. τετράγωνον a quadrangle: see tetra- and -gon. So late L. *tetragōn-um*, F. *tetragone* (14th c. in Godef. *Compl.*).]

1. *Geom.* A figure having four angles and four sides; a quadrangle considered as one of the polygons. ***regular tetragon***, a square.

1630 Lennard tr. *Charron's Wisd.* (1658) 22 In figures the Pentagone contains the Tetragone. 1690 Leybourn *Curs. Math.* 588 Half the Angle of the Tetragon or Square. 1827 Hutton *Course Math.* I. 283 An Equilateral Triangle is also a Regular Figure of three sides, and the Square is one of four: the former being also called a Trigon, and the latter a Tetragon.

2. A square fort; a quadrangular building or block of buildings. Cf. quadrangle *sb.* 3.

1669 Staynred *Fortification* 1 A Tetragon or Square Fort. 1698 Fryer *Acc. E. India & P.* 57 The Fort is a Tetragone from Corner to Corner. 1884 *Daily News* 5 Feb. 5/7 Populations living in immense tetragons of brick and stone.

b. A quadrangular court surrounded by buildings or walls, e.g. a college quadrangle.

3. *Astrol.* The aspect of two planets when they are 90° distant from one another relatively to the earth; the square or quadrate aspect.

*a*1626 Bp. Andrewes *Serm.* (1856) I. 185 In the horoscope of Christ's nativity... Whether a trigon or no, this tetragon I am sure there was. 1727-41 Chambers *Cycl.*, *Tetragon*,.. an aspect of two planets with regard to the earth, when they are distant from each other a fourth part of a circle or 90°... The tetragon is expressed by the character □. [1819 J. Wilson *Compl. Dict. Astrol.*, *Tetragonus*.]

B. *adj.* Four-cornered, tetragonal, quadrangular.

1794 Morse *Amer. Geog.* 553 The remains of an ancient.. fortification: it is now a regular tetragon terrace, about four feet high, with bastions at each angle.

tetragonal (tɪ'trægənəl), *a.* (*sb.*) Also (in sense 4) **-el**. [f. prec. + -al[1]. So mod.F. *tétragonal.*]

A. *adj.* **1.** Of or pertaining to a tetragon; having four angles; quadrangular.

1571 Digges *Pantom.* iv. Tjb, When any equiangle triangle, square, or Pentagonum is.. described within a circle,.. their sides are called the trigonall, tetragonall and pentagonall Cordes of that circle. 1667 *Phil. Trans.* II. 627 Two Tetragonal Prismes of Tendons. 1874 Coues *Birds N.W.* 592 An elongated pyramid with a tetragonal base.

2. *Bot.* and *Zool.* Quadrangular in section, like a 'square' rod; tetraquetrous.

1753 Chambers *Cycl. Supp.* s.v. *Leaf*, A leaf that has, instead of three ribs or edges, four or five, is.. called tetragonal, pentagonal, &c. 1853 Royle *Mat. Med.* (ed. 2) 641 Norway Spruce Fir. Leaves scattered, tetragonal. 1875 C. C. Blake *Zool.* 109 The bill is elongate,.. tetragonal, and acuminate.

†**3.** *Astrol.* = quartile *a.*, quadrate *a.* 2. *Obs.*

1646 Sir T. Browne *Pseud. Ep.* iv. xii. 213 Reckoning on unto the seventh day, the Moone will be in a Tetragonall or Quadrate aspect, that is, 4. signes removed from that wherein the disease began.

4. *Her.* Represented as quadrangular: see quot.

*c*1828 Berry *Encycl. Her.* I. Gloss., *Tetragonel Pyramids*, piles are generally considered to represent wedges,.. they are sometimes borne.. square, in which latter case they may be termed square piles, or *tetragonel pyramids reversed*. 1889 Elvin *Dict. Her.*, *Tetragonal Pyramids*.

5. *Cryst.* Applied to a system of crystallization in which the three axes are at right angles, the two lateral axes being equal, and the vertical of a different length. Also applied to (the structure and symmetry of) substances crystallizing in this system.

1868 Dana *Min.* (ed. 5) Introd. 21 Crystallography.. systems of crystallization... Having only the lateral axes equal. The Tetragonal and Hexagonal. 1878 Gurney *Crystallogr.* 38 If four symmetral planes only intersect in the same straight line it is called an axis of tetragonal symmetry. 1879 Rutley *Stud. Rocks* ix. 77 Crystals belonging to the tetragonal and hexagonal systems are singly refractive when viewed in the direction of the principal crystallographic axis. 1886 [see *grey tin* s.v. grey, gray *a.* 8c]. 1912 *Dana's Man. Mineral.* (ed. 13) 36 The cross section of a crystal when viewed in the direction of the axis of tetragonal symmetry consists usually of a square or a truncated square. 1937 A. F. Rogers *Introd. Study Minerals* (ed. 3) i. 67 Interfacial angles in the prism zone are the same for corresponding faces of all tetragonal crystals. 1973 H. D. Megaw *Crystal Structures* xii. 307 Several other modifications of the spinel structure have been reported. Cr_2CuO_4 has a different tetragonal structure, with approximately the same unit cell as Cr_2NiO_4.

†**B.** *sb.* = tetragon 1. *Obs. rare*$^{-1}$.

1684 tr. *Agrippa's Van. Arts* To Rdr., The intricate Geometrician will imprison me in his Triangles and Tetragonals.

Hence **te'tragonally** *adv.*, in a tetragonal manner or form; **te'tragonalness**.

1727 Bailey vol. II, *Tetragonalness*, the having four Corners, Squareness. 1888 *Cassell's Encycl. Dict.*, Tetragonally. 1963 *Q. Jrnl. Geol. Soc.* CXIX. 326 Tetragonally symmetrical flattened pumice lapilli. 1966 Phillips & Williams *Inorg. Chem.* II. xxv. 248 CuF_2 has a tetragonally-distorted rutile structure.

tetragonidium: see tetra- 1.

tetragonism (tɪ'trægənɪz(ə)m). ? *Obs.* [ad. Gr. τετραγωνισμός squaring, quadrature; see tetragon and -ism.] The squaring of the circle; the quadrature of any curve.

1704 J. Harris *Lex. Techn.* I, *Tetragonism*, with some Foreign Writers is the same as the Quadrature of the Circle. 1715 tr. *Pancirollus' Rerum Mem.* II. xvii. 381 [They] affirm the Invention of the Tetragonism we are speaking of. 1727-41 in Chambers *Cycl.*

So †**te'tragonist**, one who attempts the squaring of the circle; †**tetrago'nistic**, †**tetrago'nistical** *adjs.*, of or pertaining to tetragonism; ***tetragonistic(al calculus***, the differential calculus.

1674 Boyle *Excell. Theol.* i. iii. 104 Such famous writers as Scaliger, Longomontanus, and other Tetragonists. 1710 J. Harris *Lex. Techn.* II, *Tetragonistick Calculus*, is the same with the Summatory or Differential Calculus of Leibnitz. 1727 Bailey vol. II, *Tetragonistical Calculus*.

tetragonous (tɪ'trægənəs), *a.* *Bot.* [f. tetragon or late L. *tetragōn-us* tetragonal + -ous.] Having four angles; = tetragonal *a.* 2.

1760 J. Lee *Introd. Bot.* ii. xxii. (1765) 125 Seed, a single one, oblong, often tetragonous. 1870 Hooker *Stud. Flora* 245 Convolvulus arvensis,.. peduncle.. 4-gonous. 1872 Oliver *Elem. Bot.* App. 310 [Common Wheat] Inflorescence spicate,.. tetragonous.

tetragram ('tɛtrəgræm). [In sense 1, ad. Gr. τὸ τετράγραμμον (Clem. Alex. 666), 'the (word) of four letters', f. τετρα- four- + γράμμα letter; in sense 2 from γραμμή stroke, line.]

1. A word of four letters; = next.

1870 Brewer *Dict. Phrase & Fable* s.v. *Tetragrammaton*, The Greek *Zeus*, Latin *Jove* and *Deus*, Persian *Soru*, Assyrian *Adad*, Arabian *Alla*, Egyptian *Amon*, German *Gott*, and a host of other words significant of Deity, are tetragrams. 1882-3 *Schaff's Encycl. Relig. Knowl.* I. 27 The Jews pronounced the tetragram YHWH by giving to it the vowels of Adonai.

2. *Geom.* The figure composed of four straight lines in a plane and their six points of intersection: commonly called *complete quadrilateral*.

1863 R. Townsend *Mod. Geom.* I. vii. 145 Thus, for instance, in a tetrastigm or tetragram every line of connection of two points or point of intersection of two lines is said to be the opposite of that of the remaining two.

‖**Tetragrammaton** (ˌtɛtrə'græmətɒn). Pl. **-ata**. [a. Gr. (τὸ) τετραγράμματον (Philo 2. 152), 'the (word) of four letters', neut. of τετραγράμματος, adj. f. τετρα- four + γραμμα(τ- letter.] A word of four letters; *spec.* the Hebrew word written YHWH or JHVH (vocalized as Yahweh, Jahveh, or Jehovah, q.v.); often substituted for that word (regarded as ineffable), and treated as a mysterious symbol of the name of God; sometimes used as a title of the Deity (see quot. 1689).

*a*1400-50 *Alexander* 1592 Þe grettest of all gods names, Þis title, Tetragramaton. 1577 tr. *Bullinger's Decades* (1592) 608 Among all the names of God that is the most excellent, which they call *Tetragrammaton*, that is (if we may so say), the fower lettered name. 1606 N. Baxter *Sir P. Sidney's Ourania* Cjb, Some call him mightie Tetragrammaton Of letters fower in composition. 1649 Jer. Taylor *Gt. Exemp.* i. Ad Sect. v. 61 The Tetragrammaton or adoreable Mystery of the Patriarchs. 1689 T. Plunket *Char. Gd. Commander* 44 But the tremenduos Tetragrammaton Will not, not always be a looker on. 1768 Tucker *Lt. Nat.* (1834) I. 463 The Quaternion is the holy Tetragrammaton, the same awful name variously pronounced among the sons of men: whether Jeva, Isis, Jove, Θεος, Zeus, or Deus; or.. Tien, Alla, Dios, Idio, Dieu, or Lord; for these are all Tetragrammata. 1891 T. K. Cheyne *Orig. Ps.* vi. 300 The earliest Greek copies reproduced the Tetragrammaton.

b. *gen.* with *a* and *pl.* A word of four letters used as a symbol.

1656 H. More *Enthus. Tri.* (1712) 50 In a Tetragrammaton there are five Parts, four Letters, and the Tittle Jod, from which come Nephesh, Ruach, Neschamah, Chajah, and Jachidah, five Persons of the Soul. 1665 Wither *Lord's Prayer* 17 Our English tongue as well as the Hebrew hath a Tetragrammaton, whereby God may be named; to wit, Good.

†**c.** *fig.* An emblem or symbol of something sacred. *Obs. rare.*

1601 A. COPLEY *Answ. Let. Jesuit. Gent.* 79 They are so passing vain-glorious a Societie, that call ye it the verie Tetragrammaton of the Catholicke church.

†**d.** as *adj.* Consisting of four letters. *Obs.*

a **1610** BABINGTON *Exp. Cath. Faith* II. (1637) 195 O name that cannot bee expressed! O name truly tetragrammaton! **1614** SELDEN *Titles Hon.* 50 The Tetragrammaton name of the Almightie.

Hence †**tetragra'mmatical** *a.*, consisting of four letters; pertaining to the or a tetragrammaton; **tetragramma'tonic** *a.* [irreg. for *-atic*], of or pertaining to the tetragrammaton.

1759 J. YEOMANS *Abecedarian* (title-p.), A Discourse on the Word, or A-Tau, tetragrammatical. **1895** *Funk's Standard Dict.*, Tetragrammatonic.

‖**Tetragynia** (tɛtrə'dʒɪnɪə), *a. Bot.* [mod.L., f. TETRA- + Gr. γυνή woman, female, taken in sense 'female organ, pistil'.] The name of an order or division in many of the classes of the Linnæan Sexual System of plants, comprising those having four pistils. Hence **'tetragyn** (*rare*), a plant of this order; **tetra'gynian**, **tetra'gynious**, **te'tragynous** *adjs.*, belonging to this order of any class; having four pistils.

1760 J. LEE *Introd. Bot.* II. viii. (1765) 92 *Tetragynia*, comprehending such Plants as have four Styles. **1828** WEBSTER, *Tetragyn*..in botany, a plant having four pistils. *Tetragynian*, having four pistils. **1860** MAYNE *Expos. Lex.*, *Tetragynius*,..tetragynious. **1899** *Syd. Soc. Lex.*, *Tetragynous*, having a gynecium of four carpels. *Mod. Ilex*, the Holly, is an example of Tetrandria, Tetragynia.

tetrahedral (tɛtrə'hiːdrəl, -'hɛdrəl), *a.* Also 8–9 **tetraedral**. [f. late Gr. τετράεδρος (see TETRAHEDRON) + -AL[1].]

1. a. Having four sides (in addition to the base or ends); enclosed or contained laterally by four plane surfaces, as a ***tetrahedral prism*** or ***pyramid***. ***tetrahedral angle***, ***quoin***, one bounded by four planes meeting at a common apex.

1794 G. ADAMS *Nat. & Exp. Philos.* II. xiv. 46 The internal cavity is found to be lined with beautiful tetrahedral prisms. **1812** SIR H. DAVY *Chem. Philos.* 124 Four particles may compose a tetrahedron, five a tetraedral pyramid, six an octaedron. **1828** STARK *Elem. Nat. Hist.* II. 139 Body tetraedral, furrowed above. **1878** GURNEY *Crystallogr.* 85 The tetrahedral quoins..of the rhombic dodecahedron.

b. Quadrilateral, quadrangular. (Also in *comb.*)

1816 KIRBY & SP. *Entomol.* xxvii. (1818) II. 491 Cells with regular tetrahedral bottoms. *Ibid.* 494 The tetrahedral-bottomed transition cells..still preserved their usual shape of hexagonal prisms.

2. Of or pertaining to a tetrahedron; having the form of a tetrahedron; *spec.* in *Cryst.*, belonging to a division of the isometric system of which the regular tetrahedron is the characteristic form.

1805–17 R. JAMESON *Char. Min.* (ed. 3) 200 *Tetrahedral* (Haüy *tetraèdre*), when the crystal has the regular tetrahedron as a secondary form. Example, Tetrahedral blende. **1876** HARLEY *Mat. Med.* (ed. 6) 369 The spores are minute, tetrahedral granules, each presenting four facets, and are minutely ridged by a hexagonal network. **1903** A. GRAHAM BELL in *Nat. Geog. Mag.* June 225 The Tetrahedral principle in Kite Structure. When a tetrahedral frame is provided with aero-surfaces of silk or other material ..it becomes a tetrahedral kite, or kite having the form of a tetrahedron.

3. Math. ***tetrahedral numbers***, the series of integers 1, 4, 10, 20,..., the *n*th member of which is the sum of the first *n* triangular numbers.

1939 W. W. R. BALL *Math. Recreations & Ess.* (ed. 11) ii. 59 The sums of consecutive triangular numbers are the tetrahedral numbers. **1983** *Austral. Personal Computer* IV. v. 103/1 The Tetrahedral Numbers..represent the number of identical spheres that can be stacked in a complete triangular pyramid, or tetrahedron.

Hence **tetra'hedrally** *adv.*, in a tetrahedral manner or form. So **tetra'hedric**, **tetra'hedrical** *adjs.*, tetrahedral.

1860 MAYNE *Expos. Lex.*, *Tetrahedricus*,..tetrahedrical. **1864** WEBSTER, *Tetrahedrally* (citing Dana). **1882** VINES *Sachs' Bot.* 13 The four spores or pollen-grains do not lie in one plane but are arranged tetrahedrally, and have moreover a somewhat tetrahedral form. *Ibid.* 438. **1890** *Smithsonian Rep.* 367 This latter [double linking] is an immediate consequence of the tetrahedric conception.

tetrahedrane (tɛtrə'hiːdreɪn). *Chem.* [f. TETRAHEDR(ON + -ANE.] A compound whose molecule consists of four CH groups forming the corners of a tetrahedron.

1964 *Tetrahedron Lett.* No. 22. 1418 Tetrahedrane (C_4H_4), which has local C_{3v} symmetry, should have a JC-H of about 225 c.p.s. **1976** *Sci. Amer.* Feb. 106/1 If this carbene were to undergo internal addition, the product would be the hypothetical tetrahedral molecule tetrahedrane (C_4H_4). Although the reaction has been tried many times, tetrahedrane has so far eluded isolation.

tetrahedrid (tɛtrə'hiːdrɪd, -'hɛdrɪd), *a. Cryst.* [f. as TETRAHEDRAL *a.* + -ID[2].] = TETRAHEDRAL *a.* 2.

1895 STORY-MASKELYNE *Crystallogr.* 208 Tetrahedrid mero-symmetry. The second case of holo-systematic hemi-symmetry, in which every normal is represented by a single face, is that [etc.]. *Ibid.* 206, 207, 210.

tetrahedrite (tɛtrə'hiːdraɪt, -'hɛdraɪt). *Min.* [ad. Ger. *tetraëdrit* (W. Haidinger 1845), f. as prec. + *-it*, -ITE[1] 2 b.] Native sulphide of antimony and copper, with various elements sometimes replacing one or the other of these, often occurring in tetrahedral crystals; fahlerz, fahlore.

1868 WATTS *Dict. Chem.* V. 729 Large tetrahedral crystals of tetrahedrite, having mostly a rough dull surface, are found in the Cornish mines near St. Austel. **1900** L. FLETCHER in *Brit. Mus. Return* 156.

tetrahedroid (tɛtrə'hiːdrɔɪd, -'hɛdrɔɪd), *a.* and *sb.* [f. as prec. + -OID.] **a.** *adj.* Resembling or approaching the form of a tetrahedron. **b.** *sb. Geom.* The envelope of a quadric surface which touches eight given straight lines.

1889 *Cayley's Math. Papers* I. 587 *note*, The surface here considered, the Tetrahedroid, is the general homographic transformation of the wave surface. **1899** *Geog. Jrnl.* Mar. 251 Causes, which..would go in the direction of producing tetrahedral, or tetrahedroid, deformation.

tetrahedron (tɛtrə'hiːdrən, -'hɛdrən). *Geom.* Pl. **-a** or **-ons**. Also 6–9 **tetraedron**; 6–8 **tetra(h)edrum**. [ad. late Gr. τετράεδρον sb., prop. neut. of τετράεδρος adj. four-sided, f. τετρα- four + ἕδρα base.] A solid figure contained by four plane triangular faces, a triangular pyramid; *spec.* the ***regular tetrahedron***, the first of the five regular solids, contained by four equilateral triangles. Hence, any solid body, esp. a crystal, of this form.

orthogonal tetrahedron, one in which the opposite edges, taken in pairs, are at right angles to one another. ***polar tetrahedron***, one of which the faces are polar to the vertices of another tetrahedron.

1570 BILLINGSLEY *Euclid* XI. def. xxii. 319 A Tetrahedron is a solide which is contained vnder fower triangles equall and equilater. **1571** DIGGES *Pantom.* IV. T ij, Tetraedron.. a body Geometricall. *Ibid. margin*, Tetraedrum. **1653** H. MORE *Antid. Ath.* I. vii. §5 The notion or idea of God..is no more arbitrarious or fictitious than the notion of a cube or tetraedrum or any other of the regular bodies in Geometry. **1706** W. JONES *Syn Palmar. Matheseos* 234 The Tetraedrum of 4 solid ∠s. **1800** tr. *Lagrange's Chem.* I. 359 Susceptible of crystallizing in tetraedra. **1875** BENNETT & DYER *Sachs' Bot.* 50 They [crystalloids] appear as cubes, tetrahedra, octohedra, rhombohedra, and in other forms. **1878** GURNEY *Crystallogr.* 92 Tetrahedrons are contained by four equiangular triangles.

tetrahexa'hedron. *Geom.* [f. TETRA- + HEXAHEDRON.] A solid figure contained by twenty-four planes †**a.** See quots. 1805–17, 1860. *Obs.* **b.** = TETRAKIS-HEXAHEDRON. Hence **tetrahexa'hedral** *a.*, pertaining to, or having the form of, a tetrahexahedron.

1805–17 R. JAMESON *Char. Min.* (ed. 3) 204 [A crystal is] tetrahexahedral..when its surface consists of..four.. ranges of planes, disposed six and six above each other. **1828** WEBSTER, *Tetrahexahedral*, in *crystalography*, exhibiting four ranges of faces, one above another, each range containing six faces. **1847** *Ibid.*, *Tetrahexahedron*, a solid bounded by twenty-four equal faces, four corresponding to each face of the cube. **1860** MAYNE *Expos. Lex.*, *Tetrahexahedron*,..a figure having four ranges of bases, or faces, six in each range.

tetrahydrate: see TETRA- 2 a.

tetrahydric (tɛtrə'haɪdrɪk), *a. Chem.* [f. TETRA- + HYDRIC.] Applied to an alcohol containing four hydroxyl groups, e.g. erythrite, $C_4H_6(OH)_4$.

1888 MORLEY & MUIR *Watts' Dict. Chem.* I. 101 Erythrite is the only fatty tetra-hydric alcohol known.

tetra-icosane (tɛtrə'aɪkəʊseɪn). *Chem.* Also **tetrak-**, **tetrac-**. [f. Gr. τετρα- four + εἴκοσι twenty + -ANE 2 b.] The saturated hydrocarbon or paraffin of the 24-carbon series, $C_{24}H_{50}$ = $CH_3(CH_2)_{22}CH_3$, a solid waxy substance.

1894 MORLEY & MUIR *Watts' Dict. Chem.* IV. 673/1 Tetra-icosane, $C_{24}H_{50}$. **1895** *Funk's Stand. Dict.*, Tetrakosane. **1909** *Cent. Dict. Suppl.*, Tetracosane.

So **tetra-ico'soic** *acid*, $C_{23}H_{47}.CO_2H$, a crystalline powder, very soluble in hot alcohol, occurring in the soap got by heating carnaüba wax with aqueous NaOH.

1894 MORLEY & MUIR *Watts' Chem. Dict.* IV. 673/1.

tetrakaidekahedron. [f. Gr. τετρακαιδεκα- fourteen + ἕδρα base.] A fourteen-sided solid figure. Also *tessarescædecahedron* (Cent. Dict.).

1894 *Athenæum* 17 Feb 216/3 At the request of Lord Kelvin..Mr. J. J. Walker exhibited and described Lord Kelvin's models of his 'Tetrakaidekahedron'.

tetrakis- ('tɛtrəkɪs), formative element [f. Gr. τετράκις four times] used in *Chem.* in the names of compounds to signify four identical groups all substituted in the same way; formerly = TETRA- 2.

1850 [see TRI- 5 a]. **1912** *Jrnl. Chem. Soc.* CI. 2003 The product obtained was tetrakisazobenzene, a deep red substance. **1951** KIRK & OTHMER *Encycl. Chem. Technol.* VII. 580 Tetrakis(*p*-dimethylaminophenyl)hydrazine is dissociated to the extent of 10% in benzene solution and 21% in nitrobenzene. **1963** A. J. HALL *Student's Handbk. Textile Sci.* v. 259 The Proban flameproofing process is essentially based on the use of tetrakis-hydroxymethyl-phosphonium chloride. **1979** G. C. BARRETT in D. N. Jones *Comprehensive Organic Chem.* III. XI. iv. 77 Tetrakis(methylthio)methane, $(MeS)_4C$, undergoes exchange with dithiols.

ˌtetraki'sazo-. *Chem.* [f. Gr. τετράκις four times + AZO-.] Occurring in names of compounds containing four azo- groups.

ˌtetrakisˌdodeca'hedron. *Cryst.* [f. Gr. τετράκις four times + DODECAHEDRON.] A solid body bounded by forty-eight triangular planes; also called HEXAKISOCTAHEDRON, *octakis-hexahedron*, *tetrakonta-octahedron*, and *forty-eight scalenohedron*; esp. the variety of this described in quot.

1895 STORY-MASKELYNE *Crystallogr.* 204 The complete form has the character of a pyramidion developement of the rhomb-dodecahedron, each face of the latter figure being surmounted by a rhomb-based pyramid, to which it forms a conterminous base. These therefore are the forms that may be correctly designated as *tetrakisdodecahedra* or *dodecahedrid pyramidious*.

ˌtetrakis-hexa'hedron. [f. Gr. τετράκις four times + HEXAHEDRON.] A solid figure contained by twenty-four equal triangular planes, having the appearance of a cube with a low pyramid raised on each of its six faces. (In *Cryst.* belonging to the isometric system.) In *Geom.* the name is specially applied to the figure when the pyramids are of such a height that all the adjacent faces are equally inclined to each other, so that the figure meets the sphere circumscribing the fundamental cube at fourteen points. Also called *tetrahexahedron* (b), *cube-pyramidion*, and *fluoroid*.

1878 GURNEY *Crystallogr.* 86 A four-faced cube, or more technically a tetrakishexahedron. **1887** *Athenæum* 10 Sept. 345/2 The new crystals are sharply defined cubes, of which some have the edges replaced by faces of the rhombic dodecahedron or of a tetrakishexahedron. **1895** STORY-MASKELYNE *Crystallogr.* 195–6 The *tetrakis-hexahedron*.. presents the aspect of a cube each face of which is surmounted by an obtuse pyramid, and it may, on this account, be termed the cube-pyramidion... The figure is a twenty-four-faced isoscelohedron.

'tetrakism. *nonce-wd.* [irreg. f. Gr. τετράκις four times + -ISM.] A theory or doctrine of four (persons, aspects, etc.).

1856 EMERSON *Eng. Traits* i. 18 Coleridge..went on defining, or rather refining..talked of 'trinism' and 'tetrakism', and much more.

tetraleioclone, -lemma: see TETRA- 1.

Tetralin ('tɛtrəlɪn). Also **tetralin**. [f. TETRA- + NAPHTHA)LIN(E.] = *tetrahydronaphthalene* s.v. TETRA- 2 a. (A proprietary name in the U.S.)

1920, etc. [see DECALIN]. **1924** *Nature* 14 June 866/2 Excluding benzol..alternative fuels of greatest promise include 'tetralin' (tetrahydronaphthalene), which, mixed with benzol and alcohol, was used considerably by the Germans during the war. **1944** *Official Gaz.* (U.S. Patent Office) 18 Jan. 350/1 E. I. du Pont de Nemours and Company... *Tetralin* for tetrahydronaphthalene. **1980** *Sci. Amer.* May 89/1 Certain trialkyl tin compounds,..and acetyl-ethyl-tetramethyl tetralin, a synthetic fragrance at one time used in certain cosmetics, have also been shown to damage myelin preferentially.

†**'tetralogue.** *Obs. rare.* [f. Gr. τετρα-, TETRA- + λόγος speech, word, etc., after *monologue*, *dialogue*: cf. next.] A conversation between four persons or parties; also = TETRALOGY.

1649 ROBERTS *Clavis Bibl.* 384 This song is also digested in forme..of a Tetralogue betwixt the Bridegroom, Christ; the Bridegrooms friends,..The Bride her selfe,..And The Churches Companions. **1822** T. MITCHELL *Aristoph.* I. p. cxxvi, The works of Plato are usually divided into tetralogues.

tetralogy (tɪ'trælədʒɪ). [ad. Gr. τετραλογία, f. τετρα-, TETRA- + -λογία, -LOGY. Cf. F. *tétralogie*.]

1. a. *Gr. Antiq.* A series of four dramas, three tragic (the *trilogy*) and one satyric, exhibited at Athens at the festival of Dionysus.

1656 STANLEY *Hist. Philos.* v. (1701) 158/1 He made a compleat Tetralogy (four Drama's, as the manner was, when they contested, to be presented at four several Festivals). **1840** tr. *C. O. Müller's Hist. Lit. Greece* xxiv. §2 In the several tetralogies, however, the satyrical drama must have been lost or perhaps never existed.

b. Hence, Any series of four related dramatic or literary compositions.

a **1742** [WARBURTON] *Ricardus Aristarchus* in *Pope's Dunciad* (1743) p. xxxi, May we not then be excused, if for the future we consider the Epics of Homer, Virgil, and Milton, together with this our poem, as a complete Tetralogy, in which the last worthily holdeth the place or station of the satyric piece? **1862** GOULBURN *Pers. Relig.* IV.

xii, A Tetralogy of Parables. **1883** *St. James' Gaz.* 3 Feb. 5 Wagner's 'tetralogy' of operas.

2. A set of four speeches. Cf. TETRALOGUE.

1661 BLOUNT *Glossogr.* (ed. 2), *Tetralogie* (Gr.), a speaking or writing in four parts. **1866** FELTON *Anc. & Mod. Gr.* II. I. ix. 163 They [speeches of Antiphon] are in the form of tetralogies, each tetralogy containing a speech and a reply of the plaintiff and the defendant. **1874** MAHAFFY *Soc. Life Greece* v. 127 *note*, Discussed in Antiphon's second tetralogy.

3. *Med.* A set of four symptoms jointly characteristic of a disorder; chiefly with reference to Fallot's tetralogy (see FALLOT).

1927 [see FALLOT]. **1966** WRIGHT & SUMMERS *Systemic Path.* I. ii. 75/2 The tetralogy..consists of pulmonary stenosis.., ventricular septal defect, displacement of the aorta to the right,..and right ventricular hypertrophy. **1970** [see FALLOT].

Hence **tetra'logic** *a.*, of or pertaining to a tetralogy.

1889 HAIGH *Attic Theatre* 27 But although the generic terms trilogy and tetralogy were of relatively late origin, it was customary at a much earlier period to give a common name to groups of plays composed on the tetralogic system.

tetralophodont to **-mastigate**: see TETRA-.

tetramer ('tɛtrəmə(r)). *Chem.* [f. TETRA- + -MER.] A compound whose molecule is composed of four molecules of monomer.

1929 *Chem. Abstr.* XXIII. 3213 The dimer and tetramer have also been obtained in cryst. form. **1939** *Jrnl. Amer. Chem. Soc.* LXI. 2320/1 With the aid of a molecular still we isolated the trimer and tetramer of hexatriene. **1966** *New Scientist* 16 June 724/2 The structures of the trimer and tetramer have been determined, and it is known that the trimer is virtually flat, whereas the tetramer is puckered. **1978** *Nature* 6 Apr. 496/2 The haemoglobin molecule is a tetramer of two pairs of identical polypeptide chains, the α and β chains.

Hence **tetra'meric** *a.*; **te,trameri'zation**, the formation of a tetramer from smaller molecules.

1938 *Jrnl. Chem. Soc.* 290 The study of the trimeric and the tetrameric products of acid-catalysed polymerisation. **1962** [see DEPOLYMERIZE *v.*]. **1971** *Chem. Abstr.* LXXIII. Subject Index 3626S/3 Tetramerization catalysts. **1974** GILL & WILLIS *Pericyclic Reactions* iii. 69 In certain circumstances it might then be possible to arrange for a concerted cyclic trimerization or tetramerization to occur. **1976** *Ann. Rev. Microbiol.* XXX. 96 Each tetrameric isozyme is thought to contain the three gene products in the ratio of 2:1:1. **1979** *Nature* 29 Feb. 625/1 Stacked A_4 groups in between the cloverleaf branches are supposed to aid in lining up the protein-complexed individual cloverleaf elements for tetramerisation.

tetramerous (tɪ'træmərəs), *a.* [f. mod.L. *tetramer-us* (ad. Gr. τετραμερής four-parted, f. τετρα-, TETRA- + μέρ-ος part) + -OUS.] Having, consisting of, or characterized by four parts. *spec.* **a.** *Bot.* Having the parts of the flower-whorl in series of four. (Often written *4-merous.*) **b.** *Entom.* Having the tarsi four-jointed, as the *Tetramera* among *Coleoptera*. **c.** Having four rays, as a starfish.

1826 KIRBY & SP. *Entomol.* III. xxxv. 684 Tetramerous insects are those in which all the tarsi consist of four joints. **1835** LINDLEY *Introd. Bot.* (1848) I. 316 *Tetramerous*, if [a flower consists of organs] in fours. **1857** HENFREY *Elem. Bot.* 230 *Papaveraceæ*... Flowers regular, 2-merous or 4-merous. **1859** DARWIN *Orig. Spec.* vii. (1873) 173 All the other flowers on the plant are tetramerous. **1861** HULME tr. *Moquin-Tandon* II. III. vi. 157 A tetramerous Coleopter belonging to the family Rhyncophora.

So **te'trameral** *a.*, having parts in fours; also, belonging to the *Tetrameralia*, a subdivision of the *Hydrozoa Acraspeda* in Claus's classification; **tetrame'ralian** *a.* = TETRAMERAL; *sb.* a member of the *Tetrameralia*; **'tetramere**, a division of the fourth order in the supporting reticular skeleton of the extinct siliceous sponges (*Cent. Dict. Suppl.* 1909); **te'tramerism**, the condition of being tetramerous; division into four parts or into sets of four.

[**1888** ROLLESTON & JACKSON *Anim. Life* 789 I. *Tetrameralia*: with four radial sectors... II. *Octomeralia*: with eight sectors.] **1888** *Amer. Nat.* XXII. 941 The morphological significance of the primary subdivision into four or tetramerism of the germ-bands of *Stenobothrus* and *Œcanthus*. **1899** *Syd. Soc. Lex.*, Tetramerism.

tetrameter (tɪ'træmɪtə(r)). *Pros.* [ad. L. *tetrametr-us* sb., a. Gr. τετράμετρ-ος adj., f. τετρα-, TETRA- + μέτρον measure. So F. *tétramètre*.] A verse or period consisting of four measures.

In ancient prosody, a trochaic, iambic, or anapæstic tetrameter consisted of four dipodies (= eight feet); in other rhythms a tetrameter was a tetrapody or period of four feet. The name was given specifically to the Trochaic Tetrameter Catalectic or Septenarius, as in 'Crās a|mēt quī | nūnqu' a| māvit ‖ quīque a|māvit | crās a mēt'.

1612 SELDEN *Illustr. Drayton's Poly-olb.* iv. 67 The first are couplets interchanged of xvi. & xiiii. feet,..the second of equall tetrameters. **1693** DRYDEN *Juvenal* (1697) p. xli, He makes no difficulty to mingle Hexameters with Iambique Trimeters; or with Trochaique Tetrameters. **1837** WHEELWRIGHT tr. *Aristoph.* I. 93, I ask..what thou thinkest the most perfect measure, The trimeter or the tetrameter? **1869** TOZER *Highl. Turkey* II. 250 The metre..is the iambic tetrameter catalectic.

b. *attrib.* or as *adj.*

1770 LANGHORNE *Plutarch* V. 272 A poem, entitled Pontius Glaucus,..written by him [Cicero], when a boy, in tetrameter verse. **1811** ELMSLEY in *Edin. Rev.* Nov. 72 To introduce these refractory names into tetrameter trochaics, Aristophanes has twice used a choriambus, and once an ionic *a minore*, in the place of the regular trochaic *dipodia*. **1827** TATE *Grk. Metres* §10.

tetramethylene, tetramisole: see TETRA- 2 a.

tetramorph ('tɛtrəmɔːf). *Christian Art.* [ad. Gr. τετράμορφον, prop. neut. adj. four-shaped, f. τετρα- four- + μορφή form.] A composite figure combining the symbols of the four evangelists (derived from Rev. iv. 6–8 and Ezek. i. 5–10).

1848 MRS. JAMESON *Sacr. & Leg. Art* (1850) 80 The Evangelists, or rather the Gospels, are represented as the tetramorph, or four-faced creature. **1854** FAIRHOLT *Dict. Terms Art* 430/2 *Tetramorph.* (Gr.) In *Christian Art*, the union of the four attributes of the Evangelists in one figure, winged, standing on winged, fiery wheels; the wings being covered with eyes. **1875** R. ST. J. TYRWHITT in *Smith & Cheetham's Dict. Chr. Antiq.* I. 634/1 The most interesting 6th century representation of them [symbols of the evangelists]..is the quaintly but most grandly-conceived tetramorph of the Rabula MSS. **1898** C. BELL tr. *Huysman's Cathedral* ix. 177 With Christ enthroned.. between the winged beasts of the Tetramorph.

tetramorphic (tɛtrə'mɔːfɪk), *a.* [f. as prec. + -IC.] **a.** *Nat. Hist.* Occurring in four different forms. **b.** Of or pertaining to a tetramorph.

a. 1870 HOOKER *Stud. Flora* 79 Oxalis, Wood-sorrel... Tetramorphic flowers occur. **1901** A. G. BUTLER in *Proc. Zool. Soc.* 15 Jan. 25 *Limnas chrysippus* is tetramorphic both at Aden and on the White Nile.

b. 1901 *N. & Q.* 9th Ser. VIII. 530/1 The tetramorphic emblems..date perhaps from c. 860 A.D.

So **tetra'morphism**, the phenomenon of exhibiting four different forms; in *Chem.*, the property of crystallizing in four several forms.

1909 in *Cent. Dict., Suppl.*

tetramyrmeclone, -nephric, etc.: see TETRA-.

‖**Tetrandria** (tɛ'trændrɪə). *Bot.* [mod.L. (Linnæus, 1735), f. Gr. τετρα-, TETRA- + ἀνδρ-, stem of ἀνήρ man, male: cf. POLYANDRIA, etc.] The fourth class in the Linnæan Sexual System, comprising plants bearing hermaphrodite flowers with four equal stamens. Also an order in the classes Gynandria, Monœcia, and Diœcia, having four stamens. So **te'trander**, a plant having four stamens (Webster 1828); **te'trandrian** *a.*, having four stamens (*ibid.*); **te'trandrious** (Mayne 1860), **te'trandrous** *adjs.*, having four equal stamens; belonging to the class *Tetrandria*.

1760 J. LEE *Introd. Bot.* II. xxiii. (1765) 130 *Tetrandria*, comprehending such Plants as have four Stamina. **1806** GALPINE *Brit. Bot.* 261 Tetrandrous: spikes filiform, panicled. **1830** LINDLEY *Nat. Syst. Bot.* 72 Penæa has also tetrandrous flowers. **1872** OLIVER *Elem. Bot.* I. iv. 39 In the Nettle, then, we have..in the male flower, stamens hypogynous, tetrandrous.

tetrane ('tɛtreɪn). *Chem.* [f. TETRA- 2 + -ANE 2 b.] The saturated hydrocarbon or paraffin of the tetracarbon series, C_4H_{10}, also called *butane*, *quartane*: see TETRYL.

1893 THORPE *Dict. Applied Chem.* III. 813 Tetryl hydrides. Tetranes, butanes. I. *Normal tetrane*, *n*-butane. .. Occurs in crude petroleum.

tetrant ('tɛtrənt). [ad. L. *tetrans, tetrant-em* (Vitruv.), ad. Gr. τετρᾶς.] = QUADRANT *sb.*[1] 4 (*b*).

1860 WEALE *Dict. Terms* (ed. 2), *Tetrants*, the four equal parts into which the area of a circle is divided by two diameters drawn at right angles to each other.

tetra'nucleotide. *Biochem.* Also †-nucleotid. [f. TETRA- + NUCLEOTIDE.] An oligonucleotide composed of four (unspecified) nucleotides; orig., one composed of one each of four different bases and formerly thought to constitute the nucleic acid molecule (so ***tetranucleotide hypothesis, theory***).

1912 W. JONES in *Jrnl. Biol. Chem.* XII. 34 The writer will be permitted to suggest that the nomenclature be made conformable to that which Levene and his co-workers have adopted for the nucleic acids. The term 'tetranuclease' indicates clearly a ferment which exerts its activity upon a tetranucleotide. **1912** A. E. TAYLOR *Digestion & Metabolism* vii. 429 Mononucleotids and tetranucleotids are definitely known; the most common of the tissue nucleic acids are tetranucleotids. **1914** *Jrnl. Biol. Chem.* XVII. 73 Yeast nucleic acid is a *tetra*-nucleotide and is composed of four mono-nucleotide groups. **1931** LEVENE & BASS *Nucleic Acids* II. ix. 289 The tetranucleotide theory is the minimum molecular weight and the nucleic acid may as well be a multiple of it. **1952** *Biochem. Jrnl.* LII. 566/1 The core is composed of the tetra- and penta-nucleotides and possibly some of the trinucleotides. **1960** L. PICKIN *Organization of Cells* iv. 108 Simultaneously in 1948, several groups of workers independently put forward evidence throwing doubt on the old tetranucleotide hypothesis, according to which the four nitrogenous bases present: adenine, guanine, cytosine, and thymine, were combined in equimolecular proportions in a tetranucleotide. This itself was supposed to consist of four nucleotides, each bearing a molecule of one of the four bases. **1974** *Nature* 26 Apr. 783/1 The tetranucleotide hypothesis..asserted that DNA and RNA had a molecular weight of about 1,300, and contained one of each of the four bases (adenine, guanine, cytosine and thymine in DNA; adenine, guanine, cytosine and uracil in RNA). Because these bases were found to be present in the form of nucleotides (sugar-phosphate + base) the molecule was called a tetranucleotide.

tetraodon, etc.: see TETRODON.

tetraonid (tɪ'treɪəʊnɪd), *a.* (*sb.*) *Ornith.* [f. mod.L. *Tetraōnidæ*, f. L. *tetrao* (-*ōnem*), a. Gr. τετράων, applied by Pliny to the Black Grouse and Capercailye, perh. also to other birds: see -ID[3].] Pertaining to the family *Tetraonidæ* of gallinaceous birds, including the grouse and allied forms; also as *sb.* a member of this family. (The term has also been used more widely to include the partridges, quails, and other birds.) So **te'traonoid**, *a.* allied in form to the *Tetraonidæ*; *sb.* a tetraonoid bird (*Funk's Stand. Dict.* 1895); **te'traonine** *a.*, belonging to the *Tetraoninæ*, as a subfamily of the *Tetraonidæ*: see above and GROUSE *sb.*[1] 1.

1847 WEBSTER, *Tetraonid*, a term denoting a bird belonging to the tribe of which the *tetrao* is the type, as the grouse, partridge, quail, etc. **1862** D. WILSON *Preh. Man* I. iii. 63 The name of the English partridge..is applied to one American tetraonid (*Tetrao umbellus*), the pheasant..to another, *T. cupido*. **1868** HUXLEY in *Proc. Zool. Soc.* 14 May 299 The great series of Galline, Pavonine, Phasianine, and Tetraonine birds. **1885** NEWTON in *Encycl. Brit.* XVIII. 333/1 *note*, *Caccabis* lies 'on the Galline side of the boundary', while *Perdix* belongs to the Tetraonine group.

Tetra Pak ('tɛtrəpæk). Also **Tetra pack** and as one word. [f. TETRA- + PACK *sb.*[1]] A proprietary term in the U.S. for a tetrahedral carton used for packing milk and other drinks. Hence as *v. trans.* (nonce-wd.), to sell in such a pack.

1953 *Official Gaz.* (U.S. Patent Office) 16 June 616/2 Ser. No. 623,384. Aktiebolaget Tetra Pak, Lund, Sweden. Filed Jan. 10, 1952. *Tetra Pak.* **1958** *Mod. Packaging Encycl. 1959* in *Mod. Packaging* Nov. 232 (*caption*) Triangular milk packs are formed, filled from a single roll of paper by this machine. ('Tetra Pak' machine.) **1963** *Economist* 10 Aug. 535/2 Express Dairies only 'tetra-packs' its milk for vending machines and half-pints. **1973** *Times* 29 Oct. 15/8 Just take a look at the Channel Islands, they don't use *any* bottles, not one, they use Tetrapacks; so why can't we. They are cheap, there is no disposal problems [*sic*] as with plastic.

'tetra-paper. *Chem.* [Abbrev. of the full descriptive name: see quot.] A kind of test-paper.

1899 CAGNEY *Jaksch's Clin. Diagn.* v. (ed. 4) 160 This [masking of the result] may be prevented by the use of tetra-paper (tetramethyl-paraphenyl-diamine). *Ibid.* vii. 382 Tetra-paper..immersed in the fluid will show the presence of ozone by taking a blue colour.

tetraparental to **-paretic**: see TETRA- 1.

†**tetra'petalose**, *a.* *Bot. Obs.* [f. as next: see -OSE[1].] = TETRAPETALOUS.

1694 *Phil. Trans.* XVIII. 278 Tetrapetalose deformed Flowers coming out of the Scales of the Leaves. *c* **1711** PETIVER *Gazophyl.* x. 96 Scarlet and blew tetrapetalose Flowers.

tetrapetalous (tɛtrə'pɛtələs), *a.* *Bot.* [f. mod.L. *tetrapetalus* (f. Gr. τετρα- four- + πέταλον PETAL *sb.*) + -OUS.] Having four petals.

1697 *Phil. Trans.* XIX. 435 A wonderful strange Heath-leaf'd Tetrapetalous..Plant. **1704** J. HARRIS *Lex. Techn.* I, *Tetrapetalous Flower*..is that which consists of but four single coloured Leaves (which the Botanists call *Petala*). **1837** KEITH *Bot. Lex.* 80 If the petals of a tetrapetalous corolla are so disposed on their receptacle as to spread out in the form of a cross, they are said to be cruciform.

tetraphalangeate to **-phyllous**: see TETRA-.

†**tetra'phyline.** *Min. Obs.* [ad. Ger. *tetraphylin* (Berzelius, 1836), f. TETRA- + Gr. φυλή tribe: see -INE[5].] An obs. name for TRIPHYLITE.

1836 *R. D. & T. Thomson's Rec. Gen. Sci.* III. 477 *Tetraphylline*. This appears to be a variety of the preceding [Triphylline]. **1896** CHESTER *Dict. Names Min.*, *Tetraphyline*... An obs. syn. of triphylite, the name given when a fourth base was discovered in it.

‖**tetrapla** ('tɛtrəplə). Also 7–8 anglicized **tetraples.** [a. Gr. τετραπλᾶ, neut. pl. of τετραπλοῦς fourfold, f. τετρα-, TETRA- + -πλοος -fold. Cf. F. *tétraples* (Littré).] A text consisting of four parallel versions, esp. that of the Old Testament made by Origen. Cf. HEXAPLA, OCTAPLA.

1684 N. S. *Crit. Enq. Edit. Bible* xviii. 178 He maintains that the Tetraples and Hexaples of Origen..were call'd Tetraples, because they contain'd a fourfold Version; Hexaples because they comprehended six Versions. **1705** HICKERINGILL *Priest-cr.* IV. (1721) 242 Origen's Tetraples, Hexaples, and Octaples. **1831–3** E. BURTON *Eccl. Hist.* xxiv. (1845) 516 Origen appears at first to have published the three versions of Aquila, Theodotion, and Symmachus, together with the Septuagint: they were arranged in four parallel columns, and the work was called Tetrapla.

tetraplegia (tɛtrə'pliːdʒɪə). *Path.* [f. TETRA- + PARA)PLEGIA.] = QUADRIPLEGIA.

1911 F. S. ARNOLD tr. *Bing's Compendium of Regional Diagnosis* IIA. ii. 105 The pyramids are in such close apposition to each other in the medulla, that minimal lesions may cause a condition of tetraplegia. **1964** J. J. WALSH *Understanding Paraplegia* ii. 6 When the arms are involved it is more correct..to use the term 'tetraplegia' or 'quadriplegia', and throughout this book the former word will be adopted. **1974** A. HENRY in R. M. Kirk et al. *Surgery* xvi. 349 The incidence of tetraplegia is high in this injury as the spine may have angled acutely..and thus severely pinched the spinal cord.

Hence **tetra'plegic** *a.* and *sb.* = QUADRIPLEGIC *a.* and *sb.*

1911 F. S. ARNOLD tr. *Bing's Compendium of Regional Diagnosis* IA. iii. 36 In a complete transverse lesion of the [spinal] cord in the upper cervical region the simultaneous paralysis and anæsthesia affect the four extremities and trunk (tetraplegic type). **1939** W. HAYMAKER *Bing's Textbk. Nervous Dis.* xix. 523 The contractures give way to flaccid paralyses. The latter may be monoplegic, hemiplegic, paraplegic, even tetraplegic. **1964** J. J. WALSH *Understanding Paraplegia* xvi. 110 Many tetraplegics..are capable of driving a properly converted car with automatic gear box. **1977** *Lancet* 7 May 1013/2 A strain *Ps[eudomonas] æruginosa* was isolated from a catheter specimen of urine from a tetraplegic patient. **1979** *Daily Tel.* 27 Jan. 18 As a tetraplegic may I thank your Health Services Correspondent..for continued interest in what he describes as the 'shambles' at Stoke Mandeville.

tetrapleuron (tɛtrə'plʊərɒn). Pl. **-a** or **-ons**. [a. Gr. τετράπλευρον a figure with four sides, f. τετρα-, TETRA- + πλευρόν rib, side.]

1. A square column.

1837 *Penny Cycl.* IX. 315/1 Square pillars or tetrapleurons, with either a statue, or a caryatid figure standing before.

2. *Morphol.* Pl. **tetra'pleura**: Organic forms with bilateral symmetry having four antimeres or corresponding opposite parts. Cf. DIPLEURA.

1883 [see DIPLEURA].

Hence **tetra'pleural** *a.*, *Morphol.*, zygopleural with four antimeres.

1891 in *Cent. Dict.*

tetraplocaulous, etc.: see TETRA-.

tetraploid ('tɛtrəplɔɪd), *a.* (and *sb.*) *Biol.* [f. TETRA- + -PLOID.] (Made up of somatic cells) containing the diploid chromosome complement twice over. Also as *sb.*, a tetraploid organism.

1914 *Proc. R. Soc.* B. LXXXVII. 484 In the tetraploid giants the chromosomes are 2*x*(24) in the gametic and..4*x*(48) in the somatic cells. **1921** *Amer. Naturalist* LV. 261 Few-noded tetraploids, however, are less easily distinguished. **1932** [see QUADRUPLEX *a.* 3]. **1952** *New Biol.* XIII. 38 It is necessary, before tetraploid rye can be introduced for general cultivation, to see that no normal rye is grown in the locality where the tetraploid is to be grown. **1974** E. STACEY *Peace Country Heritage* ii. 90 Clover..breeders also have concentrated some of the better features, such as leaf retention and plant vigor, into 'tetraploids' by doubling the usual number of chromosomes. **1982** *Sci. Amer.* May 118/3 Potato plants are tetraploid.

Hence **'tetraploidy**, the state of being tetraploid.

1918 BABCOCK & CLAUSEN *Genetics* xiv. 263 The doubling of the number of chromosomes typical of the species is known as tetraploidy. **1941** *Amer. Naturalist* LXXV. 321 In many ornamental plants there is a definite need for new types with larger flowers, later blooming habit, and other characteristics usually associated with tetraploidy. **1970** *Sci. Jrnl.* June 78/3 In lower animal forms both triploidy and tetraploidy are compatible with normal development.

tetraplous ('tɛtrəpləs), *a.* [f. Gr. τετραπλόος, -πλοῦς fourfold + -OUS.] Fourfold, quadruple.

1899 *Proc. Zool. Soc.* 16 May 684 Down the centre of the back is a series of tetraplous bright red spots.

tetrapod ('tɛtrəpɒd), *a.* and *sb.* [ad. mod.L. *tetrapod-us*, ad. Gr. τετράπους, τετραποδ- four-footed, f. τετρα-, TETRA- + ποῦς (ποδ-) foot. Cf. F. *tétrapode.*] **A.** *adj.* Having four feet or four limbs; *spec.* in *Entom.*, belonging to the *Tetrapoda*, a division of butterflies having only four perfect legs, the anterior pair being unfitted for walking.

B. *sb.* **1.** A four-footed animal; one of the *Tetrapoda*, applied by Credner to all vertebrates higher than fishes; in *Entom.*, a butterfly belonging to the *Tetrapoda*.

1826 KIRBY & SP. *Entomol.* IV. xlvi. 343 *Tetrapod*,..an insect having only four perfect legs.

2. (See quot. 1962.)

1962 *Newsletter Brit. Petroleum Co. Ltd.* No. 314. 1 An ingenious type of concrete block will next year be helping to protect the harbour at Das Island off the Arabian coast against storms. Known as Tetrapods, these blocks..may be visualised as a central sphere around which are equally spaced four truncated cone-shaped legs. When a number of Tetrapods are placed in position these legs interlock. **1980** *Citizen* (Ottawa) 3 Dec. 43/1 The tetrapods, which look like children's playing jacks, are designed to break up heavy waves in the event of a hurricane.

Hence **tetrapodichnite** (-'ɪknaɪt), *Geol.* [ICHNITE], the fossil footprint of a four-footed beast; **tetrapo'dology**, a treatise on quadrupeds; **te'trapodous** *a.* = sense A. above.

1835-6 *Todd's Cycl. Anat.* I. 265/2 No species of Bird ever deviates..from the tetrapodous type of formation. **1844** PAGE *Rudim. Geol.* §215 (1851) 126 *note*, Professor Hitchcock adds a third class, *tetrapodichnites*, or the footsteps of some unknown four-footed animal. **1860** MAYNE *Expos. Lex.*, *Tetrapodologia*.., term for a treatise on quadrupeds; tetrapodology.

tetrapody (tɪ'træpədɪ). *Pros.* [ad. Gr. τετραποδία, f. τετραποδ-: see prec.] A group of four metrical feet; a verse of four feet. So **tetra'podic** *a.*, consisting of four metrical feet.

1846 WORCESTER, Tetrapody. **1889** *Amer. Jrnl. Philol.* July 225 The Bactrians and Indians..appear to have found the tetrapody short enough. *Ibid.*, It seems more natural to assume the tetrapody as the primitive march-verse, and the tripody as an intentionally differentiated form for purposes of recitation. **1891** *Harper's Mag.* Mar. 570/2 Most folk-songs are constructed upon tetrapodic periods. *Ibid.* [see DIPODY]. **1895** GILDERSLEEVE *Lat. Gram.* (ed. 3) 458 Dipody ..Tripody..Tetrapody.

tetrapolar: see TETRA- 1.

‖**tetrapolis** (tɪ'træpəlɪs). [a. Gr. τετράπολις of four cities; also sb.] A district of four cities; a state or political division consisting of four towns.

1846 GROTE *Greece* I. v. I. 141 The inhabitants of the insignificant tetrapolis of Doris Proper. **1884** BOSCAWEN *Lect.* in *Builder* 6 Dec., It was a tribe called the Akkadians who..founded the tetrapolis of Nimrod.

tetrapolitan (tɛtrə'pɒlɪtən), *a.* [ad. mod.L. *tetrapolitān-us* of four cities, f. prec., after *metropolitan*.] Of or pertaining to four cities. ***Tetrapolitan Confession***, a confession of faith drawn up by the four cities Strasburg, Memmingen, Constance, and Lindau, presented to the diet of Augsburg (1530).

1847 PRANDI tr. *Cantù's Reform. Europe* I. 103 Those who were unwilling to admit the real presence, drew up another 'tetrapolitan confession'. **1906** C. G. M'CRIE *Beza's Portr. Reformers* 82 This symbol, generally styled the Tetrapolitan from the four cities.., is also called the Strasburg Confession.

tetrapous to **tetraprionid**: see TETRA-.

tetrapterous (tɪ'træptərəs), *a.* [f. mod.L. *tetrapter-us* (a. Gr. τετράπτερος four-winged, f. τετρα- four- + πτερ-όν wing) + -OUS. Cf. F. *tétraptère.*] Having four wings; *spec.* in *Entom.* applied to four-winged flies; in *Bot.* having four wing-like appendages, as certain fruits. So **te'trapter** (see quot. 1846); **te'trapteran** *a.*, tetrapterous; *sb.* a four-winged insect.

1826 KIRBY & SP. *Entomol.* III. xxix. 66 A Tetrapterous insect, the genus of which is uncertain, is said, when it is taken, to discharge its eggs like shot from a gun. *Ibid.* IV. xlvii. 376 A substance intermediate between that of the elytra of *Coleoptera* and that of the wings of the Tetrapterous Orders. **1842** BRANDE *Dict. Sc.* etc., *Tetrapterans, Tetraptera*,..applied by some entomologists to the insects which have four wings, and which thus constitute an extensive primary division of the class. **1846** SMART Suppl., *Tetrapters*, insects with four wings; fossil fishes having four fins. **1860** MAYNE *Expos. Lex.*, *Tetrapterus*..*Bot.*, having four wings, as the fruit of *Tetragonia tetraptera*. **1866** *Treas. Bot.*, *Tetrapterous*, four-winged.

tetraptote to **-quetrous**: see TETRA-.

tetrarch ('tɛt-, 'tiːtrɑːk), *sb.* Forms: 4 **tetrarke**, 5 **-arche**, 5- **tetrarch**; also 4-6 in L. form **tetrarcha**. [ad. late L. *tetrarcha* (Vulgate), cl. L. *tetrarchēs*, a. Gr. τετράρχης, f. τετρα- four- + -αρχης ruling, ruler. Cf. F. *tétrarque* (13th c.).]

1. *Rom. Hist.* The ruler of one of four divisions of a country or province; at a later period applied to subordinate rulers generally, esp. in Syria.

[*c* **1050** *Byrhtferth's Handboc* in *Anglia* VIII. 299 Quadrans on lyden on grecisc ys gecweden tetrarcha.] **1382** WYCLIF *Matt.* xiv. 1 Eroude tetrarcha [*gloss* that is, prince of the fourthe part; **1388** tetrarke], herde the fame of Jhesu. **1432-50** tr. *Higden* (Rolls) IV. 233 He and his breþer were made tetrarches, as hauenge the iiij^the^ parte of a realm, from proctors. **1480** CAXTON *Chron. Eng.* IV. (1520) 28/1 The Emperoure..the halfe of the Iury and Idumea gaue to Archylaus vnder name of Tetrache. **1526** TINDALE *Matt.* xiv. 1 Herod the tetrarcha. **1611** B. JONSON *Catiline* I. i, All the earth, Her kings, and tetrarchs, are their tributaries. **1718** ROWE tr. *Lucan* VII. 334 Kings and Tetrarchs proud, a purple Train. **1877** C. GEIKIE *Christ* lx. (1879) 735 The tetrarch Antipas had come up from Tiberias, to show how devoutly he honoured the law.

2. *transf.* and *fig.* **a.** A ruler of a fourth part, or of one of four parts, divisions, elements, etc.; also a subordinate ruler generally.

1610 *Histrio-m.* II. 19 For this abboundance pour'd at Plenties feet You shall be Tetrarchs of this petty world. **1651** DAVENANT *Gondibert* Pref. 45 The heads of the Church (where ever Christianity is preach'd) are Tetrarchs of Time; of which they command the fourth Division. **1671** MILTON *P.R.* IV. 201 If I..have propos'd What both from Men and Angels I receive, Tetrarchs of fire, air, flood, and on the earth Nations besides. **1797** BURKE *Regic. Peace* iii. Wks. VIII. 307 It is not to the Tetrarch of Sardinia..that we mean to prove [etc.].

attrib. **1642** FULLER *Holy & Prof. St.* III. xxi. 209 Men in whose constitutions one of the tetrarch Elements, fire, may seem to be omitted.

b. One of four joint rulers, directors, or heads.

a **1661** FULLER *Worthies, Cornw.* (1662) I. 213 This was he who was one of the first four Tetrarchs or Joint-managers in chief of Marshall matters in Cornwall. **1902** BARING in *Encycl. Brit.* XXVIII. 496/2 The Parnassian school [had] as their tetrarchs and judges Théophile Gautier, Leconte de Lisle, Baudelaire, and Banville.

3. a. The commander of a subdivision of an ancient Greek phalanx. (The quot. may belong here or to sense 1.)

1846 LANDOR *Imag. Conv.*, *Scipio, Polyb., & Pan.* (1853) 351 His bringing into the front of the center, as became some showy tetrarch rather than Hannibal, his eighty elephants.

b. In Fourier's social organization: A ruler of the fourth (ascending) rank.

1848 *Tait's Mag.* XV. 706 There will be duarchs for four phalanx, triarchs for 12, tetrarchs for 48.

'tetrarch, *a.* *Bot.* [f. TETRA- + Gr. ἀρχή beginning.] Proceeding from four distinct points of origin: cf. DIARCH.

1884 BOWER & SCOTT *De Bary's Phaner.* 363 Triarch and tetrarch bundles sometimes occur in thick roots of species which are usually diarch. *Ibid.* 354 In the case of diarch and tetrarch structure of the main root. *Ibid.*, The phloem-groups of triarch and tetrarch roots of Papilionaceæ. **1895** VINES *Students' Text-bk. Bot.* 179 The stele may have—in different structures—one to many protoxylem (primitive wood) groups, and is accordingly described as monarch.. diarch..triarch..tetrarch..polyarch. **1900** W. WALLACE in *Ann. Bot.* Dec. 643 The tetrarch or triarch root [of *Actinostemma*] has no pith and..no internal phloem.

tetrarchate ('tɛtrəkeɪt). Also 7 **-at**. [f. TETRARCH *sb.*[1] + -ATE[1]: cf. *exarchate* and F. *tetrarchat*.] The office or position of a tetrarch.

1651 C. CARTWRIGHT *Cert. Relig.* I. 102 Your tetrarchate would be a gain for you to lose it. **1709** STANHOPE *Paraphr.* IV. 90 Agrippa, Herod's Successor in the Tetrarchate of Galilee. **1874** H. R. REYNOLDS *John Bapt.* i. §5. 41 It was Herod's feverish desire to emulate the title of King..that cost him his tetrarchate.

tetrarchic (tɪ'trɑːkɪk), *a.* [ad. Gr. τετραρχικός of a tetrarch: see -IC.] Of or pertaining to four rulers; pertaining to a tetrarch or to a tetrarchy.

1818 W. TAYLOR in *Monthly Rev.* LXXXV. 528 The tetrarchic government is criticized. **1898** W. M. RAMSAY in *Expositor* Aug. 132 Now began tetrarchic and then monarchic rule.

tetrarchical (tɪ'trɑːkɪkəl), *a.* Now *rare.* [f. as prec. + -AL[1].] = prec.; also †of a country: Ruled by tetrarchs; divided into tetrarchies (*obs.*).

1638 SIR T. HERBERT *Trav.* (ed. 2) 21 The whole Ile is Tetrarchicall, 4 severall Kings swaying their Ebony Scepters in each Toparchy. **1646** SIR T. BROWNE *Pseud. Ep.* v. x. (1650) 212 The Tetrarchicall or generall banners, of Judah, Ruben, Ephraim and Dan. *a* **1751** BOLINGBROKE *Ess. Author. Matters Relig.* xxxii, The patriarchs had a sort of tetrarchical, or ethnarchical authority, for I suppose it is not easy to distinguish them.

tetrarchy ('tɛtrɑːkɪ). [ad. L. *tetrarchia*, a. Gr. τετραρχία, f. τετράρχης TETRARCH *sb.*[1] Cf. F. *tétrarchie* (15th c. in Godef. *Compl.*).]

1. The district, division, or part of a country or province ruled by a tetrarch; the government or jurisdiction of a tetrarch.

1432-50 tr. *Higden* (Rolls) IV. 291 Wherefore Octouian ..ȝafe to Archelaus the halfe parte of the Iewery, and Ydumea, in the name of a tetrarchye. **1591** G. FLETCHER *Russe Commw.* (Hakl. Soc.) 3 These shires and provinces are reduced all into foure jurisdictions, which they call chetfyrds (that is), tetrarchies, or fourth-parts. **1656** BLOUNT *Glossgr.*, *Tetrarchy*, the government of the fourth part of a countrey [**1674** *adds*] or a government of the whole by four persons. **1862** MERIVALE *Rom. Emp.* VI. lix. 540 The tetrarchy of Agrippa..menaced Galilee on its eastern flank.

2. *transf.* and *fig.* A government by four persons jointly; a set of four tetrarchs or rulers; a country divided into four petty governments.

c **1630** RISDON *Surv. Devon* (1810) 3 The Danish tetrarchy. **1641** MILTON *Reform.* II. Wks. 1851 III. 53 Hee ought to suspect a Hierarchy..to bee as dangerous and derogatory from his Crown as a Tetrarchy or a Heptarchy. **1716** M. DAVIES *Athen. Brit.* III. *Diss. Physick* 12 The honourable Tetrarchy of Physicians, or Doctors,.. Chirurgians, Apothecaries, and Chymists. **1862** RAWLINSON *Anc. Mon.* I. i. 19 In each of these districts we have a sort of tetrarchy, or special pre-eminence of four cities. **1885** *Spectator* 8 Aug. 1033/2 Mr. Chamberlain's proposal for a tetrarchy in the guise of Local Government.

tetrascele to **-skelion**: see TETRA-.

tetrasome ('tɛtrəsəʊm). *Cytology.* [f. TETRA- + -SOME[4].] A chromosome which is represented four times in a chromosomal complement; also, a tetrasomic individual.

1921 [see *hexasome* s.v. HEXA-]. **1944** *Genetics* XXIX. 232 Through selfing of plants possessing these aberrations, the corresponding nullisomes and tetrasomes have been obtained. **1958** C. P. SWANSON *Cytol. & Cytogenetics* vi. 192 Trisomes (6*n* + 1) and tetrasomes (6*n* + 2) have also been found..in *T[riticum] vulgare*. **1973** [see NULLISOME].

tetrasomic (tɛtrə'səʊmɪk), *a.* (*sb.*) *Cytology.* [f. as prec. + -IC.] Of or pertaining to a tetrasome. Also as *sb.*, a tetrasomic chromosome, cell, or individual.

1922 A. F. BLAKESLEE in *Amer. Naturalist* LVI. 19, I have suggested..the terms disome [etc.]..with the adjectives disomic, trisomic, tetrasomic. **1923** *Bot. Gaz.* LXXVI. 345 Since in the somatic cells of a tetraploid *Datura* each of the 12 chromosomal sets consists of 4 homologous chromosomes instead of only 2 as in diploids, it is obvious that in dealing with the transmission of Mendelian characters we have to do with tetrasomic rather than with the disomic inheritance more familiar to students of heredity. **1937** C. D. DARLINGTON *Rec. Adv. Cytol.* 325 Tetrasomics (whether of fragments or whole chromosomes) are more markedly abnormal.. than the corresponding trisomics. **1946** *Nature* 21 Sept. 418/1 Lucerne.., having also given segregation ratios which can best be interpreted as tetrasomic, may be regarded as an autotetraploid. **1961** *Lancet* 7 Oct. 789/1 His father was in effect tetrasomic for that chromosome. **1974** *Nature* 19 Apr. 714/3 The book is then divided into two main parts, the first dealing with trisomics, with some mention of tetrasomics, and the second dealing mainly with monosomics but also mentioning nullisomics.

So **'tetrasomy**, tetrasomic state.

1961 *Lancet* 23 Sept. 724/1 Monosomy, trisomy, or even tetrasomy have very little functional effect. **1977** ZELLWEGER && SIMPSON *Chromosomes of Man* p. xii, Trisomy = 46 + 1 chromosome. Tetrasomy = 46 + 2 chromosomes of the same type.

‖**tetraspo'rangium.** *Bot.* Pl. **-ia.** [mod.L., f. TETRA- + SPORANGIUM; or f. TETRASPORE + Gr. ἀγγεῖον receptacle.] A sporangium producing or containing tetraspores. Rarely anglicized as **'tetraspo,range** (*Cent. Dict.* 1891).

1890 *Athenæum* 21 June 805/2 On the Development of the Tetrasporangia in *Rhabdochorton rothii.*

tetraspore ('tɛtrəspɔə(r)). *Bot.* [f. TETRA- + SPORE.] A group (usually) of four asexual spores, resulting from the division of a mother cell, in the *Florideæ*, a group of *Algæ*.

1857 BERKELEY *Cryptog. Bot.* §88. 108 Tetraspores, mostly immersed in the fronds. **1867** BRANDE & COX *Dict. Sc.*, etc. III. 754/2 *Tetraspore* [is] one of the forms of fructification found in some sea-weeds. It consists of little clusters of spores, in most cases four in number, but very rarely eight. **1875** J. H. BALFOUR in *Encycl. Brit.* I. 508/2 Spores have a tendency to divide into four; such compound spores are called tetraspores.

Hence **tetrasporic** (-'spɒrɪk), **tetrasporous** (tɛtrə'spɔərəs, tɪ'træspərəs) *adjs.*, composed of or producing tetraspores.

1857 BERKELEY *Cryptog. Bot.* §172. 195 Distinguished by their almost constant production of tetrasporic, instead of polysporic, moniliform threads. **1874** COOKE *Fungi* 26 [He] has demonstrated that they are habitually tetrasporous.

tetraster (tɪ'træstə(r)). *Biol.* [mod.L., f. TETRA- + Gr. ἀστήρ star.] A karyokinetic figure formed in the modification of a cell-nucleus by the combination of four star-like masses of chromatin united by spindles or filaments.

1890 BILLINGS *Nat. Med. Dict.*, *Tetraster*, the figure presented when there are four centres of radiation during the indirect division of a nucleus into four daughter-nuclei. **1909** J. W. JENKINSON *Exper. Embryol.* 128 In the case where two sperm-nuclei unite with the egg-nucleus a tetraster is formed, that is four asters united by spindles in a square or rhombus.

tetrastich ('tɛtrəstɪk, tɪ'træstɪk). *Pros.* Also 7–9 **te'trastic(h)on**, (pl. **-a**); 7–8 **tetrastic**, **-sticke**, 7–9 **-stick**. [ad. L. *te'trastichon* a quatrain, a. Gr. τετράστιχον, neut. of τετράστιχος containing four rows, f. τετρα-, TETRA- + στίχος row, line of verse. Cf. F. *tétrastiche, -ique.*] A stanza of four lines.

1580 SPENSER *Let. to Harvey* Wks. (Globe) App. ii. 709/1 Here I let you see my olde use of toying in Rymes turned into your artificial straightnesse of Verse by this Tetrasticon. **1625** USSHER *Answ. Jesuit* 325 Therefore doth Theodorus Prodromus begin his Tetrastich upon our Saviours Resurrection. **1702** *Burlesque of R. L'Estrange's Vis. Quev.* 62 What Man though always in the Pouts The following Tetrastick doubts? **1779** JOHNSON *L.P.*, *Milton* Wks. II. 92 Selvaggi praised him in a distich, and Salsilli in a tetrastick: neither of them of much value. **1824** JOHNSON *Typogr.* I. 330 The last page, on which are an Epistle and Tetrastichon in Roman. **1865** R. PALMER *Bk. Praise* 489 The two tetrastichs composing the first stanza are transposed.

Hence **te'trastichal**, **tetra'stichic** *adjs.*, of, pertaining to, or of the nature of a tetrastich, or consisting of tetrastichs; **te'trastichism**, the formation of tetrastichs.

1882–3 *Schaff's Encycl. Relig. Knowl.* III. 1955 The alphabetical psalm (XXXVII).. is almost entirely tetrastichic. **1890** G. BICKELL in *Athenæum* 22 Nov. 700/3 There are hexastichic strophes throughout Prov. xxx.. and tetrastichic ones in i. 7–ix. 18. **1895** *Q. Rev.* Jan. 128 A tetrastichal metre should be chosen. **1898** R. ELLIS in *Classical Rev.* XII. 120 The process which Rutherford.. aptly calls tetrastichism, i.e. reduction of a larger original to a total of four verses.

tetrastichous (tɪ'træstɪkəs), *a.* *Bot.* and *Zool.* [f. mod.L. *tetrastich-us* (a. Gr. τετράστιχος: see prec.) + -OUS.] Having organs or parts in four rows.

1866 *Treas. Bot.*, *Tetrastichous*, having a four-cornered spike.

tetrastigm ('tɛtrəstɪg(ə)m). *Geom.* [f. Gr. τετρα-, TETRA- + στίγμα prick, mark, point.] The complete figure composed of four points in a plane and their six connecting straight lines; commonly called *complete quadrangle.*

1863 [see TETRAGRAM 2].

‖**tetrastoön** (tɪ'træstəʊɒn). *Arch.* Pl. **-oa.** [a. Gr. τετράστοον, neuter of τετράστοος having four porticos (f. τετρα- + στοά porch).] A court-yard having open colonnades on each of its four sides.

1838 BRITTON *Art & Archæol. Mid. Ages*, *Tetrastoön*,.. a court-yard with porticos, or open colonnades on each of its four sides. **1908** W. M. RAMSAY in *Expositor* Nov. 411 This atrium is what Eugenius calls a tetrastoon.

tetrastyle ('tɛtrəstaɪl), *sb.* and *a.* *Arch.* [ad. L. *tetrastȳl-os* adj., *tetrastȳl-on* sb., a. Gr. τετρά-στῦλος (neut. -ον) with four pillars, f. τετρα-, TETRA- + στῦλος pillar. Cf. F. *tétrastyle.*]

A. *sb.* A structure having four pillars or columns; a group of four pillars.

1704 J. HARRIS *Lex. Techn.* I, *Tetrastyle*.. is a Building which hath four Columns in the Faces before and behind. **1769** *De Foe's Tour Gt. Brit.* I. 369 An Organ of very good Workmanship, and supported by a Tetrastyle of beautiful Gothic Columns. **1842** FRANCIS *Dict. Art*, etc., *Tetrastyle*, a building having four columns in front.

B. *adj.* Having or consisting of four columns.

1837 *Antiq. Athens* 42 Including the tetrastyle portico and that of the Caryatides. **1838** J. L. STEPHENS *Trav.*, *Russia* 85/1 A tetrastyle Ionic temple of the purest white marble. **1842–76** GWILT *Archit.* Gloss. s.v. *Colonnade*, If the columns are four in number, it is called tetrastyle.

So **tetrastylic** (-'stɪlɪk) *a.* = B.; also **tetra'stylous** *a.* *Bot.*, having four styles or pistils.

1860 MAYNE *Expos. Lex.*, *Tetrastylus*,.. having four styles ....: tetrastylous. **1895** *Funk's Stand. Dict.*, Tetrastylic.

tetrasyllable (tɛtrə'sɪləb(ə)l), *sb.* (*a.*) [f. TETRA- + SYLLABLE; cf. Gr. τετρασύλλαβος of four syllables.] **a.** *sb.* A word of four syllables. **b.** *adj.* Tetrasyllabic.

1589 PUTTENHAM *Eng. Poesie* II. iii. (Arb.) 82 Euery sillable being allowed one time, either short or long, it fell out that euery tetrasillable had foure times, euery trissillable three, and the bissillable two. **1749** J. MASON *Numbers in Poet. Comp.* 17 Any two.. joined together in a different Position make a different tetrasyllable Foot.

So **tetrasy'llabic**, **tetrasy'llabical** *adjs.*, consisting of four syllables.

1656 BLOUNT *Glossogr.*, *Tetrasyllabical*, that hath or contains four syllables. **1775** ASH, *Tetrasyllabic*, containing four syllables. **1804** MITFORD *Inquiry* 343 *note*, Describing the antient feet, classing them as dissyllabical, trissyllabical, and tetrasyllabical.

tetrasymmetry to **-theite:** see TETRA-.

tetrate: see TETRIC *a.*[2]

tetrathionic (tɛtrəθaɪ'ɒnɪk), *a.* *Chem.* [f. TETRA- + Gr. θεῖον sulphur + -IC: see -THIONIC.] In ***tetrathionic acid***, $H_2S_4O_6$, a colourless, inodorous, very acid liquid, containing four atoms of sulphur in the molecule. Hence **tetra'thionate**, a salt of tetrathionic acid.

1848 *Chem. Gaz.* 1 Jan. 13 A double salt of the pentathionate and tetrathionate of potash. *Ibid.* 15 Sept. 369 Under the name of polythionic acids the author [F. Kessner] comprises the trithionic, tetrathionic and pentathionic acids. **1852** *Fownes' Chem.* (ed. 4) 140 Tetrathionic Acid.. was discovered by.. Fordos and Gélis [1843]. **1854** J. SCOFFERN in *Orr's Circ. Sc.*, *Chem.* 285 Bisulphuretted hyposulphuric acid (Tetrathionic acid). **1868** WATTS *Dict. Chem.* V. 641 Tetrathionic Compounds. *Ibid.*, Tetrathionate of Barium, $Ba''S_4O_6$ 2 H_2O,.. is obtained in large tabular crystals.

tetrathlon (tɛ'træθlən). [f. TETRA- + Gk. ἄθλον contest, after PENTATHLON.] An athletic contest comprising a series of four events, esp. one (for juveniles) comprising riding, shooting, swimming, and running.

1959 in *Chambers's 20th Cent. Dict.* Add. **1961** *Times* 29 May 4/4 The 1961 Schools tetrathlon competition, organized by the Modern Pentathlon Association of Great Britain and the R.M.A. Sandhurst, was won by Whitgift. **1973** *Daily Mail* 4 Sept. 33/5 Recently winning the British Horse Society's Pony Club tetrathlon in Warwickshire. **1979** *Daily Tel.* 2 Oct. 19/4 In the recent Pony Club Tetrathlon championships (pentathlon minus fencing) more than 100 girls.. competed.

tetratomic (tɛtrə'tɒmɪk), *a.* *Chem.* [f. TETR(A)- + ATOMIC.] Containing four atoms in the molecule. †**b.** = TETRAVALENT, QUADRIVALENT. *Obs.* †**c.** = TETRAHYDRIC. *Obs.*

1862 MILLER *Elem. Chem.* (ed. 2) III. 52 Tetratomic, or Tetrabasic elements, each atom of which in combination is equivalent to H_4, or four atoms of hydrogen. **1865** *Reader* 1 Apr. 372/3 Carbon has been shown by Kekulé [1857 *Annalen der Chemie* 104, p. 133] to be tetratomic. **1872** WATTS *Dict. Chem.* VI. 237 Carbon, which combines with 4 atoms of hydrogen, is tetratomic, tetradic, or quadrivalent. **1880** CLEMINSHAW *Wurtz' Atom. The.* 120 Both vapours are tetratomic, or, in other words, the molecules of phosphorus and arsenic are formed of four atoms.

tetratone to **-top:** see TETRA-.

tetratricontane (tɛtrətraɪ'kɒnteɪn). *Chem.* [f. TETRA- + Gr. τρι(ά)κοντα thirty + -ANE.] The saturated hydrocarbon or paraffin of the 34-carbon series, $C_{34}H_{70}$.

tetravalent (tɪ'trævələnt, tɛtrə'veɪlənt), *a.* *Chem.* [f. Gr. τετρα-, TETRA- + L. *valēnt-em*, pr. pple. of *valēre* to be worth.] Combining with four atoms of hydrogen or other monovalent element, or with four monovalent radicals, or capable of replacing four atoms of monovalent elements in a compound; thus the atoms of carbon and of lead are tetravalent in the compounds CH_4, $Pb(C_2H_5)_4$; = QUADRIVALENT *a.* 1. So **tetravalence**, the quality or fact of being tetravalent; quadrivalence; also **tetra'valency**.

1868 WILLIAMSON *Chem. for Students* 124 Oxygen is.. called a divalent element. A similar reasoning shows nitrogen to be trivalent; and carbon is tetravalent. **1887** *Athenæum* 13 Aug. 217/1 Proof is thus afforded that these elements [sulphur and selenium] are at least tetravalent in function. **1887** *Trans. R. Soc. Edin.* XXXII. 456 The tetravalence of Carbon unsatiated by the bivalence of Oxygen. **1913** *Phil. Mag.* XXVI. 495 The observed trivalency and tetravalency respectively of these elements. **1976** *Sci. Amer.* Dec. 33/1 In the solvents that were used.. tetravalent plutonium ions, Pu^{4+} (plutonium atoms from which four electrons have been removed), are soluble. **1982** *Nature* 25 Nov. 386/1 Organic chemistry, thanks to the tetravalency of carbon and the stability of its incestuous bonds, is responsible for most of the compounds.

tetrawickmannite to **-axonian:** see TETRA- 1.

tetrazole ('tɛtrəzəʊl). *Chem.* [f. TETRA- + AZ(O- azote + L. *oleum* oil.] A colourless compound of carbon, nitrogen, and hydrogen, N_4CH_2 = $N\!\!\!\diagup\!\!\!\!/ CH.NH$, $\diagdown N = N$ having acidic properties, crystallizing in lustrous prisms or plates.

1892 BLADIN in *Jrnl. Chem. Soc.* LXII. 1009 Tetrazole.. is obtained as a yellowish, crystalline mass, and is purified by crystallisation from alcohol.

tetrazolium (tɛtrə'zəʊlɪəm). *Chem.* [f. TETRAZOL(E + -IUM b.] **a.** The ion or radical $N_4CH_3^{(+)}$ derived from tetrazole. **b.** Any of various derivatives of this, esp. triphenyl tetrazolium chloride, a reagent used as a test for viability in biological material. Usu. *attrib.*

1895 *Jrnl. Chem. Soc.* LXVIII. I. 574 (*heading*) Constitution of tetrazolium bases. *Ibid.*, When tetrazolium derivatives are oxidised, the phenyl radicle is not eliminated. **1947** *Nature* 31 May 748/1 (*heading*) Tetrazolium salt as a seed germination indicator. **1969** J. LEVITT *Introd. Plant Physiol.* ii. 13/1 Tetrazolium dyes.. are converted from the colorless to the colored (e.g., red) form by freshly cut surfaces of living cells. **1980** *Nature* 8 May 80/1 The resulting recombinants are Mal^- when scored on maltose tetrazolium agar.

tetrazomal, tetrazooid: see TETRA- 1.

'tetrazone. *Chem.* [f. TETRA- + AZ(O- + -ONE.] Name of a class of basic compounds containing four nitrogen atoms, with the formula $R_2NN{:}NNR_2$, in which R is any monovalent group. ***ethyl tetrazone***, $(C_2H_5)_2NN{:}NN(C_2H_5)_2$, is a basic liquid of alliaceous odour.

1895 in *Funk's Standard Dict.* **1899** in *Syd. Soc. Lex.*

tetrazotize (tɛ'træzətaɪz), *v.* *Chem.* [f. TETRA- + AZOTE + -IZE: cf. DIAZOTIZE *v.*] *trans.* To convert (a compound) into one that contains two diazo groups. Hence **te,trazo'tizable** *a.*, **te'trazotized** *ppl. a.*; **te,trazoti'zation**, the process of tetrazotizing.

1908 J. C. CAIN *Chem. of Diazo-Compounds* 165 Benzidine, when tetrazotized, becomes [etc.]. *Ibid.* 166 This explains why the tetrazotization does not proceed normally. **1933** *Jrnl. Amer. Chem. Soc.* LV. 4540 The technical importance of a method of tetrazotizing *p*-phenylenediamine.. in a quantitative way has been shown. *Ibid.* 4541 It appears that *o*-phenylenediamine is tetrazotizable. **1940** [see CONGO 3]. **1972** *Science* 9 June 1132/2 Tetrazotized benzidine spray.. aided in the identification of the four major components.

tetremimeral (tɛtrɪ'mɪmərəl), *a.* *Pros.* [f. Gr. τετρα- four- + ἡμιμερ-ής half, halved (f. ἡμι- half + μέρ-ος part) + -AL[1]; after *penthemimeral.*] Occurring at the end of four half feet.

1906 SAINTSBURY *Hist. Eng. Pros.* I. 270 He mainly observes the tetremimeral cæsura, which is really important in rhyme-royal, very carefully.

‖**tetrevangelium** (,tɛtrɛvæn'dʒɛlɪəm, -'gɛlɪəm). [After med.L. *tetrevangelia*, pl. f. Gr. τετρα- four- + εὐαγγέλιον gospel, EVANGEL.] The four gospels collected into one manuscript or book.

1898 *N. York Independent* 27 Jan. (Cent. Suppl.) Codex Bezæ goes back not into a tetrevangelium, but into a detached collection.. in which the Lucan writings were a separate factor, unconnected with the rest. **1905** *Expositor* Aug. 123 We find it in the Tetrevangelium, a collection which was very probably made in Asia.

†**'tetric**, *a.*[1] *Obs.* Also 6 **tetrik**, 7 **tetrick(e**. [ad. L. *tætric-us*, *tētric-us* forbidding, harsh, gloomy, f. *tæter* foul: see -IC.] = TETRICAL.

1533 BELLENDEN *Livy* I. viii. (S.T.S.) I. 45 In þe tetrik and sorowfull science vsit amang þe sabynis. **1620** VENNER *Via Recta* iii. 23 It [wine].. correcteth the tetrick qualities which that age is subiect vnto. **1682** SIR T. BROWNE *Wks.* (1835) IV. 276 Her youthful days are over, and her face hath become wrinkled and tetrick. **1811** H. MARTYN *Diary* in *Mem.* (1825) III. 378 Amongst the others who came and sat with us, was my tetric adversary, Agra Acher.

So †**te'tricity** [L. *tætricitās*], †**'tetritude** [L. *tætritūdo*], the quality of being 'tetric', harshness, sourness; †**'tetricous** *a.* = TETRIC *a.*[1]
1623 COCKERAM, *Tetricitie*, the sourenesse of the countenance. **1656** BLOUNT *Glossogr.*, *Tetricity*, sournesse or sadnesse of countenance. *Tetritude*, idem. **1727** BAILEY Vol. II, *Tetricous*, sour in Countenance, crabbed, morose.

'tetric, *a.*[2] *Chem.* [f. Gr. τετρα-, TETRA- 2 + -IC.] In ***tetric acid***, a substance described by Demarçay in 1877, now believed to be $C_{10}H_{12}O_6$, or $C_5H_6O_3$. It is a colourless body crystallizing in triclinic prisms. Its salts are **tetrates**.
1881 WATTS *Dict. Chem.* VIII. 1918 Tetric acid and its homologues,..are formed by the successive action of bromine and alcoholic potash on the ethylic ethers of aceto-acetic acid and its homologues.

tetrical ('tɛtrɪkəl), *a. Obs.* or *arch.* [f. as TETRIC *a.*[1] + -AL[1]: see -ICAL.] Austere, severe, harsh, bitter, morose.
a **1529** SKELTON *Replic.* Wks. 1843 I. 209 Touching the tetrycall theologisacioun of these demy diuines, and Stoicall studiantes. **1627–77** FELTHAM *Resolves* I. viii. 11 It is not good to be too tetrical and virulent. **1656** BLOUNT *Glossogr.*, *Tetrical*, rude, rough, unpleasant, sower, crabbish, hard to relish. **1772** NUGENT tr. *Hist Fr. Gerund* II. 81 Some so tetrical, so cross-grained, and of so corrupt a taste. **1901** M. HUME *Span. People* 488 He had none of the forbidding, tetrical Spanish form of devotion.

Hence **'tetricalness**, the quality of being tetrical.
1653 GAUDEN *Hierasp.* 170 It requires..diligence..to contend with younger ignorance, and elder obstinacy, and aged tetricalness.

tetricity, -cous, tetritude: see after TETRIC[1].

[**tetrifolie**, error in Holland (whence **tetrifoil** in Daniel) for *tre-trifoly*, i.e. *tree-trefoil*.
Tre-trifoly was applied by Turner to the *Cytisus* of the ancients (*Medicago arborea*). The black-wooded *Cytisus* of Pliny was the laburnum (*Cytisus Laburnum*).
1601 HOLLAND *Pliny* XVI. xl. I. 490 Yet the Cytisus or Tetrifolie is blacker, and seemeth most to resemble the Ebene. **1606** DANIEL *Queen's Arcadia* V. i. 85 And seek out Clouer for thy little Lambes, And Tetrifoil to cheerish vp their Dammes.]

tetrobol ('tɛtrəbɒl). Also 7–8 **tetrobolon, -um,** 9 **-us.** [ad. mod.L. *tetrobol-um*, a. Gr. τετρώβολον a four-obolus piece, f. τετρα- four + ὀβολός OBOLUS.] A silver coin of ancient Greece of the value of four oboli.
1693 tr. *Blancard's Phys. Dict.* (ed. 2), *Tetrobolon*, four Drams. **1706** PHILLIPS (ed. Kersey), *Tetrobolum*, a Coin of four *Oboli*, about four Pence half-penny of our Money. **1842** *Smith's Dict. Grk. & R. Antiq.* s.v. *Drachma*, Specimens of the tetrobolus, triobolus, diobolus, three-quarter-obol, half-obol,..are still found. **1895** *Athenæum* 23 Nov. 723/1 An Æginetic hemi-drachm of about 40 grains..was equivalent to the Corinthian drachm or Attic tetrobol.

tetrode ('tɛtrəʊd), *sb.* and *a. Zool.* [f. TETRA- + Gr. ὁδός way.]
A. *sb.* **1.** A sponge-spicule with four equal rays in the same plane.
2. *Electronics.* A thermionic valve with four electrodes.
1919, 1932 [see PENTODE]. **1942** *Electronic Engin.* XIV. 385 The valves in this section are push-pull beam tetrodes. **1943**, etc. [see KINKLESS *a.*]. **1962** D. F. SHAW *Introd. Electronics* xi. 234 The defect in the tetrode characteristics.. is eliminated by the insertion of a third grid, called the suppressor grid, between the anode and the screen. **1976** *Physics Bull.* Aug. 359/3 (*caption*) This component is a new tetrode from Thomson-CSF.
†**B.** *adj. Telegr.* Applied to a mode of multiplex telegraphy by which four messages can be transmitted along a wire simultaneously. *Obs.*
1886 [see HEXODE *a.*].

‖**Tetrodon** ('tɛtrədɒn). *Ichthyol.* Also **tetraodon, tetradon.** [mod.L. (Linnæus 1766), f. Gr. τετρα- four + ὀδούς, ὀδοντ- tooth. So F. *tétrodon.*] A genus of plectognathic fishes, typical of the family *Tetrodontidæ*, in which the jaws are divided longitudinally by a groove, giving the appearance of four large teeth; a fish of this family, a globe-fish. Hence **tetro'donic** *a.*, of, pertaining to, or derived from fishes of this genus; *Chem.* applied to a poisonous acid obtained from the roe of a fish of this genus (*Cent. Dict. Suppl.* 1909); **tetro'donin**, a crystalline base obtained with tetrodonic acid. So **'tetrodont** (also **tetraodont**), *a.* having (apparently) four teeth; belonging to the *Tetrodontidæ*; *sb.* a tetrodon or globe-fish. Hence **tetro'dontid, tetro'dontoid** *adjs.* and *sbs.*
1774 GOLDSM. *Nat. Hist.* (1776) VI. 237 These are the Sun Fish, the Tetrodon, the Lump Fish. **1822–34** *Good's Study Med.* (ed. 4) IV. 214 The genus tetradon, in one species, secretes an electric fluid. **1854** BADHAM *Halieut.* 409 The tetraodons seem as unsafe for food as the diodons. **1858** BAIRD *Cycl. Nat. Sci.* s.v. *Diodontidæ*, The true diodonts,.. the tetraodonts,..and the sun-fishes. **1883** *Spectator* 19 May 639 The tetradon, a knobbly, bladder-shaped creature, used by the Chinese as a lantern, when he has been scooped.

tetrodotoxin (ˌtɛtrədəʊ'tɒksɪn). [a. G. *tetrodotoxin* (Y. Tahara 1911, in *Biochem. Zeitschr.* XXX. 263), f. TETRODO(N + TOXIN.] A poisonous substance found in the ovaries of certain fish of the family Tetraodontidæ.
1911 *Jrnl. Chem. Soc.* C. II. 133 Tetrodotoxin is neither acid nor base, and yields on hydrolysis a base and a crystalline substance. **1938** *Chem. Abstr.* XXXII. 8582 The toxic action of tetrodotoxin is decreased by vitacamphor, coramine,..and cardiazol. **1965** *New Scientist* 18 Feb. 442/3 As deadly as tetrodotoxin from the Japanese globe or 'puffer' fish. **1977** *Lancet* 24/31 Dec. 1331/1 The electrical and mechanical consequences of stimulation are prevented by tetrodotoxin.

tetromino (tɛ'trɒmɪnəʊ). [f. TETR(A- + D)OMINO by deliberately false analogy: see quot. 1961.] Any of the five distinct planar shapes that can be formed by joining four identical squares by their edges.
1954 S. W. GOLOMB in *Amer. Math. Monthly* LXI. 678 The checker board cannot be covered with 15 L-tetrominoes and one square tetromino. **1961** [see PENTOMINO]. **1979** *Sci. Amer.* Apr. 19/1 It is when we turn to the 4-cell animals (the tetrominoes) that the project really becomes interesting.

†**tetronymal**, *a. Obs. rare*—[0]. [f. Gr. type *τετρώνυμ-ος (f. τετρα- four + ὄνομα name) + -AL[1].]
1656 BLOUNT *Glossogr.*, *Tetronimal*, that hath four names.

tetrose ('tɛtrəʊs). *Chem.* [f. TETRA- + -OSE[2].] The name of sugars containing four carbon atoms in the molecule.
1904 [see DIOSE]. **1916** [see BIOSE]. **1963** [see ERYTHROSE]. **1970** A. L. LEHNINGER *Biochemistry* xi. 218 If the carbon chains of the trioses are extended by the addition of carbon atoms, we have, successively, tetroses, pentoses, hexoses, heptoses, and octoses.

tetrous ('tɛtrəs), *a.* Now *rare.* [f. L. *tæter* (*tēter*) offensive, foul + -OUS.] Offensive, foul.
Sometimes from contiguity of form and sense confused with TETTEROUS: so in quot. 1890.
1637 BRIAN *Pisse-proph.* (1679) 133 Your heart and head are assaulted with a tetrous vapour, so that you are melancholick and cannot take your rest. **1664** EVELYN *Sylva* (1776) 411 The Decoction [of Elder buds] is admirable to assuage inflammations and tetrous humours and especially the Scorbutis. **1890** A. W. TOURGEE in *Chicago Advance* 27 Mar., A leper whose tetrous spots threaten every soul that looks upon them.

te'troxide. *Chem.* [f. TETRA- 2 a + OXIDE.] A binary compound containing four atoms of oxygen; e.g. nitrogen tetroxide, NO_4.
1866 ROSCOE *Elem. Chem.* vii. 63 The same blue body [nitric trioxide] is obtained by adding water to nitric tetroxide and drying the distillate over calcium chloride. **1872** WATTS *Dict. Chem.* VI. 239 The tetroxide..appears.. to be capable of existing in the two polymeric modifications NO_2 and N_2O_4.

tetroxy-. *Chem.* [f. as prec. + OXY(GEN).] In comb. equivalent to *tetrahydroxy-*, denoting the substitution of four hydroxyl groups (OH) in the compound to the name of which it is prefixed.

tetryl ('tɛtrɪl). *Chem.* [f. TETR(A- 2 + -YL.]
1. The monovalent radical of the tetracarbon series, C_4H_9, also called BUTYL; chiefly attrib. = *tetrylic*, as in ***tetryl hydride*** = TETRANE, ***tetryl acetate, alcohol, aldehyde, chloride, oxide, sulphide,*** etc.; ***tetryl compounds, group, series,*** etc.
1857 MILLER *Elem. Chem.* III. 195 Tetryl, Butyl, or Valyl ..is one of the products obtained during the electrolysis of the valerate of potash. *Ibid.* 33 Valerianic or Tetrylformic [acid]. **1862** *Ibid.* 248 Tetryl Glycol (Butyl Glycol). **1868** WATTS *Dict. Chem.* V. 732 None of the tetryl-compounds can be directly prepared from it [tetryl]. *Ibid.*, Tetryl forms compounds with other alcohol-radicles. Tetryl-ethyl, C_6H_{14}... Tetryl-amyl, C_9H_{20}... Tetryl-hexyl, $C_{10}H_{22}$.
2. Also **Tetryl.** [ad. G. *tetril.*] A yellow crystalline nitro-amino explosive, tetranitro-methylaniline, $(NO_2)_3C_6H_2N(CH_3)NO_2$, used esp. as a detonator and priming agent.
1909 O. GUTTMANN *Manuf. Explosives* iii. 47 The Rheinisch-Westfälische Gesellschaft of Troisdorf make now detonators of Tetranitromethylaniline (called Tetryl). **1977** D. MACKENZIE *Raven & Ratcatcher* v. 75 A box of detonating-caps, the type with tetryl booster-charges.

Hence **'tetrylamine**, an amine or compound ammonia of tetryl, also called BUTYLAMINE; **'tetrylate**, a salt of tetrylic or butyric acid; **'tetrylene**, the olefine of the tetryl group, C_4H_8, also called *tetrene* and BUTYLENE; *attrib.* as ***tetrylene-diamine***; **tetry'lenic** *a.*, pertaining to tetrylene; **tetrylic** *a.*, of tetryl, in ***tetrylic acid***, etc.
1868 WATTS *Dict. Chem* V. 737 With nitrate of silver, *tetrylamine forms a tawny yellow precipitate. **1857** MILLER *Elem. Chem.* III. 190 Hydrocarbons homologous with olefiant gas... 4. *Tetrylene, Butylene, or Oil Gas (C_8H_8).. was ascertained by Faraday to be one of the products furnished by the destructive distillation of oil. **1868** WATTS *Dict. Chem.* V. 738 Tetrylene at −18° is a colourless mobile oil, having an ethereal but peculiar and penetrating odour. *Ibid.* 739 *Tetrylenic alcohol, $C_4H_{10}O_2$, *Tetryl-* or *Butyl-glycol*..a colourless, viscid, inodorous liquid, having a mild aromatic taste. *Ibid.*, Tetrylenic bromide, $C_4H_8Br_2$.. Tetrylenic chloride, $C_4H_8Cl_2$. **1857** MILLER *Elem. Chem.* III. 127 *Tetrylic alcohol is a colourless liquid of high refracting power, lighter than water.

tett, tette, obs. forms of TEAT.

tetter ('tɛtə(r)), *sb.* Forms: 1 tetr, 1–6 teter, 4–5 tetre, 5 -yr, -ere, 6–7 -ar, 6–8 tettar, (7 teater, 9 *dial.* titter), 6– tetter. [OE. *teter*:— OTeut. **tetru-*, pre-Teut. **dedru-*, Skr. *dadru* a kind of cutaneous disease, f. *dṝ* to crack; cf. Lith. *dedervine* tetter. The simple word is not preserved elsewhere in Teut., but cf. OHG. *zitaroh* (:—**titruha*), MHG. *ziteroch*, Bav. dial. *zitt(e)roch, -en*, Tyrol *zittrich*; also mod.Ger. *zittermal, zitterflechte*, Swiss *zitterabel* tetter, ringworm.]
1. A general term for any pustular herpetiform eruption of the skin, as eczema, herpes, impetigo, ringworm, etc.
crusted, pustular, running tetter, impetigo; ***eating t.***, lupus; ***honeycomb t.***, favus; ***humid*** or ***moist t.***, eczema; ***milky t.***, milk-blotch; ***scaly t.***, psoriasis.
a **700** *Epinal Gloss.* (O.E.T.) 128 *Basis*, teter. *Ibid.* 502 *Inpetigo*, tetr. *Ibid.* 791 *Papula vel pustula*, spryng *vel* tetr. *c* **725** *Corpus Gloss.* (O.E.T.) 128 *Balsis*, teter. *c* **897** K. ÆLFRED *Gregory's Past. C.* xi. 71 Se ðonne hæfð teter on his lichoman se hæfð on his mode ʒitsunga. *c* **1000** *Sax. Leechd.* I. 150 Heo ofʒenimð þone scruf & þone teter. *a* **1050** *Liber Scintill.* xxv. 99 Teter witodlice hæfð on lichaman. **1387** TREVISA *Higden* (Rolls) II. 61 þere beeþ hoote bathes, þat wascheþ of teteres, oþer sores and scabbes. *c* **1475** *Pict. Voc.* in Wr.-Wülcker 791/14 *Hec serpedo*,..a tetere. **1584** COGAN *Haven Health* xxviii. (1636) 48 For a Tettar or Ring-worme a little Mustard laid upon it within a few dayes will cure it. **1602** SHAKS. *Ham.* I. v. 71. **1622** HAKEWILL *David's Vow* viii. 284 It is good..to kill a Tetter before it spread to a Ringworme. **1712** tr. *Pomet's Hist. Drugs* I. 66 The true Oil of Cedar is admirable for curing Tetters. **1850** BLACKIE *Æschylus* I. 125 A leprous tetter with corrosive tooth [would] Creep o'er my skin, and fasten on my flesh.
fig. **1641** MILTON *Reform.* I. Wks. 1851 III. 19 What a universall tetter of impurity had invenom'd every part, order, and degree of the Church. **1647, 1705** [see RINGWORM 1 b]. **1693** SOUTHERNE *Maid's last Prayer* I. i, The mercenary itch in an old woman; 'tis the very tetter of that sex. **1819** W. TENNANT *Papistry Storm'd* (1827) 145 In ran the airn by chance, And lat out baith the wind and matter, That lang had lodgit in that tetter.
2. A cutaneous disease in animals, esp. horses.
1552 HULOET, Tetter for horse, *herpeta.* **1575** TURBERV. *Venerie* 227 The Tettar commeth vnto many dogs naturally or by kind or by age. **1614** MARKHAM *Cheap Husb.* (1623) 119 To heale any Tetter, or drie scabbe in Goates. **1708** *Lond. Gaz.* No. 4400/4 A black Gelding..a Tetter on the off Breast. **1794** *Sporting Mag.* III. 156 A cure for warts or tetters on horses. **1819** *Pantologia*, *Tetter*, called by farriers the flying-worm, or ring-worm. It runs up and down the skin in different directions, from whence it receives its name.

'tetter, *v. rare.* [f. prec.] †**1.** *trans.* To affect with, or as with, a tetter. *Obs.*
1607 SHAKS. *Cor.* III. i. 79 So shall my Lungs Coine words ..against those Meazels Which we disdaine should Tetter vs.
2. *intr.* To crack, to disintegrate.
1911 J. MASEFIELD *Everlasting Mercy* 30 My mind began to carp and tetter. **1967** T. KENEALLY *Bring Larks & Heroes* ii. 16 In dutiful vegetable gardens, the leaves of carrots and turnips had tettered and split, shot full of holes by antipodean summer.

tetter-berry ('tɛtəbɛrɪ). The common Bryony, *Bryonia dioica*; also, the berry of this plant. Variously said to cure and to produce tetter.
1597 GERARDE *Herbal* II. cccvi. 720 In English Bryonie, white Bryonie, and tetter Berrie. **1598** FLORIO, *Vitalba*, wilde vine or tetterberrie growing in hedges with red berries ..the iuice whereof will cause the skin to blister. **1640** PARKINSON *Theatr. Bot.* II. xiii. 181 Good against all fretting and running cankers, gangrænes and tetters, and therefore the berries [are] usually called of the Country people, Tetter berries. **1886** BRITTEN & H. *Plant-n.*, *Tetter-berry*..*Hants.*, where children have an idea that the juice of the fruit will, if it touches the skin, produce tetter.

tettered ('tɛtəd), *a.* [f. TETTER *sb.*, *v.* + -ED[2], [1].] Afflicted with tetter (usu. *fig.*).
1906 W. DE LA MARE *Poems* 84, I marvelled at..this poor creature..tettered with worms of fear. **1908** G. BOTTOMLEY *Chambers of Imagery* 2nd Ser. (1912) 19 Iron misused must turn to blight And dwindle to a tettered crust. **1975** J. I. M. STEWART *Gaudy* xvi. 281 The great façade with its massive columns was crumbling, flaked and tettered.

'tetterish, *a.* [f. TETTER *sb.* + -ISH[1].] Of the nature of tetter: with quot. cf. 1758 in next.
1709 *Brit. Apollo* II. No. 36. 4/2 It..heales all Tetterish Humors.

tetterous ('tɛtərəs), *a.* [f. TETTER *sb.* + -OUS.] Of the nature of, proceeding from, or causing tetter.
In quot. 1758 perhaps an error for TETROUS, foul.
1719 QUINCY *Lex. Physico-Med.* (1726), *Noli-me-tangere*, touch me not, is a tetterous Eruption, thus call'd, from its Soreness, or Difficulty of Cure. **1750** RUTTY in *Phil. Trans.* LI. 476 Scab, tetterous eruptions, scald head, and sore eyes. **1758** J. S. *Le Dran's Observ. Surg.* (1771) 131 A tetterous Humour..shall create an Obstruction. **1977** J. I. M. STEWART *Madonna of Astrolabe* xii. 181 The lizards, darting

from crevice to crevice on a crumbling wall, were in process of shedding tetterous skins to reveal a summer green.

tetter-totter, variant of TITTER-TOTTER.

tetterworm ('tɛtəwɜːm). A cutaneous affection; = TETTER; a form of ringworm.

1622 T. SCOTT *Belg. Pismire* 28 [It] ouerspreades the face and body thereof, like a Canker or Tetter-worm. **1727** BAILEY vol. II, *Tetter-worm*, an Insect. *a* **1825** FORBY *Voc. E. Anglia*, *Titter-worm*,..a cutaneous efflorescence, a series or confluence of minute pimples,..nor is it so troublesome and obstinate an affection as the *ring-worm*. It is a miliary eruption, in form rather vermicular than annular.

tetterwort ('tɛtəwɜːt). The common Celandine, *Chelidonium majus*: so called because supposed to cure tetters.

a **1400-50** *Stockh. Med. MS.* 175 Celydonye or teterwort, *celidonie*. **1578** LYTE *Dodoens* I. xx. 31 Called..in English Celandyne, Swallowurte, and of some Tetterwurte. **1640** PARKINSON *Theatr. Bot.* v. lxx. 618 Tetterwort..the juice often applyed to tetters..will quickly kill their sharpenesse. **1879** PRIOR *Pop. Names Plants* (ed. 3) 235 *Tetter-wort*, from its curing tetters.

b. In America, The Blood-root, or Red PUCCOON, *Sanguinaria canadensis*.

1891 in *Cent. Dict.*

†'**tetterwose.** *Obs. rare*$^{-0}$. [f. TETTER *sb.* + (?) OOZE *sb.*[3]] The Common Germander, *Teucrium Chamædrys*.

a **1500** *Voc.*, Wr.-Wülcker 569/47 *Camedreos*,.. Teterwose.

'**tettery**, *a.* [f. TETTER *sb.* + -Y.] Of the nature of tetter; tetterous.

1697 R. PEIRCE *Bath Mem.* I. iv. 72 He came for a Tettery Eruption in his Neck and Chin. **1721** *Lond. Gaz.* No. 5977/4 All Leprous, Tettery, Scabby, Scaly, Scurfy, or other.. Breakings out upon the Skin.

tettigonian (tɛtɪ'gəʊnɪən). [f. mod.L. *Tettigonia* (see next) + -AN.] = next.

1842 T. W. HARRIS *Treat. Insects Injurious to Vegetation* 183 The Tettigonians, or leaf-hoppers, have the head and thorax somewhat like those of frog-hoppers.

tettigoniid (tɛtɪ'gəʊnɪɪd). Also **tettigonid**. [a. mod.L. family name *Tettigoniidæ*, f. generic name *Tettigonia* (Linnæus *Systema Naturæ* (ed. 10, 1758) I. 429), f. TETTIX + *-onia*: see -ID[3].] = *long-horn(ed) grasshopper* s.v. LONGHORN 4. Also *attrib.*, of or pertaining to an insect of this kind or the family in which it is included.

1921 H. T. FERNALD *Appl. Entomol.* xvi. 86 Some of the Tettigoniids are wingless and come out only at night. **1935** *Discovery* Nov. 317/2 Certain long-horned grasshoppers or Tettigonids..are representatives of extensive groups. **1939** M. BARR *Insect Legion* ii. 12 The big Tettigonids..are capable of biting a piece of flesh out of a finger. **1946** F. E. ZEUNER *Dating Past* xii. 365 *Platycleis occidentalis jerseyana* .., a tettigoniid grasshopper, is well distinguished in size. **1957** *New Biol.* XXIII. 31 This wing mechanism is also found in the Tettigoniids. **1972** [see *long-horn(ed) grasshopper* s.v. LONG-HORN 4].

†**tettish, teatish**, *a. Obs.* [Origin of radical part *tet* or *teat* obscure: see also TEETY *a.*] Peevish, irritable, fretful.

1567 GOLDING *Ovid's Met.* XIII. (1575) 172 And thou the selfsame Galate art more tettish for to frame, Than Oxen of the wildernesse whom neuer wyght did tame. **1592** NASHE *P. Penilesse* (ed. 2) 16 Hee is an olde man (for those yeares are most wayward and teatish). *a* **1619** FLETCHER *Wit without M.* v. ii, This Rogue, if he had been sober, sure had beaten me, is the most tettish Knave. **1621** —— *Pilgrim* I. i, Who will be troubled with a tettish girl? *a* **1625** —— *Woman's Prize* v. i, Her sicknesse Has made her somewhat teatish.

‖**tettix** ('tɛtɪks). [a. Gr. τέττιξ.]

1. The cicada or tree-cricket, a homopterous winged insect: so called by the ancient Greeks, and hence in reference to Greece, Greek poets, etc. The South European species is *Cicada orni*.

1775 R. CHANDLER *Trav. Asia M.* (1825) I. 343 The tettix or cicada in the day-time is extremely troublesome. **1816** KIRBY & SP. *Entomol.* xxiv. (1818) II. 402 One bard entreats the shepherds to spare the innoxious Tettixs, that nightingale of the Nymphs. **1871** M. COLLINS *Inn of Strange Meetings* 40 Anacreon's tettix, singing in the trees. **1900** *Daily News* 13 Dec. 5/2 The much-sung 'tettix', or cicada.

2. *Entom.* A genus of *Acridiidæ*, or short-horned grasshoppers, typical of the orthopterous subfamily *Tettiginæ*, having the pronotum horizontal and the antennæ thirteen- or fourteen-jointed. Two species are known in Britain and nine in U.S.

3. *golden tettix* (Gr. χρυσοῦς τέττιξ), an ornament worn in the hair by Athenians before Solon's time, as an emblem of their being aboriginal.

1874 MAHAFFY *Soc. Life Greece* v. 135 Fastened their hair with a golden tettix. **1875** BROWNING *Aristoph. Apol.* 441 Citizens Like Aristeides and like Miltiades Wore each a golden tettix in his hair.

tetty, variant of TEETY, easily offended.

tet-work, obs. or erron. f. TUT-WORK, piecework.

teucalli, obs. form of TEOCALLI.

teuch, teugh, Sc. forms of TOUGH.

teuchat, -it, Sc. variants of TEWHIT, lapwing.

teuchter ('tjuxtər, 'tʃu-). *Sc.* Also **teuchtar**. [Origin unknown.] A Highlander (see also quots. 1962 and 1977).

1940 R. GARIOCH *17 Poems for 6d.* 13 Thir a glaikit pair o Teuchters, an as Heilant as a peat. **1962** *Scotsman* 26 Jan. 11 There is ample evidence that she referred to him as a 'teuchter', a word which I understand to mean a country bumpkin. **1977** *Times Lit. Suppl.* 9 Sept. 1084/2 For the inhabitants of Harris are mainly what most Scots call 'teuchtars'—a word which I had never heard till I had it applied to me by a teacher in a Glasgow school. What is a teuchtar? It is a Lowland Scots imitation of a Gaelic noise, a term of now genial contempt for a crofter or, more generally, for anyone from beyond the Highland line. **1979** R. LAIDLAW *Lion is Rampant* xviii. 137, I look like the archetypal teuchter, right down to the fur-bearing cheeks.

teucrin ('tjuːkrɪn). *Chem.* [f. Bot. L. *Teucr-ium*, generic name of germander + -IN[1].]

1881 WATTS *Dict. Chem.* 3rd Suppl., *Teucrin*,..a glucoside obtained from *Teucrium fruticans*, a Sicilian plant used as a remedy for intermittent fever.

teucrium ('tjuːkrɪəm). [mod.L., a. Gr. τεύκριον, a name used by Dioscorides.] A herb or shrub of the genus of this name, belonging to the family Labiatæ; = GERMANDER.

1673 J. RAY *Obs. Journey Low-Countries* 257 On the sides of the Mountains..*Teucrium*. **1917** L. H. BAILEY *Stand. Cycl. Hort.* VI. 3324/2 The teucriums are little known in cultivation. **1962** R. PAGE *Educ. of Gardener* v. 151, I would plant grey-leaved shrubs to grow wild and make a thicket: rosemary, cistus, the grey-leaved teucrium so much used in the South of France. **1974** *Country Life* 25 Apr. 997/2 The terraced paths..take you across the hillside..between hedges of rosemary and lavender and teucrium, always aromatic in the sunshine.

teuf-teuf (tœftœf). [a. Fr.: echoic.] An imitation of the repeated sound of gases escaping from the exhaust of a petrol engine. Hence as *v. intr.*, (of a motor) to make such a sound; (of a person) to ride in a chugging motor vehicle. Now usually anglicized as TUFF-TUFF.

1902 *Daily Chron.* 22 Aug. 3/4 The 'teuf-teuf' of the rapid motor is everywhere on the splendid roads. **1904** H. G. WELLS *Food of Gods* I. iv. 125 People..used to see him almost daily teufteufing slowly about Hyde Park. **1905** *Westm. Gaz.* 9 Sept. 11/3 The teuf-teufing of the motor is drowned by the tinkle of marriage bells. **1907** G. B. SHAW *John Bull's Other Island* III. 77 His ear catches an approaching teuf-teuf. **1914** T. A. BAGGS *Back from Front* xxiv. 121 Suddenly, piercing the night stillness, came the harsh teuf-teuf of a motor-car.

teuk (tjuːk). *local.* [From its note of alarm.] The name given in East Anglia, Essex, and Kent to a bird, the Redshank, *Totanus calidris*.

1859 ATKINSON *Walks & Talks* (1892) 300 A man went with a sailor to shoot teukes. **1892** *Within an hour of Lond.* (ed. 2) 256 The redshank, pool-snipe, teuke or took. [**1910** *Westm. Gaz.* 29 Jan. 11/1 The Redshank. The clear 'teuk-teuk' will break upon the stillness that reigns around, showing your deadly presence is detected.] *Ibid.*, The 'teuk', as they call the redshank in [the Essex marshes].

Teut (tjuːt). Colloquial abbreviation of TEUTON.

1862 J. BROWN *Lett.* (1907) 152 That blue-eyed, soft and white-skinned Teut, polyandrous and heartless. **1876** BLACKIE *Lang. & Lit. Highl. Scotl.* i. 66 The Celts..delight in a peculiar use of the nasal organ, unknown to the Teut, whether in Saxony or in the British low countries.

teutenage, obs. form of TUTENAG, zinc.

teuthology (tjuː'θɒlədʒɪ). [ad. mod.L. *teuthologia*, irreg. (for **teuthidologia*) f. Gr. τευθίς (-ιδο-ς) cuttle-fish, squid + -LOGY.] That branch of zoology which deals with cephalopods. Hence **teu'thologist**.

1886 HOYLE in *Challenger Rep.* XVI. 61 More explicit information..would be very acceptable to teuthologists. **1891** *Cent. Dict.*, Teuthology. **1982** *Sci. Amer.* Apr. 82/1 Teuthologists, the specialists who study cephalopods (the group of marine animals that includes the squid, the cuttlefish and the octopus).

'**teutlose.** *Chem.* [f. Gr. τεῦτλ-ον beet + -OSE[2].]

1868 WATTS *Dict. Chem.* V. 740 *Teutlose*,..a kind of sugar, resembling glucose, said to exist, under certain circumstances, in the juice of beet.

Teuto- (tjuːtəʊ), before a vowel **Teut-**, combining form irregularly f. TEUTON, TEUTONIC.

1. Combined with other ethnic sbs. or adjs. in the sense 'That is a Teuton, or Teutonic and...', as ***Teut-Aryan, Teuto-British, -Celt, -Celtic***, etc.

1866 *Anthrop. Rev.* IV. 62 The Teuto-Celts, under Charlemagne, vanquished the pure Saxons of the fatherland. *Ibid.* 66 A Teuto-Celtic race extends from the northern shores of the Shetland Isles to the Gulf of Lyons. **1895** *Funk's Stand. Dict.*, *Teuto-Celtic*, of mixed Teutonic and Celtic blood, as the people of northern France. **1897** *19th Cent.* May 795 The early Aryan or better Teutaryan children would seem to have used another word. **1909** *Daily Chron.* 24 Mar. 4/6 Sir Rowland Blennerhasset..belonged to that class of international publicists represented by the Baron von Bunsen.., his Teuto-British contributions to our magazines will be much missed.

2. Formative of derivatives, as **Teu'tolatry**, the idolizing of Teutonic or German nationality, ideas, etc.; **Teuto'mania**, a mania for what is Teutonic or German; hence **Teuto'maniac**, one possessed with Teutomania; '**Teutophile, -phil** *sb.*, a lover or friend of Germany and the Germans; also as *adj.*; **Teuto'phobia**, an intense dread of or aversion to Germany and the Germans; hence '**Teutophobe**, one possessed with Teutophobia; '**Teutophobism**.

1893 *Chicago Advance* 17 Aug., Words of warning against the danger of '*Teutolatry' [= blind attachment to German biblical criticism]. **1848** A. HERBERT in Todd *Irish Nennius* Notes 42 That crotchet is as old as Verstegan, who says the Picts were..phichtian or fighters... This was *Teutomania. **1899** *Q. Rev.* Apr. 440 To detest the Teutomania that worked at the expense of progress and good will. **1900** *Dundee Advertiser* 16 Apr. 16/3 France, which *Teutomaniacs are wont to brand as 'Celtic'. **1904** *Jrnl. Philos. Psychol. & Sci. Meth.* 4 Feb. 58 (C.D. Suppl.) Worthy of more attention than it receives in the current *Teutophile philosophy. **1904** *Daily Chron.* 29 Mar. 4/6 The late Tsar—who, as a *Teutophobe, would never speak German. **1905** *Daily News* 9 Aug. 6 The misunderstandings ..are directly attributable to the Teutophobe Press. **1876** H. JAMES *Let.* 1 Apr. in *Parisian Sketches* (1958) x. 102 [M. Tissot's] *Teutophobia, as an exhibition of vivacity and energy, is really very fine. **1903** *Sat. Rev.* 14 Mar. 330/1 A reasoned protest against English Teutophobia. **1904** *Q. Rev.* Jan. 320 These articles, apart from their *Teutophobism, are..lucid surveys.

Teuton ('tjuːtɒn, -t(ə)n). [ad. L. *Teuton-ēs*, *Teuton-i* (rarely sing. *Teuton, -us*), ethnic name. For sense 2 see Note to TEUTONIC.]

1. In *pl.* (usually in L. form *Teutones*) applied to an ancient people of unknown race, said to have inhabited the Cimbric Chersonesus in Jutland *c* 320 B.C., who, in company with the Cimbri, in 113–101 B.C. devastated Gaul and threatened the Roman republic.

1727-41 CHAMBERS *Cycl.*, *Teutonic*, belonging to the Teutons, an ancient people of Germany, inhabiting chiefly along the coasts of the German ocean. **1839** *Penny Cycl.* XIV. 420/2 The consul Manilius and the proconsul Cæpio were defeated by the Teutones and Cimbri in Gaul. **1879** FROUDE *Cæsar* v. 41 Both Teutons and Cimbri were Germans.

2. A German; in extended ethnic sense, any member of the races or peoples speaking a Germanic or Teutonic language; in Great Britain and its colonies, and the United States, often used like 'Saxon' in opposition to 'Celt', and in avoidance of 'German' in its modern political sense.

1833 D. MACMILLAN in Hughes *Mem.* ii. (1883) 20, I am very glad that my mother is a Teuton. **1841** SPALDING *Italy & It. Isl.* III. 221 These isolated Teutons constituted under the Venetian government a sort of smuggling free state. **1900** A. LANG in *Blackw. Mag.* Apr. 543/2 He is a partisan of the pure Teuton.

Hence '**Teutondom**, the land or domain of the Teutons, Germany; the German people or state; **Teuto'nesque** *a.* [-ESQUE], of Teutonic character.

1880 STALLYBRASS tr. *Grimm's Teutonic Mythol.* I. 103 Those divinities of whom there is least trace to be found in the rest of *Teutondom. **1889** R. B. ANDERSON tr. *Rydberg's Teutonic Mythol.* 22 Did they look upon themselves as aborigines or as immigrants in Teutondom? **1839** DARLEY *Beaumont & Fletcher's Wks.* I. Introd. 38 A *Teutonesque consonantal language like ours, will, however polished, want sufficient melodiousness.

Teutonic (tjuː'tɒnɪk), *a.* and *sb.* Also 7 **Theut-**. [ad. L. *Teutonic-us*, f. *Teuton-ēs*: see Note below.]

A. *adj.* **1. a.** Of or pertaining to the Teutons; German, esp. High German. Esp., displaying the characteristics attributed to Germans. Cf. TEUTONICALLY *adv.*

c **1645** HOWELL *Lett.* (1650) II. 80 The High Dutch or Teutonic tongue is one of the prime and most spacious maternall languages of Europe. **1657** *North's Plutarch, Add. Lives* (1676) 39 He [Charlemagne] began a Vulgar Teutonick Grammar. **1719** W. OLDISWORTH *Quillet's Callipædia* IV. 746 The fam'd Teutonick Valour, priz'd in war. **1724** WATERLAND *Athan. Creed* v. 67 There is in the emperor's library at Vienna, a German, or Teutonick version of this creed. **1770** (*title*) A Compendious View of the Grounds of the Teutonic Philosophy. With considerations by way of enquiry into..the writings of J. Behmen. **1925** F. SCOTT FITZGERALD *Great Gatsby* i. 3 A little later I participated in that delayed Teutonic migration known as the Great War. **1955** *Times* 5 July 14/3 The arresting self-portrait of 1914 has a teutonic assurance of manner. **1976** *Broadcast* Dec. 18/2 He was Teutonic in appearance, and wearing what appeared to be an Army type of tunic, slate grey in colour. **1983** *Financial Times* 11 Oct. 34/5 Research has shown that Hertz has a rather Teutonic, super-efficient but cold image.

b. Of or pertaining to the ancient Teutones.

1618 BOLTON *Florus' Hist.* (1636) 117 The Cimbrian, Theutonicke, and Tigurin Warre. **1727-41** [see TEUTON 1].

2. Of or pertaining to the group of languages allied to German (including Gothic, Scandinavian, Low German, and English), forming one of the great branches of the Indo-European, Indo-Germanic, or Aryan family, and to the peoples or tribes speaking these languages: now usually called *Germanic*, and sometimes *Gothic*. (See Note below.)

1727–41 CHAMBERS *Cycl.* s.v., Teutonic language, is the ancient language of Germany, which is ranked among the mother-tongues. **1768** BLACKSTONE *Comm.* III. xxiii. 350 Stiernhook ascribes the invention of the jury, which in the Teutonic language is denominated *nembda*, to Regner, king of Sweden and Denmark. **1840** CARLYLE *Heroes* i. (1872) 22 The word *Wuotan*, which is the original form of *Odin*, a word spread..over all the Teutonic Nations everywhere. **1846** MCCULLOCH *Acc. Brit. Empire* (1854) II. 79 The Normans, as well as the Saxons, were of Teutonic extraction. **1857** MAURICE *Ep. St. John* xx. 336 He raised up the Gothic or Teutonic race. **1864** BURTON *Scot Abr.* I. i. 5 The eastern and northern parts of what now is Scotland were peopled by a race of very pure Teutonic blood and tongue. **1888** SKEAT *Etymol. Dict.* p. xviii, German, properly called High-German, to distinguish it from the other Teutonic dialects, which belong to Low-German.

3. Teutonic Knights, **Teutonic Order** (of Knights): A military order of German Knights (in med.L. *Teutonicus Ordo Militaris*, F. *l'Ordre Teutonique*, Ger. *Deutsche Ritter*, in 16th c. *Teutsche Herren*), originally enrolled *c* 1191 as the Teutonic Knights of St. Mary of Jerusalem, for service in the Holy Land.

Their first seat was at Acre; after the fall of the Latin kingdom of Jerusalem, they settled at Marienburg on the Vistula, and carried on a crusade against the neighbouring heathen nations of Prussia, Livonia, etc. Their conquests made them a great sovereign power, but from the 15th c. they rapidly declined, and were abolished in 1809. The order maintains a titular existence in Austria.

[**1586** FERNE *Blaz. Gentrie* 128 The habite and robes of a Teuch-knight was a cloake or mantell of white, with a blacke crosse vpon the same.] **1617** MORYSON *Itin.* I. 34 A house of old belonging to the Teutonike order of Knights. *Ibid.* 61 Prussen of old was subiect to the order of the Teutonicke Knights. **1645** FULLER *Gd. Th. in Bad T.* (1841) 43 Martin de Golin, master of the Teutonic order, was taken prisoner by the Prussians, and delivered bound to be beheaded. **1727** BAILEY vol. II, *Teutonick Order*... The Order is now little known, tho' there is still a Great Master of it kept up. **1845** S. AUSTIN *Ranke's Hist. Ref.* I. 163 On the eastern frontier, where [in 1503] the Teutonic knights were incessantly pressed upon by the Poles and Russians. *Ibid.* II. ii. I. 373 Maximilian wished to hold him in check, on the one side by the Grand Duke of Moscow, on the other by the Teutonic Order.

4. Teutonic cross, a cross potent, being the badge of the Teutonic Order.

1882 OGILVIE (Annandale), *Teutonic Cross.*

B. *sb.* **1.** †The language of any Teutonic race, *spec.* the German language (*obs.*); subsequently by philologists applied only to the common or primitive speech, which afterwards broke up into the languages named in A. 2; now usu. known as *Germanic*.

1631 WEEVER *Anc. Fun. Mon.* 684 Although the Teutonic be more mixed with other strange languages. **1668** WILKINS *Real Char.* I. i. §3. 3 The Teutonic or German is now distinguished into Upper and Lower. **1727–41** CHAMBERS *Cycl.* s.v. *Mother tongue*, Of mother tongues, Scaliger reckons ten in Europe, viz. the Greek, Latin, Teutonic or German, Sclavonic..Irish and British. **1755** *Gentl. Mag.* XXV. 150/1 An history of our language, in which it is regularly traced from the old Gothic and Teutonic to modern English. **1864** BURTON *Scot Abr.* I. i. 14 All the way from the border to the Highland line, the people, high and low, came to speak in very pure Teutonic. **1870** HELFENSTEIN *Teutonic Gram.* 408 The perfect of the verb *haldan* must have been *ha-hald* in the primitive Teutonic.

†**2.** = TEUTON 2. *Obs.*

1638 SIR T. HERBERT *Trav.* (ed. 2) 361 Verstegan (alias Rowley) [had not] dar'd to make us all Teutonicks. **1691** WOOD *Ath. Oxon.* II. 40 His Grandfather was by nativity a Teutonic.

†**3.** *pl.* = Teutonic Knights: see A. 3. *Obs.*

1693 tr. *Emilianne's Hist. Monast. Orders* III. 280 The Knights of Rhodes..and the Teutonicks. **1796** MORSE *Amer. Geog.* II. 238 As grand Master of the Teutonics.

[*Note.* Late Roman writers reckoned the *Teutones* among the peoples of Germania, and *Teutonicus* became a common poetic equivalent for *Germānicus*. It is now however held by many that they were not a Germanic people. But, before 900, German writers in Latin began to follow Latin poetic precedent by using *Theutonica lingua* instead of the barbarian or non-classical *Thectisca*, to render the native *tiutisch*, *tiutsch* (OHG. *diutisc*, mod. *deutsch* = OS. *thiudisc*, OE. *þeodisc*, literally 'national, popular, vulgar') as a designation of their vulgar tongue in contrast to Latin, as if this German adj. were identical with the ancient ethnic name. In 1200 *lingua Teutonica* was similarly used, and thenceforth *Teutonicus* became a usual L. rendering of *Deutsch* or *German*. Some Early German comparative philologists (e.g. Bopp in 1820) used *Teutonisch* as the name for the family of languages including Gothic, German, Scandinavian, and English; but for this *Germanisch* is now more used in German, and *Germanic* by many in English. But in English there is an awkwardness and sometimes ambiguity in using *Germanic* beside *German* (in its ordinary political sense), which does not arise in German or French, where *germanisch* and *germanique* are entirely distinct from *deutsch* and *allemand*. To avoid this, many English scholars preferred 'Teutonic' as the term for the linguistic family, and it is commonly so used in this dictionary.]

C. *Comb.*, as ***Teutonic-Edwardian*** adj.

1976 J. WHEELER-BENNETT *Friends, Enemies & Sovereigns* iii. 73 It was hideous, since neither of its previous owners seemed to have had any decorative taste at all, but comfortable in a sort of Teutonic-Edwardian way.

Teutonically (tjuːˈtɒnɪkəlɪ), *adv.* [f. prec.: see -ICALLY.] In the manner of a 'Teuton' or German; in German style.

1859 J. MARTINEAU *Ess.*, etc. (1891) III. 534 The position Teutonically proved untenable to all 'thinkers of any force'. **1895** *Athenæum* 17 Aug. 232/1 Dr. Führer justly, if Teutonically, writes [etc.].

Teutonicism (tjuːˈtɒnɪsɪz(ə)m). [f. as prec. + -ISM.] Teutonic (i.e. German) character or practice; a Teutonic expression; a Teutonism.

1842 SIR C. LYELL in *Life*, etc. (1881) II. 63 The terms bakery and bookbindery seem useful Teutonicisms. **1901** *Westm. Gaz.* 2 Oct. 4/3 Italian composers essaying the more classical forms are impelled to out-Herod Herod in the seriousness and Teutonicism of their productions.

Teutonism (ˈtjuːtənɪz(ə)m). [f. TEUTON + -ISM.]

1. An idiom or mode of expression peculiar to or characteristic of the Teutonic languages, esp. of German; a Germanism.

[**1619** KEPLER *Harmonia Mundi* IV. v. in *Opera* (1864) V. 234 Idem quod vultus, facies; quod etiam noster Teutonismus habet, qui faciem solet nominare das Angesicht.] **1889** *L.E. & D. Philos. Mag.* Nov. 425 The translator has done his part of the work well, although we detect distinct Teutonisms here and there.

2. Teutonic or Germanic character, type, constitution, system, or spirit; German feeling and action (either in the wider ethnical or the restricted national or political sense).

1854 MILMAN *Lat. Chr.* III. vii. (1864) II. 101 Teutonic Europe, or Europe so deeply interpenetrated with Teutonism. **1881** *Atlantic Monthly* XLVII. 230 During most of classic antiquity the centre of Teutonism seems to have been farther east than Germany. **1900** A. LANG in *Blackw. Mag.* Apr. 545/2 He regrets the Norman Conquest as an interference with unmixed Teutonism.

Teutonist (ˈtjuːtənɪst). [f. as prec. + -IST.]

1. One versed in the history, etc., of the Teutonic race or languages; one who makes much of Teutonic influence in the history of England.

1882 *Academy* No. 511. 112 [J. R. Green's] 'Making of England'..will probably long represent the last word of the Teutonist on the nature and extent of the primitive English settlement. **1883** T. KERSLAKE in *N. & Q.* 6th Ser. VII. 301/2 A canon of the most profound English Teutonist, the late Mr. Kemble.

2. One whose writings have a Teutonic character or style.

1894 G. ALLEN in *Westm. Gaz.* 25 July 3/1 You may divide our poets..into two great schools in this matter—the Classicists and the Teutonists, if I may venture so to style them... To this latter class belong Shakespeare, Keats, Coleridge, Burns, Rossetti, and the greater part of our romantic poets.

Teu'tonity. [f. as prec. + -ITY.] The quality or condition of being Teutonic; Teutonism.

1877 *Athenæum* 1 Dec. 696/2 The German lieutenant has dropped some of his superfluous Teutonity. **1886** *Pall Mall G.* 24 July 3/2 If any one is inclined to think that the termination *tz* must imply Teutonity, let him remember that far from any German speech he will find such names as Retz, Batz, and Biarritz.

Teutonize (ˈtjuːtənaɪz), *v.* [f. TEUTON + -IZE.] *trans.* To make or render Teutonic or German.

1845 *Blackw. Mag.* LVII. 478 After Teutonising the Hebrew in this manner, he next proceeds to the Egyptian. **1867** FREEMAN *Norm. Conq.* I. iii. 126 Those Celtic lands..had been..to a great extent Teutonized. **1882** *Sat. Rev.* 17 June 768/1 Justified in treating, for all practical purposes, as Teutonic a nation so thoroughly Teutonized.

b. *intr.* To conform to Teutonism; to play the Teuton.

1882 in OGILVIE (Annandale).

Hence **'Teutonizing** *vbl. sb.*; **Teutoni'zation**, the action or process of rendering or being made Teutonic or German.

1855 MILMAN *Lat. Chr.* IV. x. (1864) II. 435 The Franks now..shared with the Romans the great hierarchical dignities... This Teutonising of the hierarchy [etc.]. **1872** D. H. HAIGH in *Archæo. Cantiana* VIII. 18 From Kent the Teutonization of Britain began. **1878** *Fraser's Mag.* XVIII. 571 His style underwent a process of Teutonisation.

'Teutonized, *ppl. a.* [f. TEUTON + -IZE + -ED[1].] Made Teutonic; Germanized.

1866 *Anthrop. Rev.* V. 131 The Teutonized Celts of Britain. **1918** *Hist. Amer. Lit.* I. 357 The Teutonized rhapsodies of Coleridge. **1924** *Blackw. Mag.* Aug. 280/2 All Germans kept their eyes firmly fixed on a Teutonised Europe.

Teutono-, combining form of TEUTON, as in **,Teutono'mania**, **'Teutono,phobe**, **,Teutono-'phobia**: see TEUTO-.

1839 DONALDSON *New Cratylus* §97 (1850) 141 The Hellenic or Teutono-Persic language of the North. **1886** *Pall Mall G.* 18 Oct. 3/2 It was in Russia that he discovered the earthly paradise of Teutonophobia. **1897** *Current Hist.* (Buffalo, N.Y.) VII. 96 [He] is said to be neither a Teutonophobe nor a Francophil. **1905** H. PAUL in *19th Cent.* Nov. 862 Ministers..will do no good by tampering with Mr. Chamberlain's exploded Teutonomania.

'tevel, 'tavel, *v. Obs.* exc. *dial.* Forms: 3–4 **tauel, teuel,** 9 *Sc.* **tevel, tevvel.** [Origin and primary meaning obscure; it is even uncertain whether there are not here two different words.

Senses 2 and 3 suggest a possible connexion with TAVE *v.* If sense 1 was orig. 'to contend (in words)', we might compare Norw. *tevla*, Sw. *täfla*, 'to contend, cope, vie, rival, strive, struggle'; but these go back to ON. *tefla* to play at tables or draughts, = OE. *tæflian*, ME. TAVEL[1], which appears to have no connexion with this.]

†**1.** *intr.* ? To talk, converse; or perh. rather, To discuss, argue, contend in words. *Obs.*

a **1225** *St. Marher.* 13 Ich leote ham talkin ant tauelin of godlec ant treowliche luuien ham, wiðuten uuel wilnung. *a* **1225** *Leg. Kath.* 822 Þet he þet is nomecuðest & measst con cume cuðe þrof..& teueli [*v.r.* tauele] wið me. *Ibid.* 1254 Swa awundret of hire wittie wordes, & swa offearet & offruht, & alle hise feren, þet nefde hare nan tunge to tauelin a tint wið [*v.r.* teuelin a dint].

†**2.** To struggle, strive, contend; to labour. *Obs.*

13.. *E.E. Allit. P.* B. 1189 Trwe tulkkes in toures teueled [*printed* teneled] wyth-inne, In bigge brutage [= brattice] of borde, bulde on þe walles. **13..** *Gaw. & Gr. Knt.* 1514 F[or] to telle of þis teuelyng of þis trwe kny3tez, Hit is þe tytelet, token, and tyxt of her werkkez.

3. *intr.* To behave in a disorderly or violent manner; to rage. *Sc.*

1828 CARLYLE *Let. to J. Carlyle* 25 Aug. in Froude *Life* (1882) II. ii. 37 Gawn up and down the country tevelling and screeching like a wild bear.

4. *trans.* (See quot.) *Sc.*

1825 JAMIESON, *Tevvel*, to confuse, to put into a disorderly state, *Dumfr.*

†**'tevell.** *Sc. Obs. rare.* [app. a. F. *tavelle* in its obs. sense 'a small edging lace, a Crowne-lace' (Cotgr. 1611): cf. TAVELL.] Lace.

1632 in *14th Rep. Hist. MSS. Comm.* App. III. 235 Ane goun of cloth of gold, laid over with tevell of gold. *Ibid.*, Ane blak dames goun, laid over with sylver tevell.

Tevet, var. TEBETH.

tevish, var. THIVISH.

tew (tjuː), *sb.*[1] *Obs.* exc. *dial.* Also 9 tue. [f. TEW *v.*[1]]

†**1.** The tawing of leather: see TEW *v.*[1] 1. *Obs.*

c **1440** *Promp. Parv.* 489/2 Tew, or tewynge of lethyr.

†**2.** The work of preparation; labour. *Obs.*

1644 *Hartlib's Legacy* (1655) 286 Each Acre shall be worth ..at least six pound, thirteen shillings, four pence for the tew onely, and at least six pound, thirteen shillings and four pence more for the seed.

3. Constant work and bustling; a state of worry or excitement. *dial.* and *U.S.*

1825 BROCKETT *N.C. Words* s.v. *Tue*, *Sare tues*, great difficulty in accomplishing any thing. **1866** E. TABOR *Rachel's Secr.* I. vii. 103 There was no end of the tew and worry in a farm-house. **1880** TENNYSON *Northern Cobbler* ix, When we coom'd into Meeätin', at fust she wur all in a tew. **1883** HOWELLS *Woman's Reason* (Tauchn.) II. 27 My wife was always in a tew about the danger.

†**tew**, *sb.*[2] *Obs.* Also 6 **tewe**, (7 **tewgh**, **tiew**, 9 *dial.* **tow**). [Not known before 15th c.: app. corresp. to WFris. *tûch*, late MDu., mod.Du. *tuig*, MLG., LG. *tüch*, MHG. *ziuc*, Ger. *zeug*, apparatus, gear, tools, utensils, implements, tackle: f. ablaut stem *tiug-* of **tiuhan* to draw, lead (TEE *v.*[1]).]

1. Fishing-tackle; nets, fishing-lines, etc.

c **1440** *Promp. Parv.* 490/1 Tew, of fyschynge, *piscalia*, in plurali, *retiaria* [MS. *reci-*]. **1529** *Will J. Thomson* (Somerset Ho.), A mansfare of all tewe except sperlyn nett. **1619** FLETCHER *M. Thomas* I. iii, *Dor.*.. The fool shall now fish for himself. *Alice.* Be sure then His tewgh be tith and strong: ..He'l catch no fish else. **1622** MALYNES *Anc. Law-Merch.* 246 Also that they shall be honest and true..being asked concerning the length and depth of their ropes or tewes when they are in driuing; neither shall they wittingly.. suffer their tewes to flit and run over one another.

fig. **1589** WARNER *Alb. Eng.* VI. xxix. (1612) 144 She [Queen Catharine 14..] pitched Tewe, he [Owen Tudor] masshed. **1602** *Ibid.* Epit. 391 This Cardinall, conspiring with William de la Poole,..pitched their Tew to intangle the same Protector. **1603** HARSNET *Pop. Impost.* 12 The groundes of their Art [were] layde sure and a little trying of their Tooles, whether their Tew would holde or no.

2. Implements, tools, materials for work generally; stuff. Also *fig.*

1616 T. SCOTT *Philomythie* C vj b, When..all your traines and tew in order laid. *a* **1638** MEDE *Wks.* (1672) 815, I am not unwilling to communicate unto you the most of my tew, because, I perceive, you make some account of them. **1671** SKINNER, *Tew*,..Instrumentum, Materia, Arma, Armamenta. **1674** N. FAIRFAX *Bulk & Selv.* 36 Another Argument..which may happily at first blush seem to have more tiew in it than all the stands we have met with hitherto. *a* **1825** FORBY *Voc. E. Anglia*, *Tow*,..necessary tools or apparatus for any purpose (pronounced like *cow*). **1904** *Eng. Dial. Dict.*, *Tew*,..Obsol. w. Cy. Materials for work.

tew, *sb.*[3] *Sc.* [Etymol. doubtful: perh. from same root as prec.] (?) The braces of a drum, or the braces and cords by which a drum is tightened.

c **1720** in Beveridge *Culross & Tulliallan* xix. (1885) II. 90 The council..allows the drummer to get als many new tews as will serve the drum.

tew (tjuː), *v.*[1] *Obs.* exc. *dial.* Forms: 4–7 **tewe**, 5 **tewhe, tewyn**, 6 **teawe**, 6–7 **teaw**, 7 **tiew, tewgh**, 8–9 **tue**, 7– **tew**. [In branch I. app. a later collateral, derivative, or altered form of TAW *v.*[1], with which it is synonymous; the form-history is obscure. Branch II. corresponds to nothing in TAW, and may be of other origin, though sense-development from branch I. is conceivable.]

I. 1. a. *trans.* To convert skin into a species of leather, by steeping, beating, and manipulation; to dress; = TAW *v.*[1] 2.

c **1330** R. BRUNNE *Chron. Wace* (Rolls) 12453 Fful manye kynges had he [the giant Ryton] don slo, & flow þe berdes of alle þo; Til a pane, as a furour, he did hem tewe. *c* **1440** *Promp. Parv.* 490/1 Tewyn lethyr, *frunio, corrodio*. **1530** PALSGR. 754/2, I tewe leather, *je souple*. **1601** HOLLAND *Pliny* (1634) II. 473 Certaine skinnes of leather well tewed and dressed vntill they be soft. **1681** CHETHAM *Angler's Vade-m.* xxxiv. §3 (1689) 186 After the skin is tewed in the skinner's lime-pits. **1709** *Brit. Apollo* II. No. 49. 4/1 Were his Hide tew'd by Tanners.

fig. **1709** *Brit. Apollo* II. No. 29. 3/2 Tew her Hide with an Oaken Plant.

b. *intr.* for *refl.* or *passive*.

c **1880** *Northants. Dial.*, Take it [the leather] out again and let it lie and tew.

2. To work (anything) into proper consistency by beating, etc.; to temper (mortar). Now *dial.*

1641 BEST *Farm. Bks.* (Surtees) 138 Then doe wee water it [the earth] and tewe it well att the first, and soe leaue it for her that serveth to temper. **1688** R. HOLME *Armoury* III. 88/2 *Tew*, to Batter or draw out a peece of Iron. **1721** BAILEY, To *Tew*..to beat Mortar. To *Tew* Hemp..to beat or dress it. **1797** P. WAKEFIELD *Ment. Improv.* (1801) III. 2 Kneading and tewing the two earths together is the most laborious part of the work. **1883** *Almondbury & Huddersf. Gloss.* s.v., That lime wants better tewing.

3. *transf.* and *fig.* a. To deal with or employ.

1489 *Churchw. Acc. Walberswick, Suffolk* (Nichols 1797) 183 Yt 1 man, or 2 men shall rec. the town doollys of heryngs and sperlings..and to tewe them to most profyte of the town.

†b. To prepare or bring into a proper state or condition for some purpose. *Obs.*

1571 GOLDING *Calvin on Ps.* xxx. 9 No man can giue himselfe cheerfully vnto prayer, till he bee thoroughly teawed and well furbished by the crosse. *a* **1577** GASCOIGNE *Flowers* (1587) 1 These chattering teeth, this trembling toong Well tewed with careful cries. *a* **1619** FLETCHER *Wit without M.* III. i, So tewed him up with Sack that he lies lashing a But of Malmsie for his Mares.

†4. a. To beat, flog, thrash, belabour. Also *fig.* = TAW *v.*[1] 3, 3 b. *Obs.*

1598 DALLINGTON *Meth. Trav.* G ij, He left them all France, tyned and tewed, as bare as a birdes bone. **1600** HOLLAND *Livy* 716 When they saw once the bodies of their Tribunes tewed with rods. **1622** FLETCHER *Begg. Bush* III. ii, Tew 'em, swinge 'em, Knock me their brains into their breeches. **1664** J. WILSON *A. Commenius* II. i, He does so tew the Pope; That man of sin, The Whore of Babylon. **1670** NARBOROUGH *Jrnl.* in *Acc. Sev. Late Voy.* I. (1694) 75 The Trees are much weather-beaten,..and the shore-sides much tewed with the surge of the Waters.

†b. To lay on (a rod, scourge). *Obs. rare.*

1583 STOCKER *Civ. Warres Lowe C.* Ep. Ded. A ij b, Whiche roddes and scourges, when he hath in his great wisedome, teawed vpon them, for their amendement, he will surely..caste into the fire.

c. *dial.* To shake up, toss about, turn over (as hay); to tumble, rumple, crease, disarrange (dress); to pull about, pull in pieces; to discuss; to vex. Also *pass.*, to be involved or mixed *up with*.

In *Eng. Dial. Dict.*, cited as in use from Northern Counties to Warw., Northamp., E. Anglia.

1890 KIPLING *Life's Handicap* (1981) 67 Happen there was a lass tewed up wi' it. **1904** S. R. CROCKETT *Strong Mac* xxxix. 323 Ye were somedeal tewed up wi' a lass, were ye no?

II. 5. *trans.* To fatigue or tire with hard work; *refl.* = 6. *dial.*

1825 BROCKETT *N.C. Words* s.v. *Tue*, He tues himself. **1893** *Carlisle Patr.* 30 June 3/3 (E.D.D.), S—— went down before K——, who was sair tewed in the operation... The two giants could not be said to have tew'd themselves much. *c* **1895** 'FLIT' *Holderness Harvest* 84 I'se been tewing mysen a'most to deead all forenoon.

6. *intr.* To work hard, to exert oneself, to toil; to bustle *about*. Now *dial.* and *U.S.*

1787 GROSE *Provinc. Gloss.*, To *Tew*,..also to work hard. **1825** BROCKETT *N.C. Words*, *Tue*, to labour long and patiently, to fatigue by repeated or continued exertion... *A tuing life*, a laborious life. *A tuing soul*, a hard working person. **1863** TROLLOPE *St. Olaves* II. 4 Little folks like you an' me has to tew about and fend for 'em both. **1894** BARING-GOULD *Queen of L.* xii, I tew from morning till night. **1909** *Daily News* 31 May 4 Our male folk, who after 'tewing' at the mill all the week are usually allowed to take their time at the Saturday tea table.

Hence **tewed** (tjuːd) *ppl. a.*; **tewing** *vbl. sb.* (also *attrib.*) and *ppl. a.*

c **1440** *Promp. Parv.* 490/1 *Tevwyd, *frunitus*. **1488** in *Ripon Ch. Acts* (Surtees) 286, i bukskyn tewyd. **1611** COTGR., *Tracassé*, hurried, tossed, tugged, tewed; spoiled, ouerworne, or misused, by much remouing. **1863** MRS. TOOGOOD *Yorks. Dial.*, *Tewed*, tired, exhausted. **1892** CARRUTH in *Kansas Univ. Mag.* I. (U.S.) (E.D.D.), I'm tewed and fretted. **1394–6** *Cartular. Abb. de Whiteby* (Surtees) 623 Item pro *tewyng xiiii pellium luporum, i.s.ix.d. *c* **1430** LYDG. *Min. Poems* (Percy Soc.) 201 Whoos tewhyng hath coost many a crowche, Hire pylche souple for to make. **1852** R. S. SURTEES *Sponge's Sp. Tour* x, Bullfrog, whom I bought him of, is very fat..and can't stand much tewing in the saddle. **1855** ROBINSON *Whitby Gloss.* s.v., 'A tewing hay time', the season wet and unfavourable for the hay,..involving much extra labour. **1882** OGILVIE (Annandale), *Tewing-beetle*, a spade-shaped instrument for tewing or beating hemp. **1902** BARING-GOULD *Nebo the Nailer* xix, She alway was a tewin' woman.

†**tew**, *v.*[2] *Obs.* Also 8 **tue**. [app. a derivative or altered form of TOW *v.*, of much later appearance; the phonology is obscure.] *trans.* To haul, tow (a ship, net, etc.); to drag, pull, tug; = TOW *v.*

1600 HOLLAND *Livy* XXV. xxx. 571 Marcellus caused a great hulke, laden with armed souldiours, to be fastened by an haling rope unto a gallie.., and so in the night by strength of oares to bee tewed and drawne up after it into Acradina. **1612** DRAYTON *Poly-olb.* xii. 197 The goodly river Lee..By which the Danes had then their full-fraught navies tew'd. **1622** *Ibid.* xxv. (1748) 367 The toiling fisher here is tewing of his net. *a* **1693** *Urquhart's Rabelais* III. Prol. 7 He..tugg'd it, tew'd it, carry'd it [a tub]. **1706** BAYNARD in Sir J. Floyer *Hot & Cold Bath.* II. 386 A Sprain..tued, hal'd and wrested by ignorant Bone-setters. **1787** GROSE *Provinc. Gloss.*, *To Tew*, to pull or tow.

Tewa ('teɪwə), *sb.* and *a.* Also †**Tegua**. [a. Tewa *téwa*.] A. *sb.* a. An Indian people of the south-western U.S.; a member of this people. b. The Tanoan language of this people. B. *adj.* Of or pertaining to the Tewa or their language.

1865 *Rep. U.S. Bureau Indian Affairs 1864* 191 The only reliable, genuine name ascertained is that of the dialect spoken by San Juan, Santa Clara, and others included in that class, which is the *Tegua*, pronounced Té-wa. **1896** *Amer. Anthropologist* IX. 345 The Pueblo tribes..embody four linguistic stocks... The Tanoan stock is..composed of five dialectical divisions—Tano, Tewa, Jemez, and Piro. **1910** F. W. HODGE *Handbk. Amer. Indians* II. 737/2 *Tewa* ('moccasins', their Keresan name). A group of Pueblo tribes belonging to the Tanoan linguistic family. *Ibid.*, In 1598 Juan de Oñate named 11 of the Tewa pueblos. **1910** *Amer. Anthropologist* XII. 503 Tewa is rich in sentence-words. **1912** *Ibid.* XIV. 472 The Tewa-speaking Indians occupy..five villages northwest of Santa Fé. **1914** W. H. RIVERS *Kinship & Social Organization* 53 The Tewa of Hano, a Pueblo tribe, call the father's sister's son *tada*. **1937** R. H. LOWIE *Hist. Ethnological Theory* ix. 135 In the same category..belongs the Tewa Indian's diary kept at Dr. Elsie Clews Parsons' suggestion. **1959** E. TUNIS *Indians* 115/1 The Hopi still occupy three high mesas in Arizona where they have six towns, plus a seventh occupied by a band of Tewa who have lived with the Hopi for two hundred years. **1980** *Smithsonian* Oct. 87 Tesuque, a smallish pueblo of some 200 souls, was considered one of the most restive of the six Tewa pueblos north and northwest of Santa Fe.

tewch, Sc. form of TOUGH.

tewel, tuel ('tjuːəl). Now only *dial.* Forms: 4 **tuelle, tuwel**, 5 **tewelle, touele, towel**, 5–7 **tewell**, 6–8 **tuell**, 7 **tuill, tiwill**, 4–8 **tuel**, 4– **tewel**. [a. OF. *tuel, tuele*, etc. (12th c. in Godef.) a tube, pipe, tuyere, mod.F. *tuyau*, = ME. TUTEL beak, Sp., Pg., Pr. *tudel* tube:—Romanic type **tūtellum*, referred to a German word repr. by MDu. *tûte*, Du. *tuit* pipe, nipple, etc., LG. *tûte, tüte* beak, snout, pipe, etc.: cf. also ON. *túta* teat-like prominence, Sw. *tut* pipe, Da. *tud* spout. As to ulterior etymology see Franck, s.v. *tuit*.]

†1. A shaft or opening for the escape of smoke, etc.; a chimney. *Obs.*

c **1384** CHAUCER *H. Fame* III. 559 Suche a smoke gan out wende..As dothe where that men melt lede Loo alle on high fro the tuelle. **1483** *Cath. Angl.* 380/2 A Tewelle of a chymnay, *epicavsterium*. **1567** FENTON *Trag. Disc.* v. (1898) I. 236 The chamber where our Cornelio was rammed up in the tewell of a chymney.

†b. *transf.* The vent or opening in a pie-crust.

c **1420** *Liber Cocorum* (1862) 38 In myddes þo lydde an tuel þou make, Set hit in þo ovyn for to bake; ȝete take hit oute, fede hit with wyne.

†c. A conduit. *Obs. rare*[−1].

1725 PEARCE *Laws & Cust. Stannaries* Introd. 13 The said Conduit, which the Tinners commonly call a *Tuell*, and may properly descend from the Latin Word *Tutela*.

2. The anus; the rectum, or lower bowel: now chiefly of animals, esp. horses. [Not in OFr.]

c **1386** CHAUCER *Sompn. T.* 440 And whan this sike man felte this frere Aboute his tuwel [*v.rr.* tuel, tewel, touele] grope there and heere. *c* **1425** tr. *Arderne's Treat. Fistula* (E.E.T.S.) 9 þe skynne atuyx þe tewel & þe fistule. **1523** FITZHERB. *Husb.* §85 Broken wynded is a yll dysease,..and appereth at his nosethryll, at his flanke, and also at his tuell. **1578** LYTE *Dodoens* II. xcvii. 281 Swellings and inflammations of the tuell or fundement. **1601** HOLLAND *Pliny* XXI. xix. 106 Violets..a peculiar vertue they have..to helpe the procidence or falling downe both of tuill and matrice. *c* **1720** W. GIBSON *Farrier's Dispens.* x. (1734) 241 Keeping the Horses tail close to his Tuel. **1895** *Gloss. E. Anglia*, *Tewel*, the vent or fundament of a horse.

3. (See quots., and TEW-IRON, TUYERE.)

1677 MOXON *Mech. Exerc.* No. 1. 2 In the back of the Forge..is fixed a thick Iron plate, and a taper Pipe in it..called a Tewel, or (as some call it) a Tewl-Iron... Into this taper Pipe or Tewel is placed the Nose or Pipe of the Bellows. **1831** J. HOLLAND *Manuf. Metal* I. 163 A stout perforated core of..iron, called the tewel or tew-iron.

tewel(l, -e, obs. forms of TOWEL.

†**tewer**. *Obs. rare*[−0]. [f. TEW *v.*[1] + -ER[1].] One who taws leather; = TAWER.

c **1440** *Promp. Parv.* 490/1 Teware, *corridiator*. **1483** *Cath. Angl.* 380/2 A Tewer of skynnes,..*coriarius*.

tewer, corrupt form of TUYERE.

Tewesday, tewet, obs. ff. TUESDAY, TEWHIT.

tewfikose ('tjuːfɪkəʊs). *Chem.* [f. the name of Mohammed Tewfik Pasha (Khedive of Egypt 1879–92) + -OSE[2].] A peculiar sugar found (1890–1) in the milk of the buffalo of the East, *Bubalus Buffelus*, taking the place of the ordinary milk sugar. It yields glucose when hydrolysed.

1891 *Daily Chron.* 18 Mar. 8/5 A sugar of a hitherto undescribed variety—'tewfikose', as it is proposed to be called in honour of the Khedive. **1902** in WEBSTER Suppl.

tewgh, tewhe: see TEW *v.*[1], TOUGH.

tewhit, tewit ('tiːhwɪt, 'tiːwɪt, 'tjuːɪt; also 'tjuːxɪt, 'tjʌxɪt, 'tjuːfɪt). Now *local*. Forms: α. 5, 8–9 **tuchet**, 6 **tuechit**, 9 **teuchit, -at, tchuchet**; β. 7 **tuewhite, tequhyt, terwhite**, 9 **tuquheit, tewhit, teewheep, -whoap**; γ. 6 **tuwyte**, 7– **tewit** (7–9 **tewet**, 7 **teewitte**); δ. 8–9 **tewfet, tufit**, 9 **tufat, teufet, teufit, teafit**. [Orig. echoic: see PEWIT. The α and β forms are Sc.; the others are cited in the *Eng. Dial. Dict.* from Scotland to Yorks. and Chesh.] The common Lapwing or Pewit, *Vanellus cristatus*.

α. *c* **1450** HOLLAND *Howlat* 834 The Tuchet gird to the Golk, and gaif him a fall. **1549** *Compl. Scotl.* vi. 39 The tuechitis cryit theuis nek, quhen the piettis clattrit. **1746** FORBES *Dominie Deposed* III. iii, 'Tis strange what makes kirk-fouks so stupid,..Far better for them hunt the touchit. **1815** G. BEATTIE *John o' Arnha* (1826) 63 The timid teuchit slouch'd its crest. **1899** J. COLVILLE *Scot. Vernacular* 12 The teuchat..wailed out in circles round the intruder.

β. **1629** *Orkney Witch Trial* in Dalyell *Darker Superstit. Scotl.* (1834) 150 *note*, Get the bones of ane tequhyt, and carry thame in your clothes. **1824** MACTAGGART *Gallovid. Encycl.* s.v. *Pirr*, Eggs, somewhat like tewhit eggs in size and colour. **1835** J. M. WILSON *Tales Borders* I. 185/2 He was just in the situation o' a tewhit that had lost its mate—*te-wheet! te-wheet!* it cried.

γ. **1592** *Shuttleworths' Acc.* (Chetham Soc.) 76 Towe tuwytes and a snype, iij[d]. **1678** RAY *Willughby's Ornith.* 307 In the North of England they call it the Tewit, from its cry. **1688** J. CLAYTON in *Phil. Trans.* XVII. 997 The Tewits are smaller than the English, and have no long Toppins. **1828** *Craven Gloss.*, *Tewet*, a pewit or plover.

δ. **1787** GROSE *Provinc. Gloss.*, *Tewfet*, a lapwing. North. **1788** W. MARSHALL *Yorksh.* Gloss. (E.D.S.), *Tufit*,..the peewit, or green plover. **1878** *Cumbld. Gloss.*, *Teufet*.

tew-iron ('tjuːˌaɪən). Also 6 **tewe ireon**, 7 **teu iyron**, 8 *dial.* **tuiron, tuarn**, 9 *Sc.* **tö-airn**. [Represents F. *tuyère*, through the form *tewyre*, *yre* being taken as the dial. *yre, ire*, IRON: see TUYERE.] See quots. 1825, 1888, and cf. TEWEL 3.

1570 *Wills & Inv. N.C.* (Surtees) I. 329, I do gyue vnto John Dycheborne a pair of bellowis w[th]a tewe Ireon. *c* **1670** in Beveridge *Culross & Tulliallan* xxi. (1885) II. 166 To be discharged of their worke by stryking out of thair teu iyron, and thair other worklooms. *c* **1700** KENNETT (MS. Lansd. 1033, lf. 406), Four stones or walls, that next the bellows is called the Tuarn or Tuiron wall. **1825** JAMIESON, *To-airn* (*o* pron. as Gr. υ), a piece of iron, with a perforation so wide as to admit the pipe of the smith's bellows, built into the wall of his forge, to preserve the pipe from being consumed by the fire. **1840** *Civil Eng. & Arch. Jrnl.* III. 42/1, 5 inches of the end nearest the tew iron were burnt completely away. **1888** ELWORTHY *W. Som. Wordbk.*, *Tew-iron* (tùe·uy·ur), the nozzle of a smith's bellows, or of a smelting furnace... Tew-irons are regular articles of iron-mongery.

tewit, variant of TEWHIT, lapwing.

te-wit, te-whit, also 6 **teuyt, tueit**, imitations of the cry of some birds.

a **1518** SKELTON *Magnyf.* 1005 And howe styll she [hawk] dothe syt! Teuyt, teuyt! Where is my wyt? **1549** *Compl. Scotl.* vi. 39 The oxee cryit tueit. **1791** WOLCOTT (P. Pindar) *Commiss. Ep. Ld. Lonsdale* 110 Jove's bird..Turn Owl to cry Tee-whit in some old barn.

tewke, var. TUKE *Obs.*, textile fabric.

tewly ('tjuːlɪ), *a.* Now *dial.* Forms: 6–7 **tuly**, 7 **tuely**, 8 **tooly**, 7, 9– **tewly**. [Derivation uncertain: perh. from TEW *sb.*[1] or *v.*[1]; but the early spellings *tu-, too-* do not favour this.] Weak, sickly, delicate; poorly, unwell.

1538 BALE *Temptacyon* (1870) 14 Ye are but tuly, ye are no stronge persone doughtlesse. **1619** J. DYKE *Caveat* (1620) 32 Timothy was surely weake, and but a sickely, tuely man. **1691** RAY *S. & E.C. Words*, *Tewly* or *tuly*, tender, sick: *tuly* stomached, weak stomached. **1787** GROSE *Provinc. Gloss.*, *Tooly*, tender, sickly. A tooly man or woman. *Hampsh.* **1898** *Longm. Mag.* Nov. 50 His head's wise enough, if his body be tewly.

tewly, var. TULY *a. Obs.* (of silk).

tewne, Tewsdaye, obs. ff. TUNE, TUESDAY.

†**tewslite** *v. Obs. nonce-wd.* [perh. intended for *to-slite*, OE. *tóslítan* to rend asunder, distract the mind of; but that vb. is not otherwise known after 1300, so that its actual survival is unlikely.]

1590 [TARLTON] *News Purgat.* (1844) 56, I have yet left one chapter of choplodgick to tewslite you withall.

'tewsome, *a. dial.* [f. TEW *v.*[1], *sb.*[1] + -SOME.] Troublesome; restless, unquiet.

1828 *Craven Gloss.*, *Teughsome*, unquiet, restless. 'For seur, this is lile teughsome barn'. **1881** *Cornhill Mag.* Oct. 392 A mother likes most the child that's most tewsome.

TEWT (tju:t). *Army slang.* Also Tewt, etc. An acronym formed on the initial letters of *t*actical *e*xercise *w*ithout *t*roops, an exercise used in the training of junior officers.

1942 PARTRIDGE *Dict. Abbrev.* 95/2 *T.E.W.T.*, slangily, a *tewt* or *tute*. A tactical exercise without troops. **1948** PARTRIDGE *Dict. Forces' Slang* 191 *Tewt*,..on which junior officers learnt how to be generals. Invaluable according to some authorities (those who set the Tewts), a complete waste of time according to others (those who carried them out). **1952** E. WAUGH *Men at Arms* II. iii. 194 Leonard improvised 'No more TEWTS and no more drill, No night ops to cause a chill.' **1956** J. MASTERS *Bugles & Tiger* viii. 117 Above all, individual training was the time for TEWTs. **1980** *Globe & Laurel* July/Aug. 206/1 Two TEWTs were laid on for the officers and NCOs.

†**tewtaw**, *sb. Obs.* Also 8 **tewtow**, 9 *dial.* **tewter**. [Goes with next.

If the sb. was the earlier, its derivation would prob. be from TEW *v.*[1] + TAW *sb.*[1], or TOW *sb.* = 'that which tews taw or tow'; but if the vb. was the earlier, TAW would naturally be the vb., and *tew* either TEW *sb.*[1] or some other word. The origin of the second element was app. lost before the word became *tewter*. Johnson knew only the vb. which he considered a reduplicated form of *tew*.]

An implement for breaking hemp or flax.

1649 BLITHE *Eng. Improv. Impr.* (1653) 262–3 As to the working of it, you must provide your Brakes and Tewtawes both,..the brake which bruises and toughens the harl, and the Tewtaw that cuts and divides out the coare. **1727** BAILEY vol. II, *A Tew-tow*, a Tool to break or beat Flax with. **1847–78** HALLIWELL, *Tewter*, an instrument for breaking flax, as a brake for hemp. *Chesh.* **1879** MISS JACKSON *Shropsh. Word-bk.*, *Tewter*.

†**tewtaw**, *v. Obs.* Also 9 *dial.* **tewter**. [Goes with prec., q.v.] *trans.* To beat or dress (hemp or flax); = TAW *v.*[1] Hence **tewtawing** *vbl. sb.*

1601 HOLLAND *Pliny* (1634) II. 2 Before it can be occupied, it must be watered, dried, braked, tew-tawed, and with much labor..reduced..to be as soft and tender as wooll. **1669** WORLIDGE *Syst. Agric.* (1681) 333 To *Tew-taw Hemp*. **1707** MORTIMER *Husb.* (1721) I. 155 The Method and Way of Watering, Pilling, Braking, Tew-tawing, &c. of Hemp and Flax. **1755** JOHNSON, *Te'wtaw* (formed from *tew* by reduplication), to beat, to break. **1879** MISS JACKSON *Shropsh. Word-bk.*, *Tewter*, to beat and break the hemp-stalk after it had been subjected to the action of fire.

tewyre, corrupt f. TUYERE: cf. TEW-IRON.

Tex (tɛks), *sb.*[1] *U.S. colloq.* [Abbrev. of TEXAN *a.* and *sb.*] (A nickname for) a Texan.

1909 *Cent. Dict.* Suppl., *Tex*, an abbreviation (a) of Texas; (b) of Texan. **1943** R. VANCE *They made me Leatherneck* vii. 29 Call the aborigines 'Tex' and they seem to think that at least you acknowledge Texas to be in the Union and its name well circulated. **1979** P. THEROUX *Old Patagonian Express* x. 140, I could tell you were interested in poetry, Tex. *Ibid.*, That Tex is a real fun guy.

tex (tɛks), *sb.*[2] [Abbrev. of TEXTILE *a.* and *sb.*] A unit of weight used to estimate the fineness of fibres and yarns.

1953 *Textile Research Jrnl.* XXIII. 947/1 The Textile Institute recommends the tex and the British Rayon and Synthetic Fibers Federation prefers the grex. **1956** *Rev. Textile Progress* VIII. 258 A universal system for yarn count in all fibres has been adopted... The system, based on units of grammes per kilometre, is applicable to all types of yarn and is known as the Tex System. **1963** A. J. HALL *Textile Sci.* iii. 135 This is known as the Tex system and by this the count of a yarn or any other length of fibres in bundle form ..is the number of grams which 1,000 metres of the yarn weigh. **1973** *Materials & Technol.* VI. 263 Silk is a relatively strong fibre, having a tenacity which lies between 3·5 and 4·5 g/denier (31·5 and 40·5 g/tex).

†**texalte** = *to exalt*: see T'[1] and EXALT.

c **1450** *Story Alexander* in *Wars Alexander* 281 God hath sent me..for texalte and magnifye hys lawe.

Texan ('tɛksən), *a.* and *sb.* [f. next + -AN.]

A. *adj.* Of or pertaining to the State of Texas. In some specific names of animals, plants, etc.: e.g.

Texan armadillo, the PEBA; **Texan fever** = *Texas fever*; **Texan hare**, the American JACK-RABBIT; **Texan pride**, *Phlox Drummondii*, a bright-flowered annual, native in Texas; **Texan shrew-mole**, *Scalops latimanus*.

1832 W. B. DEWEES *Lett. from Early Settler Texas* (1852) 142 On arriving at that place the Texan troops put to flight seven hundred Mexicans. **1860** BARTLETT *Dict. Amer.* 218 Jackass Rabbit..known also as Mule Rabbit, Texan Hare, and Black-tailed Hare. **1888** *Cassell's Encycl. Dict.*, Texan shrew-mole.

B. *sb.* A person or animal native to or inhabiting Texas.

1837 H. MARTINEAU *Society in America* II. II. i. 81 If the government wished all possible success to the Texans, it could hardly do better than be quiet. **1868** *Trans. Illinois Agric. Soc.* (1870) VII. 138 We also put five cows and a buffalo with some Texans about the 20th of June. **1940** W. FAULKNER *Hamlet* IV. i. 246 The Texan..managed to saw the mules about and so lock the wheels. **1974** 'R. B. DOMINIC' *Epitaph for Lobbyist* ii. 14 He combined formidable intelligence with a Texan's charm.

Texas ('tɛksəs). The name of one of the United States, formerly a province of Mexico, then for a short time an independent republic.

1. Also **texas**. **a.** *Western U.S.* The uppermost structure of a river-steamer, containing the officers' quarters. Also *attrib.*

1853 *Pen & Pencil* I. 789/2 The roof of the cabin which offered a splendid promenade, and the spectacle of a second edifice of state-rooms, surrounded by a broad promenade and curiously denominated 'Texas'. **1857** F. L. OLMSTED *Journey Texas* 27 To this Texas, inveterate card-players retire on Sundays. **1872** DE VERE *Americanisms* 128 The cabins below this [the upper deck] and above the grand saloon, where the officers of the boat are accommodated, also belong to *Texas*. **1875** 'MARK TWAIN' in *Atlantic Monthly* Feb. 220/2 A tidy, white-aproned, black 'texas-tender', to bring up tarts and ices and coffee. **1883** —— *Life on Mississippi* iv. 43 The boiler deck, the hurricane deck, and the texas deck are fenced and ornamented with clean white railings. **1889** FARMER *Dict. Amer.*, *Texas tender*, the waiter on the Texas or upper deck of a Mississippi steamer. **1901** W. CHURCHILL *Crisis* xxi, He escorted the ladies to quarters in the texas.

b. 'The elevated gallery, resembling a louver or clearstory, in a grain-elevator'.

1909 in *Cent. Dict. Suppl.*

2. In names of native Texan plants, animals, etc.:

as *Texas bead-tree, blue-grass, flax, grackle, millet, snakeroot*, etc. **Texas fever**, a North American form of bovine piroplasmosis (red-water) first identified in Texas, indicated by a high fever, reddish urine, and an enlarged spleen, and caused by a protozoan parasite, *Babesia bigemina*, which is transmitted by the cattle tick; **Texas leaguer** *Baseball* (now *rare*), a fly ball that falls to the ground between the infield and the outfield and results in a base hit; **Texas longhorn**, a bull or cow belonging to a breed once common in Texas, distinguished by long horns and able to thrive in dry regions; also *transf.* (see quot. 1908); **Texas Ranger** [RANGER *sb.*[1] 3 a], a member of the state constabulary of Texas (formerly, of certain locally mustered regiments in the federal service during the Mexican War); **Texas Tower** [so called from its resemblance to a Texas oil rig], one of a chain of radar towers built along the eastern coast of the U.S.

1866 *2nd Ann. Rep. Missouri State Board of Agric.* (1867) 16 Another pest..is the *'Texas fever',..or 'Texas murrain', as it is variously known. **1902** *Westm. Gaz.* 2 June 10/2 It is officially announced that the cattle disease prevailing in Rhodesia is Texas fever which is spread by ticks. **1905** *Sporting Life* (Philad.) 7 Oct. 9/4 A bit of bad coaching euchered him out of one single the other day, when a *Texas Leaguer from his bat had to be chalked down a force out instead of a hit. **1935** J. T. FARRELL *Judgement Day* viii. 185 A dumpy texas-leaguer over third base placed runners on first and second. **1977** *Verbatim* May 5/2 We are no longer besieged with such terms as 'hot corner', 'keystone', 'Texas Leaguer', 'flyhawk', 'maskman', and 'grasscutter'. **1908** *Pacific Monthly* July 19/1 Pink got here about the same time but he come of old *Texas-longhorn stock. *a* **1918** G. STUART *Forty Years on Frontier* (1925) II. 178 None of our cattle were Texas longhorns. **1946** *Nat. Geogr. Mag.* Jan. 17/1 Cattle then were the rangy Texas longhorns—more head, horns, and tail than thick, juicy steaks. **1972** K. BONFIGLIOLI *Don't point that Thing at Me* xiii. 101 The bleached skeleton of a Texas Longhorn..beside a faint track. **1858** SIMMONDS *Dict. Trade*, **Texas Millet*, the *Sorghum cernuum*, a prolific bread-corn cultivated in the tropics. **1846** *Whig Almanac 1847* 19/1 Capt. Samuel Walker, at the head of a small company of *Texas Rangers, left Point Isabel. **1911** *Everybody's Mag.* Sept. 354/1 Two Texas rangers faced Antonio Carrasco and his seventeen thieves sometime in December of 1910. **1943** B. HOUSE *I give you Texas* 31 A city was threatened by mob violence, so a telegram was sent to the governor to rush a force of Texas Rangers to the scene. **1980** E. BEHR *Getting Even* x. 114 The Chairman was wearing a Texas Ranger hat the American President had given him. **1954** *Tuscaloosa* (Alabama) *News* 13 Aug. 3 (*caption*) Here is a closeup of a section of one of the '*Texas Towers'..being built offshore along the Atlantic coast. Towers, named for oil rigs in the Gulf of Mexico, will be built along the continental shelf. **1971** S. E. MORISON *European Discovery Amer.: Northern Voy.* xix. 653 The Gulf Stream flows within twelve miles of Cape Hatteras, and the counter-currents, strong winds, and shifting sands are a menace to navigation even today. A Texas Tower was established off Diamond Shoals, the most dangerous, in 1966.

3. Used in various depreciatory collocations.

1905, etc. [see *Texas Leaguer*, sense 2 above]. **1942** BERREY & VAN DEN BARK *Amer. Thes. Slang* §926/1 Texas butter, a gravy made with flour and water in meat grease. **1944** R. F. ADAMS *Western Words* 164/2 *Texas cakewalk*, a hanging. *Ibid.*, *Texas gate*, a makeshift gate made of barbed wire fastened to a pole. **1962** *Amer. Speech* XXXVII. 266 *Arizona stop*; *Texas stop*, *n.* Slowing down, but not making a full stop at a stop sign. **1968–70** *Current Slang* (Univ. S. Dakota) III–IV. 125 *Texas strawberries*, *n.* Red beans.—New Mexico State. **1969** *Britannica Bk. of Year* (U.S) 801/1 *Texas toast*, a thick slice of bread warmed and covered with butter. **1975** D. BAGLEY *Snow Tiger* xi. 97 A Texas nightingale isn't a bird... It's a donkey. This is a similar New Zealand joke. **1976** BOOT & THOMAS *Jamaica* 76/2 It certainly had more flair than old LBJ taking a table of journalists and staffers into the men's room, there to reduce them to awe and wonderment at the size of his whopping great Texas trouser snake. **1979** G. SWARTHOUT *Skeletons* 172 They call it a 'Texas horserace'. Blaise and his deputies sneaked the Mexicans..to the edge of town and told them to hot-foot it for the line. They'd give them an hour's head start. Then they'd come after them, mounted... If Blaise and his boys caught up with them on this side, it was their bad luck... The Mexs didn't make it.

†**'texed**, *ppl. a. Obs. rare*⁻¹. [f. L. *tex-ĕre* to weave + -ED[1]; or perh. for *text*, ad. L. *text-us*, pa. pple. of *tex-ĕre*.] Woven.

1572 BOSSEWELL *Armorie* II. 105 Mounted on the nest texed with the slipps of the vine.

Texel ('tɛksəl). The name of an island in the West Frisian group off the northern coast of the Netherlands, used *absol.* or *attrib.* to designate a hardy, hornless sheep belonging to a breed originally developed there; also, the breed itself.

1949 A. FRASER *Sheep Husbandry* ii. 118 Milch breeds—East Friesian Milch sheep and their strains, the Texel and the West Friesian. **1957** *Encycl. Brit.* XX. 475/2 The Texel is a medium-wool, white-face, hornless sheep of the Netherlands, well adapted to range conditions and very prolific. **1978** *Times* 2 Sept. 2/4 (*caption*) Record prices were paid..at the first sale in Britain of the British Texel Sheep Society.

Texian ('tɛksɪən), *a.* and *sb.* Now *rare.* [f. TEX(AS + -IAN.] = TEXAN *a.* and *sb.* (See also quot. 1943.)

1835 *Franklin Repository* (Chambersburg, Pennsylvania) 8 Dec. 1/6 Volunteers are moving from almost every section of the west to the assistance of the Texians. **1836** D. B. EDWARD *Hist. Texas* 45 The Texian farmer of the Gulf coast. *Ibid.* 74 [It] adds to the variety of a Texian landscape. **1943** *Sat. Even. Post* 11 Sept. 61 Texians are the old rock; Texans, a term which came into use only after the Civil War, are those out of the old rock; the people who live in Texas are those who are wearing the old rock away. **1955** W. FOSTER-HARRIS *Look of Old West* v. 125 The value of the Texian dollar was then descending rapidly and reached an ultimate low of around 2 cents. **1973** R. SYMONS *Where Wagon Led* I. vii. 114 All cow people like the Hesters and other Texas folk (or as they said, 'Texians').

Texican ('tɛksɪkən). [Blend of TEXAN *a.* and *sb.* and MEXICAN *a.* and *sb.*] = TEXAN *sb.* (sometimes used more narrowly).

1863 *Lawrence* (Kansas) *Republican* 16 Apr. 2/4 (*heading*) 'Texicans' and 'Injuns' again. **1937** D. COOLIDGE *Texas Cowboys* x. 149 That's one thing you'll never find around a Mormon town..you'll never find no Texicans. **1969** in *Current Trends in Linguistics* (1972) X. 596 *Texican*, a Texan of Mexican background. (Wis.). **1978** *Maledicta* II. 172 While Texas remained a part of Mexico, Anglo settlers there called themselves *Texicans* to distinguish themselves from Spanish-speaking Mexicans.

†**texile** = *to exile*: see T'[1] and EXILE *v.*

c **1430** LYDG. *Min. Poems* (Percy Soc.) 14 From [us] texile alle maner hevinesse.

Tex-Mex ('tɛksmɛks), *a.* and *sb.* [f. TEX(AN *a.* and *sb.* + MEX(ICAN *a.* and *sb.*: cf. TEX *sb.*[1] and MEX *a.* and *sb.*] **A.** *adj.* Designating the Texan variety of something Mexican; also *occas.*, of or pertaining to both Texas and Mexico.

1949 *Time* 14 Feb. 38/1 Fluent in Texmex Spanish, he had been one of the most promising rodeo riders around Tucson, Ariz... The half English, half Spanish patois of the U.S.-Mexican border region. **1973** *News* (Mexico City) (*Vistas Suppl.*) 22 July 7 It is a mistake to come to Mexico and not try the local cuisine. It is not the Tex-Mex cooking that one is used to getting in the United States. **1976** M. MACHLIN *Pipeline* xx. 246 The voice of Miss Martinez, one of Wilbur's gestures toward Tex-Mex integration, came softly over the intercom. **1977** *Time Out* 28 Jan.–3 Feb. 8/2 Cooder's current concern is the music of Southern Texas, the 'Tex-Mex' style.

B. *sb.* The Texan variety of Mexican Spanish.

1955 W. FOSTER-HARRIS *Look of Old West* vii. 211 Northern cowboys had their chance to mess up Spanish even more than had the Texas cowhands, with their Tex-Mex, which, incidentally, is a language in itself. **1969** J. MANDER *Static Society* i. 32 A hybrid, like the 'Tex-Mex' spoken in the south-west of the United States. **1981** *Verbatim* Spring 24/1 The only foreign language she knows is Tex-Mex.

text (tɛkst), *sb.*[1] Also 4 **tixte**, **tyxt(e**, 4–5 **tixt**, 4–6 **texte**, (4, 7 (9 *dial.*) **tex**, 6 **texe**, 7 **texed**). [a. F. *texte*, also ONF. *tixte*, *tiste* (12th c. in Godef.), the Scriptures, etc., ad. med.L. *textus* the Gospel, written character (Du Cange), L. *textus* (*u*-stem) style, tissue of a literary work (Quintilian), lit. that which is woven, web, texture, f. *text-*, ppl. stem of *tex-ĕre* to weave.]

1. a. The wording of anything written or printed; the structure formed by the words in their order; the very words, phrases, and sentences as written.

13.. *E.E. Allit. P.* B. 1634 Fyrst telle me þe tyxte of þe tede lettres. **13..** *Gaw. & Gr. Knt.* 1515 For to telle of þis teuelyng of þis trwe knyȝtez, Hit is the tytelet, token, & tyxt of her werkkez. *c* **1500** *Melusine* xii. 45 They delyuered to Raymondyn the ground that was gyuen to hym after the texte or tenour of hys lettres. **1560** DAUS tr. *Sleidane's Comm.* 65 b, For those wordes.., this is my body, Luther vnderstode barely and symply after the texte of the letter. **1678** CUDWORTH *Intell. Syst.* I. iv. 240 The most of Plato's Followers..offering all kind of violence to his Text. **1720** SWIFT *To Stella* 138 Say, Stella, when you copy next, Will you keep strictly to the text? **1888** BRYCE *Amer. Commw.* II. liii. 326 Without venturing to propose alterations in the text of the Constitution.

†**b.** Applied vaguely to an original or authority whose words are quoted. *Obs.*

a **1400–50** *Alexander* 214 It be-tid on a tyme þe text me recordis, Þat þe mode kynge..farne out of toune. *c* **1400** *Destr. Troy* 4007 But truly I telle as þe text sais.

c. *fig.* or in allusive use.

c **1440** *York Myst.* xxv. 535 Hayll! texte of trewthe þe trew to taste. Hayll! kyng & sire. **1589** WARNER *Alb. Eng.* VI. xxxi. 136 Ply Sir..your busie trade, you are besides the Tex. *a* **1635** NAUNTON *Fragm. Reg.* (Arb.) 23 It is not without the text, to give a short touch on the helps, and advantages of her reign.

d. The wording adopted by an editor as (in his opinion) most nearly representing the author's original work; a book or edition containing this; also, with qualification, any form in which a writing exists or is current, as a ***good, bad, corrupt, critical, received text.***

1841 MYERS *Cath. Th.* III. §8. 26 Our present Received Text has been a growth—improved from many and various sources. **1845** GRAVES *Rom. Law* in *Encycl. Metrop.* II. 770/1 Hänel, the latest editor, has not inserted these seven constitutions in his text. **1870** FREEMAN *Norm. Conq.* (1877) II. App. 658 The text seems very corrupt. **1875** SCRIVENER *Lect. Text N. Test.* 7 The vast importance of preserving a pure text of the sacred writers. **1891** *Athenæum* 15 Aug. 219/1 No attempt has been made to settle the text.

2. *esp.* The very words and sentences as originally written: **a.** in the original language, as opposed to a translation or rendering; **b.** in the original form and order, as distinguished from a commentary, marginal or other, or from annotations. Hence, in later use, the body of any treatise, the authoritative or formal part as distinguished from notes, appendices, introduction, and other explanatory or supplementary matter.

1377 LANGL. *P. Pl.* B. XVII. 12 *Dilige deum & proximum tuum, &c.* þis was þe tixte trewly..; þe glose was gloriously writen. *c* **1385** CHAUCER *L.G.W.* Prol. (MS. Gg) 86 The nakede tixt in englis to declare. **1388** WYCLIF *Prol.* xv. 57 This symple creature hadde myche trauaile,..to studie it [Latin Bible] of the newe, the text with the glose. *a* **1430** *26 Pol. Poems* xx. 1 The tixt of holy writ,..Hit sleeþ, but glose be among. **1532** MORE *Confut. Tindale* Wks. 406/1 Nowe cummeth Tyndale and..sheweth that the latine texte and the Greke may bee hys excuse and defence. **1576** FLEMING *Panopl. Epist.* 179 *margin,* τῷ λογῷ sayth the Greeke text: *Quidnam oratione,* saith the Latine interpretation. **1700** DRYDEN *Cymon & Iphig.* 18 When his broad Comment makes the Text too plain. **1749** FIELDING *Tom Jones* III. iii, Coke upon Littleton, where the comment is of equal authority with the text. **1804** WELLINGTON in Gurw. *Desp.* (1837) III. 25 As these accompaniments, or possibly the text are seldom read. **1859** TENNYSON *Vivien* 679 And none can read the text, not even I; And none can read the comment but myself. **1875** JOWETT *Plato* (ed. 2) IV. 256 There still remains an ambiguity both in the text and in the explanation. **1908** *Athenæum* 8 Aug. 147/3 All his references are to Arabic texts.

c. That portion of the contents of a manuscript or printed book, or of a page, which constitutes the original matter, as distinct from the notes or other critical appendages. In first quot. *fig.*

c **1369** CHAUCER *Dethe Blaunche* 333 And alle the wallys with colouris fyne Were peynted, bothe text and glose. **1597** MORLEY *Introd. Mus.* Annot., I haue..thought it best to set downe in Annotations, such thinges as in the text could not so commodiouslie be handled. **1778** WARTON *Hist. Eng. Poetry* (1840) II. xxiii. 304 *note,* It is not immediately formed from the Troye-boke of Lydgate, as I have suggested in the text. **1848** MILL *Pol. Econ.* I. v. §8 (1876) 48 *note,* Consequently, as shewn in the text, her labourers suffered. **1859** TENNYSON *Vivien* 669 Every marge enclosing in the midst A square of text that looks a little blot.

†**3. a.** *spec.* The very words and sentences of Holy Scripture; hence, the Scriptures themselves; also, any single book of the Scriptures. *Obs.*

13.. *E.E. Allit. P.* C. 37 For in þe tyxte, þere þyse two [Poverty and Patience] arn in teme layde. **1393** LANGL. *P. Pl.* C. III. 129 Ich theologie þe tixt knowe. *c* **1420** ? LYDG. *Assembly of Gods* 1500 Fast by Doctryne, on that oon syde, As I remembre, sate Holy Texte. **1542–3** *Act 34 & 35 Hen. VIII,* c. 1 §10 It shalbe lawfull to everye noble man..to reade..any texte of the Byble..so the same be doone quietlie. **1597** SHAKS. *2 Hen. IV,* IV. ii. 7 To heare with reuerence Your exposition on the holy Text. *a* **1668** DAVENANT *Poems* (1672) 329 Since Holy Text bids Faith to comprehend.

b. A copy of the Scriptures, or of a book of the Scriptures; *spec.* a volume containing the Gospels. *Obs.* exc. *Hist.* (See also TEXTUS.)

1387 TREVISA *Higden* (Rolls) I. 371 Iesus Crist apperede to Patrik, and took hym a staf, and þe text of þe gospel þat beeþ in þe contray in þe erchebisshops ward. *c* **1450** *St. Cuthbert* (Surtees) 4431 He bare a boke..Of gospelles..with perle and stanes preciouse þat text richely semed arayde. *Ibid.* 6800 þe text of wangels fell in þe water. *c* **1460** *Oseney Regr.* 174 Vppon the texte whee sware, both I and my wiffe. **1536** in *Antiq. Sarisb.* (1771) 201 Textus Evangeliorum. A Text after John, gilt with gold and having precious Stones and the relicks of dyvers saints. **1849** ROCK *Ch. Fathers* I. iii. 297 The curious reader has only to look at that fine text, or book of the Gospels, bound in silver parcel-gilt, and jewelled. **1883** W. H. RICH-JONES *Reg. St. Osmund* I. 117 *note,* The 'Text', also called 'Evangelarium', was a complete copy of the four gospels.

4. a. A short passage from the Scriptures, esp. one quoted as authoritative, or illustrative of a point of belief or doctrine, as a motto, to point a moral, or esp. as the subject of an exposition or sermon.

In early practice these texts or portions of the holy text were cited in Latin from the Vulgate, connecting this use with 2.

1377 LANGL. *P. Pl.* B. III. 339 *Quod bonum est tenete,* treuthe þat texte made! *Ibid.* XIII. 125 Pieres þe ploughman ..no tixte ne taketh to meyntene his cause, But *dilige deum* and *domine, quis habitabit,* &c. **1528** TINDALE *Wicked Mammon* 45 b, This texte is playner than that it neadeth to be expounded. **1579** FULKE *Heskins' Parl.* 527 The Sixtieth Chapter treateth vpon this text of S. Paule to the Hebrues: We haue an altar, &c. **1657** HEYLIN *Hist. Ref.* (1661) I. II. iv. 38 The Art of opening, or rather of undoing a Text of Scripture (as the phrase is now) was usurped by all. **1711** ADDISON *Spect.* No. 46 ¶6 A meer Sermon Popgun, repeating and discharging Texts, Proofs, and Applications. **1782** PRIESTLEY *Corrupt. Chr.* II. VIII. 125 The preacher.. named and opened his text. **1894** J. T. FOWLER *Adamnan* Pref. 10 A discourse for St. Columba's day on the text *Exi de terra tua.*

b. A short passage from some book or writer considered as authoritative; a received maxim or axiom; a proverb; an adage; in later use, esp. one used as a copy-book heading. Now *rare.*

c **1386** CHAUCER *Prol.* 177 He yaf nat of that text [*v. rr.* tixt, texte] a pulled hen That seith that hunters beth nat hooly men. —— *Manciple's T.* 132 [see TEXTUAL 1]. **1588** SHAKS. *L.L.L.* IV. ii. 168 Societie (saith the text) is the happinesse of life. **1592** —— *Rom. & Jul.* IV. i. 22 What must be shall be. *Fri.* That's a certaine text. **1862** *Sat. Rev.* 8 Feb. 156 'Recreation is good for mind and body', as the worn-out governess writes for a text at the top of her pupil's copy-book.

c. *fig.* The theme or subject on which any one speaks; the starting-point of a discussion; a statement on which any one dilates.

1605 SHAKS. *Lear* IV. ii. 37 No more; the text is foolish. **1706** E. WARD *Wooden World Diss.* (1708) 18 The grand Text they hold forth upon is the Behaviour of their Lieutenants. **1821** SCOTT *Kenilw.* xi, Is it fit for a heretic horse-boy like thee, to handle such a text as the Catholic clergy? **1847** TENNYSON *Princess* Prol. 108 Then the Maiden Aunt Took this fair day for text, and from it preach'd An universal culture for the crowd. **1870** J. BALDWIN BROWN *Eccl. Truth* 249 A fact is a text from another book, also of God's writing.

5. Short for TEXT-HAND. Also *attrib.* See also CHURCH-TEXT, GERMAN *text.* ***chapel-text,*** an elaborated kind of church-text.

1588 SHAKS. *L.L.L.* V. ii. 42 Faire as a text B. in a Coppie booke. **1610** GUILLIM *Heraldry* IV. v. (1611) 199 He beareth Gules, three Text Esses, or. **1633** FORD *Love's Sacr.* V. i, There shall be writ in text, Thy bastarding the issues of a prince. **1740** DYCHE & PARDON, *Text,*..sometimes..means a large sort of writing. **1825** J. WILSON *Noct. Ambr.* Wks. 1855 I. 10 Their names are baith down in round text in the deevils doomsday beuk. **1904** *Daily Chron.* 23 June 4/6 Burns wrote a fine, bold hand..as big as Cromwell's or Bismarck's—what is called in Scotland 'half-text'.

6. The words of a song; = TESTO.

1891 in *Cent. Dict.*

7. *attrib.* (see also sense 5) and *Comb.*, as ***text-bill, -copy, -critic, -critical*** adj., ***-criticism, editing*** vbl. sb., ***-figure, -frequency, -monger, -mongering*** vbl. sb. and ppl. adj., ***-motto, -processing*** ppl. adj. and vbl. sb., ***processor, -quoter, -quoting*** ppl. adj., ***-source, tape, -transmission, -verse;*** **text-blindness,** word-blindness; **text-cut, -engraving, -picture,** an illustration occupying a space in the text of a book; **'text-di,vider,** a preacher who didactically 'splits up' his text; so **'text-di,viding; text editor,** a machine that permits the user to alter text using a keyboard; also, a program or component for modifying text held in a computer or processor, in accordance with a user's instructions; **text-ink,** ink used for the text of a manuscript or book; **text linguistics** [G. *textliniguistik*] (see quot. 1977); hence **text linguist; text paper,** a newspaper containing serious articles; **text-title,** a half-title, at the beginning of the text of a book. See also TEXT-BOOK, -HAND, -LETTER, etc.

1610 *Histrio-m.* v. 62 *Capt.* Sirrah, what set you up there? *Bel.* *Text-bills for plays. **1909** *Cent. Dict. Suppl.* *Text-blindness. **1775** ASH, **Textcopy,*..a copy in text hand. **1870** MAGNUSSON tr. *Asgrimsson's Lilja* Introd. 27 Of no aid to the *text-critic of the present edition. **1905** *Expositor* July 22 [The Syriac N.T.] is quite invaluable from a *text-critical point of view. **1908** *Q. Rev.* July 70 Some centuries later *text-criticism arose. **1897** *Westm. Gaz.* 8 Mar. 2/1 The first number..contains two excellent plates and numerous *text-cuts. **1670** EACHARD *Cont. Clergy* 53 Not by every bungler and ordinary *text-divider. *Ibid.* 113 They have got..such a peculiar method of *text-dividing. **1972** H. S. STONE *Introd. Computer Organization & Structures* ix. 208 Another important application of the linked list is *text editing. **1975** *Business Week* 30 June 80 Vydec Corp...soon will add communications to its display *text editor. Xerox Corp. will announce the same capability for its automatic typewriter. **1983** I. FLORES *Word Processing Handbk.* vi. 170 If the last word entered does not fit on this line, then the text editor removes that word from the line and puts it at the left of the next line. **1983** *Your Computer* Sept. 21/1 The M100 runs a full Microsoft BASIC interpreter, appointment scheduler, address filer, text editor and communications utility. **1894** *Daily News* 15 Nov. 6/2 Mr. Sheppard supplies a *text engraving of mad Margaret Nicholson. **1938** *British Birds* XXXI. 359 The book is illustrated..by good, if rather infrequent *text figures and a coloured plate. **1963** T. G. E. POWELL in Foster & Alcock *Culture & Environment* vi. 169 My thanks are also due to Miss Frances Lynch for preparing the text-figure drawings. **1942** M. Joos in *Language* XVIII. 33 The Dewey count gives us a statistical picture of **text* frequencies; the Twaddell count of *list* frequencies. **1962** P. S. RAY in F. A. Rice *Study of Role of Second Languages in Asia, Africa & Latin Amer.* (Center for Applied Linguistics) 92 'Text frequency' compares two lexical forms in their repetitions within a body of discourse. **1511** in *Rel. Ant.* I. 318 To make *texte ynke. **1977** *Language* LIII. 248 For generative *text-linguists, this means that the grammar must actually generate (all and only) possible well-formed texts of the language. **1973** W. O. HENDRICKS *Essays on Semiolinguistics & Verbal Art* ii. 53 See Fries..for a discussion of the theme-rheme distinction in *text linguistics. **1977** *Language* LIII. 247 The rapidly growing school of 'text-linguistics'... The general belief shared by these scholars is that the 'natural domain' of linguistic theory consists of discourses, or texts, rather than sentences. However,..this belief is not what distinguishes text-linguistics from other discourse-oriented..trends in linguistics. *Ibid.* 248 Text-linguistics differs from these approaches in its interpretation of the claim that texts are the natural domain of linguistics. **1883** W. S. LILLY in *Contemp. Rev.* Feb. 228 He is speaking of *textmongers. **1884** —— *Anc. Relig. & Mod. Th.* 285 St. Augustine..is speaking of *textmongering. **1880** WARREN *Book-plates* xi. 122 The *text-motto occurring on Pickheimer's book-plate. **1961** *Guardian* 30 Jan. 18/2 All possible steps will be taken to make the future of the 'Daily Herald' as a *text paper more secure. **1977** *Times* 5 Sept. 12/6 Tabloid papers sell better than serious text papers. **1905** *Daily Chron.* 7 July 3/3 It has nearly twenty full-page plates, and a great many *text pictures. **1968** *Jrnl. Assoc. Computing Machinery* XV. 8 (*heading*) Computer evaluation of indexing and *text processing. **1980** *Lebende Sprachen* XXV. 10/2 Other texts ..can probably be dealt with more efficiently by an extended text-processing system, than by machine translation as such. **1983** G. LEECH et al. in *Trans. Philol. Soc.* 28 We may..proceed now to consider the kinds of text-processing that can be performed, using a computer corpus as a database. **1970** *Technical Disclosure Bull.* XIII. IV. 9 A flow chart for a text collection program which operates to collect lines of text for a *text processor is described. **1980** *Daily Tel.* 23 Apr. 3 (Advt.), If you have bought or are about to buy a small computer or text processor, you need Cave Tab to ensure you make the most of it. *a* **1837** D. McNICOLL *Wks.* 94 This *text-quoting vagabond. **1947** A. EINSTEIN *Music in Romantic Era* xvi. 265 Shakespeare..was no more novel as a *text-source for Italian opera than was Sir Walter Scott..or Victor Hugo. **1978** *Early Music* Oct. 609/1 What is described as a 'text source', the 1545 *King's Primer,* is also used. **1970** A. CAMERON et al. *Computers & O.E. Concordances* 18 The first thing of course is the production of *text tapes and the printing thereof. **1881** H. BRADSHAW in *Bibliographer* Dec. 6/2 The *text-title of Tindale's New Testament of 1534–5, as reproduced by Mr. Fry. **1908** *Q. Rev.* July 74 The common accidents of *text-transmission.

text, *sb.*² *rare*⁻¹. [ad. L. *textus* tissue: see prec.] Texture, tissue.

1854 S. DOBELL *Balder* xxviii, And, if she were..caught of morning mist, or the unseen Material of an odour, her pure text Could seem no more remote from the corrupt And seething compound of our common flesh.

text, *v.* Now *rare.* [f. TEXT *sb.*¹]

†**1.** *trans.* To inscribe, write, or print in a text-hand or in capital or large letters. Also *fig. Obs.*

1599 NASHE *Lenten Stuffe* (1871) 15 A chronographical Latin table..in a fair text hand, texting unto us, how, in the sceptredom of Edward the Confessor, the sands first began to grow into sight at low water. **1599** SHAKS. *Much Ado* v. i. 185 Yea and text vnder-neath, heere dwells Benedicke the married man. **1607** DEKKER *Wh. of Babylon* Wks. 1873 II. 265 Vowes haue I writ so deepe,..So them texted them in characters capitall, I cannot race them. *c* **1616** FLETCHER & MASSINGER *Thierry & Theod.* II. i, Condemn me for A most malicious slanderer, nay, texte it Upon my forehead. **1624** HEYWOOD *Gunaik.* VII. 315 That such as..past.. might read them as perfectly and distinctly, as if they had beene texted in Capitall Letters. **1631** T. POWELL *Tom All Trades* 1 The Scriveners at Temple-barre had no imployment, but ..texting of Bills for letting of Chambers in Chancery-lane. **1639** SHIRLEY *Maid's Rev.* III. i, Would..every character [had] Been tex'd with blood!

b. *trans.* To write in a text-hand upon. **c.** *intr.* To write in text-hand.

1660 G. TOMLYN *Patent Specif.* No. 128 A new..way to text and flourish velumes and parchments in blacke and white. **1869** *Lonsdale Gloss., Text,* to write an engrossing hand or German text. **1884** [implied in TEXTER].

†**2. a.** *intr.* To cite texts. **b.** *trans.* To cite a text at or against (a person). *Obs.*

1564–78 BULLEYN *Dial. agst. Pest.* (1888) 13 *M.*..And how like you this texte? *A.* Texte how they will texte, I will trust none of them all. **1615** SIR E. HOBY *Curry-combe* i. 11 When his wench told him that he kissed like a Clowter, he could text her with *Labia Sacerdotis custodiunt sapientiam.*

textarian (tɛk'stɛərɪən), *a. nonce-wd.* [f. TEXT *sb.*¹, after *tractarian,* etc.] Dealing with or based upon an isolated text, or texts.

1867 SEEBOHM *Oxford Reformers* i. §2. 11 The scholastic divines..had fallen into a method of exposition almost exclusively textarian. *Ibid.* 15 They [Colet's lectures at Oxford 1496–7] were not textarian.

text-book ('tɛkstbʊk). [f. TEXT *sb.*¹]

†**1.** (See quot.) *Obs.*

1730 BAILEY (folio), *Text-Book* (in Universities) is a Classick Author written very wide by the Students, to give Room for an Interpretation dictated by the Master, &c. to be inserted in the Interlines.

2. A book used as a standard work for the study of a particular subject; now usually one written specially for this purpose; a manual of instruction in any science or branch of study, esp. a work recognized as an authority (cf. TEXT-WRITER 2).

1779 *Mirror* No. 38 The letters of the immortal Earl of Chesterfield, which I intend to use as my text-book on this occasion. **1795** SEWARD *Anecd.* I. 203 Lord Bacon's Essays ..have been the text-book of myriads of Essay-Writers. **1837** SIR F. PALGRAVE *Merch. & Friar* Ded. (1844) 9 Andrew Horne, the author of our ancient legal text-book, the Mirror of Justices. *a* **1855** MANSFIELD *Salts* Pref. (1865) 32 The current vocabulary of the chemical text-books. **1894** H. DRUMMOND *Ascent of Man* 10 In almost every department [of science] the text-books of ten years ago are obsolete to-day.

3. A book containing a selection of Scripture texts, arranged for daily use or easy reference.

1861 (*title*) The Scripture Text Book and Treasury. **1877** *Bagster's Catal.* 50 The Autograph Text Book; Containing a Text of Scripture, and a Verse of Poetry.. under every Day in the year.

4. A book containing the libretto of a musical play or opera.

1891 in *Cent. Dict.*

5. *attrib.* passing into *adj.* Derived from, dependent upon, or typical of a text-book (sense 2); orig. and still occas. in a derogatory sense, implying mechanical adherence to a stereotype; now freq. used in an approbatory sense of an exemplary or classic instance of something. Cf. COPY-BOOK 2 b.

1916 [see *Middle Western* adj. s.v. MIDDLE *a.* 6]. **1927** M. SADLEIR *Trollope* iv. 183 The presentation of Greshamsbury House.. is perfunctory... Trollope.. was content to parrot text-book phrases of appreciation. **1939** G. HOUSEHOLD *Rogue Male* 230 To deny.. I was uncomfortable, but to produce hypothetical justification for getting more comfort. It was a text-book illustration good enough to take in the foreigner. **1949** 'G. ORWELL' *Nineteen Eighty-Four* III. 260 It was a perfect conversion, a textbook case. **1954** W. FAULKNER *Fable* 33 An authority.. among textbook soldiers on how to keep troops fit. **1957** see REAL *a.*[2] 2 a]. **1963** *Times* 4 May 3/6 Smith tertius (Edwin, of Derbyshire) hit a swinging six into the Mound stand and followed this with two text-book fours. **1970** *Times* 13 Feb. 25/7 The.. strike ..was a textbook example of response to loss of 'our management'. **1979** N. HYND *False Flags* xix. 173 He followed an evasive path, a textbook lesson in how to move without leaving a trace.

Hence **'text-bookish** *a.*

1914 H. G. WELLS *Englishman looks at World* 84 An educational system.. has to be grown; and in the beginning it is bound to be thin, ragged, forced, crammy, text-bookish, superficial. **1951** *Sport* 27 Apr.–3 May 3/1 Newcastle can be the more brilliant, the more dazzling, the more text-bookish on their day. **1974** *Publishers Weekly* 4 Feb. 68/2 A textbookish survey of Arab history, religion and culture since the days of Mohammed.

†**'texted,** *a. Obs.* [f. TEXT *sb.*[1] and *v.* + -ED.]

1. Skilled or learned in 'texts' or authors. *rare.*

(In this sense *texted wel* (v.r. *text wel*) appears in one group of Chaucer MSS., where another has *textuel.* The latter was prob. the original reading, but the change in some MSS. perh. implies that *texted* was known.)

14.. *Chaucer's Manciple's T.* 131 (Harl. MS.) But for I am a man not texted wel [so *Corp.*; *Lansd.* texed, *Petw.* text; 3 *MSS.* textuel] I wil not telle of textes neuer a del. *Ibid.* 212 But as I sayd, I am nought tixted wel [*Corp.*, *Petw.*, *Lansd.* text; 3 *MSS.* textuel, -eel, tixt-].

2. Written in text-hand or text-letters; engrossed.

1620 DEKKER *Dreame* 1 They beg nothing, the texted pastbord talkes all; and if nothing be giuen, nothing is spoken. **1650–66** WHARTON *Poems* Wks. (1683) 340 To write Custodes in a Texted-hand. **1695** *Lond. Gaz.* No. 3125/4 Texted Indentures for Attorneys.

texter ('tɛkstə(r)). [-ER[1].] One skilled in writing in a text-hand (sense a); an engrosser.

1884 *Law Times* 29 Mar. 2/2 Wanted, a re-engagement as Engrossing and General Clerk.. excellent writer and texter.

'text-hand. A fine large hand in writing. **a.** *orig.* One of the larger and more formal hands in which the text of a book was often written, as distinct from the smaller or more cursive hand appropriate to the gloss, etc. See also quot. 1688. **b.** Now usually applied to a school-hand written in lines about half an inch wide.

1542 UDALL *Erasm. Apoph.* 224 He had taken vp.. an instrumente written in greate letters of texte-hande. **1599** [see TEXT *v.* 1]. **1688** R. HOLME *Armoury* III. 414/2 These are the form of the Letters.. used by the Germans; and are termed the Text Hand Letters. **1796** PEGGE *Anonym.* (1809) 475 It is called text-hand and text-letter because the text was ever wrote in a large hand and the comment in a small. As text-hand is both square and round, it means little more than a large hand of each sort. **1821** SCOTT *Kenilw.* xxxi, You seem wondrous slow in reading text hand.

†**'textible,** *a. Obs. rare.* [f. L. *text-*, ppl. stem of *texĕre* to weave + -IBLE.] That may be woven; textile.

1727 in BAILEY vol. II.

textile ('tɛkstɪl, -aɪl), *a.* and *sb.* [ad. L. *textil-is* woven, *textile* (sc. *opus*) woven fabric, f. *text-*, ppl. stem of *tex-ĕre* to weave. So F. *textile.*]

A. *adj.* **1. a.** That has been or may be woven. Also, of or pertaining to a man-made fibre or filament, not necessarily woven.

1656 BLOUNT *Glossogr.*, *Textile*,.. that is weaved or wounden, embroidered. **1755** JOHNSON, *Textile*,.. woven; capable of being woven. **1852** CONYBEARE & HOWSON *St. Paul* (1862) II. xx. 240 The wine and the textile fabrics of Cos. **1868** ROGERS *Pol. Econ.* viii. (1876) 74 Cotton and wool and other textile materials.. from all quarters. **1910** MITCHELL & PRIDEAUX *Fibres used in Textile & Allied Industries* i. 8 Textile papers. (a) Spinning fibres in raw state... (b) Cotton or flax fibre previously spun. **1931** K. P. HESS *Textile Fibers & their Use* v. 232 The fourth method of dissolving cellulose and forming it into fine filaments was worked out... Textile fibres were not developed to any great extent by this method until the close of the World War. **1961** *Wall St. Jrnl.* 23 Jan. 2/3 DuPont Co. announced it will close its textile rayon operation.. by August. **1972** *Daily Tel.* 20 Nov. 11/4 One single step is.. required to convert the chemical raw material of the synthetic fibres into a finished textile cloth, no weaving or knitting being required. **1981** M. L. JOSEPH *Essentials of Textiles* ii. 9 Textile fibres.. can be manufactured from natural fibrous materials such as wood pulp (rayon) or synthesized from chemicals with no resemblance to fibrous forms (nylon, polyester).

b. *Nat. Hist.* Having markings resembling a woven surface; e.g. ***textile cone***, a species of cone-shell, *Conus textilis*, so marked; ***textile snake***.

1802 SHAW *Gen. Zool.* III. 462 Textile Snake. *Coluber Textilis*... Yellowish-grey Snake, freckled with black, and marked by numerous, undulated, transverse, bright-ferruginous stripes. **1891** *Cent. Dict.*, Textile cone.

2. Of or connected with weaving: see B. 1 b.

3. *Naturism.* Non-naturist; *spec.* applied to places, etc., prohibited to nudists. Cf. sense 3 of the sb.

1970 *Newsweek* 25 May 55/2 Its guests follow a daily routine little different from that of the 'textile tourists'—or non-nudists—in nearby hotels. **1979** P. VALLACK *Free Sun* xi. 125 The peninsula that separates textile camping from Funtona Bay designated for nudism.

B. *sb.* **1. a.** A woven fabric; any kind of cloth. Also, a synthetic material suitable for weaving; any of various materials, as a bonded fabric, which do not require weaving. (Usually in *pl.*)

1626 BACON *Sylva* §846 In the warp and woof of textiles. **1870** ROCK *Text. Fabr.* Introd. 1. 10 The word 'textile' means every kind of stuff, no matter its material, wrought in the loom. **1885** *Manch. Exam.* 5 June 5/6 Machines for the preparation of textiles. **1886** *Pall Mall G.* 3 May 4/1 The prices of textiles have fallen considerably. **1908** A. E. GARRETT *Fibres for Fabrics* iv. 100 Since the Chardonnet silk [*sc.* artificial silk] is so much more deteriorated by pure water ..it matters little, so far as its extended use in textiles is concerned. **1927** M. H. AVRAM *Rayon Industry* i. 1 'Rayon' —the first synthetic textile... We shall briefly trace the steps from its conception; through.. its struggle to gain a place as a commercially possible textile fibre. **1961** *Wall St. Jrnl.* 1 Dec. 14/2 Mead,.. in cooperation with M. Lowenstein & Sons, Inc... is working on paper 'textiles'. **1962** Z. TRAVNÍČEK tr. *Krčma's Nonwoven Textiles* i. 11 Nonwoven textiles and, particularly, adhesively bonded textiles can be manufactured by many processes. **1970** *Cabinet Maker & Retail Furnisher* 23 Oct. 173/2 The original term 'non-woven textiles' used for adhesively-bonded fabrics has grown more and more obscure as novel manufacturing technologies based on mechanical bonding processes have been introduced. *Ibid.*, As a first simplification we can say that 'non-woven' textiles do not comprise traditional textile structures made by processes other than weaving (ie knitting, braiding, lace manufacture, etc). The present meaning of 'non-woven textiles' refers to pliable and porous products from textile materials that are reinforced by mechanical or chemical means.

b. *attrib.* (or as *adj.*) Of or pertaining to weaving or to woven fabrics. Also, of non-woven fabric.

1844 G. DODD *Textile Manuf.* Introd. 6 By 'Textile manufactures' are meant those in which filaments of cotton, of flax, of silk, or of wool, are wrought into a form fitted to be used in the making of garments. **1866** ROGERS *Agric. & Prices* I. xxii. 569 The great.. centre of textile industry in England was the two north-eastern counties of Norfolk and Suffolk. **1871** TYLOR *Prim. Cult.* I. i. 7 Among textile arts are to be ranged matting, netting, and several grades of making and weaving threads. **1971** *N.Y. Law Jrnl.* 23 Nov. 1/8 Suskin was a principal in Derby Fabrics, Inc..., a textile converting and jobbing concern. *Ibid.*, Suskin entered a business relationship with Jerry Kassel, Inc..., also a textile converter. **1974** *Times* 12 Feb. 11 Louis van Praag has a theory that textiles should not be designed by textile designers. **1976** *Jrnl. R. Soc. Arts* CXXV. 21/1 Most textile conservation begins with cleaning to remove the harmful effects of atmospheric pollution, dust, dirt and undesirable or damaging stains or soiling. *Ibid.* 24/2 The Textile Conservation Centre came into being primarily to provide the foundation for new textile conservators to base their studies.

2. Fibrous material, as flax, cotton, silk, etc., suitable for being spun and woven into yarn, cloth, etc.

1641 WILKINS *Math. Magick* II. xii. (1707) 141 The Materials.. were not from any Herb, or Vegetable, as other Textiles, but from a Stone called Amiantus. **1883** *Nature* 8 Mar. 430/1 As to textiles, the origin of flax is somewhat complicated. **1889** *Science* 1 Feb. 81/2 The discovery of a new textile on the shores of the Caspian.

3. *Naturism.* A non-naturist; *spec.* one who wears a swimming costume on the beach.

1979 *Listener* 4 Jan. 20/1 The world's first naturist community.. is up for sale and will probably become a holiday resort for 'textiles'—the word naturists use for people who keep their clothes on when they could take them off. **1979** P. VALLACK *Free Sun* vii. 85 What would the sign have to do? Alert non-naturists (textiles) that they will see nude bathers if they continue in that direction. **1983** *Times* 6 July 32/2 The topless generally inhabit the more remote ends of the beach well away from the 'textiles'.

Hence **'textilist**, one engaged in the textile industry; a weaver or seller of cloth.

1855 *Ecclesiologist* XVI. 275 The handicraft of the goldsmith, stone carver, and textilist.

textless ('tɛkstlɪs), *a.* [-LESS.] Having no text.

1926 *United Free Church Missionary Record* May 225/1 What a windy textless sermon we got. **1957** J. HOLLANDER in N. Frye *Sound & Poetry* 1. 65 Plato had disapproved of textless music. **1980** *Christian Sci. Monitor* 12 May B12/4 Another textless wonder, 'Truck' [*sc.* a book] is a bold and bouncy salute to the open road.

'textlet. *rare.* [See -LET.] A short text.

1831 CARLYLE *Sart. Res.* I. xi, [The] Dingy Priest.. preaches forth (exoterically enough) one little textlet from the Gospel of Freedom.

†**'text-,letter.** *Obs.* [cf. TEXT-HAND.] A large or capital letter in handwriting.

1511 in *Rel. Ant.* I. 318 Lett yt stond iij. dayes.. and then thou hast good ynke for texte letter. **1600** E. BLOUNT *Hosp. Incur. Fooles* A iij, Where the renowmed folly of these men may be seene.. written (as it were) in Text letters. **1605** BACON *Adv. Learn.* II. iii. §3 To write it in such Text and Capital letters. **1657** W. MORICE *Coena quasi Κοινὴ* xx. 177 Hypocrisie would.. in some Polititians be written in Court-hand, but in others in text-letters. **1706** PHILLIPS (ed. Kersey), *Text-Letters*, the Capital Letters in all sorts of Hands that are usually written.

text-man ('tɛkstmən).

†**1.** One learned in scriptural texts, and apt at quoting them; also, An advocate of literal interpretation of the Bible. *Obs.*

1619 R. HARRIS *Drunkard's Cup* 26 A very iudicious Diuine, and grounded Text-man. **1624** GODWYN *Moses & Aaron* (1641) 28 The Scribes clave to the written Word, whence they were tearmed Text-men, or Masters of the Text. **1647** TRAPP *Comm. 1 Cor.* i. 20 The Text-men, those that proceed according to the literall interpretation. **1702** C. MATHER *Magn. Chr.* IV. iii. (1852) 61 He was a notable text-man, and one who had more than forty or fifty scriptures distinctly quoted in one discourse.

2. The author of a text-book. *rare.*

1900 H. G. GRAHAM *Soc. Life Scot. in 18th C.* XII. iii. (1901) 464 Bacon, Locke and Evans, Puffendorf and De Vries were welcome text-men.

textorial (tɛk'stɔərɪəl), *a.* [f. L. *textor*, *-ōrem* weaver, *textōri-us* pertaining to weaving + -AL[1].] Of or pertaining to weavers or weaving.

1774 WARTON *Hist. Eng. Poetry* Diss. iii. (1840) I. p. cxciv, The cultivation of the textorial arts among the orientals. **1875** *Nat. Hist. & Antiq. Arran* 333 They will resume their textorial occupation.

So **tex'torian** *a. rare*[—0].

1656 BLOUNT *Glossogr.*, *Textorian*,.. of, or belonging to a weaver, or to weaving.

†**'textour.** *Obs. rare.* [a. AF. *textour*, ad. L. *textōr-em* weaver.] A weaver.

[**1429** *Act 8 Hen. VI*, c. 23 Les textours.. qunt ils ount overez un drap.] **1558** *Peebles Burgh Rec.* (1872) 247 The baillies.. hes nominat four werkmen textouris.. to exame Gilbert Wilsone his sone.. and se gif he be qualifiit to wirk on the lynning lome or nocht.

'text-,pen. A pen specially suitable for writing text-hand, or for engrossing.

1589 NASHE *Pasqvils Retvrne* Wks. (Grosart) I. 134 The Painter to bewray both his abuse of the Scriptures, and his malice against the Church, hath drawne him his worde with a Text-pen. **1593** —— *Christ's T.* Ep. Ded., Your illustrate ladiship ere this (I am perswaded) hath beheld a badde florish with a Text-penne. **1594** PLAT *Jewell-ho.* III. 42 Lines drawne with a text-penne. **1858** SIMMONDS *Dict. Trade*, *Text-pen*, a metallic pen for engrossing.

†**'textrine,** *a. Obs. rare.* [ad. L. *textrīn-us*, f. *textor* weaver.] Of or pertaining to weaving.

1713 DERHAM *Phys.-Theol.* IV. xiii. 234 How so small a Creature that emits no Web, nor hath any textrine Art, can be able to convolve the stubborn leaf, and then bind it.. with the Thread or Web it weaves from its own Body. *Ibid.* VIII. vi. (1752) 388 The curious structure of all parts ministring to this textrine power.

textual ('tɛkstjuːəl), *a.* (*sb.*) Also 4–5 **-uel.** [In form *textuel*, app. a. AF. (F. *textuel* only 15th c. in Godef.), ad. L. type **textuāl-is*, f. *textu-s*: see TEXT *sb.*[1] and -AL[1]. So Sp., Pg. *textual*, It. *-ale.* The later Eng. spelling is conformed to the L. type (as in other adjs. orig. in *-el*).]

†**1.** Of a person: Well acquainted with 'texts' or authors; well-read; literally exact in giving the text. [So F. *textuel* 'qui connait les textes', 1571 in Godef. *Compl.*, also in Cotgr.] *Obs.*

c **1386** CHAUCER *Manciple's T.* 131 (Ellesm.) But for I am a man not textueel I wol noght telle of textes neuer a deel. *Ibid.* 212 But as I seyde I am noght textueel. —— *Pars. Prol.* 57 This meditacion I putte it ay vnder correccion Of Clerkes for I am nat textueel [so *Harl. & Hengwrt*; 4 *MSS.* text wel. *Textuel* was prob. Chaucer's word, which being app. unknown to some scribes was altered to *text wel* and *texted wel*: cf. TEXTED 1]. **1613** R. CAWDREY *Table Alph.* (ed. 3), *Textuall*, cunning in the text.

2. Of, pertaining to, or contained in the (or a) text, esp. of the Scriptures.

c **1470** HENRYSON *Mor. Fab.* III. *Cock & Fox* xxviii. (Charteris) ȝit may ȝe find ane sentence richt agreabill, Vnder thir fenȝeit termis textuall. **1570** LEVINS *Manip.* 15/26 Textuall, *textualis.* *a* **1638** MEDE *Wks.* (1672) 347 So the Cethib or Textual reading hath it. **1731** WATERLAND *Script. Vind.* II. 125 So stands the case, upon the foot of the Textual Reading. **1859** I. TAYLOR *Logic in Theol.* vii. 309 The admitted principles of textual criticism. **1872** MINTO *Eng. Prose Lit.* II. vi. 468 His sagacity in textual emendations.

b. Of or belonging to the text-books.

1863 EMERSON *Misc. Papers, Thoreau* Wks. (Bohn) III. 324 Though very studious of natural facts, he was incurious of technical and textual science.

†**3.** Recognizing only the text of Scripture as authoritative. Also as *sb.* one that does this. *Obs.*

1613 PURCHAS *Pilgrimage* II. viii. 123 They are called *Karraim*, because they would seeme Textuall, and Scripture-men, disallowing Traditions [*ed.* **1614**, p. 143 *Karaim*, that is, Bible-men, or Textualls, and in the Roman tongue they call them Saduces].

4. Based on, following, or conforming to the text, esp. of the Scriptures.

1614 BP. HALL *Recoll. Treat.* Ded. A ij b, Speculation interchanged with experience, positiue theologie with polemicall, textuall with discursorie. **1670** WALTON *Life Donne* 34 Incessant study of textual divinity. **1863** ROBINSON in *Macm. Mag.* Mar. 419 The textual system..

has tended to establish a persuasion that Christian doctrines can be..proved by detached quotations. **1908** *Sat. Rev.* 11 July 39/2 Possibly we have not got the quotation exactly textual.

textualism (ˈtɛkstjuːəlɪz(ə)m). [f. prec. + -ISM.]

1. Strict adherence to the text, esp. of the Scriptures; the principles or method of a textualist.

1863 M. PATTISON *Ess.* (1889) II. 286 The arbitrary textualism of the Puritan divines. **1895** *Thinker* VIII. 405 He feels unable..to burden his audience with minutiæ, subtleties, pedantries, textualisms.

2. That department of scholarship which deals with the text of the Bible; textual criticism.

1888 *Church Times* 318 Reputations..acquired merely in the field of grammar and textualism, not in theology proper. **1908** *Times, Lit. Supp.* 5 Mar. 74/2 Textualism is not a popular study.

textualist (ˈtɛkstjuːəlɪst). [f. as prec. + -IST.]

a. One learned in the text of the Bible. **b.** One who adheres strictly to, and bases his doctrine upon, the text of the Scriptures.

1629 LIGHTFOOT *Misc.* vi. 20 How nimble textualists and Grammarians for the tongue the Rabbins are, their Comments can witnes. But..these that are so great textualists, are not best at the text. **1834** SOUTHEY *Doctor* iii. (1848) 12 When I mention Arba, who but the practised textualist can call to mind that he was..the father of Anak, and that from him Kirjath-Arba took its name? **1885** SWINBURNE *Misc.* (1886) 181 A moderate Puritan and a textualist of the old Protestant school. **1903** J. MOFFAT in *Expositor* Dec. 470 One appealing to the textualist is Dr. R. Jansen's attempt to reconstruct the Greek text.

textuality (tɛkstjuːˈælɪtɪ). [f. as prec. + -ITY.]

1. = TEXTUALISM 1.

1836 *J. Martin's Discourses* Memoir 34 Textuality, he often said, appeared to him to be one of the chief excellences of a sermon. **1888** M. W. STRYKER in *Interior* (Chicago) 5 Apr., Deliverance, for those who have all their lifetimes been subject to pithiness and apothegm would come by the broadest textuality.

2. (See quot. 1970.)

1970 *Babel* XVI. 76/1 By textuality, we mean the result of the transformation of the common language of a given type of civilization into the language of a work of literature belonging to that type of civilization. **1976** G. C. SPIVAK in J. Derrida *Of Grammatology* p. lxv, Exploiting a false etymological kinship between semantics and semen, Derrida offers this version of textuality: A sowing that does not produce plants, but is simply infinitely repeated. **1979** *N. & Q.* June 285/2 *Glyph* is a 'new serial publication' concerned with 'the problems of representation and textuality'.

textually (ˈtɛkstjuːəlɪ), *adv.* [f. as prec. + -LY[2]. Cf. F. *textuellement.*]

1. In or as regards the text.

1617 COLLINS *Def. Bp. Ely* II. ix. 351 As no lesse textually, then marginally, both waies, you blaze it. **1847** DE QUINCEY *Orthographic Mutineers* Wks. 1860 XIV. 104 In our authorized version..italics are..used..exclusively to indicate such words or auxiliary forms as, though implied and virtually present in the original, are not textually expressed.

2. In the actual words of the text; verbatim.

1837 SIR F. PALGRAVE *Merch. & Friar* Ded. (1844) 10 As they only exist in manuscript, I shall place them textually before you. **1870** LOWELL *Among my Bks.* Ser. I. (1873) 205 The theory that his plays should be represented textually. **1884** *Truth* 4 Sept. 364/2 To report textually a debate from 4.30 p.m. to 2 a.m. would fill thirty columns of the *Times*.

†**ˈtextuarist.** *Obs. rare*[-0]. [f. next + -IST.] = TEXTUARY *sb.* 1.

1755 in JOHNSON.

textuary (ˈtɛkstjuːərɪ), *a.* and *sb.* [ad. mod.L. type **textuāri-us*, f. *textu-s* TEXT *sb.*[1] + *-ārius* -ARY[1]. So F. *textuaire* sb. (1680 in Hatz.-Darm.).]

A. *adj.* **1.** Of or belonging to the text; textual.

1646 SIR T. BROWNE *Pseud. Ep.* III. xvi. 145 Pliny..hath differently translated it,..whereby he extends the exclusion unto twenty dayes, which in the textuary sense is fully accomplished in one. **1817** COLERIDGE *Lay Serm.* 411 Plucking away..from the divine organism of the Bible, textuary morsels, and fragments for the support of doctrines which they had learned beforehand. **1854** W. WATERWORTH *Eng. & Rome* 62 *note*, The textuary proofs of St. Peter's supremacy. **1882** *Sat. Rev.* LIV. 639/1 It is as genuine a result of textuary accommodation as any against which this writer protests.

†**2.** That ranks as a text-book; regarded as authoritative or as an authority. *Obs.*

1632 LITHGOW *Trav.* IX. 395 Euclide the textuary Geomettrician. **1646** SIR T. BROWNE *Pseud. Ep.* 374 He..hath left sixteen books of Opticks, of great esteem with ages past, and textuary unto our daies. **1682** —— *Chr. Mor.* III. §21 Let Pythagoras be thy Remembrancer, not thy textuary and final Instructer.

†**3.** That adheres strictly to the text of Scripture: cf. B. 2. *Obs. rare*[-1].

1613 PURCHAS *Pilgrimage* III. x. 247 They hate the Persians,..like as the Traditionary Iew doth the Textuarie, and the Papist the Protestant.

B. *sb.* **1.** One learned in the text of the Bible, = TEXTUALIST a; a textual critic, scholar, or expounder; also, one well acquainted with and ready at quoting texts.

1608 BP. J. KING *Serm.* 24 Mar. 28 Is there almost a worthier and prompter textuary in the world..in that booke of the Law? *a* **1661** FULLER *Worthies, Lincoln.* (1662) II. 167 He [Doctor Tighe] was an excellent Textuary and profound Linguist, the reason why he was imployed by King James in translating of the Bible. **1677** *Spottiswood's Hist. Ch. Scot.* App. 20 He was learned in the Hebrew, and was a great Textuary. *a* **1710** BP. BULL *Visit. Serm.* (1714) 21 If by a Textuary, we mean him who hath not only a Concordance of Scriptures in his Memory, but also a Commentary on them in his Understanding; who thinks it not enough to be ready in alledging the bare Words of Scripture, with the mention of Chapter and Verse where it is written, unless he know the Sense and Meaning of what he recites. **1720** SWIFT *Let. Yng. Poet* 1 Dec., I have made it my observation, that the greatest wits have been the best textuaries; our modern poets are all..almost as well read in the Scriptures as some of our divines. **1851** G. S. FABER *Many Mansions* 223 Mr. Scott,..than whom there probably never was a more accomplished textuary, takes pretty much the same view of the question. **1879** *Q. Rev.* CXLVIII. 422 Having the Bible at their fingers' ends... They were not merely accomplished textuaries.

†**2.** One who adheres strictly to the letter of Scripture; = TEXTUALIST b; cf. TEXTUAL 3.

1727–41 CHAMBERS *Cycl.*, *Textuaries, Textuarii*, a name given the sect of the Caraites, among the Jews. Hillel shone among the traditionaries, and Schammai among the textuaries. **1828** WEBSTER, *Textualist, Textuary*... 2. One who adheres to the text.

†**3.** (See quot.) *Obs.*

1706 PHILLIPS (ed. Kersey), *Textuary*, a Law-Book, or other Treatise, that contains only the bare Text, without any Comment or Gloss upon it. **1730–6** in BAILEY (folio).

†**textuist.** *Obs.* [f. L. *text-us* TEXT *sb.*[1] + -IST.] A textual scholar; = TEXTUARY *sb.* 1.

1631 R. H. *Arraignm. Whole Creature* xii. §3. 125 Popery affording more allegorizing Origenists, then sound Textuists. **1643** MILTON *Divorce* To Parl., When I remember the little that our Saviour could prevail about this doctrine of Charity against the crabbed textuists of his time, I make no wonder. **1700** STRYPE *Lightfoot's Rem.* Pref. 3 The author designed it for some, that desired to be good textuists.

Textularian (tɛkstjuːˈlɛərɪən), *a.* and *sb.* *Zool.* [f. mod.L. *Textulāria*, generic name (f. L. *text-us* woven) + -AN.] **a.** *adj.* Belonging to *Textularia*, the typical genus of *Textulariidæ*, a family of perforate Foraminifera. **b.** *sb.* A member of this genus or family.

1862 CARPENTER *Microsc. & Rev.* (ed. 3) §317 A less aberrant modification of the Globigerine type..is presented in the two great series which may be designated..as the Textularian and the Rotalian.

textura (tɛkˈstjʊərə). *Typogr.* [a. G. *textura* (also *textur*), f. L. *textūra*: see TEXTURE *sb.*] One of a group of typefaces first used in the earliest printed books, distinguished by narrow, angular letters and a strong vertical emphasis; also, the manuscript hand on which these typefaces were based. Also *attrib.*

[**1922** D. B. UPDIKE *Printing Types* II. 323/1 (Index), Textur type.] **1929** A. F. JOHNSON in *Library* IX. 359 The term which the Germans usually employ is Textur, or Textura, meaning 'woven', from the resemblance of a page in this letter to a woven pattern. **1955** *Archit. Rev.* CXVIII. 399/3 It [*sc.* the Gothic letter] is a magnificent letter, both formal textura and Gothic cursive. **1962** [see LETTRE b]. **1969** M. B. PARKES *Eng. Cursive Book Hands 1250–1500* p. xvii, In the fourteenth century Textura became increasingly more artificial and more difficult to write. **1970** *Times Lit. Suppl.* 7 Aug. 884/5 The textura types survived in England into the eighteenth century. **1976** [see ROTUNDA 3]. **1977** *Studies in Eng. Lit.: Eng. Number* (Toyko) 7 Ad is written in a very neat *textura* hand, which differs from that which copied the rest of the MS.

textural (ˈtɛkstjʊərəl), *a.* [f. L. *textūra* TEXTURE + -AL[1].] **a.** Of or belonging to texture.

1835–6 *Todd's Cycl. Anat.* I. 67/1 The textural properties of the two sets of vessels. **1854** JONES & SIEVEKING *Pathol. Anat.* (1874) 23 The differences in textural quality, which fibrine often presents. **1886** T. HARDY *Mayor of Casterbridge* ii, Her skin had undergone a textural change.

b. *Painting*: see TEXTURE *sb.* 6.

1859 GULLICK & TIMBS *Paint.* 229 The gem-like impasto and textural richness of the old masters. **1887** *Pall Mall G.* 8 Feb. 2/2 Never has the French master shown greater textural facility, power of expression, or frankness of colour.

c. *Mus.* and *Literary Criticism.* See TEXTURE *sb.* 5.

1962 *Listener* 1 Nov. 735/3 Outward clarity of form, of rhythmic definition, and of textural contrasts, are the most striking features. **1963** *Ibid.* 3 Jan. 23/1 Joyce's *Portrait of the Artist* is characterized by organic form, both textural and structural. **1983** *Ibid.* 10 Feb. 35/4 There are no more than one and a half piano quartets whose great music does not produce textural insuperabilities for the players.

Hence **ˈtexturally** *adv.*, in or as regards texture.

1866 *Reader* 19 May 500 The mare herself, with her beautiful foal, are all, to our eye, texturally perfect. **1872** COUES *N. Amer. Birds* 22 The second class of crests—those consisting of texturally modified feathers. **1962** *Listener* 22 Nov. 885/1 The structurally and texturally elaborate *String Quartet*. **1976** *Gramophone* Mar. 1442/3 *Missa Salisburgensis* ..is texturally complex, with its seven 'choirs' of voices and instruments spread over 54 staves.

texture (ˈtɛkstjʊə(r)), *sb.* [ad. L. *textūra* a weaving: see TEXT *sb.*[1] and -URE. So F. *texture* (16th c. in Godef. *Compl.*).]

†**1. a.** The process or art of weaving. *Obs.*

1447 BOKENHAM *Seyntys* (Roxb.) 145 Mynerve hyr self wych hath the sovereynte Of gay texture, as declayryth Ovyde. **1646** SIR T. BROWNE *Pseud. Ep.* 256 Coats of skinnes..a naturall habit..before the invention of Texture. **1656** BLOUNT *Glossogr.*, *Texture*,..a weaving. **1726** POPE *Odyss.* XX. 87 Pallas taught the texture of the loom.

†**b.** *fig.* The fabricating, machinating, or composing of schemes, conspiracies, writings, etc. *Obs.*

a **1641** BP. MOUNTAGU *Acts & Mon.* iv. (1642) 275 First they began their malicious texture with secret whisperings, and giving out in corners. **1656** EARL MONM. tr. *Boccalini's Advts. fr. Parnass.* II. xciv. (1674) 247 The exquisite diligence used in the texture of those his Eternal Labours.

2. a. The produce of the weaver's art; a woven fabric; a web; cloth. *arch.*

a **1656** BP. HALL *Rem. Wks.* (1660) 260 The invaluable sumptuousness of the Temple..;..the curious celatures, and artificial textures. **1728–46** THOMSON *Spring* 642 Others ..far in the grassy dale..their humble texture weave. **1873** BROWNING *Red Cott. Nt.-cap* 407 When the dyer dyes A texture, can the red dye prime the white?

b. *transf.* Any natural structure having an appearance or consistence as if woven; a tissue; a web, e.g. of a spider. Also *fig.*

1578 BANISTER *Hist. Man* IV. 56 The notable texture of *Mesenterium*. **1615** CROOKE *Body of Man* 499 That phlegme ..which distilleth out of that texture or web into the ventricles. *Ibid.* 525 That the spirits are attenuated in the textures of the small arteries, & in the strayghtes of those passages. *a* **1774** TUCKER *Lt. Nat.* (1834) II. 43 Nor the spider entangle the heedless fly in his texture. **1877** TYNDALL in *Daily News* 2 Oct. 2/4 His physical and intellectual textures have been woven for him during his passage through phases of history and forms of existence which lead the mind back to an abysmal past.

†**c.** A 'woven' or composed narrative or story.

1611 SPEED *Hist. Gt. Brit.* VII. xxxviii. §9. 341 A peece of ancient Saxon coine of Siluer, inscribed with his name, Anlaf Cynyng, which for the antiquity of the thing, and honor of the man we haue here imprinted, and placed, though in the texture of our English Saxon Kings.

3. The character of a textile fabric, as to its being fine, coarse, close, loose, plain, twilled, ribbed, diapered, etc., resulting from the way in which it is woven.

1685 BOYLE *Salubr. Air* 79 The texture that belongs to Linen. **1791** COWPER *Odyss.* I. 556 Putting off his vest Of softest texture. **1842** in Bischoff *Woollen Manuf.* II. 176 One piece of cloth of German wool, and another piece of South Down wool..made of the same colour and texture. **1866** ROGERS *Agric. & Prices* I. xxii. 573 The linen worn by the wealthier classes differed materially in its texture.

4. In extended use: The constitution, structure, or substance of anything with regard to its constituents or formative elements. **a.** Of organic bodies and their parts.

1665 BOYLE *Occas. Medit.* IV. iv, The Leaves..of a Tree ..are of a more solid Texture, and a more durable Nature than the Blossoms. **1738** WESLEY *Ps.* CXXXIX. ix, Thou know'st the Texture of my Heart, My Reins, and every vital Part. **1797** M. BAILLIE *Morb. Anat.* (1807) 212 The cartilage is smooth and thin, and very soft in its texture. **1844** STEPHENS *Bk. Farm* III. 905 Butter assumes a texture according as it has been treated. **1882** *Garden* 18 Mar. 182/3 Flavour and texture should be our watchword in raising Apples.

b. Of inorganic substances, as stones, soil, etc.: Physical (not chemical) constitution; the structure or minute moulding (of a surface).

1660 BOYLE *New Exp. Phys. Mech.* xxii. 165 Air is.. endow'd with an Elastical power that probably proceeds from its Texture. **1663** —— *Usef. Exp. Nat. Philos.* II. v. xiii. 242 Glass acquires a more or lesse brittle Texture, according as..it is baked. **1793** SMEATON *Edystone L.* §106 The stone..in point of hardness and texture much like the Bath stone. **1811** PINKERTON *Petralogy* p. xxii, Mr. Kirwan has justly observed the inaccuracy of Werner and his disciples, who have confounded the texture with the fracture. **1813** SIR H. DAVY *Agric. Chem.* (1814) 5 Some lands of good apparent texture are yet sterile in a high degree. **1865** GEIKIE *Scen. & Geol. Scot.* viii. 220 Gneiss is too various in its texture and the rate of its decomposition. **1878** HUXLEY *Physiogr.* 63 The loose texture of snow.

5. *fig.* Of immaterial things: Constitution; nature or quality, as resulting from composition. Of the mind: Disposition, as 'woven' of various qualities; temperament, character. Also, in Literary Criticism: the constitution or quality of a piece of writing; esp. such perceptible qualities as the imagery, alliteration, assonance, rhythm, etc. (freq. opp. *structure*). In Music: the quality of sound formed by the combination of the different (orchestral, vocal, etc.) parts.

1611 SPEED *Hist. Gt. Brit.* VI. xix. §9. 104 Albeit the very texture of this Epistle carrieth with it the true Character of Antiquity. *a* **1677** HALE *Prim. Orig. Man.* 157 Hence it is that..the texture of Zeuxes or Apelles inclines him to the invention or improving of Painting. **1692** BENTLEY *Boyle Lect.* iii. 80 An argument..of so frail and brittle a texture. **1751** SMOLLETT *Per. Pic.* (1779) III. lxxxi. 272 Had her thoughts been of a more tender texture. **1771** *Misc.* in *Ann. Reg.* 161/1 The whole texture of the fable. **1812** J. MACKINTOSH in *Mem. Life Sir J. Mackintosh* (1835) II. iii. 215 This is increased when a few bolder and higher words are happily wrought into the texture of this familiar eloquence. **1827** POLLOK *Course T.* II. 538 Creeds of wondrous texture. **1895** W. D. HOWELLS *My Literary Passions* xxxi. 223 All that Mr. De Forest has written is of a texture and color distinctly his own. **1931** *Week-End Rev.* 3 Jan. 24/2 The texture of the book is much more satisfactory than its theme. **1934** M. BODKIN *Archetypal Patterns in Poetry* 320 This duality in unity, and harmonized clash, of cosmic and personal that Blake has woven into the texture of his verses. **1934** C. LAMBERT *Music Ho!* III. 165 The first symphony [of Borodin]..achieves an admirable symphonic texture. **1941** J. C. RANSOM *New Criticism* iv. 280 The texture, likewise, seems to be of any real content that may be come upon, provided it is so free, unrestricted, and large that it cannot properly get into the structure. One guesses that it is an *order* of content, rather than a *kind* of content, that distinguishes texture from structure, and poetry from prose. **1956** M. KRIEGER *New Apologists for Poetry* v. 83 The indeterminacies of meaning, into which the poet is forced by his devotion to the determinate sound, constitute the poem's texture [according to J. C. Ransom]. **1956–7** *Modern Fiction Studies* Winter 209 The birth of Lena's child means more in the texture of the story than a simple event. **1959** *Listener* 10 Dec. 1034/1 For a long time now it has been fashionable to cry after new 'textures' in sound. **1963** *Ibid.* 21 Feb. 354/1 In his last decade as an opera composer Handel..made less use of wind instruments and tended to favour sparser textures. **1980** *Dædalus* Spring 194 The thinning of texture, and the descending succession of pitches in measures 100 to 103 of Berlioz's melody all seem to foster and presage closure.

6. In the fine arts: The representation of the structure and minute moulding of a surface (esp. of the skin), as distinct from its colour: cf. 4 b.

1845 [see PEARLY *a.* 4]. **1859** GULLICK & TIMBS *Paint.* 228 Impasting gives 'texture' and 'surface'. **1877** MORLEY *Crit. Misc., Robespierre* Ser. II. 64 It is transparent and smooth, but there is none of that quality which the critics of painting call Texture.

7. *attrib.* and *Comb.*, as **texture brick**, a roughened or rough-hewn brick; **texture-counter**, a thread-counter or waling-glass: see quot.

1909 *Cent. Dict. Suppl.*, *Texture-counter*, a small magnifying-glass of low power, used in counting the number of threads, within a given space, in the texture of a fabric. **1940** *Chambers's Techn. Dict.* 843/1 *Texture brick*, a rustic brick. **1961** [see SEPTIC *sb.* 2].

† **'texture**, *v. Obs.* [f. prec.] *trans.* To construct by or as by weaving; to give a texture to (anything). Usually in *pa. pple.*

1694 R. BURTHOGGE *Reason & Nat. Spirits* 104 Now it is certain..that Matter is alter'd, figured, textur'd, and infinite ways wrought upon and moulded by means of motion. **1775** JEPHSON *Braganza* III. i. 31 This fine frame, Nerves exquisitely textur'd. **1778** [W. MARSHALL] *Minutes Agric.* 13 Sept. an. 1774, The off-horse treads that which is textured, and destroys the effect. **1835** CARLYLE *Corr.* (1883) I. vii. 65 A bright faultless vision textured out of mere sunbeams.

textured ('tɛkstjʊəd), *a.* [f. as prec. + -ED².]

a. In comb. with adj.: of a (specified) texture. Later freq. without specific adj.: Provided with a texture, esp. as opposed to smooth or plain.

1888 *Daily News* 1 May 5/7 One of the infinitely light-textured homespuns. **1901** *Westm. Gaz.* 3 Oct. 3/2 The addition of some very fine textured lace. **1905** *Ibid.* 20 Sept. 8/1 A close-textured, nutty-flavoured, easily-digested loaf. **1923** *Times Lit. Suppl.* 28 Jan. 64/1 The method of colour woodcut, with its bold lines and textured tones, suits very well an artist whose painting is apt to be a little thin. **1938** *Burlington Mag.* Apr. 200/2 Plain or 'textured' weaves. **1943** J. S. HUXLEY *TVA* 100 The textured concrete wall finish. **1959** *Times* 12 Jan. 11/5 Textured: a term frequently met with indicating a process has been used that fluffs up surface or fabric giving greater density, softness of handle and appearance, extra warmth and some degree of absorbency. **1962** *Listener* 29 Mar. 566/3 They [*sc.* the collages and picture reliefs] appear to have both an ambivalent scale, a tiny world of textured pleasure inside the larger images they set out to establish, and a somewhat suave finish. **1969** *Amateur Photographer* 21 May 56/1 These units..have black cases of plastic with simulated textured panelling. **1977** *Time* 7 Feb. 54/1 Her far-flung locations are not textured settings but flimsy sets where the author vainly attempts to stage her quiet drama of rootlessness and disaffection.

b. ***textured yarn***, a yarn which has been modified so as to give a special texture to the fabric.

1960 *Which?* Jan. 17/2 In recent years..methods of treating continuous filament synthetic yarns have been introduced that modify their properties remarkably. These modified yarns are described as 'textured'. **1964** *Ibid.* Sept. 285/1 Textured yarns are mainly of two kinds—bulked yarns and stretch yarns. **1975** C. CALASIBETTA *Fairchild's Dict. Fashion* 543/2 *Textured y[arn]*. 1. Man-made continuous-filament yarns permanently heat-set in crimped manner or otherwise modified to give more elasticity, used to make stretch fabrics. 2. Man-made filament yarns processed to change their appearance; e.g., abraded.

c. Designating protein foods derived from vegetables but given a texture that resembles meat, esp. in ***textured vegetable protein*** (cf. *TVP* s.v. T 6 a).

1968 *Manch. Guardian Weekly* 11 July 12/3 The second exciting stage was launched this May by a Minneapolis manufacturer... TVP (textured vegetable protein) 'could hardly look or taste better..', the makers claim. **1970** *New Scientist* 24 Dec. 561/2 There is already a big sale for..textured meat analogies. **1977** *Times* 23 Feb. 4/8 Mincemeat will sometimes be mixed with textured vegetable protein in 800 schools in Kent. **1983** *Listener* 21 July 23/3 Let us..settle down to textured soya sandwiches for tea.

'textureless, *a.* [f. as prec. + -LESS.] Devoid of texture; exhibiting no texture.

1851 RUSKIN *Mod. Paint.* II. III. I. v. §14 Simple patterns upon textureless draperies. **1864** *Daily Tel.* 4 May, The whole picture [is]..disagreeably smooth and textureless. **1884** SHELDON in *West. Daily Press* 24 May 3/6 A salvy and textureless mass.

texturing ('tɛkstjʊərɪŋ). [f. TEXTURE *sb.* + -ING¹.] The representation of the texture of a surface in painting or engraving. Also in other contexts (esp. corresponding to the senses of TEXTURED *a.*).

1882 HERKOMER in *Artist* 1 Feb. 38 To enable the engraver to render a disturbed surface by an ingenuity of lining or texturing of his own devising. **1958** *Listener* 18 Dec. 1055/3 Some texturing material such as sawdust, ordinary sand, or silver sand. **1960** *Times* 4 Jan. 14/1 The two Moores..both avoid the mannered type of texturing of so many of his drawings. **1960** *Wall St. Jrnl.* (Eastern ed.) 13 Jan. 1/4 This 'texturing' alters the surface of the long, continuous strands of nylon, giving them new properties such as elasticity and bulk without adding weight. **1961** G. MILLERSON *Technique Television Production* viii. 151 (*caption*) The arrangement, distribution and texturing of scenery. **1978** *Gramophone* June 85/2 It is clear that Lill's stylish performance, with its crystalline texturing and finely pulsing inner voices, is one very much to be reckoned with.

texturize ('tɛkstjʊəraɪz), *v.* [f. TEXTUR(E *sb.* + -IZE.] *trans.* To impart a particular texture to (fabrics or food). Also *fig.* Chiefly in *ppl. a.* So **'texturizing** *vbl. sb.*

1958 *Times* 26 June 15/3 We have..entered the texturized yarn field with 'Ban-Lon'. **1959** *Wall St. Jrnl.* 20 Nov. 17/2 Allied Chemical Corp's 'Caprolan' filament nylon is offered to the carpet industry, too. But to achieve the bulkiness of spun yarns, carpet mills have to have 'Caprolan' filament yarn 'texturized', or bulked. **1969** *Daily Tel.* 24 July 3/2 This involves the design and manufacture of machinery for yarn texturising and the production of texturised yarns, hosiery and knitwear. **1976** *Jrnl. R. Soc. Arts* CXXIV. 579/1 A great deal of work has been done on converting soyabeans and other high-energy substrates (even oil feedstock) into proteinaceous material that can be spun, like nylon, and given a texture like that of lean meat. This 'Texturized Vegetable Protein' (TVP) has been successfully promoted and seems likely to have a growing impact on the food market. **1976** *Times Lit. Suppl.* 13 Feb. 166/1 This selfconsciousness distinguishes the whole show from the chunks of fictionalized, texturized social history (which are to drama as TVP to steak) the BBC now seems so casually expert with.

,textu'rology. [ad. F. *texturologie*: see -OLOGY.] A term coined by Jean-Philippe-Arthur Dubuffet (b. 1901) for a kind of painting created by him, composed of minute drops of paint entirely covering a flat surface.

1959 J. A. THWAITES in *Arts Yearbk.* III. 134/2 In the *Texturologies*..he [*sc.* Jean Dubuffet] has pulverized the form and color as never before. **1964** *New Statesman* 1 May 695/2 Dubuffet's finely granulated texturologies. **1973** *Art Internat.* Mar. 30/2, I don't want to comment here on the nature of Dubuffet's 'texturologies'.

† **'textury.** *Obs. rare*⁻¹. [f. TEXTURE *sb.* + -Y.] Weaving.

1658 SIR T. BROWNE *Gard. Cyrus* ii, Which is beyond the common art of textury, and may still nettle Minerva, the goddess of that mystery.

‖ **textus** ('tɛkstəs). [L. *textus* TEXT.]

1. A manuscript or book of the Gospels; a Bible; = TEXT *sb.*¹ 3 b. ***textus-case***, a case or cover for this (*Cent. Dict.* 1891).

1874 MICKLETHWAITE *Mod. Par. Churches* 52 The gospeller having received the textus or gospel-book from the altar. **1877** J. D. CHAMBERS *Div. Worship* 275 At Salisbury, 1222, was one great Textus. **1906** *Athenæum* 21 Apr. 478 A boss of this value was originally affixed to the centre of a Textus of the Gospels,..often the chief ornament of early altars.

2. ***Textus Receptus***, literally, received text; *spec.* the received text of the Greek New Testament.

Strictly applied to the text of the second Elzevir edition of 1633, to which the publisher prefixed the assertion, 'Textum ergo habes nunc ab omnibus receptum' (Thou hast therefore the text now received by all); but commonly extended to any reprint of this (or of that of Stephanus 1550, on which it was founded) with or without slight revision, but without the aid of the early MSS. since discovered or published.

1856 T. H. HORNE *Introd. Text. Crit. N.T.* 124 From this sort of boast sprang the expression 'Textus Receptus'. **1885** *Athenæum* 5 Sept. 296/1 Pascal's..'Letters'..suffered..from..the..partiality of uncultivated admirers for an inaccurate *textus receptus*. **1901** F. G. KENYON *Handbk. Textual Crit. N.T.* 229 Some words of this re-translation..still linger in our Textus Receptus to the present day.

text-writer ('tɛkst,raɪtə(r)).

† **1.** A professional writer of text-hand, before the introduction of printing; later, an engrosser of legal documents. *Obs.*

1463 *Canterb. Corporation Acc.* (MS.), Thomas Howlet, textwriter, alias scrivener. *c* **1490** BOTONER *Itin.* (Nasmith 1778) 141 Sub custodia scriptoris text-wryter commorantis apud Seynt Mary Strond. **1491** in *York Myst.* Introd. 39 Tixt-wryters, luminers, noters, turners, and florischers.

2. *Law.* An author of a legal text-book.

1845 POLSON *Law Nat.* in *Encycl. Metrop.* II. 720/1 Text-writers of authority, an authority which they obtain whenever they record the usages and practice of nations..in a spirit of impartiality. **1863** H. COX *Instit.* I. ix. 188 The language of text-writers upon the right of the Lords to reject money bills is uniform. **1902** SIR E. E. KEKEWICH in *Law Times Rep.* LXXXVI. 346/2 In dealing with a question of this kind, one is thrown back on maxims and principles, and the exposition of them by text-writers is important. **1902** JOYCE *Ibid.* 352/1 A dictum which..is copied in the text-books, and is considered by the text-writers to be law.

† **tey**, variant of TAY *Obs.*, outer membrane of the brain, etc.

c **1350** *Nominale Gall.-Angl.* 6 *Toup canal et ceruel*, Toppe tey and the brayne.

tey, obs. f. TEA.

tey(e, obs. ff. TIE *sb.* and *v.*

teyghte, obs. pa. pple. of TIE *v.*

teyl, teyle, teylle, var. TELE *Obs.*, blame, obs. ff. TEAL, TEIL, lime-tree, TILE.

teym, Sc. f. TEEM *v.*²

teyme, obs. f. TEAM.

teyn, teynd(e, obs. ff. TEEN, TEIND, tithe.

† **teyne.** *Obs. rare.* [a. ON. *tein-n* twig, rod: cf. *gull-*, *járn-teinn* rod of gold, of iron, MSw. *tēn* 'smal stång (af metall)', Söderwall; Sw. *ten.* Cognate with OE. *tán*, MDu. *teen* twig.] A slender rod of metal.

c **1386** CHAUCER *Can. Yeom. Prol. & T.* 672 He took out of his owene sleeue A teyne of siluer Which þat was nat but an Ounce of weighte. *Ibid.* 676 He shoope his Ingot in lengthe and eek in breede Of this teyne. *Ibid.* 777 This preest took vp this siluer teyne anon And thanne seyde the Chanon let vs gon With thise thre teynes whiche þat we han wroght To som Goldsmyth and wite if they been ouht.

teyne: see TEEN *sb.*¹, TIND *v. Obs.*, to kindle.

teynt(e, teynter, -o(u)r, -ur, teynt-wort, obs. ff. TAINT, TENT, TENTER, TENTWORT.

teyre, teyrse, obs. ff. TEAR *a.* and *sb.*³, TIERCE.

teys(e, var. TEISE *Obs.*

teyser, obs. f. TEASER.

teysoure, var. TEISER *Obs.*

teytheyng, var. *tithing*, obs. f. TIDING.

tezel, tezill, tezir, obs. ff. TEASEL, TEASER.

‖ **tezkere, teskere** ('tɛzkərə). Also 7 teskeria, -caria, 9 -caré, tischera, tezkera, teskari. [Arab. *taðkirah*, in Turkish *tezkere*, lit. memorandum, record, note, f. *ðakara*, in deriv. conj. to record, relate, remember = Heb. *zākar* to remember.] A Turkish official memorandum or certificate of any kind; a receipt, order, permit, licence; *esp.* an internal passport.

1612 CORYAT in Purchas *Pilgrims* (1625) II. x. xii. 1825 A *Teskeria* (this is a Turkish word that signifieth a Certificate written vnder his hand). **1615** G. SANDYS *Trav.* 115 We could not passe without a Tescaria from the Cadee. **1817** *By-Laws Levant Company* 26 That the Company's privilege of having tescarés or certificates..be not forfeited. **1818** BLAQUIERE tr. *Pananti* xiii. 247 No [grain] can be exported without a *tischera*, or written permit, bearing the Dey's seal. **1858** SIMMONDS *Dict. Trade*, *Tescare, Teskere*, a Turkish Custom-house certificate. **1890** *Daily News* 30 June 7/7 The Porte yesterday despatched a teskere to..the Armenian Patriarch, enjoining him to dissolve the Provincial Council of Van. **1904** *Daily Chron.* 13 Jan. 5/2 A tezkera or local passport costing 4*s.* **1905** *Dundee Advertiser* 29 Nov. 11/1 The teskari or passport is an essential inexorably demanded by the Turkish official.

th, in words of Old English or Old Norse origin, and in words from Greek, is a consonantal digraph representing a simple sound, or rather (in Teutonic words), a pair of simple sounds, *breath* and *voice*, indicated in this dictionary by the letters (θ) and (ð); the former, as in *thin*, *bath* (θɪn, bɑːθ), being the breath dental spirant akin to *t*, and the latter, as in *then*, *bathe* (ðɛn, beɪð), the voiced dental spirant akin to *d*. The group (t, d, θ, ð), corresponds to the group (p, b, f, v). The breath spirant is identical with modern Greek *theta* (Θ, θ), and approximately with Spanish *z* (or *c* before *e*, *i*). The Greek letter, which corresponds etymologically to Sanskrit ध *dh* (and so, by Grimm's Law, to Teutonic and English D), was in early inscriptions represented by **TH**, and was a true aspirate; it was subsequently often written *TΘ*, *τθ*, and has prob. the sound (tθ); but by the second century B.C. it had sunk into a simple sound, = our (θ). The Romans, having neither the sound nor the symbol, represented the letter by TH, as in *Θάψος*, *Thapsus*, but app. this was pronounced, at least in late Latin (whence in all the Romanic languages), as simple *t*; cf. Greek *θεωρία*, L. *theōria*, It. and Sp. *teoria*; in Pg. *theoria*, F. *théorie*, spelt with *th*, pronounced with *t*; also Gr. *Θωμᾶς*, L. *Thōmās*, It. *Toma*, Sp. *Tomás*; Pg., F., Eng. *Thomas* all pronounced with T.

(2) In Teutonic the breath spirant (θ) was very frequent, being the regular etymological representative of Indo-Eur. *t* initially or after the stressed vowel, as in OTeut. **þrijiz*, Goth.

þreis, OE. *þreo*, Eng. *three*, = Indo-Eur. **treies*, Skr. *trayas*, Gr. *τρεῖς*, L. *trēs*; OTeut. **brôþer*, Goth. *brôþar*, OE. *brōþor*, *brōðor*, Eng. *brother*, = Indo-Eur. '*bhrātēr*, Gr. *φράτηρ* clansman, L. '*frāter*. The voiced spirant in *brōðor*, etc., was a later development (*c* 700 in English) from the breath sound between vowels or voiced consonants, as in the parallel *v* and *z* from *f* and *s*. Initially, the same change of (θ) to (ð) took place during the Middle English period in the demonstrative group of words, *the*, *that*, and their kindred, *this*, *these*, †*tho*, *those*, *there*, *then*, *than*, *thence*, *thither*, *thus*, etc., and in the pronouns of the second person singular, *thou*, *thee*, *thine*, *thy*: these constitute the only words in English with initial (ð). In the same group of words in the cognate Teutonic languages (θ) has passed through (ð) into (d); thus Ger. *das*, Du. *dat*, Da., Sw. *det* 'that'; in High Ger., Low Ger., and Du. the same has taken place even in other original *th* words which retain (θ) in English; e.g. Ger. *dach*, *denken*, *ding*, *dick*, *donner*, *drei* = Eng. thatch, think, thing, thick, thunder, three.

(3) In the demonstrative and pronominal groups of words, change of initial *þ* to *t*, by assimilation to a preceding dental (*t*, *d*, *s*), appears in earlier English. OE. *þæt þe* became *pæt-te*, *pætte*; *þe læs þe* appears in the 11th c. as *þe læste*, whence modern *lest*. In the last section of the OE. Chronicle, from 1132, *þe* after *t* or *d* regularly becomes *te* (e.g. þat *te* king, and *te* eorles). In the Ormulum and the Cotton MS. of Cursor Mundi, this assimilation is seen in all the words of the *the-thou* group (*Orm.* þatt *tatt te* goddspell meneþþ, wrohht *tiss* boc, and *tatt te* follc all þess *te* bett; *Cursor*, ne was *tar*, here and *tare*, scho serued *taim*, als sais *te* sau). So in Ancren Riwle (and *tet* is, et *tesse* uerse, þeo þet *tus* doð, and *tes* oðer, etc.). In the course of the 14th c., this assimilation was given up, and the spirant reappeared (as ð).

(4) In the Runic alphabet (*futhorc*) the breath spirant had to itself a symbol þ or þ (called *thorn*); but in the earliest known OE. writings in the Roman alphabet this was represented by *th*, the voiced spirant being often represented by *d* (*∂*) (sometimes by *th*). Before 700 probably, the character ð, formed by a bar across the stem of ∂, was introduced; it appears in a charter of Wihtræd, king of Kent, 700–715 (Sweet *Oldest English Texts* 428). Apparently it was first used to denote the voiced spirant: see the proper names in the Moore MS. of Bæda, *c* 737, and the *Liber Vitæ*, Cott. MS., *c* 800, and charters before 800 generally. But in the ninth century it was used for both spirants, as in the Vespasian Psalter, *c* 825 (e.g. iv. 5 ða ðe cweoðað), and in a West Saxon charter of 847 (*O.E.T.* 433). In the 8th century apparently, the thorn, þ, was adopted from the Runic futhorc, the earliest charter showing it being one of Coenwulf, king of Mercia, of 811 (*O.E.T.* 456); but it was not much used till late in the 9th c. A Surrey charter *a* 889 (ibid. 451) has 34 examples of ð initial, and 25 medial or final, with 49 of þ initial, and 1 medial. From the later years of the 9th c. ð and þ were used promiscuously in West Saxon works, with some preponderance of þ initially and ð finally. This continued in ME. till the 13th c. On the other hand, the Durham *Rituale* and the Lindisfarne Gospel Gloss, *c* 950, have uniformly ð in all positions (except in the compendium ꝥ for *ðæt*), as has also the East Anglian *Genesis & Exodus*, *c* 1250; while the Mercian portion of the Rushworth Gospel Gloss, *c* 975, and Ormin, *c* 1200, have only þ. After 1250 the ð speedily became obsolete; þ remained in use, but was gradually restricted more or less to the pronominal and demonstrative words. In later times its MS. form approached, and at times became identical with, that of *y* (the latter being sometimes distinguished by having a dot placed over it). As the continental type used by Caxton had no þ, its place in print was usually supplied by *th* for both sounds and in all positions. But in Scotland, the early printers, especially in the demonstrative and pronominal words, continued the þ as *y*, as in *y^e*, *yis*, *yat*, *you* (= thou), a practice also common in England in MS., and hardly yet extinct. Confusion with the modern *y* consonant, ME. ȝ, was avoided in Scotland, sometimes by writing the latter *yh*, but usually by continuing ME. ȝ in the form ʒ or z, so that *ye zeir* stood for *þe ȝeir*, i.e. *the year*. It is remarkable that, when OE. þ and ð were both in use, no attempt was made to differentiate them as breath and voice spirants, and app. no serious attempt even to distinguish them as initial and medio-final, as was done in Norwegian when the Roman alphabet was adopted, *c* 1200, and in Icelandic before 1300. At an earlier date (prob. *c* 800) the character ð was partially adopted from OE. in Old Saxon, and was used generally in the middle and end of words, while *th* was usual as the breath spirant initially.

(5) In a few compounds, as *anthill*, *outhouse*, *lighthouse*, *Chatham*, *Wytham*, *Yetholm*, etc., *t* and *h* come together but do not form a digraph; and in a few foreign words, chiefly East Indian, as *Thakoor*, *Thug*, *th* represents Skr. थ *th* or ठ *ṭh*, the sound being a *t* or *ṭ* followed by a slight aspiration (t^h, ṭ^h), in Eng. commonly reduced to *t*.

In a few proper names and other words derived from or influenced by French, as *Thomas*, *Thompson*, *thyme*, *th* is pronounced as *t*; several other words were formerly so treated, and even spelt with *t*, e.g. *theatre*, *theme*, *theology*, *throne*, *authentic*, *orthography*: *t* has become fixed in *treacle*, *treasure*. The late L. and Romanic treatment of *th* as *t* often led to the spelling *th* where *t* was etymological, as in *Thames*, *Sathan*; in *amaranth*, *amianthus*, *author*, etc., the corruption has also affected the pronunciation. See the individual words. In some ME. MSS. *th* frequently appears for *t* or for *d*: e.g. *tho* to, *thyll* till, *myghth* might, *nyghth* night, *whythe* white; *thede* deed, *theer* deer, *thegree* degree, *thepartyth* departed, *tho* do, *thogh* doth, *abothe* abode, *groundeth* grounded, *iclodeth* y-clothed, *lowthe* loud, *rothe* rood, *unther* under. Early ME. scribes (prob. Norman) often confounded the English letters þ (or ð) and ȝ, writing e.g. *ȝefinge* for *þefinge*, thieving, *wiȝ*, *worȝ*, *wroȝ* for *wiþ*, *worþ*, *wroþ* (in Auchinleck MS. of *Florice and Bl.*).

(6) Etymologically, modern Eng. *th* (ð) often represents an OE. *d*, esp. before *r* or *er*, as in *father*, *mother*, *gather*, *hither*, *together*, etc.; dialectally, this sometimes extends to other words, as *bladder*, *ladder*, *solder*; on the other hand some dialects retain original *d*, and extend it to other words, as *brother*, *further*, *rather*, *southern-wood*, *wether*. In *burden* and *murder*, *d* represents the earlier ð of *burthen*, *murther*.

Dialectally *th* is sometimes substituted for *f*, and vice versa: e.g. *thane*, *thetch*, *thistolow*, *thrail*, *thrae*, *throm*, *thurrow*, for *fane*, *fetch* (vetch), *fistula*, *frail* (flail), *frae*, *from*, *furrow*; also *fill*, *Fuirsday*, for THILL, THURSDAY. The Welsh name *Llewelyn* appears in Eng. as *Thlewelyn* (*Rolls of Parl.* I. 463/1, Edw. I or II), and *Fluellen* (Shaks. Hen. V). *Th* also occurs dialectally for *wh*, as in *thirl*, *thortleberry*, *thorl*, for *whirl*, *whortleberry*, *whorl*. Conversely, Sc. has *whaing*, *whang*, *white*, *whittle*, for *thwaing*, *thwang*, *thwite*, *thwittle*.

1. The digraph *th* and its sound.

[*c* **1400** MAUNDEV. (Roxb.) xv. 71 We hafe in oure speche in England twa oþer letters þan þai [Saracens] hafe in þaire abce, þat es to say, þ and ȝ, whilk er called *þorn* and *ȝok*.] *a* **1637** B. JONSON *Eng. Gram.* Wks. (Rtldg.) 775/2 Th Hath a double and doubtful sound. *Ibid.* 776/2 Some syllabes, as *the, then, there, that*.. are often compendiously and shortly written, as *ye y^en y^ere y^t*. **1668** O. PRICE *Eng. Orthogr.* 24 *Q.* What is the sound of *th*? *A. Th* makes a hard sound in *thunder, through, thick, thin* [etc.]. But, *th*, makes a softer sound in *that, thine, worthy, father* [etc.]. **1730–6** BAILEY (folio), *Th*, in English is..but one Letter, or a *Litera aspirata*. **1863** MELVILLE BELL *Princ. Speech* 180 We confound the two sounds [þ and ð] by using for both the same digraph [*th*].

2. Th. is an abbreviation of THORIUM, THURSDAY.

th-, th', (ME. þ-), a clipped form of some unstressed monosyllables, esp. when the following word begins with a vowel or *h*.

1. = THE.

Still *dial.* in Lancs., etc.: cf. T' 2. See also I'TH'.

1154 *O.E. Chron.*, þe munekes..on cyricen byrieden þabbot hehlice. *c* **1200** ORMIN 5937 Tatt himm ummbeshorenn wass Hiss shapp o þalde wise. *c* **1330** R. BRUNNE *Chron. Wace* 5734 þapostles holy lyf. **13..** *E.E. Allit. P.* C. 325 þacces of anguych watz hid in my sawle. **1414–15** *Plumpton Corr.* (Camden) p. cxx, Sir Marmaduke Constable thelder, knight,..on thone partie, & Sir Robert Plompton..on thother partie. **1485** *Naval Acc. Hen. VII* (1896) 8 To be levied by thands of Thomas Combes. **1533** MORE *Apol.* 283 More old than thage of eyght hundred yere. **1623** *Shaks.'s Lear* IV. vi. 238 Least that th'infection..take ..hold on thee. —— *Temp.* II. i. 120 To th'shore. *Ibid.* 131 Which end o' th'beame should bow. **1883** *Almondbury & Huddersfield Gloss.* s.v. *T*, Th' man i'th' mooin.

†**2.** = THOU. *Obs.*

c **1315** SHOREHAM i. 94 þorwe þat blod þi soule his [= is] bouȝt..And þorwe þat water i-wessche þart. *c* **1330** R. BRUNNE *Chron. Wace* (Rolls) 8015 þer wot no man of wham þart come. *c* **1500** *Debate Carp. Tools* 6 in Hazl. *E.P.P.* I. 79 Th' all neuer be thryfty man. *a* **1586** SIDNEY *Arcadia* III. *Countrie Song* 99, I rather would my sheepe Thad'st killed with a stroke. **1594** GREENE & LODGE *Looking Glasse* (Hunter. Cl.) 25 Well sirrha well, thart as thart, and so ile take thee.

†**3.** = THEY. *Obs.*

c **1540** in Weever *Anc. Fun. Mon.* (1631) 282 God grant hem euirlastyng lyff, To whom we hop thar gon. **1707** E. WARD *Hud. Rediv.* II. VII. 18 Th'ad put the holy Puppet on A Surplice.

-th, *suffix*[1], a formative of sbs. **a.** from verbs; in some words, as *bath*, *birth*, *death*, *math*, *oath*, OTeut., repr. various Indo-Eur. suffixes, as *-tos*, *-tâ*, *-tis*, *-tus*, in which the *t* following the stressed syllable regularly became *þ* in Teutonic; in others, as *growth*, *tilth*, going back to ON. or OE.; in others, as *blowth*, *spilth*, *stealth*, of later analogical formation. In many words Indo-Eur. *t* remained in consequence of its position, or *þ* was subsequently changed to *t*: see -T *suffix*[3] a.

b. from adjs. (rarely sbs.), representing Indo-Eur. *-itâ*, OTeut. *-iþô*, Goth. *-iþa*, OE. *-þu*, *-þo*, *-þ*, with prec. *i-* umlaut, forming abstract nouns of state: as *filth* (OE. *fýlþ*, OS. *fūlitha* from *fúl* foul), *health*, *length*, *mirth*, *strength*, *truth*; in ME. and also in cognate langs., *dearth*, *depth*; of later analogical formation, *breadth*, *sloth* (cf. OE. *slǽwþ*), *wealth*. In some words of this group, *þ* has, by phonetic causes, become *t*, e.g. OE. *híehþu*, ME. *heiȝþe*, now *height*, ON. *slægð*, ME. *sleiȝþe*, now *sleight*: see -T *suffix*[3] b.

-th, *suffix*[2], forming ordinal numbers; in modern literary Eng. used with all simple numbers from *fourth* onward; representing OE. *-þa*, *-þe*, or *-oða*, *-oðe*, used with all ordinals except *fifta*, *sixta*, *ellefta*, *twelfta*, which had the ending *-ta*, *-te*; in Sc., north. Eng., and many midland dialects the latter, in form *-t*, is used with all simple numerals after *third* (*fourt*, *fift*, *sixt*, *sevent*, *tent*, *hundert*, etc.). In Kentish and O. Northumbrian those from *seventh* to *tenth* had formerly the ending *-da*, *-de*. All these variations, *-th*, *-t*, *-d*, represent an original Indo-Eur. *-tos* (cf. Gr. *πέμπ-τος*, L. *quin-tus*), understood to be identical with one of the suffixes of the superlative degree. In OE. *fífta*, *sixta*, the original *t* was retained, being protected by the preceding consonant; the *-þa* and *-da* were due to the position of the stress accent, according to Verner's Law.

The ordinals from *twentieth* to *ninetieth* have *-eth*, OE. *-oða*, *-oðe*. In compound numerals *-th* is added only to the last, as $\frac{1}{1345}$, the *one thousand three hundred and forty-fifth* part; in his *one-and-twentieth* year.

2. Used in works of fiction with preceding dash or hyphen to denote an unspecified ordinal number presented as the name of an unspecified or fictitious regiment.

1847 THACKERAY *Van. Fair* (1848) xxxvi. 324 Colonel O'Dowd, of the —th regiment. **1867** 'OUIDA' *Under Two Flags* I. v. 101 The —th came back to Brighton and to barracks. **1931** S. JAMESON *Richer Dust* x. 297 Someone asked him if it were true that the —th had run like hell in front of Festubert. **1949** G. HEYER *Arabella* ii. 33 Algernon ..held a commission in the -th Regiment.

tha, þa, thaa, þaa, OE. and northern forms of THO *Obs.*

tha, dial. form of THOU, THEE.

thaarm, obs. form of THARM, intestine.

Thaborite, obs. f. TABORITE (Blount *Gl.* 1674).

thaccy ('ðækɪ), a dial. form of *that*.

Examples of related variants, *thac(k*, *thact*, *thackey*, etc., from 1814 onward, are listed in *Eng. Dial. Dict.* (Devon, Cornwall, Glos., Wilts.) s.v. *Thac(k*. See note at THILK *dem. adj.* and *pron.*

1929 H. WILLIAMSON *Beautiful Years* (rev. ed.) i. 21 He produced it [*sc.* a knife] from his pocket, and opened an enormous blade. 'Not bad, eh?' 'A gude 'un, thaccy!' **1940** J. CARY *Charley is my Darling* lxi. 332 Tis only booys badness in you and you'll grow out of thaccy.

thach, thacher, obs. ff. THATCH *v.*, -ER.

thack (θæk), *sb.* Now *dial.* Forms: 1 **þæc**, 4 **þak**, **þakke**, 4–6 (9 *dial.*) **thak**, 5 **thakk(e**, 5–6 (9 *dial.*) **thake**, 5–7 **thacke**, 6 **thecke**, **thaec**, 6– **thack** (9 *Sc.* **theck**). [Com. Teut.: OE. *þæc* = WFris. *thek*, OLG. **þak* (MDu. *dac* (*dāke*), Du., MLG., LG. *dak*), OHG. *dach*, *dah*, *thah* (MHG., Ger. *dach*) roof, ON. *þak* roof, thatch (Sw. *tak*, Da. *tag*):—OTeut. **þako^m*, f. root *þek-* to cover, Indo-Eur. *teg-*, in L. *teg-ĕre* to cover, *tog-a* covering, gown, *tug-urium* hut, cottage, Gr. *τέγ-ος*, *στεγ-ή* roof, *στέγ-ειν* to cover; Lith. *stogas* roof; OIr. *teg*, Irish and Gael. *tigh* house. See THATCH *v.*]

†**1.** The roof of a house or building. *Obs.*

a **900** CYNEWULF *Christ* 1503 þæt hi under eowrum þæce mosten in-ȝebuȝan. *c* **975** *Rushw. Gosp.* Matt. viii. 8 Drihten nam ic wyrðe þ ðu ga under þacu minne. *Ibid.* xxiv. 17 Seþe on þæce siæ ne stiȝað he niðer. *c* **1000** *Ags. Ps.* (Th.) cxxviii. 4 þam þe on huses þæce heah aweaxeð. *c* **1330** R. BRUNNE *Chron. Wace* (Rolls) 14689 In eueses þey [sparrows] crepte, & in þe þakkes. **1489** CAXTON *Faytes of A.* II. xxxvii. 156 They ought to mounte up to the wyndowes of the houses and upon the thakkes. **1513** DOUGLAS *Æneis* IV. xii. 53 Spreding fra thak to thak, baith but and ben. **1524** LD. DACRE *Let. to Wolsey* in Ellis *Orig. Lett.* Ser. I. I. 249 Ald Howses wherof the thak and covereings ar taken awey. **1526** in T. West *Antiq. Furness* (1805) 133 The said tenant to keep his hous tennantable, upon his own charges, with thake and walle.

2. That with which the roof of a house or the like is covered to protect it from the weather; *spec.* the covering of straw, reeds, or the like disposed so as to carry off the rain: = THATCH *sb.* 1.

a **900** tr. *Bæda's Hist.* III. viii. [x.] (1890) 180 þæs huses hrof.. wæs mid ȝyrdum awunden & mid þæce beþeaht. *Ibid.* xiv. [xvi.] (1890) 202 On beamum & on ræftrum & on waȝum & on watelum & on ðeacon. *c* **1000** ÆLFRIC *Hom.* II. 136 Ða tear þæt hors þæt ðæc of ðære cytan hrofe. **14..** *Nom.* in Wr.-Wülcker 732/23 *Hectectura*, thak. **1486** *Nottingham Rec.* III. 244 Thak þat the grete wynde blewe of þe house. *a* **1500** *Chaucer's Dreme* 1773 That they would ever in houses of thacke, Their lives lead. **1530** PALSGR. 280/1

Thacke of a house, *chaume*. **1578** BANISTER *Hist. Man* I 1 To be well aduised..before he lay on Thack, Tile,..or Plaster. **1641** BEST *Farm. Bks.* (Surtees) 138 One to drawe thacke, and the other to serve the thatcher. **1721** RAMSAY *Ode to Mr. F——* 30 Wa's of divots, roof'd wi' thack. **1815** SCOTT *Guy M.* viii, Ye have riven the thack off seven cottar houses. **1859** GEO. ELIOT *A. Bede* x, It puts me i' mind o' the swallows as was under the thack last 'ear. *Mod. north. dial.* Wet as thack.

(In *Eng. Dial. Dict.* from Scotl. to Oxfordsh., Berksh., and from Worcester to E. Anglia.)

b. The covering of properly disposed straw with which the sloping top of a stack of corn or hay-rick is thatched. ***thack and rape*** (*Sc.*), this thatching and the straw rope with which it is secured: often used allusively.

1786 BURNS *Brigs of Ayr* 26 An thack and rape secure the toil-won crap. **1816** SCOTT *Antiq.* xxvi, He kens..wha feeds him, and cleeds him, and keeps a' tight, thack and rape. *Ibid.* Gloss., *Under thack and rape* means snug and comfortable. **1896** *Speaker* 3 Oct. 353/1 All is secured in the cornyard under 'thack and raip'.

3. *transf.* Covering (in quot. = skin).

c **1375** *Sc. Leg. Saints* xxxvii. (*Vincencius*) 276 þane of þe frame he bad hym tak, þat hale had nothir lith na þak.

4. *attrib.* and *Comb.*, as ***thack-roof***; **thack-board**, a wooden roofing tile, a shingle; **thack-broach** = *thack-pin*, *thack-prick*, BROACH *sb.*[1] 5; **thack divot (dowat)** = *thack turf*; **thack-gate** (*Sc.*): see quot.; **thack house**, a thatched house; **thack-lead**, lead with which a roof is covered; **thack-nail, -peg, -pin**, a sharpened pin or peg used in fastening the thatch on a roof; **thack-prick, -prod**, a sharpened wand or stick for the securing of thatch; **thack-rape** (*Sc.* and *north. dial.*), a rope (usually of twisted straw) used in fixing the thatch on a rick or cottage roof; **thack-stone**, a thin flat stone (e.g. Stonesfield slate) used for roofing; **thack-tile** [OE. *þæcti3ile*; cf. G. *dachziegel*], a roofing tile; **thack turf**, a roofing turf or sod.

1354 *Mem. Ripon* (Surtees) III. 91 In ccc de *thakbord' emp. pro stauro ecclesiæ. **1375** BARBOUR *Bruce* IV. 126 (MS. E.) For fyre all cleir Soyn throu the thak [*v.r.* thik] burd can appeir. **1418** in Rogers *Agric. & Pr.* (1882) III. 402/1 Norwich, Thackboard. **1447–8** *Durham Acc. Rolls* (Surtees) 186 In repar. molendini..in Cma Thakborde. **1573** in Feuillerat *Revels Q. Eliz.* (1908) 208 Hookes & eies with *thackbroches. **1504** *Acc. Ld. H. Treas. Scot.* II. 424 For theking of divers houses with *thak dowat. **1825** JAMIESON, **Thack-gate*, the sloping edge of the gable-tops of a house, when the thatch covers them; in contradistinction from the wind-skews that are raised higher than the thatch. **1582–8** *Hist. Jas. VI* (1804) 209 He exposit..sum of his souldiors to sum *thak housses besyd the West Port, in a windie nyght, and pat the same in fyre. **1725** RAMSAY *Gentle Sheph.* II. i, A snug thack house, before the door a green. **1894** *Northumbld. Gloss.*, 'Thack hoose'—a thatched house. **1819** W. TENNANT *Papistry Storm'd* (1827) 214 Capper and *thack-lead aff were tane. **1846** BROCKETT *N.C. Words* (ed. 3), **Thack-nail*, **Thack-peg*, **Thack-pin*, a wooden pin or stob used in fastening thatch to the roof of a building. **1828** *Craven Gloss.*, **Thack-pricks*, sharpened twigs for the securing of thatch. **1876** *Whitby Gloss.*, **Thack-reeaps*, the cords for securing the thatch. **1887** *Suppl. to Jamieson*, Thack-rape. **1442** *Calverley Charters* (1904) 253, j acre of soile..where he may gett and tak *thakstone. **1621** *Sc. Acts Jas. VI*, c. 26 (1816) IV. 627/1 To thaick þe same againe wt Sklait, or skail3ee, leade, tyild, or Thackstone. **1880** A. L. RITCHIE *Ch. St. Baldred* 37 The roof of the east end of Whitekirk Church is covered with thackstones. *c* **725** *Corpus Gloss.* (O.E.T.) 1043 *Imbricibus* *þæcti3ilum. **1477** *Act 17 Edw. IV*, c. 4 Pleintile, autrement nosmer thaktile, roftile, ou crestile. **1610** W. FOLKINGHAM *Art of Survey* 4 Gallic and Thacke Tiles. *c* **1800** S. PEGGE *Anecd. Eng. Lang.* (1803) 279 In Yorkshire they call bricks wall tile, and tiles thack tile. **1576** in *Reg. Mag. Sig. Scot.* 1580. 20/1 Pro 108 oneribus focalium..et *thak turffis.

thack (θæk), *v.*[1] Now *dial.* Forms: 5–6 (9 *dial.*) thak, 6 thacke, 7 thake, *Sc.* thaick, 6– thack. [app. partly (in form *thake*) from OE. *þacian*, f. *þæc* THACK *sb.* (so MHG., Ger. *dachen* to roof, from *dach*): cf. Sc. *mak*, *tak*, for *make*, *take*; but *thak*, *thack*, may also have been a later formation from the sb. See also THATCH *v.*, THEEK *v.*]

1. *intr.* To put thatch on houses; = THATCH *v.* 5.

a **1100** *Gerefa* in *Anglia* (1886) IX. 261 Me mæcg in Agusto and Septembri and Octobri ðacian, ðecgan and fald weoxian. **1486** *Nottingham Rec.* III. 247 Paid to a thakker thakkyng on þe same barne. **1523** FITZHERB. *Husb.* §27 To mowe theyr stubble, eyther to thacke or to bren. **1523** —— *Surv.* xx. (1539) 42 He shall bothe thacke and daube at his owne coste. **1641** BEST *Farm. Bks.* (Surtees) 139 Thatchers allwayes beginne att the eize [eaves], and soe thake upwards till they come to the ridge.

2. *trans.* To cover (a roof) or roof (a house) with thatch, formerly also with lead, tiles, etc.; = THEEK *v.* 1; *spec.* to cover the top of a rick with straw or other material so laid as to carry off the rain.

c **1440** *Promp. Parv.* 490/1 Thakkyn howsys, *sartatego*, ..*sarcitego*. **1474** *Coventry Leet-bk.* 389 þat no maner man frohensfurth thak ne couer his house with strawe nor brome within this Cite. **1530** PALSGR. 754/2 Sythe I can nat tyle my house, I must be fayne to thacke it. **1552** *Inv. Ch. Goods* (Surtees No. 97) 9 The churche thacked with leade. **1611** SPEED *Hist. Gt. Brit.* v. iv. §5. 22 Houses and cottages.. Which, as Diodorus Siculus saith were vsually thacked with reed. **1621** [see *thackstone*, prec. 4]. **1671** J. FRASER *Polichron.* (S.H.S.) 496 Tirr the Kirk to thack the quire. *a* **1825** FORBY *Voc. E. Anglia*, *Thack*, v. to thatch. **1863** MRS. TOOGOOD *Yorks. Dial.*, It will take two threave of strea to thack the hay-stack.

Hence **thacked** (θækt) *ppl. a.*, thatched; **'thacking** *vbl. sb.*, the action of thatching; also *concr.* the material used for the purpose, thatch.

1530 PALSGR. 699/1 This is a mete man to sytte on a *thacked house to scarre away crowes. **1597** *1st Pt. Return fr. Parnass.* I. i. 134 Some thacked cottage or some cuntrie hall. **1602** *2nd Pt. Return fr. Parnass.* V. ii. 2091 True mirth we may enioy in thacked stall. **1828** *Craven Gloss.*, *Thack'd*, thatched. *c* **1440** *Promp. Parv.* 490/1 *Thakkynge, *sartatectum*. **1546** *Yorks. Chantry Surv.* (Surtees) 168 The reparacion of the belles, thakkyng and other necessaries pertenyng to the sayd churche. **1613** MARKHAM *Eng. Husbandman* I. I. xvii. (1635) 103 Whole Strawe Wheate.. Husbandmen esteeme it so much for their thacking. *c* **1680** H. LEIGH in Macfarlane *Geog. Collect.* (S.H.S.) III. 252 The common and ordinary thacking is of a kind of Divet [= sod].

thack (θæk), *v.*[2] *Obs.* exc. *dial.* [OE. *þaccian*, app. onomatopœic. Cf. THWACK.]

†**1.** *trans.* To clap with the open hand or the like; to pat, slap lightly. *Obs.*

c **897** K. ÆLFRED *Gregory's Past. C.* xli. 303 Swa [swa] wildu hors, ðonne we h[ie] æresð 3efangnu habbað, we hie ðacciað & straciað mid bradre hande. *a* **900** —— in Cockayne *Shrine* (1864) 185 Hine lyst bet þaccian and cyssan ðonne oðerne on bær lic. *c* **1305** *Land Cokayne* 141 To þe maid dun hi fleeþ And geþ þe wench al abute, And þakkeþ al her white toute. *c* **1386** CHAUCER *Miller's T.* 118 Whan Nicholas had doon thus euerideel And thakked [*MS. Petw.* twakked] hire aboute the lendes weel. —— *Friar's T.* 261 (Harl. MS.) This carter thakketh his hors vpon the croupe.

†**b.** *intr.* To beat, to shower blows. *Obs.*

1480 CAXTON *Chron. Eng.* ccxliv. 299 Our men of armes and archyers that thakked on hem so thikke with arewes.

†**2.** *trans.* To clap (something) *on* or *in* a place.

1542 *St. Papers Hen. VIII*, IX. 42 But here he thakked on as many wordes, as he did bifore lawes in the other parte. **1589** R. ROBINSON *Gold. Mirr.* 31 The thorny thumps that Thought did thacke Within my wofull breast.

3. *mod. dial.* To THWACK, beat, flog.

1861 QUINN *Heather Lintie* (1863) 22 (E.D.D.) Ye weel deserve a thackin' For tellin [etc.]. **1904** in *Eng. Dial. Dict.* (Norf.), He rarely thacked th' old dicky (donkey).

'thacker. Now *dial.* [prob. representing an OE. **þæcere*, f. *þacian* to thatch.] One who covers roofs with thatch; a thatcher.

1420 *Coventry Leet-bk.* 21 Item, thakker, laborer, dawber, and palyer. **1486** [see THACK *v.*[1] 1]. **1573** TUSSER *Husb.* (1878) 86 Wheat and the rie..Such strawe some saue for thacker to haue. **1590** *Shuttleworths' Acc.* (Chetham Soc.) 62 A thacker at Tyngreve thackinge three dayes, and onne to serve him iijs vjd. **1820** *Blackw. Mag.* Oct. 14/2 Hire two-three thackers to mend the thack on the roofs.

Thackerayan ('θækəreɪən, θækə'reɪən), *a.* and *sb.* [f. proper name *Thackeray* + -AN.] **a.** *adj.* Of or pertaining to, or characteristic of, William Makepeace Thackeray (1811–63) or his works. **b.** *sb.* An admirer of Thackeray or his works. So ˌ**Thackeray'esque** *a.*, **Thacke'rayian** *a.*, **'Thackerayite**. (All more or less nonce-wds.)

1857 J. BLACKWOOD *Let.* 8 June in *Geo. Eliot Lett.* (1954) II. 344 The harsher Thackerayan view of human nature. **1861** W. F. COLLIER *Hist. Eng. Lit.* 491 Those queer, delightful, rambling, thoroughly Thackerayesque Roundabout Papers. **1885** *Athenæum* 17 Oct. 497/1 All interesting enough..to the professional Thackerayite. **1887** *Illustr. Lond. News* 22 Jan. 88/2 This is..almost Thackerayian, indeed. **1888** *Scott. Leader* 3 May 7 A certain cynical humour which is almost 'Thackerayan' in quality. **1909** G. K. CHESTERTON *Thackeray* p. xxiii, Any Thackerayan must recognize my meaning. **1917** J. B. CABELL *Cream of Jest* VI. iv. 264, I am thus digressing, in obsolete Thackerayan fashion, to twaddle about love matches alone. **1958** G. N. RAY *Thackeray* II. vi. 175 Devoted Thackerayans persist in putting it at the top of their favourite's work. **1978** *Encounter* Feb. 71/1 They have trouble with the inevitable Thackerayan mother-in-law.

Also **Thackeray'ana** [-ANA *suff.*], items associated with Thackeray.

1905 *Spectator* 18 Feb. 256/2 The voracious collector of Thackerayana cannot have too much of a good thing. **1979** *Times* 27 Dec. 8/1 The cupboard was packed with Thackerayana, early and special editions of his works, bound volumes of the journals he wrote for and a pile of his pictures.

'thackless, *a.* Now *dial.* = THATCHLESS.

a **1800** *Witch Cake* in Cromek *Rem. Nithsdale Song* (1810) 284 Some priest maun preach in a thackless kirk. **1897** LD. E. HAMILTON *Outlaws* xviii. 209 The auld Redheuch tower stands thackless and woefu' this day.

thackster ('θækstə(r)). *Obs.* exc. *dial.* Also 5 thac-, thakstare, 6 thaxster. See also THATCHESTER. [f. THACK *v.*[1] + -STER.] = THACKER.

c **1440** *Promp. Parv.* 52/2 Broche for a thacstare, *firmaculum*. *Ibid.* 490/1 Thakstare, *sartitector*. **1533** in Blomefield *Hist. Norfolk* (1806) III. 206 The Reders, Thaxsters, Rede-sellers,..with their banner. **1787** W. MARSHALL *E. Norf.* Gloss. (E.D.S.), *Thackster*, a thatcher. *a* **1825** FORBY *Voc. E. Anglia*, *Thacker*, *Thackster*, a thatcher.

thad, obs. form of THAT *rel. pron.*

thae (ðeː, ðɪə), *dem. pron.* and *adj. Sc.* and *north. dial.* Forms: (1–6 þa), 6 thai, 6–7 thay, 6– *Sc.* thae, thea, 9 theae, *n. dial.* theea, thee. [Mod. Sc. and north. dial. repr. of OE. and northern ME. *þá*, *tha*, midl. and south. ME. THO. For the phonology cf. *mae*, *nae*, *sae*, *twae*, *whae*, = OE. *má*, *ná*, *swá*, *twá*, *hwá*, Eng. *mo*, *no*, *so*, *two*, *who*.]

The Sc. and north. dial. plural of THAT, = ME. *þa*, THO; mod. THOSE. **a.** *pron.*

1583 *Leg. Bp. St. Androis* 613 Gude Robert Melwene of Carnebie I shuld not racken in with thea. ? **17..** *Auld Maitland* v. in Scott *Minstrelsy Sc. Bord.*, Thou sall hae thae, thou sall hae mae. **1780** J. MAYNE *Siller Gun* I, Her exultation was exprest In words like thae. **1790** BURNS *Tam o'Shanter* 151 Now Tam, O Tam! had thae been queans. **1873** MURRAY *Dial. S. Scot.* 182 Dynna teake theae (Don't take those).

b. *adj.*

a **1584** MONTGOMERIE *Cherrie & Slae* 85 To heir thae startling stremis cleir, Me thocht it musique to the eir. **1596** DALRYMPLE tr. *Leslie's Hist. Scot.* (S.T.S.) I. 22 Pentland it was called,..evin as this day thae mountanis declairis sa named. **1603** *Philotus* lxxviii, And send to 3ow thay claithis vnsene. **1786** BURNS *Dream* ix, Thae bonny bairn-time, Heav'n has lent. **1826** J. WILSON *Noct. Ambr.* Wks. 1855 I. 186 Thae broad vine-leaves hingin in the veranda. **1837** R. NICOLL *Poems* (1843) 76 But thae hames are gane. **1904** *Eng. Dial. Dict.* (*N. Yorksh.*), Wheea's theea tweea bairns? (*Northumb.*) Thee kye; thee folk.

thæh, þæh, early ME. form of THOUGH.

thæm, þæm, OE. infl. of THE, THAT; f. THEM.

thær, þær, obs. form of THERE, THEIR.

thære, obs. infl. of THE, THAT; obs. f. THERE.

thæs, obs. var. of THES, THESE.

thafe, variant of THAVE *v. Obs.*

thaff, obs. f. THOUGH; erron. f. TEFF.

thaft, Sc. f. *thaught*, THOFT (rower's seat).

thag, thagi, var. THUG, THUGGEE.

thagh, tha3, þagh, þaih, obs. ff. THOUGH.

Thai (taɪ), *sb.* and *a.* Also 9 T'hai, Thay, T'hay. [Native name, meaning 'free': the same word as TAI *sb.*[2] and *a.*] (Occasionally used where TAI *sb.*[2] and *a.* might be expected.) **A.** *sb.* **a.** The language of the Thai people, a member of the Tai group of languages; Siamese.

1808 *Asiatick Res.* X. 173 The more ancient eastern languages, are Jawa, Bugis, T'hay, and Barma. **1880** A. H. SAYCE *Introd. Sci. Lang.* II. viii. 224 In Siamese or T'hai every word which defines another must follow it. **1963** *Time & Tide* 2 May 23/2 HRH Prince Chula-Chakrabongse of Thailand..has written more than 30 books in Thai and English. **1972** E. A. NIDA *Bk. Thousand Tongues* (ed. 2) 427/1 Thai and related languages are linguistically grouped in a class known as the Tai languages, a class that comprises tongues spoken by at least 40 million people, from Burma to south-eastern China. **1977** *Times* 15 June 16/6 McGonagall ..had just had his prolific collection of bizarre poems translated into Russian, Chinese, Japanese and..Thai.

b. A native or inhabitant of Thailand (called Siam before 1939 and again briefly between 1945 and 1948); a member of the ethnic group that constitutes the bulk of the population of Thailand. Also, the Thais collectively.

1841 *Penny Cycl.* XXI. 452/1 The Siamese call themselves Thay. **1939** *Times* 30 May 11/3 Muang-Thai is the name by which the dominant element in the country, the Thai, call their land... The newcomers amalgamated with their Lao and Thai kinsmen. **1941** *Engineer* 15 Aug. 99/1 The Thais have always been agriculturists. **1957** *Encycl. Brit.* XX. 593B/1 Of the total population [of Siam] the great majority (about 75%–80%) belongs to the Thai group of peoples. These may be divided into the southern Thai or Siamese and the northern Thai or Lao. **1962** E. SNOW *Other Side of River* (1963) lxxxv. 681 Cambodians, like the people of Thailand and Upper Burma, are mixed descendants of the same stock as the Thai and other minority peoples of China. **1978** T. WILLIAMSON *Technicians of Death* xi. 90 He was operating his own ship..with a mixed crew of Thais and Filipinos.

B. *adj.* Of or pertaining to Thailand, its people, or its language; ***Thai silk***, wild silk woven in Thailand according to traditional designs, often with bright colours; ***Thai stick*** [cf. STICK *sb.*[1] 11 h], a marijuana cigarette.

1808 [see SIAMESE *sb.* 2]. **1939** *Times* 5 July 15/7 The Siamese Legation, now officially renamed the Thai Legation, issued the following announcement yesterday:–.. The word 'Thailand' for 'Siam' and the word 'Thai' for 'Siamese' will be used from now on by the Ministries and Departments of the Thai Government. **1948** D. DIRINGER *Alphabet* II. vii. 413 The thirteenth century witnessed a general advance of the Thai or Shan race, facilitated by the fall of Pagan dynasty. **1955** *Times* 9 May 8/4 The many millions of people of Thai race considered linguistically and ethnologically now scattered across south-west China, north Viet Nam, and Burma are split into different groups, and in many cases the split dates back for hundreds of years. **1958** A. TOYNBEE *East to West* xxviii. 85 A skiff will carry the Thai housewife to a shop-front that could not be reached on foot. **1976** *National Observer* (U.S.) 25 Sept. 22/2 Cannabis connoisseurs rank Colombian marijuana alongside such Asian types as so-called Thai-sticks from Thailand. **1977** *Times* 17 May 8/1 (Advt.), Our beautiful slim-bodied hostesses in their glamorous Thai silk outfits. **1978** *Chicago*

June 245/1 Tom yum gung soup..is almost a meal in itself as is Thai fried rice, a combination of green peppers, chicken, and tiny bits of bacon, garnished with cucumber and tomato slices. **1978** [see STICK *sb.*[1] 11 h]. **1981** *Times* 22 Apr. 4/3 He had made..money through smuggling Thai sticks.

thai, obs. form of THEY; obs. Sc. f. THAE.

† **thaie, thaye,** *dem. pron.* and *adj. Obs.* Forms: 1 **þæᵹe, ðaᵹe,** 3 **þaie, þaye.** [Late OE. *þæᵹe*, of obscure origin and history.

Generally held to be ad. ON. *þeir*, with *r* dropped (as in Ormin's *þeȝȝ*, THEY), and with *-e* added, after plurals like *ealle, sume, swylce*. But the local distribution of the word does not favour a Norse origin.]

1. *dem.* (or *pers.*) *pron.* = THOSE (THEY, THEM).

c **1000** *Ags. Gosp.* John x. 16 Hit ᵹebyrað þæt ic læde þæᵹe [*Hatton G.* þa hyder] & hiᵹ ᵹehyrað mine stefne. *Ibid.* xiv. 12 He wyrcð maran þonne þæᵹe synt [*MS. A.* þa synd]. *a* **1100** *MS. C.C.C. Camb.* No. 162 Ðæᵹe wæron on fruman of Godes oroðe..ᵹesceapene. *a* **1100** *Salomon & Sat.* (Kemble) 180 Saᵹa me, hwæt hatton ðaᵹe? *c* **1275** LAY. 18474 þaie [*c* 1205 heo] were amorwe alle idon to deaþe. *Ibid.* 28516 þaie he habbe nolde. *a* **1300** *Cursor M.* 20002 (Edin.) Ful mani a torfer suffrid þaie [*C., F., G.,* þai, *Trin.* þei].

b. as antecedent.

c **1275** LAY. 4240 Alle þaie [*c* 1205 þa] þat astode hii fulde to grunde. *Ibid.* 20775 þaye þat her bi-ȝeteþ eft hii leoseþ.

2. *dem. adj.* = THOSE (sometimes = THE).

10.. *Ags. Gosp.* Luke xi. 5 (*Marg. note*) Ðis sceal to gangdaᵹon þæᵹe tweᵹen daᵹas. *c* **1205** LAY. 12644 He sende his sonde..æfter..alle þaie ihade gomes. *Ibid.* 19541 Alle þaie halȝen þa an hæfenene hæhȝe sitteð [so 15015]. *Ibid.* 20965 þaie ilærde men heo læiden on gleden. *c* **1275** *Ibid.* 4532 He..ferde..to-ȝeines þaie sipes. *Ibid.* 16008 Wat bi-tocneþ þaie drakes [*c* 1205 þa draken]?

† **thail, thayl, theil,** obs. forms of TAEL.

1662 J. DAVIES tr. *Mandelslo's Trav.* I. (1669) 68 A Theil of Silver. *Ibid.* II. 106 Black Lacque, at ten Thails the Picol. *Ibid.* 147 Forty seven thousand Thayls, or crowns.

Thailander (ˈtaɪlændə(r)). [f. *Thailand* + -ER[1].] A native or inhabitant of Thailand.

1961 in WEBSTER. **1973** P. O'DONNELL *Silver Mistress* v. 81 His personal bodyguard, the silent Thailander who stood two paces away.

thaim, -e, obs. and dial. forms of THEM.

thain, -e, obs. forms of THANE, THEGN.

thair, Sc. f. THAR *v. impers.*, to need; var. THIR *Obs.*, this, these; obs. Sc. f. THERE, q.v., also in Comb.: see THEREABOUT, etc.

thair, -e, -es, obs. or Sc. ff. THEIR, -S.

thairf, var. THARF.

thairm, Sc. f. THARM, intestine.

thais(e, thaive: see THOSE, THEAVE.

thak, thakk(e, obs. and dial. var. THACK.

Thakali (təˈkɑːliː). [Native name.] **a.** A member of one of the tribes or castes of Nepal, of Mongol origin. **b.** The language or dialect spoken by this tribe. Also *attrib.* or as *adj.*

1928 NORTHEY & MORRIS *Gurkhas* xiii. 202 Prosperous, and great traders..the Thakales are of mixed religion and are closely allied to Tibetans. **1961** L. BAJRACHARYA *Nepal 1960–61* 10/2 Of the trading tribes those next to the Newars are the Thakalis, residents of Thak in Central Nepal. **1974** M. PEISSEL *Gt. Himalayan Passage* xvii. 246 Prosperous businessmen..are attempting to obtain for the Thakali people a high rank in the Hindu caste system. **1974** *Encycl. Brit. Macropædia* XII. 954/1 The languages of the north and east belong predominantly to the Tibeto-Burman family. These include Magar, Gurung,..and a number of Bhote dialects, including Sherpa and Thakali.

Thakin (ˈθɑːkɪn), *sb.* [Burmese.] **a.** A term of respectful address used by the Burmese. **b.** A member of a militant nationalist movement that arose in Burma during the 1930s; also *attrib.*

1920 *Blackw. Mag.* June 835/1, I do not know about the deer, *thakin.* **1934** 'G. ORWELL' *Burmese Days* iv. 74 God go with you, *thakin.* **1942** J. L. CHRISTIAN *Mod. Burma* xiii. 238 A current expression of nationalism in Burma is the 'Thakin' movement. *Ibid.*, The Thakins..have done their country little good. **1957** 'F. CLIFFORD' *Ten Minutes on June Morning* (1977) 39 'Who is it?' I asked... 'A Sikh, *thakin.*' **1971** W. LAQUEUR *Dict. Politics* 66 During the 1930s popular pressure for independence led to anti-British riots, militant student strikes and the formation of political private armies, e.g. the Thakin Army which was trained in Japan. **1974** *Encycl. Brit Macropædia* III. 515/1 The young Thakins won the trust of the villagers and emerged as leaders. *Ibid.* IX 923/1 Thant was educated at the University of Rangoon, where he met Thakin Nu (afterward U Nu, who became prime minister of Burma in 1948).

† **tha-kin,** *a.*, those kind (of): see THO and KIN[1] 6.

13.. *Cursor M.* 27282 In þakin thinges. (Cf. THOSE II. 2 c.)

‖ **thakur, thakoor** (ˈtɑːkur). *East Ind.* [a. Hindī *ṭhākur*, Skr. ˈ*ṭhākkura* a deity.] A word meaning Lord, used as a title and term of respect (cf. *dominus, don, seigneur*, etc.); also applied to a chief or noble, esp. of the Rajputs.

1800 *Misc. Tracts* in *Asiat. Ann. Reg.* 312/1 Burwarrah, which belongs to a Thakur named Bickermajeet. **1844** H. H. WILSON *Brit. India* II. x. II. 429 Under an active and prudent Raja the Thakurs might be subjected to control. **1862** BEVERIDGE *Hist. India* VII. vii, The leading thakoors or chiefs. **1895** MRS. CROKER *Village T.* 125 She was married to the heir of a rich thakur. **1904** *Q. Rev.* July 234 He commended the Thakors for their consistent support.

Hence **ˈthakurate**, the district or territory pertaining to a thakur.

1901 *Mission Record United Free Ch. Scot.* Aug. 363/2 Adjoining thakurates will share the boon.

thalam, -ame (ˈθæləm). *rare.* [ad. L. *thalamus*: see THALAMUS.] A nuptial chamber.

1791 W. BARTRAM *Carolina* 446 A booth or pavilion.. formed of green boughs..was the secret nuptial chamber.. no one presuming to approach the sacred, mysterious thalame.

‖ **thalamencephalon** (ˌθæləmɛnˈsɛfəlɒn). *Anat.* [f. THALAM(O- + ENCEPHALON.] That part of the brain which develops from the posterior part of the anterior cerebral vesicle, and includes the optic thalami, optic nerves, and parts about the third ventricle. Also called *diencephalon, middle brain*, etc. Also anglicized **thalaˈmencephal**.

1875 HUXLEY in *Encycl. Brit.* I. 767/1 The optic nerves are attached, as usual, to the floor of the thalamencephalon. **1875** HUXLEY & MARTIN *Elem. Biol.* (1883) 185 The fore-brain, which..comprises three divisions; the thalamencephalon, the cerebral hemispheres, and the olfactory lobes. **1891** *Cent. Dict.*, Thalamencephal.

Hence ˌ**thalamenceˈphalic** (-sɪˈfælɪk), *a. Anat.*, of or pertaining to the thalamencephalon.

thalamic (θəˈlæmɪk, ˈθæləmɪk), *a.* [ad. mod.L. *thalamic-us*: see THALAMUS and -IC.] Of or pertaining to a thalamus; in *Anat.*, pertaining to the optic thalamus.

1860 MAYNE *Expos. Lex.*, *Thalamicus, Bot.*, applied by Lestibondois to the insertion which takes place upon the receptacle: thalamic. **1890** BILLINGS *Nat. Med. Dict.*, *Thalamic nuclei*, special collections of gray matter within the optic thalamus. **1893** W. R. GOWERS *Dis. Nerv. Syst.* (ed. 2) II. 394 Internal thalamic hæmorrhage. **1899** *Allbutt's Syst. Med.* VII. 615 Hæmorrhage in the thalamic region.

thalamifloral (ˌθæləmɪˈflɔərəl), *a. Bot.* [f. mod.L. *Thalamifloræ*, De Candolle 18.. (f. THALAMUS + L. *flōs, flōr-* flower) + -AL[1]. Cf. F. *thalamiflore*.] Belonging to the sub-class *Thalamifloræ* of dicotyledons, in which the stamens are inserted on the thalamus or receptacle; hypogynous. So **thalamiˈflorous** *a.*

1857 HENFREY *Bot.* §454 Some Thalamiflorous Orders. *Ibid.* §478 Parietal Thalamifloral Orders. **1872** OLIVER *Elem. Bot.* I. v. 58 Thalamifloral..as Buttercup and Wall-flower. **1880** GRAY *Struct. Bot.* ix. §2. 340 *Thalamiflorous*, petals (distinct) and stamens on the torus, i.e. free.

thalamite (ˈθæləmaɪt). *Gr. Antiq.* [ad. Gr. θαλαμίτης, f. θάλαμος inner chamber, one of the compartments of a ship.] In the ancient trireme, a rower in one of the tiers of rowers, generally supposed to be that which occupied the lowest bench; but the actual arrangement is disputed: see quots. Cf. THRANITE, ZYGITE.

1886 *Encycl. Brit.* XXI. 806/2 Behind the zygite sat the thalamite, or oarsman of the lowest bank. **1906** *Athenæum* 7 Apr. 429/2 The three orders of rowers..there seems little reason to doubt..refer to the parts into which the ship was longitudinally divided..the thalamites [being] in the bows.

‖ **thalamium** (θəˈleɪmɪəm). *Bot.* [mod.L. dim. of THALAMUS.] (See quot. 1866.)

1861 BENTLEY *Man. Bot.* (1870) 375 The body of the apothecium constitutes the thalamium. **1866** *Treas. Bot.*, *Thalamium*, a hollow case containing spores in algals; also the disk or *lamina prolifera* of lichens, and a form of the hymenium in fungals.

thalamo- (ˈθæləməʊ), before a vowel **thalam-**, combining form of Gr. θάλαμος THALAMUS, used as a formative in some anatomical words. **thalamocœle** (ˈθæləməʊˌsiːl) [Gr. κοιλία cavity, ventricle], the cavity of the thalamencephalon; the third ventricle of the brain. **thalamoˈcortical** *a.*, applied to nerves running from the thalamus to the cerebral cortex. ˌ**thalamoˈcrural** *a.*, of or pertaining to the optic thalamus and to the *crus cerebri* (CRUS 2 b). **thalamoˈstriate** *a.*, connecting or serving the thalamus and the corpus striatum. **thalaˈmotomy** *Surg.* [-TOMY], an operation to destroy specific groups of cells in the thalamus, used for the relief of pain or for treatment of Parkinson's disease or mental disorders. See also THALAMENCEPHALON.

1899 *Syd. Soc. Lex.*, **Thalamocœle*, cavity of thalamencephalon. The thalamic cœlia, or third ventricle. **1902** D. J. CUNNINGHAM *Text-bk. Anat.* 504 Flechsig divides the *thalamo-cortical fibres of ordinary sensation into three sensory systems. **1954** *Gray's Anat.* (ed. 31) 994 The wealth of thalamo-cortical and cortico-thalamic connexions indicate a very close functional relationship between the two. **1970** *Jrnl. Physiol.* CCX. 15P The afferent thalamo-cortical pathways to the visual cortex of the cat and monkey have been studied. **1899** *Syd. Soc. Lex.*, **Thalamocrural.* **1902** D. J. CUNNINGHAM *Text-bk. Anat.* 540 Numerous fibres from the optic thalamus pass into the anterior limb of the internal capsule and enter both the caudate and the lenticular nuclei. These may be termed the *thalamo-striate fibres. **1968** PASSMORE & ROBSON *Compan. Med. Stud.* I. xxiv. 73/1 The thalamostriate vein passes forwards between the caudate nucleus and thalamus draining both. **1948** *Time* 21 June 76/2 Last week they announced first results of their new operation, called *thalamotomy. **1955** *Sci. News Let.* 11 June 381/1 The studies were made on 30 patients who underwent a special brain operation called thalamotomy. In this operation the cutting is done on part of the thalamus, the structure in the brain that serves as the main relay center for feelings of heat, cold, pain and the like to the thinking part of the brain. **1973** *Brit. Med. Jrnl.* 15 Dec. 666/1 The movements can be abolished only with thalamotomy. **1977** J. N. WALTON *Brain's Diseases Nervous System* (ed. 8) xi. 595 The operations of pallidectomy and ventrolateral thalamotomy.

‖ **thalamus** (ˈθæləməs). Pl. **-mi** (-maɪ). Also (in sense 3) in Gr. form **thalamos**. [L. *thalamus*, a. Gr. θάλαμος an inner chamber.]

1. *Anat.* A part of the brain at which a nerve originates or appears to originate. Now *spec.* the optic thalamus (see OPTIC *a.*).

[**1704** J. HARRIS *Lex. Techn.* I, *Thalami Nervorum Opticorum*, are two Prominences of the lateral Ventricles of the Cerebrum; so call'd, because the Optick Nerves rise out of them.] **1756** *Gentl. Mag.* XXVI. 517/1 The thalami here appeared very thin, and the pia mater..was overspread with blood-vessels of an unusual size. **1856** TODD & BOWMAN *Phys. Anat.* II. 38 Each tract adheres to the outer side of its corresponding thalamus for some distance. **1879** *St. George's Hosp. Rep.* IX. 513 An abscess..in the right optic thalamus, opening just behind the tænia. **1902** D. J. CUNNINGHAM *Text-bk. Anat.* 501 The two optic thalami, in their anterior two-thirds, lie close together on either side of a deep mesial cleft, which receives the name of the third ventricle of the brain. **1947** *Sci. News* IV. 112 There is an anatomically distinct region, the thalamus, deep in the brain-stem which has something to do with the perception of pain and other sensations and the judgment of their quality. **1948** A. BRODAL *Neurol. Anat.* vi. 157 It appears.. that the thalamus is not only an important relay station in the large afferent sensory fibre systems and the optic and acoustic systems, but in addition extensive parts of it..also discharge their impulses to the cerebral cortex. **1979** *Sci. Amer.* Sept. 85/2 The rest of the forebrain is the diencephalon: the upper two-thirds comprises the thalamus (which has numerous subdivisions) and the lower third the hypothalamus.

2. *Bot.* **a.** The receptacle of a flower, on which the carpels are placed; the torus. **b.** See quot. 1842.

1753 CHAMBERS *Cycl. Supp.*, *Thalamus*, in botany, a term used to express that part of the flower..where the embryo fruits..are lodged, and where afterwards the seeds are contained. **1766** LEE *Introd. Bot.* Gloss., *Thalamus*,..the Receptacle. **1842** *Penny Cycl.* XXIV. 274/1 Thalamus is also used in Cryptogamic botany, in common with Thallus, to express the bed of fibres from which many fungi spring up. **1861** BENTLEY *Man. Bot.* (1870) 208 The extremity of the peduncle or pedicel..is called the Thalamus, or some times, but improperly, the Receptacle.

3. *Archæol.* An inner or secret chamber.

1850 LEITCH tr. *C. O. Müller's Anc. Art* §48 The thalami, secret chambers for the women. **1884** *Times* 15 Aug. 4 The same pattern as that found on the roof of the thalamos.

thalassæmia (θæləˈsiːmɪə). *Path.* Also (chiefly *U.S.*) **-emia**. [f. THALASS(O- + Gr. αἷμα blood + -IA[1].] A hereditary hæmolytic anæmia common in malarious (or formerly malarious) areas and caused by the faulty synthesis of part of the hæmoglobin molecule, with symptoms that depend on the part of the molecule affected and on whether the individual is homozygous or heterozygous for the gene concerned; so ***thalassæmia major, intermedia, minor.***

1932 WHIPPLE & BRADFORD in *Amer. Jrnl. Dis. Children* XLIV. 364 We do not like the term 'erythroblastic anemia'. .. The disease is limited almost wholly to Italians, Greeks and Syrians, i.e., to the people originating about the Mediterranean Sea. For this reason the term 'thalassemia' ..may have an appeal. **1936**, etc. [see MEDITERRANEAN *sb.* 1 b]. **1944** VALENTINE & NEEL in *Arch. Internal Med.* LXXIV. 196/2 It is suggested, on the basis of the pathologic and genetic evidence, that the full-blown disease be designated 'thalassemia major' and the milder carrier state 'thalassemia minor'. **1954** K. SINGER et al. in *Blood* IX. 1039 We have found the following simple classification very useful; it is based on the alterations of the red cell and hemoglobin levels: 1. Thalassemia major (Cooley's anemia): very severe microcytic hemolytic anemia. 2. Thalassemia intermedia, characterized by a less severe, but still marked anemia. 3. Thalassemia minor: mild anemia. **1962** [see HAEMOGLOBINOPATHY]. **1972** D. E. COMINGS in W. J. Williams et al. *Hematology* xxxi. 332/2 Although the total number of individuals with thalassemia intermedia is relatively small.., it constitutes a clinically important group, since its relatively benign course (compared to thalassemia major) allows affected individuals to live to adulthood. **1973** B. J. WILLIAMS *Evolution & Human Origins* iv. 61/2 Osteoporosis occcurs even with thalassemia minor. **1978** *Jrnl. R. Soc. Med.* LXXI. 465/1 The hepatic cirrhosis of thalassemia major. **1979** *Brit. Med. Jrnl.* 17 Nov. 1298/2 The 26-year-old Chinese with beta-thalassaemia who had been transfused with 404 units of blood in his lifetime. His total body iron was so high that it triggered the alarm at an airport security checkpoint. **1982** *New Scientist* 21 Jan. 164/1 Red blood cells in people with thalassæmia cannot carry oxygen well enough, and patients survive only with regular blood transfusions.

Hence **thala'ssæmic**, a person with thalassæmia.

1974 *Nature* 8 Feb. 380/1 The δβ-thalassaemics were Sicilian and have been previously reported. **1979** *Ibid.* 15 Nov. 317/2 In one study, the incidence of HbF Sardinia in β-thalassaemics in Italy was 90%, compared with only 40% in normal Italians.

thalassal (θə'læsəl), *a. rare.* [f. Gr. θάλασσα sea + -AL¹.] = THALASSIC (in quot. in sense 2).

1887 *Proc. Boston Nat. Hist. Soc.* 417 The time required for the accumulation of such a stratum in the thalassal seas is probably great.

thalassarctine: see THALASSO-.

thalassian (θə'læsɪən), *a.* and *sb.* [f. Gr. θαλάσσι-ος marine, f. θάλασσα sea + -AN.]

A. *adj.* Of or pertaining to the sea, marine; *spec.* applied to the marine tortoises and turtles.

1850 BRODERIP *Notebk. Nat.* x. (1852) 264 Nature has modified the Chelonian type into the Thalassian shape.

Comb. **1869** BROWNING *Ring & Bk.* IX. 893 Pompilia.. Springs to her feet, and stands Thalassian-pure.

B. *sb.* A marine tortoise or turtle.

1850 BRODERIP *Notebk. Nat.* xi. (1852) 276 And now a few words on the natural history and capture of some of these Thalassians. **1900** F. T. BULLEN *Idylls of Sea* 164 The Thalassians or oceanic tortoises, from which alone our supplies are drawn.

† **tha'lassiarch.** *Obs. rare*⁻⁰. [f. Gr. θαλάσσι-ος marine, maritime + -αρχος ruling, ruler.] Hence † **tha'lassiarchy** *Obs. rare*⁻⁰. (See quots.)

1656 BLOUNT *Glossogr.*, *Thalassiarck*, an Admiral or chief Officer at sea. **1727** BAILEY vol. II, *Thalassiarchy*, the Admiralship, or the office of the Admiral.

thalassic (θə'læsɪk), *a.* [ad. F. *thalassique* (Brongniart 1829), f. Gr. θάλασσα sea: see -IC.]

1. Of or pertaining to the sea; growing or living in, or formed in or by the sea; marine. †In *Geol.* applied after Brongniart to strata supposed to be of marine formation (*obs.*).

1860 MAYNE *Expos. Lex.*, *Thalassicus, Geol.*, applied by Brongniart to the strata of superior sediment, i.e. those found from the surface of the earth to the limestone exclusively: thalassic. **1890** *Cent. Dict.* s.v. *Littoral*, Deposits.. formed in deep water, or thalassic rocks. **1897** MARY KINGSLEY *W. Africa* 423 Agnes rouses me from my thalassic couch and suggests Mass at 5.30 a.m.

2. Pertaining to the (smaller or inland) seas as distinct from the pelagic waters or oceans.

1883 J. R. SEELEY *Expans. Eng.* 87 [see POTAMIC]. *Ibid.*, European civilization passed from the thalassic to the oceanic state. **1884** *Q. Rev.* July 140 He [Lord Dufferin] seems to have grasped the 'oceanic' rather than the 'thalassic' nature of our Empire. **1899** *Times* 9 Jan. 6 The thalassic civilization of the Mediterranean.

So † **tha'lassical** *a. Obs. rare*⁻⁰ (see quot.).

1656 BLOUNT *Glossogr.*, *Thalassical*, of a blew colour like the sea-waves, sea-green or blew.

thalassin (θə'læsɪn). *Chem.* [See -IN¹.] A poison found in the tentacles of sea-anemones.

1909 in *Cent. Dict.* Suppl.

thala'ssinian, *a.* and *sb.* [f. mod.L. *Thalassina* + -IAN.] **a.** *adj.* Of or pertaining to the *Thalassinidæ*, a family of long-tailed decapod crustaceans, the scorpion-lobsters. **b.** *sb.* A crustacean of this family. So **tha'lassinoid** *a.*

1842 *Penny Cycl.* XXIV. 274/2 Mr. Milne Edwards arranges the family of Thalassinians, or Burrowing Macrura, between the Scyllarians and the Astacians. *Ibid.*, *Cryptobranchids*,.. all the Thalassinians which are without respiratory appendages suspended under the abdomen.

thalass(o)- (θə'læs(əʊ), **tha'lassi(o)-**, from Gr. θάλασσα sea, and θαλάσσι-ος marine, formative elements of learned words. **thala'ssarctine** *a. Zool.* [Gr. ἄρκτ-ος a bear], of or pertaining to the Polar Bear, *Thalassarctos*. **thalassi'collidan** [Gr. κόλλα glue], *a.* belonging to the *Thalassicollidæ*, a family of single-celled radiolarians; *sb.* a radiolarian of this family. **tha'lassio-, tha'lassophyte** [-PHYTE], a plant of the *Thalassiophyta* (see quot.); a seaweed, a marine alga; hence **thalassi'ophytous** *a.*, belonging to the *Thalassiophyta*. **thala'sso-meter** [-METER], a tide-gauge. **thalassome-'trician** *nonce-wd.*, one who measures the sea. **thala'ssophilous** *a.* [-PHIL], fond of the sea, living in the sea. **thalasso'phobia**, a morbid dread of the sea. **thalasso'therapy**: see quot. 1899. See also THALASSOCRACY, etc.

1842 *Penny Cycl.* XXIV. 277/1 **Thalassiophytes*.. is the name given by Lamouroux to designate the vegetable productions of the ocean... It is equivalent to the term Hydrophytes of Lingbye, and the.. Marine Algæ. **1900** B. D. JACKSON *Gloss. Bot. Terms*, Thalassophyte. **1858** SIMMONDS *Dict. Trade*, **Thalassometer*, a tide-gauge. **1652** NEEDHAM tr. *Selden's Mare Cl.* 5, I have heard of a Geometrician, or one that could measure Land; but never of a *Thalassometrician, one that could measure or lay out Bounds in the Sea. **1891** *Cent. Dict.*, *Thalassophilous. **1897** tr. *Ribot's Psychol. Emotions* II. ii. 213 Every morbid manifestation of fear is immediately fitted with a Greek designation,.. and we have aïcmophobia, belenophobia, *thalassophobia, potamophobia, etc. **1899** *Syd. Soc. Lex.*, **Thalassotherapy*, treatment of disease by sea bathing, sea voyages, etc. **1910** *Index-Catal. Libr. Surgeon-General's Office, U.S. Army* 2nd Ser. XV. 362/1 Nyström (O.E.) Några ord om hafskuren eller thalassotherapien. (A few words on sea-baths and thalassotherapy.) 8°. Göteborg, 1907. **1966** *Punch* 5 Oct. 531 Thalassotherapy is sea-bathing in a warm, enclosed and controlled area... Pure sea water is pumped in from several hundred metres out. **1983** INGLIS & WEST *Alternative Health Guide* 25 Establishments which provide thalassotherapy have been springing up around the continent of Europe.. to provide a holiday in which the usual seaside ingredients.. are supplemented.. by a regime of salt-water treatments.

thalassocracy (θælæ'sɒkrəsɪ). Rarely **-craty.** [ad. Gr. θαλασσοκρατία, f. θάλασσα sea + -κρατία, -CRACY.] Mastery at sea; the sovereignty of the sea.

1846 GROTE *Greece* I. xx. II. 151 The legendary thalassocracy of Minos. **1880** B. HEAD *Guide Coins & Medals Brit. Mus.* 6 The Phocæan Thalassocracy lasted from about 602–558 B.C. **1903** *Cornh. Mag.* Feb. 258 The existence of the Phœnician thalassocracy can be proved in detail.

thalassocrat (θə'læsəkræt). [f. after prec.: see -CRAT.] One who has the mastery of the sea.

1846 GROTE *Greece* I. xii. I. 311 An attempt on the part of the great thalassocrat to conquer Sicily. **1847** *Ibid.* II. xxxiii. IV. 327 The earliest of all Grecian thalassokrats or sea kings. **1905** G. G. A. MURRAY in *Q. Rev.* Apr. 352 At present England is the thalassocrat.

thalassography (θælæ'sɒgrəfɪ). [f. THALASSO- + -GRAPHY. Cf. med.Gr. θαλασσογράφος describing the sea.] The branch of physical geography which treats of the sea, its configuration and phenomena; oceanography.

1888 A. AGASSIZ (*title*) Contribution to American Thalassography. **1888** *Times* 7 Apr. 5/2 The necessity for some such term as oceanography or thalassography is significant of the vast progress which has been made during the past 20 years in our knowledge of the ocean depths.

Hence **thala'ssographer**, a student or investigator of thalassography; **tha,lasso-'graphic, -ical** *adjs.*, of or pertaining to thalassography.

1881 GIGLIOLI in *Nature* 18 Aug. 358/1 The war-steamer of the Italian Royal Navy *Washington*,.. left Maddalena on the 2nd inst. on her thalassographic mission. **1900** *Ibid.* 4 Jan. 228/1 Thalassographic researches in the Mediterranean. **1893** *Smithsonian Inst. Rep.* (1894) 370 *note*, Biological and thalassographical investigations.

thalatto- (θə'lætəʊ), combining form from Gr. θάλαττα, Attic for θάλασσα sea, = THALASSO-, as in **thalattocracy** (-'tɒkrəsɪ), **thalattocraty** (-'tɒkrətɪ) = THALASSOCRACY. **thala'ttology**, that branch of science which treats of the sea.

1839 T. MITCHELL *Frogs of Aristoph.* Introd. 80 The first thalattocracy which the history of the world supplies. **1874** *Proc. Physical Soc. Lond.* 7 Nov. I. 53 A sufficient theory of thalattology. **1886** *Eng. Hist. Rev.* I. 626 To reduce the Kyklades and establish a thalattokraty.

thale-cress ('θeɪlkrɛs). [f. *thale*, ad. mod.L. *thāliāna* adj. (f. *Thal* the name of a German physician, 1542–83) + CRESS.] A book-name of *Sisymbrium thalianum* (*Arabis thaliana*, Linn.), N.O. *Cruciferæ*, a small herb, bearing small white flowers. Also called *Thale Rock-cress*.

1778 LIGHTFOOT *Flora Scot.* I. 358 Thale's Cress, or coded Mouse-ear. **1835** HOOKER *Brit. Flora* (ed. 3) I. 307 *S[isymbrium] thalianum*, (common Thale-cress).

thalenite ('θɑːlən-, θə'liːnaɪt). *Min.* [ad. Sw. *thalénit* (C. Benedicks 1898, in *Geol. För. Förh.* XX. 308), f. the name of T. R. *Thalén* (1827–1905), Swedish physicist: see -ITE¹.] An yttrium silicate, $Y_3Si_3O_{10}OH$, found as translucent monoclinic crystals.

1899 *Jrnl. Chem. Soc.* LXXVI. II. 766 Minerals allied to thalénite are yttrialite, rowlandite, and kainosite. **1972** *Prof. Papers U.S. Geol. Survey* No. 800-c. 63/1 The rarity of thalenite in pegmatites, in which other rare-earth minerals may be abundant, suggests that it can form only under very unusual conditions.

‖**thaler** ('tɑːlər). [G. *thaler* DOLLAR.] A German silver coin; a dollar: see DOLLAR I.

1787 MATY tr. *Riesbeck's Trav. Germ.* I. xviii. 204 Making a Baile's Dictionary.. the true price of which is five guineas, sell at Vienna for 100 thalers. **1858** SIMMONDS *Dict. Trade*, *Thaler*, a German coin of 30 silver groschen, worth about 3*s.* sterling. **1864** CARLYLE *Fredk. Gt.* XVII. v. IV. 571 'Let my ducat be a Joachimsthal one, then!'.. 'a *Joachimsthal-er*'; or for brevity, a '*Thal-er*'; whence *Thaler*, and at last *Dollar*.

thalerophagous (θælə'rɒfəgəs), *a. Entom.* [f. Gr. θαλερός blooming, fresh + -φάγ-ος eating + -OUS.] Feeding on fresh vegetable substances.

1819 MACLEAY *Horæ Entomol.* I. 27 Thalerophagous insects, or such as live on green or fresh vegetable food. **1826** KIRBY & SP. *Entomol.* III. xxxv. 604 The saprophagous tribes of Mr. W. S. MacLeay are commonly of a more dark and dismal aspect and colour than those which feed upon such as are living and fresh, denominated thalerophagous by the same learned author. **1840** SWAINSON & SHUCKARD *Hist. Insects* II. vi. 221 The thalerophagous groups.

‖**thali¹** ('tɑːlɪ). Also tali. [Tamil *tāli*.] A gold pendant that is hung round the bride's neck as part of a South Indian wedding ceremony.

1875 *Indian Antiquary* IV. 173/1, I am surprised that the opponents of the Kuḍumî have not yet commenced to put down the use of the tâli. This is the Hindu sign of marriage, answering to the ring of European Christendom... It is always tied round the Hindu bride's neck. **1957** L. DUMONT *Hierarchy & Marriage Alliance in S. Indian Kinship* (Occasional Papers R. Anthrop. Inst. No. 12) iii. 29 The tying of a string, with or without the well-known marriage badge or *tāli*, round the bride's neck has certainly a sacramental value. **1963** *Guardian* 11 Apr. 11/4 At marriage in the wealthier, and even in the not-so-wealthy, families a good deal of gold is passed over from the bride's family to the bridegroom's. And the tokens of marriage are not the miserable rings of the Christian West but gold pendants called thalis which are then hung on solid gold necklaces. **1981** *Times* 24 Jan. 11/1 The thali is a phallic symbol worn by brides in the Dravidian South.

‖**thali²** ('tɑːlɪ). [Hind. *thālī*.] In India, a metal platter or flat dish on which food is served; a meal served on it.

1969 *Times* 13 Oct. (Indian Suppl.) p. xx/4 The Apollo room in Bombay's Taj Hotel where a 'thali' platter of assorted spoonfuls of curries and sauces is a good introduction. **1978** F. OLBRICH *Desouza pays Price* xxii. 137 The little serving-boy.. brought.. a 'thali', a gleaming round metal tray with an assortment of cooked vegetables and pulses arranged in small helpings.

‖**Thalia** (θə'laɪə). [a. Gr. Θάλεια ('luxuriant, blooming', f. θάλλειν to bloom).]

1. The eighth of the Muses, presiding over comedy and idyllic poetry; also, one of the three Graces, patroness of festive meetings.

1656 in BLOUNT *Glossogr.* **1711** SHAFTESB. *Charac.* (1737) I. 317 The Thalia's, the Polyhymnia's, the Terpsychore's, the Euterpe's willingly join their parts. **1799** CAMPBELL *Pleas. Hope* II. 168 Turn to the gentler melodies that suit Thalia's harp, or Pan's Arcadian lute.

2. *Bot.* A genus of aquatic herbaceous plants, N.O. *Marantaceæ*, natives of tropical America.

1756 P. BROWNE *Jamaica* (1789) 112. **1878** DARWIN in *Life & Lett.* (1887) III. 287 In Thalia cross-fertilization is ensured by the wonderful movement, if bees visit several flowers.

† **3.** *Zool.* An old synonym of the genus SALPA².

1756 P. BROWNE *Jamaica* (1789) 384 The *Thalia*, with a square erect crest... The *Thalia*, with a rounded depressed crest. **1842** BRANDE *Dict. Sc.*, etc., *Thalidans, Thalides*.., the name of a tribe of Tunicaries, of which the genus *Salpa* or *Thalia* is the type.

b. A genus of coleopterous insects.

1838 F. W. HOPE *Coleopterist's Man.* II. 70.

4. *Astron.* The twenty-third of the Asteroids.

thaliacean (θælɪ'eɪʃ(ɪ)ən), *a.* and *sb. Zool.* [f. mod.L. *Thaliācea* (f. *Thalia*: see prec. 3) + -AN.] **a.** *adj.* Of or pertaining to the *Thaliacea*, an order of tunicates, including the *Salpidæ*, etc. **b.** *sb.* A member of this order.

[**1888** ROLLESTON & JACKSON *Anim. Life* 441 The Thaliacea are free-swimming, and more or less barrel-shaped... The test is very thin and delicate... The muscle fibres.. [are] arranged in circular hoops round the barrel-shaped body.]

Thalian (θə'laɪən, 'θeɪlɪən), *a.* [f. THALIA + -AN.] Of or pertaining to Thalia as the muse of pastoral and comic poetry; hence, of the nature of comedy, comic.

1864 in WEBSTER. **1882** J. WALKER *Scotch Poems* 100 My wit can wimple Thro' Thalian songs like Kate Dalrymple.

thalictrine (θə'lɪktraɪn). *Chem.* [f. next + -INE⁵.] A crystalline alkaloid contained in *Thalictrum macrocarpum*, in poisonous action resembling aconitin but less violent.

1881 DOASSANS in *Jrnl. Chem. Soc.* XL. 52.

‖**Tha'lictrum.** *Bot.* [L. *thalictrum* (Pliny), a. Gr. θάλικτρον.] A genus of perennial herbs (N.O. *Ranunculaceæ*), bearing panicles, corymbs, or racemes of green, white, or yellow flowers, without petals or involucre. There are several species, of which three are British, *T. flavum* being the Common Meadow Rue; *T. aquilegifolium* is an Alpine species, known as the Feather Columbine.

1664 EVELYN *Kal. Hort.*, *May* (1729) 205 Flowers in Prime,.. Prunella, purple Thalictrum. **1741** *Compl. Fam.-Piece* II. iii. (ed. 3) 373 Featherfew, Thalictrums of several kinds. **1883** *Century Mag.* Oct. 819/1, I saw the dainty thalictrum, with its clover-like leaves, standing in thickets there, fresh and green.

thalidan: see THALIA 3, quot. 1842.

thalidomide (θəˈlɪdəmaɪd). Also **Thalidomide**. [f. ph*thal*imido*glutarimide*, f. PHTHALIMID(E + -O + *glutaric* adj. s.v. GLUT- + IMIDE.]

a. A non-barbiturate sedative and hypnotic, $C_{13}H_{10}N_2O_4$, which was found to be teratogenic when taken early in pregnancy, sometimes causing malformation or absence of limbs in the fœtus.

1958 *Lancet* 1 Feb. 271 The British Pharmacopœia Commission has issued the following new supplementary list of approved names:..Thalidomide..α-Phthalimidoglutarimide. **1961** *Ibid.* 2 Dec. 1262/1 We have just received reports from two overseas sources possibly associating thalidomide ('Distaval') with harmful effects on the fœtus in early pregnancy. **1962** *New Scientist* 28 June 717/1 The tragic cost of the use of thalidomide. **1969** N. W. PIRIE *Food Resources* vii. 167 Thalidomide is the classic example of a substance that passed orthodox tests that were, as it turned out, not relevant. **1978** *Dædalus* Spring 136 Passage of the 1962 drug law might not have occurred without the public demand for stricter controls over the testing of new drugs following disclosure of deformities caused by Thalidomide. **1979** *Nature* 29 Nov. 509/1 Other agents, notably Thalidomide, are believed to be teratogenic by virtue of metabolic products rather than the parent compound.

b. *attrib.* and *Comb.*: **thalidomide baby, child,** etc., one born deformed through the effects of thalidomide.

1962 *Guardian* 31 July 14/2 There is still no information about the number of 'thalidomide babies' in the country. **1962** *Lancet* 1 Dec. 1155/2 Attempts have been made to lengthen stunted thalidomide arms by grafts from fibula and scapula. **1971** *New Scientist* 18 Mar. 613/1 The construction of a body harness for armless thalidomide children. **1973** *Daily Tel.* 9 Jan. 2/2 A Pharmaceutical Society spokesman said..that the scale of the thalidomide compensation would undoubtedly have a 'profound effect' on the manufacture of new drugs in Britain. **1977** J. D. DOUGLAS in Douglas & Johnson *Existential Sociol.* i. 26 Her highly publicized abortion in Sweden for a thalidomide-damaged fetus. **1979** T. BENN *Arguments for Socialism* ii. 49 There was also the initial refusal by Distillers to compensate the thalidomide children properly. **1980** *Nature* 1 May 54/1 The thalidomide tragedy, for example, could have been averted if this synthetic racemate had been separated into its optical isomers, for only the left-handed (s)-(−)-isomer has teratogenic properties. **1981** *Daily Tel.* 3 Feb. 2/2 This is the first known case of a thalidomide victim becoming a father, although a couple of incidences of thalidomide mothers are known.

thallene (ˈθæliːn). *Chem.* [f. Gr. θάλλ-ειν to bloom + -ENE.] (See quot. 1881.)

1872 H. MORTON in *Chem. News* 6 Dec. 272/2 The above-described body, which I may as well call thallene hereafter. **1881** WATTS *Dict. Chem.* VIII. 1918 *Thallene*, a solid hydrocarbon, isomeric with anthracene, obtained from the last products which pass over in the distillation of American petroleum. It is distinguished by a splendid green fluorescence.

thallic (ˈθælɪk), *a. Chem.* [f. THALLI-UM + -IC.] Of, pertaining to, or derived from thallium; *spec.* applied to compounds containing thallium in smaller proportion, relatively to oxygen, than *thallious* compounds. ***thallic oxide*** = Thallium trioxide, Tl_2O_3.

1868 WATTS *Dict. Chem.* V. 750 In solutions of thallic salts, the thallium may be estimated by reducing the thallic to thallious salts with an alkaline sulphite. **1873** —— *Fownes' Chem.* (ed. 11) 411 The Trichloride or Thallic Chloride.

thalliferous (θæˈlɪfərəs), *a.* [f. as prec. + -FEROUS.] Bearing or containing thallium.

1867 *Ure's Dict. Arts*, etc. III. 889 A very considerable amount of the thalliferous deposit. **1868** WATTS *Dict. Chem.* V. 742 In burning thalliferous pyrites for the purpose of manufacturing sulphuric acid.

thalliform (ˈθælɪfɔːm), *a. Bot.* [f. THALL-US + -FORM.] Having the form of a thallus.

1891 in *Cent. Dict.*

thalline (ˈθælaɪn), *sb. Pharm.* Also -in. [f. Gr. θάλλ-ειν to bloom + -INE[5].] A trade name for a colourless compound used as an antipyretic, obtained by the reduction of the corresponding chinoline derivative.

Chemically it is tetra-hydroparamethoxyquinoline, $CH_3OC_6H_3\langle^{CH_2\cdot CH_2}_{NH\cdot CH_2}$.

1885-8 FAGGE & PYE-SMITH *Princ. Med.* (ed. 2) I. 205 Thallin (the sulphate or tartrate of tetra-hydro-parachinanisol) is, I am disposed to think, as efficient or more so [than Antipyrin], and safer. **1898** *Allbutt's Syst. Med.* V. 234.

b. *attrib.* **thalline periodide, thalline sulphate**: see quots.; **thalline urine**, urine affected by the use of thalline.

1899 *Syd. Soc. Lex.*, *Thalline periodide*, *T. periodosulphate.* (Not official.) A combination of iodine and thalline sulphate. Black and crystalline... *Thalline sulphate.* .. The sulphate of a synthetically prepared base derived from chinoline... A yellowish white crystalline powder, with an odour [like] coumarin, and an aromatic bitter taste.

thalline (ˈθælaɪn), *a. Bot.* [f. THALLUS + -INE[1].] Of or pertaining to a thallus.

thalline excipulum or ***exciple***, an excipulum composed of a portion of the thallus, which surrounds it and forms a bowl-like rim. (Bennett & Dyer tr. *Sachs' Bot.* (1875) 269.)

1856 W. L. LINDSAY *Pop. Hist. Brit. Lichens* 45 This thalline fringe is very conspicuous. **1871** W. A. LEIGHTON *Lichen-Flora* 179 Thalline margin entire.

thallious (ˈθælɪəs), *a. Chem.* [f. THALLI-UM + -OUS.] Abounding in thallium; *spec.* containing thallium in greater proportion, relatively to oxygen, than *thallic* compounds. ***thallious oxide*** = Thallium monoxide, Tl_2O.

1868 WATTS *Dict. Chem.* V. 749 Thallic salts are easily distinguished from thallious salts by their behaviour with alkalis. *Ibid.* 750 [see THALLIC]. **1873** —— *Fownes' Chem.* (ed. 11) 412 Thallious Iodide, Tl I, is formed by direct combination of its elements, or by double decomposition.

†ˈ**thallite.** *Min. Obs.* [a. F. *thallite* (J. C. Delamétherie, 1792), f. Gr. θάλλ-ειν to flourish, bloom, or θαλλός young shoot (in allusion to its colour) + -ITE[1].] A rejected name for EPIDOTE occurring in yellowish-green crystals.

1802 BOURNON in *Phil. Trans.* XCII. 291 The substance called thallite (the *epidote* of the Abbé Hauy). **1868** DANA *Min.* (ed. 5) 284 *Thallite*..was rejected because it was based on a varying character, color.

thallium (ˈθælɪəm). [f. Gr. θαλλ-ός a green shoot (θάλλειν to bloom), from the brilliant green line distinguishing its spectrum + -IUM.] **a.** A rare metal, bluish white in colour with leaden lustre, extremely soft and almost devoid of tenacity or elasticity; occurring in small quantities in iron and copper pyrites. Atomic weight 204; symbol Tl.

1861 CROOKES in *Chem. News* 16 March, III. 193 On the Existence of a New Element. *Ibid.* 18 May 303, I have thought..to propose for it the provisional name of *Thallium*, from the Greek θαλλός, or Latin *thallus*, a budding twig..which I have chosen as the green line which it communicates to the spectrum recals with peculiar vividness the fresh colour of vegetation at the present time. **1871** ROSCOE *Elem. Chem.* 262 Thallium was discovered in 1861 by Crookes, by means of spectrum analysis, in the deposit in the flue of a pyrites burner. **1874** tr. *Lommel's Light* 114 The splendid green light of Thallium is more strongly refracted than the yellow light of Sodium.

b. *attrib.* and *Comb.*, as ***thallium alloy, spectrum***; **thallium-activated** *a.*, containing a small amount of added thallium so as to make the substance active as a phosphor; **thallium glass**, a variety of glass of great density and refracting power, in the manufacture of which thallium is used instead of lead or potassium; **thallium green**, the colour of the **thallium line**, the vivid green line of the thallium spectrum.

1868 WATTS *Dict. Chem.* V. 745 The length of the wave of the green thallium-line is 0·0005348 millimetre. *Ibid.*, Thallium-salts are highly poisonous. *Ibid.* 758 Thallium-glass. **1956** *Nature* 3 Mar. 413/1 A single-crystal spectrometer (thallium-activated sodium iodide crystal). **1974** *Encycl. Brit. Macropædia* XV. 397/2 The phosphor in greatest use in scintillation counters is thallium activated sodium iodide.

thallodic (θæˈlɒdɪk), *a. Bot.* [f. THALLUS + -ODE[1] + -IC.] Formed like, of the nature of, or pertaining to a thallus. So **thallodal** (-ˈəʊdəl) *a.*

1860 MAYNE *Expos. Lex.*, Thallodic. **1871** W. A. LEIGHTON *Lichen-Flora* 179 Thallodal margin persistent.

thallogen (ˈθælədʒɛn). *Bot.* [f. THALL-US + -GEN, after *exogen*, *endogen*, etc.] = THALLOPHYTE.

1846 LINDLEY *Veg. Kingd.* 2 Those simpler plants which exist without the distinction of leaf and stem, are also destitute of flowers... Among the many names that Botanists have given such plants, that of *Thallogens* is here preferred. **1857** BERKELEY *Cryptog. Bot.* §55. 69 Thallogens (plants in which there is a fusion of root, stems, and leaves into one general mass). **1858** CARPENTER *Veg. Phys.* §123.

Hence **thalloˈgenic, thaˈllogenous** *adjs.*, of or pertaining to the thallogens; of the nature of a thallogen.

1854 BALFOUR in *Encycl. Brit.* (ed. 8) V. 146/1 Lichens.. belong to the Thallogenous division of Cryptogamics. **1857** H. MILLER *Test. Rocks* i. 9 The first class..in the ascending order is this humble thallogenic class.

thalloid (ˈθælɔɪd), *a. Bot.* [f. THALL-US + -OID.] Of the form of a thallus. So **thaˈlloidal** *a.*

1857 HENFREY *Bot.* §318 A lobed, green, thalloid stem. *Ibid.* §321 The Thalloid Hepaticæ have a broad, more or less succulent lobed leaf-like expansion in place of stem and leaf. **1875** BENNETT & DYER tr. *Sachs' Bot.* 160 In Thallophytes and thalloid Hepaticæ, dichotomy is very widely prevalent. **1900** B. D. JACKSON *Gloss. Bot. T.*, Thalloidal.

thallome (ˈθæləʊm). *Bot.* [ad. mod.L. *thallōma*, f. *thall-us* + *-oma*: cf. *rhizome*.] = THALLUS.

1875 BENNETT & DYER tr. *Sachs' Bot.* 121 The thallome of Stypocaulon..shows how the apical cell of the lateral shoot grows immediately from the apical cell of the principal process as a lateral protuberance. *Ibid.* 130 It is now agreed to apply to those vegetable structures in which the morphological distinction of stem and leaves cannot be carried out..(and from which true roots are always absent), the morphological term Thallus or Thallome.

thallophyte (ˈθæləfaɪt). *Bot.* [f. mod.L. *Thallophyta*, pl. f. Gr. θαλλό-ς green twig + φυτόν plant.] A plant belonging to the lowest of the great groups in the vegetable kingdom, comprising those of which the vegetative body is a thallus, including Algæ, Fungi, and Lichens; a cellular cryptogam; = Lindley's THALLOGEN.

1854 BALFOUR in *Encycl. Brit.* (ed. 8) V. 142/2 These tribes, from having no foliaceous axis but simply a cellular expansion, have been called *Thallogens* or *Thallophytes.* **1875** BENNETT & DYER tr. *Sachs' Bot.* 207 Thallophytes. Under this term are comprised Algæ and Fungi (Lichens being also included in the latter section). **1885** GOODALE *Physiol. Bot.* (1892) 164.

Hence **thallophytic** (-ˈfɪtɪk) *a. Bot.*, of or pertaining to the thallophytes.

1891 in *Cent. Dict.*

ˈ**thallose**, *a. Bot.* = THALLOID.

1900 in B. D. JACKSON *Gloss. Bot. T.*

thallous (ˈθæləs), *a. Chem.* [f. THALL-IUM + -OUS: cf. *aluminous*, *tantalous*.] = THALLIOUS.

1888 *Encycl. Brit.* XXIII. 220/1 Thallic salts are related to thallous pretty much as manganic are to manganous... Thallous chloride.

‖**thallus** (ˈθæləs). *Bot.* [L. *thallus*, a. Gr. θαλλός a green shoot, f. θάλλειν to bloom.] A vegetable structure without vascular tissue, in which there is no differentiation into stem and leaves, and from which true roots are absent.

1829 LOUDON *Encycl. Pl.* (1836) 874 (*Lichenes*)..the thallus..is either pulverulent, crustaceous, membranous, foliaceous, or branched and shrub-like. **1846** LINDLEY *Veg. Kingd.* 2 A thallus is a fusion of root, stem and leaves, into one general mass. **1854** THOREAU *Walden* xvii. (1857) 326 The lobed and imbricated thalluses of some lichens. **1875** J. H. BALFOUR in *Encycl. Brit.* I. 508/1 Algæ..consist of a brown, red, or green, flattened, cellular, leaf-like expansion, called a *thallus*.

b. *attrib.* and *Comb.*

1861 BENTLEY *Man. Bot.* 67 Such are..termed *Cormophytes* or stem-producing plants, to distinguish them from the thallus-forming plants or *Thallophytes.* **1875** BENNETT & DYER tr. *Sachs' Bot.* 160 The flat extension of the thallus or thallus-like stem. *Ibid.* 130 In contradistinction to Thallus-plants (Thallophytes), all plants in which leaves can be..distinguished might be termed Phyllophytes.

Thalmud, -ist, obs. forms of TALMUD, -IST.

‖**thalweg** (ˈtɑːlvɛg, ‖ˈtaːlvɛç). *Geog.* Also **talweg** (after the reformed Ger. spelling). [Ger. *thalweg* bottom path of a valley, f. *thal* valley (see DALE) + *weg* WAY. Also in Fr. (1815 *Traité de Paris*, Littré).] The line in the bottom of a valley in which the slopes of the two sides meet, and which forms a natural watercourse; also the line following the deepest part of the bed or channel of a river or lake.

1831 W. WHEWELL *Let.* 22 Feb. in I. Todhunter *William Whewell* (1876) II. 113 For *thalweg* and *riggin'* I do not think you can do better than take *daleway* and *ridge-way*. **1862** WRAXALL *Hugo's Misérables* v. xxii, The grand sewer running along the thalweg of the valley. **1881** *Harper's Mag.* LXIV. 275 Thalweg..is a German geographical term, employed in the records of the congress of Berlin, which designates the line of lowest level formed by the two opposite slopes of a valley. **1894** (May 12) *Agreemt. betw. Gt. Brit. & Congo State* in *Parl. Papers Eng.* XCVI. 26 Thence it [the boundary] shall follow the 'thalweg' of the Nile southwards to Lake Albert. **1897** *Educat. Rev.* XIII. 89 This thalweg which forms a nearly continuous waterway from the Volga to the Amur. **1937** *Geogr. Jrnl.* LXXXIX. 260 The development of a terrace..involves two clearly distinguishable phases—firstly, the formation of a continuous flood plain, and secondly, the incision of the talweg below it. **1946** L. D. STAMP *Britain's Struct. & Scenery* v. 49 Soundings show that the floor of a ria, the old river talweg, slopes steadily seawards and there is no 'lip'. **1966** J. S. HARDMAN tr. *R. Boulanger's Middle East* 608 Whilst conducting excavations towards the thalweg of the Kidron valley the Franco-British expedition discovered the remains of a rampart belonging to the Canaanaean (or Jebusite) Jerusalem. **1968** R. W. FAIRBRIDGE *Encycl. Geomorphol.* 1149/1 The opposite of the talweg itself is a divide, i.e., the lines joining all high points in topography.

tham, obs. f. THEM; obs. dat. sing. and pl. of THAT, THE.

thamarike, thamarind, obs. ff. TAMARISK, TAMARIND.

thame, obs. f. TEAM; Sc. f. THEM.

Thames (tɛmz). Forms: 1 Temes, 1–5 Temese, (4–5 Th-), 5 Temze, Temeze (Tamise), 6 Temys, Temmes(se, Themes, -ys, Themise, Thamyse, 6–7 Thamise, 6– Thames. [OE. *Tęmese* :—**Tamisa*, ad. L. *Tamēsa*, *Tamēsis*, ad. Brit. *Tamēsa*: cf. Welsh *Tafwys*, F. *Tamise*.]

a. The name of the river on which London is situated: also *attrib.* and *Comb.*, as in ***Thames barge, boat, -side, valley***; ***Thames-built, -derived*** adjs.

c **893** K. ÆLFRED *Oros.* v. xii. §2 Neah þære ie þe mon hæt Temes [*v.r.* Temese]. **1377** LANGL. *P. Pl.* B. XII. 161 Take two stronge men and in themese caste hem. *c* **1450** *Sloane MS.* 73. lf. 214 (Halliw.) Put therto tweyne galones of clene Temese water that is taken at an ebbe. **1503** *Rolls of Parlt.* VI. 527/2 A Ryvere called the Thamyse, otherwyse called the Temmesse. **1649** LOVELACE *To Althea* ii, When flowing cups run swiftly round With no allaying Thames [i.e. water]. **1688** R. HOLME *Armoury* III. xv. (Roxb.) 26/1 He beareth Azure, a Skuller, or a Thamise boate, Or. **1712** ADDISON *Spect.* No. 383 ¶5 With a good deal of the like

Thames-Ribaldry. **1883** *Boats of World* 4 Who can mistake the world-renowned Thames Barge, with her long, flat side, picturesque rig, and bright-coloured sails? **1895** *Daily News* 28 Dec. 5/4 The Thames-derived waters show a marked improvement. **1902** Cornish *Naturalist Thames* 169 The crowning glory of the Thames-side flats. **1902** *Encycl. Brit.* XXVIII. 533/2 In the London district the country in the Thames valley..is as largely occupied by flower farms as it is by fruit farms. **1961** F. H. Burgess *Dict. Sailing* 207 *Thames barge*, a ketch or yawl-rigged sailing barge with a large spritsail, common on the Thames estuary. **1977** D. James *Spy at Evening* xiv. 113 He..let himself out into the early-morning Thames valley mist. **1979** D. May *Revenger's Comedy* viii. 105 Out on the estuary, a big, red-sailed Thames barge was moving.

b. Phrase. ***to set the Thames on fire*** (†***set fire to the Thames***, †***burn the Thames***), to do something marvellous, to work wonders. Usually with negative = to work no wonders, never to distinguish oneself.

A writer in *N. & Q.* of 25 Mar. 1865, p. 249, surmised that *Thames* here was orig. *temse* a sieve, which he supposed that an active fellow might set on fire by force of friction. This conjecture has no basis of fact. The phrase has also been used of the Rhine (*a* 1638) and other rivers. See *N. & Q.* 8th s. VI. 502, and Skeat *Stud. Past.* §205-6.

1778 Foote *Trip Calais* III. iii, Matt Minnikin..an honest *burgoise*,..won't set fire to the Thames, though he lives near the Bridge. **1787** [see burn *v.* 9c]. **1796** *Grose's Dict. Vulg. Tongue* s.v. *Thames*, He will not find out a way to set the Thames on fire; he will not make any wonderful discoveries, he is no conjurer. **18..** W. E. Norris (Dixon), I hardly expect him to set the Thames on fire; but I hope his mother will never have reason to be ashamed of him.

Hence **Thameser** ('tɛmzə(r)), one who is connected with the Thames in some way; **Thamesian** (tɛ'miːzɪən) *a.*, of or pertaining to the Thames.

1614 T. Gentleman *Way to Wealth* 43 By..the yong men of the Sea-coast Townes, euen as..amongst the Theamsers. **1859** Sala *Gaslight & D.* ix. 105 Floating on the muddy bosom of the Thamesian stream.

‖**thamin** (θə'mɪn). Also **-ine, -yn, -eng.** [Burmese *thămín.*] A deer (*Cervus eldi*) of Burma and Thailand, resembling the swamp deer.

1888 *Cassell's Encycl. Dict.*, *Thamyn..Rucervus eldi*, Eld's Deer, so called from Captain Eld, who discovered it in 1838. **1900** Pollok & Thom *Sports Burma* iv. 136 In the tree-jungle beyond, I shot a thamine and hung it up. **1903** *Edin. Rev.* July 197 A peculiar looking deer is the thameng.

‖**Thammuz, Tammuz** ('tæmuːz). Also 6 Thamus, 7 Thamuz, 7–9 Tamuz. [Heb. *tammūz.*] The tenth month of the Jewish civil year, and the fourth of the sacred, containing twenty-nine days, and corresponding to parts of June and July.

Also the name of a Syrian deity, identified with the Phœnician *Adôn* or Adonis, whose annual festival began with the new moon of this month.

1535 Coverdale *Ezek.* viii. 14 There sat women mournynge for Thamus. **1614** Purchas *Pilgrimage* I. xvii. 89 This is called the mourning for Thamuz, which Iunius interpreteth Osiris, whence the fourth moneth (commonly their Haruest) is called Tamuz. **1667** Milton *P.L.* I. 446. **1827** Keble *Chr. Year* 17th S. after Trin. **1853** Kingsley *Hypatia* v. **1909** *Whitaker's Almanack* 72 Jewish Calendar: June 20 New Moon, Tamuz 1. July 6 Fast of Tamuz.

‖**thamnium** ('θæmnɪəm). *Bot.* [mod.L. a. Gr. θαμνίον, dim. of θάμνος shrub.] (See quot.)

1866 *Treas. Bot.*, *Thamnium*, the branched bush-like thallus of lichens.

Thamudic (θə'muːdɪk), *a.* and *sb.* [f. *Thamūd* (Arab. *ṯamūd*) + -ic.] **A.** *adj.* **a.** Of, pertaining to, or designating a class of inscriptions in northern and central Arabia dating from the 5th to the 1st centuries B.C., or the ancient Semitic language of which they are the only evidence. **b.** Of or pertaining to the Thamūd, a tribe that lived in northern Arabia between the 4th century B.C. and the 7th century A.D.

1909 Webster, Thamudic, *a.* **1937** P. K. Hitti *Hist. Arabs* vi. 72 The Lihyānites seem also to have held..al-Hijr ..once a Thamūdic town. **1951** [see Safaitic *a.*]. **1974** *Encycl. Brit. Micropædia* IX. 921/2 Recent archaeological work has revealed numerous Thamūdic rock writings and pictures not only on Mt. Athlith but also throughout central Arabia.

B. *sb.* The Thamudic language.

1937 F. V. Winnett *Study Lihyanite & Thamudic Inscr.* 27 In view of the fact that it has the value *zāi* in both Lihyanite and Ethiopic, there is little likelihood of its having a different value in Thamudic. **1952** Harding & Littmann *Some Thamudic Inscr.* 47 In Thamudic and Safaïtic the verb ..often means 'he acquired, he bought'.

Also **Thamu'dæan, Tha'mudene, Thamu'denic** *adjs.*, **Thamudian** *a.* and *sb.*

1909 Webster, Thamudene *adj.* **1911** *Encycl. Brit.* XXIII. 956/2 The Thamudaean inscriptions are locally nearer to Phoenicia, and the letters are more like the Phoenician. **1934** J. A. Montgomery *Arabia & Bible* v. 91 A peculiar and much discussed special type of Arabic inscriptions, the Thamudene, has been discovered. **1936**, etc. [see Lihyanic *sb.*]. **1948** D. Diringer *Alphabet* II. ii. 227 The North Arabian inscriptions..can be separated into three groups: (1) Thamudene or Thamudic... (2) The Dedanite inscriptions... (3) The Safaitic or Safahitic inscriptions. **1981** *Word 1980* XXXI. 222 We have here an important isogloss for the chronological division of the Semitic languages into languages with *ś*.., languages with *h* (Amorite, Hebrew,..and Thamudian), languages with '.., and languages with *y*.

Thamudite ('θæmjuːdaɪt), *sb.* and *a.* [f. *Thamūd* (see Thamudic *a.* b) + -ite[1].] **A.** *sb.* One of the Thamūd. **B.** *adj.* = Thamudic *a.* b.

1833 A. Crichton *Hist. Arabia* I. iii. 92 The circumstance of dwelling in caves..was common to other tribes besides the Thamudites. **1881** *Encycl. Brit.* XIII. 117/2 [The graffiti] are mostly the productions of Thamudite soldiers in the Roman army.

than (ðən; as a separate word called ðæn), *conj.* Forms: α. 1–3 **ð- þonne,** (1 **ðone, ðon**); β. 1 **ðanne, þænne,** 1–4 **þanne,** 3 **þæne,** 3–4 **þane,** 4–5 **thanne;** γ. 2–5 **þenne,** 2–3 **þene,** (3 **þeone**), 3–5 **þen,** (5 **thenne,** 7 **yen**), 4–8 **then;** δ. 1 **than,** 2–6 **þan,** 3 (*Orm.*) **þann,** (4 **þain**), 4– **than** (abbrev. 7–8 **y^n, yn**); ε. 5 **an,** 9 *dial.* **'n.** [OE. *þanne, þonne, þænne*, also *þan, þon*; originally the same word as then (OE. *þanne þonne, þænne*), the adv. of time. Its employment as the connective particle after a comparative (= L. *quam*, F. *que*) is a pre-English development, existing already in WGer.: cf. OHG. *thanne, danne*, MHG. *danne, denne*, Ger. *denn* (now largely supplanted by *als*), OS. *than*, MDu. *danne, dan*, Du. *dan*, all used after the comparative. (Not so in Gothic or Scandinavian.)

How the conjunctive use arose out of the adv. of time is obscure. Some would explain it directly from the demonstrative sense 'then', taking 'John is more skilful than his brother' as = 'John is more skilful; then (= after that) his brother'. Others derive it from the relative or conjunctive use of OE. *þonne* (then 6), = 'When, when as', thus 'When as (whereas) his brother is skilful, John is more (so)'. The analogy of L. *quam* favours a relative sense.

When interrogative or demonstrative words became conjunctive or relative they lost their stress and were liable to weakening. Already in the 8th c. OE. *þanne* appears as *ðan, þan, than*, a form exemplified in nearly every century since, though down to *c* 1500 the fuller contemporary forms of the demonstrative adv., *þanne, þenne, þane, þene*, etc., were also in use. When the adv. was reduced to *þen*, from the 15th c. spelt *then*, there was a strong tendency to spell the conjunction in the same way, which during the 16th c. nearly triumphed; but in the 17th c. the tide turned, and by 1700 or a little later the conjunction was differentiated from the adv. as *than*. As the latter was, and is, pronounced (ðən), it is manifest that it might be written either *then* or *than* with equal approximation to the actual sound.]

1. a. The conjunctive particle used after a comparative adjective or adverb (and sometimes after other words: see 2–4) to introduce the second member of the comparison; the conjunction expressing the comparative of inequality (cf. as 3). In use it is always stressless, usually joined accentually to the prec. word, e.g. *more than, less than, other than* ('mɔəðən, 'lɛsðən, 'ʌðəðən)).

The two members of the comparison are most commonly of the same grammatical form, e.g. two clauses (the latter of which may be contracted in various ways, two substantives, two pronouns, two infinitives, two adjectives, two adverbs, etc., but not invariably so: see the quots. (Two infinitives connected by *than* in mod. Eng. either both have *to* or are both without it; formerly (until *c* 1800), esp. after *had rather, had better*, the second infinitive often had *to* when the first was without it.)

Instead of *than* after a comparative, *as* (like Ger. *als*) is common in Scotland, the north of England, and in parts of Ireland and the United States; *nor* (*nar, ner*) appears to be dialectal everywhere from Shetland to Hampshire and Cornwall, as well as in Ireland and America (see E.D.D.), but seems never to have been literary except in Sc., where also *na* was formerly used. In Sc. the relation is sometimes expressed by *be* (= by) as 'this field is bigger be that' (Jamieson s.v. be).

α. *c* **825** *Vesp. Psalter* li. 5 [lii. 3] Ðu lufedes.. unrehtwisnisse mae ðon spreocan rehtwisnisse. *Ibid.* lxxxiii[i]. 11 [10] Ic ȝeceas..bion in huse godes mae ðone eardian in ȝeteldum synfulra. *c* **893** K. Ælfred *Oros.* I. i. §19 Seo [sæ] is bradre þonne æniȝ man ofer seon mæȝe. *c* **1000** *Ags. Gosp.* John i. 15 He wæs ær þonne ic. *a* **1175** *Cott. Hom.* 219 þaðe hi wolde..beon betere þonne he ȝesceapen were. *c* **1205** Lay. 6515 þe mon..þe nimeð to him seoluen Mare þonne [*c* 1275 þan] he maȝen walden.

β. **831** *Charter of Eadwald* in *O.E. Texts* 445 Nis eðelmode eniȝ meȝhond neor ðes cynnes ðanne eadwald. *a* **1000** Ælfric *Colloquy* (Disc. 3) in Wr.-Wülcker 90 Leofre ys us beon beswungen for lare þænne hit ne cunnan. *a* **1175** *Cott. Hom.* 219 Wursan þanne æniȝ oðer. *c* **1205** Lay. 3030 þe king heo louede more þanne [*c* 1275 þan] ba tueie þe oðre. *Ibid.* 8916-17 Leouere him weore þane [*c* 1275 þan] al his lond, þene al his seoluer, þæne al his gold. *c* **1220** *Bestiary* 267 More ðanne man weneð. *a* **1450** *Knt. de la Tour* (1906) 24 With fairnesse rather thanne with rudenesse.

γ. *c* **1175** *Lamb. Hom.* 17 Betere hit is þet heo beon ispilled ..þenne mid alle fordon. *Ibid.* 139 þis dei is..seouensiþe brictere þene þe sunne. *c* **1205** Lay. 11954 Ma þeone [*c* 1275 þane] heo rohten. *c* **1275** *XI Pains of Hell* 121 in *O.E. Misc.* 150 þe stude is þustrore þene þe nyht. *c* **1320** *Cast. Love* 196 And raþure he dude his wyues bode þen he heold þe heste of gode. *c* **1400** *Laud Troy Bk.* 2010 That ladi..That is gentelour, then ȝe or he. *c* **1420** *Chron. Vilod.* 3195 A nother gretter miracle ȝet þenne þis. *a* **1425** *Cursor M.* 9452 (Laud) She levyd more the fend Then god. **1470–85** Malory *Arthur* IX. xxxv. 395, I am more heuy that I can not mete with hym, thenne for al the hurtes. **1535** Coverdale *Ps.* xcv[i]. 4 He is more to be feared then all goddes. **1590** Shaks. *Mids. N.* III. i. 90 A stranger Piramus, then ere plaid here. **16..** Sir W. Mure *Sonn. to Margareit* i. 13 With vertue grac'd far more yen forme of face. **1611** Bible *Ps.* lxxxiv. 10, I had rather be a doore keeper in the house of my God, then to dwell in the tents of wickednesse. **1667** Milton *P.L.* II. 745, I know thee not, nor ever saw till now Sight more detestable then him and thee. **1684** Earl Roscom. *Ess. Transl. Verse* 48 The fault is more the Languages then theirs.

δ. **735** Bæda *Death-song* 2 Naeniȝ uuiurthit thonc snotturra than him tharf sie. *c* **1200** Ormin 1985 þatt wollde bettre Drihhtin Godd..þann þatt te laffdiȝ wæ re shennd. *Ibid.* 15689 þatt wass till Crist ȝet ner bitahht þan hise posstless wærenn. **1303** R. Brunne *Handl. Synne* 6043 Ȝyt hyt ys wers þan ys þe lore. **13..** *Cursor M.* 23240 (Cott.) Herder þan [*Edin.* þain] es here irinn mell. **1393** Langl. *P. Pl.* C. II. 144 And deye raþere þan to do eny dedlich synne. *c* **1440** *Jacob's Well* 302 Ȝe are more hethyne in ȝoure werkys þan we. **1474** Caxton *Chesse* II. ii. b iv b, The chyld that so wysely contriued the lye rather than he wold discouere theyr counceyl. **1566** Painter *Pal. Pleas.* (1813) II. 538, I had rather dye than once to open my mouth. **1682** Sir T. Browne *Chr. Mor.* III. §25 Some had rather never have lived than to tread over their days once more. **1710** Addison *Tatler* No. 220 ⁋3 Water, colder than Ice, and clearer than Christal. **1732** Berkeley *Alciphr.* III. §13 The generality of mankind obey rather force than reason. **1766** Goldsm. *Vic. W.* xii, You have more circumspection than is wanted. **1774** —— *Nat. Hist.* (1776) III. 30 They..rather tread their enemies to death than gore them. **1782** Cowper *Mut. Forbearance* 20 Some people are more nice than wise. **1803** Jefferson *Writ.* (1830) IV. 3, I had rather ask an enlargement of power from the nation..than to assume it. **1832** Tennyson *To J. S.* ix, Great Nature is more wise than I. **1850** —— *In Mem.* xxvii. 16 'Tis better to have loved and lost, Than never to have loved at all. **1848** Dickens *Dombey* xxxii, Being a whit more venturesome than before. **1854** Mrs. Jameson *Bk. of Th.* (1877) 27 We all need more mercy than we deserve. **1875** Jowett *Plato* (ed. 2) I. 36 Than which nothing..can be more irrational. **1908** R. Bagot *A. Cuthbert* v. 41 She would have..accepted the results even of a *mésalliance*..rather than that Cuthbertsheugh should not pass to a son of mine. *Mod.* He likes dogs better than cats. He likes dogs better than I. That is easier said than done. He said he would sooner die than yield.

abbrev. **1689** *Col. Rec. Pennsylv.* I. 317 This may be sooner and safer done yn returning me yt sum. **1705** Hearne *Collect.* 8 July (O.H.S.) I. 2 His Latin is..better yn Salmasius's.

ε. **1463** *Somerset Medieval Wills* (1901) 197 If their title be better an myne. *c* **1900** *New Engld. dial.*, Kicked him higher 'n a kite.

b. With a personal or relative pronoun in the objective case instead of the nominative (as if *than* were a preposition).

This is app. the invariable construction in the case of *than whom*, which is universally accepted instead of *than who*. With the personal pronouns it is now considered incorrect.

1560 Bible (Genev.) *Prov.* xxvii. 3 A fooles wrath is heauier then them bothe. **1569** J. Sanford tr. *Agrippa's Van. Artes* 165 We cannot resiste them that be stronger then vs. **1718** Prior *Better Answer* 27-8 For thou art a girl as much brighter than her, As he was a poet sublimer than me. **1762** Goldsm. *Cit. W.* xxxviii, I am, not less than him, a despiser of the multitude. *a* **1774** —— *Surv. Exp. Philos.* (1776) I. 163 Others, later than him, who appeal to experience as well as he, affirm the contrary. **1792** Wakefield *Mem.* (1804) I. 108 He was much older than me. **1815** Scott *Guy M.* xvii, I..could not be expected..to be wiser than her. *c* **1825** Beddoes *Second Brother* I. i, You are old, And many years nearer than him to death. **1861** O'Curry *Lect. MS. Materials* 253 He is better than me, then, said the monarch.

1548 Udall, etc. *Erasm. Par. Mark* 67 Or els forsake them, then whome..there is nothyng more deare vnto the. **1656** Heylin *Extraneus Vapulans* 313 An eminent Antiquary, than whom none can be fitter to give Testimony. **1667** Milton *P.L.* II. 299 Bëëlzebub..then whom, Satan except, none higher sat. **1749** Fielding *Tom Jones* XI. vi, Sophia, than whom none was more capable of [etc.]. **1876** Gladstone *Homeric Synchr.* 60 Mr. Newton, than whom no one is of greater authority, refers them [etc.].

c. Followed by *that*, or by *infin.* expressing a hypothetical result or consequence.

The modern idiom would often substitute *too* with the positive followed by the infinitive, for the comparative with *than*: e.g. in quot. 1611 'the bed is too short for a man to stretch himself'; in quot. 1693 'he is too modest to deny it'. Examples occur of a confusion of the two constructions, as 'too wise than that' or 'than to be'.

1528 Tindale *Wicked Mammon* 45 b, This texte is playner than that it neadeth to be expounded. **1611** Bible *Isa.* xxviii. 20 The bed is shorter, then that a man can stretch himselfe on it. **1779–81** Johnson *L.P.*, *Prior* Wks. III. 131 Dryden had been more accustomed to hostilities, than that such enemies should break his quiet.

1611 Beaum. & Fl. *Philaster* I. i, Your nature is more constant than to inquire after state-news. **1670** Milton *Hist. Eng.* VI. Wks. (1847) 553/2 Of a higher spirit than to accept her. **1693** Congreve *Old Bach.* IV. xxii, He is more modest..than to deny it. *a* **1704–1872** [see know *v.* 9b]. **1779** *Mirror* No. 2 ⁋6 Mr. Creech..knew his business better than to satisfy their curiosity. **1802** James *Milit. Dict.* s.v. *Rifled gun*, The bullet ought to be no larger than to be just pressed by the rifles. *Mod.* He knows better than to do that. I think more highly of him than to suppose he would do that (*or*, I think too highly of him to suppose...).

a **1677** Barrow *Serm. Ephes. v. 4* Wks. 1687 I. 202 It is a good far too pretious, than to be prostituted for idle sport. **1833** I. Taylor *Fanat.* i. 4 Those..who..are far too wise than to be religious. *Ibid.* 14 The inquiry..is too momentous..than that it should be diverted.

2. a. *Than* is regularly used after *other*, *else*, and their compounds (***another***, ***otherwise***, ***elsewhere***, etc.). See also other, else, etc.

[*c* **1200** Ormin 9305 Nohht elless ne nohht mare þann þatt tatt ȝuw iss sett to don Ne do ȝe.] *a* **1300** *Cursor M.* 7319 þai ask now oþer [*v.r.* anoþer] king þan me. *c* **1320** *Cast. Love* 1237 Oþer God nis non þen he. **1426** Lydg. *De Guil. Pilgr.*

9251 Ys nat my body & I al on?.. Ys he a-nother than am I? **1551** RECORDE *Pathw. Knowl.* Pref., There neadeth none other proofe then Aristotle his testimony. **1573** G. HARVEY *Letter-bk.* (Camden) 1 If I do otherwise then I shuld do. **1587** GOLDING *De Mornay* xxiv. 408 God was not knowne and worshipped elswhere than among the people of Israell. **1666** BOYLE *Orig. Formes & Qual.* (1667) 2 The diversity.. in Bodies must.. arise from somewhat else then the Matter they consist of. **1799** HT. LEE *Canterb. T., Frenchm. T.* (ed. 2) I. 255 [He was] no other than the rightful lord. **1896** *Law Times* C. 410/1 The acts or defaults of any person other than himself.

b. Hence sometimes after adjs. or advbs. of similar meaning to 'other', as *different, diverse, opposite*, and after Latin comparatives, as *inferior, junior*: usually with clause following. Now mostly avoided.

different(ly) than is not uncommon, esp. in the U.S., but continues to be regarded by many as incorrect. See also DIFFERENT *a.* 1 b.

c **1400** MAUNDEV. (1839) viii. 109 Þei han also dyuerse clothinge and schapp.. þan oþer folk han. **1566** PAINTER *Pal. Pleas.* (1813) I. 317 If the lorde of Mendozza were inferiour in qualitie, nobility, and goods, than hee is. **1642** BAKER *Malvezzi's Disc. Tacitus* liii. 498 He was now made overseer of the building.., a much inferiour place than the other. **1754** J. HILDROP *Misc. Wks.* I. 91 They imploy their Wealth.. to quite opposite Purposes than were intended. **1822** J. YATES *Let. to Parr* 19 May, in *P.'s Wks.* (1828) VIII. 250 Such a design.. has a right to a far different head than mine. **1857** TROLLOPE *Barchester Towers* III. xiv. 248 Things were conducted very differently now than in former times. **1902** *Westm. Gaz.* 19 Aug. 2/3 How about the following sentence? 'Unless the London members behave differently about the Bill for London than the country members about the Bill for the country, reasons for postponement and consideration will begin to look weighty.' If 'than' is excluded, how is it to be said? [Put 'otherwise' for 'differently', and retain 'than'.] **1912** J. WEBSTER *Daddy-Long-Legs* (1913) 146 It's different with me than with other girls. **1962** D. LESSING *Golden Notebk.* 59 Both come from a different world than the housing estate outside London. **1970** *Amer. N. & Q.* Nov. 39/1 Geoffrey and Erasmus are concerned with classifying metaphors along quite different lines than is Quintilian. **1980** *Outdoor Life* (U.S.) (Northeast ed.) Oct. 101/1 Mule deer bucks behave differently than whitetails in a few other ways.

3. Exceptional or peculiar uses. †**a.** With ellipsis of preceding comparative: = *rather than, more than. Obs.*

[*c* **1000** *Ags. Ps.* cxvii[i]. 8 God ys on Dryhten ȝeorne to þenceanne, þonne on mannan wese mod to treowianne. *Lat.* Bonum est confidere in Domino, quam confidere in homine.] **13..** *Minor Poems fr. Vernon MS.* xxix. 46 He was Counseyled [to] hewe of his leg: þen longe to suffre so. *c* **1449** PECOCK *Repr.* III. v. 307 It spedith to thee that oon of thi membris perische than that al thi bodi go into helle. **1647** TRAPP *Comm. Epistles* 330 He did verily believe that Job was torne and tortured by his interpretations, then ever he had been by his botches and ulcers. *a* **1648** LD. HERBERT *Hen. VIII* 68 The apprentices being encouraged herewith,.. than do nothing, brake open some prisons.

†**b.** = Nor. (? ellipsis for *any more than.*) *Obs.*

13.. *Cursor M.* 17586 (Cott.) Yeitt es he þar-wit ouer all,.. And mist noiþer in heuen þen [*v. rr.* ne, ny] here. *Ibid.* 29114 Yee wate neuer dai þen night, Yur lauerd wil cum. **1472** *Surtees Misc.* (1888) 25 That no man.. bers unlawefull wepyn to the kirk then in the market. **1473** *Rolls of Parlt.* VI. 95/2 That this Acte of Resumption, then noon other Acte made or to be made.. extend not neither be prejudiciall unto [etc.].

c. = Except, besides, but. (? ellipsis for *other than, else than, otherwise than.*) *Obs.* or *arch.*

1375 BARBOUR *Bruce* I. 501 Thar is nothir man na page,.. than thai sall be Fayn to mak thaim-selwyn fre. **1585** T. WASHINGTON tr. *Nicholay's Voy.* III. iii. 74b, There is almost nothing left then a shadow therof. **1647** W. BROWNE *Polex.* I. v. 123 The service you had done.. was such as kings could not worthily acknowledge, at least, then in giving up their crownes. **1857** RUSKIN *Pol. Econ. Art* 28 There is nothing left for him than the blood that comes.. up to the horsebridles.

¶**d.** After *hardly, scarcely*: = When (by confusion with *no sooner than*).

1864 FROUDE *Short Stud.* (1867) I. 3 He had scarcely won for himself the place which he deserved, than his health was found shattered. **1903** F. W. MAITLAND in *Camb. Mod. Hist.* II. xvi. 584 Hardly had the Council been re-opened at Trent.. than Elizabeth was allying herself with the Huguenots.

†**4.** After ERE, LESS, NIGH: see these words.

¶**5.** Erroneously used (instead of *as*) in comparisons of equality; †*like than* = such as (*obs.*); *so.. than* = so.. as.

1592 WARNER *Alb. Eng.* VIII. xl. (1612) 195 A Warrior braue: But than his Sier, himselfe, one Sonne of his, Like Polititians seldome liude. **1595** *Trag. Sir R. Grenville* (Arb.) 64 Then which the like was neuer heard before. **1602** G. BLACKWELL in *Archpriest Controv.* (Camden) II. 226, I can blame none so much for defect of Almes then Mr. Collington and his adherents. **1677** R. BOYLE *Treat. Art of War* 12 Their substantial Diet, than which, none.. have so good. **1723** MANDEVILLE *Fab. Bees* (1733) II. 201 There is nothing in which our Species so far surpasses all others, than in the Capacity [etc.].

†**than,** *dem. pron. Obs.* [ME. repr. OE. *þam* dat. sing. of *se, séo, þæt*, THAT.] After a prep.: That; as in *for þan*, for that (reason), therefore; *for al þan*, for all that (FOR 23 b); *not (na) for than*, notwithstanding that. See also FOR-THAN.

1297 R. GLOUC. (Rolls) 1418 Ȝut for al þan.. Hii broȝte oure louerd ihesu crist to deþe on þe rode. *a* **1325** *Prose Psalter, Athanasian Creed* 16 And na-for-þan þer ne ben nouȝt þre goddes. *c* **1450** LOVELICH *Grail* xlv. 365 Nevertheless not for than the water In his Eyen stille was than.

than, þan, obs. and dial. form of THEN.

than, thana, thane, OE. and ME. inflexions of THAT, THE.

‖**thana, tana** ('tɑːnə). *E. Indies.* Also **tanna(h, thanna(h.** [Hindī *thāna, thānā*.]

a. A police station in India; formerly, a military station or fortified post.

1803 WELLINGTON in Gurw. *Desp.* (1837) II. 251, I give you notice, that you may have your tannahs prepared in your villages and desire them to defend them. **1834** A. PRINCEP *Baboo* II. xi. 202 (Stanf.) The Burkundazes at last came up from the Thana. **1879** LOW *Jrnl. Gen. Abbott* iii. 214 Thannahs (posts) for the protection of the Cabul were re-established. **1895** MRS. B. M. CROKER *Village Tales* (1896) 212 They were found.. near the police thana on the Futupore Road.

b. (See quot. 1961).

1936 W. H. SAUMAREZ SMITH *Let.* 5 Dec. in *Young Man's Country* (1977) ii. 45, I am making a tour of all the thanas this fortnight. **1961** L. D. STAMP *Gloss. Geogr. Terms* 450/2 *Thānā*, a political division of a district which is under the jurisdiction of a single police-station so that a thana is really a police-station area. **1975** *Bangladesh Times* 19 July 3/2 Besides forty three members of Jessore district and thana units of the defunct organisation have applied for the membership of BKSAL. **1977** *Ibid.* 19 Jan. 12/3 He made a plea for the abolition of.. divisions, districts, sub-divisions and thanas because they are.. ineffective for today's needs.

Hence ‖**thanadar** (tɑːnə'dɑː(r)) [Hindī *thānadār*], the head officer of a police station in India; formerly the commander of a military post.

1802 C. JAMES *Milit. Dict.* (1816), *Tannadar*, a commander of a small fort. **1834** A. PRINCEP *Baboo* I. xviii. 326 (Stanf.) Thou must be a Thanadar at least. **1897** L. J. TROTTER *J. Nicholson* xvii. (1908) 233 He suspended a thanadar whom he caught in an act of oppression.

thanage ('θeɪnɪdʒ). *Obs.* exc. *Hist.* Also **thenage.** [= AF. *thaynage, thanage*, in med.L. *than-, thenagium*, f. THANE (and its variants) + OF. *-age*, med.L. *-āgium*: see -AGE.] The tenure by which lands were held by a thane; the land held by a thane, a thane-land; also the rank, office, or jurisdiction of a thane.

[**1200** *Rotuli Chart.* (1837) 51/1 Sciatis nos concessisse et.. confirmasse Willelmo Bardulf et Elysabeth uxori sue et heredibus eorum totum thenagium quod.. Willelmus.. pater predicte Elysabeth tenuit in Hepedale et in Kokedale. **1228** in *Feodar. Priorat. Dunelm.* (Surtees) 224 Requisitus an tenementum Henrici sit drengagium, dicit quod non, sed thenagium, sed pater Henrici liberavit illud a thenagio. **1230** *Stat. Alex. II*, c. 5 in *Scot. Statutes* (1844) I. 399 Si vero in dominicis vel thanagiis domini Regis malefactor ille fuerit [**14..** *transl.* ibid. 400 And gif for suth þat trespassour be in þe kingis maynis or thanagis]. ? **1305** *Rolls of Parlt.* I. 471/2 La terre appropre torcenusement a vostre Thaynage de Balhelui.]

14.. [see quot. 1230 above]. **1623** in *Thanes of Cawdor* (Spalding Cl.) 260 All and haill the lands of the thanage and barony of Calder.. united into one entire and free thanage, to be called the Thanage and Barony of Calder. **1641** *Termes de la Ley* 255 The kings thanage signifieth a certain part of the kings lands, or property, whereof the rule & government appertaineth unto him, who therfore is called *Thanus*. **1807** G. CHALMERS *Caledonia* I. III. v. §3. 366 Having no such lands [in demesne], they equally appear to have had no thanages. **1872** E. W. ROBERTSON *Hist. Ess.* 126 The Scottish Gerefa was known as the Thane or Mair, his district often as a Thanage. **1883** *Ord. Surv. Gazetteer Scot.* III. 18 It gave name to an ancient thanage.

thanatic (θə'nætɪk), *a. rare*⁻⁰. [ad. Gr. *θανατικός*, f. *θάνατος* death: see -IC.] (See quot.)

1860 MAYNE *Expos. Lex.*, *Thanaticus*, of or belonging to death;.. deadly: tha'natic. **1890** in BILLINGS *Med. Dict.*

thanatism ('θænətɪz(ə)m). [f. Gr. *θάνατος* death + -ISM.] The belief or doctrine that at death the human soul ceases to exist. So '**thanatist**, a believer in thanatism.

1900 *Academy* 1 Dec. 512/1 For ourselves we prefer to say that even atheism and thanatism are speculations. **1902** J. MCCABE tr. *Haeckel's Riddle Universe* xi. 67/1 We give the name of 'thanatism'.. to the opinion which holds that at a man's death.. his 'soul' also disappears,—that is, that sum of cerebral functions which psychic dualism regards as a peculiar entity, independent of the other vital processes in the living body. *Ibid.* 69/1. **1902** W. S. LILLY in *19th Cent.* Mar. 466, I suppose that thanatists, as it is the fashion to call them, are really not very numerous.

thanato- ('θænətəʊ), before a vowel **thanat-**, combining form of Gr. *θάνατος* death, chiefly in scientific words. ˌ**thanato-bio'logic** *a.* (see quot.). ˌ**thanatocœ'nosis, -'cœnose** (also *U.S.* **-cen-**) *Ecol.* [a. G. *thanatocoenose* (E. Wasmund 1926, in *Arch. f. Hydrobiol.* XVII. 6), f. Gr. *κοίνωσις* sharing, as in BIOCŒNOSIS], a group of fossils occurring in the same location but not necessarily representing a former biocœnosis. **thanatogno'monic** *a.*, indicative or characteristic of death. **thana'tography,** *nonce-wd.* [after *biography*], an account of a person's death. **thanato'mantic** *a.* [see -MANTIC], of or pertaining to divination concerning death. **thana'tometer** (see quots.). **thanato'philia** [-PHILIA], an undue fascination with death. ‖**thanato'phobia** (also **thana'tophoby**), morbid fear of death. **thanato'phoric** *a. Path.* [ad. F. *thanatophore* (P. Maroteaux et al. 1967, in *Presse Méd.* LXXV. 2519), ad. Gr. *θανατηφόρος* death-bringing] applied to a form of dwarfism that results in death (see quot. 1977). ‖**thana'topsis** [Gr. *ὄψις* sight, view], a contemplation of death. **thanato'typhus,** malignant typhus.

1899 *Syd. Soc. Lex.*, **Thanato-biologic*, pertaining to life and death. **1953** *Amer. Jrnl. Sci.* CCLI. 25 The term '*thanatocoenosis' implies a community of death; as used by Wasmund, however, it has come to mean the aggregated remains of organisms that in many cases never constituted a biocoenosis. **1957** *Sci. News* XLIII. 71 A fossil 'community' (a thanatocoenose or death assemblage) is seldom if ever identical with the original biocoenose. **1967** *Oceanogr. & Marine Biol.* V. 452 The following (and last) regression.. left a very rich fauna which forms most of the thanatocoenoses lying under the present sea level. **1975** *Nature* 23 Oct. 667/2 It is well known that factors such as habitat preference of the animals in question,.. and the environmental setting influence the likelihood of the preservation of thanatocoenoses. **1977** *Biotropica* IX. 131 (*heading*) A small-vertebrate thanatocenosis from northern Peru. **1862** G. W. BALFOUR tr. *Casper's Forensic Med.* §55 II. vi. 239 The lungs in the more or less recent bodies of those drowned.. present an appearance so peculiar as to be truly *thanatognomonic. **1839** THACKERAY *Catherine* vi, The excellent 'Newgate Calendar'.. contains the biographies and *thanatographies of Hayes and his wife. **1841** *Fraser's Mag.* XXV. 270 The deuteroscopic or *thanatomantic faculty of the Germans. **1860** MAYNE *Expos. Lex.*, *Thanatometrum*,.. term by Nasse [of Berlin] for a means of indicating the actual presence of death; a death-measurer: a *thanatometer. **1899** *Syd. Soc. Lex.*, *Thanatometer*, a thermometer capable of being introduced into the stomach to determine whether the depression of temperature is sufficient to be looked on as a sign of death. **1974** *Time* 28 Jan. 77/2 Romantic cults seem to spring up rapidly round poets who die young. An element of *thanatophilia enters into the worship of such poets. **1979** *N.Y. Rev. Bks.* 25 Oct. 18/4 Many of Sciascia's tales have, at their heart, thanatophilia. **1860** MAYNE *Expos. Lex.*, **Thanatophobia*, term for a dread or fear of death: *thanatophoby. **1903** *Alien. & Neurol.* May 170 Pessimism is frequently associated with morbid fear of death (thanatophobia). **1971** *Lancet* 12 June 1234/1 An achondroplastic shows some cartilage formation (in fact quite a lot, even in the *thanatophoric form). **1977** *Ibid.* 16 Apr. 854/1 Thanatophoric dwarfism is a congenital chondrodystrophy characterised by short extremities, narrow thorax, a trunk of normal length, and a relatively large head... Affected infants usually die soon after birth. **1816** W. C. BRYANT (*title*) *Thanatopsis. **1860** MAYNE *Expos. Lex.*, **Thanatotyphus*. **1890** in BILLINGS *Med. Dict.*

thanatoid ('θænətɔɪd), *a. Path.* [f. Gr. *θάνατος* death + -OID. Cf. Gr. *θανατώδης*.] (See quot.)

1857 DUNGLISON *Med. Lex.*, *Thanatoid*, resembling death; apparently dead. **1890** in BILLINGS *Nat. Med. Dict.*

thana'tologist. [f. next + -IST.] **a.** A student of or a person versed in thanatology; in quot. 1901 (*nonce-use*), one who studies dead animals.

1901 E. SELOUS *Bird Watching* viii. 224 We have studied animals only to kill them, or killed them in order to study them. Our 'zoologists' have been thanatologists. **1972** *New Scientist* 2 Mar. 497 Thanatologists ask doctors.. to help the terminal patient and his family to meet his own death. **1975** *Times Lit. Suppl.* 31 Oct. 1305/4 Their real subject, as is customary with Signor Manganelli, is death. He has always been proud of introducing himself as the supreme thanatologist. **1983** *Oxf. Bk. Death* p. xiii, While to 'deny' death would sound as foolish as the lady who told Carlyle she had decided to accept the universe, I cannot say that I share the thanatologists' missionary urge to bring death out into the open.

b. An undertaker.

1972 *Daily Colonist* (Victoria, B.C.) 1 Mar. 1/8 Quebec's 450 undertakers want to be called thanatologists. **1980** *Times* 25 Apr. 6/4 He was one of 300 thanatologists, better known as undertakers, gathered in the principality [of Monaco] to discuss death in all its aspects.

thanatology (θænə'tɒlədʒɪ). [f. Gr. *θάνατος* death + -LOGY. Cf. F. *thanatologie*.] The scientific study of death, its causes and phenomena. Also (orig. *U.S.*), the study of the effects of approaching death and of the needs of the terminally ill and their families;

1842 DUNGLISON *Med. Lex.*, *Thanatology*, a description, or the doctrine, of death. **1903** MITCHELL tr. *Metchnikoff's Nat. Man* xii. (1904) 298 The scientific study of old age and of death, two branches of science that may be called *gerontology* and *thanatology*. **1912** *Jrnl. Amer. Med. Assoc.* 27 Apr. 1246/1 There is something more than mere transcendentalism in the Science of Thanatology. **1968** *Jrnl. Indiana Med. Assoc.* LXI. 1159/1 (*heading*) Thanatology resurrected. **1969** *Courier-Mail* (Brisbane) 13 Sept. 12/7 A Foundation of Thanatology is being formed in New York. **1972** *New Scientist* 2 Mar. 497/2 The most disturbing issue that has arisen anew with thanatology is the problem of what to tell the terminal patient about his illness. *Ibid.*, Another area of thanatological controversy concerns the administration of drugs to relieve the pain of the terminally ill. **1976** *Billings* (Montana) *Gaz.* 11 July 3-F/4 Workers in the new field of thanatology are encouraging parents to take their children, even small ones, to funerals. **1977** *New York Rev. Bks.* 12 May 10/1 There is now a special branch of learning called 'Thanatology', and historians of death, like Philippe Ariès or Michel Vovelle, have suddenly appeared on the scene. **1979** *Brit. Med. Jrnl.* 15 Dec. 1530/2 The near-dead are not dead; and the dead, whether surviving in some form or not, can be left to thanatology and eschatology.

So **thanato'logical** *a.*, of or pertaining to thanatology.

1862 G. W. BALFOUR tr. *Casper's Forensic Med.* II. Title-p., Thanatological division. **1881** G. R. JESSE in *Athenæum* 9 Apr. 504/1 This sums up the thanatological results of an enormous amount of cruelty in previous experiments.

‖**Thanatophidia** (ˌθænətəʊˈfɪdɪə), *sb. pl. Zool.* [f. *thanat-*, THANATO- + OPHIDIA.] A division of *Ophidia*, comprising the venomous snakes. Hence **thanatoˈphidian** *a.*, of or pertaining to the *Thanatophidia*; *sb.* a serpent of this division; **thanatophidiˈologist**, a student of the zoology of the *Thanatophidia*.

1872 FAYRER (*title*) The Thanatophidia of India, being a Description of the Venomous Snakes of the Indian Peninsula. **1884** J. DONNET in *Nature* 27 Mar. 504/1, I believe it to be a generally accepted opinion among thanatophidiologists that, from what is known of the virulent properties of snake-poison, though fatal to man and other living beings, it is innoxious in its effects to serpents of like nature. **1891** *Cent. Dict.*, Thanatophidian *a.* and *sb.*

thanatorium (θænəˈtɔərɪəm). *nonce-wd.* Pl. -oria. [Alteration of *sanatorium*, after THANATO-.] An establishment where people are received in order to be killed.

1970 *Times* 1 May 11/4 We should need public thanatoria, just as we have public crematoria and abattoirs. **1970** *New Scientist* 24 Sept. 626/2 The Thanatoria, the most negative of all the departments. **1976** *Times Lit. Suppl.* 13 Feb. 166/1 The violent jerks from excess to excess of the patients at Dr Sacks's pseudonymous New York hospital—'not a sanatorium but a thanatorium', as one of the inmates remarked.

Thanatos (ˈθænətɒs). [a. Gr. θάνατος death.] = *death-instinct* s.v. DEATH *sb.* 19.

1935 *Brit. Jrnl. Psychol.* XXVI. 283 Freud's final duality was the division of the mind into two sets of instincts which he termed life instincts and death instincts respectively—or, if one prefers the Greek names, Eros and Thanatos. *Ibid.* 284 He was inclined..to regard the voice of Thanatos as mute. **1955** [see DEFUSION]. **1967** [see EROS 1 b]. **1970** G. GREER *Female Eunuch* 148 Our life-style contains more *thanatos* than *eros.* **1979** H. SEGAL *Klein* i. 20 The fundamental conflict, between Eros—life, including sexuality—and Thanatos—self-destruction and destruction—is the deepest source of ambivalence, anxiety and guilt.

‖**thanaˈtosis.** *Path.* [a. Gr. θανάτωσις a putting to death, f. θανατοῦν to put to death.]

1860 MAYNE *Expos. Lex.*, *Thanatosis*,..term for Mortification. **1890** in BILLINGS *Nat. Med. Dict.*

thane[1] (θeɪn). *Hist.* Forms: 1 **þeʒn, þeʒen, -in,** (**þeng**), 1–2 **þén, þeiʒn** (6–7 **theigne**), 2 **þening,** 2–3 **þein** (6, 9 **thein**), 3–4 **þ-, theyn(e** (6 **theyn**), 4 **thain** (8 **-e**), 4–6 **thayn(e,** 5– **thane.** See also THEGN. [OE. *þeʒn, þeʒen, þén,* = OS. *thegan,* OHG. *degan* boy, servant, warrior, hero (MHG., G. *degen*), ON. *þegn* freeman, liegeman:—OTeut. **þegno*[z], orig. child, boy, lad:—pre-Teut. **tek-nó-* (cf. Gr. τέκνον child), f. root *tek*: *tok* to beget.

The regular modern repr. of OE. *þeʒn*, if the word had lived on in spoken use, would have been *thain* (cf. *fain, main, rain*), as it actually appears in some writers, chiefly northern, from 1300 to near 1600. But *thain* was in 15–16th c. Sc. written *thane* (in L. *thanus*), and this form, being used by Boece, Holinshed, and Shakespeare (in Macbeth), was adopted by Selden, Spelman, and the legal antiquaries and historians of the 17th c. to represent the Anglo-Saxon *þeʒn*, and became the usual form in Eng. history. Recent historians, as Stubbs, Freeman, and Green, in order to distinguish the Anglo-Saxon use from the Sc. in sense 4, have revived the OE. *þeʒn* as THEGN, q.v.]

†**1.** A servant, minister, attendant; in OE. often applied to (Christ's) disciples. *Obs.*

a **700** *Epinal Gloss* (O.E.T.) 101 *Adsaeculam* [= *assecula*], theʒn. *c* **725** *Corpus Gloss* 77 *Adsaeclum*, þeʒn. *c* **888** K. ÆLFRED *Boeth.* vii. §2, ʒif þu þonne heora þeʒen beon wilt. *a* **900** tr. *Bæda's Hist.* IV. xxv. [xxiv.] (1890) 346 þa bæd he [a monk] his þeʒn..þæt he in þæm huse him stowe ʒeʒearwode..þa wundrode se þeʒn. *c* **950** *Lindisf. Gosp.* Matt. xxiv. 45 Hwa woenes ðu is ʒeleaf-full ðeʒn & hoʒa? **971** *Blickl. Hom.* 67 Iohannes, se deora þeʒn. *Ibid.*, Lazarus þær was ana sittende mid Hælende & mid his þeʒnum. *c* **1000** *Ags. Gosp.* Matt. xx. 26 Sy he eower þen. *Ibid.* John ii. 9 þa þenas soðlice wiston þe þæt wæter hlodon. *a* **1175** *Cott. Hom.* 229 An þera twelf Christes þeiȝne se þe was iudas ȝehaten. *c* **1275** *Death* 177 in *O.E. Misc.* 179 Hwer beoþ þine þeynes þat þe leoue were? **13..** *Cursor M.* 5373 (Cott.) First he was here als our thain [*Gött.* thrall, *Trin.* þral]. **1591** LAMBARDE *Archeion* (1635) E iij, By certaine Messengers, which they tearmed Theignes; that is to say, Ministers, or Servants.

†**2.** A military attendant, follower, or retainer; a soldier. *Obs.*

Beowulf 400 Aras þa se rica ymb hine rinc maniʒ þryðlic þeʒna heap. *a* **800** CYNEWULF *Elene* 549 (Gr.) þa cwom þeʒna heap to þam heremeðle. *c* **893** K. ÆLFRED *Oros.* v. ii. §3 Ueriatuses þeʒn þæm oþrum to longe æfterfylʒende, oþ mon his hors under him ofsceat. *c* **950** *Lindisf. Gosp.* Matt. viii. 9 Ic..hæfo under mec ðeiʒnas [*Vulg.* milites]. *c* **1000** *Ags. Gosp.* ibid., Ic hæbbe þeʒnas [*c* 1160 *Hatton* þeiʒnes] under me. *c* **1000** ÆLFRIC *Voc.* in Wr.-Wülcker 119/34 *Agaso*, hors þen.

†**b.** *poet.* A warrior, a brave man. Cf. EARL 1 b.

Beowulf 2709 Swylc sceolde secg wesan, þeʒn æt ðearfe. *c* **893** K. ÆLFRED *Oros.* III. vii. §2 ʒif ʒe swelce þeʒnas sint, swelce ʒe wenað þæt ʒe sien, þonne sceoldon ʒe swa lustlice eowre aʒnu brocu aræfnan. *a* **1272** *Luue Ron* 13 in *O.E. Misc.* 93 þeos þeines þat weren bolde beoþ aglyden.

3. One who in Anglo-Saxon times held lands of the king or other superior by military service; originally in the fuller designation *cyninges þeʒn*, 'king's thane, military servant or attendant'; in later times simply *thegn*, as a term of rank, including several grades below that of an *ealdorman* or *eorl* (EARL *sb.* 2) and above that of the *ceorl* or ordinary freeman.

In this sense the name was superseded by *baron* and *knight* in the 12th c., and continued only in historical use, in which it was written *thane* in the 16th c. Recent historians have revived the OE. form as THEGN.

805 *Charter* in *O.E. Texts* 442 Beforan wulfrede arcebiscope..& esne cyninges ðeʒne. *a* **900** *O.E. Chron.* an. 897, Maniʒe þara selestena cynges þena... Eadulf cynges þeʒn..& Ecgulf cynges hors þeʒn. **971** *Blickl. Hom.* 211 Wæs his fæder ærest cyninges þeʒn, & ða..he wæs cininges þeʒna aldorman. *c* **1000** ÆLFRIC *Gram.* ix. (Z.) 50 *Optimas*, ðeʒn. *c* **1000** —— *Voc.* in Wr.-Wülcker 155/20 *Primas*, heafodman, *uel* þeʒn. *Ibid.* 155/23 *Satrapa*, þeʒn. *c* **1029–60** *Laws Ranks* c. 1 in Liebermann *Gesetze* (1903) 456 Ælc be his mæðe, ʒe eorl ʒe ceorl, ʒe þeʒen ʒe þeoden. *c* **1050** *Byrhtferth's Handboc* in *Anglia* (1885) VIII. 326 þeʒnas & ceorlas habbað landmearke. **1066** *Writ of Eadweard* in Earle *Land-Charters* 342 Eadward cyningc gret Hereman bisceop, and Harold eorl, and Godric, and ealle his þeʒenas [L. version *barones*]. *a* **1100** *O.E. Chron.* an. 1086 (Laud MS.) Ealle þa rice men ofer eall Engla land, arce biscopas, & leodbisceopas, abbodas & eorlas, þeʒnas & cnihtas. *a* **1175** *Cott. Hom.* 231 Mid ærlen and aldren, mid cnihten, mid þeinen. *c* **1300** *Havelok* 2260 Siþen drenges, and siþen thaynes, And siþen knithes, and siþen sweynes. *c* **1325** *Chron. Eng.* (Ritson) 583 Alle the theynes of Walschelonde He made bowe to ys honde. **1570–6** LAMBARDE *Peramb. Kent* (1826) 453 As for *twelf Pindman*, it was given to the Theyn or Gentleman, bicause his life was valued at Twelve hundreth shillings. **1598** HAKLUYT *Voy.* I. 126 If a Thein so thriued, that he serued the king, and on his message rid in his houshold, if he then had a Thein that followed him..he became an Earle.

1577–87 HOLINSHED *Chron.* I. 190/1 Harold..slue thirtie gentlemen of honor, or thanes (as they called them). **1614** SELDEN *Titles Hon.* 267 The neerest name for Baron was that of Thane, anciently written also Thegn. *c* **1630** RISDON *Surv. Devon* §284 (1810) 296 The thane was descended of ancient lineage, and such a one as we call gentleman. **1754** HUME *Hist. Eng.* (1761) I. App. i. 96 The nobles were called thanes; and were of two kinds, the king's thanes and lesser thanes. **1809** BAWDWEN *Domesday Bk.* 18 In *Loctvsv* (Lofthouse) two Thanes had four carucates to be taxed. **1853** JOS. STEVENSON tr. *O.E. Chron.* an. 1036, Leofric the earl, and almost all the thanes north of the Thames..chose Harold for chief of all England **1853** —— tr. *Florence of Worcester* an. 897, Ecgulf the kings horse-thane. **1875** MAINE *Hist. Inst.* v. 135 There are in the early English laws some traces of a process by which a Ceorl might become Thane. **1888** EARLE *Land-Charters* Introd. 71 These words ..eorl, gesith, thane, knight, squire, gentleman. The last two run abreast.

4. In *Scottish Hist.* A person, ranking with the son of an earl, holding lands of the king; the chief of a clan, who became one of the king's barons.

[**1220** *Stat. Alex. II*, c. 2, in *Scot. Statutes* (1844) I. 398 De terris episcoporum abbatum baronum militum et thanorum qui de Rege tenent.] **14..** *transl. of prec.*, Of þe landis of bischopis abbotis barounis knychtis and thaynis þe quhilkis haldis of þe Kyng. **1422** in *Thanes of Cawdor* (Spalding Club) 10 To spouse and til haf to your wife, the douchter of the saide Donald thayne of Caldor. *c* **1425** WYNTOUN *Cron.* VI. xviii. 1904 Lo, ȝonder þe thayne of Crumbaghty! *Ibid.* xix. 2318 Makduf of Fif þe thayne. *c* **1470** HENRY *Wallace* XI. 894 That Erll was cummyn off trew haill nobill blud, Fra the ald thane, quhilk in his tym was gud. **1535** STEWART *Cron. Scot.* (Rolls) II. 637 'The Thane of Glames, gude morne to him', said scho. [**1596** DALRYMPLE tr. *Leslie's Hist. Scot.* I. (S.T.S.) 112 *margin* The first nobils in Scotland war called Thani; thay war of the clan cheif... In ald tymes Dukes war called Thani.] **1605** SHAKS. *Macb.* I. iii. 71 By Sinells death, I know I am Thane of Glamis, But how, of Cawdor? the Thane of Cawdor liues. *Ibid.* v. iii. 50 Doctor, the Thanes flye from me. **1609** SKENE *Reg. Maj.* 73 b, *Item*, the Cro of ane Earles sonne, or of ane Thane, is ane hundreth kye. *Item*, the Cro of the sonne of ane Than, is thriescore sax kye. **1759** ROBERTSON *Hist. Scot.* I. (1802) I. 229 The ancient Thanes were the equals and the rivals of their prince. **1810** A. BOSWELL *Edinburgh* 260 Hill after hill some cunning clerk shall gain, Then, in a mendicant, behold a Thane!

b. *transf.* to modern persons, in various senses; e.g. a Scottish lord. Often in allusion to Shaks. *Macbeth* v. iii. 50. (See above.)

1750 SHENSTONE *Odes, Rural Elegance* 7 Ye rural thanes that o'er the mossy down Some panting, timorous hare pursue. *a* **1764** LLOYD *Poetry Prof.* Poet. Wks. 1774 I. 39 Hail to the Thane, whose patriot skill Can break all nations to his will. **1839** LD. BROUGHAM *Statesm. Geo. III, Dundas* I. 232 He [Pitt] held the proxies of many Scottish Peers in open opposition! Well might his colleague exclaim to the hapless Addington in such unheard-of troubles, 'Doctor, the Thanes fly from us.' **1888** BRYCE *Amer. Commw.* lxiii. II. 455 Sometimes however he is rebuffed by the powers at Washington and then his State thanes fly from him.

5. *Comb.* **thane-right**, the legal rights and privileges of a thane; **thane-wer** [OE. *þeʒn-wer*], the wer-gild of a thane (sense 3).

1008 [see THEGNWER]. **1844** LINGARD *Anglo-Sax. Ch.* (1858) II. xii. 234 *note*, His thane-wer, and thane-right in life and in the grave means the same as his worldly goods, and Christian sepulture.

Hence ˈ**thaness**, a female thane; a thane's wife.

1827 SCOTT *Surg. Dau.* iii, All the rural thanes and thanesses attended on these occasions. **1849** J. WILSON *Christopher under Canvass* No. 5 The Thaness [Lady Macbeth] is self-stayed.

thane[2], Sc. form of FANE[1].

1496 *Acc. Ld. High Treas. Scot.* I. 286 Item, for xiij dowbill platis to be thanis to the pailȝounis. **1570** *Satir. Poems Reform.* xxii. 84 Lyke wauering thane, thy proces vane Will brew the bitter gall. **1716** in *Thanes of Cawdor* (Spalding Cl.) 417 Thanes for the horse heads [at a funeral], £80. **1782** OREM *Chanonry Aberdeen* 21 With cross thanes of iron on the top of each of them.

thane, obs. f. THEN *adv.*[1]; inflexion of THE.

thanedom (ˈθeɪndəm). [f. THANE + -DOM.] The domain or jurisdiction of a Scottish thane.

c **1425** WYNTOUN *Cron.* VI. xviii. 1910 In his ȝouth heid Off þai thayndomes þe thayne wes maid. **1579** *Reg. Privy C. Scot.* III. 140 The lordschip and thanedome of Fettarcarne. **1776** PENNANT *Tour Scot.* II. Addit. 13 This thanedom was transferred into the house of the Campbels. **1807** G. CHALMERS *Caledonia* I. III. vii. 416 The titles of Glamis, and Cawdor, were borrowed by Boece from thanedoms of more recent origin. **1837** SKENE *Highlanders Scot.* (1902) II. v. 261 Thanedoms were certainly hereditary in Scotland.

†ˈ**thanehede.** *Obs.* [f. THANE[1], in sense 1 'servant' + *-hede*, -HEAD. Essentially an earlier form of next, but unconnected with it in use, being founded on an earlier sense of OE. *þeʒn*.] Service, servitude; bondage, thraldom.

a **1300** *Cursor M.* 5404 (Cott.) Land and lijth wit bodi we bede, þat þou vs tak in þin thainhede [*v. rr.* bonde-, bundhede]; In thainhed [*Fairf.* bondehede; *Gött.* & *Trin.* þraldam, -dome] tak our landes all, For sede we mai þam sau wit-all. *Ibid.* 5791, I sal þam [Israel] bring vte of thainhede [*v. rr.* þraldome, thralhede], In-till a land, a wonsun thede. *Ibid.* 6990 In thain-hede ar þai worth to be, þat wil noght thole, and mai be fre.

ˈ**thanehood.** [f. THANE (senses 3, 4) + -HOOD. Cf. THEGNHOOD.] The condition or rank of a thane.

1897 E. CONYBEARE *Hist. Cambs.* 89 Raised to the Thanehood by their own or their forefathers' merits.

ˈ**thane-land.** Now *Hist.* (See also THEGN-LAND.) Land held by a thane, or by military tenure.

a **1641** SPELMAN *Feuds & Tenures* viii, For better manifestation that Thanelands were subject to no feudal Service, consider, I pray you, the Words of the Saxon passage before mention'd, where it is said that a Thane must have three Hides at least of his..own Land. **1701** *Cowell's Interpr.*, *Thane-Lands*, Lands..granted by Charters of the Saxon Kings to their Thanes. **1809** BAWDWEN *Domesday Bk.* 370 Ulnod holds one oxgang of the same land in thaneland.

thanen, þanen, -ene, *adv.*; see THENNE.

thaneship (ˈθeɪnʃɪp). [f. THANE[1] + -SHIP: cf. OE. *þeʒnscipe*.] The office or position of a thane: esp. in the Sc. sense. (See also THEGNSHIP.)

1766 STEEVENS *Note Shaks., Macb.* I. iii. 48 The thaneship of Glamis was the ancient inheritance of Macbeth's family. **1844** LINGARD *Anglo-Sax. Ch.* (1858) I. App. 371 These lands ceasing to support an earthly thaneship or service. **1865** KINGSLEY *Herew.* xv, He shall have..a thaneship in East Anglia. **1896** MANLY *Notes on Macbeth* 101 Since Macbeth's accession to the thaneship of Cawdor.

thang (θæŋ). Repr. a Southern U.S. pronunc. of THING *sb.*[1]

1937 *Frontier & Midland* Autumn 14/2 He done one thang he ought never done. **1941** W. A. PERCY *Lanterns on Levee* xx. 259 Negroes..insisted on going to their [flooded] cabins..to see about their 'thangs'. **1971** in A. Dundes *Mother Wit* (1973) 319/2 You ain' so bad yourself, girl... I want to help a sweet thang like you all I can. **1973** *Black World* Sept. 84 Ourselves illusionize About doin our thang.

Thanga, obs. var. SANGHA.

thanist, -stry, obs. forms of TANIST, -STRY.

thank (θæŋk), *sb.* Forms: α. 1–4 **þanc,** (3 **ðhanc**), 1–5 **þank,** (3 *Orm.* **þannk**), 4 **thanc** (**thang**), 4–5 **þanke,** 4–6 **thanck(e,** 4–7 **thanke,** (6 **thangke**), 4– **thank.** β. 1 **thonc,** 1–4 **þonc,** 2 **þeonk,** 2–5 **þonk,** (3 **þong**), 3–5 **þonke,** 4 **þoncke.** [OE. *þanc, þǫnc* = OFris. *thonk*, OS. **thank* (MDu. *danc*, D. *dank*), OHG., MHG. *danc* (G. *dank*), ON. *þökk* (:—*þanku* fem.), Sw. *tack*, Da. *tak*, Goth. *þagks*:—OTeut. **þanko*[z], f. ablaut stem *þenk*: *þank*: *þunk*: see THINK. The primary sense was therefore *thought*.]

I. †**1.** = THOUGHT. *Obs.* (See also I-THANK.)

735 BÆDA *Death-song* 2 Naeniʒ uuiurthit thonc snotturra [*or* thoncsnotturra] than him thaarf sie. *a* **900** *Andreas* 557 (Gr.) Saʒa þances gleaw þeʒn, ʒif þu cunne, hu þæt ʒewurde be werum tweonum. *c* **1000** *Ags. Ps.* (Th.) lxxxvii[i]. 11 Ne on ðeostrum ne mæʒ, þances ʒehyʒdum, æniʒ wislicu wundur oncnawan. *c* **1160** *Hatton Gosp.* Matt. xv. 19 Of þare heorte cumeð þa yfele þankes [*c* **1000** ʒeþancas]. *c* **1175** *Lamb. Hom.* 3 Heo urnen on-ȝein him..mid ufele þeonke. *a* **1200** *Moral Ode* 90 He þurþsicheþ uches monnes þonc. *c* **1200** *Trin. Coll. Hom.* 9 We..folȝeð on þonke, and on speche, and on dede, þat him is iqueme. *a* **1225** *Ancr. R.* 222 He..put..a swuc[h] þonc in hire softe heorte. *c* **1300** *Prov. Hending* i. in *Sal. & Sat.*, etc. (1848) 270 Gode þonkes and monie þewes for te teche fele schrewes.

†**2. a.** Favourable thought or feeling, good will; graciousness, grace, favour. *Obs.*

a **1000** *Cædmon's Gen.* 796 (Gr.) þis is landa betst, þæt wit þurh uncres hearran þanc habban moston. *c* **1000** *Ags. Ps.* (Th.) ci. 15 [cii. 17] Oft he þearfendra bene þance ʒehyrde. **1340** *Ave Maria* in *Rel. Ant.* I. 42 Hayl Marie of thonke vol [Vulg. *Luke* i. 28 Ave! gratia plena]. **1609** BIBLE (Douay) *Ecclus.* xii. 1 If thou wilt doe good, know to whom thou doest it, and there shal be much thanke [*Vulg.* gratia multa] in thy good deedes.

†**b.** The genitive case *thanks*, ME. *thankes*, lit. 'of thought', 'of good will', was used adverbially in sense 'willingly, voluntarily', esp. with preceding possessive pronoun, e.g. ***his thankes***

= with his consent, good will, or approval: so **Godes thankes** = *Deo volente*. Cf. UNTHANKES, unwillingly. *Obs.*

*c*888 K. ÆLFRED *Boeth.* xiii, Sæȝe me nu hwæðer se þin wela [þines] ðances swa diore seo, þe for his aȝenre ȝecynde. 1008 *Charter of Bp. Theodred* in Birch *Cart. Sax.* III. 209 Mines erfes þat ic beȝiten habbe & ȝet biȝete Godes þankes and hise haleȝen. 1066 *O.E. Chron.* (MS. C.), Tostiȝ..nam of þam butse karlon sume mid him, sume þances sume unþances. 1154 *Ibid.* an. 1140 (MS. Laud), Hi of Normandi wenden alle fra þe king.., sume here þankes & sume here un þankes. *c*1175 *Lamb. Hom.* 17 Al swa þu waldest þet me dude þe þines þonkes. *a*1250 *Owl & Night.* 70 Ek for þe þe sulue mose Hire þonkes wolde þe totose. *c*1386 CHAUCER *Shipman's T.* 188 Pardee, I wol nat faille yow, my thankes. *c*1400 MAUNDEV. (Roxb.) xxxi. 140 Þis ile dare na pilgrim come in ne nere it, þaire thankes. *a*1450 MYRC *Par. Pr.* 891 Koghe þow not þenne þy þonkes.

†3. Kindly thought or feeling entertained towards any one for favour or services received; grateful thought, gratitude. Rarely in *pl.* *Obs.*

The sense of 'gratitude, kindly or loving feeling for favour or benefit' must have been developed between that of 'good will, good feeling' generally, and that of 'the expression of gratitude'. But the feeling passes so naturally into its expression that it is not easy to separate them in the quotations, except by the accompanying verbs: *to express one's thanks*, and the archaic *to con thanks*, ought to mean to express one's *feelings of gratitude*; but *to give, offer, return* or *receive thanks*, ought to mean to give or receive *the expression of gratitude*; so *to have thanks*, but this is less clear. In many instances it is impossible to say which is meant; some of the examples given here may belong to 4.

1297 R. GLOUC. (Rolls) 9379 Muche þonc were it vs of god mid him vorto fiȝte. 13.. *Gaw. & Gr. Knt.* 1380 Haue I þryuandely þonk þurh my craft serued? *c*1374 CHAUCER *Troylus* III. 1728 (1777) Þis encres of hardynesse and myght Com hym of loue, his ladyes thank to wynne. *c*1400 *Destr. Troy* 12724 The lady..þonkit hym þroly with þonks in hir hert. *c*1420 *Brut* 343 Þanne þei..went hom ayen yn-to her owne cuntre, with grete loue & moche þanke. 1500–20 DUNBAR *Poems* xvi. 19 Or the gift deliuerit be, The thank is frustrat and expyrd. *a*1677 BARROW *Wks.* (1687) I. viii. 94 It was a satyrical answer (that of Aristotle)..who being asked..What doth the soonest grow old? replied..Thanks.

4. The expression of gratitude; the grateful acknowledgement of a benefit or favour. †a. in sing. *Obs.*

† *Gode þank, God-thank* [= L. *Deo gratias*, F. *grâce à Dieu*], thanks (be) to God, thank God.

Beowulf 1779 Þæs siȝ metode þanc, ecean dryhtne, þæs ðe ic on aldre ȝe-bad. *c*888 K. ÆLFRED *Boeth.* xxxv. §4 Þa ȝesceafta næren nanes þonces ne nanes weorðscipes wyrðe. *c*897 —— *Gregory's Past. C.* 2 Gode almiehteȝum si ðonc ðætte we nu æniȝne on stal habbað lareowa. *a*1000 *Cædmon's Gen.* 1116 (Gr.) Him þæs þanc sie. *c*1375 *Sc. Leg. Saints* xxvi. (*Nycholas*) 324 Thang to al-mychtty god he ȝaulde. *c*1440 *Promp. Parv.* 490/1 Thanke, *grates, graciarum accio, gratulamen.* 1483 CAXTON *Gold. Leg.* 195/2 Thanke and glorye to god & honoure to the vyrgyne. 1534 MORE *Treat. Passion* Introd., Wks. 1271/1 Turning to god with lawde and thanke. *a*1553 UDALL *Royster D.* II. ii, *Doughtie.* He will thank you woman. *Madge.* I will none of his thanke. 1642 ROGERS *Naaman* 385 Is this the thanke which you returne to God?

*c*897 K. ÆLFRED *Gregory's Past. C.* 9 Gode ðonc. *Ibid.* i. 27. *c*1200 *Trin. Coll. Hom.* 11 Unbileue..is aiware aleid and rihte leue arered godeðonc. 1297 R. GLOUC. (Rolls) 2578 Þe King was gode þonk aboue in four batailes. *c*1300 *Havelok* 2005 Þus wolde þe theues me haue reft, But godþank, he hauenet sure keft.

b. in plural. †Formerly sometimes const. as *sing.*

1340 *Ayenb.* 18 Me..him ne yeldeþ þonkes of his guodes, þet he ous heþ ydo. 1481 CAXTON *Reynard* iv. (Arb.) 8 All hath he but lytyl thanks. 1509 HAWES *Past. Pleas.* iv. (Percy Soc.) 21 At whose encreace there is great thankes rendred. 1538 ELYOT, *Grates*, thankes. 1588 SHAKS. *Tit. A.* I. i. 215 Thankes to men Of Noble mindes, is Honourable Meede. 1592 —— *Rom. & Jul.* II. vi. 23 Else is his thanks too much. 1651 HOBBES *Leviath.* II. xxxi. 191 Prayers precede, and Thanks succeed the benefit. 1753 HANWAY *Trav.* (1762) I. II. xvi. 72 Our soldiers were fed luxuriously at the fisheries, for nothing more than thanks. 1805 R. FULTON in *Sinclair's Corr.* (1831) II. 64, I return it to you with my sincere thanks. 1871 R. ELLIS *Catullus* xlix. 4 Thanks superlative unto thee Catullus Renders. 1881 'RITA' *My Lady Coquette* iii, Yolande gives her a smile of thanks.

c. ***a thank*** (formerly also ***a thanks***): an expression of gratitude; a thanking, a thank-you. Now *rare*.

† *to pick (get, win) a thank*: see PICK *v.*[1] 8 b. *Obs.*

13.. *Gaw. & Gr. Knt.* 1984 Vche mon þat he mette, he made hem a þonke, For his seruyse. 1474 CAXTON *Chesse* III. vii. (1883) 139 To thende that they myght haue a thanke & be preysed. 1560 DAUS tr. *Sleidane's Comm.* Pref. 5 b, Verye manye of those wryters seke to pike a thanke. *a*1577 GASCOIGNE *Herbs*, etc. Wks. (1587) 119 While Pierce the plowman hopes to pick a thank. 1579–1627 [see PICK *v.*[1] 8 b β]. 1601 B. JONSON *Poetaster* IV. vii, Without a thankes, to be sent hence! 1678 R. L'ESTRANGE *Seneca's Mor.* I. xv. (1696) 81 He..contents himself with a bare Thank for a Requital. *a*1810 TANNAHILL *Poet. Wks.* (1846) 67 With his lordship's thank. 1839 LONGF. *Black Kn.* 47 The children drank, Gave many a courteous thank.

II. Phrases and phraseological uses.

5. a. *thanks*: a much abbreviated expression of gratitude for a favour received or recognition of a service; = *I give you my thanks, my thanks to you*, or the like. Also ***many thanks, best thanks.***

1588 SHAKS. *L.L.L.* v. ii. 559 If your Ladiship would say thankes Pompey, I had done. *La.* Great thankes, great Pompey. 1605 —— *Macb.* II. i. 30 *Macb.* Good repose the while! *Banq.* Thankes, Sir: the like to you! 1647 PEACHAM *Worth of a Penny* 14 He answers you with Monosyllables, ..*Yes, No, That, Thankes, True,* &c. 1803 *Forest of Hohenelbe* I. 167 Thanks, Baron, for your good wishes. 1803 PITT in *G. Rose's Diaries* (1860) II. 16 Many thanks for your letter. 1866 E. FITZGERALD *More Lett.* (1901) 82 Don't you dislike the way some People have of saying perpetually '*Thanks!*' instead of 'Thank you'?.. It is like cutting Acknowledgment as short as possible... *Thanks* [is] about one of the most hideous monosyllables, even in the English Language. 1870 MISS BRIDGMAN *Rob. Lynne* II. xiv. 299 'Would you like to read the letter, Robert?' 'No, thanks'.

b. With intensifying advbs. and phrases, as ***thanks awfully, ever so, a lot, a million*** (orig. *U.S.*), ***very much***, etc. Also used ironically.

1890 A. TUER *Thenks Awf'lly!* i. 11 He at once burst into conversation: 'Thenks awf'lly! I nurly missed the trine.' 1911 D. H. LAWRENCE *Let.* 7 Nov. (1962) I. 84 Dear Garnett: Just got your letter—I am very glad with the *Nation*—thanks very much. 1914 'SAKI' *Beasts & Super-Beasts* 217 If you lend me three pounds that ought to see me through comfortably. Thanks ever so. 1916 E. F. BENSON *David Blaize* vii. 134, I couldn't possibly. But thanks, most awfully. 1936 *Sat. Even. Post* 12 Sept. 10/1 That was a swell lunch. Thanks a million. 1942 N. BALCHIN *Darkness falls from Air* xiv. 237, I gave him a pound and said, 'Thanks a lot.' 1965 WODEHOUSE *Galahad at Blandings* i. 8 The 'Oh, thanks awfully' which betrayed the other's English origin. 1966 H. NICHOLSON *Duckling in Capri* xv. 194 'Spend it on Pam.' 'Shall I? Thanks a million.' 1967 *Plays & Players* Apr. 41/1 *Trebor*: Couldn't we go on an aeroplane, somewhere? *Webster*: No, we couldn't go on an aeroplane. *Trebor*: Thanks very much. 1972 J. MANN *Mrs Knox's Profession* ii. 15 'Thanks ever so,' he said, his voice an octave higher than usual. 1982 'J. BELL' *Innocent* ii. 16 'You'll want a tray, love.'.. 'Of course, thanks a lot.'

c. ***thanks be***: ellipt. for 'thanks be to God', as an expression of relief or satisfaction. *colloq.*

1924 D. MOORE *Fen's First Term* ix. 97 Me 'arf dye, thanks be. 1942 C. MILBURN *Diary* 7 Oct. (1979) 154 Hats are to be fewer—I seem to have many, thanks be! 1963 *Times* 4 Feb. 13/2 And thanks be, that aging design, the longer fitted jacket has not reappeared.

6. *thanks to*: Thanks be given to, or are due to; hence, Owing to, as a result of, in consequence of. (Often ironical.) So *no thanks* (†*thank*) *to*, no credit to, not by virtue or merit of; not because or by reason of.

1633 EARL MANCH. *Al Mondo* (1636) 115 It is no thankes to a man to pay that willingly, which he must doe of necessitie. 1633 BP. HALL *Medit. & Vows* (1851) 150 It is scarce any thank to me that he prevails. 1647 TRAPP *Comm. Rev.* iii. 4 No thank to the Pastour, who was a mercenary eye-servant. *a*1687 PETTY *Pol. Arith.* vi. (1691) 99 No thanks to any Laws which have been made to that purpose. 1737 POPE *Hor. Epist.* II. ii. 68 But (thanks to Homer) since I live and thrive, Indebted to no Prince or Peer alive. 1813 SCOTT *Rokeby* v. vi, It is a sight but rarely spied, Thanks to man's wrath and woman's pride. 1894 *Westm. Gaz.* 21 Aug. 3/3 The passengers—thanks, I expect, to the bitter cold—behaved more quietly at night than in the morning.

†7. *in (on) thank, to thank*, with pleased mind, with pleasure or satisfaction; pleasantly, graciously; with thanks, gratefully. *Obs.*

*a*1000 *Andreas* 1114 (Gr.) Hie þa lac hraðe þeȝon to þance. *a*1000 *Cædmon's Gen.* 2442 Hie on þanc curon æðelinges est. *a*1300 *Cursor M.* 15047 (Cott.) Þou tak to thanc þat we þe mak Sli mensking als we mai. *c*1375 *Sc. Leg. Saints* vi. (*Thomas*) 12 Þat he in grete thank vil take, And als reward hym t[h]ankfully. *c*1400 *Rom. Rose* 4577 He seyde, 'In thank I shal it take, And high maister eeke thee make'. *c*1430 *Syr Gener.* (Roxb.) 9803 If I wist to thank ye wold it take, A mariage fayne wold I make. 1513 DOUGLAS *Æneis* VII. v. 153, I grant thine axing, Troiane messinger, And ȝour rewardis ressauis in thank.

8. *to can, con, cun (great, little) thank(s*, to acknowledge or express gratitude, to make known gratitude, to give thanks, to thank. *Obs.* exc. *dial.*

See CAN *v.*[1] 10, CON *v.*[1] 4.

†9. *to have* (or *get*) *thank*: to be thanked; also, to be thought worthy of thanks, to get the credit *for*, to have the merit or honour *of* (something); hence, contextually, *thank* = thanks due or merited, recompense, reward, credit, merit, and *ironically* discredit, blame. *Obs.*

*c*950 *Lindisf. Gosp.* Luke xvii. 9 Ahne ðonc hafeð esne ðæm forðon dyde ða ðe him ȝehaten hæfde? *c*1000 *Ags. Gosp.* ibid., Hæfð se þeowa æniȝne þanc forþam ðe he dyde þæt [etc.]? *c*1020 *Rule St. Benet* v. (Logeman) 25 He for swylcere dæde æniȝne ne begitt þanc. *c*1175 *Lamb. Hom.* 137 Þa ðe doð god for to habben ðer of aȝen in þisse liue, nabbeð heo nenne þonc on eche weorlde. 1297 R. GLOUC. (Rolls) 9915 Þe wrecche luþer giwes..a riche presant.. sende þis noble kinge, ac hor þonc was lute. *a*1300 *Cursor M.* 13841 Þar-for haf he neuer thank! *c*1320 *Sir Tristr.* 2081 Maister, þank haue ȝe. For þou me þis bode brouȝt Mi robe ȝiue y þe. *c*1385 CHAUCER *L.G.W.* 452 For who so yeveth a yifte or dooth a grace, Do it by tyme, his thank ys wel the more. *c*1460 FORTESCUE *Abs. & Lim. Mon.* vii. (1885) 125 Off somme man [h]is highnes shall haue more thanke ffor money then ffor lande. 1483 *Cath. Angl.* 381/2 A Thanke, *meritum, emericio, emericium.* 1533 BELLENDEN *Livy* II. iv. (S.T.S.) I. 142 Thir twa lawis..war pronuncit allanerlie.. be auctorite of þe said valerius (þat he mycht þarethrow haue þe thank þareof). 1539 BIBLE (Great) *Luke* vi. 32 Yf ye loue them which loue you, what thanke haue ye? [so 1611, 1881; TINDALE, what thanke are ye worthy of? *Rhem.* what thanke is to you?]. 1545 ELYOT *Dict.* s.v. *Ineo, Gratiam inire*, to get thanke or frendes with some pleasure done vnto them. 1584 *Mirr. Mag.* 9 It is a work of more thank to preserue health, then to cure Sicknesse. 1600 NASHE *Summers Last Will* Introd., He..must be making himselfe a publike laughing stock, & haue no thanke for his labor. 1633 BP. HALL *Hard Texts, N.T.* 4 The thanke of this is Gods, not yours. 1669 R. MONTAGU in *Buccleuch MSS.* (Hist. MSS. Comm.) I. 424 Lord Clarendon would have the thanks and credit of it.

10. *to give thanks* (†*thank*, †*to do thank(s)*), to express gratitude; *spec.* = 'to give thanks to God'; now esp. of saying grace at a meal. *arch.*

971 *Blickl. Hom.* 39 Don we..Drihtne þancas þe us þa wæstmas sealde. *Ibid.* 191 Þanc ic do, Crist þu ȝoda hyrde. *Ibid.* 217 He..Ælmihtiȝum Gode þære ȝife þanc sæȝ de. 1477 EARL RIVERS (Caxton) *Dictes* 1 To gyue therfore synguler louynges & thankes. 1526 TINDALE *Matt.* xxvi. 26 Jesus toke breed, and gave thankes, brake it, and gave it to his disciples. 1596 SHAKS. *Tam. Shr.* IV. i. 162 Will you giue thankes, sweete Kate, or else shall I? 1765 T. HUTCHINSON *Hist. Mass.* I. 262 The general court..gave them thanks for their good services. 1808–18 JAMIESON s.v. *Grace-drink*, After the giving of thanks at the end of a meal. 1831 SCOTT *Ct. Robt.* ix, All gave me fair thanks for the knightly manner of quitting myself towards them, except one.

11. ***to return thanks***, to render thanks in return for a benefit or favour. Now chiefly used of the formal or public expression of thanks, or of grace at a meal.

1591–1780 [see RETURN *v.* 20]. 1717 LADY M. W. MONTAGU *Let. to C'tess Mar* 18 Apr., I returned her thanks, and..took my leave. 1803 D. WORDSWORTH *Jrnl.* 27 Aug. (1941) I. 269 When breakfast was ended the mistress desired ..her husband to 'return thanks'. He said a short grace. 1827 *Edin. Weekly Jrnl.* 28 Feb., He begged leave to return thanks for the honour which had been conferred on the Patrons of this excellent Institution. 1849 C. BRONTE *Shirley* vii, 'Let us return thanks', said he; which he did forthwith, and all quitted the table.

III. 12. *attrib.* and *Comb.*, as ***thank-receiver, thanks-prayer***; †***thank-picking, thanks-freighted*** adjs.; †**thank-render**, a rendering of thanks, a thanksgiving; **thanks-day**, Thanksgiving Day (*U.S.*); **thanksdoing, thanks-living** (*nonce-wds.*, after *thanksgiving*), action or conduct indicative of a thankful spirit. See also THANK-OFFERING, THANKSGIVING, etc.

1633 FORD *Love's Sacr.* IV. i, Edged on by some *thank-picking parasite. 1786 COWPER *Let. to Lady Hesketh* 31 Jan., I will constitute you my *Thank-receiver-general for whatsoever gift I shall receive hereafter. 1548 GEST *Pr. Masse* in Dugdale *Life* (1840) App. I. 98 It is a forged worship and *thankerendre. 1696 W. BATES *Serm. Forgiveness* 123 Let our thanksgiving be joined with *thanksdoing. 1882 SPURGEON *Treas. Dav.* Ps. cxix. 65 We lose ourselves in adoring thanksgiving, and find ourselves again in careful *thanks-living. 1900 *Month* Feb. 133 Passages..which seem to have reference to this primitive *Thanksprayer.

thank (θæŋk), *v.* Forms: α. 1–2 **þancian**, 2–3 **þankien**, 3–5 **þanken**, 4–6 **thanken**, 4–7 **thanke**, **thanck**, (4 **þ-**, **thanc**, 4–5 **þanky**, **thange**), 5– **thank**. β. 1 **ðoncian**, 2 **þonkien**, 3–5 **þonke(n**, (3 **þonki**, 4 **þonkke**), 4–6 **thonk**, (5–6 **thong**). [OE. *þancian*, *þoncian* = OS. *thankôn* (MDu., Du. *danken*), OHG. *dankôn* (MHG., G. *danken*), ON. *þakka* (Sw. *tacka*, Da. *takke*):—OTeut. **þank-ôjan*, f. **þanko*[z] THANK *sb.*]

†1. *intr.* To give thanks. *Obs.* exc. as *absol.* of 3.

*c*950 *Lindisf. Gosp.* Matt. xxvi 27, ȝenimmende calic ðoncunco dyde *vel* ðoncade & sealde him. *c*975 *Rushw. Gosp.* ibid., ȝenom cælic þongade & salde heom. *c*1000 *Ags. Gosp.* ibid., He ȝenam þone calic þanciende. *c*1000 ÆLFRIC *Hom.* II. 400 Drihten ðancode ærðan ðe he ða hlafas tobræce. *c*1290 *St. Brandan* 595 in *S. Eng. Leg.* 236 Iudas þonkede reufolliche. *c*1500 *Melusine* xxxvi. 247 'Fayre lordes', said Geffray..'that ought to be thanked for' [*indirect passive of* 'one ought to thank for that'].

†2. *intr.* in particular constructions. a. To give thanks *to* a person (orig. with simple *dative*, at length treated as *accusative*: see 3). *Obs.*

*c*888 K. ÆLFRED *Boeth.* v. §3 Ðonca nu Gode þæt he ðe ȝefultumade. *a*1000 *Cædmon's Satan* 536 [Hi] þanceden þeodne, þæt hit þus ȝelomp. *c*1000 *Ags. Gosp.* Luke xvii. 16 He..feoll to his foten & him þancode. *c*1175 *Lamb. Hom.* 153, Iþonked wurðe him [Let it be thanked to him]. *a*1450 *Le Morte Arth.* 1478 On knes Felle thay..And thankyd All to god. 1508 DUNBAR *Gold. Targe* 101 Syne to dame Flora ..Thay saluse, and thay thank a thousand syse. 1542 UDALL *Erasm. Apoph.* 145 That persone, to whom onely..thou art bound to thanke.

†b. *of* (= on account of, for) a thing (orig. *genitive*): see c. *Obs.*

971 *Blickl. Hom.* 43 Ne sceal he..to lyt þancian heora ælmessan. *Ibid.* 203 Hie..þancudan þæs siȝes ðe hie ȝefered hæfdon.

†c. (combining a and b) to a person (*dative*), *of* a thing (orig. *genitive*), the dative (mostly a pronoun) passing into an accusative: the usual constr. in OE. and early ME.; passing into 3 b. *Obs.*

Beowulf 1397 Se gomela gode þancode..þæs se man ȝespræc. *a*1000 *Cædmon's Gen.* 257 (Gr.) He..sceolde his drihtne þancian þæs leanes. *c*1000 ÆLFRIC *Saints' Lives* (1885) I. 104 Iulianus þa sona þæs þancode Gode. *c*1175 *Lamb. Hom.* 39 Þet þu luuie þine drihten and him þonkien alles þinges. *c*1200 *Vices & Virtues* 29 Þanke ðar-of ðine lauerde gode. *c*1200 *Trin. Coll. Hom.* 197 Iob..þonkede him of þan wowe, alse dude ar of þe wele.

3. a. *trans.* To give thanks to; to express gratitude or obligation to. (Orig. *intr.* with *dat.*: see 2 a. By 1200 the *dat.* was treated as *acc.*, and might be subject of the passive voice.) Sometimes const. *that.*

*c*1200 *Trin. Coll. Hom.* 3 Þanked be ure louerd ihesu crist. 1297 R. GLOUC. (Rolls) 1154 Vaire he þonkede is gode folc. *Ibid.* 9281 Ich þonke ȝou..Þat ȝe me so muche loue sseweþ. *a*1300 *Cursor M.* 3321 (Cott.) Thancand god, til erth he fell.

c **1350** *Will. Palerne* 2794 þat we so scaþli ar a-schaped god mowe [we] þonk. **1362** LANGL. *P. Pl.* A. XII. 48, I..þankede hure a þousand syþes. *c* **1420** *Chron. Vilod.* 461 þey thongedone god and mournedone no more. **1537** WRIOTHESLEY *Chron.* (Camden) I. 67 The maior and aldermen riding about the cittie thancking the people. **1598** SHAKS. *Merry W.* I. i. 293, I had rather walke here (I thanke you). **1648** *Hamilton Papers* (Camden) 250 Powley is returned from London. He brings a most sleevles letter.. which signifyes nothing... Judge if I thanked him. *a* **1796** BURNS *Selkirk Grace*, We hae meat and we can eat, Sae let the Lord be thankit. **1818** SCOTT *Hrt. Midl.* xxxvii, That he has subjects in Scotland, I think he may thank God and his sword. **1841** LANE *Arab. Nts.* I. 114 The young prince kissed his hand and thanked him. **1906** *Outlook* 18 Sept. 346 He who solicits a favour by letter not infrequently concludes with the phrase, 'thanking you in anticipation', which came into vogue some ten years ago.

†**b.** Const. *of* a thing. *Obs.*

The continuation of 2 c; usual in ME.

c **1175** *Lamb. Hom.* 7 3if we þonkiet ure drihten alles þinges þe he us sent. *c* **1230** *Hali Meid.* 19 To þonki godd of his grace & of his goddede. *a* **1300** *Cursor M.* 5304 Knele i sal befor þe king, And thank him of his grett mensking. *c* **1375** *Sc. Leg. Saints* v. (*Johannes*) 644 He..bad I suld.. thange 3ou of 3ore gud vyl. *c* **1412** HOCCLEVE *De Reg. Princ.* 1062 God thanke alwey of thyne ese and of thyne smert. *a* **1533** LD. BERNERS *Huon* lxi. 212, I thanke you of your courtesye. *a* **1548** HALL *Chron.*, *Edw. IV* 236 b, The Frenche kyng..thanked the kyng of Englande of his kynde offre.

c. Const. *for* a thing: now usual.

a **1591** H. SMITH *Serm.* (1637) 133 He is not thankfull before God, which thanks him only for his benefits. **1653** HOLCROFT *Procopius* I. 11 He thanckt the man much for his good will. **1715** DE FOE *Fam. Instruct.* I. i. (1841) I. 7 How must I thank him for it? **1764** GOLDSM. *Trav.* 72 And thanks his gods for all the good they gave. **1910** W. H. HUDSON *Introd. Study Lit.* Pref. 6, I have to thank my friend..for the invaluable assistance which..he has again rendered me.

d. *fig.* To make a return to a person in evidence of obligation or gratitude. (In quot. ironical.)

1821 SCOTT *Kenilw.* xxvi, I were like to be thanked with a horse-whip.

e. In the future tense, used to express a request: ***I will thank you to do so-and-so.*** Now usu. ironic, implying a rebuke or command.

1813 I. POCOCK *Miller & his Men* I. iii. 9 Cockatrice!—I'll thank you for that portmanteau. **1843** THACKERAY *Ravenswing* vi, The page..instantly thanked her to pay his wages. **1852** —— *Esmond* III. v, I want to speak with your employer, Mr. Leach. I'll thank ye go fetch him. **1907** G. C. WHITWORTH *Indian English* xii. 248 The offence is much mitigated if..the word is followed by 'if' instead of the usual infinitive, as 'I'll thank you to be quiet.' *a* **1912** *Mod.* I will thank you to hand me my field-glass. I will thank you for a glass of water. **1930** J. B. PRIESTLEY *Angel Pavement* i. 12 Just say to 'er: 'Mrs. Cross 'as seen the note left.., and.. Mrs. Cross'll thank her to keep 'er notes to 'erself in future till they're asked for.' Just you tell 'er that, boy. **1940** H. G. WELLS *Babes in Darkling Wood* II. ii. 160 No decent people are going to bother about it, Mother. And they will thank you not to be bothered about it. **1975** 'D. JORDAN' *Black Account* II. xx. 110 I'm here to sell tractors and I'll thank you to remember it.

f. Phr. ***to thank one for nothing***: esp. in (*I*) ***thank you for nothing***, an ironical expression indicating that the speaker thinks he has got or been offered nothing worth thanks.

1703 MOXON *Mech. Exerc.* 60 But perhaps these Pretenders mean the Iron or Steel shall be as soft as Lead, when the Iron or Steel is red-hot; if so, we may thank them for nothing. **1712** ADDISON *Spect.* No. 391 ¶3 Jupiter thanked him for nothing. **1754** FOOTE *Knights* I. Wks. 1799 I. 67 Part with Favourite! no, I thank you for nothing. **1848** [see THANK YOU]. **1908** A. BENNETT *Old Wives' Tale* IV. v. 559 'Thank you for nothing!' said Dick. 'I don't want it.' **1940** W. S. CHURCHILL *Second World War* (1949) I. II. xxxiv. 548 Sweden will say 'Thank you for nothing' about any offers on our part to defend the Gällivare ironfield. **1975** 'R. PLAYER' *Let's talk of Graves* v. 202 I'm not respectable. The Judge has just told everybody that—thank ye' for nothing, my Lord.

g. Ejaculatory phrases, as ***thank God*** (†***I thank God*** (obs.), ***God be thanked***, etc.), ***thank goodness, thank heaven***. Also ***thank God for that*** (now freq. in weakened use); ***thank God hold*** (Mountaineering): an easy hold at the top of a difficult climb. See also GOD 9 e. ***to thank one's*** (or ***the***) ***stars***, to congratulate oneself on one's good fortune: see STAR.

c **1330** R. BRUNNE *Chron.* (1810) 134 þanked be God of heuen. **1340** *Ayenb.* 196 God be yhered and y-þonked. **1426** *Test. Ebor.* (Surtees) I. 76, I..in gud mynd, thanket be God. *c* **1489** CAXTON *Sonnes of Aymon* xxiv. 530 Hole & sounde, thanked be god. **1530** PALSGR. 754/2, I am one of them, God be thanked! **1599** SHAKS. *Much Ado* III. v. 15 Yes I thank God, I am as honest as any man liuing, that is an old man, and no honester then I. **1614** B. JONSON *Barth. Fair* Induct., Yet I kept the Stage in Master Tarleton's time, I thanke my starres. **1730** FIELDING *Temple Beau* IV. iii, Sir Harry, you may thank your stars that conducted you to me. **1796** MME. D'ARBLAY *Camilla* III. 99 Now..I have not the gift of writing, at which, thank God, I have left off repining. **1811** L. M. HAWKINS *C'tess & Gertr.* III. 283, I was all that, thank goodness, as I always say, last grass. **1834** T. HAWKINS *Mem. Ichthyos. & Plesiosauri* 42 But I should.. thank the stars and the Cholera that it was no worse. **1840** THACKERAY *Shabby-genteel Story* ii, I am here, thank Heaven, quite alone. **1872** [see GOODNESS 5]. **1918** A. P. MCKISHNIE *Willow, the Wisp* xxi. 303 His world was at rest, once more. Thank God for that! **1949** G. DAVENPORT *Family Fortunes* III. ii. 222 'Thank God for that,' he said. **1955** S. STYLES *Introd. Mountaineering* xi. 127 The term *thank-god hold*, which has become part of British climbing jargon, originated on the third ascent of the slab on Route II, Lliwedd East Buttress, when as each climber got his hand over the good knob at the top he expressed his heartfelt gratitude in the same two words. **1978** P. GILLMAN *Fitness on Foot* v. 67 A sense of relief on reaching the top of a difficult climb to discover enormous holds to finish on. These are known as 'thank God' holds. **1978** I. B. SINGER *Shosha* i. 16 Thank God I found friends among members of the Writer's Club.

h. In negative conditional sentences as an ironical understatement, as ***he would not thank you for doing it***, he would be displeased if you did it. Cf. THANK YOU A. 3.

[**1739–40** RICHARDSON *Pamela* (1740) I. xxiv. 65 Now I did not thank her for this, as I told her afterwards (for it brought a great deal of Trouble upon me).] **1873** TROLLOPE *Phineas Redux* (1874) I. iv. 32 His party would not thank him for ventilating a measure which..might well be postponed. **1896** KIPLING *Seven Seas* 148 The things I knew was proper you wouldn't thank me to give. And the things I knew was rotten you said was the way to live. **1970** 'A. GILBERT' *Death wears Mask* i. 19 Miss Alice wouldn't thank you for tying her into a chair. **1983** M. HINXMAN *Corpse now Arriving* ii. 14 He was probably in the middle of some world-shattering story and wouldn't thank her for the interruption.

†**4. a.** With dative of person (indirect obj.) and accusative of thing (direct obj.): = 3 b or c. *Obs.* (Cf. TELL *v.* 3 (*a*).)

c **1175** *Lamb. Hom.* 5 We ahte to..þonkien hit ure drihten þe hit us lende. *a* **1300** *Cursor M.* 16219 Herod thankes þe þi sand. **1362** LANGL. *P. Pl.* A. VII. 17 We haue no lymes to labore with; vr lord we hit þonken. *c* **1475** *Rauf Coilȝear* 271 Mair the King spak nocht, Bot thankit thame thair deid.

b. With the thing as sole obj.: To return thanks for, express one's gratitude for; to repay. *rare.*

c **1470** ASHBY *Dicta Philos.* 925 A goode man thanketh euery benefete, After the yeuers possibilite. **1818** BYRON *Mazeppa* xx, Charles forgot To thank his tale. **1819** —— *Juan* I. cxii, His young lip thank'd it with a grateful kiss. **1867** MORRIS *Jason* xv. 226 And I am well aweary of it now, And of my toil, thanked with hard word and blow.

5. To give the thanks or credit *for* something to; to consider or hold responsible; esp. in ironical use, = to blame.

1560 DAUS tr. *Sleidane's Comm.* 189 Him that brought hym vp, and whome both he and his father may thanke for all theyr good fortune. **1667** MILTON *P.L.* x. 736 Who..but ..will curse My Head,..For this we may thank Adam; but his thanks Shall be the execration. **1794** MRS. RADCLIFFE *Myst. Udolpho* xxxi, She might thank herself for what happened. **1885** SIR N. LINDLEY in *Law Rep.* 14 *Q.B. Div.* 817 If..any mistake was made by the sheriff, the defendant had only himself to thank for it.

thanka, var. TANKA[2].

thankee (ˈθæŋkiː), vulgar colloq. for *thank ye*, THANK YOU. See 'EE.

1824 in *Spirit Pub. Jrnls.* (1825) 302 My friends, the Yankees, For ten such plays, I guess, wouldn't give ten thankees. **1848** DICKENS *Dombey* xl, Thankee my Lady. Lord bless you, my Lady.

thanker (ˈθæŋkə(r)). [f. THANK *v.* + -ER[1].] One who thanks.

a **1591** H. SMITH *Serm.* (1637) 132 Moe have gone away speeders, then have gone away thankers. **1800** COLERIDGE *Wallenstein* IV. ii. 111 The devil take such thankers! **1844** BROWNING *Colombe's Birthday* II, Stay, Sabyne; let me hasten to make sure Of one true thanker.

thankful (ˈθæŋkfʊl), *a.* [f. THANK *sb.* + -FUL.]

1. a. Feeling or expressing thanks or gratitude; prompted by feelings of gratitude; grateful. Phr. ***thankful for small mercies.***

971 *Blickl. Hom.* 169 Wesað þancfulle þon Hælende eoweres andleofan. **1500–20** DUNBAR *Poems* lxxvii. 72 Be thankfull to this burgh of Aberdein. **1535** COVERDALE *1 Sam.* ii. Contents, The thankfull songe of Anna. **1592** SHAKS. *Rom. & Jul.* III. v. 149 Not proud you haue, But thankfull that you haue. **1685** DRYDEN *Thren. August.* 383 Live then, thou great encourager of arts: Live ever in our thankful hearts! **1748** BUTLER *Serm.* Wks. 1874 II. 317 The generality of mankind have cause to be thankful that their station exempts them from so great temptations. **1818** SCOTT *Heart Midl.* in *Tales my Landlord* 2nd Ser. II. xii. 295 'Ye are thankfu' for sma' mercies, then,' said Mrs Howden, with a toss of her head. **1844** EMERSON *Ess.* 2nd Ser. 41, I am thankful for small mercies. **1856** FROUDE *Hist. Eng.* I. v. 430 We have reason to be thankful that the thing, well or ill, was over. **1874** GEO. ELIOT *Let.* 3 Aug. (1956) VI. 72 One has learned to be thankful for sma' mercies in this world of dreadful possibilities. **1947** A. HUXLEY *Let.* 14 Nov. (1969) 576 It is raining harder and harder and Little Rock feels.. remote. However, the Blue Bird is clean and comfortable; so let us be thankful for small mercies. **1950** C. S. FORESTER *Mr. Midshipman Hornblower* viii. 207 Then be thankful for small mercies. And even more thankful for big ones.

†**b.** Satisfied, content. *Obs.*

a **900** tr. *Bæda's Hist.* v. xxii[i]. (1890) 478 Scottas.. wæron þoncfulle heora gemærum. *c* **1050** *Gloss.* in Wr.-Wülcker 367/18 *Contentus*, ðancful.

c. *fig.* Cf. GRATEFUL *a.* 2 b.

1610 HOLLAND *Camden's Brit.* (1637) 273 The ground.. is thankefull to the husbandman, in so much as it doth afford corne to be carried forth.

†**2. a.** Worthy or deserving of thanks, gratitude, or credit; pleasing, acceptable, grateful, agreeable.

c **1000** in *Anglia* (1890) XIII. 381 We halsiaþ..god þæt þeow þin cync ure..to þe..þancfull he mæge becuman. *c* **1050** *Suppl. Ælfric's Voc.* in Wr.-Wülcker 191/15 *Gratiosus*, ðoncful. **1375** BARBOUR *Bruce* v. 278 He had done mony a thankfull deid. **1456** SIR G. HAYE *Law Arms* (S.T.S.) 68 Unrychtwis offerandis ar nocht acceptable na thankfull to his godhede. **1511** HEN. VIII *Let.* in Burton & Raine *Hemingbrough* 380 Wherby ye shall ministre unto us right singler and thankfull pleasore. **1552** HULOET, Thanckefull, *acceptus.* **1596** DALRYMPLE tr. *Leslie's Hist. Scot.* I. (S.T.S.) I. 130 The name of king was maist grate and thankful to thame al. **1611** TOURNEUR *Ath. Trag.* I. ii, His good successe shall be most thankeful to your trust.

†**b.** *Sc.* Of a payment: Giving satisfaction, satisfactory. *Obs.*

1497 *Acc. Ld. High Treas. Scot.* I. 315, I resauit..for the Erle Marschael his thankfull and reddy payment. **1527** *Caldwell Pap.* (Maitland) I. 61 Alslang and howlang ye said Johnne and his airs mak to me and my airs gud and thankful service. **1612** *Sc. Acts Jas. VI* (1816) IV. 472/1 To mak thame thankfull teynding. **1671** in *Proc. Soc. Ant. Scot.* (1892) XXVI. 194 To make tymeous and thankfull payment.

†**3.** ? Done without reward or payment; gratuitous: cf. next, 3. *Obs. rare.*

c **1380** WYCLIF *Serm.* Sel. Wks. I. 282 þe fifte manere þat prestis shulden have shulde be þankful traveilinge; for 3if þei wolen have þank of God, þei shulden here fle symonie, and neiþer sille her preching ne oþer workes þat þei done.

thankfully (ˈθæŋkfʊlɪ), *adv.* [f. prec. + -LY[2].] In a thankful manner.

I. 1. a. With thankfulness; with thanks; gratefully.

c **1000** ÆLFRIC *Saints' Lives* (1890) II. 198 þa ongeat eustachius þæt seo fore-sæde costnung him ða ær wæs and þancfullice hi under-feng. *c* **1380** WYCLIF *Serm.* Sel. Wks. I. 130 Siþ Crist suffride þus for synne of his breþeren, þei schulden suffre þancfulli for þer own synne. **1567** *Triall Treas.* (1850) 18, I cannot but thankefully render Such commendations as is requisite to be. **1611** SHAKS. *Cymb.* I. vi. 79 Yet Heauen's bounty towards him might Be vs'd more thankfully. **1725** DE FOE *Voy. round World* (1840) 248 He accepted thankfully all my presents. **1875** JOWETT *Plato* (ed. 2) V. 365 We will desire the one to give their instructions freely, and the others to receive them thankfully.

†**b.** With satisfaction; graciously. *Obs.*

1513 DOUGLAS *Æneis* I. ix. *heading*, How Eneas with all his rowt bedene War thankfullie ressavit of the quene. *a* **1578** LINDESAY (Pitscottie) *Chron. Scot.* (S.T.S.) I. 90 The king grantit the same verray thankfullie. **1597** A. M. tr. *Guillemeau's Fr. Chirurg.* *v, Receaue thankfully this my laboure.

†**2.** So as to gratify, please, or satisfy; acceptably, pleasingly; satisfactorily. *Obs.*

c **1375** *Sc. Leg. Saints* iii. (*Andreas*) 877 He liffit sa thankfully to god and mane. **1482** *Exch. Rolls Scotl.* IX. 284 *note*, That ye redily and thankfully content and pay to the said Johne..the said yerely pensioun. **1500** *Ibid.* XI. 266 *note*, That ye cause hir to be thankfullie pait of hir said pension. **1538** ELYOT, *Placabiliter*, thankefully, contentfully. **1576** in *Maitl. Cl. Misc.* (1840) I. 16 The prices tharof salbe thankfullie allowit to 3ow in 3our comptis.

†**3.** Gratuitously; for thanks alone. *Obs.*

1552 HULOET, Thanckfully, or for nothynge, or without rewarde or deserte, but onelye for gramercye, *gratim.*

II. 4. Let us be thankful (that); one is thankful to say. orig. *U.S.*

This use as a sentence adverb, like HOPEFULLY *adv.* 2, is deprecated by some writers.

1966 in W. Follett *Mod. Amer. Usage* 170/1 The 'suicide needle' which—thankfully—he didn't see fit to use. **1969** *Chatelaine* July 1/1 Thankfully there are fewer movies to endure in which the men have all the lines. **1976** *Shooting Mag.* Dec. 41/2 An alarming safety situation..caused many a raised eyebrow but thankfully nothing worse. **1980** *New Society* 3 Jan. 33/2 But thankfully social workers will plod on, hopefully with small regard for new fashions. **1982** *Daily Tel.* 30 Aug. 8/4 Thankfully, however, the old style has not entirely disappeared. **1983** *Times* 11 Nov. 2/4 Aldabra Island in the Indian Ocean, where man 'has thankfully failed to establish himself'.

thankfulness (ˈθæŋkfʊlnɪs). [f. as prec. + -NESS.] The quality or condition of being thankful.

1. Gratefulness, gratitude.

1552 in *Vicary's Anat.* (1888) App. xvi. 291 Whiche thyng, with al due thanckefulnesse, thei receiued at his maiesties handes. **1611** BIBLE *Acts* xxiv. 3 Wee accept it alwayes..with all thankfulnesse. **1741** RICHARDSON *Pamela* II. 158 O how shall I find Words to express my Thankfulness! **1856** FROUDE *Hist. Eng.* I. v. 361 Such a resolution would probably have been welcomed with passionate thankfulness.

†**b.** Contextually: Thanks. *Obs. rare.*

1647 MAY *Hist. Parl.* I. ix. 104 The Scottish Commissioners..returned thankfulnesse to the Parliament ..for that great sum of 300000*l.*

†**2.** Gratification, satisfaction. *Obs. rare.*

1500 *Reg. Privy Seal Scotl.* I. 70 The hartlie lufe..he has and beris to the said Jonet, and..the thankfulnes done be hir oft tymes to his gud grace.

thanking (ˈθæŋkɪŋ), *vbl. sb. arch.* [f. THANK *v.* + -ING[1].] The action or an act of giving thanks; the expression of gratitude; thanks.

c **893** K. ÆLFRED *Oros.* I. iv. [viii.] §2 To wundrianne þæt þa Egipti swa lytle þoncunge wiston Iosepe. *c* **950** *Lindisf. Gosp.* John vi. 23 Ðoncunge dedon Drihtne. *c* **1000** ÆLFRIC *Hom.* II. 170 He underfeng ða lac mid ðancunge. **1382** WYCLIF *Matt.* xxvi. 27 He takynge the cuppe, dede thankyngis. *c* **1420–30** *Prymer* (1895) 51 Whanne þei ben hool, þei moun 3elde þankyngis to þee in þi chirche. **1508** BP. FISHER 7 *Penit. Ps.* cii. Wks. (1876) 190 Gyuynge thankynges vnto hym. **1611** SHAKS. *Cymb.* v. v. 407 He would haue well becom'd this place, and grac'd The thankings of a King. **1851** MRS. BROWNING *Casa Guidi W.* I. 239 We thank you that ye first unlatched the door, But will not make it inaccessible By thankings on the threshold.

'thankless, *a.* [f. THANK *sb.* + -LESS.]

1. Not moved by or expressing gratitude; unthankful, ungrateful. Also *fig.* of things: Making no return, unresponsive.

1536 LYNDESAY *Answ. Kingis Flyting* 33 Full sair I rew That euer I did Mouth thankles so persew. *c* **1560** A. SCOTT *Poems* (S.T.S.) v. 65. **1598** MARSTON *Sco. Villanie* III. ix, All as thanklesse as ungratefull Thames He slinks away, leauing but reeking steames Of dungy slime behinde. **1637** MILTON *Lycidas* 66 And strictly meditate the thankles Muse. **1792** COWPER *Stanzas Bill Mortality* 1 Thankless for favours from on high. **1865** DICKENS *Mut. Fr.* I. i, How can you be so thankless to your best friend?

2. Of a task, or the like: Which brings no thanks; receiving or deserving no thanks.

a **1547** SURREY *Æneid* II. 125 But whereunto these thanklesse tales in vaine Do I reherse? **1591** SAVILE *Tacitus' Hist.* II. lix. 88 A thancklesse office and displeasing. **1690** NORRIS *Beatitudes* (1694) I. 178 Not only a thankless, but an odious, difficult and hazardous Undertaking. **1868** MISS BRADDON *Dead-Sea Fr.* i, It is but a thankless task to catalogue such a face.

3. Without thanks; unthanked. *rare.*

1638 SIR T. HERBERT *Trav.* (ed. 2) 168 The Ambassador had no patience to digest it, save by equall contempt to.. send him thanklesse back againe. **1897** *Westm. Gaz.* 22 Feb. 2/1 Prince Max comes to the Court of Ferdinand to return, thankless, a picture painted by Ferdinand.

'thanklessly, *adv.* [f. prec. + -LY².] In a thankless manner; without thanks; unthankfully.

1626 BP. HALL *Contempl., O.T.* XX. ii, The will of God may be done thanklessly. **1881** in Spurgeon *Treas. Dav.* Ps. cxix. 75 Thanklessly receiving the gifts with no thought of the Giver.

'thanklessness. [f. as prec. + -NESS.] The quality or condition of being thankless; ungratefulness, unthankfulness.

1583 GOLDING *Calvin on Deut.* vii. 41 Were it not too shamefull a thankelesnesse in vs if wee shoulde not bee [etc.]. **1628** WITHER *Brit. Rememb.* IV. 404 Thy thanklesnesse, And such like Sinnes. **1840** L. HUNT *Legend of Florence* I. ii, Friendship ends, In treachery and in thanklessness begun. **1860** PUSEY *Min. Proph.* 273 Thanklessness shuts the door to God's personal mercies to us.

† **'thanklewe**, *a. Obs. rare.* [f. THANK *sb.* + -LEWE.] ? Deserving of thanks, thankworthy; or ? grateful, agreeable.

1430 in Sharpe *Lond. & Kingd.* (1895) III. 374 In perfourming at þis tyme of our prayer ye may do unto us soo notable and þanklewe service þat we wol wel considre hit in tyme comyng.

† **'thankly**, *adv. Obs. rare*⁻¹. [irreg. f. THANK *sb.* + -LY².] Thankfully.

1591 SYLVESTER *Du Bartas* I. iii. 809 He giueth frankly what we thankly spend.

'thank-,offering. Also **thanks-offering.** [f. THANK *sb.* + OFFERING *vbl. sb.*] In the Levitical law, An offering presented as an expression of gratitude to God; hence in ordinary use, An offering or gift made by way of thanks or acknowledgement.

1530 TINDALE *Lev.* vii. 12 Yf he offer to geue thanckes, he shall brynge vnto his thanckofferynge [**1560** (*Genev.*) for his thankes offring] swete cakes myngled with oyle. **1539** BIBLE (Great) *2 Chron.* xxxiii. 16 He..sacrificed theron peace offerynges, & thank offerynges. **1839** THIRLWALL *Greece* VI. xlix. 171 He dedicated the waggon in the citadel, as a thank-offering to the king of the gods. **1888** BURGON *Lives 12 Gd. Men* I. i. 45 He sent at once a thank-offering for distribution among the poor. **1921** G. O'DONOVAN *Vocations* xi. 171 The united prayers of the nuns were a thanks-offering to God for her. **1952** C. DAY LEWIS tr. *Virgil's Aeneid* VI. 118 A thanks-offering to Phoebus. **1978** *Washington Post* 7 Mar. A13/2 Oberammergau..has performed the Passion play every 10 years for centuries as a thanks offering for the end of the plague.

'thanksgive, *v. rare.* [Back-formation from THANKSGIVING.] *trans.* and *intr.* To give thanks (for).

a **1638** MEDE *Diatribe* (1642) 55 Irenæus also affirmeth, That our Saviour, by the institution of the Eucharist had confirmed oblations in the New Testament. Namely, to thanksgive or blesse a thing in way to a sacred use, he took to be an offering of it unto God. **1908** HARDY *Dynasts* III. 353 You almost charm my long philosophy Out of my strong-built thought, and bear me back To when I thanksgave thus. **1938** O. NASH *I'm a Stranger here Myself* 227 And each Thanksgiving I Thanksgive.

'thanks,giver. [f. as next + GIVER.] One who gives thanks.

1621 AINSWORTH *Annot. Song Sol.* i. 3 Thankesgivings, in Nehem. 12. 31 [are] for companies of thankesgivers. **1690** C. NESSE *O. & N. Test.* I. 71 The life of thanksgiving is the good life of the thanks-giver. **1818** BENTHAM *Ch. Eng.* 123 Exhausted by that same grand effort, the stock of thanksgivers is gone. **1883** J. PARKER *Tyne Chylde* 270 Thankfulness elevates and ennobles the thanksgiver.

thanksgiving ('θæŋks,gɪvɪŋ). [f. *thanks*, pl. of THANK *sb.* + GIVING *vbl. sb.*]

1. a. The giving of thanks; the expression of thankfulness or gratitude; *esp.* the act of giving thanks to God.

1533 TINDALE *Supper of Lord* E iv b, One or other Psalme or prayer of thankes giuyng in the mother tongue. **1539** BIBLE (Great) *1 Tim.* iv. 4 For all the creatures of God are good, and nothing to be refused, yf it be receaued with thankesgeuynge. **1562** WINȜET *Cert. Tract.* iii. Wks. (S.T.S.) I. 29 Gyf sic zeirlie memorial in blythnes and thankisgeifing wes haldin. **1588** SHAKS. *L.L.L.* II. i. 193, I cannot stay thanks-giuing. **1658** *Whole Duty Man* v. §8 The fifth part of prayer is thanksgiving; that is, the praising and blessing God for all his mercies. **1842** MISS MITFORD in L'Estrange *Life* (1870) III. ix. 159 Think how full of thanksgiving were my prayers last night.

b. A public celebration, with religious services, held as a solemn acknowledgement of Divine favours; also, a day set apart for this purpose; *spec.* in *U.S.*, Thanksgiving Day (see 3 b).

1641 *Nicholas Papers* (Camden) 10 It was resolved that there shalbe on yᵉ 7ᵗʰ of September next a publique thanksgiving for this good accord betweene yᵉ 2 nacions. **1665** MANLEY *Grotius' Low C. Warres* 217 Publick Thanksgivings were Ordered to be given to God for this Victory. **1760** J. ADAMS *Diary* 26 Nov., Night before Thanksgiving. **1869** MRS. STOWE *Oldtown Folks* xxvii, Great as the preparations were for the dinner, everything was so contrived that not a soul in the house should be kept from the morning service of Thanksgiving. **1930** J. DOS PASSOS *42nd Parallel* I. 87 By Thanksgiving Mac had beaten his way to Sacramento. **1981** *Nordic Skiing* Jan. 50/1 The resort is situated at 7,000 feet..with a ski season extending from Thanksgiving to mid-May.

2. An act or expression of thanks; *esp.* a form of words, a prayer or religious service used to render thanks for Divine benefits.

General Thanksgiving, the first of the forms of thanksgiving in the Book of Common Prayer, that for the blessings of life in general. ***Great Thanksgiving***, in early and oriental liturgies: see quot. 1708–22.

1535 COVERDALE *Ps.* xxxix. [xl.] 3 He hath put a new songe in my mouth, euen a thankesgeuynge vnto oure God. **1552** *Bk. Com. Prayer* (*heading*), The Thankes geuing of Women after Childe birth. **1662** *Ibid.*, Prayers & Thanksgivings upon several occasions... A General Thanksgiving. **1708–22** J. BINGHAM *Chr. Antiq.* XV. iii. (1845) 770 After this the priest went on with the *εὐχαριστία* properly so called, that is the great thanksgiving to God for all his mercies, both of creation, providence and redemption. **1849** MACAULAY *Hist. Eng.* ii. I. 185 The ministers selected from that liturgy such prayers and thanksgivings as were likely to be least offensive to the people.

3. *attrib.* and *Comb.*

1641 EVELYN *Diary* Aug., The next Sunday was the thanksgiving sermons perform'd in Col. Goreing's Regiment. **1814** SOUTHEY *Carmen Triumph.* xvi, With one consent, The high thanksgiving strain to heaven is sent,.. Glory to God! Deliverance for Mankind! *a* **1859** MACAULAY *Hist. Eng.* xxiii. (1861) V. 17 They had still in their ears the thanksgiving sermons and thanksgiving anthems. **1902** I. HAMILTON *Let.* 8 June in R. S. Churchill *Winston S. Churchill* (1969) II. Compan. I. 145 We have just had our Thanksgiving Service. **1923** KIPLING *Irish Guards in Gt. War* I. 338 On the 14th a great thanksgiving-service was held in the Cathedral.

b. Thanksgiving Day, a day set apart for public thanksgiving for Divine goodness; *spec.* in the United States, an annual festival religious and social, now appointed by proclamation and celebrated (since 1941) on the fourth Thursday in November; also in Canada, celebrated on the second Monday in October; **Thanksgiving dinner** *U.S.*, a dinner, usu. consisting of traditional dishes, served on Thanksgiving Day; **Thanksgiving turkey** *U.S.*, a turkey served as a traditional part of a Thanksgiving dinner.

The first celebration was held by the Plymouth colony in 1621, in thankfulness for their first harvest in America after a year of struggle and privation, and the usage became general in New England. After the Revolution, it extended to the Middle States, and later to the West; after the Civil War gradually to the South. Its national observance has been annually recommended by the President since 1863.

1674 JOSSELYN *Voy. New Eng.* 214 Towards night I returned to Boston again, the next day being *Thanksgiving day, on Fryday the Tenth day we weighed Anchor. **1704** LUTTRELL *Brief Rel.* (1857) V. 460 Sir Christopher Wrenn is erecting a throne in St. Pauls cathedral for her majestie to sitt in on the thanksgiving day. **1714** S. SEWALL *Diary* 25 Nov., Thanks-giving day; very cold. **1844** WHITTIER *Pumpkin* iii, Ah! on Thanksgiving day..When the gray-haired New Englander sees round his board The old broken links of affection restored. **1903** *Daily Chron.* 6 Nov. 5/1 Thanksgiving Day long remained an institution peculiar to New England, but it has been observed annually in New York State since 1817. **1830** *Workingman's Gaz.* (Woodstock, Vermont) 1 Dec. 78/2 They have added to the comfort and happiness of those, whose scanty pittance would hardly allow them to enjoy the luxuries of *Thanksgiving dinner. *a* **1892** W. WHITMAN *Daybks. & Notebks.* (1978) I. 89 Took Thanksgiving dinner there Nov 26 '80. **1981** *Washington Post* 22 Nov. K-1/3 Thanksgiving dinner starts with an enormous glut of oysters. **1829** *Virginia Herald* (Fredericksburg) 25 Apr. 4/1 (*heading*) A *Thanksgiving Turkey. **1960** *American Home* Nov. 50 Who should know better how to roast a Thanksgiving turkey or bake a mince pie than the women of early America. **1981** *Washington Post* 26 Nov. B1/1 Such a small Thanksgiving turkey.

† **'thankworth**, *a. Obs.* [f. THANK *sb.* + WORTH *a.*] = next.

? **1426** *Lett. Marg. Anjou & Bp. Beckington* (Camden) 33, I quyte me soo to yow in that matere,..as were thanke worth. **1550** COVERDALE *Spir. Perle* Pref. 1 b, The more daungerous be his sores and sicknes, and the more thancke worth the cure therof. **1627–47** FELTHAM *Resolves* 30 To trust him for an estate when we have the evidences in our iron chest, is easie; and not thankeworth.

'thank,worthy, *a.* Also 6–7 **thanks-**. Worthy of thanks; deserving gratitude or credit.

1387–8 T. USK *Test. Love* Prol. (Skeat) l. 39 Although this booke be lytel thank worthy for the leudnesse in trauail. **1421** SIR H. LUTTRELL in Ellis *Orig. Lett.* Ser. II. I. 86 Wherfore..he ys thankworthy. **1533** J. HEYWOOD *Play Weather* (1903) 1125 Thy labour is ryght myche thankeworthy. **1534** TINDALE *1 Pet.* ii. 19 For it is thankeworthye yf a man for conscience towarde god endure grefe, sufferinge wrongfully. **1594** CAREW *Huarte's Exam. Wits* xiii. (1596) 202 No lesse thanks-worthie a part of Seruice. **1672** WILKINS *Nat. Relig.* 31 It would not be thank-worthy for a man to believe that which of necessity he must believe. **1891** T. K. CHEYNE *Orig. Psalter* Introd. 17 A faulty but at that time thankworthy book.

Hence **'thank,worthily** *adv.*, in a thankworthy manner; **'thank,worthiness**, the quality or condition of being thankworthy.

1553 BALE *Gardiner's De vera Obed.* C vij, To exercise our selues godly and *thankeworthyly. **1874** SWINBURNE *Bothwell* I. i. 7 And we that do it, we do it for all men's good, For the main people's love, thankworthily. **1847** WEBSTER, **Thank-worthiness*.

'thank you. [Aphetic for *I thank you.*]

A. *phr.* **1.** A phrase used in courteous acknowledgement of a favour or service. ***thank you for nothing***: see THANK *v.* 3 f. So, rarely, **thank thee.** Cf. THANKEE. Occas. with intensifying advbs. and phrases: cf. THANK *sb.* 5 b.

14.. *Why I can't be a Nun* 159 in *E.E.P.* (1862) 142 'Thanke yow, lady', quod I than. **1616** B. JONSON *Devil an Ass* IV. ii, *Eith.* Thanke you good Madame... Thanke thee, good Eyther-side. **1705** VANBRUGH *Confed.* I. i, Thank you kindly, Mrs. Amlet, thank you kindly. **1738** SWIFT *Pol. Conversat.* ii. 140 No, thank ye, Colonel. **1848** THACKERAY *Van. Fair* xxiv, It's you who want to introduce beggars into my family? Thank you for nothing, Captain. **1862** MISS YONGE *C'tess Kate* ii. 24 She..said something meant for 'No, thank you'; but of which nothing was to be heard but 'q' [*i.e.* ——k you]. **1875** JOWETT *Plato* (ed. 2) III. 206 [He] goes about learning of others, to whom he never even says Thank you. **1885** A. EDWARDES *Girton Girl* III. x. 182 Oscar Jones looked radiant. 'Thank you, awfully, Miss Bartrand.' **1967** K. GILES *Death in Diamonds* ix. 155 Thank you a million.

2. a. Used to add emphasis to a preceding expression of a wish or opinion (usu. one implying a denial or refusal).

1904 E. NESBIT *Phoenix & Carpet* xi. 212 He didn't mean stay and be roasted... No boys on burning decks for me, thank you. **1928** E. O'NEILL *Strange Interlude* IV. 148 No, I've enough guilt in my memory now, thank you! **1940** *Punch* 5 June 624/1, I still have some remnants of self-respect, thank you. **1959** *Times* 27 Apr. 11/3 It was there.. that the emissaries of Noah came to give warning of the impending flood, only to be told that the Macneils had a boat of their own, thank you. **1963** N. MARSH *Dead Water* (1964) vii. 170 'Do you mean that you confronted her?' 'Me! No, thank you!' **1974** M. FORSTER *Seduction of Mrs. Pendlebury* x. 105, I don't want to do her good, I just want to keep her out of sight and mind, thank you very much. **1983** *Listener* 27 Jan. 25/3 Those of us who felt that nuclear weapons were quite enough to be worrying about, thank you very much, were given a nasty jolt by the documentary *Overcast, with Outbreaks of Yellow Rain.*

b. Used in imitation of direct speech to imply self-satisfaction or complacency on the part of a person just referred to; chiefly in phr. ***to do very well, thank you*** and varr.

1931 S. JAMESON *Richer Dust* xix. 524 He himself was doing very well, thank you. **1969** *Guardian* 4 July 7/1 One of them was Louise Purnell, and you know she's doing very nicely, thank you. **1971** S. JEPSON *Let. to Dead Girl* viii. 85 Merchant bankers..encouraged people like John Kinnon and..did very well out of it thank you. **1972** *National Observer* (U.S.) 27 May 8/4 Pat dresses stylishly, favoring white boots, and gets around just fine, thank you.

3. In negative contexts, used like THANK *v.* 3 h.

1935 D. L. SAYERS *Gaudy Night* xvii. 365 That's what the man wants. *He* wouldn't say thank you for a critic on the hearth. **1969** W. J. BURLEY *Death in Willow Pattern* v. 56, I wouldn't say thank you for it! **1970** D. BAGLEY *Running Blind* ix. 199 Nordlinger's Chevrolet was too long... I wouldn't have given a thank you for it.

B. *sb.* (written with hyphen or as one word): An utterance of this phrase. Also, an unspoken expression of thanks.

1792 F. BURNEY *Jrnl.* May (1972) I. 174 He looked even extremely gratified..& Bowed expressively a *thank you.* **1824** J. KEBLE *Let.* in G. Battiscombe *John Keble* (1963) I. iv. 80 And so with as hearty a thank-you and farewell as ever you received I am your obliged and very faithful John Keble. **1887** *Chr. World* 4 Aug. 589 He utters a hearty 'Thank-you!' **1894** *Westm. Gaz.* 21 Aug. 3/3 The majority of passengers retreated from the tables regardless of their running fire of 'thankyous', which were thankyous for nothing. **1900** *Ibid.* 6 Sept. 2/1 We had not said nearly enough 'thank-yous'.

C. *attrib.*, designating something written or done to convey thanks (in quot. 1922, that merits thanks); esp. ***thank-you letter, note.***

1912 J. WEBSTER *Daddy-Long-Legs* 57, I meant this to be just a short little thank-you note. **1915** —— *Dear Enemy* 111, I spend my entire time composing thank-you letters that aren't exact copies of the ones I've sent before. **1922** JOYCE *Ulysses* 131 Saving princes is a thank you job. **1939** F. SCOTT FITZGERALD *Let.* 5 Apr. (1964) 55 Got a nice thank-you letter from Frances Turnbull for the check I sent her. **1948** 'P. QUENTIN' *Run to Death* x. 83 Vera and I said, 'thank-you' speeches to Mrs. Snood and left. **1979** R. JAFFE *Class Reunion* (1980) II. i. 183 After she saw his play she wrote him a thank-you note. **1981** P. DICKINSON *Seventh Raven* xiii.

189 The thank-you party..for the children—ice-cream and sausage rolls and lemonade.

thank-you-ma'am. *U.S. colloq.* Also **thank'ee-marm.** A hollow or ridge in a road, which causes persons passing over it in a vehicle to nod the head involuntarily, as if in acknowledgement of a favour; *spec.* a ridge or hollow on a hill road serving to throw off descending rain-water.

1849 LONGF. *Kavanagh* xi, We went like the wind over the hollows in the snow;—the driver called them 'thank-you-ma'ams', because they made everybody bow. **1867** O. W. HOLMES *Guard. Angel* xiv, Life's a road that's got a good many thank-you-ma'ams to go bumpin' over, says he. **1897** HOWELLS *Landl. Lion's Head* 192 At one of the thank-you-marms in the road, the sick man stopped, like a weary horse, to breathe.

thanna(h, var. THANA[1], Indian police station.

thanne, þanne, obs. ff. THAN, THEN.

† **'thannic,** *a. Chem. Obs.* [f. *Thann* (name of a town in the Vosges where Kestner the discoverer lived) + -IC.] In *thannic acid*: see quot.

1853 *Pharmac. Jrnl.* XIII. 110 Racemic acid was.. discovered by Kestner,..in the year 1820. It was called thannic acid by its discoverer.

thanx (θæŋks), commercial and informal spelling of *thanks* (see THANK *sb.* 5). orig. *U.S.*

1936 H. L. MENCKEN *Amer. Lang.* (ed. 4) viii. 406 Such forms as *burlesk*..*thanx* and *kreem*..are used freely by the advertising writers. **1977** *Zigzag* Apr. 24/1 Thanx for writing.

thape, dial. var. *fape*: see FEABERRY, gooseberry.

‖**Thapsia** ('θæpsɪə). *Bot.* Also 4-6 **tapsia.** [L. *thapsia* (*tapsia*), a. Gr. θαψία, said to mean a plant brought from Thapsus.] A genus of umbelliferous perennials, of the tribe *Laserpitieæ*, containing four species, natives of the Mediterranean region. That formerly in medical repute is *T. garganica*, also called Deadly Carrot.

c **1400** *Lanfranc's Cirurgie* 195 þe place shal be frotid in þe sunne wiþ an oynement of tapsia. *c* **1440** *Pallad. on Husb.* I. 1044 This tapsia, this wermot, and eleure, Cucumber wilde, and euery bitter kynde Of herbe is nought for hem. **1578** LYTE *Dodoens* III. xxiv. 365 The barke of the roote of Thapsia. **1586** *Rates of Custome* E viij, Tapsia the pound xij.d. **1857** DUNGLISON *Med. Lex.*, *Thapsia*... The root operates violently, both upwards and downwards.

b. *attrib.* and *Comb.*, as ***thapsia-plaster*** (*Cent. Dict.* 1890), ***-resin*** (see quot.), ***-root.***

1890 BILLINGS *Nat. Med. Dict.*, *Thapsia resin*, a soft extract prepared by digesting thapsia-root in hot alcohol.

‖**Thapsus** ('θæpsəs). *Bot.* Also 4-5 (8) **tapsus,** 8 **thapsos.** [med.L., a. Gr. θάψος a plant used for dyeing yellow (Dioscor.).] An old name of the genus *Verbascum*, esp. of *V. Thapsus*, the great mullein.

a **1387** *Sinon. Barthol.* 41/2 *Tapsus barbastus*, flosmus idem. **1578** LYTE *Dodoens* I. lxxxi. 119 Mulleyn is called.. in Shoppes *Tapsus Barbatus*. **1718** ROWE tr. *Lucan* IX. 1566 The Gummy Larch-Tree and the Thapsos there, Woundwort and Maiden-weed perfume the Air.

‖**thar** (thɑː(r)), *sb. Zool.* [Native name.]

1. The native name in Nepal of a goat-antelope, *Nemorhædus bubalina*, belonging to the same genus as the Goral (*N. goral*).

1833 B. H. HODGSON in *Proc. Zool. Soc.* 10 Sept. 105 As compared with the Ghôrâl, *Antilope Goral*, Hardw...the Thâr is a massive beast, twice the size, and has suborbital sinuses, and a mane along the back of the neck and shoulders. *Ibid.* 24 Sept. 111 A cavity also exists in the osseous core of the horns of the Thâr Antelope. **1834** *Ibid.* 12 Aug. 86. **1834** *Penny Cycl.* II. 89/2 The Thar (*A. thar*, Hodgson) was described for the first time in a paper by B. H. Hodgson, Esq., British resident in Nepaul... The thar inhabits the central region of Nepaul. **1885** *Cycl. India* III. 885/1 Thar, the forest goat, is the Nepal name of *Nemorhædus bubalina*, called Eimu and Ramu on the Sutlej and Kashmir, and Serow in the hills generally.

2. Also applied to the TAHR, or Himalayan wild goat (*Hemitragus jemlaicus*).

1896 *List Anim. Zool. Soc.* 166 *Hemitragus jemlaicus* (Hodgs.) Thar. **1902** WEBBER *Forests Upper India* vi. 52 *Hemitragus jemlaicus* is a true wild goat, here called 'thar' by the natives... The thar is gregarious. **1902** LYDEKKER in *Encycl. Brit.* XXXIII. 939/1 The discovery of a species of thar (*Hemitragus*) in southern Arabia. **1903** *Spectator* 4 Apr. 527/2 Open and high ground.. more suitable for wild sheep, such as the thar.

† **thar,** *v. Obs.*: see THARF.

thar (ðɑr, θɑr), ME., chiefly northern, form of THERE; revived to repr. U.S. pronunc. See THERE *adv.* (*a.*, *sb.*) A. γ. Also in compounds, as *ðar abutan*, etc.: see THEREABOUT and other words to THEREWITH.

thar, thare, obs. ff. THEIR; var. THIR *Obs.*, these; obs. gen. and dat. sing. fem. and gen. pl. of THE; 3 sing. and pl. pres. indic. of THARF *v. Obs.*

tharandite ('tærəndaɪt). *Min.* [a. Ger. *tharandit* (Freiesleben, 1817), f. Tharandt in Saxony (where it occurs) + -ITE[1].] A variety of dolomite occurring in greenish yellow crystals, containing a small percentage of ferrous oxide.

1850 ANSTED *Elem. Geol.*, *Min.* etc. §385. **1868** DANA *Min.* 682 Tharandite, from Tharand, near Dresden, is crystallized, and contains 4 p.c. of Fe.

tharatour, *Sc.*: see THEREATOUR.

tharborough, corrupt form of THIRDBOROUGH.

thar-cake, tharck-cake: see THARF-CAKE.

thare, obs. f. TARE *sb.*[1]; also of THERE.

† **tharf,** *sb. Obs.* Also 1 **þearf, ðærf,** 2 **þerf,** 3 (*Orm.*) **þarrfe.** [f. THARF *v.* Cf. OS. *tharf*, OHG. *darba*, ON. *þorf*.] Need, necessity.

Beowulf 1798 Sele-þegn..se for andrysnum ealle beweotede þegnes þearfe. **735** BÆDA *Death-song* 2 Thonc snotturra than him tharf sie. *c* **1000** *Sax. Leechd.* II. 84 ȝif þearf sie, sele hwilum wyrtdrenc. *c* **1175** *Lamb. Hom.* 9 Nis hit nan þerf þet me her on þisse liue for his saule bidde pater noster. *c* **1200** ORMIN 12247 Onn alle þa þatt haffdenn ned & þarrfe to þin hellpe. *c* **1330** *Arth. & Merl.* 16 And wele ysen, ȝif þai willen, þat hem no þarf neuer spillen.

tharf, *a. Obs.* or *dial.* Forms: 1 **þeorf, þearf,** (**ðorof, ðærf**), 3 (*Orm.*) **þeorrf,** 4 **þerf, -e,** 4-5 **therf,** 5 **tharf, -e.** See also THARF-CAKE. [OE. *þeorf* (:—*þerf*), unleavened, unsoured; of milk, sweet; Com. Teut. = OFris. *therf*, *derf*, MDu. *derf* (Kilian has '*derf-brood*, panis azymus'), OHG., MHG. *derp* unleavened, Ger. *derb* solid, compact, rough, coarse, ON. *þjarfr* unleavened, insipid. With sense 2, cf. the mod.Ger. sense of *derb*; app. referring to the solid, heavy, or stiff quality of unleavened bread. Pre-Teut. etymology unknown.]

† **1.** Of bread, etc.: Not prepared with leaven, unleavened. *Obs.* exc. in THARF-CAKE.

c **950** *Lindisf. Gosp.* Matt. xxvi. 17 Ða forma uutedlice doeȝe ðara ðorofra [*Rushw.* ðefra *for* ðerfa] mæta. *c* **1000** ÆLFRIC *Hom.* II. 210 þeorfe hlafas we bringað Gode to lace. *c* **1000** —— *Exod.* xii. 39 Hi..worhton þeorfe heorþbacene hlafas. *c* **1000** ÆLFRIC *Voc.* in Wr.-Wülcker 153/32 *Azimus*, ðeorf. *c* **1200** ORMIN 997 Bræd All þeorrf wiþþutenn berrme. *a* **1300** *Cursor M.* 6079 Wit therf bred and letus wild. **1382** WYCLIF *Gen.* xix. 3 He made a feest, sethede therf breed, and thei eten. —— *Mark* xiv. 1 Pask and the feeste of therf looues was aftir the secunde day. *c* **1400** MAUNDEV. (Roxb.) iii. 10 þai say we erre þat makes þe sacrement of tharf breed. *c* **1425** *Voc.* in Wr.-Wülcker 657/30 *Panis siliginius*, tharf-bred. *c* **1440** *Promp. Parv.* 490/2 Therf, wythe owte sowre dowe. **1483** *Cath. Angl.* 381/2 Tharfe, *azimus.*

2. *transf.* Lumpish, stiff, heavy, slow; hence *fig.* reluctant, unwilling, diffident, tardy. *dial.* Hence **'tharfish** *a.* in same sense; **'tharfly** *adv.*, in a tharf or tharfish manner.

1747 HOOSON *Miner's Dict.*, *Tharf* [is] when a Vein or Pipe alters from its own intrinsical Nature to another, that is more Hask, Barren, and Dry, and more bound up, and stiff. **1828** *Craven Gloss.*, *Tharf*, stark, stiff, metaphorically, backward, unwilling. **1876** *Mid-Yorks. Gloss.*, *Tharf*,.. *Thauf*, diffident; unwilling; reluctant; tardy... Also *tharfish* adj., and *tharfly* adv. **1876** *Whitby Gloss.*, *Tharf*, *Tharfish*, shy, diffident. *Tharfly*, slowly. 'The rain comes nobbut tharfly'. **1894** *Northumbld. Gloss.*, *Tharf*, *Tharfish*, lumpish, heavy-countenanced, forbidding. Applied to substances it means 'sad', heavy, like liver in texture. *Tharfly*, slowly, reluctantly.

† **tharf, thar,** *v. Obs.* exc. *Sc. dial.* Forms: see below. [A Com. Teutonic verb, belonging to the class of preterite-presents, in which the present tense is an original preterite (cf. CAN, DOW, DARE, etc.): OE. **þurfan*, pres. *þearf—þurfon*, pa. *þorfte*, = OFris. **thurva*, *thurf*(*thorf*)—*thurvon*, OS. *thurban*, *tharf—thurbun*, *thorfta*, MDu. *dorven*, *dorfte* (Du. *durven*), ON. *þurfa*, *þarf—þurfom*, *þurfta* (Sw. *tarfva*), OHG. *durfan*, *darf—durfun*, *dorfta* (MHG. *durfen*, G. *dürfen*), Goth. **þaurban*, *þarf—þaurbum*, *þaurfta* :—OTeut. **þarf-*, **þurb-*; corresp. to a pre-Teut. ablaut series **terp-*, **torp-*, **trp-*, which has not been certainly identified. The ME. β-forms had lost the *f* or *v*, app. first in the 2nd sing. present *þearft*, *þeart-tu*, *þer-tu*, leaving a stem *þar-*, *þer-*, *þor-*, *þur-*, which was afterwards often confused with the *dar-*, *dor-*, *dur-* of DARE *v.*[1], so that the latter had forms in *th*, while there are here forms in *d*, esp. in the 2nd and 3rd person singular of the present: see γ. This confusion of *tharf* and *dare* is also found in the cognate languages: see DARE *v.*[1]]

A. Inflexions.

1. *Pres. Indic.* **a.** *1st sing.* 1 **þearf.**

Beowulf 2007 Ic þæt eall ȝe-wræc swa..[ne] ȝylpan þearf grendeles maȝa. *a* **1000** *Cædmon's Gen.* 2176 (Gr.) Ne þearf ic yrfestol eaforan bytlian.

b. *2nd sing.* α. 1 **þearft,** 2 **þerft,** (3 **þerf**).

Beowulf 1675 þæt þu him on-drædan ne þearft. *c* **1000** *Sax. Leechd.* II. 180 Ne þearft þu þone wermod to don. *c* **1175** *Lamb. Hom.* 37 Soðliche ne þerft þu bidden namare. *a* **1225** *Leg. Kath.* 1160 þu wenest ȝet þæt tu wenen ne þerf.

β. 3 **þært, þert, þer**(tu), 3-4 **þers**(tou), 4 **þertes**(tow), 4-5 **tharst,** 5 **thar, thare.**

c **1205** LAY. 14482 Ne þært [*MS.* þræt] þu nauere habben kare of uncuðe leoden. *a* **1225** *Ancr. R.* 136 Ne þer tu nout dreden þe attrie neddre of helle. *c* **1300** *St. Brandan* 626 Ne therstou nothing drede. *c* **1330** R. BRUNNE *Chron. Wace* (Rolls) 4877 Of Kent ne þertestow fle þat cost. **1390** GOWER *Conf.* II. 61 Me semeth that thou tharst noght care. *a* **1450** *Le Morte Arth.* 3285 Othure warke thou thare not wene. *c* **1460** *Towneley Myst.* ii. 293 Thar thou nowther flyte ne chyde.

γ. 3 **dert,** 4 **dars**(tou, -tow).

c **1205** LAY. 22923 Ne dert [*c* 1275 þert] þu nauere adrede. *c* **1320** *Cast. Love* 975 Ne darstou on erþe þenchen elles nouht. **1377** LANGL. *P. Pl.* B. XIV. 55 Bi so þat þow be sobre ..Darstow [*v. rr.* Tharst þow, Thardestow] neuere care for corne, ne lynnen cloth ne wollen.

c. *3rd sing.* α. 1 **ðearf, þearf** (**ðorfæð, -eð**), 2 **þerf,** 3 (*Orm.*) **þarrf,** 3-4 **þarf,** 4 **tharf.**

c **888** K. ÆLFRED *Boeth.* xxiv. §4 Ne ðearf he nanes þinges. *c* **950** *Lindisf. Gosp.* John xiii. 10 Seðe ȝeðuæn is ne ðorfæð [*c* **975** *Rushw.* ðorfeð] þætte aðoa hine. *c* **975** *Rushw. Gosp.* Matt. xxi. 3 Sæcgaþ þæt dryhten heora ðearf. *c* **1175** *Lamb. Hom.* 9 Nu ne þerf na mon his sunne mid wite abuggen. *a* **1250** *Prov. Ælfred* 161 in *O.E. Misc.* 113 Monymon weneþ þat he wene ne þarf longes lyues. *c* **1330** *Amis & Amil.* 935 Tharf the neuer haue of him drede.

β. 3 **þerh,** 4 (**tar**), **thars,** 4-5 **þar, thar, þare, thare, there,** 5 **tharre, tharth,** 9 *Sc. dial.* **ther.**

a **1300** *Cursor M.* 13554 Fra nu thar him namar be ledd. *Ibid.* 19870 (Edin.) þat to do þare þe nochte lete. **1340** HAMPOLE *Pr. Consc.* 2167 He þat hates þis lyfes lykyng Thar noght drede þe dedes commyng. ? **1370** *Robt. Cicyle* 325 More then thars be an c. folde. *a* **1400-50** *Alexander* 5377 þe thare bot graunt me to geue quat guds as I craue. **1414** BRAMPTON *Penit. Ps.* (Percy Soc.) 45 Me thar no more but aske and have. *c* **1425** *Cursor M.* 10565 (Laud) For to aske there no man Yf they were glad & ioyfull þan. *c* **1475** Tharth [see B. 2].

γ. 3 **derf,** 3-4 **darf,** 4 **darh,** 4-5 **dar, dare.**

a **1240** *Ureisun* in *Cott. Hom.* 187 Hwa derf beon unsauuet þe hauep se mihti salue. **1297** R. GLOUC. (Rolls) 6471 Me ne dar noȝt esse weþer he were kene þo & prout. *a* **1300** *Floriz & Bl.* 315 Ich wene ne darf me axi noȝt. *c* **1320** *Cast. Love* 733 Ne dar he seche non oþer leche. *a* **1327** *Pol. Songs* (Camden) 250 Of gode knyhtes darh him nout fail. *c* **1425** *Cursor M.* 10461 (Laud) To myrthe me dare [*early MSS.* þar] the not wene. *c* **1440** *Sir Gowther* 615 The dare not drede of thi werkys wyld.

d. *plural.* α. 1 **þurfon, ðurfan,** 1-3 **þurfe,** 3 **þurven** (**-uen**), **þorhfe, þurve, þorve.**

c **888** K. ÆLFRED *Boeth.* xiv. §2 þa ðurfon swiþe lytles, ðe maran ne willniað þonne ȝenoȝes. *Ibid.* xxiv. §4 Hwæt þurfon [*v.r.* þurfe] we nu ma..sprecan? *c* **975** *Rushw. Gosp.* Matt. xxvi. 65 Hwæt þurfe we leng ȝewitnisse? *c* **1205** LAY. 24909 We ne þuruen [*c* **1275** þorhfe] na mare aswunden liggen here. *a* **1225** *Ancr. R.* 6. *c* **1290** *S. Eng. Leg.* I. 106/160 3e þurue [*Harl. MS.* þore] habbe of heom no kare.

β. 3 **þore,** 4 **thore,** 4-5 **thar,** 5 *Sc.* **thair.**

c **1290** *St. Brandan* 121 in *S. Eng. Leg.* I. 223 3e ne þore noþing drede. *c* **1386** CHAUCER *Melib.* ¶ 102 Yet thar ye nat accomplice thilke ordinance but yow like. *c* **1430** *Syr Gener.* (Roxb.) 6868 Ye thar not drede of hem y-wis. **1438** *Bk. Alex. Grt.* (Bann.) 9 3e thair nocht dreid na chaissing. *c* **1485** *Digby Myst.* III. 1437 Of þis cors we thar nat a-baffe. **1825** Thair [see B. 1].

γ. 4 **dorre, durre,** 5 **dar.**

1297 R. GLOUC. (Rolls) 4 Of fon hii dorre [*v.r.* heo durre] þe lasse doute bote hit be þorȝ gyle. *c* **1477** CAXTON *Jason* 42 Ye dar not be aferd of dethe.

2. *Pres. Subj. sing.* 1 **ðyrfe,** 1-2 **þurfe,** 3 (*Orm.*) **þurrfe, þurve.** *pl.* 1 **ðyrfen, þurfen.**

c **888** K. ÆLFRED *Boeth.* xxvi. §2 Sam hi þyrfen, sam hi na þurfon, hi willað peah. *c* **897** —— *Gregory's Past. C.* xliii. 312 Oft ðonne mon ma fæst ðonne he ðyrfe. *c* **1000** *Ags. Gosp.* John iv. 15 Syle me þæt wæter þæt..ic ne ðurfe [*c* **1160** *Hatt. G.* þurfe] her feccan. *c* **1200** ORMIN 7766 þatt ure nan ne þurrfe Ut off þe rihhte weȝȝe gan. *c* **1275** *Woman Samaria* 26 in *O.E. Misc.* 85 Yef me þar-of to drynke þat ich ne þurve more to þisse welle swynke.

3. *Past Indic.* and *Subj.* **a.** *sing.* α. 1 **ðorfte,** 2-5 **þurfte,** 3 (*Orm.*) **þurrfte,** 4-5 **thurfte.**

a. c **888** K. ÆLFRED *Boeth.* xiv. §3 Ne þorfte he him nænne ondrædan. *Ibid.*, Ne ðorftes þu ðe nanwuht ondrædan. *Ibid.* xxvi. §2 Ne ðorfte he no maran fultomes. *c* **1200** ORMIN 16164 Swa þatt nan mann ne þurrfte off himm. *a* **1325** *Poem Times Edw. II* 321 in *Pol. Songs* (Camden) 338 Thurfte him noht seke tresor so fer. **14..** *Sir Beues* 4219 (MS. M.) Thurfte he neuer after to aske leche, That sir Mylis myght ouer-reche.

β. 3 **þurhte, þorte,** 3-5 **þurte,** 4 **þurt, þort, þart, thourt,** 4-5 **thurt(e;** 4 **þurste,** 4-5 **þurst,** 4-5, 9 *Sc.* **thurst.**

c **1200** *Trin. Coll. Hom.* 35 He ne þurte naure þolen hunger ne þurst. *a* **1272** *Luue Ron* 95 in *O.E. Misc.* 96 Ne þurhte þe neuer rewe. *a* **1300** *Cursor M.* 23443 Ya forsoth thurt [*v.r.* thort] naman mare. *c* **1330** *Florice & Bl.* 259 Now thourt him neuere ful iwis Willen after more blisse. **1393** LANGL. *P. Pl.* C. x. 257 Ho so þurste hit segge. *a* **1425** *Chron. R. Glouc.* (Rolls) 6389 (MS. β), He ne þurst neuer eft care of drynke ne clope. *c* **1460** *Towneley Myst.* xxv. 256 For no catelle thurt the craue. **1825** Thurst [see B. 1].

b. *plural.* α. 1 **þorfton, -an.** β. 3 **þeorte(n,** 3-4 **þurte(n,** 4-5 **thurte.**

c **897** K. ÆLFRED *Gregory's Past. C.* 9 Hi his sume ðorfton. *a* **1000** *Guthlac* 423 (452) No we þus swiðe swencan þorftan. *c* **1275** LAY. 18650 For ne þeorte þe cnihtes buten biwiten þat castel ȝat. *c* **1460** *Towneley Myst.* xxx. 473 Thai thurte bot aske and haue thare boyn.

B. Signification.

1. *intr.* To be under a necessity or obligation (*to do* something): = NEED *v.*[2] 6, 8.

c **890-901** K. ÆLFRED *Laws* Introd. c. 28 ȝif..he ..ȝewitnesse hæbbe, ne þearf he þæt ȝeldan. *a* **1000** *Cædmon's Gen.* 611 (Gr.) Ic hit þe secgan ne þearf. *a* **1200** *Moral Ode* 44 þer ne þerf he habben kare of ȝefe ne of ȝelde. *a* **1225** *Juliana* 68 Arude me þat þeos unselie ne þurue nawt seggen. *c* **1230** *Hali Meid.* 5 Ha nawiht ne þarf of oðer þing þenchen. **1825** JAMIESON s.v.,'Ye thair n' fash', you need not put yourself to the trouble. *Ibid.*, 'Ye thurstn'', ye needed not.

2. *impersonally.* It needs, there is need, it is needful [= L. *opus est*, Gr. δεῖ]. Const. *dat.* of person and *inf.* **a.** without subject *it.*

c **1200** ORMIN 12886 Ne þarrf ȝuw nohht nu follȝhenn me. *c* **1200** *Trin. Coll. Hom.* 69 þanne ne þarf us noðer gramien ne shamien. *a* **1250** *Owl & Night.* 190 Ne þarf þerof beo no tale. *c* **1275** *Passion* 17 in *O.E. Misc.* 37 Ne þerfþ þer non adrede. *c* **1275** *Duty of Christians* 37 ibid. 142 Ne þarf vs neuer a-gryse. *c* **1320** *Sir Tristr.* 3053 Who wil lesinges layt, þarf him no ferþer go. *c* **1330** R. BRUNNE *Chron. Wace* (Rolls) 4145 Ne neuere þurt hem haue drad no tyde. *c* **1430** *Syr Gener.* (Roxb.) 3 Ne thar him nat be idel long. *c* **1440** *Alphabet of Tales* 361 Sho said hym þurte not be seke herfor. *c* **1475** *Rauf Coilȝear* 538 Me tharth haue nane noy of myne erand.

b. with subject *it. rare.*

c **1430** *Pilgr. Lyf Manhode* I. lxxxvii. (1869) 39 It thurt not recche to wite of this anoon. *c* **1460** *Towneley Myst.* iv. 117 Myn ase shalle withe vs, if it thar.

tharf-cake (ˈθɑːfkeɪk). Now *dial.* Forms: 4 **þerf, þerue cake,** 6 **therfe, tharffe,** *Sc.* **thraf, threfe cake,** 7 **tharck-cake,** 7–9 **tharcake.** [f. THARF *a.* + CAKE *sb.*] A cake of unleavened bread; now *spec.* a flat circular cake of oat-, rye-, or barley-meal, unleavened, and sometimes flavoured with butter and treacle; in the latter case = PARKIN.

13.. *E. E. Allit. P.* B. 635 Abraham..þrwe þryftyly þer-on þo þre þerue kakez. **1362** LANGL. *P. Pl.* A. VII. 269 A þerf Cake, And a lof of Benes and Bren I-Bake for my Children. *c* **1470** HENRYSON *Mor. Fab.* II. (*Town & C. Mouse*) xviii, Thraf caikis als, I trow, scho spairit nocht. **1560** PILKINGTON *Expos. Aggeus* (1562) 92 Elias, fleeing from Jezebel, founde a therfe cake baked in the asshes. **1634–5** BRERETON *Trav.* (Chetham Soc.) 122 The entertainment we accepted..was Tharck-cakes, two eggs, and some dried fish buttered. **1691** RAY *N.C. Words* s.v. *Bannock, Tharcakes*,.. cakes made of oat-meal,..and fair water, without yeast, or leaven, and so baked. *c* **1746** COLLIER (Tim Bobbin) *View Lanc. Dial.* Wks. (1862) 57 'Twur os thodd'n os o Thar-Cake. **1825** BROCKETT *N.C. Wds.*, *Thauf-cake.* **1828** *Craven Gl.*, *Thar-cake*, a heavy, unleavened cake. **1888** *Sheffield Gloss.* s.v., A year or two ago I noticed that a shop-keeper.. advertised tharf-cake for sale... They call it *parkin* instead of using the old word. **1893–4** *Northumbld. Gloss.*, Tharf-kyek, Thaaf-keahyk, Thaf-kyek, Tharth-kyek, Thaugh-cyek, Tharfy.

†**ˈtharfling, ˈtherfling.** *Obs. rare.* [OE. *ðeorfling*, f. *ðeorf* THARF *a.* + -LING.] Unleavened bread or loaf; also *attrib.* Unleavened.

c **1050** *Gloss.* in Wr.-Wülcker 348/28 *Azimos*, ðeorflingas. *c* **1200** ORMIN 1588 Forr þerrflinng bræd iss clene bræd, Forr þatt itt iss unnberrmedd.

tharl(e, -dom, obs. ff. THRALL *sb.*[1], THRALDOM.

tharm (θɑːm). Now *dial.* Forms: 1 Angl. **tharm, þarm,** WSax. **þearm, thearm;** 3 **þærm, þerm,** 3–4 **þarm,** 4 **þearm,** 5 **thaarme,** 5– **tharm;** (6–7 *dial.* **therm,** 8–9 *Sc.* **therm, thairm).** [OE. *þarm, þearm* = OFris. *therm* (WFris. *term*), OLG. **þarm* (MDu. *darm, darem*, Du. *darm*, OHG. *darm, daram* (MHG., MLG., Ger. *darm*), ON. *þarmr* (Sw., Da. *tarm*):—OTeut. **þarm-oz*, f. Indo-Eur. ablaut series *ter: tor: tr* to go through. Cf. Gr. τρῆμα perforation, τράμις perineum.]

1. An intestine; chiefly in *pl.*, bowels, viscera, entrails; in quot. *c* 1460 *transf.*

a **700** *Epinal Gloss.* (O.E.T.) 503 *Intestinum*, thearm. *c* **725** *Corpus Gloss.* 2140 *Viscera*, tharme, thumle. *Ibid.* 870 *Fibra*, þearm. *c* **1000** ÆLFRIC *Gram.* xiii. (Z.) 85 *Exta*, þearmas. *c* **1205** LAY. 818 Moni þusend þer flowen, þærmes heo droȝen [*c* **1275** þarmes idrowen]. **1303** R. BRUNNE *Handl. Synne* 702 Of þe chylde þat she bare..Al to-drawe were þe þarmys. *c* **1380** *Sir Ferumb.* 949 þay stykede þorȝ guttes & þearmes, so foule with hem þei ferde. *c* **1440** *Promp. Parv.* 490/1 Thaarme (or gutte), *sumen, viscus. c* **1460** *Towneley Myst.* xiii. 391, I haue..A house full of yong tharmes,..wo is hym has many barnes. **1535** COVERDALE *2 Macc.* ix. 5 There came vpon him an horrible payne of his bowels, & a sore grefe of the tharmes. **1721** KELLEY *Scot. Prov.* 137 He that has a wide Therm, had never a long Arm. **1877** *N.W. Linc. Gloss.*, *Tharm*, the colon.

2. An intestine as cleansed and prepared for some purpose: see quots. Also, in *sing.*, as a substance or material; catgut for fiddle-strings, etc.

[**1545** ASCHAM *Toxoph.* II. (Arb.) 110 Eustathius..doeth tel, that in oulde tyme they made theyr bowe strynges of bullox thermes. **1631** R. H. *Arraignm. Whole Creature* xvi. 291 The strings made of Wolves will never tune right with those made of the Thermes of Sheepe.] **1671** SKINNER *Etymol. Ang.*, *Tharm*, vox agro Linc. usitatissima pro Intestinis mundatis ad Botulos seu Farcinima paranda inflatis. **1674** RAY *N.C. Wds.*, *Tharm*, guts prepared, cleansed, and blown up for to receive puddings; Lincolnsh. **1755** JOHNSON, *Tharm*, intestines twisted for several uses. **1786** BURNS *Ordination* vii, Come, screw the pegs wi' tunefu' cheep, And o'er the thairms be tryin. **1787** —— *To Haggis* i, Aboon them a' ye tak your place, Painch, tripe, or thairm. **1816** J. CLELAND *Rise & Progr. Glasgow* (1820) 275 A work in which Therm was manufactured from the intestines of animals. **1824** SCOTT *Redgauntlet* Let. x, The best fiddler that ever kittled thairm with horse-hair. **1881** W. ANDERSON in *Mod. Sc. Poets* II. 238 Thairm, to mount a spinnin wheel.

3. *attrib.* and *Comb.*, as *tharm-band, -string.*

1786 BURNS *Brigs of Ayr* 202 O had M'Lauchlan, thairm-inspiring Sage, Been there to hear this heavenly band engage. **1788** G. TURNBULL *Poet. Ess.* 185 Therm-strings for spinning Wheels and fiddles. **1825** JAMIESON, *Thairm-band*, a string or cord of catgut for..a spinning-wheel.

†**tharn,** *v. Obs.* Forms: 3 (*Orm.*) **þarrnenn,** 4 **þarn,** 4–5 **tharn(e, (thorne).** [ad. ON. *þarna*, refl. *þarnask* to be without, lack, want, f. *þarna* (earlier **þarf-na*) sb. need, f. *þarf-*: see THARF *v.*] *trans.* To be without; to want, lack, need; to be deprived of, to lose. Hence †**ˈtharning** *vbl. sb.*, being without, lacking, want; losing, loss.

c **1200** ORMIN 10142 þatt illke þing þatt tu full wel Ne mihht te sellf nohht þarrnenn. *c* **1300** *Havelok* 2835 Hise children sulde þarne Euere more þat eritage, þat his was. **13..** *Cursor M.* 4284 (Cott.) O quat pine es herder threst, þen tharn [*Fairf.* wante] þe thing men luues best. **1340** HAMPOLE *Pr. Consc.* 7308 Right swa þe tharnyng for ever of þat syght, Es þe mast payne in helle dyght. *c* **1375** *Sc. Leg. Saints* xvi. (*Magdalena*) 443, & scho þe lyf allane [allace?] can throne Fra þat ilke barne wes borne. *c* **1440** *York Myst.* xliii. 12 The missing of my maistir trewe..Makis me to morne..For tharnyng of his company. *c* **1460** *Towneley Myst.* xiv. 272 Thy waryson shalle thou not tharne.

tharre, tharst, tharth: see THARF *v. Obs.*

tharst(e, var. ff. *thrast*, obs. pa. t. of THRUST.

thas, obs. form of THOSE; obs. abbrev. of *it has*; obs. infl. of THAT, THE: see THES.

thass (ðæs). Also **thas, thash, thazz.** Repr. *that's* in dial. pronunc. or in speech slurred through intoxication.

1919 G. B. SHAW *Great Catherine* II. 138 Thas true. Drungn ruffian... Thas whas he said. **1932** S. GIBBONS *Cold Comfort Farm* xvii. 237 Lessee, thass twenty years ago. **1951** 'J. WYNDHAM' *Day of Triffids* i. 25 'S that bloody comet... Thash what done it. **1959** E. POUND *Thrones* xcix. 52 Thazz all there is to it. **1973** C. HIMES *Black on Black* 196 Thass 'cause you's a fool. **1981** M. C. SMITH *Gorky Park* III. iii. 341 Wasn't no mink, it was differ'nt. Thass why I took it to town, to fine [*sic*] out what it was.

that (ðæt), *dem. pron.*, *adj.*, and *adv.* Forms: see below. [In OE. *þæt*, nom. and acc. singular neuter of the simple demonstrative pronoun and adjective *se, séo, þæt*, the adjectival use of which has also produced the 'definite article' THE, under which the history and obs. inflexional forms are given. *The* is the resultant form, used for all genders, numbers, and cases of the article; *that* the unweakened neuter singular, used as demonstrative pronoun and adj. for all cases of the singular. The original plural in both uses was *þá*, in ME. *þā* and THO, q.v., surviving in Sc. and north. dial. as THAE, but superseded in literary English by THOSE.

The demonstrative was also used in OE. as a relative pronoun, for which see below.]

A. Illustration of Forms.

1. In OE. inflected for gender, number, and case: see the inflexional forms under THE. Some of the inflexions remained in early ME., and in some dialects even to 1400. A few examples of these, in which the sense is demonstrative, follow here. For the plural forms see THO and THOSE.

(The masc. and fem. pronouns *se, séo*, and 14th c. Kentish *ze, zy*, were often equivalent to 'he', 'she', and 'it'.)

Beowulf (Z.) 470 Se wæs betera ðonne ic. *Ibid.* 506 Eart ðu se Beowulf se ðe wið Brecan wunne? *c* **825** *Vesp. Ps.* vii. 16 Seað [he] ontynde & dalf ðone [= *eum*]. *Ibid.* cxlv. 4 In ðæm [= *illa*] deȝe. *a* **855** *O.E. Chron.* an. 597, Her ongon Ceolwulf ricsian..Se wæs Cuþaing, Cuþa Cynricing [etc.]. *c* **893** K. ÆLFRED *Oros.* I. i. §9 Seo Ægyptus þe us near is. *Ibid.* II. iv. §8 Seo ilce burȝ Babylonia, seo ðe mæst wæs & ærest ealra burȝa. *Ibid.* v. ix, Ic..secgan scyle,..hwa þæs [= of that] ordfruman wæron. *a* **900** tr. *Bæda's Hist.* II. vii. (1890) 118 þæm [Mellitus] sona æfterfylȝde Iustus in biscophade. *c* **1000** *Ags. Gosp.* Matt. x. 23 Ðonne hi eow ehtaþ on þysse byriȝ, fleoþ on oþre, and ðonne hi on þære [*Hatton G.* þare] eow ehtaþ, fleoþ on þa þryddan. —— John iii. 29 Se ðe bryde hæfð, se is brydguma. *a* **1175** *Cott. Hom.* 235 Si [the Law of Moses] ȝeleste sume wile. *c* **1175** *Lamb. Hom.* 37 Do þine elmesse of þon þet þu maht iforðien. *c* **1200** *Trin. Coll. Hom.* 221 Se þer her doð ani god. *c* **1200** ORMIN 17621 To þann comm icc off heffne dun. *c* **1250** *Owl & Night.* 882 þat beoþ her wo is hom þes. *c* **1300** *Harrow. Hell* (MS. O.) 65 þou miȝt wel witen þe bi þon [MS. E. 79 for þan] þat ich [am] more þen ani mon. **1340** *Ayenb.* 102 Zy þet ne seruеþ bote to onlepy manne. *Ibid.* 117 Ze þet ne heþ þise uondinges.

2. Forms of the singular neuter, and, at length, general uninflected form *that.*

1–3 **ðæt, þæt, ðet,** 1–4 **þet,** (3 **ðat, þut),** 3–6 **þat,** (3–5 **ðat,** 4 **þate,** 5 **þatte,** 5–6 **thate,** 6–7 **thatt),** 4– **that.** (Also written 4–6 **yat,** 4–8 **yᵗ, yt.)**

Beowulf (Z.) 1372 Nis þæt heoru stow. **835** *Charter of Abba* (Kentish) in *O.E. Texts* 448 ȝif hiȝan ðonne oððe hlaford þæt nylle..ȝeunnan. *c* **836** *O.E. Chron.* an. 787, þæt wæron þa ærestan scipu Deniscra monna þe Angel cynnes lond ȝesohton. *c* **1134** *Ibid.* (Laud. MS.) an. 1127, þet wes eall ðurh þone kyng Heanri of Engle land. *c* **1175** *Lamb. Hom.* 33 On cristes prisune..þet is in helle. *c* **1200** þatt [see B. II. 1]. *c* **1205** LAY. 4542 þet is þere quene scip. *c* **1250** *Gen. & Ex.* 59 Ðat was ðe firme morȝen tid..Wid ðat liȝt worn angles wroȝt. **1297** R. GLOUC. (Rolls) 6773 He was glad of þut cas. *c* **1330** R. BRUNNE *Chron. Wace* (Rolls) 1926 Englysche holden þate heritage. *c* **1400** þat [see B. II. 5]. *c* **1420** *Chron. Vilod.* 840 He sayde he mervaylede muche of þatte. *c* **1460** *Towneley Myst.* i. 40 That at is dry the erth shalle be. **1533** BELLENDEN *Livy* II. i. (S.T.S.) I. 132 Tak away þat odious name tarquyne fra þe pepill. **1583** T. WATSON *Poems* (Arb.) 45 But I (alas) might curse yat dismall day. **1638** *Hamilton Papers* (Camden) 45, I had lytill hoope of uoorking of thatt by treatie.

B. Signification and uses.

The pronominal use goes back to the earliest OE. The adjectival demonstrative use in OE. corresponded to that of L. *is, ea, id*, or the unqualified French *ce, cette*, and is often indistinguishable from that of the modern definite article. But by 1200 the adjectival use of *that* began also to be more definitely demonstrative (= L. *iste, ille*, F. *ce...là*), and to be implicitly or explicitly opposed to THIS (= L. *hic*, F. *ce...ci*). As this appears first in Ormin, it may have been due to the influence of Norse, in which the adjectival use of *þat* as a demonstrative, opposed to *þetta* 'this', is of earlier appearance.

I. Demonstrative Pronoun. Pl. †THO (*obs.*), THOSE, q.v.

* *As simple demonstrative pronoun.*

1. Denoting a thing or person pointed out or present, or that has just been mentioned: cf. II. 1.

a. a thing (concrete or abstract).

Often serving instead of repetition of the name of the thing, and directing the attention back to it (thus more emphatic than *it*). Also, for emphasis, used pleonastically in apposition to the sb.; also, in mod. use, as in quot. 1880, placed (as subj.) after the predicate sb., with ellipsis of the copula. In quot. 1905, applied to a person contemptuously spoken of as a thing or creature.

Beowulf (Z.) 2200 Eft þæt ȝe-iode ufaran dogrum, hildehlæm-mum. *c* **888** K. ÆLFRED *Boeth.* xxxiii. §5 þæt eart ðu. *c* **897** —— *Gregory's Past. C.* i. 28 Soðlice ða eaȝan þæt bioð ða lareowas, & se hrycg þæt sint ða hiremenn. *c* **1000** *Sax. Leechd.* I. 346 Haran cyslyb ȝeseald on wines drince, þæt wel ȝehæleþ. **1303** R. BRUNNE *Handl. Synne* 12560 Pryue synne and sacrylage, That loue y moste. **13..** in *Hampole's Wks.* (1896) I. 108 Luk nogth efter ylke a mans wile to do it, bot luk whilke es myne & do þat. **1451** CAPGRAVE *St. Augustine* 36 But þe principal cause whech Augustin supposed to spede, þat failed. **1456** SIR G. HAYE *Law Arms* (S.T.S.) 14 And with that I sall put sik thing langand warldly understanding. **1579** W. FULKE *Heskins' Parl.* 74 The errour of Vibicus. And that was this. **1665** BOYLE *Occas. Medit.* IV. v, To serve him that can give That, and much greater. **1709** *Lond. Gaz.* No. 4599/4 It had a black Ribbon tied to it, and the Key of the Watch fastened to that. **1808** ELEANOR SLEATH *Bristol Heiress* I. 63 Rank, high life, fashionable amusement—that's the go. **1842** BROWNING *Pied Piper* iv, 'Bless us', cried the Mayor, 'what's that?' **1878** T. HARDY *Ret. Native* VI. iv, 'What noise was that?' said Clym. **1880** TENNYSON *Sisters* 14 A sweet voice that—you scarce could better that. **1905** EL. GLYN *Viciss. Evangeline* 127 'Would you like to marry Malcolm?' I asked. 'Fancy being owned by that! Fancy seeing it every day!'

b. a person. Now noting a person actually pointed out (not one just mentioned, exc. in emphatic pleonastic use as in a). Chiefly as subject of the verb *to be* in stating or asking who or what *that* (person) is. (See also 6 c.)

Colloquially used in expressions of commendation, or in mod. use of anticipatory commendation by way of persuasion or encouragement (esp. to a child). Cf. THERE *adv.* 3 b.

Beowulf (Z.) 11 þæt wæs god cyning. **1297** R. GLOUC. (Rolls) 3044 ȝif þer is Eny mon so wis þat beste red conne rede, merlin þat is. *a* **1300** *Cursor M.* 18131 þat king o blis, quat es he, þat? **13..** *Gaw. & Gr. Knt.* 2463 Ho wayned me vpon þis wyse..þat is ho þat is at home, þe auncian lady. **1470–85** MALORY *Arthur* I. xxv. 73 What damoysel is that? .. That is the lady of the lake. **1592** SHAKS. *Rom. & Jul.* II. iii. 47 That's my good Son. **1601** —— *All's Well* III. v. 81 *Hel.* Which is the Frenchman? *Dia.* Hee, That with the plume. **1606** —— *Tr. & Cr.* IV. ii. 36 Who's that at doore? **1610** —— *Temp.* I. ii. 299 After two daies I will discharge thee. *Ar.* That's my noble Master. **1652** J. WRIGHT tr. *Camus' Nat. Paradox* IX. 215 By my Soul if that bee a Lady, my Husband may bee a Lady too. **1766** GOLDSM. *Vic. of W.* vii, 'Very well', cried I, 'that's a good girl'. **1841** BROWNING *Pippa Passes* III. 276 Why, there! Is not that Pippa..under the window? **1849** T. ARNOLD *Let.* 10 Aug. (1966) 128 Do you, my dear K, have them sent to me, that's a darling. **1854** THACKERAY *Rose & Ring* viii, 'Who's that laughing?' It was Giglio laughing. *a* **1912** *Mod.* Come along, that's a good boy! That's the man for me! **1936** [see BOY *sb.*[1] 2 c]. **1956** M. DICKENS *Angel in Corner* x. 198 'Good girl.' He lay back on the pillow. 'That's my girl,' he murmured. **1964** J. P. CLARK *Three Plays* 32 *Zifa*: He must not see my tears. *Orukorere*: That's my boy. The strong weep only at dead of night. **1973** W. H. CANAWAY *Harry doing Good* II. ii. 139 'Never mind, then,' he said, and kissed her cheek. 'That's my girl.'

c. a fact, act, or occurrence, or a statement or question, implied or contained in the previous sentence: often used instead of repeating a clause or phrase (cf. a).

In OE. and in Sc. often referring to a following statement, where mod.Eng. commonly uses *this*. Cf. II. 1, and THIS B. I. 1 d.

a **855** *O.E. Chron.* an. 755, Ða on morȝenne ȝehierdun þæt þæs cyninges þeȝnas..þæt se cyning ofslæȝen wæs. *a* **900** CYNEWULF *Elene* 1168 (Gr.) þæt is ȝedafenlic, þæt þu dryhtnes word On hyȝe healde. *c* **1000** *Ags. Gosp.* John i. 19 þæt is Iohannes ȝewitnes. *a* **1131** *O.E. Chron.* an. 1122, On þone lenten tyde þær toforen for bearn se burch on Gleawe ceastre... þet wes þes dæies viii id' Mr.' **1297** R. GLOUC. (Rolls) 10348 Wan þou seist, quaþ þe king, þat þat was mi þouȝt. *c* **1420** (?) LYDG. *Assembly of Gods* 2034 Goo we hens, for that hold I best. **1526** *Pilgr. Perf.* (W. de W. 1531) 3 The iewes also se almyghty god, but that was in a more excellent maner. **1602** SHAKS. *Ham.* III. i. 56 To be, or not to be, that is the Question. **1693** J. Edwards *Author. O. & N. Test.* 154 The Pagans would jeer the Jews for that. **1738** Swift *Pol. Conversat.* ii. 140, I can just carve Pudden, and that's all. **1824** Scott *Redgauntlet* ch. xx, I will say that for the English, . . that they are a ceevéleesed people to gentlemen that are under a cloud. **1838** Ruskin *Ess. Music & Paint.* Wks. 1903 I. 285 If others do not follow their example,—the more fools they,—that's all.

d. After various prepositions, referring to a precise time just mentioned, or an act or event in relation to the precise time of its occurrence: e.g. ***after that*** = after that time, or after that happened; ***by that*** = by that time, or by the time that happened; ***upon that, with that*** = as or immediately after that was said, done, etc. See also the prepositions.

In OE. prepositions governed other cases besides the accusative, as the dative, e.g. *æfter, ær, mid, onmang, tó ðǽm*, the instrumental, e.g. *for þý, mid þý*, etc. These partly survived in early ME.; e.g. *fro þan þat* (see fro prep. 3).

13.. *Cursor M.* 2827 (Cott.) Bi þat [*v.r.* þan] began þe light o dai. *c* **1420** *Anturs of Arth.* 565 The sone was passed, by þat, mydday and mare. *c* **1425** *Cursor M.* 14360 (Laud) Fro that forth . . There folowid Ihesu folk full fele. *c* **1515** *Cocke Lorell's B.* 12 With that they cryed, and made a shoute. **1526** Tindale *Acts* xxvii. 33 In the meane tyme, bitwixt that and daye. *a* **1715** Burnet *Own Time* (1724) I. ii. 278 A proclamation was upon that issued out. **1719** De Foe *Crusoe* (1840) II. i. 17 Some time after that . ., they were . . agreeably surprised. **1802** Jefferson *Writ.* (1830) III. 496 Probably on the 24th, or within two or three days of that. **1833** T. Hook *Parson's Dau.* iii. i, My young mistress went to be about eleven, and the Count went to bed before that. **1862** Miss Braddon *Lady Audley* xl, With that the surgeon goes to fetch the envelopes.

†**e.** In apposition with a following clause introduced by *thăt* conj.; chiefly in phr. with prep., as ***for thát thăt*** = for that cause that, because; ***in thát thăt*** = in that circumstance that, inasmuch as; ***to thát thăt*** = to the end that, in order that. *Obs.*

Taking the place of OE. *þǽm, þám, þon*, or *þý*, in *for þám þe, on þám þe, to þám þe, for þon þe, to þý þe* or *þæt*.

1502 *Ord. Crysten Men* i. iii. (1506) 31 To that that he be worthely dysposed to receyue the grace. **1513** More *Rich. III* (1883) 2 In that that manye of them were dead. **1532** —— *Confut. Tindale* Wks. 659/2 The knowen catholike churche is proued to be the verye churche of Chryste, in that that from the beginning it hath . been . . kepte and contynued one. **1535** Cromwell in Merriman *Life & Lett.* (1902) I. 417 In that that the said frensh kyng hathe . . answered at all tymes on the kinges parte. *a* **1548** Hall *Chron., Edw. IV* 222 Kynge Edward in these hys last battayles was . . fortunate for that, that he at sondry . . tymes . . was persecuted . . of his enemyes.

f. ***take that!*** († ***have that!***): a phrase used in delivering a blow, etc.

a **1425** *Cursor M.* 16290 (Trin.) Wiþ his hond a buffet He ȝaf ihesus . . He seide . . Take þat to teche þe lore. *c* **1425** *Cast. Persev.* 3119 in *Macro Plays*, For þi coueytyse, haue þou þat, I schal þee bunche with my bat. **1590** Shaks. *Com. Err.* ii. ii. 23 Thinkst y^u I iest? hold, take thou that, and that. **1833** Marryat *P. Simple* xii, I must do my duty, Sir, . . so take that—and that—and that—(thrashing the man with his rattan). *Ibid.* xiii, Then I'll turn Protestant and damn the Pope—take that now, Father M'Grath.

2. Used emphatically, instead of repeating a previous word or phrase. **a.** Preceded by *and* (rarely *but*), and referring to something in the previous clause. [Cf. L. *et id, idque*, F. *et cela.*]

c **1000** *Sax. Leechd.* I. 278 On þam [berries] ys sæd and þæt sweart. *c* **1175** *Lamb. Hom* 121 Crist godes sune wes ibuhsum . . to þa deðe, and þet to swulche deðe swa [etc.]. *c* **1386** Chaucer *Friar's T.* 294, I haue been syk, and that ful many a day. *c* **1485** *Digby Myst.* iv. 1067 We shall here tidinges . ., And þat I trust shortlye. **1535** Coverdale *2 Kings* iv. 3 Borowe without of all thy neghboures emptye vessels, & that not a fewe. —— *Ps.* xlvi. 5 God helpeth her, & y^t right early. **1581** Sidney *Apol. Poetrie* (Arb.) 62 Exercise indeede wee doe, but that very fore-backwardly. **1772** Wesley *Jrnl.* 2 June, A man began to scream, and that so loud that my voice was quite drowned. **1833** L. Ritchie *Wand. by Loire* 168 It was necessary . . to act, and that promptly.

b. Representing a word or phrase in the previous clause or sentence: usually standing first in its own clause, with inverted construction (***that I will*** = I will do that). *colloq.*

c **1350** *Will. Palerne* 4161 Hete hem þider wende . . þat i wol, seide william. *a* **1450** *Cov. Myst.* xxiii. (1841) 222 Hath any man condempnyd the? *Mulier.* Nay forsothe that hathe ther nought. **1598** Shaks. *Merry W.* iv. v. 60 Was there a wise woman with thee? *Fal.* I, that there was. **1642** *Suddaine Answ. to Sud. Moderatour* 3 The Moderator is full of Rhetorick and Oratory too, that he is. **1825** T. Hook *Sayings* Ser. ii. *Man of Many Fr.* I. 196, 'I can say 'em all!' 'That you can't', said Tom. **1865** Ruskin *Sesame* i. §29 To feel with them, we must be like them; and none of us can become that without pains. **1872** 'L. Carroll' *Through Looking-Glass* vi, 'They must be very curious creatures.' 'They are that', said Humpty Dumpty. **1900** F. P. Dunne in *Westm. Gaz.* 13 June 1/3 'They'll be out here nex' week'. . . 'They will that', Mr. Dooley replied.

3. a. In opposition to *this* (cf. II. 2): esp. in phr. ***this and (or) that*** = one thing and (or) another: see this B. I. 3. Also occas. ***that . . that*** = one thing . . another thing.

c **888** K. Ælfred *Boeth.* xxxiii. §2 þonne lufað sum ðæt, sum elles hwæt. **1390-** [see this B. I. 3]. *c* **1450** tr. *De Imitatione* iii. xvi. 84 Wheþer a good spirit or an euel stire þe to desire þat or þat. *Ibid.* lv. 130 Lete oon seke þat, a noþer þat. **1818** Scott *Hrt. Midl.* xvi, Lay that and that thegither! **1842** Marryat *Perc. Keene* xiv, Young as I was, I also could put that and that together.

b. *spec.* (after Latin idiom). The former: correl. to *this* = the latter: see this B. I. 3 b. Now *arch.* and *literary*.

c **1440–1868** [see this B. I. 3 b]. **1654** Z. Coke *Logick* (1657) A iij b, Corruption of manners, and mazing Errors . . . These delude and distract that doth deboish a people.

4. As quasi-*sb.*, with pl. ***thats*** (now freq. contrasted with *whats*). Also (with capital T) as quasi-proper name: see this B. I. 3 c, d.

1656–1895 [see this B. I. 3 c, d]. **1890** W. James *Princ. Psychol.* I. xii. 466 The conception of some object as a whole . . points to and identifies for future thought a certain *that*. **1899** F. W. Maitland *Let.* 4 Dec. (1965) 205, I wander in a maze of *whiches* and *thats*. **1909** W. James *Pluralistic Universe* 342 All the *whats* as well as the *thats* of reality, relational as well as terminal, are in the end contents of immediate concrete perception. **1910** *Contemp. Rev.* Mar. 307 The immediacy of faith . . will furnish us with the *That*, whilst we may have to look to other sources for the *What*. **1933** *Mind* XLII. 27 A fundamental tenet rather insistently taught us . .; namely, that things and events, as real, are *thats*, as well as *whats*. **1975** *New Yorker* 5 May 139/1 We wish not to guess but to know more than thises and thats, to know universal truths.

5. Phrases, belonging to senses 1 and 2.

a. ***that is*** (more fully ***that is to say***, †***to wit***, etc.): (*a*) introducing (or more rarely following) an explanation of the preceding word, phrase, or statement (or a modifying correction of it); (*b*) accompanying (usu. following) an explanatory limitation or condition of a preceding statement.

c **1175** *Lamb. Hom.* 105 þe oðer mihte is *Castitas*, þet is clenesse on englisc. *a* **1225** *Ancr. R.* 348 Efter schrifte, hit falleð to speken of Penitence, þet is, dedbote. **1340** *Ayenb.* 210 Huanne þou welcest bidde god . . wisliche and diligentliche, þet is ententifliche and perseuerantliche. *a* **1440** *Relig. Pieces fr. Thornton MS.* 8 The thirde sacrement es callede penance, þat es sothefaste forthynkynge þat we hafe of oure synne. **1523** [Coverdale] *Old God & New* (1534) B j, In all poyntes, y^t is to wyte bothe in his doctryne and also in his lyuynge. **1625** B. Jonson *Staple of N.* i. i, Look to me, . . That is look on me, and with all thine eyes. **1802** Paley *Nat. Theol.* xxiii. (ed. 2) 440 Every animated being has its *sensorium*, that is, a certain portion of space, within which perception and volition are exerted. **1865** Ruskin *Sesame* i. §21 Those who 'intrude' (thrust, that is) themselves into the fold. **1945** N. Mitford *Pursuit of Love* xiii. 101 I bet the Scotsboro' boys will be electrocuted in the end, if they don't die of old age first, that is. **1956** W. Golding *Pincher Martin* x. 155 'I think finally, I shall go into the Navy.' 'You!' . 'If they'd have me, that is.' **1958** *Argosy* Sept. 30 The Buttafava household was happy as could be. All, that is, except Fiorella. **1969** R. Hutchings *Lucky in Jeopardy* iii. 99 You'll be tasting it for yourself up at the House this very evening—if you don't go missing another meal there, that is.

b. ***all that***: all that sort of thing; that and everything of the kind. ***and all that***, and so forth, *et cetera* (see all A. 8 c); freq. implying a diffident or dismissive attitude on the part of the speaker; ***and all that jazz***: see jazz *sb.* 3 b; so, in same sense, ***and that*** (now chiefly in substandard speech or representations of it). ***not so . . as all that***: not so . . as that amounts to; not quite so . . as that. ***for all that***: see for 23 a. ***like that***, of that kind. or in that manner: see like *a.* 1 ¶, *adv.* 1.

c **1440** *Jacob's Well* 76 3itt for all þat, manye of þe iewys hadden gret indignacyoun of hem. **1638** Junius *Paint. Ancients* 36 It is for all that a greater matter to expresse in Achilles his picture the very same Art. **1702** *Mouse grown a Rat* 3 My mighty Bulk does even elevate and surprize, and all that. **1719** De Foe *Crusoe* (1840) II. vi. 150 To talk of my repenting, alas! 'tis past all that with me . . It is too late. **1742** Richardson *Pamela* III. 127 If People will set up for Virtue, and all that, let 'em be uniformly virtuous. **1821** Clare *Vill. Minstr.* II. 89 Full of chat, In passing harmless jokes 'bout beaus and that. **1848** Thackeray *Van. Fair* lx, Dob reads Latin like English, and French and that. **1884** Ruskin *Let. to F. Randal* Wks. 1907 XXX. Introd. 65 What do you think I would give to be your age, and able to draw like that! **1925** E. P. Oppenheim *Wrath to Come* ii. xvi. 271 'Glad to see you and all that, Slattery,' he said. **1929** R. Graves (*title*) Good bye to all that. **1930** Sellar & Yeatman (*title*) 1066 and all that. **1934** J. Hilton *Good-Bye, Mr. Chips* xi. 80 We don't like the fellow a great deal. Very clever and all that, but a bit *too* clever. **1965** *Listener* 2 Dec. 914/1 Having a fag and talking about sex and that just like she was, you know, ordinary. **1968** *Ibid.* 20 June 801/2 Boy: What do you do then? Girl: Well, you know, typing and filing and that. **1971** D. Potter *Brit. Eliz. Stamps* iii. 43 The Battle of Hastings, 1066 and all that, was given special treatment. **1974** *Economist* 21 Dec. 26/3 Chairman Mao has formally ordered his revolutionary genie back into the bottle . . . It sounds like goodbye to all that. **1977** *Listener* 19 May 644/1 They wait outside the pubs for them, and that.

c. ***at that*** (orig *U.S.*, *colloq.* or *slang*): estimated at that rate, at that standard, even in that capacity, in respect of that; too; 'into the bargain': 'a cant phrase . . used to define more nearly or intensify something already said' (Bartlett).

Prob. extended from *dear at that, cheap at that* (*price*).

1830 *Massachusetts Spy* 28 July 2/3 The march was now hurried on, yet slow at that, for I . . could not walk fast. **1855** *Blackw. Mag.* Sept. 324/2 'Now then, mister', turning to the man at the bar, 'drinks round, and cobblers at that'. **1883** Stevenson *Silverado Sq.* 167 Yet water it was, and sea-water at that. **1884** F. M. Crawford *Rom. Singer* I. 226 A shoemaker, and a poor one at that. **1897** *Trans. Amer. Pediatric Soc.* IX. 73 The infant was under-fed, and did not receive the correct food at that.

d. ***that's what***: used to add emphasis to a preceding statement: = 'and that is the truth'; ***that's that***: indicating that a discussion is closed, a matter settled, a job finished, etc.; similarly ***that was that***; ***that's so***: that is as you say; that statement is correct; also interrog., (***is***) ***that so?*** ***that's right***: see right *a.* 7 e; ***that's it*** = ***that's that*** above. All *colloq.*

1790 F. Grose *Provincial Gloss.* Suppl., *That's what*, just so; you are right. North. **1813** E. S. Barrett *Heroine* I. ix. 95 Not a step shall she stir in our cloathes . . . So that's that. **1857** *Knickerbocker* Jan. 86 The new and popular phrase of '*That's so*', which is working its way into common parlance. **1872** S. Butler *Erewhon* vi. 45 'So that's that,' said I to myself, as I watched them scampering. **1891** M. E. Ryan *Pagan of Alleghanies* vi. 93 'That so?' she said. **1914** *Sat. Even. Post* 4 Apr. 10/2 He's a valyable road-kid, that's what, and he ain't for sale. **1924** P. Marks *Plastic Age* 24 'Well,' he exclaimed, 'that's that. At last I know where I'm going.' **1930** *Times* 26 Mar. 7/2 Martin-Smith and Bond . . raced away with 4's, 5's, and 2's; so that was that. **1937** R. Macaulay *I would be Private* ii. v. 196 I'll not be putting up with it. And, that's that. **1967** *Listener* 14 Sept. 326/1, Well, that's it. I don't want to know. **1973** *Ibid.* 15 Nov. 662/3 When I get to bed I absolutely hit the pillow and that's it, I don't know anything until the next morning. **1974** A. Fowles *Pastime* ii. 14 When she'd gone after the job . . and got it, he'd sort of thought that was that and he wouldn't be seeing any more of her. **1976** J. Lee *Ninth Man* i. 79 Ulysses S. Grant . . was a war hero, that's what. **1978** B. Parvin *Deadly Dyke* (1979) v. 25 Alright . . that's it Sergeant. Now, where's Alan Tucker's place?

e. ***that is*** or ***was***: added to give emphasis to a statement beginning with those words or the equivalent. *colloq.*

1911 C. E. W. Bean '*Dreadnought' of Darling* ix. 78 That's exac'ly how it used to be. It's all right, that is. **1911** A. Bennett *Card* xi. 278 Well, that was a bit of a lark, that was. **1963** *B.B.C. Handbk.* 1964 25 The political world of . . 'Panorama', or the eventful world of 'That Was the Week That Was'. **1977** *Film & Television Technician* Apr. 4/2 That was the boom that was—and is. **1977** N. Marsh *Last Ditch* ii. 37 He . . suddenly ran off down the street. 'That's Master Ferrant, that was,' said Ricky.

** *As antecedent pronoun.*

(= F. *celui*, Ger. *der, derjenige*.)

6. As antecedent to a relative (pron. or adv.) expressed or understood.

Here, and in 7 and 8 usually (as in II. 3) definitive rather than demonstrative, the relative clause (or dependent phrase) serving to complete the definition.

a. Of a thing, in general sense: ***that that, that which*** = the thing which, what; so ***that whereby, wherein, wherewith, whence***, etc.

Sometimes following the relative clause, which then begins with *what*: *that* being in this case now pleonastic and emphatic.

[*a* **900** tr. *Bæda's Hist.* iii. vii. [ix.] (1890) 178 Hwelc þæs cyninges ȝeleafa & modes wilsumnis in God wære, þæt æfter his deaðe . . wæs ȝecyðed.] **13..** *E.E. Allit. P.* A. 535 Wyrkez and dotz þat at ȝe moun. *c* **1375** *Sc. Leg. Saints* xvi. (*Magdalena*) 605 For-þi be sikker in þat, . . þat scho þe taucht. **1399** *Rolls of Parlt.* III. 452/1 Havyng consideration to that that was prayed by the comon, that that that was evell . . shuld be . . amended in this Parlement. *c* **1400** tr. *Secreta Secret., Gov. Lordsh.* 48 þat þat semys to ȝow yn þys matere. **1526** Tindale *1 Cor.* xi. 23 That which I gave vnto you I receaved off the lorde. **1545** Raynold *Byrth Mankynde* 127 Though the chylde reiecte and vomyte vp agayne that the whiche it receaueth. **1597** Shaks. *2 Hen. IV*, iii. ii. 226 Hah . . that thou hadst seene that, that this Knight and I haue seene. **1650** Gentilis *Considerations* 233 Coriolanus, who could not attain to that as he wanted, should have forsaken that which he had received. **1674** Grew *Anat. Trunks* ii. ii. §3 What the Mouth is, to an Animal; that the Root is to a Plant. **1875** F. Hall in *Lippincott's Mag.* XV. 341/1 There was that about the place which filled me with a sense of utter dreariness.

b. Referring to a preceding sb., and equivalent to *the* with the sb.: e.g. in first quot., *that which* = 'the bread which'.

1634 Holland *Pliny* II. 141 The Sitanian bread, *i.* that which is made of three months corn. **1693** tr. *Blancard's Phys. Dict.* (ed. 2), *Rimula Laryngis*, that which is covered by the Cartilage of the Epiglottis. **1825** Scott *Betrothed* xv, Breaking into your apartment, [he] transported you to that where I myself received you from his arms. **1825** J. Nicholson *Operat. Mechanic* 68 The proportion . . between the load at the maximum and that by which the wheel is stopped. **1859** Ruskin *Two Paths* ii. §54 Fine Art is that in which the hand, the head, and the heart . . go together.

c. Of a person. Now only as in 1 b. In quot. 1542 *that which* = 'he who' or 'one that'.

1542 Udall *Erasm. Apoph.* 35 He . . taunted Plato, as y^t whiche in rebukyng hym did committe the veraye selfe same faulte. **1591** Shaks. *Two Gent.* iv. ii. 87 Who is that that spake? *Mod.* That was our member who spoke first at the meeting.

7. With ellipsis of a following relative (subj. or obj. of the relative clause): = that person or thing (*sc.* 'that' or 'which'). Now only where *that* is definitely demonstrative or emphatic, as in 1.

In earlier use the antecedent pronoun was omitted: see that *rel. pron.* 3. From the 16th c. onwards there are examples in which it is difficult to say whether the single *that* is the antecedent or the relative. Wherever it is emphatic it may be considered the demonstrative. Cf. also that *rel. pron.* 3 and 10.

[**1523** Ld. Berners *Froiss.* I. 295 For that is myne is yours.] **1598** Shaks. *Merry W.* iii. iii. 212 May be the knaue bragg'd of that he could not compasse. **1601** —— *Twel. N.* v. i. 153 Be that thou knowest thou art, and then thou art As great as that thou fear'st. **1601** —— *Jul. C.* i. ii. 314 Thy Honorable Mettle may be wrought From that it is dispos'd.

1850 NEALE *Med. Hymns* 20 Here vouchsafe to all Thy servants That they supplicate to gain. **1852** M. ARNOLD *Tristram & Iseult* i. 7 Who is that stands by the dying fire? **1883** WHITTIER *Our Country* 12 The best is that we have to-day. **1894** H. GARDENER *Unoff. Patriot* 49 She was not of his fold! It was *that* she thought of.

8. Followed by defining words (*of* or other prep. with a sb., or a pple. or other vbl. adj.) which serve to qualify or particularize *that* in the manner of a relative clause.

a. Referring to something just mentioned, and equivalent to *the* with the sb., or *the one*. (Cf. 6 b.)

c **1400** MAUNDEV. ii. (1839) 13 ȝif alle it be so, that men seyn, that this croune is of thornes... I haue seen.. many times that of Paris and that of Costantynoble:.. thei were bothe.. made of russches of the see. **1602** CAREW *Cornwall* 54 b, So doth their Pearch exceed that of other Countries. **1707** E. CHAMBERLAYNE *Pres. St. Eng.* III. xi. (ed. 22) 387 That at Radcliff was founded by Nicholas Gibson. **1753** CHAMBERS *Cycl. Supp.* s.v. *Rubrica*, The best in England is that from several parts of Derbyshire. **1802** MAR. EDGEWORTH *Moral T.* xii, Turning from the history of meanness to that of enthusiasm. **1825** T. HOOK *Sayings* Ser. II. *Sutherl.* I. 92 The post arrived, and brought letters... That from his sister was full of tender solicitude. *Mod.* Which house? That with a verandah. That formerly occupied by Mr. A.

b. In general sense = the thing that is.., what is... (Cf. 6 a.)

1607 C. NEWPORTE in *3rd Rep. Hist. MSS. Comm.* 54/1 Not having any man to put in trust of the ship and that in her. **1844** BROWNING *Laboratory* iv, That in the mortar—you call it a gum? **1867** MORRIS *Jason* VI. 325 Careful of that stored up within our hold.

†**c.** Referring to a statement or saying cited immediately after: usually in *that of* (the author).

1662 STILLINGFL. *Orig. Sacr.* I. v. §2 The Ægyptians are supposed to have been best skilled as to the form of the year, according to that of Macrobius, *Anni certus modus apud solos semper Ægyptios fuit*. **1671** H. M. tr. *Erasm. Colloq.* 309 Perhaps the largess may be the greater, according to that, 'The booty which is sought for by many hands is quickly acquired'. **1679** T. PULLER *Moder. Ch. Eng.* (1843) 147 Alleging that of St. Bernard; 'Such a number of festivities is fitter for citizens, than for exiles and pilgrims'.

II. Demonstrative Adjective. Pl. as in I.

1. a. The simple demonstrative used (as adjective in concord with a sb.), to indicate a thing or person either as being actually pointed out or present, or as having just been mentioned and being thus mentally pointed out. (Now distinguished from the definite article THE as being *demonstrative*, i.e. pointing out, and not merely *definitive*, i.e. distinguishing or singling out.)

The use before a possessive, as in quot. 1551, is *obs.* or *arch.*, the periphrasis with *of* (see OF 44) being now substituted for the possessive.

In *Sc.* also referring to something mentioned immediately after, where mod.Eng. uses *this*. Cf. I. 1 c, and THIS B. II. 1 b.

c **1200** ORMIN 2490 Þe Laferrd haffde litell rum Inn all þatt miccle riche. *c* **1250** [see A. 2]. **1297** R. GLOUC. (Rolls) 205 Ich wille telle þat cas. *c* **1350** *Will. Palerne* 671 He wend to haue lauȝt þat ladi loueli in armes. *c* **1440** *Alphabet of Tales* 63 Joseph.. said he sulde com agayn þat day viij dayes. **1470–85** MALORY *Arthur* II. iii. 79 That gentilwoman was causar of my faders deth. **1551** ROBINSON tr. *More's Utop.* Ep. to W. Cecylle (1895) 16 Though no commoditie of that my labour.. should arise. **1661** WALTON *Angler* xix. (ed. 3) 238 [This fish] was almost a yard broad, and twice that length. **1746** P. FRANCIS tr. *Horace, Ep.* II. ii. 16 My stock is little, but that stock my own. **1794** MRS. RADCLIFFE *Myst. Udolpho* xxxiii, She hardly dared to suffer her thoughts to glance that way. **1821** BYRON *Juan* III. lxxxvi. xii, The tyrant of the Chersonese Was freedom's best and bravest friend; That tyrant was Miltiades! **1825** T. HOOK *Sayings* Ser. II. *Man of Many Fr.* I. 189 Sophy, put down that knife—Maria, that child will cut her fingers off. **1861** M. PATTISON *Ess.* (1889) I. 47 The gates were closed at nine o'clock, and on no pretext opened after that hour. **1897** *Pall Mall Mag.* Feb. 188 The wife of the that time Governor.

b. Indicating a person or thing assumed to be known, or to be known to be such as is stated. Often (esp. before a person's name: cf. L. *iste*) implying censure, dislike, or scorn; but sometimes commendation or admiration. Freq. standing before a noun or noun-phrase in apposition with another. Also *that one*, used disparagingly of a woman.

a **1300** *Cursor M.* 11815 Þis herods.. þat caitif vn-meth and vn-meke. *a* **1400** *Stac. Rome* 405 Pope pelagius, þat holy mon. *c* **1410** LOVE *Bonavent. Mirr.* (1909) 50 The aungeles songen that ioyful songe *Gloria in excelsis*. **1526** TINDALE *2 Tim.* i. 12 He is able to kepe that which I have committed to his kepynge agaynst that daye. **1563** *Homilies* II. *Gluttony* (1859) 301 Holofernes.. had his head stricken from his shoulders by that seely woman Judith. **1591** SPENSER *Tears of Muses* 401 Thy gay Sonne, that winged God of Loue. **1611** SHAKS. *Cymb.* III. iv. 15 That Drug-damn'd Italy. **1646** R. BAILLIE *Lett.* (1841) II. 349 Will that fool Johnstone never take any course for your books? **1713** STEELE *Guard.* No. 1 ¶1 Mr. Airs, that excellent penman. **1800** WORDSW. *Andrew Jones* 1, I hate that Andrew Jones; he'll breed His children up to waste and pillage. **1848** THACKERAY *Vanity Fair* liv. 486 You don't know how fond I was of that one... Damme, I followed her like a footman. **1865** G. MACDONALD *A. Forbes* 51 He's a dour crater, that Murdoch Malison. **1866** G. MEREDITH *Vittoria* xxviii, 'Ah! in that England of yours, women marry for wealth'. **1922** F. H. BURNETT *Head of House of Coombe* vii. 75 That one in the drawing-room isn't going to interfere with the Nursery. Not her! **1980** J. DRUMMOND *Such a Nice Family* v. 22, I tell you, it's her!.. I wouldn't forget that one, not if I lived to be a thousand.

c. Used with a plural sb. or numeral, instead of *those*: now only with plurals treated as singulars (e.g. *means, pains*) or taken in a collective sense.

In some Sc. dialects used before plural sbs. generally.

c **1330** *Amis & Amil.* 2492 And in on graue thei were leyde, That hende knyghtes both two. *c* **1420** *Chron. Vilod.* 3605 He come þere þat ladyes to, And tolde hem alle. **1545** RAYNOLD *Byrth Mankynde* Hh ij, From that vaynes that be not yet affixed vnto the chorion. *Ibid.* 72 Also to wasshe that partes in water. **1575** *Reg. Privy Council Scot.* II. 473 The present troublis quhairwith that cuntreis ar inquietit. **1654–66** EARL ORRERY *Parthen.* (1676) 204, I will spare thee that pains. **1710** SWIFT *Examiner* No. 16 ¶7 That ill manners.. I have been often guilty of. **1768** GOLDSM. *Good-n. Man* I, There's that ten guineas you were sending to the poor gentleman. **1861** TROLLOPE *Framley P.* I. xiii. 252 As to that five thousand pounds. **1865** MISS BRADDON *Only a Clod* xxiv, During that rainy six weeks. **1868** G. MACDONALD *R. Falconer* I. xx, Maybe ye wad like to luik at that anes.

d. *that once*, that one time: see ONCE 9 c.

e. = 'The same' (*obs. rare*). *that same*, † *that self*: see SAME A. 5, B. 2, 4, SELF B. 1, 2.

1579 LYLY *Euphues* (Arb.) 190 The Rose that is eaten with the Canker is not gathered bicause it groweth on that stalke yat the sweet doth, neither was Helen made a Starre bicause shee came of that Egge with Castor.

2. a. In opposition to *this*: properly denoting the more distant of two things, but often vaguely indicating one thing as distinguished from another. Cf. I. 3 above.

13.. [see THIS B. I. 3]. **1551-** [see THIS B. II. 2].

b. Strengthened by *there* (also abbrev. *'ere, 'air*) immediately following: see THERE B. 3 c. Cf. *this here* (HERE *adv.* 1 d). *dial.* and *vulgar*.

3. a. In concord with a sb. which is the antecedent to a relative (expressed or understood). Cf. I. 6, 7.

Usually definitive rather than demonstrative, serving for introduction or anticipation of the relative clause, which completes the description; thus often interchangeable with *the* (cf. THE *a.* 14), but usually more emphatic. (Similarly with a noun further defined by a pple., as in quot. 1813[1].)

c **1470** ASHBY *Dicta Philos.* 701 That kyng that maketh his Region To be obedient to his iuste lawe. *c* **1500** *Melusine* 24 Erle Emerye and Raymondin.. stode.. on that syde as them semyd that the stryf was. **1532** MORE *Confut. Tindale* Wks. 450/2 A manne may saye 'the man that we spake of was here', or 'that man that we spake of was here'. **1637** HEYLIN *Brief Answ.* 75 It was ordeined, that that mans tongue should be cut out which did speake any slanderous.. words. **1647–8** COTTERELL *Davila's Hist. Fr.* (1678) 21 Brought.. to that issue as was intended. **1658** DRYDEN *Cromwell* xiii, Like that bold Greek who did the East subdue. **1690** LOCKE *Govt.* I. iv. §42 By withholding that relief God requires him to afford. **1779** *Mirror* No. 50 ¶2 That listlessness and languor which attend a state of total inaction. **1813** EUSTACE *Italy* (1815) III. xi. 394 On that peninsulated rock called La Spilla, hanging over yonder deep cavern. **1813** SIR H. DAVY *Agric. Chem.* iii. (1814) 56 The root is that part of the vegetable which least impresses the eye.

b. In advb. phrases of time or place, with following relative clause (with relative usually omitted); e.g. † *by that time* (*that*).. = by the time that.. (*obs.*). (In quot. 1573 with advb. clause.) Now *rare* (replaced by *the*), unless emphatic.

c **1420** *Chron. Vilod.* 3160 Fulle seke he was By þat tyme þat he þedur þo come. **1523** LD. BERNERS *Froiss.* I. 240 By that tyme it was day, they came to the mountayne. **1573** L. LLOYD *Marrow of Hist.* (1653) 93 That night before they should sail in the morning, appeared unto Simonides the self-same man. **1598** GRENEWEY *Tacitus' Ann.* I. ii. (1622) 21 [They] beset the wood, that way the army should returne. **1656** S. HOLLAND *Zara* (1719) 65 By that time they were half over Styx, they espyed an aged Person. **1760** *Impostors Detected* IV. iii. II. 179 He.. got me a wife by that time I had attained my fifteenth year. **1805** EMILY CLARK *Banks of Douro* I. 48 Enraptured at that time the event took place.

4. Indicating quality or amount: Of that kind or degree; such, so great. Const. *that* (conj.), *as* (with finite vb. or inf.), inf. (without *as*), or rel. pron. (also with ellipsis of the conj. or rel.); rarely without correlative. Now chiefly *arch.* (or *dial.*).

(Cf. THAT *dem. adv.*)

a **1450** *Knt. de la Tour* (1906) 131 She.. wepte for her synnes, þat was the loue of God and the drede that she had for her misleuinge. **1530** TINDALE *Prol. Deut.*, When I am brought in to that extremite that I must ether suffre or forsake god. **1547** BOORDE *Introd. Knowl.* iii. (1870) 133 Saynt Partryckes purgatory.. is not of that effycacyte as is spoken of. **1602** SHAKS. *Ham.* I. v. 48 From me, whose loue was of that dignity, That it went hand in hand, euen with the Vow I made to her in marriage. **1648** MILTON *Tenure Kings* (1650) 57 With that cunning and dexterity as is almost imperceavable. **1678** WALTON *Life Sanderson* 53 An Error of that Magnitude, that I cannot but wonder. **1734** DUCHESS QUEENSBERRY in *Lett. C'tess Suffolk* (1824) II. 94 This enlivened us to that degree that we were mighty good company. **1821** SHELLEY in Lady S. *Mem.* (1859) 155, I hope that I have treated the question with that temper and spirit as to silence cavil. **1848** DICKENS *Dombey* xlvii, He.. struck her.. with that heaviness, that she tottered on the marble floor. **1865** L. OLIPHANT *Piccadilly* (1870) 241 He blushed to that degree that I felt quite shy.

†**5.** As neuter sing. of the definite article: see THE A. 1 c. *Obs.* (exc. in *that ilk*: see ILK *a.*[1]). *that one, that other* = the one, the other: see ONE 18, OTHER B. 2; also TONE, TOTHER. *Obs.*

c **893** K. ÆLFRED *Orosius* I. i. §1 Twegen dælas: Asia, and þæt oþer Europe. **1297** R. GLOUC. (Rolls) 7017 Þat þe on broþer.. in nede helpeþ þere þat oþer. *c* **1400** *Gamelyn* 305 [He] toke him by þat on arme & threw him in a welle. **1470–85** MALORY *Arthur* X. ix. 427 Two bretheren, that one hyght Aleyn, and the other hyghte Tryan. **1509** *Sel. Cas. Crt. Star Chamber* (Selden) 194 Half of that brigge appertaigneth to the said abbot and that other half to the said Town. **1576** GASCOIGNE *Steel Gl.* (Arb.) 68 That one eye winks,.. That other pries and peekes.

III. Demonstrative Adverb. **a.** [Closely related to the adjective use in II. 4.]

To that extent or degree; so much, so. (Qualifying an adj., adv., or ppl., †rarely a vb.) Now *dial.* and *Sc.*; also *colloq.* with a negative: ***not*** (***all***) ***that***, not very.

c **1450** *St. Cuthbert* (Surtees) 6279 His sekenes þat encrest, He gert beere him.. Aboute þe contre on a bere. **1616** in J. Russell *Haigs* vii. (1881) 160 If I had been that unhappy as to have such a foolish thing. *a* **1670** HACKET *Abp. Williams* II. (1693) 67 This was carried with that little noise that.. the.. Bishop was not awaked. **1803** BOSWELL *Change Edin.* 5 Gowd's no that scanty. **1852** DICKENS *Bleak Ho.* xxiv, I was on my guard for a blow, he was that passionate. **1870** —— *E. Drood* ii. **1884** MRS. RIDDELL *Berna Boyle* vii, The rooms are that small you might reach a book off the opposite wall. **1888** 'R. BOLDREWOOD' *Robbery under Arms* xxi, He was that weak as he could hardly walk. **1902** O. WISTER *Virginian* xxxv, You were that cool! *a* **1912** *Mod. Sc.* He's grown that big ye wad hardly ken him. He was that cunning! **1932** R. LEHMANN *Invit. Waltz* I. iii. 39 This weather's that treacherous, you never know. **1937** D. L. SAYERS *Busman's Honeymoon* iv. 85, I was that ashamed I didden know w'ere to look. **1962** *Harper's Bazaar* Aug. 60/3 The Spanish gypsies.. hired to do the sweeping were not all that handy with a broom. **1969** J. LEASOR *They don't make Them like That any More* i. 7, I.. looked around the stock. It wasn't all that brilliant, I must admit. **1977** *Spare Rib* May 16/1 It's not that easy in a place like Sheffield. **1980** S. BRETT *Dead Side of Mike* xvii. 173 Charles Paris found it difficult to get that excited. **1981** *Listener* 22 Oct. 462/1 The forgiveness of sin isn't just an easygoing matter, as if to say: 'Well, you sinned, but it doesn't matter all that much—I forgive you.'

b. With an adv. or adj. of quantity, e.g. *that far* (= as far as that), *that much, that high*: more definite than *so*, as indicating the precise amount.

1634 RUTHERFORD *Lett.* (1862) I. 126, I repose that much in His rich grace that He will be loath to change upon me. **1805** JEFFERSON *Writ.* (1830) IV. 39 His family, which he had sent that far in the course of the day. **1856** MRS. STOWE *Dred* i. I. 5, I never liked anything that long [= six weeks]. **1870** MISS BRIDGMAN *Rob. Lynne* II. xi. 224, 'I.. recollect you that high'—holding her hand about six inches off the table.

that (ðət), *relative pron.* Forms: see below. [An unstressed and phonetically weakened form of THAT *dem. pron.*, used to subordinate one predication to another.

The Common Indo-Eur. had no relative pronoun, which has been developed separately in the different linguistic families. In Latin it was evolved out of the interrogative, in Teutonic chiefly out of the demonstrative. But even within the Teutonic languages the relative is differently formed (see Wright *Gothic Grammar* §270, *Old Eng. Grammar* §468). In mod. English it is expressed by *thăt*, from the demonstrative pron., and by *who* (*whom*), *which*, *what* (after L. *qui, quæ, quod*, F. *qui, que, quel*) from the interrogative pronouns. In northern dialect, ME. and mod., it is commonly expressed by AT, 'AT, rel. pron. In OE. it was expressed (1) by the simple demonstrative *se, séo, þæt*; (2) by the particle *þe*; (3) by *þe* preceded by a personal pronoun or the demonstrative. For *þe*, see THE *conjunctive particle*. The use of the demonstrative as a relative appears to have come about simply by the subordination of the second of two originally consecutive sentences to the first; thus, 'he came to a river; thát (or this) was broad and deep', whence 'he came to a river thăt was broad and deep'. In OE. it is sometimes impossible to determine whether the pronoun of the second clause is still demonstrative or has become relative. Thus the words in the OE. version of *Bæda's History*, I. xii. (1890) 52 'Hi wæron Wihtgylses suna . þæs fæder wæs Witta haten . þæs fæder wæs Wihta haten . and þæs Wihta fæder wæs Woden nemned', might be read either as short consecutive sentences, 'They were sons of Wihtgyls; *his* father [lit. *that's* father] was called Witta; *his* father was called Wihta; and this Wihta's father was named Woden'; or 'They were sons of Wihtgyls *whose* father was called Witta, *whose* father was called Wihta, and *whose* (Wihta's) father was named Woden'. Bæda's Latin has *cujus* in all three places, so that the translator apparently used *þæs* as a relative. See also Wülfing *Syntax Alfreds des Grossen* I. §275. Now, and for a long time past, the relative *that* has been stressless, and consequently with obscure vowel; but this unstressing and obscuration came gradually, and was never represented in writing, so that in the written forms there is nothing to distinguish the relative from the demonstrative.]

A. Examples of early inflexional forms.

(The inflexional forms were, to begin with, those of the dem. pron. and definite article (see prec. and THE); but, as relative, *that* is now invariable for gender, case, and number.)

c **825** *Vesp. Psalter* ix. 12 Singað dryhtne se [L. *qui*] eardað in Sion. *Ibid.* 28 Ðes [*cujus*] muð awerȝednisse & bitternisse ful is. *Ibid.* cxxxii. 3 Swe swe deaw.. se astiȝeð in munt Sion. *c* **825** *Vesp. Hymns* xiii. 4 ȝehiowadas mon ðæm [*cui*] ðinre onlicnisse ondwliotan saldes ȝelicne. *c* **893** K. ÆLFRED *Oros.* I. i. §1 Oceanus.., þone man garsecg hateð. *Ibid.* §11 Rin þa ea, seo wilð of þæm beorȝe þe mon Alpis hætt. *Ibid.*, Donua þa ea, þære æwielme is neah Rines ofre. *Ibid.* II. vii. §2 An burȝ in Affrica sio [*quæ*] wæs neh þæm sæ. *a* **900** tr. *Bæda's Hist.* I. xii. [xv.] (1890) 52 Wihta.. þæs.. fæder wæs Woden nemned. *c* **950** *Lindisf. Gosp.* Matt. xxiv. 15 Unfeȝernis slitnese ðiu [*Rushw.* þe] ȝecueden wæs from ðæm witgo. *c* **1100** *O.E. Chron.* an. 1093, Anselme.. se wæs ær abbod on Bæc.

B. Signification.

The general relative pronoun, referring to any antecedent, and used without inflexion irrespective of gender, number, and case.

I. 1. a. Introducing a clause defining or restricting the antecedent, and thus completing its sense. (The ordinary use: referring to persons or things.)

Sometimes replaceable by *who* (of persons) or *which* (of things), but properly only in cases where no ambiguity results: cf. 2, and see WHO, WHICH, *rel.* (For ellipsis of *that*, see 10.)

c **825** *Vesp. Psalter* vii. 7 In bebode ðæt ðu bibude. **858** *Charter* in *O.E. Texts* 438 Đes landes boec . . ðet eðelbearht cyning wullafe sealde. *c* **888** K. ÆLFRED *Boeth.* v. §1 Ne sece ic no her þa bec ac þæt ðæt þa bec forstent. *c* **1000** *Ags. Ps.* (Th.) lxxxviii. 41 [lxxxix. 48] Hwylc manna is þæt his aȝene . . sawle ȝenerіȝe? *c* **1175** *Lamb. Hom.* 3 God [? goð] in þane castel þet is onȝein eou. *Ibid.* 79 Þes Mon þhet alihte from ierusalem in to ierico. *a* **1225** *Ancr. R.* 162 Þeo þet duden mid God al þet heo euer wolden *a* **1300** *Cursor M.* 22118 All þat he cristen finds þare. **1340** *Ayenb.* 39 Þe ualse yulemde þet vlyeþ. *c* **1374** CHAUCER *Boeth.* IV. pr. vii. 113 (Camb. MS.) Þou þat art put in the encres or in the heyhte of vertu. **1377** LANGL. *P. Pl.* B. x. 38 Þo þat feynen hem folis. **1382** WYCLIF *Matt.* iv. 16 The peple that dwelte in derknessis say grete liȝt. **1456** SIR G. HAYE *Law Arms* (S.T.S.) 244 It that was wont to be callit law. *c* **1460** FORTESCUE *Abs. & Lim. Mon.* ix. (1885) 130 The kyng of Scottis þat last dyed. **1500–20** DUNBAR *Poems* xx. 8 He rewlis weill, that weill him self can gyd. **1526** TINDALE *John* iv. 26, I thatt spake vnto the, am he. **1531** *Test. Ebor.* (Surtees) VI. 24 A distres that I toke of hyr. **1596** DANETT tr. *Comines* (1614) 173 But this was not it that grieued them. **1611** BIBLE *Ps.* lxv. 2 O thou that hearest prayer. **1712** ADDISON *Spect.* No. 512 ⁋6 A Tree that grew near an old Wall. **1798** COLERIDGE *Anc. Mar.* II. v, We were the first that ever burst Into that silent sea. **1865** SWINBURNE *Atalanta* 76 How shall I say, son, That am no sister? **1875** JOWETT *Plato* (ed. 2) I. 342 This is about all that he has to say. **1886** C. E. PASCOE *Lond. of To-day* xxx. (ed. 3) 269 The Westminster Hall that we now see . . is the building of Richard II's time.

b. As obj. of a preposition, which in this case stands at the end of the relative clause (in OE. and ME. sometimes immediately before the verb): e.g. *the cup that I shall drink of* = the cup of which I shall drink; ME. *these that I have of told* = these of which I have told.

(When *whom* or *which* is substituted for *that*, the prep. precedes the relative.)

c **1200** ORMIN 462 Þiss gode prest, þatt we nu mælenn offe, Wass . . ȝehatenn Zacaryas. *a* **1300** *Seven Sins* 44 in *E.E.P.* (1862) 19 Þe deuil is his executur of is gold and is tresure þat he so moch trist to. *c* **1400** MAUNDEV. (1839) ii. 10 The naylles that crist was naylled with on the cros. *c* **1430** *Hymns Virg.* 37/69 Theise .iij. þat y haue of toold. **1473** *Coventry Leet-Bk.* 383 The which letter . . is in kepyng in the Tour of Sent Marie hall in the same box þat the kynges generall pardon graunted to this Citee is Ine. **1526** TINDALE *Matt.* xx. 22 Are ye able to drynke off the cuppe that y shall drinke of, and to be baptised with the baptism that y shalbe baptised with? **1611** BIBLE *Judges* xx. 48 All the cities that they came to. **1678** BUNYAN *Pilgr.* I. 49 The dangers that Mistrust and Timorus were driven back by. **1818** SCOTT *Hrt. Midl.* xxix [xxx], The ship that somebody was sailing in. **1841** S. WARREN *Ten thousand a-Year* xiv, There's nothing . . that we need be afraid of. *Mod.* The play that you were talking about. The hole that the mouse ran into. The town that he came from.

c. ***that was***: added when a married woman is referred to by her maiden name; occas. also added following the name of a deceased person.

1785 A. SEWARD *Let.* 31 Dec. (1811) I. 97 Miss Jenny Harry that was, for she afterwards married. **1872** GEO. ELIOT *Middlemarch* IV. VIII. lxxiv. 201, I am not so sorry for Rosamond Vincy that was, as I am for her aunt. **1937** D. L. SAYERS *Busman's Honeymoon* 21 Her new ladyship, Miss Vane that was, went down to Oxford the day before. **1970** S. J. PERELMAN *Baby, it's Cold Inside* 178 You remember her, don't you—Luba Pneumatic that was? **1977** N. MARSH *Last Ditch* v. 135 A . . photograph displayed a truculent young woman. . . 'That's Dulce [*sic*],' said Sergeant Plank. 'That was,' he added.

2. Introducing a clause stating something additional about the antecedent (the sense of the principal clause being complete without the relative clause). Now only *poet.* or *rhet.*, the ordinary equivalents being *who* (obj. *whom*) of persons, and *which* of things.

But the relative clause is often merely descriptive, stating an attribute of the antecedent; or it may give the reason or a reason of the main statement, and thus be closely connected with it; the use in these cases approaches that in 1. There are thus many cases in which modern use allows either *that* or *who, which*, and in which poets prefer *that*. (*That* as in quot. *c* 1450 is now impossible.)

c **893** K. ÆLFRED *Oros.* I. i. §7 On Indea londe is xliiii þeoda buton þæm iȝlande Taprabane, þæt hæfð on him x byrȝ. *a* **900** tr. *Bæda's Hist.* I. i. (1890) 24 Breoton ist garsecges ealond, ðæt wæs iu ȝeara Albion haten. *c* **1000** *Ags. Gosp.* Matt. vi. 30 Æcyres weod, þæt ðe [*Rushw.* þæt] to dæȝ is & bið to morȝen on ofen asend. *a* **1240** *Ureisun* in *Lamb. Hom.* 185 Ha haueþ oþer wilneþ after cunfort on eorþe, þet is fikel and fals. *a* **1300** *Cursor M.* 9406 He wroght a felau of his ban Till Adam, þat was first allan [*v.r.* his an]. *c* **1320** *Cast. Love* 8–9 God ffader and Sone and Holigost, þat alle þing on eorþe sixt and wost, þat O God art and þrilli-hod. *c* **1386** CHAUCER *Prol.* 10 Smale foweles maken melodye, That slepen al the nyght with open eye. *c* **1450** *Godstow Reg.* 501 Yf hit happen the said priour and Covent . . to faile in the payment of þe seid yerely rente (that god for-bede). *c* **1489** CAXTON *Sonnes of Aymon* xxiv. 515 Reynaude, that sawe this harde batayll, shoved himselfe among the thickest. **1548–9** (Mar.) *Bk. Com. Prayer, Litany*, O God mercyfull father, that despysest not the sighinge of a contryte hearte. **1621** BP. MOUNTAGU *Diatribæ* 16 You are a merry man . . that tell me, your selfe, you are not within. **1678** *Gunpowder Treason* in *Select. Harl. Misc.* (1793) 252 Catesby . . thereupon engaged Sir Everard Digby, that promised to advance fifteen hundred pounds towards it; and Mr. Francis Tresham, that gave him assurance of two thousand pounds. **1824** LAMB *Let. to W. Marten* 19 July (in *Sotheby's Catal.* 5 June (1902) 66), Pity me that have been a Gentleman these four weeks and am reduced in one day to the state of a ready writer. **1843** MACAULAY *Lays Anc. Rome, Horatius*, False Sextus That wrought the deed of shame. **1885–94** R. BRIDGES *Eros & Psyche* May 4 Lazy mists, that still Climb'd on the shadowy roots of every hill.

3. As subj. or obj. of the rel. clause, with ellipsis of the antecedent.

a. Of things: *thăt* = (the thing) that, that which, what. Very common down to 16th c.; now *arch.* and *poetic*, *what* being the prose form.

In later use the single *that* may become emphatic, and is then demonstrative with ellipsis of the relative: see THAT *dem. pron.* 7.

c **888** K. ÆLFRED *Boeth.* xxvi. §1 Þonne ðu . . oððe hæfdest þæt ðu noldes oððe næfdest þæt ðu woldest. *c* **1175** *Lamb. Hom.* 5 Nu scule ȝe understonden þet hit bi-tacnet. *c* **1250** *Gen. & Ex.* 3066 Đat [h]ail ða bileaf sal al ben numen. *a* **1300** *Cursor M.* 3711 He ete and dranc þat was his will. *c* **1315** SHOREHAM vi. 11 Þou hast y-ryȝt þat was amys, Ywonne þat was y-lore. *c* **1400** *Laud Troy Bk.* 7877 Antenor did that In him was. **1477–9** *Rec. St. Mary at Hill* 91 Paid to hewe Clerk that he lackyd in his wagis. **1535** COVERDALE *Matt.* xx. 14 Take that thine is [WYCLIF that that is thine] and go thy waye. *a* **1568** ASCHAM *Scholem.* I. (Arb.) 49 Where they should neither see that was vncumlie nor heare that was vnhonest. **1600** SHAKS. *A.Y.L.* III. ii. 77, I earne that I eate: get that I weare. **1611** BIBLE *Job* xlii. 3 Therefore haue I vttered that I vnderstood not. **1887** MORRIS *Odyss.* XII. 301 In peace eat that ye have.

b. Of persons: *thăt* = (the person) that, he (or him) that, one that; *pl.* (persons) that, they (them), or those who. Now only after *there are* and the like: see THERE *adv.* 5 f.

c **1320** *Cast. Love* 1 Þat good þenkeþ good may do. ? *a* **1400** *Arthur* 1 Herkeneþ, þat loueþ honour. **1400** *26 Pol. Poems* i. 122 That taken with wrong, are goddis theues. **14..** *Why I can't be a Nun* 244 in *E.E.P.* (1862) 144 Dame chastyte . . sum her loved in hert fulle dere, And there weren that dyd not so. **1560** BIBLE (Genev.) *Prov.* xi. 24 There is that scatereth, and is more increased. *c* **1585** R. BROWNE *Answ. Cartwright* 79 There were of the princes that tooke his parte. **1605** SHAKS. *Lear* I. iv. 279 Woe [*sc.* to him] that too late repents. **1611** BIBLE *Exod.* iii. 14, I am that I am. *a* **1665** DIGBY *Priv. Mem.* (1827) 272 Of her ancestors there have been that have exalted and pulled down kings.

II. In various special or elliptical constructions, in some of which *that* passes into a relative or conjunctive adverb. (Cf. next word.)

4. After *same*: sometimes strictly the rel. pron. (1); sometimes with looser construction or ellipsis: = *as*: see SAME A. 1 a, and cf. AS B. 23.

c **1200**, etc. [see SAME A. 1 a]. *a* **1575** tr. *Pol. Verg. Eng. Hist.* (Camden No. 29) 181 William made the same awnswer that befor. **1600** SURFLET *Countrie Farme* I. xxx. 200 The mare-mule is subiect to the same diseases that the horse. **1664** H. MORE *Exp. 7 Epist.* viii. 124, I understand by φιλαδελφία the same that ἀγάπη, *universal Love.* **1690** W. WALKER *Idiomat. Anglo-Lat.* 387 They say Diana is the same that the Moon is. **1771** LUCKOMBE *Hist. Print.* 404 He grasps his left hand about the Foot end of the Page in the same posture that his right hand grasps the Head end. **1783** COLMAN *Prose on Sev. Occas., Notes Art Poetry* (1787) III. 97 Other criticks have taken the text . . in the same sense that I have here considered it. **1819** HAZLITT *Pol. Ess.* 421 If Mr. Malthus chooses to say, that men will always be governed by the same good mechanical motives that they are at present.

5. Preceded by a descriptive noun or adj., in a parenthetic exclamatory clause (e.g. *fool that he is*): = AS B. 25.

c **1374** CHAUCER *Troylus* III. 1516 (1565) Nece, how kan ye fare? Criseyde answerede, Neuere þe bet for yow, Fox þat ye ben. *c* **1440** *York Myst.* xxx. 26 Lo! sirs, my worthely wiffe, þat sche is! **1526** TINDALE *Rom.* vii. 24 O wretched man that I am. **1591** SHAKS. *Two Gent.* V. iv. 28 O miserable, vnhappy that I am. **1605** R. R. in *Sylvester's Wks.* (1880) I. 15/1 Foole that I was, I thought in younger times [etc.]. **1855** BROWNING *Popularity* 1 Stand still, true poet that you are! I know you. **1877** E. W. GOSSE *North. Stud., 4 Danish Poets* (1890) 227 A few months after Andersen—poor little forlorn adventurer that he was—left that city.

6. †**a.** = As B. 13. *Obs. rare*$^{-1}$.

c **1175** *Credo* in *Lamb. Hom.* 75 Alle ȝe kunnen leste, þet ich wene, ower credo.

b. In ***not that I know***, and similar expressions: = According to what, as far as. Cf. KNOW *v.* 18 c.

c **1460** *Towneley Myst.* xxi. 239 No word yit he spake That I wyst. **1530** PALSGR. 762/1, I never trespassed agaynst hym, that I wotte of. **1602** SHAKS. *Ham.* II. ii. 155 *Pol.* Hath there bene such a time . . That I haue possitiuely said, 'tis so, When it prou'd otherwise? *King.* Not that I know. **1776** *Trial of Nundocomar* 30/1, I was not at Mongheer; nor was he there, that I know of. **1819** SHELLEY *Cenci* I. iii, Can we do nothing? *Colon.* Nothing that I see. **1840** CARLYLE *Heroes* iv. (1872) 126 But Protestantism has not died yet, that I hear of! **1864** DASENT *Jest & Earnest* (1873) II. 343 He had never seen Hall that he knew before that day. **1886** SIR N. LINDLEY in *Law Rep. 31 Chanc. Div.* 367 An injunction to restrain such proceedings has never that I know of been granted since 1851. *Mod.* He is not here, that I can learn. No one knows anything about it, that I can find.

7. a. After the word *time*, or any sb. meaning a point or space of time: At, in, or on which; when.

Usually introducing a defining clause, as in 1: sometimes an additional statement, as in 2. For ellipsis of *that*, see 10.

Beowulf 2646 Nu is se dæȝ cumen þæt ure man-dryhten mæȝenes be-hofað. *a* **1000** *Cædmon's Gen.* 585 (Gr.) Wæs seo hwil þæs lang, þæt ic ȝeornlice gode þeȝnode. *c* **1000** ÆLFRIC *Num.* xiii. 21 Hit wæs ða se tima þæt winberian ripodon. **1303** R. BRUNNE *Handl. Synne* 862 Fro þe fryday þat he deyde, To tyme þat he ros. *c* **1386** CHAUCER *Reeve's T.* 189 Allas quod Iohn the day that I was born. **1470–85** MALORY *Arthur* VI. xvi. 209 Thyne houre is come that thou muste dye. **1525** LD. BERNERS *Froiss.* II. 53 In the meane tyme that our supper was a dressyng, this knight said to me [etc.]. **1600** SHAKS. *A.Y.L.* III. ii. 187, I was neuer so berim'd since Pythagoras time that I was an Irish Rat. **1611** BIBLE *Gen.* ii. 17 In the day that thou eatest thereof, thou shalt surely die. **1760–72** H. BROOKE *Fool of Qual.* (1809) IV. 31 You speak . . like a sage . . at an age that our young nobility scarcely begin to think. **1802** MAR. EDGEWORTH *Moral T.* xii, The night that he went to the play. **1879** GEO. ELIOT *Theo. Such* i. 10 One day that I had incautiously mentioned this interesting fact.

†**b.** = To the time that; till, until. *Obs.*

971 *Blickl. Hom.* 237 Nu þry daȝas to lafe syndon þæt hie þe willaþ acwellan. *c* **1175** *Lamb. Hom.* 33 Þah þu liuedest of adames frumðe þet come þes dei. *c* **1205** LAY. 229 Þis lond he hire lende þat come hir lifes ende. *c* **1320** *Cast. Love* 1412 From þe tyme þat he Adam wrouȝte, þat he vp-ros and vs for-bouȝ te.

†**c.** = From the time that; since. *Obs. rare*$^{-1}$.

c **1205** LAY. 26294 Hit is feole ȝere þat heore þrættes comen here.

8. Connecting two clauses loosely or anacoluthically, the relative or dependent clause being imperfect (the part omitted being suggested by the principal clause); giving the effect of the ordinary rel. pron. with ellipsis of a preposition, an infinitive, etc.: cf. 7. (Now considered slipshod.)

c **1425** WYNTOUN *Cron.* IV. xxv. 2380 Off þe nycht next gane beforn þat Iulyus was slayn on þe morn. *c* **1530** LD. BERNERS *Arth. Lyt. Bryt.* 494 Oftentimes people speketh of a thing that they knowe but lytle what the conclusyon shall be. **1596** SHAKS. *Merch. V.* II. vi. 9 Who riseth from a feast With that keene appetite that he sits downe? **1673** *Essex Papers* (Camden) I. 51 Who put this Citty into that disorder that I found it. **1779** *Mirror* No. 29 ⁋4 His fortune and his ancestry entitled him . . to appear in any shape that he pleased. **1875** DASENT *Vikings* I. 146 If you will only see things . . in the light that we see them.

9. *That* followed by a poss. pron. corresponding to the antecedent (e.g. *you that your, the man that his*, OE. *þe his*, THE particle 3 d) is an ancient mode of expressing the genitive of the relative = *whose*.

(The same idiom is used in many langs., e.g. Celtic, Semitic, etc.). Still common dialectally.

1456 *Sc. Acts Jas. II* (1814) II. 45/2 Item, it is ordanyt . . at ilk man þ[t] his gudis extendis to xx[tj] merckis be bodyn at þe lest w[t] . . a suerde and a buclare, a bow and a schaif of arrowis. **1470–85** MALORY *Arthur* VIII. xxxv. 327 There came a man that sire Tristram afore hand had slayne his broder. **1523** FITZHERB. *Husb.* §148 That man that thy horse hath eten his corne or grasse wyll be greued at the. **1602** *Ld. Cromwell* I. ii, Theres legions now of beggars . . That their originall did spring from Kings. [**1873** MURRAY *Dial. S. Scotl.* 196 When the Relative is used in the Possessive Case (*whose*) it is necessary to express it by . . *at* (*that*) and the *possessive pronoun* belonging to the antecedent; thus 'the man ăt hys weyfe's deid' . . 'the wumman ăt ye ken hyr sun'.]

¶ **10.** The relative is very frequently omitted by ellipsis, esp. in senses 1, 1 b (chiefly as obj. or pred., less freq. and now only in certain connexions as subj.); also in sense 7.

This (one of the commonest idioms in colloquial English, and largely found in the literary language) prob. began with the relative *þe*, THE. Cf. also THAT *conj.* 10.

c **1250** *Gen. & Ex.* 297 Adam ben king and eue quuen Of alle ðe ðinge in werlde ben. —— 751 Ilc ðing deieð ðor-inne is driuen. **13..** *Cursor M.* 4892 Yon er theues . . And theif es he þam hider send. *a* **1450** *Le Morte Arth.* 72, I drede we shall discouerid be, Off the loue is vs by-twene. **1578** TIMME *Caluine on Gen.* 164 When those things should follow are set before. **1592** SHAKS. *Rom. & Jul.* I. i. 212, I do loue a woman . . and shee's faire I loue. **1611** BIBLE *Gen.* iii. 5 In the day ye eate thereof, then your eyes shalbee opened. **1676** GLANVILL *Ess.* Pref. a 3 b, It shews a particular service Philosophy doth. **1690** LOCKE *Hum. Und.* II. xxi. §32 Life it self . . is a burden cannot be born under the lasting . . pressure of such an uneasiness. **1781** COWPER *Verses Alex. Selkirk* i, I am monarch of all I survey. **1850** TENNYSON *In Mem.* iv, What is it makes me beat so low? *Ibid.* v, To put in words the grief I feel. **1851** LONGF. *Golden Leg.* ii. 273 Who was it said Amen? **1855** BROWNING *Misconceptions* i, This is a spray the Bird clung to.

that (ðət), *conj.* Also 1 **þæt**, 2–3 **þet**, 2–6 **þat**. [Uses of THAT *dem.* or *rel. pron.* in which it becomes a mere relative or conjunctive particle: cf. THE *particle*. So in the other WGer. langs. Cf. Gr. ὅτι from neuter of rel. pron. ὅστις, L. *quod* from neuter of rel. *qui*, It. *che*, Sp., Pg., Fr. *que*.]

I. 1. a. Introducing a dependent substantive-clause, as subject, object, or other element of the principal clause, or as complement of a sb. or adj., or in apposition with a sb. therein.

The dependent clause as subject is most commonly placed after the verb and introduced by a preceding *it*, e.g. 'it is certain that he was there' = 'that he was there, is certain': see IT 4 b. As object, it usually follows, e.g. 'I have heard that he was there'. (For ellipsis of *that*, see 10.)

[This use of *that* is generally held to have arisen out of the dem. pron. pointing to the clause which it introduces. Cf. (1) He once lived here: we all know *thát*; (2) *That* (now *this*) we all know: he once lived here; (3) We all know *that* (or *this*): he once lived here; (4) We all know *thăt* he once lived here; (5) We all know he once lived here. In 1, 2, 3 *that* is a demonstrative pronoun in apposition to the statement 'he once lived here'; in 4 it has sunk into a conjunctive particle, and (like the relative pronoun) has become stressless; in 5 it has disappeared, and 'he once lived here' appears as the direct object of 'we know'. After *aware, certain, conscious, suspicious, assured, informed, persuaded*, etc., *of* or some other prep. seems understood before *that*: 'I am certain of that: he once lived here'. But 'I am certain that' may have arisen as another way of saying 'I know that'; and so of the other expressions.]

*c***888** K. ÆLFRED *Boeth.* v. §3 Ic wat þæt ælc wuht from Gode com. *a***900** CYNEWULF *Elene* 815 Nu ic wat þæt þu eart ʒecyðed and acenned allra cyninga þrym. *Ibid.* 1168 þæt is ʒedafenlic, þæt þu dryhtnes word on hyʒe healde. *c***1000** ÆLFRIC *Gen.* i. 4 God ʒeseah þa, þæt hit god wæs. *c***1175** *Lamb. Hom.* 111 þe sixte unþeau is..þet he for modleste ne mei his monnan don stere. *c***1205** LAY. 13 Hit com him on mode..þet he wolde of Engle þa æðelæn tellen. *c***1250** *O. Kent. Serm.* in *O.E. Misc.* 26 And herodes i-herde þet o king was i-bore. *a***1300** *K. Horn* (Camb. MS.) 272 And þe sonde seide þat sik lai þat maide. **1375** BARBOUR *Bruce* III. 481 Þen hapnyt at þat tyme..þat þe Erle of þe Leuenax was Amang þe hillis. *c***1380** WYCLIF *Sel. Wks.* III. 362 We ben certein þat Crist may not axe oþir obedience. *c***1386** CHAUCER *Prol.* 500 And this figure he added eek ther to, That if gold ruste, what shal Iren doo? *c***1440** *Generydes* 2902 What think ye best thanne..yt we shall doo? **1535** COVERDALE *Exod.* iii. 12 This shall be the token, yt I haue sent the. **1567** PAINTER *Pal. Pleas.* (1813) II. 160 That I remaine in fielde it is to me greate fame. **1611** BIBLE *Prov.* xix. 2 That the soule be without knowledge, it is not good. **1726** G. ROBERTS *Four Years' Voy.* 135 Their Opinion, that it was not real, but imaginary Land we had seen. **1784** COWPER *Task* I. 156 We have borne The ruffling wind, scarce conscious that it blew. **1809** COLERIDGE *Lett.* (1895) 555 The story is as certain as that Dr. Dodd was hung. **1873** MORLEY *Rousseau* I. vii. 284 Rousseau was persuaded that Madame d'Epinay was his betrayer.

†**b.** Introducing a clause in apposition to or exemplifying the statement in the principal clause: = in that, in the fact that. *Obs.* or *arch.* (now usually expressed by *in* with gerund).

This appears to be transitional between 1 and 2.

901–24 in Birch *Cart. Sax.* II. 236 Helmstan ða undæde ʒedyde, ðæt he Æðeredes belt forstæl. *c***1489** CAXTON *Sonnes of Aymon* iv. 119 We have don evyll that we have not taken surete. **1526** TINDALE *Phil.* iv. 14 Ye have wele done, that ye bare parte with me in my tribulacion. **1611** BIBLE *1 Kings* viii. 18 Thou diddest well that it was in thine heart. —— *Acts* x. 33 Thou hast well done, that thou art come [so CRANMER: WYCL. & *Rhem.* in coming: TINDALE & *Geneva*, for to come].

†**c.** Introducing a sb.-clause as obj. of a preceding preposition: = the fact that. *Obs.* and *rare*, exc. after certain prepositions with which *that* forms conjunctional phrases (***after that, before that, by that***, etc.), sometimes with special meanings, and chiefly *obs.* or *arch.*: see AFTER C. 1 b, BEFORE C. 1 a, BY *prep.* 21 c, FOR THAT 1, IN *prep.* 40, UNTO, WITH, WITHOUT. *Obs.*

*c***1175**— [see AFTER C. 1 b]. *c***1200**— [see BEFORE C. 1 a]. *a***1300**— [see BY *prep.* 21 c]. *c***1440**— [see IN *prep.* 40]. **1444** *Rolls of Parlt.* V. 121/1 To stonde and abyde for terme of her lyves, with that they dwell continuelli within the seid Toun or Fraunchise. **1484** CAXTON *Fables of Alfonce* ix, I shalle not leue the goo, withoute that thow hold to me that [etc.]. **1485** *Rolls of Parlt.* VI. 325/2 Contynued their possessions in the same; unto that Humfrey Stafford..entred into the said mannors. **1525** LD. BERNERS *Froiss.* II. 554 The bysshoppe and the lorde de la Ryver were joyouse of that the herytaunce shulde abyde with the Vycount. *c***1530** —— *Arth. Lyt. Brit.* 493, I am angry wyth nothynge but with that Florence shold thus escape us. **1557** NORTH *Gueuara's Diall Pr.* xx. 36 This shalbe sene by that they succour the poore.

d. In periphrastic construction, following a clause of the form *it is* (*was*, etc.) + an adv. or advb. phr., to which emphasis is given by the periphrasis: see IT 4 d. (The sense may be less emphatically expressed by omitting *it is* (*was*, etc.) and *that*, e.g. [It was] here [that] he fell.) Cf. Onions *Advanced Eng. Syntax* §15 a, 6.

Beowulf 1362 Nis þæt feor heonen mil-ʒe-mearces þæt se mere standeð. *a***1250**, etc. [see IT 4 d]. **1470–85** MALORY *Arthur* VI. viii. 194 Thou arte..lyke on knyȝt that I hate,..so be hit that thou be not he I wyl lyghtly accorde with the. **1672** MARVELL *Reh. Transp.* I. 219 Therefore it is that they are agrieved. **1736** MRS. MANLEY *Secret Mem.* II. 116 It is not always that we ought to judge by Appearances. **1780** *Mirror* No. 77 ¶6 It is owing to this circumstance, that a general lover seldom forms an attachment to any particular object. **1814** WORDSW. *Yarrow Visited* 25 Where was it that the famous Flower Of Yarrow Vale lay bleeding? **1875** CROLL *Climate & T.* 467 It is seldom that the geologist has an opportunity of seeing a complete section. **1877** MISS YONGE *Cameos* Ser. III. xv. 140 It was for his own supremacy that he fought. **1890** SIR C. S. C. BOWEN in *Law Times Rep.* LXIII. 735/1 It was because he failed to prove this that his case broke down.

e. Introducing an exclamatory clause (with or without a preceding interjection or interj. phr.) expressing some emotion, usually (now always) sorrow, indignation, or the like. (Now usually with *should*.)

Some of those with interj. or interj. phr. may be regarded as belonging to 2: cf. 'I am sorry that..', also quot. 1535 in 2.

*c***888** K. ÆLFRED *Boeth.* ix, Eala þæt nanwuht nis fæste stondendes weorces. *c***1315** SHOREHAM v. 223 O þat hy were blyþe, þo hye here seʒen So glorious alyue. *a***1350** in *Hampole's Wks.* (1895) I. 345 Whan Adam sauȝ hym comen, lord, þat he was glade! *Ibid.* II. 360 Lord, þat þe was wo bigon in þat ilke tyde! *c***1440** *Jacob's Well* 125 Allas, þat euer gadryd I monye on hepe, to trustyn þere-vpon. *c***1460** *Towneley Myst.* iv. 195 A, Lord, that I shuld abide this day! **1470–85** MALORY *Arthur* XIII. viii. 623 Allas sayd she that euer I sawe you. **1604** SHAKS. *Oth.* II. iii. 291 Oh, that men should put an Enemie in their mouthes, to steale away their Braines? **1610** —— *Temp.* I. ii. 67 That a brother should Be so perfidious. **1819** SHELLEY *Cenci* I. ii. 54 Great God! that such a father should be mine! *Mod.* That it should ever come to this! That he should turn against us, after all his professions of friendship!

II. 2. a. Introducing a clause expressing the cause, ground, or reason of what is stated in the principal clause. (See also 1 b, e.)

In OE. often *þæs* (*þe*), gen. of *þæt*. For ellipsis of *that*, see 10.

*c***1205** LAY. 9375 He wes glæd þat his ifon weoren dæd. **13..** *Sir Beues* (A.) 4059 Beues was glad, þat he was come. *c***1412** HOCCLEVE *De Reg. Princ.* 1477 þat þou art as thou art, god þanke and herie. **1445** in *Anglia* XXVIII. 273 Men..Merveileth þat thou so lowly art. **1533** BELLENDEN *Livy* II. xi. (S.T.S.) I. 169 For þe commoun pepill reiosit þat þe wolchis war cummyn. **1535** COVERDALE *Ps.* cxix. [cxx.] 5 Wo is me, yt my banishment endureth so longe. **1611** BIBLE *Isa.* lxiii. 5, I wondered that there was none to vphold. **1810** CRABBE *Borough* xviii. 208 Men..bless their God that time has fenced their heart. **1827** HALLAM *Const. Hist.* I. 697 His sincerity in this was the less suspected, that his wife..was entirely presbyterian. **1842** MACAULAY in *Life & Lett.* (1876) II. 114, I should be very sorry that it were known. **1859** GEO. ELIOT *A. Bede* xxxv, Mrs. Poyser was quite agreeably surprised that Hetty wished to go and see Dinah. **1866** READE *G. Gaunt* (ed. 2) II. 14 She..thought of them all the more that she was discouraged from enlarging on them.

(*b*) Also in constructions now *obs.* or *arch.*

*a***1000** *Andreas* 276 (Gr.) Bið þe meorð wið god, þæt þu us on lade liðe weorðe. *c***1000** *Ags. Gosp.* Matt. xvi. 8 Hwæt þence ʒe betwux eow..þæt [*Rushw.* forþon þæt] ʒe hlafas nabbað? **13..** *Coer de L.* 831 Sche..Wrong her handes that sche was born. *c***1555** HARPSFIELD *Divorce Hen. VIII* (Camden) 270 Then is there a quarrel picked against the Popes that they made such restraints. **1567** ALLEN *Def. Priesthood* 352 And S. Augustin excommunicated County Bonifacius that he tooke from the Churche an offender. *a***1657** R. LOVEDAY *Lett.* (1663) 83 Honest J. is ready to beat his wife that she forces his promise to so slothful a performance. **1790** COWPER *Let.* 27 Feb., I am crazed that I cannot ask you all together. **1829** CARLYLE in *For. Rev. & Cont. Misc.* IV. 109 Neither should we censure Novalis that he dries his tears.

b. ***not that..*** (ellipt.): = 'I do not say this because..'; or 'It is not the fact that..', 'One must not suppose that..' (sense 1): see NOT *adv.* 6 a.

1601 [see NOT *adv.* 6 a]. **1681** DRYDEN *Abs. & Achit.* 381 Such virtue's only given to guide a throne. Not that your father's mildness I contemn. **1878** T. HARDY *Ret. Native* I. ix, Where is she staying now? Not that I care. **1878** HUXLEY *Physiogr.* 185 Not that a particle of this substance is annihilated.

3. a. Introducing a clause expressing purpose, end, aim, or desire: with simple subjunctive (*arch.*), or with *may* (pa. t. *might*), *should*, rarely *shall*.

Formerly also preceded by *as* (AS B. 21 b). See also MAY *v.*[1] B. 8 a. The meaning is now more fully expressed by *in order that*: see ORDER *sb.* 29. After *will, wish, pray, beseech*, and the like, the function of *that* seems to combine senses 1 and 3.

*a***900** tr. *Bæda's Hist.* II. xi. [xiv.] §1 þær se biscop oft..wæs, þæt he fulwade þæt folc in Swalwan streame. *c***1000** *Ags. Gosp.* Mark xiv. 38, ʒebiddað þæt ʒe on costnunge ne gan. *a***1018** *O.E. Chron.* an. 1009, We ʒyt næfdon þa ʒeselða..þæt seo scipfyrd nytt wære ðisum earde. *a***1200** *Moral Ode* 313 Ac drihte crist he ʒiue us strencþe, stonde þat we mote. **1303** R. BRUNNE *Handl. Synne* 3742 3yf þou 3aue euer cunsel or rede For yre, þat a man were dede. *c***1410** LOVE *Bonavent. Mirr.* (1908) 106 Besy that al thing were wele and couenably done. *c***1440** *Jacob's Well* 121 Turne þi face fro no pore man, þat god turne noȝt his face fro þe. **1683** MOXON *Mech. Exerc., Printing* x. ¶8 This cutting down..is made..that the Cramp-Irons..joggle not on either side off the Ribs. **1683** *Trial Ld. Russell* in *Lady R.'s Lett.* (1807) p. xlvi, We pray for the King that the challenge may be over-ruled. **1708** *Lond. Gaz.* No. 4454/3 This is to Advertise all Persons, that they do not lend her any Mony. *a***1774** GOLDSM. *Surv. Exp. Philos.* (1776) I. 75 The bones of animals..calcined in such a manner as that all their oil should be exhausted. **1816** J. WILSON *City of Plague* I. ii. 67 Give me one look, That I may see his face so beautiful. **1874** A. J. CHRISTIE in *Ess. Rel. & Lit.* Ser. III. 50 Christ.. had prayed that Peter's faith should not fail.

†**b.** Introducing a parenthetic clause of purpose. *Obs.* (Now expressed by the inf., e.g. 'that we speak of no more' = to speak of no more.)

13.. *Pol. Rel. & L. Poems* (1866) 221 Hit beoþ þreo tymes on þo day, þat soþe to witen me mai. **1611** BIBLE *Transl. Pref.* 1 Synods & Church-maintenance (that we speake of no more things of this kinde) should be as safe as a Sanctuary.

c. In exclamations of desire or longing: with verb in subjunctive.

Now always with vb. in *past subj.* (indicating improbability of fulfilment), usually with preceding interj. (see also O *int.*), also (*arch.*) with *would* or *would God* (sense 1: see *would* s.v. WILL *v.*). Formerly also with vb. in pres. subj. (indicating possibility of fulfilment), where *that* is now omitted. In quot. 13.. expressing a command (*that he war* = let him be).

1297 R. GLOUC. (Rolls) 6189 A duc þer was..þat was traytour..þat god ȝiue him ssame. **13..** *Seuyn Sag.* 651 Goth, he seigh, to the prisone, And fechcheth forht mine sone, And quik that he war an-honge. *c***1350** *Will. Palerne* 2795 God mowe we þonk, & oure worþi werwolf þat wel him by-tyde. **1535** [see O *int.*]. **1618** CORBET *Poems* (1807) 99 O that I ere might have the hap To get the bird which in the map Is called the Indian Ruck! **1790** COWPER *Rec. Mother's Picture* 1 Oh that those lips had language! **1850** TENNYSON *In Mem.* xli, Deep folly! yet that this could be—That I could wing my will with might [etc.]. **1855** —— *Maud* II. IV. i, O that 'twere possible..To find the arms of my true love Round me once again!

d. Introducing a clause expressing a hypothetical desired result: with verb in subjunctive or its equivalent.

[**1601**: see 10.] **1610** SHAKS. *Temp.* V. i. 150 Oh heauens, that they were liuing both in Naples The King and Queene there, that they were, I wish My selfe were mudded in that oozie bed. **1760–72** H. BROOKE *Fool of Qual.* (1809) III. 114, I would give a thousand pounds that he may prove the man. **1821** BYRON *Wks.* (1835) V. 216, I would gladly have given a much greater sum..that he had never been hurt. **1861** DASENT *Burnt Njal* II. 118, I would give all my goods that it had never happened.

4. Introducing a clause expressing the result or consequence of what is stated in the principal clause: with verb usually in indicative.

a. With antecedent *so* or *such*, either in the principal clause, or immediately before *that* in the dependent clause (see SO, SUCH).

Also (*arch.*) preceded by *as*: see AS B. 19 c. For ellipsis of *that*, see 10.

*c***1000** *Ags. Gosp.* Matt. xiii. 54 He lærde hiʒ..swa þæt hiʒ wundredon. *a***1300** *Cursor M.* 9730 Sa wel i am ya luued wit þe þat þi wisdom man clepes me. **1387** TREVISA *Higden* (Rolls) I. 419 Men lyueþ so longe in þat hurste, þat þe eldest deiʒeþ furst. *c***1489** CAXTON *Sonnes of Aymon* iv. 119 So longe they rode..that they came there as they were borne. **1564** P. MARTYR *Comm. Judges* 272 To aske, not in deede so apertely that his voice should be hearde. **1667** MILTON *P.L.* To Rdr., This neglect..of Rime so little is to be taken for a defect,..that it rather is to be esteem'd an example. **1705** FARQUHAR *Twin-Rivals* I. ii, The poor Creature is so big with her Misfortunes, that they are not to be born. **1731** *Gentl. Mag.* I. 391/1 This put Bluster into such a Passion, that he quitted the Surgery in a pet. **1849** MACAULAY *Hist. Eng.* vi. II. 85 He was a man of morals so bad that his own relations shrank from him.

b. Simply, without antecedent: = so that. *arch.*

*c***1175** *Lamb. Hom.* 27 þe deofel..rixat in-nan him þet he nulle nefre forleten his sunne. *c***1205** LAY. 1867 Forð com Corineus..þat alle hit bi-heolden. **1297** R. GLOUC. (Rolls) 2690 þun king hii bounde uaste ynou þat reulich he gan crie. **1377** LANGL. *P. Pl.* B. XIV. 64 Heuene was yclosed, þat no reyne ne rone. **1470–85** MALORY *Arthur* XVI. xvii. 687 Thenne were they sore affrayed that they felle bothe to the erthe. **1542** UDALL *Erasm. Apoph.* 136 b, Suche as bee naught I byte, that thei smart again. **1611** SHAKS. *Wint. T.* V. i. 65 Then I'ld shrieke, that euen your eares Should rift to heare me. **1719** DE FOE *Crusoe* (1840) I. v. 96 The fear..made me that I never slept. **1858** G. MACDONALD *Phantastes* xix, I struck one more sturdy blow..that the forest rang. **1868** TENNYSON *Lucretius* 66 A fire..scorch'd me that I woke.

c. Introducing a clause expressing a fact (with vb. in indic.), or a supposition (with vb. in subj.), as a consequence attributed to the cause indicated by the principal clause (which is most commonly interrogative): sometimes nearly = in consequence of which; or (with indic.) = since, seeing that.

*c***1000** ÆLFRIC *Exod.* v. 2 Hwæt ys se drihten, þæt ic hym hiran scile and Israela folc forlætan? *c***1205** LAY. 30280 Whæt is þe..þat þu swa wepest to-dæi? *c***1420** *Chron. Vilod.* 2769 What deseysse is come þe to þat þou art now so sorwefulle? **1535** COVERDALE *Ps.* viii. 4 Oh what is man, yt thou art so myndfull of him? *Ibid.* cxiii. [cxiv.] 5 What ayled the (o thou see) that thou fleddest? **1591** SHAKS. *Two Gent.* IV. ii. 40 Who is Silvia? what is she? That all our Swaines commend her? **1598** —— *Merry W.* I. iv. 43, I doubt he be not well, that hee comes not home. **1611** BIBLE *Isa.* liii. 2 There is no beautie that we should desire him. **1787** COWPER *Stanzas Bill Mortality* 8 Did famine or did plague prevail, That so much death appears? **1842** TENNYSON *Lady Clare* vi, Are ye out of your mind..that ye speak so wild? **1885** *Sat. Rev.* 21 Feb. 242/2 We are not pigeons that we should eat dry peas.

5. With a negative in the dependent clause (the principal clause having also a negative expressed or implied): = But that, but (= L. *quin*): see BUT *conj.* 12. (Now expressed by *without* with gerund: e.g. in quot. 1809, 'without her hearing'.)

Quots. *c* 1320, 1375 may belong to THAT *rel. pron.* 8.

*c***1000** ÆLFRIC *Saints' Lives* (1885) I. 378 Man ʒecwæman ne mæʒ twam hlafordum æt-somne þæt he ne forseo þone oðerne. *c***1290** *Beket* 2128 in *S. Eng. Leg.* I. 167 For ȝwane men peyntiez an halewe, ȝe ne seoth it nouȝt bi-leued þat þere nis depeint a Roundel al-a-boute þe heued. *c***1320** *Cast. Love* 6 Ne neuer was wrouȝt non vuel þing þat vuel þouȝt nas þe biginnyng. **1375** BARBOUR *Bruce* XVI. 280 Thar is no man That he ne will rew vp-on voman. *c***1440** *Alphabet of Tales* 293 A long tyme sho mot nowder luke on þe crucifyx nor speke..of þe Passion..þatte nevur sho fell in swone as sho had bene dead. **1773** GOLDSM. *Stoops to Conq.* v, I never attempted to be impudent yet, that I was not taken down. **1809** SOUTHEY *Let. to Lieut. Southey* 19 Sept., He never turned in his bed during that whole time that she did not hear. **1837** S. R. MAITLAND *Six Lett.*, etc. 69, I have hardly ever..turned it over for five minutes, that some gross error has not presented itself.

6. a. Added to relatives or dependent interrogatives (*who, which, what, when, where, how, why*, etc.). †Also after the demonstrative advbs. *then, there*, etc., when used as relatives. *Obs.* or *arch.*

*c***888** K. ÆLFRED *Boeth.* xvi. §2, ʒif ʒe nu ʒesawan hwelce mus þæt wære hlaford ofer oðre mys. **13..** *Cursor M.* 1247 (Cott.) Yai, sir, wist i wyderward [*v.r.* queþirward] þat [*v.r.* þere] tat vncuth contre were. *c***1374** CHAUCER *Troylus* II. Prol. 36 Euery wyght wheche þat to rome wente. *c***1386** —— *Prol.* 41 To telle yow..in what array that they were Inne. —— *Can. Yeom. Prol. & T.* 17 And in myn herte to wondren

I bigan What þat he was. **14..** in *Hist. Coll. Citizen London* (Camden) 112 Faste be-syde ther that the batelle was done. **1450** *Rolls of Parlt.* V. 202/1 In whos handes that ever they were founde. *c* **1465** *Eng. Chron.* (Camden) 98 A wommanne the whiche that knewe hym. **1470–85** MALORY *Arthur* XVII. xxii. 723 Wotest thou wherfor that he hath sente me? **1601** SHAKS. *Jul. C.* III. ii. 96 When that the poore haue cry'de, Cæsar hath wept. **1613** —— *Hen. VIII*, III. ii. 32 Wherein was read How that the Cardinall did intreat his Holinesse [etc.]. *a* **1814** *Spaniards* IV. i. in *New Brit. Theatre* III. 234 When that the crown..shall bind the brows Of my unnatural brother.

†**b.** *That* alone had formerly the force of 'when that', 'when', after *hardly, scarcely*, or some equivalent. So †*just that* (quot. 1648) = just when, just as. ***now that***: see NOW 12 b.

13.. *Cursor M.* 8160 Vnnethes had he moned his mode, þat [*v.r.* quen] a lem fra þe wandes stode. ? *a* **1380** *St. Ambrosius* 488 in Horstm. *Altengl. Leg.* (1878) 16/1 Vnneþe Ambrose and his meyne, Weoren passed out from þat citee þat sodeynliche opened þe eorþe. **1480** CAXTON *Chron. Eng.* ccvii. 189 The kyng had not yet fullych eten that ther come in to the halle another messagyer. **1530–** [see NOW 12 b]. **1648** CROMWELL in Carlyle *Lett. & Sp.* (1871) II. 56 Until just that we came. **1780** *Mirror* No. 95 ¶ 1 We spent our time as happily as possible, till about half a year ago, that my ill stars directed me to [etc.].

7. Formerly added with a conjunctive force to various words that are now commonly used conjunctionally without it; e.g. *because, if, lest, only, the* adv., *though, till, while* (see these words). *arch.* or *Obs.*

(Cf. the OE. similar use of *þe*; also prec. sense.)

c **1200** [see IF 5]. *a* **1300** *Cursor M.* 14458 Bot al þat he wit luue þam soght, Enentis þe Iuus al was for noght. *Ibid.* 22167 Þai sal be studiand in þair thoght, Queþer þat he be crist or nai. **1505** in *Mem. Hen. VII* (Rolls) 267 The kynge ..remembrithe that mater as efectually as that hit were his aune proper cause. **1590** SPENSER *F.Q.* I. i. 30 The knight.. Who faire him quited, as that courteous was. **1602** DOLMAN *La Primaud. Fr. Acad.* (1618) III. 736 The property thereof is to mount alwaies vpwards, vntill that it hath attained to the place destinated vnto it. **1656** A. WRIGHT *Five Serm.* 201 The reason is, cause that Ordinances are nothing without the Lord. **1800** COLERIDGE *Lett.* (1895) 325 As to my schemes of residence, I am as unfixed as yourself, only that we are under the absolute necessity of fixing somewhere. **1805** tr. *Lafontaine's Hermann & Emilia* III. 97 Hermann likewise trembled, because that their early friendship was awakened in his breast.

8. Used (like Fr. *que*) as a substitute instead of repeating a previous conjunction, or conjunctive adverb or phrase. Now *rare* or *arch.*

c **1175** *Lamb. Hom.* 17 Þenne were þu wel his freond..Gif þu hine iseȝe þet he wulle asotte to þes deofles hond..þet þu hine lettest, and wiðstewest. *c* **1489** CAXTON *Blanchardyn* xix. 58 When they..had seen the manere & the rewle of their enemyes, and that all wyth leyser they had seen their puyssance. *Ibid.* 59 So began he to be..all annoyed of hym self by cause he was not armed tyl his plesure, and that he myght not yssue out. *c* **1520** BARCLAY *Sallust* 55 Whan he had assayed many wayes, and that nothing came to purpose. **1535** COVERDALE *Esther* ii. 14 She must come vnto the kynge nomore, excepte it pleased the kynge, and that he caused her to be called by name. **1569** J. SANFORD tr. *Agrippa's Van. Artes* 174 b, When sleepe falleth vpon men, & that they be in bed. **1596** SHAKS. *Merch. V.* IV. i. 9 Since he stands obdurate, And that no lawful meanes can carrie me Out of his enuies reach. [Also 27 other examples.] **1611** BIBLE *1 Chron.* xiii. 2 If it seeme good vnto you, and that it be of the Lord our God, let vs send abroad vnto our brethren. [COVERD. Yf..yf...] —— *Job* xxxi. 38 If my land cry against me, or that the furrowes likewise thereof complaine. [COVERD. Yf case be that..or yᵗ...] **1655** M. CASAUBON *Enthus.* (1656) 126 Because I desire not to be over-long, and that I would not glut the Reader. **1700** TYRRELL *Hist. Eng.* II. 823 So soon as the Death of King John was..known, and that the Earls..could agree where to meet. **1797** BURKE *Regic. Peace* iii. Wks. VIII. 330 When one of the parties to a treaty intrenches himself..in..ceremonies,..and that all the concessions are upon one side. **1829** SIR W. NAPIER *Penins. War* IX. iii. (Rtldg.) II. 16 Although the rear was attacked,..and that 50 men..were captured.

†**9.** After a comparative: = THAN. (Cf. Fr. *que.*) *Obs. rare.* (See also THE *part.* 1 b.)

c **1305** *St. Kenelm* 108 in *E. Eng. P.* (1862) 50 For noman nemai þan oþer bet trecherie do þat [*Laud MS.* þane] þulke þat is him next, & he trist mest to. *c* **1330** R. BRUNNE *Chron. Wace* (Rolls) 10602 More worschip of hym [Arthur] spoke þer was þat of any of þo þat spekes Gildas. **1422** tr. *Secreta Secret., Priv. Priv.* 175 He had Slayne by trayson two prynces bettyr that he was. *c* **1450** LOVELICH *Grail* xlviii. 35 And but þe holyere man he be þat I konne wit, Elles schal there non Man here syt.

¶ **10.** The conjunction *that* is very frequently omitted by ellipsis, esp. in sense 1.

(The omission prob. began with the rel. conj. *þe*, THE.)

a **1250–1650** [see IT 4 b]. *a* **1300** *Cursor M.* 3665 (Cott.), I dred me sare, for benison He sal me giue his malison. **1390** GOWER *Conf.* I. 263 Joab..slowh Abner, for drede he scholde be [etc.]. *c* **1460** *Towneley Myst.* ix. 137 Go grete hym well,..say hym I com. **1526** TINDALE *Jas.* ii. 14 Though a man saye he hath fayth. **1591** SHAKS. *1 Hen. VI*, II. v. 37 Direct mine Armes, I may embrace his Neck. **1599** —— *Hen. V*, v. i. 54 Thou dost see I eate. **1601** —— *All's Well* II. iii. 66 I'de giue bay curtall, and his furniture My mouth no more were broken then these boyes. **1611** BIBLE *Luke* xx. 13 It may bee they will reuerence him. **1678** BUNYAN *Pilgr.* I. 3, I think I do. **1737** POPE *Hor. Ep.* II. ii. 266 There are who have not—and thank heav'n there are. **1805** SCOTT *Last Minstr.* VI. xxv, So bright, so red the glare, The castle seemed on flame. **1847** TENNYSON *Princess* VII. 281, I fear They will not. *a* **1912** *Mod.* We were sorry you couldn't come.

III. 11. *'that'-clause*: a clause introduced by the word 'that' (as conjunction or, less commonly, as relative pronoun).

1955 J. L. AUSTIN *How to do Things with Words* (1962) vi. 70 Although we have in this type of utterance a 'that' clause following a verb..we must not allude to this as 'indirect speech'. **1964** E. BACH *Introd. Transformational Gram.* v. 102 The rules for *that* clauses..must be made less general. **1978** *Language* LIV. 67 None of the (a) sentences would be appropriate if the proposition expressed in the *that*-clause were part of the undisputed background of already-held belief common to all the participants in the conversation.

thataboy (ˈðætəbɔɪ), *int. slang* (chiefly *U.S.*). Also **that a boy, thatta boy**, etc. [Corruption of *that's the boy* (cf. THAT *dem. pron.* B. 1 b), or alteration of ATTABOY *int.*] An exclamation of encouragement or admiration; = ATTABOY *int.*

1936 J. DOS PASSOS *Big Money* 287 'All right, let's go,' he said. 'Thataboy,' roared Farrell. **1975** M. BOSSE *Man who loved Zoos* iv. 96 'What should I tell Hopkins?' 'Tell him.. I'm not up a blind alley yet.' 'Thatta boy.' **1978** M. PUZO *Fools Die* xi. 114 Frank patted me on the shoulder. 'That a boy,' he said.

that-a-way (ˈðætəweɪ), *adv.* Chiefly *dial.* and *U.S.* Also **thataway, that a way**, etc. [f. THAT *dem. adj.* + AWAY *adv.*]

1. In that direction.

1839 *Southern Lit. Messenger* V. 378/2, I expect, Tommy, you're *a* sparking that *a* way. **1847** *Paddiana* I. 139 It's very careless I hear they are that aways. **1866** H. JACKSON *Gilbert Rugge* II. xii. 174 Down in the marsh lands, that-a-way. **1901** J. PRIOR *Forest Folk* iv. 41 It's out o' my road or I'd show yer; that-away. **1920** M. WEBB *House in Dormer Forest* vii. 89 'I canna see as it's to be found out,' he nodded sideways towards the murmur, 'that-a-way.' **1973** *Washington Post* 13 Jan. B8/7 'Bonanza', the Western series that went thataway a couple of weeks ago after a 14-year ride on the NBC network. **1978** G. MCDONALD *Fletch's Fortune* (1979) xviii. 127 He went thet-away.

2. In that manner; like that.

1887 *Scribner's Mag.* Sept. 366/1, I hadn' 'a' thought ye'd 'a' evidenced agin me that-a-way. **1889** *Spectator* 26 Oct. 549/2 Whin I sees him that a way the second time, your Reverence. **1938** M. K. RAWLINGS *Yearling* v. 46 'You want to tote lunch?' she called after him. 'I'd not insult my neighbors that-a-way. We'll noon with them.' **1959** *Times Lit. Suppl.* 9 Jan. 15/3, I didn't mean to treat her that-a-way. **1973** K. GILES *File on Death* iii. 72 You bloody well don't do it thataway.

thatch (θætʃ), *sb.* Forms: 4–5 **þacche**, 5–6 **thacche, thecche, thetche**, 7– **thatch**. [A late collateral form of THACK *sb.*, conformed to THATCH *v.*, which has superseded *thack* in literary use.]

1. Material used in thatching; straw or similar material with which roofs are covered; particularly **b.** that actually forming a roof, the thatching.

palmetto thatch: see PALMETTO.

1398 TREVISA *Barth. De P.R.* XVII. clxvii[i]. (Bodl. MS.), þe rafters beþ stronge and square..& beþ charged wᵗoute wᵗ sclatte and tile oþre wᵗ strawe and þacche [*ed.* **1495** thetche]. **1555** EDEN *Decades* 159 Theyr houses..are..couered with reede & thetche. **1600** J. PORY tr. *Leo's Africa* Introd. 20 Their houses are built round, al of earth, flat-roofed, and couered with a kind of thatch. **17..** POPE *Imit. Spenser* iv, Hard by a Sty, beneath a roof of thatch, Dwelt Obloquy. **1850** PRESCOTT *Peru* III. viii. II. 161 The roofs of their dwellings, instead of tiles, were only of thatch. **1878** BATES *Centr. Amer.* iv. 41 Everywhere the palms yield an abundance of poles and thatch available for building purposes.

b. 1693 EVELYN *De la Quint. Compl. Gard.* 5 The Cieling and Floor above ought to be..clad in Winter with a Thatch of Hay or Straw. **1816** in *Life W. Havergal* (1882) 13 The pretty thatch and white walls so common hereabouts. **1867** D. G. MITCHELL *Rural Stud.* 77 The roof a neat thatch of wheat straw. **1889** DOYLE *Micah Clarke* 228 They shelter the walls from the rain..by great overhanging thatches.

c. *transf.* A thatched dwelling.

1693 S. HARVEY in *Dryden's Juvenal* ix. (1697) 233 The Poor Inhabitants of yonder Thatch Call'd me their Lord. *a* **1790** T. WARTON *Ode* viii. *Morning*, Up mounts the mower from his lowly thatch. **1793** W. HODGES *Trav. India* 67 For constant residence, these would be improved into the various thatches and huts which I have seen.

2. *fig.* Covering; often *humorously* the hair of the head.

a **1633** AUSTIN *Medit.* (1635) 284 The very Top and Cover, my Thatch above..growes gray. **1634** S. R. *Noble Soldier* II. i. in Bullen *O. Pl.* (1882) I. 276 Had my Barbour Perfum'd my louzy thatch here and poak'd out My Tuskes more stiffe. **1821** CLARE *Vill. Minstr.* I. 129 'Neath the hazel's leafy thatch. **1888** LOWELL *Heartsease & Rue* 193 We..Who've paid a perruquier for mending our Thatch. **1894** MRS. DYAN *All in a Man's K.* (1899) 27 The damage he had done to his 'thatch', as he graphically styled his hair.

b. orig. and chiefly *U.S.* A matted layer of plant debris, moss, etc., on a lawn; the material of this layer.

1955 *How to install & care for Your Lawn* 59/1 Opening up a thatch of interwoven stolons and stems can be difficult. **1964** *Book of Lawn Care* (N.Y. Times) iii. 15 Because of its rapid growth, this grass has a tendency to form a heavy mat or thatch. **1977** *Western Living* (Vancouver) Apr. 61/1 Power raking for the removal of moss 'thatch' in spring often does harm to the turf. **1980** *Amat. Gardening* 4 Oct. 16/3 Another cause of moss is 'thatch', a layer of dead, moisture retentive grass and debris that builds up on the lawn's surface.

3. a. Name in the West Indies for several species of palms, the leaves of which are used for thatching: see quot. and *thatch-palm* in 4.

1866 *Treas. Bot.*, Thatch, *Calyptronoma Swartzii*, and *Copernicia tectorum*. Palmetto Thatch, *Thrinax parviflora*. Silver Thatch, *Thrinax argentea*.

b. *U.S.* Tall, coarse grass.

1622 *Relation Eng. Plantation Plimoth, New England* 25 Some of our people being abroad, to get and gather thatch, they saw great fires. **1695** in *Early Rec. Providence, Rhode Island* (1894) VI. 156 That Parcell of Meadow marsh & thatch..belongeth to me. **1797** B. TRUMBULL *Compl. Hist. Connecticut* I. iii. 24 There grew bent grass, or as some called it, thatch, two, three and four feet high. **1863** D. G. MITCHELL *My Farm of Edgewood* 49, I gave them [*sc.* bees] a warm shelter of thatch. **1951** E. GRAHAM *My Window looks down East* iv. 34 Salt hay and thatch, or evergreens, are piled around the houses to insulate against the cold.

4. *attrib.* and *Comb.*, as ***thatch-eave, -roof, -straw, -work*** (also *attrib.*); ***thatch-browed, -roofed*** adjs.; **thatch-cloak**, a cloak of any thatching material; **thatch-grass**, a grass or similar plant used for thatching, as Cape T., *Restio chondropetalus*; **thatch-hook**: see quot.; † **thatch-house**, a thatched house; **thatch-palm**, name for various palms of which the leaves are used for thatching: in W. Indies, the genus *Thrinax*; in southern U.S., the genus *Sabal*, esp. *S. umbraculifera*; in Brazil, *Euterpe montana* (*Funk's Stand. Dict.* 1895); in Lord Howe's Island, *Howea forsteriana* (*Cent. Dict.* 1891); **thatch-peg, -pin, -prick**, a stick sharpened at one end to fasten down thatch; **thatch-rake**, an implement with curved teeth for straightening the thatching material as it is laid on the roof; **thatch-rod** = *thatching-rod*; **thatch-tree** (see quot. 1866); **thatch-wood**, brushwood arranged as thatch: see quot.

1863 W. BARNES *Poems in Dorset Dial.* 61 An'by a house, where rwoses hung avore The *thatch-brow'd window, an' the open door. **1844** B. MAYER *Mexico* xxiii. 166 An Indian shepherd-boy in his long *thatch-cloak of water-flags. **1819** KEATS *Ode to Autumn* 4 The vines that round the *thatch-eaves run. **1884** MILLER *Plant-n.*, *Grass, Cape Thatch. [**1858** HOGG *Veg. Kingd.* 802 The houses at the Cape of Good Hope are commonly thatched with *Restio tectorum*,.. sometimes whole huts are built with it.] **1886** *Cheshire Gloss.*, **Thatch-hooks*, iron hooks, driven into the spars, to hold down the first layers of straw in thatching a house. **1521** in *10th Rep. Hist. MSS. Comm.* App. v. 399 No man shall buld, make or repayre anny straue or *tache housse, for fear of fyre and burninge.., unlesse they be covered with sklattes. **1609** *Ev. Wom. in Hum.* IV. ii. in Bullen *O. Pl.* IV, He that has not a tilde house must bee glad of a thatch house. **1866** *Treas. Bot* 1147/1 *Thrinax*..In Jamaica these palms are commonly known by the name of *Thatch-palms. *Ibid.*, The Silver Thatch-palm is usually said to yield..Palmetto Thatch,..extensively employed for making palm-chip hats, baskets, and other fancy articles. **1897** GILCHRIST *Peakland* 62 Busily whittling *thatch pegs. **1688** R. HOLME *Armoury* III. 266/1 Thatching, is to cover..with Straw, Ferne, Rushes or Gorst, which is bound and held together by Laths, Windings, and *Thatch Pricks. **1847–94** PARKER *Gloss. Her.* s.v. *Rake*, The *thatch-rake or thatcher's rake. **1903** *Q. Rev.* July 12 They were its *thatch-rods. **1901** *Westm. Gaz.* 15 Aug. 1/3 The *thatch roof of a West-country cottage. **1774** J. TRUMBULL *Poet Wks.* (1820) II. 210 The *thatch-roof'd hamlet and defenceless shed..are their fate. **1847** LONGF. *Ev.* I. Prel. 9 Where is the thatch-roofed village, the home of Acadian farmers? **1844** STEPHENS *Bk. Farm* III. 1095 To give the *thatch-straw a smoothness, it should be stroked down with a long supple rod of willow. **1756** P. BROWNE *Jamaica* 344 The *Thatch Tree. The leaves..used for thatch. **1866** *Treas. Bot.*, *Thatch-tree*, a name applied to palms generally in the West Indies. **1877** KNIGHT *Dict. Mech.*, **Thatch-wood Work*,..a mode of facing sea-walls with brushwood. Under-brush..is cut down, fagoted at its full length, and spread over the face of the banks. It is kept down by strong stakes, which have cross pins at their upper ends to rest upon the brush. **1895** WORKMAN *Algerian Mem.* xi. 113 Villages with *thatch-work houses.

thatch (θætʃ), *v.* Forms: α. 1 **þecc(e)an**, 4 **thecche**, 4–6 **theche**, 5 **thetche**, 6–7 **thetch** (7 *dial.* **thesh**). β. 4 **þacchen**, 5–6 **thacche**, 5–7 **thach(e**, 6 **thatche**, 6– **thatch**. [OE. *þecc(e)an* (pa. t. *þeahte*, *þęhte*, Vesp. Ps. *þæhte*, pa. pple. *ȝeþeaht*), Common Teutonic vb.; in OFris. *bi)thękk(i)a*, OS. *bi)thęccian* (MDu., MLG. *decken*, Du., LG. *dekken*), OHG. *dęcchan* (MHG., Ger. *decken*), ON. *þekja* (Sw. *täcka*, Da. *tække*):—OTeut. **þakjan*, f. **þakoᵐ* covering, roof, THACK *sb.* The regular etymological form is *thetch*: the literary *thatch* has app. taken its vowel from THACK *sb.* Cf. also the cognate THACK *v.*¹, THEEK *v.*]

†**1.** *trans.* To cover. (Only *O.E.*)

Beowulf 514 Þa ȝit on sund reon þær ȝit eagor-stream earmum þehton. *a* **1000** *Cædmon's Gen.* 877 (Gr.) For hwon wast þu wean & wrihst sceome, ȝesyhst sorȝe & þin sylf þecest lic mid leafum. *c* **1000** *Ags. Ps.* (Th.) cxlvi. 8 Se þe heofen þeceð hadrum wolcnum.

2. *spec.* To cover or roof (a house) with straw, reeds, palm-leaves, heather, or the like, laid so as to protect from the weather; also, to cover the top of (a rick or wall) in a similar way. †Formerly also, to roof (a house) with slates, tiles, or similar roofing material.

1398 TREVISA *Barth. De P.R.* XVII. xxxi. (Tollem. MS.), In þe norþe londe men þacchen [*ed.* **1495** thetche] here houses with reed. ? *c* **1500** *How Plowman lerned his Pater-Noster* 19 in Hazl. *E.P.P.* I. 210 He coude theche a hous, and daube a wall. **1555** EDEN *Decades* 101 Their houses are.. thetched with the stalkes of certayne towghe herbes. **1610**

HOLLAND *Camden's Brit.* (1637) 491 Reed for to thatch their Houses. **1623-4** *Althorp MS.* in Simpkinson *Washingtons* (1860) App. 53 To Phipp one daie theshing the dove house. **1698** FRYER *Acc. E. India & P.* 66 The Houses are low, and Thatched with Oleas of the Cocoe-Trees. **1774** PENNANT *Tour Scot. in 1772* 135 Many of the churches are thatched with heath. **1865** PARKMAN *Huguenots* iv, The buildings of the fort were all thatched.. with leaves of the palmetto.

3. *fig.* To cover as with thatch.

1589 *Pappe w. Hatchet* C iv, If that Martin could thatch vp his Church, this mans scabship should bee an Elder. **1604** MIDDLETON *Father Hubburd's T.* Wks. (Bullen) VIII. 89 My chin was well thatched with a beard. **1614** GORGES *Lucan* v. 166 Mount Æmus now was thatch't with snow. **1662** HIBBERT *Body of Div.* II. 135 Their faces thatcht over with impudence. **1683** OWEN *Serm. Chamb. Imagery* Wks. 1855 VIII. 584 One lie must be thatched with another, or it will quickly rain through. **1816** SCOTT *Bl. Dwarf* i. *note*, His head.. was thatched with no other covering than long matted red hair. **1857** EMERSON *Poems* 26 What if Trade.. thatch with towns the prairie broad. **1858** CARLYLE *Fredk. Gt.* I. v. (1872) I. 45 As if there was cloth enough.. to thatch the Arctic Zone.

4. Of a thing: To serve as a covering or roof to; to cover, to roof.

c **1000** *Sax. Leechd.* II. 242 Sio filmen [of the milt] biþ þeccende & wreonde þa wambe & þa innofaran. **1663** GERBIER *Counsel* d vj b, Leaves of Trees do thatch their Domiciliums. **1852** MRS. STOWE *Uncle Tom's C.* ix, The shock of hair that thatched his head.

5. *intr.* To do thatching; to thatch houses.

1377 LANGL. *P. Pl.* B. XIX. 232 Somme he tauȝte to tilie to dyche & to thecche. **1591** SPENSER *M. Hubberd* 264 To hedge, to ditch, to thrash, to thetch, to mowe. **1795** AIKIN & BARBAULD *Evenings at Home* vi. 105 *Gubba.* Can you thatch? There is a piece blown off the cow-house. *Alfred.* Alas! I cannot thatch.

thatch, variant of THETCH *dial.*, vetch.

thatched, thatcht (θætʃt), *ppl. a.* [f. THATCH *v.* (q.v. for Forms) + -ED[1].] Covered or roofed with thatch.

1467 in *Eng. Gilds* (1870) 372 That no chimneys of tre ner thached houses be suffred wᵗyn the cyte. *a* **1548** HALL *Chron., Hen. VI* 94 The newe Constable.. destroyed two or thre.. litle poore thetched villages. *c* **1640** [SHIRLEY] *Capt. Underwit* I. in Bullen *O. Pl.* (1883) II. 327 Does this thatchd cottage head hold still in fashion? **1653** WALTON *Angler* i. 2 Sir, I know the thatcht house very well: I often make it my resting place. **1867** MISS BRADDON *Aur. Floyd* Road-side inns with brown thatched roofs.

b. *fig.* Covered as with thatch (in quot. 1606, with reference to its inflammability). ***thatched-head***, one who has matted hair.

1606 *Sir G. Goosecappe* III. i. in Bullen *O. Pl.* (1884) III. 44 Such sparkes were good enough yet to set thacht dispositions a fire. **1613** BEAUMONT & FL. *Coxcomb* II. iii, Ere you go, Sirrah Thatch'd Head! wouldst not thou be whipt, and think it justice? **1889** DOYLE *Micah Clarke* 128 A pair of great thatched eyebrows.

thatcher (ˈθætʃə(r)). [f. THATCH *v.* (q.v. for Forms) + -ER[1].] One who thatches; *esp.* one whose business it is to thatch houses, corn or hay ricks, etc.

c **1440** *Jacob's Well* 40 Alle men of crafte, as wryȝtes, smythes,.. baxterys, thaccherys, cordewanerys.. owyn to payin þe tythe. **1562-3** *Act 5 Eliz.* c. 4 §30 Tharte or Occupation of a.. Thatcher or Shingler. **1641** BEST *Farm. Bks.* (Surtees) 145 A thatcher hath usually two folkes to waite on, viz. one to drawe out the thatch and make it into bottles, and the other to make morter and serve him. **1879** JEFFERIES *Wild Life in S. Co.* 123 The wind never blew that was strong enough to please the thatcher.

So † **ˈthatchester** (**ˈthachester**), in same sense.

1583-4 *Shuttleworths' Acc.* (Chetham Soc.) 18 Vnto a thachester for thachinge.. towe dayes and a halffe xijᵈ.

Thatcherite (ˈθætʃəraɪt), *sb.* and *a. Pol.* [f. the name *Thatcher* (see def.) + -ITE[1].] **A.** *sb.* One who supports the views or policies of Mrs. Margaret Thatcher (b. 1925), British (Conservative) politician, who became Leader of the Opposition in 1975 and Prime Minister in 1979. **B.** *adj.* Of, pertaining to, or characteristic of Mrs. Thatcher or Thatcherism.

1976 *Economist* 17 Apr. 13/2 Tory constituency rooms were by 1974 fuller of anti-Butler Thatcherites than Mr Heath dreamed. **1977** *Times* 16 May 11/7 The Thatcherite philosophy can be summed-up in two words, 'non-interference'. **1980** J. BOYD-CARPENTER *Way of Life* xxiv. 265 The Thatcherite view accepts the.. thesis that 'equality of opportunity means equal opportunity to be unequal'. **1982** *Daily Tel.* 3 Apr. 18/4 The Thatcherites.. are genuinely trying to restore the private sphere, to bring back a world fit for gentlemen. *Ibid.* 11 Aug. 8/1 With the exception of that large part of the Labour party which is now authentically Bennite, we are all, to a greater or lesser extent, Thatcherites now.

So **ˈThatcherism**, the political and economic policies advocated by Mrs. Thatcher, esp. as contrasted with those of earlier Conservative leaders.

1979 *Times* 24 Nov. 2/2 The party was fighting off the shrill divisiveness of Thatcherism, with its simple monetarist policies. **1981** GLYN & HARRISON *Brit. Econ. Disaster* v. 138 Many workers.. see Thatcherism as an outmoded nineteenth century ideology with little relevance to contemporary economic reality. **1982** *Daily Tel.* 11 Aug. 8 At heart, Thatcherism is a liberal economic reaction to the collectivism and corporatism of the past 40 years.

thatching (ˈθætʃɪŋ), *vbl. sb.* [f. THATCH *v.* (q.v. for Forms) + -ING[1].] The action of THATCH *v.*

1. The action or process of covering a building with thatch (†formerly, with any roofing material).

1393 LANGL. *P. Pl.* C. IX. 199 Tho.. peers.. putte hem alle to werke,.. In þresshynge, in þecchyng. **1520** *Maldon, Essex, Liber B.* lf. 95 b, Circa le thechynge unius orei apud Sabernes. *c* **1683** M. MACKAILE in Macfarlane *Geog. Collect.* (S.H.S.) III. 6 Gremsie affordeth only slates for thatching of houses. **1760** FOOTE *Minor* II. Wks. 1799 I. 250 Fine old hay,.. damag'd a little last winter, for want of thatching. **1846** *J. Baxter's Libr. Pract. Agric.* (ed. 4) II. 316 The Somersetshire mode of thatching is preferable to all others. It consists in using unbruised straw, provincially called reed, instead of bruised straw with the ears on it.

2. *concr.* = THATCH *sb.* 1.

1671 H. M. tr. *Erasm. Colloq.* 311 The very rafters themselves which bear up the thatching. **1703** T. N. *City & C. Purchaser* 260 This kind of Thatching will indure 40, 50, or 60 Years. **1844** STEPHENS *Bk. Farm* II. 405 Long straw ropes, which bound down the thatching of stacks.

3. *attrib.* and *Comb.*, as ***thatching work***; **thatching-beetle**, a thatcher's mallet; **thatching-fork**, (*a*) a forked stick used for carrying straw to the roof for thatching; (*b*) see quot. 1882; **thatching-rod**, a long flexible rod laid on the thatch to hold it down, and tied or pinned to the framework of the roof; **thatching-spale**: see quot. 1882; **thatching-stake**, a pointed stake with which the thatch is pinned down.

1641 BEST *Farm. Bks.* (Surtees) 139 If thatchinge worke come in hande in haytime. **1703** T. N. *City & C. Purchaser* 259 In some parts of Kent they use no Withs to bind on their Thatching-rods, but.. they use Rope-yarn. **1874** HARDY *Far from Madding Crowd* II. vi. 77 Where's your thatching-beetle and rick-stick and spars? **1879** JEFFERIES *Wild Life in S. Co.* 123 His small sharp billhook to split out his thatching stakes. **1882** OGILVIE, *Thatching-fork, Thatching-spale*, an implement with a forked blade and a cross handle at one end for thrusting home the tufts of straw in thatching. **1887** MOLONEY *Forestry W. Afr.* 438 The leaves.. are used.. for thatching purposes.

ˈthatchless, *a.* [f. THATCH *sb.* + -LESS.] Having the thatch of the roof missing or destroyed.

1882 *Century Mag.* XXIII. 912 Hingeless doors and shutters, crooked and thatchless roofs.

ˈthatchy, *a.* Abounding in thatch; like thatch. Also *Comb.*

1864 CARLYLE *Fredk. Gt.* XV. xii. (1872) VI. 88 Thatchy Trautenau, wooden too in the upper stories of it, takes greedily to the fire. **1944** E. BLUNDEN *Cricket Country* v. 61 The sweetest of hamlets and thatchiest of little old inns. **1952** L. MACNEICE *Ten Burnt Offerings* 30 Like a sick bird.. Its thatchy feathers moulting. **1973** T. PYNCHON *Gravity's Rainbow* I. 28 The flooded quarries and logged-off hillsides they'd left.. across all that thatchy-brown, moldering witch-country.

Thathanabaing (θə,θɑːnəˈbaɪŋ). [a. Burmese, f. *thathana* teaching, instruction (f. Pali *śāsana*) + *baing* to possess.] The chief Buddhist dignitary in Burma.

1839 H. MALCOM *Trav. S.-E. Asia* I. II. vi. 315 The highest functionary is the *Tha-thena-byng*, or archbishop. **1858** P. BIGANDET *Life Gaudama* 252 In our days, the power of the Thathana-paing is merely nominal. **1912** *Rangoon Gaz.* 31 Oct. 19/1 A rectangular pandal, the central position of which was assigned to the Thathana-baing (Buddhist Archbishop) and his learned sadaws. **1934** 'G. ORWELL' *Burmese Days* xv. 234 A big heathen idol.. fell down on top of the thathanabaing, that is Buddhist bishop. **1972** A. T. Q. STEWART *Pagoda War* xiii. 151 The *Thathanabaing*, the hierarch whom the English generally referred to as 'the Buddhist Archbishop', had formerly been recognized throughout Burma as the Head of the Buddhist Church.

that'n (ˈðæt(ə)n), *adv. dial.* Also 9 **that-en, thatn, that'ns.** [perh. for an earlier **thatkin(s* of that kind, f. THAT *dem. adj.* + KIN *sb.*[1] 6 b: cf. THISKIN, THISSEN. But no instance of *thatkin* has been cited, and the termination may have a different origin.] More fully ***a that'n, -s***, in that way, in that manner, like that.

1695 CONGREVE *Love for L.* III. iii, An you stand astern a that'n, we shall never grapple together. *a* **1796** PEGGE *Derbicisms*, Thatn. *a* **1825** FORBY *Voc. E. Anglia*, *That'ns*,.. in that manner. **1879** MISS JACKSON *Shropsh. Word-bk.*, *Athatn, athatns... Thatn*,.. *adv.* that way.., as of the manner of doing a thing.

thatness (ˈðætnɪs). *Philos.* [f. THAT *dem. pron.* + -NESS.] The quality or condition of being 'that', i.e. of existing as a definite thing.

1643 DIGBY *Observ. Relig. Med.* (1644) 86 It is evident that samenesse, thisnesse, and thatnesse, belongeth not to matter by it selfe,.. but onely as it is distinguished and individuated by the forme. **1889** MIVART *Truth* 211 It apprehends what kind of a thing the object perceived may be—its 'thatness', so to speak. **1891** E. B. BAX *Outlooks fr. New Standpoint* III. 183 The phenomenon or sign of the being or of the thatness which itself ever eludes us. *Ibid.* 191 Imparting to whatness a thatness. **1904** *Athenæum* 24 Dec. 868/2 The investing of the content, which is in Bradleian language a 'what', with self-existent reality or 'that-ness'.

thattaboy, thatta boy, varr. THATABOY *int.*

† **thau**, obs. form of TAU.

1483 CAXTON *Gold. Leg.* 317/1 A little staf that he helde whiche hadde the signe of thau. **1701** C. WOLLEY *Jrnl. New York* (1860) 31 That Rabbinical Critick the Oxford Gregory upon Cain's Thau.

thau, þau, þauȝ, þauh, obs. ff. THOUGH.

thauel, obs. form of THOLE *sb.*[1]

thaught, variant of THOUGHT, rower's bench.

thaumasite (ˈθɔːməsaɪt). *Min.* [mod. (Nordenskiöld, 1878), f. Gr. θαυμάσι-ος wonderful, marvellous + -ITE[1]: so named 'on account of its unusual composition'.] 'A white, amorphous mineral composed of silicate, carbonate and sulphate of calcium, and water' (Chester).

1881 in WATTS *Dict. Chem.* VIII. 1921.

thaumatin (ˈθɔːmətɪn). *Biochem.* [f. *Thaumat(ococcus*, mod.L. generic name (f. THAUMATO- + COCCUS) + -IN[1].] Either or both of two related sweet-tasting proteins isolated from the fruit of the African plant *Thaumatococcus daniellii.*

1972 VAN DER WEL & LOEVE in *European Jrnl. Biochem.* XXXI. 221/1 This paper deals with the isolation and characterization of the sweet principles we call thaumatin I and II. *Ibid.* 225/2 The thaumatins are the first sweet-tasting proteins that have been found in nature. **1973** [see MONELLIN]. **1980** *Nature* 24 Apr. 653/2 Tate and Lyle.. are to apply recombinant DNA techniques to improve production of the protein thaumatin—a substance 2,500 times sweeter than a 10% sugar solution.

thaumato- (θɔːmətəʊ), combining form of Gr. θαῦμα, θαυματ-, wonder, marvel. **thaumaˈtogenist**, a believer in or advocate of thaumatogeny. **thaumaˈtogeny**, [-GENY], the origination of life as a miraculous process: opposed to *nomogeny*. **thaumaˈtography** [-GRAPHY: mod.L. *thaumatographia*], a writing concerning the wonders of nature. **thaumaˈtolatry** [-LATRY], excessive reverence for the miraculous or marvellous. **thaumaˈtology** [-LOGY], an account of miracles; the description or discussion of the miraculous.

1891 *Cent. Dict.*, *Thaumatogenist (citing Owen). **1868** OWEN *Vertebr. Anim.* III. 814 Nomogeny or *Thaumatogeny? **1869** MOZLEY *Ess.* (1878) II. 394 Independent of all theories of elementary formation—Evolution, Epigenesis, Nomogeny, Thaumatogeny. [**1632** J. JOHNSTON (*title*) *Thaumatographia Naturalis.] **1891** *Cent. Dict.*, Thaumatography. **1827** HARE *Guesses* (1859) 98 The *thaumatolatry by which our theology has been debased. **1851** J. H. NEWMAN *Cath. Eng.* 296 In the Protestant's view.. who assumes that miracles never are, our *thaumatology is one great falsehood. **1904** *Edin. Rev.* Jan. 163 In which [volume] the work of thaumatology is carried to its furthest extreme.

thaumatrope (ˈθɔːmətrəʊp). [irreg. f. Gr. θαῦμα (see THAUMATO-) + -τροπος turning.] A scientific toy illustrating the persistence of visual impressions, consisting of a card or disk with two different figures drawn upon the two sides, which are apparently combined into one when the disk is rotated rapidly; also applied to a disk or cylinder bearing a series of figures which, on being rapidly rotated and viewed through a slit, produce the impression of a moving object (= PHENAKISTOSCOPE, ZOETROPE).

1827 J. A. PARIS *Philos. in Sport* III. i. 5 This toy is termed the Thaumatrope. **1839** BREWSTER *Optics* xviii. (ed. 4) 338 Thaumatrope [is] the name given by Dr. Paris to an optical toy, the principle of which depends on the persistence of vision. **1872** HUXLEY *Phys.* x. 245 The thaumatrope,.. by the help of which, on looking through a hole, one sees images of jugglers throwing up and catching balls.

Hence **thaumaˈtropical** *a.*, pertaining to or having the nature or effect of a thaumatrope.

1829 *Blackw. Mag.* XXV. 82 Having read Emerson on this thaumatropical proceeding.

thaumaturge (ˈθɔːmətɜːdʒ). Also 8-9 **-turg** (-tɜːg). [ad. med.L. *thaumatūrg-us*, ad. Gr. θαυματουργός wonder-working, a conjurer, f. θαυματ- wonder + -εργος working; in form *-urge*, conformed to F. *thaumaturge* (1663 in Hatz.-Darm.).] A worker of marvels or miracles; a wonder-worker.

1715 M. DAVIES *Athen. Brit.* I. 125 Petavius.. attainted.. Origen's wonder-working Scholar Gregory the Thaumaturg, with Præarianisme. **1760** WESLEY *Jrnl.* 20 Dec., You throw out a hard word,.. Thaumaturg. **1826** SOUTHEY *Vind. Eccl. Angl.* 479 The Thaumaturge.. knelt before the Image to intercede for them. **1860** *Sat. Rev.* X. 269/2 The half-maudlin, half-cheating thaumaturg. **1881** *Athenæum* 12 Mar. 363/2 Pious mythologists have made out that she [St. Frideswide] was a thaumaturge of the first order.

thaumaturgic (θɔːməˈtɜːdʒɪk), *a.* and *sb.* [f. as prec. + -IC.]

A. *adj.* **1.** That works, or has the power of working, miracles or marvels; wonder-working.

1680 *Dial. between Pope & Phanatick* 11 The Thaumatergick word of Protestant Religion have done our Cause such eminent service. **1818** G. S. FABER *Horæ Mosaicæ* I. 356 The thaumaturgic and inspired prophet Moses. **1831** CARLYLE *Sart. Res.* II. iv, The grand thaumaturgic art of Thought. **1889** PATER *G. de Latour* 65 The witchery, the thaumaturgic powers, of Virgil, or..of Shakespeare.

2. Of, pertaining to, or involving thaumaturgy. **1825** CARLYLE *Schiller* II. (1873) 73 Various thaumaturgic feats. **1894** STEVENSON *Let. to Miss A. Boodle* 14 July, Never expect..thaumaturgic conversions.

B. *sb.* †**a.** The art of constructing marvellous or apparently magical devices. *Obs.*

1570 DEE *Math. Pref.* Aj, Thaumaturgike, is that Art Mathematicall, which giueth certaine order to make straunge workes,..of men greatly to be wondred at.

b. *pl.* **thauma'turgics** [see -IC 2]: feats of magic, conjuring tricks.

1730 [see THAUMATURGY, quot. 1727]. **1824** MISS MITFORD *Village* Ser. I. 290 Mr. Moon, the very pearl of all conjurors,..with his 'wonderful..exhibition of Thaumaturgics, Tachygraphy, mathematical operations, and magical deceptions'.

thaumaturgical (θɔːmə'tɜːdʒɪkəl), *a.* [f. as prec.: see -ICAL.] = prec. adj.

1621 BURTON *Anat. Mel.* II. ii. IV. (1676) 179/1 Mills to move themselves, Archita's Dove, Albertus Brazen head, and such Thaumaturgical works. **1841** D'ISRAELI *Amen. Lit.* (1867) 642 Artful impostures..practised..by the dealers in thaumaturgical arts. **1904** R. J. CAMPBELL *Serm. Individuals* v. 74 The modern mind would..repudiate the thaumaturgical element here.

thaumaturgist ('θɔːmətɜːdʒɪst). [f. THAUMATURGY + -IST.] = THAUMATURGE.

1829 CARLYLE *Misc., Germ. Playw.* (1872) II. 91 No conjuror..can any longer pass for a true thaumaturgist. **1837** *Ibid. Diamond Necklace* xvi. V. 190 Cagliostro, Thaumaturgist, Prophet and Arch-Quack. **1879** FARRAR *St. Paul* I. 530 *note*, The city was visited by the thaumaturgist Apollonius. **1882** —— *Early Chr.* I. 116 Rome abounded in Oriental thaumaturgists and impostors.

So **'thauma,turgism**, thaumaturgy (*Cent. Dict.* 1891); **'thaumatur,gize** *v. intr.*, to act the thaumaturge, perform wonders.

1891 *19th Cent.* Nov. 825 We find Father Anquieta thaumaturgising (if I may use the expression) on the slightest occasions.

‖**thaumaturgus** (θɔːmə'tɜːgəs). Pl. -i. [med.L.: see THAUMATURGE.] = THAUMATURGE.

1730 BAILEY (folio), *Thaumaturgus*,..a Worker of Miracles, a Title which the Roman-Catholicks give to several of their Saints. **1849** CDL. WISEMAN *Ess., Mirac. N. Test.* (1853) I. 188 Nor is there reason to suppose, that every simple faithful was a Thaumaturgus. **1886** *Edin. Rev.* July 283 Nature, the great Thaumaturgus, has in the Vocal Memnon propounded an enigma.

thaumaturgy ('θɔːmətɜːdʒɪ). [ad. Gr. θαυματουργία wonder-working, conjuring, f. THAUMATO- + -εργος working: see -Y. So F. *thaumaturgie* (1878 in *Dict. Acad.*).] The working of wonders; miracle-working; magic.

1727 BAILEY vol. II, *Thaumaturgy* [1730 (folio) also *Thaumaturgicks*],..any Art that does, or seems to do Wonders, or as it is defin'd by Dr. Dee [cf. THAUMATURGIC *sb.* a], a mathematical Science, which gives a certain Rule for the making of strange Works to be perceiv'd by the Sense, yet to be greatly wonder'd at. **1778** WARTON *Hist. Eng. Poetry* xv. (1840) II. 178 This art, with others of the experimental kind, the philosophers of those times were fond of adapting to the purposes of thaumaturgy. **1831** CARLYLE *Sart. Res.* III. viii, A World of Miracles, wherein all fabled or authentic Thaumaturgy, and feats of Magic, were outdone. **1872** MINTO *Eng. Prose Lit.* I. i. 38 Magic,—both black and white,—thaumaturgy, and necromancy.

†**thave**, *v. Obs.* Forms: 1 **þafian, þeafian**, 2 **þeafen**, 3 **þeauien, þauien, ðauen, þafe**, 3–4 **þaue**. [OE. *þafian*: etymology unascertained; not known in the cognate langs.] *trans.* To consent to; to allow, permit; to submit to, suffer, endure; to tolerate. Cf. I-THAVE.

835 *Kentish Charter of Abba* in *O.E. Texts* 448 Ic ciolnoð mid godes ȝefe ærcebiscop ðis write and ðeafie. *c* **888** K. ÆLFRED *Boeth.* xxxviii. §6 Þonne þe ðincð se earmra se þæt yfel deð ðonne se þe hit þafað. *c* **1000** *Ags. Gosp.* Matt. vii. 4 Broþur þafa [*c* **1160** þafe] þæt ic ut ado þæt mot of þinum eaȝan. *a* **1023** WULFSTAN *Hom.* iii. (Napier) 23 Eal þæt he for us and for ure lufan þafode and ðolode. [*c* **1175** *Lamb. Hom.* 121 God iþeafede þet to alesendnesse alles ileffulles moncunnes.] *c* **1200** ORMIN 5457 Godd ne þole nohht Ne þafe laþe gastess To winnenn oferhannd off uss þurrh heore laþe wiless. *c* **1250** *Gen. & Ex.* 3139 Euerilc hus-folc ðe mai it ðauen On ȝer sep oðer on kide hauen. *c* **1300** *Havelok* 2696 Was neuere non þat mouhte þaue Hise dintes, noyþer knith ne knaue.

Hence †**'thaving** (in 4 **þafung**, etc.) *vbl. sb.*, permission, consent.

13.. *Ancr. R.* 344 (MS. Cott. Cl.) þurch min þafunge [*MSS. Corpus, Ti.* þeafunge, *Ca.* þauunge].

thave, variant of THEAVE.

thavel, -il, thavvle, dial. forms of THIVEL.

thaw (θɔː), *sb.* Also β. 5 **thowe**, 5– **thow** (now *north. dial.* and *Sc.*). [f. THAW *v.*: cf. ON. *þá* thawed ground; also ON. *þeyr*, ONorw. *þøyr*, Sw. *tö*, Da. *tø* thaw; also Du. *dooi* thaw.]

1. The melting of ice and snow after a frost; the condition of the weather caused by the rise of temperature above the freezing point.

14.. *Voc.* in Wr.-Wülcker 586/9 *Gelicidium*, thawe. *a* **1552** LELAND *Itin.* V. 68 The Lake of Brecnok ons frosen over, and than in a Thaue breking maketh marvelus Noise. **1568** GRAFTON *Chron.* II. 441 Vpon a sodaine thawe, the floodes agayne encreace. **1634–5** LAUD *Diary* Wks. 1853 III. 223 The Thames was frozen over,..A mighty flood at the thaw. **1686** tr. *Chardin's Trav. Persia* 349 It becomes so furious when swell'd by the Thaws of the Snow. **1726–46** THOMSON *Winter* 990 The frost resolves into a trickling thaw. **1878** HUXLEY *Physiogr.* 142 By heavy rainfall, or by rapid thaw of snow.

β. **1412–20** LYDG. *Chron. Troy* II. 5079 Newe flodis of þe sodeyn þowe þe grene mede gan to ouerflowe. *c* **1440** *Promp. Parv.* 492/1 Thowe, of snowe, or yclys or yce,..*degelacio*. **1725** RAMSAY *Gentle Sheph.* I. ii, Thick-blawn wreaths of snaw, or blashy thows. **1786** BURNS *Brigs of Ayr* 119 Arous'd by blust'ring winds an' spotting thowes; In mony a torrent down his sna-broo rowes. **1876** *Whitby Gloss.*, *Thow*, thaw.

2. *transf.* and *fig.*

1598 SHAKS. *Merry W.* III. v. 119 A man of my Kidney..that am as subiect to heate as butter; a man of continuall dissolution, and thaw. **1684** BUNYAN *Pilgr.* II. 113 If the Sun of Righteousness will arise upon him, his frozen Heart shall feel a Thaw. **1794** BURNS *The Auld Man* ii, But my white pow, nae kindly thowe Shall melt the snaws of age. **1817** BYRON *Manfred* II. ii. 202 Now I tremble And feel a strange cold thaw upon my heart.

b. *spec.* A becoming less cold, formal, or reserved.

1840 M. EDGEWORTH *Let.* 30 Dec. (1971) 575 Lord Monteagle seated himself..beside Miss Edgeworth who had..made him rather a drawback stand-off curtsey... He seemed determined there should be a thaw. **1848** DICKENS *Dombey* v, Such temporary indications of a partial thaw that had appeared with her, vanished with her. **1873** BROWNING *Red Cott. Nt.-cap* III. 326 That thaw Of rigid disapproval into dew Of sympathy.

c. *Pol.* A relaxation of control or restriction; a lessening of harshness, hostility, etc.; *spec.* that which occurred in the U.S.S.R. after the death of Stalin in 1953.

1950 *Times* 13 June 5/3 The statement on foreign policy is the latest symptom of a thaw in Labour doctrine. **1956** R. MACAULAY *Towers of Trebizond* ii. 19 She had started..working away at Russian visas..some time before the Great Thaw. **1957** *Economist* 30 Nov. 787/2 When the Polish thaw made emigration again possible, some of these 'autochthons' joined the queue. **1969** A. G. FRANK *Latin Amer.* xxi. 338 In the countries that took the Marxist road there was an increase in freedom or a noticeable thaw after a relatively short period of time. **1971** *Guardian* 13 Sept. 10/1 Krushchev inaugurated the thaw that mitigated some of the harsh intolerance of Stalinist communism. **1981** *Times* 2 Nov. 8/7 Andrei Voznesensky, arguably Russia's greatest living poet..mirrored the hopes and naivety of the post-Stalin thaw.

3. *attrib.* and *Comb.*, as *thaw-rain*, *-time*, *-water*, *-wind* (cf. G. *tauwind*); *thaw-cold*, *-cloven*, *-swamped* adjs.

a **1715** BURNET *Own Time* II. an. 1672 (1823) I. 582 In the minute in which they began to march [on the ice], a thaw wind blew very fresh. **1814** BYRON in L. Hunt *Autobiog.* (1850) II. 318, I have been snow-bound and thaw-swamped..for nearly a month. **1819** SHELLEY *Prometh. Unb.* II. iii. 34 A howl Of cataracts from their thaw-cloven ravines. **1820** —— *Vision of Sea* 36 It splits like the ice when the thaw-breezes blow. **1852** DICKENS *Bleak Ho.* iii, She gave me one cold parting kiss upon my forehead, like a thaw-drop from the stone porch. **1890** STEVENSON *Let. to H. James* 29 Dec., My theories melt, and..the thaw-waters wash down my writing. **1917** D. H. LAWRENCE *Look! We have come Through!* 156 They are the flowers of ice-vivid mortification, thaw-cold, ice-corrupt blossoms. **1947** K. M. WELLS *Owl Pen Reader* (1969) i. 38 He bumped and slithered over the ice the thaw had laid bare. He splashed through thaw water. **1976** *Times Lit. Suppl.* 23 July 926/3 Lush new green and blue sky reflected in the thaw-waters.

thaw (θɔː), *v.* Forms: 1 **þawian**, (4 **þewe**), 5–6 **thawe**, 6 **thau**, 6– **thaw**. β. 4 **þowe, thoue**, 4–5 **thowe**, 5– **thow** (now *north. dial.* and *Sc.*). *Pa. t.* and *pa. pple.* **thawed** (*dial.* **thowed**, *pa. t.* also **thew**); *pa. pple.* also 8–9 **thawn**. [OE. *þawian*, ME. *þawen*; also ME. *thōwe*; cognate with OFris. **thâia* (:—**þawian*), whence WFris. *teije*, NFris. *tuai*; OLG **þawian*, whence MLG. *doien*, LG. *däuen* (Dähnert), Du. *dooien*, EFris. *deien, deuen, doien*; OHG. *douwen, dewen* (cf. mod.Ger. *verdauen* to digest), ON. *þeyja* (:—**þauja*), ONorw. *þøya*, Sw. *töa*, Da. *tøe*. The late ME. and Sc. *thōwe* does not answer to OE. *þawian*, but seems to require **þówan* or **þáwan*, unrecorded. Ulterior history obscure.]

1. a. *trans.* To reduce (a frozen substance, as ice or snow) to a liquid state by raising its temperature above the freezing point; to melt (a frozen liquid). Also *thaw out* (orig. U.S.).

c **1000** *Sax. Leechd.* III. 274 Se wind [Zephirus] towyrpð and ðawað ælcne winter. **1530** PALSGR. 755/1 Sette the potte to the fyre to thawe the water. **1596** SHAKS. *Merch. V.* II. i. 5 Where Phœbus fire scarce thawes the ysicles. **1625** N. CARPENTER *Geog. Del.* II. v. (1635) 79 Riuers..by a remission of the cold are thawed. *a* **1704** T. BROWN *Lond. & Lacedem. Oracles* Wks. 1709 III. III. 138 After the Snow is thawn. **1790** BURKE *Fr. Rev.* 349 Mr. Bailly will sooner thaw the eternal ice of his atlantic regions, than restore the central heat to Paris. **1878** HUXLEY *Physiogr.* 64 Until the warmth of summer returns to thaw it [the snow].

β. *c* **1384** CHAUCER *H. Fame* III. 53 They [letters] were almost ithowed so That of the lettres oon or two Was molte away of euery name. *c* **1440** *Promp. Parv.* 492/1 Thowyn or meltyn, as snowe and other lyke, *resolvo*. **1596** DALRYMPLE tr. *Leslie's Hist. Scot.* (S.T.S.) I. 46 To thow the pypes and schokles of yce. **1894** A. REID *Songs Heatherl.* 107 Storms that time had thowed.

b. *fig.*

1591 SHAKS. *Two Gent.* II. iv. 200 Iulia that I loue, (That I did loue, for now my loue is thaw'd..like a waxen Image 'gainst a fire..). **1615** SIR W. MURE *Misc. Poems* viii. 43 Lat beuties beames then thau away..The ycinesse of loues delay. **1725** RAMSAY *Gentle Sheph.* III. iii. Prol., To whisper out his melting flame, And thow his lassie's breast. **1785** M. CUTLER in *Life*, etc. (1888) II. 228 This cold snowy winter has considerably cooled my zeal, but when I get thawed out, in the spring, perhaps it may return. **1821** SHELLEY *Adonais* i, O, weep for Adonais! though our tears Thaw not the frost which binds so dear a head!

2. a. *intr.* Of ice, snow, or other substance: To pass from a frozen to a liquid or semi-liquid state; to melt under the influence of warmth: esp. by rise of temperature after frost. Also *thaw out* (orig. U.S.).

c **1325** *Gloss. W. de Bibbesw.* in Wright *Voc.* 147 *Après gelé vent remoyl* [gloss] thowyng. **1387** TREVISA *Higden* (Rolls) VII. 453 Many brugges..were i-broke of þe þowynge [*v.r.* þewinge] of þe yse. **1530** PALSGR. 755/1, I thawe, as snowe or yce dothe for heate. **1552** HULOET, Thawe as yse dothe, *egelidor*. **1610** HOLLAND *Camden's Brit.* (1637) 628 As often as the Yce thereon doth thaw. **1656** M. BEN ISRAEL *Vind. Jud.* 9 The pond thawd. **1703** MAUNDRELL *Journ. Jerus.* (1732) 140 Abundance of Snow; which thawing in the heat of Summer [etc.]. **1835** J. H. INGRAHAM *South-West* I. 33 When vessels in their winter voyages..become coated with ice,..they seek the genial warmth of this region to 'thaw out'. **1880** HAUGHTON *Phys. Geog.* iv. 195 The water freezes in November and thaws in May. **1887** I. R. *Lady's Ranche Life Montana* 33 Before I can begin to write this letter the ink must be put down by the fire to thaw out, as it is frozen solid.

b. *transf.* and *fig.*

1602 SHAKS. *Ham.* I. ii. 130 Oh that this too too solid Flesh, would melt, Thaw, and resolue it selfe into a Dew. **1849** MISS MULOCK *Ogilvies* xxix, He..thawed into positive enthusiasm beneath the sunshine of her influence. **1865** SWINBURNE *Atalanta* 2104, I would that as water My life's blood had thawn. **1905** A. C. BENSON *Upton Lett.* (1906) 293 The dreariness of my heart thawed and melted into peace and calm.

3. *impers.* *it thaws*: said of the cessation of a frost, when the ice, snow, etc. begin to melt.

c **1325** *Gloss. W. de Bibbesw.* in Wright *Voc.* 160 *Ore gele*, freset; *Ore remet*, thouet. *c* **1425** *Voc.* in Wr.-Wülcker 665/2 *Degelat*, thowes. **1530** PALSGR. 755/1 It thaweth a pace. **1709** *Lond. Gaz.* No. 4507/3 This Morning it began to thaw. *Mod.* The frost seems to be giving way; I expect it will thaw before night.

4. a. *trans.* To free from the physical effect of frost; to unfreeze; said usually in reference to a non-liquid substance rigid with frost, also to a person or animal affected by extreme cold.

1596 SHAKS. *Tam. Shr.* IV. i. 9 My very lippes might freeze to my teeth,..ere I should come by a fire to thaw me. **1665** *Phil. Trans.* I. 48 The frozen Bodies will be harmlessly thawed. **1728** RAMSAY *Anacreontic on Love* 21, I..his handies thow'd. **1829** LYTTON *Devereux* v. ii, After I was lodged, thawed, and fed, I fell fast asleep. **1883** W. AITKEN *Lays* 98 (E.D.D.) The whusky thowed their Hielan' bluid. **1887** I. R. *Lady's Ranche Life Montana* 144 You have to thaw a bit before you can put it in a horse's mouth.

b. *nonce-use.* To make limp (anything stiff).

1821 SCOTT *Kenilw.* xl, Speak..at farther distance, so please you; your breath thaws our ruff.

5. *intr.* To become unfrozen; to become flexible or limp by rise of temperature.

1596 DALRYMPLE tr. *Leslie's Hist. Scot.* (S.T.S.) I. 46 Gif ony frosin thing be put athir in the loch or in the riuer, it thowis fra hand. **1687** A LOVELL tr. *Thevenot's Trav.* II. 122 We found it worse when the Sun was up, and the ground began to Thaw. **1850–6** O. W. HOLMES *Spring* 25 The bog's green harper, thawing from his sleep, Twangs a hoarse note.

6. *fig.* **a.** *trans.* To soften to sympathy or geniality; to break down coldness and reserve.

1582 STANYHURST *Æneis* II. (Arb.) 48 Wee thawde with weeping doo pardon francklye the villeyn. **1677** GILPIN *Demonol.* (1867) 92 An extraordinary occasion melts and thaws down the natural affections of men. **1741** RICHARDSON *Pamela* (1824) I. 102 She is a charming girl, and may be thawed by kindness. **1883** GILMOUR *Mongols* (1884) 201 Tea even fails to thaw completely their reserve. **1889** J. JEFFERSON *Autobiog.* xii. (1891) 329 A hopeless endeavor to thaw him out.

b. *intr.* Of a person, his feelings, manner, etc.: To become softened or 'melted' in feeling; to throw off coldness and reserve; to unbend.

1598 BP. HALL *Sat.* IV. iv. Dj b, He thaw's like Chaucers frosty Ianiuere; And sets a Months minde vpon smyling May. *a* **1631** DONNE *Valediction my Name* ix, And thou begin'st to thaw towards him for this, May my name step in. **1827** POLLOK *Course of T.* IX. 722 Pride of rank And office, thawed into paternal love. **1900** EL. GLYN *Visits Eliz.* (1906) 18 He..went on talking in the friendliest way, but I would not thaw.

7. The verb-stem in combination forming sbs., as *thaw-house*, *thaw point*.

1892 *Pall Mall G.* 30 Aug. 7/2 Dynamite..is received at the work in a frozen state, and stored in a big magazine. From this receptacle it is taken to the thaw-house as needed. **1902** *Daily Chron.* 28 May 8/5 When 'thaw' points were needed, through which steam was forced into the hard ground, they were improvised out of rifle barrels.

Hence **thawed** (θɔːd) *ppl. a.*, warmed so as to melt (as ice), softened; ***thawed out***, also, put out of work or action by a thaw; **'thawing** *ppl. a.*, that thaws, melting.

1652 CRASHAW *Mary Magd.* Wks. (1904) 259 Thawing crystall! snowy hills, Still spending, never spent! **1774** GOLDSM. *Nat. Hist.* (1776) I. 247 Clefts, from whence the thawed water trickles out. **1800** HENRY *Epit. Chem.* (1808) 37 The temperature of melting snow, or of thawing ice. **1885** *Harper's Mag.* Dec. 86/2 The now thawed-out and almost genial Miss Lisle. **1894** *Westm. Gaz.* 19 Jan. 7/2 The thawed-out skaters equalised matters by holding a carnival on wheel skates at the Wandsworth Rink last night. **1942** W. FAULKNER *Go down, Moses* 238 Out of the wet and thawing woods. *Ibid.* 240 They plunged down the bank, slipping and sliding in the thawed earth.

thaw, þaw, þawe, obs. forms of THOUGH.

thawer ('θɔːə(r)). [f. prec. vb. + -ER[1].] One who or that which thaws; *spec.* in *Mining*, a device or apparatus for thawing frozen ground.

1630 *R. Johnson's Kingd. & Commw.* 7 Even in that continuall neighbourhood of that great Thawer [i.e. the sun] have you hils perpetually covered with frost and snow. **1900** *Pop. Sci. Monthly* Feb. 461 The introduction of mining machinery, such as.. thawers.. has given fresh impetus.

thawing ('θɔːɪŋ), *vbl. sb.* [f. as prec. + -ING[1].] The action of the verb THAW (*lit.* or *fig.*). Also in *pl.* (in quot. 1886 *concr.*). Also *attrib.*, and with *out* (or *up*).

c **1325**, **1387** [see THAW *v.* 2]. **1586** HOLINSHED *Chron.* III. 20/2 At their dissoluing or thawing, manie bridges both of wood and stone were borne downe. **1681** FLAVEL *Meth. Grace* vii. 152 Thawings of the heart under the apprehensions of grace. **1861** THORNBURY *Turner* (1862) II. 135 The occasional thawings of natures, however frozen by habit. **1886** M. K. MACMILLAN *Dagonet* 154 The first thawings of the hard-bound road clung impedingly to our shoes. **1905** *Kynoch Jrnl.* Oct.–Dec. 200 Many consumers.. put frozen cartridges in thawing pans several hours before they are required. **1946** KOESTLER *Thieves in Night* 150 Ellen was engaged in a serious and measured conversation... Dina took no part in the thawing-up proceedings. **1973** 'R. MACLEOD' *Nest of Vultures* v. 97 A large whisky gently completing the thawing-out process.

thawless ('θɔːlɪs), *a.* [f. THAW *sb.* or *v.* + -LESS.] That does not thaw, or that never thaws.

1813 W. TAYLOR *Eng. Synonyms* 30 Thawless unmelting obstinacy. **1838** MARY HOWITT *Birds & Fl., Sunshine* v, Where rests the thawless snow. **1886** RUSKIN *Præterita* I. ix. 291 The winter gives them [flowers] rest under thawless serenity of snow.

thawrtouer, erron. form of THWARTOVER.

thawt, variant of THOUGHT[2], rower's bench.

thawy ('θɔːɪ), *a.* [f. THAW *sb.* + -Y.] Characterized by thaw; of or pertaining to a thaw.

1728 T. SMITH *Jrnl.* (1849) 266 There has been no thawy weather. **1809–10** COLERIDGE *Friend* (1866) 314 Thoughts brisk as beer and pathos soft and thawy. **1892** *Longm. Mag.* Dec. 206 If the day is a fine frosty one and the previous one happens to have been warm and 'thawy'.

thay, þay, obs. forms of THAE, THEY, THOUGH.

thayffe, obs. form of THEAVE.

thayl: see THAIL, obs. f. TAEL.

thaym, thayme, obs. forms of THEM.

thayn, obs. form of THANE.

thayr, -e, -es, obs. forms of THEIR, -S[1].

the (*bef. cons.* ðə; *bef. vowel* ðɪ; *emph.* ðiː), *dem. adj.* ('*def. article*') and *pron.* Forms: see below. [The reduced and flexionless stem of the OE. demonstrative *se*, *séo* (later *þe*, *þéo*), *þæt*, the neuter sing. of which has come down as the dem. pron. and adj. THAT. Com. Teut. and Indo-Eur.: = OFris. *thi*, *thiu*, *thet*, OS. (*se*), *th*(*i*)*e*, *thiu* (*the*), *that* (*the*), (MLG., MDu. *de* (*die*), *dat*, LG., Du. *de*, *dat*), OHG. *der* (*de*), *diu*, *daz* (mod.Ger. *der*, *die*, *das*), ON. *sá*, *sú*, *þat*, Goth. *sa*, *sô*, *þata*, also Gr. ὁ, ἡ, τό, Zend *ho*, *hā*, *tat*, Skr. *sa*, *sā*, *tat*; all the inflexional parts exc. the nom. sing. m. and f. having the stem *þa-*, Lith., Slav. *to-*, Gr. το-, Zend, Skr. *ta-*, Indo-Eur. *to-*, found also in L. in *tam*, *tum*, *tunc*, *is-te*, *is-tud*, etc. The nom. sing. m. and f. in OTeut., as in Skr., Zend, Gr., belong to another demonst. stem *sa-*, I.-Eur. *so-*, found also in Ir., Gael., Gaulish *so* this, L. *-se* in *ip-se*. But in OHG., OS. (in most dialects), and in late OE. (10th c. in Northumbrian, and at length everywhere) the *s-* forms were superseded by forms in *þ-* (OHG. *d-*), from the same stem as the neuter *þæt* and the oblique cases, as well as the pl. *þá*, later *þō*, THO. After the middle of the 13th c. the *s-* forms are no longer found, exc. as a belated survival (*ze* m., *zy* f.) in the Kentish dial. of the Ayenbite (1340). The only surviving reprs. of the OE. forms are *the* and *that*, Du. and LG. *de*, *dat*; but while LG. *dat* (besides its other uses) is still the neuter article, the Eng. *that* has ceased to be any part of the article. In the following illustration of Forms all the inflexions are illustrated, but the special history of *þæt* and *þá* pl. will be found under THAT, THO.

(The nom. fem. *sío*, *séo* corresponds in form not to Goth. *sô*, ON. *sú*, I.-Eur. **sā*, but to OS., OHG. *siu* 'she'. Some identify it with Skt. *syā* fem. of the 'extended' demonstrative *sya*, *syā*, *tyat*; others regard it as a special WGer. formation related to Goth. *sī* 'she'.)]

A. Illustration of Forms.

The OE. demonstrative and definite article was thus inflected:

SING.	MASC.	FEM.	NEUT.	PLURAL.
Nom.	se, *later* þe	sío, séo, *later* þío, þíu	þæt	þá
Acc.	þone, þæne	þá	þæt	þá
Dat.	þǽm, þám	þǽre	þǽm, þám	þǽm, þám
Gen.	þæs	þǽre	þæs	þára(þǽra)
Instr.	þý, þon		þý, þon	

The variants and later forms were:

I. Sing. **1. a.** *Nom. masc.* α. 1–3 **se** (1 **sæ**, 2 **seo**) [4 **ze** *antec. pron.*].

805 *Charter of Cuðred* in *O.E. Texts* 442 Æðelnoð se ȝerefa to Eastoreȝe. *c* **825** *Vesp. Psalter* ix. 25 Bismerað dryhten se synfulla. *c* **950** *Lindisf. Gosp.* Mark x. 24 Sæ [*Rushw.* ðe] hælend.. cuoeð. *c* **1000** *Sax. Leechd.* III. 84 Sa ruwa ȝealle byð wexenda on þan innoþe. *Ibid.*, Se blace ȝealle. *a* **1154** *O.E. Chron.* (Laud MS.) an. 1135, On þis ȝære for se king Henri ouer sæ. *a* **1175** *Cotton Hom.* 235 Þis is seo king. *c* **1250** *O. Kent. Serm.* in *O.E. Misc.* 26 Se king of gyus. [**1340** *Ayenb.* 117 Ze þet ne heþ þise uondinges.]

¶ Abnormal uses of *se* in oblique cases, and of *sa* pl., *ses* gen. sing. (In some of these, *s* may be a scribal error for *þ*.)

c **1121** *O.E. Chron.* (Laud MS.) an. 1114, Þæt duȝeð þæt wæs.. mid se cyng. *a* **1131** *Ibid.* an. 1123, Ðis wæs eall ear ȝedon ðurh se biscop of Seresbyriȝ, & þurh se biscop of Lincolne. *Ibid.*, Hi.. brohten him toforen se kyng. *Ibid.*, ȝebletsod to biscop fram se biscop of Lundene. *a* **1175** *Cott. Hom.* 235 Ures hlafordes to-cyme ses helendes ihesu cristes. **1200–25** *Peri Didaxeon* in *Sax. Leechd.* III. 94 To ðan sare þe abutan sa earan wycst. *Ibid.* 112 Wurm þanna sa handa & smyra þar mið.

β. 1–2 **ðe** (**ðy**), 1–4 **þe** (2–4 **te**); 2–3 **þa**, 3–5 **þo**.

The *O.E. Chron.* 1122–31 has for the nom. masc. *se*, the section 1132–54 has (exc. once, anno 1135) *þe* (and *te*).

c **950** *Lindisf. Gosp.* Matt. ii. 3 Herodes ðe cynig. *Ibid.* ix. 15 Cueð to him ðe hælend. *a* **1154** *O.E. Chron.* (Laud MS.) an. 1132, Was it noht suithe lang þer efter þat te king sende efter him. *Ibid.* an. 1135, Þat ilc ȝær warth þe king ded. *c* **1175** *Lamb. Hom.* 3 Hu þe helend nehlechede toward ierusalem. *c* **1205** LAY. 1327 Ne beo þa dai na swa long. *a* **1240** *Sawles Warde* in *Cott. Hom.* 267 Þe feder an te sune an te hali gast. *a* **1300** *Floriz & Bl.* 739 Þe Admiral.. chaungede his chere. **13..** *Cursor M.* 6282 (Cott.) Þe lauerd o might. *Ibid.* 20185 Þan said te angel. *a* **1325** *MS. Rawl. B.* 520 lf. 31 3if þat te on [Iustise] be Clerke.

b. *Nom. fem.* α. 1 **séo, sío, síu,** (**sa**), 1–3 **se,** 2 **sie, syo,** 2–3 **si,** [4 **zi, zy** *antec. pron.*].

c **888** K. ÆLFRED *Boeth.* xxxix. §5 Sio godcunde ȝesceadwisnes. *c* **893** —— *Oros.* II. iv. §8 Seo ilce burȝ Babylonia, seo ðe mæst wæs.. seo is nu læst. *c* **975** *Rushw. Gosp.* Matt. xii. 13 Swa siu oþeru [hond]. *c* **1000** *Ags. Gosp.* Mark xv. 40 Seo [*c* **1160** *Hatton G.*, sie] magdalenisce maria. *a* **1131** *O.E. Chron.* (Laud MS.) an. 1122, On þone lenten tyde.. forbearn se burch. *c* **1160** *Hatton Gosp.* John xii. 17 Syo menio þe wæs mid him. *a* **1175** *Cott. Hom.* 233 Hwat deð si moder hire bearn? *c* **1250** *O. Kent. Serm.* in *O.E. Misc.* 28 Si Mirre signefiet uastinge. [**1340** *Ayenb.* 102 Zy þet ne serueþ bote to onlepy manne.]

β. 1 **ðío, ðíu,** 1–3 **ðéo, þéo,** (3 **þæ,** 2–3 **þa,** 2–4 **þo**).

c **950** *Lindisf. Gosp.* John ii. 1 Uæs ðiu [*Rushw.* ðio] moder and ðe hælend ðer. *Ibid.* v. 25 Cymmes ðio tid & nu is. **971** *Blickl. Hom.* 65 Þeo deaþ-berende uncyst us is eallum to onscunienne. *c* **975** *Rushw. Gosp.* John xix. 20 Neh ðær cæstre wæs ðio stow. *c* **1000** *Ags. Gosp.* ibid., Þeo stow wæs ȝehende þære ceastre. *c* **1175** *Lamb. Hom.* 15 Hit wes þa laȝe. *Ibid.* 87 Þo tid to estertide. *c* **1205** LAY. 4010 Þeo uniseli moder. *Ibid.* 9815 Þæ quene spac wið him þus. *a* **1225** *Ancr. R.* 282 Þeo heorte ne ethalt none wete of Godes grace. *a* **1250** *Owl & Night.* 26 Þo vle song hire tide.

c. *Nom.* and *accus. neuter.* 1 **ðæt,** 1–3 **þæt,** 2–4 **þet,** 2–5 **þat, that,** (3 **þut**): see also THAT.

c **893** K. ÆLFRED *Oros.* I. i. §8 Þæt land Cilia. *Ibid.*, Irnende on þæt sond, & þonne besince eft on þæt sand. *c* **1000** ÆLFRIC *Hom.* I. 264 Þæt ðridde ȝebed is. *c* **1175** *Lamb. Hom.* 7 Þat ebreisce folc sungen heore leof-song. *c* **1205** LAY. 297 Þat child was ihaten Brutus. *Ibid.* 7843 Þæt weder heom strongliche drof. *a* **1225** *Ancr. R.* 186 Nis þet child fulitowen þet schrepeð aȝean? *a* **1250** *Owl & Night.* 1259 Þah ic hi warny al þat yer. **1297** R. GLOUC. (Rolls) 12014 Þo was þut lond in pes. *c* **1320** *Cast. Love* 139 To delen þat vuel from þe good. **1340** *Ayenb.* 2 Þet oþer heaued of þe beste of helle.

2. *Accus.* **a.** *masc.* 1–2 **þone,** (1 **þæne**), 2 **þana,** 2–3 **þene,** 2–4 **þane, þan, þen,** (3 **þun**), 3–4 **þon,** 4 **þanne.**

c **825** *Vesp. Psalter* iv. 4 ȝemiclað dryhten ðone halȝan his. *c* **1121** *O.E. Chron.* (Laud MS.) an. 1016, Eadric ealdormann ȝewende þa ðæne cyng onȝean. *a* **1131** *Ibid.* an. 1122, Þa com se fir on ufen weard þone stepel. *a* **1175** *Cott. Hom.* 223 He worhte þa þane man mid his handen. *c* **1175** *Lamb. Hom.* 7 Þurh þene halie gast. *Ibid.* 99 Crist ableow þana halȝa gast ofer þa apostlas. *c* **1200** *Trin. Coll. Hom.* 53 Ure helende.. makede þen heuenliche fader sehte mid mankin. **1297** R. GLOUC. (Rolls) 2184 To rere þon stronge wal. *Ibid.* 7954 He.. þen castel bisette. **1340** *Ayenb.* 187 He ne may naȝt þolye þane guode smel.. namore þanne þe boterel þanne smel of þe vine. *c* **1380** *Sir Ferumb.* 2419 Ate laste þan gurdel he fond. *c* **1400** *Sowdone Bab.* 108 To Egremoure þon riche Cite.

b. *fem.* 1–3 **þá,** 2–3 **þeo,** 3 **þie, þo.**

a **900** tr. *Bæda's Hist.* III. xii. [xiv.] (1890) 196 Se biscop þa ȝeseah þa eaðmodnesse þæs cyninges. *c* **1000** *Ags. Gosp.* John xix. 17 On þa stowe. *c* **1175** *Lamb. Hom.* 9 On þa ealde laȝe. *Ibid.* 49 [Þes put] bitacneð þeo deopnesse of sunne. *c* **1200** *Trin. Coll. Hom.* 107 Þie giue god giueð ech man. *Ibid.*, Þeo giue he giueð mid þe holi husel. *c* **1205** LAY. 31 He nom þa Englisca boc þa makede seint Beda. *c* **1250** *O. Kent. Serm.* in *O.E. Misc.* 29 We mowe habbe þo blisce of heueriche.

3. *Dative.* **a.** *masc.* and *neut.* 1 **þǽm,** 1–2 **þám,** (2 **þa**), 2–4 **þen, þon, thon, þan, than,** (3 **þæn**), 3–4 **þo** (**ten**).

Beowulf 143 Se þæm feonde æt-wand. *c* **975** *Rushw. Gosp.* Matt. viii. 24 On þæm sæ. *c* **1000** ÆLFRIC *Gen.* vi. 16 Binnan þam arce. *c* **1121** *O.E. Chron.* (Laud MS.) an. 1087, Innan þam castele. **1131** *Ibid.*, On þa tun þa wæs tenn ploȝes. *a* **1175** *Cott. Hom.* 227 Mid þan hefonlice feder. *c* **1175** *Lamb. Hom.* 41 On þon deie. *Ibid.* 121 Ibuhsum þan heuenliche federe to þa deðe. *c* **1200** *Trin. Coll. Hom.* 25 For þo þe he us shop. *c* **1205** LAY. 8157 Þu me smiten bi þon rugge. *Ibid.* 127 On þan londe. *Ibid.* 9266 He redde al þæn kæisere. *a* **1225** *Ancr. R.* 66 Al þat lescun.. of þen epple. *c* **1250** *O. Kent. Serm.* in *O.E. Misc.* 26 To-janes þo sunne risindde. *Ibid.*, Bi þo sterre. *c* **1315** SHOREHAM v. 184 Fram þan tyme he was ybore. **1340** *Ayenb.* 12 At þo daye. *c* **1386** CHAUCER *Friar's T.* 51 To.. make hym grete feestes atte nale [= at ten ale].

b. *fem.* 1–3 **þǽre** (2 **þara**), 2–3 **þere, þer,** 2–4 **þare, þar.**

c **888** K. ÆLFRED *Boeth.* xli. §3 Mid þære ilcan spræce. *c* **1000** *Ags. Gosp.* John xvii. 11 On ðære tide. *c* **1000** *Sax. Leechd.* III. 86 Byd hy to þare wunda. *a* **1175** *Cott. Hom.* 225 Binnan þara birie. *Ibid.* 235 To þar sawle. *c* **1175** *Lamb. Hom.* 3 He com to þere dune. *Ibid.* 31 Cume þenne to þer ilke chirche. *c* **1205** LAY. 1233 Mid þære sæ. *Ibid.* 4528 To þere sæ. *a* **1225** *Ancr. R.* 36 Ualleð to ðer eorðe. *a* **1250** *Owl & Night.* 31 Þe Nightegale.. þuhte wel ful of þare vle. *c* **1315** SHOREHAM ii. 118 Þe sonne dym By-come in þare tyde.

4. *Genitive.* **a.** *masc.* and *neut.* 1–3 **ðæs, þæs,** 3 **þeos,** *Orm.* **þess,** 2–4 **þes, þas.** See also THES *adv.*

c **893** K. ÆLFRED *Oros.* I. iv. §2 On þæs cyninges daȝum. *c* **1000** ÆLFRIC *Hom.* I. 240 For ðæs folces hreddinge. *a* **1131** *O.E. Chron.* an. 1122, Þet wes þes dæies viii idus Mr. *c* **1160** *Hatton Gosp.* Luke i. 10 Eall wered þas folkes. *c* **1200** *Trin. Coll. Hom.* 23 He sit on rihthalf þes almihtie faderes. *c* **1205** LAY. 713 To þas [*c* 1275 þis] kinges ferde. *Ibid.* 806 To telde þæs [*c* 1275 þis] kinges. *Ibid.* 7560 Þurh þeos [*c* **1275** þes] sweordes wunde. *a* **1250** *Owl & Night.* 338 Þu adunest þas monnes eren þar þu wunest.

b. *fem.* 1–2 **þǽre,** 2–3 **þere, þare,** 2–4 **þer.**

c **893** K. ÆLFRED *Oros.* I. i. §14 On oþre healfe þære eas. *c* **1205** LAY. 331 Þere quene cun Heleine. *a* **1250** *Owl & Night.* 28 Hit wes þare vle erdingstowe. *c* **1315** SHOREHAM i. 79 Mannys blod Hys [= ys] ryȝt þer saule ȝiste.

5. *Instrumental*: see THE *adv.*, THON, THY *adv.*

II. *Plural.* **6.** *Nom.* and *acc.* 1–4 **þá,** (2–3 **ta**), (3 **þea**), 3–5 **þo** (**to**); 3 **þeo,** 4 **theo.** (See also THO *adj.*)

a **700** *Epinal Gl.* (O.E.T.) 439 *Funestissima*, tha deat[h]licostan. *c* **725** *Corpus Gl.* 942 Ða deadlicustan. *c* **825** *Vesp. Psalter* v. 6 Ða unrehtwisan. *a* **1200** *Moral Ode* 103 Þa swicen and ta forsworene. *c* **1200** *Trin. Coll. Hom.* 35 On þa wurhliche weden. *c* **1205** LAY. 2020 He.. scæwede þea [*c* 1275 þe] leoden. *Ibid.* 2326 Þa hehste of þan hirde. *Ibid.* 5654 Þeo [*c* 1275 þe] cnihtes weoren vnwepned. **12..** *Moral Ode* (Egert. MS.) 192 He scal deme þo quike & to dede. *a* **1300** *Cursor M.* 861 Amang þa trees. *a* **1400** *K. Alis.* 4108 Theo maydenes lokyn in the glas.

7. *Dative.* 1 **þǽm, þám,** 2–3 **þam, þon, þan,** 3 **þen.**

c **893** K. ÆLFRED *Oros.* I. i. §28 Be þæm ȝesetenum iȝlandum. *c* **1000** *Ags. Gosp.* Mark v. 2 Of þam byrȝenum. *c* **1175** *Lamb. Hom.* 27 For þan deoflan. *Ibid.* 139 To alle ðon monnen. *c* **1205** LAY. 714 To þon cnihten. *Ibid.* 747 Cuð he wes þen cnihten. *a* **1225** *Ancr. R.* 50 Þe blake cloð.. deð lesse eile to þen eien.

8. *Genitive.* 1–2 **þára, þǽra,** 2 **þera,** 2–3 **þere,** 3 **þare, þer.**

971 *Blickl. Hom.* 35 Ne bið þara fæstendaȝa na ma þonne syx & þritiȝ. *c* **1000** ÆLFRIC *Hom.* I. 12 Ealra þæra þinga [*a* **1175** *Cott. Hom.* 221 þara þinge]. *a* **1175** *Cott. Hom.* 229 An þera twelf Christes þeiȝne. *c* **1175** *Lamb. Hom.* 133 Þurh ðere clerkene muðe. *c* **1200** *Trin. Coll. Hom.* 121 Þer apostlene lore. *Ibid.* 129 Nan þere prophete þe ȝe wenen.

III. 9. General uninflected form, as definite article in all cases, genders, and numbers.

This had come to be *þe*, *the* by *c* 1150 in the East Midland dialect, and may have been so even earlier in the Northern dial., where *þe* was the nom. masc. for *se a* 950. The nom. masc. and fem. had become *þe* almost everywhere by 1300, but the neuter *þat*, *þet* remained longer before a vowel (see 1 c); and inflected forms of some oblique cases survived in some southern dialects till 1400 (cf. 2 a and 3 above).

2–5 **þe,** 2, 4– **the** (also written 5–8 **ye, y[e]**). (Also 2–3 **þa,** 2–4 **te** (see T 8), 3–5 **þo,** 4 **þi,** 4 **thee,** 4–5 **þeo, theo,** 5 **þey,** 6 **they,** 8–9 *dial.* **ta, te, da, de, 'ee;** *abbrev.* 2 **þ-,** 5–6 **th-,** 7–9 (now *dial.* and *poet.*) **th';** 5–6 (8–9 *dial.*) **t'** (see T'[2]), 8–9 *dial.* **d'.**

a **1131** *O.E. Chron.* (Laud MS.) an. 1122, Þa com se fir.. and forbearnde ealle þe minstre. *Ibid.*, Se fir weax.. up to þe heouene. *Ibid.* an. 1123, He com æfter þe Rome scot. *Ibid.*, In þe lenten ferde se ærcebiscop to Rome. *a* **1154** *Ibid.* an. 1132, To þe king.. þe muneces.. þurh þe biscop of Seresberi & te b' of Lincoln and te oþre ricemen. *Ibid.* an. 1137, Þe land was al fordon.. In the hus.. on þe circe.. alle þe landes. *Ibid.* an. 1140, Þe kynges dohter Henries.. Wyd þemperice. *Ibid.*, And te cuen of France to dælde fra þe king, and scæ com to þe iunge eorl Henri. *c* **1200** ORMIN 1485, & gaddresst swa þe clene corn All fra þe chaff togeddre. *c* **1250** *Gen. & Ex.* 2949 But if it were in ðe lond gersen, ðor-inne woren ðe ebrisse men. *Ibid.* 2962 For to bi-tournen ðe kinges ðoȝt. **13..** *Cursor M.* 6859 (Cott.) Suilk was þi lessun and þi lare [*v.r.* þe.. þe]. *c* **1400** *Rule St. Benet* 12 Sua sais te prophete. *c* **1420** *Chron. Vilod.* 1910 In þe whyche water hurre to wasshe. *a* **1425** *Cursor M.* 9908 (Laud) The man that thedirward is fled. *Ibid.* 10005 Thee iiij[e] turret þer e-sette. **1436** *Coventry Leet Bk.* 185 Þat þey prior be not suffered to make no more off þe Stan wall vndur þey priory. **1470–85** MALORY *Arthur* II. xiii. 91 No thyng but thold custome. **1496** *Plumpton Corr.* p. ci, The said lands.. & t'ofice of the Steward. **1529** CROMWELL in Merriman *Life & Lett.* (1902) I. 58 Kept to thuse of my saide Soonne. **1529** in *Vicary's Anat.* (1888) App. II. 100 Mr Whittington, scolmaster to thenxmen. *a* **1533** LD. BERNERS *Huon* vi. 13 Out of temperours fauore. *Ibid.* lxxxviii. 278 His vncle themperour of Almayne. *a* **1548** HALL *Chron., Rich. III* 27 b, Lo ye honorable courage of a kyng. **1603** SHAKS. *Meas. for M.* V. iii. 241 Come, come, to' th' purpose. **1632** MILTON *Penseroso* 60 Gently o're th' accustom'd Oke. **1742** YOUNG

Nt. Th. VI. 465 Th' Almighty Fiat, and the Trumpet's Sound.

dial. c **1746** COLLIER (Tim Bobbin) *View Lanc. Dial.* Wks. (1862) p. xxxix, By th' Miss, th' owd story ogen. **1884** J. C. EGERTON *Sussex Folks & Ways* iii. 34, I can't swallow it nohows in de wurreld. **1888** ADDY *Sheffield Gloss.* 13 T' beeas has got into t' corn. **1890** BICKLEY *Surrey Hills* xxix, Let 'ee words as did vor vather do vor son. **1892** M. C. MORRIS *Yorks. Folk-talk* ii. 19 Gan inti d' hoos.

B. Signification.

I. Referring to an individual object (or objects).

* Marking an object as before mentioned or already known, or contextually particularized (e.g. 'We keep a dog. We are all fond of *the* dog').

1. The ordinary use.

805–a 1154 [see A. I. 1 a *a*]. c **950** *Lindisf. Gosp.* Matt. ii. 9 Stearra..ȝestod ofer ðer (*vel* hwer) wæs ðe cnæht [*Rushw.* se cneht]. c **1000** *Ags. Gosp.* Matt. ii. 11 And gangende into þam huse hi ȝemetton þæt cild. —— John ii. 7 þæt hiȝ þa fatu mid wætere ȝefyldon. c **1175** *Lamb. Hom.* 133 Sum of þe sede feol an uppe þe stane..sum bi þe weie. c **1200** ORMIN 1082 He toc þe recless & te blod & ȝede upp to þatt allterr. **13..** *Gaw. & Gr. Knt.* 405 Quod þe gome in þe grene to Gawan þe hende. **1340** *Ayenb.* 186 Wel ssolle we habbe reuþe..þe on of þe oþre. c **1386** CHAUCER *Prol.* 845 (Corp.) þe soþ is þis, þe Cut fel to þe kniȝht. c **1425** *Seven Sag.* (P.) 10 The emperour and is wif Loveden the child as hare lyf. **1530** PALSGR. 45 Where they saye in frenche *le maistre, la dame*, we saye in our tonge *the mayster, the lady*; so that this word *the*, with us, counter vayleth bothe *le* and *la*. **1695** CONGREVE *Love for Love* IV. iv, What's the matter now? **1818** CRUISE *Digest* V. 494 That the recovery enured to the uses of the settlement, and therefore that the purchaser had no title. **1902** GAIRDNER *Hist. Eng. Ch. 16th Cent.* viii. (1903) 149 He re-considered the matter.

b. Placed before the relative pron. *which* (*whilk*) (*arch.*): see WHICH. ***the one, the other***: see ONE, OTHER, TONE, TOTHER.

2. Used before a word denoting time, as ***the time, day, hour, moment***: the time (etc.) in question, or under consideration; the time (now or then) present. ***the while***: see WHILE.

[c **897** K. ÆLFRED *Gregory's Past. C.* xlvi. 348 Hie nanwuht godes ne maȝon ða hwile Gode brengan to ðances.] a **1425** *Cursor M.* 3889 (Trin.) þe while holde lya in bedde þenne shal þou rachel wedde. **1533** BELLENDEN *Livy* V. xxiii. (S.T.S.) II. 227 þe said voce was contempnit and necleckit in þe tyme. **1616** J. LANE *Cont. Sqr.'s T.* viii. 213 And, iust at thinstant, all the canons plaien From towne to Campe, from Camp to towne againe. **1780** *Mirror* No. 76 ¶3 He comes there only as he does to the coffee-house, to enquire after the news of the day. **1848** DICKENS *Dombey* liv, At the moment, the bell rang loudly in the hall. **1864** TENNYSON *Aylmer's F.* 194 A tongue that ruled the hour. **1866** NEWMAN *Gerontius* ad fin., And I will come and wake thee on the morrow.

b. Used before numerals denoting years.

Now only with abbreviation, either in reference to certain historical events (see FIFTEEN A. 2, FORTY-FIVE), or in expressions denoting a particular decade of a century or of a person's life (see EIGHTY 2 b, FIFTY B. 2 b, etc.).

1724 R. WODROW *Life J. Wodrow* (1828) 60 Elizabeth died ..about the 1684 of a consumption. a **1776** LD. AUCHINLECK in *Scotch Acts* (1844) I. Pref. 188, I take this Manuscript to have been wrote before the 1500, and it is clear it was not wrote before the 1455. a **1797**, **1814** [see FIFTEEN A. 2]. **1824** SCOTT *Redgauntlet* ch. xi, Ye have heard of a year they call the Forty-five. **1862** BURTON *Bk. Hunter* III. 261 Dispersed over the Highlands to keep them in order after the '45. **1880**, **1889** [see FIFTY B. 2]. *Mod.* I think it was in the early eighties.

c. ***the day, the morn, the night***, in *Sc.* and *north. dial.* = to-day, to-morrow, to-night.

a **1300** [see MORN 3 c, d]. **13..** *Cursor M.* (Cott.) 702 þe sun was þat time..Seuen sith brighter þen þe dai [*so Fairf.*; *Gött.* to-day]. c **1475** *Rauf Coilȝear* 301 Cum the morne to the Court. a **1692** in 'J. Curate' *Sc. Presb. Eloq.* iii. 106, I have brought him to you the day. a **1800** in *Burns' Wks.* (1800) I. 363 For he's far aboon Dunkel the night. **1814** [see DAY *sb.* 13 b (*b*)].

3. Before the name of a unique object or one so considered, or of which there is only one at a time; e.g. *the sun, the earth, the sea, the sky, the air, the world, the universe, the Almighty, the Lord, the Messiah, the Saviour, the Gospel, the Bible, the abyss, the pit, the Devil, the Emperor, the Pope, the Kaiser, the Sultan, the Shah*, etc.

c **975** *Rushw. Gosp.* John iv. 6 Ðe hælend forðon woeriȝ wæs of gonge. a **1000** *Boeth. Metr.* xxvi. 6 Aulixes under hæfde þæm casere cynericu twa. c **1000** *Sax. Leechd.* III. 254 Seo eorðe stent on ælemiddan. *Ibid.* 268 Seo sæ and se mona ȝeþwærlæcað him betweonan. *Ibid.* 274 Seo lyft, þonne heo astyred is, byð wind. a **1225** *Ancr. R.* 82 þe deouel..is leas, and leasunges feder. a **1240** *Ureisun* in *Cott. Hom.* 185 Iwend me from the worlde. c **1400** *Brut* xxxvi. 33 þe Emperoure..he..ordeynede a stronge power. c **1400** *Apol. Loll.* 28 Bi lawe..of þe kirk,..ilk prest haþ þe same power to vse þe key in to ani man in þo poynt of deþ, as þe pope. **1580** in *Cath. Rec. Soc. Publ.* I. 69 To the Tuission of Thallmightie. **1590** SPENSER *F.Q.* I. i. 32 The Sunne, that measures heaven all day long. **1611** BIBLE *Ps.* xxiv. 1 The earth is the Lords, and the fulnesse thereof. **1748** CHESTERFIELD *Lett.* 31 May, Sixtus the Vth..raised himself to the Popedom by his abilities. **1842** TENNYSON *Beggar Maid* ii, As shines the moon in clouded skies.

b. With names of rivers, as *the Amazon, the Thames*; of mountains, groups of islands, or regions, in the plural, as *the Alps, the Azores, the Indies*; of places or mountains, in the sing., now only when felt to be descriptive, as *the Land's End, the Lizard, the High Street, the Oxford Road, the Jungfrau, the Matterhorn*, or when *the* has come down traditionally, as *the Lennox, the Merse*; exceptionally in *the Tyrol*. Formerly often used more widely. Also forming part of the present and former names of certain countries, as *the Argentine, the Congo, The Gambia, the Lebanon, the Sudan, the Yemen*; with the names of streets, *locally* with ellipsis of the word *Street*.

c **893** K. ÆLFRED *Orosius* I. i. §21 Seo Wisle is swyðe mycel ea... Seo Wisle lið ut of Weonodlande, and lið in Estmere. **1297** R. GLOUC. (Rolls) 164 þat oþer wonder is Vpe þe hul of þe pek. *Ibid.* 4740 Wippe was king of þe march, & adelfred of humberlond. **1632** MASSINGER & FIELD *Fatal Dowry* II. i, I would they were at the Bermudas! **1653** HOLCROFT *Procopius, Goth. Wars* II. 43 When the Vesuvius casts out cynders. **1761** *Char.* in *Ann. Reg.* 52/1 The Devizes. **1784** COWPER *Task* III. 583 Th' Azores send Their jessamine. **1814** SCOTT *Wav.* xxxix, The travellers now..reached the Torwood. **1822** —— *Nigel* x, I should like to see the broad Tay once more before I die; not even the Thames can match it, in my mind. **1842** PRICHARD *Nat. Hist. Man* (ed. 2) 467 The Tupi, or native inhabitants of the Brazils. **1853**, etc. [see HIGH *sb.* 1 c]. **1855** MACAULAY *Hist. Eng.* xviii. IV. 119 From the Land's End to the Straits of Dover. **1920** G. BELL *Let.* 14 Mar. (1927) II. xviii. 484 On my way home I went to see Frank Balfour..and heard from him the afternoon's news which was that Faisal had been crowned King of Syria and Abdullah King of the Iraq. **1951** DUKE OF WINDSOR *King's Story* xii. 209 Britain had an investment of £400,000,000 in the Argentine. **1959** *Chambers's Encycl.* VIII. 431/2 In internal affairs the Lebanon had to face considerable economic and financial difficulties after the end of the 1939–45 war. *Ibid.* XIV. 796/1 In March 1958 a federal link was established between the Yemen and the United Arab Republic. **1959** *Even. Standard* 31 Dec. 8/6, I am home from the Argentine and would like to link up with some of my old friends. **1975** J. I. M. STEWART *Gaudy* xii. 225 The industrious little whirr of his camera was for a moment the only sound in the Broad. *Ibid.* 228, I had crossed Broad Street and was walking down the Turl. **1981** *Church Times* 6 Nov. 14/5 The Hoopoe had nested in his walls when he was in the Yemen. **1984** *Times* 18 Feb. 1/2 Princess Anne's four-day visit to The Gambia brings an extra air of festivity and importance to a tiny African country.

c. With names of natural phenomena, seasons, etc., as *the spring, the summer, the autumn, the winter, the day, the night; the wind, the cold, the clouds*, etc.; of the points of the compass, as *the north, the east* (in OE. usually without article).

c **1000** *Sax. Leechd.* III. 274 Se wind hæfð mistlice naman on bocum. a **1300** [see EAST *sb.* 2]. **13..** *E.E. Allit. P.* B. 953 þe rayn rueled adoun, ridlande þikke. **1382** WYCLIF *Matt.* ii. 2 We han seyn his sterre in the este. c **1440** *Alphabet of Tales* 106 Vppon a fayr day, whar þe wynde blew. **1697** DRYDEN *Virg. Georg.* III. 378 They That wing the liquid Air, or swim the Sea, Or haunt the Desart. **1784** COWPER *Task* I. 749 God made the country, and man made the town. **1791** —— *Odyss.* IX. 194 The rosy-finger'd daughter of the dawn.

†**d.** Formerly sometimes used before abstract sbs. See also DEATH *sb.* 2, 12, LIFE 7, 7 b. *Obs.*

c **888** K. ÆLFRED *Boeth.* iii. §3 þa se Wisdom þa and seo Gesceadwisnes þis leoð asungen hæfdon. c **897** —— *Gregory's Past. C.* iii. 35 On ðære ȝesundfulnesse mon forȝiett his selfes. *Ibid.* xxxiii. 214 Ða ȝeðylde þe is modur ..ealra mæȝena..[he] forlett. c **1450** tr. *De Imitatione* III. lxiii. 146 þe pes stondiþ more in very mekenes þan in propre exaltacion. **14..** *Pol. Rel. & L. Poems* (1903) 257 Ase.. roust on þe knife, and ase deþ to þe life. c **1489** CAXTON *Blanchardyn* xxi. 70 The prouost..cam sone toward the proude mayden in amours, and made to her the reuerence. *Ibid.* xxiii. 74 So cam he toward blanchardyn..And gaff hym the goode nyght. **1525** LD. BERNERS *Froiss.* II. ccxxiii. [ccxix.] 695 If Lamorabaquy wolde gyue them the herynge. **1588** ALLEN *Admon.* 11 A verie fable to the posterite.

4. With a class-name, to indicate the individual example most familiar to one, or with which one is primarily or locally concerned, e.g. *the King, the Emperor* (in mod. use), *the Lord Mayor, the Town, the House, the Court, the Tower, the Abbey, the River, the Channel, the Flood, the Reformation, the Revolution; the Gospel, the Epistle* (for the day).

c **1121** *O.E. Chron.* (Laud MS.) an. 1106, To Eastran wæs se cyng æt Baðan. *Ibid.* an. 1120, An se arcebiscop Turstein ..wearð þurh þone papan wið þone cyng acordad. a **1154** *Ibid.* an. 1140, Sume helden mid te king and sume mid þemperice. c **1175** *Lamb. Hom.* 3 Seggeð þet þe lauerd haued þar-of neode. *Ibid.* 5 Ȝe iherden er on þe godspel hu ure drihten sende his .ii. apostles. a **1300** *Cursor M.* 20502 þan spac þat leuedi..to þapostlis euerilkan. a **1568** ASCHAM *Scholem.* I. (Arb.) 68 Ye great ones in ye Court. **1621** ELSING *Debates Ho. Lords* (Camden) 16 To make his answere here at the barre. **1666** EVELYN *Diary* 13 Sept., The Queene was.. in her cavalier riding habite. **1689** LUTTRELL *Brief Rel.* (1857) I. 557 The house of commons..ordered..that the then judges should attend the house. **1837** SIR F. PALGRAVE *Merch. & Friar* Ded. (1844) 1 Any bibliopolist, in or out of the Row. **1845** [see HOUSE *sb.*[1] 4 d]. **1875** TENNYSON *Q. Mary* I. i, He swears by the Rood.

5. Formerly with names of branches of learning, arts, crafts, games, and pursuits. Now chiefly *dial.* Also generally with gerundial vbl. sbs. (*arch.*).

c **1325** [see CHESS *sb.*[1] 1]. **1470–85** MALORY *Arthur* IX. xvii. 363 On a day kynge Mark played at the chesse. **1596** SHAKS. *Tam. Shr.* I. i. 37 The Mathematickes, and the Metaphysickes Fall to them. c **1643** LD. HERBERT *Autobiog.* (1824) 89 Any man thought worth the looking on. **1739** CHESTERF. *Lett.* (1774) I. 122 As you are now reading the Roman History. **1768** H. ST. JOHN in Jesse *Selwyn & Contemp.* (1843) II. 309, I regret the badness of our climate, and the being obliged to pass the remainder of my life in [it]. **1824** MRS. CAMERON *Pink Tippet* IV. 22 What was the use of my getting you taught the dress-making? **1887** *Wellington Weekly News* 3 Feb. (E.D.D.), Apprentices and improvers wanted to the millinery, to the dressmaking, to the currying. **1901** *Union Mag.* Apr. 150/1, I wad raither hae seen ye at the joinerin' like masel'.

6. With names of literary or musical compositions, as plays, poems, anthems, etc.; also of newspapers and periodicals. Also with names of paintings and sculptures.

a **1225** *Ancr. R.* 18 þus doð..et te biginnunge of þe Venite. **1705** ADDISON *Remarks on Several Parts of Italy* 349, I have seen on coins..the Hercules Farnese, the Venus of Medicis, the Apollo in the Belvidere, and the famous Marcus Aurelius on Horseback. a **1706** EVELYN *Diary* an. 1693 (1955) V. 147, I..saw & indeede admired the Venus of Coreggio. **1780** *Mirror* No. 99 ¶7 The *Orestes* of the Greek poet. **1810** SCOTT *Let.* in Smiles *Mem. J. Murray* (1891) I. 190 'Kehama'..will get it roundly in the Edinburgh Review. **1845** GOSSE *Ocean* iv. (1849) 159 Plato, in the Timæus, gives the fullest account. **1845** *Encycl. Metropolitana* IX. 408 The Apollo Belvidere, the Venus de Medicis, and the Laocoon, have for ages been regarded as the highest possible models of excellence. a **1912** *Mod. The Times* has a leading article on the subject. **1984** *Times* 13 Sept. 13/4 Difficult to think of an art theft with greater sex appeal than that of the Mona Lisa.

7. Formerly with names of languages; now only in consciously elliptical phrases, as *from the German* (sc. *language* or *original*).

The degree of ellipsis is not easy to determine.

1593 NASHE *Four Lett. Confut.* Wks. (Grosart) II. 263 To borrowe some lesser quarry of elocution from the Latine. **1596** SHAKS. *Merch. V.* I. ii. 77 You will..sweare that I haue a poore pennie-worth in the English. **1760** *Portia, Polite Lady* xi. 28 Let not your studying the French make you neglect the English. **1795** SOUTHEY *Lett. fr. Spain* xxii. (1799) 294 Every advantage that..a complete knowledge of the Arabic could afford. **1823** COBBETT *Gram. Eng. Lang.* XIX. 131 It is the same word, you see, in both instances; but you will see it different in the French. a **1912** *Mod.* A new translation directly from the Hebrew. **1922** CHESTERTON *Eugenics & Other Evils* I. i. 11, I am content to answer that 'chivalrous' is not the French for 'horsy'. **1934** WEBSTER p. lxxxii/1, The modern descendants of the Latin are called the Romance languages. They include the Italian, the Spanish, the Portuguese [etc.]. a **1965** B. HIGGINS *Northern Fiddler* (1966) 34 'I'm corrupt' he said to me in the French, 'I think I live in corruption's stench.'

8. a. With names of diseases, ailments, etc.

Still in common use side by side with forms without the definite article.

c **1000** *Sax. Leechd.* II. 314 Wið þære ȝeolwan adle ..ȝenim þæs scearpan þistles moran and betonican. a **1300** *Cursor M.* 11819 In his heued he has þe scall þe scab ouergas his bodi all. *Ibid.* 11825 þe gutte þe potagre. **1377** LANGL. *P. Pl.* B. XIII. 325, I cacche þe crompe, þe cardiacle. c **1400** *Lanfranc's Cirurg.* 281 It is myn entencioun to speke of þe dropesie. *Ibid.* 293 Of þe cancre and þe mormole. **1480**, **1500–20** [see POCK *sb.* 2 a]. **1660** GAUDEN *Brownrig* 225 Sharp fits of the stone. **1671** C'TESS WARWICK *Autobiog.* (Percy Soc.) 9, I..fell..ill of the measles. **1743–1831** [see INFLUENZA]. **1787** [J. BEATTIE] *Scoticisms* 91 He has got the cold, the fever. **1809** SOUTHEY *Let. to Landor* 23 Apr., in *Life* (1850) III. 228, I instantly recognised the sound of the croup. **1839** —— *Let. to Mrs. Hodson* 18 Feb. *ibid.* VI. 381 A serious attack of the influenza. a **1912** *Mod.* (*familiar*) I have the toothache. **1961** I. FLEMING *Thunderball* i. 10 His secretary had gone down with the flu. **1972** *Time* 17 Apr. 41/2 Shortly before he was scheduled to make his first space flight aboard Apollo 13 two years ago, the longtime bachelor ..was accidently exposed to the German measles.

b. With colloq. or humorous names of afflictions, as *the blues, collywobbles, creeps, D.T.'s, habdabs, heebie-jeebies, jitters*, etc., q.v. Hence in analogous nonce-expressions.

1976 *Publishers Weekly* 11 Oct. 90/3 The case of the 'cutes' infecting text and pictures. **1976** *Listener* 11 Nov. 626/2 The whole story, like the chateau, has an unmistakable touch of the Enid Blytons.

9. Elliptically with the names of ships, as *the* (*ship*) *Nicholas*, and of taverns, as *the Mermaid* (*tavern*), theatres, and other well-known buildings.

1450 *Paston Lett.* I. 125 He was yn the Nicolas tyl Saturday next folwyng. **1480** WARKWORTH *Chron.* (Camden) 13 Casten in presone in the Marchalse at London. **1521** in *Essex Rev.* XIII. 221 Out of the Barbara and the Mayflower, if God send them well home. a **1616** BEAUMONT *To Ben Jonson* , What things have we seen Done at the Mermaid! **1710** SWIFT *Jrnl. to Stella* 15 Oct., Prior and I.. sat at the Smyrna till eleven. **1779** *Mirror* No. 32 ¶5 Stopping at the *George* on his way home. **1905** *Daily Chron.* 24 Oct. 3/4 *heading*, Playlet at the Coliseum. *Mod.* The *Mauretania* has made a record passage.

10. Before higher titles of rank, as *the Emperor, King, Prince, Grand Duke, Marquess, Earl, Count* (but exc. in formal use not now when followed by the name, as *King George, Prince Edward, Duke Humphrey, Earl Grey, Earl Simon*), and with the corresponding female titles *Queen, Duchess*, etc.; also with some courtesy titles, as *the Right Honourable, the Honourable, the Reverend*, etc. See further LORD, LADY, and the other titles.

c **1121** *O.E. Chron.* (Laud MS.) an. 1090, Se eorl of Normandiȝe. *Ibid.* an. 1117, Se cyng of France and se eorl of Flandra. **1340** *Ayenb.* 76 þe leuedy fortune went hare hueȝel eche daye. **1472** SIR J. PASTON in *P. Lett.* III. 39 Robert of Racclyff weddyd the lady Dymmok. **1553** in *Rutland Papers* (Camden) 119 Therle of Oxford claymeth thoffice of great chamberlayne of England. **1603** SIR R. WILBRAHAM *Diary* (Camden) 60 The lord Thomas Howard made erle of Suffolk. **1613** SHAKS. *Hen. VIII*, II. iii. 94 The Marchionesse of Pembrooke. **1707** E. CHAMBERLAYNE *Pres.*

St. Eng. II. xv. (ed. 22) 188 The Lord Chief Justice. **1794** MRS. RADCLIFFE *Myst. Udolpho* l, 'The Chevalier Valancourt!' said Emily, trembling extremely. **1827** *Edin. Weekly Jrnl.* 28 Feb., The absence of the Right Hon. the Lord Provost. **1935** C. HAMILTON *Pillion* 25 He was the third son of Colonel the Hon. Almeric Sounds Sharnal Piers Clement Piers, late of the Rifle Brigade. **1939** E. BAX *Miss Bax of Embassy* xviii. 238 Someone is always dashing in to ask me questions like...is Lady V. *The* Lady or only Lady? **1943** H. SAUNDERS *Combined Operations* vii. 52 Admiral of the Fleet Sir Roger Keyes was succeeded as Director of Combined Operations by Captain the Lord Louis Mountbatten. **1981** *Daily Tel.* 5 Nov. 16/2 Her Majesty's Body Guard of the Honourable Corps of Gentlemen-at-Arms under the command of the Lord Denham.

b. With the surnames of some Irish and Scottish chiefs of clans, as the O'Gorman Mahon, the Chisholm, the MacNab.

1561 *Inverness Sheriff Crt. Records* II. 15 Apr. (MS.), [Sederunt] the Dollace of Cantray. **1562** *Ibid.* 7 Apr., The jugis hes consignit hir to produce the samyn and to wairne the Dollace upon ane xv dayis warning. **1847** THACKERAY *Mrs. Perkins's Ball* i. 4, I became acquainted with the Mulligan through a distinguished countryman..who..did not know the chieftain himself. **1880** A. M. SHAW *Mackintoshes* p. xxvii, Moy Hall, the residence of The Mackintosh. **1910** *Daily Chron.* 1 Feb. 4/6 Three 'Thes' have sat in the House of Commons in our time—The O'Conor Don, The O'Donoghue of the Glens, and The O'Gorman Mahon. The MacDermott, K.C.,..was an Irish law officer in Liberal Governments.

c. Before names and titles of men, often in ME. a corruption of F. *de*, as in *Robert the Bruce*, *Sir Simon the Montfort*, *the Mortimer*, etc. *arch.*

1297 R. GLOUC. (Rolls) 11134 Sir Roger þe Mortimer. **1375** BARBOUR *Bruce* I. 67 That..Robert the brwys, Erle of carryk Aucht to succeid to the kynryk. *Ibid.* 435 The Clyffurd sall thaim haiff. *c* **1450** *Brut* 427 The Erle of Somersette and his brothir, and the Fytz-Watir. **1591** SHAKS. *1 Hen. VI*, III. iii. 37 *Charles.* A Parley with the Duke of Burgonie. *Burg.* Who craues a Parley with the Burgonie? **1814** SCOTT *Ld. of Isles* III. xxvii, As heroes think, so thought the Bruce.

d. Before the names of well-known singers, actresses, etc., in imitation of French and Italian usage. Also *slang* and sometimes *derogatory*, with a woman's surname or nickname. Cf. LA, LA.

1730 O. SWINY *Let.* 29 July in R. B. Peake *Mem. Colman Family* (1841) I. 18 If he does not, then we must provide a soprano man, and a contr'alto woman (though the Merighi stays). **1786** MRS. A. M. BENNETT *Juvenile Indiscretions* V. 32 The Siddons. **1796** *Publ. Advert.* 18 Nov. in T. Campbell *Life Mrs. Siddons* II. viii. 201 Last night the Siddons and the Kemble, at Drury Lane, acted to vacancy. **1822** in *Byron's Wks.* (1846) 585/1 The Guiccioli was present. **1845** DISRAELI *Sybil* v. vii, Well, what do you think of the Dashville, Fitz? **1922** *Dialect Notes* V. 143[At] Somerville ..'The Pen' is the Lady Principal, Miss Penrose, 'The Darb', Miss Derbyshire, etc. **1930** WODEHOUSE *Very Good, Jeeves!* iv. 96 The Bellinger..had sung us a few songs before digging in at the trough. **1973** —— *Bachelors Anonymous* xii. 155 The Fitch was at the hair stylist's having a permanent.

11. *spec.* Used emphatically, in the sense of 'the pre-eminent', 'the typical', or 'the only.. worth mentioning'; as 'Cæsar was *the* general of Rome', i.e. the general *par excellence*; the being often stressed in speech (ðiː), and printed in italics.

1824 L. MURRAY *Eng. Gram.* (ed. 5) I. 257 In the history of Henry the fourth, by Father Daniel, we are surprised at not finding him *the* great man. **1829** CARLYLE *Misc., Germ. Playwr.* (1872) II. 97 Dr. Klingemann..so superlative is his vigour..we might even designate him *the* Playwright. **1863** R. B. KIMBALL *Was he Successful?* vi. (Cent.), Joel Burns was a rich man, as well as *the* man of the place. **1865** LUBBOCK *Preh. Times* 131 The axe was the pre-eminently *the* implement of antiquity. **1904** S. G. TALLENTYRE *Life Voltaire* II. xxxv. 144 His Commentary remains unrivalled, and is still *the* text-book on Corneille.

12. With any part of the body of a person previously named or indicated, instead of the corresponding possessive pronoun; as 'he took him by the hand', i.e. *his* hand. So with *heart*, *soul*, used *fig.*; also with parts of personal attire.

1154 *O.E. Chron.* an. 1137, Me henged [heom] up bi the fet..bi the þumbes, other bi the hefed. **13..** *K. Alis.* (Bodl. MS.) 2276 Fulbor he smoot upon þe rygge. **1390** GOWER *Conf.* II. 213 That love..Ne schal noght take hem by the slieve. *c* **1460** *Towneley Myst.* xxiv. 115, I shall knap hym on the crowne That standys in my gate. **1583–93** GREENE *Mamillia* II. Wks. (Grosart) II. 220 Ruffes of a Syse, stiffe starcht to the necke. **1590** SHAKS. *Com. Err.* II. ii. 206 To put the finger in the eie and weepe. **1789** MRS. PIOZZI *Journ. France* I. 306 Heavy lace robbins ending at the elbow. **1838** DICKENS *O. Twist* lii, To be hanged by the neck, till he was dead. **1847** TENNYSON *Princess* vii. 209–12 Pale was the perfect face..And the voice trembled and the hand.

b. Used colloquially with names of relatives, as *the wife*, *the mother* = my (your) wife, mother.

1838 J. M. WILSON *Tales Borders* No. 210 (1839) V. 9/1 What shall I say to the wife? **1853** 'C. BEDE' *Verdant Green* I. vii, 'It's a long while since the governor was here', remarked Mr. Charles Larkyns, very unfilially. **1888** The Mater [see MATER 3]. **1891** DUNCAN *Amer. Girl in Lond.* 82 The mother and sisters would like to call upon you. **1900** The pater..the mater [see PATER 3]. **1901** W. CHURCHILL *R. Carvell* xliv, [I] sent off an express to Patty and the Mother last night.

c. Before OWN (*a.* 2 b) and SELF (C. 1 c), q.v.

13. Used before names of weights and measures, in stating a rate: as (*so much*) *the pound*, *gallon*, *yard*, *day*, etc. Cf. A *adj.*[2] 4, PER III. 2.

1426–7 *Rec. St. Mary at Hill* 65, iiij[c] hert latthe, pris þe hondrid, vij d..ij[ml] traunsum, þe m[l] x d. **1488–9** *Act 4 Hen. VII*, c. 22 Sold for iij li. sterling the pack. **1551–2** *Act 5 & 6 Edw. VI*, c. 6 §1 That all colored Clothes..shall waye fourscore pounde the pece at the lest. **1596–7** S. FINCHE in *Hist. Croydon* App. (1783) 153 Brick-layers..have xv d. apeece the day. **1631** WEEVER *Anc. Fun. Mon.* 418 Appointing them xii d. the weeke to each person. **1796** SOUTHEY *Lett. fr. Spain* (1799) 118 They are very dear, ten reales the couple. **1851** MAYHEW *Lond. Labour* II. 284/2 The sherds run about 250 pieces to the bushel.

b. So with prepositions *by*, *in*, †*on*.., chiefly with reference to time, as (*so much*) *by the day* = (so much) each day.

1477–8 *Rec. St. Mary at Hill* 79 Paid to Sir Iohn Colyns ..at viij s. iiij d. by the quarter. **1530** TINDALE *Answ. More* III. i. Wks. (1572) 304/2, I finde in all ages that men..haue suffred death by the hundred thousandes in resisting their doctrine. **1533** *Acc. Ld. High Treas. Scot.* VI. 151 To Thomas Scott passing in Ingland with writtingis and credence to the King..to him on the day iij li. **1613** SHAKS. *Hen. VIII*, v. iv. 33 What should you doe, But knock 'em downe by th' dozens? **1632** LITHGOW *Trav.* VI. 298 The Dromidory..will ride aboue 80 miles in the day. **1727** POPE, etc. *Art Sinking* xiii. 116 It may be..let out by the day. **1848** DICKENS *Dombey* xxxix, He would sit and avail himself of its accommodations..by the half-hour together. **1883** SIR J. C. DAY in *Law Rep. 12 Q.B. Div.* 206 Etymologically considered, a journeyman is one who is employed by the day.

** Marking an object not before mentioned, but now identified by a clause, phrase, or word.

14. Where the object is defined by a relative clause, *the* stands before the object. (The relative pronoun may be suppressed: cf. THAT *rel. pron.* 10.)

In mod. Eng. more emphatically expressed by *that*: see THAT *dem. adj.* 3. The OE. form did not distinguish these: *þæt spell* may be rendered 'that story' or 'the story'.

a **900** tr. *Bæda's Hist.* Pref. (1890) 2 Ic ðe sende þæt spell, þæt ic niwan awrat be Angel ðeode & Seaxum. **971** *Blickl. Hom.* 71 Seo menigo þe þær beforan ferde. *c* **975** *Rushw. Gosp.* Mark ii. 4 þa bere in ðære þe eorð-crypel læʒ. *c* **1000** *Sax. Leechd.* III. 104 þæt sindon þe teþ þe þane mete brecaþ. *c* **1200** *Trin. Coll. Hom.* 3 þe holie tid þat me clepeð aduent. *c* **1250** *O. Kent. Serm.* in *O.E. Misc.* 26 Te dai ase ure louerd ..i-bore was. *a* **1300** *Cursor M.* 14705 þe werckes þat i werc in his nam. **1382** WYCLIF *Matt.* ii. 9 Loo! the sterre, the whiche thei sayen in este, wente bifore hem. **1472** J. PASTON in *P. Lett.* III. 75, I am not the man I was. **1596** SHAKS. *Merch. V.* v. i. 83 The man that hath no musicke in himselfe ..Is fit for treasons [etc.]. **1697** T. BROWN *Dispens.* I. Wks. 1709 III. III. 67, I have known the Time, when I could go out and pick up 10 or 12 l. in a Morning. **1715–20** POPE *Iliad* XXIV. 256 Let us give To grief the wretched days we have to live. **1784** COWPER *Task* III. 141 The man, of whom His own coevals took but little note. **1805** WORDSW. *On Peele Castle*, The light that never was, on sea or land. **1850** J. H. NEWMAN *Diffic. Anglic.* I. ii. (1891) I. 48 But the passage I have quoted suggests a second observation.

15. Where the object is defined by a following phrase with prep. (esp. *of*, repr. an OE. genitive).

971 *Blickl. Hom.* 55 þeh he..ʒehyre þa word þæs halʒan godspelles. *c* **1121** *O.E. Chron.* (Laud MS.) an. 1116, On þisum ylcan ʒeare bærnde eall þæt mynstre of Burh. **1122** *Ibid.*, Se burch on Gleaweceastre. *c* **1175** *Lamb. Hom.* 53 Heo habbeð þe nome of cristene. *c* **1290** *Edmund Conf.* 387 in *S. Eng. Leg.* I. 442 In þe toun of wyricestre bi-tidde þat selue cas. **1387** TREVISA *Higden* (Rolls) II. 41 Tweie perilous places in þe see of myddel erþe. **1426–7** *Rec. St. Mary at Hill* 65 Also þe thorisday in þe Whitson weke. **1513** DOUGLAS *Æneis* IX. Prol. 7 Honeste is the way to worthynes. **1605** SHAKS. *Macb.* I. vii. 45 Like the poore Cat i' th' Addage. *a* **1734** NORTH *Exam.* I. i. §23 (1740) 26 In the telling of this Story. **1764** GRAY *Candidate* 12 Just like the picture in Rochester's book. **1824** BENTHAM *Bk. Fallacies* Introd. vii, The Sir Charles Sedley of political morality. **1870** MORRIS *Earthly Par.*, *Jan.* 42 Midmost the time 'twixt noon and dusk. **1908** R. BRIDGES *Sel. Poems R. W. Dixon* (1909) p. xii, The Oxford of 1850 was singularly unsympathetic.

b. With an object defined by an infinitive phrase with *to* (where *the* may sometimes be rendered 'that..needed or proper..').

c **1384** CHAUCER *H. Fame* III. 966 Alle the folke that ys a lyve Ne han the kunnynge to discryve The thinges that I herde there. **1642** MILTON *Sonn.* viii. 13 The power To save th' Athenian Walls from ruine bare. **1687** A. LOVELL tr. *Thevenot's Trav.* I. 225 We had the Comfort to be pittied. **1780** COWPER *Progress of Error* in *Wks.* (1905) 29 The creature is so sure to kick and bite, A muleteer's the man to set him right. **1813** JANE AUSTEN *Pride & Prej.* I. xiii. 142, I shall not be the person to discourage him. **1850** J. H. NEWMAN *Diffic. Anglic.* I. iii. (1891) I. 80, I am not the person to be jealous of such facts.

c. With an object particularized by a pple.

1658 PHILLIPS, *Salii*, the 12 Priests of Mars instituted by Numa Pompilius. **1876** ROGERS *Pol. Econ.* (ed. 3) ix. 81 The privileges accorded..to the merchants of the Hanse Towns. *a* **1912** *Mod.* The book lying on your table.

16. *The* stands before a sb. defined by another sb. (usually a proper name) in apposition, as *the poet Virgil.*

c **893** K. ÆLFRED *Oros.* I. i. §8 Se hehsta beorʒ Olimpus. *Ibid.* §9 On westende Affrica, neh þam beorʒe Athlans. **1070** *O.E. Chron.*, Toforan þam papan Alexandre. *c* **1175** *Lamb. Hom.* 73 Of clene liflade spec þe prophete isaias. *c* **1200** ORMIN Ded. 257 þatt..boc..Apokalypsis..Uss wrat te posstell Sannt Johan. **1297** R. GLOUC. (Rolls) 7956 þe king ..made..þe bissop ode..vorsuerie engelond. **1529** CROMWELL in Merriman *Life & Lett.* (1902) I. 325 The Jentylwoman your wyff. **1634** MILTON *Comus* 442 The huntress Dian.

b. More usually the proper name precedes. (Regularly so when the whole phrase becomes a recognized appellation, as *William the Conqueror.*)

c **950** *Lindisf. Gosp.* Matt. xii. 39 Becon iones ðæs witʒo [*Rushw.* tacen Ionas se witʒa]. *c* **1000** *Ags. Gosp.* Matt. iii. 1 On þam daʒum com iohannes se fulluhtere. *c* **1175** *Lamb. Hom.* 73 And dauid þe prophete spekeð in an salm. **13..** *Stac. Rome* (Vernon MS.) 238 Seint Ion þe Ewangelist. *c* **1400** *Brut* 299 About seint Lukes day þe euangglist. **1599** NASHE *Lenten Stuffe* (1871) 23 Their barony by William the Conqueror, conveyed over to them. **1906** *Edin. Rev.* Oct. 334 Bourdalone the physician was another favourite.

c. With a sb. characterizing the trade or profession of the person whose name precedes. *local* (esp. in Wales).

1894 SOMERVILLE & 'ROSS' *Real Charlotte* I. iv. 40 Norry the Boat, daughter of Shaunapickeen, the ferry-man (whence her title). **1951** W. MORUM *Gabriel* II. vii. 230 He thought Larry the Groan far worse. The effeminate singer ..was positively embarrassing. **1974** *Times* 27 Apr. 15/8 The Welsh tradition of referring to people by the names of their jobs, as Jones the Post or Davis the Bread. **1980** R. H. LEWIS *Cracking of Spines* vii. 113 'The prospective client,'.. I assumed a Welsh accent. 'Matt the Book.'

17. *The* is used with a sb. particularized or described by an adjective. The adj. usually precedes, but sometimes follows the sb.: in either case *the* stands first as *the good man*, *the church militant*.

(An adj. or pple. with a modifying addition regularly follows the sb., as 'the grass wet with dew', 'the tools needed for the work': cf. 15 c.)

A particularizing adj. often becomes a permanent epithet, as in *the Black Prince*, *the Lesser Bear*, *the Red Campion*, *the Great Exhibition*, *the Green Park*, *the Yellow Sea*, *the Count* or *County Palatine*, *the Prince Imperial*; the adj. and sb. may then be treated as name of a unique object, as in 3.

c **860** *O.E. Chron.* an. 853, þy ilcan ʒeare sende Æþelwulf cyning Ælfred his sunu to Rome. **885** *Ibid.*, Se fore sprecena here. *c* **888** K. ÆLFRED *Boeth.* xl. §4 Her endað sio fiorðe boc ..and onginð sio fifte. **971** *Blickl. Hom.* 5 Se heofonlica cyning. **1008–11** *Laws of Æthelred* VI. c. 22 §1 On þam halʒan dæʒe. *c* **1175** *Lamb. Hom.* 5 þa oðre men..stiʒen uppeon þe godes cunnes treowe. *c* **1386** CHAUCER *Knt.'s T.* 1491 Among the goddes hye it is affermed..Thou shalt [etc.]. *c* **1400** *Brut* 26 She was þe ryʒt heire of þis lande. **1413** *Pilgr. Sowle* (Caxton) v. vi. (1859) 76 The chirche militant, that laboureth here in erthe. *a* **1536** *Calisto & Melibæa* in Hazl. *Dodsley* I. 64 The mighty and perdurable God be his guide. **1575** GASCOIGNE *Making of Verse* in *Steele Gl.*, etc. (Arb.) 37 Vse your verse after thenglishe phrase. **1662** PEPYS *Diary* 20 Oct., Saw the so much desired by me picture of my Lady Castlemaine. **1710** STEELE *Tatler* No. 203 ¶1 They had the quite contrary Effect. **1750** GRAY *Elegy* xiv, The dark unfathom'd caves of ocean. **1819** SHELLEY *Prometh. Unb.* III. iii, The progeny immortal Of Painting, Sculpture, and rapt Poesy. **1863** H. COX *Instit.* I. xi. 262 The Long or Pensionary Parliament of Charles II. **1866** S. J. STONE *Hymn*, '*The Church's one Foundation*' iv, And the great Church victorious Shall be the Church at rest.

b. So with proper names of persons or places: e.g. *the judicious Hooker*. **c.** But when the adj. becomes a permanent epithet, *the* and the adj. usually follow: e.g. *Alfred the Great*; so with ordinal numerals following names of sovereigns or popes, as *Edward the Seventh.*

b. *c* **893** K. ÆLFRED *Oros.* I. i. §8 þæt land þe mon hætt seo læsse Asia. *c* **1420** ? LYDG. *Assembly of Gods* 269 Sate the good Iupyter. **1513** DOUGLAS *Æneis* x. i. 39 The fresch goldyn Venus. **1632** MILTON *L'Allegro* 86 Their savory dinner..Which the neat-handed Phillis dresses. **1743** EMERSON *Fluxions* Pref. 13 The divine Newton (whose Works will last as long as the Sun and Moon). **1906** F. THOMPSON *To Eng. Martyrs* 163 That utterance..Of the doomed Leonidas.

c. *c* **897** K. ÆLFRED *Gregory's Past. C.* iv. 36 Be ðæm cwæð Salomon se snottra. **971** *Blickl. Hom.* 15 Hit is Hælend se Nazarenisca. *a* **1000** *Byrhtnoth* 273 (Gr.) þa ʒit on orde stod Eadweard se langa. **1297** R. GLOUC. (Rolls) 1861 Seint eleyne þe gode. *c* **1400** GOWER *In Praise of Peace* 1 O worthi noble kyng, Henry the ferthe. **1484** CAXTON *Curial* 5 For to them whom fortune the variable hath most hyely lyfte up. **1558** *Cal. Anc. Rec. Dublin* (1889) 475 Patrick Fitz Symon, theldor, and William Byrsall, the yonger. **1686** [ALLIX] *Dissert.* i. in W. Hopkins *Ratramnus' Body & Bl.* (1688) 8 Charles the bald chose to consult him. *Mod.* George the Fourth's Bridge in Edinburgh.

18. *spec.* When a sb. is particularized by a superlative, or by an ordinal number (see also 17 c), the latter is regularly preceded by *the.*

c **893** K. ÆLFRED *Oros.* I. i. §22 Se man se þæt swiftoste hors hafað. **971** *Blickl. Hom.* 5 Deofol..beswac þone ærestan wifmon. *c* **1000** *Ags. Gosp.* John i. 39 Hit wæs þa seo teoðe tid [*Lindisf.* ðio teiʒða]. *c* **1000**–*a* **1225** [see FIFTH]. *a* **1225** *Ancr. R.* 60 Eien beoð..te ereste armes of lecheries pricches. *c* **1300** *Havelok* 9 He was þe wic[h]teste man at nede. **1601** SHAKS. *Jul. C.* III. ii. 187 This was the most vnkindest cut of all. **1626** C. POTTER tr. *Sarpi's Hist. Quarrels* 110 The most Potent Princes of Italy. **1748** SMOLLETT *Rod. Rand.* l, In terms the most hyperbolical. **1759** SARAH FIELDING *C'tess of Dellwyn* I. 149 Ready to take fire at every the least Provocation. **1848** MRS. GASKELL *M. Barton* ix, Th'longest lane will have a turning. **1890** LD. ESHER in *Law Times Rep.* LXIII. 692/1 The case..is of the greatest possible weight. *a* **1912** *Mod.* The first Consul; the hundredth time.

b. *The* also stands before the same adjs. when used absolutely.

c **1000** ÆLFRIC *Gram.* xlix. (Z.) 282 *Sextus*, se sixta. *c* **1175** *Pater Noster* in *Lamb. Hom.* 69 þet ðridde is þes monnes wil. **1340** *Ayenb.* 33–4 þer byeþ zix poyns [of sloth]..þe uerste is onbo3samnesse..þe pridde is grochynge. **1470–85** MALORY *Arthur* XX. viii. 811 Amonge the thyckest of the prees. **1526** TINDALE *Matt.* xviii. 1 Who is the greatest in the kyngdom of heven? **1622** in Seton *Life Earl of Dunfermline* vi. (1882) 141 *note*, [He] took sickness the first of June 1622. **1779** *Mirror* No. 27 ¶1 With the best and most affectionate of husbands. **1779** WARNER in Jesse *Selwyn & Contemp.* (1844) IV. 14 Your letter of Tuesday the 19th, was brought to me on Monday. **1799** SOUTHEY *Let. to T. Southey* 5 Jan. in *Life* (1850) II. 3 These vile taxes will take twenty pounds from me, at the least. **1852** M. ARNOLD *Youth of Nat.* 71 Too deep for the most to discern. *a* **1912** *Mod.* The third appears to be the best.

II. Referring to a term used generically or universally. * *With a singular sb.*

19. Before the name of an animal, plant, or precious stone, used generically.

Not now used with *man* or *woman*, exc. as opposed to *child, boy, girl*, or the like: cf. *the dog* is the friend of *man, man* has tamed *the dog*; *the child* is father of *the man*; you can see *the woman* in *the little girl*. Formerly *se mann, séo fæmne*: cf. Ger. *der mensch*, F. *l'homme*.

c **888** K. ÆLFRED *Boeth.* xli. §6 Ac se mann ana gæþ uprihte. *c* **893** —— *Oros.* III. xi. §3 Þonne seo leo bringð his hungregum hwelpum hwæt to etanne. *c* **1175** *Lamb. Hom.* 53 Þe tadde..ne mei itimien to eten hire fulle. *a* **1225** *Juliana* 20 Hire leofliche leor..rudi as þe rose. **13..** *K. Alis.* (Bodl. MS.) 1819 Men dreden hym..So chalf þe bere, & shep þe wolf. *c* **1440** LYDG. *Hors, Shepe, & G.* 344 The Goos may gagle, the hors may prike & praunce..A-geyn the lamb. **1553** EDEN *Treat. Newe Ind.* (Arb.) 14 The Diamande is engendred in the mynes of India, Ethiopia,..and Cyprus. *a* **1584** MONTGOMERIE *Cherrie & Slae* 21 The hart, the hynd, the dae, the rae, The fowmart, and the foxe. **1622** DRAYTON *Poly-olb.* xx. 45 The Colewort, Colifloure, and Cabidge in their season. **1727–46** THOMSON *Summer* 147 At thee the ruby lights its deepening glow. **1797** HOLCROFT *Stolberg's Trav.* (ed. 2) II. xliv. 93 They sell the heifer to the butcher. **1832** MACAULAY *Ess., Burghley* (1887) 236 Burleigh..was of the willow, and not of the oak. **1854** BUSHNAN in *Circ. Sc.* I. 290/2 It purrs like the Cat.

b. Generally, with the name of anything used as the type of its class; e.g. with the names of musical instruments, tools, etc.

c **1000** *Ags. Gosp.* Matt. iii. 10 Ys seo [*Hatton* syo] æx to ðæra treowa wurtrumum aset. *c* **1300** *Havelok* 2329 Þer mouhte men here..þe gleymen on þe tabour dinge. *c* **1450** HOLLAND *Howlat* 759 The rote, and the recordour,..The trumpe, and the talburn. **1589** PUTTENHAM *Eng. Poesie* I. xix. (Arb.) 57 To be..song to the harpe. **1592** SHAKS. *Ven. & Ad.* 454 A red morne that..betokend, Wracke to the seaman, tempest to the field. **1614** B. JONSON *Barth. Fair* III. ii, A notable hot Baker 'twas when hee ply'd the peele. **1711** STEELE *Spect.* No. 52 ¶3 The renowned British Hippocrates of the pestle and mortar. **1746** FRANCIS *Horace, Epist.* I. x. 7 You keep the Nest, I love the rural Mead, The Brook, the mossy Rock and woody Glade. **1784** COWPER *Task* II. 629 The rout is folly's circle. **1814** SCOTT *Ld. of Isles* III. xxiii, The lad can deftly touch the lute, And on the rote and viol play. **1839** LYTTON *Richelieu* II. ii. 308 The pen is mightier than the sword. **1906** *Edin. Rev.* Oct. 448 Zola has democratised the novel in another fashion.

c. Before *body, mind, soul*, or parts, functions, and attributes of these. (See also BODY *sb.* 1, MIND *sb.* 17.)

c **888** K. ÆLFRED *Boeth.* xxiv. §3 Seo fægernes..þæs lichoman. *c* **1000** *Ags. Gosp.* Matt. vi. 25 Hu nys seo sawl selre þonne mete. *c* **1175** *Lamb. Hom.* 153 Ine þe eren. *a* **1225** *Ancr. R.* 4 Þe oðer riwle is al wiðuten, & riwleð þe licome. **13..** *K. Alis.* (Bodl. MS.) 6245 A folk..rouȝ as bere to þe honde. *c* **1380** WYCLIF *Serm.* Sel. Wks. I. 103 Rychesse..ryven þe soule. *c* **1400** tr. *Secreta Secret., Gov. Lordsh.* 85 His effect is properly to comforte þe brayn, þe herte, and þe stomak. **1500–20** DUNBAR *Poems* xlvii. 6 Trew luve rysis fro the splene. **1594** R. ASHLEY tr. *Loys le Roy* 24 Nothing offending, or displeasing the eare. **1692** SOUTH *Serm.* (1697) I. 361 How accidentally oftentimes does the thing..offer it self to the mind. **1736** BUTLER *Anal.* I. i. 30 To think the eye itself a percipient. **1841** THACKERAY *Men & Pict.* 109 [They] pall on the palate.

d. With names of days of the week, as *on the Monday*, i.e. on Monday of any or every week, on Mondays generally.

1340 *Ayenb.* 213 Þe zonday is more holy þanne þe zeterday. *c* **1450** CAPGRAVE *Life St. Augustine* 16 Þat sche used to fast þe Satirday. *c* **1500–1671** [see SATURDAY 1]. **1854** MACAULAY *Speeches* 409 On the Sunday he goes perhaps to Church. *Ibid.* 553 He returns to his labours on the Monday.

20. Before a word of individual meaning used as the type of a class of persons.

c **897** K. ÆLFRED *Gregory's Past. C.* xii. 74 Ðæs biscepes weorc..ðæs hierdes life. *Ibid.* xiii. (heading), Hu se lareow sceal beon clæne on his mode. *a* **900** tr. *Bæda's Hist.* Pref. ii. (1890) 6 Ðone leornere ic nu..bidde and halsige. *c* **1175** *Lamb. Hom.* 27 Ah þenne þe preost hit deð in his muþe. *a* **1225** *Ancr. R.* 84 Þe vikelare ablent þene mon. **1388** WYCLIF *Ps.* xxxi[i.] 10 Many betyngis ben of the synnere. **1535** COVERDALE *Isa.* xliv. 13 The carpenter (or ymage caruer) taketh me the tymbre, and spredeth forth his lyne. **1600** W. WATSON *Decacordon* (1602) 334, I..craue patience of the catholike Reader. **1660** HEXHAM *Eng. Dutch Dict.* (title-p.), A compendious Grammar for the Instruction of the Learner. **1681** DRYDEN *Abs. & Achit.* 655 But where the witness failed, the prophet spoke. **1720** WATTS *Mor. Songs* I. i, 'Tis the voice of the Sluggard. **1787** 'G. GAMBADO' *Acad. Horsemen* (1809) 35 To ride with a lash whip; it shews the sportsman. **1843** MACAULAY *Ess., Addison* (1887) 791 Steele..was much of the rake and a little of the swindler. **1859** TENNYSON *Enid* 1280 As careful robins eye the delver's toil.

b. esp. in phr. *to act, be, play the man, the soldier*, etc. = to sustain the character of a man, a soldier, etc.; to do that which is manly, soldier-like, etc.: see PLAY *v.* 34.

1426 AUDELAY *Poems* (Percy Soc.) 29 Thai play not the fole. *c* **1530** H. RHODES *Bk. Nurture* in *Babees Bk.* 84 Saue thy selfe, play the man, being compelde. **1642** W. PRICE *Serm.* 40 Playing the drugsters or hucksters with it for gaine. **1719** DE FOE *Crusoe* (1840) I. iii. 47 To act the rebel. **1748** RICHARDSON *Clarissa* Wks. 1883 VII. 486, I will contrive to be the man. **1809–10** COLERIDGE *Friend* iv. (1865) 93 To act the knave is but a round-about way of playing the fool.

21. With an adjective used absolutely, usually denoting an abstract notion: e.g. *the beautiful*, that which is beautiful. Also forming phrases with the preposition *on*, as *on the cheap, quiet, sly*, etc., q.v.

c **1420** ? LYDG. *Assembly of Gods* 882 In stede of the bettyr the worse ther they chese. **1596** SHAKS. *Tam. Shr.* IV. iii. 80, I will be free, Euen to the vttermost. **1748** SMOLLETT *Rod. Rand.* xxii, A nose inclining to the aquiline. **1756** BURKE (*title*) Enquiry into the Origin of our Ideas of the Sublime and Beautiful. **1850** TENNYSON *In Mem.* cvi. 8 Ring out the false, ring in the true. **1878** T. HARDY *Ret. Native* VI. iii, There is too much reason why we should do the little we can to respect it now.

** *With a pl. sb. used universally.*

22. With a sb. in the plural, chiefly the name of a nation, class, or group of people, where *the* = 'those who are'; 'the...taken as a whole'. Also with family surnames, as 'the *Joneses* are of Welsh origin'.

c **1200** ORMIN 188 He shall turrnenn þurrh hiss spell þe trowwþelæse leode. **1297** R. GLOUC. (Rolls) 87 Þe saxons..Seve kynges made in engelond. **1548** W. PATTEN *Exped. Scot.* Pref. cij b, Neyther the Grekes [nor] the Ruthens. **1613** PURCHAS *Pilgrimage* (1614) 246 The bodie..was afflicted on the East by the Persians, on the West by the Gothes. **1783** JUSTAMOND tr. *Raynal's Hist. Indies* III. 380 The Rima..is not yet well know'n to the botanists. **1816** CRABB *Eng. Synonymes* 139/2 The Tarquins were banished from Rome. **1906** *Edin. Rev.* Oct. 429 These laws of sight the Greeks made it their business to analyse.

23. Before an adjective or participle having a plural application (usually of persons), as *the poor*, those who or such as are poor.

c **897** K. ÆLFRED *Gregory's Past. C.* xxiii. 175 Ða woroldwisan..ða dysegan. *a* **1300** *Prayer* 26 in *O.E. Misc.* 193 Ȝieue þe hungrie mete and te nakede iwede. **1362** LANGL. *P. Pl.* A. Prol. 18 Alle maner of men þe mene and þe riche. **1426** AUDELAY *Poems* 7 Vysyte the seke. **1526** TINDALE *John* xii. 8 The povre all wayes shall ye have with you. **1671** MILTON *P.R.* IV. 157 Nothing will please the difficult and nice. **1742** GRAY *Ode Spring* ii, How low, how little are the Proud, How indigent the Great! **1812** BYRON *Ch. Har.* I. xxxiv, Here ceased the swift their race, here sunk the strong. **1817–18** SHELLEY *Rosalind & Helen* 254–5 He was a coward to the strong: He was a tyrant to the weak.

b. A pa. pple. so used may retain its verbal construction or complement. (In this case *those* is now more used than *the*.)

c **1000** *Ags. Gosp.* Matt. xxii. 3 He..clypode þa gelaðodan to þam gyftum. **1600** W. WATSON *Decacordon* (1602) 49 Dignities which intitle the inuested with them, with a preheminence aboue all other persons. **1728** CHAMBERS *Cycl.* s.v. *Jesuit*, The professed of this order renounce..all preferment, and especially prelacy. **1817–18** SHELLEY *Rosalind & Helen* 474 Thou knowest what a thing is Poverty Among the fallen on evil days.

C. As Demonstrative (or *quasi*-personal) pronoun. In late OE. and early ME., when *þe* was substituted for the earlier masc. *se*, and subsequently became the general form of the definite article (see A. 1 a *β* and 9), it was also used for some time as demonstrative pronoun, = the (man), that, he, esp. as antecedent to a relative; thus early ME. *þe þe* or *þe þet* for OE. *se þe*, = that (man) that, he that. The fem. was *þéo þe* (for OE. *séo þe*) she that; the pl. *þá þe* those that, they that. (The neuter was commonly *þet þe* or *þette*.)

c **950** *Lindisf. Gosp.* Matt. iii. 3 Ðes is forðon ðe ðe [*Rushw.* seþe] gecuoeden wæs ðerh esaias. *Ibid.* xv. 24 Ðe *vel* he [L. *ipse*] soðlice onduearde. *c* **1175** *Lamb. Hom.* 95 Þe þet bið mid þen halia gast itend. *Ibid.* 109 Þe ðe deleð elmessan for his drihtnes luuan, þe bihut his gold hord on hecuene riche. *a* **1200** *Moral Ode* 217 (MS. Eg.) Þe ðe [*MS. J.* þe þat] godes milce secheð, iwis he mai is [*v. rr.* ha, hi] finde. *Ibid.* 219 Þe ðe [*v. rr.* Se þet, þe þat] deð his wille mest, he haueð wurst mede. *a* **1225** *Ancr. R.* 52 Mesire, þeo deð also þeo is betere þen ich am. *Ibid.* 86 Ase þe þe seið to þe knihte þet robbeð [etc.].

D. as *sb.* with pl. *thes.*

1882 'MARK TWAIN' *Stolen White Elephant* 269 You [English] say 'out of window'; we always put in a *the*. **1907** —— *Chr. Sci.* II. viii. 229, I uncover to that imperial word. .. The rare and..exclusive company of the THE's of deathless glory..*the* Saviour..*the* Bible. **1959** *Amer. Speech* XXXIV. 111 The Syrian student tends to put in *the*'s where they are not needed. **1977** *Guardian Weekly* 4 Dec. 4/1 If you are really serious about something and want to be taken seriously yourself, never, ever, under any circumstances, sully its name by putting a 'the' in front of it.

†**the**, *particle* (*conj., adv.*), *relative pron. Obs.* Forms: 1–4 **ðe, þe**, (2 **þæ**, 2–3 **þa**). [OE. *þe*, app. an unstressed or worn-down case or derivative formation from the stem *þa-* of THAT *demonst.* and *rel. pron.* Thought by some to be a worn-down locative case. Cf. Goth. *þê-ei, þei*, conj., similarly used.]

1. Used as a conjunction introducing clauses of various kinds: = THAT *conj.*

Beowulf 1334 Heo þa fæhðe wræc þe þu gystran niht grendel cwealdest. *Ibid.* 1436 He on holme wæs sundes þe sænra ðe hyne swylt fornam. *c* **1000** *Ags. Ps.* (Th.) cxliii. 4 Hwæt is se manna, mihtig Drihten, þe þu him cuðlice cyþan woldest? *a* **1250** *Owl & Night.* 941 Þe Nihtegale..wiste wel ..þe wraþþe binymeþ monnes red.

b. *spec.* After comparatives: Than.

c **897** K. ÆLFRED *Gregory's Past. C.* xliv. 318 Ne hie selfe ðy betran ne talien þe ða oðre. **971** *Blickl. Hom.* 215 Ða he þa hæfde twæm læs þe twentig wintra. *c* **1000** ÆLFRIC *Hom.* I. 154 Þeos woruld..nis..ðe geliccre ðære ecan woruld, þe is sum cweartern leohtum dæge. *c* **1175** *Lamb. Hom.* 151 If ȝe beoð strengre þe heo. *c* **1200** *Trin. Coll. Hom.* 119 Þe holi gost com..and alihte hem of brihtere and of festere bileue þe hie hedden er. *a* **1250** *Owl & Night.* 564 Na more þe deþ a wrecche wranne.

c. As correlative conjunction: '*hwæþer..þe..*', '*þe..þe..*', 'whether..or..'.

c **888** K. ÆLFRED *Boeth.* xxxiv. §6 Hwæþer þincð þe þonne þæt þa þincg sien, ðe ðara soðena gesælða limu, þe sio gesælð self? **971** *Blickl. Hom.* 97 Hwyder he gelæded sy, þe to wite, þe to wuldre. *c* **1000** ÆLFRIC *Hom.* II. 120 Ða Gregorius befran, hwæðer þæs landes folc cristen wære ðe hæðen. *c* **1205** LAY. 16812 Do þine iwille Whaðer swa þu wult don, þa us slan þa us an-hon. *a* **1250** *Owl & Night.* 1064 Hweþer þu wilt wif þe meyde. *Ibid.* 1408 Sei me soþ if þu hit wost Hweþer doþ wurse fleys þe gost. **1297** R. GLOUC. (Rolls) 4507 In woch half turne he nuste, þo weþer est þe west.

2. Relative particle. **a.** Appended to adverbs and adverbial expressions of time, place, etc., to make them relative or conjunctive. Cf. THAT *conj.* 6. Also in *for þan þe* because that, *ær þan þe* before that, and the like.

835 *Charter of Abba* in *O.E. Texts* 447 Ða hwile ðe hia hit mid clennisse gehaldan wile. *c* **1160** *Hatton Gosp.* Mark viii. 24 Þa þæ he hine be-seag. *c* **1175** *Lamb. Hom.* 87 Þa þe heo comen on midden þere se. *c* **1200** *Trin. Coll. Hom.* 35 Þe fiffeald mihten þe god him gef þo þe he him shop. *a* **1240** *Ureisun* 36 in *Cott. Hom.* 193 Þer ðe neure deað ne com.

b. Hence as a temporal adverb (= *þá, þá þe*): When.

c **1205** LAY. 263 Þeos ȝunge wiman iwerd hire mid childe, þe ȝet leouede Asscanius. *Ibid.* 4150 Þe [*c* 1275 Þo] Dunewale hauede isæd, al his folc luuede þene ræd. *a* **1300** *Harrow. Hell* (MS. L.) 42 Þe [*MS. E.* þan] he com þere þo [*MS. E.* þan] seyd he sere y shal nouþe telle þe.

3. As relative pronoun: That, who, which.

In OE. repr. any case or number. Also with ellipsis of antecedent, = he who, that which, what, = THAT *rel. pron.* 3.

805–31 *Charter of Oswulf* in *O.E. Texts* 444 Ic ðe ðas gesettnesse sette. **847** *Charter of Æðelwulf* in *O.E. Texts* 434 Ðonon to ðæm beorge ðe mon hateð æt ðæm holne. *c* **888** K. ÆLFRED *Boeth.* xxxiv. §3 His sio hea goodnes þe he full is. *Ibid.* xxxvi. §4 (3) Þæt ðu mæge ðy bet gelefan ðe ic ðe.. recce. *c* **893** —— *Oros.* II. i. §4 Þy ilcan geare þe Romana rice weaxan ongann. *a* **1000** *Boeth. Metr.* v. 11 Seo þe ær gladu onsiene wæs. *c* **1000** *Ags. Gosp.* Matt. vi. 9 Fæder ure þu þe eart on heofonum. —— John i. 26 Tomiddes eow stod þe [*Lindisf.* ðone] ge ne cunnon. **1154** *O.E. Chron.* an. 1140, Alle þe men þe mid him heoldon. *a* **1175** *Cott. Hom.* 221 Ælra þara þinge þe on paradis beoð. *c* **1200** *Trin. Coll. Hom.* 45 Þe þre kinges þe comen of estriche. *c* **1205** LAY. 41 Wace wes ihoten þe wel couþe writen. *a* **1250** *Owl & Night.* 1386 (Cott. MS.) For heo beoþ wode, þe [*v.r.* þat] bute nest goþ to brode. *a* **1300** *Harrow. Hell* (MS. L.) 24 Moyses, þe holy wyht [*MS.* whyt], þe heuede þe lawe to ȝeme ryht. **13..** *Cursor M.* 24317 (Edin.) Wit hard thrauis þe [*other MSS.* þat] he þrow þai sau þat he to ded him drew. *c* **1350** *Will. Palerne* 4422 Sche..went Into a choys chaumber þe clerli was peinted. *c* **1460** *Oseney Regr.* 166 He Bryngeth also Anoþer charter..the witnyssith [*orig.* Cartam..que testatur] that the Same Nicoll yafe [etc.]. *Ibid.* 170 For þe Sowle of my ffadur Robert Doylly þe þat same church foundid.

b. When the relative was governed by a preposition, the latter followed before the verb.

a **900** *O.E. Chron.* an. 885, He sende him..þære rode dæl þe Crist on þrowude. *c* **1000** *Ags. Gosp.* Mark ii. 4 Þæt bed þe se lama on læg.

c. In Old English the relative was also expressed by adding *þe* to the demonstrative pronoun *se, séo, þæt*; thus, *se-þe, séo-þe, þæt-þe* or *þætte, þæs-þe, þæm-þe*, etc.; but this combination scarcely survived after 1100.

835 *Charter of Abba* in *O.E. Texts* 448 Swælc monn se ðe to minum ærfe foe. *c* **893** K. ÆLFRED *Oros.* II. iv. §8 Seo ilce burg..seo ðe mæst wæs. *c* **1000** ÆLFRIC *Gen.* vi. 2 Hig.. namon him wif of eallum þam, þa þe hig gecuron. *c* **1000** *Ags. Gosp.* Matt. iii. 3 Dys ys se be ðam ðe gecweden ys. *a* **1175** *Cott. Hom.* 227 Se soðe sceppende se þe ane is god. *c* **1175** *Lamb. Hom.* 5 He is iblesced þe þe her cumet on drihtenes nome.

d. To express the genitive case *whose, of which, þe* or *se ðe* was followed by a possessive pronoun: cf. THAT *rel. pron.* 9.

a **800** CYNEWULF *Elene* 162 Se God..þe þis his beacen wæs. *c* **850** *O.E. Martyrol.* 118 þære fæmnan tid þe hire noma wæs sancta Anatolia. *a* **900** *Psalm* xxxii. 11 (Thorpe) Eadig byþ þæt kynn, þe swylc God byð heora God. *a* **1122** *O.E. Chron.* (Laud MS.) an. 1011, Ælmær..þe se arcb. Ælfeah ær generede his life.

the (ðə), *adv.* Also 3 **þæ**. [OE. *þé*, originally locative or instrumental case of the demonstrative and relative pron. *se, séo, þæt*. In OE. interchanging with *þý*: see THY *adv.*]

1. Preceding an adjective or adverb in the comparative degree, the two words forming an adverbial phrase modifying the predicate.

The radical meaning is 'in or by that', 'in or by so much', e.g. 'if you sow them now, they will come up the sooner'; 'he has had a holiday, and looks the better', to which the pleonastic 'for it' has been added, and the sentence at length turned into 'he looks the better for his holiday'.

c **897** K. ÆLFRED *Gregory's Past. C.* xvii. 122 Oft sio wund bið ðæs þe wierse & ðy mare. *c* **1175** *Lamb. Hom.* 87 Þa cleopede god þe ner Moyses him to. *c* **1205** LAY. 30597 Of þere brede he æt sone þer after him wes þæ bet. *c* **1290** *Beket* 1252 in *S. Eng. Leg.* I. 142 He chaungede is name, þe sikerloker forto go. *a* **1300** *Cursor M.* 3651 (Cott.) Þat he þe mai þe less mistru, Þou sal sai þou ert esau. **1398** TREVISA *Barth. De P.R.* v. xxxviii. (Bodl. MS.), He [the stomach] is rowȝe..to holde þe better þe mete þat he fongiþ. *c* **1430** *How Gd. Wife taught Dau.* 191 in *Babees Bk.* 41 Þe work is þe sonner do þat haþ many handis. **1526** TINDALE *John* xix. 8 When Pilate herde that sayinge, he was the moare afrayde [**1388** WYCLIF, he dredde the more]. **1596** SPENSER *F.Q.* VI. ii. 33 That..I may beare armes,..The rather, since that fortune hath this day Given to me the spoile of this dead knight. **1621** FLETCHER *Wild Goose Chase* IV. i, 'Tis not to be help'd now. *Lil.* The more's my Miserie. **1782** COWPER *Mut. Forbearance* 24 Your fav'rite horse Will never look one hair the worse. **1838** RUSKIN *Ess. Painting & Music* §24 Wks. 1903 I. 285 And if others do not follow their example, —the more fools they. **1883** *Law Times* 27 Oct. 425/1 What student is the better for mastering these futile distinctions?

†**b.** In phrase ***the less*** (***the***), (= L. *quominus*), OE. *þe-læs þe*, Early ME. (*þe*) *læste*, now LEST *conj.* q.v.

[*c* **825** *Vesp. Psalter* ii. 12 Ðyles hwonne eorsie dryhten.] **971** *Blickl. Hom.* 65 þe læs hi us besencean on helle grund. *c* **1000** *Ags. Gosp.* John v. 14 Ne synga þa, þe-læs þe þe on sumon þingon wyrs ȝetide. *a* **1100** in Napier *O.E. Glosses* i. 3675 þe læste ȝehremde. [**1175**: see LEST *conj.*]

2. ***the..the..***: by how much..by so much; in what degree..in that degree..[= L. *quo..eo..*, Gr. ὅσῳ..τοσούτῳ..]: denoting proportional dependence between the notions expressed by two clauses, each having *the* + a comparative; one *the* being demonstrative, and the other relative. The relative clause usually comes first, e.g. 'The more one has, the more one wants'; but the order may be reversed, as 'One wants the more, the more one has'; and in either order the comparative in the relative clause is sometimes followed by *that*, e.g. 'the more that one has'. In OE. commonly *þý*; ME. *þi*, *þe*: see THY *adv.*

c **897** K. ÆLFRED *Gregory's Past. C.* Pref. 5 Ðæt her ðy mara wisdom on londe wære, ðy we ma ȝeðeoda cuðon. **1297** R. GLOUC. (Rolls) 7547 þe more þat a mon can, þe more wurþe he is. **13..** *Minor Poems fr. Vernon MS.* LV. xii. 95 þe more we trace þe Trinite, þe more we falle in fantasye. *c* **1400** MAUNDEV. (Roxb.) v. 14 Ay þe elder it es, þe whittere it waxes. *c* **1440** *Alphabet of Tales* 1 Yitt þai er ay þe langer þe wers. **1596** SHAKS. *1 Hen. IV*, II. iv. 445 Though the Camomile, the more it is troden, the faster it growes; yet Youth, the more it is wasted, the sooner it weares. **1690** T. SAUNDERS in *11th Rep. Hist. MSS. Comm.* App. VII. 111 As to our sea affairs..the lesse I say the better. **1771** in J. Watson *Jedburgh Abbey* (1894) 98 The bells must be removed, and the sooner the better. *c* **1790** IMISON *Sch. Art* I. 208 The smaller a lens is, and the more its convexity, the nearer is its focus, and the more its magnifying power. **1855** KINGSLEY *Westw. Ho!* iv, The less said the sooner mended. **1874** MICKLETHWAITE *Mod. Par. Churches* 26 The higher the windows are from the ground the better.

Proverbial expression. The more, the merrier.

‖**thé** (te), *sb.* [Fr., = tea.] †**1.** A tea-party. *Obs.*

1788 H. MORE *Let.* 22 May (1925) 123 A *Thé* is among the stupid new follies of the winter. You are to invite fifty or a hundred people to come at eight o'clock..tea and coffee are made by the company,..and what constitutes the very essence of a *Thé*, an immense load of hot buttered rolls and muffins. **1802** C. WILMOT *Let.* 3 Jan. in T. U. Sadleir *Irish Peer* (1920) 22 We have had..Plays, Balls, Soirees, Thés, &c.; the first Thé was at Monsieur Amoulin's. **1827** E. GROSVENOR in G. Huxley *Lady Elizabeth & Grosvenors* (1965) vii. 136 On Friday we are to have a thé at the Viceroy's.

2. Phrases. **thé complet** [Fr., lit. 'complete tea'], a light meal including tea and usu. bread and cake; cf. *café complet* s.v. CAFÉ 3; **thé dansant**: see DANSANT, DANSANTE *a.*

1951 E. COXHEAD *One Green Bottle* v. 113 She darted away with another *thé complet*. **1967** N. FREELING *Strike out where not Applicable* 113 The Dutch 'thé complet' accessories.. sandwiches. Glacé fours. Dry petits fours. Fan wafers.

the, obs. form of THEE *pers. pron.*, THEE *v.*[1], to prosper, THEY, THIGH, THOUGH.

the, thé, thea, obs. forms of TEA.

thead (θiːd). Now *dial.* Also 4 **þede**, 5–6 **thede**. [Etymology unascertained.] A brewer's strainer; = TAP-HOSE: see quot. *a* 1825.

13.. *E.E. Allit. P.* B. 1717 Bifore þy borde hatz þou broȝt beuerage in þede. *c* **1440** *Promp. Parv.* 490/1 Thede, bruarys instrument, *qualus*. **1530** PALSGR. 280/1 Thede a brewars instrument. *a* **1825** FORBY *Voc. E. Anglia*, *Thead*, the tall wicker strainer placed in the mash-tub over the hole in the bottom, that the wort may run off clear. *c* **1850** *Catalogue* in *Leicester Gloss.* (1881), Spiggot and thead. **1881** *Ibid.*, *Thead*, a 'tap-whisk'.

theaf(e, theaft, obs. ff. THEAVE, THEFT.

theak, variant of THEEK *v.*, to thatch.

†**theal, thele.** *Obs.* Forms: (1 **þelu, þel, þell**), 6 **thele, thel, theall,** 7 (9 *dial.*) **theal.** [In 16th c. *thele*, corresp. to OE. *-þelu* fem. occurring in comb. *bencþelu* (also neuter pl.) 'bench-floor', and *buruhþelu* 'castle-floor', agreeing in sense with *þel*, *þell*, neut., board, plank, floor, in one place '(iron) plate'. These point to OTeut. forms **pelâ* fem., **pelo*[m] neuter, whence also **peljon*, **piljōn*, WGer. **pilljō*, OE. *pille*, ON. *pilja* fem. deal, plank, OHG. *dilla* board, MLG. *dele*, Du. *deel* deal, plank: cf. also the Finnish borrowed word *teljo*. The long gap between the latest OE. example of *-þelu* and the Eng. *thele*, after 1500, is noteworthy; perh. the word came down within a limited district. Cf. the place-name *þelwæl* (*O.E. Chron.* an. 923), *Thelwall* in Cheshire.]

1. (OE.) A floor.

a **900** *Beowulf* 487 Eal benc-þelu blode bestymed. Cf. *Ibid.* 1239 Benc-þelu beredon: hit ȝeond-bræded wearð beddum ond bolstrum.] *a* **1000** *Fight at Finnesburg* 30 Buruhðelu dynede.

2. A board, plank, deal. Cf. DEAL *sb.*[3]

1517 in *Market Harborough Rec.* (1890) 220, I wyll y[t] Richard Page..shall have a lede, a mawnger, a rake and thelys, beynge at ye sygne of Swanne in Harborow. **1521** *Nottingham Rec.* III. 355 Item anoyer pres borde and a thele yat ley at the kychyn dore. **1562** *Ludlow Churchw. Acc.* (Camden) 110 For thele to mende the churche dore. **1586** *Churchw. Acc. St. Martin, Leicester* in *N. & Q.* 6th Ser. VII. 249/2 Too plancke and too thels [for the library]. **1618** in *Archæologia* XLIV. 402 Item 4 greate theales of 30 foot a piece 3 foot 3 inches broad and three inches thicke. **1624** *Althorp MS.* in Simpkinson *Washingtons* App. p. lvii, Aug. 7. To Butlin 3 daies sawing theales, & 2 daies making a dore for M[ris] Segrave's house 00 05 00. **1847–78** HALLIWELL, *Theal*, a board; a plank; a joist. *Leic.*

theam, theame, obs. ff. TEAM, THEME.

[† **theaming** *ppl. a.* ? Some error.
1599: see ARSEDINE.]

theandric (θiːˈændrɪk), *a.* [ad. eccl. Gr. θεανδρικός, f. θεάνδρος god-man (f. θεός god + ἀνήρ man): see -IC.] Of or pertaining to both God and man; partaking of both the human and the divine.

1612 T. TAYLOR *Comm. Titus* ii. 14 It was..neither meerely diuine, nor meerely humane, but (as Diuines speake) theandrike. **1828** E. IRVING *Sermons* I. 140 + p. lxix, A class of heretics..asserting, that there was only one operation, Theandric or Godmanly. **1843** J. B. ROBERTSON tr. *Möhler's Symbolik* iii. §11 (ed. 3) 83 So that this regeneration constitutes one theandric work.

So †**theˈandrical** *a. Obs.* [see -ICAL].

1656 JEANES *Fuln. Christ* 36 To performe them as God man, is appropriate to Christ... As ascribed unto him, they are, say Divines; Theandrical, that is, divinely humane. **1693** OWEN *Holy Spirit as Comforter* i. Wks. 1855 IV. 358 He who worketh them [his mediatory operations] is God, and He worketh them all as God-man; whence they are theandrical.

theangeline (θiːˈændʒəlaɪn). *rare*[−1]. [f. Gr. θεάγγελις (-ιδ-) an intoxicating herb (Pliny) + -INE.] Name of a plant said by Pliny to grow on Libanus.

1855 BAILEY *Mystic* 33 The bruised theangeline, which gives Prophetic sense.

theanthropic (θiːænˈθrɒpɪk), *a.* [f. eccl. Gr. θεάνθρωπος, THEANTHROPOS + -IC.] Pertaining, relating to, or having the nature of both God and man; at once divine and human.

1652 BENLOWES *Theoph.* I. lxxviii, The Theanthropick Word, That Mystick Glasse of Revelations. **1864** in WEBSTER. **1868** GLADSTONE *Glean.* (1879) III. 55 The theanthropic idea, the idea of God made man without ceasing to be God, was..familiar..to the old mythology. **1879** —— in *19th Cent.* Oct. 765 An anthropomorphic or theanthropic system of marvellous imaginative splendour. **1882** CAVE & BANKS tr. *Dorner's Chr. Doctr.* 197 An image of Christ..which is actually and truly human and Divine at once, that is theanthropic.

So **theanˈthropical** *a. rare* [see -ICAL].
1846 WORCESTER cites *Bib. Rep.*

theanthropism (θiːˈænθrəpɪz(ə)m). [f. as prec. + -ISM.]

1. *Theol.* The doctrine of the union of the divine and human natures, or of the manifestation of God as man, in Christ.

1817 COLERIDGE *Biog. Lit.* xxiv. (1882) 301 Speaking theologically and impersonally, i.e. of Psilanthropism and Theanthropism as schemes of belief. **1867** WESTCOTT in *Contemp. Rev.* VI. 417 If we might venture to use a word not wholly without ancient precedent, it [Christianity] might be described as *Theanthropism*. It proclaims not a conception of God, but a manifestation of God. **1875** LIGHTFOOT *Comm. Col.* (ed. 2) 119 The monotheism of the Old Testament is supplemented by the theanthropism of the New.

2. *Mythol.* The attribution of human nature or character to the gods.

Cf. ANTHROPOPHUISM, which word Mr. Gladstone, writing to the Editor in July 1883, said he had given up and had 'taken refuge in theanthropism'.
1878 GLADSTONE *Prim. Homer* iii. 50 Greatly out of keeping with the anthropomorphism, or, as I would rather call it, theanthropism, of the Olympian system.

So **theˈanthropist**, a believer in theanthropism (also *attrib.* or as *adj.*); **theanthroˈpology** = theanthropism.

1816 COLERIDGE in *Lit. Rem.* (1836) I. 394 This is evident, that if the *theanthropist is a Christian, the psilanthropist cannot be so. **1887** *Dublin Rev.* Apr. 248 The theanthropist or Christian doctrine. **1845** F. BARHAM *A* 9 *Theanthropology, or the doctrine of God in man and the form of man.

‖**Theˈanthropos.** *Obs.* [a. eccl. Gr. θεάνθρωπος god-man, f. θεός God + ἄνθρωπος man.] A title given to Jesus Christ as being both God and man.

1635 QUARLES *Emblems* i. *Invoc.* 33 Thou great Theanthropos, that giv'st and crown'st Thy gifts in dust. *a* **1704** T. BROWN *Dial. Dead, Friendship* Wks. 1711 IV. 54 When this great Deliverer came, they [the Jews] very fairly Murder'd him; and from this Theantropos it is that the Christians derive..their Religion. **1730** BAILEY (folio), Thea'nthropos.

Hence **theanthropophagy** (-ˈɒfədʒɪ) [-PHAGY]: see quot.; **theanthroposophy** (-ˈɒsəfɪ) [-SOPHY], a system of belief concerning the God-man; **theanthropy** (-ˈænθrəpɪ) [ad. eccl. Gr. θεανθρωπία], the fact of being God-man, the union of divine and human natures (in Christ).

1654 JER. TAYLOR *Real Pres.* xii. §14. 281 Cardinal Perron ..says, that they deny anthropophagy, but did not deny *Theanthropophagy, saying, that they did not eat the flesh, or drink the bloud of a meer man, but of Christ who was God and man. **1817** COLERIDGE *Lett., to J. H. Green* (1895) 683 Of Schelling's Theology and *Theanthroposophy, the telescopic stars and nebulæ are too many for my 'grasp of eye'. **1658** J. ROBINSON *Endoxa* i. 19 Christ..by his *Theanthropy..knew Judas to be one [a hypocrite]. **1689** NORRIS *Refl.*, etc. (1691) 198 Here also we meet with a new Theanthropy, a strange Composition of God and Man.

thearchic (θiːˈɑːkɪk), *a.* [ad. eccl. Gr. θεαρχικός, f. θεαρχία: see next and -IC. In late L. *thearchicus* (Scotus Erigena, *c* 860).] Of or pertaining to thearchy.

1855 MILMAN *Lat. Chr.* XIV. ii. (1864) IX. 63 Jesus..is the Thearchic Intelligence, the super-substantial Being. **1890** HATCH *Hibbert Lect.* x. 304 Initiated in the thearchic mysteries.

thearchy (ˈθiːɑːkɪ). [ad. eccl. Gr. θεαρχία, f. θεός God + -αρχία a ruling.]

1. The rule or government of God or of a god; a theocracy.

1643 *Subject of Supremacie*, etc. 42 There ends Monarchy as a Thearchie, or divine dynastie. *c* **1643** *Maximes Unfolded* 8 Thearchie, or Gods Government in Families, a Nation, and all Nations. **1863** WHYTE MELVILLE *Gladiators* I. 254 His [the Jew's] belief in that direct thearchy, to which he was bound by the ties of gratitude.

2. An order or system of deities. (Cf. HIERARCHY 1, 3.)

1839 BAILEY *Festus* i. (1852) 11 From rank to rank in Thearchy divine, We angel raylets gladden in thy sight. **1876** GLADSTONE *Homeric Synchr.* 245 Pan was one of the younger gods in the Hellenic thearchy. **1899** *Literary Guide* 1 Dec. 178/1 When Jesus entered upon his ministry, the Olympian thearchy..was already tottering to its fall.

thear(e), thearme, obs. ff. THERE, THARM.

theat (θiːt). *Sc.* Also 5–9 **thete**, 6 **theatt, (tyghte)**, 8–9 **theet.** [Etymology obscure: derivation from ON. *þétt-r* tight, has been suggested; cf. *tyght* in quot. 1573.] *pl.* 'The ropes or traces, by means of which horses draw in a carriage, plough, or harrow' (Jam.): now chiefly of the plough.

1496 *Acc. Ld. High Treas. Scot.* I. 293 Item, for xiij stane and a pund of towis to be thetis. **1513** DOUGLAS *Æneis* XII. ix. 77 The renis and the thetis, Quharwyth hys stedis ȝokkit war in thretis. [**1573** *Lanc. Wills* (Chetham Soc.) III. 61 Twoo payre of tyghtes or trases for horses wth withes of iren.] **1599** *Aberdeen Regr.* (1848) II. 183 Cutting with his knyff the theattis of the said pleucht. **1792** *Statist. Acc. Scot.* IV. 395 The rashen theets [are supplanted] by the iron traces. **1844** STEPHENS *Bk. Farm* II. 694 The sort of harness with which he is first invested is that of the plough, consisting of a bridle, collar,..and back-band and chains, or theats, as these are called in some parts of the country.

b. In fig. and allusive expressions: cf. *traces*. ***out of theats*** (also ***out of theet***), out of bounds: see quot. 1710, and cf. 'to kick over the traces' (KICK *v.*[1] 1 c).

1682 PEDEN in *Life & Proph.* (1868) 13 Good Lord, cut their theets, that their swingle-trees may fall to the ground. **1710** RUDDIMAN *Gloss. Douglas* s.v. *Thetis*, Ye are out of theet, i.e. ye are extravagant or in the wrong. **1731** T. BOSTON *Mem.* v. 53 They were going to call a new upstart, one that broke the thetes. **1871** W. ALEXANDER *Johnny Gibb* ii, Keep baith laird an' tenan' straucht i' the theets.

theater, variant spelling of THEATRE.

Hence †**theaˈterian**, one connected with the stage; an actor (*obs.*).

1602 DEKKER *Satirom.* Wks. 1873 I. 244 One of these part-takers..(Players I meane) Theaterians, Stage-walkers.

Theatine (ˈθiːətaɪn), *sb.* (*a.*) *R.C. Ch.* Also 7 **Tiatine**, 7–9 **Theatin.** [ad. mod.L. *theatīnus*, f. *Teate*, ancient name of *Chieti* in Italy: see -INE[1]. So F. *théatin*, obs. It. *theatini* pl. (Florio).] A member of a congregation or order of 'regular clerks' founded in 1524 by St. Cajetan in conjunction with John Peter Caraffa (till then Archbishop of Chieti, whence the name, and later Pope Paul IV). A corresponding order of nuns was founded *c* 1600.

1597–8 BP. HALL *Sat.* IV. vii. 32 Like to a false dissembling Theatine. **1632** LITHGOW *Trav.* x. 472 The Tiatines would twice a day visite mee. **1658** PHILLIPS, *Theatins*. **1686** tr. *Bouhours' St. Ignatius* II. 136 The great correspondence which Ignatius held with Caraffa,..thence ..the People in those times called Ignatius and his Companions, Theatins. **1736** CHANDLER *Hist. Persec.* 291 Those who are to die have two monks or Theatins, as they call them, walking by them. **1889** BRIDGETT & KNOX *Q. Eliz. & Cath. Hierarchy* ix. 215 The aim of the Theatines was the reformation of the secular clergy and the sanctification of the faithful.

b. as *adj.* Of or pertaining to the Theatines. **1693** tr. *Emilianne's Hist. Monast. Ord.* xviii. 186 They had in some countries the name of Theatin Jesuits. **1885** *Cath. Dict.* 793/1 The Theatine nuns were founded by the B. Ursula Benincasa. **1903** *Eng. Hist. Rev.* Apr. 277 The terrible personality of the Theatine bishop.

theatral (ˈθiːətrəl), *a.* Now *rare.* [ad. L. *theātrāl-is*, f. *theātrum* THEATRE: see -AL[1]. So F. *théâtral* (16th c.).] Of, pertaining to, or connected with the theatre; theatrical; dramatic. **1594** R. ASHLEY tr. *Loys le Roy* 76 They pardoned Roscius, the Authour of the law Theatral. **1665** BRATHWAIT *Comment Two Tales* 23 He [Absolom]..in Theatral actions personates Herod in his Majesty. **1755** in JOHNSON. **1904** *Times* 16 Aug. 5/2 Impressiveness..depends..on the vast extent and theatral disposition of the whole.

Hence **ˈtheatralize** *v.*, *trans.* to adapt for performance on the stage. **1825** CARLYLE *Schiller* App. 270 Schiller had engaged to theatralize his original edition of the *Robbers*.

theatre, theater (ˈθiːətə(r)), *sb.* Forms: 4–5 **teatre**, 4– **theatre**, 5– **theater**. [ad. (directly, or through OF.) L. *theātrum*, a. Gr. θέατρον, a place for viewing, esp. a theatre, f. θεᾶσθαι to behold (cf. θέα sight, view, θεατής a spectator). The word was completely naturalized in L., whence It., Sp. *teatro*, Pg. *theatro*, OF. *teatre*, *theatre* (12–13th c.), whence perh. the ME. forms, mod.F. *théâtre*; also Ger., Du., Da. *theˈater*, Sw. *teˈater*.

The earliest recorded Eng. forms, *c* 1380, are *theatre* and *teatre*; from *c* 1550 to 1700, or later, the prevalent spelling was *theater* (so in Dictionaries from Cawdrey to Kersey), but *theatre* in Holland, Milton, Fuller, Dryden, Addison, Pope; Bailey 1721 has both, '*Theatre, Theater*': and between 1720 and 1750, *theater* was dropped in Britain, but has been retained or (?) revived in U.S. The pronunciation (θiːˈetə(r)), or its accentuation, appears in Lydgate, and is still in vulgar use; '*théater* is found as early as 1591.]

1. a. *Gr.* and *Rom. Antiq.* A place constructed in the open air, for viewing dramatic plays or other spectacles.

It had the form of a segment of a circle; the auditorium was usually excavated from a hill-side, the seats rising in tiers above and behind one another; the orchestra, occupied by the chorus, separated the stage from the auditorium.

c **1374** CHAUCER *Boeth.* I. pr. i. 2 (Camb. MS.) Comune strompetes of swich a place þat men clepyn the theatre. **1382** WYCLIF *Acts* xix. 29 Thei maden a sawt with oon ynwit, or wille, in to the teatre [*gloss* or comune biholdyng place]. **1412–20** LYDG. *Chron. Troy* III. 5442 In compleynynge, pitously in rage, In þe theatre, with a ded visage. **1540–1** ELYOT *Image Gov.* 69 Many woulde resorte to the common houses called Theatres, and purposing some matter of philosophy, wold there dispute openly. **1591** SPENSER *Ruins of Time* 92 High towers, faire temples, goodly theaters. **1697** POTTER *Antiq. Greece* I. viii. I. 37 Ὠδεῖον was a Musick-Theater, Built by Pericles. **1840** ARNOLD *Hist. Rome* xxxvii. II. 477 The whole Tarentine people were assembled in the theatre.

†**b.** An amphitheatre. *Obs.*

c **1386** CHAUCER *Knt.'s T.* 1027 Swich a noble Theatre as it was, I dar wel seyn in this world ther nas. *a* **1548** HALL *Chron., Hen. IV* 2 b, Then he graunted them the battaill & assigned the place to be at the citee of Coventree..where he caused a sumpteous theatre and listes royal..to be prepared.

c. A natural formation or place suggesting such a structure.

1652 *Donne's Epigr.* Poems 102 O wilt thou be Diana, haunt these fields, This Theater both woods and fountains yeelds? **1667** MILTON *P.L.* IV. 141 Shade above shade, a woodie Theatre Of stateliest view. **1697** DRYDEN *Æneid* v. 377 A native theatre, which rising slow, By just degrees o'erlook'd the ground below. **1727–46** THOMSON *Summer* 720 Mid the central depth of blackening woods, High-rais'd in solemn theatre around. **1818** BYRON *Ch. Har.* IV. xlviii, Girt by her theatre of hills. **1886** RUSKIN *Præterita* I. ix. 288 In Jura is a far retiring theatre of rising terraces.

†**d.** A circular basin of water. *Obs.*

1645 EVELYN *Diary* 5 May, A streame precipitating into a large theater of water. *Ibid.*, In one of these theaters of water is an Atlas spouting up the streame to a very great height.

2. a. In modern use, An edifice specially adapted to dramatic representations; a playhouse.

Its essential parts, as in sense 1, are the stage for the actors, and the auditorium (the latter consisting of ranges of seats, one above another); the stage is furnished with movable scenes and more or less elaborate stage machinery for their production and removal. In 16–17th c. the building was only partially roofed; it is now entirely under cover.

At first apparently the proper name of a particular playhouse in Shoreditch, outside the City of London, built 1576: see Arber, *Gosson's Schoole of Abuse*, Introd. 8, and early quots.

patent theatre, a theatre established or licensed by royal letters patent (the first two of which were granted in 1603). Their exclusive privileges were abolished in 1843. ***saloon theatre*** (*obs.* exc. *Hist.*), ***variety theatre***: see quots. 1892, 1902. ***picture theatre***, a hall in which cinema films are shown, a 'picture palace'.

1577 NORTHBROOKE *Dicing* (1579) 29 b, Those places.. which are made vp and builded for suche Plaies and Enterludes, as the Theatre and Curtaine is. **1578** J. STOCKWOOD *Serm. Paul's Cross* 24 If you resorte to the Theatre, the Curtayne, and other places of Playes in the Citie. *Ibid.* 134 The gorgeous Playing place erected in the fieldes..as they please to haue it called, a Theatre. **1593** SHAKS. *Rich. II*, v. ii. 23 As in a Theater, the eyes of men After a well grac'd Actor leaues the Stage, Are idlely bent on him that enters next. **1603** DRAYTON *Odes* vii. 56 Till with shrill Claps the Theater doe shake. *a* **1658** CLEVELAND *Christchurch Windows* 215 Those that before our Glass Scaffolds prefer Would turn our Temple to a Theater. **1701** *Lond. Gaz.* No. 3750/4 The Patentees of the Theater-Royal in Covent-Garden. **1738** *Act 28 Geo. III*, c. 30 Such Trajedies, Comedies,..Plays, or Farces, as now are, or hereafter shall be acted, performed, or represented at either of the Patent or Licensed Theatres in the City of Westminster. **1864** DORAN *Ann. of Stage* II. xi. Suppl. 186 List of the principal Dramatic Pieces produced at the Patent Theatres, from the Retirement of Garrick to the End of the Eighteenth Century. **1864** G. A. SALA *Robson* 14 Early in 1844 he accepted an engagement at the Grecian Saloon Theatre, in the City Road. **1888** WILLIAMS in *Encycl. Brit.* XXIII. 227/1 In the provinces patent theatres were established at Bath by 8 Geo. III. c. 10. *Ibid.* 227/2 The exclusive rights of the patent theatres were also recognized in the Music Hall Act of 1752. **1892** *Daily News* 26 Sept. 2/4 To erect a roomy theatre of varieties—which seems to be modern English for music hall. **1902** *Encycl. Brit.* XXXI. 45/2 (s.v. *Music Halls*) The 'saloon theatres' of the 'thirties were the music halls of to-day, and they owed their form and existence to the restrictive action of the patent theatres. *Ibid.* 46/2 The saloon theatres rarely offended the patent houses, and when they did the law was soon put in motion. **1911** *London Opinion* 13 May 248/1 A picture theatre [where] such films as Foxhunting..the Boat Race..or the Derby are being shown.

b. *N. Amer.* and *N.Z.* A picture theatre, cinema.

1923 H. CRANE *Let.* 5 Oct. (1965) 149 [Chaplin] is here in New York..to see that the first film he has produced in it [*sc.* a new studio] gets over profitably... It's running now..at the 'Lyric' theatre. **1956** H. KURNITZ *Invasion of Privacy* ii. 20 Do I want to book that man's pictures in my theatres? **1966** G. W. TURNER *Eng. Lang. in Austral. & N.Z.* viii. 176 'Theatre' nearly always a 'picture theatre' or cinema in New Zealand. **1977** *Chicago Tribune* 2 Oct. (TV Week Suppl.) 2/1, I went to the theater and saw George Segal and Goldie Hawn in 'The Duchess and the Dirtwater Fox'.

†**3.** *transf.* **a.** The stage or platform on which a play is acted. *Obs.*

1589 RIDER *Bibl. Schol.* 1484 A theater, or scaffold whereon musitions, singers, or such like shew their cunning, *orchestra*. **1647** TRAPP *Comm. Rom.* i. 20 Clearly seen: As in a mirrour, or as on a theatre. **1659** STANLEY *Hist. Philos.* III. III. 23 Some plead in the Forum, others act on the theater. *a* **1774** GOLDSM. *Nat. Hist.* (1776) IV. 93 Like the ghost on a theatre.

b. A theatreful of spectators; the audience, or 'house', at a theatre. (Cf. HOUSE *sb.* 4 g.)

1602 SHAKS. *Ham.* III. ii. 31 The censure of the which One [the judicious], must in your allowance o'reway a whole Theater of Others. **1634** HEYWOOD *Maidenhead lost* I. Wks. 1874 IV. 112 'Twas a glorious sight, Fit for a Theater of Gods to see. **1894** GLADSTONE *Hor., Odes* xvii. [xx.] 29 The theatre thrice clapped you then.

c. Dramatic performances as a branch of art, or as an institution; the drama. Also, the drama of a particular time or place; dramatic art as a craft, the theatrical profession.

1668 DRYDEN *Ess. Dram. Poesy* Ess. (ed. Ker) I. 56 By his encouragement, Corneille, and some other Frenchmen, reformed their theatre, which before was as much below ours, as it now surpasses it. *a* **1859** L. HUNT *Shewe Faire Seeming* v. Poems (1860) 178 For much the stage he lov'd, and wise theatre. **1880** *Scribner's Mag.* June 286 Their chief delight is the theater or opera. **1908** E. TERRY *Story of my Life* xiv. 332 The life of an actress belongs to the theatre. *Ibid.* 333, I have had many friends outside the theatre, but I have had very little time to see them. **1938** R. G. COLLINGWOOD *Princ. of Art* xiv. 323 In the Renaissance theatre collaboration between author and actors on the one hand, and audience on the other, was a lively reality. **1955** G. GORER *Exploring English Character* ii. 14 Of the theatre I know of, only the Burmese drama of the second half of the nineteenth century approaches the Elizabethan in its search for horror. **1976** J. ARCHER *Not a Penny More, Not a Penny Less* xvi. 174 Harvey recognized Dame Flora Robson, the actress, who was being honoured for a distinguished lifetime in the theatre. **1977** S. BRETT *Star Trap* IV. xiii. 143 He is a hard-working performer with a great belief in the live theatre.

(*b*) Phrases: ***theatre-in-the-round***: see ROUND *sb.*[1] 5 d; ***Theatre of Cruelty*** [tr. F. *théâtre de la cruauté* (A. Artaud (1932) *Manifeste du théâtre de la cruauté*)], a collective term for plays in which the dramatist seeks to communicate a sense of pain, suffering, and evil through the portrayal of extreme physical violence; ***Theatre of the Absurd***, a collective term for plays (chiefly French) portraying the futility and anguish of man's struggle in a senseless and inexplicable world (cf. ABSURD *sb.*); also *fig.*; ***Theatre of Fact***, documentary drama.

1954 E. BENTLEY *In Search of Theater* II. vii. 198 Antonin Artaud's 'theatre of cruelty', that theater of Dionysian energy and visionary power. **1958** M. C. RICHARDS tr. *Artaud's Theater & its Double* vi. 79 '*Theater of cruelty*' means a theatre difficult and cruel..on the level of performance, it is not the cruelty we can exercise upon each other..but the much more terrible and necessary cruelty which things can exercise against us. **1964** *Punch* 21 Oct. 627/3 To watch the 'Theatre of Cruelty' season safely on the audience side. **1973** J. ELSOM *Erotic Theatre* x. 190 The one adjective which cannot be used to describe the Theatre of Cruelty evening is, however, *unexpected*. **1961** M. ESSLIN *Theatre of the Absurd* 17 The Theatre of the Absurd strives to express its sense of the senselessness of the human condition and the inadequacy of the rational approach by the open abandonment of rational devices and discursive thought. **1962** [see ABSURD *sb.*]. **1963** *Sunday Times* 24 Feb. 24/5 They deserved to win, but two of the goals they scored came straight from the theatre of the absurd. **1977** P. JOHNSON *Enemies of Society* xix. 253 We must not be surprised to find that the United Nations.. should have become the World Theatre of the Absurd, a global madhouse where lunatic falsehood reigns. **1966** *Punch* 7 Dec. 864/1 Together they make up the most successful example so far of the Theatre of Fact, a gripping story, the clash of widely different personalities and many sharp remarks on the relationship between Science and Government. **1970** *Times* 9 Feb. 5 *Murderous Angels* is another example of the Theatre of Fact... The two main characters are Dag Hammarskjold and Patrice Lumumba. **1974** *Encycl. Brit. Macropædia* XVIII. 232/2 The Brecht approach to stage presentation has something in common with the Theatre of Fact.

d. Dramatic works collectively.

1640 C. G. in Brome *Antipodes* To Censuring Criticks, He [Jonson] was often pleas'd, to feed your eare With the choice dainties of his Theatre. **1703** ADDISON *Prol. to Steele's Tender Husb.* 9 But now Our British Theatre can boast Drolles of all kinds, a Vast Unthinking Hoast! **1880** *Cornh. Mag.* Aug. 156 Any two plays in the whole Shakespearian theatre. **1881** SAINTSBURY *Dryden* iii. 38 Except in Congreve's two editions and in the bulky edition of Scott, Dryden's theatre is unattainable.

e. Without article or pl. (chiefly predicatively). With a descriptive adjective: theatrical or dramatic entertainment (of a specified quality); esp. in ***good theatre*** (see GOOD *a.* 1 f); also used *transf.* of an action or work of art that has the quality of (good, etc.) drama or theatrical technique; hence *fig.*, dramatic effect or sensation, spectacle, outward show without serious inward intent.

1926, etc. [see GOOD *a.* 1 f]. **1927** *Sunday Times* 27 Feb. 6/4 'The Letter' is superb theatre throughout. **1934** *Sun* (Baltimore) 1 June 12/1 Superb tennis and 'good theater' have never been so generously mixed in the performance of any other player. **1939** A. THIRKELL *Before Lunch* iv. 96 It would have been rather too much theatre to awaken heroine with soft music, don't you think? **1948** A. J. P. TAYLOR *Habsburg Monarchy* i. 12 Austrian Baroque civilisation.. was grandiose, full of superficial life, yet sterile within: it was theatre, not reality. **1951** in M. McLuhan *Mech. Bride* (1967) 89 They bring real 'theater' to a sales presentation. **1955** W. W. DENLINGER *Compl. Boston* II. 9 Some of the competition exercises are almost useless; some I consider pure 'theatre' and others are practical. **1958** *Listener* 2 Oct. 499/2 You have to admit that the Old City is good theatre. **1965** *Ibid.* 21 Oct. 630/2 Standing spotlit at the end of a great black-draped room all by itself, it [*sc.* a piece of sculpture].. was above all dramatic. It was, in its way, even great theatre. **1975** J. O'FAOLAIN *Women in Wall* xii. 211 She encourages zeal and all she gets is theatre... This sort of thing was new to the convent.

4. A temporary platform, dais, or other raised stage, for any public ceremony.

1587 FLEMING *Contn. Holinshed* III. 1334/1 It was found better for them by the aduise of the prince of Orange..to tarie for his highnesse vpon a theater which was prepared for him. [**1621** *Execution at Prague* in *Harl. Misc.* (Malh.) III. 410 The theatrum, or scaffold of timber, which was to be erected, and whereupon the..execution of the prisoners.. was to be performed.] **1680** *Lond. Gaz.* No. 1475/3 Then his Lordship conducted their Royal Hignesses to the Hall, at the South end whereof, was erected a Theater of 42 Foot in length, and 40 in breadth, covered with Carpets and rising five steps from the ground. **1696** PHILLIPS (ed. 5), *Theater*, ..said in general, of any Scaffold erected for the performance or sight of any publick Ceremony. **1820** A. TAYLOR *Glory of Regality* 178 A large platform called the Theatre; in the midst of this are placed the royal thrones. **1838** *Order Coron. Q. Vict.*, The Queen..passes up through the Body of the Church,..and so up the Stairs to the Theatre. **1902** *Westm. Gaz.* 11 Aug. 4/2 According to the original order of service the King and Queen would have ascended the steps to the 'Theatre'—a square platform which had been erected in the central space under the 'Lantern'.

5. a. A room or hall fitted with tiers of rising seats facing the platform, lecturer's table, or president's seat, for lectures, scientific demonstrations, etc.

the (Sheldonian) Theatre (at Oxford), the building in which the great assemblies of the University are held, and honorary degrees are given at the annual Commemoration.

1613 PURCHAS *Pilgrimage* VI. xi. 521 That is now rather become a Sepulcher of Sciences, then a Theater, there being not above five Students. **1669** WOOD *Life* 9 July (O.H.S.) II. 165 Theater consecrated. The Archbishop's [Sheldon's] letter in English (read in Convocation) wherby he tells the vice-chancellor and Convocation that he had layd by 2000 li. for a purchase to keep the Theater in repayr. **1721** Sheldonian theatre [see TERRÆ FILIUS 2]. **1910** *Kelly's Directory of Oxford* 52 Of the many ceremonials and receptions which have taken place in the theatre, the most imposing..were the visit of the allied sovereigns in 1814, and the installation of the last five chancellors.

b. A room in a hospital specially designed for surgical operations (orig. one resembling a theatre, for the performance of such operations before observers); = *operating-theatre* s.v. OPERATING *vbl. sb.* b.

1641 EVELYN *Diary* 28 Aug., I was much pleased with a sight of their Anatomy schole, theater, and repository adjoyning. **1766** ENTICK *London* IV. 264 The surgeons erected a theatre in the Old-bailey. **1823** *Lancet* 5 Oct. 3/1 At half-past Seven this Theatre was crowded in every part, by upwards of four hundred Students, of the most respectable description; in fact we never before witnessed so genteel a Surgical class. **1910** *Kelly's Directory of Oxford* 37/2 The Radcliffe Infirmary and County Hospital... A new operating theatre was erected in 1898. **1935** MARSH & JELLETT *Nursing-Home Murder* iii. 38 In the anteroom of the theatre two nurses and a sister prepared for the operation. **1976** J. ARCHER *Not a Penny More, Not a Penny Less* xii. 129 Although the hospital had only some 200 beds, the theatre was of the highest standard.

6. *fig.* Something represented as a theatre (in sense 1 or 2) in relation to a course of action performed or a spectacle displayed; *esp.* a place or region where some thing or action is presented to public view (literally or metaphorically).

1581 in *Confer.* II. (1584) K iv, They..are set before all mens eyes, and in the middest of the Theatre of the whole world. **1600** SHAKS. *A.Y.L.* II. vii. 136 This wide and vniuersall Theater Presents more wofull Pageants then the Sceane Wherein we play in. **1639** FULLER *Holy War* V. x. 246 Asia, the theatre whereon they were acted, is at a great distance. **1684** T. BURNET *Th. Earth* I. 173 Earth was the first theater upon which mortals appear'd and acted. **1713** YOUNG *Last Day* I. 51 Wide theatre! where tempests play at large. **1769** ROBERTSON *Chas. V*, XI. III. 267 A theatre on which he might display his great qualities. **1798** WASHINGTON *Lett.* Writ. (1893) XIV. 21 The propriety..of my again appearing on a Public theatre, after declaring the sentiments I did in my Valedictory Address. **1855** BREWSTER *Newton* II. xvi. 104 An event..which..placed him in a noble position on the theatre of public life. **1877** BRYANT *Ruins of Italica* ii, A tragic theatre, where Time Acts his great fable.

b. A place where some action proceeds; the scene of action. Cf. SCENE, STAGE.

1615 G. SANDYS *Trav.* Ded. A vj, The most renowned countries and kingdomes:..the theaters of valour and heroicall actions. **1654** tr. *Martini's Conq. China* 198 Which Country was the Theater of all his Brutalities. **1720** OZELL *Vertot's Rom. Rep.* II. XI. 194 The Theatre of a Civil War. **1774** J. ADAMS in *Fam. Lett.* (1876) 26 To-morrow we reach the theatre of action. **1830** LYELL *Princ. Geol.* I. 199 The theatre of violent earthquakes. **1879** MENDELL *Art of War* iii. 75 The theater of operations of an army embraces all the territory it may desire to invade and all that it may be necessary to defend.

c. A particular region or one of the separate regions of the world in which a war is being fought. Also ***theatre of war***.

1914 W. S. CHURCHILL *Let.* 15 Oct. in M. Gilbert *Winston S. Churchill* (1972) III. Compan. I. 193 The hand of war will I expect be heavy upon us in the Western Theatre during the next four weeks. **1928** BLUNDEN *Undertones of War* xv. 160 (*heading*) Theatre of War. **1940** W. S. CHURCHILL *Into Battle* (1941) 261 Far larger operations no doubt impend in the Middle East theatre. **1958** E. BIRNEY *Turvey* vii. 76 Turvey straightened his helmet and marched down the gangplank into the European Theatre of War. **1961** G. F. KENNAN *Russia & West* viii. 118 Real fighting took place between Allied and Bolshevik forces only in one theater, in the Russian north. **1977** C. MCCULLOUGH *Thorn Birds* xv. 352 The biggest and most decisive battle of the North African theater had been fought.

†**7.** A book giving a 'view' or 'conspectus' of some subject; a text-book, manual, treatise. (Chiefly in titles of such books.) *Obs.*

? **1566** J. ALDAY tr. *Boaystuau* (*title*) Theatrum Mundi, the Theatre or rule of the world, wherein may be sene the running race and course of euerye mans life, as touching miserie and felicity. **1599** R. ALLOT (*title*) Wits Theater of the little World. **1611** SPEED (*title*) The Theatre of the Empire of Great Britaine: Presenting an exact Geography of the Kingdomes of England, Scotland, Ireland, and the Iles adioyning. **1640** PARKINSON (*title*) Theatrum Botanicum, The Theater of Plantes, or An Universall and Compleate Herball. **1657** S. PURCHAS (*title*) A Theatre of Politicall Flying-Insects. **1704** R. MONTEITH (*title*) A Theater of Mortality; Or, the Illustrious Inscriptions..upon the several Monuments..within the Grey-friars Church-Yard [etc.] of Edinburgh.

†**8.** *transf.* A thing displayed to view; a sight, scene, spectacle; a gazing-stock.

1606 SYLVESTER *Du Bartas* II. iv. I. *Tropheis* 343 All cast their eyes on this sad Theater. **1640** *Petit. A. Leighton* in Chandler *Hist. Persec.* (1736) 370 He was made a Theatre of Misery to Men and Angels. **1646** EVANCE *Noble Ord.* 38 If there be any that are made a Theature unto the world,..it is such as Paul [cf. *1 Cor.* iv. 9].

9. *attrib.* and *Comb.*, as ***theatre audience, -bill, coat, hat, -house, -haunter, -light, man, people, -pit, -poster, stall, -ticket, -train, -tram, -wrap,*** etc.; ***theatre-like*** adj. and adv., ***theatre-loving*** adj.

1936 *Vogue* 18 Mar. 101/2 The London *theatre audience is still all dressed in black and white. **1977** S. BRETT *Star Trap* xiii. 143 It doesn't bear comparison with the contact you can get with a live theatre audience. That's electrifying. **1895** G. B. SHAW *Our Theatres in Nineties* (1932) I. 1 It is not a work of art at all: it is a mere contrivance for filling a *theatre bill. **1897** *Globe* 18 Feb. 6/3 The fashionable *theatre bodice. *Ibid.*, Very handsome *theatre coats and jackets are worn at the play in London. **1611** COTGR., *Coeste*, ..vsed by the auncient Grecians in their *Theater combats. **1930** *Theatre hat [see JULIET]. **1856** KINGSLEY *Misc.*, *Plays & Purit.* (1859) II. 137 *Theatre-haunters were turning Romanists. **1577** T. W[ILCOCKS] *Serm. Pawles Crosse* 46 Beholde the sumptuous *Theatre houses. **1977** *N.Y. Rev. Bks.* 29 Sept. 12/4 On the rickety stages of a thousand provincial theater houses, alternative worlds blazed like magic by limelight. **1873** *Routledge's Yng. Gentl. Mag.* Apr. 282/2 *Theatre lights are lime-light jets fitted into square boxes. **1626** BACON *Sylva* §253 Some hills that stand encompassed *theatre-like. **1846** GEO. ELIOT *Let.* 1 June (1954) I. 219 Please to come in a very mischievous, unconscientious, *theatre-loving humour. **1933** P. GODFREY *Back-Stage* viii. 112 Every experienced *theatre-man knows that there is ample room for criticism inside the theatre. **1961** *Guardian* 6 Mar. 9/4 Some knowing theatre-men say it would have flopped..even a few years ago. **1952** E. WILSON *Shores of Light* 382, I did not want to see the *theater people again; I could not face another evening. **1907** G. B. SHAW *Let.* Dec. (1972) II. 739 With..society out of town during the parliamentary recess, *theatre stalls have been empty. **1846** THACKERAY *L. Blanchard* Wks. 1900 XIII. 477 The young fellow,..*theatre-stricken, poetry-stricken. **1902** A. C. HEGAN *Mrs. Wiggs of Cabbage Patch* vi. 73 Couldn't you use a whole load [of kindling], if I was to take it out in ..*theayter tickets? **1980** P. G. WINSLOW *Counsellor Heart* v. 94 Up for a day in town, to get theatre tickets..and then go shopping. **1905** *Longm. Mag.* Apr. 501 The people you meet in buses and trams and *theatre-trains.

b. Special combs.: **theatre club**, a theatre for which tickets are sold only to members (esp. in order to circumvent the censorship of public performances); **theatre-floor**: see quot.; **theatre-goer**, one who frequents theatres; so **theatre-going** *sb.* and *adj.*; **theatre-land**, the district of a town (spec. of London) in which most of the theatres are situated; **theatre-list** *Med.*, a list of patients about to undergo surgical operations; **theatre nurse** *Med.*, a hospital nurse qualified to assist in the operating theatre; **theatre organ** = *cinema organ* s.v. CINEMA c; hence **theatre organist**; **theatre party** (orig. *U.S.*), a party in which the guests, besides being entertained at dinner or supper, are taken to a theatre; **theatre-restaurant**, a restaurant where theatrical entertainment is provided for customers; **theatre seat**, (*a*) a seat of which the bottom is made to fold back when not occupied, so as to leave a wider passage; a tip-up seat used in theatres, also on tram-cars, etc.; (*b*) a seat that may be booked for a performance at a theatre; **theatre sister** *Med.*, in a hospital, nursing-home, etc., a sister qualified to assist in the operating theatre; **theatre suit** *Fashion* (see quot. 1969); **theatre workshop**, a non-commercial theatre company concerned esp. with experimental and unconventional theatrical productions; orig. and *spec.* a company founded by Joan Littlewood and others in 1945 and based in the East End of London from 1953 to 1973.

1961 R. WILLIAMS *Long Revolution* II. vi. 267 The growth of 'free theatres' and *theatre-clubs. **1978** R. HOLLES *Spawn* iv. 31 Marianne had met him..at a theatre club in Notting Hill Gate. **1895** *Funk's Stand. Dict.*, *Theater-floor, an inclined floor in a public building, as a lecture-hall, affording a better view of the platform from rear seats. **1870** *Boston Transcript* 1 Nov. 2/4 If the theatre is not crowded.., we shall be much disappointed in our estimation of the taste of Boston *theatre-goers. **1874** *Macm. Mag.* Aug. 281 Theatre-goers..who have long winced over the pale and unwholesome jokes of patchy vaudevilles. **1846** B. I. LANE *Mysteries of Tobacco* 11 The classical theological, feat-haunting, *theatre-going, card-playing Reverend Gentleman. **1852** GEO. ELIOT *Let.* 15 June (1954) II. 36 Between theatre-going and proof-reading, my spiritual eyes are burning as dim and bleared as gas-lights. **1853** *Household Words* VI. 63 The Parisians..are evidently a more theatre-going people than the Londoners. **1883** *Harper's Mag.* June 126/1 Theatre-going and..card-playing are..permitted. **1905** *Daily Chron.* 28 Dec. 4/7 [St. Martin's parish] Bishop Burnet described as 'the greatest cure in England'. '*Theatreland' we name it now. **1907** H. WYNDHAM *Flare of Footlights* xxxvi, The comfortable little house [the Sheridan theatre], situated in the very heart of theatre-land. **1964** G. L. COHEN *What's Wrong with Hospitals?* i. 17 A student will undertake the pre-medication of patients on *theatre-list. **1934** P. BOTTOME *Private Worlds* xxxi. 302 Matron..is a first-rate surgical nurse... The *theatre nurse is about too, in case we want her. **1959** T. S. ELIOT *Elder Statesman* II. 45, I fell in love with him During an appendicitis operation! I was a theatre nurse. **1930** R. WHITWORTH *Electric Organ* xvi. 156 The building of *theatre organs has..helped to bring electric..actions to their present state of efficiency. **1977** *Lancashire Life* Nov. 101/1 The story of Ronald Curtis and theatre organs is in effect the chronicle of a love affair which began in his childhood. **1932** R. WHITWORTH *Cinema & Theatre Organ* ix. 105 The cinema or *theatre organist fills a very important role. **1883** *Cent. Mag.* Sept. 787/1 A report..of Mrs. Dash's *theater party. **1884** L. TROUBRIDGE *Life amongst Troubridges* (1966) 170 To a theatre party on the 15th and supper after. **1885** A. FORBES *Souvenirs of Continents* 239 A New York 'theatre party'. **1903** *Smart Set* IX. 145/1 I've given theatre-parties to them, and watched them rustle in and fill box after box. **1962** J. F. POWERS *Morte d'Urban* viii. 164 The Cathedral curates..wangled an invitation to the Saturday-morning theatre-parties. **1958** *Hotel & Catering Rev.* Oct. 35/1 The only *theatre restaurant of its size and type in the world. *a* **1911** D. G. PHILLIPS *Susan Lenox* (1917) II. xviii. 421 A clever play that'll draw the damn fools who buy *theater seats. **1982** C. CASTLE *Folies Bergère* vii. 254 As a student..the only theatre seat he could afford was in the gallery. **1935** MARSH & JELLETT *Nursing-Home Murder* iii. 37 Tell the *theatre sister I'll operate as soon as they are ready. **1976** C. STORR *Unnatural Fathers* i. 10 The staff nurse on the surgical side who deputised for the theatre sister. **1964** MRS. L. B. JOHNSON *White House Diary* (1970) 202, I changed into my black *theater suit en route. **1969** R. T. WILCOX *Dict. Costume* 107/2 *Dinner* or *theater suit*, the feminine 'covered-up' look for evening of the 1930's and '40's, consisting generally of a long black skirt, a delicate blouse, a cummerbund and short jacket. **1945** *Westmorland Gaz.* 4 Aug. 4/9 Addresses were given by Miss Joan Littlewood..now in Westmorland with the *Theatre Workshop, a new venture aimed at furthering the arts in local towns. **1962** *Guardian* 7 Nov. 7/6 A theatre workshop is about to be started in Dublin. **1973** E. BULLINS *Theme is Blackness* 10 Some of the Black Arts approaches and techniques that Marvin X and I had developed in revolutionary theater and literature workshops on the Coast. **1981** *Sunday Tel.* 20 Dec. 16/5 The Arts Council refuses it [*sc.* the D'Oyly Carte Company] a grant— preferring its own East End revolutionary theatre workshops.

c. *attrib.* Designating nuclear weapons for use within a 'theatre' (at present thought of as Europe) as opp. to intercontinental or strategic weapons (cf. STRATEGIC *a.* 2), or their targets.

1977 *Observer* 3 Apr. 12/4 In a tactical role, Backfire..is ideally suited to attacking local or 'theatre' targets in Western Europe. **1978** *Orbis* XXII. 309 The United States has deployed a varied array of theater-nuclear weapons and delivery systems in Europe. **1980** *Daily Tel.* 18 June 1/2 Theatre nuclear missiles..have a longer range than battlefield weapons but cannot be fired as far as inter-continental missiles. **1983** *Chicago Sun-Times* 26 Nov. 5/2 'What worries us is the buildup of theater nuclear forces in Europe,' Defense Undersecretary Fred C. Ikle said.

Hence **'theatre** *v.*, *intr.* to go to the theatre; **'theatredom**, the domain or sphere of things theatrical and persons connected therewith; also, the district in which theatres are situated; **'theatreful**, as many as a theatre will hold; **'theatreless** *a.*, without a theatre or theatrical entertainments; **'theatrewards** *adv.*, towards a theatre; **'theatre-wise** *adv.*, in the manner of a theatre.

1896 *Pall Mall Mag.* 495 If a woman dances, and drives, and *theatres,..she keeps herself too chronically tired to think. **1906** *Daily Chron.* 26 June 4/7 Our round of entertainments..[does] not cease till we have lunched, motored, tea'd, dined, theatred, and supped. **1890** *Daily News* 29 Dec. 3/1 London *theatredom,..—if we may be allowed the expression—is, roughly speaking, about ten miles wide by six miles deep. **1904** *Westm. Gaz.* 5 May 1/3 Those versed in the inner life of London theatredom. **1902** *19th Cent.* Aug. 284 Get together a *theatreful of people to hear it. **1853** *Chamb. Jrnl.* XX. 409/2 The dreary prospect of a supperless, *theatreless Lent. **1897** *Daily News* 3 May 8/6 Walking slowly *theatrewards. **1629** MAXWELL tr. *Herodian* (1635) 164 A goodly spacious Plaine..lying under a row of Hills, *Theatre wise. **1737** [S. BERINGTON] *G. di Lucca's Mem.* (1738) 227 Two Rows of young Men and Women, placed Theatre-wise one above another.

theatrette (ˌθiːətəˈrɛt). [f. THEATR(E *sb.* + -ETTE.] A small theatre.

1927 *Melody Maker* Sept. 849/3 Things soon went wrong at his Leicester Square Theatrette. **1972** *Malay Mail* 27 May 1/7 The building..will house a theatrette for 200.

theatric (θiːˈætrɪk), *a.* and *sb.* [ad. late L. *theātric-us*, ad. Gr. θεᾱτρικός, f. θέᾱτρον THEATRE: see -IC. So F. †*theatrique* (15–16th c. in Godef.).]

A. *adj.* **1. a.** Of, belonging to, or of the nature of the theatre; = THEATRICAL *a.* 1.

1706 STEELE *Prol. Vanbrugh's Mistake* 29 By him theatric angels mount more high, And mimic thunders shake a broader sky. **1809** W. IRVING *Knickerb.* VI. ii. (1849) 318 Two buskined theatric heroes. **1812** *Examiner* 21 Sept. 603/1 Theatric amusements might be made objects of taxation. **1855** MILMAN *Lat. Chr.* XIV. iv. (1864) IX. 183 Councils denounced these theatric performances [the Mysteries].

b. Resembling a theatre or amphitheatre in shape or formation.

1764 GOLDSM. *Trav.* 108 Its uplands sloping deck the mountain's side, Woods over woods in gay theatric pride. **1781** MASON *Eng. Gard.* IV. 225 Two broad Piazzas in theatric curve. **1819** W. S. ROSE *Lett.* I. 27 Imagine..a city with something of a theatric form. **1819** WORDSW. *Malham Cove*, Oh, had this vast theatric structure wound With finish'd sweep into a perfect round.

2. = THEATRICAL *a.* 2.

1816 J. GILCHRIST *Philos. Etym.* 208 A poor, dull, servile, imitative, theatric set of artificial creatures, strutting about the stage of life in pompous insignificance.

3. Suggestive of the theatre; = THEATRICAL *a.* 3.

1656 *Artif. Handsom.* 168 What is there in any civill order ..which doth not put on something Theatrick and pompous? **1760** WALPOLE in *Four C. Eng. Lett.* (1880) 267 It was very theatric to look down into the vault, where the coffin was, attended by mourners with lights. **1788** MME. D'ARBLAY *Diary* (1876) IV. IV. 343 So theatric an attitude. **1879** MCCARTHY *Own Times* II. xxii. 139 He was picturesque and perhaps even theatric in his dress and his bearing.

B. *sb.* **1.** In *pl.* = *theatricals* (THEATRICAL *sb.* 2).

1807 W. IRVING *Salmag.* (1824) 9 Our theatrics shall take up but a small part of our paper.

2. orig. *U.S.* Doings of a theatrical character; theatrical behaviour, effects, or mannerisms; theatricality.

1929 W. FAULKNER *Sartoris* i. 3 With his race's fine feeling for potential theatrics he drew himself up. **1958** A. MILLER *Coll. Plays* iii. 18 Plays..had been written for a theatrical performance, when they should have been written as a kind of testimony whose relevance far surpassed theatrics. **1964** L. HANSBERRY in J. H. Clarke *Harlem* 136 The..little committees..have dragged on their particular obscene theatrics for all these years. **1972** *Time* 2 Oct. 52/2 A desperate device intended to lend a little spine to the sponge-cake theatrics [in a film]. **1977** *Daily Tel.* 12 July 17/6 The 'theatrics' of the Church are important to many Catholics and, in a way, this is what Lefebvre offers. **1983** *Times* 24 Aug. 5/2 Today's so-called peace movement—for all its modern hype and theatrics—makes the same old mistake.

Hence **the'atricable** *a.* (*nonce-wd.*), capable of being made theatric, i.e. dramatized.

1901 HOWELLS in *N. Amer. Rev.* CLXXII. 798 It is the subordinate affair of the actor to adapt himself to the poet's conception, and find it theatricable.

theatrical (θiːˈætrɪkəl), *a.* and *sb.* [f. as THEATRIC + -AL[1]: see -ICAL.]

A. *adj.* **1. a.** Pertaining to or connected with the theatre or 'stage', or with scenic representations.

1558 PARKER in Burnet *Hist. Ref.* (1681) II. *Collect. Records* II. III. viii. 355 To dispense God's Word..in poor destitute Parishes..more meet for my decayed Voice..than in Theatrical and great Audience. **1603** HOLLAND *Plutarch's Mor.* 19 The straunge fables and Theatricall fictions. **1637–50** ROW *Hist. Kirk* (Wodrow Soc.) 6 There were also some theatricall playes. **1730** A. GORDON *Maffei's Amphith.* 335 The Power and Extent of the Theatrical Law. **1905** A. C. BENSON *Upton Lett.* (1906) 72 He drifts up to London and joins a theatrical company.

†**b.** = THEATRIC *a.* 1 b. *Obs.*

1766 AMORY *Buncle* (1770) IV. 22 In a theatrical space of about two hundred acres, which the hand of nature cut, or hollowed out, on the side of a mountain.

2. That 'plays a part'; †representing or exhibiting in the manner of an actor (*obs.*); that simulates, or is simulated; artificial, affected, assumed.

1649 J. H. *Motion to Parl. Adv. Learn.* 37 Man in businesse is but a Theatricall person, and in a manner but personates himselfe. **1691** BOYLE *Greatn. Mind* I. 6 Philosophers..can easily distinguish betwixt that real Greatness..and that Theatrical one, that Fortune may have annext to his Condition. **1711** SHAFTESB. *Charac.* VI. iii. (1737) III. 368 The good Painter must..take care that his Action be not theatrical, or at second hand; but original and drawn from Nature her-self. **1830** MACAULAY *Ess., Moore's Byron* (1887) 169 How far the character in which he [Byron] exhibited himself was genuine, and how far theatrical, it would probably have puzzled himself to say.

3. Having the style of dramatic performance; extravagantly or irrelevantly histrionic; 'stagy'; calculated for display, showy, spectacular.

1709–10 STEELE & ADDISON *Tatler* No. 136 ¶3 His Theatrical Manner of making Love. **1751** *Affect. Narr. of Wager* 60 [He] read it to the Captain in a theatrical Tone. **1856** FROUDE *Hist. Eng.* II. viii. 277 The signal..was given with a theatrical bravado. **1883** MRS. OLIPHANT *Sheridan* ii. 57 Sheridan's art, from its very beginning, was theatrical, if we may use the word, rather than dramatic.

4. Special collocations, as ***theatrical agency, agent***, an agency, agent whose business is to act as an intermediary between actors and actresses seeking parts and producers offering them.

1825 P. EGAN *Life of Actor* ii. 62 We are engaged at the Harp to meet Mr. Schemer, the theatrical agent, to-morrow night. **1828** J. EBERS *Seven Yrs. King's Theatre* vii. 196 Been actively engaged in theatrical concerns, and the business of theatrical agency. *a* **1911** D. G. PHILLIPS *Susan Lenox* (1917) II. v. 126 She read an advertisement of a theatrical agency. **1973** D. RAMSAY *Deadly Discretion* 111 Why not go to Actors' Equity and theatrical agencies and dance studios? **1978** *Detroit Free Press* 2 Apr. 13C/5 Marco talks Mrs. Hopkins into letting him stay on as boarder by becoming her theatrical agent.

B. *sb.* **1.** *pl.* The performance of stage plays; now, dramatic performance by amateurs (usu. ***amateur theatricals***); formerly in a private house (***private theatricals***). Also *fig.* doings of a theatrical character; 'acting', pretence.

1657–83 EVELYN *Hist. Relig.* (1850) II. 291 Turning their ..services and ceremonies into theatricals. **1804** *Miniature* No. 21 (1806) I. 280 Private theatricals, when many of the first personages in the land choose to make themselves fools for the good of a large company. **1808** HAN. MORE *Cœlebs* (1809) II. xxxiii. 116 What the news-papers pertly call *Private Theatricals.* *a* **1849** H. COLERIDGE *Ess.* (1851) II. 12 If Charles had not carried his love of theatricals to church. **1873**, etc. [see AMATEUR 3 a]. **1892** G. & W. GROSSMITH *Diary of Nobody* viii. 118, I..totally disapproved of amateur theatricals. **1897** MRS. E. L. VOYNICH *Gadfly* (1904) 30/2 It's only the usual theatricals, because he's ashamed to face us. **1965** *Listener* 23 Sept. 462/3 He proved..fond of.. amateur theatricals.

2. *pl.* Matters pertaining to the stage and acting; in quot. 1855 *concr.* = stage properties. Also *transf.*, the theatrical column of a newspaper.

1763 D. GARRICK *Let.* 8 Oct. in R. B. Peake *Mem. Colman Family* (1841) I. iii. 84 God bless you! my dear Colman, and have a corner of your eye upon my theatricals. **1815** W. H. IRELAND *Scribbleomania* 106 *note*, He..dedicated his mind to the study of theatricals. **1819** KEATS *Let.* 22 Sept. (1958) II. 176, I purpose living in town in a cheap lodging, and endeavouring, for a beginning, to get the theatricals of some paper. **1829** *Censor* 224 The depressed state of theatricals. **1855** DICKENS *Lett.* (1880) I. 397, I have some theatricals at home.

3. A professional actor.

1859 SALA *Gaslight & D.* i. 18 How hard-working..and persevering theatricals..generally are. **1863** DICKENS *Let.* 1 May in Holman-Hunt *Pre-Raphaelitism* (1905) 238 That half-gipsy life of our theatricals. **1888** *Harper's Mag.* Nov. 945/2 All the theatricals went there.

the'atricalism. [f. prec. + -ISM.] The practice of what is theatrical; theatrical style or character; 'staginess'.

1854 LD. COLERIDGE in *Life* I. 220 The dangers of sentimentalism and theatricalism in religion. **1884** J. W. HALES *Notes & Ess. Shaks.* 73 There is nothing normal or calm, but incessant eccentricity and theatricalism. **1908** *Westm. Gaz.* 18 Apr. 2/3 The phrase has just enough of the declamatory quality in it to give it that touch of theatricalism which was dear to the heart of the man who spoke it.

So †**the'atricalist** *nonce-wd.*, one who takes part in private theatricals.

1802 in *Spirit Pub. Jrnls.* VI. 181 Pic-nic Theatricalists.

theatricality (θiːˌætrɪˈkælɪtɪ). [See -ITY.]

1. The quality or character of being theatrical; theatricalness. With *a* and *pl.* an instance of this.

1837 CARLYLE *Fr. Rev.* II. I. ix, By act and word he strives to do it; with sincerity, if possible; failing that, with theatricality. **1880** R. L. NETTLESHIP *Hellenica* 112 A tendency to theatricality and effusiveness. **1889** *Times* 27 Feb. 9/2 The absurd theatricalities with which the.. campaign is now mainly carried on.

b. *transf.* A theatrical personage.

1840 CARLYLE *Heroes* ii, This Mahomet..we will in no wise consider as an Inanity and Theatricality. **1892** *Review of Rev.* Jan. 657 Two such theatricalities as Lord Beaconsfield and Lord Lytton.

2. A theatrical matter; a dramatic performance.

1866 CARLYLE *Remin.* (1881) II. 164, I remember once taking her to Drury Lane Theatre... Of the theatricality itself that night, I can remember absolutely nothing.

theatricalize (θiːˈætrɪkəlaɪz), *v.* [f. THEATRICAL + -IZE.]

1. *trans.* To make or render theatrical.

1778 MME. D'ARBLAY *Diary* Sept., I shall occasionally theatricalize my dialogues. **1899** *Westm. Gaz.* 2 June 2/1 The scene in which the unhappy hero has his epaulettes.. torn from him, and his sword broken, though a little too 'theatricalised', is really very moving. **1909** *Daily Chron.* 9 Sept. 5/3 As Lamb has said, any attempt to theatricalise the grandeur of Shakespeare's conception must fail.

2. *intr.* **a.** To act on the stage. **b.** To attend or frequent theatrical performances.

1794 COLERIDGE *Lett., to Southey* (1895) 86 It is an Ipswich Fair time, and the Norwich company are theatricalizing. **1833** E. FITZGERALD *Lett.* (1889) I. 20 He and I have been theatricalizing lately. We saw an awful Hamlet the other night.

Hence **theˌatricali'zation**, the process of making theatrical; dramatization; also *fig.*

1875 HOWELLS *Foregone Concl.* iii, Ferris was an uncompromising enemy of the theatricalisation of Italy. **1890** *Judy* 1 Oct. 160/1 *Ravenswood*, as Herman Merivale calls his dramatization, or theatricalization, of the story of 'The Bride of Lammermoor'.

theatrically (θiːˈætrɪkəlɪ), *adv.* [f. as prec. + -LY².]

1. In a theatrical manner or style; in relation to the theatre; dramatically; as a public spectacle.

1647 TRAPP *Comm. Epistles* 637 The Pharisees..did all theatrically, histrionically, hypocritically, 'to be seen of men'. **1669** BP. HOPKINS *Serm. 1 Pet.* (1685) 71 Here royal and sacred blood is theatrically spilt. *c* **1702** POPE *Imit. Earl Dorset, Artemisia* iii, Her voice theatrically loud. **1813** *Examiner* 29 Mar. 205/1 Whether good taste considers such a deformity as theatrically picturesque. **1878** BOSW. SMITH *Carthage* 407 Some forty years after Caius Marius had so theatrically taken his seat amidst its ruins.

†**2.** In rising terraces, like an amphitheatre. *Obs.*

1768 *Misc.* in *Ann. Reg.* 174/2 It has a strong appearance of benches; which never rise theatrically in these buildings abroad. **1778** *Eng. Gazetteer* (ed. 2) s.v. *Woburn*, On one side of this water..there are high hills, that are planted theatrically with evergreens.

theatricalness (θiːˈætrɪkəlnɪs). [f. as prec. + -NESS.] The quality or condition of being theatrical.

1727 BAILEY vol. II, *Theatricalness*, the being according to the Custom or Manner of the Theatre. **1865** BAGEHOT in *Fortn. Rev.* No. 1. 15 A change of government..is one of those marked events which by its suddenness,..its theatricalness, impresses men more even than it should. **1890** *Spectator* 8 Feb., The thorough reality and absence of affectation in her character make an admirable foil for the innate theatricalness of that of her *fiancé*.

theatricism (θiːˈætrɪsɪz(ə)m). [f. THEATRIC *a.* + -ISM.] A mannerism or mode of action suited to the stage; artificial manner; = THEATRICALISM.

1872 *Daily News* 12 Apr. 4/6 The superb theatricisms (if we may employ such a word) of the elder Pitt, and the sonorous solemnities of the younger. **1880** MCCARTHY *Own Times* IV. lxi. 357 The monstrous excesses, the preposterous theatricism of the Paris Commune.

So **the'atricize** *v.*, *trans.* to make or render theatric or 'stagy'; to make like stage scenery.

1852 *Fraser's Mag.* XLV. 664 Theatricized Stolzenfels is a glaring example of the monstrosity which may be bred from restoration, with its pasteboard battlements and tawdry gothic ornaments.

theatrified (θiːˈætrɪfaɪd), *a.* *nonce-wd.* [f. THEATR(E *sb.* + -IFY + -ED¹.] Deluded by the conventions of popular drama.

1902 G. B. SHAW *Mrs. Warren's Profession* p. xxiv, People with completely theatrified imaginations tell me that no girl would treat her mother as Vivie Warren does.

theatrist (ˈθiːətrɪst). *rare.* [f. THEATRE *sb.* + -IST.] A lover or frequenter of the theatre; an expert in theatrical matters.

1889 E. DOWSON *Let.* 24 Dec. (1967) 120 Last night—lo what a theatrist I am becoming—I went to Benson's 'Midsummer Night's Dream'. **1905** M. BEERBOHM in *Sat. Rev.* 13 May 623/1, I do not mean that 'Salomé' has less dramatic than literary fibre. Mr. Wilde was a born dramatist —a born theatrist, too.

theatrize (ˈθiːətraɪz), *v.* [ad. Gr. θεατρίζ-ειν to make a spectacle of, f. θέᾱτρον in the sense 'show, spectacle'; also intr. as in 2: see -IZE.]

†**1.** *trans.* To make a spectacle or show of. *Obs.*

1678 J. BROWN *Life of Faith* (1824) I. i. 13 They were exposed to..public shame..when made open spectacles and theatrized. **1679** *Ibid.* II. xiv. 297 We read of some.. who were theatrized, brought to open scaffolds. **1711** HICKES *Two Treat. Chr. Priesth.* (1847) I. 279 He endeavours to expose and theatrize us.

2. *intr.* To act theatrically, play a part.

1839 *Watchman* 18 Sept., The Pope's militia..can splendidly theatrize in Protestant England.

3. *trans.* To make theatrical or dramatic: to dramatize. *rare.*

1888 *Scribner's Mag.* Oct. 439/1 It became necessary to 'theatreize' or idealize history.

theatro- (ˈθiːətrəʊ, θiːˈætrəʊ), combining form of Gr. θέατρον THEATRE. **thea'trocracy** [Gr. θεατροκρατία], absolute power exercised by the ancient Athenian democracy, as exhibited at their assemblies in the theatre; ochlocracy. **'theatrograph** [-GRAPH]: see 2nd quot. **ˌtheatro'mania** [-MANIA: cf. Gr. θεατρομανής mad after plays], excessive fondness for theatre-going; so **ˌtheatro'maniac**, one who is 'mad' on theatre-going. **'theatrophil** [-PHIL], a lover of the theatre; a theatre-goer. **ˌtheatro'phobia** [-PHOBIA], horror of theatres and theatre-going. **'theatrophone** [-PHONE]: see quot. 1891. **thea'tropolis** [Gr. πόλις city], a town or district famous for its theatres. **'theatroscope** [-SCOPE] = KINEMATOGRAPH.

1820 T. MITCHELL *Aristoph.* I. p. cxi, They form the best comment on what Plato somewhere calls the *theatrocracy of Athens. **1877** RUSKIN *Fors Clav.* lxxiii. 18 Instead of aristocracy..rose up a certain polluted theatrocracy. **1896** *Daily Chron.* 23 Mar. 3/4 At Olympia..the large audiences have been greatly pleased with Mr. Paul's '*Theatrograph', comprising realistic scenes from popular plays. **1896** *Daily News* 2 Dec. 10/5 The theatrograph, now so popular at the music-halls... The effect of the theatrograph is produced by means of an ingenious apparatus, which causes an intermittent light to fall upon the living performers, who thus assume the hazy, tremulous appearance of the animated pictures. **1891** *Cent. Dict.*, *Theatromania. **1903** *Times, Lit. Supp.* 17 July 226/2 Your theatromania will lead to the production of the very worst type of bad play. *Ibid.*, Lamb was a *theatromaniac..without the dramatic faculty. **1901** *Referee* 26 May 7 (Cass. Supp.) A point for *theatrophiles. **1839** DARLEY in *Beaum. & Fletcher's Wks.* I. Introd. 29, I must acknowledge this sect justified..in its most reasonable *theatro-phobia. **1889** *Telephone* I. 406/1 A '*theatrophone'..is an adaptation of the telephone, by which any one can be put into communication with a certain theatre. **1891** *Pall Mall G.* 29 May 6/2 The theatrophone (writes a Paris correspondent) is intended to transmit, by means of a clever adaptation..of the ordinary telephone, everything audible which goes on upon the stage of the various..theatres. *Ibid.* 10 Dec. 6/3 The theatrophone has found its way from Paris to London, and a preliminary trial has been made at the Savoy Hotel with complete success. **1897** 'OUIDA' *Massarenes* xviii, A modern woman of the world. As costly as an ironclad and as complicated as a theatrophone. **1899** E. CALLOW *Old Lond. Tav.* II. 302 The Gaiety commences what may be termed the *Theatropolis of London. **1904** *Edin. Rev.* Oct. 298 Paris has not been theatropolis all these years for nothing. **1896** *Daily News* 31 Mar. 7/6 A *theatroscope, the animated photography of which gives the audience specimens of burlesque, contortionist, and other scenes.

‖**theatrum** (teɪˈɑːtrəm). [L.: see THEATRE, THEATER.] Theatre, playhouse.

1786 [see ORCHESTRA 1 c]. **1890** E. DOWSON *Let.* 23 Feb. (1967) 139 We must try & work a theatrum this week. **1967** *Oxf. Compan. Theatre* (ed. 3) 36/1 The line of general development followed the 'Theatrum' of the Lyon Terence, absorbing on the way the lessons learned in the temporary spectacle-theatres.

‖**theatrum mundi** (teɪˈɑːtrəm ˈmʊndiː). [L., = theatre of the world.] The theatre thought of as a presentation of all aspects of human life; *spec.* (see quot. 1932).

1566 J. ALDAY tr. P. Boaistuau (*title*) Theatrum Mundi, the Theatre or rule of the world, wherein may be sene the running race and course of everye mans life, as touching miserie and felicity, wherein is contained wonderfull examples, learned devices, to the overthrow of vice, and exalting of vertue. **1932** J. NICOLL tr. *von Boehn's Dolls & Puppets* II. i. 261 Gottfried Hautsch, who died in 1703,.. constructed in Nürnberg a mechanical automaton with many figures, which was nicknamed his 'little world'. This is a kind of automaton which, to distinguish it from the others, is technically indicated by the term *theatrum mundi.* The *theatrum mundi* for centuries provided the traditional afterpiece of the wandering marionette theatres; by means of small movable figues running on rails it showed a diversity of scenes. **1953** W. R. TRASK tr. *Curtius's European Lit. & Lat. Middle Ages* vii. 140 A *theatrum mundi*, then, with men as actors, Fortune as the stage director, and Heaven as spectator. **1966** H. B. HAWKINS in *Shakespeare Q.* XVII. 174 The idea of the *theatrum mundi* was widely known in the Renaissance, and a number of themes..came to be associated with this concept. The idea that the world itself was God's theater gave cosmic significance to the contemporary stage. **1967** *Listener* 8 June 744/1 Television offers an almost Elizabethan comprehension of the world; it is the new *theatrum mundi.* **1979** C. E. SCHORSKE *Fin-de-Siècle Vienna* v. 227 Klimt..presents the world to us as if we were viewing it from the pit, a *theatrum mundi* in the Baroque tradition... The Baroque *theatrum mundi* was clearly stratified into Heaven, Earth, and Hell.

†**theatry.** *Obs.* [app. an erroneous formation for *theatre.*] = THEATRE.

1513 DOUGLAS *Æneis* IV. viii. 128 Or lyk Orestes, son of Agamemnone On theatreis, in farcis mony one. *Ibid.* V. vi. 7 A playing place wes markit on the ground, Sic as that clepit bene a theatry. **1567** FENTON *Trag. Disc.* i. (1898) I. 47 The monument of your vertues being..advaunced to the height of the highest theatrey in the worlde. **1571** *Satir. Poems*

Reform. xxvii. 121 The throne of tryall and theatrie [*v.rr.* trettie, theatre] trew Is ffor to reigne.

theats, traces: see THEAT.

theave, thaive (θiːv, θeɪv). *local.* Forms: α. 6 thayffe, 7 theafe, 8 theaf, thief. β. 7–9 **theave,** 8–9 **thaive,** 9 **thave.** *Pl.* 5–6 **theyves,** 6–7 **theves,** 7 **theives,** 6– **theaves.** [Known from 15th c.: etymology unascertained.] The name given in the midland and some southern counties of England to a female sheep of a particular age: most generally applied to a ewe of the first or second year, that has not yet borne a lamb; in some parts to a ewe between the first and second shearing: see quotations.

In Eng. Dial. Dict. cited in use from S.W. Yorkshire to the Thames, and from Hereford to Essex; also in Berks, Wilts, Dorset. In some districts app. identified with *teg* or *hog*, in others with the age succeeding this.

1465 *Paston Lett.* III. 437 Item,..iiij^xx hoggys and xl theyves. **1517** in *Eng. Hist. Rev.* (1897) XII. 234, 60 young ewes or theaves. **1523** FITZHERB. *Husb.* §53 The ewes by them-selfe, the share-hogges and theyues by them selfe. **1544** (Dec. 13) *Will of J. Borow of S. Stoke* (MS.), A thayffe youe. **1596** *Unton Invent.* (1841) 9 Two hundred tegges and theves. **1607** TOPSELL *Four-f. Beasts* (1658) 495 The first year we call it in English a Lamb.., the second year, a Hog, Lam-hog, or Teg if it be a female, the third year, Hoggrils and Theives. **1614** MARKHAM *Cheap Husb.* III. i. (1668) 87 The second year the male is a Weather, and the female a Theafe, and then she may be put to the Ram; but if you let her go over that year also, then she is a double Theafe. **1669** WORLIDGE *Syst. Agric.* (1681) 323 A *Theave*, an Ew of the first year. [So **1691** RAY *S. & E.C. Words*, Essex.] **1736** W. ELLIS *New Exper. Husb.* 52 (E.D.S.) The first year we call the ewe a lamb; the second year a ewe pug or teg; the third year a thaive; and the fourth year a sheep. **1799** A. YOUNG *Agric. Lincoln.* 314 Theaves; ewe hogs. **1841** *Penny Cycl.* XXI. 356/1 After being shorn, she is a *shearing ewe* or *gimmer*, or *theave* or double-toothed ewe; and after that, a *two* or *three* or *four shear ewe* or *theave.* **1844** STEPHENS *Bk. Farm* II. 39 Gimmers are called theaves until they bear the first lamb. **1863** MORTON *Cycl. Agric.* (E.D.S.), *Theaves* (*West Engl.*), ewes that have been shorn once. **1879** MISS JACKSON *Shropsh. Word-bk.* 437 *Thave*, a ewe sheep of the first year. **1886** C. SCOTT *Sheep-Farming* 18 From first to second shearing... Gimmer, Theave, Shearling ewe. **1904** *Eng. Dial. Dict., Theave. Wiltsh.* A ewe of the third year. *Dorset.* A sheep three years old and therefore having six incisors.

the'baia. *Chem.* [f. Gr. Θῆβαι Thebes + -IA[1] (after *ammonia*): see THEBAIC[2].] = THEBAÏNE.

1857 MILLER *Elem. Chem.* III. 282 **Thebaia*, or *Paramorphia* ($C_{38}H_{21}NO_6$). This alkali crystallizes from its solution in alcohol or in ether, in square plates of silvery lustre, which have a styptic, acrid taste. **1869** *N. Syd. Soc. Bienn. Retrospect* 443 Thebaia is the first of the opium alkaloids in toxic activity.

Thebaic (θiː'beɪɪk), *a.*[1] [ad. L. *Thēbaic-us*, ad. Gr. Θηβαϊκός, f. Θῆβαι, Θήβη Thebes.] Of or pertaining to the ancient city of Thebes on the Nile, formerly a centre of Egyptian civilization; *spec.* noting the Sahidic version of the Bible.

Thebaic marble, stone, the syenite of Thebes and Upper Egypt, famed in ancient times as material for columns, pillars, vases, etc.

1687 A. LOVELL tr. *Thevenot's Trav.* I. 123 The Vault [in old wall towers of Alexandria] is supported by great Pillars of Thebaick Stone. **1773** *Gentl. Mag.* Aug. 399/1 Thebaic stone, from waste ev'n yet secure, With hieroglyphic learn'd inwrought. **1830** TATTAM *Egypt. Gram.* Pref. 7 The terms Coptic and Sahidic have been adopted in this work, instead of Memphitic and Thebaic. **1839** *Civil Eng. & Arch. Jrnl.* II. 453/1 It seems to be the Syenite of the ancients, or perhaps..their Thebaic marble. **1884** H. M. SCOTT in *Chicago Advance* 31 Jan., Two, perhaps three, translations of the Scriptures, the Memphitic, for the Lower Egyptian Churches, and the Thebaic, for those of Upper Egypt.

the'baic, *a.*[2] *Pharm. Chem.* [f. as prec., in reference to the fact that Egypt was a chief source of the opium of commerce.] Of or derived from opium; *thebaic extract, tincture*, laudanum.

1746 H. PEMBERTON *Dispensatory* 153 Opium strained, otherwise called the Thebaic Extract. **1783** W. KEIR in *Med. Commun.* I. 129 An eighth part of thebaic tincture. **1797** *Encycl. Brit.* (ed. 3) XIV. *Pharmacy* §558 Thebaic powder. *Ibid.* §604 Thebaic electuary.

So **the'baïcine,** *Chem.*, a yellow amorphous alkaloid, described by Hesse 1870, formed by boiling thebaïne with concentrated hydrochloric acid; **thebaïne** ('θiːbeɪaɪn) [-INE[5]], a highly poisonous alkaloid, $C_{19}H_{21}NO_3$, obtained in colourless leaflets or prisms from opium; formerly also called *paramorphine* and THEBAIA; also *attrib.*; **thebaïsm** ('θiːbeɪɪz(ə)m), *Path.*, the toxic action of thebaïne; **'thebenine,** *Chem.*, an amorphous crystalline alkaloid, isomeric with thebaïne, from which it is formed by boiling with hydrochloric acid.

1875 WATTS *Dict. Chem.* VII. 1152 *Thebaïcine. **1894** MUIR & MORLEY *Watts' Dict. Chem.* IV. 681 Boiling [in] dilute H_2SO converts it [Thebaïne] into thebenine and thebaïcine. **1835** *R. D. & T. Thomson's Rec. Gen. Sc.* II. 381 Ammonia is next poured into the purified liquid, by which means, Morphine and *Thebaine are precipitated. **1868** WATTS *Dict. Chem.* V. 759 Thebaine-salts do not crystallise from aqueous solution. **1871** ROSCOE *Elem. Chem.* 429 It appears that thebaine is the most powerful of the alkaloids. **1875** WATTS *Dict. Chem.* VII. 1153 *Thebenine.

Thebaïd ('θiːbeɪɪd), *a.* and *sb.* [ad. Gr. Θηβαΐς, -ιδ-, L. *Thēbais, -id-.*] **a.** *adj.* Pertaining to Thebes; usually **b.** *sb.* the territory belonging to (*a*) Egyptian, or (*b*) Bœotian Thebes; the name of certain poems, esp. that of Statius relating to Bœotian Thebes.

[**1687** LOVELL tr. *Thevenot's Trav.* I. 175 Captos, a Town of the Thebais (the Ruines whereof are still to be seen betwixt Cossir and Chana).] **1727–41** CHAMBERS *Cycl.*, *Thebaid, Thebais*, a famous heroic poem of Statius. **1776** MICKLE tr. *Camoens' Lusiad* Introd. 146 The Iliad, the Eneid, and all those poems which may be classed with the Thebaid. **1839** *Civil Engin. & Arch. Jrnl.* II. 453/2 Thebaid [porphyry] red ground, with yellow spots. **1854** WHITTIER *Hermit of Thebaid* 115 Its holiest saint the Thebaid lost, And found a man! **1876** GLADSTONE *Homeric Synchr.* 241 Ammon was the god especially of the Thebaid.

Theban ('θiːbən), *a.* and *sb.* (also 7 **-ean,** 8 **-æan.**) [ad. L. *Thēbān-us*, f. *Thēbæ*, Gr. Θῆβαι, Thebes.]

A. *adj.* **1.** Of or belonging to Thebes, capital of ancient Bœotia in Greece.

c **1374** CHAUCER *Anel. & Arc.* 85 This theban knyght.. Was yonge. *c* **1374** —— *Troylus* v. 601 So cruwel..vn-to þe blood Thebane. **1746** FRANCIS tr. *Horace, Art Poetry* 533 Thus rose the Theban Wall; Amphion's Lyre, And soothing Voice the listening Stones inspire. **1762** FALCONER *Shipwreck* III. 227 To curb thy spirit with a Theban chain. **1861** PALEY *Æschylus* (ed. 2) VII. *Agst. Thebes* 240 *note*, The association of Theban gods..Pallas, Hera, Artemis,.. Poseidon, Aphrodite, &c.

2. Of or belonging to Thebes, ancient capital of Upper Egypt; = THEBAIC *a.*[1]

Theban drug, opium or laudanum; ***Theban marble, porphyry*** = THEBAIC *stone*; ***Theban year***, the Egyptian year of $365\frac{1}{4}$ days.

1645 EVELYN *Diary* 21 Feb., The architrave of the portico [of the Roman Pantheon] sustain'd by 13 pillars of Theban marble. [**1753** CHAMBERS *Cycl. Supp., Thebanus ophites*.. that species of the..serpentine marble more commonly called *ophites niger*, the black serpentine.] **1768** C. SHAW *Monody* xvi, Come, Theban drug, the wretch's only aid, To my torn heart its former peace restore. **1831–3** E. BURTON *Eccl. Hist.* xxviii. (1845) 596 The martyrdom of the Theban legion..may be said to have taken place about the year 286, when Herculeus was on his march into Gaul. **1839** *Civil Eng. & Arch. Jrnl.* II. 435/2 Theban Porphyry was black with yellow spots. **1962** E. COLLEDGE *Mediæval Mystics of England* 15 The hermit settlements of the Theban desert.

B. *sb.* **1.** (also † **Thebien**). A native or inhabitant of Bœotian Thebes, a Bœotian.

c **1374** CHAUCER *Anel. & Arc.* 60. *c* **1386** —— *Knt.'s T.* 1712 Thise two Thebans vp on either side. *c* **1420** *Wars Alex.* (Prose) 34 þe Thebienes also þat were so wyse, and so grete exercyse hadde in armes. **1605** SHAKS. *Lear* III. iv. 162 Ile talke a word with this same lerned Theban. **1770** LANGHORNE *Plutarch* (1851) I. 320/2 They proclaimed liberty to the Thebans. **1822** T. MITCHELL *Aristoph.* I. 103 Flute-music..was stigmatised as Theban-like, and consequently unfit for a gentleman. **1880** SWINBURNE *Study Shaks.* 183 To the simpler eyes of less learned Thebans than these—Thebes, by the way, was Dryden's irreverent name for Cambridge.

2. The variety of Greek spoken in Bœotian Thebes. *poet. rare.*

1820 SHELLEY *Oedipus Tyrannus* (1904) II. ii. 451 In plain Theban, that is to say, My name's John Bull.

thebe ('θeɪbeɪ). Pl. **thebe.** [a. Setswana, lit. 'shield'.] A currency unit in Botswana, equal to $\frac{1}{100}$ of a PULA (sense 2). Also, a coin of this value.

1976 *Botswana: Ten Years of Progress 1966–76* 17 The Bank of Botswana will ultimately perform all of the functions of a modern central bank. Its first task has been to conduct the issuance of the new notes (Pula) and coins (Thebe) in 1976. **1976** *N.Y. Times* 15 Aug. 6/1 The new unit —the pula, which will be divided into 100 thebe—will have the same value, however, as the rand, which ceases to become legal tender in this country as of Aug. 23.

thebe, *dial.*: see FEABERRY, gooseberry.

thebenine: see THEBAIC[2].

†**Thebes,** *sb. pl. Obs.* Also 5 Tebes, (Thebies). [? a. OF. **Thebes*, f. L. *Thēbæ, -ās*, the city *Thebes.*] = Thebans; see THEBAN *sb.*

13.. *K. Alis.* 2819 Mawgre the Thebes everichon. *Ibid.* 2824 Theo Thebes stoden aboute his harme. *a* **1400–50** *Wars Alex.* 2333 (MS. A.) þe Thebies [*MS. D.* tebes] þam tiȝt þe toun to defende.

Thebesian (θiː'biːsɪən), *a. Anat.* [f. *Thebesius*, name of a German anatomist (1686–1732) + -AN.] Applied to structures in the heart discovered or investigated by Thebesius:

Thebesian foramina, small openings into the right auricle, believed to be the orifices of the Thebesian veins; ***Thebesian valve***, the coronary valve; ***Thebesian veins***, small veins bringing blood from the substance of the heart into the right auricle.

1871 HUXLEY *Anat. Vertebr. Anim.* 407 In the heart [of the porpoise] the fossa ovalis is distinct, but there is neither Eustachian nor Thebesian valve.

thebolactic (θiːbəʊ'læktɪk), *a. Chem.* [f. THEBAIC *a.*[2] + LACTIC.] In *thebolactic acid*: see quots. Hence **thebo'lactate,** a salt of this acid.

1867 *N. Syd. Soc. Bienn. Retrospect* 477 Messrs. T. and H. Smith give directions for the preparation of thebolactic acid, a new body discovered by them in opium... The process depends on the ready solubility of the thebolactate of lime. **1874** GARROD & BAXTER *Mat. Med.* (1880) 191 Thebolactic acid ($C_3H_6O_3$), isomeric, or perhaps identical with lactic acid. Turkey opium contains 2 per cent. of it.

‖**theca** ('θiːkə). Pl. **thecæ** ('θiːsiː). [L., ad. Gr. θήκη case, cover.]

1. A receptacle, a cell; *spec.* (*Eccl.*) = BURSE 1 b.

1662 J. BARGRAVE *Pope Alex. VII* (1867) 121 Some of these underground streets were for their burials,..the corps were..immuralld in *thecas*, or, as it were, in hollow shelves dug into the wall. **1682** LISTER tr. *Gœdart's Insects* 95 In this Nest they [Bees] make a *Theca*, or small Cell... Every Bee lays 9. little Worms in this *Theca*, or Cell.

2. *Bot.* A part of a plant serving as a receptacle; a sac, cell, or capsule; *spec.* (*a*) an anther cell, containing pollen; (*b*) a vessel containing spores in various cryptogamous plants, as the capsule of a moss, the sporangium of a fern, or the fructification in certain lichens.

1676 GREW *Anat. Flowers* II. iii. §9 These Parts [anthers] are all hollow; each being the *Theca* or Case of a great many extream small Particles. **1829** LOUDON *Encycl. Pl.* (1836) 874 *Musci*... Thecæ many-seeded, solitary, furnished with an operculum and columella. *Ibid.* Gloss., *Thecæ*, the cases that contain the sporules of Cryptogamic plants. **1830** LINDLEY *Nat. Syst. Bot.* 307 *Sporules*, which are enclosed in particular cases called *thecæ*. **1880** GRAY *Struct. Bot.* vi. §6 (ed. 6) 251 The best technical name for anther-sac is that of *Theca*. **1897** WILLIS *Flower. Pl. & F.* I. 77 The anther has typically two main lobes or thecae.

3. *Zool.* and *Anat.* A case or sheath enclosing some organ or part: as

(*a*) the horny case of an insect pupa; (*b*) the loose sheath investing the spinal cord; (*c*) one of the fibrous sheaths in which the digital tendons glide; (*d*) the sheath of the proboscis of dipterous insects; (*e*) a cup-like or tubular structure in corals, containing a polyp.

1665–6 *Phil. Trans.* I. 89 It becomes a *Papilio* or Butterfly, in the *Theca* or Case. **1670** *Ibid.* V. 2099 Some of these Maggots I took out of their *Theca* or bagg. **1807** *Med. Jrnl.* XVII. 308 The theca or sheath which encloses the femoral artery, nerve and vein. **1826** KIRBY & SP. *Entomol.* III. xxxiv. 467 In all [mouths of Dipterous insects], the *theca* or sheath is present. **1840** E. WILSON *Anat. Vade-M.* (1851) 239 In the thecæ of the fingers several small tendinous fasciculi are generally found. **1875** HUXLEY in *Encycl. Brit.* I. 130/2 In the simple aporose corals the calcification of the base and side walls of the body gives rise to the cup or *theca*. **1899** *Allbutt's Syst. Med.* VII. 536 The water-cushion which surrounds the cord within the spinal theca.

b. In full ***theca folliculi***. A layer of hormonally active cells enclosing a tertiary (vesicular) or a mature (Graafian) ovarian follicle, consisting of an inner, vascular layer (***theca interna***) and an outer, fibrous layer (***theca externa***). [So named in Ger. by C. E. von Baer (*Über Entwickelungsgeschichte der Thiere* (1837) II. III. xv. 23).]

1857 DUNGLISON *Dict. Med. Sci.* (rev. ed.) 400/1 *Folliculi Graafiani*, small spherical vesicles in the stroma of the ovary, which have at least two coats; the outer termed ovicapsule.. and theca folliculi. **1859** R. B. TODD *Cycl. Anat. & Physiol.* V. 551/1 The external or vascular coat [of the Graafian follicle]..constitutes the tunic of the ovisac of Barry, the tunica fibrosa, S. theca folliculi of Baer. **1929** [see LUTEINIZED *ppl. a.*]. **1930** MAXIMOW & BLOOM *Text-bk. Histol.* xxxii. 640 There is no sharp limit between the two layers of the theca or between the theca externa and the stroma. **1966** *McGraw-Hill Encycl. Sci. & Technol.* XI. 474/1 A growing follicle has several layers of follicular cells, or granulosa cells.., and a surrounding capsule of connective tissue, the theca folliculi. **1978** D. B. & W. J. WILSON *Human Anat.* xvi. 388/2 The inner layer is the theca interna, which secretes the hormone estrogen into the vascular system.

4. Special Comb.: **theca cell tumour** *Path.*, an œstrogen-secreting ovarian tumour that consists of cells resembling those of the theca folliculi and is sometimes malignant; = THECOMA.

1937 *Amer. Jrnl. Obstetr. & Gynecol.* XXXIV. 988 It was not until 1932 that the last member of this interesting group of tumors was reported by Loeffler and Priesel, to which they gave the name of 'fibroma theca cellulare xanthomatodes ovarii', more commonly known as the theca cell tumor. **1974** PASSMORE & ROBSON *Compan. Med. Stud.* III. xxviii. 50/1 Luteinization of the cells of granulosa cell and theca cell tumours may occur.

Hence **'thecal** *a.*, of, pertaining to, or of the nature of a theca; **'thecate** *a.*, having a theca, sheathed.

1847 DRUITT *Surg. Vade M.* (ed. 4) 544 The tendinous whitlow, or thecal abscess. **1861** J. R. GREENE *Man. Anim. Kingd., Cœlent.* 160 A thecal corallum, in other *Actinozoa*, at length comes to be formed. **1876** TOMES *Dental Anat.* 107 The tissue whence the dentine papillæ arise blends insensibly with that making up the substance of the thecal fold. **1877** HUXLEY *Anat. Inv. Anim.* iii. 159 The thecal canals of the Millepores. **1891** *Cent. Dict.*, Thecate.

thecaphore, etc., erron. forms: see THECO-.

thecche, theche, obs. forms of THATCH.

theci- (θiːsɪ), combining form of L. THECA, esp. in botanical words. **the'ciferous** [-FEROUS], †**the'cigerous** [-GEROUS] *a.*, bearing thecæ or asci. **'theciform** *a.*, having the form of a theca.

1860 MAYNE *Expos. Lex.*, Thecigerous. **1877** HUXLEY *Anat. Inv. Anim.* iii. 152 The theciform projections of the Graptolite stem. **1891** *Cent. Dict.*, Theciferous.

‖**thecitis** (θiːˈsaɪtɪs). *Path.* [f. THEC-A + -ITIS.] Inflammation of a tendon and its sheath; = TENO-*synovitis*.

1857 in DUNGLISON *Med. Lex.*

‖**thecium** (ˈθiːsɪəm). *Bot.* [mod.L., a. Gr. θηκίον, dim. of θήκη THECA.] The HYMENIUM of a lichen.

1882 J. M. CROMBIE in *Encycl. Brit.* XIV. 554/1 The two principal parts of which an apothecium consists are the *hypothecium* and the *thecium*. *Ibid* 554/2 The thecium, or as it is more frequently termed the *hymenium*, is that part of the apothecium which contains the organs of the fruit.

theck, Sc. variant of THEEK, to thatch.

theclan (ˈθɛklən), *a. Entom.* [f. mod.L. *Thecla* generic name + -AN.] Belonging to the genus *Thecla* of butterflies, comprising the Hair-streaks.

1884 *Stand. Nat. Hist.* (1888) II. 478 Among the grandest of the group are *T*[*hecla*] *coronata*, *T. imperialis*, and *T. regalis*, which are Brazilian species, and, as their names imply, are the regnant beauties of the Theclan court.

theco- (θiːkəʊ), erroneously **theca-**, combining form of Gr. θήκη case, receptacle (see THECA), used in Botany and Zoology. **thecoˈdactyl(e** [Gr. δάκτυλος digit], *a.* having thick toes whose transverse scales furnish a sheath for the claw, as in some lizards; *sb.* a gecko of this type (Ogilvie 1882); so **thecoˈdactylous** *a.* **thecoˈglossate** *a.* [Gr. γλῶσσα tongue], having a smooth tongue furnished with a sheath, as the *Thecoglossæ*, a group of lizards. **ˈthecophore** [-PHORE], (*a*) a surface or receptacle bearing a theca or thecæ (Webster 1864); (*b*) the stalk which in some flowers supports the ovary; = GYNOPHORE 1. **thecoˈsomate, thecoˈsomatous** *adjs.* [Gr. σῶμα body], belonging to the *Thecosomata*, a group of pteropods having the body sheathed in a mantle-skirt; so **ˈthecosome**, a thecosomatous pteropod. **ˈthecospore**, a spore produced in a theca, an ascospore; hence **theˈcosporal** *a.*, pertaining to a theospore; **ˈthecospored, theˈcosporous** *adjs.*, having thecospores. **ˈthecostome** [Gr. στόμα mouth], the orifice of the hydrotheca in calyptoblastic hydroids. **theˈcostomous** *a.*, having the sucking parts of the mouth enclosed in a sheath.

1891 *Cent. Dict.*, *Thecodactylous..*Thecoglossate. **1832** LINDLEY *Introd. Bot.* I. ii. §10. 139 Sometimes the ovarium..is seated upon a long stalk... This stalk is often called the *thecaphore or gynophore. **1878** BELL *Gegenbaur's Comp. Anat.* 321 The velum is largest in the Gastropoda and the *thecosomatous Pteropoda. **1888** PELSENEER in *Challenger Rep.* XXIII. 2 The Habits of the Thecosomatous Pteropods. **1890** *Athenæum* 12 July 66/2 The *thecosomes being tornatellids modified for a swimming life. **1891** *Cent. Dict.*, *Thecasporal. **1858** CARPENTER *Veg. Phys.* §405 The Lichens produce conceptacles,..called apothecia,..which develope in their interior little bodies, called *thecaspores. **1882** J. M. CROMBIE in *Encycl. Brit.* XIV. 555/2 In various *thecaspored fungi. **1879** WEBSTER *Supp.*, **Thecasporous*. **1883** *Challenger Rep.* VII. xx. 7 On either side of the hydrotheca, nearly on a level with its orifice or *thecostome. **1891** *Cent. Dict.*, *Thecostomous.

thecodont (ˈθiːkədɒnt), *a.* and *sb.* *Zool.* [f. THECO- + Gr. ὀδούς, ὀδοντ- tooth.] **a.** *adj.* Of or belonging to the *Thecodontes*, an extinct order of primitive reptiles having the teeth fixed in sockets in the jaw-bone. **b.** *sb.* A reptile having this character.

1840 OWEN *Odontogr.* II. iv. §110. 266 (*heading*) Thecodonts. *Ibid.*, A third mode of fixation is presented by some extinct Saurians,..the teeth being implanted in sockets..: these may be termed the 'thecodont' Lacertians: the most ancient of all Saurians belong to this group. **1876** PAGE *Adv. Text-bk. Geol.* xv. 282 The thecodont saurians seem peculiar to the Permian. **1877** LE CONTE *Elem. Geol.* III. (1879) 404 In the coal, are also found now some Thecodont (socket-toothed) reptiles, allied to Crocodilians. **1933** A. S. ROMER *Vertebr. Paleontol.* viii. 170 An overgrown offshoot from the early thecodont stock was..a large South African Lower Triassic form. *Ibid.*, Confined exclusively to the Triassic, the history of the thecodonts was a brief one. **1980** N. ORRISS tr. *Babin's Elem. Palaeontol.* xviii. 327 In the classical conception, birds originated directly from the Triassic thecodonts.

So ˌ**thecodontoˈsaurian**, *adj.* belonging to or characteristic of the thecodont reptiles; *sb.* a member of this genus.

[**1840** OWEN *Odontogr.* II. iv. §112. 267 In the same formation as contained the jaw and teeth of the *Thecodontosaurus*.] **1869** HUXLEY in *Q. Jrnl. Geol. Soc.* XXVI. 44 The Thecodontosaurian ilium. *Ibid.*, I shall speak of the bones as those of Thecodontosaurians.

thecodontian (θiːkəˈdɒntɪən), *sb.* and *a.* [f. mod.L. order name *Thecodontia* (R. Owen 1859, in *Rep. Brit. Assoc. Adv. Sci.* 163) + -AN: cf. THECODONT.] = prec.

1974 *Nature* 8 Mar. 168/2 The Saurischia and Ornithischia, are usually interpreted as independent derivatives of primitive thecodontian reptiles of the Triassic, but all known Triassic dinosaurs can be distinguished from typical thecodontians. **1979** *Ibid.* 17 May. 234/2 Dinosaurs apparently lacked a fenestra pseudorotunda, as did the early thecodontians, eosuchians and captorhinomorphs.

thecoma (θɪˈkəʊmə). *Path.* [f. THEC(A + -OMA.] = *theca cell tumour* s.v. THECA 4.

1937 *Amer. Jrnl. Obstetr. & Gynecol.* XXXIV. 988 The luteoma, like the thecoma, is also a rare tumor. **1966** WRIGHT & SYMMERS *Systemic Path.* I. xxvii. 869/1 Although they may occur at any age, thecomas are most frequent in women between 50 and 60. **1981** A. D. T. GOVAN et al. *Path. Illustrated* xiii. 685 It has been suggested that fibromas found in ovaries are thecomas which have undergone fibrous degeneration.

‖**thecomeˈdusa**. *Zool.* [f. THECO- + MEDUSA.]

1878 BELL *Gegenbaur's Comp. Anat.* 98 The Thecomedusæ are polypoid Coelenterata provided with a test, and allied to the Hydriformes.

thedam, thedom, varr. THEEDOM *Obs.*

theddre, obs. form of THITHER.

†**thede**. *Obs.* Forms: 1 **þiod**, 1–3 **þeod**, 2 **þiode**, 2–4 **þeode, þede**, 4–5 **thede**. (4 **þedd**, 5 *Sc.* **theid**). [OE. *þíod, þéod* = OS. *thioda, thiod*, OFris. *thiade*, OHG. *diota*, MHG. *diet*, ON. *þióð*, Goth. *þiuda*:—OTeut. **þeuðô*, by Verner's Law:—Indo-Eur. **teutā-* fem.; cf. Lith. *tautà*, OIr. *túath*, Osc. *touto*, Sabine *touta* people.]

1. A people, race, nation.

855 *O.E. Chron.* an. 527 Her Edwine kyning wæs ʒefulwad mid his þeode on Eastron. *a* **1000** *Hymns* viii. 9 (Gr.) We þe..panciað, þioda waldend. *c* **1000** *Ags. Gosp.* Luke xxi. 10 þeod arist aʒen þeode. *a* **1175** *Cott. Hom.* 237 þurh false godes þe ælc þiode ham selfe macede. *c* **1175** *Lamb. Hom.* 115 Wa þere þeode þer þe king bið child. *c* **1200** ORMIN 3438 Tatt þeod wass hæþene þeod. *Ibid.* 16057 To spekenn wel Wiþþ alle þede spæchess. *c* **1250** *Gen. & Ex.* 2302 Quene he comen in vnkinde ðeden. *a* **1300** *Cursor M.* 4177 (Cott.) Marchands of an vncuth thede. *c* **1400** *Melayne* 1008 The chefe of hethyn thede.

b. *pl.* (biblical.) The nations, the Gentiles.

c **975** *Rushw. Gosp.* Matt. x. 18 To kyningum & ʒeroefum ʒe bioþ ʒelædde..in cypnisse [h]eora & þeodum. *c* **1000** ÆLFRIC *Hom.* I. 96 Se þeoda lareow Paulus. *a* **1175** *Cott. Hom.* 241 Ur hlaford sanctes paulus þe is þeoden lareaw.

2. The district occupied by a people; a country.

c **888** K. ÆLFRED *Boeth.* xxxv. §7 An hearpere wæs on ðære ðiode ðæt Đracia hatte. *a* **1300** *Cursor M.* 5792 (Cott.), I sal þam bring..In-till a land, a wonsun thede. **13..** *K. Alis.* (Bodl. MS.) 7947 þou shalt haue Perce, & Mede, And Babiloyne, þis riche þede. *a* **1400–50** *Alexander* 1803 In thorps & in many thede þar ʒe þurʒe ride. *c* **1470** *Golagros & Gaw.* 174 All the wyis and welth he weildis in theid.

3. *Comb.*, as **thede-folk** (OE. **þéod-folc*), people of a country, natives. (The OE. combinations and derivatives were very numerous.)

c **725** *Charter of Nunna* in Birch *Cart. Sax.* I. 211 On ðeodweʒ norð ofer þone weʒ. *c* **1000** *Boeth. Metr.* xxix. 92 þæt hi þiowien swilcum þiodfruman. *c* **1205** LAY. 26494 þusende of þan þeod-folke.

thede, obs. form of THEAD.

theder, -ere, -ir(re, -ur, -yr, obs. ff. THITHER.

†**thee**, *sb. Obs. rare*⁻¹. [f. THEE *v.*¹] *evil thee*: Evil speed; bad luck. (Cf. THEEDOM b.)

1509 BARCLAY *Shyp of Folys* (1570) 25 Downe he commeth with an euill thee.

thee (ðiː, ðɪ), *pers. pron.* Forms: 1 (acc.) **þec** (*Northumb.* **ðeh, ðech**); 1–6 (dat. and acc.) **þe**, 3 (te), **þeo**, 3–4 **þi**, 4–5 **þee**, 4–7 **the**, 4– **thee** (7 *dial.* **they**). For mod. dialect forms see *Eng. Dial. Dict.* [(1) Acc. OE. *ðec, ðeh*, later *ðē, þē* = OFris. *thi*, OS. *thic, thî* (MDu. *di*, MLG. (*dik, dek*) *dî*, LG. *dî*), OHG. *dih* (MHG., Ger. *dich*), ON. *þik* (Norw. *deg, de*, MSw. *þik, tik, tig, thig*, MDa. *thek, theg, deg*, Sw., Da. *dig*), Goth. *þuk*:—OTeut. **þeke*, pre-Teut. **tege*: cf. L. *tē*, Gr. σέ, Doric τέ. (2) Dat. (later also acc.) OE. *ðē, þē* = OFris. *thi* (NFris. *di*, WFris. *dy*), OS. *thî* (MDu., MLG., LG. *dî*); (dative only) OHG. (MHG., Ger.) *dir*, ON. *þér* (Norw. *deg* (*der*), MSw. *þær, þir*, Sw., Da. *dig*), Goth. *þus*:—OTeut. **þez*, pre-Teut. **tes*. The original OE. acc. *ðec* still remained in Mercian in the 9th c. and in North Anglian (*þec, þeh, þech*) late in the 10th; in WSax. it ran together early with the dative *ðe, þe*, and thenceforth (as in LG. and Scand.) the two cases have had the same form, so that the direct and indirect object are only distinguishable by position or by context. On the original endings of the acc. and dat., cf. ME. The *e* was orig. short, but was lengthened under stress.]

1. The objective case of the pronoun THOU, representing the OE. accusative and dative.

As to restriction of use see note to THOU *pers. pron.* 1.

a. *Accusative*, as direct object of a verb.

c **825** *Lorica Prayer* in *O.E. Texts* 174 Đonne ʒehereð he ðec ðorh hiora ðingunge. *c* **888** K. ÆLFRED *Boeth.* xxvii. §2 Ic ascige ðe..hwi þu swa maniʒfeald yfel hæfde? *c* **950** *Lindisf. Gosp.* Mark v. 31 Đu ʒesiist ðæt ðreat ðringende ðec. *c* **1160** *Hatton Gosp.* ibid., þas meniʒeo..þrungen þe. *c* **1200** ORMIN 670 To beldenn & to frofrenn þe 3iff he þe seþ forrgloppnedd. *a* **1225** *Ancr. R.* 98 Hwo haueð ihurt te, mi deore? *c* **1375** *Cursor M.* 5064 (Fairf.), I saghe þe [*Cott.* yow] neuer be-for þis day. **1382** WYCLIF *Matt.* v. 41 Whoeuere constrayneth thee a thousand pacis, go thou with hym other tweyne. *c* **1440** *Jacob's Well* 258 þe feende schal pursewe þe, & sle þe in soule. **1535** COVERDALE *1 Sam.* viii. 7 They haue not refused the, but me. **1548–9** (Mar.) *Bk. Comm. Prayer, Communion*, We praise thee, we blesse thee, we worship thee, we glorifie thee. *a* **1660** *Contemp. Hist. Irel.* (Ir. Archæol. Soc.) II. 157 They [= thy] credulitie bringe they [= thee] within distance of his reache. **1784** COWPER *Task* v. 460 Thee I account still happy. **1842** TENNYSON *Locksley H.* 30 Dost thou love me, cousin?..I have loved thee long.

b. *Dative*, as indirect object = to thee; also in dependence on certain impersonal verbs.

c **825** *Vesp. Psalter* cxix. 3 Hwet bið sald ðe oððe hwet bið toseted ðe? *c* **1000** *Ags. Gosp.* John viii. 53 Hwæt þincð þe þæt þu sy? *c* **1200** ORMIN 210 Hiderr amm icc sennd to þe þiss blisse þe to kiþenn. *a* **1225** *Ancr. R* 12 Ich chulle scheawe þe soðlice hwat is God. *a* **1300** *Cursor M.* 4424 Ful iuel es yolden þe [*Gött.* ye] þi mede. *Ibid.* 20185, I sai it te [*v.r.* þe]. **1423** JAS. I *Kingis Q.* cxxix, Gif the ne list on lufe thy vertew set. *c* **1430** *Two Cookery-bks.* 6 As þe semyth best. **1584** R. W. *Three Ladies Lond.* in Hazl. *Dodsley* VI. 323 What avantageth it thee to win the world, and lose thy soul withal? **1610** SHAKS. *Temp.* I. ii. 248 I haue..Told thee no lyes, made thee no mistakings. **1743** FRANCIS tr. *Hor.*, *Odes* I. xxxviii. 1, I tell thee, boy, that I detest The grandeur of a Persian feast. **1808** SCOTT *Marmion* VI. xiv, And, Douglas, more I tell thee here..I tell thee, thou 'rt defied! **1864** (*dial.*) TENNYSON *N. Farmer, O. Style* 68 Git ma my äile I tell tha.

c. As object of a preposition.

In OE. *accus.* or *dative*.

c **950** *Lindisf. Gosp.* Luke i. 35 Gaast haliʒ ofer-cymeð on ðeh [*Rushw.* ðec]. *c* **1000** *Ags. Gosp.* John iii. 26 Se ðe mid þe [*Lind.* ðec] wæs. *a* **1200** *Vices & Virtues* 35 3if godd wuneð on ðe. *c* **1275** *Passion our Lord* 138 in *O.E. Misc.* 41 þeyh alle of-schomed beo Ne schal me neuer schomye louered for þeo. **13..** *Cursor M.* 27483 If þou man gas þin offrand to mak, And þi broþer haf gain þi [*v.r.* þe] sak. **1470–85** MALORY *Arthur* I. xxiii. 70 Ther maye no knyght ryde this wey but yf he Iuste wyth the. **1535** COVERDALE *Isa.* lx. 2 His glory shal be sene in the. **1592** SHAKS. *Rom. & Jul.* IV. v. 57 By cruell, cruell thee, quite ouerthrowne. **1656** in *Jrnl. Friend's Hist. Soc.* (1911) VIII. 20 To..lay before yᵉ Henry Cromwell: who art Commander in Cheife..the ground of my Sufferings. **1667** MILTON *P.L.* IV. 35 To thee I call, But with no friendly voice, and add thy name. **1733** POPE *Ess. Man* III. 31 Is it for thee the lark ascends and sings? **1820** SHELLEY *To Skylark* 1 Hail to thee, blithe Spirit! Bird thou never wert.

2. *Reflexive*: = thyself. **a.** *Accus.*, as direct object.

c **950** *Lindisf. Gosp.* Matt. iv. 6 ʒif sunu godes arð ðu send ðeh [*Rushw.* þec] ufa hidune. *c* **1000** *Ags. Gosp.* ibid., Asend þe þonne nyðer. *a* **1225** *Ancr. R.* 104 Holt te i þine chaumbre. *a* **1300** *Cursor M.* 529 If þow wil þe vm-think. **13..** *Ibid.* 26575 Sua þou mate noght wasch þi [*v.r.* þee] wite. *a* **1518** SKELTON *Magnyf.* 303 Go shake the, dogge. **1560** BIBLE (Genev.) *Matt.* xvi. 23 Get thee behinde me, Satan. **1594** SHAKS. *Rich. III*, I. iii. 143 High thee to Hell..Thou Cacodemon. **1678** OTWAY *Friendship in F.* 26 Get thee gone for an Arch-wagg. **1887** *S. Cheshire Gloss.* 69 Get thee dressed wheil I wesh me.

b. *Dative*, as indirect object; or as object of a preposition.

a **1000** *Cædmon's Gen.* 518 (Gr.) Nim þe þis ofæt on hand. *a* **1100** *Leg. Rood* 15 þu ʒetuʒe to þe ealle þa sawla. *c* **1300** *Harrow. Hell* (MS.L.) 103 Heouene ant erþe tac to þe. *c* **1470** HENRY *Wallace* I. 395 Thow sall haiff leiff to fysche, and tak the ma. **1599** SHAKS *Much Ado* II. i. 20 Thou wilt neuer get thee a husband, if thou be so shrewd of thy tongue. **1611** BIBLE *1 Kings* xx. 25 Number thee an armie like the armie that thou hast lost.

c. After some intr. verbs of motion and posture; esp. *sit*; see SIT *v.* 30.

1593 SHAKS. *3 Hen. VI*, III. iii. 16 Be thou still like thy selfe And sit thee by our side. **1599** —— *Much Ado* III. i. 1 Good Margaret runne thee to the parlour, There shalt thou finde my Cosin [etc.]. **1606** —— *Ant. & Cl.* IV. vii. 16 Come thee on. **1867** E. WAUGH *Tufts* 252 Sit tho down. **1892** WRIGHT *Gram. Windhill* 120 Kum forᵊd lad ᵊn sit ðe dān.

3. Used as *nominative*, instead of *thou*.

Often so used dialectally, and, in recent times, usually by Quakers, esp. with vb. in 3rd pers. sing.; but *thĕ* or *thă* unemphatic often represents both *thou* and *thee*. Now *rare*.

c **1375** *Sc. Leg. Saints* vi. (*Thomas*) 617 þe venys þat my god wrath wil be with me. *c* **1470** HENRY *Wallace* II. 93 Go hens, the Scot, the mekill dewill the speid. *a* **1590** *Marr. Wit & Wisd.* (1846) 12 Didest the nere se man before? **1596** SHAKS. *1 Hen. IV*, I. ii. 127 How agrees the Diuell and thee about thy Soule? **1605** —— *Lear* I. iv. 204 And yet I would not be thee, Nunckle. **1684** BUNYAN *Pilgr.* II. 83 What canst thee earn a day, quoth he? **1687** W. HITCHCOCK in *Jrnl. Friends' Hist. Soc.* IV. 74 If thee canst sell 250 acres of it & yᵉ house. **1852** MRS. STOWE *Uncle Tom's C.* xiii, 'What does thee want, father?' said Rachel. *Ibid.* xvii, 'Friend, thee isn't wanted here'. **1861** E. WAUGH *Birtle Carter's T.* 15 An' mind te tells no lies abeawt th' lad i' thy talk. **1926** *Amer. Speech* I. 638/1 Even in my boyhood in New England I heard very few Quakers who habitually said *thee*. **1950** B. RUSSELL *Let.* 6 Mar. in B. Strachey *Remarkable Relations* (1980) xxi. 312 What thee says about our marriage is very generous. **1964** *Friend* 10 Apr. 453/1 Perhaps thee has noticed the comment on this point in our *Friends Journal* on February 15. **1980** B. STRACHEY *Remarkable Relations* xxi. 314 Alys [Russell (1867–1951)] had been the last of the older ones; the last to say Thee and Thy.

4. As *sb.* **a.** The person or 'self' of the individual addressed. Cf. THOU *pron.* 2 a.

c **1600** SHAKS. *Sonn.* vi, That's for thy selfe to breed an other thee. **1831** CARLYLE *Sart. Res.* I. ix, A warm movable House, a Body round thy Body, wherein that strange Thee of thine sat snug. **1859** E. FITZGERALD *Rubáiyát* xxxiv, Then of the Thee in Me who works behind The Veil, I lifted up my hands to find A Lamp amid the Darkness.

b. The word itself as used in addressing a person; esp. in phr. ***thee and thou***. Also *attrib.* in ***thee and thou Quaker***.

1694 [see THOU 2b]. **1774** J. ADAMS *Diary* 7 Sept., This plain Friend and his plain though pretty wife, with her Thees and Thous, had provided us the most costly entertainment. **1847** LONGF. *Evang.* II. v. 13 Her ear was pleased with the Thee and Thou of the Quakers. **1894** HALL CAINE *Manxman* 405 When he spoke it was always with the thees and thous and in the high pitch of the preacher. **1896** *Peterson Mag.* VI. 265/1 Whose head-master was Benjamin Hallowell, a 'thee' and 'thou' Quaker of the strictest sect.

†**thee** (θiː), *v.*[1] *Obs.* Forms: 1 **þion**, 1–3 **þeon**, 3–4 **þen**, **þe**, 4– 5 **then**, 4–6 **the**, 5 **thene**, **theen**, 5–6 **þee**, (6 **thye**), 4– **thee**. *Pa. t.* 1 **þah**, **þaȝ**, **þæh**, 1–2 **þeah**, 1–3 **þeh**, 2–3 **þeaȝh**, 3 **þeȝ**, **þeu**, (5 **thee**); *pl.* 1 **þungon**; **þiȝon**; **þuȝon**. *Pa. pple.* 2–3 **þungen**; **þiȝen**; **þoȝen**, **þowen**, **þowuen**, 4 **thowen**. [OE. *þíon*, *þéon*, contr. from **þíhan* (:—**þíohan*, **péohan*) = OS. *thîhan*, *thêh*—*thigun*, *githigan* (Du. *gedigen*), OHG. (*gi*)*dîhan*, *dêh*—*digun*, *digan* (MHG. (*ge*)*dîhen*, G. *gedeihen*), Goth. *þeihan*—*þáih*—*þaihun*—*þaihans* to thrive :—OTeut. **þiŋχ-*, earlier **þeŋχ-* (**þaŋχ-*, **þuŋg-*) of the 3rd ablaut series:—Indo-Eur. root *tenk*. With the elimination of the nasal before χ the verb came in prim. Germ. to be assimilated to the 1st ablaut series (*ī*—*ai*—*i*—*i*); but traces of the primitive conjugation survive in the OS. pa. pple. *githungan*, and the OE. forms *þungon*, *-en*. The OE. contracted form *þéon* began to follow the inflexional type of *téon*:—**teuhan* (TEE *v.*[1]), whence *þéah*, *þuȝon*, *þoȝen*.]

1. *intr.* To grow; to thrive, prosper (*arch.* in 16th c. use).

Beowulf 8 He..weox under wolcnum, weorð-myndum þah. *c* **888** K. ÆLFRED *Boeth.* xix, þeah hwa wexe..and þeo on eallum welum. *c* **1000** ÆLFRIC *Hom.* II. 104 His wæstmas ȝenihtsumlice þuȝon. *c* **1000** *Ags. Gosp.* Luke ii. 52 Se hælend þeah on wisdome and on ylde. *a* **1050** *Liber Scintill.* lxxxi. 221 Sume soþlice on æȝþrum þeoþ. *c* **1200** *Trin. Coll. Hom.* 161 And hit wacxs and wel þeaȝh. *Ibid.* 177 Here tuder swiðe wexeð and wel þieð. *c* **1250** *Gen. & Ex.* 2012 Vnder ioseph his welðe ðeȝ. *c* **1275** LAY. 24272 þe borh suþþe ne þeh. **1297** R. GLOUC. (Rolls) 240 þe child wax & wel iþeȝ [*v.rr.* thee, ythei]. *Ibid.* 7086 þis chyld wax so wel & þeu. *c* **1300** *Beket* 149 He fond his sone..þeoinge [*pr.* Theonige] fair and manliche. *a* **1310** in Wright *Lyric P.* 23 ȝef he beth thryven ant thowen in theode. **13..** *Pol. Rel. & L. Poems* 238 Ho þat me louit ssal þe no more. *c* **1400** *Gamelyn* 234 Come þou ones in my hond þou shalt neuer the. **1426** AUDELAY *Poems* 4 Thai schal have grace to thryve and thene. *c* **1440** *Promp. Parv.* 490/1 Theen, or thryvyn, *vigeo*. **1509** BARCLAY *Shyp of Folys* (1874) II. 94 [He] is seldome sen to thye. *a* **1518** SKELTON *Magnyf.* 862 Abusyon Forsothe I hyght;..That vseth me,—He can not thee. **1573** TUSSER *Husb.* (1878) 19 Giue ouer to sudgerne, that thinkest to thee.

b. In imprecations and asseverations.

a **1300** *Cursor M.* 5150 'Sais þou soth?' 'yaa, sa mot i the'. **13..** *Sir Beues* 2753 A swor, alse he moste þen, He nolde him neiþer hire ne sen. ? *a* **1366** CHAUCER *Rom. Rose* 1067 Wel yvel mote they thryve and thee, And yvel achyved mote they be. **1377** LANGL. *P. Pl.* B. v. 228 Ac I swere now, so the ik, þat synne wil I lete. *c* **1386** CHAUCER *Can. Yeom. Prol. & T.* 376 By cause our firne was nat maad of Beech, That is the cause, and oother noon, so theech. *c* **1425** *Seven Sag.* 1548 (P.) Quod the kyng, 'So mot I the, Astow wylt hyt schal bee. *c* **1450** *Mankind* 297 in *Macro Plays* 12 Gode let hym neuer thene! [*rime* sene]. **1586** FERNE *Blaz. Gentrie* 22 Full ill mought they both thee. **1598** E. GILPIN *Skial.* (1878) 19 (*Lydia*) So mote I thee thou art not faire, A plaine brownetta when thou art at best. ? *a* **1600** *Old Robin of Portingale* xiv. in Child *Ballads* III. (1885) 241/1 If it be not true,..God let me neuer thye. **17..** in Ritson *Songs* (1794) II. 132 He that spares, ne'er mote he thee. *a* **1800** in *Edinb. Mag.* June (1819) 527/1 But wearie fa' the fairy wicht..May he never thee.

2. *trans.* To cause to prosper; to prosper. *Obs.*

c **1250** *Prayer* in *Rel. Ant.* I. 22 þe lavird þieh þe in hevirilk place.

Hence †**thowen**, **þoȝen**, **þowun** *ppl. a.*, thriven; grown up, adult.

c **1200** *Trin. Coll. Hom.* 39 Mid-niht ðe bilimpeð to frumberdligges, hanecrau þe bilimpeð þowuene men. *Ibid.* 41 Ðese herdes..wakieð biforen euen, þanne þe childre wuel þewuen..he þo ful þoȝene turneð to godes bihouþe. *Ibid.* 127 Alse wat se he was þoȝen on wintre and on wastme.

thee (ðiː), *v.*[2] [f. THEE *pron.*] To use the pronoun 'thee' to a person: see THOU *v.* Also ***to thee and thou*** (cf. F. *tutoyer*). **a.** *trans.* **b.** *intr.* (or *absol.*). Hence '**theeing** *vbl. sb.*

a. **1662** TATHAM *Aqua Tri.* 6 Though I Thee Thee, and Thou Thee, I am no Quaker. *a* **1690** G. FOX *Jrnl.* (1827) I. 103, I was required to Thee and Thou all men and women, without any respect to rich or poor, great or small. *a* **1739** JARVIS *Quix.* I. IV. li, With the utmost arrogance he would thee and thou his equals and acquaintance. **1836** T. HOOK *G. Gurney* v, There I saw..two quaker children playing about the place, thee'ing and thou'ing each other, with perfect French familiarity. **1884** A. DOHERTY *N. Barlow* 28 Familiarly he 'thee'd' and 'thou'd' the men, And cheekily they 'thee'd' and 'thou'd' again.

b. **1679** [see THOU *v.* b]. **1696** C. LESLIE *Snake in Grass* p. xv, This was the Bottom upon which the Quakers first set up, to run down all worldly Honour..; to Thee and Thou; to call no Man Master, or Lord, and not to take off their Hats, or Bow to any. **1760** J. RUTTY *Spir. Diary* (ed. 2) 148 At meeting..was seen my insincerity in Theeing, inconsistent with my writing. **1894** DU MAURIER *Trilby* I. (1901) 19/2 There were ladies too *en cheveux*..some of whom thee'd and thou'd with familiar and friendly affection.

thee, obs. and dial. form of THIGH.

†'**theedom**, **thedom**. *Obs.* Also 4 **þeodam**, 5 **thedam**, **-dame**, **þeedom**. [f. stem of THEE *v.*[1] + -DOM.] Thriving; prosperity.

1362 LANGL. *P. Pl.* A. x. 105 þruft or þeodam with hem selden is I-seye. **1393** *Ibid.* C. VIII. 53 And ȝede a-bowte in my ȝouthe and ȝaf me to no þedom. *c* **1430** *How the Good Wife*, etc. 209 (*Babees Bk.* 47) Now þrift and þeedom mote þou haue. **1522** *World & Child* in Hazl. *Dodsley* I. 261 My thedom is near past.

b. ***evil theedom***, ill success, bad luck: used as a maledictory phrase.

c **1386** CHAUCER *Shipman's T.* 405 What! yuel thedam [*v.r.* thedom] on his Monkes snowte. *c* **1450** *Cov. Myst.* xiv. (Shaks. Soc.) 139 Evyl Thedom com to thi snowte!

theef(e, obs. forms of THIEF.

theek, **theik** (θiːk), *v.* *Sc.* and *north. dial.* Forms: 4–7 **theke**, 5 **thicke**, 6 *Sc.* **thik**, **thyk**, 6–9 *Sc.* **theik**, **thick**, 7–9 **theak(e**, **thake**, 8–9 *Sc.* **theck**, **theek**. [A collateral form of THATCH *v.* in use before 1400, of somewhat uncertain history. Perhaps from OE. *þęccan*, the forms of the imperative *þece* and the 2nd and 3rd pers. sing. present *þecest*, *þeceð* being extended to the verb as a whole: cf. *streek*, Sc. and north. form of STRETCH, OE. *stręccan*.]

†**1.** *trans.* To roof (a building) *with* stone, slate, tiles, shingles, lead, or the like. *Obs.*

1387 *Charters &c. of Edinb.* (1871) 35 (St. Giles) The forsayde v chapellys sal be thekyt abovyn with stane. *c* **1400** MAUNDEV. (Roxb.) x. 38 A full faire kirk..thekid wele with leed. **1535** STEWART *Cron. Scot.* (Rolls) II. 568 Rycht clene thickit was than all this tour, Weill gilt with gold. *Ibid.* III. 190 Sanct Androis kirk..That thekit wes with coper in tha dais. **1559** *Burgh Rec. Edinb.* (1875) III. 57 To thik the southe syde of the towlbuyth with new sklait. **1572** *Satir. Poems Reform.* xxxiii. 192, I se ȝour tempills cassin downe and reuin: The maist part are bot theikit with the heuin. **1628** *Extracts Burgh Rec. Glasgow* (1876) I. 365 [To] theik the samyn [ruiff] with leid. **1710** SIBBALD *Hist. Fife* II. v. §2. 78 They (as the Proverb has it) tirr'd the Kirk, to theek the Quire. **1777** J. ROBERTSON in McKay *Kilmarnock* (1880) 177 Water is gude for mony a purpose, although ye're a' aware we canna theek Kirks wi't.

b. *spec.* To cover the roof of (a house) *with* thatch of straw or the like; also, to protect the top of (a corn or hay rick) with straw laid so as to carry off the rain.

1399 *Mem. Ripon* (Surtees) III. 130 In v^xx travis de stramine ordii emp. 5s.,..in salario j hominis tegentis,..thekand prædictam domum per v dies. *c* **1440** *Pallad. on Husb.* I. 474 Thy berne also..to thicke hit, thou ne lette. *c* **1450** *Life St. Cuthbert* (Surtees) 7649 And thekyd it with hay and thak. **1513** DOUGLAS *Æneis* VIII. xi. 30 Quhais rufis laitly full rouch thykyt war Wyth stra or gloy by Romulus the wycht. **1637–50** Row *Hist. Kirk* (Wodrow Soc.) 417 The fabrick of the kirk wes in so evill a condition, being theiked with heather. **1672** T. WHITTINGHAM *Diary* 30 Aug. in Best *Farm. Bks.* (Surtees) 138 *note*, Wheatley of Saiston ye theaker is to theake Leonords' Barn. **1721** RAMSAY *Bessy Bell & Mary Gray* i, They bigg'd a bower..And theck'd it o'er with rashes. **1863** MRS. TOOGOOD *Yorks. Dial.*, I want you to theak my rick. **1895** CROCKETT *Men of Moss-Hags* 283 The roof was daintily theeked with green rushes and withes.

2. *transf.* To cover in general (but often with allusion to thatching a roof).

1667 in Campbell *Balmerino* (1899) 414 To men that thickit a holl in the kirk with divite. **1719** RAMSAY *To Arbuckle* 117, I theck the out, and line the inside Of mony a douce and witty pash. *a* **1800** *Twa Corbies* iv. in Scott *Minstr. Scot. Bord.*, Wi' ae lock o' his gowden hair, We'll theek our nest when it grows bare. *a* **1810** TANNAHILL *Rab Roryson's Bonnet* Poems (1846) 116 This bonnet that theekit his wonderful head. **1896** CROCKETT *Cleg Kelly* xlii. 283 A pump theekit frae the frost wi' strae rapes.

3. *absol.* or *intr.* (from 1 or 2).

a **1518** SKELTON *Magnyf.* 1027 For it is I that other whyle Plucke down lede and theke with tyle. **1876** *Whitby Gloss.* s.v., 'You mun theeak weel, this caud weather', put on extra clothing.

Hence '**theeked**, **-it** *ppl. a.*, thatched; '**theeking** *vbl. sb.*, the action (*concr.* the material or product) of thatching; *ppl. a.*, that thatches or covers.

1792 BURNS *Bessie & her Spinnin Wheel* ii, On ilka hand the burnies trot, And meet below my *theekit cot. *a* **1801** R. GALL *Poems* (1819) 28 She reached the theeked byre. **1393** *Regist. de Aberbrothoc* (Bann.) II. 43 For the quhilkis *thekyn and gutteryn the abbot..sal pay till hym xxxv marcis. **1579** *Burgh Rec. Edinb.* (1882) IV. 104 Wynd tycht, watter tycht, in thyking, slating,..and vther necessaris. **1617** *Mem. St. Giles', Durham* (Surtees) 47 To Nycholas Sparke for thekin 4 days, viij a day. *a* **1835** HOGG *Tales, Sheph. Cal.* xvii, Bread for the belly and theeking for the back. **1846** BROCKETT *N.C. Words* (ed. 3) s.v. *Theaker*, A 'theaking snow' quietly but continuously falling, so as to cover thickly, as a thatch does, a house.

theeker ('θiːkə(r)). *Sc.* and *n. dial.* [f. THEEK *v.* + -ER[1].] A thatcher; in early use, a roofer of houses.

14.. *Voc.* in Wr.-Wülcker 650/27 *Hic architector*, thekare. **1483** *Cath. Angl.* 382/2 A Theker, *architector, tector* (A.). **1554–5** *Burgh Rec. Edinb.* (1871) II. 360 Item, to ane thekar to theik the thre choippis,..xij^s. **1658** *N. Riding Rec.* VI. 4 To a Theaker by the day... With meate 6^d. Without meate 12^d. **1887** J. SERVICE *Dr. Duguid* I. xx. 132 Robin Rigging the theeker. **1904** in *Eng. Dial. Dict.* (from Caithness to N. Lincolnsh.).

theelin ('θiːlɪn). *Biochem.* [f. Gr. θῆλυς female + -IN[1].] = ŒSTRONE.

1930 C. D. VELER et al. in *Jrnl. Biol. Chem.* LXXXVII. 357 The isolation of the crystalline hormone seems to justify the selection of a new name... Accordingly, we suggest the term 'theelin'. **1935** [see OESTRIN]. **1936** *Jrnl. Amer. Med. Assoc.* 10 Oct. 1222/2 The term theelin has not been widely accepted. *Ibid.* 1223/1 The Council [on Pharmacy and Chemistry of the American Medical Association]..decided (1) to adopt the system of nomenclature based on the root *estr-*; (2) to retain *theelin, theelol*..as synonyms for..*estrone, estriol*. **1947** *Sci. News* IV. 137 Among the substances administered to plants..are: the juice of leaves subjected to the 'right' length of day; yeast extract;..theelin.

So '**theelol** [-OL] = ŒSTRIOL.

1931 DOISY & THAYER in *Jrnl. Biol. Chem.* XCI. 642 We propose now, in view of the facts that the new substance is a trihydroxy compound and that it shows physiological and possibly chemical similarities to theelin, to name it theelol. **1936** [see above]. **1977** *Martindale's Extra Pharmacopoeia* (ed. 27) 1419/1 Oestriol. Estriol; theelol.

theeself (**þe** self, etc.): see THYSELF.

theetsee, var. THITSI, black-varnish tree.

theeward, in phr. ***to theeward***: see -WARD 6c.

†**thef.** *Obs. rare.* In 3 **ðef.** [a. ON. *þefr* smell, mod.Icel. *þefur*, Fær. *tev*, Norw. dial. *tev*, Sw. dial. *täv*, Da. *tøv*. Cf. THEVE *v.*] A smell.

c **1250** *Gen. & Ex.* 3340 To dust he it [the manna] grunden and maden bread, ðat huni and olies ðef he bead.

theft (θɛft). Forms: α. 1 **þéofð**, **þíefð**, **þýfð**; 2–4 **þeofþe**, **þefþe**, 3–5 **þufþe(ü)**, 4 (*Ayenb.*) **þiefþe**, **þyefþe**, 5 **thifthe**. β. 1 **þýft**, **þéoft**, 4–5 **þift**, **þeft**, 4–7 **thift**, 5 **thyft**, 6 **theaft**, **thieft**, 4– **theft**; 3–5 **þefte**, 4–6 **thefte**, (4 **þifte**, **þyfte**, 5 **theefte**, 6 **thifte**). [OE. WSax. *þíefð*, *þýfð*, later *þýft*, non-WSax. *þéofð*, later *þéoft*, = OFris. *thiufthe*, *thiufte* (obs. Du. *diefte*), ON. *þýfð*, later *þýft*, Goth. **þiuƀiþa*:—OTeut. **þeuƀiþā*, f. **þeuƀo*^z, THIEF + suffix *-iþa* = L. *-itāt-em*: see -TH[1] b, -T[3] b. OE. showed two main dial. types: WSax. *þíefþ*, later *þýfþ* with umlaut; non-WS. *þéofþ*. In both, final *þ* after *f* became *t* by dissimilation; *þeoft* became *þeft*, *theft*. In ME. the various forms often had final *-e* from the oblique cases; north. dial. and Sc. had *þift*, *þyft*, *thift* from ON. *þýfð*, *þýft*.]

1. The action of a thief; the felonious taking away of the personal goods of another; larceny; also, with *a* and *pl.*, an instance of this.

α. **688–95** *Laws of Ine* c. 28 Be þeofes onfenge æt ðiefðe [*MSS. B., H.* ðyfðe]. *Ibid.* c. 73 ȝif hit bið niht eald þiefð, ȝebeten þa þone gylt þe hine ȝefengon. **695–6** *Laws of Wihtræd* c. 25 ȝif man leud ofslea an þeofðe, licge buton wyrgelde. *c* **1000** *Sax. Leechd.* III. 186 þyfð ȝestrangað. *c* **1175** *Lamb. Hom.* 13 Ne do þu þeofðe. *a* **1225** *Ancr. R.* 202 þe Vox of ȝiscunge haueð þeos hweolpes: Tricherie & Gile, þeorðe, Reflac. *c* **1290** *Beket* 445 in *S. Eng. Leg.* I. 119 ȝif a clerk hath ane Man a-slawe, oþur strong þeffþe i-do. **1297** R. GLOUC. (Rolls) 10361 þe king..let prisouns vorþ bringe, þat uor þufþe were inome, & uor oþer þinge. **1340** *Ayenb.* 37 þe oþer boȝ of auarice ys þyefþe. **1393** LANGL. *P. Pl.* C. III. 92 In bargeyns and in brocages with þe borghe of þufþe [*v.rr.* þefþe, þefte]. *a* **1450** *Knt. de la Tour* (1906) 60 The theef dothe..delite hem in thifthe tille thei be taken and putte to dethe.

β. *c* **1250** *O. Kentish Serm.* in *O.E. Misc.* 31 þo grete sennen þet biedh diadliche Ase so is..þefte. *a* **1300** *Cursor M.* 15973 Iudas..Of his thift and his felunni, His moder al he tald. **1382** WYCLIF *Matt.* xv. 19 Of the herte gon out yuel thouȝtis, mansleayngis, auoutries, fornicaciouns, theftis. **1387** TREVISA *Higden* (Rolls) V. 383 Mauricius..fondede to forbede his knyȝtes þifte [*v.rr.* þefþe, þeofþe]. *c* **1450** *Brut* 443 For treason & for þift þat thei had done to þe Kynge & to his liege peple. **1489** CAXTON *Faytes of A.* IV. ix. 251 To haue committed a smal theefte. **1552** HULOET, Theaft in stealynge cattell, *abigeatus*. **1570** LEVINS *Manip.* 52/44 Theft, *furtum*. *Ibid.* 118/5 Thift, *furtum*. **1577** HOLINSHED *Chron., Hist. Scot.* I. 440/1 Accused of theft, and of receiuing and mainteining of theeues. **1605** SHAKS. *Macb.* II. iii. 151. **1629** SIR W. MURE *True Crucifixe* 1133 To hide the thift. **1771** *Junius Lett.* lxv. (1820) 328 The thief was taken in the theft. **1909** *Q. Rev.* July 176 His borrowings were not thefts but prolific suggestions.

†**b.** ***by theft***, stealthily, furtively, by secret craft. *Obs. rare*[−1].

c **1470** HENRY *Wallace* XI. 592 Thai be thyft hecht to put Wallace doun.

2. *concr.* That which is or has been stolen; the proceeds of thieving. Now *rare*.

962–3 *Laws of Edgar* IV. c. 2 §2 To ðy þæt..þeof nyte, hwær he þyfþe [*MS. C.* þeofte] befæste. *c* **1175** *Lamb. Hom.* 57 Ne þu naȝest for to stele, Ne nan þefþe for to heole. *a* **1300** *Cursor M.* 6754 þat he mai yeild again his thift, He sal be saald. **1340** *Ayenb.* 38 þe pyeues be uelaȝrede byeþ þo þet parteþ of þe þyefþe. **1413** *Pilgr. Sowle* (Caxton 1483) III. v. 53 The theft which they haue stolen ye haue you self receyued. **1530** TINDALE *Exod.* xxii. 4 Yf the thefte [WYCLIF, that that he hath stoln] be founde in his hande alyue..he shall restore double. **1665** G. HAVERS *P. della Valle's Trav. E.I.* 145 We found the theft in his breeches ty'd to his naked flesh. **1864** KINGSLEY *Rom. & Teut.* x. 284 If a free man be caught thieving,..he replaces the theft, and pays 80 solidi, or dies.

3. *attrib.* and *Comb.*, as ***theft-guilty*** adj.

1613–16 W. BROWNE *Brit. Past.* II. i, What store of houres theft-guilty night had spent. **1907** *Westm. Gaz.* 19 Oct. 9/2 The Police Commissioner..gave it as his opinion that the theft theory was the most probable.

theft-boot, -bote. *Obs.* exc. *Hist.* Also 3, 6 thef-, 6 theefe-, 6–7 theif(e-. [orig. *thef-bote*, f. *thef*, THIEF + *bote*, BOOT *sb.*[1] Afterwards altered (app. first by Scottish writers) to *theftbote*: cf. THEFTDOM, THEFTLY.

The early form suggests an OE. **þéof-bót*, but this has not been found; the nearest equivalent in the Ags. Laws being *þéof-gyld* in Laws of Æthelred I. c. 1 §2, III. c. 4, and of Cnut II. c. 30 §1.]

The taking of some payment from a thief to secure him from legal prosecution; either the receiving back by the owner of the stolen goods or of some compensation, or the taking of a bribe by a person who ought to have brought the thief to justice.

Nichols (1865) in *Britton*, in note to quot. 1292, suggests that the word 'originally signified the legal *bote* or composition for theft', and was then 'applied to the illegal compounding of theft, or taking money to maintain or connive at such offenders'. But all our quotations refer to illegal payment, a form of compounding a felony.

α. **1284** *Stat. Wall.* an. 12 Edw. I, c. 4 De Thefbote, hoc est de emenda furti capta sine consideracione Curiæ Domini Regis. **1292** BRITTON I. xxi. §11 Et puis soit enquis de ceux qi ount pris thefbote. **1369** *Liber Assisarum* §5 (1606) 258b, Et les Iustices disoient q' vn home q' reprist son chattel emblee dun laron ne fuit pas thefbote, eins thefbote fuit proprement ou vn home prist ses chattels dun laron de luy fauourer & mainteiner, et nemy auterment. **1579** *Expos. Termes Law* 177b/2 *Thefbote*, is when a man taketh any goodes of a theefe to fauour and mainteine him. And not when a man taketh his owne goodes that were stollen from him &c.

β. *a* **1450** *Sc. Acts Robt. I*, c. 9 (1844) I. 109/2 (*heading*) Of þe takyn of thyftbute [*orig.* rechatum de latrone]. **1515** *Sc. Acts Jas. V* (1814) II. 282/2 Gif this complenar..wald concord with the said theif and tak thiftbute and put him fra the Law, in that caice he sall vnderly the Law. **1597** [see next]. **1619** DALTON *Country Just.* cviii. (1630) 288 Some other seeme to take this for theeftboot and so to be punishable..onely by ransome and imprisonment. **1678** SIR G. MACKENZIE *Crim. Laws Scot.* I. xx. §i. (1699) 106 Theft-boot is committed by securing a Thief against the punishment due by Law. **1745** *Univ. Spect.* 10 Aug., Yorkshire Tom was committed to Clerkenwell-Bridewell.. for Theft-boot, accepting of 17 Guineas and a half, not to prosecute John Ditcher, a notorious Pick-pocket. **1769** BLACKSTONE *Comm.* IV. x. 133 The offence of theftbote, which is where the party robbed not only knows the felon, but also takes his goods again, or other amends, upon agreement not to prosecute. **1814** SCOTT *Wav.* xv, The Bailie opined that this transaction would amount to theft-boot, or composition of felony. **1885** *Law Times* LXXX. 115/2 The offence of compounding a felony was really the old crime of theft-bote.

'theftdom. *Sc.* [Altered from **thefdom*, THIEFDOM.] The action or practice of stealing; theft; thievery.

1566 *Sc. Acts Jas. I*, c. 154 That nouther Lord of Regalitie, Schiref, Barrone, na vthers sell ony theif, or fyne with him of thiftdome done [*Record ed.* (1814) of thift done]. **1597** SKENE *De Verb. Sign.* s.v. *Bote*, Thieft-bote..quhen ony sellis onie thiefe, or finis with him for thieft-dome done, or to be done. **1854** MRS. OLIPHANT *Magd. Hepburn* I. 221 Gentle or simple maunna tell me that God's will is for villany and theftdom.

†**'theftfully,** *adv. Obs. rare.* In 5 thift-. [f. THEFT + -FUL + -LY[2].] By stealth: = THEFTLY.

c **1400** *Sc. Trojan War* II. 1591 Vlixes..frome Troy is passit thiftfully With all þaim of his company.

thefthorn, variant of THEVE-THORN *Obs.*

'theftless, *a. rare.* [f. THEFT + -LESS.] **a.** That is not a theft. **b.** Not liable to be stolen.

1656 S. H. *Gold. Law* 68 How punisht he poor Achan for a theftless theft to see to? **1803** LEYDEN *Scenes Infancy* iv. 362 Teviot's sons..devoid of fear Bind to the rush by night the theftless steer.

†**'theftly,** *adv. Sc.* and *north. dial. Obs.* [Altered from ME. *þefly*, THIEFLY.] By stealth, furtively.

c **1400** *Sc. Trojan War* II. 271 He gyffande thiftely ws till The palladinar at our will. *Ibid.* 623 Bycause þe palladinar was Out of þe temple tone thyftly. *a* **1485** *Promp. Parv.* (MS. S), Stelyngly (thefely), *furtive, latrocinaliter*. **1498** *Reg. Privy Seal Scot.* I. 23/1, ix catell thiftly tane fra Thomas Sowtar. **1515** *Nottingham Rec.* III. 343 Reyseyvng off oder menys goodes theyftely.

theftuous ('θɛftjuːəs), *a.* Originally *Sc.* Forms: α. 5 thiftwis, 5–6 thiftuis, 6 thiftewus. β. 6–7 thifteous, (7 thiefteous, 6 thiftius). γ. 6 thiftuus, 6–7 -uous, 7 theftous, 6– theftuous. [ME. *thiftwis*, f. THEFT + WISE *sb.*: cf. RIGHTEOUS from *rihtwis*.]

1. Of the nature of theft, thievish.

c **1400** [implied in THEFTUOUSLY]. **1491** *Reg. Privy Seal Scot.* I. 2 For the thiftwis owtputtin and awaytakin of the gudis. **1502** *Ibid.* 117/1 The thiftewus distruction of Johne Mans gudis. **1569** *Reg. Privy Council Scot.* II. 22 In thiftuous maner. **1593** *Sc. Acts Jas. VI* (1814) IV. 43/2 Pairttakaris in thair thifteous ard wicked deidis. **1678** SIR G. MACKENZIE *Crim. Laws Scot.* I. xx. §3 (1699) 108 Whosoever..assists them in their theftous Stealings. **1837** B. H. HODGSON in *Jrnl. Asiat. Soc. Bengal* VI. 367 It is.. remarkable..for its theftuous propensities. **1880** MUIRHEAD *Gaius* Digest 506 Theftuous removal of property.

b. *transf.* Furtive, secret, sneaking.

1881 MASSON *De Quincey* xi. 138 A theftuous hope to amuse an hour for you after dinner.

2. Of the nature of a thief; given to theft.

1632 LITHGOW *Trav.* (1906) 363 The Hungarians have ever beene thiftuous, treacherous and false. **1859** M. NAPIER *Visct. Dundee* I. p. x, That theftuous animal a cheap book-seller's hack. **1883** *Century Mag.* XXVII. 183 Pettily theftuous, like the English gypsies. **1885** *St. James' Gaz.* 28 Mar. 6/1 No man ever saw the most theftuous sparrow ashamed of himself.

b. *fig.* Said of an animal or vegetable parasite.

1883 H. DRUMMOND *Nat. Law in Spir. W.* (ed. 2) 342 By means of its twining and theftuous roots it [*Sacculina*] imbibes automatically its nourishment ready-prepared from the body of the crab. **1883** R. TURNER in *Gd. Words* July 470/2 Some [plants]..living by theftuous practices alone.

theftuously ('θɛftjuːəslı), *adv.* Chiefly *Sc.* [f. prec. + -LY[2].] In a theftuous manner; by or as by theft; stealthily, secretly.

c **1400** *Sc. Trojan War* II. 1637 Vlixes stall thiftuisly Away, as grauntand him gilty. **1567–8** *Reg. Privy Council Scot.* I. 609 The leid upoun the Cathedrall Kirkis..is thiftuouslie stowin and takin away. **1653** URQUHART *Rabelais* II. xiv, One little villainous Turkie..rogue came thiefteously to snatch away some of my lardons. **1880** MUIRHEAD *Ulpian* vii. §2 If a husband have theftuously abstracted anything of his wife's in prospect of divorce. **1882** *Chamb. Jrnl.* XIX. 73 On a late occasion, the tomb of a noble family was theftuously rifled of its contents.

thefysch, obs. f. THIEVISH.

thegh, obs. f. THOUGH, THIGH.

thegither, Sc. f. TOGETHER.

thegn (θeın). *Hist.* A form used by some recent historians to represent the OE. *þegn* (*þeȝen, þén*), THANE[1], in its sense of tenant by military service, and as a term of rank below the *ealdorman* or *eorl* and above the *ceorl*, corresponding in its various grades to the post-conquest *baron* and *knight*.

The purpose of this spelling is to distinguish the Anglo-Saxon from the Scottish use of THANE[1] (sense 4), made familiar by Shakespeare.

1848 LYTTON *Harold* I. i, A Thegn forfeited his rank if he lost his lands. **1867** FREEMAN *Norm. Conq.* I. vi. 428 *note*, The signatures are no doubt those of local Thegns. **1874** STUBBS *Const. Hist.* I. vi 155 Closely connected with the *gesith* is the *thegn*... The thegn seems to be primarily the warrior *gesith*; in this idea Alfred uses the word as translating the *miles* of Bede. But he also appears as a landowner. *Ibid.* 156 The name of thegn covers the whole class which after the Conquest appears under the name of knights, with the same qualification in land and nearly the same obligations. **1890** GROSS *Gild Merch.* I. 185 The merchant who made three voyages across the ocean at his own cost became a thegn.

Hence **'thegn-born** *a.*, of noble or gentle birth. **'thegndom,** the position or rank of thegn. **'thegnhood,** the condition or position of a thegn; the order of thegns, thegns collectively. **'thegn-land,** land held by a thegn. **'thegnly,** *a.* and *adv.* [OE. *þeȝnlíc, -líce*], (*a*) *adj.* of or pertaining to, or becoming a thegn; (*b*) *adv.* in a manner becoming a thegn. **'thegn-right,** the legal rights and privileges of a thegn. **'thegn-ship** [OE. *þeȝnscipe*], the office, function, or position of a thegn (in various senses). **'thegn-wer** [OE. *þeȝnwer*], the wer-gild of a thegn. **'thegn-worthy** *a.*: see quot.

? *c* **935** *Dunsæte* c. 5 in Liebermann *Gesetze* (1903) 376 Sy he *ðeȝenboren, sy he ceorlboren. **1874** STUBBS *Const. Hist.* I. vi. 156 The thegn-born are contrasted with the ceorl-born. **1897** RAMPINI *Hist. Moray & Nairn* ii. 46 The principle of comradeship..underlay English *thegndom. **1867** FREEMAN *Norm. Conq.* I. iii. 95 The growth of the *Thegnhood was, on the whole, depressing to the Ceorls. **1881** S. R. GARDINER *Introd. Stud. Eng. Hist.* ii. 34 The thegnhood pushed its roots down, as it were, amongst the free classes. *a* **1100** *Charter of Will. II* in *Tabularis Ramesiensi* clxxviii (Du Cange), Si terra de Isham..si vero *Teinlanda tunc fuisse inveniatur. **1628** COKE *On Litt.* 86 In the book of Domesday land holden by knight's service was called *Tainland*. **1876** DIGBY *Real Prop.* i. §2 (ed. 2) 13 Tain- or thegn-land. This seems to mean not a particular species of tenure, but land which was as a fact held or owned by a king's thegn. *c* **1000** ÆLFRIC *Hom.* I. 586 Andreas..is ȝereht *ðeȝenlic. *a* **1038** *Charter of Eanwene* in Kemble *Cod. Dipl.* IV. 55 Heo..to ðam þeȝnon cwæð: Doð þeȝnlice and wel! Abeodað mine ærende to ðam ȝemote. **1876** FREEMAN *Norm. Conq.* V. xxiv. 450 The words of Eanwene, when she bade the Scirgemót of Herefordshire to 'do thegnly and well'. **1897** MAITLAND *Domesday & Beyond* 53 The men..are usually men of thegnly rank. *Ibid.* 165 Each..will be entitled to a thegnly wergild and swear a thegnly oath. *c* **1000** *Oaths* in Liebermann (1903) 464 Se mæssepreost.. bið *þeȝenrihtes wyrþe. **1872** E. W. ROBERTSON *Hist. Ess.* 118 None could pretend to the privileges of full thegn-right without the possession of at least a township. **959–62** *Laws of Edgar* III. c. 2 Se dema, se ðe oðrum on woh ȝedeme ..polize a his *þeȝnscipes. *c* **1000** ÆLFRIC *Saints' Lives* (1890) II. 82 Beoð nu ȝehyrte..and healdað mid ðeȝen-scipe ða halȝan Godes æ. **1897** MAITLAND *Domesday & Beyond* 163 We begin by thinking of thegnship as a relation between two men... Then the thegnship becomes more than a relationship, it becomes a status. **1008** *Laws of Ethelred* V. c. 9 þæt he sy *þeȝenweres & þeȝenrihtes wyrðe. **1874** STUBBS *Const. Hist.* I. vi. 155 The ceorl who has acquired five hides of land,..with other judicial rights, becomes *thegn-worthy; his oath and protection and wergild are those of a thegn.

thegosis (θı'gəʊsıs). *Zool.* [f. Gr. θηγός sharp + -OSIS.] Tooth-grinding in animals as a means of sharpening the teeth.

1971 EVERY & KÜHNE in D. M. & K. A. Kermack *Early Mammals* 25 While shear edges are used in mastication, they lose their feature which they develop during a powerful and short action of sharpening. This action we call active wear and thegosis. **1974** *Nature* 30 Aug. 730/1 In mammals thegosis wear is accompanied by a second type of tooth wear, dental abrasion, which occurs at food/tooth interfaces during mastication.

thei, þei, obs. f. THEY, THOUGH.

theic ('θiːık). [f. mod.L. *the-a* TEA + -IC 3: cf. THEISM[2].] One addicted to immoderate tea-drinking, or who suffers from such excess; a tea-drunkard.

1886 *Medical News* (U.S.) XLIX. 305 It is possible to be a 'theic' by profession or a 'theic' by passion. **1899** in *Syd. Soc. Lex.*

theid, Sc. var. THEDE *Obs.*

theie, theiȝe, obs. ff. THIGH.

theif, obs. f. THIEF.

theiform ('θiːıfɔːm), *a.* [ad. mod.L. *theiform-is*, f. *thea* TEA: see -FORM.] Resembling the tea-plant.

1846 WORCESTER, *Theiform*, being in the form of tea. *Everest.* **1860** in MAYNE *Expos. Lex.*

theigh, þeiȝ, þeigh, þeiȝt, obs. ff. THOUGH.

theight, obs. f. TIGHT.

theign(e, obs. ff. THANE, THEINE *v.*

theik, var. THEEK, to thatch.

theil, var. THAIL, tael.

theileria (θaı'lıərıə). Also Theileria. [mod.L. (A. Bettencourt et al. 1907, in *Archives R. Inst. Bacteriol. Camara Pestana* I. 343), f. the name of Sir Arnold *Theiler* (1867–1936), South African zoologist + -IA[1].] A tiny, tick-borne protozoan parasite of the genus of this name, which includes those causing theileriasis.

1910 *Parasitology* III. 127 Observations on *Theileria* are fraught with considerable difficulty owing to the minuteness of the parasite. **1927** HALDANE & HUXLEY *Animal Biol.* xii. 279 Smallest parasitic Protozoa (Theileria in ox blood-corpuscle). **1979** *Nature* 5 July p. xiii (Advt.), The research will include the infection and transformation of bovine lymphocytes and other cell types by theileria parasites.

theileriasis (θaılə'raıəsıs). Also theileri'osis [f. THEILERIA + -IASIS, -OSIS.] An acute, usually fatal, feverish disease of cattle, sheep, and certain other vertebrates caused by a protozoan of the genus *Theileria* or a closely related genus and transmitted by ticks; cf. *East Coast fever* s.v. EAST D. 1 b.

1944 *Indian Jrnl. Vet. Sci.* XV. 149 (*title*) Control of cattle theileriasis in calves in the Punjab. **1959** *Adv. Vet. Sci.* V. 241 The name theileriosis has come to designate any member of a group of diseases of vertebrates produced by several species of protozoan parasites belonging to the genera *Theileria, Gonderia*, and *Crytauxzoon*. **1962** J. A. SMYTH *Introd. Animal Parasitol.* ix. 109 This organism [sc. *Theileria parva*] is the cause of the deadly 'theileriasis' or East-Coast Fever in cattle. **1979** *Protozool. Abstracts* III. 38/1 A good review is given of theileriasis of cattle in India. **1979** *Nature* 5 July p. xiii (Advt.), There are in the laboratory of the Director of ILRAD two vacancies for immunologists to work on theileriosis.

theim, obs. ff. THEM.

thein, þein, obs. f. THANE; var. THYNE *Obs.*, thence.

theine ('θiːaın), *sb. Chem.* Also †'theina. [f. mod.L. *thea* TEA + -INE[5].] A vegetable alkaloid, originally thought to be a principle peculiar to tea, but found to be identical with CAFFEINE.

1838 T. THOMSON *Chem. Org. Bodies* 295 Oudry has.. announced that he has discovered in tea a salifiable basis, to which he has given the name of *theina*. **1842** *Penny Cycl.* XXIV. 304/2 Thein, or Theina, the peculiar principle of tea. **1853** URE *Dict. Arts* II. 834 Theine was obtained from coffee by the same process slightly altered. **1863–72** WATTS *Dict. Chem.* I. 707 Oudry.., in 1827, found in tea a crystalline substance, which he called theine. **1881** A. GRIFFITH in *Science Gossip* No. 203. 248 Tea contains from a half to five per cent. of theine.

†**theine, theign,** *v. Obs.* Forms: 1–2 **þeȝnian** (1 **ðæȝn-**), **þénian,** 2 **þeiȝnen,** 3 **þæinen, þeine**(n. [OE. *þeȝnian*, f. *þeiȝn*, THANE = ON. *þegna*, OHG. *deganôn*:—OTeut. **þegnôjan*, f. **þegno*= THANE.] *intr.* To be a servant or minister, to perform the duties of an office. With *dative*: To minister to, wait or attend upon, serve. (a person); hence, quasi-*trans.*

Beowulf 561 Ic him þenode deoran sweorde swa hit ȝedefe wæs. *a* **900** tr. *Bæda's Hist.* III. xvii. [xxiii.] (1890) 232 þa he ða moniȝ ȝer..biscophad þeȝnade. **971** *Blickl. Hom.* 33 He wæs soþ God, þe him englas þeȝnedon. *c* **975** *Rushw. Gosp.* Matt. viii. 15 Hiu aras & ðæȝnade heom. *c* **1000** *Ags. Gosp.* ibid., Ða aras heo & þenode him. *c* **1160** *Hatton Gosp.* ibid., þa aras hyo & þeiȝnede hym. *a* **1175** *Cott. Hom.* 239 Mid al þan þe..laȝelice her him þenið. *c* **1175** *Lamb. Hom.* 109 Vnwurðe bið þe on elde þet him oðer men þenien. *c* **1205** LAY. 24595 þer weoren a þusen cnihtes bald..þat þeineden þan kinge. *Ibid.* 24621 A þusend hire eode biuore..to þæinen þere quene. *a* **1225** *St. Marher.* 23 þeos þreo in an iþeinet of engles. *a* **1250** *Prov. Ælfred* 499 in *O.E. Misc.* 132 Loke þat þu him þeine mid alle þeuues þines.

Hence †**theining** (**þeiȝnung, þening**), ministration, service, office.

c **888** K. Ælfred *Boeth.* xxxvii. §1 ȝif him mon þonne awint of þa claþas, & him oftihð þara þenunga & þæs anwealdes. *a* **900** tr. *Bæda's Hist.* II. xiv. [xvi.] (1890) 144 Nænig..hrinan dorste ne ne wolde buton his nedþearflicre þeȝnunge. **971** *Blickl. Hom.* 209 Englas beoð to ðeȝnunge gæstum fram Gode hider on world sended. *c* **1000** *Ags. Gosp.* Matt. xxvi. 19 Hiȝ ȝe-ȝearwodon him easter-þenunga. *a* **1175** *Cott. Hom.* 233 His water [us werpð] drench and fiscynn his fer manifeald þeninge.

their (ðɛə(r)), *poss. pron.* Forms: see below. [In existing form *their*, in Ormin *þeȝȝre*, a. ON. *þeir(r)a*, genitive pl. of simple demonst. *sá, sú, þat* (= OE. *se, séo, þæt*), used in ON. also as pl. of 3 pers. pron. The *β*-forms *þer, þar, þere*, etc., were prob. due mainly to the unstressed pronunciation of *their, thair*, confused sometimes with that of the adv. *þær, thare*, THERE; but they may sometimes represent OE. *þǽra*, late form of *þára*, gen. pl. of *þá* those, substituted for the same case of the personal pronoun. Cf. THEM.]

A. Illustration of Forms.

α. 3 (*Orm.*) **þeȝȝre, (teȝȝre), 4 þeir(e, þeyr, þayre, þayire, þaier, 4–5 þair, þaire, 5 þeire; 4–5 thaire, 5 thayre, 5–7 theire, theyr, 6 thayr, (thier, 6–7 yair), 4–** *Sc.* **thair, 5– their.**

c **1200** Ormin Ded. 84 All þurrh þeȝȝre sinne. *Ibid.* 3933 þatt teȝȝre genge shollde ben þurrh hallȝhe sawless ekedd. **1303** R. Brunne *Handl. Synne* 874 þarefore þat day al holy cherche þeyr seruyse of here þey werche. **13..** *Cursor M.* 794 (Cott.) Al þaier kin. *Ibid.* 21800 (Edin.) Mani man ..þate thair [*v.r.* þair] hele hauis getin þare. *a* **1340** Hampole *Psalter* lxxvii. 51 He gaf..þaire trauails til þe locust. *c* **1400** *Destr. Troy* 6738 Menelaus, and Thelamon,.. with theire tite batels. *c* **1440** *Pallad. on Husb.* I. 116 Oute of thaire [*v.r.* their] kynde eke seedes wol renewe. **1470–85** Malory *Arthur* VII. xviii. 240 All they felle vpon their knees. **1522** *Rutland Papers* (Camden) 84 To putt all thier stuf of householde in euery office. **1538** Starkey *England* I. iv. 120 To tempur and refrayne thayr malyce. **1549** *Baxter-bks. St. Andrews* (1903) 5 Thomas mortowne To be yair Decane. *a* **1568** *Wyfe of Auchtermuchty* xii, That straik dang baith thair harnis owt. **1620** Sir R. Naunton in *Fortescue Papers* (Camden) 139 Theyr general aunswer to his Majesties commandement. **1641** Best *Farm. Bks.* (Surtees) 126 Holes, of that bignesse that one may thrust in theire neafe.

β. (1 **þæra, þeora**) 4 **þer, þar, (þur), 4–5 þere, 4–6 þare, thar, 5 thare, 5–6 ther, 6–8 there, 7 thir** (used by Milton as unstressed form of *their*).

[? *a* **1100** *O.E. Chron.* (Laud MS.) an. 449, On þeora daȝum ȝelaðode Wyrtȝeorn Angelcin hider. *Ibid.* an. 1086, þæt þa godan men niman æfter þeora godnesse.] *c* **1330** R. Brunne *Chron.* (1810) 127 þe popille him bisouht þer kyng forto be. **13..** *Cursor M.* 476 (Cott.) þat sithen þar [*v.rr.* þair(e, her] sted was neuer sene. *Ibid.* 666 Bath he sette in þare [*v.rr.* þair(e, her] fre will. *Ibid.* 13900 Moyse þur lagh þaim broght. *c* **1400** *Destr. Troy* 12467 Trees, thurgh tempestes, tynde hade þere leues. *c* **1450** *Godstow Regr.* 491 Ther heires lawfully I-be-gote of ther bodies. *c* **1460** *Towneley Myst.* ix. 119, I shalle fownd to crak thare crowne. **1513** Douglas *Æneis* IV. ix. 33–4 The ryning fludis thar wattir stop can scho mak, And eik the sternis turne ther cours abak. **1526** There [see B. 1]. **1533** Bellenden *Livy* II. xix. (S.T.S.) I. 205 þai obeyit weill eftir to þare capitanis. **1663** Chas. II in Julia Cartwright *Henrietta of Orleans* (1894) 139 They will shew there affections to me. **1671** Milton *P.R.* II. 235 He ceas'd, and heard thir grant in loud acclaim. **1757** Mrs. Griffith *Lett. Henry & Frances* (1767) I. 56 Rogueries..which, they thought, brought a disgrace on there bruteships.

B. Signification.

1. *Poss. adj.* (orig. *gen. pl.* of *pers. pron.*) Of, belonging, or pertaining to them; also *refl.* of or belonging to themselves.

c **1200** Ormin 127 Naffdenn þeȝȝ þurrh þeȝȝre streon Ne sune, child, ne dohhterr. *c* **1330** R. Brunne *Chron. Wace* (Rolls) 1115 Brutus wiþ his folk..wente þer weye. **1340** Hampole *Pr. Consc.* 3884 Prelats..Sal account yhelde..Of þair suggets undir þair powere. **1526** Tindale *Matt.* vi. 5 Vereley I saye vnto you they have there rewarde. **1589** Puttenham *Eng. Poesie* I. vi. (Arb.) 27 Vnder the conduict of Totila and Atila and other their generalles. **1617** Moryson *Itin.* II. 219 Consider the inward motiues of their crauing mercy. **1640** tr. *Verdere's Rom. of Rom.* I. xviii. 78 With that they tooke their leaves of her. **1774** Goldsm. *Nat. Hist.* (1776) VI. 222 The great agility of these animals prevents their often being taken. **1797** Godwin *Enquirer* I. vi. 41 We must dwell upon their every word. **1847** De Quincey *Orthogr. Mutineers* Wks. 1860 XIV. 105 When.. he [Milton] wishes to direct a bright jet of emphasis upon the possessive pronoun *their*, he writes it as we now write it. But when he wishes to take off the accent, he writes it *thir*. [Cf. A. *β* 1671.] **1853** M. Arnold *Empedocles* II. 19 With men thou canst not live; Their thoughts, their ways, their wishes, are not thine. **1858** O. W. Holmes *Aut. Breakf.-t.* iv, Long after the frost and snow have done their worst with the orchards. **1864** Tennyson *Aylmer's F.* 383 These old pheasant-lords..Who had mildew'd in their thousands, doing nothing Since Egbert.

b. *Obj. gen.* Of (for, to) them. (Cf. HIS B. 2.)

1553 T. Wilson *Rhet.* (1580) 77 For a tyme your grace muche bewailed their lacke. **1579** [see 5]. **1590** Spenser *F.Q.* III. iii. 43 Shall..quite from off the earth their memory be raste? **1607** Topsell *Four-f. Beasts* (1658) 66 Yet can there not be in any nation a neglect of oxen; and their reverence was so great that, in ancient time [etc]. **1780** Beckford *Biog. Mem.* 108 Humanity pleads strongly for the abridgment of their relation. *a* **1912** *Mod.* We mourn their loss.

c. Const. with gen. pl. of *all, both*: ***their aller, their bother, beyre*** (obs.); also ***all their, their both, both their, each of their*** (arch.): meaning 'of all, both, or each of them'. See ALL D. 4, BOTH 4 b, BO *a.* c.

a **1250** *Owl & Night.* 1584 þe louerd..Vareþ vt on þare beyre neode. *a* **1300** *Cursor M.* 18766 He stei up in þair aller sight. *c* **1380** Wyclif *Serm.* Sel. Wks. I. 289 þe fend..is þer alþer kyng. *c* **1465** *Eng. Chron.* (Camden) 48 Be thair bothe assent. **1559** *Mirr. Mag.* (1563) D v, Lo thus fond hope dyd theyr both lyues abrydge. *a* **1568** [see A. *α*]. **1589** Puttenham *Eng. Poesie* I. viii. (Arb.) 35 Saying thus in all their hearings. **1654–66** Earl Orrery *Parthen.* (1676) 550 With both their helps I was carried to a Chamber. **1672** Temple *Misc.* I. 64 According to each of their hunger or need. **1874** Swinburne *Bothwell* II. i, Mine and all their free and sovereign king.

2. Used of a thing with which a number of persons have to do, or which is assumed to be the common possession of a class; e.g. 'These boys know their Greek syntax'. Cf. HIS *poss. pron.* 1 b.

1785 Burns *Halloween* ii, To burn their nits, an' pou their stocks, An' haud their Halloween. **1905** *Daily Chron.* 2 Sept. 3/1 All those who love their Devon and especially their Dartmoor.

3. Often used in relation to a singular sb. or pronoun denoting a person, after *each, every, either, neither, no one, every one*, etc. Also so used instead of 'his or her', when the gender is inclusive or uncertain. Cf. THEY *pron.* 2, THEM *pron.* 2; NOBODY 1 b, SOMEBODY. (Not favoured by grammarians.)

13.. *Cursor M.* 389 (Cott.) Bath ware made sun and mon, Aiþer wit þer ouen light. *c* **1420** *Sir Amadace* (Camden) l, Iche mon in thayre degre. **14..** *Arth. & Merl.* 2440 (Kölbing) Many a Sarazen lost their liffe. **1533** [see THEMSELVES 5]. **1545** Abp. Parker *Let. to Bp. Gardiner* 8 May, Thus was it agreed among us that every president should assemble their companies. **1563** Winȝet *Four Scoir Thre Quest.* liv, A man or woman being lang absent fra thair party. **1641** [see A. *α*]. **1643** Trapp *Comm. Gen.* xxiv. 22 Each Countrey hath their fashions, and garnishes. **1749** Fielding *Tom Jones* VII. xiv, Every one in the House were in their Beds. **1771** Goldsm. *Hist. Eng.* III. 241 Every person..now recovered their liberty. *a* **1845** Syd. Smith *Wks.* (1850) 175 Every human being must do something with their existence. **1848** Thackeray *Van. Fair* xli, A person can't help their birth. **1858** Bagehot *Lit. Studies* (1879) II. 206 Nobody in their senses would describe Gray's 'Elegy' as [etc.]. **1898** G. B. Shaw *Plays* II. *Candida* 86 It's enough to drive anyone out of their senses.

†**4.** After a sb. (usually a proper name), instead of the genitive inflexion. Cf. HIS *poss. pron.* 4, HER *poss. pron. 3rd pl.* 3. *Obs.* or *rare arch.*

1551 Robinson tr. *More's Utop.* II. (1895) 172 Vntyll the vtopians their creditours demaunde it. **1600** *Shakspere's Titus A.* (title-p.), As it hath sundry times beene playde by the Right Honourable the Earle of Pembrooke,..and the Lorde Chamberlaine theyr Seruants. **1642** Featley *Dippers Dipt* (1646) 11 These travellers their report, and the testimony of those witnesses. **1642** Drumm. of Hawth. *Skiamachia* Wks. (1711) 193 An answer to the parliament of England their declaration. **1667** Pepys *Diary* 3 Jan., The House of Lords their proceedings in petitioning the King. **1681** R. Burthogge *Argt. for Inf. Bapt.* (1684) 6 From the Children of Believers their being Abraham's Spiritual Seed.

5. Serving as antecedent to a following relative; equivalent to 'of those'. (Now usually avoided.)

1579 Tomson *Calvin's Serm. Tim.* 134/2 Under their obedience whome God hath set ouer us. **1593** in J. Morris *Troubles Cath. Forefathers* Ser. III. (1877) 124 The chiefest favour must be procured by their means that have spoiled us before. **1655** Fuller *Ch. Hist.* IX. vii. §14 This prediction.. yet miss'd their meaning, who both first reported, and most believed it.

†**6.** *absol.* = THEIRS. Cf. HER *poss. pron. 3rd pers. pl.* 4. *Obs.*

13.. *Cursor M.* 7465 (Cott.) A man o þair gains an of vr. **1592** G. Harvey *Four Lett.* Wks. (Grosart) I. 216, I offer them my hande: and request their. **1618** Wither *Motto* C iij b, My clothing keeps me full as warm as their [*rime* are]. *Ibid.* C iv, And my esteeme I will not change for their.

their(e, obs. ff. THERE, THIR *dem. pron.*, etc. = these.

†**theirkin**, *a. Obs.* Their kind of, of their kind. (Cf. THAKIN, THISKIN.)

13.. *Cursor M.* 12346 (Cott.) þe leons..Honur him on þairkin wise [*F.* þaire kin; *G.* opon þair wise].

theirn, a midl., south., and U.S. dial. form for THEIRS, on the analogy of *ourn, yourn, hisn, hern*. See also *Eng. Dial. Dict.*

1836 T. C. Haliburton *Clockmaker* 1st Ser. x. 50 When other folks lost theirn from the boys, hisn always hung there like bait to a hook. **1896** 'Mark Twain' in *Harper's Mag.* Sept. 532/1, I hain't ever seen eyes bug out..the way theirn did. **1930** *Amer. Speech* V. 267 Such possessive forms as *ourn, yourn, hisn, hern* and *theirn* are almost universal in the Ozarks.

theirs (ðɛəz), *poss. pron.* Forms: 4–5 **þayres, thayres, þair(e)s, thaires, 4–6 þairis, thairis, þeires, theires, 5 þers, therys, 5–6 theyr(e)s, theyr's, 6 therse, 8–9 their's, 5– theirs** (*Sc.* **thairs**). [In form a double possessive, f. THEIR + *-es* (cf. *hers, ours, yours*). Of northern origin.] The form of the possessive pron. THEIR, used when no sb. follows, i.e. either absolutely or predicatively: That or those belonging to them. (= F. *le, la leur, les leurs*; G. *der, die, das ihrige, die ihrigen*.)

a **1300** *Cursor M.* 22578 (Edinb.) Vntil hir channel sal sco [the sea] turne And als til þayres [*Cott.* þairs, *Gött.* þairis, *Trin.* hores, *Laud* heris] ilk a burne. *Ibid.* 14132 A castel was bath his and þairs [*Fairf. & Gött.* þairis, *Trin.* þeires]. **13..** *R. Brunne's Chron. Wace* (Rolls) 11632 (Lamb. MS.) þer nis no power to þeires liche [*Petyt MS.* non is þer þere ne to þam]. **13..** *E.E. Allit. P.* B. 1527 Heyred hem as hyȝly as heuen wer þayres. **1375** Barbour *Bruce* III. 745 That thai and thairis..Suld be in all thing at his will. **1425** *Rolls of Parlt.* IV. 296/2 Yat any of the said parties, by yayme or yaires, procede. *c* **1430** *Life St. Kath.* (1884) 27 Folowe our faders lyke as þey blessedly folewede thayres. *c* **1440** *Generydes* 2989 This day is therys, A nother shalbe ourez. **1484** Caxton *Fables of Æsop* v. iii, Telle to them that it is thyn and not theyrs. **1526** Tindale *Matt.* v. 10 Theirs ys the kingdome off heven. **1674** Boyle *Excell. Mech. Hypothesis* 7 [They] have no recourse to any peculiar agency of theirs to account for Eclipses. **1719** De Foe *Crusoe* (1840) II. iii. 50 The island was theirs. **1853** Whewell *Grotius* III. 377 Theirs is the sounder opinion, who hold that such a grant continues. **1855** Tennyson *Charge Light Brigade* ii, Their's not to make reply, Their's not to reason why, Their's but to do and die.

b. ***of theirs***: see OF 44.

c **1400** *Laud Troy Bk.* 3521 That he scholde euere be on of thaires. *c* **1400** Love *Bonavent. Mirr.* xxxix. (1908) 197 A frende of theires. **1555** Eden *Decades* 134 A childe of therse. **1564** *Brief Exam.* **, This gaye booke of theyrs. **1692** Bentley *Boyle Lect.* ii. 63 These Atoms of theirs. **1831** *Society* I. ii. 16 An old acquaintance of theirs.

†**c.** Used instead of THEIR (*rare*); in 17–18th c. when followed by another possessive, e.g. 'theirs or our country', now 'their country or ours'. *Obs.*

c **1200** Ormin 2506 And all onn ane wise fell Till eȝȝþerr þeȝȝress herrte. **1560** *Inchaffray Charters* (S.H.S.) 167 Als fre as..ouris or thairis granitaris or chalmirlanis..Josit brukit or intromettit with. **1562** Turner *Baths* Ded., For theyrs sake that are honest and vertuous men. **1652** Gaule *Magastrom.* 274 The event fell out contrary to theirs, and according to the Apostles prediction. **1667** Marvell *Corr.* lxxviii. Wks. (Grosart) II. 223 Upon the importation..into theirs or our country. *a* **1774** Goldsm. tr. *Scarron's Com. Romance* (1775) II. 54 He thought it both theirs and his duty to mount immediately.

†**d.** ***maugre theirs***: in spite of them, against their will: see MAUGRE *prep.* 1 c. *Obs.*

c **1330** R. Brunne *Chron. Wace* (Rolls) 12811 Maugre þeires he dide þem go In to þe wode. *Ibid.* 15336. **1375** Barbour *Bruce* x. 118 Magre thairis he it wan. **1480** *Coventry Leet Bk.* 427 Wheder we shall make the people to abide styll here.., magre theirs, or els let hem departe.

theirself, -selves: see THEMSELVES III.

theis, *adv.* [Cf. THIS *adv.* and DYCE.] THUS.

a **1818** M. G. Lewis *Jrnl. W. Ind.* (1834) 5 Sea terms.— ..*theis* (*thus*) you are near enough.

theism[1] (ˈθiːɪz(ə)m). [mod. f. Gr. *θε-ός* god + -ISM. Cf. F. *théisme* (Voltaire).] **a.** *gen.* Belief in a deity, or deities, as opposed to *atheism*. **b.** Belief in one god, as opposed to *polytheism* or *pantheism*; = MONOTHEISM. **c.** Belief in the existence of God, with denial of revelation: = DEISM. **d.** *esp.* Belief in one God as creator and supreme ruler of the universe, without denial of revelation: in this use distinguished from *deism*.

1678 Cudworth *Intell. Syst.* Pref., Nor indeed out of a meer Partiall Regard to that Cause of Theism neither, which we were engaged in. **1711** Shaftesb. *Charac.* (1737) II. 209, I consider..that to be a settled Christian, it is necessary to be first of all a good theist. For theism can only be oppos'd to polytheism, or atheism. *a* **1774** Tucker *Lt. Nat.* (1834) II. 323 We find the introduction of theism, that is, the doctrine of an intelligent Agent, the Author of nature,.. claimed for Pythagoras. **1841** Elphinstone *Hist. India* I. 163 The theism inculcated by the Védas..has been supplanted by a system of gross polytheism and idolatry. **1877** R. Flint *Theism* i. 18 Theism is the doctrine that the universe owes its existence, and continuance..to the reason and will of a self-existent Being... It is the doctrine that nature has a Creator and Preserver. **1888** F. L. Patton *Syllabus Lect. Theism* 1 (Funk) Theism may be considered religiously [as embracing] polytheism, pantheism, monotheism (theism par excellence).

theism[2] (ˈθiːɪz(ə)m). *Path.* [f. mod.L. *the-a* TEA + -ISM.] A morbid condition characterized by headache, sleeplessness, and palpitation of the heart, caused by excessive tea-drinking.

1886 *Science* VIII. 132 It is customary to speak of acute, subacute and chronic 'theism', a form that has no connection with theological matters. **1906** *Daily News* 14 Sept. 6 It is well to keep an eye on 'acute caffeism' and 'chronic theism'.

theist[1] (ˈθiːɪst). [mod. f. Gr. *θε-ός* god + -IST. Cf. F. *théiste* (Voltaire).] One who holds the doctrine of theism: in earlier use = DEIST; in later use, esp. as distinguished from this: see note s.v. DEIST.

1662 E. Martin *Five Lett.* 45 To have said my office.. twice a day..among Rebels, Theists, Atheists, Philologers, Wits, Masters of Reason, Puritanes [etc.]. *a* **1679** W. Owtram *Serm.* (1682) A v, What theist was ever known to live according to the principles of natural religion? *a* **1734** North *Exam.* III. viii. §11 (1740) 590 He [Oates] did but use the Privilege of a Theist or Freethinker, of which Crew, or worse, he plainly declared himself. **1820** Polwhele in *Lavington's Enthus. Meth. & Papists* Introd. 135 The highly-polished preacher, whose audience are theophilanthropists or theists. **1870** J. H. Newman *Gram.*

Assent v. §2. 120 No one is to be called a Theist, who does not believe in a Personal God.

b. *attrib.* and *Comb.*

1711 HICKES *Two Treat. Chr. Priesth.* (1847) I. 267 His atheist-ridden, or theist-ridden..mind. **1755** AMORY *Mem.* (1766) II. 107 The writings of the old theist philosophers.

'theist[2]. *nonce-wd.* [f. mod.L. *thea* TEA: cf. THEISM[2].] A person addicted to tea-drinking.

c **1818** SHELLEY in Medwin *Life* (1847) II. 47 [Shelley.. was a lover of tea, calling himself..humourously a] Theist.

theistic (θiː'ɪstɪk), *a.* [f. THEIST[1] + -IC.]

1. Of or pertaining to theists or theism.

1780 WARTON *Sir T. Pope* vi. (ed. 2) 208 From an abhorrence of superstition, he appears to have adopted the most distant extremes of the theistic system. **1875** VOYSEY *Revised Prayer Bk.* (ed. 2) Pref., This modest attempt to adapt the Liturgy of the venerable Church of England to a purely Theistic worship. **1876** GLADSTONE in *Contemp. Rev.* June 5 Those who, professedly rejecting all known expressions of dogma, are nevertheless believers in a moral Governor of the Universe... I denominate the Theistic school.

2. Used in the sense: Of or pertaining to a god or gods; divine. *rare.*

1854 BRIMLEY *Ess., Comte's Pos. Philos.* 324 A region of phenomena where Will.., quite apart from all consideration of theistic interference, introduces a disturbing element that baffles the previsions of science. **1878** GLADSTONE *Prim. Homer* vi. §2. 66 Zeus..combines, more than any other deity, the human and the theistic quality.

theistical (θiː'ɪstɪkəl), *a.* [f. as prec. + -AL[1]: see -ICAL.] = prec. 1. Hence **the'istically** *adv.*, in a theistical manner.

1697 C. LESLIE *Short Meth. w. Deists* I. §11 (1699) 45 *note*, The Theistical Clubb have set this up as a Principle. **1738** WARBURTON *Div. Legat.* III. ii. 304 That future State, which, I suppose, the Theistical Philosophers did not believe. **1841** ELPHINSTONE *Hist. India* I. 223 The work of Patanjali..is the text-book of the theistical sect. **1881** MAX MÜLLER tr. *Kant's Critique Pure Reason* II. 635 On one side, theistically, that there is a Supreme Being.

theive, obs. form of THEAVE, THIEVE.

theivil, Sc. var. THIVEL, pot-stick.

theke (θiːk). *Bot.* [ad. Gr. θήκη.] = THECA 2.

1872 TUCKERMAN *N. Amer. Lichens* 30 [Spores] occurring in eights in the thekes. **1882** *Ibid.* I. Introd. 8 The hymenium, consisting of thekes (thecæ, the spore-bearing organs). **1900** in B. D. JACKSON *Gloss. Bot. Terms.*

theke, obs. form of THEEK, THILK.

thel, thele, variants of THEAL *Obs.*, a board.

† **thele'matic**, *a.* *Obs. rare.* [f. Gr. θεληματ-, stem of θέλημα will + -IC.] Of or pertaining to will or volition; voluntary.

1813-21 BENTHAM *Ontology* Wks. 1843 VIII. 207/2 Thelematic [motions], those in the production of which volition..is seen to be concerned.

thelemic (θɛ'liːmɪk), *a.* [f. Gr. θέλημα will + -IC, with reference to the abbey of Thelème in Rabelais; see THELEMITE.] That permits people to do as they wish; *spec.* designating the Satanist activities of Aleister Crowley (1875–1947).

1926 T. E. LAWRENCE *Seven Pillars* (1935) V. lix. 335 The Catholic Christians would counter them by demanding European protection of a thelemic order, conferring privileges without obligation. **1951** J. SYMONDS *Great Beast* III. xvi. 151 The intention of these two founders [*sc.* Sir Francis Dashwood and Aleister Crowley] of Thelemic Abbeys was different. *Ibid.* 152 Five rooms were planned around a central hall, the Sanctum Sanctorum, or the temple, of the Thelemic mysteries. **1956** —— *Ibid.* (rev. ed.) 155 Those *Orgia* which so shocked the readers of the *Sunday Express* and *John Bull*; although through ignorance of magic ..these two papers could only hint at the nature of the Thelemic ceremonies. **1973** K. GRANT *Aleister Crowley & Hidden God* v. 73 Elaborate ceremonial and the establishment of fixed Lodges in specific localities would be superseded by a fluid and far-flung web comprised of Thelemic power-zones.

thelemite ('θɛlɪmaɪt). *rare.* [a. F. *thelemite* (Cotgr.), f. Gr. θέλημα will + -ITE[1], with reference to the abbey of Théléme in Rabelais, the only law of which was *Fay ce que vouldras*, Do what thou wilt.] (See quots.)

1656 BLOUNT *Glossogr.*, *Thelemite*, a libertine, one that does what he list. **1908** *Nation* 24 Oct. 144/1 We will..take our oath to observe the Thelemite rule of 'Do what thou wilt', because, as its founder said, 'men that are free, well-born, well-bred, and conversant in honest companies have naturally an instinct and spur that prompts them unto virtuous actions'. **1973** K. GRANT *Aleister Crowley & Hidden God* v. 77 Thelema represents a necessary stage in the spiritual development of the individual. Paradoxically, no one can create or contribute anything original, or bring more to life than he takes from it, unless he is already a Thelemite. The term 'Thelemite' has a wider connotation than its hitherto exclusive use in Crowleian literature might suggest. The artist, the scientist,..the poet, is such only to the degree that he expresses his true will.

thelephoroid (θɪ'lɛfərɔɪd), *a.* *Bot.* [f. mod.L. *Thelephora* (f. Gr. θηλή a teat + -φορος bearing) + -OID.] Resembling or having the form of the genus *Thelephora* of hymenomycetous fungi. So **thele'phoreous** *a.*, of or pertaining to this genus.

1860 MAYNE *Expos. Lex.*, *Thelephoreus*,..applied by Persoon to a Family..of the *Exosporii Sarcomyci*..: thelephoreous. **1891** *Cent. Dict.*, Thelephoroid.

thelke, obs. form of THILK.

† **thellich**, *a.* and *pron.* *Obs.* Forms: α. 1 **þyslic, þyllic, þillic, þilic**, 2 **þellic**, 3 **þullich** (*ü*), **þulli** (*ü*), 4 **þellich**. β. 1 **þylc, þilc**. [OE. *þyllíc*, by assimilation from *þyslíc* (beside *puslíc, pullíc*), f. *þus, þys*, THUS + *-lic*, -LY[1]. See also THILK.]

A. *adj.* Of this or such a kind; suchlike, such.

Beowulf 2637 ȝif him þyslicu þearf ȝelumpe. *a* **890** tr. *Bæda's Hist.* II. ix. [xii.] (1890) 130 Se ðe þyslice ȝife & swa micle..forecwið. *c* **897** K. ÆLFRED *Gregory's Past. C.* xliii. 314 Ðyllic fæsten ic ȝeceas. *c* **1000** ÆLFRIC *Saints' Lives* xxxiii. 142 Ac þyllic lif nis na ȝewunelic on ure ceastre. *c* **1000** *Ags. Gosp.* Matt. xviii. 5 Swa hwylc swa anne þyllicne [*v.r.* þilicne, *Hatt. G.* þellicne, *Lindisf.* ðuslic] lytling on minum naman onfehþ, se onfehþ me. —— Mark vii. 8 Maneȝa oþre þyllice [*v.r.* þylce, *Hatt. G.* þellice] ðing ȝe doð. *c* **1050** *Liber Scintill.* 33 Ac swyþe feawa synd þa þylce ȝebedu habban. *Ibid.* 80 þes þylc fela spycð. *a* **1225** *Ancr. R.* 8 þeos & swuche oþre [*MS. C.* þullich oðere] beoð alle ine freo wille to donne. *c* **1230** *Hali Meid.* 9 þe þohtes þat.. leareð þe and eggeð toward þulli þeowdom. *a* **1240** *Sawles Warde* in *Cott. Hom.* 255 Of þulliche nesche wepnen ich mahte carien summes weis. *Ibid.* 265 Sikere ha beoð of al þis of þulli lif, of þulli wit, of þulli luue..ant of þulli blisse. **1340** *Ayenb.* 27 Of þelliche þinges him gledeþ ine his herte.

B. *pron.* [absol. or ellipt. use of the adj.] A thing or things of this, that, or such a kind; such.

a **890** tr. *Bæda's Hist.* III. xvi. [xxii.] (1890) 228 þyslic wæs seo syn, þe se cyning fore ofsleȝen wæs. *c* **893** K. ÆLFRED *Oros.* IV. iv. §2 Nu Romane him self þyllic writon. *a* **1000** *Ecgbert's Confess.* c. 15 ȝif..he awiht þylces do. *c* **1000** ÆLFRIC *Colloquy* in Wr.-Wülcker 96/42 þylces fela, *his similia.* *c* **1000** *Ags. Gosp.* Luke ix. 9 Hwæt is þes be þam ic þilc [*Hatt.* þellic, *Lind.* ðuslico] ȝehyre? *a* **1225** *Leg. Kath.* 849 Low! þullich is al þæt ȝe þencheð to dei for to weorrin me wið. **1340** *Ayenb.* 7 þe þridde heste is þellich.

Thelphusian (θɛl'fjuːsɪən), *a.* (*sb.*) *Zool.* [f. mod.L. *Thelphūsa* + -IAN.] Of or pertaining to the genus *Thelphusa* of fresh-water crabs, as *T. fluviatilis*, which burrows in river banks. **b.** *sb.* A crab of this family.

1842 *Penny Cycl.* XXIV. 305/2 *Thelphusa, Thelphusians*, M. Milne Edwards's name for a tribe of brachyurous crustaceans belonging to his family of *Catometopes*. *Ibid.*, Many of the Thelphusians.

thelyblast ('θɛlɪ-, 'θiːlɪblæst). *Biol.* [f. Gr. θῆλυς female + -BLAST.] The female element of a sexual cell. Hence **thely'blastic** *a.*

1877 C. S. MINOT in *Proc. Boston Soc. Nat. Hist.* XIX. 170 The sexual generation may be called *genoblasts*, the male *arsenoblasts*, the female *thelyblasts* (direction cells, nucleoli of Infusoria and spermatozoa). **1890** BILLINGS *Nat. Med. Dict.*, *Thelyblasts*, term proposed by Minot to include mature ova and sperm-blastophores or seminal mother-cells.

‖ **thelycum** ('θiːlɪ-, 'θɛlɪkəm). Pl. **thelyca**. [mod.L., ad. Gr. θηλυκόν, neuter of θηλυκός feminine, f. θῆλυ-ς female.] Name for a structure on the ventral surface of the thorax in the female of certain macrurous crustaceans.

1888 C. S. BATE in *Challenger Rep.* XXIV. 244 The ventral plate or thelycum in the female [*Penæus canaliculatus*]. *Ibid.* 245 The peculiar formation of the complementary external female apparatus which I propose to call thelycum.

the'lygenous, *a.* *Bot.* [f. Gr. θῆλυ-ς female + -GEN + -OUS.] Producing the female element.

1900 B. D. JACKSON *Gloss. Bot. Terms* 270/1 *Thelygenous*, inducing the female element, as thelygenous castration, the production of pistils in the male-flowers of a host by *Ustilago*.

thelykaryotic (ˌθɛlɪ-, ˌθiːlɪkærɪ'ɒtɪk), *a.* *Biol.* [irreg. f. Gr. θῆλυ-ς female + κάρυον nut, kernel + -OTIC, after *mitotic*.] Having a female nucleus.

1909 J. W. JENKINSON *Experim. Embryol.* 267 In the two-celled stage one blastomere has a male and a female nucleus, ..while the other has only a female (thelykaryotic).

† **thelyph'thoric**, *a.* *Obs. nonce-wd.* [f. mod.L. *thelyphthora* (M. Madan 1780), f. Gr. θῆλυ-ς female + φθορά corruption: cf. Gr. φθορικός corrupting.] That corrupts or ruins women.

[**1780** M. MADAN (*title*) Thelyphthora; or, A Treatise on Female Ruin, in its Causes, Effects, Consequences, Prevention, and Remedy.] **1794** MATHIAS *Purs. Lit.* I. 160 Must I with Madan, bent on gospel truth, In Thelypthoric lore instruct our youth.

thelytokous (θiː'lɪtəkəs), *a.* *Zool.* Also *erron.* **thelyotokous** (-'ɒtəkəs). [f. Gr. θηλυτόκος bearing females (f. θῆλυ-ς female + -τόκος bearing) + -OUS.] Producing only female offspring, as the parthenogenetic females of some species: opposed to *arrenotokous*. So **the'lytoky** (also **thely'otoky**), the production of females only in parthenogenesis.

1877 HUXLEY *Anat. Inv. Anim.* vii. 446 The terms arrenotokous and thelytokous have been proposed by Leuckart and Von Siebold to denote those parthenogenetic females which produce male and female young respectively. **1895** D. SHARP *Cambr. Nat. Hist.* V. iv. 141 The result of parthenogenesis in some species is the production of only one sex, which in some Insects is female, in others male; the phenomenon in the former case is called by Taschenberg Thelyotoky, in the latter case Arrhenotoky. *Ibid.* xxii. 498 Thelyotokous parthenogenesis is common in sawflies.

them (ðɛm, ðəm), *pers. pron.* Forms: see below. [Three types are found in ME. α. *þeȝȝm, þeym*, a. ON. *þeim* 'to those', 'to them', dat. pl. of the demonst. *sá, sú, þat*, the plural of which also supplies that of the 3rd pers. pron. (see THEY). This came down to the 16th c. in Eng. in the form *theim*, and still exists in north. dial. and in Sc. as *thaim*. β. Northern Eng. *þam*, app. bef. 1300; this appears to represent *þǽm, þám*, dat. pl. of OE. *se, séo, þæt*, pl. *þá* (see THAT, THO), found already as accus. in the Rushworth Gospels, where Lindisf. has *hía*, Ags. Gosp. *híȝ*, Hatton *hyo*, all in the sense 'them'. This came down in Sc. as *thame* to 16th c. γ. The existing form *them*, found in R. Brunne *c* 1330. This may have originated as an unstressed form (ðəm) of *þeim* or (?) *þam*, or it may actually have represented the OE. Anglian *þæm* of the Rushworth Gospels.

Although the form from Norse is not known before Ormin, it must have been current in the Danelaw much earlier, since it was only dative in Norse, and must have been taken into OE. as dative, and have shared in the peculiar English change by which the accusative and dative of the pronouns were levelled under the dative form. In the singular *hine, him*, instances of this change are seen in the Rushworth Gospel Gloss *c* 975 (see HIM 1 d); and it is noteworthy that the same Gloss shows the use of *þæm* as acc., = *hia, hiȝ, hyo*, as mentioned above. This use of *þæm* as pers. pron. may itself have been due to Norse influence, the OE. word being used in the same sense as the Norse *þeim*

The commoner pron. of 3rd pers. pl. obj. (dat. and acc.) in OE. and ME. was HEM, surviving colloq. and dial. as '*em*.]

A. Illustration of Forms.

α. 2–3 (*Orm.*) **þeȝȝm**, 4–6 **þeym, þeim, theym(e, theim**, 6 **theime**; 4 **þaime, þaym**, 4–6 **þaim**, (4 **þaem**, 4–5 **taim**), 4–6 (4– *Sc.*) **thaim**, 4–6 **thaym(e**, 6 **thaime**.

c **1200** ORMIN 1751 þatt he þeȝȝm ȝife blisse. *Ibid.* 1768 And hellpe þeȝȝm..To winnenn eche blisse. *a* **1300** *Cursor M.* 47 (Cott.) A saumpul her be þaem [*Gött.* þaim, *F.* ham, *T.* hem] I say. *Ibid.* 19378 (Edin.) þai lerid at taim to suffer harde. *c* **1330** R. BRUNNE *Chron. Wace* 13072 Wawayn.. smot aboute, & made þeym rounn. *c* **1375** *Sc. Leg. Saints* xxvii. (*Machor*) 724 He betwene þaym pes can ma. *c* **1400** tr. *Secreta Secret., Gov. Lordsh.* 58 Worschippe..þayme þat þou seez þat doon to be worschipped. **1523** LD. BERNERS *Froiss.* I. clxxxvi. 220 A stryfe fell bytwene theym and they of Parys. **1533** GAU *Richt Vay* (S.T.S.) 3 Thay quhilk red thayme or buyr thaime. **1534** CROMWELL in Merriman *Life & Lett.* (1902) I. 374 They..make not so muche for your purpose as ye allege thaim for. **1536** WRIOTHESLEY *Chron.* (Camden) I. 43 Great lamentation that the poore people made for theim. **1537** *Adm. Crt. Exemplif.* I. No. 174 Seeing a ship coming somewhat rome with theym. **1565** ALLEN *Def. Purg.* xv. 272 Sumwhiles by thabasing of theime. **1873** Thaim [see B. 5].

β. 1 **þæm**, 3–4 **þam**, 4–6 **þame** (6 **yame**), 4–7 **thame, tham**.

c **975** *Rushw. Gosp.* Matt. xx. 25 Hælend þa ceiȝde þæm [*Lind.* hia, *Ags.* hiȝ, *Hatt.* hyo] to him. **13..** *Cursor M.* 4900 (Cott.) þe sargantz..Ran and ouertok þam [*Gött.* þaim] þare. *Ibid.* 7120 A redel þam vndo he badd. *c* **1330** R. BRUNNE *Chron.* (1810) 2 Iuor & Ini were disconfite þat day, þe Iris & þe Wals with þam fled away. **1357** *Lay Folks Catech.* (MS. T.) 39 That..suld teche thame. *Ibid.* 65 To lere tham. *a* **1400** *Isumbras* 122 For thame es alle my kare. **1513** DOUGLAS *Æneis* XIII. x. 88 Gyf thame happynis careit for to be Tyll ony wther sted. **1577** HOLINSHED *Chron., Hist. Scot.* I. 371/2 To yame that receyuit thy noble father ye Duke of Longcastell. **1641** in Row *Hist. Kirk* (Wodrow Soc.) p. xliii, Being found qualifeit be thame.

γ. 4 **þem**, 4– **them**, (5–6 **theme**).

c **1330** R. BRUNNE *Chron. Wace* (Rolls) 15336 Oure kynde ..Schal do þem bowe, maugre þayres. **13..** *Cursor M.* 13725 (Cott.) Him for to tak bituix þem tua. *c* **1430–** Them [see B. 4]. **1482** in *Eng. Hist. Rev.* XXV. 123 If ye wylle not, we bene purveyde of theme yat wylle. **1573** *Satir. Poems Reform.* xl. 21 To theme that was his fais.

B. Signification. **I.** Personal pronoun.

1. As pronoun of the third person plural, objective, direct and indirect (accusative and dative) of THEY. Also as antecedent pron. followed by relative, or prepositional phrase, and having then a demonstrative function, equivalent to *those* but less emphatic.

a. Direct object or accusative. (= L. *eos, illos*, G. *sie.*)

c **975** [see A. β]. *c* **1200** [see A. α]. *a* **1300** *Cursor M.* 1228 He þam for-soke in all þer nedis. *Ibid.* 8118 He heild þam to þaim for to kys. *c* **1330** [see A. γ]. **1470–85** MALORY *Arthur* x. lxix. 533 The grene knyghte hath..beten all them of Orkeney. **1474** *Coventry Leet Bk.* 389 To bye theym in þe Croschepyng. **1552** LYNDESAY *Monarche* 4822 Unoccupyit thay hald thame in thare neif. **1560** BIBLE (Genev.) *1 Sam.* ii. 30 Them that honour me, I wil honour. **1586** T. B. *La Primaud. Fr. Acad.* I. (1589) 383 Have them in great estimation and admiration. **1667** MILTON *P.L.* IX. 420 By Fountain or by shadie Rivulet He sought them both. **1864** J. H. NEWMAN *Apol.* iv. (1904) 125/1 Charges..which..I fully believed at the time when I made them.

b. Indirect object or dative. (= L. *eis, illis*, G. *ihnen.*)

c **1200** ORMIN 1142 þatt he þeȝȝm..Forrȝæfe þeȝȝre gilltess. *a* **1300** *Cursor M.* 667 Witte and wisdam he þam gaue. **1375** BARBOUR *Bruce* I. 79 þis ordynance þaim thocht þe best. *c* **1400** *Rule St. Benet* 20 And by-kenne it taim þat best can serue god & te cuuent. *c* **1500** *Merch. & Son* 269 in Hazl. *E.P.P.* I. 151 The maryage of them ij. ys made. **1523** LD. BERNERS *Froiss.* I. ccxli. 353 He sent..and made alyaunces with them thre. **1535** COVERDALE *Jer.* xxxv. 2 Geue them wyne to drynke. **1656** EARL MONM. tr. *Boccalini's Advts. fr. Parnass.* I. i. (1674) 2 If their Lord..do but cast an artificial smile them, they take it as..a reward. **1779** *Mirror* No. 23 ¶2 To show them what they are to understand. **1812** CRABBE *Tales* xviii, Men..whose pains, Credit, and prudence, brought them constant gains. *Mod.* I give them credit for good intentions.

c. As the object of a preposition.

c **1300** *Harrow. Hell* 29 (MS. E) Crist loked þaim vnto. *c* **1340** HAMPOLE *Prose Tr.* 28 þou will noghte tente to thaym. **1474** CAXTON *Chesse* 7 Take not from them that is theyres. **1535** COVERDALE *Ps.* xvii[i]. 48 Thou shalt lift me vp from them that ryse agaynst me. **1663** GERBIER *Counsel* f viij, Letters, which the Ægiptians did attribute unto them. **1780** *Mirror* No. 96 ¶2 They are neither of them niggardly. **1847** TENNYSON *Princess* Concl. 68 Too solemn for the comic touches in them. *Mod.* What will he do with them?

d. Sometimes *indefinitely*, as objective case of THEY 3 a. *colloq.* or *dialectal*.

e. As objective case of THEY 3 b. Hence phr. ***them and us*** used *attrib.*

1924 W. HOLTBY *Crowded Street* iii. 27 The magic circle of 'Them', the great ones. 'They' were the élite, the prefects and the games captains. **1945** H. NICHOLSON *Let.* 27 May (1967) 465 People feel, in a vague and muddled way, that all the sacrifices to which they have been exposed..are all the fault of 'them'—namely the authority or the Government. **1957** R. HOGGART *Uses of Literacy* iii. 62 To the very poor, especially, they compose a shadowy but numerous and powerful group affecting their lives at almost every point: the world is divided into 'Them' and 'Us'. **1962** *Listener* 8 Mar. 439/1 It is this feeling of being in a world that belongs to 'them' and not to 'us' that puts a strain on working-class children. **1966** *Guardian* 11 Oct. 3/1 The 'ordinary people' who looked on, who made..the Them and Us division [between cripples and other people]. **1980** A. CORNELISEN *Flight from Torregreca* x. 230 The vicious estrangements of a two-class, a Them-and-us society.

2. Often used for 'him or her', referring to a singular person whose sex is not stated, or to *anybody, nobody, somebody, whoever*, etc. Cf. THEY 2.

1742 RICHARDSON *Pamela* III. 127 Little did I think..to make a..Complaint against a Person very dear to you,..but dont let them be so proud..as to make them not care how they affront everybody else. **1853** MISS YONGE *Heir of Redclyffe* xliv, Nobody else..has so little to plague them. **1874** DASENT *Half a Life* II. 198 Whenever any one was ill, she brewed them a drink.

3. Used for the nominative *they*. **a.** As antecedent or demonstrative pronoun: = THOSE. Now only *dial.* or *illiterate*. Also in phr. ***them's my sentiments*** (now freq. used humorously).

c **1489** CAXTON *Sonnes of Aymon* iii. 78 All the foure brethern, and all theym of theyr companye arayed them selfe. *c* **1530** LD. BERNERS *Arth. Lyt. Bryt.* 393 Blessyd be them that hath brought that about. **1581** MARBECK *Bk. of Notes* 150 Such are them to whom yᵉ Lord doth giue his holy spirit. **1632** LITHGOW *Trav.* VII. 333 In a moment, them of the Villages came downe on horse and foote. *a* **1825** FORBY *Voc. E. Anglia* Introd. 141 Them are the women I meant. **1847** THACKERAY *Van. Fair* (1848) xxi. 179 The sooner it is done the better, Mr. Osborne; them's my sentiments. *c* **1864** BROUGH & 'HALLIDAY' *Area Belle* 8 Cold mutton to begin with... Cut near the knuckle, with a little currant jelly if you've got it. Them's my sentiments. **1873** MURRAY *Dial. S. Scotl.* 184 Thaim at dyd it. **1877** L. J. JENNINGS *Field Paths* iii. 47 Them be my two children. **1891** BARRIE *Little Minister* iii, Them as says there's no has me to fecht. **1900** F. NIGHTINGALE *Let.* in C. Woodham-Smith *Florence Nightingale* (1951) xxiv. 590 'Drat' hockey and long live the horse! Them's my sentiments. **1901** N. LLOYD *Chronic Loafer* i. 11 Them wasn't our only troubles. **1924** E. M. FORSTER *Passage to India* v. 48 We're out here to do justice and keep the peace. Them's my sentiments. **1972** 'J. & E. BONETT' *No Time to Kill* viii. 100 'Them's my sentiments too,' he said. 'As Thackeray wrote,' she exclaimed in delight.

b. As personal pronoun after *than, as*, and in the predicate after the verb *to be*. Common *colloq.*, but considered incorrect grammatically.

1654–66 EARL ORRERY *Parthen.* (1676) 708 It was an impossibility that these could be them. **1777** MICKLE *Cumnor Hall* xix, How far less blest am I than them! **1845** E. WARBURTON *Crescent & Cross* I. 331 It was not them we wanted. **1888** 'J. S. WINTER' *Bootle's Childr.* xiv, It was them told me about her. **1888** 'R. BOLDREWOOD' *Robbery under Arms* xxxiv, It was them or us..now. **1901** THEO. W. WILSON *Bacca Queen* xi. 89 Such as them enjoys thersells.

c. As nominative case of sense 1 e above.

1957 R. HOGGART *Uses of Literacy* iii. 62 'Them' is a composite dramatic figure, the chief character in modern urban forms of the rural peasant-big-house relationships. **1962** *Listener* 14 June 1044/2 With their use of Christian names in accusing one another of wilful misrepresentation they impressed me most with being collectively Them trying to get power from Us. **1970** *Guardian* 19 Nov. 1/4 In ..the Talk of the Town restaurant, 'them' and 'us' dined last night to earn money for the world's wildlife.

II. 4. As reflexive pron. = themselves. (= L. *se, sibi*, G. *sich.*)

As direct or indirect obj. of vb. (*arch.*), or obj. of prep. **13..** *Cursor M.* 1713 þe meke be þam ai tua and tua, þe wild do be þam-self al-sua. *Ibid.* 15757 (Cott.) þai fell þaim don vn-to þe grund. **1375** BARBOUR *Bruce* I. 205 Gyff þat ony man þaim by Had ony thing þat wes worthy. *c* **1430** *Syr Tryam.* 770 The knyghtes gyed them fulle gay, And proved them fulle preste. **1535** COVERDALE *Exod.* xxxii. 8 They haue made them a molten calfe. *a* **1550** *Christis Kirke Gr.* xi, To dans thir damysellis thame dicht. **1565** COOPER *Thesaurus, Rubriceta*,..roset colour that women vse to paynte them. **1794** MRS. RADCLIFFE *Myst. Udolpho* lvii, Superior attainments of every sort bring with them duties of superior exertion. **1848** J. H. NEWMAN *Loss & Gain* II. xx. (1904) 254 What a way those fellows have with them! **1855** MACAULAY *Hist. Eng.* xxii. IV. 697 They then bethought them of a new expedient.

III. 5. As demonstr. adj. = THOSE. Now only *dial.* or *illiterate*.

a. Qualifying an objective (direct or indirect). Also strengthened by adding *there* (*'ere, air*).

1596 H. CLAPHAM *Bible Hist.* 92 To Samaria and them partes. **1598** BARRET *Theor. Warres* I. i. 4 The warres and weapons are now altered from them dayes. **1621** AINSWORTH *Annot. Pentat.* Gen. xviii. 6 Foure of them Logs make a Kab. **1726** CAVALLIER *Mem.* III. 231 If I had but one of them Hangmen. **1809–12** MAR. EDGEWORTH *Absentee* xii, I hope, then, the agent will give you encouragement about them mines. **1840** THACKERAY *Catherine* vii, It was a rare rise we got out of them chaps. **1878** MRS. STOWE *Poganuc P.* i, He don't believe in keeping none of them air prayer-book days.

b. Qualifying a nominative.

1607 TOPSELL *Four-f. Beasts* (1658) 126 Them few [dogs] which be kept must be tyed up in the day time. **1610** HEALEY *Vives' Comment St. Aug. Citie of God* XII. xvi, Augustine..saith that them times were called eternall. **1778** J. CRANE in F. Chase *Hist. Dartmouth* (Mass.) *Coll.* (1891) I. 389 The major part tories, or them sort of creatures called neuters. **1842** S. LOVER *Handy Andy* xxviii, Them ribbons of yours cost a trifle, Kitty. **1889** TENNYSON *Owd Roä* viii, 'Faaithful an' True' Them words be i' Scriptur. **1901** M. E. FRANCIS *Fiander's Widow* II. v. 255 'Them there legs o' yourn should be pretty well stretched by now.'

‖**thema** ('θɛmə, 'θi:mə). Pl. **themata** ('θɛmətə). [mod.L. *thema*, a. Gr. θέμα THEME.]

†**1.** The theme or subject of a declamation or discourse; a position to be maintained or demonstrated; a thesis. *Obs.*

1531 ELYOT *Gov.* I. xiv, A case is appoynted to be moted by certayne yonge men, contaynyng some doubtefull controuersie, which is in stede of the heed of a declamation called *thema*. *a* **1734** NORTH *Exam.* I. i. §8. (1740) 18 His grand *Thema* or Historical Position is, That King Charles II. was a concealed Papist. *Ibid.* ii. §47. 53 Another of the Author's *Themata* or Positions.

2. The stem-form of a word; = THEME 5.

1615 BEDWELL *Arab. Trudg.*, *Alkoran*, the thema is not *Karana*,..as they would make vs beleeue: but *Kara*, which signifieth, to reade. **1883** *Athenæum* 6 Jan. 15/2 Scholars are still divided as to what thema or base to refer certain forms [of Icelandic nouns].

3. *Mus.* = THEME 4.

1801 BUSBY *Dict. Mus.* **1871** GRAEME *Beethoven* ii. (1876) 27 Beethoven..requested a thema for an improvisation.

4. A dissertation or thesis submitted for a degree; cf. THEME 3.

1888 *Athenæum* 28 July 129/3 'The Conflict of East and West in Egypt'..appears to be an enlargement of a *thema* for the doctorate of Columbia College.

thematic (θɪ'mætɪk), *a.* (*sb.*) [ad. Gr. θεματικ-ός, f. θέμα THEME: see -IC.] **A.** *adj.* Of or pertaining to a theme or themes.

1. a. Of or pertaining to a subject or topic of discourse or writing.

1871 tr. *Lange's Comm. Jer.* 104 These introductory verses thus acquire a thematic character. **1957** N. FRYE *Anatomy of Criticism* 367 Thematic; Relating to works of literature in which no characters are involved except the author and his audience, as in most lyrics and essays, or to works of literature in which internal characters are subordinated to an argument maintained by the author..opposed to fictional. **1974** R. QUIRK *Linguist & Eng. Lang.* iv. 75 There is formulaic and thematic structure..yielding striking if controversial theories about the composition of early English poetry. **1979** *N. & Q.* Feb. 63/2 The orientation of this anthology is essentially thematic.

†**b.** *Logic.* Relating to or connected with the matter or subject of thought. *Obs.*

1697 tr. *Burgersdicius his Logic* I. i. 2 A System of Logical Precepts consists of two Parts, Thematick and Organic... The first is that which is imploy'd about Theams, and their various Affections, and second Notions, as about the Matter of the Instruments of Logick.

c. *Psychol.* ***Thematic Apperception Test***: a projective test designed to reveal a person's actual social drives or needs by means of the theme common to the interpretations which he gives to each of a standard series of pictures.

1935 MORGAN & MURRAY in *Arch. Neurol. & Psychiatry* XXXIV. 289 (*title*) Method for investigating fantasies. The Thematic Apperception Test. **1938** H. A. MURRAY et al. *Explorations in Personality* vi. 531 As the subjects who took this test were asked to interpret each picture—that is, to apperceive the plot or dramatic structure exhibited by each picture—we named it the 'Thematic Apperception Test'. **1957** P. LAFITTE *Person in Psychol.* 120 The Thematic Apperception Test is more abstract because of the deliberate vagueness of its pictures as well as the fantastic nature of some. **1981** L. KRISTAL et al. *ABC Psychol.* 189 Two of the best known projective tests are the Thematic Apperception Test..and the Rorschach Inkblot Test.

d. *Philately.* Applied to the collecting of stamps with designs which relate to the same subject, or to such a collection.

1951 R. J. SUTTON *Stamp Collector's Encycl.* 231 Thematic Collecting: Collecting to a theme or subject. **1965** E. H. SPIRE *Adventures in Stamp Collecting* ix. 111 It was..only a logical development from selected collecting that brought about the advent of Thematic Philately. *Ibid.*, Collections of stamps depicting animals, flowers, ships, railways..and so on, are described as 'thematic'. **1972** *Police Rev.* 1 Dec. 1558 The American Topical Society has recorded more than one thousand subjects for thematic stamp collecting.

e. *Linguistics.* Of, pertaining to, or designating the theme of a sentence: see THEME *sb.* 1 d.

1959, etc. [see RHEMATIC *a.* 2]. **1969** K. H. WAGNER *Generative Grammatical Studies in Old Eng. Lang.* i. 52 In interrogative clauses..the initial constituent must be regarded as rhematic rather than thematic. **1977** J. LYONS *Semantics* II. xii. 506 *John Smith I haven't seen for ages.* Here the grammatical subject is 'I', but the thematic subject is 'John Smith'.

2. *Mus.* Of, pertaining to, or constituting themes or subjects (see THEME 4); relating to themes and their contrapuntal development. In ***thematic catalogue, index, summary***, = containing the opening themes or passages of musical pieces.

1864 *Reader* 21 May 660 A handy thematic summary of the work is given in the 'Orchestra' for last week. **1878** C. F. POHL in Grove *Dict. Mus.* I. 66/2 The thematic catalogue which Mozart himself had kept of his works. **1906** *Athenæum* 1 Sept. 250/2 The thematic material has been carefully chosen, and its treatment shows thought and skill.

3. *Gram.* Of or pertaining to the theme or stem-form of a word: see THEME 5. Hence, of verb-forms: having a connecting vowel between the verb-stem and the suffixes or inflections.

thematic vowel, a vowel which comes between the root and the inflexions in a verb or sb., as the ε and ο in φέρ-ο-μεν, φέρ-ε-τε, the *i, e*, and *a* in OE. *ber-i-þ, ber-e-þ, luf-a-ð*.

1861 GOLDSTÜCKER *Pánini* 257 There must be reasons for this variety of thematic forms which constitute the declension of the same base. **1877** PAPILLON *Man. Comp. Philol.* viii. (ed. 2) 167 Curtius..explains the vowel in question as a 'thematic vowel', i.e. a suffix to or increase of the stem or 'theme' previous to the reception of the inflections. **1887** COOK *Sievers' O.E. Gram.* 143 The thematic *w* being sometimes retained and sometimes lost. **1888** KENNEDY *Revised Lat. Primer* §148 (1900) 94 Verbs... In which the Verb-Stem was formed by a so-called Thematic vowel added to the root. **1894** [see ATHEMATIC *a.* 1]. **1933** *Language* IX. 82 The athematic verbs were primarily durative in aspect, while the thematic were momentary. **1933, 1955** [see NON-THEMATIC *a.* 1 a]. **1972** *Language* XLVIII. 389 Except for certain 'thematic verbs', which are exceptional, the presence of a post-position is mutually implicative with the presence of an ind. obj. morpheme.

4. Of or pertaining to the division of the Byzantine Empire into 'themes' or provinces.

1911 E. FOORD *Byzantine Empire* xi. 203 The army—The thematic system and its development—Organization, arms, equipment, and tactics. **1933** S. RUNCIMAN *Byzantine Civilisation* iv. 90 The thematic tax-gatherers took orders directly from the central government. **1980** C. MANGO *Byzantium* I. ii. 46 The accepted view is that the 'thematic' reform was accompanied by a general fragmentation of the large estates.

B. *sb.* **1.** That part of logic which deals with themes or subjects of thought.

1891 in *Cent. Dict.*

2. *Gram.* A thematic verb-form.

1968 *Language* XLIV. 717 The conventional view of the distribution of athematics and thematics seems to be that both types existed even in quite early Proto-Indo-European.

3. *Philately.* A collection of stamps with designs which relate to the same subject.

1972 *Police Rev.* 1 Dec. 1572/3 It was known as United Kingdom Thematics 1972, open to thematic entries from anywhere. **1979** *West Lancs. Even. Gaz.* 6 Apr. 18 (Advt.), Stamp collectors world-wide approvals and thematics.

4. *pl.* const. as *sing.* A body of subjects or topics of discussion or study.

1975 *Amer. Speech 1973* XLVIII. 125 Conklin's unique credentials..allow him to be catholic in his approach, both in terms of thematics and in his world-wide coverage. **1977** A. SHERIDAN tr. *J. Lacan's Écrits* v. 149 The thematics of this science is henceforth suspended, in effect at the primordial position of the signifier and the signified. **1980** *Encounter* May 34/2 Even if Dr Henry Kissinger's picture of a world of 'multi-polarity' is more a neo-Bismarckian fiction than a reality, the confrontation of two Super-powers describes neither the thematics nor the structure of world politics today.

So **the'matical** *a.* = *thematic*; **the'matically** *adv.*, in a thematic manner; with respect to a theme or themes; †'**thematism** *Obs. nonce-wd.* [ad. Gr. θεματισμός a laying down], a placing, arrangement; '**thematist**, one who composes or writes themes (Ogilvie, 1882).

1890 *Athenæum* 3 May 579/1 The *thematical material in the four movements of the work is..interesting, and..the music is pleasantly unconventional. *Ibid.* 25 Jan. 125/2 Structurally as well as *thematically we note a welcome advance towards clearness. **1729** SHELVOCKE *Artillery* v. 334 The first then shall be the **Thematism* (from the Greek Word θεματισμός) which signifies the Decorum and Gracefulness of any Pile.

thematization (ˌθi:mətaɪ'zeɪʃən). [f. THEMATIZE *v.* + -ATION.] **1.** The action of THEMATIZE *v.* 2.

1955 T. BURROW *Sanskrit Lang.* iv. 153 This tendency to thematisation had already been operating in the prehistoric period. **1972** *Language* XLVIII. 399 The thematization process..is triggered by violations of canons of permissible plus and minus values of pronominal features for non-ergator and indirect object. **1977** *Ibid.* LIII. 50 Thus the form **somos* can be regarded as a partial thematization of the copula.

2. The action of THEMATIZE *v.* 1.

1959 J. FIRBAS in *Brno Studies in English* I. 52 Whereas only two elements ([*the*] *girl* and *broke*) of the three in *The girl broke a vase* allow of thematization, any of the three elements occurring in *The girl broke the vase* can be thematized. **1969** K. H. WAGNER *Generative Grammatical Studies in Old Eng. Lang.* i. 50 In the abstract structure *Th* and *Rh* are empty places, i.e. they will not be expanded by subsequent rules. These places will be filled with constituents from the nucleus by transformation rules which may be termed rules of *thematization* and *rhematization*, respectively. **1977** J. LYONS *Semantics* II. xii. 507 It is certainly true that the processes that different languages make available for the thematization of one expression rather than another frequently involve putting the expression earlier rather than later in the utterance.

thematize (ˈθiːmətaɪz), *v. Linguistics.* [f. Gr. θεματ-, stem of θέμα THEME *sb.* + -IZE.]

1. *trans.* To convert (part of a sentence) into a theme: see THEME *sb.* 1 d.

1959 J. FIRBAS in *Brno Studies in English* I. 43 When thematic elements..occur in basically transitional or basically thematic positions, they communicatively weaken them, or so to speak, 'dedynamize', 'thematize' them. **1969** [see RHEMATIZE *v.*]. **1976** *Archivum Linguisticum* VII. 145 The following functional constituents (derived from the mood system) may be thematized by fronting them.

2. To modify (a verb-form) by the addition of a thematic vowel: see THEMATIC *a.* 3.

1966 E. P. HAMP in Birnbaum & Puhvel *Anc. Indo-Europ. Dial.* 115 **ĝhé(s)r-om*, thematized from **ĝhēsr*. **1977** *Language* LIII. 50 In addition, Isg. **esmi* was thematized.

Hence ˈ**thematized** *ppl. a.*

1972 *Language* XLVIII. 402 We would expect **n-mi-* at the beginning of the relationship terms; instead we get the thematized form, a transitive construction. **1976** *Ibid.* LII. 68 Kuno proposes..that the deep structure of every relative clause in Japanese contains a thematized sentence.

Thembu *sb.* and *a.*, var. TEMBU *sb.* and *a.*

theme (θiːm), *sb.* Forms: α. 4–6 **teme**, (4–5 **teeme**, 5 **teem**, 5–6 **tyme**). β. 4– **theme**, (6–7 **theame**, 6–8 **theam**). [a. OF. **teme* (not in Godef.: but cf. *tesme*, with graphic *s* indicating vowel-length (13th c. in Godef. *Compl.*); also *teume, thieume*); in β conformed to L. *thema*, a. Gr. θέμα proposition, f. θε-, root of τιθέναι to put, set, place, lay down. In 16–17th c. commonly spelt *theam* (θeːm). Cf. ANTETHEME.]

1. a. The subject of discourse, discussion, conversation, meditation, or composition; a topic.

α. *a* **1300** *Cursor M.* 18495 (Cott.) Bot lenthius yald up his teme Bath to ioseph and to nichodeme. **13..** *E.E. Allit. P.* C. 358 þe trwe tenor of his teme he tolde on þis wyse. *c* **1380** WYCLIF *Serm.* Sel. Wks. I. 306 Crist..toke þe same word for his teme þat Baptist toke whanne he prechide.

β. **13..** *E.E. Allit. P.* A. 943 þe nwe [Herusalem] þat lyȝt of godez sonde, þe apostel in apocalyppce in theme con take. *c* **1386** CHAUCER *Pard. Prol.* 5 My theme [teeme, teme, teem, tyme] is alwey oon and euere was Radix malorum est Cupiditas. **1485** CAXTON *Paris & V.* Prol., I vndertake this theme..because I haue all my life taken pleasure in the reading of Romances. **1570** GOOGE *Pop. Kindg.* IV. 44 b, Now to my theame again. *a* **1600** [see THESE *sb.*]. **1649** MILTON *Eikon.* ix, The overworn theme, and stuffing of all his discourses. **1708** *Brit. Apollo* No. 18. 3/2 And Love and Pleasure be my Endless Theam [*rime* name]. **1804** WELLINGTON in Gurw. *Desp.* (1837) III. 81 His Highness's notorious treachery,..the theme of all the public dispatches. **1870** BRYANT *Iliad* VI. I. 200 A theme of song for men in time to come.

†**b.** *transf.* A subject treated by action (instead of by discourse, etc.); hence, that which is the cause *of* or *for* specified action, circumstance, or feeling; matter, subject. *Obs.*

1588 SHAKS. *Tit. A.* v. ii. 80 See heere he comes, and I must play my theame. **1602** —— *Ham.* v. i. 289 *Ham.* Why I will fight with him vppon this Theme... *Qu.* Oh my sonne, what Theame? *Ham.* I lou'd Ophelia [etc.]. **1634** SIR T. HERBERT *Trav.* 110 An infallible Theame of endlesse troubles. **1713** SWIFT *Cadenus & Vanessa* 298 In vain..You form'd this project in your brain..Nor shall Vanessa be the theme To manage thy abortive scheme. **1806** H. SIDDONS *Maid, Wife, & Widow* I. 179 His son grew up to man's estate, and gave him farther theme for uneasiness.

†**c.** *Logic.* That which is the subject of thought.

1620 T. GRANGER *Div. Logike* 1 The externall is euery Theme, or matter propounded, whereof a man discourseth, or may discourse by his reason. **1697** tr. *Burgersdicius his Logic* I. ii. 2 A Theme is whatsoever may be propos'd to the Understanding to be known. Themes are either Simple or Compounded. **1725** WATTS *Logic* I. ii. §1 Every object of our idea is called a theme, whether it be a being or not-being; for not-being may be proposed to our..thoughts, as well as that which has a real being.

d. *Linguistics.* That part of a sentence which indicates what is being talked about. Cf. RHEME.

1959, etc. [see RHEME]. **1966** J. VACHEK *Linguistic School of Prague* ii. 18 'Functional' elements, the most important of which appear to be the *theme* and the *rheme* (the first being the basis of the statement, known from the context or situation.) *Ibid.* v. 89 The *theme*, is that part of the utterance which refers to a fact or facts already known from the preceding context. **1969** K. H. WAGNER *Generative Grammatical Studies in Old Eng. Lang.* i. 48 There is evidence supporting the hypothesis that O.E. is a *theme-rheme* language. That is to say that unless certain factors intervene the most natural order of the elements of a sentence is that progressing from what is known to what is unknown, or rather from what has already been mentioned to what is newly introduced into discourse. **1977** *Language* LIII. 444 Like the article by Cinque, this one gets into the theme/rheme distinction.

†**2.** *spec.* The text of a sermon; also, a proposition to be discussed. *Obs.* (or merged in 1).

α. **1362** LANGL. *P. Pl.* A. III. 86 A Sarmoun he made,..And tolde hem þis teeme [*v.r.* teme]. *Ibid.* VIII. 122 Thou mihtest preche whon þe luste, *Quoniam literaturam non cognoui* mihte be þy Teeme! *c* **1440** *Promp. Parv.* 488/1 Teme, of a sermone, *thema.* **1513** MORE *Rich. III*, Wks. 60/2 He toke for his tyme *spuria vitulamina non agent radices altas.* That is to say bastard slippes shal neuer take depe roote. **1530** PALSGR. 281/1 Tyme of a sermonde, *thesme.*

β. **1387** TREVISA *Higden* (Rolls) VIII. 151 (MS. a) He took a theme [L. *sumpto themate*] of holy writt, and gan to preche. **1432–50** tr. *Higden* ibid., This theme of scripture. *c* **1530** L. COX *Rhet.* (1899) 44 The theme of Tullyes oracyon or plee for Milo was thys, that he had slayne Clodius laufully. **1560** DAUS *Sleidane's Comm.* 367 The deuines had Themes geuen them to discusse and reason vpon. *c* **1566** *Merie Tales of Skelton* S.'s Wks. 1843 I. p. lxi, He dyd take that for hys antethem, the which of late dayes is named a theme, and sayde, *Qui se exaltat* [etc.]. **1594** T. B. *La Primaud. Fr. Acad.* II. 590 In the ende all woulde be but vanitie, according to Salomons theame, which hee handleth in his booke of the Preacher. **1618** HALES *Rem., Lett. fr. Synod of Dort* II. 50 He took for his Theme the 122 Psalm.

3. An exercise written on a given subject, *esp.* a school essay; an exercise in translation. Now *U.S.*

1545–7 in *Archæologia* XXXIV. 41 After none they [form III] have a theme to be made in Laten. **1581** PETTIE *Guazzo's Civ. Conv.* II (1586) 59 Like a schoolemaister, which doth dictate or rehearse to his schollers some Theame or Epistle. **1644** MILTON *Areop.* (Arb.) 56 The theam of a Grammar lad. **1739** CIBBER *Apol.* (1756) I. 7, I remember I was once whipp'd for my theme. **1824** in Grant *Burgh Sch. Scotl.* (1876) II. iv. 154 The Rector dictated an English theme to be translated into Latin. **1878** BOSW. SMITH *Carthage* 263 In Juvenal's time Roman schoolboys declaimed upon it in their weekly themes. **1924** [see DRIP *sb.* 3 b]. **1955** E. B. WHITE *Let.* 1 Apr. (1976) 406 If you are engaged in writing a theme about my works, I think your best bet is to read them. **1976** *National Observer* (U.S.) 14 Feb. 17/3 In my spare time I go to college and the real reason is that it is here that this small flutter comes alive... Late at night when an English theme, which an hour ago had seemed impossible, starts to jell, I feel it.

4. *Mus.* The principal melody, plainsong, or *canto fermo* in a contrapuntal piece; hence, any one of the principal melodies or motives in a sonata, symphony, etc.; a subject; also, a simple tune on which variations are constructed.

[**1597** MORLEY *Introd. Mus.* 86 Your plainsong is as it were your theme, and your descant as it were your declamation.] **1674** PLAYFORD *Skill Mus.* III. 2 It was usual with them to have a Tenor as a Theam, to which they were compelled to adapt their other Parts. **1854** *Cherubini's Counterpoint* 63 The subject, or theme of the fugue, should neither be too long nor too short. **1866** ENGEL *Nat. Mus.* iii. 103 A manifold and clever treatment of the motives of which the theme consists, contributes especially to the oneness and clearness of a musical composition.

5. *Philol.* The inflexional base or stem of a word, consisting of the 'root' with modification or addition; thus in Gr. λείπειν and τέμνειν, the roots are λιπ, τεμ, the present themes or stems λειπ-, τεμν-; in τέκνον, the root is τεκ, the theme τεκνο-.

Formerly applied to the 1 pers. sing. pres. indic. of a verb; later identified with *root* (as in Greek); the modern application began with Curtius.

1530 PALSGR. Introd. 31 The fyrst [conjugation]..hath his thre chefe rotes..his theme, his preterit participle, and his present infynityve ever of many syllables. *Ibid.*, The thyrde [conjugation] hath his theme most commenly in *S*..as *je voys*..*je prens*..*je dis.* **1580** HOLLYBAND *Treas. Fr. Tong*, I call the Theame, speaking to the vnskilfull in the Latine tong, whereby we begin to decline a Verbe. **1615** BEDWELL *Index Assuract.* O iij, The theame or roote, as they call it, from whence it [*Koran*] is deriued, is..*Kara'*, to reade. **1741** WATTS *Improv. Mind* I. vii. §6 In reducing the words to their original or theme. **1870** F. A. MARCH *Compar. Gram. Ags.* §60 The variable final letters of a noun are its case-endings, the rest is its theme. **1875** WHITNEY *Life Lang.* x. 207 In the derivative theme or base.

6. *Astrol.* The disposition of the heavenly bodies at a particular time, as at the moment of a person's birth. Cf. HOROSCOPE *sb.* 1.

1652 GAULE *Magastrom.* 293 Augustus had..such a confidence in this fatidical praesagition, that he divulged his natalitial theme. **1727–41** CHAMBERS *Cycl.*, *Theme*, among astrologers, denotes the figure they construct when they draw the horoscope; representing the state of the heavens for a certain point, or moment required; *i.e.* the places of the stars, and planets, for that moment. **1775** ASH *Dict.*, *Theme*, ..a horoscope in astrology. [**1819** WILSON *Dict. Astrol.*, *Thema cœli*, a figure of the heavens.]

7. *Anc. Hist.* Each of the twenty-nine provinces into which the Byzantine empire was divided.

1788 GIBBON *Decl. & F.* xlviii. V. 13 The Anatolian *theme* or province. *Ibid.* liii. 464 An accurate survey of the provinces, the *themes*, as they were then denominated, both of Europe and Asia. **1864** BRYCE *Holy Rom. Emp.* ix. (1889) 135 Nicephorus demanded the 'theme' or province of Rome as the price of compliance.

8. *attrib.* and *Comb.*, as *themebook, -maker*; **theme music**, music which recurs in a film, television programme, or the like; also = *signature tune* s.v. SIGNATURE *sb.* 9; cf. *theme song, tune* below; **theme park** chiefly *U.S.*, an amusement park organized round a unifying idea or group of ideas; similarly **theme pub, restaurant**; **theme song, tune**, a song or tune which recurs in a musical play, film, or the like; also = *signature tune* s.v. SIGNATURE *sb.* 9; also *fig.*; cf. *theme music* above.

1916 JOYCE *Portrait of Artist* (1969) i. 47 Father Arnall gave out the *themebooks and he said that they were scandalous. *a* **1661** HOLYDAY *Juvenal* To Rdr., Surely thou wilt acknowledge Juvenal to be a poet, but Horace to be some poor *theme-maker. **1957** MANVELL & HUNTLEY *Technique Film Music* 226 Martin and Gaston (1954). '*Theme Music'... Sound-track recording of the music from the English version of the French film on children's drawings. **1967** *Listener* 17 Aug. 222/3 Electronic music..is certainly not restricted to the novel presentation of sounds in familiar patterns, like the theme music of *Dr Who.* **1976** A. DAVIS *Television: First Forty Years* 136 The commercial was a favourite with viewers and with advertising men. It won awards and its theme music was issued on record. **1960** *Amer. Peoples Encycl. Year Bk.* 881 While most established parks and kiddielands were profitable, the *theme parks, seeking to duplicate Disneyland's success, were often in trouble. **1967** *Encycl. Brit. Bk. of Year* 335/2 American-type theme parks around the world included Edenlandia Fun Park, Naples, Italy; Prater Fun Park, Vienna; and a new park, Centro de Diversion, opened at Puerto Rico's Isla Verde. **1983** *Times* 16 Aug. 15/3 The acquisition of a tourist attraction in London and a theme park outside the capital. *Ibid.* 19 July 17 A growth segment of the pub trade is emerging..*theme pubs. Their hall mark is a design concept to create a particularly individual atmosphere (the theme) with varying combinations of restaurant, cocktail bar and normal bar service. Various theme restaurants have emerged in the past five years. *Ibid.* 4 Nov. 17/3 Grand Metropolitan's Host Group..is to spend well over £100m over the next three years on converting its outlets to a wide range of theme pubs. **1983** *9,000 Words* 196/2 *Theme restaurants that look like railroad cars or Polynesian villages. **1929** *Theme song [see RELEASE *sb.*[1] 7 b]. **1946** KOESTLER *Thieves in Night* 348 The theme-song of all evolution is the trend towards greater articulateness. **1949** 'G. ORWELL' *Nineteen Eighty-Four* II. 149 The new tune which was to be the theme-song of Hate Week..had already been composed. **1977** J. FLEMING *Every Inch a Lady* III. vi. 141 Nathaniel returned to his theme-song..murder must have a plan, a blue-print. **1950** *Sport* 24–30 Mar. 15/4 'This couldn't happen again!' should be the *theme-tune of Doncaster Rovers' fans. **1983** *Listener* 21 Apr. 30/3 The furore over the *Today* theme-tune..perfectly illustrates the BBC attitude.

Hence **theme** *v. trans.*, to furnish with a theme or subject; **themed** *a.*, having a theme; ˈ**themeless** *a.*, without a theme, having no theme; ˈ**themer**, one who sets or proposes a theme; **themester** (ˈθiːmstə(r)), one who labours at a theme (*contemptuous*).

1594 R. SOUTHWELL *St. Peters Compl.*, etc. To Rdr., This *theames my heavie penne to plaine in prose. **1641** J. JACKSON *True Evang. T.* I. 10 [Points] capable to be spread out so as to theame the Preachers speech. **1979** S. BRETT *Comedian Dies* iii. 32 Great Expectations..was a concept restaurant, themed wittily around the works of Dickens. **1963** *Observer* 29 Sept. 7/4 A *themed sequence on summer holidays. **1977** *Broadcast* 28 Nov. 12/2 There are..possibilities for ethnic themed radio services. *Ibid.* 12/3 He continued the themed service subject. **1840** GALT *Demon of Destiny* VI. 41 The *themeless babble of his idiot child. **1611** TARLTON *Jests* (1844) 28 Such commendations Tarlton got, that hee supt with the bailiffe that night, where my *theamer durst not come, although he were sent for. **1843** *Blackw. Mag.* LIV. 105 Where now, base *themester?

theme, obs. f. TEAM (sense 8); also of THEM.

themel, -elle, obs. forms of THIMBLE.

‖**Themis** (ˈθɛmɪs, ˈθiːmɪs). [a. Gr. Θέμις, goddess of law and order, Justice personified.]

1. Name of the ancient Greek goddess of law and justice; hence, Law or Justice personified.

1656 BLOUNT *Glossogr.*, *Themis*, the Godesse of Justice, that gave out Oracles at Bœotia. **1784** COWPER *Task* III. 257 Such thine, in whom Our British Themis gloried with just cause, Immortal Hale. **1880** J. PAYN *Confid. Agent* iv, She found a rival, not in Themis, but in Isabel Thurlow.

2. *Astron.* Name of the twenty-fourth of the Asteroids, discovered 5 April 1853 by De Gasparis.

Themistian (θɪˈmɪstɪən). *Ch. Hist.* [f. *Themistius*, name of the founder of the sect (see quot. 1882–3) + -AN.] In plural: A sect of the MONOPHYSITES who attributed to Christ imperfect knowledge. Cf. AGNOITES.

1874 in BLUNT *Dict. Sects, Heresies, &c.* **1882–3** *Schaff's Encycl. Relig. Knowl.* I. 36 The second sect (founded in the sixth century by Themistius, deacon of Alexandria), sometimes called the Themistians. **1883** *Cath. Dict.* (1885) 598/1 The Themistians, or Agnoetæ, held that the human element in Christ before his resurrection was subject to ignorance.

themselves (ðəmˈsɛlvz), *pron. pl.* Forms: see THEM and SELF. [The original construction was nom., acc. *hí, héo selfe*, dat. *heom selfum*, whence ME. *hemselve(n*, etc. In 14th c. this was superseded in north. dial. by *þaim self(e, þaim selven*, and in Standard Eng. *themself* was the normal form to *c* 1540, but disappeared *c* 1570. *Themselfs, themselves* appears *c* 1500, and became the standard form *c* 1540. For *theirself, theirselves*, see III.]

I. Emphatic. = Those very persons or things.

1. Standing in apposition with the pronoun *they* (rarely *them*), or with a sb., or adj. used subst.

α. 13.. Cursor M. 3708 (Cott.) All þaa þat blisses þe Sal þam-self blessed be. Ibid. 8131 (Gött.) þaim-selue again þai tok þair sty [Cott. þamself a-gain tok þai sti], And went þaim þan to ethiopy. c1460 Towneley Myst. xxx. 566 Thare neghburs thai demyd Thaym self as it semyd. 1533 More Apol. 7 b, They se full well them selfe, that they saye not trew.

γ. 1502 in Lett. Rich. III & Hen. VII (Rolls) II. 107 Thei them selves coulde not acertayne us of the tyme. 1555 Eden Decades To Rdr. (Arb.) 53 More monstrous then the monsters theim selues. 1561 T. Hoby tr. Castiglione's Courtyer II. (1577) I vij b, Oftentimes to them themselues, they thrust out filthy and most dishonest wordes. 1651 Howell Venice 143 Approv'd of by the Popes Breve's themselfs. 1779 Mirror No. 54 ¶7 You tell us the effects of your feelings, child; but you don't distinguish the feelings themselves. 1810 Crabbe Borough ii. 110 Monuments themselves memorials need. 1872 Hardy Under Greenw. Tree Pref., Music-paper (which they mostly ruled themselves). 1876 Gladstone Glean. (1879) II. 295 Themselves knowing nothing of difficulty, or of obscurity, ..they are liable to be intolerant of other men who stumble.

2. Used alone for emphasis as a simple nominative. *arch.*

α. 1512 Helyas in Thoms Prose Rom. (1828) III. 30 Thiniuries that them self had made. 1549 Coverdale, etc. Erasm. Par. Rom. 38 Vnlearned people.., whiche thinke nothing rightful, but that them selfe do.

β. 13.. Cursor M. 23517 (Edin.) God..louis þaim als his auen sonis, Mar þan þaim-selwin lof þair driht [Cott. Mare þan þam-seluen luue þai dright].

γ. 1542 Udall Erasm. Apoph. 105 Theimselfes by great pielage..dooe growe dayly & encrease in welthe. 1624 Bedell Lett. x. 135 Themselues doe vtterly denie it. 1701 Swift Contests Nobles & Com. Wks. 1755 II. I. 51 To remember how themselves sate in fear of their persons. 1853 Lynch Self-Improv. ii. 44 People's timorousness..shows how insecurely grounded themselves are.

b. *to be themselves*: to be in their normal condition of mind, body, or behaviour: see SELF D. 1.

1698 Lister in Phil. Trans. XX. 247 They came so out of their Fits, that they were also well and as much themselves as ever. 1698 Fryer Acc. E. India & P. 379 Yet those..are always as lean as Skeletons, and seldom themselves.

3. As emphatic objective. Now chiefly as object of a preposition.

1375 Barbour Bruce XIII. 234 Ane of them-selwyne that wes thar Capitane of thame all thai maid. c1400 Destr. Troy 1582 To selle and to se as þaim selfe lyked. c1430 Lydg. Min. Poems (Percy Soc.) 108 But yt move of themselfe, for sothe they thynke yt ryghte nowghte. 1711 Addison Spect. No. 26 ¶5 The Monuments of their [Dutch] Admirals..represent them like themselves. 1764 Reid Inquiry i. §1 If we would know the works of God, we must consult themselves with attention and humility. 1825 Scott Betrothed xxvi, They have..sacked the houses of the Flemings, spoiled their goods, misused their families, and murdered themselves. 1827 —— Surg. Dau. iv. You are one of themselves, you know—Middlemas of that Ilk.

II. Reflexive: = L. *sibi, se*; F. *se, soi*; G. *sich*.

4. As direct obj. (accusative), indirect obj. (dative), or object of a preposition.

α. 13.. Cursor M. 386 (Cott.) Alkin things grouand..in þam self þaire seding bere. Ibid. 16455 þai ches þaim-self dampnacion. c1489 Caxton Sonnes of Aymon xxiv. 518 They putte themself so to flighte. 1493 Beverley MSS. in Rep. Hist. MSS. Comm. XLVI. 620 That the Drapers shall have a confraternite emong thame self..as other crafts hafe. a1548 Hall Chron., Edw. IV 239 Hys heyres and successors ..by them self, or their deputie should offer a hart of lyke weight and value. c1550 R. Bieston Bayte Fortune B iv b, All men..Enforce them selfe to please him.

β. 13.. Cursor M. 801 (Gött.) þan þai sau þaim seluen bare. Ibid. 3455 (Cott.) Til þay had o þam seluen might [Gött. þaim seluen; Fairf. ham-seluen; Trin. hem self]. 1375 Barbour Bruce I. 502 Fayn to mak thaim-selwyn fre. 1419 in Ellis Orig. Lett. Ser. II. I. 73 Thay kepe this good emonge thaim selven.

γ. 1502 in Lett. Rich. III & Hen. VII (Rolls) II. 107 Thei wold confesse them selves to be there as commissioners. a1548 Hall Chron., Hen. VIII 135 b, The remnant..lept ouer the castle wal, and so saued themselfes. 1565 Stapleton tr. Bede's Hist. 163 [They] did cast lotts equally amongst them selfs. 1611 Bible Gen. iii. 7 They..made themselues aprons. 1617 Moryson Itin. III. 70 The dores.. by waights are made to shut of themselves. 1647 Trapp Comm. 2 Thess. iii. 11 Whose whole life is to eat..and laugh themselves fat. 1779 Mirror No. 17 ¶15 Not to make fools of themselves. 1818 Scott Rob Roy xxvi, These Hielands of ours..are but a wild kind of warld by themsells. 1885 Manch. Exam. 16 Sept. 5/2 The points on which they differ among themselves.

5. In concord with a singular pronoun or sb. denoting a person, in cases where the meaning implies more than one, as when the sb. is qualified by a distributive, or refers to either sex: = himself or herself. Cf. THEY 2, THEM 2.

α. 1464 Rolls of Parlt. V. 513/2 Inheritements, of which any of the seid persones..was seised by theym self, or joyntly with other. c1489 Caxton Sonnes of Aymon i. 39 Eche of theym sholde..make theymselfe redy. 1533 More Apol. 55 b, Neyther Tyndale there nor thys precher..hath by theyr maner of expounynge..wonne them self mych wurshyp.

γ. 1600 Shaks. Lucr. 125 Euery one to rest themselues [ed. 1594 himselfe] betake. 1654–66 Earl Orrery Parthen. (1676) 147 All that happened, which every one assured themselves, would render him a large sharer in the general joy. 1874 Dasent Half a Life 3 Every one likes to keep it to themselves as long as they can.

III. From the 14th c. there has been a tendency to treat *self* as a sb. (= person, personality), and substitute *their* for *them* (cf. *his self*, HIMSELF IV.).

This is prevalent dialectally, but in literary Eng. has place only where an adj. intervenes, as *their own, sweet, very selves*. See SELF C. 1 a, and cf. OURSELF, OURSELVES.

α. 13.. Cursor M. 5378 (Cott.) To ches þam ware þair-self will neuen. Ibid. 6968 (Fairf.) Ilka kinrede of þa twelue Had an ouer-man be þaire [v.rr. ham, þaim, hem] selue. c1440 Alphabet of Tales 110 þai þat will commend þer selfe vnto þe devull. c1490 Caxton Rule St. Benet xxxiii. 129 Nor it is leefull ony to haue a thyng to theyrself propre. 1545 Ascham Toxoph. (Arb.) 101 They may hit a nother I trow and neuer take blow theyr selfe. a1912 Mod. Sc. Thai offert to dui't thersel. c1926 'Mixer' Transport Workers' Song Bk. 92 Their ambition is theirself. 1969 in Halpert & Story Christmas Mumming in Newfoundland 159 They used to work theirself from all shapes. They have a couple of pillows up their back and another one on their stomach. 1979 N. Mailer Executioner's Song I. xxvii. 422 All they want to do is leave theirself a case for appeal.

β. 13.. Cursor M. 3708 (Fairf.) Alle þa atte blessis þe Sal þaire-seluen [Cott. þam-self, Gött. þaim seluen] blessed be.

γ. 1500–20 Dunbar Poems xxiii. 27 Quhen thair baggis ar full thair selfis ar bair. 1525 Ld. Berners Froiss. II. 473 They had gret desyre to prove their selfes. c1560 A. Scott Poems (S.T.S.) xxx. 20 Till thay mischeif þair sellis. a1568 Ascham Scholem. (Arb.) 97 Liking it well their selues. 1659 Gauden Slight Healers (1660) 47 To commend their skill to the publique, by giving some good experiments on their selves. 1728 Morgan Algiers I. Pref. 22 They aver that they theirselves have been no less scandalized than I myself. a1836 Boothroyd Bible Ps. xxxvii 2 They theirselves stumbled and fell. 1901 M. Franklin My Brilliant Career xxxiii. 277 A new fowl-house which 'Horace and Stanley built all by theirselves'. 1907 G. B. Shaw Major Barbara II. 241 Arf the street prayed; an the tother arf larfed fit to split theirselves. a1912 Mod. Sc. Thai beikit thersel's in the sun. 1955 F. O'Connor Wise Blood x. 167 The unredeemed are redeeming theirselves and the new jesus is at hand! 1965 C. Brown Manchild in Promised Land xiii. 314 Them damn junkies take care of theirselves twice as good as you can.

themyl, -ylle, obs. (ME.) ff. THIMBLE.

then (ðɛn), *adv.* (*conj., adj., sb.*) Forms: see below. [OE. *þanne, þonne, þænne, þenne*, ME. *þenne, þan, þen*, = OFris. *thenne, thanne, than*, OS. *thanna, than* (MDu. *danne, dan*, Du. *dan*), OHG. *danne, denne* (MHG. *danne, denne*, G. *dann*); cf. also Goth. *þan*; adverbial formations from the demonstr. root *þa-*: cf. THAT, THE.

See also THAN *conj.*, orig. the same word, which in both senses varied in ME. and 16th c. between *then* and *than*. So Mod.Ger. now has *dann* adv. 'then', *denn* conj. 'than'. Du. has *dan* in both senses. The history in OTeut. presents many points of difficulty: see Per Persson in Indog. Forsch. II. 206, Van Helten in Paul & Br. Beitr. XXVIII. 564–5.]

A. Illustration of Forms.

α. 1–3 (5) **þonne.**

898 þonne [see B. 1]. 971 Blickl. Hom. 11 Ond þæt ȝeweorþeþ on domes dæȝe..þonne forhtiaþ ealle ȝesceafta. c1205 Lay. 711 þonne [c 1275 wane] men gað to bedde. [a1425 Cursor M. 7961 (Trin.) Dauid gat ȝitt a son þonne [rime salomonne].

β. 1–5 **þanne,** (3–4 **tanne**), 3–4 **þane,** 4 **thane,** 4–5 **thanne.**

871–89 Charter of Ælfred in O.E. Texts 451 þanne ȝeselle he cc peninga eȝhwylce ȝere. Ibid. 452 Ðanne ann ic ðem.. alles mines erfes to brucenne. c1200 Ormin 221, & tanne comm he siþþenn ut. Ibid., þanne [see B. 1]. c1205 Lay. 1546 þane [c 1275 wane] he wule..scaðe werc wrchen. a1300 Cursor M. 153 (Cott.) Hit sal be reddynn þanne [G. þane, F. þan]. Ibid. 21618 (Edin.) Ilke paskis..þis croce was tanne man wont to se. c1330 Assump. Virg. 767 But þei sawe in þat stede þana Liand as it were amana [= manna]. c1375 Sc. Leg. Saints xii. (Mathias) 353 þane kyste [= cast] þai cuttis til assay. c1440 Jacob's Well (E.E.T.S.) 191 þanne þis heued preyere doth þe no profyȝt.

γ. 1–3 **þænne.**

c1000 Ags. Ps. (Th.) xcv[i]. 5 Heofonas þænne worhte haliȝ Drihten. a1050 Byrhtferth's Handboc in Anglia VIII. 306 Swa fela tida beoð þænne on þam dæȝe & on þære nihte. c1205 Lay. 9521 þænne beoð hit þe wurse.

δ. 2–5 **þenne,** (3 **þeonne**), 4 **þene,** 4–6 **thenne,** 5 **þeyne, þynne, thynne, theynne.**

c1175 Lamb. Hom. 135 Ðenne þeȝs folkes larþew his sed wule sawen. c1205 Lay. 12037 [They] iseȝen scipen an & an ..þeonne [c 1275 þan] feowere þenne fiue. c1375 Sc. Leg. Saints xxxi. (Eugenia) 106 þe oure-men þat þe cite gouernyt þene. c1420 Avow. Arth. xxx, Thenne waknut the king. c1420 Chron. Vilod. 2078 Alle þey þenne for hurre gret sorwe þey made. Ibid. 2095 And sore weptone and snobbedone þeyne. Ibid. 3253 He was kyng of Englonde ȝet þynne. 1600 St. Papers Eliz., Domestic CLXXVIII. No. 78 (P.R.O.) Thenne he was at the same play.

ε. 2–4 **þann,** 3–4 **þan (tan),** 4–7 (*dial.* –9) **than** (5 **þon**); 4–5 **þen,** 5– **then.**

c1200 Ormin 4197 Domess daȝȝ, þann all mannkinn shall risenn. c1275 Lay. 6396 Morbidus þe bolde warþ þan a-bolwe. 13.. Cursor M. 367 (Gött.) þe world..þat ȝeit was þan [Cott. tan] of forme vnschapin. Ibid. 3860 (Cott.) Fra þan [c 1375 F. þen] wit laban duelled he. c1400 Ywaine & Gaw. 805 Hastily þan went þai all And soght him. a1425 Cursor M. 6152 (Trin.) þei were whenne þei to go bigon Six hundride þousonde fote men þon [all other MSS. bigan ..þan]. c1440 Then [see B. 4]. c1450 St. Cuthbert (Surtees) 1503 It falles oft þen and þen. a1568 Ascham Scholem. Pref. (Arb.) 17, I was glad than and do rejoice yet. 1643 Denham Cooper's H. 135 Than did Religion in a lazy Cell, In empty, aery Contemplations dwell.

B. Signification.

* *Demonstrative adverb of time.*

1. a. At that time. (Referring to a specified time, past or future: opposed to NOW 1.)

† *then as*, at the time that, when (= sense 6): see AS B. 27.

Beowulf 1456 Næs þæt þonne mætost mæȝen-fultuma þæt him on ðearfe lah ðyle hroð-gares. 898 O.E. Chron. an. 894 Swa hit þonne fierdleas wæs. c1200 Ormin 4200 Whase þanne [at doomsday] wurrþiȝ beoþ To takenn eche blisse. a1300 Cursor M. 14506 (Cott.) Biscops war þai þan [Trin. þo] a-bute. c1330 R. Brunne Chron. (1810) 2 In Westsex was þan a kyng, his [name] was Sir Ine. 1424 in Picton L'pool Munic. Rec. (1883) I. 22 That we should go with him to Liverpull, then as the said congregation and riots were ordained to be. c1449 Pecock Repr. I. xi. 55 The al hool Bible was not thanne. 1582 Allen Martyrd. Campion (1908) 85 Naming one but newly cummen then into the realme. 1605 Shaks. Macb. I. vii. 49 When you durst do it, then you were a man. 1632 Lithgow Trav. x. 492 Sir Walter Aston, then Leiger Ambassadour there. 1763 J. Brown Poetry & Mus. v. 67 Melody had then its greatest Power, when the Melody was most confined in its Compass. 1796 Lamb Let. to Coleridge 13 June, I hope to be able to pay you a visit (if you are then at Bristol) some time in..August. 1857 Buckle Civiliz. I. xiii. 717 History, as it was then written.

† b. Strengthened by *as* preceding: see AS B. 34 a.

1456 Sir G. Haye Law Arms (S.T.S.) 126 The autoritee of the grete officer slokis as than..the autoritee of the smallare officer. c1470 Henry Wallace I. 375 Off that labour as than he was nocht sle. 1523–1653 [see AS B. 34 a].

c. At the time defined by a relative or other clause (with verb in pres. tense). (Cf. NOW 4.)

1340 Hampole Pr. Consc. 468 þan has a man les myght þan a beste When he es born. 1456 Sir G. Haye Law Arms (S.T.S.) 120 It folowis nocht na the vertu of force..is alswele in his curage than as before. 1567 Maplet Gr. Forest A vij, As it is with yse which dissolueth, then when it vanisheth away. a1644 Quarles Sol. Recant. Sol. xii. 49 Give him the firstlings of thy strength, even than When fading Childehood seeks to ripen man Vpon thy downy cheeks. 1772 Toplady Hymn, 'Your harps, ye trembling saints' vii, When we in darkness walk,..Then is the time to trust our God. 1908 [Miss E. Fowler] Betw. Trent & Ancholme 43 Then is the time to turn our backs upon the sun.

d. *then and there* (†*then there*), at that precise time and place; immediately and on the spot. (Also *there and then*: see THERE *adv.* 13.)

1436 Rolls of Parlt. IV. 498 Ye said William..putte hir in a stronge chaumbre till nyght; and yen yere..felonousely.. ravysshed ye said Isabell. 1442 Ibid. V. 42/1 Which entre.. was thenne and there graunted. 1587 in Picton L'pool Munic. Rec. (1883) I. 63 It was then and there concluded by a general consent. 1600 Abp. Abbot Exp. Jonah 220 To be brought to the pits brinke, and then and there to be stayed. 1825 Scott Betrothed xxxi, The Constable De Lacy..was then and there to deliver to the Flemings a royal charter of their immunities. 1889 Jerome Three Men in Boat 212 We had insisted..that the things should be sent with us then and there.

2. *now and then*, † *then and then* (obs.), at one time and at another, at various times, at intervals, occasionally (cf. *here and there*). *now ..then..*, at one time..at another time. (See also NOW 6 b, 7 b.)

c1205 [see A. δ]. 13.. Cursor M. 1848 (Fairf.) þai..wende ay þan and þan to droun. 1398 Trevisa Barth. De P.R. XI. vii. (Bodl. MS.) lf. 108 b/2 It [rain]..comeþ doune thanne and thanne. c1450 St. Cuthbert (Surtees) 1467 He walde it tell' þan and þan. c1550 R. Bieston Bayte Fortune B iij, The ryche peraduenture oppresseth nowe and than. a1555 Philpot Exam. & Writ. (Parker Soc.) 334 If that those at any time, then and then, be deceived. 1670 Eachard Cont. Clergy 26 Now and then in an age, one miraculously, beyond all hopes, proves learned. 1763 C. Johnston Reverie II. 239 She listened to him.., asking him every now and then such questions as should [etc.]. a1825 Forby Voc. E. Anglia s.v. Tan, Than..loses the aspirate in one phrase only, 'now and tan' for 'now and then'. 1894 Baring-Gould Deserts S. France II. 245 Restive, now sullen, then in boisterous revolt.

** *Of sequence in time, order, consequence, incidence, inference.*

3. a. At the moment immediately following the action, etc. just spoken of; upon that, thereupon, directly after that; also in wider application, indicating the action or occurrence next in order of time: next, after that, afterwards, subsequently (often in contrast to *first*).

Sometimes, in narrative, introducing a speech with ellipsis of *said* (now *poet.* or *rhet.*).

971 Blickl. Hom. 21 Se mon se þe gód onginneþ & þonne ablinneþ. a1000 Phœnix 216 Bæl bið onæled þonne brond þeceð heoredreorges hus. a1225 Ancr. R. 36 þeonne valleð adun, & siggeð, 'Christe audi nos', twie. 13.. Cursor M. 3904 (Cott.) Rachell bare..First ioseph, þan beniamin. 1362 Langl. P. Pl. A. XII. 139 And þanne I kneled on my knes and kyste her wel sone. a1400–50 Alexander 95 þen Anec onane riȝt efter þire wordis, A lowde laȝter he loȝe. c1440 Alphabet of Tales 196 And þe bisshop sayd; 'Nay, son, þer is none now in all þis land'..And þan þis Malchus: 'In þis I hafe a great mervayle, ffor [etc.]'. 1526 Tindale Mark iv. 28 First the blad, then the eares, after that [R.V. 1881 then] full corne in the eares. a1533 Ld. Berners Huon lxxxvii. 277 He..sayd how he wolde slee Huon, & than haue Esclaramounde to his wyfe. 1627 Hakewill Apol. (1630) 214 He cast high in the aire, then received it againe in his armes. a1654 Selden Table-T (Arb.) 49 First we Fast, and then we Feast. 1776 Trial of Nandocomar 23/1 He was at first very ill, then got better; he is now worse. 1859 Tennyson Enid 300 Then Yniol, 'Enter therefore and partake [etc.]'. 1895 Law Times Rep. LXXIII. 21/2 The annuity was regularly paid up to 1878, then Mr. Harle got into difficulties.

b. In the next place, next (in a series of any kind, or esp. in order of narration); beyond that, more than that, in addition, besides. Phr. *and then some*: see SOME *indef. pron.* 4 f.

c1290 St. Michael 511 in S. Eng. Leg. I. 314 þat fuyr is hext,..þe eir is þanne next bi-neothe. 1297 R. Glouc. (Rolls) 64 Viue & þritti ssiren..Barcssire, & hamptessire, &

þanne middelsex. **1588** PARKE tr. *Mendoza's Hist. China* III. xxvi. 406 Then forwards on there are other two small kingdoms. **1596** SHAKS. *Tam. Shr.* II. i. 358 First,..my house within the City Is richly furnished..then at my farme I haue a hundred milch-kine. **1652** NEEDHAM tr. *Selden's Mare Cl.* 32 Then, it is added next, concerning the West-border [etc.]. **1707** FARQUHAR *Beaux Strat.* I. i, *Aim*[*well*]... What other company have you in Town? *Bon*[*iface*]. A power of fine Ladies; and then we have the French Officers. **1828** SCOTT *F.M. Perth* vi, Then there are the minstrels, with their romaunts and ballads. **1847** C. BRONTE *J. Eyre* xvi, And then she had such a fine head of hair.

4. a. In that case; in those circumstances; if that be (or were) the fact; if so; when that happens. Often correl. to *if* or *when*. ***what then?*** (ellipt.) what happens (or would happen) in that case? what of that?

695-6 *Laws of Wihtræd* c. 26 ʒif man friʒne man..ʒefo, þanne wealde se cyning ðreora anes [etc.]. **971** *Blickl. Hom.* 41 ʒif ʒe þonne ʒelyfaþ..þonne biþ hit eow nyt ʒeseald. *c* **1175** *Lamb. Hom.* 137 Đenne bið þes monnes wile ibeht mid þere elmisse. *c* **1205** LAY. 9521 þænne beoð hit þe wurse. *a* **1250** *Owl & Night.* 508 (Cott.) Wane þi lust is ago, þanne is þi song ago also. *c* **1374** CHAUCER *Troylus* II. 536 (585) Be ȝe wys as ȝe ben fayr to se, Wel in þe ringe than is the ruby set. *c* **1440** *York Myst.* iv. 69 An ye do, then shall ye dye. **1533** GAU *Richt Vay* (S.T.S.) 32 For quhy if he is owr fader thane ar we his barnis and aris. **1564** *Brief Exam.* ****ij, What then? Did he not appoynt temperall rites? **1593** SHAKS. *Lucr.* 380 O had they in that darkesome prison died, Then had they seene the period of their ill. *a* **1677** HALE *Prim. Orig. Man.* I. iii. 86 Then he could never have ridden out an eternal period. **1782** MISS BURNEY *Cecilia* v. ix, Suppose you..had never a farthing but of your own getting; where would you be then? **1826** *Art of Brewing* (ed. 2) 203 The screw is sometimes made of wood, and then it is mostly nine or ten inches diameter. **1925** L. ABERCROMBIE *Idea of Great Poetry* i. 8 We have busied ourselves, it not on our own account, then vicariously in the newspapers, with the appreciation of these poets in their several qualities. **1956** A. J. AYER *Probl. Knowledge* i. 7 Can it reasonably be held that knowledge is always knowledge that something is the case? If knowing that something is the case is taken to involve the making of a conscious judgment, then plainly it cannot. **1972** M. KLINE *Math. Thought* li. 1194 This is the principle of *reductio ad absurdum*. In words, if the assumption of *p* implies that *p* is false, then *p* is false.

b. ***but then*..**: but, that being so; but at the same time; but on the other hand, but: introducing a statement (rarely a phrase) in some way contrasted with or limiting the preceding.

1445 in *Anglia* XXVIII. 279 But than thi soule..right benygne to othir, A Juge grevous for shamefastnes is felt vnto thi selfe. **1599** SHAKS. *Much Ado* v. i. 205 He is then a Giant to an Ape, but then is an Ape a Doctor to such a man. **1672** VILLIERS (Dk. Buckhm.) *Rehearsal* III. i, It is not very necessary to the Plot..But then it's as full of Drollery as ever it can hold. **1774** GOLDSM. *Nat. Hist.* (1776) VI. 286 The Fishing Frog..very much resembles a tadpole or young frog, but then a tadpole of enormous size. **1826** DISRAELI *Viv. Grey* I. iv, There was..some difficulty in keeping all things in order, but then Vivian Grey was such an excellent manager! **1887** BIRRELL *Obiter Dicta* Ser. II. *Pope* Ess. 1899 I. 182 Pope knew next to no Greek, but then he did not work upon the Greek text.

c. ***or then*** = or, if not, then..; or failing that; or else, or otherwise; or even. *Sc.*

1375 BARBOUR *Bruce* I. 217 Gud Knychtis..For litill enchesoune or than nane, Thai hangyt be the nekbane. **1513** DOUGLAS *Æneis* I. vi. 43 Quhiddir thou be Dyane,..Or than sum goddes of the nymphis kynd. **1596** DALRYMPLE tr. *Leslie's Hist. Scot.* (S.T.S.) I. 7 Verie conuenient to feid horse or nout, or flockis of scheip or gait, or than grett harte and hyne. **1634** RUTHERFORD *Lett.* (1881) 500 Pray Him to tarry, or then to take us with Him. **1636** *Ibid.* 320 They are ..valuing Him at their unworthy halfpenny or else exchanging and bartering Christ with the miserable old fallen house of this vain world, or then they lend Him out upon interest. **1825** JAMIESON s.v., Come hame sune, or than I'll be angry.

5. (As a particle of inference, often unemphatic or enclitic.) That being the case; since that is so; on that account; therefore, consequently, as may be inferred; so. ***now then***: see NOW 9 b.

971 *Blickl. Hom.* 39 Us is þonne mycel nedþearf þæt we ʒebuʒon to him. *c* **1230** *Hali Meid.* 5 Nis ha þenne sariliche ..akast & in to þewdom idrahen. **1297** R. GLOUC. (Rolls) 2491 Sire graunte me þanne..As moche place as mid a þuong ich may aboute tille. **13..** *Cursor M.* 5987 (Gött.) Wend on þann, siþen ȝe wil ga. *c* **1400** *Apol. Loll.* 4 It is certayn þan, þowe he be his seruaunt. ? *a* **1500** *Wycket* (1828) p. v, Why shoulde it then be taken awaye frome us. **1539** BIBLE (Great) *2 Sam.* iii. 18 Now then do it. **1598** SHAKS. *Merry W.* II. ii. 35 *Fal.* Good-morrow, good-wife. *Qui.* Not so, and't please your worship. *Fal.* Good maid then. **1600** —— *A.Y.L.* IV. iii. 176 Well then, take a good heart, and counterfeit to be a man. **1668** MILTON *P.L.* The Verse, This neglect then of Rime so little is to be taken for a defect..that [etc.]. **1773** GOLDSM. *Stoops to Conq.* v. ii, *Hast.* This is a riddle. *Tony.* Riddle me this then. **1821** SCOTT *Kenilw.* xx, 'Ha!' said the Countess, hastily; 'that rumour then is true, Janet'. **1884** W. C. SMITH *Kildrostan* 86 We give up our cruise, then, after all?

*** *As relative or conjunctive adv. of time.*

†**6.** At the time that; when. *Obs.*

971 *Blickl. Hom.* 17 þonne se mona wanað, þonne tacnað he ure deaþlicnesse. *c* **1000** ÆLFRIC *Colloq.* in Wr.-Wülcker 88/13 Swyþe waxʒeorn eart þu, þonne [L. *cum*] þu ealle þingc etst. **1056-66** *Inscr. Kirkdale Ch., Yorks.*, Orm.. bohte scs Gregorivs minster ðonne hit wes æl tobrocan & tofalan. *c* **1175** *Lamb. Hom.* 35 Ne beo he nefre swa riche, forð he scal þenne is dei cumeð. *c* **1200** ORMIN 8401 He wass, þanne he þiderr for, Neh off an ȝeress elde. *a* **1250** *Owl & Night.* 420 (Cott.) þu forbernest welneȝ for onde þane ure blisse cumeþ to londe. *c* **1300** *Harrow. Hell* (MS. E.) 37 þan ihesu hadde spilt his blod For our sinnes on þe rode, He nam him þe riȝt way Vnto helle. *c* **1425** *Eng. Conq. Irel.* 4 Than hir lord hit herde, he was ther-of tened swith stronge. *a* **1440** *Sir Eglam.* 286 Then hys howndys began to baye, That harde [= heard] the jean there he laye.

**** *As sb. or adj.*

7. a. Preceded by a preposition, as *by*, *since*, *till*, etc. (= by, etc. that time). (Cf. NOW 13.)

a **1300** *Cursor M.* 10953 (Cott.) Als he forwit [*Gött.* bifore] þan was wont. **1340** HAMPOLE *Pr. Consc.* 4647 Fra þan Til þe day of dome. *a* **1400** *R. Glouc.'s Chron.* (Rolls) App. G. 258 King belin after þan to þis lond gan wende. *c* **1430** *Chev. Assigne* 143 By þenne was þe hermyte go in-to þe wode. **1509** BP. FISHER *Funeral Serm. C'tess of Richmond* Wks. (E.E.T.S.) I. 294 The matrynes of our lady, which kepte her to then. **1667** MILTON *P.L.* I. 93 Till then who knew The force of those dire Arms? **1794** MRS. RADCLIFFE *Myst. Udolpho* xlii, All the time between then and now seems as nothing. **1884** *Punch* 26 Apr. 197/2, I used your Soap Two Years ago; since then I have used no other. **1905** *Daily News* 5 Jan. 6 The little man..had by then recovered himself.

b. ***by then that***, by the time that; ellipt. ***by then*** (as relative), by the time: see BY A. 21 c. Now *arch.* or *dial.*

? *a* **1400** *Morte Arth.* 99 By than that endyd was the fight, The fals were feld. **1470-85** MALORY *Arthur* I. x. 49 By than they were redy on horsbak, there were vij C knyghtes. *c* **1500** *Robin Hood* 1737 By than the yere was all agone, He had no man but twayne. **1634** MILTON *Comus* 540 This evening late by then the chewing flocks Had ta'n their supper on the savoury Herb..I sate me down. **1788** T. TAYLOR *Proclus' Comm.* (1792) I. 12 By then he was twenty-eight years of age he composed a multitude of works. **1863** READE *Hard Cash* I. v. 157 By then he had folded and addressed it, she returned. **1906** *Graphic* 29 Dec. 892/1 By then ye've been church-cried, I'll be in t' chimney corner like any proper old gaffer.

8. That time; the time referred to (esp. a past time): often contrasted with *now*. Cf. NOW 14, 15.

1549-50 PAGET *Let.* 22 Feb. in Strype *Eccl. Mem.* II. App. II, The tyme is tourned then was then, and now is now. **1601** SHAKS. *All's Well* III. ii. 62 When thou canst get the Ring vpon my finger, which neuer shall come off,..then call me husband: but in such a (then) I write a Neuer. **1674** N. FAIRFAX *Bulk & Selv.* 161 God could bring forth the world at that *then*, wherein or when he had cast with himself the world could afterwards be made. **1847** W. THOM in *Whistlebinkie* (1890) II. 234 Companion of my happy then! **1901** *Daily News* 19 Mar. 6/3 He reveals a corresponding contrast between the then and the now.

9. a. In sense 1, followed by a participle or adjective forming an adj. phrase, as *the then existing system* = the system then existing. (See also 10 a.)

1653 BAXTER *Saints' R.* II. vi. §2 (ed. 4) 257 That the extirpation of Piety was the then great design. **1827** SCOTT *Highl. Widow* ii, The then unwonted circumstance..of a passenger being seen on the high-road. **1870** LOWELL *Among my Bks.* Ser. I. (1873) 6 The trivium..and the quadrivium..of the then ordinary university course. **1888** BRYCE *Amer. Commw.* (1889) I. xlvi. 548 The then existing Constitution.

b. *attrib.* or as *adj.* That existed or was so at that time; *the then ruler* = the ruler that then was. (Cf. NOW 16.)

1584 ? SIDNEY *Earl of Leicester* Misc. Wks. (1829) 263 He saith they are no gentlemen, affirming, that the then duke of Northumberland was not born so. **1620** E. BLOUNT *Horæ Subs.* 367 To the then Bishop of Rome. *a* **1647** PETTE in *Archæologia* XII. 255 The most noble prince, my then master. **1765** BLACKSTONE *Comm.* I. ii. 157 A bill..was countenanced by the then ministry, for limiting the number of the peerage. **1876** L. STEPHEN *Hist. Eng. Th. 18th C.* I. 203 In the then state of critical enquiry.

***** **10.** *Comb.* **a.** *adv.*, with pples. or adjs., as ***then-current***, ***-instant***, ***-known***, ***-ruling***, ***-united*** (cf. 9 a); **b.** *attrib.*: **then-clause**, the apodosis in a conditional sentence; †**then-skill**, a reason belonging to the particular time or occasion (cf. SKILL *sb.* 3): ***for a then-skill***, for the occasion; **then-time**, the time that was then, the past time referred to.

1602 WARNER *Alb. Eng.* Epit., The said Edmund (whom the Duke's faction for a then-Skill surnamed Crook backe). **1605** SYLVESTER *Du Bartas* II. iii. III. *Law* 198 While the then-Time's hideous face and form Boads them (alas!) nothing but wrack and storm. **1621** G. SANDYS *Ovid's Met.* VIII. (1626) 165 Whose waues..That then-vnited masse of earth dis-ioyne. *a* **1656** BP. HALL *Rev. Unrevealed* §11 The expectation of the then-instant appearing of Christ. **1750** S. RICHARDSON *Let.* 4 June (1964) 161 From robbery to robbery they proceeded, till they had enlarged their den so as to take in the greatest part of the then-known world. **1848** C. C. CLIFFORD *Aristoph., Frogs* 40 Without the leave Of the then-ruling powers. **1905** G. B. SHAW *Let.* 28 Sept. (1972) II. 563 She subscribed to the philosophy of a then-current song, 'I Want What I Want When I Want It'. **1927** G. A. GRIERSON *Ling. Survey India* I. I. 376 If the conditional sentence is such a one as we would require the use of 'would' or 'would have' in English, the word *sik* is appended to the apodosis, or then-clause. **1962** *John o' London's* 22 Feb. 188/3 *Would* is often used to express a wish..as in..the *then*-clause of a conditional sentence, as in 'You would enjoy it if you went'. **1976** *Scotsman* 24 Dec. (Weekend Suppl.) 3/2 The military republic of Julius Caesar that ruled the then-known world. **1978** *Detroit Free Press* 5 Mar. c 24/5 (Advt.), The interest..will be recalculated..at the then-current regular passbook interest rate.

Hence **then** *v.* (*nonce-wd.*), in phr. ***to now it and then it***: see NOW.

then, obs. f. THAN; obs. inflexion of THAT, THE.

then, variant of THENNE *Obs.*, thence.

thenabouts (ˈðɛnəˈbaʊts), *adv.* Also (rarely) **thenabout**. [f. THEN *adv.*, after *thereabouts*.] About that time.

1589 PUTTENHAM *Eng. Poesie* I. vi. (Arb.) 27 For then aboutes began the declination of the Romain Empire. **1842** R. OASTLER *Fleet Papers* II. 344, I was mentioned more than once thenabouts. **1843** DICKENS *Martin Chuzzlewit* (1844) xiii. 164 Five year ago, or thenabout. **1844** TUPPER *Crock of G.* xxiv, Then, or thenabouts, the devil hinted 'steal it'. **1922** *Times Lit. Suppl.* 19 Oct. 664/2 If Archdeacon Brandon.. must go down, it is then or thenabouts that go down he will. *a* **1967** A. RANSOME *Autobiogr.* (1976) i. 18 When I first came to fish the Beela..in 1930 or thenabouts.

thenad (ˈθɛn-, ˈθiːnæd), *adv. Anat.* [f. THEN-AR + *-ad*: see DEXTRAD.] Towards the thenal aspect.

1803 BARCLAY *New Anat. Nomencl.* 166 Ulnad will signify towards the ulnar aspect... Thenad..towards the thenal. **1808** —— *Muscular Motions* 397 The pronators rolling them thenad and radiad. **1857** DUNGLISON *Med. Lex.*, *Thenad* is used adverbially..to signify 'towards the thenal aspect'.

then-a-days (ˈðɛnədeɪz), *adv. rare.* [f. THEN *adv.*, after *nowadays*.] In those days, at that (past) time.

1688 R. L'ESTRANGE *Brief Hist. Times* III. 9 At Length, through a Wonderful Providence (as Providence went Then-a-Days) both these Wants were supply'd. **1768** ROSS *Helenore* II. 87 'Bout then a days we never met wi' cross. **1844** *N. Brit. Rev.* II. 56 Then-a-days one could acquire a very complete knowledge of chemistry..in a very short space of time. **1898** M. B. EDWARDS in *Westm. Gaz.* 20 July 2/3 Then-a-days, ah! then-a-days, All the months were merry Mays.

†**then ˈafter, theˈnafter**, *adv. Obs.* After then, after that time: = THEREAFTER.

1470-85 MALORY *Arthur* X. i. 494 And thenne after he gaf hym a drynke. **1485** *Rolls of Parlt.* VI. 285/2 Unabled fro thenceforth for ever, to claime, have or enjoy, any of the premisses, by him thenne after. **1605** T. SPARKE *Brotherly Perswasion* (1607) 6 Homilies then published and authorised, or to be then after published and authorised. **1791** *Selby Bridge Act* 14 At all times for ever thenafter.

So † **then afterward(s** *adv. phr.* in same sense.

a **1485** FORTESCUE *Wks.* (1869) 486 Thanne afterward he ..destroied the Reame of Assury. **1597** BEARD *Theatre God's Judgem.* (1612) 99 He..was condemned for an Heretike by the Nicene Councell, and his books burned: and then after-wards making shew before Constantine the Emperour, with a solemne oath to recant his old errours. **1671** H. M. *Erasm. Colloq.* 226 What didst thou then afterward?

thenal (ˈθiːnəl), *a. Anat.* [f. THEN-AR + -AL[1].] Of or pertaining to the thenar.

1803 BARCLAY *New Anat. Nomencl.* 125 We may use the terms Radial and Ulnar to signify the two lateral parts... To the other two sides we may give the epithets Anconal and Thenal. **1808** —— *Muscular Motions* 398 Being thenal flexors of the carpus. **1823** J. LIZARS *Syst. Anat. Plates* I. v. 94 The muscles on the palmar or thenal aspect.

thenar (ˈθiːnə(r)). *Anat.* Also 8 **tenar, thenor, tenor.** [mod.L., a. Gr. θέναρ palm of the hand, sole or flat of the foot. Cf. OHG. *tenar*, MHG. *tener*; F. *thénar* (16th c.).] The ball of muscle at the base of the thumb; the palm of the hand; the sole of the foot.

1672 SIR T. BROWNE *Let. to Friend* §10 The Thenar or Muscle of the Thumb. **1704** J. HARRIS *Lex. Techn.* I, *Tenar*, .. *Thenor*, or *Tenor*, according to some, is the Name for an abducent Muscle which draws the Thumb from the Fore-finger. **1857** DUNGLISON *Med. Lex.*, *Thenar*, the palm of the hand, or sole of the foot.

b. *attrib.* or as *adj.* ***thenar muscles***, the muscles which form the ***thenar eminence***, the ball at the base of the thumb.

1857 DUNGLISON *Med. Lex.*, *Thenar* or *Thenal Muscle*, Riolan and Winslow give this name to the fleshy mass, formed of the abductor brevis. **1898** P. MANSON *Trop. Diseases* xiv. 224 So may the thenar, the hypothenar, and the arm muscles [be found tender]. **1899** *Allbutt's Syst. Med.* VII. 209 A distinct flattening of the thenar eminence.

thenardite (θɛˈnɑːdaɪt, tɛ-). *Min.* [Named in honour of L. J. Thénard, French chemist: see -ITE[1].] Anhydrous sodium sulphate occurring in white or brown translucent crystals.

1842 *Penny Cycl.* XXIV. 310/2 Thenardite—(Anhydrous Sulphate of Soda)—occurs crystallized... It is used in the preparation of carbonate of soda. **1868** DANA *Min.* 616 The water exudes during winter from the bottom of a basin, and becoming concentrated in the summer season, deposits crystals of thenardite.

Thénard's blue (ˈteɪnɑːz bluː). The name of a bright blue pigment of considerable stability invented by the French chemist Louis-Jacques *Thénard* (1777–1857), consisting essentially of cobalt aluminate; cobalt blue.

1837 *Penny Cycl.* VII. 301/1 Phosphate of Cobalt..is used in making a pigment known by the name of Thenard's or Cobalt Blue. **1911** *Encycl. Brit.* XXI. 599/1 Several mixed cobalt compounds..represented by cobalt violet and Thénard's blue. **1958** *Listener* 2 Oct. 514/2 With their vivid Thénard's blue, the gleaming black of some of the boots and of Dick Turpin's horse..they have a place with the painted fair-ground horses and round-abouts. **1974** *Encycl. Brit. Micropædia* IX. 930/3 In 1799 he [*sc.* Thénard] made a discovery that assured him prosperity—Thenard's blue, a pigment used in the colouring of porcelain.

† **the'nasmon**, var. TENASMON *Obs.*

c **1400** *Lanfranc's Cirurg.* 290 þou schalt acese þe akynge wiþ þis medicyn, & is good for thenasmon.

thence (ðɛns), *adv.* Forms: 3–4 **þannes**, 4 **þ-**, **thennus**, 4–5 **þ-**, **thennes**, **-is**, **-ys**, **þens**, 4–6 **thens**, 5 **þenns**, 5–6 **thense**, 6– **thence**. [ME. *þannes*, *þennes*, f. THENNE *adv.*, with adverbial genitive suffix *-es*, *-s*. The later spelling *thence* for *thens* was to preserve the breath sound of *s* when final inflexional *s* became (z); as in *hence*, *pence*, *defence*, *once*, *twice*, *mice*, *price*, etc.]

1. From that place; from there. (Now chiefly *literary*.)

c **1290** *S. Eng. Leg.* I. 50/137 And bad heom of þulke holie bodi: þat huy it þannes bere. **1340** *Ayenb.* 12 Ha [Christ] wente into helle..uor to draȝe þannes..þe zaules of þe holi uaderes. **1340–70** *Alex. & Dind.* 98, I..am temted ful tid to turne me þennus. **13..** *Cursor M.* 164 (Gött.) Hu þat he was þennis [*Trin.* þennes; *Cott.* theþen] ledd. *c* **1386** CHAUCER *Frankl. T.* 232 Er they thennes [*v.rr.* þennes, þens, thens] wente..They fille in speche. *c* **1400** *Brut* 103 Þat men myȝt hit nouȝt remeve ne bere þenns. *Ibid.* 114 Or he departede þens. **1526** TINDALE *Mark* vi. 1 He departed thens and cam in to his awne countre. **1536** WRIOTHESLEY *Chron.* (Camden) I. 51 The Kinge with his companye departed thense. **1667** MILTON *P.L.* I. 12 If Sion hill Delight thee more,..I thence Invoke thy aid. **1867** LADY HERBERT *Cradle L.* iv. 123 Thence..the pilgrims came to the beautiful low shrine. **1895** *Law Times Rep.* LXXIII. 156/2 The 'Kirkmichael' left Liverpool..on a voyage thence to Melbourne.

b. Preceded by redundant *from* († *fro*).

1382 WYCLIF *Mark* vi. 1 And Jhesus gon out thennis [*v.r.* fro thennes]. **1388** *Ibid.*, And he ȝede out fro thennus. *c* **1400** *Destr. Troy* 13270 To a perellus place past I fro thens. **1535** COVERDALE *Baruch* vi. 2 After that wil I bringe you awaye peaceably from thence. **1609** HOLLAND *Amm. Marcell.* XXI. x. 177 He commanded Victor the Hystoriographer, whom he saw at Sirmium, to come from thence unto him. **1703** POPE *Thebais* 383 Begin from thence, where first Alpheus hides His wand'ring stream. **1867** GEO. ELIOT in Cross *Life* (1883) III. 9 Making our way homeward from thence by easy stages.

†**c.** As a relative (also *thence that*): From which place, whence. *Obs. rare.*

a **1450** *Knt. de la Tour* (1906) 36 Y must to the erthe thennes that y come fro.

2. At a place distant or away from there; distant; absent. Now chiefly in stating distance.

c **1290** *Beket* 1780 in *S. Eng. Leg.* I. 157 To longe ich habbe þannes i-beo. *c* **1384** CHAUCER *H. Fame* II. 530 Lat a man stond..A myle thens and here hyt route. **1450–1530** *Myrr. our Ladye* 28 Though they..haue leue to be thense yet yt suffysyth not. **1489** CAXTON *Faytes of A.* IV. x. 257 True proues that all that day he was ferre thens. *a* **1548** HALL *Chron., Edw. V* 13 While one manne is there, which is neuer thence. *Mod.* Two miles thence is a fine waterfall.

3. From that time or date; thenceforward; thenceforth. Mostly with *from*. ? *Obs.*

c **1374** [see THENCEFORTH 1]. **1382** WYCLIF *Isa.* xvi. 13 The wrd that the Lord spac to Moab fro thennys [1388 fro that tyme]. *c* **1449** PECOCK *Repr.* II. ix. 197 He seid that peple schulde frothens after worschipe. **1606** G. W[OODCOCKE] *Hist. Justine* xx. 78 That no subiect of Carthage should from thence learne Greeke letters. *a* **1751** BOLINGBROKE *Stud. Hist.* (1752) I. vi. 236 From thence down to the present day. *a* **1832** BENTHAM *Mem. & Corr.* Wks. 1843 X. 62, I must have seen him..more than once at Romilly's, and thence afterwards at my own house.

4. From that, as a source, origin, or cause; (as an inference) from those premisses or data; therefrom. Also preceded by *from*.

1652 NEEDHAM tr. *Selden's Mare Cl.* 2 Next are premised som things, for explaining the terms of the Question, that it may bee clearly thence understood. **1692** E. WALKER *Epictetus' Mor.* ix, Weigh every Circumstance, each Consequence, And usual Accident arising thence. **1796** H. HUNTER tr. *St.-Pierre's Stud. Nat.* (1799) II. 409 It would thence follow, that..the number of women would daily go on [etc.]. **1817** JAS. MILL *Brit. India* II. v. ix. 702 They could present to parliament every thing which favoured their own purposes, keep back every thing which opposed them; and thence more effectually deceive the nation.

thence-'after. *rare.* After that time; thereafter.

1593 *Tell-Troth's N.Y. Gift* (1876) 18 Thence after they must sit no more in the shoppes. **1864** NEALE *Seaton. Poems* 187 Those blessed feet, thenceafter nailed Fast to the bitter cross! **1921** B. JARRETT *English Dominicans* ix. 180 The boy finished what remained of his noviciate..and thenceafter was no longer interfered with. **1932** BELLOC *Napoleon* iii. 182 Thenceafter, for a week or more, it was intrigue upon intrigue.

thenceforth ('ðɛnsfɔəθ, ðɛns'fɔəθ), *adv.* [Orig. two words: THENCE and FORTH *adv.*]

1. From that time onward. Also with *from* (†*fro*).

c **1374** CHAUCER *Boeth.* IV. Pr. iii. 86 (Camb. MS.) For no wiht as by Ryht fro thennes forth þat hym lakketh goodnesse ne shal ben clepyd good. **1526** TINDALE *John* xix. 12 From thence forthe sought Pilate meanes to loose hym. **1536** WRIOTHESLEY *Chron.* (Camden) I. 55 To be observed and kept from thencefourth through all this realme. **1590** SPENSER *F.Q.* I. ii. 40 Thensforth I tooke Duessa for my Dame. **1812** SOUTHEY *Omniana* II. 231 He makes a law, that from thenceforth there shall be only two lawyers in England. **1870** MORRIS *Earthly Par.* I. I. 396 Thenceforth her back upon the world she turned.

2. From that place or point onward. *rare.*

c **1449** PECOCK *Repr.* V. xi. 540 Rede there and frothens forth into the eende of the argument. **1887** MORRIS *Odyss.* XII. 429 Night-long thenceforth was I carried.

thence'forward, *adv.* [Orig. two words: THENCE and FORWARD *adv.*] = prec. Also with *from* (†*fro*).

1457 *Cal. Anc. Rec. Dublin* (1889) 294 Fro thens forward al thos that ben abyll to be jurys. **1472–3** *Rolls of Parlt.* VI. 30/2 To be from thensforward true Liegemen. **1677** CARY *Chronol.* II. II. III. ii. 226 From thence-forward they might safely betake themselves to their Labours. **1732** BERKELEY *Alciphr.* IV. §14 As an artist leaves a clock, to go thenceforward of itself for a certain period. **1856** FROUDE *Hist. Eng.* II. x. 430 No monks, thenceforward, were to leave the precincts of the monastery.

† **thence'forwards**, *adv. Obs.* [f. as prec. + FORWARDS.] = prec.

1684 T. BURNET *Th. Earth* I. 180 A new order then setled in nature, which should continue thence forwards so long as the earth endur'd. **1727** *Bradley's Fam. Dict.* s.v. *Hen*, Let them continue so for two Days without touching them, and from thenceforwards to the twentieth turn them.

thence-from, *adv. arch.* [An inversion of *from thence*: cf. *hence-from*.] From that place or source; thence.

a **1618** SYLVESTER *Wood-man's Bear* lxxi, Thence-from crafty Cupid shot All the Arrows of his quiver. **1666** J. SMITH *Old Age* (1676) 240 They flow not thence-from. **1856** PATMORE *Angel in Ho.* II. II. i, My life is hid with him in Christ, Never thencefrom to be enticed.

† **thence-'out**, *adv. Obs.* [f. THENCE + OUT *adv.*] Out of that place; out from there.

1614 RALEIGH *Hist. World* II. 401 Adad..inuaded Damascus, and thrust Rezon thence-out.

† **'thenceward**, *adv. Obs.* [f. THENCE *adv.* + -WARD.] From that direction; thence.

c **1440** CAPGRAVE *St. Kath.* III. 1015 (MS. Arundel) But this noble Adryan..had blisse I-now assigned to his part, He had so moche he was ful looth thens-wart. *c* **1440** *Alphabet of Tales* 291 He delyverd þe Holi Lande oute of Saracens handis, and come fro thens-ward be Constantynople. **1600** ABP. ABBOT *Exp. Jonah* 566 Whatsoever was to come, being to come from thence-ward.

thenche, þenche, obs. ff. THINK *v.*[1] and [2].

thend, -e, pr. pple. of THEE *v.*[1], to prosper.

thene, þene, obs. forms of THAN, THEN; obs. acc. sing. masc. of THAT, THE.

thenforth, -forthward: see THENNE.

thenk(e, þenk(e, obs. ff. THINK *v.*[1] and [2].

† **thenne, then**, *adv. Obs.* Forms: α. 1 **þanon(n)e**, **þonane**, **þonone**, 2–3 **þonene**, 2–5 **þanane**, 3 **þanene**, **þeonene**, **þenene**. β. 3 **þonne**, 3–4 **þanne**, **þeonne** (3 **þeone**), 3–5 **þenne** (3 **þene**), 4–5 **thenne**. γ. 1 **þanan**, **-on**, **-un**, **þonan**, **-on**, 2 **þenen**, **þeonen**, 2–3 **þanen**. δ. 1 **þona**. ε. 4–5 **þen**, **þan**, 5 **then**. See also THYNE. [OE. *þanone*, *þanon*, *þonan*, etc. = OFris. *thana*, OS. *thanana*, *thanân*, ODu. **panna* (MDu. *danne*, *dan*, Du. *dan*), OHG. *thanana*, *than(n)ân*, *dan(n)ân* (MHG., Ger. *dannen*), Goth. type **þanana*: all formed by the addition of particles to the stem *þa-* of the demonstrative THAT.

As to the relations of the OE. forms, the β group may have arisen from the α, with loss of the middle vowel: *þan(o)ne*, *þanne*, etc. From the β forms, loss of the final *e* gave *than*, *then*, as in THEN *adv.* The δ *þona* is app. the northern form of *þonan* in γ. But the prehistoric development in OTeut. and the relation of the preh. forms to those of THEN, is very obscure: see the articles referred to under THEN.]

1. Of motion: **a.** From that place; = THENCE 1.

α. *a* **900** CYNEWULF *Judith* xi. 132 Eodon ða geġnum þanonne þa idesa ba ellenþriste. *c* **1000** *Ags. Gosp.* Matt. v. 26 Ne gæst þu þanone [*Lindisf.* ðona, *Rush.* þonan, *Hatton* þanen] ær þu aȝylde þone ytemestan feorðlingc. *c* **1175** *Þe Lesse Crede* in *Lamb. Hom.* 217 þonene he kumeð to demen ðe quike and ðe deade. *c* **1205** LAY. 235 Sone he þonene [*c* **1275** þanene] iuatte. *Ibid.* 1297 þeonene [*c* **1275** þanene] he ferde forð. **1297** R. GLOUC. (Rolls) 1050 Brut..þat his fader slow, & þeruore was þenene [*later v.rr.* þenne, þanne, þens, þennys] idriue.

β. *c* **1205** LAY. 654 Nolde he þonne [*c* **1275** þanne] fare. *Ibid.* 5971 þæ Belin þeonne [*c* **1275** þanne] wende. *Ibid.* 31362 To fleomen hine þenne. *c* **1230** *Hali Meid.* 43 þeone godd warþ hire. *a* **1250** *Owl & Night.* 132 Euer he cuþ þat he comme þenne [*v.r.* þonne]. *c* **1300** *Havelok* 1185 þer to dwellen, or þenne to gonge. **1362** LANGL. *P. Pl.* A. I. 71 Er heo þeonne ȝeode. *c* **1440** *Pallad. on Husb.* XII. 325 Pike all the filthes thenne.

γ. *Beowulf* (Z.) 1806 Wolde feor þanon cuma collen-ferhð ceoles neosan. *c* **725** *Corpus Gloss.*, *Illinc*, þanan. **971** *Blickl. Hom.* 67 He.. þa halȝan sauwla þonon alædde. *c* **1000** *Ags. Gosp.* Matt. xi. 1 He for þanun [*c* **1160** *Hatton G.* for þanen]. *a* **1131** *O.E. Chron.* an. 1123, þeonen he ferde to Wudestoke. *Ibid.*, Ða ferde se kyng þenen to Portesmuðe. *a* **1175** *Cott. Hom.* 241 þanen hit was ibroht up into heofene.

δ. *c* **950** *Lindisf. Gosp.* Luke xii. 59 Ne gæs ðu ðona oðð [etc.].

ε. **13..** *Cursor M.* 8945 (Cott.) þe tre þai vte o þe temple drogh..þai drou it þen [*v.rr.* þeiþen, þennes]. *c* **1425** *Ibid.* 6676 (Laud) Men shall hym þan draw to die. *Ibid.* 16908 Er they then went. *c* **1420** *Chron. Vilod.* 3000 þat þulke relekes nolde neuer go þen a-way.

b. With redundant *from*: = THENCE 1 b.

1297 R. GLOUC. (Rolls) 7743 Fram salesburi to wiȝt He wende & fram þanene to normandie riȝt. *Ibid.* 8224 Fram þanene hii wende.

c. As a relative adverb: Whence, from where.

c **950** *Lindisf. Gosp.* Matt. xii. 44 Ic willo cerre in hus min ðona [L. *unde*] ic cuom. **13..** *Cursor M.* 2768 (Cott.) Loth ..Gayns þam ras fra þen [*v.r.* þar] he sate.

2. Of position: = THENCE 2.

1297 R. GLOUC. (Rolls) 5845 A toun..þat bote þre myle þanne nas. **13..** *Coer de L.* 2947 Saladyn was ten myle thenne. *a* **1375** *Joseph Arim.* 25 Neuer more come aȝeyn whon þei weore enes þenne. *c* **1450** LOVELICH *Merlin* 9866 Wers wylen they don, and we ben thenne.

3. = THENCE 3. (Only OE.)

c **888** K. ÆLFRED *Boeth.* xxx. §2, & þonan wyrð anæþeled oð ðæt he wyrð unæþele. *a* **1000** *Gloss.* in Wr.-Wülcker 220/43 *Dehinc*, *i.deinde*, *abhinc*, *rursum*,..*dein*, *uel* þonane, *uel* forþan.

4. From that source, origin, cause; = THENCE 4.

Beowulf 1265 þanon woc fela ȝeo sceaft gasta. *Ibid.* 1961 þonon ȝeomor woc, hæleðum to helpe. *c* **897** K. ÆLFRED *Gregory's Past. C.* xl. 289 Ðonne wierð ȝehnescad ðonone sio ðreaung ðæs anwaldes. *c* **1000** *Ags. Ps.* (Th.) lxvii[i]. 8 þanon eorðe byð eall onhrered. *c* **1400** *Rule St. Benet* 4 þanane byhouis þam feȝte þam ane, at god es tar best help.

Hence †**thenforth**, **-forthon** *adv.* = THENCEFORTH; †**thenforthward** *adv.* = THENCEFORWARD; †**thenward**, **-wards** *adv.* = THENCEWARD.

c **875** *Sax. Genealogies* 23 in *O.E. Texts* 179 *Ðonan forð. *a* **1023** WULFSTAN *Hom.* i. (1883) 1 He ða syððan..þanonforð ȝeseon ne mihte. **13..** *Cursor M.* 6357 (Cott.) Fra þan forth heild sir moyses þis wandes bath. **1426** in *Surtees Misc* (1888) 9 þat þe sayd John Lyllyng fra þan furth suld be of gude governaunce. *c* **1477** CAXTON *Jason* 6 Fro *thenne forthon he named him his broder. **1484** —— *Fables of Æsop* III. xx. *c* **1200** *Trin. Coll. Hom.* 189 And *þanen-forðward he bereȝeð him wið sinne. *a* **1225** *Ancr. R.* 296 Hie him so *þeoneward, & ascur him so scheomeliche. *c* **1230** *Hali Meid.* 43 As ha nuste hwuch wei ha come þeneward; ne con ha neauer ifinden na wei aȝainward. **13..** *S. Eng. Leg.* (MS. Bodl. 779) in Herrig's *Archiv* LXXXII. 313/40 Franceys al naked þenwardis gan gon.

thenne, þenne, obs. form of THAN, THEN, THIN.

† **then-to'fore**, *adv. Obs. rare.* [f. THEN *adv.*, after *theretofore*.] Before then, before that time: = THERETOFORE.

1626 L. OWEN *Spec. Jesuit.* (1629) 7 According to many graces and priuiledges then-tofore granted. **1706** *Col. Rec. Pennsylv.* II. 268 Complaints made of the excessive charge thentofore of obtaining Lycences. **1785** J. DISNEY *Mem. A. A. Sykes* 130 Bishop Atterbury had thentofore written largely in support of the power of the convocation.

thenward, *adv.*: see under THENNE *adv.*

theo, þeo: see THE, THIGH, THO *pron.* and *a.*

theo- (θiːəʊ), or, before a vowel, **the-**, repr. Gr. θεο-, stem of θεός God; in many compounds adopted from, or formed on the analogy of, Greek, or from Greek (rarely Latin or other) elements. See in their alphabetical places THEANTHROPIC, THEOCRACY, THEOLOGY, THEOSOPHY, etc. **ˌtheo-anthropo'morphic** *a.*, pertaining to gods in human form; so **ˌtheo-anthropo'morphism**: cf. *anthropomorphic*, *anthropomorphism*. **ˌtheo-astro'logical** *a.*, of or pertaining to astrology theologically treated. **theo'centric** *a.*, centring or centred in God; having God as its centre. **theo'centrism**, theocentric doctrine or belief, also (occas.) **theo'centricism**. **theo'christic** *a.* [Gr. θεόχριστ-ος], anointed by God (Webster 1864). **ˌtheo-co'llectivist**, of the nature of collectivism as divinely instituted. **ˌtheo-de'mocracy**, a democracy under divine rule. **theo-'drama**, a drama in which the actors are gods. **ˌtheogeo'logical** *a.*, of or pertaining to geology as accommodated to theological tenets. **theo'gnostic** [after AGNOSTIC; cf. Gr. θεόγνωστος known of God], one who holds that God is knowable. **theo'human** *a.*, both divine and human; that is God as well as man. **theoktonic** (-'ktɒnɪk) *a.*, of or pertaining to theoktony. **theoktony** (θiː'ɒktənɪ) [Gr. θεοκτονία (*Eccl.*)], killing or death of the gods. **theo'mammonist** (see quot.). **theo'mania** [Gr. θεομανία madness caused or inspired by God], religious mania; also, demonomania. **theo'maniac**, one affected with theomania. **theo'mastix** [-MASTIX], the scourge of (i.e. appointed by) God. **'theometry** [-METRY], measurement or estimation of God. **theomicrist** (θiː'ɒmɪkrɪst) [Gr. μικρός little], one who belittles God. **ˌtheomi'santhropist** (*nonce-wd.*, after THEOPHILANTHROPIST), one who hates God and man. **theo'monism**, a monism which recognizes God. **theo'panphilist** (see quot.). **theo'pantism** [Gr. πᾶς, παντ- all], (*a*) see quot. 1864; (*b*) the doctrine that God is all that exists: = PANTHEISM. **'theophile** [Gr. θεοφιλής dear to the gods], one beloved of God; also, one who loves God; so **the'ophilist**. **ˌtheophilo'sophic** *a.*, that applies philosophy to theology. **theophoric** (-'fɒrɪk), **theophorous** (θiː'ɒfərəs), *adjs.* [Gr. *θεοφόρος*, f. *φέρειν* to bear], bearing or containing the name of a god. **theo'physical** *a. nonce-wd.*, physical, but ordered by God. **theo'psychism** [Gr. *ψυχή* soul], ascription of a divine nature to the soul. **theo'taurine** *a.* [Gr. *θεόταυρος* god-bull, a title of Zeus], of or pertaining to a god in the form of a bull. **ˌtheotele'ology**, the doctrine of the divine direction of nature to an appointed end; hence **ˌtheoteleo'logical** *a.*

1873 FAIRBAIRN *Stud. Philos. Relig. & Hist.* (1876) 349 The Hellenic mind..created those *theo-anthropomorphic doctrines. *Ibid.* 348 The one contributed the Monotheism, the other the *Theo-anthropomorphism, which lie at the basis of Christianity. **1833** *Fraser's Mag.* VIII. 572 Their *theo-astrological mythologies, and their symbolical mysteries. **1886** M. VALENTINE in *Homilet. Rev.* Oct. 283 The old *Theocentric Calvinism, in which every thing was made to revolve about the divine sovereignty. **1893** FAIRBAIRN *Christ in Mod. Theol.* II. i. 301 This theology must..be as regards source Christocentric, but as regards object or matter Theocentric. **1925** E. UNDERHILL *Mystics of Church* x. 205 The best traditions of French spirituality, its lofty *theocentricism. **1930** *Monument to St. Augustine* viii. 272 The apparent *theocentrism of the Calvinist 'glory of God'. **1941** Theocentrism [see ANTHROPOCENTRICISM, ANTHROPOCENTRISM]. **1901** *Daily Chron.* 30 Aug. 3/4 Massachusetts with its township government centreing round the church, its *theo-collectivist modes of thought. **1830** *Hist. Eur.* in *Ann. Reg.* 244/2 The cajolery or intimidation..employed by the priests to make their flocks join the faction of (what one of them called) the *theo-democracy. **1853** LIEBER *Civil Liberty* xxiv. 242 The Mormons themselves call their government a theo-democracy. **1801** W. TAYLOR in Robberds *Mem.* I. 389 A *theo-drama or..an epic poem, where all the actors are gods. **1852** R. KNOX *Gt. Artists & Gt. Anat.* 43 A theory or two was forced on him [Cuvier] by the *theo-geological school of England, which were not his. **1898** *Chicago Advance* 14 Apr. 491/3 Is man by..his powers..an Agnostic or a *Theo-gnostic? **1839** BAILEY *Festus* x. (1852) 139 Thou art and livest, man-god, Christ!.. The *Theohuman Being. **1875** R. B. ANDERSON *Norse Mythol.* iii. 60 The Eddas have a *theoktonic myth. *Ibid.*, Ends with a *theoktony (death of the gods). **1804** COLERIDGE *Lett., to T. Poole* (1895) 455 Such men I aptly christen *Theo-mammonists, that is, those who at once worship God and Mammon. **1857** DUNGLISON *Med. Lex.*, **Theomania*, demonomania. **1890** BILLINGS *Nat. Med. Dict.*, *Theomania*, religious monomania. **1863** C. READE *Hard Cash* III. ii. 53 Dr. Wycherley..put down any man a lunatic, whose intellect was manifestly superior to his own... Nor did the dead escape him entirely. Pascal, according to Wycherley, was a madman with an illusion about a precipice... Joan of Arc a *theomaniac. **1879** SWINBURNE *Stud. Shaks.* iii. 214 The brutallest unwashed theomaniac of the Thebaid. **1633** T. CAREW *Cœl. Brit.* Wks. (1824) 154 My offices and title are, supreme *theomastix, hupercrittique of manners. **1881** ROSSETTI *Soothsay* xii, The Power that fashions man Measured not out thy little span For thee to take the meting-rod In turn, and so approve on God Thy science of *Theometry. **1834** DE QUINCEY in *Tait's Mag.* I. 688 He had defended Christianity against the vile blasphemers and impotent *theomicrists of the day. **1831** SOUTHEY in *Q. Rev.* Jan. 113 Those who (in reference to the appellation of a sect, not more presumptuous, and somewhat less impious) deserve to be called the *Theomisanthropists. **1906** F. BALLARD (*title*) *Theomonism True: God and the Universe in Modern Light. **1908** *Daily News* 7 Feb. 4/2 Mr. Ballard ..calls it sometimes theism and sometimes theomonism. **1833** *Fraser's Mag.* VIII. 570 The *initiati* called themselves *Theopanphilists, those who believed in the universal exhibition of the Divinity in characters of love. **1864** N. WEST in *Homilet. Rev.* (1886) May 407 It is true to teach *Theopantism, or that God is in all things. **1873** FAIRBAIRN *Stud. Philos. Relig. & Hist.* (1877) 392 It may evolve an Akosmism or Theopantism which is but the apotheosis of nature. *c* **1645** HOWELL *Lett.* (1650) II. xlii. 54 Afflictions are the portion of the best *Theophiles. **1677** GALE *Crt. Gentiles* II. III. 84 Virtuose persons..are *Theophilists, or beloved of God. **18..** MILMAN is cited by Worcester as using **theophilosophic*. **1901** W. MACINTOSH *Rabbi Jesus* 182 With the dawn of Christianity the theophilosophic train of thought was carried onward and upward into a higher, nobler, purer channel. **1891** CHEYNE *Orig. Psalter* vi. 303 Such shortened forms of *theophoric names as Ahaz for Jehoahaz. **1903** *Expositor* May 323 We are left for conjecture to the *theophorous names of her kings. **1908** *Ibid.* Jan. 95 Yahu..is familiar enough from Hebrew theophorous names. **1775** ADAIR *Amer. Ind.* 129 By the time that this *theo-physical operation is performed on a patient [i.e. breaking his neck on pretence that it is the Divine will]. **1896** DK. OF ARGYLL *Philos. Belief* vi. 253 It may be said..that '*theopsychism' attributed to man, is the real explanation of what is called the anthropomorphism attributed in the Hebrew scriptures to the mind and will of God. **1814** SOUTHEY *Lett.* (1856) II. 368 When..prepared for the food of man, it..resembleth entirely in its appearance the *theo-taurine compost from whence it sprung. **1903** L. F. WARD *Pure Sociol.* III. xvi. 465 A doctrine that afterwards took the name of *teleology*,..would be better called **theoteleology*, since it simply postulates a power outside of nature directing it toward some end.

‖**Theobroma** (θiːəʊ'brəʊmə). *Bot.* [mod.L., f. Gr. *θεός* god + *βρῶμα* food.] A genus of low trees, of which one species, *Theobroma Cacao*, a native of tropical America, and now naturalized in other warm countries, is the source of cocoa and chocolate. Hence **theo'bromic** *a. Chem.* in *theobromic acid*: see quots.; **theobromine** (θiːəʊ'brəʊmaɪn), a bitter volatile alkaloid, $C_7H_8N_4O_2$, resembling caffeine, contained in the seeds of the cacao tree.

[**1737** LINNÆUS *Genera Plant.* 367 Polyadelphia. I. Pentandria. *Theobroma.] **1760** LEE *Introd. Bot.* App. (1788) 331/2 Chocolate-nut, *Theobroma.* **1785** MARTYN *Rousseau's Bot.* xxxi. (1794) 478 In..Theobroma, or Chocolate..it [the nectary] is Bell-shaped. **1871** GARROD *Mat. Med.* (ed. 3) 194 Oil of Theobroma... Cacao Butter. A concrete oil obtained by expression and heat from the ground seeds of Theobroma Cacao. **1878** KINGZETT in *Jrnl. Chem. Soc.* XXXIII. 44, I propose for it the name of **Theobromic acid*, which recalls the source from which it is obtained, namely, the fat of the seeds of *Theobroma Cacao.* **1881** WATTS *Dict. Chem.* VIII. 1922 *Theobromic acid*, $C_{64}H_{128}O_2$. This acid, the highest known member of the fatty series, has been obtained..from cacao-butter. **1842** *Penny Cycl.* XXIV. 313/2 The analysis of *Theobromine by Wosresensky shows..that this article [chocolate]..must be highly nutritious. **1887** MOLONEY *Forestry W. Afr.* 165 They contain a very appreciable quantity of theobromine, which assists the action of caffein and possesses similar properties to that base.

theocracy (θiː'ɒkrəsɪ). Also 7 **-craty**, 7–8 **-crasie, -crasy**. [ad. Gr. *θεοκρατία* (Josephus): see THEO- and -CRACY: cf. F. *théocratie* (1704 in Hatz.-Darm.).] A form of government in which God (or a deity) is recognized as the king or immediate ruler, and his laws are taken as the statute-book of the kingdom, these laws being usually administered by a priestly order as his ministers and agents; hence (loosely) a system of government by a sacerdotal order, claiming a divine commission; also, a state so governed: esp. applied to the commonwealth of Israel from the exodus to the election of Saul as king.

1622 DONNE *Serm.* (ed. Alford) V. 209 The Jews were only under a Theocraty, an immediate Government of God. *a* **1652** J. SMITH *Sel. Disc.* VII. iv. (1821) 346 Josephus.. properly calls the Jewish government *θεοκρατιαν*, 'a theocracy', or 'the government of God himself'. **1737** WHISTON *Josephus, Agst. Apion* II. §17 (1814) IV. 340 He [Moses] ordained our government to be what, by a strained expression, may be termed a Theocracy [*ὡς δ' ἄν τίς εἴποι, βιασάμενος τον λόγον, θεοκρατιαν*]. **1741** WARBURTON *Div. Legat.* v. ii. II. 365 Thus the Almighty becoming their King, in as proper a Sense as he was their God, the Republic of the Israelites was properly a Theocracy; in which the two Societies, Civil and Religious, must..be intirely incorporated. **1811** PINKERTON *Mod. Geog., Peru* (ed. 3) 694 The government of the incas was a kind of theocracy. **1836** J. H. NEWMAN *Par. Serm.* (ed. 2) II. xxi. 283 When they tired of the Christian Theocracy, and clothed the church with 'the purple robe' of Cæsar. **1863** STANLEY *Jew. Ch.* vii. 155 The 'Theocracy' of Moses..was a government by God Himself, as opposed to the government by priests or kings. **1864** BURTON *Scot Abr.* I. v. 276 It [the Church of Calvin] was a theocracy, dictating to all men the rule of the Deity as to their daily life. **1878** MACLEAR *Celts* ii. (1879) 17 The Druids were at once the ministers of a theocracy and the judges and legislators of the people.

b. *transf.* A priestly order or religious body exercising political or civil power.

1825 WELLINGTON *Desp.* (1867) II. 597 The Roman Catholic clergy, nobility, lawyers, and gentlemen having property, form a sort of theocracy in Ireland, which in all essential points governs the populace.

theocrasia (θiːəʊ'kreɪzɪə). Also **-krasia**. [a. Gr. *θεοκρᾱσία*, a mingling with God.] = THEOCRASY 1.

1913 *Encycl. Relig. & Ethics* VI. 422/1 The working of the *theokrasia* in the domain of religion and religious art. **1920** H. G. WELLS *Outline Hist.* 496/2 A sort of theocrasia went on between Christianity and Judaism..and other competing cults. **1971** R. E. WITT *Isis* xi. 146 Bast was the intermediary when the process of theocrasia began.

theocrasy ('θiːəʊˌkreɪsɪ, θiː'ɒkrəsɪ). [ad. Gr. *θεοκρᾱσία*, f. *θεό-ς* god + *κρᾶσ-ις* mingling: see -Y.]

1. *Anc. Mythol.* A mingling of various deities or divine attributes into one personality; also, a mixture of the worship of different deities.

1816 G. S. FABER *Orig. Pagan Idol.* II. 248 The mystic theocrasy of the old mythologists, by which all their deities were ultimately resolved into one person. **1831** KEIGHTLEY *Mythol.* I. ii. 16 The system of theocrasy..or mixing up, as we may call it, of the gods together.

2. (See quot.)

1842 BRANDE *Dict. Sc.*, etc., *Theocrasy*, in ancient Philosophy, a term invented to signify the intimate union of the soul with God in contemplation, which was considered attainable by the newer Platonists.

Hence **theocrasical** (-'kræsɪkəl) *a.*, pertaining to or involving theocrasy.

1816 G. S. FABER *Orig. Pagan Idol.* I. p. xxxviii, Theocrasical identity of Osiris and Typhon.

theocrat ('θiːəʊkræt). [f. next: see -CRAT. Cf. mod.F. *théocrate* (Littré).]

1. One who rules in a theocracy as the representative of the Deity; a divine or deified ruler.

1827 G. S. FABER *Orig. Expiat. Sacr.* 234 This mode of administering temporal sanctions on the part of the temporal theocrat of Israel. **1854** MILMAN *Lat. Chr.* VI. iii. (1864) III. 482 Admirers of the great theocrat [Pope Gregory]. **1862** *Westm. Rev.* Jan. 269 Mahomet gradually degenerated..ultimately into a voluptuous tyrant and oppressive theocrat. **1874** REYNOLDS *John Baptist* viii. 490 The haughty theocrats of Persia dared to call on their subjects to adore them.

2. One who believes in or favours theocratic government; an advocate of theocracy.

1843 EMERSON *Misc. Papers, Carlyle* Wks. (Bohn) III. 313 Though no theocrat..Mr. Carlyle..finds the calamity of the times not in bad bills of Parliament, nor the remedy in good bills. **1895** *Q. Rev.* Oct. 355 Disraeli..was a born theocrat. **1897** GOLDW. SMITH in *Amer. Hist. Rev.* Oct. 138 For all but the aristocracy and extreme theocrats they must have been about the best years that Scotland had known.

¶ **b.** See quot. (? erroneous use).

1864 WEBSTER, *Theocrat*, one who obeys God as his civil ruler. **1882** OGILVIE (Annandale), *Theocrat*, one who lives under a theocracy; one who is ruled in civil affairs directly by God.

theocratic (θiːəʊ'krætɪk), *a.* [f. Gr. *θεοκρατία* THEOCRACY + -IC: cf. *aristocratic*, etc.] Of, pertaining to, or of the nature of theocracy.

1741 WARBURTON *Div. Legat.* v. ii. II. 375 The true Reasons of the Theocratic Form of Government. **1841** TRENCH *Parables* ii. (1877) 29 We may say generally of the parables.. that St. Matthew's are more Theocratic; St. Luke's more ethical. **1865** LECKY *Ration.* (1878) II. 120 This Church and State theory..forms the last vestige of the old theocratic spirit that marks the earlier stages of civilisation.

theocratical (θiːəʊ'krætɪkəl), *a.* [f. as prec. + -AL[1]: cf. *aristocratical.*] = prec.

1690 C. NESSE *O. & N. Test.* I. 180 A new commonwealth with a theocratical government. **1755** WARBURTON *Div. Legat.* v. iv. Wks. 1788 III. 123 Temporal rewards and punishments administered by the hand of God, followed, as a consequence, from the Jewish Government's being Theocratical. **1837** *Foreign Q. Rev.* XIX. 187 The prophetic books were preserved in writing by a theocratical people. **1863** E. V. NEALE *Anal. Th. & Nat.* 201 The original form of all governments appears to have been theocratical.

theo'cratically, *adv.* [f. prec. (or THEOCRATIC): see -ICALLY.] In a theocratic manner; from a theocratic point of view.

1827 G. S. FABER *Orig. Expiat. Sacr.* 234 Even the precept of a perfect love to God, when viewed theocratically, was part and parcel of the statute law of Israel.

Theocritean (θɪɒkrɪ'tiːən), *a.* [f. L. *Theocritus*, a. Gr. *Θεόκριτος* Theocritus, a Greek poet of Sicily, of the 3rd c. B.C.: cf. SOPHOCLEAN *a.*] Of, pertaining to, or characteristic of Theocritus or his writings, esp. his pastoral poetry; of the style of Theocritus; hence pastoral, idyllic. Also **The'ocritan** *a.*

1846 T. KEIGHTLEY *Notes Bucolics Virgil* 73 He [*sc.* Virgil] was thoroughly imbued with the Theocritean poetry. **1879** [see BUCOLICISM]. **1896** *McClure's Mag.* VI. 467/2 With his [*sc.* Corot's] Theocritan spirit, he could see the fountain of Jouvence in the woods of Sèvres. **1910** *Daily News* 17 Oct. 3 All this is more real and more grim than Arcadia, but even Arcadia had its reality, and there is something of Theocritean sweetness penetrating the intimate truth of this book. **1935** L. MACNEICE *Eclogue by Five-Barred Gate* in *Poems* 24, I am a shepherd of the Theocritean breed. **1969** V. DE S. PINTO *City that Shone* xii. 293 A Theocritean flavour was given to our courtship by the fact that Irène had two white goats.

theod, theode, var. THEDE *Obs.*, people.

theo-democracy: see THEO-.

theodicaea (θiːɒdɪ'siːə). *rare.* [App. an erron. Latinization of Fr. *théodicée* in the title of a work by Leibniz: see THEODICY.] = THEODICY.

1845 *Encycl. Metrop.* II. 659/1 Leibnitz fancied that..he could construct a *Theodicæa*, in which the doctrines of theology should be reconciled with philosophy. **1883** J. SIBREE tr. *Hegel's Lect. on Philos. of Hist.* 16 Our mode of treating the subject is, in this aspect, a Theodicæa [rendering G. *Theodicee*],—a justification of the ways of God ..in indefinite abstract categories. **1974** *Times Lit. Suppl.* 18 Oct. 1161/2 The mysterious 'Spirit' which presides over, or constitutes, reality in the Hegelian scheme of things is supposed..to be pursuing in history a plan of which historical agents are largely or wholly unaware: that is why Hegel can claim to be offering a theodicaea.

theodicy (θiː'ɒdɪsɪ). Also 9 **theodice, -ee**. [ad. F. *théodicée*, the title of a work of Leibniz (1710), f. Gr. *θεό-ς* God + *δίκη* justice.] The, or a, vindication of the divine attributes, esp. justice and holiness, in respect to the existence of evil; a writing, doctrine, or theory intended to 'justify the ways of God to men'. Cf. OPTIMISM 1.

1797 D. STEWART in *Encycl. Brit.* (ed. 3) XI. 481/2 Metaphysical theology, which Leibnitz and some others call theodicy. **1825** COLERIDGE *Aids Refl.* (1848) I. 120 All the theodices ever framed by human ingenuity, before and since the attempt of the celebrated Leibnitz. **1875** WHITE *Life in Christ* v. xxix. (1878) 500 Their theodicy is based on the belief that out of all evil God will bring eternal good.

Hence **theodi'cean**, one who frames or maintains a theodicy.

1873 MORLEY *Rousseau* I. 322 All things are for the best, said Rousseau and the theodiceans.

theodidact ('θiːəʊdɪˌdækt), *a.* and *sb.* [f. THEO- + Gr. *διδακτ-ός* taught.] **a.** *adj.* Taught by God. **b.** *sb.* One taught by God.

1715 M. DAVIES *Athen. Brit.* I. 66 Pretended Theodidacts, and self-knowing Gnosticks. **1865** tr. *Strauss's New Life Jesus* I. I. xxx. 262 The young Theodidact was able ..to give some advice to the most learned. **1894** LOUISE S. HOUGHTON tr. *Sabatier's St. Francis* Introd. 16 Owing nothing to church or schools he [St. Francis] was truly theodidact.

† **'theodisc**, *a. Obs. rare.* [OE. *þéodisc* = OS. *thiudisc*, OHG. *diutisc*:—OTeut. **þeudisko-*[z], f. OE. *þéod*, THEDE. Cf. DUTCH. If the word had survived in later ME., its form would have been

*theedish.] Of or belonging to a nation or people; native, national, popular; in biblical use, Gentile; in quot. 1715 used for Old German.
c **1000** *Aldhelm Gl.* viii. 350 in Napier *O.E. Gloss.*, *Gentiles*, þeodisce. *c* **1205** LAY. 5838 Wende þa þeodisce men [*c* 1275 þe Romanisse] þat Belin wolde þenne. **1715** M. DAVIES *Athen. Brit.* I. 197 Who turn'd the Gospels into Theodisck or old Francick Rhyme.

theodolite (θiːˈɒdəlaɪt). Forms: 6–7 **theodelitus,** 7 **theodelite, -dolit, -dilit,** 8 **-dolet,** 7– **theodolite.** [Origin unknown: see Note below.]

A portable surveying instrument, originally for measuring horizontal angles, and consisting essentially of a planisphere or horizontal graduated circular plate, with an alidad or index bearing sights; subsequently variously elaborated with a telescope instead of sights, a compass, level, vernier, micrometer, and other accessories, and now often with the addition of a vertical circle or arc for the measurement of angles of altitude or depression.

The original *theodelitus* of Digges was for horizontal angles only, and many quots. down to 19th c. use the name in this sense; Digges also describes a compound instrument having also a vertical semicircle for taking altitudes, but he calls that his *topographicall instrument*, restricting the name *theodelitus* to the horizontal circle.

1571 DIGGES *Pantom.* I. xxvii. H iij, The composition of the instrument called Theodelitus. It is but a circle diuided in 360.. degrees, or a semicircle parted in 180 portions, and euery of those diuisions in 3 or rather 6 smaller partes... The index of that instrument with the sightes &c. are not vnlike to that whiche the square hath: In his backe prepare a vice or scrue to be fastned in the top of some staffe. *Ibid.* I ij, [In the figure] GEFO [is] *Theodelitus*, GF his *Alhidada* or index with sightes. *Ibid.* xxix. I j b, Describing also within the same square the Planisphere or circle called Theodelitus. **1607** J. NORDEN *Surv. Dial.* III. 127 It [Circumferentor] is a new name giuen to the very Theodelite, used in a sort otherwise then the Theodelite. **1611** A. HOPTON *Speculum Topogr.* vi. 27 The Theodelitus is an instrument consisting of a Planisphere and an Alhidada. *Ibid.* Table D d 2 b, To take a plat at one station by the Theodelite. **1669** STURMY *Mariner's Mag.* II. 46 Any Instrument, as the Plain Table, the Theodolit or Circumferenter. **1701** MOXON *Math. Instr.* 20 *Theodolet*, a whole Circle made of Brass, containing 360 degrees, diagonally or otherwise divided, with an Index and sights moving on the Center, and a box and Needle in the middle. **1790** ROY in *Phil. Trans.* LXXX. 136 It is a brass circle, three feet in diameter, and may be called a great theodolet, rendered extremely perfect. **1833** HERSCHEL *Astron.* ii. §155 The zenith sector and the theodolite are peculiar modifications of the altitude and azimuth instrument. **1842** *Penny Cycl.* XXIV. 314/2 *Theodolet*, or *Theodolite*.. the name generally given to the instrument used for measuring horizontal angles. [*Ibid.* 315/2 The problem is to measure the horizontal angle between two objects. *Ibid.* 316/2 If the vertical angles are to be measured as accurately as the horizontal angles, the instrument becomes an altitude and azimuth circle.] [Cf. ALTAZIMUTH.]

b. *attrib.*, as **theodolite-goniometer**, a goniometer with horizontal and vertical graduated circles; **theodolite-magnetometer**, an instrument for measuring magnetic declination, and for observations of magnetic force; **theodolite-needle**, the needle of the compass of a theodolite.
1820 SCORESBY *Acc. Arctic Reg.* I. 333 A theodolite needle .. performed ten vibrations in sixty seconds. **1877** KNIGHT *Dict. Mech.*, Theodolite-magnetometer. **1909** *Cent. Dict. Suppl.*, Theodolite-goniometer.

Hence **theodoˈlitic** *a.*, of, pertaining to, done or made with a theodolite (Webster 1864).

[*Note.* The name, alike in the Latinized form *theodelitus* and the vernacular *theodelite* (subseq. *-dolite*), originated in England, and is not known in French and German until the 19th c. Its first user, and probable inventor, L. or T. Digges, has left no account of its composition, as to which various futile conjectures, incompatible with its early history and use, have been offered; such is the notion that it arose in some way out of *alhidada* or its corruption *athelida* occurring in Bourne's *Treasure for Travailers* 1578, which an examination of the works of Digges and Bourne, where both words occur in their proper senses, shows to be absurd. *Theodelite* has the look of a formation from Greek; can it have been (like many modern names of inventions) an unscholarly formation from θεάομαι 'I view' or θεῶ 'behold' and δῆλ-ος 'visible, clear, manifest', with a meaningless termination?]

theodom: see THEOWDOM.

Theodosian (θiːəʊˈdəʊsɪən, -ˈdəʊʃ(ɪ)ən), *a.* and *sb.* [f. the name *Theodosi-us*: see -AN.]

A. *adj.* Of or pertaining to one named Theodosius; *esp.* of or pertaining to the Roman emperor Theodosius II (A.D. 408–450).

Theodosian code, a collection of laws made by direction of Theodosius II, and published A.D. 438.
1765 BLACKSTONE *Comm.* I. Introd. iii. 81 Which Theodosian code was the only book of civil law received as authentic in the western part of Europe till many centuries after. **1802** RANKEN *Hist. France* II. II. iii. §2. 251 The Gothic gave way to the Theodosian code. **1833** *Encycl. Brit.* (ed. 7) V. 713/2 In the novel which sanctions the Theodosian Code, the emperor evidently admits that the compilers whom he had employed were not mere copyists. **1864** BRYCE *Rom. Emp.* iii. (1889) 29 Revised editions of the Theodosian code were issued by the Visigothic and Burgundian princes.

B. *sb.* **1.** A follower of Theodosius, a rhetorician of Alexandria, who became (A.D. 535) the leader of a division of the MONOPHYSITES.
1788 GIBBON *Decl. & F.* xlvii. IV. 611 *note*, The Gaianites and Theodosians. **1797** *Encycl. Brit.* (ed. 3) I. 797/2 Theodosians.. held that the persons of the Trinity are not the same; that none of them exists of himself, and of his own nature; but that there is a common god or deity existing in them all, and that each is God, by a participation of this deity. **1874** J. H. BLUNT *Dict. Sects* (1886), *Theodosians*, the Alexandrian section of the sect of the Phthartolatræ.

2. A member of a sect founded by Theodosius, a Russian monk: see quot. 1860.
1860 J. GARDNER *Faiths World, Theodosians*, a sect of dissenters from the Russo-Greek Church who separated some years since from the Pomoryans, partly because they neglected to purify by prayer.. articles.. purchased from unbelievers. **1874** in J. H. BLUNT *Dict. Sects*, etc.

Theodotian (θiːəʊˈdəʊʃ(ɪ)ən, -ˈdəʊtɪən). [f. the name *Theodot-us*: see -IAN.] A follower of Theodotus ('the Tanner') of Byzantium, who (*c* 200 A.D.) taught the antitrinitarian doctrine of the MONARCHIANS; also, a follower of Theodotus ('the Banker') who promulgated a similar heresy in the 3rd c. A.D. Hence **Theoˈdotianism**.
1853 W. E. TAYLOR *Hippolytus* II. iv. 102 Disputes occurring among the Theodotians, he became the head of a new sect. **1874** J. H. BLUNT *Dict. Sects, Heresies*, etc. (1886) s.v., Epiphanius writes that the Theodotians held Christ to be a mere man, and begotten of the seed of man... Hippolytus and Theodoret state that they had their beginning from Theodotus the Banker. **1876** A. PLUMMER tr. *Döllinger's Hippolytus & Callistus* iv. 287 *note*, A full denial of the divinity of Christ or Theodotianism.

theo-drama: see THEO-.

theody (ˈθiːəʊdɪ). [ad. It. *teodía*, ad. L. **theōdia*, *Gr. θεῳδία, f. θεό-ς God + ᾠδή song: cf. MELODY.] A song of praise to God; a psalm.
1867 LONGF. *Dante, Paradiso* xxv. 73 '*Sperent in te*', in the high Theody He sayeth, 'those who know thy name' [*orig.* Sperino in te, nell'alta Teodia, dice, color che sanno il nome tuo].

theof, theofthe, obs. ff. THIEF, THEFT.

theogeological, -gnostic: see THEO-.

†**theˈogonal,** *a.* [irreg. f. THEOGONY.] = next.
1727 A. HAMILTON *New Acc. E. Ind.* I. p. vii, Opportunities to know some topographical, historical, and theogonal Parts of this Work, from the Natives. *Ibid.* p. xxi, The theogonal and moral Parts may without Doubt, deserve some serious Thoughts or Attention.

theogonic (θiːəʊˈgɒnɪk), *a.* [f. as THEOGONIST + -IC.] Of or pertaining to theogony; of the nature of theogony. So **theoˈgonical** *a.*
1840 tr. *C. O. Müller's Hist. Lit. Greece* xvi. §4. 234 They show that by this time the character of the *theogonic poetry had been changed, and that Orphic ideas were in vogue. **1846** GROTE *Greece* I. xvi. I. 493 The acts described in the old heroic and theogonic legends. **1880** GLADSTONE in *19th Cent.* Apr. 720 The probable forms of theogonic and anthropomorphic evolution. **1702** *Lives of Anc. Philosophers* p. xxvi, A Magus.. was imploy'd to sing a *theogonical hymn, as a powerful enchantment. **1854** MILMAN *Lat. Chr.* (1863) II. 30 To reconcile the doctrines of the Gospel with the theogonical system of Asia.

theogonist (θiːˈɒgənɪst). [f. next + -IST. (In sense 2, f. Gr. θεόγονος born of God.)]

1. One who is versed in or treats of theogony.
1678 CUDWORTH *Intell. Syst.* I. iii. §13. 114 Such Theologers as these, who were Theogonists, and Generated all the Gods.. out of Sensless and Stupid Matter. **1845** MAURICE *Mor. & Met. Philos.* in *Encycl. Metrop.* (1847) II. 635/1 Plato, the cosmogonist and theogonist, is another man altogether from Plato the seeker of hidden truths in the facts which lay before him. **1880** E. MYERS *Æschylus* in E. Abbott *Hellenica* 16 If Pindar and Aeschylus treated the primitive theogonies with reverence, it was not the reverence of a primitive theogonist.

¶**2.** *erron.* One who is born of God.
1833 *Fraser's Mag.* VIII. 570 [In] Genesis.. it is.. stated that the aboriginal races of just men distinguished themselves by this.. title, Alibenim, theogonists, or God's sons, from the atheistical Sathanists, or evil-seekers.

So **theˈogonism**, a system or theory of theogony; **theˈogonite** = sense 2.
1678 CUDWORTH *Intell. Syst.* Pref. 34 That strange kind of Religious Atheism, or Atheistick Theogonism, which asserted.. Beings.. called by them Gods;.. Generated at First out of Night and Chaos.. and Corruptible again into the same. *Ibid.* Contents I. v. 726 A certain kind of Atheistick Theism, or Theogonism, which acknowledging a God or Soul of the World,.. supposed Him.. to have emerged out of Night and Chaos. **1831** *Fraser's Mag.* IV. 94 He [Lord Brougham] assumes too much of the theogonite to be wise.

theogony (θiːˈɒgənɪ). Also 8–9 *erron.* **-geny.** [ad. Gr. θεογονία generation or birth of the gods, f. θεός god + -γονία a begetting. So F. *théogonie.*] The generation of the gods; *esp.* an account or theory, or the belief or study, of the genealogy or birth of the deities of pagan mythology.
1612 SELDEN *Illustr. Drayton's Poly-olb.* xi. 183, I imagine many of their descents were iust as true as the Theogonie in Hesiod. **1656** BLOUNT *Glossogr.*, *Theogonie*, the beginning or generation of the gods. **1748** HARTLEY *Observ. Man* II. ii. 87 There were many Cosmogonies and Theogenies current amongst the Pagans. **1853** MAX MÜLLER *Chips* (1880) I. iii. 73 In the Veda,.. a theogony of which that of Hesiod is but the last chapter. **1859** I. TAYLOR *Logic in Theol.* 253 Theogenies, and theories of the universe.

theohuman, theoktonic, -ny: see THEO-.

theolatry (θiːˈɒlətrɪ). [ad. Gr. θεολατρεία worship of God, f. θεός God + λατρεία worship: see -LATRY.] The worship of a deity or deities.
1806 *Edin. Rev.* VII. 487 The distinction between herolatry and theolatry, or the sacred rites of heroes and the sacred rites of Gods, was perfectly well known in Greece. **1887** J. C. MORRISON *Service of Man* 265 The worship of deities has passed into the service of man. Instead of Theolatry we have anthropolatry.

theolepsy (ˈθiːəʊlɛpsɪ). *rare.* [ad. Gr. θεοληψία, f. θεός god + -ληψία, f. λῆψις seizure, f. λαμβάνειν, root λαβ- to take.] Seizure or possession by a deity, inspiration. So **theoˈleptic** [Gr. θεοληπτικ-ός adj.], one possessed or inspired by a deity.
1881 W. ALEXANDER *Speaker's Comm. N.T.* IV. 332/2 The streets of Ephesus were full of theoleptics and convulsionaries. **1886** MAUDSLEY *Nat. Causes & Supernat. Seemings* 222 The incoherent utterances which.. the theoleptic.. poured out under divine compulsion. *Ibid.* 315 Neither theolepsy, nor diabolepsy, nor any other lepsy in the sense of possession of the individual by an external power.

theolog, obs. form of THEOLOGUE.

theologal (θiːˈɒləgəl), *a.* and *sb.* [a. F. *théologal* adj. and sb. (14th c. in Hatz.-Darm.), f. Gr.-L. *theolog-us* theologian: see -AL[1].]

†**A.** *adj.* in **theologal virtues** [OF. *vertus théologales* (14th c.)]: see THEOLOGICAL *a.* 1. *Obs.*
1484 CAXTON *Chivalry* 71 Of the seuen vertues thre ben theologale or deuyne and the other four ben cardynal. The theologal ben fayth, hope and charyte. **1502** *Ord. Crysten Men* (W. de W. 1506) I. v. 48 There ben thre vertues theologales & infuses. **1610** DONNE *Pseudo-martyr* 190 Theologall vertues, Faith, Hope, and Charity, are infus'd from God. *Ibid.* 210 This is not meant onely of Charitie, as it is a Theologall vertue.

B. *sb. R.C. Ch.* A lecturer on theology and Holy Scripture attached to a cathedral or collegiate church. Also called *theologus* and *canon theologian.*
1638 BAKER tr. *Balzac's Lett.* (vol. III) 173 To Monsieur Senne, Theologall of the Church of Saints. **1872** JERVIS *Gallican Ch.* I. xi. 389 *note*, The theologal enjoyed a canonry by virtue of his office.

†**theˈologant.** *Obs. rare*[−1]. [ad. med.L. *theologānt-em*, pres. pple. of *theologāre, -ārī* (Du Cange) to theologize: see -ANT.] = THEOLOGER.
1678 MARVELL *Def. J. Howe* Wks. (Grosart) IV. 169 The Theologants of former and later times.. have attempted to clamber [etc.].

theologaster (θiːɒləˈgæstə(r)). [a. med.L. *theologaster* (Luther 1518), f. *theolog-us* theologian: see -ASTER.] A shallow or paltry theologian; a smatterer or pretender in theology.
1621 BURTON *Anat. Mel.* II. ii. III, The like measure is offered unto God himself by a company of theologasters. **1642** H. MORE *Song Soul* Interpr. Words, Superficiall conceited Theologasters.. having but the surface and thin imagination of divinity. **1744** WARBURTON *Rem. Occas. Refl.* I. App. 134 This sorely distresses our Theologaster. **1888** SCHAFF *Hist. Chr. Ch.* VI. III. lix. 322 The furious decree of the Parisian theologasters.

Hence **theoloˈgastric** *a.*, of or pertaining to a theologaster; in quot. as *sb.* a theologaster.
1894 FROUDE *Erasmus' Life & Lett.* iv. 65, I am speaking merely of the theologastrics of our own time, whose brains are the rottenest.

theologate (θiːˈɒləgət). *R.C. Ch.* [ad. mod.L. *theologāt-us*, f. *theolog-us* theologian: see -ATE[1].]

1. The course in theology prescribed for candidates for the priesthood.
1889 in WORCESTER *Suppl.*

2. A theological college or seminary.
1879 H. FOLEY *Records Eng. Province Soc. of Jesus* V. 944 *The College of St. Beuno*... This extensive pile of building was erected in 1848–9 for a Theologate, or House of Divinity, by the late Father Randal Lythgoe, then Provincial. **1884** *Mrs. Calderwood's Jrnls.* v. 169 *note*, The Jesuit College at Liège, the theologate of the English Province. **1898** *Month* Oct. 439 The Professor of Holy Scripture at the great Jesuit Theologate of Woodstock. **1906** *Tablet* 15 Sept. 401 Ditton Hall, not far from Liverpool, where the exiled German province then had its theologate.

theologe, obs. form of THEOLOGUE.

theologer (θiːˈɒlədʒə(r)). Now *rare.* [f. stem of Gr.-L. *theolog-us* or Eng. *theolog-y* + -ER[1]: see -LOGER.] One who studies or busies himself with theology; = THEOLOGIAN (but now with less implication of scholarship). **a.** In reference to Christianity or other monotheistic religion.
1588 J. HARVEY *Disc. Probl.* 37 After which last maner may our diuines, or Theologers be termed prophets, but not otherwise. **1653** H. MORE *Conject. Cabbal.* (1713) 39 Supposing them [conclusions] true,.. till such time as some able Philosopher or Theologer shall convince me of their falshood. **1756** AMORY *Buncle* (1770) II. 126 To make me a theologer, that I might be an able defender of the Creed of St. Athanasius. **1849** O. BROWNSON *Wks.* VII. 16 The theological speculations of theologers, as he [Dr. Bushnell] contemptuously calls them.

b. In reference to pagan religions.

1609 HOLLAND *Amm. Marcell.* 166 That..Goddesse Themis, whom..the antient Theologers have shrined in the verie bed and throne of Jupiter. **1678** CUDWORTH *Intell. Syst.* Pref. 38 The Pagan Theologers..acknowledged one Sovereign..Deity, from which all their other Gods were Generated or Created. **1724** COLLINS *Grounds Chr. Relig.* I. xi. 83 Allegory was in use among the Pagans; being cultivated by many of the Philosophers themselves as well as by Theologers. **1876** BLACKIE *Lang. & Lit. Highl. Scot.* ii. 79 The 'Works and Days' of the old Bœotian theologer [Hesiod].

theologian (θiːəʊˈləʊdʒɪən). Also 5–6 **-yen**. [a. F. *théologien* (14th c. in Hatz.-Darm.), f. *théologie* or L. *theologia* THEOLOGY; subseq. assimilated to L. spelling: see -LOGIAN.] **a.** One who is versed in theology; *spec.* one who makes a study or profession of theology; a divine. Also *attrib.*

1483 CAXTON *Cato* F j b, The phycycyen was..ryght good Theologyen or knowyng the dyuyne scryptures. **1509** FISHER *Funeral Serm. C'tess Richmond* Wks. (1876) 303 Whiche thinge not onely the theologyens wytnesse, but the phylosophers also. *a* **1627** HAYWARD *Edw. VI* (1630) 84 Some theologians..desteining their professions..by publishing odious vntruths. **1667** MILTON *P.L.* v. 436 The common gloss Of Theologians **1769** ROBERTSON *Chas. V*, XI. III. 352 The abilities or zeal of theologians long exercised in disputation. **1836** H. ROGERS *J. Howe* ii. (1863) 23 Professed theologians were not the parties for whom the Bible was exclusively, or even principally intended. **1897** *Scotsman* 26 May 10/6 My theologian judges and my lay judges.

b. In reference to pagan religions: = THEOLOGER b. *rare.*

1603 HOLLAND *Plutarch's Mor.* 1047 The olde Theologians and Divines..have put into the hands of the images of the gods, musicall instruments. **1904** BUDGE *3rd & 4th Egypt. Rooms Brit. Mus.* 127 Under the New Empire the votaries of Rā formed a numerous and powerful body, and their theologians and priests endeavoured to impress their views on the country in general.

c. ***canon theologian*** (R.C. Ch.) = THEOLOGAL B.

1885 *Cath. Dict.* (ed. 3) s.v. *Canon Theologian*, The Council of Trent directed..that..in..cathedral..or even collegiate churches..a Canon Theologian..should be appointed.

d. In sense 1 d of THEOLOGY.

1968 *Listener* 10 Oct. 469/2 To speak well of the past was a mortal sin and got you into trouble with the party theologians and eventually with the police. **1982** 'I. I. MAGDALEN' *Search for Anderson* II. ii. 147 We had the ideologists and the purists and the theologians.

theologic (θiːəʊˈlɒdʒɪk), *a.* (*sb.*) [ad. F. *théologique* (14th c. in Hatz.-Darm.), ad. L. *theologicus*, a. Gr. θεολογικός, f. θεολογία THEOLOGY.]

1. Of or belonging to theology; = next, 2.

1477 EARL RIVERS (Caxton) *Dictes* 78 Aristoteles..lerned of plato..Ethikes and the iiij sciences theologikes. **1669** GALE *Crt. Gentiles* I. Introd. 4 Plato..derived the choisest of his contemplations, both Physiologic, and Theologic..from the Jewish Church. **1678** CUDWORTH *Intell. Syst.* I. iv. 323 It was customary with the Egyptian Priests, to entitle their own Philosophick and Theologick Books, to Hermes. **1780** H. WALPOLE *Let. to Cole* 4 July, I hate theologic or political controversy. *a* **1876** M. COLLINS *Th. in Garden* (1880) II. 237 These young theologic adepts fancy they know everything.

†**2.** = THEOLOGICAL *a.* 1. *Obs. rare.*

1605 DRAYTON *Man in Moone* 488 Those Hierarchies..Whose Orders..Make up that holy Theologicke nine: Thrones, Cherubin, and Seraphin [etc.]. **1637** HEYWOOD *London's Mirr.* Wks. 1874 IV. 314 The Theologicke vertues, the three Graces, And Charities have here their severall places.

B. *absol.* as *sb.* (*pl.*) Theological matters. *rare.*

1728 YOUNG *Love Fame* v. 374 These..who thus excell In Theologicks.

theological (θiːəʊˈlɒdʒɪkəl), *a.* (*sb.*) [ad. med.L. *theologicālis* (Duns Scotus *a* 1308), f. L. *theologicus* (see prec.) – *-ālis*, -AL[1]: see -ICAL.]

1. Of or pertaining to the word of God, i.e. the Bible; scriptural: cf. THEOLOGY 2; in ***theological virtues*** [*virtutes theologicæ*, Albertus Magnus], applied to faith, hope, and charity (1 Cor. xiii. 13), as distinct from the earlier four *cardinal virtues* of Plato and the Stoics (cf. TEMPERANCE, *Note*).

(From the contemporary senses of *theologia*, this seems to have been the original meaning; but other reasons for and explanations of the name were current from Aquinas onward: see the quots.; cf. also *c* **1380** WYCLIF *De Eccl.* ii. Sel. Wks. III. 340 þes two godliche virtues [faith and hope]. The ancient pre-Christian virtues were called *virtutes cardinales* A.D. 379, by Ambrose *Exc. Satyri* i. 57.)

[**1484**: cf. THEOLOGAL.] **1526** *Pilgr. Perf.* (W. de W. 1531) 142 The rofe y[t] couereth all is the theologicall vertue, hope. **1588** A. KING tr. *Canisius' Catech.* 184 The vertues (quhilk I hawe called theological and cardinal). **1607–12** BACON *Ess.*, *Goodness* (Arb.) 198 Goodnes aunswares to the Theologicall vertue, Charitie, and admittes not excesse, but errour. **1616** BULLOKAR *Eng. Expos.*, *Theologicall vertues*, Faith, Hope and Charity are so called, because they haue their obiect and end in God. **1660** R. COKE *Power & Subj.* 14 By Theological virtues I do not mean only those three most eminent virtues of Faith, Hope, and Charity, but all those actions of obedience due to them..; to whom I owe my obedience not by any Law of Nature, but as commanded by God in the Scriptures. **1875** MANNING *Mission H. Ghost* iii. 82 Faith is called a theological virtue, because it unites the soul with its Maker. **1909** OTTLEY *Chr. Ideas & Ideals* I. vi. 98 Faith, hope, and love are commonly called 'theological virtues', for reasons which Aquinas briefly enumerates. They have, he says, God for their object; they [etc.].

2. Of, pertaining to, or of the nature of theology; dealing with or treating of theology.

1603 HOLLAND *Plutarch's Mor.* 1304 The Theologicall interpretations that the Stoicks give out: for they holde, that the generative and nutritive Spirit, is Bacchus. **1664** JER. TAYLOR *Dissuas. Popery* II. I. ii. (1667) 89 It is cited..in the decrees of the Popes, and in the Theological sums of great Divines. **1780** HARRIS *Philol. Enq.* Wks. (1841) 541 Among their [the Arabians'] theological works, there are some upon the principles of the mystic divinity. **1780** BENTHAM *Princ. Legisl.* Introd. ii. §18 The theological principle; meaning that principle which professes to recur for the standard of right and wrong to the will of God. **1833** HT. MARTINEAU *Charmed Sea* i, Frederick was a theological student in the university at Wilna. **1861** STANLEY *East. Ch.* i. (1869) 23 The Athanasian controversy..is, strictly speaking, theological; unlike the Pelagian or the Lutheran controversies, it relates not to man, but to God. **1904** *Times* 4 May 2/6 The abolition of all theological tests and sectarian teaching during school hours.

3. *transf.* In trivial or disparaging use: of, pertaining to, or characterized by dogma or abstract principles (as opposed to practical considerations); doctrinaire, academic.

1959 *Times Lit. Suppl.* 5 June 329/4 The 'theological' approach to Soviet Marxism..proves in the long run unsatisfactory. **1964** S. BRITTAN *Treasury Under Tories* II. vi. 196 The three Treasury ministers played straight into the Prime Minister's hands, by their theological stress on permitting no increase at all on government expenditure for the coming financial year in money terms (which meant cutting it in real terms). **1964** *Listener* 30 July 148/2 Mr Walt Rostow..referred to 'the whole insoluble theological issue' of control... 'Theological' has two senses... He was clearly using the second or vernacular meaning, which is 'as impractical and as irrelevant to the matter in hand as the study of the nature of God'. **1968** *Observer* 28 Apr. 8/3 The doctrinal arguments which used to involve Labour in theological warfare. **1979** H. KISSINGER *White House Years* xviii. 719 It was a reflection on the theological nature of our China debate that many experts still regarded the 'solution' of the UN issue, liturgically, as the absolute precondition of any improvement in our relations with Peking. **1980** *Spectator* 2 Feb. 5/3 The dispute..nominally involves theological distinctions between 'News' and 'Current Events'.

B. *sb.* †**1.** *pl.* The theological virtues. *Obs.*

1600 W. WATSON *Decacordon* (1602) 138 Three speciall *principia* or causes..called of Diuines the three Theologicals,..faith,..charitie,..hope.

†**2.** *pl.* Theological matters or principles. *Obs.*

a **1626** W. SCLATER *Exp. 4th ch. Rom.* Ep. Ded., The greatest patterne, and example for men to live by:..whether in your Naturalls, or in your Morals, or in your Theologicalls. **1774** J. HUTTON in *Mme. D'Arblay's Early Diary* (1889) I. 303, I have found much pleasure in Madame de Maintenon's Letters (except in Theologicals and Spirituals).

3. A man trained at a theological college.

1866 S. B. JAMES *Duty & Doctr.* (1871) 18 University clergy are rarer, and theologicals and literates more numerous.

theologically (θiːəʊˈlɒdʒɪkəlɪ), *adv.* [f. THEOLOGICAL + -LY[2].] In a theological manner; from a theological point of view; according to the principles of theology; as regards theology. Also in sense 3 of prec.

1611 COTGR., *Theologalement*, Theologically, diuinely. **1617** MORYSON *Itin.* II. 165 To speake theologically, God preserves us, but stil in our waies. **1681** FLAVEL *Meth. Grace* v. 95 Though a man be physically a living man,..yet his soul having no union with Christ, he is theologically a dead man. **1773** JOHNSON 7 May, in Boswell, He may be morally or theologically wrong in restraining the propagation of opinions, which he thinks dangerous, but he is politically right. **1845** FORD *Handbk. Spain* I. 70 It was long a disputed point in Spain whether chocolate did or did not break fast theologically. **1874** P. BAYNE in *Contemp. Rev.* Oct. 708 He liked them to be theologically in sympathy with the Reformation. **1905** W. SANDAY *Crit. Fourth Gosp.* v. 145 The simple peasants of Galilee needed moral teaching; whereas the theologically minded inhabitants of Judaea called out more of a theology. **1973** *Times* 13 Oct. 14 There is a fundamental fascism of the left which is the real problem in the universities: they are theologically right, as they believe, and you are so wrong that you should even be denied the freedom to speak. **1978** *Guardian Weekly* 5 Feb. 5/5 The Government is no longer theologically wedded to it [*sc.* free trade].

theologician (θiːɒləʊˈdʒɪʃən). Now *rare.* Also 7 **-itian**. [f. L. *theologic-us* THEOLOGIC + -IAN: see -ICIAN.] = THEOLOGIAN.

c **1560** in *500 Yrs. Chaucer Criticisms* (Chaucer Soc.) 95 Geffery Chaucer..was a sharpe Logician, a sweete Rhetorician, a pure Poett, a graue Philosopher, and a sacred theologician. **1647** W. BROWNE tr. *Polexander* I. III. 60 Though I am a weake Theologitian I dare assure my selfe [etc.]. **1757** MRS. GRIFFITH *Lett. Henry & Frances* (1767) II. 110 The same error..which theologicians attribute to the heathen Romans. **1898** ADAMSON *Life J. Morison* xv. 171 Mr. Meikle was pre-eminently the theologician of the group.

theologico- (θiːəʊˈlɒdʒɪkəʊ), combining form from Gr. θεολογικό-ς THEOLOGICAL: 'theologically-, theological and..'; as in ***theologico-astronomical***, ***-ethical***, ***-historical***, ***-metaphysical***, ***-military***, ***-moral***, ***-natural***, ***-political*** adjs.; also with sbs., as in ***theologico-politician***.

1800 COLERIDGE *Lett., to Southey* (1895) 323 A *theologico-astronomical hypothesis. **1837** LEWIS *Lett.* (1870) 85 *Theologico-ethical opinions. **1842** BARHAM *Ingol. Leg.* Ser. II. *Lay St. Cuthbert* Introd., The extracts..may be considered as *theologico-historical. **1855** H. MARTINEAU *Autobiogr.* (1877) I. 120 Trying my hand at a sort of *theologico-metaphysical novel. **1897** *Daily News* 21 Oct. 8/3 A theologico-metaphysical speculator of no mean capacity. **1827** G. S. FABER *Sacr. Calend. Prophecy* (1844) III. 229 The *theologico-military exploits of the Saracens and the Turks. *c* **1644** *An Enquiry*, etc. in *Harl. Misc.* (Malh.) V. 498 The *theologico-moral design of convincing unnatural sinners. **1782** BECKFORD *Italy*, etc. (1834) I. iii. 330 A *theologico-natural history of birds, beasts, and fishes. **1680** R. MANSELL *Narr. Popish Plot* Addr. b j b, These *Theologico-Political Quacks. **1657–83** EVELYN *Hist. Relig.* (1850) II. 271 The *Theologico-politician Spinosa.

theologism (θiːˈɒlədʒɪz(ə)m). [f. THEOLOGIST or THEOLOGIZE: see -ISM; cf. F. *théologisme* (Littré).] The action or product of theologizing; theological speculation or system: usually in a derogatory sense.

1867 WESTCOTT in *Contemp. Rev.* VI. 407 The potential creed of the mass, springing out of spontaneous polytheism and tending to theologism. **1901** J. K. INGRAM in *Academy* 28 Sept. 256/2 Theologism, especially in its monotheistic form. **1908** *Hibbert Jrnl.* July 924 Dr. White's book..has opened Mr. Tyrrell's eyes to all the vileness of theologism.

theologist (θiːˈɒlədʒɪst). [ad. med.L. *theologista* (Luther 1519 *Wks.* (1884) II. 161), agent-n. f. *theologizāre*: see THEOLOGIZE and -IST.]

A professed theologian. **a.** In reference to pagan religions: = THEOLOGER b. (Used of ancient or modern writers on these.) Now *rare.*

a **1638** MEDE *Apostasy Later Times* (1641) 19 Their Theologists bring in another kinde of Daemons more high and sublime. *a* **1638** —— *Wks.* (1672) 626, I take the word Δαιμόνιον..in the better..sense, as it was..taken among the Theologists and Philosophers of the Gentiles. **1755** *Gentl. Mag.* XXV. 58/1, I am informed by a most learned..theologist, that Tantalus did not incur the displeasure of Jupiter till after the accident which happened to his son. **1816** G. S. FABER *Orig. Pagan Idol.* II. 102 The other philosophizing theologists of the east.

b. In reference to Christianity or other monotheistic religion: = THEOLOGER a.

1641 EARL MONM. tr. *Biondi's Civil Warres* v. 109 The schoole of Theologists who say that by sinning hee lost what hee had received by favour. **1668** FRANCO *Truth Springing* 1 The generally-received Opinion amongst the Jews Theologists,..That the Lord governeth onely the people of Israel with his peculiar and particular Providence. **1774** WARTON *Hist. Eng. Poetry* I. Diss. II. 42 Anselm, an acute metaphysician and theologist. *Ibid.* 75 These visionary theologists never explained or illustrated any scriptural topic. **1857** BADEN-POWELL in *Oxford Ess.* 181 The generality of these later natural theologists.

c. In derogatory sense: cf. THEOLOGISM.

1900 A. M. CHRISTIE tr. *Hist. Germ. People Mid. Ages* III. 57 His opponents were not theologians but theologists.

‖**theologium** (θiːələʊˈdʒaɪəm). *Gr. Antiq.* Also in Gr. form **theologeion** (-ˈgaɪən). [mod.L., ad. Gr. θεολογεῖον (see def.), f. θεο-, THEO- + λογεῖον speaking-place.] In the ancient theatre, a small balcony above the stage, from which those impersonating the gods spoke.

1888 in *Cassell's Encycl. Dict.* **1889** A. E. HAIGH *Attic Theatre* iv. §8. 193 Another appliance for exhibiting gods in a supernatural manner was the theologeion.

theˌologiˈzation. *rare.* Also 6 **-sacioun**. [f. as next, perh. through a med.L. **theologizātio*: see -ATION.] The action of theologizing.

a **1529** SKELTON *Replyc.* Wks. 1843 I. 209 The tetrycall theologisacioun of these demy diuines, and Stoicall studiantes.

theologize (θiːˈɒlədʒaɪz), *v.* [In sense 1, ad. med.L. *theologizāre* (Albertus Magnus *c* 1250; also in Aquinas, Duns Scotus, Wyclif, etc.), f. *theologia* THEOLOGY: see -IZE. So F. *théologiser* (Godef. *Compl.*). But the trans. senses may have been formed later directly from *theology*.]

1. *intr.* To play the theologian; to discourse or reason theologically; to speculate in theology.

1656 BLOUNT *Glossogr.*, *Theologize*, to preach or play the Divine. **1662** H. MORE *Philos. Writ.* Pref. Gen. (1712) 6 My Design, which is not to Theologize in Philosophy. **1721** EARL NOTTINGHAM *Answ. to Whiston* 57 As we Christians have been taught to Theologize of Him. **1826** G. S. FABER *Diffic. Romanism* (1853) 158 Justin..theologises in manner following. **1875** E. WHITE *Life in Christ* Pref. (1878) 4 When they do theologise..on the question whether the existing human race owes its being to law or to grace.

2. *trans.* To render theological; to conform to theology; to treat theologically.

1649 V. WEIGELIUS (*title*) Astrologie Theologized: wherein is set forth what Astrologie, and the light of Nature is. **1873** H. ROGERS *Orig. Bible* vii. (1875) 295 Voltaire said that Pascal had illustrated..his genius..by theologising two things that seemed not made for theology—wit and pleasantry.

†**3.** To attribute divinity to; to treat as of divine or spiritual nature. Also *intr.* or *absol.* *Obs.*

1678 CUDWORTH *Intell. Syst.* I. i. §33. 40 The same persons did..both Atomize in their Physiology, taking away all Substantial Forms.., and also Theologize or

Incorporealize, asserting Souls to be a Substance really distinct from Matter and Immortal. *Ibid.* iv. §17. 298 In which Orphick Fables, not only the Things of Nature, and Parts of the World were all Theologized, but also all manner of Humane Passions..attributed to the Gods.

Hence **the'ologizing** *vbl. sb.* and *ppl. a.*; also **the'ologizer**, one who theologizes, a theologer.

1685 BOYLE *Enq. Notion Nat.* iv. (1686) 93 The ancient Ægyptian *Theologizers..look'd upon the Sun and Moon ..as the chief Gods. **1693** J. EDWARDS *Author. O. & N. Test.* 92 Epicharmus, Thales, Plato, and all the Greek theologizers. **1857–8** SEARS *Athan.* 8 Theologizers of the school we describe. **1677** GALE *Crt. Gentiles* II. III. 136 Origen's allegoric mode of *Theologising. **1833** J. H. NEWMAN *Arians* II. iv. (1876) 190 The introduction of a subtle and irreverent question, whenever the theologizing Sophists should choose to raise it. **1881** G. A. SIMCOX in *Academy* 7 May 330 An instructive contrast to much fashionable theologising.

theologo- (θiːˈɒləgəʊ), combining form repr. Gr. θεολόγο-ς a theologian: as in **the'ologo-inquisi'torial** *adj.*, of or pertaining to a theological inquisitor; **the'ologo-'jurist**, a jurist who treats of theology.

1802–12 BENTHAM *Ration. Judic. Evid.* (1827) I. 555 The character of theologo-inquisitorial despotism. *a* **1843** SOUTHEY *Doctor* clxxii. (1848) 448/2 'The title of Christ to Eternal Life is become absolute,—by absolute',—says this theologo-jurist [J. Asgill],—'I mean discharged from all tenure or condition, and consequently from all forfeiture'.

‖**theologoumenon** (θiːələʊˈgaʊmɪnən, -ˈguːmɪnən). Pl. **-a** (-ə). [a. Gr. θεολογούμενον, neut. of pr. pple. pass. of θεολογεῖν to theologize, f. θεολόγος theologian.] A theological statement or utterance on theology: distinguished from an inspired doctrine or revelation.

1891 *Brit. Weekly* 29 Oct. 1 What gives this dubious theologoumenon its importance in Dr. Dale's system is the connection into which he brings it with the doctrine of propitiation. **1895** J. DENNEY *Stud. Theol.* iii. 52 His utterances on this point may be disregarded as private theologoumena. **1906** D. W. FORREST *Author. Christ* VI. ix. 330 It can only rank as a theologoumenon of Peter.

theologue (ˈθiːəlɒg). Also 5–7 **theologe**, 6–9 **theolog**. [ad. L. *theolog-us*, a. Gr. θεολόγος one who treats, or gives an account, of the gods (e.g. Hesiod, Orpheus), or of God; f. θεός God + λέγειν to discourse: see -LOGUE. Before *c* 1600 app. only Sc.: cf. ASTROLOGUE.]

1. = THEOLOGIAN. Now *rare*.

c **1425** WYNTOUN *Cron.* IX. xxi. 2237 (MS. Cott.) Master Henry of Wardlaw..A theologe solempneȝ was he Kende, and knawyn of gret bownte. *c* **1470** HENRYSON *Orpheus & Eur.* 422 Doctor nycholas Quhilk in his tyme a noble theologe was. **1508** DUNBAR *Lament for Makaris* 38 Art, magicianis, and astrologgis, Rethoris, logicianis, & theologgis. **1605** TIMME *Quersit.* Ded. 1 Moses, that auncient theologue. **1682** H. MORE *Annot. Glanvill's Lux O.* 62 The dry Dreams..of earthly either Philosophers or Theologs. **1693** *Phil. Trans.* XVII. 807 A bad Astronomer, a worse Theologe, and the worst of all Physiologers. *a* **1734** NORTH *Exam.* III. ix. §7 (1740) 652 It is not for a Layman to act the Theologue. **1859** I. TAYLOR *Logic in Theol.* 147 The writings of the great theologue of Bethlehem, Jerome.

2. A theological student. *U.S. colloq.*

(Prob. after Ger. *theolog.*)

1663 BLAIR *Autobiog.* ii. (1848) 42 My refusal would very much grieve all the young theologues. **1810–16** O'CONOR *Columbanus' Lett.* vi. 111 Barrister Theologues of the poddle! **1884** *Jrnl. Educ.* XIX. 327 The theologs who graduate from Lombard will stand high in their profession.

theology (θiːˈɒlədʒɪ). Also 4 **teologye**, 4–7 **theologie** (5 -i, 6 -ye). [a. F. *théologie* (14th c. in Hatz.-Darm.), ad. L. *theologia*, a. Gr. θεολογία, abstr. sb. f. θεολόγ-ος: see prec. and -LOGY. For the early sense-history see Note below.]

1. a. The study or science which treats of God, His nature and attributes, and His relations with man and the universe; 'the science of things divine' (Hooker); divinity.

Biblical theology: orig. theology as a non-dogmatic description of the religious doctrines contained in the Bible, following J. P. Gabler's distinction, in 1787, between biblical and dogmatic theology; now usu. the exposition of biblical texts (both O.T. and N.T.), based on the presupposition that there is a common biblical way of thinking which informs the Bible as a whole.

dogmatic theology, theology as authoritatively held and taught by the church; a scientific statement of Christian dogma. *natural theology*, theology based upon reasoning from natural facts apart from revelation. *pastoral theology*, that branch of theology which deals with religious truth in its relation to the spiritual needs of men, and the 'cure of souls': see PASTORAL *a.* 4.

1362 LANGL. *P. Pl.* A. XI. 136 Bote Teologye [B. x. 180, C. XII. 129 theologie] haþ teoned me ten score tymes; For þe more I muse þeron þe mistiloker hit semeþ. *c* **1386** CHAUCER *Pars. T.* ¶969 The exposicion of this hooly preyere..I bitake to thise maistres of Theologie. **1552** ABP. HAMILTON *Catech.* (1884) 1 Doctours of Theologie and Canon law. **1594** HOOKER *Eccl. Pol.* III. viii. §11 The whole drift of the scripture of God, what is it but only to teach Theologie? Theologie, what is it, but the Science of things Divine? *c* **1698** LOCKE *Cond. Underst.* xxii, Theology, which, containing the knowledge of God and His creatures, our duty to him and our fellow-creatures, and a view of our present and future state, is the comprehension of all other knowledge, directed to its true end. **1742** YOUNG *Nt. Th.* IV. 73 Were I as plump, as stall'd theology, Wishing would waste me to this shade again. [**1787** J. P. GABLER *Kleinere Theologische Schriften* (1831) II. 179 (*title*) De iusto discrimine theologiae biblicae et dogmaticae regundisque recte utriusque finibus.] **1837** HALLAM *Hist. Lit.* (1847) I. i. § 81. 72 Peter Lombard, the founder of systematic theology in the twelfth century. **1845** CORRIE *Theol.* in *Encycl. Metrop.* 857/1 Under the..term Theology we comprehend all the knowledge which man can obtain respecting God, whether concerning His nature and attributes, or concerning the relation in which man stands to Him. **1846** C. W. BUCH tr. *Hagenbach's Compendium Hist. of Doctrines* I. 5 In our opinion biblical theology is only to be regarded as the *foundation-stone* of the edifice..and dogmatic theology as the builder. **1874** J. DUNCAN *Pulpit & Commun. Table* 73 Polemical theology is the defence, Practical theology the application, of Dogmatic theology, which again rests upon Exegetical. **1888** *Encycl. Brit.* XXIII. 264/2 Biblical theology is the delineation of a section of religious ideas,—that section of which the traces and records remain in the Bible. **1904** A. B. DAVIDSON *Theology of O.T.* i. 1 In Biblical Theology the Bible is the source of the knowledge, and also supplies the form in which the knowledge is presented. **1951** H. H. ROWLEY *Old Testament & Modern Study* xi. 312 Since the publication of Gabler's famous address in 1787, the correctness of the distinction which he drew between biblical and dogmatic theology has been accepted as axiomatic by the majority of scholars. **1958** *Listener* 14 Aug. 241/1 A new subject has appeared called Biblical Theology. This means that the Bible, or rather the New Testament, is now subjected to analysis in order to see what is the total message or picture that it contains. **1969** A. RICHARDSON *Dict. Christian Theol.* 36/2 The question.. remains whether there can be a completely presuppositionless interpretation of any historical documents (as tended to be assumed by those who regarded biblical theology as a purely descriptive science).

b. A particular theological system or theory. Also *fig.* ***liberation theology, theology of liberation***: see LIBERATION THEOLOGY.

1669 GALE *Crt. Gentiles* I. III. iv. 53 Aristotle wonderfully agrees with the Mosaic Theologie herein. **1796** H. HUNTER tr. *St.-Pierre's Stud. Nat.* (1799) III. 734 Among those questions, two hundred referred to the theology of the Hebrews. **1830** MACKINTOSH *Eth. Philos.* Wks. 1846 I. 81 Clarke..considered such a scheme as the only security against Hobbism, and probably also against the Calvinistic theology. **1837** HALLAM *Hist. Lit.* (1847) I. i. §18. 13 The scholastic theology..was, in its general principle, an alliance between faith and reason. **1874** J. B. BROWN *Higher Life* xx. 408 There lies a meaning in these glorious words..for which there is no room that I can see in any of our theologies. **1899** C. K. PAUL *Mem.* iv. 130 There [at Eton] in 1841 [some] of us..became conscious of the great stir which was going on at Oxford; a few of our masters were falling under the influence of the new theology. **1907** *Standard* 19 Jan. 9/4 Latest development of 'New Theology'. **1956** P. A. LARKIN *Less Deceived* 36 Our garden, first: where I did not invent Blinding theologies of flowers and fruit, And wasn't spoken to by an old hat.

c. Applied to pagan or non-Christian systems.

1662 STILLINGFL. *Orig. Sacr.* I. ii. §8 Had we no other demonstration of the greatness of mans Apostacy and degeneracy, the Ægyptian Theology would be an irrefragable evidence of it. **1677** GILPIN *Demonol.* (1867) 201 The Gentile theology of demons is the thing which Paul prophesies should be introduced into Christianity. **1712** ADDISON *Spect.* No. 471 ¶8 Our Forefather, according to the Pagan Theology, had a great Vessel presented him by Pandora. **1841** ELPHINSTONE *Hist. India* II. iv. (1845) I. 211 Their theology, mythology, philosophy,..are almost entirely of the Hindú family.

d. In trivial or disparaging use: a system of theoretical principles; an (impractical or rigid) ideology. Cf. THEOLOGICAL *a.* (*sb.*) 3.

1962 *Listener* 29 Mar. 551/2, I would also like to see a couple of first-class philosophers, who would..check the new brand of strategists, who have produced a complete theology, not only about the deterrent but about conventional weapons, and about morale and everything else. I think the spectacle of Whitehall trying to keep up with American theologies is too sad for words. **1973** *Times* 3 Oct. 14/4 There were also a few rival interpretations of Marxist theology. *a* **1974** R. CROSSMAN *Diaries* (1976) II. 391 At S.E.P., this morning, we were discussing Paper 105, a brilliant demolition of the theology of PESC. **1980** *Times Lit. Suppl.* 8 Feb. 134/2 Like the farmers of Iowa in relation to China in a later period, they were impatient with the theology of diplomatic recognition.

†**2. a.** Rarely used for Holy Scripture. So late Gr. θεολογία (Pseudo-Dion. *de Cæl. Hier.* 9 §3), med.L. *theologia*. *Obs.*

[Cf. *a* **1149** *Hugo de S. Victore* (in Migne 1091 C), Theologia, id est divina scriptura.] **1494** FABYAN *Chron.* VII. ccxx. 242 This Lamfranke..was perfytely lerned in the scyence of theologie or holy wrytte. [Cf. **1653** MILTON *Hirelings* (1659) 98 The study of Scripture (which is the only true theologie).]

†**b.** Hence, ***virtues of theology*** (also *vertues theologyes*, (?) *theologycs*) = 'theological virtues': see THEOLOGICAL 1. *Obs.*

1422 tr. *Secreta Secret., Priv. Priv.* 124 The prologe of the iiij^e. Cardynale vertues, declarynge the .iij^e. vertues of theologie, and foure maner of goodis. *Ibid.* 145 Ther byth thre Vertues pryncipalle of theologi or dyuynte, y-callid in lateyne Fides, Spes, Caritas. **1502** *Ord. Crysten Men* (W. de W. 1506) II. i. 85 The thre vertues theologyes or diuynes.

†**3.** Metaphysics. (See Note below.) *Obs.*

1390 GOWER *Conf.* III. 86–7 Theorique..stant departed upon thre, The ferste..Is cleped in Philosophie The science of Theologie, That other named is Phisique, The thridde is seid Mathematique. Theologie is that science Which unto man yifth evidence Of thing which is noght bodely. *c* **1425** (?) LYDG. *Assembly of Gods* 859 Arsmetry, Geometry with Astronomy,..Nobyll Theology, and Corporall Physyk.

[*Note.* Gr. θεολογία meant 'an account of the gods, or of God (whether legendary or philosophical)'. Varro, following the Stoics, distinguished three kinds of *theologia*, mythical, natural (rational), and civil, the last being the knowledge of the due rites and ceremonies of religion. This threefold division is referred to also by Tertullian and St. Augustine. In Christian Greek, the vb. θεολογεῖν was used = 'to speak of as God, to attribute deity to', whence θεολογία had the specific sense of 'the ascription of a divine nature to Christ', in contrast to οἰκονομία, the doctrine of his incarnation and human nature. Another patristic Gr. use, arising out of the primary sense, was 'the account of God, or record of God's ways, as given in the Bible', whence the late Gr. and med.L. use of *theologia* for the Scriptures themselves. In the 12th c. (1121–40) Abelard applied the term to a philosophical treatment of the doctrines of the Christian religion, which, though at first strongly condemned, became current, and, in this sense, 'theologia' came to designate a department of academic study, the text-books of which were the Bible and the Sentences (from the Fathers) of Peter Lombard. Hence the earliest Eng. use. (The passage from Gower in sense 3 is derived ultimately from Aristotle's division of the theoretic forms of philosophy into μαθηματική, φυσική, θεολογική, the last being what we should call metaphysics, which included his doctrine of the divine nature.)]

†ˈ**theolony.** *Obs. rare*⁻¹. [ad. med.L. *theolōneum* tax, impost, corruption of late L. *telōnium* (-*eum*), in Vulg., ad. Gr. τελώνιον toll-house, custom-house.] Payment of taxes, tolls, or imposts.

1610 W. FOLKINGHAM *Art of Survey* III. iv, Immunities and Exemptions from Theolonie, Pontage, Picage, Murage [etc.].

theomachy (θiːˈɒməkɪ). Also 6 in Gr.-L. form **theomachia** (θiːəʊˈmækɪə). [ad. Gr. θεομαχία, f. θεός god + -μαχία fighting.]

†**1.** A striving or warring against God; opposition to the will of God. **b.** *spec.* See quot. *Obs.*

1570–6 LAMBARDE *Peramb. Kent* (1826) 327 The whole religion of Papistrie..is Theomachia and nothing else. **1598** BACON *Sacr. Medit.* xi. (Arb.) 127 Atheisme and Theomachie rebelleth and mutineth against the power of God. **1633** T. ADAMS *Exp. 2 Peter* ii. 3 A theomachy, a desperate war against heaven. **1690** C. NESSE *O. & N. Test.* I. 134 This theomachy or rebelling against God.

b. 1656 BLOUNT *Glossogr.*, *Theomachy*, a warring or fighting against the gods, as the old Giants are feigned to have done.

2. A battle or strife among the gods: esp. in reference to that narrated in Homer's Iliad.

1858 GLADSTONE *Homer* II. ii. 77 When we come to discuss the position of Latona, both generally and in the Theomachy. **1865** —— *Farewell Addr. Edin. Univ.* 29 Xanthos, a river god, appears in the Theomachy. **1878** —— *Prim. Homer* vi. §27. 83 Artemis..is sorely belaboured, in the Theomachy, by the strong arm of Hera.

Hence [or from Gr. θεομάχ-ος] **theomachist** (θiːˈɒməkɪst), one who fights against God.

1794 MATHIAS *Purs. Lit.* (1798) 18 The continued labours of the arch Theomachist of the age,..that..conflict which he maintained, during..a long and impious life, against the spiritual 'kingdoms of God and of his Christ'. **1871** T. HARDY *Desperate Remedies* viii, To resist fate with the vindictive determination of a Theomachist.

†**theo'magic,** *a.* (*sb.*) *Obs. rare.* [f. THEO- + MAGIC.] Of or pertaining to magic claiming to be wrought by divine aid. **b. theo'magics** *sb. pl.*, the principles and practice of 'theomagic' art. So †**theo'magical** *a.*; †**theoma'gician**, one who practises 'theomagics'.

1650 H. MORE *Observ.* in *Enthus. Tri.*, etc. (1656) Fj, The ..Magicall Multiplication, or Theomagical fecundity of your Divine Writings. *Ibid.* 72 Anthroposophus would be a rare Theomagician indeed. *Ibid.* 76 We will set the saddle on the right Horse; and this Theomagick jade shall bear the blame. *Ibid.* 127 His strange mysteries of his Theomagick stone. **1651** —— *Second Lash* ibid. 170 A publick professor of Theomagicks. **1656** BLOUNT *Glossogr.*, *Theomagical*, pertaining to the wisdome of God, or that works wonders by his help.

theomammonist: see THEO-.

theomancy (ˈθiːəʊmænsɪ). [ad. Gr. θεομαντεία spirit of prophecy, f. θεός god + μαντεία divination: see -MANCY.] A kind of divination: see quots.

1651 HOBBES *Leviath.* I. xii. 56 These kinds of foretelling events were accounted Theomancy, or Prophecy. **1807** ROBINSON *Archæol. Græca* III. xii. 257 Theomancy is distinguished from oracular divination, which was commonly limited to a fixed and stated time, and always to a certain place; whilst the θεομάντεις were free and unconfined, and able to offer sacrifices, and perform other prophetic rites, at any time, and in any part of the world. **1842** BRANDE *Dict. Sc.*, etc., *Theomancy*, a name..given to that species of divination which was drawn from the responses of oracles.., or from the predictions of sibyls and others supposed to be immediately inspired by some divinity.

Hence **theo'mantic** *a.*, pertaining to theomancy.

1620 MIDDLETON & ROWLEY *World Tost at Tennis* 258 Strike, by white art, a theomantic power, Magic divine. **1684** tr. *Agrippa's Van. Arts* xlvii. 122 This part..is twofold: Arithmantick..and Theomantick, which searches into the mysteries of the Divine Majesty.

theomania, -iac, to **theomonism**: see THEO-.

†**theomeny.** *Obs. rare*⁻⁰. [ad. Gr. θεομηνία the wrath of God, f. θεός God + μῆνις wrath.]

1623 COCKERAM, *Theomenie*, the wrath of God. **1656** BLOUNT *Glossogr.*, Theominy.

theomorphic (θiːəʊˈmɔːfɪk), *a.* [f. Gr. θεόμορφος of divine form (f. θεό-ς god + μόρφη form) + -IC.] Having the form or likeness of God; of or pertaining to theomorphism.

1870 J. H. BLUNT *Dict. Theol.* 324/2 Although the Creator thus made man theomorphic, we are not to think of God as anthropomorphic. **1889** A. MOORE *Christian Doctr. God* in *Lux Mundi* 64 A theomorphic view of man is of the essence of his faith. **1894** J. R. ILLINGWORTH *Personality Hum. & Div.* viii. (1895) 214 Our anthropomorphic language follows from our theomorphic minds. **1897** OTTLEY *Aspects O. Test.* vii. 340 Mosaism recognizes, so to speak, the theomorphic structure of man.

So **theo'morphism**, the doctrine that man has the form or likeness of God; **theo'morphize** *v., trans.* to form in the image of God.

1822 tr. *Malte-Brun's Universal Geogr.* I. 576 *Theomorphism*, the religion of the Hindoos, is the best supported of all the ancient systems of worship; it still exists. **1886** MIVART in *Fortn. Rev.* Jan. 63 A natural and innocuous Anthropomorphism of the intellect—which..may be more properly called Theomorphism. **1897** T. STEPHENS in *Evang. Mag.* June 289 Theomorphism in the doctrine of man has gone on side by side with anthropomorphism in the doctrine of God. **1905** J. ORR *Probl. O. Test.* v. 118 God, in creating, theomorphises man.

ˌtheo-myˈthology. [f. THEO- + MYTHOLOGY. (Cf. Gr. θεομυθία divine lore, mythology.)] A combination of theology and mythology. Hence **ˌtheo-myˈthologer.**

1858 GLADSTONE *Homer* II. i. 2 That which, following German example, I have denominated the Theo-mythology of Homer. By that term it seems not improper to designate a mixture of theology and mythology. *Ibid.* v. 366, I have a lively conviction that Homer was (so to speak) the theomythologer who moulded these materials into system. **1868** —— *Juv. Mundi* ix. (1870) 349 The will and power of the Olympian deities..may be described, from its mixed character of truth and fable, as the Theomythology of the poet.

theonomy (θiːˈɒnəmɪ). [f. Gr. θεό-ς God + -νομία, -NOMY, after Ger. *theonomie* (1838 in Heyse).] Administration or government by God; the condition of being ruled or governed by God.

1890 J. F. SMITH tr. *Pfleiderer's Developm. Theol. since Kant* i. 14 His autonomy must therefore..be an actual (not merely subjectively conceived) theonomy. **1905** P. T. FORSYTH in *Contemp. Rev.* Oct. 578 The God who rules us in Christ is not a foreign power. Theonomy is not heteronomy. He, our law, becomes also our life.

theopanphilist, -pantism: see THEO-.

Theopaschite (θiːəʊˈpæskaɪt). *Ch. Hist.* Also 6 -paschit, 7 -passit. [ad. eccl. L. *theopaschīta*, ad. Gr. θεοπασχίτης, f. θεό-ς god + πάσχ-ειν to suffer: see -ITE[1] 1 a.] A member of a Monophysite sect of the 6th c., who held that the divine nature of Christ suffered on the Cross. Also *attrib.*

1585 T. ROGERS *39 Art.* ii. §2 (1625) 11 Most wicked were the opinions of those men which held..that..Christ had a bodie without a soule; as thought..the Theopaschites. *Ibid.* §4. 14 That Christ really and indeed, hung not on the crosse: for his passion was in showe onely, said the Cerdonites..and the Manicheans: and another man, saide the Theopaschits, ..suffered, and hung on the crosse. **1625** GILL *Sacr. Philos.* IV. 32 The errours..of the Theopaschites, who held that the God-head of Christ did suffer, while His body was nayled on the Crosse. **1874–86** J. H. BLUNT *Dict. Sects*, etc., *Theopaschites*, a sect of the Monophysites who maintained that Christ having only one Nature, and that the Divine, it was therefore the Divine Nature which suffered..at the Crucifixion. **1882–3** *Schaff's Encycl. Relig. Knowl.* III. 2346 Theopaschites..a by-name applied to such as accepted the formula, that..'God had suffered and been crucified'. **1914** W. E. BEET *Medieval Papacy* 15 Uncompromising was the attitude of Hormisdas with reference to the so-called Theopaschite formula. **1971** R. BROWNING *Justinian & Theodora* iii. 102 His [*sc.* Justinian's] new 'Theopaschite' doctrine in the end contributed nothing to the religious unity of the empire.

Hence **Theopaschitally** (-ˈpæskɪtəlɪ) *adv.*, in the manner of, or in accordance with the doctrine of the Theopaschites; **Theopaschitic** (-pæˈskɪtɪk) *a.*, of or pertaining to the Theopaschites or their doctrine; **Theopaschitism** (-ˈpæskɪtɪz(ə)m), the doctrine or tenets of the Theopaschites. So **Theopaschist** (-ˈpæskɪst), a Theopaschite.

1887 RICHTER *Levana* ix. 154 Theologians are active *Theopaschists. **1882** CAVE & BANKS tr. *Dorner's Chr. Doctr.* 209 In this respect it speaks quite *Theopaschitally. **1893** E. K. MITCHELL tr. *Harnack's Hist. Dogma* 299 The carrying out of the *theopaschitic formula. **1882–3** *Schaff's Encycl. Relig. Knowl.* I. 463 A revival of..Patripassianism, or *Theopaschitism.

theopathetic (θiːəʊpəˈθɛtɪk), *a.* (*sb.*) [f. THEOPATHY, after *pathetic.*] Of, pertaining to, or characterized by theopathy: see quots.

1748 HARTLEY *Observ. Man* II. iii. §7. 316 To deduce practical Rules concerning the Theopathetic Affections, Faith, Fear, Gratitude, Hope, Trust, Resignation, and Love. **1830** W. TAYLOR *Hist. Surv. Germ. Poetry* II. 5 All these publications..tend to assuade a benevolent sensibility, theopathetic affections, and evangelical doctrines. **1856** R. A. VAUGHAN *Mystics* (1860) I. I. v. 27 There are three kinds of mysticism, theopathetic, theosophic, theurgic. *Ibid.* 31 The mystic of the theopathetic species is content to contemplate, to feel, or to act, suffering under Deity, in his sublime passivity. **1878** DOWDEN *Stud. Lit.* 197 Studying the phenomena of morbid theopathetic emotion.

b. *sb.* (See quot.)

1860 GARDNER *Faiths World* II. 899/2 *Theopathetics*, those mystics who have resigned themselves more or less passively to an imagined divine manifestation.

theopathic (θiːəʊˈpæθɪk), *a.* [f. next.] = prec.

1846 WORCESTER cites *Q. Rev.* **1864** *Edin. Rev.* July 249 One of those rare beings..whose temperament, so to speak, is theopathic. **1899** *Q. Rev.* July 101 The theopathic and contemplative quietism of the East.

theopathy (θiːˈɒpəθɪ). [f. THEO- + -PATHY. Cf. Gr. θεοπάθεια the suffering of God.] Sympathetic passive feeling excited by the contemplation of God; susceptibility to this feeling; sensitiveness or responsiveness to divine influence; pious sentiment. Cf. THEOPATHETIC.

1748 HARTLEY *Observ. Man* I. iv. §5. 486 The Pleasures and Pains of Theopathy: under this Class I comprehend all those Pleasures and Pains, which the Contemplation of God and his Attributes, and of our Relation to Him, raises up. **1816** SOUTHEY *Ess.* (1832) I. 235 In the order of nature, what Hartley calls theopathy, is not, and ought not, to be looked for, as the predominant feeling of youth. **1837** HALLAM *Hist. Lit.* III. ii. §73 The writings..of St. Teresa..are..full of a mystical theopathy. **1881** *Ch. Q. Rev.* 60 The Sufi School, the 'Methodists of the East', as Martyn calls them, in reference to their creedless theopathy.

theophagous (θiːˈɒfəgəs), *a.* [f. THEO- + -PHAGOUS.] Of, pertaining to, or marked by theophagy; God-eating. So **theˈophagy** (-dʒɪ), (*a*) the eating of God (in the mass or communion rite); (*b*) *Anthrop.*, the eating of meals at which the participants believe that they ingest a deity with the consecrated food. **theˈophagite** (-dʒaɪt), (*nonce-wd.*) a God-eater (in quot. *attrib.*).

1805 *Monthly Mag.* XX. 35 The theophagite cannibalism of the communion-rite. **1875** SWINBURNE *Lett.* (1960) III. 49 Would the exalted privilege of theophagy be conceded to a believer in the identity of those two Beings? **1880** —— in *Fortn. Rev.* June 762 In the bosom of a deicidal and theophagous Christianity. *Ibid.*, A creed..based on deicide and sustained on theophagy. **1903** G. B. SHAW *Revolutionist's Handbk.* viii. in *Man & Superman* 209 We have relapsed into disputes about transubstantiation at the very moment when the discovery of the wide prevalence of theophagy as a tribal custom has deprived us of the last excuse for believing that our official religious rites differ in essentials from those of barbarians. **1907** *Hibbert Jrnl.* Apr. 684 The origin of the rites of Theophagy or Communion. **1912** *Encycl. Relig. & Ethics* V. 136/1 The chief among the reasons given for the correlated rite of theophagy. *Ibid.* 137/1 A more detailed account supplies a valuable type of such theophagous ceremonies. **1937** *Jrnl. Theol. Stud.* XXXVIII. 97 Notable also is the demonstration how slight evidence we have, not only that any one ever associated theophagy with the Dionysiac omophagy, but even that any one in the centuries with which we are concerned ever celebrated an omophagy at all. **1956** C. WINICK *Dict. Anthropol.* (1957) 533/2 *Theophagy*, the practice of ingesting the god. It probably stemmed from the ancient habit of eating the sacred animal to secure blessing, grace, and identity with the deity.

theophany (θiːˈɒfənɪ). [ad. L. *theophania* (*c* 400 in Rufinus), a. Gr. θεοφάνεια and θεοφάνια (neut. pl.), f. θεός god + φαίνειν to show: see -PHANY. So F. *théophanie*. Cf. TIFFANY.] **a.** A manifestation or appearance of God or a god to man. Also *transf.*

a **1633** AUSTIN *Medit.* (1635) 56 First, the Starre manifested him..from the Heavens. That's, the Epiphany: Secondly, it manifested him from God (in Trinity): for hee sent the Starre. There's, the Theophany. And lastly; It manifested him on Earth (in Domo):..There's the Bethphany. **1677** GALE *Crt. Gentiles* II. III. 193 Neither was the name Theophanie, which signifies the apparition of God or the Gods, unusual even among the Gentiles. **1854** MILMAN *Lat. Chr.* VIII. v. III. 352 The universe is but a sublime Theophany, a visible manifestation of God. **1894** F. WATSON *Genesis a true Hist.* vi. 141 In the records of the Theophanies to Joshua, Gideon, and Manoah. *Ibid.*, The Theophany to Elijah at Horeb. **1962** AUDEN *Dyer's Hand* (1963) 256 The practical joker desires to make others obey him without being aware of his existence until the moment of his theophany.

b. A festival celebrating the manifestation of a deity. (Sometimes spec. applied to Christmas.)

1745 A. BUTLER *Lives Saints* (1836) I. 26 *note*, The Greeks still keep the Epiphany with the birth of Christ on Christmas-day, which they call *Theophany*, or the manifestation of God. [**1753** CHAMBERS *Cycl. Supp.*, *Theophania*, θεοφάνεια, . a festival observed by the Delphians upon the day whereon Apollo first manifested himself to them.]

Hence **theoˈphanic** *a.*, of or pertaining to theophany; **theˈophanism**, theophany; also, belief in theophanies; **theˈophanous** *a.*, characterized by theophany.

1882–3 *Schaff's Encycl. Relig. Knowl.* III. 2346 No vision is without a *theophanic element. **1886** C. A. BRIGGS *Messianic Proph.* I. vi. §10. 20 It is the theophanic manifestation of God in forms of time and space and the sphere of physical nature. **1849** LADY WILDE tr. *Meinhold's Sidonia Sorc.* III. xiii. II. 184 *note*, All the *theophanisms (God-manifestations) recorded in the Old Testament. **1938** S. BECKETT *Murphy* v. 81 An adherent (on and off) of the extreme theophanism of William of Champeaux. **1970** R. MANHEIM tr. *Corbin's Creative Imagination Ṣūfism* 52 Not to understand..Ibn 'Arabī's conscious intention..of expressing a divine love, would be..to close one's eyes to the theophanism on which this book insists. **1909** *19th Cent.* Oct. 676 This *theophanous land.

theophilanthropist (ˌθiːəʊfɪˈlænθrəpɪst). [f. THEO- + PHILANTHROPIST, after F. *théophilanthrope*, erron. employed to express 'loving God and man', though etymologically it ought to mean 'a divine philanthropist'.] A member of a sect of Deists which appeared in France in 1796.

1797 W. TAYLOR in *Monthly Rev.* XXIV. 554 It is satisfactory to observe how nearly the Theophilanthropists agree with the more thinking Christians. **1798** HEL. M. WILLIAMS *Tour Switzerl.* I. v. 79 This sect, distinguished by the name of Theophilanthropists, the friends of God and man. **1801** BELSHAM *Geo. III*, an. 1797 (R.), The Directory gave great encouragement to a new sect recently established under the name of theo-philanthropists.—These religionists, rejecting all revelation, confined their worship to one Supreme Being. **1897** *Daily News* 16 Jan. 6/2 The Society of Theophilanthropists, whose first public meeting was held in Paris, January 16, 1797, was of purely religious origin.

attrib. **1823** SOUTHEY in *Q. Rev.* XXVIII. 502 The proffered service of the Theophilanthropist lecturers. **1882–3** *Schaff's Encycl. Relig. Knowl.* III. 2347 God, virtue, and the immortality of the soul, formed the three articles of the Theophilanthropist creed.

So **theoˈphilanthrope** [as in F.] in same sense; **ˌtheophilanˈthropic, -ical** *adjs.*, of or pertaining to theophilanthropy or theophilanthropists; **ˌtheophiˈlanthropism** = next.

1801 W. DUPRÉ *Lexicographia Neologica Gallica* 275 *Théophilantrope*,..a *theophilanthrope. **1803** in *Spirit Pub. Jrnls.* VII. 254 We give and bequeath to our friend the Elector of Bavaria, the Bible of the Theophilanthropes. **1843** tr. *Custine's Empire of Czar* III. 64 Their whole adjustment reminds one of the theophilanthropes of the French republic. **1797** W. TAYLOR in *Monthly Rev.* XXIII. 560 The illuminated or *theophilanthropic sect..who are supposed to reject the Old and to socinianize the New Testament. **1895** PÉRONNE *Veil of Liberty* 389 Jean..had now transformed his Huguenot church into a Theophilanthropic temple. **1801** W. DUPRÉ *Lexicographia Neologica Gallica* 276 *Théophilantropique*.., *theophilanthropical. **1804** LARWOOD *No Gun Boats* 32 Having revolted from the Goddess of Reason, and the scheme of *Theophilanthropism. **1860** GARDNER *Faiths World* II. 899/2 An attempt was made by Lamennais to revive Theophilanthropism in 1840, but it utterly failed.

ˌtheophiˈlanthropy. [a. F. *théophilanthropie*, intended to express 'love to God and man': cf. prec.] The deistic system of the theophilanthropists, based on a belief in the existence of God and in the immortality of the soul.

Theophilanthropy was adopted in France as a substitute for Roman Catholicism. It died out *c* 1801–2.

1798 W. TAYLOR in *Monthly Rev.* XXVII. 500 The rise of Martinism and of Theophilanthropy. **1847** J. HARE *Vict. Faith* 7 His Christianity..has been stunted and enervated, ..into a sort of sentimental theophilanthropy. **1895** PÉRONNE *Veil of Liberty* 395 The pastor of Versailles closed his church..and reopened it to preach Theophilanthropy.

theophile, -ist, -philosophic: see THEO-.

‖**theophobia** (θiːəʊˈfəʊbɪə). [f. THEO- + -PHOBIA. Cf. F. *théophobie* (*a* 1784 in Littré *Suppl.*).] Anxious fear of God; dread of divine anger; rarely, aversion to or hatred of God. So **theophobist** (-ˈɒfəbɪst), one who is affected with theophobia.

1870 O. W. HOLMES *Mechanism* (1888) 105 Pascal, whose reverence amounted to *theophobia. **1885** SWINBURNE *Misc.* (1886) 239 His..masterpiece of *Cain*,..might seem to a devout spirit to have been dictated by actual theophobia. **1899** *Expositor* Oct. 317 Those men laboured under a terrible disease—it is called Theophobia. **1885** MRS. H. WARD tr. *Amiel's Jrnl.* II. 134 A *theophobist, whom faith in goodness rouses to a fury of contempt.

theophoric, -ous, -physical: see THEO-.

Theophrastian (θiːəʊˈfræstɪən), *a.* Also -an, -ean. [f. L. *Theophrastus*, a. Gr. Θεόφραστος, a Greek philosopher of Eresus in Lesbos (4th c. B.C.) + -IAN.] Of, pertaining to, or characteristic of Theophrastus or his writings, esp. his *Characters*, a set of thirty sketches on disagreeable aspects of human behaviour. So **Theoˈphrastic**, † **Theoˈphrastical** *adjs.*

1662 J. SPARROW tr. J. Boehme in *Remainder of Bks.: Apol. conc. Perfection* 132 Not Tinctured, according to the Cabalisticall, Theophrasticall, Roso-Crucian kind. **1924** *Public Opinion* 18 Jan. 53/2 Some charming little essay or Theophrastan Study. **1926** *Glasgow Herald* 8 Apr. 4 One of the earliest [Characters] which has the true Theophrastian ring. **1928** *Observer* 12 Feb. 4 Some of these Theophrastic 'characters' are very charming. **1962** W. & M. KNEALE *Devel. Logic* iv. 190 Any account of modal syllogisms, either Aristotelian or Theophrastean.

theophylline (θiːəʊˈfɪlaɪn). *Chem.* [irreg. f. mod.L. *thea* TEA + Gr. φύλλον leaf + -INE[5].] A colourless alkaloid, $C_7H_8N_4O_2$, found in tea-leaves.

1894 in MORLEY & MUIR *Watts' Dict. Chem.* IV. 682/2. **1899** *Syd. Soc. Lex.*, *Theophyllin*,..an alkaloid discovered in tea. It is isomeric with the base obtained from cacao (theobromine) and with paraxanthin, but differs from them in its reactions. **1957** [see ORAL *a.* 4 b]. **1976** *Lancet* 20 Nov. 1115/2 Theophylline..and caffeine have been shown to be strong prostaglandin antagonists and weak agonists. **1983** *Daily Tel.* 18 Aug. 8/6 The council found that tea has three bracing ingredients—caffeine which stimulates the nervous system, and theophylline and theobromine which relax muscles and stimulate the heart.

theoplasm (ˈθiːəʊplæz(ə)m). *rare.* [f. THEO- + PLASM.] (See quot. 1901.)

1901 E. S. HARTLAND in *Folk-lore* XII. 27 *Tilo*,..like the Siouan *Wakanda*, is found to be theoplasm, god-stuff, not a god fully formed and finally evolved. **1941** R. R. MARETT *Jerseyman at Oxford* xi. 161 My conception of the process whereby both magic and religion had evolved out of the same 'theoplasm or god-stuff', as Hartland was for calling it.

theopneust (ˈθiːəʊpnjuːst), *a.* [ad. Gr. θεόπνευστος, f. θεό-ς God + -πνευστος inspired, f. stem πνευ- of πνεῖν to breathe, blow.] Divinely inspired.

1647 HAMMOND *Power of Keys* iii. 30 Which delivers down all the books which make up our Canon of Scripture, for Canonicall, and Theopneust. **1806** G. S. FABER *Diss. Prophecies* (1814) II. 314 The promotion of image-worship, the purpose for which this misnamed *theopneust assembly* met together. **1885** tr. *Wellhausen's Hist. Israel* I. iii. 48 Their polemic is a purely prophetic one, i.e. individual, theopneust,..independent of all traditional..opinions.

So **theoˈpneustic** *a.* in same sense; **theoˈpneusty** [Ger. *theopneustie* (Heyse 1837), F. *théopneustie* (Littré)], ‖**theoˈpneustia** [Gr. θεοπνευστία], divine inspiration; also **theopneustian**.

1894 *Thinker* VI. 67 According to this theory, the writers of the books of Kings and Chronicles needed and received less of *theopneustia than the prophet Isaiah or the Evangelist John. **1660** S. FISHER *Rusticks Alarm* IV. i. Wks. (1679) 592 Denying any such *Theopneustian [*sic*], Divine Inspiration, Revelation, Motion, immediate Mission. **1827** HARE *Guesses* Ser. I. (1873) 209 Its [Christianity's] anthropomorphism is *theopneustic. **1847** J. W. DONALDSON *Vind. Protest. Princ.* 50 If man is, in his higher nature, a theopneustic being. **1847** WEBSTER, **Theopneusty*, divine inspiration.

theoˈpolitics, *sb. pl. rare.* [f. THEO- + POLITICS.] Politics based on the law of God. So **theopoliˈtician**, one who bases his politics on conformity to the will of God or the divine law; †**theoˈpolity**, a polity based on the law of God.

1736 BAILEY (folio) Pref., *Theopoliticks*..godly or divine Politics. *Ibid.*, *Theopolity*..a godly or divine Administration of the Republick. **1867** *Union Rev.* July 346 He is not so much a politician as a theopolitician. **1945** in J. H. Whyte *Church & State in Mod. Ireland* (1980) iii. 71 The Catholic press. A study in theopolitics.

theopsychism: see THEO-.

theor (ˈθiːɔː(r)). *Gr. Antiq.* Also in L. form **theˈorus**. [mod. ad. Gr. θεωρ-ός spectator, one who travels in order to see things, also an envoy, ambassador: see THEORY[2].] An ambassador or envoy sent on behalf of a state, esp. to consult an oracle or perform a religious rite. (Cf. THEORY[2].)

1847 GROTE *Greece* II. ix. III. 37 The Theors or sacred envoys..appeared with ostentatious pomp. **1849** *Ibid.* II. lv. VII. 73 The tent which the Athenian theôrs provided for their countrymen visitors to the games. **1873** SYMONDS *Grk. Poets* iii. 90 He went as a Theorus to the shrine of Delphi.

theorbo (θiːˈɔːbəʊ). Also 7 **theorboe**, 7–8 **-orba**; 7 **theorb'**, 7–8 **-orb**, 8–9 **-orbe**. [ad. F. *téorbe*, *théorbe* (17th c.), ad. It. *tiorba* 'a kind of musicall instrument used among countrie people' (Florio 1598), Sp. *tiorba*. The spelling with *th* appears first in Eng. (prob. after the THEO- group); the ending *-o* for It. and Sp. *-a* occurs in other words: see -ADO. Origin of the It. word unknown: some suggest that it was named after the inventor.] A large kind of lute with a double neck and two sets of tuning-pegs, the lower holding the melody strings and the upper the bass strings; much in vogue in the 17th century. (Cf. ARCHLUTE.)

1605 CHAPMAN *All Fooles* Plays 1873 I. 144 *Cor.* Take thy Theorbo for my sake a little. *Val.* By heauen, this moneth I toucht not a Theorbo. **1611** CORYAT *Crudities* 252 Two singular fellowes played together vpon Theorboes. **1652** BENLOWES *Theoph.* I. lv, There sweet Religion strings and tunes, and skrues The Souls Theorb', and doth infuse Grave Dorick Epods. **1690** SHADWELL *Am. Bigot* IV. i, I had provided this drum to sing to, which is better than a Theorb, or Harpsychord. **1697** tr. *C'tess D'Aunoy's Trav.* (1706) 258, I never saw any Virginals or Theorba's here. **1899** E. GOSSE *J. Donne* i. 28 A madrigal for the theorbo. **1906** *Blackw. Mag.* Sept. 338/2 The whole household purchased Theorbes.

attrib. and *Comb.* **1657** J. GAMBLE (*title*) Ayres and Dialogues. To be Sung to the Theorbo-Lute or Bass-Viol. **1676** T. MACE *Musick's Monum.* 236 A Stop..which my Work-man calls the Theorbo Stop. **1688** PLAYFORD (*title*) Harmonia Sacra..: with a Thorow-bass for the Theorbo-Lute, Bass-Viol, Harpsichord, or Organ. **1880** SHORTHOUSE *J. Inglesant* xxii, He found a young man,..playing on a double-necked theorbolute.

Hence **theˈorboed** (-əʊd) *ppl. a.*, converted into a theorbo; **theˈorbist**, a player on the theorbo.

1611 CORYAT *Crudities* 252 These two Theorbists concluded the night's musicke. **1889** A. J. HIPKINS in Grove *Dict. Mus.* IV. 100/2 Early in the 17th century many large lutes had been altered to theorbos by substituting double necks for the original single ones... The theorbo engraved in Mersenne's 'Harmonie Universelle' (Paris, 1636) is really a theorboed lute. **1976** *Early Music* Oct. 414/2 Quantz wrote that the theorbist should sit behind the second harpsichord, between two cellists. **1980** *Ibid.* Jan. 50/1 A lutenist and theorbist are shown in the orchestra in two contemporary drawings of the performance of *Teofane*.

theorem (ˈθiːərɪm), *sb.* Also 6–7 **-eme**. [ad. late L. *theōrēma* (Gellius), a. Gr. θεώρημα, -ματ-, spectacle, speculation, theory, (in Euclid) a proposition to be proved, f. θεωρεῖν to be a spectator (θεωρός), to look at, inspect. Perh. directly a. F. *théorème* (*téorème* in Rabelais).]

1. A universal or general proposition or statement, not self-evident (thus distinguished from an AXIOM), but demonstrable by argument (in the strict sense, by necessary reasoning); 'a demonstrable theoretical judgement' (Abp. Thomson).

a. In Mathematics and Physics; *spec.* in Geometry, a proposition embodying merely something to be proved, as distinguished from a PROBLEM (sense 4), which embodies something to be done.

Particular theorems are usually named after their discoverers or investigators, as *Boole's*, *Carnot's*, *Cauchy's*, *Cayley's*, *Clifford's*, *Euler's*, *Fermat's*, *Feuerbach's*, *Galileo's*, *Lagrange's*, *Lambert's*, *Maclaurin's*, *Newton's*, *Pappus's*, *Pascal's*, *Ptolemy's*, *Riemann's*, *Sylvester's*, *Taylor's*, *Wallis's*, *Wilson's* (etc.) *theorem*; sometimes by defining adjectives, as the BINOMIAL, EXPONENTIAL, MULTINOMIAL *theorem*.

1551 RECORDE *Pathw. Knowl.* Argts., The Theoremes, (whiche maye be called approued truthes) seruinge for the due knowledge and sure proofe of all conclusions..in Geometrye. **1570** BILLINGSLEY *Euclid* I. Introd. 8 A Theoreme, is a proposition, which requireth the searching out and demonstration of some propertie..of some figure. **1612** SELDEN in Drayton *Poly-olb.* A iij, His Geometricall Theorem in finding the squares of an Orthogonal triangles sides. **1752** FRANKLIN *Lett.* Wks. 1887 II. 253, I thank you for communicating the illustration of the theorem concerning light. **1806** HUTTON *Course Math.* I. 2 A Theorem is a demonstrative proposition; in which some property is asserted, and the truth of it required to be proved... A set or collection of such Theorems constitutes a Theory. **1816** tr. *Lacroix's Diff. & Int. Calculus* 22 This formula is called Taylor's Theorem, from the English geometer by whom it was discovered. **1862** H. SPENCER *First Princ.* II. xvi. §136 Geometrical theorems grew out of empirical methods.

b. In general sense, or in reference to any particular science or technical subject. (In quot. 1697 applied to an axiom.)

1597 HOOKER *Eccl. Pol.* V. lxxvi. §2 The first being a Theoreme both vnderstood and confest of all, to labour in proofe thereof were superfluous. **1615** CROOKE *Body of Man* 27, I call it a Science, because it hath vniuersall or generall Theoremes or Maximes, and common Notions. **1649** JER. TAYLOR *Gt. Exemp.* I. Ad Sect. vi. 105 Christian Princes can-not be restrained [from war] with the engagements and peaceful Theoremes of..a holy Religion. **1676** COLEY *Astrol.* 143 Note that by the word Theorem is understood a Speculation or an undoubted Rule or Principle in any Science or Art, and is that which respects Contemplation more than Practice. **1697** tr. *Burgersdicius his Logic* I. xxii. 90 *Ax*[*iom*] 10... *Ax.* 11... These Theorems..the Sense of them is manifest enough. **1766** BECCARIA *Ess. Crimes* xiv. (1793) 51 The following general theorem is of great use in determining the certainty of facts. **1835** I. TAYLOR *Spir. Despot.* iii. 101 In working the abstract theorem of a church polity. **1864** BOWEN *Logic* xi. 374 A demonstrable judgment, or one which is announced as needing proof, if theoretical, is called a Theorem.

2. A stencil. Also *transf.*, a design executed by means of a stencil. *Obs.* exc. *Hist.*

1824 *Federal Gaz.* 29 Apr. 1/5 Theorem painting on velvet..varnished theorems or theorems cut from any design..may be had. **1832** L. M. CHILD *Girl's Own Book* (ed. 4) 137 After all the parts are in readiness, lay your theorem upon your drawing paper, take a stiff brush of bristles..fill it with the colour you want. **1968** *Canad. Antiques Collector* June 21/1 Theorem Painting, designs painted on white cotton velvet, was an art introduced to America from England. Also known as Formula or, if on silk, Poonah painting. **1973** *New Yorker* 3 Feb. 40/3 Old theorems (stencilled paintings or watercolors done on velvet or paper by genteel housebound girls in the nineteenth century).

Hence **ˈtheorem** *v.*, *trans.* to express in or by means of a theorem.

1840 CARLYLE *Heroes* i. (1872) 23 They are matters which refuse to be theoremed and diagramed. **1891** G. MEREDITH *One of our Conq.* I. vii. 121 Euclid would have theorem'd it out for you at a glance.

theorematic (ˌθiːərɪˈmætɪk), *a.* [ad. Gr. θεωρηματικός, f. θεώρηματ-, THEOREM + -ικος, -IC. Cf. *problematic*.] Pertaining to, by means of, or of the nature of a theorem. Also †**theoreˈmatical** *a.* Hence **theoreˈmatically** *adv.*, in the way of or by means of a theorem. So **theorematist** (-ˈrɛmətɪst), one who discovers or formulates a theorem. Also †**theoˈremic** *a.* = *theorematic*; †**ˈtheoremist** = *theorematist*.

1656 BLOUNT *Glossogr.*, **Theorematick* or *Theoretick*, belonging to a theoreme, or to contemplation. **1879** W. E. FORSTER in T. W. Reid *Life* (1888) II. 224 The old principle was the Theorematic rule of the Sultan. **1908** *Hibbert Jrnl.* Oct. 102 Theorematic Demonstration. **1730** BAILEY (folio), **Theorematical*, of Theorems. **1755** JOHNSON, Theorematical, Theorematick, Theoremick. **1652** URQUHART *Jewel* Wks. (1834) 291 *Theorematically to infer consequences from infallible maximes. **1788** T. TAYLOR *Proclus* I. 109 We ought to conceive all those theorematically, but not problematically. **1727** BAILEY vol. II, **Theorematist*,..a Finder out or Producer of Theorems. **1701** GREW *Cosm. Sacra* II. v. 52 *Theoremick Truth, or that which lies in the Conceptions we have of Things. **1656** BLOUNT *Glossogr.*, **Theoremist*, a professor of Theoremes.

theoretic (θiːɒˈrɛtɪk), *a.* and *sb.* [ad. late L. *theōrētic-us* (*a* 397 Ambrosius *Exameron* I. 5 §17, *theoreticæ artes* opposed to *actuosæ*), a. Gr. θεωρητικός contemplative, f. θεωρητ-ός that may be seen, f. θεωρεῖν to look at, contemplate, inspect. So F. *théoretique* (1721 in Hatz.-Darm.).]

A. *adj.* †**1.** Speculative. *Obs.*

1656 STANLEY *Hist. Philos.* V. (1701) 180/2 Of Theoretick Philosophy one part enquires into things immutable..and the first causes of things. **1706** PHILLIPS, *Theoretick*, *Theorical*, or *Theorick*, belonging to Theory; Speculative.

2. (Rendering Gr. θεωρητικός in Aristotle.) Contemplative, as opposed to active or practical (πρακτικός): cf. CONTEMPLATIVE A. 3. *rare.*

1907 J. SETH in *Hibbert Jrnl.* Oct. 117 In Aristotle we find the affirmation of the superior value..of the 'theoretic' or spiritual life to the practical life.

3. a. = THEORETICAL 2.

a **1661** FULLER *Worthies, Cornw.* (1662) I. 202 Attaining to great perfection in the Theoretick, and practicall parts of those professions. **1750** JOHNSON *Rambler* No. 77 ¶7 Few men, celebrated for theoretick wisdom, live with conformity to their precepts. **1773** *Life N. Frowde* 65, I soon reduced my Theoretic Knowledge to Practice. **1862** TYNDALL *Mountaineer.* ii. 10 Our master minds built their theoretic edifices upon the rock of fact.

b. = THEORETICAL 2 b.

1790 BURKE *Fr. Rev.* Wks. V. 234 Is it then true, that..it was of absolute necessity the whole fabrick should be.. pulled down, and the area cleared for the erection of a theoretick experimental edifice in its place? **1837** CARLYLE *Fr. Rev.* II. I. ii, Plots which cannot be executed; which are mostly theoretic. **1856** EMERSON *Eng. Traits, Universities* Wks. (Bohn) II. 91 Seven years' residence is the theoretic period for a master's degree.

c. Of persons, their minds, etc.: Versed in or proceeding by the scientific theory of the subject; opposed to *empirical*; also, Given to theories; speculative; theorizing: sometimes opp. to *practical*; = THEORETICAL 3 a, b.

1727–41 CHAMBERS *Cycl.* s.v., The theoretic physicians were such as went on the foot of reason, in opposition to the empirical physicians, who went wholly on experience. **1783** POTT *Chirurg. Wks.* II. 435 To which theoretic and whimsical people have assigned this disease. **1872** GEO. ELIOT *Middlem.* i, Her mind was theoretic, and yearned by its nature after some lofty conception of the world. *Ibid.* lxxxvi, Distinguished in his side of the county as a theoretic and practical farmer.

4. Relating to the moral perception of beauty. (Used in this sense by Ruskin, in preference to *æsthetic*: see quot., and cf. THEORIA 2.)

1846 RUSKIN *Mod. Paint.* II. III. I. i. §10 The Theoretic faculty is concerned with the moral perception and appreciation of ideas of beauty. And the error respecting it is..calling it Æsthetic, degrading it to a mere operation of sense.

5. As the second element of parasynthetic adjs. formed from compound sbs. of the type *quantum theory*.

1930 *Acta Math.* LIV. 81 (*heading*) A maximal theorem with function-theoretic applications. **1971** E. C. DADE in Powell & Higman *Finite Simple Groups* viii. 249 To use the minimum of ring-theoretic machinery. **1973** *Times Lit. Suppl.* 9 Mar. 267/5 (Advt.), The systems are approached from two directions—proof-theoretic and model-theoretic.

B. *sb.*

1. Usually *pl.*: Theory (as opposed to *practic*, practice); theoretical matters (= next, B.).

1656 STANLEY *Hist. Philos.* V. (1701) 180/1 The Science of things that are is called Theoretick; of those which pertain to Action Practick. **1706** PHILLIPS (ed. Kersey), *Theoreticks*, those things that belong to the Speculative part of Physick. **1860** H. B. WILSON in *Ess. & Rev.* 160 Morals come before contemplation, ethics before theoretics. **1865** HODGSON *Time & Space* II. ix. §68. 566 The three functions are conation, cognition, and feeling. The three branches of knowledge founded on these are Technic, Theoretic, and Teleologic.

2. A person devoted to a life of contemplation. (See quot.; cf. 2 above, and THEORIC *sb.* 4.)

a **1832** BENTHAM *Deontology* (1834) I. 54 A band of men, whom..he [the Moralist] calls theoretics. These men look ..to contemplation alone for the summum bonum... To reach the summit of human felicity, a man has nothing to do but to contemplate. Who would not be a theoretic?

theoretical (θiːɒˈrɛtɪkəl), *a.* and *sb.* [f. as prec. + -AL[1]: see -ICAL.]

A. *adj.* †**1.** (In sense of Gr. θεωρητικός, L. *theōrēticus*.) Of or pertaining to contemplation, contemplative.

1616 BULLOKAR *Eng. Expos.*, *Theoretical*, that which belongeth to contemplation or inward knowledge of a thing.

1623 COCKERAM, *Theoreticall*, belonging to studie or contemplation.

2. Of, pertaining or relating to theory; of the nature of or consisting in theory. Often opp. to *practical*.

a **1652** J. SMITH *Sel. Disc.* vi. 207 They fall into great confusions in many theoretical matters of no small moment. **1700** C. NESSE *Antid. Armin.* (1827) 99 The persons..had merely escaped..through a theoretical knowledge of the Lord. **1727–41** CHAMBERS *Cycl.* s.v. *Theoretic*, The sciences are ordinarily divided into theoretical, as theology, philosophy, &c., and practical, as medicine, law, &c. **1770** COOK *Voy. round World* II. x. (1773) 477 The theoretical arguments which have been brought to prove that the existence of a southern continent is necessary to preserve an equilibrium between the two hemispheres. **1830** MACKINTOSH *Eth. Philos.* Wks. 1846 I. 177 In the strictly theoretical part his exposition is considerably fuller. **1860** MAURY *Phys. Geog. Sea* (Low) viii. §381 These observations agree with the theoretical deductions. **1860** ABP. THOMSON *Laws Th.* §129. 274 Judgments that relate to speculation only are called theoretical; those which refer to practice are practical.

b. That is such according to theory; existing only in theory, ideal, hypothetical.

1826 HENRY *Chem.* II. 699 The theoretical numbers not agreeing with the experimental results, which are those of Dr. John Davy. **1883** SIR N. LINDLEY in *Law Rep. 11 Q.B. Div.* 556 The attachment was granted for something more than a mere theoretical contempt. **1883** GILMOUR *Mongols* xvii. 204 A man..whose existence is evidently..theoretical.

3. a. Of the mind or intellectual faculties: Having the power of forming theories; speculative.

a **1652** J. SMITH *Sel. Disc.* iv. 115 As for the mind and theoretical power. **1863** E. V. NEALE *Anal. Th. & Nat.* 117 The intuitions of space and time, and the conceptions of relation drawn from the theoretical reason.

b. Of persons: Addicted to theory; constructing or dealing with theories; speculative.

1840 CARLYLE *Heroes* vi. (1872) 211 What is to be done?.. a question which theoretical constitution-builders may find easy to answer. **1859** DARWIN *Orig. Spec.* i. (1860) 12 Doubts have been thrown on this principle only by theoretical writers. **1902** J. DENNEY *Death of Christ* iii. 121 The simplest preacher and the most effective is always the most absolutely theoretical. **1922** *Glasgow Herald* 30 Oct. 10 He was a brilliant theoretical chemist. **1936** *Proc. IRE* XXIV. 353 In our search for good emitters, very little aid can be obtained from the theoretical physicist. **1951** C. P. SNOW *Masters* I. v. 48 One of the earliest theoretical chemists. **1958** J. CLEUGH tr. *Jungk's Brighter than Thousand Suns* i. 17 Rutherford for his part did not hesitate to declare that it was the theoretical, not the experimental, physicists who were to blame for the confusion. **1968** J. J. C. SMART *Betw. Sci. & Philos.* 13 Theoretical physicists have far outstripped philosophers in their imaginativeness. **1980** *English World-Wide* I. 251 The importance of this book is that it is by a scholar who is generally considered to be a 'theoretical' linguist, but who is sympathetic to socio-linguistics and its implications for theory.

4. Used as THEORETIC *a.* 5.

1920, etc. [see QUANTUM-THEORETICAL *a.*]. **1934** [see FIELD-THEORETICAL *a.*].

B. *sb.* (*pl.*) Theoretical points or matters.

1860 H. B. WILSON in *Ess. & Rev.* 181 It is..strange..to expect all ministers..to be of one opinion in theoreticals.

theo'retically, *adv.* [f. prec. + -LY².] In a theoretic or theoretical manner.

a. In the way of or by means of theory; in relation to theory. (In quot. 1701 perh. = contemplatively, speculatively.)

1701 NORRIS *Ideal World* I. v. 235 As they [the Divine Ideas] are thus independent upon the existence of things in nature, so also upon all mind or understanding.., that is, I mean, as conceptive, or theoretically considered. **1748** HARTLEY *Observ. Man* I. iii. 343 This lessens the Difference theoretically also. **1831** BREWSTER *Optics* xxxiii. §163. 274 Huygens..investigated the subject, both experimentally and theoretically. **1886** *Manch. Exam.* 6 Jan. 3/1 Questions which are theoretically interesting to thoughtful people and practically interesting to every one.

b. According to theory, in theory, ideally; hypothetically (as opp. to actually).

1790 C. C. PINCKNEY in Sparks *Corr. Amer. Rev.* IV. 341 One great advantage, that might not attend a Constitution theoretically perfect. **1853** LYTTON *My Novel* III. ix, The position was not quite so pleasant as, theoretically, he had deemed it. **1875** WHITNEY *Life Lang.* iv. 67 The possible number of human articulations is theoretically infinite.

theoretician (ˌθiːərɪˈtɪʃən). [f. THEORETIC + -IAN: see -ICIAN.] One who treats of or studies the theoretical side of a subject; = THEORIST 1.

1886 *Q. Rev.* Jan. 284 Not a mere theoretician or 'statist'. **1891** *Athenæum* 29 Aug. 299/2 Among musical theoreticians Mr. Prout occupies a distinguished position. **1931** *Times Lit. Suppl.* 26 Mar. 255/2 The most articulate theoretician among the Russian film producers. **1954** [see ACTIVIST]. **1959** K. R. POPPER *Logic of Sci. Discovery* v. 107 The theoretician..shows the experimenter the way. **1970** *Physics Bull.* Apr. 150/2 These results..provide an incentive for theoreticians to tackle the much more complex problem posed by real finite nuclei. **1980** 'M. FONTEYN' *Magic of Dance* 288 He was by no means a dry, boring theoretician even though he wrote extraordinarily advanced books on dance.

theoreticism (θiːɒˈrɛtɪsɪz(ə)m). [f. THEORETIC *a.* (*sb.*) + -ISM.] (See quot. 1974.) So **theo'reticist** *a.*

1970 B. BREWSTER tr. L. Althusser in *Althusser & Balibar's Reading Capital* 8 One of the theses I advanced as to the nature of philosophy did express a certain 'theoreticist' tendency. More precisely, the definition of philosophy as a theory of theoretical practice..is unilateral and therefore inaccurate. **1974** *Science & Society* XXXVIII. 404 After 1965..Althusser responded to 'theoreticist' and 'positivist' readings of his texts by reformulating in particular his concept of 'philosophy' and its relationship to 'science'. *Ibid.* 421 This dialectical understanding..preserves method against three forms of reductionism and their corresponding ideologies: historical empiricism (historicism)..; structural idealism/empiricism..; and speculative idealism (theoreticism), which radically separates historical and structural analysis. **1981** *Times Lit. Suppl.* 6 Feb. 136/4 They were..saturated in what would have been called—had the word not borne the double taint of 'jargon' and 'theory'—theoreticism.

theoretico- (θiːɒˈrɛtɪkəʊ), combining form from Gr. θεωρητικό-ς THEORETIC, THEORETICAL, as in **theoˌretico-hiˈstorical** *a.*, pertaining to both the theoretical and the historical sides of a subject; **theoˌretico-ˈpractical** *a.*, pertaining to or skilled in the theory as well as the practice of a subject.

1832 AUSTIN *Jurispr.* (1879) II. 1122 A theoretico-practical lawyer extensively versed in law..and in the sciences related to law. **1922** D. AINSLIE tr. *Croce's Aesthetic* (ed. 2) II. vi. 241 Cesarotti purposed (1762) bringing out a great theoretico-historical book. **1970** B. BREWSTER tr. *Althusser & Balibar's Reading Capital* II. i. 73, I intended to interrogate Marx himself, to see where and how he had theoretically reflected the relationship between his work and the theoretico-historical conditions of its production.

‖**theoria** (θiːˈɔːrɪə). *rare.* [a. Gr. θεωρία a looking at, contemplation, f. θεωρεῖν to look at.]

†**1.** ? Contemplation, survey. *Obs. rare.*

1590 MARLOWE *2nd Pt. Tamburl.* IV. iii, My love, In whom the learned Rabbis of this age Might find as many wondrous miracles As in the theoria of the world!

2. The perception of beauty regarded as a moral faculty. (Used in this sense by Ruskin, in contradistinction to *æsthesis*: cf. THEORETIC *a.* 4.)

1846 RUSKIN *Mod. Paint.* II. III. I. ii. §1 The impressions of beauty..are neither sensual nor intellectual, but moral; and for the faculty receiving them..no term can be more accurate..than that employed by the Greeks, 'Theoretic', which I pray permission..to use, and to call the operation of the faculty itself, Theoria. *Ibid.* §6 The mere animal consciousness of the pleasantness I call Æsthesis; but the exulting, reverent, and grateful perception of it I call Theoria.

theoric (ˈθiːərɪk), *sb.* and *a.*¹ *Obs.* or *arch.* Also 4–5 **-ik**, 4–7 **-ike**, 4–9 **-ique**, 5–6 **-yke**, **-yque**, 6–7 **-icke**, **-icque**, 6–8 **-ick**. [ME. *theorique* in Gower, a. OF. *theorique* (13th c. in Godef., opposed to *pratique* practice), prob. repr. a med.L. *theōrica*, Gr. θεωρική (not recorded in this sense): cf. med.L. *theōricus* adj. (13th c. in Du Cange) in *vita theorica* the contemplative life. The place of the stress, as in '*catholic*, is due to Fr. derivation.

(L. **theōricē* sb., attributed in the Dicts. to Jerome, is now eliminated as an error, the word being θεολογικήν.)]

A. *sb.* **1.** = THEORY¹ 4, 5: chiefly in sense 4 b; often opposed to *practic* or *practice*. *Obs.* or *arch.*

1390 GOWER *Conf.* III. 85 The nature of Philosophie, Which Aristotle..Declareth..As of thre points in principal. Wherof the ferste in special Is Theorique. **1483** CAXTON *Gold. Leg.* 389 b/2 Phylosophye is deuyded in thre in theoryque in practyque and in logyque. **1565** J. HALLE *Hist. Expost.* (Percy Soc.) 42 Chirurgerye cannot be perfectlye learned wythoute theorike. **1599** SHAKS. *Hen. V*, I. i. 52 So that the Art and Practique part of Life, Must be the Mistresse to this Theorique. **1601** HOLLAND *Pliny* II. Explan. Words, *Theoricke*, or *Theoretique*, contemplative knowledge without action and practise. **1604** SHAKS. *Oth.* I. i. 24. **1720** STRYPE *Stow's Surv.* (1754) I. I. vi. 32/2 The great French Philosopher Des Cartes..telling us, that, from the Theorique of the Moon, the Moon moves so in her elliptical Orb [etc.]. **1830** MISS MITFORD *Village* Ser. IV. 195 These.. matters..may rather be termed the theorique than the practique of reform. **1853** [see PRACTIC *sb.*¹ 1].

†**b.** A theoretical treatise or discourse. *Obs.*

c **1391** CHAUCER *Astrol.* Prol. 3 The .4. partie shal ben a theorik to declare the Moeuynge of the celestial bodies with [þe] causes.

†**c.** *pl.* **theorics**: theoretical statements or notions; theory; often opp. to *practics* or *practice*.

1551 RECORDE *Pathw. Knowl.* I. Defin., As they in theyr theorikes (which ar only mind workes) do precisely vnderstand these definitions. **1602** BLUNDEVILLE (*title*) The Theoriques of the seuen Planets, shewing all their diuerse motions. **1637** WOTTON *Lett.* (1907) II. 371 He was..a rare mathematician even..in algebra and the theoriques. *a* **1661** FULLER *Worthies, Cornw.* (1662) I. 202 Atwell..was well seen in the Theoricks of Physick, and happy in the practise thereof.

†**2.** A (mental) view or survey; a conspectus.

1591 LAMBARDE *Eiren.* Proheme 2 A summarie consideration & Theorique of the whole office belonging to this Iustice. *Ibid.* I. 4 (*heading*) The First Booke, conteining a Theoricqve [*ed.* 1602, or insight] of the office of the Iustices of Peace.

†**3.** A mechanical device theoretically representing or explaining a natural phenomenon. *Obs.*

1592 DEE *Comp. Rehears.* (Chetham Soc.) 28 Divers other instrumentes as the theorick of the eighth spheare, the nynth and tenth, with an horizon and meridian of copper. **1594** BLUNDEVIL *Exerc.* VI. Introd. (1636) 608 In the Limbe of the backe part is described the Theorique of the Sun, to know therby in what signe and degree the Sun is every day..by laying the Diopter thereto. **1657** W. RAND tr. *Gassendi's Life Peiresc* I. 145 He caused a mechanicall Theoric [*printed* Theorie; the L. is *theoricen mechanicam*] or Instrument to be made..that..the Places of the..Stars might be calculated.

†**4.** A man devoted to contemplation or speculation; a member of a contemplative sect of Essenes. (Cf. PRACTIC *sb.*²) *Obs.*

1625 T. GODWIN *Moses & Aaron* I. xii. 62 Of these Essenes there were two sorts, some Theorikes, giuing themselues wholly to speculation; others Practicks, laborious..in..handy-crafts. *a* **1641** BP. MOUNTAGU *Acts & Mon.* vii. (1642) 430 The one sect hee names Theoriques or Contemplators. **1798** W. TAYLOR in *Monthly Rev.* XXVII. 212 To the theorics, or instructors, a supper only.

†**B.** *adj.* **1.** = THEORETIC 3, THEORETICAL 2. (Often opp. to *practic* = practical.) *Obs.*

1551 RECORDE *Pathw. Knowl.* I. Defin., This exactnes of definition is more meeter for onlye Theorike speculacion, then for practise and outwarde worke. **1662** PLAYFORD *Skill Mus.* I. i. (1674) 5 A true Rule of the Theorick part of Musick. **1726** *Adv. Capt. R. Boyle* (1768) 25 Gardening.. I always took Delight in, both Theoric and Practic. **1804** W. TAYLOR in *Crit. Rev.* Ser. III. III. 528 These were daily instructed..both in the theoric and practic parts of the Pythagorean philosophy.

†**2.** Knowing or studying the theory of things; theorizing; contemplative, speculative; = THEORETIC *a.* 2, 3 c, THEORETICAL 1, 3. *Obs.*

1599 B. JONSON *Cynthia's Rev.* II. iii, According to our subdivision of a courtier, elementary, practique, and theorique. Your courtier theoric, is he that hath arrived to his farthest, and doth now know the court rather by speculation than practice. **1602** PLAT *Delightes for Ladies* Epist. (1605) 3 By fancie framde within a theorique braine. **1632** MASSINGER & FIELD *Fatal Dowry* II. i, A man but young, Yet old in judgment; theoric and practic In all humanity.

theoric (θiːˈɒrɪk), *a.*² *Gr. Antiq.* [ad. Gr. θεωρικός pertaining to spectacles, f. θεωρία viewing, beholding.] Pertaining to or connected with public spectacles, religious functions, and solemn embassies: applied esp. to a fund provided for these purposes from the public treasury at Athens. (Cf. THEORY².)

1727–41 CHAMBERS *Cycl.* s.v., By the law of Eubulus, it was made a capital crime to pervert the theoric money to any other use; even to employ it in the occasions of war. **1852** GROTE *Greece* II. lxxv. IX. 526 The Theoric Board, or Paymasters for the general expenses of public worship and sacrifice. **1884** *Q. Rev.* Oct. 342 Pericles..by his theoric largesses, helped to swell the city mob of idlers.

†**'theorical**, *a. Obs.* [f. as THEORIC *a.*¹ + -AL¹: see -ICAL.]

a. = THEORIC *a.*¹ 1. (Often opp. to *practical.*)

1571 DIGGES *Pantom.* Epist. *ij b, A Discourse Geometricall..containing sundry Theoricall and practicall propositions. *a* **1619** FOTHERBY *Atheom.* II. viii. §5 (1622) 292 Wee must..ioyne theoricall and practicall vertues together. **1651** BIGGS *New Disp.* §230 Theoricall or practicall phlebotomy. **1730** MALCOLM (*title*) A new system of Arithmetick Theorical and Practical.

b. = THEORETICAL 3.

1594 PLAT *Diuerse new Sorts Soyle* 26, I thinke that those ..did not obteine this skil by any true theoricall imagination, but..they did fynde the same without any seeking. **1663** COWLEY *Verses & Ess., Disc. O. Cromwell* (1669) 76, I see you are a Pedant, and Platonical Statesman, a Theorical Common-wealths-man, an Utopian Dreamer. **1730** MALCOLM *Syst. Arith.* Pref. 6 The Theorical writers have treated Arithmetick as a Science.

c. Contemplative, speculative. *rare.*

1612 T. TAYLOR *Comm. Titus* i. 15. 281 Their cheife and eminent inward parts are defiled, whether we consider the theoricall part, that is, the minde and vnderstanding,..or the practicall facultie (included in the conscience). **1734** WATERLAND *Doctrine Holy Trinity* 513 That Three-fold Method of commenting which St. Jerome lays down; namely, the Historical, Tropological, and Theorical; or, in more familiar Terms, the literal, moral, and sublime.

†**'theorically**, *adv. Obs.* [f. prec. + -LY².] In theory; = THEORETICALLY a.

1571 DIGGES *Pantom.* IV. xxv. Ggj, Hitherto haue I onely intreated of the fiue regulare bodies, Theorically and practically opening sundrie meanes to search out the proportion [etc.]. **1640** QUARLES *Enchirid.* 22 It is most requisite for a Prince to prepare against..Warre, both Theorically in reading Heroick Histories; and practically, in maintaining Martiall discipline. **1680** AUBREY *Lives, W. Holder* (1898) I. 404 He is very musicall, both theorically and practically.

theorician (θiːɒˈrɪʃən). [f. (after F. *théoricien*) on THEORIC *sb.* + -IAN; cf. *logician, physician*, etc.] A holder of a theory; = THEORIST.

1841 *Blackw. Mag.* L. 16 To examine Mr. Porter the statistician, to discover a decisive refutation of Mr. Porter the free-trade theorician. **1895** *Westm. Gaz.* 1 Oct. 3/1 Some editors..believed, at the promptings of jealous theoricians, that the Pasteur system was a fallacy. **1905** *Athenæum* 16 Sept. 365/1 Two other poets..are..considered in these pages; and then some theoricians.

‖**theoricon** (θiːˈɔːrɪkən). *Gr. Antiq.* Also **-kon.** [a. Gr. θεωρικόν, neut. of θεωρικός THEORIC *a.*²] The theoric fund in ancient Athens: see THEORIC *a.*²

1828 tr. *Boeckh's Public Econ. Athens* I. 294 The payment of the Theoricon out of the public money was first introduced by Pericles... This distribution of the Theoricon filled the theatre. **1842** BRANDE *Dict. Sc.*, etc., *Theoricon*, in ancient Attic History, the name given to that portion of the revenue of the state which was..reserved for the purpose of theatrical representations. **1850** GROTE *Greece* II. lxvi. VIII. 424 The manager of the Theôrikon or religious festival-fund.

theorism (ˈθiːərɪz(ə)m). *rare.* [f. as next + -ISM.] Theorizing, speculation.

1820 T. CAMPBELL *Let.* 14 July in W. Beattie *Life Thomas Campbell* (1849) II. 370 At times, perhaps, there is a little German theorism in it [*sc.* Arndt's conversation]. **1856** H. R. REYNOLDS in *Life* v. (1898) 125 The lynx-eyed theorism of Lepsius. **1906** *Contemp. Rev.* July 60 Dead, dry-as-dust theorism.

theorist (ˈθiːərɪst). [f. THEORY (or its Gr. or L. source) + -IST.]

1. An adept in the theory (as distinct from the practice) of a subject. Often with mixture of sense 2.

1594 CAREW *Huarte's Exam. Wits* xii. (1596) 177 It is a miracle to find out a Phisition, who is both a great Theorist, and withall a great Practitioner. **1664** POWER *Exp. Philos.* Pref. 16 The Theorists in Conical Sections. **1784** *Cook's Voy. Pacific Ocean* v. vii. III. 144 *note*, Burney..perhaps the greatest musical theorist of this or any other age. **1855** MACAULAY *Hist. Eng.* xx. IV. 492 It is..curious..that a man who, as a theorist, was distinguished..by the largeness of his views..should, in practice, have been distinguished..by the obstinacy with which he adhered to an ancient mode of doing business.

2. One who theorizes; one who frames or propounds a theory or theories, a theoretical investigator or writer; one who holds or maintains a theory; sometimes, a framer or maintainer of a mere hypothesis or speculation (cf. THEORY[1] 6).

1646 SIR T. BROWNE *Pseud. Ep.* 115 That a Brock or Badger hath his legs of one side shorter then of the other,..an opinion..received not only by theorists and unexperienced beleevers, but assented unto by most who..behold and hunt them dayly. **1692** BENTLEY *Boyle Lect.* vii. 204 It [gravitation] is lately demonstrated..by that very excellent and divine theorist Mr. Isaac Newton. **1735** JOHNSON *Lobo's Abyssinia, Descr.* x. 106 Some of these Theorists have been pleas'd to declare it as their favourite Notion. **1884** *Spectator* 4 Oct. 1309/1 As a theorist on law, he has a distinctive place of his own.

theorize (ˈθiːəraɪz), *v.* [f. as prec. + -IZE: cf. med.L. *theōrizāre* (Scotus Erigena *a* 880).]

†**1.** *trans.* To contemplate, survey. *Obs. rare.*

1638 SIR T. HERBERT *Trav.* (ed. 2) 223 Hitherto wee have beene practicall; let mee now draw your eyes to theorize in generall the severall properties and fashions of this great Empire.

2. *intr.* To form or construct theories.

1638 SIR T. HERBERT *Trav.* (ed. 2) 6 Let us theorize a little upon the Mathematiques. **1797** GILLIES *Aristotle's Ethics* x. vii. I. 397 Even unassisted and alone, though perhaps better with assistants, he [the sage] can still think and theorize. **1809–10** COLERIDGE *Friend* I. iv. (1865) 118 The meanest of men has his theory, and to think at all is to theorize. **1845** JEBB *Gen. Princ. Law* in *Encycl. Metrop.* II. 677/1 He did not theorize without regard to facts and experience. *a* **1862** BUCKLE *Misc. Wks.* (1872) I. 16.

3. *trans.* To construct a theory of or about.

a **1848** W. A. BUTLER *Hist. Anc. Philos.* (1856) I. 40 [Mechanics] theorizes the forces and motions of the masses; [Chemistry] the intimate structure of each.

b. To suppose, or assume, in the way of theory. (With simple obj. or obj. clause.)

1838 G. S. FABER *Inquiry* 107 We can scarcely theorise a lower depth than this glaring and scandalous prostitution of justice. **1863** COWDEN CLARKE *Shaks. Char.* xx. 507 He theorised that the difference between a pea and nothing could make no difference to the poor beast.

c. To make or constitute in theory; to bring *into* or *out of* some condition theoretically.

1843 *Blackw. Mag.* LIII. 697 He had..theorized himself into the future husband of his ward. **1864** LOWELL *McClellan's Rep.* Prose Wks. 1890 V. 97 The one thing that cannot be theorized out of existence..is a lost campaign. **1886** J. KER *Serm.* Ser. II. (1887) xi. 171 Men theorise it into a thing of natural growth.

Hence ˈ**theorized** *ppl. a.*; ˈ**theorizing** *vbl. sb.* and *ppl. a.*; also ˌ**theoriˈzation**, the action of theorizing, construction of a theory or theories; ˈ**theorizer**, one who theorizes.

1820 JEFFERSON *Writ.* (1830) IV. 325 The misconstructions, interpolations, and *theorizations of..fanatics. **1854** E. G. HOLLAND *Mem. J. Badger* 417 Men who have no tendency to speculative theorization. **1975** *Amer. Economic Rev.* LXV. 416/1 It is not obvious whether the net effect of all these shortcomings necessarily exaggerates the regression results in favor of the *theorized results. **1979** *Internat. Jrnl. Sociol. of Law* VII. 319 The material that is reproduced here would undoubtedly be of considerable use in some more theorized or general analysis. **1829** CARLYLE *Crit. & Misc. Ess., Novalis* (1872) II. 197 A great and original plan, very different..from that of our idle *theorisers and generalizers. **1870** PROCTOR *Other Worlds* 3 Not..the mere fanciful theoriser.., but men of the highest eminence in science. **1817** COLERIDGE *Biog. Lit.* I. xii. 258 The necessity of *theorising. **1818** HALLAM *Mid. Ages* (1872) I. Pref. 6 A fault too common,..that of theorising upon an imperfect induction. **1849** NOAD *Electricity* (ed. 3) 127 One fact is worth a volume of theorizing. **1792** J. BELKNAP *Hist. New Hampsh.* III. 229 The inconsistent conclusions of these *theorising philosophers. **1891** *Athenæum* 5 Dec. 753/2 We find the utmost scorn expressed [by Moltke] for..theorizing demagogues.

theory[1] (ˈθiːərɪ). Also 7 -ie, -ee. [ad. late L. *theōria* (Jerome in Ezech. XII. xl. 4), a. Gr. θεωρία a looking at, viewing, contemplation, speculation, theory, also a sight, a spectacle, abstr. sb. f. θεωρός (:—*θεαορός) spectator, looker on, f. stem θεα- of θεᾶσθαι to look on, view, contemplate. In mod. use prob. from med.L. transl. of Aristotle. Cf. It. *teoria* (Florio 1598 *theoría*), F. *théorie* (15.. in Godef. *Compl.*).]

†**1.** A sight, a spectacle. *Obs. rare.*

1605 BP. ANDREWES *Serm., Passion* (1631) 365 Saint Luke ..calleth the Passion θεωρίαν a Theory or Sight... Of our blessed Saviour's whole life or death, there is no part but is a Theorie of it selfe, well worthie our looking on.

†**2.** Mental view, contemplation. *Obs.*

[**1598–1611** FLORIO, *Theoría*, contemplation, speculation, deepe study, insight or beholding.] **1611** COTGR., *Theorie*, theorie, contemplation, deepe studie; a sight, or beholding, speculation. **1643** SIR T. BROWNE *Relig. Med.* I. §45 Nor can I thinke I have the true Theory of death when I contemplate a skull, or behold a Skeleton with those vulgar imaginations it casts upon us. **1646** —— *Pseud. Ep.* VII. xix. 385 As they encrease the hatred of vice in some, so doe they enlarge the theory of wickednesse in all. **1653** W. HARVEY *Anat. Exercit.* Pref. ¶v, All their theory and contemplation (which they count Science) represents nothing but waking mens dreams, and sick mens phrensies. **1710** NORRIS *Chr. Prud.* ii. 65 Speculative Knowledge contemplates Truth for itself, and accordingly stops and rests in the Contemplation of it, which is what we commonly call Theory.

3. A conception or mental scheme of something to be done, or of the method of doing it; a systematic statement of rules or principles to be followed.

1597 HOOKER *Eccl. Pol.* v. xxix. §8 If they had been themselves to execute their owne Theorie in this Church. **1643** BP. HALL *Devout Soul* i, It will hardly be believed, how far some of their contemplative men have gone in the theory hereof. **1674** DRYDEN *Prol. Univ. Oxford* 11 Your theories are here to practice brought, As in mechanic operations wrought. **1798** MALTHUS *Popul.* III. ii. (1806) II. 103 A theory that will not admit of application cannot possibly be just. **1832** AUSTIN *Jurispr.* (1879) II. 1133 Theory of what is and theory of what ought to be are perpetually confounded. **1853** BRIGHT *Sp. India* 3 June (1876) 4 The theory of the old Government of India was one which could not be defended. **1879** M. PATTISON *Milton* xiii. 219 Even the calm and gentle author of the Christian Year..deliberately framed a theory of Poetic for the express purpose, as it would seem, of excluding the author of Paradise Lost from the first class of poets.

4. a. A scheme or system of ideas or statements held as an explanation or account of a group of facts or phenomena; a hypothesis that has been confirmed or established by observation or experiment, and is propounded or accepted as accounting for the known facts; a statement of what are held to be the general laws, principles, or causes of something known or observed.

1638 SIR T. HERBERT *Trav.* (ed. 2) 127 Or whether from subterranean fires,..I dare not conclude, but leave such theories to those that study Meteors. **1684** BURNET (*title*) The Theory of the Earth. **1706** PHILLIPS (ed. Kersey), *Theories of the Planets*, certain Hypotheses, or Suppositions about the Motions of the Heavens, according to which, Astronomers explain..the Phænomena or Appearances of the Planets. **1727–41** CHAMBERS *Cycl.* s.v., We say..theory of the rainbow, of the microscope..the motion of the heart, the operation of purgatives, etc. **1812** PLAYFAIR *Nat. Phil.* (1819) I. 3 A theory is often nothing else but a contrivance for comprehending a certain number of facts under one expression. **1850** GROVE *Corr. Phys. Forces* (ed. 2) 105 Were a theory open to no objection it would cease to be a theory, and would become a law. **1879** M. PATTISON *Milton* xiii. 180 The Copernican theory, which placed the sun in the centre of our system, was already the established belief of the few well-informed. **1890** A. R. WALLACE *Darwinism* 7 The truest and most complete theory would not enable us to solve all the difficult problems which the whole course of the development of life upon our globe presents to us.

b. That department of an art or technical subject which consists in the knowledge or statement of the facts on which it depends, or of its principles or methods, as distinguished from the *practice* of it.

1613 R. CAWDREY *Table Alph.* (ed. 3), *Theorie*, the contemplation, or inward knowledge of any art. **1626** BACON *Sylva* §327 The means, hitherto propounded, to effect it, are in the practice, full of error and imposture, and in the theory, full of unsound imaginations. **1660** R. COKE *Power & Subj.* Pref. 5 A Musitian, who Composes well, yet understands but little in the theory of Musick. **1795** HUTTON *Math. Dict.* s.v., To be learned in an art, &c., the Theory is sufficient; to be a master of it, both the Theory and practice are requisite. **1827** WHATELY *Logic* (ed. 2) 205 Logic being concerned with the theory of Reasoning. **1828** J. S. MILL in *Westm. Rev.* IX. 155 A prodigious step in the theory of naming. *a* **1854** —— *Early Draft Autobiogr.* (1961) 135, I pushed on..to try whether I could do anything further to clear up the theory of Logic generally. **1884** GROVE *Dict. Mus.* IV. 101/1 *Theory*, a term often used..to express the knowledge of Harmony, Counter-point, Thorough-bass, etc., as distinguished from the art of playing, which is..called 'Practice'. **1885** *Encycl. Brit.* XVIII. 793/2 Epistemology (theory of knowledge, Erkenntnisstheorie). **1927** B. RUSSELL *Outl. Philos.* xxiii. 248 Descartes..inaugurated two movements, one in metaphysics, one in theory of knowledge. **1966** R. M. CHISHOLM (*title*) Theory of Knowledge.

c. A systematic statement of the general principles or laws of some branch of mathematics; a set of theorems forming a connected system: as ***the theory of equations***, ***of functions***, ***of numbers***, ***of probabilities***.

1799 W. FREND (*title*) The Principles of Algebra..; or the true Theory of Equations established by mathematical demonstration. **1806** [see THEOREM 1 a]. **1811** P. BARLOW (*title*) An Elementary Investigation of the Theory of Numbers. **1838** [see PROBABILITY 3]. **1893** FORSYTH (*title*) Theory of Functions.

5. In the abstract (without article): Systematic conception or statement of the principles of something; abstract knowledge, or the formulation of it: often used as implying more or less unsupported hypothesis (cf. 6): distinguished from or opposed to *practice* (cf. 4 b). ***in theory*** (formerly ***in the theory***): according to theory, theoretically (opp. to *in practice* or *in fact*).

1624 T. MACARNESSE in Capt. Smith *Virginia* Pref., That thou mightst read and know and safely see, What he by practice, thou by Theoree. **1692** SIR W. HOPE *Fencing-Master* (ed. 2) 164 Theorie without Practice will serve but for little. **1769–72** *Junius Lett.* Pref. (1820) 17 Theory is at variance with practise. **1776** J. ADAMS *Wks.* (1854) IX. 375 It is certain, in theory, that the only moral foundation of government is, the consent of the people. **1821** J. Q. ADAMS in Davies *Metr. Syst.* III. (1871) 175 A compromise between philosophical theory and inveterate popular habits.

6. In loose or general sense: A hypothesis proposed as an explanation; hence, a mere hypothesis, speculation, conjecture; an idea or set of ideas about something; an individual view or notion. Cf. 4.

1792 BURKE *Corr.* (1844) IV. 13 Whether I am right in the theory or not,..the fact is as I state it. **1794** PALEY *Evid.* (1825) II. 347 Theories which have, at different times, gained possession of the public mind. **1829** JAS. MILL *Hum. Mind* (1869) II. xxv. 403 The word theory has been perverted to denote an operation..which..consists in supposing and setting down matters supposed as matters observed. Theory in fact has been confounded with Hypothesis. **1864** BOWEN *Logic* xi. (1870) 375 A Theory, sometimes incorrectly used as a synonyme for Hypothesis. **1867** LADY HERBERT *Cradle L.* iii. 95 So varied are the theories as to the origin of these wonderful sepulchres. **1880** T. A. SPALDING *Eliz. Demonol.* 35 This was not a mere theory, but a vital active belief.

7. *Comb.*, as ***theory-making*** adj. and sb., ***-building***, ***-monger***, ***-spinning***; ***theory-bigoted***, ***-mad***, ***-ridden*** adjs.; **theory-blind** *a.*, (*a*) blinded by a theory, so as to be unable to see the facts truly; (*b*) blind to a theory, i.e. unable to see or apprehend it (cf. *colour-blind*); **theory-laden** *a.*, applied to a term, statement, etc., the use of which implies the acceptance of some theory; contrasted with ***theory-free***, ***-neutral*** adjs.; **theory-man** (*nonce-wd.*), a theorist; **theory-tailor**, contemptuously for a shaper of theories.

1884 *Q. Rev.* Apr. 337 More *theory-bigoted than Mr. ——. **1892** W. S. LILLY *Gt. Enigma* 230 You cannot help recognising, unless you are *theory-blind,..the law of correlation. **1902** *Q. Rev.* Apr. 359 No one who is not theory-blind—a very common form of blindness. **1780** *Mirror* No. 107 ¶2 There is something..so delightful in this art of *theory-building. **1964** *Language* XL. 225 Spelling out..how its results have been incorporated into other experiments and theory-building. **1977** A. GIDDENS *Stud. in Social & Polit. Theory* i. 49 As Feigl says, most positivistically inclined authors today..recognize that observation statements cannot be entirely '*theory-free'. **1958** N. R. HANSON *Patterns of Discovery* i. 19 There is a sense..in which seeing is a '*theory-laden' undertaking. Observation of *x* is shaped by prior knowledge of *x*. **1977** A. GIDDENS *Stud. in Social & Polit. Theory* 12 The theory-laden character of observation-statements in natural sciences entails that the meaning of scientific contexts is tied-in to the meaning of other terms in a theoretical network. **1850** E. A. POE in *Sartain's Union Mag.* Oct. 233/1 He must be *theory-mad beyond redemption who, in spite of these differences, shall still persist in attempting to reconcile the obstinate oils and waters of Poetry and Truth. **1931** A. HUXLEY *Music at Night* 77 The *theory-making mind. **1964** I. L. HOROWITZ *New Sociology* 31 Problems of this kind can be multiplied..in every sphere of sociology from poll-taking to theory-making. **1727** DE FOE *Syst. Magic* I. i. (1840) 9 What our learned *theory-men insist to have been the causes of the deluge. **1905** *Academy* 4 Feb. 105/1 It is high time that protest be made..against the master's works being made the prey of *theorymongers. **1968** J. J. C. SMART *Betw. Sci. & Philos.* iii. 80 Observation reports can not be couched in *theory-neutral language. **1977** A. GIDDENS *Stud. in Social & Polit. Theory* iii. 150 The 'orthodox view' has an answer which Habermas has apparently (although..not finally) rejected: correspondence to sensorily apprehended reality, grounded in the descriptions of a theory-neutral observation language. **1922** R. FRY *Let.* 6 Mar. (1972) II. 522, I don't take it to heart when you say that my pictures are the utterly dismal performances of a *theory-ridden painter. **1904** WINDLE *Prehist. Age* Pref. 13 There has been a vast amount of *theory-spinning in connexion with the early epochs. **1876** MEREDITH *Beauch. Career* xxxvii, These men are *theory-tailors not politicians.

theory[2] (θiːˈɔːrɪ). *Gr. Antiq.* [ad. Gr. θεωρία, the same word as in THEORY[1], in a specialized sense.] A body of THEORS sent by a state to perform some religious rite or duty; a solemn legation.

1842 *Smith's Dict. Grk. & Rom. Antiq.* s.v. *Salaminia*, They conveyed theories, despatches, &c. from Athens. **1850** GROTE *Greece* II. lv. VII. 72 Curiosity..to see what figure the Theôry of Athens would make as to show and splendour.

1853 *Ibid.* II. lxxxiii. XI. 38 He sent thither his Theôry, or solemn legation for sacrifice, decked in the richest garments.

theos, early ME.: see THIS, THESE.

theosis (θiːˈəʊsɪs). *Theol. rare.* [a. med.L. *theōsis*, ad. Patristic Gr. θέωσις deification.] Deification.

1875 J. W. DRAPER *Hist. Conflict between Relig. & Sci.* v. 126 The return of the soul to the universal Intellect is designated by Erigena as Theosis, or Deification. **1934** *Theology* XXVIII. 24 Both natures, therefore, can be correlated positively through the communion of qualities, *communicatio idiomatum*, in the theosis of the created by the Divine. **1967** *Eastern Churches Rev.* I. 246 This is a kind of *theosis* whereby the symbols become life-giving.

theosoph (ˈθiːəsɒf). [= Fr. *théosophe* (*a* 1784 Diderot in Littré), ad. med.L. *theosophus* (Scotus Erigena *a* 880), a. late Gr. θεόσοφ-ος (*a* 500, Pseudo-Dionysius *De Div. Nom.* §6) wise concerning God, f. θεός God + σοφός wise.]

One who pursues THEOSOPHY (sense 1).

(The med.L. *theosophus* was often used for *theologian*, in contrast with *philosophus*.)

1822 SOUTHEY in *Q. Rev.* Jan. 37 This Theosophe was too poor, too religious, and too insane to have any share in establishing the seminary..at Avignon. **1838** *Fraser's Mag.* XVII. 27 The Theosophs were right in separating entirely the mind from the soul. **1878** MORLEY *Diderot* I. v. 203 The article on Theosophs would hardly have been so disproportionately long as it is, merely for the sake of Paracelsus. **1880** *Chambers' Encycl.* IX. 400/1 Within the Christian period we may number among Theosophs, the Neo-Platonists..; the Hesychasts of the Greek Church [etc.].

theosopheme (θiːˈɒsəfiːm). *rare.* [ad. Gr. type *θεοσόφημα: cf. *philosopheme*.] A theosophical speculation or conclusion.

1856 C. J. ELLICOTT in *Cambr. Ess.* 162 Some appear to have been gospels..others the wildest and most unhistorical theosophemes. **1873** SYMONDS *Grk. Poets* vii. 231 The colossal theosophemes of Aeschylus called for profound reflection.

theosopher (θiːˈɒsəfə(r)). [f. THEOSOPH(Y, or med.L. *theosoph-us* (Scotus Erigena *a* 880) THEOSOPH + -ER[1]: cf. PHILOSOPHER.] = THEOSOPHIST. (Applied spec. to Jacob Boehme, 'the Teutonic Theosopher', and his followers.)

1647 WARD *Simp. Cobler* (1843) 18 Have an extraordinary care..of the late Theosophers, that teach men to climbe to heaven upon a ladder of lying figments. **1653** H. MORE *Conject. Cabbal.* (1713) 72 Laying down such Conclusions as the Naturalists and Theosophers in all Ages have looked upon as the choicest and most precious. **1755** AMORY *Mem.* (1766) II. 73 *note*, Jacob Behemen, the reverend theosopher. **1782** *Gentl. Mag.* LII. 329/1 The true and infallible ground of what he there advanced was to be found in the Teutonic Theosopher, in his three first Properties of Eternal Nature. **1850** MAURICE *Mor. & Met. Philos.* I. viii. §2. 234 These books..which have procured him [Boehme] the name of the Theosopher. **1881** OVERTON *W. Law* 269 Hitherto Law has been presented to us in this chapter rather as a theosopher than as a mystic proper.

theosophic (θiːəʊˈsɒfɪk), *a.* [f. THEOSOPH(Y + -IC. Cf. F. *théosophique* (Diderot).] Of, pertaining to, or of the nature of theosophy; versed in theosophy. (Chiefly in reference to the school of Boehme; more recently = THEOSOPHICAL b.)

1649 ELLISTONE tr. *Behmen's Epist.* vii. §24 He is a young companion of the Theosophic school. **1691** E. TAYLOR (*title*) Jacob Boehmen's Theosophick Philosophy Unfolded. **1710** R. WARD *Life H. More* 128 Such most Noble Truths, and Theosophick Mysteries are deliver'd in it. **1828** CARLYLE *Misc.*, *Werner* (1872) I. 79 His French scepticism had got overlaid with wondrous theosophic garniture. **1856** R. A. VAUGHAN *Mystics* I. v. (1860) I. 31 The mysticism I term theosophic aspires to know and believes itself in possession of a certain supernatural divine faculty for that purpose. **1902** *Encycl. Brit.* XXVII. 60/2 Christian Science, a system of theosophic and therapeutic doctrine,..was originated..about 1866 by Mrs. Mary Baker Eddy.

theosophical (θiːəʊˈsɒfɪkəl), *a.* [f. as prec. + -AL[1]: see -ICAL.] = prec.

1642 H. MORE *Song of Soul* I. ii. III. iii. Argt., That th' earth doth move, proofs Physicall Unto us do descrie; Adde reasons Theosophicall, Als' adde Astronomie. **1697** *State Philadelph. Soc.* 13 The Title Page of the Theosophical Transactions. **1830** PUSEY *Hist. Enq.* II. 351 To the theosophical fanatics, or a D. Hoffman, such a man, as he was, could not possibly assent. **1866** G. MACDONALD *Ann. Q. Neighb.* xii, He had..often some theosophical theory to bring forward. **1886** *Manch. Exam.* 17 Feb. 3/3 Boehme is anything but a dealer in mere theosophical enigmas.

b. Of or belonging to THEOSOPHY, in sense 2. *Theosophical Society*, an association founded at New York, 1875, by Col. H. S. Olcott, Madame Blavatsky, and W. Q. Judge, its professed objects being: 1. to form the nucleus of a universal brotherhood; 2. to promote the study of Aryan and other Eastern literature, religions, and sciences; 3. to investigate the unfamiliar laws of nature and the faculties latent in man.

1881 SINNETT *Occult World* 35 Assisted by some other persons whose interest in the subject was kindled by occasional manifestations of her extraordinary powers, and notably by Colonel Olcott, its life-devoted President, she [Madame Blavatsky] founded the Theosophical Society. **1885** OLCOTT *Theosophy* Pref. 10 The Theosophical spirit of conceding to the people of all creeds the right of enjoying their religious convictions unmolested.

theo'sophically, *adv.* [f. prec. + -LY[2].] In a theosophical manner; by means of theosophy.

1689 TRYON (*title*) A Treatise of Dreams and Visions, wherein The Causes Natures and Uses of Nocturnal Representations, and the Communications both of Good and Evil Angels, as also departed Souls, to Mankinde, Are Theosophically Unfolded. **1855** SMEDLEY, etc. *Occult Sciences* 135 The doctrine of Bœhmen,..worked out theosophically.

b. By means of or in accordance with theosophy (in sense 2).

1896 *Columbus* (Ohio) *Dispatch* 21 July 4/3 C. B...says: Theosophically I know that W. J. Bryan is the reincarnation of Andrew Jackson, and spiritually I see around him the forms of Washington, Lincoln and the lamented Polk.

theosophico- (θiːəʊˈsɒfɪkəʊ), combining form of assumed Gr. *θεοσοφικό-ς theosophic.

1851 CARLYLE *Sterling* I. viii. (1872) 50 The moaning sing-song of that theosophico-metaphysical monotony.

theosophism (θiːˈɒsəfɪz(ə)m). [f. as THEOSOPH + -ISM. Cf. F. *théosophisme* (Diderot).] The theory and practice of theosophy; theosophizing.

1791 ENFIELD *Hist. Philos.* IX. iii. II. 489 Many traces of the spirit of Theosophism may be found through the whole history of philosophy; in which nothing is more frequent, than fanatical and hypocritical pretensions to divine illumination. **1797** W. TAYLOR in *Monthly Rev.* Dec. 526 The ardent, zealous, and exalted enthusiast aspires to super-human excellence, and clings to the prospects of theosophism.

b. In reference to THEOSOPHY in sense 2.

1896 *Chicago Advance* 1 Oct. 449 Theosophism, spiritualism, Christian Science,..are all modern instances of ways in which men are led astray.

theosophist (θiːˈɒsəfɪst). [f. as prec. + -IST.]

1. One who professes or believes in THEOSOPHY (in sense 1). **a.** With specific reference to Boehme. **b.** In a more general sense.

a. **1656** H. MORE *Enthus. Tri.* a viij, A promiscuous Collection of divers odd Conceits out of severall Theosophists and Chymists. *Ibid.* 40 This disease many of our Chymists and several Theosophists, in my judgement, seem very obnoxious to who dictate their own Conceits and Fancies so magisterially and imperiously, as if they were indeed Authentick messengers from God Almighty. **1791** ENFIELD *Hist. Philos.* IX. iii. II. 488 The Theosophists.. neither contented with the natural light of human reason, nor with the simple doctrines of scripture understood in their literal sense, have recourse to an internal supernatural light, superior to all other illuminations, from which they profess to derive a mysterious and divine philosophy, manifested only to the chosen favourites of heaven. **1817** COLERIDGE *Biog. Lit.* I. ix. 139 How dare I be ashamed of the Teutonic theosophist, Jacob Behmen?

b. **1814** SHELLEY *Deism* Pr. Wks. 1880 II. 77 The God of the rational Theosophist is a vast and wise animal. **1834** SOUTHEY *Doctor* ccix. (1862) 562/1 Certain theologians, and certain theosophists, as men who fancy themselves inspired sometimes affect to be called. **1837–9** HALLAM *Hist. Lit.* (1847) II. III. ii. §74. 361 The principal mystics or theosophists have generally been counted among philosophers. **1856** VAUGHAN *Mystics* I. v. (1860) I. 31 The theosophist is one who gives you a theory of God, or of the works of God, which has not reason, but an inspiration of his own for its basis. **1882** *Pall Mall G.* 30 Aug. 4 Of late years we have heard and learned a great deal about that interesting Oriental theosophist, the ideal Buddhist.

2. A professor or adherent of THEOSOPHY (in sense 2); a member of the Theosophical Society; name of a magazine, the organ of that society.

1881 *Sat. Rev.* 3 Sept. 298/2 The *Theosophist* is full of translations from the works of ancient 'theurgists'. **1881** SINNETT *Occult World* 37 The natives [of India] were flattered at the attitude towards them taken up by their new 'European' friends, as Madame Blavatsky and Colonel Olcott were no doubt generally regarded in spite of their American nationality, and showed a shallow eagerness to become Theosophists. **1885** OLCOTT *Theosophy* Pref. 11 We are..the same thing to all men—viz., Theosophists, who believe in the essential identity of all men, race, caste, and creed to the contrary notwithstanding. *Ibid.* 144 The Theosophist is a man who, whatever be his race, creed, or condition, aspires to reach this height of wisdom and beatitude by self-development.

theosophistic (θiːɒsəˈfɪstɪk), *a.* [f. prec. + -IC.] Of the nature of or pertaining to a theosophist or theosophy (in sense 1).

1849 LADY WILDE tr. *Meinhold's Sidonia Sorc.* III. xiii. II. 184 *note*, The theosophistic, cabalistic Dr. Joel. **1856** C. J. ELLICOTT in *Cambr. Ess.* 169 The main facts of Christianity ..interwoven with the theosophistic speculations, the mystical doctrines..that were so dear to the hybrid Christian of Alexandria. **1857** —— *Comm. Col.* Introd. (1861) 111 To warn the Colossians against a system of false teaching, partly Oriental and Theosophistic in its character, and partly Judaical and ceremonial. **1897** *Daily News* 5 Feb. 6/7 The theurgic and theosophistic obscurities of Kabbalistic writings.

b. Of or pertaining to THEOSOPHY (in sense 2).

1886 *Athenæum* 9 Jan. 68/3 Mr. Cumberland..in India is studying theosophistic philosophy on the spot.

So **theoso'phistical** *a.*, in same sense (but with disparaging implication).

1814 SHELLEY *Refut. Deism* Prose Wks. 1888 I. 292 To shew how much the cause of natural and revealed Religion has suffered from the mode of defence adopted by Theosophistical Christians. **1894** *Westm. Gaz.* 16 Nov. 4/2 The disingenuousness of this very Theosophistical letter.

theosophize (θiːˈɒsəfaɪz), *v.* [f. as THEOSOPH + -IZE.] *intr.* To practise or pretend to theosophy; to reason or discourse theosophically. Hence **the'osophizing** *ppl. a.*

1846 in WORCESTER citing M. STUART. **1858** *Chamb. Jrnl.* X. 265/2 We owe, indirectly, the greatest scientific impetus of the modern world to a theosophising shoemaker [Behmen]. **1875** M. ARNOLD in *Contemp. Rev.* XXVI. 685 These things are not at all in the manner of Jesus. Jesus never theosophized.

theosophy (θiːˈɒsəfɪ). [ad. med.L. *theosophia* (Scotus Erigena *a* 880), a. late Gr. θεοσοφία (*a* 500 Pseudo-Dion. *Myst. Theologia* i. §1) wisdom concerning God or things divine, abstr. sb. from θεόσοφος THEOSOPH. So F. *théosophie* (18th c. in Littré).]

The word was revived early in the 17th c. in Latin and vernacular forms, to denote a kind of speculation, such as is found in the Jewish Cabbala and is illustrated by the writings of Cornelius Agrippa (1486–1535), Paracelsus, Robert Fludd, and others, which sought, usually by the doctrine of the macrocosm and microcosm, to derive from the knowledge of God contained in sacred books, or traditions mystically interpreted, a profounder knowledge and control of nature than could be obtained by the methods of the Aristotelian or other current philosophy. The name *theosophy* was often applied specifically to the system of Jacob Boehme (1575–1624), which, though not claiming to the same degree traditional authority, was largely expressed in language borrowed from writers of the school in question. The word has then and since been applied to more ancient and more recent views having more or less affinity to those already mentioned.

1. Any system of speculation which bases the knowledge of nature upon that of the divine nature: often with reference to such authors as those above mentioned, and more particularly to Boehme.

1650 'EUGENIUS PHILALETHES' (= T. Vaughan) *Anthroposophia Theomagica*, Author to Reader 13 The Ancient, reall Theosophie of the Hebrewes and Egyptians. **1678** CUDWORTH *Intell. Syst.* I. iv. §20. 377 Xenophanes, philosophizing concerning the supreme Deity, was wont to call it ἓν καὶ πᾶν, *one and all*... Xenophanes his Theosophy, or divine philosophy, is most fully declared by Simplicius. **1681** H. MORE in Glanvill *Sadducismus* I. Postscr. (1726) 29 The sound Principles of Theosophy and true Divinity. **1691** E. TAYLOR *Behmen's Theos. Philos.* 171 What is all Sacred Theosophy, but the very understanding of a certain Divine Art? **1831** CARLYLE *Early Germ. Lit.* in *Misc. Ess.* (1872) III. 194 That..devout temper, now degenerating into abstruse theosophy..was awake in this era. **1837** HALLAM *Hist. Lit.* I. I. vii. §17. 397 His own models were the oriental reveries of the Cabbala, and the theosophy of the mystics. *Ibid.* §20 The theosophy of Paracelsus. **1841** W. SPALDING *Italy & It. Isl.* III. 19 The Italians furnished few converts to the theosophy of Lepaux, they numbered very many quiet and contemptuous unbelievers. **1852** CONYBEARE & HOWSON *St. Paul* I. xiii. 483 There was a strong affinity between the Neo-Platonic philosophy of Alexandria and the Oriental theosophy which sprang from Buddhism and other kindred systems. **1856** R. A. VAUGHAN *Mystics* I. v. (1860) I. 30 Among the Germans I find mysticism generally called *theosophy* when applied to natural science. Too narrow a use of the word, I think. **1871** FARRAR *Witn. Hist.* iii. 102 Porphyry and Hierocles met them with haughty mysticism and intellectual theosophy. **1877** E. CAIRD *Philos. Kant* ii. 17 The philosophies or theosophies that close the record of Greek speculation.

2. Applied to a system of recent origin, resembling the above in its claim to a knowledge of nature profounder than is obtained from empirical science, and contained in an esoteric tradition of which the doctrines of the various historical religions are held to be only the exoteric expression. Sometimes called Esoteric Buddhism. See *Theosophical Society*, under THEOSOPHICAL b.

1881 SINNETT *Occult World* 172 They have shown that Theosophy, or Occult Philosophy, is no new candidate for the world's attention, but is really a restatement of principles which have been recognized from the very infancy of mankind. **1884** *Chr. World* 16 Oct. 788/3 Theosophy is really another name for Esoteric Buddhism. **1885** OLCOTT *Theosophy* Pref. 13 Theosophy is the complement both of science and of philosophy, and as such is entitled to the respectful examination of the *savant* and the theologian. *Ibid.* 256 That priceless knowledge of divine things which we call Theosophy. **19..** MRS. BESANT *Meaning of Theosophy* 1 What is the essence of Theosophy? It is the fact that man, being himself divine, can know the Divinity whose life he shares. *Ibid.* 4 Theosophy has no code of morals, being itself the embodiment of the highest morality.

3. In etymol. sense: Wisdom or knowledge concerning things divine. *nonce-use.*

1836–7 SIR W. HAMILTON *Metaph.* I. 416 An organ of Imagination is intimately connected with that of Theosophy or Veneration.

theotaurine: see THEO-.

theotechny (ˈθiːəʊtɛknɪ). [f. Gr. θεός god + τέχνη art.] The introduction of divine or supernatural beings in the construction of a drama or epic; such beings collectively.

1858 GLADSTONE *Homer* II. iii. 268 It is not difficult to understand why..Dionysus does not appear in the theotechny of the Iliad. **1869** —— *Juv. Mundi* vii. 206 The personages of the Homeric Theotechny, under which name I include the whole of the supernatural beings, of whatever rank, introduced into the Poems. *Ibid.* xiv. §1. 491 The Theotechny, or divine movement of the Poem [the Iliad].

So † **theo'technal** *a. Obs. rare*[−1], of the nature of divine art; **theo'technic** *a.*, pertaining to the invention or making of gods; also, belonging to theotechny; **theo'technist**, one who invents gods.

1651 BIGGS *New Disp.* Pref. 9 Those Arts we speak of are Theotechnal, the Arts of God. **1874** PIAZZI SMYTH *Inher. Gt. Pyramid* v. (ed. 2) 64 At Thebes..those temples and tombs..speak lamentably to human theotechnic inventions. *Ibid.* xxii. 425 The original inventor and theotechnist of animal and other gods for his countrymen. **1878** GLADSTONE *Prim. Homer* vi. (1889) 67 Behind the complex and ever-active theotechnic machinery of the poem,..there is still the presence and operation of an august personage.

theoteleological, -logy: see THEO-.

†**theoten**, *v. Obs.* Forms: 1 **ðeotan, ðiotan, ðutan**, 3 **þeoten**, (*Orm.*) **þutenn**. [OE. *þéotan*, (pa. t. *þéat, þuton*) = ON. *þjóta* to whistle, etc., OHG. *diozan* to howl:—OTeut. **þeutan* (*þaut-, þut-*). OE. had also another pres. stem *þútan*, whence *þútende* pr. pple. and *þutenn* in Ormin; so Da. *tude*:—**þúta* to howl. Cf. *búȝan*, BOW *v.*[1]] *intr.* To howl.

*c*888 K. ÆLFRED *Boeth.* xxxviii. §1 Sume wurdon to wulfan; þa ðuton, þon hi sprecan sceoldon. *a*1000 *Boeth. Metr.* xxvi. 80 Ac hio præȝmælum ðioton ongunnon. *c*1000 ÆLFRIC *Hom.* I. 374 Ðeotende swa swa wulf. *c*1000 *Ags. Gloss.* in Wr.-Wülcker 195/17 *Bombosa*, hlowende, þutende. *a*1225 *St. Marher.* 22 Þa bigunnen to þeoten ant to ȝellen. *a*1225 *Ancr. R.* 120 Ne deð heo bute þeoteð.

b. *trans.* To howl at.

*c*1200 ORMIN 2034 Mann wollde tælenn þatt & hutenn hire & þutenn. *Ibid.* 4875 Icc hutedd amm & þutedd.

theothe, etc., for *teoþe*, obs. f. TITHE, etc.

Theotiscan (θiːəʊ'tɪskən). *rare.* [f. med.L. (8th–9th cent.) (*lingua*) *theotisca* (the) German (language), reflecting early forms of OHG. *diutisc*, G. *deutsch* (see DUTCH) + -AN.] (See quot.)

1817 COLERIDGE *Biog. Lit.* I. x. 203, I read through..the most important remains of the Theotiscan, or the transitional state of the Teutonic language from the Gothic to the old German of the Swabian period.

‖**theotokion** (θiːə'tɒkɪɒn). *Eastern Church.* [eccl. Gr., f. θεοτόκος: see THEOTOKOS.] A *sticheron* or *troparion* addressed to the Mother of God; usu. the last in a series of stanzas.

1850 J. M. NEALE *Hist. Holy Eastern Church* I. 832 The theotokion is simply a sticheron or troparion addressed to the Mother of God. **1880** *Encycl. Brit.* XII. 580/1 A 'theotokion', or ascription of praise to the mother of our Lord. **1961** D. ATTWATER *Christian Churches of East* I. 225 *Theotokos* (*Gk., tokos*, childbirth), the Mother of God. *Theotokion*, a hymn in her honour.

‖**Theotokos** (θiː'ɒtəkɒs). [a. Gr. θεοτόκος adj., f. θεό-ς God + -τοκος bringing forth, f. stem τεκ-, τοκ- of τίκτειν to bear.] A title of the Virgin Mary as 'Mother of God'; = DEIPARA.

1874 PUSEY *Lent. Serm.* 206 By this the lowly Virgin became Theotokos, 'the Mother of God'. **1879** SIR G. G. SCOTT *Lect. Archit.* xvii. II. 257 The Church of the Holy Theotokos, or of the Mother of God, is of much later date. **1896** *Trans. St. Paul's Eccles. Soc.* IV. i. 175 The devout orison to our Lady..said in honour of the Blessed Theotokos.

So **The'otoky**, the divine motherhood of Mary.

1899 *Westm. Gaz.* 24 Apr. 4/3 The Mysteries of..the Virginity of the Blessed Virgin, the Theotoky.

theow, thew, *sb.* and *a.* Now only *Hist.* or *arch.* Forms: α. 1 **þeow** (*fem.* **þeowe**, *pl.* **þeowas**), **ðiow**, 2–3 **þeu**, 3 **þeou**, (*Orm.*) **þeoww, þeww**, (9 theow(e). β. 1 **þeowa** (*fem.* **þeowe**, *pl.* **þeowan**), **ðiowa, ðiuwa, ðiua, ðeua, ðea**, 2–3 **þeowe**, 3 **þeue**, 4 **þewe**. [OE. *ðíow, þéow, þéo*, str. masc., = OHG. *deo, dio*, ON. (Runic) *þewaR*, Goth. *þius*:—OTeut. **þewo*[z]; beside OE. *þeow* str. fem., = OS. *thiu, thiwi*, OHG., MHG. *diu*, ON. *þý*, Goth. *þiwi*:—OTeut. **þewjô*. Also weak sbs. *þéowa* (masc.), *þéowe* (fem.); cf. OS. *thiwa*. *þéowa, -e* have the weak inflexion of the adj.]

A. *sb.* A slave, bondman, thrall.

*c*893 K. ÆLFRED *Oros.* I. i. §22 Þa þeowan drincað medo. *c*897 —— *Gregory's Past. C.* Pref. 4 Micel meniȝu Godes ðeowa [*Hatton MS.* ðiowa]. *a*950 *Rituale Dunelm.* (Surtees) 170 Besih ofer vsiȝ ðea ðino [L. *famulos tuos*]. *c*950 *Lindisf. Gosp.* Matt. viii. 9 Ic cueðo..ðeua [*Rushw.* ðeow] minum do ðis & does. *c*1000 *Ags. Gosp.* Matt. xviii 28 Þa se þeowa [*Hatton* þeowe] ut-eode he ȝemette hys efen-þeowan. *Ibid.* xx. 27 Sy he eower þeow [*Lindisf.* ðea *vel* ðeȝn, *Rushw.* esne]. *c*1200 *Trin. Coll. Hom.* 181 Ðus was adam þeu, þo godes muð cursede eorðe. *c*1200 ORMIN Introd. 31 Adam wass wurrþenn deofless þeoww. *Ibid.* 7454 An defless þeww. *c*1205 LAY. 29390 Þenne moste he libben þeou a þisse londe. *c*1320 *Cast. Love* 249 Þeuwe and þral may not craue þorw riht non heritage to haue.

Hist. and *arch.* **1819** SCOTT *Ivanhoe* xxxii, Theow and Esne art thou no longer. **1839** KEIGHTLEY *Hist. Eng.* I. 75 Beneath these orders of freemen were the Theowes or slaves... This word *ðeow* seems to have left no trace in the modern languages. **1865** LECKY *Ration.* II. vi. 260 All the civil laws for the protection of the theows, or Saxon slaves, appear to have been preceded by, and based upon, the Canon law. **1874** STUBBS *Const. Hist.* I. v. 78 The *theow* or slave simple, whether *wealh*—that is, of British extraction..or of the common German stock.

b. A female slave, a bondwoman.

*a*900 tr. *Bæda's Hist.* IV. xii. [ix.] (1890) 290 Seo foresprecene Cristes þeowe. *c*950 *Lindisf. Gosp.* Matt. xxvi. 69 An ðiua [*Rushw.* menen *vel* þeowæ] cueð. —— Luke xii. 45 ȝife..esne..onginneð..slaa ða cnæhtas & ðiuwas [*Rushw.* ða ðiowe, *Vulg.* pueros et ancillas]. **1398** TREVISA *Barth. De P.R.* VI. xii. (Tollem. MS.), Sche is þewe and þralle er he be bore.

†**B.** *adj.* [OE. *þéow*, pl. *þéowe*; later pl. *þewe, thue.*] Servile, slavish; 'bond'. *Obs.*

*c*888 K. ÆLFRED *Boeth.* xli. §2 ȝif him sceolden þiowe men þenian. *c*893 —— *Oros.* III. vi. §3 Hit þurh ænne þeowne mon ȝeypped wearð. *c*1000 ÆLFRIC *Gram.* ix. (Z.) 67 *Hic manceps*, þes ðeowa mann. *Ibid.* xv. 101 *Meis mancipiis diuido denarios*, minum ðeowum mannum ic dæle peneȝas. *a*1023 WULFSTAN *Hom.* xxxix. (Napier) 181 Þeowemen þa ðriȝ daȝas beon weorces ȝefreode. *c*1205 LAY. 334 Al heo weren þeowe [*c*1275 þeue]. *a*1225 *St. Marher.* 4 Cuð me..ȝef þu art foster of freo monne oðer þeow wummon. *c*1290 *Beket* 279 in *S. Eng. Leg.* I. 114 Þat word was sone wide couth among þeuwe and freo. **1297** R. GLOUC. (Rolls) 9657 Þuman ne may nowȝt be imad aȝen is louerdes wille fre. *c*1300 *Havelok* 2205 Alle samen, þeu and fre. *c*1400 *St. Alexius* (Laud 463) 2 Ȝong & olde, thewe & freo.

†**theow, thew**, *v. Obs.* Forms: 1 **þeowian**, 1–2 **þewian**, 2 **þowie, þeowien**, 3 **þiwien**. [OE. *þéowian*, f. *þéow*, THEOW *sb.*] *trans.* To be a serf or servant to; to serve, minister. (In OE. *intr.* with *dat.*, or *absol.*)

*c*888 K. ÆLFRED *Boeth.* xxi. §1 Þa ðeowiað ealle þa þe ðeowiað, ȝe ða þe cunnon ȝe þa þe ne cunnon. *Ibid.* xxxix. §13 Hi ne mihton elles bion, ȝif hi ne ðiowedon hiora fruman. *c*975 *Rushw. Gosp.* Matt. iv. 10 To dryhtne þinum gode ðu to ȝebidde & him anum ðewiȝe. *c*1000 *Ags. Gosp.* Luke xvi. 13 Ne mæȝ nan þeow twam hlafordum þeowian [*c*1160 *Hatton G.* þewian]. *a*1175 *Cott. Hom.* 241 Nan ne mai twan hlaforde..samod þowie. *c*1205 LAY. 10015 Heo him wolden þiwien [*c* 1275 he þeouwe].

'theowdom, 'thewdom. *Obs.* exc. *Hist.* Also 4 **þedome**, 5 **theudome**, 7, 9 **theodom.** [OE. *þéowdom*, f. *þéow*, THEOW *sb.* + -DOM.] The condition of a 'theow' or slave; slavery, bondage, thraldom. (In OE. also in sense 'service', without connotation of servility.)

*c*893 K. ÆLFRED *Oros.* I. x. §6 Þæt men hie mehten aliesan mid feo of þeowdome. *a*950 *Rituale Dunelm.* (Surtees) 6 In nedhernisse vel in ðeadome ic beȝo. *c*1000 ÆLFRIC *Hom.* II. 524 Eȝe is twyfeald, and ðeowdom is twyfeald. *c*1122 *O.E. Chron.* an. 675 (Laud MS.), Hi hit heafden ȝefreod..of ealle þewdom. *Ibid.* an. 963, Hi hit freodon..wið ealle weoruld þeudom. *c*1175 *Lamb. Hom.* 99 Men weren alesde from deofles ðeowdome. *c*1200 ORMIN 3611, I þeowwdom unnderr laferrd. *Ibid.* 14779 Ut off þewwdomess bandess. *c*1205 LAY. 454 Dardanisc kun..woneð in þisse londe..inne þeowe-dome [*c*1275 þeudome]. *a*1225 *Ancr. R.* 32 Summe ine prisune, summe ine alse muchele ðeudome alse oxe is oþer asse. *c*1320 *Cast. Love* 247 Whon he him serwede in þewdome [*v.rr.* thewdome, þedome]. *c*1425 *Eng. Conq. Irel.* 138 Nether al to be vndone, ne fully I-broght yn-to theudome. [**1658** PHILLIPS, *Theodom* (Sax.), servitude. **1833** GALT in *Fraser's Mag.* VIII. 497 Too fond of literature to relish the distasteful theodom of a tutor.]

†**'theowlike, 'thewlike,** *a. Obs. rare.* [f. THEOW *sb.* + -LIKE.] Servile, slavish; base.

*c*1200 ORMIN 4177 Itt iss Ressteda33 Off all þewwlike dede. *Ibid.* 4181 Uss birrþ wel uss ȝemenn..All fra þewwlike dede, þatt iss, fra sinnfull word & werrc.

†**'theowten,** *v. Obs. rare.* In Ormin **þeowwtenn, þewwtenn.** [f. OE. *þeowot, -(e)t* service, f. THEOW *sb.*] *trans.* and *intr.* To serve, minister.

*c*1200 ORMIN Introd. 43–4 Forr all swa summ þu þeowwtesst himm, Swa shall þin sune himm þeowwtenn. *Ibid.* 546 To þewwtenn i þe temmple.

thepe, dial. var. *fape*: see FEABERRY, gooseberry.

ther, inflexion of THARF *v.*; obs. f. DARE *v.*[1] (A. 9); obs. f. THEIR, THERE; obs. var. THIR; obs. inflexion of THAT, THE.

theralite ('θɪərəlaɪt). *Petrogr.* [ad. G. *theralith* (H. Rosenbusch *Mikrosk. Physiogr.* (ed. 2, 1887) II. 248), f. Gr. θηρᾶν to hunt, pursue: see -LITE, -LITH.] Any of a group of mafic, intrusive, igneous rocks that contain nepheline and calcic plagioclase.

1898 *Bull. U.S. Geol. Survey* No. 150. 197 This feldspar was determined as in part ordinary sanidine, in part a soda-lime feldspar, and the rocks were therefore made the types of a plutonic rock characterized by the mineral combination nephelite, soda-lime feldspar, and named theralite by Professor Rosenbusch. **1938** A. JOHANNSEN *Descr. Petrogr. Igneous Rocks* IV. 222 Among rocks difficult to place are the shonkinites, theralites, and teschenites. On the basis of their limited extent and mode of occurrence as sills, small intruded masses, and border facies, the rocks are hypabyssal; on the character of their usual textures, they are plutonic. **1978** S. R. NOCKOLDS in S. R. Nockolds et al. *Petrol. for Students* xvi. 177 Theralites appear to be rather rare but occur, for instance, as dykes cutting nepheline syenite in the Khibina complex, Kola Peninsula, U.S.S.R. .. Theralites are found also in the Lugar sill, Ayrshire.

‖**therapeusis** (θɛrə'pjuːsɪs). [mod.L., a. Gr. type *θεράπευσις healing, f. θεραπεύειν to tend, heal (a sick person).] Therapeutic treatment.

1857 DUNGLISON *Dict. Med. Sci.*, *Therapeusis*, therapeutics. **1875** H. C. WOOD *Therap.* (1879) 679 In regard to therapeusis, the first point to be determined in acute cases is..when to commence electrical treatment. **1897** *Allbutt's Syst. Med.* IV. 211 Effecting a more scientific and direct therapeusis.

‖**Therapeutæ** (θɛrə'pjuːtiː), *sb. pl.* Also 9 in anglicized form **therapeuts**. [eccl. L., a. Gr. θεραπευταί servants, attendants, ministers.] A sect of Jewish mystics residing in Egypt in the first century A.D., described in a book attributed to Philo.

1681 S. PARKER *Demonstr. Law Nat.* II. xviii. 247 These Therapeutæ read the ancient Writings of the Authours of their Sect. **1856** R. A. VAUGHAN *Mystics* (1860) I. 53 The *Therapeutæ*, a sect similar to the Essenes, number many among them whose lives are truly exemplary. **1865** tr. *Strauss's New Life Jesus* I. I. xxix. 235 He took the Egyptian branch of the Essenes, the so-called Therapeuts, for regular Christians.

therapeutic (θɛrə'pjuːtɪk), *sb.* Also 6 tera-. [In sense 1, ad. mod.L. *therapeutica*, a. Gr. θεραπευτική (sc. τέχνη) the art of healing, fem. sing. of θεραπευτικός: see THERAPEUTIC *a.* In Fr. *thérapeutique* (16th c.). In senses 2 and 3 recent absolute uses of the adj.]

1. That branch of medicine which is concerned with the remedial treatment of disease; the art of healing. **a.** In the singular. Now *rare*.

(Quot. 1890 may belong to 2 b.)

1541 R. COPLAND *Galyen's Terap.* 2 A j, The fourth boke of the Terapeutyke or Methode curatyfe of Claude Galyen. **1547** BOORDE *Brev. Health* Pref. 2 b, Galen, prince of phisicions, in his Terapeutike doth reprehende and disproue [it]. **1625** HART *Anat. Ur.* I. ii. 19 Who did likewise deuide Physicke..into two parts, to wit, that which we commonly call Therapeuticke..: and..that part which we call Diagnosticke. **1890** S. P. LAMBROS in *Athenæum* 30 Aug. 294/2 The modern therapeutic is far from having used all the sources of the ancients.

b. Now usually in the plural **therapeutics**.

1671 SALMON *Syn. Med.* III. i. 324* The Therapeuticks, or active part of Physick, is either Material, or Relative. **1707** FLOYER *Physic. Pulse-Watch* p. ii, The Chinese also have made that a part of their Therapeutics. **1843** MILL *Logic* VI. vi. §1 Students in politics..attempted to study the pathology and therapeutics of the social body, before they had laid the necessary foundation in its physiology.

2. a. A curative agent. **b.** A medical man.

1842 ABDY *Water Cure* (1843) 123 M. Roche acknowledges..that cold water has long been known as a therapeutic. **1858** HOGG *Life Shelley* II. 429 Medical society... Some of the therapeutics were tolerably good company.

3. *pl.* = THERAPEUTÆ. *rare.*

1847 WEBSTER, *Therapeutics*,..a religious sect described by Philo. They were devotees to religion.

thera'peutic, *a.* [In sense 1, ad. mod.L. *therapeutic-us*, a. Gr. θεραπευτικός, f. θεραπευτής, agent-n. from θεραπεύ-ειν to minister to, treat medically, f. θέραψ, θεραπ- attendant, minister. In sense 2, from the name of the *Therapeutæ*.]

1. Of or pertaining to the healing of disease. Also *loosely* in weakened use.

1646 SIR T. BROWNE *Pseud. Ep.* IV. xiii. 230 Therapeutick or curative Physick, we term that, which..taketh away diseases actually affecting. **1678** PHILLIPS (ed. 4) s.v., The Therapeutick part of Medicine, is that which treats of the healing or curing of diseases. **1800** *Med. Jrnl.* III. 577 Here the fundamental therapeutic principles are proposed. **1857** MILLER *Elem. Chem.* (1862) III. 196 It has long been used as a therapeutic agent. **1970** *Daily Tel.* 11 Feb. 15 She doesn't get bad-tempered; she merely picks up the piece of patchwork she is working on. 'It is so peaceful and relaxing, quite therapeutic.' **1982** L. CHAMBERLAIN *Food & Cooking of Russia* 253 Bread-making in the last century was a continuous process rather than a therapeutic exercise on a wet afternoon.

2. Of or pertaining to the Therapeutæ.

1681 S. PARKER *Demonstr. Law Nat.* II. xviii. 248 Philo affirms that this Therapeutick Sect prayed onely twice a day. **1727–41** CHAMBERS *Cycl.* s.v. *Therapeutæ*, Josephus..does not say one word of the *Therapeutæ*, or the therapeutic life. **1875** *Expositor* 429 Members of the Essene or Therapeutic communities.

3. Special collocations: ***therapeutic community***, a residential unit comprising staff and certain classes of mentally or behaviourally disturbed patients run in a deliberately informal manner to encourage social reintegration and rehabilitation; ***therapeutic index***, the ratio of the lethal or toxic dose of a drug to the therapeutically effective dose.

1964 G. L. COHEN *What's Wrong with Hospitals?* viii. 167 In the past decade, reformers have gone a step further, attempting to put inmate and authority on the same level: partners in a '*therapeutic community'. This endearing phrase originated at Belmont. **1977** *Lancet* 24/31 Dec. 1344/2 Common-milieu therapy, used by most therapeutic communities, is probably best regarded as re-educative psychotherapy. **1942** H. R. ROSENBERG *Chem. & Physiol. Vitamins* 150 The *therapeutic index [of vitamin B_1]..is extremely high. **1973** J. J. MCKELVEY *Man against Tsetse* iii. 200 It had a narrow therapeutic index, that is, a small difference between the 'curative' dose that would kill trypanosomes in human blood and the 'tolerated' dose beyond which the host would suffer damage.

therapeutical (θɛrə'pjuːtɪkəl), *a.* (*sb.*) [f. as prec. + -AL[1].] **a.** = prec. 1. (In first quot. *absol.*)

1605 DANIEL *Queen's Arcadia* III. ii, We must now Descend unto the Therapeutical. **1640** CHILMEAD tr. *Ferrand's Love Melanch.* xxxvii. 336 This Remedy..should rather be Prophylacticall, for Prevention of the disease, then Therapeuticall, for the Cure of it. **1657** [see PROPHYLACTICAL]. **1703** T. S. *Art's Improv.* p. xxv. **1843** R.

J. Graves *Syst. Clin. Med.* Introd. Lect. 21 Observation of the progress of symptoms and the effects of therapeutical agents. **1950** G. B. Shaw *Farfetched Fables* Pref. 90 Such a public department should be manned not by chemists analyzing the advertized wares and determining their therapeutical value, but by mathematicians criticizing their statistical pretentions. **1952** E. Hobsbawm in *Granta* 15 Nov. 12/1 We did not take to politics for therapeutical or aesthetic reasons.

b. *sb.* A therapeutic substance, a medicine.
1845 Ford *Handbk. Spain* II. xiii. 967/2 Mineral therapeuticals still remain a..dead letter.

Hence **thera'peutically** *adv.*, in a therapeutic manner; in relation to therapeutics.
1875 H. C. Wood *Therap.* (1879) 97 Dr. Leand affirms that the oxide of manganese is therapeutically equivalent to the preparations of bismuth except in that it does not constipate. **1885** G. H. Taylor *Pelv. & Hern. Therap.* 28 The local parts are by no means independent, therapeutically, as local therapeutics seem to imply.

thera'peutism. [f. Therapeut-æ + -ism.] The system or practice of the Therapeutæ.
1854 Milman *Lat. Chr.* I. 129 The Essenism or Therapeutism of the Jews.

therapeutist (θɛrə'pjuːtɪst). [f. therapeut(ic *sb.* + -ist. Cf. F. *thérapeutiste.*] One skilled in therapeutics; a physician.
1816–30 Bentham *Offic. Apt. Maximized, Extr. Const. Code* (1830) 63 This little work of the illustrious Therapeutist. **1886** W. T. Gairdner in *Life Sir R. Christison* II. vii. 138 Many..are now accomplished therapeutists.

theraphim, -in, -ym, -yn, obs. ff. teraphim.

theraphose ('θɛrəfəʊs), *a.* and *sb. Zool.* [f. mod.L. *Thērăphōsæ* (Walckenaer), irreg. f. Gr. θηράφιον a little 'beast' or insect, f. θήρ beast.]
a. *adj.* Of or pertaining to the *Theraphosæ*, a division of latebricole spiders, as the mygalids and trap-door spiders. **b.** *sb.* A spider of this group. So **thera'phosid** *a.* and *sb.*; **thera'phosoid** *a.*
1891 *Cent. Dict.*, Theraphose. **1898** *Proc. Zool. Soc.* 29 Nov. 892 A characteristic feature in these arboreal Theraphosids..the long feathery fringes on the legs. **1895** *Funk's Standard Dict.*, Theraphosoid.

'therapist. [f. Gr. θέραψ, θεραπ- attendant (see therapeutic *a.*), or f. therap(y + -ist.] One who practises in therapy, now esp. psychotherapy.
1886 *Medical News* (U.S.) XLIX. 510 The results..will be much more satisfactory to the therapist. **1917** G. B. Shaw in *Eng. Rev.* Dec. 490 A homœopath, or a bonesetter, or a serum therapist. **1937** *Brit. Jrnl. Psychol.* XXVIII. 109 He describes how the therapist..is able through unconscious observation to conjecture the nature of the patient's unconscious processes. **1978** *Listener* 5 Oct. 430/3, I would describe psychotherapy..as a treatment in which the doctor or therapist uses talking: first, to establish a relationship with the patient; secondly, to help him understand what is happening to him.

‖**Therapon** ('θɛrəpɒn). *Ichthyol.* [mod.L., a. Gr. θεράπων attendant.] A genus of fishes, the type of the family *Theraponidæ*, allied to the perch; a fish of this genus. So **'theraponid**, a member of the *Theraponidæ*; **'theraponoid** *a.*, resembling the *Theraponidæ*.
1891 *Cent. Dict.*, Theraponoid. **1895** *Funk's Standard Dict.*, Theraponid.

therapsid (θɛ'ræpsɪd), *sb.* (and *a.*) [*a.* the name of the order *Therapsida* (R. Broom 1905, in *Rec. Albany Museum* I. 269), f. thero- + apsis: see -id[3].] A mammal-like fossil reptile of the order Therapsida; also as *adj.*, of or pertaining to an animal of this kind.
1912 *Rep. Brit. Assoc. Adv. Sci.* 581 The humble Therapsid-like mammal felt the impetus of its new-found power of adaptation. **1933** A. S. Romer *Vertebr. Paleontol.* xi. 229 The limbs in advanced therapsids are greatly changed from the primitive sprawling position. **1966** E. Palmer *Plains of Camdeboo* vi. 95 The first of the mammal-like reptiles, or Therapsids as these famous fossil reptiles of the Karoo are known, had been discovered in 1838. **1971** J. Z. Young *Introd. Study Man* xxix. 408 Probably we shall never know whether the therapsid reptiles possessed the features of the soft parts that are so characteristic of mammals. **1973** B. J. Williams *Evolution & Human Origins* vii. 103/1 The therapsids had developed mammal-like features in locomotion and in their dentition. **1979** C. Kilian *Icequake* i. 14 His sermons on President Wood..had been as boring as his lectures on therapsid endothermy.

therapy ('θɛrəpɪ). [ad. mod.L. *therapīa*, a. Gr. θεραπεία healing: cf. θεραπεύ-ειν to attend medically. Cf. F. *thérapie.*] **1.** The medical treatment of disease; curative medical or psychiatric treatment. See also *group therapy* s.v. group *sb.* 6 b, *occupational therapy* s.v. occupational *a.*
1846 Worcester cites *Month. R.* **1873** Wagner tr. *Teuffel's Hist. Rom. Lit.* II. 26 The second [treats] of..general pathology and therapy. **1881** Virchow in *Nature* 11 Aug. 348/1 It will be pointed out to us..that therapy is to be replaced by hygiene. **1894** *Lancet* 3 Nov. 1044 Serum therapy..is a discovery belonging to M. Behring.

2. As the final element in words denoting treatment by means expressed in the first element, as actinotherapy, chemotherapy, psycho-therapy, radiotherapy, *roentgeno-therapy* s.v. roentgen-, roentgeno-, etc.

Theravada (θɛrə'vɑːdə). [a. Pali, lit. 'doctrine of the elders'.] = Hinayana.
[**1875** R. C. Childers *Dict. Pali Lang.* 545/1 The adj. *theravādī* (*theravāda*..) means holding the orthodox doctrine.] **1882** W. Hoey tr. *Oldenberg's Buddha* I. i. 75 The Church of Ceylon remained true to the simple, homely, 'Word of the Ancients' (Theravâda). **1923** Ld. Ronaldshay *Lands of Thunderbolt* vi. 48, I shall refer to it as the Thera Vada—'the way of the Elders'—because this is the title which its adherents themselves prefer, the term Hinayāna being objectionable to them. **1959** *Encounter* Jan. 19 Theravada Buddhism stems directly from the Indian tradition. **1978** C. Humphreys *Both Sides of Circle* xii. 132 My own list, however, was far wider than Olcott's 'Fourteen Fundamental Principles', which were largely confined to the Canon of the Southern or Theravada school.

therblig ('θɜːblɪg). [Anagrammatic formation by partial reversal of the name of its inventor, F. B. *Gilbreth* (1868–1924), American engineer and pioneer of time-and-motion studies.] In time-and-motion study, a unit of work or absence of work into which an industrial operation may be divided (see quot. 1921); a symbol representing such a unit.
1921 F. B. Gilbreth in *Bull. Taylor Soc.* June 128/2 We believe that there are but sixteen sub-divisions of a cycle of motions. They are called therbligs. They are as follows: 1. Search, 2. Find,..13. Transport, empty, 14. Rest for overcoming fatigue [etc.]. **1930** *Movie Makers* Nov. 687/1 The motions of the operator are broken down into fundamental motions known as 'therbligs' (Gilbreth spelled backwards). **1947** [see micromotion]. **1948** Ghiselli & Brown *Personnel & Industrial Psychol.* xi. 279 The therblig type of classification of movements is important principally in such problems as changing the sequence of movements and in the elimination of unnecessary movements. **1963** *Engineering* 27 Dec. 826/3 Maynard intended to allocate time values to Gilbreth's therbligs. **1964** A. Battersby *Network Analysis* ii. 13 Two main sets of symbols are used: Gilbreth's 'therbligs' for motion study and the standard ASME (American Society of Mechanical Engineers) symbols for method study. **1975** *Daily Tel.* 11 Dec. 14/5 There are 18 therbligs altogether. Each has its own symbol and colour (e.g. 'search' is black, 'grasp' is red, 'use' is purple) and these can be used to construct simultaneous motion charts. **1976** W. H. Canaway *Willow-Pattern War* vii. 82 She was skilled..in lovemaking, and only now and then did you get the feeling that..in her mind there was a stopwatch and a work-study chart covered with therbligs.

therdde, obs. form of third.

there (ðɛə(r), *unstressed* ðə(r)), *adv.* (*a.*, *sb.*) Forms: see below. [OE. *þǽr, þár, þér*, cognate with OS. *thâr*, OFris. *thêr, dêr*, MLG. *dār*, MDu. *daer*, Du. *daar*, OHG. *dâr* (MHG. *dâr, dâ*, Ger. *da*); cf. also Goth. *þar*, ON. *þar* (Sw., Da. *der*); all derivatives of the demonstrative stem *þa-*, pre-Teut. *to-* (that, the). The adverbial suffix *-r* appears also in OE. *hwǽr, hwér, hwar*, where.
Besides *þǽr*, etc., OE. had also a rare form *þāra*, prob. an emphatic deriv., like OHG *dāra, dāre*, and not cognate with OHG. *dara*, MHG. *dare, dar*, 'thither'. In ME. all the variants *þār, þǽr, þēr, þōr* appear also with final *-e*, perh. taken from the advb. *-e* in *inne, uppe, ūte, fore*, etc. The later forms *thare* and *there* may represent ME. *þāre, þêre*, or the final *e* may merely indicate the long vowel.]

A. Illustration of Forms.
α. 1 **þára.**
c **888** K. Ælfred *Boeth.* xxxiii. §5 Ac hit is þeah þara. *c* **1000** *Ags. Gosp.* Mark xiv. 15 ȝe ȝe-earwiað us þara [*Hatton* þare, *Lindisf.* & *Rushw.* ðer].

β. 1–3 **þǽr,** 2 **þǽre.**
c **888** K. Ælfred *Boeth.* xxxiii. §5 Swa is eac þær fyr on ðam stanum and on ðam wætere. *a* **900** tr. *Bæda's Hist.* I. i. (1890) 28 Swa þæt ðær seldon snau leng ligeð þonne ðry dagas. *c* **1000** *Ags. Gosp.* Matt. xiv. 23 He wæs ana þær. *a* **1131** *O.E. Chron.* an. 1123, Ða..ferde se king to Winceastre and wæs ealle Eastren tyde þære. *c* **1200** Ormin 2789 þe laffdiȝ Marȝe comm Till Zacariȝess bottle, And spacc þær wiþþ Elysabæþ.

γ. 1–2 **þár,** 2–5 **þar, þare,** 3–5 *north.* **þaire,** 4– **thar** (now U.S. *dial.* and *colloq.*: see also sense B. 2 c(*c*) below), 4–6 **thare** (4–5 **tare**), 6 *Sc.* **thair, yare, yair.**
c **893** K. Ælfred *Oros.* I. i. §22 ȝyf þar man an ban findeð unforbærned. *c* **1000** *Ags. Gosp.* Matt. xxi. 17 He..lærde hi þar [*A.* þær, *Hatt.* þar, *Lind.* ðer, *Rushw.* þær] be godes rice. *c* **1275** Lay. 27474 Cnihtes þar aswalten; blodes vt hurnen. *Ibid.* 25651 þare. **13..** *Cursor M.* 5420 (Cott.) Iacob þaire [*Gött.* þar] liued seuenten yeir. *Ibid.* 21655 (Edin.) Thare dide him driȝtin to resune. ? *a* **1400** *Morte Arth.* 3603 Thare the false men fletyde, and one flode lengede. *c* **1400** *Rule St. Benet* 21 þai sal be broȝt by-fore þe cuuent and tare amende hir faute. **1483** *Cath. Angl.* 381/2 Thare, *ibi, ibidem, illic.* **1535** Stewart *Cron. Scot.* (Rolls) I. 33 Greit slauchter oftymes wes maid yair. **1562** *Reg. Privy Council Scot.* I. 226 Williame Gordoun in Wigtoun, Johne Martine thair, Robert Johnestoun thair. **1859** Bartlett *Dict. Amer.* (ed. 2) 477 A person wishing to imply that he is perfectly at home in any thing, says he is *thar*; a good hunter or fisher is also *thar*. **1885** *Weekly New Mexican Rev.* 29 Jan. 4/5 The Santa Rifles had their first drill at Alhambra hall last night... Nearly all the boys have 'been thar' before, and as a consequence, catch up the command very readily. **1887** [see tchick *sb.*]. **1937** W. Blair in B. A. Botkin *Treas. S. Folklore* (1949) IV. iii. 645 Hello, thar, gin us 'Forked Deer', old fiddle-teazer. **1980** 'D. Shannon' *Felony File* i. 27 Thar's a big store, with a lot of different departments.

δ. 1–2 **þér,** 3–5 **þer, þere** (4 tere), 5 **þeer, theer,** 4–6 **ther,** 4– **there.**
c **950** *Lindisf. Gosp.* Matt. v. 24 Forlet ðer [*Rushw.*, *Ags. G.*, *Hatt.* þær] ðing ðin to wiȝbed. —— Mark iv. 15 Seðe ymb woeȝ ðer [*Ags. Gosp.* þar, *Hatt.* þær] bið ȝesauen. *c* **1205** Lay. 10 þer he bock radde [*c* **1275** þer heo bokes radde]. *Ibid.* 25651 Nes he þere [*c* 1275 þare] buten ane niht. *Ibid.* 29876 Alle..þa þer icumen weoren. *c* **1275** *Ibid.* 8 Merie þer [*c* 1205 þar] him þohte. *Ibid.* 582 þere [*c* 1205 þer] Brutus nam Antigo[num]. **1297** R. Glouc. (Rolls) 1796 An vrninde water þat ȝut is þer, ich wene. *Ibid.* 3519 þere he huld is parlement. **13..** *Cursor M.* 21104 (Cott.) His bodi is birid tere [*rime* sper; *other MSS.* þere]. *c* **1400** *Destr. Troy* 3719 Ermonia þe myld maynly was ther. **1412–20** Lydg. *Chron. Troy* II. 4189, I was not þere. *c* **1420** There [see B. 12]. *a* **1425** *Cursor M.* 22980 (Trin.) Men wene þe doom shal be þeer. **1430–40** Lydg. *Bochas* IX. xxxi. (1558) 32 b, Clement theer concludyng if he may. **1432–50** tr. *Higden* (Rolls) VII. 401 The sedes..whiche hade bene sawen þer of olde tyme. *c* **1440** There [see B. 9].

ε. (variants of δ *þer, there*) 2 **þeor,** 3 **þear, þiar,** 5–7 **their,** 6 **thear,** 6– *dial.* **theare.**
a **1200** *Moral Ode* 273 (Lamb. MS.) þeor beð naddren and snaken. *c* **1200** *Ibid.* 165 (Trin. Coll. MS.) Ne sal þeih no man samie þiar. *c* **1205** Lay. 607 Brutus hefde þa men..idon into þan castle & þear heom quic heolde. *a* **1225** *Leg. Kath.* 8 Constantin..wunede summe hwile þear. *c* **1425** *Cursor M.* 10042 (Laud) Their buxumnes holt her state. **1535** Coverdale *Josh.* xxi. 45 Their myssed nothinge of all the good that the Lorde had promysed. **1563** B. Googe *Cupido* Eglogs, etc. (Arb.) 117 And..thear, for succour thus doth call. **1570** —— *Pop. Kingd.* II. (1880) 13 Togither stande they theare [*rime* weare]. **1616** Purchas *Pilgrimage, India* (1864) 49 Three of the Gallions driuen on ground,..and had beene their left but for the Frigates. **1655** Stanley *Hist. Philos.* I. 53/2 For their's no order in Equality.

ζ. 3–4 **þôr,** 3–5 **þôre,** 4–5 **thôre.**
c **1250** *Gen. & Ex.* 1844 He droȝ ðider and wunede ðor. *Ibid.* 2270 Ðat riche louerd ðore. *c* **1300** *Havelok* 922 Go þu yunder and sit þore [*rime* more]. *Ibid.* 1044 For neuere yete ne saw he or Putten the stone, or þanne þor. *c* **1300** *Harrow. Hell* (Harl. MS.) 30 Ihesu crist..seide he wolde vacche hem thore [*rime* sore]. *c* **1330** R. Brunne *Chron. Wace* (Rolls) 1021 He..wende haue founde Brutus þore. *c* **1380** *Sir Ferumb.* 544 þe Sarsyn þat was þor. *c* **1420** *Chron. Vilod.* 2040 To make alle thyngus redy þore [*rime* byfore]. *a* **1425** *Cursor M.* 409 (Trin.) He vs ȝaf ensaumple þore [*rime* more; *earlier MSS.* þare..mare]. *c* **1470** Harding *Chron.* III. iv, Seleucus than was the first kynge þore [*rime* afore].

B. Signification.
I. As a demonstrative adverb.
* *Expressing locality or position.*

1. a. In or at that place; in the place (country, region, etc.) pointed to, indicated, or referred to, and away from the speaker; the opposite of *here*.
c **888** [see A. α, β]. *a* **900** [see A. β]. *c* **950** [see A. δ]. *c* **1050** *Byrhtferth's Handboc* in *Anglia* (1885) VIII. 303 þonne beoð þær swa fela concurrentes. *c* **1205** Lay. 716 þær þu findest seouen houndred. *c* **1400** *Three Kings Cologne* 118 þei ȝede to þe cite of Sewill..and þere þei leuyd .ij. ȝere. **1523** Ld. Berners *Froiss.* I. cv. 126 The erle of Derby went to Pelagrue, and ther was sixe dayes. **1673** Ray *Journ. Low C.* 23 At our being there it was held with a strong Garrison. **1786** Cowper *Let. to Lady Hesketh* May, I have walked there, but have never walked thither. **1827** Scott *Highl. Widow* iii, The cloudberry..which is only found on very high hills, and there only in very small quantities. **1874** Bosw. Smith *Mohammed*, etc. (1876) 322 There if anywhere, will be the Armageddon of Islam.

b. *there* (in emphatic use) may be defined by a relative clause, following or preceding, introduced by *where* (†*there*) or an equivalent.
c **950** *Lindisf. Gosp.* Matt. vi. 21 Ðer *vel* huer forðon is strion ðin ðer is and hearta ðin. *c* **1000** *Ags. Gosp.* ibid., þær ðin gold is þær is ðin heorte. *a* **1300** *Cursor M.* 20258 þar i sal be, quar mi sun is. *c* **1500** *Melusine* xxxvi. 294 There where he passed by he enquyred after guedon. **1591** Harington *Orl. Fur.* Pref. ¶ij b, Where the hedge is lowest, there doth euery man go ouer. **1810** Crabbe *Borough* iii. 195 Where Time has plough'd, there Misery loves to sow. **1850** McCosh *Div. Govt.* II. i. (1874) 138 Wherever we find law, there we see the certain traces of a lawgiver. **1850** Tennyson *In Mem.* cxxiii, There rolls the deep where grew the tree.

2. a. Appended, unstressed, to the name of a person or thing to whose presence attention is called: = Who or that is there, whom or which you see there.
1590 Shaks. *Com. Err.* V. i. 275 He din'de with her there, at the Porpentine. **1606** —— *Tr. & Cr.* II. i. 91, I would haue peace.., but the foole will not: he there. **1611** —— *Wint. T.* II. iii. 160 You that haue beene so tenderly officious With Lady Margerie, your Mid-wife there. **1794** Mrs. Radcliffe *Myst. Udolpho* xlii, There she lay,..her face was upon the pillow there! *Mod.* Hand me that book there, please.

b. As a brusque mode of address (often in commands) to a person or persons in the place or direction indicated; = you (that are) there. Now also appended casually to exclamations of greeting, etc., as *hi* (or *hello*) *there!*, with varying purpose: freq. to attract attention or to express cordiality.
1589 [see hollo, hollow *int.*]. *a* **1596** *Sir T. More* I. ii. 97 Silence there, hoe! **1605** Shaks. *Lear* IV. vii. 25 Louder the music there! *a* **1619** Fletcher *Mad Lover* III. ii, Put to the doors a while there. **1676** Dryden *Aurengzebe* II. i. 24 Your fury hardens me:..A Guard there; seize her. **1840** [see hallo, halloa *int.*]. **1859** *Habits Gd. Soc.* v. 200 He will..use some such phrase as: 'May I trouble you for that ball, sir?' not 'Ball, you there', as one sometimes hears it. **1885** [see hi *int.* 2]. *a* **1912** *Mod.* Hurry up there! Do you hear there? Pass along there, please! **1924** *Dialect Notes* V. 270 *Hi there*, (call or warning). **1945** T. Williams *Battle of Angels* II. i. 33 *A girl*: Hello! *Val*: (amiably) Hello there. **1962** J. Braine *Life at Top* xv. 188 'Hello there,' I said, 'What's new?'

c. Emphatically appended to the demonstrative *that*. *dial.* and *vulgar*. (Cf. HERE *adv.* 1 d.) Also ***that 'ere, that 'air***.

1742 RICHARDSON *Pamela* III. 404 On leaving yours and Mr. B.'s hospitable House, because of that there Affair. **1778** MISS BURNEY *Evelina* (1791) II. xxxvii. 244 Did you ever get a ducking in that there place? *Ibid.* 245 'For the matter of that there', said the Captain, 'you must make him a soldier'. **1818** SCOTT *Hrt. Midl.* xli, That trunk is mine, and that there band-box, and that pillion mail. **1825** J. NEAL *Bro. Jonathan* I. 244 Is that 'air fellow gone yet? **1840** THACKERAY *Catherine* vi, How came you by that there horse? **1863** *Literary Times* 20 June, The 'this here' and 'that there' (euphonically contracted into 'that 'ere') of the Cockney.

(*b*) ***that there***. Used adjectivally and absolutely, often in *euphem.* reference to sexual activity, esp. in catch-phrase ***you can't do that there 'ere*** (see quot. 1933).

1819 BYRON *Let.* 26 Oct. (1976) VI. 232 As to 'Don Juan' confess—confess—you dog—and be candid—that it is the sublime of *that there* sort of writing—it may be bawdy—but is it not good English? **1933** SQUIERS & WARK *You can't do that there 'Ere* in *Feldman's 41st Song & Dance Album* 37 As they took a kiss, The keeper shouted this: You can't do that there 'ere, so there! You can't do that there 'ere. You'd ought to know you 'ad, I'm sure, That that there 'ere's agin the law. **1937** *Even. News* 13 Apr. 8/3 The British Government gives vent to a 'John-Bullism', and says, after the abduction of a Hindu girl from within the border, 'You can't do that there 'ere!' **1962** AUDEN *Dyer's Hand* (1963) 406 How suitable, too, for a that-there poet that the room in which his 'Memoirs' were burned should now be called the Byron Room. **1974** P. WRIGHT *Lang. Brit. Industry* xi. 96 Long before the song 'You can't do that there here', Northerners used *that there* as a euphemism for the sexual act. It is a standard phrase in the north when youngsters of both sexes are 'educating' themselves by discussing sex matters.

(*c*) Phr. ***there's gold in them there*** (freq. ***thar***) ***hills***, with reference to a potentially profitable enterprise or activity. Also allusively. orig. *U.S.*

1941 C. B. KELLAND *House of Cards* xiv. 159 She heard him chuckle. 'Thar's gold in them thar hills.' **1961** J. L. AUSTIN *Philos. Papers* vi. 129 There is gold in them thar hills. **1965** E. GUNDREY *Foot in Door* xxxiii. 189 There's money in them thar pills—but very little else. **1976** *New Society* 16 Sept. 607/1 There's gold in them there sand-dunes, about 10 million people enjoyed a naturist holiday last year.

3. a. Pointing to something as present to the sight or perception, chiefly in ***there is, there are*** ('ðεərɪz, ðεəz; 'ðεərə(r)); also, calling attention to something offered (often *absol.*; cf. 7).

1535 LYNDESAY *Satyre* 1355 Tak, thair, ane vther [i.e. blow] vpon thy peild harne-pan. **1597** SHAKS. *2 Hen. IV*, v. ii. 117 There is my hand, You shall be as a Father, to my Youth. **1601** —— *Twel. N.* IV. i. 27 *And.* Now sir, haue I met you again: ther's for you. *Seb.* Why there's for thee, and there, and there. **1728** RAMSAY *There's my Thumb* ii, There's my thumb I'll ne'er beguile thee. **1742** RICHARDSON *Pamela* IV. 375 There's for you, dear Sir! See what a Mother can do, if she pleases! **1890** 'L. FALCONER' *Mlle. Ixe* v, There was that lazy Mr. Lethbridge lounging in the doorway. *Mod.* There is the dinner-bell; make haste. See, there comes the train. Hark! there goes the bugle.

b. Pointing out a person or object with approval or commendation, or the contrary. Also in anticipatory commendation of the person addressed; cf. THAT *dem. pron.* B. I. 1 b.

1595 SHAKS. *John* II. i. 163 It grandame will Giue yt a plum, a cherry, and a figge; There's a good grandame. **1596** —— *Tam. Shr.* v. ii. 180 Why there's a wench: Come on, and kisse mee Kate. **1741** RICHARDSON *Pamela* II. 224 There's a Word for a Lady's Mouth! **1780** *Mirror* No. 97 ¶26 'Quantity of syllables', exclaimed the Captain, 'there is modern education for you!' **1825** T. HOOK *Sayings* Ser. II. *Man of Many Fr.* I. 191 Tom,..go and fetch the wine for your sister, there's a dear love. **1870** DICKENS *E. Drood* ii, Don't moddley-coddley, there's a good fellow. **1872** 'L. CARROLL' *Through Looking-Glass* vi. 123 There's glory for you! *Mod.* There's a fine horse! all skin and bones.

c. ***there is***, usu. contracted to ***there's*** (with succeeding adj.): used in statements or exclamations in place of standard English *that is* or HOW *adv.* 7. *Welsh dial.*

1939 R. LLEWELLYN *How Green was my Valley* ii. 23 'Go on, boy,' Cedric whispered, 'there is soft you are to eat old cake.' **1951** E. COXHEAD *One Green Bottle* v. 113 There's tantalising! Plenty of company and no time for a word. **1968** A. LASKI *Keeper* vi. 68 There's sad, about Japhet; that was a good man. **1971** 'H. CALVIN' *Poison Chasers* ix. 123 There's selfish you are, I had him saved up for myself.

4. Used unemphatically to introduce a sentence or clause in which, for the sake of emphasis or preparing the hearer, the verb comes before its subject, as *there comes a time when*, etc., *there was heard a rumbling noise*. In interrogative sentences *there* comes between the verb and subject, as *Breathes there the man*, etc.?, or follows the first word of a compound verb, as *Does there breathe a man?, Shall there be any notice taken of it?* The same order was formerly observed after an introductory adv. or clause, as *Then came there a voice, Soon shall there arise a prophet*.

Grammatically, there is no difference between *There comes the train!* and *There comes a time when*, etc.; but, while in the former *there* is demonstrative and stressed, in the latter it has been reduced to a mere anticipative element occupying the place of the subject which comes later. Preceding or following a main verb, or following any verb, *there*, thus used, is stressless (proclitic or enclitic: e.g. *there-'came, 'breathes-there, 'is-there, 'will-there*), but preceding *be* or an auxiliary, *there* has a slight stress, and the verb is enclitic (e.g. *'there-is, 'there-was, 'there-will*).

a. with intransitive verbs.

c **888** K. ÆLFRED *Boeth.* iii. §1 þa com þær gan in to me heofencund Wisdom. *c* **1000** *Ags. Gosp.* Matt. vii. 25 þa com þær ren and mycele flod and þær bleowun windas. *c* **1250** *Gen. & Ex.* 3863 And ðer ros wreððe and strif a-non Aȝen moysen and aaron. *a* **1300** *Cursor M.* 19867 Als petre þan bigan til hon [*Fairf., Gött.* hone] þar com anoþer voice alson. *c* **1320** *Cast. Love* 736 In þulke derworþe feire tour þer stont a trone wiþ muche honour. *c* **1386** CHAUCER *Melib.* ¶537 Ne neuere cam ther a vileynous word out of his mouþ. **1470–85** MALORY *Arthur* I. xxiii. 70 Ther maye no knyght ryde this wey but yf he Iuste with the. *c* **1477** CAXTON *Jason* 22 For to sle a man..ther behoueth but one stroke wel sette. *c* **1566** J. ALDAY tr. *Boaystuau's Theat. World* K viij b, There died an infinite number of people. **1590** SPENSER *F.Q.* II. ix. 59 There chaunced to the Princes hand to rize An auncient booke. **1609** HOLLAND *Amm. Marcell.* 47 In these Cottian Alpes..there peaketh up a mightie high mount. **1611** BIBLE *Numb.* xxiv. 17 There shall come a starre out of Iacob, and a Scepter shall rise out of Israel. **1761–2** HUME *Hist. Eng.* (1806) V. lxx. 247 There want not sufficient materials on which to form a true judgment. **1805** SCOTT *Last Minstr.* VI. i, Breathes there the man with soul so dead, Who never [etc.]? **1812** BYRON *Ch. Har.* II. lxxxii, Lurk there no hearts that throb with secret pain? **1857** BUCKLE *Civiliz.* I. vii. 399 From all these things there resulted consequences of vast importance.

†**b.** with transitive verbs: usually before an auxiliary of tense or mood. *Obs.*

13.. *Cast. Love* (Halliw.) 306 Withoute these..Ther may no kyng lede gret lordship. **1387** TREVISA *Higden* (Rolls) I. 223 Whan it was ones i-tend..þere couþe no man it aquenche wiþ no craft. **14..** HOCCLEVE *Compl. Virgin* 54 Ther may no martirdom me make smerte. **1548** UDALL, etc. *Erasm. Par. Acts* 43 b, Peter, knowing..that there woulde some Iewes reproue this his doing.

c. with a verb in the passive voice.

a **1533** LD. BERNERS *Huon* cxi. 385 There coude not be founde a more goodlyer man. **1584** R. SCOT *Discov. Witchcr.* x. vii. (1886) 147 Whilest the treasure is a digging, there must be read the psalmes [etc.]. **1691** T. H[ALE] *Acc. New Invent.* 99 There's nothing said herein. **1877** RUSKIN *St. Mark's Rest* i. §4 There were no plenipotentiaries sent to the East, and back again. *Mod.* Here, there were found various relics of Franklin's expedition.

d. especially with the verb *to be*: cf. BE B. 1, 1 b, 5 b. ***there is, there are***, are equivalent to F. *il est, il y a*, Ger. *es ist, es sind, es giebt*, Sp. *hay*. (For such phrases as ***there is no saying*** = 'it is impossible to say', see NO *a.* 4.)

c **893** K. ÆLFRED *Oros.* I. i. §22 þær is mid Estum an mæȝð. **1297** R. GLOUC. (Rolls) 7551 þer nas prince in al þe world of so noble fame. *a* **1300** *Cursor M.* 17787 Vp risen [he] es, dut es þar nan. *Ibid.* 20123 Ne was tar noiþer seke ne fere. **13..** *Cast. Love* (Halliw.) 275 Ther wes a kyng of myche myȝht. *c* **1330** R. BRUNNE *Chron. Wace* (Rolls) 5467 Waster [was there] non þat wolde hym feyne. *c* **1380** WYCLIF *Wks.* (1880) 147 As þouȝ þer were no lif but only in þis wrecchid world. *a* **1415** LYDG. *Temple of Glass* 179 And some þer were..That pleined sore. **1456** SIR G. HAYE *Law Arms* (S.T.S.) 1 Into the quhilk buke thare salbe foure partis. **1485** CAXTON *Malory's Arthur* Pref., Dyuers men holde oppynyon that there was no suche Arthur. **1531** in J. Bulloch *Pynours* (1887) 59 Considering thair has bene and is dalie besynes and ado with the pynouris. **1605** SHAKS. *Lear* II. iv. 305 For many Miles about There's scarce a Bush. **1657–83** EVELYN *Hist. Relig.* (1850) I. 79 Epicurus and his scholars of old.. make this an argument of there being no God. **1782** COWPER *Alex. Selkirk* 2 My right there is none to dispute. **1823** F. CLISSOLD *Ascent Mt. Blanc* 22 There being no moon. **1842** TENNYSON *Lady Clare* xi, I will know If there be any faith in man.

e. When a relative clause follows, the relative pron. (*that, who*, or *which*) is often omitted. Now chiefly *colloquial* or *archaic*, as in ballad style.

Cf. THAT *rel. pron.* 10, of which this is a case.

? *a* **1366** CHAUCER *Rom. Rose* 1239 Ther is no cloth sitteth bet On damiselle, than doth roket. **1470–85** MALORY *Arthur* XIII. iii. 616 There was no knyȝt knewe from whens he came. **1596** SHAKS. *1 Hen. IV*, II. iv. 568 There are two Gentlemen Haue in this Robberie lost three hundred Markes. **1806** WORDSW. *Address to Child* 8 But how he will come, and whither he goes, There's never a scholar in England knows. *Mod. colloq.* There's a man at the door wants to see you.

f. The antecedent, when a simple pronominal word (usu. pl., e.g. *they, those, some*, rarely sing., e.g. *he, she, that*), is sometimes omitted. (App. a Latinism, after *sunt qui dicunt*, and the like.) Cf. THAT *rel. pron.* 3.

c **1400** *Destr. Troy* 12860 There come out of castels & of cloise townes..þat hom bale wroght. **14..** *Why I can't be a Nun* 244 in *E.E.P.* (1862) 144 There weren that dyd not so. *a* **1533** LD. BERNERS *Gold. Bk. M. Aurel.* K k iv, There were that saied, that this ambassadour should be chastised. **1560** BIBLE (Genev.) *Prov.* xi. 24 There is that scatereth, and is more increased. **1569** J. SANFORD tr. *Agrippa's Van. Artes* 101 b, There are of them whiche accompte it a greate offence to touche monie. **1628** FELTHAM *Resolves* II. [I.] xiii. 35 There are, to whom Death doth seeme no more then a blood-letting. **1657–83** EVELYN *Hist. Relig.* (1850) I. 9 There have been..who pretend [etc.]. **1736** WELSTED *Wks.* (1787) 455 There are, I know, who have strong prejudices to opinions of this sort. *a* **1849** H. COLERIDGE *Ess.* (1851) I. 236 Waller called Milton the old blind schoolmaster, and there are who have spoken of Wordsworth as the stamp-master. **1864** BROWNING *Abt Vogler* v, There wanted not who walked in the glare and glow.

5. a. At that point or stage in action, proceeding, speech, or thought; formerly sometimes referring to what immediately precedes or follows: at that juncture; on that; on that occasion; then.

a **1400** *Relig. Pieces fr. Thornton MS.* 77 At myn endynge ..I pray þe lady helpe me þare. *a* **1450** *Le Morte Arth.* 2388 The kynge Arthur Answerys thore Wordys that were kene and throo. *Ibid.* 3480 'A! false traytor' he sayd thore. **1596** SHAKS. *Merch. V.* II. viii. 46 And euen there his eye being big with teares, Turning his face, he put his hand behinde him. **1602** —— *Ham.* II. i. 19 And there put on him What forgeries you please. **1647** MAY *Hist. Parl.* I. vii. 76 There we are at this instant. **1706** FARQUHAR *Recruit. Officer* I. i, Brother! hold there, friend; I am no kindred to you that I know of yet.

b. ***and there('s) an end***: and that is the end of the matter or the last word on the subject; 'and that's all'. *Obs.* or *arch.*

1591, 1615 [see END *sb.* 23]. **1596** SHAKS. *1 Hen. IV*, v. iii. 64 If not, honour comes vnlook'd for, and ther's an end. **1650** TRAPP *Comm. Exod.* vii. 25 As the dog, who getting out of the water, shakes his ears, and there's an end. **1872** RUSKIN *Fors Clav.* xvi. §5 Confirmed by the signature of any person whom the Queen might appoint.., and there an end.

6. †**a.** In that case; then. *Obs.*

c **888** K. ÆLFRED *Boeth.* xvi. §2 Hu ne is se anweald þon þær nauht? **1362** LANGL. *P. Pl.* A. IX. 32 þer [B. VIII. 37 þanne] weore þe Monnes lyf I-lost þorw lachesse of himselue.

b. In that thing, matter, or business; in that fact or circumstance; in that respect, as to that.

c **1386** CHAUCER *Prol.* 259 In loue dayes ther koude he muchel helpe, For there he was nat lyk a Cloystrer. **1585** T. WASHINGTON tr. *Nicholay's Voy.* II. xx. 57 b, If the moneye ordayned for the poore is not there bestowed. **1592** SHAKS. *Rom. & Jul.* III. iii. 137 Thy Iuliet is aliue,..There art thou happy. **1602** —— *Ham.* III. i. 65, I, there's the rub. **1605** —— *Lear* IV. vi. 148 Oh ho, are you there with me? **1613** —— *Hen. VIII*, III. ii. 408 There was the waight that pull'd me downe. **1855** BROWNING *Bp. Blougram's Apol.* 85 You would be all, I would be merely much; you beat me there. **1884** H. JAMES in *Eng. Illustr. Mag.* Dec. 248/2 It was beastly awkward certainly; *there* I could quite agree with him. **1896** *Daily News* 17 June 5/4 There is where the Japanese differ from us.

c. Referring to something said or done: In those words, in that act.

a **1596** *Sir T. More* I. i. 176 *Wil.* My maisters..lets.. sweare true secrecie vppon our liues. *Geo.* There spake an angell. Come, let vs along, then. **1603** SHAKS. *Meas. for M.* III. i. 86 There spake my brother: there my fathers graue Did vtter forth a voice. **1829** *Blackw. Mag.* XXV. 558 There you have hit the nail on the head, James. *Mod. colloq.* You have me there! I cannot tell you.

7. Used interjectionally, usually to point (in a tone of vexation, dismay, derision, satisfaction, encouragement, etc.) to some fact, condition, or consummation, presented to the sight or mind. Hence ***there-there*** vb. trans., to soothe or comfort by saying these words.

1535 COVERDALE *Ps.* xxxiv. [xxxv.] 21 They gape vpon me with their mouthes, sayenge: there, there [1611 Aha, aha!]: we se it with oure eyes. **1596** SHAKS. *Merch. V.* III. i. 87 Why there, there, there, there, a diamond gone cost me two thousand ducats. **1606** —— *Tr. & Cr.* v. v. 43 *Ajax.* Troylus, thou coward Troylus. *Diom.* I, there, there. **1788** J. O'KEEFFE *Prisoner at large* I. vi, There, sir, the bed's ready. **1798** JANE AUSTEN *Lett.* (1952) 42 There! I may now finish my letter and go and hang myself. **1824** SCOTT *St. Ronan's* xxx, 'There now', said Touchwood, 'there was a rencontre between them—the very thing I wanted to know'. **1840** T. C. HALIBURTON *Clockmaker* 3rd Ser. xx. 284 It's no such thing, says mother, quite snappishly; Sam is only twenty-one last Thanksgiving-day, and he was born just nine months and one day arter we was married, so there now. **1856** MRS. CARLYLE *Lett.* (1883) II. 295 There! I have put my foot in it! **1872** *Routledge's Ev. Boy's Ann.* 514/1 'There, there', my poor father answered, 'it is not that'. **1875** L. TROUBRIDGE *Life amongst Troubridges* (1966) 101 There now, if I haven't entirely forgotten to say anything about the boys. **1876** STEVENSON *Lett.* (1901) I. iii. 115 There, that's your prophecy did that! **1878** BROWNING *La Saisiaz* 49 There, the dread descent is over. **1888** 'J. S. WINTER' *Bootle's Childr.* ix, And, indeed—but there, what's the good of talking about it. **1893** BURRELL & CUTHELL *Indian Mem.* 210 But there! I was not going to tell you how you felt. **1894** 'J. S. WINTER' *Red-Coats* 55 My life's my own to do what I like with, and I'm going to 'em now; so there! **1903** *Daily Chron.* 28 Oct. 7/1 She showered blows upon the lad's head and shoulders, with the words,..'There now, how do you like it?' **1924** R. MACAULAY *Orphan Island* xxi. 280, I suppose you think I'm in love with you. Well, I'm not, so there. **1938** D. RUNYON *Furthermore* viii. 159 He.. starts whispering, 'There, there, there, my itty oddleums.' **1948** 'J. TEY' *Franchise Affair* iv. 39 Only one thing your Aunt Lin makes better than me..hot cross buns, and that's only once a year. So there! **1968** J. SANGSTER *Touchfeather* xv. 180, I was sobbing my heart out on his chest and he was there there-ing me all over the place. **1969** *Listener* 15 May 698/1 But Gwen was going to marry her lecherous tutor, so there. **1977** 'E. CRISPIN' *Glimpses of Moon* xii. 240 There, There, sir. **1977** C. DEXTER *Silent World N. Quinn* 254 Joyce took the baby..and lovingly there-thered his raucous cries.

** *Expressing motion to a place.*

8. To that place: now taking in ordinary use the place of THITHER.

there and back, to that place and back again; also as a catch-phrase reply (see quot. 1937). ***to get there*** (colloq. or slang): see GET *v.* 31 c.

a **900** *O.E. Chron.* an. 894, Wæs Hæsten þa þær cumen mid his herȝe. *c* **1205** LAY. 29876 Alle ut wenden þa þer [*c* 1275 þider] icumen weoren. **13..** *Cursor M.* 1780 (Gött.) Quen þai cam þar [*v.rr.* þare, þere] was þar na bote. *a* **1425** *Ibid.* 9929 (Trin.) Waried wiȝt comeþ þere neuer. *c* **1440** *Alphabet of Tales* 122 þis clerk denyed hym & sayd he come nott þer. **1592** SHAKS. *Ven. & Ad.* 780 And will not let a false sound enter there. **1610** —— *Temp.* II. i. 99 And the rarest that ere came there. **1663** GERBIER *Counsel* 41 Strangers that come there. **1772** in S. Rosenfeld *Temples of Thespis* (1978)

v. 78 Pd Mr. Richards..at 2 Guineas pr Day & expenses there & Back £62.5.0. **1803** G. COLMAN *John Bull* III. ii. 32 Aye, he might have been there and back, over and over again; but my husband is slow enough in his motions. **1830** M. EDGEWORTH *Let.* 18 Oct. (1971) 419 This 'Trip to the Viaduct'..five shillings apiece there and *back*. **1858** J. H. NEWMAN *Mission Bened. Ord.* Sel. Ess. 211 When St. Hubert was brought there. **1871** MRS. H. WOOD *Dene Hollow* xxviii, We shall go only there and back, grandpapa. **1907** *Westm. Gaz.* 7 June 12/1 The 'there-and-back' distance between 'Auld Reekie' and Inverness is but eight miles less. *a* **1912** *Mod.* Going to the meeting?—I am on my way there. **1937** PARTRIDGE *Dict. Slang* 874/2 *There and back*, a c.p. reply to an impertinent or unwelcome inquiry 'where are you going (to)?': late C. 19–20. **1977** *Transatlantic Rev.* LX. 191 'Where are we going?' 'Oh, there and back,' said the cabbie, giggling.

II. As a relative or conjunctive adverb.

†**9.** In, on, at, or into which place; = WHERE.

a. with a sb. as antecedent.

a **800** *O.E. Chron.* an. 755, On þære byriȝ..þær se cyning ofslæȝen læȝ. *c* **950** *Lindisf. Gosp.* Matt. vi. 20 Strionas..iuh striona in heofnum, ðer [*Rushw.* þær] ne hrust ne ec mohðe ȝespilles. *c* **1000** *Ags. Gosp.* John xviii. 20 Ic lærde..on temple þar [*Hatt.* þær] ealle iudeas togædere comon. *c* **1175** *Lamb. Hom.* 91 Bi þere stret þere petrus forð-eoðe. *a* **1272** *Luue Ron* 122 in *O.E. Misc.* 97 Hit stont vppon a treowe mote þar hit neuer truke ne schal. **1297** R. GLOUC. (Rolls) 7683 In þe tresorie at westmunstre þere it ȝut is. *c* **1300** *Cursor M.* 2904 (Cott.) þai sink in þat wele þar neuer man sank þat was o sele. *c* **1386** CHAUCER *Frankl. T.* 347 In to hir owene dirke Regioun Vnder the ground ther Pluto dwelleth Inne. *c* **1440** *Pallad. on Husb.* I. 21 In places there thow wilt have the culture. **15..** *Merch. & Son* 92 in Hazl. *E.P.P.* I. 139 The erthe tremelyd there Wyllyam stode.

b. with *there* also as antecedent: *there there* = there where, in that place where.

c **1000** ÆLFRIC *Gen.* ii. 21 God..ȝefilde mid flæsce, þær þær þæt ribb wæs. *c* **1000** ÆLFRIC *Saints' Lives* xiii. 67 Man mot..hine ȝebiddan, beo þær-þær he beo. *c* **1175** *Lamb. Hom.* 85 He..scal þer þer hit is ful, makien hit clene. *a* **1250** *Owl & Night.* 295 Loke þat þu ne beo þare þar changling beoþ. *a* **1400** *Relig. Pieces fr. Thornton MS.* 24 Lecherye..mase manes herte to melte, and to playe thare þare his herte lykes.

c. with *there* serving as both antecedent and relative: (In) the place in which; = mod. *where*, as in 'I found it where I left it'.

c **888** K. ÆLFRED *Boeth.* xxxii. §1 He nænne ne mæȝ ȝebringan þær he him ȝehet. *c* **1175** *Lamb. Hom.* 35 Ga to þine feder burinesse oðer þer eni of þine cunne lið in. *c* **1220** *Bestiary* 10 Ðe leun..Draȝeð dust wið his stert ðer he steppeð. **1303** R. BRUNNE *Handl. Synne* 851 And þere men haunted þat custome lest, Falleþ oft tyme grete tempest. *c* **1340** HAMPOLE *Prose Tr.* 5 For þare he es he sekes hym noghte. **13..** *Cursor M.* 2768 (Gött.) Again þaim he ras fra þar [*Trin.* þere] he sate. *c* **1400** *Laud Troy Bk.* 2926 Thei sayled alle on a rawe, Til thei were ther thei were knawe. *c* **1440** CAPGRAVE *St. Kath.* I. 506 Wyth a G set there C shuld stond. *c* **1500** *God Speed the Plough* 22 Than cometh the clerk..To haue A shef of corne there it groweth. *a* **1533** LD. BERNERS *Huon* lxiv. 221 It had been better for hym to haue taryed there he was. **1594** T. BEDINGFIELD tr. *Machiavelli's Florentine Hist.* (1595) 182 Your laughing there you are, is the occasion I weep not where I am.

†**10.** In the very case or circumstances in which; where on the other hand, or on the contrary; whereas, while. (Cf. 6.) *Obs.*

c **1200** *Trin. Coll. Hom.* 219 For nu is euerihc man ifo þare he solde fren[d] be. *c* **1380** WYCLIF *Wks.* (1880) 32 þei han ..welfare of mete and drynk, þere þei myȝtten unneþe before have bene-bred and watir or feble ale. *c* **1380** *Antecrist* in Todd *3 Treat. Wyclif* 134 þei putten grete penaunce unto men þere Cristis charge is liȝt. **1393** LANGL. *P. Pl.* C. XVII. 88 For pouerte haþ bote pokes to putten yn hus goodes, Ther auarice haþ almaries and yre-bounden cofres.

III. 11. as *sb.* That place; the (or a) place yonder.

1588 R. PARKE tr. *Mendoza's Hist. China* 202 They.. kneeled downe right ouer against there whereas the Viceroye sate in a chaire. **1857–8** SEARS *Athan.* 19 [Motion] requires a here and a there. **1888** J. MARTINEAU *Stud. Relig.* I. I. i. 68 In the Space-field lie innumerable other theres that never have been here. **1907** *Outlook* 16 Mar. 339/2 We.. draw, laboriously, a small circle in the dark and say, 'We are here', forgetful that there is no 'here' nor 'there'. *Mod.* We shall stay in Birmingham overnight, and go on from there next day. He left there last night.

IV. Phrases. (from I.)

12. a. *to be there*: to be at or in the place in question; to be present or at hand.

a **1300** *Cursor M.* 1248 þou wat þat i was neuer þare. *c* **1400** *Brut* ccxxv. 295 He wolde be þer him-self in al þe haste þat he myȝt. *c* **1420** *Avow. Arth.* xxiii, Kay callut on Gauan, ȝorne Asshes 'Quo is there?' **1600** *St. Papers Eliz., Domestic* CCLXXVIII. No. 78 (P.R.O.), Whether Sr John davyes were ther or not thys examinate can not tell. **1602** SHAKS. *Ham.* I. i. 1 Who's there? **1722** RAMSAY *Three Bonnets* II. 43 Ha, ha! ye Judas, are ye there? **1818** LADY MORGAN *Autobiog.* (1859) 49 The Duke of Sussex was there, with Lady Arran,..and the whole family of Gore. **1881** LADY HERBERT *Edith* 17 The 'little rift within the lute' was still there.

b. *to be all there* (colloq.): to have all one's faculties or wits about one; to be smart or on the alert; hence, *not all there* = not quite right in the head.

1864 MRS. GATTY *Parab. fr Nat.* Ser. IV. 3 Hans Jansen was what is commonly called *not all there*. **1883** PAYN *Thicker than Water* xx, It was his excusable boast..that when anything was wanted he was 'all there'. **1889** MRS. L. B. WALFORD *Stiff-necked Generation* 325 'Was he there after dinner last night?' 'Very much there'. **1900** *Daily News* 23 Apr. 8/1 But they were of the real Lancashire type, and were, as the phrase goes, 'all there'.

c. *to have been there* (*before*) (colloq.): to have had previous experience of the activity or thing under review; to be fully conversant with or know something at first hand. orig. *U.S.*

1877 *Sat. Even. Post* in J. R. Ware *Passing Eng.* (1909) 24/1 Some reasons why I left off drinking whiskey, by one who has been there. **1913** A. BENNETT *Great Adv.* I. ii. 46 But I'm not a young girl. If it's a question of the male sex, I may say that I've been there before. **1977** J. WAMBAUGH *Black Marble* (1978) viii. 106 Philo Skinner's been in this racket thirty years. Philo Skinner's *been* there, baby!

d. *in there* (U.S. slang): excellent, superlative (esp. of a jazz musician's performance); well-informed, *au fait*.

1944 D. BURLEY *Orig. Handbk. Harlem Jive* 104 Now, this skull was in there, Jack. **1945** L. SHELLEY *Jive Talk Dict.* 26 *In there*, superlative performance. **1955** SHAPIRO & HENTOFF *Hear me talkin' to Ya* vii. 101 The Lincoln Gardens, of course, was still in there. **1958** J. KEROUAC *On Road* I. i. 6 It took him just a few months..to become completely *in there* with all the terms and jargon. **1962** *Down Beat* 13 Sept. 37 A guy playing a horn has..gotta get in there.

13. a. *there and then* (†*there then*), at that precise place and time; on the spot, forthwith. Also *attrib.* (Also *then and there*: see THEN *adv.*[1] 1 d.)

1428 in *Surtees Misc.* (1888) 8 And þar þan he was asked. **1496** *Coventry Leet Bk.* 580 Wheruppon þe seid Laurence was there & then commyt vnto þe Flete. **1600** ABP. ABBOT *Exp. Jonah* 564 Although God do not say before, that there and then he will strike. **1848** MRS. GASKELL *M. Barton* xxxviii, Going on the search there and then. **1908** *Daily Chron.* 16 July 3/5 Happily..a there-and-then agreement was come to on their behalf.

b. *here and there, here..there, here, there and everywhere, neither here nor there*: see HERE *adv.* 9–12.

14. *there or* (†*and*) *thereabouts*: primarily in the literal local sense; hence also = that or very nearly that (amount); something like that; approximately. See also THEREABOUTS.

a **1696** AUBREY *Lives* (1898) II. 226 (*Shakspere*) He left 2 or 300*li.* per annum there and thereabout to a sister. **1819** SCOTT *Leg. Montrose* xiii, 'Speak plainly, will there be five thousand men?' 'There and thereabouts', answered Dalgetty. **1825** T. HOOK *Sayings* Ser. II. *Passion & Princ.* i. II. 248 A close, or field, containing eight acres, there or thereabouts. **1890** 'R. BOLDREWOOD' *Col. Reformer* (1891) 431 You'll mostly find him there or thereabouts, as long as he's alive. **1890** BP. LIGHTFOOT in *Expositor* Feb. 91 Forty-six years there or thereabouts had actually elapsed.

15. *there he* (or *she*) *goes, there you, they, go*, is primarily literal, the person going being pointed to (as in 3); but it also calls attention to the way in which a person goes on, acts, talks, etc., usually expressing surprise or disapproval. *there it goes!* is a common exclamation when a thing falls, disappears, goes off, breaks, bursts, or the like.

1780 *Mirror* No. 97 ¶32 'There she goes, the travelled lady', cried the Captain; 'she must always have a fling at her catechism'. **1837** DICKENS *Pickw.* ii, 'They're beginning up-stairs..fiddles tuning—now the harp—there they go'. The various sounds..announced the commencement of the first quadrille.

16. a. *there you are!* (colloq.) (*a*) = *there you go!* in 15; (*b*) expressing or drawing attention to the simplicity or ready consummation of a process or action; = There it is for you, there you have it, the thing is done; (*c*) = What did I tell you? (*d*) expressing resignation to an unpleasant fact.

1857 DICKENS *Dorrit* II. xxv. 536 All the people who had tried to make money and had not been able to do it, said, There you were! [**1863** H. E. P. SPOFFORD *Amber Gods* 133 She couldn't hire him a nurse, and there he was.] **1883** 'MARK TWAIN' *Life on Mississippi* xlii. 431 The immortelle requires no attention: you just hang it up, and there you are. **1894** A. CONAN DOYLE *Mem. Sherlock Holmes* 142 'There you are!' said Holmes smiling. **1907** *Westm. Gaz.* 22 May 3/1 Tables, setting out in a there-you-are! fashion the declining percentage to the total of British imports into certain countries for two contrasted decades. *a* **1912** *Mod.* Can't find the waiter? That's quite easy; just press that button and there you are! Accidents are common in Alpine ascents; one false step, and there you are! **1915** CONRAD *Victory* IV. x. 373 'There you are!' Ricardo shrugged his shoulders philosophically. 'Can't be helped.' **1937** M. SHARP *Nutmeg Tree* xix. 250 '*We've* no business to talk about him. But there you are,' said Julia harshly, 'I'm the sort of woman any one talks to about anything.' **1926** S. JAMESON *Three Kingdoms* i. 49 I'm sure that's a revolting sentiment, and revoltingly sentimental, but there you are. **1953** L. P. HARTLEY *Go-Between* xiv. 173 It's a pity we have to shoot so many of them but there you are.

b. *there it is* = sense 16 a (*d*) above. Also with past tense.

1857 TROLLOPE *Barchester T.* III. i. 10 There it is. If they haven't the spirit to enjoy it, the fault shan't be mine. **1884** 'MARK TWAIN' *Huck. Finn* xxxiii. 345 So there it was!—but I couldn't help it. **1904** H. JAMES *Golden Bowl* I. xviii. 311 'It's not, at any rate,' she went on, 'my fault. There it is.' **1932** 'A. BRIDGE' *Peking Picnic* xxiii. 296 He had been hurt hideously, and it made her cry; she was nearly as much surprised as he, but there it was. **1954** R. MACAULAY *Last Lett. to Friend* (1962) 196, I feel a little mean about the dear Chapel, but there it is. **1973** C. SAGAN *Cosmic Connection* xxii. 150 We would not ordinarily consider the flatulence of cattle as a dominant manifestation of life on Earth, but there it is.

V. 17. *there* (in branch I) in combination with adverbs and prepositions.

For the history of these, see note s.v. HERE *adv.* 16. 'The compounds of *there* meaning *that*, and of *here* meaning *this*, have been for some time passing out of use, and are no longer found in elegant writings, or in any other than formulary pieces' (Todd's *Johnson* 1818, s.v. *Therewithall*). But see the Main words THEREABOUT, THEREAFTER, etc.

a. With adverbs, as *there all-about, there east, there-without*; †**there-gates**, in that manner; †**there-thence**, thence; †**there-whyne** (*-quhyne*), from whence. Also THEREAWAY, etc. **b.** With prepositions: = that, that place, matter, etc., as *there-among* (†*-imong*), *there-below, there-between*; **thereamid** (†*-emid*), amid that; †**therebout** (*-buten*) = THEREABOUT; †**therebove** (*-buve*(*n*) = THEREABOVE; †**therenext**, next to that; †**thereoffen** = THEREOFFE; †**thereouten**, out of that; †**there-ovenon** (*-ufenen*), above that; †**there-toforn**, before that (time). Originally mostly written as two words. See also the main words from THEREABOUT to THEREWITHIN.

1422 tr. *Secreta Secret., Priv. Priv.* 198 Noone god of al that weryn *ther al aboute in al regions. *a* **1300** *Cursor M.* 11988 Mani childer was *þar emid. **1901** G. GISSING in *Literature* 21 Dec. 572/1 Thereamid stood a girl, her eyes fixed upon the prospect of city roofs. *c* **1220** *Bestiary* 601 He ðe swiken *ðer imong. **1899** *Westm. Gaz.* 18 Apr. 2/1 It is a real joy to know that the pilot-fish does hide itself within the capacious throat, or some snug harbourage *therebelow, when danger threatens. **1876** MORRIS *Sigurd* III. 194 And lingering flecks of the cloud-host are tangled *therebetween. **1885–94** R. BRIDGES *Eros & Psyche, October* 9 She ..sweeping therebetween a passage wide, Made clear of corn and chaff the temple space. *c* **1250** *Gen. & Ex.* 3625, .vii. moneð *ðor buten he ben. **1297** R. GLOUC. (Rolls) 11614 Bruggen hii breke oueral hii ne beleuede ssip non ..þer boute [*C.* aboute]. *c* **897** K. ÆLFRED *Gregory's Past. C.* viii. 52 *Ðærbufan is ȝeteald hwelc he beon sceol. *a* **1300** *Floriz & Bl.* 294 Aboue þe walle stant a treo..lef and blosme beoþ þer buue. **1639** BAILLIE *Lett.* 28 Sept. (Bann. Club) I. 201 The Tables *there East thought meet they should not conjoyne, bot divided them in foure. *c* **1440** *York Myst.* xii. 48 þus may *þer-gatis be mente. **13..** *Cursor M.* 141 (Cott.) *þar neist [*F.* þar next] sal be sythen tald How þat ioseph was boght and sald. **1387** TREVISA *Higden* (Rolls) VII. 71 Under a treen brugge þat was þere next. *c* **1450** LOVELICH *Merlin* 6294 The wheche child to hire schal ben browht; but *there-offen the peple may weten nowht. *c* **1250** *Gen. & Ex.* 3364 And he smot wið his wond ðor on, And water gan *ðor vten gon. *c* **1205** LAY. 12423 Heo bigunnen..ane swiðe deope dich & *þer ouen on ouer al ænne strongne stanene wal. *Ibid.* 17696 þer ufenen he hæfde Ane ladliche here. *c* **1475** *Partenay* 3125 *Ther thens to uavuent [Vauvent] A man sent in message, Which full courtois was, inly wise also. *a* **1425** *Cursor M.* 12479 (Trin.) [He] wende þe maistir were of lyue As oþere *þer to forn were. **1456** SIR G. HAYE *Law Arms* (S.T.S.) 77 And *thairquhyne cumis this? *a* **1500** *Flower & Leaf* 71 Al tho that yeden *there without.

there, obs. gen. and dat. sing. fem. of THE; obs. var. of THEIR, THIR; inflexion of THARF *v. Obs.*

thereabout (ðɛərəˈbaʊt, ˈðɛərəbaʊt), *adv.* Forms: see THERE and ABOUT. [OE. *þǽr abútan*, two words, viz. *þǽr*, THERE 17 and *abútan*, ABOUT.]

1. About (orig. outside) or near that place: = THEREABOUTS 1.

a **925** *O.E. Chron.* an. 917 (Parker MS.) Æt Hocneratune, and þær onbutan. *c* **1000** ÆLFRIC *Saints' Lives* xxv. 595. *c* **1000** *Ags. Gosp.* Mark xiv. 69 Heo ongan cweðan to þam þe ðar abutan stodon. **1131** *O.E. Chron.* an. 1124 (Laud MS.) Ealla þa casteles ða þær abuton wæron. *c* **1290** *Beket* 2126 in *S. Eng. Leg.* 167 And al round þare a-bouten it lay. *c* **1400** MAUNDEV. (Roxb.) Pref. 3 Ierusalem, and the haly placez þat er þare aboute. **1451** *Paston Lett.* I. 196 To all yowr frendes and tenauntes ther abowtyn. **1517** TORKINGTON *Pilgr.* (1884) 56 The Cityes in the Countre ther a bowght. **1562** *Reg. Privy Council Scot.* I. 220 To remane within the samin and foure mylis thairabout. **1692** RAY *Disc.* II. v. (1732) 215 The Alteration of the sea thereabout. **1864** BURTON *Scot Abr.* I. iii. 120 Quartered in the different villages thereabout. **1908** [MISS E. FOWLER] *Betw. Trent & Ancholme* 67 From somewhere thereabout our garden gravel came.

†**b.** Around that object (a pillar, or the like).

1340–70 *Alex. & Dind.* 1136 He bad bulden of marbre A piler..& þat þei wrouhten a wrytte & writen þer aboute.

c. *fig.* About that; near to that state or action: cf. THEREABOUTS 1 c. *Obs.* or *rare.*

1664 DRYDEN *Rival-Ladies* IV. iii, *Amid*... I feel already My stout Heart melts. *Hip.* Oh! Are you thereabout?

2. a. About or somewhere near that time or date. **b.** About that number, quantity, size, space of time, etc. = THEREABOUTS 2. (Chiefly after *or*.)

1297 R. GLOUC. (Rolls) 8984 Hit biuel þer aboute þat þe erl thebaud..destourbede þe peys. **1465** J. PASTON in *P. Lett.* II. 236 The xxii yere of Kyng Herry or ther abought. **1534** in *Rep. Hist. MSS. Comm., Var. Coll.* IV. 217 Amountyng to the some of 30*l.* or therabout. **1564** *Brief Exam.* *****ij b, Referred to the Prophetes tymes, and thereabout. **1612** DAVIES *Why Ireland*, etc. (1787) 15 A company of volunteers, in number four hundred, or thereabout. **1727** DE FOE *Syst. Magic* I. ii. (1840) 51 At the distance of less than two hundred years, or thereabout. **1908** [MISS E. FOWLER] *Betw. Trent & Ancholme* 369 She has walked 221,490 miles, or thereabout.

3. About, concerning, or with reference to that matter or business; thereanent. *to go* or *be* *thereabout*, to occupy or busy oneself therewith: cf. ABOUT B. 10, 11. Now *arch.* or *rare.*

a **1300** *Cursor M.* 22885 (Edin.) Þe mar man swink him þar aboutin Fra sped þe ferre he sal ben outin. *c* **1350** *Will. Palerne* 972 But i were busi þer a-boute to blame i were. *c* **1386** CHAUCER *Sompn. T.* 129 What wol ye dyne? I wol go ther-aboute. *c* **1400** *Ywaine & Gaw.* 2698 Thar-obout wil i be bayn. *c* **1440** *Jacob's Well* 56 Here resonable expensys þere abowte awȝte ferst to be takyn vp. **1450–1530** *Myrr. our Ladye* 51 All that wyll do theyr besynes there aboute. **1534** MORE *Treat. Passion* Wks. 1289/2 How much payn so euer himselfe tooke thereabout. **1611** BIBLE *Luke* xxiv. 4 They were much perplexed thereabout. **1657** W. RAND tr. *Gassendi's Life Peiresc* II. 77 Peireskius..congratulated with him thereabout.

therea'bouts, *adv.* [f. prec. with advb. *-s.*

Of later appearance than prec., but now in southern Eng. more frequent in senses 1 and 2.]

1. About, or in the neighbourhood of, that place; in the district, region, etc. round about there.

c **1400** MAUNDEV. (Roxb.) xiv. 63 Þare aboutes er many gude hilles and faire. **1522** *Rutland Papers* (Camden) 83 The noblemen belongyng to themperor that be lodged in the chanons howses of Paules and ther aboutes. **1585** T. WASHINGTON tr. *Nicholay's Voy.* I. xii. 14 Theeues..there abouts do lye secretly hidde too entrappe them that came therabouts. **1662** J. DAVIES tr. *Olearius' Voy. Ambass.* 6 Flies, Gnats, and Wasps, which the Fens thereabouts produce in such quantity. **1797** MME. D'ARBLAY *Let. to Burney* 13 Sept., It is the best house thereabouts..in a broad street. **1860** HAWTHORNE *Marb. Faun* xvi, A homeless dog, that haunted thereabouts. **1909** *Times* 23 July 10/1 In the streets thereabouts men and women gathered in crowds.

†**b.** After a preposition. *Obs. rare.*

1491 CAXTON *Vitas Patr.* (W. de W. 1495) I. xxxvi. 38 b/1 All the others..departed all fro there abowtes. **1568** GRAFTON *Chron.* II. 673 In the Countie of Yorke, and other places, nere therabouts. **1654** EARL MONM. tr. *Bentivoglio's Warrs Flanders* 427 The Town of Groll is not far from thereabouts.

c. *fig.* About that; near to that state or action: see ABOUT *adv.* 13. *Obs.* or *rare.*

1606 SHAKS. *Ant. & Cl.* III. x. 29, I, are you thereabouts? Why then goodnight indeede. **1611** —— *Wint. T.* I. ii. 378. **1697** VANBRUGH *Æsop.* II. i, *Euph.* Unlace me, or I shall swoon. *Dor.* Unlace you! why, you are not there abouts, I hope? **1732** FIELDING *Debauchees* II. iv, Hoity-toity—Are you thereabouts, good father?

2. Transferred to time, quantity, quality, degree, etc. Mostly preceded by *or.*

a. About or near to a specified date or time.

1561 T. NORTON *Calvin's Inst.* I. viii. 17 Cyrus was borne in the hundreth yere or there aboutes after the death of Esaie. **1631** WEEVER *Anc. Fun. Mon.* 139 Which happened since the dissolution here in England, or much what thereabouts. **1769** BURKE *Corr.* (1844) I. 177 The meeting is put off until..the twelfth of September, or thereabouts. **1878** HUXLEY *Physiogr.* 10 From the year 1660 or thereabouts.

b. About or not far different from a stated number, sum, quantity, space of time, degree, condition, etc.; very nearly so; approximately so. *there or thereabouts*: see THERE *adv.* 14.

1413 *Pilgr. Sowle* (Caxton 1483) IV. xvii. 64, I wyl that man lyue in..tribulacion fyue thousand yere or neyhe ther aboutes. **1581** in *Cath. Rec. Soc. Publ.* V. 20 William Tharley aged thirtie yeares or theraboutes. **1601** SHAKS. *All's Well* IV. iii. 171 Fiue or six-thousand horse I sed..or thereabouts. **1704** *Lond. Gaz.* No. 3987/4 A lighter Bay, 13 hands and half high, or thereabouts. **1719** DE FOE *Crusoe* (1840) II. viii. 191 In three hours, or thereabouts. **1794** SULLIVAN *View Nat.* II. 17 Mont Blanc is 15,562 feet or thereabouts. **1818** KEATS *Lett.* Wks. 1889 III. 127 Write to me and tell me that you are well, or thereabouts. **1878** HUXLEY *Physiogr.* 210 The pavement..was at the sea-level or thereabouts. **1898** *Pall Mall G.* 20 Jan. 2/2 You may be sure the original statement was thereabouts, if not quite there.

†**3.** About or concerning that; = prec. 3. *Obs.*

1586 DAY *Eng. Secretary* II. (1625) 71, I would haue you to conferre with my Cosen T. R. thereabouts. **1611** W. SCLATER *Key* (1629) 306 Colour..cannot be said to be *obiectum actu*, till some act of sight be exercised thereabouts. **1631** GOUGE *God's Arrows* III. §61. 298 Mens conjectures thereabouts are various. **1657** W. RAND tr. *Gassendi's Life Peiresc* I. 178 He concludes a passage there-abouts in these words.

thereabove (ðɛərə'bʌv), *adv.* [Orig. two words, THERE 17 and ABOVE *adv.*] †**a.** Above or on the top of that (*obs.*). †**b.** Above or more than that (*obs.*). **c.** Up above there; up yonder (in heaven). *rare.*

1382 WYCLIF *1 Kings* vii. 35 In the cop..was a maner roundnes,..so forgid, that the watir vessel myȝte be sette there aboue. **1439** in *Fenland N. & Q.* July (1905) 221 To the somme of xl. m¹. marc or yer above. **1891** C. E. NORTON *Dante's Hell* i. 5 That Emperor who reigneth thereabove [I. 124 quello Imperador, che lassù regna]. **1892** —— *Paradise* i. 4 Beatrice was standing with her eyes wholly fixed on the eternal wheels, and on her I fixed my eyes from there-above removed [I. 66 Le luci fisse di lassù rimote].

thereafter (ðɛə'rɑːftə(r), -æ-), *adv.* [OE. *þǽr æfter*, two words, viz. *þǽr*, THERE 17 and *æfter*, AFTER; ME. *þer after*. Cf. OS. *thar after* (Du. *daarachter*); ON. *þar epter* (Sw., Da., Norw. *derefter*).]

1. After that in time, order, or sequence; subsequently; afterwards. (Now somewhat formal.)

c **897** K. ÆLFRED *Gregory's Past.* C. xix. 144 Hie..ne ondrædað ðone dom þe ðær æfter fylȝeð. *c* **1000** *Sax. Leechd.* III. 244 Þonne byð se sunnan dæȝ þær æfter easter dæȝ. **1154** *O.E. Chron.* an. 1132 (Laud MS.) Was it noht suithe lang þer efter þatte king sende efter him. *c* **1205** LAY. 1220 He gon slomnen & þer æfter to slepen. **1297** R. GLOUC. (Rolls) 8277 Ȝut sone þer after an oþer com al so. **1375** BARBOUR *Bruce* I. 591 And the King A parlyament Gert set thareftir hastely. **1445** in *Wars Eng. in France* (1861) I. 465 At Witsontide next thereaftere. **1535** COVERDALE *Luke* xv. 13 Not longe therafter, gathered the yonger sonne all together. **1632** LITHGOW *Trav.* III. 84 A little thereafter the Generall of the Galleys came to the Monastery. **1760–72** H. BROOKE *Fool of Qual.* (1809) III. 50 This prerogative..was thereafter..discontinued. **1898** *Allbutt's Syst. Med.* V. 513 A year thereafter she must be re-examined.

†**b.** After that in place or position. *Obs.*

c **1000** *Ags. Gosp.* Matt. xxi. 9 Ðæt folc þæt þar beforan ferde, and þæt þær æfter ferde. *c* **1250** *Gen. & Ex.* 3644 Ðat briȝte skie bi-foren hem fleȝt, And ðis folc ðor after teȝ.

†**2.** Conformably thereto, accordingly; ***thereafter as***, according as; ***to be thereafter***, to be conformable or agreeable thereto. *Obs.*

c **1175** *Lamb. Hom.* 133 Euric mon þe lusteð luueliche godes wordes and ledeð his lif rihtliche þer efter. *c* **1200** *Vices & Virt.* 65 Þis is godes ȝiue, ȝif ðu ðus ðe beþencst and ðar after wercst. *c* **1380** WYCLIF *Sel. Wks.* III. 360 Ȝif oþer men wolden be preestis, lyve þei þerafter. **1470–85** MALORY *Arthur* IV. xii. 134 Ye shalle be a knyghte of myne, and yf your dedes be there after I shall so proferre yow [etc.]. *a* **1533** LD. BERNERS *Huon* xlii. 140 He was .xvii. fote of length, & of bygnes he was therafter. **1535** COVERDALE *Ps.* cx. 10 A good vnderstondinge haue all they that do thereafter. **1551** T. WILSON *Logike* (1580) Epist., The presente of a true faithfull subiecte, whiche would haue brought better if his power had been thereafter. **1584** COGAN *Haven Health* (1636) 198 The Physitian, in dyeting, should regard chiefly two things..and thereafter to prescribe lesse or more to be received. **1597** SHAKS. *2 Hen. IV*, III. ii. 56. **1618** BP. HALL *Righteous Mammon* Wks. (1628) 723 Because these are but flowers,..wee regard them thereafter. **1671** MILTON *P.R.* II. 321. **1727** GAY *Begg. Op.* II, That, Madam, is thereafter as they be.

†**3.** With verbs const. with *after*, as *cry*, *gaze*, *look*, *wish*, *yearn*: cf. AFTER B. 5 e. *Obs.*

c **1200** *Trin. Coll. Hom.* 5 Alle bileffulle men þe waren þo and ðar biforen wissede swiðe ðar after. *a* **1300** *Cursor M.* 486 For godd aght not gif þam mercy, þat þar efter wil not cri. **1393** LANGL. *P. Pl.* C. VIII. 225 Leue hem in þy lift hand and loke nouht þer-after.

4. quasi-*adj.* (with n. of action). Subsequent.

1830 GALT *Lawrie T.* IV. xii, Supposing no thereafter increase.

the'reafterward, *adv. rare.* [f. THERE *adv.* 17 + AFTERWARD.] = prec. 1.

1867 LONGF. *Dante's Paradiso* XXIV. 70 And I thereafterward; 'The things profound [etc.]'. **1884** J. PAYNE *1000 Nts.* VIII. 8 The day thereafterward for weariness thou'lt pine.

†**thereagain**, *adv. Obs.* Forms: α. 1 **þæronȝen**, 3 **þer aȝen**, (*Orm.*) **þær onnȝæn**, 4 **þer aȝeyn(e**, **þer oȝein**. β. 3–4 **þar again, -egain, -agayn(e**, 4 **þer agayn(e, again**, 5 **therageyn**. [OE. *þǽr onȝé(a)n*, two words, viz. *þǽr*, THERE 17 and *onȝéan*, ME. *onȝen*, *aȝen*, subseq. *ogain*, AGAIN.]

1. = THEREAGAINST 1.

α. [*a* **1023**: see 2.] *c* **1200** ORMIN 5304 Þa birrþ þe stanndenn þær onnȝæn. **1297** R. GLOUC. (Rolls) 8881 Þis mayde was þer aȝen, & wiþ sede it longe. *a* **1300** *Cursor M.* 3094 (Cott.) We sal neuer do þer again [*F.* þar a-gayne, *G.* þar egain, *T.* þer aȝayn]. **13..** *Guy Warw.* (A.) 977, & who so þer oȝain sey ouȝt. **1387** TREVISA *Higden* (Rolls) VII. 157 It is byholdinge to hym..þat he goo þere agayne wiþ tonge and hond. **1393** LANGL. *P. Pl.* C. XXI. 312 And neuere was þer aȝeyn. *a* **1425** *Cursor M.* 17034 (Trin.) Þer is no mon.. may say þer aȝeyne. **1430–40** LYDG. *Bochas* IX. xviii. (MS. Bodl. 263) 422/1 Yet ther was sume that gruchched therageyn.

2. = THEREAGAINST 2.

a **1023** WULFSTAN *Hom.* xlviii. (Napier) 248 Englas.. cyðað þine dæda..and deofol awrit þæronȝen ealle þine misdæda. **13..** *Cursor M.* 20789 (Fairf.) Bot þar againe [*C.* þar egain] sais Ieronim He wille take na charge on him. *a* **1350** *St. Stephen* 109 in Horstm. *Altengl. Leg.* (1881) 29 Bot þarogayn to þam he kend On thre maners þaire mys to mend.

3. = THEREAGAINST 3.

c **1330** *Arth. & Merl.* 5152 Wawain it seiȝe sone on hast, His scheld þer oȝein gan cast.

thereagainst (ðɛərə'gɛnst, -ə'geɪnst), *adv.* Now *arch.* Forms: α. 4 **þerageyns**, 5 **therayeines, -ayeynes, þer-aȝens, þar-agaynys, there aȝens.** β. 5 **ther agenst, ageynste, ther(eayenst(e**, 6 **ther agenst, -ageinst**, 6– **thereagainst.** [f. THERE 17 + *againes*, AGAINST *prep.*]

1. Against or in opposition to that.

α. *c* **1380** WYCLIF *Sel. Wks.* III. 367 No mon may distrie hit, or dispense þerageyns. *c* **1402** LYDG. *Compl. Bl. Knt.* 533 Ther ayeines shal I never stryve. *c* **1449** PECOCK *Repr.* 75 If the gretter laboure be mad thereaȝens.

β. **1450–1530** *Myrr. our Ladye* 10 Remedyes..to be used there ageynste. *Ibid.* 69. **1528** TINDALE *Obed. Chr. Man* 93 b, I will not stryue nor saye thar agenst. *c* **1647** SANDERSON *Episcopacy* (1673) 9 Remedy provided there-against by an Act of Parliament. **1870** MAGNÚSSON & MORRIS *Völsunga Saga* xx. 71 But thereagainst I vowed a vow, that never would I wed one who knew the name of fear.

†**2.** As a set-off thereto; contrariwise; on the other side. *Obs.*

a **1400–50** *Alexander* 1264 Ser Beritinus þe bald þai bretned to dethe, And Sampson on þis side was slay þar agaynys. *c* **1407** H. SCOGAN *Moral Ballad* 158 Seeth, there ayenst, how vertuous noblesse..Dryveth away al vyce. **1422** tr. *Secreta Secret., Priv. Priv.* 141 Of the wynde comyth good... But ther ayeynes dyuers Perillis..and destourbaunce fallyth. **1558** PHAER *Æneid.* II. E iv b, In his purpose still he fixt remainyd fast. We therageinst with streaming teares.

3. In pressure or impact against that.

1863 SALA in *Temple Bar Mag.* VII. 496 From the bobbing and rasping of watch-spring crinolines thereagainst. **1884** C. T. DAVIS *Manuf. Bricks & Tiles*, etc. ix. (1889) 285 Its ends are passed through the side pieces of the frame and tightened there-against by nuts.

thereamong (ðɛərə'mʌŋ), *adv.* Now *rare* or *arch.* [Orig. two words, THERE 17 and AMONG *prep.*] Among that, those, or them.

1399 LANGL. *Rich. Redeles* Prol. 57 If ȝe ffynde ffables or ffoly þer amonge. **1482** *Rolls of Parlt.* VI. 222/1 And thereamonge put Thokes and broken belyed fissh. **1836** *Fraser's Mag.* XIII. 12 There is neither fruit, nor appearance of fruit, there-among. **1869** TENNYSON *Pelleas* 92 Three knights were thereamong; and they too smiled.

So **therea'mongst** *adv. rare*, in same sense.

1599 A. M. tr. *Gabelhouer's Bk. Physicke* 10/1 Mixe theramongste Cubebes, Mace, Cloves. **1606** G. W[OODCOCK] *Hist. Iustine* II. 11 b, They might perceiue a multitude of women to be there amongst.

thereanent (ðɛərə'nɛnt), *adv.* Orig. and chiefly *Sc.* and *north.* [Orig. two words, THERE 17 and ANENT *prep.*] About, concerning, or in reference to that matter, business, etc.; relating thereto.

c **1340** *Cursor M.* 20789 (Gött.) Bot þar enent [*v.r.* there-again], sais Ieronim, He wil noght take þe boke on him. **1562** *Reg. Privy Council Scot.* I. 218 For satisfying of hir Hienes thairanent. **1578** *Ibid.* II. 700 Ordour to be takin thairanent with expeditioun. **1681** *Sc. Acts Jas. II* (1820) VIII. 243/2 According to the tenour of the respective acts of Parliament thereanent provided. **1726** *Wodrow Corr.* (1843) III. 243 To hear the state of this affair..and bring in an overture thereanent. **1819** SCOTT *Leg. Montrose* xii, I will gage my life upon his making my words good thereanent. **1853** C. BRONTE *Villette* xxi, The reader would not care to have my impressions thereanent. **1868** VISCT. STRANGFORD *Select.* (1869) II. 311 The public prints of an earlier date in this year ..may be consulted thereanent with propriety.

Hence (with advb. genitive) †**therea'nents (-anentis, -anendes)** *adv.*, in same sense; in quot. *c* 1400 app. = THEREABOUTS 1.

c **1400** MAUNDEV. (Roxb.) viii. 30 It [þe Reed See] is þer anentes vi. myle brade. **1552** *Reg. Privy Council Scot.* I. 133 [We sall] leif nocht behind that lyis in our possibiliteis thairanentis. **1564** *Child-Marriages* 26 Procured the Counselles lettres theranendes. *c* **1568** REG. MURRAY in H. Campbell *Love Lett. Mary Q. Scots* (1824) 218 My Lord of Argyll..spak largely..theiranents to the Queen herself.

†**thereas**, *conj. Obs.* [Originally a conjunctive phrase: see THERE 9, 10 and AS 27.]

1. In that place (or case) in which; where; = THERE 9.

a **1225** *Ancr. R.* 12 Þer ase þeos þinges beoð þer is riht religiun. **13..** *Cast. Love* (Halliw.) 444 Þes ne bydyth in no londe, Ther as werre is nyȝh-honde. **1493** *Festivall* (W. de W. 1515) 6 To go to an hous ther as is a corps. **1550** COVERDALE *Bk. Death* II. i. 178 The comfortable promes of Chryst, there as he sayth: I am the resurreccion and yᵉ lyfe.

2. Whereas; = THERE 10.

c **1385** CHAUCER *L.G.W.* 1282 (*Dido*) Sche hath..hire reame ȝeuyn In to his hand, there as she myghte haue been Of othere landys than of cartage quien. *c* **1460** FORTESCUE *Abs. & Lim. Mon.* xix. (1885) 155 Þer as oþer kynges haue ffounded byshopriches..þe kyng shall þan haue ffounded an holl reaume. **1470–85** MALORY *Arthur* XX. xi. 815 There as ye say I haue slayn your good knyghtes, I wote wel that I haue done soo, and that me sore repenteth.

thereat (ðɛər'æt), *adv.* Now formal or *arch.* [OE. *þǽr æt*, two words: see THERE 17 and AT.]

1. At the place, meeting, etc., mentioned; there.

a **900** tr. *Bæda's Hist.* IV. vii. §2 Moniȝe untrume..þær æt hælo onfengon. **1297** R. GLOUC. (Rolls) 9526 Hii hulde a parlement..& þe king him sulf was þerate. **13..** *Seuyn Sag.* (W.) 2358 Whan he com to Rome yate, And wolde wenden out therate. *c* **1400** MAUNDEV. (Roxb.) xvi. 74 Sum saise þai hafe bene þare att. **1526** TINDALE *Matt.* vii. 13 Many there be which goo yn there att. **1611** SHAKS. *Wint, T.* IV. iv. 500 Not for Bohemia, nor the pompe that may Be thereat gleaned. **1885** *Act 48 & 49 Vict.* c. 78 §30 He shall..hold a sitting..and shall thereat take and receive any evidence.. offered.

b. With a verb of motion or aim: cf. AT 13.

1517 TORKINGTON *Pilgr.* (1884) 27 He cast a stonne ther att.

c. Expressing attachment to a thing: cf. AT 7.

1566 tr. *Sc. Acts Jas. III*, c. 87 Our Souerane Lord.. annexis till his Crowne the Erldome of Ros with the pertinentis, to remane thairat for euer. **1567** in *6th Rep. Hist. MSS. Comm.* 643/2 Ane tabled hyngand with ane grytt rubye and ane grytt hingand perle thairatt. **1650** BULWER *Anthropomet.* xi. 109 A broad plate..and the Jewel they hang thereat. **1688** R. HOLME *Armoury* III. 161/2 A Leather Girdle..with a strong Rope..hanging thereat.

2. On the occasion or occurrence of that, thereupon, because of that: cf. AT 34, 35.

a **1300** *Cursor M.* 2722 Sarra..Herd þis word and logh þar at. *a* **1450** *Knt. de la Tour* 98 His wyff..dysdeyned thereatte, and had scorne therof. **1490** CAXTON *Eneydos* xviii. 68 For to take theratte som comforte. **1590** SPENSER *F.Q.* II. vii. 34 Thereat the feend his gnashing teeth did grate. **1605** SHAKS. *Lear* IV. ii. 75 Bending his Sword To his great Master, who, thereat enrag'd Flew on him. **1869** TENNYSON *Pass. Arthur* 462 Thereat once more he moved about. **1870** MORRIS *Earthly Par.* II. III. 253 Thereat the silver trumpet's tuneful blare Made music strange.

3. At or in connexion with the thing or process on which action is brought to bear: cf. AT 17.

13.. *Cursor M.* 11674 (Fairf.) My hande þer at may naþing do. *c* **1440** *Alphabet of Tales* 198 When he fand gude wyne on a tyme, he seld his slavyn & drank it þer-att. *c* **1556** R. COCKES in *Archæologia* XXXV. 20, I trust this weke that cometh we shall do a good chare therat [at the hay-making]. **1581** *Exch. Rolls Scot.* XXI. 551 The saidis parties oblissis thame to.. abyid thairat bot any reclaming.

† **therea'tour**, *adv. Sc. Obs.* In 5 tharatour, 5–6 **thairattour.** [f. THERE 17 + ATOUR *prep.*] Over or beyond that; about or concerning that: see THEREOVER.

1457 *Sc. Acts Jas. II*, c. 25 (1814) II. 51/1 Gif he dois ony thing þairattour furth with to arreist his persoun. **1473** *Rental Bk. Cupar-Angus* (1879) I. 173 Tharatour tha sal do thar det lelaly and truly to our myl.. bath in fre multur and thyrl. **15..** *Priests Peblis* I. in Pinkerton *Scot. Poems* (1792) I. 14 Than spak the King, your conclusion is quaint; And thairattour ye mak to us a plaint.

thereaway ('ðɛərəweɪ), *adv.* Chiefly *Sc.* and *north. dial.* [Orig. two words, THERE 17 and AWAY *adv.*]

†**1.** Of motion: Away thither, or in that direction. ***hereaway, thereaway***: see HERE-AWAY. *Obs.*

1375 BARBOUR *Bruce* x. 32 (MS. E.) For gif the king held thar away, He thoucht he suld soyn vencust be. *c* **1400** MAUNDEV. (Roxb.) v. 15 Schippes.. commes þer away for to fraght þam with þat salt. *c* **1450** *Life St. Cuthbert* (Surtees) 5102 þare away to fare. *a* **1500** *Smith & his Dame* 30 in Hazlitt *E.P.P.* III. 202 Ovr lorde came there away. **1549, 1793**, etc. [see HEREAWAY 2]. **1601** in Foley *Rec. Eng. Prov. S.J.* (1880) VI. 735 For such English as come thereaway to Loreto. **1659** W. GUTHRIE *Chr. Gt. Interest* II. vi. (1724) 207 Confirming the same by many mighty Works in Scripture tending there-away.

2. Of situation: Away in that direction or region; in those parts; thereabouts.

1551 R. ROBINSON *More's Utop.* II. (1895) 253 There be fewe warres there awaye, wherin is not a greate numbre of them in bothe partyes. *c* **1670** PENN *Let.* in *Life* Wks. 1726 I. App. iii. 156 Among the Carnal and Historical Christians there-away. **1816** SCOTT *Bl. Dwarf* viii, All evil comes out o' thereaway.. and we'll e'en away there. **1840** CAROLINE FOX *Old Friends* (1882) 60 The Duke of Wellington.. in some mighty action thereaway showed his wondrous power in animating masses.

3. Somewhere about that (number, amount, age, etc.); = THEREABOUTS 2.

1824 SCOTT *Redgauntlet* ch. xi, Swaggering about the country.. for five or six months, or thereaway. **1830** MISS MITFORD *Village* Ser. IV. 328 An old batchelor of fifty-five, or there-away. **1862** MRS. GROTE *Coll. Papers* 261 A hundred thousand pounds or there-away.

Hence † **thereaway-abouts** *adv.*, thereabouts.

1828 MOIR *Mansie Wauch* xxii. (1849) 169 The martyrs had been buried thereaway-abouts.

'**thereaways**, *adv.* Now *dial.* [f. prec. with advb. genitive *-s*: cf. AWAYS.] = prec.

1575 *Gamm. Gurton* IV. ii, He intends this same night to slip in there awayes. **1682** in *Jrnl. Friends' Hist. Soc.* IV. 151, I would have yᵉ to mynd my love to friends there-aways and at Darnton. **1791** 'G. GAMBADO' *Ann. Horsem.* xvii. (1809) 137 Come from Lapland, or thereaways. *a* **1825** FORBY *Voc. E. Anglia* s.v., Is the horse worth twenty pounds? There and there-aways. **1902** BUCHAN *Watcher by Threshold* 73 What's taking ye thereaways?

† '**therebe'fore**, *adv. Obs.* Forms: see THERE and BEFORE. [Late OE.; two words.]

1. Before that in position or order; in front.

c **1000** *Ags. Gosp.* Matt. xxi. 9 Ðæt folc þæt þar beforan [*c* **1160** *Hatton Gosp.*, þær be-fore] ferde.

2. Before that (time); formerly, previously.

c **1200** [see THEREAFTER 3]. *c* **1275** *Passion our Lord* 218 in *O.E. Misc.* 43 As vre louerd þer by-vore heom iseyd hedde. *c* **1386** CHAUCER *Man of Law's T.* 99 In sterres many a wynter ther biforn Was writen the deeth of Ector Achilles. *c* **1430** *Freemasonry* 302 3ef he nulle okepye hem no more, As he hath y-done ther by-fore. **1592** in J. Morris *Troub. Cath. Forefathers* (1877) 34 And the priest there before dead.

there'ben, *adv. Sc.* [See BEN *adv.* c.] 'Ben' there, within there.

[**13..** *Cursor M.* 2721 (Cott.) Sarra þar bin quare sco satt Herd þis word and logh þar-at.] *c* **1500** ROWLL *Cursing* 124 in *Bannatyne Poems* (Hunter. Cl.) 302 And thow art scho that stall the hen And put hir in the pot thair ben. *a* **1568** *Wowing Jok & Jynny* 21 ibid. 388 Ane pig, ane pot, ane raip thair ben. **1604** *Acts Sederunt* 11 Jan. (1790) 36 For removing of that impediment of proceeding in the Utter-house, (that the procurator is thair ben) it is appointit.. that [etc.]. **1728** RAMSAY *Monk & Miller's Wife* 144 'Hout I', quoth she, 'ye may well ken, 'Tis ill brought but [= out] that 's no there-ben'.

therebe'side, *adv.* Now only *arch.* and *poet.* [Orig. two words: see THERE 17, BESIDE *prep.*] By the side of that; next to that; near by.

a **1250** *Owl & Night.* 25 Þo stod on old stoc þar biside. **13..** in Horstmann *Altengl. Leg.* (1875) 91 He hedde þer is asse an is oxe, iteiȝed þer biside In a cracche. *c* **1400** MAUNDEV. (Roxb.) iii. 9 Þare be syde es a fayre place ordaynd for iustyng. **1470–85** MALORY *Arthur* II. xvi. 94 Ther besyde satte a fayr knyght on the ground. **1870** MORRIS *Earthly Par.* III. IV. 339 When I stood therebeside Methought its likeness ever would abide Within my mind.

So †, **therebe'sides** *adv.*, in same sense.

1470–85 MALORY *Arthur* I. x. 48 There bysydes were viij knyghtes that aspyed them.

therebinthe, obs. form of TEREBINTH.

thereby (ðɛə'baɪ, 'ðɛəbaɪ), *adv.* Forms: see THERE and BY. [OE. *þǽrbi*, f. *þǽr*, THERE 17 + *bi*, BY *prep.*, *adv.* (*a.*, *sb.*) Cf. G. *dabei*, Du. *daarbij*.]

1. By that; by means of, or because of, that; through that. Cf. BY A. 30–33, 36.

c **897** K. ÆLFRED *Past. C.* v. 42, ȝif he ðonne bearn ðærbiȝ [*v.r.* -bie, *Hatt.* -biȝ] ȝestriene. *a* **1225** *Ancr. R.* 160 He.. feste.. one iðe wildernesse vorte scheawen þerbi þet [etc.]. *a* **1300** *Cursor M.* 107 Þar bi man mai hir helping kenn. **1413** *Pilgr. Sowle* (Caxton) IV. xxxviii. (1859) 63 Supposyng therby for to geten honoure and fame. **1551** CRANMER in Strype *Life* (1694) App. 158 God shal therby be glorified. **1588** A. KING tr. *Canisius' Catech.* i vij, Ye sall haiff yairby ye hicht of ye æquinoctiall lyne. **1600** HAMILTON *Facile Tr.* in *Cath. Tractates* (S.T.S.) 220 Desyrous to ressaue thairbe, thair eternel felicitie in heauin. **1607** TOPSELL *Four-f. Beasts* (1658) 83 They cannot abide the savour of ointments, but fall mad thereby. **1703** MOXON *Mech. Exerc.* 126 Of the Ten-foot Rod, and thereby to measure and describe the Ground-plot. **1809** PINKNEY *Trav. France* 93 The rooms were so full as to render our stay unpleasant, and we thereby lost an anatomy lecture. **1896** R. S. S. BADEN-POWELL *Matabele Campaign* vi, For fear of having my attention distracted.. and of my thereby losing my bearings.

2. Beside, adjacent to, or near that. (In quot. *c* 1220, Up against that.) Now *arch.* and *dial.*

c **1220** *Bestiary* 634 A tre he sekeð.. ðat is strong.. and leneð him.. ðer bi. *c* **1250** *Gen. & Ex.* 3361 It was a stede henden ðor bi, On a syde of munt synay. *a* **1300** *Cursor M.* 13765 þar bi lai many [man] vn-fere. *c* **1449** PECOCK *Repr.* II. iii. 151 Ȝondir is the Holi Goost and therbi is Marie with Seint Peter. *c* **1450** *St. Cuthbert* (Surtees) 3915 He duelt in a place þare by. **1590** SPENSER *F.Q.* II. vii. 32 A couetous Spright.. Who thereby did attend. **1641** HEYLIN *Hist. Episc.* I. (1657) 23 The twelve fountaines of Elim, and the seventy Palmes that grew thereby. **1719** DE FOE *Crusoe* (1840) II. iv. 94 At the foot of a tree thereby. **1875** MORRIS *Æneid* Proem 2 Fields that are thereby. **1888** ELWORTHY *W. Somerset Wordbk.* s.v., Nif I baint there, you'll vind me thereby.

b. With verbs of motion, in sense of BY A. 16.

a **1300** *Cursor M.* 15634 Quer i sal þis calice drinc, Or i sal pass þar bi. **1526** *Pilgr. Perf.* (W. de W. 1531) 3 Whan my glory shall passe therby, thou shalt se my hynder partes. **1606** G. W[OODCOCKE] *Hist. Ivstine* IV. 21 The tales of Scylla and Charibdis, which made men beleeve in sailing thereby that they heard the continuall barking of doggs.

c. ***to come thereby*** = to 'come by' or get possession of that: see COME *v.* 39 b and BY A. 15.

c **1386** CHAUCER *Wife's T.* 128 Whan that he saugh he myghte nat come therby This is to seye what wommen loue moost. *c* **1430** [see COME *v.* 39 b]. **1567** *Gude & Godlie B.* (S.T.S.) 27, I traist eternall glore to se; Christ grant that I may cum thairby.

†**3.** Besides, together with, or in addition to that.

13.. *Minor Poems fr. Vernon MS.* xxxii. 524 Wȝuche ben þe seuen synnes dedly, And þe seuen vertuwes þerby. **14..** *Tundale's Vis.* 803 All ȝif god be fulle of mercye, Ryghtwysnesse behoves go þer by. ? *a* **1500** *Chester Pl.* (E.E.T.S.) 388 That he would revive them sone in hye, With flesh and Sinew and Skynn therby, Which sone he can them geue.

4. In reference to a number or quantity: Very nearly so; somewhere about that; = THERE-ABOUTS 2, 2 b. *Sc.*

[*c* **1425** WYNTOUN *Cron.* IX. xiv. 1568 A thousande and thre hundyr ȝhere Nynti and v. or þar by nere.] **1557–75** *Diurn. Occur.* (1833) 82 At xij houris at evin or thairby. **1563** *Reg. Privy Council Scot.* I. 245 To the nowmer of fourtie personis or thairby. **1582–8** *Hist. Jas. VI* (1804) 172 Thair were takin prisoneris 9 scoire and ten gentillmen or thairby. **1726** *Wodrow Corr.* (1843) III. 271 The spurious paper.. dully written, two years or thereby after Mr. Henderson's death. **1821** SCOTT *Kenilw.* x, There was one maiden of fifteen or thereby. **1863** A. B. GROSART *Small Sins* Pref. (ed. 2) 8 It is my intention.. to print half-a-dozen or thereby of small books.

†**5.** With reference thereto; *apropos* of that; thereanent. *Obs.*

a **1250** *Owl & Night.* 244 Aday [= by day] þu art blynd oþer bisne, þar by men seggeþ a vorbisne. **1303** R. BRUNNE *Handl. Synne* 3999 Seynt Gregory telleþ a tale þar by.

b. ***thereby hangs a tale***: see TALE *sb.* 3.

†**6.** In accordance with that. *Obs.*

1512 *Act 4 Hen. VIII*, c. 19 *Preamble*, The seid Frensche kyng.. the Decree of the enterdiccion dispysyng will not therby reforme himself.

7. quasi-*adj.* Consequent. *nonce-use.*

1661 FELTHAM *Resolves* II. xl. 262 The chiefest Knowledg that we get, is that of our thereby guilt and misery.

† **there'down**, *adv. Obs.* [In ME. two words, THERE 17 and DOWN *adv.* q.v. for Forms.] Down there; down: in reference to direction or position.

1297 R. GLOUC. (Rolls) 9791 þe brain orn al abrod in þe pauiment þer doune. *Ibid.* 9797 Nou he liþ þer doune. *c* **1305** *St. Kenelm* 206 in *E.E.P.* (1862) 53 And falsliche as heo com anheȝ, also heo ful [= fell] þerdoune. *c* **1325** *Poem Edw. II* 37 in *Pol. Songs* (Camden) 325 Certes holi churche is muchel i-brouht ther doune. **1375** BARBOUR *Bruce* XI. 300 The sykis alswa thair doune Sall put thame to confusioune. *a* **1550** *Freiris of B.* 178 in *Dunbar's Poems* (S.T.S.) 291 All that thay did thair doun he micht weill se.

therefore ('ðɛəfə(r)), **therefor** (ðɛə'fɔː(r)), *adv.* (*sb.*) Forms: α. 2–3 **ðer-**, 2–5 **þerfore**, (2 **þaruore**, 2–4 **þeruore**, 3 **ðor-**, **þar-fore**, 3–4 **þervore**), 5–6 **therfore**, (6 *Sc.* **thair-**, **yair-**, **theirfore**). β. 2–5 **þerefore**, (2–3 **þereuore**, 4 **þarefore**), 5– **therefore**. γ. 3–5 **þerfor**, (3 **þeruor**, 4 **þar-**, **tarfor**, 4–5 **þer-for**, **yarfor**), 5–7 **therfor**, (6 *Sc.* **thair-**, **yairfor**, **-foir**, 7 **therfoer**). δ. 6– **therefor**, (9 **there-for**). [Early ME. *þerfore*, *þerefore* (often written as two words), f. *þǽr-*, *þer-*, THERE + *fore*, OE. and early ME. collateral form of *for*: see FORE *adv.* and *prep.* After final *e* became mute, *fore* prep. was gradually levelled with *for*, and *ther(e)fore* was often written *therfor*, *therefor*. In mod. Eng. (since *c* 1800) *therefore* and *therefor* are almost always differentiated in spelling and stress in accordance with meaning: see below.]

I. (Now stressed (ðɛə'fɔː(r)), and usu. spelt *therefor* for distinction from 2.) *formal* or *arch.*

1. For that (thing, act, etc.); for that, for it. **a.** In various senses of FOR *prep.*

c **1175** *Lamb. Hom.* 9 His festen.. and chirc-ȝong and god to donne þeruore. *c* **1220** *Bestiary* 377 God giueð ðer fore mede. *a* **1300** *Cursor M.* 610 (Cott.) He gaf it him, als in heritage, To yeild þerfor [*v.rr.* þare fore, þar for, þerfore] na mar knaulage. *c* **1386** CHAUCER *Sqr.'s T.* 169 Born anon in to the heighe Tour, With certeine officers ordeynd therfore [*v.rr.* ther fore, there fore, þerfore]. *c* **1440** *Alphabet of Tales* 97 Shoársswerd agayn & sayd.. sho wold not delyver it or he & his felow bothe samen come þerfor. **1477** EARL RIVERS (Caxton) *Dictes* 1 To gyue therfore synguler louynges & thankes. **1561** NORTON & SACKV. *Gorboduc* V. i, Speede must we vse to levie force therefore. **1622** CALLIS *Stat. Sewers* (1647) 86 To erect new Walls, Banks and other Defences, and what sums of Money to Raise and Levy therefore. **1824** MEDWIN *Convers. Byron* II. 186, I.. have.. continued here .. in the hope of seeing things reconciled, and have done all in my power there-for. **1856** R. A. VAUGHAN *Mystics* VI. iv. (1860) I. 184 If the emperor sins, he must give account to God therefor. **1861** *Evening Star* 4 Oct., 100lbs. of potatoes or a substitute therefore thrice a week. **1870** MORRIS *Earthly Par.* II. III. 344 The love I had therefor. **1877** F. HALL *Eng. Adj. in -able* 39 Argument being at an end, recourse was then had to the common substitute therefor, ridicule. **1885** *Act 48 & 49 Vict.* c. 70 §7 He shall supply a copy of such report .. on payment of the sum of one shilling therefor.

b. By reason of that; for that reason, on that account: cf. FOR *prep.* 21, 22.

c **1175** *Lamb. Hom.* 5 þa ȝe [*MS.* þaȝ] habbe wele to ouer stohwennesse on þisse liue ne beo þu þereuore prud. *c* **1200** *Trin. Coll. Hom.* 143 þaruore hire sinne hire bicome swiðe laðe. *c* **1220** *Bestiary* 509 Vt of his ðrote it smit an onde, .. ðer-fore oðre fisses to him draȝen. *c* **1250** *Gen. & Ex.* 1215 Ysmael pleide hard gamen; Sarra was ðor-fore often wroð. **1297** R. GLOUC. (Rolls) 5348 Vre louerd mid is eyen of milce on þe lokeþ þeruore. *a* **1300** *Cursor M.* 287 þerfor is he cald trinite For he es anfald godd in thre. **13..** *Ibid.* 2894 (Gött.) God forbede ȝe do þat sin þat ȝe in hell þarfor [*Trin.* þerfore] brin. *c* **1385** CHAUCER *L.G.W.* 1863 (*Lucrece*) That Tarquyny shulde ybanysshed be ther-fore. **1533** MORE *Debell. Salem* Wks. 954/1 When he saith himself that they haue punished many therfore, that is to wit, for thesame cause. **1605** CAMDEN *Rem.* 181 If that any Iew did buy any Christian for his slave, hee should bee fined therefore. **1805** SCOTT *Last Minstr.* IV. vi, They crossed the Liddle.. And burned my little lonely tower; The fiend receive their souls therefor! **1848** LOWELL *Lett.* (1894) I. 151 Tell Briggs that his ticket came safely, and that I am thankful therefor. **1868** HAWTHORNE *Amer. Note-Bks.* (1879) II. 173 They would all be.. healthier men therefor. **1899** F. T. BULLEN *Log Sea-waif* 149 The ill-used crew promptly refused to do any more in her, and were, of course, clapped in jail therefor.

II. (Now always spelt *therefore*, and stressed ('ðɛəfə(r), 'ðɛəfɔː(r)).)

2. In consequence of that; that being so; as a result or inference from what has been stated; consequently. Formerly sometimes unemphatic (esp. in versions of N.T.) = THEN 5.

In early use often indistinguishable from 1 b, where see earlier examples; now distinguished as expressing a general relation of consequence or inference. Sometimes classed as a conjunction.

a **1400** *Prymer* (1891) 45 Lo ther fore alle generations schulle seye y am blessed. **1526** TINDALE *Matt.* xiii. 18 Heare ye therfore the similitude off the sower. **1533** CRANMER *Misc. Writ.* (Parker Soc.) II. 260, I trust, therefore, you will not so hardly regard my first request herein. **1548–9** (Mar.) *Bk. Com. Prayer*, *Communion*, It is very mete.. that we shoulde.. geue thankes to thee, O Lorde... Therefore with Angelles and Archangels.. we laud [etc.]. **1552** HULOET, Therfore,.. *cum accent. in penult.*, *eo, ergo, idcirco, ideo, igitur,.. propterea, propter hoc.* **1555** EDEN *Decades* 202 Manate.. is the thyrde [fish] whereof I haue promysed to entreate. Manate therefore, is a fysshe of the sea, of the byggest sorte [etc.]. *c* **1600** SHAKS. *Sonn.* xli, Gentle thou art, and therefore to be wonne, Beautious thou art, therefore to be assailed. *Ibid.* cxxiii, Our dates are breefe, and therefor we admire, What thou dost foyst vpon vs that is ould. **1611** BIBLE *John* iv. 6 Now Iacobs Well was there. Iesus therefore [TINDALE then], being wearied with his iourney, sate thus on the Well. **1660** BARROW *Euclid* I. xv. Schol., Because the angle AEC + AED + CEB + DEB = 4 right angles, therefore the angle AEC + AED = CEB + DEB = to two right angles, therefore CED and AEB are strait lines. **1735** BERKELEY *Freethink. in Math.* §2 Things obscure are not therefore sacred. **1845** M. PATTISON *Ess.* (1889) I. 15 The Franks were the stronger, and therefore the masters. **1849** MACAULAY *Hist. Eng.* vi. II. 80 The refugees were zealous for the Calvinistic discipline... James therefore gave orders [etc.].

B. as *sb.* The word 'therefore' as marking a conclusion; an expressed conclusion or inference.

1641 'SMECTYMNUUS' *Vind. Answ.* xiii. 144 Let him first answer our *Therefores*, and wee will quickly answer his *Wherefores.* **1674** HICKMAN *Hist. Quinquart.* (ed. 2) 185 The Article having made a (*therefore*), its strange that any one should draw any other conclusion from it, than what it self hath drawn. **1874** GEO. ELIOT *Coll. Breakf. P.* in *Jubal*, etc. 232 A faith Defying sense and all its ruthless train Of arrogant 'therefores'.

† **there'forne**, *adv. Obs.* In 3–4 **þer-, þar-**. [app. an alteration of THEREFORE, in imitation of words in *-forne* from OE. *-foran*, e.g. *beforne*.] = THEREFORE 1.

a **1300** *E.E. Psalter* xvii[i]. 3 Mi schelder.. And mi fonger ai þer forne. *Ibid.* xxxi[i]. 4, I am torned in mi sorw þar forn, Whiles þat pricked es þe thorn. **13..** *Gaw. & Gr. Knt.* 1107, & quat chek so ȝe acheue, chaunge me þer forne. *c* **1400** *Cato's Mor.* 260 in *Cursor M.* p. 1672 (Fairf.) If þi gode be lorne Sorou noȝt þar forne To double þi harme.

† **there'forth**, *adv. Obs.* [f. THERE 17 + FORTH *adv.*]

1. a. Forth from thence; away from that place. **b.** Along that way; by that place.

1297 R. GLOUC. (Rolls) 5704 þis king also at glastingbury as he þeruorþ com, Seint aþelwold þat was þere monek, out of þe house he nom. **1387** TREVISA *Higden* (Rolls) V. 299 þe kyng passede þerforþ, and wolde wite what it were. *c* **1450** LOVELICH *Grail* xliii. 312 Hem he took vpe thanne Everychon, and with hym bar þereforth Anon.

2. Out, outside; in the open; = THEREOUT 2.

1536 BELLENDEN *Cron. Scot.* II. xi. (1541) 17 b/1 He punist theiffis.. and othir criminabyll personis with sic seuerite.. that the bestiall & gudis lay thairfurth but ony trubyl. *Ibid.* v. iv. 56 b/1 Thay wer ane rude vndantit pepill, and lay thair furth all wynter nochtwithstanding yᵉ cauld frostis.

† **there'fro**, *adv. Obs.* Also *Sc.* **þar-fra.** [Orig. two words, THERE 17 and FRO *prep.*] = next.

13.. *Cursor M.* 1316 (Gött.) þar fra [*C.* þat oute of, *F.* þer-out] renis four grete stremis. **1340** HAMPOLE *Pr. Consc.* 5214 Lo! here þe sepulcre a lytil þar fra. ? *a* **1366** CHAUCER *Rom. Rose* 1660 Whan I was not fer therfro. *c* **1380** WYCLIF *Wks.* (1880) 364 With-owten addynge þer to or abregynge þer fro. **1413** *Pilgr. Sowle* (Caxton 1483) IV. x. 62 The juse that yssueth ther froo. **1565** in *Reg. Mag. Sig. Scot.* 1575. 656/1 Passand thairfra up ane dyke betuix Kippelaw and Bowdane. **1588** A. KING tr. *Canisius' Catech.* g viij b, Bot in this our age throwch ye anticipation of ye æquinoxe is distant yairfra almaist 4 dayes. **1622** MABBE tr. *Aleman's Guzman d'Alf.* II. 59, I would.. desist there-fro. **1678** SIR G. MACKENZIE *Crim. Laws Scot.* II. xxiii. §4 (1699) 248 They are not excluded therefrae by the foresaid act of Parliament.

therefrom (ðɛəˈfrɒm), *adv. arch.* or *formal.* [Orig. two words, THERE 17 and FROM *prep.*] From that; from that place; away from there.

a **1250** *Owl & Night.* 137 þeyh he beo þar from bicume He cuþ hwenene he is icume. *c* **1300** *St. Brandan* 512 The ȝut hi were fur ther fram. **1387** TREVISA *Higden* (Rolls) VIII. 89 þe schap of þe cros was i-seie forsake þe baner and passe somwhat of space þerfrom [*MS. γ.* þarvram]. *c* **1610** SIR J. MELVIL *Mem.* Author to Son (1735) 18 Debarring therefrom all honest, true, and plain Speakers. **1660** SHARROCK *Vegetables* 24, I much doubt of any effect therefrom. **1728** CHAMBERS *Cycl.* s.v. *Circus*, They took their name therefrom. **1850** NEALE *Med. Hymns* (1867) 102 The streams that flow therefrom. **1885** *Law Times* LXXX. 132/1 Nor was the doctrine contended for.. logically deducible therefrom.

† **there'gain**, *adv. Obs.* Forms: 3 **ðor ȝen, þer yen,** 5 **ther geyn.** [f. THERE 17 + GAIN *prep.* Cf. THEREAGAIN.] Against or in opposition to that.

c **1250** *Gen. & Ex.* 2797 If he it werne and be ðor ȝen, Ic sal ðe techen hu it sal ben. *c* **1300** *Havelok* 2271 þer yen ne wolde neuer on striue. *c* **1400** *Rom. Rose* 6555 If men wolde ther geyn appose The naked text.

So † **there'gains** *adv.* [GAINS], on the side opposite to that; over against there.

c **1330** R. BRUNNE *Chron. Wace* (Rolls) 13538 O syde toke þe Romayns, & Arthur þat oþer euen þer gayns.

therehence, *adv. Obs.* exc. *dial.* Forms: α. 4–5 **þerhenne,** (4 **therhanne**). β. 4 **þer hannes,** 6– **there(-)hence,** (6 **therence** (9 *dial.*), **therehens,** 7 **therhence**). [f. THERE 17 + HEN, HENNE *adv.*, and *hennes, hens*, HENCE *adv.*]

1. From or out of that place; from there: = THENCE 1. Now *dial.*

α. *c* **1300** *Beket* 1145 Therhanne he wende to Eystrie. ? *a* **1400** *Arthur* 591 Muche folke þerhenne he toke þo.

β. *c* **1400** *R. Gloucester's Chron.* (Rolls) App. AA. 2 He nolde þer hannes passi. **1548** UDALL *Erasm. Par. Luke* viii. 89 Therehens as.. out of a chaire or pulpite he taught the multitude. **1600** HAKLUYT *Voy.* (1904) X. 101 The famous voyage of Sir Francis Drake into the South sea, and therehence about the whole Globe of the earth, begun in 1577. **1724** R. WELTON *Chr. Faith & Pract.* 367 The waves toss the ships up to the very clouds, and the winds therehence drive them to the deep abyss. **1898** T. HARDY *Wessex Poems* 46 Stone-deaf therence went many a man.

† **2.** From that source or origin; from that fact or circumstance: = THENCE 4. *Obs.*

1528 TINDALE *Parable Wicked Mammon* 16 *Hamon*, in the Ebrewe speche sygnyfyeth a multytude or abundaunce... And therhence commeth *mahamon* or *mammon*, abundaunce or plenteousnes of goodes or ryches. **1597** J. KING *On Jonas* (1618) 10 Therehence, they say, he was named the son of Amittai; that is, the sonne of truth. **1623** W. C. *Fatall Vesper* 4 Those vnreuealed attributes, which doe flow therehence. **1718** SWIFT *To Sheridan* 3, I have a great esteem for Plautus; And think your boys may gather there-hence More wit and humour than from Terence.

† **3.** Distant from that place: = THENCE 2. *rare.*

1611 CORYAT *Crudities* 10 A countrey village.. fourteene miles therehence distant. *Ibid.* 68 A parish tenne miles therehence.

therein (ðɛərˈɪn), *adv.* Now *formal*, *arch.*, or *dial.* Forms: see THERE and IN; also 3 **þrin.** [OE. *þǽrin*, f. *þǽr* THERE 17 + IN *prep.*]

1. In that place or (material) thing.

a **1000** *Boeth. Metr.* xi. 4 Wealdend.. heofones & eorðan.. & ealra ðara þe ðærin wuniað. *a* **1300** *Cursor M.* 15895 (Cott.) A knaun freind he had þare in [*v.rr.* þar ine, þerin]. **1398** TREVISA *Barth. De P.R.* XIII. xxvi. (Bodl. MS.), þerin is a maner kinde of beestes Dolphyns wiþ rugge itoþed as a sawe. *c* **1450** *St. Cuthbert* (Surtees) 789 þai sailed þar in merualously. **1535** COVERDALE *Ps.* xxiv. 2 The compasse of the worlde, and all yᵗ dwell therin. **1676** RAY *Corr.* (1848) 123 If you have observed any errors or mistakes therein. **1875** JOWETT *Plato* (ed. 2) III. 688 The universe, and the things that are and move therein. **1911** *Act 1 Geo. V*, c. 1 Sched. (Paisley Corp. Order Confirm. Act), The late Robert Brodie.. by his trust disposition.. conveyed his entire property to trustees therein named.

b. In or during that time.

1539 BIBLE (Great) *Exod.* xxxi. 14 Kepe my Sabbath.. whosoeuer worketh therin, the same soule shalbe roted out from amonge hys people.

2. In that affair or matter; in that thing, circumstance, or particular.

c **1230** *Hali Meid.* 3 Maken þe to þenchen hwuch delit were þrin. *a* **1300** *Cursor M.* 13759 (Cott.) Lok þi will bi noght þar in. **1526** *Pilgr. Perf.* (W. de W. 1531) 2 That ye neuer.. be besy to attempte ony persone therin. *c* **1555** HARPSFIELD *Divorce Hen. VIII* (Camden) 83 Therein we do find no fault. **1588** A. KING tr. *Canisius' Catech.* 130 All perdition had the beginning thairin [in pride]. **1631** HEYWOOD *2nd Pt. Maid of West* IV. Wks. 1874 II. 391 Thou therein hadst much hyperboliz'd. **1882** SPURGEON *Treas. Dav.* Ps. cxix. 17 The more will he be driven towards God for help therein.

3. Inside, in the house, within doors. *mod. Sc.*

1822 HOGG *Perils of Man* III. vii. 202 Bessy Chisholm —Heh! Are ye therein? **1828** BUCHAN *Ballads* I. 113 If ye'll work therein as we thoreout, Well borrow'd shou'd your body be.

4. Into that place or (material) thing.

a **1240** *Sawles Warde* in *Cott. Hom.* 263 þu most al gan þrin ant al beon bigotten þrin, for in þe ne mei hit nanesweis neomen in. *a* **1300** *Cursor M.* 8852 þair in [*Trin.* þerynne] þan was þair relikes don. **1398** TREVISA *Barth. De P.R.* III. xviii. (W. de W. 1495) 65 Somtyme grauel and powder falleth therin. **1526** R. WHYTFORD *Martiloge* 135 b, Than made they a grete fyre.. and cast therin pytche and rosyne. **1747** WESLEY *Prim. Physick* (1762) 90 Smell to a Spunge dipt there-in.

† **5.** = THEREON 2: cf. IN *prep.* 32 a. *Obs.*

1535 COVERDALE *1 Sam.* xxxi. 4 Then toke Saul yᵉ swerde, and fell therin. [Cf. *Germ.* (Luther) fiel darein; *Vulg.* super eum; *next verse has* vpon his swerde.]

† **6.** As *relative adv.*: In which; into which; = WHEREIN. *Obs.*

971 *Blickl. Hom.* 73 He wæs on Simones huse.. þærin ʒeat þæt wif þa deorwyrþan smerenesse on his heafod. **13..** *Cast. Love* (Halliw.) 56 This castel Marie bodi wes, Therin he alyght and his in ches [chose his inn]. **13..** *Cursor M.* 396 (Gött.) In þe heiest element of all, þar in þe fire has his stall. **1422** tr. *Secreta Secret., Priv. Priv.* 167 The Seete therin as he was woned to sitte.

7. therein 'after, therein be'fore, therein 'under, = after, before, below in that document, statute, etc. (Usually written as single words: cf. *herein after*, etc., s.v. HEREIN.)

1818 CRUISE *Digest* (ed. 2) II. 276 Upon trust to preserve the contingent remainders thereinafter limited. **1827** JARMAN *Powell's Devises* (ed. 3) II. 105 A general residuary devise of real and personal estate not thereinbefore disposed of. **18..** A. BAIN in B. Stewart *Conserv. Force* (1873) viii. 221 He gave 'mental work' as one heading, but declined to make an entry thereinunder.

† **there'inne**, *adv. Obs.* Forms: see THERE and INNE: also 4–5 **thrynne.** [OE. *þǽrinne*, f. *þǽr*, THERE 17 + INNE.] = THEREIN.

(In late instances perh. only a var. spelling of *therein*.)

c **897** K. ÆLFRED *Gregory's Past.* C. xvi. 100 He wæs ðǽrinne ʒetoʒen to ðære godcundan sceawunge, & ðærute [*v.r.* ðærut] he wæs abisʒod ymb ðæs folces ðearfe. *c* **1200** *Vices & Virt.* 137 All ðat folk ðe þerinne was. *c* **1200** ORMIN 1651 ȝiff þatt iss þatt mann wile itt don Wiþþ witt & skill þærinne. *c* **1250** *Gen. & Ex.* 1104 Non ðing ne mai ðor inne liuen. **1382** WYCLIF *Luke* xix. 45 He.. bigan to caste out men sellinge ther ynne and biggynge. *c* **1400** *Gamelyn* 314, I wil not that this compaignye parten a-twynne, And ye wil doon after me, whil eny sope is thrynne. *c* **1400** *Sowdone Bab.* 335 Thai slough all, that were ther Inne. *c* **1450** *Merlin* i. 10 She wende to haue founde hym thar ynne.

† **therein'till**, *adv. Sc. Obs.* [f. THERE 17 + INTILL.] Therein; thereinto.

1507 in *Charters, &c. Edinb.* (1871) 192 To mak ony stop or impediment to thame thairintill. **1533** BELLENDEN *Livy* II. xiii. (S.T.S.) I. 175 The faderis, quhen þis mater wes brocht afore þame, mycht nocht ordourlie gif þare consultacioun þareintill. **1650** *Acts Sederunt* 29 Jan. (1790) 66 All bands and actis of caution.. heirefter, shall bear this clause insert thereintill. **1700** in A. McKay *Kilmarnock* (1880) 61 To give furth and pronounce.. sentences thereintill.

thereinto (ˌðɛərɪnˈtuː, ðɛəˈrɪntuː), *adv. arch.* [f. THERE 17 + INTO.]

1. Into that place, matter, condition, etc.

a **1300** *Cursor M.* 23222 (Edinb.) Cald sa ken.. þat þoh a firin fel war mad, And þoru a chance þar into slad [etc.]. **1611** BIBLE *Luke* xxi. 21 Let not them.. enter thereinto. **1652** KIRKMAN *Clerio & Lozia* 178 No Victualls could be carried thereinto. **1695** WOODWARD *Nat. Hist. Earth* Pref., The Ways whereby I got Light thereinto. **1867** KINGSLEY in *Life* (1877) II. 249, I have been drawn there-into because I find every one talking about it [Darwinism]. **1887** MORRIS *Odyss.* XI. 36 And the black blood flowed thereinto.

† **2.** = THEREIN 2. Cf. INTO 22. *Obs.*

1581–2 *Reg. Privy Council Scot.* III. 452 The said compliner hes differrit the samin unto the tyme he knew his Hienes and Lordschippis myndis thairinto. **1676** OWEN *Nat. & Causes Apost.* Wks. 1851 VII. 4 On such principles of difference in judgment as have no considerable influence thereinto.

† **'there-mid, ther-mid**, *adv. Obs.* [Orig. two words, THERE 17 and MID *prep.*[1]] With or by means of that; = THEREWITH 3.

c **888** K. ÆLFRED *Boeth.* xvi. §2 (MS. B.) þa forceaw he his aʒene tungan and wearp hine ðær mid on ðæt neb foran. *c* **1000** ÆLFRIC *Saints' Lives* xxiii B. 767 Ongan þa þær mid delfan. *c* **1175** *Lamb. Hom.* 63 We hit aȝen to ȝeme and god solf þer mid iqueme. *c* **1330** R. BRUNNE *Chron. Wace* (Rolls) 16450 ȝyf any had leyd a cors in pyt, Hym self fel þanne ded þer myt [the plague]. **1393** LANGL. *P. Pl.* C. IV. 253 To do þer myd here beste.

† **ther(e)-mide, -mydde**, *adv. Obs.* [f. as prec. + *-e*, after THEREINNE, etc.] **a.** Along with that; together with that; at the same time. **b.** = prec.

a. *c* **1175** *Lamb. Hom.* 75 Ic ou wile seggen word efter word and þermide hwat þet word bi-queþ. **1377** LANGL. *P. Pl.* B. XVI. 262 þe pouke it hath attached, And me þere myde. *c* **1425** *Seven Sag.* (P.) 2171 He went don a[nd] bare uppe a cole, And a torche up ther myde.

b. *c* **1220** *Bestiary* 615 Siðen he bigeten on, and two ȝer he ðer mide gon. *a* **1250** *Prov. Ælfred* 392 in *O.E. Misc.* 126 Ne myhte he þar myde his lif none hwile holde. *c* **1250** *Gen. & Ex.* 2656 Hise tunges ende is brent ðor mide. *c* **1350** *Will. Palerne* 5358 Eche man þer mide miȝt hold him a-paied. **1377** LANGL. *P. Pl.* B. VI. 69 Make hem mery þere mydde.

theremin (ˈθɛrəmɪn). Also **thérémin,** and with capital initial. [f. the name of its inventor, L. *Thérémin* (b. 1896), Russian engineer.] An electronic musical instrument in which the tone is generated by two high-frequency oscillators and the pitch controlled by the movement of the performer's hand towards and away from the circuit (see quot. 1971).

1927 *Times* 12 Dec. 11/1 Professor Theremin and his collaborator play duets for two 'theremins' and piano. **1934** S. ROBERTSON *Devel. Mod. Eng.* x. 418 Miscellaneous examples.. of the taking over of a surname.. and using it as a common noun are *boycott*,.. *theremin*, and *zeppelin*. **1950** BLESH & JANIS *They all played Ragtime* x. 199 And then those long metal cylinders, different lengths. The players wore gloves and would pull on them and make weird sounds like a Theremin. **1971** *Daily Colonist* (Victoria, B.C.) 13 Feb. 25/5 Greenway, of Vancouver, will play a theremin. The instrument was developed and introduced to the public in 1920 by Leo Theremin, a Russian scientist. A box-like apparatus, it produced musical tones from two electric circuits running through vibrating radio tubes. The player stands in front of the theremin and moves his hands through the air... The left hand controls volume or tone, and the right hand raises pitch as it nears the instrument and lowers pitch as it moves away. **1974** *Times* 5 Feb. 11 Most illuminating of all were the live performances of Varèse's *Ecuatorial*,.. its original thérémin part now played by two ..*ondes Martenot*. **1982** *New Scientist* 16 Dec. 753 Moog recently recorded her playing the theremin.

therence, variant of THEREHENCE.

thereness (ˈðɛənɪs). [f. THERE + -NESS.] The condition or quality of being there; existence in a defined place. (Sometimes opposed to *hereness*.)

1674 N. FAIRFAX *Bulk & Selv.* 11 The all-fillingness of God, the herenesses and therenesses of ghosts, have been too much interwoven and twisted together. *Ibid.* 45 The thereness or hereness was nothing belonging unto God. **1887** W. JAMES in *Mind* XII. 18 Could that possibly be the feeling of any special whereness or thereness? **1899** J. CAIRD *Fundamental Ideas Chr.* II. ix. 13 Hereness and thereness are incessantly passing out of and into each other. **1929** D. H. LAWRENCE *Paintings D.H.L.* (Introd.) fo. 7 *verso*, All the host of other defiant.. cats that have come back.. to form and substance and *thereness*, instead of delicious nowhereness. **1958** *Listener* 20 Nov. 822/2 The immense Thereness of someone else. **1976** I. MURDOCH *Henry & Cato* I. 196 All those would-be deep explanations are so abstract and so simple when confronted with the awful complex thereness of a relationship which has gone wrong. **1983** J. JONES *Dostoevsky* i. 7 Its absurd yet maddening thereness like that of the pea under the mattress of the princess.

† **there-'nigh**, *adv. Obs.* Forms: see THERE and NIGH. [OE. *þǽr néah*: *þǽr*, THERE 17, *néah* near, NIGH.] Near that place or thing.

971 *Blickl. Hom.* 139 Ceʒende ealle hire maʒas þa þe þær neah wæron. *c* **1175** *Lamb. Hom.* 43 þar neh ne mihte nan liuende mon gan. *c* **1290** *Beket* 929 in *S. Eng. Leg.* I. 133 Ich ov hote þat ȝe þare neiȝ ne beon. *a* **1300** *Cursor M.* 767 (Cott.) If we com þer nei [*F.* þer neye; *G.* þar ney; *T.* þer nyȝe]. **13..** *Ibid.* 7589 (Cott.) þe sarzins war þar neigh beside All fled.

thereof (ðɛəˈrɒf, ðɛərɒv *with shifting stress*), *adv.* Now *formal* or *arch.* Forms: see THERE and OF; also 3 **þrof** (trof), 5 **throf.** [OE. *þǽr of*: see THERE 17 and OF.]

1. Of that or it: in various current senses of OF.

c **1000** *Sax. Leechd.* I. 196, ʒenim þas ylcan wyrte, wyrc clyþan þærof. *c* **1200** ORMIN 9867 þa staness þatt he spacc þærofф, þeȝȝ wærenn rihhte staness. *a* **1240** *Sawles Warde* in *Cott. Hom.* 253 To a rudden him ut þrof. *Ibid.* 265 þat tu hauest ibeo þear ant soð hauest iseid trof. **13..** *Cursor M.* 22722 (Cott.) þar of wit trout he broght þam vte. *c* **1400** MAUNDEV. (Roxb.) v. 16 Men makes þerof gude glasse. **1486** *Bk. St. Albans* C v, Make throf .iij. pellettis. **1526** *Pilgr. Perf.* (W. de W. 1531) 116 A sage persone.. wyll be well ware therof. **1588** SHAKS. *L.L.L.* III. i. 130, I.. in lieu thereof, impose on thee nothing but this. **1599** HAKLUYT *Voy.* II. 186, I.. tooke oute thereof a iarre of oyle. **1611** BIBLE *John* vi. 50 That a man may eate thereof, and not die. **1678** WANLEY *Wond. Lit. World* v. ii. §79 Having lived about fifty two years, and thereof Reigned thirty one. *a* **1761** LAW

Comf. Weary Pilgr. (1809) 61 But instead thereof, he was left solely to the light and spirit of this world.

b. = *of it*, as objective genitive.

c1175 *Lamb. Hom.* 3 þe lauerd haueð þar of neode. c1250 *Gen. & Ex.* 1132 Maniman ðor of holdet litel tale. a1300 *Cursor M.* 1287 (Cott.) Quen [he] þar of son had a sight. c1380 WYCLIF *Wks.* (1880) 69 þei ben consenteris & fautouris þer of. c1400 *Ywaine & Gaw.* 762 For tharof had he grete myster. 1568 GRAFTON *Chron.* II. 105 To the spedy execution thereof. 1590 SHAKS. *Com. Err.* IV. i. 38 Disburse the summe, on the receit thereof. 1600 J. PORY tr. *Leo's Africa* II. 62 At last [he] vsurped the gouernment thereof. 1665 in De Foe *Plague* (1840) 41 Give notice thereof to the examiner of health. 1698 TYSON *Anat. Opossum* 3 Find out some Name, that might be most expressive thereof. 1818 CRUISE *Digest* (ed. 2) III. 304 Nor should the heir be occupant thereof.

c. = *of it, its*, as possessive genitive.

Many examples in Biblical use; a few occur in the later Wycliffite version; they increase in the 16th c. versions, and become very numerous in the Rhemish and in 1611.

1388 WYCLIF *2 Kings* ii. 12 The chare of Israel, and the charietere therof [1382 of it; Cov. and his horsmen; *Genev.*, 1611, and *R.V.* and the horsemen thereof]. —— *Prov.* iii. 16 Lengthe of daies is in the riȝthalf therof, and richessis and glorie ben in the lifthalf therof [1382 [1]his, [2]of it]. —— *Matt.* ii. 16 And slowe alle the children, that weren in Bethleem, and in alle the coostis therof [1382 in alle the eendis of it; TINDALE in all the costes there of; *Genev.*, *Rhem.* therof; 1611 thereof; 1881 *R.V.* in all the borders thereof]. 1594 SHAKS. *Rich. III*, I. iii. 154 As little ioy you may suppose in me, That I enioy, being the Queene thereof. 1611 BIBLE *Joshua* xv. 47 Vnto the riuer of Egypt and the great sea and the border thereof. [So R.V.] 1623 COCKERAM III, *Ignavus*.. He runneth up trees, and his desire is to sit there on the tops thereof. 1632 SANDERSON *Serm.* 129 Esay, speaking of Christ and his kingdome, and the righteousnesse thereof. 1825 J. NEAL *Bro. Jonathan* III. 401 He tottered away to a rock as to.. an altar; clung to it, as to the horns thereof. 1910 *Act 10 Edw. VII*, c. 38 §3 The schedules.. shall be deemed to be part of this Act in the same manner as if they had been contained in the body thereof.

2. From or out of that, as source or origin.

c1230 *Hali Meid.* 5 Al þat muchele lure þat ter of ariseð. 1399 *Rolls of Parlt.* III. 451/2 So mykel harme and meschief felle therof. c1400 MAUNDEV. (Roxb.) Pref. 2 þeroff þai hafe grete solace and comforthe. c1440 *Pallad. on Husb.* I. 5 What cam therof? 1542 UDALL *Erasm. Apoph.* 324 It is thought that one Caluus a poete brought it firste vp on Pompeius, & thereof the same to haue been taken vp in a prouerbe. 1590 SHAKS. *Com. Err.* V. i. 68 And thereof came it, that the man was mad. 1667 MILTON *P.L.* XII. 476 Much more good thereof shall spring. 1888 RICKABY *Moral Philos.* I. x. 181 Better is the activity.. than the pleasure which comes thereof.

†**3.** Answering to various obsolete uses of OF: in quots. = *thereat, therefor, therefrom, thereanent*, etc.

a1200 *Vices & Virt.* 29 And ðanke ðerof gode swiðe ȝierne. 13.. *Guy Warw.* (A.) 4656 Now, sir, take þerof pite. c1386 CHAUCER *Pars. T.* ⁋240 For soothly he.. sholde.. yeuen his body and al his herte to the seruice of Ihesu crist and ther-of doon hym hommage. 1390 GOWER *Conf.* I. 112 Gret offence He tok therof. c1400 MAUNDEV. (Roxb.) xxix. 131 þai meruailed þam gretely þeroff. c1400 *Brut* ccxxv. 293 þe lordez of eny toun.. shulde ansuere to þe King þerof. c1440 *Alphabet of Tales* 113 He þankid almighti God þeroff. c1450 *Godstow Reg.* 424 Doyng therof seruyce as hit is I-conteyned in the Charter. c1500 *Melusine* xxiv. 183 By my feyth, lady,.. doo your wyll therof. 1594 CAREW *Huarte's Exam. Wits* (1616) 99 If Lazarus had carried to him a pitcher of fresh water, hee should haue taken great refreshment thereof. 1669 MARVELL *Corr.* Wks. (Grosart) II. 276 If there be any particular that may more nearly relate to your affaires, you will be pleas'd to consider thereof.

Hence †**there-'offe, the'roffe** *adv.* [with final -*e*, after THEREINNE, etc.], in same senses.

c1400 MAUNDEV. (1839) ii. 13 He þat bereth A braunche ..þereoffe. *Ibid.* xiv. 156 So cold þat noman may drynke þere-offe. a1461 *How Gd. Wif taught hir Doughter* 53 in Hazl. *E.P.P.* I. 183 Mesurely take ther offe [*v.r.* (*Babees Bk.* 36) þer-of], that the falle no blame.

thereology (θɛrɪˈɒlədʒɪ). *rare*⁻¹. [erron. f. Gr. θέρ-ειν to heat, in Nicander 'to foment or apply a fomentation to (a wound)', hence θέρων is glossed by a scholiast by ἰώμενος healing, curing: see -OLOGY.] The healing art. (See quot.)

1841 R. PARK *Pantology* XII. iii. (1847) 418 In the branch of Thereology, we include the study of diseases, and the practice of Medicine. The name is derived from the Greek, Θερεω, I cure, or take care of.

So **there'ologist**, one skilled in thereology.

1882 in OGILVIE (Annandale).

thereon (ðɛərˈɒn, ˈðɛərɒn), *adv. formal* or *arch.* Forms: see THERE and ON; also 3 **þron**, 4 **þran**. [OE. *þǽron*, f. *þǽr*, THERE 17 + ON *prep.*]

1. Of position, *lit.* or *fig.*: On or upon that or it.

971 *Blickl. Hom.* 71 His þeȝnas.. læddon him to þone eosol, & ȝedydon þæt he þær on ȝesittan mihte. c1220 *Bestiary* 83 Đanne goð he to a ston, and he billeð ðer on. a1300 *Cursor M.* 2472 (Cott.) Quar-for þar on [*T.* þeron] godd tok his wrac. c1400 *Lanfranc's Cirurg.* 181 If þe place be whijt & neische and miche moisture þeron. a1533 LD. BERNERS *Huon* lxxxiii. 259 He toke his cuppe and made theron .iii. crosses. 1606 SHAKS. *Ant. & Cl.* v. ii. 133 If thereon you relye, I'll take my leaue. 1786 JEFFERSON *Wks.* (1859) I. 570 To confer with him thereon. 1809–10 COLERIDGE *Friend* I. iv. (1865) 125 All our notion of right and wrong is built thereon. 1896 *Law Times* C. 358/2 After payment of all charges thereon.

†**b.** as *relative adv.* On which: = WHEREON.

c1330 *Assump. Virg.* (B.M. MS.) 600 Foure of þe apostles schal bere þe beere Ther on schal ligge me modre deere.

2. Of motion or direction: On or upon that or it; onto that.

a1300 *Cursor M.* 10776 A duu.. þare lighted dun, and þar on lend. c1315 SHOREHAM iii. 158 þenche þou most wel bysyly, And þy wyȝt þran by-stowe. c1400 MAUNDEV. (Roxb.) ii. 7 þe Iews.. set a coroun on his heued and thrast it þeron so fast þat þe bluode ran doune. c1475 *Rauf Coilȝear* 374 Thairun my lyfe dar I layd [= lay it]. 1593 SHAKS. *Lucr.* 1139 Who, if it winke, shall thereon fall and die. 1728 CHAMBERS *Cycl.* s.v. *Glass*, By reason of the Sand strew'd thereon. 1887 MORRIS *Odyss.* XI. 591 When up reached the elder his hands thereon to lay.

3. As soon as that happened, was done, or was said; immediately after that; = THEREUPON 2 b.

a1300 *Cursor M.* 5872 (Cott.) And taron [*v.rr.* þar on, þer on] sett he men at ask Cf ilk dai to yeild þair task. 1618 WITHER *Motto, Nec Curo* Wks. (1633) 545, I care not greatly what succeed thereon. 1783 in Cruise *Digest* (1818) V. 319 Any non-claim which had ensued thereon. 1870 MORRIS *Earthly Par.* II. III. 243 Slowly thereon he gat unto his feet.

†**4.** From some obsolete uses of ON: **a.** In that, therein. **b.** Into that, thereinto. **c.** About that, thereof. **d.** At that, thereat. *Obs.*

a. c897 K. ÆLFRED *Gregory's Past. C.* li. 399 Hio is an lytel [burȝ], & ðeah ic mæȝ ðæron libban. c1000 ÆLFRIC *Hom.* II. 410 Aplanta þæron þa soðan lufe. c1205 LAY. 7275 þer Bruttus bi-com and to his liue he wunede þer an. c1290 *St. Michael* 453 in *S. Eng. Leg.* I. 312 Men seoth þar on liȝt. 1513 DOUGLAS *Æneis* I. iii. 82 Bid Eolus.. clois the presoun of wyndis, and thairon ring. 1525 LD. BERNERS *Froiss.* II. xxvi. 71, I had brought with me a boke... And euery night after supper I reed theron to hym.

b. c1000 ÆLFRIC *Deut.* xxxii. 52 þu scealt ȝeseon þæt land and þu ne cymst þær on. c1275 LAY. 7274 þar on Brutus bicom.

c. c1000 ÆLFRIC *Gen.* xxxix. 23 He ne cuðe nan þing þar on.

d. c1400 *Brut* lxviii. 64 He wondrede þeron gretly, what it myȝt bitoken.

Hence †**there'onne** (**þerone**, also 3 **þronne**) *Obs.* [after *þærinne*, etc.; in later use sometimes only a variant spelling of *thereon*] = THEREON.

c1200 ORMIN 957 þa twellfe namess ec þatt wærenn don þæronne. c1200 *Trin. Coll. Hom.* 89 Ure helende rod þerone. *Ibid.* 217 Ich wille ew segge þat ich þronne understonde. c1400 *Rowland & O.* 416 Ther-one was sett a Sercle of golde. c1420 *Anturs of Arth.* 171 þere one hertly take hede. a1425 *Cursor M.* 1938 (Trin.) Noe.. let reise an autere swiþe, þeronne [*C.* þar-on] made he sacrifise.

Also **there'onto** *adv.*, onto or upon that. *rare.*

1898 *Blackw. Mag.* Mar. 406 Thereonto throw nine hairs from the head.

thereout (ðɛərˈaʊt), *adv.* Forms: 1 **þǽr út**(**e**, ME. **þar, þer out**(**e**: also 4–5 (9 *Sc.*) **throut**(**e**. [OE. *þærút*(*e*: see THERE 17 and OUT, OUTE.]

1. Outside of that place, etc.; without. Now *rare.*

c893 K. ÆLFRED *Oros.* II. viii. §4 Nahton hie naþer ne þærinne mete ne þærute freond. c897 [see THEREINNE]. c1000 *Ags. Gosp.* Mark iii. 31 His modor and his ȝebroðra ..þar ute stodon. c1175 *Lamb. Hom.* 33 þe mon þe leie .xii. moneð in ane prisune halde he ȝefen al þet he efre mahte biȝeten wið þet he moste .xii. beo ðer ut of. c1205 LAY. 1179 Bruttus ferde in to þere temple.. & lette al his folc bilæuen þer vte. a1300 *Cursor M.* 1333 (Cott.) He.. stod þer oute [*v.rr.* þar oute, þar vte] And sagh þe thing. *Ibid.* 15934 He ..Fain wald ha ben þer vte. c1470 HENRY *Wallace* IV. 488 The ȝett he wor..; he held na man tharout. 1881 J. T. BENT *Genoa* vi. 127 A.. story current in Roman Catholic circles, but not much accredited thereout.

2. Out of doors; in the open. Now *Sc.*

a1300 *Cursor M.* 3928 Iacob.. On þe feild þar oute he lai. c1325 *Body & Soul* 214 in *Map's Poems* 349 For alle owre toures heye, ligge we shule throute In forstes ant in snowes. c1400 MAUNDEV. (Roxb.) xxvii. 125 þe comouns.. er all hird men and lyez þeroute in logez. c1440 *Pallad. on Husb.* I. 896, x crabbes yf thou kest with watir in an erthen potte ywrie, Ten dayis throut [L. *subdivo*], vntil the vapur die. 1483 *Cath. Angl.* 382/1 Tharovte, *subdiuo .i. sub nudo Aere.* 1572 *Satir. Poems Reform.* xxxiii. 300 Lang time thay lay thairout. 1808–18 JAMIESON s.v. *To lie thairout*, to lie in the open air during night.

b. Abroad; in existence; = OUT 26 c. *Sc.*

a1300 *Cursor M.* 1977 Quils þou may se mi rainbou þar oute, Of suilk a flod haue man na doute. c1560 A. SCOTT *Poems* (S.T.S.) xxxiv. 25 The wysest woman þairout Wt wird may be wyllt To do þe deid. 1725 RAMSAY *Gentle Sheph.* III. ii, Greater liars never ran thereout.

3. Of motion: Out of that; out from that place, etc.; forth from thence. Now *Sc.*

a1300 *Cursor M.* 4542 þe boteler to þe prisun lep, And suith þar-out he broght ioseph. 13.. *Ibid.* 2567 (Fairf.) Come now þer-oute, ȝe-halde þou þe lift a-boute. c1489 CAXTON *Sonnes of Aymon* xvi. 371 He went to the couffres, and toke ther-out all the treysour. 1533 GAU *Richt Vay* (S.T.S.) 4 Blissit be god quhilk hes helpit me thair owt. c1750 J. NELSON *Jrnl.* (1836) 58 They had better never have known the way of salvation than, after knowing it, be turned thereout.

4. From or out of that (it, them), as source or origin; thence. *arch.*

c1375 *Sc. Leg. Saints* i. (*Petrus*) 391 þe fals fend in his liknese Vith þe pupill wald spek þarowte [out of the figure]. 1535 COVERDALE *Ps.* lxxii[i]. 10 And there out sucke they no small auauntage. 1650 EARL MONM. tr. *Senault's Man bec. Guilty* 36 They teare up the bowels of the earth to learn secrets thereout. 1783 JEFFERSON *Wks.* (1859) II. 353 On condition that he may retain thereout one hundred and eighty thousand guilders. 1865 KINGSLEY *Herew.* ix, With the divine instinct of freedom, and all the self-help and energy which spring thereout. 1871 B. TAYLOR *Faust* (1875) I. viii. 120 As oft as he drank thereout.

thereover (ðɛərˈəʊvə(r)), *adv. arch.* [OE. *ðǽrofer*, ME. *þer, þar ouer*: see THERE 17 and OVER *prep.*]

1. Over or above that, in position (or in transit; also in charge, rank, number or amount).

c897 K. ÆLFRED *Gregory's Past. C.* xlv. 336 Ne he self nanne wæstm ðærofer ne bireð. c1000 *Ags. Gosp.* Matt. xxvii. 35 Hiȝ to-dældon hys reaf and wurpon hlot þær ofer. c1220 *Bestiary* 64 Đer ouer he fleȝeð. a1300 *Cursor M.* 4157 þer ouer standes a mikel tre. c1400 MAUNDEV. (Roxb.) xviii. 85 He berez it to þe kyng and makes þar ower many blissings. 1535 COVERDALE *1 Chron.* xxiv. [xxiii.] 17 But yᵉ children of Rehabia were many therouer. 1558 PHAER *Æneid* VI. Qj, Therouer dare no bird attempt to flie, for deadly dout. 1870 MORRIS *Earthly Par.* III. IV. 235 In a dark blue kirtle was he clad, And a grey cloak thereover. 1905 *Contemp. Rev.* Feb. 208 To drive Man out of Paradise, and to keep watch thereover.

2. *fig.* In reference to that (which is under consideration or observation, or is the object of occupation, discourse, or attention: see OVER *prep.* 4).

1535 COVERDALE *Ecclus.* xxxiv. 12, I.. came oft in parell of death therouer, tyll I was delyuered from it. —— *John* vi. 41 Then murmured the Iewes ther ouer, that he sayde: I am yᵗ bred which is come downe from heauen. 1870 MORRIS *Earthly Par.* II. III. 355 He.. smiled to see his deep-set eyes and grave Gleam out with joy thereover.

thereright (ðɛəˈraɪt), *adv. Obs.* exc. *dial.* [OE. *'þǽr rihte* (two words): see THERE 17 and RIGHT *adv.* 7 b. Cf. HERERIGHT.] Straightway, forthwith; there on the spot.

971 *Blickl. Hom.* 221 þa eode he ðær rihte biȝ on sume stowe. c1000 ÆLFRIC *Gram.* xxxviii. (Z.) 233 *Statim*, þar rihte. c1205 LAY. 25676 Nu fulle feowertene niht þe feond heo hafueð ilaðet þer riht [*c* 1275 forþ riht]. 1628 HOBBES *Thucyd.* (1822) 92 Because their virtue was thought extraordinary [they] were therefore buried thereright. a1656 USSHER *Ann.* vi. (1658) 392 And they with their naked swords threatened to kill them there-right, unless they returned to the fight. 1675 HOBBES *Odyss.* 112 On me.. Bestow'd a ram, which on the sand there-right I made a sacrifice to mighty Jove. 1896 *Cheltenham Exam.* 12 Feb. 8 (E.D.D.) Er picked un up thurrite un went. 1898 T. HARDY *Wessex Poems* 204 Till he comes to the orchet, when crooping there-right.. His lonesome young Bartree appears.

So †**there'rights** *adv.*, OE. **þǽr rihtes** [with advb. genitive], in same sense.

a1100 *Ags. Hymns* (Surtees) 92 Pacemque dones protinus [*gloss*] & sibbe þu selle þær rihtes. *Ibid.* 113 Ascendant.. protinus Ad thronum..[*gloss*] Astiȝan.. þær rihtes to þrymsetle. c1175 *Lamb. Hom.* 33 þerihtes he ne bið.

Theresian, variant of TERESIAN.

†**there'teken, þer'teken**, *adv. Obs.* [OE. *þǽr tó éacan*, i.e. *þǽr*, THERE 17 and *tó éacan*, TEKE, TEKEN.] In addition to that; besides that.

c1000 ÆLFRIC *Hom.* II. 84 Hu he urum gyltum miltsað, and ðær to eacan þæt heofenlice rice behæt. a1120 *O.E. Chron.* an. 1091, þær to eacan. a1225 *Ancr. R.* 174 þe nome of Hester ne seið nout one, 'abscondita',.. auh deð þer teken, 'eleuata in populis'. a1300 *Havelok* 2878 She is fayr, and she is fre,.. þertekene she is wel with me.

therethrough (ðɛəˈθruː), *adv. arch.* Forms: see THERE and THROUGH. [Early ME. *þer þurh*: see THERE 17, THROUGH *prep.*]

1. Of place: Through that, it, or them.

c1175 *Lamb. Hom.* 83 þet gles.. þe sunne schineð þer þurh. a1325 *MS. Rawl. B.* 520 lf. 32 b, [They] sullen wite þe toune.. ȝif ani vncouz passez þere þoru sal be aresteid for te amorue. 13.. *Cursor M.* 12872 (Gött.) þe fader steuen þar thoru it brast, Right als it war a thonir blast. 1495 *Trevisa's Barth. De P.R.* v. v. (W. de W.) giv/1 The glasy humour [of the eye] is.. bryghte as glasse, soo yᵗ we maye se ther thorugh. 1594 BLUNDEVIL *Exerc.* III. II. xxvii. (1636) 423 To make therethrough a navigable passage. 1672 MARVELL *Reh. Transp.* I. 55 Its Waters would not mix with this Lake ..but ran theere thorow without ever touching it. 1870 MORRIS *Earthly Par.* II. III. 232 He hurried on until he reached again The outer door, and, sighing, passed therethrough. 1873 M. COLLINS *Miranda* I. 73 The musical moan of the water as the ship cuts its way therethrough.

2. By means, or by reason, of that; thereby.

c1200 *Trin. Coll. Hom.* 189 þat he haueð þer þurh forloren heuene wele. c1200 ORMIN 2325 þatt ȝho.. shollde wurrþenn Wiþþ childe swa þatt ȝho þærþurrh Ne shollde nohht ben wemmedd. c1300 *Beket* 75 And therthurf me taȝte hire the wei: so that heo thider com. c1412 HOCCLEVE *De Reg. Princ.* 2667 His lorde þe kyng withe venym wolde he fede, So þat ther-þurgh he steruen shulde nede. 1535 COVERDALE *Ecclus.* Prol., Therfore they that.. reade it, shulde not onely them selues be wyse there thorow, but serue other also with teachinge and wrytinge. 1678 R. BARCLAY *Apol. Quakers* v. xxi. 161 Every Man.. may come there-through to believe. 1818 SCOTT *Hrt. Midl.* xliii, Ye maun be minded not to act altogether on your ain judgment, for therethrough comes sair mistakes. 1894 F. T. ELLIS *Reynard Fox* 257 Winning renown and fame therethrough.

theretill (ðɛəˈtɪl), *adv. north. dial.* and *Sc.* [ME. *þar till*: see THERE 17 and TILL *prep.*] = THERETO (in all its senses).

a1300 *Cursor M.* 887 'þe worm', sco said, 'me draf þar till'. *Ibid.* 15638 All þi wil it sal be dun, þar til i am redi. a1300 *Havelok* 1443 Castles ten, And þe lond þat þor til longes. c1330 R. BRUNNE *Chron.* (1810) 110 Heyre was he non, no þertille had resoun; þe Emperice sonne Henry he had right þertille. c1400 MAUNDEV. (Roxb.) vii. 26 By cause of þe perilous wayse þertill. c1425 WYNTOUN *Cron.* III. ix. 1080 A thousand and thre hundyr yhere And ten thare tyll. c1470 HENRY *Wallace* v. 516 Gret strenth he has, bathe wyt and grace thartill. 1562 BP. PILKINGTON *Burn. Paules Ch.* §7 It is a commen true sayinge: he that wil do no yl, must do nothinge that longes there til. a **1577** GASCOIGNE *Dan Bartholomew* Wks., *Hearbes, Weedes, &c.* (1587) 96 And signe it with my simple hand and set my seale theretil. **1819** TENNANT *Papistry Storm'd* II. (1827) 63 Wi' angry bill, and wing theretill. **1832** HENDERSON *Scot. Prov.* 158 A shower of rain in July.. Is worth a plough of owsen, and a' belangs theretill.

thereto (ðɛə'tuː, 'ðɛətʊ), *adv.* Now *formal* or *arch.* [OE. *þǽr tó, þǽrtó*: see THERE 17 and TO *prep.*] To that (or those things), to it (or them).

1. To that place, thing, affair, etc. in various senses of TO *prep.*

c **1000** ÆLFRIC *Hom.* II. 378 þæt he us ȝebringe to his ecan ȝebeorscipe, seðe þurh his to-cyme us ðærto ȝelaðode. c **1000** —— *Saints' Lives* xxv. 227 Mathathias.. ofsloh.. þæs cyningces ðeȝn þe hine ðær to neadode. a **1225** *Ancr. R.* 6 Hwoa se nimeð þing on hond and bihat hit.. to donne, heo bint hire þerto. a **1250** *Owl & Night.* 103 His nest.. þar to þu stele in o day & leydest þar on þi fule ey. **1377** LANGL. *P. Pl.* B. XVIII. 178 Moyses and meny mo mercy shullen synge; And I shal daunce þer to. c **1400** *Apol. Loll.* 34 Ne to put more þer to, ne to draw þer fro. c **1440** *Pallad. on Husb.* I. 40 Smell also therto in cas it stynke. **1445** tr. *Claudian* in *Anglia* XXVIII. 275 Where he þat is worthy is callid therto. a **1533** LD. BERNERS *Huon* lxxxi. 247 Nere therto there was a lytell wode. **1538** STARKEY *England* I. ii. 53 Such as haue byn long vsyd therto. **1611** BIBLE *Isa.* xliv. 15 He maketh it a grauen image, and falleth downe thereto. **1794** G. ADAMS *Nat. & Exp. Philos.* IV. xxxviii. 59 The edge of the disk will be perpendicular thereto. **1875** F. HALL in *Lippincott's Mag.* XVI. 749/2 All circumstances of the provocation thereto being dispassionately considered. **1892** *Law Times Rep.* LXV. 582/1 The posts.. are fixed thereto by iron dogs and dowels.

2. With words denoting pertinence, suitability, etc., expressed or implied: (Belonging, pertinent, suitable, needful) to that matter or thing; (according) therewith; for that matter, purpose, etc.

c **1000** ÆLFRIC *Hom.* II. 494 On oðre healfe stod ðæs monan cræt.. and ða oxan ðærto. c **1000** —— *Saints' Lives* xxix. 129 Ures hælendes ȝerip mæniȝ-feald is.. and feawa wyrhtan þæ r-to. c **1305** *St. Andrew* 33 in *E.E.P.* (1862) 99 Hou miȝte hit beo, þat his wille were þerto? c **1425** *Eng. Conq. Irel.* 6 His hert was mych there-to. **1454** *E.E. Wills* (1882) 133 My bed of grene sylke, wiþ the testour & Canape ther-to. c **1485** *Digby Myst.* I. 24 If our cunnyng be ther-too. **1539** TONSTALL *Serm. Palm Sund.* (1823) 86 Hauynge tyme therto. **1556** *Aberdeen Regr.* (1848) I. 294 All materiallis neidfull therto. **1626** GOUGE *Serm. Dignity Chivalry* §4 Preparation for Warre, Exercises thereto. **1748** G. WHITE *Serm.* (MS.), Nothing more is needful thereto. **1871** BROWNING *Pr. Hohenst.-Schw.* 643 Now for the means thereto.

3. Added to that, in addition to that; besides, also, moreover. Now *arch.* and *poet.*

a **900** tr. *Bæda's Hist.* III. xiv. [xvii.] (1890) 202 Nowiht agnes.. butan his cyricean and þær to feower æceras. c **1000** ÆLFRIC *De Vet. Test.* (Gr.) 14 Ic ȝesett hæbbe.. wel feowertiȝ larspella on Engliscum ȝeorde and sumne eacan þær to. a **1121** *O.E. Chron.* an. 1102, Se eorl Rotbert.. hæfde þone eorldom her on lande on Scrobbesbyriȝ.. & micel rice þær to. c **1175** *Lamb. Hom.* 67 His apostles.. and monie oðre þere to. c **1386** CHAUCER *Prol.* 153 A Prioresse.. Hir mouth ful smal, and ther to softe and reed. *Ibid.* 353. —— *Squire's T.* II. a **1450** *Knt. de la Tour* 103 To falle from richesse into lowe astate, and thereto pouerte. **1587** GOLDING *De Mornay* xi. (1592) 160 Man reasoneth and discourseth, because he is Man: and were he thereto vnchangeable, he were a God. **1633** P. FLETCHER *Purple Isl.* XI. xlvi, Thereto of substance strange, so thinne and slight. **1830** TENNYSON *Talking Oak* 196, I would have paid her kiss for kiss, With usury thereto. **1887** MORRIS *Odyss.* XI. 287 As Cromius and Nestor,.. And thereto the glorious Pero.

theretofore (ˌðɛətʊ'fɔə(r)), *adv.* Now *formal.* [ME. *þer tofore*: see THERE 17 and TOFORE *adv.*] Before that time; previously to that.

c **1350** *Will. Palerne* 2611 þei.. wist þat þai in wast wrouȝt þer to-fore. **1430–40** LYDG. *Bochas* VIII. i. (MS. Bodl. 263) 368/2 Emperors reknid for ther toforn was non. **1791** in Picton *L'pool Munic. Rec.* (1886) II. 205 The By-laws theretofore made. **1851** GLADSTONE *Glean.* (1879) VI. 4 A judgment that alienated dissenting endowments from purposes to which they had theretofore been applied. **1894** *State Trials* (N.S.) VI. 410 According to the canonical practice theretofore observed in England.

there'toward, *adv. rare.* [ME. *þertoward*, f. THERE 17 + TOWARD *prep.*] Toward that (place, thing, matter, etc.).

a **1225** *Leg. Kath.* 1484 þat alle þ..t ter bi gað.. buhe þer toward. a **1225** *Ancr. R.* 52 Eue.. turnde hire lust þer toward, & nom & et þerof, & ȝef hire louerd. **1908** *Daily News* 29 Feb. 4 The matter of Signor Nasi's conduct, with the popular attitude theretoward.

†**thereto'yens**, *adv. Obs.* Forms: 1 **þær toȝeanes, þar toȝenes,** 3 **þer to ȝenes, þertoȝeines, þerteyens.** [Orig. two words: OE. *þær*, THERE 17, *toȝenes*, TO-GAINS; if the compound had survived till 15th c. it would have become *theretogainst.*]

1. Against or in opposition to that.

c **1000** ÆLFRIC *Hom.* I. 236 Swilce hi wislice sprecon! Ac we cweðað þær toȝeanes, þæt God is Ælmihtiȝ. a **1225** *Ancr. R.* 80 Nu we schullen sumhwat speken.. aȝein vuel speche þæt ȝe þertoȝeines tunen ower earen. **1340** *Ayenb.* 11 Huo þet deþ þerteyens be his wytinde zenȝeþ dyadliche.

2. In return for that; in exchange therefor.

1066–9 in Thorpe *Charters* (1865) 436 We habbaþ heom ȝeunnen.. and hi us þar toȝenes ȝifeþ. c **1200** *Trin. Coll. Hom.* 203 Ech man þe for mine name.. folȝeð me he shal fon þer to ȝenes hundredfeld mede.

thereunder (ðɛə'rʌndə(r)), *adv.* Now *formal.* [OE. *ðærunder*: see THERE 17 and UNDER *prep.*]

1. Under that or it; below or beneath that.

c **897** K. ÆLFRED *Gregory's Past. C.* xviii. 130 Ealle ða þe ofer oðre beoð, beoð heafdu ðara þe ðærunder beoð. c **1220** *Bestiary* 314 He draȝeð ðe neddre of ðe ston.. for it wile ðerunder gon. **13..** *Cursor M.* 28731 þe berer.. behouis it [the burden] cast him fra, Quen he mai noght þar vnder ga. c **1440** *Sir Gowther* 313 There under he made his sete. **1579** W. WILKINSON *Confut. Family of Love, Heret. Affirm.* b b, Not that they should alwayes remaine as subject thereunder. **1630** SANDERSON *Serm.* (1681) II. 311 There is no way but to submit, and to humble our selves thereunder. **1862** SMILES *Engineers* III. 358 A contract with owners of land.. for the working of the coal thereunder.

2. Under that title, heading, etc.; under the provisions, or by the authority, of that.

1617 MINSHEU *Ductor* Title-p., The Nature, Propertie, Condition.. of things there-vnder contayned. **1640** BP. HALL *Episc.* I. v. 21 The cause of those, who there-under have reformed France. **1706** in *Parish Accts. St. Julian's, Shrewsbury* II. 43 (MS.) The Assessors thereunder named or the major part of them. **1885** H. REED in *Law Rep.* 15 *Q.B. Div.* 160 The intention is that s. 125.. and the rules to be made thereunder shall constitute a complete and separate code. **1908** *Times* 6 May 17/3 Royalties paid thereunder were to be paid to the publishers.

3. Under or less than that (number, age, etc.).

1535 COVERDALE *1 Chron.* xxvii. 23 Them that were twentye yeare olde and there vnder.

†**thereun'till**, *adv. Obs.* [f. THERE 17 + UNTIL *prep.*] = THEREUNTO.

13.. *Cursor M.* 1066 (Gött.) Vr lauerd loked noght þar vntill [*Cott.* þar till].

thereunto (ðɛərʌn'tuː, -'ʌntʊ), *adv. arch.* [f. THERE 17 + UNTO *prep.*]

1. Unto or to that place; unto that thing, matter, subject, etc.

13.. *Cursor M.* 3717 (Gött.) Hir moder consail was þar vnto [*rime* do; *v.r.* þar to]. **1474** *Rolls of Parlt.* VI. 113/1 The said sommes.. shuld be restored.. to every persone.. that had payed therunto. **1568** GRAFTON *Chron.* II. 395 To make the offense the greater, he added much therevnto. a **1661** FULLER *Worthies, Surrey* (1662) III. 87, I am affraied that our Infidel Age will not give credit thereunto. **1713** WARDER *True Amazons* (ed. 2) 105 Many cannot attain thereunto. **1875** MYERS *Poems* (ed. 4) 89 When God had brought me thereunto.

†**2.** In addition to that; = THERETO 3. *Obs.*

1567 DRANT *Horace, Epist.* To Rdr. *v, A sillye translator rythmical and thervnto an harde wryter. **1678** WANLEY *Wond. Lit. World* v. ii. §79. 472/1 Of an exceeding courage and strength, of a sharp wit, and thereunto very fortunate.

†**there'up**, *adv. Obs.* Forms: see THERE and UP; also 3 **þruppe.** [Late OE. *þǽr uppan* (*þǽr* there, *uppan* upon, on) would give ME. **þer uppen, þeruppe*, and in 14th c. *þerup*; but these might also be new formations from *uppe*, UP.]

1. Up on that, upon that (place or thing); up in or into that place; up there, up above. In quots. c 1230, above (on the page or in the document).

α. c **1000** ÆLFRIC *Saints' Lives* xxx. 200 Him wæs his myxen forlæten þæt he þær uppan sittan mihte. c **1230** *Hali Meid.* 39 Ich habbe ihalden mine beheaste þruppe. *Ibid.*, Forsac þi fader hus as hit is þeruppe iopenet. c **1250** *Gen. & Ex.* 1609 Ðe louerd ðor uppe a-buuen Lened ðor on. c **1300** *St. Brandan* 123 Bord and cloth i-sprad, And bred and fisch ther uppe. c **1315** SHOREHAM i. 41 Howe mey þat be? wo dar þer oppe steiȝe?

β. **1572** BUCHANAN *Detect. Q. Mary* U iij, I haue wakit laiter thairvp [Fr. *là haut*] then I wald haue done, if it had nat bene [etc.]. **1829** A. CLARKE in *Life* xiii. (1840) 478 Collectors.. to take silver from all who should go thereup.

2. = THEREUPON 2, 3.

α. a **1225** *Ancr. R.* 42 Hwo se wule mei a-stunten þeruppe anon rihtes efter þe uorme ureisun. c **1290** *Beket* 447 in *S. Eng. Leg.* I. 119 Heo wollez þanne mis-don al day and beon þare-oppe wel bolde. **1297** R. GLOUC. (Rolls) 8084 [Robert] borewede þer uppe [*v.r.* c 1400 þer vpon] of him an hondred þousend marc. a **1325** *MS. Rawl. B.* 520 lf. 32 þat a non riȝt.. be i-mad so uers siute þer oppe fram toune to toune.

β. **1375** (*MS.* 1487) BARBOUR *Bruce* x. 433 Sic melle tharup can he mak. **1430** W. PASTON in *P. Lett.* I. 30 And there up to graunte your worthy lettres.

3. Over and above that, in addition to that.

1297 R. GLOUC. (Rolls) 716 3if þou wole ȝut þer vppe more esse [= ask] & wite of me. *Ibid.* 1085 þanne aȝt it be inou.. Loue & frendssipe to aski us.. þei þou ne askedest þer vppe þralhede euere mo.

thereupon (ðɛərə'pɒn, 'ðɛərəpɒn), *adv.* Forms: see THERE and UPON. [In ME. two (or three) words.]

1. Upon that or it (of position or motion, *lit.* or *fig.*). *arch.* or *formal.*

c **1175** *Lamb. Hom.* 53 þes riche men.. liggeð þer uppon alse þe tadde deð in þere eorðe. a **1225** *St. Marher.* 21 Cume þe sunfule mon ant legge his mud þer up on. a **1300** *Cursor M.* 18565 þar apon þai did þair sele. c **1400** *Brut* 103 þat euery man miȝt.. pereoppon loke. c **1400** *Destr. Troy* 8447, Yche lede, þat leuys þerapon. **1588** A. KING tr. *Canisius' Catech.* h ij b, Ye sonday.. callit ye day of our Lord, because of his resurrection yairvpon. **1716** *Lond. Gaz.* No. 5480/1 The Goods and Merchandizes laden thereupon. a **1774** TUCKER *Lt. Nat.* (1834) II. 679 If any man thinks he has.. formed his own speculative plan thereupon.

†**b.** Alongside of that. *Obs.*

c **1275** LAY. 12423 Hii bi-gonne.. anne swiþe deope dich, and þar vp on oueral one stonene wal. **1652** NEEDHAM *Selden's Mare Cl.* To Rdr., Divers Potent Princes.. who have.. large territories lying thereupon [on the sea].

†**c.** = THEREABOUTS 2 b. *Sc. Obs.*

1649 BP. GUTHRIE *Mem.* (1702) 72 Standing in the Close, with 60 Gentlemen or thereupon about him.

2. Upon that (in time or order); on that being done or said; (directly) after that.

13.. *Cursor M.* 4945 (Gött.) Mete and drinck i gaf þaim bath,.. And þar apon [*C.* þar on] stale [*C.* þai] þus mi thing. c **1400** [see THEREUP 2, quot. 1297]. **1499** BP. R. FOX in *Lett. Rich. III & Hen. VII* (Rolls) II. 85 [He] wilbe with you at Michaelmas or soone thereupon. **1526** *Pilgr. Perf.* (W. de W. 1531) 1 b, Thervpon I begon after my poore maner to wryte in latyn. **1651** HOBBES *Leviath.* II. xxvii. 159 If thereupon he accept Duell. **1891** *Law Times* XCII. 104/2 For the purposes of the argument and the decision following thereupon.

b. On that ground; in consequence of that. *arch.*

1534 STARKEY *Let. to Cromwell* in *England* (1878) p. x, So therapon wyth your beneuolent mynd you may set forward somewhat better my purpos. **1590** SHAKS. *Com. Err.* v. i. 388, I was tane for him, and he for me, And thereupon these errors are arose. **1766** BLACKSTONE *Comm.* II. xviii. 281 In some particular countries, by local custom, where other trees [than oak, ash, and elm] are generally used for building, they are thereupon considered as timber. **1851** RUSKIN *Stones Ven.* I. Pref. 5 It had been fitted up for somebody's reception, and been thereupon fresh painted.

3. On that subject or matter; with reference to that (it, them); thereanent. *arch.* or *formal.*

1414 *Rolls of Parlt.* IV. 22/2 That ther never be no Lawe made ther uppon. **1439** in *Archæologia* XXI. 35 After þe.. Kynges lettres patentz ther upon made. a **1557** *Diurn. Occur.* (1833) 34 The erle Bothwell.. tuke thame to Abirlady, and disponit thairvpone at his pleasour. **1695** *Enq. Anc. Const. Eng.* 39 Upon a legal process issued out thereupon. **1781** H. GATES in Sparks *Corr. Amer. Rev.* III. 420, I should have been happy to know your sentiments thereupon. **1905** *Sat. Rev.* 23 Dec. 814/2 As the.. reports.. interest.. teachers I venture to address you thereupon.

'thereward, *adv. rare*$^{-1}$. [f. THERE *adv.* + -WARD.] = THERETOWARD *adv.*

1922 JOYCE *Ulysses* 378 Thereward carrying desire immense among all one another.

†**there'while**, *adv. Obs.* Forms: see THERE and WHILE. [ME. *þer hwile*, analysis not certain, but app. repr. an OE. (*on*) *þǽre hwíle* 'in that time', and thus, practically = the more usual *the while*, OE. *þá hwíle.*

þer hwile had evidently come to be apprehended as a whole, and taken as an adv. before 1250, when it appears with advb. genitive *-es, -s*: see next. Cf. *the while* (OE.), *the whiles* c 1300, and the later *while, whiles*, advbs., both c 1300.]

a. During the time that; whilst; so long as. **b.** During that time; the while; meanwhile.

c **1220** *Bestiary* (in *O.E. Misc.*) 784 Ne dar he stiren, ne noman deren, Ðer wile he laȝe and luue beren. **1340** *Ayenb.* 213 þer huile þet ich me solaci an playe, iche ne þenche none manne kuead. a **1400–50** *Alexander* 157 Many was þe bald berne at banned þar quile þat euer he dured þat day. c **1430** *Life St. Kath.* Cont. (1884) 3 How þe Emperour.. ther whyle sent pryue lettres. **1575** Q. ELIZ. in *Harington's Nugæ Ant.* (ed. Park 1804) I. 126 Their-while I prepair my selffe to welcome deathe. **1617** HIERON *Wks.* II. 66 What becommeth of the Spirit of God therewhile? Is it lost?

†**there'whiles, -'whilst**, *adv. Obs.* [f. prec. with *-s* of advb. genitive, subseq. made *-st*: see WHILST.] = prec.

α. c **1250** *Gen. & Ex.* 1282 Ðor quiles he wunede in bersabe, So was ysaaces eld [etc.]. c **1320** R. BRUNNE *Medit.* 367, Y kepte hem þyrwhylys y was with hem. **1340** *Ayenb.* 194 Offre to god worþi offringe þerhuyls þet þou leuest. **1377** LANGL. *P. Pl.* B. VII. 8 What sholde we wommen worche þere whiles? c **1491** CAXTON *Chast. Goddes Chyld.* 28 There whiles he may not be unied to god by cause he liueth in all contraryousnes. a **1557** MRS. M. BASSET tr. *More's Treat. Passion* M.'s Wks. 1376/2 Which is priuely emplied in euery thing he doth therwiles.

β. a **1541** WYATT *Penit. Ps.* xxxvii. 57 Therewhilst shall fail these wicked men therefore. **1587** FLEMING *Contn. Holinshed* III. 976/1 The lord Greie.. bad him repeat his message, and therwhilest made a clearke.. to write the same *Verbatim.* **1603** FLORIO *Montaigne* I. xxx. (1632) 103 Their women busie themselves therewhil'st with warming of their drinke.

therewith (ðɛə'wɪθ, ðɛəwɪð *with shifting stress*), *adv.* Now *formal* or *arch.* [OE. *þǽr wiþ, ðærwið*, f. *þǽr*, THERE 17 + *wið*, WITH *prep.*]

†**1.** Against that (or those); in opposition to that; in return for that. *Obs.*

c **1000** ÆLFRIC *Gen.* xlvii. 16 Drifað hider eowre orf,.. and ic sylle eow þær wið mete. a **1200** *Moral Ode* 300 Warnie [elc man] æc his frend þer wið so ic habbe mine. c **1220** *Bestiary* 383 Mikel ned, ðat we ðar wið ne dillen. c **1300** *Cursor M.* 28109, I said not ans þar wit nai.

2. With that (or those) as accompaniment, adjunct, etc.; together or in company with that (and in allied senses of *with*).

c **888** K. ÆLFRED *Boeth.* xxxiii. §5 Swaþeah hi sint ðærwið ȝemengde. a **1300** *Cursor M.* 7262 [Samson] slogh his faas, him-self þar with. **1340** HAMPOLE *Pr. Consc.* 1751 þai sal fele þar many a ded brayde, Bot þai sal ay lyf þar with. **1599** DAVIES *Immort. Soul* I. xxiii, All things.. We seeke to know, and how therewith to do. **1885** *Law Rep.* 14 *Q.B. Div.* 246 At right angles therewith. **1886** SPURGEON *Treas. David* Ps. cxxxii. 10 Every person connected therewith. **1907** ILLINGWORTH *Doctr. Trin.* iii. 44 The.. historical accuracy of the Acts has been amply revindicated.., and therewith the value of its evidence. **1910** *Act 10 Edw. VII*, c. 38 Sched. B, For Old Age Pensions.. and for certain Administration Expenses in connection therewith £500,000.

b. In addition to that; besides, withal.

a **1300** *Cursor M.* 2204 Nembrot.. O babilon king, stijf in stur, And þer wit [*v.rr.* þar-wid, -wiþ] was he gret werrur. *c* **1400** MAUNDEV. (Roxb.) xii. 50 þe water of þis see es full bitter and salt þarwith. **1886** KIPLING *Departm. Ditties*, etc. (1899) 41 Pagett, M.P., was a liar, and a fluent liar therewith.

c. With that (word, act, or occurrence); that being said or done; thereat, thereupon, forthwith.

c **1369** CHAUCER *Dethe Blaunche* 275 Y fil aslepe, and therewith evene Me mette so ynly swete a swevene. **1377** LANGL. *P. Pl.* B. XIX. 479 þe vyker.. toke his leue, And I awakned þere with. *a* **1425** *Cursor M.* 10462 (Trin.) Vtayne þer wiþ [*G.* wid þis word] gon to tene. **1512** R. COPLAND *Helyas* (1827) 76 Therwith the king and the quene went and kyssed theyr sonne Helias. **1517** TORKINGTON *Pilgr.* (1884) 33 And ther with they con ner hym. **1868** MORRIS *Earthly Par.*, *Man born to be King* 107 Therewith he rose And led the way unto a close.

3. With that as instrument; by means of that.

c **1250** *Gen. & Ex.* 379 Two pilches weren.. to Adam and to Eue broȝt, Ðor wið he ben nu boðen srid, And here same sumdel is hid. **1297** R. GLOUC. (Rolls) 3828 Is suerd he drou þere Vor to asaile him þerwiþ. *c* **1400** *Brut* ccviii. 238 þai toke stone, and made þerwiþ þe tour. **1526** TINDALE *Jas.* iii. 9 The tonge.. Therwith blesse we God the father and therwith cursse we men which are made vnto the similitude off God. **1579** LANGHAM *Gard. Health* (1633) 437 Whether fish or birds be taken therewith. **1725** *Bradley's Fam. Dict.* s.v. *Mint*, If you bathe the affected Part therewith.

b. With that as cause or occasion; on account of or because of that; in consequence of that.

c **1440** *Jacob's Well* 300 Whan þe flesch sufferyth penauns or hardnesse, it grucchyth þer wyth. *c* **1500** *Melusine* 360 Hys bretheren and the baronnye þere were abasshed ther-with. **1526** TINDALE *1 Tim.* vi. 9 When we have fode and rayment, let vs theirwith be content. **1579** SPENSER *Sheph. Cal.* Mar. 94 Therewith affrayd I ranne away. **1792** COWPER *Let. to J. Johnson* 5 Nov., I have finished the Sonnet.. and sent it to Hayley, who is well pleased therewith.

therewithal (ðɛəwɪˈðɔːl), *adv. arch.* [Orig. two words, THERE 17 and WITHAL *adv.*]

1. Along with or together with that; besides, or in addition to that (fact, circumstance, etc.); with all that; over and above that; = THEREWITH 2, 2 b.

c **1330** R. BRUNNE *Chron. Wace* (Rolls) 11915 Nys non on lyue... þat semeþ so wel his beryng, Ne so curteys þer wyþ-al. *c* **1386** CHAUCER *Wife's Prol.* 773 And ther with al he knew of mo prouerbes Than in this world ther growen gras or herbes. **1490** CAXTON *Eneydos* xxix. 112 A whyte coloure, with a bryght hew there with alle. **1591** SHAKS. *Two Gent.* IV. iv. 90 Giue her that Ring, and therewithall This letter. **1620** VENNER *Via Recta* vi. (1637) 113 A couple of potched Egges, ..eating therewithall a little Bread and Butter. **1809** MALKIN *Gil Blas* XI. xi. (Rtldg.) 414 He was to make a voyage, and as he hoped, his fortune there-withal. *a* **1850** ROSSETTI *Dante & Circ.* I. (1874) 250 False hopes, true poverty, and therewithal The blinded judgment of a host of friends.

2. That being said or done; = THEREWITH 2 c.

a **1300** *Cursor M.* 1117 Caym.. wend [h]a scaped þar wit alle [*G.* þar wid all]. **1375** BARBOUR *Bruce* v. 252, 'I grant', he said; and thar with all He lowtit, and his leyf has tane. *c* **1475** *Rauf Coilȝear* 151 He stakkerit thair with all Half the breid of the hall. *c* **1570** *Pride & Lowl.* (1841) 20 What then? .. Quoth he; and therewithal he swore an oath. **1663** BLAIR *Autobiog.* iii. (1848) 55 Therewithal, stretching out both his arms, drew in my head to his bosom. **1801** WORDSW. *Troilus & Cr.* 8 And therewithal to cover his intent A cause he found into the Town to go. **1879** BUTCHER & LANG *Odyss.* xv. 255 He had signed silently to the woman and therewithal gat him away to the hollow ship.

†**3.** With that; = THEREWITH 3. *Obs.*

1490 CAXTON *Eneydos* lx. 159 He toke hys hand fulle of erthe.. and fylled hys throte therwithalle. **1577** B. GOOGE *Heresbach's Husb.* I. (1586) 43 Make plaister, and washe therewithall the walles within. **1656** EARL MONM. tr. *Boccalini's Advts. fr. Parnass.* I. xxvi. (1674) 28 [He] throwing off his Royal Cloak.. would therewithall have covered that beautiful Lady.

therewithin (ðɛəwɪˈðɪn), *adv. arch.* [Early ME. two words, *þer wiðinnen, wiþinne*, = THERE 17 and OE. *wiðinnan*, WITHIN: cf. THEREINNE, THEREIN.] Within or into that place; within there.

c **1200** *Trin. Coll. Hom.* 115 þe engles þe þer wiðinnen weren. *c* **1320** *Cast. Love* 771 Neuer synne þer wiþ Inne com. **1375** BARBOUR *Bruce* III. 446 þai na mete þar within had. **1447** *Shillingford Lett.* (Camden) 104 Eny persone dwelling there withynne. **1885** TENNYSON *Prol. to Gen. Hamley* 15 Therewithin a guest may make True cheer. **1892** C. E. NORTON *Dante's Paradise* v. 27.

therf, therf-cake: see THARF, THARF-CAKE.

therfor(e, -fro, -from, (-geyn), -hence, obs. ff. THEREFORE, -FRO, -FROM, -GAIN, -HENCE.

theriac (ˈθɪərɪæk), *sb.* (*a.*) *arch.* Forms: α. (1 tyriaca); 6– theriace, 7–8 theriace. β. 5 tiriake, tyriake. γ. 6– theriac, 7 -ack, -aque. See also THERIACLE. [a. late L. *thēriaca, thēriacē* (med.L. *thēriacum*), a. Gr. θηριακή (ἀντίδοσις), θηριακὸν (φάρμακον), fem. and neut. of θηριακός pertaining to wild beasts or poisonous reptiles, f. θηρίον, dim. of θήρ wild beast, poisonous reptile. So F. *thériaque* (16th c. in Godef.), whence the last γ form; It., Sp. *teriaca*, Sp. *triaca*, Pr. *tiriaca*; MHG. *triak*, G. *theriak*, Du. *teriaak*: see also THERIACLE.] An antidote to poison, esp. to the bite of a venomous serpent; = TREACLE *sb.* 1.

The flesh of the viper was formerly held to be a necessary ingredient of the antidote to its bite (see quot. 1608); hence many references in the fig. uses of *theriac* and *treacle*.

α. [*c* **1000** *Sax. Leechd.* II. 175 Tyriaca is god drenc wiþ innoþ tydernessum. *Ibid.* 290 Nime þonne ane lytle snæd þæs tyriacan & ȝemenge.] **1562** BULLEYN *Bulwark, Dial. Soarnes & Chir.* (1573) 59 Take Theriaca of the making of Andromachus,.. which is a Triacle incomperable. **1601** HOLLAND *Pliny* XXIX. i. 343 See what account there is made of a composition called Theriace [*mispr.* Theriall: *corrected in list of errata*]. **1608** TOPSELL *Serpents* (1658) 810 *Theriace*, or Triacle, not only because it cureth the venomous bitings of Serpents, but also because the Serpents themselves are usually mingled in the making thereof. **1765** *Univ. Mag.* XXXVII. 237/1 He.. took.. a large dose of theriaca with wine. [**1811** HOOPER *Med. Dict.* s.v., *Theriaca Andromachi*, the Venice or Mithridate treacle... *Theriaca communis*, common treacle, or molasses... *Theriaca Londinensis*, a cataplasm of cummin seed, bay-berries, germander, snake-root, cloves and honey.]

β. *c* **1440** *Pallad. on Husb.* III. 1100 Vyn tiriake [*v.r.* Vyntariake] is also now to make.. The bite of euery best me shal escape. *Ibid.* 1118 Also tiriake [*v.r.* Tyriake] Ys good to take and.. Heeld on theyr rootes ofte.

γ. **1568** SKEYNE *The Pest* (1860) 24 One half vnce of guid auld theriac. **1658** ROWLAND *Moufet's Theat. Ins.* 1005 Oyl of Quinces is commended as the certain Theriack for this disease. **1665–6** *Phil. Trans.* I. 160 The great number of Vipers, brought to the Grand Duke of Toscany for the composing of Theriac or Treacle. **1674** JEAKE *Arith.* (1696) bij b, As when the skilful Artist to compose His mighty Theriaque; Weighs the Critick Dose. **1751** *Student* II. 344 When the disease was young, it was mitigated with.. crabs eyes;.. theriac and vinegar. **1862** BEVERIDGE *Hist. India* I. I. v. 108 Tiriak of Khutta, a medicine.. then in high repute as an antidote. **1890** *Athenæum* 19 Apr. 496/3 Such tisane or theriac as the science of the time could furnish.

B. *adj.* = THERIACAL.

c **1440** Vyn tiriake [= med.L. *vīnum tiriacum*; see β above]. **1857** DUNGLISON *Med. Lex.* s.v. *Theriaca*, 'Theriac' and 'Theriacal' have been used adjectively for 'medicinal'.

theriacal (θiːˈraɪəkəl), *a.* [f. THERIAC + -AL¹. Cf. F. *thériacal* (15th c. in Godef. *Compl.*).] Pertaining to or of the nature of theriac; antidotal.

1603 HOLLAND *Plutarch's Mor.* 703 Who confound and mixe together minerals, herbs, theriacall trochists, made of the parts of venemous serpents, for the composition of their treacles. *Ibid.* Explan. Words, *Theriacal Trochisks*, Trosches made of vipers flesh. **1607** TOPSELL *Four-f. Beasts* (1658) 215 The heart of a Hair hath in it a theriacal virtue also. **1756–7** tr. *Keysler's Trav.* (1760) II. 131 To carry a spunge moistened with spirits of wine and a theriacal vinegar, and often to smell to it. **1857** [see prec. B].

Hence †**theriaˈcality**, theriacal quality. *rare*⁻¹.

1657 TOMLINSON *Renou's Disp.* 331 Mesucus uses it in the Electuary.. because there is some theriacality in it.

†**theˈriacle.** *Obs.* Forms: 5 tiriacle, 6 tyriakle, 7 theriacle, -cal. [a. OF. *tiriacle, ter(i)acle* (15th c. in Godef. *Compl.*), beside OF. *triacle* (12th c.); popular alterations of *tiriaque, thériaque*, THERIAC: see also TREACLE.] = THERIAC, TREACLE *sb.* 1.

c **1400** MAUNDEV. (Roxb.) xxi. 94 Tiriacle may noȝt helpe ne nan oþer medecyne. **1561** HOLLYBUSH *Hom. Apoth.* 29 Geue him.. a penyweyght of fyne Tyriakle. **1647** TRAPP *Comm. Acts* xxviii. 5 A wholesome theriacle.., or treacle, as we call it. **1681** tr. *Willis' Rem. Med. Wks.* Vocab., *Theriacal*, or treacle, a medicine.. invented against poysons. **1730–6** BAILEY (folio), *Theri'aca, Theri'ace, Theri'acle*, Treacle.

[**therial**, in recent Dicts., error for THERIAC.

Founded upon a misprint in Holland's *Pliny*, corrected in the *Errata* and in subsec. editions, but correction missed by Richardson: see quot. 1601 in THERIAC α.]

therian (ˈθɪərɪən), *a.* (*sb.*) *Zool.* [a. mod.L. *Theria* (Parker & Haswell *Textbk. Zool.* (1897) II. 448), f. Gr. θήρ, θηρίον wild beast.] Of or pertaining to the subclass Theria, one of the four subclasses into which the class Mammalia is commonly divided. Also as *sb.*, a placental or marsupial mammal belonging to this subclass.

1960 *McGraw-Hill Encycl. Sci. & Technol.* XIII. 549/2 Therian mammals are characterized by the distinctive structural history of the molar teeth. **1971** *Nature* 23 Apr. 506/1 The 'cochlea' in birds and reptiles is only slightly curved, in contrast to the tightly coiled cochlea of therian mammals. **1974** D. & M. WEBSTER *Compar. Vertebr. Morphol.* v. 99 The more generalized therians have a clavicle, extending ventromedially and articulating with the anterior portion of the sternum. **1977** *Sci. Amer.* Aug. 79/3 The marsupials have retained the basic ancestral therian reproductive pattern.

Thericlean (θɛrɪˈkliːən), *a.* [f. L. *Thēriclē-us* adj., a. Gr. Θηρίκλει-ος made by Thericles, a famous Corinthian potter: see -AN.] Of Thericles; of the form or kind made by Thericles, as a cup.

1692 R. L'ESTRANGE *Josephus, Antiq.* IX. i. (1733) 278 Vessels that Nebuchadnezzar carry'd away from the Temple at Jerusalem to be sent back and restor'd; that is to say.. fifty golden Vessels all thericlean Cups, and four hundred silver ones. **1703** ROWE *Ulyss.* Prol. 13 They sent her Billets doux, and presents many Of ancient Tea and Thericlean China. [**1857** BIRCH *Anc. Pottery* (1858) II. 107 The *Thericleios* was a kind of cup invented by Thericles, a Corinthian potter, the contemporary of Aristophanes.]

‖**Theridion** (θiːˈrɪdɪən), **-ium** (-ɪəm). *Zool.* [mod.L. a. Gr. θηρίδιον little animal, dim. of θήρ wild beast.] A genus of spiders, many of which spin webs of irregularly intersecting threads.

1861 HULME tr. *Moquin-Tandon* II. v. ii. 261 Spiders... The most important are—1, the Mygales;..2, the Clubiones;..3, the Theridions, especially the Malmignatte of Corsica and Italy, and the Mactans of South America.

therin, -inne, etc.: see THEREIN.

therio- (θɪərɪəʊ), before a vowel **theri-** (θɪərɪ), representing Gr. θηριο-, combining form of θηρίον, dim. of θήρ wild beast; forming the first element in some scientific and other words. **therianˈthropic** *a.* [Gr. ἄνθρωπος man], combining the form of a beast with that of a man; of or pertaining to deities represented in the combined forms of man and beast, as dog- or eagle-headed divinities. **theriˈanthropism**, representation or worship of therianthropic deities (*Funk's Stand. Dict.* 1895). **ˈtheriodont** [Gr. ὀδούς, ὀδοντ- tooth], a fossil reptile with teeth of a mammalian type, *spec.* one of the order *Theriodontia*; also *attrib.* or as *adj.* **theriˈolatry**, the worship of beasts, or of theriomorphic deities. †**therioˈlogic**, †**-ical** *adjs. rare*, of or pertaining to the scientific study of beasts; zoological. **ˈtheriomancy** [-MANCY], divination from the movements of animals. **therioˈmaniac**, *nonce-wd.*, one who has a mania for hunting wild beasts. **ˈtheriopod** *a.* and *sb.* = THEROPOD (*Cent. Dict.* 1891). **theriˈotomy** [Gr. τομή cutting], the dissection or anatomy of beasts; zootomy. **therioˈtrophical** *a.* [Gr. τροφικ-ός nursing], concerning the nursing or rearing (of man) by beasts. **therioˈzoic** *a.* [ZOIC], of or belonging to a period in human history anterior to the domestication of animals.

1886 C. P. TIELE in *Encycl. Brit.* XX. 367/2 Religions, in which animistic ideas still play a prominent part, but which have grown up to a *therianthropic polytheism. **1876** OWEN in *Q. Jrnl. Geol. Soc.* XXXII. 352 (*title*) Evidences of *Theriodonts in Permian Deposits elsewhere [etc.]. *Ibid.* 356 It is to the Theriodont, not the Labyrinthodont order that such humerus must be referred. **1877** LE CONTE *Elem. Geol.* (1879) 410 Remarkable reptiles,.. which from some mammalian characters, especially in the teeth, he [Owen] calls Theriodonts (beast tooth). **1905** *Athenæum* 25 Feb. 246/3 On.. the Anatomy of a Theriodont Reptile. **1897** *Edin. Rev.* July 239 He rightly declines to trace back all *theriolatry to totemism. [**1620** ALSTED *Encycl.* 625 Physiognomia *theriologica est bestiarum.] **1697** EVELYN *Numism.* viii. 296 Compares this Theriologic Physiognomy and resemblance of Brutes. **1653** R. SANDERS *Physiogn.* b ij, I have dispatcht all the parts of Physiognomie except the *Theriological part. **1652** GAULE *Magastrom.* xix. 165 *Theriomancy, [divining] by Beasts. **1845** FORD *Handbk. Spain* II. xi. 751/2 Portraits of *theriomaniac Austrian royalty. **1857** DUNGLISON *Med. Lex.*, **Theriotomy*, zootomy. **1845** FORD *Handbk. Spain* I. vii. 535/1 These *theriotrophical legends are of all countries; thus Habis, king of Spain, was reared by a doe. **1898** SIR H. HOWORTH in *Nat. Sc.* Apr. 269 To separate the *Theriozoic beds into two series.

theriodic (θɪərɪˈɒdɪk), *a. rare*⁻⁰. [f. Gr. θηριωδία brutality, savagery + -IC.] Of ulcers, etc., Malignant.

1899 in *Syd. Soc. Lex.* **1909** in *Cent. Dict.*, *Suppl.*

theriomorph (ˈθɪərɪəʊmɔːf), *sb.* and *a.* [f. THERIO- + -MORPH; cf. THERIOMORPHIC *a.*]

A. *sb.* **a.** A representation of an animal form in art.

1913 [see ANTHROPOMORPH]. **1928** V. G. CHILDE *Most Anc. East* iv. 84 Some theriomorphs are made of just those variegated stones.

b. = THEROMORPH. Also *fig.*

1920 H. G. WELLS *Outl. Hist.* I. vi. 24/1 These little Theriomorphs, these ancestral mammals, developed hair. **1934** A. J. TOYNBEE *Study of Hist.* III. 194 But he [*sc.* Wells] comes to grief in the recent annals of our own Western history when he has to size up that singularly etherialized theriomorph William Ewart Gladstone.

B. *adj.* Having the form or characteristics of a beast.

1969 H. ARENDT *On Violence* (1970) 60 Why should we, after having 'eliminated' all anthropomorphisms from animal psychology (whether we actually succeeded is another matter), now try to discover 'how "theriomorph" man is'?

theriomorphic (θɪərɪəʊˈmɔːfɪk), *a.* [f. THERIO- + Gr. μορφή form + -IC: cf. MORPHIC.] Having the form of a beast; also *transf.* of or pertaining to a deity worshipped in the form of a beast.

1882 *Sat. Rev.* 21 Jan. 71 The process by which Theriomorphic became Anthropomorphic Gods is.. sufficiently illustrated in early religions. **1884** E. H. PLUMPTRE in *Expositor* July 4 The 'abominations' of the Egyptian theriomorphic worship. **1890** L. R. FARNELL in *Oxf. Phil. Soc. Tr.* 7 Feb. 9 The perfectly human God, the transition from a.. vaguer and often theriomorphic conception of him. **1898** *Q. Rev.* July 103 An elaborate cult of bestial gods, or at least a theriomorphic ritual.

So **theriomorphosis** (-ˈmɔːfəʊsɪs, -mɔːˈfəʊsɪs), transformation into the shape of a beast; **therioˈmorphous** *a.*, (*a*) = THERIOMORPHIC;

(*b*) *Zool.* of or pertaining to the *Theriomorpha*, in Owen's classification, a suborder of *Batrachia*; also in *Palæont.* resembling a quadruped or mammal, as 'the theriomorphous reptiles of the Permian period'.

1865 BARING-GOULD *Werewolves* x. 172 The phase of transition from theriomorphosis to anthropomorphosis.

theriomorphism (ˌθɪərɪəʊˈmɔːfɪz(ə)m). [f. THERIO- + -MORPHISM; cf. THERIOMORPHIC *a.*] The ascription to God or to a god of the form or characteristics of a beast.

1908 *Encycl. Relig. & Ethics* I. 538/1 The Annamese believes in .. beings who can pass from one genus or species to another under certain conditions of space and time. Hence theriomorphism and totemism. **1912** H. M. CHADWICK *Heroic Age* vi. 125 It may be remarked in passing that theriomorphism plays a very prominent part in the religious practices and conceptions of primitive peoples, and .. we hear not unfrequently of a struggle between a god or national hero and some theriomorphic being whose sanctuary or attributes he appears to have taken over. **1930** A. S. PRINGLE-PATTISON *Stud. Philos. of Relig.* vi. 75 Theriomorphism seems .. to precede anthropomorphism, and it is only gradually that the gods are humanized. **1969** *Times Lit. Suppl.* 11 Dec. 1431 The Charollais becomes the focal-point for a manic, if short-lived, cult of theriomorphism. **1982** *Jrnl. Indo-European Stud.* X. 159 Volos is subsumed by theriomorphism .. heavenly bodies .. fertility .. and the realm of life.

† **therk**, *a.* *Obs.* Forms: 3 **ðherk**, 4–5 **þerke**, 5 **therk, thirke, thyrke**, 7 **thurck, thurk**. [app. a variant of ME. *derk*, DARK; but the change of initial *d* to ð, þ, is abnormal and unexplained: cf. however OS. *thimm*, beside OE. *dim*(*m*), OFris. *dimme* DIM.] = DARK *a.*

c **1250** Ðherk [see THERKNESS below]. **13..** *Sir Beues* (A.) 2790 Til it was þe þerke niȝt. *c* **1430** LYDG. *Min. Poems* (Percy Soc.) 204 Your byl clothyd thirke and on clene. *c* **1440** *Jacob's Well* 219 Ffyve cytees schal be in þe lond of thirknes spekyng wyth a chaungyng tunge. Þis is for to saye, ffyve citees schal be in the therk body of man. *c* **1450** *Cov. Myst.* xvii. (1841) 170 To marre ȝow in a thyrke myste. *a* **1682** SIR T. BROWNE *Tracts* viii. (1684) 146 Words .. of common use in Norfolk .. as .. *Thurck*. **1691** RAY *S. & E.C. Words*, *Tharky* adj., 'very *tharky*', very dark. *Suff.*... *Thurk*, *Norf.* *Ibid.* Pref. 5 *Thurk* is plainly from the Saxon *deorc*, dark.

Hence † **therk** *v.* *Obs.* (3 **þirk**) = DARK *v.*; † ˈ**therkness** *Obs.*, darkness.

c **1275** LAY. 11973 Þirkede vnder sonne þustrede þe wolkne. *c* **1250** *Gen. & Ex.* 3102 Ðhikke ðherknesse cam on ðat lond. *c* **1440** [see above]. *c* **1485** *Digby Myst.* III. 773 Owt of þe ded slep of therknesse de-fend vs aye!

therl, obs. form of THIRL *sb.*[1] and *v.*[1]

therm (θɜːm), *sb.*[1] *arch.* Also 6–8 **therme**. [prob. a. F. *therme* (13th c. in Godef. *Compl.*) in pl., ad. L. *thermæ*, a. Gr. θέρμαι hot baths, pl. of θέρμη heat.] A public bath or bathing establishment.

1549 THOMAS *Hist. Italie* (1549) 28 b, A noumbre of hote-houses in euerie Therme. **1606** SYLVESTER *Du Bartas* II. iv. I. *Trophies* 1112 O cleer Therms, If so your Waves be cold; what is it warms, Nay burns my heart? **1613** DANIEL *Hist. Eng.* I. 25 Britaine .. could not but partake of the magnificence of their goodly structures, Thermes, Aquaductes, High wayes. **1629** MAXWELL tr. *Herodian* (1635) 175 The Theaters, Therms, and all the splendor and glory thereof. **1726** LEONI *Alberti's Archit.* II. 74/1 A public Bath or Therme. **1890** BRIDGETT *Blunders & Forg.* ii. 32 The same author describes the therms at Paris.

therm (θɜːm), *sb.*[2] *Physics.* [mod. f. Gr. θερμός hot, warm, θέρμη heat.]

† **1.** A proposed unit of heat: the quantity of heat required to raise the temperature of one gramme of water at its maximum density one degree centigrade; = CALORIE b. *Obs.*

1888 *Rep. Brit. Assoc.* 56 It was resolved, on the motion of Mr. W. H. Preece, to adopt the name 'Therm' for the Gramme-Water-Degree-Centigrade Unit of Heat. **1888** *Nature* 13 Dec. 159 *Electrical Notes*... The term 'therm', in place of *calorie*, for the unit of heat in the C.G.S. system, has not met with general approbation. **1889** *Rep. Brit. Assoc.* 514 The *Therm* as the unit of heat .. did not commend itself to the French members [of the Electrical Congress in Paris, 1889]. They preferred for the present to retain the word *Calorie*. **1899** EDSER *Heat for Adv. Students* Pref. 1 Following the nomenclature used in the *Smithsonian Physical Tables* the term *therm* has been [here] used [etc.].

2. A quantity of heat equal to 100,000 British thermal units, used in Britain as the statutory unit in expressing the quantity of gas supplied.

1920 *Act 10 & 11 Geo. V* c. 28 §1 (2) A standard or maximum price for each hundred thousand British thermal units (in this Act referred to as 'a therm'). **1922** *Westm. Gaz.* 18 Oct. 8/5 The new method of charging by therm. **1955** *Times* 20 July 8/3 A 'substantial increase' was forecast by the chairman of the South Eastern Gas Board when he announced recently an increase of 2d, a therm in the price of gas. **1982** *Daily Tel.* 26 Apr. 2/8 The average price being paid by British Gas for existing and new supplies is 10p–12p a therm.

therm (θɜːm), *sb.*[3] [erron. f. TERM *sb.* (sense 15)]

1. See quot. 1846.

1727–41 CHAMBERS *Cycl.*, *Terms, Termes, Termini*... Some write the word *thermes*, from *hermes*, a name the Greeks gave the god Mercury; whose statue .. was placed in several of the cross-ways. **1811** W. COOKE *Thames* Sign. 39, lf. 3 The first object is the bust of Flora, on a therm. **1846** WORCESTER, *Therm* .., a pedestal increasing upwards for the reception of a bust.

2. In 18th.-c. cabinet-making, a rectangular, tapering leg or foot of a chair, table, or the like. Also *attrib.* or as *adj.*

1788 *Cabinet-Makers' London Bk. Prices* (1803) No. 7, If the plinth of the Therms is work'd hollow [price, extra, 1½d]. **1925** PENDEREL-BRODHURST & LAYTON *Gloss. Eng. Furnit.* 173 *Therm foot*, a rectangular tapering foot to the legs of chairs and tables, also called a spade or taper foot, often used by the brothers Adam and Hepplewhite, and to a lesser degree by Sheraton. *Therm leg*, the taper or therm leg was a favourite feature of Hepplewhite and later designers. **1952** J. GLOAG *Short Dict. Furnit.* 475 (*caption*) Ten designs for therms for claws.

† **therm** (θɜːm), *sb.*[4] Colloq. abbrev. of THERMOMETER. *Obs.*

1791 J. WOODFORDE *Diary* 11 Dec. (1927) III. 318 It froze all day long even within doors very quick Therm at 52. **1799** MALTHUS *Diary* 21 July (1966) 173 Yesterday his therm was 18, & mine in a deep shade was 71. **1877** W. WHITMAN *Daybks. & Notebks.* (1978) I. 58 *Very hot*—therm 90–96.

therm (θɜːm), *v.* [f. THERM *sb.*[3]] *trans.* In 18th.-c. cabinet-making, to turn (a leg or foot of a chair, table, or the like) to a rectangular, tapering form; also *absol.* Hence **thermed** *ppl. a.*, ˈ**therming** *vbl. sb.*

1788 *Cabinet-Makers' London Bk. Prices* (1803) No. 12, The Price of Therming Legs... The Price of Therming in the Neck... When the legs are therm'd at the top only, the tapering to be paid for extra. **1907** G. O. WHEELER *Old Eng. Furnit.* 461 *Therming*, a process of conferring a delicate taper, especially applied to the feet of chairs, sideboards, and tables of the Sheraton order. **1925** PENDEREL-BRODHURST & LAYTON *Gloss. Eng. Furnit.* 173 *Therming*, a process in use towards the end of the eighteenth century, before circular and band saws were invented, by which the legs of chairs and tables were thermed or tapered, by means of a lathe provided with a cylinder about six feet in diameter, on which the legs were placed and turned down one side at a time. **1952** J. GLOAG *Short Dict. Furnit.* 470 *Taper leg*, a leg of square section, sometimes called a thermed leg, gradually diminishing towards the foot, introduced in the second half of the 18th century for chairs, tables and sideboards.

therm, obs. and Sc. form of THARM, intestine.

‖ **thermæ** (ˈθɜːmiː), *sb. pl.* *Cl. Antiq.* [L. = 'baths': see THERM *sb.*[1]] One of the public bathing establishments of the ancient Romans and Greeks; also, hot springs (? *obs.*).

1600 HOLLAND *Livy, Summ. Mar.* IV. XXV. 1382 Those places where they built these baines and hote houses, they call Thermæ. **1695** WOODWARD *Nat. Hist. Earth* III. i. 144 Thermæ, Natural Baths, or Hot-Springs. **1832** GELL *Pompeiana* I. iv. 47 The baths or thermae. **1908** *Westm. Gaz.* 31 Dec. 4/1 Unlike the thermæ of the *élégants* of Pompeii .. the R.A.C. baths will have ample window space.

‖ **thermæsthesia** (θɜːmɪsˈθiːsɪə). *Path.* [mod.L., f. Gr. θέρμη heat + αἴσθησις perception.] Sensitiveness to heat or cold; the sense of heat. Hence **thermæsthesiˈometer**: see quot. 1885.

1885 *Buck's Handbk. Med. Sc.* I. 85/2 *Thermæsthesiometer*, for measuring the sensibility to differences of temperature, Weber used two long glass phials filled with oil. *Ibid.* 86/1 In 1866, Eulenburg described his thermæsthesiometer. **1899** *Allbutt's Syst. Med.* VIII. 169 Thermæsthesia.—There are two disorders of subjective sensation of heat and cold.

thermal (ˈθɜːməl), *a.* [= F. *thermal* (Buffon), f. Gr. θέρμη heat + -AL[1].]

1. Of, pertaining to, or of the nature of *thermæ* or hot springs; of a spring, etc., (naturally) hot or warm; also, having hot springs.

1756 C. LUCAS *Ess. Waters* III. 69 These thermal waters are absolutely colorless. **1800** W. SAUNDERS *Min. Waters* Pref. 17 The thermal waters of Bath or Buxton. *Ibid.* iv. 352 Enriched with several thermal springs. **1859** R. F. BURTON *Centr. Afr.* in *Jrnl. Geog. Soc.* XXIX. 81 Detached boulders, blackened, probably, by the thermal fumes. **1876** M. COLLINS *From Midn. to Midn.* III. ix. 169 The thermal city's [Bath's] superb crescents. **1898** *Allbutt's Syst. Med.* V. 1000 Simple thermal baths at 90° F. or under commonly tend to reduce the pulse-rate.

2. a. Of or pertaining to heat; determined, measured, caused, or operated by heat. ***thermal agitation***, the motion of atoms or the like due to their thermal energy; ***thermal analysis***, analysis of a substance by examination of the way its temperature falls on cooling or rises on heating; ***thermal barrier*** (Aeronaut.) = *heat barrier* s.v. HEAT *sb.* 14d; ***thermal bremsstrahlung***, electromagnetic radiation produced by the thermal motion of charged particles in a plasma; ***thermal capacity***, the capacity of a body (cf. CAPACITY 1 c, HEAT *sb.* 2 d) measured by the quantity of heat required to raise its temperature one degree; ***thermal column*** (Nucl. Physics), a body of moderator inside or projecting from a reactor such that it serves as a source of thermal neutrons for experimental purposes; ***thermal cycle***, a cycle in which the temperature of a substance rises or falls and then returns to its initial value; ***thermal cycling***, the periodic heating and cooling of a substance; ***thermal death point***, the lowest temperature at which a micro-organism is killed under specified conditions; ***thermal diffusion***, diffusion occurring as a result of the thermal motion of atoms or molecules, esp. as a technique for separating gaseous compounds of different isotopes of an element (which diffuse at different rates in a temperature gradient); ***thermal diffusivity***, the thermal conductivity of a substance divided by the product of its density and its specific heat capacity; ***thermal efficiency***, the efficiency of an engine measured by the ratio of the work done by it to the heat supplied to it; ***thermal imaging***, the technique of using the heat given off by objects or substances to produce an image of them; so ***thermal imager***; ***thermal lance*** = *thermic lance* s.v. THERMIC *a.*; ***thermal noise*** (Electronics), noise arising from the random thermal motion of electrons; ***thermal pollution***, the production of heat, or the discharge of warm water, esp. into a river or lake, on a scale that is potentially harmful ecologically; ***thermal printer***, a printer having a matrix of fine pins as the print-head, which are selectively heated to form a character on heat-sensitive paper; ***thermal runaway*** (Electronics), a dramatic or destructive rise in the temperature of a transistor as a result of an increase in its temperature causing an increase in the current through it, and vice versa; ***thermal shock*** (cf. SHOCK *sb.*[3] 2); ***thermal storage*** a system of storing water at high pressure and temperature in vessels above the boilers during hours of low load in electric generating stations; also used *attrib.* to designate appliances which store heat in other ways; ***thermal unit***, a unit of heat; the ***British thermal unit*** is the amount of heat required to raise the temperature of a pound of water at its maximum density through one degree Fahrenheit (abbrev. B.Th.U., B.T.U., B.t.u.).

1837 BREWSTER *Magnet.* 267 The thermal and the magnetic equators are connected .. with the thermal and magnetic poles. **1853** *Trans. R. Soc. Edin.* XX. 170 The mechanical equivalent of the ordinary thermal unit. **1870** TYNDALL *Lect. Electr.* §10 To produce both magnetic and thermal phenomena. **1876** *Catal. Sci. App. S. Kens. Mus.* §1056 The heat is calculated as follows, either in calories or British thermal units. **1880** W. THOMSON in *Encycl. Brit.* XI. 558/2 Regnault's measurements of the thermal capacity of water at different temperatures. *Ibid.* 578/1 The thermal conductivity of the substance is not generally the same at different temperatures. *Ibid.* 581/2 It is *k*/*c*, not merely *k*, that expresses the quantity of the substance on which the phenomenon chiefly depends. We therefore propose to give to *k*/*c* the name of thermal diffusivity. **1884** KNIGHT *Dict. Mech.*, *Suppl.* 891/1 Thermal Alarm for Hot Boxes. **1898** *Public Health Papers & Rep.* (Amer. Public Health Assoc.) XXIII. 86 In determining the thermal death point cultures should always be moist. **1910** J. G. HORNER in *Encycl. Brit.* IV. 148/2 In some cases where the work required is very intermittent, thermal storage is employed. **1910** H. L. CALLENDAR *ibid.* V. 61/1 The specific heat of a substance is sometimes defined as the thermal capacity of unit mass. *Ibid.* XIII. 137/1 English Engineers usually state results in terms of the British Thermal Unit (B. Th. U.). *Ibid.* 138/1 The improvement in thermal efficiency obtained by expansive working. **1916** S. CHAPMAN in *Proc. R. Soc.* A. XCIII. 10 We may call D_{12}, D_{12}', D_p, and D_T respectively the coefficients of diffusion, forced diffusion, pressure diffusion, and thermal diffusion. The definition of D_{12} agrees with that usually given for the coefficient of diffusion. The other coefficients seem to be defined here for the first time. **1925** *Jrnl. Iron & Steel Inst.* CXII. 489 Thermal analysis was followed by determination of the hardness and a study of the micro-structure of the test-pieces. **1925** Thermal shock [see PULPAL *a.*]. **1927** *Physical Rev.* XXIX. 367 Ordinary electric conductors are sources of random voltage fluctuations, as a result of thermal agitation of the electric charges of the conductor. **1930** F. B. LLEWELLYN in *Proc. IRE* XVIII. 244 The importance of this noise, which will be termed 'thermal noise', in high-frequency radio receiving circuit design will be discussed. **1932** HARDY & PERRIN *Princ. Optics* 142 Thermal radiation is characteristic of the temperature of the radiating body rather than the material of which it is composed. **1933** *Archit. Rev.* Oct. p. xl/1 During the last two or three years an entirely new kind of cooking appliance has made its appearance in England. It is known as the thermal storage or stored heat cooker. **1935** *Discovery* July 214/2 Barometric depressions are discussed .. in their modern guise as interacting air masses, the forced ascent necessary to give rain being related to dynamical instability instead of to thermal instability as in the older theories. **1936** W. L. NELSON *Petroleum Refinery Engin.* xvii. 304 The thermal decomposition or cracking of oil was called to our attention by Silliman in 1871. **1943** *Gloss. Terms Electr. Engin.* (*B.S.I.*) 14 A B.t.u. is equivalent to 1054 joules. **1950** *Sci. News* XV. Plate 16 (*caption*) Slip-lines in pure zinc after exposure to 50 thermal cycles between 30°C and 150°C (× 500). **1950** *Canad. Jrnl. Res.* A. XXVIII. 434 The thermal column of the Chalk River pile was used as a large block of scattering material with a high flux of thermal neutrons. **1951** *Jrnl. R. Aeronaut. Soc.* LV. 757/2 A new barrier is faced after 'climbing' the sonic barrier, namely the Thermal Barrier. **1954** R. STEPHENSON *Introd. Nucl. Engin.* vi. 249 The X-pile has no thermal shield... After 10 years operation there is no material damage of the concrete, which would indicate that the possibility of failure of concrete due to thermal stress may be much less severe than is generally assumed. *Ibid.*, A thermal shield is an inner wall .. which is placed between the reactor and the biological shield. Its function is to remove most of the heat energy of the gammas and thermal neutrons .. and thereby protect the biological shield from damage. **1955** *Sci. Amer.* July 58/1 Coal supplied only 34 per cent of the nation's total B.T.U.'s (British thermal units). **1957** *Times* 12 Nov. (Canada Suppl.) p. iii/2 A 1,200,000 h.p. thermal power station is to be built near Vancouver, using natural gas. *Ibid.* 11 Dec. 16/4 It has been necessary to increase the capacity of the distillation unit and provide a thermal cracker. **1958** C. C. ADAMS *Space Flight* 265 The MA-2 is a special suit that is ventilated for travel through the thermal barrier, and the MA-1 is a new ARDC helmet. **1960** CHALMERS & QUARRELL *Physical Examination of Metals* (ed. 2) iii. 183 The simplest method of carrying out a thermal analysis is to place the specimen in a furnace which is arranged to have a negligible temperature gradient over a zone somewhat greater than the length of the specimen. **1961** *Guardian* 12 June 6/6 A domestic thermal storage heater is now available. **1962** *Research* XV. 80/1 Uranium polycarbide..is much more resistant to thermal shock and thermal cycling. **1962** SIMPSON & RICHARDS *Physical Princ. Junction Transistors* ix. 210 In extreme cases this positive feedback may lead to a catastrophic increase in temperature—a phenomenon commonly called 'thermal runaway'. **1962** *Newnes Conc. Encycl. Nucl. Energy* 357/2 The separations achieved in a convection-free system are small, and are only used to determine the magnitude of the thermal diffusion effect and to provide information on intermolecular force fields. **1963** B. FOZARD *Instrumentation Nucl. Reactors* xiii. 166 A count rate from the fission chamber of 10^5 c/s..is produced by a neutron flux, in the thermal column, of about 5×10^6 neutrons cm^{-2} sec^{-1}. *Ibid.* 170 Thus the reactor can be operated under virtually isothermal conditions over a wide range of load, with consequent constancy of steam conditions and absence of thermal cycling. **1964** H. S. HVISTENDAHL *Engin. Units* vii. 110 The legal definition of the Btu is the amount of heat required to raise 1lb of water from 60 to 61°F at standard atmospheric pressure. **1965** R. G. KAZMANN *Mod. Hydrol.* iv. 109 The so-called thermal pollution of streams has resulted primarily from the installation of steam-electric generating plants along our rivers. **1966** C. R. TOTTLE *Sci. Engin. Materials* v. 117 The mean free path *l* depends on the thermal agitation of the lattice. *Ibid.*, In less regular lattices, such as those of amorphous materials, there is a reduced probability of attenuation of the thermal wave, by virtue of the variable distances between the atoms. **1968** R. R. ERNST in Lawrence & Block *Disinfection, Sterilization & Preservation* VII. xliii. 707/2 The thermal death point is the lowest temperature at which a suspension of bacteria is killed in 10 minutes. This standard has been almost abandoned. **1969** Thermal pollution [see POLLUTION 1 a]. **1970** *Nature* 19 Sept. 1182/1 The technique of thermal imaging—picking up infrared radiation from the human body and displaying the resulting thermal image on an oscilloscope—..has been used to map the flow of warm arterial blood into, for example, tumours and varicose veins. **1971** *Gloss. Soil Sci. Terms* (Soil Sci. Soc. Amer.) 21/1 *Thermal analysis* (*differential thermal analysis*), a method of analyzing a soil sample for constituents, based on a differential rate of heating of the unknown and standard samples when a uniform source of heat is applied. **1972** *Sci. Amer.* July 33/3 This combination of conditions is all that is needed to produce the X rays, since accelerated charges are a source of electromagnetic radiation. A compact name for the process is 'thermal bremsstrahlung'. **1972** *Oxf. Univ. Gaz.* CII. Suppl. No. 8. 3 Work has begun on the installation of a second thermal storage boiler. **1973** 'K. ROYCE' *Spider Underground* viii. 119 Someone must be on tap to answer awkward questions if Old Bill [*sc.* the police] arrives. The thermal lance men will be below. **1973** J. G. TWEEDDALE *Materials Technol.* I. iv. 95 Thermal diffusivity (*a*) is important when it is necessary to consider the effects of temperature differences set up in a material during transfer of heat. *Ibid.*, Both thermal conductivity and diffusivity cease to have much meaning for the liquid state since in that state the principal mechanism of transfer becomes convective mixing. **1974** *Sci. Amer.* Dec. 95/2 They are not die-cast in significant quantity now because the thermal shock to the metal components, including the mold, is so severe that the life of the components is short. **1975** *McGraw-Hill Yearbk. Sci. & Technol.* 44/2 Some kind of thermal shield had to be designed, fabricated, and deployed quickly if Skylab was to be saved. **1975** G. J. KING *Audio Handbk.* iv. 106 Since f.e.t.s are less temperature sensitive than bipolar transistors, temperature compensation is not necessary, neither can thermal runaway occur, for I_o tends to fall with increasing temperature. **1975** D. G. FINK *Electronics Engineers' Handbk.* XXII. 60 Thermal noise for the most part originates in the first stages of the radio receiver and sets the minimum signal amplitude acceptable for a given signal-to-noise ratio. **1977** F. WEBB *Go for Out* vii. 125 A modern peterman needs explosives—else thermal lances. **1977** I. M. CAMPBELL *Energy & Atmosphere* v. 86 There is unlikely to be a thermal pollution problem of any importance on a global basis within the forseeable future. **1978** *Jrnl. R. Soc. Arts* CXXVI. 683/1 Structures of supersonic aircraft are subject to thermal stresses due to temperature gradients. **1980** *Times* 4 Aug. 17/2 Thermal imaging..involves the visualization of objects and scenes by detecting and processing the infra-red energy they emit. **1982** *Daily Tel.* 20 Aug. 5/2 Their passive infra-red viewers, image intensifiers, and thermal imagers were excellent. **1982** *Sci. Amer.* Dec. 93/1 Thermal printers, which cost less than $500, burn an image into a special paper at a rate of some 50 characters per second.

b. Nucl. Physics. ***thermal neutron***, a neutron which is in thermal equilibrium with its environment (see quot. 1966); so ***thermal speed, velocity***, the speed characteristic of such a neutron; ***thermal reactor***, a nuclear reactor in which the fission process relies upon thermal neutrons. Cf. *slow neutron*, *slow reactor* s.v. SLOW *a.* 13 c.

1936 *Physical Rev.* XLIX. 520/1 It is therefore not necessary to ascribe all large cross sections to neutrons of thermal velocities. **1938** *Ibid.* LIV. 235/1 (*heading*) Collimated, variable energy beam of pure thermal neutrons. **1945** H. D. SMYTH *Gen. Acct. Devel. Atomic Energy Mil. Purposes* viii. 79 We now introduce a factor f, called the thermal utilization factor, which is defined as the probability that a given thermal neutron will be absorbed in the uranium. **1949** H. ETHERINGTON in S. C. Rothmann *Constructive Uses of Atomic Energy* v. 76 In a thermal reactor fission is produced by neutrons that have been slowed approximately to thermal velocities. **1959** *Listener* 19 Nov. 872/1 At slow or 'thermal' speeds neutron capture by nuclei of Uranium 238 is less important. **1966** C. R. TOTTLE *Sci. Engin. Materials* x. 236 Fast neutrons may be moving at speeds of the order of 10^{10} cm sec^{-1} with an energy of 1 to 10 MeV. When slowed down to a similar order of energy to that of the thermal vibration of atoms (hence called thermal neutrons) the speed is about 10^5 cm sec^{-1} at an energy of 1 eV. **1971** *Nature* 23 July 211/1 The companies say that they have between them a good deal of experience in building thermal reactors of several types.

c. Promoting the retention of heat. Usu. of clothes, esp. underwear. ***thermal pane*** = *Thermopane* s.v. THERMO-.

1970 *Toronto Daily Star* 24 Sept. 16/2 (Advt.), Quilted thermal suits. **1973** *Times* 9 Aug. 5/6 He has thermal underwear for use at high altitudes. **1974** H. MACINNES *Climb to Lost World* viii. 122, I had taken the precaution of carrying my pair of calf-length thermal boots with me... They proved very useful in this swampy ground. **1978** *Detroit Free Press* 16 Apr. E5/1 In addition to long johns, thermal socks and two caps, Harwell wore a tee shirt. **1978** T. GIFFORD *Glendower Legacy* 39 He..glanced out the wide thermal-pane window. **1982** *Oxford Star* 4–5 Feb. 10/7 Tartan Cottage, Oxfordshire's crashed mail order clothing firm, has been rescued by a thermal underwear company.

3. *fig.* Heated with passion; erotic, passionate, impassioned.

1866 *Lond. Rev.* 18 Aug. 178 Instead of the establishment in England of a thermal school of poetry; instead of the revivification of a grand (and wicked) old Paganism.

Hence **ther'mality**, thermal condition; **'thermally** *adv.*, in a thermal manner; by means of or with regard to heat.

1884 tr. *L. Brachet's Aix-les-bains* 1. 74 We must pay special attention to the thermality, which is the sole bond of union [etc.]. **1871** TYNDALL *Fragm. Sc.* (1879) I. xvii. 449 The experiments proved rock-salt to be coloured thermally.

thermal ('θɜːməl), *sb.* [f. prec. adj.] A rising current of relatively warm air, used by gliders and birds to gain height.

1933 *Jrnl. R. Aeronaut. Soc.* XXXVII. 678 Herr Hirth had gained a great deal of experience regarding 'thermals', that is to say, ascending currents of warm air which can be used for soaring as distinct from soaring in the currents beneath clouds. **1950** 'N. SHUTE' *Town like Alice* 229 She rolled over on her back and watched a seagull soaring in the thermals from the island. **1962** *Amer. Scientist* L. 180 Thermal soaring is the method most commonly used by soaring birds. **1974** 'G. BLACK' *Golden Cockatrice* iii. 60 He had been using that moving water belt beyond the harbour as a bird uses a thermal.

Hence **'thermalling** *vbl. sb.*, soaring in thermals.

1936 *Archit. Rev.* LXXIX. 255/3 For greater heights the second and more interesting method is employed; what is known as 'thermalling.' This is the utilization of the columns of rising air that are always in existence under certain weather conditions. **1974** *Reader's Digest* Feb. 89 With a Rogallo you can also do another type of soaring, called thermaling, where you circle in chimney-like updrafts of warm air that rise from sun-heated ground.

Thermalite ('θɜːməlaɪt). Also with small initial. [f. THERMAL *a.* + -ITE[1].] The proprietary name of a type of cellular concrete building block with good insulating qualities.

1949 *Trade Marks Jrnl.* 3 Aug. 690/1 *Thermalite*... Concrete products included in Class 19. **1955** *Archit. Rev.* CXVII. 117/2 The construction is cavity brick walls with inner skin of thermalite blocks, with a roof of ¾ inch asphalt on rafters at 5° pitch, and 2 inch cork insulation. **1960** *Times* 3 Oct. (Suppl.) p. ii/2 External walls are of cavity construction with brick facing and Thermalite inner leaf. **1977** *Reader's Digest Bk. of Do-It-Yourself Skills & Techniques* 201/1 Aerated blocks, e.g. Celcon or Thermalite, are also easy to work and have better insulation qualities [than lightweight aggregate blocks] but are more expensive and are unsuitable for exposed garden walls.

thermalize ('θɜːməlaɪz), *v. Physics.* [f. THERMAL *a.* + -IZE.] **a.** *trans.* To bring into thermal equilibrium with the environment.

1956 *Ann. Rev. Nucl. Sci.* VI. 317 The coolant..slows down the neutrons, acting as a 'moderator' and tending to thermalize the assembly. **1961** G. R. CHOPPIN *Exper. Nuclear Chem.* viii. 116 It is necessary to surround the source with paraffin or water to thermalize the neutrons. **1979** *Nature* 29 Nov. 456/1 The hypothetical Oort cloud should be thermalised by weak stellar encounters on a time scale ~ 1 Myr.

b. *intr.* Of sub-atomic particles, etc.: to attain thermal equilibrium with their environment.

1966 *New Scientist* 17 Mar. 707/1 It has been predicted that a positron in a metal should 'thermalize'—that is, reach the kinetic energy characteristic of the temperature of the metal—in about 10^{-12} s. **1973** *Physics Bull.* Nov. 652/3 The density was so high that any radiation generated would have readily thermalized. **1978** *Nature* 11 May 133/2 If the infalling protons thermalise just at the surface of the compact object, the radiation will be in the form of γ rays.

Hence **'thermalized, 'thermalizing** *ppl. adjs.*; also **thermali'zation**, the process of thermalizing.

1950 GLASSTONE *Sourcebk. Atomic Energy* xi. 294/1 The process of reducing the energy of a neutron to the thermal region by elastic scattering is sometimes called thermalization or, more commonly, slowing down. **1971** *Nature* 16 Apr. 450/1 A more likely possibility..is that electron thermalization during trapping produces local heating of the matrix. **1971** *Engineering* Apr. 34/2 Moderating materials are often an integral part of the structure of nuclear reactors so that thermalized beams can be obtained directly. **1979** *Nature* 30 Aug. 749/2 The major issue remaining is whether sputtered atoms escape Io or are merely supplied to a thermalising atmosphere for later escape.

thermammeter (θɜː'mæmɪtə(r)). [f. THERM(O- + AMMETER.] A device whereby the ampere-strength of an electric current is measured by the quantity of heat that it generates.

1891 in *Cent. Dict.*

‖**thermanæsthesia** (,θɜːmænɪs'θiːsɪə). *Path.* [mod.L. f. as prec. + ANÆSTHESIA.] Absence or loss of heat-perception; insensibility to heat.

1885 *Buck's Handbk. Med. Sc.* I. 86/2 By extremes of heat or cold a thermanæsthesia is produced. **1899** *Allbutt's Syst. Med.* VII. 355 Cases..in which there have been complete analgesia and thermanæsthesia.

ther'mantic, *a.* (*sb.*) *Med.* Now *rare* or *Obs.* [ad. Gr. θερμαντικός, f. θερμαίνειν to heat. Cf. F. *thermantique* (15th c. in Hatz.-Darm.).] That promotes warmth; heating, calefacient.

1748 tr. *Renatus' Distemp. Horses* 175 The Animal must be warmed with thermantick Drenches. **1768** [W. DONALDSON] *Life Sir B. Sapskull* II. xii. 81 He then pulled out of his pocket a large phial of thermantic ingredients, which he had prepared..the night before. **1860** MAYNE *Expos. Lex.*, *Thermanticus*, promoting warmth;.. thermantic.

B. as *sb.* A heating medicine, a calefacient.

1706 PHILLIPS (ed. Kersey), *Thermanticks*, Medicines that cause Heat.

thermantidote (θɜː'mæntɪdəʊt). [f. Gr. θέρμη heat + ANTIDOTE.] An antidote to heat.

1. A rotating fan fixed in a window-opening and incased in wet tatties, used in India to drive in a current of cooled air. (Introduced in 1831.)

'[It] is in fact a winnowing machine fitted to a window aperture' (Yule).

1840 W. G. OSBORNE *Crt. & Camp Runjeet Sing* 132 The thermometer at 112 all day in our tents, notwithstanding tatties, thermantidotes, and every possible invention..to lessen the stifling heat. **1898** P. MANSON *Trop. Diseases* xii. 214 Rooms should be kept dark during the day, and cooled by means of punkahs, thermantidotes, tatties.

2. *Med.* A cooling medicine. *rare*⁻⁰.

1860 MAYNE *Expos. Lex.*, *Thermantidotum*, term for a medicine..: a thermantidote. **1890** BILLINGS *Med. Dict.*, *Thermantidote*, a remedy against excessive heat or fever.

thermatology (θɜːmə'tɒlədʒɪ). *rare*⁻⁰. [f. Gr. θέρμα, θερματ- = θέρμη heat: see -LOGY.] Properly = THERMOLOGY; but given in Dicts. as = *thermotherapy* (see THERMO-).

1891 in *Cent. Dict.* **1899** *Syd. Soc. Lex.*, *Thermatology*, science of treatment of disease by heat, or specifically by thermal baths.

therme, obs. form of THARM, THERM *sb.*[1]

†**thermefy,** *v. Obs. rare*⁻⁰. [irreg. f. Gr. θερμός hot + -FY.]

1656 BLOUNT *Glossogr.*, *Thermefy*, to chafe or make one hot with outragious eating and drinking hot things.

thermelæometer: see THERMO-.

thermic ('θɜːmɪk), *a.* [f. Gr. θέρμη heat + -IC: cf. F. *thermique*.] Of or pertaining to heat; of the nature of heat; = THERMAL 2. ***thermic balance*** = BOLOMETER. ***thermic fever***, fever resulting from external heat, esp. heat-stroke, insolation. ***thermic lance***, a steel pipe packed with steel wool through which a jet of suitable gas may be passed in order to burn away metal, concrete, or the like using heat generated by the burning of the pipe; cf. LANCE *sb.*[1] 8 a, *thermal lance* s.v. THERMAL *a.* 2 a.

1842 J. F. W. HERSCHEL *Let.* Nov. in *Phil. Trans. R. Soc.* (1843) CXXXIII. 5 If the restriction to these rays of the term *thermic* as distinct from *calorific* be not..a sufficient distinction, I would propose the term *parathermic rays* to designate them. **1846** GROVE *Corr. Phys. Forces* 39 The definite thermic effects produced by chemical changes, have been lately much studied. **1849** MRS. SOMERVILLE *Connex. Phys. Sc.* xxv. 266 Those rays of the spectrum, whether luminous or thermic. **1890** BILLINGS *Med. Dict.*, *Thermic fever*, heat-stroke. **1896** *Allbutt's Syst. Med.* I. 499 In thermic fever or insolation the object is to reduce the temperature. **1897** *Ibid.* II. 313 Simple continued, thermic, and enteric fevers. **1899** *Ibid.* VIII. 706 Tactile, thermic, and pain sensibility. **1970** P. LAURIE *Scotland Yard* x. 251 The thieves..penetrate the wall of the vault with a thermic lance. **1982** *Daily Tel.* 7 Sept. 3/3 He planned to break into the bank with a thermic lance.

So **'thermical** *a.* in same sense; hence **'thermically** *adv.*, in a thermic manner; thermally; **'thermics** *sb. pl.*, the study of heat, thermotics (*rare*).

1851 CARPENTER *Man. Phys.* (ed. 2) 44 This Power.. manifests itself in those phenomena which we call electrical, magnetical, chemical, thermical, optical, or mechanical. **1854** Thermics [see *palæometeorology* s.v. PALÆO-, PALEO-]. **1859** R. F. BURTON *Centr. Afr.* in *Jrnl. Geog. Soc.* XXIX. 261 There are no unhealthy exhalations..., no thermical extremes nor surprises. **1877** ROSENTHAL *Muscles & Nerves* 109 A portion of the nerve may be heated, that is, it may be thermically irritated. **1953** *Archit. Rev.* CXIV. 195/2 (*heading*) Kitchen thermics.

thermid: see THEREMID *adv.*

Thermidor (θɜːmɪˈdɔː(r), ‖tɛrmidɔr). [Fr. (1793), f. Gr. θέρμη heat + δῶρον gift.]

1. The eleventh month of the French revolutionary calendar, extending (in 1794) from July 19 to August 17.

1801 W. DUPRÉ *Neological French Dict.* 276 *Thermidor*,.. hot month... The 9th Thermidor answers to the 27th of July. **1802** C. WILMOT *Let.* 30 July in *Irish Peer* (1920) 75 Paris, 30th July, 1802. 9 Thermidor. **1827** SCOTT *Napoleon* Introd., The 9th Thermidor, or 27th July. **1842** BRANDE *Dict. Sc.*, etc. s.v. *Thermidor*, It was the month signalized by the overthrow of Robespierre and the Reign of Terror; thence commonly called the Revolution of Thermidor, and those who boasted of having participated in it called themselves Thermidorians.

b. *lobster thermidor*: see LOBSTER[1] 5.

2. A moderate reaction following a revolution. [Cf. quot. 1842, sense 1.]

1938 C. BRINTON *Anatomy of Revolution* viii. 244 We shall have to call Thermidor a convalescence from the fever of revolution. **1960** *Commentary* June 508/1 The retreat from 'war communism'..did not lead to the revolutionary regime's overthrow by a new Thermidor. **1974** tr. *Wertheim's Evolution & Revolution* 341 Should all such symptoms be taken as evidence that the Cultural Revolution ..got stuck in a kind of Thermidor, and that consequently the fight of Mao and his allies against a Thermidor was a last stand, a losing battle? **1981** *Times* 30 June 15/1 Iran is about to enter its Thermidor.

Thermidorian (θɜːmɪˈdɔərɪən), *sb.* and *a.* Also **-ean.** [a. F. *thermidorien*, f. THERMIDOR + *-ien*, -IAN.]

A. *sb.* **a.** *Fr. Hist.* One of those who took part in the overthrow of Robespierre on the 9th Thermidor (27 July) 1794.

1801 W. DUPRÉ *Neological French Dict.* 276 Un thermidorien, spéculateur révolutionnaire—A thermidorian, and speculator in revolutions. **1827** SCOTT *Napoleon* Introd., The *Thermidoriens*, as the actors in Robespierre's downfall termed themselves. *Ibid.* III. 58 The Thermidoreans, who had killed Robespierre and now reigned in his stead. **1842** [see THERMIDOR 1].

b. A moderate opponent of a revolutionary movement; a counter-revolutionary.

1981 *Encounter* Dec. 34/1 The Thermidorians..are themselves not easy to define..and the Thermidorian régime..is so fragmented as to defy any simple analysis.

B. *adj.* **a.** Of, pertaining, or appropriate to the month Thermidor. **b.** Of or pertaining to the Thermidorians: see A.

1891 T. HARDY *Tess* xxii, June passed, and the Thermidorean weather which came in its wake seemed [etc.]. **1895** *Edin. Rev.* Oct. 391 The Thermidorian leader [Barras].

c. Of, pertaining to, or designating a moderate reaction following a revolution.

1938 C. BRINTON *Anatomy of Revolution* viii. 244 The ensuing slow and uneven return to quieter, less heroic times has long been known to French historians as the Thermidorean reaction. **1974** tr. *Wertheim's Evolution & Revolution* 333 It is against the background of these Thermidorian tendencies in the Soviet Union that we have to view the so-called 'Great Proletarian Cultural Revolution' in China. **1978** *Pacific Affairs* LI. 474 For them the Thermidorian effects of the bureaucratic restoration were much mitigated by the emergence at the helm of the enlightened Chou En-lai. **1981** [see sense b of the *sb.* above].

thermion (ˈθɜːmɪɒn). *Physics.* [f. THERM(O- + ION.] An electron or ion emitted from an incandescent surface.

1909 O. W. RICHARDSON in *Phil. Mag.* XVII. 814 The substantive Thermionics furnishes naturally the further substantive Thermion. **1922** J. MILLS *Within Atom* vii. 73 An electron which is emitted in this way is sometimes called a 'thermion'. **1973** H. A. ENGE *Introd. Atomic Physics* iii. 81 In 1899, J. J. Thomson showed that the thermions in this effect are electrons.

thermionic (θɜːmɪˈɒnɪk), *a. Physics.* [f. prec. + -IC.] Of, pertaining to, or employing electrons emitted from an incandescent surface; *thermionic valve*, an electronic device consisting of an evacuated envelope containing two or more electrodes, such that a current can flow only in one direction as a result of thermionic emission from one electrode.

1909 O. W. RICHARDSON in *Phil. Mag.* XVII. 814 Here we have two currents: the current used to heat the wire and the thermionic current away from the surface of the latter. **1915** *Electrician* 21 May 241/1 The thermionic current.. increased at first. **1917** *Wireless World* June 152 The invention by the writer [*sc.* J. A. Fleming] of this article of the thermionic detector. *Ibid.* 158 Known by various titles, such as Fleming valve, vacuum valve,..thermionic valve, and audion valve, it is the result of experiments extending over a large number of years. **1920** *Glasgow Herald* 9 July 10 What with the high-frequency alternator, and..the thermionic valve, wireless practice has been very much revolutionised. **1933** *Jrnl. Exper. Biol.* X. 293 (*heading*) A thermionic potentiometer for measuring light intensity with photo-electric cells. **1956** G. A. MONTGOMERIE *Digital Calculating Machines* xi. 216 By using thermionic valves and similar devices, the speed of automatic computors can be made very much higher. **1957** *Times* 26 Nov. 10/6 A new 'thermionic converter'..takes advantage of the fact that electrons can be 'boiled out' of a hot metal surface and used to produce an electric current directly. **1975** D. G. FINK *Electronics Engineers' Handbk.* XXVII. 18 In a thermionic generator..electrons are emitted from the heated cathode.. and collected by a cooler anode.

So **thermiˈonically** *adv.*; **thermiˈonics** *sb. pl.*, the branch of science and technology concerned with thermionic emission.

1909 O. W. RICHARDSON in *Phil. Mag.* XVII. 814 The author ventures to suggest that the word 'Thermionics'..is very suitable for the purpose. **1922** J. MILLS *Within Atom* vii. 74 When electrons are being thermionically emitted from a heated wire. **1933** E. L. CHAFFEE *Theory of Thermionic Vacuum Tubes* i. 8 Early experimenters in the field of thermionics believed that the emission of electricity from hot bodies..was the result of some sort of chemical reaction. **1940** *Times* 31 Aug. 7/4 New branches of knowledge like..photo-electricity, and thermionics sprang up out of the fertile soil. **1947** *Jrnl. Optical Soc. Amer.* XXXVII. 424/2 Associated with this component of the dark current is a shot noise resulting from random thermionically emitted electrons. **1966** *McGraw-Hill Encycl. Sci. & Technol.* XII. 542*a*/1 In thermionics, power densities of 25 watt/cm² at emitter temperatures of 1700°C have been obtained with hardware which is suitable for [space] flight.

thermistor (θɜːˈmɪstə(r)). [Contraction of *therm(al res)istor*.] A small piece of semi-conducting material the resistance of which falls with increasing temperature, enabling it to be used for the sensitive measurement and control of the latter.

1940 G. L. PEARSON in *Physical Rev.* LVII. 1065/2 Thermistor is a contraction of the words 'thermal resistor' and designates an electrical resistance whose value is markedly dependent on its temperature. **1955** *Sci. Amer.* Oct. 50/3 The heart of the instrument is a flake of metallic oxides called a thermistor, whose conduction of electric current is increased when it is heated. An amplifying and recording system translates this conductivity into a temperature reading. **1962** *New Scientist* 15 Mar. 638/3 The usual method of measuring the temperature in a borehole from the surface involves the use of thermistor probes. **1973** *Sci. Amer.* Feb. 42/3 The thermistor that sensed the muscle temperature was in the tip of the harpoon and the one that sensed the water temperature was attached to the transmitter, outside the fish's body on the harpoon shaft. **1979** *Guardian* 8 Sept. 20/2 When the water in the panels becomes warm enough, a thermistor produces a signal which is interpreted by the control unit, so that a standard central heating pump takes the hot water from the panel to the bulk storage tank, and from there to the radiators.

thermite (ˈθɜːmaɪt). Also **thermit.** [ad. Ger. *thermit*, f. Gr. θέρμη heat, θερμός hot + *-it* = -ITE[1].] **1.** A mixture of finely divided aluminium and oxide of iron or other metal, which produces on combustion a very high temperature (*c* 3000° C.)

Invented by Mr. Claude Vauten of London; named subsequently by Dr. H. Goldschmidt of Essen.

1900 *Engineering Mag.* XIX. 756/2 A mixture called 'thermit' consisting essentially of iron oxide and aluminium. **1901** *Westm. Gaz.* 2 May 4/2 The application of 'thermite', as the mixture has been named, to welding steel tubes and rails was illustrated. **1901** *Nature* 8 Aug. 362/1 To this mixture the name of 'thermit' has been given, and several varieties of it, adapted to various kinds of work, are used. **1906** *Dundee Advertiser* 26 June 10/1 The heat developed in the combustion of thermit,..which makes it possible to mend iron castings weighing tons. **1918** *Nature* 14 Nov. 217/2 Thermit, now an important munition of war, is in a class by itself. It is used for charging incendiary bombs and sometimes in a kind of shrapnel. **1971** B. SCHARF *Engin. & its Lang.* xi. 115 The thermite is ignited and the hot metal allowed to flow into the mould, where it fills the gap between the two parts and forms a collar around them. **1973** R. DENTRY *Encounter at Kharmel* xi. 198 The third explosion.. set off thermite positioned under the big transceiver.

2. *attrib.* and *Comb.*, as ***thermite method, reaction, shell, weld***; **thermite process**, the reduction of finely divided oxides of iron or other metals by means of an exothermic reaction with finely divided aluminium; also, thermite welding; **thermite welding**, fusion welding in which the heat and the weld metal are produced by the thermite process.

1929 *Times* 16 Jan. 12/4 The *thermit method of welding has proved its worth in long-continued use. **1905** *Chambers's Jrnl.* Dec. 78/2 A perfectly successful joint..has been made by utilising the *thermite process. **1910** C. H. DESCH *Metallography* vi. 109 The great reducing power of aluminium at high temperatures has been utilized in what is known as the Thermit process to produce metals and alloys free from carbon. **1930** *Engineering* 14 Mar. 349/2 The Thermit process, the oxy-acetylene and similar blowpipes, ..have all attained to a usefulness and convenience applicable..to single jobs. **1958** [see ALUMINOTHERMIC *a.*]. **1980** *Daily Tel.* 19 Feb. 6/8 British Rail uses two main welding techniques. One, the thermit process used along the Bushey track, involves welding long stretches of rail together at the site. **1915** *Chambers's Jrnl.* July 558/1 The *thermit reaction is used largely in the preparation of metals from their oxides. **1923** KIPLING *Irish Guards in Gt. War* I. 219 Oil-drums, gas and *thermit shells were added to the regular allowances sent over. **1980** *Times* 19 Feb. 3/3 There are at least 700 track welds, called *thermit welds, similar to the one that failed. **1906** *Jrnl. Iron & Steel Inst.* I. 452 Experiments with electric and *thermite welding for tramway rails. **1927** [see METALLIC *a.* 1 h]. **1952** FUCHS & BRADLEY *Welding Practice* II. ii. 39 It must be remembered that Thermit welding can only be carried out successfully by specially trained and experienced personnel.

thermo- (ˈθɜːməʊ), before a vowel usually **therm-** (but often in full form), repr. Gr. θερμο-, combining form of θερμό-ς hot, θέρμη heat; entering into many scientific and technical terms, as THERMOCHEMISTRY, THERMODYNAMIC, THERMOGRAPH, THERMOMETER, THERMOSCOPE, etc., q.v., and their derivatives; also in the following words of less frequent use or more recent formation. (In some of these *thermo-* is used as an abbreviation of THERMO-ELECTRIC.)

ˌthermelæˈometer [Gr. ἔλαιον oil: see -METER], an apparatus for measuring the heat evolved by mixing concentrated sulphuric acid with various fixed oils; ‖**ˌthermo-æsˈthesia** = THERMÆSTHESIA; ‖**ˌthermo-anæsˈthesia** = THERMANÆSTHESIA; **thermoˈaqueous** *a.*: see quot.; **thermoˈbarograph**, an instrument which simultaneously records temperature and atmospheric pressure; **thermobaˈrometer**, a name given to two distinct modifications of the barometer: see quots.; **thermo-ˈbattery**, short for *thermo-electric battery*; **thermo-ˈcalcite** [CALCITE], a name for non-crystalline limestones; **ˈthermo-call**, (*a*) a fire-alarm operated by a thermo-electric battery; (*b*) an electric fire-alarm in which the circuit is closed automatically when the temperature reaches a certain point; **thermo-ˈcautery**, any form of actual cautery; *spec.* a hollow platinum cautery in which heat is maintained by means of benzine or gasolene vapour; **ˈthermo-cell**, a thermo-electric cell or couple; **thermochaˈotic** *a.*, of or pertaining to disintegration or dissolution by heat; **ˈthermocline** [Gr. κλίνειν to incline], a temperature gradient; *esp.* an abrupt temperature gradient occurring in a body of water; also, a layer of water marked by such a gradient, the water above and below being at different temperatures; **ˌthermocoaguˈlation** *Surg.*, the coagulation of tissue, esp. in the brain, by means of heat; so **thermocoˈagulated** *ppl. a.*, **-coˈagulative** *a.*; **thermocomˈpression**, the simultaneous application of heat and pressure; usu. *attrib.*; **ˈthermo-current**, the electric current produced in a thermo-electric battery; also (*nonce-use*) a stream of warm air or water; **thermo-diˈffusion**, diffusion of heat; **thermoˈduric** *a. Biol.* [L. *dūr-āre* to hold out, last] (of bacteria, etc.) capable of surviving high temperatures, esp. those of pasteurization; **ˌthermodynaˈmometer**, a sensitive thermometer in which the thermometric substance is the saturated vapour of some volatile liquid supporting a column of mercury; **thermo-eˈlastic** *a.*, pertaining to elasticity in connexion with heat; **ˌthermo-elecˈtrometer**, an instrument for measuring the heating power of an electric current, or for determining the strength of a current by the heat produced; **ˌthermo-electroˈmotive** *a.*, of, pertaining to, or of the nature of electromotive force produced by heat; = THERMO-ELECTRIC 1; **thermo-eˈlectroscope**, an instrument for indicating temperature electrically, as a thermopile; **ˈthermo-ˌelement**, a thermo-electric couple as an element of a battery; **thermo-exˈcitory** *a.*: see quot. 1899; **thermo-exˈpansive** *a.*, expanding under the influence of heat; **thermo-ˈfocal** *a.*, of or pertaining to the focal length of a lens as influenced by heat; **ˈthermoformer**, a person who carries out thermoforming; **ˈthermoforming** *vbl. sb.*, the process of heating a thermoplastic material and shaping it in a mould; so **ˈthermoform** *v. trans.*; **thermo-galvaˈnometer**, a thermo-electric instrument for measuring small electric currents; **ˈthermo-gauge**, a form of pyrometer (*Cent. Dict., Suppl.*); **thermo-geoˈgraphical** *a.*, pertaining to the geographical distribution and variation of temperature; so **thermo-geˈography**, the study of this; **thermoˈhaline** *a. Oceanogr.* [Gr. ἅλς, ἁλι- salt + -INE[1]], of or pertaining to the temperature and salinity of seawater; **thermo-ˈhalocline** *Oceanogr.* [after *thermocline*], a narrow layer of water separating layers of differing temperature and salinity; **thermo-ˈharden** *v. trans.*, to harden permanently by subjection to heat; **thermo-ˈhardening** *ppl. a.*, rendered permanently hard by heat; **thermo-hyˈdrology** [Gr. ὕδωρ water], the scientific study of thermal waters; **thermo-hyˈdrometer**, a combined instrument showing the temperature and density of a liquid; **thermo-ˈhygrograph** [Gr. ὑγρός moist], a combined instrument recording the temperature and the humidity of the air; **thermo-ˈhygroscope** [-SCOPE], a combined instrument indicating the temperature and humidity of the air; **thermo-inˈhibitory** *a.*, pertaining to the prevention of undue heat in the body; applied to a part or function of the nervous system (Billings 1890); **thermo-'isopleth** [Gr. *ἰσοπληθ-ής* equal in quantity, number, etc.]: see quot.; **'thermo-junction**, the junction of two metals in a thermo-couple; **'thermokarst** [a. Russ. *termokárst* (M. M. Ermolaev 1932, in *Trudȳ Soveta po Izuch. proizv. Sil*: *Ser. yakutsk.* 211)], topography in which the melting of permafrost has produced hollows, hummocks, and the like reminiscent of karst; **thermokine'matics**, the theory of the motion of heat; **'thermo-lamp**: see quot.; **thermo'lysin** *Biochem.* [Gr. *λύσις* a parting], a heat-stable proteolytic enzyme found in some thermophilic bacteria; **thermo-mag'netic** *a.*, pertaining to or of the nature of thermo-magnetism; **thermo-'magnetism**, magnetism caused or modified by the action of heat; **thermo-ma'nometer** [MANOMETER], an instrument for measuring at the same time the temperature and elasticity of vapour; **thermo-meta'morphic** *a.*, of or pertaining to thermo-metamorphism; **thermo-meta'morphism**, *Geol.*, metamorphism produced by the action of heat; **thermo-'motive** *a.*, of, pertaining to, or caused by heat applied to produce motion, as in a thermo-motor; **thermo-'motor**, an engine driven by the expansive power of heated air or gas; **thermo'nasty** *Bot.* [NASTY *sb.*[2]], a nastic movement caused by a change in temperature; so **thermo'nastic** *a.*; **'thermo-pair** = *thermo-couple*; **thermo-pal'pation**: see quot. 1899; **'Thermopane** *N. Amer.*, a proprietary name for an openable double-glazed window unit; **thermopegology** (-piː'gɒlədʒɪ) [Gr. *πηγή* spring], the scientific study of thermal springs; **ther'mophagy** [-PHAGY]: see quot. 1899; **'thermophore** [-PHORE], a portable heating apparatus: see quots.; **thermophyllite** (-'fɪlaɪt), *Min.* [Gr. *φύλλον* leaf; A. E. Nordenskiöld, 1855, in Swedish], a light brown variety of serpentine which exfoliates when heated, found in aggregate masses of small scaly crystals; **thermo'physics**, the branch of physics dealing with the physical properties of substances at high temperatures; so **thermo'physical** *a.*; ‖**thermoplegia** (-'pliːdʒɪə) *Path.* [Gr. *πληγή* stroke], heat-stroke; **'thermopower** *Electr.* [f. *thermo*(*electric power*)], the thermo-electric e.m.f. developed by a substance per degree difference in temperature; **thermo-radi'ometer**: see quot.; **thermo'remanent** *a.*, pertaining to or being magnetism acquired, esp. by rock, as a result of cooling or solidifying in a magnetic field; so **thermo'remanence**; **thermo'sensitive** *a.*, possessing or relating to sensitivity to heat; so ˌ**thermosensi'tivity**; **thermo'synthesis**, chemical combination due to the action of heat; **thermosy'staltic** *a.*, of or pertaining to systaltic motion due to heat; † **thermo-tank**, a tank containing pipes through which water, air, or the like circulates for heating or cooling, esp. as a heating or ventilating system (*obs.*); **thermo'telephone**, a thermo-electric telephone; **thermo-'tensile** *a.*, of or pertaining to cohesive power as affected by temperature; **thermo-'tension**, tension or strain applied to material at a specified temperature to increase or test its tensile power; **thermo-'therapy** (also in Gr.-L. form **-thera'peia**) [Gr. *θεραπεία* medical treatment], treatment of disease by heat; **thermo'tolerant** *a.* (see quot. 1940); **thermo'toxin**, a poison developed in the body by heat; ˌ**thermo-un'stable** *a.* = THERMOLABILE; **thermo-vol'taic** *a.*, of or pertaining to the thermal effects of voltaic electricity, or to heat and voltaic electricity.

1890 *Jrnl. Soc. Chem. Industry* IX. 113 The heat evolved by mixing the oil with sulphuric acid is determined by means of the . . apparatus named by the author [F. Jean in *J. Pharm. Chim.* (1889) XX. 337] '*Thermeleometer'. **1909** *Cent. Dict.* Suppl., *Thermoæsthesia. **1890** BILLINGS *Nat. Med. Dict.*, *Thermo-anæsthesia. **1899** *Allbutt's Syst. Med.* VII. 47 There was complete thermo-anæsthesia below the second rib. **1881** RAYMOND *Mining Gloss.*, **Thermo-aqueous*, produced by, or related to, the action of heated waters. **1891** *Cent. Dict.*, *Thermobarograph. **1864** WEBSTER, **Thermobarometer*, a barometric instrument graduated for giving altitudes by the boiling point of water. **1868** WATTS *Dict. Chem.* V. 761 *Thermobarometer*... Applied by Belloni to a syphon-barometer having its two wide legs united by a narrow tube, so that it could be used either in its ordinary position as a barometer, or in the reversed position as a thermometer. **1849** NOAD *Electricity* (ed. 3) 427 In order to effect the decomposition of water, Mr. Watkins employs a massive *thermo-battery, with pairs of bismuth and antimony. **1888** *Cassell's Encycl. Dict.*, *Thermo-calcite. **1895** *Funk's Standard Dict.*, *Thermo-call. **1902** SLOANE *Stand. Electr. Dict.*, *Thermo Call*, (*a*) An electric alarm or call bell operated by thermo-electric currents... (*b*) See *Thermo-electric Call.* **1879** BRYANT *Pract. Surg.* II. 6 The galvano-caustic or *thermo-cautery is superior to any. **1907** *Daily News* 13 Nov. 11/1 The adoption of this method of telephony was made possible by the invention of a *thermo-cell for use in the receiving circuit. **1895** *Funk's Stand. Dict.*, *Thermochaotic. **1898** *Nat. Science* May 297 As regards the production of the *Thermocline, Prof. Birge believes that, in Lake Mendota at least, it is due to the concurrence of gentle winds and hot weather. **1902** *Nature* 6 Nov. 16/1 Throughout the circulating water above the thermocline, oxygen was abundant, but carbonic acid was absent... Just below the thermocline both gases were present. **1955** *Sci. News Let.* 2 Apr. 217/1 Investigations off the coast of California showed that skin divers can spot thermoclines, the layers of water which mark the sharp change in water temperature, in three different ways. **1973** *Sci. Amer.* Feb. 42/3 The coastal waters of Nova Scotia are characterized by a marked thermocline (a sharp drop in temperature as the depth increases), so that a free-swimming fish might encounter a wide range of water temperature. **1973** P. A. COLINVAUX *Introd. Ecol.* xxxiii. 470 The animals have to feed in the warm surface waters . . but they go down to cold water below the thermo-cline in daytime. **1938** *Yale Jrnl. Biol. & Med.* X. 575 The *thermocoagulated layers are completely 'resorbed' within four months. **1933** J. G. DUSSER DE BARENNE in *Science* 2 June 547/1 This method of laminar *thermo-coagulation of the cerebral cortex, as it might be called, results . . in a sharply localized, selective destruction of the nervous elements. **1974** *Nature* 4 Jan. 58/2 The destruction of the area postrema was performed by sight through the occipital foramen by thermocoagulation. **1976** *Ibid.* 22 Apr. 660/2 The *thermocoagulative lesions were aimed at various limbic tracts, and each estimated at 6 mm in diameter. **1965** *Wireless World* July 337/2 Typically this is done by *thermo-compression bonding of extremely thin gold or aluminium wires to the electrodes and terminal posts. **1972** *Physics Bull.* Mar. 154/1 Circuits can now be made with . . active components subsequently soldered or thermocompression bonded to the microstrip. **1979** A. L. LYDERSEN *Fluid Flow & Heat Transfer* xi. 323 The waste heat is often available at a temperature which is too low for direct use in the process. However, it may be utilized in conjunction with thermocompression. **1849** NOAD *Electricity* (ed. 3) 428 Dr. Andrews . . succeeded in obtaining chemical decompositions, by this peculiar *thermo-current. *a* **1859** G. WILSON *Relig. Chem.* (1862) 16 A sleeper in a confined chamber could gain nothing from the winds, or thermo-currents, or the far-off sea. **1899** *Syd. Soc. Lex.*, **Thermo-diffusion*, diffusion (of gas) by inequalities of temperature. **1927** *Techn. Bull. N.Y. State Agric. Exper. Station* No. 130. 6 *Thermoduric spore-forming bacteria are common types in pasteurized, sterilized, and boiled milk. **1946** *Nature* 23 Nov. 755/1 Working with suspensions of *Staph. aureus*, thermoduric micrococci, and spores of *B. subtilis*, we found that . . solutions [of hypochlorite] of low *p*H were more germicidal than at higher *p*H. **1975** CAMPBELL & MARSHALL *Sci. of providing Milk for Man* xxiii. 501 Bacteria that survive specific heat treatments are usually said to be thermoduric (heat-tolerant). **1909** *Cent. Dict.*, Suppl., *Thermodynamometer. **1903** *Science Abstracts* VI. 130 To represent the *thermo-elastic properties of gases, liquids, and solids as the statical properties of monocyclic systems. **1842** FRANCIS *Dict. Arts*, etc., *Clarke's . . *Thermo-Electrometer*, . . an instrument which professes to ascertain the deflagrating, or heating power of an electric current. **1849** NOAD *Electricity* (ed. 3) 247 The instrument employed was a Harris's thermo-electrometer. **1890** *Lond., Edin. & Dubl. Philos. Mag.* Feb. 146 *Thermoelectromotive forces are . . expressed in terms of a fixed standard, the torsional rigidity of the platinum wire. **1895** *Funk's Stand. Dict.*, *Thermo-electroscope. **1888** *Cassell's Encycl. Dict.*, *Thermo-element. **1891** *Cent. Dict.*, *Thermo-excitory. **1899** *Syd. Soc. Lex.*, *Thermo-excitory*, having the function of exciting the production of heat. **1854** J. SCOFFERN in *Orr's Circ. Sc., Chem.* 118 A *thermo-expansive material. **1903** *Science* 27 Feb. 333 A study of the *thermo-focal changes in long focus lenses. **1958** *Times Rev. Industry* Aug. 57/2 Machine . . for *thermoforming . . industrial parts. **1972** *Sci. Amer.* Aug. 9 (Advt.), By helping the *thermoformer with mold modifications and adjustments to equipment and operating conditions which enabled him to produce high quality parts economically. **1978** *Detroit Free Press* 5 Mar. C-14/7 (Advt.), Machinist assembler, parts and stock man, and a thermo-former. **1963** SIMONDS & CHURCH *Conc. Guide to Plastics* (ed. 2) vii. 182 There are seven basic techniques for the *thermo-forming of plastics sheet. **1972** *Sci. Amer.* Aug. 9 (Advt.), By supplying the sheet extruder with a high molecular weight Marlex thermoforming resin ideally suited for the production of large thick sheet. **1978** *N.Y. Times* 30 Mar. B-19/1 (Advt.), We are seeking manager for our model-making dept. in thermoforming. **1867** *Chambers' Encycl.* IX. 401/2 Special galvanometers . . in which the coil wire is short . . and thick . . are called *thermo-galvanometers. **1902** SLOANE *Stand. Electr. Dict.* App., *Thermo-Galvanometer*, a galvanometer whose needle is suspended in a special form of thermo-electric couple . . used to measure small amounts of radiant energy. **1895** C. L. MADSEN (*title*) *Thermo-geographical Studies: General Exposition of the Analytical Method applied to Researches on Temperature and Climate. **1897** *Ibid.* Advt., Articles on the subject of *Thermo-Geography will be most thankfully received. **1942** H. U. SVERDRUP et al. *Oceans* xiii. 509 When examining the circulation [of the waters of the oceans] that arises because of the external factors influencing the density of the surface waters, one must take changes of both temperature and salinity into account, and must consider not the thermal but the *thermohaline circulation. **1963** G. L. PICKARD *Descriptive Physical Oceanogr.* vii. 107 The ocean circulation can be divided into two parts, the thermohaline and the wind-driven components. **1978** *Nature* 13 July 151/1 The observed distribution patterns of late Quaternary sapropels favour the hypothesis of periodically altered basin-wide thermohaline circulation entrained by regionally important climatic and eustatic changes. **1964** *Oceanogr. & Marine Biol.* II. 135 When a basin is permanently stagnant, the redox discontinuity may rise to the level of the *thermo-halocline, as is well known in the Black Sea. **1976** *Nature* 2 Sept. 23/1 Mechanism and rate of molecular exchange across a well developed thermo-halocline have been studied thoroughly. **1949** R. J. W. REYNOLDS in J. M. Preston *Fibre Science* xvii. 318 The final products may be *thermo-hardened by a suitable cross-linking treatment. **1933** *Archit. Rev.* LXXIII. 266/1 The elaborate laboratory researches into the nature of thermo-plastic and *thermo-hardening materials. **1961** J. N. ANDERSON *Appl. Dental Materials* (ed. 2) xxi. 220 The Bakelite type of resin is called thermohardening or thermoset as . . heat is applied to cure the resin. **1881** PEALE in *12th Rep. U.S. Geol. & Geog. Survey* II. (1883) 355 *Thermo-hydrology. **1884** *Athenæum* 16 Aug. 211/2 The chapters on 'Thermo-hydrology' give evidences of a thoroughly scientific observer. **1894** *Brit. Jrnl. Photogr.* XLI. 43 Mr. W. E. Hales exhibited Fletcher's *Thermo-hydrometer. **1901** *Pop. Sc. Monthly* Dec. 186 An interesting figure shows the '*thermo-isopleths' for Berlin, these lines indicating, in one drawing, both the diurnal and the annual march of the air temperature. **1889** *L.E. & D. Philos. Mag.* Sept. 213 If the heat generated were immediately communicated to the *thermo-junction. **1903** *Times* 10 Sept. 10/4 A number of thermo-junctions of the platinum metals for use up to the highest temperatures have also been studied. **1943** S. W. MULLER *Permafrost or Permanently Frozen Ground* 84 Phenomena of *thermokarst. a. Cave-in lakes. b. Settling lakes. c. Cave-in and settling funnels. **1970** *Globe Mag.* 17 Jan. 4/3 Even south of the Alaska Range there is much permafrost within the forested areas which will create further problems of heat loss, permafrost melt and thermokarst development. **1871** CLERK MAXWELL *Heat* Introd. 9 The theory of the equilibrium of heat might be called Thermostatics, and that of the motion of heat *Thermokinematics. **1828** WEBSTER, **Thermolamp*, an instrument for furnishing light by means of inflammable gas. *Med. Repos.* **1965** H. MATSUBARA et al. in *Biochem. & Biophysical Res. Communications* XXI. 242 A proteolytic enzyme with the commercial name 'Thermoase' was isolated by Endo . . from cultures of *Bac. thermoproteolyticus* Rokko... It was recently reported that the enzyme had a strong elastase-like activity... We propose the trivial name **thermolysin* for this enzyme. **1979** *Nature* 29 Feb. 667/1 The determination of the three-dimensional structure of the thermostable protease thermolysin showed that heat-stable proteins do not contain unusual structural features absent from less stable proteins. **1823** T. S. TRIALL in *Ann. Philos.* N.S. VI. Dec. 449 Having been lately engaged in some *thermomagnetic experiments. **1954** *Jrnl. Geomagnetism & Geoelectricity* VI. 6 This simple apparatus could be used for the study of the thermomagnetic analysis of ferromagnetic mineral with a fair accuracy. **1828** F. WATKINS *Electro-Magnetism* 22 Experiments in *thermo-magnetism teach us that magnetical phænomena will arise from a disturbance in the equilibrium of temperature of metals. **1860** MAYNE *Expos. Lex.*, *Thermo-magnetism*, the same as Thermo-electricity. **1864** in WEBSTER. **1883** *Athenæum* 9 June 736/1 The use of a *thermo-manometer, which would indicate whether the vapour pressure is below that to be expected from the temperature of the water. **1889** HARKER in *Geol. Mag.* VI. 17 The interpolation of *thermo-metamorphic rocks. *Ibid.* 16 High temperature and low pressure (**thermo-metamorphism*). **1936** L. J. F. BRIMBLE *Intermediate Bot.* xx. 294 Examples of *thermonastic movements are seen in the flowers of the crocus and tulip. **1976** BELL & COOMBE tr. *Strasburger's Textbk. Bot.* (rev. ed.) 365 Repeated thermonastic curvatures may cause an increase in length. **1936** J. B. HILL et al. *Bot.* ix. 228 The rapid opening of certain flowers when brought into a warm room from a cold place is a *thermonasty. **1951** Thermonasty [see NASTIC *a.*]. **1976** BELL & COOMBE tr. *Strasburger's Textbk. Bot.* (rev. ed.) 365 Many flowers . . open or close according to the temperature. Such a phenomenon is referred to as thermonasty. **1807** JOYCE *Sci. Dial., Electr.* vi. (1846) 424 Delicate *thermo-pairs have been used to obtain the temperature of the human body. **1891** *Cent. Dict.*, *Thermopalpation. **1899** *Syd. Soc. Lex.*, *Thermo-palpation*, palpation of the surface of the body, with a view of determining local or general variations of temperature. **1941** *Official Gaz.* (U.S. Patent Office) 14/2 **Thermopane*. For multiple glass sheet glazing units . . Claims use since May 1, 1931. **1968** *Globe & Mail* (Toronto) 13 Jan. 42/8 (Advt.), Large brick and cut stone bungalow . . 2 fireplaces, drapes, thermopane windows etc. **1974** *Whig-Standard* (Kingston, Ontario) 9 Feb. 15/1 Modernisation of the whole interior of the present building, including modern heating, thermopane, air-conditioning and elevator service. **1978** *N.Y. Times* 29 Mar. B8/1 (Advt.), Builder's custom built 72′ hi ranch, 2 acs, circ driveway, thermopane windows. **1888** *Cassell's Encycl. Dict.*, *Thermo-pegology. **1860** MAYNE *Expos. Lex.*, *Thermophagy. **1899** *Syd. Soc. Lex.*, *Thermophagy*, the habit of swallowing very hot food. **1900** *Brit. Med. Jrnl.* 5 May 1105 To sterilise this instrument [i.e. a catheter] . . with a small pocket *thermophore. **1901** *Lancet* 9 Nov. 1297/2 The introduction of a ring-shaped thermophore. **1868** DANA *Min.* 465 *Thermophyllite. **1957** *New York Times* 25 Aug. IV. 9/3 Perdue University has established a *thermophysical properties research center. **1976** *Physics Bull.* Dec. 561/3 The symposium is concerned with both theoretical and experimental aspects of thermophysical properties of all matter in solid, liquid, gaseous and plasma states. **1962** A. L. KING (*title*) *Thermophysics. **1966** G. B. HELLER *Thermophysics & Temperature Control of Spacecraft* p. xi, The modern field of thermophysics rests on some of the oldest branches of physics, namely, thermodynamics, heat transfer, and electromagnetic radiation. **1909** *Cent. Dict.* Suppl., *Thermo-plegia. **1963** *Canad. Jrnl. Physics* XLI. 1080 The *thermopower of the special copper was measured carefully at the low-temperature end. **1976** *Physics Bull.* June 248/2 In figure 4 are plotted the conductivity and thermopower of the magnesium-bismuth alloy as a function of composition. **1876** *Catal. Sci. App. S. Kens. Mus.* §1056 *Thermo-radiometer, [an instrument] for measuring losses of heat by radiation from walls of furnaces, sides of steam boilers, etc. **1938** J. G. KOENIGSBERGER in *Terrestr. Magnetism & Atmospheric Electr.* XLIII. 120 The full apparent remanence acquired by cooling in a given field from *Tc* . . may be denoted the *thermoremanence. **1967** *Nature* 28 Oct. 359/2 The mean directions [of magnetization] . . are . . fairly well grouped, and are believed to represent the direction of thermo-remanence acquired when the rocks cooled. **1951** *Proc. Jap. Acad.* XXVII. 643 The remanent magnetism thus produced has been called the *thermo-remanent magnetism. **1958** *Antiquity* XXXII. 124 Measurement of the thermoremanent magnetism in the clay. **1971** *Physics Bull.* Aug. 476/3 Half the papers.. were concerned with the analysis of contact printing processes, both the anhysteretic transfer method with γ Fe_2O_3 slave tapes and the thermoremanent method with chromium dioxide tapes. **1975** *Nature* 27 Feb. 701/2 Stable remanent magnetisation discovered in lava samples collected during the Apollo 11 mission has been interpreted as thermoremanent magnetisation acquired when the lava flows cooled through the Curie point 3·6 Gyr ago. **1918** *Jrnl. Exper. Zool.* XXV. 279 The animal is *thermosensitive. **1952** *Archit. Rev.* CXI. 278/3 Suitable safety devices operated by a thermosensitive bi-metal strip are fitted. **1978** *Nature* 2 Feb. 470/1 Our results indicate that temperature control of reproduction in an ectothermic thermosensitive species may also be mediated in part by circadian systems. **1918** *Jrnl. Exper. Zool.* XXV. 281 This method.. demonstrated the *thermosensitivity of the species, because the animals gave an ejection reflex when brought into a region of higher temperature. **1981** *Pflügers Archiv: European Jrnl. Physiol.* CCCXCI. 66/2 It turns out that in the goose a minor fraction only of total body thermosensitivity can be attributed to the spinal cord. **1895** *Funk's Standard Dict.*, *Thermo-systaltic. **1899** *Syd. Soc. Lex.*, *Thermosystaltic*, muscular contraction due to heat. **1909** WEBSTER, *Thermo-tank. **1920** *Lancet* 25 Sept. 666/2 Eight thermo-tanks. **1928** *Observer* 15 July 9/4 A new Thermo-Tank heating system. **1884** KNIGHT *Dict. Mech.* Suppl., *Thermo-telephone. **1891** *Cent. Dict.* s.v. *Thermotensile*, Elaborate *thermotensile experiments on iron and steel, especially with reference to boiler-iron. **1847** WEBSTER, *Thermotension. **1860** E. WILSON (*title*) *Thermo-therapeia: the heat cure. *Ibid.* 3 Thermo-therapeia is the application of atmospheric air at a high temperature to the surface of the body, for the relief of pain and disease. **1899** *Syd. Soc. Lex.*, *Thermotherapy. **1902** W. WINTERNITZ (*title*) Hydrotherapy, Thermotherapy, Heliotherapy, and Phototherapy. **1940** *Chambers's Techn. Dict.* 846/1 **Thermotolerant*, able to endure high temperatures, but not growing well under such conditions. **1964** COONEY & EMERSON *Thermophilic Fungi* 161 [Fungi] which may grow at or near 50°C but which also grow well at temperatures below 20°C, are considered thermotolerant and are excluded from the true thermophilic fungi. **1973** *Nature* 16 Mar. 203/2 Many species of thermophilic and thermotolerant fungi isolated from natural thermal habitats similarly occur in man-made heated habitats. **1902** *Brit. Med. Jrnl.* 5 Apr. 846 To demonstrate two very different forms of complement—one a *thermo-unstable, and the other a thermo-stable. **1895** *Funk's Stand. Dict.*, *Thermo-voltaic.

thermo-æsthesia to **-chaotic**: see THERMO-.

thermo'chemistry. [f. THERMO- + CHEMISTRY.] That branch of chemical science which deals with the quantities of heat evolved or absorbed when substances undergo chemical change or enter into solution; e.g. the amount of heat evolved when hydrogen burns in oxygen or when sodium hydroxide is neutralized by sulphuric acid. Also sometimes used in a wider sense to include all relations of heat to substances, such as conductivity, specific heat, etc.

1844 JOULE in *L.E. & D. Philos. Mag.* (1845) May 382 The phænomena described in the present paper, as well as most of the facts of thermo-chemistry, agree with this theory. **1880** CLEMINSHAW *Wurtz' Atom. The.* 330 It is useless to bring forward in opposition to the hypothesis of atoms considerations drawn from thermo-chemistry. **1901** *Westm. Gaz.* 16 Dec., Up to the war of 1870 his [Berthelot's] time was mainly spent on researches in the region of physical chemistry, culminating in the foundation of a new science—that of thermo-chemistry.

So **thermo'chemic, thermo'chemical** *adjs.*, of or pertaining to thermochemistry; **thermo'chemically** *adv.*, by means of or with reference to thermochemistry; **thermo'chemist**, one who is skilled in thermochemistry.

1871 THOMSEN in *Jrnl. Chem. Soc.* XXIV. 878 On the Inaccuracy of Favre and Silbermann's *Thermochemical Determinations made with the Mercury Calorimeter. **1880** CLEMINSHAW *Wurtz' Atom. The.* 330 Thermo-chemical facts agree perfectly with the atomic hypothesis. **1901** *Nature* 24 Oct. 644/1 A thermochemical comparison of the action of acids upon oxide of silver before and after the action of hydrogen peroxide. **1890** *Ibid.* 18 Dec. 165/2 *Thermochemists.. attempt to draw an impossible distinction between chemical and physical changes.

thermochromism (θɜːməʊˈkrəʊmɪz(ə)m). [ad. G. *thermochromie* (H. Stobbe 1904, in *Ber. d. Deut. Chem. Ges.* XXXVII. 2239), f. Gr. χρῶμα colour: see THERMO- and -ISM.] The phenomenon whereby certain substances undergo a reversible change of colour or shade when heated or cooled. Also **'thermochromy**, in the same sense.

1911 *Chem. Abstr.* V. 2087 Characteristics of 'thermochromy'. **1914** *Ibid.* VIII. 2387 The corresponding salts of the thiourethans.. are colorless and do not exhibit thermochromism. **1960** *New Scientist* 2 June 1424/1 In all cases where the substance was both thermochromic and photochromic the colour formed either by heat (thermochromism) or by ultra-violet irradiation at low temperature (photochromism) was spectroscopically identical. **1963** [see PHOTOCHROMY c]. **1965** *New Scientist* 14 Jan. 102/1 Thermochromy.. may well be a quite general property of solids containing trivalent chromium ions. **1974** *Inorg. Chem.* XIII. 2512/2 The thermo-chromism of these compounds involves a gradual change in color from gold to yellow to light green as the temperatures are lowered from 100° down to liquid nitrogen temperature.

So **thermo'chromic** *a.*, of, pertaining to, or displaying thermochromism.

1904 *Jrnl. Chem. Soc.* LXXXVI. I. 672 (*heading*) Thermochromic properties of dibenzylidensuccinic anhydride. **1953** [see PHOTOCHROMIC *a.*]. **1965** *New Scientist* 14 Jan. 102/1 Heating has the same effect and the higher the chromium content, the lower the temperature required for the 'thermochromic' transition. **1974** *Inorg. Chem.* XIII. 2106/1 This salt is thermochromic: green at 25° and yellow at 80°.

thermochrosy (ˈθɜːməʊkrəʊsɪ, θəˈmɒkrəsɪ). Also **thermochrose** (*erron.* -crose), **-'chrosis.** [f. THERMO- + Gr. χρῶσις colouring. Cf. F. *thermochrose* (Melloni).] The 'coloration' of heat-rays; the property possessed by radiant heat of being composed of waves of different lengths and degrees of refrangibility (thus corresponding to the different colours of light-rays). So **thermo'chroic** *a.*, of or pertaining to thermochrosy; **ˌthermochro'ology**, the science of thermochrosy.

1847 WHEWELL *Hist. Induct. Sc.* x. i. §8 (ed. 2) II. 594 M. Melloni.. has proposed for this part of thermotics the name Thermochroology. **1864** WEBSTER, *Thermochrosy.* **1866** ATKINSON tr. *Ganot's Physics* (ed. 2) §379 Different luminous rays being distinguished by their colours, to these different obscure calorific rays Melloni gave the name of thermocrosis [*ed.* **1877** thermocrose] or heat coloration. **1867** MILLER *Elem. Chem.* I. 296 Thermochrosis or calorific tint.. is analogous to a difference in colour. **1895** *Funk's Standard Dict.*, Thermochroic. **1899** *Syd. Soc. Lex.*, *Thermo-chroic*, pertaining to a quality of certain substances that transmit some thermal radiations, but absorb or change others. **1909** *Cent. Dict.* Suppl., *Thermochroic*, of or pertaining to the differences in wave-length of heat-waves, and to the phenomena resulting therefrom.

thermocline to **thermocompression**: see THERMO-.

'thermocouple. Formerly also **thermo-couple.** [f. THERMO- + COUPLE *sb.*] A thermoelectric device for measuring temperature, consisting of two different metals joined at a point so that the junction develops a voltage dependent on the amount by which its temperature differs from that of the other end of each metal.

1890 *Lond., Edin. & Dubl. Philos. Mag.* Feb. 141 A practical method for the calibration of thermocouples by aid of boiling-points. **1901** *Nature* 23 May 92/2 The temperatures were measured with the thermocouple. **1934** *Jrnl. R. Aeronaut. Soc.* XXXVIII. 618 Twenty-two thermocouples were installed on the heads and bases of all rear-bank cylinders.. for temperature tests. **1953** *Brit. Jrnl. Psychol.* XLIV. 41 A thermocouple was used [for recording respiration]. It converted temperature variations in front of the nostrils into electrical variations. **1966** *McGraw-Hill Encycl. Sci. & Technol.* XIII. 562/2 Two dissimilar wires welded together at one end form the basic thermocouple. **1977** J. L. HARPER *Population Biol. Plants* v. 145 Emerged seedlings were recorded and marked every week. Surface temperatures were measured with thermo-couples.

thermod (ˈθɜːmɒd, -əʊd). [f. THERM(O- + OD².] The odic or odylic force of heat; heat 'od': see OD² b.

1891 in *Cent. Dict.*

thermode (ˈθɜːməʊd). [f. THERMO-, after *electrode*.] An object that is introduced into a medium, esp. living tissue, as a means by which heat may enter or leave it.

1938 *Yale Jrnl. Biol. & Med.* X. 573 A simple coagulator was used, the one inconvenience of which was that only the heating surface, the 'thermode' proper, could be sterilized. **1951** *Jrnl. Neurophysiol.* XIV. 424 A metal thermode.. was applied on the tongue and kept there at constant pressure during the total experiment. **1967** *New Scientist* 16 Mar. 553/1 About 10 cu. cm of clean mercury is placed in a Perspex boat with mild steel 'thermodes' at either end, one electrically heated, the other water-cooled. **1975** *Nature* 1 May 72/1 Unilateral water-perfused thermodes with thermistors fixed to the tips were placed stereotaxically into the POA [*sc.* preoptic area]. **1978** *Sci. Amer.* Aug. 91/1 In classic experiments conducted by Henry G. Barbour in 1912 silver thermodes were implanted in the hypothalamus.

thermodin (ˈθɜːmədɪn). *Pharm.* [? Arbitrarily f. Gr. θερμώδης lukewarm + -IN.] Trade name: see quot.

1899 *Syd. Soc. Lex.*, *Thermodin*, acetyl-para-ethoxy-phenylmethane. (Not official.) It forms colourless crystals, almost insoluble in cold, and very slightly soluble in warm water. It is recommended.. as a mild antipyretic.

thermoduric: see THERMO-.

ˌthermody'namic (see DYNAMIC), *a.* [f. THERMO- + DYNAMIC.] Of or relating to thermodynamics; operating or operated by the transformation of heat into motive power.

1849 THOMSON (Ld. Kelvin) in *Trans. R. Soc. Edin.* XVI. 545 A perfect thermo-dynamic engine. **1851** *Ibid.* XX. 261 In some conceivable 'thermo-dynamic' engines. **1853** RANKINE in *Phil. Trans.* (1854) 125 Third Corollary (of Thermo-Dynamic Functions). *Ibid.* 126 This function which I shall call a Thermo-dynamic Function. **1875** J. D. EVERETT *C.G.S. Syst. Units* ix. 54 By thermodynamic principles, the heat converted into mechanical effect in the cycle of operations is [etc.]. **1882** G. H. DARWIN in *Nature* 16 Feb. 361/1 He shows that the sun and earth together constitute a thermodynamic engine whereby the earth's rotation is accelerated.

So **thermody'namical** *a.*, in same sense; **ˌthermody'namically** *adv.*, in a thermodynamical manner; **ˌthermodyna'mician, ˌthermody'namicist, thermo'dynamist**, one versed in thermodynamics.

1860 MAURY *Phys. Geog. Sea* (Low) ii. §129 By no means the only body of warm water that the *thermo-dynamical forces of the ocean keep in motion. **1901** *Nature* 27 June 210/2 If the equilibrium between the jelly substance and the water was of a purely thermodynamical character. **1889** THURSTON in *Jrnl. Franklin Inst.* Dec. 467 The quantity so wasted varies with the weight of steam worked *thermodynamically each stroke. **1892** *Cambr. Univ. Corresp.* 15 Mar. 14/1 He failed to make any mark as a '*thermodynamician' during his lifetime. **1889** *Academy* 26 Oct. 273/3 The mechanical equivalent of heat—the familiar 'J.' of *thermodynamicists. **1901** THURSTON in *Smithsonian Rep.* (1902) 267 Prof. De Volson Wood, the greatest of American *thermodynamists of the nineteenth century.

thermody'namics, *sb. pl.* [f. as prec. + DYNAMICS.] The theory of the relations between heat and mechanical energy, and of the conversion of either into the other.

1854 *Phil. Trans.* 116 (*heading*) Mr. Macquorn Rankine on Thermo-dynamics. [Word not in article.] **1854** THOMSON (Ld. Kelvin) in *Trans. R. Soc. Edin.* XXI. 123 Fundamental Principles of General Thermo-dynamics recapitulated. **1867** MURCHISON *Siluria* xx. (ed. 4) 499 The principles of thermo-dynamics. **1871** CLERK MAXWELL *Heat* viii. 152 The principle of the conservation of energy, when applied to heat, is commonly called the First Law of Thermodynamics.

thermodynamometer, -elastic: see THERMO-.

ˌthermo-e'lectric, *a.* (*sb.*) [f. THERMO- + ELECTRIC.]

1. Of or pertaining to thermo-electricity; characterized or operated by an electric current produced by difference of temperature. ***thermo-electric battery, current, pair, pile***: see quot. 1876.

1823 CUMMING in *Ann. Philos.* Sept. 177 (*heading*) A List of Substances arranged according to their Thermoelectric Relations, with a Description of Instruments for exhibiting Rotation by Thermoelectricity. **1832** *Nat. Philos.* II. *Electro-Magnet.* xiii. §305. 93 (Usef. Knowl. Soc.) The electrical current thus excited has been termed Thermo-electric, in order to distinguish it from the common galvanic current. **1842** FRANCIS *Dict. Arts*, etc., Thermo-Electric Circuit,.. Piles,.. Thermometer. **1863** TYNDALL *Heat* i. (1870) App. 77 A thermo-electric pair or couple. *c* **1865** J. WYLDE in *Circ. Sc.* I. 29/1 We observe the thermo-electric battery. **1876** PREECE & SIVEWRIGHT *Telegraphy* 298 A current of electricity will continue to flow so long as a difference of temperature is maintained between the junction and the extremities. This current is named a thermo-electric current, and the two metals form what is known as a thermo-electric pair; a combination of these pairs forms the thermo-electric pile or battery. **1878** GURNEY *Crystallogr.* 115 Crystals sometimes acquire different electrifications when two ends are.. differently heated... These crystals are called thermo-electric. **1902** SLOANE *Stand. Electr. Dict.*, *Thermo-electric Telephone*, a telephone transmitter including a thermo-electric battery placed in circuit with the line.

2. Of or pertaining to heat and electricity; ***thermo-electric alarm*** or ***call***, a device in which a rise or fall of temperature to a pre-arranged point closes an electric circuit so as to cause a bell to ring.

1877 KNIGHT *Dict. Mech.*, *Thermo-electric-Alarm*, an apparatus designed to indicate the rise of temperature in bearings for shaftings, or in any kind of machinery or any branch of manufacture where a fixed temperature is desirable. **1902** SLOANE *Stand. Electr. Dict.*, *Thermo-electric Call*, a thermostat arranged to ring a bell or give some indication when the temperature rises or falls beyond certain points.

†**B.** *sb.* (See quot. 1842.) *Obs.*

1823 CUMMING in *Ann. Philos.* Sept. 179 The motion of the thermoelectrics on the approach of a magnet. **1842** FRANCIS *Dict. Arts*, etc., *Thermo-Electrics*, metallic bodies, the union of which show[s] the effects attributed to thermo-electricity.

So **thermo-e'lectrical** *a.*; hence **thermo-e'lectrically** *adv.*, in a thermo-electric manner; by means of thermo-electricity.

1830 *Edinb. Encycl.* XVIII. 584/1 Professor Oersted has proposed to call the current discovered by Dr. Seebeck the thermo-electrical current. **1878** CHRYSTAL in *Encycl. Brit.* VIII. 94/2 A thermoelectric series, any metal in which is thermoelectrically related to any following one. **1881** *Athenæum* 29 Jan. 169/3 A thermo-electrical pile, one end of which is exposed to the heat, the other end being kept cool. **1895** *Electrician* 13 Sept. 637/1 He also considered the possibility of the back E.M.F. being produced thermo-electrically. **1979** *Nature* 11 Oct. 498/1 (*caption*) Photo-multiplier in.. thermoelectrically cooled housing.

ˌthermo-eˌlec'tricity. [f. THERMO- + ELECTRICITY.] Electricity generated in a body by difference of temperature in its parts; *esp.* an electric current produced in a closed circuit composed of two dissimilar metals when one of the points of union is kept at a temperature different from that of the rest of the circuit. Also, that branch of electrical science which treats of currents produced by means of heat.

1823 [see THERMO-ELECTRIC 1]. **1827** CUMMING *Man. Electro-Dynamics* 189 On the electro-dynamic effects of heat, or thermo-electricity. **1830** HERSCHEL *Nat. Philos.* 341 The curious relations of electricity to heat, as exhibited in the phenomena of what has been called thermo-electricity. **1834** *Edin. Rev.* LIX. 167 The new branches of magneto-electricity and thermo-electricity. **1871** TYNDALL *Fragm. Sc.* (1879) II. xiv. 347 In 1826 Thomas Seebeck discovered thermo-electricity.

thermo-electrometer to **-expansive:** see THERMO-.

Thermo-Fax (ˈθɜːməʊfæks). Also Thermofax. [f. THERMO- + FACS(IMILE *sb.*] The proprietary name of a process for copying documents by means of infra-red radiation, and of a type of overhead projector employing copies made by this process.

1953 *Official Gaz.* (U.S. Patent Office) 17 Mar. 574/1 *Thermo-Fax.* For electrically operated machine employing infrared light source for producing copies of printed or pictorial matter by means of heat-sensitive paper. Claims use since November 1949. **1956** *Trade Marks Jrnl.* 18 Apr. 236/2 *Thermo-fax...* Reproducing (copying) apparatus for office use. Minnesota Mining and Manufacturing Company .., manufacturers. **1962** A. GÜNTHER *Microphotogr. in Library* (Unesco) 16 Some microfilm readers have special accessories for the occasional production of enlarged prints. Either a dry process such as 'Thermofax' is used or a semi-dry process such as diffusion printing (e.g. 'Copy-rapid') or stabilization techniques. **1964** *Times* 7 Feb. (Advt. Suppl.) p. ii/5 This is the situation the Thermo-Fax overhead projector is designed to overcome... It uses large transparencies which are inexpensive and simple to make—a Thermo-Fax infra-red copying machine takes just 4 seconds to produce one.

thermofocal to **-gauge:** see THERMO-.

†ˈ**thermogen.** *Obs. rare*⁻⁰. [f. THERMO- + -GEN.] A name for the fluid formerly supposed to exist as the material substance of heat; = CALORIC *sb.* 1.

1847 in WEBSTER.

Thermogene (ˈθɜːməʊdʒiːn). Also thermo-, †-gène. [ad. F. *thermogène* THERMOGENIC *a.*] A proprietary name for medicated cotton wool.

1902 *Official Gaz.* (U.S. Patent Office) 18 Mar. 2357/2 Absorbent wadding. Vandenbroeck & Cie., Brussels, Belgium... *Thermogène.* **1905** *Trade Marks Jrnl.* 22 Nov. 1449 Thermogène absorbent wadding... Medicated wadding for human use. Thomas Other Windsor, trading as the Thermogène Co., Invermay, Lucastes Avenue, Hayward's Heath, Sussex; manufacturer. **1907** *Yesterday's shopping* (1969) 520/1 Thermogene..pkt. 1/0. **1928** A. HUXLEY *Point Counter Point* xviii. 327 What you need..is a good rubbing with camphorated oil and a wad of Thermogene. **1939** M. SPRING RICE *Working-Class Wives* iv. 75 The doctor told her to keep the parts warm, so she used thermogene wool. **1958** W. SANSOM *Cautious Heart* 157 Pinkish brown clouds flew across the cold iron sky like tufts of thermogene loose in the night. **1962** C. WATSON *Hopjoy was Here* xv. 173 I'd been downstairs for some Thermogene.

thermogenesis (θɜːməʊˈdʒɛnɪsɪs). [f. THERMO- + -GENESIS.] The generation or production of heat, esp. in the animal body.

1891 in *Cent. Dict.* **1896** *Allbutt's Syst. Med.* I. 143 The nervous system presides over thermogenesis no less directly than over thermolysis. **1899** *Nature* 10 Aug. 360/1 Thermogenesis and use of energy by man in raising and lowering his own weight.

So **thermogeˈnetic, thermoˈgenic** *adjs.*, of or pertaining to thermogenesis; **thermogenous** (-ˈɒdʒɪnəs) *a.*, produced by or producing heat; **therˈmogeny,** thermogenesis (*Cent. Dict., Suppl.* 1909).

1860 MAYNE *Expos. Lex., Thermogenus, Min.*, applied by Haüy to a quartz agate which is deposited near the sources of silicious thermal springs..: thermogenous. **1877** FOSTER *Phys.* II. v. (1878) 377 Indications of the existence of what may be called 'thermogenic' nerves and thermogenic nervous mechanisms. **1879** WEBSTER Suppl., *Thermogenous,* producing heat. **1896** *Allbutt's Syst. Med.* I. 151 The thermogenetic chemical processes to which the taking in of food gives rise. **1899** *Ibid.* VIII. 244 In these children thermogenic powers are deficient. **1898** SALTER tr. *Lafar's Techn. Mycol.* I. 165 Thermogenic Bacteria.

thermo-geographical, etc.: see THERMO-.

thermogram (ˈθɜːməgræm). [f. THERMO- + -GRAM: cf. next.] **1.** = next, 2.

1883 R. H. SCOTT *Elem. Meteorol.* 38 The thermograms, as such curves are called, are measured every hour. **1901** *Nature* 28 Mar. 522/2 During each winter the Vienna thermograms show some anomalous jumps of temperature, amounting to 3° to 5° C.

2. A photograph or image produced by infra-red radiation emanating naturally from the subject under study.

1957 *Canad. Services Med. Jrnl.* 523 (*caption*) Thermogram lower left showed an area of increased heat. **1964** *Amer. Jrnl. Roentgenol.* XCI. 919/2 The normal breast in the thermogram can be recognized by its size, shape and the heat pattern of the overlying skin. **1967** *Idle Moments* (Austral.) Oct. 5/2 Thermograms..are taken in total darkness, since they are photographic reproductions of infra-red radiations of longer wavelength emitted by the object itself. **1968** *New Scientist* 1 Feb. 263/3 A pair of 'thermograms' of the crater Tycho.

thermograph (ˈθɜːməgrɑːf, -æ-). [f. as prec. + -GRAPH: cf. F. *thermographe.*]

1. A figure or tracing produced by the action of heat, esp. of the heat-rays of the spectrum upon a prepared surface.

1840 HERSCHEL in *Proc. Roy. Soc.* 3 Mar. 209 He has discovered a process by which the calorific rays in the solar spectrum are made to affect a surface properly prepared..so as to form what may be called a *thermograph* of the spectrum. **1865** *Reader* 28 Jan. 105/2 His drying paper presented to him a thermograph of the spectrum, and showed the heating power to extend far beyond the red. **1871** TYNDALL *Fragm. Sc.* (1879) I. ii. 48 The light is cut away,..but an invisible thermograph remains. **1906** *Athenæum* 23 June 768/3 Such experiments..will yield valuable 'thermographs', as the resulting parti-coloured 'prints' are named.

2. A graphic record of variations of temperature; a heat register; = THERMOGRAM 1.

1843 *Mech. Mag.* XXXIX. 128 Obtained..by the aid of the pyrometer,..with the addition of the thermograph, or heat-register, which I have added to it. **1878** T. BRYANT *Pract. Surg.* I. 55 These points are well seen in the following thermographs.

3. A thermometric instrument which automatically records variations of temperature; a self-registering thermometer.

1881 *Nature* 15 Sept. 470/2 Bowkett's New Thermograph,..an instrument for recording changes of temperature, which are measured by the action of heat upon a hollow circular metallic ring connected with a circular vessel. **1883–4** *Med. Ann.* 78 *Thermograph*—an ingenious instrument..for recording in permanent diagrams all variations in temperature occurring in any patient.

4. a. = THERMOGRAM 2. **b.** An apparatus for obtaining thermograms.

1964 *New Scientist* 16 July 163/1 Personal thermographs can sometimes with practice be recognised individually. **1964** *Amer. Jrnl. Roentgenol.* XCI. 919/2 This thermograph has been in daily use in this institution for over a year and has quite recently been replaced by a new model. **1970** *New Scientist* 5 Feb. 260/3 Thermographs of a person's finger before and after smoking show significant changes in the heat pattern.

thermographic (-ˈgræfɪk), *a.* [f. as prec. + -GRAPHIC, or f. prec. + -IC.] Of, pertaining to, or obtained by a thermograph or thermography.

1848 *Art-Union Jrnl.* Mar. 72 We have much satisfaction in recording the Thermographic processes. **1879** *St. George's Hosp. Rep.* IX. 688 In none..was there anything specially remarkable in the thermographic tracings. **1964** *Amer. Jrnl. Roentgenol.* XCI. 925/2 Their experience with thermographic scanning using electro-chemical paper was limited, but suggested a promising future. **1975** J. TAYLOR *Superminds* vii. 116 The general features of the aura seem very comparable to pictures obtained by the thermographic camera.

Hence **thermoˈgraphically** *adv.*, in a thermographic manner; by means of thermography.

1840 *Phil. Trans. R. Soc.* CXXX. 59 The focal image.. had acquired the power of imprinting itself thermographically on the paper. **1964** *New Scientist* 16 July 163/2 It now seems clear that most cancers of the breast raise the skin temperature and can be demonstrated thermographically.

thermography (θəˈmɒgrəfɪ). [f. as prec. + -GRAPHY: cf. F. *thermographie.*]

1. Any process of writing or drawing effected or developed by the influence of heat.

1840 HUNT in *Philos. Mag.* Oct. 268 A new..field of.. inquiry, which may..end in..the establishment of the new art of Thermography. **1842** *Ibid.* Dec. 466, I..proposed the name of Thermography, to distinguish it from Photography. **1848** *Art-Union Jrnl.* Mar. 71 From the circumstance that all the results..exhibit a very close relation between the surfaces employed and their powers of radiating heat, the term *Thermography* or Heat-drawing has been employed. **1875** *Ure's Dict. Arts,* etc. (ed. 7), *Thermography,* a term proposed..to express the 'Art of Copying Engravings, &c. on Metal Plates'; the effect being due..to the influence of heat-radiations. **1883** J. F. CAMPBELL *Thermography* i. §3. 11. *Ibid.* 12 Because light does not act upon the materials used, dark cameras are not needed in thermography.

2. The taking or use of infra-red thermograms, esp. to detect tumours.

1957 R. LAWSON in *Canad. Services Med. Jrnl.* XIII. 519 It was apparent that 'thermography' or heat imaging by suitable equipment might have a very important place in the early diagnosis of breast lesions. **1963** *Science* 24 May 873/2 The human body is an ideal subject for thermography. **1969** *New Scientist* 8 May 276/1 Thermography is a completely harmless method in which the patient is 'photographed' by her own body heat. **1971** *Daily Tel* (Colour Suppl.) 22 Jan. 22/2 Aerial thermography has been used to locate old mineshafts, and coal seams burning underground. **1977** *Time* 20 June 48/1 Thermography, or heat scanning, concentrates on looking for infra-red radiation to find tumors.

thermogravimetry (θɜːməʊgrəˈvɪmɪtrɪ). *Physical Chem.* [f. THERMO- + GRAVIMETRY.] The technique of chemically analysing substances by measuring changes in weight as a function of increasing temperature.

1951 *Chem. Abstr.* XLV. 2274 (*heading*) Thermogravimetry and automatic gravimetry. **1953** *Nature* 22 Aug. 365/1 The advantage of the differential thermogravimetry over differential thermal analysis is that it is quantitative. **1975** H. L. FRIEDMAN in I. M. Kolthoff et al. *Treat. Analytical Chem.* III. III. D-1. 401 In thermogravimetry (TG), one generally records the weight of a sample continually as it is heated through a preselected rate of temperature rise.

Hence ˌ**thermograviˈmetric** *a.*

1953 C. DUVAL *Inorg. Thermogravimetric Analysis* i. 3 The investigations of Honda.., and the construction by Chevenard of automatic recording instruments, have all combined to give birth to a new science which we may perhaps call thermogravimetric analysis. **1972** *Nature* 15 Dec. 418/1 According to our thermogravimetric analyses compounds (III)–(V) contain one molecule of lattice water per formula unit. **1977** *Proc. R. Soc. Med.* LXX. 518/2 If the stone has been passed or removed it should be analysed. This may be by wet chemistry..or by physical methods such as infra-red spectroscopy..X-ray crystallography..or thermogravimetric analysis.

thermohaline to **-kinematics:** see THERMO-.

thermolabile (θɜːməʊˈlæbɪl, -ˈleɪbɪl), *a.* [f. THERMO- + LABILE.] Liable to destruction at moderately high temperatures, as certain toxins and serums: opposed to *thermostable.* Hence ˌ**thermolaˈbility,** thermolabile quality.

1904 *Brit. Med. Jrnl.* 10 Sept. 557 [see THERMOSTABLE]. *Ibid.* 561 The hæmolysis being due to the co-operation of a thermolabile complement—also called alexin—and thermostable immune body, otherwise amboceptor. *Ibid.* 563 This thermolabile serum feast preparer is called by Wright and Douglas opsonine. *Ibid.* 561 Buchner has drawn special attention to the characters of the alexins—their thermolability [etc.]. **1907** *Jrnl. Med. Research* May 288 (C.D., Suppl.) The digestive ferment of these organs in solution is..thermolabile at 56° C.; the entire extract..is thermolabile at slightly higher temperatures.

thermology (θɜːˈmɒlədʒɪ). [ad. F. *thermologie*: see THERMO- and -LOGY.] The science of heat; that department of physics which treats of heat; thermotics.

1838 tr. A. Comte in *Edin. Rev.* July 284 It remained only [for Comte]..to tack to Hydrodynamics the sciences of Magnetism, Electricity, Galvanism and Thermology. **1840** WHEWELL *Philos. Induct. Sc.* I. p. lxxii, The science which treats of heat has hitherto had no special designation... M. Le Comte terms it *Thermology* (i.e. the science of heat). In the History of the Sciences, I have named it *Thermotics.* **1843** MILL *Logic* II. iv. §5 (1846) I. 246 Thus mechanics, hydrostatics, optics, acoustics, and thermology, have successively been rendered mathematical. **1858** H. SPENCER *Ess.* I. 215 Thus acoustics was arrested until thermology overtook and aided it.

Hence **thermoˈlogical** *a.*, of or pertaining to thermology.

1838 tr. A. Comte in *Edin. Rev.* July 282 The most important and precise laws of thermological phenomena are developed without the slightest enquiry into the intimate nature of heat. **1871** PROCTOR *Sun* iv. 193 So high an authority in meteorological and thermological questions.

thermolumiˈnescence. [f. THERMO- + LUMINESCENCE.] Luminescence resulting from exposure to high temperature; *spec.* as used as a means of dating ancient pottery and other material.

1897 J. J. THOMSON in *Smithsonian Rep.* (1898) 158 The phenomenon called by its discoverer, Prof. E. Wiedemann, thermoluminescence. **1898** SIR W. CROOKES *Addr. Brit. Assoc.* 22 Fluor-spar, which by prolonged heating has lost its power of luminescing when re-heated, regains the power of thermo-luminescence when exposed to Röntgen rays. **1906** J. B. BURKE *Orig. Life* xiii. 241 Many substances, when warmed, possess the power of radiating energy which they had previously stored up in some other way: a phenomenon which is known as Thermoluminescence. **1967** *New Scientist* 26 Oct. 206/3 Proposals for thermo-luminescence on the Moon are not new. **1968** *Ibid.* 21 Mar. 644/1 Methods of using the natural thermoluminescence of minerals in fired ceramics to find out when they were made have been investigated..for several years. **1968** *Times* 14 Oct. 8/1 Archaeological fakes, some so convincing that they have deceived experts, are being exposed by a new scientific technique developed for dating ancient pottery. The results of one test, known as thermoluminescence dating, are to be used in a court case in America. **1977** G. CLARK *World Prehistory* (ed. 3) p. xx, The degree of thermoluminescence given out by a sample of pottery or stone under heat is proportional to the amount of radiation accumulated since the sample was last fired.

thermolumiˈnescent, *a.* [f. THERMO- + LUMINESCENT.] Characterized by or pertaining to thermoluminescence. Also used *spec.* of a means of dating ancient pottery and other material; abbrev. *TL* s.v. T 6a.

1899 A. S. HERSCHEL in *Nature* 11 May 29/2 A very moderate degree of heat suffices to expel completely from minerals..all the store of thermo-luminescent energy which ..they more or less abundantly possess. **1962** *Oxf. Univ. Gaz.* 9 Mar. 788/2 *Thermoluminescent Dating.* The principle of this technique is that radiation damage accumulates in all clay due to the natural radio-activity of uranium and thorium impurities [etc.]. **1968** *New Scientist* 21 Mar. 644/2 The initial thermoluminescent measurements are capable of good accuracy and reproducibility. **1970** *Daily Tel.* 25 Apr. 11/6 The thermo-luminescent method is based on the fact that many minerals when heated to temperatures around 500°C. emit light, additional to the ordinary red-hot glow. **1971** *Physics Bull.* Oct. 579/1 Nearly all acidic rocks and sedimentary carbonates are thermoluminescent.

thermolysin: see THERMO-

thermolysis (θəˈmɒlɪsɪs). [f. THERMO- + Gr. λύσις loosing, solution, etc., after Ger. *thermolyse* (F. Mohr, 1874).]

1. *Chem.* The separation of a compound into its elements by the action of heat; decomposition or dissociation by heat.

1875 WATTS *Dict. Chem.* VII. 636 Decomposition by heat. Dissociation—Thermolysis (F. Mohr, Ann. Ch. Pharm. clxxi. 361). *Ibid.* 637 An essential condition of thermolysis is that the constituents of the compound shall, in combining, have given out heat. **1884** A. DANIELL *Princ. Physics* xiii. 319

The heat.. has the effect of throwing the molecule into such agitation that the mutual affinity of the atoms cannot retain them in union. This is the process of Dissociation or Thermolysis.

2. *Physiol.* The dissipation or dispersion of heat from the body.

1896 *Allbutt's Syst. Med.* I. 143 [see THERMOGENESIS]. *Ibid.* 159 In Dr. Macalister's.. Goulstonian Lectures on Fever it is suggested that thermogenesis, thermolysis, and thermotaxis must be regarded as three separate functions of the nervous system. **1899** *Syd. Soc. Lex., Thermolysis*, the dissipation of heat.

Hence **thermo'lytic** *a.*, pertaining to or producing thermolysis; *sb.* a thermolytic agent or substance; **'thermolyse, -yze** *v., trans.* to subject to thermolysis; to decompose by the action of heat.

1890 BILLINGS *Nat. Med. Dict., Thermolytic*, heat-discharging. **1896** *Allbutt's Syst. Med.* I. 150 Able to influence 'thermolytic' or thermogenetic processes. **1891** *Cent. Dict.*, Thermolyze. **1899** *Syd. Soc. Lex., Thermolytic*, ..[also] an agent promoting the discharge of heat from the body.

thermo-magnetic to **-metamorphism**: see THERMO-.

thermome'chanical, *a.* [f. THERMO- + MECHANICAL *a.* and *sb.*] **a.** *Physics.* Designating or referring to an effect observed in helium II in which the liquid tends to flow from a region of lower to one of higher temperature.

1939 H. LONDON in *Proc. R. Soc.* A. CLXXI. 484 By maintaining a temperature gradient along the capillary, it is thus possible to produce a flow of helium against a pressure gradient... The phenomenon which we shall call the 'thermomechanical effect' reveals a new mechanism by which heat can be transformed into mechanical work. **1959** K. R. ATKINS *Liquid Helium* i. 11 The thermo-mechanical pressure difference Δp arising from a temperature difference ΔT is given by $\Delta p/\Delta T = Q^*/TV$, where Q^* is the heat transfer associated with the transfer of unit mass.. and V is the volume of unit mass. **1964** [see *mechanocaloric* adj. s.v. MECHANO-]. **1974** D. R. & J. TILLEY *Superfluidity & Superconductivity* i. 9 These manifestations of the thermomechanical effect show clearly that heat transfer and mass transfer in the II are inseparable.

b. *gen.* Both thermal and mechanical; *spec.* in *Metallurgy*, involving simultaneous thermal and mechanical treatment to achieve results not obtained when they are applied separately.

1974 *Sci. Amer.* June 34/3 The less energetic ions (thermal deuterons and tritons).. are capable of producing sharp thermomechanical stresses in a thin skin of the first wall. **1975** *Nature* 7 Aug. 455/3 The uncertainty in geochemical characteristics, especially of the radiogenic isotopes, leaves many degrees of freedom in predicting the present thermo-mechanical state of the interior [of Mercury]. **1976** *Ibid.* 22 July p. iii. (Advt.), The journal will welcome papers concerned with the relevant areas of materials technology and metallurgy, e.g. thermomechanical treatments.

thermometer (θəˈmɒmɪtə(r)). Also 7 -tre. [mod. f. Gr. θέρμ-η heat, θερμό-ς hot + μέτρον measure: see -METER. In F. *thermomètre* (1624). The name *thermoscopium* appears somewhat earlier: see THERMOSCOPE.]

An instrument for measuring temperature (see TEMPERATURE 7) by means of a substance whose expansion and contraction under different degrees of heat and cold are capable of accurate measurement.

For the history of the instrument and its names, see H. C. Bolton *The Evolution of the Thermometer* (Easton Pa. 1900), Renou *Hist. du Thermomètre* (Versailles 1876), Burckhardt *Zur Geschichte des Thermometers*, 1902.

The earliest form was an air-thermometer invented and used by Galilei *a* 1597, for indicating the temperature of the atmosphere; alcohol thermometers were used *c* 1650; the device of a fixed zero (orig. the freezing-point) was introduced by Hooke, 1665. The fixing of the zero at an arbitrary point below the freezing point is attributed to FAHRENHEIT of Amsterdam, who made mercurial thermometers *c* 1720, and his scale has been in general use in England since *c* 1724. The zero of REAUMUR (1730), and of the CENTIGRADE thermometer of Celsius (1742), now largely used in science, is (like that used by Hooke and Sir I. Newton) the freezing-point. The ordinary form is now a slender hermetically sealed glass tube with a fine bore, having a bulb at the lower end filled with mercury, or with alcohol or other liquid, and adjusted to a graduated scale; variations of temperature being indicated by the varying heights of the column of liquid in the tube, due to its expansion and contraction.

air-, centigrade, clinical, differential, Fahrenheit, gas-, maximum-, minimum-, Réaumur, register thermometer: see the first elements. ***metallic*** (or ***bimetallic***) ***thermometer***, a thermometer which indicates temperature by differential expansion and contraction of composite metal bars.

[**1624** 'H. VAN ETTEN' (J. Leuréchon) *Récréation mathématique* (1626) 99 Thermomètre ou instrument pour mesurer les degrez de chalour ou de froidure qui sont en l'air.] **1633** W. OUGHTRED tr. *van Etten's Math. Recr.* 110 Of the Thermometer: or an instrument to measure the degrees of heat and cold in the aire. **1646** SIR T. BROWNE *Pseud. Ep.* 227 The same is evident from the Thermometer. **1665** HOOKE *Microgr.* vii. 38 Sealed Thermometers, which I have, by several tryals, at last brought to a great certainty and tenderness:.. for graduating the stem, I fix that for the beginning of my division where the surface of the liquor in the stem remains when the ball is placed in.. water, that is so cold that it just begins to freeze.. (which I mark with an [o] or nought). **1687** A. LOVELL tr. *Thevenot's Trav.* II. 30 It is very hot in Aleppo,.. the first day of June at Noon I found by my Thermometre, that the heat was at the thirtieth Degree. **1744** *Phil. Trans.* XLIII. 32 Fahrenheit,.. so well known by his Mercurial Thermometers. **1782** *Phil. Trans.* LXXII. I. 72 Account of an improved Thermometer. By Mr. James Six. **1799** *Monthly Rev.* XXX. 9 In Pennsylvania, on the 14th of March,.. Fahrenheit's thermometer stood at 65° at noonday, though it had been at 14° but a week before. **1820** Register thermometer [see REGISTER *sb.*[1] 12]. **1878** HUXLEY *Physiogr.* 71 Dry-and-wet bulb Thermometers... One of the instruments has its bulb free, whilst the other is covered with muslin. *Ibid.* 199 If a thermometer be buried in the ground.., it is found to be affected by all superficial changes of temperature. **1898** P. MANSON *Trop. Diseases* viii. 158 The tongue now begins to moisten, the pulse-rate and the thermometer to fall.

b. *fig.*

1801 A. HAMILTON *Wks.* (1886) VII. 224 No bad thermometer of the capacity of our Chief Magistrate for government is furnished by the rule which he offers for judging of the utility of the Federal Courts. **1824** BYRON *Juan* XVI. xlviii, Taste.. now-a-days is the thermometer By whose degrees all characters are class'd. **1883** H. SMITH in J. G. Butler *Bible Work* II. 825/1 The true missionary spirit in the Church is.. the test and thermometer of her piety.

c. *attrib.* and *Comb.*, as ***thermometer bulb, piece, reading, scale, tube***; **thermometer-gauge**, a steam-gauge which indicates the pressure in a boiler by the expansion of a fluid at the temperature due to the pressure; **thermometer-stove**, a stove automatically regulated by means of a thermometer.

1784 WEDGWOOD in *Phil. Trans.* LXXIV. 367 Some of the clay thermometer pieces were set on end upon the silver piece. **1834** MRS. SOMERVILLE *Connex. Phys. Sci.* xv. 125 A glass tube of extremely fine bore, such as a small thermometer-tube. **1838** *Civil Eng. & Arch. Jrnl.* I. 129/2 The self-regulating fire, or thermometer-stove. **1841** *Ibid.* IV. 13/1 The four instruments employed.. to determine the pressure of steam,.. the barometer-gauge, the air-gauge, the thermometer-gauge, and the spring-gauge or indicator. **1901** *Daily Chron.* 26 Nov. 5/1 The downward tendency in yesterday's thermometer readings.

thermometric (θɜːməʊˈmɛtrɪk), *a.* [f. prec. + -IC: cf. Gr. μετρικός of or for measuring. So F. *thermometrique* (18th c.).] = next.

1784 *Phil. Trans.* LXXIV. 367 The stage of extension.. always precedes the thermometric diminution. **1826** HENRY *Chem.* I. 86 The absolute zero, or point of total privation of heat on the thermometric scale. **1860** TYNDALL *Glac.* II. xiii. 296 His own thermometric experiments show us that the body of the glacier is at a temperature of 32° Fahr.

thermometrical (θɜːməʊˈmɛtrɪkəl), *a.* [f. as prec. + -AL[1]: see -ICAL.] Of or pertaining to the thermometer or its use; made with or involving the use of the thermometer.

1664-5 BOYLE *Exper. & Obs. Cold* (heading), New Thermometrical Experiments and Thoughts. **1715** CHEYNE *Philos. Princ. Relig.* v. §21 (ed. 2) 233 His Heat raises the Liquor in the Thermometrical Tubes. **1820** SCORESBY *Acc. Arctic Reg.* I. 352 A series of thermometrical observations, continued through the space of a few years. **1880** HAUGHTON *Phys. Geog.* iii. 90 Making so many fixed points on the earth's thermometrical scale.

b. That acts as a thermometer; indicating rise or fall of temperature.

1823 J. BADCOCK *Dom. Amusem.* 40 Thermometrical Ink.

Hence **thermo'metrically** *adv.*, according to or by means of the thermometer or its indications.

1828 in WEBSTER. **1856** G. WILSON *Let.* 10 Apr., in *Mem.* x. (1860) 427 For a month.. the wind has blown geographically from Araby the blest, but thermometrically from Iceland the accursed. **1881** SULLIVAN in *Macm. Mag.* XLIV. 342 A very heated term, thermometrically speaking.

thermometrograph (θɜːməʊˈmɛtrəgrɑːf, -æ-). [f. THERMOMETER + -GRAPH.] A self-registering thermometer.

1837 MACDOUGALL tr. *Graah's E. Coast Greenland* 20 Mr. Vahl, having.. let down his thermometrograph, found the temperature of the sea, at the depth of 110 fathoms, to be 5°·50, while that at the surface was 6°·3. **1877** KNIGHT *Dict. Mech., Thermetograph* [*sic*], a self-registering thermometer, recording the maximum and minimum of temperature in a given time.

thermometry (θəˈmɒmɪtrɪ). [f. THERMOMETER: see -METRY.] The department of science which deals with the construction of thermometers; the scientific use of the thermometer; the measurement of temperature.

1858 LARDNER *Hand-bk. Nat. Phil.*, etc. 240 Chap. II. Thermometry. **1871** MAXWELL *Theory of Heat* Pref., The whole science of heat is founded on Thermometry and Calorimetry. **1878** LOCKYER *Stargazing* 376 He attaches a thermo-pile to his telescope and establishes a celestial thermometry.

thermo-motive, -motor: see THERMO-.

ˌthermo-ˈmultiplier. [f. THERMO- + MULTIPLIER 4.] Early name for a THERMOPILE: so called in reference to the multiplying effect of the numerous cells in the battery.

1835 FARADAY tr. Melloni in *Philos. Mag.* VII. 475 In order to experiment under these circumstances, it is clearly necessary to employ an extremely delicate thermoscope, such as well-constructed thermomultipliers. **1854** J. SCOFFERN in *Orr's Circ. Sc., Chem.* 276 The thermo-multiplier of Nobili consists of about fifty pairs of antimony and bismuth bars. **1879** NEWCOMB & HOLDEN *Astron.* 495 In the case of the brighter stars the heat radiated has been made sensible in the foci of our telescopes by means of the thermo-multiplier.

So **ˌthermo-ˈmultiple** in same sense.

1895 in *Funk's Stand. Dict.*

thermonastic, -nasty: see THERMO-.

thermonatrite (θɜːməʊˈneɪtraɪt). *Min.* [a. Ger. *thermonatrit* (Haidinger 1845), 'because it results from the drying out of natron' (Chester), f. THERMO- + NATRON: see -ITE[1].] Hydrous carbonate of soda, found in various saline lakes, about some mines and volcanoes, and as an efflorescence in many dry regions.

1859 PAGE *Handbk. Geol. Terms* s.v., According to Haidinger, a saturated solution of soda at a temperature of 77° to 99° Fahr., and cooling slowly, forms crystals of thermonatrite. **1863-72** WATTS *Dict. Chem.* I. 795 Na_2CO_3 + aq. formed from the deca-hydrate by efflorescence, is found native as thermonatrite, in the same localities as natron.

thermo'neutral, *a.* [f. THERMO- + NEUTRAL *a.* and *sb.*] **1.** *Biol.* Of an environment or its temperature: such that an organism is in thermal equilibrium without thermoregulation.

1961 in WEBSTER. **1966** *Respiration Physiol.* I. 30 The thermoneutral skin temperature zone for fasting adult sheep has been found to be 33-35°C as determined by immersion in a water bath. **1976** *Nature* 13 May 134/1 Neonates and infants were tested using a tight-fitting face mask with minimal dead space while the subjects were asleep in a thermoneutral condition. **1977** *Lancet* 7 May 988/1 The incubator should if possible be kept at the lower end of the thermoneutral range.

2. *Chem.* Of a reaction: accompanied by neither the absorption nor the emission of heat.

1970 *Nature* 12 Sept. 1097/1 Because the translational energies of the reactant ions are approximately thermal, these two reactions must be thermoneutral or exothermic. **1971** *Sci. Amer.* Dec. 57/3 The first and second reactions are strongly endothermic; the third is exothermic; the fourth is essentially thermoneutral. **1977** I. M. CAMPBELL *Energy & Atmosphere* v. 106 It appears probable that this depends upon the attack of radicals like CH upon N_2 in a near thermoneutral elementary reaction.

So **ˌthermoneuˈtrality**, the condition of being thermoneutral.

1881 WATTS *Dict. Chem.* VIII. 985 The term thermo-neutrality is employed.. to express the fact that the quantity of heat evolved or absorbed when a salt is dissolved in water already containing equivalent quantities of other salts, is, for the most part, the same that it would be if the former salt were dissolved in pure water. **1960** K. SCHMIDT-NIELSEN *Animal Physiol.* iii. 43 Thus, man has a narrow range of thermoneutrality between 27°C and 31°C. **1979** *Nature* 24 May 322/1 The abnormal thermoregulatory thermo-genesis quantitatively accounts for most of the metabolic efficiency of the obese animals as pair feeding at thermo-neutrality rather than at 23°C reduces the excess fat deposited by 65%.

'thermonous, *a. rare*[−1]. [a. Gr. θερμό-νους heated in mind, f. θερμός hot + νοῦς mind.]

1888 G. MEREDITH *Reading of Earth* Poems 1898 II. 200 Not as Cybele's beast will thy head lash tail So præter-determinedly thermonous.

thermonuclear (θɜːməʊˈnjuːklɪə(r)). Also **thermo-nuclear.** [f. THERMO- + NUCLEAR *a.*]

a. Derived from, utilizing, or being a nuclear reaction that occurs only at very high temperatures (such as those inside stars), viz. fusion of hydrogen or other light nuclei.

[**1937** G. GAMOW *Struct. Atomic Nuclei* 232 The first calculations concerning thermal nuclear reactions were carried out by Atkinson and Houtermans.] **1938** *Physical Rev.* LIII. 595/1 The behavior of a star with a thermo-nuclear energy source.. is studied. **1942** B. BLIVEN *Men who make Future* xi. 202 This perhaps represents a struggle between two almost unbelievably powerful forces within each star—what is called the 'thermo-nuclear reaction' and gravitation. **1954** *Ann. Reg. 1953* 377 *Pravda* described the results of a 'thermo-nuclear' explosion. **1958** *New Statesman* 1 Feb. 123/2 Thermo-nuclear energy depends on building up atoms of hydrogen into atoms of helium. **1962** F. I. ORDWAY et al. *Basic Astronautics* vi. 284 A new star not yet hot enough to initiate thermonuclear reactions obtains its luminosity from gravitational contraction. **1964** M. GOWING *Britain & Atomic Energy 1939–1945* ix. 260 Thermonuclear fusion of light elements would provide infinitely more powerful reactions than fission of heavy elements. **1969** *Times* 20 Feb. 17/5 It implied that their calculations of the sun's thermonuclear fuel budget were considerably in error. **1976** *McGraw-Hill Yearbk. Sci. & Technol.* 342/1 In controlled thermonuclear reactors the nuclear reaction D + T→^{4}He + n + 17·6 MeV occurs in a plasma at temperatures of 100–500 × 10^6 kelvins.

b. Pertaining to, characterized by, or possessing weapons that utilize thermonuclear reactions.

1953 *Time* 19 Oct. 25/3 Secretary of Defense Wilson, at his press conference, cast doubt on a suggestion that the Russians had a thermonuclear bomb 'in droppable form'. **1955** *Ann. Reg. 1954* 169 Mr. Adlai Stevenson.. inquired whether the 'New Look' meant leaving the country with 'the choice of inaction or a thermo-nuclear holocaust'. **1955** *Times* 13 July 9/5 They draw attention to the possibility that a thermo-nuclear war might put an end to the human race. **1958** *Listener* 7 Aug. 207/3 So long as Britain makes her own nuclear weapons, and particularly the thermo-nuclear weapon, there is no possibility of dissuading France or Germany or Sweden from developing theirs. **1959** *Times Lit. Suppl.* 16 Jan. 27/3 In the Thermo-nuclear age, if civilization is not to disintegrate.., the premises of Gandhi have an immediate relevance. **1959** *Daily Tel.* 4 Mar. 8 With the thermo-nuclear cloud overshadowing the world no statesman, not even a Soviet Prime Minister, can afford to disregard mankind's longing for peace. **1965** H. KAHN *On*

Escalation ii. 42 In a thermonuclear balance of terror, both nations will be reluctant to start a crisis. **1966** J. W. BURTON in de Reuck & Knight *Conflict in Society* xxiii. 380 In the relations of the two thermo-nuclear States, tensions arise from unacceptable enactments of their respective roles. **1972** M. H. HALPERIN *Contemporary Mil. Strategy* i. 7 One has only to recall Mr. Khruschev's statements during the Cuban missile crisis about the world being close to thermo-nuclear war.

Thermopane: see THERMO-.

thermophil, -phile ('θɜːməfɪl), *a.* and *sb.* [f. THERMO- + -PHIL.] **a.** *adj.* Requiring a high temperature for development, as certain bacteria. **b.** *sb.* A thermophil organism. So **thermophilic** (-'fɪlɪk), **thermophilous** (-'ɒfɪləs) *adjs.*

1894 MACFADYEN & BLAXALL in *Jrnl. Path. & Bacteriol.* III. 88 To those organisms that grow best at very high temperatures we have applied the name of thermophilic bacteria. **1896** *Allbutt's Syst. Med.* I. 513 There is a class of microbes which refuse to grow at any temperature below 50° C.; such organisms are called 'thermophile'. **1899** *Nature* 15 June 147/1 Facts regarding the existence of thermophilous organisms. **1900** *Ibid.* 22 Feb. 388/2 Thermophilic bacteria ..are specially important as regards the fermentation in ensilage and the digestion of cellulose. **1909** H. W. CONN *Agric. Bacteriol.* (ed. 2) i. 16 A few species..grow best at unexpectedly high temperatures, some having been found flourishing at 140° or even higher. These peculiar bacteria are called thermophiles. **1964** COONEY & EMERSON *Thermophilic Fungi* i. 6 To the algologist a thermophile may have a maximum between 60° and 80°C..to the bacteriologist..55° to 80°C, and the acarologist 35° to 45°C. **1965** BELL & COOMBE tr. *Strasburger's Textbk. Bot.* III. 774 The wood and fruits of thermophilous trees and shrubs have been repeatedly found some hundreds of metres above their present altitudinal limits. **1975** J. G. EVANS *Environment Early Man Brit. Isles* ii. 49 The Allerød Interstadial..was the first zone to see the appearance of thermophilous land snails. **1977** *Time* 26 Dec. 20/3 Their droppings will be placed into fermenter tanks filled with thermophilic (heat-loving) bacteria. **1981** *New Scientist* 10 Sept. 667/2 The plasmid may be of value..for transferring genes into thermophiles (bacteria that like high temperatures).

thermophone ('θɜːməʊfəʊn). [f. as prec. + Gr. φωνή voice, sound, after TELEPHONE.] An apparatus in which sonorous vibrations of a diaphragm are produced by heat-rays.

1878 TH. WIESENDANGER in *Engineer* XLVI. Nov. 335 The Thermophone. A new source of sound for the telephone. **1881** A. G. BELL in *Nature* 12 May 44/1 We have decided to adopt the term 'radiophone'..limiting the words thermophone, photophone, and actinophone to apparatus for the production of sound by thermal, luminous, or actinic rays respectively. **1902** SLOANE *Stand. Electr. Dict.* 537 *Thermophone*, an apparatus for reproducing sounds telephonically by the agency of heat; a receiving-telephone actuated by heat.

thermophore to **-physics**: see THERMO-.

thermopile ('θɜːməpaɪl). [f. THERMO- + PILE *sb.*[3] 5.] A thermo-electric battery, used in connexion with a galvanometer, for measuring minute quantities of radiant heat; also called THERMO-MULTIPLIER.

1849 NOAD *Electricity* (ed. 3) 424 Thermo-piles are now constructed by soldering together at their alternate edges, bars of antimony and bismuth, with squares of cardboard or thick paper intervening. **1871** B. STEWART *Heat* §165 A square block, containing altogether 25 couples of bismuth and antimony is generally employed, and such an arrangement is called a thermo-pile. **1891** *Times* 2 Oct. 3/1 A thermopile..is an apparatus for direct conversion of heat into electricity.

thermoplastic (θɜːməʊ'plæstɪk), *a.* and *sb.* [f. THERMO- + PLASTIC *a.*] **A.** *adj.* Becoming soft when heated and rigid when allowed to cool, and capable of being repeatedly reheated and reshaped without loss of properties; made of such a substance.

1883 *Fisheries Exhib. Catal.* 63 Thermoplastic Splints, likewise Splints for Fractures and Broken Bones. **1909** *Chem. Abstr.* III. 2063 Thermo-plastic composition containing keratin. Keratin is mixed with β-naphthol and the compn. subjected to heat and pressure, to form a subst. for rubber, celluloid, etc. **1937** *Jrnl. R. Aeronaut. Soc.* XLI. 525 Some kinds of synthetic resins and to a limited extent one natural resin (shellac) have the valuable characteristic of being 'thermosetting', i.e., when once moulded they set to permanently infusible products. Most resins are 'thermoplastic', i.e., they become soft whenever the temperature exceeds a certain value. **1951** [see *benzyl* s.v. BENZO-]. **1958** *Listener* 4 Dec. 967/1 Thermoplastic tiles and rubber floors. **1976** J. FLEMING *To make an Underworld* xi. 128 These small thermo-plastic boats..were safer than houses, kids could play with them.

B. *sb.* A thermoplastic substance.

1929 *Brit. Plastics & Moulded Products Trader* June 25/1 Thermoplastics are divided into pheno-plastics..and amino-plastics. **1945** *Electronic Engin.* XVII. 516 It is frequently used in association with polythene and other thermoplastics. **1967** *Times Rev. Industry* May 75/3 Other thermoplastics, including polyvinyl chloride (PVC), polypropylene and polyvinylidene chloride comprise about 10 per cent..of the total weight of plastics used in packaging. **1976** *Shooting Mag.* Dec. 33/2 (Advt.), Lightweight muff-type ear protector... Earcups are manufactured from thermoplastic with soft sponge-filled ear cushions.

Hence ˌ**thermopla'sticity**, the quality of being thermoplastic.

1935 C. ELLIS *Chem. Synthetic Resins* II. lvi. 1150 The thermoplasticity of the resins is a disadvantage. **1962** J. T. MARSH *Self-Smoothing Fabrics* x. 141 Some of these mixed products can be used to reduce the solubility and swelling of the linear polymer but the thermoplasticity will be reduced. **1980** *Nuclear Engin. & Design* LVII. 323 (*heading*) Coupling phenomena in thermoplasticity.

‖**thermopolion, -ium** (θɜːməʊ'pəʊlɪɒn, -ɪəm). *Antiq.* [a. Gr. θερμο-πώλιον (L. *thermopōlium*, Plaut.) a tavern where hot drinks were sold.] (See quot. 1753.) Hence †**ther'mopolist**: see quot. 1656; **ther'mopolite**, the keeper of a thermopolion.

1656 BLOUNT *Glossogr.*, *Thermopolist*.., a Cook that sells hot meat. **1753** CHAMBERS *Cycl. Supp.*, *Thermopolium*, a name for a sort of public houses among the ancients, in which hot liquors were sold. **1832** GELL *Pompeiana* I. ii. 8 The shops of a thermopolite. *Ibid.* II. xii. 10 An ordinary wine shop or thermopolion.

†'**thermopot, -pote.** *Obs. rare*$^{-0}$. [ad. Gr. θερμο-πότης drinker of hot liquids, f. θερμο-, THERMO- + πότης drinker.] (See quot.)

1727 BAILEY vol. II, *Thermopote*, a Drinker of hot Liquors.

So ‖**thermopotis** (θə'mɒpəʊtɪs), *Class. Archæol.* [a. Gr. θερμο-πότις cup for hot drinks.]

1857 BIRCH *Anc. Pottery* (1858) II. 90 The thermopotis was a vase also used for warming wine.

thermopower: see THERMO-.

Thermopylae (θɜː'mɒpɪliː, -pɪlaɪ). The name of a narrow pass on the north-east coast of Greece between Thessaly and Locris, the scene of a battle in 480 B.C. in which a small Greek force temporarily withheld a Persian invasion; used *transf.* and *fig.* with reference to heroic resistance against strong opposition.

1928 A. HUXLEY *Point Counter Point* xxix. 471 E. talked a lot about Thermopylae and the Spartans. But my resistance was even more heroic. Leonidas had three hundred companions. I defended my spiritual Thermopylae single-handed against E. and his Freemen. **1929** J. BUCHAN *Courts of Morning* III. iii. 335 I'm going to try the Themopylae stunt... Our Thermopylae is going to be a more cunning affair than the old one. **1955** in R. Megarry *Second Miscellany-at-Law* (1973) 157 It courageously held the line of reason at the Thermopylae of logic and did not give way at the Gettysburg of fact. **1967** C. SETON-WATSON *Italy from Liberalism to Fascism* iii. 125 A column of 500 Italian troops had been wiped out by several thousand Ethiopians at Dogali, after fighting almost to the last man and the last round. This 'Italian Thermopylae' caught the public imagination. **1972** V. G. KIERNAN *Lords of Human Kind* (ed. 2) p. xxiv, The consequence has been Vietnam's Thermopylae of twenty years.

thermo-radiometer: see THERMO-.

thermoreceptor ('θɜːməʊrɪˌseptə(r)). *Physiol.* [f. THERMO- + RECEPTOR.] A nerve ending that is sensitive to stimulation by heat and cold.

1937 L. V. HEILBRUNN *Outl. Gen. Physiol.* xli. 506 Animals in general are sensitive to heat and cold but, except in higher animals, thermoreceptors are rare, or at any rate not well known. **1951** *Jrnl. Neurophysiol.* XIV. 423 Knowledge of the intracutaneous depth of the thermo-receptors is of very great importance. **1961** *Lancet* 9 Sept. 610/1 Professor Hensel will lecture on the electrophysiology of thermoreceptors. **1971** D. J. AIDLEY *Physiol. of Excitable Cells* xv. 307 The sense organs themselves can be classified according to the type of stimulus which normally excites them. Thus mechanoreceptors are excited by mechanical stimuli, photoreceptors are sensitive to light, thermoreceptors are temperature sensitive.

thermoregulation ('θɜːməʊrɛgjʊ'leɪʃən). [f. THERMO- + REGULATION.] Regulation of temperature, esp. body temperature in an animal or human.

1927 *Jrnl. Exper. Zool.* XLVII. 156 We deal in nest-building with a behavior pattern definitely adapted to the thermoregulation of the organism. **1932** *Jrnl. Gen. Physiol.* XVI. 9 The machine described above is kept in a thermoregulated room. The thermoregulation of a room for such purposes has been regarded..as a difficult and expensive undertaking. **1962** *Lancet* 8 Dec. 1207/1 Most of the research into human problems of thermoregulation in hot surroundings has been sponsored by the Government and the Services. **1972** *Sci. Amer.* June 74/2 Understanding of the physiology of the sphinx moth's thermo-regulation requires..an examination of the levels of body temperature maintained during flight.

So **thermo'regulate** *v. intr.*, to regulate temperature, esp. body temperature; **thermo-'regulated, -'regulating** *ppl. adjs.*; **thermo-'regulative** (*rare*), ˌ**thermoregu'latory** *adjs.*, of, pertaining to, or effecting thermoregulation; **thermo-'regulator**, an apparatus for regulating temperature; a thermostat.

1875 WATTS *Dict. Chem.* VII. 1153 An automatic thermo-regulator for use in the preparation of nitrous oxide and other gases. **1899** CAGNEY *Jaksch's Clin. Diagn.* x. (ed. 4) 446 Of these [thermostats] the author uses the thermo-regulator of L. Meyer. **1917** T. SOLLMAN *Man. Pharmacol.* 449 (*heading*) The hypothetical thermoregulating centres. **1927** *Jrnl. Exper. Zool.* XLVII. 152 Nest-building may be considered a thermoregulative activity. **1932** Thermoregulated [see above]. **1949** KOESTLER *Insight & Outlook* xi. 168 Animals..develop techniques such as nest building..and, in the case of the termites, even contriving thermo-regulatory devices. **1972** *Science* 12 May 601/3 Bumblebees, which can also thermoregulate, occur on the neotropical and Asian mountains. **1973** *Brit. Med. Jrnl.* 22 Dec. 727/2 Some degree of thermoregulatory failure is common in old age. **1974** M. C. GERALD *Pharmacology* xiv. 265 Aspirin..does increase heat loss from the body by its action on the thermoregulatory centers in the hypothalamus. **1978** *Nature* 19 Oct. 646/2 Reptiles which thermoregulate behaviourally..are subject to considerable daily fluctuations in body temperature.

thermoremanence, -remanent: see THERMO-.

Thermos ('θɜːmɒs). [a. Gr. θερμός warm, hot.] A registered trade term noting a flask, bottle, or the like capable of being kept hot or cold by the device (invented by Sir James Dewar) of surrounding the interior vessel with a vacuum jacket to prevent the conduction of heat. Hence (freq. with small initial) applied loosely to any vacuum flask. Also *absol.*, and designating a liquid which has been kept in a Thermos flask.

Patented 1904, No. 4421; not named. Name (Trade Mark No. 289,470) adv. in *Trade Marks Jrnl.* 20 March, 1907. Still (1984) a proprietary term in Great Britain.

1907 *Eng. Mech.* 18 Oct. 246 This invention [of Sir James Dewar] is utilised in the thermos flask. **1909** *Ladies' Field* 28 Aug. 511/2 A Thermos bottle filled with hot coffee was not forgotten. **1909** *Westm. Gaz.* 16 Sept. 5/2 Lieutenant Shackleton testified to the fact that the Thermos flask helped him to perform his wonderful feats in the Antarctic. **1910** *Repts. Patent Cases* XXVII. 396 This was the *Dewar* vessel... In 1904 it occurred to a Mr. Burger that this vessel could be adapted for use as a flask..the result..was the production of the well known *Thermos* flask. **1922** S. LEWIS *Babbitt* xx. 255 Say, could I borrow your thermos—just dropped in to see if I could borrow your thermos bottle. **1923** R. FRY *Let.* 21 June (1972) II. 541 I'd got my thermos filled the day before. **1938** C. G. NORRIS *Bricks without Straw* 350 He poured a glass of water from his thermos jug. **1950** *Time* 3 Apr. 24/3 Simon began to pack blankets and Thermoses for a fishing trip. **1960** E. L. WALLANT *Human Season* (1965) v. 55 'Let me pour you some coffee.' He poured a cupful from the big Thermos. **1977** *New Yorker* 27 June 53/1 Stoical munching forms in mackintoshes taking a swig of something hot out of thermoses. **1978** P. GRACE *Mutuwhenua* vii. 40 The others had home-made biscuits in their parcels or fruit. Oranges, apples, and reeking bananas. Chocolates, a thermos of soup. **1979** *Church Times* 14 Sept. 12/4 No registration is necessary, but please bring sandwiches and a thermos. **1979** *Nature* 15 Nov. 227/1 Sipping green tea poured out of a large thermos flask, we discussed differences between Chinese and UK science. **1979** *Beautiful Brit. Columbia* Winter 6 Relaxing with a hot cup of thermos coffee. **1980** P. FITZGERALD *Human Voices* ii. 47 Workers off work, each with their own thermos.

thermoscope ('θɜːməskəʊp). [ad. mod.L. *thermoscopium* (Bianconi, 1617): see THERMO- and -SCOPE. Cf. F. *thermoscope.*] An instrument for indicating changes of temperature, of which there are various forms.

a. An early name for the thermometer, esp. in its earlier forms. **b.** Count Rumford's name for a differential thermometer for detecting minute differences of temperature. **c.** An electric or magnetic apparatus, as a thermopile, for detecting and measuring minute differences of temperature. **d.** Any substance or device used to indicate excessive heat in machinery, variations of bodily temperature, rate of radiation of heat, or the like.

a. [**1617** GIUS. BIANCONI *Sphæra Mundi, seu Cosmographia Demonstrativa*... Thermoscopium.] **1656** tr. *Hobbes's Elem. Philos.* (1839) 531 This organ is called a thermometer or thermoscope, because the degrees of heat and cold are measured and marked by it. **1672** BOYLE in *Phil. Trans.* VII. 5110 The Air by the seal'd Thermoscope appeared hot for the season. **1778** *Phil. Trans.* LXVIII. 484 The first inventors..called..their instruments.. Baroscopes, Thermoscopes, Microscopes. **1790** DE LUC *ibid.* LXXXI. 32 The thermoscopes of quicksilver and water. **1842** BRANDE *Dict. Sc.*, etc. s.v. *Thermometer*, The thermometer of Drebbel and Sanctorio..had no scale, and was therefore merely an indicator of changes of temperature, or a thermoscope.

b. 1804 CT. RUMFORD in *Phil. Trans.* XCIV. 101 An instrument I contrived for measuring, or rather for discovering, those very small changes of temperature in bodies, which are occasioned by the radiations of other neighbouring bodies, which happen to be at a higher, or at a lower temperature. This instrument..I shall take the liberty to call a thermoscope. **1842** BRANDE *Dict. Sc.*, etc. s.v., The modification of the air thermometer, called by Leslie a differential thermometer, was claimed by Count Rumford as one of his own inventions, under the name of thermoscope. **1850** GROVE *Corr. Phys. Forces* (ed. 2) 42 With the most delicate thermoscope, he could detect no indications of transmitted heat. **1860** MAYNE *Expos. Lex.*, *Thermoscopium*, term for an instrument by Rumford for measuring the difference of temperature by dilatation of dry air contained in two balls, which a long tube, twice bent, separates from each other: a thermoscope.

c. 1835 [see THERMO-MULTIPLIER]. **1879** tr. *Du Moncel's Telephone* 195 It is therefore a microphone as well as a thermoscope. **1881** *Nature* 17 Feb. 372/2 The magnetic thermoscope is intended to indicate differences of temperature by showing differences between the magnetic moments of steel magnets.

d. 1877 KNIGHT *Dict. Mech.* 2550/1 Barker and Mayer's thermoscope..is designed to indicate..the existence of excessive heat in journal-bearings... Marcy's thermoscope ..is particularly designed for experiments on animal heat. **1884** *Ibid.* Suppl. 892/2 The varied changes of tint..may serve..as a rough index of the temperature of surrounding bodies, thus constituting the little instrument a thermoscope.

thermoscopic (θɜːməʊˈskɒpɪk), *a.* [f. prec. + -IC.] Of, pertaining to, or of the nature of a thermoscope.

1730 *Phil. Trans.* XXXVI. 254 The Severity of the Weather did not cease;..the Spirit of Wine, in the English Thermometer, in a Morning always stood at, or under the 80th Deg. of the Thermoscopick Scale. **1843** GROVE *Corr. Phys. Forces* (1846) 17 Of which heat no evidence can be afforded by any thermoscopic test. **1854** J. SCOFFERN in *Orr's Circ. Sc., Chem.* 121 Thermometric and thermoscopic instruments.

So **thermoˈscopical** *a.*, in same sense; whence **thermoˈscopically** *adv.*

1670 *Phil. Trans.* V. p. iv, The Thermoscopical Measures of Warmth and Frigidity. **1730** *Ibid.* XXXVI. 254 From Thermoscopical Observations. **1895** *Funk's Stand. Dict.*, Thermoscopically.

thermosensitive, -sensitivity: see THERMO-.

thermoset (ˈθɜːməʊsɛt), *a.* and *sb.* [f. THERMO- + SET *ppl. a.*] **A.** *adj.* Incapable of being softened or melted by heat like a thermoplastic; also = THERMOSETTING *ppl. a.*

1947 [see CURE *v.*[1] 10]. **1972** *Physics Bull.* Nov. 663/2 Epoxy resins are polymers with one or more epoxide groups ..which can be converted to a thermoset stage by reaction with appropriate curing agents. **1973** *Sci. Amer.* July 42/3 Today the matrix in glass-reinforced composites may be either a thermoset plastic, such as polyester, phenolic or epoxy, or any of a number of thermoplastic resins, such as nylon, polyethylene or polystyrene. **1973** J. M. G. COWIE *Polymers* i. 19 The thermoset plastics generally have superior abrasion and dimensional stability characteristics compared with the thermoplastics which have better flexural and impact properties. In contrast to the thermoplastics, thermosetting polymers..are changed irreversibly from fusible, soluble products into highly intractable crosslinked resins which cannot be moulded by flow.

B. *sb.* A thermoset substance.

1955 in M. Reifer *Dict. New Words.* **1958** *Times Rev. Industry* Aug. 57/1 Thermoplastics have gained a..market at the expense of thermosets. **1970** *New Scientist* 19 Mar. Suppl. 9/1 Reinforced thermosets are used in many high-strength applications from boat hulls to aircraft radomes. **1975** *Sci. Amer.* July 63/1 Nonmetals such as thermoplastics, thermosets, polytetrafluoroethylene and carbon-graphites are successful bearing materials because of their excellent resistance to scoring and erosion.

thermoˈsetting, *ppl. a.* [f. THERMO- + SETTING *ppl. a.*] Of a plastic: solidifying and becoming thermoset when heated; also, = THERMOSET *a.*

[**1929** *Brit. Plastics & Moulded Products Trader* June 24/2 Thermoplastic mouldings..comprise substances which go through a process of thermo-setting on the application of heat and pressure.] **1931** *British Plastics Yearbk.* 74 *Thermo-setting plastics*, those compositions that though thermo-plastic in the first instance, harden off rapidly under the influence of heat. **1937** [see THERMOPLASTIC *a.*]. **1951** *Archit. Rev.* CIX. 166/2 Hardness and resistance to scratching and heat..is one of the main advantages of the thermo-setting plastics. **1973** [see THERMOSET *a.*]. **1982** M. DUKE *Flashpoint* xviii. 134 The thermosetting polyurethane plastic floor. **1983** *Daily Tel.* 12 Dec. 19/3 The inclusion of fillers, particularly metallic ones, in thermosetting plastics is a known and recognised practice for reducing and dissipating exotherm.

thermo-ˈsiphon. [f. THERMO- + SIPHON.] A siphon attachment by which the circulation in a system of hot-water pipes is increased or induced. Also *attrib.* So **thermo-siˈphonic** *a.*

1834 LOUDON *Encycl. Gard.* §2142 Fowler's method of circulating hot water in his thermosiphon. **1904** A. B. F. YOUNG *Compl. Motorist* iii. 55 Circulation is maintained either by a centrifugal pump driven by a chain off the engine shaft, or, automatically, by means of what is known as the 'Thermo-Syphon' system, in which advantage is taken of the fact that hot water rises to the top of a tank and cold water sinks to the bottom. **1906** *Daily Chron.* 3 Mar. 3/6 Water from a reservoir is circulated around the cylinder, in the water-jacket, either by a pump worked by the engine, or on the thermo-syphon system. **1920** *Autocar* 7 Feb. 251/1 Water is circulated by thermo-syphonic action. **1963** R. F. WEBB *Motorists' Dict.* 210 *Thermo syphon cooling*, a type of liquid cooling for an automobile engine where there is no mechanical assistance for the flow of the liquid through the system. **1968** G. N. GEORGANO *Compl. Encycl. Motorcars* 473 Cooling was by thermo-syphon, the hallmark of the Renault being the huge dashboard radiator. **1982** *Solar Energy* (Shell Internat. Petroleum Co.) 3/2 (*caption*) Typical solar water heater thermo-syphon system.

thermosphere (ˈθɜːməʊsfɪə(r)). [f. THERMO- + SPHERE *sb.*] **1.** †**a.** (See quot. 1924.) *Obs. rare*⁻¹. **b.** The part of the atmosphere between the mesopause and the height at which it ceases to have the properties of a continuous medium, characterized throughout by an increase of temperature with height.

1924 S. N. SEN in *Q. Jrnl. R. Meteorol. Soc.* L. 29 Up to an approximate height of 8 km. above the ground the air density is chiefly controlled by the temperature. The name 'thermosphere' is proposed to denote this layer of the atmosphere. **1950** S. CHAPMAN in *Jrnl. Geophysical Res.* LV. 396, I propose the name..thermosphere for the layer of upward increasing temperature above that level [i.e. of the mesosphere]. **1967** R. W. FAIRBRIDGE *Encycl. Atmospheric Sci.* 731/2 At the top of the thermosphere, the temperature approaches a constant value of ~ 1500°K. **1981** *Sci. Amer.* July 46/3 On the earth the thermosphere is present day and night; the large-scale rotation of the atmosphere with the planet carries the heated day-side upper atmosphere to the night side of the planet. On the night side of Venus, however, the thermosphere disappears.

2. The warmer, upper part of the oceans.

1956 *Nature* 16 June 1106 (*in figure*) Thermosphere. **1957** [see *psychrosphere* s.v. PSYCHRO-].

Hence **thermosˈpheric** *a.*

1971 *Nature* 29 Jan. 333/2 Calculations suggest that the thermospheric winds may produce some net rotation [of the atmosphere] at low latitudes. **1979** *Ibid.* 8 Feb. 458/2 Rocket measurements of mesospheric and thermospheric nitric oxide concentrations revealed strong enhancements during auroral particle precipitation events.

thermostabile (θɜːməʊˈsteɪbaɪl), *a. Biol.* [f. THERMO- + L. *stabilis* STABLE *a.*] = THERMOSTABLE *a.*

1908 *Practitioner* Feb. 249 In the proglottides of tapeworms..there exists a lipoid substance..which..is thermo-stabile and is similar to proteolytic ferment. **1947** *Ann. Rev. Microbiol.* I. 92 Mottling type strains are more thermostabile than the ringspot type strains.

thermostable (θɜːrməʊˈsteɪb(ə)l), *a.* [f. THERMO- + STABLE *a.*] Retaining its character or active quality at moderately high temperatures: opposed to *thermolabile*. Hence **thermostaˈbility**, the quality of being thermostable.

1904 *Brit. Med. Jrnl.* 10 Sept. 557 The killing of the bacteria is associated with the presence in the serum of an immune animal, of two substances, one thermolabile (complement) which naturally occurs in the serum of the animal species involved, and the other thermostable (immune body), which either is present in normal serum in very small amount or is altogether absent. *Ibid.* 561 [see THERMOLABILE]. **1907** *Science* 13 Sept. 346 The high stability of opsonins against desiccation and the high thermostability of dried opsonins are very striking.

thermostat (ˈθɜːməʊstæt), *sb.* [f. THERMO- + Gr. στατός standing: cf. HELIOSTAT.]

a. An automatic apparatus for regulating temperature; *esp.* a device in which the expansive force of metals or gas acts directly upon the source of heat, ventilation, or the like, or controls them indirectly by opening and closing an electric circuit.

1831 URE in *Proc. Roy. Soc.* 16 June 67 On the Thermostat or Heat Governor, a self-acting physical Apparatus for regulating Temperature. **1835** —— *Philos Manuf.* 26 The instrument, for which I have obtained a patent, under the name of the heat-governor, or thermostat. **1877** W. THOMSON *Voy. Challenger* I. i. 34 The size of the iron frame was arranged so as to receive one of Bunsen's thermostats in ordinary use in laboratories. **1899** CAGNEY *Jaksch's Clin. Diagn.* ii. (ed. 4) 107 The test-tube containing the infected serum is now placed in a thermostat, maintained at 36·5°–37° C.

b. An apparatus which gives notice of undue increase of temperature; an automatic fire-alarm.

1881 *Philad. Record* No. 3462. 4 The thermostat, which gives an alarm as soon as the temperature of the room where it may be rises to 100°. **1908** *Daily Chron.* 24 Aug. 6/3 The thermostat is usually attached to the ceiling, and immediately an abnormal and dangerous rise of temperature occurs the metal bars expand.

Hence as *v. trans.*, to regulate the temperature of (a substance or a piece of apparatus) by means of a thermostat; **ˈthermostat(t)ed** *ppl. a.*; **thermoˈstatic** *a.*, of, pertaining to, or of the nature of a thermostat; **thermoˈstatically** *adv.*, by means of a thermostat; **thermoˈstatics** *sb. pl.* [after *hydrostatics*], name suggested for the theory of the equilibrium of heat.

1839 URE *Dict. Arts*, etc. 1237 A single thermostatic bar, consisting of two or more bars or rulers of differently expansible solids..firmly riveted or soldered together, face to face... A thermostatic hoop. **1871** Thermostatics [see *thermokinematics*, THERMO-]. **1877** KNIGHT *Dict. Mech.*, *Thermostatic Alarm*, a device to give a signal when a certain temperature is attained. **1883** *Cassell's Fam. Mag.* Aug. 537/2 Frost tell-tales..can be readily constructed by employing a thermostatic spring. **1891** *Cent. Dict.* s.v., A thermostatically adjusted radiator. **1940** *Brit. Jrnl. Psychol.* July 63 The tests were done in a roughly thermostated water-bath. **1950** W. J. MOORE *Physical Chem.* xv. 424 The cell must be well thermostated since the conductivity increases with the temperature. **1962** *Plant & Cell Physiol.* III. 212 The temperature of the algal suspension was controlled by flowing thermostated water on the surface of the vessel. **1963** G. L. PICKARD *Descriptive Physical Oceanogr.* vi. 86 This necessitates thermostating the samples to ± 0·001C° during measurement. **1967** MARGERISON & EAST *Introd. Polymer Chem.* ii. 94 The data..were obtained using solutions of polystyrene in benzene illuminated by light of 5461Å and thermostatted at 25°C. **1979** *Nature* 25 Jan. 291/2 The complete reaction chamber was heated in a thermostatted oven.

thermosynthesis, etc.: see THERMO-.

thermoˈtactic, *a.* [f. THERMO- + Gr. τακτικ-ός arranging, f. τακ-, root of τάσσ-ειν to arrange: see THERMOTAXIS] Of or pertaining to thermotaxis.

1896 *Allbutt's Syst. Med.* I. 150 To this [the nervous] system must be assigned the thermotactic function. *Ibid.* 151 The question where the thermotactic centre or centres are to be found, and how they act in fevers. **1899** *Ibid.* VI. 860 The so-called heat fibres, that is the thermotactic.

thermo-tank: see THERMO-.

‖**thermotaxis** (θɜːməʊˈtæksɪs). [mod.L., f. THERMO- + Gr. τάξις arrangement: see TAXIS.]

1. *Physiol.* That function of the nervous system on which the normal temperature of the body depends; the regulation of the bodily heat.

1891 in *Cent. Dict.* **1896** *Allbutt's Syst. Med.* I. 150 It may be assumed that thermotaxis is conducted by a 'centre' or 'centres'. *Ibid.* 156 What they do not prove is that fever is nothing more than a disorder of thermotaxis. **1899** *Ibid.* VII. 341 The tuber cinereum, which he regards as the true centre of thermotaxis.

2. *Biol.* Movement or stimulation in a living body caused by heat: cf. TAXIS 6.

1900 B. D. JACKSON *Gloss. Bot. Terms*, *Thermotaxis*, changes produced by warmth. **1902** MAX VERWORN in *Encycl. Brit.* XXXI. 715/1 Cases of directive stimulation.. have been designated..positive or negative Chemotaxis, Phototaxis, Thermotaxis, Galvanotaxis, and so forth.

Hence **thermoˈtaxic** *a.* = THERMOTACTIC.

1877 FOSTER *Phys.* II. v. (1878) 378 This at first sight looked like the indication of a thermotaxic mechanism, rendered inactive by the condition of fever. **1899** *Syd. Soc. Lex.*, *Thermotaxic*, same as *Thermotactic*.

thermotelephone, etc.: see THERMO-.

thermotic (θɜːˈmɒtɪk), *a.* [f. Gr. θερμωτικός (Plutarch *Q. Conv.* 715 C) warming, calorific: used in modified sense to match *acoustic*, *optic*, etc.] Of or pertaining to heat; *esp.* relating to thermotics. So **therˈmotical** *a.*, in same sense (hence **therˈmotically** *adv.*); **therˈmotics** *sb. pl.*, the science of heat, thermology.

1831 W. WHEWELL *Let.* 18 Sept. in I. Todhunter *William Whewell* (1876) II. 132 It is very true that we very much want a name for the part of science which treats of *light*.. also..that which treats of *Heat*... [In my MSS.] I have called one *Photistics* and the other *Thermotics*. **1837** —— *Hist. Induct. Sc.* VIII. Introd. II. 293 Acoustics, Optics, and Thermotics. *Ibid.* x. Introd. 465, I employ the term Thermotics, to include all the doctrines respecting Heat. *Ibid.* x. i. §4. 481 They require the light of thermotical calculations. **1858** BUCKLE *Civiliz.* (1869) II. vii. 362 Fourier..employed himself in raising thermotics to a science. **1874** tr. *Lommel's Light* 201 In the spectrum of a flint-glass prism the apex of the thermotic curve is situated outside the apparent spectrum in the ultra-red region. **1879** S. HIGHLEY in *Cassell's Techn. Educ.* IV. 234/1 Optical, acoustic, and thermotic demonstrations in the lecture-room. **1895** *Funk's Stand. Dict.*, Thermotically.

thermotolerant: see THERMO-.

thermotropic (θɜːməʊˈtrɒpɪk, -ˈtrəʊpɪk), *a. Bot.* [f. Gr. θερμο-, THERMO- + -τροπ-ος turning + -IC: cf. HELIOTROPIC.] **1.** Turning or bending under the influence of heat; of, pertaining to, or exhibiting thermotropism.

1885 GOODALE *Physiol. Bot.* (1892) 394 Curvatures dependent upon temperature are called thermotropic.

2. *Physical Chem.* Brought about or effected by a change in temperature: used esp. with reference to mesophases and their phase transitions.

1909 SENIER & SHEPHEARD in *Jrnl. Chem. Soc.* XCV. II. 1945 Phototropic and thermotropic reactions are more probably due to isomeric changes affecting the aggregation of molecules in solids than to intramolecular change. **1962** G. W. GRAY *Molecular Structure & Properties of Liquid Crystals* i. 5 Mesophases are most commonly observed when a suitable compound is heated to a temperature above that at which the crystal lattice is stable. This type of mesomorphism is called thermotropic. **1966**, etc. [see LYOTROPIC *a.* 2]. **1972** *Physics Bull.* May 279/3 This article will be concerned only with those liquid crystals, known as thermotropic, where the phase transitions are induced by a change in temperature. **1978** *Nature* 13 Apr. 646/1 The membrane lipids of cells cultured in these conditions show a greatly sharpened thermotropic gel-to-liquid crystalline phase transition.

thermotropism (θəˈmɒtrəpɪz(ə)m). *Bot.* [f. as prec. + -ISM.] The property possessed by growing plant-organs of turning or bending towards (***positive thermotropism***) or away from (***negative thermotropism***) the sun or other source of heat. In *Biology*, The bending or growth of any organism dependent upon temperature (*Cent. Dict.*, *Suppl.*).

1898 tr. *Strasburger's Text-Bk. Bot.* I. ii. 263 Thermotropism..and Aerotropism..stand in direct relations to certain vital requirements of plants.

thermotype (ˈθɜːmətaɪp). [f. THERMO- + -TYPE.] Name proposed for an impression obtained from an object by means of heat. Hence **thermoˈtypic** *a.*, of or pertaining to thermotypes or thermotypy; **ˈthermotypy**, the process or art of making thermotypes.

1864 WEBSTER, Thermotype; Thermotypy. **1877** KNIGHT *Dict. Mech.*, *Thermotype*, an impression (as of a slice of wood) taken by means of wetting with dilute acid, pressing on the object, and subsequently heating the impression. **1909** *Cent. Dict.* Suppl., Thermotypic.

thermo-unstable, -voltaic: see THERMO-.

† **therne.** *Obs.* Also 4 tharne, (tarne), þierne. [a. ON. *þerna* (Sw. *tärna*, Da. *terne*) = OS. *thiorna* (Du. *deern*), OHG. *diorna* (MHG. *dierne*, Ger. *dirne*).] A girl, maid, young woman.

c **1300** *Havelok* 298 Sholde ic yeue a fol, a þerne, Engelond, þou sho it yerne? **1303** R. BRUNNE *Handl. Synne* 7353 Two vnweddyd..sengle knaue and sengle tarne [*v.r.* tharne]. *c* **1315** SHOREHAM *Poems* i. 1726 þet knaue child fortene ȝer Schel habbe, ane tuel þe þerne. **1340** *Ayenb.* 129 þe þierne [of] saynt abraham [i.e. Hagar].

thero- (θɪərəʊ), repr. Gr. θηρο-, combining form of θήρ wild beast; hence THEROID, THEROPOD, etc.; also the following: **therocephalian** (-siːˈfeɪlɪən) [Gr. κεφαλή head], *a.* belonging to an extinct order of carnivorous reptiles having a skull of the mammalian type; *sb.* a reptile of this order. **therocrotaphous** (-ˈkrɒtəfəs) *a.* [Gr. κρόταφος the temple], having the temporal bone resembling that of mammals. **ˈtherodont** *sb.* and *a.*, = *Theriodont* (*Cent. Dict.* 1891): see THERIO-. **theˈrolatry** [-LATRY], beast-worship, worship of animals. ˌ**theromorphoˈlogical** *a.*, of or pertaining to the morphology of the lower animals.

1904 *Amer. Nat.* Feb. 103 These cynodonts have lost several of the other more primitive characters of the *therocephalians, such as teeth in the palate. **1907** *Science* 6 Dec. 796 Three new Therocephalian genera have been discovered in beds which are probably Middle Permian. *Ibid.*, The discovery of this new reptile, *Galechirus*, strongly favors the descent of the Therocephalians from an early Rhyncocephaloid ancestor. **1907** WILLISTON in *Proc. U.S. Nat. Mus.* XXXII. 488 The plesiosaurs have a larger temporal vacuity, larger indeed than is to be found in any other reptiles of the *therocrotaphous (I coin the word) type. **1873** W. CORY *Lett. & Jrnls.* (1897) 311 Mahomet's alteration of a national character, the complete obliteration of *therolatry. **1885** HARTMANN *Anthropoid Apes* iii. 111 Virchow and W. Gruber have agreed in representing this frontal process as *theromorphological—that is, as a characteristic of the lower animals, and more especially of apes.

theroid (ˈθɪərɔɪd), *a.* [f. THERO- + -OID; cf. Gr. θηροειδής.] Like or having the form of a brute; of bestial nature or character.

1867 MAUDSLEY *Physiol. Mind* 291 The theroid degenerations of mankind are pathological specimens. **1870** —— *Body & Mind* 47 There is a class of idiots which may justly be designated theroid, so like brutes are the members of it. **1886** N. PEARSON in *19th Cent.* Sept. 353 The animal mind of the theroid idiot is accompanied by appropriate animal peculiarities of body.

therology (θiːˈrɒlədʒɪ). [f. THERO- + -LOGY. Proposed as a substitute for the irregular but established *mammalogy*.] The science of beasts or mammals; mammology. Hence **therologic** (θɪərəʊˈlɒdʒɪk), **theroˈlogical** *adjs.*, of or pertaining to therology, mammalogical; **theˈrologist**, one versed in therology; a mammalogist.

[Cf. **1620** ALSTED *Encycl.* 572 Irrationale animal est, quod formâ brutâ est præditum, & dicitur bestia. Ejus doctrina dicitur Therologia.] **1877** *Academy* 25 Aug. 199/3 A gentleman who, to use a newly-coined transatlantic word, is certainly one of the first 'therologists' of his country. **1882** OGILVIE (Annandale), Therology. **1891** *Cent. Dict.*, Therologic, Therological, Therology.

theromorous (θɪərəʊˈmɔərəs), *a.* *Palæont.* [f. mod.L. *Thērōmōra* (see def.), f. Gr. θηρο-, THERO- + μωρ-ός sluggish, stupid, foolish: see -OUS.] Of or belonging to the *Theromora* (Cope), a synonym of *Theromorpha* (see next). So **theroˈmoran** *a.*, in same sense.

1889 NICHOLSON & LYDEKKER *Palæontol.* liii. II. 1053 Theromorous Branch.—The Reptiles included in this branch or alliance. **1895** *Funk's Stand. Dict.*, Theromoran.

theromorph (ˈθɪərəʊmɔːf). *Palæont.* [f. mod.L. *Thērōmorpha* neut. pl. (see def.), f. Gr. θηρο-, THERO- + μορφή form.] A reptile of the extinct order *Theromorpha*, of Permian and Trias age, having certain mammalian characters. So **theroˈmorphic** *a.*[1], **theroˈmorphous** *a.*, belonging to or having the characters of the *Theromorpha*.

1887 COPE *Orig. Fittest* xi. 317 The Mammalia have been traced to the theromorphous reptiles through the Monotremata. **1891** *Cent. Dict.*, Theromorph, Theromorphic. [**1901** H. GADOW in *Cambr. Nat. Hist.* VIII. viii. 303 Many of the Theromorpha reached a considerable size, massive skulls of one foot in length being not uncommon. *Note.* Cope, the inventor of this most appropriate name (Theromorpha, or 'beast-shaped' animals), soon changed it, unnecessarily, into Theromora.]

‖**theromorphia** (θɪərəʊˈmɔːfɪə). [mod.L. a. Gr. θηρομορφία = θηριομορφία, f. θηριόμορφος having the form of a beast: see prec.] (See quot. 1890.) So **theroˈmorphic** *a.*[2], of or pertaining to theromorphia; **theroˈmorphism** = *theromorphia*.

1890 BILLINGS *Nat. Med. Dict.*, *Theromorphia*, an abnormity in human anatomy resembling the normal structure in lower animals. **1891** *Cent. Dict.*, Theromorphic. **1899** *Syd. Soc. Lex.*, *Theromorphism*, an apparent reversion to an animal of lower type in the human subject.

therophyte (ˈthɪərəʊfaɪt). *Bot.* [ad. Da. *therofyte* (C. Raunkiaer 1904, in *Bot. Tidsskrift* XXVI. p. xiv) f. Gr. θέρο(ς summer + -PHYTE.] (See quot. 1960.)

1913 *Jrnl. Ecol.* I. 18 Therophytes, or plants of the favourable season, live through the unfavourable season as seeds; hence they are annual plants. **1932** FULLER & CONARD tr. *Braun-Blanquet's Plant Sociol.* i. 13 Many communities of the subtropics begin their annual development with a therophyte aspect. **1952** P. W. RICHARDS *Trop. Rain Forest* i. 10 Therophytes are entirely absent, except in clearings. **1960** N. POLUNIN *Introd. Plant Geogr.* iii. 93 Therophytes (annuals)..complete their life-cycle, from germination to ripe seed, within a single limited vegetative period, surviving the unfavourable times as seeds, spores, or other special (usually resistant) reproductive bodies. They are especially abundant in deserts.

theropodous (θiːˈrɒpədəs), *a.* *Palæont.* [f. mod.L. *Thērōpoda* (O. C. Marsh 1881, in *Amer. Jrnl. Sci.* CXXI. 423) neut. pl. (f. Gr. θηρο-, THERO- + πούς, ποδ- foot) + -OUS.] Of or belonging to the *Theropoda*, an order of carnivorous dinosaurs in Marsh's classification, having feet like those of mammals. So **theropod** (ˈθɪərəʊpɒd), *a.* = *theropodous*; *sb.* a dinosaur of this order.

1889 *Q. Jrnl. Geol. Soc.* XLV. i. 44 Axis of a (? Theropodous) Dinosaur from the Wealden. **1891** *Cent. Dict.*, Theropod. **1901** H. GADOW in *Cambr. Nat. Hist.* VIII. x. 425 The whole hind-limb of the Theropodous *Compsognathus* is far more ornithic than that of any three-toed Ornithopoda. **1933** A. S. ROMER *Vertebr. Paleontol.* ix. 181 The theropods (using this term in a broad sense) include all the characteristic terrestrial reptilian carnivores of the late Triassic, Jurassic, and Cretaceous. **1970** *Nature* 11 Apr. 109/1 Theropod dinosaurs normally walked on three toes on each hind foot, leaving birdlike tracks. **1981** *Sci. Digest* Aug. 36 (*caption*) The most complete theropod found in China, *Yangchuanosaurus shangyouensis* (discovered 1977, described in 1978).

therosaur (ˈθɪərəsɔː(r)). *Palæont.* [f. Gr. θηρο-, THERO- + σαῦρος lizard.] One of the *Therosauria*, an extinct order of herbivorous dinosaurs having the mammalian form and bird-like feet. Hence **theroˈsaurian** *a.*, of or pertaining to the *Therosauria*, or having their characters; *sb.* a dinosaur of this order.

therrepylle, obs. f. THRIPPLE, cart-shelving.

thers, therse, obs. forms of THEIRS.

Thersitical (θɜːˈsɪtɪkəl), *a. rare.* [f. Gr. Θερσίτης Thersites ('the Audacious'), an ill-tongued Greek at the siege of Troy + -ICAL.] Like Thersites in language or address; abusive, reviling, scurrilous. So **Thersitean** (θɜːsɪˈtiːən) *a. rare*[−1].

1650 BULWER *Anthropomet.* 4 With a Thersitical head and heart. **1767** STERNE *Tr. Shandy* IX. xiv, There is a pelting kind of Thersitical satire, as black as the very ink 'tis wrote with. **1908** *Daily Chron.* 28 July 4/4 Adding a string of Thersitean scurrilities unfit for publication.

therst(e, obs. form of THIRST.

therst(e: see DARE *v.*[1] A. 9, THARF *v.*

therve-cake: see THARF-CAKE.

therwe, þerwe, obs. form of THROUGH.

†**thes**, *adv.* (*conj.*). *Obs.* Forms: 1–3 **þæs**, 2–4 **þes, þas**, 3 (*Orm.*) **þess**. [OE. *þæs*, gen. sing. masc. and neut. of *se, séo, þæt*: see THE A. 4a, THAT A. 1. Retained in certain adverbial and conjunctive uses, after its simple genitive use became obsolete.]

1. a. Because of or on account of that; because. **b.** From that time, after that; from the time that, after. **c.** In the way that, according as, as. **d.** To that extent, so: cf. THAT *dem. adv.*

a. *c* **897** K. ÆLFRED *Gregory's Past. C.* xlix. 379 Waa me ðæs [L. *quia*] ic swigode. *c* **1205** LAY. 2743 Wa wes Lumbardisce folc þes [*c* **1275** þas]. *Ibid.* 5989 Wel wes Romanisce folc þes [*c* **1275** þas]. *a* **1300** *XI Pains of Hell* 208 in *O.E. Misc.* 153 Þat weren her, wo is ham þes.

b. *c* **893** K. ÆLFRED *Oros.* IV. vi. § 12 þæs ymb iii ȝear..þa consulas foran..on Africe. *a* **900** *O.E. Chron.* an. 894, þæt wæs ymb twelf monað þæs þe hie ær hider..comon. *a* **900** tr. *Bæda's Hist.* I. ix. [xii.] (1890) 44 Sona þæs ðe hi on þis ealond comon. *c* **1380** *Sir Ferumb.* 1387 Olyuer wax hol sone þas.

c. *c* **888** K. ÆLFRED *Boeth.* xxiv. § 3 Men secað anfealde eadignesse ðæs ðe him ðincð. *a* **900** tr. *Bæda's Hist.* I. xiv. [xxv.] (1890) 60 þæs þe me ȝeþuht is & ȝesewen. *c* **1000** ÆLFRIC *Gen.* xliii. 7 We him andswaredon þæs þe he us axode. *c* **1000** *St. Andrew & Veronica* 26 Ðæs ðe bec secgaþ.

d. *a* **1000** *Cædmon's Gen.* 832 Nære flod þæs deop, nære stream þæs micel.

2. ***thes the, þes þe*** (***þess te***), before a comparative: For that the (more, etc.); so much the more, etc.); = OHG. *desde*, MHG. *deste*, Ger. *desto* (*mehr*, etc.).

c **897** K. ÆLFRED *Gregory's Past. C.* xvii. 123 Sio wund bið ðæs ðe wierse. *c* **1000** *Ags. Gosp.* Matt. xx. 31 þa clypodon hiȝ þæs ðe ma. *c* **1160** *Hatton Gosp.* ibid., þa clepedon hyo þæs þe mare. [So Mark x. 48.] *c* **1200** ORMIN 444–5 þatt hise frend mihhtenn off himm All þess te mare blissenn, & tatt te follc all þess te bett Hiss lare shollde folljhenn. *a* **1275** *Prov. Ælfred* 436 in *O.E. Misc.* 129 þanne sal þe child þas þe bet worþen.

thes, obs. f. THESE; gen. sing. of THAT, THE.

†**ˈthesaur, -aure.** Chiefly *Sc. Obs.* [ad. L. THESAURUS: cf. Prov. *thesaur*, OCat. *tesor*, Sp., It. *tesoro*, Pg. *thesouro*.] = TREASURE.

1491 *Sc. Acts Jas. IV* (1814) II. 230/1 Stelaris [and] concelaris, of the said gold or thessaure. *a* **1510** DOUGLAS *K. Hart* II. 340 Quhair is the thesaure now that ȝe have woun? **1532** *Addr. fr. Convoc.* (MS. Cleop. E. VI. lf. 274 b), The thesaure of this realme hath beene carried and conueyhed beyond the mountaines to the coort of rome. **1596** DALRYMPLE tr. *Leslie's Hist. Scot.* (S.T.S.) I. 7 Mony hidd thesauris. *Ibid.* v. 303 Quhat proffit sa euir cumis of that feild..sall cum in to the kingis Thesaur.

b. *Comb.* **ˈthesaurhouse**, treasury.

1488 *Acc. Ld. High Treas. Scot.* I. 85 *margin*, Thir boxis put in the Thesaurhous in the grete kist nerrest the windo. **1596** DALRYMPLE tr. *Leslie's Hist. Scot.* x. (S.T.S.) 264 The palice of Halyruidhous..the Thesaurhous, and vtheris places.

thesaurarial (θiːsɔːˈrɛərɪəl), *a.* [f. L. *thēsaurāri-us* (see next) + -AL[1].] Of or pertaining to the office of treasurer.

1881 *Athenæum* 2 July 15/2 He was invariably to be found ..in his thesaurarial chair at the evening meetings. **1896** *Trans. Roy. Hist. Soc.* X. 42 The addition of the judicial to the thesaurarial functions..of the Court of Exchequer.

†**theˈsaurary, -ie.** Chiefly *Sc. Obs.* [ad. med.L. *thēsaurāria* 'thesaurarii dignitas' (Du Cange), fem. of *thēsaurāri-us* adj., f. *thēsaur-us* treasure: see -ARY[1]; cf. Pr. *thezauraria*, Sp. and It. *tesoreˈria*, mod.F. *trésorerie* treasury.]

1. The office of treasurer; treasurership. *Sc.*

1473–4 *Acc. Ld. High Treas. Scot.* I. 1 Compt of a reuerennd fader in God..of the office of Thesaurary. *a* **1557** *Diurn. Occur.* (1833) 11 Archibald was depryvit of the thesaurarie. **1596** DALRYMPLE tr. *Leslie's Hist. Scot.* x. (S.T.S.) 291 The Cardinal..put him fra the office of the Thesaurarie.

2. *transf.* A treasury; also = THESAURUS 2.

1592 *Sc. Acts Jas. VI* (1814) III. 558/1 The ordinar fies.. sall nawayis be gevin out of his Maiesties thesaurarie. **1597** A. M. tr. *Guillemeau's Fr. Chirurg.* C iij b/2 The end of the thesaurarye or storehouse of the Instrumentes of Chyrurgerie.

3. *attrib.* **thesaurary house**, treasury.

1495 *Acc. Ld. High Treas. Scot.* I. 268 To turs it to the Thesaurary hous in the Castell.

†**ˈthesaurer.** Chiefly *Sc. Obs.* Also 5–6 **thesaurair, -are**, 5–7 **-ar**, 6 **thesorar, -uerer, -awrar**, 7 **-orer**. [ad. L. *thēsaurārius* treasurer, f. *thēsaurus* treasure: see -AR[2], -ER[2] 2. Cf. Pr. *thesaurier*, Sp. *tesorero*, It. *tesoriere*; also TREASURER.] An officer in charge of treasure, or of a treasury; = TREASURER. ***thesaurer deput***, deputy treasurer: see quot. 1708.

c **1450** HOLLAND *Howlat* 209 Apon the sand ȝit I sawe, as thesaurer tane,..schir Gawane the Drak. **1473** *Acc. Ld. High Treas. Scot.* I. 32 Pait be the Thesaurair. **1489** *Ibid.* 125 Takyne be the Kyng..out of the Thesorarris purs. **1544** in Gross *Gild Merch.* II. 75 The othir halfe to the thesuerer of the sayde sytty [Dublin]. **1557–75** *Diurn. Occur.* (1833) 180 Iohne Cunnynghame..wes maid half thesaurer, with Mr. Robert Ritchartsone that wes thesaurer of befoir. **1685** *Lond. Gaz.* No. 2031/1 The Earl of Kintore Lord Thesaurer Deput. **1707** *Narr. Jas. Nimmo* (1889) 103, I was chosen Town Thesaurer. **1708** J. CHAMBERLAYNE *St. Gt. Brit.* II. II. iv. (1737) 376 The Officers of State [of Scotland] before the late Union... The Lord Thesaurer Depute, whose Commission ran in the same Terms with that given to the Thesaurer Principal, or the Commissioners of Thesaury. **1711** *Countrey-Man's Let. to Curat* 21 The Lord Thesaurer Burleigh and Sir Francis Walsingham Secretary,..were professed Friends to the Non-conformists.

b. *attrib.* **thesaurer house**, treasury.

1489 *Acc. Ld. High Treas. Scot.* I. 110 Item, the thrid da of May, takin be the King furth of the Thesaurare Houss himself, foure score of demyss, lvj li.

†**ˈthesaurize**, *v.* *Obs.* [ad. late L. *thēsaurizāre*, ad. Gr. θησαυρίζ-ειν, f. θησαυρ-ός treasure: see -IZE; cf. F. *thésauriser* (14th c. in Godef. *Compl.*).] *trans.* To hoard, as treasure. Mostly *fig.*

1594 *Zepheria* vi, My heart prepares anew to thesaurize Sighs and loue options. *a* **1610** SIR J. SEMPLE in *S. Ballatis* (1872) 244, I was resoluit to thesaurize my greeife. *Ibid.* 247 ȝet durst I not behold [? be bold]..But thesawriz'd my hiddin harmes. **1623** COCKERAM, *Thesaurize*, to gather riches. (Also in BLOUNT, BAILEY, etc.)

thesaurosis (θɪsɔːˈrəʊsɪs). *Path.* [f. Gr. θησαυρ-ός store + -OSIS.] A disorder of the lungs caused by the accumulation in them of inhaled material.

1958 *New England Jrnl. Med.* 6 Mar. 475/1 Evidence concerning the etiology of the pulmonary lesion of Case 2 is ..less compelling, but we believe that..this, too, was a case of thesaurosis due to hair-spray constituents. **1975** *New Yorker* 7 Apr. 56/3 For at least fifteen years, it has been suspected that the plastic resins in hair sprays cause a restrictive-lung-storage disease called thesaurosis, as well as abnormal lung cells that may be the precursors of lung cancer.

thesaurus (θiːˈsɔːrəs). Pl. -i. [L., a. Gr. θησαυρός a store, treasure, storehouse, treasury.]

1. *Archæol.* A treasury, as of a temple, etc.

1823 in CRABB *Technol. Dict.* **1846** in WORCESTER. **1847** GROTE *Greece* II. ix. III. 44 Myrôn.. built at the same holy place [Olympia] a thesaurus..for the reception of commemorative offerings.

2. A 'treasury' or 'storehouse' of knowledge, as a dictionary, encyclopædia, or the like.

[**1565** COOPER (*title*) Thesaurus Linguæ Romanæ et Britannicæ [etc.]. **1736** AINSWORTH (*title*) Thesaurus Linguæ Latinæ compendiarius; or.. Dictionary of the Latin Tongue.] **1840** MILL *Diss. & Disc.* (1859) II. 461 A thesaurus of commonplaces for the discussion of questions. **1862** MARSH *Lect. Eng. Lang.* iii. 49 In a complete thesaurus of any language, the etymology of every word should exhibit both its philology and its linguistics. **1906** *Westm. Gaz.* 18 Dec. 2/2 This work is one of five thesauri published under the auspices of Kang Hsi, the second Emperor of the present dynasty. **1910** *Spectator* 20 Aug. 279/2 A thesaurus of critical learning.

b. A collection of concepts or words arranged according to sense; also (*U.S.*) a dictionary of synonyms and antonyms.

1852 ROGET (*title*) Thesaurus of English Words and Phrases classified and arranged [etc.]. **1898** 'MARK TWAIN' *Autobiogr.* (1924) I. 172 The fact that the writer's balance at the vocabulary bank has run short and that he is too lazy to replenish it from the thesaurus. **1942** BERREY & VAN DEN BARK (*title*) The American thesaurus of slang. **1960** W. NAYLOR *Silver Birch Anthol.* 8, I know how you have to polish and repolish, alter words, delete others, change sentences, consult the dictionary and the thesaurus, before you are satisfied. **1962** U. WEINREICH in Householder & Saporta *Probl. Lexicogr.* 30 The grouping of synonyms along a continuum yields a thesaurus, like Roget's. **1975** (*title*) Family word finder: a new thesaurus of synonyms and antonyms in dictionary form.

c. A classified list of terms, esp. key-words, in a particular field, for use in indexing and information retrieval.

1957 H. BROWNSON in *Proc. Internat. Study Conference on Classification for Information Retrieval* 100 The best answer ..may be the application of a mechanized thesaurus based on networks of related meanings. **1961** *Aslib Proc.* XIII. 265 We decided to..designate the analytical compilation a 'thesaurus'. **1965** *Revue Internat. de Documentation* XXXII. 21/1 It has become commonplace to hear of retrieval systems embodying a thesaurus. In this context a thesarus usually means an arrangement of a vocabulary of terms in each group being connected in some defined way. **1974** *Encycl. Brit. Macropædia* IX. 572/2 The second stage should be a fully automatic selection and matching process, preferably using a thesaurus.

† ˈ**thesaury.** Chiefly *Sc. Obs.* [ad. med.L. *thēsauria* 'locus ubi thesaurus reconditur, gazophylacium' (Du Cange), f. THESAUR-US + *-ia*: see -Y.] The treasury; the treasurership.

a **1639** SPOTTISWOOD *Hist. Ch. Scot.* VII. (1677) 517 His Uncle..was made Deputy in the Office of Thesaury. **1688** *Addr. Sc. Privy C.* in *Lond. Gaz.* No. 2388/2 They..have got Pay for the Month of October instant out of Your Majesties Thesaury. **1708** [see THESAURER].

† **these,** *sb. Sc.* [a. F. *thèse* (1579 in Godef. *Compl.*), or ad. med.L. *thesis.*] = THESIS 4, 5.

a **1600** MONTGOMERIE *Sonn.* lxiv. 11 Fy! I refuse sik filthie these or theam. **1640** R. BAILLIE *Canterb. Self-Convict.* 29 The Authour..avowes..that the These alleadged, and all the rest of his booke doeth perfectly agree with the English Articles. **1648** —— *Lett. & Jrnls.* (1841) III. 63 The generall These which he professed to maintain.

these (ðiːz), *dem. pron.* and *adj.* (*plural*). Forms: see below. [This word has a complicated history. The OE. pl. of *ðes, ðéos, ðis*, was *ðás*, less commonly *ðǽs* (:—OTeut. **þai-se, -si*), dat. *ðiosum, ðis(s)um*, gen. *ðissa, ðisra*. The form *ðás* remained in ME. as *þās*, which was duly retained in the north, and by regular phonetic development became *þōs* in midland and south. The OE. *ðǽs* gave ME. *þǣs, þēs, þeos*, and their local variants, including s.w. *þüs*. A frequent form of *þēs* from the 12th to the 16th c. was *þis*, identical with the sing.: see γ below. The two forms *þēs* and *þās* became differentiated in use after 1250–1300, *þēs* and its variants remaining in the south as plural of THIS, while *þās* became synonymous with *þā*, the plural of *se, séo, þæt*, THAT. This was prob. due to assimilation, *þēs, þis*, etc. being more like the singular and the dat. and gen. pl., while *þās* was in vowel like *þat* and *þā*. Apparently the assumption of *þās* as pl. of *þat* began in the north, and slowly spread to the south in the form *þōs*: see THOSE. But from the 12th c. there was evidently a tendency in the midl. dialects to differentiate the plural of *this* by adding *-e*, as in the plural of adjs. (*al, alle, sum, sume, his, hise*, etc.), so that from *c* 1200 to 1500 a frequent midland form was *þis-e* (2 syllables in Ormin, etc.); in e. midl. also *þese* appears *c* 1200. Even the s.w. *þüs* varied with *þüse*. Of all these varieties, *these* was the survivor. Also, of *thō* and *thōs*, the two plurals of *that*, the former was finally dropped in the course of the 16th c.; so that there now remain in standard English only the two forms *these* and *those* (*thoos, thōs*)—both in their origin plurals of *this*; the original plural of *that* being lost in standard English, though in Scotland and the northern counties of England it survives dialectally as *thae, theä, theeä*: see THAE. In the same district *these* has been superseded by THIR (*thur, thor*). (The original pl. *þās, þōs* is treated under THOSE, to which it belongs in form, though in meaning it belongs here.)]

A. Illustration of Forms.

α. 1–3 **ðás, þás, þōs**: see THOSE.

β. 1 **ðǽs,** 1–3 **þǽs,** 2–5 **þēs,** 3 **ðēs,** 3–4 **þeos,** (**teos, þeors**), 5 **þies, thees,** 5–6 **thes, thies,** 6 **thyes, thez, theis.** *Early inflexions*: *dat.* 1 **ðisum; ðiosum, ðissum, ðassum,** 2 **þison, -an,** 2–3 **þissen, þisse,** 2–4 **þisen,** 3 **þesse.** *gen.* 1 **ðissa; ðeossa, ðassa, þisra,** 2–3 **þisse, þissere.**

c **888** K. ÆLFRED *Boeth.* xxxii. §2 Hwelc þæs flæslican good sien. **971** *Blickl. Hom.* 5 þeos haliʒe fæmne..brohte eallum ʒeleaffullum þæs bletsunga. *c* **1175** *Lamb. Hom.* 11 Moyses þe hehte heom feste þes daȝes uppon þe munte of synai. *c* **1200** *Trin. Coll. Hom.* 19 Nu ich eu habbe opened þes fif word... Hereð nu þes oðre. *c* **1205** LAY. 1038 þæs [*c* **1275** þeos] tiðende him weren læðe. *Ibid.* 4621 We..nuten næuere þæs gume [*c* **1275** þis gomes]. *c* **1230** *Hali Meid.* 5 þeos þohtes warp ut of þin heorte. *c* **1250** *Gen. & Ex.* 1643 Iacob ðes hirdes freinen gan. *a* **1375** *Lay Folks Mass Bk.* App. IV. 175 þeos Auctours alle. *c* **1380** WYCLIF *Serm.* Sel. Wks. II. 113 Studie þes wordis. *c* **1400** *Destr. Troy* 1454 All thies maters. **1490** CAXTON *Eneydos* xvi. 65 By what wayes he maye notyfye thees thynges to Dydo. *c* **1500** *New Not-br. Mayd* 235 Ayenst thyes thre. **1529** CDL. WOLSEY in *Four C. Eng. Lett.* (1880) 10 Thes thyngs consyderyd. **1556** *Chron. Gr. Friars* (Camden) 74 Theis iiij. knyghttes. *a* **1596** *Sir T. More* II. ii. 26 Fier the howses Of theis audatious strangers.

dat. *c* **825** *Vesp. Psalter* xvii[i]. 18 From ðissum ða fiodon me. *c* **893** K. ÆLFRED *Orosius* II. ii. §2 He þa Romulus æfter þiosan underfeng Cirinensa ʒewinn. *c* **897** —— *Gregory's Past. C.* xviii. 138 Betweox ðissum. *Ibid.* xxi. 162 Be ðiosum ʒit is swiðe ryhtlice ʒecweden. *c* **1000** *Ags. Gosp.* Matt. iii. 9 Of þysum stanum. *Ibid.* xxvii. 21 Hwæþerne..of þisum twam? [*c* **1160** *Hatt. G.* ibid. of þisen stanen..Of þisan twam?]. *c* **1175** *Lamb. Hom.* 11 On þisse gastliche daȝen. *Ibid.* 37 Summe of þisse þinge. *c* **1200** *Trin. Coll. Hom.* 217 On þesse fewe litele wored... Ac ich ne mai ne ich ne can þesse [*pr.* þosse] on openi. *c* **1205** LAY. 26356 No aȝæf þissen [*c* **1275** to þeos] eorlen. **1340** *Ayenb.* 218 Of þisen we habbeþ ane uorbisne ine þe godspelle.

gen. *c* **897** K. ÆLFRED *Gregory's Past. C.* xiv. 82 Mid nanum ðissa. *c* **950** *Lindisf. Gosp.* Matt. xxi. 3 Hlaferd ðisra nytt hæfeð. *c* **1000** ÆLFRIC *Lives of Saints* xxiii. 137 Menn ..þisra seofona ʒeorne heddon. *c* **1000** *Ags. Gosp.* Matt. xiii. 22 Leasung þissa woruld-welena. *c* **1160** *Hatton Gosp.* ibid., Leasunge þissere worlde welen. *c* **1205** LAY. 14829 Ich æm þissere leodene king.

γ. 2–5 **þis,** 5–7 **this,** (5–6 **thys**).

c **1200** *Trin. Coll. Hom.* 211 On þis fuwer laȝes. **1297** R. GLOUC. (Rolls) 320 þes men of þis wilde bestes slowe & caȝte inowe. **1477** EARL RIVERS (Caxton) *Dictes* 30 Thou hast ben in all this dangers. **1534** in *Lett. Suppress. Monasteries* (Camden) 11 Yn thys thynges I desyryd you to do that you thowht metyst. **1622** S. WARD *Christ All in All* (1627) 13 This Eagles feathers will not abide blending with others.

δ. 3–5 **þus** (ü), **þuse, thus(e.**

1297 R. GLOUC. (Rolls) 11950 þus sixe iwis. *a* **1300** *Fragm. Pop. Sc.* (Wright, 1841) 135/124 Of thuse four elementz ech quik best y-maked is. *c* **1300** *Beket* 890 Thuse kniȝtes ich lovie more. *c* **1380** *Sir Ferumb.* 1012 þus þay prikede, þuse two baroun hure frendes to rescowe. *c* **1420** *Chron. Vilod.* 41 And hade þuse foure in his gouernynge. *Ibid.* 1359 And dred þus laudable wordus.

ε. 2–5 **þise,** 4–5 **thise,** 5 **thyse.**

c **1200** ORMIN 4573 Whas itt iss þatt follȝheþþ wel & filleþþ þise mahhtess. *c* **1220** *Bestiary* 514 Đis cete ðanne..ðise fisses alle in sukeð. *c* **1386** CHAUCER *Wife's Prol.* 560 Thise wermes, ne thise Motthes, ne thise mytes. *c* **1450** *Merlin* i. 23 Whan alle thise thynges were don. **1494** FABYAN *Chron.* VII. 359 The best men of ye cytie by thyse ryotous persones were spoyled & robbid.

ζ. 3 **ðese,** 4–5 **þese,** 4– **these,** (4 **þeose, þiese,** 5 **þeese,** 6 **theese, theise**).

c **1200** *Trin. Coll. Hom.* 13 Đese six werkes..ben cleped lihtes scrud. *c* **1250** *Gen. & Ex.* 3697 Forð was gon al ðese oðer ȝer. **13..** *Cursor M.* 16767+65 (Cott.) These ilk wordez said he. *c* **1425** *Ibid.* 4597 (Trin.) þeese oþere seuen woful neet. *c* **1550** *Disc. Common Weal Eng.* (1893) 139 In consideration of theese thinges. *Ibid.*, At theise days.

B. Signification.

The plural of THIS *pron.* and *adj.*

I. Demonstrative pronoun.

1. Denoting things or persons actually or ideally present or near; esp. those that have just been mentioned.

a. things: plural of THIS B. I. 1 a.

c **893** [see A. β]. *c* **1205** LAY. 26044 Ær þe king hæfde þæs ful isæide. **1303** R. BRUNNE *Handl. Synne* 11112 þese are þo yche twey verse þat to holynes are reuers. **1340** *Ayenb.* 97 þise byeþ þe seve ruieles of holy lyf þet þe soþe salomon tekþ to his children. *a* **1425** *Cursor M.* 10115 (Trin.) Lecchory and gloteny, þourȝe þese am I doun dryuen. **1474** *Coventry Leet Bk.* 397 If he do the contrary to any of thies his fyne is at euery tyme xl d. **1581** CAMPION in Allen *Martyrd.* (1908) 2 These are the wordes of S. Paule. **1624** WOTTON *Archit.* in *Reliq.* (1651) 211 Such conceipts as these seem somewhat too fine among this Rubbage. **1790** BURKE *Fr. Rev.* 56 For want of these, they have seen the medicine of the state corrupted into its poison. **1862** RUSKIN *Unto this Last* iv. §78 (1901) 158 His [man's] race has its bounds also; but these have not yet been reached.

b. persons.

Still used without the restriction to which the singular *this* is now subject: see THIS B. I. 1 b.

c **825** [see A. β]. **1297** R. GLOUC. (Rolls) 547 þes were as þre kinges. *c* **1330** R. BRUNNE *Chron. Wace* (Rolls) 13395 Bifore Arthur schuld þeos alle wende. **1382** WYCLIF *Rev.* vii. 13, 14 Who ben thes..and of whennus camen thei?.. Thes ben thei, that camen fro greet tribulacioun. *c* **1400** *Destr. Troy* 14022 (heading) Thez Paris slogh in the ffeld. *c* **1440** *Gesta Rom.* lxiii. 274 (Harl. MS.) þees ben þei, that sleith hire soulis. **1526** TINDALE *John* xxi. 15 Lovest thou me more then these? **1610** SHAKS. *Temp.* II. ii. 91 These are diuels; O defend me. *a* **1715** BURNET *Own Time* (1823) I. 342 One of these being taken, and apprehending he was in danger. **1869** TENNYSON *Coming of Arthur* 52 He..rode a simple knight among his knights, And many of these in richer arms than he.

c. Referring to things mentioned or enumerated immediately after: pl. of THIS B. I. 1 d; cf. II. 1 b.

a **1225** *Ancr. R.* 36 þe vreisuns beoð þeos. 'Deus qui sanctam crucem' [etc.]. *c* **1380** *Lay Folks Catech.* 349 These ben also þy fyue Inwyttys, Wyl, Resoun, Mynd, ymaginacioun, and thogth. *c* **1400** tr. *Secreta Secret., Gov. Lordsh.* 68 þes er þe tokenys of a good stomak—lightnes of body, clernes of vnderstondynge, stiryng appetyt. **1526** TINDALE *Gal.* v. 19 The dedes of the flesshe are manyfest, whiche are these, advoutrie, fornicacion [etc.]. **1678** BUNYAN *Pilgr.* I. 190 Such sayings as these: All our righteousnesses are as filthy rags [etc.]. **1847** TENNYSON *Princess* II. 55 Then an officer Rose up, and read the statutes, such as these: Not for three years to correspond with home [etc.].

2. In opposition to †*tho, those* (of things or persons); sometimes *spec.* = 'the latter': plural of THIS B. I. 3, 3 b. Also † ***these..they*** = some ..others (quot. *c* 1450).

c **893** K. ÆLFRED *Oros.* I. xi, ʒeþence þonne þara tida and nu þissa. *c* **1450** in Aungier *Syon* (1840) 266 Other sustres.. nowe these, now thei, owe of pyte..to visitte suche prysoners. **1611** BIBLE *Ezek.* i. 21 When the liuing creatures were lift vp from the earth, the wheels were lift up... When those went, these went, and when those stood, these stood. **1674** tr. *Scheffer's Lapland* 15 The Russians are generally tall, the Laplanders..very short; those are fat and corpulent, these lean and slender. **1734** POPE *Ess. Man* IV. 22 Some place the bliss in action, some in ease, Those call it Pleasure, and Contentment these. **1902** *Westm. Gaz.* 20 Feb. 2/1, I left the skaters flitting to and fro, these with their hockey sticks, those with their sledges.

II. Demonstrative adjective.

1. Indicating things or persons present or near (actually, or in thought, esp. as having just been mentioned): plural of THIS B. II. 1.

c **888**, etc. [see A. β]. *c* **1175** *Lamb. Hom.* 107 Hu þes halie mihten ouercumað þa sunnan. *c* **1205** LAY. 29786 þæs [*c* **1275** þeos] tiðende come to Austine sone. *c* **1290** *Beket* 308 in *S. Eng. Leg.* I. 115 þis wise men þat weren is Messagers. **1340** *Ayenb.* 7 þise þri hestes diȝteþ ous to gode specialliche. **1390** GOWER *Conf.* I. 34 Yet these clerkes alday preche And sein, good dede may non be. **1411** *Rolls of Parlt.* III. 650/2, I..dyd assemble thise persones that here been. *c* **1440** *Alphabet of Tales* 42 Nowder of þies two did itt; I did it my selfe. **1526** TINDALE *Matt.* xx. 21 These my two sonnes. **1557** NORTH *Gueuara's Diall Pr.* 50 This daungerous and perillous warres. **1653** WALTON *Angler* ii. 69 I'l give you another dish of fish one of these dayes. **1869** LOWELL *Yussouf* ii, His who buildeth over these Our tents His glorious roof of night and day. **1872** TENNYSON *Gareth & Lynette* 798 Well that ye came, or else these caitiff rogues Had wreak'd themselves on me.

b. Referring to something immediately following: plural of THIS B. II. 1 b.

a **1225** *Ancr. R.* 16 Efter þis ualleð acneon..mid teos vif gretunges. 'Adoramus te Christe [etc.]'. *c* **1275** LAY. 688 And þeos [*c* **1205** þas] word seide: Brutus þe sele, Niþinc þou art dead. **1377** LANGL. *P. Pl.* B. Prol. 184 A mous..to þe route of ratones reherced þese wordes: 'Thouȝ we culled þe catte [etc.]'. *c* **1420** *Chron. Vilod.* 2454 And þuse wordus to hym dude say. **1589** PUTTENHAM *Eng. Poesie* III. iv. (Arb.) 159 Also ye finde these words, *penetrate, penetrable, indignitie.* **1678** BUNYAN *Pilgr.* I. 80 Then was he glad, and that for these reasons: First [etc.]. **1737** *Gentl. Mag.* VII. 182/2 Under the Inscription are these Words, in Greek Letters, *Kairos 'o Pandamatôr.*

c. Referring to things or persons familiarly known, esp. to the whole class of such things or persons: plural of THIS B. II. 1 d.

c **1325** *Poem Times Edw. II* 49 in *Pol. Songs* (Camden) 326 Thise ersedeknes that ben set to visite holi churche. *c* **1386** CHAUCER *Frankl. Prol.* 1 Thise olde gentil Britons. **1591** SHAKS. *1 Hen. VI*, I. ii. 123 These women are shrewd tempters with their tongues. **1602** —— *Ham.* II. ii. 223 These tedious old fooles. *a* **1704** T. BROWN *Misc., Match for Devil* Wks. 1711 IV. 149 These Husbands are such very Drones. **1766** GOLDSM. *Vic. W.* iv, These rufflings, and pinkings, and patchings, will only make us hated. **1820** BYRON *Mar. Fal.* IV. ii. 17 These city slaves have all their private bias. *Mod.* Do you approve of these old age pensions? Who are these Manchu's in China?

d. Used instead of *this* with a sing. noun of multitude (formerly with *company, number*; now only with collectives in pl. sense, as *vermin*); or esp. with *kind, sort* (†*form*, †*manner*) followed by *of* with pl. sb. (cf. KIND *sb.* 14 b, THOSE II. 2 c).

a **1533** LD. BERNERS *Gold. Bk. M. Aurel.* Let. xii. (1535) Oo ij b, As I say of these smalle nombre, I myght say of many other. **1583** STUBBES *Anat. Abus.* I. (1879) 147 Then, marche these heathen company towards the Church. *a* **1643** J. SHUTE *Judgem. & Mercy* (1645) 108 All the land was covered with these vermin. **1796** SOUTHEY *Lett. fr. Spain* (1799) 328 A faithful picture of these vermin.

e. With a numeral (definite or indefinite) in expressions of time referring to a period immediately past or immediately future.

c **1386** CHAUCER *Merch. Prol.* 22, I haue ywedded bee Thise Monthes two. **1552** ASCHAM in *Lett. Lit. Men* (Camden) 11 Any thing that hapt vnto me, thies many years. **1600** SHAKS. *A.Y.L.* IV. i. 180 For these two houres Rosalinde, I wil leaue thee. **1641** R. BAILLIE *Lett. & Jrnls.* (1841) I. 313 These three or four years bygone. **1655** *Nicholas Papers* (Camden) II. 209 Att the French Court they expect not the conclusion these 4 monthes. **1738** SWIFT *Pol. Conversat.* 44 Where has the Wench been these Three Hours? **1764** FOOTE *Patron* III. Wks. 1799 I. 357, I warrant he won't shew his head for these six months. **1782** COWPER *Gilpin* ii, Though wedded we have been These twice ten tedious years. **1852** THACKERAY *Esmond* II. x, Dan Chaucer's, who's dead these ever so many hundred years.

1865 WHEWELL in *Life* (1881) 549 As I have done any time these twenty years and more.

f. ***these days*** advb. phr., nowadays, at present.

1936 R. LEHMANN *Weather in Streets* I. v. 97 An estate like this must be a terrible problem these days. **1948** M. DICKENS *Joy & Josephine* I. iv. 132 'Play golf?' Mr. Gray asked George, who answered: 'Not these days,' as if he ever had. **1960** S. BARSTOW *Kind of Loving* II. iii. 181 He looks as though he's walked out of an American picture. It's all Yankeeland these days. **1981** *Woman* 5 Dec. 5/1 These days women are educated to expect some choice in how they spend their lives.

2. In opposition to *those*: pl. of THIS B. II. 2.

1641 HINDE *J. Bruen* xxxiii. 104 O how great is the difference betwixt those holy exercises of Religion..and these prophane exercises of corruption and lust! **1660** BARROW *Euclid* v. xv, The number of these parts is equal to the number of those. **1810** CRABBE *Borough* iv. 54 And these fair acres, rented and enjoy'd, May those excel by Solway-moss destroy'd. *Mod.* Do you think these scissors sharper than those you had yesterday?

III. *Comb.* **these-like** *a.*, like these, such as these: cf. *this-like* s.v. THIS B. III.

1644 MILTON *Areop.* (Arb.) 57 Every acute reader upon the first sight of a pedantick licence, will be ready with these like words to ding the book a coits distance from him, I hate a pupil teacher [etc.]. **1819** KEATS *Hyperion* I. 50 Some mourning words, which in our feeble tongue Would come in these like accents.

Thesean (θiːˈsiːən), *a.* Also †**Theseian**. [f. L. *Thēsē-us* adj. + -AN.] Of or belonging to Theseus, a legendary hero-king of Athens. So **Theseid** (θiːˈsiːɪd) [ad. L. *Thēsēïs*, *-idem*, Gr. *Θησηΐς, -ΐδα*], the title of a poem on the exploits of Theseus; *transf.* a poem of the same character as the 'Theseid of hoarse Codrus' referred to by Juvenal. **Theseium** (θiːˈsiː(ɪ)əm), **Theseum** (θiːˈsiːəm), **Theseion** (θiːˈsaɪɒn) [a. L. *Thēsēum*, Gr. *Θησεῖον*], the temple of Theseus at Athens, or the Doric building to which the name is now applied (generally held to be the temple of Hephæstus).

1815 B. R. HAYDON *Jrnl.* 6 Nov. in T. Taylor *Life Haydon* (1853) I. xv. 294 Lord Elgin's steward..thus entirely ruined the moulds of the *Theseian bas-reliefs, which had cost Lord Elgin so much. **1902** *Speaker* 26 June 370/1 These..should go far to explain the old Thesean legends. **1725** *Pope's Odyss.* I. *View Epic Poem*, etc. iv. 10 Poets..who composed their *Theseids, Heracleids, and the like. *a* **1822** SHELLEY *Def. Poetry* Ess. & Lett. (Camelot) 39, I confess myself..unwilling to be stunned by the Theseids of the hoarse Codri of the day. **1873** HAYMAN *Odyss.* XI. 260 *note* II. 205 An Amazon of the Theseid legend. **1819** E. DODWELL *Tour Greece* I. xii. 362 The *Theseion impresses the beholder more by its symmetry than its magnitude. **1837** *Antiq. Athens* 68 Unlike the lavish decoration of the temple of Minerva, the *Theseium was ornamented with a sparing hand. **1854** tr. *Hettner's Athens & Peloponnese* 152 The monument of Aristion in the *Theseum at Athens.

†**thesial**, *a.* *Obs. rare*⁻¹. [irreg. f. THESI-S + -AL¹.] Relating to a thesis or theses.

1654 VILVAIN *Epit. Ess.* App. 191 One hundred Thesial Verses are here rendred.

ˈ**thesicle.** *nonce-wd.* [f. THESIS + *-cle*, dim. suffix: see -CULE.] A little insignificant thesis.

1863 RUSSELL *Diary N. & S.* I. 232 Their paltry thesicles on the divine origin and uses of slavery. **1864** in WEBSTER.

thesis (ˈθiːsɪs, ˈθɛsɪs). Pl. **theses** (ˈθiːsiːz). [a. Gr. *θέσις* putting, placing; a proposition, affirmation, etc., f. root *θε-* of *τι-θέ-ναι* to put, place.]

I. In *Prosody*, etc.: opposed to ARSIS.

1. Originally and properly, according to ancient writers, The setting down of the foot or lowering of the hand in beating time, and hence (as marked by this) the stress or *ictus*; the stressed syllable of a foot in a verse; a stressed note in music.

[**1855** WEIL & BENLOEW *Théorie générale de l'accentuation latine* 98. **1861** R. WESTPHAL *Fragm. der griech. Rhythmiker* 98. **1880** P. PIERSON *Métrique Naturelle du Lang.* 32.] **1864** HADLEY *Ess.* (1873) 81 The name *feet* for rhythmic elements, *arsis* (raising of the foot), *thesis* (setting down of the foot), have primary reference to orchestic. **1891** *Cent. Dict.*, *Thesis*... In musical rhythmics, a heavy accent, such as in beating time is marked by a down-beat.

2. By later Latin writers (e.g. Martianus Victorinus *a* 400, Priscian *c* 500) used for the lowering of the voice on an unstressed syllable, thus practically reversing the original meaning; hence in prevalent acceptation (from the time of Bentley, 1726): The unaccented or weak part of a foot in verse (classical or modern), or an unaccented note in music; *spec.* in Old English prosody and in the prosody of other Germanic languages.

1398 TREVISA *Barth. De P.R.* XIX. cxxxi. (1495) 941 *Arsis* is rerynge of voys and is the begynnyng of songe. *Thesis* is settynge and is the ende. [**1726** BENTLEY *Terence* p. i.] **1830** J. SEAGER tr. *Hermann's Metres* I. ii. 4 After the example of Bentley, we call that time in which the ictus is, the *arsis*, and those times, which are without the ictus, the *thesis*... Other writers on metres, together with ancient musicians,..call that thesis which we call arsis, and that arsis, which we call thesis. **1844** [see ANACRUSIS]. **1846** KEIGHTLEY *Notes Virg., Bucol.* I. 47 (Fŏrtūnātĕ sĕnĕx, ĕrgō tŭă rūră mănēbŭnt!) He [Wagner] adds, that the emphasis should therefore be on *tua*, and not on *manebunt*. But this was not possible to a Roman, for *tua* here (like *mea* ix. 4) is in the *thesis* of a dactyl. **1870** F. A. MARCH *Introd. Anglo-Saxon* 147 The regular Germanic epic line has four..arses in each section, each of which may have a thesis or not. **1876** KENNEDY *Pub. Sch. Lat. Gram.* §258 Each simple Foot has two parts, one of which is said to have the ictus upon it, and is called arsis..; the other part is called thesis. **1879** OUSELEY in Grove *Dict. Mus.* I. 95/2 The terms arsis and thesis may be regarded as virtually obsolete, and are practically useless in these days. **1888** A. H. TOLMAN in *Trans. Mod. Lang. Assoc. Amer.* III. 20 Only one accented syllable, out of the first sixteen in this poem [sc. *Beowulf*], has a syllable expressed as its thesis or senkung. **1910** J. SCHIPPER *Hist. Eng. Versification* 28 Syllables with this secondary accent are necessary in certain cases as links between the arsis and the thesis. **1938** A. CAMPBELL *Battle of Brunanburh* 18 A dissyllabic second thesis seems not to be found in lines of type A. **1942** J. C. POPE *Rhythm of Beowulf* 49 We fill the down-beat or thesis of this measure with a rest.

‖**3.** *Mus.* ***per arsin et thesin*** (= 'by raising and lowering'): used of a fugue, canon, etc. in which the subject or melody is inverted, so that the rising parts correspond to the falling ones in the original subject and *vice versâ*: the same as *by inversion*.

1597 MORLEY *Introd. Mus.* II. 114 If therefore you make a Canon *per arsin & thesin*, without anie discorde in binding maner in it. **1706** PHILLIPS (ed. Kersey) s.v. *Arsis*, A Point being inverted or turned, is said, To move *per Arsin* and *Thesin*, that is to say when a Point rises in one Part, and falls in another; or on the contrary, when it falls in one Part, and rises in another. **1879** [see ARSIS 3].

II. In *Logic*, *Rhetoric*, etc.

4. A proposition laid down or stated, esp. as a theme to be discussed and proved, or to be maintained against attack (in *Logic* sometimes as distinct from HYPOTHESIS 2, in *Rhetoric* from ANTITHESIS 2); a statement, assertion, tenet.

1579 DIGGES *Stratiot.* aiv, The vulgare Thesis of the Earthes Stabilitie. **1600** W. WATSON *Decacordon* Pref. (1602) A v b, By way of a Quodlibet or Thesis proposed. **1651** *Life Father Sarpi* (1676) 8 He was sent to dispute against the Theses that were then given in. **1697** tr. *Burgersdicius his Logic* II. xxiii. 112 A Thesis, whose Truth is not known by the meer Signification of the Words only; but by the Judgment of the Senses, or some other way of Declaration. **1727–41** CHAMBERS *Cycl.* s.v., The maintaining a thesis, is a great part of the exercise a student is to undergo for a degree. *Ibid.*, Every proposition may be divided into thesis and hypothesis, thesis contains the thing affirmed or denied, and hypothesis the conditions of the affirmation or negation. Thus,..If a triangle and parallelogram have equal bases and altitudes (is the hypothesis), the first is half of the second, the thesis. **1833** COLERIDGE *Table-t.* 3 July, The style of Junius is a sort of metre, the law of which is a balance of thesis and antithesis. **1860** COLLIER *Gt. Events Hist.* vi. 182 [Luther] Shaping his belief on the subject of the indulgences into ninety-five theses or propositions. **1879** FARRAR *St. Paul* II. 96 In the Epistle to the Romans he established the thesis that Jews and Gentiles were equally guilty.

b. *spec.* distinguished from HYPOTHESIS 1, q.v. quots. 1620–*a* 1647.

c. A theme for a school exercise, composition, or essay.

a **1774** TUCKER *Lt. Nat.* (1834) II. 624 Whether among the theses given to declaim upon, it might not be profitable sometimes to choose those wherein the boys will be heartily interested. **1786** JEFFERSON *Writ.* (1859) II. 42 On such a thesis, I never think the theme long.

5. A dissertation to maintain and prove a thesis (in sense 4); esp. one written or delivered by a candidate for a University degree.

1653 *Munim. Univ. Glasgow* (1854) II. 323 Theologicall theses. **1659** OWEN *Consid. Bibl. Polygl.* 205 The Thesis prefering this or that translation above the originall. **1673** RAY *Journ. Low C.* 36 He makes Theses upon the Subject he intends to answer, which Theses are printed. **1741** WATTS *Improv. Mind* I. xiii. §3 It is the business of the respondent to write a thesis..or short discourse on the question proposed. **1837** LOCKHART *Scott* vi, Scott's thesis was, in fact, on the Title of the Pandects, 'Concerning the disposal of the dead bodies of criminals'. **1864** BURTON *Scot Abr.* I. v. 266 There was an instruction that each should write his name on his thesis.

6. *Comb.*: ***thesis-monger*** (see MONGER¹ 2); **thesis-novel** = *roman à thèse* s.v. ROMAN *sb.*⁴; **thesis-play**, a play composed with the purpose of maintaining a thesis, a tendency-play; so ***thesis-playwright***.

1932 *Essays & Stud.* XVII. 75 The aimless burrowings of a *thesis-monger. **1959** *Listener* 13 Aug. 255/1 Subjects like the Henrician Reformation..have been far too much in the hands of thesis-mongers. **1934** WEBSTER, *Thesis novel. **1954** K. TILLOTSON *Novels of Eighteen-Forties* I. 117 Novelists who..avoided the thesis-novel. **1979** S. WEINTRAUB *London Yankees* vii. 233 Elizabeth Robins..continued writing thesis-novels on euthanasia, prostitution, women's rights. **1904** *Edin. Rev.* Oct. 299 The use of '*thesis play' as a term of reproach is not without a certain justification. **1905** *Daily Chron.* 14 June 5/2 'L'Adversaire' is one of those brilliantly specious thesis-plays with which M. Capus has been wont to astonish both the philosophic and dramatic worlds. **1902** *Edin. Rev.* July 199 The conscious, deliberate *thesis-playwright was Dumas *fils*.

thesˈmophilist. *nonce-wd.* [f. Gr. *θεσμός* law (f. root *θε-* to lay down) + *-φιλ-ος*, -PHIL + -IST.] A lover of law.

1644 SIR E. DERING *Prop. Sacr.* e iij b, His Bishop [Bp. Wren], that great Thesmophilist.

Thesmophoric (θɛsməʊˈfɒrɪk), *a.* *Gr. Antiq.* [f. Gr. (*τὰ*) *θεσμοφόρια*, neut. pl. (f. *θεσμοφόρος*, f. *θεσμός* law + *-φορος* -bearing, an epithet of the goddess Demeter) + -IC.] Of or pertaining to the **Thesmophoria**, an ancient Greek festival held by women in honour of Demeter. So **Thesmoˈphorian** *a.*, in same sense.

1788 J. LEMPRIERE *Bibliotheca Classica* s.v. *Thesmophora*, The Thesmophoria were instituted by Triptolemus, or according to some by Orpheus, or the daughters of Danaus. *Ibid.*, Such as were initiated at the festivals of Eleusis assisted at the Thesmophoria. **1884** W. M. RAMSAY in *Encycl. Brit.* XVII. 127/2 Thesmophoric rites are so obscure that no sure idea can be gained of the relation between them and the simpler Arcadian cultus. **1890** J. G. FRAZER *Golden Bough* II. iii. 46 The casting of the pigs into the vaults at the Thesmophoria formed part of the dramatic representation of Proserpine's descent into the lower world. **1891** *Cent. Dict.*, Thesmophorian. **1940** M. P. NILSSON *Gr. Folk Relig.* 24 Best known is the festival of the autumn sowing, the Thesmophoria. **1978** *Times Lit. Suppl.* 18 Aug. 922/4 The regular female festival of fertility, the Thesmophoria, was entirely confined to women.

thesmothete (ˈθɛsməʊθiːt, -θɛt). Also in Gr. form **thesmothetes** (θɛsˈmɒθɪtiːz), *pl.* **-thetæ**. [ad. Gr. *θεσμοθέτης*, pl. *-θέται* (see def.), f. *θεσμός* law + *-θετης*, forming agent-nouns from root *θε-* to place, lay down.] Each of the six inferior archons in ancient Athens, who were judges and law-givers; hence *transf.* one who lays down the law.

1603 HOLLAND *Plutarch* Explan. Words, *Thesmothetæ*, were six of the nine Archontes or chiefe rulers in Athens during their free popular estate. **1727** BAILEY vol. II, *Thesmothete*, a Law-giver. **1819** H. BUSK *Tea* 18 Without thee thesmothetes their laws enacted. **1874** T. HARDY *Far fr. Madding Crowd* x, Then this small thesmothete stepped from the table, and surged out of the hall.

thesocyte (ˈθɛsəʊsaɪt). *Biol.* [irreg. f. Gr. *θέσις* putting, deposit + -CYTE.] (See quot.)

1887 SOLLAS in *Encycl. Brit.* XXII. 420/2 Reserve cells or *thesocytes* have been described in several sponges as well as amylin and oil-bearing cells.

thesorar, -er, variant of THESAURER *Obs.*

thesp (θɛsp), colloq. abbrev. of THESPIAN *sb.*

1962 *New Statesman* 23 Feb. 274/3 Like all tales about thesps, [it] seems to involve us just that much less in their fate. **1976** *Times Lit. Suppl.* 5 Mar. 262/2 More commonly than not, Shakespeare productions by Eng Lit dons involving undergraduate actors come with terrific programme notes but scrawny thesps. **1978** *Guardian Weekly* 15 Jan. 21/4 Hero and heroine—actors both..a famous pair of Budapest thesps.

Thespian (ˈθɛspɪən), *a.* and *sb.* [f. Gr. proper name *Θέσπις* + -AN.]

A. *adj.* Of or pertaining to Thespis, the traditional father of Greek tragedy (6th c. B.C.); hence, of or pertaining to tragedy, or the dramatic art; tragic, dramatic.

1675 COCKER *Morals* 39 Nectar, Ambrosia, and the Thespian Spring, May all avant, for Mony is the Thing. **1748** THOMSON *Cast. Indol.* I. 463 Oft they snatch the pen, As if inspir'd, and in a Thespian rage; Then write and blot, as would your ruth engage. **1847** (*title*) Theatrical Times, a Weekly Magazine of Thespian Biography. **1855** KINGSLEY *Westw. Ho* ii, To extemporise a pageant,..or any effort of the Thespian art. **1906** *Athenæum* 3 Mar. 256/2 The Chorus was a reminiscence of the old Thespian drama.

B. *sb.* A tragedian; an actor or actress.

1827 W. KENNEDY *Poems* 42 The Thespian's outward guise Of happiness, her secret mood belies. **1864** DORAN *Ann. Eng. Stage* I. v. 121 The..Lord Chamberlain..clapped the unoffending Thespian..in the Gate House.

Thespianism (ˈθɛspɪənɪz(ə)m). [f. THESPIAN *sb.* + -ISM.] The art of acting, dramatic art.

1914 C. MACKENZIE *Sinister Street* II. III. viii. 664 Scarcely ever did the Academic Muse enter the O.U.D.S... She must greatly dislike Thespianism with all that it connoted of mildewed statuary in an English garden. **1928** *Daily Express* 79 Oct. 9 He still wraps round him..the rags of a tattered toga of Thespianism.

Thessalian (θɪˈseɪlɪən), *a.* and *sb.* *Gr. Antiq.* [f. L. *Thessalius*, *Thessalus* (Gr. *Θεσσάλειος*, *Θεσσαλός*) adjs. f. *Thessalia* (*Θεσσαλία*) Thessaly: see -AN, -IAN.] **A.** *adj.* Of or pertaining to Thessaly, a region in northern Greece.

1590 SHAKS. *Mids. N.* IV. i. 127 Crooke kneed, and dew-lapt, like Thessalian Buls. **1667** MILTON *P.L.* II. 544 As when Alcides..tore Through pain up by the roots Thessalian Pines. **1757** J. DYER *Fleece* II. 56 When, o'er the deep by flying Phryxus brought, The fam'd Thessalian ram enrich'd her plains. **1842** TENNYSON *Talking Oak* 292 Or that Thessalian growth, In which the swarthy ringdove sat, And mystic sentence spoke. **1888** *Encycl. Brit.* XXIII. 299/1 These Thessalian passes were of the utmost importance to southern Greece. **1973** R. LANE-FOX *Alexander* I. iii. 47 Demeratus the Corinthian..had bought the horse from his Thessalian breeder.

B. *sb.* An inhabitant of Thessaly; the dialect of Greek spoken there.

1608 E. TOPSELL *Serpents* 5 One Aleua a Thessalian, who feeding his Oxen in Thessaly..there fell in loue with him a Serpent. **1704** S. PARKER tr. *Tully's Old Age* 34 When Cineas the Thessalian told him of it. **1888** *Encycl. Brit.* XXIII. 299/2 In race, as in geographical position, the Thessalians held an intermediate place between the non-Hellenic Macedonians and the Greeks of pure blood. **1910** C. D. BUCK *Gr. Dial.* I. 3 Thessalian is of all dialects the most closely related to Lesbian, and at the same time shares in some of the characteristics of the West Greek dialects. **1973** R. LANE-FOX *Alexander* I. iii. 60 Philip's heir was ruler of the Thessalians, a people essential for his army. **1978** *Language* LIV. 179 Thereafter Thessalian underwent some influence from Northwest Greek.

thessaure, var. THESAUR *Obs.*, treasure.

thessel, -downe, obs. form of THISTLE, -DOWN.

†**thester**, *sb. Obs.* Forms: 1 **ðiostru, -tro, þeostru, ðiestru, þystru, -o,** 2 **þeostre,** 3 **þuster,** 4 **þustre,** 4 **þestri, þester,** 4–5 **thestre,** 5 **thestur.** [OE. *ðiestru, þéostru*, fem. (orig. of the *-î* decl.) = OS. *thiustrî*; also OE. *ðíestre, þéostre*, pl. *-ru*, neut.; f. THESTER *a.*] Darkness. *lit.* and *fig.*

Beowulf 87 Seþe in þystrum bad. *c* **897** K. ÆLFRED *Gregory's Past. C.* xxxv. 244 Se dæᵹ bið ierres dæᵹ & ðiestra ðæᵹ. *a* **900** tr. *Bæda's Hist.* v. xiii. [xii.] (1890) 426 He mec forlet in middum þæm þeostrum. *c* **1000** *Ags. Gosp.* Matt. xxii. 13 Wurpaþ hyne on þa uttran þystro [*c* **1160** *Hatton G.* þeostran, *Rushw.* ðiostre, *Lindisf.* ðiostrum]. *c* **1175** *Lamb. Hom.* 131 He ledde heom of þeostran and of scadewe. *a* **1250** *Owl & Night.* 230 Hit luuyeþ þuster & hateþ lyht. *c* **1315** SHOREHAM v. 130 þaȝ hyt were þustre of nyȝt. **13..** *E.E. Allit. P.* B. 1775 þay þrongen þeder in þe þester. *c* **1400** *Destr. Troy* 4629 Thunret in the thestur throly with all. *a* **1400–50** *Alexander* 4627 Quen it walows & wannes all oure thestres.

Hence †'**thesterful, þeosterful** *a.*, full of darkness; †**theosterleyk** (*Orm.* **þeossterrleȝȝc**), darkness.

c **1000** ÆLFRIC *Hom.* II. 350 Se engel me lædde..to anre þeostorfulre stowe. *c* **1000** *Ags. Gosp.* Matt. vi. 23 Eall þin lic-hama byð ðysterfull [*c* **1160** *Hatton G.* þeosterful]. *c* **1200** ORMIN 2964, I þiss lifess þeossterrleȝȝc.

†**thester**, *a. Obs.* Forms: 1 **ðiostre, *ðiestre, þystre, þiostor,** 1–2 **þeoster (-or, -ur),** 1–3 **þeostre,** 2 **þiestre, þostre,** 2–3 **þestre,** 2–4 **þester,** 3 **þuster, -re, þestere,** (*Orm.* **þessterr**), 4 **þyestre, þister, þyster,** 4–5 **thester, -ir,** 5 **thestur.** [OE. *þíostre, þéostre*, in WS. (with umlaut) *þíestre, þýstre*, = OS. *thiustri*, OFris. *thiustere*, MDu. *dûster* (Du. *duister*, MLG., LG., G. *düster*), :—OTeut. **þiustr-jo-*. Ulterior etymology uncertain.] Dark. *lit.* and *fig.*

Beowulf 2332 Breost innan weoll þeostrum ᵹeþoncum. *a* **900** tr. *Bæda's Hist.* v. xiii. [xii.] (1890) 426 Under ðæm scuan þære ðeostran nihte. *c* **1000** *Ags. Ps.* (Th.) xvii[i]. 11 þa hangode swiðe þystru wæter on þam wolcnum. *c* **1175** *Cott. Hom.* 233 H[e] sweueð hus mid þiestre nicht. *c* **1200** *Trin. Coll. Hom.* 39 Al þis lif..is to nihte iefned, for þat it is swa þester of ure ateliche synnes. *c* **1200** ORMIN 16774 Nicodem, þatt comm till ure Laferrd O þessterr nahht. ?*a* **1300** *XI Pains Hell* 121 in *O.E. Misc.* 150 þe stude is þustrore þene þe nyht. *Ibid.* 225 þustrur þane þe nyht. *c* **1315** SHOREHAM v. 146 Be hyt þyster, be hyt lyȝt. **1340** *Ayenb.* 45 þise zelleres of cloþ þet chieseþ þe þyestre stedes huer hi zelleþ hare cloþ. *c* **1400** *Destr. Troy* 2362 He þrong into þicke wodes, þester within. ?*a* **1500** *Chester Pl.* (Shaks. Soc.) I. 226 He maie goe no thester waie.

†**thester**, *v. Obs.* Forms: 1 **ð-, þeostrian, þiestrian, þystrian,** 2 **þestrian,** 2–3 **þ(e)ostren,** 3 **þustren,** 4 **þester.** [OE. *þéostrian, þíestrian*, f. *þéostre*, THESTER *a.* Cf. G. *düstern.*]

1. *intr.* To become dark, grow dim.

a **900** tr. *Bæda's Hist.* v. xiii. [xii.] (1890) 426 þa ᵹeseah ic ..onginnan ðeostrian ða stowe. *c* **1000** ÆLFRIC *Gen.* xlviii. 10 Israheles eaᵹan þystrodon for þære miclan ylde. **1154** *O.E. Chron.* an. 1135 (Laud MS.) þa þestrede þe dæi ouer al landes. *c* **1175** *Lamb. Hom.* 143 Steorren sculen þeostren. *c* **1205** LAY. 4574 þeostrede [*c* **1275** þustrede] þa wolcne.

2. *trans.* To make dark, darken; to dim.

c **888** K. ÆLFRED *Boeth.* xxxviii. §5 Se dæᵹ blent & þiostrað heora eaᵹan. *c* **950** *Lindisf. Gosp.* Mark xiii. 24 Sunna bið ᵹe-ðiostrod. *a* **1225** *Ancr. R.* 94 þet heo her þeostreð nu ham suluen.

†'**thesterly**, *a.* and *adv.* Forms: 1 **þeosterlic** (*adj.*), 4 **þiesterliche** (*adv.*). [f. THESTER *a.*: see -LY[1], [2].] **a.** *adj.* Dark. **b.** *adv.* Darkly.

c **1000** ÆLFRIC *Hom.* I. 504 þæs muntes cnoll mid þeosterlicum ᵹenipum eal oferhangen wæs. **1340** *Ayenb.* 244 þe clene of herte þet hier ssole ysy him be byleaue, ac alneway þiesterliche.

†'**thesterness.** *Obs.* Forms: see THESTER *a.* [OE. *þéosternes*, etc., f. *þéostre*, THESTER *a.* + -NESS.] Darkness. *lit.* and *fig.*

c **888** K. ÆLFRED *Boeth.* xxxiv. §8 þesternes. *c* **893** —— *Oros.* VI. ii. §3 Wearð micel þeosternes ofer eallne middanᵹeard. *c* **1000** *Ags. Hom.* (ed. Assmann 1889) 203 þa com..þære nihte þysternys. *c* **1175** *Lamb. Hom.* 61 þe engles a-dun follon in to þe þosternesse hellen. *a* **1200** *Moral Ode* 277 Eure þer is vuel smech, þusternesse and eie. *c* **1200** ORMIN 16737, & menn ne lufenn nohht te lihht Acc lufenn þessterrnesse. *c* **1250** *Gen. & Ex.* 1942 Quiles he slep, In ðis ðisternesse, old and dep. *c* **1300** *Havelok* 2191 Gon was þisternesse of þe nith. **1377** LANGL. *P. Pl.* B. XVI. 160 On a thoresday in thesternesse þus was he taken. ?*a* **1500** *Chester Pl.* ii. 12 Twynned shalbe throughe my mighte the lighte from Thesternes.

†**thestri**, *a. Obs.* Forms: 1 **ðiostriᵹ, þystriᵹ,** 3 **þeostri,** 4 **thestri.** [OE. *þiostriᵹ*, f. *þíostre, þéostre*, THESTER *a.* + *-iᵹ*: see -Y.] Dark (*lit.* and *fig.*); = THESTER *a.*

a **900** WÆRFERTH *Gregory's Dial.* (1900) 76 þonne bið þin lichama eall þystriᵹ. *c* **950** *Lindisf. Gosp.* Mark viii. 17 Ðiostriᵹ..ᵹie habbað hearta iuer. *a* **1240** *Ureisun* in *Cott. Hom.* 200 Aliht mine þeostri heorte. *c* **1325** *Body & Soul* in *Map's Poems* (Camden) 346 In a thestri stude y stod.

thesuerer, variant of THESAURER *Obs.*

thet, þet, obs. f. THAT; obs. neut. sing. of THE.

theta ('θiːtə). [a. Gr. θῆτα: see def.]

1. a. The eighth letter of the Greek alphabet, Θ, θ (see TH).

In ancient Greece, on the ballots used in voting upon a sentence of life or death, θ stood for θάνατος, death; hence in allusive use.

1603 DANIEL *Def. Ryme* H iv, Setting his *Theta* or marke of condemnation vppon them. **1616–61** HOLYDAY *Persius* iv. 317 And the black theta, signe of deadly shame, Thou can'st prefix 'fore an offenders name. **1682** SIR T. BROWNE *Chr. Mor.* I. §22 At the Tribunal..wherein iniquities have their natural Theta's, and no nocent is absolved by the verdict of himself. **1789** M. MADAN tr. *Persius* (1795) 103 Able to fix the black theta to vice.

b. *attrib.* and *Comb.*, as ***theta-sounding*** adj.; **theta-function**, in *Math.*, a name for two different functions: (*a*) the sum of a series from $n = -\infty$ to $n = +\infty$ of terms denoted by $\exp(n^2a + 2na)$; also extended to a similar function of several variables; (*b*) a function occurring in probabilities, expressed by the integral $\int\exp(-t^2)dt$; **theta-phi diagram**, the temperature-entropy diagram, which represents the heat-units converted into work per pound of working fluid (θ = absolute temperature, and ϕ = entropy).

1871 M. COLLINS *Mrq. & Merch.* III. iii. 88 You [English] are a theta-sounding people. **1879** CAYLEY *Coll. Math. Papers* X. 475 We have thus an addition-with-subtraction theorem for the double theta-functions. **1901** *Pract. Engineer Pocket Bk.* 166 The temperature-entropy diagram is usually called the θφ (theta-phi) diagram.

2. *Biol.* Used to designate rhythmic activity of the brain recorded by an electroencephalograph and having a frequency of between four and seven cycles per second.

1944 WALTER & DOVEY in *Jrnl. Neurol., Neurosurg., & Psychiatry* VII. 64/1 In the case of the 4–7 c/s. waves the term we suggest is 'theta'. *Ibid.* 65/1 It is suggested that rhythms at about 6 c/s. should be termed 'theta' rhythms and that such rhythms are characteristic of the resting, immature or isolated parieto-temporal complex. **1953** *Brit. Jrnl. Psychol.* XLIV. 320 The excessive theta rhythm.. found in some aggressive psychopaths. **1961** *Lancet* 26 Aug. 465/1 An E.E.G. recorded when fasting showed some abnormality, with rhythmic 6 c.p.s. theta activity in the resting tracing. **1972** *Sci. Amer.* Feb. 85/3 Subjects with a great deal of experience in meditation showed other changes: the alpha waves slowed..and rhythmical theta waves at six to seven cycles per second appeared. **1975** J. TAYLOR *Superminds* vii. 121 In states of extreme emotion, theta waves of four to seven cycles and up to thirty microvolts occur.

3. In Scientology: creative energy or spirit. Also '**thetan**, the embodiment of this spirit in the individual. (See quots. 1965.)

1951 L. R. HUBBARD *Handbk. for Preclears* 77/1 *Theta.* The mathematical symbol for the static of thought. By *theta* is meant the static itself. **1952** —— *Scientology: 8-80*, 83 The thetan, or theta being, takes over a body only a few days or a week before birth. **1957** J. F. HORNER *Summary of Scientol.* iv. 56 In Scientology, the specialized term, 'theta', is used to refer to thought and spirit. The term, 'Thetan', refers to the single unit of beingness which each person is. **1965** L. R. HUBBARD *Scientol. Abridged Dict.* 33 *Theta*, energy peculiar to life or a thetan which acts upon material in the physical universe. *Ibid.*, *Thetan*, the person himself ..; that which is aware of being aware; the identity that is the individual. **1971** [see SCIENTOLOGY]. **1977** C. MCFADDEN *Serial* (1978) xxvii. 60/2 Marlene said Theta taught you how to overcome Specific Negatives. **1977** *Times Lit. Suppl.* 13 May 582/5 The gnosis centres on the 'thetan', the true self. .. The core task of the cult ought to be to cleanse and return the thetan to its immortal, pristine, form.

4. Chem. ***theta*** (or ***θ, Θ***) ***temperature***, the temperature of a polymer solution at which it behaves ideally as regards its osmotic pressure; so ***theta condition, solvent***, etc.

1953 P. J. FLORY *Princ. Polymer Chem.* xii. 523 Frequently it is preferred to use as a parameter the 'ideal' temperature Θ... At the temperature $T = \Theta$, the chemical potential due to segment-solvent interactions is zero... Hence the temperature Θ is that at which the excess chemical potential is zero and deviations from ideality vanish. *Ibid.* xiv. 612 An ideal solvent, or Θ-solvent. *Ibid.*, The intrinsic viscosity usually changes rapidly with temperature in the vicinity of the Θ-point. **1966** BRANDRUP & IMMERGUT *Polymer Handbk.* IV. 163 Theta-solvents (θ-solvents) are solvents in which, at a given temperature, a polymer molecule is in the so-called theta-state, where it behaves like an ideal statistical coil. **1973** J. M. G. COWIE *Polymers* vii. 138 Above the theta temperature expansion of the coil takes place, caused by interactions with the solvent, whereas below Θ the polymer segments attract one another, the excluded volume is negative, and eventual phase separation occurs. **1974** *Sci. Amer.* Dec. 60/2 At that temperature, which varies for different polymers and solvents, the measured properties of the polymer can be usefully compared with those of other polymers at their theta temperature.

5. *Particle Physics.* Freq. written θ. A meson that decays into two pions, now identified with the kaon. Also ***theta meson.***

1954 *Physical Rev.* XCIV. 1732/1 A large fraction of these V^0 decays are consistent with the decay scheme $\theta^0 \rightarrow \pi^\pm + \pi^\pm$ (or $\mu^\mp$). **1955**, etc. [see TAU].

6. ***theta pinch*** (Nucl. Physics): a toroidal pinch (PINCH *sb.* 13) in which the magnetic field follows the axis of the plasma and the current-carrying coils encircle it. [θ, the symbol of the angle of the radius vector of the circular path of the current.]

1959 *Nucleonics* Oct. 82/2 The conference topic that aroused greatest interest was the theta pinch. **1967** *New Scientist* 9 Nov. 369/1 The simplicity of the theta pinch as a means of achieving that sought after goal of power from thermonuclear reactions had led to considerable studies of its real effectiveness in confining and heating up a plasma. **1974** *Nature* 20 Sept. 193/2 In the theta-pinch design, the compression coils are not superconducting and no special measures are taken to reduce neutron heating.

thetatron ('θiːtətrɒn). *Nucl. Physics.* Also Thetatron. [f. THETA + -TRON.] A fusion reactor employing a theta pinch in which the plasma is compressed axially by causing the current in the coils, and hence the axial magnetic field, to increase suddenly.

1959 *Nucl. Instruments & Methods* IV. 323/1 At A.W.R.E. both straight and toroidal magnetic compression devices ('Thetatron') have been examined. **1962** W. B. THOMPSON *Introd. Plasma Physics* iv. 63 Much interest has been shown in the axial compression devices, or thetatron, in which a cylindrical plasma is compressed by a rapidly rising axial field. **1964** *Times Sci. Rev.* Autumn 14/1 Thetatrons produce hot dense plasmas for..a few microseconds. **1980** W. M. GIBSON *Physics Nucl. Reactors* x. 200 At the Culham laboratory..magnetic mirror and bottle systems have received thorough investigation in experiments with Thetatron and Phoenix devices.

thetch (θɛtʃ). *dial.* [A dial. form of *fetch* = VETCH: cf. *thane*[2], and see TH (6).]

1733 W. ELLIS *Chiltern & Vale Farm.* 50 Waggon Loads of Peas, Thetches, Chaff and other Grain. **1759** in *Q. Jrnl. Economics* Nov. (1907) 77 To be sowed Wheat as soon as the thetches are tyed off. **1893** *Wilts. Gloss.*, *Thetches, Thatches*, vetches. *Lent thetches* are an early spring kind.

thetch(e, obs. variants of THATCH.

thete (θiːt). *Gr. Antiq.* [ad. Gr. θής, θητ-, orig. a villein, slave.] In ancient Athens, by the constitution of Solon, a free man of the lowest class, whose property in land was assessed at less than 150 medimni.

1652 L. S. *People's Liberty* ix. 17 Such whose revenue amounted not to so much as 200 measures of aride and liquide fruicts (who were called Thetes). **1846** GROTE *Greece* I. xx. II. 131 Poor freemen called Thetes, working for hire. *Ibid.* 132 The condition of a slave under an average master may have been as good as that of the free Thête.

thete, variant of THEAT.

Thetford ('θɛtfəd). The name of a town in Norfolk, England, used *attrib.* to designate Saxo-Norman pottery of a type made there and in other parts of East Anglia. Usu. as ***Thetford ware.***

1949 *Archaeological News Let.* Feb. 3/1 Until quite recently the origin and affinities of St. Neots (or Thetford) pottery have been misunderstood. **1956** *Proc. Cambridge Antiquarian Soc.* XLIX. 46 There is also evidence that Thetford ware was made at Norwich and Ipswich. **1966** *Daily Tel.* 31 Oct. 14/5 The kilns themselves and the finds of pottery may shed new light on Thetford ware which is known all over East Anglia... This is the first time that a good specimen of a Thetford ware kiln has been available for examination. **1971** *Canad. Antiques Collector* Apr. 17/2 Thetford Ware which is very frequently found at North Elmham is well made, fired hard and has a very characteristic 'feel' which is sandy, but not as friable as the shell-gritted St. Neots Ware also found in this region.

thethe, thething, erroneous spelling of *tethe, tething*, = TITHE, TITHING.

†**thethen**, *adv. Obs.* Forms: 2–3 (*Orm.*) **þeþenn,** 3 **ðeðen,** 4 **þi-, þei-, þeyþen, þeiþin, thythen, þeden, -in,** 4–5 **þeþen, -þin, -thyn, theþen, -then, -thyn,** 5 **þ-, -thethin, -thyne.** [Early ME., a. ON. *þeðan*, Icel. *þaðan* (MSw. *thædhan*, obs. Da. *deden*), f. root of THE with suffix of 'motion from', as in HETHEN, WHETHEN; cf. Gr. -θεν.] From that place; = THENCE.

c **1200** ORMIN 1098 Siþþenn ȝede he þeþenn ut. *c* **1220** *Bestiary* 727 in *O.E. Misc.* 23 Ðeðen he sal cumen eft. *a* **1300** *Cursor M.* 6190 þai suld his banes þeþen bring. *Ibid.* 8945 (G.) þai drow it þedin [*F.* þeiþen]. *c* **1400** *Melayne* 519 The myghte of god..Had broghte tham thethyn a way. *c* **1450** *St. Cuthbert* (Surtees) 548 Sho hyed her þeþin fast.

b. Preceded by *fro* (= from).

1340 HAMPOLE *Pr. Consc.* 1018 þe ayre fra þeþen, and þe heat of þe son Sustayns þe erthe here, þar we won. *c* **1400** *Destr. Troy* 8790 Fro thethen the lycour belyue launchit doun evyn. *c* **1420** *Wars Alexander* (Prose) 66 Fra thethyn, Alexander remowede his Oste & come to þe ȝates of Caspee.

Hence †'**thethenforth** *adv.* = THENCEFORTH; †'**thethenward** *adv.* = THENCEWARD.

c **1200** ORMIN 10786 Iwhillc mann þatt..Iss laȝhelike fullhtnedd Birrþ stiȝhenn dun fra þeþennforþ Off modiȝnessess lawe. *Ibid.* 18176, & teþennforrþ to þewwtenn Crist. *c* **1200** *Trin. Coll. Hom.* 69 Ðe ðeðen forð shal wexen alse he seide. **13..** *Cursor M.* 6357 (Fairf.) Fra þeiþen forþ sir moises þer wandes bare. *Ibid.* 14557 (Cott.) In effraym dueld he..And þeþen ward son can he funde.

thether, -ur, obs. forms of THITHER.

†**thethey**, obs. ? scribal error for TEETHY *a.*[1]

c **1400** *Rowland & O.* 1032 Gude sir, ryde my lemmane nere, the knyghte es full thethey.

thethorn, variant of THEVE-THORN *Obs.*

thethy: see TETHY.

thetic (ˈθɛtɪk), *a.* (*sb.*) [ad. Gr. θετικ-ός such as is placed or is fit to be placed; positive, affirmative, f. θέτος placed, f. root θε- to place.]

1. Characterized by laying down or setting forth; involving positive statement: cf. THESIS 4.

1678 GALE *Crt. Gentiles* III. Pref., To render our Discourse the lesse offensive, we have cast it into a thetic and dogmatic method, rather than agonistic and polemic. **1837** E. BICKERSTETH *Life Francke* iv. 61 Thetic and historical divinity were not the fields which Francke had chosen to lecture upon. **1882** A. M. FAIRBAIRN in *Contemp. Rev.* Dec. 862 His [Mohammed's] genius was not thetic, but synthetic, not creative but constructive.

2. *Pros.* That bears the thesis; stressed.

1815 J. GRANT in *Monthly Mag.* XXXIX. 303 The first syllable of each being thetic or emphatic and the remainder of the foot being in arsis or remiss.

b. 'Beginning with a thesis' (*Cent. Dict.* 1891).

B. *sb.* (*pl.*) **thetics** (nonce-wd.), the art of laying down principles or putting forth propositions.

1864 CARLYLE *Fredk. Gt.* XVI. v. (1873) VI. 182 Polemics, Thetics, Exegetics.

thetical (ˈθɛtɪkəl), *a.* [f. as prec. + -AL[1]: see -ICAL.] Of the nature of or involving direct or positive statement; laid down or stated positively or absolutely; positive; dogmatic; arbitrary.

1653 H. MORE *Conject. Cabbal.* (1713) 66 This Law..was merely Thetical or Positive, not Indispensable and Natural. **1678** CUDWORTH *Intell. Syst.* Pref. 2. **1718** J. CHAMBERLAYNE *Relig. Philos.* Pref. (1730) 4 The Thetical Way..must not appear imperfect to them. **1873** W. HUMPHREY *Div. Teacher* p. iii, A thetical exposition of the Catholic doctrine.

thetically (ˈθɛtɪkəlɪ), *adv.* [f. THETICAL + -LY[2].] In a thetical manner; by way of assertion or positive statement; positively.

1657 W. MORICE *Coena quasi Κοινὴ* v. 58 Why should the same thing be true when proposed thetically, generally.., and false when applyed hypothetically, particularly? **1697** G. K. *Disc. Geom. Problems* 12, [I] have proposed it rather Problematically than Thetically. **1870** M. J. EVANS *Oosterzee's Theol. N.T.* 305 The doctrine of justification is in the Epistle to the Romans presented more thetically (i.e. by way of statement), in Galatians more polemically.

Thetis (ˈθɛtɪs). [a. Gr. Θέτις, proper name.]

1. *Gr.* and *Rom. Mythology.* One of the Nereids or sea-nymphs, the mother of Achilles; poetically, the sea personified.

1422 LYDG. *Min. Poems* (Percy Soc.) 14 Thetes wiche is of water chef Goddes. *c* **1620** T. ROBINSON *Mary Magd.* 14 Neptune too, and Thetis greene, In my palace may bee seene. **1711** SHAFTESB. *Charac.* (1737) II. 396 The bridegroom-doge, who in his stately Bucentaur floats on the bosom of his Thetis, has less possession than the poor shepherd, who from a hanging rock..admires her beauty. **1840** BARHAM *Ingol. Leg.* Ser. I. *Witches' Frolic* 87 If..he laid his head In Thetis's lap beneath the seas.

2. *Astron.* Name of the seventeenth asteroid.

Hence †**'Thetisie**, *obs. nonce-wd.*, the abode of Thetis and the Nereids; the watery realm.

1600 TOURNEUR *Transf. Metam.* xl, The Treasure-house of Neptune's Thetisie. *Ibid.* lxxiv, When fatall Neptune.. hal'd him to his Thetisie.

thetsee, var. THITSI, black-varnish tree.

theu, theue, var. THEOW, THEW.

theurgic (θiːˈɜːdʒɪk), *a.* (*sb.*) [ad. L. *theurgicus*, a. Gr. θεουργικός magical: see THEURGY and -IC. So F. *théurgique* (14th c.).] Of or pertaining to theurgy.

1610 HEALEY *St. Aug. Citie of God* X. ix. 371 Certaine Theurgike consecrations called *Teletae*. **1718** BP. HUTCHINSON *Witchcraft* 35 A Golden Image of Jupiter, prepared by the Theurgic Art. **1834** LYTTON *Pompeii* II. viii. [see GOETIC A.]. **1861** —— *Str. Story* (1862) I. 313 Every secret..which the nobler, or theurgic, magic seeks to fathom. **1895** FARRAR *Gathering Clouds* ii. 38 Whatever skill ..of medicine he possessed, he eked it out with theurgic pretences.

†**B.** *sb.* A theurgist. *Obs. rare.*

1610 HEALEY *St. Aug. Citie of God* X. xvi. (1620) 362 Let the Platonists, Theurgikes (or rather Periurgikes..) or any other Philosophers answer. *Ibid.* 395 They whom the malicious Theurgike bound from purging the soule of the good one.

theurgical (θiːˈɜːdʒɪkəl), *a.* [f. as prec. + -AL[1]: see -ICAL.] = prec. adj.

1569 [see THEURGY I]. **1610** HEALEY *St. Aug. Citie of God* 395 The true Angels..differ from them that descend unto men that use Theurgicall conjurations. **1652** [see GOETICAL]. **1678** CUDWORTH *Intell. Syst.* I. iv. §16. 286 This Divine Magick of Zoroaster..degenerated..into the Theurgical Magick. *a* **1834** COLERIDGE *Lit. Rem.* (1839) III. 159 A corrupt mystical theurgical pseudo-Platonism.

Hence **the'urgically** *adv.*

1854 MAURICE *Mor. & Met. Philos.* II. 71 The author proposes to discuss..theurgical [questions] theurgically.

theurgist (θiːˈɜːdʒɪst). [f. THEURG(Y + -IST. Cf. F. *théurgiste* (18th c.).] One who practises or believes in theurgy; a magician.

1652 GAULE *Magastrom.* xxvi, The sacrilegious theurgist will consecrate my head to the crows. **1678** CUDWORTH *Intell. Syst.* I. iv. §15. 269 One of those more refined [magicians], who have been called by themselves Theurgists. **1856** R. A. VAUGHAN *Mystics* (1860) I. I. iv. 24 The mysticism of the theurgist, who will pass the bounds of the dreaded spirit world..to seize one of its thrones.

theurgy (θiːˈɜːdʒɪ). [ad. L. *theūrgia*, a. Gr. θεουργία sorcery, f. θεός god + -εργος working. So F. *théurgie* (14th c. in Godef. *Compl.*).]

1. A system of magic, originally practised by the Egyptian Platonists, to procure communication with beneficent spirits, and by their aid produce miraculous effects; in later times distinguished as 'white magic' from GOETY or 'black magic'.

1569 J. SANFORD tr. *Agrippa's Van. Artes* 59 b, Porpherie who doth muche dispute of this Theurgie or Magicke of thinges deuine doth finally conclude that with Theurgicall consecrations mans mince may be made apte to receaue Spirites and Angels. **1584** R. SCOT *Discov. Witchcr.* XV. xlii. (1886) 392 There is yet another art, which is called Theurgie; wherein they worke by good angels. **1652** GAULE *Magastrom.* xxvi, Of ceremoniall magick there are two parts, goetie and theurgie. **1751** [see GOETY]. **1899** W. R. INGE *Chr. Mysticism* vii. 267 The turbid streams of theurgy and magic flowed into the broad river of Christian thought by two channels—the later Neo-platonism, and Jewish Cabbalism.

2. The operation of a divine or supernatural agency in human affairs; the effects produced among men by direct divine or spiritual action.

1858 GLADSTONE *Homer* III. 564 We stand here at a juncture in the poem, where its theurgy supersedes its human mechanism. **1873** M. ARNOLD *Lit. & Dogma* (1876) 167 The constant tendency of popular Christianity to add to the element of theurgy and thaumaturgy, to increase and develope it. **1878** GLADSTONE *Prim. Homer* 86 The Olympian court is the masterpiece of the whole theurgy of Homer.

Theutonicke, obs. form of TEUTONIC.

†**theve**, *sb. Obs. rare*[−1]. The first element of THEVE-THORN, of uncertain derivation: app. Brush-wood, bush, shrub; = BRUSH *sb.*[1] 2.

c **1440** *Promp. Parv.* 490/2 Theve, brusch [*v.r.* brush: no Latin equivalent given].

†**theve**, *v. Obs.* Also 4 **thef.** [ME. a. ON. *þefa* to smell, to sniff. Cf. THEF.] *trans.* To smell.

13.. *Cursor M.* 23456 (Gött.) In þis lijf has man gret liking..Suete spiceri to theue [*Edin.* thef, *Cott.* fell (= fele), F. tast] and smell.

theves, obs. pl. of THEAVE, THIEF.

†**'theve-thorn, 'the-thorn.** *Obs.* Forms: 1 **thebanthorn, þefan-, þeofe-, þife-, þyfe-,** 1–3 **þefeþorn,** 3–5 **theve-,** 4 **theoue, thef-,** 4–5 **thethorn(e;** (5 **thewe-, threw-thorn**). [Cogn. with OHG. *depandorn* (*Ahd. Glossen* I. 237, 34). Etymology of first element uncertain.

Grimm, *Kl. Schr.* I. 246, renders *depandorn* 'brenndorn', comparing '*deba, diba* incendium', in the Malb. Gloss. This might refer to thorns used for burning or kindling a fire. See also Van Helten in *P. & B. Beitr.* XXV. 348.]

Name of some thorny shrub.

a. In OE. and ME. glossaries commonly rendering L. *rhamnus*, which was sometimes in late and med.L. applied to the bramble or blackberry-bush, and was sometimes glossed by whitethorn or hawthorn.

The sense 'bramble' or 'blackberry-bush' is supported by L. *mōrus* in *Metr. Voc.* (which has this sense sometimes in Pliny, and still in Romanic langs.); that of 'hawthorn' by the *red* fruit of *Sinon. Barthol.* (*Thevethorn* could not be buckthorn, the late botanical identification of *Rhamnus* with buckthorn being merely a caprice of Linnæus, without any ancient warrant.)

a **700** *Epinal Gloss.* (O.E.T.) 880 *Ramnus*, thebanthorn. *c* **725** *Corpus Gloss.* 1710 *Ramnus*, ðeofeðorn. *c* **1000** *Sax. Leechd.* II. 312 Wiþ bite wyrc sealfe; nim..þefan þorn. *Ibid.* III. 56 Nim..ðefeþorn. *c* **1000** *Ags. Voc.* in Wr.-Wülcker 269/21 *Ramnus*, coltetræppe, þefanðorn. *c* **1000** ÆLFRIC *Voc.* ibid. 139/20 *Ramnus*, þifeþorn. *Ibid.* 149/32 *Ramnus*, *uel sentix ursina*, ðyfeþorn. *a* **1300** *E.E. Psalter* lvii[i]. 10 Ar-til þai undre-stande bi-forn Of youre thornes of theve-thorn [**1382** WYCLIF theue thorne, Vulg. *rhamnum*]. **13..** *Heber MS.* 8336 in *Promp. Parv.* 490 *note*, Nym the floures of theoue-thorn. *a* **1340** HAMPOLE *Psalter* lvii. 9 Rammyn, þat þai call thefthorne, has swilke a kynd, þat it is first soft, and sithen turnys it in til thornes. *a* **1387** *Sinon. Barthol.* (Anecd. Oxon.) 36 *Rampnus* est frutex spinosus ferens rubeos fructus, i. thethorne. **1388** WYCLIF *Judg.* ix. 14 And alle trees seiden to the ramne [*gloss* ether theue thorn; *Vulg.* ad rhamnum; 1382 to the thorn], Come thou, and be lord on vs. **14..** *Metr. Voc.* in Wr.-Wülcker 629/6 *Morus*, thewe-thornys. **14..** *Nom.* ibid. 715/35 *Hec ramnus*,..a thethorntre. *c* **1450** *Medulla* in *Cath. Angl.* 382 *note*, *Ramnus*, a whyte thorne or a thepe [? theve] bushe. **1483** *Cath. Angl.* 382/2 A Thethorne, *rampnus*.

b. Sometimes applied to the gooseberry.

In Ps. lvii. 9, the two 12th c. Anglo-Norman Psalters (ed. Fr. Michel, 1860, 1876) render *rhamnus* by *groseiller*, *groselier*, gooseberry, and this identification is found in some ME. glossaries, and was also adopted by Theodore Gaza, *c* 1450. Cf. also FEABERRY, DAYBERRY, possibly dialectal alterations of *the-berry* from *thethorn*.

c **1265** *Voc.* in Wr.-Wülcker 558/29 *Ramni*, *i.* [Fr.] grosiler, *i.* [Eng.] þefeþorn. *c* **1450** *Alphita* (Anecd. Oxon.) 156 *Rampnus*, *gallice* griseler, *anglice*, threwthorn. [**1862** WRIGHT *Hist. Domest. Mann.* 296 In the dialect of Norfolk, gooseberries are still called *theabes*.] [Cf. *Thapes*, *thepes* gooseberries (Eng. Dial. Dict.).]

†**'thevis 'nek.** *Sc. Obs.* = 'Thief's neck', one fit for the gallows: a term of opprobrium.

In quots. represented as the cry of the tewhit or lapwing.

c **1450** HOLLAND *Howlat* 823 The Tuchet and the gukkit Golk... Callit him [the Rook] thryss thevisnek, to thrawe in a widdy. **1549** *Compl. Scot.* vi. 39 The tuechitis cryit theuis nek, quhen the piettis clattrit.

thew (θjuː), *sb.*[1] Forms: 1–3 **þeaw, þeau,** (1 **ðeow**), 2–3 **þæw,** 2–5 **þew, þewe,** 3 **þeauw, þeuw, þeæw, þeu,** 4 **theaw,** 4–5 **theu, thue,** 4–9 **thewe,** (5 **thegh**), 4– **thew.** [OE. *þéaw* = OS. *thau* usage, custom, habit, OHG. *thau* (*dau*) discipline. Not recorded outside WGer. langs. Ulterior etymology uncertain.]

†**1. a.** A custom, usage, general practice (e.g. of a people, community, or class). *Obs.*

Beowulf 360 Cuþe he duȝuðe þeaw. *c* **893** K. ÆLFRED *Oros.* I. x. §2 Sippan wæs hiera þeaw. *c* **950** *Lindisf. Gosp.* John xix. 40 Sua ðeau Iuðeum [*Rushw.* ðeow iudea, *Ags. Gosp.* iudea þ[e]aw, *Hatton G.* iudea þæw] is bybyrȝe. *c* **1200** *Trin. Coll. Hom.* 47 Wich þeau was on þe olde laȝe. *Ibid.*, Swich þeu wes bi þan daȝen.

†**b.** *pl.* Customs ordained; ordinances. *Obs.*

13.. *E.E. Allit. P.* B. 544 In de-voydynge þe vylanye þat venkquyst his þewez. *Ibid.* 755. **1624** QUARLES *Job* vii. 7 Thy sacred Thewes, and sweet Instructions, did Helpe those were falling, rays'd up such as slid.

†**2. a.** A custom or habit of an individual; manner of behaving or acting; hence, a personal quality (mental or moral); a characteristic, attribute, trait. Chiefly in *pl. Obs.*

c **888** K. ÆLFRED *Boeth.* xxvii. §2 Wisdom..ælces godes þeawes he ȝefyllð þone þe hine lufað. *c* **893** —— *Oros.* VI. xiv. §1 He wæs swiþe yfel monn ealra þeawa. **971** *Blickl. Hom.* 217 Wæs he swiðe ȝeþungen on his ðeawum. *c* **1000** ÆLFRIC *Gen.* xxxi. 5 Ic ȝeseo on eowres fader þeawum, þat he nys swa wel wið me ȝeworht. *c* **1200** ORMIN 7328, I dærne unnclene þohht & þæw. *c* **1205** LAY. 6361 Morpidus.. Monnene strengest Of maine and of þeauwe. *c* **1230** *Hali Meid.* 3 Euch meiden þat haueð meidene peawes. *a* **1300** *Cursor M.* 1947 (Cott.) To doghty thues lok þou þe gif. **1382** WYCLIF *I Cor.* xv. 33 Forsoth yuele spechis corumpen (or distroyen) goode thewis (or vertues). **1422** tr. *Secreta Secret.*, *Priv. Priv.* 211 A man may not fynde in no beste, custume ne thegh, wyche is noght in a man. **1456** SIR G. HAYE *Law Arms* (S.T.S.) 120 The vertues cardinalis..reule of all vertues and gude thewis as kingis. **1508** DUNBAR *Tua Mariit Wemen* 119 Full of eldnyng..and anger, and all euill thewis. **1559** *Mirr. Mag.*, *Dk. Clarence* xviii, In vertuous thewes. **1590** SPENSER *F.Q.* II. x. 59 Helena..in all godly thewes and goodly prayse Did far excell. **1805** SOUTHEY *Madoc* II. xviii, In martial thewes and manly discipline, To train the sons of Owen.

†**b.** Without qualification: A good quality or habit; a virtue; courteous or gracious action. *Obs.*

c **1205** LAY. 300 Þis child leuede & wel iþei, & þeweas [*c* **1275** þeuwes] hit luuede. *a* **1225** *Ancr. R.* 278 Þes þeau [humility] is alre þeauwene moder. *c* **1250** *Gen. & Ex.* 2757 Hu a ȝunge man, at te welle[n] Ðewe and wursipe hem dede. **13..** *Cursor M.* 20996 (Cott.) A man o mekenes and o theu. **1357** *Lay Folks Catech.* 406 The third vertu or thew is charite. *c* **1400** *Emare* 58 She thawȝth [= tawȝt] hyt curtesye and thewe, Golde and sylke for to sewe. **1575** GASCOIGNE *Notes Instr.* in *Steele Gl.* etc. (Arb.) 37 This poeticall license ..turkeneth all things at pleasure, for example, *ydone* for *done*..*thewes* for good partes or good qualities.

3. *pl.* Physical good qualities, features, or personal endowments. †**a.** *generally* (e.g. the fair features or lineaments of a woman). *Obs.*

1567 TURBERV. *Ovid's Epist.* xv. N iv b, Doost thou thinke ..that doltish silly man, The thewes of Helens passing forme, may iudge, or throughly scan? *Ibid.* xviii. Q vj, I leaue her thewes vntoucht, Wherein she may compare With heauenly peeres, such feature fals On earthlie creatures rare.

b. The bodily powers or forces of a man (L. *vires*), might, strength, vigour; in Shaks., bodily proportions, lineaments, or parts, as indicating physical strength; in modern use after Scott, muscular development, associated with *sinews*, and hence materialized as if = muscles or tendons. Also in *sing.* and *fig.*

1566 NUCE tr. *Seneca's Octavia* I. iv. B iij b, Ere while thilke wretch recoyleth backe againe, And to my thews for ayde retyres amaine. **1597** SHAKS. *2 Hen. IV*, III. ii. 276 Care I for the Limbes, the Thewes, the stature, bulke, and bigge assemblance of a man? giue mee the spirit. **1601** —— *Jul. C.* I. iii. 81 Romans now Haue Thewes, and Limbes, like to their Ancestors. **1602** —— *Ham.* I. iii. 12 Nature cressant does not grow alone, In thewes and Bulke. **1791** COWPER *Odyss.* XVII. 271 He should on bulkier thewes Supported stand [cf. POPE ibid. 264 If any labour those big joints could learn]. **1818** SCOTT *Rob Roy* iii, My fellow-traveller, to judge by his thewes and sinews, was a man who might have set danger at defiance. **1843** LYTTON *Last Bar* I. vi, A man who values his kind mainly by their thews and their sinews. **1850** TENNYSON *In Mem.* ciii. 31, I felt the thews of Anakim, The pulses of a Titan's heart. *c* **1863** E. DICKINSON *Poems* (1955) II. 512 Thigh of Granite—and thew—of Steel. **1873** G. M. HOPKINS *Jrnls. & Papers* (1959) 233 A floating flag is like wind visible and what weeds are in a current; it gives it thew and fires it and bloods it in. **1876** —— *Wr. Deutschland* xvi, in *Poems* (1967) 56 He was pitched to his death at a blow, For all his dreadnought breast and braids of thew. **1887** MISS BRADDON *Like & Unlike* i, Nature has been kinder to your brother in the matter of thew and sinew. **1930** R. CAMPBELL *Adamastor* 77 A Hercules of matchless thew Whose body is the breath of flowers. **1977** *N.Y. Rev. Bks.* 15 Sept. 40/3 By 'language' he means not the whole body of speech, the thew and sinew of the language.. but a precursor's language.

c. *fig.* Applied to cords or ropes.

1851 MELVILLE *The Whale* xvi. I. 111 (*Descr. of a ship*), Bulwarks.. garnished.. with the long, sharp teeth of the sperm whale,.. to fasten her old hempen thews and tendons to. Those thews ran not through base blocks of land wood, but deftly travelled through sheaves of sea-ivory.

† **thew** (θjuː), *sb.*[2] *Obs.* Also 3–4 **theu**, 3–6 **thewe**. [Known before 1250: etymology obscure; app. from THEW *v.*, in sense 'chastise'; but OE. *þýwan, þéowan* 'to press, squeeze, compress' is also a possible source. The forms are identical with contemporary ones of THEW *sb.*[1]]

Name of an instrument or apparatus of punishment ordained, instead of the pillory, for women; often identified with the CUCKING-STOOL. Also in comb. ***thewpenny*** (cf. BURGHAL-PENNY).

The med.L. equivalent was *collistrigium*, i.e. an iron collar compressing and confining the neck.

1275 *Rot. Hundred.* (1818) II. 302/2 (Bassetlaw, Notts) Tempore domini Walteri de Gray [*a* 1256].. levatum fuit le theu primo in villis ejusdem Archiepiscopi.. jam xxx annis elapsis. **1287** *Plac. de Quo Warranto* (1818) 11/1 Ibi habet tantummodo tumberellum et thewe. *Ibid.* 11/2 Cum soca et saka.. boruhapeny et theupeny. **1290–1** *Ipswich Domesday* lxxiv. in *Blk. Bk. Admir.* (Rolls) II. 164 Femmes qe sunt communs tenceresses.. seyent eles chastiez par la juyse qe [est] apele le theu. **1364** *Lett.-Bk. G. London* lf. 137 Consideratum fuit.. quod præfata Alicia subhiat judicium cullistr' pro mulieribus inde ordinat' vocata la Thewe [tr. Riley *Mem.* (1868) 319 That the said Alice should undergo the punishment of the pillory for women ordained, called the thewe.] **1391** *Ibid. H.* lf. 258b, Quod eadem Isabella ponatur super le Thewe pro mulieribus ordinat'.. ibidem moratura per unam horam diei [tr. *ibid.* 526, that she should be put upon the thewe, for women ordained, for one hour of the day]. *c* **1440** *Promp. Parv.* 490/2 Thewe, or pylory, *collistrigium*. *c* **1450** *Surtees Misc.* (1888) 60 Y^{e} sayd Burgese schall.. ordan a pelory and a thew, lawfull and strang. **1483** *Cath. Angl.* 382/2 A Thewe, *tripotheum* (A. *Collistrigium, et cetera*). **15..** in *MS. Harl. 2115* lf. 77 Punire per iudicium de Thewe, hoc est ponere eas super Scabellum vocatum Cokestolle. **1533** *Surtees Misc.* (1888) 34 She shalnot chyde ne flyte,.. oppen ridyng of the jebit, or thew, aboute the towne. **1577** HARRISON *England* II. xix. (1877) I. 310 It is not lawfull for anie subiect.. to.. set vp furels, tumbrell, thew, or pillorie. **1696** PHILLIPS (ed. 5), *Thew*, an old Word for a Cucking Stool.

thew, *sb.*[3] and *v.*[1] ME. form of THEOW *sb.* and *v.*

† **thew**, *v.*[2] *Obs.* In early ME. **þæwen**, pa. pple. **i-þæwed, i-þeuwed**. [app. f. OE. *þéaw*, THEW *sb.*[1]] *trans.* To instruct in morals or manners; to discipline, train, instruct, chastise.

(In quots. *a* 1225 and *c* 1305 it may possibly represent or be influenced by OE. *þýwan, þýȝan, þéowan* to press, oppress, repress, threaten, rebuke, which otherwise does not appear to have come down into ME.)

c **1200** ORMIN 6217, & ȝunnc birrþ nimenn mikell gom To þæwenn ȝunnkerr chilldre. *a* **1225** *Ancr. R.* 268 (MS. T.) Tu ne schuldest nout tuhten, ne chasten þi meiden uor hire gultes, ne þeawe þine servanz. *c* **1305** *Pilat* 57 in *E.E.P.* (1862) 112 þo þ'emperour ihurde þat he miȝte þat liþere folc so þewe, He ne huld non so queynte man as he huld þe schrewe. *c* **1422** HOCCLEVE *Learn to Die* 83 And thee the bettre for to thewe, The misterie of my lore y shal the shewe. **1625** GILL *Sacr. Philos.* iv. 53 Although some Fathers were no better Cosmographers then to think this; yet for the most part they were better thewed [? instructed, or mannered].

thewed (θjuːd), *ppl. a.* Also 2 **þeaud**, 3–4 **þeu(e)d**, 3 **i-þæwed, i-þeuwed**. [Orig. pa. pple. of THEW *v.*, but app. often treated as f. THEW *sb.*[1] + -ED[2].]

† **1.** Trained, instructed in morals or manners; having qualities or manners (of a specified kind). Chiefly in compounds, as ***ill-thewed***, WELL-THEWED, etc., -mannered, -conditioned, -natured.

c **1200** *Trin. Coll. Hom.* 41 þe wise man and þat wel þeaud child habbeð boðe on laȝe. *c* **1205** LAY. 6536 He wes swiðe soðfest and swiðe wel iðæwed [*c* **1275** i-þeuwed]. *c* **1374** CHAUCER *Compl. Mars* 180 My lady is.. so wel fortuned and thewed That thorow the worlde her goodnesse is yshewed. *c* **1440** *Pallad. on Husb.* IV. 856 [Foals] So thewed that from high quyete & reste Anoon they may be stered forto prike. **1456** SIR G. HAYE *Law Arms* (S.T.S.) 150 Men.. full of vicis, ryotous and evil thewit. **1590** SPENSER *F.Q.* II. vi. 26 Yet would not seeme so rude, and thewed ill As to despise so curteous seeming part. **1596** —— *Hymne in Hon. Beautie* 138 A beauteous soule, with faire conditions thewed.

† **b.** *spec.* Having good qualities or manners.

a **1300** *Cursor M.* 8425 þe child es theud [*v.rr.* theued, þewed] and mild o mode, Lok þat he haf maister god. **13..** *Ibid.* 27632 (Fairf.) If þou be þewed al-so curtaise, þen atte first I wille þe praise. **13..** *E.E. Allit. P.* B. 733 A.a.! blessed be þow,.. so boner & þewed. [*a* **1601** ? MARSTON *Pasquil & Kath.* III. 16 Nay, good Thewte hart: good kind lacke, stay.]

2. Having thews or muscles (of a specified kind).

1864 WEBSTER s.v., A well-thewed limb. **1865** SWINBURNE *Chastelard* I. ii. 34 Do you know that lord With sharp-set eyes? and him with huge thewed throat? *Ibid.* IV. i. 116 You have a heart thewed harder than my heart. **1881** C. DE KAY *Vis. Nimrod* iv. 71 A fearful beast.. Amazing thewed, with fourfold plate-like horns.

† **'thewedly**, *adv. Obs. rare*[−1]. [f. prec. + -LY[2].] In a well-mannered way; virtuously.

13.. *Cursor M.* 28663 (Cott.) Charite.. biddes vs bath in gode and ill Theudli [*v.r.* trewly] thole vr lauerds wille.

† **'thewful**, *a. Obs.* [f. THEW *sb.*[1] + -FUL.] Full of or characterized by good qualities; good, virtuous, moral.

c **1205** LAY. 1797 Heo godd thonkeden mid þeu-fulle worden. *a* **1225** *Ancr. R.* 422 Talkeð mid ouer meidenes and mid þeaufule talen schurteð ou to-gederes. *c* **1230** *Hali Meid.* 45 Wiðute oðer god & þawfulle mihtes. **13..** *Cursor M.* 2337 (Cott.) For [Abram] was theuful [*F.* curtays, *G.*, *Tr.* meke] bath and hind. *Ibid.* 2665 A theuful [*G.*, *Tr.* holy] takynyng for to ken At tuin yow wit fra oþer men.

thewless ('θjuːlɪs), *a.* Now only *Sc.* [f. THEW *sb.*[1] + -LESS. Cf. THOWLESS.]

† **1.** Destitute of morals or virtue; vicious, immoral: = THOWLESS 1. *Obs.*

a **1327** *Pol. Songs* (Camden) 255 For lust hath leve, the lond is theweles. **1513** DOUGLAS *Æneis* IV. Prol. 163 Sic thewles lustis [sall returne] in bittir pane and wo.

2. Without energy, inert, spiritless: = THOWLESS 2.

1895 CROCKETT *Men of Moss-Hags* l, He was a quiet, thewless, pleasantly conforming man. **1896** SNOWDEN *Web of Weaver* vi. 72, I seemed to stand thewless. **1900** C. MURRAY *Hamewith* 85 Like some puir dwinin' thewless wicht Wi' death in view. **1904** *Dundee Advertiser* 13 June 8/1 That the 'thewless' and 'wastrel' class be relegated to labour colonies there to work out their own salvation.

'thewness. *rare.* [f. THEW *sb.*[1] + -NESS.]

† **a.** Virtue. *Obs.* **b.** Vigour, robustness.

c **1200** *Trin. Coll. Hom.* 177 Wunderful is ure louerd on þeunesse. **1860** W. J. C. MUIR *Pagan or Christian* 274 Real wealth lies in the sinewy force of moral thewness.

thewtill, obs. variant of THWITTLE.

thewy ('θjuːɪ), *a. rare.* [f. THEW *sb.*[1] 3b + -Y.] Having well-developed thews; muscular, brawny.

1845 S. JUDD *Margaret* I. x, There were.. broad, hard hands in kid gloves; thewy, red elbows.. in lace ruffles.

they (ðeɪ), *pers. pron.* Forms: see below. [Early ME. *þei* (in Ormin *þeȝȝ*), a. ON. *þei-r*, nom. pl. masc. of the simple demonstrative *sá, sú, þat* (= OE. *þá*, ME. *þā, þō*), which in ON. filled the place of the lost plural of the 3rd pers. pron.: cf. Norw., MSw., Sw., MDa., Da. *de*, 'they'. In OE. the 3rd pers. pron. had its own plural *hí, híe, híᵹ, héo*, which continued in extreme southern dialect to about 1400, and in the oblique cases a century longer: see HI[2], HEM *pron.*, HER *poss. pron.*[2] But even in OE. the function of *hí* was largely shared by the pl. demonstrative *þá* 'those', ME. northern *þā*, midl. and south. *þō*: see THO *dem. pron.* 1. The Trin. Coll. Homilies, *c* 1200, have both *hie* and *þei*, but only *hem, her(e* for 'them, their'. Ormin, *c* 1200, has always *þeȝȝ* in the nom., but often *hemm* and *heore, here*, beside *þeȝȝm* and *þeȝȝre*. Between 1200 and 1500 the Norse forms gradually displaced the original pronominal: in Caxton's earlier works we find *thei, hem, hir*, and in the later *thei, theim, their*. See HE, HI[2], THO *dem. pron.*]

A. Illustration of Forms.

3 (*Orm.*) **þeȝȝ**, (**teȝȝ**), 3 **ðei**, 3–5 **þei, þai** (**tai**), **þey**, 4 (**þi, þy**), 4–6 **thei, thai** (*unstressed* **þe, the**), 4–7 (*Sc.* -9) **thay**, (5 **þeȝe, dey**, 5–6 **yei**, 6–7 **thee**), 4– **they**.

c **1200** ORMIN 125–7, & swa þeȝȝ leddenn heore lif Till þatt teȝȝ wærenn alde, þatt naffdenn þeȝȝ þurrh þeȝȝre streon Ne sune child ne dohhterr. *c* **1200** *Trin. Coll. Hom.* 189 For þan þe þei nehȝie wunien. *c* **1250** *Gen. & Ex.* 573 Mete quorbi ðei miȝten liuen. *a* **1300** *Cursor M.* 19044 (Edin.) Ilkane als tai saȝ mistir haue. *c* **1300** *Havelok* 414 In þe castel.. þer þei sperd wore; þer he greten ofte sore. *c* **1300** *E.E. Psalter* xxi. 5 Oure fadres in þe hoped þai. *c* **1330** R. BRUNNE *Chron. Wace* (Rolls) 2745 þey ȝede spiande her & þer. *Ibid.* 2747 þay wyste alle at ones. *c* **1375** *Cursor M.* 2243 (Fairf.) Quen thay.. had fest þe gronde, þe werke thai raised. **1382** WYCLIF *Matt.* vi. 5 Thei han resseyued her meede. *c* **1386** CHAUCER *Prol.* 40 To telle yow al the condicion Of ech of hem.. whiche they were and of what degree. *c* **1400** *Rule St. Benet* 10 Yeme þaim, þat tay folȝ þe wordis of god. *c* **1400** *Brut* 83 Thei of Normandye, Gascoigne & Spaigne. *c* **1400** *Destr. Troy* 8008 When the knewen all the cause, þo kynges bydene, All denyede it anon. *a* **1425** *Cursor M.* 5042 (Trin.) Into egipte soone coom þey. **14..** in *Hist. Coll. Citizen London* (Camden) 213 To set the pavys where the lykyd. *c* **1440** *Generydes* 2633 So fought y^{ei} still. *c* **1550** CHEKE *Matt.* xxvi. 15 Yei appointed him 30 silverlinges. **1559** BP. SCOT in Strype *Ann. Ref.* (1709) I. App. vii. 12 Thei be joyned as in one. *c* **1560** A. SCOTT *Poems* (S.T.S.) ii. 101 Than to Dalkeith thai maid thame boun. *a* **1584** MONTGOMERIE *Cherrie & Slae* 541 Thay get na credit quhair we come.

B. Signification.

I. 1. a. As pronoun of the third person plural, nom. case; the plural of *he, she*, or *it*: The persons or things in question, or last mentioned.

c **1200–** [see A.]. *c* **1200** *Trin. Coll. Hom.* 39 Here orf þe þei leswueð on halie larspelle. *c* **1330** R. BRUNNE *Chron. Wace* (Rolls) 4990 þritty oþer wyþ hym þey went. **13..** *Cursor M.* 800 (G.) For scham þay stode bath and quakid. *c* **1489** CAXTON *Sonnes of Aymon* xii. 301 Lete theym shyfte hardely, they two togyder. *c* **1550**–*a* **1584** [see A.]. **1707** E. WARD *Hud. Rediv.* II. v. 27 They're Rogues, as sure as Light's in Heaven. **1838** RUSKIN *Ess. Music & Paint.* §24 Wks. 1903 I. 285 If others do not follow their example,—the more fools they. **1846** GROTE *Greece* I. xxi. II. 175 They two were the framers of all Grecian theogony. **1909** J. W. JENKINSON *Experim. Embryol.* 28 The plane in which they all lie.

b. Sometimes used where literary Eng. has the objective THEM. Now only *dial.* or *illiterate*. Also as ***theyselves*** (var. ***theysel(l)s***) for *themselves*.

[*c* **1380** WYCLIF *Wks.* (1880) 391 No man lawfully may.. minystre hem save þai. Cf. SAVE *prep.* 1 b.] **1681** T. FLATMAN *Heraclitus Ridens* No. 37 (1713) I. 239 An Officer, who is sworn not to permit any Person to speak with them, or they with any Body. **1688** LD. DELAMER *Wks.* (1694) 27 That will only tend to render both you and they uneasie. **1882** *Century Mag.* Apr. 892 They're pretty peart at the game theyselves. **1890** A. GISSING *Vill. Hampden* I. iv. 102, I don't understand anything about they. **1890** A. C. BICKLEY *Surrey Hills* I. i. 12 It 'ud be a sight better if 'ee kept they to hissen. **1893** P. H. EMERSON *On English Lagoons* xlii. 256 Those gents expect you to keep as clean as theysels. **1901** C. HARE *Dinah Kellow* 255 Passon didn' like for they to be locked in by theysells. **1974** *Black World* Apr. 8 He was presenting the street nigguhs in all they glory without no overt exhortation to them to git theyselves togetha.

c. ***they are*** (or ***were***) was formerly used (instead of the earlier *it are, it were*, mod. *it is, it was*: see IT B. 2) to introduce a plural sb. about which some statement is made by a relative clause following. Now *rare*.

a **1716** SOUTH *Serm.* (1823) I. 437 The scripture vouches Solomon for the wisest of men: and they are his Proverbs that prove him so. *Ibid.* IV. 420 They were the sins and apostasies of their souls, for the reformation of which he plagued them. **1748** RICHARDSON *Clarissa* (1811) IV. 375 They are the abandoned people in the house who keep thee up to a resolution against her. *a* **1838** PUSEY *Paroch. Serm.* (1883) III. 223 They are our own self-chosen employments, .. which hinder prayer. **1889** A. LANG in *Scribner's Mag.* Sept. 265/2 They are small-minded and small-hearted people who are most shocked by what they call 'vanity' in the great. **1899** L. C. CORNFORD *R. L. Stevenson* vi. 140 Alan Breck Stewart is the central figure, and they are his sayings and deeds of arms that go to make the chief interest.

2. Often used in reference to a singular noun made universal by *every, any, no*, etc., or applicable to one of either sex (= 'he or she').

See Jespersen *Progress in Lang.* §24.

1526 *Pilgr. Perf.* (W. de W. 1531) 163b, Yf.. a psalme scape ony persone, or a lesson, or else y^{t} they omyt one verse or twayne. **1535** FISHER *Ways perf. Relig.* ix. Wks. (1876) 383 He neuer forsaketh any creature vnlesse they before haue forsaken them selues. **1749** FIELDING *Tom Jones* VIII. xi, Every Body fell a laughing, as how could they help it. **1759** CHESTERF. *Lett.* IV. ccclv. 170 If a person is born of a .. gloomy temper.. they cannot help it. **1835** WHEWELL in *Life* (1881) 173 Nobody can deprive us of the Church, if they would. **1858** BAGEHOT *Lit. Stud.* (1879) II. 206 Nobody fancies for a moment that they are reading about anything beyond the pale of ordinary propriety. **1866** RUSKIN *Crown Wild Olives* §38 (1873) 44 Now, nobody does anything well that they cannot help doing. **1874** [see THEMSELVES 5].

3. a. As indefinite pronoun: People in general; any persons, not including the speaker; people. (Cf. ONE *pron.* 21, and OE. *man*, ME. *men, me*, G. *man*, F. *on*.) Often in phrase ***they say*** = people say, it is said.

Much used colloquially and dialectally instead of the passive voice.

1415 SIR T. GREY in 43 *Dep. Kpr.'s Rep.* 583 A man.. yay calle Skranby toke me a lettre. **1565** COOPER *Thesaurus* s.v. *Basis*, Suche a foote as they set chafing disshes on. **1582** ALLEN *Martyrd. Campion* (1908) 111 Sent to prison upon suspition of Papistry, as they terme the Catholike faith. **1599** SHAKS. *Much Ado* IV. i. 254 To strange sores strangely they straine the cure. *a* **1637** B. JONSON *Goodwife's Ale* (*Athenæum* 1 Oct. 1904), My pock-hold Face, they say, appeared to some Just like a dry and burning hony combe. **1671** LADY MARY BERTIE in *12th Rep. Hist. MSS. Comm.* App. v. 23 They say the King hath put out a Proclamation to forbid maskerades. **1756–7** tr. *Keysler's Trav.* (1760) II. 64 They still shew here the three cells in which Cosmo.. used frequently to retire. **1884** *Manch. Exam.* 17 May 5/1 In India and in Holland they 'cure' tobacco fairly well. **1896** M. FIELD *Attila* II. 49 He shall be scourged With the iron-knotted lash they use for slaves. *a* **1912** *Mod.* They do the passage to America now in 5 days.

b. *colloq.* Used to refer collectively to people in authority, regarded as impersonal and oppressive.

1886 KIPLING *Delilah* in *Definitive Verse* (1940) 7 One day, *they* [*sc.* people in power] brewed a secret... It related to Appointments. **1939** AUDEN in *Times Lit. Suppl.* 25 Mar. (Spring Books Suppl.) p. i, The legions of cruel inquisitive 'They' Were so solid and strong, like dogs. **1945** H. NICOLSON *Let.* 27 May (1967) 465 People.. believe that 'they' mean the upper classes, or the Conservatives. **1947** 'G. ORWELL' *Eng. People* 24 English political thinking is much governed by the word 'They'. 'They' are the higher-ups, the mysterious powers. **1967** G. F. FIENNES *I tried to run a Railway* iii. 25 'They' shifted me to York. **1976** *Leicester Chron.* 26 Nov., 'They' are always doing you down. **1981** I. BOLAND tr. *Ginzberg's Within Whirlwind* II. v. 228 How could I go and work in a children's establishment, where 'they' would be able to keep tabs on me?

II. 4. a. As demonstrative pronoun, chiefly as antecedent: = THOSE I. 2, 4. Somewhat *arch.*

1382 WYCLIF *Matt.* v. 10 Blessid be thei that suffren persecucioun for riȝtwisnesse, for the kyngdam of heuenes is herun. *c* **1400** *Brut* lxxiii. 69 þai wiþin kepte þe toune. **1470–85** MALORY *Arthur* XVII. i. 689 They within were putte to the werse. **1539** BIBLE (Great) 2 *Kings* vi. 16 For they that be with vs, are moo then they that be with them. **1630** *R. Johnson's Kingd. & Commw.* 130 The shops.. nothing so full of wares, nor so rich, as they of London. **1691** tr. *Emilianne's Observ. Journ. Naples* 290 They are they that have all the Nobility at command. **1803** WORDSW. *Rob Roy's*

Grave 39 The good old rule Sufficeth them, the simple plan, That they should take, who have the power, And they should keep who can. **1847** TENNYSON *Princess* I. 143 And they that know such things . . would call them masterpieces.

b. Also obj., instead of *them*: cf. 1 b. (Now *dial.*)

c **1489** CAXTON *Sonnes of Aymon* iii. 90 Reynawde . . made all they that were wyth hym . . to be hanged. *a* **1553** UDALL *Royster D.* III. v. (Arb.) 57 And as for all they that woulde do you wrong. **1900** NORWAY *Parson Peter* iv. 108 The devil damn they that keeps me here.

5. As demonstrative adj. = THOSE II. 2, 4; but often in weaker sense, = THE (*pl.*). Now *dial.* (In the Sc. quots. perh. meant for *þa*, *tha*, mod.Sc. THAE.)

a. Qualifying a sb. in the nominative case.

1297 R. GLOUC. (Rolls) 2091 So þei [*v.r.* þe] ssrewe robeours abbe hor wille. **13..** *Cursor M.* 1423 (Cott.) Stil ai stod þai [*G.* þa, *T.* þo] wandes thre. *c* **1375** *Sc. Leg. Saints* v. (*Johannes*) 180 þai men . . þat sa set þar appetyte In Riches. **1567** *Satir. Poems Reform.* iv. 76 How that thay bucheouris blew me in the air. **1877** L. J. JENNINGS *Field Paths* iii. 45 They rooks as you see on bärson's pläce.

b. Qualifying a sb. in the objective case.

c **1375** *Sc. Leg. Saints* iv. (*Jacobus*) 324 And folow þai bese [[oxen], till þai blyne Of þar awne wil. *c* **1400** *Destr. Troy* 1024 þen he lacches his leue and þai lordes þonkit. **1422** tr. *Secreta Secret., Priv. Priv.* 160 Fore thay thre causis, I leue of that matiere. **1456** SIR G. HAYE *Law Arms* (S.T.S.) 82 For the occasioun of thai weris. *c* **1470** HENRY *Wallace* I. 57 Thai landis thane he clamde as heretage. **1552** *Reg. Privy Council Scot.* I. 136 He suld be Commissar in they pairtis. **1596** DALRYMPLE tr. *Leslie's Hist. Scot.* (S.T.S.) I. 10 The inhabitours of thay pairtes. **1885** G. M. FENN *Patience Wins* (1886) 130 A set o' fullish boys as plays they tricks. **1905** F. YOUNG *Sands Pleas.* I. iii, Some o' they Cockney labourers began grumbling.

6. As possessive pronoun: = THEIR *poss. pron.* 1. *U.S. dial.*

1928 J. PETERKIN *Scarlet Sister Mary* 162 When dey is worried in dey mind. **1929** W. FAULKNER *Sartoris* i. 23 They was a-settin' behind a table with they pistols layin' on the table. **1935** in Z. N. Hurston *Mules & Men* I. ii. 45 They all brought they rocks and Christ turned 'em into bread. **1974** *Black World* Nov. 58 Just because all the pussy they can snatch is what they can lick off they goddam fingers.

III. 7. As advb.: = THERE *adv.* 4 d. *U.S. dial.*

1874 'MARK TWAIN' in *Atlantic Monthly* Nov. 592/2 Dey was de biggest dey *is*. **1889** J. W. RILEY *Pipes o' Pan at Zekesbury* 41 They's music in the twitter of the bluebird and the jay. **1920** [see *monkey suit* s.v. MONKEY *sb.* 18 a]. **1949** H. HORNSBY *Lonesome Valley* 185 They's more ways than one to skin a cat. **1973** *Black World* Aug. 61/2 They was ten packets looked like Horse.

they, obs. f. THIGH, THOUGH.

theyf, obs. f. THIEF.

theyfage, error for *theyfish*, THIEVISH.

† **theyght**, i.e. the eighth: see TH-^{1}, TH' 1.

1536 *Cal. Anc. Rec. Dublin* (1889) 400 Kyng Henri theyght.

theyn(e, theynne, obs. ff. THANE, THEN.

theynt, þ-, obs. 3rd pers. sing. of THINK *v.*^{1}

theyrd, theyves: see THIRD, THEAVE.

thi, þi, obs. form of THE, THEY, THIGH, THY.

thiabendazole (θaɪə'bɛndəzəʊl). *Vet. Med.* and *Pharm.* [f. *thia*(*zole* s.v. THIO- 1 + *ben*(*zimi*)*dazole* f. BENZ(ENE + IMID(E + AZO- + -OLE.] An anthelmintic used in veterinary and human medicine, esp. against intestinal nematodes.

1961 H. D. BROWN et al. in *Jrnl. Amer. Chem. Soc.* LXXXIII. 1765/1, 2-(4'-Thiazolyl)-benzimidazole (I, generic name: thiabendazole) was outstanding in anthelmintic activity. **1970** W. H. PARKER *Health & Dis. in Farm Animals* xx. 265 New worm medicines are appearing frequently. At the present time the choice is likely to be either thiabendazole or tetramisole. **1978** R. B. SCOTT *Price's Textbk. Pract. Med.* (ed. 12) II. 236/2 Thiabendazole has been shown to destroy adult female worms [*sc.* *Trichinella spiralis*] and larvae but must be used with extreme caution because it may precipitate serious reactions with anorexia, nausea, headache, giddiness, and drowsiness, possibly as a result of allergy to dead larvae.

thiacetate to **thiamide:** see THIO-.

thiamine ('θaɪəmiːn). [f. THI(O- + AMINE.]

† **1.** *Chem.* (See quot.) *Obs. rare.*

1886 C. A. BENNERT *Brit. Pat. 13,466* 3 This invention has for its object the manufacture or production of a new class of organic coloring compounds or materials by reactions between certain amines of the aromatic series and the dioxide of sulphur group, which organic colouring compounds or materials so obtained I designate 'Thiamines'.

† **2.** *Chem.* Generic name for amines containing the group NHSH, as *ethylthiamine*, C_2H_5.NHSH. *Obs. rare.*

3. *Biochem.* **a.** Also **thiamin.** Vitamin B_1; a water-soluble, heat-labile, sulphur-containing compound that is present in many foods (esp. whole cereal grains, pork, and liver) but absent from fats and is necessary for carbohydrate metabolism, its dietary deficiency resulting in disturbances of the nervous system.

1937 *Jrnl. Amer. Med. Assoc.* 18 Sept. 952/1 Dr. Jansen has been very cooperative in discussing the matter of nomenclature for vitamin B1 and suggested . . that Dr. R. R. Williams . . propose a name based on the chemical structure. Dr. Williams . . proposed the term Thiamin Chloride. **1939** A. HUXLEY *After Many a Summer* II. vi. 234 With a course of thiamin chloride and some testosterone I could have made him as happy as a sand-boy. **1951** A. GROLLMAN *Pharmacol. & Therapeutics* xxvii. 597 Thiamine contains thiazole and pyrimidine rings. **1952** *New Biol.* XIII. 111 The role of thiamin in cell metabolism is to provide a portion of certain enzyme systems. **1972** *Materials & Technol.* V. xix. 674 In Great Britain, all bread except wholemeal must be fortified with thiamin . . to compensate for the losses of the natural vitamin consequent on milling. **1980** D. MADDEN *Food & Nutrition* i. 23/2 After vitamin C, thiamine is probably the most unstable vitamin.

b. thiamine pyrophosphate, the active form of thiamine in which it acts as a co-enzyme: = COCARBOXYLASE.

1949 *New Biol.* VII. 108 These include thiamine pyrophosphate, nicotinamide nucleoside and riboflavine, all of which are involved in systems through which carbohydrates are oxidised. **1960** [see DIPHOSPHOTHIAMINE]. **1973** YUDKIN & OFFORD *Comprehensive Biochem.* (1980) xvii. 297 Transketolase needs as co-factor the vitamin derivative thiamine pyrophosphate, which . . is also involved in the transfer of a two-carbon fragment from pyruvate to lipoic acid.

Hence **thi'aminase** [-ASE], an enzyme that destroys thiamine, splitting the thiazole and the pyrimidine rings.

1938 BONNER & BUCHMAN in *Proc. Nat. Acad. Sci.* XXIV. 437 It has been shown . . that the pea root synthesizes vitamin B_1 . . from a mixture of the pyrimidine and thiazole components of the vitamin molecule. . . This must . . be a synthesis in which a specific enzyme, a 'thiaminase' . . , takes part. **1972** L. HANCOCK *There's a Seal in my Sleeping Bag* ii. 23 Herring is a fish that contains an enzyme called thiaminase, which breaks down thiamin in the body.

‖ **thiasus, thiasos** ('θaɪəsəs, -ɒs). *Gr. Antiq.* [L. *thiasus*, a. Gr. *θίασος* the Bacchic dance.] A company assembled to celebrate the festival of one of the gods (esp. of Bacchus) with dancing and singing. So **thiasarch** ('θaɪəsɑːk) [ad. Gr. *θιασάρχης*], the leader of the thiasus; **'thiasite** (-aɪt), **'thiasote** (-əʊt) [ad. Gr. *θιασίτης, θιασώτης*], a member of the thiasus.

1820 W. TOOKE tr. *Lucian* I. 569 *note*, The president of it was styled a thiasarch. **1850** LEITCH tr. *C. O. Müller's Anc. Art* §390 (ed. 2) 507 Representations of Dionysus and his thiasotes . . were got up. *Ibid.* §367. 460 Dionysus bringing back Hephæstus in the thiasus (at which are also Marsyas and Comœdia). **1873** *Contemp. Rev.* XXI. 568 The 'eranists' are termed 'thiasotes' or 'thiasites'.

thiazide ('θaɪəzaɪd) *Pharm.* [f. THI(O- + AZ(INE + OX)IDE, elements in the systematic name of the parent compound.] Any of a class of drugs derived from 1,2,4-benzothiadiazine-1,1-dioxide that increase the excretion of sodium and chloride and are used as diuretics and as auxiliary hypotensive agents.

1959 *Jrnl. Amer. Med. Assoc.* 22 Aug. 2052/2 When the thiazide derivatives are first administered to hypertensive patients being treated with other drugs, it is advisable to continue giving Rauwolfia derivatives. **1961** *Lancet* 12 Aug. 334/1 The use of guanethidine in combination with one of the thiazide group of diuretics extends the application of these drugs in the management of patients with high blood-pressure. **1974** M. C. GERALD *Pharmacol.* xxii. 399 When used alone, the thiazides have only weak anti-hypertensive effects. **1980** *Brit. Med. Jrnl.* 18 Oct. 1053 Vasodilators are used mainly as additional treatment in patients who are not controlled by thiazides and beta-blockers.

thiazolidine (θaɪə'zɒlɪdiːn). *Chem.* and *Pharm.* [f. *thiazole* s.v. THIO- 1 + -IDINE.] **a.** A liquid, C_3H_7NS, whose molecular structure is that of thiazole with an additional hydrogen atom attached to the nitrogen and each carbon atom. **b.** Any compound containing this ring structure in its molecule.

1916 *Chem. Abstr.* X. 3647/2 (Index), Thiazolidine (tetrahydrothiazole). **1945** *Science* 21 Dec. 628/2 Penicilloic acids are undoubtedly thiazolidines. **1949** E. CHAIN in H. W. Florey et al. *Antibiotics* II. xxii. 823 Penicillamine and its esters react readily with aldehydes or ketones to form thiazolidines. **1951** A. GROLLMAN *Pharmacol. & Therapeutics* xxii. 443 Penicillin is a monocarboxylic acid with β-lactam and thiazolidine rings attached through a CONH linkage to a prosthetic group. **1979** *Nature* 25 Oct. 716/2 The chemical assay based on the behaviour of the fused thiazolidine-β-lactam ring consistently gave higher results than the bioassay which required the full penicillin molecule for biological activity.

Thibet, Thibetan: see TIBET, etc.

thible, dial. variant of THIVEL.

thic, obs. form of THICK; dial. var. of THILK.

thich, thicht, Sc. forms of THIGH, THIGHT.

thick (θɪk), *a.* (*sb.*) Forms: 1 ðicce, (3 þihk), ðhikke, þeck, (9 *dial.* theck), 3–5 þ-, thikke, 3–6 þ-, thycke, 3–7 þ-, thicke, 4 thic, thikc, 4–5 þ-, thyk(e, thykke, þik, 4–6 thik, thikk, 5 thek, þ-, thike, 5–6 thyck, (7 thigge), 4– thick. [OE. *þicce* = OS. *thikki* (Du. *dik*), OHG. *dicchi* (G. *dick*), ON. *þykkr*, beside *þjokki* (Da. *tyk*, Sw. *tjok*, tjock), Goth. **þiqus*:—OTeut. **þik*(*k*)*uz*, *fem.* *þik*(*k*)*wī*-; cf. Ir., Gael. *tiugh* (< **tigu*-); ulterior etymology uncertain.]

A. *adj.* **I. 1. a.** Having relatively great extension between the opposite surfaces or sides; of comparatively large measurement through: as a thick wall, board, or plank, a thick stem, post, or stick; a thick stratum or seam of coal, a thick layer of fat or coating of paint, thick cloth, etc. Opposed to *thin*; distinct from *long* and *broad*: cf. sense 2.

c **888** K. ÆLFRED *Boeth.* xxxv. §4 Hi woldon witan hu heah hit wære to ðæm heofone, & hu ðicce se hefon wære & hu fæst. *c* **1000** *Sax. Leechd.* II. 200 Leȝe on þone þiccestan clað opðe on fel. *c* **1020** *Rule St. Benet* lv. (Logeman) 91 Culam [[= cowl] on wintre þicce on sumere þinne. *a* **1225** *Ancr. R.* 50 þe blake cloð . . is þiccure aȝein þe wind. *c* **1375** *Sc. Leg. Saints* vii. (*Jacobus*) 753 He saw a wal wes fow thyke. *c* **1440** *Promp. Parv.* 490/2 Thykke clothe. **1535** COVERDALE 1 *Kings* xii. 10 My litle fynger shall be thicker then my fathers loynes. **1552** HULOET, Thicke leafe, *carnosum folium.* **1687** A. LOVELL tr. *Thevenot's Trav.* I. 6 The Grapes that grow there . . have a thick skin. **1776** WITHERING *Brit. Plants* (1796) III. 206 Stems several, the central one thickest; leafy. **1809** *Med. Jrnl.* XXI. 335 The individuals belonging to the Austrian branch have thick lips. **1845** TALFOURD *Vac. Rambles* I. 174 The dull gleam through the thick glass of my small round peep-hole.

fig. *a* **1571** JEWEL *Sacram.* in *Serm.* etc. (1583) X v b, I neede not speake more hereof, the errour is so grosse, so thicke, so sensible and palpable.

† **b.** Extending far down from the surface; deep.

c **893** [see sense 2]. **1676** W. ROW *Contn. Blair's Autobiog.* ix. (1848) 138 Riding the water of Belfast, it being thicker than he apprehended. **1693** EVELYN *De la Quint. Compl. Gard.* II. 58 A thick Frost would kill the Roots, as well as the Head.

c. Of a person or animal: Thickset, stout, burly. *Obs.* exc. *dial.*

a **1250** *Owl & Night.* 580 Ne þu nart þikke ne þu nart long. **1297** R. GLOUC. (Rolls) 8570 þikke mon he was ynou, round && noȝt wel long. *c* **1385** CHAUCER *L.G.W.* 1198 (*Dido*) Vp on a thikke palfrey . . Sit Dido. **1486** *Bk. St. Albans* a vj b, A longe hawke, a short thike hawke. **1570** FOXE *A. & M.* (ed. 2) 2252/1 She was . . of a very litle and short stature, somwhat thicke. **1643** BAKER *Chron., Will. II.* 49 He was but meane of stature, thick and square bodied. **1819** W. TENNANT *Papistry Storm'd* ii. (1827) 69 Thick Jamie Bud, lang Sandy Kay.

† **d.** *transf.* Having substance all through; solid, not hollow. *Obs.* $rare^{-1}$.

a **1400–50** *Alexander* 4073 Imagis . . He made his pepill þaim to perse, to proue þam with-in, Quethire þai ware hologhe or hale, & hale he þam fyndis, Saȝe þaim thike þurȝe-out.

2. a. Used (with words of measurement, or in the comparative or superlative) to express the third dimension of a solid, which has a direction at right angles at once to the length and the breadth: Having a (specified) thickness. (Sometimes equivalent to *deep*, but not now said of a body of water or other fluid.) Commonly following the words stating the measure, as *ten feet thick*, *paper* $\frac{1}{10}$ *of a millimeter thick.*

In this sense not opposed to *thin*; for the thinnest substance has some thickness, as the shortest line has some length, and the narrowest surface some breadth or width.

c **893** K. ÆLFRED *Oros.* I. iii. §1 Ælce ȝeare þæt land middeweard oferfleow mid fotes þicce flode. *Ibid.* IV. xiii. §2 Se weall wæs xx fota ðicce, & XL elna heah. *c* **1384** CHAUCER *H. Fame* III. 245 Men myght make of hem a bible xx^{ti} foote thykke. **1493** *Litt. Red Bk. Bristol* (1900) II. 134 Whiche wall we Fynde xxij yenchis thycke by the grownde. **1602** SHAKS. *Ham.* V. i. 214 Let her paint an inch thicke, to this fauour she must come. **1682** WHELER *Journ. Greece* I. 70 The Front is thick Fourteen foot. **1703** MOXON *Mech. Exerc.* 88 One Inch thick, and three Inches broad. **1812** *New Bot. Gard.* I. 61 Some very rotten dung put in the bottom six inches thick. **1825** J. NICHOLSON *Operat. Mechanic* 69 When a sheet of water is not a quarter of an inch thick before it meets the float [of a mill-wheel].

† **b.** Standing one behind the other; = DEEP *a.* 2 b. *Obs.*

1604 E. GRIMSTONE *Hist. Siege Ostend* 56 They discouered their Gabions nine thicke. **1605** B. JONSON *Volpone* I. i. ad fin., There is a guard of spies ten thick upon her. **1650** RUDD *Geom. Questions* 130 The Pikes are invironed with shot four men thick, round about.

3. *fig.* Excessive in some disagreeable quality; too much to manage or to stand; *spec.* too gross, indecent, or indelicate. Often in phrase ***a bit thick.*** Cf. *to lay it on thick. slang.*

1884 *Standard* 6 June 6/3, I know it is thick in Brum. [Birmingham] for you, so that we must meet in London. **1902** G. W. E. RUSSELL *Londoner's Log-bk.* iii. 46 These manifold exercises of culture are characterized by our curate as 'a bit thick', and he owns himself 'fairly out of it'. **1902** *Daily Chron.* 9 Sept. 7/3 Guardsmen who have been drinking are a thick lot, . . and gentle methods will not always prevail with them. **1907** H. WALES *The Yoke* xii, They hinted more than once that Christopher was 'a bit thick'. **1907** H. WYNDHAM *Flare of Footlights* x, 'By the way, what's the piece like?' . . 'A bit thick, my dear? I should just think it was! It's an adaptation from the French, you know'. *Ibid.* xxii, 'It's a bit thick', he said indignantly, 'when a man of my position is passed over for a beginner like young Merrick'.

b. ***the thick end of the stick*** = *the dirty end* (*of the stick*) s.v. DIRTY *a.* 1 e.

1957 *Times* 22 Nov. 8/3 Sir Ralph Richardson has the thick end of the stick. . . He has to represent an ordinary city insurance clerk. **1960** *Woman's Own* 13 Feb. 17/2 I'm the one to get what Father used to call 'the thick end of the stick'.

II. In general sense of *dense*.

4. a. Closely occupied, filled, or set with objects or individuals; composed of numerous individuals or parts densely arranged; dense, crowded. Of hair: Bushy, luxuriant.

c **888** K. ÆLFRED *Boeth.* xxxv. §5 Ðu..lædst me hidres & ðidres on swa þicne wudu. *a* **900** *O.E. Martyrol.* 148 Þa ȝewat he in þone þiccestan wudu. *c* **1000** *Sax. Leechd.* II. 156 ȝif hær to þicce sie, ȝenim [etc.]. *c* **1205** LAY. 27525 Amidden þan þrunge þer heo þihkest weoren. *a* **1250** *Owl & Night.* 17 In ore vaste þikke hegge. **13..** *K. Alis.* 4067 (Bodl. MS.) Of þe draweyng of bowȝes & stykke, Þe eyre bicom trouble & þicke. *c* **1330** R. BRUNNE *Chron. Wace* 13925 Mikel was þe pres, ful þykke þe þro. *c* **1400** *Destr. Troy* 12496 A thoner and a thicke rayne þrublet in the skewes. *c* **1440** *Promp. Parv.* 490/2 Thykke, as wodys, gresse, or corne, or other lyke, *densus*. **1500–20** DUNBAR *Poems* xxxiii. 89 This was the clud of kayis and crawis. **1612** *Proc. Virginia* 61 in *Capt. Smith's Wks.* (Arb.) 424 He had a thicke blacke bush beard. **1620** T. GRANGER *Div. Logike* 166 A thick multitude of people. **1658** DRYDEN *Stanzas to O. Cromwell* xiv, Thick as the galaxy with stars is sown. **1711** ADDISON *Spect.* No. 56 ¶3 A thick Forest made up of Bushes, Brambles, and pointed Thorns. **1855** MACAULAY *Hist. Eng.* xii. III. 199 The women..were seen amidst the thickest fire serving out water and ammunition to their husbands and brothers. **1872** TENNYSON *Last Tourn.* 213 Then fell thick rain. **1899** *Westm. Gaz.* 24 Nov. 8/2 After..the high grass and thick country is entered.

fig. **1387** TREVISA *Higden* (Rolls) I. 355 Þey makeþ..melody wiþ wel þicke tunes, werbeles, and nootes. **1655** FULLER *Ch. Hist.* III. iv. §24 His reign was not onely long..but also thick for remarkable mutations happening therein.

b. Const. *with*, †*of*.

c **1386** CHAUCER *Knt.'s T.* 217 A wyndow thikke of many a barre Of Iren. **1535** COVERDALE *Ps.* lxiv. [lxv.] 13 The valleys stonde so thicke with corne yᵗ they laugh and synge. **1558** PHAER *Æneid* VII. Siij, This Laurel bushe full thick of browse. **1660** F. BROOKE tr. *Le Blanc's Trav.* 22 The Red Seas coast towards Aden is thick of good towns. **1700** DRYDEN *Sigism. & Guiscardo* 102 A mount of rough ascent, and thick with wood. **1871** FREEMAN *Norm. Conq.* IV. xviii. 154 The whole range of walls and towers was thick with defenders.

5. a. Of the individual things collectively: Existing or occurring in large numbers in a relatively small space, or at short intervals; densely arranged, crowded; hence, numerous, abundant, plentiful. (Usually *predicative*, rarely *attrib.*) Also in colloq. phr. *thick on the ground*: (chiefly of persons) numerous, abundant; closely concentrated or crowded. Cf. THIN *a.* 2 e.

c **893** K. ÆLFRED *Oros.* I. i. §9 Heo ȝedeð mid þæm flode swiþe þicce eorþwæstmas on Ægypta lande. *c* **1386** CHAUCER *Wife's T.* 12 Hooly freres..As thikke as motes in the sonne beem. *c* **1400** MAUNDEV. (Roxb.) xxxiv. 152 Gude tounes er þare so thikk þat [etc.]. *c* **1400** *Destr. Troy* 6626 He segh þe troiens so tore, & turnyt so þik, All pyght in a place on a playn feld. **1560** DAUS tr. *Sleidane's Comm.* 136 Rotman..running amonges his ennemies where they were thickest was slayne. **1667** MILTON *P.L.* I. 303 His Legions..Thick as autumnal leaves that strow the brooks In Vallombrosa. **1726** LEONI tr. *Palladio's Archit.* (1742) I. 97 Thick columns..distant from each other..at the most two diameters. *c* **1813** MRS. SHERWOOD *Stories Ch. Catech.* xxxvi. (1816) 367 We are pretty thick..in this berth. **1836** BROWNING *Paracelsus* v. 369 Lay me..within some narrow grave..But where such graves are thickest. **1849** MACAULAY *Hist. Eng.* v. I. 629 Among the thick graves of unquiet and aspiring statesmen, lie more delicate sufferers. **1893** J. SALISBURY *Gloss. Words S.E. Worcestershire* 42 *Thick on the ground* = crowded. **1919** J. BUCHAN *Mr Standfast* xii. 218, I see you're some kind of general. They're pretty thick on the ground here. **1964** C. WILLOCK *Enormous Zoo* viii. 133 Where animals are thick on the ground as with the herds, often three hundred strong, of topi [etc.]. **1978** 'E. PETERS' *Rainbow's End* i. 24 Willing workers are not so thick on the ground these days.

†**b.** Of actions: Occurring in quick succession; rapid, frequent. Also *transf.* of an agent. *Obs.*

c **1450** *St. Cuthbert* (Surtees) 8319 Þe bischops prayers þik Made him to take þe bischopryk. **1552** HULOET, Thycke speaker, *tolutiloquus*. *Ibid.*, Thycke speakynge, *tolutiloquentia*. **1573–80** BARET *Alv.* T 154 A thicke and feeble beating of the pulse. **1611** SHAKS. *Cymb.* I. vi. 67 He furnaces The thicke sighes from him. *a* **1631** DONNE *Lett.* (1651) 149 If you make not so thick goings as you used. **1665** DRYDEN *Ind. Emperor* I. ii, Thick breath, quick Pulse and heaving of my Heart.

6. a. Having great or considerable density, either from natural consistence or from containing much solid matter; dense, viscid; stiff. (Said of liquids, semi-liquids, and plastic or easily liquefiable solids; formerly sometimes of solids generally.)

c **888** K. ÆLFRED *Boeth.* xxxiii. §5 Sio eorþe þon is hefiȝre & þiccre þon oðra ȝesceafta. *c* **897** —— *Gregory's Past. C.* xliv. 329 Ðonne ðæt mon gadriȝe ðæt ðicce fenn on hiene. *c* **1000** *Sax. Leechd.* II. 74 Wæter..swa þicce swa huniȝes tear. *Ibid.* 314 Hrer on blede oþ þ hit sie þicce swa þynne briw. **1377** LANGL. *P. Pl.* B. xix. 398, I can..drawe..at on hole þikke ale and þinne ale. **1398** TREVISA *Barth. De P.R.* XIX. lxiii. [xlviii.] (Bodl. MS.), Þᵉ more þik melke is þᵉ more chese is þerin. *c* **1440** *Promp. Parv.* 490/2 Thykke, as lycure, *spissus*. **1552** HULOET, Thicke as dregges, *turbidus*. **1605** SHAKS. *Macb.* IV. i. 32 Make the Grewell thicke, and slab. **1674** N. FAIRFAX *Bulk & Selv.* 86 So as the surface might not be some airsom body, but all such thick or fast body. **1875** DARWIN *Insectiv. Pl.* v. 78 A mixture about as thick as cream. **1877** HUXLEY *Physiogr.* x. 161 Not..a clear bright spring, but..a thick stream laden with detritus. **1893** HODGES *Elem. Photogr.* (1907) 106 It should solidify into a thick jelly.

fig. **1596** SHAKS. *Tam. Shr.* v. ii. 143 A woman mou'd, is like a fountaine troubled, Muddie, ill seeming, thicke, bereft of beautie. **1602** —— *Ham.* IV. v. 82 The people muddied, Thicke and vnwholsome in their thoughts.

b. Of air: Foul from admixture of fumes, vapours, etc., stuffy, close; also, dense, not rare or thin. Now *rare* or *Obs.* (Cf. 7.)

1626 BACON *Sylva* §143 When the aire is more Thin,..the Sound pierceth better; But when the Aire is more Thicke, (as in the Night) the Sound spendeth and spreadeth abroad lesse. **1756–7** tr. *Keysler's Trav.* (1760) I. 330 Thick fogs..continually rising from the Po, and other waters, by which the air is rendered thick and moist, and consequently unhealthy. **1819** SHELLEY *Peter Bell the Third* III. xxiii, They breathe an air Thick, infected, joy-dispelling.

7. a. Of mist, fog, smoke, etc.: Having the component particles densely aggregated, so as to intercept or hinder vision. Hence of the weather, etc.: Characterized by mist or haze; foggy, misty. Also *dial.* or *colloq.* in phr. (*to be*) *thick o' fog*.

a **1000** *Boeth. Metr.* v. 6 Se þicca mist þynra weorðe. *Ibid.* xx. 264 Todrif þone þiccan [mist]. *c* **1000** ÆLFRIC *Exod.* xix. 16 Liȝetta & þunor & þicce ȝenip [*nubes densissima*] oferwreh þone munt. *c* **1290** *St. Michael* 621 in *S. Eng. Leg.* 317 Þanne freost þe þicke Myst, and cleouez an heiȝ on þe treo. *c* **1384** CHAUCER *H. Fame* II. 400 Or ellis was the aire so thikke That y ne myght not discerne. *c* **1400** *Song Roland* 848 Thik, and clowdy, and evyll wedur thene. **1594** T. B. *La Primaud. Fr. Acad.* II. 211 Like to a thick smoke ascending out of a great fire which would dim the eies. **1654** WHITELOCKE *Jrnl. Swed. Emb.* (1772) II. 328 The fogge..was so thicke, that we could not see two ships length before us. **1745** P. THOMAS *Voy. S. Seas* 18 The Weather proving thick and hazy. **1836** MARRYAT *Midsh. Easy* xxvi, The horizon was so thick that the vessels ahead were no longer to be seen. **1884** Q. VICTORIA *More Leaves* 128 A very dull, dark thick morning..Still, no rain. **1935** L. LUARD *Conquering Seas* ii. 19 Thick o' fog—can't see whaleback. **1972** E. STAEBLER *Cape Breton Harbour* xvii. 148 We wanted to go back next day but thought we better wait till it was thick-a-fog and nobody'd see us.

b. *transf.*, esp. of darkness: Difficult to penetrate; dense, deep, profound.

a **900** tr. *Bæda's Hist.* v. xiii. [xii.] (1890) 426 Ða þeostro..swa micel & swa ðicco wæron, þæt ic noht ȝeseon meahte. *c* **1000** ÆLFRIC *Hom.* II. 194 Ðicce ðeostru and eȝeslice. *c* **1250** *Gen. & Ex.* 3102 Ðhikke ðherknesse cam on ðat lond. **1340** HAMPOLE *Pr. Consc.* 6566 Swa mykel myrknes, þat it may be graped, swa thik it es. **1605** SHAKS. *Macb.* I. v. 51 Come thick Night, And pall thee in the dunnest smoake of Hell. **1611** BIBLE *Exod.* xx. 21 Moses drew neere vnto the thicke darkenes, where God was. **1781** *Sc. Paraphrases* I. ii, Thick darkness brooded o'er the deep.

III. In transferred senses.

8. Of the voice, etc.: Not clear; hoarse; having a confused or husky sound; indistinct, inarticulate; also, of low pitch; deep; guttural; throaty.

1398 TREVISA *Barth. De P.R.* XIX. cxxxi. (1495) 942 The voyces ben fatte and thycke whanne moche spyryte comyth out as the voys of a man. **1556**, etc. [implied in THICK *adv.* 4]. **1748** J. MASON *Elocut.* 17 To cure a thick confused cluttering Voice. **1844** MRS. CARLYLE *Lett.* (1883) I. 283 His speech is..so thick that I have great difficulty in catching what he says. **1881** ROSSETTI *Ballads & Sonn.* (1882) 325 The young rooks cheep 'mid the thick caw o' the old. **1887** HALL CAINE *Deemster* xxxiii, The thick boom of the sea that came up from the rocks. **1889** MORFILL *Gram. Russian Lang.* 4 The sound of the vowel ы is a thick guttural *e*.

9. a. Of or in reference to hearing: Dull of perception; not quick or acute. Also of sight. (See also *thick-eyed* in 12 b, THICK-SIGHTED.) Now *dial.*

1526 TINDALE *Acts* xxviii. 27 The hert off this people is wexed grosse and their eares wexe thycke of hearinge. **1594** T. B. *La Primaud. Fr. Acad.* II. 81 Many become deafe by hearing ouergreat soundes, whereof wee haue experience in Smithes, amongest whome many are thicke of hearing. **1597** SHAKS. *2 Hen. IV*, III. ii. 336 His Dimensions (to any thicke sight) were inuincible. **1601** —— *Jul. C.* v. iii. 21 My sight was euer thicke. **1720** *Col. Rec. Pennsylv.* III. 97 But we find their Ears are thick. **1888** ELWORTHY *W. Somerset Gloss.* s.v., 'Thick o' yearin'' (hearing).

b. Of mental faculties or actions, or of persons: Slow (or characterized by slowness) of apprehension; dense, crass, thick-headed; stupid, obtuse. Now chiefly *colloq.* of persons. Also emphatically, *as thick as two planks*, etc. Cf. THICK-HEADED *a.* b.

(In quot. 1597 with play on sense 6.)

1597 SHAKS. *2 Hen. IV*, II. iv. 262 Hang him Baboone, his Wit is as thicke as Tewksburie Mustard. **1603** HAYWARD *Answ. to Doleman* iv. Mj, I omit your thicke error in putting no difference betweene a magistrate and a king. **1670** PENN *Liberty of Consc.* v. 32 What if you think our Reasons thick, and our ground of Separation mistaken? *a* **1800** PEGGE *Suppl. Grose, Thick*... Also stupid. North. **1824** BYRON *Juan* XVI. lxxxiii, To hammer a horse laugh from the thick throng. **1865** *Harper's Mag.* Dec. 133/2 [He] is nevertheless slow to see the point—in fact, 'thick' otherwise than crosswise. **1961** S. CHAPLIN *Day of Sardine* ii. 53 Free rides on trains and trolleys were routine stuff; and the thickest character in the school could find a buckshee road into a cinema. **1974** G. HONEYCOMBE *Adam's Tale* I. ii. 27 'He must be as thick as two planks,' said Nick. **1976** J. I. M. STEWART *Memorial Service* iii. 40 You might expect to become P.M. if you hadn't been so thick as to accept your idiotic life peerage. **1980** 'J. GASH' *Spend Game* xiii. 130 Rough-mannered and a bit greedy... Corporal's thick as a plank.

IV. 10. (*fig.* from 5.) Close in confidence and association; intimate, familiar; often in similes (with allusion to other senses), e.g. *as thick as glue, as inkle-weavers, as peas in a shell, as* (*two*) *thieves, as three in a bed*, etc. *colloq.*

c **1756** BP. LAW in J. Nichols *Lit. Anecd. 18th C.* (1812) II. 70 'Yes', said he, 'we begin now, though contrary to my expectation, and without my seeking, to be pretty thick; and I thank God who reconciles me to my adversaries'. **1781** TWINING in *Select. Papers T. Family* (1887) 100 He and I were quite 'thick'. We rode together frequently. **1803** LAMB *Let. to Manning* Feb., Are you and the first consul thick? **1820** SCOTT *Monast.* Introd Ep., That's right, Captain,..you twa will be as thick as three in a bed an ance ye forgather. **1833** T. HOOK *Parson's Dau.* II. ii, She and my wife are as thick as thieves, as the proverb goes. **1836** LADY GRANVILLE *Lett.* (1894) II. 199 He is thick with all the new Ministers. **1869** *Routledge's Ev. Boy's Ann.* 593 We soon grew as thick as inkle-weavers.

V. 11. Phrases. *thick and threefold*: see THICK *adv.* 6; THICK AND THIN, q.v.

12. a. Combinations. Chiefly parasynthetic adjectives; these can be formed at pleasure; the following are specimens: *thick-ankled* (having thick ankles), *-barred* (having thick bars), *-billed, -blooded, -bodied, -bottomed, -brained* (in sense 9 b), *-coated, -fingered, -fleeced, -foliaged, -haired, -hided* (hence *-hidedness*), *-knobbed, -legged, -lensed, -lugged, -necked, -piled, -ribbed, -rimmed, -rinded, -shelled, -shouldered, -soled, -stemmed, -topped, -voiced, -walled, -wooled.* Also *thick-looking* (looking or seeming thick). See also THICK-HEADED, -SKINNED, -SKULLED, etc.

1853 TENNYSON in Ld. Tennyson *Mem.* (1897) II. 505 [In these, he would say] 'Wordsworth seemed to him *thick-ankled'. **1753** YOUNG *Brothers* v. i, Ye *thick-barr'd sunless passages for air. **1855** J. R. LEIFCHILD *Cornwall Mines* 96 Slate abounding in tin is uniformly of a *thick-bedded, deep-blue colour. **1770** G. WHITE *Let.* 21 May in *Nat. Hist. Selborne* (1789) II. vi. 131 The bird you kept..abides all the year, and is a *thick-billed bird. **1783** LATHAM *Gen. Syn.* III. 148 Thick-billed Gr[osbeak]. Size of a Bulfinch: length five inches three quarters. **1897** W. R. OGILVIE-GRANT *Game-Birds* II. 151 The Thick-billed Partridges. Genus Odontophorus. **1939** F. C. LINCOLN *Migration Amer. Birds* 103 As an exemplar of vagrant migration from south to north, the Thick-billed Parrot may be cited. **1980** CYRUS & ROBSON *Bird Atlas of Natal* 274 Thick-billed Weaver..inhabits coastal bush. **1888** DOUGHTY *Arabia Deserta* I. 471 A little of that *thick-blooded unforbearing, which was in her family, with her own elder son. **1752** J. HILL *Hist. Anim.* 110 The long-legged and *thick-bodied, small, green Lacerta. **1868** *Rep. U.S. Commission. Agric.* (1869) 314 Small, thick-bodied butterflies. **1844** MRS. BROWNING *Duchess May* Concl. v, Though in passion ye would dash..Up against the *thick-bossed shield of God's judgment in the field. **1619** DRAYTON *Sacr. Apollo* vii, The *thick-brained audience lively to awake. **1620** VENNER *Via Recta* vi. 106 It..is for them that be short and *thicke breathed, the..greatest remedy. **1626** BACON *Sylva* §318 A Pomegranate or some such *thick-coated fruit. **1874** 'MARK TWAIN' *Let.* 9 Dec. (1917) I. xiv. 238, I am so *thick-fingered that I miss the keys. **1864** G. M. HOPKINS *Poems* (1967) 136 *Thick-fleeced bushes like a heifer's ear. **1924** E. SITWELL *Sleeping Beauty* xxvi. 95 As lovely as the thick-fleeced waters. **1828** P. CUNNINGHAM *N.S. Wales* (ed. 3) II. 170 Clumps of *thick-foliaged trees. *c* **1386** CHAUCER *Knt.'s T.* 1660 Somme helden with hym with the blake berd, Somme with the balled, somme with the *thikke herd. *c* **1611** CHAPMAN *Iliad* II. 40 The thick-hair'd Greeks. **1861** KINGSLEY in *Lett.*, etc. (1877) II. 132 But the mass will not have ——'s courage or *thick-hidedness. **1689** *Lond. Gaz.* No. 2415/4 A Young Slender Horse 5 years old,..*thick Jawed. **1861** DICKENS *Gt. Expect.* xxviii, Their keeper..carried a *thick-knobbed bludgeon. **1873** J. BROWN *Let.* 23 June (1912) 280 Uig is a pretty snug little bay, with its tidy Inn and its *thick-legged, humorous landlord, John Urquhart. **1946** E. O'NEILL *Iceman Cometh* I. 4 He has black eyes which peer near-sightedly from behind *thick-lensed spectacles. **1973** J. GOODFIELD *Courier to Peking* ii. 23 A short, squat person with thick-lensed glasses. **1849** *Sk. Nat. Hist., Mammalia* III. 197 Forster's Sea-Lion..everywhere equally *thick-looking, as Buffon describes it, like a great cylinder. **1922** JOYCE *Ulysses* 319 The curse of a goodfornothing God light sideways on the bloody *thicklugged sons of whores' gets! **1591** PERCIVAL *Sp. Dict.*, *Cervigudo*, *thicke necked. **1840** CARLYLE *Heroes* v. (1872) 176 There is the same burly thick-necked strength of body as of soul. **1853** M. ARNOLD *Sohrab & Rustum* in *Poems* 6 Upon the *thick-pil'd carpets in the tent. **1976** *Sounds* 11 Dec., His hair, short at the sides and thickpiled high on top, makes him look faintly ridiculous. **1603** SHAKS. *Meas. for M.* III. i. 123 To recide In thrilling Region of *thicke-ribbed Ice. **1976** 'R. GORDON' *Doctor on Job* iii. 18 A small, round, well-scrubbed looking man in a grey business suit and *thick-rimmed glasses. **1590** GREENE *Orl. Fur.* Wks. (Rtldg.) 95/2 And thick-shadow'd groves. **1649** G. DANIEL *Trinarch.* The Author 8 To stoope at the *thick-Shell'd Dorrs of Obiection. **1804** BEWICK *Brit. Birds* (1847) II. 272 The female..lays..six or seven thick-shelled white eggs. **1965** J. A. MICHENER *Source* (1966) 564 And he knelt in the boat, a *thick-shouldered, heavy-necked, sandy-haired German seeking God. **1815** SCOTT *Guy M.* l, His rough coat and *thick-soled boots. **1840** EMERSON *Woodnotes* in *Dial* (Boston) Oct. 244 You ask..what guide Me through trackless thickets led, Through *thick-stemmed woodlands. **1851** MANTELL *Petrif.* i. §3. 70 *Thick-toed tridactylous birds. **1552** HULOET, *Thycke tothed, or stronge tothed, *dentatus*. **1859** CORNWALLIS *New World* I. 63 A very stout, thick-set, *thick-voiced Yorkshireman. **1820** M. EDGEWORTH *Let.* 26 Dec. (1971) 231 Old *thick-walled mansions. **1875** BENNETT & DYER *Sachs Bot.* 484 The very thick-walled mother-cells do not become isolated. **1913** W. DE LA MARE *Peacock Pie* 85 Roasting a *thick-wooled mountain sheep Upon an iron spit.

b. Special combinations and collocations: **thick-back**, in full *thickback sole*, a flat-fish, *Microchirus variegatus*, found in the

Mediterranean and off western European coasts; **thick-bill**, a local name of the bullfinch; **thick coal**: see quot.; hence *thick-coalman*; **thick ear**, an ear swollen or numbed by a sharp blow; usu. in phrases, as *to give* (someone) *a thick ear*; also *spec.* used *attrib.* to designate literature, etc., marked by rough violence and horseplay, or the writers of such material; **thick end**, the greater part *of* anything (*colloq.* and *dial.*); **thick-eyed** *a.*, having obscure vision, dim-sighted; **thick intestine**, *Entom.*, in some insects, a dilatation of the posterior end of the ileum, forming a large blind sac turned back towards the ventricules; **thick-knit** *a.*, designating a garment knitted from wool of greater thickness than double knitting; also *absol.* as *sb.*, a thick-knit sweater; **thick-leaf**, a name of plants of the genus *Crassula*; †**thick letter** *Typogr.*, type cast too thick: see quot.; †**thick listed** *a.* [LIST *sb.*[1]], hard of hearing; **thick register**, the lowest register of the voice; **thick sandwich (course)**, a sandwich course (see SANDWICH *sb.*[2] 1 b) with an extended theoretical component between two periods of practical instruction (see quot. 1978); **thick seam**, a seam of 'thick coal'; also *attrib.*; **thick space** *Typog.*, a third of an em space used in separating words; cf. *thin space* s.v. THIN *a.* D b; hence **thick-spaced** *a.*; **thick-stamen** (see quot.), a small genus of prostrate euphorbiaceous plants, the Alleghany Mountain Spurge; **thick-stuff**: see quot. *c* 1850; **thick tea**, high tea (*local*); **thick-tongued** *a.*, speaking thickly; **thick wind**, in *Farriery*, laborious breathing, usually due to previous inflammation; hence *thick-winded* adj; **thick woods** *Canad.* = *strong wood(s* s.v. STRONG *a.* 12 b. Also THICK-HEAD, THICK-KNEE, etc.

1864 J. COUCH *Hist. Fishes Brit. Isles* III. 203 The *Thickback seldom exceeds the length of eight or nine inches. **1896** J. T. CUNNINGHAM *Nat. Hist. Marketable Marine Fishes Brit. Isles* 259 The Thickback... Pectoral fins very small. **1925** J. T. JENKINS *Fishes Brit. Isles* 198 The Thickback Sole..is brownish-red, with six or seven dark bands running across the body. **1969** A. WHEELER *Fishes Brit. Isles & N.-W. Europe* 557/1 The thickback sole is found rather more offshore. *Ibid.* 557/2 The thickback makes a very minor contribution to fishery landings of 'soles', but its flesh is of high quality. **1847–78** HALLIWELL, **Thick-bill*, the bullfinch. *Lanc.* **1883** GRESLEY *Coal Mining Gloss.*, **Thick Coals* or *Thick Seams*, coal seams of greater thickness than (say) 8 or 10 feet... The *Thick coal* of South Staffordshire is about 28 or 30 feet thick. **1894** *Daily News* 7 May 8/4 The new scale will give 1d per ton rise in *thick-coalmen's wages for every 1½d advance in the price of thick coal. **1909** J. R. WARE *Passing Eng.* 243/2 *Thick ear. **1916** 'TAFFRAIL' *Pincher Martin* ii. 28, I sed I'd give yer a thick ear if yer went on worryin' me. **1922** A. HADDON *Green Room Gossip* ix. 248 'A thick-ear play' was Sir Gerald du Maurier's description of 'Bull-dog Drummond'. **1943** *Gen* 2 Jan. 28/1 A member of the thick-ear fraternity. **1978** *Lancashire Life* Oct. 83/2 Ah geet a reyt thick ear yon time Ah tarned sheets in a tangle! **1981** N. TUCKER *Child & Book* v. 133 One particular favourite type of comic—referred to in the trade as the 'thick-ear market'—is chiefly concerned with crude, knockabout humour. **1847–78** HALLIWELL s.v., 'The *thick-end of a mile'. *Linc.* **1865** W. WHITE *E. Eng.* II. 66 When he spoke of the *thick end of a mile*, it reminded me of the 'thick league' of a certain rustic whom I once accosted on the sandy wastes of Friesland. **1877** *N.W. Lincs. Gloss.* s.v., I've gotten th' thick end o' th' job finished wi'. **1938** 'N. SHUTE' *Ruined City* x. 195 It would be the thick end of that sum before we're cracking as a proper yard again. **1965** P. O'DONNELL *Modesty Blaise* xviii. 196 Willie..tested the weight. 'It's the thick end of a hundredweight..But I could manage one on me own all right.' **1971** D. LEES *Rainbow Conspiracy* i. 13 It will take them the thick end of half an hour to get to the Travellers from here. **1596** SHAKS. *1 Hen. IV*, II. iii. 49 *Thicke-ey'd musing, and curst melancholly. **1684** *Lond. Gaz.* No. 1976/4 A gray Horse, Milk white about the Mouth and Tail,..all his Paces, thickeyed. **1961** *Thickknit [see COVER-UP]. **1976** J. FLEMING *To make Underworld* xii. 138 The three Irishmen, ill-disguised as sailors or fishermen in their thick-knits. **1884** MILLER *Plant-n.*, **Thick-leaf*, the genus *Crassula*. **1683** MOXON *Mech. Exerc.*, *Printing* 392 A Fount of Letter that Rubs not high enough into the Neck is called **Thick Letter*; and consequently will Drive out Matter. [*c* **1200** *Trin. Coll. Hom.* 129 Deue we ben, oðer *þicke liste, þanne we heren speke godes word and nimeð þer to litel geme.] **1579** TWYNE *Phisicke agst. Fort.* II. xcvii. 289 They that are thicke listed, seeme in a maner to be out of their wittes. **1905** J. HEYWOOD *Music in Churches* 17 Average choir boys cannot recite on a low note without being liable to use the *thick register or chest voice instead of the medium register, and the use of their lower mechanism is usually accompanied with.. coarseness of tone. **1962** *Engineering* 13 July 57/2 The 1-3-1 type of '*thick sandwich' course (one year in industry, three years at university, and one year in industry again). *Ibid.* 26 Oct. 555 A pre-university year in industry (as in 1:3:1 thick sandwiches). **1978** *Jrnl. R. Soc. Arts* CXXVI. 549/1 A sandwich course such as the 'thick' sandwich, where you do one year in industry, three years at university and then one year back in industry. **1883** *Thick seam [see *thick coal*]. **1892** *Daily News* 25 Jan. 2/6 The leading thick-seam pits are sending a large tonnage to Hull and Grimsby. **1683** MOXON *Mech. Exerc.* II. 99 Some [letters] are Space thick; that is, one quarter so thick as the Body is high; though Spaces are seldom Cast so,..and therefore..we shall call these Spaces, *Thick Spaces. **1808** C. STOWER *Printer's Gram.* iii. 90 Of Spaces... They are cast to various thicknesses... Three to an m—or three thick spaces. **1967** E. CHAMBERS *Photolitho-Offset* ii. 12 The *thick space* and *middle space* are a third and a quarter respectively of the width of the *em quad*. **1824** J. JOHNSON *Typographia* II. 132 A *d* and an *h*..will admit an addition, but not more than a middle and thin space to a *thick spaced line. **1893** HART *Rules for Compositors* 22 When the last line but one of a paragraph is widely spaced and the first line of the following paragraph is also more than thick-spaced. **1878** T. MEEHAN *Native Fl. & Ferns U.S.* I. 30 The stamens have remarkably thick filaments, and this suggested its botanical name Pachysandra, which is the Greek for '*thick-stamen'. **1884** MILLER *Plant-n.*, American Thick-stamen, *Pachysandra procumbens*. **1769** FALCONER *Dict. Marine* (1789) H iij, The **thick stuff*, or strong planks of the bottom withinboard. *c* **1850** *Rudim. Navig.* (Weale) 155 *Thickstuff*, a name for sided timber exceeding 4 inches, but not being more than 12 inches, in thickness. **1886** S. COOLIDGE *What Katy did Next* xi. 305 The month's housekeeping wound up that night with a '*thick tea'. **1893** *Daily News* 1 June 5/2 Perhaps something might have been said for the compromise of a thick tea. **1896** *Ibid.* 18 Dec. 3/6 The 'thick teas' of Lancashire have long been celebrated for their eccentricity. **1887** *Poor Nellie* (1888) 370 Though *thick-tongued still, she spoke more clearly. **1831** [YOUATT] *Horse* x. 193 *Thick-wind consists in short, frequent, and laborious breathing, especially when the animal is in exercise. *a* **1694** *Life M. Robinson* (1856) 35 He was *thickwinded and ungovernable. **1704** *Lond. Gaz.* No. 3981/4 A..Mare,..thick Winded. **1831** [YOUATT] *Horse* x. 193 Heavy draught-horses are..thick-winded. **1754** A. HENDRY *Jrnl.* 2 Dec. in *Trans. R. Soc. Canada* (1907) I. II. 343 Strong gale with Snow & Sleet. Obliged to remove into *thick woods. **1865** MILTON & CHEADLE *N.W. Passage by Land* xii. 223 We had thirteen horses to pack and drive through the thick woods. **1957** C. HARRIS *Cariboo Trail* 137 The gold-seekers had arrived at the fort after making their way through the thickwoods.

B. *absolute* use of *adj.*, passing into *sb.*: That which (rarely, one who) is thick, in any sense.

I. Only in *sing.* **1. a.** The most densely occupied or crowded part (*of* a wood, an assemblage, etc.).

a **1250** *Owl & Night.* 1626 Me may vppe smale sticke Me sette a wude ine þe þikke. *c* **1400** MAUNDEV. (1839) xxi. 226 Ʒif ony of hem had ben hid in the thikke of the wodes. *a* **1548** HALL *Chron.*, *Edw. IV* 221 Some fledde for succor in the thyck of the parke. *a* **1610** KNOLLES (J.), In the thick of the dust and smoke presently entered his men. **1637** RUTHERFORD *Lett.* (1671) 28 If I could yoke in amongst the thick of Angels, and Seraphims. **1714** *Spect.* No. 625 ¶22 In the Anti-chamber, where I thrust my Head into the thick of the Press. **1857** LADY CANNING in Hare *Two Noble Lives* (1893) II. 328 The Residency buildings and its gardens are in the thick of the town. **1890** C. MARTYN *W. Phillips* 192 Mr. Phillips was constantly out in the thick and throng of the world.

b. *fig.* The position, time, stage, or state in which activity is most intense; the midst, the height (of an action). Always *in the thick of*.

1681 FLAVEL *Meth. Grace* x. 214 Something they enjoy.. in the very thick of troubles. **1821** BYRON *Sardan.* III. i. 111 Where a soldier should be. In the thick of the fight. **1849** C. BRONTË *Shirley* i, They are in the thick of a revival. **1870** BURTON *Hist. Scot.* (1873) V. lv. 105 The bishop was in the thick of these splendid projects. **1885** DUNCKLEY in *Manch. Exam.* 15 June 6/2 We are now in the thick of a Cabinet crisis.

2. a. The more turbid or viscid part of a liquid, which usually subsides to the bottom. *rare.*

? *c* **1400** LYDG. *Æsop's Fab.* ii. 39 He was wont my water here to trouble, To meue þe thyk þat lay low doune. **1707** MORTIMER *Husb.* (1721) I. 78 This he dissolved in Water, and poured off the thick into another Bason, till all was gone but the Sand.

b. A beverage of thick or heavy consistency, as cocoa, porter, etc. *slang.*

1887 J. W. HORSLEY *Jottings from Jail* i. 26 A somewhat.. despairing view of prison life is indicated by 'Lads, your only friend here is your brown lofe [*sic*] and pint of thick'. **1903** FARMER & HENLEY *Slang* VII. 99/1 *Thick*, (common). —porter: ironically said to be 'a decoction of brewers' aprons'. **1923** J. MANCHON *Le Slang* 309 *Thick*, le café, le *jus*. **1947** W. DE LA MARE *Coll. Stories for Children* 222 The mugs of thick proved to be cocoa.

3. The thick part of a limb or of the body.

c **1400** *Destr. Troy* 9021 He..braid out a big sword,..& derit hym full euyll Throgh the thicke of the thegh. **1470–85** MALORY *Arthur* VII. xxii. 248 He smote hym with a foyne thorou the thycke of the thyȝ. **1880** TENNYSON *Northern Cobbler* xv, An' blacksmith 'e strips me the thick ov 'is airm, an 'e shaws it to me.

4. So '**thickest** (the superl. adj. used *absol.* as *sb.*): the thickest part (in any of prec. senses).

c **1470** HENRY *Wallace* II. 56 Throuch oute the thikest of the pres he ȝeid. **1548** UDALL *Erasm. Par. Luke* iii. 37 Puttyng himself in coumpaignie emong the thickest of the people. **1617** MORYSON *Itin.* II. 24 Valiantly fighting among the thickest of the Rebels. **1868** FREEMAN *Norm. Conq.* II. viii. 259 Henry was..soon again in the thickest of the fight.

II. *sb.* with *pl.* **5.** (from 1) = THICKET. *Now rare.*

c **825** *Vesp. Psalter* xxviii [xxix]. 9 Stefn dryhtnes ȝearwienden heoretas & biwrah ða ðiccan [*Vulg.* revelavit condensa]. *c* **1430** *Pilgr. Lyf Manhode* II. cxxxii. (1869) 126 He may not sette the wacches in the thikke ther thei ben. *a* **1547** SURREY *Æneid* IV. 708 Among the bushy thickes of bryar. **1612** DRAYTON *Poly-olb.* iii. 118 Where mists and rotten fogs Hang in the gloomie thicks, and make vnstedfast bogs. **1812** *Sporting Mag.* XXXIX. 200 A fox..made good his retreat to Sir Thos. Beauchamp's thicks. **1836** L. HUNT in *New Monthly Mag.* XLVII. 20 The lusty bee..dances in the bloomy thicks with darksome antheming.

6. *colloq.* and *slang* (orig. *Schoolboys'*). A thick-headed or stupid person.

1857 HUGHES *Tom Brown* I. vii, What a thick I was to come! *Ibid.* II. viii, I'm such a thick, I never should have had time for both. **1891** WRENCH *Winchester Word-bk.* s.v., He is not a thick, but he won't mug. **1925** S. O'CASEY *Juno & Paycock* III, in *Two Plays* 97 The thick made out the Will wrong. **1960** B. MOORE *Luck of Ginger Coffey* vii. 123 Ha, Ha! cried all the countrified young thicks he had gone to school with. **1970** G. LORD *Marshmallow Pie* iii. 28 Some of those thicks in Earls Court would do it just for the kicks.

7. A thick fog. Cf. sense 7 a of the adj. *slang.*

1936 J. BUCHAN *Island of Sheep* ii. 35 Out of the marshes a fog crept which the gunners call a 'thick'. **1961** PARTRIDGE *Slang* Suppl. 1463/1 *Thick, in the*, in, esp. caught in, a thick fog: R.A.F. (operational 'types'): since ca. 1930.

thick (θɪk), *adv.* Forms: see the adj. [OE. *þicce* = OS. *thikko*, OHG. *diccho*: see THICK *a.*] In a thick manner, thickly. (After many verbs as *come*, *fall*, *lie*, *stand*, *sow*, etc., when *thick* expresses the accompanying or resulting condition, it is often rather an adj. than an adv.; cf. L. *pinus prona cadit*; *supinus cadere*.)

1. a. So as to be thick; to a great depth.

c **1000** ÆLFRIC *Voc.* in Wr.-Wülcker 151/22 *Pauidensis*, ðicce ȝewefen hræȝel. *a* **1300** *Cursor M.* 3377 (Cott.) Suilk er in þis liue ful thike, Forgetes þe deid for þe quick. **1670** H. STUBBE *Plus Ultra* 136 We found the passage crusted very thick. **1713** ADDISON *Cato* I. iii, Cato has piercing eyes, and will discern Our frauds, unless they're cover'd thick with art. **1860** TYNDALL *Glac.* I. x. 67 The snow..lay thick upon the glacier.

†**b.** *fig.* Deeply, severely. *Obs. rare.*

13.. *E.E. Allit. P.* C. 6 Quo for þro may noȝt þole, þe þikker he suffers.

c. *to lay it on thick*, (*fig.*) to do something with vehemence or excess. Cf. LAY *v.*[1] 55 f. Also, *to put* (*spread*, etc.) *it on thick*.

1740 *Champion* 29 Jan. (1741) I. 225 You may lay on Honour and Beauty, and all Manner of Virtues as thick as you please. **1806–7** J. BERESFORD *Miseries Hum. Life* (1826) I. Introd., Lay it on thick, I beg, while your hand is in. **1818** SCOTT *Br. Lamm.* xi, Lay it on thick, and never mind expenses. **1865** 'MARK TWAIN' in *Californian* 6 May 9/3 Don't you think he is spreading it on rather thick? **1888** MRS. H. WARD *R. Elsmere* xviii, Henslowe lays it on thick —paints with a will. **1929** A. CHRISTIE *Seven Dials Mystery* xviii. 148, I thought Bundle was laying it on a bit thick myself... But Codders is such an ass he'd swallow anything. **1955** W. C. GAULT *Ring around Rosa* xiv. 165 Now she was putting it on as thick as a starlet at a producer's party. **1976** *Times* 24 Mar. 3/2 (Advt.), If we are laying it on a bit thick it's only because we want you to volunteer out of a mature realisation of what the Army can be like.

†**d.** After a sum of money: To the extent of (so much), 'deep'. *Obs.*

1570 FOXE *A. & M.* (ed. 2) 2142/2 Which then cost the Vniuersitie an hundreth pound thicke. **1592** GREENE *Blacke Bks. Messenger* Wks. (Grosart) XI. 31 My couetous maister is cheated fortie or fiftie pound thick at one clap. **1592** —— *Repentance* ibid. XII. 177.

2. In a thick, dense, or crowded state; closely, densely, compactly; in crowds or throngs; numerously, abundantly. (See also *thick and threefold* in 6.)

971 *Blickl. Hom.* 203 Ða fluȝon þa leȝetu swylce fyrene strælas..toðæm þicce þæt [etc.]. *c* **1000** *Sax. Leechd.* III. 234 Eall swa þicce is þeo heofon mid steorrum afylled on dæȝ swa on niht. *a* **1175** *Cott. Hom.* 237 Of þe folce we siggeð þat hit..elce deȝie þicce þringeð. *c* **1290** *S. Eng. Leg.* I. 26/72 Þut folk a-boute heom cam ase þicke ase huy miȝten go. *c* **1305** *St. Lucy* 12 in *E.E.P.* (1862) 101 Þat folc wende þider þicke. *c* **1400** *Brut* lxxviii. 79 Þai deide wonder þik wiþin the citee for hunger. *c* **1500** *Melusine* 289 Quarelles & arowes, that flewh so thyk. **1523** FITZHERBERT *Husb.* §12 The beste propertie..is, to sowe all maner of corne thycke ynough. *a* **1687** PETTY *Pol. Arith.* (1690) 73 When England shall be thicker peopled. **1772–84** *Cook's Voy.* (1790) V. 1683 The woods in many places..so thick intersected with boughs and matted with leaves. **1855** MACAULAY *Hist. Eng.* xiv. III. 454 Doubts came thick upon him.

3. In close or rapid succession; frequently; quickly; fast. Often *thick and fast*. (See also *thick and threefold* in 6.)

a **1000** *Cædmon's Gen.* 684 (Gr.) Hio spræc him þicce to. *c* **1385** CHAUCER *L.G.W.* 655 (*Cleopatras*) Ffor strokys whiche that wente as thikke as hayl. *c* **1450** in Aungier *Syon* (1840) 255 She schal nothing say butte '*Mea culpa*, I wylle amende', whiche sche schal reherse thykke and many tymes. **1540** *Act 32 Hen. VIII*, c. 43 The sayd apparaunce & attendaunce commeth so often and thicke together. **1573** TUSSER *Husb.* (1878) 165 Cock croweth at midnight, times few aboue six,..At three a clock thicker. **1642** FULLER *Holy & Prof. St.* III. xxi. 210 Great talkers discharge too thick to take alwayes true aim. **1706** E. WARD *Wooden World Diss.* (1708) 98 He and his Brother-Jacks..toss Jests and Oaths about as thick and fast as Boys do Squibs. **1729** LAW *Serious C.* xx. (1732) 378 It will perhaps be thought..that these hours of prayer come too thick. **1869** FREEMAN *Norm. Conq.* III. xi. 66 Thick and fast indeed came the events.

4. With confused and indistinct articulation; also, with a husky or hoarse voice.

1556 W. TOWSON in Hakluyt *Voy.* (1589) 102 These wordes they speake very thicke. **1597** SHAKS. *2 Hen. IV*, II. iii. 24 Speaking thicke (which Nature made his blemish) Became the Accents of the Valiant. **1686** *Lond. Gaz.* No. 2143/4 He speaks so thick that he is scarce to be understood. *a* **1791** *Tom Line* xiii. in Child *Ballads* (1884) II. 343/2 Out then spak her father dear, He spak baith thick and milde.

5. With density or thick consistence; densely.

a **1711**, **1746** [implied in *thick-clouded*, *-streaming* in 7]. *Mod. colloq.* The syrup runs thick. The porridge stirs thick.

6. Phrases. *to lay it on thick*: see 1 c. *thick and fast*: see 3. **thick and threefold**, *advb.* (*sb.*, *adj.*) *phr.* **a.** In large numbers; in quick succession; with rapid iteration. *arch.* and *dial.*

a **1548** HALL *Chron.*, *Hen. VIII* 186 When mo newe Testamentes were Imprinted thei came thicke and threfold into Englande. **1560** DAUS tr. *Sleidane's Comm.* 134 There dwell deuylles thycke and threfolde. *a* **1592** GREENE

Alphonsus I. Wks. (Rtldg.) 225/2 How that such clients cluster'd to thy court, By thick and threefold. **1613** DAY *Dyall* ix. (1614) 218 Our Antipodes of Rome that so much boast of the Fathers, and how they are theirs, thicke and threefold. **1710** tr. *Werenfels's Disc. Logom.* 3 Scoffs and Reproaches come thick and threefold. **1872** DE MORGAN *Budget of Paradoxes* 163 A.. writer.. who threw aspersions on his opponents thick and threefold.

†**b.** With vehemence; fervently, ardently, impetuously. *Obs. rare*[−1].

1627 W. SCLATER *Exp. 2 Thess.* (1629) 295 So thicke and threefold he falls vpon his deuotion.

†**c.** as *adj.* Abundant and frequent. *Obs.*

1614 DAY *Festivals* xi. (1615) 302 The Commendations given Anna here are thicke and threefold. **1809** MALKIN *Gil Blas* v. i. ¶4 This thick and threefold companionship with [the] birch was not the only rub.

7. In combination with participles (with hyphen, or as single words); forming adjs., usually of obvious meaning, unlimited in number; as **a.** in sense 1, as *thick-blown, -mined, -plied, -spread, -tangled, -woven, -wrought*; **b.** in senses 2 and 3, as *thick-beating, -coming, -drawn, -flaming, -growing, -jewelled, -laid, -packed, -rustling, -spreading, -starred*, etc.; **c.** in sense 4, as *thick-speaking*; **d.** in sense 5, as *thick-clouded, -plotting, -scarred, -streaming*.

1690 DRYDEN *Don Sebast.* IV. i, The trampling of *thick-beating feet. **1725** RAMSAY *Gentle Sheph.* I. ii, The *thick-blawn wreaths of snaw. *a* **1711** KEN *Edmund* Poet. Wks. 1721 II. 355 Your now *thick-clouded Mind. **1605** SHAKS. *Macb.* V. iii. 38 Troubled with *thicke-comming Fancies. **1715–20** POPE *Iliad* III. 6 With piercing frosts, or *thick-descending rain. **1777** J. MOUNTAIN *Poet. Reveries* (ed. 2) 6 His children watch his *thick-drawn breath. **1757** DYER *Fleece* IV. Poems (1761) 184 While flames, *thick-flashing in the gloom. **1865** TROLLOPE *Belton Est.* xxxi, Wide fields and *thick-growing woods. **1593** SHAKS. *3 Hen. VI*, III. i. 1 Vnder this *thicke growne brake. **1833** TENNYSON *Lady of Shalott* III. iii, All in the blue unclouded weather *Thick-jewell'd shone the saddle-leather. **1698** NORRIS *Pract. Disc.* (1707) IV. 191 So *thick-laid are the Temptations of the World. **1957** C. DAY LEWIS *Pegasus* 35 The rescuer plunging through some *thick-mined region Who cannot rescue and is not to die. **1599** SHAKS. *Much Ado* I. ii. 10 Walking in a *thick pleached alley. **1840** CARLYLE *Heroes* vi. (1872) 204 The *thick-plied perversions which distort our image of Cromwell. **1922** JOYCE *Ulysses* 35 They swarmed loud.. their heads *thickplotting under maladroit silk hats. **1969** G. MACBETH *War Quartet* 59 Its enormous back, *thick-scarred From under-water struggles. **1861** W. F. COLLIER *Hist. Eng. Lit.* 114 The *thick-speaking, shambling,.. pedant. **1740** SOMERVILLE *Hobbinol.* I. 9 On the large Bough Of a *thick-spreading Elm. **1676** DRYDEN *Aurengzebe* I. i, Of *thick-sprung Lances in a waving Field. *c* **1391** CHAUCER *Astrol.* II. §23 In some wynters nyht, whan the firmament is clere & *thikke-sterred. **1860** EMERSON *Cond. Life, Worship* Wks. (Bohn) II. 408 Thick-starred Orion was my only companion. **1746** FRANCIS tr. *Hor., Sat.* I. viii. 47 They.. fill'd a magic Trench profound With a black Lamb's *thick-streaming Gore. **1738** WESLEY *Psalms* CXVIII. iv, Hosts of Enemies Vexatious as *thick-swarming Bees. **1956** D. GASCOYNE *Night Thoughts* 15 The shadows drift in tattered velvet bunches, *Thick-tangled rags of shadow are set swaying. **1595** *Locrine* II. v. 39 Amongst the dangers of the *thick throngd pikes. *c* **1410** *Master of Game* (MS. Digby 182) ii, Whan þe heed is of gret beemes and is wele afeeted and *thike tynded. **1671** MILTON *P.R.* IV. 246 Where the Attic Bird Trills her *thick-warbl'd notes. **1865** *Q. Rev.* Apr. 329 The *thick-wove paper, and the brilliant type. **1667** MILTON *P.L.* IX. 437 Now hid, now seen Among *thick-wov'n Arborets and Flours. **1743** FRANCIS tr. *Hor., Odes* I. vii. 28 Whether.. Tibur holds thee in its *thick-wrought Shade.

thick (θɪk), *v.* Now *rare* or *Obs.* (In the current senses THICKEN is the usual verb.) [OE. *þiccian*, f. *þicce*, THICK *a.* (cf. OHG. *dicchên*, MHG. *dicken*).]

1. *trans.* To make dense in consistence. *arch.*

c **1000** ÆLFRIC *Gram.* xxxvii. (Z.) 220 *Denso*.. and *denseo*.., ic ðiccige. **1398** TREVISA *Barth. De P.R.* IV. ii. (Tollem. MS.), It [melancholy] þikkeþ þe blood, þat it fleteþ nouȝt from digestion by clernesse and þinnesse. *c* **1440** *Anc. Cookery* in *Househ. Ord.* (1790) 430 Let hit boyle and thyck hit with floure of ryse. **1526** *Grete Herball* cxliv. (1529) I ij b, A moysture that by the heet of the sonne is thycked,.. and torned to a gommy substaunce. **1611** SHAKS. *Wint. T.* I. ii. 171 Thoughts, that would thick my blood. **1642** H. MORE *Song Soul* I. I. xxvii, You thick that veil, and so your selves array With visibility. **1798** COLERIDGE *Anc. Mar.* III. xi, The Night-Mare Life-in-Death was she, Who thicks man's blood with cold.

†**2.** To make (cloth, etc.) close in texture by fulling; = THICKEN 5. *Obs.*

1482 *Rolls of Parlt.* VI. 223/2 Made, wrought, fulled and thikked, by the myghte and strengh of men. **1511–12** *Act 3 Hen. VIII*, c. 6 §1 The Walker and Fuller shall truely walke fulle thikke and werke every webbe of wollen yerne. **1566** *Act 8 Eliz.* c. 11 §2 That no person.. shall thicke or full in any Myll.. any Cappe vntyll suche tyme as the same Cappe be first.. half thicked.. in the Footestocke. **1719** D'URFEY *Pills* VI. 92 The Water.. over-thicks my Cloth.

3. *intr.* To become thick, in various senses; = THICKEN *intr.* Now *dial.* or *arch.*

a **1000** *Gloss.* in Wr.-Wülcker 219/7 *Densescit, spissat*, þiccaþ. *c* **1290** *St. Michael* 714 in *S. Eng. Leg.* 320 Hit þickez to Nye dawes.. þanne it tornez formest to flesch. **13..** *K. Alis.* 3841 (Bodl. MS.) Þe erþe quaked of her rydyng: þe weder þicked of her crieyng. *c* **1450** *Two Cookery-bks.* 91 Lete hit not boyle til hit thikke. **1579** SPENSER *Sheph. Cal.* Mar. 115 But see the Welkin thicks apace. **1876** *Mid-Yorks. Gloss.* s.v., T'day's thicking (getting cloudy). **1879** J. D. LONG *Æneid* II. 374 The sounds grow clear, The noise of battle thicks.

†**b.** ? To become frequent or prevalent. *Obs.*

13.. *Cursor M.* 17476 (Cott.) Ful wa þam was þaa wreches wick, Quen þis tiþand bigan to thik.

†**4.** *intr.* To move thickly or in crowds; to flock, crowd. *Obs. rare.*

c **1000** in Cockayne *Shrine* (1864) 38 Þa þiccodan þider semninga þa ismaheli. **1513** DOUGLAS *Æneis* VI. v. 30 Als gret number thiddir thikkit in feir As.. Levis of treis. *Ibid.* x. vii. 31 Quhar ȝondir sop of men thikkis in a rout.

†**5.** *refl.* [f. THICK *sb.* 5.] To get into the thick of any place; to hide. *Obs. rare*[−1].

1574 HELLOWES *Gueuara's Fam. Ep.* (1584) 144 Hauing past three daies and three nightes, forsaking al high wayes, thicked myself in the great desart, and being vtterly tyred with great and extreame heat.

Hence **thicked** (θɪkt) *ppl. a.*, thickened; †fulled; **'thicking** *vbl. sb.*, thickening; †fulling.

c **1440** *Anc. Cookery* in *Househ. Ord.* (1790) 435 Stere hit tyl hit be thyk, and in the thikkynge do the rosted felettes therto. **1482** *Rolls of Parlt.* VI. 223/2 To forfaite and lose xl *s.*, as ofte as eny such persone shall putt to fullyng or thikkyng, or to sale, eny suche Huers, Bonettes or Cappes. **1552–3** *Act 7 Edw. VI*, c. 8 (*title*) An Acte for the true fulling and thicking of Cappes. **1604** *Compt Bk. D. Wedderburne* (S.H.S.) 45, xij ellis & a quarter bred thickit blew worzet clayth. **1759** *Compl. Letter-writer* (ed. 6) 53 The thicking or fulling-mill.

thick, Sc. var. THEEK, to thatch; dial. var. THILK.

thick and thin, 'thick-and-'thin, *phr.* Also **thick or thin, (neither) thick nor thin.**

Cf., for the mere collocation, *a* **1000** *O.E. Riddles* xli. 36 Eal ic under heofones hwearfte recce.. þicce and þynne.

A. as *sb.*

1. Phr. ***through thick and thin*** (†***in thick and thin***): through everything that is in the way; without regard to or in spite of obstacles or difficulties; under any circumstances. *lit.* and *fig.* (app. orig. with reference to 'thicket and thin wood'.)

c **1386** CHAUCER *Reeve's T.* 146 The hors.. gynneth gon.. Forth with wehee, thurgh thikke and thurgh thenne [*v.r.* thurgh thikke and thenne]. **1426** LYDG. *De Guil. Pilgr.* 22682 A smale posterne I may pace, And, thorough thykke and thynne trace. *c* **1450** J. METHAM *Wks.* 41/1101 Forth yn thyk and thyn He gan lepe. **1543** GRAFTON *Contn. Harding* 544 Kyng Richard.. purposed to goo thorow thicke and thinne in this mater. **1590** SPENSER *F.Q.* III. i. 17 His tyreling Jade he fiersly forth did push Through thicke and thin, both over banck and bush. **1627** DRAYTON *Mooncalf* 1317 And tag and rag through thick and thin came running. **1681** DRYDEN *Span. Friar* v. ii, A thorough-paced liar, that will swear through thick and thin. **1782** COWPER *Gilpin* 40 Six precious souls, and all agog To dash through thick and thin. **1894** HALL CAINE *Manxman* v. vi, There's five hundred men here to back you up through thick and thin.

2. a. *sb.* Adherence to some course, principle, or party, under all circumstances. **b.** *attrib.* or *adj.* (usually hyphened): That adheres or is ready to follow in all circumstances; constant, steadfast, unwavering. **c.** Hence **thick-and-thinnite** (*nonce-wd.*), one who supports a 'thick-and-thin' or resolute policy regardless of consequences. (*Political* and *journalistic slang.*)

1822 M. EDGEWORTH *Let.* 1 Feb. (1971) 339 Mr. Ellice is a *thick and thin* friend of Lord Byron's and defends him.. against his wife and all the world. **1884** *Pall Mall G.* 14 Feb. 1/1 He would have been denounced as a traitor by the hidebound partisans of thick and thin. **1886** J. PAYN *Heir of Ages* xxxv, It would have been difficult to find a more thick-and-thin admirer of its excellences. **1890** *Spectator* 18 Oct. 515/2 In his thick-and-thin advocacy of the democratic policy. **1898** DR. FARQUHARSON *Sp. Ho. Com.* 9 May, [On these matters he was a] thick and thin-ite. **1900** A. J. BALFOUR *Sp. Manchester* 9 Jan., I felt as if I was before this speech tarred with the brush of being a 'thick-and-thinnite'. **1900** *Westm. Gaz.* 11 Jan. 2/2 There does not exist a thick-and-thinner party man than Mr. Balfour.

†**B.** as *adv.* ***either thick or thin***: in any case, under any circumstances; ***neither thick nor thin***, in no circumstances. *Obs. rare.*

1486 *Bk. St. Albans* e vij b, Thyk nor thynne [see GARGILON]. **1546** *St. Papers Hen. VIII*, XI. 254 The Dolphyn spared not, thyck nor thynne.

C. as *adj.* **1.** *Naut.* Of a tackle-block: Having one sheave larger than the other; cf. FIDDLE-*block*.

1815 BURNEY *Falconer's Dict. Marine* s.v. *Block, Thick and thin*, or, *Quarter Block*, is a double block with one sheave thicker than the other, and is used to lead down the topsail-sheets and clew-lines. **1841** DANA *Seaman's Man.* Gloss., *Thick-and-thin Block*, a block having one sheave larger than the other. Sometimes used for quarter-blocks.

2. See A. 2 b.

thicke, obs. form of THEEK, THICK, THILK.

thicken ('θɪk(ə)n), *v.* [f. THICK *a.* + -EN 5. Cf. ON. *þykkn-a*, f. *þykk* adj. THICK.] To make or become thick or thicker.

1. *trans.* To make dense in consistence; to coagulate, inspissate. Also *fig.*

c **1425** tr. *Arderne's Treat. Fistula* 30 Vnto þat þe watrynes of þe Iuyse be somewhat þikned. **1552** HULOET, Thycken or congeale, *congelo.* **1616** SURFL. & MARKH. *Country Farme* 64 Heat doth safegard and thicken the milk. **1698** FRYER *Acc. E. India & P.* 353 By indulging his Body he thickens his Understanding. **1771** MRS. HAYWOOD *New Present* 44 It is a very good thing to thicken gravy with. **1801** C. DIBDIN *Tour* I. 356 The illuminati, who generally thicken in the clear, so as to confound the business, that a man of plain sense can make nothing out of them. **1866** ROGERS *Agric. & Prices* I. xiii. 221 Oatmeal was used scantily, but generally for thickening soup.

b. *intr.* To increase in density or consistence; also, to become turbid or cloudy. Also *fig.*

1598 *Epulario* I j b, Set it all night to thicken.. in a cold place. **1660** F. BROOKE tr. *Le Blanc's Trav.* 19 A licquor, or gumme, which thickens of it selfe. **1718** PRIOR *Solomon* I. 355 Water stopt gives birth To grass and plants, and thickens into earth. **1888** BESANT *50 Years Ago* vii. 121 There comes a time when the brow clouds, and the speech thickens, and the tongue refuses to act.

2. *intr.* To become dark, obscure, or opaque; of the weather: to become misty.

1605 SHAKS. *Macb.* III. ii. 50 Light thickens,.. Good things of Day begin to droope, and drowse. **1606** —— *Ant. & Cl.* II. iii. 27 Thy Luster thickens, When he shines by. **1670** DRYDEN *1st Pt. Conq. Granada* II. i, I'll face this Storm that thickens in the Wind. **1784** *Cook's Voy. Pacific* VI. iii. III. 239 The weather still thickening, and preventing a nearer approach to the land. **1860** TYNDALL *Glac.* I. xxv. 189 As we approached the summit the air thickened more and more.

3. *trans.* To make close or dense in disposition of parts or in texture; to fill up the interstices or intervals of. ? *Obs.*

1575 LANEHAM *Let.* (1871) 8 Seauen posts on a side, that stood a twelue foot a sunder, thikned betweene with well proportioned Pillars turnd. **1620** T. GRANGER *Div. Logike* 30 The clouds are not thickned in the skie: therfore it will not be raine. **1755** JOHNSON *Dict.*, *Thicken*, v.,.. to make frequent, to make close or numerous. **1812** BRACKENRIDGE *Views Louisiana* (1814) 116 It is perhaps good policy in our government.. to thicken the frontier, and to suffer the intermediate space to fill up gradually.

4. *intr.* To become crowded, numerous, or frequent; to gather thickly. Also †To move in great numbers, to flock, troop (*obs. poet.*).

1726 POPE *Odyss.* XVIII. 49 Well pleased they spring Swift from their seats, and thickening form a ring. **1771** *Junius Lett.* liv. (1820) 286 Honours shall.. thicken over him. **1789** MME. D'ARBLAY *Diary* 19 Nov., The crowd every instant thickening. **1838** DICKENS *Nich. Nick.* liv, Misfortune and discovery are thickening about your head.

5. a. *trans.* To increase the substance between opposite surfaces of; to make thicker in measure.

c **1611** CHAPMAN *Iliad* XIII. 123 Lance was lin'd with lance; Shields thickned with opposed shields. **1777** SHERIDAN *Trip to Scarborough* I. ii, The calves of these stockings are thicken'd a little too much. **1858** GLENNY *Gard. Everyday Bk.* 244/1 The earth in the alleys [is to be] thrown up to thicken the soil above them a little. **1884** BOWER & SCOTT *De Bary's Phaner.* 229 In most cases the walls are thickened by spiral fibres.

b. *intr.* To become thicker in measurement; to increase in girth or bulk.

1763 MILLS *Syst. Pract. Husb.* IV. 35 That their roots.. may have full room to thicken and run downward. **1805** PIKE *Sources Mississ.* (1810) 42 Ice in the river thickening. **1872** R. B. SMYTH *Mining Statist.* 21 The seams.. thicken in one place and thin out in another.

c. *trans. fig.* To make more substantial; to strengthen, confirm.

1604 SHAKS. *Oth.* III. iii. 430 This may helpe to thicken other proofes, That do demonstrate thinly. **1893** C. W. WENDTE in *Reasonable Relig.* 73 The philosophers.. are thickening up their systems.. with scientific facts.

6. *intr. fig.* To become more complex or intricate (esp. said of a plot); to increase in intensity.

1671 VILLIERS (Dk. Buckhm.) *Rehearsal* III. ii. (Arb.) 81 Ay, now the Plot thickens very much upon us. **1697** DRYDEN *Æneid* IX. 908 The combat thickens, like the storm that flies. **1810** SCOTT *Lady of L.* I. ii, The cry, That thickened as the chase drew nigh. **1859** KINGSLEY *Misc.* I. i. 16 As the quarrel thickened and neared.

Hence **thickened** ('θɪk(ə)nd) *ppl. a.*, that is made thick or thicker, in various senses.

c **1611** CHAPMAN *Iliad* XIX. 368 A bright thickned bush of golden haire. **1667** MILTON *P.L.* XI. 742 The thick'nd Skie Like a dark Ceeling stood. **1697** DRYDEN *Virg. Georg.* IV. 386 Mix it with thicken'd Juice of sodden Wines. **1861** BENTLEY *Man. Bot.* 401 Plants with succulent or thickened leaves. **1900** *Daily News* 17 Apr. 7/4 With solids and pneumatics [tyres], both of the wired-on and thickened-edge varieties.

thickener ('θɪk(ə)nə(r)). [f. prec. vb. + -ER[1].] That which (or one who) thickens; in *Dyeing*, a substance used to increase the consistence of the colours or mordants.

1652 FRENCH *Yorksh. Spa* iv. 46 The body is to be annointed with oyle, with spissaments or thickeners. **1732** ARBUTHNOT *Rules of Diet* in *Aliments*, etc. 261 Thickeners of the Humours. **1883** R. HALDANE *Workshop Receipts* Ser. II. 206/2 The next step.. is the removal of the thickeners.

thickening ('θɪk(ə)nɪŋ), *vbl. sb.* [f. as prec. + -ING[1].] The action of the verb THICKEN; the process of making or becoming thick or thicker; *concr.* the result of this action or process; a thickened substance or part.

1580 HOLLYBAND *Treas. Fr. Tong*, *Espessissement*, a thickening. **1603** HOLLAND *Plutarch's Mor.* 998 Mists, fogs, and clouds are no congealations, but onely gatherings, and thickenings of a moist and vapourous aire. **1822** J. PARKINSON *Outl. Oryctol.* 159 A subglobose univalve; the opening longer than wide;.. no thickening of the left lip. **1893** TUCKEY tr. *Hatschek's Amphioxus* 154 He was misled by a thickening of the alimentary canal in front of the gland. **1899** *Allbutt's Syst. Med.* VIII. 511 Eczema of the palms very frequently leads.. to great thickening of the epidermis. *c* **1900** *Beeton's Everyday Cookery Bk.* 209/2 By the addition of various store sauces, thickening and flavouring, good stock may be converted into good gravies.

b. A substance used to thicken something; *spec.* in *Dyeing*. = THICKENER.

1839 URE *Dict. Arts*, etc. 222 Several circumstances may require the consistence of the thickening to be varied. **1874** W. CROOKES *Dyeing & Calico-print.* ii. 17 Only two mineral thickenings are at present employed, namely, kaolin and pipe-clay.

c. *Foundry* = THICKNESS 8.

1872 ELLACOMBE *Bells of Ch.* i. 200 When thoroughly dried, the outer mould is removed, and the thickening (the *fac-simile* of the bell) destroyed.

d. *Bot.* ***thickening layer, mass, ring*** (Ger. *verdickungsring*): see quots.

1875 BENNETT & DYER tr. *Sachs's Bot.* 27 A wider cavity, which is bounded on the sides by the narrow part of the thickening-masses, on the outside by the primary cell-wall. *Ibid.* 108 Generating ring of tissue, corresponding to Sanio's thickening ring. **1900** B. D. JACKSON *Gloss. Bot. Terms* 270/2 *Thickening Layer*, an apparent layer of cellulose on the inner face of a cell-wall; *Thickening Ring*, Sanio's term for a ring of meristem in which the first fibro-vascular bundles originate.

thickening (ˈθɪk(ə)nɪŋ), *ppl. a.* [f. as prec. + -ING².] That thickens: **a.** That grows thicker; **b.** That makes something thick or thicker.

1721 J. DART *Westminster Abbey* 57 When Learning was with thick'ning Mists o'erspread. **1784** COWPER *Task* IV. 330 Earth receives Gladly the thickening mantle [snow]. **1860** TYNDALL *Glac.* I. xii. 88 At the close of the day thickening clouds warned me off. **1880** BROWNING *Dram. Idyls, Pan & Luna* 10 Fast-thickening poppy-juice. **1895** *Model Steam Engine* 69 The thickening piece is soldered to the boiler.

†**ˈthicker.** *Obs.* [f. THICK *v.* + -ER¹.] One who 'thicks' or fulls cloth; a fuller. Also as second element in comb., as ***cap-thicker, say-thicker.***

1520 WHITINTON *Vulg.* (1527) 16 b, In the strete vpon the backe halfe, be drapers..cappers, thyckers of cappes. **1570** FOXE *A. & M.* (ed. 2) 944/2 One Walker a thicker of S. Clementes. **1641** Saye-Thickers [see SAY *sb.*¹ 3].

thicket (ˈθɪkɪt). Also 1 þiccet, 6 thykette, 7 thickett. [OE. *þiccet*, neut., f. *þicce* thick + *-et*, denominative suffix (as in *emn-et* plain, *rýmet* space).] A dense growth of shrubs, underwood, and small trees; a place where low trees or bushes grow thickly together; a brake. Cf. THICK *sb.* 5.

a **1000** *Ps.* (Spelm.) xxviii[i]. 9 Stefn drihtnes awrihþ þiccettu [*Lamb.* þiccetu]. **1530** TINDALE *Gen.* xxii. 13 A ram caught by the hornes in a thykette. **1530** PALSGR. 280/1 Thicket or a forest, *boscaige*. **1555** EDEN *Decades* 57 They founde a greate thicket of reedes. **1593** SHAKS. *3 Hen. VI*, IV. v. 3 Leaue off to wonder why I drew you hither, Into this cheefest Thicket of the Parke. **1667** MILTON *P.L.* IV. 681 How often from the steep Of echoing Hill or Thicket have we heard Celestial voices to the midnight air..Singing. **1711** ADDISON *Spect.* No. 56 ¶3 This huge Thicket of Thorns and Brakes was designed as a Kind of Fence. **1855** KINGSLEY *Heroes* III. (1868) 32 They sang like nightingales among the thickets.

b. *transf.* and *fig.*

1582 STANYHURST *Æneis* II. (Arb.) 54, I run forward too rush throgh thicket of armoure. **1612** WEBSTER *White Devil* II. i. 79 I'le meete thee Even in a thicket of thy ablest men. **1657** S. PURCHAS *Pol. Flying-Ins.* xvii. 111 They are quickly be-wildred in a thicket of errors. **1698** FRYER *Acc. E. India & P.* 45 A Thicket of twenty Sail of our Enemies were discovered. **1821** SCOTT *Kenilw.* xiii, His wild and overgrown thicket of beard was now restrained to two small mustachios. **1866** J. MARTINEAU *Ess.* I. 52 We entangle ourselves in a thicket of ever-growing problems.

c. *attrib.* and *Comb.*, as ***thicket-maze, -haunting.***

1813 SCOTT *Rokeby* IV. ii, Where the thicket-groupes recede. **1837** STANLEY *Gipsies* 136 Or track old Jordan through his thicket maze. **1850** ALLINGHAM *Poems, Music-master* II. xv, The thicket-tangling, tenderest briar-rose. **1892** *Guardian* 11 May 706/2 Along the courtly mere of thicket isles.

Hence **ˈthicketed** *a.*, occupied or covered by thickets; **ˈthicketful**, as many or as much as fills a thicket; **ˈthickety** *a.*, abounding in thickets.

c **1624** CHAPMAN *Homer, Hymn to Bacchus* 140 In ivies and in baies All over *thicketed. **1835** W. IRVING *Tour Prairies* xxxiii, The same kind of rough, hilly, thicketed country. **1887** J. SERVICE *Dr. Duguid* 270 Sweet sounds..From out the *thicketful of singing throats. **1640** in *Maryland Hist. Mag.* (1910) V. 374 The Neck of land..lyeing between *thicketty Creek on the North, hog pen Creek on the South. **1740** J. E. OGLETHORPE *Jrnl.* 14 May in *Coll. S. Carolina Hist. Soc.* (1887) IV. 152 They got into such thickety ground that they could not overtake them. **1846** MRS. MARSH *Emilia Wyndham* (1848) 349 Very fine timber and thicketty woods. **1865** W. G. PALGRAVE *Arabia* I. 238 Broken and thickety ground in front.

†**ˈthickfold**, *adv.* (*adj.*) *Obs.* Chiefly *north.* [f. THICK *a.*: see -FOLD.] Thickly together; in great numbers, in crowds.

a **1300** *Cursor M.* 11258 Þas oþer [angels] lighted dun thicfald. *c* **1400** *Rowland & O.* 1108 Full thikke folde gan Sarazenes dy. *c* **1440** *Bone Flor.* 871 Many myrakyls for hur he wroght, Many a oon and thyck folde. **1513** DOUGLAS *Æneis* XIII. ii. 68 O ȝe my feris..Throu mony hard perrellis and thikfald..Hiddir now careit to this cost with me. **1535** STEWART *Cron. Scot.* (Rolls) III. 98 Thikfald to him all in the tyme tha drew.

ˈthick-head. One who or that which has a thick head.

1. a. One who is dull of intellect; a blockhead.

1824 H. WILSON *Mem.* I. ii. 41 'Don't you know,' said thickhead, '..that I am blind as well as deaf?' **1871** CARLYLE in *Mrs. Carlyle's Lett.* (1883) I. 103 *note*, Ambitious thickhead. **1882** H. SEEBOHM *Siberia in Asia* 32 One of the greatest thickheads that I have ever met with.

b. *attrib.* or *adj.* = THICK-HEADED b.

1873 BROWNING *Red Cott. Nt.-cap* II. 235 Who ever has his speech in readiness For thick-head juvenility at fault. **1894** F. S. ELLIS *Reynard Fox* 187 I'll shortly sow strife among Those thick-head folks.

2. A name given in different localities to various birds: e.g. **a.** Any bird of the subfamily *Pachycephalinæ*, the Thick-headed Shrikes of the Australian region. **b.** A scansorial barbet of the subfamily *Capitoninæ* (*Cent. Dict.* 1891).

1837 SWAINSON *Nat. Hist. Birds* II. 250 Vireoninæ.. Pachycephala..Thickhead. **1890** *Victorian Stat., Game Act* Sched. iii. (Morris), Thick-heads. [Close season] From the first day of August to the twentieth day of December. **1894** NEWTON *Dict. Birds* 621 Native-Thrush, *Pachycephala olivacea* (Thickhead). **1896** *Ibid.* 958 The name Thickhead is..given in other parts of the world to very different birds, and in South Africa especially to *Œdicnemus capensis*.., the Stone Curlew of that country.

ˈthick-ˈheaded, *a.*, [Parasynthetic f. prec. + -ED².] Having a thick head. **a.** *lit.*; esp. in names of animals, as **thick-headed mullet**, *Moxostoma congesta*; **thick-headed shrike** = THICK-HEAD 2 a.

1707 MORTIMER *Husb.* (1721) I. 314 Make a Trail..so as to bring it near some thick-headed Tree. **1752** J. HILL *Hist. Anim.* 569 The thick-headed Hippopotamus, with no tail. The Copy-Bara.

b. *fig.* Dull of intellect; slow-witted, obtuse.

1801 MAR. EDGEWORTH *Gd. French Gov.* (1895) 7 He was so 'thick-headed at his book', that Mrs. Grace..affirmed that he never would learn to read. **1860** GEN. P. THOMPSON *Audi Alt.* III. cxxv. 80 A thick-headed idea of law is, that it is a machine for getting men hanged. **1891** LOUNSBURY *Stud. Chaucer* II. vi. 481 Something of the feeling..which represents the members of the nobility as being good-hearted but also thick-headed.

Hence **thickˈheadedness**, obtuseness, crassness.

1889 *Voice* (N.Y.) 14 Feb., He..failed to estimate the thickheadedness of the party addressed. **1892** *Spectator* 23 Jan. 126/2 Bumptious, bullying thickheadedness.

thickie (ˈθɪkɪ). *colloq.* [f. THICK *a.* (*sb.*) + -IE.] = THICK-HEAD 1 a. Cf. THICK *sb.* 6

1968 B. EARNSHAW *At St. David's a Year* 52 When I hear that one of our Sixth Form boys Has been kicked-up by a Haverfordwest thickie For stealing his girl friend, I think 'Good'. **1976** J. I. M. STEWART *Memorial Service* v. 74 Just one more grouse-slaughtering thickie like my father. **1983** *Times* 5 Sept. 3/1 Teachers still think that engineering is a subject for 'thickies'.

thicking, *vbl. sb.*: see THICK *v.*

thickish (ˈθɪkɪʃ), *a.* [f. THICK *a.* + -ISH¹.] Somewhat thick.

1545 RAYNOLD *Byrth Mankynde* 141 Also her vryne waxeth spysse and thyckysshe. **1713** *Lond. Gaz.* No. 5178/4 Thickish of Hearing. **1737** BRACKEN *Farriery Impr.* (1757) II. 23 Horses that are a little thickish about the Shoulders. **1894** *Cornh. Mag.* Mar. 269 Two thickish quarto volumes.

thick-knee (ˈθɪkniː). Also **thicknee**. A name for any bird of the genus *Œdicnemus*, esp. the Stone Curlew, Norfolk or Great Plover, *Œ. scolopax* (*Œ. crepitans*, Temminck); so called from the enlargement of the tibio-tarsal joint.

1816 LEACH *Cat. Mamm. & B. in Brit. Mus.* 28 *Fedoa Œdicnemus* Common thicknee, Wiltshire. **1840** *Penny Cycl.* XVI. 402/1 The..Thick-knee. Thick-kneed Bustard. **1866** OWEN *Vertebr. Anim.* xiv. II. 26 The 'Thick-knees'..and Bustards..have the four-notched sternum. **1896** *List Anim. Zool. Soc.* 520 *Œdicnemus grallarius*, Australian Thicknee... *Œ. superciliaris*, Peruvian Thicknee.

So **ˈthick-ˌkneed** *a.*, having thick knees; esp. in ***thick-kneed bustard*** or ***plover***, the Stone Curlew.

1776 PENNANT *Zool.* (ed. 4) I. 244 Bustard, thick-kneed. **1840** [see THICK-KNEE]. **1893** NEWTON *Dict. Birds* 129 The Curlew of inlanders, or Stone-Curlew—called also..most wrongly..the Thick-knee or Thick-kneed Bustard.

ˈthick-leaved (-liːvd), **-leafed** (-liːft), *a.* [See LEAVED, LEAFED.] **a.** Having or covered with dense foliage; thickly set with leaves.

1582 STANYHURST *Æneis* I. (Arb.) 28 Shaded with thick-leaued arbours. **1660** BLOUNT *Boscobel* 32 The colonel made choice of a thick-leafed oak. **1847** TENNYSON *Princess* III. 159 The thick-leaved platans of the vale.

b. Having thick fleshy leaves.

1707 MORTIMER *Husb.* (1721) I. 31 Where thick-leav'd Weeds are amongst the Grass, they will need more drying than ordinary Grass doth. **1860** *Merc. Marine Mag.* VII. 199 A thick leafed..plant.

thick-lipped (ˈθɪkˈlɪpt: stress var.), *a.* Having thick or full lips.

a **1529** SKELTON *E. Rummyng* 467 She was vgly hypped, And vgly thycke lypped. **1588** SHAKS. *Tit. A.* IV. ii. 175 Come on you thick-lipt-slaue. **1682** *Lond. Gaz.* No. 1685/4 John Wilmote,..of a pretty Ruddy Complexion, and something thick Lipped. **1838** JOHNSTON in *Proc. Berw. Nat. Club* I. No. 6. 171 *Mugil chelo*,..the Thick-lipped Grey Mullet. **1867** BAKER *Nile Tribut.* xx. (1872) 352 A real thick-lipped flat-nosed nigger.

So **ˈthick-lips**, one who has thick lips; a contemptuous appellation for a Negro.

1604 SHAKS. *Oth.* I. i. 66 What a full Fortune do's the Thick-lips owe If he can carry't thus?

thickly (ˈθɪklɪ), *adv.* [f. THICK *a.* + -LY².] In a thick manner; so as to be thick, in various senses; densely; closely; abundantly; frequently; deeply; obscurely, indistinctly.

c **1400** *Laud Troy Bk.* 5672 Thei died thanne thikly. *c* **1430** *Pilgr. Lyf. Manhode* II. lvii. (1869) 98 Sum time thou shalt see me thikkeliche and derkeliche. **1573–80** BARET *Alv.* T 151 Thicklie: groslie: clubbishlie, or blockishlie. *c* **1611** CHAPMAN *Iliad* XV. 440 His helmet, thickly plum'd. **1630** DRAYTON *Noah's Flood* 83 Your sins..so thickly throng. **1770** COOK *Voy. round World* III. ii. (1773) 519 Lofty hills, all thickly clothed with wood. **1860** TYNDALL *Glac.* I. xviii. 123 Mont Cervin gathered the clouds more thickly round him. **1883** LD. R. GOWER *My Remin.* I. iii. 35 The walls of the principal apartments are thickly hung with paintings.

b. In comb. with ppl. or other adjs.

1797 T. PARK *Sonn.* 7 Clouds, thickly-driving, veil the face of day. **1832** MOTHERWELL *Poet. Wks.* (1847) 8 Those thickly-timbered shores. **1900** *Westm. Gaz.* 7 Sept. 4/1 A thickly-inhabited district.

thicknee, variant of THICK-KNEE.

thickness (ˈθɪknɪs). [OE. *þicness* = OHG. *diknissa*, f. THICK *a.* + -NESS.]

I. The quality or condition of being thick.

1. Relatively large measurement through, or between opposite surfaces; stoutness, bulkiness; the opposite of *thinness* or *slenderness*. Also *fig.*

c **1000** *Ags. Gloss.* in *Haupt's Zeitschr.* (1853) IX. 519 *Elephantina callositate*, hreoflicre þicnesse. **1538** ELYOT, *Crassamentum*, thyckenesse... *Crassities & crassitudo*, fatnesse, thicknes, grossenes. **1577** B. GOOGE *Heresbach's Husb.* II. (1586) 80 b, The equall medley of..thicknesse and thinnes. **1613** HAYWARD *Norm. Kings* 23 As he grew in yeeres, so did he in thicknesse and fatnesse of body. **1641** EVELYN *Diary* 7 Aug., Walls..of prodigious thicknesse. **1885** J. PAYN *Luck of Darrells* xx, His companion's astounding thickness of skin [cf. THICK-SKINNED 2].

2. Measurement or extension of anything between its opposite surfaces; the third (and commonly least) dimension, distinct from length and breadth.

a **900** WÆRFERTH *Gregory's Dial.* (1900) 44 He ȝewænde þæs wæteres ȝecynd on eles þicnesse. **1387** TREVISA *Higden* (Rolls) I. 45 Þe þiknesse of þe erþe þorw oute is almest sexe þousand and fyue hondred myle. **14..** *Tundale's Vis.* (Wagner) 1314 Fourti cubytes on brede he hadde And nine on theknes was he made. *a* **1548** HALL *Chron., Hen. VIII* 33 The Frenchmen came on in .iii. ranges, xxxvi. mens thickenes [i.e. thirty-six deep]. **1570** BILLINGSLEY *Euclid* I. def. ii. 2 A point..neither hath length, breadth, nor thickenes. **1683** MOXON *Mech. Exerc., Printing* xxiv, It is Quadrat high, of several Thicknesses, viz. a Nonparel, Brevier, Long-primmer, Pica, etc. **1735** JOHNSON *Lobo's Abyssinia, Descr.* x. 103 The Crocodile is very ugly, having no Proportion between his Length and Thickness. **1815** J. SMITH *Panorama Sc. & Art* I. 7 In half an hour it will scarcely be the thickness of a sixpence. **1854** *Pereira's Polariz. Light* 134 The resulting tint depends on the difference of the thicknesses. **1884** BOWER & SCOTT *De Bary's Phaner.* 411 They there attain a thickness which amounts to ½ or even more than ⅔ of the entire thickness of the leaf.

3. The quality or condition of being consistent or viscous (also, degree of consistence); of the air, the condition of being laden with impurities.

c **1000** *Sax. Leechd.* I. 126 Cnuca mid wine on huniȝes þicnysse. **1398** TREVISA *Barth. De P.R.* III. xvii. (W. de W. 1495) d iv b/1, Yf it is all clere & w^t^out thyknesse as the ayere is, thenne y^t^ is not seen. *c* **1425** tr. *Arderne's Treat. Fistula* 36 Medled togidre in suche þiknes þat it may be ȝetted in by a nastare of tree. **1663** GERBIER *Counsel* 27 Morter..unequall in thicknesse. **1737** WHISTON *Josephus, Antiq.* II. xiv. §5 Whereby their sight being obstructed, and their breathing hindered by the thickness of the air, they died miserably. **1747** WESLEY *Prim. Physick* (1762) 109 Mix juice of Celandine with Honey to the Thickness of Cream.

4. Of the air, etc.: Misty or hazy condition; obscurity, opacity.

c **1000** *Ags. Ps.* (Spelm.) xcvi. 2 ȝenipu and þicnæs, *nubes et caligo*. *c* **1000** *Sax. Leechd.* III. 232 We ne maȝon for ðære fyrlynan heahnysse & þæra wolcna ðicnysse..hi næfre ȝeseon. **1426** LYDG. *De Guil. Pilgr.* 11036 And off the owgly ffoul thyknesse,.. Thow shalt lese the syht off me.

5. Dense or crowded condition; closeness of collocation or growth.

1398 TREVISA *Barth. De P.R.* v. xv. (Bodl. MS.), Þiknes of berd is signe and tokenne of heete and of substancial humour and of strengþe. **1433** LYDG. *St. Edmund* II. 838 A couert, shrowded with thyknesse Of thornys sharpe. *c* **1440** *Promp. Parv.* 491/1 Thykkenesse, as of wodys, gresse, corne, or other lyke, *densitas*. **1825** SCOTT *Talism.* vi, His hair in thickness might have resembled that of Samson.

6. Want of clearness in breathing, hearing, or utterance; indistinct articulation.

1538 ELYOT *Dict.* Addit., *Daseia*, thyckenes of brethe. **1669** HOLDER *Elem. Speech* 168 Being at sometimes subject to thicknes of Hearing. **1686** BURNET *Lett.* (1708) 249 Her Nurse had an extraordinary Thickness of Hearing. **1863** A. M. BELL *Princ. Speech* 183 The inarticulate confusion of speech which results is commonly called 'thickness'. **1908** R. BAGOT *A. Cuthbert* iii, His few observations being characterised by a decided thickness of utterance.

II. That which is thick or has thickness.

7. That which is thick, in any sense; the part (of anything) which is thick; the thick (of anything); the space between opposite surfaces (e.g. of a wall).

c **1000** *Ags. Gloss.* in *Haupt's Zeitschr.* (1853) IX. 499 *Sulphureis flammarum globis*, sweflenum þicnyssum. *a* **1000** *Lambeth Ps.* cxvii[i]. 27 On þyccetum *vel* on ðicnessum, *in* *condensis.* **1382** WYCLIF *Isa.* ix. 18 It shal be brend vp in the thickenes of the wilde wode. **1560** BIBLE (Genev.) *Ezek.* xlii. 10 The chambres were in the thickenes of the wall of the court. **1687** A. LOVELL tr. *Thevenot's Trav.* II. 82 They go down..by steps made in the thickness of the Walls. **1796** MORSE *Amer. Geog.* II. 477 Incumbered with unwholesome marshes..and impenetrable thicknesses. **1859** JEPHSON *Brittany* vii. 93 The wall is here about five yards thick, and in its thickness are stone benches. **1905** R. BAGOT *Passport* iii. 19 There was only the thickness of a floor between them.

8. A layer (of cloth, paper, etc.). In *Foundry*, A layer of loam in a mould which represents the object to be cast (e.g. a pipe, bell), and is broken away from the completed mould to make room for the molten metal.

1815 J. SMITH *Panorama Sc. & Art* II. 807 Place several thicknesses of paper upon the glass. **1853** SIR H. DOUGLAS *Milit. Bridges* (ed. 3) 325 The whole six thicknesses of planks..are then well drawn together, and fastened to each other, by the trenails. **1884** N. E. SPRETSON *Casting & Founding* 215 In the absence of patterns, however, for these and for other varieties of short piping, they are swept up in loam, the core within the 'thickness'. **1889** *Anthony's Photogr. Bull.* II. 237 On top..a single thickness of common felt cloth is placed.

Hence **'thicknessing** *vbl. sb.*, the action of reducing (boards, etc.) to a given thickness; **'thickness** *v. trans.*, **'thicknessed** *ppl. a.* (back-formations).

1870 *Eng. Mech.* 4 Feb. 497/2 That side of the machine employed for tenoning, planing, thicknessing, or moulding. **1901** *Daily Chron.* 9 May 1/6 Planing and Thicknessing Machine, 20in. **1915** Thicknessed [see *spindle machine* s.v. SPINDLE *sb.* 17]. **1978** *Early Music* Oct. 506 The marks on the inside of the belly..have contributed to the theory that the central strip was first thicknessed and then bent to the long arch, the outer strip being glued to this solid and then carved in the usual way.

thicknesser ('θɪknɪsə(r)). [-ER[1].] A thicknessing machine.

1920 F. T. HILL *Pract. Aeroplane Constr.* 103 Another machine is the surfacer and thicknesser, in which one set of cutters is used for both operations, the top table for the truing-up process..and the bottom table for thicknessing. **1930** *Times Educ. Suppl.* 20 Sept. 400/1 Panel planer and thicknesser. **1959** *Times* 29 Oct. 13/4 A planing machine, which reduces sawn timber to specified dimensions, or sometimes merely smoothes the surface, is frequently referred to as a thicknesser. **1977** *West Briton* 25 Aug. 8/6 (Advt.), Carpenter's universal planer, thicknesser.

thicko ('θɪkəʊ). *colloq.* [f. THICK *a.* (*sb.*) + -O[2].] = THICK-HEAD 1 a.

1976 *Oxford Diocesan Mag.* Nov. 8/2 You have mixed ability teaching throughout, which means..having the thickos in with the brainy and the in-betweens. **1981** P. THEROUX *Mosquito Coast* xiv. 176 Where's the camp store, thicko?

thicksell, dial. variant of THIXIL, an adz.

thick-set, *a.* and *sb.* [f. THICK *adv.* + *set*, pa. pple. of SET *v.*[1]]

A. *adj.* (Stress variable, *'thick-'set*, *ˌthick-'set*, *'thick-ˌset*; cf. note under ILL *adv.* 3.)

1. Composed of individuals or parts arranged in close order; thickly studded or planted (*with* something).

?*a* **1366** CHAUCER *Rom. Rose* 1419 By the stremes.. Sprang up the gras, as thikke sette And softe as ony velvet. **1610** HOLLAND *Camden's Brit.* (1637) 627 Thicker set with high Hilles. *c* **1665** MRS. HUTCHINSON *Mem. Col. Hutchinson* (1846) 22 His hair of light brown, very thick set in his youth. **1697** DRYDEN *Æneid* I. 617 Thick-set with trees, a venerable wood. **1869** TOZER *Highl. Turkey* II. 220 A wild hilly country..thick-set with bushes of prickly palluria.

c **1410** *Master of Game* (MS. Digby 182) xxiv, He [a hart] bereth a thykesette heede [HEAD *sb.* 6]. **1638–48** G. DANIEL *Eclog.* ii. 2 The Covert of yond' thickset Thorne. *a* **1700** DRYDEN *Ovid's Met.* XIII. *Acis*, etc. 156 A thick-set underwood of bristling hair. **1819** CRABBE *T. of Hall* VI. 132 That thickset alley by the arbour closed.

2. Set or placed close together; closely arranged.

1570–6 LAMBARDE *Peramb. Kent* (1826) 181 The place hath in it sundry villages, although not thicke set, nor much inhabited. **1765** *Museum Rust.* V. xxiv. 118 Its flowers are yellow, and thick-set.

1612 DRAYTON *Poly-olb.* i. 447 Where Corineus ran With slaughter through the thick-set squadrons of the foes. **1848** BUCKLEY *Iliad* 457 They made a great fence around, with thick-set stakes.

3. a. Having a dense or close-grained nap: cf. B. 2. b. ***thick-set wheat***: see quot. 1808.

1709 *Lond. Gaz.* No. 4608/4 A pair of thickset Fustian Breeches. **1769** *Public Advertiser* 25 Sept. 3/1 Dressed in Fustian or Thickset Cloaths. **1808** BATCHELOR *Agric.* 362 Velvet-eared wheat, which is called in this county white-chaffed led wheat, and thick-set wheat.

4. Of close compact build; *esp.* short and strongly made; square-built; stocky. (This is now the commonest use.)

1724 *Lond. Gaz.* No. 6251/3 He is a thick-set Boy. **1777** *Charact.* in *Ann. Reg.* 43/1 A short thick-set man, with a very honest ingenuous countenance. **1824** L. M. HAWKINS *Annaline* I. 86 Distinguished by thickset limbs. **1830** MARRYAT *King's Own* xix, He was short and thick-set. **1893** H. VIZETELLY *Glances back through Seventy Years* I. viii. 165 Captain Marryat was tall,..but broad shouldered and thick set. **1977** N. ADAM *Triplehip Cracksman* xiv. 143 A thickset ..guy in a thick woollen polo-neck sweater.

B. *sb.* ('θɪksɛt).

1. A thicket; a thick-set plantation.

1766 AMORY *Buncle* (1825) III. 108 The first spring of this water is..in the middle of a thick-set of shrubs. **1844** *P. Parley's Ann.* V. 191 Tungee had more than once threaded this maze of wood and thickset.

2. a. A stout twilled cotton cloth with a short very close nap; a kind of fustian; also, a garment of this material. ? *Obs.*

1756 TOLDERVY *Hist. 2 Orphans* II. 105 The latter having on his back his common grey frock, and the former a Manchester thickset. **1796** MORSE *Amer. Geog.* I. 440 Jeans, fustians, denims, thicksets, velvets. **1822** GALT *Sir A. Wylie* i, His breeches, of olive thickset, were..carefully preserved from stains. **1882** BECK *Draper's Dict.* 142 Corduroy and thickset are also coarser varieties of fustian.

b. Short for *thick-set wheat* (see A. 3 b).

1875 *Encycl. Brit.* I. 354/1 The red-straw white [wheat] and Piper's thick-set have properties similar to the Fenton.

'thick-'sighted (stress var.), *a.* ? *Obs.* Not seeing clearly; having obscure or dim vision.

1592 SHAKS. *Ven. & Ad.* 136 Were I..Thick-sighted, barren, leane, and lacking iuyce. **1628** FELTHAM *Resolves* II. [I.] xcii. 269 Shee is thick-sighted, and cannot see them. **1775** SHERIDAN *St. Patr. Day* II. iii, We are but blind guessers... Thick-sighted mortals. **1863** MRS. GASKELL *Sylvia's Lovers* xxi, Too thick sighted to see through a board.

thickskin ('θɪkskɪn). One who has a thick skin; a person dull or slow of feeling. Also *attrib.*

1582 STANYHURST *Æneis* Ded. (Arb.) 9 What thinck you of thee thick skyn, that made this for a fare wel for this mystresse? **1597** BP. HALL *Sat.* I. i. 8 Nor can I bide to pen some hungry Scene For thick-skin eares, and vndiscerning eyne. **1611** COTGR., *Ceruelle à double rebras*, a..ioulthead, thicke-skinne, dull fellow. **1893** H. M. DOUGHTY *Wherry in Wendish L.* 53 We..should have made a fair distance but for those slugs and thickskins of bridge-keepers.

'thick-'skinned (-skɪnd: stress var.), *a.*

1. Having a thick skin; of plants, fruits, etc., having a thick outer coat or peel.

1545 ELYOT, *Callosus*, thicke skynned. **1601** HOLLAND *Pliny* I. XI. xxxix. 346 Men..who are thicke skinned..be more grosse of sence and understanding. **1813** SIR H. DAVY *Agric. Chem.* (1814) 152 In the South of Europe, hard or thin-skinned wheat is in higher estimation than soft or thick-skinned wheat. **1831** CARLYLE *Sart. Res.* II. ii, Did not these bristly thick-skinned beings [hogs] here manifest intelligence? **1884** BOWER & SCOTT *De Bary's Phaner.* 38 The superficial position of the stomata is the rule for herbaceous less thick-skinned parts.

2. *fig.* Dull of sensation or feeling; obtuse, stolid; now *esp.* not sensitive to criticism or rebuff; the opposite of *thin-skinned.*

1602 *2nd Pt. Return fr. Parnass.* III. iv. 1383 The Seruile current of my slyding verse, Gently shal runne into his thick skind eares. **1658** SIR T. BROWNE *Hydriot.* Introd. (1736) 8 They who are so Thick-skinned as still to believe the Story of the Phœnix. **1828** SCOTT *Jrnl.* 26 June, He would be thick-skinned if he stands the clamour. **1885** *American* IX. 387 He is too thick-skinned to mind eloquent and indignant criticism.

'thick-'skulled (-skʌld: stress var.), *a.* Having a thick skull; hence *fig.* slow or dull of apprehension; dense, dull-witted; = THICK-HEADED.

a **1653** G. DANIEL *Idyll.* v. 140 As the thick-Skull'd Turke .. It baffles vs, with our owne Instrument. **1673** *Ess. Educ. Gentlewom.* 32 Every thick-skull'd Fellow that babbles this out, thinks no Billingsgate Woman can Answer it. **1755** SMOLLETT *Quix.* I. IV. xxi. (1803) II. 258 Is it possible that your worship can be so thick-skulled and brainless, as not to perceive the truth of what I alledge? **1821** SCOTT *Let. to Cunningham* 27 Apr., The common class of readers..are thick-skulled enough. **1860** EMERSON *Cond. Life, Fate* Wks. II. 317 Thick-skulled, small-brained, fishy..quadruped.

So **'thick-skull**, a thick-skulled person.

1755 JOHNSON, *Dolt*, a heavy stupid fellow; a blockhead; a thickscul; a loggerhead. **1838** JAS. GRANT *Sk. Lond.* 223 Says I, 'You lie, you stupid thickskull!' **1894** CROCKETT *Raiders* 346 Such a thick-skull was I.

'thick-'sown, *a.* Also 8 **thick-sowed.** Sown thickly or with little interval between the seeds. Also *fig.* So **thick-sow** *v.* (*rare*), to sow thickly.

1683 NORRIS *Coll. Misc.* (1687) 429 A little Plot of ground thick-sown. **1712** ADDISON *Spect.* No. 285 ⁋8 Metaphors are not so thick sown in Milton. **1728** MORGAN *Algiers* I. Pref. 14 Many were more inclined to fall on the well-laden thick-sowed English than any others. **1742** YOUNG *Nt. Th.* IX. 1234 To count The thick-sown glories in this field of fire. **1896** *Harper's Mag.* Apr. 671/2 The distances, thick-sown with the faint yellow candle-flames. **1898** *Westm. Gaz.* 7 Oct. 3/1 It is useless to thick-sow your dialogue with 'ess fay' and 'thicky', and 'pretty vitty',..and omit the breath of life and..expression of character.

thick 'un ('θɪkən). *slang.* Also **thick one.** [f. THICK *a.* + UN, 'UN[2] (= ONE *pron.*).] Formerly, a gold sovereign (***half a thick 'un***, ten shillings); ***to smash a thick 'un*** (see SMASH *v.*[2] 2). Also, a crown or five-shilling piece, and rarely in mod. use applied *loosely* to a pound.

1848 *Sessions Papers Cent. Criminal Court* (Kent cases) 7 Mar. 847 Would not a *thick* one or two be very serviceable this cold weather? **1862** *Cornh. Mag.* Nov. 648 If you like.. I will send a few thickuns. **1888** J. PAYN *Eavesdropper* II. ii. 79 'Can you smash a thick un for me?' inquired one, handing his friend a sovereign. **1897** HALL CAINE *Christian* IV. iv. 376 A 'thick 'un'? Oh, that was a sovereign, half a thick'un half a sovereign. **1926** 'SAPPER' *Final Count* iii. 66 Done with you, your Graces; a thick 'un it is. **1968** *Gloss. Brit. Argot* (Paramount Pictures), Quid, nicker, thick 'un, one pound.

†**'thickways**, *adv. Obs. rare.* [f. THICK *a.* + -WAYS.] In the direction of the thickness.

1644 DIGBY *Nat. Bodies* xviii. §1. 158 The ayre..not.. admitting to be diuided thickewayes so much as is necessary to fill the first growing distance, between the two stones. *Ibid.* xxv. §2. 227 If the externe causes had pressed vpon this droppe, only broadwayes and thickewayes..then it would haue proued a cylinder.

'thick-'witted (stress var.), *a.* Having 'thick' wits; dull of intellect, stupid.

1634 W. WOOD *New Eng. Prosp.* To Rdr., I decline this sort of thick-witted readers. **1642** MILTON *Apol. Smect.* Wks. 1851 III. 256 The conceit that all who are not Prelaticall, are grosse-headed, thick-witted, illiterat, shallow. **1821** SCOTT *Kenilw.* xxxv, He is..thick-witted enough to adopt any belief that is thrust on him.

So **'thickwit**, a thick-witted person.

1904 M. HEWLETT *Queen's Quair* III. ii. 376 She cheapened herself in Love's honour and was held cheap by Scotch thickwits.

†**'thicky**, *a. Obs.* [f. THICK *a.* + -Y.] Of a thick nature; inclined to be thick.

1587 A. DAY *Daphnis & Chloe* (1890) 112 Since Ceres first these thickie groues pursued. **1590** GREENE *Mourn. Garm.* Wks. (Rtldg.) 304/2 It was near a thicky shade, That broad leaves of beech had made. **1598** Q. ELIZ. *Plutarch* iv. 26 Fly thou this darke and thikky mysty folded Cloude. *c* **1868** G. M. HOPKINS *Poems* (1967) 211 And light us, Lord, with Thy day-break. Beat from our brains the thicky night And fill the world up with delight.

thicky, *dem. adj.* (*dial.*): see THILK.

thidder, -ir, etc., obs. ff. THITHER.

thie, obs. form of THIGH.

thief (θiːf). *Pl.* **thieves** (θiːvz). Forms: 1 **theb, þíof, þéof,** (**þéaf, þæf**), 2 **þof** (*dat.* **þove**), 2–5 **þeof,** (3 *dat.* **þeve**), 3–4 **þief,** 3–5 **þef, þeef,** 4 **þyef, þefe,** 4–5 **thef, -ff, thif, theyf,** 4–6 **thefe,** 4–7 **theif, theef, -ffe,** 5 (**þeue**), **thife, thyf(e,** 5–6 **theyff,** 5–7 **theefe,** 6 **theaf, theiff, thieffe,** 6–7 **thiefe,** 6– **thief.** *Pl.* also 4 **þewes; þeifs, þefs, theffes,** 4–6 **thefes.** [OE. *þíof, þéof* (North. *þéaf*). Com. Teut.; in OFris. *thiaf*, OS. *thiof* (MDu., Du. *dief*, MLG. *dief, dêf*, LG. *dêf*, pl. *dêven*), OHG. *diob, diup* (MHG. *diep*, Ger. *dieb*); ON. *þiófr* (Sw. *tiuf*, Da. *tyv*), Goth. *þiufs, þiub-*:—OTeut. **þeubo-*, pointing to an Indo-Eur. ablaut-series **teup-, toup-, tup-*: cf. Lith. *tupėti* to crouch down.

The final consonant represents an unvoicing of the stem consonant, which appears in the inflected forms and the derivatives, as pl. *thieves, thievery*, etc.]

1. One who takes portable property from another without the knowledge or consent of the latter, converting it to his own use; one who steals.

a. *spec.* One who does this by stealth; esp. from the person; one who commits theft or larceny.

688–95 *Laws of Ine* c. 12 ȝif ðeof sie ȝefongen. ?*a* **900** *Durh. Adm.* in *O.E.T.* 176 Wið netena ungetionu & ðiofum. *c* **975** *Rushw. Gosp.* Matt. vi. 19 Ne hydeþ eow hord..þær ðiofes [*Lindisf.* ðeafas, *Ags. Gosp.* ðeofas, *Vulg.* fures] adelfaþ ne forstelaþ. *c* **1000** *Ags. Gosp.* John x. 1 Se þe ne gæð æt þam gete into sceapa falde, ac styhþ elles ofer he is þeof [*Lind.* ðeaf, *Rush.* ðæf] & sceaða [*Vulg.* fur et latro]. *c* **1175** *Lamb. Hom.* 29 Rubberes and þa reueres and þa þeoues. *a* **1200** *Moral Ode* 43 (Lamb. MS.), For þer ne þerf he bon of-dred of fure ne of þoue [*v.r.* þeve]. *c* **1200** *Trin. Coll. Hom.* 61 Oðer þurh fur, oðer þurh þiefes, oðer þurh roberie. *c* **1250** *Gen. & Ex.* 1773 Ðu me ransakes als an ðef. *a* **1300** *St. Gregory* 997 in Herrig's *Archiv* LVII. 69 þou þeefes fere, þou ne dost bote make men of þe speke. *a* **1300** *Cursor M.* 4891–2 (Cott.) Yon er theues we lelmen wend, And theif [*v.rr.* thefe, þeof] es he þam hider send. *Ibid.* 15970 Iudas was iesu aumnere, Bath theif [*v.r.* þeef] and traitur bald. *c* **1386** CHAUCER *Doctor's T.* 83 A theef [*v.rr.* theefe, þeef, þef, þeof] of venyson..Kan kepe a fforest best of any man. **1390** GOWER *Conf.* I. 52 So that an yhe is as a thief To love, and doth ful gret meschief. *c* **1420** *Chron. Vilod.* 2923 Bot þe Iaylardes folowedone þis theff fulle fast. *a* **1425** *Cursor M.* 7234 (Trin.) Þer is noon so myche may greue As traitour derne & priue þeue. **14..** *Nom.* in Wr.-Wülcker 694/1 *Hic..fur*, a theffe. *c* **1470** HENRY *Wallace* II. 392, I trow thow be sum spy, Or ellis a theyff. **1532–3** *Act 24 Hen. VIII*, c. 5 An Acte where a Man kyllyng a Theffe shall not forfayte his Goodes. **1596** SHAKS. *Merch. V.* III. i. 97 The theefe gone with so much, and so much to finde the theefe, and no satisfaction, no reuenge. **1605** CAMDEN *Rem.* 229 When thou commest into a strange place, thinke all men there to be theeves. **1643** SIR T. BROWNE *Relig. Med.* I. §46 How comes He then like a theefe in the night? **1678** BUNYAN *Pilgr.* I. 163 Thou art a Theif and a Robber. *Ibid.* 165 He did hang his head like a Thief. **1769** COOK *Voy. round World* I. x. (1773) 100 The people of this country [Otaheite],..are the errantest thieves upon the face of the earth. **1878** STUBBS *Const. Hist.* III. xviii. 243 There is more spirit and a better heart in a robber than in a thief. **1879** JEFFERIES *Wild Life in S.C.* 160 The robin is accused of being a terrible thief of currants.

b. In more general sense, comprehending such as rob with violence; e.g. robbers, freebooters, pirates, etc.; now *rare* exc. as a general designation of one who obtains goods by fraudulent means, over-reaching, deceit, etc.

border thieves, the freebooters of the Scottish Border, whose depredations were so notorious in the 16th century. † ***thief of the sea***, a pirate, SEA-THIEF.

In the Revised Version of the N.T., in all cases where *thief* in the 1611 version renders λῃστής, Vulg. *latro*, it is changed to *robber*, and *thief* only retained where it renders κλέπτης, Vulg. *fūr*.

a **700** *Epinal Gloss* (O.E.T.) 630 *Mimoparo*, thebscib. *c* **950** *Lindisf. Gosp.* Matt. xxi. 13 ȝie worhton ða ilca cofa (*vel* græfe) ðeafana [*Vulg.* latronum *c* **975** *Rushw. Gosp.* ibid., ȝescræfe ðiofas (*vel* scaþena), *c* **1000** *Ags. Gosp.* þeofa cote]. *c* **1000** *Ags. Gosp.* Matt. xxvi. 55 Eall-swa to þeofe [*Lindsif.* mor-sceaðe, *Rushw.* scaþe, *Vulg.* latronem] ȝe synt cumene mid swurdum. —— John xviii. 40 Witodlice barrabbas wæs þeof [*Lindisf.* morsceaðe, *Rushw.* sceaða, *Vulg.* latro, Gr. λῃστής, WYCLIF, *Rhem.* theef, theefe, TINDALE, 1611 robber]. *c* **1200** *Vices & Virt.* 51 Betwenen twa þieues. *a* **1300** *Cursor M.* 10297 (Cott.) Stalworth men..þat moght again þe theues [*v.r.* thefes] fight. *c* **1330** R. BRUNNE *Chron. Wace* (Rolls) 6631 þise Sarsynes þeues þey drof awey. **1340** *Ayenb.* 37 þer ys a þyef open and a þyef ywreȝe, a þief priue and a þyef uelaȝe. **13..** *E.E. Allit. P.* B. 1142 Hit were rafte wyth vnryȝt & robbed wyth þewes. **1382** WYCLIF *Matt.* xxvii. 38 Thanne two theeues [*Vulg.* latrones] ben crucified with him. **1387** TREVISA *Higden* (Rolls) I. 329 þe men of þat lond beeþ schipmen and þeues of þe see. **1436** *Libel Eng. Policy* in *Pol. Poems* (Rolls) II. 164 The grettest rovers and the grettest thevys That have bene in the see many oone yere. **1533** GAU *Richt Vay* (S.T.S.) 93 The tirannis and oppressours and theyffis. **1567** SIR R. MAITLAND *Complaynt* i, Of Liddisdaill the commoun theifis Sa pertlie steillis now and reifis, That nane may keip Hors, nolt, nor scheip: Nor yit dar sleip, For thair mischeifis. *Ibid.* iv, Thay thiefis have neirhand herreit haill Ettricke forest and Lawderdaill. **1651** HOBBES *Leviath.* I. x. 45 Till there were constituted great Commonwealths, it was thought no dishonour to be..a High-way Theefe. **1678** R. L'ESTRANGE *Seneca's Mor.* II. vii. (1705) 150 Nothing is more Common, than for Great Thieves to ride in Triumph, when the Little ones are punish'd. **1712** tr. *Arab. Nights* (1785) 561/2 The Story of Ali Baba, and the Forty Thieves. **1892** KIPLING *Ballad of East & W.* 24 Who rides at the tail of a Border thief, he sits not long at his meat.

c. In proverbial expressions.

c **1230** *Hali Meid.* 17 Man seið þat eise makeð þeof. **1539** TAVERNER *Erasm. Prov.* (1552) 65 Aske my felowe if I be a thefe. **1546** J. HEYWOOD *Prov.* (1867) 20 A paterne, as meete as a rope for a theefe. **1562** *Ibid.* 151 When theeues fall out, trewe men come to their goode. **1670** RAY *Prov.* 129 Opportunity makes the thief. *Ibid.* 148 Set a thief to take a thief. **1791** BENTHAM *Panopt.* Wks. 1843 IV. 225 A sort of honour may be found (according to a proverbial saying) even among thieves. **1833** [see THICK *a.* 10].

d. *fig.* That which steals or furtively takes away.

1742 YOUNG *Nt. Th.* I. 393 Procrastination is the thief of time. **1838** L. HUNT *Rondeau* 3 Time, you thief, who love to get Sweets into your list, put that in.

2. a. As a general term of reproach or opprobrium: Evil man, villain, scoundrel. (Still *dial.*)

1297 R. GLOUC. (Rolls) 5621 þis þef þat lay bi neþe..smot þen king..in þe brust. *a* **1300** *K. Horn.* 323 Hennes þu go, þu fule þeof. **13..** *Cursor M.* 736 (Fairf.) He sayde þaire ioy walde be mykel þis fals þefe þat was so fikel. *c* **1400** *Laud Troy Bk.* 15271 This wicked theff Achilles Thi bretheren hath sclayn with-oute les. *c* **1425** *Cast. Persev.* 1137 in *Macro Plays* 111 For ilke man callyth oþer 'hore & thefe'. *a* **1548** HALL *Chron., Hen. IV.* 12 b, Thou trayter thefe, thou hast bene a traitour to kyng Richard. **1653** HOLCROFT *Procopius, Goth. Wars* III. 107 These Theeves alledge, to provoke you to a War, our holding Syrmium, and some other places in Dacia. *a* **1800** PEGGE *Suppl. Grose, Thief*, a general term of reproach, not confined to stealing. **1893** STEVENSON *Catriona* ix. 102 Yon thief of the black midnight, Simon Fraser.

b. *old* (*auld*), *ill thief*: the Devil. *Sc. dial.*

1789 BURNS *To Dr. Blacklock* ii, The ill-thief blaw the Heron south! **1822** HOGG *Perils of Man* III. 38 Cuffed about by the 'auld thief' as they styled him. **1893** *Westm. Gaz.* 21 Feb. 9/2 What does D stand for?—The first letter o' the Auld Thief's name.

3. *transf.* †**a.** Applied to a goshawk (*obs.*). †**b.** A kind of wild bee said to rob hives (*obs.*). **c.** A shoot from the root of a vine, rose-bush, or other trained shrub, which robs the main stem of its strength. **d.** *Mod. slang.* A horse that does not run up to form in a race.

1486 *Bk. St. Albans* d ij, A Goshawke shulde not flie to any fowle of the Ryuer with bellis in no wise, and therfore a Goshawke is calde a theef. **1608** TOPSELL *Serpents* (1658) 650 Some have thought that Theeves are one proper sort of Bees, although they be very great, and black, having a larger belly or bulk then the true Bee, and yet lesser then the drones. **1658** ROWLAND *Moufet's Theat. Ins.* 920 The Theeves being naturally odious to the Bees, steal upon their labours when they are absent, wasting and spoyling their provision of honey. **1669** J. ROSE *Eng. Vineyard* (1675) 28 Rubbing off the thieves which sprung from the roots of the plant. **1896** J. PORTER *Kingsclere* 127 Gay Hampton.. turned out a terrible 'thief', and a savage.

4. 'An excrescence in the snuff of a candle' (J.) which causes it to gutter and waste.

1628 MAY *Virg. Georg.* I. 436 Theeues about the snuffe doe grow. *a* **1633** FLETCHER & SHIRLEY *Night-Walker* II. i, Methinks the light burns blew, I prethee snuff it, There's a thief in't I think. **1642** HOWELL *For. Trav.* (Arb.) 77 If there bee a theefe in the Candle, (as wee use to say commonly) there is a way to pull it out. **1665** BOYLE *Occas. Reflect.* II. x, Upon a Thief in a Candle. **1796** MME. D'ARBLAY *Camilla* II. 407 [He] perceived a thief in the candle, which made it run down..over his hand and the sleeve of his coat. **1824** LAMB *Let. to Barton* 9 Jan., My wick hath a thief in it, but I can't muster courage to snuff it.

5. *attrib.* and *Comb.*, as *thief-catching*, *-colony*, *-craft*, *-den*, *-detector*, *-maker*; *thief-proof*, *-resistant*, *-resisting*, *-stolen* adjs.; **thief and reever bell**: see quots.; **thief-ant**, a small ant of the genus *Solenopsis* which raids the nests of other ants to steal food; **thief-bote**: see THEFT-BOOT; **thief-catcher**, (*a*) one who catches thieves; = THIEF-TAKER; (*b*) a device used formerly in apprehending thieves; **thief-key**, a skeleton key; †**thief-land**, a name for Botany Bay; †**thief-leader**, a thief-taker; **thief-tube**: see quot.; †**thef-wyke**: see quot. Also with *thieves'*, as **thieves' cat**: see quots.; **thieves' hole**, a dungeon reserved for thieves; **thieves' kitchen**: see KITCHEN *sb.* 1 b; **thieves' Latin**, cant used by thieves; **thieves' market**, a street market of a type found in many Eastern cities and elsewhere, at which cheap (sometimes, stolen) goods are offered for sale; cf. *flea market* s.v. FLEA *sb.* 6; **thieves' vinegar**, an infusion of rosemary tops, sage leaves, etc. in vinegar, formerly esteemed as an antidote against the plague. Also THIEF-LIKE, -TAKER.

1777 BRAND *Pop. Antiq.* 17 A Bell, usually called the *Thief and Reever Bell, proclaims our two annual Fairs. **1825** BROCKETT *N.C. Words*, *Thief and Reever-Bell*, the name given to the tolling of the great bell of Saint Nicholas, Newcastle, which is rung at 8 o'clock of the evening preceding every fair. **1904** W. M. WHEELER in *Amer. Naturalist* XXXVI. 952 The walls of the galleries in some of the formicaries were tenanted by teeming colonies of the ..*thief ant. **1971** E. O. WILSON *Insect Societies* xix. 357/1 Colonies of the 'thief ants'..often nest next to larger ant species. **1732** *Hist. Litteraria* IV. 83 The Draper, to engage the *Thief-catcher to his Interests, made him a Present of a Suit of Clothes. **1851** H. MELVILLE *Moby Dick* III. xxii. 150 What art thou thrusting that thief-catcher into my face for, man? Thrusted light is worse than presented pistols. **1891** *Daily News* 6 Nov. 3/1 The thief-catcher..is a shrewd piece of work, from which no head, leg, or arm could extricate itself once caught. **1737** *Gentl. Mag.* VII. 592/1, I do not know that the Army has ever been employed in any sort of *Thief-catching, except with respect to those Thieves called Smugglers. **1786** A. DALRYMPLE (*title*) A Serious Admonition to the Publick, on the Intended *Thief-Colony at Botany Bay. **1859** W. ANDERSON *Disc.* (1860) 291 Adepts in the fashionable *thief-craft. **1844** POE *Marginalia* in *Wks.* (1902) XVI. 20 A race of dolts..whose clumsily stolen bulls never fail of leaving behind them ample evidence of having been dragged into the *thief-den by the tail. **1909** *Cent. Dict. Suppl.*, **Thief-detector*..a delicate microphone designed for seismological studies, but so arranged by Milne that it gives notice of tremors produced by the gentlest footstep in its neighborhood. **1820** *Examiner* No. 614. 39/2 Inauspicious unliterary *Thiefland. **1692** R. L'ESTRANGE *Fables* cccclxvii. 441 A Wolf had the Fortune to pass by, as the *Thief-Leaders were Dragging a..Fox to the Place of Execution. **1856** G. PRICE (*title*) A Treatise on Fire & *Thief-proof Depositories. **1963** *B.S.I. News* June 9/1 It was the insurance companies and police who first asked the British Standards Institution to lay down a standard for locks for outside doors which really should be *thief-resistant. **1968** *Observer* 22 Dec. 22/2 Locks should be built in and made to British Standard 3621, which ensures that they are thief-resistant although not thief-proof. **1904** *Daily Chron.* 29 Sept. 1/6 Safes.., fire and *thief-resisting. **1551** ROBINSON tr. *More's Utop.* I. (1895) 66 The Kynge; whome they thynke to haue no more ryghte to the *thefe stolen thynge than the thieffe himselfe hath. **1611** SHAKS. *Cymb.* I. vi. 5 Had I bin Theefe-stolne. **1877** KNIGHT *Dict. Mech.*, **Thief-tube*, a tube for withdrawing of liquids from casks, etc. A sampling-tube; a ve-linche. *c* **1350** in *Eng. Gilds* (1870) 350 þer sholde be twey baylyues y-swore in þe Citee, and treweleche þe *þef-wyke wytye.

1867 SMYTH *Sailor's Word-bk.*, **Thieves' Cat*, a cat-o'-nine-tails having knots upon it..used for the punishment of theft. **1899** *Daily News* 19 Sept. 6/3 The 'cat' used at Macquarie Harbour..was called 'the thief's cat', or 'double cat o' nine-tails'. **1578** *Burgh Rec. Edinb.* (1882) IV. 86 For ..dichting of the new wall, clenging of the *thevis hoill, and the vther the commoun affaris. **1864** A. MCKAY *Hist. Kilmarnock* (1880) 45 A loathsome dungeon called the Thieves'-hole. **1821** SCOTT *Kenilw.* xxix, A very learned man..and can vent Greek and Hebrew as fast as I can *thieves'-Latin. **1840** *Comic Lat. Gram.* 16 Thieves' Latin, more commonly known by the name of slang... Examples, to prig a wipe—to steal a handkerchief [etc.]. **1873** TROLLOPE *Eustace Diamonds* II. xlvii. 278 If such a lot of diamonds had been through the *thieves' market in London, they would have left some track behind them. [**1927** B. DIQUI *Visit to Bombay* 62 Null Bazaar is..a big market... An interesting section..is the Chor Bazaar. Chor really means 'thieves.' Chor Bazaar, then, means the bazaar of thieves. Probably in the past thieves disposed of their stolen property here. In this bazaar—the Petticoat Lane of Bombay—you can buy secondhand articles of any description.] **1953** S. BEDFORD *Sudden View* I. xi. 103 The Thieves' Market at Mexico City..where thieves offer goods for sale during a limited time to give the owners a chance. **1979** P. DRISCOLL *Pangolin* xiv. 114 Upper Lascar Row, better known as Cat Street, the thieves' market of Hong Kong. **1802** MRS. J. WEST *Infidel Father* III. 5 Conversation was for some days confined to ipecacuanha, '*thieves' vinegar, and smoked tobacco.

Hence **'thiefwise** *adv. rare* = THIEF-LIKE *adv.*

1898 W. J. LOCKE *Idols* vi. 75 Creeping thiefwise up the stairs. **1904** HARDY *Dynasts* I. IV. iii. 114 Stealing up to us Thiefwise, by our back door.

thiefdom, thievedom ('θiːfdəm, 'θiːvdəm). [f. THIEF + -DOM.]

1. The practice of theft; thieving, robbery. *rare.*

α. **1548** HOOPER *Declar. Commandm.* xi. 180 The grettist thyffdomme of all is Sacrilege, in robbing of the goodes appointid to an holye vse.

β. **1562** PHAER *Æneid* x. Dd iij, Who did their league by theuedom breke? **1887** P. M'NEILL *Blawearie* 153 A' we made by our thievdom, was—I lost a tooth and had my dowg's tail destroyed.

2. The realm or domain of thieves.

α. **1864** *Sat. Rev.* 27 Aug. 272/1 A narrative illustrative of London thiefdom. **1888** A. WARDROP *Poems & Sk.* 193 Literary thiefdom and Yankeedom are now synonymous.

β. **1862** *Cornh. Mag.* Nov. 645 A fiddler to play at the thievedom carnivals. **1870** H. W. HOLLAND in *Gd. Words* 1 June 391/2 In the interior of thievedom they have public-houses, beer-houses, shops, and lodging-houses, almost entirely to themselves.

thief-like ('θiːflaɪk), *a.* and *adv.* [f. THIEF + LIKE *a.* and *adv.*] **a.** *adj.* Like or resembling a thief. **b.** *adv.* In the manner of a thief.

1621 FLETCHER *Pilgrim* II. ii, But since thou stealst upon me like a spie, And thief-like thinkst that holy case shall carry thee Through all my purposes. **1760–72** H. BROOKE *Fool of Qual.* (1809) IV. 25 Each of them, thief-like, wished to steal an unobserved gaze at the other. **1847** EMERSON *Poems* (1857) 143 And thief-like step of liberal hours Thawing snow-drift into flowers.

†**'thiefly**, *a.* and *adv. Obs.* [ME. *þeoflich*(*e*, *þevelich*:—OE. **þéoflic*, *-líce*: see THIEF and -LY[1,2].]

A. *adj.* Thief-like, stealthy, underhand.

1395 PURVEY *Remonstr.* (1851) 11 It is theefli, fals and symonient. *c* **1422** HOCCLEVE *Learn to Die* 115 Ful vnwaar was Y of thy theefly breid.

B. *adv.* In a thievish or thief-like manner; by stealth; stealthily, furtively.

c **1290** *St. Brandan* 284 in *S. Eng. Leg.* I. 227 ȝwan it is ov i-brouȝt, þane ȝe it þeofliche nomen. **1377** LANGL. *P. Pl.* B. XVIII. 336 Theuelich þow me robbedest. **1382** WYCLIF *Gen.* xl. 15 Theuelich [**1388** theefli] Y am had a wey fro the loond of Hebrew. **1387** TREVISA *Higden* (Rolls) VI. 63 (MS. α) Seynt Oswald his arm..was þeefliche [*v.rr.* þeevelich, þuefliche; CAXTON theefly] i-stole out of þe olde restynge place. **1568** SKEYNE *The Pest* A ij b, Ane feuir most wikit quietlie and thieflie strikis the patient.

thieft, thiefthe, obs. forms of THEFT.

'thief-,taker. One who detects and captures a thief; *spec.* one of a company who undertook the detection and arrest of thieves.

1535 STEWART *Cron. Scot.* (Rolls) I. 87 The theif takar suld haif the forder spald. **1700** T. BROWN *Amusem. Ser. & Com.* viii. (1709) 84 Serv'd the State in the Quality of Marshal's Men, and Thief-Takers. **1718** C. HITCHIN (*title*) A True Discovery of the Conduct of Receivers and Thief-takers in and about the City of London. **1761** *Chron.* in *Ann. Reg.* 76/2 Two thief-takers, in hopes of entrapping the highwayman.., set out..like travellers. **1840** DICKENS *Barn. Rudge* lxi, A body of thief-takers had been keeping watch in the house all night.

So **thief-taking** (in quot. *attrib.*).

1771 SMOLLETT *Humph. Cl.* (1815) 188 He had been for some time in the snares of the thief-taking society.

thiefteously, obs. form of THEFTUOUSLY.

thien, þien, var. THYNE *adv. Obs.*, thence.

thier, obs. form of THEIR, THIR (these).

Thiersch (tiːəʃ). *Surg.* The name of Karl *Thiersch* (1822–95), German surgeon, used *attrib.* and formerly in the possessive with reference to a split-skin graft including only superficial layers, so that regeneration of the donor area can occur (described by him in *Verhandl. d. Deutsch. Ges. f. Chir.* (1874) III. 69).

1890 W. J. WALSHAM *Surgery* (ed. 3) I. 35 New method of skin-grafting (Thiersch's). **1892** KEEN & WHITE *Amer. Text-bk. Surg.* IV. iii. 1095 (*heading*) Thiersch's method of skin-grafting. **1911** F. S. KOUE *Plastic & Cosmetic Surg.* xi. 180 The remaining raw surface is either allowed to heal by granulation or is covered immediately with Thiersch grafts. **1977** *Brit. Med. Jrnl.* 29 Jan. 278/1 Simple division with a Thiersch graft to the raw areas suffices.

thiethe, obs. erron. form of TITHE.

thieve (θiːv), *v.* [In OE. *þéofian*, f. *þéof*, THIEF. The verb is rare in OE., after which it does not appear till the 17th c. The vbl. sb. *thieving* occurs from 1530. (For the *v.* see note to THIEF.)]

1. *intr.* To act as a thief, commit theft, steal.

[*a* **901** *Laws of Ælfred* c. 6 ȝif hwa on ciricean hwæt ȝeðeo-fiȝe.] *c* **920** in Thorpe *Charters* (1865) 177 Se ðe..ða are þænce to þeofiȝenne. **1530, 1598** [see THIEVING *vbl. sb.* and *ppl. a.*]. **1627** DRAYTON *Mooncalf* 1067 And there this monster sat him down to thieve. **1656** S. H. *Gold. Law* 11 Thus to Traytorize, Murther, and Thieve it. **1691–2** WOOD *Life* 13 Jan. (O.H.S.) III. 380 Foot-soldiers..rob and theeve in Oxon. **1848** DICKENS *Dombey* xxii, I never did such a thing as thieve.

2. *trans.* To steal (a thing).

a **1695** WOOD *Oxford* (O.H.S.) III. 172 A brass plate having been theeved away. **1760–72** H. BROOKE *Fool of Qual.* (1809) IV. 7 He endeavoured to thieve from me the only friend I had. **1867** *Pall Mall G.* 27 July 9 The prisoner ..said it was the first time he had 'thieved' anything. **1901** *Academy* 23 Mar. 243 Goods to the value of a quarter of a million..were annually thieved out of ships in the Pool.

Hence **'thievable** *a.*, that may be stolen; **'thiever**, one who thieves, a thief.

1615 J. STEPHENS *Ess. & Char.*, *Warrener*, Where he hath many night-spels, to the hazard of much Pullen, and indeed all things thieve-able. **1899** LUMSDEN *Edinburgh Poems & Songs* 105 Wha hack'd an' hash'd an' stole, Like reivers an' thievers.

thievedom: see THIEFDOM.

thieve-friend. *nonce-wd.* A friend of thieves. So **'thieveland**, a land of thieves; a district full of thieves; whence **'thievelander** [-ER[1] 1].
1599 PORTER *Angry Wom. Abingd.* I iij, Let not this theefe friend misty vale of night, Incroach on day. **1642** SHIRLEY *Sisters* I. i, Ye are all valiant, honest Thievelanders, And I will be your prince again.

thieveless ('θiːvlɪs), *a. Sc.* [Of uncertain origin; first in Ramsay, ? misreading of earlier *theueles*, THEWLESS, to which it answers in sense.] Void of energy, ineffectual, aimless; spiritless, not serious; cold, without warmth of manner.
1725 RAMSAY *Gentle Sheph.* I. i, She cam wi a right thieveless errand back. **1786** BURNS *Brigs of Ayr* 89 Wi' thieveless sneer to see his modish mien, He, down the water, gies him this guid-e'en. **1835** CARRICK *Laird of Logan* 289 (E.D.D.) She answered in a gay, thieveless-like way. **1897** R. M. FERGUSSON *Vill. Poet* xiii. 80 He..appeared listless, or, as he himself expressed it, 'rale thieveless'.

b. 'Applied to weather in a sort of intermediate or uncertain state. Thus, a thieveless day is one that has no decided character, neither properly good nor bad' (Jamieson, s.v. *Thewles*).

thievely, variant of THIEFLY *Obs.*

thievery ('θiːvərɪ). [f. THIEF, *thiev-* (see note in etym. s.v.), or THIEVE *v.* + -ERY.]
1. The committing or practice of theft; stealing. With *a* and *pl.*, An act of thieving.
1568 FULWELL *Like Will to Like* E j b, Yet better it is to beg moste shamefully, Then to be hanged and to theeuery our selues frame. **1580** *Apol. Pr. Orange* in *Pœnix* (1721) I. 479 Their Thieveries and Sackings. **1623** T. SCOT *Highw. God* 21 But the Theefe proceedes in his theeuery till he brings himselfe to the gallowes. **1722** DE FOE *Col. Jack* vii, They were whipped so for picking pockets, and other petty thieveries. **1840** CARLYLE *Heroes* iv. (1872) 138 We do not 'tolerate' Falsehoods, Thieveries, Iniquities. **1871** R. ELLIS *Catullus* xlvii. 2 The greedy Piso's Tools of thievery, rogues to famish ages.
2. The result or produce of thieving; stolen property. Cf. PILFERY 3.
1583 STOCKER *Civ. Warres Lowe C.* IV. 23 b, The Spaniardes departed Mastright, with their butin and theeuerie. **1606** SHAKS. *Tr. & Cr.* IV. iv. 45 Now with a robbers haste Crams his rich theeuerie vp, he knowes not how. **1873** BROWNING *Red Cott. Nt.-cap* II. 720 A veriest trap of twigs On tree-top, every straw a thievery.

thieving ('θiːvɪŋ), *vbl. sb.* [app. f. THIEVE *v.* + -ING[1]; but perh. f. THIEF *sb.*]
1. The action of a thief; the committing of theft; stealing. Also *attrib.*
1530 PALSGR. 699/2 A nyghtes he gothe a thevyng. **1571** GOLDING *Calvin on Ps.* x. 8 They made royall palaces theyr theeuing-places, too cut silie mens throtes in. **1634** SIR T. HERBERT *Trav.* 185 These Mallabars..excell in theeuing. **1892** SYMONDS *Michel Angelo* (1899) II. xi. 54 Your failure to discharge your obligations is regarded as an act of thieving.
2. *concr.* A thing obtained by theft.
1861 THORNBURY *Turner* (1862) I. 328 The Louvre, at that time full of Napoleon's magnificent thievings.

'thieving, *ppl. a.* [f. as prec. + -ING[2].] That thieves or acts like a thief.
1598 MARSTON *Pygmal.* v 157 Theeuing Mercury That euen in his new borne infancy Stole faire Apollos quiuer. **1823** SCOTT *Quentin D.* vi, I will teach these misbelieving, thieving sorcerers, to interfere with the King's justice. **1897** MARY KINGSLEY *W. Africa* vi. 107 Canoes..drawn up out of the reach of the ever-mischievous, thieving sea.
†**b.** *thieving nutmeg*: see quot. *Obs.*
1668 *Phil. Trans.* III. 863 The Nutmeg called Theeving; because that being put among a whole room full of good Nutmegs, though it be but one, it will corrupt them all. **1681** GREW *Musæum* IV. iii. 376 The Fruit..of..the Thieving-Nutmeg, because it infects and spoils the good ones where it lies. **1693** SIR T. P. BLOUNT *Nat. Hist.* 45.
Hence **'thievingly** *adv.*, by way of thieving, theftuously.
1880 RUSKIN *Fors Clav.* lxxxix. 144 Every pleasure got.. cheaply, thievingly, and swiftly.

thievish ('θiːvɪʃ), *a.* Forms: α. 5 **thef-**, 6 **theaffish.** β. 5–6 **theu-**, 6 **thev-**, 6–7 **theeu-**, 6–8 **theev-**, 6– **thievish.** [f. THIEF, *thiev-* (see note in etym. s.v.) + -ISH[1].]
†**1.** Infested or frequented by thieves. *Obs.*
1483 *Cath. Angl.* 382/2 Thefyische (*A.* A Thefis place), *crebrifurus, spoliatorium.* **1535** COVERDALE *1 Macc.* i. 35 Thus became it a theuysh castell. **1541** BIBLE (Cranmer) *Ps.* x. 8 He syteth lurkyng in yᵉ theuish corners of the stretes. **1592** SHAKS. *Rom. & Jul.* IV. i. 79 Or walke in theeuish waies. **1632** LITHGOW *Trav.* VII. 335 Three French murderers set vppon me in a theeuish Wood.
2. Inclined or given to thieving; dishonest.
1538 ELYOT, *Furax, acis*, theuyshe, a great picker. **1552** HULOET, Theaffyshe and thieuyshe, *furax, cis.* **1555** EDEN *Decades* 300 A theeuysshe kynd of men. **1575** *Gamm. Gurton* v. ii, A theeuisher knaue is not on liue. **1634** SIR T. HERBERT *Trav.* 236 Rashboots a theeuish but valiant people in India vnder the Mogul. **1748** *Anson's Voy.* III. x. 414 Their Magistrates are corrupt their people thievish. **1883** J. GILMOUR *Mongols* xxxi. 363 The Mongol is despised as ignorant, dirty, stupid, and thievish.
3. Of, pertaining to, or characteristic of a thief or thieves; thief-like; furtive, stealthy.
c **1450**, *c* **1460** [implied in THIEVISHLY, -NESS]. **1587** TURBERV. *Trag. T.* (1837) 152 Yet wrought it not so well, For all their theevish pace. **1600** SHAKS. *A.Y.L.* II. iii. 33 Enforce A theeuish liuing on the common rode. *c* **1600** —— *Sonn.* lxxvii, Times theeuish progresse to eternitie. **1691** HARTCLIFFE *Virtues* 95 According to the manner of Thievish War, the Conqueror by Proclamation gave away the Houses and Possessions of such as were vanquished. **1735** THOMSON *Liberty* III. 399 Corruption's Thievish Arts. **1837** W. IRVING *Capt. Bonneville* III. 8 Their extortion, and their thievish propensities.

thievishly ('θiːvɪʃlɪ), *adv.* [f. prec. + -LY[2].] In a thievish manner; as a thief; furtively, by stealth.
c **1450** in Aungier *Syon* (1840) 265 Any instrumente,..by the whiche sche myghte escape theueschely out of pryson. **1628** WITHER *Brit. Rememb.* IV. 664 Some, theevishly, purloyned from the sick. **1708** *Brit. Apollo* No. 64. 2/2 A Woman so thievishly inclined. **1855** SINGLETON *Virgil* I. 128 Fire..thievishly beneath the fatty bark At first concealed, hath on the timber seized.

thievishness ('θiːvɪʃnɪs). [f. as prec. + -NESS.] The quality or condition of being thievish.
c **1460** METHAM *Wks.* 94 Yt sygnyfyith onstabylnes and ontrwth and theuyschnes. **1727** BAILEY Vol. II, *Thievishness*, Addictedness to Stealing. **1907** *19th Cent.* Apr. 567 Attacking the spite, frivolity, vanity,..thievishness and similar endearing qualities of the sex.

†**'thievously**, *adv. Obs.* = THIEVISHLY.
1658 BROMHALL *Treat. Specters* I. 92 [They] thievously stole to the shore through rough and hard rocks.

thif(e, thift(e, -th(e, obs. ff. THIEF, THEFT.

thife-thorn, variant of THEVE-THORN *Obs.*

thig (θɪg), *v.* Now *Sc.* Forms: 1 **þicg(e)an,** 2 **þigg(i)en,** 3–5 **thigge,** 3–8 **thigg,** 4–5 **thygg,** 5–6 **thyg,** (6 **thige**), 4– **thig.** [OE. *þicg(e)an, þeah, þáh-, þǽȝon, þeȝen* to take, esp. as food; also as a weak vb., pa. t. *þiȝ(e)de.* ME. *thigge*, a. ON. *þiggja, þá-, þǫ́gum, þágum, þegen* to receive (Sw. *tigga*, Da. *tigge* to beg); cf. OS. *thiggian* to beg, OHG. *dikken*, etc. (MHG. *digen*) to beg; :—OTeut. **þigjan* (with *j* suffix as in **ligjan* LIE *v.*[1], **sitjan* SIT *v.*), f. root **þig-*: *þag-*: *þǣg-*:—Indo-Eur. **tegh*: *togh-*: *tēgh.*
The OE. vb., which would have given *thidge* or perh. *thie, thy* in mod. Eng. (cf. LIE, SAY), was lost *a* 1150, and its place was taken in the north by the Norse form, with modification of sense.]
†**1.** *trans.* To take, receive, accept; *esp.* to take (food), to consume by eating or drinking.
a **864** *O.E. Chron.* an. 755 (Parker MS.) And hiera se æþeling ȝehwelcum feoh and feorh ȝebead and hiera næniȝ hit ȝeþicgean [*Laud MS. c* **1100** þicgan] nolde. *c* **1000** *Ags. Gosp.* Mark vii. 5 Hwi..þine leorning-cnihtas.. besmitenum handum hyra hlaf þicgað [*c* **1160** *Hatton Gosp.*, þiggieð]. *c* **1000** *Sax. Leechd.* III. 92 Þiȝe þar of anne cuppan fulle on ærne morȝe and oþerne on niht. *c* **1175** *Lamb. Hom.* 105 Temperantia þet is metnesse on englisc, þet mon beo imete on alle þing and to muchel ne þigge on ete and on wete.
2. To receive by begging; to beg (alms, one's food, etc.); in mod. *Sc.*, to solicit gifts on special occasions, esp. on setting up housekeeping, etc.: cf. THIGGING *vbl. sb.* quots. 1827, 1872.
c **1300** *Havelok* 1373 He haueth me do[n] mi mete to thigge, And ofte in sorwe and pine ligge. *c* **1375** *Sc. Leg. Saints* xxiv. (*Alexis*) 169 [He] Ilke day thigyt his lyf-led. *c* **1400** *Destr. Troy* 13549 Now me bus, as a beggar, my bred for to thigge. **1561** *Maitl. Club Misc.* III. 282 My brother is and salbe Vicar of Crayll quhen thow sal thyg thy mayt fals smayk. **1887** J. SERVICE *Dr. Duguid* III. iv. 262 He gaed to the gaits' hoose to thig 'oo' [= wool]. **1894** P. H. HUNTER *J. Inwick* xi. 145 Syne thig a' they can get aff the pairish.
b. *intr.* To beg, cadge.
a **1300** *E.E. Psalter* cviii. [cix.] 10 Drecchand his sones be outborne awai, And thigg mote þai, night and dai. *c* **1470** HENRYSON *Mor. Fab.* IV. (*Fox's Conf.*) xiv, I eschame to thig, I can not wirk. **1665** J. FRASER *Polichron.* (S.H.S.) 281, I will not goe begg nor thigg amongst my friends. **1818** SCOTT *Rob Roy* xxvi, Lang-legged Hieland gillies that..maun gang thigging and sorning about on their acquaintance. *Note. Thigging* and *sorning* was a kind of genteel begging, or rather something between begging and robbing, by which the needy in Scotland used to extort cattle, or the means of subsistence, from those who had any to give. **1895** CROCKETT *Men of Moss-Hags* 166 Ye see it's treason to hae sic a thing, and rank conspiracy to thig and barter to get it back.
c. *trans.* To take, borrow (as a quotation).
1728 RAMSAY *Epist. to D. Forbes* xi, I'll frae a Frenchman thigg a fable, And busk it in a plaid. **1728** —— *Adv. to Mr. —— on his Marriage* 22 And blaw ye up with windy fancies, That he has thigit frae romances.
†**3.** To crave, request, ask (a boon, a favour, leave); in quot. *c* 1470[2] with the person as obj. *Obs.*
c **1450** *St. Cuthbert* (Surtees) 3565 Bot of thi grace we thyg To vouche safe with us to ligg. *c* **1470** HENRY *Wallace* II. 260 Scho..thyggyt leiff away with him to fayr. *c* **1470** HENRYSON *Mor. Fab.* IX. (*Wolf & Fox*) xiii, Thocht we wald thig 3one verray Churlische chuf, He will not gif vs ane hering of his Creill. **1513** DOUGLAS *Æneis* VII. x. 75 Thay thyg vengence at the goddis. *a* **1568** BALNAVES in *Bannatyne Poems* (Hunter. Cl.) 391 To tar and tig, syne grace to thig, That is ane petouss preiss.
†**b.** *intr. Obs.*
c **1375** *Sc. Leg. Saints* I. (*Katerine*) 1144 Graunt þaim þar bowne, I thig at þe. *a* **1578** LINDESAY *Chron. Scot.* (S.T.S.) I. 125 They war faine to thige and cry for peace.
Hence **thig** *sb.*, begging, mendicancy.
1898 *Blackw. Mag.* July 82/1 Master Brown sat.. studying through horn specks the tale of thig and theft which the town officer had made up a report on.

thigger ('θɪgə(r)). *Sc.* [f. THIG *v.* + -ER[1].] One who thigs; a beggar, a cadger; an exactor of contributions; one who plants himself on others for assistance; 'one who draws on others for subsistence in a genteel sort of way' (Jamieson); a gaberlunzie or licensed beggar who went his regular rounds, and received a night's lodging and food at particular houses; also, any one who begged or solicited presents on certain recognized occasions, e.g. wedding-presents.
1424 *Sc. Acts Jas. I* (1879) II. 8 þat na thiggar be thollyt to thyg noþer in burghe nor to land. *a* **1733** *Shetland Acts* 4 in *Proc. Soc. Ant. Scot.* (1892) XXVI. 196 That all thiggers of wool, corn, fish and others be apprehended wherever they come. **1822** SCOTT *Pirate* v, Ye wadna have me waste our substance on every thigger or sorner that has the luck to come by the door in a wet day? **1824** MACTAGGART *Gallovid. Encycl.*, *Thiggers*..are those who beg in a genteel way; who have their houses they call at in certain seasons, and get corn, and other little things. **1828** SCOTT *F. M. Perth* ix, Such exaction, which more resembles the masterful license of Highland thiggers and sorners.
So **'thigster** [-STER] in same sense.
1710 *Dict. Feudal Law* 151 *Thigsters*, are a sort of gentle Beggars.

thigging ('θɪgɪŋ), *vbl. sb.* [f. THIG *v.* + -ING[1].] The action of the verb THIG; begging.
1331 *Chester Plea Roll* 4 & 5 *Edw. III* m. 15 (P.R.O.) Bedelli non debent habere offringes thiggynges fulcenale nec aliquod aliud proficuum nisi tantummodo puturam de illis certis tenementis que vocantur warelondes. *c* **1440** *Promp. Parv.* 490/2 Thyggynge, or beggynge, *mendicacio.* **1513** DOUGLAS *Æneis* VIII. Prol. 74 Scho..waistis hir tym In thiggin, as it thrift war. **1827** J. ANDERSON *St. Soc. & Knowl. in Highlands* 73 *note*, Sometimes the young people [about to be married] made the round of their relatives and neighbours to try fortune's smiles. This was called *thigging.* **1872** MICHIE *Deeside T.* xv. 132 The bridegroom gaed a thiggan' among the friends, an got presents o' corn an' ither gear in token o' their well wishes.
So **thigging** *ppl. a.*, that thigs.
a **1300** *E.E. Psalter* xxxix. 18 [xl. 17] And thiggand and pouer am I [WYCLIF, I forsothe a beggere am and pore].

thigh (θaɪ), *sb.* Forms: see below. [OE. *þíoh, þéoh*, Anglian *þéh* = OFris. *thiach*, neuter, OLG. **thioh*, ODu. *thio* (MDu. *diē, diege, dieghe, dijge*, Du. *dij*), ON. *þjó*, OHG. *dioh* (MHG. *diech*):—OTeut. **þeuh-oᵐ*, from Indo-Eur. ablaut-series **teuk-, tauk-, tuk-*; cf. Lith. *taukas*, OSlav. *tukŭ*, Russ. *tukᵘ* fat of animals, Lith. *tukti* to become fat. The regular representative of OE. *þéoh* was ME. *þeh, þeȝ, þee*, which still remains as *thee* in Sc. and north. dialect; but in the 12–13th c. *þeȝ* became narrowed to *þiȝ, thigh* (as *heȝ, neȝ, deȝen* became *hiȝ, niȝ, diȝen, high, nigh, die*).]
1. The upper part of the leg, from the hip to the knee (in man).
α. 1 **théoh, þéoh, þíoh** (**ðeeoh, þyoh**), *Angl.* **thegh,** 1–3 **þeh, þeo,** 3 **þeȝ,** 3–5 **þe,** 4–5 **þee, thegh,** 4–6 **they, the,** 5 **peie, theȝe, theiȝe;** 4–7 (*Sc.* and *north.* -9) **thee.** Pl. 1 **þéoh,** 2–3 **þeȝ,** 2– **þeos,** etc.
c **725** *Corpus Gloss.* (O.E.T.) 556 *Coxa*, thegh. *a* **800** *Erfurt Gloss.* 295 Theoh. *c* **893** K. ÆLFRED *Oros.* I. vii. §1 Hy crupon þæm mannum betuh þa þeoh. *c* **897** —— *Gregory's Past. C.* lvi. 433 Be his ðio. *a* **900** *O.E. Martyrol.* 130 Wund on oðrum þeo. *c* **1000** *Lorica Gl.* in *Sax. Leechd.* I. Pref. 70 Ðeeoh, *bathma. Ibid.* 74 Ðyoh. *Ibid.* I. 78 ȝif men his ðeoh acen. *c* **1200** ORMIN 8079 Fet & þeos Tobollenn. *c* **1250** *Hymn to God* 24 in *Trin. Coll. Hom.* 258 Bind him honden, fet, & þeȝ. *c* **1275** LAY. 30581 He cutte his owe þeh. *a* **1300** *Havelok* 1903 He broken shankes, he broken thes. *a* **1300** *Cursor M.* 3941 Þe maister sinu of his the. *a* **1340** HAMPOLE *Ps.* xliv. 4 With þi swerd abouen þi thee. *c* **1375** *Sc. Leg. Saints* xxviii. (*Margaret*) 430 Vpwart til his theis. **1422** tr. *Secreta Secret., Priv. Priv.* 177 Woundid in the thegh. *c* **1450** *St. Cuthbert* (Surtees) 1525 In his the þar was a byle. *c* **1475** *Pict. Voc.* in Wr.-Wülcker 750/28 *Hoc femur*, a they. **1513** DOUGLAS *Æneis* II. viii. [vii.] 56 Ane Gregioun swerd doun by his thee. **1685** *Lintoun Green* (1817) 168 The miller ..stands Wi' his untheeked thees. *a* **1869** C. SPENCE *Fr. Braes of Carse* (1898) 71, I wade the ditches to the thees.
β. 2–3 **þih,** 2–4 **þi, þy,** 4–5 **þiȝ, þiȝe, þigh(e, þyghe, þyhe, thyȝe,** 4–6 **þie, þye, thie,** 5–6 **thy, thyghe,** 5–7 **thye,** 6 **thighe,** *Sc.* **thich,** 6– **thigh.** Pl. 2–3 **þih;** 3–6 **þyes,** etc.; 6– **thighs.**
11.. *Fragm. Ælfric's Gram.* (1838) 2 *Femur* vel *coxa*, þih. *c* **1200** *Trin. Coll. Hom.* 211 þih and shonkes and fet. *c* **1275** *Passion Our Lord* 490 in *O.E. Misc.* 51 þat heore þyes beon to-broken. **13..** *Minor Poems fr. Vernon MS.* xxv. 337 þi boþe þhiȝes. *c* **1380** WYCLIF *Serm.* Sel. Wks. I. 143 þe knyȝtis broken not Cristis þies. **1387** TREVISA *Higden* (Rolls) I. 425 As hit were a manis þyghe. *Ibid.* II. 203 Somme haueþ þighes with oute hammes. *a* **1400** *R. Gloucester's Chron.* 4921 + 110 (Harl. MS.) A gret pece of ys owe þy [*v. rr.* þiȝ, þiȝe, thyȝe, þye] he kerf out wyþ a knyf. **1484** CAXTON *Fables of Avian* xiii, He..hytte hym on the thye. *c* **1532** DU WES *Introd. Fr.* in *Palsgr.* 903 The thighe, *la cuisse.* **1545** T. SCALON *Treat. Astron.* (MS. Ashm. 391), Mars the hed, Sol the thyg[h]es or hamme. *a* **1584** MONTGOMERIE *Cherrie & Slae* 114 By his naked thyis. **1590** SPENSER *F.Q.* III. v. 20 The wicked steele stayd not till it did light In his left thigh. **1596** DALRYMPLE tr. *Leslie's Hist. Scot.* VIII. (S.T.S.) 125 His thich bane is brokne. **1615** CHAPMAN *Odyss.* XVIII. 105 Through his thin Garment, what a Thigh he showes. **1865** KINGSLEY *Herew.* x, Hereward..owned..no mistress save the sword on his thigh.
†**b.** The part of a garment covering the thigh.
1533 *Acc. Ld. High Treas. Scot.* VI. 184 To draw the theis of the saidis gray hois. **1550** *Ibid.* IX. 405 Theis of hose.

2. In lower vertebrate animals, The part of the hind leg which is homologous with the human thigh, or which is popularly regarded as corresponding to it in position or shape; in certain quadrupeds, as the horse, applied to the tibia; in birds to the tarsus; hence in insects, etc., the third section of the leg.

a **1300** *Thrush & Night.* 68 in Hazl. *E.P.P.* I. 53 Fowel, me thinketh thou art les, They thou be milde and softe of thes. **1387** TREVISA *Higden* (Rolls) V. 355 Liche to mares wiþ white legges up to þe þiȝes. *c* **1440** *Promp. Parv.* 490/2 Thy, lymme of a beeste, *femur*. **1604** DRAYTON *Owle* 121 Each Bee with Honey on her laden thye. **1737** *Ochtertyre House Bks.* (1907) 66 For a thigh of beefe for the hawks £0. 1. 1. **1834** McMURTRIE *Cuvier's Anim. Kingd.* 374 The posterior thighs are strongly inflated in one of the sexes, where the antennæ are usually long and smaller at the extremity. **1866** B. W. HAWKINS *Anat. Horse* 23 The bones of the leg ('thigh' of horsemen) are the *tibia* and *fibula*.

3. *transf.* e.g. the stem of a plant, the lower trunk of a tree, the lower slopes of a mountain.

c **1440** *Pallad. on Husb.* III. 255 About his thegh let no thyng growyng be, But if hit axe to be reuocate. **1758** *Phil. Trans.* L. 632 Ribs, like what we call the thighs of certain trees. **1889** C. EDWARDES *Sardinia* 232 The burly thighs of [mount] Gennargentu as an impenetrable barrier between us and the south.

4. *attrib.* and *Comb.*, as ***thigh-ache***, ***-joint***, ***-muscle***, ***-percussion-sound***, ***-socket***, ***-wound***; ***thigh-slapping***; ***thigh-born***, ***-deep***, ***-fraughted***, ***-high***, ***-long***, adjs.; † **thigh-belly-less** *a.*, having neither thighs nor belly (*nonce-wd.*); **thigh-boot**, a boot with uppers reaching to the thigh; **thigh-hole**, †(*a*) the groin (*obs.*); (*b*) a hole for the thigh in bathing-drawers or the like; **thigh-length** *a.*, (of a garment, boot, etc.) extending down or up to the thigh; **thigh lift**, a dance movement or gymnastic exercise in which the thigh is raised; the lifting of the thigh in this; **thigh-piece** (†**the-pess**), a piece of armour for the thigh; **thigh roll**, a roll of padding on a saddle, designed to prevent the girths from slipping backwards and to support the rider's legs in jumping and dressage; **thigh-slapper** *colloq.*, an exceptionally funny joke, description, or the like; **thigh-tongue**: see quot.

c **1000** *Sax. Leechd.* II. 6 Læcedomas wiþ *þeohece. **1579** LANGHAM *Gard. Health* (1633) 655 Thighache, anoint with sheepes doung and vinegar often. *a* **1649** DRUMM. OF HAWTH. *Shadow Judgm.* Wks. (1711) 34 *Thigh-bellyless, most gastly to the sight. **1840** DICKENS *Barn. Rudge* lxiv, Great *thigh-boots smoked hot with grease and blood. **1630** J. TAYLOR (Water P.) *Triumphall Verses* Wks. III. 122/2 His braine-bred Daughter, and his *thigh-borne Sonne. **1655** tr. *Com. Hist. Francion* v. 7 Bacchus the thigh-born Infant. **1851** MAYNE REID *Scalp Hunt.* xli, We fought *thigh-deep in the gathering flood. **1615** BRATHWAIT *Strappado* (1878) 87 When the *thigh-fraughted Bee gathered her thyme. **1893** *Scribner's Mag.* June 734/1 Bamboo grass, *thigh-high. *c* **1425** tr. *Arderne's Treat. Fistula* 11 þe armeholes, þe *þeholes, þe chawellez, &c. **1895** *Thigh-length [see *knee-length* s.v. KNEE *sb.* 13]. **1979** S. SMITH *Survivor* xvii. 177, I wore a thigh-length Indian-print chemise. **1949** SHURR & YOCOM *Mod. Dance* v. 113 Do not allow body to tip forward on *thigh lift. *c* **1973** J. CHOLERTON *Acrobatic Section Syllabus* (Assoc. Amer. Dancing) (ed. 6) 2 Thigh Lifts.—sit: legs straight in front—hands on the floor behind, lean slightly back. **1899** *Allbutt's Syst. Med.* VII. 191 The knee-jerk is uniformly absent when the *thigh-muscles are paralysed. **1853** MARKHAM *Skoda's Auscult.* 10 The completely empty percussion-sound—the *thigh-percussion-sound—heard at any yielding part of the walls of the thorax, or the abdomen. *c* **1470** HENRY *Wallace* VIII. 265 On the *the pess a felloun strak him gaiff. **1828** TYTLER *Hist. Scot.* (1864) I. 322 Arm-plates, thigh-pieces, greaves for the legs. **1963** E. H. EDWARDS *Saddlery* xiv. 101 The Continental panel is similar, but with..the addition of a *thigh roll at the rear... The thigh roll is rarely evident to the rider unless it is very heavily stuffed, and its real use is to prevent the girth straps moving back off the flap. **1976** *Horse & Hound* 3 Dec. 31 (Advt.), Colombo the unique jumping saddle... The exterior thigh roll is an unusual but effective feature. **1965** *Wall St. Jrnl.* 13 Sept. 14/4 The *thigh-slapper..the President got off to reporters when Lynda Bird showed up in a billowy muu-muu dress. **1932** V. WOOLF *Common Reader* 2nd Ser. 216 [Meredith] overdoes the pith and the sap; the fist-shaking and the *thigh-slapping. **1979** *Dance Mag.* Feb. 32/3 'Lovesick Blues' unexpectedly serves as the up-beat, thigh-slapping finale. **1812** A. PLUMTRE *Lichtenstein's S. Afr.* I. 97 The great muscle of the thigh [of the eland] smoked... These.. from the resemblance they then bear to bullocks' tongues, are called *thigh tongues.

† **thigh** (θaɪ), *v.* *Obs.* [f. THIGH *sb.*]

1. *trans.* To carve (a small bird): see quots.

c **1470** in *Hors, Shepe, & G.* etc. (Caxton 1479 Roxb. repr.) 33 Alle smale birdes thyed. **1508** *Bk. Keruing* Aj, in *Babees Bk.* 265 Thye that pegyon..thye that wodcocke, thye all maner of small byrdes. **1675** HAN. WOOLLEY *Gentlewom. Comp.* 113 In cutting up all manner of small Birds, it is proper to say, Thigh them. **1796** MRS. GLASSE *Cookery* xxvi. 382 So you thigh curlews, plover, or snipe.

2. *intr.* To cower down, squat. *rare*$^{-0}$.

1611 FLORIO, *Accosciare*, to thigh, to coure down [1598 to ioyne thighes].

'**thigh-bone.** Also 5 *north.* **the-bane.** The bone of the thigh; the femur; in quot. 1825 as an emblem of death: cf. *cross-bones*.

c **1450** *St. Cuthbert* (Surtees) 5849 Men wend his the bane had bryst. **1615** CROOKE *Body of Man* 999 On the foreside at the roote of the necke the thighbone is large and rough. **1825** J. NEAL *Bro. Jonathan* III. 295, I begin to see a thighbone or two, now. **1889** MIVART *On Truth* 148 The girdle to which the thigh-bones are articulated.

thighed (θaɪd), *a.* Also 7 **thyght.** [f. THIGH *sb.* + -ED^{2}.] Having thighs (of a specified kind); often in parasynthetic combinations.

c **1600** HARINGTON *Nugæ Ant.* (1779) II. 181 To seeme.. smaller wasted, and fuller thyght, then wee are. **1737** BRACKEN *Farriery Impr.* (1757) II. 38 If he [a horse] is Thigh'd down to the Hough, as the Expression is. **1860** RUSKIN *Mod. Paint.* V. IX. iii. 220 Thighed and shouldered like the billows. **1881** R. BUCHANAN *God & Man* I. 160 Bee-hives, with gold thighed swarms hovering near them.

transf. *c* **1440** *Pallad. on Husb.* III. 226 Diuerse kynde of vynys: The best is lyke a bosh ythied breef [cf. THIGH *sb.* 3, quot. *c* 1440].

thight (θaɪt), *a.* Now *dial.* Forms: 4 **thycht** (*Sc.*), 5 **thyght, thyht,** 6 **thicht** (*Sc.*), (**theight**), 7 (9 *dial.*) **thite, thyte,** 7–8 (9 *dial.*) **thight,** (9 *dial.* **theet, theat**). [Found *c* 1375: the earlier form of the word TIGHT. App. a. early ON. **þéhtr*, in later ON. *þéttr* tight, water-tight, close in texture, solid (Norw. *tjett*, *tett*, Sw. *tät*, Da. *tæt* tight, compact, close). Corresponding in form and meaning to WFris. *ticht*, MDu. and MLG. *dicht* (whence also mod. Ger. *dicht* in same sense), also to MHG. *dîhte* close (whence mod. Ger. dial. *deicht* in Livonia and Esthonia). Not known in the earlier stage of any WGer. lang., but would be in OHG. **dîht*, OS. and OFris. **thicht*, OE. **þíht*, Goth. **þeihts*:—OTeut. **þîhto*^{z} from earlier **þiŋχto*^{z}, f. verbal root **þiŋχ-* to grow: see THEE *v.*[1] Though not evidenced before 1375, the word was doubtless in use in the Danelaw from early times. See also TIGHT.]

1. Set or growing closely together; thick-set, dense: said of rain, growing crops, reeds in a marsh, etc. Now *dial.*

c **1375** *Sc. Leg. Saints* xl. (*Ninian*) 574 Þare-with fel þe rane sa thycht, þat [etc.]. **1787** W. MARSHALL *Norfolk Gloss.*, *Thight*, applied to turneps or other crops,—close, thickset. [*Ibid.* I. 271 There are men who are fully aware that the 'proof' of their turnep-crop depends more on its thightness than on the size of the plant.] **1895** EMERSON *Birds*, etc. *Norfolk Broadland* I. xx. 56 The happy pair [of reed-pheasants] fly about the 'thyte (thick) reed', plucking reed-feathers.

†**2.** Solid, not hollow, whole. *Obs.*

c **1440** *Promp. Parv.* 491/2 Thyht, hool fro brekynge, not brokyn.., *integer*. Thyht, not hool wythe-in, *solidus*. *Ibid.*, Thyhtyn, or make thyht, *integro*, *consolido*, *solido*.

†**3.** Close, compact, or dense in structure or texture, as a membrane. *Obs.*

In quot. 1539 the sense differs little from 1. In some uses also with the notion of being impermeable to moisture, as in 4.

1539 *Will T. Samson* (Somerset Ho.), A thyght nett. **1615** CROOKE *Body of Man* 86 It is harder then the true skin and more thight. [*Ibid.* 88 Wherefore they referre the cause of the concretion or congealing with Aristotle, to the fastnesse and thightnesse of the Membranes.] *Ibid.* 387 The coates of the veines are thicke and thight, that nothing but that which is very thinne may sweate out. **1678** PHILLIPS (ed. 4), *Thight*, (old word) well compacted or knit together.

4. So close in texture or structure as to keep water out; *esp.* of a ship or boat, so closely compacted and well caulked as to be water-tight. Now *dial.*

1501 *Acc. Ld. High Treas. Scot.* II. 24 Item, for vij pund of rosait to mak the clath thicht..xiiij *d.* **1587** GREENE *Penelope's Web* Wks. (Grosart) V. 150 Causing his weather beaten shippes to be warped out of the Hauen as soone as they were made theight. *a* **1625** *Nomenclator Navalis* (Harl. MS. 2301) s.v., When the Shipp is staunch and makes but little water, she is thight. **1628** DIGBY *Voy. Medit.* (Camden) 27 Shee was so leakie as was a great cumber..till shee were vnladen and mended thyte. *Ibid.* 37 The boate seemed to be a fine one and thite, but with long driuing was halfe full of water. *a* **1825** FORBY *Voc. E. Anglia*, *Thite*, compact, not leaky, water-tight. **1866** EDMONDSTON *Gloss. Shetl. & Orkney*, *Thight*, close, so as not to admit water. **1877** *Holderness Gloss.* s.v., A theet roof, a theet cask.

5. Tight, close-fitting, as apparel. *dial.*

a **1825** in FORBY *Voc. E. Anglia*.

Hence †'**thight** *v.*, *trans.* to make 'thight'; '**thightness**, closeness, denseness, tightness.

c **1440** Thyhtyn [see 2]. **1615**, **1787** Thightness [see 3, 1].

thigmokinesis (ˌθɪgməʊkaɪ'niːsɪs, -kɪn-). *Zool.* [f. Gr. *θίγμ-α* touch + *o* + KINESIS.] A kinesis in which the stimulus is absence of touch or body contact.

1940 FRAENKEL & GUNN *Orientation of Animals* ii. 23 It seems probable, therefore, that the contact is the positive stimulus involved and that its action is inhibitory. In that case, *thigmo-kinesis* (*θίγμα*, touch) is the appropriate name for the reaction. **1954** *New Biol.* XVII. 49 There is..a low thigmokinesis, causing the animals to assume positions in which as much as possible of their surface is in contact with another surface. **1961** *Listener* 21 Sept. 439/3 The earwig.. displays marked thigmokinesis. **1976** *Acta Neurobiol. Exper.* XXXVI. 579 Crickets attain their ethological praeferendum of resting site owing to their innate photo- and thigmo-kinesis, which are supplemented by hygrophilia and thermophilia.

‖**thigmotaxis** (θɪgməʊ'tæksɪs). *Biol.* [mod.L. f. Gr. *θίγμα* touch + *τάξις* arrangement, disposition.] The way in which an organism moves or disposes itself in response to a touch stimulus, i.e. by being attracted (positive thigmotaxis) or repelled (negative thigmotaxis).

1900 B. D. JACKSON *Gloss. Bot. Terms* 270/2 *Thigmotaxis* ..is a synonym [of Thigmotropism]. **1905** *Nature* 31 Aug. 426/2 The 'Thigmotaxis' exhibited by an oxytrocha moving round a spherical egg, unable to leave its surface. **1909** J. W. JENKINSON *Experim. Embryol.* 272 Thus we have positive and negative heliotropism, galvanotaxis, geotropism, galvanotropism, thigmotaxis, and so on.

So **thigmo'tactic** *a.* [Gr. *τακτικ-ός* pertaining to arrangement], of, pertaining to, or exhibiting thigmotaxis; hence **thigmo'tactically** *adv.*

1900 in *Amer. Jrnl. Psychol.* XII. 141 One is the thigmotactic reaction. Starting with the moving infusorian, we find that it reacts to contact with solid bodies of a certain physical texture by suspending part of the usual ciliary motion. **1901** *Ibid.* 229 A definite rat-hole consciousness that acts, as it were, thigmotactically. **1903** *Science* 8 May 738 The ventral surface of planarians is strongly positively thigmotactic, whereas the dorsal surface is negatively thigmotactic.

thigmotropism (θɪg'mɒtrəpɪz(ə)m). *Biol.* [f. Gr. *θίγμα* touch + *τρόπη* a turning + -ISM.] The movement of some part of any organism in response to a touch stimulus; the habit of turning towards or away from a foreign body on coming into contact with it. So **thigmo'tropic** *a.*, of, pertaining to, resulting from, or exhibiting thigmotropism.

1900 B. D. JACKSON *Gloss. Bot. Terms* 270/2 *Thigmotropism*, curvature induced in climbing plants by the stimulus of a rough surface. **1908** M. F. WASHBURN *Animal Mind* iii. §12. 57. **1909** J. W. JENKINSON *Experim. Embryol.* 275 The outgrowth of the ciliated ring into the arms is due to a stimulus—thigmotropic, perhaps,—exerted by the tip of the spicule.

thik, var. THEEK, THILK; obs. form of THICK.

thilc, þ-, variant of THELLICH *Obs.*

† **thild.** *Obs.* [ONorthumb. *þyld* (= general OE. *ȝeþyld*) = OHG. *dult*,:—OTeut. **þul-di-*, nominal derivative of verb-stem **þul-* in Goth. *þulan* to endure: see THOLE *v.*] Patience, endurance.

c **950** *Lindisf. Gosp.* Luke xxi. 19 On ðyld [*Rushw.* ðylde] iuera ȝie byeð sauelo iuero. *c* **1200** ORMIN 2613 For þild birrþ ben wiþþ iwhillc mahht To beoldenn itt & strengenn. *a* **1300** *E.E. Psalter* ix. 19 Þild ofe pouer [WYCLIF the pacience of pore men] ouer alle Noght in ende forworth salle.

Hence †'**thildi** (OE. **þyldiȝ**, early ME. **þuldi** (*ü*)) *a.*, patient; whence †'**thildiliche** *adv.*, patiently.

a **950** *Rituale Dunelm.* (Surtees) 101 Crist' ðv ðe arð doeme soðfæst strong and *ðyldiȝ. *a* **1225** *Leg. Kath.* 177 Ha wes þuldi and þolemod. *c* **1200** ORMIN 1186 Ure Laferrd Jesu Crist..Toc *þildiliȝ wiþþutenn bracc, þatt mann himm band wiþþ woȝhe. *a* **1225** *Ancr. R.* 106 He þolede þuldeliche þet te Giws dutten..his deorewurde muð mid hore dreori fustes. *a* **1225** *Juliana* 28 Þuldeliche heo hit þolede.

thilk (ðɪlk), *dem. adj.* and *pron.* *arch.* or *dial.* Forms: α. 3–5 **þilke,** 3–7 **thilke,** 4–5 **þylke, þilk,** 4–7 **thylke,** 5 **thylk,** (6 **thailk**), 4– **thilk.** β. 3–5 **þulke** (*ü*), 5 **þulk,** 4–5 **þelke.** γ. 3–5 **þike,** 4 **þyke, þeke, þuke,** 4–5 **thike, thyke, theke,** 5 **thik,** 6 **þieke;** 9 *dial.* **thik, thic, thick, thek, thuck, thicky.** [ME. *þilke*, known *a* 1300; app. f. *þe*, THE + *ilce*, ILK same, meaning *the* or *that same*; in some of the quots. *þe ilke* or *þet ilke* occurs as a MS. variant.

This analysis suits the form *þilke*, but does not explain the early southern *þülke* and the Kentish *þelke*, which naturally indicate an OE. **þylce*. Can there have been a confusion in the south between *þilke* and late OE. *þylc* for *þyllic*, THELLICH?

(*Thick* (ðɪk) is in dialect use from Cornwall and Hants to Worcester and Hereford; and also in Pembroke, Glamorgan, and Wexford. In many parts it has also the form *thicky*, *thickee*, or *thicka*. It generally means 'that', but in some parts 'this', in which case it is contrasted with *thuck*, *thock*, or *thack* = that. It is sometimes indefinite, and has to be made definite, as *thick here*, this, *thick there*, that. In Somerset and Dorset, *thick* and *theäse* are used only of individual shaped things, as a man or tree, while *that* and *this* are used of formless substances in the mass, as flour, milk, marble. See *Eng. Dial. Dict.*)]

A. *adj.* The very (thing, person, etc.) mentioned or indicated; the same; that; this.

a **1225** *Ancr. R.* 68 Iðen ilke huse [*MS. C.* in þilke hus]. *a* **1300** *Floriz & Bl.* 54 So blisful him þuȝte þilke steuene. *c* **1330** R. BRUNNE *Chron. Wace* (Rolls) 381 Ascaneus..gat a child Cycillius; þylke Cycylli gat þat man Brutus. *c* **1374** CHAUCER *Boeth.* III. pr. x. 73 (Camb. MS.) It semeth þat þilke same thing be most desyred. *a* **1425** *Cursor M.* 11386 (Trin.) And comen to crist þilke day [*C.*, *G.* þat ilk dai]. *c* **1449** PECOCK *Repr.* 235 Neither in thilk hil neither in Ierusalem. **1513** DOUGLAS *Æneis* I. Prol. 134 Thilk werk tuelf ȝeris first was in making eik. **1579** SPENSER *Sheph. Cal.* Jan. 61, I loue thilke lasse, (alas why doe I loue?). *a* **1643** CARTWRIGHT *Ordinary* II. ii, Dan Cupido Sure sent thylke sweven to mine head. **1724** DE FOE *Mem. Cavalier* (1840) 236 Says he, in a broad north-country tone, 'whar hast thou thilk horse?'

β. *c* **1290** *St. Brandan* 519 in *S. Eng. Leg.* 234 Þo tornede þe wynd in-to þe North,..In þulke side stronge Inouȝ. *a* **1300** *Floriz & Bl.* 432 Þulke terme him þuȝte long. *c* **1315** SHOREHAM vii. 133 And þelke sone ȝet naþeles Ryȝt ase þe fader hys endeles. **1387** TREVISA *Higden* (Rolls) V. 83 (MS.

γ) þulke Decius. *Ibid.* VI. 303 Unlawful wedlok.. with þelke Iuditha. *c* **1400** *R. Gloucester's Chron.* (Rolls) 3771 þe men of norweye.. adde ymade anoþer mon king of þe [*MS.* a þelke] londe. *a* **1425** *Cursor M.* 11417 (Trin.) þulke [*Laud* thilk, *Cott.* & *Gött.* þis ilk] sterre hem coom to warn.

γ. **1303** R. BRUNNE *Handl. Synne* 6151 Syn þat þyke pore ermyte was yn drede for so lyte. *c* **1320** *Cast. Love* (Halliw.) 747 Ne never wes but thyke [*v.r.* þulke] oon. *c* **1410** *Master of Game* (MS. Digby 182) xxxv, Hemm þat shulde haue parte of þike deere. **1432–50** tr. *Higden* (Rolls) II. 449 Theke parte scholde haue þe victory. **1439** in *Ancestor* July (1904) 16 That every day in thik month the vij tapres brenne. *c* **1440** LOVELICH *Merlin* 12104 The tothyr cyte.. hindicam hyghte at thyke tyme tho. **1553** *Respublica* III. iii, þieke same waie goeth the hare. **1820** COBBETT *Gram. Eng. Lang.* xvii. (1847) 109 When we hear a Hampshire plough-boy say '[She] have giv'd I thick handkercher'. **1874** T. HARDY *Far fr. Madding Crowd* II. 289 To ho and hanker after thik woman in the way a do. **1898** E. PHILLPOTTS *Child. of Mist* I. iii. 28 'Tis thicky auld Muscovite duck, roostin' on his lil island. **1909** *Westm. Gaz.* 7 Aug. 2/2 Do 'e mind thic time, Daddy, when you an' me catched gert lobsters?

†**b.** With plural sb.: These; those. *Obs.*

c **1275** LAY. 1284 þe strengest þe weren in þilke daies [*c* 1205 o þon dawen]. **1387** TREVISA *Higden* (Rolls) I. 49 Of þilke mouþes þe see of myddel erþe bygynneþ. *c* **1420** *Chron. Vilod.* 3000 þat þulke relekes nolde neuer go þen a-way. *c* **1489** CAXTON *Sonnes of Aymon* xxviii. 577 Wyth-oute ye had more helpe than thilke knaves.

B. *pron.* That (or this) person or thing.

c **1275** *Passion our Lord* 110 in *O.E. Misc.* 40 Mayster am ich þilke þat þe wile so dyhte. *c* **1300** *Harrow. Hell* 135 þilke þat nulleþ aȝeyn hem stonde. *c* **1386** CHAUCER *Pars. T.* ¶ 32 Pryuee penaunce is thilke that men doon alday for priuee synnes. **1413** *Pilgr. Sowle* (Caxton) I. xix. (1859) 19 Ful oftymes haue I warned the.. as thylk that loueth the. *c* **1449** PECOCK *Repr.* II. xx. 273 Therfore chese the reder.. whether this or thilk or bothe he wole holde. **1867** ROCK *Jim & Nell* vii, Britting o' thick an' crazing thack. **1880** JEFFERIES *Gt. Estate* x. 188 Thuck's our feyther's. **1885** *Househ. Words* 20 June 141/2, I cowd ha' told thee thilk.

†**b.** *pl.* Those. *Obs.*

c **1330** R. BRUNNE *Chron. Wace* (Rolls) 7341 þulke of twenty wynter elde. **1370–80** *XI Pains of Hell* 113 in *O.E. Misc.* 226 þo þat weren vp to þe briȝes In þat flod.. þulke weore glade of þe mischeef. **1401** J. SKYDMORE in Ellis *Orig. Lett.* Ser. II. I. 20 To all thilke that ye suppose wol take this mater to hert. *a* **1450** MYRC *Par. Pr.* 687 Al thilk that with hold eny fredomes.

thill[1] (θɪl). Also 5 **þylle, thyl,** 6 **thyll.** Cf. also FILL *sb.*[2] [Of uncertain origin: the 14th c. *þille, þylle* is identical in form with OE. *þille*, glossed *tabulāta, tabulāmen, tabulāmentum*, i.e. 'board, deal, boarding, flooring', but the sense 'pole or shaft' is so different that, without further evidence, it seems unsafe to connect them.

For the OE. *þille* see THEAL: none of the cognate words there cited show any approach to the mod. sense of *thill*.]

a. The pole or shaft by which a wagon, cart, or other vehicle is attached to the animal drawing it, *esp.* one of the pair of shafts between which a single draught animal is placed. Applied (*a*) in *sing.* to the single pole, rarely to the pair of shafts (now only *U.S.*); (*b*) in *pl.* to the pair of shafts.

(*a*) **14..** *Voc.* in Wr.-Wülcker 615/35 *Temo*, a thylle. **14..** *Metrical Voc.* ibid. 628/20 *Reda*, thylle. *c* **1440** *Promp. Parv.* 491/1 Thylle, of a carte, *temo.* **1530** PALSGR. 280/2 Thyll of a carte, *le lymon.* **1611** COTGR., *Alimonner*, to put into.. the thill of a cart. *Ibid.*, *Limon*,.. the Thill of a waine, wagon, &c.; In which sense (because a Thill consists of two beames) it is most vsed in the Plurall number. **1688** R. HOLME *Armoury* III. xviii. (Roxb.) 139/1 The two side shafts make one thill. **1770** LANGHORNE *Plutarch* (1879) I. 256/2 That piece of wood with which they supported the thill of a waggon. *c* **1873** E. DICKINSON *Poems* (1955) III. 869 Elijah's wagon has no thill—Was innocent of wheel. **1901** *Century Mag.* Jan. 452/1 I'm like a bronco in a buggy. I want to bust a thill every time I feel the rein. **1944** *Sun* (Baltimore) 16 May 10/3 An old slave cabin and an old ox thill.

(*b*) *c* **1325** *Gloss. W. de Bibbesw.* in Wright *Voc.* 168 *Les lymouns*, the thilles. *c* **1400** *Laud. Troy Bk.* 12820 Fals fortune of him now filles, He put him riȝt In hir thilles. *c* **1425** *Voc.* in Wr.-Wülcker 665/30 *Hic limo*, thyllys. **1707** MORTIMER *Husb.* (1721) I. 360 If the fore Wheels were as high as the hinder Wheels, and if the Thills were fixed under the Axis. **1890** O. CRAWFURD *Round the Cal. in Portugal* 104 The mule and the horse work between the thills of the cart and of the plough.

b. *attrib.* and *Comb.*, as **thill hame, harness, pin; thill-coupling, -jack, -tug**: see quot. 1877; **thill-saddle** = SADDLE *sb.* 3. Also THILL-HORSE.

14.. *Nom.* in Wr.-Wülcker 727/33 *Hic limarillum* a thylpyn. **1549** *Rutland MSS.* (1905) IV. 570 Thill hames, xl pare. **1776** in Hughes *Scour. White Horse* v, The same time a Thill harness will be run for by Cart-horses, &c. **1807** A. YOUNG *Agric. Essex* (1813) I. 107, 3 thill saddles, breechins, cruppers, &c. **1859** HUGHES *Scour. White Horse* v, Varmer Mifflin's mare.. won a new Cart-saddle and thill-tugs. *Ibid.* vi, The great horses in their thill harness. **1877** KNIGHT *Dict. Mech.*, *Thill-coupling*, a device for fastening the shafts to the fore-axle. *Ibid.*, *Thill-jack*, a tool for attaching the thills of a carriage to the clips of the axle. *Ibid.*, *Thill-tug*, a leathern loop depending from the harness saddle to hold the shaft of a carriage.

thill[2] (θɪl). [A local term of unknown origin; cf. TILL *sb.*, boulder-clay.] The thin stratum of fire-clay, etc. usually underlying a coal-seam; underclay; the floor or bottom of a seam of coal.

1329–30 *Durham Acc. Rolls* (Surtees) 515 Quatour bayardours portantibus Thill et focale in abbathiam per x septimanas, xxiij s. vj d. **1454–5** *Ibid.* 634 Operanti circa le ryddyng ac adquisicione de le Thill pro eodem furno. **1500–1** *Ibid.* 657 Pro iiij[or] plaustr. de lez thillstone, xvj d. **1708** J. C. *Compl. Collier* (1845) 39 Sometimes a Pit may happen to have a Hitch or Dipping of the Thill or Bottom of the Way. **1851** GREENWELL *Coal-trade Terms Northumb. & Durh.* 54 *Thill*, the floor of a seam of coal. **1867** W. W. SMYTH *Coal* 25 The floor, thill, or seat.., of the coal is an underclay. **1878** LEBOUR *Geol. Northumberland & Durh.* (1886) iii. 12 There is a strict analogy between these peat-marls and clays and the 'thills' or 'underclays' of many coals. **1881** *Borings & Sinkings* II. 4 (E.D.D.) Grey thill with water. **1887** WOODWARD *Geol. Eng. & Wales* (ed. 2) 179 The Underclay is known as 'Spavin' in Yorkshire; as 'Thill' in Durham; as 'Warrant' or 'Seat-earth' in Lancashire; and as 'Bottomstone' or 'Pouncin' in South Wales. **1894** HESLOP *Northumb. Gloss.* s.v., The underlayer of a coal seam frequently consists of a thin bed of fireclay; hence thin strata of that material are called *thill*, irrespective of their position with regard to a seam of coal.

thiller ('θɪlə(r)). Also 9 *dial.* **tiller**: see also FILLER[2]. [f. THILL[1] + -ER[1].] = next. Also *attrib.*

1552 HULOET, Thyller of a carte, *veredus, di.* **1573** TUSSER *Husb.* (1878) 36 Hole bridle and saddle, whit lether and nall, With collers and harneis, for thiller and all. **1607** TOPSELL *Four-f. Beasts* (1658) 330 His Thiller fell and put his shoulder clean out of joynt. **1640** HEXHAM *Princ. Art Milit.* III. 5 A halfe Canon.. vpon its carriage, drawne with seven couple of horse, and a Thiller horse. **1733** TULL *Horse-Hoeing Husb.* xxiii. 363 Limbers,.. also called Shafts, Sharps, and Thills; from whence the Horse that goes in them is call'd a Thiller. **1893** *Stratford-on-Avon Herald* 24 Feb. 4/2, 3 Sets of Harness, Thillers' and Trace Gears.

thill-horse ('θɪlhɔːs). See also *fill-horse* s.v. FILL *sb.*[2] [f. THILL[1] + HORSE.] The shaft-horse or wheeler in a team.

c **1325** *Gloss. W. de Bibbesw.* in Wright *Voc.* 168 En lymouns [*gl.*] thilles va ly limounere [*gl.*] the thillo-hors. *c* **1425** *Voc.* in Wr.-Wülcker 665/32 *Hic uiredus*, thylhors. **1483** *Funeral Edw. IV* in *Lett. & Pap. Rich. III*, etc. (Rolls) I. 7 Upon the fore horse, and the thil horse sat ij chariot men. **1543** *Will J. England* (Somerset Ho.), Oon Carte, a Tyll horsse & foure Oxen. **1704** W. DERHAM in *Phil. Trans.* XXV. 1583 The Thill-Horse in Charles's Wain, called Alioth. **1876** BROWNING *Pacchiarotto* xxi, A Spare-Horse? Be rather a thill-horse.

'**thilly**, *a.* [f. THILL[2].] Of the nature of thill.

1894 HESLOP *Northumbld. Gloss.* s.v. *Thill*, Any stone partaking of the nature of indurated clay is called *thilly*.

thimble ('θɪmb(ə)l), *sb.* Forms: α. 1 **þýmel**, 5–6 **thymelle, -yl(le, thymle, themel, -elle, -yl(le,** (5 **thomelle, timmele),** 9 *dial.* **thimmel.** β. 5 **thymbyl(l, thomble,** 6 **thymble, -bel(l, -bil(l, thumble, (tymble),** 6–7 **thimbell,** 6– **thimble.** [OE. *þýmel*, f. *þúma* THUMB + *-el*, -LE, suffix forming names of instruments: cf. *handle*. The later Eng. form has developed a *b* after *m*, as in *humble*, *nimble*, etc. ON., *þumall* meant the thumb of a glove; perh. a leather thumbstall was the earliest form of thimble; metal thimbles were app. introduced in the 17th c.]

†**1.** A sheath or covering for the thumb or finger; a fingerstall. *Obs.* (Only OE.)

c **1000** *Sax. Leechd.* II. 150 Wyrc þonne þymel to.

2. a. A bell-shaped sheath of metal (formerly of leather) worn on the end of the finger to push the needle in sewing.

tailor's, upholsterer's, etc. *thimble*, a similar metal sheath open at both ends; *sail-maker's thimble* = PALM *sb.*[2] 5. *knight of the thimble*, a tailor: see KNIGHT *sb.* 12 c.

α. *c* **1412** HOCCLEVE *De Reg. Princ.* 682 Look whedir In þis purs þer be any croyse or crouche, Sauf nedel and þrede, & themel [*MS. Reg.* thymelle] of leþer. **14..** *Voc.* in Wr.-Wülcker 578/29 *Digitale*, a themyl. **1483** *Cath. Angl.* 383/1 A Themelle (*A.* Thymbylle, Thymle). **1488** *Acc. Ld. High Treas. Scot.* I. 80 A thing of gold with a top like a timmele. *a* **1568** in *Bannatyne Poems* (Hunter. Cl.) 396 With elwand, scheir and thymmill.

β. *c* **1440** *Promp. Parv.* 491/1 Thymbyl, *theca*,.. (digita). **14..** *Debate Carpenter's Tools* 18 in Hazl. *E.P.P.* I. 80 ȝis, ȝis, seyd the wymbylle, I ame als rounde as a thymbyll. **1530** PALSGR. 280/2 Thymble to sowe with, *deyl.* **1591** FLORIO *2nd Fruites* 5, I haue neither needle, thred, nor thimble. **1664** POWER *Exp. Philos.* I. 5 The Common Fly.. her eyes are.. most neatly dimpled with innumerable little cavities like a small grater or thimble. **1700** CONGREVE *Way of World* III. iii, Hast thou ne'er a brass thimble clinking in thy pocket? **1793** *Girlhood M. J. Holroyd* (1896) 253, I have worked with my Thimble, and like it extremely. **1812** [see KNIGHT *sb.* 12 c]. **1841** MOORE *Young Jessica* i, The safest shield against the darts Of Cupid, is Minerva's thimble.

b. ***Thimble and Bodkin Army*** (Eng. Hist.): a nickname of the Parliamentary Army of the Civil War: see quots.

1647 MAY *Hist. Parl.* II. vi. 97 The poorer sort, like that Widow in the Gospel, presented their Mites also; insomuch that it was a common Jeer of men disaffected to the Cause, to call it the Thimble- and Bodkin-Army. **1884** DOWELL *Taxes in Eng.* II. i. 3 On the parliamentary side the subscriptions of silver offerings included even such little personal articles as those that suggested the term, the 'Thimble and Bodkin' army.

c. A thimble or similar article as used by a thimblerigger: see THIMBLERIG I.

1716 GAY *Trivia* II. 166 Nor try the Thimble's Cheats. **1742** FIELDING *Jos. Andrews* II. iii, A person travelling to a neighbouring fair with the thimble and button. **1838** DICKENS *Nich. Nick.* l, Gathered round a pea and thimble table. **1909** *Q. Rev.* July 173 A conjuror.. astonishing a simple audience with the pea-and-thimble trick.

3. The ring or socket in the heel of a gate which turns on the hook or pin in the gate-post. *local.*

1550 *Hawkhurst Ch. Acc.* in *Archæol. Cantiana* V. 64 For a thymble to the churche gate ij[d]. **1627** *MS. Acc. St. John's Hosp., Canterb.*, For ij thimbles for the beane garden gate xvj d. **1804** *Trans. Soc. Arts* XXII. 83 The upper thimble should be fixed.. nearer the farther side of the heel of the gate than the lower thimble. **1881** *Leicestersh. Gloss.*

4. *Naut.* A broad ring of metal, having a concave outer surface, around which the end of a rope is spliced, so that the thimble forms an eye to the rope.

1711 W. SUTHERLAND *Shipbuild. Assist.* 132 Thimbles, large.. 34. Ordinary.. 118. **1775** FALCK *Day's Diving Vessel* 50 Each cable has a large thimble spliced in at one end, through which each alternate cable is reeved. **1860** *Merc. M. Mag.* VII. 113 A leach-line is.. carried through thimbles.

5. In various technical applications. **a.** *Mech.* A ring, tube, or similar part, e.g. a sleeve, bushing, ferrule, etc.; often in comb., as ***thimble-coupling, -joint***, etc.: see 9. **b.** The outer casing of a rifle-ball. **c.** *Pottery*: A rest for placing the ware during glost-firing. **d.** *Dentistry*: see quot. **e.** A cone of fat-free paper used in a fat-extraction apparatus. **f.** = *thimble-rubber* in 9. **g.** See quot.

a. **1789** *Trans. Soc. Arts* VII. 179 Thimbles made of wire, twisted in the slit of the harpoon. **1831** J. HOLLAND *Manuf. Metal* I. 184 Fitting into the holes bushes or thimbles to give them the greater strength. **1877** KNIGHT *Dict. Mech.*, *Thimble*... 3. (*Machinery.*) *a.* A sleeve or tube through which a bolt passes, and which may act as a stay. *b.* A ferrule to expand a tube; specifically, a ferrule for boiler-tubes. 4. A sleeve around a stove-pipe when it passes through a wall or ceiling. **1881** GREENER *Gun* 84 The charge is put in a small steel thimble.

b. *c* **1860** H. STUART *Seaman's Catech.* 11 The thimble expands and rifles the ball. **1900** *Brit. Med. Jrnl.* No. 2053. 1156 The thimble or shell of the Mauser and Lee-Metford. *Ibid.*, The core is of hardened lead, and the thimble composed of copper and nickel.

c. **1901** [see *thimble-picker* in 9]. **1910** *Rep. Lead Comm.* (Parl. Pap. Eng.), Placing the ware on rests with pointed projections..'Thimbles' similar in shape to a sewing thimble,.. provided with a single horn.

d. **1877** KNIGHT *Dict. Mech.* 2554/1 The extension thimble of the dentist is a prong on the end of the thimble, used to reach into the mouth to hold the foil or a compress, while operating on the teeth.

e. **1901** *Jrnl. Exper. Med.* 25 Mar. 515 This residue was then ground up with sand, placed in a fat-extraction thimble and extracted again.

f. **1909** *Cent. Dict. Suppl.*, *Thimble*,.. *pl.*, a tradename for crude india-rubber from the lower Kongo and Loanda in small balls of a gray color, darker outside.

g. **1541** R. COPLAND *Guydon's Quest. Chirurg.* L iij, Thyrdly a seame incarnatyfe is made with egal themylls made of towe well wrythen & sklenderly.

6. Applied (usually in *pl.*) to certain flowers and plants, or parts of them, e.g. (*a*) the Foxglove, also known as *Fairy* or *Witches' Thimbles*; (*b*) the Sea Campion; (*c*) the Harebell; (*d*) the cup of an acorn. See also *Lady's Thimble*, LADY *sb.* 18 b.

1873 BROWNING *Red Cott. Nt.-cap* I. 150 Nor its fine thimble fits the acorn top. **1878** BRITTEN & HOLLAND *Plant n.*, Fairy Thimbles, *Digitalis purpurea.* **1881** J. A. SIDEY in *Mod. Scot. Poets* 396 Whaur the witch thummles bloom. **1886** BRITTEN & H. *Plant-n.*, *Thimble*, (1) *Digitalis purpurea*.. (2) *Silene maritima.* **1894** *Daily News* 28 Apr. 6/5 The tall foxglove, with its graduated 'thimbles'.

7. *Thieves' slang.* A watch.

1812 in J. H. VAUX *Flash Dict.* **1834** W. H. AINSWORTH *Rookwood* III. v, My thimble of ridge. **1901** W. S. WALKER *In the Blood* xiii. 138 Silver money, and a watch and chain, or, in thieves' language, 'white-lot' and 'thimble and slang'.

8. = THIMBLEFUL.

1841 HOOD *Tale of Trumpet* xii, [They] never swallowed a thimble the less Of something the Reader is left to guess. **1865** BUSHNELL *Vicar Sacr.* Introd. (1868) 24 Such thimbles of meaning as can be confidently managed.

9. *attrib.* and *Comb.*, as ***thimble-case, -finger, -maker, -top; thimble-crowned, -like, -sealed, -shaped, -sized*** adjs.; **thimble-belt**, a kind of cartridge-belt; **thimble-berry** (**thimble blackberry**), the black raspberry of America, *Rubus occidentalis*, so called from the shape of its receptacle; any of several other North American raspberries having thimble-shaped fruit; **thimble-coupling**: see quot.; **thimble-grater**, a species of gastropod shell; **thimble-joint**: see quot.; **thimble lily**, a name of the Australian liliaceous plant *Blandfordia nobilis*, with flowers in racemes; **thimble-limpet**, a West Indian species of limpet, so called from its shape; **thimble-man** = THIMBLERIGGER; **thimble-picker**, a young person employed in a pottery to pick from among the used thimbles (see sense 5 c) those that can be used a second time: so *thimble-picking*; **thimble-pie**: see quots.; **thimble-plating**, the formation of a cylindrical boiler-shell or a flue by successive slightly overlapping rings of plate; **thimble-rubber**: see quots.; **thimble-screwer** *Criminals' slang*, one who steals watches or 'thimbles' (sense 7); cf. SCREWER 2; **thimble-shift, -shifting**, the shifting of the pea from one thimble to another by a thimblerigger; also *fig.*; **thimble-skein**, a skein for an axle made in tubular form; **thimble-surface**, *Ceramics*, a surface of raised dots produced by closely pitting the interior of the mould; **thimble-weed**: see quot.

1901 *N. Amer. Rev.* Feb. 231 The *thimble belt, used only by the Americans, is still preferred to the cartridge pouches of the others. **1789** R. HASWELL *Jrnl.* 16 Mar. in F. W. Howay *Voy. Columbia to Northwest Coast* (1941) 60 We frequently met with gooseberrys rousberrys currants blackberries strawberries and *thimble berries. **1847** [see BLACK-CAP 5]. **1854** THOREAU *Walden* xiv. (1886) 262 Strawberries, raspberries, thimble-berries. **1883** STEVENSON *Silverado Sq.* iii, A bower of green and tangled thicket..where thimbleberry played the part of our English hawthorn. **1886** [see BLACK-CAP 5]. **1946** T. M. STANWELL-FLETCHER *Driftwood Valley* 219 Here the devil's-club gave way..to a dense growth of alders, azaleas, and thimbleberry. **1715** LADY M. W. MONTAGU *Basset-Table* 34 A myrtle foliage round the *thimble-case. **1882** OGILVIE, *Thimble-coupling.... In *mach.* a kind of permanent coupling, of which the coupling-box consists of a plain ring of metal, supposed to resemble a tailor's thimble. **1876** H. GARDNER *Sunflowers, Dream of Noon* 48 Then she Raising a slender finger, *thimble-crowned, Beckoned him onwards. **1796** BURNEY *Mem. Metastasio* III. 277 A whitloe in the stitching or *thimble finger. *c* **1711** PETIVER *Gazophyl.* VI. liv, Borneo *Thimble Grater... The outside is rough like a Grater, and hollow like a Cap or Thimble. **1877** KNIGHT *Dict. Mech.*, *Thimble-joint, a sleeve-joint, with an interior packing to keep the joints of pipes tight during expansion and contraction. **1899** *Allbutt's Syst. Med.* VIII. 602 The minute honey-combed, *thimble-like appearance of its surface. **1883** GUILFOYLE *Catal. Plants Melbourne Bot. Gard.* 22 *Blandfordia nobilis*..*Thimble Lily. *c* **1711** PETIVER *Gazophyl.* Dec. viii. Tab. 80 Barbadoes *Thimble Limpet. **1654** *Nicholas Papers* (Camden) II. 116 For other his undertakinges [he] is a *thimble-maker.., a mere cheat that rambles up and doun, not worth on farthing. **1830** GEN. P. THOMPSON *Exerc.* (1842) I. 192 The army of *thimble-men from Doncaster is upon you. **1901** *Scotsman* 28 Mar. 9/1 Persons are returned..as *thimble-pickers, without mentioning that they are directly engaged in making.. earthenware. **1828** *Craven Gloss.*, *Thimble-pie, a fillip with the thimble. **1882** MOZLEY *Remin.* II. cviii. 245, I had to sit under the lady's three-legged work table, receiving 'thimble-pie', that is a sharp rap with a thimble on the crown of my head. **1881** *Rep. Kew Gardens* 39/2 W. African rubber ..appears as..agglutinated masses of small cubes of which there are specimens in the Kew Museum under the name of *Thimble rubber. **1862** H. MAYHEW *London Labour* Extra vol. 25 '*Thimble-screwers', those who wrench watches from their guards. **1932** Thimble-screwer [see RAMPSMAN]. **1840** THACKERAY *Catherine* i, The dirty scrap of paper, *thimble-sealed. **1867** *Thimble-shaped [see THIMBLE-EYE]. **1905** *Daily News* 1 Aug. 4 [A bee's] thimble-shaped cell. **1834** *Hist.* in *Ann. Reg.* 90/1 About twenty per cent. was to be deducted from the tithe-owner [etc.]. This was *thimble-shift the first. **1834** STANLEY in *Hansard's Parl. Deb.* 4 July XXIV. 1154 How was this deficiency to be made good to the State? Here, then, was one instance of his right hon. friend's *thimble-shifting. **1895** CLIVE HOLLAND *Jap. Wife* (ed. 11) 121 The little silver pipe with its *thimble-sized bowl. **1874** KNIGHT *Dict Mech.* 144/2 *Arm*..the *axle-spindle*. When of wood, it is strengthened by metallic straps called skeins, and sometimes by a conical sheath called a *thimble-skein. **1879** H. DRUMMOND in *Life* vii. (1899) 166 The spurts come up in little domes, some only the size of a *thimble-top. **1860** BARTLETT *Dict. Amer.*, *Thimble-weed. (*Rudbeckia*.)..Like the Thimble-berry, its receptacle resembles a thimble.

b. More generally applied *attrib.* or as *adj.* to various objects considered to resemble a thimble in size or shape, esp. as ***thimble cup***, ***glass***. Also *fig.*

1843 *Ainsworth's Mag.* III 470 Having now taken a lump of sugar..and thrown the same into a thimble glass. **1899** H. B. CUSHMAN *Hist. Indians* 501 The monotonous tinkling and rattling of the thimble bells..could be heard. **1907** G. O. WHEELER *Old Eng. Furnit.* xv. 390 The feet [in Sheraton's chairs] were of the thimble-toe or thermed variety. **1933** N. WALN *House of Exile* i. 24 Warm rice-wine, served in thimble cups. **1955** M. ALLINGHAM *Beckoning Lady* xi. 157 The comfortable landlady brought two thimble-glasses, frighteningly overfilled. **1962** *Flight International* LXXXII. 354/1 The new thimble blower is believed to be the world's smallest pressure blower. **1971** *Daily Colonist* (Victoria, B.C.) 24 Nov. 2/1 The thimble-brains who perpetrate the law-breaking know the police are so manacled. **1983** *Times* 16 Dec. 6/4 The thimble measure should be filled to the top.

Hence **thimble** *v.*, *intr.* to use a thimble, to sew; **'thimbling** *vbl. sb.* and *ppl. a.*, using a thimble in sewing; also = *thimblerigging*.

1659 H. M. *Pair Spectacles Nation* 4 Cobling Hewson, Cooper, thimbling Barkstead, Bury, and the rest of their Confederates. **1780** BECKFORD *Italy* (1834) I. v. 38 Pretty sempstresses, warbling melodious hymns as they sat needling and thimbling at their windows above. **1856** J. BALLANTINE *Poems, Wee Raggit Laddie* xiv, Ilk thimblin' thievin' gamblin' diddler..Chase thee like fire. **1857** BORROW *Rom. Rye* xliv, If you have not sufficient capital, why do you engage in so deep a trade as thimbling?

thimbled ('θɪmb(ə)ld), *a.* [f. THIMBLE + -ED[2].] Having, or furnished with, a thimble; in *thieves' slang*, wearing a watch.

1812 J. H. VAUX *Flash Dict.*, *Thimbled*, having or wearing a watch. **1851** HAWTHORNE *Snow Image* (1879) 21 With her thimbled finger. **1884** *Pall Mall G.* 10 Dec. 3/2 Long before either Dutch or English thought of thimbles Chinese ladies were thimbled when they worked at their embroidery.

thimble-eye ('θɪmb(ə)laɪ). [f. THIMBLE + EYE.] **a.** *Naut.* See quots. 1867, 1877. **b.** A fish, the Chub Mackerel, *Scomber colias.* So **thimble-eyed** *a.*, having eyes like thimbles, as this fish.

1815 *Trans. Lit. & Philos. Soc. N.Y.* I. 422 Thimble eyed, bull eyed, or chub mackerel..comes occasionally in prodigious numbers to the coast of New-York in autumn. **1867** SMYTH *Sailor's Word-bk.*, *Thimble-eyes*, are thimble-shaped apertures in iron-plates where sheaves are not required; frequently used instead of dead-eyes for the top-mast-rigging, futtock-plates, and backstays in the channels. **1877** KNIGHT *Dict. Mech.*, *Thimble-eye*,..an eye in a plate through which a rope is rove without a sheave. A dead-eye. **1888** GOODE *Amer. Fishes* 196 The only other spotted fish which has been known to frequent our coast is the 'chub mackerel' or 'thimble eye'. **1891** *Cent. Dict.*, *Thimble-eyed*, ..used of the chub-mackerel.

thimbleful ('θɪmb(ə)lfʊl). [f. THIMBLE + -FUL.] As much as a thimble will hold; hence, a small quantity, esp. of wine or spirits; a dram; also *fig.* of something immaterial.

1607 MARKHAM *Caval.* II. (1617) 120 Take halfe a thimble-ful of Gunpowder. **1622** MABBE tr. *Aleman's Guzman d'Alf.* I. 23 By eating by ounces, and drinking by thimble-fuls, they liue by crams. **1760** FOOTE *Minor* I. Wks. 1799 I. 248 Wou'd you take another thimbleful, Mrs. Cole? **1789** WOLCOTT (P. Pindar) *Expost. Odes* xi, Now can't I give a thimblefull of Praise. **1889** JESSOPP *Coming of Friars* ii. 93 Cordials were..on special occasions dealt out in thimble-fuls. **1894** HELEN M. GOUGAR in *Voice* (N.Y.) 31 May, Anybody with a thimbleful of political or reform sense knows.

thimblerig ('θɪmb(ə)lrɪg), *sb.* [f. THIMBLE + RIG *sb.*[5] 2; *lit.* 'thimble-trick'.]

1. A swindling game usually played with three thimbles (see THIMBLE 2 c) and a pea which was ostensibly placed under one of them; the sharper then challenging the bystanders to guess under which the pea had been placed, and to bet on their choice; a cheat similar to the *three-card trick*.

1825 HONE *Every-day Bk.* I. 768 An unfair game known among the frequenters of races and fairs by the name of 'the thimble rig'. **1836** T. HOOK *G. Gurney* vii, I will start alone, and appear to know no more of you, than one of the cads of the thimble-rig knows of the pea-holder. **1856** J. D. CHAMBERS *Strictures on Judgm. in Westerton v. Liddell* 139 *note*, The manipulations of a sharper with cups and balls on his gambling table, commonly called *thimblerig*. **1893** LELAND *Mem.* I. 13.

attrib. and *Comb.* **1834** LITTLETON in *Hansard's Parl. Deb.* 4 July, XXIV. 1206 His right hon. friend (Mr. Stanley).. had chosen to describe him (Mr. Littleton) as a thimble-rig player, in consequence of the changes that he had made in the clauses of that Bill. **1856** T. A. TROLLOPE *Girlhd. Cath. de Med.* Notes 352 A good deal of confusion as to the dates of these thimblerig-like transactions exists in the narratives of the historians. **1886** C. E. PASCOE *London of To-day* xviii. (ed. 3) 157 Epsom Downs... There are..tumblers, jugglers, boxers, thimble-rig men.

2. = THIMBLERIGGER.

1839 *Fraser's Mag.* XX. 355 Greatly applauded by all the thimblerigs of the fauxbourgs.

'thimblerig, *v.* [f. prec.: app. first used in vbl. sb. and pr. pple.] *intr.* To practise the cheat of the thimblerig; also *fig.* to cheat in a juggling manner or as with sleight of hand. **b.** *trans.* To manipulate (a matter or thing) in this manner. So **'thimblerigged** (-rɪgd) *ppl. a.*, duped by the game of thimblerig; disturbed or affected by thimblerigging, as a market; = RIGGED *ppl. a.*[2]; **'thimblerigging** *vbl. sb.* and *ppl. a.*

1839 THACKERAY *Catherine* i, Don't let us have any juggling and thimblerigging with virtue and vice. **1840** —— *Cruikshank* Wks. 1900 XIII. 310 The different degrees of rascality, as exhibited in each face of the thimblerigging trio. *Ibid.*, Is any man so blind that he cannot see the exact face that is writhing under the thimblerigged hero's hat? **1887** FRITH *Autobiog.* I. xxi 271 Gambling tents and thimble-rigging..had not then been stopped by the police. **1889** MIVART *Orig. Hum. Reason* 92 That 'intellectual thimble-rigging' which all men of the sensist school..must perform. **1892** *Labour Commission* Gloss., *Thimblerigged*, an expression in general use descriptive of speculative operations in the stock produce, or other markets by combination for other than legitimate trade or market requirements. **1899** *Daily News* 31 Jan. 5/3 M. Lebret passes quickly over the legal aspect of the case—thimblerigs it so to speak.

thimblerigger ('θɪmb(ə)l,rɪgə(r)). [f. THIMBLERIG *sb.* + -ER[1].] A professional sharper who cheats by thimblerigging; also *transf.* one who cheats by means of tricks, or juggles with phrases, etc.

1831 *Lincoln Herald* 7 Oct. 4/4 An altercation took place between some countrymen and the thimble-riggers, on a charge of cheating. **1871** L. STEPHEN *Playgr. Eur.* ix. (1894) 202 A cross between a prizefighter and a thimble-rigger. **1891** T. HARDY *Tess* xvii., A firm believer—not as the phrase is now elusively construed by theological thimble-riggers in the Church and out of it.

Hence **'thimble riggery**, thimblerigging.

1841 *Blackw. Mag.* L. 178 Lying and thimbleriggery assume high privilege. **1841** R. OASTLER *Fleet Papers* I. I. 399 The noble art of 'thimble-riggery'.

thimbling, *vbl. sb.* and *ppl. a.*: see THIMBLE *v.*

thime, obs. form of THYME.

thin (θɪn), *a.* (*sb.*) and *adv.* Forms: 1 þynne, þinne, þyn, þin, 3–5 þunne, 3–6 thyn, 4 þenne, 4–6 thynne, (4 thyne, 5 thynn), 4–7 thinn(e, (4–5 thine), 6– thin. [OE. *þynne* = OFris. **thenne*, **thinne* (WFris. *ten*, *tēn*, *tin*); OLG. **þunni* (MLG. *dunne*, MDu. *dunne*, *dinne*, Du. *dun*), OHG. *dunni* (MHG. *dünne*, G. *dünn*), in Gothic **þunnu-s*, ON. *þunnr* (Sw. *tunn*, Da. *tynd*):—OTeut. **þunnu-z*, fem. **þunnī*, with *nu* from *nw*, in Indo-Eur. **tnús*, fem. **tnwī*, from weak grade of ablaut stem *ten-*, *ton-*, *tn-* to stretch (cf. Skr. *tanús*, L. *tenuis*).]

A. *adj.*

I. 1. a. Having relatively little extension between opposite surfaces; of little thickness or depth. Opposed to THICK *a.* 1.

a **900** tr. *Bæda's Hist.* v. vi. (1890) 400 Stan..mid ðinre tyrf bewrigen. *c* **1000** *Sax. Leechd.* I. 288 Ðeos wyrt..hafað þynne leaf. *c* **1020** *Rule St. Benet* lv. (Logeman) 91 Culam on wintre þicce on sumere þinne. *a* **1300** *Cursor M.* 1673 (Cott.) Wit pike þou lok it be noght thyn [*v.rr.* þinne, thine, þynne]. *a* **1310** in Wright *Lyric P.* x. 37 Betere is were thunne boute laste, Then syde robes aut synke into synne. **1387** TREVISA *Higden* (Rolls) I. 405 Brook cakes, round and þynne. **1508** DUNBAR *Tua Mariit Wemen* 23 With curches..of kirsp cleir and thin. **1530** PALSGR. 280/2 Thyn skynne, *tenue peau*. **1638** JUNIUS *Paint. Ancients* 227 We doe not make our plate so thinne as to break it. **1710** J. CLARKE *Rohault's Nat. Phil.* (1729) I. 215 A Glass that is thinner in the Middle than at the Edges. **1802** PLAYFAIR *Illustr. Hutton. Th.* 294 The thinnest part of that rock..is still covered by the strata. **1887** B. V. HEAD *Hist. Numorum* 697 The coins of the Sassanian monarchs are thin, flat, and neatly executed.

b. Of small cross section in proportion to length; slender, tenuous, attenuated. (Usually said of a thing more or less cylindrical, as a wire, rod, branch, stem, stock, trunk, limb.)

a **1425** tr. *Arderne's Treat. Fistula* 59 If it be bi reson of þe membre, þat is for þe membre is to ouer þinne. **1570** LEVINS *Manip.* 133/24 Thinne, *gracilis, tenuis*. **1665** SIR T. HERBERT *Trav.* (1677) 303 Their Harquebuz is longer than ours, but thinner. **1776** WITHERING *Brit. Plants* (1796) IV. 118 Branches..of equal thickness, nay rather thinner at their origin. **1884** BOWER & SCOTT *De Bary's Phaner.* 426 In the cortex of the thin stem. **1885** WATSON & BURBURY *Math. Th. Electr. & Magn.* I. 95 The connection between them being a very thin wire.

c. *spec.* Having little flesh; lean, spare, not fat or plump. Also of ears of corn.

c **1000** *Sax. Leechd.* II. 206 Ne mæg him se lichoma batian ac he bið blac & þynne & acolod. *c* **1050** *Gloss.* in Wr.-Wülcker 415/27 *Galbus*, þynne monn. *a* **1327** *Maximon* iv. in *Rel. Ant.* I. 120 Care and kunde of elde Maketh mi body felde..Ant mi body thunne Such is worldes wunne. **1382** WYCLIF *Gen.* xli. 6 Seuene eerys..thinne and smytun with meldew, weren growun. **1535** COVERDALE *Gen.* xli. 3 Seuen kyne,..thynne euell fauoured, and leenfleshed. **1617** MORYSON *Itin.* II. 46 His face grew thinne, his ruddy colour failed. **1697** DRYDEN *Virg. Past.* III. 156 My Flocks..yet look so thin, Their Bones are barely cover'd with their Skin. **1794** MRS. RADCLIFFE *Myst. Udolpho* xlix, You look so pale now, and so thin, too. **1805–6** COLERIDGE *Three Graves* IV. xi, Oft she said, I'm not grown thin! And then her wrist she spanned. **1865** MISS BRADDON *Sir Jasper* iv. 37 To have long thin white hands, all aglitter with diamond rings.

d. Penetrable by light or vision, like a thin veil; *fig.* easily 'seen through', transparent, flimsy, as a pretext or excuse. (Cf. some uses in 4 a.)

1613 SHAKS. *Hen. VIII*, v. iii. 125, I come not To heare such flattery now, and in my presence They [commendations] are too thin. **1662** HIBBERT *Body Div.* I. 252 A lie is of a thin and transparent nature. **1851** BRIMLEY *Ess., Wordsw.* 103 Under a thin disguise of name. **1860** TYNDALL *Glac.* I. xiv. 94 Over the glacier hung a thin veil of fog. *a* **1904** A. ADAMS *Log Cowboy* xviii, He put up a thin excuse just like the rest. Any one could see through it.

e. Phr. ***the thin end of the wedge***: see WEDGE *sb.* 2 b.

II. 2. a. Consisting of or characterized by individual constituents or parts placed at relatively large intervals; not thick, dense, or bushy. Opposed to THICK *a.* 4. Also ***thin on top***: of a man, having little hair on the (top of the) scalp, balding. Also, of the hair itself.

849 in Birch *Cart. Sax.* II. 40 In..sceaɡan ðær he ðynnest is. *c* **1000** ÆLFRIC *Hom.* II. 466 Oft of ðinnum renscurum flewð seo eorðe. *c* **1290** *S. Eng. Leg.* I. 48/44 Bote þornes and þunne boskes. *c* **1400** MAUNDEV. (Roxb.) xxvi. 126 Þe Tartarenes hase..lytill berdes and thynne. *c* **1440** *Promp. Parv.* 491/1 Thynne, as gresse, corne, wodys,..*rarus*. **1573–80** BARET *Alv.* T 166 Thinne,..not thicke growen, or set,..*rarus*. **1617** MORYSON *Itin.* II. 45 [Lord Mountjoy's] haire was..thinne on his head. **1796** MORSE *Amer. Geog.* I. 77 Indian population is thin; vast tracts..are uninhabited. **1868** TROLLOPE *He knew He was Right* (1869) I. xxxi. 243 'You are not bald at all.'..'I am beginning to be thin enough at the top.' **1894** DOYLE *Mem. S. Holmes* 49 A thin rain began to fall. **1921** G. B. SHAW *Back to Methuselah* v. 217 Getting a little hard set and flat-chested and thin on the top, wasn't she? **1933** W. S. MAUGHAM *Sheppey* I. 2 'Air's very dry, sir..getting a bit thin on top. **1950** J. CANNAN *Murder Included* vi. 124 There 'e goes—thin on top, ain't 'e? **1978** L. MEYNELL *Papersnake* vi. 77 At forty-one his hair was definitely receding and getting thin on top.

†**b.** Of the members of a collective group or class: Not numerous or abundant; scarce, rare, few, scanty. Opposed to THICK *a.* 5. *Obs.*

1508 KENNEDY *Flyting w. Dunbar* 350 Corspatrik..Thy forefader maid Irisch and Irisch men thin. **1573–80** BARET *Alv.* T 166 Thinne:..seld and not often, *rarus*: to waxe thin, to waxe a small number. **1638** JUNIUS *Paint. Ancients* 188 Artificers also grew thinner and thinner, till none at length were left. *c* **1645** HOWELL *Lett.* (1650) I. 95 Gentry amongst them is very thin,..and coming to dwell in towns, they soon mingle with the merchants, and so degenerate. **1725** T. THOMAS in *Portland Papers* VI. (Hist. MSS. Comm.) 109 Churches are very thin in this part of the World. [**1863** W. C. BALDWIN *Afr. Hunting* ix. 405 Game of all sorts is as thin as deal boards.]

†**c.** Of a place: Sparsely occupied or peopled; with *of*, sparsely furnished or supplied with; thinly occupied or attended by. *Obs.*

1621 BURTON *Anat. Mel.* Democr. to Rdr. (1628) 52 Many Kingdomes are fertile, but thin of inhabitants. **1673** *Essex*

Papers (Camden) I. 65 How thinn of Soldrs are ye Few Garrisons we keepe. **1693** *Humours Town* 51 You must be content with such as your thin Neighbourhood affords. **1711** Swift *Jrnl. to Stella* 24 Aug., The town being thin, I am less pestered with company. **1733** Tull *Horse-Hoeing Husb.* xi. 124 Both these Rows were Thin of Plants. **1797** *Encycl. Brit.* (ed. 3) VII. 528/1 Galicia..is but thin of people. **1800** Ht. Lee *Canterb. T.* (ed. 2) III. 89 Summer was now fast approaching, and the town was thin.

d. Of an assembly or body of people: Scantily furnished with members; thinly attended; not full.

1647 Clarendon *Hist. Rev.* v. §361 What had been..in a full House, rejected, was many times in a thin House.. resumed, and determined contrary to the former conclusions. **1660** Pepys *Diary* 2 Oct., There I found but a thin congregation already. **1703** *Lond. Gaz.* No. 3904/1 Their Battalions are thin and sickly. **1713** S. Sewall *Diary* 27 Oct., Buried with a very thin Funeral. **1746** Francis tr. *Horace's Art Poetry* 297 The little Theatre..To which a thin and pious Audience came. **1860–70** Stubbs *Lect. Europ. Hist.* I. ix. (1904) 119 In a very thin meeting, Ferdinand stated his view.

e. ***thin on the ground***: (chiefly of persons) few in number, widely scattered; scarce, and therefore difficult to find. Also of a group, having few members. Cf. thick *a.* 5 a.

1951 W. S. Churchill *2nd World War* IV. I. vi. 86 There was very heavy fighting and many craft were sunk, but the Australians were thin on the ground and enemy parties got ashore at many points. *a* **1957** A. Brooke in A. Bryant *Turn of Tide 1939–43* (1957) ii. 115, I got up early..and started with the 3rd Division, which I found well established but infernally thin on the ground. **1964** 'A. Gilbert' *Knock, knock, who's There?* i. 14 The customers were still pretty thin on the ground. **1976** A. Hill *Summer's End* ii. 22 Work was a bit thin on the ground everywhere, wi' long dole queues. **1980** *Times Lit. Suppl.* 25 July 850/1 Even now, when the Anglo-Irish are precariously thin on the ground, people among them who don't like horses can be miserable in certain counties.

f. *Mountaineering.* Of or pertaining to a rock face on which good climbing holds are hard to find.

1955 S. Styles *Introd. Mountaineering* 144 *Thin*, generally used of steep rock, meaning 'smooth; having few or very small holds'. **1963** A. Greenbank *Instructions in Rock Climbing* vi. 73 When a guidebook says '*strenuous*', it usually means steep, fierce-looking rock; '*delicate*' or '*thin*', the footholds and/or handholds are tiny. **1970** R. James *Rock Climbing in Wales* 161 Climb this buttress up the L. side, centre and R. side respectively, each giving a thin lower pitch followed by a short artificial section. **1981** *Fell & Rock Jrnl.* XXIII. II. 199 To its left Wafer Thin gives some very thin climbing up flaky pockets to a final smooth slab.

g. ***thin red line***: see red line *sb. phr.* Similarly ***thin blue line***: a line of policemen, esp. one which holds back a surging crowd; also *transf.*, the defensive barrier of the law.

1962 *Sunday Times* 16 Dec. 17/2 (*caption*) The 'thin blue line' at an anti-nuclear demonstration. **1970** G. Jackson *Let.* 17 Apr. in *Soledad Brother* (1971) 222 You've heard the patronizing shit about the thin blue line that protects property and the owners of property. **1979** 'M. Underwood' *Smooth Justice* ii. 45 The sort of protection we can give..isn't even a thin blue line.

3. a. Of a liquid or a pasty substance: Of slight density or consistence; fluid; of air or vapour: not dense; rare, tenuous, subtile. Opp. to thick *a.* 6.

a **900** tr. *Bæda's Hist.* III. xix. [xxvii.] (1890) 244 Nemne medmicel hlafes mid þinre meolc. *a* **1000** *Boeth. Metr.* v. 6 Ær se þicca mist þynra weorðe. *c* **1000** *Sax. Leechd.* II. 314 Hrer on blede oþ þ hit sie þicce swa þynne briw. *c* **1375** *Sc. Leg. Saints* xxxii. (*Iustin*) 735 Vndir it a fyre gert ma Til þat mater [pitch and brimstone] wes moltyne thyne. *c* **1430** *Two Cookery-bks.* 12 Late it be nowt to þikke ne to þinne, but as potage shulde be. **1530** Palsgr. 280/2 Thyn cloude in the ayre. **1621** Burton *Anat. Mel.* II. ii. I. i. (1651) 232 Pure, thin, light water. **1667** Milton *P.L.* viii. 348 Fish..cannot change Thir Element to draw the thinner Aire. **1744** Berkeley *Siris* §121 An exceeding thin volatile oil. **1850** *Young's Patent* in *Law Times Rep.* X. 862/1 Chalk, ground up with a little water into a thin paste.

b. *transf.* and *fig.* Wanting body or substance; unsubstantial; intangible. Also in phr. ***to vanish*** (***melt***, etc.) ***into thin air***: to disappear completely from sight or existence (formerly only of spirits). More rarely ***to come*** (etc.) ***out of thin air***. Now chiefly *colloq.*

1610 Shaks. *Temp.* iv. i. 150 These our actors..were all Spirits, and Are melted into Ayre, into thin Ayre. **1671** Milton *P.R.* i. 499 Satan bowing low His gray dissimulation, disappear'd Into thin air diffus'd. **1705** Addison *Italy* 3 The lab'ring Plow-man oft with Horror spies Thin airy Shapes that o'er the Furrows rise. **1724** R. Welton *Chr. Faith & Pract.* 120 All the thin and airy delights of the world. *c* **1800** Blake *Vala* v, in *Compl. Writings* (1966) 305 As plants wither'd by winter..Melt into thin air. **1892** Westcott *Gospel of Life* 108 Man cannot live in the thin atmosphere of abstractions. **1904** Conrad *Nostromo* I. i. 4 Vapours that..vanish into thin air. **1907** *Edin. Rev.* Oct. 402 Logic is too thin and bloodless a thing to govern life. **1918** L. Strachey *Eminent Victorians* 223 The Ever Victorious Army..was an ill-disciplined, ill-organised body..constantly on the verge of mutiny..and, at the slightest provocation, melting into thin air. **1932** W. Faulkner *Light in August* ix. 204 Having apparently materialised out of thin air. **1951** *Sport* 7–13 Jan. 16/2 Speed, confidence, shooting ability, all seemed to have vanished into thin air. **1977** 'E. McBain' *Long Time no See* xi. 181 The recurring nightmares hadn't come out of thin air.

c. Wanting depth or intensity; faint, weak, dim, pale. Formerly of light (*arch.*): in mod. use, of colours, painting, or the like.

1649 Lovelace *Poems* 90 Yet its Glory did appeare But thinne, because her eyes were neere. **1655** Stanley *Hist. Philos.* II. (1701) 61/2 The Moon hath a light of her own: but very thin. **1875** Fortnum *Maiolica* xiv. 156 The use of a bright yellow..in imitations of the golden lustre, and a thin green. **1893** Hodges *Elem. Photogr.* (1907) 102 Thin and rather weak negatives. **1894** *Athenæum* 3 Mar. 285/3 The figures are half-lengths, and executed in a thin, hard, and laborious manner.

d. Of sound: Wanting fullness, volume, or depth; weak and high-pitched; shrill and feeble.

16.. Dryden (J.), I hear the groans of ghosts; Thin, hollow sounds, and lamentable screams. **1726** Pope *Odyss.* xxiv. 8 Trembling the Spectres glide, and plaintive vent Thin, hollow screams. **1824** Lamb *Elia* Ser. II. *Capt. Jackson*, Be dumb, thou thin accompanier of her thinner warble! *a* **1895** W. Morris in Mackail *Life* (1899) II. 314, I heard..the trowels fall Upon the stone, a thin noise far away. **1901** *Scotsman* 15 Mar. 7/4 The possessor of the thinnest treble in the Irish quarter..piped tremulously.

4. *fig.* Deficient in substance or quality; poor; unsubstantial. **a.** Of immaterial things: Wanting in fulness, breadth, force, or vigour; scanty, insufficient; weak, feeble; slight; of little worth.

[*a* **900** tr. *Bæda's Hist.* v. xvii. [xix.] (1890) 462 Nemne ðynre eðunge anre ætywde þæt he lifes wæs. *c* **1000** *Sax. Leechd.* II. 84 Hwilc þ mægen sie & sio ȝecynd þæs lichoman, hwæþer hio sie strang.., þe hio sie hnesce & mearwe & þynne.] *a* **1225** *Ancr. R.* 144 Vre god þet is þunne —vre sunnen þet beoð so monie. *c* **1315** Shoreham iii. 272 Hare wyȝt [= wit] hys al to þenne. *c* **1330** R. Brunne *Chron. Wace* (Rolls) 113 My witte was oure thynne So strange speche to trauayle in. *c* **1374** Chaucer *Boeth.* II. Met. vii. 47 (Camb. MS.) The thynne fame yit lastynge of hir ydel names, is marked with a fewe letterys. *c* **1425** ? Lydg. *Assembly of Gods* 1591 My brayne ys so thynne. **1545** Ascham *Toxoph.* (Arb.) 28 As thinne invention, as other poore men. **1580** H. Gifford *Posie Gillowflowers, Merrie Jest*, Yet was her wit but thin. **1658–9** *Burton's Diary* (1828) IV. 65 They are gallant in their persons, but thin in relations. **1844** Kinglake *Eöthen* vii. (1878) 96 Engaged in very thin conversation. **1888** *Daily News* 9 July 4/8 The apology is a very lame one—what our American cousins call 'thin'. **1890** *Spectator* 16 Aug. 221/2 This is about the thinnest travel-book we have ever read. **1894** *Westm. Gaz.* 5 Feb. 1/2 Really, has not this laudation of the old at the expense of the new become a little too thin?

b. Of diet or supplies: Scanty, meagre, spare; not full or rich; poor, low. Now *rare.*

c **1374** Chaucer *Former Age* 36 Ther as vitayle is ek so skars and thinne [*v.r.* thynne]. *c* **1450** *St. Cuthbert* (Surtees) 5264 Bot vytayls were ful thynn. *c* **1485** *Digby Myst.* III. 1733 Yower spendyng is thyn. **1535** Stewart *Cron. Scot.* (Rolls) II. 618 Becaus he wes in his substance so thyn. **1596** Shaks. *Tam. Shr.* iv. iv. 61 At so slender warning, You are like to haue a thin and slender pittance. **1648** Crashaw *Steps to Temple* Wks. (1904) 82 Nor hath God a thinner Share. **1707** Floyer *Physic. Pulse-Watch* 196 In these Fasting is necessary, or a thin Diet. **1826** Disraeli *Viv. Grey* vi. i, Thin entertainment here, kind Sir.

c. *spec.* Of liquor: Without body; not strong or rich; of low alcoholic strength; weak. (Cf. 3.)

[**1377** Langl. *P. Pl.* B. xix. 398, I can selle Bothe dregges & draffe, and drawe it at on hole, þikke ale and þinne ale.] *c* **1440** *Alphabet of Tales* 6, I may not drynk your thyn ale. **1560** Pilkington *Expos. Aggeus* (1562) 90 Loke howe many of youre poore neighbours..drink thin drink. **1597** Shaks. *2 Hen. IV*, iv. iii. 134 To forsweare thinne Potations, and to addict themselues to Sack. **1691** Ray *N.C. Words* 138 Thin drink, small Beer, *Cerevisia tenuis.* **1859** Dickens *T. Two Cities* II. xv, Monsieur Defarge sold a very thin wine at the best of times.

d. Phr. ***a thin time***: a wretched period of experience. *colloq.*

1924 A. J. Small *Frozen Gold* iv. 108 Yes, sure, you go... If you don't, she will give me such a thin time. **1935** *Economist* 17 Aug. 326/1 Dairy farming and lumbering and doing poorly; while the mountain peasantry especially are having a thin time. **1955** *Times* 22 Aug. 3/3 The London sides in the Championship had a thin time. Not one of them won.

e. *Econ.* Of or pertaining to a stock market (or to stocks, shares) in which trading is light.

1931 *Economist* 28 Feb. 441/2 Prices were marked up to 10 cents a pound in the hope of attracting buyers who had refused to take metal at 9½ cents, but the market remains thin. **1946** *Sun* (Baltimore) 17 Jan. 12–0/1 Some of the 'thin' shares tacked on around six points. **1964** *Financial Times* 3 Mar. 19/2 Further speculative buying in a thin market led to a fresh rise. **1981** *Times* 30 June 20/1 Dealers described turnover as thin.

B. *absol.* as *sb.*: mostly elliptical or nonce-uses. ***thin and thick***: see thick and thin.

c **1350** *St. Jacob* 173 (xix.) in Horstmann *Altengl. Leg.* (1881) 99/1 þai suld noght leue for thin ne thik Till þai war broght bath ded or quik. **1426** Lydg. *De Guil. Pilgr.* 11135, I [Youth] passe bothe thorgh thynne & thykke. **1895** G. Allen *Woman who did* (1906) 184 This very fact that she had always lived in the Thick of Things made a change to the Thin of Things only the more enchanting.

C. *adv.* **1. a.** = thinly 1. †***to go thin***: to wear thin clothing, to be thinly clad (*obs.*).

a **1250** *Owl & Night.* 1529 Wel þunne isrud & ived wroþe. *a* **1610** Healey *Theophrastus* (1636) 11 Why hee goes so thinne, and why hee will not go better cloth'd? *a* **1631** Donne *Serm.* xlv. 450 Spread we this a little thinner, and we shall better see through it. **1633** Herbert *Temple, Praise* vii, My heart, Though press'd, runnes thin. **1652–62** Heylin *Cosmogr.* iv. (1682) 31 The people go extreme thin in the sharpest Winter. **1738** Swift *Pol. Conversat.* p. xliii, They ought to be husbanded better, and spread much thinner. **1806** A. Hunter *Culina* (ed. 2) 194 Cut the chops very thin.

†**b.** In a poor or sparing manner. *Obs.*

1607 Topsell *Four-f. Beasts* (1658) 325 Let the Horse be thin dieted, during his curing time.

2. = thinly 2.

1375 Barbour *Bruce* iv. 685 Bot þai prophetis so thyn ar sawin, þat [etc.]. *c* **1386** Chaucer *Knt's Prol.* 679 But thinne it lay, by colpons oon and oon. **1573–80** Baret *Alv.* T 167 Seldome: not oft: thinne: not thicke, *rare.* **1649** Blithe *Eng. Improv. Impr.* (1653) To Husbandm., The earlier thou sowest, the thinner thou maiest sow thy winter corn. **1707** Mortimer *Husb.* (1721) I. 34 To sow something thinner than ordinary. **1886** C. Scott *Sheep-Farming* 37 The thinner sheep are pastured the healthier they are.

D. Combinations. **I.** Of the adj.

a. Chiefly parasynthetic adjectives, as ***thin-bedded***, ***-bladed***, ***-blooded***, ***-brained*** (in sense A. 4 a), ***-cheeked***, ***-faced***, ***-flanked***, †***-gaskined*** (gaskin[1] 2), ***-haired***, ***-leaved***, ***-lipped***, ***-rinded*** (†***rined***), ***-soled***, ***-stemmed***, etc. See also thin-gutted, -skinned, -walled..

1859 Murchison *Siluria* iv. (ed. 3) 75 We reach the *thin-bedded..flags. **1855** Whyte Melville *Gen. Bounce* ix, A *thin-bladed knife and two-pronged fork. **1934** Webster *Thin-blooded. **1959** *Times* 10 June 7/3 The rest of the programme, though it sometimes achieved a sort of thin-blooded distinction, was really rather disappointing. **1598** Marston *Sco. Villanie* III. x, *Thin-brain'd Idiots, dull, vncapable. **1596** R. L[inche] *Diella* (1877) 74 In my *thin-cheekt face thou well maist see. **1633** T. Adams *Exp. 2 Peter* ii. 1 Away with that *thin-dawned profession. **1601** Shaks. *Twel. N.* v. i. 213 A *thin fac'd knaue, a gull **1899** Crockett *Kit Kennedy* xii. 88 A thin-faced..woman, with an air of being perpetually tired. **1649** G. Daniel *Trinarch., Hen. V* clxiv, The *thin-film'd Bladder breakes. **1894** Kipling *Seven Seas* (1896) 148 Till you married that *thin-flanked woman. **1737** Bracken *Farriery Impr.* (1757) II. 102 Some Horses are so *thin Gascoign'd, that they will never look plump. **1398** Trevisa *Barth. De P.R.* xviii. xv. (Bodl. MS.), The Bugle is..*þynne hered. **1697** Dryden *Virg. Georg.* II. 96 The *thin-leav'd Arbute Hazle Graffs receives. **1897** *Daily News* 2 Oct. 2/3 Cranes and herons and ibis and other *thin-legged water fowl. **1681** Grew *Musæum* I. vi. i. 130 The *Thin-Lip'd Wilk. **1907** H. Wyndham *Flare Footlights* vii, An unpleasant smile playing about the corners of his thin-lipped mouth. **1677** Yarranton *Eng. Improv.* 120 Our Wheat is large, full-brested, and *thin-rined. **1805** Dickson *Pract. Agric.* I. 572 The most plump and thinnest-rinded grain. **1682** Otway *Venice Preserved* III. ii, Cathars and Tooth Ach got By *thin-sol'd shoos. **1869** Tozer *Highl. Turkey* I. 315 An Albanian with his long *thin-stocked gun.

b. Special combinations and collocations: **thin-belly**, one who has a thin belly; in quot. *attrib.*; so **thin-bellied** *a.*, lean, hungry-looking; **thin coal**, coal found in shallow beds or seams: cf. *thick coal* s.v. thick *a.* 12 b; **thin-film** *a.*, applied to processes and devices that employ or involve a very thin solid or liquid film; **thin-headed** *a.*, having a thin or narrow head; *fig.* shallow-pated, silly; **thin-layer chromatography** *Chem.* [tr. G. *dünnschicht-chromatographie* (E. Stahl 1956, in *Pharmazie* XI. 633)], chromatography in which compounds are separated on a thin layer of adsorbent material such as charcoal or silica gel; **thin-minded** *a. rare*−1, narrow-minded, prejudiced; **thin-miner**, see quot.; **thin seam** (also *attrib.*), see quots.; **thin section**, a thin, flat piece of rock or tissue prepared with a thickness of about 0·03 mm. for examination with an optical microscope; also, a piece of tissue of the order of 30 nm. thick prepared for electron microscopy; hence **thin-sectioning** *vbl. sb.*, the making of thin sections; **thin space** *Typogr.*, a piece of metal used for separating words, cast five to an em of its own body; cf. *thick space* s.v. thick *a.* 12 b; **thin-worn** *a.*, made thin by wear.

1588 Shaks. *L.L.L.* III. i. 19 Your armes crost on your *thinbellie doublet. **1591** Percival *Span. Dict.*, *Trasijado*, lanke, *thinne bellied. **1855** J. Phillips *Man. Geol.* 188 Strata and *thin coals. **1900** *Engineering Mag.* XIX. 717 In days gone by thin seams were worked by special thin coal miners. **1956** *Nature* 24 Mar. 571/2 *Thin-film lubrication. **1963** *New Scientist* 21 Mar. 632/3 Thin-film memories and logic devices. **1966** D. G. Brandon *Mod. Techniques Metallogr.* ii. 90 Variations in absorption with crystalline perfection contribute significantly to the contrast in thin-film transmission microscopy. **1970** *Brit. Printer* July 69/2 The advent of thin-film inks gave the screen printer a choice which had not previously existed. **1603** Dekker *Wonderfull Yeare* A iij b, *Thin-headed fellowes that liue vpon the scraps of inuention. **1804** Shaw *Gen. Zool.* V. 237 Thin-headed Carp, *Cyprinus Leptocephalus.* **1957** *Chem. Abstr.* LI. 6948 (*heading*) *Thin-layer chromatography (the method, affecting factors, and a few examples of application). **1961** *Jrnl. Amer. Oil Chemists' Soc.* XXXVIII. 313/1 Two procedures for the analysis of mixtures of mono-, di-, and triglycerides. One employs..thin-layer chromatography. **1967** *Oceanogr. & Marine Biol.* V. 267 Thin layer chromatography can pinpoint some inaccuracies in the interpretation of spectra and give a more adequate image of the variety of pigments. **1978** H. H. Bauer et al. *Instrumental Analysis* xxi. 626 Appreciation of the full advantages of planar chromatography then led to thin-layer chromatography (TLC). **1864** Trollope *Small House at Allington* I. ii. 11 Such *thin-minded men can hardly go to the proof of any matter without some pre-judgment in their minds. **1892** *Labour Commission* Gloss., **Thin miners*, miners who get coal out of thin seams. **1883** Gresley *Gloss. Coal-mining*, **Thin Seams*,..coal seams (say) less than 3 feet in thickness. **1887** *Pall Mall G.* 5 Sept. 12/1 The coal-mining industry in the thin-seam districts. **1858** *Q. Jrnl. Geol. Soc.* XIV. 469 For some purposes, however, *thin sections are quite indispensable. **1872** F. Delafield *Handbk. Post-Mortem Examinations* I. 21 The proportion of alcohol is to be afterward increased until the mucous membrane is hard enough to be cut into thin sections. **1916** JORDAN & FERGUSON *Text-bk. Histol.* xx. 734 Thick sections may be obtained from the firmer tissues by free-hand sectioning with a razor, but for the satisfactory preparation of thin sections a microtome is a necessity. **1956** *Nature* 14 Jan. 98/1 Although electron microscope contrast may be increased by the use of objective apertures, accurate focusing in thin-section work is still difficult. **1970** *Ibid.* 17 Oct. 251/2 Petrological analysis by thin section has enabled the locality of origin of axes made from hard rock to be identified. **1964** G. H. HAGGIS et al. *Introd. Molecular Biol.* v. 135 The pellet which contains them [*sc.* mitochondria] can be identified, and its purity assessed, by *thin-sectioning of the osmium-fixed embedded pellet. **1978** *Sci. Amer.* May 141/2 There are two principal specimen-preparation methods for rendering cells suitable for examination in the electron microscope: thin-sectioning and freeze-fracturing. **1683** *Thin space [see SPACE *sb.*[1] 15 b]. **1808** C. STOWER *Printer's Gram.* iii. 90 Of Spaces... Five to an m—or five thin spaces. **1968** J. R. BIGGS *Basic Typogr.* 76/2 Space between words is achieved by means of tiny bricks of metal... They are.. thin space.. thick space.. hair space. **1823** MRS. GRANT *Mem. & Corr.* (1844) III. 31 Easily she threw off the *thin-worn robe of mortality.

II. Of the adverb: with participles or adjectives, to which *thin* is now joined by a hyphen, or as a single word; forming adjs., usually of obvious meaning, unlimited in number, as, in sense 1, *thin-cut, -frozen, -laid, -lined, -pervading, -veiled, -wrought*; in sense 2, † *thin-bred, -descending, -flowing, -grown, -officered, -peopled, -set, -shot*, etc. **thin-clad** *a.*, wearing thin clothes; also (*U.S. colloq.*) *absol.* as *sb.*, an athlete. See also THIN-SOWN, THIN-SPUN.

a **1400–50** *Alexander* 320 A berd as a besom with *thyn bred haris. **1690** LOCKE *Hum. Und.* IV. xvii. §4 'Tis not safe ..to go abroad *thin clad. **1947** *Sun* (Baltimore) 30 Oct. 19/2 (*heading*) Maryland thinclads beat navy. **1974** *Anderson* (S. Carolina) *Independent* 24 Apr. 5B/1 Cliff Satterwhite.. has been coaching the few Trojan thinclads. **1851** CARLYLE *J. Sterling* I. ii. (1872) 11 A light *thin-flowing style of mirth. **1865** W. J. LINTON 3 *Englishmen, Alfred*, He.. breaks a way through the *thin-frozen sludge. **1908** *Westm. Gaz.* 29 Sept. 4/2 Prices that need not stand in the way of the *thinnest-lined of purses. *a* **1687** PETTY *Pol. Arith.* i. (1690) 11 In *thin peopled places. **1647–9** G. DANIEL *Poems* Wks. (Grosart) II. 130 Hee, poore Swaine, in bare And *thin-Set Shades did Sing. **1812** CRABBE *Tales* x. 351 The burning sand, the fields of thin-set rye. **1642** H. MORE *Song of Soul* II. iii. I. xxiii, Their *thin-shot shadowings And lightned sides. **1538** ELYOT *Dict.*, *Leuidensis*, *thynne wrought, and of small substance.

thin (θɪn), *v.*[1] [OE. *þynnian*, f. *þynne*, THIN *a.* Cf. OHG. *dunnên*, Ger. *dünnen*, MLG. *dunnen*, MDu. *dunnen, dinnen*, Du. *dunnen*, ON. *þynna* to thin.]

1. *trans.* To make thin; to reduce in thickness or depth; to spread or draw *out* in a thin layer or thread. *to thin off, down*: to diminish gradually to vanishing point.

c **900** *Bede Glosses* 80 in *O.E. Texts* 182 *Obtenueraṫ* (*t*), ðynnade. *c* **1000** ÆLFRIC *Saints' Lives* xxxiii. 236 And ne oncneow hi na for-þam heo wæs swiðe ȝeþynnod. **1482** *Monk of Evesham* (Arb.) 41 For the stature and forme of some of them was as hyt had be lessyd or thynnyde by tormentys. **1608** TOPSELL *Serpents* (1658) 616 To smooth and thin the skin. **1684** R. WALLER *Nat. Exper.* 117 The battered Silver (which being so little Ductile did not at all thin, and distend it self). **1727** *Philip Quarll* (1816) 56 Having resolved, as the summer approached, to thin his clothing by degrees. **1793** *Trans. Soc. Arts* V. 204 The two ends are to be thinned off in form of a wedge. **1891** G. MEREDITH *One of our Conq.* III. iv. 66 She.. had thinned her lips for utterance of a desperate thing.

b. *fig.* (In quot. 1382 a literalism of translation.)

1382 WYCLIF *Jer.* xxx. 19, Y shal glorifie them, and thei shuln not be thynned [*Vulg.* non attenuabuntur]. **1670** EACHARD *Cont. Clergy* 33 By this means he has usually so thinn'd his judgment. **1787** JEFFERSON *Writ.* (1859) II. 117 Real friends, whose affections are not thinned to cob-web. **1874** H. R. REYNOLDS *John Bapt.* viii. 497 To thin down the distinction between the mission, character, education, and position of John and those of Christ.

2. *intr.* To become thin or thinner; to decrease in thickness or depth. *to thin out* (*off, away*): to become gradually thinner until it disappears, as a layer or stratum. Also *fig.*

1804 COLERIDGE *Lett., to D. Stuart* (1895) 475 A rock which thins as it rises up. **1830** LYELL *Princ. Geol.* I. 341 When a number of beds thin out gradually, and at different points. **1833** HERSCHEL *Astron.* viii. 256 The half-moon becomes a crescent, which thins off. **1851** *Jrnl. R. Agric. Soc.* XII. II. 473 In which direction the boulder clay appears to thin off. **1874** HARDY *Far fr. Madding Crowd* xxii, Men thin away to insignificance and oblivion. **1899** J. HUTCHINSON in *Arch. Surg.* X. 155 Their usual course is to cause the nail over them to thin and break down.

b. *spec.* To lose flesh; to become spare or lean.

1870 *Pall Mall G.* 7 Sept. 11 During this troubled period he had thinned so as to seem a different man. **1893** *Chamb. Jrnl.* 19 Aug. 523/2 Her fresh comeliness left her; her face thinned down.

3. *trans.* To render less crowded or close by removing individuals; hence, to reduce in number.

a. With an assemblage of individuals as object.

c **1440** *Promp. Parv.* 491/1 Thynnyn, or make thynne, as wodys, cornys, gresse. **1687** DRYDEN *Hind & P.* II. 243 As when the cause goes hard, the guilty man Excepts, and thins his jury all he can. **1699** S. SEWALL *Diary* 28 Dec., Our Meeting was pretty much thin'd by it. **1832** HT. MARTINEAU *Homes Abroad* i. 12 To thin our population. **1855** MACAULAY *Hist. Eng.* xvi. III. 681 The malady which had thinned the ranks of Schomberg's army at Dundalk.

b. With the individuals as object.

1697 DRYDEN *Virg. Georg.* II. 554 T' unload the Branches, or the Leaves to thin, That suck the Vital Moisture of the Vine. **1786** ABERCROMBIE *Gard. Assist.* 257 Hoe and thin turneps. **1850** *Florist* Aug., Thin out superfluous shoots. **1856** DICKENS *Lett.* (1880) I. 439 Your friend.. has thinned the trees. **1890** *Spectator* 19 Apr., For reducing the new expenditure on drink, and for thinning-off the public-houses in the rural districts.

c. To render (a place) less closely or numerously occupied by the removal *of* occupants.

1743 BLAIR *Grave* 213 Who.. in a cruel wantonness of power Thinn'd states of half their people. **1774** GOLDSM. *Nat. Hist.* (1776) III. 400 It would soon thin the forest of every other living creature. **1856** MERIVALE *Rom. Emp.* IV. xl. 507 The Forum and other public places were deliberately thinned of their overgrowths of sculpture. **1905** *Daily Chron.* 24 Aug. 4/7 A head already thinned of hair.

4. *intr.* Of a place: To become less full or crowded; of a crowd: to become less numerous.

1779 EARL CARLISLE in Jesse *Selwyn & Contemp.* (1844) IV. 180 The town begins to thin, though Parliament is still sitting. **1805** HAN. MORE in Roberts *Mem.* (1835) III. 240 No resident minister;.. the church of course thins. **1828** *Examiner* 129/1 The band.. is steadily thinning. **1848** DICKENS *Dombey* iv, 'The streets have thinned', as Mr. Gills says, 'very much'. *c* **1860** FABER *Hymn*, '*After a Death*' xvii, My world of friends thins round me fast. **1897** H. DRUMMOND *Ideal Life* 101 The crowd thinned.

5. *trans.* To make less thick, dense, or viscid; to dilute. Also *fig.*

c **1000** *Sax. Leechd.* II. 194 þæt ofstandene þicce slipiȝe horh þu scealt.. wyrman & þynnian. *a* **1340** HAMPOLE *Psalter, Cant.* 497 Myn eghyn ere thynyd, that is.. purgid of vile lustis.. and made sutil. *c* **1440** *Promp. Parv.* 491/2 Thynnyn, or make thynne, as lycurys, *tenuo.* **1605** TIMME *Quersit.* III. 182 This water.. cutteth and thinneth grosse matters. **1796** MRS. GLASSE *Cookery* xxi. 336 Mix half a pound of best flour, and thin it with damask-rose-water. **1880** J. CAIRD *Philos. Relig.* ii. 60 By thinning down the idea of God to an abstraction which would embrace under a common head the rudest fetishism and the spiritual theism of Christianity. **1890** ABNEY *Photogr.* (ed. 6) 76 The.. liquid is.. thinned down to proper fluidity.

6. *intr.* To become less dense or consistent; to grow fluid, tenuous, or rare.

1834 M. SCOTT in *Blackw. Mag.* XXXV. 900 Gradually the figure, without changing its position, thinned, and anon ..the stars were seen through it. **1884** S. COX *Miracles* 63 The haze of difficulty which enshrouds them thins.

† **thin**, *v.*[2] *Obs. rare.* [f. OE. *þennan* (*þænnan*) and *þenian* = OS. *thennian*, OHG. *dennen, denen* (G. *dehnen*), ON. *þenja*, Goth. *uf)þanjan* :—OTeut. **þanjan-*, factitive vb. from Indo-Eur. root **ten-* to stretch.] *trans.* To stretch out, extend.

The existence of this in ME. is doubtful: the OE. form would properly give ME. *penne or pene*; *pinne* is perh. an error.

c **1000** *Ags. Ps.* (Th.) cxlii[i]. 6 Ic mine hande to þe holde þenede. *c* **1000** *Sax. Leechd.* III. 22 Þænne þone swiðran earm swa he swiþast mæȝe. *a* **1300** *E.E. Psalter* cvii. 10 [cviii. 9] In Ydume sal i þinne [WYCLIF strecchen] mi scho.

thin, obs. f. THINE; var. THYNE, *Obs.*, thence.

thine (ðaɪn), *poss. pron.* Forms: 1–4 **ðín, þín**, 4–5 **þyn, þine, þyne. thin, thyn**, 4–6 **thyne**, (2, 4 **tin**, 3 **ten**, 3–4 **tine**, 5 **tyn**), 4– **thine.** [OE. *ðín, þín*, used as genitive case of *ðú*, THOU, and as possess. adj. = OFris., OS. *thîn* (MDu. *dijn*, MLG., LG. *dîn*), OHG. *dîn* (MHG. *dîn*, G. *dein*), ON. *þin* (*þín-*, etc.) (Norw., Sw., Da. *din*), Goth. gen. *þeina*, poss. pron. *þeins*, etc.:—OTeut. **þîno-*, deriv. of stem *þe-*: see THEE.]

For restriction of use see note to THOU *pron.* I.

† **I. 1.** Genitive case of the pronoun THOU: = of thee, thee. *Obs.*

971 *Blickl. Hom.* 233 Hie woldon to eorþan astiȝan, & þin þær onbidan. *c* **1300** *Havelok* 1128 Ye sholen ben weddeth, And, maugre þin, to-gidere beddeth. *Ibid.* 1789. *c* **1500** *Lancelot* 115 Al magre thine a seruand schal yow bee.

II. The possessive adjective or pronoun of the second person sing.: Belonging to thee.

In OE. an adj. *þín, þine, þín*, with strong inflexions, remains of which survived in Early ME., as sing. masc. acc. *þinne* (*þine*), dat. *þínum* (*-an, -en, -e*), gen. *þínes*; f. nom. *þíne*, gen. and dat. *þínre* (*þire, þine*); pl. nom., acc. *þíne*, dat. *þínum* (*-on, -en, -e*), gen. *þínra* (*-re, þire*). The final *n* of *þín* began to be dropped before a cons. *a* 1200, leaving *þí*, later written *þy*, THY, q.v. At last *thin, thine*, was restricted to the position in which the possessive is not followed by a sb. Cf. MINE.

2. *Attributively* (= Ger. *dein*, F. *ton*). Now *arch.* or *poet.* before a vowel or *h*, or when following the sb.: otherwise superseded by THY.

c **825** *Vesp. Psalter* ci[i]. 29 Bearn ðiowa ðinra ineardiað ðer. *Ibid.* cxviii[i]. 125 Ðiow ðin ic eam. *c* **1000** *Ags. Ps.* (Th.) xlix. 21 [l. 20] þu sæte onȝean þinne broþor, and tældest hine. *c* **1000** *Ags. Gosp.* Matt. vi. 10 ȝewurþe ðin willa on eorðan. *c* **1175** *Lamb. Hom.* 13 Þenne beoð þine daȝes ilenged.. in eorðan. *c* **1200** ORMIN 6727 Þurrh þine gode þæwess. *c* **1205** LAY. 3093 Þine sustren sculen habben mi kinelond. *a* **1240** *Ureisun* 149 in *Cott. Hom.* 199 Uor ðire mild-heortnesse. *a* **1250** *Owl & Night.* 429 Al so þu dost on þire side. *c* **1250** *Gen. & Ex.* 3556 Go ðu nu dun ðin folc to sen. *a* **1300** *Cursor M.* 923 (Cott.) Al þe dais on þin eild. *Ibid.* 11340 (Gött.) Do me to rest nu seruand þine. *Ibid.* 24675 (Edin.) For qui his moder was tin ant. **1382** WYCLIF *Matt.* vi. 22 Ȝif thin eiȝe be symple, al thi body shal be liȝtful. **14**.. *Chaucer's Astrol.* II. §2–3 (MS. L.) To knowe the degre of thyn sonne in thyn zodiak. *c* **1440** *Pallad. on Husb.* I. 56 No doute is in thi watir ner thyn aier. **15**.. HUNNIS *Psalms* vi. 59 Yet, O Lord, in rigour thine Forbeare thy heauie stroke. **1615** BEDWELL *Moham. Imp.* II. §47, I am amazed at this thine answer. **1616** B. JONSON *Forest, To Celia* i, Drink to me only with thine eyes. **1784** COWPER *Task* v. 782 Thine eye shall be instructed, and thine heart, Made pure, shall relish [etc.]. **1864** PLUMPTRE *Hymn*, Thine arm, O Lord, in days of old Was strong to heal and save.

3. *Predicatively.* (= Ger. *der deinige*, F. *le tien.*)

c **1000** *Ags. Gosp.* John xvii. 6 Hiȝ wæron þine [*Lind.* ðino ueron]. *a* **1240** *Wohunge* in *Cott. Hom.* 271 Al is tin mi sweting. *a* **1300** *Floriz & Bl.* 4 Whil he is þin ne dute noþing. **13**.. *Cursor M.* 2601 If ani barn of hir war þine. **13**.. HAMPOLE *Medit. Passion* Wks. 1895 I. 93 Swete Ihesu, I biseche þee to.. make me al þin. **1390** GOWER *Conf.* I. 74 Fro this day forth I am al thin. *c* **1475** *Rauf Coilȝear* 56 Sum part salbe thyne. **1534** TINDALE *Matt.* vi. 13 For thyne is the kyngedome and the power, and the glorye. **1605** SHAKS. *Lear* I. i. 265 Let her be thine. **1667** MILTON *P.L.* v. 154 Almightie, thine this universal Frame. **1707** WATTS *Hymn*, '*Come let us join*' iii, And blessings more than we can give Be, Lord, for ever thine. **1869** TENNYSON *Grail* 449 'Take thou my robe', she said, 'for all is thine'.

4. *Elliptically*, equivalent to THY with a sb. to be supplied from the previous context.

c **1430** *Freemasonry* 328 Ny by thy felows concubyne [lie], No more thou woldest he dede by thyne. *c* **1440** *Alphabet of Tales* 316, I thank þe at þou hase giffen me my son agayn, & behold, lo, I bryng þe thyne agayn. **1601** LYLY *Love's Met.* I. ii, Of what colours or flowers is thine made of, Niobe? **1749** CHESTERF. *Lett.* (1792) II. 220 *S.* Tastes are different, you know... *E.* That's true; but thine's a devilish odd one.

5. *absol.* **a.** That which is thine; thy property. (= Ger. *Deines, das deinige*, F. *le tien.*)

a **1000** *Cædmon's Gen.* 2144 (Gr.) Nis.. sceat ne scilling, þæs ic.. þines ahredde. *c* **1175** *Lamb. Hom.* 79 Ȝif þu mare spenest of þine, hwan ic aȝen cherre al ic þe ȝelde. **13**.. *Cursor M.* 2428 (Cott.) O þine wil i not haue a dele. *Ibid.* (Gött.) Of þin wil i neuer a dele. **1555** EDEN *Decades* 17 b, That amonge them [Cubans], the lande is as common as the sonne and water: And that Myne and Thyne (the seedes of all myscheefe) haue no place with them.

b. (*pl.*) Those who are thine; thy people, family, or kindred. (= Ger. *die deinigen*, F. *les tiens.*)

c **1000** *Ags. Gosp.* John xvii. 10 Ealle mine synt þine & þine synt mine. *c* **1000** *Sax. Leechd.* I. 328 Þonne þu & þine beoð alysde. *a* **1300** *Cursor M.* 2386 (Cott.) Abram þis es þi land þar þou and tine [*v.r.* þine] sal be weldand. *c* **1440** *Jacob's Well* 201 To restoryn as myche as was don harme be þe or be þine. **1593** SHAKS. *Lucr.* 1630 Lasting shame On thee and thine this night I will inflict. **1776** TOPLADY in *Sacr. Poetry* (1868) 109 Thou Feeder and Guardian of Thine.

c. *of thine*: that is (or are) thine; belonging to thee: see OF *prep.* 44.

1390 GOWER *Conf.* I. 47 Ma dame, I am a man of thyne, That in thi Court have longe served. **1526** *Pilgr. Perf.* (W. de W. 1531) 300 b, Spyttynge in that blessed face of thyne. **1605** SHAKS. *Macb.* v. iii. 16 Those Linnen cheekes of thine Are Counsailers to feare. **1877** TENNYSON *Harold* I. ii, Thou hast misread this merry dream of thine.

thine, þine, var. THYNE *adv. Obs.*, thence.

thing (θɪŋ), *sb.*[1] Forms: 1–3 **ðing**, 1–5 **þing**, 3–4 **þyng**, 4–5 **þinge, þynge**, (**thyngge**), 4–6 **thyng**, 5–6 **thinge, thynge**; 4– **thing.** (*β.* 1 **þingc, þincg**, 3 **þinc**, 3–4 **þink**, 4 **þynk**, 4–6 **think**, 5–6 **thynk**(**e.**) Pl. 1–3 **ð-, þing**, 3–5 **þinges** (3 **þingues**), 5–7 **thinges**, 5– **things.** [OE. *þing* (see below), Com. Teut.: cf. OFris. *thing, ting* assembly, council, suit, matter, thing (WFris., NFris. *ting* assembly); OS. *thing* assembly for judicial or deliberative purposes, conference, transaction, matter, affair, thing, object (MDu. *dinc* court-day, suit, plea, concern, affair, thing, Du. *ding* thing; MLG. *ding, dink*, LG. *ding* affair, thing, object); OHG. *ding, dinc* public assembly for judgement and transaction of business, law-court, lawsuit, plea, cause, matter, affair, thing, mod.G. *ding* affair, matter, thing; ON. *þing* public assembly, meeting, parliament, council; also in pl., objects, articles, valuable things, Norw. *ting* neut. public assembly, creature, being; masc. affair, thing, object, Sw. *ting* assize, thing; Da. *ting* court, court of justice, thing. Gothic had the cognate *þeihs* n.:—**þiŋχ-s* fixed time, time appointed for something, whence it is thought by some that the original sense of N. and WGer. *þing* was 'day of assembly'. With the sense-history, as shown in OE. and more fully in the cognate langs., cf. that of Ger. *sache*, Du. *zaak* affair, thing, orig. strife, dispute, lawsuit, cause, charge, crime, and F. *chose*, It., Sp. *cosa* thing, from L. *causa* judicial process, lawsuit, cause; also L. *rēs* affair, thing, also a case in law, lawsuit, cause.]

I. † **1.** (Only in *OE.*) A meeting, assembly, *esp.* a deliberative or judicial assembly, a court, a council. Phr. *þing ȝehéȝan*, to hold a meeting.

685–6 *Laws of Hlothær & Eadric* c. 8 ȝif man oþerne sace tihte and he þane mannan mote an medle oþþe an þinge. *Beowulf* 426 [Ic] nu wið Grendel sceal.. ana ȝeheȝan ðing wið þyrse. *a* **800** CYNEWULF *Christ* 926 Þonne he frean ȝesihð ealra ȝesceafta andweardne faran mid mæȝen-wundrum monȝum to þinge. *a* **1000** *Andreas* 157 Swa hie symble ymb þritiȝ þing ȝehedon nihtȝerimes. *a* **1000** *Gnomic Verses* 18 þing sceal ȝeheȝan frod wið frodne, bið hyra ferð ȝelic.

†**2. a.** A matter brought before a court of law; a legal process; a charge brought, a suit or cause pleaded before a court. *Obs.* or passing into 3.

a **1000** *Ags. Psalms* (Th.) xxxiv. 22 [xxxv. 23] Drihten, min God, aris to minum þinge. *Ibid.* cviii. 30 [cix. 31] þær he þear-fendra þinga teolode. *c* **1122** *O.E. Chron.* an. 1022 (Laud MS.) [He] hine þær ælces þinges ȝeclænsode þe him mann on sæde. [**1534** CROMWELL in Merriman *Life & Lett.* (1902) I. 387 Ye..shall repayre hither to answer unto suche thinges as then shalbe leyed and obiected to you. *a* **1548** HALL *Chron., Hen. VI* 151 The duke..sufficiently answered to all thynges to hym obiected.]

†**b.** Hence, Cause, reason, account; sake. *Obs.*

c **1000** ÆLFRIC *Saints' Lives* xxxiii. 129 þonne nimð he me neadunga þanon for mines bryd-guman þingan. *c* **1000** *Ags. Gosp.* Luke viii. 47 For hwylcum þinge heo hit æt-hran. *c* **1175** *Lamb. Hom.* 67 Luue him for godes þing. *a* **1250** *Owl & Night.* 434 Ech wiht is glad for mine þinge. **13..** *Guy Warw.* (A.) 7306 + st. 86 Wiltow fiȝt for mi þing..? *c* **1386** CHAUCER *Prol.* 276 He wolde the see were kept for any thyng Bitwixe Middelburgh and Orewelle. *c* **1425** *Eng. Conq. Irel.* 8 Robert was a trew man, & for no tynge wold do thynge wher-of he myght be þer-after I-wyted of wntrowth. **1581** [see NOTHING A. 9 a].

3. a. That with which one is concerned (in action, speech, or thought); an affair, business, concern, matter, subject; *pl.* affairs, concerns, matters. (In early use sometimes *sing.* in collective sense.)

c **897** K. ÆLFRED *Gregory's Past. C.* xviii. 128 Sio ȝeornfulnes eorðlicra ðinga abisȝað ðæt ondȝit. **971** *Blickl. Hom.* 13 No on ȝesundum þingum anum, ac..on wiðer weardum þingum. *c* **975** *Rushw. Gosp.* Matt. xviii. 19 ȝif tweȝen eower ȝeþafiȝaþ on eorþan be ænȝum þinge. *c* **1200** ORMIN 3640 All þiss middellærdess þing Aȝȝ turneþþ her & wharr-feþþ Nu upp, nu dun. *Ibid.* 8954 Me birrþ beon hoȝhefull Abutenn hise þingess. **1375** BARBOUR *Bruce* xx. 142 Quhill [= till] thai had wit to steir thar thing. *c* **1400** *Laud Troy Bk.* 2724 That thei with Paris to Grece schulde wende, To brynge this thyng to an ende. **1550** *Acts Privy Counc.* (1891) III. 84 The Lord Admirall desired licence to go into Lincolnshire for a moneth to see his thinges that he had not seen of a long tyme. **1598** SHAKS. *Merry W.* IV. v. 126 You shall heare how things goe. **1622** MABBE tr. *Aleman's Guzman d' Alf.* I. 11 These things (I meane your Law-suites) will require a great deale of care. **1743** BULKELEY & CUMMINS *Voy. S. Seas* 190 He acquainted us, that the Brigadier had order'd Things in another Manner. **1844** DICKENS *Mart. Chuz.* xii, How have things gone on in our absence? **1867** FREEMAN *Norm. Conq.* I. iv. 252 *note*, Things changed greatly in the course of a year.

b. With possessive adj. One's particular interest, speciality, or talent. *spec.* in colloq. phr. ***to do one's (own) thing***: to do what one wants, to follow one's interest or inclination.

Evidence for this sense is patchy into the early-twentieth cent. The phrase had become a cliché (often associated with the 'hippie' culture) by the late nineteen-sixties.

1841 EMERSON *Essays* ii. 54 But do your thing and I shall know you. Do your work, and you shall reinforce yourself. **1861** R. W. DIXON *Christ's Company* 98 Go thy way, all things say, Thou hast thy way to go..Do thy thing. **1909** H. G. WELLS *Ann Veronica* xvi. 328 Every human being.. exists to do new things... Well, this is *our* thing. **1914** *Egoist* 1 June 216/1, I cannot picture the spring of the editor's actions as being a..desire to do the decent thing. I think, rather, she insists on doing her own thing—what it pleases or suits her to do. **1951** 'M. INNES' *Operation Pax* VI. vi. 285 Roof-climbing used to be one of my things, rather. **1962** I. MURDOCH *Unofficial Rose* xxii. 214 Mummy won't be happy, it's not her thing. **1968** [see FREAK *v.* 3]. **1968** *Melody Maker* 23 Nov. 23/6 No one is right and no one is wrong as long as they say what they feel—as long as they do their thing. **1970** E. BULLINS *Theme is Blackness* (1973) 165 Anything that anybody wants to do is groovy with me... Go ahead and do your thing, champ. **1971** M. SPARK *Not to Disturb* ii. 49 'What are they doing here, anyway in this world?' Heloise, pink and white of skin, fresh from her little sleep, says, 'Doing their own thing.' **1974** K. MILLETT *Flying* (1975) II. 207 She knows her thing. And I am doing mine. **1981** R. BARNARD *Sheer Torture* x. 109 A ghastly warning against..aiming at total self-fulfilment, doing your own thing regardless.

c. *Loosely*, with qualifying adj. or noun (phrase): matter, business; preoccupation (influenced by next sense).

1906 'H. MCHUGH' *Skiddoo!* vii. 94 When it comes to that poetry thing he thinks he can make Hank Longfellow beat it up a tree. **1909** ST. J. LUCAS *First Round* III. xxxiii. 320, I shall have to stay there I suppose; they spoke of giving me a fellowship at Balliol, and of course there is the All Souls thing later on.

1968 T. WOLFE *Electric Kool-Aid Acid Test* i. 11 Thousands of kids were moving into San Francisco for a life based on LSD and the psychedelic thing. **1969** *Listener* 27 Mar. 434/1 The male fashion thing. **1976** *National Observer* (U.S.) 7 Aug. 13/1 You can write the nostalgia thing, but it's been done a thousand times before. It's so easy. **1977** A. SHERIDAN tr. *J. Lacan's Écrits* iv. 131 The psychoanalytic thing has become an accepted thing.

d. A preoccupation or obsession. *spec.* (*a*) ***to make a thing about*** or ***of*** (something), to preoccupy oneself greatly with (a matter); to make an issue out of (something), or to (over)-exaggerate its importance; (*b*) ***to have a thing about*** (occas. *for*) (a person or thing), to be obsessed by (something); to harbour a prejudice or fear about. *colloq.*

1934 E. WAUGH *Handful of Dust* ii. 32, I know we aren't going. I'm not making a thing about it. I just thought it might be fun. **1936** 'J. TEY' *Shilling for Candles* xix. 201 You got a 'thing' about astrology? **1938** D. SMITH *Dear Octopus* II. i. 59 It's one of my things like turning bath-taps off. **1940** N. MITFORD *Pigeon Pie* ii. 25, I nearly fainted. I can't bear knees, I've got a thing about them. **1952** E. GRIERSON *Reputation for Song* (1955) 22 Steady on, Laura... Don't let's make a thing of it. **1955** 'E. C. R. LORAC' *Ask Policeman* ii. 19 Connie's got a 'thing' about police. 'Never trust a policeman' is her motto. **1958** E. H. CLEMENTS *Uncommon Cold* viii. 185 Remin was her 'thing' at the moment. **1967** T. WOLFE in *N.Y. Mag.* 29 Jan. 6/1 The plainclothes men are beginning to pick up on all that, but they still fog up on the shoes. The heads have a thing about the shoes straight people wear. **1971** 'A. BURGESS' *M F* ii. 22 There was an American thing against knives. **1973** R. PARKES *Guardians* ii. 49 He's made a thing of championing cultural minorities.

e. *spec.* a love affair, a romance; esp. in phr. ***to have a thing*** (***with*** someone). *colloq.*

1967 M. SHARMAN *Face of Danger* viii. 77 'Are you—er —sort of having a—thing—with Madalena?'..'I'm interested in her,' he said. 'But not sexually.' **1970** 'D. HALLIDAY' *Dolly & Cookie Bird* v. 61 Janey..had obviously just finished a thing with Guppy Collins-Smith and was looking for new material. **1978** R. LEWIS *Uncertain Sound* v. 128, I know Sandy Kyle, had a thing going with her.

4. That which is done or to be done; a doing, act, deed, transaction; an event, occurrence, incident; a fact, circumstance, experience. ***(the) first thing*** (advb.): as that which is first done or to be done; in the first place, firstly: see FIRST A. 2 d. So ***(the) next thing***, in the next place, next; ***(the) last thing***, in the last place, lastly; also ***last thing at night***.

c **1000** ÆLFRIC *Exod.* ix. 5 Tomorȝen deþ Drihten þas þing on eorþan. *c* **1000** *Sax. Leechd.* I. 112 Drince þonne fæstende niȝon daȝas, binnan þam fæce þu onȝytst on ðam wundorlic ðingc. *c* **1205** LAY. 265 Vnder-ȝetene weren þe þinges þat þeo wimon was mid childe. *Ibid.* 16042 Sæie me of þan þinge þe me to cumen sonden. **1382** WYCLIF *1 Cor.* xvi. 14 Be alle ȝoure thingis don in charite. **1449** in *Calr. Proc. Chanc. Q. Eliz.* (1830) II. Pref. 55 In witnes of which thyng the forseid parties to these endentures chaungeable haue sette her seales. **1525** LD. BERNERS *Froiss.* (1812) II. cciv, The fyrst thynge he dyd he wente to the Churche of saynt Peter. **1651** HOBBES *Leviath.* III. xl. 252 When two of them Prophecyed in the Camp, it was thought a new and unlawfull thing. **1712** STEELE *Spect.* No. 284 ¶4, I hate writing, of all Things in the World. **1809** MALKIN *Gil Blas* I. xvii. ¶9 Have not I done the thing genteelly? **1841** HELPS *Ess., Pract. Wisd.* (1842) 4 Men who have done great things in the world. **1848** TROLLOPE *Kellys & O'Kellys* II. xii. 281, I must see her the last thing,—about nine. **1871** *Routledge's Ev. Boy's Ann.* June 370 He often goes round the last thing ..to make sure that all is right. **1875** JOWETT *Plato* (ed. 2) V. 512 Theft is a mean, and robbery a shameless thing. **1902** *Munsey's Mag.* XXVI. 602/2 The great thing was to get there. *a* **1912** *Mod.* A pretty thing to have your own children rounding on you! **1935** *Discovery* Apr. 95/2 It [*sc.* the pump] is run last thing at night. **1966** 'C. AIRD' *Religious Body* viii. 74, I do a round of doors and windows last thing at night.

5. a. That which is said; a saying, utterance, expression, statement; with various connotations, e.g.: a charge or accusation made against a person (see 2); †a form of prayer (*pl.* prayers, devotions); a story, tale; a part or section of an argument or discourse; a witty saying, a jest (usu. ***good thing***).

13.. *Cursor M.* 17288 + 375 (Cott.) In alle thinkez þat þe prophetz han spoken. *c* **1386** CHAUCER *Pard. Prol.* 39 Lat hym telle vs of no ribaudye Telle vs som moral thyng. —— *Shipm. T.* 91 Dann Iohn..hath hise thynges [prayers, offices] seyd ful curteisly. **1551** T. WILSON *Logike* (1580) 40 This manne is no Rhetoricien, because he can not place his thynges in good order. **1686** tr. *Chardin's Trav. Persia* 122 The first thing she said to me. **1738** SWIFT *Pol. Conversat.* i. 34, I never heard a better Thing. **1766** GOLDSM. *Vic. W.* xvi, All the good things of the high wits. **1771** *Misc. Ess.* in *Ann. Reg.* 184/2 This Greek spoke many handsome things of Marseilles, and of our colonies. **1859** SALA *Tw. round Clock* (1861) 132 The people who went about saying things. **1909** *Nation* 3 Apr. 13/2 The right thing will say itself—and will say itself with awful precision.

b. That which is thought; an opinion; a notion; an idea.

1765 A. DICKSON *Treat. Agric.* (ed. 2) 76 With equal reason we may infer the same thing of earth. **1842** TENNYSON *Dora* 56 Mary sat..and thought Hard things of Dora. **1885** ANSTEY *Tinted Venus* i. 8 Putting things in the poor girl's head.

†**6.** Formerly used *absol.* (without article or qualifying word), also *a thing*, in indefinite sense: = anything, something. (With various meanings: see prec. senses.) *Obs.*

a **1300** *Cursor M.* 14952 þai wil me neuer luue, i-wiss, For thing i mai þam tell. **1382** WYCLIF *1 Sam.* xiv. 12 Stieth vp to vs, and we shulen shewe ȝou a thing. **1413** *Pilgr. Sowle* (Caxton 1483) IV. xxv. 70 Neuer ne dyde the body thyng withouten thyn assent. *c* **1500** *Melusine* 24, I pray you to telle it to me, yf it is thinge that I may knowe. **1525** LD. BERNERS *Froiss.* II. lxxxvi. [lxxxii.] 255 They neuer dyd thynge that they wolde haue ben gladder. **1588** SHAKS. *L.L.L.* v. i. 152 Shall I tell you a thing? **1678** BUNYAN *Pilgr.* I. 142 Ho, turn aside hither, and I will shew you a thing.

II. An entity of any kind.

7. That which exists individually (in the most general sense, in fact or in idea); that which is or may be in any way an object of perception, knowledge, or thought; a being, an entity. (Including persons, when personality is not considered, as in quots. *c* 888, 1380, 1539, 1597, 1732.) **a.** In unemphatic use: mostly with adj. or other defining word or phrase (the two together corresponding to the absol. use of a neuter adj. in Latin or Greek).

Cf. also *anything*, *nothing*, *something*, in 17.

c **888** K. ÆLFRED *Boeth.* xxxiii. §1 þonne þa fif þing..eall ȝegadorede bioð, þonne bið hit eall an þing, & þæt an ðing bið God. **1044-7** *Charter of Eadweard* in Kemble *Cod. Dipl.* IV. 115 On ealweldendes drihtnes naman ðe ealle þing ȝewrohte. *c* **1200** ORMIN 1839 Niss nani þing þatt muȝhe ben Wiþþ Godd off efenn mahhte. *c* **1250** *O. Kentish Serm.* in *O.E. Misc.* 28 Wer-bi we moue hatie þo ileke þinges þet he hatedh,..and luuie þo ilek þinkes þat he luued. *a* **1300** *Cursor M.* 695 Ilkin thing, on serekin wise ȝeld til Adam þar seruise. **1380** *Lay Folks Catech.* 530 þer ys but O god in trinite..This god is most myȝty þyng þat may be. **1388** WYCLIF *Ps.* cxlviii. 5 For he seide, & þingis weren maad; he comaundide, & þingis weren maad of nouȝt. **1539** TONSTALL *Serm. Palme Sund.* (1823) 8 He said in the tenth chapiter of John, I and my father are one thynge, that is to say, one substance. **1549** LATIMER *5th Serm. bef. Edw. VI* (Arb.) 147 All thynges are solde for mony at rome. **1594** GREENE *Selimus* I. A iij b, He knowes not what it is to be a King, That thinks a scepter is a pleasant thing. **1597** SHAKS. *2 Hen. IV*, v. v. 60 Presume not, that I am the thing I was. **1667** MILTON *P.L.* II. 922 To compare Great things with small. **1732** BERKELEY *Alciphr.* I. §11 A man of parts is one thing, and a pedant another. **1788** J. MILNER in *Life I. Milner* iv. (1842) 44 Regencies are generally turbulent things. **1818** KEATS *Endym.* I. 1 A thing of beauty is a joy for ever. **1843** MILL *Logic* I. iii. §5 What is an action? Not one thing but a series of two things: the state of mind called a volition, followed by an effect. **1879** GEO. ELIOT *Theo. Such* xiii. 266 The latest thing in tattooing.

b. Applied to an attribute, quality, or property of an actual being or entity; hence sometimes (in such phrases as *in all things*) = point, respect.

971 *Blickl. Hom.* 13 þa wæs heo on eallum þingum þe eaþ moddre. *c* **1200** *Trin. Coll. Hom.* 15 Ðre þing ben þat elch man habben mot..þat on is rihte bileue, þat oðer is fulohtninge, þe þridde þe faire liflode. *a* **1300** *Cursor M.* 295 In þe sune þat schines clere Es a thing and thre thinges sere; A bodi rond, and hete and light. **1340** *Ayenb.* 194 þe oþer þing þet behoueþ ine elmesse is þet me hit do zone and hasteliche. *c* **1520** BARCLAY tr. *Sallust* (ed. 2) 47 Their enmies myght lytell thynge preuayle agaynst them. **1558** KNOX *First Blast* (Arb.) 26 Augustine defineth ordre to be that thing, by the whiche God hath appointed and ordeined all thinges. **1644** EVELYN *Diary* 10 Nov., The whitenesse and smoothnesse of the pargeting was a thing I much observ'd. **1705** BERKELEY *Commonplace Bk.* Wks. 1871 IV. 420, I side in all things with the mob. **1838-9** FR. A. KEMBLE *Resid. in Georgia* (1863) 132 Ignorance is an odious thing.

c. Used indefinitely to denote something which the speaker is not able or does not choose to particularize, or which is incapable of being precisely described; a something, a somewhat. Also (often with initial capital) applied to some particular supernatural or other dreadful monster (i.e. ***the Thing***). Hence *transf.* (sometimes *humorously*) of persons.

1602 SHAKS. *Ham.* I. i. 21 What, ha's this thing appear'd againe to night? **1804** WORDSW. *To Cuckoo* iv, No Bird, but an invisible thing, A voice, a mystery. **1822** BYRON *Heaven & Earth* I. iii, Thou..awful Thing of Shadows, speak to me! **1842** TENNYSON *Walking to the Mail* 36 'Yes, we're flitting,' says the ghost (For they had pack'd the thing among the beds). **1888** KIPLING *Smith Administration* (1891) 64 The burning-*ghât*, where a man was piling logs on some Thing that lay wrapped in white cloth. **1893** STEVENSON *Catriona* xv, Wi' the bang and the skirl the thing had clean disappeared. **1917** CONRAD *Shadow-Line* vi. 197 The hair of my head stirred... I could see It—that Thing! **1954** L. M. BOSTON *Children of Green Knowe* 126 The Thing..gave a silent yell... Then it went fumbling round the room. **1973** 'B. MATHER' *Snowline* i. 7, I find The Thing hard to take. He's blind,..he can only make mewing noises, and he has no legs and only one arm.

d. In emphatic use: That which has separate or individual existence (e.g. as distinct on the one hand from the totality of being, on the other from attributes or qualities). See also 8.

1817 COLERIDGE *Biog. Lit.* xii. I. 267 An infinite independent thing, is no less a contradiction, than an infinite circle or a sideless triangle. **1820** BYRON *Mar. Fal.* v. i. 288 True words are things, And dying men's are things which long outlive, And often times avenge them. **1862** H. SPENCER *First Princ.* I. iii. §15 (1875) 47 While, on the hypothesis of their objectivity, Space and Time must be classed as things, we find, on experiment, that to represent them in thought as things is impossible. **1884** tr. *Lotze's Logic* 58 The doctrine of Kant, who represented the relation of a thing to its property, or of substance to its accident, as the model upon which the mind connects *S* and *P* in the categorical judgment. **1910** CHRISTIE in *Contemp. Rev.* Feb. 194 'Things'..are, as Lotze tried to show, but the activities of the One everlasting Spirit.

8. *spec.* **a.** That which is signified, as distinguished from a word, symbol, or idea by which it is represented: the actual being or entity as opposed to a symbol of it. † ***in thing***, in reality, really, actually (opposed to *in name* = nominally).

c **1450** *Bk. Curtesye* 343 (Oriel MS.) His [Chaucer's] longage was so feyre and pertinent, That semed vnto mennys heryng, Not only the worde, but verrely the thing. **1482** *Rolls of Parlt.* VI. 208/2 That the Deane..and Chanons..be oon body corporate in thyng and name. *a* **1533** FRITH *Answ. More* (1548) G iij, But the thinge it selfe, whose sacrament thys is, is receyued. **1534** MORE *Treat. Passion* Wks. 1332/2 The thyng of a sacrament is properly called that holye thinge that the sacrament betokeneth. **1663** BUTLER *Hud.* I. I. 804 Bear-baiting is an Antichristian Game Unlawful both in thing and name. **1705** BERKELEY *Commonplace Bk.* Wks. 1871 IV. 440 The supposition that things are distinct from ideas takes away all real truth. **1725** WATTS *Logic* I. iv. §1 The World is fruitful in the Invention of Utensils of Life, and new Characters and Offices of Men, yet Names entirely new are seldom invented; therefore old Names are almost necessarily us'd to signify new Things. **1827** ROBINSON *Archæol. Græca* x. (ed. 2) p. lxiii, The philosophy of Aristotle is rather the philosophy of words than of things. **1850** TENNYSON *In Mem.* lxxv. 6 What practice howsoe'er expert In fitting aptest words to things.. Hath power to give thee as thou wert? **1876** JEVONS *Logic Prim.* vi. 22 The meaning of a word is that thing which we think about when we use the word.

b. *esp.* A being without life or consciousness; an inanimate object, as distinguished from a person or living creature. (See also 11, 12.)

1689–90 TEMPLE *Ess. Learn.* Wks. 1731 I. 302 Things.. such as have been either of general Use or Pleasure to Mankind. **1729** LAW *Serious C.* iv. (1732) 47 Things.. are all to be used according to the Will of God. **1766** [see 12 b]. **1840** DICKENS *Barn. Rudge* iii, Consideration of persons, things, times and places. **1850** LYNCH *Theo. Trin.* viii. 149 'He that getteth a wife getteth a good thing'; that is at least, if his wife be more than a *thing*. **1853** MAURICE *Proph. & Kings* xvi. 279 The human being was sacrificed; the *person* was given up for the *thing*.

9. Applied (usually with qualifying word) to a living being or creature; occasionally to a plant.

c **1000** *Sax. Leechd.* II. 146 For þon þonne ealle æterno þing fleogaþ. *c* **1000** ÆLFRIC *Gen.* vii. 22 Ælc þing, þe lif hæfde. *c* **1275** LAY. 25656 He saide þat þar was icome A luþer þing to londe.. A wel loþliche feond. *a* **1300** *Cursor M.* 385 Alkin things grouand sere.. in þam self paire seding bere. *c* **1440** *Pallad. on Husb.* I. 935 For eddris, spritis, monstris, thyng of drede. **1580** FRAMPTON *Monardes' Med. agst. Venome* 138 Least any venomous thing fall therein, as spyders. **1667** MILTON *P.L.* IX. 194 When all things that breath,.. send up silent praise To the Creator. **1819** SHELLEY *Prometh. Unb.* I. 305, I wish no living thing to suffer pain. **1858** GLENNY *Gard. Every-day Bk.* 120/1 Nemophila, Coreopsis, and other free-growing things.

10. Applied to a person, now only in contempt, reproach, pity, or affection (esp. to a woman or child); formerly also in commendation or honour. Cf. CREATURE 3 b, c. **a.** with qualifying word. Also in phrases: *dear old thing*, an expression of affection applied esp. to an elderly person; *old thing*, a jocular or affectionate form of address (not necessarily to an elder). *colloq.*

c **1290** *St. Lucy* 150 in *S. Eng. Leg.* I. 105 Ȝwan he ne miȝte þis clene þing [St. Lucy] ouer-come mid al is lore. *a* **1300** *Cursor M.* 2077 Fle me fra, þou wared thing. *Ibid.* 7285 Samuel.. was a selcuth dughti thing, þe first þat smerld man to king. *c* **1330** *Arth. & Merl.* 6482 Þe kinges steward.. wedded þat swete þing. *c* **1450** *Guy Warw.* (C.) 26 A may ȝynge, The Erlys doghtur, a swete thynge. **1533** J. HEYWOOD *Play Wether* (1903) 1097 A goodly dame, an ydyll thynge iwys. **1542** UDALL *Erasm. Apoph.* 241 b, Augustus beeyng yet a young thyng vnder mannes state. *a* **1568** ASCHAM *Scholem.* I. (Arb.) 53 If he be bashefull, and will soone blushe, they call him a babishe and ill brought vp thyng. **1607** SHAKS. *Cor.* IV. v. 122 But that I see thee heere Thou noble thing, more dances my rapt heart [etc.]. **1689** MRS. BEHN *Novels* (1871) I. 70 The worst-natur'd, incorrigible, thing in the world. **1711** STEELE *Spect.* No. 4 ¶5 At a Play.. looking.. at a young thing in a Box before us. **1758** JOHNSON *Idler* No. 13 ¶3 My wife often tells me that boys are dirty things. **1838** DICKENS *Nich. Nick.* xxvii, Why don't you go and ask them to walk up, you stupid thing? **1852** *Punch* 31 July 55/2 Aunt Ratchet and I had quietly sat down, I to read and she to listen to a new novel—the greatest pleasure the dear old thing can experience. **1864** C. M. YONGE *Trial* II. xiv. 273 I'll do anything for you.. you know that, you old thing! **1865** 'L. CARROLL' *Alice's Adventures in Wonderland* ix. 130 'You can't think how glad I am to see you again, you dear old thing!' said the Duchess, as she tucked her arm affectionately into Alice's, and they walked off together. **1898** FLOR. MONTGOMERY *Tony* 12 The very smallest and youngest thing that had ever worn an Eton jacket. **1905** KIPLING *Actions & Reactions* (1909) 18 No, thanks, old thing! Isn't that quite English? *a* **1912** *Mod.* Poor thing! I pity her. **1921** [see CLEVER-CLEVER *a.*]. **1975** J. DRUMMOND *Slowly the Poison* 13 Don't worry, old thing. It may not be as bad as it sounds.

b. without qualification, in contempt or reproach, implying unworthiness to be called a person: cf. 8 b.

1610 SHAKS. *Temp.* III. ii. 63 Reuenge it on him, (for I know Thou dar'st) But this Thing dare not. **1611** —— *Wint. T.* II. i. 82 O thou Thing. **1633** BP. HALL *Occas. Medit.* (1851) 143 What can we make of this thing? man, I cannot call him. **1756** LADY M. W. MONTAGU *Let. to C'tess of Bute* 8 Nov., By what accident they have fallen into the hands of that thing Dodsley I know not. **1860** MOTLEY *Netherl.* ii. I. 37 To accept the sovereignty of a thing like Henry of Valois.

11. a. A material object, a body; a being or entity consisting of matter, or occupying space. (Often, a vague designation for an object which it is difficult to denominate more exactly.)

971 *Blickl. Hom.* 91 Heofon & eorþe, & sæ, & ealle þa þing þe on þæm syndon. *c* **1200** ORMIN 18825 þatt arrke þatt iss wrohht off tre.. iss whilwendlike þing. *a* **1300** *Signa ante Judicium* 102 in *E.E. Poems* (1862) 10 Þe iren sul blede.. þe þing þat bodi no flesse nap non. *a* **1300** *Cursor M.* 9383 Alking thing was þan.. Wel pithier þan þai ar now. *c* **1400** *Lanfranc's Cyrurg.* 141 Woundis.. maad wiþ a swerd or wiþ sum dinge ellis þat woundiþ. **1547** HOOPER *Declar. Christe* viii. H vij, Mens yeyes be obedient unto the creatour that they may se on think and yet not a nother. **1570** BILLINGSLEY *Euclid* I. post. i. 7 Thinges equall to one and the selfe same thyng are equall also the one to the other. *c* **1595** CAPT. WYATT *R. Dudley's Voy. W. Ind.* (Hakl. Soc.) 16 Leavinge behinde us certaine letters inclosed in a thinge of wood provided of purpose. **1709** BERKELEY *Ess. Vision* §135 Things perceivable by touch. **1719** DE FOE *Crusoe* (1840) I. xvi. 273 A three-cornered.. thing, like.. a shoulder-of-mutton sail. **1842** TENNYSON *Vis. Sin* IV. vii, Callest thou that thing a leg? **1875** JOWETT *Plato* (ed. 2) III. 509 Stones and shells and things of earth and rock.

b. A material substance (usually of a specified kind); stuff, material; in mod. use chiefly applied to substances used as food, drink, or medicine.

c **1000** *Sax. Leechd.* II. 210 Eal þa wætan þing.. & eall swete þing.. ȝe þa scearpan afran þing sint to fleonne. **13..** *E.E. Allit. P.* B. 819 Loth þenne.. his men amonestes mete for to dyȝt, Bot þenkkez on hit be þrefte what þynk so ȝe make, For wyth no sour ne no salt seruez hym neuer. *c* **1400** *Destr. Troy* 7856 Þai wold stuf hom full stithly.. with mete .. & mony othir thinges. *a* **1500** in Arnolde *Chron.* (1811) 91 Yf ony persone caste or put ony rubyes, dunge.. or ony other noyos thinge in Thamys at Walbrok. **1589** J. CHILTON in Hakluyt *Voy.* 590 Annele.. is a kinde of thing to dye blew withall. **1631** R. BYFIELD *Doctr. Sabb.* 204 We drinke some warme thing. **1694** SALMON *Bate's Dispens.* (1713) 169/1 It is a most excellent Thing in Fevers. **1737** WHISTON *Josephus, Antiq.* XI. viii. §7 Accused by those at Jerusalem of having eaten things common. *Mod.* Sour things are bad for the stomach.

c. *euphem.* Privy member, private parts; usu. preceded by possessive pron.

c **1386** CHAUCER *Wife's Prol.* 121. *c* **1440** *Voc.* in Wr.-Wülcker 632/12. **1508** DUNBAR *Tua Mariit Wemen* 389. **1610** B. JONSON *Alch.* v. i. **1700** FARQUHAR *Constant Couple* IV. iii. **1762** BRIDGES *Burlesque Homer* (1772) 62. **1955** J. P. DONLEAVY *Ginger Man* (1957) vi. 38 Men wagging their things at you from doorways. Disgusting. **1969** L. HELLMAN *Unfinished Woman* ii. 23 One.. had opened his pants and was shaking what my circle called 'his thing'. **1981** P. TURNBULL *Deep & Crisp & Even* vi. 110 'His coat was open and his thing...' 'Thing?' 'You know, between his legs... Penis.'

d. With capital initial. Substituted (esp. after a title, as *Miss Thing*, etc.) for the proper name of a person which the speaker cannot recall. Cf. THINGUMMY, WHAT'S-HIS-NAME. *colloq.*

1920 J. M. BARRIE *Kiss for Cinderella* I. 12 She was called something else when she came—Miss Thing, or some such name. **1954** M. RIDDELL *M for Mother* x. 44 Mrs. Thing had absolutely washed her hands of him and my mother was never going to speak to her again. **1977** M. KENYON *Rapist* vi. 70 Keane could not remember the name of.. the colonel. Too many names. Colonel Thing.

12. †**a.** A collective term for that which one possesses; property, wealth, substance. *Obs.*

c **1000** ÆLFRIC *Hom.* II. 506 Him eallum wæron heora ðing ȝemæne. *a* **1200** *Moral Ode* 263 Þer inne boð.. þe þet is oðers monnes þing louie. *c* **1200** ORMIN 4520 þatt tu nan oþerr manness þing Ne ȝeorne nohht to winnenn. *c* **1250** *Gen. & Ex.* 3378 He let bi-aften de more del, To kepen here ðing al wel. **1297** R. GLOUC. (Rolls) 10196 Persones þing he solde men þat mest wolde þeruore ȝiue. **13..** *Minor Poems fr. Vernon MS.* xxxvii. 719 For he wolde haue offryng And liue bi oþur mennes þing. **1432–50** tr. *Higden* (Rolls) I. 35 Composicion of a commune thynge, the disposicion of a thynge familier. **1513** DOUGLAS *Æneis* VI. xiv. 93 That art full mychty bot of lytle thing.

b. A piece of property, an individual possession; usually in *pl.*, possessions, belongings, goods; *esp.* (*colloq.*) those which one has or carries with one at the time, e.g. on a journey; *impedimenta.*

things real, things personal (in Law) = real property, personal property: see REAL *a.*[2] 6, PERSONAL *a.* 6 b.

c **1290** *S. Eng. Leg.* I. 14/459 Mid þat gold and þe riche þingues þat he fond al-so þere þe churchene.. þare with he liet a-rere. *c* **1460** *Towneley Myst.* vi. 83 Where ar oure thyngis, ar thay past Iordan? **1481** CAXTON *Godeffroy* xlv. 85 They had born theder alle theyr thynges. **1560** DAUS tr. *Sleidane's Comm.* 119 b, The parson and vicar wyll haue for a mortuary.. the best thynge that is about the house. **1585** T. WASHINGTON tr. *Nicholay's Voy.* I. v, [They] lost the most part of theyr apparrel, & things. **1603** KNOLLES *Hist. Turks* (1621) 599 Busie in packing vp his things against his departure. **1662** J. DAVIES *Mandelslo's Trav.* 17 We.. went .. to the Custome House to have our things search'd by the Officers there. **1759** JOHNSON *Let. to Miss Porter* 23 Mar., in *Boswell*, I have this day moved my things, and you are now to direct to me at Staple-inn. **1766** BLACKSTONE *Comm.* II. ii. 16 The objects of dominion or property are things, as contradistinguished from persons: and things are by the law of England distributed into two kinds; things real, and things personal. **1865** TROLLOPE *Belton Est.* xxvi, She packed up all her things.

c. *spec.* (*pl.*) Articles of apparel; clothes, garments; *esp.* such as women put on to go out in, in addition to the indoor dress. *colloq.*

1634 W. WOOD *New Eng. Prosp.* (1865) 56 A long coarse coate, to keepe better things from the pitched ropes and plankes. **1713** STEELE *Guardian* No. 10 ¶5, I know every part of their dress, and can name all their things by their names. **1748** RICHARDSON *Clarissa* (1811) V. xxiv. 257 But having her things on, (as the women call every thing).. she thought it best to go. **1774** FOOTE *Cozeners* I. Wks. 1799 II. 157, I have had but just time to huddle on my things. **1833** T. HOOK *Parson's Dau.* (1847) 239 Take off your things—and we will order.. tea. **1885** ANSTEY *Tinted Venus* vi. 66, 'I haven't bought my winter things yet', said Matilda. **1902** R. BAGOT *Donna Diana* viii. 100 Diana left the room to put on her things for driving.

d. *pl.* Implements or equipment for some special use; utensils. Chiefly *colloq.*

1698 VANBRUGH *Prov. Wife* III. i, Here, take away the things; I expect company. **1738** *Ochtertyre House Bks.* (1909) 154 For mending the Kitchen things. **1844** *Mem. Babylonian Princess* II. 304 With the breakfast things the waiter brought the morning paper. **1891** C. JAMES *Rom. Rigmarole* 156, I hadn't any proper hunting things. **1898** G. B. SHAW *Plays* II. *Man of Destiny* 160 Clearing the table and removing the things to a tray on the sideboard.

13. An individual work of literature or art, a composition; a writing, piece of music, etc.

c **1386** CHAUCER *Prol.* 325 Ther-to he [the Sergeant of the Law] koude endite and make a thyng. —— *Sqr.'s T.* 70 Herknynge hise Mynstrals hir thynges pleye. **1581** PETTIE *Guazzo's Civ. Conv.* I. (1586) 17 b, Yt they haue imploied all their time in reading some good thing or other. **1589** PUTTENHAM *Eng. Poesie* III. xxii. (Arb.) 265 One of our late makers who in the most of his things wrote very well. **1591** SHAKS. *Two Gent.* IV. ii. 71 You would haue them alwaies play but one thing. **1731** SWIFT *Let. to Pope* 12 June, I have a thing in prose, begun above twenty-eight years ago, and almost finished. **1831** *Examiner* 213/2 A dozen things of Handel's;.. some things of Avison's, one of the poorest of musicians. **1902** BESANT *5 Yrs. Tryst* 26 You'll pass your exams with distinction; you'll get appointments; you'll write things.

III. Phrases, special collocations, and combinations.

14. a. *... and things* (colloq., unstressed): and other things of the same kind; and the like, *et cetera*. **b.** *for one thing*: as one point to be noted; in the first place. So *for another thing*. **c.** *to make a good thing of*: to turn to profit, make gain out of. **d.** *no great things* (used predicatively, usually of a person or thing): nothing great, nothing much, of ordinary quality or character. *colloq.* or *dial.* (Cf. *no great shakes.*) **e.** *thing in itself* (rendering Ger. *ding an sich* (Kant)), *Metaph.*: a thing regarded apart from its attributes; a noumenon. **f.** *to know a thing or two*: see KNOW *v.* 15; so *to learn, to show, to tell* (or *teach*) (a person) *a thing or two*; similarly, *to be up to a thing or two*, to be knowing or shrewd. **g.** *one thing.. another* (*thing*): see ONE *numeral a.* 17 c. **h.** (*the*) *things of the mind*, matters of a specifically intellectual character. Cf. *life of the mind* s.v. LIFE *sb.* 12 e. **i.** *of all things*: of all conceivable possibilities (often parenthetically implying that the eventuality is surprising or unexpected). **j.** (*just*) *one of those things*: see ONE *pron.* 31 f. **k.** *like one thing*, 'like anything'. *Austral. colloq.* and *U.S. dial.* **l.** With reference to a previous statement: *to do that* (*small*, etc.) *thing*, to act in the manner indicated (esp. when taking up a suggestion). *colloq.*

a. 1596 SHAKS. *Tam. Shr.* IV. iii. 56 With Ruffes and Cuffes, and Fardingales, and things. **1841** S. C. HALL *Ireland* I. 30 Grace would mend her father's nets and things. **1894** *To-day* 13 Jan. 14 The Japanese supper with the Japanese room and mats and things.

b. 1790 *Bystander* 139 For one thing, he [Garrick] knew that in delivering the text of an author, if he endeavoured to give his meaning a new colouring,.. it would be considered as pedantic. **18..** KEBLE [see FOR *prep.* 19 d]. **1878** MORLEY *Diderot* I. v. 173 For one thing, physical science had in the interval taken immense strides. *Mod.* I didn't care much for his speech; for one thing, his delivery was very bad; for another thing, the subject was not particularly interesting.

c. 1819 SHELLEY *P. Bell the Third* VI. xxxv, I have found the way To make a better thing of metre Than e'er was made. **1873** GREENWOOD in *St. Paul's Mag.* XII. 657 These dealers in ragged merchandize make a good thing of it.

d. 1816 'QUIZ' *Grand Master* VII. 184 Now I shall give, —'the Governor,'—He's no great things, between us, Sir. **1842** THACKERAY *Miss Tickletoby's Lect.* vi, His scholarship .. I take it, was no great things. **1890** 'R. BOLDREWOOD' *Col. Reformer* (1891) 352 That old place at Bowning.. I don't believe it was any great things.

e. [**1659** H. MORE *Immort. Soul* I. ii. §2. 6 What ever things are in themselves, they are nothing to us, but so far forth as they become known to our.. Cognitive powers.] **1798** A. F. M. WILLICH *Elem. Crit. Philos.* 21 The position of the sufficient ground, in general, depends.. upon *things in themselves.* **1817** COLERIDGE *Biog. Lit.* I. x. 195 Of this sheet of paper.. as a thing in itself, separate from the phænomenon or image in my perception. **1867** [see NOUMENON]. **1871** FRASER *Life Berkeley* ii. 41 He recognises substance, or, as we might say, the thing-in-itself. *a* **1881** A. BARRATT *Phys. Metempiric* (1883) 39 We have had to conclude that the doctrine of Realism or Things-in-themselves cannot be proved. **1891** E. B. BAX *Outlooks fr. New Standp.* III. 182 This is the truth at the bottom of the 'thing-in-itself', so much decried by the orthodox Hegelians.

f. 1792, 1817 [see KNOW *v.* 15]. **1816** *Sporting Mag.* XLVIII. 173 The training-groom was up to a thing or two. **1856** READE *Never too late* lii, Jackey showed Robinson a thing or two. **1859** HOTTEN *Dict. Slang* 113. **1859** THACKERAY *Virgin.* xviii, I think I have shown him that we in Virginia know a thing or two. **1897** MARY KINGSLEY *W. Africa* 673 Does any one.. feel inclined to tell me that those old palm-oil chiefs have not learnt a thing or two during their lives? **1930** WODEHOUSE *Very Good, Jeeves!* vi. 143 'Listen, Bertie,' said Aunt Dahlia earnestly, 'I'm an older woman than you are—well, you know what I mean—and I can tell you a thing or two.' **1932** L. GOLDING *Magnolia St.* III. ix. 592 It's taught us both a thing or two. **1973** M. BENCE-JONES *Palaces of Raj* xi. 191 Simla could teach Naini Tal a thing or two as regards dances.

h. [**1902** H. JAMES *Wings of Dove* II. iii. 44 All the high, dim things she lumped together as of the mind.] **1903** G. K. CHESTERTON *Robert Browning* iii. 61 She.. lived her second and real life in literature and the things of the mind. **1965** *New Society* 15 July 10/3 The superiority of the things of the mind over the externals of bodily appearance and success in competitive enterprises. **1980** T. MORGAN *Somerset Maugham* III. 222 Syrie.. had no interest in things of the mind. She was the sort who says 'how extraordinary' when a book is being discussed.

i. 1925 T. DREISER *Amer. Tragedy* II. II. xii. 170 Well, well, of all things! Well, I'll be damned! **1958** A. HUXLEY *Let.* 22 June (1969) 851 There have been endless contretemps, including, as a last straw, the collapse of the publicity woman with, of all things, chickenpox. **1977** MCKNIGHT & TOBLER *Bob Marley* ix. 110 Keyboard instrument effects.. which sound like a harmonium of all things.

k. 1946 B. JAMES in Murdoch & Drake-Brockman *Austral. Short Stories* (1951) 249 No good for crops,.. but it would 'grow cherries like one thing'. **1948** D. BALLANTYNE *Cunninghams* xiv. 75 He saw Phil.. and some other.. jokers skiting like one thing. **1972** J. S. HALL *Sayings from Old Smoky* 136 *Like one thing*, said of something very well done or in large quantity. 'He can mimic Windy Bill just like one thing.'

I. **1958** I. MURDOCH *Bell* xiv. 186 'I'm going to have a bath.' 'Darling, you do that small thing!' **1960** K. AMIS *Take Girl like You* vi. 83 'Grab one with us.'..'I'll do that small thing if I may.' **1963** N. FREELING *Because of Cats* i. 23 'I'll plan that.' 'You do that thing.' **1967** N. MARSH *Death at Dolphin* iii. 57 'Will you bear me in mind, then?' 'I'll do that thing,' said Peregrine. **1977** J. TARRANT *Rommel Plot* ix. 89 'I'll be there in twenty minutes.' 'You do that small thing.'

15. ***the thing*** (colloq., emphatic). **a.** (predicatively) The correct thing; what is proper, befitting, or fashionable; also of a person, in good condition or 'form', 'up to the mark', fit (physically or otherwise).

1762 GOLDSM. *Cit. W.* lxxvii, [The silk] is at once rich, tasty, and quite the thing. **1775** MME. D'ARBLAY *Early Diary* 3 Apr., Mr. Bruce was quite the thing; he addressed himself with great gallantry to us all alternately. **1781** JOHNSON 12 Apr., in *Boswell*, Why, Sir, a Bishop's calling company together in this week [Passion Week] is, to use the vulgar phrase, not the thing. **1802** MRS. J. WEST *Infidel Father* II. 123 This behaviour was certainly the very thing. **1832** J. ROMILLY *Diary* 20 Sept. (1967) 19 Better today: tho not quite the thing: dined at home. **1841** THACKERAY *Gt. Hoggarty Diamond* ii, He really looked quite the genteel thing. **1854** C. M. YONGE *Heartsease* I. II. i. 115 And how are you? You don't look quite the thing. **1864** MEREDITH *Sandra Belloni* xix, Wilfrid took his arm and put it gently down on the chair, saying: 'You're not quite the thing to-day, sir.' **1897** *Boston* (Mass.) *Jrnl.* 12 Jan. 5/1 They are used in the long gold chains which are so pre-eminently the thing. **1901** 'L. MALET' *Sir R. Calmady* v. vii, I am not quite the thing this morning.

b. The special, important, or notable point; *esp.* what is specially required. Also *colloq.* in weakened use (*the thing is*..), the truth or the fact of the matter.

1850 THACKERAY *Pendennis* lxxv, But he has got the rowdy, which is the thing. **1873** M. ARNOLD *Lit. & Dogma* Pref. 11 The question [of a state church]..is..so absolutely unimportant! The thing is, to recast religion. **1892** SYMONDS *Michel Angelo* (1899) I. VI. x. 290 The thing about Michel Angelo is this: he is not..at the head of a class, he stands apart by himself. **1971** C. BONINGTON *Annapurna South Face* xiv. 175, I think the thing is that we want to start pushing out the route as fast as possible because the faster we can push the route out the less oxygen we need to use. **1976** 'A. HALL' *Kobra Manifesto* xv. 208 They've struck some kind of problem... The thing is they've seized a TWA Boeing.

16. †**a.** ***all thing*** (obs.): everything, all things; also *advb.* altogether, wholly: see ALL A. 3, C. 2 b. **b.** ***that*** (***this, what,*** etc.) ***kind*** (or ***sort***) ***of thing***: see KIND *sb.* 14, SORT *sb.* **c.** ***a thing of nothing*** or ***of nought***: see NOTHING A. 3 b, NOUGHT A. 4 c. †**d.** ***public thing, thing public*** (obs.) = L. *res publica*: see PUBLIC *a.* 2 a. **e.** ***such a thing, no such thing***: see SUCH.

f. ***any old thing***: any thing whatever. *slang* (orig. *U.S.*).

1900 ADE *More Fables in Slang* 205 An Author was sitting at his Desk trying to..grind out Any Old Thing that could be converted into Breakfast Food. **1911**, etc. [see *any old*.. s.v. ANY *a.* 1 e].

17. ***any thing, every thing, no thing, some thing*** (in which *thing* is an unemphatic stressless use of sense 7 or 11), are now written each as one word (see ANYTHING, EVERYTHING, NOTHING, SOMETHING).

18. *attrib.* and *Comb.*, as ***thing-aspect, -element***; ***thing-creating*** adj.; ***thing-like*** adj., like a material or impersonal thing (hence ***thing-likeness***); **thing-word**, a substantive referring to some material object; after Jespersen, *spec.* a countable noun.

1663 BOYLE *Usef. Exp. Nat. Philos.* I. 123 Matter cannot move it self, but requires to be mov'd by a Tectonic thing-creating Power. *c* **1854** FABER *Old Labourer* iii, Such a thing-like person. **1877** H. SWEET in *Trans. Philol. Soc.* 1875–6 487 'Snow'..is both a thing-word and a noun, 'white' is a quality-word and an adjective, 'whiteness' a quality-word and a noun. **1895** POLLOCK & MAITLAND *Hist. Eng. Law* II. iv. §6 II. 133 Annuities..in course of time..assumed the guise of merely contractual rights; but in the earlier Year Books their thinglikeness is visible. **1909** G. TYRRELL in *Q. Rev.* July 108 Those..who, as priests..are interested in the 'thing-aspect' of religion. *Ibid.*, His tendency to cleave to this 'thing-element' in religion. **1914** O. JESPERSEN *Mod. Eng. Gram.* II. v. 115 Another difference in the adjuncts of mass-words and thing-words: the former have *what*, the latter *what a* in exclamatory quasi-questions. **1937** A. SMEATON tr. *R. Carnap's Logical Syntax Lang.* v. lxxvii. 297 'Thing' is a universal word (provided that the designation of things constitutes a genus)... 'Moon' is a thing-word..; 'five' is not a thing-word, but a number-word.

Hence (chiefly *rare* or *nonce-wds.*) **thingal** (ˈθɪŋəl) *a.*, pertaining to things (= REAL *a.*[2] 7 b); in first quot. *absol.*; **ˈthinghood**, the state or character of being a thing (in quot. 1888, as distinct from a person); existence as a thing, reality, substantiality; **thingification** = REIFICATION; hence **ˈthingify** *v. trans.*, **ˈthingifying** *vbl. sb.*; **thingish** (ˈθɪŋɪʃ) *a.*, having the nature of a thing: = THINGY a; **ˈthingism** *Fr. Lit.* [tr. Fr. *chosisme*] (see quot. 1966); **thingless** (ˈθɪŋlɪs) *a.*, destitute of the character of a thing, insubstantial (whence **ˈthinglessness**); **thinglet** (ˈθɪŋlɪt), a little thing, a diminutive object or creature; **thingliness** (ˈθɪŋlɪnɪs), the quality of being *thingly*; existence as a thing, essence; **thingling** (ˈθɪŋlɪŋ) = *thinglet*; **thingly** (ˈθɪŋlɪ) *a.*, having the nature of a thing: = THINGY a; **ˈthingness**, the fact or character of being a thing (in quot. 1902, as distinct from a person); reality; so †**ˈthingship**, †**ˈthingsomeness**.

1857 J. HINTON in *Life* vii. (1885) 132 This love might lead us away from thoughts of the real or *thingal. **1884** *Mind* July 398 What he [James Hinton] would probably call 'thingal beauty'. **1865** J. GROTE *Moral Ideals* ii. (1876) 28 Any form of *thinghood or reality. **1872** *Contemp. Rev.* XX. 76 The conception of an external thinghood, and..of a permanent substantiality as basis of the qualities. **1880** *Mind* V. 141 Thinghood, Substantiality, Existence, are synonymous terms. **1888** L. ABBOTT in *Century Mag.* Aug. 624/1 The materialism that puts thinghood above manhood. **1919** A. N. WHITEHEAD *Princ. Natural Knowledge* II. vi. 73 Events appear as indefinite entities without clear demarcations and with mutual relations of baffling complexity. They seem..deficient in thinghood. **1950** A. HUXLEY *Themes & Variations* 55 A completer deification of the State, accompanied by a completer reification, or reduction to thing-hood, of individual persons. **1972** L. HUDSON *Cult of Fact* 76 To know about nature, and especially about people, in a way that reduces them to thing-hood, is to pursue knowledge in a way that is inimical to the proper growth of human self-awareness. **1947** *Partisan Rev.* XIV. 456 Everything in this icy landscape must be adapted to the *things* of cold steel. The organic must fuse with the mechanical, the **thingification* of man be pushed to its extreme, and the world of the workers become functional and naked. **1979** E. P. THOMPSON in *PN Rev.* No. 9 (Suppl.) p. xxvi, He had fallen on the 1844 MSS, was high on alienation and reification (which he insisted upon rendering as 'thingification'), and he had put Marx and Freud together in the bed of a single book. **1931** *Thingify [see REIFY *v.*]. **1972** *Guardian* 7 Feb. 12/8 The thingifying of anything else on the road—whether it's another competitor or..a stray pedestrian. **1890** *Open Court* (U.S.) 5 June 2316/2 Yet is space no *thingish entity, no tangible object. **1961** *Guardian* 7 Feb. 9/6 M. Robbe-Grillet..hears his method described as '*thingism' because he concentrates on..things. **1966** H. T. MOORE *Twentieth Cent. French Lit.* II. v. 116 They often produce the antiroman (antinovel) or indulge in chosisme (which might be literally translated as thingism)... In their novels and manifestoes, the antinovelists emphasize their escape from the conventional novel's preoccupation with straight-line plot, psychological analysis, and moral involvements. The group of chosistes concentrate on material objects because, in the words of one of their practitioners and spokesmen, Alain Robbe-Grillet, 'things *are there*'. **1599** T. M[OUFET] *Silkwormes* 1 What breth embreath'd these almost *thingles things. **1874** F. H. LAING in *Ess. Relig. & Lit.* Ser. III. 270 How thing came out of *thinglessness. **1890** *Australian Girl* I. xv. 203 Creatures on foot and on wing—*thinglets that fly one moment and fall down helplessly the next. **1662** J. CHANDLER *Van Helmont's Oriat.* 69 That man was ignorant of the *thingliness of a Gas ..and..of the properties of cold in the Air. *Ibid.* 343 The essential thingliness of a thing. **1652** BENLOWES *Theoph.* v. xxiv, Poor *thingling Man! **1950** O. NASH *Family Reunion* 45 I'd rather shake hands with Mr. Ringling And tell him his circus is a beautiful thingling. **1860** J. W. PALMER tr. *Michelet's Love* II. iv. 101 Things have cast off their **thingly* qualities. **1900** *Westm. Gaz.* 25 July 2/3 The words 'real presence' (he adds) meant originally the presence of (*res*) a thing—if one may say so, a 'thingly' presence—*i.e.*, presence as a thing. **1896** FRASER *Philos. Theism* Ser. II. vi. 150 Personality instead of *thingness is the highest form under which man..can conceive of God. **1902** GREENOUGH & KITTREDGE *Words* 35 *note*, A New-England philosopher was much ridiculed for using the 'thing-ness of the here' for 'the actuality of the present'. **1930** 'WYNDHAM LEWIS' *Apes of God* IX. 288 Health as intended by Kalman is '*thingness*' right enough! It is vegetable bulk, it is unconsciousness. **1967** S. BECKETT *No's Knife* 34 Into what nightmare thingness am I fallen? **1975** *New Yorker* 2 June 90/1 Clouseau finds himself forced into unkind collision with the thingness of things. **1697** J. SERGEANT *Solid Philos.* 239 We can have..a Notion of the Thing..precisely according to its *Thingship (as we may say) or Reality. **1674** N. FAIRFAX *Bulk & Selv.* 19 He that gives it a little reality or *thingsomeness, cannot..be so sparing as to..give it no more.

Thing (θɪŋ), *sb.*[2] Also ting. [a. ON. *þing* (mod.Scand. *ting*); the same word as THING *sb.*[1], but taken independently from ONorse.]

1. In Scandinavian countries (or settlements, as in parts of England before the Conquest): A public meeting or assembly; *esp.* a legislative council, a parliament; a court of law. Cf. ALTHING, STORTHING. (Usually with capital T.)

1840 *Iceland, Greenland,* etc. 99 They had been accustomed to assemble at the *Thing*, near the idol temples. **1857** DUFFERIN *Lett. High Lat.* xii. (ed. 3) 387 These landed proprietors were called the Bonders... On stated occasions they met together, in a solemn assembly, or Thing, (*i.e.* Parliament,)..for the transaction of public business. **1860** LONGF. *Wayside Inn, Saga K. Olaf* XVII. vi, The Swedish King Summoned in haste a Thing, Weapons and men to bring In aid of Denmark. **1861** PEARSON *Early & Mid. Ages Eng.* 150 Next year, 1014 A.D., while Sweyn, in the midst of his ting, was blaspheming St. Edmund, the saint appeared armed. **1865** KINGSLEY *Herew.* xxvii, We shall see what thou sayest to all this, in full Thing at home in Denmark. **1886** CORBETT *Fall of Asgard* I. xi. 137 He was proclaimed King of Norway by the Thing. *Ibid.* II. vii. 92 The judges went out to try the causes... It was the greatest suit of which notice had been given for that Thing.

transf. **1888** *Pall Mall G.* 3 Oct. 11/1 This morning..the twenty-eighth Church Congress began work... Those who remember..the third Congress..are remarking how the great Thing of the Church-folk has grown in popularity.

‖**2.** (See quot.)

1874 STUBBS *Const. Hist.* I. iii. §26 Iceland is divided into four fiordungs [ON. *fjorðungar*] or quarters... Each fiordung was divided into three things, and each thing into three godords or lordships.

3. *attrib.* and *Comb.*: **Thing-day**, a day on which a Thing is held; **Thing-dues**, fees payable to a chief who presides at a Thing; **Thing-field, -hall, -hill, -stead**, a field, hall, hill, or place where a Thing meets. See also THINGMAN.

c **1856** *Denham Tracts* (1895) II. 207 The thingstead for determining the controversies among the rude tribes. **1886** CORBETT *Fall of Asgard* I. xiii. 168 They skirted the Thing-field. *Ibid.* II. i. 7 All that were gathered that day upon the Thing-hill. *Ibid.* vii. 98 Till the end of the Thing-days. *Ibid.* ix. 127 Thorkel found himself rich. Nor was it from the Thing-dues alone. *Ibid.* xiv. 195 To Olaf's great Thing-hall went Thorkel,..on the day appointed.

thing, *v.* [OE. *þingian*, as sense 1 below, also to make terms, come to terms, settle, determine, speak, discourse, address; Com. Teut. = OFris. *thingja* to plead (WFris. *tingen*, NFris. *tingje*), OS. *thingôn* to confer, transact business, deal (MDu. *dinghen*, Du. and LG. *dingen* to bargain, etc.), OHG. *dingôn* to hold a court, conduct a process or suit, negotiate, come to an agreement, arrange a compromise or terms of peace, to stipulate, etc. (Ger. *dingen* to discuss, bargain, hire, engage on terms), ON. *þinga* to hold a (public) meeting, confer, consult, discuss terms (Sw. *tinga* to agree as to terms, engage, Da. *tinge* to bargain, etc.):—OTeut. *þingôjan*, f. *þingo*[m] THING *sb.*[1], the original sense being more distinctly retained in the vb.]

†**1.** *intr.* To plead a cause, supplicate, intercede, make intercession (with *dative* = for); *trans.* to bring to reconciliation. *Obs.*

a **1000** *Ecgberti Poenitentiale* IV. c. 62 Gif he wyle..him sylfum þingian [L. *supplicare*]. *c* **1000** *Cædmon's Satan* 510 Ic [Christ] eow þingade, þa me on beame beornas sticedon. *c* **1200** *Trin. Coll. Hom.* 15 Þe lauerd sainte poul..þingie us to þe holie fader of heuene, þat he geue us mihte. *Ibid.* 43 Do we ec mid ure wel dede þingen us wið ure helende. *c* **1200** ORMIN 8997 To þingenn uss wiþþ ure Godd þurrh bedess & þurrh lakess. *Ibid.* 18124 Ure Laferrd Jesu Crist Iss Prest.. Hiss follc to þingenn wel inoh Towarrd Drihhtin off Heffne.

2. To represent by things, i.e. concrete objects. Hence **thinger** (ˈθɪŋə(r)).

1883 G. MASSEY *Nat. Genesis* I. i. 16 Symbolism was not a conscious creation of the human mind; man..did not begin by thinging his thoughts in intentional enigmas of expression. *Ibid.*, Things were pourtrayed before thoughts by those who were thingers rather than thinkers.

thing, obs. form of THINK *v.*[1] and [2].

thingal to **thingly**: see after THING *sb.*[1]

thinger: see THING *v.* 2.

thingman (ˈθɪŋmən). Pl. -men. [ad. ON. *þingmaðr*, in pl. *þingmenn*.] A member of a Scandinavian Thing; *spec.* = HOUSECARL.

[**1862** LD. BROUGHAM *Brit. Const.* x. 137 The Danish Princes..keeping on foot a guard called *Thingmann* or *Thinglate*, of 3,000 men.] **1870** FREEMAN *Norm. Conq.* (ed. 2) I. vi. 440 Cnut now organized a regular paid force... These were the famous Thingmen, the Housecarls. **1886** CORBETT *Fall of Asgard* II. x. 130 The bonders came and laid their hands in Thorkel's, swearing themselves his Thingmen. **1890** HALL CAINE *Bondman* III. iv, Who were these men? They were Thingmen..the law-makers.

thingness to **thingsomeness**: see after THING *sb.*[1]

thingum (ˈθɪŋəm). *colloq.* ? *Obs.* exc. *dial.* Also 9 thing'em. [f. THING *sb.*[1], with meaningless suffix.] = THINGUMMY. (In first quot. in reduplicated form ***thingum thangum***: cf. CRINKUM-CRANKUM.)

1680 OTWAY *Atheist* IV. i, With a deep Point Thingum Thangum over her Shoulders. **1681** T. FLATMAN *Heraclitus Ridens* No. 45 (1713) II. 38 Is there no News from the Thingum in the Old Baily? **1741** CHESTERF. *Let. to Son* 6 Aug., To speak of Mr. What-d'ye-call-him, or Mrs. Thingum, or How-d'ye-call-her, is excessively awkward and ordinary. **1793** FITZGERALD in *Europ. Mag.* XXIII. 387 All your bunch of thingums. **1808** MRS. C. KEMBLE *Day after Wedding* 11 What were you saying, Mr. Thing'em?

So in extended forms **thingumary** (ˈθɪŋəmərɪ), (thingummarie, thing-a-merry), **thingumajig** (ˈθɪŋəmədʒɪg), (thingymyjig, etc.). See also next two words.

1819 'R. RABELAIS' *Abeillard & Heloisa* 146 Deep pond'ring—in a reverie On some dubious thingummarie. **1824** *Casket* June 76 I'd a lot of cousins, that 'com'd all the way down from Varmount to larn the fashions, and to hear and see all the cute and curious thingumajigs of the Old Colony'. **1827** HONE *Every-day Bk.* II. 58 That clever fellow, 'Thing-a-merry', or that stupid dog, 'What-d'ye-call-um'. **1876** 'L. CARROLL' *Hunting of Snark* I. ix, He would answer..To 'What-you-may-call-um?' or 'What-was-his-name!' But especially 'Thingum-a-jig!' **1889** *Century Mag.* Apr. 913/1 He got ther critter propped up an' ther thingermajig stropped on ter 'im. **1902** ELIZ. L. BANKS *Newspaper Girl* 149, I would drive through Hyde Park in a victoria,..and everybody would say, 'There goes the editress of the Thingymygig Magazine!'

thingumbob (ˈθɪŋəmbɒb). *colloq.* Also 8–9 **thing(-)em(-)bob**, 9 **thing'em bob, thingamobob, thingumebob.** [Arbitrary extension of prec., the last syllable now meaningless.] = next.

1751 SMOLLETT *Per. Pic.* ii, In a laced doublet and thingumbobs at the wrists. **1778** MISS BURNEY *Evelina* (1791) II. xxxvii. 240 Pray, is one Miss Anville in any of them thingembobs? **1788** BENTHAM *Mem. & Corr.* Wks. 1843 X. 181 One is composed of the thingumbobs called Cinq-foils, which you will find in your seal. **1832** LYTTON *Eugene A.* I. ii, A lonely grey house with a thingumebob at the top; a servatory they call it. **1870** MISS BRIDGMAN *Rob. Lynne* II. v. 107 We're going to try him for thingamobob—bigamy.

thingummy ('θɪŋəmɪ). *colloq.* Also 8 **thing-o-me, thing-o'-me,** 9 **thing-o-my, thingamy, -ammy, -ummie, -umy.** [f. THINGUM + -Y (?dim.).] Used (in undignified speech) to indicate vaguely a thing (or person) of which the speaker cannot at the moment recall the name, or which he is at a loss or does not care to specify precisely; a 'what-you-may-call-it'. Also in extended form **thingummytight (-tite,** etc.).

1796 MME. D'ARBLAY *Camilla* III. 259 Poor miss thing-o'-me's hat is spoilt already. **1803** FESSENDEN *Terr. Tractor.* IV. (ed. 2) 174 *note,* The little whalebone thingamy which the Duke of Queensbury run at New Market. **1807** W. IRVING *Salmag.* (1824) 38, I mean only to tune up those little thing-o-mys, who represent nobody but themselves. **1819** 'R. RABELAIS' *Abeillard & Heloisa* 101 A passport to a brilliant court Where all great thingummies resort. **1862** THACKERAY *Philip* viii, What a bloated aristocrat Thingamy has become! **1904** *Times* 11 Jan. 12/2 Mr. So-and-so has..'entrusted' its little carcase to Mr. Thingummy, birdstuffer. **1937** G. FRANKAU *More of Us* xvii. 177 Quick. The small green phial. It's in my bathroom. In the thingummytight—The corner cupboard. **1939** J. CARY *Mister Johnson* 23 What's the trouble? Why, it's thingummytite, aren't you? **1977** D. CLARK *Gimmel Flask* viii. 147 We've got a thingumitite with us...a sort of visionary. Young cops with fantouche ideas! **1980** D. BOGARDE *Gentle Occupation* i. 21 Nothing in the taps of course because the terrorists had buggered up the hydroelectric thingummytites.

† **'thin-gut.** Now *Obs.* or *vulgar.* [f. THIN *a.* + GUT *sb.*] One who has a thin belly; a lean starved-looking person: a starveling.

1602 MIDDLETON *Blurt, Master Constable* I. ii, Sirrah thin-gut, what's thy name? **1607** ROWLANDS *Diog. Lanth.* 6 'Tis Mounsieur Vsury, what a leane lanke thin-gut it is. **1631** MASSINGER *Believe as You List* III. ii, Does it soe, you thinnegut? Thou thinge without moysture.

So † **'thin-'gutted** *a.*, thin-bellied, lank, lean.

1625 MASSINGER *New Way* I. ii, I am out of charity With none so much as the thin-gutted squire. **1735** R. GALE in *Mem. W. Stukeley* (Surtees) III. 111 A thin-gutted dog, like a grey-hound. **1746** FRANCIS tr. *Hor., Sat.* I. v. 93 Methinks, a single Pound of Bread a day Might such a sleek thin-gutted Rogue content.

thingy ('θɪŋɪ), *sb.* Also **thingie,** (occas. **-ee**). [-Y[6], dim. suff.; cf. -IE.]

1. *Sc.* A little thing.

1888 BARRIE *When a Man's Single* (1900) 11/2 A speerity bit thingy she was.

2. = THING *sb.*[1] (in various senses); cf. THINGUMMY. *colloq.*

1933 GREEN & STEPT *(song-title)* Swingy little thingy. **1968** M. RICHLER *Cocksure* v. 32 It was going to be the rage. A thingee. Like TW3. **1977** *Spare Rib* June 26/3 Then there are those women who make men wear things on their thingies. **1981** J. BARNETT *Firing Squad* xiii. 184 We don't do crime here... Contracts, copyright, companies floated, that's our thingie.

thingy ('θɪŋɪ), *a.* [-Y[1].]

a. Having the nature or character of a thing; real, actual, objective, substantial; in quot. 1894, ?consisting of separate, independent, or unconnected things. **b.** Devoting oneself to or concerned with actual things, practical, matter-of-fact.

1891 *Cent. Dict.*, Thingy, *adj.* **1894** M. SCHUYLER in *Forum* (N.Y.) July 617 The government buildings have become more and more 'thingy', more and more compilations of 'features' that fail to make up a physiognomy.

So **thinginess** ('θɪŋɪnɪs), the quality of being thingy; (*a*) reality, actuality, objectivity; (*b*) devotion to things, practical or matter-of-fact character.

1891 *Cent. Dict.*, Thinginess. **1914** *Morning Post* 26 Feb. 2/2 Let us hear the second-hand eloquence of one of those second-rate authorities in his vain attempt to get at the thinginess of such things. **1962** W. NOWOTTNY *Lang. Poets Use* v. 107 The 'thinginess' even of what we call 'concrete objects' is so inaccessible to the probe of our common language. **1976** *New Yorker* 15 Mar. 118/2 The very thinginess of the contemporary city life in the film shows—the fast cars, the unobtrusive chic, the small cafes—seems to deprive us of any illumination. **1982** T. GUNN *Occasions of Poetry* I. 22 He was in love with the bare fact of the external world, its thinginess.

† **'thinhead.** *Obs. rare*[−0]. [f. THIN *a.* + *-hede*, -HEAD.] = THINNESS.

*c*1440 *Promp. Parv.* 491/1 Thynnesse, or thynhede of licurys, as ale, water, and oþer lyke, *tennitas.*

† **think,** *v.*[1] *Obs.* (exc. in METHINKS, q.v.) Forms: see below. [OE. *þync(e)an, þûhte, ʒeþûht* = OS. *thunkian, thûhta* (Du. *dunken*), OHG. *dunchan, dûhta* (MHG. *dunken,* G. *dünken, däuchte*), ON. *þykkja, þótta* (:—**þunkja, *þúhta*) (Sw. *tycka,* Da. *tykkes*), Goth. *þugkjan, þûhta*,:—OTeut. **þuŋkjan, *þuŋχta* to seem, appear. Although in Gothic and all the Teutonic langs. *þuŋkjan* is inflected as a weak verb, with forms parallel to those of *þaŋkjan* (THINK *v.*[2]), it is generally held to have been originally a strong vb., the present stem of which was formed with *-ja* suffix, like **ligjan, *sitjan,* etc., on the weak grade of an original ablaut series **þiŋk-, *þaŋk-, *þuŋk-* (see THINK *v.*[2]), which subseq. passed into the first class of weak vbs. (cf. *brûkjan, brûhte, bugjan, bauhte,* etc.). In OE., as in the cognate langs., the forms of this vb. and THINK *v.*[2] remained quite distinct; but in ME., owing to the fact that both *þync-* and *þenc-* gave ME. *þink-*, and both *þúht* and *þóht* appeared in ME. as *þouȝt, thought,* they became confused and finally fell together. The contiguity of sense also helped: see THINK *v.*[2]]

A. Illustration of Forms.

1. *Inf.* and *Pres. t.* α. 1 **þyncan, -cean;** *3rd pers. sing.* 1 **ðynceþ, ðyncþ,** 4 **thunceth(*ü*);** 3 **puncþ (þunþ).**

*a*800 CYNEWULF *Elene* 541 (Gr.) Do swa þe þynce. *c*897 K. ÆLFRED *Gregory's Past. C.* xxxvi. 255 Hwelc wite sceal us ðonne to hefig ðyncan [*v.r.* ðyncean]? *c*1250 *Owl & Night.* 1592 Ek steape hire þun[c]þ a mile. *Ibid.* 1649 Me þunch. *Ibid.* 1672 þuncþ [*Jesus MS.* þinkþ].

β. 1 **þincan, þincean,** 3-5 **þink(e,** 4 **þynke, thinc,** 4-6 **thynk(e,** 4-7 **thinke,** 5 **thynck,** 6 **thincke,** 4-6 (7-9 *arch.* in METHINKS) **think;** *3rd pers. sing.* 1 **þinþ,** 1-3 **þincþ,** 3 **þinkþ,** 4 **thinkt;** 3 (*Orm.*) **þinnkeþþ.**

*c*888 K. ÆLFRED *Boeth.* xxxiii. § 2 ðif he hine þonne beȝit, þonne þincð him þæt he næbbe ȝenoȝ. *c*1000 *Sax. Leechd.* II. 74 Swa micel swa þe þince. *c*1200 ORMIN 11807 Ne þinnke ȝuw nan wunnderr. *c*1325 *Spec. Gy Warw.* 588 þouh þe þinke, hit greue þe. *c*1350 *Will. Palerne* 384 Lordes, lusteneþ her-to, ȝif ȝou lef þinkes. **13..** *Cursor M.* 18966 (Gött.) Gret selcuth here-of thinces vus. *Ibid.* 2602 (Fairf.) Me walde þink þat hit ware myne. *a*1400 HYLTON *Scala Perf.* (W. de W. 1494) I. xxxiv, Hym shall thynke that his synnes are..so fowle. *c*1400 MAUNDEV. (1839) xxvii. 278 þanne wolde hem thinken gretter delyt. **1531** *Dial. on Laws Eng.* I. xxix. 70 It thynketh more resonable. **1577** HARRISON *England* II. i. (1877) I. 18 Adding what him thinketh good of his owne knowledge.

Irreg. **13..** *Cursor M.* 225 (Cott.) Notful me thinc it ware to man. *Ibid.* 16389 Selcuth vs thinc o þe. *c*1400 MAUNDEV. (Roxb.) xxi. 96 þis think me ane of þe grettest meruailes. **1530** CROME in Strype *Eccl. Mem.* (1721) III. App. x. 20 But my thynk theye hurt purgatorye sore. *c*1572 GASCOIGNE *Fruites Warre* Wks. (1831) 212 Me thinke if then their cause be rightly scande.

γ. 2-3 **þinche(n,** 2-4 **þunche(n;** 3 **þenche(n,** 4 **thynche(n.**

*c*1175 *Lamb. Hom.* 33 Nalde hit þe þinchen na mare bute [etc.]. *Ibid.* 35 ȝet hit wald me þunchen þet softeste beð..þat ic efre ibad. *Ibid.* 59 þet puncheð gode swiðe god. *a*1200 *Moral Ode* 62 Eiðer to lutel and to muchel scal þunchen [*v.r.* þunche] eft hom baþe. *c*1230 *Hali Meid.* 7 Tah hit þunche oðre men þat ha drehen harde. *c*1250 *A lutel soth Sermun* 80 in *O.E. Misc.* 190 An eue to go mid him Ne þunchet [*v.r.* þincheþ] hire no schome. *c*1300 *Harrow. Hell* (Harl. MS.) 140 Me þuncheþ he is a coward. **1399** *Pol. Poems* (Rolls) I. 397, I say ffor my self, and schewe, as me thynchith.

δ. 3-4 **þenke(n,** 4-5 **thenke(n,** 5 **thenck;** *3rd pers. sing.* 4 **thenkth.** (Belonging in form to THINK *v.*[2])

*c*1330 [see B. 3]. *c*1374 CHAUCER *Anel. & Arc.* 105 But no thing thenkith þe fals as doth the trewe. **1390** GOWER *Conf.* II. 8 So that him thenketh of a day A thousand yer, til he mai se The visage of Penolope. **1419** in *Proc. Privy Council* (1834) II. 247 þus us thenkiþ þer was grete negligence in sum persone.

ε. *3rd pers. sing.* 3-4 **þingþ,** 4 **thingth;** 5 **thyngyt; thing.**

*a*1300 *Fragm. Pop. Sc.* (Wright) 96 The sonne is more than the mone,. The mone thinȝth the more, for heo so neȝ ous is. **1340** *Ayenb.* 166 Suo dede þe martires ase hit þingþ ine hare liue. *c*1420 *Anturs of Arth.* xxv, Vs thing [*v.r.* thynke] a masse as squete, As any spyce that euyr thou ete.

2. *Pa. t.* α. 1-3 **þuhte,** 3 **þuȝte, ðhuȝte,** (*Orm.*) **þuhhte,** 4 **puȝt,** 5 **thught.**

*a*800 CYNEWULF *Christ* 1424 Lytel þuhte is leoda bearnum. *c*1200 *Trin. Coll. Hom.* 119 Hit þuhte here ech sunderlepes þat it was his landes speche. *c*1200 ORMIN 15324 Itt himm þuhhte swiþe god. *c*1250 *Death* 186 in *O.E. Misc.* 180 Hit þuȝte [*v.r.* þuhte] þe ful god. *c*1250 *Gen. & Ex.* 1849 To sen de werld ðhuȝte hire god. **13..** *Cursor M.* 750 (Fairf.) If ham gode þuȝt [*v.rr.* thoght, þouȝt].

β. 3 **þohte,** 3-4 **þoȝte,** 3-5 **þouȝte,** 4 **thoȝte, þoȝt, þoht, thouht, (þouȝth),** 4-5 **þouȝt, thoght,** 4-6 *Sc.* **thocht,** 5 **thoghte, thoȝt, þowht,** *Sc.* **thoucht,** 5-7 (8-9 *arch.* in *methought*) **thought;** 3-4 **þoute,** 4 **thout, (thouth),** 4-5 **þout,** 5 **thowt.** (Coinciding in form with THINK *v.*[2])

*c*1290 *St. Kenelm* 123 in *S. Eng. Leg.* I. 348 Him þouȝte he clam op-on þat treo. *a*1300 *Cursor M.* 19040 (Edin.) þar of to don quat taim god þoȝte [*C., G.* thoght, *L.* thoȝt, *Tr.* þouȝt]. *Ibid.* 1339 (Cott.) Him thoght [*Gött.* thout, *F.* þoȝt, *Tr.* þouȝte]..þat to þe sky it raght þe toppe. **13..** *E.E. Allit. P.* B. 562 Hard hit hym þoȝt. **1375** BARBOUR *Bruce* I. 79 þis ordynance þaim thocht þe best. *c*1430 *Hymns Virg.* 83 Al þat y dide, it þouȝte me swete. **1513** DOUGLAS *Æneis* XI. vi. 15 The Goddis wraik, hym thocht, Schew that by fait Ene was thiddir brocht. **1632** HOLLAND *Cyrupædia* 205 Him thought that one came unto him.

B. Signification. *intr.* To seem, to appear.

1. With expressed subject (sometimes *it*) and complement; often also with dat. pron.

*c*888 K. ÆLFRED *Boeth.* xxxii. §2 þonne ne ðuhte he him no innon swa fæȝer swa he utan þuhte. *c*897 [see A. 1 α]. *c*975 *Rushw. Gosp.* Matt. xvii. 25 Hwæt ðynceþ þe simon petre? *a*1000 *Boeth. Metr.* xxviii. 63 Ne þincð þæt wundor micel monna æneȝum. *c*1175 *Lamb. Hom.* 119 Monie þewas beoð..þe monnen þuncheð rihte. *c*1200 *Trin. Coll. Hom.* 109 þe sunne þinkeð ful of liht..þe sunne þincheð ful of hete. *c*1275 *Woman of Samaria* 19 in *O.E. Misc.* 84 Hwat artu þat drynke me byst, þu þinchest of iude-londe. *c*1386 CHAUCER *Knt.'s T.* 2183 Thanne is it wysdom, as it thynketh me To maken vertu of necessitee. **1437** EARL WARWICK in *Wars Eng. in France* (Rolls) II. Pref. 67 Such as shall think unto youre lordship necessarie and sufficient. *a*1450 *Le Morte Arth.* 3829 That lyffe hym thought no-thyng longe.

2. Impersonal, i.e. without expressed subject, or with following clause as implicit subject: It seems. (Always with dat. pron., *me, him, her,* etc.)

After *c* 1300 sometimes irreg. put into the person or number of the dative pron., by confusion with THINK *v.*[2]: thus *methink,* for *methinks,* after *I think.* Cf. A. 1 β *irreg.*

a. With complement, as in 1; also with following inf. clause as implicit subject.

Beowulf 1748 þinceð him to lytel þæt he lange heold. *c*888 K. ÆLFRED *Boeth.* xiv. §2 Ac þincð him ȝenoȝ on þam þe hi binnan heora æȝenre hyde habbað. *c*1200 ORMIN 5030 ȝiff himm þinnkeþþ god, he maȝȝ þe ȝifenn heoffness blisse. *a*1300 *Cursor M.* 636 (Cott.) þar for thoght þam þe na scham. *Ibid.* 868 Vs thoght scam þe to bide. *c*1425 *Ibid.* 16827 (Laud) Dothe hym doune as you thenckyth best. *c*1460 *Towneley Myst.* ii. 158 Cry on, cry, whyls the thynk good. *c*1520 BARCLAY *Jugurth* (1557) 28 b, Whan he had.. such compani as him thought competent for an army. **1556** *Aurelio & Isab.* (1608) D iv, Take that nombre of men and women as shall thincke you goode.

b. Followed by a sb. clause (constituting the logical subject), or parenthetic. See also METHINKS.

*c*888 K. ÆLFRED *Boeth.* xxix. §1 Him selfum ðincð þæt he nænne næbbe. *c*1200 ORMIN 10299 Hemm þuhhte þatt he mihhte ben Helysew þe profete. **1297** R. GLOUC. (Rolls) 7597 To bete þulke robberie, þat him þoȝte he adde ydo. *c*1386 CHAUCER *Knt.'s T.* 100 Hym thoughte þat his herte wolde breke. *c*1470 HENRY *Wallace* v. 998 Say quhat ye will, this is the best, think me. **1530** TINDALE *Pract. Prelates* I vij, The maryage of the brother with the sister is not so greuouse agenst the lawe of nature (thinketh me) as the degrees aboue rehersed. **1635** HEYWOOD *Hierarch.* IV. 198 Him thought that in his depth of sleepe he saw A Souldier arm'd.

c. With adverb (*as, how, so, thus*), usually representing a clause.

[*Beowulf* 1341 ðe feor hafað fæhðe ȝestæled þæs þe þincean mæȝ þeȝne moneȝum.] *c*1000 *Ags. Gosp.* Matt. xxi. 28 Hu þincð eow? *a*1300 *Cursor M.* 639 (Cott.) 'Adam', he said, 'how thinkt [*v.rr.* thinkes, þinkeþ] þe, In þis stede es fair to be?' *c*1385 CHAUCER *L.G.W.* Prol. 248 Therfore may I seyn, as thynketh me, This songe in preysyng of this lady fre. *c*1440 *Alphabet of Tales* 175 We hard a grete noyse of armyd men, & as vs thoght, of harnessid hors. **1570-6** LAMBARDE *Peramb. Kent* (1826) 333 The which may (as me thinketh) be broken in-to foure severall portions.

3. Phr. *think long,* to seem long, to be wearisome (to one): cf. THINK *v.*[2] 10 c.

*a*1000 *Boeth. Metr.* x. 66 þeah hit lang ðince. *c*1200 *Trin. Coll. Hom.* 183 Hire þuncheð lang, þat hie on him bileueð. *c*1330 *Assump. Virg.* (B. M. MS.) 121 Alle him þenkeþ swiþe longe Til þou comest hem amonge. *c*1430 *Hymns Virg.* 9/49 After his loue me þenkiþ long.

think (θɪŋk), *v.*[2] Pa. t. and pple. **thought** (θɔːt). Forms: see below. [OE. *þenc(e)an, þóhte, (ȝe)þóht,* = OFris. *thinka* (WFris. *tinkje, tinze*); OS. *thenkian, thâhta* (Du., LG. *denken*), OHG. *denchen, dâhta* (MHG., Ger. *denken, dachte*), ON. *þekkja, þátta* (**þeŋkja, *þâhta*), (Sw. *tänka,* Da. *tænka*), Goth. *þagkjan, þâhta* (:—**þaŋχta*). In form, a factitive vb. f. *þaŋk-*, strong grade of ablaut series *þiŋk-, þaŋk-, þuŋk-*:—pre-Teut. **teng-, *tong-, *tng-*: cf. THINK *v.*[1] The original meaning may thus have been 'to cause (something) to seem or appear (to oneself)'. In ME., *þenk* (as was normal with the groups *-eng, -enk*) became *þink,* with the result of confusing this in the present stem with the prec. vb., of which the pa. t. *þúhte* was also from 13th c. written *þoughte, thought(e,* so that the forms of the two verbs became completely identical. The practical equivalence of sense between *me thinks, him thought,* etc., and *I think, he thought,* etc., also contributed to this result, there being no difference of import between 'such compani as *him thought* [= OE. *him þúhte*] competent' (see THINK *v.*[1] B. 2 a) and 'such company as *he thought* [= OE. *he þóhte*] competent'.]

A. Illustration of Forms.

1. *Inf.* and *Pres. t.* α. 1 **þencan,** 2 **þence,** 2-4 **þenken,** (3 *Orm.* **þennkenn, ðenke(n,** 4 **þengke),** 4-5 **þenke, thenke, þenk,** 4-5 **thenk.**

*c*888 Hwæt he þencð [see B. 1]. ?*a*1100 *O.E. Chron.* an. 995 (MS. F) Nan mann ne mihte ðencan embe naht elles butan. *a*1175 þence [see B. 8 b]. *c*1200 *Trin. Coll. Hom.* 49 þe man þe..ne þencð no þing. *c*1250 *Gen. & Ex.* 2072 Of me ðu ðhenke ðan it sal ben. *Ibid.* 3563 And ðenk, louerd, quat ben bi-foren Abram, and ysaac, and iacob sworen. *c*1290 *St. Gregory* 50 in *S. Eng. Leg.* I. 357 þou þencst.. with þi conseil al rome to bi-traiȝe. **1382** Thenk [see B. 2]. *c*1440 *Promp. Parv.* 490/2 Thenkyn, *cogito.*

β. 2-3 **þenchen,** 3-4 **þenche,** 4 **thenche.**

*c*1175 *Lamb. Hom.* 61 þet we ne þenchen ufel to don. *c*1200 *Moral Ode* 118 (Trin. Coll. MS.) He sal hit þenche þanne. *c* **1205**, *c* **1275** þench, þinche [see B. 2 b (*b*)]. *c* **1330** *Arth. & Merl.* (Kölbing) 6534 Eten & drink men schal on benche And after mete in chaumber þenche. *c* **1386** Thenche [see B. 4].

γ. 4 **þink-, þinc-, thinc-,** 4–5 **þinke,** 5 **þynke;** 4–6 **thynk, thynke, (thincke),** 4–7 **thinke, (thinck,** 6 **thyncke),** 4– **think.**

13.. *Cursor M.* 14187 (Cott.) Sir quat thinckes þou? *Ibid.* 21630 (Edin.) Mar.. Than ani man mai þinc [*Cott.* thing] in thoȝt. *a* **1340** HAMPOLE *Psalter* cxlv. 1 þe purere part of mannys saule, þat thynkis þe wisdom of god. *c* **1425** *Eng. Conq. Irel.* 22 Other, that wors is.. vs tynken vndo that god shild. **1552** HULOET, Thyncke often, *reputo, as.* **1648** tr. *Senault's Paraphr. Job* 360 To thinke.. on their domesticke affaires. **1653** Thinck [see B. 2 b (*b*)].

δ. 3–4 *imper.* **þeng,** 4 *inf.* **thing.**

a **1275** *Prov. Ælfred* 518 in *O.E. Misc.* 133 Ne þeng þu neuere þi lif. **13..** Thing [see γ]. *a* **1400** þeng [see B. 5 a].

2. *Pa. t.* 1–4 **ð-, þóhte,** 3 **þoȝte, (þochte, þoute, þuhte,** *Orm.* **þohhte),** 3–5 **þouȝte, þouȝt,** 4 **þouhte, þoughte, þoȝt, þoght, (þout, þuȝt), thoȝte, thoȝt, thouȝte,** *Sc.* **thowcht,** 4–5 **þought,** *Sc.* **thoucht,** 4–6 **thoght,** 4– *Sc.* **thocht,** 5 **þowȝt(e, (þowȝth), thouȝt, thowght(e, (thught),** 6 **thoughte, (***dial.* 8–9 **thoft,** 9 **thowt),** 4– **thought.**

971 Ðohte [see B. 2 b]. *c* **1200** ORMIN 7312 Herode ..þohhte þohh to cwellenn himm. *c* **1205** LAY. 1255 He þoute [*c* **1275** þohte] of his swefne. *Ibid.* 24190 þuhte [see B. 10]. **1297** R. GLOUC. (Rolls) 2652 Hengist þoȝte þe king & is bytraye. **13..** *Cursor M.* 3352 (Cott.) He.. thoght on thing he had to done. *Ibid.* 2039 (Fairf.) þe ȝonger broþer þuȝt ful wa. *c* **1350** *Will. Palerne* 855 Sche þout þroly in herte þat leuer hire were. **13..** *Gaw. & Gr. Knt.* 848 Wel hym semed for soþe, as þe segge þuȝt. *c* **1375** *Sc. Leg. Saints* iii. (*Andreas*) 928 Fore-þi I thowcht I wald nocht dwell. **1375** BARBOUR *Bruce* II. 69 He Thoucht that suld pass ane othir way. *c* **1400** *Destr. Troy* 3189 Fele of þe folke febull it thughten. **1450** W. LOMNER in *Four C. Eng. Lett.* (1880) 4 He thowghte he was desseyvyd. **1535** STEWART *Cron. Scot.* (Rolls) I. 90 Tha thocht it greit folie. **1604** E. G[RIMSTONE] *D'Acosta's Hist. Indies* III. ix. 146, I thought good to speak this. **1749** FIELDING *Tom Jones* VII. xiii, I thoft he had been an officer himself. **1864** MRS. LLOYD *Ladies Polc.* 102 I thoft, if so be you would be so handsome as to spake a word for me. **1864** TENNYSON *Northern Farmer, Old Style* v, I niver knaw'd whot a meän'd but I thowt a 'ad summat to saäy.

3. *Pa. pple.* 3 **iþoht, -e, (yþout), þoht, (***Orm.* **þohht),** 3–4 **iþoȝt,** 4 **i-þouȝt, yþouȝt, i-thought, þoȝt, -e, þouȝte,** *Sc.* **thowcht, thocht,** 4–5 **thought,** 5 **þouȝt, þought,** 5–6 **thowght,** 6–7 *Sc.* **thocht(e,** 7 **thoughte, (**5–9 *dial.* **thoft(e),** 5– **thought.**

c **1200** *Trin. Coll. Hom.* 71 Ure ateliche sinnes þe we hauen don and queðen and þoht. *c* **1200** ORMIN 2364 Wel haffde þohht to libbenn. *c* **1205** LAY. 13468 þat he hæfde iþoht ær. **13..** *Cursor M.* 20092 (Edin.) Quat hauis tu þoȝte [*v.r.* thoght]? *c* **1330** *Arth. & Merl.* 513 Ich haue y-þouȝt. *c* **1375** *Sc. Leg. Saints* ii. (*Paulus*) 380 To do þis, hafe I thowcht. *Ibid.* x. (*Mathou*) 135 As men.. thocht had. **1377** LANGL. *P. Pl.* B. XIII. 268 þis wil be þouȝte longe. **1387–8** T. USK *Test. Love* I. ii. (Skeat) I. 162 If I coud haue made chere to one, and ithought an other. **1482** *Ord. Gild Exeter* in *Eng. Gilds* (1870) 314 To have a sustenans.. as cane be thofte.. resounabyll. **1560** DAUS tr. *Sleidane's Comm.* 276 This was thought to be done for this intent.

B. Signification. **I.** To conceive in the mind, exercise the mind, etc.

1. *trans.* To form in the mind, conceive (a thought, etc.); to have in the mind as a notion, an idea, etc.; to do in the way of mental action.

a. with simple obj. (sb. or pron.).

c **888** K. ÆLFRED *Boeth.* xxxix. §9 þeah hwa mæȝe onȝitan hwæt oðer do, he ne mæȝ witan hwæt he þencð. *a* **1200** *Moral Ode* 79 He wat wet þenkeð and hwet doð alle quike wihte. **13..** *Cursor M.* 27101 (Cott.) Vr thoghtes ar þai be thoght. *c* **1400** *Rom. Rose* 2541 They in herte cunne thenke a thing And seyn another, in hir speking. *a* **1548** HALL *Chron., Edw. IV* 224 Whatsoeuer he thought in his Imaginacion. **1596** SHAKS. *Merch. V.* II. vii. 50 To thinke so base a thought. **1651** HOBBES *Leviath.* II. xxx. 180 Any man that sees what I am doing, may easily perceive what I think. **1871** SMILES *Charac.* i. (1876) 22 They think great thoughts. **1895** *Cornh. Mag.* Mar. 303 Don't begin to think hard things now.

b. with a direct statement, question, or exclamation as obj. (For constructions with indirect statement, etc., see 2 b, 4 a, 5 a, 8 a, 9.)

971 *Blickl. Hom.* 21 þæt mæȝ beon þæt sume men þencan oþþe cweþan, 'hu mæȝ ic secan þæt gastlice leoht [etc.]?' *c* **1386** CHAUCER *Man of Law's T.* 939 Parfay, thoghte he, fantome is in myn heed. *c* **1440** *Gesta Rom.* xxxi. 112 (Harl. MS.) And he thought to him selfe 'how many this be..?' **1611** BIBLE *2 Kings* v. 11, I thought, He will surely come out to me. **1634** MILTON *Comus* 566 O poor hapless Nightingale thought I. **1692** BENTLEY *Confut. Atheism* III. (1693) 16 If any one shall think with himself, How then can any thing live in Mercury and Saturn? **1832** TENNYSON *Miller's Dau.* 93 My mother thought, What ails the boy? **1842** —— *Dora* 4 He.. often thought, 'I'll make them man and wife'.

c. To conceive, feel (some emotion): as, †*to think wonder* (*ferly*), to wonder (*obs.*); *to think scorn* (*of*, or *to do* something), to scorn (*arch.*); *to think shame*, to be ashamed (now *dial.*). See also SCORN *sb.* 4, SHAME *sb.*

a **1300** *Cursor M.* 10601 (Cott.) Hir freindes.. Thoght ferli hou sco þider wan. *c* **1425** *Eng. Conq. Irel.* 16 Many hadden gret enuy, and mych wonder toght of Robert de barr. *c* **1430** [see SCORN *sb.* 4]. *c* **1440** *Alphabet of Tales* 85 When þe preste hard þis, onone he thoght shame. *a* **1533** LD. BERNERS *Huon* lxxxiii. 259 He thinkes scorne to speke to me. **1681** R. KNOX *Hist. Ceylon* 49 These gifts.. he thinks scorn to receive. *a* **1791** GROSE *Olio* (1796) 108 He ought to think shame of himself for such treatment. **1886** STEVENSON *Kidnapped* i, Can you forget.. old friends..? Fie, fie; think shame!

†**2. a.** (with simple obj.) To meditate on, turn over in the mind, ponder over, consider. *Obs.*

c **1000** *Ags. Ps.* (Th.) cxviii. [cxix.] 117 And ic þine soðfæstnysse symble þence. *c* **1200** *Moral Ode* 118 (Trin. Coll. MS.) Al þat a fri man haueð idon.. he sal hit þenche þanne. *a* **1300** *E.E. Psalter* i. 2 And his lagh þincke he night and dai. **13..** *Cursor M.* 24064 (Cott.), I thinc it euer and ai. **1382** WYCLIF *1 Tim.* iv. 15 Thenk thou thes thingis. **1486** *Bk. St. Albans* e ij b, Thynke what I say my sonne nyght and day. **1605** SHAKS. *Macb.* II. ii. 33 These deeds must not be thought After these wayes.

b. with indirect question as obj.: (For const. with direct question see 1 b.) (*a*) in reference to a fact or possibility.

971 *Blickl. Hom.* 7 Maria.. ðohte hwæt seo halettung wære. *a* **1300** *Cursor M.* 1323 (Cott.) Seth bigan to thinc for-qui, þat þis tre bi-com sua dri. **1881** TROLLOPE *Dr. Wortle's School* v. iv, Mrs. Wortle began to think whether the visitor could have known of her intended absence.

(*b*) In reference to something to be done, with implication of purpose or design. (Cf. 7, 8.)

971 *Blickl. Hom.* 241 And hie þohton hu hie hine acwellan meahton. *c* **1205** LAY. 8555 And þench [*c* **1275** þinche] mid wulche deden þu miht werien þine leoden. *c* **1386** CHAUCER *Melib.* ¶761 Thinkinge how she myghte brynge this nede vnto a good conclusion. **1474** CAXTON *Chesse* IV. viii. (1883) 184 He began to thynke in what maner he myght escape the deth. **1653** HOLCROFT *Procopius* I. 10 Thinck Sir! how you may avenge us and the Persians. **1778** MISS BURNEY *Evelina* (1791) I. xxxiii. 178 A-thinking what he should do. *Mod.* I am thinking what to do next.

c. To have one's thoughts full of, imbued with, or influenced by; to think in terms of. Also, with adj. as quasi-obj. or used quasi-advb., to think in terms of, prefer, have in view (things that are——), esp. ***to think big***, to be ambitious.

1821 BYRON *Diary* 29 Jan., They.. think and dream Dante. **1859** *Habits Gd. Soc.* Pref., A horse-dealer.. if he thinks nothing but horses, he cannot be good society. **1865** KINGSLEY *Herew.* ii, Unless thou hast been drinking beer and thinking beer. **1889** *Pall Mall G.* 24 Oct. 7/2 The present generation of Greeks talks French but thinks German. **1960** J. CARSWELL *South Sea Bubble* vi. 100 Even Blunt, though his maxim was certainly to 'think big', would hardly have suggested anything so obviously unacceptable. **1962** A. LURIE *Love & Friendship* xv. 300 Living in a small town had subtly affected my mind, and I had begun to Think Small. **1970** in M. Pei *Words in Sheep's Clothing* ii. 14 For those who think old! **1972** D. HASTON *In High Places* xii. 139 With people pulling off tricks like the West Ridge, Dhynenfurth was not day-dreaming in thinking tall. **1978** *National Geographic* Nov. 615/2 When people think apple, ..they usually think red. **1979** *Now!* 21–27 Sept. 134/3 Simple, uncluttered and tubular they illustrate fashion's new mood of 'think thin'. **1981** *Daily Tel.* 21 Dec. 2/3 (*heading*) 'Think British' call to CBI firms.

3. a. *intr.* To exercise the mind, esp. the understanding, in any active way; to form connected ideas of any kind; to have, or make, a train of ideas pass through the mind; to meditate, cogitate. (The most general verb to express internal mental activity, excluding mere perception of external things or passive reception of ideas.)

think aloud: to express one's thoughts by audible speech as they pass through the mind; ***to think for oneself***: to form independent judgements, not to be overinfluenced by preconceptions or received opinions; ***to think out loud*** = *to think aloud*; ***to think straight***: see STRAIGHT *adv.* 1 g.

c **1000** ÆLFRIC *Gen.* xxiv. 63 þe eode ut on þæt land þencende. *c* **1320** *Cast. Love* 17 He leue vs þenche and worchen so, þat he vs schylde from vre fo. **1382** WYCLIF *1 Cor.* xiii. 11 Whanne I was a litil child.. I thouȝte as a litil child. **1552** HULOET, Thinke muche, *reputo.* **1603** SHAKS. *Meas. for M.* II. iv. 1 When I would pray, and think, I thinke, and pray To seuerall subiects. **1673** DRYDEN *State Innocence* II. i, That I am I know, because I think. **1690** LOCKE *Hum. Und.* II. i. §10 There is something in us, that has a Power to think. *c* **1714** POPE *Lett.* (1735) I. 151 The Freedom I shall use in this Manner of Thinking aloud. **1735** BERKELEY *Defence of Free-Thinking in Math.* xix. 19 The only advantage I pretend to, is that I have always thought and judged for myself. **1764** GOLDSM. *Trav.* 372 Those who think must govern those that toil. **1853** DICKENS *Let.* 28 Nov. (1938) II. 522 One of the great uses of travelling is to encourage a man to think for himself. **1864** BOWEN *Logic* i. 10 To think is to make clear through Concepts something already otherwise represented or known to consciousness. **1870** J. P. SMITH *Widow Goldsmith's Daughter* vi. 90 The merry mischief in his eyes.. made her feel her absurdity in thinking out loud. **1974** *Times* 1 May 6/6 Those matters were thoroughly probed.. the President often taking the role of devil's advocate; sometimes merely thinking out loud. **1974** D. L. EDWARDS *What Anglicans Believe* xii. 100 Anglican laymen have been encouraged to think for themselves.

b. with *about*, *of*, (*on*, *upon* arch.), *over*, †*to* (obs. rare): To exercise the mind upon, or have the mind occupied with; to meditate on; to consider, attend to mentally, apply the mind to.

to give (one) ***furiously to think***: see GIVE *v.* 38.

971 *Blickl. Hom.* 57 Myccle swiðor we sceolan þencan be þæm gastlicum þingum. *c* **1000** *Ags. Ps.* (Th.) cxvii[i]. 8 God ys on Dryhten ȝeorne to þenceanne. *c* **1000** *Institutes of Polity* c. 14 Riht is þæt munecas.. a to Gode þencan and ȝeornlice clypian. *c* **1200** *Vices & Virt.* 17 Ac ðu.. noldest þenchen of ðine for[ð]siðe. *a* **1300** *Floriz & Bl.* 32 Ac floriz þencheþ al on oþer. *c* **1340** HAMPOLE *Prose Tr.* 36 Thow may ..thynke ouer thi synnes be-fore donne. **13..** *Cursor M.* 15612 (Gött.) To thinc apon his care. *a* **1380** *Minor Poems fr. Vernon MS.* xxxix. 138 Nou is deþ a wonder þing And grislich for to þenken on. *a* **1425** *Cursor M.* 9977 (Trin.) [She] þouȝte neuer to wicked dede. **1477** EARL RIVERS (Caxton) *Dictes* 11 Think & loke wele vpon your werkis without hasting you. **1641** EVELYN *Diary* 2 Jan., Who now thought of nothing but the pursuite of vanity. **1706** E. WARD *Wooden World Diss.* (1708) 100 It makes him think upon Pay-Day. **1782** MISS BURNEY *Cecilia* VIII. vi, Think of it well ere you proceed. **1804–6** SYD. SMITH *Mor. Philos.* (1850) 89 He began thinking about lances. *Mod.* I'll think over the matter, and let you know my decision in a day or two. [Cf. 16.]

4. To form or have an idea of (a thing, action, or circumstance, real or imaginary) in one's mind; to imagine, conceive, fancy, picture. **a.** *trans.* with simple obj. or obj. cl.; also *absol.* in colloq. phrases ***only think! you can't think!***

c **1200** ORMIN 1761 Unnseȝȝenndlike mare inoh þann aniȝ wihht maȝȝ þennkenn. *a* **1300** *Cursor M.* 647 Es nan.. wit hert mai think,.. þe mikel ioy þat þam es lent. *c* **1386** CHAUCER *Miller's T.* 67 There nas no man so wys þat koude thenche So gay a popelote, or swich a wenche. **1415** *Rolls of Parlt.* IV. 85/1 As free.. as hert may thynk, or eygh may see. **1590** SHAKS. *Mids. N.* V. i. 431 Thinke but this.. That you haue but slumbred heere. **1656** STANLEY *Hist. Philos.* VIII. (1701) 303/1 Thou seest not what thou thinkst before thy eye. **1782** MME. D'ARBLAY *Diary* 8 Dec., You can't think how I'm encumbered with these ruffles! **1864** MRS. CARLYLE *Lett.* III. 220 Only think! I get my new milk again, at eight.

b. *intr.* with *of* (*on* obs. or arch.), in same sense. (Often imperative in colloq. phrases.)

a **1300** *Cursor M.* 18802 (Cott.) Quat hert mai thinc o suilk honur. *c* **1400** MAUNDEV. (1839) xxvii. 278 He had.. all maner of foules & of bestes that ony man myghte thenke on. **1598** SHAKS. *Merry W.* III. v. 116 And then to be stopt in like a strong distillation with stinking Cloathes, that fretted in their owne grease: thinke of that, a man of my Kidney; thinke of that. **1653** WALTON *Angler* ii. 41 The gloves of an Otter are the best fortification for your hands against wet weather that can be thought of. **1741** H. WALPOLE *Lett. to Mann* (1834) I. vi. 12 Do but think on a duel between Winnington and Augustus Townshend. **1842** TENNYSON *Locksley Hall* 73 Can I think of her as dead? **1844** E. FITZGERALD *Lett.* (1889) I. 125 Think of the *rocococity* of a gentleman studying Seneca in the middle of February 1844 in a remarkably damp cottage. **1861** J. PYCROFT *Agony Point* xlvi, Think of me ever being rich! **1875** JOWETT *Plato* (ed. 2) IV. 264 The ancient philosophers.. thought of science only as pure abstraction. **1885** J. PAYN *Talk of Town* I. 7 She always thought of him.. as a very young man.

c. *trans.* with simple obj. To form a definite conception of (something real) by a conscious mental act; to picture in one's mind, apprehend clearly, cognize (with or without direct perception).

1864 BOWEN *Logic* i. 5 We.. are thus enabled *to think* the landscape as a whole. **1885** J. MARTINEAU *Types Eth. Th.* (ed. 2) I. I. xi. §8. 212 When you think this equation [surface of a sphere = area of circle of twice its diameter]. **1890** W. JAMES *Princ. Psychol.* II. xx. 203 We think the ocean as a whole by multiplying mentally the impression we get at any moment when at sea.

II. To call to mind, take into consideration.

5. a. *trans.* (with obj. clause, often indirect interrogative): To call to mind; to consider, reflect upon; to recollect, remember, bear in mind. ***to think that——!*** (int.): introducing a statement of a fact thought of as remarkable or surprising.

c **1020** *Rule St. Benet* lxiii. (Logeman) 104 Ac he þænce simle þæt he beo eallum his domum & weorcum be his is to ȝildanne. *c* **1230** *Hali Meid.* 3, & maken þe to þenchen hwuch delit were þrin. *a* **1400** *Pol. Rel. & L. Poems* (1903) 258 þeng wat þou art, & wat þou was. **1474** CAXTON *Chesse* I. iii. (1883) 15 Yf thou be a man thinke that thou shalt dye. **1605** SHAKS. *Macb.* II. ii. 51, I am afraid, to thinke what I haue done. **1667** MILTON *P. L.* VI. 135 Fool, not to think how vain Against th' Omnipotent to rise in Arms. **1818** SHELLEY *Rosalind & Helen* 188 Helen smiled.. To think that a boy as fair as he.. The like sweet fancies had pursued. **1906** BELLOC *Hills & Sea* 30 To think that you can get to a place like that for less than a pound! **1919** G. B. SHAW *Heartbreak House* II. 60 And to think that I actually condescended to fascinate that creature there to save you from him! **1946** M. PEAKE *Titus Groan* 337 To think that an hour earlier she had been helping to plait those locks.

b. *intr.* To consider the matter; to reflect.

Beowulf 290 Æȝ hwæþres sceal scearp scyld-wiȝa ȝescad witan worda & worca seþe wel þenceð. *a* **1800** COWPER *Inscr. Tomb Hamilton* 1 Pause here, and think. **1842** TENNYSON *Dora* 27 Consider, William: take a month to think. **1862** E. FITZGERALD *Lett.* (1889) I. 286, I somehow fancy a line of nonsense will catch you at Ely: and yet, now I come to think, you will have left Ely, probably. **1879** J. BLACKWOOD *Let.* 14 Jan. in *Geo. Eliot Lett.* (1956) VII. 94, I have been reading it all with great interest, and it does make one think. **1933** M. LOWRY *Ultramarine* i. 41, I wonder why it [*sc.* a carrier pigeon] had a message from Swansea... Makes you think, that, doesn't it? **1968** G. MITCHELL *Three Quick & Five Dead* ii. 67 'But young Otto is a psychopath!' said Laura. 'Makes you think a bit, that does,' agreed the Superintendent. **1976** 'D. HALLIDAY' *Dolly & Nanny Bird* x. 127 Remember how Comer came bursting in one evening?.. It makes you think, doesn't it?

c. *intr.* with *of* (arch. *on*, *upon*), or *inf.*: To call to mind, remember, bethink oneself (of), hit upon mentally. (See also 7 b.) Also, ***to think back*** (*on* or *to*), to recall, reflect on; (***when one***) ***come(s) to think of it***: see COME *v.* 24 b.

c **1175** *Pater Noster* 96 in *Lamb. Hom.* 59 He walde þet he of him þohte. *a* **1300** *Cursor M.* 1860 (Cott.) Our lauerd þan on noe thoght. *c* **1400** *Emare* 951 The emperour.. þowȝt on hys synne; Of hys þowȝtyr Emare, That was putte yn-to þe see. *a* **1536** TINDALE *Declar. Sacraments* a vj b, God.. promysed that thei shuld be thoght vpon before the lord yir god & saued from their enemies. **1552** HULOET, Thynke vpon me, *memento mei.* **1611** SHAKS. *Wint. T.* IV. iv. 547 Haue you thought on A place whereto you'l go? **1613** ——

Hen. VIII, II. ii. 138 The most conuenient place, that I can thinke of..is Black-Fryers. 1712 ARBUTHNOT John Bull II. iv, There is a small concern of a thousand pounds; I hope you think on it, Sir. 1844 MACAULAY Ess., Earl Chatham (1887) 838 In his distress, he thought on Pitt. a1912 Mod. Did you think to ask him how his father is? No, I didn't think of it. 1960 Times Lit. Suppl. 17 June 387/1, I think back to the sixth forms of the twenties. 1965 H. GOLD Man who was not with It iii. 29 Goombye, I thought back to him. 1976 Times Lit. Suppl. 22 Oct. 1327/2 When I think back on it now, that was the best thing I could have done.

d. *intr.* with *on* (adv.), To remember. Now *dial.*

1671 H. M. tr. Erasm. Colloq. 226, I much wonder that now thou thinkest on at last to ask me that. a1800 PEGGE Suppl. Grose, Think on, think of it, as I will if I think on. 1828 Craven Gloss., Think-on, to remember. 'Be sure to mind to think-on'.

e. *refl.* To bethink oneself. *rare.*

1556 Aurelio & Isab. (1608) G j, I thinckes me never the lesse that you have saide an exemple of the peacock. 1890 W. A. WALLACE Only a Sister 325, I thought me at last of the vestry window.

f. ***to think better of***: see BETTER *adv.* 6.

g. ***to think twice*** (const. *about* or *absol.*): to hesitate, change one's mind (about), decide against (something); also, in a negative context: (not) to take any notice of or worry about.

1898 G. B. SHAW Philanderer III. 119 He thinks twice before he commits himself. 1910 G. F. HILL in Archæologia LXII. 140, I confess that had I come across this MS. at the beginning of my search, I should have thought twice before going on. 1936 W. H. SAUMAREZ SMITH Let. 21 Nov. in Young Man's Country (1977) ii. 43 When they find that I am neither a Blue..nor a bridge-player, they may think twice about offering the appointment to me. 1955 M. HASTINGS Cork & Serpent v. 67 Don't worry. Nobody here thinks twice about me. 1956 A. HUXLEY Let. 13 Aug. (1969) 805 He thought I had been wise to think twice about talking on TV about mescalin. 1979 R. RENDELL Make Death love Me i. 8 The rule was made to be broken and no one ever thought twice about breaking it. 1981 P. SALWAY Roman Britain 705 This must make us think twice before attributing reasons to any funerary or religious practice from the ancient world for which we have no written evidence.

h. ***to think again***: to realize that one is mistaken, to change one's mind, to have second thoughts. Cf. THOUGHT¹ 2c.

1911 G. B. SHAW Getting Married 291 So youre not coming home with me. Hotchkiss..: Yes I am. Mrs. George: No. Hotchkiss: Yes. Think again. 1935 C. S. FORESTER African Queen ii. 35 It would blow this ole launch..to Kingdom Come. You think again, miss. 1958 P. SHORE in N. Mackenzie Conviction 37 Those who imagine that the problem of the public schools will disappear..will have to think again. 1974 M. GILBERT Flash Point xiii. 109 It was a put-up job. If they think I'm going to sit down under it, they can think again.

6. To take into consideration, have regard to, consider. †**a.** *trans.* with simple obj. *Obs. rare.*

c1175 Lamb. Hom. 15 Þet we sculden þenchen nu ȝef we weren iseli. 1382 WYCLIF Prov. iii. 6 In alle thi weies thenc [1388 thenke on] hym. c1450 tr. De Imitatione I. xxiv. 32 þenke no þinge but þi soule helpe; charge onely þo þinges þat longiþ to þi soule.

b. *intr.* with *of*, arch. *on* (*upon*).

a1300 Cursor M. 10435 (Cott.) Qui ne wil þou on þi seluen thinc, þat þou wil noiþer ete ne drinc? 1340 HAMPOLE Pr. Consc. 2652 And whyles he lyffes..Thynk he suld ay of his lyfes hende. c1380 WYCLIF Serm. Sel. Wks. I. 65 Wolde God þat preelatis wolde þenke on þis now. 1387 TREVISA Higden (Rolls) V. 181 To þinke [v.r. þengke] on þe comyn profit. 1532 TINDALE Expos. Matt. v-vii vii. II. 89 If thou repente..he promyseth that he will not thynke on thy synnes. 1735 JOHNSON Lobo's Abyssinia, Descr. xi. 112 Nothing was thought of, but how to save ourselves, and the little goods we had. 1827 SCOTT Surg. Dau. x, 'That is the last matter to be thought on', said Hartley. 1875 JOWETT Plato (ed. 2) IV. 35 If..we begin by thinking of ourselves first, we are easily led on to think of others.

7. To bethink oneself of something in the way of a plan or purpose; to find out or hit upon (a way to do something) by mental effort; to contrive, devise, plan, plot. (Cf. *think out*, 15. See also 8.) **a.** *trans.* with simple obj. or inf.

c1330 R. BRUNNE Chron. Wace (Rolls) 1075 Brutus by-þoughte hym of queintise: Queyntise bihouede [v.r. behoues] hym nedly þenke, þat his enemy schold waite a blenk. 1483 CAXTON Gold. Leg. 181b/1 Thou cursyd wretche now thynke to saue thy lyf. 1602 MARSTON Antonio's Rev. IV. v, Let's thinke a plot. 1852 THACKERAY Esmond I. ix, It was this lady's disposition to think kindnesses..and to scheme benevolence.

b. *intr.* with *of* (*on*, *upon*, obs. or arch.).

1598 SHAKS. Merry W. IV. iv. 46 What shall be done with him? What is your plot? Mist. Pa. That likewise haue we thought vpon. 1630 in Picton L'pool Munic. Rec. (1883) I. 158 His Majesty..hath thought of a way. 1699 LISTER Journ. Paris 49 'Tis..their Misfortune not to have Thought of an Alphabet. a1715 BURNET Own Time (1766) II. 31 She ..took all the ways she could think on to ruin him. a1774 GOLDSM. Surv. Exp. Philos. (1776) II. 121 Derham..was the first who thought upon this method of measuring the heights..by the barometer.

c. ***to think on one's feet***: to react to events, etc., quickly and effectively.

1935 WODEHOUSE Luck of Bodkins xvi. 202 PS. Think on your feet, boy! 1960 Analog Science Fact/Fiction Oct. 73/2 Your records show that you can think on your feet. 1976 J. ARCHER Not a Penny More x. 116 'James,' said Jean-Pierre, thinking on his feet for not the first time in his life. 'You take a taxi immediately.' 1981 T. WRIGHT in Believing in Church v. 112 Reports approved by Synod (the Church thinking on its feet).

8. To conceive or entertain the notion of doing something; to meditate, contemplate, intend, purpose, design, mean, 'have a mind', 'have thoughts (of)'. In early use often not distinguishable from 7; in later use mostly denoting an imperfect, temporary, or ineffective intention: cf. THOUGHT *sb.* 3 d. **a.** *trans.* with *inf.* or *obj. cl.*

Beowulf 1536 Swa sceal man don þonne he æt guðe ȝegan þenceð long-sumne lof. 971 Blickl. Hom. 151 þa Iudeas ..þohton þæt hie woldan ofslean þa apostolas. c1175 Lamb. Hom. 61 Þet we ne þenchen ufel to don. c1220 Bestiary 455 He..ðoȝte he wulde him fordon. 1297 R. GLOUC. (Rolls) 1181 Iulius þe emperour..þoȝte to sle al þat folc. 1375 BARBOUR Bruce XI. 532 To the castell thai thoucht to fair. c1400 Brut xii. 16 Ferst he þougt assaye whiche of ham louede him most and best. 1535 COVERDALE 2 Chron. ii. 1 Salomon thoughte to buylde an house vnto the name of the Lorde. 1585 ABP. WHITGIFT in Lett. Lit. Men (Camden) 44 This Paper..which I had thowght to have delivered unto you my self yesterday. 1681 DRYDEN Abs. & Achit. 510 With them joined all the haranguers of the throng, That thought to get preferment by the tongue. 1833 TENNYSON Lady Clara V. de Vere i, You thought to break a country heart For pastime. 1878 T. HARDY Ret. Native IV. ii, He.. thought he would send for his mother; and then he thought he would not.

b. *trans.* With simple obj. (usually an action).

a1175 Cott. Hom. 221 Ne yfel to þence, ne to donne. c1220 Bestiary 449 Wo so seieð oðer god, & ðenkeð iuel on his mod, Fox he is & fend iwis. a1300 Cursor M. 4124 To stint wald he..þe foly þat his breþer thoght. c1320 Cast. Love 1 þat good þenkeþ, good may do. a1450 Le Morte Arth. 1655 How in an Appelle he dede the galle And hadde it thought to syr gawayne. 1553 ASCHAM in Lett. Lit. Men (Camden) 14 To whom yow never intended to think any harm. 1667 MILTON P. L. I. 661 Peace is despaird, For who can think Submission? 1819 SHELLEY Cenci I. i. 97 While yet Manhood remained to act the thing I thought.

c. *intr.* with *of* (also *upon*, ? arch. or dial.).

1698 FRYER Acc. E. India & P. 9 We began to think of returning. 1749 FIELDING Tom Jones Ded., It was by your Desire that I first thought of such a Composition. 1760-72 H. BROOKE Fool of Qual. (1809) III. 138 You must not think of going till you take a dinner with us. 1812 CRABBE Tales xviii, Each thought of taking to himself a wife. 1861 KINGSLEY in Lett. & Mem. (1877) II. 133, I hear you think of getting into Parliament. 1894 J. T. FOWLER Adamnan Introd. 60 He thought of going to Rome and Jerusalem, and did go to Tours.

d. *spec.* with *of*: To consider (a person) in view of some vacancy or *esp.* of marriage; to cherish the notion or intention of marrying.

1670 LADY CHAWORTH in 12th Rep. Hist. MSS. Comm. App. v. 17 Lady Exeter..could heartily wish that you thought of her niece Lady Betty. 1802 MAR. EDGEWORTH Moral T. (1816) I. xx. 187, I trust to your prudence, not to think of Flora..; for you can't..marry a girl with so small a fortune. 1856 PATMORE Angel in Ho. II. II. iii, You, with your looks and catching air, To think of Vaughan!

†**e.** *intr.* or *ellipt.* To purpose or intend to go; to direct one's course. *Obs.*

c893 K. ÆLFRED Oros. IV. ix. §2 He þara ælces ehtend wolde beon,..þe þæs wordes wære þæt from Romebyrg þohte. a1023 WULFSTAN Hom. xlii. (Napier) 200 On ða wisan, þe man hors ȝewæpnað, þonne man to wiȝe þencð. c1330 R. BRUNNE Chron. Wace (Rolls) 12501 [Arthur] passed Burgoyne..Vntil Hostum, þyder he þought. 1377 LANGL. P. Pl. B. XVI. 175, I frayned hym..of whennes he were, and whider þat he þouȝte. a1400-50 Alexander 1121 Now airis he furthe with his ost, to Egist he thinkes.

†**f.** *fig.* To seem likely (*to do* something): *thought to* = 'was like to', was on the point of, nearly did... Cf. F. *penser à*. *Obs.*

1578 N. BAXTER Calvin on Jonah 9 The shyppe thought to be broken. 1585 T. WASHINGTON tr. Nicholay's Voy. II. xi. 45b, A Northerly wynde..thought to haue made vs turne backe agayne. 1599 NASHE Lenten Stuffe 46 With so ill a will hee went, that hee had thought to haue topled his burning carre..into the sea (as Phaeton did).

III. To be of opinion, deem, judge, etc.

9. a. *trans.* with *obj. cl.* (or pronoun substitute), or parenthetic: To be of opinion, hold the opinion, believe, deem, judge, apprehend, consider; usually, to believe without any great assurance, to regard it as likely, to have the idea, to suppose; in reference to a future event, to expect (coinciding partly in sense with 12).

who do you think? what do you think? (colloq.) phrases used, esp. parenthetically, to introduce a surprising statement.

Beowulf 691 Nænig heora þohte þæt he þanon scolde eft eard lufan æfre ȝesecean. c1175 Lamb. Hom. 67 Þos ilke bode, wisliche þing, of oðre is ful festning. a1300 Cursor M. 950 Þou sal thinc þou liues to lang. c1386 CHAUCER Sompn. T. 322 Thanne thoughte they it was the beste reed To lede hem bothe to the Iuge agayn. 1450 W. LOMNER in Four C. Eng. Lett. (1880) 4 He thowghte he was desseyvyd. a1548 HALL Chron., Hen. VIII 170 Who would haue thought that our Uncle of Englande would haue made warre on vs? 1592 MORYSON Let. in Itin. (1617) I. 25 Each of vs went to our taske, he (as I thought) to goe, I to sleepe. 1601 HOLLAND Pliny (1634) I. 188 Thrason was the first builder of towne wals: of towers & fortresses, the Cyclops, as Aristotle thinketh. 1610 SHAKS. Temp. I. ii. 40 Canst thou remember ..? I doe not thinke thou canst. 1615 G. SANDYS Trav. 38 Fresh water, some say brought thither by art, I rather think from a naturall fountain. 1616 B. JONSON Epigr., Voyage itself 135 But 'mongst these Tiberts, who do you think there was? Old Banks the juggler. 1726 SWIFT Gulliver I. vii, A country, governed, as I thought, by very different maxims from those in Europe. 1790 Tom Tit's Song Bk., There was an old woman, And what do you think, She lived upon nothing, But victuals and drink. 1849 MACAULAY Hist. Eng. vi. II. 15 It was thought that the flocks, thus separated from the evil shepherds, would soon return to the true fold. 1875 JOWETT Plato (ed. 2) I. 97, I think that I understand him.

b. ***I don't think*** (slang): used after an ironical statement, to indicate that the reverse is intended. ***that's what you think*** (cliché, with stress on *you*): an expression of emphatic, sometimes scornful, disagreement.

1837 DICKENS Pickw. xxxviii, 'You're a amiably-disposed young man, sir, I don't think', resumed Mr. Weller, in a tone of moral reproof. 1853 'C. BEDE' Verdant Green III. iv, 'Well! you're a grateful bird, I don't think!' said Mr. Bouncer. 1857 HUGHES Tom Brown II. ii, Hark how he swears, Tom. Nicely brought-up young man, ain't he, I don't think. 1911 KEBLE HOWARD Cheerful Knave xvi, Breakfast? Yer a credit to yer calling, I don't think. 1934 J. O'HARA Appointment in Samarra ii. 31 'I can handle that.' 'That's what you think.' 1973 P. MOYES Curious Affair of Third Dog xi. 148 'We're going to have the pleasure of your company for several days at least.' 'That's what you think.'

c. *intr.* To hold the opinion (indicated by context). ***to think so***, to be of that opinion; ***to think from*** (quot. 1625), to dissent from, to disagree with; ***to think with***, to be of the same opinion as.

a1200 Moral Ode 149 Al he walde and oðerluker don and oðerluker þenchen Wenne he bi-þohte on helle fur. 1552 HULOET, Thyncke contrarye, absentio, is. 1560 DAUS tr. Sleidane's Comm. 425b, He said he spake as he thought. 1591 SHAKS. Two Gent. II. vii. 62, I feare me it will make me scandaliz'd. Luc. If you thinke so, then stay at home. 1625 F. MARKHAM Bk. Hon. I. vi. §2 The Holy Ghost (from whose rule we dare not thinke) mentioneth but two Sonnes. 1820 BYRON Mar. Fal. II. i. 302, I did not Think with him, but would not oppose the thought. 1877 Smith & Wace's Dict. Chr. Biog. I. s.v. Atticus, Those who thought with him found in him a warm friend.

d. ***I thought as much***: see AS C. 1.

e. ***I should think*——**, introducing emphatic assent: certainly, assuredly, indeed. Also *ellipt.* in neg., ***I should think not***.

1894 A. JESSOPP Random Roaming iv. 160 Fish? I should think there was fish! There was fish enough to come to at least £15 of our money. 1903 G. B. SHAW Man & Superman IV. 167 Promise me that you wont. Violet (very decidedly) I should think not indeed. 1944 L. P. HARTLEY Shrimp & Anemone iv. 41 'Do you know..Nancy Steptoe?' 'I should think I did.'

10. a. *trans.* with complement (with or more often without *inf.*): To believe, consider, or suppose (to be..); to look upon as.

†Also (quot. 1607) with *for* (cf. *take for*, and 12d).

c1205 LAY. 24190 For he heom þuhte wurðe. a1250 Prov. Ælfred 60 in O.E. Misc. 106 We [read þe] hine her on worlde wrþie þenchep [c1275 þenket]. 1340 HAMPOLE Pr. Consc. 4250 He sal thynk hym loverd of alle. c1459 Regist. de Aberbrothoc (Bann. Cl.) II. 107 Thynkand it onkyndle tyll thole ane nominatioun of lardschipe of sic ane man. a1548 HALL Chron., Hen. VII 7 They were thought to haue been confederates. 1593 SHAKS. Rich. II, v. ii. 26 Thinking his prattle to be tedious. 1607 —— Cor. IV. v. 62 If..not yet thou know'st me, and..dost not thinke me for the man I am. 1610 —— Temp. IV. i. 120 May I be bold To thinke these spirits? 1651 HOBBES Leviath. II. xxv. 135 Some, that have the ambition to be thought eloquent. 1728 YOUNG Love of Fame VI. 205 Think nought a trifle, tho' it small appear. 1834 JAMES J. Marston Hall vii, Lord Masterton thought himself bound to act the part of an elder brother. 1865 RUSKIN Sesame ii. §94 You think that only a lover's fancy.

b. with complement immediately following (with ellipsis of obj. *it*, or with inf. or clause as obj. placed after the complement). Now chiefly in ***think fit*** (see FIT *a.* 2b), ***think proper***.

c1375 Cursor M. 14096 (Fairf.) Martha þuȝt il ho [Mary] ne help hir walde. c1400 Laud Troy Bk. 3426 Wherfore I rede, if ȝe thenke right, That we sende som messanger To Delos. c1460 SIR R. ROSS La Belle Dame 190 Whan he þought tyme to dance with her. a1500 Debate Carpenter's Tools 208 in Hazl. E.P.P. I. 86 Alle the ȝerne that I may spynne, To spend at ale he thinkes no synne. 1560 in Feuillerat Revels Q. Eliz. (1908) 51 As the said Edmunde.. shall thinke behoofefull & expedient. 1611-1875 [see FIT a. 2b]. 1692 SIR T. P. BLOUNT Ess. 37, I thought good to go to the Philosophers. 1831 SCOTT Chron. Canongate Introd., The little narrative which I thought proper to put forth in October, 1827.

c. ***think*** (*it*) ***long***: to grow weary with waiting; to weary, to be impatient; to long, yearn. In quot. c1380 ***think long by*** = to weary of. See also LONG *a.*¹ 9b. *Obs.* exc. *dial.*

A perversion of the earlier *think long* (THINK *v.*¹ B. 3) 'to seem or appear long to', by substituting the nom. for the (uninflected) dative. In the first quot. 'þat Crist þouȝte longe' may be = that to Christ seemed long (cf. 'that him thoughte long').

c1380 WYCLIF Serm. Sel. Wks. II. 59 Þe Jewis þouȝten þat Crist þouȝte longe bi his liif, and wolde..slee himsilf. 1450 MARG. PASTON in P. Lett. I. 178, I thynk ryth longe tyll I have some god tydyngys fro yow. a1533 LD. BERNERS Huon xciii. 303 My wyfe..thynkethe longe for my comynge. 1592 G. HARVEY Four Lett., etc. Sonn. xviii, These hungry wormes thinke longe for their repast. 1631 RUTHERFORD Lett. (1862) I. 75 Behold I come..; think not long. I shall be with you at once. 1650 TRAPP Comm. Exod. x. 3 God think's long of the time that men misspend..in wicked courses. 1788 CLARA REEVE Exiles I. 195 We think long till we see you. 1895 FRASER Whaups xi. 152 Ye maunna bide lang away, for I'll be thinkin' lang till I see ye again.

†**d.** ***think*** (*it*) ***much***: to think it a great or serious matter; to make objection, object, grudge; to be shy, hesitate (*to do* something, or *of* something); to be surprised, wonder (*that* ...). See also MUCH B. 2g, and cf. 11. *Obs.*

Perh. altered from 'it thinks me much' (THINK *v.*¹).

1610 SHAKS. Temp. I. ii. 252 Thou..thinkst it much to tread yᵉ Ooze Of the salt deepe. 1656 EARL MONM. tr. Boccalini's Advts. fr. Parnass. I. i. (1674) 1 Menante thinks not much to acquaint you here with the chiefest of them. **1669** R. MONTAGU in *Buccleuch MSS.* (Hist. MSS. Comm.) I. 465 Mr. Grey nor Mr. Treasurer will not think much of my sharing with them. **1678** TILLOTSON *Serm., 1 John v. 3* I. 221 If we consider our infinite obligations to God, we have no reason to think much to sacrifice to him our dearest interests.

†**e.** *pass.* To seem, appear (*to* a person): = THINK *v.*[1]; also *ellipt.* to seem good. *Obs.*

Perh. originally for THINK *v.*[1]: 'it thinks (= appears) to the king' being changed by way of correction to 'it is thought to the king'; hence the retention of *to*.

1425 *Rolls of Parlt.* IV. 290/2 Hit is thoght to the Kyng.. that there is provision. **1427** *Ibid.* 326/2 Alleggyng..such groundes..as it was þought to youre discretion. **1558** Q. MARY in J. M. Stone *Life* (1901) 512 As to hys godly wysdome shall be thowght mete and convenyent. **1577** J. KNEWSTUB *Confutation* (1579) 86 It was thought good vnto almighty God, that the Scriptures shoulde be penned.

11. a. *intr.* To have a (good, bad, or other) opinion with regard to a person or thing; to value or esteem something (highly or otherwise). Const. with adv. (*much, little, well, ill*, etc.), or adverbial accusative (in fig. phrases, as ***to think the world of, small beer of***, etc.: see also the sbs.); and with *of* († *by*, † *at*, dial. *to, on*) before the name of the person or thing.

c **1375** *Cursor M.* 14669 (Fairf.) þai loked on him & loured grim & heþeli þai þu3t be him. *c* **1489** CAXTON *Sonnes of Aymon* xii. 298 'What thynke you by hym?' 'Certes', sayd rowlande, 'reynawd is a sage knyght'. **1535** COVERDALE *Haggai* ii. 3 But what thinke ye now by it? **1579** TOMSON *Calvin's Serm. Tim.* 111/1 To constraine vs to thinke better on our selues. **1581** MULCASTER *Positions* iii. (1887) 11 This man wrote thus, and was verie well thought of. **1598** SHAKS. *Merry W.* II. i. 85 What doth he thinke of vs? **1601** —— *Twel. N.* IV. ii. 59, I thinke nobly of the soule. **1711** STEELE *Spect.* No. 104 ¶ 1 To be negligent of what any one thinks of you, does not only shew you arrogant but abandoned. **1813** *Sk. Character* (ed. 2) I. 55, I didn't think much of her. **1902** O. WISTER *Virginian* ix, Mrs. Tayler..thought the world of her. *a* **1912** *Midl. dial.* I don't think much to him. What do you think to the book? **1974** *Amer. Speech 1971* XLVI. 117 We should think on each student as unique. **1978** R. HILL *Pinch of Snuff* ix. 85 I've known Charlie for years. I asked what he thought on it.

b. ***think nothing of***: (*a*) to have a very low opinion of, set no value upon, esteem as worthless; (*b*) to make light of, make no difficulty or scruple about (cf. *make nothing of*, NOTHING 11 a); so ***to think no more of..than***; ***think nothing of it***: *imp.* phr. deprecating proffered thanks or apology.

[**1640** DK. NEWCASTLE *Country Capt.* II. i, Betweene, us too, what thinke you of a wench? *Court.* Nothinge.] **1802** BEDDOES *Hygeia* VIII. 76 A pint of wine in two hours is nothing thought of. **1872** O. W. HOLMES *Poet Breakf.-t.* v, The Lady thanked him..but said she thought nothing of the walk. **1888** *Harper's Mag.* Mar. 565/2 The Western people..think no more of throwing down a railroad..than a conservative Easterner does of taking an unaccustomed walk across country. **1948** M. ALLINGHAM *More Work for Undertaker* vii. 87 'We did not disturb you, I hope?' 'Think nothing of it,' murmured the torchbearer magnanimously. **1950** [see PLEASURE *sb.* 3]. **1980** F. OLBRICH *Desouza in Stardust* iv. 41 'Thank you for giving up so much of your time, Mr. Chiknis.' 'Think nothing of it, Chief Inspector.' **1982** W. J. BURLEY *Wycliffe's Wild-Goose Chase* i. 17 'Sorry to bother you on a Sunday morning.'.. 'Think nothing of it.'

12. To believe possible or likely; to suspect; to expect, anticipate. **a.** *trans.* with simple obj.

c **1400** *Destr. Troy* 11837 Priam..& his prise knightes, Sweryn all swiftly, & no swyke thoghtyn. **1604** SHAKS. *Oth.* III. iii. 339, I saw't not, thought it not: it harm'd not me. **1719** DE FOE *Crusoe* (1840) I. ii. 25 He, thinking no harm, agreed.

b. with *inf.* To expect.

c **1400** *Ywaine & Gaw.* 549 He thoght to be wele on hys way Or it war passed the thryd day. **1597** SHAKS. *2 Hen. IV*, IV. v. 92, I neuer thought to heare you speake againe. **1613** —— *Hen. VIII*, III. ii. 429 Cromwel, I did not thinke to shed a teare In all my Miseries. **1765** G. COLMAN *Terence, Step-Mother* IV. vi, And do you think To find a woman without any fault? **1769** BICKERSTAFFE *Dr. Last* III. xi, O, don't think to humbug me so. **1823** SOUTHEY *Lett.* (1856) III. 392, I thought to have seen you ere this. *Mod.* I little thought to find you here!

c. *intr.* with *of*, †*on* (*upon*), †*to*: To have a notion, anticipation, or expectation; to suspect; to expect, look for.

1483 CAXTON *G. de la Tour* d iv b, She..answerd withoute remembrynge her ne thynkyng to no harme. **1594** SHAKS. *Rich. III*, I. iv. 244 When that our Princely Father..Blest his three Sonnes.., He little thought of this diuided Friendship. **1650** GENTILIS *Considerations* 234 He stumbles at some evill which hee did not think upon. **1706** E. WARD *Wooden World Diss.* (1708) 98 He may meet with both when he least thinks on 't.

fig. **1868** MORRIS *Earthly Par., Man born to be King* 298 Staring out into the night Where yet the woods thought not of light.

d. *intr.* with *for* (†*of*, †*on*), after *as* or *than*, and with the preposition at the end of the clause: To expect, suppose. (Cf. *look for*, LOOK 15 a.)

c **1530** LD. BERNERS *Arth. Lyt. Bryt.* 239, I thinke ye should not reioyse her so easily as ye thynke of. **1596** SHAKS. *Tam. Shr.* IV. iii. 163 Oh sir, the conceit is deeper than you think for. **1658** GURNALL *Chr. in Arm.* verse 14. ix. (1669) 93/2 A godly Servant is a greater blessing than we think on. **1751** R. PALTOCK *P. Wilkins* (1884) I. 141, I have not made so bad a hand of my time as I thought for. **1821** SCOTT *Kenilw.* xv, They hear farther than you think of. **1852** LYTTON *My Novel* XII. xiv, It is of more importance to him than I even thought for.

13. *trans.* To judge or consider to exist; to believe in the existence of. *rare.*

1532 CROMWELL in Merriman *Life & Lett.* (1902) I. 351 He..percase might thinke sum unkyndenes and also presumpcyon in yow so to handell hym. **1671** MILTON *Samson* 295 Unless there be who think not God at all. **1872** *Contemp. Rev.* XX. 92 Whatever its limits in a given percept be, there must be thought corresponding limits in its external sphere.

IV. With adverbial extension.

14. *trans.* To bring by thinking, or in thought, into or out of some specified condition.

1599 SHAKS. *Much Ado* III. iv. 84 Indeed I cannot thinke, if I would thinke my hart out of thinking, that you are in loue. **1666** SOUTH *Serm., Tit.* ii. 15 (1715) I. 199 He that thinks a Man to the Ground, will quickly endeavour to lay him there. **1784** COWPER *Task* VI. 85 Meditation here May think down hours to moments. **1849** *Tait's Mag.* XVI. 376/2 He thinks away every proposition he has been taught to believe. **1865** BUSHNELL *Vicar. Sacr.* II. iv. (1868) 187 We hardly dare think them into our finite molds.

15. ***think out***: (*a*) To find out, devise, or elaborate by thinking, to construct intellectually; (*b*) to arrive at a clear understanding of by continued thinking; to solve by a process of thought; (*c*) to think to the end, finish or complete in thought.

1382 WYCLIF *Ecclus.* xvii. 31 Or what wers than that flesh tho3te out and blod? [*Vulg.* quid nequius quam quod excogitavit caro et sanguis?] **1847** HELPS *Friends in C.* I. iii. 40 Too mean a subject for despair, or, at least, unworthy of having any remedy..thought out for it. **1849** MACAULAY *Hist. Eng.* iv. I. 519 He meditated deeply on the philosophy of trade, and thought out by degrees a complete..theory. **1862** MISS BRADDON *Lady Audley* xxxiii, She did not finish the thought in words. She did not even think out the sentence. **1885** ANSTEY *Tinted Venus* ii. 25 Oh, don't bother me... I don't want to be uncivil, but I've got to think this out.

16. ***think*** (a thing) ***over***: to give continued thought to (it); to apply the mind steadily to, with the view of coming to a decision.

1847 MARRYAT *Childr. New Forest* ix, He would think the matter over. **1873** BLACK *Pr. Thule* xxii, She had thought it well over beforehand. **1884** [see OVER *adv.* 12].

17. ***think through*** = *think out* (sense 15) (*b*) or (*c*).

1922 HARDY *Late Lyrics* 150 I've been thinking it through, as I play here to-night. **1934** T. N. WILDER *Heaven's my Destination* iii. 42 During the journey he..'thought through' the matter of capital punishment. **1961** *Observer* 8 Oct. 10/3 It is doubtful if Mr. Gaitskell himself had thought through the problem of inner-party democracy. **1979** B. HEBBLETHWAITE in M. Goulder *Incarnation & Myth* iv. 97 A remarkable attempt to think through what it means for our concept of God to say that Christ's cross is God's cross in our world.

18. ***think up***: to make up or compose by thinking; to devise, invent, contrive, or produce by thought or cogitation. Orig. *U.S.*

1855 MRS. STOWE *Tales & Sk. New Eng. Life* 79 Christmas is coming..and I have got to think up presents for everybody. **1872** S. HALE *Lett.* (1918) iv. 83 He asked our plans at once, took right hold and thought up what we had better do. **1885** *Century Mag.* XXIX. 350/1, I believe she is thinking up another poem. **1901** MERWIN & WEBSTER *Calumet 'K'* vii. 108, I had him pretty busy there for a while thinking up lies. **1930** *G. K.'s Weekly* 15 Nov. 146/1 If Mr. Lloyd George can think up a good ticket. **1956** *People* 13 May 8/6 In America the magic new process—it was thought up over there—is being developed in all sorts of wonderful ways. **1977** J. WAINWRIGHT *Nest of Rats* I. xii. 103 There's a way round it... There *has* to be. Some brainy type thought it up.

V. *Comb.* **19.** (It is not clear in every case whether the verbal or the nominal sense of *think* is dominant.) **think(s) balloon, bubble**, in a comic-strip cartoon, a circle resembling a balloon or bubble floating above a character's head and containing (the word 'thinks' followed by) the character's thought in direct speech; **think book**, a book containing the writer's thoughts, opinions, observations. etc.; one that makes the reader think; **think box** *colloq.* or *joc.*, the brain; **think factory** *U.S. colloq.*, a research institution; **think-fest** [FEST], an intellectual treat; **think group**, a group of people that meets to thrash out a subject or problem; **think-man** = *idea(s) man* s.v. IDEA *sb.* 12; **think-piece** chiefly *Journalism*, a general article containing discussion, analysis, opinion, etc., as opp. to fact or news. See also THINK TANK.

1959 *Spectator* 31 July 133/3 In a 'thinks' balloon are the words: 'Rock Hanson..looks an awful wolf'. **1977** *Times* 31 May 7/6 Roy Lichtenstein's *Girl at the Piano* has a nice verbal irony in the 'thinks balloon' as she muses. **1962** *Listener* 25 Oct. 694/2 People who want a short, quick holiday from newspapers, problems, and 'think' books. **1917** *Dialect Notes* IV. 330 Brain. Also *think tank, think box.* **1937** *Daily Express* 5 Feb. 10/6 I do not believe that their brains, or think-boxes, are of sufficient calibre to understand what they are preaching. **1964** C. HODDER-WILLIAMS *Main Experiment* I. viii. 95 A drawing of a computer with a think-bubble coming out of it with the caption, 'Computers'. **1981** N. TUCKER *Child & Book* v. 141 The self-proclaiming speech styles of the main characters [in comics], and their periodic 'thinks' bubbles. **1959** *Nation* 24 Jan. 62/2 Other think-factories are Johns Hopkins University Operations Research Office... Johns Hopkins thinks for the Army. Stanford Research Institute..does the bulk of its thinking for a variety of government agencies. **1947** AUDEN *Age of Anxiety* (1948) i. 28 Assembled again For a Think-Fest. **1958** *Sunday Times* 21 Dec. 12/3 The most stimulating think-fest in my week was Sir Kenneth Clark's lucid lecture on the revolting subject, 'Can Art Be Democratic?'. **1967** *Guardian* 26 Sept. 8/1 Think groups, in which scientists frighten one another with visions of a not too distant future. **1967** *Economist* 15 July 187/1 Nor is Mr Brezhnev the think-man who throws up bright new ideas to keep his colleagues on the ball. **1947** *Partisan Rev.* XIV. 478 Rapid withering of talent, as shown in slick formula novels or plays or 'think-pieces' for periodicals, has more often than not been the fate of the intellectual. **1966** E. WEST *Night is Time for Listening* iv. 120 I'm not reporting stories... I'm in the think piece business these days. *a* **1974** R. CROSSMAN *Diaries* (1977) III. 546 They are producing various think-pieces, including one on industrial relations, one on social services and one on poverty, discussion papers out of which will be boiled one policy paper to be presented at Conference.

think, *sb. dial.* or *colloq.* [f. THINK *v.*[2]]

1. a. An act of (continued) thinking; a meditation.

1834 *Tait's Mag.* I. 426/1 We lie lown yonder..and have time for our ain think. **1870** MRS. WHITNEY *We Girls* ii, Ruth did talk..when she came out of one of her thinks. **1891** FENN *Mahme Nousie* II. v. 73 Let's have a cigar and a quiet think.

b. *nonce-use.* An idea, a thought.

1886 MAUDSLEY *Nat. Causes & Supernat. Seemings* 33 To every one a thing is..what he thinks it—in effect, a think. **1887** G. MACDONALD *Home Again* iv, A thing must be a think before it be a thing.

2. a. What one thinks about something; an opinion.

1835 LADY GRANVILLE *Lett.* (1894) II. 187 My own private think is that he will execute another voluntary. **1861** J. BROWN *Horæ Subs.* Ser. II. 355 The cobbler..dispenses his 'think'..to all comers on all subjects.

b. ***to have another think coming***: to be greatly mistaken.

1937 *Amer. Speech* XII. 317/1 Several different statements used for the same idea—that of *some one's making a mistake*...[e.g.] you have another think coming. **1942** T. BAILEY *Pink Camellia* xxvii. 199 If you think you can get me out of Gaywood, you have another think coming. **1979** *Jrnl. R. Soc. Arts* CXXVII. 221/2 Any design consultant who thinks he is going to get British Leyland right by himself on his own has got another think coming.

3. *attrib.* and *Comb.* (*nonce-wds.*), as **thinkache**, pain of thought, mental suffering; **think-room**, a room or apartment for meditation.

1892 BRIDGER *Depression* p. v, Each separate thinkache enumerated by my depressed patients. **1906** *Month* July 72 Castle, work-room, think-room.

think, þink, obs. form of THING.

thinkable (ˈθɪŋkəb(ə)l), *a.* (*sb.*) [f. THINK *v.*[2] + -ABLE. Cf. UNTHINKABLE *c* 1430, etc.]

1. Capable of being thought; such as one can form a notion or idea of; cogitable. Also (*rare*) as *sb.*, a thing that can be thought of, a thinkable thing.

1854 H. SPENCER in *Brit. Q. Rev.* July 137 A corresponding progress in language, by which greater varieties of objects are thinkable and expressible. **1883** H. DRUMMOND *Nat. Law in Spir. W.* Introd. (1884) 3 To marshal the discrete materials..into thinkable form. **1890** W. JAMES *Princ. Psychol.* I. xiii. 529 As 'thinkables' or 'existents' even the smoke of a cigarette and the worth of a dollar-bill are comparable. **1907** —— *Pragmatism* iv. 140 *Absolute* generic unity would obtain if there were one *summum genus* under which all things without exception could be eventually subsumed. 'Beings', 'thinkables', 'experiences', would be candidates for this position.

2. That can be deemed real or actual; conceivable or imaginable as an existing fact.

1805 CARLYLE *Fredk. Gt.* XX. vi. (1872) IX. 109 How charming that you should make thinkable to us..what we were all inclined to think. **1908** *Times* 10 Sept. 8/4 It is thinkable that considerate driving may render legal enactments unnecessary.

Hence **'thinkableness**; **'thinkably** *adv.*, in thought, according to thought; conceivably.

1895 A. J. BALFOUR *Found. Belief* 286 'Ultimate' scientific ideas may be unthinkable without prejudice to the 'thinkableness' of 'proximate' scientific ideas. **1935** *Mind* XLIV. 325 For finitists, 'to exist' means 'to be thinkably constructible'. **1966** *Listener* 9 June 840/3 Death is thinkably of two sorts—(i) the physical break-up of animate entities,..and (ii) our own projected death.

†**'thinkative**, *a. Obs.* [f. THINK *v.*[2] + -ATIVE: cf. *talkative*.] Consisting in mere thinking, speculative.

1662 J. CHANDLER *Van Helmont's Oriat.* 343 The knowledge of Observation, doth not introduce an understanding into the essential thingliness of a thing, but erecteth only a thinkative knowledge.

thinker (ˈθɪŋkə(r)). [f. THINK *v.*[2] + -ER[1].]

1. One who thinks. **a.** *gen.* A person or being engaged in thinking, or having the power to think; also, one who thinks out or devises something.

c **1440** *Promp. Parv.* 490/2 Thenkare, *cogitator, pensator.* **1548** UDALL, etc. *Erasm. Par. Matt.* xii. 73 Noysome onely vnto the thynker. **1678** CUDWORTH *Intell. Syst.* I. v. §2. 761 The Democriticks and Epicureans did indeed suppose all humane cogitations to be caused..by the incursion of corporeal atoms upon the thinker. **1841** SPALDING *Italy & It. Isl.* III. 208 He stands forth..as the thinker, the inventor, the actor of the scene. **1879** J. COOK *Lect. Conscience* vi, The universe exhibits thought. There cannot be thought without a thinker.

b. with qualifying adj.: One who thinks in the way expressed by the adj.; with commendatory words (e.g. *able*, *deep*, *original*, etc.) often practically coinciding with next sense.

c **1698** LOCKE *Cond. Underst.* §4 You may as well hope to make a good..Musician..by a Lecture..in the Arts of Musick..as a coherent Thinker, or strict Reasoner, by a Set of Rules. **1703** ATTERBURY *Serm.* (1734) IV. iv. 114 He was able..to delude a superficial Thinker with his new Terms and Reasonings. **1807** G. CHALMERS *Caledonia* I. II. i. 227 Lloyd..was an original thinker, rather than the collector of the opinions of others. **1874** L. STEPHEN *Hours in Library* (1892) I. ix. 300 Two of the ablest thinkers whom America has yet produced. **1903** *Church Times* 11 Dec. 749/3 Mr. Spencer showed another weakness of the abstract Thinker.

c. *spec.* One who has special or well-trained powers of thought, esp. abstract thought; a person of skilled or powerful mind; also, one who devotes himself to thinking, as distinguished from action or practical affairs.

1830 CARLYLE in Froude *Life* (1882) II. 128 Neither is his [Jeffrey's] arguing like that of a thinker, but of the advocate. **1849** MACAULAY *Hist. Eng.* I. i. 20 English thinkers aspired to know, or dared to doubt, where bigots had been content to wonder and to believe. **1880** E. WHITE *Cert. Relig.* 30 Not one of them makes the slightest pretension to be a scholar or a thinker.

2. *Theatr. colloq.* An actor who plays in 'thinking parts' (see THINKING *vbl. sb.* 3).

1886 *Stage Gossip* 70 The gentlemen who play the most subordinate parts are..called 'thinkers' on account of their having little or nothing to say and lots of time wherein to think.

3. *nonce-use.* That which thinks; thinking organ or faculty; mind.

1835 ANN F. TYTLER *Mary & Fl.* i. 6 What should we do about our thinkers? would one thinker do for two Tongues? **1883** J. PARKER *Tyne Ch.* 279 'If God did not intend I should think, why did He give me a "thinker"?' Probably a more childish inquiry was never made by a full-grown man. **1899** MISS A. ROBERTSON in *Educat. Rev.* Aug., So this unnecessary 'finger accuracy' is really the result of a sluggish unwillingness to use one's 'thinker'.

thinkful ('θɪŋkfʊl), *a. rare.* [f. THINK *v.*² + -FUL; cf. *wakeful*.] Full of or given to thinking; thoughtful. Hence **'thinkfulness**, quality or faculty of thinking.

1674 N. FAIRFAX *Bulk & Selv.* 16 As sure, as I am of my own thinkfullness. **1864** 'MARK TWAIN' in *Californian* 1 Oct. 9/3 There is a handsome portrait in the Art Gallery of a pensive young girl... Says she, 'I like it—it is so sad and thinkful.' **1910** *Weekly Westm. Gaz.* 23 Apr. 6/3 A thinkful man, and one of eloquent silences.

think-in. [f. THINK *v.*² + -IN³ (after SIT-IN *a.* and *sb.*, TEACH-IN, etc.).] A meeting, conference, etc., for thoughtful discussion.

1966 *Newsweek* 19 Sept. 30/3 The think-ins..produced only a few flickers of..anti-war sentiment. **1973** *Belfast Tel.* 23 Feb. 4 The Social Democratic and Labour Party is to have a major 'think-in' this weekend to prepare the party and its supporters for the White Paper.

thinking ('θɪŋkɪŋ), *vbl. sb.* [f. THINK *v.*² + -ING¹.] The action of THINK *v.*²

1. a. Thought, cogitation, meditation, mental action or activity, etc.: see various senses of the verb. ***high thinking***, idealistic opinions on or attitudes to social, moral, or religious questions; ***good*** (or ***nice***) ***thinking***: an expression of approval of a neat, ingenious, or well-thought-out plan, explanation, observation, etc.

a **1300** *E.E. Psalter* xviii. 15 [xix. 14] And thinginge of herte mine, Ever mare in sight þine. **1382** WYCLIF *ibid.*, The swete thenking of myn herte in thi si3te euermore. *c* **1460** ASHBY *Dicta Philos.* 16 Bethink in the nyght of goode ordennance, And in the day execute thy thynkyng. **1598** SHAKS. *Merry W.* III. ii. 31 Has Page any braines? Hath he any eies? Hath he any thinking? **1690** LOCKE *Hum. Und.* II. ix. §1 Thinking..signifies that sort of operation of the Mind about its Ideas, wherein the Mind is active. **1802** WORDSW. *Sonn.*, 'O *Friend! I know not*', etc., Plain living and high thinking are no more. **1885** J. MARTINEAU *Types Eth. Th.* I. I. i. §3. 159 Thinking is the very essence of mind, as extension is of matter. **1910** J. LONDON *Let.* 5 June (1966) 307 Bourgeois circles where he expected to find refinement, culture, high-living and high-thinking. **1959** *Manch. Guardian* 11 Aug. 5/2 For all the high thinking that goes with a branch of the United Nations Association and with folk dancing..there is not much sign of hard living. **1968** *Listener* 26 Dec. 848/2 Marc's *Trendy Ape* saw the final disappearance of high thinking in our new Bloomsbury before the onslaught of the Colonel's cry: 'Good thinking!' **1974** L. DEIGHTON *Spy Story* xx. 214 'They might be security police holding your friend Remoziva in custody.' 'Nice thinking, Pat,' said Schlegel. **1977** D. BAGLEY *Enemy* ix. 65 'We need to keep in his good books.' 'Very good thinking,' said Ogilvie.

b. *pl.* Thoughts; meditations, courses of thought.

1382 WYCLIF *Isa.* lxv. 2 A puple..that goth in a wei not good, after ther thenkingus. **1491** CAXTON *Vitas Patr.* (W. de W. 1495) II. 192 b/2 So oryson with fastyng casteth out..the foule thoughtes & vayne thynkynges. **1548** UDALL *Erasm. Par. Luke* v. 70 The secrete thinkynges of theyr hertes. **1601** SHAKS. *All's Well* v. iii. 128, I am wrap'd in dismall thinkings. **1812** SOUTHEY *Lett.* (1856) II. 283 Put together all your recollections and memoranda, I will put together my gleanings and thinkings. **1840** DICKENS *Old C. Shop* viii, All these sayings and doings and thinkings..affected him not in the least.

†**c.** *spec.* Imagination, fancy; idle fancy. *rare.*

c **1420** *Chron. Vilod.* 1702 þe sweuene Of þe tweyn appullon þat fellon from þe tre in to þe water in his thenkyng. **1502** *Ord. Crysten Men* (W. de W. 1506) I. iii. 23 These wordes..be not made for no thynge and with thynkynge.

d. With various constructions: see the verb. ***there is no thinking***, one cannot or need not think.

1638 BAKER tr. *Balzac's Lett.* (vol. II.) 111 There is no thinking therefore to deceive you by a shew of good. **1669** R. MONTAGU in *Buccleuch MSS.* (Hist. MSS. Comm.) I. 436 Without her ever thinking of it. **1849** CLOUGH *Dipsychus* II. ii. 195 My pleasure of thought is the pleasure of thinking How pleasant it is to have money.

2. The holding of an opinion or opinions; judging, mental viewing; opinion, judgement, belief; phr. ***to*** (†***after, in***) ***my thinking*** = in my opinion.

c **1410** *Master of Game* (Digby MS. 182) Prol. 13 What shalbe in euery sesoun moste durable and, to my thynkynge, ..oftenest most desportfull of all games. **1490** J. KAY tr. *Caoursin's Siege of Rhodes* (1870) ¶10 That hyt was impossible, after hys thynkyng, to fynde in all the world such instruments of werre. **1597** SHAKS. *2 Hen. IV*, v. v. 114, I heare a Bird so sing, Whose Musicke (to my thinking) pleas'd the King. **1599** DALLAM in *Early Voy. Levant* (Hakl. Soc.) 11 In my thinkinge it seemed not to be above 3 myles. *c* **1775** BURKE *Addr. to King* Wks. IX. 177 In..opposition to the..confirmed sentiments and habits of thinking of an whole people. **1879** E. TAYLOR *Stud. Germ. Lit.* 143 Frauenlob, the last, and, to my thinking, the poorest of the Minnesingers.

3. *attrib.* and *Comb.*, as ***thinking-material***, ***-party***, ***-place***, ***process***, ***-room***, ***-substance***; **thinking-box**, *colloq.* (*a*) = *think box* s.v. THINK *v.*² 18; (*b*) a study; **thinking-cap** (see CAP *sb.*¹ 9, and cf. *considering-cap*, CONSIDERING *vbl. sb.* 2b); **Thinking Day**, 22 February, the joint birthday of the first Chief Scout and Chief Guide, kept by members of the Girl Guides Association for thinking of other Guides all over the world; **thinking distance**, the distance travelled by a motor vehicle from the time when the driver first decides to stop until the time when he begins to apply the brake; cf. *stopping-distance* s.v. STOPPING *vbl. sb.* 7; **thinking-machine**, (*a*) a person whose thinking consists (merely) in mechanical response to symbols; (*b*) *colloq.*, an electronic computer; **thinking-out** [f. vbl. phr. *to think out* s.v. THINK *v.*² 15], the activity of reaching an understanding or a solution of (some problem) by a process of thought; **thinking part** (*Theatr. colloq.*), a part in which the actor has no words to speak, a silent part; **thinking-shop** (*humorous*), a building or institution for study, as a university; **thinking-through** [f. vbl. phr. *to think through* s.v. THINK *v.*² 17] = *thinking-out* above; **thinking-time**, **-while**, time to think, a short space of time.

1911 'SEPHARIAL' *Kabala of Numbers* I. vii. 75 The *thinking-box of a scientific man [*sc.* Newton]. **1915** GALSWORTHY *Bit o' Love* I. 10 He'm in his thinkin' box. **1951** N. G. ANNAN *Leslie Stephen* i. 29 Stephen wanted to appear..as an athlete who incidentally owned a competent thinking-box. **1874** COUES *Birds N.W.* 527 Startled in his retreat while his *thinking-cap is on, he [the bittern] seems dazed, like one suddenly aroused from a deep sleep. **1903** *Daily Chron.* 21 Jan. 5/4 It is satisfactory to know that the Post Office Department has its 'thinking-cap' on. **1927** *Girl Guide Gaz.* Feb. 33/1 At the World Conference in America it was suggested by one of the French delegates that there should be an international '*Thinking Day', on which the Guides of all our different countries should remember each other. **1977** *Guider* July 327/2 The colours of the Retford Unit of Ranger Guides were dedicated on Thinking Day this year. **1947** *Highway Code* (*recto rear cover*), Think in terms of overall stopping distance... *Thinking distance = Distance travelled before driver reacts. **1980** J. W. HILL *Intermediate Physics* iii. 20 The Highway Code shows that for a car travelling at 70 m.p.h...the 'thinking distance' travelled is 70ft..before the brakes are applied. **1943** H. READ *Politics of Unpolitical* iii. 46 We teach them [*sc.* children]..to master abstract symbols and the processes of conceptual thought, and by the age of eleven or twelve we have produced a *thinking-machine of sorts. **1948** BLUNDEN *Shakespeare to Hardy* ii. 47 His [*sc.* Francis Bacon's] danger was to turn himself into a thinking-machine. **1950** *Mind* LIX. 436 The present interest in 'thinking machines' has been aroused by a particular kind of machine, usually called an 'electronic computer' or 'digital computer'. **1842** POE in *Graham's Mag.* Jan. 68/2 With the increase of the *thinking-material comes the desire..of abandoning particulars for masses. **1971** B. Z. DE FERRANTI *Living with Computer* ix. 80 The amount of 'thinking material' in the brains of a number of fishes was doubled by transplantation from other fishes. **1934** H. G. WELLS *Exper. Autobiogr.* II. ix. 654, I was using my prestige and possibilities as an imaginative writer, to do the *thinking-out of this problem of human will and government, under fantastic forms. **1946** R. G. COLLINGWOOD *Idea of Hist.* 196 This thinking-out of the meaning of a concept is philosophy. **1890** 'B. HALL' *Turnover Club* i. 17 Then he uses this man to play *thinking parts, like the *Bleeding Officer* and the two armies. **1898** *Daily News* 12 Mar. 6/3 The great Benefit which is to be given to Nellie Farren next week at Drury Lane... Some of the most famous [actresses] are content with what are humourously called good 'thinking' parts. **1908** *Greenroom Bk.* 667 He made his professional debut in 1867 in a 'thinking part'. **1897** *Q. Rev.* Apr. 348 That remarkable series of reading-parties (or more truly of *thinking-parties). **1883** JEFFERIES *Story of my Heart* 74 This..was a favourite *thinking-place. **1899** *Allbutt's Syst. Med.* VII. 423 These kinæsthetic images..play only a small part in *thinking processes. **1862** THOREAU *Yankee in Canada* i. (1866) 13 When every house..will have not only its sleeping-rooms, and dining-room, and talking-room or parlor, but its *thinking-room also. **1836–48** B. D. WALSH *Aristoph., Clouds* I. ii, I am come To be a Scholar in the *Thinking-shop. **1890** *Spectator* 19 Apr., It turned Oxford into an aristocratic boarding-school from a democratic thinking-shop. **1884** J. TAIT *Mind in Matter* (1892) 99 The etherialised medium of force, which probably connects the brain with the *thinking-substance. **1971** *Listener* 16 Dec. 838/2 An inadequate *thinking-through of what those fine phrases will mean in practice. **1667** DRYDEN & DK. NEWCASTLE *Sir Martin Mar-all* v. i, I'll put you upon something, give me but a *thinking time. *Ibid.* III. i, As a whiff of tobacco..[used] in the midst of a discourse for a *thinking-while.

'thinking, *ppl. a.* [f. as prec. + -ING².]

1. That thinks; having, or exercising, the faculty of thought; cogitative.

1678 DRYDEN & LEE *Œdipus* III. i, A thinking soul is punishment enough. **1709** STEELE & ADDISON *Tatler* No. 111 ¶1 What was the proper Employment of a thinking Being? **1800** *Med. Jrnl.* III. 281 According to the laws of the thinking faculty, the understanding and reason. **1864** BOWEN *Logic* i. 2 The Thinking or Elaborative faculty,—i.e. the Understanding.

2. Given to thinking; habitually exercising one's mind; having special or well-trained powers of thought; thoughtful, reflective, intellectual. (Cf. THINKER 1 c.)

1681 *Let. to Person of Hon.* in *Select. Harl. Misc.* (1793) 461 To have an account of the sense of the thinking-men about the town concerning it. **1799** *Mirror* No. 16 ¶3 Those moments of deeper pensiveness to which every thinking mind is liable. **1837** W. IRVING *Capt. Bonneville* III. 225 The senior chief..was a thinking man, and a man of observation.

3. *fig.* Said of very life-like sculpture: cf. BREATHING *ppl. a.* b.

1732 M. GREEN *Grotto* 57 The thinking sculpture helps to raise Deep thoughts, the genii of the place.

Hence **'thinkingdom** (*nonce-wd.*), a realm of thinking persons; **'thinkingly** *adv.*, in a thinking manner, in the way of thought; with thought, consciously, deliberately; in (one's own) thought or supposition (quot. 1894); **'thinkingness**, thinking quality; thoughtfulness, intellectuality; the essence of a thinking being (quot. 1865).

1880 *Q. Rev.* Oct. 415 Christendom..is far enough as yet from having been replaced by the Utopian *Thinkingdom (*Cogitantenthum*), to which one of the modern German apostles of materialism..looks forward. **1847** WEBSTER, **Thinkingly*, by thought. **1887** MARY LINSKILL *In Exchange for Soul* xlviii, Quite thinkingly he sent the message in his wife's name. **1673** O. WALKER *Educ.* v. 43 Contrary to that seriousnes and *thinkingnes requisite to prudence and gallantry of spirit. **1838** *New Monthly Mag.* LIII. 118 All men say..good things of the courage of Englishmen, the chastity of English women, the thinkingness of both sexes. **1865** J. GROTE *Explor. Philos.* I. 140, I recognise two manners of existence,..thinkingness and thoughtness.

thinkling ('θɪŋklɪŋ). *nonce-wd.* [f. THINK *v.*² + -LING.] A petty or inferior thinker.

1815 J. GILCHRIST *Labyrinth Demolished* 22. **1816** —— *Philos. Etym.* 247 A proper Etymological Dictionary, which petty thinklings—quackish pretenders affect to despise.

'think-so. *nonce-wd.* [The phr. (*I*) *think so* (THINK *v.*² 9c) used as a sb.] A mere opinion.

1666 BUNYAN *Grace Ab.* §97 How if all our Faith, and Christ, and Scriptures, should be but a Think-so too? **1675** —— *Saved by Grace* Wks. (1692) I. 568/1 He thinks former encouragements were Fancies, Delusions or meer Think-so's. **1887** HALL CAINE *Deemster* xxxix, All the dread I had felt hitherto..was no more than a thinkso.

'think-tank. orig. *U.S.* [f. THINK *v.*² + TANK *sb.*¹] **1.** *colloq.* The brain. *U.S.*

1905 A. L. STILLMAN in A. H. Shearer *Little Bk. Rutgers Tales* 51 There's too much scrapping in the Joint... Your Think-tanks are getting to be Air-tight Compartments. **1910** [see MAVERICK *v.* b]. **1964** *St. Louis Post-Dispatch* 8 May 2A/3 Truman..said he hoped to live to be 90 but only 'if the old think-tank is working'.

2. A research institute or other organization providing advice and ideas on national or commercial problems; an interdisciplinary group of specialist consultants. Also in extended (usu. facetious) use.

1959 *Times Lit. Suppl.* 6 Nov. p. xix/2 Even the Institute of Advanced Studies at Princeton does not quite meet the bill, nor does the 'think tank', the Center for Behavioral Sciences at Palo Alto. **1963** *Business Week* 13 July 61 There are many others..in the special groups—or 'think tanks'—that do analytical work for the armed forces, such as the Air Force's RAND Corp., the Navy's Operations Evaluation Group, the Army's Research Analysis Group, the Defense Dept.'s Institute for Defense Analysis. **1967** MRS. L. B. JOHNSON *White House Diary* 8 Oct. (1970) 577 Mt. Hope Farm..will be the site for the environmental planning center—a sort of a 'think tank' for city-planning experts. **1968** *Sunday Times* 25 Feb. 10 The private research corporations, or 'think tanks' (in the current American terminology) which are paid, mostly by departments of Government, to think about problems. **1968** *Economist* 13 Apr. 29/3 'Think tank' work is usually secret. **1969** *Sunday Mail Mag.* (Brisbane) 4 May 2/7 He's pretty busy as a 'Business Doctor' there—runs a 'think-tank'. **1970** *Daily Tel.* 22 Jan. 3/5 P & O, the world's largest shipping group, have formed a special company to exploit the inventions of their technical staff. A 'think tank' of 40 graduate engineers and naval architects will work on ideas and suggestions sent in by the sea-going and shore staffs. **1971** *Ann. Reg. 1970* 36 Lord Rothschild..described the task of the new organization (or, as it was nicknamed, the 'think-tank') as being to 'weigh up the pros and cons and consequences' of a proposed policy and to advise the Cabinet on it. **1973** *Listener* 26 Apr. 534/3 It has become the fashion among heads of governments and chiefs of state in the parliamentary democracies to equip themselves with a special staff of personal advisers—a think-tank, an entourage ..—whose views supplement and sometimes run counter to the processed findings of civil servants. **1976** H. WILSON *Governance of Britain* iv. 95 In addition to establishing the Central Policy Review Staff (the Think Tank),.. he [*sc.* Edward Heath] initiated the practice of the Cabinet Office Units, which has been developed since. **1978** R. HILL *Pinch of Snuff* xiv. 146 He leaves the service, possibly under a cloud.. The inference in the rugby club think-tank was that the cloud was sexual. **1981** *Daily Tel.* 15 Dec. 13/2 The Rand Corporation, a 'think tank' which undertakes various studies for the Pentagon, completed an analysis of all the Communist-bloc armies. *Ibid.* 29 Dec. 10/4 Lean times are looming for the private consulting firms, 'think tanks' and universities.

3. A meeting or conference of experts, scholars, specialists, etc.

1976 T. SHARPE *Wilt* iv. 39 She had been accepted by people who flew to California or Tokyo to conferences and Think Tanks as casually as she took the bus to town. **1978** *Washington Post* 8 May A14/2 The meeting here, which one official called the NAACP's first 'think tank', was an effort to develop new positions for the association.

Hence **think-tanker**, a member of a think-tank.

1971 *New Scientist* 2 Sept. 536/2 Throughout this century think-tankers have been confidently predicting the imminent exploitation.. of the seas. **1975** 'J. LYMINGTON' *Spider in Bath* vii. 124 A brief report from our Think Tankers on hypnotising the village people.

thin-laid, -leaved, etc.: see THIN *a.* D.

thinly ('θɪnlɪ), *adv.* [f. THIN *a.* + -LY².] In a thin manner.

1. With little thickness or depth; with thin clothing. Also *fig.*

13.. *K. Alis.* 5906 (Bodl. MS.) Thynnelich hy beþ y-hatered. **1746** FRANCIS tr. *Hor., Sat.* II. vi. 94 This Morning Air is very bad For them, who go but thinly clad. **1770** *Phil. Trans.* LXI. 334, I covered the bottom with it thinly. **1855** MACAULAY *Hist. Eng.* xxi. IV. 570 The scheme of assassination, thus thinly veiled, was communicated to James. **1859** GULLICK & TIMBS *Paint.* 229 Pictures in oil.. may, of course, be thinly painted throughout.

b. *fig.* Poorly, meagrely. ? *Obs. rare.*

1537 CROMWELL in Merriman *Life & Lett.* (1902) II. 75 Your neighbours, without whom.. all the rest of you would live full thynnely.

2. With large intervals of space or time; sparsely; not closely or thickly.

c **1545** in Dugdale *Monast.* (1821) III. 283, v. acrez di. thinly growyne with olde bechez and some oke. **1667-8** SIR T. BROWNE *Brampton Urns* Wks. 1835 III. 500 Great ones were but thinly found. *a* **1727** NEWTON *Chronol. Amended* i. (1728) 178 He found that country.. peopled but thinly. **1827** HONE *Every-day Bk.* II. 106 The market was.. thinly attended.

3. In combination with pa. pples. or adjs. used attributively; now usually hyphened.

1757 DYER *Fleece* I. Wks. (1761) 60 The thinly-scatter'd meal. **1797** GODWIN *Enquirer* II. xii. 454 Ten thinly printed pages. **1862** ANSTED *Channel Isl.* I. ii. (ed. 2) 26 Thinly-bedded grey rocks. **1890** 'R. BOLDREWOOD' *Col. Reformer* (1891) 70 An open, thinly-timbered, well-grassed country. **1902** *Daily Chron.* 25 Jan. 3/2 He makes thinly-veiled love to the young lady.

† **'thinmost**, *a. Obs. rare*⁻¹. [f. THIN *a.*: see -MOST.] Thinnest.

1644 NYE *Gunnery* (1670) 83 If this Peece were fortified.. onely so much, as the thinmost part of the metall is.

thinned (θɪnd), *ppl. a.* [f. THIN *v.*¹ + -ED¹.] Made thin or less thick, in senses of THIN *v.*¹; reduced in thickness, density, frequency, number, etc.

1710 J. CLARKE *Rohault's Nat. Phil.* I. xxvii. (1729) I. 210 The Superficies of the thinned Body, where it is of any one Thickness. **1857** LD. DUFFERIN *Lett. High Lat.* xii. (ed. 3) 359 The thinned ranks on board the '*Iron Beard*' are constantly replenished. **1899** *Allbutt's Syst. Med.* VIII. 695 Pigment is irregularly accumulated in the thinned epidermis.

'thinner. [agent-n. from THIN *v.*¹: see -ER¹.]

1. One who thins; a machine for thinning plants, seeds, etc.

1832 *Planting* 63 in *Libr. Usef. Knowl., Husb.* III, Leaving them to press upon each other more severely than vigorous thinners would permit. **1889** *Pall Mall G.* 2 July 2/2 The case of the little turnip-thinners in Saxony. **1943** [see PELLETED *ppl. a.* 2]. **1962** *Times* 21 May 18/4 More use of mechanical beet thinners.

2. (Also in colloq. pl. form.) A liquid used to dilute paint, printing-ink, etc., to a suitable consistency.

1904 *Jrnl. Franklin Inst.* July 17 The painter then adds thinners until the paint will work under his brush. **1958** B. BEHAN *Borstal Boy* III. 338 He.. told me where I'd find an extra can of turps, if I wanted thinners. **1967** *Gloss. Paper/Ink Terms for Letterpress Printing (B.S.I.)* 9 *Thinner*, a fluid for addition to a printing ink to reduce its consistency. **1973** J. G. TWEEDDALE *Materials Technol.* II. ii. 33 A viscous liquid constituent may present particular problems, perhaps requiring.. thinning by solution with a volatile thinner, to make it fluid enough for mixing and pouring. **1980** *New Scientist* 23 Oct. 244/1 This bottle of correction fluid.. would be all right if I.. added thinners.

thinness ('θɪnnɪs). [f. THIN *a.* + -NESS.] The quality or condition of being thin.

1. a. Narrowness of dimension between opposite surfaces; absence of thickness or depth.

1577 B. GOOGE *Heresbach's Husb.* II. (1586) 80 b, Fulnesse and emptinesse, or thicknesse and thinnes. **1617** MORYSON *Itin.* III. 175 Cotton cloth.. for thinnesse not vnlike our boulting cloths. **1715** DESAGULIERS *Fires Impr.* 113 Where you cannot dig in the Back-Wall of a Chimney by reason of its thinness. **1807** VANCOUVER *Agric. Devon* (1813) 54 The thinness of the seam [of coal]. **1863** LYELL *Antiq. Man* iii. 34 The extreme thinness of the film of matter.

b. Lean or spare habit of body; spareness.

1827-35 WILLIS *Leper* 65 There, alone, Wasted to ghastly thinness, Helon knelt. **1932** G. GREENE *Stamboul Train* I. i. 5 Her mackintosh showed the thinness of her body.

c. *fig.* Deficiency, poverty, meagreness, feebleness; lack of depth or fullness.

c **1000** *Sax. Leechd.* I. 134 Hit ȝehælð þa þynnysse þære ȝesihðe. **1623** W. BALCANQUAL *Serm. St. Maries Spittle* 98 The thinnesse of our Ioy, because we did sowe our teares too thin. **1903** *Daily Chron.* 20 Feb. 3/6 That there was much 'intellectual thinness' among young men.

2. The condition of being thinly arranged, occupied, or attended; want of fullness; sparseness.

c **1440** *Promp. Parv.* 491/1 Thynnesse, of wodys, cornys, and oþer lyke, *raritas.* **1573-80** BARET *Alv.* T. 166 Thinnesse: seldomnesse, *rarité.* **1690** LOCKE *Govt.* II. vi. §74 The Thinness of People gives Families Leave to separate into unpossessed Quarters. **1774** A. GIB *Pres. Truth* II. 40 None of these brethren opened a mouth about the thinness of the meeting. **1826** F. REYNOLDS *Life & Times* II. 200 Expressing my surprise at the.. thinness of the house.

3. Absence or lack of density, consistence, or viscosity; fluidity, tenuity, rarity.

c **1000** *Sax. Leechd.* II. 199 þonne þara metta meltung biþ & þynnes. **1398** TREVISA *Barth. De P.R.* XI. i. (Tollem. MS.), Eyer haþ more þinnesse and clerenesse þan oþer elementis. *c* **1440** *Promp. Parv.* 491/1 Thynnesse, or thynhede of licurys. **1582** STANYHURST *Æneis* I. (Arb.) 37 From earthly thicknesse, too thinnesse vannished ayerie. **1684-5** BOYLE *Min. Waters* 26 Of the thinness or viscosity of the Mineral Water. *a* **1854** CAROLINE B. SOUTHEY *Poet. Wks.* (1867) 67 Milk.. tempered down To wholesome thinness.

† **'thinnify**, *v. Obs. rare*⁻¹. [f. THIN *a.* + *-ify*, -FY.] *trans.* To make thin; = THIN *v.*¹ 5.

a **1693** *Urquhart's Rabelais* III. iv. 49 The Heart doth in its left side Ventricle so thinnifie the Blood.

'thinning, *vbl. sb.* [f. THIN *v.*¹ + -ING¹.] **a.** The action of THIN *v.*¹, in various senses; reduction or decrease in thickness, closeness, number, density, etc. Also with *out, off, away, up*, etc. spec. in *Forestry*, removal of some of the trees in an immature stand, or removal of part of the crown of an individual tree. Also *attrib.*

c **1000** *Sax. Leechd.* II. 260 Læcedomas þa þe þynnunge mæȝen hæbben. **1398** TREVISA *Barth. De P.R.* XIX. xi. (Bodl. MS.), White mater is igendred of thynnynge and spredinge of aier. **1799** J. ROBERTSON *Agric. Perth* 257 Weeded down by various thinnings. **1800** W. PONTEY *Profitable Planter* 33 It is not to be wondered at, if, even before thinning, the soil should be nearly exhausted, and the trees checked in their growth. **1822** J. C. LOUDON *Encycl. Gardening* III. iii. 1108 Autumn, or very early in spring, are the proper seasons for thinning where the trees are to be taken up by the root and replanted elsewhere. **1839** URE *Dict. Arts* 1269 The thinning up, or quantity of turpentine required to bring it to its proper consistence. **1851** CARPENTER *Man. Phys.* (ed. 2) 268 By the thinning-away of its wall at its most projecting part. **1868** *Rep. U.S. Commissioner Agric.* (1869) 423 Upon thinning out, enough plants were cast away to have run at least twelve rows additional. **1880, 1922** [see COPPICING *vbl. sb.* b]. **1970** H. L. EDLIN *Collins Guide to Tree Planting & Cultivation* xi. 170 The thinning cycle, or interval of years between thinnings, can be short.. or long. *Ibid.*, In regular thinnings a definite proportion of the growing stock of trees is taken out.

b. *concr.* usually *pl.* That which is removed in the process of thinning. (Cf. *sweepings.*)

1771 *Usef. Proj.* in *Ann. Reg.* 115/2 Sir John.. never receives less than a guinea an acre in thinnings throughout his plantations. **1805** R. W. DICKSON *Pract. Agric.* I. Pl. xxx. 110 A fir paling of the horizontal kind, made from the thinning of trees of that kind. **1893** *Jrnl. R. Agric. Soc.* Dec. 826 Thinnings and rubbish should be immediately removed and burnt.

'thinning, *ppl. a.* [f. THIN *v.*¹ + -ING².] That thins, in various senses of the verb.

1550 BALE *Eng. Votaries* II. 81 To confirme the thynynge shewe of hypocresye. **1790** WOLCOTT (P. Pindar) *Rowland for Oliver* 92 Art thou a Doctor? Yes, of thinning skill. **1888** *Pump Court* 31 Oct. 5/2 His gradually thinning hair. **1899** MACKAIL *Life Morris* II. 154 A mere thinning remnant between two divergent and increasing camps.

thinnish ('θɪnɪʃ), *a.* [f. THIN *a.* + -ISH¹.] Somewhat thin; tending to thinness.

1545 RAYNOLD *Byrth Mankynde* 139 Her vryne shall appeare whyte and thynnyssh. **1780** C. A. BURNEY in *Mme. D'Arblay's Early Diary* (1889) II. 289 The Masquerade at the Pantheon was rather thinnish. **1827** F. COOPER *Prairie* I. ii. 30 They told us.. we should find settlers something thinnish hereaway. **1884** *Century Mag.* XXIX. 138/1 My somewhat slight figure and thinnish legs.

thinnye, obs. form of TUNNY.

thinocorine (θaɪ'nɒkəraɪn), *a. Ornith.* [f. mod.L. *Thinocorus* (properly *-ys*), f. Gr. θίς, θῑν- beach, sea-shore + κόρυς lark: see -INE¹.] Of, pertaining to, or characteristic of the *Thinocoridæ* or quail-snipes, a family of South American wading birds, typified by the genus *Thinocorus.*

1885 *Stand. Nat. Hist.* IV. 92 The Thinocorine palate, in which the vomer is connected with the nasal cartilages in a manner recalling that of the Ægithognathæ.

thinolite ('θaɪnəlaɪt). *Min.* [f. Gr. θίς, θῑν- (see prec.) + λίθος stone: see -LITE.] 'A variety of calcite, occurring in pseudomorphous crystals, the original mineral being still in doubt' (Chester *Dict. Min.* 1896).

1879 C. KING *Geol. 40th Parallel* I. 508 (Chester).

thin-skinned (-skɪnd: stress var.), *a.*

1. Having a thin skin or rind.

1598 CHAPMAN *Blinde Begger of Alexandria* Wks. 1873 I. 11 Round faces and thinne skinde are happiest still. **1707** MORTIMER *Husb.* (1721) II. 155 Chuse the large, round, white, and thin-skinned ones. **1875** BENNETT & DYER *Sachs' Bot.* 539 A stony endocarp surrounding the thin-skinned seed.

2. *fig.* Sensitive to criticism, ridicule, or abuse; easily hurt or offended; touchy.

1680 BAXTER *Answ. Stillingfl.* lxxviii. 99, I.. never was so thin Skin'd as to be unable to bear a Cholerick breath. **1771** SMOLLETT *Humph. Cl.* 8 June, My apothecary, who is a proud Scotchman, very thin skinned. **1818** COBBETT *Pol. Reg.* XXXIII. 311 The professional gentlemen in Pennsylvania are.. extremely thin-skinned, when they are the party attacked. **1894** FROUDE *Life & Lett. Erasmus* xvii. 328 Erasmus.. was thin-skinned as ever.

Hence **'thin-'skinnedness**, the condition or quality of being thin-skinned; sensitiveness.

1882 SALA *Amer. Revis.* (1883) I. iii. 43 *note*, A very gratifying proof of the diminution of what may be termed 'thin-skinnedness'. **1897** *Spectator* 23 Oct. 552/1 This thin-skinnedness among experienced public men.

thin-sown (θɪnsəʊn: stress var.), *a.* Also 7 **thin-sowed.** Sown or planted thinly; *lit.* said of plants, or a crop; *fig.* scattered at wide intervals, scarce; also, of a field or territory: scantily furnished *with* (†*of*).

1589 R. HARVEY *Pl. Perc.* (1590) 18 Good deeds, which are now both thin sowne.., and thinner growne. *a* **1631** DONNE *Lett.* (1651) 159 This Countrie is so thin sowed with such persons, as he comes to seek; that he will scarce know, where to find a corn to peck at. **1698** NORRIS *Pract. Disc.* IV. 60 Very good Men.. were always very thin sown. *a* **1846** in J. Baxter *Libr. Pract. Agric.* (ed. 4) II. 398 In the early stages .. the appearance of thick-sown corn is much superior to that of the thin-sown.

'thin-,spun, *a.* (stress var.) Spun thinly; drawn out in spinning to a slender thread. Also *fig.*

1637 MILTON *Lycidas* 76 Comes the blind Fury with th' abhorred shears, And slits the thin spun life. **1642** H. MORE *Song of Soul* II. iii. IV. ix, Thin-spun reason and exile discourse. **1821** CLARE *Vill. Minstr.* I. 93 How thin-spun clouds glide swiftly by. *Ibid.* 120 Nor broken seam, nor thin-spun screen.

'thin-walled (-wɔːld), *a.* Having thin walls.

1854 OWEN *Skel. & Teeth* (1855) 7 The thinnest-walled and widest air-bone of the bird of flight was first solid. **1875** BENNETT & DYER *Sachs' Bot.* 90 Alternate layers of narrow thick-walled and broad thin-walled cork-cells are formed. **1875** HUXLEY & MARTIN *Elem. Biol.* (1877) 184 Posteriorly, the oviducts dilate into capacious thin-walled chambers.

thio- (θaɪəʊ), also before a vowel **thi-**, repr. Gr. θεῖον sulphur; a formative element in names of things containing or connected with sulphur.

1. in *Chem.* (See also THIOL-, THION-.) In names of compounds containing sulphur = *sulpho-.*

In systematic nomenclature restricted to those in which one or more atoms of sulphur take the place of one or more of oxygen in the substance designated by the rest of the name; e.g. *thiacetic* acid $C_2H_3O.SH$, from acetic acid $C_2H_3O.OH$, *tri-thiocarbonic* acid H_2CS_3, from carbonic acid H_2CO_3. So *thio-acid, -alcohol, -aldehyde, -ether, -salt*; also ***thio-anti'monic, -anti'monious, -ar'senic, -ar'senious, -lactic, -phosphoric, -phosphoryl, -stannic, -tungstic***, etc. But many names do not conform exactly to this systematic use.

The following are the chief combinations of *thio-.*

thi'acetate, a salt of thiacetic acid. **thia'cetic** *a.*, in ***thiacetic acid*** ($C_2H_3O.SH$), a colourless liquid boiling at 93°C. **thi-'acid** = *thio-acid.* **thi'aldine** [ALD(EHYDE + -INE⁵], a crystalline substance, $NH{:}2(CHCH_3.S){:}CHCH_3$, produced by passing hydrogen sulphide into a solution of aldehyde ammonia. **'thialol** [AL(COHOL + -OL 3], a name for diethyl disulphide, $(C_2H_5)_2S_2$, a colourless oily compound, having an odour like garlic. **'thiamide**, generic name for substances formed by replacing the oxygen of an amide by sulphur, as ***thiacetamide***, $CH_3CS.NH_2$, from acetamide, $CH_3CO.NH_2$. **'thiazine** [AZINE], any of a class of dyes that contain a ring of one nitrogen, one sulphur, and four carbon atoms in the molecule, such as thionine and methylene blue. **thiazole** [AZO- + *-ole*, -OL 3; ad. G. *thiazol* (Hantzsch & Weber 1887, in *Ber. d. Deut. Chem. Ges.* XX.

3118)], N(//CH.S. | \CH:CH), a liquid boiling at 117°C.; also, any of the substituted derivatives of this compound. **ˈthienyl** [contr. of *thiophenyl*, proposed 1883 by V. Meyer], the radical C_4H_3S contained in *thiophene*, C_4H_4S. **ˈthio-ˌacid**, **ˈthi-ˌacid**, an acid in which oxygen is replaced by sulphur. **thio-ˈalbumose**, a deutero-albumose containing a large amount of sulphur. **thio-ˈalcohol**, a compound of the nature of an alcohol in which sulphur takes the place of oxygen, as mercaptan, $C_2H_5.SH$, analogous to ethyl alcohol, $C_2H_5.OH$. **thioˈcarbamate**, a salt of thiocarbamic acid. **thiocarˈbamic** *a.*, in ***thiocarbamic acid***, $NH_2.CO.SH$ and $NH_2.CS.OH$: now distinguished as *thiolcarbamic* and *thioncarbamic* acids: see THIOL-, THION-. **thioˈcarbamide**, $CS(NH_2)_2$ or $HS.C(NH_2){:}NH$, a crystalline substance melting at 170°C. **thioˈcarbonate**, a salt of thiocarbonic acid. **thiocarˈbonic** *a.*, in ***thiocarbonic acid***: in derivatives, as ***mono-***, ***di-***, ***tri-thiocarbonic acid***: the last, H_2CS_3, is a dark yellow strongly smelling oil, very easily decomposed by heating into CS_2 and H_2S; esters of ***dithiocarbonic acid***, H_2COS_2, and of ***monothiocarbonic*** acid, H_2CO_2S, are known. **thioˈcarbonyl**, the radical (CS)″, in which the oxygen of carbonyl (CO)″ is replaced by sulphur. **thioˈcarbylamine** = *iso-thiocyanic* acid, CHNS, = C≡N.SH. **thioˈcholine**, the sulphur analogue of choline, $HS{\cdot}CH_2CH_2N(CH_3)_3OH$, or a derivative in which the hydroxyl group is replaced by an organic radical. **thiocresol** (θaɪəʊˈkresəl), a compound with the formula $CH_3{:}C_6H_4SH$, of which there are three modifications, two crystalline and one liquid. **thioˈcyanate**, a salt of thiocyanic acid. **thiocyˈanic** *a.*, in ***thiocyanic acid***, $N{:}C.SH$ = cyanic acid, $N{:}C.OH$, in which oxygen is replaced by sulphur; a liquid with a penetrating odour. **thiocyˈanogen**, the radical CNS of thiocyanic acid; in comb. *thiocyano-*. **thio-ˈester**, the sulphur analogue of an ester, containing the group –CO·S–. **thio-ˈether**, any compound in which an atom of sulphur is bonded to two organic radicals. **thioˈformic** *a.*, in ***thioformic acid***, H_2COS, a crystalline substance melting at 120°C. **thioglyˈcollic** (also **-glycolic**) **acid** [tr. G. *thioglycolsäure* (P. Claesson 1877, in *Ann. d. Chem.* CLXXXVII. 113): see GLYCOLLIC, GLYCOLIC *a.*], a colourless liquid, $CH_2(SH){\cdot}COOH$, that is a strong reducing agent used as a reagent for detecting ferric iron; so **thioglyˈcol(l)ate**, a salt or ester of this acid, esp. the sodium salt, used in culture media to produce anaerobic conditions. **thioˈketone**, a sulphur analogue of a ketone, containing the group >CS. **thioˈnaphthene**, a colourless crystalline compound, C_8H_6S, consisting of benzene, C_6H_6, of which two atoms of H are replaced by CH:CH.S. **ˈthionate**, a salt of a thionic acid. **thionic** (θaɪˈɒnɪk) *a.*, in ***thionic acids***, group name for the acids represented by the formula $H_2S_nO_6$, where n = 2, 3, 4, 5, and perhaps 6. These acids are called ***dithionic***, ***trithionic***, ***tetrathionic***, ***pentathionic***, and ***hexathionic*** acid. **ˈthionine**, a brownish-black dye, $SC_{12}H_9N_3$, crystallizing in plates, called *phenylene violet*, or *Lauth's v.*, and largely used to stain microscopic objects. **thioˈnurate**, a salt of thionuric acid. **thionuric** (θaɪəˈn(j)ʊərɪk) *a.* [f. Gr. θεῖον + URIC], in ***thionuric acid***, $CO{:}2(NH.CO){:}CH.NH.SO_3H$, formed by the action of ammonia and sulphurous acid on alloxan in aqueous solution. **ˈthionyl** [-YL], the radical (SO)″: so named in 1857 by Schiff (*Annalen der Chem. und Pharm.* CII. 113). **ˈthiophene**, C_4H_4S, a colourless liquid with an odour like benzene, occurring in benzene from coal-tar to the extent of about 0.5 per cent.; also **thiophen**; hence **thioˈphenic** *a.*, in ***thiophenic acid***, $C_4H_3S.CO_2H$, derived from thiophene. **thioˈphenol**, a colourless liquid, C_6H_5SH (= PHENOL with S in place of O), with the odour of garlic. **ˈthiophthene** [NA)PHTHENE], a colourless oily compound, $C_6H_4S_2$, obtained by the distillation of citric acid with P_2S_3. **ˌthioreˈsorcin**, also **thioreˈsorcinol**, $C_6H_4(SH)_2$, a yellowish-grey substance, used medicinally as a substitute for iodoform. **ˌthiosaliˈcylic** *a.*, in ***thiosalicylic acid***, $HOC_6H_4CO(SH)$, a brownish-yellow amorphous substance, used in medicine as an antiseptic. **thio-salt**, a salt of a thio-acid, as a thiosulphate. **ˌthiosemiˈcarbazide** [SEMICARBAZIDE], a colourless crystalline compound, $H_2N{\cdot}CS{\cdot}NH{\cdot}NH_2$, used esp. as a rodenticide and as a stabilizer in organic liquids. **ˌthiosemiˈcarbazone**, any of a class of compounds analogous to the semicarbazones, the oxygen being replaced by a sulphur atom. **thioˈsinamine** [L. *sinapis* mustard + AMINE] = *allyl-thio-urea*, $C_3H_5NH.CS.NH_2$, a crystalline substance produced by the action of ammonia on allyl mustard oil. **thioˈsulphate**, a salt of thiosulphuric acid; formerly called *hyposulphite*. **thiosulˈphuric** *a.*, in ***thiosulphuric acid***, $H_2S_2O_3$, an acid only known in solution and soon decomposing, the salts of which are stable, and are applied in bleaching and photography; it is sulphuric acid, H_2SO_4, in which one atom of oxygen is replaced by sulphur; formerly called *hyposulphurous* acid. **thioˈtepa**, **-TEPA** [TEPA], the thio analogue, $PS(N(CH_2)_2)_3$, of tepa, used in the treatment of cancer. **thioˈtoluene** [TOLUENE] = *methylthiophene*, $C_4H_3(CH_3)S$, a colourless oily compound, found as an impurity in crude toluene; two isomeric forms are known. **thioˈuracil**, a mercapto derivative of uracil that has been used to depress the activity of the thyroid gland; 4-hydroxy-2-mercaptopyrimidine, $C_4H_4N_2OS$. **thio-urea** (θaɪəʊˈjʊəriːə), $CS(NH_2)_2$ or $HS.C(NH_2){:}NH$ = *thiocarbamide*. **thioˈxanthene**, †**-en**, a tricyclic crystalline compound, $C_{13}H_{10}S$, that is the sulphur analogue of xanthene; also, any of a class of derivatives of this that includes several antipsychotic tranquillizers similar to the phenothiazines. **thioˈxanthone** [XANTHONE], $C_{13}H_8OS$, crystallizing in yellow needles. **thioxene** (θaɪˈɒksiːn), **thioxylene** (θaɪˈɒksɪliːn) [named *thioxene* by Victor Meyer (*Ber. Deut. Chem. Ges.* 1884, XVII. 789)] = *dimethylthiophene*, $C_4H_2(CH_3)_2S$, found as an impurity in xylene; there are several isomeric forms.

1854 KEKULÉ in *Proc. Roy. Soc.* VII. 38 **Thiacetic Acid*, —*Sulphuretted Acetic Acid*—has been obtained by me by acting on monohydrated acetic acid with tersulphide of phosphorus. **1847** WÖHLER & LIEBIG in *Mem. Chem. Soc.* III. 303 A new organic alkali free from oxygen..which we call *thialdine..contracted from θεῖον and aldehyde. **1881** WATTS *Dict. Chem.* VIII. 1952 *Thiamides..may be conveniently prepared by the action of phosphorus sulphide ..on amides. **1893** *Jrnl. Soc. Chem. Industry* 31 Jan. 4 The original colour quickly reappears on exposure to air: Azine-, Oxazine-, *Thiazine- and Acridine-Colours. **1971** R. L. M. ALLEN *Colour Chem.* viii. 130 Thiazine dyes are used on cellulosic fibres, silk, bast fibres, leather and paper. **1888** HANTZSCH & WEBER in *Jrnl. Chem. Soc.* LIV. 256 *Thiazole is the name given to [these] isomeric compounds. *Ibid.* LIV. 574 Thioamides condense with α-halogen-substituted ketones to form thiazoles. **1956** I. L. FINAR *Org. Chem.* II. xii. 451 A general method for preparing thiazoles is the condensation between α-halogenocarbonyl compounds.. and thioamides. **1885** PETER *Jrnl. Chem. Soc.* XLVIII. 141 **Thiënylmethylacetoxime* $C_4H_3S.CMe{:}NOH$..forms a white crystalline mass. **1882** WILL *Ibid.* XLII. 1088 *Thiocarbamates... A continuation of the author's researches. **1878** GUARESCHI *Ibid.* XXXIV. 860 **Thiocarbamide* CS $(NH_2)_2$ [etc.] when oxidised by permanganate likewise yield all their sulphur in the state of sulphuric acid. **1891** *Anthony's Photogr. Bull.* IV. 397 Prof. J. E. Reynolds, who was the original discoverer of the rinsing sulphur urea, now known as *thio-carbamide*. **1883** *Jrnl. Chem. Soc.* XLIV. 405 The use of potassium *thiocarbonate as a remedy against phylloxera. **1887** *Ibid.* LI. 272 The conversion of *thiocarbonyl chloride into thiocarbonyl tetrachloride by the assimilation of two atoms of chlorine takes place at ordinary temperatures. **1929** *Bull. Chem. Soc. Japan* IV. 176 *Thio-choline bromide was prepared by heating bromocholine bromide with 2-thio-uracil or 4-methyl-2-thio-uracil with water. **1980** *Sci. Amer.* Apr. 37/3 Nerve gas in the sampled air inhibits the enzyme, just as it would in the human body, resulting in a drop in the thiocholine level, which triggers the alarm. **1877** *Jrnl. Chem. Soc.* XXXII. 859 *Thiocyanates of the acid radicles are prepared by the action of acid chlorides on dry lead thiocyanate. *Ibid.* 423 Action of Nascent *Thiocyanic Acid on Alcohol. **1952** *Jrnl. Biol. Chem.* CXCVI. 545 These results thus confirm the conclusions of Lynen and Reichert that the acetyl group of acetyl CoA is attached, in *thioester linkage, to the thioethanolamine portion of the CoA molecule. **1979** *Nature* 1 Mar. 86/1 The role of ATP and other energy-rich phosphates is considered in detail and this is followed by a study of thioesters including coenzyme A derivatives. **1889** G. M'GOWAN tr. *Bernthsen's Text-bk. Org. Chem.* iv. 94 The *Thio-ethers, also termed alkyl sulphides, *e.g.* ethyl sulphide, $(C_2H_5)_2S$, are..neutral volatile liquids. **1979** *Nature* 20–27 Dec. 808/2 Each haem is linked, as in cytochrome *c*, to the apoprotein by two thioether bonds. **1857** *Jrnl. Chem. Soc.* IX. 185 *Thioformic acid crystallises from formic acid, or from boiling alcohol, in slender needles. **1877** *Jrnl. Chem. Soc.* XXXII. 595 Carius obtained an acid of the formula $H.C_2H_2(HS)O_2$, which he called monosulphoglycollic acid. Some uncertainty was attached, however, to the constitution of the product of this reaction, and the author now shows that both *thioglycollic acid, $H.C_2H_2(HS)O_2$, and thiodiglycollic acid..are produced. **1980** A. L. SMITH *Microbiol. & Path.* (ed. 12) v. 64/1 Thioglycollate broth, a special medium containing thioglycollic acid, supports the growth of anaerobes.. without special seal. **1877** *Jrnl. Chem. Soc.* XXXII. 595 Potassium *thioglycollate..crystallises in masses of small needles, and is readily soluble in water and alcohol. **1976** *Nature* 24 June 652/1 Much early work was concerned with the evaluation of different methods for breaking disulphide bonds, and procedures were developed using..sodium thioglycollate. **1889** G. M'GOWAN tr. *Bernthsen's Text-bk. Org. Chem.* 542/1 (Index), *Thio-ketones. **1965** *New Scientist* 30 Dec. 921/2 The thioketones (compounds containing the > C = S group) are in general red oils with intense nauseating smells. **1878** *Chem. News* 20 Dec. 294/2 (*heading*) Notes on certain *thionates. **1938** *Thorpe's Dict. Appl. Chem.* (ed. 4) II. 574/2 All thionates are decomposed by heat, yielding generally sulphates, sulphur dioxide, and, except with dithionates, sulphur. **1880** *Jrnl. Chem. Soc.* XXXVII. 593 A qualitative reaction, by which pentathionic acid is clearly distinguished from any other of the *thionic acids. **1886** *Jrnl. Chem. Soc.* L. 53 The addition of strong hydrochloric acid does not turn the solution blue, as is the case with *thionine. **1956** *Thorpe's Dict. Appl. Chem.* (ed. 4) XI. 590/1 Lauth had already indicated that bright blue dyes could be obtained by methylating thionine but such a process was not economic. **1976** *Nature* 1–8 Jan. 60/2 Feulgen reaction carried out on the specimens treated with ..thionin and exposed to light gave differential staining. **1839** THOMSON *British Ann.* 377 *Thionurate of zinc. *Ibid.*, *Thionuric acid. **1874** WATTS *Dict. Chem.* V. 779 Thionuric acid..forms a crystalline mass, consisting of fine needles. **1866** *Chem. News* 9 Mar. 117/1 M. Wurtz presented a note 'On the Synthesis of Chloride of *Thionyle'. **1874** WATTS *Dict. Chem.* V. 780 Thionyl. SO.—The radicle of the sulphurous compounds: e.g., sulphurous chloride, $(SO)''Cl_2$ = chloride of thionyl. **1883** MEYER in *Jrnl. Chem. Soc.* XLIV. 1091 A substance contained in Coal-tar Benzene..to which the author has given the name of **thiophene*. **1903** A. J. WALKER tr. *Hollemans' Textbk. Org. Chem.* 500 Thiophen can be synthesized by various methods, the most important being the interaction of succinic acid and pentasulphide of phosphorus. **1932** I. D. GARARD *Introd. Org. Chem.* xiii. 183 Coal tar benzene always contains thiophene, C_4H_4S, which boils at 85° and is therefore not readily removed by distillation. **1951** *Engineering* 23 Nov. 667/3 Thiophen cannot be removed from [town] gas by any practical chemical method. **1967** M. J. JANSSEN *Organosulfur Chem.* i. 10 Benzene derivatives are much less readily hydrogenated than thiophene. **1899** *Syd. Soc. Lex.*, **Thiophenol*,..phenyl mercaptan. *Ibid.*, **Thioresorcin*,..a popular substitution of resorcin... Used as a dusting powder. **1894** *Jrnl. Chem. Soc.* LXVI. I. 76 (*heading*) Derivatives of *thiosemicarbazide. **1971** *Chem. Abstr.* LXXIV. 74835 Thiosemicarbazide.. given i.p. to mice did not affect the incorporation of intraventricularly administered..putrescine-2HCl..into γ-aminobutyric acid in the brain. **1902** *Jrnl. Chem. Soc.* LXXXII. 572 The *thiosemicarbazones of aldehydes and ketones readily yield insoluble copper, silver and mercury derivatives, which can be used for the purpose of isolating these compounds. **1979** *Cancer Res.* XXXIX. 4601/1 The isoquinoline thiosemicarbazone derivatives have been shown to be potent inhibitors of ribonucleotide reductase. **1853** URE *Dict. Arts* I. 32 *Thiosinnamine. **1881** PIESSE & STANSELL in *Jrnl. Chem. Soc.* XL. 207 *Thiosinamine* is an oily substance at 100°, but gradually solidifies when cold. **1873** WATTS *Fownes' Chem.* 198 The solution of a *thiosulphate. **1874** *Jrnl. Chem. Soc.* XXVII. 771 The close relation between the thiosulphates and sulphates is shown by the formulæ—$SO_2{}^{SNa}{}_{ONa}$ and $SO_2{}^{ONa}{}_{ONa}$. **1873** WATTS *Fownes' Chem.* 204 *Thiosulphuric Acid is scarcely known. **1874** *Jrnl. Chem. Soc.* XXVII. 770 On the Constitution of Hyposulphurous (Thiosulphuric) Acid. **1953** *Arch. Internal Med.* XCII. 629 The purpose of this communication is to present our preliminary experience in the treatment of.. human leukemias..with triethylene thiophosphoramide (*ThioTEPA). **1976** *Nature* 13 May 135/1 Criticism of the use of the alkylating agent thiotepa (triethylene thiophosphoramide) to sterilise mosquitoes, as part of an eradication programme in India, focused on its toxicity and the possibility that it or its breakdown products would harm other animal components of the food chain. **1885** *Jrnl. Chem. Soc.* XLVIII. 251 A Simple Method of obtaining *Thiotolene. **1905** WHEELER & BRISTOL in *Amer. Chem. Jrnl.* XXXIII. 458, 2-*Thiouracil... This compound was first obtained.. when pseudoethylthiourea, containing some thiourea, was condensed with ethyl sodium formylacetate. **1977** *Martindale's Extra Pharmacopœia* (ed. 27) 304/1 Thiouracil was formerly used in the control and treatment of thyrotoxicosis and in the preparation of patients for thyroidectomy. **1894** MUIR & MORLEY *Watts' Dict. Chem.* IV. 710 Formed by adding Br to an alcoholic or cold aqueous solution of *thio-urea. **1911** *Jrnl. Chem. Soc.* XCIX. 145 In order to obtain this sulphoxide [*sc.* diphenylmethane *o*-sulphoxide], *thioxanthen was oxidised with hydrogen dioxide in acetic anhydride solution. **1924** '*Chem. Age*' *Chem. Dict.* 148/2 *Thioxanthenes*, derivatives of thioxanthene. **1945** *Jrnl. Chem. Soc.* 659 (*heading*) Action of oxygen in sunlight on thioxanthen. **1885** *Ibid.* XLVIII. 251 A simple method of obtaining..*thioxylene.

2. In pharmaceutical and other terms.

thiaˈcetazone [ACET(YL + SEMICARB)AZONE], a semicarbazone used as a bacteriostatic drug in the treatment of tuberculosis and leprosy; 4-acetamidobenzaldehyde thiosemicarbazone, $C_{10}H_{12}N_4OS$. **ˈthiobacillus** *Biol.* [mod.L., coined in Ger. (M. W. Beijerinck 1904, in *Centralbl. f. Bakteriol.* II Abt. 597)], a rod-shaped Gram-negative autotrophic bacterium deriving energy from the oxidation of sulphur and certain sulphur compounds, and belonging to the genus *Thiobacillus*. **thiobacˈteria**, name proposed by Migula for sulphur and iron bacteria mostly found in seawater and soils. **ˈthiocamph** [CAMPH(OR)], a fluid disinfectant, used for fumigation, formed by the action of sulphur dioxide on camphor. **ˈthiochrome** *Biochem.* [ad. G. *thiocrom* (R. Kuhn et al. 1935, in *Zeitschr. f. physiol. Chem.* CCXXXIV. 196), f. Gr. χρῶμα colour], a yellow basic solid, $C_{12}H_{14}N_4OS$, that has a strong blue fluorescence in solution and is formed when thiamine is oxidized in a procedure for the estimation of the latter. '**thiocol** [GUAIA)COL], a preparation of guaiacol, used in lung diseases. '**thioform** [after *chloroform*], trade-name of a basic bismuth di-thiosalicylate, as an antiseptic for wounds. **thio'genic** *a.* [-GEN 1 + -IC], producing sulphur, *spec.* applied to bacteria which produce free sulphur by the oxidization of sulphuretted hydrogen. **Thi'ogenol**, trade-name of a solution of sodium sulphonate as a medical wash. **Thiokol**, a proprietary name for various polysulphide rubbers and liquids. '**thiolin** [L. *līnum* flax], trade-name of a dark-green substance prepared from linseed oil by the action of sulphur; hence ***thio'linic acid.*** **thio'mersal** [MER(CURY *sb.* + SAL(ICYLATE *sb.*], a bacteriostatic and fungistatic organomercury compound used as a disinfectant for the skin and internally and as a preservative for biological products; sodium ethylmercurithiosalicylate, $H_5C_2{\cdot}Hg{\cdot}S{\cdot}C_6H_4COONa$; cf. MERTHIOLATE. **thio'nazin** [*pyr*)*azin*(*yl* in the systemic name, f. PYR(O- + AZ(O- + -IN[1] + -YL], an insecticide and nematocide, $(C_2H_5O)_2{\cdot}PS{\cdot}O{\cdot}C_4N_2H_3$. **thioridazine** (-rɪ'deɪziːn) [f. PIPE)RID(INE + AZINE], a phenothiazine derivative, $C_{21}H_{26}N_2S_2$, that is a white or yellow powder and is given orally as a tranquillizer, esp. in cases of schizophrenia and mania. **Thio'sapiol, -sapol** [L. *sapo* soap], **-'savonal**, trade-names of soap containing sulphur in chemical combination. **thio'thixene** [f. *thi*(*o*)*x*(*anth*)*ene*], a derivative, $C_{23}H_{29}N_3O_2S_2$, of thioxanthene given orally as an anti-psychotic drug. ‖'**Thiothrix** [Gr. θρίξ hair], a genus of sulphur bacteria found in sulphur springs.

1952 *Lancet* 1 Mar. 436/2 Para-acetamidobenzaldehyde Thiosemicarbazone. [*Note*] This substance..is marketed under various names;..*thiacetazone, &c. **1976** MACGILLIVRAY & HALL in G. S. Avery *Drug Treatment* xiv. 382/2 Massive breast enlargement has been seen with isoniazid regimens containing thiacetazone. **1951** *Biol. Abstr.* XXV. 811/2 It was possible to isolate *thiobacilli capable of changing hyposulfides into sulfates. **1973** *Nature* 11 May 99/2 Thiobacilli, iron bacteria and algae can survive in acidic water of about pH 2. **1900** A. C. JONES tr. *Fischer's Str. & Funct. Bacteria* 65 The sulphur bacteria, **Thiobacteria*, whose cells are often crammed full of spherical refringent masses of pure sulphur, occur in nature in places where free sulphuretted hydrogen is present. *Ibid.*, Thiobacteria can be found at any time of the year, but are most abundant in the early spring and late autumn. **1899** *Syd. Soc. Lex.*, **Thiocamph*..on exposure evolves sulphur dioxide in steady fumes. **1935** *Chem. Abstr.* XXIX. 6242 When crude lactoflavin is made alk., the fluorescence changes from yellowish green to blue. This phenomenon is due to the presence of a S-contg. pigment for which the name *thiochrome is proposed. **1963** STEYN-PARVÉ & MONFOORT in Florkin & Stotz *Comprehensive Biochem.* XI. i. 16 The thiochrome method is based on the observation.. that oxidation with alkaline ferricyanide converts thiamine into a compound with intense blue fluorescence: thiochrome... The thiochrome is extracted..and the fluorescence of the extract measured. **1899** *Syd. Soc. Lex.*, **Thioform*..a light yellowish powder, without odour or taste..has..been introduced into surgery with promising success. **1910** BRICKDALE *Guide Newer Remedies* 60 A dithiosalicylate..has been..named Thioform. **1930** *Official Gaz.* (U.S. Patent Office) 20 May 555/2 **Thiokol* for sulfur-containing plastic material used in the manufacture of gaskets,..protective coatings, and like products. **1936** *Industr. & Engin. Chem.* Mar. 275/1 Various olefin-polysulfide reaction products.., under the trade name of Thiokols, have been presented to the industry. **1943** *Trade Marks Jrnl.* 8 Dec. 525/1 *Thiokol...* Thermo-setting or thermo-plastic condensation products of the nature of rubber, being compounds of or containing sulphur, and articles (not included in other Classes) made therefrom. Thiokol Corporation.., Trenton, New Jersey. **1972** *Materials & Technol.* V. xiv. 491 All thiokols are originally obtained in latex form, and as such they have found some industrial applications as an impregnant for textiles and leather. **1894** REMINGTON *Pract. Pharm.* (ed. 3) 1433 **Thiolin.* Salts of thiosulphonic acid. Salt of thiolinic acid. Sulphonated and sulphurated linseed oil. **1899** *Syd. Soc. Lex.*, Thiolin, *thiolinic acid. **1958** *Brit. Pharmacopœia* 675 *Thiomersal should be protected from light. **1968** WILSON & SCHILD *Appl. Pharmacol.* (ed. 10) xxxvi. 671 Phenylmercuric nitrate, thiomersal (merthiolate), and other organic mercurials, have a better therapeutic index than mercuric chloride. **1964** *B.S.I. News* Mar. 23 *Thionazin. **1974** MARTIN & WORTHING *Pesticide Man.* (Brit. Crop Protection Council) (ed. 4) 488 Thionazin is a soil insecticide and nematicide effective against..nematodes,.. root maggots and..aphids. **1959** *Jrnl. Pharmacol. & Exper. Therapeutics* CXXVI. 312 (*heading*) Some neuro-pharmacological properties of *thioridazine hydrochloride (Mellaril). **1899** *Syd. Soc. Lex.*, **Thiosa·piol*, a sulphuretted soap, containing 10 per cent. of sulphur, obtained by heating sulphur and oleic acid together... A successful application to many skin diseases. **1965** SIMPSON & IQBAL in *Current Therapeutic Res.* VII. 697 (*heading*) A preliminary study of *thiothixene in chronic schizophrenics. **1976** SMYTHIES & CORBETT *Psychiatry* x. 194 Thiothixene is a potent and effective antipsychotic agent in acute and chronic schizophrenia.

3. Used *attrib.* as an independent word (without hyphen), denoting the presence of a sulphur atom, usu. in place of one of oxygen.

1879 *Chem. News* 24 Oct. 204/2 (*heading*) Organic thio compounds. **1926** *Chem. Abstr.* XX. 364 An investigation of the chemistry of the thio ketones as compared with that of the ordinary O ketones. **1955** KIRK & OTHMER *Encycl. Chem. Technol.* XIV. 61 Thio amides may react in either the thiono form, RC(:S)NH_2, or the tautomeric thiol form, RC(:NH)SH. **1980** J. W. COOPER *Spectroscopic Techniques Organic Chemists* vi. 186 Amino, cyano, and thio groups.

thioctic (θaɪ'ɒktɪk), *a. Chem.* [f. THIO- + OCT(A- + -IC.] ***thioctic acid***: any of the sulphur-containing acids with the formula

$$\underbrace{S-S-CH_2(CH_2)_x}CH(CH_2)_{5-x}COOH,$$

where x = 1, 2, 3, 4, or 5; *spec.* 6,8-dithio-*n*-octanoic acid (x = 1), = *α-lipoic acid* s.v. LIPO-.

1952 J. A. BROCKMAN et al. in *Jrnl. Amer. Chem. Soc.* LXXIV. 1868/2 The name 'thioctic acid' is proposed for this structure (x = 2), a sulfur-containing organic acid with 8 carbon atoms. **1953** FRUTON & SIMMONDS *Gen. Biochem.* xxxviii. 900 Recent work has assigned to α-lipoic acid..the structure of 6,8-dithio-*n*-octanoic acid ('6-thioctic acid'). Isomers of this compound such as the 4,8-dithio acid ('4-thioctic acid') or the 5,8-dithio acid ('5-thioctic acid') have less POF [*sc.* pyruvate oxidation factor] activity. **1975** *Sci. Amer.* Mar. 98/2 In the 1950's thioctic acid had been proposed as a remedy for liver damage caused by heavy-metal poisoning.

thioindigo (θaɪəʊ'ɪndɪgəʊ). [f. THIO- + INDIGO *sb.* (*a.*).] A red vat dye in which the two imino groups of indigotin are replaced by sulphur atoms; also, any of various derivatives of this also used as dyes.

1906 *Textile Colorist* XXVIII. 321/1 Messrs. Kalle & Co., Aktiengesellschaft, have placed upon the market, under the name of Thio Indigo Red B, a new coloring matter, which like Indigo is admirably suited for dyeing the various textile fibres and for calico printing. **1923** THORPE & INGOLD *Vat Colours* vi. 131 The following aromatic bases have been converted..into the corresponding aromatic thioglycollic acids, which have been transformed..into thioindigos. **1951** KIRK & OTHMER *Encycl. Chem. Technol.* VII. 823 Thioindigo..forms brownish-red metallic crystals when recrystallized from xylene or other organic solvents... On reduction with sodium hyposulfite in the presence of alkali, it forms a pale yellow leuco compound, Thioindigo White. **1961** COCKETT & HILTON *Dyeing Cellulosic Fibres* v. 185 Thio-indigo is an important basic structure for a number of useful vat dyes.

So **thio'indigoid**, any of a class of vat dyes that are substituted derivatives of thioindigo and are used esp. in textile printing; also *attrib.* or as *adj.*

1943 *Thorpe's Dict. Appl. Chem.* (ed. 4) VI. 454/1 This process has been applied..for preparing the orange thio-indigoid dye from *p*-phenetioline. **1951** KIRK & OTHMER *Encycl. Chem. Technol.* VII. 824 Although the fastness of thioindigoids does not in general approach that of the anthraquinone vat dyes, the brightness and clarity of shade are in many cases considerably superior. **1952** [see INDIGOID *a.* (*sb.*)]. **1970** K. VENKATARAMAN *Chem. Synthetic Dyes* III. i. 36 With the exception of halogenated indigo and a few thioindigoids..the indigoid group is steadily declining in commercial importance. **1972** *Materials & Technol.* V. xi. 358 Thioindigoid reds and maroons are vat dyestuff pigments with good light-fastness in full colours and reduced shades and excellent acid and alkali resistance.

thiol ('θaɪɒl). *Chem.* [f. next.] **a.** = MERCAPTAN.

1900 *Jrnl. Chem. Soc.* LXXVIII. I. 163 Methods used for the preparation of aromatic thiols. **1971** *Nature* 31 Dec. 507/1 This interpretation is supported by the restoration of the equilibrium..when an extraneous thiol, mercaptoethanol, is added.

b. = MERCAPTO(-) b, SULPHYDRYL

1951 C. R. NOLLER *Chem. Organic Compounds* xiv. 265 The—SH group is known as the thiol or sulfhydryl group, or more commonly as the mercapto group. **1973** *Sci. Amer.* Apr. 60/3 All the simplest organic molecules have been found in interstellar space, whereas many of the even simpler nonorganic species such as nitric oxide (NO), sulfur monoxide (SO) and the thiol radical (SH) have not been detected in spite of sensitive searches.

thiol- ('θaɪəl). *Chem.* [f. THI(O- + -OL.] A name for the group SH in combination, analogous to hydroxyl, OH.

It indicates the presence of an -SH group (or an -SR group, where R is an alkyl radical), as in *methyl-thiolcarbamate*, $H_2N.CO.SCH_3$, as distinguished from *methyl carbamate*, $H_2N.CO.OCH_3$, and also from *methyl-thioncarbamate*, $H_2N.CS.OCH_3$: see THION-. Also, in those cases in which *hydroxy-* would mean the presence of an -OH group, *thiol-* indicates the presence of an -SH group; and where *methoxy-*, *ethoxy-*, etc., would indicate CH_3O-, C_2H_5O-, RO- groups, *methylthiol-*, *ethylthiol-*, *R-thiol-*, indicate CH_3S-, C_2H_5S-, RS- groups; thus, the sulphur compound corresponding to *sodium ethoxyacetate* $C_2H_5O.CH_2.CO_2Na$ is *sodium ethylthiolacetate* $C_2H_5S.CH_2.CO_2Na$. Cf. THION-.

1899 *Jrnl. Chem. Soc.* LXXVI. I. 797 The authors adopt the Geneva nomenclature, *thion* being used to denote compounds containing the group .CS.OR, and *thiol* those containing the group .CO.SR. **1905** *Ibid.* LXXXVIII. I. 626 α-Thiolbutyric acid, SH.CHEt.CO_2H, is an oil boiling at 118–122° under 19 mm. pressure.

thion- ('θaɪən). *Chem.* [a. Gr. θεῖον sulphur: cf. THIO-.] A name for sulphur taking the place of oxygen in a compound and joined by two bonds to carbon.

e.g. in *methyl thioncarbamate*, $H_2N.CS.OCH_3$, as distinct from methyl carbamate and methyl-thiolcarbamate: see THIOL-. (Certain words beginning with *thion-* do not conform to this system: see THIONIC, etc. under THIO-.)

1899 *Jrnl. Chem. Soc.* LXXVI. I. 797 [see THIOL-]. **1904** *Ibid.* LXXXVI. I. 990 The crude ester..is best converted directly into thionoxanilic acid, NHPh.CS.CO_2H.

thiopental (θaɪəʊ'pɛntəl). *Pharm.* Chiefly *U.S.* [f. next + -AL (cf. PENTAL).] = next. Also called ***thiopental sodium.***

1947 *U.S. Pharmacopœia* 572 Thiopental Sodium occurs as a yellowish white, hygroscopic powder. **1955** GOODMAN & GILMAN *Pharmacol. Basis Therapeutics* (ed. 2) v. 60/2 Ether (as well as cyclopropane and thiopental) causes renal vasoconstriction.

thiopentone (θaɪəʊ'pɛntəʊn). *Pharm.* [f. THIO- + PENTO(BARBIT)ONE.] A sulphur analogue of pentobarbital sodium that is given intravenously as a short-acting general anæsthetic; sodium 5-ethyl-5-(1-methylbutyl)-2-thiobarbiturate, $C_{11}H_{17}N_2O_2SNa$. Also called ***thiopentone sodium.*** Cf. PENTOTHAL.

1945 *Brit. Pharmacopœia 1932* Add. VII. 65 (*heading*) Soluble thiopentone. **1952** [see HEXOBARBITONE]. **1965** J. POLLITT *Depression & its Treatm.* iv. 50 It [*sc.* electro-convulsive treatment] is usually administered after the patient has been anæsthetised with thiopentone sodium. **1977** *Proc. R. Soc. Med.* LXX. 782/1 Generalized reactions were not seen for the first twenty years after the introduction of thiopentone.

thir (ðɪr, ðɜː(r)), *dem. pron.* and *adj. Sc.* and *north. dial.* Forms: 3 ?, 4– **thir**; also 4 (**þeir, þier**), **þer(e, þar(e, there**, 4–5 **þir(e**, 4–7 **ther**, 5 **thire, theire, thair**, (8–9 *north. dial.* **ther, thor, thoor, thur**). [Origin obscure. The introduction of the word app. coincided with the change of *þās* in the north from being plural of *this* to being synonymous with *þā*, pl. of *that*: see THESE, THOSE, THO. The earliest evidence is that of Cursor Mundi and the northern works of 1300–1350, in which *þās* and *þā* appear as plural of *that*, and *thir* in various spellings is the established plural of *this*, = southern *thēs*, midland *thise*, *these*. Some suggest its adoption from ON. *þeir*, *þǽr* 'those', pl. masc. and fem. of the simple demonstrative *sá*, *sú*, *þat*, of which the plural was used also as 3rd pers. pron. pl. 'they'. Others have suggested a combination of *þe* with *hēr* 'here', as if = the here, those here. Both suggestions present difficulties. See Note.]

A. *pron.* = THESE *dem. pron.*

13.. *Cursor M.* 6291 (Cott., Gött.) þir [*F.*, *Tr.* þes] er þe folk of israel. *Ibid.* 6481 (Cott.) þir [*F.* þer, *G.* þis, *Tr.* þese] er þe coma[n]mentes ten. *Ibid.* 23053 (Edin., Gött.) Gret lauerdschip sal þir [*Cott.* þar, *F.* ham] be lent. *Ibid.* 23643 (Edin. Gött.) þir sal worsip al creature. *a* **1340** HAMPOLE *Psalter* iii. 2 þere ere leghers, and þai say to bigile þe. **13..** *Evang. Nicod.* 28 in Herrig's *Archiv.* LIII. 392 We, whatkyn godes er þire [*rimes* syre, ire, desyre]? *c* **1450** *St. Cuthbert* (Surtees) 3521 þir [five onions], he saide, has bene my mete. **1456** SIR G. HAYE *Law Arms* (S.T.S.) 85 Of all thir, thare is nane sa gude as..defens of gude rycht. **1552–3** *Reg. Privy Council Scot.* I. 137 Thir ar the artikills of the Lordis. **1637–50** ROW *Hist. Kirk* (Wodr. S.) 197 Any one of thir requyrs a wholl man. **1825** BROCKETT *N.C. Words*, *Thur*, these. **1828** *Craven Gloss.*, *Thur*, *thir*, these.

B. *adj.* = THESE *dem. adj.*

13.. *Cursor M.* 4085 (Cott.) þeir [*Gött.* þir, *F.* þes, *T.* þese] breþer, þat i said of are. *Ibid.* 5938 'Yee prai your lauerd', he said, 'þat he Wald do þier frosses [*F.* þere froskis, *G.* þir froskis, *T.* þese frogges] a-wai fra me'. *Ibid.* 19391 þir [*F.* þer, *Tr.* þese] seuen were Sett be-fore þe aposteles sere. **1340** HAMPOLE *Pr. Consc.* 1682 Als þir clerkes fyndes writen. *c* **1400** MAUNDEV. (Roxb.) Pref. 2 þir werldly lordes. *c* **1420** *Anturs of Arth.* 575 Witturly ther weys [*Douce MS.* þes wighte mene] thayre weppuns thai weld. **1423** JAS. I *Kingis Quair* li, I..said thir versis sevin. *c* **1440** *Alphabet of Tales* 55 He lukid evur when þir fendis suld com agayn. **1490** *Exch. Rolls Scotl.* X. 663 To quhais knauleg thire our letterris salcum greting. **1553** KENNEDY *Compend. Tract.* in *Wodrow Soc. Misc.* (1844) 109 Sen the tyme of the Apostolis to thir our dayis. **1678** *Contract* in *Proc. Soc. Ant. Scot.* (1896) XXX. 21 Both pairties are content that ther present[s] be insert. **1715** *Wodrow Corr.* (1843) II. 33 Thir two men have bred trouble enough. **1790** BURNS *Tam o' Shanter* 155 Thir breeks o' mine, my only pair. **1790** MRS. WHEELER *Westmld. Dial.* Pref. 11 Thor Men hed been at a College, coad Cambridg.

[*Note.* Difficulties of derivation from ON. *þeir*, *þǽr* are: (1) The retention of inflexional *-r*, otherwise unexemplified, and the fact that *þei-r* had already been adopted in its pronominal sense as *þeȝȝ*, *they*, *thei*, in the north *þai*, *þay*, and was in full use in Cursor M. and other northern works: see THEY. Moreover, neither *thir* nor *ther* appears to represent *þei-r* phonetically, as Ormin's *þeȝȝ* and E. Midl. *þei* did. (2) The sense is quite different; the ON. word means 'those' or 'they', distinct from *þesser*, *-ar* 'these'; while *thir* has been from the beginning emphatically 'these', as distinct from *þā*, *þās* 'those'. The explanation 'the here', 'those here' suits the sense; but (1) no trace has been found of these in an uncombined form; and (2) the addition of *here* to a demonstrative, common in the midlands and south of England (see HERE 1 d), is not known as a northern idiom.]

thir, obs. unstressed form of THEIR.

thiram ('θaɪræm). *Chem.* [f. *thi*(*u*)*ram* in the systematic name (see def.), f. *thi*(*o*)-*ur*(*ea* s.v. THIO- 1 + CARB)AM(IC *a.*] Tetramethylthiuram disulphide, $[(CH_3)_2N{\cdot}CS{\cdot}S-]_2$, used as a fungicide and a seed protectant.

1950 *Phytopathology* XL. 118 The Subcommittee on Fungicide Nomenclature of The American Phytopathological Society, cooperating with the Interdepartmental Committee on Pest control, has selected common names for five commercially-available fungicidal chemicals... The coined common names and designations are:..*Thiram* for the fungicidal chemical tetramethylthiuram disulfide. **1962** *Amateur Gardening* 10 Feb. 10 The chemical known as thiram..remarkably increases the percentage of germination of most garden seeds. **1975** *Daily Tel.* 15 Nov. 8/2 A refinement would be to dust them over with antiseptic thiram powder before putting them in a box of peat..to await another spring for replanting.

third (θɜːd), *a.* (*adv.*), *sb.* Forms: see below. [OE. *þridda, -e, þird(d)a, -e*, Comm. Teut. and Indo-Eur.; = OFris. *thredda*, OS. *thriddio* (MLG. *drudde, derde*, Du. *derde*), OHG. *dritto* (MHG., G. *dritte*), ON. *þriðe, -i* (Sw. *tredje*, Da. *tredie*), Goth. *þridja*,:—OTeut. **þriđjó-*, :—Indo-Eur. **tritjós*: cf. Gr. *τρίτος*, L. *tertius*, Skr. *trtīyas*.

The metathesis of *third* for *thrid* appears already in ONorthumb. *c* 950, but *thrid* was the prevalent type down to the 16th c.]

A. Illustration of Forms.

α. 1 (3) **þridda**, 2–5 **þridde**, 3 **þride**, 4 **þryd(e, threid, þred**, 4–5 **thrydde, thride, þrid, thridd**, 4–6 **thridde, thryd, thredde**, 4–7 **thred**, 4–6, *Sc.* -8 **thrid**, 5 **thryde, thrudde, (tryd)**.

a **800** CYNEWULF *Christ* 726 Wæs se þridda hlyp. *c* **1000** *Sax. Leechd.* II. 298 þridde mæȝen is. *c* **1200** ORMIN Ded. 6 Broþerr min i Godess hus, ȝet o þe þride [*elsewhere* þridde] wise. *c* **1250** *Gen. & Ex.* 3516 Đe ðridde moneð in is cumen. *a* **1300** *Cursor M.* 8471 (Cott.) þe thride boke efter þa tua. *Ibid.* 16892 To rise þe thrid [*Gött.* thred] dai. *Ibid.* 18646 To þe thrid [*G.* threid] morn. **13..** *E.E. Allit. P.* B. 300 The Iolef Iapheth watz gendered þe þryd. **1382** WYCLIF *Acts* xx. 9 He ledd by sleep fel down fro the thridde stage. *c* **1450** *Two Cookery-bks.* 113 (Laud MS.) Ye thrudde perty shal be sugar. **1588** A. KING tr. *Canisius' Catech.* Kalendar 1 Feb., S. Ignatius bischop of Antioch threid efter S. Peter. **1606** *Sc. Acts Jas. VI* (1816) IV. 279/2 The thrid day of this instant. *c* **1730** Thrid [see B. I. 1].

β. 1 (*Northumb.*) **ðirda, ðirdda**, 2 **þerdde**, 4 **þirde**, 5–6 **thyrd(e**, 5–7 **thirde**, 6 **theyrd, thurd**, 5– **third.**

c **950** *Lindisf. Gosp.* Luke xii. 38 ȝif on ða ðirdda wacan ȝecymeð. *a* **1200** *Moral Ode* 138 (Lamb. MS.) Nolde he for al middenerd þe þerdde [*v.r.* þridde] [dei] þer abiden. **1393** LANGL. *P. Pl.* C. XXII. 264 And matheu þe þirde. **1446** LYDG. *Nightingale Poems* i. 299 Ye that are in the third age Of your lyfe ande passed morow & prime. **1473** WARKW. *Chron.* (Camden) 3 In the thyrde ȝere of the reygne of Kynge Edwarde. **1552** HULOET, Thyrde fayre or market proclaymed.

B. Signification. **I.** *adj.*

As with other ordinals, usually ***the third***: see THE *def. art.* B. 18.

1. The ordinal numeral corresponding to the cardinal three: last of three; that comes next after the second. **a.** with sb. expressed.

a **800** [see A. *α*]. **971** *Blickl. Hom.* 15 þy þriddan dæȝe he of deaþe ariseþ. *a* **1225** *Ancr. R.* 14 þe þridde dole. **1340** HAMPOLE *Pr. Consc.* 1664 Here bigynnes þe thred part. **1497** *Naval Acc. Hen. VII* (1896) 141 The thryde day of Marche. **1533** BELLENDEN *Livy* III. xi. (S.T.S.) I. 292 To be haldin þe thrid day eftir þe nundinis. **1552** HULOET, Thyrde sillable, *ante penultima*. **1597** A. M. tr. *Guillemeau's Fr. Chirurg.* 30/1 The finger called *Medicus*, or thirde finger. *c* **1730** BURT *Lett. N. Scotl.* (1818) I. 20 Inquire for such a launde.., where the gentleman stayd, at the thrid stair, that is three stories high. **1847** HELPS *Friends in C.* I. vi. 92, I prefer real life..where there is no third volume [as in a novel] to make things straight.

b. Following the names of sovereigns, popes, etc.: cf. SECOND A. 1 b.

1414 *Rolls of Parlt.* IV. 59/2 Kyng Henry the Thridde. **1550** BALE *K. Johan* (Camden) 42 Pope Innocent the thred. **1735** JOHNSON *Lobo's Abyssinia, Descr.* v. 73 King John the Third [of Portugal].

c. with sb. understood.

c **950** *Lindisf. Gosp.* Matt. xxii. 26 ȝelic ðe æftera..& ðe ðirda [*Rushw.* þridde]. *c* **1175** *Lamb. Hom.* 133 Đreo þing ..þet oðer is goddes word and þet ðridde is weldede. *a* **1300** *Cursor M.* 358 (Cott.) þ e thrid es air, and fir þe ferth. **1382** WYCLIF *Dan.* v. 7 Shal be the thrid in my rewme. *c* **1440** *Gesta Rom.* xv. 51 (Harl. MS.) And so he wrote to the thrid, þat seid she lovid him. **1552–3** *Inv. Ch. Goods, Staffs.* in *Ann. Lichfield* (1863) IV. 7c, iij vestements, one of whyte fustian, another of blacke chamblet, & the thryd of blewe sarsynet. **1662** PLAYFORD *Skill Mus.* II. (1674) 92 Six strings, ..the first..is called the Treble; the second, the Small Mean; the third, the Great Mean. **1821** SCOTT *Kenilw.* xxxviii, 'Hush! thou knave!' said a third; 'how know'st thou who may be within hearing?'

d. *Gram.* In ***third person***: see PERSON *sb.* 8. Also in ***third declension, conjugation***, and in names of tenses, as ***third future, preterite***, where the reference is to a conventional order of enumeration adopted by grammarians.

1530 PALSGR. 93 In verbes of theyr thyrde conjugation I fynde a litell more difficultie. *a* **1586** SIDNEY *Arcadia* II. (Sommer) 137 He had..forgotten in speaking of him selfe to vse the third person. **1764** W. PRIMATT *Accentus Rediv.* 111 Provided they were third persons plural. **1848** J. T. WHITE *Xenophon's Anab.* II. iv. §5 Notes (1872) 116 Sometimes.. the third future is used, instead of the common future, to point out more forcibly all but immediate occurrence of some future action. **1857** WILLIAMS *Sanskrit Gram.* §415 Fortunately..the third preterite occurs but rarely in the better specimens of Hindú composition.

e. In proverbial phr. (***the***) ***third time('s) lucky***.

[*c* **1840** BROWNING *Lett.* (1933) 5 'The luck of the third adventure' is proverbial.] **1862** A. HISLOP *Proverbs Scotl.* 194 The third time's lucky. **1882** R. L. STEVENSON *New Arabian Nights* II. 59 'The next time we come to blows——' 'Will make the third,' I interrupted... 'Ay, true... Well, the third time's lucky.' **1942** N. MARSH *Death & Dancing Footman* vii. 123 It was a glancing blow..but..it might have been my head... One of them's saying to himself: 'Third time lucky'. **1979** J. TATE tr. *Blom's Limits of Pain* ix. 82 Lars Westerberg discovered that the expression third time lucky had something in it.

2. a. Additional to and distinct from two others already known or mentioned. ***third person*** (in *Law*) = THIRD PARTY. † ***third place***, a place which is neutral ground to two persons (*obs.*).

c **1290** *Beket* 415 in *S. Eng. Leg.* I. 118 þat þridde þing ȝeot mest of alle and sonest in wraþþe hem brouȝte. *c* **1400** *Apol. Loll.* 3 And þe þrid, if he be moost obedient to God and to His lawe. **1579** W. WILKINSON *Confut. Familye of Loue* 17 b, Incorporall and immateriall essences cannot be coupled in the same third matter. **1709** E. WARD tr. *Cervantes* 189 Any thing is easily believ'd that is to the Disreputation of a third Person. **1757** CHESTERF. *Lett.* 31 Dec., I could neither visit, nor be visited by, the Ministers of those two Crowns; but we met every day, or dined at third places. **1818** CRUISE *Digest* (ed. 2) I. 444 The clause..extends..to third persons only; not to the persons conveying, or those to whom lands are conveyed to uses. **1865** KINGSLEY *Herew.* xvii, Martin Lightfoot..was as a third hand and foot to him all day long. **1878** STEWART & TAIT *Unseen Univ.* iv. §122. 133 There can be no third thing besides body and void. [Cf. TERTIUM QUID.]

†**b.** ***third tongue***, a backbiter; a slanderer. Used by Wyclif and Coverdale to render *lingua tertia* of the Vulgate, in LXX. γλῶσσα τρίτη. *Obs.*

1382 WYCLIF *Ecclus.* xxviii. 16 The thridde tunge manye men stirede. **1388** *Ibid.* 19 *margin*, The tunge of the preuey bacbiter is clepid the thridde tunge..and the bacbiter him silf hath the thridde tunge, for he, as the thridde, makith debate betwen a man and his neiȝbore. **1535** COVERDALE *Ecclus.* xxviii. 14–15 The thirde tonge hath disquieted many one, and dryuen them from one londe to another... The thirde tonge hath cast out many an honest woman, and robbed them of their labours.

3. ***third part*** = B. II. 1. Now *rare*: see PART *sb.* 5.

a **1300** *Cursor M.* 973 (Cott.) þe half parte gladli or þe thrid We wil þe giue. **1375** BARBOUR *Bruce* II. 305 þe thrid part went to þe forray. **1483** *Cath. Angl.* 385/2 þe Thryd parte of a halpeny, *trissis*. **1570–6** LAMBARDE *Peramb. Kent* 228 The Monkes should enioy the whole tongue, and two third partes of the rest of the body. **1611** BIBLE *Rev.* viii. 8 The third part of the sea became blood.

4. a. The last of each successive group of three; one in every three, i.e. one third of the whole. ***third penny***: one third of the whole sum; *spec.* (see quot. 1706). ***third sheaf and teind***: see *third and teind*, II. 1.

c **1400** MAUNDEV. (Roxb.) xix. 87 Sum..at ilke a thridd passe knelis doune apon þe erthe. **1423** *Cal. Letter Bk. I. Lond.* (1909) 295 Have he, for his labour, the tryd peny that shal be recovered. *a* **1578** LINDESAY (Pitscottie) *Chron. Scot.* (S.T.S.) II. 315 Thair come in be sie sa meikill victuallis that it come downe the thrid penny. **1597** [see EVERY 1 e (*c*)]. **1627** *Rep. Parishes Scotl.* (Bann. Cl.) 3 Ten landis..payis presentlie the thrid scheiff and teind led. **1706** PHILLIPS (ed. Kersey), *Third-penny*, the third part of Fines and Profits, arising from Law-Processes, which in every County was heretofore allow'd to the Sheriff; the other two Parts being appointed for the King's Use. **1727** SWIFT *Poisoning E. Curll* Wks. 1755 III. I. 152 You shall have your third share of the Court poems. **1904** [see QUARTAN A. 1, def.].

b. ***third-day ague***, tertian ague.

1817–18 COBBETT *Resid. U.S.* (1822) 319 You would frighten him into a third-day ague.

5. With following superlative: having two superior in the specified attribute; third in point of quality, position, etc.

1375 BARBOUR *Bruce* XIII. 321 He was the thrid best knycht, perfay, That men wist liffand in his day. **1859** *Habits Gd. Soc.* iii. 155, I am wondering whether everybody arranges his wardrobe as our ungrammatical nurses used to do ours, under the heads of 'best, second-best, third-best', and so on. **1962** E. SNOW *Other Side of River* (1963) lxvii. 508 In 1960 it was the world's third-greatest reservoir. *Ibid.* lxxv. 577 The most significant additions to China's third-largest educational center are the T'ung Chi Medical College and hospitals. **1979** *Dædalus* Winter 62 Pursuing policies that would be optimal in a first-class world when one actually lives in a..third-best world can be highly inefficient.

6. Combinations, collocations, or phrases with special meaning (some of which may be used *attrib.* or as *adj.*), as ***third base, baseman, cousin, cousinship, form*** (hence ***third-former***), ***heir, -level, magnitude, person, realm, -stage, story, term*** (hence ***third-termery***): see the sbs.; **third ague**, tertian ague; **third-day**, the Quaker name for Tuesday, as being the third day of the week; **third dimension**, the dimension of thickness or depth (see DIMENSION *sb.* 3 a); hence **third-dimensional** *a.*; **third ear** esp. in *Psychoanal.*, a figurative ear which listens intuitively for what lies behind the words heard by the actual ears; **third estate**, the Commons: see ESTATE *sb.* 6; **third eye** *Hinduism* and *Buddhism*, the eye of insight or destruction located in the middle of the forehead of the god Siva; hence *transf.*, the power of inward or intuitive sight occasionally gained by humans; **third eyelid**, the nictitating membrane of many animals; **third floor**, (*a*) in England, the floor or story of a building separated by two from the ground floor; (*b*) in *Sc.*, *U.S.*, etc., the third story, counting the ground floor as the first; **third flute** *Mus.*, a flute pitched a minor third above the ordinary flute (see quots.); **third force, Third Force** [after Fr. *Troisième Force*], a political party or parties standing between two extreme or opposing parties (formerly, esp. between the French Gaullists and Communists); also *loosely*, any neutral power or third body; **third-generation** *attrib.*: see GENERATION 4 b; **third-grader** *N. Amer.*, a pupil in the third grade (GRADE *sb.* 4 c) at school; **third hour**, (*a*) among the Jews, the third of the twelve equal divisions of time between morning and evening; the hour between 8 and 9 a.m.; (*b*) in *R.C.Ch.*, the hour of TIERCE; **third house**, (*U.S. polit. slang*): see quot. 1889; **Third International**: see INTERNATIONAL *sb.* b; **third man**, (*a*) *Cricket*, a fielder placed between point and short slip, but further out; an additional short slip; also, the position occupied by him; (*b*) *Lacrosse*, a defence player placed behind the centre; the position occupied by him; (*c*) *Philos.* [Gr. τρίτος ἄνθρωπος], a term from Aristotle (*Metaphysics* Bk. A 990b 17) for a third element (or man) which, in the paradox stated in Plato's *Parmenides*, seems to be needed in arguments from the particular instance (of a man) to the ideal form (of Man); hence *attrib.*, as ***third-man argument***; (*d*) *Boxing slang*, the referee; (*e*) an unidentified third participant in a crime; **third market** *U.S.*, trade in stock undertaken outside the stock exchange; cf. OFF-BOARD *a.*; **third order**: see TERTIARY A. 5; **third penny**: see 4 above; † **third place**: see 2 above; **third point**, *Arch.* = TIERCE *point*: see quot.; hence **third-pointed** *a.*; **Third Position**, a name applied to the political stance of Juan Domingo Perón (1895–1974), President of Argentina (1944–55 and 1973–4), being neither capitalist nor communist, but a combination of Fascism and socialism; cf. JUSTICIALISM, PERONISM; **Third Programme**, (from 1946 to 1967, when its name was changed to 'Radio 3': see RADIO *sb.* 2 d) one of the three national radio networks of the BBC, broadcasting programmes of a predominantly cultural nature; often used allusively to qualify what is considered intellectually superior or 'highbrow'; **third rail**, (*a*) in some systems of electric railways, an additional rail which conveys the current; cf. *conductor rail* s.v. CONDUCTOR 12 d; an additional rail for the accommodation of trains with a wider gauge; (*b*) *U.S. slang*, used *attrib.* to designate highly intoxicating liquor; **third reading, Third Reading**, the third and final presentation of a parliamentary bill after amendments have been made, sometimes allowing for a final debate before it is voted on; cf. READING *vbl. sb.* 2 c; **third rime, rhyme**, = TERZA RIMA; **third season man**, = *third year man*; **third sex**: see SEX *sb.* 1 d; **third slip**: see SLIP *sb.*[3] 14 c; **third staff**, = *third stave*; † **third state**, = *third estate*; **third stave**: see quot.; **third stream** (also hyphenated and with capital initials), a style of music which combines elements of jazz and classical music (see quots.); † **third tongue**: see 2 b above; **third ventricle**, that portion of the central cavity of the brain that lies between the optic thalami; **third wave** [in allusion to Plato's metaphor (*Republic* 472 a) τὸ μέγιστον τῆς τρικυμίας 'the greatest of the three waves'], the last and most forceful of three successive arguments or propositions; **third way, Third Way**, used in a variety of contexts to designate a third possible ideology or solution to a problem (see quots.); **Third World War**, a hypothetical third war involving the majority of the world's nations (cf. *First World War* s.v. FIRST *a.* C. 2; *Second World War* s.v. SECOND *a.* 7 a); **third year man**, a student who has entered upon the third (often the last) year of a course of study; see also YEAR[1] 3 b.

1674 N. FAIRFAX *Bulk & Selv.* 131 In the very fit of a *Third Ague. **1845** in *Appleton's Ann. Cycl. 1885* (1886) XXV. 77/2 A ball knocked outside the range of the first or *third base is foul. **1946** *Chicago Sun* 2 July 25/3 He can start a club that would have a Red Sox star at every position except third base and right field. **1857** *Spirit of Times* 7 Feb. 373/1 Mr. Scott, their *third base man is always at his post. **1936** O. NASH *Primrose Path* 38 Long have I wondered why a locomotive engineer should be so much nicer than an ambassador or a novelist or a banker or a third-baseman or a quartermaster or a lancer. **1978** *Detroit Free Press* 16 Apr. (Detroit Suppl.) 23/3 Phil spent all of 1977 with Tigers and figures to be the club's 3rd baseman of the future. **1840** LYTTON *Money* I. ii. 7 You are very, very, very distantly connected with the deceased—a *third cousin, I think? **1921** G. B. SHAW *Back to Methuselah* II. 65 They are all third cousins of somebody with a title or a park. **1901** *Daily News* 31 Jan. 7/3 The *third-cousinships of German Princes. **1677** in Penn *Trav. Holland* (1694) 9 A Monthly Meeting.. upon the third *third day of the Month. **1858** *Third dimension [see DIMENSION 3 a]. **1923** H. CRANE *Let.* 20 Jan. (1965) 116, I prefer Egyptian sculpture to the Greek, and this book makes me feel that the Greeks had more to express in line and design than they had in the third dimension. **1964** M. MCLUHAN *Understanding Media* (1967) I. i. 28 He acquires the illusion of the third dimension. **1934** H. C. WARREN *Dict. Psychol.* 277/1 *Third-dimensional. **1937** *Univ. Calif. Publ. Mod. Philol.* XX. 188 Only with such a spray [*sc.* lipiodol] can the third-dimensional aspect be brought out, giving vivid pictures of the epiglottis and tongue. **1954** *Ann. Reg. 1953* 365 Third dimensional (3-D) or stereoscopic films viewed through polaroid spectacles were no novelty in London. **1907** H. ZIMMERN tr. *Nietzsche's Beyond Good & Evil* viii. 202 What a torture are books written in German to a reader who has a **third* ear... These were my thoughts when I noticed how.. unintuitively two masters in the art of prose-writing have been confounded. **1948** T. REIK *Listening with Third Ear* II. xv. 144 The psychoanalyst has to learn how one mind speaks to another beyond words and silence. He must learn to listen 'with the third ear'. **1979** F. KERMODE *Genesis of Secrecy* i. 5 The best psychoanalysts are admired.. for their powers of divination, for the acuteness of their third ear. **1604** in Rymer *Fœdera* XVI. 562/1 Knightes and Burgesses..doe present the Bodie of the *Thirde Estate. **1855** F. B. WELLS tr. *Thierry* (*title*), The Formation and Progress of the Tiers État, or Third Estate in France. **1875** STUBBS *Const. Hist.* II. xv. 185 That portion of the third estate which was represented by the knights of the shire. **1810** E. MOOR *Hindu Pantheon* 36 He [*sc.* Siva] has a *third eye in his forehead, pointing up and down. **1921** [see SATORI]. **1936** DYLAN THOMAS *Twenty-Five Poems* 38 No third eye probe into a rainbow's sex That bridged the human halves. **1978** S. GOOCH *Paranormal* v. 202 It is the pineal gland to which the Hindu mystics of 3000 years ago gave the name of 'the third eye'—the 'eye' of clairvoyance and second sight. **1822–34** *Third eyelid [see NICTITATING *ppl. a.*]. **1892** C. S. MINOT *Human Embryol.* (1897) xxviii. 727 The third eyelid is well developed in birds, etc., but is rudimentary in man. **1983** *Sci. Amer.* Apr. 86/2 When a cat falls asleep.. its eyes close, and the nictitating membrane (the 'third eyelid') covers part of the eye under the outer eyelids. **1908** *Daily Chron.* 14 Aug. 8/6 Immediately after the arrival of the *third-floor-back lodger a transformation takes place. **1876** STAINER & BARRETT *Dict. Mus. Terms* 433/2 *Third flute. [Terzflöte]. **1906** GOODCHILD & TWENEY *Technol. & Sci. Dict.* 434/2 There is also a flute in E♭ (often spoken of as the third flute in F, but tuned to E♭), which transposes a minor third higher. **1954** *Grove's Dict. Mus.* (ed. 5) III. 168/1 In the 18th century this [*sc.* the Flute in F] was known as the 'third' flute or 'tierce', since it stood in pitch a minor third above the ordinary flute, whose lowest note at that time was most usually d'. **1687** SETTLE *Refl. Dryden* 63 So old a Phrase,..that it has been in twenty *third-Form School-Boys Exercises. **1869** BLACKMORE *Lorna D.* ii, A *third-former nearly six feet high. [**1933** *Esprit* 1 Sept. 718 Le projet qui suit a été établi par le Comité économique du mouvement de la Troisième Force et adopté par son Congrès National, à Tours, les 28 et 29 juillet.] **1936** E. BURNS tr. *Thorez's France To-day & People's Front* IV. xxv. 228 The 'new economic régime' proposed in the '*Third Force' plan is dressed up in anti-Capitalist garb to make it capable of attracting and winning over the masses. **1951** N. MITFORD *Blessing* II. xi. 256 Mr Clarkley, more interested in French politics than English elegance, began asking a few questions about the Third Force. **1955** G. GREENE *Quiet American* II. iii. 160 There was always a Third Force to be found free from Communism and the taint of colonialism—national democracy he called it. **1956** *Foreign Affairs* XXXV. 60 An armed 'third force'. **1963** *Listener* 31 Jan. 194/2 Some Europeans have a vision of a great power arising to take its place alongside the Soviet Union and the United States—a third force, possibly armed with a separate European deterrent free of American control. **1971** *Irish News* 31 Aug. 1 What was needed was an immediate increase in the strength of the UDR—or if necessary the formation of a 'third force'. **1974** *Times* 27 Feb. 6/2 A doubling of the vote for the third-force candidates would still leave the relative positions of the Conservative and Labour parties unaffected on current evidence from the polls. **1981** *Daily Tel.* 24 Nov. 1/4 The 'third force' which Loyalist hardliners have formed as their own anti-IRA vigilante group made its first significant appearance on the streets during a commemoration service for terrorist victims. **1962** A. LURIE *Love & Friendship* i. 19 You make me sound like a *third-grader. 'I learned simple division, Mummy, and drew a picture of an Eskimo.' *c* **1400** *20 Pol. Poems* xxvi. 208 Men seyen 'good geten vntrewly, The *iij^de eyre browke hit ne may'. **1484** CAXTON *Fables of Auian* xviii, Of the thynge wrongfully and euylle goten, the thyrd heyre shalle neuer be possessour of hit. **1382** WYCLIF *Acts* ii. 15 It is the *thridde our of the day. **1706** tr. *Dupin's Eccl. Hist. 16th C.* II. v. 43 Called Tierce, because it began at the Third Hour of the day. **1849** *Alta California* (San Francisco) 31 Dec. 1 The solicitude manifested by the members of the legislature to ascertain where they are to get their mileage and per diem, is a subject of much jocularity among the **third house*. **1889** FARMER *Dict. Amer.* s.v. *Lobby*, The lobby is also called the 'Third House'. **1950** *Look* 31 Jan. 24/1 In a state where the Third House, the lobbyists,..spend millions every year.., a legislator going on a payroll for 75 bucks a week is looked upon as just a precedent-setting price-cutter, undermining the foundations of a fine profession. **1959** M. SCHLAUCH *Eng. Lang. in Mod. Times* iv. 121 These deviations from strictly completed structure, occurring in formal discourse, are obviously very different from the rambling repetitions, the loose pleonasms and unfinished statements of *third-level speech as exemplified in Juliet's nurse. **1975** *Cork Examiner* 30 May 10/4 About 55,200 students were expected to leave the primary, post-primary and third-level education this year. **1905** *Westm. Gaz.* 13 Feb. 10/1 In the constellation of the Twins, near the *third-magnitude star Mu. **1801** T. TAYLOR tr. *Aristotle's Metaphysics* I. vii. 26 Some make ideas of things relative, of which we do not say there is an essential genus, and some assert that there is a *third man. **1851** F. LILLYWHITE *Guide to Cricketers* 23 If Long-slip is required, take the Third man away. **1871** HOPPE, *Third man*, einer der *fielders* im Cricket. **1881** *Standard* 14 June 3/8 The catch that dismissed him was an easy one at third man. **1891** W. G. GRACE *Cricket* 260 Third man must ask the bowler whether he should stand rather fine or square. **1897** E. T. SACHS in S. Christopherson et al. *Hockey & Lacrosse* 104 In third man I like a powerful player, and a tall. **1916** A. E. TAYLOR in *Proc. Aristotelian Soc.* XVI. 255 What I propose to show is that the appeal to the regress..is certainly not what Aristotle usually has in mind when he speaks of a certain type of argument as the 'third man'. **1920** S. ALEXANDER *Space, Time, & Deity* I. II. iii. 218 This objection..is analogous to one of the kinds of objection taken in ancient Greece to the Forms under the name of the argument of the 'third man'. **1924** W. D. ROSS *Aristotle's Metaphysics* I. 195 Other forms of the 'third man' argument. **1927** J. PALMER *Recoll. Boxing Referee* i. 2, I have acted as third man in the ring on at least three thousand occasions. **1949** G. GREENE in *Amer. Mag.* Mar. 142 (*title*) The 3rd Man. *Ibid.* 149/2 And the third man? Who was he? **1954** *Philos. Rev.* LXIII. 342 Plato could neither convince himself that the Third Man Argument was valid, nor refute it convincingly. **1960** M. GOLESWORTHY *Encycl. Boxing* 171/2 Corri..was the third man in the ring for the middleweight bout. **1964** *Lacrosse* ('Know the Game' Ser.) 34/2 Third Man should mark Third Home closely. **1977** M. GREEN *Children of Sun* (rev. ed.) ix. 434 Kim Philby was finally identified as the 'Third Man', in 1963, when he too fled to Moscow. **1964** *Wall Street Jrnl.* 15 Jan. 1/6 A 10-man Big Board committee..is..studying the expanding role of off-board trading, or the '*third market' as it has come to be known. (The other two are the exchange markets and the over-the-counter market in unlisted securities.) **1629** WADSWORTH *Pilgr.* vii. 72 There is besides another Nunnery of the *third Order of St. Francis. **1753** CHALLONER *Cath. Chr. Instr.* 184 Besides these there are the..Nuns of the third Order of St. Francis. **1908** *Westm. Gaz.* 24 Dec. 6/3 The..version of the Rule of the Third Order found..in the Capistran Convent in the Abruzzi. **1727–41** CHAMBERS *Cycl.*, **Third Point*, or *Tierce-point*, in architecture, the point of section in the vertex of an equilateral triangle. Arches or vaults of the third point..are those consisting of two arches of a circle, meeting in an angle a-top. **1868** G. M. HOPKINS *Jrnls. & Papers* (1959) 186 The nave is very long, the roof, *Third-Pointed, very low... The Third-Pointed altar-screen..and the choir screen..were beautiful in design and proportion. **1953** *Third Position [see PERONISM]. **1971** Third Position [see JUSTICIALISM]. **1946** *Times* 1 July 8/3 The future of broadcasting and television was outlined by Sir William Haley... He said that a *third programme was planned and awaited only the completion of the Brookman's Park high mast. **1946** *Whitaker's Almanack 1947* 349/2 The *Third Programme*, introduced on Sept. 29, 1946, is broadcast on 203·5 metres and 514·6 metres. **1946** *Lancet* 21 Dec. 921/1 Oh yes, I've met *him*, of course—awfully decent fellow and all that, but frightfully Third Programme! **1951** J. B. PRIESTLEY *Festival at Farbridge* II. i. 145 She had fine eyes but a rather ugly despairing sort of mouth, as if she came out of one of those Greek tragedies on the Third Programme. **1960** *Guardian* 22 July 6/3 The lectures—one of the 'Third Programme' ventures that Radio Eireann manages to squeeze in to its narrow broadcasting hours. **1966** H. OGDON in 'H. MacDiarmid' *Company I've Kept* ii. 56 In England, of course, it [*sc.* an Indian *naga*] is esoteric, 'Third Programme'; a thesis could be written on it. **1980** *Daily Tel.* 29 May 14/6 MacNeice's most famous two plays..had an impact on a mass Home Service audience before he and his work disappeared into the Third Programme. **1867** *Commercial & Financial Chron.* 29 June 808 It is throughout a double track road, and a *third rail is laid..for the accommodation of the wide cars of that line. **1890** *Jrnl. Franklin Inst.* CXXIX. 268 In 1879, Dr. Werner Siemens constructed and operated an exhibition railway... A third rail centrally placed between the other two was used as the outgoing conductor. **1901** *Westm. Gaz.* 23 July 4/3 A new electric railway..built on the 'third rail' system, which is believed to represent a great economy as compared with the overhead system. **1905** *Daily Chron.* 2 Feb. 3/4 Avoiding the dangers which had been experienced with the third-rail system. **1916** *Gazette-News* (Asheville, N. Carolina) 7 Jan. 1/2 This recipe is for fourteen and one-half gallons of the 'third-rail' liquor. **1929** J. CALLAHAN *Man's Grim Justice* i. 4 A shot of the third-rail booze that the Silver Alley joints peddled. **1972** *Modern Railways* Sept. 331/3 Invalides is the terminus of the Western Region 750V third-rail service to Versailles Rive Gauche. *Ibid.* 332/3 From October 1, the third-rail electric trains from Paris St Lazare to St Germain will be replaced by 1500V dc RER trains. **1656** H. PHILLIPS *Purch. Patt.* (1676) A iv b, An house of the *third rate. ? **1571** *House of Commons Orig. Jrnls.* 14 Apr. II. 16 The Bill for Seweres the *thirde readinge. **1878** W. STUBBS *Constitutional Hist. England* III. xx. 466 It [*sc.* a bill] is brought up for a third reading, debated again if necessary, read a third time and passed. *a* **1974** R. CROSSMAN *Diaries* (1976) II. 407 Though we had 116 to start with there were only ninety-nine left when the Third Reading vote came. **1908** W. JAMES *Let.* 9 Jan. in R. B. Perry *Tht. & Char. W. James* (1935) II. 485 Surely truth can't inhabit a *third realm between realities and statements or beliefs. **1957** G. RYLE in M. Black *Importance of Lang.* (1962) 167 It is..positively misleading to speak as if there existed a Third Realm whose denizens are Meanings. **1820** BYRON *Let. to Murray* Wks. (1846) 505/1 You will find..in *third rhyme (*terza rima*),..Fanny of Rimini. *a* **1860** ALB. SMITH *Lond. Med. Stud.* (1861) 17 His mentor is ready in the shape of a *third-season man. **1961** *Lancet* 5 Aug. 321/1 We had a total of 236 calls, of which 177 were for *third-stage complications. **1967** J. H. SUDD *Introd. Behaviour Ants* vi. 125 Large third-stage larvae are fed more often than small ones of the same stage. **1667** E. CHAMBERLAYNE *Pres. St. Eng.* I. xix. (1684) 322 Of the *Third State, or Commons of England. **1898** STAINER & BARRETT *Dict. Mus. Terms*, **Third Stave*, a name given to the stave upon which pedal music is written for the organ. **1679** MOXON *Mech. Exerc.* vii. 130 Your Ground-plot, or second or *third Story. **1930** W. B. YEATS *Wild Apples* 16 The third-story skylarks are singing again. **1960** *N.Y. Times* 17 May 44 Gunther Schuller..has been heralding the arrival of what he calls a '*third stream' of music—a music that is neither jazz nor 'classical' but that draws on the techniques of both. **1962** W. BALLIETT *Dinosaurs in Morning* 214 'What about the third stream?' I asked. 'I [*sc.* Gunther Schuller] coined the term as an *adjective*, not a noun... This music is only *beginning*. I conceive of it as the result of two tributaries—one from the stream of classical music and one from the other stream, jazz—that have recently flowed out toward each other. **1977** *Times Lit. Suppl.* 11 Feb. 144/5 The heady days of the 'Third Stream' of the late 1950s, when it seemed possible that string quartets and free-form saxophonists might sit down and make common cause together. **1890** *Cincinnati Commerc. Gaz.* 30 June, There would be no *third termery in it, as he [Pres. Cleveland] had not two consecutive terms. **1866** SWINBURNE *Poems & Ballads* 43 Who swims in sight of the great *third wave That never a swimmer shall cross or climb. **1933** *Mind.* XLII. 175 We come now to the 'third wave' of the discussion. **1965** *Observer* 4 Apr. 31/3 The third wave in the tide of emancipation. **1949** *Third way [see PHENOMENOLOGY b]. **1956** *Sun* (Baltimore) 11 Oct. (B ed.) 16/2 People 'in the know' in Holland have been talking about the influence over the Queen held by a faith-healer... The healer..professes to be uninterested in politics, but she is closely connected with a movement called 'The Third Way', something like the 'Third Force' which swept Europe after the war. The movement is strongly neutralist and pacifist..and is opposed to Holland's commitments to NATO. **1972** *Times* 13 Aug. 16/2 At present, the only possible alternative route for the big tanker lies some 1,200 miles to the south... The idea of a 'third way', as it is often called here, could be attractive to the Japanese. **1947** *Civil & Mil. Gaz.* 27 May 16/3 Sir John Boyd Orr..said in an interview..that a *Third World War would be in the making unless some sort of world food plan was established. **1976** *Glasgow Herald* 26 Nov. 6/4 He is correct when he says that 'dreaming of a world free from conflict will get nowhere', but working for such a world is a different proposition, and unless people are prepared to devote time and energy to that end there can only be a third world war.

II. *sb.*

1. A third part (B. I. 3) *of* anything; any one of three equal parts into which a whole may be divided.

third and teind, one-third of the produce and one-tenth of the remainder (making two-fifths of the whole) paid as rent.

1382 WYCLIF *1 Macc.* x. 29 Nowe Y assoile ȝou..of tributis, and I forȝeue to ȝou the pricis of salt, and forȝeue crownys, and the thriddis [1388 thridde part] of seed. **1479** *Act. Dom. Conc.* (1839) 32/2 þat þe schiref..deliuer þe said vmfra & his tennandis ane evinly thrid þarof. **1611** SHAKS. *Cymb.* v. iv. 19 Men, Who of their broken Debtors take a third, A sixth, a tenth, letting them thriue againe. **1705** ADDISON *Italy* 136 No Sentence can stand that is not confirm'd by Two Thirds of this Council. **1799** J. ROBERTSON *Agric. Perth* 139 In most parts of Strathallan, the land is kept in thirds, (i.e.) one third in tillage for three year, and two thirds always grass. **1852** R. F. BURTON *Falconry in Vall. Indus* vi. 71 One will require at least a third more breaking than another. **1884** J. TAIT in *U.P. Mag.* Apr. 156 The Master was to have the third and teind shorn and set up. **1893** *Law Times* XCIV. 504/1 Whether such a gift..would be divisible into moieties or thirds.

2. *Law.* (Mostly *pl.*) The third of the personal property of a deceased husband allowed to his widow. Also, the third of his real property to which his widow might be legally entitled for her life (*obs.* exc. *Hist.*). Cf. TERCE 2.

1396 in *Scott. Antiq.* XIV. 318 Swa mykyl as pertenys to the modyr of the forsaid Erle..be resone of hir thryd. **1540** *Test. Ebor.* (Surtees) VI. 106 She [the wife] to be fullie content with hir thirds. **1596** BACON *Use of Law* Wks. 1879 I. 585/1 By this course of putting lands into use there were many inconveniences, as..The wife was defrauded of her thirds; the husband of being tenant by courtesy [etc.]. **1609** SKENE *Reg. Maj.* I. 113. **1636** in *Crt. & Times Chas. I* (1848) II. 239 Having renounced her jointure and thirds, she may be so utterly undone. **1664** *Early Rec. Groton, Mass.* (1880) 145 Vnto which alienation the wiues of them both doe giue their consent to the giuing vp their thirds. **1709** S. SEWALL *Diary* 18 Nov., 30*l.* more to Grace, and 12. to her Brother, to come out of their Mothers Thirds now to be divided. **1767** [see DOWER *sb.*[2] 1]. **1864** THOREAU *Maine W.* (1894) 207 There you are never reminded that the wilderness which you are threading is, after all, some villager's familiar wood-lot, some widow's thirds.

†**3.** A third of the proceeds of captures, or of certain fines, forfeitures, etc., of which two thirds were due to the king. *Obs.*

1429 in Rymer *Fœdera* X. 422 Eny Thriddes, or other Gaines of Werre. **1444** in *Coll. Hist. Staff.* (1891) XII. 319 The thrides of the thrides of all maner Prisoners, Prises, and wynynges. **1627** in *Crt. & Times Chas. I* (1848) I. 234 A commission to proceed against recusants for their thirds due to his majesty by law.

4. *Sc. Eccl. Hist.* See quot. 1838.

1573 *Satir. Poems Reform.* xlii. 812 Thir thriddis, I say, but stopping ony, The Kirkis Collectouris suld vptane, Syne vnto the Excheker gane. *c* **1575** *Balfour's Practicks* (1754) 143 The teindis, landis, maillis, fermis, and dewteis of landis assumit in the thriddis of benefices. **1586** in *Dunfermline Regr.* (Bann. Cl.) 449 The haill prelaceis of our reallme ar bund and obleissit to warrand their thridis to ws fra thair awin deidis. **1838** W. BELL *Dict. Law Scot.*, *Thirds.* .. Before the annexation of the year 1587, the King, in order to prevent the entire abstraction of their provisions from the acting clergy,..assumed into his own hands a third of the revenues of all ecclesiastical benefices, which he intrusted to the Commissioners of Plat, who assigned to the ministers respectively sufficient provisions, and reserved the remainder for the King. [See PLAT *sb.*[3] 6.]

†**5.** *pl.* The sum paid by an incoming freshman for the furniture, etc. of his college rooms, usually assessed at two thirds of the amount paid by the preceding tenant. *Obs.*

1687 WILDING in *Collect.* (O.H.S.) I. 255 Reced of my Chum for thirds. **1826** C. WORDSWORTH *Let.* in *Ann. Early Life* I. 38 Tell my father that I expect he will hear something about 'the thirds' which we pay for furniture, &c. **1853** 'C.

BEDE' *Verdant Green* I. iv, Mr. Filcher then explained the system of thirds, by which the furniture.. was to be paid for. **1858** HOGG *Shelley* I. 69 Transferring the.. movables to the successor on payment of thirds, that is, of two-thirds of the price last given.

6. *Mus.* A note three diatonic degrees above or below a given note (both notes being reckoned); also (usually) the interval between this and the given note, equivalent either to two tones (***major third***), or to one tone and one diatonic semitone (***minor third***); also, the harmonic combination of two such notes.

diminished third, an interval equal to two diatonic semitones, being less by a chromatic semitone than a minor third.

1597 MORLEY *Introd. Mus.* 70 Which distances make a Concord or consonant Harmony?.. A third, a Fift, a Sixt, and an eight. **1662** PLAYFORD *Skill Mus.* I. v. (1674) 20 You will tune from Sol to Mi which is a Third. **1752** tr. *Rameau's Treat. Musick* 34 Those Notes, which are a Third above, are deemed Thirds. **1855** BROWNING *Toccata of Galuppi's* vii, Those lesser thirds so plaintive. **1855** —— *Lovers' Quarrel* xviii, We shall have the word In a minor third There is none but the cuckoo knows. **1884** PARRY in Grove *Dict. Mus.* IV. 102 *Third*, one of the most important intervals in modern music... Three forms are met with in modern music—major, minor, and diminished.

7. a. The third of the subdivisions of any standard measure or dimension which is successively subdivided in a constant ratio; the subdivision next below seconds: see PRIME *sb.*[2] 2. †Formerly, in Scotland, a weight of account = the 13,824th part ($1 \div 24^3$) of a grain (*obs.*).

1594 J. DAVIS *Seaman's Secr.* (1643) D j b, Euery degree.. doth containe 60 minutes, and euery minute 60 seconds, and euery second 60 thirds, &c. **1604** in Moryson *Itin.* I. (1617) 282 (Tables of Scottish Weights cf Coins), xx. s. [sterling] = 06 pennyweights, 10 graines, 16 mites, 18 droits, 10 periots, English Weight; 07 deniers, 21 graines, 07 primes, 01 seconds, 09 thirds, 19 fourths, Scottish Weight. **1694** HOLDER *On Time* ii. 32 To divide.. an Hour into 60' (Minutes), a Minute into 60'' (Second Minutes), a Second Minute into 60''' (Thirds). **1840** LARDNER *Geom.* 56 This system of division is sometimes carried even further, a second being divided into sixty equal parts called thirds; but it is more usual to express small angles or arcs in decimal parts of a second.

†**b.** In decimal fractions: see quots. *Obs.*

1660 J. MOORE *Arith.* 10 Some call their Tenth part Primes, the Hundereth parts Seconds, the 1000 parts Thirds. **1766** HUTTON *School Master's Guide* 55 The 1st, 2d, 3d, 4th, &c. places of decimals.. are denominated the places of primes, seconds, thirds, and fourths, &c. respectively.

8. *Comm. pl.* Goods of the third degree of quality.

1768 J. WEDGWOOD *Let.* June (1965) 66 All our thirds shall be saved for you. **1823** J. BADCOCK *Dom. Amusem.* 163 Flour or bread,.. of the usual London manufacture, as *seconds*, *thirds*, and *browns*. **1832** G. R. PORTER *Porcelain & Gl.* 186 Crown glass is sold, according to its quality, under four different denominations—firsts, seconds, thirds, and fourths. **1888** *Times* (weekly ed.) 14 Sept. 19/1 Fruit should be sorted into bests and seconds and in some cases into thirds. **1903** *Daily Chron.* 21 Apr. 2/6 Cork butter.—Firsts, 86s.; seconds, 80s.; thirds, 78s.

9. Elliptical uses of the adj. passing into sb.

a. ***third of kin*** (*Sc.*): one related in the third degree of consanguinity.

1535 STEWART *Cron. Scot.* (Rolls) III. 260 The erle of Arrane, lord of Hammiltoun, Evin thrid and thrid to him [that] weiris the croun. **1569** *Reg. Privy Council Scot.* II. 39 The said Erll and the said umquhile Johnne Suthirland quha wes slane thrid and ferdis of kin [the Earl's father was cousin to John's grandmother]. **1583** *Ibid.* III. 622 Quha and he ar secundes and thriddes of kin. **1892** G. STEWART *Shetland Fireside T.* ix. (ed. 2) 71 Auld Ibbie Bartley, dat wis trids o' kin to my wife's foster midder, an' her oey.

b. Elliptical for third person (in Grammar); third day (of the month); third chapter (of a book of the Bible); third year (of a reign).

1530 PALSGR. Introd. 33 The thyrde syngular [endeth].. most commenly in T. **1536** CROMWELL in Merriman *Life & Lett.* (1902) II. 1 From Eltham thridde of Janua[ry]. **1539** TONSTALL *Serm. Palm Sund.* (1823) 86 It is written in the thirde of Matthewe. **1747** *Gentl. Mag.* May 247/1 On Sunday the 3d of May. **1857** WILLIAMS *Sanskrit Gram.* §330 It is the only conjugation that rejects the nasal in the 3d. plur.

c. A card of the third size; also ***thirds card***: see quots.

1891 *Cent. Dict.* s.v., *Thirds card*, a card 1½ by 3 inches, the size most used for a man's visiting-card. (Eng.). **1892** *Chiswick Press Calendar*, Sizes of Cards.. Extra Thirds 3 × 1⅞. Thirds 3 × 1½ in.

d. ***third of exchange***: the last of a set of three bills of exchange of even tenor and date: see EXCHANGE *sb.* 5.

e. Generally, the word omitted being usually obvious from the context; esp. in familiar use.

a **1635** SIBBES *Confer. Christ & Mary* (1656) 104 He must be a friend or enemy; there is no third in God. **1859** *Habits Gd. Soc.* (new ed.) 44 In the third [class railway-carriage] he will have to sit next to an odoriferous ploughboy. **1864** BOWEN *Logic* iii. 49 The Axiom which is usually called the Law of Excluded Third. **1889** LINSKILL *Golf* iii. (1895) 15 Odd No. 1. 'Stroke a hole'... Sometimes a 'third' is given, which means the application of Odd No. 1 at every third hole. **1891** *Cent. Dict.*, *Third*... In *base-ball*, same as *third base*. **1900** *Monthly Rev.* I. 46 The Russian peasant who travels third is not accustomed to luxuries. **1902** J. E. FLECKER *Let.* in J. Sherwood *No Golden Journey* (1973) iii. 37, I have got a third in Mods! **1903** *Westm. Gaz.* 30 Dec. 11/1 It is of course the Third Preference stock which is directly affected... Some operators are anticipating that the Thirds will get a half per cent. more than for last year. **1908** *Ibid.* 25 Apr. 2/3 Off they went into the stokehole, where the Third put two of them to mind the feed-checks. **1909** J. S. V. BICKFORD *Faults & how to find Them* §1173 Let us now consider a change from a lower gear to a higher (neutral to first, first to second, second to third, etc.). *c* **1912** *Mod.* Mr. A. did badly; he only got a third in Greats. **1924** C. CONNOLLY *Let.* 21 Sept. in *Romantic Friendship* (1975) 13, I have run out of money and have to spend three nights Third in the train. **1942** *Horizon* Nov. 297 For the polished word of an Oxford Third Has left them cheerfully chastened. **1952** *Radio Times* 4 Jan. 7/3 The 'Third' is continuing a series of programmes on Dvořák. **1970** N. FLEMING *Czech Point* viii. 107 Melanie flipped the car deftly into third and tramped on the accelerator. **1972** P. BLACK *Biggest Aspidistra in World* III. iv. 173 The job of the Home was to reflect.. the life of the whole community... The Third's was to broadcast only those things that had artistic value and serious purpose. **1979** 'G. BLACK' *Night Run from Java* i. 9 'I've my Second Mate's papers,' 'And you sail as that?' 'No. A Third.'

10. a. *pl.* Esp. in phr. ***on thirds***. An agreement whereby an owner of sheep has them grazed and cared for by another person who in return receives one third of the profits (see quots.). *Austral.* and *N.Z.*

1824 E. CURR *Account Van Diemen's Land* 78 It is a common practice for persons who have not sufficient land, or who cannot attend personally to their flocks, to give them in charge to another party, who receives one third of the increase for his trouble.. and if the party taking them [*sc.* the flocks] for 'the thirds' be careful and trust-worthy, it is beneficial to both parties. **1852** G. C. MUNDY *Our Antipodes* I. viii. 282 One may buy stock,.. or take stock on the system of 'thirds', in which the working partner gets one third of the wool and of the increase while the proprietary partner.. follows some other profession. **1878** E. JOLLIE *Reminisc.* 18 [Watts].. agreed to take my sheep on 'thirds' for three years. On 'thirds' meant that he was to have one third of the wool each year and I had to have two thirds. **1930** L. G. D. ACLAND *Early Canterbury Runs* 1st Ser. viii. 206 For five years part of the run and sheep were let on thirds to a man named Thomas.

b. ***third(s)-and-fourth(s)***: in cotton and corn farming, a system whereby the tenant contributes towards the cost of seed and fertilizer and the landowner receives a proportion of the crops (see quots. 1964, 1967, 1976). *U.S.*

1940 W. FAULKNER *Hamlet* I. i. 8 'What rent were you aiming to pay?' 'What do you rent for?' 'Third and fourths,' Varner said. **1964** *Amer. Folk Music Occasional* I. 62 He could take advantage of the new system of farming rented land. 'You call that third-and-fourths, now. I do my own furnishing and then the man that owned the land would get [e]very third bale of cotton, every fourth load of corn.' **1967** G. W. WALTON in *Publ. Amer. Dial. Soc.* XLVII. 29 *Thirds and fourths*,.. a method of tenant farming whereby the following practices are common: the landowner furnishes the land and a house for the tenant; the tenant furnishes his own plow animals and tools and does all the work; the tenant then pays for one-fourth of the seed and fertilizer for growing the cotton and receives one-fourth of the cotton grown; the tenant pays for one-third of the seed and fertilizer for growing corn and receives one-third of the corn. **1976** C. S. BROWN *Gloss. Faulkner's South* 198 *Third and fourth*,.... One who pays at this rate is a 'share tenant'... He supplies his own equipment... Then he pays one third of the seed and fertilizer for cotton, and pays one fourth of his crop as rent.

third, *v.* [f. prec.]

1. *trans.* To divide (anything) into three equal parts; to reduce to one third of the number or bulk.

1455 *Sc. Acts Jas. II* (1814) II. 44/2 þ^t^ na man gang away w^t^ na maner of gudis quhill it be thriddyt, and partyt befor þe chiftane. **1612** *Two Noble K.* I. ii, What man Thirds his owne worth? **1747** FRANKLIN *Lett.* Wks. 1887 II. 97 That celerity doubled, tripled, &c., or halved, thirded, &c. **1874** FURNIVALL in *10th Rep. Committee E.E.T.S.* 16 Such a course would have halved or thirded the number of our subscribers.

†**b.** To buy or sell (college furniture, etc.) at two thirds of its last selling price: see THIRD *sb.* 5. *Obs.*

1811 [R. FENTON] *Tour Genealogy* 157 The same.. tale.. is always worse told by him that tells it last; till like college furniture, too often thirded, it becomes too threadbare for credit.

2. To speak in favour of (a motion, proposition, etc.) as third speaker; to support the seconder.

1656 *Burton's Diary* (1828) I. 90 It has been firsted, seconded, and thirded. **1707** LUTTRELL *Brief Rel.* (1857) VI. 233 A motion of the lord Wharton, seconded and thirded by the lords Somers and Hallifax. **1893** E. H. BAKER in *King's Business* (New Haven, Conn.) 174 That resolution.. was seconded by a theological professor... It was thirded by a pastor in the Episcopal Church.

†**b.** To support or back up in the third place: cf. SECOND *v.* 2. *Obs.*

1602 CAREW *Cornwall* 84 b, The next Captains should forthwith put themselves with their companies into their assigned sea coast townes, whom the adjoyning land-forces were appoynted to second and third.

†**3.** To hoe (turnips), clean (wheat), etc., the third time. *Obs.*

1683 J. ERSKINE *Jrnl.* 20 Sept. (1893) 17, I was winding and thirding some corn. **18..** *Moor's Suffolk MS.* (Halliw.), 'Ar them there tahnups done woth?' 'No, we are thirding 'em.'

'thirdborough, 'thridborrow. *Obs.* exc. *Hist.* Also 5–6 (7–8) thrid-, 6 thred-, thur-, thar-, 6–7 therd-; 5 -borro, 6 -bourogh(e, -borow(e, 6–7 -barow(e, -barrow, 7 -borrow, -bearer. [In 15th c. *thridborro*, 16th c. *thridborowe*, later *third-borow*; and with both elements variously corrupted. Early evidence of origin scanty; but, as pointed out by Professor Skeat, prob. a ME. corruption of *fridborgh*:—OE. *friðborȝ* peace-pledge, peace-surety: see FRITHBORH, FRANK-PLEDGE. The corruption may have been due to Norman scribes, but not necessarily so: cf. TH (6). See Note below, and cf. BORROWHEAD, BORSHOLDER, HEADBOROUGH.]

Formerly, The head man of a frithborh or frank-pledge; hence, the conservator of peace or peace-officer of a tithing, the petty constable of a township or manor.

? *c* **1475** *Hunt. Hare* 199 Jac of Bonam he was constabull. .. Hobb Andrw he was thridborro; He bad hom, 'Pesse! God gyff hom sorro! For I may arrest yow best'. **1512** *Act 4 Hen. VIII*, c. 19 §6 Preceptes to the Constables Hedbouroghes Thirdbouroghes Subconstables Tythingmen Borsalders. **1523** FITZHERB. *Surv.* 20 b, The othe of all maner of Offycers generally... I shall true constable be, trewe thridborowe, trewe reue, trewe frankelege [etc.].. and truely and duely do and kepe all thynges that belongeth to myne offyce to do. **1536** *Act 28 Hen. VIII*, c. 10 §6 Euery.. Hedborowe, Thredborough, Borsolder, and euery other Lay Officer. **1547** in J. H. Glover *Kingsthorpiana* (1883) 84 If any customery tenant or suter.. do rebuke, revyle, or dysobey the constables, thurbarowes, ale-tasters, haywarde, or other officers sworne in doyinge their offyce. **1581** LAMBARDE *Eiren.* I. iii. (1588) 15 Where each third Borow only hath a Constable, there the officers of the other two Borowes, be called Third-borowes. **1588** SHAKS. *L.L.L.* I. i. 185, I my selfe reprehend his owne person, for I am his graces Tharborough. **1596** —— *Tam. Shr.* Induct. i. 12 *Host.* I know my remedie, I must go fetch the Head-borough. *Beg.* Third, or fourth, or fift Borough, Ile answere him by Law. **1607** COWELL *Interpr.*, *Thridborow*, is vsed for a constable.. which seemeth to be corruptly vsed for the Saxon *freoborh* i. *ingenuus fideiussor.* **1610** NORDEN *Spec. Brit.*, *Cornw.* (1728) 30 The hundreds haue Constables, Tythinges haue Therd-barows, in some places Hedborows, in some Borowsheds, and in the weste partes a tythingman. *a* **1625** SIR H. FINCH *Law* (1636) 336 The conseruator of peace.. is called.. In a Tything, a petie Constable, Borsholder, Headborough, Thirdborough, Boroughhead, Tything-man, or Chiefe pledge. **1634–5** *Althorp MS.* in Simpkinson *Washingtons* (1860) App. p. lxix, March 5. To the third bearers of Brington for cryeing and prayseing a baye straye nagg taken up. **1645** *MS. Rec. Court Leet Castle Donington, Leicester.* 25 Apr., They present R. R., J. B., R. W. and T. T. to serve the kinge and the lord of this mannor in the office of Thirdborrow for one whole year which they refused. **1658** PHILLIPS, *Thridborough* or *Thirdborough*, a word used in some old Acts, for a Headborough or Constable. **1755** JOHNSON, *Thirdborough*,.. an under-constable. **1831** CARLYLE *Sart. Res.* III. i, Some prospect of.. an honourable Mastership in Cordwainery, and perhaps the post of Thirdborough in his Hundred.

[*Note.* The *friðborh* or *frithborgh* was orig. the 'association of ten men in common responsibility' to prevent crime and breach of the peace. In ME. legal use the word was worn down to *fridborgh*, *friborg*, and *freoborg*, and, the first element being associated with *freo* 'free', was rendered in Anglo-Fr. *frank plege*, Anglo-L. *francum plegium.* The head man of the frithborh was in the 12th c. called *friðborgheved* or *frithborges heved*, 'head of the frithborh' (*Laws of Edw. Conf.* 20 (or 19), §3), and was later known as *bor(r)owhead*, *head-bor(ou)gh*, *bor(h)s-holder*, and *burrow-elder* (:—**borh-ealdor*), also in Anglo-L. *plegius capitalis* 'head or chief pledge'. In Fleta I. xlvii. §10, it is said, 'frithborgh [*printed* frich-] est laudabilis homo astrarius testimonii... per quem omnes iuxta ipsum commorantes firmiori pace sustententur sub stabilitate fideiussionis eius vel alterius per denarium numerum, unde quilibet est quasi plegius alterius'. In this we see the transition of *frithborh* from the association to its individual members, and esp. to the headborough. In certain cases the latter acted with two of his fellows, 'duos de melioribus suorum frithborgorum' (*Laws of Edw.* 20 (or 19), §3), and this association of three may have contributed to the change of name from *fridborgh* to *thridborgh* and *thirdborough.* The probable connexion of *thridborow* with *freoborh* was suggested by Cowell: see quot. 1607.]

third class, third-class, *phr.* (*sb.* and *a.*)

1. *sb. phr.* The class next below the second; esp. of railway carriages; also in an examination list; hence, a place in the third class in an examination.

1844 *Punch* VII. 258/2 *Third class.* Make up your mind for unmitigated hail, rain, sleet, snow and lightning... Do not expect the luxury of a seat. **1845** *Bradshaw's Railway Guide* Aug. 5 Fares between London and Brighton.. by.. third class, 5s. *Mod.* Mr. A. got a third class in History.

2. *attrib.* or *adj.* Of or belonging to the class next below the second.

1839 *Bradshaw's Railway Time Table* 19 Oct., Children under seven years of age.. for Second Class Carriages [charged] Third Class price. **1840** *Bradshaw's Railway Comp.*, Third class passengers are conveyed by the 6 a.m. and 8 p.m. Down Trains. **1852** R. S. SURTEES *Sponge's Sp. Tour* (1893) 76 The introduction of railways, whose worst third-class accommodation is far better than the old coaches' best. **1859** *All Year Round* No. 30. 78 The third-class carriages, as a rule, were the mere seatless and unsheltered cattle-trucks that still linger on the road from London to Greenwich. **1871** M. COLLINS *Marq. & Merch.* III. iv. 127 The train was third class. **1886** C. E. PASCOE *London of To-day* xix. (ed. 3) 186 The economical traveller will find many a worse resting-place than its third-class carriages provide. **1891** *Cent. Dict.*, *Third-class matter*, in the postal system of the United States, printed matter other than newspapers or periodicals, sent through the mails by the publishers.

3. quasi-*adv*. By a third-class conveyance.
1864 TREVELYAN *Compet. Wallah* (1866) 24 Natives almost invariably travel third-class.

third degree, third-degree, *phr.* (*sb.* and *a.*)
A. *sb. phr.* **1.** *gen.* The third step or stage in succession, intensity, or amount.
1578 [see DEGREE *sb.* 6 c.]. **1601** SHAKES. *Twel. N.* I. v. 145 For he s in the third degree of drinke: hee's drown'd: go looke after him. **1716** POPE tr. *Homer's Iliad* II. v. 48 He got *Orsilochus, Diöcleus* He, And these descended in the third Degree. **1966** TACHERON & UDALL *Job of Congressman* ix. 250 House Rule XIX prohibits amendments in the third degree. An amendment to an amendment is permitted, but not an amendment to an amendment to an amendment.
2. *Freemasonry.* The highest grade in freemasonry, that of master-mason. Cf. DEGREE *sb.* 7 b.
1772 W. PRESTON *Illustrations of Masonry* 205 (*heading*) A charge, to be delivered at Initiation in the Third Degree. **1865** J. HOW *Freemason's Man.* (ed. 2) 138 The Third Degree, or the Master Mason. *Ibid.*, The Fellow-Craft who is duly qualified by time, on presenting himself as candidate for the third Degree, has to submit himself to an examination of his qualifications as a Craftsman. **1901** *Scotsman* 5 Apr. 6/4 In the third degree in [Free] Masonry a skull and cross-bones are employed.
3. *U.S. Law.* In defining the extent of criminality, the least serious grade of a particular crime. Cf. DEGREE *sb.* 6 d.
1865 *Penal Code State of New York* xv. i. 192 Maliciously burning in the day time a building, the burning of which in the night time would be arson in the second degree, is arson in the third degree. *Ibid.* ii. 195 Every person who breaks into any dwelling house in the night time, with intent to commit a crime, but under such circumstances as do not constitute the offense of burglary in the first degree, is guilty of burglary in the third degree. **1949** BRANHAM & KUTASH *Encycl. Criminology* 20/2 Assault in the third degree.
4. In many classifications of burns, the deepest variety, resulting in the death of all layers of skin.
Today a twofold classification tends to be used (see quot. 1961).
[**1832** G. DUPUYTREN *Leçons Orales* I. xvi. 209 Nous avons divisé les brûlures en six degrés ainsi caractérisés:..3° destruction d'une partie de l'épaisseur du corps papillaire.] **1866** C. H. FAGGE tr. *Hebra's On Diseases of Skin* I. xiii. 317 For all practical purposes, the three grades which I have described are sufficient... We may include under burns of the third degree those forms which Dupuytren and others have spoken of as burns of the fourth, fifth and sixth degrees. **1930** J. J. MORTON in E. A. Graham *Surgical Diagnosis* II. 136 Injuries of the first and second degree will leave practically no scarring but serious deformities may result from the third degree burns. **1961** *Brit. Med. Dict.* 231/2 Classification of burns. Dupuytren's classificaton: 1st degree..3rd degree..6th degree... Modern classification: superficial burn or partial thickness skin destruction; deep burn or whole thickness skin destruction.
5. An interrogation of a prisoner by the police involving the infliction of mental or physical suffering in order to bring about a confession or to secure information. orig. *U.S.*
[**1880** *Harvard Lampoon* 6 Feb. 166/1 He met the large and celebrated brother of one of his houries. He stopped to greet him, and was surprised at receiving a clip over the head from the brother's cane. This was followed by a personal chastisement in the third degree.] **1900** *Everybody's Mag.* Nov. 406 From time to time a prisoner..claims to have had the Third Degree administered to him. **1930** G. B. SHAW *Apple Cart* I. 15 *Boanerges.* What do you mean? put me through it? Is this a police office? *Pliny.* The third degree is not unknown in this palace, my boy. **1976** T. SHARPE *Wilt* xiii. 136 'You don't think they're giving him third degree or anything of that sort?' 'My dear fellow, third degree? You've been watching too many old movies on the TV. The police don't use strong-arm methods in this country.'
B. *attrib.* or *adj.* Of or belonging to the third step or stage (in the senses above).
1926 *Scribner's Mag.* Aug. 193/1 Everybody at Police Headquarters agreed that it was ominously dull that night. There was scarcely a third-degree assault to disturb the city. **1930** J. J. MORTON in E. A. Graham *Surgical Diagnosis* II. 136 Serious deformities may result from the third degree burns. **1972** MILLER & KEANE *Encycl. & Dict. Med. & Nursing* 155/1 Third-degree burns damage the epidermis, dermis and subcutaneous tissue. **1976** 'E. MCBAIN' *Guns* (1977) iv. 86 They'd charged Colley with..second-degree assault... Even better than that, Colley's lawyer thought, would be for him to plead guilty to the lesser charge of *third*-degree assault.
Hence **third-degree** *v. trans.*, to subject to an intensive or violent interrogation; **third-degreeing** *vbl. sb.*
1928 W. GILLETTE *Astounding Crime Torrington Rd.* v. 260 They third-degreed Jimmy Dreek good and plenty. *Ibid.* 269 The fools in Boston had third-degreed an innocent man to his death. **1944** 'G. ORWELL' in *Horizon* Oct. 237 The third-degreeing of the gangster. **1979** C. WATSON *Blue Murder* xiii. 111 He third-degreed me about Birdie... The man just goes on and on.

† **'thirdel.** *Obs.* Forms: 3 thriddedel, 4 **þ**ridde deel, 5 thryddele, 6 thirdle, thirdel. [ME. *thriddedel*:—OE. *þridda dǣl* third part: see DEAL *sb.*[1] Cf. Ger. *drittel.*] A third part (*of* anything); = next.
1297 R. GLOUC. (Rolls) 283 þe þriddedel mi kinedom ich ȝiue þe to be mi fere. **1387** TREVISA *Higden* (Rolls) III. 169 þe quene hadde i-sent hire ȝong sone wiþ þe þridde deel [*MS. β.* thriddel, CAXTON thryddele] of heere oost aȝenst Cirus. **1542** RECORDE *Gr. Artes* K vj b, There bee tertians (that is to say thirdles) of pypes, of hogges heddes, and of barels. *Ibid.* L iij, Take awaye 2 thyrdeles frome any summe, and you muste needes graunt, that that whyche remayneth, is 1 thyrdele of the summe laste before.

† **'thirdendeal.** *Obs.* Forms: 1 **þriddan dǣl**; 4 **þridden-**, 4–5 thridden-, 5 threden-, thredden-, thryden-, thyrdyn-, 6 thirdin-, thyrden-, (thirding-, 7 thurron-), 6–8 thirden-; 4–5 -del, 5–7 -dele, 6 -deale, deall, 7 -dell, 7–8 -deal; 4–6 (9 *dial.*) -dale. [OE. (*þone*) *þriddan dǣl*, accus. case of (*se*) *þridda dǣl* the third part (see THIRDEL, DEAL *sb.*[1], DALE[2]). Cf. HALFENDEAL, FARTHINGDEAL.]
1. The third part of anything; a third.
c **1000** *Sax. Leechd.* I. 98 Seoþe on wætere to þriddan dæle. *Ibid.* II. 120 Bewyl oþ þriddan dæl. **13..** *Guy Warw.* (A.) 7306 + st. 65 þriddendel his lond haue he schold. **14..** *E.E. Misc.* (Warton Cl.) 72 With the thyrdyndele of gume, and twyse so mych of water. *a* **1500** in Arnolde *Chron.* (1811) 147 Euery Sonday a soule out of purgatory and the thredden dele of al synnes releced. **1558** WARDE tr. *Alexis' Secr.* I. I. (1580) 37 b, Drinke thereof two thirdendales of a glassefull. **1581** J. BELL *Haddon's Answ. Osor.* 459 b, A thyrdendeale of the Crowne of Thornes is shewed at Paris in the Holy Chappell there.
2. A third of a tun; = TERTIAN B. 2.
1423 *Rolls of Parlt.* IV. 256/1 Thredendels and hoggeshedes so aftur lesse mesure. **14..** *MS. Cantab. Ff.* 5. 48, lf. 55 *b* (Hartshorne *Anc. Metr. T.* (1829) 54), Hit holdis a gode thrydendele Ful of wyne euery mele.
3. (See quots.)
1571 in *Shaks. Jahrbuch* (1896) 142 The hooped pot commonly called a thirdindeale and a half thirdindeale. **1590** [TARLTON] *News Purgat.* (1844) 114 When Tapsters.. Fill thirdingdeall pots till the drinke run ouer. **1620** MELTON *Astrolog.* 32 Many of them dare not goe to bed without a Thurrondell Pot of six shillings Beere. **1678** PHILLIPS (ed. 4), *Thirdendeal*, a Liquid Measure used in Salisbury containing three Pints. **1721** in BAILEY.

'thirder. *rare*$^{-1}$. [f. THIRD *sb.* + -ER[1].] In *thirder and teinder*, one who pays by way of rent the 'third and teind' (see THIRD B. II. 1).
1884 J. TAIT in *U.P. Mag.* Apr. 156/2 Another case resembles the arrangement of thirders and teinders described by Arthur Young as existing in some parts of France.

third hand, third-hand. [THIRD B. 1 and HAND *sb.* 10 c, after SECOND-HAND.]
1. In advb. phrase *at* (†*the*) ***third hand***: from a second middleman or intermediary; at the second remove from the original source.
1553 *Reg. Privy Council Scot.* I. 141 Na maner of gudis can be had nor coft bot at the thrid hand. *a* **1635** SIBBES *Confer. Christ & Mary* (1656) 67 We have it at the third hand. **1895** in *Bookman* Oct. 23/1 The illustrations..were reproduced from inferior German copies at third-hand.
2. *attrib.* or as *adj.* Obtained, copied, or imitated from a second-hand source; further away from the original source, and so more stale, less authoritative, etc., than the second-hand.
1599 MARSTON *Sco. Villanie* I. iv, Laboring with third-hand iests, and Apish skips. **1862** LATHAM *Channel Isl.* III. xiv. (ed. 2) 348 The second-hand and third-hand text-books. **1866** *Macm. Mag.* Apr. 521 Resting on mere second-hand, nay, often third-hand information.
b. ***third-hand dealer***, one who deals in third-hand articles.
1864 TREVELYAN *Compet. Wallah* (1866) 104 Cheated in the purchase of his first buggy by a third-hand dealer in Calcutta.

† **'thirding,** *sb. Obs. rare*$^{-0}$. [f. THIRD *sb.* + -ING[3].] = RIDING *sb.*: cf. TRITHING.
1847–78 HALLIWELL, *Thirdings*, the Ridings. This word is given by Urry, in his MS. Additions to Ray.

'thirding, *vbl. sb.* [f. THIRD *v.* + -ING[1].] (See quots.)
1670 BLOUNT *Law Dict.*, *Thirdings*, the third part of the Corn or Grain growing on the Ground at the Tenants death, due to the Lord for a Heriot within a certain Mannor,.. belonging to the Chappel of Turfat in Com. Heref. [So **1706** in PHILLIPS; **1721** in BAILEY; and in mod. dicts.] **1847–78** HALLIWELL, *Thirding...* (2) A custom practised at the universities, where two thirds of the original price is allowed by the upholsterers to the students for household goods returned to them within the year.

thirdling ('θɜːdlɪŋ). *nonce-wd.* [f. THIRD *a.* + -LING.] Something that comes third.
1884 BROWNING *Ferishtah* Prol. 18 First, food—then, piquancy—and last of all Follows the thirdling.

thirdly ('θɜːdlɪ), *adv.* [f. THIRD *a.* + -LY[2].] In the third place.
1509 HAWES *Past. Pleas.* viii. (Percy Soc.) 30 Thyrdly, they had suche a fantasy In this hyghe arte to be intelligible. **1662** STILLINGFL. *Orig. Sacr.* I. ii. §12. **1877** A. MACEWEN *Serm.* xvii. 217 Thirdly, we need a firm conviction of the sufficiency of Divine grace.

thirdness. *Philos.* [f. THIRD *a.* + -NESS.] The quality or state of belonging to a third category or of being a third element, *spec.* in the philosophy of C. S. Peirce (1839–1914), that which connects, mediates between, etc., the ontological categories that he designated as firstness and secondness (cf. SECONDNESS).
c **1875** C. S. PEIRCE *Coll. Papers* (1931) I. §337. 170 (*heading*) Examples of thirdness. *Ibid.* 171 Continuity represents Thirdness almost to perfection. **1914** W. DE MORGAN *When Ghost meets Ghost* I. xx. 219 The first person plural pronoun, used as a dual by a lady to a gentleman, sometimes makes hay of the thirdness of their respective persons singular. **1934** *Mind* XLIII. 490 Thirdness includes the meaning of signs, the conception of general laws, 'infinity, continuity, diffusion, growth, and intelligence'... It is the category that is concerned with connecting, and it is involved in all reflective thought. **1978** *Sci. Amer.* July 19/3 Thirdness concerns two things 'mediated' by a third, for example an apple falling from a tree. The tree and the apple are linked by the relation 'falling from'.

'third ˌparty.
1. A party or person besides the two primarily concerned, as in a law case or the like. Also *attrib.*
1818 SCOTT *Rob Roy* xiii, Speak as you would to an unconcerned third party. **1853** MAURICE *Proph. & Kings* xx. 343 It appears to be a narrative written by a third party. **1883** *Wharton's Law Lex.* s.v., 'A Third party' may be introduced into an action by a defendant claiming an indemnity, or any other remedy over against him, under Jud. Act, 1873, s. 24. sub. 3, and Order XVI., Rules 17, 19. **1883** *Law Times* 20 Oct. 407/2 The rules relating to third-party procedure..are a great improvement upon the former rules. **1905** *Daily Chron.* 12 Sept. 3/2 The largest third-party vote, with one exception, since the Civil War.
2. *spec.* **a.** Used *attrib.* to designate insurance arranged against injury to persons other than the insured.
1901 C. H. GREEN in A. W. Tarn *Insurance Guide & Handbk.* (ed. 3) 254 Indemnity or Third Party Insurance, dealing with the Common Law Liability of the individual with regard to the general public and their property. **1910** E. M. FORSTER *Howards End* x. 84 As we've insured against third-party risks, it won't so much matter. **1931** *Daily Express* 5 Sept. 9/1 Each man was fined £5 with an additional £2 for Dougson for driving without a third party insurance. **1978** *Dumfries Courier* 13 Oct. 15/4 Clark was fined £5 and licence endorsed in two other charges—using the car without a third party risks insurance and using it while the handbrake was defective.
b. ***third party adoption***, an adoption of a child arranged by a third party who is a private individual rather than an adoption agency.
1965 HALL & HOWES *Church in Social Work* iii. 57 That social worker's bane, the 'third party' adoption.

'third-ˌrate, *a.* and *sb.* [See RATE *sb.*[1] 9, 9 b.]
A. *adj.*
† **1.** Of the third 'rate' (esp. of ships). *Obs.*
1649 CROMWELL *Let.* 14 Nov. in *Carlyle*, The Garland, one of your third-rate ships, coming happily into Waterford Bay. **1666** PEPYS *Diary* 9 Mar., Mr. Castle's new third-rate ship, which is to be called the Defyance. **1693** *Lond. Gaz.* No. 2857/3 This day was Launched a New Third Rate Ship of 80 Guns, called the *Norfolk*.
2. Of the third class in point of quality; usually *depreciative*, below 'second-rate'; of decidedly poor or inferior quality. Also *absol.*
1814 *Theatrical Inquisitor* IV. 357 Allusions, which have long constituted the commonplaces of poetry among third-rate makers of verse. **1816** JANE AUSTEN *Emma* II. i. 2 In danger of falling in with the second rate and third rate of Highbury. **1838** THIRLWALL *Greece* V. xliv. 327 An actor of third-rate parts. **1850** GROTE *Greece* II. lxi. VII. 491 A town of second-rate or third-rate magnitude. **1855** MACAULAY *Hist. Eng.* xix. IV. 354 The poor thoughts and poor words of a thirdrate pamphleteer.
B. *sb. Naut.* A war-vessel of the third rate.
1666 PEPYS *Diary* 4 July, Ten great ships..none to be under third-rates. **1695** *Lond. Gaz.* No. 3061/1 A Third Rate of 62 Guns. **1790** BEATSON *Nav. & Mil. Mem.* I. 65 The fleet.., consisting of but one third rate, five fourth rates, and one sixth rate.
Hence **'third-'rateling, 'third-ˌrater,** a third-rate person or thing.
1816 SOUTHEY *Ess.* I. 245 The second and third-ratelings compose works of perishable stuff. **1820** *Blackw. Mag.* VIII. 89 Where is there a Whig in England..that, as a literary man, is fairly out of the class of third raters?

Third Reich (θɜːd raɪç, raɪk). [Partial tr. of (med.) G. *drittes Reich*: see REICH.] The German state under the rule of Hitler and the Nazi party, 1933–45; the regime of Hitler.
Of the sequence *First, Second* (etc.) *Reich*, only *Third Reich* forms part of recognized English historical terminology.
[**1923** A. MOELLER VAN DEN BRUCK (*title*) Das dritte Reich.] **1930** *Times* 26 Sept. 12/2 Asked to give some idea of the 'Third Reich', Herr Hitler said the old Germany was a State of great honour and of glorious events, but the conception of 'the people' was not the central pillar of its structure. The second State had placed democracy and pacificism in the centre. They hoped for the Third Reich, which would have as its keystone the conception of the people and the national idea. **1933** L. STOWE *Nazi Germany means War* i. 9 On October 18th, four days after he had led the Third Reich out of the League of Nations..Adolf Hitler made the following peace declaration before eight hundred of his party leaders in Berlin. **1946** J. FLANNER *Janet Flanner's World* (1980) I. 105 It was odd to..hear young Dr. Horn..state that it might well have been the international London Naval Conference of 1935 that drove Hitler's hypersensitive Third Reich into rearmament. **1966** *Listener* 3 Nov. 659/2 In the early years of the Third Reich, certain ideological ambiguities in Mann's attitude aroused Lukacs's apprehension. **1981** S. DUNMORE *Ace* 6 The good old days when the flyers of the Third Reich could do no wrong.

thirdsman ('θɜːdzmən). A third person or party; *esp.* one called in as an intermediary, mediator, or arbiter.
1818 SCOTT *Hrt. Midl.* xxiv, There was risk of Andro Ferrara coming in thirdsman. *Ibid.* xlviii, If I come in thirdsman among you at the kirk-sessions, you will be all in

a tamn'd pad posture indeed. **1887** SAINTSBURY *Hist. Elizab. Lit.* x. (1890) 386 Herrick and Carew.. with Crashaw as a great thirdsman, called themselves 'sons' of Ben Jonson.

†'**thirdsome**, *a. Obs. rare.* In 5 **thryd-, þridde-, thyrd(e)-.** [f. THIRD *a.* + -SOME.] Being one of three; accompanied by two others.

c **1425** *Eng. Conq. Irel.* 14 Othere thwey cantredes he yaf heruy of Mountmorthy,.. a knyght þat com in that same flote, hym þriddesum [*v.r.* thyrdesum] of knyghtes. *Ibid.* 32 Heruy of Mountmorthy, that to ham was ycome, hym thrydsome [*v.r.* thyrdsome] of knyghtes.

Third World, third world, *sb.* (and *a.*) [tr. Fr. *tiers monde.*] The countries of the world, esp. those of Africa and Asia, which are aligned with neither the Communist nor the non-Communist bloc; hence, the underdeveloped or poorer countries of the world, usu. those of Africa, Asia, and Latin America. Cf. *Second World* s.v. SECOND *a.* 7a. Also *attrib.* or as *adj.*, and in extended use.

[**1956** G. BALANDIER *Tiers Monde* 369 La conférence tenue à Bandoeng en avril 1955, par les délégués de vingt-neuf nations asiatiques et africaines.. manifeste l'accès, au premier plan de la scène politique internationale, de ces peuples qui constituent un 'Tiers Monde' entre les deux 'blocs', selon l'expression d'A. Sauvy.] **1963** *Economist* 26 Oct. 353/1 Relations between Europe and the third world nowadays. **1964** *Ibid.* 18 Jan. 178/2 The ingredients common to most 'third world' countries (poverty, ignorance, love-hate of the former colonial powers). **1967** A. A. MAZRUI in *Jrnl. of Politics* XXIX. 792 The concept of the Third World in the sense of the economically underprivileged sector of mankind must include Latin America, as well as the Asian-African countries. But in this paper we use the word, 'the Third World' in a more restrictive sense, meaning the world of the new states. **1969** *Wall St. Jrnl.* 15 May 14/2 By 'Third world' students Jerry means Orientals, Latins and American Indians. **1970** D. CAUTE *Fanon* v. 65 The 'Third World'.. means 'positive neutralism' and 'non-alignment' between the Western and Soviet camps. **1974** *Globe & Mail* (Toronto) 29 Jan. 13/1 The First World Development was Capitalist... The Second World was Communism, in particular Russian Communism. The Third World takes in all the other countries that are not developed. Everyone counts China in the Third World... It includes the whole of Africa, Asia, Latin America. It has to do with income and low standard of living and so this takes in such countries as Greece, Yugoslavia, and some include Spain and Portugal. **1978** *Poland* May 1/2 You will find statements and articles written by Poles, people from other socialist and from capitalist countries as well as from the countries of the Third World. **1978** *Listener* 14 Sept. 322/1 The long ride into town underlines just how Third World, poor and underdeveloped Vietnam still is. **1980** *Times* 6 May 12/8 Andalusia, often described as Spain's 'third world', with its high crime rate and unemployment.

Hence **Third 'Worlder**, an inhabitant of the Third World; **Third 'Worldism**, an ideology or policy of support for the Third World.

1970 *New Scientist* 29 Oct. 227/2 Skills which the average 16-year-old western youth would have little difficulty in mastering apparently pose almost insoluble problems for the average Third Worlder. **1970** *New Yorker* 26 Dec. 46 The revolutionary Third Worldism of large sections of Sweden's politically active youth and intellectuals. **1975** *New Left Rev.* Nov.–Dec. 13 It comes down to little more than a more sophisticated justification of romantic nationalism, now transformed in 'Third Worldism'. **1978** G. VIDAL *Kalki* v. 119 We have a superb military machine second to none, not to mention a standard of living that is the envy of every commie and the despair of every Third Worlder. **1980** *Encounter* Nov. 40/1 Third-Worldism will not continue to be a one-sided problem for the West.. but will also.. be embarrassing.. the East.

†'**thirkin**, *a. Obs.* [f. THIR + KIN *sb.*[1] 6b. Cf. THAKIN: which is the antithetic word.] These kind of; of this kind.

13.. *Cursor M.* 28576 Man þat o þirkin sinn es scriuen, on seuen maners ar þai for-giuen.

thirl (θɜːl), *sb.*[1] Now *dial.* Forms: 1 **þyrel, -il, þyrl,** 3 **þirl, þurl,** 4 **therl,** 9 **thurl,** 4– **thirl.** See also THRILL *sb.*[1] [OE. *þýrel*, for older **þyrhil*, **þurhil*, f. *þurh* THOROUGH + -EL[1]. Cf. OHG. *dur(i)hhil*, MHG. *dürchel, dürkel*, OE. *þýrel* adjs., pierced, perforated.]

1. A hole, bore, perforation; an aperture.

a **900** tr. *Bæda's Hist.* IV. iii. (1890) 272 þonne is on þæm medmicel þyrel ȝeworht. *c* **950** *Lindisf. Gosp.* Matt. xix. 24 Ðerh ðyril nedles. *c* **1000** ÆLFRIC *Voc.* in Wr.-Wülcker 113/29 *Orificium*, ælces kynnes muð *vel* ðyrl. *a* **1225** *Ancr. R.* 202 He.. þet lette makien swuche þurles in him uorte huden us inne. *a* **1300** *Cursor M.* 528 Mans hefd has thirls seuen. **1513** DOUGLAS *Æneis* VII x. 59 A thyrll or aynding stede Of terribyle Pluto. *a* **1640** JACKSON *Creed* XI. xxxviii. §10 They could not peck the least hole in the mitre, or make the least thirl in the surplice, without working [etc.]. **1866** BROGDEN *Provinc. Wds. Lincoln.* s.v., Fetch a nail passer and make a thirl through this board.

b. Each of the two holes or orifices of the nose; a nostril: see NOSE-THIRL.

a **1350** *St. Barthol.* 89 in Horstm. *Altengl. Leg.* (1881) 120 His nese es euyn, with thirles small. **1382** WYCLIF *Job* xli. 11 Of his nose therlis goth forth smoke. **1513** DOUGLAS *Æneis* XII. Prol. 29 The flambe owtbrastyng at his neys thyrlys. **1560** DAUS tr. *Sleidane's Comm.* 222b, With her wyde mouthe and nose thirlles. **1828** *Craven Gloss.*, *Thirl*, the orifice of the nose; nose-thirl, alias nostril.

2. An aperture or opening in a wall or the like; e.g. a door or window in a house (*obs.*), a sheep-hole in a wall, etc. Also *fig.*

a **1050** *Liber Scintill.* xxxviii. 140 Hwæt framað þæt onȝean feonda searwa eal ceaster byþ ȝehealden ȝif an þyrl open byð forlæten. *a* **1225** *Ancr. R.* 62 þe kerneaus of þe castel beoð hire huses þurles. *Ibid.* 96 ȝif eni.. worpe his hond forð touward þe þurl cloð, swiftliche anonriht, schutteð al þet þurl [*MS. T.* windohe] to, & letteð hine iwurden. **1340** *Ayenb.* 204 Huerby þe dieuel geþ in ofte ine þe vif þerles of þe house. **14..** *MS. Lincoln A.* i. 17, lf. 241 (Halliw.) If.. alle the thirlles, dores and wyndows ware stokyne that na sone myght enter. **1794** W. HUTCHINSON *Hist. Cumbld.* I. 64 *Thirl*.. of common acceptation in the north, for an opening left in moor fences, for sheep to pass to and from the commons adjacent to inclosed grounds. **1904** *Eng. Dial. Dict.* s.v. (n. Yorks.), A lot c' sheep.. wantin' to go threw a thirl at yance.

†**3.** A small cavity or recess: in quot. a closet.

a **1300** *E.E. Psalter* civ. [cv.] 30 He forth-broght froskes þe land of þa, In thirles [L. *in cubilibus*] of þar kinges ma.

4. See quots. and cf. THIRLING *vbl. sb.*[1] 2.

1847–78 HALLIWELL, *Thurl*, a long adit in a coal-pit. **1871** *Trans. Amer. Inst. Mining Engin.* I. 304 These would be thurled (cross-cut) at every forty or sixty feet, or at such a distance as the air could be induced to pass the last thurl made. **1899** PREVOST *Cumbld. Gloss.*, *Thirls*, openings made between a pair of exploring places or drifts, for the purpose of ventilation.

5. = THRILL *sb.*[3] 1

1879 J. WHITE *Jottings* 226 (E.D.D.) Yer sang.. gied me a thirl. **1897** W. BEATTY *Secretar* xlii. 343 'I kend that', she said with a thirl of gladness in the words.

thirl (θɜːl), *sb.*[2] *Sc.* Also 6 **thyrile, thyrll,** 6–8 **thirle.** [f. THIRL *v.*[2]]

1. a. Astriction (usually to a particular mill; in quot. 1564 to a smithy): see THIRLAGE 2. **b.** The duty and liability of tenants in thirlage. **c.** The astricted lands or district, = SUCKEN.

1564 in *Reg. Mag. Sig. Scot.* (1586) 301/2 Cum astrictione fabricandi ferrum infra terras suas de Angus (the haille thirle of the irne werk of oure landis of Angus usit and wont). **1582** *Calr. Laing Charters* (1899) 258 In primis, The thyrile, the haile toun.. to haif twa chaldyr of schilling. *Ibid.* 259 This is the just thyrll that we fermoraris of Crummy aw to our mile. **1681** STAIR *Inst. Law Scot.* xvii. §19. 351 A Clause of thirlage granted by a Town to a Miln.. found to be extended to all Corns Kilned or Steeped within the Thirle. *a* **1722** FOUNTAINHALL *Decisions* (1759) I. 276 That the building a mill within his thirle could be interpreted to be done with no other design but *in aemulationem vicini.* **1773** ERSKINE *Inst. Law Scot.* II. ix. §20 The astricted lands are called *the thirl*, or *the sucken*; and the persons subjected to the astriction get the name of *suckeners.* **1821** SCOTT *Pirate* xi, Plaguing themselves about baron's mills, and thirls.

2. A bondsman, a thrall. *rare.*

1871 WADDELL *Ps.* lxxix. 11 Lat the sigh o' the weary thirl win ben afore yer sight.

3. *Comb.* **thirl-band**, chain or bond of servitude; **thirl-folk**, bondmen; **thirl-man**, bondman, serf; **thirl-service** (see THIRL *v.*[2] 2, quot. 1609).

1871 WADDELL *Ps.* ii. 3 Lat's rive their thirlbans syndry. *Ibid.* lxxxix. 50 O Lord hae min' o' yer thirlfolk's pine. *Ibid.* lxxviii. 70 He lightit on David his thirlman.

thirl (θɜːl), *a. Sc.* [? attrib. use of THIRL *sb.*[2] 1.] Bound in thirlage *to.*

1582 *Calr. Laing Charters* (1899) 258 Ouir mile that we ar thyrll to. **1897** SARAH TYTLER *Witch-wife* vi. 82 Malt and meal from the mill to which he was 'bound thirl'.

thirl (θɜːl), *v.*[1] *Obs.* exc. *dial.* and *local.* Forms: 1 **þyrlian, þirlian,** 2–4 **þurle(n** (ü), 3–4 **þorle,** 4 **þerle, thirll,** 4–5 **therle, þirle, thurle,** 4–7 **thyrl(e,** 4–8 **thirle,** 5 **thorle,** 5–6 **thyrll,** 7–9 **thurl,** 4– **thirl.** See also THRILL *v.*[1] [OE. *þyrlian*, f. *þýr(e)l* THIRL *sb.*[1]: cf. MHG. *dürkeln.*]

1. *trans.* To pierce, to run through or into (a body) as a sharp-pointed instrument does; to pierce (anything) with such an instrument; to bore a hole in or through; to perforate.

c **1000** ÆLFRIC *Exod.* xxi. 6 þirlie his eare mid anum æle. *c* **1205** LAY. 4541 þer wes moni breoste mid brade spere i-þurlud [*c* **1275** iþorled]. *c* **1320** *Cast. Love* 1151 He lette boþe þurlen his feet and honden. *c* **1386** CHAUCER *Knt.'s T.* 1852 Namely oon That with a spere was thirled his brest boon. **1398** TREVISA *Barth. De P.R.* XVIII. cvi. (Bodl. MS.), These wormes beþ icleped Terodenes for þey þorleþ & eteþ trees. *c* **1440** *Pallad. on Husb.* I. 925 They thurle a nutte, and stuffe hit so withynne With brymstoon, chaf, and cedria, this thre. **1578** in *Scot. Poems 16th C.* (1801) II. 127 Remember the speir that thirlit my hart. **1674** RAY *N.C. Words*, To *Thirl*, to bore a hole. **1706** SIBBALD *Hist. Picts* in *Misc. Scot.* I. 118 Being thirled or pierced in many places. **1825** BROCKETT *N.C. Words*, *Thirl*, to pierce, to perforate. **1878** *Cumbld. Gloss.*, *Thirl*, *Thurl*, to bore through.

†**b.** With the weapon or instrument as object.

a **1400** *Prymer* (1891) 41 A spere in to his syde was therled of a knyȝt. *a* **1400** *Stac. Rome* 568 There is.. A thorne thyrlyd in crystis hed, when he suffyrde for us.

c. To make (a hole) by piercing, to bore. *Obs.*

1609 HOLLAND *Amm. Marcell.* XXIV. ii. 244 The forcible and violent push of the Ram had thirled an hole through a corner-tower.

†**d.** To fix with a nail or the like; to transfix.

c **1450** *Mirour Saluacioun* 2506 Thai.. thirlid thaym to the crosse with one naille cruwelly.

e. *fig.* To 'pierce'.

c **1315** SHOREHAM iv. 194 Hy beþ men,.. Wyþ sennes al þorȝ-þerled. *a* **1340** HAMPOLE *Psalter* xliv. 7 þi wordis ere sharpe þat thirlis mennys thoghtis. *c* **1470** HENRY *Wallace* x. 394 The pytuous payn so sor thyrllyt his thocht. *c* **1560** A. SCOTT *Poems* (S.T.S.) xviii. 34 Throw langour of my sueit So thirlit is my spreit. **1742** R. FORBES *Ajax* xxix, Whare now thy groans in dowy dens The yerd-fast stanes do thirle.

†**2.** *transf.* To pass right through, penetrate, traverse (anything). *Obs.*

c **1175** *Lamb. Hom.* 85 þet corn þet þurleð þe wind, þet smal chef þet flið forð mid þe winde. *a* **1350** *Peter & Paul* 492 in Horstm. *Altengl. Leg.* (1881) 70 Goddes sun now hardily es he; He thyrles heuyn. **1496** *Dives & Paup.* (W. de W.) I. xv. 47/2 The prayer of hym that loweth hym in his prayer thyrleth the clowdes. **1541** R. COPLAND *Guydon's Quest. Chirurg.* F ij b, The Meri otherwyse called Ysophagus.. commeth out of the throte and thyrleth the mydryfe vnto yᵉ bely or stomacke. *c* **1560** A. SCOTT *Poems* (S.T.S.) xiv. 1 Rycht as þe glass bene thirlit thruᵗ wᵗ bemis Off Phebus.. visage bricht.

†**3.** To make a hole in (the earth); to excavate.

a **1000** *Voc.* in Wr.-Wülcker 201/32 *Cauantur, euacuantur*, þyrliaþ. **1577** STANYHURST *Descr. Irel.* in *Holinshed* (1808) VI. 9 The toad.. began to thirle and as it were to dig the earth, where finding an hole, it slunke awaie.

4. *spec. Coal Mining.* To cut through (a wall of coal, etc.). Also *absol.* or *intr.*

1686, 1797 [cf. THIRLING *vbl. sb.*[1] 2]. **1839** URE *Dict. Arts* 987 The stenting walls 6 or 8 yards thick,.. are holed or thirled at such a distance as may be most suitable for the state of the air. **1871** [see THIRL *sb.*[1] 4]. **1881** MISS JACKSON *Shropsh. Word-bk.* s.v., We'n thirled out o' our Top-end into Smith's Level to-day. **1883** GRESLEY *Coal Mining Gloss.*, *Thirl*,.. to cut away the last web of coals, etc., separating two headings or other workings.

†**5.** *intr.* or *absol.* To pierce, penetrate (as a sharp instrument). Also *fig. Obs.*

c **1374** CHAUCER *Anel. & Arc.* 214 So thirlleþe with þe poynt of Rememberaunce þe swerde of sorowe. **1398** TREVISA *Barth. De P.R.* VIII. xxviii. (Bodl. MS.), Light is a bodilich substaunce.. moste meuable and passinglich þorling. *Ibid.* IX. xix, þis moneth [November] for his coldenes þorleþ inward and greueþ bodies wele sore. **1513** DOUGLAS *Æneis* X. viii. 114 Quhill throu the cost thyrlit the deidly pryk. *Ibid.* XI. xvii. 26 A wofull wyfly cry Went to the starnys and thyrlyt throw the sky. *a* **1600** MONTGOMERIE *Misc. Poems* xv. 26 Ten thousand dairts.. Thirlis throu my hevy hart.

†**6.** *intr.* To pass through or penetrate (*into* or *to* a place or thing). *Obs.*

a **1300** *Cursor M.* 21098 (Cott.) Thomas.. soght þat estrin thede, And thirlid intil haiþen-hede. **1398** TREVISA *Barth. De P.R.* IV. ii. (Tollem. MS.), þat oon abideþ with blood, and þurleþ þerwith in to þe membris. *Ibid.* v. v. (Bodl. MS.), For þe spirite of siȝt may not þurle and come þereto, for þe lette þat is bitwene. **1565** GOLDING *Ovid's Met.* III. (1567) 31 The piercing dart.. Whereas the ioynts doe knit the backe it thirled through the skin.

7. = THRILL *v.*[1] in various constructions. *dial.*

1725 RAMSAY *Gentle Sheph.* I. ii, His words they thirle like music thro' my heart. **1785** BURNS *Epist. to J. Lapraik* iii, It thirl'd the heart-strings thro' the breast, A' to the life. **1819** R. ANDERSON *Cumbld. Ball.* 60 A single luik will thirl ye thro; A single word ensnare ye! **1868** J. SALMON *Gowodean* I. iv. 27 Yon roof-tree, which had sae often dirled As Willie's gladsome voice around it thirled.

Hence **thirled** *ppl. a.*[1], pierced, perforated.

c **1200** *Trin. Coll. Hom.* 199 Neddre.. cumeð to ane þurlede ston, and criepeð nedlinge þureh nerewe hole, and bileueð hire hude baften hire. **1398** TREVISA *Barth. De P.R.* XVII. cxcvi. (1495) X iv b/1 Not thyrllyd nother hoolyd. *c* **1440** *Pallad. on Husb.* IV. 821 Their nasis thorlid wide and patent be. *c* **1560** A. SCOTT *Poems* (S.T.S.) xviii. 26 My thirlit hairt dois bleid. **1610** HOLLAND *Camden's Brit.* I. 387 And now the pipes of thyrled box On euery side resound.

thirl (θɜːl), *v.*[2] Chiefly *Sc.* Also 6 **thirll,** 6–7 **thirle.** [A metathetic variant of THRILL *v.*[2]]

†**1.** *trans.* To reduce to or hold in bondage or servitude; to enslave (a person, country, etc.).

1535 STEWART *Cron. Scot.* (Rolls) I. 538 This land.. wes thirlit and ouirthrawin Be this tirrane that now is laitlie deid. **1536** BELLENDEN *Cron. Scot.* (1821) I. 109 That daye, behuffit thay othir to recover thair liberte, or ellis be thirlit to perpetual servitude. **1567** *Gude & Godlie B.* (S.T.S.) 35 Father gif me my part of geir,.. I will na mair be thirlit heir.

†**b.** To subject or bind *to* some condition. *Obs.*

1541 BELLENDEN *Descr. Albion* i. in *Cron. Scot.* B j b, All thyngis (quhilkis ar comprehendit within the speir of the mone) ar sa thirlit to deith & alteration, yᵗ [etc.]. **1586** *Reg. Privy Council Scot.* IV. 102 To.. thirll him to the pament of certane ministeris stipendis to be modifeit be thame.

2. *Sc. Law.* To bind or astrict (lands or tenants) to a servitude, esp. *to* a particular mill (usually that of the landlord or superior) for the grinding of their corn: see THIRLAGE 2.

[**1480**: see THRILL *v.*[2] 2.] **1574** *Reg. Privy Council Scot.* II. 384 Quhilk haill lordschip is thirlit to the mylne of Mabroule. **1609** SKENE *Reg. Maj.* I. 113 No.. Fermour may thirle his Lord of his frie tenement, althought he within his time haue done thirle seruice [*seruicium*].. not aught be him... For the law sayes, that the deedes of the Fermour may not thirle, nor make prejudice to his Lords right. **1773** ERSKINE *Inst. Law Scot.* II. ix. §21 Thirlage.. may be constituted.. by the proprietor thirling his tenants to his own mill. **1805** G. BARRY *Orkney Isl.* (1808) 356 Mills, to which almost all the lands are thirled or astricted.

fig. **1834** *Tait's Mag.* I. 428/2 Earnest-money given by the Church, in sign that he has thirled himself to her mill.

b. with the corn as object.

1881 J. RUSSELL *Haigs of Bemersyde* v. 115 On the other part, Robert Haig [in contract of 1592].. 'thirles' the whole of the corns of the lands of Bemersyde to the mill of Dryburgh,.. the said corns to be thirled for all time coming.

†**3.** To mortgage (land, etc.). *Obs.*

1582 *Reg. Privy Council Scot.* III. 521 Thay.. have spendit and warit thair commoun gude and rentis that the samin ar yit thirlit and not fre. **1582–3** *Ibid.* 554 His saidis landes.. wilbe altogither thirlit and engadgit. **1587** *Ibid.* IV. 170 They have thirllit ane uthir parte of thair commoun gude.

4. To bind or oblige (a person) to give his work, service, or custom to one particular party.

1871 A. S. HARVEY in *Gd. Words* 614 Till this account is cleared off, the hapless knitter is hopelessly bound or 'thirled' to the merchant. **1890** H. HALIBURTON *In Scot. Fields* 125 The inhabitants were not, of course, 'thirled' to any particular tailor, as they used to be to a district mill.

b. *fig.* To bind, confine, or restrict in service or action *to* (some party or thing); to tie *to*.

1864 W. ARNOT *Parab. our Lord* iv. (1874) 119 The serpent, as a metaphor, was in practice as completely thirled to the indication of evil, as leaven had been. **1888** BRYCE *Amer. Commw.* IV. lxxix. (1889) II. 266 Great is their power, because they are deemed to be less 'thirled' to a party or leader, because they speak from a moral standpoint. **1902** *Union Mag.* June 246/2 We don't 'thirl' ourselves enough to our duties. **1903** W. DICKIE *Chr. Ethics Soc. Life* 18 God does not encourage us to be thirled to this world and its material things.

Hence **thirled** (θɜːld) *ppl. a.*[2], bound in servitude, service, or duty.

1567 *Gude & Godlie B.* (S.T.S.) 59 Till Christ.. I gif my thirlit hart in gouernance. *a* **1722** FOUNTAINHALL *Decisions* (1759) I. 276 The defender ought not to have built a mill upon the thirled lands. **1898** CROCKETT *Standard Bearer* iv. 36 As a thirled labourer serves for his meat.

†**thirl**, *v.*[3] *Obs.* [Chiefly of 16th c.: origin obscure. Sense 1 might possibly arise out of THIRL *v.*[1], and give origin to the intr. sense 2. But sense 3 appears to have some connexion with *whirl*: cf. note in etym. of THIRLEPOLL.]

1. *trans.* To hurl (a missile, etc.), esp. with spinning or revolving motion. Hence **thirled** *ppl. a.*[3]

1567 TURBERV. *Epitaphs*, etc. C ij b, First shall you see the shiuering shafts and vewe the thirled darts. **1587** *Mirr. Mag.* (1610) 477 These..who deem'd themselues in skies to dwell, She [Fortune] thirleth downe to dread the gulfes of gastly hell. **1603** FLORIO *Montaigne* I. iv. (1632) 9 On whom a Moore hath thirl'd his slinged speare. *Ibid.* xlviii. 157 With monstrous buzzing came a fire-dart thirled, As if a thunder-bolt had there beene whirled.

2. *intr.* To pass or fly with darting or spinning motion.

1565 GOLDING *Ovid's Met.* VIII. 98 b, He tooke the Chaplet from hir head, and vp to Heauen it threw, The Chaplet thirled through the Aire [l. 179 *tenues volat illa per auras*] and as it gliding flew [etc.]. **1567**–*a* **1593** [see THIRLING *ppl. a.*[2]].

3. *trans.* To whirl, twirl, roll or wind round.

1582 STANYHURST *Æneis* II. (Arb.) 59 [The adder] hym self now youthfulye bleacheth, His tayle smoog thirling, slyke breast to Titan vpheauing [*Lubrica convolvit sublato pectore terga*]. **1594** NASHE *Unfort. Trav.* 16 Like a countrie huswiues banskin, which she thirles her spindle on.

†**thirl**, *v.*[4] *Sc. Obs.* [Dialectal form of FURL *v.*: see TH initial (6).] *trans.* = FURL *v.* 1.

1549 *Compl. Scot.* vi. 41 Tak in ȝour top salis, and thirl them. **1632** LITHGOW *Trav.* VII. 328 [We] thirle our Sailes, if Pirats but appeare.

†**'thirlable**, *a. Obs. rare*[−0]. [f. THIRL *v.*[1] + -ABLE.] That may be thirled or pierced; penetrable.

1483 *Cath. Angl.* 383/2 Thirleabylle, *penetrabilis.*

thirlage ('θɜːlɪdʒ). *Sc.* [A metathetic variant of THRILLAGE. Cf. THIRL *v.*[2]]

†**1.** Thraldom, bondage, servitude; also, thirl-service. *Obs.*

1513 DOUGLAS *Æneis* XI. iv. 61 This mysfortoun is myne of ald thirlage. **1536** BELLENDEN *Cron. Scot.* (1821) I. 170 The Romanis contending to saif thaim fra thirlage of barbar pepill. **1549** *Compl. Scot.* xi. 93 ȝe sal lyf in mair thirlage nor brutal bestis. **1560** ROLLAND *Crt. Venus* Prol. 171 To hald thair Realme and land out of thirlage. **1578** *Gude & Godlie B.* (S.T.S.) App. 236, I haue the fred from all thirlage. **1609** SKENE *Reg. Maj.* I. 113 Gif any frie-halder..does to that ilk Ladie any service..or for her lifdayes does any thirlage.

†**b.** A lien on land or property; mortgage. *Obs.*

1578 *Sc. Acts Jas. VI* (1814) III. 100/2 The said vmquhile erll of Mar..spendit and debursit.., besydis the thirlage of his awin Leving, and the rentis of his proper dependance for the advancement of our souerane Lordis seruice.

2. *Sc. Law.* A condition of servitude or state of obligation, in which the tenants of certain lands, or dwellers in certain districts, are bound to restrict their custom to a particular mill, forge, or the like. In later times, spec. the obligation to grind their corn at a particular mill (orig. that of the lord or his assignee), and pay the recognized consideration (multure), or at least to pay the dues in lieu thereof.

In early times there were other forms of thirlage, e.g. the obligation on tenants to get all their ironwork done at a particular forge or smithy: see THIRL *sb.*[2] 1, quot. 1564.

1681 STAIR *Inst. Law Scot.* xvii. §15. 348 The chief and most frequent Servitude in Scotland is Thirlage, or a restriction of Lands to Milns, wherein the Miln is Dominant, and the Lands astricted are servient. **1773** ERSKINE *Inst. Law Scot.* II. ix. §18 Thirlage is that servitude by which lands are astricted or thirled to a particular mill, to which the possessors must carry the grain of the growth of the astricted lands to be grinded. **1799** J. ROBERTSON *Agric. Perth* 396 Thirlage is a grievous bondage; and its pernicious influence on the improvement of the country is severely felt, in every place where it prevails. **1812** SIR J. SINCLAIR *Syst. Husb. Scot.* I. 5 A recent law, by which the servitude of thirlage, or bondage to any particular mill, may be legally commuted. **1820** SCOTT *Monast.* xiii, Those of the *Sucken*, or enthralled ground, were liable in penalties, if, deviating from this thirlage,..they carried their grain to another mill.

b. The multure exacted under this system.

1799 J. ROBERTSON *Agric. Perth* 396 At every mill, the present amount of the thirlage is by far more than an adequate value for the labour, to which it is supposed to be the price. **1898** CROCKETT *Red Axe* (ed. 4) 235 The smile of a shrewd miller casting up his thirlage upon the mill door when he sees the fields of his parish ripe to the harvest.

†**'thirldom.** *Sc. Obs.* [A metathetic variant of THRILDOM: cf. THIRL *v.*[2], THIRLAGE.] Thraldom, bondage, servitude.

1489 *Barbour's Bruce* I. 236 (MS. E.) The angyr, na the wrechyt dome, That is cowplyt to foule thyrldome [*Ibid.* 265 threldome; 269 thryldome]. **1552** ABP. HAMILTON *Catech.* (1884) 23 Thair..miserable thirldome in Babylone [*Ibid.* 38 thrildome]. **1567** *Gude & Godlie B.* (S.T.S.) 114 On the sauch treis our harpis we hang, Quhen thay requyrit vs ane sang, That held vs in sic thirldome. **1609** SKENE *Reg. Maj.* I. 24 Gif he be made ane professed Monke, he sall be made frie from bondage and thirldome.

thirled, *ppl. a.*[1], [2], [3]: see THIRL *v.*[1], etc.

†**thirlepoll, -pole, -poole.** *Obs.* Forms: α. 5 thorle-, thurlepolle, 6 thurle-, thyrlepole, thirlepolle, -poole. β. 6 thir-, thorpole. γ. 7 thorn(e)pole, thornpool. See also WHIRLPOOL. [perh. f. THIRL *sb.*[1] + POLL *sb.*[1], from the blow-holes or nostrils in the head: cf. quot. 1603.

If this was the etymology the name would be applicable to the Cetacea generally, although from the quots. it was, at least often, specifically applied. But the etymology is itself rendered doubtful by the synonyms WHIRLPOOL (1552: see quot. 1538) and HURLPOOL (1556), which show that in the 16th c. the first element was sometimes taken as THIRL *v.*[3] to hurl, whirl, and the name thus app. identified with WHIRLPOOL, a vortex, from the commotion caused by its spouting or blowing. See however THURLHEAD.]

A whale, or some species or kind of whale.

c **1460** J. RUSSELL *Bk. Nurture* 837 Salt Thurlepolle, salt whale, is good with egre wyne. **1513** *Bk. Keruynge* in *Babees Bk.* (1868) 281 Samon, congre, sturgyon, turbot, thorpole, thornebacke, hounde-fysshe, & halybut. **1533** ELYOT *Cast. Helthe* (1541) 67 b, Greatte fyshes of the sea, as thurlepole, porpyse, and sturgeon. **1538** —— *Dict.*, *Balæna*, a greatte fishe, which I suppose to be a thurlepoll [*edd.* **1545, 1548** thirlepoole; 1552 whirlepoole]. **1550** BALE *Eng. Votaries* II. 105 By the sea coast a she fish was founde of a wonderfull greatnesse, called a thirlepoole. **1570** LEVINS *Manip.* 160/41 A Thirlepoole, *balena*. A Hurlepoole, *idem*. **1577–87** HOLINSHED *Chron.* (1807) II. 390 There were eleauen whales or thirlepooles cast on land. **1591** HARINGTON *Orl. Fur.* VI. xxxvi, The Dolphin strong, the Tunny good of tast ..With Porpose, Seales, and Thornpooles. **1603** OWEN *Pembrokeshire* (1892) 127 The thornepole is of like forme.. to the Porpisse..having a great round hole in the pole of his head, thoroughe the w[ch] he vseth to spoute out water.

†**'thirler.** *Sc. Obs.* [f. THIRL *v.*[2] + -ER[1].] A person under thirlage.

1656 *Burgh Rec. Culross* 18 Aug., They war his thirleris this hundrethe and halfe yeir.

thirling ('θɜːlɪŋ), *vbl. sb.*[1] Forms: see THIRL *v.*[1] [f. THIRL *v.*[1] + -ING[1].]

1. The action of THIRL *v.*[1]; piercing, boring.

a **1225** *Ancr. R.* 166 þet, ȝif ȝe weren iðe worldes þrunge, mid a lutel hurlunge [*MS. T.* hurtlinge; *MS. C.* þurlunge] ȝe muhten al uor leosen. **1443** *Durham Acc. Rolls* (Surtees) 713 Cum thirlyng unius shafte, ut patet per bill. 10*li.*

2. *Coal Mining.* See quots. and cf. THIRL[1] 4.

1686 PLOT *Staffordsh.* 148 Between the wallings there were ribbs left, and passages through them called thurlings. **1797** *Encycl. Brit.* (ed. 3) V. 101/1 The workings called rooms, turned off at right angles from the others,..the workings called *throughers* or *thirlings*, 9 feet wide, wrought through at right angles from one room to another. **1839** URE *Dict. Arts* 976 Let fig. 840 be a small portion of the pillars, rooms, and thirlings formed in a coal-field.

thirling ('θɜːlɪŋ), *vbl. sb.*[2] [f. THIRL *v.*[2] + -ING[1].] A bringing into subjection or bondage.

1535 STEWART *Cron. Scot.* (Rolls) II. 444 Rycht hevelie he buir into his hart The grit ouirthraw and thirling of his ring [= realm]. **1871** A. S. HARVEY in *Gd. Words* 615 As in the hosiery trade, so in the fishery, the 'thirling' begins with the boy, and is never subsequently thrown off.

b. *thirling mill*, a mill to which certain lands, etc. are astricted in thirlage.

1773 FERGUSSON *Farmer's Ingle* xi, How big a birn maun lie on bassie's back, For meal and multure to the thirling mill. **1824** MACTAGGART *Gallovid. Encycl.* s.v. *Thirlage*, All [mills] erected by such compactions are thirling mills.

thirling ('θɜːlɪŋ), *ppl. a.*[1] [f. THIRL *v.*[1] + -ING[2].] That thirls; piercing.

c **1380** WYCLIF *Sel. Wks.* III. 27 þoru liȝt of þin arrowis, þat is, of þi þurlinge wordis. **1398** [see THIRL *v.*[1] 5]. *a* **1547** SURREY *Æneid* IV. 91 [The hind which] the Shepheard smiteth at unwares And leaves unwist in her the thirling head. **1566** DRANT *Horace, Sat.* iii. F vij, What thirlinge thrawes doth twitche thy harte? *a* **1618** DAVIES *Eglogues* Poems (1772) 116 To let in thirling notes of noted laies. **1801** W. BEATTIE *Parings* (1873) 28 Really this night's thirlin'; I never maist fan sic a frost.

†**'thirling**, *ppl. a.*[2] *Obs.* [f. THIRL *v.*[3] 2 + -ING[2].] Flying like something hurled; darting; whirling.

1567 TURBERV. *Ovid's Epist.* 22 Where thou with thy nymble arme a thyrling launce doth cast. **1579** *Remedy agst. Love* B iij b, To hunt, to hawke, to throwe the thyrling darte. *a* **1593** MARLOWE *Hero & Leander* I. 108 Nor that night-wandering, pale, and watery star (When yawning dragons draw her [Diana's] thirling car From Latmus' mount up to the gloomy sky).

†**thirl-'multure.** *Sc. Law. Obs.* Also 5 thrill-, thryl-, threll-. [See THIRL *sb.*[2], THRILL *sb.*[2], and MULTURE.] The insucken multure paid by tenants of astricted lands to the mill having the right of thirlage; also, the right to exact this multure.

α. **1423** *Charters, &c. of Edinb.* (1871) 55 With the suckins, thryl multuris, and al freedomes langand thairto. **1471** *Acta Audit.* (1839) 21/1 The actioune..twiching þe thrill multer of þe landis of Carnfyne & Carnebro. **1488** *Ibid.* 124/2 þe wrangwis w[t]halding of þe threll multure & sukkin awing to þe said Alexandris mylne.

β. **1537** *Reg. Mag. Sig. Scot.* 374/1 Astricta multura, vulgariter *thirle multer.* **1617** *Sc. Acts Jas. VI* (1816) IV. 579/2 His Maiestie..dissolvis fra the Croun..the said Burgh of Abirdene with all and sindrie thair landis,.. salmond fischeingis..milnes, thirle multeris [etc.]. **1882** J. WALKER *Scot. Poems* 122 Quoth the man o' dust an' thirl-mouter.

thirs, thirse, var. THURSE *Obs.*, goblin.

thirse, obs. form of THYRSE.

thirsill, obs. Sc. form of THISTLE.

thirst (θɜːst), *sb.* Forms: α. 1–4 **þurst**, 3–5 **þorst**, 4–5 **thurste**, 4–6 **thurst**; 3 (*Orm.*) **þirrst**, 3–5 **þirst**, 4 **þerst(e**, 5 **þirste**, 5–6 **thyrst(e**, 6 **thirste**, 4– **thirst.** β. 3 (*Orm.*) **þrisst**, 3–5 **þrist**, 4 **threist, threste, þrust(e, þrest (þrast)**, 4–5 **threst, thryst**, 4–6 **thriste, thrust, thruste**, 4–7 **thrist**, 5 **þreste**, 5–6 **thryste.** γ. 4 **first, ferst, furst, vurste.** [OE. *þurst* = OFris. **thurst*, **thorst* (mod.Fris. *torst, toarst*, EFris. *thurst*), OS. *thurst* (Du. *dorst*), OHG. (G.) *durst*:—OTeut. **þurs-tus*; cf. ON. *þorsti* masc. (Sw., Da. *törst*), Goth. *þaurstei* fem.; all formed, with nominal suffix, from a verbal stem **þurs-* (cf. Gothic *þaurseiþ mik* I thirst):—Indo-Eur. **trs*, weak grade of **ters*: **tors*: **trs*. Cf. L. *torrēre* to dry, Skr. *trš* to thirst.

The change from *thurst* to *thirst* was prob. an assimilation of the sb. to the form of the vb. The metathetic *thrist, thrust*, was in use from *c* 1200 to 1590.]

1. a. The uneasy or painful sensation caused by want of drink; also, the physical condition resulting from this want.

α. *c* **1000** *Sax. Leechd.* II. 192 Do þis wið maȝan bryne & þurste. *c* **1050** *Byrhtferth's Handboc* in *Anglia* (1885) VIII. 336 Win & beor eall to ecum þurste awend. *c* **1175** *Lamb. Hom.* 79 He hefde þurst and hunger. *c* **1200** *Trin. Coll. Hom.* 75 He ne mai þolen hunger ne þirst ne oðer pine. *c* **1200** ORMIN 14602 þatt maȝȝ þe slekkenn wel þin þirrst. *a* **1225** *Ancr. R.* 114 He..mende him ase of þurst. *c* **1330** R. BRUNNE *Chron. Wace* (Rolls) 10176 þey deyde for hunger & þirst. **1340** *Ayenb.* 139 He soffreþ and honger an þorst. **1377** LANGL. *P. Pl.* B. xx. 19 He dronke at eche diche ar he for thurste deyde. *c* **1380** *Sir Ferumb.* 2810 Feynt & pal for hungre & for þerst. *c* **1440** *Promp. Parv.* 491/2 Thyrste, or thryste, *sitis.* **1489** CAXTON *Faytes of A.* I. xiii. 34 They ouercome theyre enemyes more by thurst than by armes. **1508** FISHER *Penit. Ps.* cii. Wks. (1876) 179 That may suffre & endure grete labours, watchynge, pouerte, thurst, hungre, colde, & hete. **1697** DRYDEN *Virg. Georg.* III. 470 Let thy Goats..be..led to living Streams, to quench their Thirst. **1738** GRAY *Propertius* iii. 89 The long thirst of Tantalus allay. **1858** O. W. HOLMES *Aut. Breakf.-t.* ix. 79 Thirst belongs to humanity, everywhere, in all ages.

β. *c* **1200** ORMIN 1615, & pinenn þær þi bodiȝ a Wiþþ chele & þrisst & hunngerr. *c* **1220** *Bestiary* 320 He haueð ðrist. *c* **1300** *Harrow. Hell* 50 (MS. E.) Seþþen haue y fond & wist Hot & cold, hunger & þrest. **13..** *Sir Beues* (A.) 2791 Beues hadde þanne swich þrast. *a* **1340** HAMPOLE *Psalter* cxlii. 7 Slokyn my threst. *c* **1375** *XI Pains of Hell* 156 in *O.E. Misc.* 215 þai schil haue hongir and þrust wereeuer þai gon. *c* **1400** MAUNDEV. (Roxb.) viii. 30 þai made murmuracion agaynes him by cause of thrist. *c* **1440** *Jacob's Well* 147 Be þe weye thedyrward, he hadde thrust. **1530** PALSGR. 163 *Soyf*, thrust. **1535** STEWART *Cron. Scot.* (Rolls) II. 219 Vter drank for to cuill his thrist. **1590** SPENSER *F.Q.* II. vi. 17 Him..that ..Will die for thrist, and water doth refuse.

γ. **13..** *S. Eng. Leg.* in Herrig's *Archiv* LXXXII. 395/68 For drede of gret hongir & ferst. *c* **1325** *Song of Mercy* 53 in *E.E.P.* (1862) 120 Ne neuer my furst ne woldestou slake. **1387** TREVISA *Higden* (Rolls) VI. 269 He brende for first [*v.r.* vurste].

†**b.** (See quot.) *dial. Obs.*

1741 *Compl. Fam.-Piece* III. (ed. 3) 504 Swine..are subject to a Distemper which is called the *Thirst*, or *Lungs*, according to some Farmers.

c. Short for *thirstland*: see 3.

1906 *Blackw. Mag.* Sept. 394/2 Getting a span of oxen through the long 'thirsts', as the waterless stretches of road are expressively called.

2. *fig.* A vehement desire (*of* (arch.), *for*, *after* something, *to do* something).

c **1200** ORMIN 5688 All hiss hunngerr & hiss þrisst Shall ben þurrh Drihhtin sleckedd. *c* **1374** CHAUCER *Boeth.* II. met. ii, The more ay brenneth in Hem the thurst of hauynge. *c* **1450** *Mirour Saluacioun* 219 Thi thrust to shedde mans blode was neuer wery. *a* **1541** WYATT *Penit. Ps.* cxxx. 27 To quench of sleep the thrust. **1554** KNOX *Faythf. Admon.* D vj, An earnest thrist..of your saluacion. **1607** SHAKS. *Cor.* I. i. 25 Not in thirst for Reuenge. **1669** GALE *Crt. Gentiles* I. I. i. 2 Those infinite thirsts after truth. **1751** JOHNSON *Rambler* No. 83 ⁋1 That thirst after curiosities, which often draws contempt and ridicule upon itself. **1812** CARY *Dante, Paradise* IV. 121 Our mind can satisfy her thirst to know. **1831** SCOTT *Ct. Robt.* xiii, The more lofty-minded..despise the thirst of gold. **1849** MACAULAY *Hist. Eng.* v. I. 657 It may be distinctly traced..either to thirst for money or to thirst for blood. **1851** DIXON *W. Penn* xxxi. (1872) 296 In his thirst for knowledge he was in the habit of studying every sect.

3. *attrib.* and *Comb.*, as ***thirst-fever, -longing, -quencher; thirst-abating, -creating, -inducing, -mad, -making, -quenching, -scorched,***

-tormented adjs.; **thirst-country, -land,** a waterless tract of country, spec. in S. Africa; **thirst-serpent** (see quot.).

1708 J. PHILIPS *Cyder* II. 63 The Root For *Thirst-abating Sweetness prais'd. **1895** J. G. MILLAIS *Breath fr. Veldt* (1899) 170 If you are in a '*Thirst' country, you take, of course, a water-bottle. **1781** COWPER *Conversat.* 262 The riotous abuse Thy *thirst-creating steams at length produce. **1829** T. HOOK *Bank to Barnes* 49 These cows had just finished their *thirst-inducing meal. **1878** P. GILLMORE (*title*) The great *thirstland: a trek through Natal, Transvaal, Orange Free State and the Kalahari Desert. **1889** FARMER *Americanisms* 532/1 The region of extinct lakes and inland seas of Southern Nevada and South-eastern California is the great thirstland of the continent. **1895** J. G. MILLAIS *Breath fr. Veldt* (1899) 184 We entered the great forest Thirstland... In this expanse of some hundred square miles there is but one waterhole. **1908** J. WELLS *Stewart of Lovedale* xviii. 182 Without crossing the Karoo and great Thirst-land of Unbelief. *c* **1614** CAMPION *Wks.* (1909) 179 A heate I finde, Like *thirst-longing, that doth bide Where they say my heart doth moue. **1969** G. MACBETH *War Quartet* 68 They..lived As beasts, *thirst-mad. **1952** J. CANNAN *Body in Beck* ii. 41 Will you excuse me if I beetle through for another pint?.. That's a *thirst-making rock if ever there was one. **1908** *Daily Chron.* 3 Jan. 3/6 He prefers pure water as a *thirst-quencher. **1895** *Westm. Gaz.* 19 Mar. 8/2 This orange wine is most refreshing and *thirst-quenching. **1861** W. F. COLLIER *Hist. Eng. Lit.* 443 In view of the *thirst-scorched seamen. **1731** MEDLEY tr. *Kolben's Cape G. Hope* II. 165 The Dipsas or *Thirst-Serpent is so call'd from its bite causing a burning thirst.

thirst (θɜːst), *v.* Forms: α. 1 ð-, þyrst, 2-4 þirst-, 3-4 þurst- (ü), (4 furst-), 4-6 thurst-, 5-6 thyrst-, 5- thirst. β. 4 þryst-, þrist-, þrest-, 4-6 thrust-, 5 thryst-, 5-6 threst-, thrist-. [OE. *þyrstan*, f. *þurst* THIRST *sb.* Cf. OS. *thurstian* (Du. *dorsten*), OHG. *dursten* (G. *dürsten*), ON. *þyrsta* (Sw. *törsta*, Da. *törste*).]

†**1.** *impers.* as in *me thirsteth*, 'it thirsts me', I am thirsty. (In OE. with accus. of person and gen. of thing, or with dat. of person.)

c **897** K. ÆLFRED *Gregory's Past. C.* ii. 30 Ðeah ðæt folc ðyrste ðære lare. *c* **1000** *Ags. Gosp.* John xix. 28 þa cwæð he, me þyrst. *c* **1000** *Sax. Leechd.* II. 194 þa men ne þyrst. *c* **1200** ORMIN 14603 ʒiff þatt iss þatt te þirrsteþþ. *c* **1200** *Trin. Coll. Hom.* 199 Hire þurst swiðe. *a* **1300** *Cursor M.* 23085 Me thristed sare, drinc yee me broght. *c* **1386** CHAUCER *Monk's T.* 49 So thursted hym, that he Was wel ny lorn. *c* **1440** *York Myst.* xxxvi. 221 A! me thristis sare.

2. *intr.* To feel or suffer thirst; to be thirsty. Also *transf.*, e.g of parched ground or plants. Somewhat *arch.*

c **950** *Lindisf. Gosp.* John xix. 28 Cuoeð ic ðyrsto. *c* **975** *Rushw. Gosp.* John iv. 14 Seðe wutudlice drinceð of wætre ðæt ic selo him ne ðyrstet in ecnisse. **1340** HAMPOLE *Pr. Consc.* 5771, I thrested, and yhe me na drynk bedde. **1382** WYCLIF *1 Cor.* iv. 11 We hungren, and thirsten, and ben nakid. **1398** TREVISA *Barth. De P.R.* v. xliv. (Bodl. MS.), Euerich beeste with lunges þrusteþ moche. **14..** *Lybeaus Disc.* (1890) 1426 Sir Libeaus þursted sore And seide.. To drinke let me go. **1530** PALSGR. 757/1, I Thrust, I want drinke. **1577** B. GOOGE *Heresbach's Husb.* III. (1586) 146 You shall gyue them water as oft as they thirst. **1611** BIBLE *Isa.* lv. 1 Ho, euery one that thirsteth, come ye to the waters. **1649, 1770, 1820** [see THIRSTING *ppl. a.*]. **1871** R. ELLIS *Catullus* lxviii. 79 Bloodless of high sacrifice, Now thirsts each desolate altar! **1875** [see THIRSTY 1].

3. *fig.* To have a longing, craving, or strong desire. Const. in OE. with gen., = of; later *after*, *for* (†*to*) something, *to do* something.

c **893** K. ÆLFRED *Oros.* II. iv. §10 þu þe þyrstende wære monnes blodes. *c* **1375** *Sc. Leg. Saints* xlii. (*Agatha*) 87 Scho thristyt.. for till cume til hewynnis kyng. **1388** WYCLIF *Ps.* lxii. 2 [lxiii. 1] Mi soule thirstide to thee; my fleisch thirstide to thee ful many foold. **1419** in Sharpe *Lond. & Kingd.* (1894-5) III. 363 Your poure lieges þat have loong thrusted after knowlech of your prosperite. *a* **1548** HALL *Chron., Hen. VII* 25 b, The Frenche nacion.. thrusted for the blood.. of the poore Brytones. **1601** R. JOHNSON *Kingd. & Commw.* (1603) 157 The Turkish Emperor.. thirsting to open a way into Moscouie. **1791** BURKE *App. Whigs* Wks. VI. 203 It is not necessary to teach men to thirst after power. **1858** G. MACDONALD *Phantastes* v. (1878) 75, I entered, thirsting for the shade which it promised.

†**4.** *trans.* To desire vehemently; to long for. *Obs.*

c **950** *Lindisf. Gosp.* Matt. v. 6 Eadge biðon ða ðe hyncgrað & ðyrstas soðfæstnisse. *c* **1000** *Ags. Gosp.* ibid., Eadige synt þa ðe rihtwisnesse hingriað & þyrstað. *c* **1050** *Liber Scintill.* x. 49. *a* **1340** HAMPOLE *Psalter, Cant.* 506 Erthly kyngis þat threstis mannys blode. **1382** WYCLIF *Matt.* v. 6 Blessid be thei that hungren and thirsten riʒtwisnesse, for thei shuln ben fulfillid. **1432-50** tr. *Higden* (Rolls) III. 471 Ye thruste golde.. and couette honoure. **1527** TINDALE *Obed. Chr. Man* To Rdr. 20 b, Sufficient vnto them that thirst the trueth. **1593** Q. ELIZ. *Boeth.* I. iv. 11 Wicked men, that thursted the blud of all the senate. **1718** PRIOR *Solomon* I. 203 He seeks his keeper's flesh, and thirsts his blood.

Hence †'**thirsted** *ppl. a.*, longed for.

c **1611** CHAPMAN *Iliad* XXII. 277 His bright and sparkling eyes.. sought through all that prise The next way to his thirsted life.

thirster ('θɜːstə(r)). [f. THIRST *v.* + -ER[1].] One who thirsts; *fig.* one who craves or longs (*for*, *after* something).

1382 WYCLIF *Isa.* xxxii. 6 Drinc to the thristere he shal don awei. *a* **1578** LINDESAY (Pitscottie) *Chron. Scot.* (S.T.S.) I. 100 Ane fallis wngodlie thrister of innocent bloode. **1624** F. WHITE *Repl. Fisher* 112 The Pope was.. an insatiable.. thirster after monie. **1779-81** JOHNSON *L.P., Prior* Wks. III. 139 He was by nature no thirster for blood. **1883** *Cambridge Staircase* ii. 28 The thirster after knowledge.

thirstful ('θɜːstfʊl), *a. rare.* [f. THIRST *sb.* + -FUL.] Full of thirst; thirsty.

1865 *Reader* No. 151. 563/1 A dry, arid, thirstful land. **1871** G. MEREDITH *H. Richmond* xxix, My other eager thirstful self I shook off like a thing worn out.

thirstily ('θɜːstɪlɪ), *adv.* [f. THIRSTY + -LY[2].] In a thirsty manner; with thirst. Also *fig.*

1549 COVERDALE, etc. *Erasm. Par. 1 Peter* 7 Not to be supped lothesomly, but gredily, yea and thrustily. *a* **1586** SIDNEY *Arcadia* III. Wks. 1724 II. 427 Which she.. had drunk up thirstily. *c* **1665** MRS. HUTCHINSON *Mem. Col. Hutchinson* (1846) 408 A kinsman of his who thirstily aspired after preferment. **1831** CARLYLE *Sart. Res.* II. iii, From such Fountain he draws, diligently, thirstily.

thirstiness ('θɜːstɪnɪs). [f. THIRSTY + -NESS.] The quality or condition of being thirsty; thirst.

1583 GOLDING *Calvin on Deut.* clxvii. 1035 There is no man but he is vexed with diuerse chaunges and sortes of thirstinesse. **1619** R. HARRIS *Drunkard's Cup* 3 It.. causes a dropsie and.. thirstinesse. **1649** BLITHE *Eng. Improv. Impr.* (1653) 107 That Thirstiness in me after the Common good. **1872** *Daily News* 15 July, Streams of sightseers, whose curiosity is accompanied by a general thirstiness. **1897** *Ibid.* 19 July 3/1 The terrible and undoubted thirstiness of the season.

thirsting ('θɜːstɪŋ), *vbl. sb.* [f. THIRST *v.* + -ING[1].] The condition denoted by the verb THIRST; thirst; *fig.* longing, craving.

c **1500** KENNEDY *Passion of Christ* 739 Bitter wyne myxt with gall.. þai him gaif to slokin his thristing. **1653** CROMWELL *Sp.* 14 July in *Carlyle*, We have had many desires, and thirstings in our spirits, to find out ways and means. **1701** STANHOPE *Augustine's Medit.* xxxv. 82 What impatient thirstings ought I to bring! **1861** *Times* 22 Aug., A thirsting for political liberty.

'**thirsting,** *ppl. a* [f. as prec. + -ING[2].] That thirsts, thirsty; *fig.* longing.

1382 WYCLIF *Prov.* xxv. 25 Cold watir to the threstende soule. **1552** HULOET, Thyrstynge, or beynge a thyrste, *sitiens.* **1649** BLITHE *Eng. Improv. Impr.* (1653) 25 Keep thy Land rather in a thirsting condition. **1770** WESLEY *Jrnl.* 26 June, They drank in the words of life, just as the thirsting earth the showers. **1820** SHELLEY *Cloud* i, I bring fresh showers for the thirsting flowers. **1857-8** SEARS *Athan.* II. iii. 195 His marvellous tale.. has fallen into thirsting ears.

Hence '**thirstingly** *adv.*, longingly.

1619 W. SCLATER *Exp. 1 Thess.* (1630) 570 The will.. so thirstingly inclined to wickednesse.

thirstless ('θɜːstlɪs), *a.* [f. THIRST *sb.* + -LESS.] Having no thirst; not thirsty.

1591 SYLVESTER *Du Bartas* I. vii. 648 Th' officious Kids.. sip (self thirst-less) of the River's brink, Which in their mouthes they bring them [their Parents old] home to drink. **1856** DOBELL *Lyrics in War Time, Home Wounded*, Among the thirstless dead. **1883** *Half-hours in Many Lands* 4 This great thirstless teetotal abstainer [the camel].

b. Not impelled by thirst. *nonce-use.*

1706 BAYNARD in Sir J. Floyer *Hot & Cold Bath.* II. 330 Unnecessary and thirstless Epotations.

Hence '**thirstlessness**.

1822-34 *Good's Study Med.* (ed. 4) I. 102 Cases of thirstlessness are not by any means frequent.

†'**thirstlew,** *a.* [f. THIRST *sb.* + -LEWE.] Thirsty.

c **1425** *Orolog. Sapient.* i. in *Anglia* X. 327/9 þe whiche qwenchede not fullye here thriste, but hit.. made hem more thristlewe. *c* **1430** LYDG. *Min. Poems* (Percy Soc.) 75 Drye in the see, and wete upon the stronde;.. In reveris thurstlew, and moyst upon the londe. **1430-40** —— *Bochas* I. xv. (MS. Bodl. 263) lf. 69/2 He was.. wonder thrustleuh afftir trauailyng.

thirsty ('θɜːstɪ), *a.* Forms: see THIRST *sb.* [OE. *þurstiʒ*, *þyrstiʒ*, f. *þurst*, THIRST *sb.* + -*iʒ*, -Y. Cf. OS. *thurstig*, OHG. *durstag*.]

1. a. Having the sensation of thirst; feeling desire or craving for drink.

c **950** *Lindisf. Gosp.* Matt. xxv. 35 Ic wæs ðyrstiʒ and ʒe saldon me dringe. *c* **1000** *Ags. Ps.* (Th.) lxi[i]. 4 Wide urnon; þurstiʒe muðe. *c* **1200** ORMIN 6163 Forr þe birrþ fedenn hunngriʒ mann & þrisstiʒ ʒifenn drinnke. *a* **1300** *Cursor M.* 1020 (Cott.) Suld he neuer threst [*F.* þristy, *G.* thristi, *Tr.* fursti] be. **1426** AUDELAY *Poems* 7 The thorste ʒif dryng. *c* **1440** *Alphabet of Tales* 460 Hym thoght in his slepe þat hym was passand thrustie. *a* **1533** LD. BERNERS *Huon* xxii. 66, I fele my selfe nother hungry nor thrusty. **1549** *Compl. Scot.* v. 34 Quhen ve ar thirsty, ve seik drynk. **1590** SPENSER *F.Q.* I. x. 38 His office was the hungry for to feed, And thristy give to drinke. **1697** DRYDEN *Virg. Past.* v. 38 The thirsty Cattel.. abstain'd From Water. **1703** MAUNDRELL *Journ. Jerus.* 79 The Fountain being.. very inviting to the thirsty Passenger. **1875** JOWETT *Plato* (ed. 2) III. 319 The thirsty one, in that he thirsts, desires only drink.

b. *transf.* Of earth or plants: Greatly wanting moisture; dry, parched, arid.

1388 WYCLIF *Isa.* xxxv. 7 That that was drie, is maad in to a poond, and the thirsti.. in to wellis of watris. **1471** RIPLEY *Comp. Alch.* III. iv. in Ashm. *Theat. Chem. Brit.* (1652) 140 Dry up thyne Erth tyll hyt be thrysty. **1577** B. GOOGE *Heresbach's Husb.* II. (1586) 80 b, The salte, bitter, and thirstie ground. *c* **1586** C'TESS PEMBROKE *Ps.* LXXIV. xiv, Thou wondrously didst cause.. From thirsty flynt a fountayne flow. **1743** FRANCIS tr. *Hor., Odes* I. xxii. 16 The tawny lion reigns Fierce on his native Afric's thirsty plains. **1878** BOSW. SMITH *Carthage* 254 The country was parched and thirsty.

2. *fig.* Having or characterized by a vehement desire or craving; eager, greedy.

c **888** K. ÆLFRED *Boeth.* xii, Swa swylcð seo ʒitsung þa dreosendan welan.. forþam hio hiora simle bið þurstegu. *c* **1400** tr. *Secreta Secret., Gov. Lordsh.* 56 It semys bettir þat þe eres of þe folk be thristy to þe wordes of þe kyng. **1577** HARRISON *England* II. i. (1877) I. 17 The thirstie desire of the people.. to heare the word of God. **1697** DRYDEN *Virg. Georg.* III. 727 When the thirsty Fire had drunk Their vital Blood. **1760** FRANKLIN *Lett.* Wks. 1840 VI. 230 She has a mind thirsty after knowledge. **1831** LAMB *Elia, Newspapers 35 Yrs. ago*, Refreshing to the thirsty curiosity of the traveller.

b. Of a motor vehicle, engine, etc.: that has a high fuel-consumption rate.

1977 *Jrnl. R. Soc. Arts* CXXV. 364/1 Larger and quieter aeroplanes and less thirsty engines. **1980** *Daily Tel.* 9 July 12/5 It should.. appeal to motorists wishing to move up from the normal run of mass-produced saloons without.. running a bigger and thirstier model.

3. *transf.* That causes thirst. (Now *colloq.*)

1599 SANDYS *Europæ Spec.* (1632) 152 Troubled with the dropsie.. caused.. or accompanied with a thirstie infirmitie. **1603** SHAKS. *Meas. for M.* I. ii. 134 Our Natures doe pursue Like Rats that rauyn downe their proper Bane, A thirsty euill, and when we drinke, we die. **1812** W. TENNANT *Anster F.* IV. xlviii, Slices of the thirsty ham. **1897** F. T. JANE *Lordship*, etc. i. 2 A thirsty walk up and down terrible bad roads. *Mod.* Thirsty weather and thirsty work.

4. *Comb.*, as ***thirsty-cupped, thirsty-looking*** adjs.; **thirsty frog, thirsty snake**: see quots.

1567 MAPLET *Gr. Forest* 70 b, There is.. fiue kindes of Aspis. The first named *Dipsas* in Greeke, in Latine *Situla*, Thristie Snake. **1802** SHAW *Gen. Zool.* III. 115 Thirsty Frog, *Rana Sitibunda*.. Native of desert places about the river Ural:.. has the habit of a toad. **1875** LANIER *Poems, Symphony* 132 Marsh-plants, thirsty-cupped for rains. *Mod.* A thirsty-looking man standing outside a public-house.

thirteen (ˌθɜːˈtiːn, ˈθɜːtiːn: see -TEEN). Forms: α. 1 þreotiene, -tene, -tyne, þreottene, -tyne, 1-4 þrettyne, 2-5 þrit-, 3 þre-, þreat-, 4 thrat-, þrot-, thrittene, þritten, 4-7 thret-, 5 throt-, (thred-), thryttene, thretten, 6 thretene, 7 threteen(e, thretein. β. 5 þirt-, 5-6 thyr-, thurtene, 6 thirtene, -tine, thurteyn, 6-7 thirteene, 8 therteen, 7- thirteen. [OE. *þréotíene, -téne* = OS. *thriutein, thrutein*, OFris. *thretten* (MLG. *druttein*, Du. *dertien*), OHG. *drîzehan* (G. *dreizehn*), ON. *þrettán* (Da. *tretten*, Sw. *tretton*); f. *þréo*, THREE + *tíene, téne*, pl. -TEEN, TEN.] The cardinal number composed of ten and three, represented by the symbols 13 or XIII.

A. *adj.* **1.** In concord with a sb. expressed.

α. *a* **900** tr. *Bæda's Hist.* I. xiii. [xxiii.] (1890) 54 þreotteno ʒer & syx monað & tyn daʒas. *Ibid.* IV. xxiv. [xxiii.] 342 þær seondon betweoh þæm mynstrum twæm þreottyne mila ametene. *c* **1200** ORMIN 11071 ʒe muʒhenn uppo ʒure ʒer þrittene moneþþ findenn. *c* **1205** LAY. 7771 þreottene monðes wunede Julius in Oðeres. *a* **1225** *Ancr. R.* 234 Seinte Sare, nes heo fulle þreattene ʒer itented of hire vlesche. **1297** R. GLOUC. (Rolls) 652 Brut is sone king was þrettene [*v.rr.* þrottene, thryttene] ʒer. **13..** *Guy Warw.* (A.) 7305 + st. 279 For þritten pouer men & ʒete mo. **1610** *Mem. St. Giles's Durham* 39 Everie housholder shall pay to the bakehouse man for everie threteene cakes one cake and no more. **1661** *Reg. Privy Counc. Scotl.* I. 26 Threttein.

β. *c* **1430** *R. Gloucester's Chron.* (Rolls) 8666 (MS. *ε.*) He adde be kyng þirttene ʒer. **1531** in *Sel. Cases Crt. Requests* (1898) 34 To haue for his waiges only thurteyn shillinges and foure pence by the yere. **1538** ELYOT, *Tredecim*, thyrtene. **1561** DAUS tr. *Bullinger on Apoc.* Pref. (1573) 14 Thirtine yeares past. **1588** *Holy Bull*, etc. (title-p.), Pardon and Indulgence of their Sinnes: and that for.. two Spanish Realls, viz. Thirteen Pence. **1659** BAXTER *Key Cath.* xxxii. 205 One Kingdom hath thirteen Arch-bishops. **1776** *Declaration of Independence*, The unanimous Declaration of the thirteen united States of America. **1776** in *Huntington* (N.Y.) *Town Rec.* (1889) III. 6 Yesterday the Freedom and Independence of the Thirteen United Colonies was.. proclaimed. **1901** *N. Amer. Rev.* Feb. 162 Fines amounting to thirteen times the amount of the indemnity. **1941** S. V. BENÉT *Listen to People* (1942) 471 There are the pretty girls with their hair curled Who represent the Thirteen Colonies. **1950** *Chicago Tribune* 23 Feb. 4/4 Our 13 original states found that survival and progress depend on closer association and common effort.

2. Absolutely (or sb. implied in context).

spec. with reference to the original thirteen states (previously colonies) of the U.S.A.

c **1000** *Menologium* (Gr.) 116 Ymb þreotyne [tida lange].. tyn mihtum eac. **1297** R. GLOUC. (Rolls) 10377 In þe ʒer of grace ywis Tuelf hundred & þretene ido was al þis. **1362** LANGL. *P. Pl.* A. v. 128, I.. putte hem in a pressour.. Til ten ʒerdes oþer twelue tolden out þrettene. **1562** in W. H. Turner *Select. Rec. Oxford* (1880) 289 Called before the Mayre and the thurtene. **1725** in Warden *Burgh Laws Dundee*, etc. (1872) 356 Non shall give no more butt therteen for the duson of bread, except that it be to Baxteris or Baxters wifs. **1834** H. M. BRACKENRIDGE *Recollections* vii. 69 Fort Fayette, surmounted by the stripes and stars of the old thirteen. **1865** S. EVANS *Bro. Fabian's MS., Charm* v, If thirteen sit down to sup And thou first have risen up, Goodman, turn thy money! **1884** *Harper's Mag.* Nov. 889/1, I do not know as to their feelings regarding thirteen at table. **1904** *Hartford* (Conn.) *Courant* 30 Aug. 10 We want to see the Old Thirteen draw closer and closer together.

†**3.** As ordinal: = THIRTEENTH. *Obs.*

c **1375** *Sc. Leg. Saints* ii. (*Paulus*) 72 [He] prechit þare.. till of nero þe thrattene ʒere. *c* **1430** *Freemasonry* 239 The threttene artycul.. Ys [etc.]. **1503** *Rolls of Parlt.* VI. 527/2 The thretene day of Marche. **1551** RECORDE *Pathw. Knowl.* I. Defn., In the thirtene conclusion. **1603** KNOLLES *Hist. Turks* (1638) 30 He.. died the thirteen of November, Anno 1142. **1640-1** *Kirkcudbr. War-Comm. Min. Bk.* (1855) 60 The threttene day of October, 1640.

4. *Comb.*, forming attrib. phrases, as ***thirteen-day***, ***-inch***, ***-stone***; ***thirteen-ringed***, ***-square*** adjs.; †**thirteen-penny** *sb.* = B. 2; **thirteen-year cicada, locust**, a periodical cicada that reappears every 13 years rather than every 17.

1517 TORKINGTON *Pilgr.* (1884) 30 A fayer Tower xiij Sqware. **1798** *Hull Advertiser* 6 Oct. 2/1 The two thirteen-inch mortars. **1828** LANDOR *Imag. Conv.* Wks. 1846 I. 305/2 A half-crown contents me..and, just for the peg-polisher, a thirteen-penny. **1846** *Dollar Newspaper* (Philad.) 17 June 2/3 The locusts are said to be thirteen years' locusts, having made their appearance before this time in 1833. **1897** MARY KINGSLEY *W. Africa* 263 Getting these twelve to thirteen-stone gentlemen up. **1898** P. MANSON *Trop. Diseases* xxxvii. 589 A thirteen-ringed larva is hatched out from each egg. **1904** *Westm. Gaz.* 8 Feb. 5/2 The thirteen-story Continental Trust building. **1964** BORROR & DELONG *Introd. Study Insects* (ed. 2) xx. 204 There are at least 13 broods of 17-year cicadas and 5 of 13-year cicadas.

†**b.** ***thirteen-pence-halfpenny***, alleged to have been the wage of a hangman. ***thirteen-pence-halfpenny piece***, the name of the Scottish merk (= 13*s.* 4*d.* Scots money) current during the 17th century. *Obs.*

[*c* **1470** *Miners' Laws* in C. Walters *Bygone Somerset* (1897) 41 If any..doth pick or steal any lead or Oare to the value of thirteen pence halfpenny the lord or his Officers may Arrest all his Lead-works.] **1604** DEKKER *2nd Pt. Honest Wh.* Wks. 1873 II. 171 Why should I eate hempe-seed at the Hangmans thirteene-pence halfe-penny Ordinary? **1608** DAY *Hum. out of Br.* IV. F iij, He could not hang me for't; tis not worth thirteen pence halfe penny. **1722** DE FOE *Col. Jack* (1840) 46 A paper of old thirteen-pence-halfpenny pieces, half and quarter pieces, with nine-pences, and four-pence-halfpennies, all old crooked money, Scotch and Irish coin. **1796** PEGGE *Anonym.* (1809) 460 Thirteen-pence halfpenny is Hangman's wages, because there was a piece of money of this sort, as likewise six-pence three-farthings, the half of it, both of them Scotch pieces, brought to us by James the First. I have seen them both.

B. *sb.* (With plural *thirteens.*)

1. a. The abstract number; also, a symbol or the figures representing this.

That the number is unlucky is a widespread superstition (cf. quots. 1865, 1884 in A. 2); hence such applications as *thirteen club*: see quots. 1883, 1905.

a **1400** in Halliwell *Rara Mathem.* (1841) 30 Nombrys.. componyd of a digyt and of an article as fourtene fyftene thrittene and suche other. **1599** MINSHEU *Span. Dict.* s.v. *Tréze, Estárse en sus Tréze*, to be in his thirteenes, to be obstinate, to stand still in his purpose. **1883** *St. James's Gaz.* 26 Oct., The social crusade against the venerable superstition respecting the number 13... Last year, a Thirteen Club was established [in America]. **1905** *Daily News* 6 Feb. 9 Where is the Thirteen Club and its campaign to shame the superstitious public out of their dread of the number 13?

b. A thing distinguished by the number thirteen, as an article of a certain size so called.

1799 *Hull Advertiser* 20 Apr. 2/3 Wine bottles, thirteens, fourteens, and fifteens, at 2s. 6d. per dozen. *Mod.* This gentleman takes a thirteen in boots.

†**2.** The name formerly current in Ireland for a silver shilling, as being worth thirteen pence of Irish copper currency. *Obs.*

c **1720** SWIFT *Dean's Answ.* 8 Restore..My twelve thirteens and sixpence ha'penny. **1762** FOOTE *Orators* II. (1780) 57 I'll wager you three thirteens to a rap, that it is no such matter at all, at all. **1810** *Naval Chron.* XXIV. 151 Oft was his pocket without a thirteen. **1830** MARRYAT *King's Own* xxi, He says that it's two thirteens that must be paid for it'... 'Have you two shillings?'

thirteener (θɜː'tiːnə(r)). [f. prec. sb. + -ER[1].]

1. A silver shilling; = THIRTEEN B. 2. ***thirteener and a baubee***: see prec. A. 4 b.

1762 *Naval Chron.* XXIV. 369 Cheat the sheriff out of his thirteener and a baubee! **1811** *Henry & Isabella* I. 289, I have scraped together a few thirteeners honestly, for my old age. **1836** T. HOOK *G. Gurney* ii, Says the padré, 'tip us the thirteeners, and you are as clean as a whistle for the next twelve months'.

2. a. *Cricket.* A hit for thirteen runs. **b.** See quot. 1891: esp. in the game of bridge.

1893 *Black & White* 29 July 139/2 Of cricket there are anecdotes galore; how a 'thirteener' was once run out on the Marlborough ground. **1900** *Westm. Gaz.* 5 July 3/2 But F. P. Miller once hit a 'thirteener' at single wicket, which is considered a record. **1891** *Cent. Dict.*, *Thirteener*,..the thirteenth one of any number of things; specifically, in whist, the last card of a suit left in the hands of a player after the other twelve have been played. **1914** M. C. WORK *Auction Developments* 611 *Thirteener*, the last card of any suit. **1964** FREY & TRUSCOTT *Official Encycl. Bridge* 614/2 *Thirteener*, the card remaining in a suit when all other cards in that suit have been played on the first three tricks of the suit.

thirteenth (ˌθɜː'tiːnθ, 'θɜːˌtiːnθ: see -TEEN), *a.*, *sb.* (*adv.*). Forms: see below. [Of this there have been many forms, the earlier reflecting the various types of TENTH, the later the two types of THIRTEEN. In OE. (Anglian **þríteoȝeða, -e, -teȝða*) WSax. *þrie-, þréotéoða*, etc., whence early southern ME. *þretteþe*. Northern ME. had *þrett-, þrittēnd(e* from ON. *þrettánde*. From these arose *a* 1400 *þrett-, þrittenþ(e*, and by metathesis (as in *thirteen*), *ther-, thyr-, thirtenth*, and finally in 16th c. *thirteenth*, as if formed at once from *thirteen* + -TH[2]. Cf. in the cognate langs. OFris. *threttinde* (Du. *dertiende*), OHG. *drittozehanto* (Ger. *dreizehnte*), ON. *þrettánde* (Sw. *trettonde*, Da. *trettende*).]

A. *adj.* in concord with sb. expressed or implied. **1.** The ordinal numeral belonging to the cardinal thirteen: the last of thirteen.

α. 1 **þreoteȝþa, þrie-, þreo-, þryteoða**, 1–3 **þreott-, þrytteoða**, 3 **þrett-, þritteþe.**

a **900** *O.E. Martyrol.* 13 Mar. 38 On þone þreoteȝðan dæȝ þæs monðes. *c* **1000** *Ags. Gosp.* Matt. xi. 20 *margin*, On þære þrytteoðan wucan ofer pentecosten. *c* **1000** ÆLFRIC *Hom.* II. 520 Paulus is se ðreotteoða ðyses heapes. *c* **1275** *Shires & Hundreds* in *O.E. Misc.* 146 þe þreotteoþe on lyncholne. **1297** R. GLOUC. (Rolls) 5933 In þe þritteþe [*MS.* aþretteþe] ȝer.

β. 3 (*Orm.*) **þrittennde**, 4 **thritt-, thretend(e, thritteind, thritend**, 4–5 **þrettend(e.**

c **1200** ORMIN 11062 Itt iss þe þrittennde daȝȝ. *a* **1300** *Cursor M.* 11373 (Cott.) Fra he was born þe dai thritteind. *Ibid.* 29330 (Cott. Galba) þe thritend case. **1447** BOKENHAM *Seyntys* (Roxb.) 34 Of Octobyr the thretend day.

γ. 4 **þrett-, þrittenþe, þritteneþ**, 4–5 **threttenethe; 6 threttent.**

c **1380** WYCLIF *Serm.* Sel. Wks. II. 268 þe þrittenþe condicioun. *c* **1420** *Chron. Vilod.* 2395 þe threttenethe ȝere. *a* **1425** *Cursor M.* 22671 (Trin.) þe prettenþe day shal be snelle. **1581** N. BURNE *Disput.* in *Cath. Tractates* (S.T.S.) 142 Gregorius the threttent quha is now bischop of Rome.

δ. 5 **þirttenth (þirdtenth), thertenth (-tenst)**, 6 **thyrd-, thyr-, thirtenth**, 6– **thirteenth.**

1483 CAXTON *Gold. Leg.* 78 b/2 The thertenst day. **1530** PALSGR. 372/1 *Treiziesme*, thyrteenth. **1538** ELYOT, *Terdenus, na, num*, the thyrdtenth. **1552** HULOET, Thyrtenth. **1579** FULKE *Heskins' Parl.* 180 The thirteenth Chapter. **1624** BEDELL *Lett.* i. 42 This thirteenth Article, of the thirteenth Apostle,..it seemes you haue learned. **1711** *Lond. Gaz.* No. 4903/2 On the Thirteenth the Artillery.. was discharg'd. **1759** *Walton's Angler* ii. (ed. 7) 38 The wise Statutes made in the 13th of Edward the First. **1878** VILLARI *Machiavelli* (1898) II. ii. 73 The literature of the thirteenth century.

2. ***thirteenth part***: one of thirteen equal parts into which anything may be divided.

1790 BURKE *Fr. Rev.* 178 About a thirteenth part of their clear income. **1857** MILLER *Elem. Chem.* (1862) III. 157 Exactly twelve thirteenth parts of an equal measure of distilled water.

B. *sb.* **1.** A thirteenth part.

1611 COTGR., *Treziesme*, a thirteenth. *Mod.* A lunar month is very nearly a thirteenth of a year.

b. *Eng. Hist.* A thirteenth part of the value of movables, or of the rent of the year, formerly granted or levied as a tax.

[**1206–7** *Patent Roll 8 John* m. 3 dorso in *Lanc. & Chesh. Rec. Soc.* (1893) XXVII. 35 M. CC. vij, Hoc anno assisa de terciodecimo facta est ad opus regis universaliter a clericis et laicis et per vim laicalem.] **1893** J. A. C. VINCENT *ibid.* 36 The method of collecting this thirteenth is laid down in the king's letters patent. Every layman to give 12-pence out of every mark's (13*s.* 4*d.*) worth of annual rent, or out of such moveable chattels of like value as he had on the Octaves of the Purification (9 February), being the date of the council. **1874** STUBBS *Const. Hist.* I. xiii. 586 The assessment of the thirteenth in A.D. 1207 was..not made by juries, but by the oath of the individual payer taken before the justices; the contribution of the clergy being a matter of special arrangement made by the archdeacons.

2. *Music.* A note thirteen diatonic degrees above or below a given note (both notes being counted); the interval between, or consonance of, two notes thirteen diatonic degrees apart; a chord containing this interval.

1597 MORLEY *Introd. Mus.* 71 Which distances do make vnperfect consonants?.. A third, a sixt, and their eightes: a tenth, a thirteenth [etc.]. **1609** DOULAND *Ornith. Microl.* 79 An eight doth agree in sound with an vnison,..and a thirteenth with a sixt. **1880** STAINER *Composition* §14 The third degree of the scale..also forms part of the well-known cadential $^6_4$ chord, and dominant thirteenth.

C. *adv.* Thirteenthly.

1526 *Pilgr. Perf.* (W. de W. 1531) 292 b, Thyrtenth, they be mortifyed from all property of wyll.

Hence **thir'teenthly** *adv.*, in the thirteenth place; also as *sb.* (*nonce use*) the thirteenth head or section of a discourse, etc.

a **1642** SIR W. MONSON *Naval Tracts* III. (1704) 322/1 Thirteenthly, They ought to take a yearly account. **1887** J. SERVICE *Life & Recoll. Duguid* iii. 22 Mr. McClumpha..was toilin' on to his thirteenthly. **1893** STEVENSON *Catriona* xvi, Thirteenthly, my brethren,..the law itself must be regarded as a means of grace.

thirtieth ('θɜːtɪɪθ), *a.* (*sb.*) Forms: *α.* 1 **ðritiȝoða, þrittiȝoþa, þriteȝoða, þritteoȝoða, þreotteoȝaþa, þríteȝða**, 2–3 **þrittuþe**, 3–4 **þrittiþe**, (3 **-teþe**), 4 **þrittyþe, thretyd,** (*Ayenb.*) **þrittaȝte**, 4–5 **thrittyde, threttithe, -yth**, 5 **thrydtythe, thryddyþ.** *β.* (5 **thyrttyest**), 6 **thyrteth, -ieth, thirteth, -ith, therttieth**, 6– **thirtieth.** [OE. *þritiȝoða, -e*, f. *þritiȝ* + *-oða, -oðe* (see -TH[2]), becoming in ME. *þrittyþe, threttyth*, in 16th c., by assimilation to the current form of the cardinal, *thirtith, therttieth, thirtieth*. Cf. ON. *þrítugande, -tugunde, -tegunde*, later *þrítugti*. The WGer. langs. have a form in *-ésta, -esta*, OFris. *thritegesta*, OHG. *drîzugôsto*, Ger. *dreissigste*; so mod.Icel. *þrítugasti*: cf. Caxton's *thyrttyest*.]

A. *adj.* The ordinal numeral belonging to the cardinal thirty; the last of thirty. ***the thirtieth man***, the last man, or any one man, of thirty.

thirtieth part, one of the thirty equal parts into which anything may be divided.

a **900** tr. *Bæda's Hist.* v. xxii. [xxiii.] (1890) 482 þy ðritiȝoðan [ȝere mines lifes]. *a* **900** *Martyrol.* 88 On þone an ond þriteȝðan dæȝ. *c* **1000** ÆLFRIC *Gram.* xlix. (Z.) 283 *Tricesimus*, se þrittiȝoða [ðritoȝoða, þritteoȝoða]. *c* **1200** *Trin. Coll. Hom.* 47 On þe two and þrittuðe dai. **1297** R. GLOUC. (Rolls) 9129 In þe sixe & þrittiþe ȝer. *c* **1330** R. BRUNNE *Chron. Wace* (Rolls) 1418 þe þrittyþe day, lesse ne mo. **1340** *Ayenb.* 234 þo þet byeþ ine spoushod..habbeþ þet þrittaȝte frut. *c* **1375** *Sc. Leg. Saints* xxvi. (*Nycholas*) 560 He ..syne þe thretyd psalme can say. *c* **1400** MAUNDEV. (Roxb.) xxxiv. 155 In þe foure and thrittyde ȝere. *c* **1420** *Chron. Vilod.* 2182 In þe same thryddyþ day. **1483** CAXTON *Gold. Leg.* 350 b/2 The monke that was dede appierid on the thyrttyest day. **1530** PALSGR. 372/2 *Trentiesme*, thyrteth. **1579** FULKE *Heskins' Parl.* 390 The thirtieth Chapter beginneth the exposition. **1587** GOLDING *De Mornay* xvi. (1592) 258 Which of all the beastes hath so much as the thirtith part of them in his body? **1596** DALRYMPLE tr. *Leslie's Hist. Scot.* (S.T.S.) I. 167 The threttieth ȝeir of his regne. *Mod.* Term ends on the thirtieth of June.

B. *sb.* A thirtieth part; in *Eng. Hist.* a thirtieth part of movable goods payable as an aid.

1800 YOUNG in *Phil. Trans.* XCI. 59 A thirtieth of an inch. **1825** J. NICHOLSON *Operat. Mech.* 662 An addition of one-twentieth or one-thirtieth to the mass. **1893** J. A. VINCENT in *Lanc. & Chesh. Rec. Soc.* XXVII. 44 The great council, in which the king required a Thirtieth from the whole nation.

thirtover, dial. form of THWARTOVER.

thirty ('θɜːtɪ), *a.* and *sb.* Forms: *α.* 1 **ð-, þrítiȝ, þrittiȝ, ðrít(e)ih, ðrittih**, (2 **þrihti**), 2–3 **þrittiȝ, þritti**, 3 **þrittie, þrytti, þriȝti**, 3–4 **þritty**, 3–5 **þrytty**, 4 **þritte, þrutty, thriti**, 4–5 **thritte, thritti**, 4–6 **thritty**; also 4 **þretti, þretty, threti, threiti**, 4–5 **thretti**, 5 **threty**, 6–7 **threttie**, 4–6 (–9 *dial.*) **thratty.** *β.* 5 **thirtti (derty)**, 5–6 **thyrty**, 6 **thurty, thyrtye**, 6–7 **thirtie**, 6– **thirty.** [OE. *þrítiȝ*, f. *þrí*, THREE + *-tiȝ* (= Goth. **tigus* decade: see -TY); = OFris. *thritich*; OS. *thritig* (LG. *dörtig*, Du. *dertig*); OHG. *drîzzug* (MHG. *drîzec*, G. *dreissig*); ON. *þrírteger* (*-tigir*), later *þrjátigi, þrjátíu* (Sw. *trettio*, Da. *tredive*); Goth. *þreis tigjus* 'three tens'. The metathetic form *thirty* appears in literature in 15th c. and has prevailed since 16th c.

In the oldest Eng., *ðrítiȝ* was a neuter sb. sing. construed with a genitive pl., e.g. *he ȝenam þritiȝ þeȝna* he took (a) thirty (of) thanes (Beowulf 123), *he wæs ðritiȝes ȝeara eald* he was of (a) thirty (of) years old (*Past. C.* xlix). Later it was construed as an adj. pl., with dat. *þrittiȝum*, gen. *þrittiȝ(r)a*, e.g. *þara þrittiȝra manna* of those thirty men. Few traces of these inflexional forms remained in early ME.]

A. *adj.* **1. a.** The cardinal number equal to three tens, represented by the symbols 30, or XXX, xxx. In concord with a sb. expressed or implied.

α. *Beowulf* 123 [He] ȝenam þritiȝ þeȝna. *c* **950** *Lindisf. Gosp.* Luke iii. 23 Hælend wæs onginnende suelce wintra ðrittih [*Rushw.* ðritiȝ, *Ags. G.* þrit[t]iȝ, *Hatt.* þrittiȝ(e. *c* **1000** ÆLFRIC *Gen.* vi. 15 þreohund fæðma..on lenge..and þrittiȝ on heahnisse. *Ibid.* xviii. 30 Hwæt, ȝif þær beoð þrittiȝ? *a* **1175** *Cott. Hom.* 225 þritti fedme [*OE.* þrittiȝ fæðma] heah. *c* **1200** ORMIN 3207 Neh Off þrittiȝ winnterr elde. *c* **1205** LAY. 26631 After þan þreom cnihten þritti þer comen; after þan þrittie heo iseȝen þreo þusende. **1297** R. GLOUC. (Rolls) 7055 He was fleme & frendles mo þan þritty [*MS. B.* þrutty, *C.* pretty] ȝer. **13..** *Cursor M.* 1216 (Fairf.) Vs telles of adam þis story Of sones he had ful þretty [*Cott.* thritti, *G.* thritti, *Tr.* þritty]. **1375** BARBOUR *Bruce* IX. 640 Quhar ay for ane thai var thretty. *c* **1400** *Apol. Loll.* 53 Judas sold Him onis..for þritty penies. *a* **1450** MYRC *Festial* 22 And duret soo þrytty wyntyr. *c* **1489** CAXTON *Blanchardyn* xxi. 71 Hath he not taken this daye..threty coursers? **1579** SPENSER *Sheph. Cal.* Feb. 17 Selfe haue I worne out thrise threttie yeares. **1818** SCOTT *Hrt. Midl.* xii, 'Ye may ca' the twenty punds thretty', said Dumbiedikes.

β. **1413** *Pilgr. Sowle* (Caxton) v. v. (1859) 76 The sterres.. were sette by thyrty and by thyrty, in suche a maner wyse, that in euery thyrty was sette a grete sonne. **1526** TINDALE *Luke* iii. 23 And Iesus..was about thirty yere of age when he began. **1530** PALSGR. 367/2 *Trente*, thurty, xxx. **1552** HULOET, Thyrtye tymes, *tricies.* **1671** MILTON *Samson* 1197 Your ill-meaning Politician Lords..Appointed to await me thirty spies. **1837** HT. MARTINEAU *Soc. Amer.* II. 33 Lenders of money into Vermont received thirty per cent. interest from farmers.

b. In comb. with the numerals *one* to *nine*, to express numbers between thirty and forty, as *thirty-one, thirty-six*, also (now less commonly) *one-and-thirty, six-and-thirty*, etc., and the ordinals *thirty-first, thirty-second, thirty-ninth*, etc., now less usually *one-and-thirtieth, five-and-thirtieth*, etc. Also as a multiple of higher numbers, as *thirty thousand, thirty-six millions.*

971 *Blickl. Hom.* 35 Ne bið þara fæstendaȝa na ma þonne syx & þritiȝ. *c* **1000** *Ags. Gosp.* John v. 5 Ðær wæs sum man eahta and þrittiȝ [*c* **950** *Lind.* ðrittih, *c* **975** *Rushw.* ðritiȝ] wintra on his untrumnysse. *c* **1200** *Vices & Virt.* 51 þrie and þrihti wintre and an half. **13..** *Sir Beues* (A.) 4532 þe nombre was, veraiment, To and þretti þosent. **13..** *Cursor M.* 2158 (Gött.) Thre hundrid and eyt and thriti ȝere. *c* **1425** *Craft of Nombrynge* (E.E.T.S.) 5 Rede forth þus, 9 thousand sex hundryth thritty & foure. **1536** CROMWELL in Merriman *Life & Lett.* (1902) II. 26 In the yere of our Lorde god a thousande five hundreth syxt and thritty. **1610** HOLLAND *Camden's Brit.* (1637) 696 Thirty thousand Englishmen were that day left dead in the field. **1711** *Lond. Gaz.* No. 4903/2 On the Thirty-first of the last Month. **1731** MILLER *Gard. Dict.* s.v. *Aloe*, The fifth,..thirty-fourth, and thirty-fifth Sorts require a greater Share of Heat. **1797** *Encycl. Brit.* (ed. 3) XVIII. 659/1 In the 39th degree of latitude. **1837** Southey *Let.* 24 Nov., The difference of five and thirty years between me and Bertha. **1884** *Harper's Mag.* Feb. 471/2 One-thirty-sixth of their..area.

c. Phrases. ***the Thirty*** (***Tyrants***): the thirty magistrates imposed by Sparta upon the Athenians at the end of the Peloponnesian war (403 B.C.). ***the Thirty Years' War***: the religious wars of 1618–48 fought chiefly on German soil. ***like thirty cents*** and varr., cheap, worthless (*U.S. slang*).

1842 *Penny Cycl.* XXIV. 382/1 This conquest was the last important event of the Thirty Years' War, which began and ended at Prague. **1875** Jowett *Plato* (ed. 2) I. 266 Anytus.. had joined Thrasybulus in the conflict with the Thirty. **1896** [see Reub, Rube]. **1906** J. London *Let.* 24 Nov. (1966) 225 You made my exposition look like thirty cents. **1944** *Chicago Daily News* 31 July 3/6 (*heading*) Sues to make Uncle Sam feel like a 30-cent refund. **1973** T. Tobin *Lett. G. Ade* 2 Feeling 'like thirty cents' and 'the cold gray dawn of the morning after' became part of the American idiom.

2. *spec.* (*ellipt.*) **a.** The age of thirty; thirty years (of age, old, etc.). So *thirty-one*, etc.

c **1000** in *Anglia* XI. 3/77 Se hælend wæs þrittiȝ þa hine mann fullude. **1618** Chapman *Hesiod's Georg.* II. 486 Thy selfe, if well in yeares; thy wife take home, Not much past thirtie; nor haue much to come. *a* **1715** Burnet *Own Time* III. (1724) I. 373 A cooler and elder man than I was, being then but thirty. **1780** Mme. D'Arblay *Diary* 7 Apr., Conversable as he could have been at thirty-two. **1859** Geo. Eliot *A. Bede* xxxi, She might well die o' th' inflammation afore she war thirty.

b. In stating the time of day, thirty minutes; as in *six-thirty* = 6.30 o'clock, half-past six; also *attrib.* as *the 6.30 train.*

1870 Miss Bridgman *Rob. Lynne* xvi, Mr. Lynne had come down..by the 7.30, and departed by the 9.45. **1899** *Westm. Gaz.* 23 Dec. 6/3 He who came a moment after eleven-thirty stood very small chance of getting anywhere near the carriage door.

†**3.** As ordinal: = thirtieth. So *thirty-two* for *thirty-second*, etc. *Obs.*

c **1380** Wyclif *Last Age of Chirche* p. xxiv, þe þre and þritty sermon. **1540** Hyrde tr. *Vives' Instr. Chr. Wom.* (1592) Cc vij, In the hundred and thirtie Psalme. **1594** *Contention* I. i. 50 Ere the thirty day of the next month. **1606** G. W[oodcocke] *Lives Emperors* in *Hist. Ivstine* Ff ij, He died the thirty two year of his age. **1609** Skene *Reg. Maj., Stat. K. William* 3 The sextene veshell, or the tuentie or threttie.

B. *sb.*

1. The abstract number; also, a symbol representing this. So *thirty-one*, *thirty-six*, etc.

c **1050** *Byrhtferth's Handboc* in *Anglia* (1885) VIII. 302 Fif siðon seofon beoð fif & þrittiȝ. *c* **1425** *Craft of Nombrynge* (E.E.T.S.) 4 The figure of 3... betokens ten tymes more þen he schuld & he stode þere þat þe figure of 4. stondes, þat is thretty. **1501** in *Exch. Rolls Scotl.* XII. 236 *note*, The nomir threttynyne. *Mod.* A Roman thirty is written thus: xxx. Twice thirty are sixty.

2. ***the thirties***: the years of which the numbers begin with 30; the fourth decade of a century.

1880 G. Meredith *Tragic Com.* xvi, His forty years.. matched the twenties and thirties of other men. **1883** Seeley *Expansion Eng.* 288 Dating only from about the thirties of the present century. **1892** A. E. Lee *Hist. Columbus, Ohio* II. 73 The company..maintained its primary organization until some time in the early thirties.

b. *attrib. spec.* Of, pertaining to, or characteristic of the 1930s.

1967 *Observer* 10 Sept. 24/3 Heaven knows, you can peg people by their opinions—'thirties communist' or '*New Statesman* type' seems as hard a definition as 'whisky priest' or 'teacher's pet'. **1969** 'J. Munro' *Innocent Bystanders* xiv. 205 The whole thing was as English as a Thirties farce: sandwiches and tinkling spoons. **1971** G. Charles *Destiny Waltz* v. 149 It was...furnished in a heavy, thirties style. **1976** S. Hynes *Auden Generation* iii. 82 *New Signatures*.. was the first anthology of 'thirties poets. **1981** C. Leopold *Night Fishers of Antibes* ii 15 His Thirties forehead with the thin black hair brushed back from a parting precisely dead centre.

3. (See quot. 1895.) *U.S.* Also in journalism, broadcasting, and wider slang use.

1895 *Funk's Standard Dict.*, *Thirty*..among printers and telegraphers, the last sheet, word, or line of copy or of a despatch; the last; the end. **1929** *Amer. Speech* IV. 290 '30' or 'Thirty' indicates the end of a shift or of the day's work, and has come to mean, also, death. **1938** *Sun* (Baltimore) 20 Jan. 2/8 Newsmen..mourned today at the bier of Edward J. Neil,..who was killed by shrapnel while covering the civil war..in Spain. Prominent..was a shield of white carnations with a red-flowered figure '30'—the traditional 'good night' in the lore of the fourth estate. **1941** J. Smiley *Hash House Lingo* 58 *30*, end of anything. **1945** J. O'Hara in *New Yorker* 27 Jan. 22/3 'I say thank you and thirty.' This last, the word 'thirty', is the traditional signing-off signal of the newspaper business. **1973** R. Ludlum *Matlock Paper* xxix. 251 The number 30 at the bottom of any news copy meant the story was finished. **1978** G. Vidal *Kalki* iv. i. 88 'When we know those two things, it's fat thirty time.' Bruce had obviously been impressed by journalism school.

4. *Thirty* and its compounds in elliptical uses: e.g. *thirty-four*, port-wine of the year 1834; *thirty-eight*, a revolver of ·38 calibre; ammunition for such a revolver; *thirty-three* (*and a third*), *33(⅓)*, 33⅓ revolutions per minute; a gramophone record to be played at this speed; *thirty-two*, a thirty-two-pound gun; a flower-pot of which there are 32 in a 'cast' (see cast *sb.* 15); a revolver of ·32 calibre; see also thirtytwomo.

1802 W. Forsyth *Fruit-Trees* viii. 114 *note*, [Flower] pots are denominated by the number contained in what the Potters call a Cast... [The] 5 [size, cf] 32 [in the Cast is called] Thirty-two's. **1860** *All Year Round* No. 66. 378 'Toasts are almost out of date', I replied; 'but the 'thirty-four must pay for this'. **1870** *Routledge's Ev. Boy's Ann.* Feb. 85 They..could knock the thirty-twos about in the style characteristic of British sailors. **1903** D. McDonald *Gard. Companion* Ser. ii. 70 They choose pots of various sizes—those called thirty-twos (6 in.) seem to be most liked. **1942** L. Hughes *Shakespeare in Harlem* 3 Gonna go get my pistol, I mean thirty-two. **1951** Sackville-West & Shawe-Taylor *Record Guide* 716 While we in England cannot say how bad were the worst of the early Columbia 33s, or how good the best of the Victor 45s, the difference would have to be great to justify..the Victor system. **1953** W. Burroughs *Junkie* i. 20 Jack's voice..went on and on... 'Give me a thirty-eight every time. Just flick back the hammer and let her go. I'll drop anyone at five hundred feet.' **1959** I. Jefferies *Thirteen Days* iv. 46 Mostly I filled up with nine-milli..but I threw in some thirty-eights and three-oh-three. **1968** *Melody Maker* 22 June 2 This is the EP which is recorded at 33⅓ and plays for 18 minutes. **1974** R. B. Parker *Godwulf Manuscript* iii. 17 The girl's voice..was thick and very slow, almost like a 45 record played at 33. **1978** R. Thomas *Chinaman's Chance* III. xxix. 291 We need a couple of pieces... Revolvers. No smaller than a thirty-two, no larger than a thirty-eight.

C. *Comb.* **a.** With sbs. forming attrib. phrases, as ***thirty-acre, -day, -foot, -hour, -knot, -pound, -ton, -word, year***; hence ***thirty-footer, -miler, -tonner***, etc. (a...of thirty feet, miles, tons, etc.). So with the compounds *thirty-one, thirty-nine*, etc., as ***thirty-two-horse*** (power), ***-months-old; thirty-three-year; thirty-two-celled, thirty-four-seated, thirty-eight-volumed*** adjs.; ***thirty-five-tonner, thirty-six-pounder***, etc. (a...of thirty-...tons, pounds, etc.); ***thirty-five millimetre, mm., mil(l)***. (photographic film, camera).

1666 J. Davies *Hist. Caribby Isles* 200 These French Servants, by reason of the three years service they are engaged to, are commonly called the *Thirty-six-months-men*. **1733** Tull *Horse-Hoeing Husb.* xiv. 176 Drill Double Rows with Eight-Inch Partitions, and Thirty-Inch Intervals. **1775** *Chron.* in *Ann. Reg.* 163/2 They are about the size of a thirty-six shilling piece. **1825** J. Nicholson *Operat. Mechanic* 491 The great wheel..pulley on its axis, over which the cord goes (as in a common thirty-hour clock). **1876** Blackmore *Cripps* xxxv, A May cold is a thirty-day cold. **1880** J. F. Carll *Geol. of Oil Regions* III. 197 Sand shells and slate, '30' Rock'. **1890** W. J. Gordon *Foundry* 13 Where the mighty thirty-five-tonner is shaking the earth. **1907** *Westm. Gaz.* 21 Mar. 9/1 The working expenses of thirty-four-seated petrol motor-omnibuses. **1909** *Ibid.* 8 Mar. 12/2 A thirty-six holes match has been arranged between..one-armed golfers. **1909** *Times Lit. Suppl.* 18 Mar. 101/2 This thirty-eight-volumned behemoth. **1938** R. M. Fanstone *Colour Photogr.* i. 17 Agfacolor... 35 mm. film for miniature cameras. **1969** 'H. Pentecost' *Girl Watcher's Funeral* (1970) iii. i. 123 'What kind of a camera was it, Morrie?' I asked. 'Leica—thirty-five millimeter,' he said. **1971** O. Norton *Corpse-Bird Cries* vi. 116 'He couldn't have—well turned the film back, or anything?' 'On a thirty-five mil Paxette? No, he couldn't.' **1972** I. Hamilton *Thrill Machine* xxii 102 It's a low-quality blow-up from thirty-five mill. movie film. **1978** F. Maclean *Take Nine Spies* vi. 196 His visitor brought out two rolls of 35 mm film. **1978** S. Sheldon *Bloodline* xxxviii. 341 The thirty-foot police boat..had been built for service, not comfort.

b. Special Combs.: †**thirty-cross**, one of the transverse bars of a cross staff, viz. that used for about 30°; **Thirty-nine Articles**: clauses of a doctrinal statement drawn up by the Church of England in the sixteenth century, to which those taking orders in that Church have to assent; **thirty-penny nail**, a size of nail: see penny 10; †**thirty-perforce**, name of an old card game: see quot.; **thirty-pounder**, a gun throwing a shot of thirty pounds: so *thirty-six-pounder*, etc.; †**thirty-pound knight**, one alleged to have obtained his knighthood for a payment of thirty pounds; **thirty-second-note** (*Mus.*), a note of the length of $\frac{1}{32}$ of a semibreve, a demisemiquaver; **thirty-year rule**, a rule that public records should normally be open to inspection after a lapse of thirty years from their compilation.

1726 G. Roberts *Four Yrs. Voy.* 102 They left my Fore-staff, with only the *Thirty-cross, having as I suppose, flung the other Crosses over-board. **1607** T. Rogers *Faith, Doctrine, & Relig. in Realme of Eng. expressed in 39 Articles* 3 The purpose of our church is best knowne by the doctrine which shee doth professe; the Doctrine by the *39. Articles established by Act of Parliament. **1739** (*title*) Thirty nine articles of constitutions & canons of Church of England. **1903** G. B. Shaw *Man & Superman* viii. 211 Straightforward public lying has reached gigantic developments, there being nothing to choose..between.. the clergyman subscribing the thirty-nine articles, and the vivisector who pledges his knightly honor that no animal operated on in the physiological laboratory suffers the slightest pain. **1969** A. Richardson *Dict. Christian Theol.* 336/1 In their revised form the Thirty-nine Articles were passed by Convocation in 1571 and the text finally determined in 1604... Subscription is still required from clergymen on their ordination. *c* **1850** *Rudim. Navig.* (Weale) 135 Nails of sorts are..*30, and 40-penny nails. **1599** Minsheu *Sp. Dict.* Dial. iii. 25 Behold here are the cards, let vs play at *thirtie perforce, or Albures [*Sp.* juguemos treinta por fuerça, o los albures], for these are good plaies. **1812** R. Hall in *Examiner* 12 Oct. 648/1 Two batteries of..*thirty-six pounders commanded the beach. **1769** Falconer *Dict. Marine* (1789) I iv, A thirty-two-pounder. **1605** Chapman, etc. *Eastward Hoe* iv. i. F j b, I ken the man weel, hees one of my *thirty pound knights. **1966** *Times* 11 Aug. 13/2 In two years' time the *30-year rule will be operating. **1979** *N.Y. Rev. Bks.* 25 Oct. 52/2 British Foreign Office papers recently opened under the thirty-year rule verify Butterfield's point.

†'**thirty-day.** *Obs.* A commemoration of a deceased person thirty days after his death: = month's mind 1.

1479 *Bury Wills* (Camden) 51, I will that euery poure man that comyth to my threty day haue j d. **1537** *Ibid.* 129 A thyrty daye kepte wythe mete..money, and a yere daye lekwyse. **1546** Langley *Pol. Verg. De Invent.* vi. viii. 128 In England the custome is to kepe the thirty daie or moneth mynde with like Obites, as wer dooen on the buriall daies.

'**thirty,fold**, *a.* (*adv.*) [See -fold.] Thirty times as great or as much; increased thirty times.

c **1000** *Ags. Gosp.* Matt. xiii. 8 Sume..sealdon weastm sum hund-fealdne..sum þrittiȝ-fealdne. *c* **1230** *Hali Meid.* 23 Wedlac haueð hire frut þrittifald in heuene. **1382** Wyclif *Matt.* xiii. 8 Sume an hundred fold, another sexti fold, another thritti fold. **1871** Proctor *Light Sci.* 132 An increase of width not less than thirtyfold. **1898** *Allbutt's Syst. Med.* V. 450 Mixing..equal volumes of, say, thirty and forty-fold diluted normal acid and titrating with the resulting thirty-five-fold acid solution.

thirtyish ('θɜːtɪɪʃ), *a. colloq.* [f. thirty *a.* + -ish[1] 4.] **1.** Of about thirty years of age.

1925 F. M. Ford *No More Parades* i. i. 20 A very thin man; thirtyish. **1926** A. Bennett *Lord Raingo* ii. lxxi. 320 The..little thirtyish nurse. **1979** 'J. Ross' *Rattling of Old Bones* vii. 63 'How old was he?' 'Thirty-ish. Perhaps less, perhaps more.'

2. Characteristic of or reminiscent of the 1930s; = thirty *sb.* 2 b.

1962 *Times* 8 Mar. 16/7 Stuart Davis's hard, bright, 'Thirtyish' cubism. **1976** S. Hynes *Auden Generation* x. 355 The Berlin that their lives express..belongs to the 'thirties. .. And what makes it 'thirty-ish is that it can define its hell in political terms. **1978** *Broadcast* 20 Nov. 8/1 The decor is full of thirty-ish touches.

thirty-one. The name of a game (or games) of cards. Also *one-and-thirty*: see one 2 b.

Cf. F. *trente et un*: 'il consiste à compléter 31 points; qui passe perd' (Littré).

[**1549** Latimer *5th Serm. bef. Edw. VI* (Arb.) 149 It is like he gaue one to his man for his laboure to make vp the game, and so ther was xxxi. **1596**, **1632**, **1654**: see pip *sb.*[2] 1 b.] **1834–43** Southey *Doctor* cxlii. (1848) 356/1 A Frenchman ..published a Treatise upon the game of Thirty-One. **1903** in Hoffmann *Card & Table Games* (ed. 3) 249 Thirty-one (the German *Schnautz*)... The primary object of the game is to hold three cards of the same suit, which shall together make 'thirty-one'; the ace counting eleven, court cards ten each.

thirtytwomo (-'tuːməʊ). [English reading of the symbol 32mo or xxxiimo, for L. (*in*) *tricesimo secundo*: cf. *twelvemo*, *sixteenmo*.] The size of a book, or of a leaf of a book, formed of sheets each folded five times, making thirty-two leaves; hence, a book of this size. Also **thirty-twos**. So **thirty'sixmo** (**thirty-sixes**).

1771 Luckombe *Hist. Print.* 403 Sixteens, Twenty-fours, Thirty-two's, are but the Octavo's and Twelves doubled, or twice doubled and Imposed in Half Sheets. *Ibid.* 424 A half sheet of thirty-six's without cutting. **1787** *Smith's Printer's Gram.* 210 A Sheet of Thirty-twos, with Four Signatures. **1841** Savage *Dict. Printing* 796 A sheet of paper folded into thirty-six leaves, seventy-two pages, is termed thirty-sixmo .., a sheet of paper folded into thirty-two leaves, sixty-four pages, is termed thirty-twomo.

this (ðɪs), *dem. pron.* and *adj.* Pl. these, q.v. [Orig. the sing. neuter, nom. and acc., now the sole singular form of the OE. demonstrative *þes, þéos, þis*, corresp. to OFris. **this, thius* (*thisse*), *thit*, OS. **these, thius* (*thesu*), *thit*, OHG. *dese, -er* (later *diser, dirro*), *desiu* (*disiu*), *diz*, ON. m. and f. *þesse, þessi*, neut. *þetta*; a Norse and WGer. formation, produced by adding *se, si* (prob. = Goth. *sai* 'see, behold') to the simple demonstrative represented by the and that, as shown by the early ON. Runic forms *sá-si, sú-si, þat-si*, acc. sing. *þan-si, þá-si, þat-si*, dat. *þaim-si*, pl. neuter *þau-si*. Later the compound was felt as a single word and inflected at the end, the initial *þ* being also extended to the m. and f. nom. sing., making **þá-si*, **þú-si*, in ON. *þesse, -i*, in OE. *þe-s, þío-s* or *þéo-s*. Gothic expressed the sense differently, viz. by adding to the demonstrative *sa, sô, þata*, the strengthening particle *-uh*, making *sah, sôh, þatuh*, pl. m. *þáih*. The OE. nom. pl. was *þás*, less commonly *þǽs*, ME. *þēs*; the former now represented by those (which functions as pl. of *that*), the latter by these q.v. In OE. the word was thus inflected:

Sing.	Masc.	Fem.	Neut.	Plural
Nom.	þes	þéos, þíos	þis	þás, þǽs
Acc.	þisne	þás	þis	þás, þǽs
Dat.	þis(s)um	þisse	þisum	þisum
Gen.	þis(s)es	þisse	þis(s)es	þisse
Inst.	þýs, þis		þýs, þis	

In ME. these forms were gradually eliminated or reduced, until by 1200 in some dialects, and by 15th c. in all, *þis* alone remained in the sing.]

A. Forms and Inflexions. (For plural see THESE.)

1. *Sing. Nom.* α. *masc.* 1–4 **þes,** (1 **þæs, þis**), 2–3 (*Orm.*) **þiss, -tiss,** 3–5 **þis,** (3 **þus,** 4 **þeos**); 4– **this.** β. *neut.* 1–3 **þis,** (1 **þæs**), (*Orm.*) **þiss, -tiss,** 3–4 **þes.** γ. *fem.* 1 **ðios,** (**ðius, ðyus**), 1–4 **þéos,** 2 **þies, þyos,** 2–3 **þas,** 3–4 **þis,** 4 **þues.**

α, β. ?**670** *Bewcastle Column* in *O.E. Texts* 124 þis sigbecn þun setton. *a* **800** *Beowulf* 1703 þæt ðes eorl wære geboren betera. *c* **950** *Lindisf. Gosp.* John i. 30 Ðæs is of ðæm ic cuæð. *Ibid.* vi. 42 Ahne is ðis se hælend? *c* **1175** *Lamb. Hom.* 49 þes put bitacneð deopnesse of sunne. *Ibid.* 81 Nu is þes prest uorþe. *c* **1205** LAY. 16937 þa þus [*c* **1275** þes] dom wes isæid. **1297** R. GLOUC. (Rolls) 1902 þoru þes signe. **1340** *Ayenb.* 41 þes boȝ heþ manie tuygges. **1387** TREVISA *Higden* (Rolls) III. 253 (MS. γ) þeos Salon his lawes.

γ. *c* **825** *Vesp. Psalter* cviii[i]. 27 Ðæt witen ðætte hond ðin ðeos is. *c* **950** *Lindisf. Gosp.* John xii. 30 Ne fore mec stefn ðius [*Rushw.* ðios] cuom. *a* **1000** *Boeth. Metr.* xx. 118 þios eorðe. *c* **1000** *Ags. Gosp.* John xii. 30 þeos stefen. *c* **1160** *Hatton Gosp.* ibid., þyos stefne. *Ibid.* vii. 36 Hwæt ys þies spræce þe he sprecð? *c* **1175** *Lamb. Hom.* 35 Nis þas weorld nawiht. *Ibid.* 103 Ðeos sunne forðeð eiðer ȝe saule ȝe lichoma. *c* **1205** LAY. 261 þeos ȝunge wiman. *Ibid.* 2061 þus is þas burh i-uaren. **1297** R. GLOUC. (Rolls) 5579 To wonye þer as in hor owe, & a þis alf [*MS.* α (*c* 1350) a þeos half] noȝt. **1387** TREVISA *Higden* (Rolls) III. 13 (MS. γ) þeos queene. *Ibid.* VI. 421 In preysinge of þis [γ þues] Elfleda.

2. *Accus.* α. *masc.* 1–4 **þisne,** (1 **þysne, þeosne**), 2–3 **þesne,** 3 **þusne,** 4 **þerne.** β. *neut.* as nom.; (also 3 **þæs**). γ. *fem.* 1–3 **þás,** 3 **þes,** (*Orm.*) **þiss.**

α, β. *c* **897** K. ÆLFRED *Gregory's Past. C.* xliv. 324 gehieren men ðisne cwide. **971** *Blickl. Hom.* 11 He gelfylde þysne middangeard. *Ibid.* 15 Eal þæt folc þe þis wundor gesean. *c* **1000** ÆLFRIC *Saints' Lives* (1890) II. 38 Oþ þeosne andweardan dæg. *c* **1122** *O.E. Chron.* an. 1012, þet hi woldon þisne eard healdan. *c* **1175** *Lamb. Hom.* 5 Al þe hebreisce folc . . sungun þisne lofsong. *Ibid.* 27 þesne mon ic habbe itaken. *c* **1205** LAY. 216 Asscanius heold þis drih[t]liche lond. *Ibid.* 827 Iche wlle þesne king læden mid me seolfan. *Ibid.* 4081 þis wes þe feiruste mon þe æuere æhte ær þusne kinedom. **1297** R. GLOUC. (Rolls) 5104 þis auisyon þat þe aungel him sede. *c* **1315** SHOREHAM vii. 716 For þou areredst þerne storm. **1340** *Ayenb.* 94 þerne gardyn zette þe greate gardyner þet is god þe uader. **13..** *R. Gloucester's Chron.* (Rolls) App. H. 145 þe king . . þisne heiȝe man igrop.

γ. *c* **897** K. ÆLFRED *Gregory's Past. C.* 2 (*heading*) Hu S. Gregorius ðas boc gedihte þe man Pastoralem nemnað. *c* **975** *Rushw. Gosp.* Matt. xv. 15 Arecce us gelicnisse þas. *a* **1175** *Cott. Hom.* 235 þer efter arerde god þas laȝe. *c* **1205** LAY. 2044 þas [*c* **1275** þes] burh he luuede swiðe.

3. *Dative.* α, β. *masc.* and *neut.* 1 **þisum, þysum, ðissum,** 2 **þisen, ðise, þis,** 2–3 **þissen, þisse,** 3–5 **þis.** γ. *fem.* 1–3 **þisse, þissere,** (**þysse**), 1–2 **þisser,** 2 **þesser, þeser,** 2–4 **þusse,** 3 **þese, þis,** 3–4 **þise,** 4 **þyssere.**

α, β. *c* **1000** *Ags. Gosp.* Matt. xxi. 21 Eac þeh ge cweþan to þisum [*Lindisf.* ðissum, *Hatton* þisen] munte, Ahefe þe upp. *a* **1131** *O.E. Chron.* an. 1124, Sende se papa of Rome to ðise lande. *c* **1205** LAY. 9912 A þisse londe.

γ. *c* **1000** *Ags. Gosp.* Matt. xii. 32 Ne on þisse worulde ne on þære toweardan. *a* **1175** *Cott. Hom.* 235 Wið-ute þeser laȝe. *Ibid.*, Ærndraces of þisser laȝe. *Ibid.*, An þesser laȝe. *c* **1175** *Lamb. Hom.* 9 Heo is unbunden in þisse newe laȝe. *Ibid.* 91 On þissere tide. *a* **1200** *Moral Ode* 342 Fared bi þusse strete. *c* **1200** *Trin. Coll. Hom.* 59 On þese wise. *c* **1205** LAY. 5320, I þissere [*c* **1275** þisse] burh. *c* **1290** *S. Eng. Leg.* I. 292/148 Criede in þusse place. *c* **1315** SHOREHAM *Poems* i. 1449 Inne þe elde lawe þe ordre a-gan, Ine tokne of þyssere newe. *a* **1325** *MS. Rawl. B.* 520 lf. 48 On þusse manere ant in þilke forme sal þe writ ben idressed.

4. *Genitive.* α, β. *masc.* and *neut.* 1 **þises, þys(s)es,** 1–3 **þisses,** 3 **þesses,** 4 **þisis.** γ. *fem.* 1–2 **þisse,** 2–3 **þissere.**

α, β. *c* **893** K. ÆLFRED *Oros.* I. i. §1 þisne ymbhwyrft þises middangeardes. *a* **1000** *Boeth. Metr.* xxiv. 3 Ofer heane hrof heofones þisses. *c* **1200** *Trin. Coll. Hom.* 230 Wið þesses wreches woreldes luue. *c* **1205** LAY. 823 Ich habbe þisses [*c* 1275 þis] folkes king. *a* **1225** *Ancr. R.* 198 þisses hweolpes nurice. **1382** WYCLIF *Tobit* vii. 5 Tobie, of the whiche thou askest, is thisis fader [1388 the fadir of this man].

γ. *c* **975** *Rushw. Gosp.* Matt. xiii. 22 Be-hygdnis weorulde þisse. *c* **1000** *Ags. Gosp.* ibid., Eornfullness þisse worulde. *c* **1175** *Lamb. Hom.* 21 For þisse weorlde lewnesse. *Ibid.* 105 þa sorinessen þissere sterke worlde.

5. *General uninflected form.* 3 (*Orm.*) **þiss, tiss,** 3–5 **þis,** (3–4 **tis, þes,** 4–5 **thus,** 4–6 **thys**), 4– **this.**

c **1200** ORMIN Ded. 95, & whase wilenn shall þiss boc Efft oþerr siþe writenn. *Ibid.* 303, & tohh þatt tiss Elysabæþ . . Wass þuss off Aaroness kinn. *Ibid.* 411, & ȝet tiss Godd-spell seȝȝþ off hemm [etc.]. *c* **1220** *Bestiary* 88 Al is man so is tis ern. *Ibid.* 276 Ðis little wile ðe we on ðis werld wunen. *a* **1440** *Sir Degrev.* 387 Her is comen to thus walle, . . Sire Degrevvant the gode knyȝt. **1478** J. PASTON in *P. Lett.* III. 219 To handyll well . . thys mater now thys Lent. **1551** R. ROBINSON tr. *More's Utopia* Transl. Ep., This my poore present. **1552** HULOET, Thys, *hic, hæc, hoc.*

B. Signification.

I. Demonstrative Pronoun.

1. Indicating a thing or person present or near (actually in space or time, or ideally in thought, esp. as having just been mentioned and thus being present to the mind); *spec.* as being nearer than some other (hence opposed to *that*, or in earlier and dial. use to *yon*: see 3, also THAT B. II. 2).

a. a thing (concrete or abstract).

Sometimes, for emphasis (in mod. use), placed (as subj.) after the noun (as pred.) with ellipsis of *is*: cf. THAT B. I. 1 a.

a **900** tr. *Bæda's Hist.* Pref. i. (1890) 2 For þinre ðearfe & for þinre ðeode ic þis awrat. *c* **1000** *Ags. Gosp.* Mark i. 27 Hwæt ys þis? **1056–66** *Inscr. on Dial. Kirkdale Ch. Yorks.*, þis is dæges sol merca. **1297** R. GLOUC. (Rolls) 110 Al þis was ȝwile icluped þe march of walis. *a* **1300** *Cursor M.* 22476 (Edin.) þe toþer day . . it sal be wel wer þan þiis. **1477** *Paston Lett.* III. 186 Thes beyng the vj. letter that I have send yow. *a* **1575** *Wife lapped*, etc. 1100 in Hazl. *E.P.P.* IV. 225 This yong man was glad, ye may be sure, That he had brought hys wyfe to this. **1610** SHAKS. *Temp.* II. ii. 148 O Stephano, ha'st any more of this? **1622** FLETCHER *Beggar's Bush* III. iii, This is the wood they live in. **1654–66** EARL ORRERY *Parthen.* (1676) 131 The greatness of its horror had this of advantageous, that it made Death a Comparative Good. **1699** VANBRUGH *False Friend* II. i, A very humdrum marriage this. **1748** RICHARDSON *Clarissa* (1811) VIII. lxxvi. 362 This of Bavaria is a gallant and polite court. **1809** WINDHAM *Let.* 23 July, in *Sp.* (1812) I. 108 Terrible news this from Germany! **1837** CARLYLE *Fr. Rev.* III. III. v, It has grown to be no country for the Rich, this. **1864** TENNYSON *Aylmer's Field* 240 A gracious gift to give a lady, this! *Mod.* This is what I like.

b. a person. Now indicating a person actually present, or a person speaking or (interrog.) being spoken to on a telephone, etc., and always as subj. of the verb *to be*, with the person as predicate; in which position the neuter *þis* was used in OE. (so Ger. *dies* ist mein bruder). (Cf. THAT B. I. 1 b.)

† *he this, she this*, this man, this woman: see also 3. *Obs.*

c **825** *Vesp. Psalter* xxiii[i]. 5 Ðes onfoeð bledsunge from dryhtne. *c* **950** *Lindisf. Gosp.* Matt. iii. 17 Ðis is sunu min leof [*c* **975** *Rushw.* þis is min sune]. *Ibid.* xxi. 10–11 Hua is ðis? . . ðis is ðe hælend. *c* **1000** *Ags. Gosp.* ibid., Hwæt is þes? . . þis ys se hælend. *Ibid.* xiv. 2 þes [*Lind.*, *Rushw.* þis *Hatton* þes] is iohannes se fulluhtere. *c* **1275** *Passion our Lord* 244 in *O.E. Misc.* 44 þer arysen tweyne and bigunne to speke, þes seyde hwat he wolde þe temple al to-breke. *a* **1300** *Cursor M.* 11351 Quen þat sco þis can iesus se. *Ibid.* 18209 A ded man suilk als tis es an. *c* **1374** CHAUCER *Troylus* III. 855 (904) This is so gentil and so tender of herte. *c* **1380** WYCLIF *Serm.* Sel. Wks. II. 52 More þan Jonas is he þis. *c* **1400** MAUNDEV. (Roxb.) vi. 19 He þis, by cause he was ane aliene, . . was putte oute of þe land. **1451** CAPGRAVE *Life St. Gilbert* 77 And þis þat schuld be his successour he lerned for to do lich as he saide. **1588** SHAKS. *L.L.L.* v. ii. 640 Hector was but a Troyan in respect of this. **1601** —— *Jul. C.* I. ii. 299 What a blunt fellow is this growne to be! *c* **1633** MILTON *Arcades* 5 This, this is she To whom our vows and wishes bend. **1808** SCOTT *Marm.* I. xxiv, Here is a holy Palmer come... This were a guide o'er moor and dale. **1864** TENNYSON *En. Ard.* 28 This is my house and this my little wife. *a* **1912** *Mod.* This is our new inspector. **1947** *Sun* (Baltimore) 8 Jan. 17 (*caption*) Very well, we'll expect you at nine this evening. Who did you say this was?

c. Referring to a fact, act, or occurrence, or a statement or question, mentioned or implied in the preceding context. (Cf. THAT B. I. 1 c.)

c **893** K. ÆLFRED *Oros.* I. viii. §1 þa þis gedon wæs. *Ibid.* II. i. §3 On þæm ilcan geare þe þiss wæs. *a* **1123** *O.E. Chron.* an. 1101, And þis þa mid aðe gefæstnodan. *c* **1200** ORMIN 1340 All þiss wass don forr heore ned. *a* **1300** *Cursor M.* 14776 (Cott.) Quen iesus had said tis [*other MSS.* þis] and mare, He left all his disciplis þar. *c* **1425** WYNTOUN *Cron.* IX. xxv. 2910 Fore þis þane rais þe gret debaite. *c* **1500** *Melusine* 368 Euer thinking vpon this that Melyor had said to hym. **1591** SHAKS. *Two Gent.* v. ii. 49 Why this it is, to be a peeuish Girle. **1693** J. EDWARDS *Author. O. & N. Test.* 152 They said this as a jeer to the Jews. **1825** L. MURRAY *Eng. Gram.* (ed. 5) I. 325 Bodies which have no taste, and no power of affecting the skin, may, notwithstanding this, act upon organs which are more delicate. **1868** BROWNING *Ring & Bk.* VI. 234 This was years ago, Four hundred, full. **1954** G. KERSH in D. Knight *100 Yrs. Sci. Fiction* (1969) 223 So you came back to life—more than four hundred years ago! Is this right? **1965** *Times* 16 Mar. 13/4, I cannot refrain from a violent protest against the ever increasing use of 'this' instead of 'that': e.g., 'Will you come to supper tomorrow?' Answer: '*This* would be very nice.' **1970** *Nature* 4 Apr. 47/2 The reader . . may come to think that this new approach to mathematics is not worth while. This would be a shame.

d. Pointing to a statement, proposal, or question which immediately follows. Cf. II. 1 b.

c **1000** *Ags. Gosp.* Luke viii. 11 Soðlice þis is þæt bigspell, þæt sæd ys godes word. **1297** R. GLOUC. (Rolls) 8719 He bihet god & þat folc an biheste þat was þys, To alegge alle luþer lawes . . & þe betere make. *c* **1400** *Gamelyn* 603 My reed is now this, Abide we no lenger. **1451** CAPGRAVE *Life St. Aug.* 42 The question disputed amongis hem was þis, Fro whens þat euel comith. **1535** COVERDALE *Dan.* v. 25 This is the scripture, that is written vp: Mane, Thetel, Phares. **1602** SHAKS. *Ham.* I. iii. 78 This aboue all: to thine owne selfe be true. **1664** BUTLER *Hud.* II. II. 255 Yet all of us hold this for true, No faith is to the Wicked due. **1858** M. ARNOLD *Merope* 895, I speak no word of boast, but this I say: A private loss here founds a nation's peace.

e. After various prepositions (*after, before, by, ere*, etc.), = 'this time'; i.e. either, the present time, the time of speaking or writing; or, in narrative, the time just mentioned. (Cf. THAT B. I. 1 d; also NOW 13, THEN 7.)

c **897** K. ÆLFRED *Gregory's Past. C.* Pref. 6 Hu sio lar Lædengeðeodes ær ðysum [*Hatt. MS.* ðissum] oðfeallen wæs. *a* **900** tr. *Bæda's Hist.* I. vii. (1890) 40 Ða wæs se dema æfter ðyssum . . gedrefed. *c* **1000** *Ags. Ps.* (Th.) cxx. 7 Of þisson forð awa to woruld. *c* **1250** *Gen. & Ex.* 925 After ðis spac god to abram. *a* **1300** *Floriz & Bl.* 430 Ihc wulle fonde what i do may Bituene þis and þe pridde day. *a* **1300** [see BY *prep.* 21 b]. **13..** *Cursor M.* 7252 (Fairf.) Be þis [*Cott.* wit þis] his hare was waxin new. **1390** GOWER *Conf.* I. 21 For it hath proeved ofte er this. **1571–2** *Reg. Privy Council Scot.* II. 130 Frome this furth I sall and will beare fayth and trew allegeance. **1607** SHAKS. *Cor.* IV. iii. 43, I shall betweene this and Supper, tell you most strange things. **1654–66** EARL ORRERY *Parthen.* (1676) 683 My Soldiers having (during this) taken a little refreshment. **1719** DE FOE *Crusoe* (1840) II. i. 17 Some time after this, . . they fired three muskets. **1818** KEATS *Endym.* I. 988 By this the sun is setting. **1922** YEATS *Player Queen* I. 20 The basket-makers and the sieve-makers will be out by this. **1971** in *Sc. Nat. Dict.* (1974) IX. 283/2 I'll hae plenty adee atween this and Whitsunday.

f. After a preposition, or as obj. of a verb: = 'this place'. (Now (in colloq. use) more usually *here*: cf. HERE *adv.* B.)

c **1460** [see HERE *adv.* 1 d]. **1535** LYNDESAY *Satyre* 2191 Betwixt this and Dumbartane. **1802** JEFFERSON *Writ.* (1830) III. 496, I shall leave this on the 21st. **1841** LYTTON *Money* II. v, The finest player . . between this and the Pyramids. **1868** W. S. GILBERT *Bab Ballads, Bob Polter* xiv, You filthy beast, get out of this.

g. Strengthened by *here* immediately following (cf. II. 1. i): see HERE *adv.* 1 d. *dial.* and *vulgar.*

†**2.** In OE. and early ME., used (like THAT) with the verb *to be* in the plural in reference to a plural predicate.

(This was a collective use of the singular neuter.)

c **888** K. ÆLFRED *Boeth.* iii. §4 Sint þis nu þa god & þa edlean þe þu ealne weg gehete. *c* **893** —— *Oros.* III. i. §7 þiss wæron ealle Creca leode. *c* **1000** ÆLFRIC *Exod.* i. 1 Thys synd Israela bearna naman. *c* **1205** LAY. 25387 þis weoren þa sixe.

3. In contrast to *that*: now almost always of things; esp. in phr. *this and* (*or*) *that* = one thing (or person) and (or) another. So † *he this . . he that* = this (or the one) man . . that (or the other) man (quot. 1426). Also occas. *this . . this* = one thing (or person) . . another; also *this . . the other. this, that, and* (or *or*) *the other*, every sort (of), every possible or imaginable.

[**13..** *Cursor M.* 8502 (Cott.) þat [the forbidden] tre was ded [*v.r.* deþ], þis sal be lijf.] **1390** GOWER *Conf.* II. 210 In ech of hem he fint somwhat That pleseth him, in this or that. **1426** LYDG. *De Guil. Pilgr.* 20110 He thys ys wroth, he that ys glad. **1526** TINDALE *Jas.* iv. 15 For that ye ought to saye: yff the lorde will . . , let vs do this or thatt. **1581** E. CAMPION in *Confer.* II. (1584) L iv, It shalbe reported that I sayd this and that, and my wordes shalbe depraued. **1629** DONNE *Serm.* xxxi. (1640) 308 A Ruby will conduce best to the Expressing of This & an Emeraud of This. **1693** DRYDEN *Persius' Sat.* iv. 19 This is not fair; nor profitable that; Nor t'other Question proper for Debate. **1800** MRS. HERVEY *Mourtray Fam.* II. 227 Because one man did this, that truly I must do that. **18..** M. ARNOLD *Epil. to Lessing's Laocoon* 116 This through the Ride upon his steed Goes slowly by, and this at speed. **1824** SCOTT *St. Ronan's* II. i. 24, I am sure I aye took your part when folk miscaa'd ye, and said ye were this, that, and the other thing. **1870** MORRIS *Earthly Par.* I. I. 381 At their . . feast they sat Thinking their thoughts, and spoke of this or that. **1918** *Nation* (N.Y.) 7 Feb. 161/1 They . . offered us a contract in this, that, or the other company, whose dividend-paying record had been thus and so. **1938** N. MARSH *Artists in Crime* xvii. 255 It's a bit awkward what with this and that and the other thing.

b. *spec.* (after Latin idiom.) The latter: in contrast to *that* = the former (THAT B. I. 3 b).

c **1440** *Pallad. on Husb.* IV. 21 Ffor sunne & wynde hem make a tegument, Lest they in this be shake, in that to brent. **1591** FRAUNCE (*title*) The Countesse of Pembrokes Yuychurch. Conteining the affectionate life, and vnfortunate death of Phillis and Amyntas: That in a Pastorall; This in a Funerall. **1627–47** FELTHAM *Resolves* I. lxxxvii. 271 Travaile . . makes a wise man better, and a foole worse. This gains nothing but the gay sights, vices, . . and the Apery of a Countrey. **1740** BERKELEY *Siris* §72 Warm water . . mixed with hot and cold, will lessen the heat in that, and the cold in this. **1868** S. J. STONE *Hymn*, '*The old year's long campaign is o'er*' ii, Go forth! firm faith in every heart, Bright hope on every helm, Through that shall pierce no fiery dart, And this no fear o'erwhelm.

c. With *That*, as quasi-proper names (with capital T), indefinitely denoting one person and another. So 'No. [= number] This . . No. That'.

1824 BYRON *Juan* XVI. xliv, Miss That or This, or Lady T'other. **1864** J. H. NEWMAN *Apol.* i. (1904) 9/2 He . . placed me between Provost This and Principal That.

d. As quasi-*sb.*: *a this or a that* = one thing or another (in quot. 1656, one or other person of consequence); also nonce-pl. *thises and thats.*

1656 CROMWELL *Sp.* 17 Sept., in *Carlyle*, A company of mean fellows, . . not a lord, nor a gentleman, nor a man of fortune, nor a this nor that, among them. **1865** RUSKIN *Ethics of Dust* v. (1883) 100 You . . begin to think that it is a chastisement or a warning, or a this or that or the other of profound significance. **1895** *Harper's Mag.* Nov. 952/1 There were many thises and thats put together.

4. Phrases. *all this*: cf. *all that* s.v. THAT B. I. 5 b; *for all this*, notwithstanding this: cf. FOR 23 a. *like this*, of this kind; in this manner, thus: cf. *like that* (LIKE *a.* 1 ¶, *adv.* 1; THAT B. I. 5 b).

c **1122** *O.E. Chron.* an. 1006 (Laud MS.), Ac for eallum þissum se here ferde swa he sylf wolde. *c* **1250** *Gen. & Ex.* 3791 For al ðis, oðer day ðor was nest, Aȝenes moyses and is prest Gan al ðis folc wið wreðe gon. *a* **1774** GOLDSM. *Surv. Exp. Philos.* (1776) I. 288 Yet the friction shall not for all this become four times as great. **1858** J. H. NEWMAN *Sel. Ess.* 213 The monks were not so soft as all this, after all. **1881** DUFFIELD *Don Quix.* II. 548 To go like this . . is like looking for . . the bachelor in Salamanca. **1881** W. S. GILBERT *Patience* II, You hold yourself like this, You hold yourself like that, By hook or crook, you try to look, both angular and flat. **1889** C. C. R. *Up for Season* 76 Of what could we talk on an evening like this?

II. Demonstrative Adjective.

1. a. Used in concord with a sb., to indicate a thing or person present or near (actually or in thought), esp. one just mentioned: cf. I. 1.

The use before a possessive pron. (e.g. *this my son*) is *arch.*, the periphrasis with *of* being now substituted, as with *that*: cf. THAT B. II. 1.

this morning, this afternoon, this evening now always mean 'the morning (etc.) of to-day' (whether past, present, or future): cf. MORNING *sb.* 3 d.

c **893** K. ÆLFRED *Oros.* II. viii. § 1 þysne nyttan cræft, þeh he arlic næ re, funde heora ticiator, Camillis hatte. *c* **897** —— *Gregory's Past. C.* 3 (Hatton MS.) *heading*, Ðeos boc sceal to wiogora ceastre. *a* **900** tr. *Bæda's Hist.* I. v. (1890) 32 þes casere framlice rehte ða cynewisan. *c* **1000** *Ags. Gosp.* Matt. xiv. 15 Ðeos stow ys weste. **1154** *O.E. Chron.*, On þis gær wærd þe king Stephne ded. *c* **1200** *Trin. Coll. Hom.* 141 þes wimmannes name. *c* **1200** ORMIN 273, & he, þiss Zakaryas, wass Bitwenenn oþre prestess..to serrfenn sett. *a* **1240** *Ureisun* in *Cott. Hom.* 199 Ich habbe i-sungen þe ðesne englissce lai. *c* **1250** *Gen. & Ex.* 3951 Al-so leun is miȝtful der, So sal ðis folc ben miȝtful her. **1340** *Ayenb.* 12 þis article zette saynt andreu. **1382** WYCLIF *Luke* xv. 24 For this my sone was deed, and hath lyued aȝen. *c* **1400** *Brut* 100 þis Elfride hade a sone þat me callede Edwynne. **1432-50** tr. *Higden* (Rolls) II. 285 Whiche consuetude peple of that cuntre vse to this tyme presente. **1518** in *Peebles Burgh Rec.* (1872) 46 This last Sonday he send his..men. **1554** J. CHRISTOPHERSON in Maitland *Ess.* (1849) 302 He had bene better a great deale to have lived amonge Turkes & Saracenes then amonge this kind of folke. **1600** SHAKS. *A.Y.L.* II. i. 15 And this our life exempt from publike haunt. **1632** SIR T. HAWKINS tr. *Mathieu's Unhappy Prosperitie* 163 This five yeares Consulship intoxicated him. *a* **1648** LD. HERBERT *Hen. VIII* (1683) 471 To omit the same for this present. **1711** ADDISON *Spect.* No. 18 ¶ 1 It is my Design in this Paper to deliver..a faithful Account of the Italian Opera. **1772** *Sheridaniana* (1826) 47, I have this moment heard that Sheridan is returned. **1819** SCOTT *Ivanhoe* xliv, To do battle for her in this her cause. **1851** TENNYSON *To the Queen* v, Take, Madam, this poor book of song.

b. Referring to something which is mentioned immediately after. (Cf. the use of *that* for something mentioned before: see THAT B. II. 1.)

c **897** K. ÆLFRED *Gregory's Past. C.* xliv. 324 ȝehieren men ðisne cwide: Hald ðine ælmessan, ðylæs ðu hie forweorpe. *a* **1175** *Cott. Hom.* 225 Ic wille settan mi wed betwuxe me and eow to þisan behate, þat is [etc.]. *a* **1225** *Ancr. R.* 44 And sigge, stondinde, þesne vreisun. 'Uisita quesumus, Domine, habitationem istam'. *c* **1440** *Alphabet of Tales* 186 He began to syng þis antem, 'O! pastor eterne'. **1509** HAWES *Past. Pleas.* xxxv. (Percy Soc.) 180 In a russet banner..There was wrytten this worde, Detraction. **1681-6** J. SCOTT *Chr. Life* (1747) III. 48 Upon this account indeed they had great cause to rejoice, because now they knew they had a sure Friend in Heaven. **1703** THORESBY *Let. to Ray* (E.D.S.), This additional list of local words is larger than I expected. **1864** J. H. NEWMAN *Apol.* 63, I..confine myself to this one consideration, viz. [etc.].

c. In phrases denoting or referring to the present state or stage of existence; esp. *this life*, THIS WORLD (q.v.).

c **1000-** [see LIFE *sb.* 12 b]. *c* **1200** *Trin. Coll. Hom.* 187 To freurende þo forsineȝede of þis wrecche woreld. **1526** TINDALE *1 Cor.* xv. 53 For this corruptible must putt on incorruptibilite: and this mortall must put on immortalite. **1709** KEN *Hymn*, '*All Praise to Thee my God this night*' iii, That this vile Body may Rise Glorious at the awful day.

d. Referring to something as known, talked about, or (as in quot. 1610) inferred; esp. (*colloq.*) to something now in vogue or recently introduced. (Cf. THAT B. II. 1 b.) Also, the present or existing.

1533 BELLENDEN *Livy* I. viii. (S.T.S.) I. 46 Numa, this civil and Illustar prince. **1582** ALLEN *Martyrd. Campion* (1908) 16 Raised and upholden by this new religion. **1585** T. WASHINGTON tr. *Nicholay's Voy.* II. xiii, This lamentable losse of Constantinople. **1596** SHAKS. *Tam. Shr.* I. ii. 160 Oh this learning, what a thing it is. **1599** —— *Much Ado* III. iv. 73 Get you some of this distill'd *carduus benedictus*. **1610** —— *Temp.* v. i. 280 Where should they Finde this grand Liquor? **1785** BOSWELL *Jrnl. Tour Hebrides* 86 We were told this Mr. Waller was a plain country gentleman. **1788** H. WALPOLE *Let.* 26 July (1918) Suppl. II. 24 Do you know the medals of gold belonged to this Lord Pembroke's grandfather? *a* **1912** *Mod. colloq.* What do you think of this wireless telegraphy? This railway strike is a serious business. *a* **1933** *Mod.* I knew the last doctor very well. I don't get on with this one.

e. Used before a date, esp. (now only) in legal or formal documents.

1582 L. KIRBY in Allen *Martyrd. Campion* (1908) 77, I bid you farewell, this x of Januarie, 1582. **1603** PARSONS *Let.* 6 July, in *Cath. Rec. Soc. Publ.* (1906) II. 218 And with this I byd you most hartely farewell..this 6 of July 1603. **1648** CROMWELL *Procl.* in Carlyle *Lett. & Sp.* (1871) II. 55 Given under my hand, this 20th September, 1648. **1739** in J. O. Payne *Rec. Eng. Cath. of 1715* (1889) 53, I, William Plowden, being this 31st March, 1739, full 70 years of age.

f. Used instead of THESE in concord with a plural sb. or numeral; esp. (now only) with a plural treated as a singular (e.g. *means*, *odds*), or with a numeral expression denoting a period of time taken as a whole (in this case usually = 'just past or completed', or more rarely 'just beginning'). So also *this many a day* (*year*, etc.) = these many days, this period of many days (etc.) just past.

The earlier evidence is often doubtful from the fact that *this* was long one of the forms of *these*: see THESE A γ.

[*c* **1275** LAY. 26320 þis [*c* 1205 þeos] þreo cnihtes bolde.] *c* **1420** *Avow. Arth.* lxix, Thoȝhe þe sege this seuyn ȝere, Castelle gete ȝe none here. *c* **1450** *Cov. Myst.* xiv. (1841) 132 More..Than evyr ther was this thowsand ȝere. **1523** LD. BERNERS *Froiss.* I. ix. 7 Whan the quene hard thys tidyngis. **1550** CRANMER *Defence* To Rdr., Where-with they haue this many yeares deluded and bewitched the world. **1578-1600** *Scot. Poems 16th C.* II. 164 This lang and mony ane day. **1592** SHAKS. *Rom. & Jul.* v. ii. 25 Within this three houres will faire Iuliet wake. **1596** DANETT tr. *Comines* (1614) 206 Which will bleed this many a yeare. **1779** *Mirror* No. 55. ¶ 7 By this means..even the worthiest men..may be led into fatal errors. **1810** SOUTHEY *Ess.* (1832) I. 9 Unless there be something to weigh against this fearful odds. **1867** RUSKIN *Time & Tide* xv. § 86 (1904) 109 The silence has kept my own heart heavy this many a day. **1883** L. OLIPHANT *Altiora Peto* II. 261 This last six months.

† **g.** *this bearer* (*bringer*) = the bearer of this.

1493 *Plumpton Corr.* (Camden) 106, I pray you that I may be answered by my servant, this bearer. *c* **1495** *Ibid.*, I desire ..you to send me a copple with my servant, this bringer. **1533** CRANMER *Let. to Ld. Rochford* in *Misc. Writ.* (Parker Soc.) II. 259 This bringer P. M. sueth unto me to write unto you in his favour. **1623** USSHER *Lett.* (1686) 91, I received your Graces Letter brought by this Bearer. **1630** W. BEDELL *ibid.* 440 These things I write now in exceeding post-haste, in respect that this Bearer goes away so presently.

h. *this once*; *this same* (*ilk*); *this side*: see ONCE 9 c, SAME A. 5, B. 2, 4 (ILK), SIDE *sb.* 13 b.

13.. *Cursor M.* 15928 (Cott.) þis ilk es an of his felauscep for-soth. *c* **1375** *Sc. Leg. Saints* xxxiii. (*George*) 931 þis sammyne aray, þat now þou seis me haf. **1513** DOUGLAS *Æneis* IV. vi. 36 This ilk cursit fame. *c* **1542** UDALL in Flügel *Neuengl. Leseb.* I. 352 Be good maister to me this oons. **1769** *De Foe's Tour Gt. Brit.* I. i. 4 A little on this Side the Whalebone, a Place so called, because [etc.].

i. Strengthened by *here* immediately following: see HERE *adv.* 1 d. (Cf. *that there*, THERE B. 2 c.) Now *dial.* or *vulgar*.

c **1380** WYCLIF *Sel. Wks.* III. 203 God forbede þat ony Cristene man understonde, þat þis here synsynge and criynge..be þe beste servyce of a prest. **1762-** [see HERE *adv.* 1 d].

† **j.** *this other* = 'the other' (OTHER A. 3 b).

1300-1596 [see OTHER A. 3 b (*b*), (*c*)].

k. In unliterary narrative: referring to a person, place, etc., not previously mentioned or implied. orig. *U.S.*

1922 S. LEWIS *Babbitt* viii. 116 Did you read about this fellow that went and paid a thousand dollars for ten cases of red-eye that proved to be nothing but water? **1946** K. TENNANT *Lost Haven* (1947) ii. 41 They dug this great big trench with bull-dozers. **1969** FABIAN & BYRNE *Groupie* (1970) xvi. 111 The rest of the letters were all written on small sheets of blue notepaper in this really childish handwriting. **1976** *Drive* Nov.–Dec. 24/1 It was on the Chester road, in Birmingham. I saw this car with the keys in the ignition.

2. In contrast to *that*: properly denoting the nearer of two things, but often vaguely indicating one thing as distinct from another, esp. in phr. *this and* (*or*) *that*.. = one and (or) another.. So also † *this..this..* (quots. *c* 1460, 1624); *this..the other..* (quot. 1717); *this..the next..* (quot. 1768). Cf. I. 3 above.

c **1460** *Towneley Myst.* ii. 251 Thou wold I gaf hym this shefe, or this sheyfe. **1551** T. WILSON *Logike* (1580) 33 Shewyng it to be true in this substaunce, and that substance. **1560** DAUS tr. *Sleidane's Comm.* 40 b, The cause of this or that precept. **1588** SHAKS. *L.L.L.* v. ii. 942 You that way; we this way. **1597** A. M. tr. *Guillemeau's Fr. Chirurg.* 5 j b, Those turne this way and that way in the hande. **1624** DONNE *Serm.* ii. (1640) 16 How Rheubarb, or how Aloes came by this, or this vertue, to purge this, or this humour. **1697** DRYDEN *Æneid* I. 82 This way and that the impatient captives tend. **1717** PRIOR *Alma* III. 494 This man pursues What if he gain'd he could not use: And t'other fondly hopes to see What never was, nor e'er shall be. **1732** BERKELEY *Alciphr.* I. § 16 Truth..must not be measured by the convenience of this or that man. **1768** GOLDSM. *Good-n. Man.* I. i, He laughs this minute with one, and cries the next with another. **1842** [see DIVIDE *v.* 8 e]. **1867** FREEMAN *Norm. Conq.* I. iii. 128 The temporary..superiority of this or that Bretwalda. **1930** R. GRAVES *Ten Poems More* 11 Neat this-way-that-way and without mistake. **1937** C. DAY LEWIS *Starting Point* I. iii. 53 The field was scored..with streaking, ..incessant this-way that-way movement.

III. Combinations and special collocations.

this child: see CHILD *sb.* 7 b; † **this gate**, (in) this way, thus (cf. THUS-GATE); † **'this half** (*obs.*), this side (HALF *sb.* 1, 2); *a* (*on*) *this half* = on this side of (see also A-THIS-HALF); **'this-how** *adv.* (*nonce-wd.* after *somehow*), in this manner, thus (in quot. as sb.); **'this-like** *a.*, like this, such as this, of this kind (cf. *these-like*, THESE, B. III); **'this-way-ward** *adv.*, towards this way, in this direction; † **this while** *advb. phr.* (also † *this whiles*), during this time, or the time in question; meanwhile; the while. See also THISKIN, THISWISE, THIS WORLD.

1513 DOUGLAS *Æneis* XII. xi. 28 Turnus, lat ws persew Troianys *this gayt. **1872**, **1893** [see GATE *sb.*[2] 2]. *c* **1205** LAY. 14018 A *þas hæ f [*c* **1275** a þis half] þere Humbre. **1387-8** T. USK *Test. Love* I. ix. (Skeat) l. 39 Is not euery thyng a thiss-halfe God; Made buxome to mannes contemplacion? **1476** SIR J. PASTON in *P. Lett.* III. 162, xij myle on thysehalff Roome, the Lorde Ryverse was robbyd off alle hys jowelles. **1868** BROWNING *Ring & Bk.* I. 706 The somehow may be *thishow. **1880** W. WATSON *Prince's Quest* Poems 1905 II. 153 The passion..voiced itself in *this-like monotone. **1662** PEPYS *Diary* 7 May, He left the Queen and fleet in the Bay of Biscay, coming *this wayward. **1594** CAREW *Huarte's Exam. Wits* xiii. (1596) 236 A thousand inconueniencies come into his fancie, which hold him in suspense, and *this-while the occasion of the remedie passeth away. **1644** DIGBY *Nat. Soul* Conc. 455 Making roome for this soule rauishing contemplation, by remouing this whiles all other images of things farre from me. **1660** F. BROOKE tr. *Le Blanc's Trav.* 3 This while the greatest part of us perished on the shallowes.

this (ðɪs), *adv.* [In I. prob. OE. *þýs*, *þís*, instrumental case of THIS *dem. pron.*; in II. app. advb. use of accus. sing. neuter (cf. THAT *adv.*). In some instances, perhaps an alteration of THUS *adv.*]

I. † **1.** In this way or manner; like this; thus.

c **1375** *Sc. Leg. Saints* i. (*Petrus*) 729 And þis he ȝalde þe spyrit. *c* **1420** *Chron. Vilod.* 3123 When þis lomb had þis y ron þrye þe tomb abouȝt. *a* **1518** SKELTON *Magnyf.* 1043, I wyll not haue it so, I wyll haue it this. *a* **1578** LINDESAY (Pitscottie) *Chron. Scot.* (S.T.S.) I. 368 And this the King of Scottland depairtit out of France. **1592** SHAKS. *Ven. & Ad.* 205 What am I that thou shouldst contemne me this?

II. † **2. a.** To this extent or degree; as much as this; thus. *Obs.* exc. as in b. (Cf. THAT *adv.*)

c **1460** *Wisdom* 936 in *Macro Plays* 66 To clense þe soull wyche ys þis fowll. ? *a* **1500** *Chester Pl.* (Shaks. Soc.) II. 11 Elles this boulde durste he not be, To make such araye. **1523** LD. BERNERS *Froiss.* I. ccclxxviii. 631 Let vs go forwarde, let vs nat be this a colde to make warr. **1567** *Gude & Godlie B.* (S.T.S.) 60 This vmbeset I am on eurie syde.

b. Qualifying an adj. or adv., orig. chiefly of quantity, esp. *this much* (where *this* is perh. felt as the pronoun = 'as much as this'; cf. THAT *adv.* b.); now also qualifying other adjs. and advs. (grading into an intensive).

c **1460** *Wisdom* 982 in *Macro Plays* 67, I be-gyn awake, I that þis longe hath slumberyde in syne. **1586** SIR F. WALSINGHAM in *Leycester's Corr.* (Camden) 230 This myche have I receyved from her majestye. **1596** DALRYMPLE tr. *Leslie's Hist. Scot.* (S.T.S.) I. 62 And this far of the Iles called Hebrides. **1675** BAXTER *Cath. Theol.* II. viii. 190 Having said this much preparatorily. **1763** C. JOHNSTON *Reverie* I. 23 He might have spared himself the trouble even of this much. **1877** RUSKIN *Fors Clav.* lxxxii. 324 Perhaps this much of Plato is enough for one letter. **1884** J. P. NORRIS in *Shakespearian* May 181 None of the portraits mentioned by Walpole are dated this early. **1885** J. J. MURPHY in *Brit. Q. Rev.* July 100 The Agnostic argument..must go this far if it is to be valid. **1932** J. LEATHAM *Fisherfolk* 13 A'm this aul', an' I never had a sy-ystem! **1967** *Boston Sunday Herald* 30 Apr. (Mag.) 34/2, I have a stack of telegrams this thick. **1971** *Where* Dec. 376/3 Yet the picture is usually not even this good. Most teachers..talk much more than half the time in their classes, and the time that is left is not all used for children talking. **1972** *Real Estate Rev.* Winter 8/2 Keep in mind, however, that no existing property is this typical. **1976** *Woman's Day* (U.S.) Nov. 154/2, I haven't felt this well in years.

thisan(e, obs. var. PTISAN, barley-water, etc.

this-a-way ('ðɪsəweɪ), *adv. dial.* and *U.S.* Also **thisaway**, **this a-way**, **this-away**, **thisserway**. [Repr. pronunc. of THIS *dem. adj.* + intrusive *-a-* + WAY *sb.*[1]: cf. THAT-A-WAY *adv.*]

1. In this manner or respect.

1834 S. LOVER *Legends & Stories of Ireland* 2nd Ser. 54 Don't ruinate me this-a-way. **1901** A. C. HEGAN *Mrs Wiggs* v. 58 Did I ever tell you 'bout how Jim brought our other hoss to town?.. It was this a-way. **1938** M. K. RAWLINGS *Yearling* xxiv. 310 He's mean, at best. He's been this-a-way ever since Oliver takened his gal away from him. **1939** *Best Short Stories* 53 Why can't it last? We're sitting pretty, thisserway. **1956** H. GOLD *Man who was not with It* (1965) xix. 166 Boy, if I wanted to tell you that, I would say it this-away: Git! My dotter's too green for screwing! **1978** J. A. MICHENER *Chesapeake* xii. 728 'I jes' cain't believe it,' he said.. 'Goddamnit, he's my own brother-in-law and he hadn't oughta behave thisaway.'

2. In this direction.

1903 *Dialect Notes* II. 333 Was he coming this-a-way when you seed him? **1955** F. O'CONNOR *Wise Blood* iii. 57 I'm going thisaway too. **1959** *Observer* 11 Oct. 6/4 Politically, Chataway can run thisaway or thataway.

thisen, this-en: see THISSEN.

† **'thiskin**, *a. Sc. Obs.* Also **thiskins**. [f. THIS *dem. a.* + KIN *sb.*[1] 6 b; repr. an OE. **þises cynnes*, early ME. **þis cunnes* = L. *hujus generis*.] Of this kind; *on thiskin wise*, on this wise, in this way.

a **1300** *Cursor M.* 3292 (Cott.) He..said til hir o þiskin wise. **1375** BARBOUR *Bruce* XVI. 49 Kyng robert, upon thiskyn wiss, In-till Irland arivit is. *c* **1420** *Sir Amadace* (Camden) xxix, Qwen he was gone on this kin wise, Thenne iche mon sayd thayre deuise.

thisne: OE. and ME. inflexion of THIS.

thisness ('ðɪsnɪs). [f. THIS + -NESS: rendering med. (Scholastic) L. *hæcceitās*.] The quality of being 'this' (as distinct from anything else): = HÆCCEITY.

1643 [see THATNESS]. **1837** WHEWELL *Hist. Induct. Sc.* (1857) I. 244 Which his school called Hæcceity or thisness. **1895** RASHDALL *Universities* II. 532 An individuating form called by the later Scotists its *hæcceitas* or 'thisness'.

thissell-cok: see THROSTLE-COCK.

thissen ('ðɪs(ə)n), *adv. dial.* Also 9 **this'ne**, **this(-)en**, **thisn**, **this'ns**. [perh. reduced from THISKIN: cf. dial. *siccan* = *swilk-kin*, *that'n what'n* = WHATKIN.] In this way or manner. Usually *a thissen* or *thissens*, in this way, thus.

(Some so understand Bottom's *Thisne* in SHAKS. *Mids. N.* I. ii. 54.)

a **1652** BROME *Eng. Moor* III. ii, *Ed.* An Idiote is it. *Buz.* Yes: A very natural; and goes a thissen. **1707** MRS. CENTLIVRE *Platonick Lady* IV. i, If old Roger Dowdy were alive and zeen me thissen. **1790** MRS. WHEELER *Westmld. Dial.* 89 Tae gang on a thisen is a fearful Thing. *a* **1825** FORBY *Voc. E. Anglia*, *This'ns, thus'ns, that'ns*..in this or that manner.

thister, þister, variant of THESTER *Obs.*, dark.

thistle ('θɪs(ə)l), *sb.* Forms: 1 **thistil**, **þistel**, **þystel**, 4–6 **thistel**, **thystle**, 5 **thestel**, **thystelle**, **-tylle**, 5–6 **thistell**, **thystell**, 6 **thystel**, **thistyll**,

thessel, 7 thissel, 5- thistle. *β.* (chiefly *Sc.*) 5 thristelle, 5-7 thrissill(e, 6 thirsill, thyrsill, 6-9 thrissel, thrisle, 8-9 thrissle, 9 thristle. *γ.* 9 *dial.* fissle, fistle. [OE. *þistil*, *-el* m. = OHG. *distil* masc., *distila* fem. (MHG. *distel* m., f., Ger. *distel* f.), Du. *distel*, ON. *þistell*, *-ill* m. (Sw. *tistel*, Da. *tidsel*). Modern dialects point to an original long *ī* in the stem-syllable (cf. Somersetsh. *dəis'l*, *deiʃ'l*, *dāʃ'l*; also LG. *diestal*, *dīstel*, *dîssel*, beside *dəistələ*, *deussl*, *duissl*, in various German dialects. Of OTeut. **pistil-o²* m., **pīstil-a* f., the ulterior history is unknown.
Sc. *thristell* may have been influenced by *thrist* vb.]

1. a. The common name of the prickly herbaceous plants of the genus *Carduus* (N.O. *Compositæ*, suborder *Cynarocephalæ*) and several closely allied genera (*Cnicus*, *Cirsium*, *Onopordum*, etc.), having the stems, leaves, and involucres thickly armed with prickles, the flower-heads usually globular, and the flowers most commonly purple; many species are abundant as weeds.

Formerly (and in scriptural or rhetorical language) applied vaguely, including various prickly plants: cf. 2, 3.
c725 *Corpus Gloss.* (O.E.T.) 384 *Carduus*, þistel. **a800** *Erfurt Gloss.* 271 *Carduus*, thistil. **c1050** *Gloss.* in Wr.-Wülcker 379/23 *Carduus orrens*, se onscunienda þystel. **a1327** *On Dreams* in *Rel. Ant.* I. 264 Ȝef thou etest of thystles ȝurne, Thy fomon the freteth on uche hurne. **c1400** *Rom. Rose* 1835 Thornes sharpe..Ther were, and also thistels thikke, And breres, brimme for to prikke. **1481** CAXTON *Reynard* xxxii. (Arb.) 86, I haue nothyng but thystles and nettles. **1535** COVERDALE *Gen.* iii. 18 Cursed be yᵉ earth for thy sake... Thornes and thistles shall it beare vnto the. **1562** TURNER *Herbal* II. 145 b, Spina in Latin is properly called a thistel. **1650** BAXTER *Saint's R.* I. vii, Doubts are like the Thistle, a bad weed, but growing in good ground. **1758** R. BROWN *Compl. Farmer* II. (1760) 31 Thistles, docks, and all sorts of rank weeds. **1890** A. R. WALLACE *Darwinism* 28 Hundreds of square miles of the plains of La Plata are now covered with..species of European thistle.
β. **c1400** MAUNDEV. (1839) xi. 130 A gode contree to sowen Inne thristelle & breres & broom & thornes. **1503** DUNBAR *Thistle & Rose* 129 Vpone the awfull Thrissill scho beheld. **1548** H. BALNAUES *Conf. Faith* (1584) 132 May yee gather grapes of thornes, or figges of thrisles? **1806** A. DOUGLAS *Poems* 145 (E.D.D.) Nae thrisles here your thumbs to prick. **1815** SCOTT *Guy M.* iii, The thristles by the road-side.
γ. **1809** T. BATCHELOR *Orth. Anal. Eng. Lang., Bedford Words* 123/2 Provincial Pronunciations, *fislz*. **1848** B. EVANS *Leicestersh. Words*, *Fistle*, var. pron. of 'thistle'. **1886** BRITTEN & HOLLAND *Plant-n.*, *Fissle*, *Fistle*, a thistle.

b. As the heraldic emblem of Scotland; also, a figure of a thistle as such. Cf. ROSE *sb.*[1] 6 b, 12 c.
1488 *Acc. Ld. High Treas. Scot.* I. 85 A couering of.. purpir tartar browdin with thrissillis and a vnicorne. **1507** *Ibid.* III. 261 Thre thrissilles of coppir gilt. **1562** A. SCOTT *Poems* (S.T.S.) i. 3 Welcum, oure thrissill with þe Lorane grene! **1786** BURNS *Earnest Cry & Prayer* vii, Paint Scotland greeting owre her thrissle. **1831** SCOTT *Cast. Dang.* xiii, She seeks the Black Douglas, or some such hero of the Thistle. **1853** [see ROSE *sb.*[1] 12 c].

c. As a part of the insignia of the ***Order of the Thistle***, the distinctively Scottish order of knighthood (instituted by James II in 1687 and revived by Queen Anne in 1703) conferred on noblemen of that country; hence *transf.* the order itself, or membership in it; ***Knight of the Thistle***, a member of this order.
1687 *Lond. Gaz.* No. 2251/2 His Majesty having been Graciously Pleased the 29th of May last, to Sign a Patent to be past under the Great Seal of Scotland, for Reviving and Restoring [*sic*] the most Ancient and most Noble Order of the Thistle. **1710** *Ibid.* No. 4694/3 The Earl of Stair was invested..with the most Noble Order of the Thistle. **1732** *Gentl. Mag.* June 827/1 The E. of Portmore, made a Kt of the Thistle in the Room of the E. of Loudoun, dec. **1828** N. H. NICOLAS *Statutes of Order of Thistle* 21 After its [*sc.* Order of the Thistle's] Revival by King James, the Knights of the Thistle were Installed in the Chapel of Holyrood House. **1852** THACKERAY *Esmond* III. iv, Having the Thistle already originally bestowed on him by King James the Second, his Grace was now promoted to the honour of the Garter. **1898** *Westm. Gaz.* 10 Jan. 1/1 The Duke of Argyll ..received his Thistle from Lord Palmerston in 1851. **1911** J. WARRACK *Knights of Most Noble Order of Thistle* 29 The King, after consulting the Chapter of the Knights of the Thistle, ordered a letter to be sent. **1963** *Times* 30 Apr. 10/7 Sir Robert Menzies, the Prime Minister, is expected to visit Britain and the United States in June,..later going to Edinburgh to be installed as a Knight of the Thistle.

d. *transf.* Something resembling a thistle in form or appearance.
1891 J. W. HARRISON *Mackay of Uganda* i. 2 Thistles of frost garnished the window-panes.

e. *fig.* or in figurative context, with reference to the thistle as a noxious or prickly weed.
1563 WINƷET *Vincent. Lirin.* xxviii. Wks. (S.T.S.) II. 59 God forbid that the rose plantis of the catholik sense be turnit in thrissillis and thornis! **1642** FULLER *Holy & Prof. St.* v. xiv. 415 He snatcheth at the thistle of a project, which first pricks his hands, and then breaks. **1797-1803** FOSTER in *Life & Corr.* (1846) I. 163 Adversity! thou thistle of life. **1840** CARLYLE *Heroes* ii, His knowledge is a pedantry, and dead thistle, otherwise.

†2. a. Applied (definitely) to other prickly plants, as artichoke, sea-holly (*Eryngium*), teasel, etc.
1398 TREVISA *Barth. De P.R.* XVII. cxxvii. (Bodl. MS.), Paliurus is a þistel moste rowȝe & scharp with prikkes and growiþ..wiþ certeyne hedes ful of certeyne prickes. **14..** [see TEASEL *sb.* 1]. **1545** ELYOT, *Scolymus*, a thystell nowe called Arkechoke, of some men is taken for the.. cowethystell. **1577** B. GOOGE *Heresbach's Husb.* II. (1586) 64 A Thistell is the Hartichoch; that euerie where dooth grow. **1578** LYTE *Dodoens* IV. lviii. 519 The first kinde of these Thistels is called..in Latine *Eryngium*:..in Englishe,..Sea Holly. *Ibid.* lx. 522 Of the Teasel... This kinde of Thistel is called..in Englishe, Fullers Teasel, Carde Thistell.

b. = TEASEL *sb.* 2.
1839 URE *Dict. Arts* 1322 The large side [of the frame], against which the tops of the teasels rest, is hollowed out... There are..cross-bars, which serve..to form short compartments for keeping the thistles compact.

3. With qualifying words, applied to various species of *Carduus* and allied genera, and to some prickly plants of other orders: as **bull thistle**, a local name (in Ireland and U.S.) for *Carduus lanceolatus*; **Californian thistle** (*N.Z.*), **Canada thistle** (*U.S.*), **corn-thistle, creeping thistle, cursed thistle**, *Carduus arvensis* (*Cirsium arvense*), a troublesome weed with creeping rootstocks; **dog thistle**, 'apparently *Carduus arvensis*' (Britten & Holland); **dwarf thistle**, *Carduus* (*Cnicus*) *acaulis*; **gentle thistle**, *Carduus anglicus*; **green thistle**, **herring-bone thistle** (also called ***fish-bone thistle***: see FISH *sb.*[1] 7), *Chamæpeuce* (*Cirsium*) *Casabonæ*; **holy thistle**, (*a*) *Centaurea benedicta* (*Cnicus benedictus*), with yellow flowers and weak prickles on the leaves, formerly in repute as an antidote; also called ***blessed thistle***; (*b*) erron. applied to *Carduus Marianus*, with white veins on the leaves; also called ***Our Lady's thistle*** or ***milk thistle***; **hundred-headed thistle** (abbrev. ***hundred thistle***), *Eryngium campestre* (N.O. *Umbelliferæ*); **Jersey thistle**, *Centaurea Isnardi* (*C. aspera*); **Mexican thistle**, a prickly composite plant, *Erythrolæna conspicua*, cultivated in gardens, having yellow florets surrounded with scarlet involucral scales; **Russian thistle** (*U.S.*), a species of saltwort, *Salsola Tragus*, with prickly stems, introduced from Russia into S. Dakota with flax-seed, and now abundant as a weed in that and neighbouring States; **Scotch thistle**, a name for the species supposed to be that figured as the emblem of Scotland, variously identified as the spear-thistle (*Carduus lanceolatus*), the musk thistle (*C. nutans*), the milk thistle (*C. Marianus*), and the cotton-thistle (*Onopordum Acanthium*); **silver thistle**, a name for the cotton-thistle; **smooth thistle**, a name for SOWTHISTLE (*Sonchus*); **Syrian thistle**, *Notobasis Syriaca*; **welted thistle**, *Carduus acanthoides*; **woolly thistle**, the cotton-thistle; **woolly-headed thistle**, *C. eriophorus*; **yellow thistle**, (*a*) a species of thistle with pale-yellow or purple flowers (*Cnicus horridulus*), found in the eastern U.S.; (*b*) a name for the prickly poppy (*Argemone mexicana*): see POPPY *sb.* 3. See also ARGENTINE *thistle*, *St.* BARNABY'S *t.*, BLESSED *t.*, BOAR *t.*, BUR *t.*, CARD *t.*, CARLINE *t.*, COTTON-THISTLE, DISTAFF *t.*, FRIAR'S *t.*, FULLERS' *t.*, GLOBE *t.*, GOLDEN *t.*, GUM *t.*, HARE'S *t.*, HEDGEHOG *t.*, HORSE *t.*, LADY'S THISTLE, *St. Mary's t.*, MELANCHOLY *t.*, MELON *t.*, MILK *t.*, MUSK *t.*, OAT *t.*, PINE *t.*, PLUME *t.*, SAFFRON *t.*, SEA-THISTLE, SOWTHISTLE, SPEAR *t.*, STAR-THISTLE, SWINE'S *t.*, THOWTHISTLE, TORCH *t.*, WAY *t.*, WOLF'S *t.*
1878 BRITTEN & HOLLAND *Eng. Plant-n.*, *Bull Thistle, *Carduus lanceolatus. Irel.* (Belfast). **1891** R. WALLACE *Rural Econ. Austral. & N.Z.* xxii. 310 One of the most recent importations..is that of the 'Canadian' or '*Californian' thistle. **1948** D. W. BALLANTYNE *Cunninghams* I. ii. 10 It's been awful with Californian thistle up there. **1884** MILLER *Plant-n.*, *Cirsium arvense*, *Canada Thistle, Creeping Thistle, 'Cursed Thistle', of N. America. **1878** BRITTEN & HOLLAND *Eng. Plant-n.*, *Corn Thistle, *Carduus arvensis.* **1845** *Gard. Chron.* 20 Dec. 864/1 Will any of your correspondents inform me the most effectual way to eradicate the *Dog Thistle? **1846** SOWERBY *Eng. Bot.* (ed. 3), *Dwarf Thistle, *Carduus acaulis.* **1760** J. LEE *Introd. Bot.* App. 329 *Gentle Thistle. **1882** *Garden* 3 June 391/3 A large oval-shaped bed of Ricinus Gibsoni..edged with Chamæpeuce Casabonæ or *Green Thistle. **1884** MILLER *Plant-n.*, *Chamæpeuce Casabonæ*, Fish-bone or *Herring-bone Thistle. **1587** MASCALL *Govt. Cattle, Horses* (1627) 190 Take the soft downe of the stalks of the hearb *Cardus Benedictus*, called the *holy-thistle, and therewith fill the wounds. **1599** SHAKS. *Much Ado* III. iv. 80 Get you some of this distill'd *carduus benedictus*.., it is the only thing for a qualm... I meant plaine holy thissell. **1793** A. B[ISANI] *Pict. Tour Europe*, etc. 52 Sciato... The hills..are covered with holy thistle, centaury, thyme, sage, and calamint. **1866** *Treas. Bot.* 222 The Holy Thistle (*Carduus Marianus*) is well marked by the white veins on its large shiny leaves. **1893** MCCARTHY *Red Diamonds* II. 42 Here was holy thistle, which of old its admirers called Benedictus for its supposed astonishing virtues. **1578** LYTE *Dodoens* IV. lviii. 519 The other kinde is called..the *Hundred headed Thistel... This without doubt is a kinde of Eringium. **1880** BRITTEN & HOLLAND *Eng. Plant-n.*, Hundred Thistle, *Eryngium campestre.* **1866** *Treas. Bot.* 468 *E*[*rythrolæna*] *conspicua*.. was introduced to English gardens about 1838, and is commonly known as the Scarlet *Mexican Thistle. **1705** tr. *Cowley's Plants* Wks. 1711 III. 367 Whilst the *Scotch Thistle, with audacious Pride, Taking Advantage, gores your bleeding Side. **1861** MISS PRATT *Flower. Pl.* III. 240 The handsome Cotton Thistle..is often cultivated under the name of the Scotch Thistle. **1888** *Encycl. Brit.* XXIII. 307/1 The common *C*[*arduus*] *lanceolatus* seems to be the most suitable prototype for the Scotch Thistle. **1578** LYTE *Dodoens* IV. lxiv. 526 In Latine *Acanthium*;..in Englishe White Cotton Thistell, Wilde white Thistell, and Argentine, or *Siluer Thistel. **1633** *Gerarde's Herbal* II. xx. 292 The stalk of Hares Lettuce or *smooth-Thistle. **1866** *Treas. Bot.* 794 The *Syrian Thistle, *N*[*otobasis*] *syriaca*,.. is distinguished from other thistles by the central florets of the flower-head only being fertile. **1846** SOWERBY *Eng. Bot.* (ed. 3), *Welted Thistle, *Carduus crispus.* **1884** MILLER *Plant-n.*, Thistle, Welted, *Carduus acanthoides.* **1760** J. LEE *Introd. Bot.* App. 329 Thistle, *Woolly, *Onopordon.* **1867** BABINGTON *Man. Brit. Bot.* (ed. 6) 200 *C*[*arduus*] *eriophorus*. .. Heads very large; involucre covered with a dense white web... *Woolly-headed Thistle. **1866** *Treas. Bot.* 1145 Thistle.., *Yellow, *Argemone mexicana.*

4. *attrib.* and *Comb.*, as ***thistle-clock*** [CLOCK *sb.*[1] 8], ***-flower***; ***thistle-topped*** adj.; **thistle-ball**, the globular head of feathery seeds of the thistle; **thistle-beard** = THISTLE-DOWN; **thistle-bird**, a bird that feeds on thistle-seeds (cf. THISTLE-FINCH); *spec.* the American goldfinch, *Chrysomitris* (*Spinus*) *tristis*; **thistle-butterfly**, the 'painted lady', *Vanessa* (*Pyrameis*) *cardui*, whose larva feeds on the thistle; **thistle-cock** (*dial.*), the corn bunting, *Emberiza miliaria*; (see also THROSTLE-COCK); **thistle-cropper** = *thistle-eater* (*b*); **thistle-crown**, (*a*) a name for a Scottish gold coin of James VI, bearing the figure of a thistle on the reverse, and worth about 4 shillings; cf. *thistle noble*; (*b*) the flower-head of the thistle; **thistle cup**, a silver cup with an outward-turning rim, of a type formerly manufactured in Scotland; **thistle-cutter**, a machine for cutting down thistles or other weeds; **thistle-digger**, a tool for rooting up thistles; **thistle dollar**, (*a*) a name for a Scottish silver coin of James VI, also called *double merk*, bearing the figure of a thistle on the reverse, and worth 26*s.* 8*d.* Scotch (2*s.* $2\frac{2}{3}$*d.* English); (*b*) a silver coin of the reign of Charles II; **thistle-eater, thistle-feeder**, (*a*) a bird that eats thistle-seeds (cf. THISTLE-FINCH); (*b*) a beast that eats thistles, as a donkey; so **thistle-feeding** *a.*; **thistle-fly**, an insect (*Urophora cardui*) infesting a species of thistle; **thistle funnel**, a kind of funnel used in chemical operations, having a large bulb between the conical flaring part and the tube, so as to suggest the form of a thistle-head upon its stalk; **thistle-gall**, a gall produced by the *thistle-fly* or **thistle-gall fly**; **thistle glass**, a drinking glass with a round bowl and an outward-turning rim; **thistle-head**, the flower-head or *capitulum* of the thistle (in quot. 1839, that of the teasel = 2 b above); **thistle-like** *a.*, resembling a thistle; also, of the thistle kind, of the suborder *Cynarocephalæ* of *Compositæ*, comprising the thistles and allied plants; **thistle merk** [MARK *sb.*[2]], collectors' name for a Scottish silver coin of James VI, bearing the figure of a thistle on the reverse, and worth 13*s.* 4*d.* Scotch ($13\frac{1}{3}$*d.* English); **thistle noble**, a Scottish gold half-merk of James VI, bearing the figure of a thistle on the reverse; **thistle-plume** [PLUME *sb.* 5], *U.S.*, 'a plume-moth, *Pterophorus carduidactylus*, whose larva feeds on thistle-heads' (*Cent. Dict.*); **thistle-saffron**, the safflower = *saffron-thistle* (see SAFFRON 6 c); **thistle-seed**, the feathery or pappose 'seed' or achene of the thistle; **thistle-spud** = *thistle-digger*; **thistle-stamped** *a.*, stamped with the figure of a thistle; **thistle-teasel** = TEASEL *sb.* 2; **thistle-top**, (*a*) = THISTLE-DOWN; (*b*) = *thistle-head*; **thistle-tube** = *thistle funnel*; **thistle-tuft** = THISTLE-DOWN; **thistle-whipper** (*Hunting slang*), a nickname for a hare-hunter.
1855 BROWING *Two in Campagna* xi, Must I go Still like the *thistle-ball..Onward, whenever light winds blow? **1797** COLERIDGE *Foster-mother's T.* 20 A baby wrapt in mosses, lined with *thistle-beards. **1872** COUES *N. Amer. Birds* 131 American Goldfinch. Yellowbird. *Thistlebird. **1893** *Scribner's Mag.* June 763/1 The goldfinch or wild canary is seen, perched on a thistle-top... 'Thistle bird' is another name that he bears, on account of his fondness for thistle-seeds as food, and thistle-down for the lining of his nest. **1836** PRICHARD *Phys. Hist. Man.* (ed. 3) I. 58 The *thistle-butterfly, termed 'La Belle Dame'. **1948** C. DAY LEWIS *Poems 1943-47* 63 *Thistle-clocks fly. **1866** EDMONSTON *Shetl. & Orkney Gloss.* 127 **Thistle-cock*, common bunting (*Emberiza miliaria*). **1726** LEAKE *Nummi Brit. Hist.* 83 *Thistle Crowns..4*s.* $4\frac{1}{2}$*d.* **1878** M. A. BROWN *Nadeschda* 20 Plucked a thistle-crown and fastened it As a breast-knot. **1899** *Daily News* 12 July 8/3 To watch the goldfinch clinging to the silken thistle-crown. **1947** W. C. WALLIS *Silver, Glass & Pott.* 4 Another type of vessel, unique in Scotland, which made its appearance during the last twenty years of the seventeenth century, is the little mug known, from its supposed resemblance to a thistle, as a '*thistle' cup. **1968** *Canadian Antiques Collector* July 17/1 Late in the seventeenth century appear two forms of secular silver unique to Scotland. One is a drinking cup of a type

often called a 'thistle' cup, though it has little resemblance to a thistle. **1901** *Dundee Advertiser* 30 June 3 A capital display of the *thistle cutter's powers on a rank growth of bracken.., the rapidly whirling knives..made short..work of the bracken. **1877** KNIGHT *Dict. Mech.* s.v. *Spade*, The *thistle-digger is a pronged tool, intended to catch the root below the crown, and then pry out of the plant. **1562** TURNER *Herbal* II. 145 b, Aristotel..wryteth..: τὰ δὲ τοία ἀκανθοφάγα... That is to saye, these are spiniuora, that is *thistel eaters... Aristotell sayeth that Linetes and Goldfinches, and Grenefinches, are acanthophage. **1904** *Daily News* 20 June 5, I did not see either the bullfinch or the goldfinch,..either the detested bud-plucker or the pretty *thistle-feeder. **1906** *Outlook* 24 Mar. 404/2 In Hertfordshire, a county notable for the high-farming that was supposed to have exiled the *thistle-feeding birds, goldfinches were singing about their nests. **1552** HULOET, *Thystle floure, *scholymos.* **1908** [MISS FOWLER] *Betw. Trent & Ancholme* 107 No Thistle flowers as yet. **1753** CHAMBERS *Cycl. Supp.*, **Thistle Fly*, a small fly produced from a flyworm, hatching in the protuberances of the carduus hæmorrhoidalis. **1849** D. CAMPBELL *Inorg. Chem.* 17 Sometimes a small funnel (called a *thistle funnel) passes through the cork, and reaches nearly to the bottom of the bottle. **1753** CHAMBERS *Cycl. Supp.*, **Thistle-Galls*, a name given..to the protuberances on the stalks of a species of Thistle, called..*carduus hæmorrhoidalis*, from these tubercles, which are supposed to resemble those of the hæmorrhoidal veins. **1864-5** WOOD *Homes without H.* xxvi. (1868) 505 The Thistle-gall Fly (*Urophora Cardui*)..produces large and hard woody galls upon the thistle. **1935** M. MITCHISON *We have been Warned* II. 138 Alex..got a bottle of hock and poured it out into *thistle glasses. **1973** *Times* 20 Oct. 14/3 The 'thistle' glass, with its outward-angled rim. **1839** URE *Dict. Arts* 1322, 16 frames bearing the teasels which are to act upon the cloth,..their breadth only large enough to contain two *thistle-heads set end to end. **1896** *Spectator* 31 Oct. 588/2 He [a bee] returned to the inviting thistle-head. **1857** HENFREY *Bot.* 320 The *Cynareæ*, or *thistle-like Compositæ. **1866** *Treas. Bot.* 225 *Carlina*, a genus..distinguished among the thistle-like group of compound flowers by having the inner leaves of the..involucre coloured. **1590-1** *Reg. Privy Council Scot.* IV. 574, [200 oz. weight of] utter fyne gold [shall be coined] in the *thrissill noblis. **1603** *Ibid.* VI. 529 Thrissill noblis of gold. **1782** COWPER *Progr. Err.* 555 They..Like *thistle-seeds, are sown by every wind. **1896** MRS. CAFFYN *Quaker Grandm.* 105 Why should Mr. Ince lag behind with the dogs, and his *thistle-spud? **1882** J. WALKER *Jaunt Auld Reekie* 41 *Thistle-stampit auld Scotch bodles. **1835** URE *Philos. Manuf.* 202 Preparing *thistle-teasels for the workman. **1552** HULOET, *Thystle toppe, whyche is lyke plume, *pappus.* **1606** [see THISTLEWARP]. **1893** [see *thistle-bird* above]. **1903** *Westm. Gaz.* 29 Dec. 10/1 Carved thistles ornament his dining-room chairs; and a *thistle-topped railing lends novelty to the front of the house. *a* **1847** ELIZA COOK *Song of Wind* iii, I grasped an airy *thistle-tuft. **1801** *Sporting Mag.* XIX. 114 This North-Country *Thistle Whipper. **1856** 'STONEHENGE' *Brit. Sports* (ed. 2) §1 A brace of hares, or a single fox, will serve for the amusement of a large field of fox-hunters or thistle-whippers.

Hence **'thistle** *v., trans.* to clear of thistles, to weed out the thistles from (whence **'thistling** *vbl. sb.*); **thistled** ('θɪs(ə)ld) *a.*, covered or overgrown with thistles; adorned with figures of thistles; **'thistlery** ('θɪs(ə)lrɪ), a plantation of thistles; **'thistlish** *a.*, resembling or suggesting a thistle.

1766 *Compl. Farmer* s.v., In France, a farmer may sue his neighbour who neglects to *thistle his land at the proper seasons. **1745** in Motherwell *Harp of Renfrewshire* (1819) 319 The *Thistled banners far were streaming. **1797** MRS. M. ROBINSON *Walsingham* I. 72 The upland mead, and thistled down. **1893** CHR. G. ROSSETTI *Poems* (1904) 123/2 Our thorned and thistled plot. **1889** MARY E. BAMFORD *Up & Down Brooks* 97 Do not his folk make such '*thistleries' in Paraguay that robbers can hide among them? **1766** *Compl. Farmer*, **Thistling*, the action of cutting or pulling up thistles. **1858** MOTLEY *Corr.* 17 June, Like his tongue and his mind, it [his visage] is eminently Scotch, sharp, caustic, rugged, *thistle-ish.

thistle, obs. variant of THIXEL, an adz.

thistle-down ('θɪs(ə)ldaʊn). [f. THISTLE *sb.* + DOWN *sb.*[2]] The down or pappus which crowns the 'seeds' or achenes of the thistle, and by means of which they are carried along by the wind: either collectively, or that of a single 'seed'.

1561 [see c]. **1585** HIGINS *Junius' Nomencl.* 112/1 *Pappus*, the downe of flowers which the wind bloweth about: as thistle downe. **1591** SPENSER *M. Hubberd* 634 As a thistle-downe in th' ayre doth flie. **1723** MANDEVILLE *Fab. Bees* 277 If it were a hard Winter, they mingled some Thistle down with their Rushes to keep them warm. **1879** JEFFERIES *Wild Life in S. Co.* 206 Thistledown is sometimes gathered to fill pillow-cases. **1894** MISS F. WILLARD in *Chicago Advance* 4 Oct., One sees a thistledown borne on the breeze.

b. As a type of lightness, flimsiness, or instability; hence *fig.*

1868 W. CORY *Lett. & Jrnls.* (1897) 251 The thistle-down of sentiment hung about me all the time. **1904** R. HICHENS *Gard. Allah* x, Forgive my malice... It was really a thing of thistledown. **1908** *Outlook* 27 Nov. 880/1 That is not to say that Christianity is to be a thistledown to be blown hither and thither at the breath of every fad and whim.

c. *attrib.* Of or like thistle-down (*lit.* and *fig.*).

1561 *Will M. Langrygge* (Somerset Ho.), Thesseldowne bed. **1889** *John Bull* 2 Mar. 149/3 The train was of thistle-down brocade, that being the design brocaded, or rather embossed, upon the snowy surface of the silk. **1897** *Westm. Gaz.* 12 Feb. 2/1 The thistle-down character of Miss Hart.

'thistle-finch. [f. as prec. + FINCH; cf. G. *distelfink*, OHG. *distilvinko*, Du. *distelvink.*] Any one of several species of finches which feed on the seeds of the thistle; *spec.* the goldfinch, *Carduelis elegans.*

1589 FLEMING *Virg. Georg.* III. 48 The singing thistle-finch. **1678** RAY *Willughby's Ornith.* 256 The Goldfinch, or Thistle-finch. **1736** AINSWORTH *Lat. Dict.* III. s.v. *Aëdon*, She is feigned to have died for grief, and to be turned into a linnet, or thistlefinch. **1851** BRODERIP *Leaves fr. Note Bk. Nat.* (1852) 230 The goldfinch or thistlefinch passes much of its time among flowers.

† **'thistle-tack.** *Obs.* exc. *Hist.* [Origin obscure: connexion with THISTLE *sb.* is doubtful; the second element is TACK *sb.*[2]] The name in some localities of a due levied upon the owners of pigs by the lord of the manor, as a charge for pannage. Cf. quot. 1523 for *tack-swine*, s.v. TACK *sb.*[2] 6.

1303-5 *York Vac. Roll* (Ministers Accts. 1144/1, P.R.O.), Et de xs. vijd. de operibus custumariorum..cum pannagio quod dicitur thistiltak. **1327** *Inquis. Death Thomas Earl Lancaster* (I.P.M. Edw. III, File 6 (m. 3), P.R.O.) (Yorks., Soureby), Et de quadam consuetudine porcorum ibidem vocata Thistletack ad terminum Sancti Andree xviij d. **1377** *Halymote of Halton*, etc. (Court Rolls 50 Edw. III, Bundle 2. No. 27), Et de iij s collectis de pannagio vocato Thistletak pro porcis diversorum tenencium domini apud Runkorn. **1419** *Excheq. Accts.* 7 *Hen. V*, Bundle 131. No. 14 (Forest of Galtres, Yorks.) Sed de Thistiltak nichil quia nullum tale proficuum accidit hoc anno.

¶ The following accounts of the term are given by 17th c. writers:

1677 THOROTON *Nottinghamshire* 308/1 If any Native or Cottager [at Fiskerton, Nottinghamshire] having a Swine above a year old, should kill him, he was to give the Lord 1[d]. and it was called Thistletak. **1691** *Blount's Law Dict.* (ed. 2), *Thistle-take*,..a Custom in the honor of Halton,..That if in driving Beasts over the Common, the Driver permits them to graze or take but a Thistle, he shall pay a half-peny a Beast to the Lord of the Fee. **1906** N. J. HONE *Manor & Manor. Recds.* 112 'Thistle-take' was claimed by the lords [of Manors] in Lancashire and Yorkshire, as an acknowledgment of the hasty crop taken by droves of beasts passing over a common, and similar payments.

(The statement in quot. 1691 (whence in 1906) was evidently 'popular etymology'.)

† **'thistlewarp.** *Obs.* [f. THISTLE *sb.* + WARP *v.*, to throw, turn, twist; cf. MOULDWARP.] The goldfinch: = THISTLE-FINCH.

1606 MARLOWE & CHAPMAN *Hero & Leander* VI. 277 Neptune for pity..Flung them into the air, and did awake them Like two sweet birds, surnamed th' Acanthides, Which we call Thistle-warps, that..feed on thistle-tops. **1624** BURTON *Anat. Mel.* II. iii. VII, An asse flung downe a Thistlewarpes neast, the little bird pecked his gaul'd backe in revenge.

thistly ('θɪs(ə)lɪ), *a.* [f. THISTLE *sb.* + -Y.]

1. Of the nature of or resembling a thistle; spiny, prickly; consisting of or consituted by thistles. (In 1611, made of 'thistles', i.e. teasel-heads.)

1598 SYLVESTER *Du Bartas* II. ii. IV. *Columnes* 625 That shell [of the chestnut] incas't in a thick thistly fell. **1611** COTGR., *Applaneur de draps*, the Cloathworker; who with his thistly cards doth smooth, and stroake downe clothes. **1784** COWPER *Task* VI. 768 The land..Exults to see its thistly curse repealed. **1845** G. STRUTHERS in *Ess. Chr. Union* vii. (1851) 416 The plant of schism has put forth its thistly spines wherever it has been carried.

2. Full of, abounding or overgrown, with thistles.

1710 *Tusser Redivivus* in *T.'s Husb.* (1878) 129 *note*, Where the Wheat is thistly. **1727-46** THOMSON *Summer* 1658 Wide o'er the thistly lawn, as swells the breeze, A whitening shower of vegetable down Amusive floats. **1900** HUDSON *Nat. in Downland* 41 Thistly and weedy wastelands.

3. *fig.* (from 1 and 2).

1784 COWPER *Task* IV. 335 A world, so thorny,..where none Finds happiness..Without some thistly sorrow at it's side. **1866** HOWELLS *Venet. Life* 342 Converted into a fortress..all thistly with bayonets. **1889** *Harper's Mag.* Mar. 661/1 Wandering..into thistly byways of dissent.

† **'thistolow.** *Obs. rare.* Altered form of *fistolow*, FISTULA: see TH (6).

1684 HANNAH WOOLLEY *Queen-like Closet* (ed. 5) Supp. 25 When you dress any Wound or Thistolow with it, you must warm it very hot. *Ibid.*, I did cure a Gentlewoman of a Thistolow in the Eye with it.

thiswise ('ðɪswaɪz), *adv.* Now *rare.* [Short for *a* (*on*) *this wise.*] In this manner, thus.

13.. *Cursor M.* 11971 (Cott.) 'Sun', sco said '[wirk] noght þis wise'. **1509** BARCLAY *Shyp of Folys* (1570) 244 Howe darest thou wretched men this wise abuse? **1530** TINDALE *Answ. More* Wks. (1572) 254/2 Whiche text may this wise be vnderstand. **1846** H. W. TORRENS *Rem. Milit. Hist.* 166 This-wise they slowly pursued their journey.

this world. a. The present world; the present state or stage of existence, as distinguished from another, esp. a future one. (Cf. OTHER WORLD.)

c **950** *Lindisf. Gosp.*, Luke xvi. 8 Suno ðisses woruldes [*c* **1000** *Ags. Gosp* ðisse worulde bearn]. *a* **1175** *Cott. Hom.* 231 He cumð an ende þisser wrld. *c* **1175** *Lamb. Hom.* 7 þeos world is whilende. **1382** WYCLIF *John* xvi. 11 The prince of this world is now demyd. **1470-85** MALORY *Arthur* XIII. vii. 621 They alle shalle neuer mete more in thys world. **1583** J. MUNDEN in J. B. Wainwright *Two Eng. Mart.* (C.T.S.) 24 Biddinge you farewell for ever in this worlde. **1705** STANHOPE *Paraphr.* III. 332 The perishing possessions of this World. **1883** MISS BRADDON *Gold. Calf* xiv, What higher office can a man hold in this world than to form the minds of the rising generation?

b. *attrib.* Pertaining to this world; mundane.

1889 J. TITSWORTH in *Chicago Advance* 7 Feb., [To] appreciate the this-world sphere of the Kingdom of Heaven.

Hence ˌ**this-'worldian**, a man of this world, a wordling; **'this-ˌworldism**, ˌ**this-'worldliness**, devotion to the things of this world; **'this-worldly** *a.*, concerned with the things of this world or the present state of existence; **'this-worldness** = THIS-WORLDLINESS.

1830 COLERIDGE *Ch. & St.* (1839) 77 Those..that separate the Christian from the this-worldian. **1872** HOWELLS *Wedd. Journ.* (1892) 269 A spiritual-worldiness which was the clarified likeness of this-worldiness. **1883** W. M. ADAMSON in *Evang. Union Worthies* 319 This-worldism ignored God, if it did not deny His existence. **1883** 'MARK TWAIN' *Life on Mississippi* xlviii. 480 The guests were always this-worldly, and often profane. **1887** *Pall Mall G.* 19 Oct. 2/1 The Need of 'This-worldliness'... Evangelical Christians have been too often guilty of 'other-worldliness'. **1928** C. H. DODD *Authority of Bible* IV. xii. 268 Hard experience revealed the insufficiency of the robust 'this-worldliness' of the classical Hebrew religion. **1930** G. GREENE *Two Witnesses* 92 His sensitively spiritual soul could make no truce with any thisworldness. **1944** J. S. HUXLEY *On Living in Revol.* xv. 187 The Churches..feel themselves threatened by the rise of an outlook more concerned with social planning for this-worldly improvement than with individual concern for other-worldly salvation. **1957** *Times Lit. Suppl.* 20 Dec. 776/1 Our civilization acquired its secular, scientific, anti-theological character, its 'this-worldliness'. **1978** J. SKORUPSKI in Hookway & Pettit *Action & Interpretation* 83 It treats the magical and, by and large, the religious practices as 'instrumental': as attempts to control the course of events in such a way as to bring about this-worldly ends which the actors seek.

thite, obs. and dial. form of THIGHT.

thither ('ðɪðə(r)), *adv.* (*a.*) Forms: see below. [OE. *ðider*, *þider*, earlier *þæder* (Lindisf. *ðadder*): corresp. in form to ON. *þaðra* there; f. *þa-*, stem of THAT, THE + suffix, denoting motion towards, Goth. *-drē*, Vedic *-trā*: cf. *hither*, OE. *hider*, Goth. *hidrē*, and *whither*, OE. *hwider*:—*hwæder*, Goth. *hwadrē*; a form corresp. to OE. *þæder* is wanting in Goth. (which uses *jaindrē* thither, yonder); cf. Vedic *tatrā* there, thither. The OE. *þæder*, *hwæder* became *þider*, *hwider*, app. under the influence of *hider*, HITHER, in which the *i* was original. For the later ME. *-ther* for *-der* in all three words (first in MSS. of *Cursor Mundi*, but rare bef. 1525), as in *gather*, *mother*, etc., see TH (6), and Note s.v. FATHER. In Sc. *thidder* came down to 1600. The extended ME. *þidere*, *þidre*, was app. influenced by ordinary adverbs in *-e*.]

1. To or towards that place (with verb of motion expressed or implied). (Now almost exclusively literary; in ordinary speech superseded by THERE.)

α. 1 **þæder, ðadder.**

a **900** *O.E. Martyrol.* 190 On merȝen com se biscop þæder. *Ibid.* 222 þa Thome þæder ineode. *c* **950** *Lindisf. Gosp.* John vii. 35 Ðadder ðes færende is [*mistr.*]. *c* **1000** ÆLFRIC *Exod.* xxxii. 34 Ga þu and læde þis folc þæder, þe ic þe ær sæde.

β. 1-3 **ðider,** (1 **ðieder**), 1-4 **þidder,** 1-5 **þider,** 3 (*Orm.*) **þiderr** (**tiderr**), 4 **thidur, þyder, -ir,** (**tyder**), 4-5 **þidur, -ir, thider,** 5 **thidir, -yr, thyd(d)ur,** 5-6 **thyder,** 6 **thidder, -ir.**

a **900** tr. *Bæda's Eccl. Hist.* III. vi. [viii.] (1890) 174 þæt ȝyldne mynet..þætte þider of Cent cwom. *c* **950** *Lindisf. Gosp.* John xi. 8 Eftersona ðu faeris ðidder [*c* **975** *Rushw.* ðider]. *c* **1000** ÆLFRIC *Deut.* i. 37 Ne færst þu þider. *c* **1175** *Lamb. Hom.* 61 Crist us ȝife þider to cumen. *c* **1200** ORMIN 17924, & tiderr comm þe follc till himm. *c* **1250** *Gen. & Ex.* 1959 Ðan ruben cam ðider a-ȝen. **13..** *Cursor M.* 746 (Fairf.) Selcuþ was how he þidder [*v.r.* þider] wan. *c* **1375** *Sc. Leg. Saints* iii. (*Andreas*) 23 He knew nocht [t]hydir þe way. *Ibid.* 1008 þare-for had he þidder socht. *c* **1386** CHAUCER *Frankl. T.* 763 They ne wiste why she thider wente. **1388** WYCLIF *John* xviii. 3 He cam thidur with lanternys, and brondis, and armeris. **14..** *Voc.* in Wr.-Wülcker 588/46 *Illuc*, thydur. *c* **1450** *St. Cuthbert* (Surtees) 347 How þe kyng sent hir thider. **1559** *Mirr. Mag.* (1563) Hiv, Thyder they came wyth kynge Henry out of Skotlande. *a* **1600** MONTGOMERIE *Misc. Poems* xi. 28 Thidder did I drau For to refresh my werynes.

γ. 1 **þyder,** 3-5 **þuder(ü).**

Beowulf 3086 Wæs þæt ȝifeðe to swið þe ðone þyder ontyhte. **971** *Blickl. Hom.* 29 þæt he þyder come..mid his wyllan. **12..** *Moral Ode* 396 (Egerton MS.) Crist ȝyue us ..þat we moten þuder [*v.r.* þider] come. **1297** R. GLOUC. (Rolls) 2509 þis king com þuder priueliche. **1387** TREVISA *Higden* (Rolls) III. 455 Moche folk was iflowe þider [*MS. γ.* þuder]. *Ibid.* IV. 445 Men..com þider [*γ.* þuder].

δ. 4-5 **þedir, -yr,** 4-6 **þeder,** 5 **-ur, þeoder.**

13.. *Cursor M.* 1700 (Cott.) Al þeir filth sal þedir [*Gött.* þeder] fall. *c* **1350** *Will. Palerne* 2235 Whanne þei þeder come. *c* **1400** *R. Gloucester's Chron.* 8078 (MS. *a*) Hii þeoder ne wende. *c* **1400** *Destr. Troy* 13454 Thedur kyngis wold come. **1447** BOKENHAM *Seyntys* (Roxb.) 165 Of hire thedyr goyng this was the entent. **1464** *Nottingham Rec.* II. 375 At their first ridyng thedir. **1536** WRIOTHESLEY *Chron.* (Camden) I. 50 After dynner the Kinges grace came theder in a maske.

ε. 4 **þeþir,** 5 **thethur,** 6-7 **thether.**

a **1400** *Cursor M.* 17566 (Gött.) þat iesus be noght rauist þeþir [*Cott., Trin.* þider]. *c* **1420** *Avow. Arth.* xxii, Wold ȝe thethur be bowne. **1526** *Pilgr. Perf.* (W. de W. 1531) 14 By bothe wayes man may come thether. **1560** DAUS tr. *Sleidane's Comm.* 307 b, Thether came none at all; and hether but very fewe. **1653** HANE *Jrnl.* (1896) 1 A ship..which I made use of for my transportacion thether.

ζ. 4 **þiþer, -ir, 6 thyther, 6- thither.**
a **1400** *Cursor M.* 13692 (Gött.) þiþer [*v. rr.* þidder, þidur] ȝode he ai..þar to prai. **1523** LD. BERNERS *Froiss.* I. ccliii. 376 Thyther syr Eustace was ryght wellcome to all the company. **1548–9** (Mar.) *Bk. Com. Prayer, Collect Ascension Day,* We may also in heart and mind thither ascende. **1585** T. WASHINGTON tr. *Nicholay's Voy.* I. iv, Merchauntes comming thyther too lade salte. **1605** SHAKS. *Macb.* II. iv. 36 Will you to Scone?.. No, Cosin, Ile to Fife... Well, I will thither. **1709** STEELE & ADDISON *Tatler* No. 88 ¶12 The Gentlewoman of the next House begged me to step thither. **1872** JENKINSON *Guide Eng. Lakes* (1879) 256 The road thither leaves the main road at right angles.

η. 3–4 **þidere, þudere(ü), 4 þedire, þid(d)ire, þeodre, 4–5 þ-, thedere, þ-, thidere, 5 thed(d)re, thidre, thidyre, 6 thiddre.**
c **1205** LAY. 8171 He wes þudere icumen. **1340–70** *Alex. & Dind.* 2 Ryndinge þedirre. *Ibid.* 156 Drawen hem þiddire. **1393** LANGL. *P. Pl.* C. VIII. 292 Now most ich þudere, To loke how me lykeþ hit. *c* **1400** *R. Gloucester's Chron.* (Rolls) 827 (MS. *a*) Þur meseise him þeodre [*v.r.* theder] drof. *Ibid.* 5721 Þe monekes out of abendone verst were þedere yuet. *c* **1400** MAUNDEV. (1839) ii. 13 Grete Lordes that comen thidre. **1448** *Lett. Marg. Anjou & Bp. Beckington* (Camden) 101 To resorte thedre. **1473** WARKWORTH *Chron.* (Camden) 9 The Lorde Scales..was sent thedere. **1483** *Cath. Angl.* 382/2 Thidyre, *illo, illuc.* **1490** CAXTON *Eneydos* xxii. 81 Yf she went thidre. **1492** in *10th Rep. Hist. MSS. Comm.* App. v. 323 Nor to goo theddre. **1507** in Leadam *Sel. Cas. Star Chamber* 252 He..resorted thiddre.

θ. (chiefly *north.*; perh. scribal errors.) 4 **didir dydur, dedur, 5 -yr; 4 diþer, deþir(e, -er, -ur.**
a **1400** *Cursor M.* 2383 (Gött.) Als suith als þai diþer cam. *Ibid.* 14573 For didir gas sua mani man. *Ibid.* 14596 Deþir. *Ibid.* 17352 Deþire. *a* **1400** *Stac. Rome* 66 To alle þat wylle deþur goo. **1482** *Monk of Evesham* (Arb.) 75 Al that..whent not dedyr.

ι. 4 *Sc.* **yd(d)ir, -yr(e, -ire.** (app. for *þdir,* etc.)
c **1375** *Sc. Leg. Saints* xvi. (*Magdalena*) 784, & yddir ewinely can hyr mark. (So xxxii. 352, xxxiii. 65, xl. 119; xxix. 347 ydir; xviii. 864 ydyr; vii. 616 yddyre; xvi. 384 yddire.)

†**b.** Followed by *in, out*: In or out thither.
971 *Blickl. Hom.* 207 Hie þyder inwæron to ðæm lofsangum ȝesamnode. *c* **1000** ÆLFRIC *Saints' Lives* xxiii B. 500 Ic becom to sanctes iohannes cyrcan..and ic me þyder inneode. *c* **1205** LAY. 31599 Ah Penda ga þider ut anon. *c* **1300** *Cursor M.* 22643 It sal..dump þe deuls þider in.

c. Defined by a relative clause introduced by *þe* or *þæt* (see 2), *whither, where,* or equivalent.
The relative clause with *whither,* etc., often precedes.
[*c* **897**, **1393**, **1496**: see 2.] *c* **1380** WYCLIF *Serm.* Sel. Wks. II. 37 Wherever þe bodi be, þiþer shal þe eglis be giderid. For whidir ever comeþ Cristis bodi, þidir shal his seintis come. **1482** *Monk of Evesham* (Arb.) 35 They wondrid howe ..he myght comme thedyr to that place, where the couent was. **1548–9** (Mar.) *Bk. Com. Prayer, Communion,* That where he is, thither might we also ascende. **1650** T. B. *Worcester's Apoph.* 27 The meanes of bringing her thither, where now she had but little way to go. *a* **1700** DRYDEN *Ceyx & Alcyone* 440 She..thither by her destiny was brought, Where last he stood.

d. *hither and thither*: see HITHER *adv.* 5.

†**2.** With relative *particle* (*þe, that, as*) = WHITHER *rel. adv.* (See THE *particle* 2, THAT *conj.* 6, AS 27.)
c **897** K. ÆLFRED *Gregory's Past. C.* xi. 65 (Hatton MS.) Ðonne ne maȝon ðider fullice becuman ð a stæpas ðæs weorcas ðieder ðe he wilnað. **1393** LANGL. *P. Pl.* C. II. 119 For þider as þe fend flegh, hus fote for to sette, Ther he failede & ful. **1496** *Dives & Paup.* (W. de W.) VI. v. 237/1 Theder that the hede ledeth thyder sholde the bodye folowe.

†**3.** *transf.* **a.** Up to that time; until then. **b.** To or towards that end, purpose, result, or action.
13.. *Cursor M.* 5181 (Cott.) Yee sal ha lijf langer þen þider. **1600** SHAKS. *A. Y. L.* I. i. 179 This wrastler shall cleare all: nothing remaines, but that I kindle the boy thither.

B. *adj.* Lying on that side or in that direction, i.e. the side or direction away from *this*; the farther or more remote (of two things). A recent use, introduced as the opposite of HITHER *a.*
1830 LAMB *Let. to Wordsworth* 22 Jan., These all came in ..on the thither side of innocence. **1857–8** SEARS *Athan.* 5 Death is not a transition to another existence on the thither side of nature. **1868** HAWTHORNE *Amer. Note-Bks.* (1879) II. 166 Between the hither and the thither row of houses. **1890** KIPLING in *Fortn. Rev.* XLVII. 165, I doubt that a double is to be found on the thither side of hell.

'thither, *v.* Used in 'to hither and thither': see HITHER *v.*
1837 MRS. CARLYLE *Let. to Carlyle* 29 Aug. in *Lett. & Mem.* (1903) I. 61 Waiting for certainties; hithering and thithering being a condition under which I find it almost impossible to write. **1856, 1864** [see HITHER *v.*].

thitherto (ðɪðəˈtuː, ˈðɪðətuː), *adv.* [f. THITHER *adv.* + TO *prep.*: after *hitherto.*]

1. Up to that time; until then. Now *rare.*
c **1449** PECOCK *Repr.* I. iv. 19 The Iewis weren chargid with alle the lawis..with whiche the peple fro Adam thidir to weren chargid. **1529** MORE *Dyaloge* III. Wks. 205/2 All the men in effecte yt any faith had from Adam thetherto. **1654–66** EARL ORRERY *Parthen.* (1676) 655 Usage..which thitherto I had considered as an invitation. **1822** O'CONOR *Chron. Eri* I. p. vi, The thitherto one and only language. **1900** H. G. GRAHAM *Soc. Life Scot. in 18th C.* XIII. i. (1901) 476 Young men who had thitherto thronged to Holland.

†**2.** To that condition, point, or result. *Obs.*
1659 WHARTON *Cabal 12 Ho. Astrol.* Wks. (1683) 208 Although it be indeed new, and hitherto unheard of, yet it is firmly established upon Physical Reasons, and..is thither-to reduced. **1662** J. CHANDLER *Van Helmont's Oriat.* 313 The manner of comming thitherto..is moreover far remote.

thitherward (ˈðɪðəwəd), *adv.* (*a.*) *arch.* [OE. *þiderweard*: see THITHER and -WARD.]

1. Towards that place; in that direction; thither.
hitherward and thitherward: see HITHERWARD.
c **893** K. ÆLFRED *Oros.* I. i. §20 Ða he þiderweard seȝlode. *c* **1000** ÆLFRIC *Josh.* x. 7 Iosue þa ferde mid his fyrde þiderweard. *c* **1205** LAY. 1662 Swiðe he fusde þider ward kene his ferde. **1297** R. GLOUC. (Rolls) 9183 Anon he wende þuderward wiþ vair compainie. *a* **1300** *Cursor M.* 9908 (Cott.) Þe man þat þider-werd [*v.rr.* þiþer-ward, thedir-ward] es fledd. **1340** HAMPOLE *Pr. Consc.* 979 Þider sal we com..If we þederward hald þe right way. **1393** LANGL. *P. Pl.* C. VIII. 205 This ys þe heye weye þyderwarde. **1433** *Rolls of Parlt.* IV. 425/1 His passage from hens thither-ward. *a* **1533** LD. BERNERS *Huon* lx. 208 Huon..saw a shyppe comynge thether warde. **1560** BIBLE (Genev.) *Jer.* l. 5 They shal aske the waye to Zion, with their faces theitherward. **1624** CAPT. SMITH *Virginia* v. 196 He..instantly made thitherward in person. **1823** SCOTT *Quentin D.* viii, Were thy vocation in truth thitherward! **1884** ROE *Nat. Ser. Story* viii, All eyes turned thitherward.

†**2.** On the way thither; going thither. *Obs.*
c **1000** ÆLFRIC *Saints' Lives* xxx. 200 Þa he ðyderweard wæs, ȝeseah he þæt an wulf ȝenam þæt [child]. *c* **1175** *Lamb. Hom.* 3 Þa wes hit cud..þet þe helind wes þider-ward, heo urnen on-ȝein him. *a* **1300** *Cursor M.* 2956 (Cott.) Þiderward þair wonnyng was. *a* **1400** *Stac. Rome* 242 Ȝyf þou dye dydurward, Heuenne blys shalle be þy part. **1634** SIR T. HERBERT *Trav.* 28 He dared not to..plead his defence..in our Company and thitherward.

B. quasi-*adj.* Moving or directed thither. *rare.*
1795 SOUTHEY *Joan of Arc* VI. 49 The sentinel, soon as he heard Thitherward footsteps,..Challenged the darkling travellers.

'thitherwards, *adv. arch.* [f. prec.: see -WARDS.] = prec. 1.
c **888** K. ÆLFRED *Boeth.* xxxix. §5 He..tiohhode hit ðeah þiderweardes. *c* **1000** ÆLFRIC *Saints' Lives* xxiii. B. 724 Heo ..ofer þa hnescan yða þæs wæteres eode swa swa heo ær dyde þyder-weardes. **13..** *Sir Beues* (A.) 125 Þeder-wardes he gan gon Wiþ outen demere. **1484** *Cely Papers* (Camden) 149 On Tewysday nexte they schall departe theder warddes. **1592** MARLOWE *Edw. II,* v. ii, So, now away! post thitherwards amain. **1756** *Phil. Trans.* LV. 189 The air of the lower regions [is] flowing thitherwards. *a* **1850** ROSSETTI *Dante & Circ.* I. (1874) 40, I had occasion to..go thitherwards where she abode. **1886** *Cornh. Mag.* July 43 A number of rough labouring men..strolling thitherwards.

†**'thitherways,** *adv. Obs. rare.* [f. THITHER + -WAYS: cf. *sideways,* etc.] On the way thither, in that direction, thitherwards.
1630 *R. Johnson's Kingd. & Commw.* 41 Suppose an enemie..be discovered at Sea upon the coast of Kent, thitherwayes presently make the Land forces.

[**thitling,** spurious word; a misprint for TITHING, cited by Richardson from an ed. of Milton's Prose Wks., and thence in recent American Dictionaries.]

‖**thitsi, thitsee** (ˈθɪtsiː). *East Ind.* Also **thet-, theet-, thietsee, thyt-si.** [Burmese *þitsī, þissī* (written *sachchē*), f. *þit* tree, wood + *asī*, in comb. *-sī* gum: cf. *sē* to be sticky.] The 'black varnish tree', *Melanorrhœa usitatissima,* N.O. *Anacardiaceæ,* of Burma; also applied to the varnish obtained from it.
1832 DON *Gen. Syst. Gard.* II. 67/1 *M*[*elanorrhœa*] *usitata*... Native of Hindostan..where it is called *Theet-tsee* or *Zitsi.* **1839** ROYLE *Bot. Himalayan Mts.* I. 178 *Melanorrhœa usitata* of Dr. Wallich,..the *theet-see,* or varnishing-tree of the Burmese,..abounds in a thick and viscid, greyish-brown fluid, which turns black soon after coming into contact with the air. **1858** HOGG *Veg. Kingd.* 244 The Black Varnish-Tree..grows..in the Burmese empire, on the banks of the Irrawadi, where it is called Theet-tsee, or Zit-si. **1858** SIMMONDS *Dict. Trade, Thetsee,* a varnish obtained from *Melanorrhœa usitata,* in Arracan, and used for lacquering. **1890** HALLETT *1000 Miles* 284 A plain in which many great *thyt-si* (black-varnish trees) were growing.

thiuret (ˈθaɪ(j)ʊərɛt). *Chem.* [f. Gr. θεῖον sulphur (see THIO-) + -URET.] A light odourless crystalline powder, $C_8H_7N_3S_2$, used as a substitute for idioform as an antiseptic.
1899 *Syd. Soc. Lex.* s.v., Sulphur separates out from thiuret in presence of alkalies, even at low temperatures. It owes its antiseptic properties to the separation of sulphur in a nascent state.

thivel, thible (ˈθɪv(ə)l, ˈθaɪv(ə)l; ˈθɪb(ə)l, ˈθaɪb(ə)l). *Sc.* and *north. dial.* Forms: α. 5 **thyvelle,** 6 **thyvil,** 7– **thivel,** (9 *dial.* **thyvel, theevil, thieval,** etc.); β. 7– **thible,** (9 *dial.* **thibble, thybel,** etc.); γ. 9 *dial.* **thavel, thaivel, thabble,** etc.; δ. 9 *Sc.* **theedle**; for other forms see E.D.D. [Of obscure origin and history. The forms with *v* are app. the original, being found two centuries earlier, and used both in Scotland and the north of England, while the later forms with *b* are confined to n. Engl. The stem vowel is found variously as (ɪ), (iː), (ɛ), (eː), (a), (ɑː), (ɔː), and (aɪ); the earliest spellings have *y* (? ɪ or iː), but the phonological development is not easy to trace.
In form, *thivel* seems to correspond to OE. *þyfel* 'bush, leafy plant', but no links of connexion between this and the modern sense have been found. In its various current forms the word is in use from N. of Scotl. to S. Lancashire, W. and E. Yorksh.; this localization suggests a Norse origin, and it has been referred to OIcel. *þefja* (ˈθɛvja); but this is a very rare word of doubtful standing, and in any case meant 'to thicken by beating or stamping' rather than 'to stir'. The actual ONorse name for a stirring-stick was *þvara,* between which and *thivel* there is of course no connexion.]

1. A stick for stirring porridge or anything cooked in a pot; a potstick. (See also quot. 1876, γ.)
α. **1483** *Cath. Angl.* 383/2 A Thyvelle, *spatula, vertimella.* **1570** LEVINS *Manip.* 126/17 A Thyuil, *rubicula.* **1768** ROSS *Helenore* 138 The thivel on the pottage pan, Shall strick my hour to rise. **1785** *Spanish Rivals* 8 He's a queer stick to make a thivel on. **1815** G. BEATTIE *John o' Arnha* (1826) 35 An' ay's they steer'd them wi' a thivel, They mummelt 'crowdy for the devil'. **1880** EDWARDS *Mod. Scot. Poets* I. 362 Soup ladles and theevils. **1889** BARRIE *Window in Thrums* vi, Nearly a foot having been cut..from the original ..to make a porridge thieval. **1894** HESLOP *Nthbld. Gloss., Thivel, Thybel,* a round stick,..about fifteen inches long and three-quarters of an inch in diameter; used to stir porridge.
β. **1674** RAY *N.C. Words,* A *Thible* or *Thivel,* a Stick to stirre a Pot. **1764** ELIZ. MOXON *Eng. Housew.* (ed. 9) 109 With a paste-pin or thible stir in your flour to the butter. **1847** EMILY BRONTË *Wuthering Heights* xiii, The quicker the thible ran round..the faster the handfuls of meal fell into the water. **1863** E. WAUGH *Lancash. Songs* 54 Wi' th' edge o' th porridge thible [*rime* Bible].
γ. **1876** *Whitby Gloss., Thabble,* the plug in the leaden milk-trough, which draws out and lets off the milk, while the cream is left behind.
δ. **1864** A. LEIGHTON *Myst. Leg. Edinb.* (1886) 68 The stirring utensil called a 'theedle'. **1884** C. ROGERS *Soc. Life Scot.* I. vii. 233 Stirred with a wooden spurtle or theedle.

†**2.** = DIBBLE *sb. Obs.* (perh. an error in RAY).
1691 RAY *N.C. Words, Thible, Thivel*... Also a dibble, or setting-stick. Hence **1787** in GROSE *Provinc. Gloss.*

thivish (ˈθaɪvɪʃ). *Anglo-Ir.* Also **tevish.** Pl. **-es;** also **tevishies, thevshi.** [ad. Ir. *taibhse,* pl. *taibhsí.*] A ghost, apparition, or spectre.
1852 W. WILDE *Irish Pop. Superstitions* i. 14 Thivishes or thoushas (shadowy apparitions) are literally ghosts. *Ibid.* iii. 71 (*heading*) Reminiscences of the West.—The Welshes.—The Thivish or Fetch. *Ibid.* 111 'Mother,' said he, gazing steadily upon the pale anxious face that was bent upon him, 'I've seen the *thivish.*' **1888** W. B. YEATS *Fairy & Folk Tales of Irish Peasantry* 128 Ghosts, or as they are called in Irish, *Thevshi* or *Tash* (*taidhbhse, tais*), live in a state intermediary between this life and the rest. They are held there by some earthly longing or affection. **1892, 1963** [see SOWLTH].

thixel, thixle (ˈθɪks(ə)l). Now *dial.* Forms: 4 **þixil, -el,** 5 **thyxyl, -le, -ill, -ille, -elle, (tyxhyl, tixil), thyxtyll, -ill, thistill,** 7 **thistle,** 8–9 **thi-, thyzle,** 9 **thixle, thicksell.** [ME. *þixil, þixel,* known *c* 1300, not yet found in OE. = MDu. *dessel, dissel* (Du. *dissel,* LG. *dessel*), OHG. *dehsala, dehsla,* MHG. *dehsel, dichsel,* Ger. *deichsel,* in Upper Ger. dialects *dechsel, dächsel*; from OTeut. root **þehs-* (by-form **þihs-*), Indo-Eur. **teks-*: cf. OSlav. *tes-ati* to hew, *tesla* axe, Lith. *tasz-ýti* to hew or shape with the axe. See Kluge *Etym. Wbch.,* and Schade.] An adze.
c **1300** *E.E. Psalter* lxxiii. 7 [lxxiv. 6] Als in wodes of trees ..In ax and in thixil [*MS. E.* þixel] þai ite dounecaste. **1404** *Durham Acc. Rolls* (Surtees) 396, j thyxtyll..j thyxtyll goug. **14..** *Nom.* in Wr.-Wülcker 726/37 *Hec acia,* a thyxylle. *c* **1440** *Promp. Parv.* 491/2 Thyxyl, instrument (*S.* twybyle, *P.* thyxill), *ascia.* **1468** *Medulla Gram.* (MS. Cant.), *Ascia,* a thyxelle... *Celtes,* a cheselle or a thyxelle [*Harl. MS.* tixil]. **1562** *Wills & Inv. N.C.* (Surtees) I. 207, j mattoche, j thistill,..iij woumbles. **1611–12** *Knaresb. Wills* (Surtees) II. 34 One thistle, all my chissils. **1796** PEGGE *Derbicisms* (E.D.S.), *Thizle,* an adze. **1847–78** HALLIWELL, *Thixille,* an axe, or hatchet. **1888** *Sheffield Gloss., Thicksell,* an adze... It has a crooked handle, and is used by wheelwrights, and for making spouts hollow, etc. [*E.D.D.* gives the forms thixle, thicksell, thizle, thyzle.]

thixotropy (θɪksəˈtrɒpɪ). [ad. G. *tixotropie* (T. Péterfi 1927, in *Arch. f. Entwicklungsmech.* CXII. 689), f. Gr. θίξ-ις touching + -O + Gr. τροπ-ή turning: see -Y³.] The property of certain gels of becoming fluid when agitated and of reverting back to a gel when left to stand.
1927 *Chem. Abstr.* XXI. 1391 Thixotropy is the phenomenon that a coagulated sol can be liquefied by merely shaking and always again coagulated to a gel by stopping agitation. **1949** P. C. CARMAN *Chem. Constitution & Properties Engin. Materials* xiii. 379 This type of reversible gelation is known as thixotropy and is particularly strongly marked in montmorillonite clays. **1971** *New Scientist* 19 Aug. 435/2 How to demonstrate thixotropy with custard.
Hence **thixo'tropic** *a.,* exhibiting or pertaining to thixotropy; **thixo'tropically** *adv.*
1927 *Chem. Abstr.* XXI. 1391 (*heading*) Thixotropic behavior of aluminum hydroxide gels. **1947** *Nature* 11 Jan. 70/2 The range of thixotropic materials extends from the hardest solids, through doughs and pastes to liquids such as blood or milk. **1958** *Woman* 22 Feb. 11/2 Thixotropic paint is the non-spill type. **1963** *Geol. Mag.* C. 209 Nodules.. produced by allowing a thin layer of sand to sink into thixotropically mobilized mud. **1971** *Nature* 30 July 328/1 A thin layer of grey silt covered a 20 cm layer of black thixotropic mud.

‖**Thlaspi** (ˈθlæspɪ). *Bot.* Also 7 **thlaspe,** 8 **thlaspy.** [mod.L., a. Gr. θλάσπι, -ις, 'a sort of cress, the seed of which was bruised and used like mustard' (L. and Sc.).] A genus of cruciferous plants (tribe *Thlaspideæ*), containing about thirty species, chiefly annuals, bearing insignificant white, pink, or purplish flowers, succeeded by flattened orbicular seed-pods. *T. arvense*, Penny-cress, was formerly in repute for its medicinal qualities.

Formerly including *Capsella* or Shepherd's Purse, and loosely applied to Candytuft, etc.

1562 TURNER *Herbal* II. 152 Thlaspi is named..in English triacle mustard, boures mustard, or dishe mustarde. **1579** LANGHAM *Gard. Health* (1633) 634 Thlaspi seeds eaten, purge choller. **1597** GERARDE *Herbal* II. xix. 207 The seede of Thlaspi..helpeth the sciatica. **1640** PARKINSON *Theat. Bot.* VII. xii. 839 That Thlaspi that the best do allow for the truest Thlaspi to be used in Treakle and Mithridate. **1725** *Bradley's Fam. Dict.* s.v. *Shepherds Purse*, Some-what like the Leaves of Thlapsi. **1842** *Penny Cycl.* XXIV. 384/2 The genus Thlapsi is known by its silicles being emarginate at the apex with the valves winged at the back.

‖**thlipsis** ('θlɪpsɪs). *Path.* [a. Gr. θλῖψις pressure, compression, from θλῖβ-ειν to press, squeeze.] (See quots.)

1693 tr. *Blancard's Phys. Dict.*, Thlipsis. **1704** J. HARRIS *Lex. Techn.* I, *Thlipsis*, is a Compression of the Vessels in an Animal Body. **1857** DUNGLISON *Med. Lex.*, *Thlipsis*, compression, and especially constriction of vessels by an external cause. Oppression. [Hence in mod. Dicts.]

So ‖**thlipsencephalus** (ˌθlɪpsɛn'sɛfələs) [Gr. ἐγκέφαλος brain]: see quot.; hence ˌ**thlipsen'cephalous** *a.*, of or pertaining to a thlipsencephalus.

1857 DUNGLISON *Med. Lex.*, *Thlipsencephalus*,..a monster in whom the skull is open, not merely in the frontal and parietal, but also in the occipital regions. **1860** MAYNE *Expos. Lex.*, Thlipsencephalous.

thlummery, obs. variant of FLUMMERY.

thnetopsychism (θniːtəʊp'saɪkɪz(ə)m). [f. eccl. Gr. θνητόψῡχος maintaining the mortality of the soul (f. θνητός mortal + ψῡχή soul) + -ISM.] The doctrine (based on 1 *Tim.* vi. 16, 'who only hath immortality') held by the *Thnētopsȳchītæ*, a Christian sect which arose in Arabia in the third century, who believed that the soul dies with the body, and is recalled to life with it at the Day of Judgement.

[**1625** GILL *Sacr. Philos.* IV. 63 The *Thnatopsychitæ*, which thought that the soule of man came to nought, as the soules of the beasts.] **1882–3** W. F. TILLETT in *Schaff's Encycl. Relig. Knowl.* III. 2218 The still grosser error of soul-death, or thnetopsychism.

†**tho**, *dem. pron.* and *adj.* (*rel. pron.*), *pl. Obs.* Forms: see below. [OE. *þá*, nom. and acc. pl. of *se, séo, þæt*, simple demonstrative, THAT, and definite article, THE; = OFris. *thâ*, OS. *thia* (also m. *thie, the*, f. *the*, n. *thiu*, OHG. m. *die, dia, dê*, f. *dio, dia, dê*, n. *diu, dei*, ON. m. *þeir*, f. *þǽr*, n. *þau*, Goth. m. *þai*, f. *þôs*, n. *þô*. The original form *þá*, *thā* remained in the northern dialect, where it still exists as Sc. *thae, theae*, N. Yorksh. *theeä*: see THAE. In midl. and south of England *þā* became reguarly *þō* (found in Kentish *a* 1200), and remained in use as *tho* (*thoo, thoe*) to *c* 1550. As early as 1300 it began to be supplanted in the north by *þās*, which finally took its place in Standard Engl. as THOSE, q.v.]

A. Illustration of Forms.

α. 1–3 **ðá**, 1–5 **þá**, (3 **þæ**), 4 **þaa**, 4–6 **tha**, *Sc.* **þai, thai, thay** [6– *Sc.* THAE, q.v.]. *Early inflexions*: *dat.* 1 **þǽm, þám**, 2–3 **þan, þon**, 3 **þen**. *gen.* 1 **þára, þǽra, ðeara**, 2–3 **þare, þere**.

c **825** *Vesp. Psalter* ii. 10 Alle ða ðe doemað eorðan. *c* **1000** *Ags. Gosp.* Mark iv. 10 þa twelfe þe mid him wæron. *c* **1200** ORMIN 429 Swa ne didenn nohht ta twa þatt we nu mælenn ummbe. *Ibid.* 2796 þa menn þatt wel himm follȝhenn. *c* **1205** LAY. 9180 Seoððe him comen þæ [*c* 1275 þe] tiðinde of Crist godes childe. **1340** HAMPOLE *Pr. Consc.* 6435 Aparty of þa paynes sere. **13..** *Cursor M.* 6448 (Cott.) To þaa þat gret birþin bar. *c* **1375** *Sc. Leg. Saints* iv. (*Jacobus*) 317 To þai discipulis þe kynge Had granttit..par askine. *c* **1560** A. SCOTT *Poems* (S.T.S.) ii. 16 Tha stalwart knychtis. [**1583**–: see THAE.]

dat. c **893** K. ÆLFRED *Oros.* I. i. §7 Betux þæm twæm ean sindon þas land Arocasia & Parthia. *Ibid.* II. vii. §2 On þæm daȝum. *c* **1000** *Ags. Gosp.* Matt. iii. 1 On þam [*Rushw.* In þæm] daȝum com iohannes se fulluhtere. *c* **1160** *Hatton Gosp.* Matt. v. 44 Doð wel þan [*Ags. G.* þam] þe eow yfel doð. *c* **1200** *Trin. Coll. Hom.* 47 Swich þeu wes bi þan daȝen. *c* **1205** LAY. 747 Cuð he wes þen cnihten [*c* 1275 þeos cniþtes]. **1340** *Ayenb.* 11 To alle þon þet wyleþ by yborȝe. *Ibid.* 30 Of þan þet hi byeþ yhealde uor te amendi.

gen. c **825** *Vesp. Psalter* xiii. 3 Ðeara [*L. quorum*] muð awerȝednisse & bitterniss ful bið. *c* **893** K. ÆLFRED *Oros.* I. i. §16 þara wæron syx stælhranas. *c* **1000** *Ags. Ps.* (Th.) ii. (*heading*) Ælc þæra þe þysne sealm singð. *c* **1175** *Lamb. Hom.* 135 On ðere monne heorte. *c* **1205** LAY. 1776 þere Freinsce monnen [*c* 1275 of þe Frense mennene]. *Ibid.* 3346 Heo sende..to þare cnihtene inne. *a* **1250** *Owl & Night.* 1584 (Cott.) On þare beire nede.

β. 2–3 **þeo**.

c **1175** *Lamb. Hom.* 47 Alle þeo þe ihereð godes weordes. *c* **1205** LAY. 9056 þeo cudden Kinbeline. *a* **1225** *Leg. Kath.* 360 Cleopest þeo [*MS. C.* þoa] þinges godes. *c* **1300** *Beket* 721 Nameliche theo for alle other.

γ. 2–4 **þo**, (3 **to**), 3 **þoa**, 4 **þoo**, 4–6 **tho, thoo**, (5 **thow**), 6 **thoe**.

c **1175** *Lamb. Hom.* 79 þo þet weren imakede engles. *c* **1200** *Trin. Coll. Hom.* 139 And bi þo daȝes luuede herodes.. his broðer wif. **1388** WYCLIF *Prov.* iv. 22 For tho ben lijf to men fyndynge thoo. *c* **1460** *Wisdom* 689 in *Macro Plays* 58 Now wyll we thre do make a dance Off thow þat longe to owur retenaunce. **1521** FISHER *Wks.* (1876) 316 In thoo causes that perteyne vnto god. **1526** TINDALE *Rev.* ii. 10 Feare none off thoo [COVERD. tho; *Gt. Bible* those] thynges which thou shalt soffre. **1553** BECON *Reliques of Rome* (1563) 238 All thoe that fraunches of holye Churche breake.

B. Signification.

I. Dem. pron.: pl. of THAT B. I.; = THOSE I. (they, them).

Often indistinguishable from 3rd pers. pron. *they*. The ME. north. and Sc. *þa* often ran together with *þai, þay*, they.

1. In general sense.

c **893** K. ÆLFRED *Oros.* I. i. §21 þa habbað him sylf cyning. *Ibid.* I. i. §11 Binnan þæm sindon moneȝa þeoda. *c* **1000** *Sax. Leechd.* I. 290 Heo hafaþ leaf sinewealte and ða bittere on byrgincge. [Cf. THOSE I. 2 b.] *c* **1205** LAY. 6403 þeo [*c* 1275 hii] fihten wið þone duke. *a* **1300** *E.E. Psalter* cxxiii[i]. 6 þat noght gaf us swa In taking of tothe of þa. *a* **1310** in Wright *Lyric P.* vii. 29 Ne lete for non of tho. **13..** *Cursor M.* 8817 (Gött.) þus þa [*C., F.* þai, *Tr.* þei] proued it thre days. **1388** WYCLIF 1 *Kings* vi 12 If thou..kepist alle my comaundementis, and goist bi tho [1382 hem; L. *per ea*]. **1390** GOWER *Conf.* I. 52 Tho be proprely the gates, Thurgh whiche..Comth alle thing. **1434** MISYN *Mending Life* II. vi. 116 Be þame þa wote endles lyfe to wynn. *c* **1440** *Generydes* 888 Peraventour I myght be on of thoo. **1573** *Satir. Poems Reform.* xliii. 231 Quhair ar tha? **1596** DALRYMPLE tr. *Leslie's Hist. Scot.* x. (S.T.S.) II. 298 Sa tha facht that betueine thame was amissing a thousand or thairabout. *a* **1600** MONTGOMERIE *Misc. Poems* xiv. 9, I am not one of tho.

2. As antecedent pronoun followed by a relative clause or its equivalent: = THOSE B. I. 4.

c **825** *Vesp. Psalter* cxxxiv. 2 Ða ðe stondað in huse dryhtnes. *c* **1000** *Ags. Ps.* (Th.) v. 5 þu hatast ealle þa þe unriht wyrcað. *a* **1175** *Cott. Hom.* 219 Heo ȝescop ȝesceafte þaða he wolde. *c* **1200** ORMIN 53 þa þatt wærenn gode menn. *c* **1205** LAY. 6420 þeo [*c* 1275 þaie] þat hit iseȝen. *a* **1225** *Ancr. R.* 32 Habbeð reouþe of þeo þet beoð ine. *c* **1300** *Harrow. Hell* 82 Alle þo þat bueþ heryne. *c* **1330** R. BRUNNE *Chron. Wace* (Rolls) 1903 Seide Arthur þen to þo þer ware. **13..** *Cursor M.* 1529 (Cott.) þaa [*v. rr.* þai, þei] þat þa [þer, þir] wonders werkes wroght. *c* **1385** CHAUCER *L.G.W.* 1531 (*Hypsiphyle*) Alle tho that lyuyn & been dede. *c* **1400** *Rule St. Benet* 12 Of þe þridde maner o mekenes spekys sain benet to þa in his ruel wyl be. *c* **1400** MAUNDEV. (Roxb.) iii. 10 þa þat schafes þaire berdes. **1463** *Bury Wills* (Camden) 29 The chymes, as wel tho that been in Seynt Marie stepill as tho that been [etc.]. *c* **1475** *Rauf Coilȝear* 802 The maist man of all tha That euer he had sene. **1509** FISHER *Wks.* (1876) 271 Blessyd are tho whiche haue made vertuous ende. *a* **1533** LD. BERNERS *Huon* lvii. 193 All tho in your company. **1553** BECON *Reliques of Rome* (1563) 238 b, All thoe yt be common robbers.

II. Dem. adj.

3. Plural of THAT B. II.; = THOSE II.

c **893** K. ÆLFRED *Oros.* I. i. §16 þa deor hi hatað hranas. *Ibid.* §17 On þæm morum eardiað Finnas. *a* **1123** *O.E. Chron.* an. 1119, þa tweȝen cyngas..mid heoran folcan. *c* **1200** *Trin. Coll. Hom.* 51 þo word muneȝeð us. *c* **1330** R. BRUNNE *Chron. Wace* (Rolls) 461 Custume was bi þo dawes. **13..** *Cursor M.* 2590 (Cott.) Als it was hight befor þaa [*v.rr.* þa, þas] dais. *c* **1386** CHAUCER *Prol.* 500 Out of the Gospel he tho wordes caughte. **1412–20** LYD. *Chron. Troy* I. 1755 Al-þei he were a paynym in þo dawes. **1502** ARNOLDE *Chron.* (1811) 146 Whoo kysseth thoo crosses hath v. C. yere of pardon. **1526** TINDALE *Acts* xviii. 17 Gallio cared for none of tho thynges. **1553** KENNEDY *Compend. Tract.* in *Wodrow Soc. Misc.* (1844) 108 The juge that wes in tha days.

b. In concord with a sb. antecedent to a relative.

c **893** K. ÆLFRED *Oros.* I. i. §22 Ealle ða menn ðe swyftoste hors habbað. *Ibid.* §25 þa land þe man hæt Gallia Bellica. *c* **1000** *Ags. Ps.* (Th.) iii. (*heading*), Ælc þæra manna þe þisne sealm singð. **1122** *O.E. Chron.*, Ealle þa gersumes þe þær binnen wæron. *c* **1175** *Lamb. Hom.* 125 Ða songes þa we nu singeð. **1382** WYCLIF *Prov.* i. 22 Tho thingus that ben noȝesum to them. **1418** HEN. V in *Proc. Privy Counc.* (1834) II. 244 Al þoo personnes þat been oure sugettes. *c* **1450** tr. *De Imitatione* III. i. 64 Blessid be þo eres þat receyueþ of goddys rounynge. **1526** [see A. γ]. **1579** SPENSER *Sheph. Cal.* Sept. 32 In tho countryes, whereas I haue bene.

4. Plural of definite article THE.

c **825** *Vesp. Psalter* v. 6 Ne ðorhwuniað ða unrehtwisan biforan eȝum ðinum. *c* **850** *O.E. Chron.* an. 2, And þa cild on Bethlem of slæȝene wærun for Cristes ehtnesse from Herode. *c* **893** K. ÆLFRED *Oros.* I. i. §15 þa Finnas, him þuhte, and þa Beormas spræcon neah an ȝeþeode. *c* **1000** *Ags. Gosp.* Matt. v. 5 Eadiȝe synt þa liðan [*Lindisf.* ða milde], forþam þe hi eorðan aȝun. *a* **1123** *O.E. Chron.* an. 1116, Eallæ þa husas. *Ibid.* an. 1117, þurh þa renas. *c* **1175** *Lamb. Hom.* 11 þa halie daȝes. *c* **1200** *Moral Ode* (Egerton MS.) 192 He scal deme þo quike and to dede. *a* **1300** *Cursor M.* 861 (Cott., Gött.) He wend to hide him amang þa [*F., Tr.* þe] tres.

III. 5. Relative pron., plural of THAT *rel. pron.*

c **825** *Vesp. Psalter* viii. 4 Steorran ða ðu ȝesteaðulades. *c* **1000** *Ags. Ps.* (Th.) cxliii. 9 Fremdra bearna, and frecenra, þara [L. *quorum*] muðas sprecað man-idel word. *c* **1175** [see 3 b]. *c* **1200** *Trin. Coll. Hom.* 21 Us..and alle þo nede habbeð. *c* **1205** LAY. 7121 For uncuðe leoden þeo þis londe habbeð bi-wunnen. *Ibid.* 6415 Alle þa [*c* 1275 þe] he funde. *Ibid.* 7789 He sette reuwen stronge & hæȝen þo fengen þa lond-gauel. **1422** tr. *Secreta Secret., Priv. Priv.* 160 His Sonnes tha wickyd men were. *a* **1425** *Cursor M.* 5237 (Trin.) Manassen and effraym þo [*earlier MSS.* þat] in egipte his wif him bare whiche [*v. rr.* þat, þe quilk] þe kyng had geten him þare.

tho, *adv.* (*conj.*) *Obs.* exc. *dial.* Forms: 1–4 **þá**, (1 **ðá, tha**), 2–5 **þo**, (5 **þoo**), 3 **þeo, þeoa, ðoa** (**ta, to**), 4 **þaa, þae**, 4–5 **thoo**, 4–7 (*dial.* -9) **tho**, (5–6 **thoe**). [OE. *ðá*, *þá* = ON. *þá* (Norw. *daa*, Sw. *då*, Da. *da*) then, when; orig. a case-form of the demonstr. stem *þa-* of THE, THAT; either the actual acc. sing. fem., OE. and ON. *þá*, or (as some think) a stressed form of the orig. acc. masc.; meaning 'that time', the sb. being omitted: cf. L. *tum, tam*. (But cf. also the sense-equivalent OS. *thô, thuo*, OHG. *dô, duo*.) In ME. *þā* remained in the north, but *c* 1200 regularly became *þō, thō* in midland and south. *Tho, thoa* still remains = then, at that time, in the south-west.]

1. As demonstrative adv.: Then. a. At that time: = THEN *adv.* 1. Now *dial.* (In quot. *c* 1385 preceded by a prep.: = THEN *adv.* 7.)

c **893** K. ÆLFRED *Oros.* I. i. §14 þa for he norþryhte be þæm lande. *c* **897** —— *Gregory's Past. C.* 2 Hu ȝesæliȝlica tida þa wæron ȝeond Angelcynn. *c* **1000** ÆLFRIC *Hom.* II. 378 Hit mæȝ eow nu fremian swa micclum swa hit ða mihte. *c* **1200** *Trin. Coll. Hom.* 51 Nimeð forbisne efter þe olde men þe þo weren. *a* **1225** *Juliana* 9 As me luuede þa. *a* **1300** *Cursor M.* 6383 (Cott.) þis mete þat þai war fed of þaa [*v.rr.* þo, þan] þai cald it..manna. *c* **1330** R. BRUNNE *Chron. Wace* (Rolls) 7936 þe kyng þankede God þo. *Ibid.* 16261 þider cam nought þo Osewy. *c* **1385** CHAUCER *L.G.W.* 1060 (*Dido*) The queene..had herde ofte of Eneas er thoo. **1390** GOWER *Conf.* I. 6 Tho was the lif of man in helthe, Tho was plente, tho was richesse. *c* **1420** *Chron. Vilod.* 46 Fiue maner of pepull here dwellyd þo. **1513** DOUGLAS *Æneis* I. vi. 68 As was the maner tho. **1549–62** STERNHOLD & HOPKINS *Ps.* lxxviii. 6 They and their posteritie, Which were not sprong up tho. **1600** *Sheph. Slumber* in *Eng. Helicon* (1887) 222 In peascod time..I went to gather strawberries tho. **1888** ELWORTHY *W. Som. Words*, *Tho*, adv. of time, then. Still the usual form here... 'Her told'n he should have his money, but her 'adn a-got it *tho*.'

†b. (Next) after that, upon that, thereupon: = THEN *adv.* 3. *Obs.*

c **700** CÆDMON *Hymn* 7 He aerist scop..heben til hrofe.. Tha middunȝeard [etc.]. *c* **893** K. ÆLFRED *Oros.* I. ii. §1 þa æt nyhstan he wæs feohtende wið Sciððie. *a* **1000** *Juliana* 594 þa se dema wearð hreoh & hyȝegrim. **1131** *O.E. Chron.* (Laud MS.) an. 1127, Siððen þa nam he þes kynges wifes swuster of France to wife. *a* **1175** *Cott. Hom.* 225 þo warð god toðan swiðe ȝegremed þurh manna mandede. *c* **1200** ORMIN 225, & ta þeȝȝ wisstenn sone anan Forr whatt he dwelledd haffde. *a* **1225** *Ancr. R.* 428 Ette mete no word, oðer lut, & þeo beon stille. *c* **1275** LAY. 3616, þo [*c* **1205** þon] nam Leir þe king his leofeste cnihtes. *c* **1386** CHAUCER *Sompn. T.* Prol. 18 Vn-to this Angel spak the frere tho. **1470–85** MALORY *Arthur* XVII. i. 689 Whanne Galahad had rescowed Percyual..he yede tho in to a waste foreste. **1579** SPENSER *Sheph. Cal.* Jan. 11 Tho to a hill his faynting flocke he ledde. **1642** H. MORE *Song Soul* I. II. xxxv, Tho I gan closely on his person look.

†2. As relative or conjunctive adv.: When, at the time that. (Often correlative to *þa* in sense 1.)

Beowulf (Z.) 462 Ða hine gara cyn,..habban ne mihte. *c* **893** K. ÆLFRED *Oros.* I. i. §20 Ða he þiderweard seȝlode ..þa wæs him on þæt bæcbord Denamearc. **971** *Blickl. Hom.* 19 Hwæt he dyde þa hine seo meneȝo þreade. **1154** *O.E. Chron.*, þa þe king was ded þa was þe eorl beionde sæ. *c* **1175** *Lamb. Hom.* 11 þa ten laȝe þe þa israelisce folc sceolde halden þa he heom ledde of egipte londe. *a* **1225** *Ancr. R.* 314 He was lutel child þeoa he hit dude. *a* **1250** *Owl & Night.* 1690 Ah hit was unker uoreward, þo we come hiderward. *c* **1250** *Death* 20 in *O.E. Misc.* 168 We weren poure þa we hider come. **13..** *K. Alis.* 1648 (Bodl. MS.) Afterward þoo it was niȝth, Hij founden [etc.]. **1377** LANGL. *P. Pl.* B. Prol. 176 Ac þo þe belle was ybouȝt..þere ne was ratoun..þat dorst haue ybounden þe belle aboute þe cattis nekke. *c* **1425** *Seven Sag.* (P.) 183 Uppon morwen, tho it was day, The childe awakid.

†b. Also followed by *the* conj. (*þa þe*), in same sense: = When that, when. See THE *particle* 2 a.

c **1000** *Ags. Psalter* (Surtees) xlviii. 21 Ða ðe he in are wes. *a* **1175** *Cott. Hom.* 219 þaðe hi wolde mid modinesse beon betere þonne he ȝesceapen were. *Ibid.* 223 þaðac he slep þa ȝename he ribb of his sidan. *c* **1175** *Lamb. Hom.* 79 þa þe he heuede scome aȝeines his scuppende þa he hefde þurst and hunger.

tho, þo, obs. inflexions of THE.

tho, tho', abbrev. forms of THOUGH.

thoan ('θəʊən), *a. Zool.* ? *Obs.* [f. THO-US + -AN.] Of or pertaining to canine beasts of or akin to the subgenus *Thous*; in a restricted application including certain African jackals, but often extended as in THOOID.

1839 C. H. SMITH *Dogs* I. iv. 193 The Thoan group represents in form the wolf on a reduced scale. **1842** *Penny Cycl.* XXIV. 240/2 A race of..dogs..in Arabia..of Thoan form.

thoch, thocht, obs. Sc. forms of THOUGH.

thocht, Sc. f. THOUGHT[1], and pa. t. and pple. of THINK *v.*[1] and [2]; so THOCHTFUL, THOCHTY.

†**thode**. *Obs. rare.* Forms: 1 **þoden**, 3 **þode**, **þodde**, 7 **thode**, (9 **thod**). [OE. *þoden* str. masc., ? f. stem *þud-* of OE. *þyddan* (:—**þudjan*), pa. t. *þudde*, to strike, thrust, push, THUD.] A violent wind, a whirlwind. With quot. 1684 cf. THUD *sb.* 1.

c **725** *Corpus Gloss.* (O.E.T.) 136 *Alcanus* [? Altanus], þoden. *c* **897** K. ÆLFRED *Gregory's Past. C.* xviii. 128 Sio ȝeornfulnes..ablent ðæs modes eaȝan..suæ suæ dust deð ðæs lichoman eaȝan on sumera mid ðodene [*v.r.* ðodne]. *a* **1000** *Ags. Voc.* in Wr.-Wülcker 203/5 *Ceruleis turbinibus*, laȝeflodum þodenum. *c* **1000** ÆLFRIC *Gram.* ix. (Z.) 37 *Turbo*, ðoden. *c* **1012** *O.E. Chron.* an. 793 (MS. D.) Her wæron reðe forebecna cumene ofer Norðanhymbra land

...þ[æt] wæron ormete þodenas & liȝrescas. *c* **1205** LAY. 27645 He þraste to þan fihte swa þode. [*c* **1275** þodde] doþ on felde. **1684** BUNYAN *Seasonable Counsel* 206 Those thodes, gusts, blasts, or battering storms that beat against thy wall. [**1867** SMYTH *Sailor's Word-bk.*, *Thods*, an old northern term for sudden gusts of wind.]

thoe, var. THO *pron.*, *adj.*, and *adv. Obs.*

thoes, pl. of THOS, a canine beast; obs. f. THOSE.

thof(e, thoff(e, obs. or dial. ff. THOUGH.

thof, thoft, obs. and dial. ff. THOUGHT[1]; see also THINK *v.*[2]

thoft (θɒft). Now *north. dial.* Forms: 1 **þofta**, 4 **thofte**, 4– **thoft**, 9 *Sc.* **thaft** (*Shetl.*, *I. of Man* **taft**, **taff**). [OE. *þofte* (wk. fem.), = ON. *þopta* (Norw., Da. *tofte*), OHG. *dofta*; MLG., LG. *ducht*, whence Ger. *ducht* (*duft*), MDu. *dofte*, *dochte*, Du. *doft*:—OTeut. **puftô*:—Indo-Eur. **tuptâ*, f. root **tup* to squat, sit low. Also Gaelic *tobhta* from Lowland Sc. or Norse. See also THOUGHT[2].

þofta in quot. *c* 1000 is either a scribal error for *þoftan*, or pl. of a str. fem. *þoft*.

It is remarkable that this word, which must have lived on in the north, should appear only once between 1336 and the 19th c.]

A rower's bench; = THWART *sb.*[2]

c **1000** ÆLFRIC *Voc.* in Wr.-Wülcker 166/17 *Transtra*, scipsetl. *Transtra*, uel *juga*, þofta. *c* **1050** *Suppl. Ælfric's Voc.* ibid. 182/5 *Transtra*, þoftan. **1307–8** *Acc. Exch. K.R.* Bd. 14 No. 14 (P.R.O.), In .C. bordis extrinsis emptis..ad faciendum inde Thoftes, Hurdys, et cotes pro dicta Bargia ..xv. s... In .vj. bordis emptis..ad ponendum sub Thoftis ..iij. s. **1336** *Acc. Exch. K.R.* Bundle 19. No. 31. m. 6 Et in xiiij lignis emptis pro Thofftes inde faciendis precium cuiuslibet .vj. d. **1513** DOUGLAS *Æneis* v. iii. 63 (Camb. MS.) The remanent of ye rowaris..Apon yair scyttis and thoftis all atanys Yair placis hynt. [Cf. Virg. v. 136 *considunt transtris*.] **1808–18** JAMIESON, *Thafts*, the benches of a boat, on which the rowers sit. **1827** *Blackw. Mag.* XXI. 859 This waterman on one 'thoft' presenting the breadth of his oar before the wind and with the stream. **1834** H. MILLER *Scenes & Leg.* xvii. (1857) 251 One of the poor fellows tumbled over the thaft. **1876** *Whitby Gloss.*, *Thofts*, the thwarts, or plank-seats across a boat. **1885** RUNCIMAN *Skippers & Sh.* 21 Leapt lightly on the thoft. **1887** T. E. BROWN *Doctor* 18 (I. of Man) Sortin them out On the taff. **1891** BURGESS *Rasmie's Büddie* 51 (Shetl.) Strik rouwin faider frae his taft. **1904** *Eng. Dial. Dict.* s.v. (Shetl.), In a boat the thoft where the mast stands is called the sailing thoft.

Comb. **1847–78** HALLIWELL, *Thoft-fellow*, a fellow oarsman. [Cf. 1874 VIGFUSSON *Icel. Dict.*, *þópti*, a bench-fellow.]

thogh, þoȝ, þogh, thoght, obs. ff. THOUGH.

thoȝen, þoȝen, pa. pple. of THEE *v.*[1] *Obs.*

thoght, þoȝt, etc., obs. ff. THOUGHT[1]: see also THINK *v.*[1] and [2].

thoil(l, obs. Sc. f. THOLE *v.*; erron. f. TOLL *sb.*

thoke (θəʊk), *a.* and *sb.* Now *dial.* [Late ME.; origin unascertained.]

†**A.** *adj.* Not firm or solid; unsound. *rare*$^{-0}$.

c **1440** *Promp. Parv.* 491/2 Thoke, as onsadde fysche, *humorosus*.

B. *sb.* †**1.** An unsound fish: see quots. *Obs.*

1482 *Rolls of Parlt.* VI. 222/1 That tale fish shuld not be pakked with the lesse fish called Grilles, nor there shuld be pakked therwith neither Thokes nor broken belied fissh. [Cf. 1482–3 *Act 22 Edw. IV*, c. 2 §3 Saunz mixture & pakkur dez chosez et [*v.r.* thokes ou] pessons rompez le ventre.] **1494–5** *Act 11 Hen. VII*, c. 23 Without medling and packing of Thokys or broken belied fisshe with the seid tale fisshe or small fisshe. **1758** *Descr. Thames* 259 Of barrelled Fish. Grills, Thokes, &c.

2. *dial.*, *School slang.* (See quots.)

[*a* **1485** *Promp. Parv.* (Winch. MS., ed. 1908) 97 Cowerde, herteles, long choke [*suggested reading* 582 thoke], *vecors*.] **1891** WRENCH *Winchester Word-bk.*, *Thoke*,..a rest, a lying in bed, an idling.

Hence **thoke** *v.* 'to lie late in bed, to be idle; *thoke on*, to look forward to; '**thokester**, an idler' (*Winchester Word-bk.*); '**thokish, thoky** *adjs.* *dial.*: see quots.

a **1682** SIR T. BROWNE *Tracts* viii. (1684) 146 Words..of common use in Norfolk..as..Thokish. **1691** RAY *S. & E.C. Wds.* Pref. *ad fin.*, *Cothish*, morose, and *thokish*, slothful, sluggish, I have no account to give of. **1847–78** HALLIWELL, *Thokish*, slothful; sluggish. *East.* In Lincolnshire it is usually *thoky*.

†'**tholance.** *Sc. Obs.* [f. THOLE *v.* + -ANCE; cf. *sufferance*.] Sufferance, toleration; cf. THOLING *vbl. sb.* 2.

1456 SIR G. HAYE *Law Arms* (S.T.S.) 171 Throu the permissioun and tholaunce of God. **1470** *Regr. Aberbrothoc* (Bann. Cl.) 162 Suppos the said abbot and conuent dois ws fauor in the sasyng of the said anwellis.., of thar gracious tholance and prestance. **1479** *Act. Dom. Conc.* (1839) 39/1 Gife..his predecessouris occupijt þe said acris.., and quheþir as malaris, or tholance or propirte to þe chapellanery. **15..** *Brechine Reg.* lf. 92 (Jam.) Hed ony richt to the said tak bot allanerly off tholance.

thole (θəʊl), *sb.*[1] Forms: 1 thol, ðoll, þol; 5–6 tholle, 6–8 thoule, 7–8 thowle, 8 thoul, 9 thowel(l, thowl, (thauel), 7– thole. [OE. *þol(l*, corresp. to ON. *þollr*, Norw. *toll*, *tulle*, Sw. (*år*) *tull*, Da. (*aar*) *tol*; MLG. *dolle*, *dulle*, *dole*, *doule*, LG. (Brem. Wbch.) *dolle*, *dulle*, EFris. *dolle*, *dol*, MDu. *dolle*, Du. *dol(l*. Ulterior etymology uncertain. In ON. *þollr* was also 'fir-tree', poet. 'tree' generally: the connexion of sense is not clear. The history of the Eng. word also shows a hiatus during nearly the whole ME. period.

The late altered forms *thoule*, *thowle*, and 19th c. *thowel*, may be influenced by *doule*, *dowle*, DOWEL.]

1. A vertical pin or peg in the side of a boat against which in rowing the oar presses as the fulcrum of its action; *esp.* one of a pair between which the oar works; hence, a rowlock.

c **725** *Corpus Gloss.* (O.E.T.) 1820 *Scalmus*, thol. *c* **1000** *Voc.* in Wr.-Wülcker 289/9 *Scalmus*, ðoll. **1611** COTGR., *Scalme*, a Thowle; the little peg whereby the oare of a Skiffe is staied. **1624** CAPT. SMITH *Virginia* 62 In stead of thoules wee made stickes like Bedstaues. **1697** DAMPIER *Voy. round World* (1699) 35 Straps..through which they put their Oars in rowing, instead of tholes or pegs. **1769** FALCONER *Dict. Marine* (1789), *Autarelles*, the thoules or rowlock-pins of a galley. **1827** ROBERTS *Voy. Centr. Amer.* 178 These oars are secured to the thowel by straps of raw hide. **1847** LONGF. *Evang.* II. ii. 102 The sound of their oars on the tholes had died in the distance. **1857** P. COLQUHOUN *Comp. Oarsman's Guide* 29 The row-lock is composed of 3 parts; the thauel, against which you row [etc.]. **1862** WHITTIER *Cry Lost Soul* iv, The guide..drops his oar against the gunwale's thole.

2. A pin or peg in general: *spec.* **a.** A pin by means of which the shafts are fastened to the carriage or axle of a cart, etc. **b.** The handle or 'nib' of a scythe-snathe.

c **1440** *Promp. Parv.* 492/1 Tholle, carte pynne (or tolpyn, *infra*), *cavilla*. **1530** PALSGR. 280/2 Tholle a cartpynne, *cheuille de charette*. **1707** SLOANE *Jamaica* I. p. lii, The use of..drums made of a piece of a hollow tree, covered on one end with any green skin, and stretch'd with Thouls or Pins. **1828** WEBSTER, *Thole*, 2. the pin or handle of a sythe-snath. **1880** R. S. CHARNOCK *Essex Gloss.*, *Thole*, the two pieces or handles of a scythe. **1910** H. BELLOC *Mr. Clutterbuck's Election* iv, The woodwork..was designed in the Cheshire fashion, with drawpins, tholes, and spring-heads tinctured to a sober brown.

†**thole**, *sb.*[2] *Obs. rare*$^{-1}$. [f. THOLE *v.*] Patience, forbearance, endurance.

c **1250** *Gen. & Ex.* 3496 Ic am god, gelus and strong, Min wreche is hard, min ðole is long.

†**thole**, *sb.*[3] *Obs. rare.* [Anglicized f. L. *thol-us*: see THOLOS.] See quot. 1656, and cf. THOLOS.

1633 [J. FISHER] *True Trojans* III. ii. Eij, Let Altars smoake, and Tholes expect our spoiles. **1656** BLOUNT *Glossogr.*, *Thole* (*tholus*),..that place in Temples, where donaries and such gifts as were presented there, are hung up.

thole (θəʊl), *v.* Now *north. dial.* or *arch.* Forms: 1 **þolian**, 2–3 **-ien**, (2 **þale(n)**, 2–4 **þolye**, **-ie**, **-en**, 3 (*Orm.*) **þolenn**, 3–4 **-yen**, 4 **þoole**, **tholen**, **-y**, 4–5 **þole**, **tholie**, 4– **thole**. (Also 4, 6 *Sc.* **thol**, 4 (5–6 *Sc.*) **thoile**, 4–6 *Sc.* **thoill**, 5 **poliȝe**, **þol(l**, **thoole**, **thowle**, **tholl**, 6 (7–8 *Sc.*) **thoell**, 8 *n. dial.* **thoyl**, 6– *Sc.* and *n. dial.* **thoil.**) [OE. *þolian* = OS. *tholôn*, *tholian*, OHG. *dolôn*, *dolên* (MHG. *dolen*, *doln*; cf. Ger. *gedul-d*), ON. *þola* (Da. *taale*, Sw. *tåla*), Goth. *þulan*, f. OTeut. stem **pul-*:—weak grade of root **tel*: **tol*: **tl* to bear, suffer: cf. L. *tuli*, *tolerare*, *toll-ere*, Gr. τλῆναι.]

1. *trans.* To be subjected or exposed to (something evil); to be afflicted with; to have to bear, suffer, undure, undergo.

Beowulf 832 Hie..for þreanydum þolian scoldon torn unlytel. *c* **897** K. ÆLFRED *Gregory's Past. C.* xxviii. 197 Dauid ..lange ær his [Saul's] ehtnesse earfoðlice ðolode. *a* **1000** *Cædmon's Gen.* 2240 (Gr.) þeowdom þolian. **1154** *O.E. Chron.* (Laud MS.) an. 1137, Suilc & mare þanne we cunnen sæin we þoleden xix wintre for ure sinnes. *c* **1175** *Lamb. Hom.* 75 His halie fif wunden þa he þolede for us ine þe halie rode. *c* **1200** ORMIN Ded. 201 He ȝaff hiss aȝhenn lif..To þolenn dæþþ o rodetre. *c* **1290** *Beket* 2316 in *S. Eng. Leg.* I. 173 þis holi man..þolede martyrdom. *c* **1320** *Cast. Love* 410 He scal euere þolyen deþ. **13..** *Cursor M.* 9636 (Cott.) Ded he aght to thole. **1375** BARBOUR *Bruce* IV. 659 Feill anoyis thoill ȝhe sall. *c* **1386** CHAUCER *Friar's T.* 248 So muche wo as I haue with yow tholed. *c* **1450** *Mirour Saluacioun* 212 All y[t] oure lord Ihū soeffred in his passionne Oure ladie tholed in sawle. **1530** LYNDESAY *Test. Papyngo* 175 Off bitter deth now mon I thole the schouris. **1599** PORTER *Angry Wom. Abingd.* in Hazl. *Dodsley* VII. 370 What a winter of cold fear I thole. **1717** RAMSAY *Elegy on Lucky Wood* i, What loss, what crosses dost thou thole! **1884** FREEMAN in Stephens *Life* (1895) II. x. 321 They that believed nothing were to thole all revealed punishments. [*Affected archaism.*]

absol. **1357** *Lay Folks Catech.* 132 [Christ] tholed [*v.r.* suffryd] bodily for synful man kynd. *c* **1394** *P. Pl. Crede* 90 þe cros þat crist opon þolede. *c* **1430** LYDG. *Min. Poems* (Percy Soc.) 227 How ever thou thole ore thryfe, Alwey thonk God of alle. **1718** RAMSAY *Christ's Kirk Gr.* III. xvi, Ye's thole for this, ye scaul. **1880** A. FORBES in *19th Cent.* Jan. 190 To be told how our countrymen..toil and thole.

b. *to thole an assize*, *judgement*, *the laws*, etc., to undergo trial. *Sc.*

1425 *Sc. Acts Jas. I* (1814) II. 9/2 þe king..forbiddis þat ony man..be aponne his assise þat sall thole þe law. **1508** DUNBAR *Flyting* 78 For quhilk, brybour, ȝit sall thow thoill a breif. *a* **1578** LINDESAY (Pitscottie) *Chron. Scot.* III. iv. (S.T.S.) I. 223 The lordis..quhilk was..thair to thoill ane syse conforme to thair ditta. **1609** SKENE *Reg. Maj.* I. 93 b, It is statute, that na man sould thoill judgement, or be judged, be ane man of inferiour estate then his awin peir. **1678** SIR G. MACKENZIE *Crim. Laws Scot.* I. xx. §4 (1699) 108 The Receptor with us cannot be punished, or thole an Assize, till the principal Thief be first convict. **1886** *St. James' Gaz.* 16 Dec. 3 Mr...would probably by this time have tholed an assize before the High Court of Justiciary.

2. To endure without resistance or complaint; to submit with patience to; to bear with, 'abide'; to put up with, tolerate. Also with *inf.* or *subord. cl.*

c **950** *Lindisf. Gosp.* Mark ix. 19 Ða huile mið iuh ic beom, ða huile iuih ic ðola. *a* **1000** *Cædmon's Gen.* 597 (Gr.) þæt is micel wundor þæt hit ece god æfre wolde, þeoden, þolian. **1297** R. GLOUC. (Rolls) 9479 So luþer & prout heo was, þat me ne miȝte it þolie noȝt. *c* **1330** R. BRUNNE *Chron. Wace* (Rolls) 15976 Al þer trauaille & al þer ylle þat þey had þoled wiþ gode wille. **1393** *Rec. Elgin* (New Spald. Cl) I. 7 þis as before wyt al men we wil nocht thole. *c* **1430** *Syr Gener.* (Roxb.) 8490 He might the betre thoole Thurgh gile to les a little ring, Whan [etc.]. **1552** ABP. HAMILTON *Catech.* (1884) 81 Thai that tholis nocht thair father and mother, suppose thai do thame iniuris and be cummersum. **1584** HUDSON tr. *Du Bartas' Judith* III. 179 For thee, we frankly shall pursue and thole Th'eternall heat and colde of either Pole. **1786** BURNS *Twa Dogs* 96 Poor tenant bodies, scant o' cash, How they maun thole a factor's snash. *c* **1800** *Newcastle Prov.* in Brockett *N.C. Gloss.* (1846) II. 178 He that has a good crop may thole some thistles. **184.** in *Contemp. Rev.* (1905) July 64 'I com' away,' said he, 'for I couldn't thoil to see good food wasted.' **1889** BARRIE *Window in Thrums* 38, I canna thole 'im.

absol. **1154** *O.E. Chron.* an. 1140 §6 (Laud MS.) þa hi ne leng ne muhten þolen, þa stali hi ut & fluȝen. *c* **1200** *Trin. Coll. Hom.* 79 þe man..þe þoleð and forbereð and ne wile seche after wreche. *a* **1340** HAMPOLE *Psalter* ix. 41 þaire hert redy to serue þe and to thole. *c* **1470** HENRY *Wallace* VIII. 663 ȝeit Wallace tholyt, and leit thaim say thar will. **1560** ROLLAND *Seven Sages* 77 Better it is to thoill heir patientlie, Nor euer mair in hell condampnit be. **1880** A. FORBES in *19th Cent.* Feb. 234 The British soldier can thole as well as can the Russian soldier.

†**b.** To endure or bear without giving way; to withstand; to stand. *Obs.*

c **1200** ORMIN 9399 þa maȝȝ itt [the eye] siþþenn þolenn wel þe sunness brihhte leome. **13..** *Cursor M.* 7312 (Gött.) It es wel worthi þat qua May thole na wele, to thole þe wa. *c* **1400** *Destr. Troy* 9674 No buerne vpon bent his buffettes might thowle. **14..** *Songs Costume* (Percy Soc.) 60 Her mantill of humilitie, To tholl bayth wind and weit.

c. To bear, stand, admit of, be capable of; to have room for; esp. in phrase ***to thole amends***, to admit of improvement. *dial.*

1770 JAS. WATT *Let. to Small* 3 Jan., Health and spirits beyond what I commonly enjoy..; though they would still thole amends. *a* **1774** FERGUSSON *Cauler Oysters* Poems (1845) 7 Fling owre your craig sufficient doses; You'll thole a hunder. **1808** SCOTT *Let. to G. Ellis* 23 Feb., in *Lockhart*, The style would..*thole amends*, i.e. admit of improvement. **1871** in *N. & Q.* 4th Ser. VIII. 156/2 It'll thole a drap mair watter.

†**3.** To allow, suffer, permit. (With obj. clause, obj. and inf., or equivalent pron.) *Obs.*

c **1070** *Charter of Leofgifu* in Kemble *Cod. Dipl.* IV. 269 Ic bidde mine leuedien for Godes louen ðat ðu [ne] þolie ðat ani man mine quide awende. *c* **1175** *Lamb. Hom.* 71 þole us to bi-wepen ure sunne. *c* **1200** ORMIN 12089 ȝiff Crist itt nollde þolenn himm Naffde he þærto nan mahhte. **1297** R. GLOUC. (Rolls) 1583 þe toun folc..nolde namore þolie þan ssrewe among hom a wede. **13..** *Gaw. & Gr. Knt.* 1859 þenne he þulged with hir þrepe, & þoled hir to speke. *c* **1400** *Apol. Loll.* 59 þei be þolid to minister prestly oþer sacraments. **1466** *Dunfermline Regr.* (Bann. Cl.) 356, I sall nocht thole, graunt nore gyff leiffe..to na man..to draw na drauchtis of wateris throu my landis. **1513** DOUGLAS *Æneis* IX. vii. 89 Thoil me to trubble this gret rout of men. **1552** ABP. HAMILTON *Catech.* (1884) 35 God will nocht thoile you want your dailie sustentatioun. **1575** CHURCHYARD *Chippes* (1817) 193 God would not thoell, for one mans sake alone: That broyles should cause a million make their mone. **1721** RAMSAY *Prospect of Plenty* 83 They'll never thole this great design to tak.

4. *intr.* To be patient, have patience, wait patiently. *dial.*

1674 RAY *N.C. Words* 48 *Thole* a while, i.e. stay a while. **1766** A. NICOL *Poems* 58 (E.D.D.), I do bid them thole a while Till ance the spring come in again. **1896** [J. LUMSDEN] *Poems* 7 (ibid.) Great is our drouth—but thole a wee.

5. *trans.* To bear to give; to afford or grant willingly. *dial.*

1703 THORESBY *Let. to Ray* Gloss. (E.D.S.), *Thoyl*, to afford. **1828** *Craven Gloss.* s.v., I could thole him t' meat out o' my mouth. **1863** MRS. TOOGOOD *Yorksh. Dial.* (MS.), He is so covetous he cannot thoil his servants enough food.

thole, obs. erron. f. TOLL, in *thole and theam*, 'toll and team'.

†'**tholeburde**, *a.* *Obs. rare.* Forms: 1 **þolebyrde**, (**þoli-**, **þolo-**), 3 **þoleburde**. [Late OE. *þolebyrde*, f. stem of THOLE *vb.* + *byrd* bearing.] Bearing patiently; forbearing, submissive. Hence †'**tholeburdness** *Obs. rare*, patience, submission.

a **1050** *Liber Scintill.* i. 3 To þolibyrdnysse þrowunga strange, *ad tolerantiam passionum fortes*. *Ibid.* ii. 13 þolobyrde mann, *patiens homo*. *Ibid.*, Wer soðlice þolebyrde, *uir enim patiens*. *c* **1200** *Trin. Coll. Hom.* 79 [To] ben swo þoleburde to-ȝenes his wissinge to forleten þat he forbet, and don þat he bit. *Ibid.*, *Tanta est uirtus paciencie*.., swo holie mihte is þoleburdnesse. *a* **1250** *Orison* 51 in *O.E. Misc.* 140 Ihesuc ich þe grete..For þe muchel þoleburne [? -burnesse] ..þat þu schawedest mon-kunne, þo þu þoledest deþ.

tholeiite ('θəʊlɪaɪt). *Petrogr.* Also 9 **tholeite.** [ad. G. *tholeiit* (J. Steininger *Geognostische Beschreibung des Landes zwischen der unteren Saar und dem Rheine*: *Nachträge* (1841) 26), f. *Tholei* (now *Tholey*), name of a village in N.E. Saar, W. Germany: see -ITE[1].] Formerly, a basaltic rock containing plagioclase feldspar, pyroxene, and glass, with little or no olivine, and having an intersertal texture; in recent use, any basaltic rock typically containing augite and a calcium-poor pyroxene (pigeonite or hypersthene), and distinguished from alkali basalts by a higher silica and lower alkali content.

1866 P. H. LAWRENCE tr. *von Cotta's Rocks Classified & Described* II. i. 138 Steininger has given the name of Tholeite to a rock found at the Schaumberg near Tholei, which he took for a compound of albite and titanite. But according to Bergemann's analysis this rock consists of 70 labradorite, 5 augite... It must therefore from its composition be considered a dolerite or basalt unless indeed it be considered as plutonic and classed with melaphyre. **1893** [see INTERSERTAL *a.*]. **1922** *Q. Jrnl. Geol. Soc.* LXXVIII. 229 The rocks were described as being..of one type: namely, olivine-free dolerites or tholeiites. **1924** THOMAS & BAILEY in E. B. Bailey et al. *Tertiary & Post-Tertiary Geol. Mull* xxv. 280 Olivine-free and olivine-poor plagioclase-augite rocks with intersertal structure are classed by Rosenbusch as tholeiites. **1962** *Jrnl. Petrol.* III. 352 The two planes identified in Fig. 1..divide the basalts into five unique groups..: 1. Tholeiite (oversaturated): normative quartz and hypersthene. 2. Tholeiite (saturated; hypersthene basalt): normative hypersthene. 3. Olivine tholeiite (undersaturated): normative hypersthene and olivine. 4. Olivine basalt: normative olivine. 5. Alkali basalt: normative olivine and nepheline. **1967** *Geol. Mag.* CIV. 337 Significant use of the term tholeiite dates from 1887 when Rosenbusch redefined Steininger's Schaumberg, Saar tholeiite (1840) from Tholey as a melaphyre with intersertal texture... Bailey and Thomas (1924) in setting up their non-porphyritic central magma type of Mull recognized its 'tholeiitic' character using..Rosenbusch's definition of 1887... A more precise petrographic and chemical definition was to follow in Kennedy's important papers of 1931 and 1933 in which the non-porphyritic central magma type was redefined as the Tholeiitic Magma Type... Paramount in this definition was the recognition of the presence of an enstatite-augite or pigeonite series pyroxene in the ground-mass of tholeiitic lavas. **1978** *Nature* 13 July 128/1 The two principal Icelandic basalt types are evolved tholeiites, mostly quartz-normative, with Mg/Mg + Fe^{2+} atomic ratio of 0·40 to 0·50, associated with fissure swarms and central volcanoes; and second, olivine tholeiites with Mg/Mg + Fe^{2+} in the 0·60–0·70 range and predominantly associated with monogenetic shield volcanoes.

Hence **tholeiˈitic** *a.*

1922 *Q. Jrnl. Geol. Soc.* LXXVIII. 237 The tholeiitic intrusions have produced little thermal alteration of the rocks into which they have been ultimately injected. **1933** [see *plateau basalt* s.v. PLATEAU 4]. **1933** *Amer. Jrnl. Sci.* CCXXV. 247 The general thesis is..advanced that the olivine-basalt magma-type is the parent of the alkaline line of descent while the tholeiitic magma-type occupies a similar position with respect to the calc-alkaline rock suite. **1967** [see THOLEIITE above]. **1970** *Nature* 12 Dec. 1030/2 Geochemists have known for some time that [ocean] ridge basalts tend to be tholeiitic whereas alkali basalts are more likely to be found away from ridges. **1972** F. H. HATCH et al. *Petrol. Igneous Rocks* (ed. 13) vii. 364 Alkali olivine-basalt magmas can differentiate towards alkali-enrichment; but tholeiitic magmas differentiate towards silica-enrichment.

†**ˈtholemode**, *a.* and *sb.* *Obs.* Forms: 1–4 **þolemod, þolmod,** (1 **þolo-**), 2–4 **þolemode,** 4 **tholemod, tholmod, -moud, -mud,** (**-mound**), 4–5 **tholemode, tholmode;** *Sc.* 5 **tholemude,** 6 **thoilmude, -muide,** (8 **tholemoody**). [OE. *þolemód*, f. *þole-* (see THOLEBURDE *a.*) + *mód*, MOOD *sb.*[1] Cf. ON. *þolin-móðr*, Da. *taal-modig.*]

A. *adj.* Patient, submissive, meek.

c **1000** *Ags. Hom.* (Assmann) 127 (Gr.) Heo wæs þolemod and ʒestæððiʒ on hire ʒebæran. *c* **1000** ÆLFRIC *Saints' Lives* xvii. 56 And beo ʒesibsum, ʒeðyldiʒ and ðolmod. *a* **1050** *Liber Scintill.* ii. 8 þolomod, *patiens.* *a* **1100** *O.E. Glosses* (Napier) I. 1319 *Longanimem*, þolemod. *c* **1175** *Lamb. Hom.* 105 þet þe mon beo ipuldi and þolemod. *a* **1225** *Leg. Kath.* 177 Ha wes þuldi & þolemod. *a* **1300** *Cursor M.* 10187 (Cott.) Was neuer..nan tholmoder in chastite. *c* **1450** *Mirour Saluacioun* 4607 In alle aduersitees y[t] I so tholemode ay be. **1513** DOUGLAS *Æneis* v. vii. 48 In vane that name thow beris,..Geif thow, sa thoilmuide, sufferis leid away Sa greit a price. **1710** RUDDIMAN *Gloss. to Douglas' Æneis*, *Thoilmude*, Scot. Bor. say *tholemoody*, i.e. patient.

B. *sb.* = THOLEMODENESS. *rare.*

c **1000** ÆLFRIC *Saints' Lives* xvi. 334 (MS. D.) Se feorðe mihte is patientia, þæt is ðolmod ʒecweden. *c* **1175** *Paternoster* 266 in *Lamb. Hom.* 69 Edmodnesse and þolemod þet þuncheð gode swiðe god.

†**ˈtholemodely**, *adv.* *Obs.* [f. prec. + -LY[2].] Patiently, submissively, meekly.

a **1225** *Ancr. R.* 46 Nime hire sicnesse nout one þolemodliche, auch do swuð gledliche. *a* **1340** HAMPOLE *Psalter* xxiv. 2 All þat tholmodly beris þe birþin of tribulacioun. *c* **1375** *Sc. Leg. Saints* iii. (*Andreas*) 403 Gyf þu wil her me tholmodly. *c* **1450** *Mirour Saluacioun* 3195 The swerde of sharpest tonges herd of crist tholemodely.

†**ˈtholemodeness.** *Obs.* [f. as prec. + -NESS.] Patience, submissiveness, meekness.

c **1000** ÆLFRIC *Saints' Lives* xvi. 334 (MS. J.) Patientia þæt is ʒeðyld and þolmodnys ʒecwæden. *a* **1225** *Ancr. R.* 276 Wreððes salue [is] þolemodnesse. **1303** R. BRUNNE *Handl. Synne* 5831 Moche he louede þolmodnesse. *c* **1375** *Sc. Leg. Saints* xxxvi. (*Baptista*) 433 Of tholmudnes als sic wes he þat he with-stud in na degre Agane þame þat..til hyme mysded. **1456** SIR G. HAYE *Law Armys* (S.T.S.) 285 The prince suld be..of gude tholemudenes, to suetely here the caus.

ˈthole-pin. Forms: see THOLE *sb.*[1]; also 5 **tolpyn.** [f. THOLE *sb.*[1] + PIN *sb.*]

1. A peg used as a fastening; = THOLE *sb.*[1] 2.

c **1440** *Promp. Parv.* 496/1 Tolpyn, *idem quod* tholle, *supra.* **1881** *Isle of Wight Gloss.*, *Thole-pin*, the pin that goes into the shafts of the roller by which the horse draws. **1884** *19th Cent.* Feb. 244 A coffin..having a thong-hinged cover..fastened by a thole pin. **1893** INGLIS *Ain Folk* vii, The thole-pin which kept the loft folding-door in position.

2. = THOLE *sb.*[1] 1.

1598 FLORIO, *Schelma*..a..peg in a boate whereat the rowers stay their oares when they rowe, called a thoule pin. **1725** DUDLEY in *Phil. Trans.* XXXVI. 264 An Oar..not so much as lifted up out of the Thole-Pin. **1859** W. H. GREGORY *Egypt* I. 293 It scorched our hands to touch at midday the iron plates in which the thowl-pins were fastened.

tholing (ˈθəʊlɪŋ), *vbl. sb.* [f. THOLE *v.* + -ING[1].]

1. The action of THOLE *v.*; suffering, enduring.

a **1300** *Cursor M.* 15684 (Cott.) Thoru mi bodi most it pass þe tholing o þis pine. *c* **1400** *Apol. Loll.* 5 Petir..fillid þe office of Crist, in liuing, and in teching, and in þoling. **1562** TURNER *Baths* 10 b, According to the complexion of the sicke, and after the suffrance or tholling of the stomack. **1884** FREEMAN in Stephens *Life & Lett.* II. x. 322 But then that entitles me to the unrevealed tholings [*affected archaism*].

†**2.** Sufferance, permission, allowance, leave. *Obs.*

c **1375** *Sc. Leg. Saints* xxx. (*Theodera*) 6 þo þar-to he haf mycht Thru godis tholyne & gret slycht. **1457** *Dunfermline Regr.* (Bann. Cl.) 344 Rechart be goddis tholyng Abbote of Donfermlyn. **1466** *Ibid.* 356, I giff and grauntis..full leiffe and tholing and gude will to þe saidis Abbot..to mak land stell and Dame forganis my said landis.

ˈtholing, *ppl. a.* [f. THOLE *v.* + -ING[2].] That tholes; enduring; patient.

1340 *Ayenb.* 167 þe holy gost..him makeþ strang and þolyinde uor to þolye huanne hi comeþ. *c* **1425** tr. *Arderne's Treat. Fistula* 58 Men now of daiez bene vnpacient and yuel tholyng.

tholl, obs. erron. f. TOLL *sb.*

tholnie, tholoney, var. TOLNE *Sc. Obs.*, toll.

tholobate (ˈθɒləbeɪt). *Arch.* [f. Gr. θόλ-ος THOLOS + -βατης one who goes, f. βαίνειν to go.] (See quots.)

1831 HOSKING in *Encycl. Brit.* (ed. 7) I. 471/1 *Tholobate*, ..that on which a dome or cupola rests... A term not in general use... What is generally termed the attic above the peristyle and under the cupola of St. Paul's, would be correctly designated the tholobate. A tholobate of a different description..is the circular substructure to the cupola of the London University. **1838** BRITTON *Dict. Archit.* 457. **1845** PARKER *Gloss. Archit.* (ed. 4), *Tholobate*, the substructure on which a dome or cupola rests.

tholoid (ˈθəʊlɔɪd). *Geol.* [f. Gr. θόλος see THOLOS + -OID.] A dome-shaped, steep-sided extrusion of hardened lava plugging the vent of a volcano.

In quot. 1912 repr. a Ger. form.

1912 *Jrnl. Geol.* XX. 85 'Tholoides' have slopes of over 35° and are convex upward. **1939** *Nature* 25 Nov. 913/2 Of the latter [*sc.* new volcanoes] there were two:..(*b*) Iōzima-Sintō, south of Kyûsyû.., which was of the tholoid type. **1976** P. FRANCIS *Volcanoes* iv. 151 Even when the tholoid is shrouded in mist and invisible, as it often is in the afternoon, the dry clattering continues, with every now and then a much larger collapse taking place.

‖**tholos** (ˈθɒlɒs). *Arch.* Pl. **tholoi** (-ɔɪ). Also in Latin form (esp. in sense 1) **tholus** (ˈθəʊləs), pl. **tholi** (-aɪ). [L. *tholus*, Gr. θόλος, a round building with a conical or vaulted roof.] **a.** A circular domed building or structure; a dome, cupola; a lantern.

1644 EVELYN *Diary* 7 Nov., A pretty odd fabriq, with a Tribunal, or Tholus within. *a* **1668** LASSELS *Voy. Italy* (1698) I. 188 On the top of it [the Domo of Florence] stands mounted a fair Cupola (or Tholus). **1730–6** BAILEY (folio), *Tholus*, the Roof of a Temple or Church, the Centre, Scutcheon, or Knot in the middle of an arched Roof, the Lanthorn or Cupola of a publick Hall. **1832** GELL *Pompeiana* I. iv. 47 A circular or polygonal tholos. **1841** *Civil Eng. & Arch. Jrnl.* IV. 117/2 The tholus, or concave dome.

b. *Gr. Antiq.* An excavated circular tomb of the Mycenæan age, domed and lined with masonry. Also ***tholos-tomb.***

1885 *Athenæum* 12 Dec. 773/2 Mr. Pullan..was astonished to find that the lower cell of the so-called prison of St. Peter at Rome was part of a tholus. **1896** Tholoi [see DROMOS]. **1910** *Edin. Rev.* Apr. 479 Among the forms sepulchre are the great bee-hive *tholos* [etc.]. **1957** [see *beehive tomb* s.v. BEEHIVE 3]. **1975** *Times Lit. Suppl.* 14 Mar. 282/1 The megalithic architecture of Britain..had no conceivable ancestry in the Mycenaean *tholoi.*

attrib. **1902** R. C. BOSANQUET in *Ann. Brit. Sch. at Athens* VIII. 305 Tholos-burial was introduced in eastern Crete towards the close of the Minoan Age. **1921** *Discovery* Feb. 33/1 The principle of the tholos-tomb was most in use in Mycenæan times. **1983** *Times* 10 Feb. 1/3 The underground *tholos* tomb, shaped like a giant beehive, lies in a fifteenth-century BC cemetery..three miles south of Argos.

tholsel, -l, var. TOLSEL, TOLZEY. *Obs.*

tholus, var. THOLOS.

Thomæan (təʊˈmiːən), *a.* and *sb.* Also **Thomean.** [app. f. med.L. *Thōmæ-us* (f. the name *Thōmā-s*) + -AN.] **a.** *adj.* Of or pertaining to the Christian church traditionally said to have been founded by St. Thomas the Apostle, which has existed from early times on the Malabar coast. **b.** *sb.* A member of this church. Also called *Thomite, Christian of St. Thomas.*

1727–41 CHAMBERS *Cycl.*, *Thomæans, Thomeans, Thomites*, or *Christians of St. Thomas*, a people of the East-Indians, who, according to tradition, received the gospel from the apostle St. Thomas. *Ibid.*, A great part of the Thomæan church relapsed, and thus still continues partly Roman, partly Thomæan. **1842** BRANDE *Dict. Sci., Lit.*, etc., *Thomæans*, or *Thomites.*

Thomaism, variant of THOMISM, q.v.

thoman, -and, obs. variants of TOMAN.

Thomas (ˈtɒməs). [a. L. *Thōmās*, Gr. Θωμᾶς.]

1. A Greek, Latin, and common Christian name; well known as that of the 'doubting apostle' (see John xx. 25), and hence used allusively; also used as a representative proper name for one of the populace taken at random. Familiarly abbreviated to TOM *sb.*[1], the dim. or pet form of which is TOMMY[1].

c **1000** *Ags. Gosp.* John xx. 24 Thomas an of þam twelfon þe ys ʒecweden didimus..næs mid him þa se hælend com. *c* **1275** *O.E. Misc.* 90 Haly thomas of heoue[n]riche. *c* **1412** HOCCLEVE *De Reg. Princ.* 5080 ȝe, so I drede me, by seynt Thomas. *c* **1620** ROBINSON *Mary Magd.* 1519 O, that I might, with wauering Thomas, dippe The finger of my faith within his side. **1656** BLOUNT *Glossogr.*, *Thomas* (*Hebr.*) signifies twin, or as some will have it, bottomlesse deep. **1848** MRS. GASKELL *M. Barton* xii, Mary, don't let my being an unbelieving Thomas weaken your faith. **1883** *Harper's Mag.* June 93/1 Doubting Thomases, who will only believe what they see, must wait awhile.

2. Generic name for a footman or waiter.

1846 MRS. GORE *Eng. Char.* (1852) 78 The gossip of one fashionable dinner-table alone, within ear-shot of three or four first-rate Thomases, is sufficient to disperse throughout the town rumours enough to set a hundred families of consideration into a ferment. **1901** *Daily Graphic* 23 Feb., The 'men' are not any less 'splendid' because they are known by this diminutive term [Tommy], any more than waiters are heroic because we give them their full title of 'Thomas'.

3. Thomas Atkins (also *Thomas*): a familiar name for the typical private soldier in the British Army; arising out of the casual use of this name in the specimen forms given in the official regulations from 1815 onward: see quots.

In some of the specimen forms other names are used; but 'Thomas Atkins' being that used in all the forms for privates in the Cavalry or Infantry, is by far the most frequent, and thus became the most familiar. Now more popularly TOMMY ATKINS or TOMMY[1] q.v.

1815 (Aug. 31) Warr Office, *Collection of Orders, Regulations, etc.* 75 (Form of a Soldier's Book in the Cavalry when filled up). Description, Service, &c. of Thomas Atkins, Private, No. 6 Troop, 6th Regt. of Dragoons. Where Born... Parish of Odiham, Hants... Bounty, £6. Received, Thomas Atkins, his x mark. *Ibid.* 76 Clothing Account of Thomas Atkins, Private, No. 6 Troop, 6th Dragoons... Clothing Account of William Jones, Trumpeter, No. 2 Troop, 9th Light Dragoons... Clothing Account of John Thomas, Serjeant, No. 8 Troop, 15th Hussars. [So Forms on pp. 78–81 all 'Thomas Atkins, Private'.] *Ibid.* 82 Form of Soldier's Book in the Infantry, when filled up. Description, Service, etc. of Thomas Atkins, Private, No. 6 Company, 1st Batt. 23d Regt. Foot. Where born [etc.]... Bounty £7 7s. Received, Thomas Atkins, his x mark. [So Forms on pp. 83–87, all signed 'Thomas Atkins, his x mark'.] **1837** (June 1) *King's Regulations & Orders for the Army* 204, Form No. 2, No. 55 Thomas Atkins, Serjeant, Born in the Parish of St. Mary in or near the Town of Portsmouth, in the County of Hants, by Trade a Labourer. *Ibid.* 206–9 [Various Forms, all filled up or subscribed 'Thomas Atkins' (who no longer signs by 'his mark')]. *Ibid.* 210 Character: Thomas Atkins has been a well-conducted Soldier; was wounded at ——, and has distinguished himself by several acts of bravery. Signed ——, Commanding Officer. **1864** *Stand. Orders Roy. Reg. Artill.* 89 Thomas Atkins. Enlisted..on the 9th April, 1857. *Ibid.*, We certify that the above is a correct Statement of the Services of Thomas Atkins, to the 10th June 1887. **1888** KIPLING *From Sea to Sea* (1899) I. 185 Every Thomas is interesting, except when he is too drunk to speak. **1890** *Times* 6 Dec. 12/4 Mr. Thomas Atkins..can break it [a rifle] down in half-a-dozen ways in the course of his musketry instruction. **1897** *Allahabad Pioneer* in *Westm. Gaz.* 14 Dec. 7/3 'You take my advice, Bill', remarked one Thomas to another,..'don't you never stand near no white stone or yet near no horcifer'.

4. St. Thomas', in composition. **St. Thomas' balsam** = *balsam of* TOLU. †**St. Thomas' coin** (also **St. Thomas**), ? an East Indian coin. **St. Thomas' tree,** *Bauhinia tomentosa* or *B. variegata* of the E. Indies, the pale yellow petals of which are spotted with crimson, fabled to be the blood of St. Thomas. **St. Thomas worsted**: see SAINT *a.* 4 c.

1559 in Marsden *Court Adm.* (Selden) II. 110 Novem pecias auri vulgo dictas *Saintte Thomas coyne. **1698** FRYER *Acc. E. India & P.* 53 Their Coins are of Gold; a St. Thomas, 10s. a Fanam, 7 and ½ of which go to a Dollar, or Petacha. **1866** *Treas. Bot.*, *St. Thomas' Tree, *Bauhinia tomentosa.* **1887** MOLONEY *Forestry W. Afr.* 332 St. Thomas' Tree... Shrub or small tree. **1518** *N.C. Wills* (Surtees 1908) 95 A jaket of tawny *Saint Thomas worsted.

5. *Surg.* The name of H. O. *Thomas* (1834–91), English surgeon, used *attrib.* and in the possessive to designate a splint that he invented for immobilizing the hip, consisting of a rigid bar that extends from the back to the calf and is bandaged to the leg, and with rings attached that partly encircle the chest and leg;

also (now the usual sense), a splint consisting of a soft ring encircling the thigh from which two rigid rods extend on each side of the leg and meet beyond the foot, allowing traction to be applied to the leg via the cross-piece or the knee to be immobilized.

1884 W. PYE *Surg. Handicraft* xxiii. 291 There are many other ways of treating acute hip disease... By Thomas' splint. **1940** N. MITFORD *Pigeon Pie* vi. 102 If..real casualties were brought in and found all the personnel tied up in Thomas's splints. **1961** *Countryman* LVIII. III. 600 The M.O... fixed my fractured leg in a Thomas splint. **1974** PASSMORE & ROBSON *Compan. Med. Stud.* III. iv. 11/2 The Thomas' splint is designed so that when the traction tapes are tightened over the end of the splint, a counter thrust is exerted through the padded ring against the bony prominence of the ischium.

6. The name of S. G. *Thomas* (1850–85), English metallurgist and inventor, used *attrib.* to designate a steel-making process like the Bessemer process but using a converter with a basic instead of an acid lining, so that phosphorus is removed (invented by Thomas in 1878). Also ***Thomas-Gilchrist*** [P. *Gilchrist* (1851–1935), cousin and collaborator of Thomas].

1881 *Encycl. Brit.* XIII. 346/1 Owing to the success of these operations, the 'basic' process has been more frequently spoken of as the 'Thomas-Gilchrist process'. **1925** *Jrnl. Iron & Steel Inst.* CXII. 523 Notwithstanding prognostications as to the supersession..of the Bessemer acid and basic (Thomas) process by the open-hearth process, it is certain that..the Bessemer process will long continue to hold its own. **1948** H. W. BAKER *Mod. Workshop Technol.* I. 22 In the Thomas process the necessary amount of lime..is charged into the converter..before the iron..is poured in. **1973** [see SIEMENS a].

Thomas-Fermi (tɒməs'fɜːmɪ). *Physics.* The names of L. H. *Thomas* (b. 1903), English physicist, and E. FERMI, used *attrib.* with reference to a model of the electronic charge distribution in an atom in which the electrons are treated as a gas of independent particles obeying Fermi-Dirac statistics and the exclusion principle is taken into account, proposed by them in 1927 and 1928 respectively.

1931 *Phil. Mag.* XII. 111 The Thomas-Fermi method of approximating to the atomic charge distribution. **1955** J. LINDHARD in W. Pauli *Niels Bohr* 190 If we ask for the behaviour for heavier atoms,..a Thomas-Fermi treatment should again be preferable. **1970** G. K. WOODGATE *Elem. Atomic Struct.* vi. 101 The Thomas-Fermi potential does serve as a trial potential for self-consistent field methods.

Thomasing ('tɒməsɪŋ). *dial.* [f. THOMAS + -ING[1].] The begging of alms on St. Thomas's day (21 Dec.). Also called *corning, doling,* or *gooding.*

1847–78 HALLIWELL, *Thomasing*, a custom in Derbyshire, going from house to house on St. Thomas's day with a basket and can to beg milk, wheat, oatmeal, or flour. **1866** W. HENDERSON *Folk Lore* ii. 50 The widows ask and commonly receive at the farmers' houses a small measure of wheat, and they call it 'going a Thomasing'. **1900** *Daily Chron.* 3 Nov. 3 (Cass. Supp.) The maying, processioning, Thomasing, carolling, and other junketings.

Thomasite ('tɒməsaɪt). [f. as prec. + -ITE[1].] = CHRISTADELPHIAN, from the name of the founder, Dr. John Thomas.

1888 in *Cassell's Encycl. Dict.*

thomb(e, thome, obs. forms of THUMB.

thomble, thomelle, obs. forms of THIMBLE.

thomble toe, etc.: see THUMBLE-TOE.

Thomism ('təʊmɪz(ə)m). *Theol.* [f. THOM-AS + -ISM. So F. *thomisme* (Roquefort, 1829).] The doctrines of Thomas Aquinas or of the Thomists.

1727–41 CHAMBERS *Cycl.*, *Thomism*, or *Thomaism. Ibid.*, The Thomism..which Alvarez embraces, admits a physical premonition, or predetermination. **1731** BAILEY vol. II, *Thomism*, the doctrine of Thomas Aquinas,..chiefly with respect to his opinions on predestination and grace. **1883** *Schaff's Encycl. Relig. Knowl.* III. 2354 The Jesuits opposed Thomism,..but it prevailed at the Spanish Universities of Salamanca, Coimbra, and Alcala.

Thomist ('təʊmɪst), *sb.* (*a.*) *Eccl.* [ad. med.L. *Thōmista* (Wyclif, 1359), f. *Thōm-ās*: see below. Cf. F. *thomiste* (Pascal).] A follower of Thomas Aquinas (known as 'The Angelical Doctor'), a scholastic philosopher and theologian of the 13th c. (Cf. SCOTIST.)

[**1359** WYCLIF *Wks.* (1905) 127 Thomiste qui sanctum Thomam secuntur.] **1533** TINDALE *Supper of Lord* B iij *margin*, Thomistes be the schole docters. **1669** T. GALE *True Idea Jansenisme* 58 No doubt there are such small Graces, as the Thomists call sufficient. **1709** POPE *Ess. Crit.* 444 Scotists and Thomists now in peace remain Amidst their kindred cobwebs in Duck-lane. **1842** BRANDE *Dict. Sc.*, etc. s.v., The Thomists continued as a sect to the commencement of the 17th century. **1882–3** *Schaff's Encycl. Relig. Knowl.* I. 658 The controversy between Thomists and Scotists..concerning the exemption of Mary from hereditary sin.

b. *attrib.* or as *adj.*

1845 S. AUSTIN *Ranke's Hist. Ref.* I. 485 She was that same thomist aristotelic church, with which he was engaged in a mortal struggle. **1884** *Mind* IX. 159 The Thomist philosophy, now again authoritatively proclaimed to be the sheet-anchor of Catholic doctrine.

Thomistic (təʊ'mɪstɪk), *a.* [f. prec. + -IC.] Of or pertaining to the Thomists or their doctrines.

1881 *Nature* XXIII. 235 On the recent restoration of the scholastic and tomistic philosophy. **1882–3** *Schaff's Encycl. Relig. Knowl.* I. 358 [Cajetan] was generally considered the real head of the Thomistic school. **1889** E. H. DERING (*title*) On Universals: an Exposition of Thomistic Doctrine. By Father Matteo Liberatore, S.J.

So **Tho'mistical** *a.* = prec.; **Tho'misticate** *v.* (*nonce-wd.*) *intr.* to argue or discourse in the manner of the Thomists; to 'split hairs', use over-refined arguments.

1533 TINDALE *Supper of Lord* C v b, Howe farre lo, M. More is thys your straunge *thomystical sense from the flate letter? **1642** J. EATON *Honey-c. Free Justif.* 120 The Thomisticall distinctions of the Schoolemen. **1715** M. DAVIES *Athen. Brit.* I. 171 The rigorous Calvinistical and Thomistical Opinion of Predestination. **1730** LEWIS *Life of Fisher* (1855) I. 194 In defence of the mass's being a sacrifice, the king thus *Thomisticates.

Thomite ('təʊmaɪt). *rare*$^{-0}$. [f. THOM-AS + -ITE[1].] = THOMÆAN *sb.* (q.v. quot. 1727–41).

Thompson ('tɒm(p)sən). *Mil.* (orig. *U.S.*). The name of John T. *Thompson* (1860–1940), U.S. general, used *attrib.* and *absol.* to designate a type of sub-machine-gun which was conceived by him and financed by his company, and named after him in 1919 at the insistence of its designer, O. V. Payne. Cf. TOMMY GUN.

1920 *Army & Navy Jrnl.* 2 Oct. 120/1 Colonel Thompson is now connected with the Auto-Ordnance Corporation of New York City, which has put the Thompson sub-machine gun on the market. **1921** M. THOMPSON *Let.* 26 Apr. in W. J. Helmer *Gun that made Twenties Roar* (1969) iv. 69 We came back with a tentative agreement on their part to purchase 50,000 Thompsons. **1933** 'J. SPENSER' *Limey* ii. 27 There was a Thompson sub-machine gun, universally known in gangland as a 'Tommy gun'. **1946** D. M. WARD *Other Battle* xxi. 140 An order was placed in America for Thompsons, but by the time the first few were delivered it was realized that not enough ·45 ammunition could be made. **1970** E. K. WALKER in W. King *Black Short Story Anthol.* (1972) 54 Captain Bull..carried a Thompson submachine gun at high port. **1978** D. MURPHY *Place Apart* ii. 22 Kerins had a Thompson under the bed but he never had a chance to use it.

Thompsonian (tɒm(p)'səʊnɪən), *sb.* and *a.* [f. the name *Thompson* (see below) + -IAN.]

A. *sb.* An admirer of the work of Francis Thompson (1859–1907), English poet and writer. **B.** *adj.* Of, belonging to, or characteristic of Thompson or his work.

1913 T. HARDY in V. Meynell *Francis Thompson & Wilfrid Meynell* (1952) xiii. 198 You may be sure I am a Thompsonian. ?**1921** J. THOMSON *Remarks on Francis Thompson's Hound of Heaven* 9 Nearer than either to the Thompsonian *Hound of Heaven*..comes the *heaven's wingèd hound* of Shelley. **1927** *Observer* 19 June 8 The next in the series is a choice from Francis Thompson's prose... This Thompsonian addition to the 'handy Harraps' is no end of a shillingsworth. **1948** *Tablet* 30 Oct. 282/2 Answering the letters of the growing army of Thompsonians all over the world. **1962** J. BRODRICK in F. Thompson *St Ignatius Loyola* p. xii, He made one precious contribution to Thompsonian psychology.

thomsenolite ('tɒmsənəʊlaɪt). *Min.* [Named, 1868, after Dr. Julius Thomsen of Copenhagen: see -LITE.] Hydrous fluoride of aluminium, calcium, and sodium, found with pachnolite on the cryolite of Greenland.

1868 DANA *Min.* 129 Thomsenolite..was first noticed by Dr. Julius Thomsen of Copenhagen, the originator of the cryolite industry, after whom it is here named. **1883** *Science* I. 331/2 It is distinguished from thomsenolite by its absence of water.

Thomsen's disease. *Path.* [Named after Dr. Thomsen of Schleswig-Holstein, who first described it, from his own case.] See quot. 1890. So **'Thomsen-like** *a.*

1890 BILLINGS *Nat. Med. Dict.*, *Thomsen's disease, Myotonia congenita*, a peculiar congenital affection characterized by inability to relax the muscles immediately after contraction. **1899** *Allbutt's Syst. Med.* VI. 471 The Thomsen-like contractions are due to the action of phosphate of soda on the muscular fibres themselves.

Thomson ('tɒmsən). Also (*erron.*) Thompson.

1. *Physics.* [The name of Sir William *Thomson*: see KELVIN, KELVIN.] ***Thomson effect***: the effect an electric current has, when flowing in the direction of a temperature gradient, of absorbing or giving out heat independently of the Joule heating; so ***Thomson coefficient***, a numerical measure of this effect for a material.

1878 *Encycl. Brit.* VIII. 98/1 This anomaly led Tait to the discovery..that the Thomson effect in iron changes its sign ..at a temperature near low red heat. **1906**, etc. [see SEEBECK]. **1930** *Engineering* 9 May 596/2 The Thomson and Peltier coefficients were given values of the right general order of magnitude. **1966** C. R. TOTTLE *Sci. Engin. Materials* vi. 130 By choosing appropriate values of the Peltier and Thomson coefficients, two dissimilar materials can be arranged to produce a substantial e.m.f. if one junction is maintained at a high temperature and the other at a lower one. **1975** D. G. FINK *Electronics Engineers' Handbk.* XXVII. 3 At large values of dT/dx the Thompson effect may be comparable with the Seebeck effect and must be taken into account in the design of generators and refrigerators.

2. *Zool.* The name of Joseph *Thomson* (1858–94), Scottish explorer, used in the possessive (rarely *attrib.*) to designate an East African gazelle with a broad black lateral stripe, *Gazella thomsoni*, first collected by him and named in his honour by A. Günther in 1884 (*Ann. & Mag. Nat. Hist.* XIV. 428).

1897 *Proc. Zool. Soc.* 454 Thomson's Gazelle does not.. extend beyond a few miles north of Lake Nakuru. **1906** [see TOMMY[1] 3 c]. **1915** ROOSEVELT & HELLER *Life-Hist. Afr. Game Animals* II. xviii. 600 The Thomson gazelle is essentially a highland antelope. **1969** *Daily Tel.* 13 Aug. 17/3 A Thomson's gazelle, born at Whipsnade Zoo, brings the number in the herd..to 20. **1980** R. W. HAYMAN tr. *Haltenorth & Diller's Field Guide Mammals Afr.* 94 Thomson's Gazelle..horns lyre-shaped and weakly S-formed.

3. *Physics.* [The name of Sir J. J. *Thomson* (1856–1940), British physicist.] ***Thomson scattering***: scattering of light by free charged particles, *spec.* electrons, in accordance with classical mechanics.

1935 COMPTON & ALLISON *X-Rays in Theory & Exper.* (ed. 2) iv. 298 This classical scattering from a free electron is often called 'J. J. Thomson scattering'. *Ibid.* 827/2 (Index), Thomson scattering. **1962** *Sci. Survey* III. 123 Knowing the brightness of the corona and, from the theory of Thomson scattering, the proportion of sunlight scattered towards the observer by each electron, we can calculate the number of electrons per cubic centimetre. **1978** *Nature* 19 Jan. 220/1 One..expects that up to a certain radial distance from the accretion column the neutron star surface is covered by a dense atmosphere and represents a 'tarnished mirror', reflecting quasi-isotropically by Thomson scattering.

Thomsonian (tɒm'səʊnɪən), *a.* (*sb.*) [f. *Thomson*, proper name (see definitions) + -IAN.]

1. Of or pertaining to the system of medicine practised by Dr. Samuel Thomson, of Massachusetts (1769–1843). Also as *sb.* One who follows this system. (Often erroneously spelt *Thompsonian.*)

1833 C. THOMSON (*title*) A plain historical Statement of facts respecting the Thomsonian plan of medicine, as originated by Samuel Thomson. **1857** DUNGLISON *Med. Lex.*, *Thompsonian*, one who practises or believes in Thompsonianism. *Ibid.* s.v., *Thompsonianism*, The Thompsonians are Botanical Doctors. **1860** BARTLETT *Dict. Americanisms, Thompsonian Doctor*, a physician who follows the Thompsonian practice; also called Steam Doctor. *Thompsonian Practice*, a peculiar treatment of diseases.

2. Of, pertaining to, or characteristic of the poet James Thomson, author of 'The Seasons'.

1890 TENNYSON in *Mem.* (1897) I. i. 11, I covered two sides of a slate with Thomsonian blank verse in praise of flowers. **1908** *Westm. Gaz.* 5 Feb. 4/2 One is apt..to over-estimate the difference between the Wordsworthian 'Nature' and the Thomsonian 'Nature'.

Hence **Thom'sonianism**, the Thomsonian medical system: see sense 1.

1857 [see sense 1 above]. **1890** BILLINGS *Nat. Med. Dict.*, *Thomsonianism.* **1894** *Outing* (U.S.) XXIV. 332/1 Do you believe in the mind cure—Thompsonianism—metallic tractors—Christian science? **1899** *Syd. Soc. Lex.*, *Thomsonianism*.., a form of empiric medicine introduced by Samuel Thomson (1769–1843), of Massachusetts. Sweating, lobelia, and capsicum, were the principal agencies relied on.

thomsonite ('tɒmsənaɪt). *Min.* [Named, 1820, after Dr. Thomas Thomson (1773–1852), professor of chemistry at Glasgow: see -ITE[1].] Hydrous silicate of aluminium, calcium, and sodium, found often in fibrous radiated masses, white to reddish-brown in colour; = COMPTONITE.

1820 H. J. BROOKE in *Ann. Philos.* Sept. 193, I shall call the Auvergne variety, Mesotype; that from Iceland and Ferro, Needlestone; and that from Dumbarton, Thomsonite, after the editor of this journal [Dr. T. Thomson]. **1843** PORTLOCK *Geol.* 215 Thomsonite..is rarely met in Irish trap. **1869** PHILLIPS *Vesuv.* x. 294 Thomsonite, or Comptonite [occurs] in ejected blocks of gray lava.

thon (ðɒn), *dem. pron.* and *a.*, *dial.* [app. a comparatively recent alteration of *yon*, the initial consonant being assimilated to *this* and *that*. (A suggestion that it arose from misreading the written *y* as the compendious form of *th*, as in *y*[e], *yis, yat, yem, yairof*, etc., is, in view of the wide popular diffusion of *thon* and *thonder*, inadequate.)]

= YON: the demonstrative pron. and adj., pointing to something more remote in place or time than *that*: = L. *ille*, Sp. *aquello.*

Used in Scotland, Ulster, and the four northern English counties. Written examples not found before 1800; app. not in Ramsay nor in Burns.

1804 TARRAS *Poems* 96 (Jam.) Leuk down the gate, what squabble's thon, That ca's the thrang's attention? **1808**

JAMIESON *Sc. Dict.*, *Thone*, yonder, yon. **1818** MISS FERRIER *Marriage* I. ii. 18 'Hoose!' repeated the driver, 'ca' ye thon a hoose? Thon's gude Glenfern Castle'. **1886** R. L. STEVENSON *Lett.* (1901) II. viii. 39 Strange conduc' o' thon man Rankeillor. **1893** —— *Catriona* 136 I'll no forget thon of the cinnamon water. **1894** HESLOP *Northumbld. Gloss.* 727 Whe's thon? Whe's thon chep? De ye see thon hoose ower there? [**1904** in *Eng. Dial. Dict.* from Scotland (Aberdeen to Roxb.), Ulster, Northumberland, Durham.]

So **thonder** ('ðɒndə(r)) *adv.* and *a. dial.* (also **thaander, thander, thender, thinder**) = YONDER.

Used in Scotland, Ulster, England from north border to Hereford, Leicester, E. Anglia.

a **1825** FORBY *Vocab. E. Anglia*, *Thinder*, adv., v. Yinder. *c* **1847** [Common in Roxburghsh.] *Thonder* adv. **18..** ROBSON *Bards of Tyne* (1863) 44 Then at last, aw heard her say, O! thonder is the Gardens. **1854** MISS BAKER *Northampt. Gloss.* s.v., He lives over thender. **1876** BOUND *Provinc. Herefordsh.* (E.D.D.), Thander one is the man. **1879** MISS JACKSON *Shropsh. Word-bk.* Introd. 50 Yander, thander, *adj.* **1887** DARLINGTON *Folk-sp. S. Cheshire* 70 *Yonder* has the forms *yondur, yaandur*, and *dhondur*. **1899** *Blackw. Mag.* Feb. 168, (*Sc.*) I didna mak verra muckle o' the fairming up-bye thonder.

thon, þon, obs. f. THAN, THEN; obs. inflexion of THE.

-thon, *suffix.* Var. -ATHON used in some words, as TELETHON.

1954 *Amer. Speech* XXIX. 229 The word *moviethon* is merely the most recent in what promises to be a long list of words created arbitrarily by means of the *-thon* suffix. **1963** R. I. MCDAVID *Mencken's Amer. Lang.* 228 *Rockerthon, poolathon* and *pianothon* appeared in Canada in 1955.

thonder, -dre, etc., obs. ff. THUNDER.

†**thone,** coalesced form of *the one*, frequent in 16th c.: see TH-[1], TH'.

Chiefly used in contrast with THOTHER = the other.

1542 UDALL *Erasm. Apoph.* E.'s Pref., He had mingled the saiynges..thone with thother. *c* **1566** *Merie Tales of Skelton* in *Wks.* (1843) I. p. lix, If any scoler had fallen out thone with thother, the one woulde call thother Swanborn. **1594** WEST *2nd Pt. Symbol.* §43 Because thone hath trespassed more than thother, he shall pay to thother, x.s.

thoner, thonewonge, obs. forms of THUNDER, THUNWANG.

thong (θɒŋ), *sb.* Forms: α. 1 **ðwong, ðuong, ðwangc, þwæng, ðuuencg,** 1–3 **þwang;** 4 **thuang,** 4–5 (*Sc.* and *north.* –9) **thwang** (5 **thwange, twange,** 6 **thwangue**), 5–7 *Sc.* **thwayng** (*dial.* 7–9 (with *hw, wh-*, for *þw-*) **whaing, whang**). β. 3–4 **þwong, þuong(e,** 4–5 **thwong(e** (*dial.* **twonge**). γ. 3–5 **þong,** 4– **thong,** (4–5 **þonge, thongh,** 6–7 **thonge,** 6 **thongue**). δ. 5 **thownge, thowyng;** *dial.* 8–9 **thung, thunk, thonk.** [OE. *þwang, þwong* str. masc. (also fem.); also, ONorthumb. pl. *ðuuencgu*, N. Anglian *þwænga*, agreeing with ON. *þvengr* (:—*þvaŋgi*[z]); all from ablaut stem **þwing-*, **þwang-*, **þwung-*, to restrain:—Indo-Eur. root **twenk*: cf. Ger. *zwingen*: see TWING, TWINGE *v.*, and cf. the dial. form WHANG.]

1. a. A narrow strip of hide or leather, for use as a lace, cord, band, strap, or the like.

In early use, esp. the lace or 'latchet' of a shoe.

α. *c* **950** *Lindisf. G.* John i. 27 Ic ne am wyrðe þætte ic undoe his ðuong scoes [*Rushw.* ðwong ʒiscoes, *Ags. Gosp.* sceoþwang]. *c* **1000** *Ags. Gosp.* Mk. i. 7 His sceona þwanga [*Lindisf.* ðuongas scóe his, *Rushw.* þwongas ʒescoas his]. *c* **1000** ÆLFRIC *Gen.* xiv. 23 (Gr.) þæt ic ne underfo furðon anne þwang of eallum þisum þingum. *c* **1050** *Gloss.* in Wr.-Wülcker 379/32 *Corrigie*, olþwongas. *a* **1100** *Ibid.* 332/12 *Corrigia*, ðwangc. *c* **1275** LAY. 22295 Somme makede þwanges. *a* **1300** *Cursor M.* 12823 (Cott.) To lese þe thuanges of his sco. *c* **1425** WYNTOUN *Cron.* VIII. xxviii. 4599 A royne lanȝhare..And schare a thwayng at all laysere. **1513** DOUGLAS *Æneis* IX. xi. 5 Dartis..Quhilk thai with lyamis and thwangis lang owt threw. **1570** LEVINS *Manip.* 23/42 A Thwangue, *lorum.* **1641** *Ferguson's Sc. Prov.* No. 647 Mony ane tines the haff-merk whinger for the halfpenny whang. **1703** THORESBY *Let. to Ray* Gloss. (E.D.S.), 'A thwang for a shoe', the latchet. **1894** HESLOP *Northumbld. Gloss.* 779 The end..of a flail is lashed to the wood with a whang.

β. *c* **1200** *Trin. Coll. Hom.* 137 Ich nam noht ne for ðen wurðe þat ich un-cnutte his sho þuong. *c* **1205** LAY. 22295 Sum makede þwonges. **1297** R. GLOUC. (Rolls) 2492 As moche place as mid a þuong ich may aboute tille. **13..** *Gaw. & Gr. Knt.* 194 Syþen þrawen wyth a þwong a þwarle knot alofte. **1387** TREVISA *Higden* (Rolls) I. 369 þey usede hiȝe schone unto þe kne, i-slitte to fore, and i-laced wiþ þwonges. **1485** CAXTON *Paris & V.* 27 Henge a lytel keye by a thwonge.

γ. *c* **1205** LAY. 14221 þa al islit wes þe þong he wes wunder ane long. *c* **1350** *Will. Palerne* 1720 Sche..festened hire in þat fel wiþ ful gode þonges. **1480** CAXTON *Chron. Eng.* lvi. 40 Engyst prayd hym..of as moche place as he myght compasse with a thong of a skynne. **1563** GOLDING *Cæsar* v. (1565) 138 He aduised him to tie the letter to the thong of a Iaueling, & so to throw it into his camp. **1570** LEVINS *Manip.* 167/2 A Thongue, *lorum.* **1610** HOLLAND *Camden's Brit.* (1637) 339 A beasts hide cut into thongs. **1649** G. DANIEL *Trinarch., Hen. V* clxxix, Another girds his Frock, with a sure Thonge [*rime* strong]. **1703** MOXON *Mech. Exerc.* 179 The Noose of a Leather Thong. **1867** PARKMAN *Jesuits N. Amer.* xvii. (1875) 246 Subsisting on the bark of trees or the thongs of raw hide.

δ. *c* **1425** *Eng. Voc.* in Wr.-Wülcker 656/1 *Hec corigia*, thowyng. *c* **1440** *Promp. Parv.* 492/1 Thownge, or lanere. *a* **1800** PEGGE *Suppl. Grose*, *Thunk*, Lancashire pronunciation of Thong. **1881** MISS JACKSON *Shropsh. Word-bk.* s.v. *Thung*, 'I give the cobbler a penny fur two thunks'. **1886** *Cheshire Gloss.*, *Thonk*, a thong, a bootlace; also *Thunk*.

†**b.** A phylactery. Only *OE. rare.*

c **950** *Lindisf. Gosp.* Matt. xxiii. 5 Hia ʒebrædas forðon ðuuencgu hiora. *c* **975** *Rushw. Gosp.* ibid., þwænga.

c. Such a strip used as an instrument of flagellation; also as the lash of a whip; hence *spec.* a whip-lash of plaited hide.

1592 LYLY *Midas* IV. iii. A boy was beaten on the taile with a leathern thong. **1728–46** THOMSON *Spring* 809 The trembling steed..Nor heeds the rein, nor hears the sounding thong. **1782** COWPER *Progr. Err.* 360 Man's coltish disposition asks the thong. **1832** LYTTON *Eugene A.* II. vi, A gentleman..left the whip to have a new thong put to it. **1876** GRANT *Burgh Sch. Scot.* II. v. 195 Horace prayed for a settled standard of punishment, lest any one should be subjected to the horrible thong, who is only deserving of a slight whipping.

d. *transf.* A similar strip of other material, as a tough pliant plant-stem, etc.; *spec.* a root or root-cutting of horse-radish or sea-kale.

1665 HOOKE *Microgr.* 6 Bound together with thongs of Brambles. **1838** T. THOMSON *Chem. Org. Bodies* 696 Take a thong of this substance [india-rubber]. **1875** T. W. HIGGINSON *Yng. Folks' Hist. U.S.* iii. 17 The edges were sewed with thongs cut from the roots of the cedar. **1927** *Smallholder* 26 Mar. 105 Plant [horseradish] each year.. fresh pieces..made from the side roots or thongs. *Ibid.*, It is now time to plant out thongs of seakale. **1951** *Dict. Gardening* (R. Hort. Soc.) IV. 1916/2 Cuttings [of seakale], or thongs as they are frequently called, are clean straight pieces of the side roots. **1961** *Amat. Gardening* 21 Oct. 9/3 The thick roots [of seakale] or 'thongs'..are not needed for forcing.

e. *fig.*; esp. in phrase ***to cut a large thong*** (or ***large thongs***) ***of another man's leather, thongs of other men's hides***, to be lavish with that which is another's.

c **1380** WYCLIF *Serm.* Sel. Wks. I. 76 þis ordre is a þuonge to bynde mennis willes togidere. **1465** MARG. PASTON in *P. Lett.* II. 226 Men cut large thongs here of other mens lether. **1784** COWPER *Task* III. 26 What chance that I..Should speak to purpose, or with better hope Crack the satiric thong? **1865** KINGSLEY *Herew.* i, As long as I could cut long thongs out of other men's hides. **1878** *Masque Poets* 149 The silken tie became a thong Wherewith she pinioned him in bondage strong.

f. *Austral.* and *U.S.* = FLIP-FLOP f. Cf. *thong-sandal*, sense 2 below.

1967 *Coast to Coast 1965–6* 87 Her feet, in scuffed leather thongs, were none too clean. **1976** *New Yorker* 17 May 35/2 Please, no clogs, Earth Shoes, or thongs. **1981** H. ENGEL *Ransom Game* (1982) xxx. 197 She..handed me a pair of Japanese thongs. I slipped them on and felt the skin between my first two toes protest.

2. *attrib.* and *Comb.*, as ***thong-point, -wearer***; ***thong-hurled*** adj.; **thong-drill,** a drill rotated by means of a thong or cord wound round its stem; **thong-man,** a man who wields the thong or lash; in quot., a critic; **thong sandal** *Austral.* and *U.S.* = sense 1 f above; **thong-seal,** a name sometimes given to the bearded seal, *Erignathus barbatus*, the hide of which is cut into a continuous strip for use as a line; **thong weed** = *sea thong* s.v. SEA *sb.* 23 e.

1865 TYLOR *Early Hist. Man.* ix. 242 The *thong-drill with the mouthpiece. **1685** COTTON tr. *Montaigne* (1877) I. 23 The bear, made fiercer by the wound from the Lybian's *thong-hurled dart. **1876** G. MEREDITH *Beauch. Career* xxxiv, Self-appointed *thongmen who walk up and down our ranks flapping their leathern straps. **1897** *Blackw. Mag.* Nov. 593/2 A leather sporran tagged with *thong points tied in knots. **1965** *Times Lit. Suppl.* 25 Nov. 1057/2 Supporting activities, like teaching and editing and selling *thong-sandals. **1972** J. AIKEN *Butterfly Picnic* iii. 59 He wore a magenta tussore shirt..burnt-orange shorts, and local-made thong sandals. **1901** *Athenæum* 2 Nov. 589/1 It is the cord-wearer [Franciscan] rather than the *thong-wearer [Dominican] who is the hero of the more scandalous anecdotes. **1958** *Listener* 31 July 179/2 With *I-Spy at the Seaside* I shall look for..some *thong weed. **1966** *Oxf. Bk. Flowerless Plants* 4/2 *Himanthalia elongata* ('Thong Weed') is to be found attached to rock surfaces.

Hence **thongy** ('θɒŋɪ) *a. dial.*: see quots.

1847–78 HALLIWELL, *Thongy*, ropy, viscid. *Somerset.* **1885** *Reports Provinc.* (E.D.D.), Cider is often said 'to be thongy', when it gets into the peculiar state known as 'reamed' or 'ropy'.

thong (θɒŋ), *v.* Forms: see prec. [f. THONG *sb.* Cf. ON. *þvengja* (*skó*) to furnish (shoes) with a thong.]

1. *trans.* To furnish with a thong; to fasten or secure with a thong or thongs; to bind with thongs.

a **1225** [implied in THONGED]. **1483** *Cath. Angl.* 388/1 To Thwange [*v.r.* Twange], *corrigiare.* **1723** R. MILLAR *Hist. Propag. Chr.* II. vii. 302 Their Habits are Sheep Skins undressed thonged together. **1861** *Life of Bacon* xx. 414 He too is thonging the scourge for his own back.

2. To flog or lash with a thong. Also *absol.*

1746 *Exmoor Scolding* 77 (E.D.S.) Chell [= ich will] thong tha,..chell pummel tha,..chell lace tha. **1855** THACKERAY *Newcomes* I. ii. 23 Mrs. Newcome thonged him with the lash of her indignation. **1866** *Cornh. Mag.* Dec. 743 'Stick to them, my lads', shouts Captain Blake, double-thonging with a hunting-whip like a maniac. **1890** 'R. BOLDREWOOD' *Miner's Right* vii, He..was quite capable of raising a wale upon that epidermis which it suited him to thong.

3. *dial.* (See quot.)

1888 *Berksh. Gloss.*, *Thong*, to twine or twist together.

4. *dial. intr.* To become viscous or 'ropy'.

1847–78 HALLIWELL, *Thong*, to rope; to stretch out into viscous threads or filaments.

Hence **thonged** (θɒŋd) *ppl. a.*, furnished or fastened with thongs; esp. ***thonged sandal***; '**thonging** *vbl. sb.*, flogging with a thong.

a **1225** *Ancr. R.* 362 And me ne mei nout..two þongede scheon habben, wiðuten buggunge. *a* **1847** J. T. HURLOCK in *Essex Rev.* XVII. 56 Scourge not with thonged whips. **1860** THACKERAY *Round. Papers, Small-beer Chron.*, Is there no enemy who would be the better for a little thonging? **1880** BROWNING *Dram. Idyls* II. *Echetlos* 22 The large limbs thonged and brown. **1958** N. MARSH *Singing in Shrouds* (1959) ix. 189 She had high-heeled thonged sandals on her feet. **1972** D. BLOODWORTH *Any Number can Play* xv. 135 Fashionable accessories, including thonged sandals. **1982** J. ELLIOTT *Country of her Dreams* ii. 15 Rosa Treadwell, in thonged sandals and sweat-stained smock, flumped herself down.

Thonga, var. TSONGA[4].

thonir, obs. f. THUNDER.

thonk(e, obs. ff. THANK.

thonne, þonne, obs. f. THEN, THENNE.

†**thonneliche, þ-,** *adv. Obs. rare*[−1]. [f. ME. *þonne*, THEN + *-liche*, -LY[2]. (The modern form, if the word had survived, would be *thenly*.)] In that case: = THEN 4.

1340 *Ayenb.* 31 Kueade anginnynge heþ þe sleuuolle be zix zennes. þe uerste is þonneliche huanne þe man loueþ lite and lheucliche oure lhord.

thonner, thonor, etc., obs. ff. THUNDER.

thonwange, -wonge, var. THUNWANG *Obs.*

thoo, þoo, variant of THO *pron.* and *adv. Obs.*

thooid ('θəʊɔɪd), *a.* (*sb.*) *Zool.* [f. Gr. θώ-ός, THOUS + -OID.] Resembling in form, or related to, the sub-genus *Thous*; in an extended use applied to a division of the genus *Canis* including the wolf, dog, and jackal; as distinct from the alopecoid, typified by the fox. **b.** *sb.* A beast of this division.

1880 HUXLEY in *Proc. Zool. Soc.* 6 Apr. 278 Thooids and Alopecoids, similar to those which exist at present, inhabited Europe during the Quaternary epoch. *Ibid.* 286, I am disposed..to regard *Otocyon* and the Thooid and Alopecoid series respectively as genera, retaining for the two latter the old names of *Canis* and *Vulpes*. **1891** FLOWER & LYDEKKER *Mammals* xi. 548 Thooid or Lupine Series [of Canines].

thoole, þoole, obs. form of THOLE *v.*

thoom, obs. and dial. form of THUMB.

Thor (θɔː(r)). *Mythol.* [a. ON. *þórr*:—*þunro*[z] thunder: see THURSDAY.] The proper name of the strongest and bravest of the Scandinavian deities, the god of thunder, whose weapon was a hammer; his belt doubled his strength; hence in allusive use.

a **1020** WULFSTAN *Hom.* xlii. (21 a) Napier 197 þór and Owðen, þe hæðene men herjað swiðe. **1605** VERSTEGAN *Dec. Intell.* 74 Description of the great Idol Thor. **1817** BYRON *Beppo* lxi, Crush'd was Napoleon by the northern Thor, Who knock'd his army down with icy hammer. **1841** EMERSON *Ess.* Ser. I. ii. (1876) 63 Let us enter into the state of war, and wake Thor and Woden, courage and constancy, in our Saxon breasts. **1898** *Daily News* 6 May 8/1 The din of a thousand Thors at their forges, the hubbub of the workshop.

b. *attrib.*, as ***Thor-hammerer***; ***Thor-like*** adj.; **Thor-barley** (see quot. 1755).

1755 tr. *Pontoppidan's Nat. Hist. Norway* I. iv. §5. 105 This barley..the peasants term Thor-barley, possibly from the opinion of the ancients, who..imagined this corn to be fit for the banquets of the gods. **1865** DE MORGAN in *Athenæum* 14 Oct. 729/2 The Thor-hammerer does nothing but grumble. **1866** M. C. TYLER *Glimpses Eng.* (1898) 159 The splendor of his [John Bright's] Thor-like eloquence.

thor, dial. variant of THEIR, and THIR, these.

Thora, variant of TORAH, the Mosaic law.

thoracabdominal, etc.: see THORACO-.

thoraci- (θɒ'ræsɪ), combining form of L. *thōrāx, -ācem*, in same sense as THORACO-. **tho'raciform** *a.*, having the form of a thorax, thorax-shaped. **tho'racipod** [Gr. ποδ- foot] *a.*, of or pertaining to the *Thoracipoda*, a division of crustaceans having ambulatory thoracic limbs; *sb.* a crustacean of this division; so **thora'cipodous** *a.* (*Cent. Dict.* 1891). **tho,raci'spinal** *a.*, pertaining to the thoracic portion of the spinal column.

1826 KIRBY & SP. *Entomol.* IV. xlvi. 331 Orismology... Mesothorax...β. Dorsolum. *Thoraciform,..when it forms the principal part of the upper surface of the trunk. **1887** COUES in *Cent. Dict.*, *Thoracispinal. **1899** *Syd. Soc. Lex.*, Thoracispinal.

thoracic (θɒ'ræsɪk), *a.* (*sb.*) Also 7 **thorachique, -cique.** [ad. med.L. *thōrăcic-us*, a. Gr. θωρακικ-ός,

f. θώρᾱξ, θωρᾱκ-: see THORAX and -IC. In Blount from obs. F. *thorachique* (A. Paré in Cotgr.).]

1. *Anat.* Of, pertaining to, or contained in the thorax; pectoral.

thoracic aorta (also called *pectoral aorta*), that part of the aorta which traverses the thorax. ***thoracic artery***, any one of the branches arising from the axillary artery. ***thoracic cage***, the skeleton of the thorax with its ligaments (Billings, 1890). ***thoracic cavity***, the space enclosed by the ribs, spine, and diaphragm, containing the heart, lungs, etc. ***thoracic duct***, the main trunk of the lymphatic system, through which the chyle and lymph are conveyed to the blood. ***thoracic limb***, in a vertebrate, a fore-limb; in man, the arm; in quadrupeds, the fore-leg; in birds, the wing; in fishes, a thoracic or pectoral fin; in invertebrates, a member appended to the thorax. ***thoracic vertebra***, a vertebra which articulates with a rib; a dorsal vertebra.

1656 BLOUNT *Glossogr., Thorachique*,..belonging to the breast or stomack. *Ibid.* s.v. *Vein.* **1658** PHILLIPS, *Thoracique*,..belonging to the stomack or brest. **1727–41** CHAMBERS *Cycl.* s.v., The thoracic arteries... Thoracic veins... Thoracic duct..is..a continuation of the exit or mouth of the receptaculum chyli. **1793** BEDDOES *Lett. Darwin* 56 No sooner does it touch the lungs than..the functions of all the thoracic organs go on easily and pleasantly again. **1793** M. BAILLIE *Morb. Anat.* Pref. (1807) 10 The thoracic and abdominal viscera. **1876** BRISTOWE *The. & Pract. Med.* (1878) 13 In our own country, thoracic inflammations are most frequent during the cold seasons of the year.

b. Pertaining to, attached to, or forming part of the thorax (of an insect or crustacean).

1817 KIRBY & SP. *Entomol.* (1818) II. 413 The light emitted by the two thoracic tubercles alone is so considerable [etc.]. **1880** HUXLEY *Crayfish* i. 22 The crayfish ..walks by means of the four hinder pairs of thoracic limbs.

2. *Ichthyol.* Having the ventral fins situated directly beneath the pectoral; belonging to the *Thōrācicī*, the third order of fishes in the Linnæan system. Cf. ABDOMINAL *a.* 3.

1769 PENNANT *Zool.* III. 216 That section of bony fish, termed Thoracic. **1774** GOLDSM. *Nat. Hist.* (1862) II. III. i. 294 The ventral fins placed directly under the pectoral fins, ..and then it is called a Thoracic fish. **1854** OWEN *Skel. & Teeth* in *Orr's Circ. Sc.* I. *Org. Nat.* 183 The fins called 'ventral'..indicate by their position the orders of fishes called 'abdominal', 'thoracic', and 'jugular', by Linnæus.

3. Having a thorax (as a distinguishing character); belonging to the *Thoracica*, a sub-order of cirripeds, in which the body consists of six thoracic segments, with a rudimentary abdomen.

1891 in *Cent. Dict.*

4. As a specific distinction in *Nat. Hist.*: Having the thorax conspicuously marked or coloured.

c **1812** SHAW *Natur. Misc.* XXII. 969 Thoracic Wagtail [*Motacilla thoracica*]. **1819** STEPHENS in Shaw *Gen. Zool.* XI. 322 Thoracic Francolin [*Francolinus thoracicus*].

5. Comb., as **thoracic-abdominal** *a.*, of the combined thorax and abdomen.

1835–6 *Todd's Cycl. Anat.* I. 214/1 A..band which commences at the thoracic-abdominal constriction. **1854** OWEN *Skel. & Teeth* in *Orr's Circ. Sc.* I. *Org. Nat.* 191 The ribs..do not encompass the thoracic-abdominal cavity.

B. *sb.* †**1.** A medicine acting on the thorax; a pectoral. *Obs.*

[**1706** PHILLIPS (ed. Kersey), *Thoracica*, medicines proper for Diseases of the Breast.] **1710** T. FULLER *Pharm. Extemp.* 249 In a word it is a most excellent Thoracic.

2. A thoracic fish: see 2 above.

1828 WEBSTER, *Thoracics*,..an order of bony fishes,..the ventral fins are placed underneath the thorax, or beneath the pectoral fins.

3. A thoracic organ or structure.

1857 DUNGLISON *Med. Lex.* s.v., *First of the Thoracics*, mammary superior external artery.

†**tho'racical**, *a.* *Obs.* [f. as prec. + -AL[1]: see -ICAL.] = THORACIC.

1664 POWER *Exp. Philos.* III. 191 We had yet never known the Mesenterical and Thoracical *Lacteæ*. **1669** W. SIMPSON *Hydrol. Chym.* 65 The thoracical vessels. **1830** *Fraser's Mag.* I. 354 Medicinal in all matters thoracical, if I may use the expression.

tho'racically, *adv.* [f. THORACIC *a.*: see -ICALLY.] In the thorax.

1901 W. JAMES *Let.* 13 Apr. (1920) II. 143, I find myself much more comfortable thoracically already than when I came. **1977** *Archivum Linguisticum* VIII. 87 Syllables with long vowels are 'thoracically arrested'.

thoracico- (θɒˈræsɪkəʊ), combining form of THORACIC *a.*, used to form adjs. in sense 'pertaining to the thorax and (some other part)', as ***thoracico-abdominal*** (also *thoracicabdominal*: see also THORACIC 5), ***thoracicoacromial*** (also *thoracicacromial*), ***thoracico-humeral***, ***thoracico-lumbar***.

1870 ROLLESTON *Anim. Life* 30 The internal aspect of the *thoracico-abdominal cavity. **1891** *Cent. Dict.*, *Thoracicacromial. **1895** *Funk's Standard Dict.*, Thoracicoacromial. **1891** *Cent. Dict.*, *Thoracicohumeral. **1899** *Syd. Soc. Lex.*, **Thoracico-lumbar*, pertaining to the thoracic and lumbar regions.

†**tho'racious**, *a.* *Obs.* *rare*[−1]. [irreg. f. L. *thōrāx, thorāci-*, THORAX + -OUS.] = THORACIC *a.* 1.

1681 tr. *Willis' Rem. Med. Wks.* Voc., *Thoracious*, belonging to the breast or thorax, or medicines good to help the diseases of the thorax.

‖**thoraco-** (θɒˈreɪkəʊ), before a vowel **thorac-**, combining form of Gr. θώρᾱξ, θωρᾱκ-, THORAX; used in forming terms of anatomy, zoology, etc. **thoracab'dominal** *a.* = *thoracico-abdominal*. **thoraca'cromial** *a.* = *thoracico-acromial*. **thoracen'tesis** = *thoracocentesis*. ‖**thoracetron** (-ˈsiːtrɒn) [Gr. ἦτρον abdomen], Owen's name of the second division of the body in certain crustaceans, as the king-crab (cf. PLEON[1]); hence **thora'cetral** *a.*, of or pertaining to the thoracetron. **tho,raco-a'cromial** = THORACICO-ACROMIAL. ‖**thoraco-centesis** (-sɛnˈtiːsɪs) [Gr. κέντησις pricking], the perforation of the chest-wall to draw off morbid accumulations of fluid. ‖**thoracocyllosis** (-sɪˈləʊsɪs) [Gr. κύλλωσις curvature], deformity of the thorax (Billings, 1890). ‖**thoracocyrtosis** (-səˈtəʊsɪs) [Gr. κύρτωσις crookedness], abnormal curvature of the chest. ‖**thoracodynia** (-ˈdɪnɪə) [Gr. ὀδύνη pain], pain in the thorax; also in English form †**'thoracodyne**. **thoraco'lumbar** *a.*, pertaining to the thoracic and lumbar parts of the spine; *spec.* an epithet of the sympathetic nervous system (see quot. 1948). **thoracometer** (-ˈkɒmɪtə(r)), an apparatus for measuring the movement of the chest-wall in respiration; a stethometer. **thoracopagous** (-ˈɒpəgəs) *a.*, pertaining to or of the nature of a thoracopagus. ‖**thora'copagus** [Gr. πάγος that which is fixed, f. πηγνύναι to fasten], a double or twin monster joined at the thorax. **thoracopathy** (-ˈɒpəθɪ), disease in the thoracic region. **'thoraco,plasty** [-PLASTY]: see quot. **tho'raco,scope** [-SCOPE], an instrument for sounding the chest, a stethoscope. **thora'coscopy**, the sounding or exploration of the chest. **thora'costracous** [Gr. ὄστρακον hard shell] *a.*, of or pertaining to the *Thoracostraca*, a division of crustaceans, including the Decapoda and other series, having a cephalo-thoracic shield and (usually) stalked eyes. ‖**thoraco'theca** *Entom.* [THECA], that part of the pupa-case which covers the thorax of the pupa (*Cent. Dict.* 1891). **thora'cotomy** [Gr. τομή cutting], incision into the thorax.

1891 *Cent. Dict.*, *Thoracabdominal. **1899** *Syd. Soc. Lex.*, *Thoracabdominal*, pertaining to, or common to, the thorax and abdomen. **1887** COUES in *Cent. Dict.*, *Thoracacromial. **1857** DUNGLISON *Med. Lex.*, *Thoracentesis. **1866** A. FLINT *Princ. Med.* (1880) 147 Thoracentesis..is admissible whenever the pleural cavity remains filled with liquid after a brief trial of the measures designed to promote absorption. **1872** OWEN in *Trans. Linnean Soc.* XXVIII. 467 The succeeding *thoracetral appendages are 4-articulate. *Ibid.* 465 This segment..belongs to the category of 'thoracetral' plates: it is cephaletral only by confluence. *Ibid.* 463, I venture to hope that the term 'cephaletron' may meet with some acceptance.., and that the term '*thoracetron' may have the same fortune in relation to the second division of the body. *Ibid.* 467 The ventral surface of the thoracetron. **1857** DUNGLISON *Med. Lex.*, *Thoracocentesis. **1903** *Westm. Gaz.* 10 July 7/1 Professor Rossoni..and Dr. Mazzoni went to the Vatican at half-past eight this morning, and repeated the operation of thoraco-centesis. **1860** MAYNE *Expos. Lex.*, *Thoracocyrtosis. **1857** DUNGLISON *Med. Lex.*, **Thoracodyne*, pleurodynia. **1860** MAYNE, Thoracodyne, Thoracodynia. **1918** STEDMAN *Med. Dict.* (ed. 5) 999/1 *Thoracolumbar. **1935** J. C. WHITE *Autonomic Nervous System* iv. 52 The tendency to asphyxia, acidosis, dehydration, and loss of body heat which follow general anæsthesia and prolonged operations are all combated by the thoracolumbar division of the autonomic nervous system. **1948** A. BRODAL *Neurol. Anat.* xi. 340 The preganglionic efferent neurons of the sympathetic nervous system in man have their perikarya in the spinal cord, more precisely in all the thoracic and the uppermost two lumbar segments... Synonymous designations for the sympathetic and para-sympathetic system therefore are the thoraco-lumbar and cranio-sacral systems. **1957** *Jrnl. Nervous & Mental Disease* CXXV. 462/2 Cannon's distinction between the thoraco-lumbar and the cranio-sacral division of the autonomic nervous system deals with the same sort of temporal division. **1967** G. M. WYBURN et al. *Conc. Anat.* i. 2/2 Latissimus dors; arises from the spines of the lower six thoracic vertebrae, the thoracolumbar fascia, [etc.]. **1974** PASSMORE & ROBSON *Compan. Med. Stud.* III. ix. 3/2 The thoracic spine is relatively immobile... The most mobile part..is the thoracolumbar junction and this is damaged most commonly. **1877** S. GEE *Auscult. & Percuss.* I. ii. (ed. 2) 35 Instruments which have been invented for registering the respiratory movements and powers: stethographs, stethometers, *thoracometers, spirometers, pneumatometers. **1886** A. GAMGEE in *Encycl. Brit.* XX. 477/1 Apparatuses for measuring the excursion of a given point of the chest wall during respiration are called thoracometers or stethometers. **1894** BATESON *Variation* xxiv. 560 Eichwald examined the evidence as to *thoracopagous double monsters. **1902** *Brit. Med. Jrnl.* 15 Mar. 672 The Greeks in their deity-construction seem to have made no use of..the various types of united twins—for example, the thoracopagous and dicephalic monstrosities. **1894** BATESON *Variation* xxiv. 560 There are..a few cases even of *thoracopagi where neither body exhibits any transposition. **1890** BILLINGS *Nat. Med. Dict.*, **Thoracoplasty*, plastic operation on the thorax, as excision of portions of ribs to close an abscess; Estlander's operation. [**1857** DUNGLISON *Med. Lex.*, *Thoracoscopium*, stethoscope.] **1895** *Funk's Standard Dict.*, *Thoracoscope. **1890** BILLINGS *Nat. Med. Dict.*, **Thoracoscopy*, exploration of the chest. **1902** *Cassell's Encycl. Dict.* Suppl., *Thoracostracous. **1857** DUNGLISON *Med. Lex.*, **Thoracotomy*, thoracocentesis. **1890** BILLINGS *Nat. Med. Dict.*, *Thoracotomy*, cutting into the chest; Estlander's operation. **1944** *Lancet* 26 Aug. 265/1 A right anterior thoracotomy exposed the bleeding-point. **1976** *Proc. R. Soc. Med.* LXIX. 851/1 Subcutaneous midline sternotomy is a method whereby an upper abdominal vertical incision may be extended into the chest without performing a formal thoracotomy and without opening the pleura.

Thorah, variant of TORAH, the Mosaic law.

†**tho'rakial**, *a.* *Obs.* *rare*[−1]. [f. Gr. θωρακ-, THORAX + -IAL.] = THORACIC *a.* 1. *T. canal*, the thoracic duct.

1716 M. DAVIES *Athen. Brit.* III. *Diss. Physick* 5 Speaking more at large of the Thorakial Canal, than a Roman Physician..near an Age before.

†**'thoral**, *a.* *Obs.* *rare.* [f. *thor-us* (cf. '*Thoral, thorāle*, culcitra' in Du Cange), med. spelling of L. *torus* couch, marriage + -AL[1].] Of or pertaining to the marriage-bed.

1696 PHILLIPS (ed. 5), *Thoral Line*, otherwise call'd in Palmistry the Mensal Line, or the Line of Venus. **1726** AYLIFFE *Parergon* 48 The second Punishment..is a Thoral Separation or a Dissolution of Matrimony.

thorax (ˈθɔəræks). Pl. **'thoraxes** (*rare*), or in L. form **thoraces** (θɒˈreɪsiːz). [a. L. *thōrāx*, a. Gr. θώραξ breast-plate, cuirass, also breast, chest.]

1. *Anat.* and *Zool.* That part of the body of a mammal between the neck and the abdomen, comprising the cavity enclosed by the ribs, breastbone, and dorsal vertebræ, and containing the chief organs of circulation and respiration; the chest; also the corresponding part in the lower vertebrates, as birds, serpents, and fishes.

c **1400** *Lanfranc's Cirurg.* 161 Thorax is maad of .vij. boonys & euery boon at þe eende is cartilaginosum. **1548–77** VICARY *Anat.* vii. (1888) 54 The Brest or Thorax is the Arke or Chest of the spirituall members of man. **1653** H. MORE *Antid. Ath.* II. xii. §5 Enlarging the Thorax, that the Lungs may have play. **1692** LOCKE *Educ.* (1693) 12 The Thorax, wherein is placed the Heart and Seat of Life. **1704** F. FULLER *Med. Gymn.* (1711) 7 Laughing..proves so beneficial by the playing of the Muscles of the Thorax. **1855** HOLDEN *Human Osteol.* (1878) 228 The Thorax is the framework which contains the heart and lungs.

2. *Zool.* The middle region of the body of an arthropod, between the head and the abdomen.

In insects, the thorax consists of three somites, the prothorax, mesothorax, and metathorax, and bears the legs, and wings if any exist. In arachnids and some crustaceans, the thorax is joined to the head, forming the CEPHALOTHORAX.

1750 *Phil. Trans.* XLVII. viii. 40 The thorax drops its breast-plate, and then the legs quit their crustaceous coverings. **1842** BRANDE *Dict. Sc.*, etc., *Thorax*, the second segment of insects is so called by Latreille and Audouin; the term is restricted to the upper surface of the trunk by Linné and Fabricius. **1868** DUNCAN tr. *Figuier's Insect World* Introd. 7 The thorax, the second primary division of the body of insects, plays almost as important a part as the head. **1888** ROLLESTON & JACKSON *Anim. Life* 491 A head region.. either remains distinct..or becomes continuous with a part or whole of the thorax, forming a cephalo-thorax... A thorax is not marked off in the *Myriapoda*.

‖**3.** *Gr. Antiq.* A cuirass, corselet: see quots.

1842 BRANDE *Dict. Sc.*, etc., *Thorax*, in Grecian Antiquities, a piece of defensive armour consisting of two parts, one defending the back, and the other the belly; called *lorica* by the Romans. **1845** C. H. SMITH in *Kitto's Cycl. Bibl. Lit.* s.v. *Arms*, In Egypt..a more ancient national form [of cuirass] was a kind of thorax, tippet, *shereyon*, or square, with an opening in it for the head, the four points covering the breast, back, and both upper arms. **1857** BIRCH *Anc. Pottery* (1858) I. 410 They wear Corinthian helmets, often crested; *thoraces*, or breast-plates, under which is a tunic, and greaves.

Hence **thoraxed** (ˈθɔərækst) *a.*, having a thorax (of a specified kind).

1907 *Nation* 24 Aug. 923/1 The yellow-thoraxed species [of insects].

Thorazine (ˈθɔərəziːn). *Pharm.* Also **thorazine**. [f. parts of the systematic name, 2-chl*or*o-N, N-dimethyl-10-H-pheno*thiazine*-10-propanamine, rearranged: see CHLORO-[2], THIO-, AZINE.] A proprietary name for CHLORPROMAZINE.

1954 *Official Gaz.* (U.S. Patent Office) 9 Mar. 299/1 Smith, Kline & French Laboratories... *Thorazine* for central nervous system depressant. **1968** J. HUDSON *Case of Need* II. x. 164 Thorazine is a tranquilizer universally used as an antidote to LSD and employed to end bad trips. **1972** *Trade Marks Jrnl.* 20 Sept. 1873/2 *Thorazine*... Pharmaceutical and veterinary preparations and substances, all consisting of or containing azine compounds. Smith Kline & French Laboratories Limited. **1979** *Time* 2 Apr. 46/2 The stronger antipsychotic drugs like Thorazine are useful for handling schizophrenics, whose behavior is characterized by hallucinations and severely disordered thinking.

†**thore**. *Obs.* *rare*[−1]. App. an anglicization of *thorus*, med. spelling of L. *torus* nuptial couch.

1649 LOVELACE *Lucasta* Ded. 7 To the Taper of the Thore Which the God himselfe but bore; To the Sea of Chast Delight Let me cast the Drop I write.

thore, obs. var. of DARE *v.*[1] (A. 9).

thore, þore, obs. 3 pl. indic. pres. of THARF *v.*, to need; obs. f. THERE.

thoreaulite ('θɒrəʊlaɪt). *Min.* [a. F. *thoreaulite* (H. Buttgenbach 1933, in *Bull. Soc. géol. Belgique* LVI. 328), f. the name of J. Thoreau, 20th-c. Belgian geologist: see -ITE[1].] A monoclinic oxide of tin and tantalum, $SnTa_2O_6$, found as rough brown prismatic crystals that are transparent in thin splinters.

1934 *Chem. Abstr.* XXVIII. 6658 Thoreaulite (new) is monoclinic with high *n* and birefringence. **1959** *Mineral. Abstr.* XIV. 107/1 Two flat veins break off from the north of the dyke of pegmatite at Manono (Katanga)... The heavy minerals are: cassiterite, tantalo-columbite, thoreaulite, löllingite, pyrite, galena. **1974** *Amer. Mineralogist* LIX. 1036/1 It is necessary to justify the choice of $SnTa_2O_6$ as the ideal composition of thoreaulite, since the ideal formula is usually given as $SnTa_2O_7$.

Thoreauvian (θə'rəʊvɪən), *sb.* and *a.* [f. *Thoreauv-ius*, Latinized form of *Thoreau* (see below) + -IAN.] **A.** *sb.* One who admires the writings or shares the philosophy of Henry David Thoreau (1817–62), U.S. naturalist and writer. **B.** *adj.* Resembling or characteristic of Thoreau's writing or philosophy.

1927 *Observer* 14 Aug. 8 There was a fair sprinkling of conscious or sub-conscious Thoreauvians among bygone seamen. **1964** *Sat. Rev.* (U.S.) 10 Oct. 70/2 Thoreauvians favor solitude. **1971** D. CONOVER *One Man's Island* 142, I am a Thoreauvian by thought and by deed. **1975** *Yankee* Oct. 113/2 In case any reader wishes to test his own ability to distinguish the true Thoreauvian style from the 'ghost-written'. **1977** *Time* 21 Feb. 59/1 It is a relaxed Thoreauvian journal of a year spent dismantling and rebuilding a 1950 Dodge pickup.

†**Thores even, ene.** *Obs.* [After *Thores-day* THURSDAY.] The eve of (Holy) Thursday (Ascension Day).

1297 R. GLOUC. (Rolls) 394 Hii bygonne an holy Thore's ene þen toun asaly þere. *Ibid.* 8120 An hal[i] þores euen [*v.rr.* þors, þours, þorsdai, Thursday eue].

thorfe, inflexion of THARF *v.*, to need.

thorgh, þorgh, -3, thorght, thorghoute, obs. ff. THROUGH, THROUGHOUT.

‖**thoria** ('θɔərɪə). *Chem.* [f. as THORIUM + *-a*, after *alumina, magnesia, silica*, etc.] An oxide of thorium, ThO_2; a very heavy white substance discovered in the mineral thorite by Berzelius, 1828, and named by him in Swedish, *Thorjord*, Ger. *Thorerde*, lit. Thor-earth. Now important in the manufacture of incandescent gas mantles. Also *attrib.*

1847 in WEBSTER. **1881** WATTS *Dict. Chem.* VIII. 1967 Thorium Oxide, or Thoria,..is insoluble in dilute acids. **1899** *Westm. Gaz.* 10 June 6/3 The expiry of the master patent this year, and the thoria patent next spring. **1904** *Ibid.* 16 Apr. 7/1 About [1888] experiments on incandescent mantles gave to thoria considerable commercial value. A mantle of pure thoria gives a very little light; but, on the other hand, it gives a stability to the fragile mantle which no other body yet discovered is able to do.

thorian ('θɔərɪən), *a. Min.* [f. THOR(IUM + -IAN 2.] Of a mineral: having a (small) proportion of a constituent element replaced by thorium.

1930 *Amer. Mineralogist* XV. 572 Thorian. **1974** A. R. PHILPOTTS in H. Sørensen *Alkaline Rocks* IV. vi. 303/1 Hydrothermal activity along fractures, producing biotite and enrichment of the carbonatite in thorian pyrochlore.

thorianite ('θɔərɪənaɪt). *Min.* [f. **thorian* (f. THORIA) + -ITE[1] 2b.] A mineral consisting chiefly of the oxides of thorium, uranium, and other rare metals, found in 1904 in the south-west of Ceylon, in small brownish-black crystals having a resinous lustre; a variety of pitch-blende.

1904 DUNSTAN in *Nature* 31 Mar. 510 This mineral appears to be new, and I suggest for it the name of *thorianite.* **1907** *Daily Chron.* 5 Jan. 2/5 The discovery of deposits of the very valuable mineral thorianite, containing something like 80 per cent. of the rare earth thoria, which is used in the manufacture of incandescent gas mantles.

thoriated ('θɔərɪeɪtɪd), *a.* [f. THORI(UM + -ATE[3] + -ED[1].] Of tungsten, or a valve filament made of tungsten: containing a proportion of thorium, e.g. to enhance electron emission in a valve.

1922 *Encycl. Brit.* XXXII. 1025/1 A thermionic valve of the latter type comprises a highly exhausted glass bulb having in it a filament of tungsten, or thoriated tungsten. **1951** *Engineering* 12 Oct. 459/1 The final..output stage consists of two water-cooled thoriated-filament triodes. **1973** J. G. TWEEDDALE *Materials Technol.* II. v. 118 Commonly, a non consumable electrode is made of tungsten or a tungsten alloy (notably thoriated tungsten).

thoric ('θɔərɪk), *a. Chem.* [f. THOR(IUM + -IC.] Of or derived from thorium.

1891 in *Cent. Dict.*

†**thorina** (θɒ'raɪnə). *Chem. Obs.* [ad. F. *thorine*, 1817, a bad representation of Berzelius's name *Thorjord*, Ger. *Thorerde*: see THORIA.

In the *Annales de Chemie*, etc. 1817, V. 5, the form *thorine* is erroneously attributed to Berzelius himself ('une nouvelle terre à laquelle M. Berzelius a donné le nome de thorine'). Misled by this, English chemists long used *thorina* and *thorinum* for *thoria* and *thorium*.]

1. The name given at first to a substance found by Berzelius in 1815 in various Swedish and Norwegian minerals, and named by him *Thorjord*, which afterwards proved to be yttrium phosphate.

1818 W. PHILLIPS *Outl. Min. & Geol.* (ed. 3) 29 The discovery of a new Earth by Berzelius a Swedish Chemist, has lately been announced.. This earth has been named.. Thorina, from the Scandinavian deity Thor. **1826** HENRY *Elem. Chem.* II. 695 A farther investigation by Berzelius of the substance to which, in 1815, he had given the name of Thorina [*ought to be* Thorjord]..has now satisfied him that it is merely a sub-phosphate of yttria.

2. The name formerly given to the earth or oxide to which Berzelius in 1828 transferred the name *Thorjord*, now called THORIA.

1831 T. P. JONES *Convers. Chem.* xvii. 180 Thorina [is found] in one mineral only, in Norway. **1836** BRANDE *Chem.* (ed. 4) 847 Thorina..after having been heated to redness, is white, and insoluble in the acids, with the exception of the sulphuric. **1839** URE *Dict. Arts*, etc. 1239 Pure thorina is a white powder, without taste, smell, or alkaline reaction on litmus. **1877** WATTS *Fownes' Chem.* (ed. 12) 397 Thorinum Oxide or Thorina, ThO_2.

†**tho'rinic**, *a. Chem. Obs.* [f. next + -IC.] = THORIC.

1868 WATTS *Dict. Chem.* V. 786 A precipitate of thorinic hyposulphite is then formed.

‖**thorinum** (θɒ'raɪnəm). *Chem. Obs.* [f. F. *thorine* and Eng. THORINA, in accordance with L. names of metals in *-um*, as *aurum, cuprum, plumbum.*]

1. The name originally given to a hypothetical metal of which THORINA (sense 1) was (erroneously) supposed by Berzelius, 1815, to be the oxide.

1819 CHILDREN *Ess. Chem. Anal.* §76 Oxide of Thorinium, or Thorina. **1820** URE *Dict. Chem.*, *Thorinum*, the supposed metallic basis of the preceding earth [THORINA 1], not hitherto extracted. **1826** HENRY *Elem. Chem.* I. 635 *Thorinum.* Nothing is known of the metallic base of this earth [thorina], and it is only from analogy that it is supposed to be constituted of such a base united with oxygen.

2. The name given in France and England, for several years after 1828, to the metallic element THORIUM, q.v.

1836 BRANDE *Chem.* (ed. 4) 847 Thorinum..was discovered by Berzelius in 1828, in a rare and complex mineral, found in the Syenitic rock of the Isle of Lövon, near Brevig, in Norway. It contained about 58 per cent. of thorina. *Ibid.*, By passing a current of dry chlorine over a mixture of thorina and charcoal-powder, a crystalline chloride of thorinum is obtained, which is easily decomposed by potassium, and the product is thorinum. It is of a gray colour, metallic lustre, and apparently malleable. **1873** WATTS *Fownes' Chem.* (1877) I. 397 Thorinum forms but one class of compounds, in all of which it is quadrivalent.

thorite[1] ('θɔəraɪt). *Min.* [a. Swed. *thorit* (Berzelius, 1828–9), f. *Thor* (as in *thoria, thorium*) + -ITE[1] 2b.] Hydrous silicate of thorium, occurring crystalline, massive, and compact, orange-yellow (ORANGITE) to brownish-black or black, with a vitreous or resinous lustre.

1832 [see THORIUM] **1839** URE *Dict. Arts* 1239 It [thorina] was extracted from the mineral thorite, of which it constitutes 58 per cent. **1868** DANA *Min.* 413 The brownish-black and black variety, from Lövö, Norway, was the mineral from which Berzelius obtained the metal thorium, and which received the name thorite.

thorite[2] ('θɔəraɪt). [f. THOR nitrate -ITE[1] 4.] An explosive of the ammonium nitrate class.

1899 *Westm. Gaz.* 13 July 7/2 Thorite, a new explosive invented by Dr. Tuttle, of Tacoma,..stood severe tests... A red-hot iron was plunged into a can of thorite, but it merely ignited the particles that touched the iron.

‖**thorium** ('θɔərɪəm). *Chem.* [f. THOR, the Norse deity + -IUM in other names of metals.

So named by its discoverer Berzelius 1828–9: see *Kongl. Vetenskaps-Acad. Handlingar* 1829, p. 1. The French having called the earth *thorine* (see THORINA) named the metal THORINUM, which prevailed also in England for many years.]

1. A rare metallic element discovered by Berzelius in the mineral thorite, and subsequently found in small quantities in some other rare minerals. Symbol Th. Also *attrib.*

Now noted as one of the radio-active elements.

1832 *Encycl. Brit.* (ed. 7) VI. 401/2 Thorina, which constitutes an oxide of thorium, has been hitherto found only in a black mineral.., thorite. *Ibid.* 402/1 The only known compound of thorium and oxygen is thorina. **1868** WATTS *Dict. Chem.* V. 785 *Thorinum*, or *Thorium.* Atomic Weight, 115·72; Symbol, Th. **1881** *Ibid.* VIII. 1967 Thorium..is not isomorphous with any other known element. *Ibid.*, Thorium Oxide [ThO_2]..Chloride [$ThCl_4$]..Nitrate..Sulphate [etc.]. **1898** SIR W. CROOKES *Addr. Brit. Assoc.* 24 Rays..emitted by thorium and its compounds. The thorium rays affect photographic plates through screens of paper or aluminium, and are absorbed by metals and other dense bodies. **1903** *Daily Chron.* 27 Nov. 8/3 He [Sir W. Ramsay] pointed out that the thorium emanations were an ephemeral gas which in two minutes ceased to exist. **1907** *Athenæum* 31 Aug. 244/2 Thorium.. gives no fewer than seven radio-active products, in the following order: mesothorium, radiothorium, thorium X, thorium emanation, and thorium A, B, and C.

2. Special Combs.: **thorium lead**, (*a*) the isotope lead 208, which is the final decay product of the series of radioactive transformations beginning with the common isotope of thorium; (*b*) used *attrib.* (with hyphen) to designate a method of isotopic dating, and results obtained with it, based upon measurement of the relative amounts in rock of thorium 232 and its ultimate decay product, lead 208; **thorium series**, the series of isotopes produced by the radioactive decay of thorium 232 (the major natural isotope), each member resulting from the decay of the previous one.

1914 *Phil. Mag.* XXVIII. 827 It may be concluded with reasonable certainty [*though erroneously*] that thorium lead is unstable. **1946** F. E. ZEUNER *Dating Past* x. 319 The thorium-family begins with the element thorium (atomic weight 232). In the course of its disintegration, 6 atoms of helium are given off, and thorium-lead remains. **1955** *Bull. Amer. Geol. Soc.* LXVI. 1141/2 The low thorium-lead age for the zircon could have been the result of addition of thorium to the mineral. *Ibid.*, The analysis..demonstrates that small amounts of uranium lead and major amounts of thorium and thorium lead are very loosely bound, chemically. **1971** I. G. GASS et al. *Understanding Earth* ii. 46/1 (*heading*) Uranium-lead.., lead-lead..and thorium-lead..methods. **1913** *Chem. News* 28 Feb. 97/2 The parent of ionium, the product in the uranium series corresponding with radio-thorium in the thorium series, is still experimentally unknown. **1955** I. KAPLAN *Nucl. Physics* x. 207 In the actinium and thorium series, the mass numbers are given by the expressions $4n + 3$ and $4n$, respectively. **1973** J. YARWOOD *Atomic & Nucl. Physics* viii. 246 There are three main series of radioactive elements: the uranium, thorium, and actinium series, leaving out, for the present, the comparatively recently discovered neptunium series.

thorle, þorle, obs. form of THIRL *v.*[1]

thorlepolle, variant of THIRLEPOLL *Obs.*

thorn (θɔːn), *sb.* Forms: 1–3 **ðorn**, 1–5 **þorn**, (2 **þeorn**, 3 (*Orm.*) **þorrn**, 4 **thorun**), 4–5 **þorne**, 4–8 **thorne**, 4– **thorn**. [OE. *þorn* = OS. *thorn* (Du. *doorn*), OHG. *dorn* (MHG., G. *dorn*), ON. *þorn* (Sw., Da. *torn*), Goth. *þaurnus*,:—OTeut. **þurn-uz*;:—Indo-Eur. **trnus*: cf. OSlav. *trŭnŭ* thorn.]

I. 1. A stiff, sharp-pointed, straight or curved woody process on the stem or other part of a plant; a spine, a prickle.

a **800** CYNEWULF *Crist* 1445 þa hi hwæsne beaȝ ymb min heafod heardne ȝebyȝdon..se wæs of þornum ȝeworht. *c* **950** *Lindisf. Gosp.* Matt. xxvii. 29 Ða cempo.. ymbworhton ða beȝe of ðornum, ȝesetton ofer heafud his. *c* **1000** *Ælfric's Voc.* in Wr.-Wülcker 139/21 *Spina*, þorn. *Ibid.* 139/22 *Tribulus*, þorn. *c* **1200** *Trin. Coll. Hom.* 207 He hadde..þornene helm, and þe þornes swiðe prikeden. *a* **1300** *Cursor M.* 17136 (Cott.) þe thornnes o mi hede standes. *Ibid.* 17774 (Cott.) Wit thorns crund als was he. **1382** WYCLIF *Prov.* xxvi. 9 If a thorun [**1388** thorn] be growen in the hond of the drunken. *c* **1400** *Lanfranc's Cirurg.* 166 Of woundis of þornis. **1484** CAXTON *Fables of Æsop* III. i, As he ranne, a thorne entred into his foote. **1593** SHAKS. *3 Hen. VI*, III. ii. 175 Like one lost in a Thornie Wood, That rents the Thornes, and is rent with the Thornes. **1667** MILTON *P.L.* IV. 256 Flours of all hue, and without Thorn the Rose. **1671** GREW *Anat. Plants* iv. App. §1 Thorns are of two kinds, Lignous and Cortical. **1776** WITHERING *Brit. Plants* (1796) II. 104 Capsules..awl-shaped, scored, tapering and ending in a double thorn or awn. *Ibid.* 350 Fruit-stalks forming bunches: thorns 3 together. **1867** J. HOGG *Microsc.* II. i. 324 Thorns, such as those of the rose, are aborted branches. **1880** GRAY *Struct. Bot.* iii. §3 (ed. 6) 55 A Spine or Thorn is usually..the termination of a stem or branch, indurated, leafless, and attenuated to a point. *Prov.* There is no rose without a thorn.

2. *fig.* (or in fig. context): Anything that causes pain, grief, or trouble; in various metaphors, similes, and proverbial expressions, as ***a thorn in the flesh*** or ***side***, a constant affliction, a source of continual grief, trouble, or annoyance; ***(to be, sit, stand, walk) on thorns (a thorn)***, (to be, etc.) in a painful state of anxiety or suspense.

c **1230** *Hali Meid.* 9 Ha lickeð huni of þornes: ha buggen al þat swete wið twa dale of bittre. *c* **1374** CHAUCER *Troylus* III. 1055 (1104) Ye, Nece, wole ye pulle out þe þorn [*v.r.* thorne] That stiketh in his herte. **1500–20** DUNBAR *Poems* xii. 14 Welth, warldly gloir, and riche array, Ar all bot thornis laid in thy way. **1561** T. HOBY tr. *Castiglione's Courtyer* II. (1900) 114 The poore gentilwoman stood upon thornes, and thought an houre a thousande yeare, till she were got from him. *c* **1580** JEFFERIE *Bugbears* III. ii. in *Archiv. Stud. Neu. Spr.* (1897), I sytt all on thornes till that matter take effect. **1602** SHAKS. *Ham.* I. v. 87 Those Thornes that in her bosome lodge. **1611** BIBLE *Numbers* xxxiii. 55 Those which ye let remaine of them, shall be..thornes in your sides. *Ibid.* *2 Cor.* xii. 7 Least I should bee exalted aboue measure.. there was giuen to me a thorne in the flesh [**1526** TIND. vnquyetnes of, **1557** *Gen.* a pricke in the fleshe], the messenger of Sathan to buffet me. *a* **1698** TEMPLE *Hist. Eng.* 93 No Prince ever came so early into the Cares and Thorns of a Crown. **1768** EARL CARLISLE in Jesse *Selwyn & Contemp.* (1843) II. 316, I should have been upon thorns till you had wrote. **1775** SHERIDAN *Rivals* V. i, Virtuous love.. shall pluck the thorn from compunction. **1822** GALT *Provost* xlv, The perverse views..of that Yankee thorn-in-the-side, Mr. Hickery. **1853** MRS. GASKELL *Cranford* vii. 100 Peggy wanted now to make several little confidences to her, which Miss Barker was on thorns to hear. **1864** BRYCE *Holy Rom. Emp.* xii. (1875) 191 The Eastern Church was then, as she is to this day, a thorn in the side of the Papacy. **1886** C. E.

Pascoe *Lond. of To-day* xxx. (ed. 3) 274 Not far from the grave of Elizabeth and Mary is that of the former's thorn in life, Mary of Scotland. **1913** D. H. Lawrence *Sons & Lovers* xiii. 379 He was on thorns to be gone from so trying a situation. **1923** —— *Stud. in Classic Amer. Lit.* ii. 21 Probably I haven't got over those Poor Richard tags yet. I rankle still with them. They are thorns in young flesh. **1924** E. M. Forster *Passage to India* iv. 34, I can be a thorn in Mr. Turton's flesh, and if he asks me I accept the invitation. **1929** J. Buchan *Courts of Morning* ii. iii. 187 You've given me a thorn to lie on, just when I was feeling comfortable. **1946** W. S. Maugham *Then & Now* xxxi. 187 The family that had been for so long a thorn in the flesh of the Vicars of Christ. **1977** E. Quinn tr. *Kung & Lapide's Brother or Lord* 36 Jesus was undoubtedly a thorn in the flesh for many Saducees.

3. a. A spine or spiny process in an animal.

c **1300-** [implied in thornback 1]. *c* **1711-56** [implied in thorny 1 b]. **1860** [see *thorn oyster* in 8].

b. *Histology.* (See quots.)

1899 *Allbutt's Syst. Med.* VI. 490 The dendrons are possessed of numerous minute lateral projections, gemmules, spines, or 'thorns' as they have been variously called. *Ibid.* VIII. 325 Dr. Alexander Hill believes the so-called 'thorns' to be organic structures, which are not shewn in their entirety by the chrome-silver method; and that a thorn is really the cell-end of an unstainable nerve filament, surrounded by a film of staining cell plasm.

c. *pl.* In *Lace-making*, Pointed projections used to decorate the cordonnet, etc., in point-lace.

1874 *Queen Lace Bk.* i. 18 Little loops, knots, or knobs.. called Pearls, Thorns, or Picots. **1882** Caulfeild & Saward *Dict. Needlework, Thorns*, used in Needlepoints to decorate the cordonnets and raised parts of the lace. See *Spines*.

d. *thorn needle* = *fibre needle* s.v. fibre *sb.* 8. (*Disused.*)

1950 *Vogue* Aug. 98/2 Intellectuals often have an E.M.G. gramophone..and they play with thorns, not steels. **1973** *Amateur Photographer* 3 Jan. 33/2 A 'thorn' needle was composed of some soft woody or fibrous substance, which was ground to a point in a special machine.

II. 4. a. A plant which bears thorns or prickles; a bramble or brier; a prickly bush, shrub, or tree; a thorn-tree or thorn-bush; esp. any species of the genus *Cratægus*; in England, *spec.* the Hawthorn or White-thorn (*C. Oxyacantha*).

In early OE. *þyrne* wk. fem.:—**þurnjōn*.

a **700-** [implied in hawthorn]. *c* **725** *Corpus Gloss.* (O.E.T.) 1834 *Sentes*, ðornas. *c* **888** K. Ælfred *Boeth.* xxiii, Swa hwa swa wille sawan westmabære land, atio ærest of ða þornas & þa fyrsas & þ fearn & ealle þa weod. *c* **950** *Lindisf. Gosp.* Matt. xiii. 7 Oðro uutedlice ʒefeollon in ðornum..& woxon ða ðornas..& underdulfon ða. *c* **1000** Ælfric *Gen.* iii. 18 þornas and bremelas heo asprit þe. **1045** *Charter Edward* in Kemble *Cod. Dipl.* IV. 98 On ðane greatan þorn ðe stynt wið Grimes dic. *c* **1200** Ormin 9219 þurrh þorrness & þurrh breress þær shulenn beon ridinngess nu. *c* **1250** *Gen. & Ex.* 1334 Faste in ðornes he saʒ a sep. **1382** Wyclif *Judg.* ix. 14 And alle the trees seiden to the thorn, Com, and comaund thow vpon us. *c* **1450** *Godstow Reg.* 34 Fowre burdyns of thornys of her wood of Cumnore. **1545** Brinklow *Lament.* (1874) 92 Do briers bringe forth figges, and thorns grapes? **1615** W. Lawson *Orch. & Gard.* (1623) Pref., Curious conceits..inoculating Roses on Thornes, and such like. **1750** Gray *Elegy* 116 Grav'd on the stone beneath yon aged thorn. **1800** Wordsw. *Hart-leap Well* 33 Dismounting, then, he leaned against a thorn. **1866** *Treas. Bot.* 344/2 The thorns [*Cratægus*] are natives of Europe, North America, and the temperate regions of Asia and Africa. **1882** *Garden* 24 June 449/1 Thorns, white, pink, and crimson..have been very beautiful.

b. (*without article*). Thorn bushes or branches collectively; also, the wood of a thorn-tree.

a **1300** *Cursor M.* 924 (Cott.) Brembel and thorn it sal te yeild. *Ibid.* 16437 þai crond him wit þorn. *c* **1330** R. Brunne *Chron.* (1810) 14 Sibriht,..þat a suynhird slouh vnder a busk of thorn. **1377** Langl. *P. Pl.* B. xii. 228 þe pyes..þere þe þorne is thikkest..buylden and brede. **1508** Dunbar *Tua Mariit Wemen* 15 Throw pykis of the plet thorne I presandlie luikit. **1592** Shaks. *Rom. & Jul.* i. iv. 26 It is too rough, Too rude, too boysterous, and it pricks like thorne. **1615** Chapman *Odyss.* xiv. 17 The inner part..Which with an hedge of Thorn he fenc't about. **1712** Pope *Messiah* 73 Sandy vallies once perplexed with thorn. *Mod.* Thorn is a hard wood, and makes good cudgels.

c. *fig.* (or in figurative language). Sometimes alluding to the parable of the sower, Matt. xiii. 7.

a **1340** Hampole *Psalter* xxxii. 12 Full of thornes & brers of synnes. **1735** Johnson *Lobo's Abyssinia, Descr.* i. 47 Little besides the Name of Christianity is to be found here, and the Thorns may be said to have choaked the Grain. **1819** Shelley *Ode West Wind* 54, I fall upon the thorns of life! I bleed! **1850** W. Irving *Goldsmith* xxxvii. 358 The thorns which beset an author in the path of theatrical literature.

5. With qualifying words used to distinguish species and varieties of *Cratægus*, and to designate various other thorny plants: as **aronia, thorn**, *Cratægus Aronia*; **buffalo thorn**, *Acacia latronum*, an Indian tree; **Egyptian thorn**, *Acacia vera*, one of the trees which produce gum-arabic; **elephant thorn**, *Acacia tomentosa* (*Treas. Bot.* 1866); **evergreen thorn**, *Cratægus Pyracantha*, an ornamental evergreen bearing a profusion of red berries in clusters during winter; **Jerusalem thorn**, *Parkinsonia aculeata*, a spiny shrub found in tropical regions; **Mysore thorn**, *Cæsalpinia sepiaria*, a leguminous plant; **Spanish hedgehog thorn**, some species of the genus *Anthyllis*. See also blackthorn, box-*t.*, buckthorn, camel('s-*t.*, christ's *t.*, Glastonbury *t.*, goat's-*t.*, hawthorn, lily *t.*, mouse-*t.*, orange *t.*, purging *t.*, sallow *t.*, scorpion's *t.*, white-thorn.

1882 *Garden* 12 Aug. 145/3 The *Aronia Thorn..is a moderate-growing tree. **1866** *Treas. Bot.*, *Buffalo Thorn, *Acacia latronum*. **1731** Miller *Gard. Dict.*, *Acacia*, *Egyptian Thorn or Binding Bean Tree. **1860** Mayne *Expos. Lex.*, Egyptian Thorn,..*Acacia vera*, the gum-arabic tree. **1731** Miller *Gard. Dict.* s.v. *Mespilus*, The Pyracantha or *Ever-green Thorn. **1866** *Treas. Bot.* 847/2 *P[arkinsonia] aculeata*, called in Jamaica the *Jerusalem Thorn. **1814** Roxburgh *Hort. Bengal.* 32 *Cæsalpinia sepiaria*, *Mysore Thorn. **1760** J. Lee *Introd. Bot.* App. 329 Thorn, *Spanish Hedgehog, *Anthyllis*.

6. (Short for *thorn-moth*.) Collectors' name for various geometrid moths.

Applied originally to species whose larvæ feed on the hawthorn or kindred plants.

1832 Rennie *Conspectus Butterfl. & Moths* 105 Geometra (Leach)... The September Thorn (*G. erosaria*). *Ibid.* 106 The Angled Thorn (*G. angularia*). **1869** Newman *Brit. Moths* 57 The September Thorn (*Ennomos erosaria*).

III. 7. The name of the Old English and Icelandic runic letter **þ** (= th); named, like other runes, from the word of which it was the initial.

c **1000** *Runic Poem* iii. (Gr.), þorn byð þearle scearp. *c* **1400** Maundev. (Roxb.) xv. 71 þ and ʒ, whilk er called þorn and ʒok. **1885** E. M. Thompson in *Encycl. Brit.* XVIII. 160/1 The English letter thorn, *þ*, survived and continued in use down to the 15th century.

IV. 8. *attrib.* and *Comb.* **a.** Attributive, as ***thorn-acacia, avenue, -bed*** (bed *sb.* 8), ***-cover*** (cover *sb.*[1] 4), ***fence, -fire, forest, grove, -holt, jungle, kloof, -prick, -puncture, scrub, stick, -sting, thicket, -twig, woodland***; objective, etc., as ***thorn-bearer, -eater***; ***thorn-like, -proof*** (also as sb., *sc.* 'material'), ***thorn-resisting*** adjs.; instrumental, as ***thorn-bound, -covered, -encompassed, -marked, -pricked, -set, -strewn, -wounded, -wreathed*** adjs. **b.** Special combs.: † **thorn-beak**, the garfish, *Belone vulgaris*; **thornberry**, (the fruit of) the hawthorn; **thorn-bill**, (*a*) a humming-bird of the South American genus *Rhamphomicron*; (*b*) any of several small warblers of the genus *Acanthiza* or a closely related genus, found in Australia, New Guinea, and New Zealand; **thorn-bird**, a South American bird, *Anumbius acuticaudatus* (allied to the oven-bird), which builds a large domed nest of thorny twigs (Webster, 1890); **thorn-bit**, ? a bit with a sharp projection which pricks the horse's mouth; also *fig.*; † **thorn-broom**, (*a*) the petty whin, *Genista anglica*; (*b*) the common furze; † **thorn-but** [butt *sb.*[1]], ? = thorn-back 1; **thorn-catcher**, a device attached to a bicycle or motor-car, to extract thorns and the like from the tire as the wheel rotates; **thorn-devil**, name of an Australian lizard, *Moloch horridus*; = Moloch 2; **thorn-fly** (also *hawthorn-fly, thorn-tree fly*), a kind of artificial fly; † **thorn-garth**, an enclosure protected by a thorn-hedge; † **thorn-grape**, the gooseberry; **thorn-head** (Webster, 1890), **thorn-headed worm**, one of the *Acanthocephala*, intestinal parasitic worms having the proboscis furnished with hooks or spines; † **thorn-hog**, a hedgehog; **thorn-hopper**, a tree-hopper, *Thelia cratægi*, which frequents thorny shrubs (*Cent. Dict.* 1891); **thorn house**, in salt-making by the graduation method, a structure in which weak brine is caused to trickle over piles or high walls of thorns and brushwood giving a large surface for evaporation; **thorn-letter**, the runic letter þ: = sense 7; **thorn-lizard** = *thorn-devil*; **thorn-locust**, the common honey-locust tree of N. America, *Gleditschia triacanthos*; **thorn-moth** = sense 6; **thorn-mussel**, a pinna; **thorn oyster**, popular name of bivalves of the family *Spondylidæ*, in which the older specimens have the lower valve spiny; also *thorny oyster*; **thorn-quick**, a young thorn-plant for a hedge; † **thorn-rone**, a brake or undergrowth of thorns; **thorn-shell**, a spiny shellfish; **thorn-stone**, a concretion deposited on the faggots in a *thorn house* (see quot. 1848); **thorn-swine**, a porcupine (*Cent. Dict.* 1891); **thorn-tail**, popular name of the humming-birds of the South American genus *Gouldia*, distinguished by a long pointed tail; **thorn-tailed** *a.*, having a tail resembling a thorn, or with thorn-like processes; *thorn-tailed agama*, an agamoid lizard of the genus *Uromastix*, having the tail cased with rings of spiny scales; **thornveld** *S. Afr.*, veld in which Acacias predominate; **thorn-wall**, in salt-making: cf. *thorn house*; **thorn-wood**, (*a*) a wood of thorns; (*b*) (*thornwood*) a South African tree (perh. *Acacia Natalitia*, the South African Wattle); also *attrib.* See also thorn-apple, thorn-bush, etc.

1570 Levins *Manip.* 207/6 A Hornbeak, fish... A *Thorn-beak. **1894** G. Allen in *Westm. Gaz.* 8 May 2/1 They [nettles] make a practice of sheltering themselves under..stouter and taller *thorn-bearers. **1844** Stephens *Bk. Farm* I. 374 The ditch is thus marked out ready for the formation of the *thorn-bed. **1766** Ld. Fife *Let.* 30 Nov. in A. & H. Tayler *Lord Fife & his Factor* (1925) ii. 36 Tell Thos. Reid that his Information as to there being no *Thornberrys this season is wrong. **1886** Britten & Holland *Dict. Eng. Plant-Names* 467 Thornberries. Fruit of *Cratægus Oxyacantha*. **1934** E. Reynard *Narrow Land* v. 248 The Dover cliff was a thornberry scratch compared with what befell Cape Cod. **1861** Gould *Humming Birds* III. Pl. 188 *Ramphomicron Ruficeps*—Red-capped *Thorn-Bill. **1870** Gillmore tr. *Figuier's Rept. & Birds* 471 The Thornbills..are American birds. **1911** J. A. Leach *Austral. Bird Bk.* 141 These birds..have been called *Thornbills by Mr. A. J. North. **1933** *Bulletin* (Sydney) 5 Apr. 27/1 The yellow-tailed thornbill constructs a double nest, the lower cavity..containing the eggs. **1964** *Courier-Mail* (Brisbane) 17 Oct. 2/1 There is a species or more of Thornbill in every mainland State. **1975** I. Rowley *Bird Life* iii. 40 The real diminutives forage..by rapid and nearly continuous searching of ground or shrub layer as by wrens and thornbills. **1886** Kipling *Departm. Ditties*, etc. (1899) 90 The colt who is wise will abstain from the terrible *thorn-bit of Marriage. **1578** Lyte *Dodoens* vi. ix. 668 *Genistilla*, Furze or *thorne Broome groweth in vntoyled places. **1597** Gerarde *Herbal* iii. xviii. 1140 In English Furze, Furzen bushes, Whinne, Gorsse, and Thorne Broome. **1668** Charleton *Onomast.* 149 *Rhombus*..Qui est vel *Aculeatus*, the *Thorn-but. **1736** Ainsworth *Lat. Dict.*, The thornbut, *Rhombus aculeatus*. **1901** *Daily Chron.* 1 June 8/7 A great many punctures can be nipped in the bud, so to speak, by employing *thorn-catchers. **1850** R. G. Cumming *Hunter's Life S. Afr.* (1902) 158/2 We halted..beside several acres of *thorn-cover. **1642** Milton *Apol. Smect.* v. Wks. 1738 I. 119 This obscure *thorn-eater of Malice and Detraction, as well as of Quodlibets and Sophisms. **1843** *Farmers' Cabinet* 15 Jan. 184/1 Our fences are either the worm, post-and-rail, or *thorn. **1946** L. G. Green *So Few are Free* 226 Deep in the mountains they discovered a high thorn fence, obviously a man-made obstruction. **1799** G. Smith *Laboratory* II. 310 *Thorn-fly. Dubbing of black lamb's wool [etc.]. **1903** W. R. Fisher tr. *Schimper's Plant-Geogr.* i. iii. 260 The *Thorn-forest..is very rich in underwood. **1960** N. Polunin *Introd. Plant Geogr.* xiv. 442 Tropical thorn-forests..are usually still more xerophilous. *a* **1340** Hampole *Psalter* lxxxviii. 39 Thou distroyd all his *thorne garthis. **1578** Lyte *Dodoens* vi. xix. 681 *Vua spina*, whiche may be Englished, *Thorne grape. **1886** Fagge & Pye-Smith *Princ. Med.* (ed. 2) II. 234 An acanthocephalous or *thornheaded worm, Echinorrhynchus sp., has only once been certainly discovered in the human intestine. **1340** *Ayenb.* 66 þe *þorn-hog þet ys al ywryʒe myd prikyinde eles. *c* **1450** *Godstow Reg.* 208 Half a rode of lond, liyng in the *thorneholte in the feldes of halso. **1866** *Tomlinson's Cycl.* II. 552/1 [At Moutiers] There are four evaporating houses called *Maisons d'Epines* or **thorn-houses*. **1879** G. Gladstone in *Cassell's Techn. Educ.* IV. 353/1 Thorn houses..are gigantic erections consisting of a skeleton of timber filled in with thorn bushes..the water trickles down over the ends of the twigs. **1913** 'Saki' *When William Came* vi. 102 We have somewhere to go to..better than the scrub and the veldt and the *thorn-jungles. **1936** *Discovery* Nov. 337/1 The City of the Lake, buried deep in thorn jungle, through which we cut a path. **1902** Skeat in *Athenæum* 22 Nov. 684/1 The words 'that' and 'this' and 'the' all begin, in the MS., with the usual *thorn-letter. **1899** Cagney *Jaksch's Clin. Diagn.* viii. 413 The resulting cultivation is marked with..*thorn-like processes projecting from it. **1860** Wraxall *Life in Sea* vi. 143 The great *Thorn-mussel (*Pinna*) of the Mediterranean. *Ibid.* viii. 208 They [species of Spondyli] are distinguished by bright colours, but more especially by the long thorns and spurs with which they are covered, and for this reason they are also called *Thorn Oysters. **1858** Chr. Rossetti *Fr. House to Home* 63, I felt no *thorn-prick when I plucked a flower. **1565** Jewel *Repl. Harding* (1611) 417 That *Thorn-prickt, Nail-boared, Speare-pierced, and otherwise wounded, rent, and torne Bodie. **1908** *Daily Chron.* 25 Apr. 9/5 A Beeston Humber bicycle, of roadster type, fully equipped with special *thorn-proof tyres and a metal gear-case. **1955** W. Gaddis *Recognitions* iii. iv. 846 Engulfed in the flow of a tartan lap robe and folds of Irish *thorn-proof, he stared fixedly at an open book. **1978** *Birds* Spring 3/2 (Advt.), *Gamefair Jacket*. .. In natural olive Beacon Thornproof. **1755** *Forfeited Estates Papers* (S.H.S.) 92 [He] has raised.. since 1740 no less than 1,676,147 *Thorn Quicks. *a* **1400** *Sc. Trojan War* ii. 2437 And has bot one small hole but dout In-to þat *thorn-rone, richt secre. **1903** Kipling *Five Nations* 54 The thickets dwined to *thorn-scrub, and the water drained to shallows. **1974** R. Adams *Shardik* lviii. 496 This is a country of thorn-scrub and fine, blowing sand. **1757** Dyer *Fleece* i. 115 Haughty trees..that weaken *thorn-set mounds. **1860** Wraxall *Life in Sea* viii. 209 A wondrously beautiful *Thorn Shell. **1857** Hughes *Tom Brown* i. ii, A stout *thorn stick in his hand. **1848** *Knapp's Chem. Technol.* I. 266 The thorns become gradually covered with a thick coating (**thorn-stone*), consisting of carbonates of lime, magnesia, manganese, and protoxide of iron. **1885** C. G. W. Lock *Workshop Receipts* Ser. iv. 153/1 [The fagots] have to be changed every 2 years or so, on account of a deposit of calcium carbonate ('thornstone') which coats them. **1783** Latham *Gen. Syn. Birds* IV. 463 *Thorn-tailed Warbler... Inhabits Terra del Fuego. **1888** *Cassell's Encycl. Dict.* s.v. *Uromastix*, Thorn-tailed Agamas..from the south of Russia ..and Central India. **1895** G. B. Shaw *Let.* 31 Aug. (1965) I. 556, I lay there looking up peacefully at the moon through ..the laced *thorntwigs of the briar. **1878** A. Aylward *Transvaal of To-Day* xii. 246 Four young men, all Africanders, nearly lost their lives in the Speckboom *thornveld. **1936** L. Herrman in N. Isaacs *Trav. & Adventures Eastern Afr.* I. ii. 19 His 'panthers' are the small dark-skinned leopards of the thornveld. **1972** Palmer & Pitman *Trees S. Afr.* I. iii. 81 In the thornveld of Zululand, *Acacia karoo, Acacia nilotica, Acacia caffra*,..and *Acacia tortilis* subsp. *heteracantha* are frequent. **1866** *Tomlinson's Cycl.* II. 554/1 The Saxon method of graduation by the use of *thorn-walls. **1850** R. G. Cumming *Hunter's Life S. Afr.* (1902) 147/1 Reducing with adzes a *thornwood tree, which was to serve as a beam. **1863** W. C. Baldwin *Afr. Hunting* vi. 148 A beautiful country of dense thornwood. **1903** W. R. Fisher tr. *Schimper's Plant-Geogr.* iii. iv. 492 *Thorn-woodland appears..on very permeable, dry, sandy soil.

1960 N. POLUNIN *Introd. Plant Geogr.* xiv. 442 Grasses are often lacking in the drier thorn-woodlands. **1819** SHELLEY *Prometh. Unb.* I. 598 Let that *thorn-wounded brow Stream not with blood.

thorn (θɔːn), *v.* Now *rare.* [f. prec. sb.]

1. *trans.* To make thorny, to furnish with thorns; *esp.* to protect (a newly planted quick-set hedge or the like) with dead thorn-bushes. Also *absol.*

1483 *Cath. Angl.* 384/1 To Thorne, *dumare, spinare, dumere esse vel fieri, -escere.* **1541** *Nottingham Rec.* III. 382 For thorns and for thornyng of wylo settes. **1579** *Mem. St. Giles, Durham* (Surtees) 1 Payde..for thornynge the wicke for saufegayrde of the shepe. **1784** ROBINSON *Let.* in *N. & Q.* 3rd Ser. IV. 342/2, [I] set a man to hedge and thorn. **1875** BROWNING *Aristophanes' Apol.* 630 Vowel-buds thorned about with consonants.

2. To prick with or as with a thorn; to vex.

1590 C'TESS PEMBROKE *Antonie* 226 And thousand thousand woes Our heau'nly soules now thorne. *Ibid.* 917 This grief, nay rage,..thornes me still. **1778** *Saberna* 16 A ruffian he!..Who stole a rose, and thorn'd the heart it blest! **1811** COLERIDGE *Let.* in J. P. Collier *Seven Lect.* (1856) p. lvii, The perplexities with which..I have been thorned and embrangled. **1877** TENNYSON *Harold* I. i. 243, I am the only rose of all the stock That never thorn'd him.

†**3.** To attach or pin together with thorns. *Obs.*

1598 SYLVESTER *Du Bartas* II. i. IV. *Handie-crafts* 140 With their sundry locks, thorn'd each to other, Their tender limbs they hide.

'thorn-,apple. The common name of *Datura Stramonium*, N.O. *Solanaceæ* (see DATURA), a coarse annual plant bearing large funnel-shaped white flowers, succeeded by large four-celled capsules covered with prickly spines; also the capsule or fruit itself. Also formerly called *thorny apple.*

1578 LYTE *Dodoens* III. lxxxvii. 440 Fruite, round as an apple.., beset rounde about with many prickley thornes, and therefore they call it Thorne apple. **1694** W. SALMON *Bate's Dispens.* (1713) 680/2 Fresh Leaves of Strammonium bearing Thorn Apples. **1846** LINDLEY *Veg. Kingd.* 619 The Thorn-apple..is a violent narcotic when taken internally. **1898** *Allbutt's Syst. Med.* V. 415 Crenation of the red-corpuscles, giving rise to the so-called mulberry and thorn-apple forms.

thornback ('θɔːnbæk). Forms: see THORN *sb.* and BACK *sb.*[1]; also 5 **-bagge**, 7 **-bage**, **-bagg**.

1. The common ray or skate (*Raia clavata*) of British seas, used as food, distinguished by having several rows of short sharp spines arranged along the back and tail. Also called †*thorny-back* (obs.).

c **1300** *Havelok* 759 Þe Butte, þe schulle, þe þornebake. *Ibid.* 832. **1392** *Earl Derby's Exp.* (Camden) 155 Pro vj thornebakkes, iiij d. *c* **1440** *Anc. Cookery* in *Househ. Ord.* (1790) 469 A codlynge or whitynge, or thornbagge, or hadok. **1594** NASHE *Unfort. Trav.* 16 My cape cloake.. ouer-spreading my backe like a thorne-backe. **1605** *Shuttleworths' Acc.* (Chetham Soc.) 170 One thornbage and fyve flokes vj[d]. **1653** H. COGAN tr. *Pinto's Trav.* xxiv. (1663) 89 We saw Fishes in the Shape of Thornbacks, that were four fathoms about, and had a Muzzle like an Ox. **1859** *Yarrell's Brit. Fishes* II. 582 The Thornback and its female the Maid. **1861** HULME tr. *Moquin-Tandon* II. III. i. 106 The Thorn-back.., from the shores of the Mediterranean, is of a brown colour, spotted with white and black. The body attains a length of twelve feet.

b. As the name of other species of ray: see quots.

1731 MEDLEY *Kolben's Cape G. Hope* II. 202 The Cape Thornback is a broad flat fish from three quarters of an inch to an inch thick. **1898** MORRIS *Austral Eng.*, *Thornback*, Name for one of the Stingrays, *Raia lemprieri*, Richards.

†**c.** *fig.* Opprobriously applied to a person.

1599 NASHE *Lenten Stuffe* (1871) 101 To be held a flat thornback, or sharp pricking dog-fish to the public weal.

2. a. Short for *thornback crab*: see 4.

1891 in *Cent. Dict.*

b. Provincial name of the stickleback.

1859 *Yarrell's Brit. Fishes* (ed. 3) II. 75 Rough-tailed Stickleback. Pinkeen..Thornback. *c* **1904** E. SMITH (*MS.*) *Warwick. Gloss.* (E.D.D.), *Thorn-back*, a small fish with a strong back fin. It abounds in the Avon, but it is not the stickleback.

†**3.** An old maid. *slang. Obs.*

The female young of the thornback is called *maid* (MAID *sb.*[1] 7), and *maiden-skate* (*Sc.*).

1694 MOTTEUX *Rabelais* V. iv, Whether when they were Maids, or Thornbacks, in their Prime, or at their last Prayers. **1709** *Brit. Apollo* II. No. 70. 2/2 Meeting with three Thornbacks.., I treated them. **1898** *Daily News* 14 Mar. 4/7 After 25, young ladies were called 'thorn-backs' by the much marrying Puritans of New England.

4. *attrib.*, as **thornback crab**, a species of spider-crab or sea-spider, *Maia squinado*, called also in U.S. king-crab; †**thornback dog**, a kind of dog-fish or shark of the genus *Galeus*; **thornback ray** = sense 1; **thornback skate** (see quot.).

1668 WILKINS *Real Char.* II. v. §3. 132 Thornback Dog, [margin] *Galeus spinax.* **1862** COUCH *Brit. Fishes* I. 99 Thornback Ray, Ray-maid... This is one of the commonest of the Rays, and the most valued. **1875** *Melbourne Spectator* 28 Aug. 201/3 A thornback skate [*Raia rostrata*],..weighing 109 lbs., has been caught..at North Arm.

Hence †**'thornbackly** *a. Obs.*, of the nature of a thornback: cf. 1 c above.

1605 *Tryall Chev.* v. ii. in Bullen *Old Pl.* (1884) III. 350 The Thornbackly slave!

'thorn-bush. Any bush that bears thorns; e.g. a hawthorn, a bramble. Also *attrib.*

c **1330** R. BRUNNE *Chron.* (1810) 9 A suynhird smote he to dede vnder a thorn busk. **1483** *Cath. Angl.* 384/1 A Thorne buske, *spinetum.* **1535** COVERDALE *Judg.* ix. 15 Then sayde all the trees vnto the thorne buszshe: Come thou, and be kynge ouer vs. **1590** SHAKS. *Mids. N.* v. i. 263, I, the man in the Moone; this thorne bush, my thorne bush; and this dog, my dog. **1896** BADEN-POWELL *Matabele Campaign* xi, I lay up during the heat of the day with a water-proof sheet spread over a thorn-bush as a shelter from the sun. **1902** *Westm. Gaz.* 3 Nov. 3/1 Crossing this thick thorn-bush country in the face of the opposition of a numerous army elated by recent success.

'thorn-crown. A crown or fillet of thorns: chiefly in reference to that placed in mockery on the head of Christ (Matt. xxvii. 29, etc.).

?*c* **1400** *Warres of Jewes* (Laud MS. 22) in Warton *Hist. Eng. Poetry* (1840) II. 106 A strange thorn crown was thraste on his hed. **1859** LD. LYTTON *Wanderer* (ed. 2) 420 The thorn-crown hath blossom'd on my brow. **1902** *Lindsey Star* 12 July 2/2 He wore the thorn-crown on His brow.

So **'thorn-crowned** *a.*, crowned with thorns, wearing a crown of thorns.

1609 J. DAVIES *Holy Roode* G j, We learne..by his Thorne-crowned head, How to adorne vs. **1792** R. CUMBERLAND *Calvary* (1803) II. 101 His thorn-crown'd head upon his breast reclin'd. **1903** *Month* Aug. 127 The thorn-crowned figure of the Redeemer.

thorne, variant of THARN *v. Obs.*, to lack.

thorned (θɔːnd), *a.* [f. THORN *sb.* + -ED[2].]

a. Having or provided with thorns. **b.** Overgrown with thorn-bushes.

1893 CHR. ROSSETTI *Songs for Strangers*, etc., Poems (1904) 123/2 Our crooked ground, our thorned and thistled plot. **1895** *Pop. Sci. Monthly* Feb. 499 The thorned plants that inhabit them. **1903** *Daily Chron.* 21 Mar. 8/4 Long trails of thorned rose stems.

†**'thornel.** *Obs. rare*[−1]. [Corruption of dial. German *darndel* = *darrling*, f. *darr-en* to dry, parch, roast.] Silver or copper ore which remains unreduced in smelting.

1683 PETTUS *Fleta Min.* I. xxviii. §9. 75 Let the Silver be dry, and when the Thornels (if there be any) and the Silver hath taken hold on the Ashes, they must be beaten down with a Hammer. *Ibid.* II. 125 *Thornels*,..a term of Art, for that which remains of the roasted Oar, unmelted.

thornen ('θɔːnən), *a. Obs.* exc. *dial.* Forms: 1 **ð-, þyrnen**, 2 **þernen**, 2–4 **þornen**, 4 (9 *dial.*) **thornen**, 9 *dial.* **tharnin**. [In OE. *þyrnen* = OHG. *durnîn*, Goth. *þaurneins*,:—OTeut. **þurnînoz*, f. **þurn-us* THORN: see -EN *suffix*[4]. ME. *þornen* (without umlaut) was assimilated to the sb.; so Ger. *dornen*.] Of thorns or thorn; thorny.

c **897** K. ÆLFRED *Gregory's Past. C.* xxxvi. 260 He ȝeðafode ðæt him mon sette ðyrnene beaȝ on ðæt heafod. *c* **1000** ÆLFRIC *Hom.* II. 252 His cempan..mid þyrnenum helme his heafod befengon. *c* **1160** *Hatton Gosp.* Mark xv. 17 þa cempen..him on setten þernene helm awundene. *c* **1175** *Lamb. Hom.* 121 Mid þornene crune his heaued wes icruned. *c* **1400** *Trevisa's Higden* (Rolls) VI. 427 He feng a party of þe holy crosse, and som of þe crowne of þorne [*MSS.* α, γ, þornene crowne; β, þornen coroun]. **1859** HUGHES *Scour. Wh. Horse* iv, The tharnin tree..As is called King Alferd's tharn. **1863** BARNES *Poems* III. 29, I pass'd the maid avore the spring, An' shepherd by the thornen tree.

'thorn-'hedge. A hedge of thorny shrubs; *spec.* a hedge composed of hawthorn 'sets'. Hence **'thorn-'hedged** *a.*, furnished with or enclosed by a thorn-hedge.

1560 BIBLE (Genev.) *Micah* vii. 4 The most righteous of them is sharper then a thorne hedge. *a* **1732** T. BOSTON *Crook in Lot* (1805) 33 It is like a thorn-hedge..in the way which that bias inclines him to. **1854** *Zoologist* XII. 4286, I discovered in a thorn-hedge the first nest that I had seen that year. **1892** A. M. CLERKE *Fam. Stud. Homer* iii. 73 Odysseus ..approached the thorn-hedged enclosure.

thornily ('θɔːnɪlɪ), *adv.* [f. as next + -LY[2].] In a thorny manner; so as to be thorny.

1887 BLACKMORE *Springhaven* xvi, Thornily crested with good stout furze.

thorniness ('θɔːnɪnɪs). [f. THORNY + -NESS.] Thorny quality or condition, prickliness; *fig.* acerbity of manner, roughness, ruggedness.

1674 R. GODFREY *Inj. & Ab. Physic* 87 The Thornyness, or bad Character imprinted on the stomach,..might be obliterated. **1721** BAILEY, *Spinosity*, thorniness, difficulty. **1868** A. R. WALLACE *Malay Archip.* 158 The most characteristic feature of the jungle was its thorniness. **1895** *Current Hist.* (Buffalo, N.Y.) V. 753 The historian's rude sallies and general thorniness. **1906** *Athenæum* 7 July 5/2 The thorniness of metre which this poet shares with Browning.

†**'thornish.** *a. Obs. rare.* [f. THORN *sb.* + -ISH[1].] Thorny, prickly.

1426 LYDG. *De Guil. Pilgr.* 11234 Me thouthe I sawh a fforkyd weye Partyng at an heg on tweyne, Thykke and thornyssh in certayne. **1577** FRAMPTON *Joyful News* II. (1596) 79 The fruite of a tree very great, after the maner of Thornish Chestnuts.

thornless ('θɔːnlɪs), *a.* [f. THORN *sb.* + -LESS.] Having no thorns; free from thorns; without a thorn.

1776 WITHERING *Brit. Plants* (1796) II. 461 [*Mespilus germanica*] Thornless: leaves spear-shaped, cottony underneath: flowers solitary, sitting. **1803** VISCT. STRANGFORD *Poems of Camoens, To Night* (1810) 66, I.. Have never yet been one of those Whose love has prov'd a thornless rose! **1825** H. ALFORD in *Life* 17 Perennial and thornless flowers bloom only in the Paradise above. **1900** L. H. BAILEY *Cycl. Amer. Hort.* I. 164/2 The Thornless or Mountain Blackberry..is not in cultivation. **1980** M. SPILLER *Growing Fruit* vii. 159 The thornless form of the parsley-leaved blackberry..can be planted a little closer than other varieties.

Hence **'thornlessness.**

1857 LIVINGSTONE *Trav.* xviii. 345 The thornlessness of the vegetation is especially noticeable.

thornlet ('θɔːnlɪt). [f. THORN *sb.* + -LET.]

a. A diminutive thorn-bush. **b.** A minute thorn.

1865 E. BURRITT *Walk Land's End* xii. 419 The Rifle Corps fired a volley over the consecrated thornlet. **1882** SLADEN in *Jrnl. Linn. Soc.* XVI. 201 The spinelets..appear like well-developed thornlets.

thornpole, -pool, var. *thorlpoll*, THIRLEPOLL.

'thorn-tree. **a.** A tree having or bearing thorns; in Great Britain, usually a hawthorn tree; in southern Africa, usually an acacia.

1483 *Cath. Angl.* 384/1 A Thorne tree, *mespula, rampnus.* **1785** G. FORSTER tr. *Sparrman's Voy. Cape of Good Hope* I. ix. 324 Being once upon a plain under the shelter of a few scambling thorn-trees, (*mimosa Nilotica*) he thought he should steal upon an elephant that was near the spot. **1798** LADY A. BARNARD *Jrnl.* 13 May in *Lives of Lindsays* (1849) III. 440, I plucked from the great thorn-trees some of their prickles. **1850** R. G. CUMMING *Hunter's Life S. Afr.* (1902) 60/1 A clump of tangled thorn-trees. **1856** STANLEY *Sinai & Pal.* x. 363 The 'Nabk', or thorn-tree,..here breaks out along the hill-sides in thick jungles. **1895** *Atlantic Monthly* July 61 The thorn-tree before me was perhaps fifteen feet high. **1970** *Stand. Encycl. S. Afr.* I. 10/2 In South Africa the indigenous members of the genus [*Acacia*] as a whole are generally referred to as 'thorn-trees' or 'acacias'.

b. *attrib.* **thorn-tree fly**, a March trout-fly, a thorn-fly or HAWTHORN-FLY, q.v.

1676 COTTON *Walton's Angler* II. vii. (1881) 285 There is also for this month [March], a fly, called the Thorn-tree fly; the dubbing is..black, mixed with eight or ten hairs of Isabella-coloured mohair. **1787** BEST *Angling* 99 March. The Thorn or Hawthorn Tree fly. **1909** *Westm. Gaz.* 4 May 2/3 Scant thorn-tree shade where white sheep flock.

thorny ('θɔːnɪ), *a.* [OE. *þorniȝ*, f. THORN *sb.* + *-iȝ*, -Y. Cf. MHG. *dornic*.]

1. a. Abounding in, characterized by, or consisting of thorns or spines; spiny, prickly.

a **1023** WULFSTAN *Hom.* xlviii. (Napier) 246 Ðeheȝa þine earan mid þorniȝum heȝe. *a* **1225** *Ancr. R.* 134 Heo makieð frommard hore nest—softe wiðuten, & þorni wiðinnen. **1398** TREVISA *Barth. De P.R.* XVIII. xix. (Bodl. MS.), Þe Cameles mete is þorny and harde. **1456** *Coventry Leet Bk.* 291 Weryng þe Thorny crowne yn worship of Jhesu. **1596** SHAKS. *Tam. Shr.* Ind. ii. 59 Daphne roming through a thornie wood. **1697** DRYDEN *Virg. Georg.* III. 490 On Shrubs they browze, and..thorny Brambles crop. **1850** TENNYSON *In Mem.* lxix. 6, I found a wood with thorny boughs.

b. Of an animal (or a part of one): Having thorn-like organs or appendages; spiny. See also 4.

c **1711** PETIVER *Gazophyl.* VI. lx, Sea Porcupine... This thorny Fish is a sort of Sea Hedge-hog. **1743** ZOLLMAN in *Phil. Trans.* XLII. 463 Those Caterpillars which, from the Figure and the Stiffness of their Hairs, have been called the Thorny ones. **1756** AMORY *Buncle* (1825) I. 250 The perch [with] the thorny fins on its back.

2. Abounding in thorn-bearing or prickly plants; overgrown with thorns or brambles. Also *fig.*

thorny ground, fig. after the parable of the sower, Matt. xiii. 7, etc. Often *attrib.*

c **1000** ÆLFRIC *Hom.* I. 342 Se yrðling lufað ðone æcer, ðe æfter ðornum..wæstmas aȝifð, swiðor þonne he lufiȝe ðone ðe ðorniȝ næs, ne wæstmbære ne bið. *c* **1325** *Metr. Hom.* 52 This gat es stany and thornye. *c* **1440** *Gesta Rom.* viii. 19 (Harl. MS.) þe wey toward þe Cite was stony, þorny, and scroggy. **1593** SHAKS. *3 Hen. VI*, v. iv. 67 The thornie Wood, Which..Must by the Roots be hew'ne vp yet ere Night. **1657** J. WATTS *Dipper Sprinkled* 93, I was a High-way side Hearer, a Thorny-ground Auditor. **1735** SOMERVILLE *Chace* I. 259 He..in the thorny Brake Torn and embarrass'd bleeds. **1799** MARY TITHERINGTON *Diary* in *Life* 13, I am but too much a thorny-ground hearer. **1863** W. C. BALDWIN *Afr. Hunting* vi. 150 There are lots of game here, and a nice thorny country.

3. *fig.* **a.** Pricking or piercing to the mind; full of points painful or wounding to the feelings; painful, distressing; harassing, vexatious, irritating.

a **1340** HAMPOLE *Psalter* xvii. 36 All þe thorny & þe lairy besynes of þis warld. *a* **1586** SIDNEY *Arcadia* III. (R.), It was easily seen it was a very thorny abode he made there. **1600** SHAKS. *A.Y.L.* II. vii. 94 The thorny point Of bare distresse, hath tane from me the shew Of smooth ciuility. **1728** YOUNG *Love Fame* v. 252 Thorny care, and rank and stinging hate. **1868** LYNCH *Rivulet* CXL. vi, That thorny cares may yield sweet fruits.

b. Full of points of contention or difficulty; difficult to handle; delicate, ticklish.

1653 tr. *Hales' Dissert. de Pace* x. 48 In these so subtil and thorny explications, if they..chance to erre, shall they presently be termed the enemies of God and Christ? **1675**

TRAHERNE *Chr. Ethics* 25 Prudence is that knowledge, by which we guide our selves in thorny and uncertain affairs. **1793** BURKE *Corr.* (1844) IV. 133 This American is an ugly and thorny affair. **1831** SCOTT *Jrnl.* 13 Mar., I have finally arranged a thorny transaction. **1907** *Athenæum* 25 May 638/1 Several of the thorniest questions which have perplexed both ancient and modern logicians.

4. a. In the names of species or varieties of plants, animals, or shells, characterized by having thorns or spines: prickly, spiny; as ***thorny acacia, asparagus, clam, germander, lobster, rest-harrow.***

Also **thorny apple** = THORN-APPLE; **thorny broom**, (*a*) the petty whin, *Genista anglica*, (*b*) the common whin, furze, or gorse; **thorny oyster** = *thorn-oyster* (THORN *sb.* 8); **thorny palm**, the prickly palm of the W. Indies, *Bactrio Plumierana*; **thorny trefoil**, a thorny shrub of the Mediterranean region, *Fagonia Cretica*; **thorny woodcock**, a shell of the Indian Ocean, *Murex tenuispina*, with long thin closely-set spines. (See also 5 b.)

1834 PRINGLE *Afr. Sk.* vii. 239 An open grassy meadow.. bordered by willow trees and groves of the *thorny acacia [*A. horrida*, Dornboom]. **1578** LYTE *Dodoens* III. lxxxvii. 441 The Names..*Thornie apples, Prickle apples, and *Stramonia*. **1832** *Veg. Subst. Food Man* 187 The *thorny asparagus,.. beset with sharp spines. **1597** GERARDE *Herbal* III. xviii. 1140 This *thorney Broome is taken for Theophrastus his *Scorpius*, which Gaza nameth *Nepa*. **1822** *Hortus Anglicus* II. 81 *T[eucrium] Spinosum*, *Thorny Germander. **1833** *Encycl. Brit.* (ed. 7) VII. 502/1 The *Palinurus vulgaris*, or *thorny lobster, sometimes also termed cray-fish. **1666** J. DAVIES *Hist. Caribby Isles* 35 The Prickly or *Thorny-Palm, having that name from the prickliness of it. **1822** *Hortus Anglicus* II. 233 *O[nonis] Spinosa*. *Thorny Rest Harrow. **1760** LEE *Introd. Bot.* App. 353/1 *Thorny Trefoil, of Candia, *Fagonia*. **1842** *Penny Cycl.* XXII. 55/1 *Murex Tribulus* (Common *Thorny Woodcock).

b. In other collocations, as †**thorny marrow**, the spinal marrow.

1662 J. CHANDLER *Van Helmont's Oriat.* 195 It is made motive in the thorny marrow or *Spina Medullæ*.

5. a. *Comb.* as ***thorny-edged, -pointed, -pricking, -thin, -twining*** adjs.

1594 KYD *Cornelia* II. 269 Whose loftie Towers (like thorny-pointed speares). **1596** *Edw. III*, I. i, Feruent desire, ..Is farre more thornie pricking than this blade. **1705** PETIVER in *Phil. Trans.* XXV. 1952 The Thorny-edged Carolina Crab. **1735** SOMERVILLE *Chace* II. 166 The thorny-twining Hedge. **1885** HEL. G. CONE in *Atlantic Monthly* Apr. 451 What lifeless laughter, crackling thorny-thin?

b. Special Combs.: **thorny-back**, (*a*) the thornback; (*b*) the stickleback; (*c*) the river perch; **thorny devil** = MOLOCH 2. **thorny-ribs** (see quot.); **thorny-shell**, a univalve mollusc, *Voluta spinosa*.

1810 P. NEILL *List Fishes* 28 (Jam.) *Thorny-back (*Raia clavata*). **1869** *Chater's Tyneside Alm.* 13 (E.D.D.) Here may be fund the thorney-back, the Poheed an' Tommy Lodjor. **1899** *Strand Mag.* June 653 The Western Australians..describe it [*sc.* the moloch lizard] familiarly as the '*thorny devil'. **1932** *Discovery* Nov. 364/2 The Thorny Devil,..a sturdy creature about a foot long, covered with horny spikes and knobs, killed a puff adder with its tail. **1975** H. G. COGGER *Reptiles & Amphibians Austral.* 226/1 Thorny devil or Moloch... An unmistakable lizard, unique in scalation and form. *c* **1711** PETIVER *Gazophyl.* VIII. lxxviii, Limington *Thorney-ribs... A sort of Fossil Murex. **1713** PETIVER *Aquat. Anim. Amboinæ* Tab. iii, *Voluta spinosa*.. River *Thorney-shell.

thoro, obs. form of THOROUGH.

thoro- ('θɔərəʊ), combining form of THORIUM, in names of compound salts, minerals, etc. e.g. **thoro'gummite** *Min.* [GUMMITE: see quot. 1889], a hydrated thorosilicate of uranium; **thoro'silicate** *Chem.*, a silicate in which part of the silicon is replaced by thorium.

1889 *Amer. Jrnl. Sc. & Art* XXXVIII. 481 We name this mineral *thoro-gummite*, because it is a gummite in which the water has been replaced by the thorite molecule. *Ibid.* 480 It seems better to regard the mineral as a hydrated thoro-silicate of uranium, rather than as a urano-silicate of thorium. **1909** *Cent. Dict. Supp.*, Thorogummite..like other native compounds of thorium and uranium, has marked radio-active properties.

thoron ('θɔərɒn). *Chem.* and *Physics.* [a. G. *thoron* (C. Schmidt 1918, in *Zeitschr. f. anorg. Chem.* CIII. 114), f. THOR(IUM + -ON[2].

Quot. 1920 represents an independent coinage.]

A radioactive isotope of radon, atomic weight 220, that is a gaseous decay product of thorium, being formed by the decay of radium 224; thorium emanation.

1918 *Jrnl. Chem. Soc.* CXIV. II. 306 A rational system of nomenclature for the radioactive elements and their degradation products is suggested. Radium emanation is given the name Radon, Ro... The other emanations become Thoron, To, and Acton, Ao. **1920** E. Q. ADAMS in *Jrnl. Amer. Chem. Soc.* XLII. 2206 The names 'radium emanation', 'actinium emanation' and 'thorium emanation' have been shortened, respectively, to 'radon', 'actinon' and 'thoron', names which suggest that the element in question is an inert gas. **1938** R. W. LAWSON tr. *Hevesy & Paneth's Man. Radioactivity* (ed. 2) xi. 132 The emanation of thorium (thoron) decays with a half-value period of 55 seconds. **1961** *New Scientist* 2 Nov. 290/3 The filter is placed in a lead cask and, after allowing four days for the decay of the 'daughter' products of natural radon and thoron, the total beta-activity of the sample is recorded. **1981** *Indian Jrnl. Earth Sci.* VIII. 1 (*heading*) On the behaviour and measurement of thoron (Rn^{220}) in soil. **1983** *Canad. Mining Jrnl.* Mar. 34/1 Measurements were carried out to estimate the radon and thoron daughter levels.

Thorotrast ('θɔərəʊtrɑːst, -æ-). *Med.* Also **thorotrast.** [a. G. *thorotrast* (A. Weiser 1930, in *Wiener med. Wochenschr.* 25 Oct. 1428/2), f. *thoro-* THORO- + *kon)trast* CONTRAST *sb.*] A colloidal solution of thorium dioxide formerly used as a contrast medium in radiography.

A proprietary name in the U.S.

1932 *Official Gaz.* (U.S. Patent Office) 5 Apr. 14/2 Heyden Chemical Corporation, New York... *Thorotrast* for medicinal preparation finding its application in the photography by X-rays for medicinal and similar purposes. **1933** [see ANGIOGRAM]. **1947** *Radiology* XLIX. 362/2 The fact that 'thorotrast' (a colloidal suspension of thorium dioxide) is frequently used in human diagnostic work. **1976** P. COLLARD *Devel. of Microbiol.* x. 136 Animals were injected intravenously with particulate materials, indian ink, colloidal iron or thorotrast. **1977** *Lancet* 18 June 1297/1 The main long-term sequelæ of thorotrast are local effects and tumours at the site of injection and/or deposit..and fatal blood dyscrasias, including leukæmia and aplastic anæmias.

thorough ('θʌrə), *prep.* and *adv.* Chiefly archaic or *Obs.* Forms: see below. [A disyllabic development of OE. *þurh*, THROUGH, when fully stressed, which appeared already in later OE. as *þuruh* (cf. OHG. *duruh, durah, durih*, OS. *thuru*), and has regularly become *thorough* in mod.Eng., as *burh* became *buruh, borough, furh furrow, borh borrow, sorh sorrow, mearh marrow. Thorough* is thus the direct representative of the full-stressed OE. *þurh*; and it is owing to the fact that *þurh* was chiefly a preposition, and thus usually proclitic and stressless, that it is now, in this use, represented by *through* (unstressed θrʊ, new-stressed θruː). The stressed form was naturally used when *þurh* was a separate word, i.e. an adv., adj., or sb., or the stressed part of a compound, as in '*thoroughfare*; and, as prepositions were sometimes emphatic and stressed, the *þuruh, thorough* form remained also as a prep. beside the unstressed *þŭrh, þŭr, prŭh, prŭ*, etc.; on the other hand, the new-stressed form *through* (θruː) of the prep. has in more recent times been taken also by the adv., while *thorough* remains in both as an archaic form, and as that of the derived adj. and sb. In the adverb its function is largely taken over by its derivative *thoroughly*.

As both *thorough* and *through* are existing words, distinct in spelling and still more in pronunciation, it seems best to make two articles, placing under THROUGH the various monosyllabic forms, including the obsolete *þurh, thurgh, þurþ, þurth*, and the now dialectal *thruff*, and treating under THOROUGH the less numerous disyllabic variants. This entails some duplication of the definition, but appears preferable to treating *thorough* merely as a variant of *through*. It must be remembered however that both *þruh*, through, and *þuruh*, thorough, developed by insensible gradations out of *þurh, thurgh*, and that therefore the *a*-forms under THROUGH belong, down to 1300 and 1400, really as much to the history of *thorough*.]

A. Illustration of Forms.

α. 1–3 **þuruh**, 3 **þureh, þuregh**, 3–5 **þoruȝ**, 4 **þoruh, þoruhe, þoroȝ, þorogh, thorogh**, 4–5 **þorouȝ, thoruȝ**, 4–6 **thorough**, 5 **thoruh, thorowh, -owgh, -ughe, -oughe**, 5– **thorough** (8– **thoro'**). *β.* 3–4 **þuru, þoru**, 4 **thoru, þorou**, 4–5 **thoro, thorou, þorow**(**e**, 4–6 **thorowe**, 4–8 (9 in comb.) **thorow**, (5 **thurow, thurrowe**, 5–6 **dorow**, 6 **thurrou(ly)**, **thorro**, 6–7 **thorrow**); *γ.* 3–4 **þorw**, 4 **þurw, þourw, thorw**, 4–5 **þorwe**; 4 **þoruth** (in *þoruthlike*, THOROUGHLY).

c **1000** *Ags. Ps.* (Th.) lxv. 11 We þuruh fyr farað, and þuruh floda þrym. *c* **1200** *Trin. Coll. Hom.* 199 Oðer kinnes neddre..criepeð nedlinge þureh nerewe hole. *Ibid.* 33 þuregh [see B. I. 6]. **1297** R. GLOUC. (Rolls) 8513 þoru godes wille. *a* **1300** *Cursor M.* 151 How crist com thoro [*v.rr.* þorow, thoru, þourȝe] propheci. **13..** *Ibid.* 20698 (B.M. Add. MS.) þorwe [*v.rr.* thoru, þorou, þourȝe] þe toun. **1377** LANGL. *P. Pl.* B. IX. 151 þus þourw cursed caym cam care vppon erthe. *Ibid.* XIV. 300 þorw þe pas of altoun Pouerte myȝte passe with-oute peril of robbynge. *c* **1380** þorouȝ [see B. I. 1 b]. *c* **1430** *Hymns Virg.* 123 Longeus hym stonge dorow þe syde. *c* **1449** PECOCK *Repr.* I. i. 7 Weelnyȝ thoruȝ al the chapiter. **1456** Thurrowe [see B. I. 6]. **1467, 1482** Thorow [see B. II. 3]. **1474** Thorough [see B. II. 4]. **1484** CAXTON *Fables of Æsop* I. xiv, Deceyued thoroughe fals counceylle. **1485** —— *Chas. Gt.* I. II. v. 30 Thorugh hys empyre. **1556** *Chron. Gr. Friars* (Camden) 40 Browte..to the tower thorrow Smythfelde and in at Newgat, rydynge soo thorrow Chepe-syde. *Ibid.* 56 Prechyng thorro alle Ynglonde agayne the sacrament of the auter. **1590** SHAKS. *Mids. N.* II. i. 3 Over hill, over dale, Thorough [*folios* Through] bush, thorough brier. **1672,** *a* **1713** Thorow [see B. II. 1]. **1725** S. SEWALL *Diary* 17 Mar., Much Water passes thorow the three Spaces left for that purpose. **1850, 1893** Thorough [see B. I. 1, 2].

B. Signification.

I. *prep.* (Still in poetic or archaic use.)

1. From side to side or end to end of; = THROUGH *prep.* 1. *arch.*

c **1000**, *c* **1200** [see A.]. **1297** R. GLOUC. (Rolls) 4277 þe erl ..mid is launce þoru þe þrote smot on. *a* **1300** *Cursor M.* 7809 Thoru his licam mi suerd i draif. **1377** [see A.]. *c* **1450** *ME. Med. Bk.* (Heinrich) 204 Let hyt renne þorow a fayre cloþ. *a* **1540** BARNES *Wks.* (1573) 212/2 You ryde thorowe streetes, and townes. **1684** R. WALLER *Nat. Exper.* 121 An hole thorough the bottom of the Vessel. **1712** tr. *Pomet's Hist. Drugs* I. 149 Such as will pass thorow an Iron Ring. **1850** BLACKIE *Æschylus* I. 191 Thorough my heart, Thorough my liver, Keen as the cold ice Shot through the river.

b. Of transmission of light or sight. *Obs.* or *arch.*

c **1380** WYCLIF *Serm.* Sel. Wks. I. 142 As þe sunne comeþ þorouȝ þe glas. **1585** T. WASHINGTON tr. *Nicholay's Voy.* II. iii. 33, I saw these bathes thorow a great hole. *a* **1636** LYNDE *Case for Spect.* (1638) 45 You begin to looke asquint thorow your Spectacles at the reformed Churches. **1705** STANHOPE *Paraphr.* II. 599 The Truth never shines so bright, as when the Oppositions, that strive to darken it, are plainly seen thorow.

†**c.** In reference to the passage of the voice through the throat, etc.: = THROUGH *prep.* 1 d.

1668 [see THROUGH B. I. 1 d].

†**d.** Of passage between the individual things of a group; = THROUGH *prep.* 1 e. *Obs.*

1535 FISHER *Wks.* (1876) 365 He must..creepe thorowe the thicke bushes. **1684** BUNYAN *Pilgr.* II. 39 The man that cut his way thorough his Enemies.

†**e.** In phrase ***thorough one's hands*** = THROUGH *prep.* 1 f. *Obs.*

1660 F. BROOKE tr. *Le Blanc's Trav.* 19 The Jewes..are such cheates, they sophisticate all that comes thorough their hands. **1710** PRIDEAUX *Orig. Tithes* v. 268 Lawyers, whose hands it passed thorough.

†**f.** In various fig. applications: see THROUGH *prep.* 1 g. *Obs.*

1543 [see THICK AND THIN A. 1]. **1581** PETTIE *Guazzo's Civ. Conv.* II. (1586) 58 b, Those of Piemount, who with the shrilnesse of their wordes goe thorow ones eares. **1619** HIERON *Wks.* II. 16 Good points of doctrine runne thorow vs as thorow a pipe. **1680** BURNET *Rochester* (1692) 127 Which the strength of his Mind would soon break thorough.

†**g.** ***thorough and thorough*** = THROUGH *prep.* 1 h. *Obs.*

13.. *Cursor M.* 24381 (Fairf.) A squorde sulde stike ouerthwert þorou and þorou [*Gött.* Toru and thoru] þine awen hert. *c* **1489** CAXTON *Sonnes of Aymon* i. 56 He shoued hym thorughe and thorughe his body.

2. Along (to any distance) within. Without implication of traversing from end to end. *arch.*

c **1050**, etc. [see THROUGH B. I. 2]. *c* **1430** *Chev. Assigne* 95 He wente þorow a foreste fowre longe myle. **1646** SIR T. BROWNE *Pseud. Ep.* v. xvi. 257 The Picture of St Christopher..with a staff in his hand, wading thorow the water. **1893** SYMONDS in H. T. Wharton *Sappho* (1895) 60 Pinion on pinion, thorough middle ether Down from heaven hurried.

3. Over the whole extent of, in or to all parts of; throughout; = THROUGH *prep.* 3. Also **b.** sometimes following the sb. *arch.* and *poet.*

c **1000** [see THROUGH B. I. 3]. ? *a* **1366** CHAUCER *Rom. Rose* 1366 Fyges, and many a date tree There wexen..Thorough the gardyn in length and brede. **1485** CAXTON *Chas. Gt.* I. II. v. 30 Charles..sente oueral thorugh hys empyre. **1535** COVERDALE *Acts* xiv. 23 Whan they had ordeyned them Elders by eleccion thorow all the congregacions. *a* **1635** BP. CORBET *Poems* (1807) 12 Send of this stuffe thy territories thorough To Ireland, Wales and Scottish Eddenborough. **1678** CUDWORTH *Intell. Syst.* I. iv. §18. 343 Which Supreme Incorporeal Deity, was..said to be All Things, because it diffused it self thorough All. **1803** WORDSW. *Yarrow Unvisited* v, O'er hilly path and open Strath We'll wander Scotland thorough.

†**b.** Phrase. ***thorough all thing***: see THROUGH *prep.* 3 c. *Obs.*

1297 R. GLOUC. (Rolls) 7549 þis noble duc willam him let crouny king At londone amidwinter day, nobliche þoru alle þing. *c* **1380** *Sir Ferumb.* 1926 Charlis, þat is of fraunce kyng ..Hoteþ þe þorw alle þyng to leuen þyn errour.

4. From beginning to end of a space of time; = THROUGH *prep.* 4. Also following the sb.

a **1000**, etc. [see THROUGH B. I. 4]. **1535** COVERDALE *Ps.* lxxvii. 14 All the night thorow with a light of fyre. **1608** DOD & CLEAVER *Expos. Prov.* ix–x. 7 Thorow the whole yeere. **1896** A. E. HOUSMAN *Shropshire Lad* xvii, Twice a week the winter thorough [*rime* sorrow] Here stood I.

†**5.** From beginning to end of a process, action, writing, etc., *esp.* to the very end of; = THROUGH *prep.* 5, 5 c. *Obs.*

c **1449** PECOCK *Repr.* I. i. 7 Weelnyȝ thoruȝ al the chapiter, Poul meeneth [etc.]. **1628** WITHER *Brit. Rememb.* 243 At the last God brought me thorow all My doubts and feares. **1632** SANDERSON *Serm.* 61, I foresaw we should not haue time to goe thorow all that was intended.

6. Indicating intermediation, means, agency, instrumentality; = THROUGH *prep.* 7. *arch.* or *Obs.*

a **800**–**1154** [see THROUGH B. I. 7]. *c* **1200** *Trin. Coll. Hom.* 33 þe engel..seweð a whilche wise and þuregh hwam þis blisse cumen sholde. *a* **1300** *Cursor M.* 1395 Thoro birth of a blisful child. **1377** [see A.]. **1456** *Coventry Leet Bk.* 289 The blessyd babe..Thurrowe whom pece & tranquilite shall take þis reme on hand. **1535** COVERDALE *Josh.* xxiv. 12 Not thorow thy swerde, ner thorow thy bowe. **1671** FLAVEL *Fount. Life* xiii. 37 By Vertue of the Mediator and thorow the Benefit of his Death. **1847** EMERSON *Poems, Sphinx*, Thorough a thousand voices Spoke the universal dame.

†**b.** Indicating the agent after a passive verb; = THROUGH *prep.* 7 b. *Obs.*

a **900**–*c* **1000** [see THROUGH B. I. 7 b]. *c* **1290** *Beket* 374 in *S. Eng. Leg.* I. 117/374 þe churche..þat..was..a-rerd þoruȝ henri þe oþur kingue. *a* **1325** *MS. Rawl. B.* 520 lf. 32 b, Hit is icomaunded þoru þe King þat eche man habbe in house wepne. **1393** LANGL. *P. Pl.* C. IV. 2 þorw bedeles and bailifs brouht by-fore þe kynge.

†**7.** Indicating cause, reason, or motive; = THROUGH *prep.* 8. *Obs.*

a **1000**–*c* **1460** [see THROUGH B. I. 8]. **1297** R. GLOUC. (Rolls) 11320 þe king hadde þer to gode wille þoru frerene rede. *c* **1374** CHAUCER *Anel. & Arc.* 271 þe swerde of sorowe byte My woofull harte þorowe your creweltee. **1596** DANETT tr. *Comines* (1614) 236 He ended his life thorow a sickenes. **1666** H. STUBBE *Mirac. Conform.* 3 His life seemed burthensome to him thorough the violence of the.. temptation.

II. *adverb.* (Now *arch.* or *dial.*)

1. From side to side, from surface to surface, from end to end (of a body or space); = THROUGH *adv.* 1.

a **1000**–*c* **1400** [see THROUGH B. II. 1]. *a* **1300**, **1330** [see *thorough-bear*, *-bore* in THOROUGH- 1]. *c* **1493** *Epitaffe*, etc. in *Skelton's Wks.* (1843) II. 392 Thorow thrylled and persyd with payne. **1638** JUNIUS *Paint. Ancients* 227 We doe not make our plate so thinne as to..cut it quite thorough with engraving. **1672** MARVELL *Reh. Transp.* I. 42 If he meet them in the dark, he runs them thorow. *a* **1713** ELLWOOD *Autobiog.* (1765) 184, I walked it thorow in a Day. **1883** SWINBURNE *Cent. Roundels, Sorrow* ii, One thought lies close in her heart gnawn thorough [*rime* furrow] With pain.

†**b.** To the end of the journey, all the way; = THROUGH *adv.* 1 b. *Obs.*

1684 BUNYAN *Pilgr.* II. 73 You should have begged me of him to have gon quite thorough with you. *Ibid.* 176 How he got thorow to whither he intended.

2. From beginning to end (of a time, process, action, work, book); = THROUGH *adv.* 2. *arch.*

a **1225** [see *thorough-fill* in THOROUGH- 1]. **1513** MORE in Grafton *Chron.* (1568) II. 777 Sithence he had once begonne, he would stoutly go thorowe. **1548–9** (Mar.) *Bk. Com. Prayer, Concern. Service*, They were onely begon, and neuer read thorow. **1670–1** MARVELL *Corr.* Wks. (Grosart) II. 371 The Committee of Conventicles have..gone thorow with their Bill. **1748** CHESTERF. *Lett.* 26 July, They..never consider it in all its different views; and, in short, never think it thorough. **1843** CARLYLE *Past & Pr.* III. xv. (tr. Goethe), The Future hides in it Gladness and sorrow; We press still thorow.

†**3.** Predicatively, after the vb. *to be*, indicating settlement; = THROUGH *adv.* 3 b. *Obs.*

1467 J. PASTON in *P. Lett.* II. 299 He is owtlawyd at Sir John Fastolfys swte..notwithstanding he is thorow with Sir T. Howys for Sir John Fastolf. **1482** *Cely Papers* (Camden) 88, I gawhe the exchetter xls for ws bothe and so whe be thorow with hym for aull matters.

4. Qualifying pa. pple. or adj.; = THROUGH *adv.* 4 a. *Obs.* or *dial.*

Now usually expressed by THOROUGHLY, except when hyphened to a pa. pple., as *thorough-bred*; see THOROUGH- 1. In 17–18th c. also hyphened to adjs.

a **1240** *Ureisun* 123 in *Cott. Hom.* 197 Mid swuþe luðere lasten mi soule is þuruh bunden. **1474** *Coventry Leet Bk.* 401 þat it be thorough tannyd and thorowe Coryed. **1531** TINDALE *Exp. 1 John* i. (1538) 14 b, Yet is it neuer thorow whole vntyll the houre of death. **1594** PLAT *Jewell-ho.* II. 38 When it is thorough hot. **1620** VENNER *Via Recta* vii. 120 The sweet Grapes..being thorow ripe. **1622** MABBE tr. *Aleman's Guzman d'Alf.* I. 37 When he [the patient] saw that he was thorow well. **1640** FULLER *Joseph's Coat, David's Punishm.* (1867) 239 Thou art not yet so thorough worn with age. **1692** R. L'ESTRANGE *Fables* ccii. (1714) 219 The Lion himself was not Thorough-Proof against this Fantastical Alarum. **1702** C. MATHER *Magn. Chr.* III. III. (1852) 560 They had thorow-good reasons for doing so. **1710** PRIDEAUX *Orig. Tithes* iv. 208 A Veteran and thorough settled Constitution of this Kingdom. **1729** BUTLER *Serm.* Wks. 1874 II. 82 A thorough honest man would..have repeated his former answer. *a* **1774** GOLDSM. *Hist. Greece* II. 112 He had a thorough good opinion of himself. **1796** C. MARSHALL *Garden.* xiv. (1813) 192 Till the earth is got thorough warm again. **1853** MISS YONGE *Heir of Redclyffe* xliv, He is a thorough great man.

†**5.** ***thorough and thorough*** = through and through: see THROUGH *adv.* 5. *Obs.*

1470–85 MALORY *Arthur* I. xvi. 58 With his swerd he broched the hors..thorow and thorow. **1526** TINDALE *John* xix. 23 The coote was with out seme woven vppon thorowe and thorowe. **1658** CLEVELAND *Rustick Ramp.* Wks. (1687) 446 Richard might have been struck thorough and thorough.

†**6.** With ellipsis of *go*, *get*, *pass*, or other vb. of motion; = THROUGH *adv.* 6. *Obs.*

1573 TUSSER *Husb.* (1878) 31 Trench hedge and forrow, that water may thorow. **1670** COTTON *Espernon* II. VII. 339 We are now come too far..to return.., we must either thorow, or dye.

thorough (ˈθʌrə, *U.S.* ˈθʌrəʊ), *adj.* and *sb.* [attrib. use of prec. adv.]

A. *adj.*

1. Used chiefly with sbs. of action or position, being a kind of elliptical use of the adv. = 'going, passing, or extending through', as ***thorough passage*** = passage through, ***thorough heat*** = heating through; cf. THROUGH *a.* 1. *Obs.* exc. in special applications. (See also THOROUGH- *in comb.* 2.)

c **1489** [see sense 2]. *c* **1566** SIR H. GILBERT in Hakluyt *Voy.* (1600) III. 20 He had heard a Fisherman..say..that he sayled very farre towards the Southeast, finding no end of the Sea: whereby he hoped a thorow passage to be that way. **1776** G. SEMPLE *Building in Water* 47 Very large Stones carefully bedded.., to guard the thorough Foundation between the Piers from..being displaced. **1799** G. SMITH *Laboratory* I. 186 Give it by degrees a thorough heat. **1843** R. J. GRAVES *Syst. Clin. Med.* v. 62 The bed-room..should be well aired, but without what is termed thorough air. *Ibid.* xxi. 251 The patient caught a fresh cold from being exposed to the thorough air of our too well ventilated ward. **1884** F. J. BRITTEN *Watch & Clockm.* 101 The holes for the train pivots are termed 'thorough holes'.

2. a. Of an action, etc.: Carried out through the whole of something; thoroughgoing; fully executed; applied to or affecting every part or detail. Hence, *gen.* That is fully what is expressed by the noun; thoroughgoing, complete, perfect, downright, entire. †In quot. 1581, Completely apt or suitable. (See also THROUGH *a.* 2.)

Formerly sometimes hyphened to the following sb., being treated as the adv. in combination (cf. THOROUGH- 2, THROUGH-).

c **1489** SIR S. HAMERTON in *Plumpton Corr.* (Camden) 63 To make a thorow search for my matter. *a* **1500** in C. Trice-Martin *Chanc. Proc. 15th C.* (1904) 6 [To] make a thurgh ende with the said Piers Hous and pay hym .xx. marcs. **1581** SIDNEY *Astr. & Stella* lvii, He forc't them out to find The thorowest words, fit for woes selfe to grone. **1615** LATHAM *Falconry* (1633) 92 To give her a thorough scowring. **1617** HIERON *Wks.* II. 110 To bring vs to this thorow and effectuall vnderstanding. **1678** BUTLER *Hud.* III. II. 850 Those who laid the first Foundation Compleat the thorow Reformation. **1719** DE FOE *Crusoe* I. 214 In the Morning, even before it was thorow Day-light. **1766** GOLDSM. *Vic. W.* xxv, A thorough knowledge of the world. **1780** in Jesse *Selwyn & Contemp.* (1844) IV. 383 Mr. Mathews.. proposed a thorough resolution..to stand by you. **1862** BURTON *Bk. Hunter* 102 The thoroughest test of active scholarship. **1893** W. LEWIN in *Bookman* June 85/2 His knowledge of English literature is extensive and thorough.

b. Of a person in reference to his action or quality.

1655 GURNALL *Chr. in Arm.* verse 13. viii. §4 (1669) 144/1 The soul effectually brought out of the love of sin as sin, will never be thorow-friends with it again. *a* **1700** DRYDEN (J.), A thorough translator must be a thorough poet. **1726** LEONI *Alberti's Archit.* II. 96/2 He is a thorow master of those elements of Painting. **1822** M. EDGEWORTH *Let.* 26 Feb. (1971) 359, I have engaged a ladys maid..and a *thorough* maid for cooking and brooming. **1829** LYTTON *Disowned* xlii, He was the finest and most thorough gentleman I ever saw. **1850** MRS. CARLYLE *Lett.* (1883) II. 129 Servants who give themselves out for 'thorough'. **1884** 'RITA' *Vivienne* I. iii, Blanche de Verdreuil was a thorough coquette.

B. *sb.* [Elliptical or absolute uses of THOROUGH *a.* or *adv.*].

1. Thorough-going action or policy: in *Eng. Hist.* (with capital T) applied to that of Strafford and Laud in the reign of Charles I, and sometimes to that of Cromwell as Lord Protector.

c **1634** LAUD in *Strafford Papers* I. 111 And for the state, indeed, my lord, I am for Thorough. **1849** MACAULAY *Hist. Eng.* i. I. 92 And now Wentworth exulted in the near prospect of Thorough. **1874** GREEN *Short Hist.* viii. §5 The dark gloomy countenance, the full heavy eye, which meet us in Strafford's portrait are the best commentary on his policy of 'Thorough'. **1900** MORLEY *Cromwell* IV. vi. 354 They had set up the Commonwealth without lords or monarch. They were deep in all the proceedings of Cromwellian Thorough.

†**2.** A channel artificially cut or dug; a trench, esp. *Agric.* one made for draining a field; = THROUGH *sb.*^{2} 1. *Obs.*

a **1555** BRADFORD *Wks.* (Parker Soc.) I. 303 If any man would alter the natural course of any water to run a contrary way, he shall never be able to do it with dams... Therefore the alteration must be from the head, by making other thoroughs and devices. **1581** *Coventry Leet Bk.* 824 Vp a thorowe betwene two Landes in the middes of the feild by certain meare-stones there sett.

3. A furrow; ***water-thorough***, a 'thorough' made for surface-draining; a water-furrow. *Agric.*

The *Eng. Dial. Dict.* has in sense 'furrow', *thurrow*, Yorksh. to Herts and Essex, also locally written *thorough*, *thurrough*, *thurrar*. Cf. TH, the initial, (6).

1733 W. ELLIS *Chiltern & Vale Farm.* 5 The Ignorance and Idleness of the Plowman, who either goes so shallow, or plows his Thoroughs so wide, or misses Part of the Ground. *Ibid.* 22 Sow them in four Thoroughs. **1744–50** —— *Mod. Husbandm.* I. I. 16 The ploughman..goes on plowing throughout the field, without making any..water-thoroughs. **1766** *Compl. Farmer* s.v. *Lucern*, Then ploughing it very narrow and sharp, he made water thoroughs with the plough. **1796** W. MARSHALL *Midl. Gloss.*, *Thorough*, an interfurrow, between two ridges. **1888** *Sheffield Gloss.*, *Thurrow*, a furrow of land.

†ˈ**thorough**, *v.*^{1} *Obs. rare*$^{-1}$. [f. THOROUGH *adv.*] *trans.* To pass through, pierce, penetrate.

1578 BANISTER *Hist. Man* I. 32 The superiour [part] is thorowed on ech side, with a large & ample hole.

ˈ**thorough**, *v.*^{2} *local.* [f. THOROUGH *sb.*] *trans.* To make 'thoroughs' or furrows in; see THOROUGH *sb.* 3. Hence ˈ**thoroughed** *ppl. a.*; ˈ**thoroughing** *vbl. sb.*

1733 W. ELLIS *Chiltern & Vale Farm.* 28 Plough them in very shallow,..thorough and harrow well. *Ibid.* 106 The Ground may be so gathered into a four Thorough'd-stitch or Ridge. **1744–50** —— *Mod. Husbandm.* V. I. 87 The land ..should be back-bouted, or what we call thoroughed-down. **1759** —— *Pract. Farmer* (ed. 5) Gloss. 5 Four-thoroughing of Land is not Clean Ploughing, but running up four Thoroughs close together with the Plough. *Ibid.*, Thoroughing down is drawing the plough once through the bought, to lay it plain for wheat or barley.

thorough- in combination. (See also THOROUGH *a.* 2, and THROUGH- *in comb.*)

1. Combinations of THOROUGH *adv.* with verbs, pples., or adjs.: †ˈ**thorough-ˈbear** *v.* [BEAR *v.*^{1} 35], *trans.* to 'bear' through, pierce, transfix, stab; ˈ**thorough-ˈbind** *v.*, *trans.* to bind or fasten (a wall, etc.) by a stone or iron, passing through from side to side (cf. *thorough-band* in 2); ˈ**thorough-ˈbore** *v.* [OE. *þurhborian*], *trans.* to bore through, perforate; †ˈ**thorough-ˈcleansing** *a.*, cleansing throughout or thoroughly; †ˈ**thorough-ˈdevilled** *ppl. adj. Obs.*, *nonce-wd.*, completely possessed by a devil; ˈ**thorough-ˈdress** *v.*, *trans.* to dress or manure (ground) thoroughly; ˈ**thorough-ˈdry** *v.*, *trans.* to dry thoroughly; ˈ**thorough-ˈfelt** *pa. pple.*, felt throughout; †ˈ**thorough-ˈfill** (*þuruh fullen*) *v.*, to fill up, complete; ˈ**thorough-ˈfought** *ppl. a.*, fought through or to the end; ˈ**thorough-go-ˈnimble** (*slang* or *dial.*): see quots.; †ˈ**thorough-ˈhumble** *v.*, *trans.* to humble thoroughly or completely; †ˈ**thorough-ˈlined** *ppl. a.*, lined throughout; †ˈ**thorough-ˈmade** *ppl. a.*, thoroughly made, made with full determination; ˈ**thorough-ˈripe** (ˈ**through-ripe**) *a.*, ripe throughout, thoroughly ripe; †ˈ**thorough-ˈrun**, *v. trans.* to run through, pierce, penetrate; †ˈ**thorough-ˈseasoned** *ppl. a.*, seasoned throughout or thoroughly; †ˈ**thorough-ˈshot** *ppl. a.*, shot through, transfixed as with an arrow; †ˈ**thorough-ˈsiping** *ppl. a.* [SIPE *v.*], oozing or trickling through; ˈ**thorough-ˈsped** *ppl. a.* (? *obs.* exc. *dial.*), thoroughly accomplished or developed; perfect, thoroughgoing, thorough-paced; †ˈ**thorough-ˈstain** *v.*, *trans.* to stain thoroughly. See also THOROUGHBRED, etc.

(In early use the adv. was often written separately before a vb., as it still is when it follows the vb.)

a **1300** *Cursor M.* 7624 þe king smat til him wit a sper In breth he wald him *thoru ber. *c* **1400** *Laud Troy Bk.* 16431 Echon other al to-bet, Sclow, & wounded, & thorow-bare. **1884** L. OLIPHANT *Haifa* (1887) 189 The crusaders used them [granite pillars] to *thorough-bind their walls. **1900** *Union Mag.* Oct. 457/2 Ancient columns are built into the walls of later castles, to thoroughbind the masonry. *c* **1000** in Cockayne *Narrat.* (1861) 20 Het hie þa *þurhborian. *c* **1330** R. BRUNNE *Chron. Wace* (Rolls) 16184 Handes, armes, þey dide þorow bore. **1703** T. N. *City & C. Purchaser* 4 They then thorough bore their Poles. **1642** H. MORE *Song Soul* II. i. I. xxi, *Thorough-cleansing virtue. **1604** PARSONS *3rd Pt. Three Convers. Eng.* 279 They were indeuilled, superdeuilled, and *thorowdeuilled. **1733** W. ELLIS *Chiltern & Vale Farm.* 31 Their vast Crops of Straws, and great Numbers of Cattle, make such Returns of Dung, as enables most of them to *thorough-dress their own Grounds. **1707** MORTIMER *Husb.* (1721) I. 184 Firing..must be long continued to *thorough-dry so many together. **1817** MOORE *Lalla R., Fire-worsh.* iv. 115 How deep, how *thorough-felt the glow Of rapture. *a* **1225** *Ancr. R.* 404 Heo..*þuruh fulleð, onont hire, Godes pine o rode. **1585–6** EARL LEYCESTER *Corr.* (Camden) 427 A gallant and a *thorow-fought assault. **1822** SCOTT *Pirate* iv, The small beer of the college, commonly there termed '*thorough-go-nimble'. **1825** BROCKETT *N.C. Words*, *Thorough-go-nimble*, a diarrhœa. **1617** HIERON *Wks.* II. 77 To bring Dauid to these two specialties: first, of *thorow-humbling himselfe; secondly, of making an acknowledgement. **1605** SYLVESTER *Du Bartas* II. iii. III. *Law* 1006 A cloak of clouds, all *thorough-lin'd with thunder. **1649** LOVELACE *To Deare Bro. Col. F. L.* v, One gallant *thorough-made Resolve Doth Starry Influence dissolve. **1669** WORLIDGE *Syst. Agric.* (1681) 153 They get more in the *through-ripe Hop by the weight, than they loose in the colour. **1707** MORTIMER *Husb.* (1721) II. 347 Cyder pressed from pulpy, or thorough-ripe, or mellow Fruit. **1658** A. FOX *Würtz' Surg.* I. iv. 18 If..sharper things should be used, they would thorough-run the Wound. **1598** SYLVESTER *Du Bartas* II. i. I. *Eden* 62 The *thorough-seasoned But Wherein the tears of death-prest Grapes are put. **1649** LOVELACE *Poems* 50 Thee and thy wounds I would bemoane Faire *thorough-shot Religion. **1642** H. MORE *Song Soul* I. III. xxiv, Here fifty Sisters in a sieve do draw *Thorough-siping water: Tantalus is here. **1730** SWIFT *Vind. Ld. Cartaret* ¶28 Our *thoroughsped republic of Whigs. **1898** T. HARDY *Wessex Poems* 63 Never upon me Had she thrown look of love so thorough-sped. **1593** NASHE *Christ's T.* Wks. (Grosart) IV. 216 Spotting and *thorow-stayning thy deere bought Spyrit.

2. Combinations with sbs. or derived adjs. (cf. THOROUGH *a.*): ˈ**thorough-ˌband** (ˈ**through-band**), a stone, etc., extending through the breadth of a wall or dyke so as to bind the sides together (cf. *band-stone*, BAND *sb.*^{1} 15); also *attrib.*; **thorough-blood** *a.*, of pure breed (said of a horse); cf. FULLBLOOD; ˈ**thorough-door**, a door leading through; the door of a passage; ˈ**thorough-draught** (ˈ**through-draught**), a draught or current of air passing through a room, etc. (in quot. 1866, a channel or passage for a draught of air); ˈ**thorough-edged** *a.*, thoroughly or perfectly edged; keen-edged; ˈ**thorough-foot**, a disarrangement in a tackle caused by one or both of the blocks getting entangled in the fall (cf. *thorough-put*); ˈ**thorough-hearted** *a.*, whole-hearted, entirely devoted; hence *thorough-ˈheartedness*; ˈ**thorough-joint** (*Anat.*), a perfectly movable joint or articulation (cf. DIARTHROSIS); ˈ**thorough-put**, a knot or tangle upon a rope formed by putting one part of it through a loop in another (cf. *thorough-foot*); †ˈ**thorough-road** = THOROUGHFARE *sb.* (in quot. *attrib.*); ˈ**thorough-shot**, see quot.; **thorough-**

souled *a.*, to one's inmost soul, downright; **thorough-stem**, see quot.; †'**thorough-touch** (†'**through-touch**), a touch that penetrates the soul, a deep spiritual impression; '**thorough-winded** *a.* (of a horse), sound in 'wind' or breathing; not broken-winded. See also THOROUGHBASS to THOROUGHWORT.

1805 DICKSON *Pract. Agric.* I. Pl. xxix, The *through band turf..being first lightly laid. **1810** S. SMITH *Agric. Surv. Galloway* vi. 88 It is essential to the durability of a dyke..that the two sides be well bound together by long stones laid across, termed throughbands. **1844** STEPHENS *Bk. Farm* III. 1007 It tends much to the stability of a dyke to have what is called a thorough-band stone..placed across it. **1829** *Sporting Mag.* XXIII. 271 Our nearly *thorough-blood hunter and carriage horses. **1827** G. DARLEY *Sylvia* 32 But you may catch his sullen roar More loud when opes the *thorough-door. **1853** C. M. YONGE *Heir of Redclyffe* II. ix. 141 Three rooms..opening into each other..so that it was possible to produce a *thorough draught. **1866** HOWELLS *Venet. Life* iii, The narrow streets are bitter thorough-drafts. **1868** *Rep. U.S. Commissioner Agric.* (1869) 438 The windows are closed and matted, and no thorough-draught is allowed. **1905** *Daily Chron.* 22 July 8/5 The drawing-room is..spared the desecrating through-draught. **1830** TENNYSON *Isabel* ii, The intuitive decision of a bright And *thorough-edged intellect to part Error from crime. **1867** *Thorough-foot [see *thorough-put*]. **1887** *Athenæum* 31 Dec. 883/3 The *thorough-heartedness with which Barnes threw himself into this. **18..** COUES (Cent. Dict.), *Thorough-joint. **1829** GEN. P. THOMPSON *Exerc.* (1842) I. 112 Knots, of different degrees of complexity, from a simple *thorow-put, to a complication of loops and twists [etc.]. **1867** SMYTH *Sailor's Word-bk.*, *Thorough-puts*, or *Thorough-foots*, are kinks or tangles in a rope; or parts of a tackle not leading fair by reason of one of the blocks having been passed round part of the fall. *a* **1661** FULLER *Worthies, Lond.* (1662) II. 224 He built at Buntingford (a *thorow-road market..) a neat and strong Chappel. **1891** *Cent. Dict.*, **Thorough-shot*, same as *thorough-pin*. **1842** POE *Lett.* (1948) I. 193, I cannot bring myself to like that man... He is too *thorough-souled a time-server. **1891** *Cent. Dict.*, **Thorough-stem*, same as *thorough-wort*. **1607** HIERON *Wks.* I. 459 Nothing which may argue a *through-touch, or a comfortable expectation of Gods fauour. **1617** *Ibid.* II. 72 Whether we haue receiued any such thorow-touch as is the ..fruit of true repentance. **1737** BRACKEN *Farriery Impr.* (1757) II. Pref. 11 You shall hear many a Horse praised for being a *thorow-winded one.

thorough-band to **-bore**: see THOROUGH-.

thoroughbass (ˈθʌrəbeɪs). *Mus.* [f. THOROUGH *prep.* or *adv.* + BASS *sb.*[5]; cf. BASSO *continuo*.] A bass part extending through a piece of music, and written by itself, with figures indicating the chords or harmonies to be played with it; a figured bass, *basso continuo*; *esp.* (formerly) an accompaniment thus written or played; hence *loosely*, an accompaniment in general (also *fig.*). Also, the method of indicating harmonies by a figured bass, or the art of playing from it; *loosely*, the science of harmony in general.

1662 PLAYFORD *Skill Mus.* I. ii. (1674) 36 The Figures usually placed over Notes in the Thorough-Bass of Songs or Ayres. **1685** EVELYN *Mem.* 10 Mar., She had an excellent voice, to which she play'd a thorough bass on the harpsichord. **1731** KELLER in *Holder's Harmony* 159 Rules for Playing a Thorow-bass. **1778** H. WALPOLE *Let. to H.S. Conway* 8 July, Tumults would be a dreadful thorough bass to speeches. **1845** E. HOLMES *Mozart* 258 He..wrote a treatise on thorough bass. **1875** STEDMAN *Vict. Poets* i. 3 Full-throated, happy minstrels, like Béranger or Burns, need no knowledge of thorough-bass and the historical range of composition.

¶ **b.** *erron.* A loud or deep bass.

1749 FIELDING *Tom Jones* v. ix, He found..his nurse snoring..at the bed's feet. He immediately took the only method of silencing this thorough bass, whose music he feared might disturb Mr. Allworthy. **1835** W. IRVING *Crayon Misc.* (1849) 30 He..had..a whiffling double voice, shifting abruptly from a treble to a thorough-bass.

thorough-bolt: see *through-bolt*, THROUGH- 2.

thoroughbrace (ˈθʌrə(ʊ)breɪs). *U.S.* [f. THOROUGH *prep.* or *adv.* + BRACE *sb.*[2] 11.]

a. Each of a pair of strong braces or bands of leather connecting the front and back C-springs and supporting the body of a coach or other vehicle.

1837 HT. MARTINEAU *Soc. Amer.* II. 175 Half a mile before reaching the place..the thorough-brace broke, and we had to walk..to the inn. **1858** O. W. HOLMES *Deacon's Masterp.* 22 In building of chaises..There is always somewhere a weakest spot,—In hub, tire, felloe, in spring or thill,..In screw, bolt, thoroughbrace.

†**b.** A vehicle whose body is supported on thoroughbraces. *Obs.*

1886 *Leslie's Pop. Monthly* Dec. 722/1 The mustangs looked worse than the thorough-brace itself. **1930** A. W. GROOM *Merry Christmas* xv. 111 The heavily laden thoroughbrace was hitched behind seven lively horses.

Hence '**thoroughbraced** (-breɪst) *a.*, suspended by thoroughbraces.

1865 *Harper's Mag.* Nov. 700/1 Preference to be given to a thorough-braced ambulance of Concord manufacture. **1884** S. O. JEWETT *Country Doctor* 19 The old-fashioned thorough-braced wagon.

thoroughbred (ˈθʌrəbrɛd), *a.* (*sb.*) Also 8 **through-bred**. [f. THOROUGH *adv.* + BRED *ppl. a.*[1]]

1. Thoroughly educated or accomplished; hence, complete, thorough, out-and-out. (Now regarded as *fig.* from 2: cf. 2 b.)

1701 GREW *Cosm. Sacra* II. vii. 77 A through-bred Soldier weighs all present Circumstances, and all possible Contingents. **1721** AMHERST *Terræ Fil.* No. 47 (1754) 253 Nothing can restrain a thorough-bred gamester. **1874** L. STEPHEN *Hours in Library* (1892) I. ix. 300 A thoroughbred utilitarian, full of sagacity. **1882** MISS BRADDON *Mt. Royal* III. i. 20 He never handled a gun like a thoroughbred sportsman.

2. Of a horse: Of pure breed or stock; *spec.* applied to a race-horse whose pedigree for a given number of generations is recorded in the studbook. Also of a dog, bull, etc.

1796 J. LAWRENCE *Treat. Horses* iv. 166 Thorough-bred hacks are the most docile and quiet, and the least liable to shy. **1825** N. H. SMITH *Breeding for Turf* 5 The pedigree of Eclipse affords a singular illustration of the descent of our thorough-bred horses from pure Eastern blood. **1840–70** BLAINE *Encycl. Rur. Sports* §930 The term thorough-bred, as relating to a horse..is neither critically nor conventionally definite. **1856** *Farmer's Mag.* Jan. 29 There are some men who prefer the cross-bred animal—the best I believe to be between the Hampshire Down and Cotswold; but..I must give a decided preference to the thorough-bred. **1887** SIR R. H. ROBERTS *In the Shires* i. 18 Mounted upon a thoroughbred..bay mare.

b. *transf.* Applied to human beings or their attributes: sometimes implying characteristics like those of a thoroughbred horse, as gracefulness, energy, distinction, etc. (Cf. B. 2.)

1820 BYRON *Juan* v. cvi, More thorough-bred or fairer fingers. **1864** TREVELYAN *Compet. Wallah* (1866) 345 It is hardly possible for a man brought up amidst European.. associations to realize the idea conceived of him..by a thorough-bred Hindoo.

Comb. **1882** MISS BRADDON *Mt. Royal* ix, Who the deuce is that thoroughbred-looking girl?

B. *sb.* **1.** A thoroughbred animal, esp. a horse.

1842 THACKERAY *Fitz-Boodle Pap.* Pref., I can't afford a thorough-bred, and hate a cock-tail. **1887** 'H. SMART' *Cleverly Won* i, Three or four thorough-breds that he had reared.

2. *transf.* and *fig.*: A well-born, well-bred, or thoroughly trained person. Also a first-rate motorcar, bicycle, or other vehicle.

1894 H. GARDENER *Unofficial Patriot* 15 There is rather a paucity of thoroughbreds among the Methodists. **1894** *Outing* (U.S.) XXIV. 281/2 An air..that made you feel sure that she could play tennis or sail a boat. In fact, she looked a thoroughbred. **1901** *Pall Mall Mag.* Sept. 67/2 A vehicle running a race must in some mysterious way be a thoroughbred. **1908** *Daily Chron.* 21 Nov. 9/4 This machine [bicycle] and all the thorough-breds..are now..treated before enamelling to the special Coslett non-rusting process, which preserves the metal from all corrosion.

Hence '**thorough,bredness**.

1894 ELIZ. L. BANKS *Camp. Curiosity* 127 As regards the thorough-bredness of my black poodle.

thorough-cleansing, etc.: see THOROUGH-.

'**thorough-drain**, *v. Agric.* [f. THOROUGH *adv.* (or *sb.* 3) + DRAIN *v.*] *trans.* To drain (a field) by means of water-thoroughs or -furrows; also, to drain thoroughly.

1844 STEPHENS *Bk. Farm* I. 489 As by this kind of draining [surface-draining] the land is thoroughly or effectually drained, it has been most appropriately called thorough-draining. *Ibid.* 593 A farmer..thorough-drained one-half of a 4-acre field. *Ibid.* 662 The subsoil will afford a sufficient quantity of stones, to thorough-drain the ground. **1847** RAYNBIRD in *Jrnl. R. Agric. Soc.* VIII. II. 311 The term thorough-draining is perhaps derived from the old word 'thorrow', which Bradley mentions as 'a distinguishing character for a trench cut purposely for carrying off of water'.

thoroughfare (ˈθʌrəfɛə(r)), *sb.* (*a.*) Forms: 4–5 **thurghfare**, 5 **thurghe-**; **thoruȝ faar**, **thoruhfare**, 6 **thorowe**, **thoroughe**, **thorough fare**, 6–8 **thorowfare**, 7–8 **thorow-**, **thorough-fare**, (7 **thorow-faire**, **thorough fair**, 7–8 **thorow-**, **thorough-fair**, 8 **thorowfair**, 8–9 **thorofare**), 7– **thoroughfare**. *β.* 5 *Sc.* **throchtfayr**, 6 **throw-fare**, *Sc.* **throuchfair**, **throuche fair**, 6–7 **through fare**, **through-fare**, 7–9 **throughfare**. [In ME. *thurghfare*, 15th c. *thoruȝ faar*, f. *þurh*, *þuruh*, THROUGH + FARE *sb.*[1], OE. *faru* passage, way, track: cf. THOROUGH- 2. Cf. Du. *doorvaart* (*deurvaerd*, Kilian) passage, esp. passage for ships (cf. 1 d below), LG. *dörfard*, MHG. *durchvart*, G. *durchfahrt*.]

1. A passage or way through.

a. In general sense; also *fig.* Now usually merged in sense c, exc. in phr. ***no thoroughfare***, no public way through or right of way here.

c **1386** CHAUCER *Knt.'s T.* 1989 This world nys but a thurghfare ful of wo, And we been pilgrymes, passynge to and fro. **1430–40** LYDG. *Bochas* I. i. (MS. Bodl. 263) lf. 11/2 This world is a thoruhfare [*ed.* 1554 throw-fare] ful of wo. **1596** SHAKS. *Merch. V.* II. vii. 41 The Hircanion deserts, and the vaste wildes Of wide Arabia are as throughfares now For Princes to come view faire Portia. **1601** WEEVER *Mirr. Mart.* B iv, Yet makes the wood my through-fare into heauen. **1641** HINDE *J. Bruen* lviii. 195 You..rather glory to have your house made a thorough-fare of profane persons. **1797–1802** G. COLMAN *Br. Grins, Elder Bro.* (1819) 117 Making their throats a thorough-fare for wine. *a* **1817** JANE AUSTEN *Persuasion* (1818) III. xi. 235 The 'no-thoroughfare of Lyme'. **1822** BYRON *Juan* VII. xi, To hint, at least, 'Here is no thoroughfare'. **1856** EMERSON *Eng. Traits, Ability* Wks. (Bohn) II. 41 They have made the island a thoroughfare; and London a shop..inviting to strangers. **1893** HUXLEY *Sci. & Chr. Tradit.* Pref. (1894) 8 Before me stood the thorny barrier with its comminatory noticeboard —'No Thoroughfare. By order. Moses'.

†**b.** *spec.* A town through which traffic passes; a town on a highway or line of traffic. *Obs.*

c **1440** *Promp. Parv.* 493/2 Thurghfare, *oppidum*. *c* **1449** PECOCK *Repr.* v. vii. (Rolls) 521 Whi in a town which is a thoruȝ faar toward Londoun ben so manye ostries clepid innes? **1530** PALSGR. 200/1 Borowe or thorowe fare, *bourc*. *Ibid.* 281/1 Throwfare, *bourgade, bourc*. *a* **1552** LELAND *Itin.* IV. 131 From Uxbridge to Southall a Village about 6 Miles. Thence to Acton a pretty Through-Fare a 4 Miles. **1619** DALTON *Country Just.* vii. (1630) 32 In Townes which are no thorow-fare the Justices shall..be sparing of allowing of any alehouse. **1769** *De Foe's Tour Gt. Brit.* I. 87 Newmarket.. being a Thorough-fare, reaps no small Advantage by that Means, as well as from the Races. **1829** SCOTT *Anne of G.* vii, The little castle and town of Ferette..served as a thoroughfare to the traffic of Berne and Soleure.

c. A road, street, lane, or path forming a communication between two other roads or streets, or between two places; a public way unobstructed and open at both ends; *esp.* a main road or street, a highway.

1540 *Act 32 Hen. VIII*, c. 17 Chauncerie lane... And.. Fewter lane, being thorough fares and passages from Fletestrete into Holborne. **1628** WITHER *Brit. Rememb.* IV. 251 The Strand, that goodly thorow-fare betweene The Court and City. **1658** W. BURTON *Itin. Anton.* 2 Those publick Through-fares, or Waies, which the Souldiers raised. **1796** W. MARSHALL *W. England* II. 54 It is a large inland Market Town; but has no thorofare to support it. **1843** BETHUNE *Sc. Fireside Stor.* 275 One of the thoroughfares to the metropolis passed through the place.

d. A piece of water, as a strait or river, affording passage for ships, etc.; an unobstructed channel. (In definite application to a particular channel, chiefly *U.S.*; otherwise a special case of the general sense.)

1699 ROBERTS *Voy. Levant* 32 There is a Thoroughfare between the Mainland..and this Isle. **1712** E. COOKE *Voy. S. Sea* 127 There is a Thorough-Fare in the Midst of it, where we rode with our Ships. **1739** *Descr. Windward Passage* (ed. 2) 6 A Thorough-fare for Shipping between some Islands, or other Land, as..the Gulf of Messina between the Island of Sicily and Italy. **1856** STANLEY *Sinai & Pal.* ii. 113 The Mediterranean was not yet the thoroughfare—it was rather the boundary..of the eastern nations.

(*b*) **1848** THOREAU *Maine W.* (1894) 46 After one mile of river, or what the boatmen call 'thoroughfare'—for the river becomes at length only the connecting link between the lakes,—..we entered the North Twin Lake. **1896** *Trans. Roy. Soc. Canada* II. ii. 210 *Thoroughfare*, a passage between lakes on the same level.

e. 'A strait of water, or neck of land connecting two bodies of water, habitually traversed by wild fowl in migrating or passing to and from their feeding-grounds' (Hallock *Sportsman's Gazetteer* 1883, Gloss.).

2. The action of going or passing through, or the condition of being passed through or traversed; passage. Now *rare* or *Obs.*

1667 MILTON *P.L.* x. 393 Ye..have..made one Realm Hell and this World, one Realm, one Continent Of easie thorough-fare. **1668** CULPEPPER & COLE *Barthol. Anat.* I. x. 23 Made hard and callous, by the continual thoroughfare of the Chylus. **1810** *Sporting Mag.* XXXVI. 57 Till custom had grown into a right of thoroughfare. **1868** STANLEY *Westm. Abb.* i. 4 The River Thames..here widening to an almost majestic size, yet not too wide for thoroughfare.

3. *attrib.* or *adj.* That is a thoroughfare; passed or travelled through by traffic; chiefly in ***thoroughfare town*** = sense 1 b.

[Cf. OE. *þurhfere* passable, in *Ags. Hymnar.* (Surtees) 112, 9 (Bosw.-T.) ȝeat þurhfere.]

1553 *Reg. Privy Council Scot.* I. 143 All villages and throuchfair townis of this realme. **1564** *Yorks. Chantry Surv.* (Surtees) 264 [Boroughbridge] being one thoroughffare towne of the Kinges strete. **1592** *Sc. Acts Jas. VI* (1814) III. 576/1 At the principall throuche fair townis and paroche kirkis. *a* **1661** FULLER *Worthies, Hartford.* (1662) II. 25 William of Ware born in that thorough fair Town twenty miles from London. **1674** N. FAIRFAX *Bulk & Selv.* 146 The two ends of the Earths throughfare line or diameter. **1841** LANE *Arab. Nts.* I. 76 Most of the great thoroughfare streets. **1908** *Westm. Gaz.* 10 June 2/1 How seldom must these ancient [Italian] walled villages communicate with the thoroughfare-valleys, or the railway, or distant Rome!

'**thoroughfare**, *v. rare.* [In early use, OE. *þurhféran* (also *þurhfaran* str. vb.) to pass through, traverse: cf. Du. *doorvaren* (*deurvaeren*, Kilian), LG. *dorfaren*; OHG. *durahfaran*, Ger. *durchfahren*. In 2 from (or after) prec. sb.]

1. *trans.* To go, pass, or travel through.

a **900** tr. *Bæda's Hist.* IV. ii. (1890) 258 He sona ðurhferde eall Breotone ealond. *a* **1225** *Leg. Kath.* 1147 Hu mei he helpen oðre..þe þurhferde deað as heo doð? [**1674**, **1895**: see *thoroughfaring* below.]

2. To pass through or traverse, as a road; to form a thoroughfare in or across.

1886 LOWELL *Progr. World* in *Latest Lit. Ess.* (1891) 163 Those..slits that thoroughfared the older town.

So †**'thoroughfared** *a. Obs.* [f. prec. sb. + -ED[2]], having a thoroughfare or passage, perforated; †**'thorough-farer** (**'through-farer**) *Obs.*, one who goes or travels through, a wayfarer; **'thorough-faring** (**'throughfaring**), a going, passing, or travelling through; **'thoroughfaresome** (**'through-faresome**) *a.*, (*a*) capable of being passed through, penetrable; (*b*) relating to passing through.

1668 CULPEPPER & COLE *Barthol. Anat.* II. vii. 111 When the Ventricles are dilated above the *through-far'd Septum ..the little holes would be shut up. **1626** in *10th Rep. Hist. MSS. Comm.* App. v. 474 [To] entertaine *through-farers and passengers. **1674** N. FAIRFAX *Bulk & Selv.* 90 There would be..no *throughfarings of the least steams or reekings of bodies. **1895** A. NUTT *Voy. Bran* I. 301 A road worn with much thoroughfaring. **1674** N. FAIRFAX *Bulk & Selv.* 138 All body being as *throughfaresom to ghost, as tis stopping to body. **1863** DE MORGAN *Let. to Whewell* in *Life* (1882) 319, I feel helped by the word διέναι, because it is a very thoroughfaresome word... It is used for going *through* a country, or for running a man *through* the body.

thorough-felt to **-fought**: see THOROUGH-.

†**'thoroughgate.** *Obs.* In 5 throgat, 6–7 thorowgate. [f. THOROUGH *adv.* + GATE *sb.*[2]] A passage through: = THOROUGHFARE *sb.* 1.

1456 *Burgh Rec. Peebles* (1872) 117 The throgat sal serf tham bath vp throu and don throu. **1598** R. BERNARD tr. *Terence, Adelphi* IV. ii, That corner is no thorow gate [*angiportum non pervium*]. **1639** HORN & ROB. *Gate Lang. Unl.* lviii. §617 Lanes most commonly are unpasseable, and have no thorow-gate.

thoroughgoing ('θʌrəˌgəʊɪŋ), *a.* [f. THOROUGH *adv.* + *going*, pr. pple. of GO *v.* See also THROUGHGOING.] Going the full length; doing things thoroughly; acting with completeness; uncompromising, thorough, extreme, out-and-out. (Of persons, actions, etc.)

1800 M. EDGEWORTH *Parent's Assistant* (ed. 3) VI. 168, I am a *thorough-going* friend at any rate. **1819** SCOTT *Leg. Montrose* xiii, A thoroughgoing friend that understands a hint is worth a million! **1838** THIRLWALL *Greece* IV. xxxi. 194 They now proceeded to bolder and more thorough-going measures. **1856** R. A. VAUGHAN *Mystics* (1860) II. 18 What seems..the thorough-going madness of the fiery Persian. **1888** BRYCE *Amer. Commw.* I. 120 Jefferson..was a thorough-going party leader.

Hence **'thorough'goingly** *adv.*; **'thorough-'goingness.** So **'thorough'goer**, a thorough-going person or animal; **'thorough,going** *sb.*, the action or habit of doing things thoroughly.

1895 *Outing* (U.S.) 388/1 The horses [polo-ponies] are such *thoroughgoers in the field that it is difficult to say this or the other is best. **1851** J. D. BURNS *Jrnl.* in *Mem.* iv. (1869) 66 Much..is said about *thoroughgoing and decision of character. **1886** *N.E.D.* s.v. Boot *sb.*[3] 1 b, *Like old boots*: vigorously, *thoroughgoingly. **1838** C. GILMAN *Recoll. Southern Matron* xxviii. 194 The gentleman had even the *thoroughgoingness to request that my brother's large, stout new slate might be exchanged for a recently-invented tablet. **1865** M. ARNOLD *Ess. Crit.* ii. 65 The newspaper, with its party spirit, its thorough-goingness. **1867** PEARSON *Hist. Eng.* I. 35 The Roman sword did its work..with terrible thorough-goingness.

thorough-go-nimble to **thorough-lined**: see THOROUGH- *in comb.* 1, 2.

'thoroughleaf. ? *Obs.* In 6 thorow-. [f. THOROUGH *adv.* + LEAF *sb.*[1]] = THOROUGHWAX.

1578 LYTE *Dodoens* I. xcv. 136 Of Thorowwaxe, or Thorowleafe. Thorowleafe hath a round, slender stalke ful of branches, yᵉ branches passing, or going thorow the leaues. **1597** [see THOROUGHWAX]. **1866** *Treas. Bot.* 181 *Bupleurum.* Hare's-ear, Thorow-wax, or Thorow-leaf.

'thorough-light. Now *rare* or *Obs.* Also **'through-light.**

a. *pl.* Windows on opposite sides of a room, so that the light passes right through.

1625 BACON *Ess., Building* (Arb.) 551 And let all three Sides, be a double House, without Thorow Lights, on the Sides, that you may haue Roomes from the Sunne, both for Fore-noone, and Afternoone. **1642** FULLER *Holy & Prof. St.* III. vii. 167 Thorow-lights are best for rooms of entertainment, and windows on one side for dormitories. **1697** DRYDEN *Æneid* VIII. 349 The doors, unbarr'd, receive the rushing day; And thorough lights disclose the ravish'd prey. **1745** P. THOMAS *Jrnl. Anson's Voy.* 230 The Houses have thorough Lights.

b. *fig.* (*sing.* and *pl.*) in reference to the 'light' of knowledge or discovery.

1605 BACON *Adv. Learn.* II. ii. §13 This great Building of the world had neuer through lights made in it till the age of vs and our fathers. **1642** FULLER *Holy & Prof. St.* II. xxi. 137 [Drake] returned safe into England, and landed at Plimouth, (being almost the first of those that made a thorow-light through the world). **1646** TRAPP *Comm. John* i. 5 The former [light of nature] is but a dim half-light... The latter [light of Scripture] is a clear thorough-light. **1698** NORRIS *Pract. Disc.* IV. 44 All shall be then open,..every Man's Heart a thorough-light to every Man. **1841** EMERSON *Lect. 'Times'* Wks. (Bohn) II. 256 Paving the earth with eyes, destroying privacy, and making thorough-lights.

So **'thorough-lighted** (**'through-**) *a.*, having thorough-lights; having the light passing through.

1624 WOTTON *Archit.* in *Reliq.* (1651) 286 Rooms windowed on both ends, which we call through-lighted. **1703** T. N. *City & C. Purchaser* 260 Rooms are said to be Through-lighted when they have Windows on both ends. **1842–76** GWILT *Archit.* Gloss., *Thorough lighted Rooms*, such as have windows on opposite sides.

thoroughly ('θʌrəlɪ), *adv.* [f. THOROUGH *adv.* or *adj.* + -LY[2]. See also THROUGHLY.]

†**1.** In a way that penetrates or goes through; right through, quite through. *Obs. rare.*

With quots. 1633, 1703 cf. THROUGHLY *adv.* 2.

c **1300** *Havelok* 680 Godard..lokede on him þoruth-like, with eyne grim. **1633** W. MULSHO in *Buccleuch MSS.* (Hist. MSS. Comm.) I. 273, I would have gone home (wet thoroughly). **1703** MAUNDRELL *Journ. Jerus.* (1732) 9 Thorowly soaked with the wet.

2. In a thorough manner or degree; in every part or detail; in all respects; with nothing left undone; fully, completely, wholly, entirely, perfectly.

1473 *Rolls of Parlt.* VI. 66/1 In cas all other things were thoroughly passed and concluded betwixt his Highnes and theym. **1522** MORE *De Quat. Noviss.* Wks. 76/2 We knew them..yet not so very thorowly as we might peraduenture. **1593** SHAKS. *2 Hen. VI*, I. i. 202 To looke into this Businesse thorowly. **1643** BURROUGHES *Exp. Hosea* iv. (1652) 77 This promise is not yet thoroughly fulfilled. **1736** BUTLER *Anal.* II. vi. 224 Whoever will weigh the Matter thoroughly. **1846** RUSKIN *Mod. Paint.* (1851) I. II. I. vii. §10 The thoroughly great men are those who have done everything thoroughly. **1878** HUTTON *Scott* iii. 35 She had a thoroughly kindly nature.

thoroughness ('θʌrənɪs). [f. THOROUGH *a.* + -NESS.] The quality of being thorough or of doing things thoroughly; the condition of being done thoroughly; completeness of execution or treatment; completeness in general, perfectness.

1843 PRESCOTT *Mexico* (1850) I. 152 A book of the highest authority, for the perspicuity, fidelity, and thoroughness, with which the multifarious topics in it are discussed. **1848** MILL *Pol. Econ.* I. vii. §3 The thoroughness of their application to work. **1862** DANA *Man. Geol.* II. 245 The exception to the thoroughness of the extinction in the Eastern border region. **1897** E. K. CHAMBERS in *Bookman* Jan. 113/1 He has emulated the Teutonic thoroughness without the Teutonic pedantry.

thoroughoute, etc., obs. forms of THROUGHOUT.

thorough-paced ('θʌrəpeɪst), *a.* Also β. 7 through-paced. [f. THOROUGH *adv.* + PACED.]

1. *lit.* Of a horse: Thoroughly trained; having all his paces. *rare.* ? *Obs.*

a **1661** FULLER *Worthies, Huntington.* (1662) II. 51 It is given to thorough-paced-Naggs, that amble naturally, to trip much whilest artificial pacers goe surest on foot.

β. **1668** *Lond. Gaz.* No. 272/4 A Baye Mare,..flat ribb'd, Roach back'd, through paced.

2. *fig.* Thoroughly trained or accomplished, perfectly skilled or versed (*in* something); hence, thoroughgoing, complete, perfect, thorough.

1646 JENKYN *Remora* 18 The thorow-pac'd Politician borrows this of the Atheist. **1678** CUDWORTH *Intell. Syst.* I. iv. §30. 382 Anaxagoras..was severely taxed..as one not thorough-paced in Theism. **1710** PALMER *Proverbs* 114 A thoro'-pac'd villain. *a* **1715** BURNET *Own Time* an. 1681 (1823) II. 278 Men of a thorough-paced obsequiousness. **1823** LAMB *Elia* Ser. II. *Old Margate Hoy*, A hearty thorough-paced liar. **1850** GROTE *Greece* II. lvi. VII. 132 Introducing more thorough-paced oligarchy into the already oligarchical Sikyônian government. **1893** *Spectator* 28 Jan. 101/2 A thorough-paced English gentleman.

β. **1655** FULLER *Church Hist.* I. iv. §13 Constantius was a through-paced Christian. **1658** PHILLIPS *Dict.* Ded., An universally through-pac't Dictionary. *a* **1661** FULLER *Worthies, Huntington.* (1662) II. 50 He was through-paced in three Tongues, Latine, Greek..and Hebrew. **1691** WOOD *Ath. Oxon.* I. 535 Robert Burton..was..a thro-pac'd Philologist.

So †**'thorough-pace** *v. Obs. intr.* of a horse; †**'thorough-,pacer**, a horse having all his paces.

1684 *Lond. Gaz.* No. 1945/4 A bay Nag..seven years old, a thorough pacer. **1690** *Ibid.* No. 2545/4 A light sorrel Gelding,..walks, thorough-paces and gallops.

thorough-passage: see THROUGH-PASSAGE.

thorough-pierce: see *through-pierce*, in THROUGH- 1.

thorough-pin ('θʌrəpɪn). *Farriery.* [f. THOROUGH- + PIN *sb.*[1] (cf. sense 10).] A swelling in the sheath of the tendon of the flexor perforans muscle in a horse's hock, appearing on both sides so as to suggest a pin passing through; also a similar swelling in the carpal joint of the fore-leg. Cf. earlier *through serewe*, etc.: s.v. THROUGH- 2.

1789 *Bath Jrnl.* 22 June Advt., [A pony] with a spavin and thorough pins. **1831** YOUATT *Horse* 265 We have spoken of wind-galls... A similar enlargement is found above the hock... As from its situation it must necessarily project on both sides of the hock, in the form of a round swelling, it is called a thorough-pin. **1906** *Daily News* 20 Apr. 6 Amitie, a very well-bred mare, is marred by a thorough-pin.

thoroughpost: see THROUGHPOST.

thorough-put to **-run**, etc.: see THOROUGH-.

†**thorough-'see**, *v. Obs.* [OE. *þurh séon*, f. *þurh* THOROUGH, THROUGH *adv.* + *séon* to SEE: cf. OHG. *durhsehen*, Ger. *durchsehen.*] *trans.* To see through (*lit.* and *fig.*: cf. SEE *v.* 24). Hence †**thorough-'seeing** *vbl. sb.*, the action of this vb.; *ppl. a.* that sees through; †**thorough-'seeable** *a.*, capable of being seen through, transparent.

c **888** K. ÆLFRED *Boeth.* xli. §1 He ȝeseohð & þurhseohð ealle his ȝesceafta ændemest. *a* **1200** *Moral Ode* 90 (Lambeth) He þurþ-sicheþ uches monnes þonc [*v.r.* þurh-sihð elches mannes þanc]. *a* **1225** *Ancr. R.* 50 Þe blake cloð ..is þiccure..& wurse to þurhseon. **1553** GRIMALDE *Cicero's Offices* (1556) 7 Whoso thorowseeth moste what in everye case is truest. *Ibid.* 68 So desireful of thorow seing and learning the nature of things. **1561** T. HOBY tr. *Castiglione's Courtyer* IV. (1577) X viij b, The eyes of the minde..then beginne to be sharp and thorough seing, when the eyes of the body lose the floure of theyr sightlynesse. **1562** TURNER *Herbal* II. 151 The rosin or turpentine [of Terebinthus]..is clere, & thorow seable, whyte, like a glasse & blewish gray.

thorough-seek, -shining: see THROUGH-SEEK, -SHINING.

'thorough-stitch, 'through-stitch, *sb., adv.* and *adj. Obs.* exc. *dial.* [f. THOROUGH *adv.* + STITCH *sb.*]

†**A.** *sb.* ? A stitch drawn right through the stuff; hence *fig.* in reference to thoroughness of action: cf. B. *Obs. rare.*

a **1569** KINGESMYLL *Man's Est.* xv. (1580) 124 Now there fore to knitte vppe the knot, and to make a through stitch. **1663** COWLEY *Cutter Colman St.* II. viii, When I do a business, I'm for through-stich; I'm through pac'd.

B. *adv.* Right through, through to the end; thoroughly, completely; almost always in phr. *to go thorough-stitch* (*with*), to perform something thoroughly, carry it out completely and effectually, go through with: 'a tailor's expression for finishing any thing once begun' (Egan *Slang Dict.* 1823).

1579 GOSSON *Sch. Abuse, Apol.* (Arb.) 68 Philippe of Macedon tooke vpon him to reason with a new Musition.. and was not able to go thorowe stitche. **1596** NASHE *Saffron Walden* 37 That wee might haue made round worke, and gone thorough stitch. **1634** FORD *Perkin Warbeck* II. iii, He that threads his needle with the sharp eyes of industry shall in good time go throughstitch with the new suit of preferment. **1685** EVELYN *Diary* 22 May, The..Cheif Justice Jefferies..went thorough stitch in that tribunal. **1694** R. L'ESTRANGE *Fables* cxxxiii. (1714) 150 'Tis Perseverance alone that can carry us Thorough-Stitch. **1723** MANDEVILLE *Fab. Bees* (1725) I. 216 A Man of Honour enters into a Conspiracy with others to murder a King; he is obliged to go thorough Stich with it. **1824** *Blackw. Mag.* XV. 147 We have gone too far to retreat,..we must e'en go thorough-stitch. **1904** *Eng. Dial. Dict.* s.v. *Thorough*, She's means to do the place up thorough-stitch.

C. *adj.* Thoroughgoing, out-and-out. ? *Obs.*

c **1685** in *Verney Memoirs* (1907) II. 396 A thorough-stitch enemy to the crown. **1786** A. GIB *Sacr. Contempl.* 402 It may not suit with his courage or his prudence to be thorough-stitch with it. **1825** HAZLITT *Spirit of Age* 335 He ..must make thorough-stitch work of it. **1828** WILSON in *Blackw. Mag.* XXIII. 785 [He] seems to have no thorough-stitch advocate in the London press.

Hence †**'thorough-stitched**, **'through-stitched** *a.* = C.

1682 MRS. BEHN *City Heiress* 35 You are resolv'd to make a through-stitcht Robbery on't. **1799** T. TWINING in *Recreat. & Stud.* (1882) 233 What a painstaking, thorough-paced, thorough-stitched man you are when you set about anything!

thorough-stone: see THROUGH-STONE[2].

thoroughte, obs. form of THROUGHOUT.

thorough-toll: see THROUGH-TOLL.

thorough-touch: see THOROUGH- 2.

thoroughwax ('θʌrəwæks). Also 6- thorow-, 6 thorowe-, 7 through-, 6–7 waxe, 6- -wax. [f. THOROUGH *prep.* and *adv.* through + WAX *v.* to grow, after G. *durchwachs*; from the branches appearing to grow through the leaves.]

A name for the umbelliferous herb *Bupleurum rotundifolium*, also called *hare's-ear*, having roundish-oval perfoliate leaves, and small greenish-yellow flowers with conspicuous bracts.

1548 TURNER *Names Herbes* 85 Perfoliata is an herbe wyth a leafe lyke a pease... The Germans cal it Durchwassz. It may be called in englishe Thorowwax, because the stalke waxeth thorowe the leaues. **1578** LYTE *Dodoens* I. xcv. 137 This herbe is now called..in English Thorowwaxe and Thorowleafe. **1597** GERARDE *Herbal* II. cxlviii. §1. 429 Thorowe waxe or Thorowe leafe, hath a..stalke, diuided into manie small branches, which passe or go thorow the leaues. **1678** PHILLIPS (ed. 4), *Thorough-wax*,..a Martial Herb, somewhat bitter and astringent and good against Ruptures. **1828** J. E. SMITH *Eng. Flora* II. 93 *B*[*upleurum*] *rotundifolium.* Common Hare's-ear. Thorow-wax. **1925** E. MELLOR tr. *Bonnier's Brit. Flora* 76 *Bupleurum*..Leaves oval, perfoliate..Throw-wax. **1971** *Country Life* 4 Nov. 1192/1 Our cornfield weed thorow wax..is virtually extinct in Britain.

thorough-winded: see THOROUGH- 2.

thoroughwort ('θʌrəwɜːt). [f. THOROUGH *prep.* or *adv.* + WORT, after THOROUGHWAX.]

a. A North American composite plant, *Eupatorium perfoliatum*, having opposite leaves, each pair united at the base so that the stem appears to grow through them (connate-perfoliate), and large corymbs of numerous white flowers; valued for its tonic properties; also called *boneset* or *crosswort*. Also used as a name for other species of *Eupatorium*.

1814 J. BIGELOW *Florula Bostoniensis* 190 Thoroughwort ..has acquired great medicinal reputation. **1828** in WEBSTER. **1842** [see *number six* s.v. NUMBER *sb.* 19]. **1845–50** MRS. LINCOLN *Lect. Bot.* 185 Florets tubulous, without rays; as, boneset, or thoroughwort (Eupatorium). **1857** GRAY *First Lessons Bot.* (1866) 100 Cases of real leaves growing together.., those of the common Thorough-wort, and the upper pairs in Woodbines or Honeysuckles. **1893** F. P. HUMPHREY *New Eng. Cactus* 27 Aromatic herbs, pennyroyal, thoroughwort, and catnip. **1906** *Harper's Mag.* Oct. 712 The boggy place where she came..for..the wild marsh-marigold, good for greens, thoroughwort, and the root of the sweet-flag. **1968** PETERSON & MCKENNY *Field Guide to Wildflowers* 46 The thoroughworts..are composites of late summer and fall with numerous small fuzzy heads in rounded or flat-topped clusters.

†**b.** = THOROUGHWAX. *Obs. rare*⁻¹.

1597 GERARDE *Herbal, Table,* Throughwoort and his kinds.

thorow, obs. f. THOROUGH.

thorowout, thorowte, etc., obs. ff. THROUGHOUT.

thorp (θɔːp). *arch.* and *Hist.* Forms: *α.* 1 **ðrop** (**þrep**), 1–5 **þrop**, (4–5 **throop-e**, **þroup**), 4, 9 *dial.* **throp** (5 **thrope**). *β.* 1–2, 4–5 **þorp**, 5– **thorpe**, 5, 7– **thorp**. [OE. and ME. *þrop* and *þorp* hamlet, village, farm, or estate; Com. Teut. = OFris. *thorp, therp* village, mod.Fris. *terp* village, village-mound (see TERP[1]); OS. *thorp* (MLG., LG., MDu., Du. *dorp*, LG. and EFris. *dörp*); OHG. (MHG., Ger.) *dorf* village (locally 'gathering of people, meeting'); ON. *þorp* village, hamlet, farmstead (Norw. *torp*, Sw. *torp* cottage, little farm, Da. *torp* farmstead, hamlet, borough), Goth. *þaurp* estate, land, field:—OTeut. **þorpoᵐ*. Ulterior etymology doubtful; original sense and its development in the Teutonic languages not clear.

ON. has (app. thence derived) *þyrpast* to crowd, throng, *þyrping* crowd; and *þorp* is by many referred to same root as L. *turba* Gr. *τύρβη* crowd, tumult. Others compare L. *tribus* tribe, and OCelt. **treb* subdivision of a people, W. *tref* town. For other suggested cognates, cf. Kluge, Franck, Doornkaat-Koolman.]

A hamlet, village, or small town; in ME. *esp.* an agricultural village: see quots.

Not a frequent word in OE., being chiefly found in Glosses and Vocabularies, in form *þrop*, which was also the prevailing form in ME. down to 1400. *þorp* appears once in late OE. and in the north in 14th c., and may really be due to Norse influence. In various forms as *Thorpe, Throop, Thrupp*, the word occurs as a place-name, and it is a frequent second element in these in the forms *-thorpe, -thrup, -trup*, chiefly in the Danelaw district. It appears to have been a 'common noun' to Langland and Chaucer; but in Caxton to be a literalism of translation. As a separate word it has been used occasionally from 1600, but is app. only literary or archaic, rarely dialectal: see *Eng. Dial. Dict.*

α. *c* **725** *Corpus Gloss.* (O.E.T.) 557 *Conpetum* [= cross-ways, Carfax], tuun, þrop. *a* **800** *Erfurt Gloss.* 307 *Conpetum*, tuun, *vel* ðrop. *a* **1000** ÆLFRIC *Voc.* in Wr.-Wülcker 147/5 *Fundus* [= farm, piece of land], þrop. *a* **1000** *Ags. Gloss.* ibid. 207/14 *Competum*..i. *uilla, uel* þingstow, *uel* þrop. *c* **1200** *Trin. Coll. Hom.* 89 Bethfage, Swo hatte þe þrop þe preste one wunien, bi sides ierusalem. *c* **1350** *Will. Palerne* 2141 To seche eche cite & alle smale þropes. **1362** LANGL. *P. Pl.* A. II. 47 For lewede, for lerede, for laborers of þropes [*v.rr.* þrepis, þorpes]. **1393** *Ibid.* C. I. 219 As barouns & burgeis and bondemen of þroupes [*v.rr.* þropus, þropes, thorpys]. *c* **1386** CHAUCER *Wife's T.* 15 Citees, burghes, castels, hye toures, Thropes, bernes, shipnes, dayeryes, This maketh that ther been no ffairyes. —— *Clerk's T.* 143 Noght fer..There stood a throope [2 *MSS.*, throop 1, thrope 3, thorpt 1] of site delitable, In which that poure folk of that village, Hadden hir beestes and hir herbergage. *c* **1440** [see *β*].

β. *a* **1122** *O.E. Chron.* an. 963 (Laud MS.), Sce. Petres mynstre Medeshamstede..and ealle þa þorpes þe ðærto lin. **13..** *E.E. Allit. P.* B. 1178 He wast wyth werre þe wones of þorpes. *c* **1381** CHAUCER *Parl. Foules* 350 (MS. Gg. 4. 27) The kok that orloge is of thorpis lyte. *c* **1440** *Promp. Parv.* 492/1 Tho(r)pe, thrope, lytylle towne. **1481** CAXTON *Reynard* viii. (Arb.) 15 The worde anone sprange oueral in the thorpe [*Orig. Flem.* die mare die spranck over al den dorp]. **1485** —— *St. Wenefryde* 18 He reteynynge his felawe with hym abode that nyght in a thorpe. **1600** FAIRFAX *Tasso* XII. xxxii. 219 Within a little thorpe I staid at last. **1613** W. BROWNE *Brit. Past.* II. iii, About whose Thorps that night curs'd Limos went. **1814** WORDSW. *Excursion* VIII. 101 Welcome, wheresoe'er he came—Among the tenantry of thorpe and vill. **1855** TENNYSON *Brook* 29, I hurry down.. By twenty thorps, a little town, And half a hundred bridges. **1864** —— *En. Ard.* (end), The little thorp had seldom seen A costlier funeral.

Hence †'**thorpsman**, a villager. *Obs. rare.*

1674 N. FAIRFAX *Bulk & Selv.* To Rdr., The inbred stock of more homely women and less filching Thorps-men. **1876** *Whitby Gloss.*, *Thorpsmen*, villagers. Old local print.

thorpole, variant of THIRLEPOLL *Obs.*

thorrocke, Thorsday, obs. ff. THURROCK, THURSDAY.

thorst, obs. f. THIRST; obs. var. *durst*, pa. t. of DARE *v.*[1]

thort, obs. pa. t. of THARF; Sc. f. THWART.

thorter ('θɔːtə(r), *Sc.* 'θortər), *adv.*, *prep.*, *adj.*, *sb. Sc.* Forms: 5 **thwortour, thuortour, thourtour,** 5–6 **thortour,** 6 **-oure, -yr, -ir, -ar,** (**thortwart**), 7 **thorture,** 6– **thorter.** [In early forms *thwortour, thuortour, thortour*, Sc. forms of THWARTOVER: cf. Sc. *a-thort* = *a-thwart*. The second element has been so weakened as to appear a mere suffix, as in *easter, wester*, etc. *Thortwart* is a deformation.]

†**A.** *adv.* Athwart, across, crosswise. *Obs. rare.*

c **1470** HENRY *Wallace* v. 1110 Feill off thaim dede fell thwortour in [= into] in fyr.

B. *prep.* Athwart, across, overthwart.

1533 BELLENDEN *Livy* I. vi. (S.T.S.) I. 39 Incontinent þe buschment foresaid come thortoure þare gate. **1609** *Sc. Acts Jas. VI* (1816) IV. 443/2 Landis..beginnand at þe watter of Tarress..To rowaneburne and thorter Ingreis ȝeattis by the fute of magilwod. **1897** LD. E. HAMILTON *Outlaws* xviii. 209 You daurna show your face thorter the water.

C. *adj.* Crossing, lying athwart, transverse. ***thorter land***, land lying across or beyond a certain area, outer land; ***thorter way***, a cross-way; so ***thorter lane, road***, etc.

c **1470** HENRY *Wallace* IV. 540 A cleuch thar was, quharoff a strenth thai maid With thuortour treis. *Ibid.* IX. 1632 A thourtour bande, that all the drawcht wpbar, He cuttyt it. *c* **1475** *Rauf Coilȝear* 569 In ane thourtour way, Seir gaitis pas thay,..Thus partit thay twa. **1533** BELLENDEN *Livy* II. xvi. (S.T.S.) I. 194 Sic thingis done, he past fordwart with thortoure passage in [= into] þe latyne way. **1535** *Aberd. Reg.* XV. (Jam.), To remoif, red, & flit out of the said inland thortyrland, yard, & forentres. **1580** *Burgh Rec. Edinb.* (1882) IV. 185 To caus mak sufficient thorter barris of irne, and infix thaim in the window of the mid hous. **1814** *North Antiq.* 404 (Jam.) To look through an elf-bore in wood, where a thorter-knot..has been taken out. *Mod.* Forming part of local names: there is in Dundee a 'Thorter Row', which 'crosses' between the Nethergate and Overgate; in Hawick 'Thorter Dykes', beyond the Loan-head, etc.

†**b.** Coming athwart; obstructing, opposing.

1533 BELLENDEN *Livy* I. v. (S.T.S.) I. 35 The sabyne ladyis..be preiss of þair thortwart cuming devidit & put sindry þe armit oistis. **1536** —— *Cron. Scot.* III. iv. (1541) 27/1 Sa agill of thair bodyis, that thay may dant all thortour and difficill gatis.

†**D.** *sb.* Opposition, obstruction, resistance.

1581 J. MELVILL *Diary* (Wodrow Soc.) 124 The thrid thortar and debat quhilk he haid was with the provist, bailyies, and counsall..about their ministerie. **1598** *Ibid.* 532 Anent quhatsoevir the thorteris and accidentis fallin out.

Hence '**thorter** *v. trans.* and *intr.*, to cross the path or way of; to thwart or oppose (a person); hence '**thortering** *vbl. sb.*, thwarting, resisting; †'**thortersome** *a.*, tending to thwart, obstructive.

1608 JAS. VI *Let.* in Calderwood *Hist. Ch. Scot.* (1678) 581 Their willingness..hath been ever *thortered and impeded by too many..Advocations. **1671** M. BRUCE *Gd. News in Evil Times* (1708) 46 There is much Thortering with, and Murdering of Light in Scotland now, but Thortering of Light shall be the drearysomest Sin that ever Scotland had. **1890** J. SERVICE *Thir Notandums* xiv. 101 They [witches] made wee maiks oot o' clay..of them that had thortered them, stappin' the maiks fu o' preens. **1606** BIRNIE *Kirk-Buriall* (1833) 30 The passage so impeshed with *thortersome throughes.

'**thorter-'ill.** *Sc.* Also **thwarter-.** [f. prec. + ILL *sb.*] A disease of sheep, characterized by distortion of the neck; louping-ill.

1791 *Statist. Acc. Scot.* I. 138 Palsy, called trembling, or thorter ill, to which those fed on certain lands are peculiarly subject. **1808** *Sporting Mag.* XXXII. 195 A sheep which had died of disease (the thorter ill) and was at the time in a state of putrescence. **1829** HOGG *Tales, Sheph. Cal.* xvi, The thwarter-ill (a sort of paralytic affection) came among them [the sheep].

†'**thortron**, *a. Sc. Obs. rare.* [f. THORTER: cf. *southron*.] Having a transverse direction.

c **1580** *Balfour's Practicks* (1754) 439 Thortron burnis in monthis hie Sall stop na heid roume, thoch thay be.

thortveitite ('θɔːtvaɪtaɪt, -veɪtaɪt, 'tɔːt-). *Min.* [ad. G. *thortveitit* (J. Schetelig 1911, in *Centralbl. f. Min.* 721), f. the name of O. *Thortveit* of Norway, its discoverer: see -ITE[1].] A silicate of scandium, $(Sc, Y)_2Si_2O_7$, found as colourless or greyish monoclinic crystals.

1912 *Jrnl. Chem. Soc.* CII. II. 56 (*heading*) Thortveitite, a new mineral. **1963** *Prof. Papers U.S. Geol. Survey* No. 475-B. 11/1 The association of thortveitite with fluorite in the deposit at Crystal Mountain represents a new type of occurrence, which contrasts strongly with the occurrences in granitic pegmatites of Norway and Madagascar.

†**thorty**, obs. form of THIRTY.

1538 *Sel. Cas. Star Chamb.* (Selden) II. 60.

thoru, þoru, thorugh, thorw, etc., obs. ff. THOROUGH, THROUGH *sb.*[1]

‖**thos** (θəʊs). Pl. thoes ('θəʊiːz). [L. *thōs*, pl. *thōes*, a. Gr. *θώς*, pl. *θῶ-ες*, a beast of prey of the dog kind.] The Greek and Latin name of a beast of the canine group; probably a jackal of some species; but variously identified or imagined by 17th c. translators. See also THOUS.

1601 HOLLAND *Pliny* x. lxiii. I. 303 Wolves, Panthers, and Thoes, kindle their young before they can see. *Ibid.* lxxiv. 308 The Thoes and the Lions doe foulely jarre and disagree. **1607** TOPSELL *Four-f. Beasts* (1658) 581 The lesser kinde of Thoes are the best, for some make two kinde of Thoes, and some three... We will therefore take it for confessed, that the Thoes is a beast engendered betwixt a Wolf and a Fox, whereof some are greater and some are smaller. **1706** PHILLIPS (ed. Kersey), *Thos*,..a Lynx, a Creature resembling a Wolf, but spotted like a Leopard. **1753** CHAMBERS *Cycl. Supp.*, *Thos*,..a name given to an animal of the wolf kind, but larger than the common wolf. **1839** C. H. SMITH *Dogs* I. v. 207 It may be, that one of the smaller Thoes of Aristotle is the true Jackal.

thos, þos, obs. form of THOSE, THUS.

Thoscan, obs. form of TUSCAN.

those (ðəʊz), *dem. pron.* and *adj.* (*pl.*) Forms: *α.* 1–3 **ðás**, 1–4 **þás**, 4 **þaas, þais**, 4–5 **þase**, (5 **þaes**); 5 **thas, thase**, 5–6 **thais.** *β.* 3–4 **þos** (3 **þosse**), 4–5 **þose, thoos,** (5, 7 **thoes**, Scotticized **thoise, thoys**), 6 **thoose**; 4– **those.** [OE. *þás, þæs*, ME. *þōs*, pl. of THIS, which during the ME. period became synonymous with *þā*, THO, pl. of *that*, which it at length superseded, and thus came to be used in its current sense. The identification of *þās* (*þaas, þase, þais(e)*) with *þā* began in the north, where it is evidenced *c* 1300–1340; the use of *þōs* (*thoos, those*) for *þō*, in midld. and south, came later. Chaucer has only *tho*; and most of the examples of *thos(e* before 1475 occur either in midld. versions of northern poems, such as the *Anturs of Arthur* and *Sir Perceval*, where the scribe transliterated *thas(e* into *thos(e*, or in the works of northern men, as Wyclif, whose native dialect had *thas(e*. In Eng. literature *those, thoos, thoes*, became common first in works printed by Caxton, and thenceforth *those* and *tho* continued to be used in the same sense, *tho* gradually becoming rarer, till *c* 1550.

The early southern ME. *þōs* = THESE, appears to have been retained longest in Kentish: see quot. 1340 in. I. 1. It was of course obsolete in Midld. Eng. before *thos, thoos, those* in the modern sense was accepted. It is doubtful whether *thase* ever found a footing in Scotland, where *þā* continued in use, and still exists as THAE pl. of *that*.]

I. Demonstrative pronoun.

†**1.** Plural of THIS B. I = THESE B. I. *Obs.*

c **825** *Vesp. Psalter* xliii. 18 [xliv. 17] Ðas all cwomun ofer usic. *a* **900** K. ÆLFRED *Laws* Introd. c. 49 §9 Ic ða Ælfred cyning þas togædere ȝegaderode. *a* **900** tr. *Bæda's Hist.* III. xix. [xxvii.] 242 Betweoh þas wæron tweȝen ȝeonge æðelingas. *c* **1000** *Ags. Gosp.* Matt. iv. 9 Ealle þas ic sylle þe. *c* **1200** *Trin. Coll. Hom.* 217 Ac ich ne mai ne ich ne can þosse [i.e. words] on openi. **1340** *Ayenb.* 10 Vor alle þos byeþ ualse wytnesses. *Ibid.* 39 þise makeþ þe ualse mariages. þise benimeþ þe heritages. þos doþ zuo moche kuead..and al þis hi doþ be hare greate couaytise.

2. Plural of THAT: indicating things or persons pointed to or already mentioned: see THAT B. I. 1.

1340 HAMPOLE *Pr. Consc.* 6556, I fynde wryten paynes fourtene,..And whilk þas er I sal yhow telle. *a* **1400** *K. Alis.* 4913 (Bodl. MS.) A folk woneþ biside þoos, þat beeþ ycleped Farangos. **1477** EARL RIVERS (Caxton) *Dictes* 33 He made diuers bookis of phisik..and of thoos, xij the most be studyed by ordre. **1591** SHAKS. *Two Gent.* III. i. 225 A Sea of melting pearls, which some call teares: Those at her fathers churlish feete she tenderd. **1599** —— *Hen. V*, III. vii. 74 The Armour that I saw in your Tent to night, are those Starres or Sunnes vpon it? **1611** BIBLE *Eccl.* vii. 28 A woman among all those haue I not found. **1653** WALTON *Angler* ii. 65 *Milk.* What Song was it, I pray? was it, Come Shepherds deck your heads: or, As at noon Dulcina rested: or Philida flouts me? *Pisc.* No, it is none of those. *a* **1822** SHELLEY *Serchio* 36 Melchior and Lionel were not among those. *Mod.* Who are those passing? Those are our neighbours Smith and Jones. I looked at all the books on the top shelf, but it was not one of those.

b. Preceded by *and*, introducing an additional qualification of the things or persons mentioned in the previous clause: plural of THAT I. 2a.

1545 ASCHAM *Toxoph.* II. (Arb.) 162 Other and those very good archers in drawyng, loke at the marke. **1590** RYTHER tr. *Ubaldino's Disc. Span. Invasion* 5 Through penurie of many and those necessarie things. **1601** HOLLAND *Pliny* (1634) I. 529 If the vineyard lie pendant vpon the hanging of an hill, it requireth deeper ditches, and those raised vp well with earth. **1697** DRYDEN *Virg. Georg.* IV. 189 Lord of few Acres, and those barren too. **1701** NORRIS *Ideal World* I. ii. 53 Other figures..and those perfect ones. *Mod.* I have only three, and those not of the best.

3. In opposition to *these*; sometimes *spec.* = 'the former': plural of THAT B. I. 3, 3b. For quots. see THESE B. I. 2, II. 2. Also in contrast to (*the*) *others*.

1653 WALTON *Angler* iv. 116 Palmer flies, not only those rib'd with silver and gold, but others that have their bodies all made of black. **1655** STANLEY *Hist. Philos.* I. I. 6 Those affirming they had bargain'd onely for the fish, the others that they bought the draught at a venture.

4. As antecedent pronoun, followed by a defining word or phrase, viz. a relative clause (with relative expressed or understood), a participle (or other vbl. adj.), or a preposition (esp. *of*) with a sb. which serves to qualify or particularize *those*: plural of THAT B. I. 6–8. (= Ger. *diejenigen* or *die*, F. *ceux*, *celles*.)

a. In general sense: chiefly, now only, of persons: *those who* = the people who; *those of* = the people of, etc. Plural of THAT B. I. 6 a, c, 8 b.

1340 HAMPOLE *Pr. Consc.* 7510 Alle þase þat wille þair syn forsake. *c* **1400** MAUNDEV. (Roxb.) xv. 67 þase þat trowes perfitely in Godd sall be sauf. *c* **1440** *Alphabet of Tales* 296 þase at sulde bere hym myght gett hym no ferrer. **1477** EARL RIVERS (Caxton) *Dictes* 115 Thoos that be nedy. *Ibid.* 129 Thoes that blame. **1535** COVERDALE *Prov.* viii. 12, I am louynge vnto those that loue me. **1548** FORREST *Pleas. Poesye* 55 Of thoise that they had too them made subiugate. **1554–9** T. WATERTOUNE in *Songs & Bal.* (1860) 11 All thoys that have years this understande. **1590** SHAKS. *Com. Err.* III. i. 48 Who are those at the gate? **1598** —— *Merry W.* v. v. 57 Those as sleepe, and thinke not on their sins. **1605** —— *Macb.* II. iii. 106 Those of his Chamber, as it seem'd, had don't. **1610** —— *Temp.* I. ii. 398 Those are pearles that were his eies. **1613** —— *Hen. VIII*, III. i. 167 Pray thinke vs, Those we professe, Peace-makers, Friends, and Seruants. **1777** ROBERTSON *Hist. Amer.* (1783) II. 216 Those who appeared more gentle and tractable. **1790** BURKE *Fr. Rev.* 50 Those from whom they are descended. **1856** GEO. ELIOT *Ess.* (1884) 232 Those among our painters who aim at giving the rustic type of features. **1896** *Law Times* C. 410/1 Any person other than himself and those claiming under him. *Mod.* Of those expected only a few turned up.

b. Referring to things or persons mentioned immediately before, and equivalent to *the* with the pl. sb.; e.g. in quot. 1593, *those* = 'the storms'. Plural of THAT B. I. 6 b, 8 a.

1477 EARL RIVERS (Caxton) *Dictes* 31 Diuerse opinions, And in especial thoos of plato. **1593** SHAKS. *Lucr.* 1589 These watergalls.. Foretell new stormes to those alreadie spent. **1611** BIBLE *Josh.* iii. 16 The waters which came downe from aboue, stood and rose vp vpon an heape.. and those that came downe toward the sea of the plaine.. failed, and were cut off. **1774** GOLDSM. *Nat. Hist.* (1790) VII. 51 The oysters.. are by no means so large as those found sticking to rocks. **1779** *Mirror* No. 6 ¶ 10 The classical writers.. were those from whose works he felt the highest pleasure. **1797** *Encycl. Brit.* (ed. 3) IV. 778/2 The larvæ, which resemble those of the wasp. **1819** KEATS *Ode Grecian Urn* ii, Heard melodies are sweet, but those unheard Are sweeter. **1874** DASENT *Half a Life* II. 76 His laws being like those of the Medes and Persians.

II. Demonstrative adjective.

†**1.** Plural of THIS B. II = THESE B. II. *Obs.*

a **900** K. ÆLFRED *Laws* Introd., Dryhten wæs sprecende ðas word to Moyse. *c* **1000** *Ags. Gosp.* Matt. vi. 32 Ealle þas þing þeoda seceað. *c* **1175** *Lamb. Hom.* 11 (*De Quadragesima*) þas daȝes beoð iset us to muchele helpe.. al swa moyses.. feste þes daȝes. *c* **1200** *Trin. Coll. Hom.* 185 Ðos feawe word .. seide ure drihten. *c* **1205** LAY. 672 Brutus hine bi-þohte .. & þas [*c* **1275** þeos] word seide. *a* **1250** *Owl & Night.* 139 (Cott.) þos [*Jes.* þeos] word aȝaf þe niȝtingale.

2. Plural of THAT B. II. 1.

a. **13..** *Cursor M.* 2590 (Gött.) As it was hite [*v.r.* hight] bifor þas [*C.* þaa, *F.* þa] dais. *Ibid.* 4948 (Cott.) þan spak ruben, þe eildest broiþer, Stilli menand til þas [*F.* þase] oþer. *Ibid.* 8187 (Cott.) He tok þaas [*G.* þa] wandes in his hand. *Ibid.* 19859 Quen petre þais [*G.*, *F.* þa: *Tr.* þo] vnbestes sagh. *c* **1440** *Alphabet of Tales* 82 With all þase candels he cursid þis fend & entirditid hym.

β. *c* **1375** *Cursor M.* (Fairf.) 7254 Bi a piler was he sette to glew þos [*C.* þaa] gomis at mete. *c* **1380** WYCLIF *Serm.* Sel. Wks. II. 112 Bifore þat tyme weren þos wordis spoken of Crist. *a* **1400** *Sir Perc.* 229 Fyftene wynter and mare He duellede in those holtes hare. **1477** EARL RIVERS (Caxton) *Dictes* Pref. 3 Ony of thoos bookes. *Ibid.* 27 Whiche was a Cyte in thoos dayes. **1491** in *Lett. Rich. III & Hen. VII* (Rolls) I. 99 Bring the said Sir Robert and thoes other oure rebelles and traitours. **1526** TINDALE *Luke* i. 39 Mary arose in thoose [COVERD. & *Gt. Bible* those] dayes. **1595** SHAKS. *John* III. iv. 61 Binde vp those tresses. **1639** *Hamilton Papers* (Camden) 90 So many men.. with thoes I haue heir, as will make up that number. **1741–2** CHALLONER *Mission. Priests* (1803) II. 19 John Sugar was born at Womborn.. of a noted family in those parts. **1845** M. PATTISON *Ess.* (1889) I. 14 A living stirring picture of the Church and State of those days.

b. Indicating things or persons as known to be such as described: plural of THAT B. II. 1 b.

1590 SHAKS. *Mids. N.* III. ii. 140 Thy lips, those kissing cherries. **1678** CUDWORTH *Intell. Syst.* I. ii. 61 As for those Romantick Monogrammous Gods of Epicurus. **1753** CHALLONER *Cath. Chr. Instr.* 178 Those two great Lights of the Church, St. Gregory Nazianzen and St. Basil. **1822** SHELLEY *Question* 10 Daisies, those pearled Arcturi of the earth. **1855** MACAULAY *Hist. Eng.* xx. IV. 494 Those worst enemies of the nation.

c. Used instead of *that* with a sing. noun of multitude (now only with collectives in pl. sense, as *clergy*, *foot* (foot-soldiers), *horse*, *vermin*); and esp. with *kind*, *sort*, followed by *of* with pl. sb. (see KIND *sb.* 14 b). Cf. THESE B. II. 1 d.

those kind (or *sort*) *of men*, is put for 'men of that kind (*or* sort)', L. *ejus generis homines*, and is grammatically anomalous: cf. THAKIN.

1560 WHITEHORNE *Ord. Souldiours* (1588) 9 b, Behind the said teeth to place those number of men which first were taken out. **1601** SHAKS. *Twel. N.* I. ii. 10 You, and those poore number saued with you. **1692** O. WALKER *Grk. & Rom. Hist.* 266 He.. chased away those Vermin of Courtiers. **1875** GLADSTONE *Glean.* VI. 126 Some of those clergy who are called Broadchurchmen.

1565 J. SPARKE in Hawkins *Voy.* II. (Hakl. Soc.) 51 Those sorte of men are eaters of the flesh of men, as well as the Canibals. **1577** NORTHBROOKE *Dicing* (1843) 99 From whence those kinde of playes had their beginning. **1608** DOD & CLEAVER *Expos. Prov.* xi–xii. 150 In those kind of trees, the root cannot defend the branches, nor bodie. **1761** H. WALPOLE *Let. to H. Zouch* 3 Jan., The little regard shown.. to those sort of things. **1798** JANE AUSTEN *Lett.* (1884) I. 187 Those kind of foolish and incomprehensible feelings. **1887** RIDER HAGGARD *Jess* 126 Those sort of reflections.

3. In opposition to *these*: plural of THAT B. II. 2; cf. I. 3 above. For quots. see THESE B. II. 2.

4. In concord with a noun which is the antecedent to a relative (expressed or omitted), or which is further defined by a participle: pl. of THAT B. II. 3.

c **1175** *Lamb. Hom.* 13 þas .x. bebode þe godalmihti seolf idihte. **1526** TINDALE *Eph.* v. 12 Those thynges which are done of them in secrete. —— *Jude* 10 Those thinges which they knowe not. In tho thynges which they knowe naturally they corrupte them selves [so COVERD. & *Gt. Bible*]. **1539** BIBLE (Great) *Rev.* i. 3 And kepe those [TINDALE & COVERD. thoo] thynges which are written therin. **1563** WINȜET *Four Scoir Thre Quest.* § 35 Wks. (S.T.S.) I. 100 Gif ȝe be nocht admittit be thais Kirkis, quhome ȝe serue. **1599** SHAKS. *Hen. V*, IV. viii. 96 The Names of those their Nobles that lye dead. **1631** MILTON *Epitaph Marchioness Winchester* 43 Those Pearls of dew she wears. **1779** *Mirror* No. 30 ¶ 2 Those national boasts which are always allowable. **1780** *Ibid.* No. 79 ¶ 5 Those useful chronicles of facts, called newspapers. **1859** GEO. ELIOT *A. Bede* xlix, Brethren and sisters.. who have none of those comforts you have.

5. = SUCH: plural of THAT B. II. 4. Now *rare.*

1605 SHAKS. *Lear* I. i. 99, I returne those duties backe as are right fit. **1611** —— *Cymb.* v. v. 338 Those Arts they haue, as I Could put into them. **1632** MASSINGER & FIELD *Fatal Dowry* III. i, Obnoxious to those foolish things As they can gibe at. **1689** LUTTRELL *Brief Rel.* (1857) I. 567 The town.. was reduced to those straights, that if not releived.. it must have surrendred in two daies time. **1827** DISRAELI *Viv. Grey* v. vi, He spoke of you in those terms that make me glad that I have met the son.

† **thost** (e. *Obs.* [OE. *þost* = OHG. *dost.*] Dung, excrement; a turd.

c **1000** *Sax. Leechd.* I. 364 Scinseocum men wyrc drenc of hwites hundes þoste on bitere lege. *a* **1300** *E.E. Psalter* lxxxii[i]. 11 [10] þai for-worthed in Endor, þai ere made als thoste of erthe þar-for. *c* **1327** *Pol. Songs* (Camden) 237 Alle weren y-haht Of an horse thoste. **1387** TREVISA *Higden* (Rolls) IV. 423 Alle men þrewe on hym drit and thost. *c* **1425** *Cast. Persev.* 2413 in *Macro Plays* 149 Al oure fare is not worth a thost. *c* **1440** *Pallad. on Husb.* IV. 348 Asse vryne & swynes thost. *c* **1440** *Promp. Parv.* 492/1 Thoste (or toord), *stercus.*

tho't, thot, repr. a U.S. pronunc. of *thought.*

1879 W. WHITMAN *Daybks. & Notebks.* (1978) I. 161 *Very bad spells*, unable sometimes to walk a block (sometimes tho't it all nearing the end). *a* **1886** E. DICKINSON *Poems* (1955) III. 1148 The right to perish might be tho't An undisputed right. **1888** W. WHITMAN *Daybks. & Notebks.* (1978) II. 453 The Calming Tho't of all. **1971** *Black World* Mar. 53/1 She wuzn't sure but she thot it had. **1975** *Budget* (Sugarcreek, Ohio) 20 Mar. 12/2 Thot: Troubled waters cleanse the garments best.

† **'thother,** coalesced form of *the other*, frequent from 14th to 17th c.; in later time also written *th' other*: see TH-[1], TH'.

Often used in contrast to THONE = the one: see THONE, ONE 18, 19, and TOTHER.

c **1300** *Beket* 466 Tho were thothere glad ynouȝ. *c* **1400** *Trevisa's Higden* (Rolls) III. 65 (MS. *γ*) þooþer wys men. **1534–5** *MS. Rawl.* D. 777 lf. 67 b, One of them in [etc.] and thoder in the hawpace. **1556** *Knaresborough Wills* (Surtees) I. 73 To my children thother half. **1633** T. STAFFORD *Pac. Hib.* I. i. (1821) 11 On thother part.

thou (ðaʊ), *pers. pron.*, *2nd sing. nom.* Forms: 1–3 **ðu**, 1–5 **þu**, (2–3 **tu**, **tou**, **-te**), 3 (**þe**, **þeou**), **ðhu**, 3–5 **þou**, 3–6 **thu**, (4 **þouȝ**), 4–5 **þow**, (**-tow**), 4–6 **thow**, 4, 6 (9 *dial.*) **th-**, **th'**, (5 **thowe**), 4– **thou**. (*Mod. dial.* **thau, thaw, thah, tha; theau, theow, thoo, thu; tau, taw, ta. tay; teau, teaw, teu, too, tou, tow; doo, dou, du,** etc.: see *Eng. Dial. Dict.*) [OE. *ðŭ*, *þŭ*; Com. Teut. and Indo-Eur.; = OFris. *thu* (*du*), OS. *thŭ* (MDu., MLG., LG. *du*), OHG. *dŭ* (MHG., Ger. *du*), ON. *þú* (Norw., Sw., Da. *du*), Goth. *þu*:—OTeut. *þŭ* = pre-Teut. *tu*: = L. *tu*, Ir. *tu*, Welsh *ti*, Gr. *σύ*, Doric *τύ*, Lith. *tu*, OSlav. *ty*, Skr. *twa-m.* The oblique cases, and the possessive, are formed on a stem *þe-* = pre-Teut. *te-*: see THEE, THINE. The pl. YE, in OE. *ȝé*, is from a different root, to which also belonged a dual *ȝit*, YIT, 'ye two', still used after 1200 in ME. The acc. and dat. sing. were levelled in OE. under the dat. form: see THEE. The OE. genitive was identical in form with a possessive adj. *þín*: see THINE, THY. The paradigm of *thou* is therefore as follows:

Old English.

	SINGULAR.	DUAL.	PLURAL.
Nom.	þú, þu	ȝit	ȝé, ȝe, ȝie
Acc.	þec; þē, þe	incit; inc	eowic; ēow (iuih, iuh)
Dat.	þē, þe	inc	ēow
Gen. / *Poss. Pron.*	þin	incer	ēower

Middle English.

Nom.	þū, þou, þow	ȝit, ȝet	ȝe, ȝie, yhe, ye
Dat. Acc.	þē, þee	inc, ȝinc, ȝunc	eow, eou, ou, ow, ȝiu, ȝu, ȝou, yhu (etc.)
Gen.	þīn	inker, ȝunker,	eower, eour, ower, ȝure, ȝour(e
Poss. Pron.	þīn, þī	unker inker, ȝunker, unker	

Modern English.

Nom.	thou	[*obs.*]	ye, you
Dat. Acc.	thee	,,	you
Poss. absol.	thine	,,	yours
Pron. adj.	thy	,,	your.]

1. The pronoun by which a person (or thing) is addressed, in the nominative singular; the pronoun denoting the person (or thing) spoken to.

Thou and its cases *thee*, *thine*, *thy*, were in OE. used in ordinary speech; in ME. they were gradually superseded by the plural *ye*, *you*, *your*, *yours*, in addressing a superior and (later) an equal, but were long retained in addressing an inferior. Long retained by Quakers in addressing a single person, though now less general; still in various dialects used by parents to children, and familiarly between equals, esp. intimates; in other cases considered as rude. In general English used in addressing God or Christ, also in homiletic language, and in poetry, apostrophe, and elevated prose. For details of dialect use, see Wright, *Eng. Dial. Dict.*, *Thou* II, *Eng. Dial. Gram.* §404.

In ME. freq. combined with its verb when this precedes, the *þ* being then absorbed in the preceding *t*, as *artow* = art thou, *hastow* = hast thou. The initial *þ* also became *t* after *s*, *t*, or *d*, as *hauis tu* = hast thou, *þat tu*, *and tu*: see T 8.

Beowulf 507 Eart þu se Beowulf? *c* **825** *Vesp. Psalter* ix. 15 Ðu uphest mec of ȝeatum deaðes. *c* **1205** LAY. 690 Niðing þou ært al dead.. Bote þu min lare do. *Ibid.* 2978 þeou [*c* **1275** þou] ært leouere þene mi lif. *a* **1225** *Ancr. R.* 240 þench ec hwat tu owust God, uor his god deden. *a* **1240** *Ureisun* in *Cott. Hom.* 199 So þu dest and so þu schalt. *c* **1250** *Gen. & Ex.* 361 For ðhu min bode-word haues broken, ðhu salt ben ut in sorȝe luken, In swinc ðu salt tilien ði mete. **1297** R. GLOUC. (Rolls) 6371 þou ne ssalt of þin liflode neuere carie noȝt. *a* **1300** *Cursor M.* 19585 (Edin.) Hauis tu [*v.rr.* þu, þou] na parte.. here. *Ibid.* 1253 (Gött.) In þat way sal yu [*Cott.* þou] find forsoth þi moþer. *Ibid.* 8306 (Fairf.) Werrour artow [*Cott.* art þow] gode in fiȝt. *c* **1391** CHAUCER *Astrol.* I. §13 Thanne hastow a brod Rewle. *c* **1440** *Pallad. on Husb.* I. 42 The better may thowe with that water holde. **1535** COVERDALE *Ps.* lxiv. [lxv.] 1 Thou, O God, art praysed in Sion. **1592** SHAKS. *Rom. & Jul.* I. v. 9 Good thou, saue mee a piece of Marchpane. **1597** —— *2 Hen. IV*, II. ii. 17 How many paire of Silk stockings yᵘ haste. **1671** H. M. tr. *Erasm. Colloq.* 326 Why shouldest thou do so, seeing how thou was not far from thine own shore? **1715–20** POPE *Iliad* XII. 69 Oh thou! bold leader of the Trojan bands, And you, confederate chiefs from foreign lands! **1741** RICHARDSON *Pamela* II. 273, I dare say thou'lt set the good Work forward. *a* **1835** MRS. HEMANS *Graves of Househ.* viii, Alas, for love! if thou wert all, And nought beyond, O Earth. **1872** TENNYSON *Gareth & Lyn.* 1210 Thou—Lancelot!—thine the hand That threw me?

Dialectal. **1579** SPENSER *Sheph. Cal.* July 33 Syker, thous but a laesie loord. **1607** BEAUMONT *Woman Hater* III. i, Heres ta, and tha [Hearest thou, if thou] wants lodging, take my house, 'tis big enough. **1802** R. ANDERSON *Cumberld. Ball.*, *Sally Gray* iv, Had tou seen her at kurk, man, last Sunday, Tou couldn't ha'e thought o' the text. **1861** E. WAUGH *Birtle Carter's T.* 32 Well neaw, mind ta does do. **1876** *Whitby Gloss.* 171/2 If thoo will gan, sithence be 't. **1886** HALL CAINE *Son of Hagar* I. i, What sayst tha, Reuben?

b. Used in apposition to and preceding a sb. in the vocative: in reproach or contempt often emphasized by being placed or repeated after the sb.

c **888** K. ÆLFRED *Boeth.* xxvii. §2 Ic ascige ðe, þu Boetius. **13..** *Cursor M.* 13632 (Gött.) 'Hald ȝe to him', said þai, 'þu caitiue'. *c* **1350** *Will. Palerne* 312 A! gracious gode god! þouȝ grettest of alle! *c* **1425** ? LYDG. *Assembly of Gods* 1394 'What' seyde Ryghtwysnes, 'thow olde dotyng foole'. *c* **1485** *Digby Myst.* III. 1399 Loke þat we have drynke, boy þou. **1590** SHAKS. *Mids. N.* v. i. 177 Thow wall, o wall, o sweet and louely wall. **1601** —— *Jul. C.* IV. iii. 301 Sleepe againe Lucius: Sirra Claudio, Fellow, Thou: Awake. **1610** —— *Temp.* III. ii. 52 Thou lyest, thou iesting Monkey thou. **1756** HOME *Douglas* III. ii, Thou riddler, speak Direct and clear. **1820** WORDSW. *Ch. San Salvador* 1 Thou sacred Pile! whose turrets rise.. Guarded by lone San Salvador. **1850** (Westmorland), Get oop, thoo lile ligabed!

2. As *sb.* **a.** The person or 'self' of the individual addressed. Cf. THEE *pron.* 4 a.

1693 DRYDEN *Persius' Sat.* i. 249 Thou, if there be a Thou, in this base Town, Who dares, with angry Eupolis, to frown. **1831** CARLYLE *Sart. Res.* II. ix, Because the Thou (sweet gentleman) is not sufficiently honoured, nourished, soft-bedded.

b. The word itself: see also THEE *pron.* 4 b.

1655 BAXTER *Quaker Catech.* 27 The Quakers.. call out for a formal Righteousnesse.., consisting in such things as these following, to wit,.. That we say (*Thou*) and no (*You*) to him we speak to. **1694** PENN in *G. Fox's Jrnl.* (1827) I. Pref. 15 They also used the plain language of Thou and Thee to a single person. **1827** HARE *Guesses* (1859) 119 When *you* came into use among the higher classes, the lower were still addrest with *thou*. **1905** *Daily Chron.* 16 Feb. 5/1 Among the concessions.. is that the men shall be addressed in the second person plural, not as is usual throughout Russia, in the case of the working classes, in the singular 'thou' (a mark of inferiority).

thou (ðaʊ), *v.* [f. THOU *pron.*] To use the pronoun 'thou' to a person: familiarly, to an inferior, in contempt or insult, or as done (formerly universally, now less frequently) on principle by Quakers: cf. note to THOU *pers. pron.* 1. Often in phr. ***to thou and thee, to thee***

and thou: cf. also THEE *v.*[2] **a.** *trans.* **b.** *intr.* (or *absol.*). Hence **thouing** *vbl. sb.* (Cf. THOWT(E *v.*)

a. *c* **1440** *Promp. Parv.* 492/1 Thowtyn, or seyn thow to a mann (*A.* thowyn or sey þu), *tuo.* **14..** *Voc.* in Wr.-Wülcker 618/7 *Tuo*, to thuy. *c* **1450** in Aungier *Syon* (1840) 297 None of hyghenesse schal thou another in spekynge. *c* **1530** *Hickscorner* (1905) 149 Avaunt, caitiff, dost thou thou me! I am come of good kin I tell thee! **1564–78** BULLEYN *Dial. agst. Pest.* (1888) 5 He thous not God, but you[s] hym. **1603** COKE in Hargrave *State Trials* (1776) I. 216 All that Lord Cobham did was by thy instigation, thou viper; for I thou thee, thou Traitor! **1664** PEPYS *Diary* 11 Jan., She [a Quakeress] thou'd him [the king] all along. **1682** R. WARE *Foxes & Firebrands* II. 103 He.. Quaker-like, thou'd and thee'd Oliver. **1805** tr. *Lafontaine's Hermann & Emilia* I. 110 When she heard the young people *thou* and *thee* each other. **1888** *Liversedge, Yorks. Dial.*, Shoo said, Art thah goin'? Yo' knaw shoo al'us thah's ma. We're owd mates.

b. **1679** *Establ. Test* 23 A.. Iesuit takes a Lodging at a Quakers, can thou and thee, and yea and nay, as well as the best of them. **1697** *State Philadelph. Soc.* 2 They were not so silly as to place Religion in Thouing and Theeing. **1883** *Globe* 24 Mar. 1/5 In this country 'thouing' is a lost art.

thou (θaʊ), *sb.* Also thou. (with point), thou'. A colloquial and familiar shortening of the word *thousand*; *esp.* a thousand pounds sterling; a thousandth of an inch; (*U.S.*) a thousand dollars; also in other senses: see quots.

1867 'OUIDA' *Under Two Flags* I. vi. 113 Losing "long odds in thou'" over the Oaks. **1869** tr. *Sue's Myst. Paris* I. xxvi, The annual amount of his betting-book reached to two or three 'thous'. **1897** *Speaker* 13 Nov. 531 The writer did not demean himself by fixing his price at so much 'per thou'. **1899** *Daily News* 23 Feb. 6/2 Fancy Wellington and Nelson coaxed for copy at the rate, say, of five hundred pounds a 'thou'. **1902** *Westm. Gaz.* 30 June 3/3 In engineering we divide the inch into one thousand parts, and the expression of dimensions in 'thous', as they are called in workshops, is far more convenient than the expression of the same dimensions in parts of millimètres. **1924** GALSWORTHY *White Monkey* III. ix. 276 If he did take a few thou. under the rose, he took 'em off the Huns. **1934** *Practical Motorist* 19 May 94/2 The width of the gap.. should not be more than 3 to 5 'thous'. **1952** M. TRIPP *Faith is Windsock* xi. 173 We're below ten thou..; you can take off your oxygen masks **1965** *New Yorker* 20 Feb. 34/3 The gesture cost me a cool ten thou, but I didn't begrudge it. **1975** *Hi-Fi Answers* Feb. 36/1 The AT21X carries an elliptical stylus of 0·3 × 0·7 thou. dimensions.

thou, þou, thouch(t, obs. forms of THOUGH.

thoucht, obs. Sc. f. THOUGHT *sb.*[1]; also of *thought* pa. t. of THINK *v.*

though (ðəʊ), *adv.* and *conj.* Forms: see below. [OE. had *ðéah, þéah, þéh*, corresp. to Goth. *þauh* (= *þau* 'in that case' + *h* = L. *-que* 'also'), OFris. *thâch* (Saterl. *dach*); OS. *thôh* (MDu., Du., LG. *doch*), OHG. *doh* (shortened fr. *dôh*), ON. *þó* (contr. fr. **þauh*), MSw., MDa. *þo, tho.* Of the numerous ME. forms, those in *α* and *β* were developments of OE. *þéah, þǽh, þáh*, with various treatment of the diphthong, and early shortening of the vowel in unstressed position (cf. Ormin's *þĕhh*, Lamb. Hom. *þăch*), with subseq. stress-lengthening, as *þeih, they*, and *þauch, thau, thaw*. The *γ* forms were from Norse, representing an ON. **þóh* (intermediate to *þauh* and *þó*), shortened in Ormin to *þŏhh*, with subseq. stress-lengthening to *þōuȝ, though, thō*. The Norse form gradually gained over the native *α* and *β* forms, which disappeared from literature before 1500. The *δ* forms show the same development of *f* from *ȝ, gh* (x), as in *laugh, cough, tough*; *thof* was occasional in literature as late as 1750, and is still prevalent in many varieties from Yorksh. and Lancash. to Hampsh. and Devon: see Wright *Eng. Dial. Gram.* In Scotl. and north of Engl. *though* is pronounced (θɔː); the Hampsh. and WSom. *thof* also is (θɔf), not (ðɔf).]

A. Illustration of Forms.

α. 1 **þéah, ðǽh,** 1–3 **þéh, ðæch, þæh,** 2–3 **þech, (þehȝ),** (*Orm.*) **þĕhh, þeih,** 3–4 **þeigh,** 3–5 **þei, þey,** 4 **þeiȝh,** 4–5 **þeyȝ, þeyh, þeiȝ, thegh, thei,** 5 **þeiȝt, theigh(e, they (the).** Also 3 **þaih, þaiȝ, þayh, þayȝ, þay,** 4 **þai.**

c **888** K. ÆLFRED *Boeth.* xix. §1 Hu neara þære eorðan stede is, þeah heo us rum þince. *c* **950** *Lindisf. Gosp.* Mark xiv. 29 ȝif *vel* ðæh alle ȝeondspyrand see.. ah.. næfre ic. —— John iv. 2 Ðæch se hælend ne fuluuade. **971** *Blickl. Hom.* 37 þeah [see B. I]. *Ibid.* 55 þeh he ȝeornlice ȝehyre þa word. *c* **1175** *Lamb. Hom.* 77 He [Christ] nis nawiht alle monne lauerd, þech alle men bon on his onwald. *c* **1200** *Vices & Virt.* 9 þeh me niede me to ðan aðe, me ne net me noht te forsweriȝen, ac soð te seggen of ðan ðe ic am bicleped. *c* **1200** *Trin. Coll. Hom.* 83 þeh [see B. II. 4]. *Ibid.* 159 Al þat man doð.. þehȝ hie ben don ec for godes luue. *c* **1200** ORMIN 395 þatt teȝȝ.. sinndenn þohh swa þehh i þohht. *c* **1205** LAY. 13002 He þus sæide, soð þæh [*c* **1275** þoh] hit nære. *Ibid.* 22736 Wunder þæh [*c* **1275** þeh] hit þunche. *c* **1290** *S. Eng. Leg.* I. 260/143 þei he fader and moder a-slouȝ. *c* **1350** *Will. Palerne* 689 As þeiȝh he gyled were. **1387** TREVISA *Higden* (Rolls) I. 213 þeyȝ þou nygh all fallynge be. *c* **1394** *P. Pl. Crede* 69 þeiȝ his felawes fayle good. **1398** TREVISA *Barth. De P.R.* III. iii. (Tollem. MS.), þey [L. *quamvis*] þe soule be onid to a body. *c* **1400** *Brut* 49 As þeiȝt Vortiger hade nouȝt wiste perof. **1400** in *Roy. & Hist. Lett. Hen. IV* (Rolls) 38 Thegh John Welle hath doon as thu aboven has certefied. *c* **1425** *Seven Sag.* (P.) 1741 He loved hit wel, the hit were bad. *a* **1450** *Le Morte Arth.* 1985 What wondyr theighe hys herte were wo. *c* **1450** LOVELICH *Grail* lv. 298 As they Alle they in the world haden ben there. *c* **1205** LAY. 2513 þaih he were ræd gold. *c* **1250** *Hymn Virgin* 62 in *Trin. Coll. Hom.* 257 Betere ne miȝte he þaiȝ he wolde. **1297** R. GLOUC. (Rolls) 3284 þei [*v.r.* þay] 30 were wif.

β. 1–3 **þah** (3 **tah**), 2 **þach, þaȝh,** 3–4 **þaȝ,** 5 **þagh, thaȝ, thaghe, thaȝhe;** 2–5 **þau,** 3 **þaue,** 3–4 **þauh (tauh),** 4–5 **þauȝ, þaw,** 5 **þawe, thau.**

c **950** *Lindisf. Gosp.* Luke xviii. 4 Ðah god ne ondredo ic ne monno sceomiȝo. *c* **1175** *Lamb. Hom.* 15 þaȝh [see B. II. 2]. *Ibid.* 147 þach his likame swiche pine ne þole. *c* **1205** LAY. 244 þa com his lifes ende, lað þah him were. *a* **1225** *St. Marher.* 4 Freo wummon ich am ant tah godes þeowe. *a* **1240** *Ureisun* in *Cott. Hom.* 203 [He] beieð adun toward þe his.. heaued, ase þauh [*v.r. Ibid.* 189 þah] he seide [etc.]. *a* **1250** *Owl & Night.* 1274 þah he habbe neole. *c* **1320** þauȝ [see B. I]. **1340** þaȝ [see B. II. 3]. **1362** LANGL. *P. Pl.* A. I. 132 No dedly sunne to do dyȝe þauȝ þou scholdest. *c* **1420** *Sir Amadace* xxviii, Quat wundur were hit, thaȝhe him were wo? **1426** AUDELAY *Poems* 15 Thaȝ Kayme his borne broder were cursid. *a* **1450** MYRC *Par. Pr.* 91 And thaghe þe chylde bote half be bore.

γ. 3 (*Orm.*) **þohh (tohh),** 3–4 **þoh (þoch,** 3 **ðhoȝ),** 4 **þoȝ, þhoh, þho, þouh, þouȝh, þouhȝ, þowh, þowgh,** 4–5 **þowȝ, þouȝ, -e, þou, þogh, þow (dow), þo,** 4–6 **thow,** 5 **þowe, thoȝe, thouȝ, thowh, thowgh, thou,** *Sc.* **thouch,** 5–6 **thoughe,** 5–7 **thogh,** 6 *Sc.* **thoch,** 5– **though;** 5–9 **tho,** 6– **tho',** (7 **thô**).

The form *tho* has been used in the U.S. as a reformed spelling, and (like *tho'*) is used informally as an abbreviation of the word.

c **1200** ORMIN Ded. 155 þohh þatt teȝȝ all forrwerrþenn itt. *Ibid.* Introd. 23, & itt wass þohh full mikell rihht. *c* **1275** LAY. 2345 He seide, soþ þoh [*c* **1205** þeih] hit neare. *Ibid.* 4264 þoh [*c* **1205** ȝef] he hadde man islaȝe. **13..** *Cursor M.* 21818 (Edin.) þat tu fande þoȝ [*Cott.* þof, *Gött.* þou] I walde it noȝte. *Ibid.* 24590 þho þu wald þai birid þi barn. *Ibid.* 73 (Gött.) þou i sumtime be untrewe. *Ibid.* 4763 (Fairf.)þo þai had siluer and golde rede. *Ibid.* 10941 (Gött.) And dow þai þar-fore murnand were. **1377** LANGL. *P. Pl.* B. VI. 40 And þowgh ȝe mowe amercy hem, late mercy be taxoure. *c* **1380** WYCLIF *Sel. Wks.* III. 328 þouȝ men ben nevere so opynly cursid. *c* **1425** *Seven Sag.* (P.) 576 Hit his no wondir tho me be wo. *c* **1425** tr. *Higden* (Rolls) VII. App. 519 (MS. *β*) Thouȝ that tale teller were as huge as a geaunt. *c* **1449** PECOCK *Repr.* II. ix. 195 ȝhe, thou tho gouernauncis.. be weel ynouȝ. **1456** SIR G. HAYE *Law Arms* (S.T.S.) 81 Thouch thai be feble of corps. *c* **1489** CAXTON *Sonnes Aymon* xxii. 481 Thoughe he dothe wronge to leve me here. *a* **1529** SKELTON *Agst. Garnesche* 124 Thow a Sarsens hed ye bere. *a* **1540** BARNES *Wks.* (1573) 281/1 Though all the worlde say naye. *a* **1550** *Christis Kirke Gr.* xvi, Thoch he wes wight, he wes nocht wyss. **1615** HIERON *Wks.* I. 628 Thogh He do not alwaies shew it. **1643** DENHAM *Cooper's H.* Poems (1703) 12 Tho deep, yet clear, tho gentle, yet not dull. **1711** SHAFTESB. *Charac.* (1737) II. 149 Tho the impatience of abstaining be greater. **1741** Tho' [see B. I]. **1796** R. BARRIE *Let.* 12 Oct. in N. Tolstoy *Half-Mad Lord* (1978) ii. 35 Tho: he sometimes might act imprudently his conduct never merited the ignominious punishment he receiv'd. **1818** M. EDGEWORTH *Let.* 8 Sept. (1971) 84 The library *tho* magnificent is a most comfortable.. room. **1842** TENNYSON *Poems* II. 91 Tho' much is taken, much abides. **1849** G. GRAY *Let.* 22 June in M. Lutyens *Ruskins & Grays* (1972) xxiii. 217, I have now taken the opportunity.. tho' without alluding to your Letter, of asking her how it was. **1879** *Proc. Amer. Philol. Assoc.* 6 The committee now present the following words as the beginning of such [a] list [of reformed spellings], and recommend them for immediate use:.. Tho. Thru. Wisht. **1906** *Simplified Spelling Board Circular* (U.S.) No. 2. 12 Tho... Thru. **1973** *Black World* June 66 Sister Habiba's party was still smokin. Tho all the good food and wine and reefer was gone now. **1982** *N.Y. Times* 22 Sept. C-2/3 Tho' the trip's less than a mile it's still a dreary, cheerless bore.

δ. 4 **þowf,** 4–5 **þof (of), þofe, thofe, thoffe,** 5 **(yof), þaf, þuff,** 5–6 **thaff,** 5–7 (*dial.* -9) **thof,** 8 *dial.* **thoff.**

13.. *Cursor M.* 698 (Cott.) þowf he was euer wittur. *Ibid.* 19648 And þof a smitt moght he not se. *c* **1340** HAMPOLE *Prose Tr.* 7 'Thofe I ware', quod he. *Ibid.* 21 Thoffe I be a wrech and vnworthi. *c* **1440** þof, yof [see B. II. 1]. *c* **1440** *Lay Folks Mass Bk.* (MS. E.) 7 þaf a M[le] [= thousand] clerkus dyd noght ellus. *c* **1440** *Alphabet of Tales* 64 þuff all he lefte it. *c* **1450** Thof [see B. II. 2]. **14..** *Kyng & Hermit* 158 in Hazl. *E.P.P.* I. 19 Thaff thou were sych thre. *a* **1565** J. HEYWOOD *Dial. Wit & Folly* (Percy Soc.) 8 As thowghff he knewe th' end of thing at begynnyng. **1695** CONGREVE *Love for L.* III. xv, A Sailor will be honest, thof mayhap he has never a Penny of Money in his Pocket. **1748** Thof [see B. II. 1]. **1803** MARY CHARLTON *Wife & Mistress* II. 149, I never mintioned it before, thof I knowed it all along!

ε. (Chiefly *Sc.*) 4–5 **þocht,** (4 **þoght, thowcht),** 4–6 **thoucht,** 4–7 **thocht,** 5–7 **thoght,** 6 **thought, thouȝght, tho[t].**

1303 R. BRUNNE *Handl. Synne* 969 Y wlde nat leue for here to werche þoght men rong noun at þe cherche. *c* **1375** *Sc. Leg. Saints* Prol. 166 Thowcht god chesit Androw firste To be ane apostill. **1375** (MS. 1489) BARBOUR *Bruce* I. 264 ȝe may weile se, thoucht nane ȝow tell. *c* **1470** HENRY *Wallace* VI. 24 Thocht Inglismen was grewyt at his repayr, ȝeit [etc.]. **1530** in W. H. Turner *Select. Rec. Oxford* (1880) 78, I wolde it had ben uppon the constabyll, thouȝght it had ben worse. **1535** Thocht [see B. II. 1]. *c* **1560** A. SCOTT *Poems* (S.T.S.) ii. 147 Tho[t] I had rycht no[t] bot a rok. **1567** *Ps.* li. in *Gude & Godlie B.* (S.T.S.) 122 Thocht [*v.r.* thoght] thow.. be Jugeit thus Full fals and wrangouslie.

B. Signification.

An adversative particle expressing that relation of two opposed facts or circumstances (actual or hypothetical) in which the one is inadequate to prevent the other, and therefore both concur, contrary to what might be expected.

I. **a.** *adv.* For all that; in spite of that; nevertheless, howbeit, however, yet. Now *colloq.*; usually enclitic, as 'he did though' (hiː ˈdɪd ðəʊ).

971 *Blickl. Hom.* 37 Ne maȝon þis þeah ealle men don. *c* **1175** *Lamb. Hom.* 119 Monie þewas beoð.. þe monnen þuncheð rihte, ac hi þah ledað to deðe on ende. *a* **1225** *Ancr. R.* 10 Ich am blac & tauh hwit, heo seið. *Ibid.* 422 Ancre ne schal nout.. turnen hire ancre hus to childrene scole. Hire meiden mei, þauh, techen sum lutel meiden. *c* **1320** *Cast. Love* 1296 Persones þreo in þrillihod, And o God þauȝ in on-hod. **13..** *Cursor M.* 5750 (Gött.) þe tre.. semid to brine, And þou [*Fairf.* ȝet] þar was na fir widin. **1590** SHAKS. *Mids. N.* III. ii. 343 Your hands then mine, are quicker for a fray, My legs are longer though to runne away. **1672** DRYDEN *Assignation* Prol. 3 Prologues like bells to Churches toll you in With chiming verse,.. With this sad difference though, of pit and pew, You damn the poet, but the priest damns you. **1741** RICHARDSON *Pamela* I. xxv. 30 Is there no Constable nor Headborough, tho', to take me out of his House? **1872** BROWNING *Fifine at the Fair* lxvii. 13 It did its duty, though. **1885** ANSTEY *Tinted Venus* vii. 81 It was in a note, but I've lost it. She told me what was inside though.

b. *colloq.* Used as an intensive after a question or emphatic statement: indeed, truly.

1905 *Eng. Dial. Dict.* VI. 102/1 'How it do rain!' indicates a heavy shower; but, 'How it do rain though!' marks a much heavier. **1906** [see GEEWHILLIKINS *int.*]. **1912** B. HARRADEN *Out of Wreck I Rise* viii. 153 'I didn't know that persons who wrote plays made thousands.' 'Don't they, though,' Hailsham answered, laughing. **1929** E. M. BRENT-DYER *Rivals of Chalet School* vi. 83 'We've got more than an hour yet!' 'Have you, though?' said Mrs Maynard's voice just behind her. 'You've nothing of the kind.' **1948** G. VIDAL *City & Pillar* I. v. 147 'What a sad story!' said Maria. 'Isn't it, though?' **1974** J. AIKEN *Midnight is Place* iv. 128 'I get enough money.. for Papa and me.' 'Did you though?' said Lucas.. with surprise.

II. *conj.* (or *conjunctive adv.*).

1. **a.** Introducing a subordinate clause expressing a fact: Notwithstanding that; in spite of the fact that, although. (Formerly with verb in subjunctive, where the indicative is now used.) Proverbial phr. ***though I say it that should not*** and varr.: see SAY *v.*[1] B. 2 b.

c **888** [see A. *α*]. **971** *Blickl. Hom.* 21 [He] bið þonne undeaþlic, þeah he ær deaþlic wære. *c* **1175** [see A. *α*]. **12..** *Moral Ode* 356 Ne mai non vuel.. beon inne godes riche ðeh þer beð wunienges fele. **13..** *E.E. Allit. P.* B. 233 For-þy þaȝ þe rape were rank, þe rawþe watz lyttel. **13..** *Gaw. & Gr. Knt.* 69 Ladies laȝed ful loude, þoȝ þay lost haden. **1362** LANGL. *P. Pl.* A. I. 10 Ich was a-ferd of hire face þauh heo feir weore [*B.* þeiȝ she faire were]. *c* **1440** *York Myst.* xxx. 45 My-selffe yof I saye itt. *Ibid.* xlviii. 344 Helpe ne holde, Hadde I none of you, þof I quaked. **1535** STEWART *Cron. Scot.* (Rolls) II. 590 The duke.. Treittit him weill thocht he was far fra hame. **1610** SHAKS. *Temp.* II. ii. 135 Though thou canst swim like a Ducke, thou art made like a Goose. **1701** DE FOE *True-born Eng.* II. 314 They are no kings, though they possess the crown. **1746** FRANCIS tr. *Horace, Art Poet.* 414 The hone Gives edge to razors, though itself has none. **1748** SMOLLETT *Rod. Rand.* vi, The French.. are very civil, thof I don't understand their lingo. **1840** DICKENS *Old C. Shop* xv, A gentle hand.. rough-grained and hard though it was. **1857** BUCKLE *Civiliz.* I. xi. 647 Though they rallied, the effort cost them dear.

b. With ellipsis in the subordinate clause: usually directly preceding an adj., pple., sb., or adj. phr. qualifying the subject of the main clause, or an adv. or adv. phr. qualifying the verb.

1592 WARNER *Alb. Eng.* IX. xlvi. (1602) 216 It was objected, though untruely, That they were ydle. **1599** SHAKS. *Much Ado* II. i. 215 The base (though bitter) disposition of Beatrice. **1711** SHAFTESB. *Charac.* I. III. ii. (1737) II. 48 Favourable to a few, tho for slight causes. **1812** CRABBE *Tales* xv. 268 For the zealous Youth Resolved, though timid, to profess the truth. **1875** JOWETT *Plato* (ed. 2) I. 256 One who, though a foreigner, has often been chosen their general. **1896** *N. & Q.* 8th Ser. IX. 160/1 Though marred by eccentricities and extravagances of language, the play has genuine dramatic fibre.

2. **a.** Introducing a subordinate clause expressing a supposition or possibility: Even if; even supposing that; granting that. (With verb. in subjunctive.)

c **888** K. ÆLFRED *Boeth.* xiii, Hwæt hæfst þu.. æt ðæm welan, þeah hy nu ec wæron? *c* **1175** *Lamb. Hom.* 15 þaȝh we suneȝhie nu on þisse liue ne scal us na mon uelien þer uore. *a* **1300** *Cursor M.* 4296 Strengh o luue.. nan mai stere, þof his hert al stillen were. *a* **1450** MYRC *Par. Pr.* 358 For þaȝ a preste be but a fonne Aske hys teyþynge welle he conne. *c* **1450** in Aungier *Hist. Syon Monast.* (1840) 385 None shal enclyne to other, thof it be the abbes that passethe by them. **1539** BIBLE (Great) *Job* xiii. 15 Though he slaye me, yet wyll I put my trust in hym. **1610** SHAKS. *Temp.* I. i. 62 Hee'l be hang'd yet, Though euery drop of water sweare against it. **1714** ADDISON *Spect.* No. 557 ¶2 He would not accept of one [witness], tho' it were Cato himself. **1884** *Leisure Hour* Oct. 611 Though knots be tied in the sunshine ..they're meant to hold in a gale.

b. With ellipsis (as in 1 b).

1591 SHAKS. *Two Gent.* III. i. 102 Though nere so blacke, say they haue Angells faces. **1703** ROWE *Fair Penit.* II. ii, No Place, tho' e'er so holy, shou'd protect him. **1792** CHARLOTTE SMITH *Desmond* III. 346 If she looks pale, though only from slight cold or.. fatigue, I fancy her about to be ill. **1875** J. P. HOPPS *Princ. Relig.* x. (1878) 32 Though punished by the rulers, [he] may be rewarded by the ruled.

3. Introducing an additional statement restricting or modifying the preceding: And yet, but yet, but still, nevertheless, however. Sometimes preceding the main statement.

(Coinciding in sense with I, but differing in construction, being conjunctive.)

a **1240** *Ureisun* 105 in *Cott. Hom.* 197 Ful wel þu me iseie þauh þu stille were. **1340** *Ayenb.* 9 Þet is on of þe zeuen dyadliches zennes, þaȝ þer by zome bronches þet ne byeþ naȝt dyadlich zenne. *c* **1400** *Destr. Troy* 1312 Tho þat left were on lyue þogh þai lite were. **1526** *Pilgr. Perf.* (W. de W. 1531) 2 Though it be necessary to all maner of religyous persones, yet moost expedient it is to prelates. **1678** BUNYAN *Pilgr.* 178 Glad shall I be, if I meet with no more such brunts, though I fear we are not got beyond all danger. **1774** MITFORD *Ess. Harmony Lang.* 16 Tho what has been printed on both sides is little red. **1810** CRABBE *Borough* vii. 48 To show the world what long experience gains, Requires not courage, though it calls for pains. **1894** *Solicitors' Jrnl.* XXXIX. 2/2 The..report..must state that fraud has been committed, though the guilty person need not be specified.

4. In more or less weakened or modified sense, often nearly coinciding with *if*, but usually retaining some notion of opposition. †**a.** After negative or interrogative phrases with *wonder*, *marvel*, *be sorry*, *care*, etc., where *if* or *that* is now substituted.

c **1200** *Trin. Coll. Hom.* 117 He forbed his apostles, þat hie neren noht sorie, þeh he hem forlete lichamliche. **1340** HAMPOLE *Pr. Consc.* 9585, I rek noght, þogh þe ryme be rude. **13..** *Cursor M.* 4122 (Gött.) Na wonder þan þow [*Fairf.* if] him was wa. **14..** *Beryn* 953 No mervell þouȝe his herte wer in grete mournyng. **1557** NORTH *Gueuara's Diall Pr.* 295, I do not merveil though they are ful of dyseases when they are old. **1637** GILLESPIE *Eng. Pop. Cerem.* Ep. A ij b, He cares not though the Church sinke.

b. In phr. *as though*: as if; as would or might be the case if; so as to suggest the supposition that. (With verb in past subjunctive (also with ellipsis), or with inf. of purpose: cf. *as if* s.v. IF 8 c.) In quot. 1297, with ellipsis of *as* (obs.). In quot. 1963, with verb in present indicative.

Here the opposition is not between the two suppositions actually denoted by the main and subordinate clauses, but between two facts, one expressed by the main clause, and the other implied; e.g. in quot. 1598, 'I thank you as much as though I did', = 'I thank you as much as I would thank you if I did eat (though I do not)'.

c **1200** *Trin. Coll. Hom.* 7 Sainte powel wrot þo a writ,.. and dude him seluen mid hem þaron, alse þeih he sunful were. **1297** R. GLOUC. (Rolls) 165 Vpe þe hul of þe pek þe wind þere iwis Vp of þe erþe ofte comþ of holes þei hit were. **13..** *Cursor M.* 19088 (Edin.) Qui wondir ȝie..Als þoȝ þis war don wiþ ur miȝt? *c* **1400** *Brut* 238 Buriede in þat sande, as þauȝ þai hade bene hondes. **1509–10** *Act 1 Hen. VIII*, c. 18 §2 The Quene [shall] have like Habilitie..as though she had orygynally ben borne within this Realme. **1583** STUBBES *Anat. Abus.* II. (1882) 72 This is as though a man should despise meane fare, bicause he cannot come by better. **1598** SHAKS. *Merry W.* I. i. 291 I'faith, Ile eate nothing: I thanke you as much as though I did. **1632** LITHGOW *Trav.* VI. 298 The Camell..hath a most slow and lazy pace.., as though he were weighing his feete in a ballance. **1794** MRS. RADCLIFFE *Myst. Udolpho* lii, I have reason to love him as though he was my own son. **1864** DASENT *Jest & Earnest* (1873) II. 239 This looks as though Magnus was more afraid of Harold than of Sweyn. *a* **1912** *Mod.* He shaded his eyes as though dazzled by the light. He raised his hand as though to take off his hat. **1963** D. STOREY *Radcliffe* xxxvi. 367 It's the sense of imitation that's so forbidding... As though it's all a deception, and the only person it doesn't deceive is me.

†**c.** *simply*. If, supposing that. *Obs. rare.*

1526 TINDALE *Acts* xxiii 9 Though a sprete or an angell hath apered to hym, lett vs not stryue agaynst God.

5. With special constructions (in sense 1, 2, or 3). †**a.** Followed by *that* (in OE. *þe*): see THAT *conj.* 7, THE *particle* 2. *Obs.*

c **1050** *Byrhtferth's Handboc* in *Anglia* (1885) VIII. 302 Ðeah ðe ealle daȝas ælce ȝeare habbon heora concurrentes. *c* **1200** ORMIN Ded. 155 Icc hafe hemm wrohht tiss boc To þeȝȝre sawle nede, þohh þatt teȝȝ all forrwerrpenn itt. *a* **1300** *Cursor M.* 1803 Bot þof þat noe was in quert, He was noght al at es in hert. *c* **1386** CHAUCER *Prol.* 729, I pray yow..That ye narette it nat my vileynye Thogh that I pleynly speke. *c* **1475** *Rauf Coilȝear* 166 Thocht that I simpill be, Do as I bid thee. **1595** SHAKS. *John* III. iii. 57 Though that my death were adiunct to my Act, By heauen I would doe it. **1605** —— *Lear* IV. vi. 219 Though that the Queen on special cause is here Her Army is mou'd on. **1711** in *10th Rep. Hist. MSS. Comm.* App. v. 160 It appears to be a mock-siege; tho' that Ginckle gained the town in earnest.

b. Strengthened by *all*, following (see ALL C. 10 a) or preceding. *Obs.* (exc. in comb. ALTHOUGH). Also by *even* preceding: see EVEN *adv.* 9 c.

even though is not used by Shakespeare nor in Bible of 1611.

c **1325** *Song Mercy* 168 in *E.E. Poems* (1862) 123 Al þauȝ i kouþe, yf þat i wolde. *c* **1330** R. BRUNNE *Chron. Wace* (Rolls) 16055 þowh al he hadde Crysten feyþ, To þo Crysten he dide ouer leyþ. **13..** *Cursor M.* 4246 (Gött.) Al þou þair treuthes sundri ware. *a* **1400** in *Hampole's Wks.* (1896) I. 200 þofe-all they know me noghte for þi sone. *c* **1400** MAUNDEV. (Roxb.) Pref. 2 John Mawndevyle, Knyȝt, þof all I be vnworthy. *c* **1450** *St. Cuthbert* (Surtees) 107 þof all' he be with outen gylte. **1697**, **1791** [see EVEN *adv.* 9 c]. **1856** J. H. NEWMAN *Serm. Var. Occas.* i. (1881) 12 Nor, even though it be told to her, can she enter into it.

†**6.** Ormin has the combination *þohh swa þehh*, lit. 'though so though', 'though so yet', in the sense 'nevertheless', 'notwithstanding'. Cf. THOUGH-WHETHER in same sense.

This is the only use of the form *þehh* in Ormin.

c **1200** ORMIN 9717, & teȝȝre name þohh swa þehh

III. as *sb.* The word used as a name for itself, or an utterance of it. *nonce-use.* (Cf. IF B.)

1634 CANNE *Necess. Separ.* (1849) 255 To answer his ifs & thoughs & whats particularly.

†**thoughless, þaȝles**, *adv.* or *conj.* *Obs.* [f. *þaȝ*, THOUGH + -LESS *adv.*] Nevertheless.

1340 *Ayenb.* 6 Oure lhord..ous uorbyet..þet me ne zuerie,..þaȝles ine guode skele me may zuerie wyþ-oute zenne. *Ibid.* 8 Þis heste uorbyet þet non ne ssel slaȝe oþren. ..þaȝles uor to slaȝe þe misdoeres,..hit is guod riȝt by þe laȝe. *Ibid.* 9.

thought[1] (θɔːt). Forms: 1–3 **ðoht**, 1–4 **þoht**, 2–4 **þouht**, 3–4 **þoȝt**, 3–5 **þouȝt**, 5– **thought**; also 3 **þoucht**, (*Orm.*) **þohht** (**ðhoȝt**), 3–4 **þoȝte**, 4 **thouȝt**, (**thouht, thouth, thout, toght**); 4–5 **þoght, thoȝt**, (**þout, þouth, thoȝth**), *Sc.* **thoucht**; 4–7 **thoght**; 5 **þowȝt, þouȝte, thoȝte**, (**thowhte, þow3th, þowth, towyth** (? **tow3th**), 5–6 **thoughte, thowte, thowthe**, 6 **thowghte, thoft**), 4– *Sc.* **thocht**. [OE. *þoht*, shortened from **þóhi*,:—**þaŋχt*-, from stem of *þencan* THINK *v.*[2] + -T *suffix*[3]. Cf. OS. *githâht* (Du. *gedachte*), OHG. *gidâht*; also ON. *þótti*, *þóttr*, Goth. *þûhtus* (:—**þuŋχtus*). In most of the senses *thought* corresponds not so much to OE. *þoht*, as to the compound *ȝeþoht*, which survived in the 12th c. as *iþoht*: see sense 2.]

1. a. The action or process of thinking; mental action or activity in general, esp. that of the intellect; exercise of the mental faculty; formation and arrangement of ideas in the mind.

In quot. *c* 1250, thinking in a specified way; nearly = feeling, emotion.

a **839** *Laws of Ecgbert* c. 5 Mid þohtes wilnunga.. besmiten. *c* **1250** *Gen. & Ex.* 2254 Quanne Iosep hem alle saȝ, Kinde ðoȝt in his herte was ðaȝ. **1377** LANGL. *P. Pl.* B. v. 513 Þise Ribaudes..repente hem..þat euere þei wratthed þe..in worde, þouȝte, or dedes. *c* **1425** *Craft of Nombrynge* (E.E.T.S.) 28 Here he teches þe to multiplie be þowȝt figures in þi mynde. *c* **1440** *Promp. Parv.* 492/1 Thowhte, or thynkynge, *cogitacio.* **1530** PALSGR. 280/2 Thought, the laboryng of the mynde, *cogitation, pensee.* **1637** MILTON *Lycidas* 189 With eager thought warbling his Dorick lay. **1704** NORRIS *Ideal World* II. iii. 102 Whether Brutes are capable of thought? **1794** PALEY *Evid.* III. viii. (1817) 393 Thought..can be completely suspended and completely restored. **1853** KINGSLEY *Hypatia* xiv. 166 The pale.. student, oppressed with the weight of careful thought. **1875** JOWETT *Plato* (ed. 2) IV. 270 Psychology..analyses the transition from sense to thought.

b. As a function or attribute of a living being: Thinking as a permanent characteristic or condition; the capacity of thinking; the thinking faculty; in early use often nearly = mind.

c **950** *Lindisf. Gosp.* Matt. xxii. 37 Lufa drihten..of alle hearte ðine & of alle sauele ðine & in alle ðoht ðinne [L. *in tota mente tua*]. —— Mark v. 15 Sittende ȝecladed..& hales ðohtes [L. *sane mentis*]. [*c* **1175** *Lamb. Hom.* 99 He onlihte ure mod mid seofanfald ȝife, þet is mid wisdom, and angite mid iðohte, and streinde [etc.].] *c* **1200** *Trin. Coll. Hom.* 71 We hauen on ure þoht, to shewen him ure sinnes. *a* **1300** *Cursor M.* 22166 (Edin.) Þai sale be studiand in þair þoȝte [*Gött.* thouth] Queþer þate he be criste ouir nai. *Ibid.* 25598 Do wickednes vte of vr thoght. *c* **1386** CHAUCER *Wife's T.* 227 Greet was the wo the knyght hadde in his thoght. *c* **1400** *Emare* 223 Alle hys hert & alle hys þowȝth, Her to loue was yn browght. *c* **1460** *Wisdom* 959 in *Macro Plays* 67 Put yt, Lorde, in-to my thowte. *c* **1470** HENRY *Wallace* I. 251 With hewy cheyr and sorowfull in thocht. **1605** SHAKS. *Lear* IV. vi. 45 Had he bin where he thought, By this had thought bin past. **1830** TENNYSON *Deserted House* i, Life and Thought have gone away. **1877** E. R. CONDER *Bas. Faith* i. 8 Thought, feeling, will, are the three strands of the triple cord of life.

c. The product of mental action or effort; what one thinks; that which is in the mind (sometimes, as expressed in language: cf. quot. 1702). *train of thought*: see TRAIN *sb.*[1] 12 b.

c **1200** ORMIN 2577 Forr hire þohht & hire word & hire weorrc wass clene. *c* **1250** *Hymn to God* 12 in *Trin. Coll. Hom.* 258 þu þe wost al ure þoucht. *c* **1290** *Beket* 1188 in *S. Eng. Leg.* I. 140 He rounede in is wiues ere, and tolde hire al is þouȝt. *c* **1375** *Sc. Leg. Saints* i. (*Petrus*) 424 Cum furth, and say þi thoucht and ded but delay. *c* **1400** MAUNDEV. (Roxb.) xiii. 59 Oure Lord takes mare hede to thoȝt þan to word. **1560** BIBLE (Genev.) *Ps.* cxxxix. 2 Thou vnderstandest my thoght afarre of. **1702** ADDISON *Dial. Medals* i. Wks. 1721 I. 439 One..may often find as much thought on the reverse of a Medal as in a Canto of Spenser. **1732** POPE *Hor. Sat.* II. ii. 129 Thus Bethel spoke, who always speaks his thought. **1822** 'B. CORNWALL' *Flood Thessaly* II. 553 Those wondrous letters..By which bright thought was in its quick flight stopp'd And saved from perishing. **1865** TYLOR *Early Hist. Man.* iv. 68 Thought is not even present to the thinker, till he has set it forth out of himself.

d. In a collective sense (with defining adj.): The intellectual activity or mental product characteristic of the thinkers of a particular class, time, or place; what is or has been thought by the philosophers or learned men of some specified country, etc. Also (without defining adj.), that of a named person [cf. G. *denken*].

a **1853** ROBERTSON *Lect.* (1858) 228 Wordsworth is the type of English thought. **1856** *N. Brit. Rev.* XXVI. 39 How old is Modern Thought?—a few years only:—we think ten years—in this country, will include the time within which this peculiar tendency and feeling has distinctly shown its characteristics... Modern Thought, regarded as the opposite and the antagonist of an unexceptive submission to the authority of Holy Scripture. **1884** F. TEMPLE *Relat. Relig. & Sc.* v. (1885) 132 The leaders of scientific thought. **1903** P. SHOREY (*title*) The unity of Plato's thought. *a* **1912** *Mod.* Plato and Aristotle, the leaders of Greek thought. **1935** R. B. PERRY (*title*) The thought and character of William James as revealed in unpublished correspondence and notes, together with his published writings. **1960** G. HARLAND *Thought of Reinhold Niebuhr* i. 13 The centrality of Christology in Niebuhr's thought is clear and unmistakable. **1964** S. J. WILSON (*title*) The thought of Cicero. **1968** in Gray & Cavendish *Chinese Communism in Crisis* 222 A force of revolutionised workers, armed with the thought of Mao Tse-tung, has been trained and tempered. **1971** D. MCLELLAN *Thought of Karl Marx* p. ix, An exposition of certain themes central to Marx's thought. **1974** *Encycl. Brit. Macropædia* IV. 395/2 Socialist education at first had a rather abstract quality, because people had to measure their lives against the 'thought of Mao Tse-tung', a slogan that was to grow in popularity.

2. a. (with *a* and *pl.*) A single act or product of thinking; an item of mental activity; something that one thinks or has thought; a thing that is in the mind; an idea, notion. (Sometimes, as expressed in writing: as in quots. 1645, 1709, 1875, 1967.)

c **975** *Rushw. Gosp.* Matt. ix. 4 And þa ȝeseende ðohtas heora cwæþ to heom forhwon þencaþ ȝe yfel in heortum eowrum? [*c* **1175** *Lamb. Hom.* 109 Ðan alden his to warniene wið uuele iþohtas.] *c* **1200** *Vices & Virt.* 11 Oðer of ðouhtes oðer of wordes oðer of weorkes. **13..** *Cursor M.* 27101 (Cott.) Vr thoghtes ar þai be thoght..he seis. **1451** CAPGRAVE *Life St. Gilbert* 86 Occupied with orisones and meditaciones to avoyde euel þoutes. **1557** N. T. (Genev.) *2 Cor.* x. 5 Wherwith we..bringe into captiuitie euery thoght, to the obedience of Christe. *a* **1568** KING H. STEWARD in *Bann. Poems* (Hunter. Cl.) 706 Gif cairfull thoftis restoir My havy hairt. **1604** SHAKS. *Oth.* III. iii. 161 *Oth.* Ile know thy Thoughts. *Iago.* You cannot, if my heart were in your hand, Nor shall not, whil'st 'tis in my custodie. **1645** FULLER (*title*) Good Thoughts in Bad Times. **1709** POPE *Ess. Crit.* 354 The last..couplet fraught With some unmeaning thing they call a thought. **1754** GRAY *Progr. Poesy* III. iii, Thoughts that breathe, and words that burn. **1803–6** WORDSW. *Intim. Immort.* xi, Thoughts that do often lie too deep for tears. **1824** L. M. HAWKINS *Annaline* I. 344, I will collect my scattered thoughts. **1875** JOWETT *Plato* (ed. 2) V. 28 A similar thought is repeated in the Laws. **1891** 'J. S. WINTER' *Lumley* i, Here I'm idle and haven't a thought in my head —there my brain positively teems with ideas. **1967** tr. Mao Tse-Tung (*title*) The thoughts of Chairman Mao Tse-Tung. **1971** [see RED BOOK, RED-BOOK 4]. **1977** 'S. LEYS' *Chinese Shadows* (1978) i. 11 'We have friends all over the world.' This Thought of Chairman Mao can be seen on many walls. **1982** *Sunday Tel.* 7 Mar. 10/2 Between 1928 and 1941 there were less than 5,000 prosecutions [in Japan] for 'dangerous thoughts'.

b. *spec.* An idea suggested or recalled to the mind; a reflection, a consideration. ***thought for the day*** (*week*, etc.): a pregnant or gnomic thought (esp. one published or broadcast) to be pondered in the course of the day.

a **1240** *Ureisun* in *Cott. Hom.* 203 Hwi ne bi-hold ich þis euer in mine heorte, and þenche ðet hit was for me... Þis þoht wolde sikerliche ontenden so soð luue on me. **1593** SHAKS. *Rich. II*, v. v. 28 Like silly Beggars, Who sitting in the Stockes, refuge their shame That many haue, and others must sit there; And in this Thought, they finde a kind of ease. **1665** BOYLE *Occas. Refl.* v. v, This..is onely to tell us, what you observ'd, not what Reflections you made upon it, and..that which I was inquisitive after, was your Thoughts. **1818** SCOTT *Hrt. Midl.* xxxvii, The thoughts that ye hae intervened to spare the puir thing's life will be sweeter in that hour..than [etc.]. **1835** J. H. NEWMAN *Par. Serm.* (1837) I. i. 15 Though this thought should never make a man despair to-day, yet it should ever make him tremble for to-morrow. **1932** R. LEHMANN *Invit. Waltz* I. ii. 6 'Remember what Mother said yesterday.' 'What?' 'She'd have to start calling you herself.' Olivia gave a hoarse chuckle. 'Thought for the day...' **1972** *B.B.C. Handbk. 1973* 82 *Thought for The Day* is broadcast as part of the morning *Today* sequence at 7.45 a.m. **1973** J. LEASOR *Host of Extras* iii. 41 Gratitude is sufficiently rare to cause surprise in those who find it, which is my thought for today. **1976** *Listener* 2 Dec. 716/3 So there, for the programme-makers' suggestion box, is a thought for the week. **1978** R. THOMAS *Chinaman's Chance* xv. 152 They pay a lot to live here and then they never get up in time to watch the sun rise... Just my thought for the day.

c. ***second thoughts***: ideas occurring subsequently; later and maturer consideration (usu. in phr. *on* or *upon second thoughts*). So ***first thoughts***.

1642 CHAS. I *Mess. to Both Houses* 28 Apr. 4 Second thoughts may present somewhat to your considerations which escaped you before. **1667** MILTON *P.L.* IX. 213 Now advise Or hear what to my mind first thoughts present. **1687** BP. CARTWRIGHT in *Magd. Coll.* (O.H.S.) 139 Are you.. willing upon better and second thoughts to submit? **1711** HICKES *Two Treat. Chr. Priesth.* (1847) II. 396, I desire you to send your second thoughts and reflections upon it. **1838** J. H. NEWMAN *Par. Serm.* (1842) IV. ii. 41 It is often said that second thoughts are best; so they are in matters of judgment, but not in matters of conscience. **1864** TENNYSON *Sea Dreams* 65 Is it so true that second thoughts are best? Not first, and third, which are a riper first?

3. Proverbial Phrases (from 1 and 2): **a.** ***as swift as thought***, etc.; so ***at, like, upon,*** or ***with a thought***, in an instant, immediately, at once. **b.** ***thought is free***: one is at liberty to think as one will.

a **1225** *Ancr. R.* 94 Ase swifte ase is nu monnes þouht, & ase is þe sunne gleam. **1572** FORREST *Theophilus* 342 in *Anglia* VII, Made in vocation, And was present in manner, at a thought. **1588** SHAKS. *L.L.L.* v. ii. 261 Fleeter then arrows, bullets, wind, thought. **1610** —— *Temp.* IV. i. 164 Come with a thought; I thank thee Ariell: come. **1611** —— *Wint. T.* IV. iv. 565 Faster then Thought, or Time. **1845** GOSSE *Ocean* iv. (1849) 168 The whole herd are gone like a thought, leaving their unhappy comrade to his fate. **1885** C. F. HOLDER *Marvels Anim. Life* 230 Quick as thought the skipper hurled his weapon.

b. 1580 LYLY *Euphues* (Arb.) 281 Thought is free my Lord quoth she. *a* **1600** [see THRALL *a.*[1] 1 (*b*)]. **1601** SHAKS. *Twel.*

N. I. iii. 73. **1673** KIRKMAN *Unlucky Citizen* 185, I would tell him that thought was free, and I should not tell him what I thought. **1690** DRYDEN *Amphitryon* II. i, I dare say nothing, but thought is free.

c. Phr. ***it is the thought that counts*** and varr.: the value (to the recipient of a gift) lies in the goodwill, affection, etc., with which it is given.

1934 D. L. SAYER *Nine Tailors* II. iv. 148 Not that I minded.. where my poor little remembrance was placed, for ..it is the thought that counts. **1961** C. MCCULLERS *Clock without Hands* iv. 78 A house-warming present..not too modern or attractive, but it's the thought that counts. **1976** L. THOMAS *Dangerous Davies* ix. 105 'He's eaten your Smarties.'.. 'Thanks for bringing them anyway... It's the thought, really.' **1982** *Preview Shopper* (London ed.) Spring 7 It's the thought that matters. When someone you care for has a special occasion to celebrate you want to choose exactly the right gift.

4. In various specialized senses (from 1 and 2): cf. various senses of THINK *v.*[2]

a. Consideration, attention, heed, care, regard. ***to take thought***, to consider, meditate (how to do something, etc.). In quot. 1602 implying indecision.

a **1250** *Owl & Night.* 492 He ne rekþ noht of clennesse, Al his þouht is of golnesse. *a* **1300** *Cursor M.* 1563 (Cott.) On al thinges was mare þair thoght [*G.* thout] þan was on drightin þat al wroght. *c* **1385** CHAUCER *L.G.W.* 373 (*Balade*) This schulde a ryghtwys lord han in his thouȝt. **1509** *Payne Evyll Marr.* 125 And wyll take thought, and often muse How he myght fynde [etc.]. **1567** *Reg. Privy Council Scot.* I. 519 Na persoun..takkis thocht quhat unhappy deid he sall tak upoun hand. **1602** SHAKS. *Ham.* III. i. 85 And thus the Natiue hew of Resolution Is sicklied o're, with the pale cast of Thought. **1684** EARL ROSCOMMON *Ess. Transl. Verse* 162 Pride..Proceeds from Ignorance, and want of Thought. **1742** GRAY *Ode Eton Coll.* x, Thought would destroy their paradise. *a* **1845** HOOD *Lady's Dream* xvi, Evil is wrought by want of Thought, As well as want of Heart! **1862** F. HALL *Hindu Philos. Syst.* 109 To realize his own wretchedness, so that he may take thought how to escape from it.

b. Meditation, mental contemplation; †perplexity, puzzled condition of mind (quot. 1387, and cf. 5); †*transf.* subject of meditation (quot. *c* 1300). ***lost in thought***: abstracted; absorbed in reverie or contemplation.

a **1300** *Floriz & Bl.* 34 On blauncheflur was al his þoȝt. *c* **1300** *E.E. Psalter* cxviii[i]. 97 Hou luued i, lauerd, þi lagh ai; Mi thoghte es it al þe dai. **1387** TREVISA *Higden* (Rolls) I. 311 To brynge here hertes out of þouȝt þat hereþ speke of laborintus, here I telle what laborinthus is to menynge. *c* **1420** *Sir Amadace* (Camden) xx, On the dede cors, that lay on bere, Ful myculle his thoȝte was on. **1611** SIR W. MURE *Misc. Poems* ii. 13 Perceauing me in thot perplex'd. **1715** POPE *2nd Ep. Miss Blount* 33 In pensive thought recall the fancy'd scene. **1806** J. PORTER *Thaddeus of Warsaw* (ed. 4) III. x. 251 Miss Beaufort..was standing by one of the windows, evidently lost in thought. **1842** TENNYSON *Lord of Burleigh* 21 From deep thought himself he rouses. **1863** W. COLLINS *No Name* I. x. 44/1 He..sat at the table, drawing lines on the blotting-paper with his pen, lost in thought. *a* **1912** *Mod.* She was lost in thought. **1926** B. A. MCKELVIE *Huldowget* iii. 35 He seemed lost in thought. **1955** L. P. HARTLEY *Perfect Woman* xxvii. 240 Jeremy stood lost in thought. 'She hasn't been away very long,' he said.

c. Conception, imagination, fancy.

a **1300** *Cursor M.* 21630 (Edin.) Mar miȝtis hauis ur lauerd wroȝt Than ani man mai þinc in thoȝt. **1413** *Pilgr. Sowle* (Caxton 1483) III. x. 56 The grete horrour therof may not be ..declared by..thought of mannes herte. **1593** SHAKS. *Lucr.* 288 Within his thought her heauenly image sits. **1602** MARSTON *Ant. & Mel.* I. Wks. 1856 I. 15, I long, beyond all thought, To know the man. **1671** MILTON *Samson* 117 O change beyond report, thought, or belief! **1742** COLLINS *Ecl.* ii. 50 When thought creates unnumber'd scenes of woe. **1832** TENNYSON *Miller's Dau.* 237 With blessings beyond hope or thought. **1850** —— *In Mem.* lxx. 8 In shadowy thoroughfares of thought.

d. The entertaining of some project in the mind; the idea or notion of doing something, as contemplated or entertained in the mind; hence, intention, purpose, design; *esp.* an imperfect or half-formed intention; with negative expressed or implied = not the least intention or notion of doing something. Also in *pl.* as '***to have thoughts*** (*of*)'. Cf. THINK *v.*[2] 8.

c **1250** *Gen. & Ex.* 1153 Ðis maidenes deden it in god ðhoȝt. *c* **1320** *Cast. Love* 4 For nas neuere good werk wrouȝt W^t-oute biginninge of good þouȝt. *c* **1425** *Cast. Persev.* 581 in *Macro Plays* 94 Of worldly good is al his þouth. **1535** COVERDALE *Jer.* xxix. 11, I knowe, what I haue deuysed for you... My thoughtes are to geue you peace, & not trouble. **1610** SHAKS. *Temp.* IV. i. 220, I do begin to haue bloody thoughts. *a* **1771** GRAY *Tophet* 6 Satan's self had thoughts of taking orders. **1818** SCOTT *Hrt. Midl.* xlix, Knock says his Grace has no thought to buy it. **1849** MACAULAY *Hist. Eng.* vi. II. 76 All thought of returning to the policy of the Triple Alliance was abandoned. *Mod.* I had some thought of going, but found I could not manage it. I had no thoughts of it then.

e. Remembrance, 'mind'. †***to hold in thought***, †***to have thought on***, to keep in mind, remember. *Obs.* or merged in the general sense.

1297 R. GLOUC. (Rolls) 6553 Of alle is proute dedes i ne may uorbere noȝt, þat i ne mot ȝou telle of on, nou it comeþ in mi þoȝt. **13..** *Cursor M.* 24042 (Gött.) To domes-dai liue if i moght, Ne ȝode it neuer vte of mi thoght. **13..** *Minor Poems fr. Vernon MS.* l. 66 Hold hem in þi þouht. *c* **1400** *Gamelyn* 474 Adams wordes he held in his thoght. *c* **1475** *Rauf Coilȝear* 257 Haue gude thocht on my Name. **1611** SHAKS. *Cymb.* IV. iv. 33, I and my Brother are not knowne; your selfe So out of thought,..Cannot be question'd.

f. Mental anticipation, expectation. (Now mostly with negative expressed or implied.)

a **1307** in *Pol. Songs* (Camden) 220 Tho [= when] he wes in Scotlond, lutel wes ys thoht Of the harde jugement that him wes bysoht In stounde. **1597** SHAKS. *2 Hen. IV*, I. iii. 30 Flatt'ring himselfe with Proiect of a power, Much smaller, then the smallest of his Thoughts. **1611** BIBLE *Ps.* xlix. 11 Their inward thought is, that their houses shall continue for euer. **1677** HALE *Contempl.* II. 127, I had thoughts to find repose there. *Mod.* I had no thought of meeting him there.

g. An opinion or judgement; a belief or supposition; what one thinks of or about a thing or person. Phr. ***perish the thought***: see PERISH *v.* 1 e; ***it's a thought*** (colloq. phr.): it is an idea worth considering.

1596 SHAKS. *1 Hen. IV*, III. ii. 131 Heauen forgiue them, that so much haue sway'd Your Maiesties good thoughts away from me. **1606** —— *Tr. & Cr.* IV. i. 53 Who in your thoughts merits faire Helen most? **1613** WEBSTER *Devil's Law-Case* II. i, You are false To the good thought I held of you. **1786** BURNS *Twa Dogs* 221 The Ladies arm-in-arm.. As great an' gracious a' as sisters; But hear their absent thoughts o' ither. **1831** SCOTT *Ct. Robt.* xxvii, What, then, are thy thoughts of the Emperor? **1855** BROWNING *Childe Roland* i, My first thought was, he lied in every word. **1967** 'S. MITCHELL' *Come, Sweet Death* vii. 63 'Possibly he'd had a key cut.' 'It's a thought.' But I gathered from his tone that he didn't think much of it. **1974** M. HASTINGS *Dragon Island* xiii. 113 'Did they..kill him?' 'Quite a thought. It hadn't occurred to me, but it's a logical explanation.' **1980** J. DITTON *Copley's Hunch* II. iii. 154 'It's a thought, sir.'.. 'If so, it doesn't help us.'

h. In negative contexts: ***not to give*** (something or someone) ***a*** (or ***another***) ***thought***, not to think at all (or any more) about, to dismiss from one's mind.

[**1864** BROWNING *Abt. Vogler* viii, One scarce can say.. That he even gave it a thought.] **1925** F. SCOTT FITZGERALD *Great Gatsby* iii. 64, I wanted..to apologize for not having known him in the garden. 'Don't mention it,' he enjoined me eagerly. 'Don't give it another thought, old sport.' **1952** M. ALLINGHAM *Tiger in Smoke* ii. 50 If it was Martin that was on the tiles I wouldn't give it another thought. **1953** H. CLEVELY *Public Enemy* xxvii. 214 'After your wife's death, didn't you miss this bag?' 'I didn't even give it a thought.' **1956** M. DICKENS *Angel in Corner* viii. 116 There will be plenty of young men in America... You won't give this Joe creature another thought. **1973** W. H. CANAWAY *Harry doing Good* I. iii. 35 I'll do that. Don't you give it another thought.

†**5. a.** Anxiety or distress of mind; solicitude; grief, sorrow, trouble, care, vexation. ***to take thought***, to trouble oneself, grieve, be anxious or distressed. *Obs.* (exc. *dial.*: see Eng. Dial. Dict.).

c **1220** *Bestiary* 682 in *O.E. Misc.* 22 He suggeden & sorȝeden & weren in ðoȝt, Wu he miȝten him helpen ovt. *c* **1250** *Gen. & Ex.* 1433 Ysaac..wunede ðor in ðoȝt and care, For moderes dead and sondes fare. *c* **1330** R. BRUNNE *Chron.* (1810) 85 Þe kyng had fulle grete þouht, his reame ageyn him ros. *c* **1425** *Cast. Persev.* 292 in *Macro Plays* 86, I stonde & stodye, al ful of þowth. **1485** CAXTON *Paris & V.* 46 Paris kyssed Vyenne wyth grete syghes and thoughtes. *c* **1500** *Nutbrown Maid* 119 in Hazlitt *E.P.P.* II. 277 To make thought, Your labur were in vayne. **1523** LD. BERNERS *Froiss.* I. ccxxxiii. 324 His wyfe..toke moche thought for his departyng. **1526** TINDALE *Matt.* vi. 31 Therfore take no thought saynge: what shall we eate? **1556** BP. PONET *Treat. Politic Power* I iij b, Wriothesley..either poisoned himself, or pyned awaye for thought. **1608** E. GRIMSTONE *Hist. France* (1611) 270 Valentine, Duchesse of Orleans (seeing her paines lost..) dies for thought within few daies after. **1613** PURCHAS *Pilgrimage* (1614) 871 Soto died of thought in Florida.

b. *transf.* A cause of distress or anxiety, a 'trouble'. *Obs.* exc. *Sc.* and *dial.*

1649 CROMWELL in Carlyle *Lett. & Sp.* (1871) II. 188 How many considerable ones we have lost, is no little thought of heart to us. **1887** *Suppl. to Jamieson, Addenda*, s.v., That wild son has been a sair thocht..to his mother. **1895** CROCKETT in *Cornh. Mag.* Dec. 569 So mony bairn's things were just a cumber and a thocht to me.

6. a. A very small amount, a very little, a trifle. (Usually, now always, adverbial.)

1581 MULCASTER *Positions* xxxix. (1887) 204 The prince is a thought aboue him for all he be his brother in respect of old Adam. **1599** SHAKS. *Much Ado* III. iv. 14, I like the new tire ..if the haire were a thought browner. **1617** HIERON *Wks.* II. 207 A wound may be giuen in a thought of time, which yet may be in healing aboue a yeere. **1628** GAULE *Pract. The. Panegyr.* 49 They are not currant, if they want the least Thought of a Graine. **1727** SWIFT *Let. to Sheridan* 12 Aug., My giddiness seized me,..I think I am a thought better. **1818** SCOTT *Rob Roy* iv, He seems a thought rash. **1897** G. ALLEN *Type-writer Girl* xvii, The champagne..was a thought too dry.

b. *U.S.* A very short length of time, a moment; usu. in advb. phr.

1912 L. J. VANCE *Destroying Angel* xi. 142 Suddenly she turned her head and intercepted his whole-hearted stare. For a thought wonder glimmered in the violet eyes. **1937** in J. S. Hall *Sayings from Old Smoky* (1972) 122 A panther was attracted by the frying venison. In just a thought or two it came out and screamed. **1949** H. HORNSBY *Lonesome Valley* 59 Johnny loved to hear the screech owl, except that when the scream came unexpectedly it was enough to scare anybody, for a thought.

7. *attrib.* and *Comb.* **a.** attrib., as ***thought-accent*** (accent of thought), ***thought-action***, ***-barrier***, ***-box***, ***-centre***, ***-construction***, ***-content***, ***-coop***, ***-defect***, ***-entity***, ***-form***, ***-habit***, ***-life***, ***-line***, ***-manufactory***, ***-mode***, ***-object***, ***-part***, ***-picture***, ***-process***, ***-product***, ***-production***, ***-relation***, ***-scheme***, ***-seed***, ***-shop***, ***-sign***, ***-structure***, ***-stuff***, ***-system***. **b.** objective and obj. gen., as ***thought-abhorring***, ***-destroying***, ***-engendering***, ***-exceeding***, ***-giving***, ***-inspiring***, ***-reviving***, ***-saving***, ***-shaming***, ***-sounding***, ***-stirring***, ***-straining***, ***-tracing***, ***-transcending*** adjs.; ***thought-catcher***, ***-conductor***, ***-maker***, ***-sprinkler***, †***-taking*** (see 5); ***thought block***. **c.** instrumental, as ***thought-bewildered*** (bewildered by thought), ***thought-burdened***, ***-fed***, ***-laden***, ***-pressed***, ***-unsounded***, ***-winged***, ***-working***, ***-worn***, ***-woven***; locative, as ***thought-bound*** (bound in thought), ***thought-fixed***, ***-free***, ***-set***, ***-tinted***; similative, as ***thought-swift***; ***thought-worthy*** (worthy of thought); limitative, as ***thought-tight*** [after *airtight*]. **d.** Special Combs.: **thought-body** (*Psychics*), see quot.; **thought-consciousness**, consciousness in the state in which it is during the process of thought; **thought control**, the control of a person's thoughts; *esp.* the attempt by a government to restrict ideas and impose opinions by such means as censorship and the control of curricula; **thought-counter**, a current symbol of a thought; **thoughtcrime**, **thought-crime**, in George Orwell's novel *Nineteen Eighty-Four*, the offence of failing in absolute loyalty to the ruling power; hence in any totalitarian system, unorthodox thinking considered as a criminal offence; **thought-executing** *a.*, (*a*) in quot. 1605, 'doing execution with the swiftness of thought' (Aldis Wright); (*b*) executing the thought or intention of a person; **thought-experiment** = GEDANKENEXPERIMENT; **thought-forms** *pl.*, chiefly *Theol.*, the combination of presuppositions, imagery, vocabulary, etc., current at a particular time or place and in terms of which thinking on a subject takes place; **thought model**, a system of related ideas or images; **thought pattern**, a set of assumptions and concepts underlying thought; an habitual way of thinking; in *pl.*, thought-forms; **thought police**, in a totalitarian state, a police force established to suppress freedom of thought; *spec.* in pre-war Japan, the Special Higher Police (*Tokubetsu Kōtō Keisatsu* or *Tokkō*); hence **thought-policing** *vbl. sb.*; **thought-provoking** *a.*, prompting serious thought; **thought reform**, a process of individual political indoctrination used in Communist China; also in extended sense; **thought-saver**, a trite expression used to save one the trouble of thinking, a cliché; †**thought-sick** *a.*, sick with 'thought' or thinking; **thought-sign**, a symbol of thought or judgement, the copula of a predication; **thought-stream**, the continuous succession of a person's thoughts, *spec.* as represented in fiction of a certain kind (cf. STREAM OF CONSCIOUSNESS 2); †**thoughtswift-flying** *a.*, that flies as swift as thought: †**thought-taking** *sb.*, the taking of thought; **thought-'transfer**, **-transference** (*Psychics*), transference or communication of thought from one mind to another apart from the ordinary channels of sense; telepathy; **thought-trans'fer** *v.*, *trans.* to convey by thought or telepathically; hence **thought-transfe'rential** *a.*, pertaining to thought-transference; **thought-wave**, (*a*) in *Psychics*, a 'wave' or undulation of a hypothetical medium of thought-transference; (*b*) a 'wave' or impulse of thought passing simultaneously through a crowd of persons or other living beings; **thoughtway**, a customary way of thinking; an unconscious assumption or idea; **thought-word**, a word conceived in the mind but not uttered; **thought-world** [cf. G. *gedankenwelt*], the amalgam of mental attitudes, beliefs, presuppositions, and concepts about the world characteristic of any particular people, time, place, etc.; **thought-writing**, the recording of thought by graphic symbols directly denoting ideas; ideography. See also THOUGHT-READING.

1835 *Woman* I. 104 An idle set, a *thought-abhorring crew. **1897** ANWYL *Greek Gram.* §40 The *Thought-Accent is the stress or emphasis laid upon a word or syllable, in order to bring out the meaning of the sentence. **1909** *Encycl. Relig. & Ethics* II. 85/2 Purely mental exercise consists in those '*thought-actions' (*Denkhandlungen* as Eucken calls them) which determine both our mental attitude and our conduct. **1935** Thought-action [see *brain-wave* s.v. BRAIN *sb.* 6]. **1958** *New Statesman* 15 Mar. 338/3 This *thought-barrier, the difficulty of re-thinking the problems of defence in nuclear terms, is a very real thing. **1969** *Listener* 24 July 98/2 It seems we are again about to ram what C. H. Rolph calls 'a thought-barrier at least as old as the Great Rebellion'. This is the instant assumption of many Englishmen that whatever they dislike ought to be put a stop to. **1796** COLERIDGE in J. Cottle *Early Recoll.* (1837) I. 199, I wandered on so *thought-bewildered, that it is no wonder I became way-bewildered. **1965** J. POLLITT *Depression & its Treatment* i. 5 Definite features of schizophrenic illness, e.g.

*thought block. **1893** H. R. HAWEIS in *Fortn. Rev.* Jan. 121–2 Assume that there is something personal about us able to manifest and arrange matter, and thus assert itself after death..suppose we call that something our *thought-body. ..Consider then the evidence; first, for the thought-body as Double, and second, for the thought-body as Ghost. **1886** TUPPER *My Life as Author* 145 The emptying out of my *thought-box.., a most necessary relief. **1892** SYMONDS *Michel Angelo* II. XII. viii. 31 This terrible *thought-burdened form. **1584** LYLY *Campaspe* v. iv, I am no *thought catcher, but I gesse vnhappily. **1846** E. A. POE in *U.S. Mag. & Democratic Rev.* Apr. 268/1 We think in cycles, and may, from the frequency or infrequency of our revolutions about the various *thought-centres, form an accurate estimate of the advance of our thought toward maturity. **1890** W. JAMES *Princ. Psychol.* I. iv. 115 But our higher thought-centres know hardly anything about the matter. Few men can tell off-hand which sock, shoe, or trousers-leg they put on first. **1904** Thought-centre [see ASSOCIATION 9]. **1889** SIR W. F. BUTLER *C. G. Gordon* vii. (1899) 188 This lightning *thought-conductor [the electric telegraph] had been used..to disseminate lies and foster gambling in stocks or horses. **1901** E. B. TITCHENER *Exper. Psychol.* I. i. 1 A *thought-consciousness, our mind as it is when we are arguing something out. **1920** S. ALEXANDER *Space, Time, & Deity* I. 161 In these *thought constructions we are dealing all the time with ideas belonging to the empirical world. **1962** *Listener* 15 Mar. 470/2 In science, no thought-construction about the real world can be taken as more than provisionally true. **1916** L. BLOOMFIELD in C. Hockett *Bloomfield Anthol.* (1970) 73 The type of sentence we have so far examined is..often used as the expression of a logical *thought-content. **1972** *Jrnl. Social Psychol.* LXXXVI. 258 A 'thought-content' unit refers to all of a subject's utterance which..seems to express a single moral idea. **1935** U. CLOSE *Behind Face of Japan* xxviii. 332 '*Thought control' in Japan is strictly constitutional. **1939** R. LEHMANN *No More Music* 87 Have you ever tried this healing by thought control?.. It seems that if you think right you'll never have an ache or pain. **1945** *Ann. Reg. 1944* 295 Mr. Chen Li-fu, who as Minister of Education had attempted to institute 'thought control' for Chinese students abroad. **1954** T. S. ELIOT *Confidential Clerk* I. 33 No, Claude, he only teaches *thought* control. Mind control is a different matter. **1980** 'J. MELVILLE' *Chrysanthemum Chain* 10 A scientist of high intellectual integrity opposed to any form of thought control. **1870** LOWELL *Study Wind.* (1886) 309 His importation of the French theory of the couplet as a kind of *thought-coop did nothing but mischief. **1899** *Allbutt's Syst. Med.* VII. 423 The auditory and visual images of words which constitute our habitual *thought-counters. **1949** 'G. ORWELL' *Nineteen Eighty-Four* I. 22 He had committed..the essential crime that contained all others in itself. *Thoughtcrime, they called it. **1954** *Encounter* May 28/1 [The Revolution] first created the 'People's Democracy' of the Terror and of compulsory unanimity, of thought-crimes, and of denunciation as the supreme duty of the citizen. **1968** *Economist* 22 June 19/1 If it were not the habit of Herr Ulbricht's government to put so many people in prison for thought-crime [etc.]. **1637** NABBES *Microcosm.* I. Bivb, Dispute not..your owne *thought-defects. **1909** G. K. CHESTERTON *Orthodoxy* iii. 62 This..summary of the *thought-destroying forces of our time would not be complete without some reference to pragmatism. **1851** H. MELVILLE *Moby Dick* I. xxxiv. 253 How could I—being left completely to myself at such a *thought-engendering altitude,—how could I but lightly hold my obligations to observe all whale-ships' standing orders, 'keep your weather eye open, and sing out every time'. **1892** *Thought-entity [see TRANSCENDENTALISTIC *a.*]. **1949** *Mind* LVIII. 340 There is present, in addition to the imagery, an entity of another kind, a thought-entity. **1593** NASHE *Christ's T.* Wks. (Grosart) IV. 61 *Thought-exceeding glorification. **1605** SHAKS. *Lear* III. ii. 4 You Sulph'rous and *Thought-executing Fires. **1819** SHELLEY *Prometh. Unb.* I. i. 387 Trampled down By his thought-executing ministers. **1945** M. WERTHEIMER *Productive Thinking* vii. 180 (*heading*) On movement, on space, a *thought experiment. **1965** P. CAWS *Philos. of Sci.* xxix. 218 The situation may be illustrated by means of the following thought experiment. **1982** *New Scientist* 14 Jan. 75/2 Bekenstein considered a 'thought experiment' in which a box full of heat radiation was slowly lowered on a rope towards the surface (the horizon) of a black hole. **1876** GEO. ELIOT *Coll. Breakf. P.* 472 The thrill..Of *thought-fed passion. **1773** BEATTIE *Tri. Melancholy* lii, The *thought-fix'd portraiture, the breathing bust. **1892** *Month* Jan. 10 The Thought-forms with which he has surrounded himself. **1890** W. JAMES *Princ. Psychol.* II. xxviii. 664 Kant ..insisted on *thought-forms with which experience largely *agrees*. **1958** E. L. MASCALL *Recovery of Unity* iv. 91 The deadlock between Catholics and Protestants..has been mainly due to their common inheritance of uncriticised.. assumptions and thought-forms from the theologically decadent late Middle Ages. **1976** *Times* 2 Aug. 14/8 Bultmann insisted on the task of re-interpreting the substance of the mythological [biblical] materials in terms of thought-forms intelligible and acceptable in the twentieth century. **1626** SHIRLEY *Brothers* v. iii, To clear myself *thought-free From any promise. **1939** P. CHRISTOPHERSEN *Articles* i. 18 The rise of new grammatical categories must be supposed to result from *thought-habits that have become so common and urgent that they demand linguistic expression. **1954** *Essays & Stud.* VII. 66 The common and ancient thought-habit that sight is the chief and most powerful of the senses. **1729** SAVAGE *Wanderer* III. 167 *Thought-inspiring Woe. *a* **1847** ELIZA COOK *Summer is Nigh* iv, My *thought-laden brow. **1884** J. PARKER *Apostolic Life* III. 267 The writing..is a kind of body in which his *thought-life lives for ever. **1909** J. WELLS *Stewart of Lovedale* xxxiv. 371 His strenuous life had deepened the *thought-lines on his strong face. **1855** *Pict. Chr. Heroism* 244 Pictures of the *thought-maker at his work. **1860** RUSKIN *Mod. Paint.* V. VIII. i. §14. 164 From the time of the Aristophanes thought-shop to the great German establishment, or *thought-manufactory. **1939** V. A. DEMANT *Religious Prospect* vi. 145 Dialectical thought has.. a kinship with traditional religious *thought-modes. **1936** WIRTH & SHILS tr. *Mannheim's Ideology & Utopia* v. 247 The next factor which may serve to characterize the perspective of thought is the so-called *thought-model; i.e. the model that is implicitly in the mind of a person when he proceeds to reflect about an object. **1942** *Mind* LI. 137 It is the perception of spatio-temporal objects, and not the conception of real entities, that is providing the thought-model. **1958** W. STARK *Sociol. of Knowl.* iv. 193 Pareto devalues, and indeed abolishes, the relative in reality; but that means..that he operates with a thought-model which is unrealistic. **1890** W. JAMES *Princ. Psychol.* I. ix. 283 It will show the relative intensities ..of the several nerve-processes to which the various parts of the *thought-object correspond. **1957** G. RYLE in M. Black *Importance of Lang.* (1962) 166 It is left to philosophy to be the science of this third domain which consists largely..of thought objects or Meanings. **1937** *Thought-pattern [see PATTERN *sb.* 8c]. **1943** *Mind* LII. 123 Those elements in the nineteenth-century thought-pattern, which are frequently referred to as Darwinism. **1962** *N. & Q.* Jan. 33/1 This strenuous attempt to convey the archaic thought-patterns of the New Testament into 'the natural vocabulary, constructions, and rhythms of contemporary speech'. **1977** T. ALLBEURY *Man with President's Mind* iii. 23 The rigid education..that surrounded all Soviet citizens..led to a thought pattern that automatically rejected anything but the Soviet official position. **1919** W. DEEPING *Second Youth* xxix. 243 The arched vestibule..and the figure of the man standing there ..reminded Laverach of the picture of the Roman sentinel ..at his post in doomed Pompeii, and the..crashing of successive bombs made the *thought-picture more vivid. **1963** *Times Lit. Suppl.* 10 May 344/4 Wesley's slowly evolving thought-picture of the nature of sin. **1945** *Sun* (Baltimore) 6 Oct. 4/1 It is an order imposing freedom of speech, thought, religion and assembly on the Japanese people, and requiring the immediate liberation of those imprisoned for political offenses by the so-called '*thought police'. **1949** 'G. ORWELL' *Nineteen Eighty-Four* I. 49 He had denounced his uncle to the Thought Police after overhearing a conversation which appeared to him to have criminal tendencies. **1969** *Guardian* 5 Feb. 3/1 The Kremlin's thought-police are moving in slowly, circumspectly, on the Soviet scientific community. **1982** *Sunday Tel.* 7 Mar. 10/2 It may be that the reviewer has confused the latter with the Special Higher Police, or 'Thought Police' as they are sometimes called. **1968** *Listener* 26 Sept. 412/3 To submit to censorship..is to submit to *thought-policing, censorship being the prevention of certain thoughts and images from entering your mind. **1973** *Howard Jrnl.* XIII. 268 The attitude develops into official self-protectiveness—restricting law books in case prisoners become litigious, for example—and downright thought-policing. **1796** T. TOWNSHEND *Poems* 69 The musing *thought-prest head. **1889** J. M. BALDWIN *Handbk. Psychol.* I. xiv. 271 We are concerned merely with the nature of the *thought process—though a full treatment would include also its logic,—its value and bearing in the mental life. **1907** J. LONDON *Iron Heel* i. 18 Each and every thought-process of the scientific reasoner is metaphysical. **1981** 'M. INNES' *Lord Mullion's Secret* ii 22 This was a well-trodden little path in Honeybath's thought-processes. **1906** J. N. KEYNES *Formal Logic* (ed. 4) 6 We may..say that psychology is concerned with *thought-processes, logic with thought-products. **1933** *Mind* XLII. 111 The..view..that there must be radical discontinuity between the antecedents of a valid thought and a valid thought-product. **1884** J. TAIT *Mind in Matter* (1892) 114 Tunnelling out a theory of *thought-production. **1916** J. DEWEY *Ess. Exper. Logic* ii. 84 It..endeavours to define *what* in the various occasions renders them *thought-provoking. **1936** *Discovery* Oct. 332/2 Mr Berenson..contributes a thought-provoking foreword. **1983** I. MURDOCH *Philosopher's Pupil* 323 This was the most thought-provoking observation John Robert had ever elicited from her. **1959** *Atlantic Monthly* Dec. 75/1 xlviii. 371 In serious cases where criminality is involved ..*thought reform and punishment are combined. **1964** M. ARGYLE *Psychol. & Social Probl.* x. 134 Great interest has been aroused by Chinese thought reform, because it has been used on a very wide scale with considerable success and because the methods used are novel. **1966** F. SCHURMANN *Ideology & Organization in Communist China* i. 47 One of the most important questions..is whether 'thought reform' (*szuhsiang kaitsao*) can produce 'correct' behavior in the individual. **1981** J. BANCROFT in Bloch & Chodoff *Psychiatric Ethics* ix. 174 'Thought reform' techniques and aversion therapy. **1887** A. SETH *Hegelianism* i. 36 It does not ..follow that the whole external world is nothing more than a complex of *thought-relations. **1825** D. L. RICHARDSON *Sonn.* 24 A calm and *thought-reviving sound. **1931** L. STEFFENS *Autobiogr.* III. i. 632 They were thoughtless conservatives..whose *thought-saver was: 'My father was a Republican, and what was good enough for him is good enough for me.' **1948** E. GOWERS *Plain Words* vii. 55 It [*sc.* the word *involve*] is used as a thought-saver because it is so faded. **1963** *Times Lit. Suppl.* 10 May 342/3 Those old thought-savers 'the imagination of England' and 'the American mind'. **1927** A. HUXLEY *Proper Stud.* 298 There are plenty of people..who feel as much enthusiasm for *thought-saving devices as for automatic dishwashers and sewing-machines. **1948** *Mind* LVII. 259 Treating existential intuitions as the perceived convergencies of complementary *thought-schemes—the sort of structures that Wittgenstein used to call 'hypotheses'. **1962** *Listener* 15 Mar. 470/2 By purely logical processes of combination, inference, and construction, [mathematics] builds up the most elaborate thought-schemes. **1839** BAILEY *Festus* xx. (1848) 245 He would his brain had died ere it conceived One half the *thought-seeds that took life in it. **1813** HOGG *Queen's Wake* 225 Still his *thought-set eye was raised To Ettrick mountains. **1605** SYLVESTER *Du Bartas* II. iii. I. *Abraham* 373 Your *thought-shaming acts. **1598** J. DICKENSON *Greene in Conc.* (1878) 109 *Thought-sicke louers haue onely reason their soueraigne refuge. **1602** SHAKS. *Ham.* III. iv 51. **1854** S. NEIL *Elem. Rhet.* 34 The *thought-sign *is*, also possesses its own specific signification. **1598** SYLVESTER *Du Bartas* II. i. IV. *Handie-crafts* 304 Reinsearching God, *thought-sounding Judge. *a* **1774** TUCKER *Lt. Nat.* (1834) II. 506 *Thought-straining fervours of prayer and devotion. **1930** WYNDHAM LEWIS *Let.* 30 July (1963) 191 The Ulyssean '*thought-stream' method is only appropriate to the depiction of children, morons, and the extremely infirm. **1948** E. BOWEN *Who do I Write?* 23 But, of course, your monologue isn't simply a thought-stream. **1960** R. ST. JOHN *Foreign Correspondent* xi. 225 Could I make it a vital memory for them and part of their thought stream for ever after? **1980** D. LODGE *How Far can You Go?* i. 5 American psychologists have..established ..that the thought stream of the normal healthy male turns to sex every other minute between the ages of sixteen and twenty-six. **1931** O. JESPERSEN in H. N. Shenton et al. *Internat. Communication* iii. 112 Collinson..has been.. driven to the view that 'it is precisely through our individual use of and reaction to our mother tongue that we can approach these general and fundamental problems of *thought-structures and realize to the full their complexity and subtlety'. **1965** *Eng. Stud.* XLVI. 371 He envisages an extremely..complicated Coleridgean thought-structure which is realized or clothed in a number of images. **1890** W. JAMES *Princ. Psychol.* II. xviii. 58 In some individuals the habitual '*thought-stuff', if one may so call it, is visual. **1915** *New Statesman* 23 Jan. 386/1 Hampered by so much ready-made reach-me-down thoughtstuff. **1595** MARKHAM *Sir R. Grinvile* xiv, In that same myd-daies hower came sayling in A *thought-swift-flying pynnase. **1900** *Month* Sept. 236 The Church has used..whatever other *thought-system she has found in vogue. **1615** HIERON *Wks.* I. 661 Exercised with a world of cares and *thought-takings. **1668** WILKINS *Real Char.* II. viii. 201 Anxiety, Discontent, thought-taking, dump, trouble, anguish. **1913** L. JERROLD *French & English* viii. 153 One is often amazed by..*thought-tight compartments in a walled-up mind. **1937** L. HART *Europe in Arms* xv. 190 Departmentalism tends to thought-tight compartments. *a* **1845** HOOD *Two Peacocks* xv, As if *thought-tinted by the stains Of gorgeous light through many-colour'd panes. **1791** COWPER *Yardley Oak* 158 The *thought-tracing quill. *a* **1711** KEN *Hymnarium* Poet. Wks. 1721 II. 101 O Great I am, enthron'd on high, Of *Thought-transcending Majesty. **1898** *Month* Sept. 232 Other perplexing instances are tortured into cases of *thought-transfer. **1901** *Westm. Gaz.* 8 Jan. 4/2 The Psychic has only got to thought-transfer his desire for telescopic verification. **1884** E. GURNEY in *Pall Mall G.* 29 May 2/2 Our conclusion as to genuine *thought-transference. **1886** MYERS *Phantasms Living* I. Introd. 43 It was thus..that thought-transference, or telepathy, was first discovered. **1905** A. R. WALLACE *My Life* II. 310 Thought, or brain-vibrations, may be carried by the ether to other brains, and thus produce thought-transference. **1890** O. LODGE in *Proc. Soc. Psych. Research* Dec. 461 The hypothesis of a direct *thought-transferential means of obtaining information. **1878** SWINBURNE *In the Bay* xxxix, The *thought-unsounded sea. *a* **1930** D. H. LAWRENCE *Last Poems* (1932) 24 A tremendous body of silence Enveloping even the edges of the *thought-waves. **1954** L. J. COHEN *Princ. World Citizenship* 4 The middle-class southern English have many thoughtways, like their conception of liberty, which they do not share with Cato. **1976** NICHOLS & ARMSTRONG *Workers Divided* 19 They provide..ready-made and well trodden thoughtways (so straightaway it appears 'natural' that 'militants' will be 'mindless' [etc.]). **1980** *Times* 13 May 16/4 Their Civil service advisers—whose thoughtways and corporate interest impel them in certain directions. **1891** *Cent. Dict.*, *Thought-wave. **1901** *Daily Chron.* 18 Sept. 3/2 The Greek idea of a thought-wave, or wind of thought, sweeping through crowds. **1818** SHELLEY *Lines Euganean Hills* 207 The sun floats up the sky, Like *thought-winged Liberty. *a* **1866** J. GROTE in *Jrnl. Philol.* (1872) IV. 66 Looking at language as it naturally presents itself, its apparently most simple units are what we call words, and therefore I describe a noem as a *thought-word. **1889** MIVART *Orig. Hum. Reason* 106 Expressing a voluminous perception by a sudden gesture far too rapid even for thought-words. **1906** *Hibbert Jrnl.* Jan. 277 The doctrine of the Logos, the Thought-Word in the Cosmos. **1816** L. HUNT *Rimini* IV. 88 His *thought-working head. **1947** N. H. BAYNES (*title*) The *thought-world of East Rome. **1958** *Spectator* 20 June 812/2 The thought-world of the laity, high and low, was in many ways pagan and magical. **1979** J. HICK in M. Goulder *Incarnation & Myth* iv. 78 No Christian who has ever lived within the evangelical thought-world can read without emotion such lines as Cowper's, There is a fountain filled with Blood [etc.]. **1846** MRS. GORE *Eng. Char.* (1852) 127 Sparing and *thought-worn, there is nothing in his gravity of brow to encourage indiscreet encroachment. **1859** LEVER *Davenport Dunn* ii, Thoughts of what alone is *thought-worthy. **1892** W. B. YEATS *Countess Kathleen* 132 The tall thought-woven sails that flap unfurled Above the tide of hours, rise on the air. **1890** *Smithsonian Rep.* 50 The monographs on sign language and pictography, having as their text the attainments of the North American Indians..may contribute to the understanding of similar exhibitions of evanescent and durable *thought-writing.

Hence (chiefly *nonce-wds.*) †'**thoughtive** *a.*, addicted to or engaged in thought, thoughtful; '**thoughtkin**, '**thoughtlet**, '**thoughtling**, a small or insignificant thought; '**thoughtsman** (*nonce-wd.*, after *draughtsman*, etc.): see quot.

1654 GAYTON *Pleas. Notes* I. ii. 5 If he be *thoughtive or cogitabund,..his lips, his eyes, his hands, goe as well as his legs. *Ibid.* IV. iii. 187 The Don is indeed a more thoughtive, inward, close, and conceal'd Cocksome. **1867** CARLYLE *Remin.* (1881) II. 148 That little *thoughtkin stands in some of my books. **1858** H. W. BEECHER *Life Th.* (1859) 74 Mosses and inconspicuous blooms hidden in the grass—*thoughtlets, the intents of the heart. **1863** *Reader* 22 Aug., Mere vendors of what may be called carefully-connected thoughtlets. **1832** J. P. KENNEDY *Swallow B.* x, A little nest of *thoughtlings about the eyes. **1842** MIALL *Non-conf. Sketch-bk.* 255 One whom we shall venture to designate a *thoughtsman for the rest..whose..business it shall be..to make himself..acquainted with truth..for for the common benefit.

thought², **thaught** (θɔːt). Now *dial.* Also 7 **thougt**, **thoat**, 8 **thout**, 9 **thawt**, *dial.* **thowt**. [Altered from the earlier THOFT, q.v. with change of (f) to (x), (the converse of what occurs in *thoft* for *thought*, THOUGHT¹ and pa. t. THINK *v.*², and *thof* for THOUGH). Cf. also MDu. *dochte* and *dofte*, Du. *doft*, MLG. and LG. *ducht*, whence mod.Ger. *ducht*, beside dial. *duft* from

OHG. *dofta*. See also the modern equivalent *thwart*.] A rower's bench; = THWART *sb.*[2]

1622 SIR R. HAWKINS *Voy. S. Sea* liv. 129 His boate fitted with Sayle, Oares, thougts, tholes, dauyd, windles and rother. **1627** CAPT. SMITH *Seaman's Gram.* vi. 27 Thoughts are the seats whereon the Rowers sit. **1633** T. JAMES *Voyage* 57 It did breake two thoughts of our Boat. **1688** R. HOLME *Armoury* III. xv. (Roxb.) 27/1 The thaughts and seats they sit on to rowe. **1697** DAMPIER *Voy. round World* (1699) 118 These Canoas were fitted with Thoats or Benches. **1704** J. HARRIS *Lex. Techn.* I, *Thaughts*, or *Thoughts*. **1725** DE FOE *Voy. round World* (1840) 341 Three muskets which were lashed under their thouts, or benches of the canoe. **1823** MOOR *Suffolk Wds.* 428 *Thowts*, the seats of rowers in a boat —the *thwarts* perhaps; or what go across. **1867** SMYTH *Sailor's Word-bk.*, *Thought*, an old spelling of *thwart*. **1886** R. C. LESLIE *Sea-painter's Log* 172 We turned-to and lashed the nets down from thawt to thawt.

thought (θɔːt), pa. t. and pple. of THINK *v.*[1] and [2].

thought, obs. Sc. form of THOUGH.

thoughted ('θɔːtɪd), *a.* [f. THOUGHT[1] + -ED[2].]

1. Having thoughts (of a specified kind): esp. in parasynthetic combinations, as ***deep-*, *high-*, *low-*, *solemn-thoughted***, etc.: see the first element.

1592, **1631** Sick-thoughted [see SICK *a.* 11]. **1599** R. LINCHE *Fount. Anc. Fict.* Iij, They should not grow insolent, prowd,..or ouer-highly thoughted. **1643** *True Informer* 23 Most of the moderate and well-thoughted Members were retired to their rest. **1886** SWINBURNE *Stud. Prose & Poetry* (1894) 167 The same high-thoughted harmony of primal and ideal emotions.

2. *Sc.* (**thochtit**) Affected with grief or anxiety; anxious, concerned. (Cf. THOUGHT[1] 5.)

1869 [McLENNAN] *Peas. Life* Ser. I. 19 She can see ne'er a door at a' for hirin', and she's sair thochted for it. *a* **1884** J. SERVICE *Dr. Duguid* II. v. (1887) 209, I was geyan thochted 'estreen, when I heard the win' risin' the way it did. *c* **1890** *Let. to Editor*, Old Scotch folks say *Thoughted* for 'sicklied o'er with the pale cast of thought'.

†'**thoughten**, *a. Obs. rare*[−1]. [irreg. form of *thought*, pa. pple. of THINK *v.*[2]; cf. *boughten*.] Having a (specified) thought or belief; thinking.

1608 SHAKS. *Per.* IV. vi. 115 For me be you thoughten That I came with no ill intent.

thoughtful ('θɔːtfʊl), *a.* [f. THOUGHT[1] + -FUL.] Full of or characterized by thought, in various senses.

1. Given to, disposed to, or engaged in thinking; absorbed in thought; meditative, contemplative; pensive, musing; full of thoughts, preoccupied in mind, hence, in quot. 1656, absent-minded. Also *transf.* of personal attributes, actions, etc.

c **1200** ORMIN 3423 Ure laffdiȝ Marȝe toc All þatt ȝho sahh & herrde,..& leȝȝde itt all tosamenn aȝȝ I swiþe þohhtfull heorrte. **1552** HULOET, Thoughtfull, *cogitabundus*, *meditabundus*. **1656** STANLEY *Hist. Philos.* IV. (1701) 152/2 He was so thoughtful, that going to put Incense into a Censer, he put it besides. **1704** POPE *Windsor Forest* 249 Wand'ring thoughtful in the silent wood. **1722** —— *1st Chorus Trag. Brutus* 7 War, horrid war, your thoughtful walks invades. **1805** H. K. WHITE *Lett., to B. Haddock* 18 Oct., My silent and thoughtful cup of tea. **1873** BLACK *Pr. Thule* iii, Her calm and thoughtful look.

b. Disposed to think about or consider matters; prudent; reflective. Also *transf.* Characterized by reflection; manifesting thought or consideration.

13.. *Cursor M.* 11404 (Cott.) þai ordeind tuelue, þe thoghtfulest a-mang þam-selue. *a* **1533** LD. BERNERS *Gold. Bk. M. Aurel.* x. (1535) Fijb, This emperour was so thoughtfull in the orderynge and teachynge of his children, that [etc.]. **1736** BUTLER *Anal.* II. viii. Wks. 1874 I. 292 Objections, which may appear very material to thoughtful men. **1879** FROUDE *Cæsar* xiv. 200 Thoughtful persons.. had heard of these doings with uneasiness. **1884** F. TEMPLE *Relat. Relig. & Sc.* i. (1885) 5 Not beyond the reach of thoughtful inquiry.

c. With *inf.*, *dependent cl.*, or *of*: (*a*) Careful, heedful; (*b*) Having the intention or purpose, aiming at or desirous *of* something; (*c*) Thinking about or meditating on something; mindful. Now *rare* or *Obs.* (See also 3.)

[*c* **1375** *Sc. Leg. Saints* xvi. (*Magdalena*) 552, I..prays [= pray] þe þat þu wil thochtful one me be.] **1597** SHAKS. *2 Hen. IV*, IV. v. 73 For this, they haue beene thoughtfull, to inuest Their Sonnes with Arts, and Martiall Exercises. **1621** T. WILLIAMSON tr. *Goulart's Wise Vieillard* 105 They are much more thoughtfull of their minde. **1715** J. CHAPPELOW *Rt. Way Rich* (1717) 138 The believer..is thoughtful to have a ..fuller view of him [Christ]. **1726** LEONI *Alberti's Archit.* I. 93/2 A Prisoner always thoughtful of his liberty and safety. **1821** *Examiner* 252/1 Thoughtful of enjoyments for ever left behind.

†**2.** Full of mental trouble; anxious; sorrowful, melancholy, moody. Also *transf. Obs.*

a **1300** *Cursor M.* 11140 He wex thoghtful and likand ill. **1387–8** T. USK *Test. Love* II. ix. (Skeat) l. 185 For her hast thou suffred many thoughtfull diseases. *c* **1430** *Diatorie* 6 in *Babees Bk.* 54 Not pensif ne þouȝtful for ony sodein chaunce. *c* **1500** *Melusine* 26 In this dolour & woo was Raymondyn a longe space of tyme, & was moche þoughtfull & wroth. **1627–77** FELTHAM *Resolves* I. v. 6 The merry soul is freer from intended mischief than the thoughtful man. **1744** M. BISHOP *Life & Adv.* viii. 117 Something to divert my Mother and Wife who were both prodigiously thoughtful.

3. Showing thought or consideration for others; considerate, kindly.

1851 BRIMLEY *Ess., Wordsw.* 155 Rich in thoughtful affection. **1863** MRS. GASKELL *Sylvia's L.* iii, In his thoughtful wish of escorting them through the streets of the rough, riotous town. *Mod.* She is very unselfish and thoughtful of others.

†**4.** Capable of thought; conscious, intelligent. *Obs. rare*[−1].

1674 N. FAIRFAX *Bulk & Selv.* 134 To think, that body may be thoughtful too, and any ways aware.

5. *Comb.*, as ***thoughtful-browed***, ***-looking***.

a **1849** MANGAN *Lay Bell* Poems (1859) 35 He alone is thoughtfulsouled. **1904** *Westm. Gaz.* 9 Dec. 6/3 Great, round, thoughtful-looking heads.

thoughtfully ('θɔːtfʊlɪ), *adv.* [f. prec. + -LY[2].] In a thoughtful manner; with thought or consideration; meditatively, musingly; reflectively; considerately, kindly.

1611 COTGR., *Songneusement*, carefully, thoughtfully. **1746** FRANCIS tr. *Horace, Epist.* I. xviii. 163 The Modest oft too dark appear, The Silent thoughtfully severe. **1860** TYNDALL *Glac.* II. App. 431 Right or wrong, a theory thus thoughtfully uttered has its value. **1885** S. H. PRESTON in *Law Times* LXXIX. 335/1 Many of the persons entitled could not be traced..so the company very thoughtfully issued advertisements.

'**thoughtfulness.** [f. as prec. + -NESS.] The quality or state of being thoughtful.

†**1.** Anxiety, concern, melancholy. *Obs.*

1574 tr. *Marlorat's Apocalips* 113 The scripture calleth vpon vs to lay away..all thoughtfulnesse for this present life. **1685** BAXTER *Paraphr. N.T.* Matt. vi. 27 Your selftroubling distrustful care and thoughtfulness. **1742** RICHARDSON *Pamela* III. 418 If he but sees the least Thoughtfulness upon my Brow, studying..to dispel it.

2. Meditativeness, pensiveness; reflectiveness; considerateness.

1697 BURGHOPE *Disc. Relig. Assemb.* Ded., These are the men that I wou'd awaken into sober thoughtfulness. **1737** WHISTON *Josephus, Antiq.* XVI. ix, Herod was silent and in great thoughtfulness. **1809** W. IRVING *Knickerb.* 85 The honest burghers smoked their pipes in profound thoughtfulness. **1876** MISS BRADDON *J. Haggard's Dau.* III. 101 A countenaunce as mysterious in its solemn thoughtfulness as the head of Memnon. **1880** 'OUIDA' *Moths* II. iv. 89 Reared in tender thoughtfulness to the poor.

thoughtiness: see after THOUGHTY.

thoughtive, thoughtkin: see after THOUGHT[1].

thoughtless ('θɔːtlɪs), *a.* [f. THOUGHT[1] + -LESS.] That is without thought, in various senses: the opposite of THOUGHTFUL.

1. Not taking thought, acting without thought or reflection; unreflecting, heedless, imprudent.

1592 KYD *Sp. Trag.* IV. i. 40 Nor thinke I thoughtles thinke vpon a meane, To let his death be vnreueng'd at full. **1611** FLORIO, *Inpensierato*, thoughtlesse, carelesse. *a* **1704** T. BROWN *Sat. agst. Woman* 39 Weak curses..For thoughtless crimes, which come out of thy kind. **1736** BUTLER *Anal.* I. ii. Wks. 1874 I. 42 Youth may be alleged as an excuse for rashness and folly, as being naturally thoughtless. **1849** B. TAYLOR in *Life & Lett.* I. vii. 149, I shall neither be rash nor thoughtless.

b. With *of* or dependent clause: Not thinking; unmindful, forgetful; heedless, careless; unsuspecting. Now *rare*.

1615 CHAPMAN *Odyss.* v. 19 He..Finds you so thoughtlesse of him, and his birth. **16..** ROGERS (J.), Without remorse for the past, and thoughtless of the future. **1697** DRYDEN *Virg. Georg.* III. 668 A Snake..Leaving his Nest..thoughtless of his Eggs. **1725** POPE *Odyss.* IV. 716 The Royal guest, Thoughtless of ill, accepts the fraudful feast. **1742** YOUNG *Nt. Th.* IV. 365 Men homage pay to men, Thoughtless beneath whose dreadful eye they bow.

†**c.** Free from care or anxiety. Also *transf. Obs.*

1742 GRAY *Eton Coll.* v, The thoughtless day, the easy night. **1764** GOLDSM. *Trav.* 255 So blest a life these thoughtless realms display. **1789** BLAKE *Songs Innoc., Night* 17 They look in every thoughtless nest.

d. Wanting in consideration for others; inconsiderate.

1794 BLAKE *Songs Exper., Fly* 3 Little fly, Thy summer's play My thoughtless hand Has brush'd away. *Mod.* It was very thoughtless of you to disturb her.

2. Deficient in or lacking thought; not given to thinking; stupid, senseless, dull-witted; destitute of ideas. Now *rare*.

1682 DRYDEN *Mac Flecknoe* 26 Shadwell never deviates into sense.., his goodly fabric..seems designed for thoughtless majesty. **1714** POPE *Epil. Jane Shore* 7 As a blockhead rubs his thoughtless skull, And thanks his stars he was not born a fool. **1879** B. TAYLOR *Stud. Germ. Lit.* 194 He was an earnest thinker in a thoughtless time.

†**b.** Of inanimate things: Devoid of thought.

1691–8 NORRIS *Pract. Disc.* (1711) III. 22 Bodies have no Thought, therefore they produce none:..for how can a thoughtless Principle produce a Thought? *c* **1705** BERKELEY *Commonpl. Bk.* Wks. 1871 IV. 469 Extension to exist in a thoughtless thing (or rather in a thing void of perception..), is a contradiction.

'**thoughtlessly**, *adv.* [f. prec. + -LY[2].] In a thoughtless manner; without thought or consideration; unreflectingly, carelessly, inconsiderately.

1714 GARTH *Dispensary* v. 59 In restless Hurries thoughtlessly they live. **1792** V. KNOX *Serm.* vi. 133 He who runs on thoughtlessly in the mad career of pleasure. **1806** HUTTON *Course Math.* I. 152 One thoughtlessly spends 10*l.* a year more than his pay. **1890** GROSS *Gild Merch.* I. 104 The arbitrary interpretation..which came to be thoughtlessly accepted as a fact.

'**thoughtlessness.** [f. as prec. + -NESS.] The quality of being thoughtless; want of thought or consideration; carelessness, inconsiderateness.

a **1704** T. BROWN *Praise Pov.* Wks. 1730 I. 96 The remains of the night [they spend] in sleep, idleness, thoughtlessness [etc.]. **1775** ADAIR *Amer. Ind.* 420 Dry wood, with which they..provide themselves, but only from day to day, through their thoughtlessness of to-morrow. *a* **1862** BUCKLE *Misc. Wks.* (1872) I. 27 Vice is often cunning and wary; but thoughtlessness is always profuse and reckless. **1884** *Manch. Exam.* 1 Oct. 3/1 The thoughtlessness of some of her actions is only equalled by their stupidity.

thoughtlet, thoughtling: see after THOUGHT[1].

thoughtness ('θɔːtnɪs). *rare.* [f. *thought*, pa. pple. of THINK *v.*[2] + -NESS.] The fact or quality of being thought or mentally discerned.

1865 J. GROTE *Explor. Philos.* I. 140, I recognise two manners of existence,..thinkingness and thoughtness, and it is the latter which, when we believe the thought correct or justified, we call phenomenal existence or matter. **1905** *Athenæum* 11 Mar. 306/3 In the dead-alive fashion of the functions of a thinking apotheosized as a thoughtness.

thoughtography (θɔː'tɒgrəfɪ). [f. THOUGHT[1] + PHOT)OGRAPHY.] The production of a visible, usu. photographic, image (supposedly) by purely mental means. Hence '**thoughtograph**, the image produced; **thought'ographer**, one who is said to practise thoughtography; **thoughto'graphic** *a.*

1931 T. FUKURAI (*title*) Clairvoyance and thoughtography. *Ibid.* x. 245 The medium can make the thoughtograph of the object presented by the sitter. **1967** *Psychic News* 20 May 4/2 Thus thoughtographic research spans more than half a century. **1968** J. EISENBUD *World of Ted Serios* xiii. 299 These [nightmares] kept up until he began his 'thoughtography'. **1976** C. WILSON *Geller Phenomenon* 33 (caption) Serios producing a thoughtograph. **1978** *Sunday Sun* (Brisbane) 5 Feb. 66/3 Professor Eisenbud ..subjected thoughtographer Serios to scientific scrutiny. *Ibid.* 66/5 Ted randomly imprinted on film a thoughtograph.

thought-out ('θɔːt'aʊt: stress variable), *ppl. a.* [pa. pple. of *think out* (see THINK *v.*[2] 15) used as adj.] Elaborated, constructed, or arrived at by thinking or mental labour; thoroughly considered.

1870 J. H. FRISWELL *Mod. Men of Lett.* vii. 129 'Paracelsus', and other hard thought-out dramatic pieces. **1907** BP. ROBERTSON in *Trans. Devon Assoc.* XXXIX. 44 A weighty and thought-out survey of the scope and nature of scientific truth.

'**thought-,reading**, *sb.* The reading of another person's thoughts; direct perception by one mind of what is passing in another, independent of ordinary means of expression or communication: a power alleged to be possessed by certain persons or by persons in certain psychic states. Hence allusively. So '**thought-read** *v.*, *trans.* to read a person's thoughts (with the person or the thought as obj.); *intr.* to practise thought-reading; '**thought-,reader**, one who practises or professes thought-reading; '**thought-,reading** *a.*, that practises thought-reading.

1855 SMEDLEY, etc. *Occult Sc.* 258 Thought-reading, in certain experiences of the somnambulist. **1880** MRS. FORRESTER *Roy & V.* I. 30 Did you ever hear of people being thought-readers? **1883** *Fortn. Rev.* 1 Aug. 275 The most recently refurbished mystery in the guise of science, viz. that of so-called 'Thought-reading'. **1891** MRS. RIDDELL *Mad Tour* 111 No thought-reader could have imagined the topic that was engaging Bobby's mind. **1892** *19th Cent.* Jan. 37 These thought readings and foretellings. **1898** L. A. TOLLEMACHE *Talks w. Gladstone* 166 One would like to have seen, or (better still) to have thought-read, Carlyle. **1899** *Daily News* 9 Dec. 6/4 Do you think your thought-reading gift could be turned to practical service in detective work —a thought-reading Sherlock Holmes? **1906** *Pall Mall G.* 4 Jan. 2 He thought-read the conditional intentions of the British commander.

thoughtsman: see after THOUGHT[1].

†'**thoughtsome**, *a. Obs. rare.* [f. THOUGHT[1] + -SOME.] **a.** Addicted to thought; thoughtful. **b.** Of the nature of thought, or having the faculty of thought; mental, spiritual. Hence †'**thoughtsomeness**.

1611 COTGR., *Mental*,..mentall, thoughtsome, belonging to the mind. *c* **1627** SCUDDER *Chr. Daily Walk* ix. §1 (1637) 219 If men report evill of you..Be not so much inquisitiue who raised it, or thought-some how to bring him to his answer. **1674** N. FAIRFAX *Bulk & Selv.* 82 A ghost being in it self not roomthy, it cannot bear any roomthy behaviour towards bodies that are so, any more than bodies that are bulky, can bear immaterial respects or thoughtsom behaviours towards ghosts that are so. *Ibid.* 34 Thoughtsomness setting full as close to the very stamp or inmostness of a thinking Being, as boak or roomthyness does to the Being that is Bodysom.

ˈ**thoughty**, *a.* *Obs.* exc. *Sc.* Forms: see THOUGHT¹. [f. as prec. + -Y.] Given to thought, thoughtful. **a.** Heedful, attentive, intent. †**b.** Pensive, melancholy, anxious.

c **1375** *Sc. Leg. Saints* xxvii. (*Machor*) 706 Besy..Til infourme ȝu in cheryte, And in sawle-hele thochty to be. **1387-8** T. USK *Test. Love* II. ix. (Skeat) l. 21 Euer is their contemplacion in ful of thoughty study to plesaunce. *c* **1412** HOCCLEVE *De Reg. Princ.* 80 Who so þat thoghty is, is wo-begon. *c* **1425** WYNTOUN *Cron.* VI. xvi. 1608 As he past apon a day In til huntynge..On his gamyn al thouchty. *c* **1430** *Pilgr. Lyf Manhode* I. cxl. (1869) 73, I was ther of wunderliche abashed and thouhti. **1823** CORBETT *Petticoat T.* II. 110 (Jam.) Fanny is two years younger than I am, and not so thoughty, as Philip says.

Hence †ˈ**thoughtiness**, melancholy, pensiveness.

1707 J. NIMMO *Narr.* (1889) 4 My father was resolved to use authoretie q^eh was not pleasing to me and increased my thoghtiness.

†**though-whether**, *adv.* *Obs.* Forms: 1 **þeah-hwæþere**, 2 **þeah-, þæh-, þahwhweðre, -weþere, -weðer**, 3 **þohhwheþþre** (*Orm.*), **þeih hweðere, þohqueþer, -ir**, 4 **þoh-, þo-, do-, þou-, þof-, þe-queþer, -ir, though whethir.** [OE. *þéahhwæþere*, f. *þéah* THOUGH + *hwæðere* WHETHER. Cf. OHG. *thoh uuidaru, thoh thiu uuidoro* (Tatian), *dhoh dhiu huuedheru* (Isidore). The analysis of the combination is not clear.] Notwithstanding, nevertheless, howbeit, however.

c **897** K. ÆLFRED *Gregory's Past. C.* xxi. 151 Moniȝe sint ..ðe mon sceal wærlice licettan, and ðeahhwæðre eft cyðan. **971** *Blickl. Hom.* 31 Nam he fif stanas..& þeah-hweþere mid anum he þone gigant ofwearp. *a* **1175** *Cott. Hom.* 223 Se lichame is deadlic..ac þeahweðer god arerð eft þane licame to ecene þingum. *c* **1175** *Lamb. Hom.* 37 þa hweþere þine saul feren scal in to eche pine. *Ibid.* 131 þah hweðre his saule wes in helle. *c* **1200** ORMIN 2459 þatt ȝho þohhwheþþre shollde ben Maȝȝdenn all þwerrt ut clene. *c* **1200** *Moral Ode* 131 (Trin. MS.) þeih hweðere we hit leueð wel. **13..** *Cursor M.* 22934 (Edin.) þohqueþir we sal understand þat [etc.]. *Ibid.* 19546 (Cott.) Thar naman þofqueþer wene. **1357** *Lay Folks Catech.* (MS. T.) 93 Thoughwhethir noght twa goddes the fadir and the son.

thoul(e, thoume, obs. ff. THOLE *sb.*¹, THUMB.

thoundre, thouner, obs. forms of THUNDER.

thour, þour, thourch, thourgh, þourȝ, thourh, þourh, thourth, obs. ff. THROUGH.

thourt, variant pa. t. of THARF *v.* *Obs.*

‖**thous** (ˈθəʊəs). *Zool.* [mod.L., a. Gr. θώς, θω-ός: see THOS.] A species or group of species of the extended genus *Canis*, canine beasts, natives of Africa and Asia; including *Thōus* (or *Canis*) *anthus* (the North African Jackal), and *T. mesomelas, variegatus*, and *Senegalensis*, African jackals.

1839 C. H. SMITH *Dogs* I. iv. 193 Section IV. Thous. *Ibid.* v. 207 By separating our group of Thous from the true Jackals, much confusion..is removed.

thousand (ˈθaʊzənd), *sb.* and *a.* Forms: 1-3 **þusend**, 2-3 **-ent**, (*Orm.*) **-ennd**, 3 **-and, -und, þousunt**, 3-4 **-end**, 3-6 **thousande**, 4 **thus(s)-, thos(s)and(e**, 4-5 **þous-, þows-, thous-, thows-, -and(e, -ant(e, -aund, -end, -ent, -ind(e, -ond(e, -ynd**, 4-7 **thowsand**, 5 **þou-, þow-, thouzand**; 4- **thousand** (*mod.Sc.* **thoozan(t)**. [OE. *þúsend*, sb. fem. and neut. = OFris. *thûsend*, OS. *thûsundig, thûsind* (Du. *duizend*), OHG. *dûsunt* (MHG. *tûsent*, G. *tausend*), Salfrank. *þûschunde*, ON. *þúsund* (*þúshund, þúshundrað*, Sw. *tusen*, Da. *tusind*), Goth. *þûsundi* sb. fem. and neut. Generally held to be cognate with Lith. *túkstanti-s*, Lett. *tûkstûts*, OPruss. **tūsimta* (acc. pl. *tūsimtons*), OSlav. *tysąšta, -ęšta*, Russ. ˈ*tysjatša*, Pol. *tysiac*, Czech *tisíc*, pointing to an orig. Slavo-Teut. **tūssontiā* or *tussntjā*, whence also OTeut. **þūsundi*. The first element is considered by many to be an Indo-Eur. **tūs* meaning 'multitude, force'; cf. Skr. *tawás* 'strong, force'; as to the rest of the word etymologists differ.

The general result is that *þūsund* was prob. an indefinite term for a 'great multitude' (cf. Gr. μυριάς, -αδ-, in its indefinite, and *myriad* in its common English use), which was used as the available equivalent of Gr. χιλιάς and L. *mille*, themselves prob. originally indefinite words, there being no general Indo-Eur. word for 'thousand'.]

1. The cardinal number equal to ten times one hundred: denoted by the symbols 1000 or M (for L. *mille*), formerly often by m̄, or ᵐ, as xxxᵐ.

a. As sb. or quasi-sb., with plural. (*a*) In singular. Usually ***a thousand***, emphatically or precisely ***one thousand***.

971 *Blickl. Hom.* 119 Nis..næniȝ mon þe..wite..hwæþer þis þusend sceole beon scyrtre ofer þæt þe lengre. *c* **1000** *Ælfric's Vocab.* in Wr.-Wülcker 110/12 *Ciliarcus*, þusendes ealdor. *c* **1205** LAY. 21401 Bi þusund & bi þusend þer feollen [*sc.* Sexes] æuere in þene grund. **1340** HAMPOLE *Pr. Consc.* 7490 Men and wymmen, many a thousand. **1398** TREVISA *Barth. De P.R.* XIX. cxxiii. (1495), Ten hundryd makyth a thousande. **1583** STOCKER *Civ. Warres Lowe C.* IV. 49 A thousande fiue hundred seuentie and nine. **1668** R. STEELE *Husbandman's Calling* x. (1672) 256 A thousand to one, they have..some gnawing care..that defeats their comfort. *Mod.* Bricks are sold by the thousand.

(*b*) In plural *thousands* (OE. *þúsendu, -o, -a*, ME. *-e, -es*).

In *Arith.* often *ellipt.* for the digits denoting the number of thousands: cf. *units, tens, hundreds*.

Beowulf 2196 He..him ȝesealde seofan þusendo. *c* **893** K. ÆLFRED *Oros.* v. iv. §2 þider for mid moneȝum þusendum. *c* **1000** ÆLFRIC *Josh.* vii. 3 Ac twa þusenda oððe þreo læt faran. *a* **1120** *O.E. Chron.* an. 694 (Laud MS.) Cantwara.. him ȝesealdon xxx þusenda. *c* **1205** LAY. 545 þider in iwenden moni þusunde [*c* **1275** mani þusend]. *c* **1275** *Ibid.* 465 Ich habbe..in þan mountes mani þusendes. *a* **1300** *Cursor M.* 19134 (Edin.) þare was conuertid thusandis [*Gött.* thousandes] v. *c* **1425** [see (*c*)]. **1542** RECORDE *Gr. Artes* 120 Then adde I ye thousandes together. **1615** MURE *Misc. P.* xiv. 12 Metamorphos'd his thowsands in milleounes. **1771** *Hist. Eur.* in *Ann. Reg.* 24/2 They amounted in all to some thousands. **1877** H. SPENCER in *Min. Evid. Copyright Comm.* (1878) 258 Now I simply have to print additional thousands as they are demanded.

(*c*) After another numeral the singular is now commonly used as a collective plural. (Cf. *dozen, hundred*.)

But in OE. the plural form was usual: see (*b*).

c **1000** ÆLFRIC *Gram.* (Z.) 282 Tweȝen îas, ȝetitelode ī ī, ȝetacniað twa þusend. *c* **1205** LAY. 83 Hire weoren..hund þousunt deade. *Ibid.* 465 Ich habbe in þane munten monie þusund [*c* 1275 þusendes]. **1297** R. GLOUC. (Rolls) 1789 þe brutons sywede after,..& slowe mani þousend. **1382** WYCLIF *Luke* xiv. 31 If he may with ten thousynd go aȝens him that cometh to him with twenty thousynd. *c* **1425** *Crafte Nombrynge* (E.E.T.S.) 29 In þe 5 place [þe schuld betoken] sexty þowsant... In þe 8 place sexty þowsant thowsantes. **1587** GOLDING *De Mornay* xviii. (1592) 288 For one that triumpheth, a hundred thousand are led in captiuitie. *Mod.* How many followers has he? He claims to have fifty thousand. The hall will seat four thousand.

(*d*) As a sb. it takes after it *of*, representing the OE. genitive pl. Now after a numeral only as a unit of quantity by which things are sold.

(*A thousand of, thousands of*, are used partitively as in the case of other numerals.)

c **893** K. ÆLFRED *Oros.* I. x. §4 On an scip mæȝe an þusend manna. *Ibid.* II. v. §2 Hie acuron endlefan þusend monna. *c* **1000** ÆLFRIC *Hom.* II. 334 Ða ȝehyrde he..sang..maneȝa ðusenda engla. *c* **1050** *Byrhtferth's Handboc* in *Anglia* (1885) VIII. 311 Eahta þusend tida. *c* **1175** *Lamb. Hom.* 35 Moni þusent monne mahte libben fele ȝere mare þenne he do. *c* **1275** *Shires & Hund.* 58 in *O.E. Misc.* 146, xxvi. þusend hida.

c **1250** *Gen. & Ex.* 4078 Godes wreche ðor haueð of-slaȝen xx.iii. ðusent of daȝen. **1398** TREVISA *Barth. De P.R.* I. (1495) A iv/2 He fedde many thousandes of peple wyth fewe looues of brede. *c* **1449** PECOCK *Repr.* (Rolls) 540 Many hundrid thousind of soulis. *c* **1450** tr. *De Imitatione* III. xi. 78 What shal I ȝeue þe for all þese þousand of godes? *c* **1475** *Rauf Coilȝear* 327 Ane thousand and ma of fensabill men. **1596-7** in Ducarel *Hist. Croydon* App. (1783) 153 Four loads of flinte..will well save one thousand of bricke. **1606** G. W[OODCOCKE] *Lives Emperors* in *Hist. Ivstine* Iij, The King of Persia with his wife Cæsarea and many thousand of their followers. **1663** GERBIER *Counsel* 52 Twenty Thousand of Bricks. **1671** S. CLARKE (*title*) A Mirrour, or Looking-Glass, both for Saints and Sinners, held forth in some Thousands of Examples. **1748** in Waghorn *Cricket Scores* (1899) 41 Some thousands of pounds were depending on this match. **1880** C. R. MARKHAM *Peruv. Bark* 51 Thousands of arrobas were..obtained.

b. As adj. or quasi-adj., followed immediately by a plural (or collective) noun.

c **1000** ÆLFRIC *Hom.* II. 458 Iob..wæron eft forȝoldene ..þusend ȝetyme oxena and þusend assan. *a* **1123** *O.E. Chron.* an. 1101, Rotbert..sceolde..þreo þusend marc seolfres habban. *c* **1200** *Vices & Virt.* 115 Mani þusend hali saules. *c* **1200** ORMIN 15510 He fedde fif þusennde menn Wiþþ fife barrliȝ lafess. *c* **1290** *S. Eng. Leg.* I. 8/243 More þane a þousend ȝer. *c* **1380** WYCLIF *Wks.* (1880) 465 þis þousinde wynter & more. **1489** WRIOTHESLEY *Chron.* (Camden) I. 2 Manye knightes with seaven thowsand men. **1523** LD. BERNERS *Froiss.* I. 672 He brought over the mountaynes a xxx. thousande fyghtinge men. **1553** T. WILSON *Rhet.* 66 b, Him..that was once worthe three thousande pounde, and is not nowe worthe three grotes. **1650** BAXTER *Saints' R.* II. vii. (1654) 269 So many thousand Christians so barbarously murdered. **1891** KIPLING *Light that Failed* xiv. (1900) 263 You've lost about a thousand pounds' worth of sketches.

2. a. Often used vaguely or hyperbolically for a large number: cf. *hundred*.

So ***ten thousand, thousands, thousands of thousands, thousand and one.***

c **1000** *Ags. Ps.* (Th.) iii. 5 Ic me nu na ondræde þusendu folces. *a* **1300** *Cursor M.* 10090 þe sunn o rightwisnes,..Hir mad a thusand sith sa bright. *c* **1385** CHAUCER *L.G.W.* 1 A Thousent sythis haue I herd men telle That there is Ioye in heuene. **1549** COVERDALE *Erasm. Par. Epist.* Ded. 2 What vayne pylgremages, what offerynges and lyghtes to stockes and stones,..with thousandes moe inconueniences. **1638** R. BAKER tr. *Balzac's Lett.* (vol. III.) 37, I give you a thousand thanks. **1700** T. BROWN *Fresny's Amusem.* v. 49 Some of them [*sc.* ladies] having Scab'd, or Pimpled Faces, wear a Thousand Patches to hide them. **1713** YOUNG *Last Day* III. 159 Ten thousand thousand fathoms still remain. **1779** *Mirror* No. 67 ¶ 11 You may do good to thousands. **1786** tr. *Beckford's Vathek* 157 A thousand ridiculous stories were propagated, at his expence. **1821** BYRON *Juan* III. lxxxvi. *Isles of Greece* iv, And ships, by thousands, lay below, And men in nations;—all were his! **1832** F. TROLLOPE *Dom. Manners Amer.* II. xxxiii. 239 Of all the thousand and one towns I saw in America, I think Buffalo is the queerest looking. **1839** E. W. LANE (*title*) The thousand and one nights, commonly called, in England, The Arabian Nights' Entertainments. A new translation from the Arabic, with copious notes. **1842** *Dumfries Herald* Oct., Clean them from the worms of the thousand-and-one flies that feed on them. **1880** W. S. GILBERT *Pirates of Penzance* I, You will find me a wife of a thousand. *a* **1895** in Baring-Gould *Nursery Songs & Rhymes* vii. 17 Ten thousand parks where deer run, Ten thousand roses in the sun. **1910** W. L. PHELPS *Essays Mod. Novelists* iii. 63 All the thousand and one details that make up the daily routine of the average person. **1962** J. WAIN *Strike Father Dead* IV. 206 Would I be likely to suggest coming along as your manager if I didn't know a thousand and one ways of making myself useful?

b. Phrases: ***a thousand times, no***: certainly not; similarly ***a thousand times, yes*** (rare); ***I believe you, thousands wouldn't*** (and similar expressions): ambiguous responses to remarks received with scepticism; ***death of*** (or ***by***) ***a thousand cuts***: a succession of minor hurts that are cumulatively very serious or annoying; ***a thousand of bricks***: see BRICK *sb.*¹ 5 a.

1896 'M. RUTHERFORD' *Clara Hopgood* v. 57 'No,' said Madge, 'a thousand times no.' **1897** H. JAMES *Spoils of Poynton* xxii. 279 A thousand times yes—her choice should know no scruple. **1926** R. H. MOTTRAM *Crime at Vanderlynden's* 46 'I did twelve months in the line, as a platoon commander. How long did you do that?' 'Twelve months about!' 'I believe you where thousands wouldn't.' **1932** A. CHRISTIE *Peril at End House* xvii. 199 Am I sure, myself, about anything at all? No, no—a thousand times, no. **1966** tr. *Quotations from Chairman Mao Tse-Tung* xxvii. 258 'He who is not afraid of death by a thousand cuts dares to unhorse the emperor'—this is the indomitable spirit needed in our struggle to build socialism and communism. **1968** C. AIRD *Henrietta Who?* x. 97 'I don't even know..what I don't know.' Bill Thorpe nodded comprehendingly. 'I follow you—though thousands wouldn't.' **1974** D. SEAMAN *Bomb that could Lip-Read* ix. 73 The head of the rocket..chips off tiny fragments of steel... The poor buggers who get in the way die the death of a thousand cuts. **1980** G. GREENE *Doctor Fischer* vii. 39 It had to be the death of a thousand cuts. He told her he forgave her..but he told her also that he could never forget her betrayal. **1980** P. MOYES *Angel Death* xx. 255 I can believe it. Thousands wouldn't. **1981** P. TURNBULL *Deep & Crisp & Even* vii. 116 'Don't you think I'm too old?' 'No, a thousand times, no!' **1982** P. INCHBALD *Sweet Short Grass* xx. 172 Oh, Franco! *Yes!* A thousand times yes!

3. Elliptical uses. **a.** A thousand of some weight, measure, or quantity; e.g. acres, pounds, cubic feet, years, pieces, packages, etc. according to the nature of the commodity, etc.

a **900** *O.E. Chron.* an. 648 (Parker MS.), Her Cenwalh ȝesalde Cuþrede his mæȝe iii þusendo londes be Æsces dune. *c* **1000** *Ags. Ps.* (Th.) cxviii[i]. 72 Me is micle betere, ..þonne mon me ȝeofe ȝeara ðusende goldes and seolfres. *a* **1300** *E.E. Psalter* ibid., Ouer thousandes ofe siluer ore golde. **1443** *Acts Privy Counc.* (1835) V. 281 To delivere Johan Dawnsonn maister of þordenances of my Lorde of Somerset iiij^ml salpetre iij^ml sulphure. **1482** in *Charters, &c. Edinb.* (1871) 169 Of the thousand irne ij s. **1840** THACKERAY *Cox's Diary* May, Instead of looking twenty, he looked a thousand. **1873** TROLLOPE *Phineas Redux* II. xxi. 172 Mere words, supplied at so much the thousand. **1884** *Sat. Rev.* 7 June 758/1 He dines at 6, plays [billiards] a thousand-up by gaslight. **1896** G. B. SHAW *Let.* 15 Feb. (1965) I. 597 Men who rattle off their copy at anything from 20/- to 40/- a thousand. **1901** *Daily Express* 28 Feb. 4/6 The price of gas in London in 1876 was 3*s.* 9*d.* per thousand. **1919** W. S. MAUGHAM *Moon & Sixpence* iii. 14 We would talk..of editors and the sort of contributions they welcomed, how much they paid a thousand, and whether they paid promptly or otherwise.

b. A thousand pounds sterling; (*U.S.*), a thousand dollars.

1547-64 BAULDWIN *Mor. Philos.* (Palfr.) 65 A merchant's compters, that is to day worth thousands. **1588** *Marprel. Epist.* (Arb.) 5 Come downe you bishopps from your thousands, and content you with your hundreds. **1609** B. JONSON *Sil. Wom.* IV. v, A man of two thousand a yeere. **1826** DISRAELI *Viv. Grey* II. xiii, A clear rental of five-and-twenty thousand per annum. **1852** THACKERAY *Esmond* I. ix, A merchant on 'Change,..having lost his thousands, embarks a few guineas upon the next ship. **1919** E. O'NEILL *Moon of Carib.* 163 Smith said he would give two thousand cash if I would sell the place to him. **1942** *Amer. Mercury* July 85 He might confidence Sweet Back out of a thousand on a plate.

†**4.** As ordinal: = THOUSANDTH. *Obs.*

c **1400** MAUNDEV. (Roxb.) xvi. 74 He knew noȝt þe thowsand parte of his gude. **14..** *Tundale's Vis.* 1923 (Edinb. MS.) Not by an hvndryþe þowsand part. **1600** SHAKS. *A.Y.L.* IV. i. 46 Breake but a part of the thousand part of a minute in the affairs of loue. **1680** N. LEE *Cæsar Borgia* Ep. Ded., My best Merits are not the ten thousand part of his smallest labours.

5. *Comb.* Forming (*a*) attrib. compounds with a sb., as ***thousand-acre, -dollar, -guinea, -mile, -pound, -round, -year*** (hence ***-year-long, -year-old***, etc.); (*b*) parasynthetic combs., as ***thousand-eyed*** (having a thousand eyes), ***-footed, -handed, -headed, -hued, -petalled, -sided, -souled, -voiced***, etc. adjs.; also **thousand-feet**, a millepede or centipede; **thousand-head(ed) kale**, a branching variety of cabbage, *Brassica oleracea* var. *fruticosa*, cultivated as fodder for sheep or cattle; **thousand island** [f. *Thousand Islands*, name of a large group of islands in the St. Lawrence River], used *attrib.* and *absol.* to designate Russian salad-dressing containing added pieces of garnishing; also **thousand isle**; **thousand-jacket** *N.Z.* = HOUHERE; **thousand-legs** = *thousand-feet*; **thousand-miler** *slang*, a dark shirt that does not show the dirt; **thousand-year(-old) egg**, a Chinese delicacy consisting of a pickled egg that has been kept in earth, lime, and chopped straw for some weeks; **thousand-yearist**, nonce-rendering of CHILIAST; **Thousand-Year Reich** [G. *tausendjähriges Reich*], the German Third Reich (1933–45), as a regime envisaged by the Nazis as established for an indefinite period.

1895 *Daily News* 30 Nov. 3/4 The attempt to turn England into a rural arcadia of *thousand acre farms. **1871** ALABASTER *Wheel of Law* 171 There the *thousand-eyed Lord..is attended by thousands of houris. *Ibid.* 209 The thousand-eyed is a common epithet of Indra. **1704** in Churchill *Collect. Voy.* III. 828/2 *Thousand Feet, called *Millepie* by the Portugueses. **1858** O. W. HOLMES *Aut. Breakf.-t.* vii, To take shelter..under one of the *thousand-footed bridges. **1894** DU MAURIER *Trilby* II. 111 Princes..who pay them *thousand-guinea fees. **1870** EMERSON *Soc. & Solit.* vii. 133 This *thousand-handed art. *a***1618** SYLVESTER *Miracle of Peace* xxiv, Thou *thousand-headed head-lesse Monster-most. **1887** *Times* 22 Oct. 8/1 This practice of making *thousand-headed kale stand down..on poor land..is likely to come rapidly into favour. **1925** Thousandhead kale [see *marrow-stem (kale)* s.v. MARROW *sb.*[1] 5]. **1929** OLDERSHAW & PORTER *Brit. Farm Crops* v. 235 Thousand-headed kale is a very useful crop to grow both for sheep- and cattle-feed. **1975** PARK & EDDOWES *Crop Husbandry* (ed. 2) xiii. 294 Marrow stem kale should be used before the new year followed by the hardier thousand head kale. **1839** BAILEY *Festus* xxxi. (1852) 490 Fluttering its wings in lightnings *thousand-hued. **1916** *Daily Colonist* (Victoria, B.C.) 19 July 6/1 (Advt.), Mrs. Porter's *Thousand Island Salad Dressing, bottle 35¢. **1945** J. L. MARSHALL *Santa Fe* 106 For years, Bill Gardner, steward on the Kansas City–Chicago run, handed out a special '1001 Dressing', an improvement on the usual Thousand Island mixture. **1962** Thousand-isle [see ROQUEFORT b]. **1981** *Times* 2 Mar. 12/5 In a year or two she will be specifying that the thousand island dressing (a pinkish salad cream with bits of vegetables in it) should be low-calorie. **1888** *Cassell's Picturesque Austral.* III. 210 Toi-toi, supplejack, *thousand-jacket, are names of things known well enough to the inhabitants of Napier and Taranaki. **1946** Thousand-jacket [see HOUHERE]. **1807** YOUNG *Agric. Essex* I. 392 The *thousand-legs eats and makes them [potatoes] scabby. **1962** GORDON & LAVOIPIERRE *Entomol. for Students of Med.* vii. 41 The class Diplopoda contains all the millipedes or '*thousand legs'. **1875** 'MARK TWAIN' in *Atlantic Monthly* Apr. 450/1 The *thousand-mile wall of dense forest. **1929** F. C. BOWEN *Sea Slang* 139 **Thousand milers*, black twill shirts. **1959** *Washington Post* 8 Oct. c3/3 A thousand-miler is a navy blue shirt which doesn't show the gravy stains and may be worn for days at a time without washing. Slim must have a wardrobe of thousand-milers. **1978** K. BONFIGLIOLI *All Tea in China* vii. 86 A 'thousand-miler' turned out to be a sort of durable shirt made of black twill; so-called..because it should be washed..after every thousand miles of the voyage. **1951** L. MACNEICE tr. *Goethe's Faust* II. ii. 204 But here at Pharsalus was fought a master model To prove how might opposes greater might and tears To shreds the lovely *thousand-petalled wreath of freedom. **1970** *Times* 10 Mar. 17/2 (Advt.), A hitherto unrecorded Baccarat 'thousand-petalled' rose weight. **1898** *Westm. Gaz.* 17 June 5/1 A *thousand-pound projectile..tore a gaping hole in the emplacement. **1902** *Lond. Mag.* June 484/1 Accused of systematically uttering forged Bank of England thousand-pound notes. **1704** NORRIS *Ideal World* II. ix. 387 Four, five, or a *thousand-sided figures..are capable of a greater number of relations..than simple triangles are. **1838–9** HALLAM *Hist. Lit.* III. III. vi. §49. 313 Coleridge has most felicitously applied to him a Greek epithet..*μυριόνους*, the *thousand-souled Shakspeare. **1898** *Westm. Gaz.* 2 Sept. 5/1 Amidst the *thousand-voiced tumult. **1886** KIPLING *Departm. Ditties*, etc. (1899) 45 So I fled with steps uncertain On a *thousand-year long race. **1961** E.-M. WONG *Chinese Cookery* v. 36 Everyone has heard of '*thousand-year-old' eggs, but in reality these eggs are only a few months old. **1972** K. LO *Chinese Food* I. 47 Thousand-Year-Old Egg (which, to be more precise, should be called Pickled Eggs)..can be incorporated into a Chinese breakfast. **1980** E. BEHR *Getting Even* xviii. 208 Seaslugs, jellyfish and thousand-year eggs appeared on the table. **1610** HEALEY *St. Aug. Citie of God* 798 The worde [Chiliasts] is greeke, and may bee interpreted, Millenaryes, or *Thousand-yere-ists. [**1934** *Times* 6 Sept. 12/4 Herr Hitler's proclamation to the rally was read... Herr Hitler declares that 'there will be no further revolution in Germany for a thousand years.'] **1946** A. HUXLEY *Let.* 27 Oct. (1969) 553 When people think of far-off communist Utopias or *Thousand-Year Reichs, they are so much dazzled by the beauty of what they see..in the unknowable future, that they are ready to commit any atrocity in the present. **1970** A. PRICE *Labyrinth Makers* vi. 89 The Wagnerian last hours of the Thousand Year Reich. **1979** J. CROSBY *Party of Year* xviii. 109 Now that the 1,000-year Reich had crumbled, what else was there?

Hence **thousand'aire** (*nonce-wd.* after *millionaire*), one who has a thousand pounds; †**'thousandly** *adv.*, thousandfold.

1896 *Eclectic Mag.* Mar. 350 To prevent their possessor from ever becoming even a thousandaire. *c* **1450** *Mirour Saluacioun* 4920 Now shalle I the rewarde innoumbrable thovzandly.

†**'thousandel.** *Obs.* [Contr. of the phr. *by a thousand deal* (DEAL *sb.*[1] 1 e).] A thousand times.

13.. *Guy Warw.* (A.) 4265 More riches þe worþ bi a þousandel Boþe of cites & of riche castel, ..þan þerl Rohaut haþ. **1390** GOWER *Conf.* I. 66 For in good feith, this lieveth wel, Mi will was betre a thousendel.

thousandfold ('θaʊzəndfəʊld), *a.*, *adv.*, and *sb.* [OE. *þúsendfeald*: see THOUSAND and -FOLD.]

A. *adj.* One thousand times as much or many; consisting of a thousand parts; a thousand times repeated or multiplied.

c **1000** ÆLFRIC *Hom.* II. 576 Salomon..ʒeoffrode him ..þusendfealde onsæʒednyssa æt anre offrunge. *a* **1023** WULFSTAN *Hom.* xlvii. (Napier) 243 Ðæt þusendfeald ʒetæl is fulfremed. *c* **1200** *Trin. Coll. Hom.* 191 Mid þusendfeld wrenches he þe herte to-wendeð. **1840** CARLYLE *Heroes* i, How such light will then shine out, and with wondrous thousandfold expansion spread itself. **1858** HAWTHORNE *Fr. & It. Note-Bks.* (1872) I. 45 This bustle and babble; this thousand-fold talk.

B. *adv.* A thousand times (in amount); a thousand times as much. (Usually *a thousandfold.*)

a **1225** *Leg. Kath.* 2323 þæt þing..schal arisen, þurh þæt fal, a þusentfalt te fehere..to lif undeðlich. *c* **1374** CHAUCER *Troylus* I. 819 A guerdoun..A þowsand folde more þan he kan deserue. ? *a* **1500** *Chester Pl.* i. 144 Brighter then god a thowsand fould. **1586** A. DAY *Eng. Secretary* II. (1625) 86 Thou hast..heaped mischiefe a thousandfold to thy selfe. **1681–6** J. SCOTT *Chr. Life* II. i. §3 Our sincere Compliance with the immutable Obligations of Piety and Vertue, is a Thousandfold more acceptable to God, than [etc.]. **1872** MORLEY *Voltaire* i. (1886) 10 The sacrifice may repay itself a thousand-fold.

†**b.** A thousand times (in succession). *rare*[−1].

1500–20 DUNBAR *Poems* xlix. 37 War the fox tane a thousand fawd, And grace him gevin als oft for frawd.

C. *sb.* A thousand times the amount or number.

a **1711** KEN *Sion* Poet. Wks 1721 IV. 370 The Son ador'd and nurs'd by the sweet Maid, A thousand-fold of Love for Love repaid.

Hence **'thousand,foldly** *adv.* = B. *rare*[−1].

1829 COLERIDGE *Improvisatore* Poems II. 130 In the person of a thousand-foldly endeared partner.

thousandth ('θaʊzəndθ), *a.* and *sb.* [f. THOUSAND + -TH[1]. Not found before 16th c.: cf. THOUSAND 4.] The ordinal numeral belonging to the cardinal THOUSAND.

A. *adj.* **1.** Coming last in order of a thousand successive individuals.

1552 HULOET, Thousandth, *millesimus.* **1656** tr. *Hobbes' Elem. Philos.* (1839) 100 Though our computation reach the fixed stars, or the ninth or tenth, nay, the thousandth sphere. **1732** POPE *Ess. Man* I. 246 From Nature's chain whatever link you strike, Tenth or ten thousandth, breaks the chain alike. **1875** BRYCE *Holy Rom. Emp.* (ed. 5) vi. 77 Modern Germany proclaims the era of A.D. 843 the beginning of her national existence, and celebrated its thousandth anniversary thirty-two years ago.

2. ***thousandth part***: one of a thousand equal parts into which anything may be divided.

1561 T. HOBY tr. *Castiglione's Courtyer* I. K ij, Ye felt not the thousandeth part of yᵉ delite. **1710** BERKELEY *Princ. Hum. Knowl.* §127 The ten thousandth part of that line. **1782** HERSCHEL in *Phil. Trans.* LXXII. 165 Pinions..so evenly divided as..to be depended upon..to perhaps the two, three, or four thousandth part of an inch. **1836** J. H. NEWMAN *Lyra Apost.* (1849) 231 Lord! Who Thy thousand years dost wait To work the thousandth part Of Thy vast plan.

B. *sb.* A thousandth part.

1793 YOUNG in *Phil. Trans.* LXXXIII. 174 In the ox's eye, the diameter of the crystalline is 700 thousandths of an inch. **1867** DENISON *Astron. without Math.* 6 Inches about a thousandth longer than our inches.

thousandweight ('θaʊzəndweɪt). *rare.* A weight of a thousand pounds.

1538 ELYOT, *Milliarius, a, um*, of a thousande weight. **1552** HULOET, Thousande weyght, *millepondium.* **1559** W. CUNNINGHAM *Cosmogr. Glasse* 176 Sulphure is there so plentifull that you may for the 4. part of a ducate, haue a thousande weight. **1667** PRIMATT *City & C. Build.* 99 A thousand weight of Lead taken up in Pipes, Gutters, and in Ridges. **1685** *Lond. Gaz.* No. 2064/4, 40 thousand weight of Powder. **1768** *Chron.* in *Ann. Reg.* 113/2 The Sherborne waggon was stopped by the populace, and about a thousand weight of butter taken away.

'thout, aphetic form of *athout*, WITHOUT.

1893 H. A. SHANDS *Some Peculiarities of Speech in Mississippi* 63 *Thout*, Negro for *without.* **1897** KIPLING *Capt. Cour.* iv. 91 Don't let's hev another [sad song] 'thout somethin' between. **1917** —— *Divers. Creatures* 341 I'm the only farmer you've got. Nothin' goes off my place 'thout it walks on its own feet. **1935** Z. N. HURSTON *Mules & Men* I. x. 205 Nobody can't mention fat 'thout you makin' out they talkin' bout you. **1979** 'E. MCBAIN' *Calypso* iv. 37 *You* ain't gettin *nothin* 'thout the forty dollars.

thout, þout, thouth, obs. ff. THOUGHT[1] and [2].

thow, obs. f. THOU *pron.*; also, occasional copyist's error for *you.*

thow, þow(e, var. THO *dem. pron.*; obs. form of THOUGH.

thowcht, obs. Sc. form of THOUGH, THOUGHT.

thowel(l, thowl(e, obs. ff. THOLE *sb.*[1] and *v.*

thowen, þoȝen, þowun, pa. pple. of THEE *v.*[1]

thowght, þowȝt, þowht, etc., obs. ff. THOUGHT.

thowless ('θaʊlɪs, 'θoʊlɪs), *a. Sc.* Forms: 4–5 **thowles,** 5 **-lace, -las, -lys, thoulass,** 8– **thowless.** [app. a collateral Sc. form of THEWLESS, with which it agrees in sense; but the phonology is unexplained.]

†**1.** Without morality or virtue; wanton, dissolute, profligate; also, thoughtless. *Obs.*

1375 [implied in THOWLESSNESS]. *c* **1425** WYNTOUN *Cron.* VIII. xxii. 3292 (MS. Cott.) He was thowlace [*v.r.* wantoun], and had in won, ..oftsyis to ly Oþir syndry women by. *Ibid.* xxxiii. 5933 Weil waxyn vp..And thowles þan, for his ȝoutheide To þat natur walde hym leide. **14..** *How the Good wife*, etc. 260 in *Barbour's Bruce* 534 And chasty thame quhen thai do myss, Or [*MS.* our] rekles thoulass wantoun is. *a* **1500** *Ratis Raving* I. 1264 This eild is thowles & wnswere, And ȝarnis play, and al blytht chere. *a* **1500** *Thewis Gd. Women* 145 in *Ratis Raving*, etc. 107 Women that has a thowlas hart.

2. Devoid of energy or spirit; inert, inactive; spiritless, listless.

1721 RAMSAY *Prospect of Plenty* 128 A poor and haughty drone, Wha thowless stands a lazy looker-on. **1728** —— *Tea-t. Misc.*, *Widow* vi, Fortune..ruins the woer that's thowless and cauld. **1801** MACNEILL *Poems* (1844) 111 Thowless, he tint his gate deep 'mang the snaw. **1818** SCOTT *Br. Lamm.* xii[i], You, ye thowless jade, to sit still and see my substance disponed upon to an idle, drunken, reprobate, worm-eaten serving man. *a* **1875** J. MURRAY in *Mod. Scot. Poets* (1881) III. 150 The kye stand thowless on the croft.

Hence **'thowlessness,** †evil or immoral conduct, bad behaviour; wantonness, vice (*obs.*); also, want of energy, ineffectiveness.

1375 BARBOUR *Bruce* I. 333 And till swylk thowlesnes he ȝeid, As the courss askis off ȝowtheid. *c* **1425** WYNTOUN *Cron.* VI. iii. 268 That thai suld noucht for ydilnes Fall intill iwill thowlysnes. **1885** 'J. STRATHESK' *More Bits* xi. (ed. 2) 206 She did not quite like some of Bell's remarks about 'wasterfu'ness' and 'thowlessness', possibly because they were only too true.

thowmbe, thowme, obs. Sc. ff. THUMB.

thown, thownyr, obs. ff. TOWN, THUNDER.

†**thowt(e,** *v. Obs.* [f. *thow*, THOU *pers. pron.* Cf. MHG. and Ger. *dutzen, duzen*, F. *tutoyer*, It. *tuizzare, tizzare*, med.L. *tuāre, tuisāre.*] *trans.* To address with the singular pronoun *thou*, to thou. Hence †**'thowting** *vbl. sb.*

c **1440** *Promp. Parv.* 535/2 þowton, or thowton [*v.rr.* þowtyn, yowtyn], *tuo.* *Ibid.*, þowtynge, or thowthynge, *tuacio, vel tuatus.*

thowt(e, obs. or dial. ff. *thought*: see THINK *v.*[1] and [2]; obs. ff. THOUGHT[2], rower's bench.

'thowthistle. Now *dial.* [OE. *þúðistel*, = OHG. *dúdistel*, MHG. *du-, dau-distel* (Grimm). Etymology of first element obscure. Perh. the original name, subseq. changed to SOWTHISTLE: see E. Schröder, *Götting. Gelehrte Nachr.* 1908, p. 28.] A herb; the sowthistle, or perh. formerly the wild lettuce.

a **700** *Epinal Gloss.* (O.E.T.) 601 *Lactuca*, þuþistel. *c* **725** *Corpus Gl.* 1175 *Lactuca*, þuðistel. *c* **1265** *Voc. Names Plants* in Wr.-Wülcker 559/5 *Andiuia*, *i.* letrun, *i.* þuȝeþistel. *c* **1440** *Promp. Parv.* 492/1 Thowthystylle, herbe (or sowthystylle). **1888** *Sheffield Gloss.*, *Sowthistle*..also called a thow-thistle, or thoo-thistle.

thra, variant of THRO *sb.*, *a.*, *adv.*

thra, thraa, dial. forms of THROW *v.*

Thracian ('θreɪʃ(ɪ)ən), *sb.* and *a.* [f. L. *Thrācius*, *Thrācus*, a. Gr. *θρᾴκιος*, f. *θρᾴκη* Thrace: see -AN, -IAN.] **A.** *sb.* **a.** A native or inhabitant of Thrace, in antiquity a region to the N.E. of Macedonia, and now comprising European Turkey, southern Bulgaria, and the region of Thrace in N.E. Greece.

1569 T. STOCKER tr. *Diodorus Siculus' Hist. Successors Alexander* 105 Aboute two thousand Mercenarie Grekes, and so many Thracians. **1618** E. BOLTON tr. *Lucius Julius Florus' Roman Hist.* (1636) 176 The Sordiscans were of all the Thracians the most savage. **1875** *Encycl. Brit.* III. 854/1 In the earliest times of history Bœotia was inhabited by various tribes, such as the Aonians, Temmicians, Thracians, [etc.]. **1949** *Oxf. Classical Dict.* 901/2 The Thracians were not without a native culture. **1976** *Daily Tel.* 31 Aug. 6 A major archaeological discovery..has been made in Bulgaria. Knowledge of the Thracians is advanced substantially. **1982** K. FOLLETT *Man from St. Petersburg* ix. 178 'I wonder how the Thracians would feel about all this.' 'They would rather belong to Russia than Turkey.'

b. The language of the ancient Thracians, an Indo-European language thought to be related to Phrygian or Illyrian.

1879 *Academy* XV. 99/1 It is still doubted by..philologists whether Albanian should be classed as an Aryan language... However.., I am quite willing to allow that it is ..a descendant of the ancient Illyrian or Thracian, and I will not quarrel with anyone who wishes to call the latter Pelasgian. **1933** C. D. BUCK *Compar. Gram. Gk. & Lat.* 14 Thracian is known from proper names and glosses, and there is one obscure inscription believed to be Thracian. **1962** A. J. BEATTIE in Wace & Stubbings *Compan. to Homer* x. 312 From the Hellespont to Chalcidice most of the inhabitants spoke Thracian. **1972** W. B. LOCKWOOD *Panorama Indo-Europ. Lang.* 172 At the time of its greatest known extent, in antiquity, Thracian was spoken throughout the eastern half of the Balkan Peninsula and stretched northwards into the Central European Plain.

B. *adj.* Of or pertaining to Thrace.

1588 SHAKS. *Tit. A.* I. i. 138 The selfe same Gods that arm'd the Queene of Troy With opportunitie of sharpe reuenge Vpon the Thracian Tyrant in his Tent. **1594** KYD *Cornelia* III. ii. 49 Stoute Thracian Mars. **1667** MILTON *P.L.* VII. 34 The Race Of that wilde Rout that tore the Thracian Bard In Rhodope. **1697** DRYDEN *Æneis* VI. 877 The Thracian bard..There stands conspicuous in his flowing vest. **1781** GIBBON *Decl. & F.* II. xxvi. 593 Orders were immediately dispatched to the civil and military governors of the Thracian diocese. *a* **1822** SHELLEY *Cyclops* in *Posthumous Poems* (1824) 343 And when the Thracian wind pours down the snow, I wrap my body in the skins of beasts. **1848** *Rep. Brit. Assoc. Adv. Sci.* 1847 266 The second family is the Thracian or Illyrian, once spread on the Dnieper, the

Hellespont, and in Asia Minor. **1920** *Glasgow Herald* 12 May 9 Several of the Thracian harbours now under Greek sovereignty..are to be free. *Ibid.* 27 July 7 To-day at dawn the Thracian Army launched its offensive. **1949** *Oxf. Classical Dict.* 901/2 Greek recruiting officers (especially in the fourth century) enlisted Thracian 'peltasto' or light-armed fighters. **1977** *Jrnl. R. Soc. Arts* CXXV. 485/1 The nearest parallels which we can refer to are two helmets of the so-called 'Thracian' type.

thrack (θræk), *v.* Now *dial.* Also 9 *dial.* **thrag.** [Etymology obscure.] *trans.* To pack full, fill, cram; to load. Also *intr.* for *passive.*

1655 GURNALL *Chr. in Arm.* verse 11. I. v. §3 (1669) 33/2 Bags that are thracked full with money. *a* **1716** SOUTH *Serm.* (1744) VIII. vi. 176 The strait gate is too narrow for any man to come bustling in, thrack'd with great possessions. **1809** BATCHELOR *Anal. Eng. Lang.* 145 *Thrag*, to throng. 'As full as it could thrag'. **1854** MISS BAKER *Northampt. Gloss.* II. 337 *Thracked*... Used..for a hamper of apples. 'It was thracked full'. **1904** in *Eng. Dial. Dict.* s.v. *Thrag*, The streets were thragged with people.

† **thracksat.** *Obs. rare.* [Origin obscure: perh. f. prec. + *sat* for *set* = 'set in compact mass'.] (See quot.)

1678 PHILLIPS (ed. 4), *Thracksat*, a Chymical term for a Metal, which is yet in the Mine. [Hence (printed *-scat*) in Bailey, Crabb, Worcester, Cassell, etc.]

Thraco- ('θreɪkəʊ), also *rarely* **Thrako-**, used as comb. form of THRACIAN *sb.* and *a.*, as in ***Thraco-Illyrian*** adj., ***Thraco-Phrygian*** adj. and sb.

1902 *Encycl. Brit.* XXV. 249/2 Albanian is peculiarly interesting as the only surviving representative of the so-called Thraco-Illyrian group of languages which formed the primitive speech of the peninsula. **1924** G. MURRAY *Rise Gk. Epic* (ed. 3) ii. 40 A great movement of Thraco-Phrygian tribes with eastern linguistic affinities. **1931** *Times Lit. Suppl.* 12 Feb. 116/4 The Thrako-Illyrian stratum which underlies all the races of the Peninsular. **1946** PRIEBSCH & COLLINSON *German Lang.* (ed. 2) i. 19 He places the prehistoric connexions of the Tokharians with the progenitors of Balts, Slavs, Armenians and Thraco-Phrygians in the steppes of South-East Russia between the Dniepr and the Urals. **1968** D. L. CLARKE *Analytical Archaeol.* ix. 391 An older, outer ring of non-Urnfield Indo-European areas—Teutonic and Baltic on one hand and Thraco-Phrygian, Greek, and Hittite on another. **1972** W. B. LOCKWOOD *Panorama Indo-Europ. Lang.* 172 Thraco-Phrygian is the term used to denote a group of languages whose earliest known homeland was South-East Europe. Three languages are distinguished: Thracian, Phrygian and Armenian.

thraf, thrafe, thraif, obs. forms of THRAVE.

thraf caike, obs. f. THARF-CAKE.

† '**thraftly,** *adv. Obs.* Forms: 3 **þræfliche,** 6 **thraftly.** [perh. f. OE. *þræft* quarrel, contention, chiding (= ON. *þrapt* quarrel: cf. OE. *þrafian* to urge, press, rebuke, censure) + -LY[2].] ? Angrily; surlily.

c **1205** LAY. 27797 Ah Bruttes him þrungen to þræfliche [*c* 1275 wroþliche] swiðe. *a* **1578** LINDESAY (Pitscottie) *Chron. Scot.* XXI. xxxvi. (MS. F. Advoc. Libr.; ed. 1728, 171), Where they were bot thraftlie receaved of the King.

† '**thrafully,** *adv. Obs.* [f. **thraful* adj. (f. THRO, THRA *sb.* + -FUL) + -LY[2].] Violently.

1535 STEWART *Cron. Scot.* (Rolls) I. 144 With sic ane reird quhill all the rochis rang, So thrafullie togidder that tha thrang.

[**thragge,** in Halliwell's ed. of Nares, misquotation of Huloet's *shragge*, SHRAG *v.*, copied in Latham's *Johnson* and some later Dicts.]

† **thrail.** *Obs.* [Alteration of *frail*: see TH (6).] = FRAIL *sb.*[1]

1694 WESTMACOTT *Script. Herb.* 164 Matt-Reed..of which also are made Matts, and Frailes, or Thrailes.

thraip, obs. and dial. variant of THREAP.

thraldom ('θrɔːldəm). Forms: see next. [f. next + -DOM.] The state or condition of being a thrall; bondage, servitude; captivity. **a.** *lit.*

c **1205** LAY. 29156 Summe heo flu3en to Irlonde..and þer wuneden þeouwe inne þraldome. *c* **1250** *Gen. & Ex.* 2322 Driuen In-to ðraldom, euermor to liuen. **1377** LANGL. *P. Pl.* B. XVIII. 103 And 3owre Fraunchise, þat fre was fallen is in thraldome. **1450–1530** *Myrr. our Ladye* 331 Theyr delyuerance oute of the thraldome of Egypte. **1590** WEBBE *Trav.* (Arb.) 14 In the midst of my thraldome in Turkie. **1617** MORYSON *Itin.* II. 25 Tyrone was among the Irish celebrated as the Deliverer of his Country from thraldome. **1756** HUME *Hist. Eng.* II. xli. 432 Elizabeth..would have been sure to detain him in perpetual thraldom. **1872** YEATS *Techn. Hist. Comm.* 165 Shoemakers were among the first to rescue themselves from the thraldom of the lords of the soil.

b. *fig.*

c **1175** *Lamb. Hom.* 139 Alle oðer da3es of þe wike beoð to þreldome to þis dei. *c* **1380** WYCLIF *Serm.* Sel. Wks. II. 53 þe moost þraldom and worst of alle is þe þraldom of synne. *c* **1450** tr. *De Imitatione* II. xii. 58 To chastise þe body, to bring it in þraldom. **1561** T. NORTON *Calvin's Inst.* I. xv. (1634) 74 This miserable estate whereunto man is now in thraldome. **1755** YOUNG *Centaur* iii. Wks. 1757 IV. 170 This thraldom to their pleasures. **1875** JOWETT *Plato* (ed. 2) I. 461 She may deliver herself up again to the thraldom of pleasures and pains.

thrall (θrɔːl), *sb.*[1] (*a.*[1]). Now *arch.* or *Hist.* Forms: α. 1 **þræl,** 2–4 **þrēl** (*pl.* **þrēles, þrelles**), 4 **þrell, þrelle, threll.** β. 2–3 **þral** (*pl.* 3–5 **þrāles, þralles**), (4 **þrale**), 4–5 **þrall,** 4–8 **thral,** 4– **thrall** (6 **thrawl, thraule,** *Sc.* **thraill**). γ. 4–5 **tharl,** 5 **tharlle.** See also THRILL *sb.*[2] [OE. *þrǽl*, a. ON. *þrǽll* (Da. *træl*, Sw. *träl*), perh.:—prehist. ON. **þrāhilaR*:—OTeut. **þrăhilo*[z], f. OTeut. root *þreh-* to run. Cf. OHG. *dregil*, *drigil* 'servant', prop. 'runner'. Branch II is from THRALL *v.*: cf. M.Da. and Norw. *træl* drudgery, f. *trælle* to drudge.]

I. 1. One who is in bondage to a lord or master; a villein, serf, bondman, slave; also, in vaguer use, a servant, subject; *transf.* one whose liberty is forfeit; a captive, prisoner of war.

α. *c* **950** *Lindisf. Gosp.* Mark x. 44 And sua huæ seðe wælle in iuh forðmest wosa bie allra ðræl. **991** *Laws of Æthelred* II. c. 5 §1 ʒyf Englisc man Deniscne ðræl ofslea, ʒylde hine mid punde. *c* **1175** *Lamb. Hom.* 47 Heo [i.e. Sunday] on eorðe 3eueð reste to alle eorðe þrelles, wepmen and wifmen of heore þrel weorkes. *Ibid.* 123 Herien we ure drihten þe..makede us freo of þeowan and of þrelan his ah3ene bern. *a* **1225** *Ancr. R.* 130 'Hwon 3e habbeð al wel idon' he seið, ..'si33eð þæt 3e beoð unnute þrelles'. **1340** *Ayenb.* 19 He deþ manhode to þe dyeule and becomþ his þrel. **1375** BARBOUR *Bruce* I. 274 Nane can tell The halle condicioun off A threll. *Ibid.* III. 220 Serwandis and threllis mad he fre.

β. *c* **1200** *Vices & Virt.* 17 Ðe ðe hlauerd betahte his þralle. *c* **1200** *Trin. Coll. Hom.* 121 To lesen þe þrales of þralshipe. **1297** R. GLOUC. (Rolls) 3010 Þe king..Nom of him sikernesse to be is þral euere mo. **1415** HOCCLEVE *To Sir J. Oldcastle* 98 Where is thy knyghtly herte, art thow his thral? **1566** DRANT *Wail. Hierim.* v, Our yonge men, lyke to vylaine thrawles, in drudgerie did grinde. **1612** T. TAYLOR *Comm. Titus* i. 4 (1619) 68 A Redeemer, purchasing us being captiues, and thralls to Sathan. **1748** THOMSON *Cast. Indol.* I. xi, Outcast of Nature, Man! the wretched thrall Of bitter-dropping sweat. **1867** BURTON *Hist. Scot.* (1873) I. xi. 362 The thralls or personal slaves.

γ. *a* **1500** *Spir. Remedies* in Halliwell *Nugæ Poet.* 65 Lorde, sende it unto the syke tharlle.

b. *fig.* One who is in bondage to some power or influence; a slave (*to* something).

c **950** *Lindisf. Gosp.* John viii. 34 Seðe wyrcas synne ðræl is synnes. *c* **1230** *Hali Meid.* 5 Þeos as flesches þralles beoð in worldes þeowdom. **1340** *Ayenb.* 86 Þet hi ne byeþ þrelles ne to gold ne to zeluer ne to hare caroyne. **1571** GOLDING *Calvin on Ps.* xxxvi. 5 They willingly yeelde themselves thralls to wickednes. **1605** SHAKS. *Macb.* III. vi. 13 Slaues of drinke, and thralles of sleepe. **1821** LAMB *Elia* Ser. I. *Imperfect Sympathies*, The veriest thrall to sympathies, apathies, antipathies.

II. 2. The condition of a thrall; thraldom, bondage, servitude; captivity.

13.. *Cursor M.* 6304 (Fairf.) Quen moises þe folk had lad ..out of þe þralle of pharaon. **14..** *Chester Pl.* I. 129 If that yow in thrall yow bringe. *a* **1578** LINDESAY (Pitscottie) *Chron. Scot.* (S.T.S.) II. 24 The nyght in prosperatie, the morne in thraill. **1592** TIMME *Ten Eng. Lepers* A ij b, To bring this noble Realme of England to thraule. **1607** DEKKER & WEBSTER *Sir T. Wyatt* Wks. 1873 III. 111 You free your Countrie from base spanish thrall. **1791** BURNS *Lament Mary Q. Scots* ii, In love and freedom they rejoice, Wi' care nor thrall opprest. **1842** TENNYSON *Sir Galahad* ii, For them I battle till the end, To save from shame and thrall.

fig. **1576** *Thanksgiving* in *Liturg. Serv. Q. Eliz.* (1847) 559 Thou didst set us free from thrall. **1633** G. HERBERT *Temple, Church-porch* xx, When wanton pleasures becken us to thrall. **1800–24** CAMPBELL *Jilted Nymph* iv, A suitor, Whose heart I have gotten in thrall. **1856** MISS MULOCK *J. Halifax* xii, The Anonymous Friend: who held him in such fascinated thrall.

† **3.** Oppression, trouble, misery, distress. *Obs.*

1560 ROLLAND *Seven Sages* 25 It is better..we all seuin suld die..Or this 3oung man suld suffer ony thrall. **1609** DANIEL *Civ. Wars* VIII. xciv, Sit downe, And rest you, after all this passed thrall. *c* **1796** MISS J. GRAHAM in Chambers *Scott. Songs* (1829) 15 As yet you've met with little thrall. *a* **1829** in Roby *Trad. Lanc.* (1867) II. 26 In my trouble and thrall.

III. 4. *attrib.* and *Comb.*, as ***thrall-folk***, ***-man*** [ON. *þræl-monni*], ***-woman***, ***-work*** [ON. *þræl-verk*]; ***thrall-like*** adj.

c **1175** Þrel weorkes [see 1 α]. *c* **1205** LAY. 455 Þat Dardanisc kun..woneð. inne þeowe-dome þrel-werkes [*c* **1275** þralle-workes] doð. **1641** MILTON *Reform.* I. 2 Instead of..cheerful boldness..came servile and thrallike fear. **1886** CORBETT *Fall of Asgard* I. 35 She was a wild-looking thrall-girl. *Ibid.* 86 The thrall-woman came to answer for herself. **1887** MORRIS *Odyss.* XI. 190 A-winter he sleeps in the feast-hall whereto the thrall-folk seek.

B. *adj.* [attrib. use of the sb.]

1. That is a thrall; subject, captive, enslaved, in bondage. **a.** in the predicate, or following the sb. (*a*) *lit.*

1297 R. GLOUC. (Rolls) 4074 To bringe hom vnder þe þat þe wolde makie þral. *c* **1330** R. BRUNNE *Chron.* (1810) 51 Hardknoute of Danmark..he was born thralle. *c* **1430** LYDG. *Chichev. & Byc.* in *Min. Poems* (Percy Soc.) 132 For we ben thralle and they be free. *c* **1510** BARCLAY *Mirr. Gd. Manners* (1570) D iij, Sparing the Citizens to him subiect and thrall. **1633** HEYWOOD & ROWLEY *Fort. by Land & Sea* IV. Wks. 1874 VI. 418 We now are captives that made others thrall. **1862** BARING-GOULD *Iceland* (1863) 252 Male or female—free or thrall.

(*b*) *fig.*

a **1225** *Ancr. R.* 370 Hweðer is betere, ine secnesse uorte beon Godes freo child, þen i flesches heale uorte beon þrel under sunne? *a* **1300** *Cursor M.* 16940 (Cott.) Thoru a tre.. was al mankind mad thrall. **1477** EARL RIVERS (Caxton) *Dictes* 1 To be subgette and thral vnto the stormes of fortune. **1548** UDALL *Erasm. Par. Luke* vi. 75 To be thrall to no vice. *a* **1600** *Scot. Poems 16th C.* (1801) II. 216 Sen word is thrall, and thoght is only free. *a* **1628** F. GREVIL *Mustapha* III. i, Those silly natures, apt to louingnesse, Which euer must in others power liue, With doubt become more fond, with wrong more thral. **1845** E. HOLMES *Mozart* 167 It would seem that he was soon thrall to the court taste.

† **b.** preceding the sb. *Obs.*

1450–1530 *Myrr. our Ladye* 213 For the delyuerance of hys thrall seruante. **1526** *Pilgr. Perf.* (1531) 208 As thrall synners bounde in captiuite. **1554–9** in *Songs & Ball.* (1860) 3 Beyng slaves to Sathan, and thrall captyves vyle.

† **2.** Belonging to or characteristic of thraldom; slave-like, slavish, servile. *Obs.*

1398 TREVISA *Barth. De P.R.* II. xii. (1495) b vj b/2 To put of thrall drede & torne to god. **1528** ROY *Rede me* (Arb.) 69 Rid vs from antichristis bondes so thrall. **1535** in Strype *Eccl. Mem.* (1721) I. App. lxiii. 155 To perceive the thral captivity under the usurped power of the Bishop of Rome.

† **thrall,** *sb.*[2] *Obs.* [app. corruption of *thraw*, THROW *sb.*[1]] A space of time, a while.

c **1450** *Cov. Myst.* xxxv. (1841) 351, I pray 3ow alle Abyde stylle a lytyl thralle. **1535** STEWART *Cron. Scot.* (Rolls) II. 522 He..schew to him into that samin thrall, Far moir kyndnes nor ony of thame all.

thrall, thrawl (θrɔːl), *sb.*[3] *dial.* Also 7 **throale.** [Origin uncertain: ? an application of THRALL *sb.*[1]] A stand or frame for barrels, milk-pans, etc.

1674 *Inv.* in *New Shaks. Soc. Trans.* (1881–3) App. II. 14†, In the Sellars..Throales, hogsheads..and Tubbs. *a* **1800** PEGGE *Suppl. Grose*, *Gantril*, a stand for a barrel. North. Called also a *Thrawl*. **1843** *Jrnl. Roy. Agric. Soc.* IV. II. 497 A barrel thrawl, or stillion, of cast-iron, furnished with a.. lever apparatus for tilting casks without shaking their contents. **1859** GEO. ELIOT *A. Bede* vi, The dairy thralls, I might ha' wrote my name on 'em. **1884** *Vaughan's Patent* No. 14432 A thrall or stand and tilter for casks.

thrall, *a.*[1]: see THRALL *sb.*[1]

† **thrall,** *a.*[2] *Obs. rare.* [Etymology obscure.] ? Strenuous, hard, severe.

c **1430** *Syr Gener.* (Roxb.) 3947 [Generides] was in hert thral; His shelde he made from him to fall. *c* **1525** in *Rel. Ant.* II. 118 At Beverley a sudden chaunce did falle, The parish chirch stepille it felle At evynsonge tyme, the chaunce was thralle, Fourscore folke ther was slayn thay telle.

thrall (θrɔːl), *v. arch.* [Early ME. *þrallen*, f. THRALL *sb.*[1]] *trans.* To bring into bondage or subjection; to deprive of liberty; to hold in thraldom, enthrall, enslave; to take or hold captive. **a.** *lit.*

c **1205** LAY. 11205 He sloh þæ eorles & þrallede þæ chærles. **13..** *Cursor M.* 9485 (Cott.) Quils he es thralled in his seruis He ne mai be fre. *Ibid.* 17209 Þus am i thrald to ma þe fre. *c* **1450** *Mirour Saluacioun* 3311 The childere of Israel be pharao thralde hoegely. *a* **1612** HARINGTON *Ps.* cxxxvii. in Farr *S.P. Eliz.* (1845) I. 116 They that thralle us thus by wrong, Amid our sorrowes aske a song. **1872** TENNYSON *Gareth & Lyn.* 348 Yet lo! my husband's brother had my son Thrall'd in his castle, and hath starved him dead.

b. *fig.*

? *a* **1366** CHAUCER *Rom. Rose* 882 The God of Love..can wel these lordis thrallen. *c* **1412** HOCCLEVE *De Reg. Princ.* 4658 He þat auaricious is, is thrallid To moneie. *a* **1533** FRITH *Disput. Purg.* Pref. (1829) 91 Fleshly lust..would subdue..and hold us thralled under sin. *a* **1649** DRUMM. OF HAWTH. *Sonn.* I. iv, That bright Cherubine which thralls my Thought. *a* **1651** CALDERWOOD *Hist. Kirk* (1843) II. 391. **1835** *Court Mag.* VI. 216/1 What right had he..to thrall her promise, and waste away her young life?

c. *refl.* To enslave, bind, or submit oneself.

a **1300** *Cursor M.* 23787 (Edin.) We thrall vs til vr ful fa In prisun for to life in wa. *c* **1412** HOCCLEVE *De Reg. Princ.* 2959 They wolden nat hem to þo lawes thralle.

Hence '**thralling** *ppl. a. rare*, enthralling.

1871 J. HAY *Pike County Ball.* (1880) 88 Wrapped in thralling memories.

thralled (θrɔːld), *ppl. a.* [f. prec. vb. + -ED[1].] Made a thrall, enslaved, held in bondage; also *transf.* thrall-like, servile.

1527 *St. Papers Hen. VIII*, I. 230 For the delyveraunce of Your Grace out of the thraulde, pensif, and dolerous lif that the same is in. *a* **1586** SIDNEY *Arcadia* II. (1622) 103 With the most submissiue behauiour that a thralled heart could expresse. **1665** *Surv. Aff. Netherl.* 179 The English spirit, that prefers an honourable death to a thralled life. **1859** A. MACMILLAN *Lett.* (1908) 11 Italy is the thralled place she is, owing to her indulgence in that luscious enfeebling vein of literature.

thraller ('θrɔːlə(r)). *rare*[−0]. [f. as prec. + -ER[1].] One who enthralls.

1887 in *Cassell's Encycl. Dict.*

† **thralless** ('θrɔːlɪs), *sb. Obs. rare.* [f. THRALL *sb.*[1] + -ESS.] A female thrall; a bondwoman.

1382 WYCLIF *Deut.* xxviii. 68 There thow shalt be sold to thin enemyes, into thrallis and thrallessis. —— *Isa.* xiv. 2 And shal welden hem the hous of Irael..in to thralles and thrallesses [1388 in to seruauntis and hand maidis].

thralless ('θrɔːllɪs), *a.* [f. THRALL *sb.*[1] + -LESS.] Having no thrall; without bondmen.

1847 in WEBSTER.

† '**thrallful,** *a. Obs. rare*[−1]. [f. THRALL *sb.*[1] + -FUL.] Full of misery: cf. THRALL *sb.*[1] 3.

1615 SYLVESTER *Job Triumphant* IV. 686 Also the Lord accepted Job, and staid His Thrall-full State.

†'**thrallhead, -hood.** *Obs.* [f. THRALL *sb.*[1] + -HEAD, -HOOD.] = THRALDOM.

1297 R. GLOUC. (Rolls) 3013 An place..To wonie þer inne in þralhede vnder þe king. *a* **1300** *Cursor M.* 18372 (Cott.) All þi peple for to bring Vte of thralhed til þi chosling. *a* **1300** *K. Horn* 439 (MS. C) þanne is mi þralhod [*MSS. L, O*, þralhede] I went in to kniȝthod.

†'**thralship.** *Obs.* [See -SHIP.] = THRALDOM.

c **1200** *Trin. Coll. Hom.* 37 þe shepisse and þe netisse men beð under cristes þralshipe. *Ibid.* 101 Ure louerd hadde maked hem fre of þe deules þralsipe. *a* **1400** *R. Glouc.'s Chron.* (Rolls) 1085 (MS. α) þei þou ne askedest þer vppe þralschipe [*MSS. β.* -scheep, δ. -schype, γ. thralschyppe; *A.* þralhede] euere mo.

thraly, thraness, var. THROLY, THRONESS.

thrammel, Sc. and dial. variant of TRAMMEL.

thraneen, Irish var. TRANEEN.

thrang, pa. t. of THRING *v. Obs.*; Sc. and n. dial. f. THRONG.

thranite ('θreınaıt). *Gr. Antiq.* [ad. Gr. θρανίτης, f. θρᾶνος bench.] In the ancient trireme, a rower in one of the tiers, as generally supposed, the uppermost tier, which had the longest oars and hardest work; but the actual arrangement is disputed. Also *attrib.*

1842 BRANDE *Dict. Sc.* etc., *Thranite*, the uppermost (or, according to some arrangements of the classical galley, the foremost) of the three classes of rowers in an Athenian trireme. **1869** 'W. BRADWOOD' *The O.V.H.* xxx, Look at that tall, sloping-shouldered, brown-bearded thranite. **1894** *Athenæum* 29 Sept. 426/3 If..the oarsmen sat in a rectangular gallery..it would seem to be impossible to have more oarsmen on the thranite bank than on the other banks. **1904** KIPLING *Traffics & Discov.* 38 The thranite now and the thalamite are [steam] pressures low and high.

Hence **thra'nitic** *a.*, of or pertaining to the thranites.

1886 WARRE in *Encycl. Brit.* XXI. 807 Supernumerary oars..probably slightly exceeding the thranitic oars in length. *Ibid.*, About the level of the thranitic benches.

thrap, *v.* [Error for or dial. var. of *frap*: cf. TH (6).] *trans.* To bind tightly; = FRAP *v.*[2]

1813 SOUTHEY *Nelson* I. 150 The hull was so damaged, that it had for some time been secured by having cables served or thrapped round.

thrapple, Sc. dial. form of THROPPLE.

thrash (θræʃ), **thresh** (θrɛʃ), *v.* Forms: see below. [OE. *þerscan* (pa. t. *þærsc, þurscon*, pa. pple. *þorscen*), rarely and late *þrescan, þryscan*; a Common Teutonic verb, = OLG. **þerscan* (MLG., MDu., Flem. *derschen*; also MDu., Du., LG. *dorschen*, LG. *drosken*, EFris. *dörsken*); OHG. *dreskan* (MHG., Ger. *dreschen*); ON. *þreskja*, weak vb. (Norw. *treskja*, Da. *tærske*, Sw. *tröska*); Goth. *þriskan* (**þrask*, **þruskans*):—OTeut. **þresk-** :—Indo-Eur. **tresk-*, exemplified also in Lith. *traszketi* to rattle, make a noise, Russ. *treskatⁱ* (refl.) to burst, crash, crackle: cf. OSlav. *tresk"* sb. a crash. The metathesis *þersk-* for *þresk-* is found in OE., LG., Du., and Da. The meaning in OTeut. was prob. 'to tramp or stamp heavily with the feet', including both the action and the noise, as shown by the senses in which the word was taken into Romanic: Prov. *tresc-ar, dresc-ar*, It. *tresc-are*, OF. *trescher* to dance, Sp., Pg. *trisc-ar* to make a noise with the feet (see Diez s.v. *trescare*). The word came to be applied esp. to the act of treading out corn by the feet of men or oxen, and thus to the action of threshing by this or any later method. This is the only sense known in Gothic, OHG., and ONorse; but within historical times the chief mode of threshing was beating with the flail, whence the word came to be applied fig. to knocking, beating, or striking generally, and esp. of a person in battle or in punishment. In English this appears already in the OE. period; in German it is later (Grimm). The historical form in Eng. is *thresh*; a dialectal variant *thrash*, faintly represented in early times, came into literary use near the end of the 16th c., and became established in the 17th c., esp. in the sense 'to beat, flog, or belabour', for which it is now the ordinary form, while *thresh* is still largely retained in reference to corn. By this means, *to thresh* (corn) and *to thrash* (an offender or an opponent) have become to a considerable extent differentiated, so as almost to be felt as distinct words, esp. since the use of the flail has become so much superseded by mechanical means. Another form *throsh*, with the vowel of the pa. pple. as in Du. and LG., was frequent in late ME., but is now only dialectal.]

A. Illustration of Forms.

1. Present stem.

α. 1 **þersc(e)an, þirsc-, ðærsc-, ðerhs-, ðearc-, ðearsc-, þearcs-, þrex-, ðryscan**; 3 **þreoschen**, 3–4 **þresch-**, 4 **threisch-, threissch-**, 4–5 **þresch-, þressch-e(n**, 4–6 **thresshe, thresche, -yn, threshe, thresse, -yn**, 5 **thraissh**, 6–7 **threash**, 6– **thresh** (*dial.* 6 **tress, drayse, draysche**, 8–9 **draish, dresh**).

a **800** CYNEWULF *Elene* 358 (Gr.) Ða wereȝan neat, þe man ..drifeð and þirsceð. *a* **850** Ðeh ðu þercce [? þersce] [see B. 1]. *c* **897** Ðerscað ðone weall [see B. 4]. *c* **950** *Lindisf. Gosp.* Mark v. 5 Cliopende & ðærscende hine to stanum. *Ibid.* xiv. 65 Ongunnun..mið fystum *vel* dyntum hine ȝeslaa *vel* ȝeðearsca [*c* 975 *Rushw.* ðarsca]. *c* **1000** To þerscenne. *a* **1100** Ðerhsan [see B. 1 b]. *a* **1100** in Napier *O.E. Glosses* 212/1 *Territat*, þearcs. *a* **1100** *Aldhelm Gloss.* I. 3433 ibid. 91/2 *Triturandos*, to þrexen[n]e. *a* **1225** *Ancr. R.* 306 þet seoruwe þreosche him wiðinne þe heorte. **1377, 1382,** *c* **1386** Thresche, threshe, threischinge, thresshe, þressche [see B. 1 b]. **14..** *Tretyce* in *W. of Henley's Husb.* (1890) 50 Let yoʳ thresers be sworne to thresse it clene. *c* **1440** *Promp. Parv.* 492/2 Threschyn, *trituro, flagello*. **1530** PALSGR. 755/2, I thresshe corne in a barne. **15..** Thressyn [see B. 1 b]. **1552** HULOET, Threshe, *flagello*,..*trituro*. **1570** LEVINS *Manip.* 91/32 To Thresh, *triturare*. **1596** DALRYMPLE tr. *Leslie's Hist. Scot.* I. (S.T.S.) I. 95 Thay thresche na stuf. **1693, 1764,** etc. Thresh [see B. 1].

β. (1 **ðarscan**), 5 **thrassh**, 6– **thrash** (8–9 *dial.* **drash**).

c **975** Ðarsca [see α, quot. *c* 950[2]]. **1591** SPENSER *M. Hubberd* 264 To..thrash, to thetch, to mowe. **1662** J. DAVIES tr. *Olearius' Voy. Ambass.* 390 The men bring it [corn] into the barn, but the women thrash and sell it. **1746** *Exmoor Scolding* 94 Chell baste tha, chell stram tha, chell drash tha. **1795** WOLCOTT (P. Pindar) *Royal Visit Exeter* II. xiv, He did zo drash about his brain, That was not over stor'd.

γ. 5 **throsch(e**, 5–6 **throsh(e, throsshe, throszshe**, (8–9 *dial.* **drosh**).

14.. *Chaucer's Prol.* 536 (MS. Cambr. Gg4, 27) He wolde throsche. **1486** [implied in Throsheris: see THRASHER[1] 1]. **1495** *Trevisa's Barth. De P.R.* XVIII. xiv. aa viij b/1 They ledyth them [oxen] abowte vpon corne to breke the strawe in throsshyng and tredynge the flour. **1526** TINDALE *1 Cor.* ix. 10 He which throssheth in hope shulde be part taker of his hope. **1535** COVERDALE *Hab.* iii. 12 Thou trodest downe the londe..and didest throsshe the Heithen.

2. Past tense.

α. 1 **ðærsc**, *pl.* **ðurscon, -un (þurcson, þurhsun)**, 2 *pl.* **þurscen**, 5 *pl.* **throsshen**; 8–9 *Sc.* **thruish, threush (-ø-)**.

a **900** *O.E. Martyrol.* 7 Mar. 36 He..corn þærsc ond þæt windwode. *c* **950** *Lindisf. Gosp.* Mark xii. 5 Sume ðurscun oðero æc ofsloȝon. *c* **1000** *Ags. Gosp.* Luke xxii. 64 þa..oferwruȝon hys ansyne & þurhsun [*v.r.* þurcson, *c* **1160** *Hatton G.* þurscen] his nebb. *c* **1430** *Pilgr. Lyf Manhode* I. lxxiv. (1869) 43 Manye..throsshen it and fanned it. **1815** Threush [B. 3 b]. *Mod. Sc.* He thruish aa' day i' the barn.

β. (*weak conj.*) 4–5 **thresched**, 6 **threashed, (throszshed)**, 6– **threshed, thrashed**.

c **1400** Thresched [see B. 4 b]. **1535** COVERDALE *1 Chron.* xxii. [xxi.] 20 Arnan throszshed wheate. **1560** BIBLE (Genev.) *Judg.* vi. 11 Gideon threashed [**1611** threshed] wheat. **1577** HOLINSHED *Chron.* II. 639/1 Sundrie..came to theyr Barnes, threshed vp theyr grayne. **1633** Thresht [see B. 2].

3. Past participle.

α. 1 **þorscen**, 2 **iþor(s)chen**; 3 **i-ðrosschen**, (*Orm.*) **þrosshenn**, 4 **ithrosshen, i-þrosschen, y-þorsse, throsshe**, 5 **throsshen, (trosshyn)**, 6 **throshen**, 9 *Sc.* **thruishen (-ø-)**.

c **1175** Iþor[s]chen [see B. 2]. *c* **1200** ORMIN 1530 þa winndwesst tu þin þrosshenn corn. *a* **1225** Iðrosschen [see B. 5]. **1340** Y-þorsse [see B. 1, 4]. **13..** *Propr. Sanct.* (Vernon MS.) in Herrig's *Archiv* LXXXI. 83/26 Hit is brouht hom til a Berne, Hard I-þrosschen in an hurne. **1584** *Shuttleworths' Acc.* (Chetham Soc.) I. 21 When the same [corn] was throshen xiijᵈ. *Mod. Sc.* When the last stack was thruishen.

β. 5–6 **thresshen**, (5 **(i)thresshe, ythrysshe**), 6 **threshoone**, 7 *Sc.* **threaschin**, 8 *Sc.* **threshen**.

1426 LYDG. *De Guil. Pilgr.* 5412 Tyl the thressherys.. Hadde thys greyn ythrysshe & bete. *c* **1450** *Godstow Reg.* 649 The corn that is wonyd to be gyf I-thresshe. *c* **1450** *Oseney Reg.* 144, I and myne heyres schall make it to Be thresshe. **1523** FITZHERB. *Husb.* §13 Whan it is thresshen, there is moche lyght corne. **1599** *Nottingham Rec.* IV. 251 All the corne..threshoone and vnthreshoone. **1629** *Orkney Witch Trial* in *County Folk-Lore* (1903) III. 77 Edward Rendall.. said thair was nane [corn] threa[s]chin. **1720** T. BOSTON *Fourfold St.* (1797) 135 The corn of my floor threshen in the floor of wrath.

γ. (*weak conj.*) 4 **threschid, threischid**, 6 **(tressyd), thresht(e**, 6– **threshed, thrashed** (7 **thrasht**).

1382 Threschid [see B. 2]. **1538** in *Lett. Suppress. Monasteries* (Camden) 176 Sum is threshte,..and mych is yit to threshe. **1544** in I. S. Leadam *Sel. Cases Crt. Requests* (1898) 76 The said Baylyf causyd the same pease to be tressyd. *a* **1625** Thrasht [see B. 5 β].

B. Signification.

I. To thresh (thrash) corn, etc. and directly derived senses.

1. To separate by any mechanical means, e.g. rubbing, shaking, trampling, stamping, beating, or intermittent pressure, the grains of any cereal from the husks and straw; esp. by beating with a flail; now (from the latter part of the eighteenth century) also by the action of revolving mechanism in a mill or machine. Also, to shake out or separate in the same way the seed of any plant.

The verb was in early times applied to the trampling and stamping of oxen, or the dragging of heavy rugged things, over the corn laid on a smooth surface or 'floor'.

a. *trans.*

α. *a* **850** *Kentish Gloss.* in Wr.-Wülcker 83/35-7 Ðeh ðu þercce [*for* þersce] swa berecorn ðerccedum [*for* ðerscendum]. *c* **1200** ORMIN 1500 þa þresshesst tu þin corn wiþþ fleȝȝl. **1340** *Ayenb.* 139 Of þe hyeape of huete y-þorsse, þe cornes byeþ beneþ e and þet chef above. *c* **1450** LYDG. *Secrees* 1436 Afftir hervest..men thresshe shevys. **1530, 1596** [see A. 1 α]. **1693** EVELYN *De la Quint. Compl. Gard.* II. 163 Cutting off all the Seed stems, and when they are dried, threshing out the Seed. **1764** *Museum Rust.* II. lxxvi. 260 How he lets his corn to thresh by the great. **1845** FORD *Handbk. Spain* I. 25 The modern system of threshing grain in Spain is extremely ancient, classical, and Oriental. **1880** W. NEWTON *Serm. Boys & Girls* (1881) 219 He had a number of men engaged in threshing wheat.

β. **1588** SHAKS. *Tit. A.* II. iii. 123 First thrash the Corne, then after burne the straw. **1603** HOLLAND *Plutarch's Mor.* 1008 Husbandmen are affraid to thrash their wheat upon a dry and sandy floore, because of ants. **1662** [see A. 1 β]. **1846** *J. Baxter's Libr. Pract. Agric.* (ed. 4) II. 337 The [turnip] seed may then be..stacked and thrashed when wanted. **1877** KNIGHT *Dict. Mech.* 2555/2 Doura, sorghum, or flax was thrashed by drawing across a comb-like instrument.

b. *absol.* or *intr.*

α. *c* **1000** *Ælfric's Voc.* in Wr.-Wülcker 147/14 *Area*, breda þiling, *uel* flor on to þerscenne. *a* **1100** *Gerefa* in *Anglia* (1886) IX. 261 Mæniȝe inweorc wyrcean, ðerhsan, wudu cleofan. *a* **1300** *Cursor M.* 4744 (Cott.) Ioseph þat was ful o pite Did thresche [*v. rr.* þresshe, threche] son in þat contre. **1377** LANGL. *P. Pl.* B. v. 553 Some tyme I sowe and some tyme I thresche. **1382** WYCLIF *Micah* iv. 13 Ryse thou, and threshe, douȝter of Syon. —— *1 Cor.* ix. 9 Thou schalt not bynde the mouth of the oxe threischinge [**1388** that threischith]. *c* **1386** CHAUCER *Prol.* 536 He wolde thresshe [*v. rr.* throsche, þressche] and ther to dyke and delue. **15..** *Ragman Roll* 53 in Hazl. *E.P.P.* I. 72 Whoo so lyst may thressyn in your berne. **1758** JOHNSON *Idler* No. 70 ¶10 He, whose task is to reap and thresh.

β. **1591** [see A. 1 β]. **1755** JOHNSON, To thrash, *v.n.*

c. *intr.* for *pass.* Of corn: To bear threshing; to be threshed.

1760 R. BROWN *Compl. Farmer* II. 72 The weeds..will.. cause it [rye] not to thrash well. *Ibid.* 81.

2. *fig.*; in earlier use sometimes with reference to ancient modes of threshing. ***to thresh (thrash) straw***, to work at what is unproductive or unprofitable; also ***to thresh over old straw***.

c **1175** *Lamb. Hom.* 85 In þe deie of liureisun hwense god almihtin wule windwin þet er wes iþor[s]chen. **1382** WYCLIF *Isa.* xxv. 10 Threschid shal ben Moab vnder hym, as ben totreden strawes in a wayn. **1633** P. FLETCHER *Purple Isl.* XI. xxiv, She..Drove farre their flying troops, and thresht with iron flail. **1777** GARRICK *Prol. Sheridan's Sch. Scand.* 11 All night at cards when threshing Strong tea and scandal. **1857** PUSEY *Real Presence* i. (1869) 144 Bruick said,..'as to the King himself [Hen. VIII] it was to thresh an empty ear'. **1871** B. TAYLOR *Faust* (1875) I. iv. 73 Why plague thyself with threshing straw forever? *a* **1876** *Binorie O an Binorie* iii. in Child *Ballads* I. (1882) 133/1 O sister, O sister, will ye go to the dams, To hear the blackbird thrashin oer his songs?

b. ***to thresh (thrash) out (a subject***, etc.), to discuss (a matter) exhaustively, to argue thoroughly; to get at the truth of (a question) by discussion or argument.

1882 PEBODY *Eng. Journalism* xxiii. 186 There is hardly a question..that is not now completely thrashed out in the Press long before it reaches Parliament. **1884** *Law Times* 15 Mar. 353/1 Every case thoroughly thrashed out. **1885** SIR C. S. C. BOWEN in *Law Rep. 29 Ch. Div.* 810 That point had been threshed out before Mr. Justice Pearson. **1893** *Spectator* 18 Mar. 349 The matter should have been thoroughly threshed out.

3. *transf.* **a.** To beat or strike as with a flail: see quots. and cf. 5.

α. **1573** TUSSER *Husb.* (1878) 180 At Shroftide to shrouing, go thresh the fat hen. **1707** J. STEVENS tr. *Quevedo's Com. Wks.* (1709) Rij, Condemn'd to thresh the Sea, that is to the Gallies. **1867** F. FRANCIS *Angling* v. (1880) 153 The angler goes on threshing the water.

β. **1638** SIR T. HERBERT *Trav.* (ed. 2) 171 Swarms of Gnats, Mus-ke-toes, and such like.., stung and pesterd us ..; they biting us, we thrashing them like mad folks. **1697** DRYDEN *Virg. Past.* II. 73 Myself will..thrash the Chesnuts in the Neighb'ring Grove. **1823** F. COOPER *Pioneers* i, The black..began thrashing his arms together, in order to restore the circulation.

b. *intr.* To deliver or inflict blows as with a flail; to strike or beat *on* or *at.* (With quot. 1693 cf. BEAT *v.*[1] 26 b.)

1693 DRYDEN *Juvenal's Sat.* x. 194, I rather wou'd be Mævius, thrash for Rhimes Like his,..Than that Philippique..should be mine. **1815** G. BEATTIE *John o' Arnha'* (1826) 33 He scourg'd the water wi' his tail, An' threush on John as wi' a flail. **1905** F. YOUNG *Sands Pleas.* III. ii, Richard..walked out of the graveyard, threshing at the nettles with his stick.

†**4. a.** *trans.* To beat, batter, strike, knock. Also *fig. Obs.* exc. as in 3.

c **897** K. ÆLFRED *Gregory's Past. C.* xxi. 160 Send ðærto ȝefylceo, & ðerscað ðone weall mid rammum. *a* **950** *Rituale Eccl. Dunelm.* (Surtees) 6 Svæ ic fehto no svoelce lyft ðerscende [*non quasi æram* (Vulg. *aerem*) *verberans*]. *a* **1000** *Sal. & Sat.* (Kemble) 148 Se ðunor hit ðrysceð mid ðære fyrenan æcxe. **1340** *Ayenb.* 266 Vram þo lyȝte byeþ y-þorsse mine eȝen. *a* **1400-50** *Alexander* 1326 He laschis out a lange swerde..Threschis doun in a thrawe many threuyn dukis.

†**b.** *intr.* To strike, inflict blows *on. Obs.*

13.. *Gaw. & Gr. Knt.* 2300 Wy þresch on, þou þro mon, þou pretez to longe. *c* **1400** *Laud Troy Bk.* 16912 Echon on other dong & thresched.

II. To beat a person, an army, etc. Now commonly thrash.

5. a. *trans.* To beat by way of punishment; to chastise by or as by beating; to flog, orig. with a stick, cudgel, whip, etc.; in mod. use also to pommel with the fists. Also *transf.* and *fig.*

α. *a* **950** *Rituale Eccl. Dunelm.* (Surtees) 43 Ðv ðe rehtlice ðv ðersces synfvllo [*qui juste verberas peccatores*]. *a* **1225** *Ancr. R.* 186 Hendi children þet cusseð þe ȝerden þet he haueð ou mid iðrosschen. *a* **1400** *Octouian* 764 With a staf Y wol the thressche. **1647** TRAPP *Comm. Epistles* 366 Gideon by threshing the men of Succoth, taught them [etc.]. **1806–7** J. BERESFORD *Miseries Hum. Life* XXI. xvii, Learning to box, too—i.e. feeing a great raw-boned fellow to thresh you as long as he can stand over you.

β. *a* **1625** FLETCHER *Nice Valour* III. iii, Oh gentlemen y'are welcom: I have been thrasht i' faith... Never was Shrove-tuesday Bird So cudgel'd gentlemen. **1733** FIELDING *Mock Doctor* iv, Take a good cudgel, and thrash him with it. **1739** 'R. BULL' tr. *Dedekindus' Grobianus* 168 A Wife, an Ass, a Walnut-tree ('tis thought) Except they're thrash'd, are never good for ought. **1833** MARRYAT *P. Simple* x, O'Brien.. was very kind to me in general, and allowed nobody to thrash me but himself. **1866** GEO. ELIOT *F. Holt* i, I always meant to.. thrash a lord or two who thrashed me at Eton. **1885** *Manch. Exam.* 11 Nov. 3/3 The deacon.. thrashes him for wasting his time.

b. In colloq. phrases, as ***to thrash one's jacket***, ***to thrash the life out of*** (cf. BEAT *v.*[1] 15).

1687 T. BROWN *Saints in Uproar* Wks. 1730 I. 74 I'll substantially thrash your jacket for you. **1873** BLACK *Pr. Thule* xvii, If you were half-a-dozen years older, I would thrash the life out of you.

6. To beat completely or thoroughly (BEAT *v.*[1] 10); to defeat or overcome with severe loss in war or fighting, or *at* a game or contest.

α. **1606** SHAKS. *Tr. & Cr.* II. i. 50 Thou scuruy valiant Asse, thou art heere but to thresh Troyans. **1721** AMHERST *Terræ Fil.* No. 13. (1754) 66 They could either thresh corn, or their country's enemies.

β. **1778** LADY SARAH LENNOX *Lett.* (1901) I. 279 Send them home to thrash the French. **1796** NELSON in Nicolas *Disp.* (1845) II. 256, I shall.. take my chance of helping to thrash Don Langara. **1841** LEVER *C. O'Malley* lxxii, We had been attacked by the French in force and devilishly well thrashed. **1863** KINGSLEY *Water Bab.* i, [He] could have thrashed Mr. Grimes himself in fair fight. **1890** 'R. BOLDREWOOD' *Col. Reformer* (1891) 276 The Colonel.. has just been thrashing me at billiards. **1903** *Westm. Gaz.* 14 Apr. 2/3 [incident of June 1815] It touched land, and a man jumped out waving his hat and exclaiming, 'Hurrah, Wellington has thrashed Boney!'

III. Transferred uses, often referring to both I and II. Usually thrash.

7. a. *intr. Naut.* To force or work one's way against opposing wind, tide, etc.; = BEAT *v.*[1] 19; said of a ship or of mariners. Also *trans.* with *way*. Also *refl.* and *fig.*

α. **1857** DUFFERIN *Lett. High Lat.* v. (ed. 3) 28 We had to return.. to our old practice of threshing to windward.

β. **1830** COL. HAWKER *Diary* (1893) II. 15 Hard labour to .. thrash for an hour through blocks of ice before we could get out. **1855** KINGSLEY *Westw. Ho.* xx, The ship thrashed close-hauled through the rolling seas. **1890** CLARK RUSSELL *Marriage at Sea* xiii, The steamer was thrashing through it at an exhilarating speed. **1900** *Daily News* 15 Oct. 6/7 The Nuddea encountered the typhoon some distance to the southward of Hong Kong, and.. had to thrash her way through it. **1939** T. S. ELIOT *Family Reunion* I. ii. 60 The fish Thrashing itself upstream.

b. *trans.* To force (a ship) forward, esp. against contrary wind or sea. Cf. BEAT *v.*[1] 19 d.

α. **1886** *Daily Tel.* 23 Apr. 2/1 The captain threshes his great structure through the deep.

β. **1891** KIPLING *Light that Failed* xv. 310 The screw began to thrash the ship along the Docks. **1893** —— *Many Invent.* 365 Carry on and thrash her out with all she'll stand.

8. *intr.* To make wild movements like those of a flail or a whip; to lash out; to throw oneself (or itself) to and fro with violence; to toss, plunge; of hair, branches, or anything free at one end: to flap, whip, lash; esp. with *about* or *around*. Also *fig.* and *trans.* (*refl.*) with *into*.

1846 *Boston Courier* 17 June 2/4 Arter I'd gone to bed & heern Him a thrashin round like a short tailed Bull in fli time. **1850** SCORESBY *Cheever's Whalem. Adv.* v. (1858) 74 [A whale] blindly thrashed and rolled about in great agony. **1875** LD. SHAFTESBURY in *Life* (1886) III. xxxiii. 354 He [a preacher] thrashed with his arms, as though he were about to strike. **1883** C. F. HOLDER in *Harper's Mag.* Jan. 186/2 The shark squirmed out, thrashing about and snapping its jaws. **1884** 'MARK TWAIN' *Huck. Finn* vi. 45 He didn't go sound asleep, but was uneasy. He groaned, and moaned, and thrashed around this way and that. **1891** KIPLING *Light that Failed* i. 13 A night-wind thrashed along the bents of the foreshore. *Ibid.* xiii. 244 The red-haired girl thrashed distressfully across the sheets. **1896** *Boston* (Mass.) *Jrnl.* 11 Jan. 4/8 The wounded bears were kicking and thrashing around me. **1897** CROCKETT *Lad's Love* xxiii, The wind unloosed the banded hair and blew it about.., till it threshed in the man's face and annoyed him. **1900** N. MUNRO in *Blackw. Mag.* Nov. 656/1 They saw the boughs thrash and the tree tops rise and fall like billows round the village. **1962** K. A. PORTER *Ship of Fools* 178 He groans and yells and thrashes about at night. **1962** K. KESEY *One Flew over Cuckoo's Nest* IV. 309 It fought a long time against having it taken away, flailing and thrashing around. **1973** *Times* 12 Nov. 11/8 His is in many ways a sad life to watch, as he thrashes around for the opening that will bring him fame. **1978** R. BARNARD *Unruly Son* xvii. 190 This little detail panicked you.. and then you started thrashing around... You did silly things.

refl. **1865** BUSHNELL *Vicar. Sacr.* III. v. (1868) 327 A broken engine by running will only thresh itself into a more complete wreck.

Hence **thrashed, threshed** *ppl. a.*

[*c* **1200** þrosshenn corn: see A. 3 a.] **1707** MORTIMER *Husb.* (1721) I. 147 They.. put some of the Chaff in first, and then their thrashed Wheat. **1805** DICKSON *Pract. Agric.* I. 48 A large quantity of thrashed grain is seldom kept. **1867** F. FRANCIS *Angling* vi. (1880) 193 One of our well-thrashed streams.

thrash, thresh, *sb.*[1] [f. prec. vb.]

†**1.** ? A threshing implement, a flail: cf. THRESHEL.

1669 PENN *No Cross* xviii §10 (1682) 368 That the Cart, the Plough, the Thrash should be in that continual Severity laid upon Nineteen parts of the Land, to feed the inordinate Lusts and delicious Appetites of the Twentieth.

2. a. An act or the action of thrashing or threshing; a blow, stroke, knock; a beat or beating.

1840 HOOD *Kilmansegg, Fancy Ball* iii, Tories like to worry the Whigs,.. Giving them lashes, thrashes, and digs. **1898** *Blackw. Mag.* Sept. 376 It [a boat's progress] was a long monotonous thresh for the rest of the afternoon. **1899** CROCKETT *Black Douglas* xlii. 305 The thresh of the rain upon the lattice casement. **1902** J. MASEFIELD *Salt-Water Ball., D Avalos' Prayer* iii, The wash and thresh of the sea-foam. **1906** *Outlook* 20 Oct. 511/2 A thrash of rain.

b. *fig.* A dash.

1870 J. K. HUNTER *Life Stud. Charac.* xxxv, I appeared in the court.. wi' a thrash, and had the case settled in a jiffy.

c. In reduplicated form ***thresh-thresh***, representing the continuous sound of threshing.

1904 *Blackw. Mag.* Apr. 485 A rhythmic thresh-thresh that had accompanied but hardly broken the silence, suddenly ceased.

3. A party, esp. one that is lavish or unrestrained. (Regularly *thrash*). *slang.*

1957 G. SMITH *Friends* 120, I think he stole away to London for an occasional thrash when it got too much for him, but in general he was a model pupil. **1968** K. AMIS *I want it Now* ii. 68 No quiet family party at all, it had turned out, but a twenty-cover thrash. **1976** *Times Lit. Suppl.* 6 Feb. 131/3 Staggering.. from his sick-bed to play host at an enormous black-tie thrash at a Belgravia mansion borrowed for the night. **1980** C. MATTHEW *Loosely Engaged* 17 Occasionally someone throws a thrash, but most of the time we just bomb round to Wedgies.. and have a bit of a giggle.

thrash, thresh, *sb.*[2] *Sc.* Also 7 thrush. [corrupt. of *rash*, *resh*, OE. *risc*, RUSH *sb.*[1]] A rush. Also *attrib.*, **thresh-bush**, a clump of rushes.

1697 CLELAND *Poems* 30 (Jam.) Their bare preaching now Makes the thrush-bush keep the cow. **1795** A. WILSON *Spouter* in *Poems & Lit. Prose* (1876) II. 335 Green thrashes were strewed on the floor. **1822** R. WILSON *Poems, Twa Mice* (E.D.D.), Wi' their teeth green threshes chackit. **1850** J. STRUTHERS *Life* vi. Poet. Wks. I. p. cxiv, The shelter of a few well-grown thresh-bushes. **1871** H. S. RIDDELL *Poet. Wks.* II. 127 (E.D.D.) Threshes formed the theekin.

thrashel, dial. form of THRESHEL.

thrasher[1], **thresher** (ˈθræʃə(r), ˈθrɛʃə(r)). Forms: see THRASH *v.*; also 6–7 tres(s)her. [f. THRASH, THRESH *v.* + -ER[1].] One who or that which thrashes or threshes.

1. a. One who separates grain from the straw by beating with a flail, or otherwise. (More usually spelt *thresher*.)

1380 in Thorold Rogers *Oxford City Doc.* (1891) 39 *De Waltero* le thressher. *c* **1400** *Laud Troy Bk.* 9333 Echon on other ffaste doth bete, Ryght as threscheres doth on whete. *c* **1440** *Promp. Parv.* 492/2 Threschare, *triturator, flagellator*. **1486** *Bk. St. Albans* Fvj b, A Thraue of Throsheris. **1535** COVERDALE *Isa.* xxi. 10 O my felowe throsshers and fanners. **1593** SHAKS. *3 Hen. VI*, II. i. 131 A lazie Thresher with a Flaile. **1616** SURFL. & MARKH. *Country Farme* 18 Your Barne, with his great dore.. to giue light to the Threshers. **1632** MASSINGER *City Madam* II. ii, To sit like a fool at home, and eye your thrashers. **1641** BEST *Farm. Bks.* (Surtees) 143 Others.. give to theire thrashers 5d. a quarter for oates. **1707** MORTIMER *Husb.* (1721) I. 36 A good Thrasher can thrash out but about six Gallons in a Day. **1784** COWPER *Task* I. 356 We may discern the thresher at his task. Thump after thump resounds the constant flail. **1859** JEPHSON *Brittany* iii. 23 The threshers.. struck the corn alternately. **1864** H. AINSWORTH *John Law* v. ix, I lays about me right and left like a thrasher.

b. (*a*) Each of the beaters in a threshing-machine. (*b*) A threshing-machine.

1805 DICKSON *Pract. Agric.* I. 30 If the unthrashed corn goes in sideways or irregularly, the thrashers can have but little power upon it. **1877** KNIGHT *Dict. Mech.* 2554/1 Meikle.. invented a machine in 1786, which is the type of modern thrashers. **1884** *Manchester Exam.* 30 Sept. 5/7 Teams of horses draw the corn to the thrasher. **1891** T. HARDY *Tess* xlvii, The hum of the thresher.. increased to a raving whenever the supply of corn fell short of the regular quantity.

2. A sea-fox or fox-shark, *Alopias vulpes*; so called from the very long upper division of the tail, with which it lashes an enemy. Also called ***thresher-*** or ***thrasher-fish***, ***-shark***.

α. **1609** *Newes fr. Bermudas* July, in Force *Hist. Tracts* II. 22 The Threasher keepeth above him, & with a mighty great thing like unto a flaile, hee so bangeth the whale, that hee will roare as though it thundered. **1630** DONNE *Progr. Soul* 351 The Flail-finn'd Thresher, and steel-beak'd Sword-fish. **1758** BORLASE *Nat. Hist. Cornw.* xxiii. §3. 265 The sea-fox, *Vulpecula*, or *Simia marina*..; this shark we call the Thresher, from the motion of its long fox-like tail with which it strikes or threshes its larger and less agile enemy the grampus. **1845** GOSSE *Ocean* iii. (1849) 146 Another Shark, often called the Thresher,.. is said to use its muscular tail.. to inflict terrible slaps on the Whale.

β. **1638** DAVENANT *Madagascar* Wks. (1673) 206 The martiall Musick might incite The Sword-fish, Thrasher, and the Whale to fight. **1712** E. COOKE *Voy. S. Sea* 173 The Spaniards say the Thrashers and Sword-Fishes often kill the Whales. **1860** J. COUCH *Brit. Fishes* I. 38 Instances are reported where a Sword fish on the one hand and a Thrasher on the other, have persecuted a large Whale.

3. One who thrashes or beats another.

1907 *Daily Chron.* 21 Mar. 5/5 A Bill.. introduced.. into the Legislature of Pennsylvania legalising the thrashing of editors.. who wrongfully comment on individuals. The Bill makes the proof of publication of a libel a complete defence if the editor sues the thrasher for assault and battery.

4. *attrib.* and *Comb.*, as ***thresher-fish***, ***-shark*** = 2; **thresher-** or **thrasher-whale**, a grampus or killer, as *Orcinus orca*.

1782 'J. H. ST. J. DE CRÈVECŒUR' *Lett. from Amer. Farmer* vi. 169 The following are.. the various species of whales known to these people... The killer, or thrasher about thirty feet; they often kill the other whales. **1865** DE MORGAN in *Athenæum* No. 1981. 504/2 As the thresher-fish behaves towards the whale. **1888** *Ayr Advertiser* 5 July 6 A very large specimen of the fox or 'thresher' shark was recently caught .. at Port-na-Luing. **1905** *Daily Chron.* 5 July 6/6 A thrasher whale, measuring 10ft., and weighing 2 cwt. **1906** *Ibid.* 11 June 5/5 Three Southwold fisherman have secured in the bay a thresher fish.

thrasher[2] (ˈθræʃə(r)). Also **thresher, thrusher.** [Perh. a survival of *thrusher*, *thresher*, an Eng. dialectal name of the THRUSH (*Turdus musicus*), in U.S. assimilated to prec.; but chronological evidence is wanting.

Cf. **1881** *Oxfordsh. Gloss., Suppl.* (E.D.S.), *Thresher* or *Thrusher*, a thrush.]

A bird of the North American genus *Harporhynchus*, resembling the Song Thrush; esp. *H.* (†*Turdus*) *fuscus*, the best known of the species, of the north-eastern U.S., called also ***brown thrasher***, ***brown thrush***.

1808–14 A. WILSON *Amer. Ornith.* (1832) I. 233 The Brown Thrush, or Thrasher, of the middle and eastern states. *Ibid.* 235 The Thrasher is a welcome visitant in spring. **1845** S. JUDD *Margaret* I. vi, She sings round after dark, like a thrasher. **1883** NEWTON in *Encycl. Brit.* XVI. 541/1 Known in the United States as Threshers.. very Thrush-like in their habits. **1896** —— *Dict. Birds* 958 *Thrasher*, *Thresher*, or *Thrusher*,.. a bird well known in the eastern part of North America, the *Turdus fuscus* of the older and *Harporhynchus fuscus* of later ornithologists.

thrashing, threshing (ˈθræʃɪŋ, ˈθrɛʃɪŋ), *vbl. sb.* [f. THRASH, THRESH *v.* + -ING[1].] The action of the verb THRASH or THRESH in various senses. (For the status of the spellings, see the vb.)

I. 1. Beating with or as with a flail; *esp.* the separation of grain from the straw by beating or otherwise.

1382 WYCLIF *Hos.* x. 11 Effraym a cow calf, tauȝt for to loue thresshyng. **1393** LANGL. *P. Pl.* C. IX. 199 In þresshynge, in þecchynge, in thwytynge of pynnes. **1601** HOLLAND *Pliny* XVIII. xxx. I. 602 The good redbearded wheat Far.. commeth hardly out of the huske, and asketh some painefull thrashing. **1877** TALMAGE *Serm.* 378 In Grace, as in farming, there is a time for threshing. **1898** *Westm. Gaz.* 31 Jan. 2/1 No break or variety in the low, dark clouds, or the steady threshing of the rain.

b. That which is threshed; the grain obtained by threshing.

1382 WYCLIF *Isa.* xxi. 10 My thressing, and the doȝter of my cornflor. **1898** *Westm. Gaz.* 21 Apr. 2/1 The British farmer who has not yet sold last year's thrashing will thus reap the benefit of the higher prices.

II. 2. Beating or flogging, esp. by way of punishment; an instance of this. (Regularly *thrashing*.)

1843 BETHUNE *Sc. Fireside Stor.* 111 The benefit of the instructions and thrashings of.. the parish schoolmaster. **1863** P. BARRY *Dockyard Econ.* 53 Gifts of that kind.. are viewed in the light of schoolboy indulgences after a severe thrashing. **1875** A. R. HOPE *Schoolboy Friends* 80 I'll give you the greatest thrashing you ever had.

b. A defeat in battle or in any contest.

1815 LD. APSLEY in Stocqueler *Wellington* (1853) II. App. 340, I think the French will get such a thrashing as they have seldom had. **1885** *L'pool Daily Post* 1 June 5/4 The county suffered a 'one innings' thrashing [at cricket] at the hands of their antagonists.

3. *transf.*: see senses 7 and 8 of the verb.

1886 R. C. LESLIE *Sea Painter's Log* 115 Much thrashing to and fro in the chops of the Channel. **1895** *Outing* (U.S.) XXVII. 50/1, I knew from the thrashing going on.. that the game was mine.

4. *attrib.* and *Comb.*, as ***thrashing-*** or ***threshing-barn***, ***-flail***, etc.

1382 WYCLIF *Gen.* l. 10 Thei camen to the thresshyng feelde of Adad. **1560** BIBLE (Genev.) *Amos* i. 3 Thei haue threshed Gilead with threshing instruments of yron. **1609** BIBLE (Douay) *Isa.* xli. 15, I have made thee as a new threshing wayne, having teeth like a saw. **1812** SIR J. SINCLAIR *Syst. Husb. Scot.* I. 15 The threshing-barn.. must be sufficiently spacious to contain one stack of grain in the straw. *Ibid.* 72 The threshing-mill has generally one set of fanners attached to it, driven by a belt from the end of the axle of the threshing drum. **1844** STEPHENS *Bk. Farm* II. 267 No corn should be presented until the mill has acquired its proper momentum, the *thrashing-motion*, as it is termed. **1865** MISS CARY *Ball. & Lyrics* 140 The.. farmer-boy Who cut my name upon his thrashing-flail. **1877** KNIGHT *Dict. Mech.* 2557/1 Rollers which carry the grain in the straw from the feed-board to the thrashing cylinder.

ˈ**thrashing,** ˈ**threshing,** *ppl. a.* [f. as prec. + -ING[2].] That thrashes or threshes; *esp.* that threshes corn, etc. In quot. 1706 in sense 'great', 'big': cf. THUMPING *ppl. a.*

1591 *Troub. Raigne K. John* (1611) 28 Base heardgroom, coward, peasant, worse than a threshing slaue. **1670**

EACHARD *Cont. Clergy* 71 He observes, that the worm Jacob was a threshing worm [cf. Isa. xli. 14, 15]. **1706** E. WARD *Wooden World Diss.* (1708) 30 In one Twelve-Month he comes to be an able, roaring, threshing Fellow. **1887** G. MEREDITH *Ballads & P.* 74 Chosen warriors, keen and hard; Grains of threshing battle-dints.

'thrashing-, 'threshing-floor. A prepared hard level surface on which corn is threshed: cf. FLOOR *sb.*[1] 6.

a. **1398** TREVISA *Barth. De P.R.* XVII. clvi. (Bodl. MS.), þe greyne þat is loweste in þe þresschinge floore is beste to sede. *Ibid.* clxxv, Feeldes and þresschinge flores. **1611** BIBLE *Gen.* l. 10 They came to the threshing floore [**1885** *Revised* threshing-floor] of Atad. **1839** LONGFELLOW *Village Blacksmith* iv, The burning sparks that fly Like chaff from a threshing-floor.

β. **1697** DRYDEN *Virg. Georg.* I. 278 In vain the Hind shall vex the Thrashing-floor, For empty Chaff and Straw will be thy Store. **1805** DICKSON *Pract. Agric.* I. 47 The size of the thrashing-floors of barns must vary according to circumstances.

'thrashing-, 'threshing-machine. A power-driven machine for separating grain or other seed from the straw or husk. Also in *Comb.*

a. **1812** SIR J. SINCLAIR *Syst. Husb. Scot.* I. 78 Oxen are at least equal..to horses, for working threshing-machines. **1812** *Examiner* 21 Dec. 813/1 W. Forrest, Shiffnal, Salop, threshing-machine-maker. **1848** MILL *Pol. Econ.* I. ix. §4 It may not answer to a small farmer to own a threshing machine, for the small quantity of corn he has to thresh.

β. **1797** *Encycl. Brit.* (ed. 3) XVIII. 505/2 The first thrashing machine attempted in modern times..was invented in Edinburgh..about the year 1732. **1834-6** BARLOW in *Encycl. Metrop.* (1845) VIII. 92/1 Where the thrashing machine supplies the place of the flail. **1861** *Times* 24 Sept., The fine farm-steading, with its stalls, barns, 12-horse fixed steam engine, thrashing machine, saw-mill, bone-mill, &c.

'thrashing-, 'threshing-mill A fixed threshing-machine; usually, one driven by water or wind power (though the name was also given to those driven by a horizontal wheel drawn round by horses or oxen).

1797 *Encycl. Brit.* (ed. 3) XVIII. 506/1 Such was the thrashing mill invented by Mr. Michael Stirling..1758. **1816** J. SCOTT *Vis. Paris* (ed. 5) 308 The Scotch threshing mill seems to be entirely unknown in France. **1825** J. NICHOLSON *Operat. Mechanic* 86 A considerable fall of water..used to give motion to a thrashing mill. **1902** R. C. MACLAGAN *Evil Eye in W. Highl.* 64 They had no threshing-mill and did it all with flails.

Thraskist, -ite, obs. ff. TRASKIST, -ITE.

‖**Thraso** ('θreɪsəʊ). Pl. **-os, -oes,** also as L., **Thrasones** (-'əʊniːz). [L., ad. Gr. Θράσων, name of a braggart soldier in Terence's *Eunuchus*, f. θρασ-ύς bold, spirited.] A braggart, a boaster.

[**1563** B. GOOGE *Eglogs* (Arb.) 85 In Countreye Venus hath defecte, In Countreye Thraso hath no grace.] *a* **1576** PILKINGTON *Expos. Nehem.* iv. 14 (1585) 62 b, These big boasting Thrasones and vaunting *Milites gloriosi.* **1580** HOLLYBAND *Treas. Fr. Tong, Vn Tevot*, a Thraso. **1650** FRENCH tr. *Sandivogius' Alchymie* Pref. A iij b, Vapouring Thrasoes or Letter-learned scoffers. **1716** BOLINGBROKE *Refl. on Exile* (1777) 351 Philosophy has her Thrasos as well as war.

thrasonic (θrə'sɒnɪk), *a.* [f. L. *Thrasōn-*, stem of THRASO + -IC.] = next.

1657 H. PINNELL *Philos. Ref.* 154 With a..Thrasonick boasting they brag that they can perfectly cure all diseases. **1778** JEFFERSON *Corr.* Wks. 1859 I. 207 Thrasonic accounts of victories they have never won. **1843** *Blackw. Mag.* LIV. 52 The last extravagance of thrasonic and impotent national arrogance. **1903** *Contemp. Rev.* Aug. 178 The 'Thrasonic' verbiage of German nautical enthusiasts.

thrasonical (θrə'sɒnɪkəl), *a.* [f. as prec. + -AL[1]: see -ICAL.] Resembling Thraso or his behaviour; given to or marked by boasting; bragging, boastful, vainglorious.

1564 COVERDALE tr. *Ridley* in *Lett. Mart.* 76 In comparison of this Thrasonicall and glorious ostentation. **1590** [see GNATHONICAL]. **1600** SHAKS. *A.Y.L.* v. ii. 34 Cesars Thrasonicall bragge of I came, saw, and ouercame. **1755** CARTE *Hist. Eng.* IV. 130 *note*, It is too thrasonical to deserve any credit. **1877** MORLEY *Crit. Misc.* Ser. II. 374 Ocular arrogance, and a rather too thrasonical complacency. **1893** MCCARTHY *Dictator* II. x. 3 Unlike the ordinary soldier of fortune, he was not in the least thrasonical.

Hence **thra'sonically** *adv.*, in a thrasonical manner.

1591 GREENE *Farewell to Folly* Wks. (Grosart) IX. 249 Such..as Thrasonically countenance themselues w^t the title of a souldior. **1626** L. OWEN *Spec. Jesuit* (1629) 59 These..fathers doe very Thrasonically brag, that their society or order, was diuinely ordained. **1755** JOHNSON s.v. *Rodomontade*, To brag thrasonically, to boast like Rodomonte. **1862** BEVERIDGE *Hist. India* II. v. viii. 509 General Stuart..had rashly and thrasonically pledged himself, that..'the army might and must move'.

†**'thrasonism.** *Obs. rare.* [f. L. *Thrasōn-*, stem of THRASO + -ISM.] Thrasonic conduct; boastfulness. So †**'thrasonist**, a boaster, a swaggerer; †**'thrasonize** *v. intr.* (in quot. const. with *it*), to play the Thraso, to boast, brag.

1596 NASHE *Saffron-Walden* Wks. (Grosart) III. 200 Hath he (as with his Thrasonisme) infected them all with his methode of Lenuoyes, Post-scripts and Preambles. **1619** H. HUTTON *Follie's Anat.* 48 Warres austere God, with stout Achilles lance..doth Thrasonize it, rage. **1626** T. H[AWKINS] *Caussin's Holy Crt.* 74 These little Thrasonists are no sooner out of the shell, but instantly they establish a iurisdiction in the family.

thrassel, obs. form of THROSTLE.

thrast, -e, early var. and pa. t. of THREST *v.*

thrat, thratte, -en, obs. pa. t. of THREAT *v.*

thratch, dial. variant of FRATCH *v.* and *sb.*

thratle, thrattell, thrattle, obs. ff. THROTTLE.

thrau(e, thrauwe, obs. forms of THROW *v.*

†**'thraupis.** *Obs.* [a. Gr. θραυπίς.] A species of finch mentioned by Aristotle as feeding on thistles; generally taken to be the Siskin.

1600 SURFLET *Countrie Farme* VII. lxx. 900 The *Thraupis* [F. *tarin*] is of the continuance of sixe yeeres or there about, according as she is kept better or woorse... Her singing is but yrkesome and tedious. **1910** THOMPSON tr. *Aristotle's Hist. Anim.* 592 The following and the like feed on thistles; to wit, the linnet, the thraupis, and the goldfinch.

thrave, threave (θreɪv, θriːv). Chiefly *Sc.* and *north. Eng.* Forms: *a.* 1 *pl.* **þreues**; 4-6, 9 **threve,** 5 **threfe,** 6 **threff, threif(f, threafe,** 7 *Sc.* **thref,** 8 *Sc.* **threive,** 9 *Sc.* **thrief, thrieve,** 7- **threave.** *β.* 5 *Sc.* **thraf,** 5-6 **thraue, thrafe,** *north.* **thrawe,** 6 **thrayf, thravffe,** *Sc.* **thraif,** 9 **thraive,** 5- **thrave.** *γ.* *Sc.* and *north.* 3 **traue,** 5 **trawe,** 6 (8- *dial.*) **trave** (cf. med.L. *trava* in Du Cange), 9 *dial.* **traeve.** [Of Scandinavian origin; in *a*, a. West Scand. **þrefe*, Icel. *þrefi*, Norw. *treve, træve*; in *β*, a. East Scand. **þrafe*, MSw. *þrave*, Sw. *trafve*, Da. *trave* (whence NFris. (Sylt.) *traav*). **þrefe* and **þrafe* were prob. ablaut variants.]

1. Two shocks or stooks of corn (or pulse), generally containing twelve sheaves each, but varying in different localities; hence used as a measure of straw, fodder, etc.

a. **963-84** in Birch *Cart. Sax.* III. 367 Swa man ær simle dide tioþunge æt ælcere sylh an foðer cornes þe eahte þreues cornes on weron. **1483** *Cath. Angl.* 384/2 (MS. A.) A Threfe [*v.r.* thrave] of corne, *traua.* **1512-13** *Durham Acc. Rolls* (Surtees) 106 Pro xl threff straminis. **1556** *Records of Elgin* (N. Spalding Cl.) I. 30 The threafe or fodder, viij d. **1572** in *Reg. Mag. Sig. Scot.* 1576. 708/2 For ane threif of custome stray. **1618-19** *N. Riding Rec.* II. 189 A Thirske woman presented for stealing six threaves of Hempe value 10/. **1716** *Parochial Rec. Stonehouse* 17 July, To cause pull sixtie threive of heather for thatching. **1812** SIR J. SINCLAIR *Syst. Husb. Scot.* I. 330 A threave of wheat, consisting of twenty-eight sheaves, each sheaf measuring thirty inches round,..a threave of barley, oats, or pease, of twenty-four sheaves, each thirty inches round. **1822** *Lights & Shadows of Sc. Life* 214 (Jam.), I have thrashed a few thrieves in the minister's barn. **1851** *Jrnl. R. Agric. Soc.* XII. I. 129 An acre of good oats generally averages 32 threves (768 sheaves).

β. **1423** *Act 2 Hen. VI*, c. 2 *Endowé..dun Thrave des blees aprendre annuelment de chescun charue...* Endowed..of a thraue of corn to be taken yerely of euery ploughe. *c* **1462** *Wright's Chaste Wife* 245 A thrafe of flex. **1537** *Stanlowe Cell Inv.* (Publ. Rec. Office), vj Thrayf of vnthrashen Barlycorne. **1551** in *Wills & Inv. N.C.* (Surtees) I. 134 A c. thrave of wheit and rye at ijs. vjd. a thrave. **1584** *Shuttleworths' Acc.* (Chetham Soc.) 19 Eighte thravffe of stroue sould at Houle viij^d. **1679** FILMER *Freeholder* 54 Their Living..consisted chiefly upon the having of a Thrave of Corn of every Plow-land. **1865** W. WHITE *E. Eng.* I. 289, Reapers got sixpence a thrave for their reaping.

γ. **1284** *Acc. Exch. K.R.* Bd. 97 No. 3 Pro .lxxij. Trauis litere emptis..pro eisdem [horses]. *c* **1447** in *Jarrow & Wearmouth* (Surtees) 242 Tho trawes and other arrerage of the said corn. **1504-5** *Durham Acc. Rolls* (Surtees) 251 Pro xxxij trave de lyng. **1764** *Museum Rust.* II. xxxiii. 107 Some shock their sheaves setting them up in traves of six sheaves of a side, and two to cap them. *Ibid.*, If the sheaves were dry when the traves were set up. **1868** ATKINSON *Cleveland Gloss.*, *Thrave, pron.* trave, treeav. **1900** *Shetland News* 22 Sept. (E.D.D.), What mak's doo o' da twartree [= two or three] traeve o' bare. **1905** *Contemp. Rev.* July 95, I learned how to build a trave (which is by interpretation a shock or stook).

2. *transf.* and *fig.* A large number; a company; a multitude, a 'heap', a 'lot'.

a. **1377** LANGL. *P. Pl.* B. XVI. 55, I have þouȝtes a threve of þis þre piles, In what wode thei woxen. **1610** B. JONSON *Alch.* v. ii, Gallants..[have] beene seene to flock here In threaues. **1635** J. JONES *Adrasta* III. i. Gj, Come, gi' me a threave of kisses. **1825** SCOTT *Betrothed* xxi, Minstrels singing ballads by the threave.

β. **1486** *Bk. St. Albans* f vi b, A Thraue of Throsheris. **1500-20** DUNBAR *Poems* lxvi. 55 Sum with ane thraif playis passage plane. *a* **1656** BP. HALL *Rev. Unrevealed* §8 Tidings ..of a thrave of Jews newly converted.

†**3.** A bundle or handful tied up like a small sheaf. *Obs.*

1606 CHAPMAN *Gentleman Usher* II. i. Plays 1873 I. 273 Lay me vm [rushes] thus In fine smoothe threaues, look you sir, thus, in threaues. **1656** SIR J. MENNIS *K. Oberon's Apparel* in *Musarum Del.* 34 His Belt was made of mirtle leaves, Plaited in small curious threaves.

Hence **'thraver, 'threaver,** a reaper who is paid according to the number of thraves he cuts; **'threaving** *vbl. sb.*, the practice of paying reapers at so much for the thraves.

1812 SIR J. SINCLAIR *Syst. Husb. Scot.* I. 329 About six years ago, another practice took place in that district, which ..is called threaving. **1813** G. ROBERTSON *Agric. Surv. Kincard.* 264 (Jam.) While a reaper cuts..at the rate of nine threaves a-day, a threaver will..cut ten threaves in the same time. **1844** STEPHENS *Bk. Farm* III. 1053 Threavers..have a strong inducement to cut the straw near the ground.

thraw (θrɔː), *v.*, the earlier form of THROW *v.*[1], retained in northern dialect in all senses of the verb, and preserving in Scottish use a group of senses in which *throw* is not in English use, or, when occasionally used by English writers, is taken in the Sc. form as a distinct word; viz. the senses: To turn, twist, turn awry, contort, distort (esp. to make a wry face or mouth, cf. THRAWN *ppl. a.*); to wrest, warp, strain, or distort (words or their meaning); to wrench; to extort; to cross, thwart, vex, manifest opposition or ill temper. For these see THROW *v.*[1], senses 1 to 5 b. So **thraw** *sb.*, northern and Sc. form of THROW *sb.*[2]: see esp. senses 1, b, c.

thraw (θrɔː), *a. Sc.* and *n. dial.* [app. shortened form of THRAWN.] Twisted, turned awry. Also in *comb.* = WRY-, as **thraw-gabbit** *a.*, wry-mouthed, peevish; **thraw-necked** *a.*, having the neck twisted.

1501 DOUGLAS *Pal. Hon.* I. 437 Thir megir bellis, Sum round, sum thraw. **18..** JOANNA BAILLIE *Hooly & Fairly* i, My wife..ca's me a niggardly thraw-gabbit carlie. **1884** MRS. J. H. RIDDELL *Berna Boyle* xi, There was nothing in his offer the best gentleman in the land need have drawn a thraw mouth over. **1894** LANG *Poems* 41 (E.D.D.) Our present Duke's nae thraw man. **1898** LD. E. HAMILTON *Mawkin* xx. 275 A pair of poor thraw-neckit corpses.

thraw, obs. f. or var. THRO, THROE, THROW *sb.*[1]

thraward ('θrɔːwəd), *a. Sc.* Also 5-9 **thrawart,** 6 **thrauard (threwart),** 7 **thrawert.** [app. altered from the earlier *fraward* (*c* 1200), FROWARD, perh. under the influence of THRAW *v.*, THRAWN, etc. But cf. mod.Sc. dial *thra, thrae*, for *fra, frae.*]

1. Disposed to turn aside from the proper way; froward, refractory, perverse, adverse. *arch.*

c **1470** HENRYSON *Mor. Fab.* XII. (*Wolf & Lamb*) vii, His exhorbetand and thrawart [*ed.* 1570 frawart] pleid. **1508** DUNBAR *Flyting* 108 In sic is sett thy thraward appetyte. *a* **1600** MONTGOMERIE *Sonn.* xxxiii. 2 Vhom suld I warie bot my wicked weard, Vha span my thriftles thrauard fatall threed? **1795** MACNEILL *Will & Jean* I, Such was Jean when Will first, mawing, Spied her on a thrawart beast. **1818** SCOTT *Hrt. Midl.* xiii, Mony a thrawart job I hae had wi' her first and last. **1901** J. MOLLESON *Poems* 48 The maister ne'er gae them a thrawart look.

2. *dial.* Twisted, crooked, wry, 'thrawn'.

1814 W. NICHOLSON *Poems* 118 Yon todlin' burn.. Still presses owre ilk thrawart turn. **1827** J. WATT *Poems* 15 (E.D.D.) Man's life's..A chain o' mony thrawart links. **1894** A. REID *Sangs Heatherland* 72 His nosie..Sae hookit, and thrawart.

Hence **'thrawartly** *adv. Sc.*, frowardly, perversely. So **'thrawart-like** *adv.*

1533 BELLENDEN *Livy* II. xxv. (S.T.S.) I. 232 þe armye consauit na litill Ire and Indignatioun in þare myndis..and did all thingis sa thrawartlie..that [etc.]. **1768** ROSS *Helenore* I. 30 Very thrawart like, I yeed in by.

'thrawardness. *Sc.* [f. prec. + -NESS.] Frowardness, perversity, 'thrawnness'.

1567 *Reg. Privy Council Scot.* I. 515 Hir Hienes clemency is commounlie abusit and recompansit with threwartnes and ingratitude. *a* **1600** *Scot. Poems 16th C.* (1801) I. 70 Remoue from mee all thrawardnesse, Als well in mynde, as into deid. **1609** SKENE *Reg. Maj., Stat. Will.* 4 b, Gif he quha leides bot ane beast..be thrawertnes, passes throw them, quha drives the many horse. *a* **1651** CALDERWOOD *Hist. Kirk* (1843) II. 538 A pitifull caus,..and yitt led by the thrawardnesse of time and our unhappe.

thrawcrook, variant of THROW-CROOK.

thrawe, obs. f. THRAVE, THRO, THROE, THROW.

thrawl, obs. f. THRALL *sb.*[1], dial. var. *sb.*[3]

thrawn (θrɔːn, θrɑn), *ppl. a. Sc.* Also 6-9 **thrawin,** (6 **throwin**). [Sc. and north. dial. form of THROWN; used in senses in which *thrown* is not now used in English. Cf. THRAW *v.*]

1. Twisted, crooked, bent from the straight; mis-shapen, drawn awry, distorted.

1513 DOUGLAS *Æneis* II. ii. (i.) 70 In jonyngis of the thrawin wame of tre Festinyt the lance. **1715** RAMSAY *Christ's Kirk Gr.* II. x, A thrawn knublock hit his heel. **1752** *Rec. Elgin* (New Spald. Cl.) I. 465 All..sowms, thramels, rigwoodies, tethers, wallropes, thrawn wawns [wands] and all other wood or work of wood, straw, bent, or rushes. *a* **1824** *Ld. Saltoun & Auchanachie* vi. in Child *Ball.* VIII. (1892) 348/1 He's bowed on the back, and thrawin on the knee. **1871** G. LAWRENCE *Anteros* xv, She had seen the husband..brought home a corpse stiff and thrawn. **1897** Thrawn thrapple [see THREAP *sb.* 2]. **1901** *Westm. Gaz.* 9 Apr. 3/1 'Dramatic idyls'..peopled by the stark 'thrawn' figures of the Pre-Raphaelite world.

b. Of the mouth or face: Drawn awry or distorted by anger, ill-temper, or the like; frowning.

1513 DOUGLAS *Æneis* III. ix. 89 His mekle E, That lurkit allane vnder his thrawn front. *Ibid.* VII. viii. 23 Alecto her thrawin vyssage dyd away. *a* **1585** POLWART *Flyting w. Montgomerie* 784 Iock Blunt, thrawin frunt! **1719, 1897** [see 3].

2. *fig.* Perverse, contrary; cross-grained, ill-tempered, crabbed, peevish, cross.

c **1450** HOLLAND *Howlat* 918 Thus wycit he the walentyne thraly and thrawin. *c* **1470** HENRY *Wallace* x. 593 Thar salusyng was bot boustous and thrawin. *c* **1475** *Rauf Coilȝear* 129 Sa mot I thriue, I am thrawin, Begin we to threip. **1585** JAS. I *Ess. Poesie* (Arb.) 39 Lyke the curr,.. sparing alwaies those are to him knowin, To them most gentle, to the others throwin. **1718** RAMSAY *Christ's Kirk Gr.* III. i, Greedy wives wi' girning thrawn, Cry'd lasses up to thrift. **1719** —— *To Arbuckle* 109 Wishing thrawn parties wad agree. **1737** —— *Sc. Prov.* v. (1750) 15 A thrawin question should have a thrawart answer. **1816** SCOTT *Bl. Dwarf* xviii, Though he was thrawn and cankered in his converse, he likeit dumb creatures weel. **1862** *Leisure Hours in Town* 13 The expressive Scotticism which says of a perverse and impracticable man that he is a thrawn person; that is, a person who has got a thraw or twist. **1889** BARRIE *Window in Thrums* xix, He cried it oot fell thrawn. **1893** CROCKETT *Stickit Minister* 117 A grummle from that thrawn stick o' a registrar.

3. *Comb.* as **thrawn-faced, -gabbit, -mowit** *adjs.*, having a 'thrawn' face or mouth (see 1, 1 b); hence, crabbed, ill-tempered, snarling.

1578 *Inv. Royal Wardr.* (1815) 229 Ane moyane of fonte thrawin mowit without armes maid be Hanis Cochrane. **1719** RAMSAY *2nd Answ. to Hamilton* vii, Thrawn-gabbit sumphs that snarl At our frank lines. **1897** CROCKETT *Lad's Love* iii, Ye thrawn-faced, slack-twisted muckle haythen ye.

Hence **'thrawnly** *adv. Sc.*, awry; perversely, ill-temperedly; **'thrawnness** *Sc.*, perversity, obstinacy, cantankerousness.

1513 DOUGLAS *Æneis* VII. vii. 133 Wyth bludy ene rowing full thrawinly. **1825** JAMIESON, *Thrawinness*, perverseness, obstinacy. **1862** *Leisure Hours in Town* 18 Perversity, or general Unpleasantness and Thrawn-ness. **1883** STEWART *Nether Lochaber* lii. 328 A perverseness of disposition and a thrawnness of temper. **1899** J. BUCHAN *Grey Weather* 250 'What bird are ye?' he asked thrawnly. **1980** *Times Lit. Suppl.* 28 Mar. 373/1 The Kilbrandon Commission found the stage army of the Scottish good solidly pro-devolution. .. Only the Labour Party remained thrawnly hostile to the whole idea.

thre, obs. form of THREE.

†**threa**, *v. Obs.* Forms: 1 **ðréaȝan, þréawian,** 1–4 **ðrean, þrean,** 3 **þraih-, þhray-, þrayh-, þrah-, þraghen;** 2 *pa. t.* **þreadde, þredde.** [OE. *þréaȝ(e)an*, wk. vb., contr. *þréan*, pa. t. *þréade* = OHG. *drewen, drowen* (MHG. *dröuwen, drouwen*, Ger. *dräuen*), Goth. **þraujan* :—OTeut. **þrawjan*; f. OE. *þrawu, þréa* sb. threatening, rebuke, chastisement, OHG. *drô*, ON. *þrá*: OTeut. **þrawā*: cf. Falk & Torp, s.v. *Traa* II.] *trans.* To rebuke, reprove, chastise; to punish; to torment, afflict.

c **897** K. ÆLFRED *Gregory's Past. C.* ii. 30 Forðon hi nan mon ne dear ðreaȝean ðeah hi agylten. *Ibid.* xxi. 150 Swiðe wel Dryhten ðreade Iudeas. *a* **900** tr. *Bæda's Hist.* II. vi. (1890) 114 Mid hu miclum swingum he þread.. wæs. *c* **950** *Lindisf. Gosp.* Luke xxiii. 22 Ic ðrea.. forðon hine & ic forleto. *c* **1000** *Ags. Gosp.* Matt. xvii. 18 þa þreade [*c* **1160** *Hatton G.* þredde] se hælend hyne. *c* **1160** *Hatton Gosp.* Luke xxiii. 40 þa andswerede se oðer & hine þreadde. *a* **1300** *E.E. Psalter* lxxii[i]. 14 In vghteninges mi þhraying ai. *Ibid.* cxvii[i]. 18 Ȝraihand [*v.rr.* þraghand, ȝrayhand] lauerd me ȝrahed he [*castigans castigavit me Dominus*].

thread (θrɛd), *sb.* Forms: 1–3 **þræd** (1 **ðréd**), 2 **þread,** 3–5 **þred,** 4–5 **þreed,** 4–7 (9 *dial.*) **threed,** (5 **tredde**), 5–6 **threde,** 5–8 **thred,** 6 **threade, thredde, thride,** 6–7 **threede,** *Sc.* **threid,** 6–8 **thrid,** 7 **thrydd,** 5– **thread.** [OE. *þræd* = OLG. **thrâd* (MDu. *draet*, Du. *draad*), OHG., MHG. *drât* (G. *draht*), ON. *þráðr* (Da. *traad*, Sw. *tråd*):—OTeut. **þrǣ-ðuᶻ*, pre-Teut. **trētús*; f. **þrǣ-* to twist (see THROW *v.*[1]) + dental suffix. Cf. *bread, seed.*]

I. 1. a. A fine cord composed of the fibres or filaments of flax, cotton, wool, silk, etc. spun to a considerable length; *spec.* such a cord composed of two or more yarns, esp. of flax, twisted together; applied also to a similar product from glass, asbestos, a ductile metal, etc.

c **725** *Corpus Gloss.* (O.E.T.) 876 *Filum*, ðred. *c* **888** K. ÆLFRED *Boeth.* xxix. §1 Hwæt ðæt bið ȝesæliȝ mon þe him ealne weȝ ne hangað nacod sweord ofer ðæm heafde be smale þræde. *c* **1000** *Sax. Leechd.* I. 218 Cnyte mid anum ðræde on anum clænan linenan. *c* **1205** LAY. 14220 Nes þe þwong.. buten swulc a twines þræd [*c* **1275** twined þred]. *c* **1400** *Sowdone Bab.* 1999 He teyde a tredde on a pole. *c* **1425** tr. *Arderne's Treat. Fistula* 9 It hath.. an yȝe like a nedel by whiche þredes ow to be drawen agayn by middez of þe fistule. **1508** DUNBAR *Gold. Targe* 62 Thair brycht hairis.. wyppit wyth goldyn thredis. **1535** COVERDALE *1 Kings* vii. 23 A threde of thirtie cubites longe. **1641** W. GASCOIGNE in *Nat. Philos.* III. *Hist. Astron.* xiii. (1834) 66/2 (Usef. Knowl. Soc.), I am fitting my sextant for all manner of observations, by two perspicills with threads. **1720** WELTON *Suffer. Son of God* II. xxii. 594 From these little Threads.. such strong Cables are form'd. **1828** J. M. SPEARMAN *Brit. Gunner* (ed. 2) 150 Hawsers (Machine made)... Of 4 Inches, or 108 Threads.. Of 10 Inches, or 648 Threads. **1832** G. R. PORTER *Porcelain & Glass* ix. 231 Glass may be spun into very long and minute threads.

b. The sacred thread with which Brahmins and Parsees are invested at initiation: see quots.

1582 N. LICHEFIELD tr. *Castanheda's Conq. E. Ind.* I. xvi. 42 b, Vpon their left sholders they had certaine number of thrids, which came vnder their right shoulders. **1860** J. BATEMAN *Life Bp. D. Wilson* I. xii. 341 Several Brahmins being manifested by their 'thread'. **1874** J. H. BLUNT *Dict. Sects*, etc. 405/2 (*Parsees*) The investiture at initiation with the sacred thread. **1903** *Times* 5 Mar. 3/5 Mrs. Ruttonjee Tata.. was.. invested with the sacred thread and *sudra* of the Parsees.

†**c.** *spec.* A fishing-line. (In quot. 1622 *fig.*) *Obs.*

1602 CAREW *Cornwall* 31 b, For catching of Whiting and Basse, they vse a thred, so named because it consisteth of a long small lyne with a hooke at the end. **1622** BACON *Hen. VII* 137 Thinking, that the King (what with his Baits, and what with his Nets) would draw them all vnto him,.. diuers came away by the Thred, sometimes one, and sometimes another.

2. a. Each of the lengths of yarn which form the warp and woof of a woven fabric; hence, any one of these as an ultimate constituent of such a fabric, and thus of one's clothing; the least part of one's dress; esp. in the phrase ***not a (one) dry thread on one.*** Also *fig.*

c **1200** *Vices & Virt.* 39 Ðar behoued to maniȝe þreades ær hit bie full wroht. *c* **1374** CHAUCER *Boeth.* I. pr. i. 2 (Camb. MS.) Hyr clothes weeren maked of riht delye thredes. *c* **1380** WYCLIF *Wks.* (1880) 316 Ilche þreed of siche cloþis þat ben tuo wast & too costliche. **1382** —— *Gen.* xiv. 23 Fro a threed of the weeft vnto a garter of an hoos I shal not take of alle thingis that ben thin. **1470–85** MALORY *Arthur* XV. ii. 699 It shalle not lye in your power nor to perysshe me as moche as a threde. *a* **1500** *Flower & Leaf* 370 The ladies ne the knightes nade o threed Drie on them. **1550** VERON *Godly Sayings* (1846) 141 Howe can you.. come to this roial feast and banket not having one thrid of this wedding rayment.. upon you? **1600** HAKLUYT *Voy.* III. 83 Hee that had fiue or sixe shifts of apparell had scarce one drie threed to his backe. **1610** SHAKS. *Temp.* IV. i. 3. **1610** B. JONSON *Alch.* III. ii, Your threescore minutes Were at the last thred. **1726** LEONI *Alberti's Archit.* III. 13/2, I take a veil made of the finest threds..: this I divide into.. squares.. by some bigger threds parallel to each other **1815** SCOTT *Guy M.* xl, There will no be a dry thread amang us or we get the cargo out. **1844** G. DODD *Textile M.* vi. 201 Plain silks, as well as most woven fabrics, consist of threads crossing each other at right angles. **1879** JEFFERIES *Wild Life in S.C.* 133 The costume is true to a thread. **1908** in *Westm. Gaz.* 1 Apr. 12/1 Till April's dead, change not a thread.

b. *bare* or ***worn to the thread***, etc. = THREADBARE.

1483–4 *Act. 1 Rich. III*, c. 8 *Preamble*, Suche course Clothes, beyng bare of threde. **1615** CHAPMAN *Odyss.* XVII. 254 His garments to a thred All bare, and burn'd. **1882** STEVENSON *New Arab. Nts.* i. 23 The furniture was scanty, and the coverings worn to the thread.

c. ***thread and thrum*** each length of the warp-yarn, and the tuft where it is fastened to the loom; hence *fig.* the whole of anything; good and bad together. Also, ***threads and thrums***, ends of warp threads, miscellaneous scraps or waste fragments.

1590 SHAKS. *Mids. N.* v. i. 291 O Fates! come, come: Cut thred and thrum. **1648** HERRICK *Hesper.*, *Upon some Women*, Learne of me what woman is. Something made of thred and thrumme; A meere botch of all and some. **1654** GATAKER *Disc. Apol.* 93 By those thrums and threds that he hath pickt and puld out of it.., the Reader may judge of the whole. **1833** CARLYLE *Diderot* in *Misc. Ess.* (1872) V. 2 The confused and ravelled mass of threads and thrums, ycleped Memoirs.

d. A lineal measure of yarn: the length of a coil of the reel, varying in amount according to the material, and also with the locality (see quots.).

1662 *Act 14 Chas. II*, c. 5 §6 Every Reel staff shall containe fourteen Leas and every Lea fourty threads. **1688** R. HOLME *Armoury* III. vi. 288/2 A knot is a Hundred Threds round the Reel. **1696** PHILLIPS (ed 5) s.v. *Lea*, Every Lea of Yarn at Kidderminster shall contain 200 Threds reel'd on a Reel four yards about. *a* **1825** FORBY *Voc. E. Anglia*, *Lea*, forty threads of hemp-yarn. **1858** SIMMONDS *Dict. Trade*, *Thread*, .. a yarn-measure, containing in cotton-yarn 54 inches; in linen-yarn 90 inches; in worsted yarn 35 inches. On the Continent 85½ Ermland inches make one thread. **1875** TEMPLE & SHELDON *Hist. Northfield, Mass.* 161 A run of yarn consisted of twenty knots, a knot was composed of forty threads, and a thread was seventy-four inches in length, or once round the reel.

e. *fig.* A single element interwoven with others in any composite fabric, mental, moral, social, political, or the like.

1836 J. GILBERT *Chr. Atonem.* vii. (1852) 190 In this, as in almost all theories.. there is indeed a thread of truth. **1851** HELPS *Comp. Solit.* xiii. (1874) 248 The threads of our poor human affairs.. might yet be interwoven harmoniously with the great cords of love and duty. **1859** KINGSLEY *Misc.* (1860) II. ii. 29 The only threads of light in the dark web of his history are clerical and theurgic. **1879** STAINER *Music of Bible* 168 The pleasure which accrues to a trained musician when he grasps in his mind many threads of delicious melody, and traces the composer's genius in interlacing them.

f. *pl.* Clothes. *slang* (orig. and chiefly *U.S.*).

1926 MAINES & GRANT *Wise-Crack Dict.* 11/2 *New set of threads*, new suit of clothes. **1959** R. BLOCH *Blood Runs Cold* (1963) 163 Mitch got into some decent threads—he had this one blue suit and he wore a white shirt and a tie too. **1972** M. J. BOSSE *Incident at Naha* ii. 64 *My friends*, who grooved the way I did... I mean, love beads, wild threads, granny glasses.. and a bit of grass. **1978** J. GARDNER *Dancing Dodo* xxiii. 175 Load it and get in on under that set of executive threads.

3. a. Without *a*, as name of the substance of which the above-mentioned things are composed, or of these things taken in the mass; woollen, silk, linen, cotton, or other fibre, or fine-drawn metal, spun into material for weaving, knitting, sewing, or fastening: often with distinctive word, as ***gold*** or ***silk thread***; sometimes *spec.* flaxen or linen thread as distinct from silk or cotton; in *pl.*, kinds of thread.

c **1386** CHAUCER *Monk's T.* 485 Nettes of gold threed hadde he greet plentee. *c* **1400** *Rom. Rose* 7369 A large coverechief of threde She wrapped alle aboute hir hede. *c* **1400** *Laud Troy Bk.* 6775 Of his hors fel that kynge, As it were a clewe of thred. *c* **1400** *Lybeaus Disc.* (Kaluza) 940 As selke þrede. **1529** MORE *Dyaloge* II. x. Wks. 195/1 He thankinge the monke for the thrid, desired him to teach him how he should knit it. **1545** *Rates of Customs* c vij b, Threde called wotenall threde. **1552–3** *Inv. Ch. Goods, Staffs.* in *Ann. Lichfield* (1863) IV. 48, ij vestements, one of grene chamblet, another of threde. **1576** in Feuillerat *Revels Q. Eliz.* (1908) 264 For a quartern of black threede. **1584** *Ibid.* 370 For iii li. of thrid of all cullers. **1588** PARKE tr. *Mendoza's Hist. China* 320 They take out of this plant.. a kinde of thride or yarne. **1596** DALRYMPLE tr. *Leslie's Hist. Scot.* I. (S.T.S.) I. 94 Wᵗ threid of silke.. al the partes of the sarke .. thay sewit. **1660** F. BROOKE tr. *Le Blanc's Trav.* 184 They have also thread from another tree called Langir. **1806** *Gazetteer Scotl.* (ed. 2) 555/2 The principal manufacture is that of linen yarn, thread, and brown linens. **1887** *Daily News* 19 Oct. 2/8 Linens and threads maintain the improvement lately reported.

†**b.** *fig.* The material or 'fibre' of which anything is composed; 'texture', quality, nature. *Obs.*

1632 SANDERSON *Serm.* 268 Hypocrisie is spunne of a fine threed, and is not easily discerneable. **1635** A. STAFFORD *Fem. Glory* (1869) 134 Of the same pure thred with the rest of her life. **1659** O. WALKER *Instruct. Oratory* 19 That the Oration may seem Continuous and all of one thread. **1718** OCKLEY *Saracens* (1848) II. Introd. 24 The language must be all of the same thread. **1746** FRANCIS tr. *Hor.*, *Sat.* II. iv. 14 The Matter nice, and wrought of subtle Thread.

4. a. Something having the slenderness or fineness of a thread: e.g. a fine ligament, an animal or vegetable fibre, a hair, a filament of a cobweb or of the byssus of a shell-fish.

1398 TREVISA *Barth. De P.R.* XVIII. xi. (Bodl. MS.), þe spiþer.. drawiþ and bringeþ ofte aȝen his þrede þwarte ouer fro pointe to pointe. *c* **1400** *Lanfranc's Cirurg.* 263 Þer is a þreed vndir sum mannes tunge þat he mai not put out his tunge as he schulde, & also it lettiþ him to speke. **1541** R. COPLAND *Galyen's Terap.* 2 A iij b, A spyder threde. **1686** GOAD *Celest. Bodies* I. ii. 2 A Fog which sometimes casts it self into Threds or Ropes, and.. furls up into Gossamere. **1693** EVELYN *De la Quint. Compl. Gard.* II. 57 Producing the least Thread of a capilar Root. **1774** GOLDSM. *Nat. Hist.* (1776) VII. 45 These threads, which are usually called the beard of the muscle. **1776** WITHERING *Brit. Plants* (1796) I. 365 The Seeds, with the elastic threads to which they are attached. *Ibid.* IV. 129 Threads when dry uniting into stiff sharp points. Conferva amphibia.

b. A 'string' of any viscid substance; a thin continuous stream of liquid, sand, etc.; a narrow strip of space; a fine line or streak of colour or light; a 'thin' continuity of sound; *spec.* in glassmaking: see quot. 1832.

1593 NASHE *Christ's T.* (1613) 126 Why breake not thunder bolts through the Clowdes in steade of thrids of raine? **1626** BACON *Sylva* §24 Stillicides of Water.. will Draw themselues into a small thred. **1674** N. FAIRFAX *Bulk & Selv.* 121 What a long thread of sand passes the neck-hole of an hour-glass in that same time. **1710** J. CLARKE *Rohault's Nat. Phil.* (1729) I. 22 If it be a fat Liquor, it will go on in a long Thread, whose Parts are uninterrupted. **1830** *Trans. Nat. Hist. Soc. Northumb.*, etc. I. 186 Sandstone roofs [in coal-mines] are subject to fissures of various sizes and extent, called threads and gullets by the colliers. **1832** G. R. PORTER *Porcelain & Gl.* 248 The name of threads is usually given to fibrous appearances in the body of the glass, which result from the vitrification of clay. **1837** P. KEITH *Bot. Lex.* 56 The infusions were absorbed by the roots, and carried up to the very summit of the stem, leaving.. traces of their ascent in the form of longitudinal streaks or threads. **1868** GLADSTONE *Juv. Mundi* xi. (1869) 432 The Trojan elders, whose volubility, and their shrill thread of voice, Homer compares to the chirp of grasshoppers. **1884** J.H. HOLLOWELL in *Congregationalist* June 498 The pale Aare.. winds its white thread through the valley. **1899** *Westm. Gaz.* 6 Apr. 2/1 Using her pleasant thread of voice agreeably. **1904** *Daily Chron.* 17 Oct. 8/1 The amazing thing is that so much good work should be done in such a mere thread of space. **1907** *Outlook* 16 Nov. 661/1 A little thread of unfrozen water which tinkles feebly over the rocks.

c. Applied to the apparent action of a feeble pulse: see quot., and cf. THREAD-LIKE b. THREADY 4.

1899 *Allbutt's Syst. Med.* VI. 49 A mere tightened thread being felt under the finger.

d. A degree of stickiness reached in boiling clarified syrup for confectionery: see quot.

1862 J. THOMAS *How to mix Drinks* 104 There are nine essential points, or degrees, in boiling sugar. They are called Small Thread, Large Thread, Little Pearl, Large Pearl [etc.]. *Ibid.*, The sugar forms a fine thread which will break at a short distance... This is termed the 'Small Thread'. *Ibid.*, A somewhat longer string will be drawn. This is termed the 'Large Thread'. **1883** R. HALDANE *Workshop Receipts* Ser. II. 152/1.

5. *transf.* The spiral ridge winding round the shank of a screw; also, each complete turn of this; a similar ridge round the inside of a cylindrical hole, as in a nut or a screwhole.

1674 PETTY *Disc. Dupl. Proportion* 116 The Force must be increased at every Turn or Thred of a Screw-Press. **1677** [see TAP *sb.*[1] 4]. **1733** TULL *Horse-Hoeing Husb.* xxiv. 402 Taper Screws made with Iron, having very deep Threads, whereby they hold fast when screw'd into Wood. **1829** *Nat. Philos* I. *Mechanics* II. xi. 48 (U.K.S.) Hunter's screw.. gives an indefinitely slow motion, without requiring a very exquisitely fine thread. **1875** [see TAP *sb.*[1] 4]. **1902** MARSHALL

Metal Tools 63 For pipes and tubes a special thread termed a gas thread is employed. **1938** [see SELF-TAPPING *ppl. a.*]. **1972** *How Things Work* III. 168 For the majority of screwed work a tap is used for internal threading (Fig. 3, showing the thread being cut in a nut) and a die head is used for external threading. **1977** *Reader's Digest Bk. Do-It-Yourself Skills & Techniques* vi. 175/2 As soon as the tap starts to cut, stop pressing down, and let the tap screw itself into the hole, cutting a thread as it goes.

II. 6. *fig.* Something figured as being spun or continuously drawn out like a thread. **a.** The continued course of life, represented in classical mythology as a thread which is spun and cut off by the Fates.

1447 Bokenham *Seyntys* (Roxb.) 8 Wil.. Attropos.. My fatal thred a sundyr smyte. *Ibid.* 43 Or than deth the threed untwyne Of oure fatal web. **1563** *Mirr. Mag., Induct.* xliii, His vitall threde. **1596** Spenser *F.Q.* iv. ii. 48 Sad Clotho held the rocke, the whiles the thrid By griesly Lachesis was spun with paine, That cruell Atropos eftsoones undid, With cursed knife cutting the twist in twaine. **1643** Sir T. Browne *Relig. Med.* i. §42 For my owne part, I would not .. beginne againe the thred of my dayes. **1696** Tate & Br. *Ps.* xc. 10 So soon the slender Thread is cut. **1704** Swift *Batt. Bks.* ⁋25 Her Son.. to whom the Fates had assign'd a very short Thred. **1829** Scott *Anne of G.* xvii, Why I should spare my own almost exhausted thread of life. **1846** H. G. Robinson *Odes of Horace* ii. iii, While.. the three Sisters' sable thread Allows you still the power. **1907** Dillon in *Contemp. Rev.* Nov. 705 So long as three such Parcae have the threads of Macedonia in their hands.

b. In various other applications: see quots.

c **1586** C'tess Pembroke *Ps.* lxxxv. ii, Wilt thou of thy wrathfull rage Draw the threed from age to age? **1588** Shaks. *L.L.L.* v. i. 19 He draweth out the thred of his verbositie finer then the staple of his argument. **1608** D. T[uvil] *Ess. Pol. & Mor.* 88 b, I will stretch the thred of my subiect to a further length. **1645** *City Alarum* 19 Consider first what a thred of time the German wars have spun out. **1670** Eachard *Cont. Clergy* 32 Fearing he should break the thread of your patience, he concludes. **1719** De Foe *Crusoe* (1840) II. vii. 159, I cut the thread of all his comforts, and shortened his days. **1736** Butler *Anal.* ii. vii. 362 To make up a continued thread of history of the length of between three and four thousand years. *a* **1774** Tucker *Lt. Nat.* (1834) II. 664 Drawing out the threads of argumentation, preventing them from entangling.

7. A thread in various mythological or legendary tales (esp. that of Theseus in the Cretan Labyrinth) is mentioned as the means of finding the way through a labyrinth or maze: hence in many figurative applications: That which guides through a maze, perplexity, difficulty, or intricate investigation: cf. CLEW *sb.*[1] 3, CLUE *sb.* 2.

1580 Lyly *Euphues* (Arb.) 312 Neither Ariadnes thrid, nor Sibillas bough, nor Medeas seede, may remedy thy griefe. **1582** T. Watson *Centurie of Loue* lv, My guiding thrid by Reason spunne. **1589** *Pasquil's Return* A iij, Hauing gotten this thred by the end, I neuer left winding til I came to the paper that made the bottom. *c* **1614** Sir W. Mure *Dido & Æneas* i. 6 Path'd wayes I trace, as Theseus in his neid, Conducted by a loyal virgin's threid. **1672** Sterry *Freed. Will* (1675) C iij, What a golden-thread of Harmony guides us through the nature of things! **1711** W. King tr. *Naude's Ref. Politics* i. 11 Having in my hand that thread of knowledge, which might extricate me thence.

8. That which connects the successive points in anything, esp. a narrative, train of thought, or the like; the sequence of events or ideas continuing through the whole course of anything; train. Esp. in phr. ***to pick*** (or ***take***) ***up the thread(s)*** (***of***), to continue (with) after an interruption or separation; *spec.* to resume an interrupted friendship; ***to lose the thread***, to cease to follow the sense of what is being said.

1642 Howell *For. Trav.* (Arb.) 23 If one read skippingly and by snatches, and not take the thread of the story along, it must needs puzzle and distract the memory. **1687** Dryden *Hind & P.* iii. 278 The matron.. then Resumed the thrid of her discourse again. **1738** Swift *Pol. Conversat.* Introd. 64 After a Pause, the grave Companion resumes his Thread, ..'Well, but to go on with my Story'. **1782** Mme. D'Arblay *Diary* Dec., We laughed so violently.. that he could not recover the thread of his harangue. **1844** Thirlwall *Greece* VIII. lxii. 201 We resume the thread of Grecian history. **1881** R. L. Stevenson *Virginibus Puerisque* 137 We shall.. take up again the thread of our enjoyment in the same spirit as we let it fall. **1907** G. B. Shaw *John Bull's Other Island* iv. 95 Eighteen years is a devilish long time, Nora. Now if it had been eighteen minutes, or even eighteen months, we should be able to pick up the interrupted thread, and chatter like two magpies. **1924** A. Christie *Poirot Investigates* v. 125 Philip Ridgeway narrated the circumstances leading to the disappearance of the bonds... When he had finished, Poirot took up the thread with a question. **1929** H. J. Laski in *Holmes-Laski Lett.* (1953) II. 1169, I don't, I suppose, see him more than once in two years; but I always find that we can take up the threads and plunge *in medias res* without any difficulty. **1944** E. S. Gardner *D.A. calls Turn* (1947) xi. 101 If it were true, he'd make some sort of a financial adjustment, but could hardly be expected to pick up the thread of a life where it had been broken ten years ago. **1956** A. Wilson *Anglo-Saxon Attitudes* ii. i. 215 He stopped and, for a moment, he appeared to have lost the thread of his remarks. **1980** D. Lodge *How Far can you Go?* vi. 226 Dennis and Angela picked up the threads of their lives together,.. a little chastened, but both hugely relieved. **1981** A. Schlee *Rhine Journey* xi. 143 He chose.. to appear to have lost the thread of the discussion and looked from one to another with a kind of cautious bewilderment.

9. Some continuous or persistent feature which runs through the pattern of anything, or combines with other features to form a pattern or texture.

1685 Mrs. Evelyn *Let.* in *E.'s Diary* (1827) IV. 440 A thred of piety accompanyed all her actions. **1823** Lamb *Elia* Ser. ii. *Some Sonn. of Sydney*, An historical thread runs through [Sydney's Sonnets]. **1875** Jowett *Plato, Introd. Phaedrus* (ed. 2) II. 86 The continuous thread which appears and reappears throughout his rhetoric. **1892** Symonds *Michel Angelo* (1899) I. vii. vii. 343 A pleasant thread runs through Michel Angelo's correspondence.

†**10.** A (fine) dividing line or boundary line. ***to cut*** (***to***) ***a thread*** (***between***), to strike the exact line of division, to 'draw the line'. *Obs.*

13.. *Gaw. & Gr. Knt.* 1771 þat prynce of pris depresed hym so þikke, Nurned hym so neȝe þe þred, þat nede hym bihoued, Oþer lach þer hir luf, oþir lodly re-fuse. **1567** Maplet *Gr. Forest* 28 To twine vp this threde of deuision [the division of plants into kinds] vpon some bottome. *c* **1591** W. Davies in Pollen *Acts Eng. Mart.* (1891) 131 It was come to that now, that a thread divided my life and death. **1598** Manwood *Lawes Forest* xx. §11 (1615) 180 Within the lists or bounds of the Forest, or within the threed (as they call it) of the Forest. **1647** Ward *Simp. Cobler* (1843) 52 To cut an exquisite thred between Kings Prerogatives, and Subjects Liberties. **1650** B. *Discolliminium* 19, I know no harder task.. than.. to cut a just thread between Gods Providence, and Mans Improvidence. **1692** R. L'Estrange *Fables* ccccxvi. 393 The Art of Pleasing is.. the Skill of Cutting to a Thrid, betwixt Flattery and Ill Manners.

11. The central line of the current of a stream, esp. as a boundary line. [Rendering med.L. *filum aquæ*: cf. F. *fil de l'eau.*]

1691 *Blount's Law Dict., Filum Aquæ* is the Thread or Middle of the Stream, where a River parts Two Lordships. [? **17..** tr. *Commission to ordain Ways to Hull*, The Jurors say that from the thread of the Water of Hull [1302 *de filo aque de Hull*] there is a certain way ordained next Alexander Cook's Mill. —— tr. *Charter 25 Hen. VI* (1447) All lands between the said ditch as far as the middle thread of the water of Humbre [*usque medium fili acque de Humber*].] **1815** J. Smith *Panorama Sc. & Art* II. 110 One part of a river is generally observed to flow with much greater velocity than any other part, and is therefore called the thread or channel of the river, which is very rarely in the middle, or at any regular distance from the banks. **1848** Wharton *Law Dict.* 255. **1886** H. Austin *Farm Law* 135 (Cent. Dict.).

12. That by which something is suspended, or upon which things hang. ***to hang by*** (***on, upon***) ***a thread***, to be in a precarious condition. Often with reference to the legend of Damocles.

[*c* **888**: see sense i.] **1538** Starkey *England* i. iv. 121 But thys hangyth only apon the wyl of the prynce—a veray weke thred in such a case. **1560** Daus tr. *Sleidane's Comm.* 63 b, There hangeth assuredly a wounderfull daunger ouer you, as a sworde dependynge ouer your neckes by a twhyne threde. **1607** H. Raymond *Ode* in Farr *S.P. Jas. I* (1848) 360 Life, ioy, and euery pleasant weede, Scarce hangeth by a slender threede. **1804** Jefferson *Writ.* (1830) IV. 19 My evening prospects now hang on the slender thread of a single life. **1869** J. Martineau *Ess.* II. 94 Hair-bridges, suspending you by a thread of logic.

13. In reference to other functions of a thread; esp. as a means of connecting or holding together.

Sometimes with mixture of sense 6 or 7.

1818 Scott *Hrt. Midl.* xxxvii, She kept in her hands the thread of many a political intrigue. **1844** A. W. Welby *Poems* (1867) 58 She was the golden thread that bound us In one bright chain together here. **1849** Robertson *Serm.* Ser. i. xv. (1866) 260 A thread runs through all true acts stringing them together. **1861** Tulloch *Eng. Purit.* i. 84 So was snapped the last feeble thread of negotiation. **1875** Jowett *Plato* (ed. 2) IV. 123 Many threads join together in the one love and dialectic of the Phædrus. **1904** Jessie Weston in *Romania* XXXIII. 334 *note*, A thread uniting all the different parts of our legend.

14. *attrib.* and *Comb.* **a.** General. (*a*) Simple attrib., 'of thread', as ***threadball***, ***-end***, ***-mill***, ***-spool***, etc. (*b*) in sense 'made of linen or cotton thread' = THREADEN, as ***thread bodice***, ***girdle***, ***glove***, ***net***, ***point***, ***ribbon***, ***shoe***, ***stocking***, etc. (often hyphened). (*c*) Objective and obj. genitive, as ***thread-maker***, ***-manufacturer***, ***-spinner***, ***-twister***, ***-winder***, etc.; ***thread-cutting***, ***-forming***, ***-making***, ***-spinning***, ***-twisting***, ***-winding***, etc. sbs. and adjs.; ***thread-wise*** adv.; similative, parasynthetic, etc., as ***thread-line***; ***thread-lettered***, ***-shaped*** adjs.

1896 G. B. Shaw *Our Theatres in Nineties* (1932) II. 252 Peer's wild run through the night over the charred heath, stumbling over the *threadballs and broken straws. **1918** G. Frankau *One of Them* xvi. 123 How the three crones must laugh as they entwine Cat's-cradle-wise our mortal threadball's tangle. *c* **1665** in *Verney Mem.* (1907) II. 275 A black *thread bodice. **1884** Knight *Dict. Mech.* Suppl., **Thread-cutting machine*.. for cutting threads in bolts, etc. **1900** W. H. Hudson *Nat. Downland* 53 Slender dry bents standing out like pale yellow *thread-ends. **1927** T. Woodhouse *Artif. Silk* 34 The tanks which supply the solution to the *thread-forming apparatus. *a* **1604** Hanmer *Chron. Irel.* (1633) 80 A linnen or *threed Girdle. **1851** *Illustr. Catal. Gt. Exhib.* 201 Fast cotton dyeing for Lisle *thread gloves. **1858** Simmonds *Dict. Trade, Lisle-gloves*, fine thread gloves. **1873** *Routledge's Yng. Gentl. Mag.* Jan. 83/2 The specific name *filigrammaria*, or *thread-lettered. **1890** Jul. P. Ballard *Among Moths & Butterfl.* 122 The quickness of the parting and closing of this narrow *thread-line. **1695** J. Edwards *Perfect. Script.* 237 Where had they thread, when the *thread-makers trade was not invented? **1878** J. Watson (*title*) Art of Spinning and *Thread-Making. **1895** Zangwill *Master* i. vii, A *thread-net confined her hair. **1635** *Voy. Foxe & James* (Hakl. Soc.) I. 42 He gave every one of them a *Threed point [= needle]. *c* **1645** Howell *Lett.* (1650) II. 34 Calicoes, *threed-ribbands, and such polldavy ware. **1713** *Lond. Gaz.* No. 5173/4 A *Thread-Sattin Night-Gown, striped red and white. **1760** Lee *Bot.* (1778) 56 An amentaceous aggregate Flower has a Filiform, *Thread-shaped Receptacle. **1660** F. Brooke tr. *Le Blanc's Trav.* 184 Strings which they pull out to make.. *thread shooes after the Spanish manner. **1892** 'Mark Twain' *Amer. Claimant* x. 102 Today, the work of.. the 2,000,000 *thread-spinners [women] is done by 1,000 girls. **1870** Emerson *Soc. & Solit.* Wks. (Bohn) III. 42 Out of blocks, *thread-spools, cards, and checkers, he [the child] will build his pyramid. *c* **1665** in *Verney Mem.* II. 275 Stirrup *thredd stockins. **1697** tr. *C'tess D'Aunoy's Trav.* (1706) 3 They.. presented me with Gloves, and Thread-Stockings, most delicately knit. **1711–12** Swift *Jrnl. to Stella* 9 Jan., I hide my purse in my thread stocking between the bed's head and the wainscot. **1725** *Lond. Gaz.* No. 6384/7 Gabriel Beale,.. *Thread-Twister. **1877** Knight *Dict. Mech.* 2560 *Thread-winding Guide.. Thread-winding Machine. **1918** Mrs. Belloc Lowndes *Out of the War?* xx. 255 The narrow, winding road which ran *thread-wise on the cliffs.

b. Special Combs.: **thread-animalcule**, a vibrionine animalcule; **thread bag** *Jamaica*, a small cloth bag, tied or drawn closed with a thread or string; **thread belay** *Mountaineering*, a belay in which the rope or sling is passed through a hole in the rock before being secured again to the climber; **thread-board**, in a ringframe, a board placed over the spindles to hold the thread-guides; **thread-carrier**, a guide through which the yarn passes in the knitting-machine (Knight *Dict. Mech.* 1877); **thread-cell**, (*a*) a stinging cell in cœlenterates; a nematocyst; (*b*) a spermatozoon (*Cent. Dict.*); **thread clips** (see quot. 1964); also *attrib.* in *sing.*; **thread-counter**, a magnifying-glass used in counting the threads within a given space in a texture; **thread-cutter**, (*a*) a small blade attached to a sewing-machine or the like for severing a sewing-thread; (*b*) a tool or machine for cutting screw-threads; **thread-drawing**, the process of ornamenting a textile fabric by drawing out some of the threads so as to form a pattern; cf. DRAWN-WORK; **thread-feather**: see quot; **thread-fin** = *thread-fish*, (*a*); **thread-finisher**, a machine by which a smooth glossy surface is given to thread (Knight, 1877); **thread-fish**, (*a*) a polynemoid fish; (*b*) the West Indian cobbler-fish, *Blepharis crinitus*; (*c*) the cutlass-fish or silvery hair-tail, *Trichiurus lepturus*; **thread-flower**, (*a*) a name for plants of the genus *Poinciana*, N.O. *Leguminosæ*, section *Cæsalpinieæ*, so called from their long thread-like stamens; (*b*) a plant of the S. American genus *Nematanthus*, N.O. *Gesneraceæ*, of climbing shrubs, bearing crimson flowers pendent on long stalks; **thread-foot**, a name of the herb *Podostemon ceratophyllus*, in reference to its finely-divided linear leaves; **thread-frame**, a machine in which linen or cotton yarn is doubled and twisted into thread; **thread-gauge**, a gauge for ascertaining the number of turns to the inch in, or the accuracy of, a screw-thread (Knight, 1877); **thread-guide**, a device in a sewing- or spinning-machine for directing the thread (ibid.); **thread-herring**, popular name of (*a*) *Dorosoma cepedianum*, also called the mud-shad or gizzard-shad (*local, U.S.*); (*b*) a clupeoid fish, *Opisthonema thrissa*, of the Atlantic coast of N. America, in which the last ray of the dorsal fin is thread-like; **thread-indicator**, a device for the accurate measurement of plant-growth, in which a thread attached to the plant passes over a pulley and actuates a registering apparatus; **thread-leaved** *a.*, having narrow filiform leaves; **threadman**, a maker or seller of thread; **thread-mark**, a distinguishing mark consisting of a highly coloured thread, incorporated in bank-note paper to prevent counterfeiting by photography; **thread-mill**, a factory actuated by water or steam power in which thread is made; **thread-moss**, a moss of the genus *Bryum* or one of its allies; **thread-oiler**, an oil vessel through which the thread was conducted in some sewing machines (Knight, 1877); **thread-petalled** *a.*, having filiform petals; **thread-plant**, any plant from which fibre for thread-making is obtained (Ogilvie, 1882); **thread rush**, *Juncus filiformis*; **thread-sister** [SISTER 7 d], the stool on which the thread-lace pillow is placed; **thread-tangle**, the seaweed *Chorda filum*, having long cylindrical fronds; sea-laces; **thread-waxer**: see quot.; **thread-wire**, a wire thread-guide in a spinning-machine; **thread-woman**: see *threadman*; **thread-work**, (*a*) a fabric consisting of or resembling threads; ornamental work formed of threads, lace-work; ***drawn thread work***: see DRAWN-WORK; (*b*) *pl.* a thread-making establishment; **thread-worn** *a.*, worn to the thread, threadbare; also, of a screw, having a worn thread. See also THREADBARE, -LACE, etc.

1924 M. W. BECKWITH *Jamaica Anansi Stories* 35 An' Goat cut her up an' put her in his *tread-bag. **1953** R. MAIS *Hills were Joyful Together* II. xii. 226 Her money gone! Somebody had robbed her while she was asleep. She carried it in a threadbag tied with a string around her neck. **1935** *Jrnl. Fell & Rock Climbing Club* X. 236 (*caption*) *Thread belay. **1941** C. F. KIRKUS *Let's go Climbing* iv. 54 Here you use a thread belay, passing a loop of your rope through a muddy hole behind a chockstone . . and tying it round the stone or on to your waist line. **1965** A. BLACKSHAW *Mountaineering* viii. 225 Because a thread belay with the main climbing rope is usually very awkward and complicated . . slings are normally used. **1892** NASMITH *Cotton Spinning* ix. 328 The yarn is taken through the wire eyes fixed in hinged boards known as '*thread boards'. **1859** HUXLEY *Oceanic Hydrozoa* 82 The distal division remains short, and acquires only small *thread-cells. **1871** ALLMAN *Monogr. Gymnoblastic Hydroids* I. p. xiv, *Thread-cells*, peculiar bodies consisting of a containing capsule and contained filament destined for urtication. **1958** *Times* 27 Dec. 4/1 *Threadclip scissors . . are employed in the weaving trade for snipping loose ends during the weaving process. **1964** *McCall's Sewing* v. 62/2 *Thread clips*, a real time-saving little clipper that can be used effectively for snipping threads and making the small clips needed for marking or for curved seams. It has one ring which fits over the little finger, and is operated by squeezing with the palm of the hand. **1911** *Thread-counter [see *texture-counter* s.v. TEXTURE *sb.* 7]. **1877** KNIGHT *Dict. Mech.*, **Thread-cutter*, a small blade attached to a thimble, to a thread-stand, or to a sewing-machine, to cut off a sewing-thread. **1872** COUES *N. Amer. Birds* 4 Filoplumes (*filoplumæ*), or *thread-feathers . . have an extremely slender, almost invisible, stem. **1896** JORDAN & EVERMANN *Check-List Fishes* 335 Polynemidæ. The *Threadfins. **1933** *Bulletin* (Sydney) 5 Apr. 27/3 Thread-fins . . rarely extend southward to the coast of N.S. Wales. **1979** *Arizona Daily Star* 5 Aug. C-5/1 He was credited with introducing threadfin shad as a forage fish for bass. **1885** HORNADAY *2 Yrs. in Jungle* xxxii. 386 All but three were *thread fishes, a stange species of *Polynemus* . . distinguished by the . . thread-like filaments . . attached to the pectoral fins. **1884** MILLER *Plant-n.*, Crimson *Thread-flower, *Poinciana* (*Cæsalpinia*) *Gilliesii*. *Ibid.*, *Thread-foot, *Podostemon ceratophyllus*. **1839** URE *Dict. Arts*, etc. 1239 The doubling and twisting of cotton or linen yarn into a compact thread . . is performed by . . the *thread-frame. **1924** LD. RONALDSHAY *India* xiii. 159 The supply from abroad of such things as bobbins, plane tree-rollers . . and porcelain *thread-guides was cut off. **1964** *McCall's Sewing* v. 69/2 On most machines, the last thread guide will indicate the direction in which the thread must enter the needle. **1888** GOODE *Amer. Fishes* 409 In the Chesapeake region it is known as the 'Mud-Shad', . . in North Carolina as the 'Hairy-back' or the '*Thread Herring'. **1875** BENNETT & DYER *Sachs' Bot.* 747 The *Thread-indicator . . in which . . a horizontal needle . . moves freely over a graduated scale as the end of the thread which is fixed to the plant rises with its growth. **1884** MILLER *Plant-n.*, *Drosera filiformis*, *Thread-leaved Sun-dew. **1663** *Canterbury Marriage Licences* (MS.), Stephen Ward of Maidstone, *thredman. **1711** *Lond. Gaz.* No. 4932/4 Benjamin Cutlove, of London, Threadman. **1799** *Hull Advertiser* 23 Feb. 3/2 A . . fire broke out . . which entirely consumed nine *thread-mills. **1907** *Daily Chron.* 2 Oct. 6/6 Exciting scenes . . in connection with the Paisley thread mill strike. **1864** M. G. CAMPBELL in *Intell. Observ.* No. 33. 155 The *thread-mosses are an interesting and numerous tribe. **1899** *Daily News* 7 Dec. 11/1 Spidery kinds [of chrysanthemums] include the *thread-petalled Mrs. Carter. **1861** MISS PRATT *Flower. Pl.* V. 291 *Thread Rush, or Slender Rush . . is remarkable for its thread-like stems. **1721** C. KING *Brit. Merch.* I. 285 *Thred Sisters. **1844** STEPHENS *Bk. Farm* II. 416 The *Chorda filum*, or *thread-tangle. **1877** KNIGHT *Dict. Mech.*, **Thread-waxer*, a bowl of heated shoemaker's wax, through which the thread is conducted in sewing-machines for boots, shoes, and leather. **1825** J. NICHOLSON *Operat. Mechanic* 398 When either of the threads break, the *thread-wire through which it passes falls down. **1753** *World* No. 4. ¶5 'The happiest in the world, madam', returned the *thread-woman. **1856** R. A. VAUGHAN *Mystics* (1860) II. VIII. ix. 97 The deftly-woven *threadwork of the tissues. **1861** LYTTON *Str. Story* (1862) II. 185 Pillows edged with the thread-work of Louvain. **1906** *Daily Chron.* 10 May 9/4 Mill girls employed in the thread works joined this organisation. **1888** *Dublin Rev.* July 69 The subject . . is *threadworn.

thread (θrɛd), *v.* Forms: 4–6 **threde**, 6 **threede**, 6–7 **thred**, 7 **thrred**, 7– **thread**; also 6– **thrid**. Pa. t. and pple. **threaded**; also 9 (*arch.*) **thrid** (*pa. pple.* **thridden**). [f. THREAD *sb.*: independently in various senses.

The spelling *thrid* is still quite common in some of the transf. and fig. uses.]

1. a. *trans.* To pass one end of a thread through the eye of (a needle) in order to use it in sewing; to furnish (a needle) with a thread; also, to treat (any perforated object) in the same way (as in quot. 1607).

? *a* **1366** CHAUCER *Rom. Rose* 99 A sylvre nedle forth I droughe, . . And gan this nedle threde anon. **1530** PALSGR. 755/2, I threde a nedell to sowe with, *je enfile*. **1570** LEVINS *Manip.* 52/29 To Threede, *acum filo inducere*. **1607** TOPSELL *Four-f. Beasts* (1658) 307 Thread all the other rings with the loose end of the rope. **1676** C. HATTON in *H. Corr.* (Camden) 124 Good for nothing but to sit in ladyes chambers and thred their needles. **1709–10** STEELE *Tatler* No. 141 ¶2 The Girl can scarce thread a Needle. **1840** HALIBURTON *Letter Bag* i. 14 He threaded my needle for me.

b. *transf.* To cause (something) to pass through something else, as a thread through the eye of a needle.

1851 MANTELL *Petrifact.* iii. §7. 341 The graphic simile . . that the Plesiosaurus might be compared to a serpent threaded through the shell of a turtle. **1894** H. GARDENER *Unoff. Patriot* 27 Nature built these mountains, and threaded that little river over the stones. **1901** WATERHOUSE *Conduit Wiring* 3 Size of Conductors which can be threaded through Simplex Conduits. **1902** *Westm. Gaz.* 28 Apr. 5/2 The [foot-]ball was . . threaded in and out among the Southampton players.

c. *fig.* To pass through, make a hole through, penetrate, pierce.

1670 PETTUS *Fodinæ Reg.* 2 When the Miners by these Shafts or Adits do strike or threed a Vein of any Metal. **1896** *Pall Mall Mag.* May 12 Tom out here will have leave to thrid you with bullets. **1899** B. CAPES *Lady of Darkness* xvi, Thridding Ned's brain as they passed with a receding sound like that made by pebbles hopping over ice.

d. Of a man: to have sexual intercourse with (a woman). *slang.*

[**1903** FARMER & HENLEY *Slang* VII. 109/1 *To thread the needle*, to possess a woman.] **1958** B. BEHAN *Borstal Boy* I. 15 Sheila would be sorry she did not let me thread her, the night we walked the canal.

2. a. To fix (anything) upon a string or wire that passes through it; *esp.* to connect (a number of things) by passing a thread through each, to string together on or as on a thread. Also *fig.*

1633 G. HERBERT *Temple, Sunday* v, The Sundaies of mans life, Thredded together on times string. **1650** EARL MONM. tr. *Senault's Man bec. Guilty* Ep. Ded., If you will adde Charity enough . . to pardon the faults escaped in the Presse, I shall thread it to the rest of my Obligations. *a* **1668** DAVENANT *Song* Wks. (1673) 321 Thy Teares to Thrid instead of Pearle, On Bracelets of thy Hair. **1705** F. HAUKSBEE in *Phil. Trans.* XXIV. 2166 Amber . . beads, about the bigness of small Nutmegs, and Threaded. **1809** SCOTT *Let.* 14 Sept., The sight of our beautiful mountains and lakes . . [has] set me to threading verses together. **1867** F. FRANCIS *Angling* vii. (1880) 268 Threading the bait upon the hook. **1874** SPURGEON *Treas. David* Ps. ciii. 3 He selects a few of the choicest pearls . . threads them on the string of memory. *Mod.* The girl was threading beads on a string of catgut.

b. To make or embellish with or as with things strung on or fastened together by a thread.

1796 MRS. M. ROBINSON *Angelina* I. 230 No blithesome groups, thridding the roseate wreath, Or tripping in fantastic measures by. **1877** S. LANIER *Tampa Robins* 11, I Will . . thrid the heavenly orange-tree With orbits bright of minstrelsy.

3. *fig.* To run or pass like a continuous thread through the whole length or course of; to pervade.

1830 *Examiner* 485/2 The melody which threads the first duet. **1858** *Eclectic Rev.* Ser. VI. III. 413 The burr of which [consonants] . . thridding the open music of the vowel-sounds. **1871** EARLE *Philol. Eng. Tongue* 259 One spirit and purpose threads the whole, and gives a sort of unity. **1905** *Westm. Gaz.* 13 Oct. 1/3 A haunting mystical vision that always threaded my slumbers.

b. *intr.* for *refl.* To connect itself as by a thread.

a **1848** R. W. HAMILTON *Rew. & Punishm.* ii. (1853) 78 It has been seen how thought can thrid with thought, and feeling flow into feeling.

4. a. *trans.* To make one's way through (a narrow place, a passage presenting difficulties or obstacles, a forest, a crowd, or the like); to pass skilfully through the intricacies or difficulties of. ***to thread out***, to pick out and follow, to trace (a path).

1593 SHAKS. *Rich. II*, V. v. 17 It is as hard to come, as for a Camell To thred the posterne of a Needles eye. **1607** —— *Cor.* III. i. 127 They would not thred the Gates. *a* **1619** FLETCHER *Bonduca* IV. ii, See where he thrids the thickets. **1633** G. HERBERT *Temple, Vanitie* i, The fleet Astronomer can bore, And thred the spheres with his quick-piercing Minde. **1751** SMOLLETT *Per. Pic.* xcvi. (1779) IV. 175 A captain of the guards, who . had threaded every station in their community. **1809** MALKIN *Gil Blas* I. vi. ¶3, I threaded all the windings of this new labyrinth. **1832** LYTTON *Eugene A.* IV. x, Events thicken, and the maze is nearly thridden. **1863** GEO. ELIOT *Romola* i, A labyrinth of narrow streets . . rarely threaded by the stranger. **1866** DORA GREENWELL *Ess.* 219 A land intersected and thridden by the channels of benevolence.

b. ***to thread one's way, course***, etc. in same sense.

1825 COLERIDGE *Aids Refl.* (1848) I. 323 He . . thrids his way through the odorous and flowering thickets into open spots of greenery. **1868** E. EDWARDS *Ralegh* I. x. 179 He . . proceeded to thread his course amidst the tortuous . . channels. **1887** BOWEN *Æneid* II. 634, I . . through foemen and flames, by the goddess's grace Thrid my way.

c. *intr.* = b.

1660 F. BROOKE tr. *Le Blanc's Trav.* 5 The other [stream] . . threds through the middle of the Town. **1872** JENKINSON *Guide Eng. Lakes* (1879) 68 Bend to the left . . and thread in an up-and-down course amongst the bare, rugged rocks. **1893** STEVENSON *Catriona* xi. 119, I . . threaded through the midst of it [the wood], and returned to the west selvage. *Ibid.* xxii. 260 We thrid all the way among shoals.

†**d.** *trans.* ***to thread the difference***: to trace out or follow the narrow dividing line. *Obs. rare.*

1627 WREN *Serm. at Whitehall* 17 Feb. 15 The Epidemiall prophanation of our times, that will thrid you a difference now betwixt this feare and perfect worship.

5. *intr.* To move in a thread-like course or manner; to flow in a slender stream; to creep, twine, wind.

1611, **1626** [see THREADING *vbl. sb.*]. *a* **1879** T. ORMOND in *Mod. Sc. Poets* II. 356 Gracefully the ivy green Did round the craprods thread.

6. a. *trans.* To weave as a thread into the texture of something; to interweave.

1853 ROCK *Ch. of Fathers* III. II. 25 These old 'tropes' . . used to be twined and threaded into the words of the daily service.

b. *passive.* To be penetrated, permeated, or interspersed as with threads.

1861 DORA GREENWELL *Poems* 215 The thrice refined gold Was thrid with baser clay. **1875** —— *Liber Human.* 108 The elements which, mixed and threaded with whatever imaginable alloy, go to make up man's moral nature. **1891** ZANGWILL *Bachelor's Club* 21 His tawny hair, too, began to be threaded with silver.

†**7.** To bring on or induce gradually, as by the gentle drawing of a thread or line; to lead on. *Obs.*

1709 WODROW *Corr.* (1842) I. 48 Our corruptions, and so our desolation for a season, are like to be threaded in gradually upon us. *Ibid.* 61 Provided we be not gradually threaded in to greater encroachments on the Church's rights this way. **1716** *Ibid.* II. 202 We are like to be threaded out of the exercise of our power as to fasts and thanksgivings by the Assembly.

8. To stretch threads across or over; to intersperse with threads so stretched.

1884 *Chr. Commw.* 20 Mar. 536/2 The devil's long lines of temptation, with which the stream of life is so thickly threaded. **1907** *Westm. Gaz.* 25 Feb. 2/3 Heavy spraying . . and threading [fruit-trees] . . he has found to be a failure. *Mod.* I am obliged to thread my crocuses and polyanthuses every spring to protect them from destructive birds.

9. To form a screw-thread on; to furnish (a bolt or the like) with a screw-thread.

1858 SIMMONDS *Dict. Trade* s.v. *Screw*, Threading is effected by a saw which [etc.]. **1877** KNIGHT *Dict. Mech.* 2074/1 Screw-threading machine. **1888** HASLUCK *Model Engin. Handybk.* (1900) 46 The extreme end is threaded for a nut, as shown in the section of cylinder. **1893** *Brit. Jrnl. Photogr.* XL. 801 A hole is bored in the neck and threaded, and the valve is screwed . . in.

10. a. To place the thread, film, or tape in its proper course in (a sewing machine, projector, etc.). Usu. with *up*. Also *absol.*

1873 *Young Englishwoman* Mar. 150/1 Thread up the machine with the same coloured silk. **1913** F. A. TALBOT *Pract. Cinematogr.* vii. 85 In threading up the camera it is only necessary to make sure that the image on the negative comes squarely and truly before the window in the gate. **1923** —— *Moving Pictures* 81 Threading the camera, as it is called, completed, the door of the exposed magazine is closed. **1932** SIMPSON & WEIR *Weaver's Craft* x. 92 Threading the Loom.—It is still an advantage for two people to work together for this. **1962** L. DEIGHTON *Ipcress File* xxiv. 155 He threaded up the 16mm projector. **1964** *McCall's Sewing* v. 69/1 Your machine simply won't work if it isn't threaded exactly according to plan. **1970** A. FOWLES *Dupe Negative* i. 8 It's [*sc.* the film's] just back from the lab. Take a couple of minutes to thread up.

b. To pass (film, etc.) *through* a projector, recorder, etc., so that it occupies the correct path; = LACE *v.* 4 f.

1915 J. B. RATHBUN *Motion Picture Making & Exhibiting* ii. 33 The loading of a motion picture camera is usually no more difficult than threading the film through a projector. **1932** SIMPSON & WEIR *Weaver's Craft* xi. 115 Thread the new piece through the correct heddle and dent of the reed, then wrap the loose end round a pin in the woven fabric. **1959** N. MAILER *Advts. for Myself* (1961) 168 Sam attempts to talk while he is threading the film. **1961** *N.Y. Times* 10 Sept. x. 15/3 The user has to thread the tape through the machine before starting, and rewind the tape after playing or recording. **1972** W. P. BLATTY *Exorcist* (1974) III. i. 279 The priest quickly set up the tape recorder; looked for an outlet; plugged it in; threaded tape.

threadbare ('θrɛdbɛə(r)), *a.* Also 5 *Sc.* **thred bar**, (8 **thread-bear**), 5– **thread(-)bare**. [f. THREAD *sb.* + BARE *a.*]

1. Of a garment, etc.: Having the nap worn off, leaving bare the threads of the warp and woof; worn to the thread; shabby; worn-out.

1362 LANGL. *P. Pl.* A. v. 113 But ȝif a lous couþe lepe I con hit not I-leue Heo scholde wandre on þat walk hit was so þred-bare. *c* **1386** CHAUCER *Prol.* 260 He was nat lyk a Cloystrer With a thredbare cope as is a poure scoler. *c* **1470** HENRY *Wallace* VI. 449 Thi ald hud, becaus it is thred bar. **1590** SPENSER *F.Q.* I. iv. 28 Thred-bare cote, and cobled shoes, hee ware. **1693** BOWLES *Juvenal* v. 193 Will any Freedom here from you be born, Whose Clothes are thread-bare? **1711** ADDISON *Spect.* No. 42 ¶2 Dresses and Clothes that were thread-bare and decayed. **1824** W. IRVING *T. Trav.* I. 196 Wit and coin are always doubted with a thread-bare coat.

2. *fig.* Resembling a threadbare garment; hence, poorly furnished or provided; meagre, scanty, poor, beggarly; contemptible, 'sorry'.

c **1412** HOCCLEVE *De Reg. Princ.* 1431 Som person is so threde-bare of konnynge. **1462** MARG. PASTON in *P. Lett.* II. 83 Yelverton is a good thredbare frend for yow. *c* **1518** SKELTON *Magnyf.* 223 Welth and Wyt, I say, be so threde bare worne. *a* **1550** *Fane wald I luve* 19 in *Dunbar's Poems* (S.T.S.) 308 Sum strykis down a threid bair cheik. **1586** DAY *Eng. Secretary* I. (1625) 44 With bad attire, and thred-bare dyet, he liued with him a pretty season. **1676** MARVELL *Mr. Smirke* 10 What Power they have, they will not wear it thred bare. **1704** SWIFT *T. Tub* Introd. ¶25 A conscience thread-bare and ragged with perpetual turning. **1864** PUSEY *Lect. Daniel* (1876) 438 We should often have had but a threadbare history.

b. *esp.* Having lost its influence, freshness, or force by much use; trite from constant repetition; commonplace, stale, hackneyed.

1598 E. GILPIN *Skial.* (1878) 26 So long he hath vsde to cry, *oh rare*, That now that phrase is growne thin & thred-bare. **1657** J. WATTS *Vind. Ch. Eng.* 107 A trite, and thredbare exception. **1746** CHESTERF. *Lett.* (1870) 23 The trite, threadbare jokes of those who set up for wit without having any. **1825** SCOTT *Let.* 29 Apr., If this quotation is rather threadbare. **1891** MRS. OLIPHANT *Jerusalem* I. iv. 157

A strange sermon upon..the fallacy of the hopes of men, which is a threadbare subject.

3. Of persons: Wearing threadbare clothes; shabby, seedy; hence, impecunious, hard up; down-at-heel, out-at-elbows. Now *rare* or *Obs.*

1577 R. WRIGHTE in Ellis *Orig. Lett.* Ser. II. III. 75 He shall not onley be thrid bare but ragged. **1628** EARLE *Microcosm., Prison* (Arb.) 82 Onely to be out at elbowes is in fashion here, and a great Indecorum, not to be thredbare. **1672** SHADWELL *Timon* I. Wks. 1720 II. 298 Honesty, Thou foolish, slender, thread-bare, starving thing. **1713** STEELE *Englishm.* No. 16. 108 You shall see him..in close Whisper with a thread-bare Philosopher. **1760–72** H. BROOKE *Fool of Qual.* (1809) IV. 136 [He] took the thread-bare Longfield..under the arm, and carried him away.

4. *Comb.*, as ***threadbare-genteel***, (cf. *shabby-genteel*).

1849 CLOUGH *Amours de Voyage* I. 130 Some Threadbare-genteel relations.

'threadbareness. [f. prec. + -NESS.] The state or quality of being threadbare.

1530 PALSGR. 280/2 Threde bareness, *deureur.* ?*c* **1600** *Distr. Emperor* I. i. in Bullen *O. Pl.* (1884) III. 169 Thou that hast worne thy selfe and a blewe coate To equall thryddbareness. **1771** MACKENZIE *Man Feel.* xxi. (1886) 60 His look..spoke of the sleekness of folly and the threadbareness of wisdom. **1870** LOWELL *Among my Bks.* Ser. I. (1873) 355 A little threadbareness in the similes.

So **thread'barity** *nonce-wd.*, in same sense.

1892 BESANT *Ivory Gate* 69 The rags and duds and threadbarity too often enter largely into the picturesque.

threaded ('θrɛdɪd), *ppl. a.* [f. THREAD *v.* (and *sb.*) + -ED.]

1. a. Furnished with a thread (as a needle); strung on or as on a thread (as beads); interlaced, twined; consisting of or ornamented with threads.

1541 COPLAND *Guydon's Quest. Chirurg.* L iij, In puttyng threded nedles in to theym [wounds]. **1758** J. S. *Le Dran's Observ. Surg.* (1771) 274, I supported the Compress with a threaded Dossil. **1821** *Sporting Mag.* VIII. 262 She [a mare] had large corns on each foot, one of which was what is termed a threaded corn. **1821** JOANNA BAILLIE *Wallace* liv, Tissue of threaded gems is worn. **1856** BRYANT *West Wind* i, And hear the breezes of the West Among the threaded foliage sigh. **1876** GEO. ELIOT *Dan. Der.* IV. xxx, Standing with her arms thrust down and her fingers threaded. **1904** FARRER *Gard. Asia* viii. 74 A threaded chain of lakes.

b. *Computers.* Of a list or tree: in which items contain a pointer to a preceding node as well as one to the following node.

1960 PERLIS & THORNTON in *Commun. Assoc. Computing Machinery* III. 196/1 This paper presents an addition to the list structure languages which is expected to add to the above advantages while simplifying machine processing of lists. This is done by the use of threaded lists. A threaded list is a structure in which the last element of each list specifies the location of the head of the list of which it is the terminal member. **1979** TREMBLAY & BUNT *Introd. Computer Sci.* xi. 583 Given the threaded representation of a binary tree with respect to inorder traversal, it is a simple matter to formulate algorithms for obtaining the inorder predecessor and successor of a designated node.

2. Having or furnished with a screw-thread.

1844 *Civil Eng. & Arch. Jrnl.* VII. 153/2 On approaching the farther or opposite end they are made irregular, commonly called 'drunken threaded'. **1884** C. G. W. LOCK *Workshop Receipts* Ser. III. 288/1 The shank and threaded part of the tap. **1898** *Cycling* 49 Working upon the threaded end of the axle.

3. [f. THREAD *sb.*] As the second element in parasynthetic combinations, as ***bare-***, ***gold-***, ***grey-***, ***small-threaded***.

1616 J. DEACON *Tobacco Tortured* 66 They make..well bred Gentelmen, but bare thredded Yeomen. **1617** MINSHEU *Voc. Hisp. Lat., Aranuelo*,..a small threaded net to catch birds. **1896** *Godey's Mag.* Feb. 211/2 Long opera wraps..of gold-threaded brocade.

threaden ('θrɛd(ə)n), *a.* Now *arch.* or *dial.* Forms: see THREAD *sb.*; (also 5 **therdyn**). [f. THREAD *sb.* + -EN⁴.] Composed or made of thread; *spec.* made of linen thread.

c **1400** *Laud Troy Bk.* 8351, I ȝeue not a threden lace Off thyn euel wil and thi manace! **1499** *Croscombe Churchw. Acc.* (Som. Rec. Soc.) 23 A therdyn cerchewe. **1590** LODGE *Euphues' Gold. Leg.* 59 b, A dosen of new thredden points of medley coulour. **1594** WILLOBIE *Avisa* (1880) 76 Not worth in proofe a threden poynt. **1610** B. JONSON *Alch.* I. i, A thin thredden cloake. **1688** R. HOLME *Armoury* III. 224/1 They went always covered with Threaden Caps or Hoods. **1780** WARNER *Let.* 24 Aug., in Jesse *Selwyn & Contemp.* (1844) IV. 366 Of his threaden sails [he] has made wings to our riches wherewith to fly away. *a* **1825** FORBY *Voc. E. Anglia* s.v., Within our memory 'threaden stockings' were an article of Sunday apparel for village servants and apprentices. **1870** ROCK *Text. Fabr.* Introd. v. 127 Very fine threaden cloths..for liturgical purposes.

threader ('θrɛdə(r)). Also 5 **thredere**, 9 **thredder**. [f. THREAD *v.* + -ER¹.] One who or that which threads; *spec.* **a.** a person employed to keep the shuttles threaded in weaving; **b.** a bodkin for threading tape or ribbon through interstices in a garment or the like; see also quot. 1877.

c **1430** *Pilgr. Lyf Manhode* IV. lviii. (1869) 204 My mooder Charitee was cordere and thredere [Fr. *fillaciere*]. **1877** KNIGHT *Dict. Mech., Threader*, a device for guiding the thread into the eye of a needle. See *Needle-threader*. **1908** *Daily News* 1 Aug. 5/1 He went, at the age of ten, into a lace mill, where he advanced from the position of a 'jacker off' to that of a 'thredder'. **1911** *Ibid.* 3 May 8 Inspecting automatic threaders and inquiring into their adaptability.

'threadiness. *rare.* [f. THREADY + -NESS.] The quality of being thready; in quot., stringiness.

c **1425** tr. *Arderne's Treat. Fistula* 82 Arsenic & auripigment bene boþe one,..but auripigment is..more disesy for to grynde for his þredinez. **1864** in WEBSTER.

'threading, *vbl. sb.* [f. THREAD *v.* + -ING¹.] The action of the verb THREAD in various senses; an instance of this.

1611 COTGR., *Filet d'huyle*, a small drop, or threading of oyle. **1626** BACON *Sylva* §293 We see in Liquors, the thredding of them in Stillicides. **1852** R. S. SURTEES *Sponge's Sp. Tour* (1893) 118 The collar..exhibited all the stitchings and threadings incident to that department of the garment. **1887** E. GURNEY *Tertium Quid* II. 45 Accurate thridding of labyrinthine things. **1889** *Pall Mall G.* 25 Nov. 7/1 The machine which does the threading [of screws] is complicated and slow. **1908** R. W. CHAMBERS *Firing Line* xxviii, Another woman awoke to take up the ravelled threadings of her life again. **1913** F. H. RICHARDSON *Motion Picture Handbk.* (ed. 2) 219 It is aggravating for the operator who has to do rapid work in threading up, to be obliged to work with reels in bad condition. **1932** SIMPSON & WEIR *Weaver's Craft* x. 92 For the threading up one person should sit at the back of the loom in such a position that the 'shed' sticks and warp threads can be easily seen. **1933** *Sight & Sound* Spring 34/2 Accessibility of the gates and sprockets for threading up. **1964** *McCall's Sewing* v. 69/1 Always check your instruction manual for proper threading. **1970** *Which?* Jan. 8/1 Threading can be a tedious and sometimes tricky business, especially if the thread has to go *through* other openings as well as the eye of the needle.

†**'threadish,** *a. Obs. rare*⁻¹. [f. THREAD *sb.* + -ISH¹.] Resembling a thread; thread-like.

1578 LYTE *Dodoens* II. i. 147 The roote is tender & of threddish strings.

'thread-lace. Lace made of linen or cotton thread as distinguished from silk lace.

1581 *Acc. Bk. W. Wray* in *Antiquary* XXXII. 117 A grose white thred lace, v s. vj d. **1785** in *Home Counties Mag.* (1902) IV. 226 One of the best thread lace-makers in England. **1821** J. SMYTH *Pract. of Customs* 118 No Thread Lace can be imported in a less quantity than 12 yards, unless of the value of £2 per yard or upwards. **1861** GEO. ELIOT *Silas M.* i, Great ladies, clothed in silk and thread-lace.

threadle ('θrɛd(ə)l), *v. dial.* Also 9 **threddle, thriddle.** [f. THREAD *sb.* + -LE 3.] = THREAD *v.*

1746 BOWLKER *Art Angling* (1833) 52 Threadle this gudgeon. **1767** J. BICKERSTAFFE *Love in City* I. ii, Here threadle my needle. **1881** *Isle of Wight Gloss., Threadle*, to thread; to string. **1887** BOWEN *Æneid* II. 454 A passage adjoined Thriddling the inner palace. **1888** *Berks. Gloss.* s.v., To 'threddle' a needle is to pass thread through the eye of it ready for sewing.

threadless ('θrɛdlɪs), *a.* [f. as prec. + -LESS.]

1. Without a thread; having no thread; unthreaded.

1822 *Blackw. Mag.* XII. 711 Threadless, knotless, endless, useless mysteries, tragedies, and dramas. **1866** T. BRUCE *Summer Queen* 14 Fancy lost in threadless maze Was running to and fro.

2. Having no screw-thread.

1886 *Cyclist* 4 Aug. 1081/1 It [a bicycle]..is made with Clarke's patent threadless spokes.

threadlet ('θrɛdlɪt). [f. as prec. + -LET.] A minute thread; a slender filament.

1882 J. PARKER in *Homil. Mag.* (N.Y.) May 459 By what threadlets is he lifted up? **1887** C. L. MORGAN *Anim. Biol.* iii. 29 A delicate dark thread, from which minute threadlets pass off.

thread-like ('θrɛdlaɪk), *a.* [f. as prec. + -LIKE.] Like a thread; also, like that of a thread.

1774 MRS. DELANY in *Life & Corr.* Ser. II. (1862) II. 47 A little brassish, copperish, goldish thread-like stuff adhering to a bit of slate or coal. **1814** SOUTHEY *Roderick* XVII. 50 The stream's perpetual flow..with its..Dimples and thread-like motions infinite. **1835–6** *Todd's Cycl. Anat.* I. 604/1 Cellular tissue formed of white thread-like filaments. **1901** *Scribner's Mag.* XXIX. 433/2 Ridges over which the white tracks wind, thread-like, toward the hazy rim of mountains.

b. Of the pulse: = THREADY 4.

a **1829** in *Good's Study Med.* (1829) II. 612 Difficulty of swallowing; thread-like pulse. **1897** *Allbutt's Syst. Med.* II. 818 The heart's action becomes extremely feeble, and the pulse threadlike and uncountable. *Ibid.* IV. 389 It may be found that a pulsation of thread-like smallness will pass in spite of almost any pressure which the finger can apply.

†**'threadmeal,** *adv. Obs. rare.* [f. as prec. + -MEAL.] Thread by thread.

1565 COOPER *Thesaurus, Filatim*,..threade meale: threade by threade. *Ibid.* s.v. *Distraho, Filatim distrahi*, to be pulled a sunder threadmeale.

'thread-ˌneedle. Also **thread-the-needle; thread the (my) needle-eye, my grandmother's, the tailor's needle;** *dial.* **grandy needles.** [f. THREAD *v.* + NEEDLE.]

1. A children's game, in which, all joining hands, the player at one end of the string passes between the last two at the other end, the rest following.

1751 *Advent. G. Edwards* 140 (Halliwell) Eight people..joining hands like children at thread-needle. **1797–1805** S. & HT. LEE *Canterb. T.* III. 450 Children..playing thread my grandmother's needle. **1825–7** HONE *Every-day Bk.* I. 692 The prettiest sight..was a game at 'Thread my needle', played by about a dozen lasses. **1856** MISS MULOCK *J. Halifax* xxv, From top to bottom, the young men and women were running in a long 'Thread-the-needle'.

2. **thread the needle**, as *verb phrase*: (*a*) in dancing, denoting the movement in which the lady passes under her partner's arm, their hands being joined; (*b*) to pass in and out in a winding course; (*c*) in shooting: see quot. 1895².

1844 DICKENS *Christmas Carol* ii, Advance and retire, both hands to your partner, bow and curtsey, corkscrew, thread-the-needle, and back again to your place. **1895** *Daily News* 12 June 7/2 The toiling oarsman..might then have to 'thread the needle' (inshore for the boat, outside for the punt, close astern). **1895** *Funk's Standard Dict.* s.v., *To thread the needle* (*Western U.S.*), to fire a rifle-ball through an auger-hole barely large enough to allow the ball to pass without enlarging the hole.

'Threadˌneedle Street. The name of the street in the City of London where the Bank of England is located, used allusively to mean the Bank or its directors. Cf. *the Old Lady of Threadneedle Street* s.v. LADY *sb.* 4 e.

1924 LD. BIRKENHEAD *Amer. Revisited* i. 10 They [*sc.* U.S. economists and financiers] lack something of the sophistication and age-long sagacity of Threadneedle Street. **1974** G. VAIZEY *Tangled Web* ii. 25 It's only a question of time..before it gets to 'the ferret's' ears in Threadneedle Street. Then, heaven help you.

'thread-ˌpaper. A strip of thin soft paper folded in creases so as to form separate divisions for different skeins of thread; the paper so folded forming a long and narrow strip.

1761 STERNE *Tr. Shandy* III. xli, What is become of my wife's thread-paper? **1796** MME. D'ARBLAY *Camilla* II. 404 [She] had lost the thread-paper from which she was to mend her gown. **1880** *Plain Hints Needlework* 57 It should be cut at each end of the skein and folded securely into a 'thread paper'.

b. *fig.* A person of slender or thin figure.

1824 MISS MITFORD *Village* Ser. I. 153 So tall and so limp, bent in the middle—a thread-paper, six feet high! **1833** MARRYAT *P. Simple* xxxix, If the common sailors were..such little thread-papers as you. **1881** HUXLEY in *Life* (1900) II. ii. 35, I was a thread paper of a boy myself.

c. *attrib.* Having the attributes of a thread-paper; long and narrow, slender, attenuated; limp, feeble, flimsy.

1746–7 MRS. DELANY in *Life & Corr.* (1861) II. 450, I expect soon to see the other extreme of thread-paper heads and no hoops, and from appearing like so many blown bladders, we shall look like so many bodkins stalking about. **1803** *Naval Chron.* X. 510 Bonaparte's thread paper flotilla. **1882** P. FITZGERALD *Recreat. Lit. Man* (1883) 186 [Landing from a Calais steamer] Singers, actresses, ladies of quality, princesses, queens, all reduced to the common thread-paper level. **1884** STEVENSON *New Arab. Nts.* 308 She was a thread-paper creature.

threadworm ('θrɛdwɜːm). A worm of threadlike form, as the GUINEA WORM, HAIR-WORM, etc.; *esp.* the pin-worm, *Oxyuris* (*Ascaris*) *vermicularis*, parasitic in the human rectum, chiefly in children.

1802 BINGLEY *Anim. Biog.* (1813) III. 400 The Indian thread-worm, or guinea-worm,..enters the naked feet of the slaves. **1822–34** *Good's Study Med.* (ed. 4) I. 274 The head of the thread-worm is subulate, nodose, and divided into three vesicles. **1879** WRIGHT *Anim. Life* 582 The Thread Worm (*Gordius aquaticus*) is viviparous, and the young differ in form from the mother. **1899** *Allbutt's Syst. Med.* VIII. 512 [Eczema] may follow the irritation of thread worms.

thready ('θrɛdɪ), *a.* [f. THREAD *sb.* + -Y.]

†1. Full of or covered with thread. *Obs.*

1594 WILLOBIE *Avisa* 37 b, When threedy spindle full was grown. **1757** DYER *Fleece* III. 135 The thready shuttle glides along the lines.

2. Of thread-like texture; composed of fine fibres; stringy, fibrous.

c **1425** [implied in THREADINESS]. **1715** tr. *Pancirollus' Rerum Mem.* I. I. iv. 12 Its threaddy Substance may be weav'd into a Web. **1750** tr. *Leonardus' Mirr. Stones* 71 Amianton is a stone of a lucid colour, and thready, like feathered alum. **1797** *Encycl. Brit.* (ed. 3) XII. 371/2 The bark [of the mulberry tree]..is rough, thick, thready, and fit for being made into ropes. **1809** tr. *Landt's Descr. Feroe Isl.* (1810) 141 Compact, thready, or radiant zeolite. **1826** CARLYLE *Early Lett.* (1886) II. 350 Abundance of grand thready peats.

b. Of liquid: Forming strings; viscid, ropy.

1733 *Ordinary of Newgate* No. 1 Advt., Urine..foul, slimy, thready. **1846** G. E. DAY tr. *Simon's Anim. Chem.* II. 182 The mucus will become very tough, and almost thready. **1897** *Allbutt's Syst. Med.* IV. 435 [The fluid of a pyonephrosis] is more or less thready and glairy.

c. Of a plant: Bearing thread-like fibres or parts; filamentous, hairy. *rare*⁻¹.

1804 CHARLOTTE SMITH *Conversations*, etc. II. Notes 204 Thready Yucca, an Aloe, I believe.

d. Having thread-like markings; veined.

1601 HOLLAND *Pliny* (1634) I. 493 Ioyners doe chuse the mistresse threadie grain that is most streight.

e. Threadbare; showing the threads.

1910 *Nation* 15 Jan. 639/2 The envelope fluttered to the thready carpet.

3. Of the nature of, consisting of, or resembling a thread or a mass of loose threads; thread-like, hair-like; of a root: fibrous.

1597 GERARDE *Herbal* I. ii. §4. 3 The roote is threddie. **1621** T. GRANGER *Comm. Eccles.* xii. 6. 325 The small and threddie rootes of a tree. **1671** MARTEN *Voy. Spitzbergen* in *Acc. Sev. Late Voy.* II. (1694) 92 Her Feathers are thready or hairy. **1698** J. PETIVER in *Phil. Trans.* XX. 405 Its Style is thready, and about an Inch long. **1733** W. ELLIS *Chiltern & Vale Farm.* 231 Here it will twist and fasten its thready Entanglements to them almost from top to bottom. **1879** G. MACDONALD *Sir Gibbie* i, Her black hair..would have revealed a thready glitter of grey. **1882** —— *Castle Warlock* xxviii, Many a thready weed.

4. Of the pulse: see quot. 1899.

1753 N. TORRIANO *Gangr. Sore Throat* 109 A frequent, and very thready Pulse. **1764** *Phil. Trans.* LIV. 239 His pulse was too quick..and withall low and thready. **1860–1** FLOR. NIGHTINGALE *Nursing* 80 The pulse becomes quick, perhaps 130, and so thready, it is not like a pulse at all, but like a string vibrating just underneath the skin. **1897** *Allbutt's Syst. Med.* III. 621 The pulse becomes small, sharp, wiry or thready. **1899** *Syd. Soc. Lex., Thready pulse*, a small, scarcely perceptible pulse found in the terminal stages of fatal diseases.

5. Of the voice, etc.: Dry and thin; wanting in fullness. (Cf. THREAD *sb.* 4 b.)

1860 *All Year Round* No. 41. 344 Incapable of knowing how exceedingly high he is pitching his thready old voice. **1874** LISLE CARR *Jud. Gwynne* I. iii. 92 Sickly pianos and thready harps. **1902** MISS BROUGHTON *Lavinia* (ed. Tauchn.) 235 A fuller sound in the thready voice.

threap (θriːp), *sb.* Now *Sc.* and *north. dial.* Forms: 3–4 **þrep**, 4–5 **þrepe**, **threp**, 4–6 **threpe**, 6 **threip**, **threype**, 7 **threape**, 8–9 **threep**, 8– **threap**. [f. THREAP *v.*]

1. The action of threaping; contradiction, contention, argument, discussion; controversy, dispute; strife, quarrel, contest.

a **1300** *Cursor M.* 13310 (Cott.) Wit-vten threp [*Gött.* ani threpe] or strijf. *Ibid.* 27609 O pride bicums throues o thrett, Hething, threp [*v.r.* þrepe], and athes grett. **13..** *E.E. Allit. P.* B. 350 Enter in þenne..& haf þi wyf with þe, Þy þre sunez with-outen þrep & her þre wyuez. *c* **1400** *Destr. Troy* 5246 Þai hade no strenght to withstonde þe striff of þe pepull, Þat were þro men in threpe. **1418** *26 Pol. Poems* xiv. 78 Stryf wiþ comons, threp, and thro, To brynge þat in amendement. **1535** STEWART *Cron. Scot.* (Rolls) I. 37 We sall make threip ȝit or we ouirthrawin. **1794** *Har'st Rig* lxi, They stop at last, but still look laith The threap to yield. **1866** CARLYLE *Let.* Apr. in Froude *Life in L.* (1884) II. xxviii. 308, I had privately a kind of threap that the brandy should be yours. **1886** *S.W. Linc. Gloss.* s.v., We had a bit of a threap about it.

2. An act of threaping; a contradictive or pertinacious assertion; a hostile charge or accusation.

1538 CROMWELL in Merriman *Life & Lett.* (1902) II. 128 To desire to conquer me by shrowde wordes, to vanquishe me by sharpe threpes of scripture. *a* **1699** J. FRASER in *Wodrow Soc. Sel. Biog.* (1847) II. 214 Let us..hear patiently all assertions and threaps. **1742** R. FORBES *Ajax* viii, At threeps I am na' sae perquire, Nor auld-farren as he. **1768** ROSS *Helenore* III. 111, I nae mair sall say this threap about,..That on my side the bargain did na fa'. **1864** CARLYLE *Fredk. Gt.* XV. xv. (1872) VI. 119 He had taken a threap that he would have it finished. **1897** SNAITH *Fierceheart* vi. 67 The threep was fause, an he..got a thrawn thrapple for a deed he didna dae.

b. Phr. *to keep (to) one's threap.*

1756 MRS. CALDERWOOD *Jrnl.* (1884) 318 Encouraging her to keep to her threap. **1818** SCOTT *Br. Lamm.* xxvii, Lady Ashton..will, as Scotchmen say, keep her threep.

†**3.** Reproof, rebuke. (Cf. THREAP *v.* 1.) *Obs. rare.*

1636 JAMES *Iter Lanc.* 276, I leaue thy heape Of bloodie crimes to God's revendge and threape.

4. *Comb.* **threap-ground, threap-land(s,** land of disputed ownership, debatable land; *spec.* applied to the Debatable Lands of the Border.

1259 *Registr. Aberdon.* (Maitl.) I. 26 Super quadam terra que dicebatur threpland inter terram de Bondyngton..et terram de Newton. **1449** in Rymer *Fœdera* XI. 245/1 As touching the Landez callid Batable Landez or Threpe Landez in the West Marchez. **1568** in H. Campbell *Love-Lett. Mary Q. Scots* App. (1824) 15 The contraversy yerely arising by occasion of certein grounds upon the frontiers in the east marches, commonly called the threap-land, or debatable. **1825** E. MACKENZIE *Hist. Northumbld.* II. 257 A long tract of land..which was formerly Debateable Land, or Threap Ground; but which, in 1552, was divided by agreement between the proper officers of both nations. **1858** DENHAM *Folk-Lore* 55 (E.D.D.) Part of Wooler Common is still undivided, owing to disputes respecting it. It is called Threap-ground. **1894** HESLOP *Northumbld. Gloss., Threap-lands, Threap-ground*,..land the ownership of which is disputed.

threap (θriːp), *v.* Now *Sc.* and *north. dial.* Forms: 1 **ðreapian**, 3 **þreape**, (*Orm.*) **þræpenn**, 3–5 **þrepe**, 3–7 **threpe**, 4–6 **threppe**, (4–5 *pa. t.* **þrappit**, **þreppit**), 5–6 **threip**, 6 **thraip**, 6–7 **threape**, 6–9 **threep**, 6– **threap**. [OE. *préapian* to rebuke, reprehend: of uncertain history.]

1. *trans.* To rebuke, reprove, chide, scold, blame.

c **897** K. ÆLFRED *Gregory's Past. C.* xxi. 165 Ðonne he to suiðe & to ðearllice ðreapian wile his hieremenn. *a* **1300** *E.E. Psalter* xciii[i]. 10 Þat vndretakes genge, noght threpe mon, Þat leres man wisedome to kun? **1582** STANYHURST *Æneis* IV. (Arb.) 106 Let not mee falslye be threpped. **1682** SHADWELL *Lanc. Witches* v. 71 Who threped and threped, and aw to becaw'd me. **1787** GROSE *Provinc. Gloss., Threap*, or *Threapen*, to blame, rebuke, reprove, or chide. **1877** *N.W. Linc. Gloss.* s.v., I wen't be threp by a little thing like thoo. **1879** CLOUGH *B. Bresskittle* 14 (E.D.D.) Th' owd lass..threap'd me foinly.

†**b.** *to threap* (a person) *with kindness* = *to threap kindness upon*: see 4 b. *Obs.*

1567 JEWEL *Let. to Harding* in *Def. Apol.* Rrr j b, Yee threape her Maiestie fondely with kindenesse.

2. *intr.* To contend in words; to inveigh *against*; to argue, dispute; to quarrel, bicker, disagree; to wrangle about terms, haggle.

c **1200** ORMIN 5744 Acc himm birrþ þræpenn aȝȝ wiþþ skill Onnȝæness alle sinness. **1303** R. BRUNNE *Handl. Synne* 4352 Whan ȝe aȝens þe prechur þrepe. *Ibid.* 6065 Aȝens mokerers wyl y þrepe. *c* **1400** *Destr. Troy* 2152 Than..priam..þonket hom þroly, þrappit no lengur. *Ibid.* 12235 He þroly with þrong wil preppit agayn. *c* **1475** *Rauf Coilȝear* 79 Thank me not ouir airlie, for dreid that we threip. **1535** STEWART *Cron. Scot.* (Rolls) III. 454 The erle of Craufurd that same tyme and he,..Begouth to threip quha than that war best peiris. **15..** *Ballad, Take thy old cloak about thee* 67 It's not for a man with a woman to threape Unless he first gave oer the plea. **1755** JOHNSON, To *Threap*, a country word denoting to argue much or contend. **1847** C. BRONTË *J. Eyre* xxix, They were so agreeable with each other—never fell out nor 'threaped'. **1871** [see THREAPING *vbl. sb.*]. **1873** LYTTON *Parisians* IX. iii, Threep and argue as we may.

†**b.** *intr.* To fight, struggle, strive, contend. *Obs.*

13.. *Gaw. & Gr. Knt.* 504 Bot þenne þe weder of þe worlde wyth wynter hit þrepez. ? *a* **1400** *Morte Arth.* 930 Of the nyghtgale notez the noisez was swette, They thrępide wyth the throstilles, thre hundreth at ones! *c* **1400** *Destr. Troy* 2003 Þre dayes þroly þai þrappit with stormys. *Ibid.* 10098 Mony thoghtes full þro þreppit in his hert. *Ibid.* 12134 In þronge and in þraldom þrepe with þe werld.

3. *trans.* (usu. with *obj. cl.*) To persist in asserting (something contradicted or doubted); to affirm positively or pertinaciously; to maintain obstinately or aggressively.

c **1386** CHAUCER *Can. Yeom. Prol. & T.* 273 Sol gold is and Luna siluer we threpe. *c* **1475** *Rauf Coilȝear* 199 Thay threip that I thring doun of the fattest. **1509** FISHER *Wks.* (1876) 299 Some other threpe that he hathe forgoten theym. **1656** BLOUNT *Glossogr., Threpe*,..to affirme positively, or to face one down with confidence, still used in the North. **1728** RAMSAY *Cameleon* 26, I say he's blue; He threaps, he's green: now what say you? *a* **1774** FERGUSSON *Drink Ecl.* Poems (1845) 53 Will ye your breedin' threep ye mongrel loun? **1816** SCOTT *Antiq.* xxiv, He threeps the castle and lands are his ain as his mother's eldest son. **1887** P. M'NEILL *Blawearie* 50 A group o' miners..threepit doon my throat that the grave..was only about four feet deep.

b. *to threap* (a person) *out of*: to move or do (him) out of (something) by persistent assertion.

1677 GILPIN *Demonol.* (1867) 168 Thus are men threaped out of their own persuasions. **1885** J. HARTLEY *Clock Alm.* 40 (Yorks.) (E.D.D.) Shoo tried to threap me aght on it.

c. with *inf.* To insist on or persist in doing something. *rare*$^{-1}$.

1827 SCOTT *Surg. Dau.* i, She threeps to keep on a black fause-face, and skirls if we offer to take it away.

4. *to threap* (something) *upon* (a person):

†**a.** To impose (an assertion) upon; to lead or try to lead one to believe by persistent assertion. *Obs.*

c **1440** *Alphabet of Tales* 482 When his servandis wolde eatt any gude meate, þai wolde threpe vppon hym at he was seke. **1530** PALSGR. 755/2, I threpe a mater upon one, I beare one in hande that he hath doone or saide a thing a mysse... This terme is..farre northren. He wolde threpe upon me that I have his penne. **1608** HIERON *2nd Pt. Def. Ministers' Reas. Refusal Subscription* 72 Slaundring the Ministers and threaping one and the same..slaunder vpon them.

†**b.** To impute, attribute, ascribe (something) to a person. *to threap kindness* or *love upon* (also *of*): to attribute kindness, etc. to; to give (one) credit for love or goodwill, to urge to the exercise of kindness. (See also 1 b.) *Obs.*

1559 BERCHER *Nobylytye Wymen* (1904) 104 In dede..you threape kindenes vppon me, and surely..I can well a way wᵗʰ yoʳ prayse. **1579** W. WILKINSON *Confut. Familye of Loue* 65 It is but a vayne kyndnes, which Theophilus in this place threapeth on God. **1589** R. BRUCE *Serm.* (1843) 129 Thou suld threep kindness of him. **1596** NASHE *Saffron Walden* 152 The baudie rymes he threapes vpon me. *a* **1603** T. CARTWRIGHT *Confut. Rhem. N.T.* (1618) 231 You do but threap kindnesse of the Hereticks, as you call them; for they acknowledge no such miracles to be done by your reliques. **1648** J. BEAUMONT *Psyche* v. ccxxvii, Behold how gross a Ly of Ugliness They on my face have threaped. **1660** DICKSON *Writings* (1845) I. 42 If any wilt threap love upon God, they shall not be disappointed. **1730** T. BOSTON *Serm. Song of Sol.* ii. 17 Wks. 1855 V. 552 It will make men very peremptory for Christ, that they will not take a refusal, to threap kindness on him and special interest in him.

c. To thrust, obtrude, press (something) upon a person; to urge upon him acceptance of or acquiescence in.

1571 GOLDING *Calvin on Ps.* xviii. 3 If Sathan threpe any feare uppon us, it may be kept farre of from enterance. **1690** C. NESSE *O. & N. Test.* I. 68 Araunah had a princely spirit ..but generous David threaps upon him fifty shekels. **1816** SCOTT *Antiq.* xv, Monkbarns had threepit on them to gang in till 't to see the wark o' the monks lang syne. **1869** 'OUIDA' *Puck* xlii, Look'ee here! These arena goods to threap.

5. *to threap down*: to put down or silence by vehement or pertinacious assertion; also, with double object (sb. and clause), *to threap* (a person) *down* (*that*...): to try to force a statement upon (a person) by strength of assertion or insistent reiteration.

1599 NASHE *Lenten Stuffe* (1871) 51 Bolingbroke,..at his removing..into banishment, as Father Froissart threaps down, was accompanied with forty-thousand men, women, and children weeping. **1674** N. FAIRFAX *Bulk & Selv.* 83 You may as well threap one down, that a ghost is heavier or lighter, colder or hotter,..whiter or blacker than a body. **1841** R. W. HAMILTON *Nugæ Lit.* 340 A man will say of a clamorous talker, he did not convince me, but he threaped me down. **1877** LEIGH *Cheshire Gloss.* s.v., He thraped me down it were noine, but I knowed it were a dozen.

Hence **'threaping** *vbl. sb.* and *ppl. a.*; **'threaper,** one who 'threaps' or persistently asserts.

c **897** K. ÆLFRED *Gregory's Past. C.* xxi. 167 ȝif him mon to unȝemetlice mid ðære ðreapunga oferfylgð. **13..** *E.E. Allit. P.* B. 183 For þeft, & for þrepyng, vnþonk may mon haue. *c* **1400** *Destr. Troy* 10847 A thowsaund full þro, þrepand in wer. *c* **1440** *York Myst.* xl. 105 Thei thraste hym full thraly, þan was þer no threpyng. *c* **1460** *Towneley Myst.* xxviii. 19 Do way youre threpyng! are ye wode? **1785** [W. HUTTON] *Bran New Wark* 38 Naa brawling or threaping is heard. **1871** W. ALEXANDER *Johnny Gibb* i, Johnny offered 'sax poun'..after much 'threepin' as his ultimatum. **1871** P. H. WADDELL *Ps.* xxxv. 11 Thar raise amang them threepers o' ill. **1899** *Leeds Merc., Suppl.* 18 Feb. (E.D.D.), Ah niver knew sich a threaper as thee.

'threapen, *v. Obs.* exc. *dial.* [app. f. THREAP *v.* + -EN⁵; but, in sense 1, perh. for *threaten*.]

†**1.** To threaten (*trans.* and *intr.*). *Obs.*

1340 *Ayenb.* 84 Naȝt ne habbeþ more of myȝte aye uirtues kueade mysfalles and zorȝes ne al þet fortune may þreapny and do: more þanne þer byeþ dropen of rayn ine þe ze. *Ibid.* 97. *Ibid.* 162 Hardyesse uor to þolie alle þe kueadnesse þet þe wordle may þreapni. **1559** BERCHER *Nobylytye Wymen* (1904) 128 Yf they be threpned [It. *se sono minacciate*] they langwyshe, yf they be cheryshed they be prowde.

2. To blame, rebuke, chide, reprove: = prec. 1.

a **1667** SKINNER *Etymologicon* (1671), To Threap or Threapen, *vox agro Linc. usitatissima*, ab AS. *Ðreapian, Redarguere, vel Ðrafian, Urgere.* **1691** RAY *N.C. Words, Threap, Threapen*, to blame, rebuke, reprove, chide. **1904** *Eng. Dial. Dict.* (E. Yorks.), *Threapen*, to reprove, rebuke, chide.

Hence **'threapening** *vbl. sb.*

1340 *Ayenb.* 65, vij. oþre boȝes. Huer-of þe uerste is strif, þe oþer chidinge, þe þridde missigginge, þe uerþe godelinge, þe uifte atwytinge, þe zixte þreapninge, þe zeuende vnonynge arere. *Ibid.* 66 Efterward zuo comeþ þe þreapnynges and beginneþ þe medles and þe werres.

threat (θrɛt), *sb.* Forms: 1–3 **þreat**, (1 **ðreot(t, ðreatt)**, 2 **þreatt**, 3 **þræt**, 3–4 **þrat**, 4 **þret**, **thrett**, 4–5 **þret(e**, **thret(e**, 6 **threte**, 6– **threat**. [OE. *préat* masc. (With sense 2 cf. ON. *praut* fem. struggle, labour, trouble):—OTeut. **prauto²*, *-ā*, from ablaut-series **preut-*, *praut-*, *prut-* (cf. OE. *préotan* to trouble, weary, Goth. *us-priutan* to trouble, threaten, OHG. *ir-driozan*, MHG. *ver-driozen*, Ger. *ver-drieszen*, Du. *ver-drieten* to trouble, vex; cf. L. *trūdĕre* to press, thrust). Sense 1 has the same form as 2 in OE. and early ME., and is commonly considered the same word; it appears to go back, like 'throng' and 'press (of people)', to the radical sense 'to press'.]

I. †**1.** A throng, press, crowd, multitude of people; a troop, band, body of men. *Obs.*

Beowulf 2406 Se wæs on ðam ðreate þreotteoða secg. *a* **800** CYNEWULF *Elene* 329 Hio..þrungon..on þreate. *c* **950** *Lindisf. Gosp.* Mark iii. 32 ȝesætt ymb hine ðreat [*c* **975** *Rushw. G.* ðe ðreatt, L. *turba*]. *Ibid.* viii. 2 Ic milsa ofer ðreat [*R.* ðreott]. *c* **1205** LAY. 9791 Riden ut to-some..þritti þusend þe þræt wes þa mare. *Ibid.* 26294 Hit is feole ȝere þat heore þrættes [*c* **1275** þretes] comen here.

II. †**2.** Painful pressure, oppression, compulsion; vexation, torment; affliction, distress, misery; danger, peril. *Obs.*

a **800** CYNEWULF *Juliana* 465 Is þeos þraȝ ful strong, þreat ormæte; ic sceal þinga ȝehwylc þolian. **971** *Blickl. Hom.* 119 Hie seoþþan ealle worlde wean & ealle þreatas oforhoȝodan. *c* **1200** *Trin. Coll. Hom.* 61 Listeð nu wich þreat dauid setted uppen us bute [we] lesten ure bihese. **13..** *E.E. Allit. P.* B. 55 Þenne þrat moste I þole. *c* **1330** R. BRUNNE *Chron.* Prol. (1810) p. xcviii, With mykelle wo, In sclaundire, in threte & in thro. **13..** *Minor Poems fr. Vernon MS.* xliv. 36 And þretes—þo beoþ vuele þre, ffurst and hunger and þesternesse. *c* **1450** LOVELICH *Grail* xiii. 606 They wenden han put him to gret thret.

3. A denunciation to a person of ill to befall him; *esp.* a declaration of hostile determination or of loss, pain, punishment, or damage to be inflicted in retribution for or conditionally upon some course; a menace. Also *fig.* an indication of impending evil.

The radical sense appears to be 'pressure applied to the will by declaration of the harm that will follow non-compliance'. It is thus indirect compulsion.

It is doubtful whether quots. *c* 1000 belong here or to sense 2.

c **1000** ÆLFRIC *Saints' Lives* xxv. 220 Ac mathathias nolde ..godes æ forgæȝan for his [the king's] gramlican ðreate. *Ibid.* xxviii. 105 Ða hæþenan..heton hine secgan mid swyðlicum þreate hweþer he cristen wære. *c* **1200** *Vices & Virt.* 87 Oðerhwile cumeð maniȝe þohtes of godes þreatt of helle pines. *a* **1250** *Owl & Night.* 58 Ne recche ich nouht of þine þrete. *c* **1325** *Song of Yesterday* 148 in *E.E.P.* (1862) 137 ȝif þi neiȝebor þe manas Oþer to culle oþer to bete..þou wold drede þi neiȝebores þrete. **1526** *Pilgr. Perf.* (W. de W. 1531) 14 b, Wherby he myght scape the menasses and threttes of god. **1601** SHAKS. *Jul. C.* IV. iii. 66 There is no terror Cassius in your threats. **1750** GRAY *Elegy* 62 The threats of pain and ruin to despise. **1874** GREEN *Short Hist.* vii. §1. 348 He met the hostility of the nobles with a threat which marked his power. **1884** *Manch. Exam.* 19 Feb. 5/4 Clouds full of the threat of rain.

4. *Zool.* Animal behaviour that keeps other animals at a distance or strengthens social dominance without physical conflict. Freq. *attrib.*

1933 R. W. G. Hingston *Meaning of Animal Colour* v. 119 Whenever a bird has threat-colours on the crown, it either lowers its head so that the colours can be seen, or erects the feathers..to make them visible above the level of the beak. *Ibid.* x. 291 Song is an exhibition of threat. 1943 D. Lack *Life of Robin* iii. 26 It is..a threat display, serving to intimidate a trespassing robin. 1949 *Brit. Birds* XLII. 234 One female called a peculiar, low, harsh, single note.. similar to a harsh growling threat-note. 1966 N. Tinbergen *Animal Behaviour* viii. 177 The signalling movements of higher animals, particularly those used in threat and courtship. 1978 P. Marsh et al. *Rules of Disorder* v. 127 Certain threat signals are evolved such that intra-specific conflicts became ceremonial in character. 1981 *Oxf. Compan. Animal Behaviour* 563/2 The opening of the mouth that precedes biting has evolved into a ritualized baring of the teeth that is characteristic of threat in many mammals.

threat (θrɛt), *v. arch.* and *dial.* Forms: see below. [OE. *þréatian* weak vb., pa. t. *þréatode*, f. *þréat*, THREAT *sb.*:—OTeut. type *þrautôjan.]

A. Illustration of Forms.

1. *Pres. stem.* α. 1 **þreatian, 3 -en, in, þretie(n, þræten, þreat, 3–5 þrete, 5 þreete, 5–6 threte, 6 threete, 6–7 threate, 6– threat.**

c888 K. Ælfred *Boeth.* xxxvii. §1 Þa..þreatiað eal moncynn mid hiora þrymme. a1225 *Leg. Kath.* 623 Me ham walde þreatin & leaden unlaheliche. a1225 *Juliana* 13 Nulle ich þe her onont þreate se þu þreate buhe ne beien. a1250 *Owl & Night.* 1609 Me myd stone & lugge þreteþ. 1483 *Cath. Angl.* 385/2 To Threte, *minari.* 1530 Palsgr. 755/2, I threete, or I thretten one to do hym harme, *je menasse.* 1600 Threat [see B. 5].

β. **4–6 thret, threte, 4–7 thrett.**

13.. *Cursor M.* 18247 Nu þai thrett [*v.r.* thret] vs sare. *Ibid.* 19181 Þar-for sal we thret þam herd. c1375 *Sc. Leg. Saints* xlii. (*Agatha*) 147 Gyf þe fyre þu threttis me. 1523 Ld. Berners *Froiss.* I. clx. 194 Whan ye be at Parys..ye do thret thenglysshmen. a1533 —— *Gold. Bk. M. Aurel.* (1546) Gg iij b, She..threteth them that be absent.

γ. **3 þrattien, -en.**

c1205 Lay. 20341 Swiðe heo gunnen þrattien [c 1275 þretie] Arður þene king. *Ibid.* 18738 þrattest [see B. 4 a].

2. *Past tense.* α. **1 th-, þreatade, -ode, 2 -ede, 3 þreated, þræted, þret-, þrætt-, þrettede, 4 þreted, 5–6 thretid, 6– threated.**

c725–c1000 [see B. 1]. c1160 [see B. 2]. c1205 Lay. 504 Þe king þræted [c1275 þretede] Brutun. *Ibid.* 27131 Summe þrætteden [c1275 þrettede] heore ueond. c1250 Ðreated [see B. 3]. 13.. *Minor Poems fr. Vernon MS.* liv. 33 Harde þei þreted me in her þouȝt. c1440 Thretid [see B. 3]. a1529 Skelton *Wofully Araid* 13 The Jewis me thretid. 1673 Wood *Life* 14 July (O.H.S.) II. 266, I threated to geld the translator.

β. **3–4 þrette, 4 þret, 4–5 thrett, 4–6 thret, threte, 5 threte, (thred).**

c1250 Ðrette, c1300 þrette [see B. 5]. 13.. *Cursor M.* 19603 Saulus..thrett [*v.rr.* þrette, þret] All þe cristen. c1330 R. Brunne *Chron.* (1810) 44 Þe corsaynt & þe kirke he threte for to brennyng. c1400 *Laud Troy Bk.* 10493 He chased the Troiens & thret. c1440 *Alphabet of Tales* 81 And þan he thred hur. c1440 *Generydes* 500 She threte hym sore. 1523 Ld. Berners *Froiss.* I. ccclxxxiii. 645 They thret them of London.

γ. **2–4 þratte, 4 þrat, 5 thrat(t, 5–6 thratte, 6 thrate.**

c1200 Ormin 15514 He þratte stirne wind o sæ & itt warrþ stille & liþe. 13.. *E.E. Allit. P.* B. 937 Þe aungelez hasted þise oþer & aȝly hem þratten. 13.. *Gaw. & Gr. Knt.* 1980 Fele þryuande þonkkez he þrat hom to haue. c1400 *Laud Troy Bk.* 6907 Thei thrat him alle, tho he was tan. 1589 R. Robinson *Gold. Mirr.* (Chetham) 37 Albion Isle he thrate.

3. *Pa. pple.*: **3 i-ðrat, 4–5 þret, -tt, -tte; 4–6 threted, 7 threat, 5– threated.**

a1225 *Ancr. R.* 304 Ich was ined [*MS. T.* iðrat] þerto. 13.. *Gaw. & Gr. Knt.* 1725 Þer he watz þreted, & ofte þef called. a1400–50 *Alexander* 707 Þik & þrathly am I thret. 1470–85 Malory *Arthur* x. lxii. 520 Ful sore are we threted. 1472 Sir J. Paston in *P. Lett.* III. 38 That poor woode is soor manashed and thrett. 1631 Threat [see B. 3].

B. Signification.

†1. *trans.* To press, urge, try to force or induce; esp. by means of menaces. (With clause or inf.)

c725 *Corpus Gloss.* (O.E.T.) 1275 *Maceratus*, þreatende. *Ibid.* 2169 *Urguet*, threatade. a900 *O. E. Martyrol.* 18 Apr. 58 Adrianus se caser[e hine] þreatade þæt he Criste wiðsoce. c950 *Lindisf. Gosp.* Matt. v. 42 Ðæm nedende *vel* ðæm ðreatende [*Vulg.* uolenti] huerfa ðec ne acerre. c1000 Ælfric *Hom.* I. 416 Þa cempan..hine ðreatodon þæt he ðære deadan anlicnysse his lac offrian sceolde. a1225 *Ancr. R.* 248 Ne mei he [the devil] buten scheawe þe uorð sumhwat of his apeware, & oluhnen, oðer þreaten þet me bugge þerof. 13.. [see A. 2 γ]. c1470 Ashby *Dicta Philos.* 308 Who that wol nat be feire entreted, Must be foule & rigorously threted. 1501 *Plumpton Corr.* (Camden) 157 Ever they thratte me that I shold goe to London. 1638 *Hamilton Papers* (Camden) 4 They..thrett privatt men to singe the Covenatt.

†2. To rebuke, reprove. *Obs.* Cf. THREAP *v.* 1.

a1000 *Ags. Ps.* (Th.) lxvii. 27 [lxviii. 30] On wuda þu wildeor wordum þreatast. c1160 *Hatton Gosp.* Luke ix. 55 And he be-wente hine and hyo þreatede. c1200 [see A. 2 γ]. a1300 *E.E. Psalter* vi. 1 Lauerd, ne threte me in þi wreth.

3. To hold out threats against; = THREATEN 2.

a1000 *Ags. Ps.* (Th.) ix. 29 [x. 8] And þreatað þone earman mid his eaȝum. c1205 Lay. 641 He..þreateð þene castel & þat folc þer inne. c1250 *Gen. & Ex.* 4125 And wrot an canticle..Ðat ðreated ðo men bitter-like Ðe god ne seruen luue-like. 1428 in *Surtees Misc.* (1888) 3 Wham he thret with bodily harm. c1440 *Alphabet of Tales* 439 Sho apperid vnto hym & thretid hym att he was ferd for hur. c1489 Caxton *Sonnes of Aymon* xvii. 390 It becometh not to suche a knighte as ye be, for to threte me thus. 1526 *Pilgr. Perf.* (W. de W. 1531) 66 He that thretteth a dogge for his barkyng prouoketh hym to more felnesse. 1631 R. H. *Arraignm. Whole Creature* x. §2. 84 The Apostles glad, that they were threat, and beat for the Name of Christ. 1781 *Hist. Europe* in *Ann. Reg.* 25/2 The Spaniards sent out so great a force.. as seemed sufficient..to threat the British fleets and islands with the most imminent danger. 1848 Lytton *Harold* I. iv, Send for me if danger threat thee.

b. With inf. or clause as complement.

a1330 *Otuel* 736 Hou þei..þratten roulond to die. c1330 R. Brunne *Chron. Wace* (Rolls) 8294 [The Britons] þretten Hengist to wake hys wough. c1440 *Alphabet of Tales* 32 Þe devull come aforn hym with a byrnand stake, and thretid hym þat he sulde þruste itt in at his mouthe. 1461 *Paston Lett.* II. 25 She is thret if that she myght be take, she shuld be slayne. a1517 in G. P. Scrope *Castle Combe* (1852) 295 He..thret hym that he schulde make hyme aper before my lordys grase. 1611 *Coryat's Crudities* Panegyr. Verses c iij, All the Sophists he did threat Their problemes to confound. 1642 J. Eaton *Honey-c. Free Justif.* 475 It would be a foolish part to set it [a kettle] beside the fire, and then charge it to be hot, and to threat it that else it shall be spilt.

c. *fig.* Said of things; = THREATEN 4.

1422 [see THREATING *vbl. sb.*]. c1590 Marlowe *Faust.* vii. 18 A sumptuous temple..That threats the stars with her aspiring top. 1634 Milton *Comus* 39 This drear Wood, The nodding horror of whose shady brows Threats the forlorn and wandring Passinger. a1717 Parnell *Bookworm* 70 To see what dangers threat the year. 1800 Coleridge *Piccolom.* I. iii. 46 This tempest, which..threats us from all quarters. 1832 *Fraser's Mag.* IV. 764 The fate which threats kingdoms.

4. To hold forth (something) by way of a threat; = THREATEN 3. a. with inf. or clause as obj.

c1205 Lay. 17300 He gon þretien swiðe þat al he wolde heom to-driue. *Ibid.* 18738 Þu..þrattest hine to slænne. c1250 *Lutel Soth Sermun* 82 in *O.E. Misc.* 190 Hire sire & hire dame þreteþ hire to bete. 1375 Barbour *Bruce* vi. 536 Vmbeset With fayis þat to slay hym thret. c1557 Abp. Parker *Ps.* D ij, If the adversaries flocke to-gether..and threate to destroy the house of God. 1633 Bp. Hall *Hard Texts, O.T.* 413 Who is this..that threats to sweep all before him? 1681 Dryden *Abs. & Achit.* 801 If ancient fabrics nod and threat to fall. 1724 Ramsay *Royal Archers* 25 And seems to threat,..'No man unpunish'd shall provoke my rage'.

b. With sb. or pron. as obj.

c1386 Chaucer *Parson's T.* ¶572 He threttith more þan he may parfourme. 1526 *Pilgr. Perf.* (1531) 61 What payne & turment is thrette to the wycked & euyll lyuers. 1581 Mulcaster *Positions* vi. (1887) 47 Where thickning threates harme, there thinning fines the substance. 1594 Shaks. *Rich. III*, v. iii. 205 Euery one did threat To morrowes vengeance on the head of Richard. 1633 Bp. Hall *Hard Texts, N.T.* 17 Let the Tyrants..threat what they please. 1795 Burns *Dumfries Volunteers* i, Does haughty Gaul invasion threat? 1821 Clare *Vill. Minstr.* I. 4 Where black neglect..threats her constant winter cold and chill.

5. *absol.* or *intr.* To offer threats; = THREATEN 5.

c1250 *Gen. & Ex.* 2023 Often ȝhe ðrette, often ȝhe scroð. c1300 *Havelok* 1163 Sho was adrad, for he so þrette. 1390 Gower *Conf.* III. 57 Bot they with proude wordes grete Begunne to manace and threte. c1491 *Chast. Goddes Chyld.* 14 She..spekyth somtyme sharply somtyme she threteth. a1541 Wyatt *Penit. Ps.* vi. 30 That drede of deathe, of deathe that ever lastes, Threateth of right. 1600 Holland *Livy* viii. xxxii. 304 Some were heard to intreat, others to threat. 1605 Shaks. *Macb.* ii. i. 60 Whiles I threat, he liues. 1725 Pope *Odyss.* ii. 231 Threat on, O prince! elude the bridal day, Threat on, till all thy stores in waste decay. 1822 Byron *Werner* ii. ii. 266 Threat'st thou? 1901 Savage-Armstr. *Ball.* 64 (E.D.D.) Whun danger threats, return.

Hence †**threat** *ppl. a.*, obtained by threats, forced, compulsory.

c1375 *Cursor M.* 26944 (Fairf.) Wiseli loke þou be shriuin & noȝt wiþ strenght þer-to driuen For þret shrift mai haue na mede. c1375 *Sc. Leg. Saints* xi. (*Symon & Judas*) 1338 God wald one na wyse Of ony man haf thret seruice.

threaten (ˈθrɛt(ə)n), *v.* Forms: 1 **þreatnian, 3 þret(t)ne(n, þretni, 4–5 þret(t)en, 4–6 threten, thretne, 6 thretten,** *Sc.* **threiten, (6–8 thretn-), 6– threaten.** [OE. *þréat-n-ian*, f. *þréat*, THREAT *sb.* + -EN[5] 2.]

†1. *trans.* To press, urge, force; = THREAT *v.*[1] 1. Only in OE.

c1000 Ælfric *Hom.* I. 424 Neadað se deofol eow þæt ȝe cristene men to his biȝgengum ðreatniað?

2. a. To try to influence (a person) by menaces; to utter or hold out a threat against; to declare (usually conditionally) one's intention of inflicting injury upon (in quot. 1816, one's certainty that some specified injury will fall upon); to menace. Const. *with* the thing; also with compl. clause (with finite vb. or inf.).

c1290 *S. Eng. Leg.* I. 35/41 He þrettnede faste hermogenes. 1297 R. Glouc. (Rolls) 2391 Þe picars were wroþe ek & þretnede him ynou. 1387 Trevisa *Higden* (Rolls) III. 419 Alisaundre þrettneþ þe Iewes. 14.. *Sir Beues* 3341 (MS. N.) He me thretenyd for to slen. [15.. *Ibid.* (Pynson) 3001 He threteneth me to be slayne.] 1474 Caxton *Chesse* ii. v. (1883) 68 A tyrant dide do tormente Anamaximenes & thretenyd hym for to cutte of his tonge. 1526 *Pilgr. Perf.* (W. de W. 1531) 177 b, Traian commaunded hym to speke no more of it, thretnynge hym, that yf he dyd, he sholde lese his heed. 1651 Hobbes *Leviath.* ii. xxxi. 186 Threatning them with Punishment. 1715 De Foe *Fam. Instruct.* i. iv. (1841) I. 83, I won't be threatened neither. 1816 Scott *Old Mort.* xliv, In vain his wife..hung by his skirts, threatening him with death..for meddling with other folks' matters. 1834 *Picture of Liverpool* 39 All classes were threatened to be overwhelmed in one universal ruin.

†b. To charge or command with threats of punishment or displeasure; to command sternly or strictly. (Chiefly in biblical versions.) *Obs.*

1382 Wyclif *Mark* viii. 30 And he thretenyde hem, that thei schulden nat seie to ony man of him. 1526 Tindale *Acts* iv. 17 Lett vs threten and chaurge them that they speake hence forth to noo man in this name. 1555 Eden *Decades* 158 They..threatned them to auoyde the lande excepte they woolde bee distroyed euery manne. 1582 N. T. (Rhem.) *Mark* i. 25 And Iesvs threatened him, saying, Hold thy peace, and goe out of the man.

c. *fig.* (chiefly of impersonal agents or objects): To be likely to injure; to be a source of danger to; to endanger actively.

1638 R. Baker tr. *Balzac's Lett.* (vol. II.) 34 Perhaps the tempest that threatens my head will fall but at my feet. 1725 De Foe *Voy. round World* (1840) 302 The wind..blew very hard, threatening us with a storm. 1781 Gibbon *Decl. & F.* xix. II. 139 The Persian monarch, elated by victory, again threatened the peace of Asia. 1835 Thirlwall *Greece* x. I. 381 Where one threatens the existence of another. 1877 Froude *Short Stud.* (1883) IV. i. ii. 23 France and England had been..drawn together by a special danger which threatened Christendom.

3. To hold out or offer (some injury) by way of a threat; to declare one's intention of inflicting. a. with infin. or clause as obj.

1297 R. Glouc. (Rolls) 11209 Þe burgeis were þo bolde, & þretnede to nime mo. 1567 *Satir. Poems Reform.* vi. 71 The Propheit threitnit..That war and battell sould his land pas throw. 1649 Bp. Reynolds *Serm. Hosea* iv. 59 God threatneth terribly to shake the earth. 1682 Bunyan *Holy War* 49 They threatned also what men they would be. 1748 *Anson's Voy.* ii. iii. 146 Threatning to murder all who should oppose them. 1855 Macaulay *Hist. Eng.* xxi. IV. 663 He was at last forced to threaten that he would immediately make the whole matter public.

b. with sb. or pron. as obj.

1297 R. Glouc. (Rolls) 9383 Mid word he þretneþ muche & lute deþ in dede. c1450 *R. Gloucester's Chron.* (1724) 483/1 *note* (MS. Coll. Arms), He meketh prout men, and he thretneth werre. 1590 Marlowe *2nd Pt. Tamburl.* v. iii, These cowards..threaten conquest on our sovereign. 1649 Bp. Reynolds *Serm. Hosea* i. 43 They..should unwillingly suffer what he threatneth. 1774 Burke *Corr.* (1844) I. 498 The party that has lost the election threatens a petition. 1844 H. H. Wilson *Brit. India* ii. xii. II. 585 Reluctant to inflict the penalty that had been threatened.

4. *fig.* Of things, conditions: To give ominous indication of (impending evil); to presage, portend.

1611 Shaks. *Wint. T.* iii. iii. 4 The skies looke grimly, And threaten present blusters. 1644 Evelyn *Diary* 22 Oct., Another pendant Towre like that at Pisa, always threatning ruine. 1818–20 E. Thompson tr. *Cullen's Nosol. Method.* (ed. 3) 247 A sense of hunger threatening syncope. 1863 W. C. Baldwin *Afr. Hunting* viii. 339 The weather constantly threatens rain.

intr. (for *pass.*). 1850 D. G. Mitchell *Reveries Bachelor* 175 Hostilities would sometimes threaten between the school and village boys.

b. with infin.: To appear likely *to do* some evil.

1780 *Mirror* No. 81 ¶9, I am sometimes..frightened with dangers that threaten to diminish it [my estate]. 1848 Dickens *Dombey* iv, It threatens to be wet to night. 1899 'A. Hope' *King's Mirr.* ix, Age had not bent, but it threatened to break him. *Mod.* The new drainage scheme threatens to be an expensive undertaking.

5. *absol.* or *intr.* To utter or use threats; to declare one's intention of injuring or punishing in order to influence. a. *lit.* (absol. use of 2 or 3).

1297 R. Glouc. (Rolls) 10308 Nou sir clerc quaþ þe king ȝe mowe þretni ynou. c1450 tr. *De Imitatione* iii. xviii. 86 Þou shalt not þreten euerlastingly. 1602 Shaks. *Ham.* iii. iv. 57 An eye like Mars, to threaten or command. 1774 Goldsm. *Nat. Hist.* (1776) VII. 221 If too closely pursued, they [snakes] hiss and threaten. 1864 in Ellacombe *Ch. Bells Devon*, etc. (1872) 267 Do not threaten,..never let down your dignity by one single word of violence.

b. *fig.* (absol. use of 2 c or 4). To portend evil.

1610 Shaks. *Temp.* v. i. 178 Though the Seas threaten they are merciful. 1725 Pope *Odyss.* ii. 6 A two-edged faulchion threatened by his side. 1793 Mann in *Lett. Lit. Men* (Camden) 437 Our political horizon blackens and threatens more and more. *Mod.* The weather threatens.

¶6. *to threaten kindness* (*upon* a person): app. an altered form of the phrase *to threap kindness*: see THREAP *v.* 4 b. *Obs.*

1560 Daus *Sleidane's Comm.* 247 The byshop of Rome sendeth his letters to the Swisses, & threatning vpon them kindnes, for the frenship that had ben betwene them & his predecessours. 1577–87 Holinshed *Chron.* (1807) II. 249 The moonks being overcome with the kings words, threatning kindnesse upon them, fulfilled his request. 1579 Lyly *Euphues* (Arb.) 84 Philautus..threatneth such kindenesse at my handes, and suche curtesie at yours, that he shoulde accompt me his wife before he woe me.

7. In weakened use: to express an intention *to do* something, not necessarily evil.

1925 *Dialect Notes* V. 344 *Threaten, v.i.*, promise; as, he threatened to give me money. 1928 A. Huxley *Let.* 1 May (1969) 296 [He] was lunching here today and broached a notion about a preliminary limited edition... He threatens to come and talk to you about it.

Hence **ˈthreatenable** *a.*, that may be threatened.

1841–4 Emerson *Ess., Exper.* Wks. (Bohn) I. 186 The chagrins which the bad heart gives off..take form..and threaten or insult whatever is threatenable and insultable in us.

threatened ('θrɛt(ə)nd), *ppl. a.* [f. prec. + -ED[1].]

1. a. That is the object of a threat; assailed by menaces. Proverb ***threatened men live long***.

1533 LADY ELIZ. WHEATHELL in Mary A. E. Wood *Lett. Roy. & Illustr. Ladies* (1846) II. 91 There is an old saying,—'threatened men live long'. *a* **1642** SIR W. MONSON *Naval Tracts* II. (1704) 287/1 It is an old Saying, That a threaten'd Man eats Bread. **1855** MACAULAY *Hist. Eng.* xx. IV. 401 He took his post near Louvain, on the road between the two threatened cities. **1894** *Westm. Gaz.* 27 Nov. 5/3 The best-hated and the most threatened man in Germany.

b. Of a wild animal or plant: in danger of becoming rare or extinct.

1960 *Oryx* V. 381 (*heading*) Australia's threatened mammals. **1966** *Red Data Bk.* II. 2 The object of these lists and sheets of threatened species is not only to draw universal attention to the dangers facing some unique creatures,..but also to provide the factual information necessary for action. **1972** *Ibid.* (new ed.) I. Preamble 1 The threatened species include those that are in immediate danger of extinction (endangered species), those that are likely to enter this category (vunerable species), and those that are rare and at risk (rare species). **1976** *New Yorker* 12 Jan. 58 Seven hundred and sixty-one plants were designated as 'endangered', meaning their survival was in serious doubt, twelve hundred and thirty-eight were listed as 'threatened' and an even one hundred were declared extinct. **1979** *Birds* Summer 56/1 The most authoritative and comprehensive reference book published on the world's rare, endangered and threatened birds. **1979** *Red Data Bk.* (ed. 2) II. Preamble 3 *Endangered* (E)..Taxa in danger of extinction and whose survival is unlikely if the causal factors continue operating... *Vulnerable* (V)..Taxa believed likely to move into the endangered category in the near future if the causal factors continue operating... *Rare* (R)..Taxa with small world populations that are not at present endangered or vulnerable, but are at risk... A taxon at subspecific level which might qualify for the V..category has not been included if no other subspecies of the species concerned is in a threatened (E, V, R or I) category.

2. Of evil: Held out or presented as impending.

1567 GOLDING *Ovid's Met.* VI. (1593) 129 Neptunus standing striking with his long threatned blade Upon the ragged rocke. **1660** SOUTH *Interest Deposed* (title-p.) In the threatned and expected Ruin of the Laws. **1794** MRS. RADCLIFFE *Myst. Udolpho* xxxi, She determined to brave the threatened vengeance. **1831** SCOTT *Ct. Robt.* xxiv, The Turks..had resolved to prevent the threatened attack of the crusaders.

threatener ('θrɛt(ə)nə(r)). [f. as prec. + -ER[1].] One who threatens.

a **1541** WYATT *Song of Iopas* 46 The starre of Saturne olde, A threat'ner of all liuing things with drought. **1595** SHAKS. *John* v. i. 49 Threaten the threatner, and out-face the brow Of bragging horror. **1630** *R. Johnson's Kingd. & Commw.* A ij b, That Enemie and Threatner of our English Nation. **1748** RICHARDSON *Clarissa* (1810) III. ii. 10 Threateners.. were seldom to be feared. **1867** JEAN INGELOW *Story Doom* VII. 140 A feeble threatener with a foolish threat.

threatening ('θrɛt(ə)nɪŋ), *vbl. sb.* [f. as prec. + -ING[1].] The action of the verb THREATEN; menacing; also, an instance of this, a threat.

c **1290** *St. Kenelm* 242 in *S. Eng. Leg.* I. 352 So gret þretningue for him heo made. **1388** WYCLIF *Acts* iv. 29 And now, Lord, biholde in to the thretnyngis [1382 thretingis] of hem. **1489** CAXTON *Faytes of A.* I. xvi. 46 By thretnyng he shal also fraye hem. *a* **1548** HALL *Chron., Hen. IV* 7 b, The said kyng..menaced theym with sore thretenynges. **1611** BIBLE *Eph.* vi. 9 Doe the same things vnto them, forbearing threatning. **1719** DE FOE *Crusoe* (1840) II. iii. 54 The Spaniards, despising their threatening. **1865–6** H. PHILLIPS *Amer. Paper Curr.* II. 12 The threatenings of war were then only heard at a distance.

'**threatening**, *ppl. a.* [f. as prec. + -ING[2].] That threatens; conveying or indicating a threat or menace; portending some impending evil.

1530 in W. H. Turner *Select. Rec. Oxford* (1880) 83 Gevyng hym many thretenyng and opprobryous words. **1656** EARL MONM. tr. *Boccalini, Pol. Touchstone* (1674) 287 With threatning countenances they said [etc.]. **1724** DE FOE *Mem. Cavalier* (1840) 48 If Tilly did but write a threatening letter. **1829** SCOTT *Anne of G.* xxx, There muster yonder in the west some threatening clouds. **1898** *Allbutt's Syst. Med.* V. 118 The fever is high, and the condition of the patient is threatening.

'**threateningly**, *adv.* [f. prec. + -LY[2].] In a threatening manner; menacingly.

1601 SHAKS. *All's Well* II. iii. 85 The honor sir that flames in your faire eyes, Before I speake too threatningly replies. **1819** WORDSW. '*Departing summer hath assumed*' vii, Woe! woe to Tyrants! from the lyre Broke threateningly. **1857** W. COLLINS *Dead Secret* v. iii, The booming of the surf sounding threateningly near in..the fog.

So '**threateningness**.

1891 ATKINSON *Last of Giant Killers* 239 The suddenness of the action, and the threateningness of it.

† '**threater.** *Obs. rare*—[0]. [f. THREAT *v.*[1] + -ER[1].] = THREATENER.

c **1440** *Promp. Parv.* 492/2 Thretare, *minator.*

threatful ('θrɛtfʊl), *a.* [f. THREAT *sb.* + -FUL.] Full of threats; threatening.

c **1557** ABP. PARKER *Ps.* E iij, The thretfull warninges of the judgement. **1611** SPEED *Hist. Gt. Brit.* IX. viii. (1623) 582 By their threatfull letters. **1760–72** H. BROOKE *Fool of Qual.* (1809) IV. 129 A threatful and agile whirl of his staff. **1882** FARRAR *Early Chr.* II. 6 Not the threatful Law of Moses,.. but the royal Law, the perfect Law of liberty. **1895** G. MACDONALD *Lilith* viii. 53 The eagle, perched with outstretched wings on the top, appeared threatful. **1922** E. R. EDDISON *Worm Ouroboros* xxxi. 391, I have read signs in heaven: nought clear, but threatful unto both you and me. **1923** M. SADLEIR *Desolate Splendour* 199 He felt a desire still further to ingratiate himself with this threatful lord. **1932** W. FAULKNER *Light in August* ii. 42 It still lingers about her ..something dark and outlandish and threatful.

Hence '**threatfully** *adv.*, threateningly.

1565 STAPLETON tr. *Bede's Hist. Ch. Eng.* 50 S. Austen thretfully proficied, that, if they would not take peace..with their brethern, they should receaue..warre from their enemies. **1634** SIR T. HERBERT *Trav.* 190 [A] flaming Semiter (threatfully held against him). **1822** HOOD *Lycus* vi, The spirits of sin..that..threatfully warr'd with the light.

threating ('θrɛtɪŋ), *vbl. sb. Obs.* or *arch.* [f. THREAT *v.*[1] + -ING[1].] The action of the verb THREAT; threatening; a threat.

1046 *O.E. Chron.* (MS. D), On þam ȝeare ȝegaderade Eadward cyng mycele scypferde on Sandwic þurh Magnus þreatunge on Norwegon. *a* **1225** *Ancr. R.* 156 Vre Louerd hefde ifuld him of his þreatunge. **1382** [see quot. 1388 s.v. THREATENING *vbl. sb.*]. **1422** tr. *Secreta Secret., Priv. Priv.* 152 Seneca..wriet the hede atte the t[h]retyngis of the Swerde. **1482** *Monk of Evesham* (Arb.) 96 Whenne he herde ..this thretyng he was sore aferd. **1562** J. HEYWOOD *Prov. & Epigr.* (1867) 129 Not to wag their beardes in brawlyng and threatyng. **1643** BP. H. LESLIE *Serm. St. Mary's, Oxford* 9 Feb. 4 None of his threatings could fall to the ground.

'**threating**, *ppl. a. Obs.* or *arch.* [f. as prec. + -ING[2].] That threats; threatening, menacing.

13.. *K. Alis.* 930 (Bodl. MS.) Wiþ cryeyng & þretyng wordes. **1483** *Cath. Angl.* 385/2 Threthynge, *minans, minax.* **1510** *Sel. Cas. Crt. Star Chamber* (Selden) 205 With thretyng wordes [they] Caused the Carpynders to leve ther werke. **1641** A. SCOTT *Journ.* in *Sc. Hist. Soc. Misc.* (1904) 278 The threating danger of the Scottish mist.

threatless ('θrɛtlɪs), *a. rare.* [f. THREAT *sb.* + -LESS.] Devoid of threats; not threatening.

1605 SYLVESTER *Du Bartas* II. iii. IV. *Captaines* 201 Threat-lesse their brows, and without braves their voyce.

threave, variant of THRAVE.

thred(e, thredde, obs. ff. THIRD, THREAD.

three (θriː), *a.* and *sb.* Forms: see below. [OE. *þrí* (*þríe*), *þrío*, *þréo*, Com. Teut. and Indo-Eur.; = OFris. *thre* m., *thria* f., *thriu*, *thria* n.; OS. *thrie* (*thria*, *threa*) m., *threa* f., *thrua* (*thriu*, *thria*) n. (MLG., LG. *drê*, *dru* n., MDu., Du. *drie*); OHG. *drî*, *drio*, *driu* (MHG. *drî*(*e*, Ger. *drei*); ON. *þrír*, *þrjár*, *þrjú* (Norw., Sw., Da. *tre*); Goth. **þreis*, *þrija*;—OTeut. **þrí*[z] (:—**þrijiz*), **þrijā*:—Indo-Eur. *treies*, *treja*. Cf. Skr. *trayas*, Zend *θri*, Gr. τρεῖς, τρία, L. *trēs*, *tria*, Lith. *trýs*, OSlav. *trĭje*, *trije*, Irish and Welsh *tri*. The masc. has the form of a plural -*i* stem.]

A. Illustration of Forms.

α. nom. and *acc.* 1 masc. **þrí, þríe, þrý (þréo)**, fem. and neut. **þrío, þréo,** (*O North.* **ðríu, ðría, ðréa**); 2–4 **þreo**, 1–5 **þre**, (2 **þru** (? *ü*), 2–3 **þri, þro**, 2–4 **þrie**), 4 **þree**, (tre), 4–6 **thre** (6 **threy, thrie**), 5– **three.**

803 *Charter Cuðred* in *O.E.T.* 442 þisses londes earan ðrie sulong. *c* **825** *Vesp. Hymns* v. (*O.E.T.* 405), Ðreo foeðan [*ternos statores*]. *c* **891** *O.E. Chron.* an. 891, þrie Scottas comon. *c* **950** *Lindisf. Gosp.* Mark viii. 2 Ðrio doȝor ȝeabidas mec. *Ibid.* ix. 5 Ðrea [*c* **975** *Rushw.* ðria] husa. —— Luke xi. 5 Sel me ðreo [*Rushw.* ðria] hlafas. **971** *Blickl. Hom.* 145 þa þre fæmnan. *c* **1000** ÆLFRIC *Gen.* xl. 12 þa þreo clystru þæt sind..þri daȝas. *c* **1000** *Ags. Gosp.* Matt. xii. 40 þry daȝas and þreo niht. **11..** *Sax. Leechd.* III. 134 Leȝe þarto þru dæȝes & þre niht. *a* **1175** *Cott. Hom.* 237 þri ampres were an mancyn. *c* **1175** *Lamb. Hom.* 73 þro þing boð þet ech Mon habbe mot. *c* **1200** *Trin. Coll. Hom.* 3 On þesse þre wuken. *Ibid.* 27 þese þrie þing. *c* **1205** LAY. 53 þa þre boc. *Ibid.* 391 He ȝef Assaracun..þreo [*c* **1275** þre] castles. *c* **1275** *Ibid.* 16589 þreo daȝes and þreo niht. **13..** *Cursor M.* 5469 (Cott.) þar of tre yeir was him wan. *Ibid.* 9192 (Gött.) þat was vmgang jornays thrie. **1340** *Ayenb.* 88 þe þri greteste guodes. **1362** LANGL. *P. Pl.* A. I. 20 þreo [**1377** B. þree, **1393** C. þre] þinges. **1483** *Cath. Angl.* 385/1 Three, *tres & tria.* **1552–3** *Inv. Ch. Goods Staffs* in *Ann. Lichfield* (1863) IV. 46 Stoles & fannes for threy vestiments. **1596** Thrie [see B. I. 3]. **1600** in *Shaks. Cent. Praise* (Shaks. Soc.) 36 The L. montegle with some thre more.

β. dative, 1 **þrim, þrym, þriim, þrém**, 1–3 **þréom** (3 **þrom**); *genitive*, 1 **þríora, þréora**.

c **893** K. ÆLFRED *Oros.* Contents IV. vi, On þriora consula dæȝe. *Ibid.* III. ix. §5 On ðæm þrim ȝearum..on þrim folc ȝefeohtum. *c* **950** *Lindisf. Gosp.* Matt. xxvi. 61 Æfter ðrim [*c* **1000** *Ags. Gosp.* þrym; *c* **1160** *Hatt. Gosp.* þrem] daȝum. —— Mark xv. 29 On ðriim caȝum. *c* **1000** *Ags. Gosp.* John ii. 6 Ælc wæs on tweȝra sestra ȝemete oððe on þreora. *c* **1100** *O.E. Chron.* an. 1078, þreom nihton ær Candelmæssan. *c* **1205** LAY. 8059 þas dæies æn þreom [*c* **1275** a þreo] wiken. *Ibid.* 10034 Wið innen þan þrom ȝeren.

B. Signification.

The cardinal number next above two, represented by the symbols 3, III, or iii.

I. as *adj.* **1. a.** In concord with a sb. expressed.

803–*c* **1000** [see A]. *c* **1175** *Lamb. Hom.* 11 Nu weren þas þreo laȝe ȝe-writen inne þa oðre table breode sunderlipes. *c* **1250** *Gen. & Ex.* 557 Noe and hise ðre sunen. *a* **1300** *Cursor M.* 182 Fiue thossand men..he Fedd wyt fiue laues and fisses thre. *c* **1412** HOCCLEVE *De Reg. Princ.* 1801 Of thre conclusions moot I cheese one: Or begge, or stele, or sterue. *c* **1460** *Wisdom* 293 in *Macro Plays* 45 Ye haue iij enmyes:.. The worlde, þe flesche, & þe fende. **1526** *Pilgr. Perf.* (W. de W. 1531) 1 This treatyse..is..diuyded in to thre bokes. **1753** CHALLONER *Cath. Chr. Instr.* 2 The three Divine Virtues of Faith, Hope and Charity. **1775** SHERIDAN *Rivals* IV. ii, Like Cerberus, three Gentlemen at once. **1871** TYNDALL *Fragm. Sci.* (1879) I. xii. 358 Rocksalt cleaves in three directions.

b. Standing alone as predicate, or in concord with and following a pronoun, or pronominal adj.

c **1050** *Charter of Eadwine* in Kemble *Cod. Dipl.* IV. 260 Ðise write sinden þre. *c* **1200** ORMIN 18657, & tohh þeȝȝ sinndenn alle þre An Godd. **1362** LANGL. *P. Pl.* A. IX. 100 As þei þreo assenten. **13..** *Pol. Rel. & L. Poems* 228 Reuthþe and treuthþe and charite, Beþ out of lond alle þreo. *c* **1470** *Golagros & Gaw.* 400 Our souerane Arthour..Has maid ws thre as mediatour. *a* **1548** HALL *Chron., Edw. IV* 199 b, Wee were all three one mannes sonnes. **1678** DRYDEN & LEE *Œdipus* III. i, *Tir*[*esias*]... By the Fates that spun thy thread! *Cho*[*rus*]. Which are three. **1845** BROWNING *How they brought the Good News* 2, I galloped, Dirck galloped, we galloped all three.

c. Forming compound numerals with multiples of ten; originally placed first, as ***three and thirty*** (rarely ***thirty and three***), now usually ***thirty-three***. So also ***three and thirtieth*** (arch.: now ***thirty-third***), etc.

c **1000** ÆLFRIC *Exod.* xxxii. 28 þreo and twentiȝ þusendra manna. *c* **1205** LAY. 3870 þer of he wes lauerd þro and þritti wintere. *c* **1380** WYCLIF *Sel. Wks.* III. 340 Aboute þree and þritti ȝeer. *c* **1470** *Golagros & Gaw.* 247 The roy rekinnit on raw Thretty and thre. **1579** FULKE *Heskins' Parl.* 204 The three and twentieth Chapter endeth the exposition. **1588** PARKE tr. *Mendoza's Hist. China* 301 So they departed..and the three and twentie day of Ianuarie. **1725** DE FOE *Voy. round World* (1840) 168 A true oriental pearl..I sold it for three-and-fifty pounds.

d. Followed by *dozen*, *score*, and by *hundred*, *thousand*, etc., or the ordinals of these.

971 *Blickl. Hom.* 75 To þrim hunde peneȝa. *a* **1123** *O.E. Chron.* an. 1101, Rotbert..sceolde..þreo þusend marc seolfres habban. *c* **1220** *Bestiary* 616 Ðre hundred ȝer. **1388**– [see THREESCORE]. *c* **1475** *Rauf Coilȝear* 757 Ilk ȝeir thre hundreth pund assigne the I sall. **1483** *Cath. Angl.* 385/1 Threhundrethe, *tricentesimus.* **1634** SIR T. HERBERT *Trav.* 205 Seuenty Temples, in one of which are set three thousand three hundred thirty three gilded Idols. **1839** URE *Dict. Arts* 583 With about..a three-thousandth part of arsenic. *Mod.* I can find room for three dozen begonias.

e. ***three fourths***: three out of four equal parts or portions into which a whole is or may be divided; three quarters. Often *loosely* or *hyperbolically*, the greater part, most *of*.

1600 HOLLAND *Livy* VIII. ii. 289 Two acres in the Latine countrie, with a supplement of three foure parts out of the Privernates land to make up the whole. **1777** ROBERTSON *Hist. Amer.* (1783) III. 279 About three-fourths..of it belongs to the holder of the grant. **1779** *Mirror* No. 23 ⁋5 He was called a good-hearted man by three-fourths of his acquaintance. **1849** D. J. BROWNE *Amer. Poultry Yd.* (1855) 28 They do not get perfectly feathered till they are three fourths grown. **1866** FROUDE in Sir H. Brackenbury *Some Mem. My Spare Time* (1909) 41 The sailor's rule for grog —three-fourths spirit and all the water you add spoils it— applies pre-eminently to writing on practical questions. **1890** *Anthony's Photogr. Bull.* III. 200 A block of wood has a three-fourth inch hole bored in it.

†**f.** Rarely used for the ordinal THIRD. *Obs.*

1521 in *Test. Ebor.* (Surtees) VI. 4 Witnesses, Rober Gibson..and many other, the three daye of Auguste. **1598** SHAKS. *Merry W.* I. i. 142 The three party is..mine Host of the Garter.

g. In special collocations. ***problem of three bodies*** (Dynamics): the problem of ascertaining the movements of three particles attracting one another under the law of gravitation (as yet only approximately solved for special cases). ***three acres and a cow***: regarded as the requirement for self-sufficiency. ***three ages*** (Archæol.), the Stone, Bronze, and Iron Ages (see also *three-age*, sense III. 1 a below). ***the Three Bishoprics*** (Hist.), Metz, Toul, and Verdun. ***the three chapters*** (Ch. Hist.), the writings, etc., condemned by an edict of Justinian issued 544 A.D.: see quot. ***three cheers***, three successive cheers in unison, freq. *for* someone or something. ***three musketeers***, [tr. Fr. *les trois mousquetaires* (title of a novel (1844) by Alexandre Dumas père] three close associates. †***the three tongues***, the three inscribed on the Cross, and primarily requisite to the theologian, viz. Latin, Greek, and Hebrew. †***three trees***, the gallows. ***three vowels*** (slang), an IOU. ***the three wise men*** = *the three Kings* s.v. KING *sb.* 1 c; *transf.*, three men who act as advisers or arbitrators.

See also *three* (†*blue, golden*) *balls* (BALL *sb.*[1] 20); *the three* (*Holy*) *Children* (CHILD *sb.* 2 b); *three faces under a* (*one*) *hood* (FACE *sb.* 1 d); *the three kings* (KING *sb.* 1 c); *the three Persons* (PERSON *sb.* 7); *three sheets in the wind* (SHEET); *the three sisters* (SISTER *sb.* 4 b); *three sticks* (STICK *sb.*).

1885 J. CHAMBERLAIN in *Times* 17 Nov. 10/2 This man.. reported..that wherever the labourer had land and kept a cow—'*three acres and a cow' (loud laughter)..the poor rates were reduced. **1889** G. N. CURZON *Russia in Central Asia* vii. 239 The majority of residents would seem to have attained the ideal of Arcadian bliss expressed elsewhere in the historical phrase, 'Three acres and a cow'. **1964** *English Studies* XLV. (Suppl.) 214 Chesterton the Distributist and advocate of 'three acres and a cow'. **1866** J. CRAWFURD in *Trans. Ethnol. Soc. London* IV. 1 The theory which supposes three different ages of civilisation, marked respectively by the use of arms and implements of stone, of bronze, and of iron, seems to have originated in the discoveries recently made by the examination of the refuse heaps of Denmark and the pile buildings of the Swiss lakes. .. There can be little doubt but that the *three ages above indicated did really exist. **1944** V. G. Childe *Progress & Archæol.* i. 5 Of course Thomsen's three 'Ages' are just periods of this relative kind and would be better designated *Stages.* **1794** A. Young *Trav. France* II. xix. 420 The provinces of Loraine, Alsace, the *three Bishoprics, and the West Indies, not included. **1910** H. N. Williams *Henri II* xxi. 271 The princes..authorised him to take possession of the towns of Toul, Metz and Verdun—the 'Three Bishoprics'. **1964** C. Duffy *Wild Goose & Eagle* viii. 111 Conti..might be tempted to harry the Three Bishoprics and the Austrian-garrisoned Duchy of Luxemburg. **1816** Playfair *Nat. Phil.* II. 263 Mayer has also sought to determine the Sun's parallax from one of the lunar equations, as deduced from the solution of the problem of the *three bodies. **1858** Cayley *Math. Papers* III. 97 The problem of three or more bodies is considered by Sir W. R. Hamilton in his two..memoirs on a general method in Dynamics, *Phil. Trans.* 1834 and 1835. **1885** *Cath. Dict.* s.v. *Three Chapters,* The condemnation of the *three chapters means the condemnation of (1) Theodore of Mopsuestia, his person, and his writings, (2) of Theodoret's writings against Cyril and the Ephesine Council, (3) of a letter from Ibas to Maris the Persian, also against Cyril and the Council. **1751** *Three chears [see cheer *sb.* 8]. **1840** *Brother Jonathan* 10 Oct. 4/6 They gave him three cheers. **1907** G. B. Shaw *John Bull's Other Island* ii. 30 Three cheers for ould Ireland, is it? **1970** G. F. Newman *Sir, You Bastard* vi. 174 Three cheers for any good publicity we can get. **1887** Kipling in *Civil & Mil. Gaz.* 11 Mar. (*title*) The *three musketeers. **1903** G. B. Shaw *Man & Superman* p. xxviii, He and I and Mr Sidney Webb were sowing our political wild oats as a sort of Fabian Three Musketeers. **1923** Three musketeers [see blow *v.*[1] 1 b]. **1979** *Nature* 8 Nov. 136/2 Those were the three musketeers who soon agreed that in publishing their joint work they would always share the credit for all ideas, whoever had thought them up. **1582** Allen *Martyrd. Campion* (1908) 36 He was also very skilful in the *three tongues. **1561** T. Hoby tr. *Castiglione's Courtyer* ii. (1577) M iij, To play your Comedye yee shall neede..as much wood as is in Sclauonia..and for preparation of the Tragedie *three trees is enough. **1582** Breton *Toyes Idle Head* (Grosart) 28/2 For commonly, such knaues as these Doe ende their lyves vpon three trees. **1822** Scott *Nigel* xvii, The captain, who was in the habit..of paying his losses with *three vowels. **1867** *Chambers's Encycl.* IX. 419/2 The visit of the three magi or *wise men of the East. **1904** Three wise men [used s.v. Magus 2]. **1961** *Ann. Reg. 1960* 467 The conference decided that three wise men (who later became four) should recommend the best means of co-ordinating Western economic policies. **1976** *Hansard Commons* 9 June 1578 The three wise men..who make up the Programme Complaints Commission. **1979** G. St. Aubyn *Edward VII* iv. 185 The Prince of Wales decided..to submit the negotiations to the Prime Minister, the Lord Chancellor and Lord Hartington... These three wise men produced a memorandum.

h. With letters of the alphabet, as *the three B's, the three C's, the three H's,* etc., referring to alliterative collocations.

See also *the three F's* (F III. 2); *the three L's* (L 7); *the three R's* (R II. 2b).

1909 J. R. Ware *Passing Eng.* 244/2 *Three B's, the (Clerical),* bright, brief, and brotherly—the modern protest against the sleepy nature of a majority of the 19th century church services. **1934** Webster s.v., *Three B's, Music,* the three great composers, Bach, Beethoven, and Brahms. **1969** Three B's [see off *adj.* 4]. **1885** *Three C's [see C I. 1]. **1976** *Casper* (Wyoming) *Star-Tribune* 29 June 3/3 Q. In money matters, what's meant by 'The Three Cs'? A. That's a term used by the credit experts. Capital, capacity to pay and collectibility. Of the three, capacity to pay is generally thought to be the most important, capital the least. **1974** P. Wright *Lang. Brit. Industry* xii. 105 Alliteration, slang and a desire to hide the meaning all contribute to the *three Hs, standing for 'high, hot, and a hell of a lot', and used when a soft soap and water enema has to be applied. **1976** *Guardian Weekly* 10 Oct. 12/4 Women's groups rebelling against the old commandment of the '*Three Ks'—Kinder, Kirche, Küche (children, church and kitchen). **1938** J. Daniels *Southerner* 136 It was impressive how directly the town's merchants made their appeal to poverty with the heavy necessities of living—the *three M's, meat, meal and molasses. **1955** D. W. Maurer in *Publ. Amer. Dialect Soc.* xxiv. 187 Excuses for *missing meets* are sometimes delicately referred to as the **three esses: shit, shave,* and *shine.* **1929** F. C. Bowen *Sea Slang* 140 Three Ss, The. The old naval rule to promotion, to mind your three Ss. That is to say, to be Sober, Silly and Civil.

2. Used vaguely for a small or trifling number; a few. So *three or four.* Cf. Two *or three.*

1534 More *Comf. agst. Trib.* iii. Wks. 1247/2 So very a childishe fantasy, that in a matter almost of three chippes..neuer should mooue any man. **1596** Harington *Apol. Ajax* (1814) 39 After they have roved three or four idle wordes. **1638** R. Baker tr. *Balzac's Lett.* II 39 If they have but three words of latin. **1825** T. Hook *Sayings* Ser. ii. *Man of Many Fr.* I. 182 But as to his anger..I don't care three of his sugar-loaves. **1842** Borrow *Bible in Spain* xli. (Pelh. Libr.) 283, I but said three words to the alcayde of the prison.

3. Absolutely or with ellipsis of sb. (most often *persons*; otherwise to be supplied from context).

More specifically, short for *three years* (of age); *three tines* (of a stag's horns); also for *three pounds, shillings, pence, farthings, inches,* etc., as *three ten* = £3. 10; *three and three* = 3*s.* 3*d.*; *one and eleven-three* = 1*s.* 11¾*d.*; *three foot three* = 3 ft. 3 in.

1382 Wyclif *Matt.* xviii. 20 For where two or three shulen be gedrid in my name, ther am I in the midil of hem. **1412–20** Lydg. *Chron. Troy* iv. 4640 Þis þre han made a suggestioun Vn-to þe kyng touchynge þe trete. *c* **1489** Caxton *Sonnes of Aymon* xvi. 377 The other thre he broughte to the dongeon. **1596** Dalrymple tr. *Leslie's Hist. Scot.* (S.T.S) I. 13 Fresche water lochis..; that abundes in mony kyndes of fische, cheiflie in thrie, Killine, Skait, and Makrell. **1675** *Essex Papers* (Camden) I. 319 That Trear. had lately procured from King thirteen thousand pounds for Essex, of which Trear. was to have three for himselfe. **1683** J. Mason *Spir. Songs* xxiii. iv, The Three, when Christ did make the Fourth, Found Fire as meek as Air. **1688** R. Holme *Armoury* ii. 131/2 Hares, 2 a Brase, 3 a Lease. *Mod.* Which three do you choose? Any three you please.

c **1425** *Seven Sag.* (P.) 55 Er ther passe thre and fyve, Yf he have wyt and his on lyve. **1840** Thackeray *Barber Cox* Jan., Sold in pots at two-and-three, and three-and-nine. **1872** H. Kingsley *Hornby Mills,* etc. II. 40 'How much money have you got, my lord?'..'Three-and-sixpence'. **1884** Jefferies *Red Deer* iv. 69 At the upper end the antler divides into three points, called three on top. **1906** C. Mansfield *Girl & Gods* v, You told me yesterday you could not afford a pug bitch you wanted, and she was only three ten. **1909** *Lady's Realm* Mar. 554/2 The chubby, dirty-faced child of three. **1913** J. Vaizey *College Girl* ii. xxvi. 360, I paid eleven-three for it. **1947** *Vogue* Apr. 73/1 Three-and-eleven-three is much less than four shillings. **1962** M. Duffy *That's how it Was* ii. 33 The girls would buy a few yards of stuff at two-and-eleven, three, a yard. **1965** *Canad. Jrnl. Linguistics* Spring 121 A three-by-five card was made out for each address. **1978** W. Stovall *Presidential Emergency* v. 119 Solving his problems on three-by-five index cards.

II. *sb.* (With plural *threes.*)

1. a. The abstract number.

c **1200** Ormin 11266 3iff þu sammnesst þreo till þreo þa findesst tu þær sexe. *a* **1300** *Cursor M.* 21747 O four and thre qua tels euen He sal þe numbre mak o seuen. **1387–8** T. Usk *Test. Love* iii. i. (Skeat) l. 3 Among all nombres thre is determined for moste certain. **1588** Shaks. *L.L.L.* v. ii. 495 By Ioue, I alwaies tooke three threes for nine. **1597** Hooker *Eccl. Pol.* v. lxxix. §7 Three, being the mysticall number of Gods unsearchable perfection within himselfe. **1825** T. Hook *Sayings* Ser. ii. *Passion & Princ.* vi. III. 53 It would be..useless..to expatiate upon the qualities attributable to the number Three, or quote the Graces, the Fates [etc.].

b. The figure (3) denoting this number. Also, a figure resembling that denoting the number three, *esp.* in *Skating.*

1895 *Outing* (U.S.) XXVII. 204/1 Granted control of the outside and inside edges, and the many eights, threes, loops, etc. are simplified at once. **1903** [see grape-vine 2 c]. **1938** J. Cary *Castle Corner* 378 He cut a three. **1975** *Oxf. Compan. Sports & Games* 522/1 The three, a two-lobed figure, so named because the turn involved at the extreme end of each circle leaves a tracing on the ice resembling the numeral '3'.

2. A group or set of three things or persons. *spec.* **a.** A card, a domino, or the side of a die marked with three pips or spots. † *three, two, and ace*: name of an old card game. **b.** *Cricket.* A hit for which three runs are obtained.

c **1540** J. Heywood *Four P.P.* E ij, Take thre of the yongest and thre of the eldest... And when all these threes be had a sunder, Of eche three, two..Shall be founde shrewes. **1578** Timme *Caluine on Gen.* 196 By seven and seven, understand not so many pairs of every kind, but threese, to the which one beast is added over and above. **1587** Saunders *Voy. Tripolie* B iv b, Wee were cheaned three and three to an oare. **1599** Minsheu *Span. Dict., Dial.* iii. 25 Games of chiefest price, as the Reynado, the three, two and ace, still trumpe. **1607** Shaks. *Cor.* ii. iii. 47 We are ..to come by him where he stands, by ones, by twoes, and by threes. **1755** Johnson, *Kayle,* a kind of play..in which nine holes ranged in three's are made in the ground. **1830** Lindley *Nat. Syst. Bot.* 137 Flowers solitary, or in pairs or threes. **1836** in 'Bat' *Cricket Man.* (1850) 100 Threes, fours, and fives appear as easy for him to get. **1870** Hardy & Ware *Mod. Hoyle* 77 Fifteen can be made in several ways [in cribbage]; for example, ten and five,..three fours and a three. **1889** W. B. Yeats *Wanderings of Oisin* 130 Children sing in twos and threes. **1953** R. Chandler *Long Goodbye* xix. 117 Three shots, three misses. I hate it when they come in threes. **1977** 'M. Yorke' *Cost of Silence* xvi. 130 'First Pedro—then Emma Widnes—now Jamie Renshaw. Who'll be next?'..'Things do go in threes, don't they?'

c. in military drill, when each three men form a unit for the purpose of wheeling.

1796 *Instr. & Reg. Cavalry* (1813) 63 When a division wheels to a flank rank by three's. **1832** *Regul. Instr. Cavalry* 14 The Threes wheel at once, upon the word 'Threes Right', 'Threes Left', or 'Threes about'. **1847** *Infantry Man.* (1854) 61 The company..may form threes.

3. a. *ellipt.* for *three parts* or *divisions*; as *to divide a thing in(to) three.*

13.. *Cursor M.* 10178 (Gött.) In thre [*Cott.* thrin] his godis did he dele. *c* **1400** *Destr. Troy* 1146 Þat oþer part of our pupull put we in thre! *c* **1425** Wyntoun *Cron.* i. ix. 534 As men may be a roundall se Merkit to be delt in thre. *c* **1435** *Torr. Portugal* 686 He brast hys schyld on thre. *c* **1450** *Songs, Carols,* etc. (E.E.T.S.) 20/79 They clave my harte in III. **18..** G. Macdonald *Ballads, Leg. Corrievrechan* xiii, The hemp was broken in three.

b. With omission of *hours* (of the day): *three o'clock* (also *attrib.*), also simply *three*; *half-past three*; *three fifteen,* 3.15 = a quarter past three.

c **1460** *Wisdom* 797 in *Macro Plays* 61 At þe parvise I wyll be,..be-twyn ij ande iij. **1530** Palsgr. 714/1 We shal nat set in tyll to morowe thre of the clocke. **1762** Foote *Orator* i. Wks. 1799 I. 191 We shall be sure to find them at three at the Shakspeare. **1814** Scott *Diary* 17 Aug., in *Lockhart,* On board at half-past three. **1902** Eliz. L. Banks *Newspaper Girl* 42, I want you to go out at once and report that three o'clock meeting at the Methodist Church. *Mod.* Our train starts at three fifteen.

c. In phrases and specific uses. *Three in One,* (*a*) = the Trinity, the Triune God (also *One in Three,* and simply *Three*), (*b*) *attrib.* as *three-in-one,* combining three items, functions, etc., in one whole; (*c*) *Three in One* (attrib. also *Three-in-One*), the proprietary name of a lubricating oil. *three to one,* three chances to one; †in the ratio of three to one, three times (in amount) (quot. 1683). *three-o(h)-three* (usually printed ·303), a rifle of ·303 calibre; also, ammunition manufactured for use in such a rifle. *three times three,* i.e. cheers; hence as a verb (*nonce-use*), to utter nine times. *rule of three*: see rule *sb.* 8 b.

a **1711** Ken *Hymnarium* Poet. Wks. 1721 II. 68 Most holy, holy, holy *Three, Harmonious Unity. **1849** Rorison *Hymn,* Three in One, and One in Three, Ruler of the earth and sea. **1909** *Grocery Catal.* (T. Eaton & Co.) 26/2 Three-in-One Hand Saw..combining in one tool a saw, 2 ft. rule and square. **1928** *Trade Marks Jrnl.* 22 Aug. 1354/1 '*Three in One*'... Lubricating oil. Three in One Oil Co..., 130, William Street, City, County, and State of New York, United States of America; manufacturers. **1931** *Advertiser* (Adelaide) 7 Oct. 10 (Advt.), A three-in-one garment, comprising vest, bloomers, and underskirt. **1962** E. Snow *Other Side of River* (1963) xxxii. 245 We call it a three-in-one technique. It combines, in all grades, teaching, practical research work, and actual production. **1967** N. Marsh *Death at Dolphin* i. 14 The key..refused to turn... 'You want a touch of the old free-in-one... Oil, mate. Loobrication.' **1970** W. Klatt in D. J. Dwyer *China Now* (1974) xviii. 341 Lin Piao gave high priority to the task of 'struggle—criticism—transformation' which is apparently being carried out by the chief organ of the new order, i.e. the 'three-in-one combination' of the Revolutionary Committees, embracing representatives of the revolutionary cadres, of the People's Liberation Army and of the revolutionary masses. **1977** O. Schell *China* (1978) i. 104 And those old factories with pollution problems must form three-in-one groups to solve their problems. **1979** T. Gifford *Hollywood Gothic* (1980) xxiv. 240 The lock had gotten rusty, but..Three-in-One oil did the job. **1683** Penn *Let. to Comm. Free Soc. Traders Pennsylv.* 1 The Back-Lands being generally *three to one Richer than those that lie by Navigable Waters. **1766** Earl March in Jesse *Selwyn & Contemp.* (1843) II. 28 The odds are three to one on my side. **1903** *Kynock Jrnl.* Aug.–Sept. 128/1 The ·303 Sporting Rifle. The *·303 is used a great deal as a sporting rifle, and being the Government arm is quoted in comparison with Express rifles. **1928** E. Blunden *Undertones of War* xix. 202, I was at least more skilful with the shots of epigram than with the three-o-three of the small-arms factory. **1959** [see *thirty-eight* s.v. thirty *sb.* 4]. **1981** J. Barnett *Firing Squad* viii. 79 Firearm certificate holders on ·303 Lee Enfields..were mostly rifle clubs. **1789** *Loiterer* 19 Sept. 4 My health has been drank in a bumper, with *three times three, by every Club of Tradesmen in the City. **1813** *Chron.* in *Ann. Reg.* 51/2 Next followed 'The King', drank standing, and with three times three. **1850** Tennyson *In Mem.* Concl. xxvi, Again the feast, the speech, the glee,..The crowning cup, the three-times-three. **1829** E. Elliott *Jacobin's Prayer* iv, And when pale Freedom's champions fell, He three-times-three'd his carnage yell.

d. *threes,* short for three per cent stock, or three per cents (so *three-and-a-halfs*); for three-quarter-backs (in Football); for three-pennyworth (of liquor).

1850 Thackeray *Pendennis* xxxvi, I'm told she has six hundred thousand pounds in the Threes. **1891** *Daily News* 27 Apr. 3/2 People who had 'threes' of beer and 'large lagers', both of which were over half a pint. **1895** *Ibid.* 30 Sept. 2/6 French Threes rose on the day 15 c., to 101 for money. *Ibid.* 30 Dec. 7/4 Three-and-a-Halfs declined 25 c., to 105.45 for money. **1905** *Westm. Gaz.* 12 Dec. 9/2 Another run by the Cambridge 'threes' took them down to the Oxford line once more.

III. Combinations (unlimited in number, of which the following are examples):

1. a. Adjectives formed of *three* and a sb. (usually in singular), meaning 'of, pertaining to, consisting of, containing, measuring, etc. three of the things named', as *three-act* (consisting of three acts), *three-bout* (formed by three bouts of the plough), *three-age, -alarm, -bean, -blade, -bushel, -car, -cent, -class, -colour, -core, -cylinder, -dollar, -electrode, -fathom, -foot (-feet), -guinea, -hand, -horse, -hour(-s), -island, -judge, -lane* [lane *sb.* 2 d], *-level, -line, -member, mile, -minute, -month(-s), -party, -person, -phase* (phase *sb.* 3), *-pin, -pint, -place, -plait, -ply, -point, -position, -pound, -rail, -row, -shilling, -speed, -stage, -stairs, -story, -strand, -syllable, -term, -throw, -tier, -volume, -wheel, -word.* **b.** Parasynthetic adjs. formed on similar collocations + -ed[2], = 'having or characterized by three of the things named', as *three-aisled* (having three aisles), *three-angled, -armed, -bladed, -bodied, -bolted, -branched, -chinned, -coloured, -coned, -corded, -crowned, -dayed, -dimensioned, -dropped, -eared, -engined, -eyed, -faced, -fanged, -fingered, -floored, -formed, -grained, -groined, -handed, -heeled, -hooped, -lettered, -mouthed, -necked, -nooked, -numbered, -phased, -pointed, -pronged, -ribbed, -roomed, -shaped, -soled, -storied, -stranded, -suited, -syllabled, -tailed, -tiered, -toothed, -wheeled, -wormed,* etc.; *spec.* in botanical and zoological adjs., as *three-capsuled, -celled, -fibred, -flowered, -jointed, -lobed, -nerved, -petalled, -seeded, -valved,* etc. (now largely superseded by terms derived from Latin, as *tricapsular, trilocular, trivalvular,* etc.); also with other endings, as †*three-dayen* (of three days), *three-dimensional,* †*three-shapen, three-weekly.* **c.** Parasynthetic sbs. in *-er* [see -er[1] 1], as *three-miler* (one who goes three miles), *three-mover* [mover[1] 7], *three-acter, -alarmer, -hitter, -railer, -tonner, -volumer, -wheeler.*

1825 H. WILSON *Memoirs* II. 76, I..fixed, upon Moliere's comedy of the Malade Imaginaire, which I hastily transformed into an English *three-act piece! **1905** CHESTERTON *Heretics* 280 Some absurd shrill and affected voice, such as we only hear from a duchess in a three-act farce. **1948** C. MCCULLERS in *Mademoiselle* Sept. 257/1 By autumn I was writing a *three-acter about revenge and incest. **1957** G. BIBBY *Testimony of Spade* 31 He [*sc.* Christian Thomsen] was constrained to write a short account of his arrangement of the Copenhagen museum and of his *Three Age system. **1970** BRAY & TRUMP *Dict. Archaeol.* 231/2 *Three Age System*, the scheme for dividing prehistory into a stone age, bronze age and iron age. It was first formulated by C. Thomsen 1816–19. **1766** ENTICK *London* IV. 204 Making a *three-isled cathedral. **1932** *Amer. Speech* VII. 337 *Three alarm fire, used with negative to indicate mediocrity. *a* **1975** WODEHOUSE *Sunset at Blandings* (1977) xii. 80 Lord Emsworth entered looking like a refugee from a three-alarm fire. **1950** O. NASH *Family Reunion* 80 The author's attention has been called to a type of conflagration known as a *three-alarmer. **1865** *Cornh. Mag.* July 34 The thrice *three-angled beech nut shell. **1976** *Billings* (Montana) *Gaz.* 17 June 7-B/1 Create a picnic-like atmosphere with such favorites as potato salad and *three bean salad. **1931** D. ROSE *J. de la Cierva's Wings of Tomorrow* vi. 92 For certain purposes the *three-blade rotor may prove the most efficient. **1967** *Jane's Surface Skimmer Systems 1967–68* 9 (*caption*) A. Turboméca Artouste IIC drives..two three-blade variable-pitch propellers for thrust. *c* **1830** *Glouc. Farm Rep.* 32 in *Libr. Usef. Knowl., Husb.* III, Cut with a *three-bladed knife. **1574** HELLOWES *Gueuara's Fam. Ep.* (1577) 336, I giue my condemned soule and life to the infernall *three bodyed Pluto. **1667** MILTON *P.L.* VI. 764 Beside him hung his Bow And Quiver with *three-bolted Thunder stor'd. **1770–4** A. HUNTER *Georg. Ess.* (1803) IV. 38 Suppose..the field to be formed into *three-bout ridges. **1617** HIERON *Wks.* II. 352 This treble or *three-branched sufficiencie. **1860** *All Year Round* No. 69. 448 A hectolitre contains a trifle more than a *three-bushel English corn-sack. **1881** C. E. TURNER in *Macm. Mag.* XLIV. 307 A gray riding-coat, with a *three-caped collar. **1944** R. CHANDLER *Lady in Lake* iv. 23 Outside the wall to the left was the *three-car garage. **1980** J. MCNEIL *Spy Game* ix. 93 There was..a three-car garage. **1793** MARTYN *Lang. Bot.*, *Three-celled Pericarp. **1851** *Statutes at Large U.S.A.* IX. 587 No ingots shall be used for the coinage of the *three-cent pieces herein authorized, of which the quality differs more than five-thousandths from the legal standard. **1898** P. L. FORD *Hon. Peter Stirling* 281 The three-cent papers..abuse me. **1946** *Publ. Amer. Dial. Soc.* VI. 37 To feel like a three-cent piece with a hole in it. (To feel worthless and do-less.) **1910** *Westm. Gaz.* 14 Feb. 6/4 [Germany] The detested *three-class system..and..the system of promotion of certain classes of electors from one class to another on other than property qualifications. **1980** *Jrnl. R. Soc. Arts* June 411/1 Gone are..the limitations on political rights of a 'three-class franchise'. **1741** *Compl. Fam.-Piece* II. iii. 403 *Three colour'd Violet or Heart's Ease. **1649** *Lanc. Tracts* (Chetham Soc.) 277 A *three-corded scourge. **1922** *B.I. Hand-bk.* (Brit. Insulated & Helsby Cables Ltd.) (ed. 3) 106 *Three-core cables. **1958** *Spectator* 8 Aug. 190/2, 3-core electric wiring. **1604** HIERON *Wks.* I. 576 To maintaine the state Of your *three-crowned potentate. **1904** *Westm. Gaz.* 28 Dec. 3/1 The best work on the Midland [Railway] was accomplished with *three-cylinder compounds. **1422** tr. *Secreta Secret., Priv. Priv.* 200 God Sente..Ionas to the grete Cite of Nynyvee, wyche was a *thre-dayen Iornay. **1904** KIPLING *Traffics & Discoveries* 212 'Heaven is beautiful, Earth is ugly,' The *three-dimensioned preacher saith. **1858** J. H. HICKCOX *Hist. Acct. Amer. Coinage* 56 *Three Dollar gold coins were coined..under an act passed in 1853. **1618** CHAPMAN *Hesiod, Georg.* II. 426 A *three-ear'd tripod. **1918** *Wireless World* VI. 144 De Forest was experimenting with a *three-electrode valve. **1932** *Discovery* July 216/1 The starting point of modern wireless is what is known as the three-electrode thermionic valve. **1931** *Nineteenth Cent.* Feb. 159 The *three-engined types. **1967** *Economist* 16 Sept. 1022/1 What might happen to passenger traffic if one's competitor should advertise 'three engined safety'. **1598** Q. ELIZ. *Plutarch* x. 30 Axing for..*thre yead men. **1689** *Lond. Gaz.* No. 2510/4 A *Three faced Steel Seal. **1915** D. H. LAWRENCE *Let.* 15 July in *Let. to B. Russell* (1948) 53 Liberty, Equality & Fraternity is the *three-fanged serpent. **1828** G. W. BRIDGES *Ann. Jamaica* II. xiv. 183 *Three-fingered Jack, the notorious rebel. **1793** MARTYN *Lang. Bot.*, *Three-flowered Peduncle. **1861** MISS PRATT *Flower. Pl.* V. 298 Three-flowered Rush. **1567** GOLDING *Ovid's Met.* VII. (1593) 157 Our *threeformed Goddesse. **1766** *Compl. Farmer* s.v. *Meadow*, With a shovel, hoe, or *three grained fork. **1719** HAMILTON *Ep. to Ramsay* 24 Aug., in *R.'s Poems*, The pleasure..snoovt away like *three-hand ombre. **1680** COTTON *Compl. Gamester* x. 83 Some play at two handed, or *three handed Whist. **1792** J. WOODFORDE *Diary* 10 Feb. (1927) III. 335 After Coffee and Tea we got to Cards to three-handed Cribbage. **1907** W. M. COCKRUM *Pioneer Hist. Indiana* xiv. 344 Dancing was the principal amusement ..three- and four-handed reels and jigs. **1937** G. GREENE *19 Stories* (1947) 57 They had played their usual rubber of three-handed bridge. **1976** 'TREVANIAN' *Main* (1977) ii. 23 They were playing three-handed cut-throat. *a* **1889** G. M. HOPKINS *Poems* (1967) 180 Yet Arthur is a Bowman: his *three-heeled timber'll hit The bald..gold. **1976** *Billings* (Montana) *Gaz.* 30 June 3-E/1 John Candelaria fired a *three-hitter and tripled in two runs during an eight-run first inning. **1593** SHAKS. *2 Hen. VI*, IV. ii. 72 The *three hoop'd pot, shall haue ten hoopes. **1812** SIR J. SINCLAIR *Syst. Husb. Scot.* I. 75 A *three-horse power does very well for potatoe-oats, when the corn is fed in by a careful hand. **1906** KROPOTKIN *Mem. Revolutionist* (1908) I. v. 23 A three-horse carriage. **1592** SHAKS. *Rom. & Jul.* III. ii. 99, I, thy *three houres wife. **1920** *Blackw. Mag.* July 1/1 The *Ulidia* was a typical '*three-island' tramp steamer. **1962** A. G. COURSE *Dict. Naut. Terms* 198 *Three island ship*, a vessel with a raised forecastle forward, a raised bridge deck amidships, and a raised poop aft. **1837** *Penny Cycl.* IX. 13/2 [The antennæ] are generally..*three-jointed. **1944** *Mod. Lang. Notes* Dec. 515, *3-judge court. **1981** *Times of India* 30 Aug. 4/5 A three-judge bench. **1929** *Sat. Even. Post* 16 Nov. 41/2 On a *three-lane boulevard a local driver generally keeps well toward the center. **1972** M. JONES *Life on Dole* xii. 88 This road..was eventually completed not as a dual carriageway but as a three-lane road. **1653** R. SANDERS *Physiogn.* 69 The *three-lettered name of the 72 Angels. **1956** J. LOTZ in L. White *Frontiers of Knowledge* xiv. 221 This multistage, *three-level construction involving phonemes, morphemes, and sentences characterizes natural language. **1979** *Guardian Weekly* 28 Oct. 18/4 A three-level promenade. **1793** MARTYN *Lang. Bot.*, *Three-lobed leaf. **1833** *Penny Cycl.* I. 77/1 Leaves.., three-lobed. **1944** *Mod. Lang. Notes* Dec. 515 The *three-member compound is peculiarly modern. **1957** LD. HAILEY *African Survey 1956* vi. 303 Such elections..might be tried as an experiment in two three-member constituencies. **1889** *Cent. Dict.*, *Three-mile limit. **1895** *Outing* (U.S.) XXVI. 459/1 In the three-mile run England has a decided advantage. **1911** *Daily Colonist* (Victoria, B.C.) 14 Apr. 15/4 The schooners were well within the three-mile limit, poaching on the British Columbia fisheries grounds. **1977** G. V. HIGGINS *Dreamland* xii. 151 Small freighters. Plying ..between Scotland and the three-mile limits, until Repeal, they easily returned their cost of purchase. **1899** *Daily News* 19 July 6/5 The *three-milers were the next to appear. **1838** E. B. BROWNING *Seraphim & Other Poems* 160 In the eyes all undefiled Of a little *three months' child. **1861** *Chicago Tribune* 26 May 1/3 So shameful has been the treatment of many of the three month volunteers, that most of them will certainly return home as soon as their terms expire. **1977** J. M. JOHNSON in Douglas & Johnson *Existential Sociol.* viii. 251 The three-month period when the events occurred. **1697** DRYDEN *Virg. Georg.* IV. 692 The gaping *three-mouth'd Dog forgets to snarl. **1881** *Brentano's Chess Monthly* June 86 The sacrifice of Queen is very much the same as in the 'Welcome' *three-mover. **1891** *Athenæum* 31 Jan. 148/2 The current runs..in favour of short [chess] problems; nothing beyond three-movers is even looked at. **1799** H. GURNEY *Cupid & Psyche* xx. (1800) 51 Charm the *three-neck'd dog of Hell! **1793** MARTYN *Lang. Bot.*, *Three-nerved Leaf. **1606** SHAKS. *Ant. & Cl.* IV. vi. 6 The *three nook'd world. **1876** G. M. HOPKINS *Wr. Deutschland* ix, in *Poems* (1967) 54 Be adored among men, God, *three-numberèd form. **1925** J. A. SPENDER *Public Life* II. xix. 27 The difficulties of the *three-party system. **1978** A. GILCHRIST *Cod Wars* viii. 66 As a result of the 1956 election [in Iceland], the conservative-dominated coalition of the Independence and Progressive parties gave way to a three-party coalition from which the Independence Party was excluded. **1964** I. L. HOROWITZ *New Sociol.* 33 Models devised to deal with two- or *three-person groups need not lead to the trivialization of sociology. **1892** *Lightning* 3 Mar. *Gloss. Electr. Terms*, **Three phase system*, a system of distribution of electrical energy in which three alternating currents, each differing from the two others by one third of the period, are used. **1922** Three-phase system [see BIAS *v.* 5]. **1926** *Jrnl. Iron & Steel Inst.* CXIV. 77 These solutions of the important problem gave a simple and comparatively cheap installation, without transforming the three-phase current to direct current or..regulating the speed of the generator. **1961** *Listener* 9 Nov. 767/2 The normal three-phase alternating current system. **1868** J. C. ATKINSON *Gloss. Cleveland Dial.* 325 *Merls*, sb... Other names are.. Five-pin, Nine-pin, *Three-pin, Morris or Merels. **1940** *Chambers's Techn. Dict.* 848/1 *Three-pin plug*, a plug with three contact pins, two for the main circuit and one for the earth connexion. **1974** A. ROSS *Bradford Business* 75 A length of insulated cable..snaked across the floor to a three-pin socket. **1522** in *Bury Wills* (Camden) 115 A *thre pynt pott of pewter. **1947** H. REICHENBACH *Elem. Symbolic Logic* §17. 83 A *three-place function is given by the verb 'gives' in the sentence 'Peter gives Paul a book'. **1964** R. H. ROBINS *Gen. Linguistics* viii. 330 English plosive and nasal consonants fall into a three-place..system, bilabial, alveolar, velar. **1868** *Rep. U.S. Commissioner Agric.* (1869) 51 Carpets, treble ingrain, *three-ply, and worsted chain Venetian. **1905** *Timber Trades Jrnl.* 21 Jan. 72/1 Date cases, made entirely of three-ply wood. **1910**, etc. Three ply [see PLY *sb.* 1]. **1797** *Encycl. Brit.* (ed. 3) XIV. 606/1 One dog-tooth, and five or six *three-pointed grinders. **1921** *Daily Mail Year Bk.* 112/2 The new..railway is..equipped with *three-position signals. **1971** *Gloss. Electrotechnical, Power Terms* (*B.S.I.*) I. iii. 16 *Three-position relay*, a relay which has one unenergized and two energized conditions. **1866** CRUMP *Banking* x. 223 Edward VI. Gold. *Three-pound piece, sovereign [etc.]. **1711** *Lond. Gaz.* No. 4915/4 A small *three prong'd silver Fork. **1944** T. H. WISDOM *Triumph over Tunisia* vi. 54 Jerry..dropped a load of three-pronged spikes on the runway. **1968** N. MITCHELL *Sir George Cunningham* vii. 138 A Punjabi called Khurshid Anwar.. was on the Hazara border organising a three-pronged drive into Kashmir. **1890** 'R. BOLDREWOOD' *Col. Reformer* (1891) 283 The Colonel..rode his horse over a stiff *three-railer [fence]. **1828** SIR J. E. SMITH *Eng. Flora* II. 93 Partial bracteas five, ovate, acute, *three-ribbed. **1844** *Port Phillip Patriot* 11 July 1/3 A *three-roomed hut. **1593** G. HARVEY *Pierce's Super.* 109 The *three-shapen Geryon. *a* **1817** JANE AUSTEN *Persuasion* (1818) IV. vi. 116 She has a blister on one of her heels, as large as a *three shilling piece. **1640–1** *Kirkcudbr. War-Comm. Min. Bk.* (1855) 149 The inch of *thrie-solled schoes, of the best leather, be sold at twa shillings twa pennies. **1895** *People* 6 Jan. 4/5 The *three-speed gear bicycle invented by Messrs. Lindley and Biggs. **1902** *Daily Chron.* 21 Nov. 11/4 The Sturmey-Archer three-speed gear,..an elaboration of the well-tried 'Hub' two-speed gear, is exhibited by the Raleigh Cycle Company. **1977** *New Yorker* 9 May 34/1 A..young woman..had just bought a three-speed Raleigh. *Ibid.* 34/2 Why did I buy a three-speed? **1977** *Lancs. Life* Nov. 138/2 Her bike had broken down—something to do with the three-speed. **1980** J. L. CARR *Month in Country* 69 You can have Dad's bike... It's a three-speed and the chain has an oil bath. **1936** *Discovery* Sept. 299/2 The proposed *three-stage rocket-ship. **1965** *Language* XLI. 117 A three-stage process of increasing deprovincialization in Russian linguistics. **1852** W. WICKENDEN *Hunchback's Chest* 330 In his *three-stairs back, Grove Street. **1814** SCOTT *Diary* 22 Aug., in *Lockhart*, There is a decent *three-storied house, belonging to the laird. **1939** *Oxoniensia* IV. 127 No. 2 is part of a 'three-storeyed' pitcher, showing a combination of various decorative ideas. **1963** J. ROBINSON *Honest to God* i. 13 The traditional language of a three-storeyed universe. **1832** G. LONG *Egypt. Antiq.* I. ix. 199 To the height of 60 feet, which is considerably above the ordinary elevation of *three-story houses. **1841** CATLIN *N. Amer. Ind.* I. xxi. 147 Its string was *three stranded. **1605** SHAKS. *Lear* II. ii. 16 A base,.. beggerly, *three-suited, hundred pound, filthy woosted-stocking knaue. **1886** *Amer. Jrnl. Philol.* VII. 246 In early Latin this energetic stress-accent was not bound by the *three-syllable limit. **1964** W. S. ALLEN in D. Abercrombie et al. *Daniel Jones* 4 It [*sc.* stress] falls..on a light antepenultimate only because of the overriding three-syllable rule, which will not permit it to recede further. **1718** M. W. MONTAGU *Let.* 19 May (1965) I. 413 'Tis common for the Heirs of a great *three-tail'd Bassa not to be rich enough to keep in repair the House he built. **1802–12** BENTHAM *Ration. Judic. Evid.* (1827) I. 11 A three-tailed instead of a five-tailed bandage. **1848** THACKERAY *Bk. Snobs* iii, A three-tailed Pasha. **1957** E. B. JONES *Instrument Technol.* III. II. 72 (*caption*) Response of a *three-term controller to an artificial disturbance. **1977** *Time* 21 Nov. 28/2 In Cleveland, scrappy Dennis Kucinich, 31, a former three-term city councilman, edged out Edward Feighan, 30, the candidate of the regular Democratic organization. **1883** *Heal & Son Catal.: Dining Rm., Libr., & Drawing Rm. Furnit.* 215 *Three-tier Whatnot, in Walnut or Ebonised. **1957** LD. HAILEY *African Survey 1956* viii. 467 In form this constituted a 'three-tier' system of Councils, but it was the District Council which was to form the focal point in it. **1977** *Guardian Weekly* 23 Oct. 8/3 The three-tier agreement is to be made up of a treaty limiting the numbers of certain strategic weapons for the period of eight years, a protocol imposing certain limits on other weapons for three years, and a statement of principles looking toward major arms reductions in the future. **1822** GALT *Provost* xliii, Wearing ..a white three-tiered wig. **1973** 'M. INNES' *Appleby's Answer* xv. 129 A three-tiered contraption loaded with pastries and éclairs. **1883** J. D. J. KELLY in *Harper's Mag.* Aug. 445/2 Diminutive *three-tonners..were cruising. *a* **1944** K. DOUGLAS *Alamein to Zem Zem* (1946) 38 This necessitated sweating about to find a three-tonner or a tank to tow us out. **1971** B. W. ALDISS *Soldier Erect* 39 We marched off the platform in good order..and transferred our kit to a line of three-tonners standing waiting for us outside the station. **1382** WYCLIF *1 Sam.* ii. 13 The child.. hadde a flesh hook *thre tothid in his hoond. **1793** MARTYN *Lang. Bot.*, *Three-valved pericarp. **1877–84** F. E. HULME *Wild Fl.* p. viii, Capsule obtusely three-angled and three-valved. **1844** R. P. WARD *Chatsworth* I. 115 The fee-simple of this estate in *three-volume-noveldom. **1864** G. MEREDITH *Let.* Oct. (1912) I. 162 My 'plain story' is first to right me and then the *3 volumer will play trumpets. **1927** *Daily Tel.* 27 Sept. 5/1 When the 'three-volumer' went out it was thought we had ceased to ask for literary quantity. **1889** *Athenæum* 10 Aug. 184/3 He has made clear the distinction between the 'racionabilis secta' and suit to the *three-weekly court. **1936** *Discovery* Nov. 351/1 An 1888 Benz *three-wheel motor car. **1973** *Times* 30 Oct. 4/1 A new three-wheel car, the Robin, for which an average fuel consumption of 50 miles to the gallon is claimed. **1656** EARL MONM. tr. *Boccalini's Advts. fr. Parnass.* I. xxxi. (1674) 35 A *three-wheel'd Charret. **1900** W. S. CHURCHILL in *Morning Post* 1 Jan. 5/7 Suddenly three-wheeled things appeared on the crest. **1981** *London Mag.* July 69/1 We were rattled and rocked in our three-wheeled *samlor*. **1886** *Cyclist's Tour. Club Gaz.* IV. 123 The safeties and *three-wheelers [tricycles]. **1958** C. FREMLIN *Hours before Dawn* iv. 41 She saw Mrs Henderson's miniature three-wheeler drawn up in front of the house. **1975** *Times* 22 Dec. 3/1 Their three-wheeler disintegrated in collision with another car. **1880** 'MARK TWAIN' *Tramp Abroad* xxx. 321 They know a *word* here and there, of a foreign language, or a few little beggarly *three-word phrases, filched from the back of the Dictionary. **1978** R. LUDLUM *Holcroft Covenant* xiii. 154 He had sent Sam a three-word cablegram from the airport in Lisbon. **1683** MOXON *Mech. Exerc., Printing* xi. ¶1 A *Three-Worm'd Spindle.

2. Special combinations and collocations: **three-address** *a. Computers*, (employing instructions) having three addresses, two that specify the location of the two operands and one that specifies where the result is to be stored; †**three-aged** *a.*, living through three generations; **three-anti** *China* = SANFAN; **three-awned** *a.*, having three awns, as in ***three-awned grass***, the name of several American grasses of the genus *Aristida*; also called *beard-grass* (*Cent. Dict.* 1891); **three-axis** *a.*, having or involving an ability to be rotated about each of three mutually perpendicular axes; **three-ball** *a.*, of a golf match: involving three players, each playing his own ball; **three-ball(s)**, a three-ball golf match; **three-banded** *a.*, having three bands, as in ***three-banded armadillo***, an armadillo of the genus *Tolypeutes*, distinguished by the shell consisting of three bands; **three-bar** *a.*, (*a*) *Geom.* applied to a curve generated by the motion of three bars pivoted together; (*b*) of an electric fire: having three heating elements; **three-bearded** *a.*, having three beards (BEARD *sb.* 3 a) or barbels, as ***three-bearded cod*** or ***rockling*** (see ROCKLING); **three-birds**, (*a*) a showy garden species of toad-flax, *Linaria triornithophora*, from Spain; (*b*) name of two American orchids, *Pogonia pendula* and *Triphora trianthophora*, also called *nodding cap* (*Cent. Dict.* 1891, and *Suppl.* 1909); **three-body** *a. Math.* and *Physics*, involving or pertaining to three objects or particles; ***three-body problem*** = *problem of three bodies* (see sense I. 1 g); **three-bottle** *a.*, applied to one who can drink three bottles of wine at a sitting; **three-card** *a.*, pertaining to or played with three cards, as ***three-card monte*** (see MONTE); ***three-card trick***, a trick popular with race-course sharpers, also known as *find the lady*, in which a queen and two other cards are spread out face downwards, and bystanders invited to bet which is the queen;

three-centre *a. Chem.*, applied to a bond in which the orbital of the two electrons forming it is spread over three contributing atoms; **three-circle diagram**, a Venn diagram in which there are three circles; **three-cleft** *a.*, cleft or divided into three segments, trifid; **three-coat** *a.*, requiring three coats, as work in plastering and painting; **three-cocked** *a.*, having three cocks, as *three-cocked hat* (COCKED *ppl. a.*[2]); also absol. as *sb.*; † **three-corned** [CORNED[2] 2], three-cornered; **three-crop** *a.*, of a ewe: that has borne lambs in three successive years; **three-cushion** *a.*, designating a type of billiards in which the cushion must be struck at least three times by a ball at each play (see quot 1957); **three-D, 3-D, 3D** *a.*, three-dimensional, used *esp.* of a stereoptic process of filming; also *ellipt.* as *sb.*, a three-dimensional realization or state; **three-day** *a.*, extending over three days, that takes three days to complete or come to an end, as *three-day event*, a tripartite equestrian competition, usu. with the first day given over to dressage, the second to cross-country riding, and the third to show-jumping in a ring (hence *three-day eventer*, a horse that participates in such competitions), *three-day week*, a reduced working week of only three days; **three-day(s) fever** = DENGUE; **three-dimensional** *a.*, having, or appearing to have, the three dimensions of length, breadth, and depth (cf. DIMENSION *sb.* 3 a); = TRI-DIMENSIONAL *a.*; also *fig.*; hence **three-dimensionality**; **three-dimensionally** *adv.*; **three-eight** (usually 3/8) *Mus.*, denoting a 'time' or rhythm with three quavers in a bar; **three estates**: see ESTATE *sb.* 6, 7; † **three-fallow** *v.*, to fallow threefold: cf. THRY-FALLOW; **three-field** *a.*, noting a method of agriculture in which three fields are worked on a three-course system of two crops and a fallow; **three-figure** *a.*, consisting of three digits; one hundred or more (pounds, runs, miles per hour, etc.); calculated to three decimal places; **three-four** (usually 3/4) *Mus.*, denoting a 'time' or rhythm with three crotchets in a bar; **three-halves power**, the square root of the cube of a number; in *Electronics* used *attrib.* to designate a law that the anode current of a valve is proportional to the three-halves power of the anode voltage; **three-high** *a.*: see quots.; **three-holes**, a boys' game of marbles; **three-horned** *a.*, having three horns; esp. applied to particular species of animals; **Three Hours** (or **Hours'**) **Service**, a devotional service lasting from 12 to 3 o'clock in the afternoon of Good Friday, designed to cover the hours of the crucifixion of Jesus Christ; also *ellipt.*; **three-in-hand**, three horses drawing a vehicle, driven by one person; **three-iron** *a.*, welded together from three strands of iron; **three-letter man**, (*a*) *U.S.*, a person awarded a mark of distinction (cf. LETTER *sb.*[1] 1 e) in three different sports; (*b*) *colloq.*, an obnoxious person; **three-life** *a.*, applied to a system of tenure under which (till 1854) land (esp. ecclesiastical and college estates) was held during the joint lives of three persons or the longest liver of them; **three-light**, (*a*) *adj.* having three lights: see LIGHT *sb.* 10; also *ellipt.*; (*b*) *sb.* 'a chandelier or candelabrum with three lamps for candles' (*Cent. Dict.* 1891); † **three-like** *a.*, having three equal sides, equilateral (of a triangle); **three-line, three-lined** *a.*, having, consisting of, or marked with three lines; in *Printing*, extending through three lines, as a large capital letter; also, *three-line* (occas. *-lined*) ***whip***, a written notice, underlined three times to indicate great urgency, requesting the attendance of members of Parliament at a particular parliamentary session; the discipline of such a notice; **three-martini lunch** *U.S.*, a lavish lunch, esp. one charged to a business expense account; **three-minute** *a.*, that occupies, or completes or is completed within, three minutes (in quot. 1833, that completes a mile in three minutes); that indicates the passage of three minutes; **three-nines** *a.*, (*a*) (see quot. 1927); (*b*) of a telephone call: made to an emergency service, for which in the U.K. 999 is dialled; **three-out**: see OUT *sb.* 1 b; **three-pipe problem**, a problem which requires considerable thought (for the duration of the smoking of three pipes of tobacco); **three-pounder**, a thing weighing three pounds; a gun firing a three-pound ball; **three-putt** *v. intr.* (Golf), to take three putts to hole the ball on a particular green; *trans.* to play (a green or hole) taking three putts; **three-ring, -ringed circus**, a circus having three rings; hence *fig.*, a showy or extravagant spectacle; a scene of confusion or disorder; cf. *one-ring circus* s.v. ONE *numeral a.* 33; † **three-shafted** *a.* [cf. Ger. *dreischäftig*], of cloth, woven with treble web-shafts (see SHAFT), three-stranded; **three-shear**, a sheep between its third and fourth shearing; **three-sixty**, in various sports, aerobatics, etc.: a turn through three-hundred-and-sixty degrees; **three-space**, three-dimensional space; **three-spined** *a.*, having three spines, as ***three-spined stickleback***, the commonest species of STICKLEBACK *Gasterosteus aculeatus*; **three-spot**, a three-pipped playing card; **three-star** *a.*, having, displaying, bearing as insignia, or being designated by three stars as a mark of quality, rank, etc., usu. in a four- or five-star grading system (see STAR *sb.*[1] 10 c, d); *spec.* used to designate: (*a*) a good quality French brandy; (*b*) a highly-rated hotel or restaurant; (*c*) *U.S.*, a lieutenant general (in rank below a general, above a major general); (*d*) a grade of petrol; (*e*) *transf.*, anything of high quality or in a high degree characteristic; also *ellipt.* as *sb.*, three-star brandy, petrol, etc.; **three-striper**: see STRIPER 1; **three-thorned** *a.*, having three thorns, or triple thorns, as ***three-thorned acacia***, a name for the honey-locust (*Gleditschia triacanthos*), a N. American tree having thorns in groups of three; = *honey locust* s.v. HONEY *sb.* 7 b; † **three-threads**, a mixture of common ale, porter, and double (or twopenny) beer, popular *c* 1700: see quots.; **three-throw** *a.*, having three throws (see THROW *sb.* [2] 2), as a ***three-throw crank***; hence, having such a crank, as ***three-throw pump*** or ***engine***, one worked by a three-throw crank-shaft; **three-time** *a.*, that has occurred or been done three times; of a person, to whom something has happened, or who has achieved something, three times; spec. *three-time loser*, a person who has served three prison sentences; **three-two** (usually 3/2) *Mus.*, denoting a 'time' or rhythm with three minims in a bar; **three-up**, a game resembling pitch and toss; **three-valued** *a.*, having three values; *spec.* in *Philos.*, designating a logical system or technique which incorporates a third value such as indeterminacy, uncertainty, half-truth, etc., in addition to the values of truth and falsehood customary in two-valued systems; **three-water** *a.*, *Naut.* diluted with three times its bulk of water, as ***three-water grog*** or ***rum***; also *absol.*; **three-went way**, *dial.* a point where three roads meet without intersecting; cf. FOUR-WENT; **three-wire** *a.*, (*a*) applied to a system of distributing electric power, involving three mains and two dynamos, the two outer mains being joined to the free terminals of the dynamos, and the central main to a conductor joining the two; (*b*) applied to a system of mooring used to keep an airship or balloon at a constant height from the ground; **three-wood**, (*a*) *Archery*, a bow made of three pieces of wood; also *attrib.*; (*b*) *Golf*, a wooden club providing medium loft, formerly called a spoon (SPOON *sb.* 4 c).

1948 *Math. Tables & other Aids to Computation* III. 69 The control of this machine is accomplished, for the most part, by means of *three-address orders. In contrast, the 'Mark I' at Harvard uses a two-address system. **1970** O. DOPPING *Computers & Data Processing* vi. 103 A three-address machine. **1976** BANKS & DOUPNIK *Introd. Computer Sci.* vii. 242 The principal disadvantage of three address instructions is their great length and consequent excessive use of memory space. **1697** CREECH tr. *Manilius* I. 30 Great Atreus Sons,.. With *three-ag'd Nestor. **1966**, etc. *Three-anti [see SANFAN]. **1975** A. WATSON *Living in China* iv. 90 The 'three anti' campaign which opposed the three evils of corruption, waste and excessive red tape in the Party and government. **1962** V. GRISSOM in *Into Orbit* 78 We had to learn from scratch.. how to manipulate the new *three-axis control stick and make the precise adjustments in yaw, pitch and roll. **1977** *Dædalus* Fall 52 Some [satellites] are provided .. with three-axis stabilization, so that their instruments can be pointed steadily, for long periods of time, to a chosen target. **1839** *Rules of Hon. Co. Edin. Golfers* in C. B. Clapcott *Rules of Ten Oldest Golf Clubs* (1935) 69 In a *Three-ball match, the Ball nearest the hole, and within the prescribed distance, must be lifted, if the third party require it, where the Player does so or not. **1890** H. G. HUTCHINSON *Golf* ix. 241 The three-ball match;.. these matches are of two kinds, that wherin each plays against each, and that wherin two are in combination against a third, though each play his individual ball. **1901** *Rules of Golf* 5 Three players may play against each other, each playing his own ball, when the match is called 'a three-ball match'. **1952** *Chambers's Jrnl.* May 299/1 The Major introduced them without enthusiasm and Basil promptly attached himself to the party, much to the Major's annoyance, for he hated *three-balls. **1976** *Webster's Sports Dict.* 450/1 *Three-ball*, a golf match in which 3 players compete against each other with each playing his own ball. **1800** SHAW *Gen. Zool.* I. 188 *Three-banded Armadillo.. may be considered.. as the most elegant of the whole genus;.. it is a native of Brazil. **1956** G. DURRELL *Drunken Forest* iv. 75 Inside the hat, curled into a tight ball, lay.. a three-banded armadillo. **1966** E. PALMER *Plains of Camdeboo* xii. 196 A three-banded plover was paddling in the furrow. **1875** S. ROBERTS in *Proc. Lond. Math. Soc.* 11 Nov. 14, I propose to extend.. to general *three-bar motion a discussion.. of some particular cases. **1876** CAYLEY *Math. Papers* IX. 551 The Three-Bar Curve is derived from the motion of a system of three bars.. pivoted to each other, and to two fixed points. **1973** 'H. CARMICHAEL' *Too Late for Tears* vi. 81 In the hearth stood a *3-bar electric fire. **1979** T. WISEMAN *Game of Secrets* iv. 49 A three-bar electric heater. **1936** *Physical Rev.* L. 638/2 The procedure for the *three-body problem. **1968** M. S. LIVINGSTON *Particle Physics* iv. 74 Evidence that this is a three-body decay is that the electrons have a wide distribution in energy. **1972** *Sci. Amer.* Jan. 85/1 The Herzberg bands of O_2 and the atmospheric infrared bands probably both owe their origin to three-body association: $O + O + X \rightarrow O_2^* + X$, where X, the third atom.. is unchanged in the process. **1806** SURR *Winter in Lond.* III. 121 Metamorphosed from a *three-bottle man to the image of temperance. **1854** T. PARKER in Weiss *Life* (1863) II. 134 *Three-card-monte men, and gambling-house keepers. **1887** LOWELL *Tariff Reform* Wks. 1890 VI. 187 They.. play their three-card trick. **1920** C. SANDBURG *Smoke & Steel* 175 Pick-pockets, yeggs, three card men. **1938** [see BROAD *sb.* 6]. **1973** *Times* 19 Jan. 3/8 Three-card tricksters are a nuisance. They have someone posted to watch for the police, then they invite people to lay down money on which of three cards.. is the 'lady'. **1979** W. H. CANAWAY *Solid Gold Buddha* xxii. 145 Sam was as confused as a yokel watching a three-card artist. **1954** W. H. EBERHARDT et al. in *Jrnl. Chem. Physics* XXII. 989/1 In our approach, the only new, or rather, unfamiliar concept is that which we call the '*three-center bond'. **1978** *Further Perspectives Organic Chem.* (CIBA Symp.) 61 The short S–O bonds in the thioimine may reflect a three-centre bond. **1883** J. VENN in *Proc. Cambr. Philos. Soc.* IV. 51 Both Drobisch and Schröder have used what I have called.. the *three-circle diagram. **1952** W. V. QUINE *Methods of Logic* I. 79 We set up a three circle diagram as usual. **1793** MARTYN *Lang. Bot.*, *Three-cleft, *trifidus*. *Ibid.*, Three-cleft-palmate leaf. **1875** MORRIS *Æneid* II. 475 Three-cleft tongue. **1842** BRANDE *Dict. Sc.*, etc., **Three-coat Work*. In Architecture. **1877** KNIGHT *Dict. Mech.*, *Three-coat Work*. (Plastering.) The first is called *pricking-up* on lath... The second coat is called *floating*; the third, *set* or *finishing-coat*. **1813** LD. PALMERSTON in *Parl. Deb.* 8 Mar., To see the troops in the small *three cocked hats which they formerly wore. *a* **1608** DEE *Rel. Spirits* I. (1659) 83 The books be green, bright, and they be *three-corned. **1946** J. CARY *Moonlight* viii. 53 One heard first a single 'aw-aw' from some old *three-crop mother, followed at once by a hearty 'mey' from her stout lamb. **1960** *Farmer & Stockbreeder* 1 Mar. 77/3 Mr. McIlwraith also paid.. £180 for a three-crop ewe. **1910** *Encycl. Brit.* III. 939/2 There is also *Three-Cushion Carom.. and the Bank-Shot game. **1957** *Ibid.* III. 569/1 A count is validly made in three-cushion billiards in any one of four ways: (1) when the cue ball strikes an object ball and then strikes three or more cushions before striking the second object ball; (2) when the cue ball strikes three or more cushions before contacting the two object balls; (3) when the one ball strikes a cushion, then the first object ball, then two or more cushions and then the second object ball; (4) when the cue ball strikes two or more cushions, then the first object ball, then one or more cushions and finally the second object ball. **1974** *Mark Twain Jrnl.* Summer 3/1 Cure and Cutler played a game of three cushion billiards, a novelty at the time [*sc.* 1906]. **1952** *Jrnl. Soc. Motion Picture & Television Engineers* Oct. 249/1 Up to now the production of three-dimensional (*3-D) films has been sporadic. **1953** *Sun* (Baltimore) 5 Feb. 14/1 We receive with mixed reaction the news that three-dimensional motion pictures, coyly called '3-D', will shortly come into general distribution. **1953**, etc. 3-D, 3D [see D., dimensional, s.v. D III. 3]. **1955** W. GADDIS *Recognitions* III. v. 914 She's terrific, even in 3-D she'd be terrific. **1966** *T.V. Times* (Austral.) 7 Dec. 10/2 Three-D Television is now the subject of experiment in several overseas countries, particularly Russia. **1971** 'D. HALLIDAY' *Dolly & Doctor Bird* x. 130 Monopoly would maybe do. Or three-D noughts and crosses? **1983** *U.S.A. Today* 20 May 5D/4 But in a 3-D comic, futility flattens the actors even as the visual gimmick pops them out. **1890** *Pall Mall G.* 18 Aug. 2/1 Whether you go by a two-day or a *three-day coach. **1937** S. CLOETE *Turning Wheels* ix. 143 Three day sickness, which as a rule animals recovered from if left alone, meant abandoning beasts since there was no time to wait for them to recover. **1965** *N.Y. Herald Tribune* 18 Apr. 3 An annual three-day.. walk. **1976** *Times* 21 May 2/5 The committee's three-day conference on negotiated independence.. has been postponed. **1952** *Rules & Reg. governing One-Day Events* (Brit. Horse Soc.) 5 One Day combined Tests.. lead up to the Olympic *Three Day Event. **1963** E. H. EDWARDS *Saddlery* vii. 69 This is not of importance by the time one's horse is sufficiently advanced to perform Three Day Event tests. **1982** BARR & YORK *Official Sloane Ranger Handbk.* 152/1 The easiest house parties are for a sport—racing, three-day event, shooting. **1976** *Horse & Hound* 10 Dec. 57/1 (Advt.), An ideal type to sire top quality point-to-pointers and *three-day-eventers. **1974** *Times* 16 Feb. 1/1 The *three-day week will carry unemployment to a very high level. **1977** M. WALKER *National Front* vi. 147 The state of national emergency and the three-day week. **1897** *Allbutt's Syst. Med.* II. 376 Synonyms [of Dengue].. polka fever (Brazilian), *three days fever. **1878** *Three-dimensional [see DIMENSION *sb.* 3 a]. **1882** [see DIMENSIONAL *a.* 2]. **1920** W. W. STRONG *New Philos. of Mod. Sci.* xvi. 142 In gravitational phenomena a small disturbance leaves a circular trajectory finite in a three dimensional space. **1923** H. CRANE *Let.* 2 Mar. (1965) 129 O yes, the 'background of life'—and all that is still there, but that is only three-dimensional. **1925** B. DOBRÉE in W. Congreve *Comedies* p. xvii, Congreve.. made his people three-dimensional. **1953** *N.Y. Times* 19 Feb. 20 This much touted picture.. is advertised as the first feature made in the three-dimensional Natural Vision process. **1971** A. DRUMMOND *Auckland Jrnls. Vicesimus Lush* 22 His children .. emerge from the pages of his journals as sufficiently three-dimensional figures to be of interest to readers a century later. **1926** H. READ *Eng. Stained Glass* I. 11/2 *Three-dimensionality. Perspective and shading give the proper spatial relations of the various details represented. **1956** E. H. Hutten *Lang. Mod. Physics* vi. 208 This.. suggests that causal action exemplified by the inverse-square law is connected with the three-dimensionality of space. **1977** *Jrnl. Playing-Card Soc.* Nov. 69 The three-dimensionality of 19th- and 20th-century German cards is one of their distinguishing features. **1958** C. Smith in 'E. Crispin' *Best SF Three* 210 Light.. allowed the ships to reform *three-dimensionally.. as they moved from star to star. **1979** *Nature* 29 Mar. 439/2 The method for producing these three-dimensionally interconnected fibrous structures is described here. **1577** B. Googe *Heresbach's Husb.* i. (1586) 22 b, For some seede, you must not only twyfallowe and *threefallowe your ground, but also fourefallow it. **1868** *Rep. U.S. Commissioner Agric.* (1869) 156 The Polish *three-field farming. **1907** M. C. F. Morris *Nunburnholme* 251 Supposing the three-field system to be adopted. **1855** J. Lang *Forger's Wife* xv. 44 'There is not a really good placard on the walls—tens, and fifteens, and twenties; but not a single *three-figure gentleman' (he meant £100) 'among 'em.' **1861** C. Knight *Eng. Cycl.: Arts & Sci.* VII. 1007 A. De Morgan. Three-figure logarithms: three figures of numbers to three of logarithm, complete, on a sheet of 7½ by 6 inches. **1929** *Star* 21 Aug. 12/1 A three-figure stand. **1973** J. Wainwright *Devil you Don't* 5 It was a great car—a Jag. Mark II—well capable of three-figure speeds. **1978** R. V. Jones *Most Secret War* xxi. 174 Assuming.. that the three-figure entries were bearings. **1902** *Westm. Gaz.* 14 June 4/3 The new waltz,.. the 'Military Dip', is in *three-four waltz time, and has one dip to each three counts. **1920** *Proc. Inst. Radio Engineers* VIII. 70 At low plate voltages.. the measured values of the amplification constant are lower and the *three-halves power law does not appear to hold. **1963** B. Fozard *Instrumentation Nucl. Reactors* xi. 138 As the anode voltage is raised the equation to the anode characteristic takes the commonly assumed three-halves power law. **1877** Knight *Dict. Mech.*, **Three-high Roll* (Metal-working), a rolling-apparatus in which three rollers are arranged in a vertical series. **1881** Raymond *Mining Gloss.*, *Three-high train*, a roll-train composed of three rolls, the bar being entered on one side between the bottom and the middle roll, and on the other side between the middle and the upper roll. **1853** Lytton *My Novel* i. xi, Keep off the other boys from.. playing *three-holes and chuck-farthing. **1681** Grew *Musæum* i. vii. §2. 163 The little *Three-Horned Beetle, *Scarabæus Triceros minor.* **1887** Morris *Odyss.* xii. 135 Unto the Three-horned island she sent them aloof to dwell. [**1864** *Guardian* 30 Mar. 299/2 The English Church is indebted to Mr. Mackonochie for the revival of.. the admirable ancient Office in Commemoration of the Three Hours.] **1898** (*title*) The *three hours' service for Good Friday. **1923** *Spectator* 5 May 753/2 Two hours afterwards I went to the Three Hours at a church in a residential southern suburb. **1976** *Oxford Mission Q. Paper* July/Sept. 5 The little church was packed from beginning to end of the Three Hours. **1816** 'Quiz' *Grand Master* vii. 198 When Jove had found that *three in hand This Jehu did not understand. **1892** Greener *Breech-Loader* 5 Processes of Barrel Welding. (1) *Three-Iron Damascus; (2) Two-Iron Damascus. **1929** R. H. Barbour *Tod Hale on Nine* xxiv. 264 He wanted to be a '*three-letter man', and until a few days ago his chance had looked very bright. **1941** *Amer. Speech* XVI. 190 Three-letter man, F-A-G. **1946** J. Irving *Royal Navalese* 81 A three-letter man is a 'cad'. **1972** *Sci. Amer.* Feb. 114/2 A boxer of almost professional caliber; a three-letter man in college, a Rhodes scholar, he passed the bar examination but after only a year of practice decided 'to chuck the law for astronomy'. **1898** A. F. Leach *Beverley Act Bk.* I. p. xlv, In 1300, one of the Canons leased, on the usual *three-life system, some of the lands of his prebend. **1618** in Willis & Clark *Cambridge* (1886) I. 208 One *three light window and two single light windowes. **1853** in *Notes on Cheshire Churches* (Chetham Soc.) (1894) 10 Each side of the porch having open three-light windows. **1908–9** H. R. Barker *E. Suffolk Illustr.* 330 The east window is a Transitional three-light, and in the side walls are very good two-lights in square heads. **1937** *Burlington Mag.* Mar. 149/1 The three-light Peter de Dene window of the Minster. **1551** Recorde *Pathw. Knowl.* i. Defin., That the Greekes doo call *Isopleuron*, and Latine men *æquilaterum*: and in english it may be called a *threlike triangle. **1683** Moxon *Mech. Exerc., Printing* xxii. ¶ 5 He begins his Chapter.. with a.. *Three or Four-lin'd Letter. *a* **1912** *Mod.* A three-lined whip has been issued for to-night's division in the House of Commons. **1939** W. I. Jennings *Parliament* iii. 78 A 'three-line whip' indicates that all other engagements should be put aside. **1958** *Spectator* 27 June 826/3 A debate sufficiently important to warrant a three-line whip. **1975** J. P. Morgan *House of Lords & Labour Govt.* iv. 127 Labour Peers took their own vote on the question of the vote in the Lords, choosing a free vote, unlike M.P.s who agreed to submit to a three-line whip. **1972** G. McGovern in W. Safire *Polit. Dict.* (1978) 727/1 The rich businessman can deduct his *three-martini lunch, but you can't take off the price of a baloney sandwich. **1977** *Time* 26 Sept. 49/2 Carter has railed so vehemently against the 'three-martini lunch' that his staff has to come up with something. **1833** *Knickerbocker* I. 160 The present Mrs. S. admired his *three minute roan. **1857** *Uncle Jack the Fault Killer* ix. 131 My three-minute glass lets the sand run through just in three minutes, which is time to boil an egg. **1958** Three minute [see long-playing *a.*]. **1927** W. Collinson *Contemp. Eng.* 89 The house-agent's repulsive terminology e.g... a *three nines agreement (i.e 999 years). **1982** P. Turnbull *Dead Knock* i. 11 Tango Delta Foxtrot.. responded to a three-nines call for a fire appliance. **1891** A. Conan Doyle in *Strand Mag.* Aug. 197/2 It is quite a *three-pipe problem, and I beg that you won't speak to me for fifty minutes. **1976** *Lancet* 20 Nov. 1131/2 Appraising and comparing the effectiveness of what we do has certainly up to now proved to be what Sherlock Holmes would have called 'a 3-pipe problem'. **1684** J. Peter *Siege Vienna* 109 *Three pounders of Iron. **1872** H. Kingsley *Hornby Mills*, etc. II. 232 One three-pounder is worth fishing all day for. **1876** Bancroft *Hist. U.S.* V. xx. 568 The Hessians captured two brass three-pounders, which had lately arrived from France. **1946** *Sun* (Baltimore) 2 July 17/6 Joe Kirkwood.. scored a 74,.. *three-putting the last green. *Ibid.*, Lawson Little overshot the greens and three-putted frequently. **1978** *Detroit Free Press* 16 Apr. E7/3 McLendon.. three-putted the 18th about the same time. **1898** B. Matthews *Outlines in Local Color* 145 What good is a three-ringed circus to anybody, except the boss of it? **1904** *Everybody's Mag.* Aug. 161/2 A Barnum *three-ring circus compared to Henry H. Rogers's exhibitions. **1904** 'O. Henry' in *McClure's Mag.* Apr. 613/2 They commenced to scramble down, and for awhile we had a three-ringed circus. **1914** Kipling *Divers. Creatures* (1917) 394, I can see lots of things from here. It's like a three-ring circus! **1951**, **1955** [see circus 2 c]. **1981** D. Clark *Roast Eggs* viii. 159 Don't m'lud me... You turned my court into a damned three-ring circus. *c* **1440** *Promp. Parv.* 492/2 (MS. A.) *Thre schaftyd clothe, *trilix.* **1770–4** A. Hunter *Georg. Ess.* (1803) IV. 593 Under the necessity of wintering some of their *three-shears before they are marketable. **1886** C. Scott *Sheep-Farming* 18 After the third shearing, three-shear or four-shear, three or four year olds, are the definitions employed. **1927** C. A. Lindbergh *We* v. 82 One of the first lessons was the '*three sixty'—so named because its completion required a total change in direction of three hundred and sixty degrees. **1977** *Skateboard Special* Sept. 7/1 The first really difficult stunt I learned then was a three-sixty. That.. is a stunt where you spin the board through a full circle on its back wheels. **1972** *Sci. Amer.* Dec. 102/2 A Möbius strip, for example, has a handedness in *3-space that cannot be altered by twisting and stretching. **1977** *New York Rev. Bks.* 12 May 29/1 A plane is infinite and unbounded. Bend it through 'three-space' (i.e., three-dimensional space) and it can be the closed surface of a sphere. **1769** T. Pennant *Brit. Zool.* III. 217 The *three spined s[tickle] back... These are common in many of our rivers. **1836** W. Yarrell *Hist. Brit. Fishes* I. 77 The Three-spined Stickleback was first described by Belon. **1971** *Nature* 23 Apr. 536/2 The three-spined stickleback.. found sanctuary in the Atlantic. [**1871** G. H. Lewes *Let.* 27 Aug. in *Geo. Eliot Lett.* (1955) V. 180 Will you meanwhile order for me from the Stores.. 3 bottles of Martorell's three stars Brandy at 5/-.] **1879** R. J. Atcherley *Trip to Boërland* ii. 32 In the up-country towns of the Transvaal.. common brandy is retailed at 1*s.*, and '*Three Star' at 1*s.* 6*d.* per glass. **1929** *Amer. Speech* IV. 387 A little *three-star Hennessey* brought overland from Detroit. **1931** S. Cooke *This Motoring* xvii. 172 The.. Lion at Guildford.. is a typical three-star A.A. hotel. **1939** [see S.A.E., s.a.e. s.v. S 4 a]. **1944** *Mod. Lang. Notes* Dec. 526 Whereas once a sword, a ship, was given an epithet fit for a hero or a goddess, today a warrior is labelled in the manner of a manufactured product:.. *3-star general.* **1960** *Harper's Bazaar* July 19/1 The number of three-star restaurants in France has just dropped from 11 to 10. This reduction has been effected by the *Guide Michelin.* **1968** *Listener* 28 Mar. 405/3 Courvoisier V.S.O.P., he croaked, none of your rotten Three Star. *Ibid.* 1 Aug. 159/3 To ask for.. two gallons of three-star. **1973** J. Burrows *Like an Evening Gone* xvii. 220 'I'd respect any decent woman.' 'What about Tamara Tayne?' 'That three star whore? That's a different category.' **1973** H. Gilbert *Hotels with Empty Rooms* xiii. 114 He.. poured himself a glass of three-star cognac. **1977** *Air Mail* Spring 45/2 (Advt.), Six-berth luxury caravan for hire on three-star site with all amenities. **1977** A. Sampson *Arms Bazaar* xvii. 288 He is a stocky three-star general from Alabama.. on his tie was a three-star tie pin. **1979** *Country Life* 13 Sept. 807/2 The typical three-star menu.. of foie gras and truffles with everything... And still, in too many three-stars, foie gras with everything. **1982** S. Wilson *Dealer's Wheels* ix. 85 We filled up with three-star.. and I went to check the oil and tyres. **1818** *Mass Agric. Repository & Jrnl.* V. 56 Gleditsia Triacanthos. It is also called *Three-Thorned Acacia in the catalogues of nurserymen. **1822** *Hortus Angl.* II. 573 *Gleditschia Triacanthos.* Three thorned Acacia, or Honey Locust Tree. **1698** W. King tr. *Sorbière's Journ. Lond.* 35 He had a thousand such Sort of Liquors, as.. *Three Threads, Four Threads. *a* **1700** B. E. *Dict. Cant. Crew*, *Three-threads*, half common Ale, and the rest Stout or Double Beer. **1802** [see entire A. 2 b]. **1829** *Nat. Philos.* I. *Hydraulics* ii. 12 (Usef. Knowl. Soc.) Keeping two or.. three pumps constantly at work by what is called a triple or *three-throw crank. **1900** *Engineering Mag.* XIX. 726 Three-throw ram pump for dip workings. **1908** J. Kelley *Thirteen Yrs. Oregon Penitentiary* vii. 81 Pat came back again; he was a *three-time loser. **1914**, etc. Three-time [see loser 4]. **1943** P. Cheyney *You can always Duck* vi. 96 He's a three-time killer. **1979** *Tucson* (Arizona) *Citizen* 20 Sept. 6D/1 The Cats.. will be led into tomorrow's meet by three-time All-America selection Thom Hunt and 1978 All-American choice Dirk Lakeman. **1851** Mayhew *Lond. Labour* I. 12/1 'Shove-halfpenny' is another game played by them [costermongers]; so is '*Three up'. **1932** Lewis & Langford *Symbolic Logic* vii. 213 One such alternative is the *Three-valued Calculus, developed by Lukasiewicz and Tarski. *Ibid.*, If, in addition, the number ½ is taken, then we have the matrix of the three-valued system. **1934** *Mind* XLIII. 104 Professor Lukasiewicz is sole author of these systems, having originated the three-valued system in 1920, and *n*-valued systems in 1922. **1946** *Nature* 14 Sept. 356/2 This decisive step opens the way for the construction of a new non-Aristotelian logic, a 'three-valued logic' as it is called. **1965** N. Chomsky *Aspects of Theory of Syntax* 232 Thus we can regard.. gender as a three-valued.. dimension. **1967** *Encycl. Philos.* VII. 118/1 With this way of reconstructing quantum mechanics, use must be made of a three-valued logic. **1974** tr *Wertheim's Evol. & Revol.* i. 100 Three-valued prestige models were used by people who placed themselves in the middle class. **1840** *P. Parley's Ann.* I. 295 A large lump of salt beef, with some *three water grog. **1905** *Daily Chron.* 25 May 4/7 Rum and water came to be called 'grog' likewise, being 'two-water' or 'three-water' grog, according to the proportions of the mixture. **1787** *Kentish Trav. Comp.* 49 He gets to a *three-went way. **1898** *Westm. Gaz.* 9 July 7/2 There was some discussion as to the particular kind of electrical equipment to be used, but eventually the *three-wire system was adopted. **1933** *O.E.D. Suppl.*, Three wire mooring. **1934** J. A. Sinclair *Airships in Peace & War* ix. 186 Then came the three-wire system, which was first employed on the rigid airship No. 9 in 1917... To steady the bow, three wires were taken from the mooring point and attached to three bollards set in a triangle... A three-wire mooring was prepared at Pulham. **1875** *Encycl. Brit.* II. 376/1 Bows.. made of three pieces.. are called *three-woods... Three-wood bows being made a little reflex, should retain their shape. [**1938** R. A. Whitcombe *Golf's no Mystery* xiii. 80 The spoon—or as it is called the No. 3 wood—is one of the golfer's greatest friends.] **1949** B. Hogan *Power Golf* ii. 15 Three wood.. 235 [yards]. **1960** *Times* 24 June 19/2 Second shots with a three-wood and a one-iron at these two holes brought him just short of the green in each case.

three-colour (stress variable), *a.* [three *a.*]

1. Utilizing or involving three distinct colours or wavelengths of light, usu. as a means of reproducing any desired colour by a combination of three primary colours in appropriate proportions. Cf. trichromatic *a.*

1893 *Jrnl. Soc. Arts* 19 May 669/1 This three-colour print, a reproduction of a chromo-lithograph. **1898** *Daily News* 15 Oct. 6/3 A very cheap way of producing.. necessary block for three-colour printing. **1902** *Daily Chron.* 10 Jan. 6/6 Methods of colour-photography,.. the 'three-colour process' invented by Professor Lippman. **1906** [see additive *a.* c]. **1932** R. C. Bayley *Compl. Photographer* xxiv. 291 The amateur who makes his own three-colour prints. **1972** [see psychophysical *a.*]. **1978** Pasachoff & Kutner *University Astron.* iii. 55 Thousands of stars have had their colors measured with this UBV set of filters; we call the process three-color photometry... A four-color system, uvby, has ultraviolet, violet, blue and yellow filters.

2. Designating *san ts'ai* ware; also *ellipt.* as *sb.*

1933 *Burlington Mag.* Nov. 211/1 The early Ming three-colour ware. **1959**, **1972** [see san ts'ai].

'three-'corner (stress var.), *a.* Of or pertaining to three corners (quot. *a* 1548); having three corners, three-cornered, triangular.

a **1548** Hall *Chron., Hen. VI* 122 The Frenche kyng, perceiuyng this toune [Laigny], to be the thre corner key, betwene the territories of the Englishemen, the Burgonyons, and his awne. **1683** Wood *Life* 3 Dec. (O.H.S.) III. 84 He pointed to the dore, and bid me 'be gone', with his three corner cap. **1902** Marshall *Metal Tools* 38 Three-corner files are very useful for cleaning out the sharp corners of square holes,.. for sharpening saw teeth, or for filing nicks in a piece of steel before breaking it off.

So **three-cornerism** (*nonce-wd.*), the fact or system of having 'three-cornered' constituencies; **three-corner jack** *Austral.* = *three-cornered jack* s.v. three-cornered *a.* 3; **three-corner-ways, -wise** *advs.*, with three corners, triangularly.

1884 *Edin. Rev.* Jan. 294 No diagnosis will discover *three-cornerism to be the cause of the disease. **1919** G. E. A. Russell *Wild Life in Bushland* 32 Springing from the centre or core of each burr are three long spikes or prongs, often half an inch in length—an uninviting thing to sit upon. Most bushmen will recognise the seed—it is the Centralian-famed '*three-corner jack'. **1748** H. Glasse *Art of Cookery* (ed. 3) ix. 199 Toast some thin Slices of Bread cut *three-corner ways. **1862** T. A. Trollope *Marietta* I. xii. 228 Kerchief folded *three-cornerwise.

three-cornered ('θriːˈkɔːnəd: str. var.), *a.*

1. a. Having three corners or angles; triangular (in plan or in cross-section).

c **1400** Maundev. iii. 15 Costantynoble.. is iij cornered. *c* **1400** *Lanfranc's Cirurg.* 36 Haue a nedle þre cornerid. **1594** Blundevil *Exerc.* iii. i. (1636) 274 Of Triangles or three-cornerd figures. **1668** Culpepper & Cole *Barthol. Anat.* i. xviii. 49 Somtimes they are three-corner'd, seldom round. **1833** T. Hook *Parson's Dau.* ii. i, Immediately following.. came a three-cornered note from Lady Gorgon. **1855** O. W. Holmes *Poems* 86 The old three-cornered hat.

b. *transf.* Applied to a constituency represented by three members.

Such constituencies were a feature of the electoral system for the House of Commons from 1867 to 1885; each elector having the right to vote for not more than two candidates, which enabled a strong minority to elect one of the representatives.

1882 Ogilvie, Three-cornered constituency. **1883** *Manch. Guard.* 22 Oct. 5/2 What shall be done with the three-cornered constituencies?

c. Applied to a contest, discussion, or the like, between three persons.

1891 Kipling *Light that Failed* xii. (1900) 197 Let us rather.. consider whether Torp's three-cornered ministrations are exactly what Dick needs just now. **1894** H. Gardener *Unoff. Patriot* 59 They had a three-cornered fight with Bradley's mulatto, Ned. *Mod.* The election in Kilmarnock Burghs was a three-cornered fight.

2. a. Of a horse: Awkwardly shaped. *colloq.*

1861 Whyte Melville *Mkt. Harb.* iv. 28 The grey.. and the bay, with a little three-cornered jumping hack. **1890** 'R. Boldrewood' *Col. Reformer* (1891) 386 And the horses? Sell every three-cornered wretch of 'em.

b. *fig.* Awkward, cross-grained, peevish; cf. angular *a.* 4. (Also quasi-*adv.*)

c **1850** E. Farmer *Scrap Bk.* (1869) 96 Matters run three-cornered. **1876** Geo. Eliot *Dan. Der.* xxxiii, A three-cornered, impracticable fellow. **1879** F. W. Robinson *Coward Consc.* iii. xviii, This hard, three-cornered family.

3. three-cornered jack *Austral.*, the spiny burr of the annual weed, *Emex australis.*

1953 A. Upfield *Murder must Wait* xxv. 223 'You lie there.'.. 'But not on the three-cornered jacks.'.. Her husband.. swept the place clean of the skin-piercing burrs.

Hence **'three-'corneredness**, triangularity; **'three-'corneredwise** *adv.*, triangularly.

1682 T. Flatman *Heraclitus Ridens* No. 68 (1713) II. 169 A Place in Egypt, call'd *Delta*, from the Three-corner'dness of its Shape. **1580** Hollyband *Treas. Fr. Tong*, *Triangulaire*, three cornerdwise, or after three corners.

'three-deck, *a. rare.* = next.

1692 Luttrell *Brief Rel.* (1857) II. 636, 3 three deck ships were lately launched at Brest. **1708** *Lond. Gaz.* No. 4423/7 The Boyn, a three Deck Ship of 80 Guns. **1797** *Encycl. Brit.* (ed. 3) XVII. 403/1 The middle deck in three-deck ships.

'three-decked (-dɛkt), *a. rare.* Having three decks; ***three-decked ship*** = next, 1.

1692 DELAVAL in *Lond. Gaz.* No. 2769/3, I found 3 three Deck'd Ships of the Enemies. **1834** *Encycl. Metrop.* (1845) VI. 343/1 The Royal Navy is divided into the following classes and denominations. 1. Rated ships, *viz. First rate*, all three-decked ships.

'three-'decker. [f. *three-deck*: see DECKER².]

1. a. A three-decked ship; formerly *spec.* a line-of-battle ship carrying guns on three decks.

1792 A. YOUNG *Trav. France* 181 The bason of Toulon, with ranges of three deckers, and other large men of war. **1795** [see DECKER²]. **1797** *Encycl. Brit.* (ed. 3) XVII. 403/1 In three-deckers it [the fire hearth] is..on the middle deck. **1855** TENNYSON *Maud* I. I. xiii, If..the rushing battle-bolt sang from the three-decker out of the foam.

b. *fig.* Applied to a thing (or person) of great size or importance.

1835 E. FITZGERALD *Lett.* (1889) I. 34 Pray do write to me: a few lines soon are better than a three-decker a month hence. **1836** E. HOWARD *R. Reefer* xlv, Three deckers—words of Latin or Greek derivation. **1877** BLACK *Green Past.* xxiv, He went over to Mrs. Blythe,..and sat down by that majestic three-decker. **1886** DOWDEN *Shelley* (1887) I. iii. 115 Some great three-decker of orthodoxy.

2. *transf.* Something consisting of three ranges or divisions: *spec.* **a.** Nickname for the three-storied pulpit formerly in use, consisting of the desk for the clerk, the reading desk, and the pulpit proper, one above another. **b.** A skirt with three flounces. **c.** A three-volume novel. **d.** A three-storey building. *U.S. local.*

1852 A. MOZLEY in *Christian Remembrancer* July 92 In the midst of the church stands, elaborately carved, the offensive structure of pulpit, reading-desk, and clerk's desk; in fact, a regular old three-decker in full sail westward. **1874** MICKLETHWAITE *Mod. Par. Churches* 56 The Georgian three-decker, the few surviving examples of which are now such objects of scorn. **1894** KIPLING in *Sat. Rev.* 14 July 44/1 The old three-decker. And the three-volume novel is doomed. **1895** *Westm. Gaz.* 26 Apr. 2/1 The long-winded novel of our forefathers—what you may call the old three-decker of fiction. **1909** *Daily Chron.* 3 May 7/4 That graceful form of skirt, which consists of three flounces (known sometimes to the irreverent as a 'three-decker'). **1910** GATHORNE-HARDY *Mem. 1st Earl Cranbrook* I. 115 In the place now occupied by the present one [chancel arch] the old 'three-decker' stood [in 1858]. **1942** BERREY & VAN DEN BARK *Amer. Thes. Slang* §83/1 *Three-* (or more) *decker*, a building of three, or more, stories. **1961** L. MUMFORD *City in History* xv. 465 Vast wooden firetraps called three-deckers in New England, happily blessed with open-air porches. **1978** J. CARROLL *Mortal Friends* II. iii. 151 The flat, the top floor of a Southie three-decker, was large enough.

3. *attrib.* (in senses 1 b and 2).

1860 O. W. HOLMES *Prof. Breakf.-t.* ii, A boy..with a three-decker brain. **1890** *John Bull* 5 Apr. 229/1 In the latter part of the eighteenth and first part of the nineteenth centuries..great 'three-decker' pulpits blocked up the chancels. **1898** *Daily News* 29 Sept. 3/4 The 'three-decker' skirt is supplemented by a three-decker cape. **1904** *Daily Chron.* 27 Apr. 7/4 The winding rope attached to the three-decker cage parted, and it dropped a distance of 2,000 ft. **1926** G. ADE *Let.* 8 Sept. (1973) 110 While some of us have been building chicken coops.., Mr. Dreiser has been creating sky-scrapers. He makes the old three-decker novel look like a pamphlet. **1981** *N. & Q.* June 271/1 The widespread circulation of Evangelical tracts and sermons helped to create a sympathetic readership for the voluminous three-decker novel.

† **'three-ˌdouble,** *a. Obs.* 'Doubled' or folded in three; consisting of three layers, courses, thicknesses, etc.; threefold.

1541 R. COPLAND *Guydon's Quest. Chirurg.* Qj, Ouer that a lynnen cloth thre dowble. **1613** *Uncasing of Machivils Instr.* 16 A Falling-band, or a three-double ruffe. **1653** H. COGAN *Pinto's Trav.* xxxii. (1663) 129 Having a chain of Pearl three double about his neck. **1658** J. ROWLAND *Moufet's Theat. Ins.* 953 Terrible for biting,..piercing through a three double stocking and boots likewise. **1728** E. SMITH *Compleat Housewife* (ed. 2) 128 Butter Papers three double, one white, and two brown. **1874** HARDY *Far from Madding Crowd* I. viii. 105 'And he's growed terrible crooked, too, lately,' Jacob continued, surveying his father's figure, which was rather more bowed than his own. 'Really, one may say that father there is three-double.'

So † **three-double** *v.*, to treble; † **three-doubled** *a.*, threefold, triple.

1558 PHAER *Æneid* VII. U iij b, Threedubbeld shyrtes Of golde. **1580** HOLLYBAND *Treas. Fr. Tong*, *Tripler*, to three double.

'three-'edged (-ɛdʒd: stress var.), *a.* Having three edges. Also *fig.*

1398 TREVISA *Barth. De P.R.* XVII. xxxv. (Bodl. MS.), Segge..is acounted amonge kindes of rissches, as Sias seiþ, and cleped it a þre egged ruyssche. **1541** R. COPLAND *Guydon's Quest. Chirurg.* L iij b, Nedles..euen and smoth, and thre edged at the poynte. **1685** *Lond. Gaz.* No. 2085/4 Lost.., a large Silver Hilted Sword, with..a long three edged blade. **1793** MARTYN *Lang. Bot.*, Three-cornered or Three-edged, *trigonus*. **1898** G. W. E. RUSSELL *Collect. & Recoll.* xix. (1903) 178 This three-edged compliment has seldom been surpassed. **1900** B. D. JACKSON *Gloss. Bot. Terms* 270/2 *Three-edged*, with three sides,..and three acute angles, triquetrous.

'three-'farthings. In the literal sense: see FARTHING. Also, money of the value of three farthings; hence the name of a silver coin of that value issued by Queen Elizabeth.

1561 Q. ELIZ. *Proclam.* 15 Nov., Because a halfpeny cannot be made of such finenesse to beare any conuenient bulke, an other small peece shall also be coyned of three farthynges..whiche..shalbe of meere fine starling syluer. **1588** SHAKS. *L.L.L.* III. i. 140 Remuneration, O, that's the Latine word for three-farthings. *Ibid.* 150 Threefarthings worth of Silke. **1598** B. JONSON *Ev. Man in Hum.* II. i, He values me at a crack'd three-farthings, for aught I see. *a* **1616** BEAUM. & FL. *Scornf. Lady* III. i, Whip'd and then crop'd, For washing out the roses in three farthings, To make 'em pence. **1898** G. B. RAWLINGS *Brit. Coinage* 65 The threefarthings..was the least of all the coins having a rose behind the ear. *Ibid.* [see THREE-HALFPENCE].

Hence **three-'farthing** *a.*, of the value of three farthings; hence, paltry, insignificant.

c **1600** *Timon* III. v. (Shaks. Soc.) 56 Away, away, thou poore three farthing Iacke! **1656** EARL MONM. tr. *Boccalini, Pol. Touchstone* (1674) 276 They had put to arbitriment the salvation of mens souls upon a three-farthing business. **1822** tr. *Aristoph., Plutus* 15 Do you suppose the despotism.. would be worth a three-farthing piece, were you [Plutus] to recover? **1898** G. B. RAWLINGS *Brit. Coinage* 64 Two new denominations in silver are introduced in this [Elizabeth's] reign, namely, the threehalfpenny and threefarthing pieces. *Mod.* A three-farthing bun.

threefold ('θriːfəʊld), *a.*, *adv.* (*sb.*) Forms: see THREE and -FOLD. [OE. *þrífeald*, *þrýfeald*: = OFris. *thrífald*, obs. Du. *drijvoud*, OHG., MHG. *drivalt*, ON. *þrífaldr*: see THREE and -FOLD.]

A. *adj.* **1.** Consisting of three combined in one, or one thrice repeated; comprising three kinds, parts, divisions, or branches; triple.

c **1000** ÆLFRIC *Hom.* II. 606 Nis se Ælmihtiȝa God na ðryfeald, ac is Ðrynnys. *c* **1200** *Twelfth Cent. Hom.* 136 Crist arerde þreo men of deaþe to life, & þa þreo tacnoden þene ðreofealde deaþ þare sunfule sawle. *c* **1200** *Trin. Coll. Hom.* 65 God bad us turnen to him, and þat us bihoueð to don on þrefold wise. **13..** *Cursor M.* 25943 (Cott.) And for we sin on maners thre, Vr scrift aght thrifald for to be. **1434** MISYN *Mending Life* i. 107 Þis is þe threfold rope þat vnnethis may be brokyn. *a* **1600** *Scot. Poems 16th C.* (1801) II. 192 His popish pride, and threefald crowne. *c* **1709** PRIOR *1st Hymn Callimachus* 66 The three-fold empire Of Heaven, of ocean, and deep hell beneath. **1793** MARTYN *Lang. Bot.*, *Terna folia*, three-fold leaves, in threes, or three and three. **1857** TOULMIN SMITH *Parish* 104 Highways, bridges, and military defence, constituted the three fold conditions (*trinoda necessitas*) always..attached to the tenure of land.

2. Three times as great or numerous.

c **1200** ORMIN 14034 Twafald oþerr þrefald mett Þa fetless alle tokenn. **1858** LARDNER *Hand-bk. Nat. Phil.* 158 If the compressing force be increased in a threefold proportion, the volume of the air compressed will be diminished in a threefold proportion. **1870** BRYANT *Iliad* I. v. 140 A threefold courage now Inspired him.

B. *adv.*

1. In a threefold manner, triply; †in threes, three together (*obs.*); †in three ways (*obs.*); in or into three parts (now *rare*).

c **1020** *Rule St. Benet* i. (Logeman) 10 Þa twyfealde þreofealde oððe soðes anlepie gangende butan hyrde. **13..** *Cursor M.* 26069 (Cott.) Als þe sin es wroght Thre-fald, wit word, dede, and thoght. **1486** *Bk. St. Albans, Her.* C vij b, Rather it shall be calde a cros threfolde partitid flurri. **1558** PHAER *Æneid* IV. L j, On the threefoldshapen dame, And on Diana's virgins faces three she doth exclame. **1855** TENNYSON *Brook* 73 The chestnut, when the shell Divides threefold to show the fruit within.

2. Three times, thrice (in amount); three times or thrice as much. See also THICK *adv.* 6.

c **1400** *Brut* 299 3et were þey threfold so meny of hem as of Englisshe men. **1591** SHAKS. *Two Gent.* I. i. 116 'Tis threefold too little. **1594** —— *Rich. III*, II. ii. 86 Alas! you three, on me threefold distrest: Power all your teares.

C. *sb.* A name for the plant buckbean (*Menyanthes trifoliata*), from its threefold leaves. *dial.*

1788 W. MARSHALL *Yorksh.* II. Gloss. (E.D.S.), *Threefold, Menyanthes trifoliata*, bogbean, buckbean. **1876** in ROBINSON *Whitby Gloss.*

Hence **'threeˌfolded** *a.* (*rare*), threefold (whence **three'foldedness** = *threefoldness*); **'threefoldly** *adv.*, in a threefold manner; **'threefoldness**, the quality or condition of being threefold.

1528 ROY *Rede me*, etc. (Arb.) 29 Fye on his golden *three folded crowne. **1553** T. WILSON *Rhet.* 6 b, Quintilian giueth warnyng to vse this threfolded order. **1905** *Chr. Progress* Feb. 22 The word Trinity means *Threefoldedness. *a* **901** *Laws of Ælfred* c. 39 §2 ȝif syxhyndum þissa hwæðer ȝelimpe, *ðriefealdlice arise be ðære cierliscan bote. **13..** *Cursor M.* 25939 (Cott.) Man he sinnes threfaldli, Þat es in thoght, in word, in wark. *c* **1450** *Mirour Saluacioun* 1591 How the feend temptede crist threfaldelye. **1901** R. C. MOBERLY *Atonem. & Person.* viii. 154 The Three Persons [in the Trinity] are neither Three Gods, nor Three parts of God. Rather they are God Threefoldly. **1856** FABER *Creator & Creature* II. i. (1886) 110 The *Threefoldness of Persons and the Unity of Essence.

'three-foot, *a.* † **a.** = THREE-FOOTED. *Obs.* **b.** Measuring three feet in length, breadth, or other dimension.

1590 SHAKS. *Mids. N.* II. i. 52 The wisest Aunt.. Sometime for three-foot stoole, mistaketh me. **1675** HOBBES *Odyss.* 155 A caldron, or a three-foot pot of brass. **1870** MRS. RIDDELL *A. Friars* iv, The usual three-foot passage leading from the front door to the kitchen. **1880** A. A. COMMON in *Mem. Roy. Astron. Soc.* XLVI. 173 Particulars of the Mounting of a Three-Foot Reflector.

'three-ˌfooted, *a.* Having three feet; *esp.* having three supports, tripod, as a ***three-footed stool***.

c **1000** ÆLFRIC *Gram.* xlix. (Z.) 287 *Tripes*, þryfete [*MS. W.* þrifotede]. —— *Voc.* in Wr.-Wülcker 124/6 *Trisilis*, þryfotad fæt. *c* **1425** *Cast. Persev.* 2599 in *Macro Plays* 154 Worldis wele is lyke a iij-foted stole; It faylyt a man at hys most nede. **1555** EDEN *Decades* 195, I named the mountayne where these trees grow, the mountayne of three footed trees. **1671** H. M. tr. *Erasm. Colloq.* 436 If we believe Oedipus, there are found fourfooted, and threefooted, and twofooted men. **1821** SCOTT *Kenilw.* x, So saying he approached to the fire a three-footed stool.

'three-forked (-fɔːkt, *poet.* -ˌfɔːkɪd), *a.* Having three forks or prongs; trifurcate.

1535–1887 [see FORKED *ppl. a.* 1 f]. **1615** CROOKE *Body of Man* 375 Within these vesselles are certaine values or leafe-gates... Some of these are three-forcked, some like halfe Moones. *a* **1678** MARVELL *Horatian Ode*, Like the three-forked lightning. **1822** *Hortus Angl.* II. 165 *C. Tricuspidatus.* Three-forked Stock. Leaves lyre-shaped; pods three toothed at the tip.

three-halfpence (θriː'heɪpəns). Money of the value of three halfpennies, or a penny and a halfpenny (1½*d.*); a silver coin of this value issued by Queen Elizabeth; also, a silver coin of William IV and Victoria, issued for use in Ceylon.

1483 *Cath. Angl.* 385/1 Threhalpenys, *trissis* (A.). **1562** J. HEYWOOD *Prov. & Epigr.* (1867) 151 They take three halfpence. **1654** WHITLOCK *Zootomia* 181 To the Philosopher, three halfpence. **1872** *Punch* 9 Mar. 105/1 The fee for the hire of a chair with arms will be reduced to three-halfpence. **1898** G. B. RAWLINGS *Brit. Coinage* 65 The sixpence, threepence, threehalfpence, and threefarthings [of Q. Elizabeth], are distinguished by having a rose behind the head.

three-halfpenny (-'heɪpənɪ), *a.* (*sb.*) That is worth, or costs, three-halfpence; often depreciatory epithet of anything held in small esteem: paltry, vile, contemptible. Also *sb.* a three-halfpenny piece: see prec.

1552 GILPIN *Serm.* in *Life*, etc. (1636) 258 A great number ..keep them [the livings] as their owne lands, and give some three halfe-peny Priest a Curates wages. **1587** FLEMING *Contn. Holinshed* III. 1287/1 To let it perish in threehalfe-penie pamphlets, and so die in obliuion. **1638** SANDERSON *Serm.* (1657) 142 We laugh't at the silliness of the poor Indians..for parting with a massie lump of Gold-ore for a three halfpenny knife. **1726–31** TINDAL *Rapin's Hist. Eng.* XVII. (1743) II. 157 The Three Half-penny Piece (coined by this queen only). **1898** G. B. RAWLINGS *Brit. Coinage* 66 The threehalfpennies, pennies and threefarthings have as their obverse legend *E D G Rosa sine spina. Ibid.* 200 William IV also coined silver three-halfpenny pieces for Ceylon and the West Indies.

three-halfpennyworth, usually contr. **-ha'porth** (-'heɪpəθ). [Cf. HALFPENNYWORTH.] As much as is worth, or costs, three-halfpence.

c **1440** *Promp. Parv.* 492/2 Thre halpworthe, *trissis.* **1692** SOUTHERNE *Wives Excuse* I. i, Three halfperth of farthings. **1901** *Essex Weekly News* 15 Mar. 6/1 Deceased only had three ha'porth of beer.

† **'threehead.** *Obs.* [f. THREE + -HEAD.] The being three (in one); trinity.

a **1225** *Juliana* 78 Þet rixleð in þreohad & þah is an untweamet. *a* **1240** *Sawles Warde* in *Lamb. Hom.*, etc. 267 His hali milce..rixleð in þreo-had a buten ende. *a* **1400** *Relig. Pieces fr. Thornton MS.* 59 A God and ane Lord yn threhed, And thre persons yn anehed.

three-headed ('θriːˌhɛdɪd), *a.* [f. *three head*(*s* + -ED².] Having three heads.

c **1000** ÆLFRIC *Gram.* ix. (Z.) 67 *Triceps*, þryheafdede. *c* **1400** *Destr. Troy* 300 He highyt vnto helle yates, A þre hedet hounde in his honnd coght. **1567** GOLDING *Ovid's Met.* VII. (1593) 157 And thou three-headed Hecat. **1839** BAILEY *Festus* xxvi. (1852) 456 The dog three-headed, by the gates of woe. **1905** W. T. PILTER *Bible & Babylon* 116 The woman was first tempted by the three-headed Serpent.

'three-inch, *a.* Measuring three inches in length, thickness, etc. (in first quot. *humorous*). Also in *comb.*, as ***three-inch-thick***, ***-wide***. So **three-inched** (-ɪnʃt) *a. rare.*

1596 SHAKS. *Tam. Shr.* IV. i. 27 Away you three inch foole, I am no beast. **1626** CAPT. SMITH *Accid. Yng. Seamen* 9 All the Orlope to be layd with square three inch plancke. **1839** URE *Dict. Arts*, etc. 927 A three-inch-thick plank. **1845** STOCQUELER *Handbk. Brit. India* (1854) 399 A formidable knife..tapering from a three-inched hilt to the finest point. **1846** *J. Baxter's Libr. Pract. Agric.* (ed. 4) I. 153 In Suffolk they are hoed..with three-inch hoes, having handles not above two feet in length.

† **'three-leaf.** *Obs.* [f. THREE + LEAF: cf. TREFOIL.] A three-leaved or trifoliate plant.

a. The wood-sorrel; so called from its ternate leaves. **b.** A species of orchid (? *Habenaria*) with three root-leaves.

c **1000** ÆLFRIC *Voc.* in Wr.-Wülcker 133/22 *Trifolium*, ȝeacessure, *uel* þrilefe. **1562** TURNER *Herbal* II. 128 Satyrion whiche som call Threleafe, because it hath thre leaues, bowing doune toward the earth.

'three-leaved (-liːvd), *a.* Also **-leafed**. [See LEAVED and LEAFED.] Having three leaves, or leaves consisting each of three leaflets; trifoliate. **three-leaved grass**, an old name for clover; in quot. 1634 app. wood-sorrel (cf. prec. a); **three-leaved ivy**, an American name for the poison ivy

(*Rhus toxicodendron*); **three-leaved rush**, *Juncus trifidus*.

14.. *Voc.* in Wr.-Wülcker 595/33 *Melilotum*, thre-leued-gras. **1562** TURNER *Herbal* II. 41 Among so many thre-leued herbes as we haue. **1634** SIR T. HERBERT *Trav.* 18 Such as haue the Scuruy,..eat three-leafed-grasse, fresh meate, or the like. **1772** FORSTER in *Phil. Trans.* LXII. 55 The threeleaved Hellebore. **1861** MISS PRATT *Flower. Pl.* V. 296 Three-leaved Rush... This rare species,..has crowded, erect, thread-like stems, from four to six inches high. **1884** J. TAIT *Mind in Matter* (1892) 329 Saint Patrick..employed the three-leaved clover to illustrate the Unity of Nature, and Plurality of Persons in the Deity.

'three-legged (-lɛgd, -ˌlɛgɪd), *a.* Having three legs, as ***a three-legged stool***.

† ***three-legged mare***, a nickname for the gallows; ***three-legged race***, a race run by couples, the right leg of one person being bound to the left leg of the other; † ***three-legged staff***, a tripod for supporting surveying instruments, etc.

1596 SHAKS. *Tam. Shr.* I. i. 64 To combe your noddle with a three-legg'd stoole. **1685** T. BROWN *Advice Dr. Oates* 26 From Fear Of being mounted on a Three-legg'd-Mare. **1694, 1834** [see MARE[1] 2 a]. **1701** MOXON *Math. Instr.* 21 *Three-Leg'd Staff*, made with Joynts to shut together, and take off in the middle for the better carriage: to support Instruments for Astronomy, Surveying, etc. **1764** MASKELYNE in *Phil. Trans.* LIV. 350 The wooden three-legged stand, which supports the sector. **1863** W. C. BALDWIN *Afr. Hunting* i. 3 Quill-driving was not my particular vocation, nor a three-legged stool the..range to which I was willing to restrict myself. **1876** *N.Y. Times* 21 May 2/5 The three-legged race of 100 yards was won by the Brown-Hammond team. **1909** *Mission Field* July 118 How the boys did enjoy the 'three-legged' race and the sack races!

'threelihood. *nonce-wd.* [app. f. THREE + -LY[1] + -HOOD; perh. after ME. THRILLEHOD.] The Trinity; threefoldness.

1839 BAILEY *Festus* xx. (1848) 250 To shew the holy God, in three scenes, first And last in Threelihood, and midst in One.

'three-man, *a.* Requiring three men; managed, worked, or performed by three men; esp. in ***three-man('s) song, glee*** (also ***three men's song***), a convivial part-song for three men; a trio for male voices. (Corrupted to *freeman's song*: see FREEMAN 4.)

c **1425** *Cast. Persev.* 2336 in *Macro Plays* 147, xxx[ti] thousende..þat had leuere syttyn at þe ale, iij mens songys to syngyn lowde, þanne to-ward þe chyrche for to crowde. *c* **1440** *Promp. Parv.* 492/2 Thre mannys songe, *tricinnium*. **1597** SHAKS. *2 Hen. IV*, I. ii. 255 If I do, fillop me with a three-man-Beetle. **1611** —— *Wint. T.* IV. iii. 44 Three-man song-men, all, and very good ones. **1600** HEYWOOD *1st Pt. Edw. IV*, Wks. 1874 I. 51 Weele haue a three-men song, to make our guests merry. **1857** KINGSLEY *Two Y. Ago* xxi, An old seventeenth-century ditty, of the days of 'three-man glees'. **1865** —— *Hereward* v.

'three-mast, *a.* Having three masts. So **'three-'masted** *a.*; **'three-'master** [MASTER *sb.*[2]], a three-masted ship.

1775 DALRYMPLE in *Phil. Trans.* LXVIII. 392 Two three-mast vessels with latine sails. **1798** *Connecticut Jrnl.* 23 May 3/1 New York... May 14. Loss of the armed three masted schooner Harmony, captain Price, who sailed on Saturday the 5th inst. from this port for Surinam. **1827** F. WITTS *Diary* 26 Apr. (1978) 70 One of these ships was a three-master. **1839** MARRYAT *Phant Ship* vi, A three-masted vessel. **1861** *Mitchell's Maritime Register* 28 Sept. 1241/1 On the 21st inst. was launched from the yard of Messrs. Thomas Harvey & Sons, Wivenhoe, a three-masted brigantine. **1883** DE FOREST in *Harper's Mag.* Mar. 519/2 This ghost of a great three-master. **1970** E. J. MARCH *Inshore Craft* II. iii. 144 Mention should also be made of the big three-masted lugger *New Moon*.

ˌthree-'monthly, *a.* (*sb.*) Of or pertaining to three months; appearing every three months, as a periodical; quarterly. **b.** *sb.* A quarterly magazine or review.

1818 BYRON *Juan* I. ccxi, Magazines,..Daily, or monthly, or three monthly. **1830** GEN. P. THOMPSON *Exerc.* (1842) I. 233 Writing in a three-monthly Review. **1846** MRS. GORE *Eng. Char.* (1852) 13 Convinced that all the weekly, monthly, and three-monthly critics cannot be in the wrong. **1886** TUPPER *My Life as Author* 179, I was editor..of an extinct three-monthly, the *Anglo-Saxon*.

threen, obs. form of THRENE.

threeness ('θriːnɪs). [f. THREE + -NESS; cf. OE. *þrynes, þriȝnes*: see THRINNESS.] The fact, quality, or condition of being three or threefold; *spec.* said of the Godhead.

[*a* **900** tr. *Bæda's Hist.* IV. xix. [xvii.] (1890) 312 We ondettað..þriȝnisse in Annisse efenspedelice, ond Annesse in þære þriȝnesse.] **1829** JAS. MILL *Hum. Mind* (1869) II. 92 Abstract terms merely; in place of which, the words oneness, twoness, threeness, might be substituted. **1855** LYNCH *Lett. to Scattered* v. (1872) 65 That in the Oneness there is Threeness, that the One God is Triune. **1899** *Month* Jan. 14 Threeness in person with oneness in nature.

three-one, *a.* (*sb.*) Being three in one, triune. **b.** *absol.* or as *sb.* The triune God, the Trinity.

1638-56 COWLEY *Davideis* I. 371 Who shall describe thy throne, Thou great Three-One? **1719** J. T. PHILIPPS tr. *Thirty-four Confer.* 174 This glorious Three-One God had created all Things. **1772** T. OLIVERS *Hymn*, '*The God of Abraham praise*', Before the great Three-One They all exulting stand. **1802** J. JAMIESON *Use Sacr. Hist.* II. III. ii. 53 The love of a three-one God is displayed.

threep, variant of THREAP.

'three-pair, *a.* In full, ***three pair of stairs*** (see PAIR *sb.*[1] 6 b). Of or belonging to the third floor, as in ***three-pair room, back, front, window***.

1788 *Phil. Trans.* LXXVIII. 217 Out of a three-pair-of-stairs window. **1818** SCOTT *Hrt. Midl.* xli, Like a squirrel in his cage, hung out of a three pair of stairs window. **1838** DICKENS *Nich. Nick.* xxi, In the two-pair back of the house ..or in the three-pair front. **1883** MRS. PLUNKETT in *Harper's Mag.* Jan. 236/2 Kate was established in the little 'three pair back'.

three-part, *a.* (*adv.*) Containing, consisting of, having, or involving three parts.

1854 *Cherubini's Counterpoint* 20 It is prohibited in three-part-counterpoint, as in two-part-counterpoint, to make concealed fifths. **1884** F. J. BRITTEN *Watch & Clockm.* 255 [A] Three Part Clock [or] Three Train Clock..[is] a clock with three trains: the going train, the striking train, and the quarter or chiming train. **1910** TOVEY *Encycl. Brit.* III. 129/2, 15 three-part symphonies.

b. *adv.* (in comb.) = THREE-PARTS.

1840 BLAINE *Encycl. Rur. Sports* § 1282 A three-part-bred mare.

So **three-parted** *a.*, divided into or having three parts, tripartite.

1553 GRIMALDE *Cicero's Offices* III. (1558) 117 A threeparted deuision. **1793** MARTYN *Lang. Bot.*, Three-parted leaf,..divided into three parts down to the base, but not entirely separate. **1900** JACKSON *Gloss. Bot. Terms* 270/2.

three parts. Three out of four equal parts, three quarters. Hence as *advb. phrase*, To the extent of three quarters; well-nigh, almost.

1711 SWIFT *Jrnl. to Stella* 30 June, Patrick comes early, and wakes me.., though I am three parts asleep. **1842** BORROW *Bible in Spain* vii. 45 He was half-intoxicated, and soon became three-parts so. **1871** M. COLLINS *Mrq. & Merch.* x, He rides a three-parts thorough-bred. **1877** BROWNING *La Saisiaz* 72 There's the stoppage at the inn Three-parts up the mountain. **1887** STEVENSON *Mem. & Portraits* xv. 250 Conduct is three parts of life, they say; but I think they put it high.

threepence ('θrɪpəns, 'θrɛpəns). [f. THREE + PENCE, collective pl. of PENNY.]

1. A sum of money equal in value to three pennies.

1605 B. JONSON *Volpone* II. i, What monstrous.. circumstance Is here, to get some three or four gazettes, Some three-pence in the whole! **1701** CIBBER *Love makes Man* v. ii, *Ang*...Fortune, once again, is kind; but how it comes about—*D. Lew.* Does not signify Three pence. **1849** *Sk. Nat. Hist., Mammalia* IV. 12 In Pennsylvania an old law existed offering threepence a head for every squirrel destroyed.

2. *Hist.* A coin of this value, originally of silver, and later of nickel brass and dodecagonal in shape; a threepenny piece.

At the time it was discontinued, the silver threepence was the smallest silver coin of Great Britain.

1589 *Hay any Work* (1844) 11 A round threepence serueth the turn. **1675** *Lond. Gaz.* No. 987/4 One Purse.., and therein..about 18 new Groats, Three-pences, and Two-pences. **1712-13** SWIFT *Jrnl. to Stella* 23 Jan., Dr. Pratt and I..with the Bishop of Clogher,..played at ombre for threepences. **1824** MISS MITFORD *Village* Ser. I. (1863) 235, I would venture the lowest stake of gentility, a silver three-pence, that [etc.]. **1898** G. B. RAWLINGS *Brit. Coinage* 53 Edward VI coined..a silver crown, half-crown, sixpence, and threepence.

threepenny ('θrɪpənɪ, 'θrɛpənɪ), *a.* (*sb.*)

1. Of the value or price of threepence.

a. ***threepenny nail***, a nail of the size which originally cost threepence a hundred. (See PENNY 10.)

1429-30 *Rec. St. Mary at Hill* 73 Also for d[c] iij peny nayll, j d ob. **1481, 1484** [see PENNY 10]. **1486** *Naval Acc. Hen. VII* (1896) 16, ccc iij peny nailes ix[d]. **1494-5** in Swayne *Sarum Churchw. Acc.* (1896) 43 De clauis vocatis threpenynayle precii centene iij d.

b. ***threepenny bit*** (BIT *sb.*[2] 8 c), ***piece*** = THREEPENCE 2; also *fig.* (in reference to the size of the silver coin) something very small. Also ellipt. *threepenny*.

1729 *Evelyn's Kal. Hort.* 199 A Leaf as broad as a Three-penny Piece. **1879** *St. George's Hosp. Rep.* IX. 311 Pieces of ..bone, varying in size from that of a threepenny-piece to half-a-crown. **1884** W. BLACK in *Harper's Mag.* Dec. 21/2 A small threepenny-bit of a creature. **1892** A. MACLAREN *Paul's Prayers*, etc. (1893) 289 Only a threepenny bit and not a talent. **1905** *Daily Chron.* 8 Nov. 6/7 Threepennies, indeed, are as characteristic of the provinces as the farthing is peculiar to London.

c. Costing or involving an outlay of threepence.

1698 *Christ Exalted* 55 No more shaken than a pair of Three-penny Bellows can shake down the Monument. **1712-13** SWIFT *Jrnl. to Stella* 17 Feb., I play but threepenny ombre. **1825** T. HOOK *Sayings* Ser. II. *Passion & Princ.* viii. III. 126 The letter which had arrived by the threepenny post from Hackney. **1902** *Westm. Gaz.* 25 Apr. 7/3 The 7.3 from Hoe-street, Walthamstow, commonly known as 'the last threepenny train' (largely used by workmen).

d. *transf.* Of or pertaining to threepence or to something worth threepence; able or willing to pay threepence.

1630 J. TAYLOR (Water P.) *Navy Land Ships* Wks. I. 79/1 Some Men (being borne vnder a threepeny planet) can neither by paines..or any industry be worth a groat. **1895** *Daily News* 13 Dec. 7/1 Consigned to the threepenny boxes of the second-hand booksellers. **1898** *Daily Chron.* 14 Oct. 3/4 What in magazine parlance may be called..the 'threepenny' public. **1899** J. PENNELL in *Fortn. Rev.* LXV. 113 It is useless to discuss any matter with the threepenny populace.

2. *fig.* as a disparaging epithet: Of little worth; trifling, paltry, cheap, worthless.

1613 ROWLAND *Four Knaves* (Percy Soc.) 47 Like threepenie watch-men..Each with a rustie browne-bill in his hand. **1651** C. CARTWRIGHT *Cert. Relig.* I. 76 Such men ..were permitted to excommunicate for a threepeny matter. **1823** SCOTT *Peveril* xxvii, Down to that three-penny baggage, Mistress Nelly.

3. *sb.* A length of rod used in basket-making.

1912 [see *long-small* s.v. LONG *a.*[1] A. 18]. **1953** A. G. KNOCK *Willow Basket-Work* (ed. 5) 9 Three feet, Tacks;.. six feet, Threepenny.

threepennyworth (ˌθriːˈpɛnɪwəθ), contr. **-penn'orth** (-'pɛnəθ). The quantity that is worth, or costs, threepence.

[**1340** *Ayenb.* 37 Hi habbeþ þri paneworþes of worke uor ane peny.] **1617** *MS. Acc. St. John's Hosp., Canterb.*, For thre penneard of wax candelles iij d. **1700** CONGREVE *Way of World* v. i, With your Three-penny-worth of small Ware. **1865** DICKENS *Mut. Fr.* III. x, 'Threepenn'orth Rum', said Mr. Dolls.

'three per ˌcent, *adj.* and *sb. phr.*

A. as *adj.* **a.** Yielding 3 per cent. interest (see B.). **b.** Containing three parts in every hundred.

1753 *Bank of Eng. Dividend Bk.* 5 Jan., 3 per cent. consolidated annuities. **1796** CNT. RUMFORD in *Phil. Trans.* LXXXVII. 215 In the three per cent. consolidated public funds of this country. **1880** BARWELL *Aneurism* i. 12, I.. placed them in a three-per-cent. solution of carbolic acid.

B. as *sb.* (*absol.* use of A. a). In pl. **three per cents**, the Government securities of Great Britain, consolidated in 1751 into a single stock paying 3 per cent. interest: see CONSOLIDATED 1 b.

In 1888 the interest on the consolidated stock (*consols*) was reduced to $2\frac{3}{4}$ per cent., and in 1903 to $2\frac{1}{2}$ per cent., so that the name, so long familiar, ceased to be applicable.

1794 G. ROSE *Diaries* (1860) I. 195 We borrow in the Three Per Cents. **1823** SCOTT *Quentin D.* Introd., There were two thousand three per cents as much lost to my family as if the sponge had been drawn over the national slate. *a* **1839** PRAED *Poems* (1864) I. 266 Annuities and Three per Cents., Little cares he about them. **1905** *Harmsw. Encycl.* 1562/2 In 1888..the 3 per cents. outstanding were ..£549,094,000.

'three-piece, *a.* and *sb.* **A.** *adj.* **1.** Of a suite of furniture: comprising three separate items; freq. of a lounge suite: (usu.) comprising two armchairs and a sofa.

1908 *Sears, Roebuck Catal.* 455 Five-piece parlor suite... Three-piece parlor suite. **1952** *New Statesman* 5 July 10/1 Thankfully home, not to sink onto the centre couch of a three-piece suite. **1976** G. MOFFAT *Short Time to Live* ix. 82 The bathroom held..the usual three-piece suite. **1978** E. MALPASS *Wind brings up Rain* xi. 109 A three-piece suite in blue moquette for the front room.

2. Of a suit of clothes: comprising three separate garments; freq. of a man's suit: comprising trousers, jacket, and waistcoat.

1909 in C. W. Cunnington *Eng. Women's Clothing in Present Cent.* (1952) iii. 91 New Three Piece Suit. **1923** *Queen* 26 July p. viii, The three-piece coat-frock. **1965** F. SARGESON *Memoirs of Peon* vi. 134 Three-piece suits were the rule. **1980** *TWA Ambassador* Oct. 84/2 We try to be a little lively, just to get out of that staid, gray, three-piece-suit mold.

3. *Mus.* Of a band: comprising three instruments or players.

1939 C. R. COOPER *Designs in Scarlet* ii. 13 A three-piece string band or a full orchestra. **1959** WALLIS & BLAIR *Thunder Above* xii. 125 The band struck up again. The three-piece combination..played German dance music. **1978** M. RUSSELL *Daylight Robbery* i. 20 The assortment of dance-floor routines that were accompanying the pulsation of a three-piece Latin-American group.

B. *sb.* **1.** A three-piece suit.

1931 W. HOLTBY *Poor Caroline* 18 Oh, Mums, I *must* show you my new blue three-piece. **1982** BARR & YORK *Official Sloane Ranger Handbk.* 42/1 There are a few basic lines that continue practically for ever, like..the basic City three-piece.

2. A three-piece suite.

1966 G. BURNETT *Dead Account* iv. 27 The room looked more expensive..a grey/red three-piece that wouldn't show much change out of two hundred guineas. **1977** *Times* 24 Dec. 16/6 What suburban child is going to believe that.. Santa would be allowed..to put his great sooty footmarks all over the Dralon three piece and the wall to wall?

Hence **three-piecer** *U.S.*, a three-piece suit.

1964 *N.Y. Post* 9 Nov. 13 Orlon® cardigan three-piecer a-glitter with trim. **1976** *Billings* (Montana) *Gaz.* 20 June 5-E (Advt.), Our all polyester knit shirt is great for leisure suits, a three piecer, even tucked into a pair of casual pants.

'three-'pile, *a.* (*sb.*) [See PILE *sb.*[5] 2.] Applied to velvet in which the loops of the pile-warp (which constitutes the nap) are formed by three threads, producing a pile of treble thickness; so of carpets; also *absol.* or as *sb.* = three-pile velvet.

[**1603** SHAKS. *Meas. for M.* IV. iii. 11 Master Three-Pile the Mercer.] **1607** DEKKER *Westw. Hoe* I. i. Wks. 1873 II. 283 My..maister hath sent you a veluet gowne heare:.. three pile. **1611** SHAKS. *Wint. T.* IV. iii. 14, I haue seru'd Prince Florizell, and in my time wore three pile. **1827** HARE *Guesses* Ser. I. (1847) 1 A cloak should be of three-pile, to keep its gloss in wear. **1844** WILLIS *Lady Jane* I. 208 This delicate alarum is worth while, More 'specially with carpets of three-pile.

'three-piled (-paɪld), *a.*[1] [f. prec. + -ED[2]. Cf. PILED *ppl. a.*[3] 2.]

1. = THREE-PILE. Also *transf.* of grass, Growing thickly with a soft surface like velvet.

1603 SHAKS. *Meas. for M.* I. ii. 35 Thou art good veluet; thou'rt a three pild peece I warrant thee. **1605** *Lond. Prodigal* I. i. 140 Sixe peeces of vellet...a peece of Ash-colour, a three pilde blacke [etc.]. **1610** *Chester's Tri.* (Chetham Soc.) 41 Our verdant pastures three pil'd greene in graine. *a* **1861** MRS. BROWNING *Nature's Remorses* ii, On three-piled carpet of compliments.

2. *fig.* Of the highest quality, refined, exquisite; also, of very great degree, excessive, extreme, intense (cf. *threefold*, *treble*, *triple*). ? *Obs.*

1588 SHAKS. *L.L.L.* v. ii. 407 Taffata phrases, silken tearmes precise, Three-pil'd Hyperboles. *a* **1616** BEAUM. & FL. *Scornf. Lady* III. i, You, tender sir, whose gentle blood ..makes you snuff at all But three-piled people. **1690** DRYDEN *Don Sebastian* III. ii, She has made my pious father a three-piled cuckold.

'three-piled, *a.*[2] [See PILED *ppl. a.*[2]] Consisting of three things piled one upon another; also *fig.* threefold.

1656 J. HARRINGTON *Oceana* (1700) 59 As under Herod, Pilat, and Tiberius, a threepil'd Tyranny. **1661** COWLEY *Disc. Cromwell* Wks. 1710 II. 637 The Son of Earth,.. Upon his three-pil'd Mountain stands, 'Till Thunder strikes him. **1908** *Daily Chron.* 21 Nov. 9/5 The work under the mark of the three piled arms of the B.S.A. Co.

'three-point, *a.* **1.** Marked with three points; *spec.* designating a grade of point blanket (see POINT *sb.*[1] B. 14).

1855 [see *point blanket* s.v. POINT *sb.*[1] B. 14]. **1921** [see POINT *sb.*[1] A. 32]. **1948** *Beaver* June 21/2 The simple voyageur Leger lost only a three-point blanket..a portage strap, a pair of French shoes.

2. At three points; with contact or support at three points; *spec.* of an aircraft landing: in which all three wheels, or two wheels and the tail skid, touch the ground simultaneously.

1909 *Westm. Gaz.* 9 Nov. 5/1 What is actually achieved by the Rolls-Royce plan is to make a three-point suspension without complication. **1918** R. FROST *Let.* 24 Oct. (1972) 39 You have to learn to make a 'three-point landing' that is on your two wheels and skid simultaneously. **1953** C. A. LINDBERGH *Spirit of St. Louis* II. vi. 266 Boy, *he* always makes 'em three-point! **1960** *Farmer & Stockbreeder* 15 Mar. 103 It connects to any modern tractor by the three-point hitch..and the category shaft. **1969** *Gloss. Terms Dentistry* (*B.S.I.*) 78 *Three-point contact*, a term used to indicate that when the jaws are in eccentric position there is a minimum of three points of occlusal contact, as widely spaced as possible. **1971** *Power Farming* Mar. 15/4 Hitching up an implement to the three-point-linkage could be both difficult and dangerous. **1977** *New Yorker* 4 July 42/1 He came in on final, flared, and made a three-point full-stall landing.

3. In surveying, navigation, etc.: involving the measurement of three known points to determine one's position.

1900 H. M. WILSON *Topographic Surveying* ix. 185 The three-point problem calls for the finding of distances from an unknown and occupied point to three others whose relative positions and distances are known. **1960** E. L. DELMAR-MORGAN *Cruising Yacht Equipment & Navigation* 18 The best..fix obtainable in coastal navigation is the three-Point Fix... Here three identified objects are required, and either the sextant is used to measure the angles or, less accurately, by [*sic*] compass bearings.

4. ***three-point turn***, a method of turning a vehicle round in a narrow space, whereby the vehicle moves in three arcs, forwards, backwards, then forwards again.

1957 C. SMITH *Case of Torches* xiii. 152, I switched on the motor..and did a three-point turn. **1976** 'Z. STONE' *Modigliani Scandal* III. i. 114 He did a three-point turn on the narrow road.

Hence **three-pointer**, (*a*) a three-point landing; (*b*) a three-point turn.

1932 D. GARNETT *Rabbit in Air* III. 106 This time the wind took off the extra height just as planned and with an almost dead machine made a perfect three-pointer. **1965** P. M. HUBBARD *Hive of Glass* i. 12, I did a copy-book three-pointer, drove back to the main street. **1976** B. LECOMBER *Dead Weight* i. 21 The Gemini rumbles on to the ground in a neat three-pointer.

three-'quarter, -'quarters, *sb.*, *adj.*, and *advb. phr.*

A. as *sb.* **1.** ***three quarters***, three of the four equal parts into which anything is or may be divided; *loosely*, the greater part of anything.

1470, 1650 [see QUARTER *sb.* 1]. **1886** C. E. PASCOE *London of To-day* i. (ed. 3) 29 A modest luncheon of grilled chops and boiled potatoes is ordered. In three-quarters of an hour these appear. **1900** STODDARD *Evol. Eng. Novel* 191 That three-quarters of life which is called conduct.

2. ***three-quarter*** (pl. **-*quarters***), in *Football*, short for *three-quarter back* (see D.).

1889 H. VASSALL *Rugby Football* 13 If he [the captain] is playing four three-quarters and finds that his eight forwards are swamped by the opposing nine, he must make his extra three-quarter go forward. **1897** *Whitaker's Alm.* 645/1 The English halves and three-quarters were run out before they had a chance of getting away.

B. as *adj.* **a.** ***three-quarter*** (rarely **-*quarters***). Amounting to three quarters of the whole; one quarter less in magnitude or dimension than that which is complete or full; three-fourths of the ordinary; also vaguely (cf. A. 1).

1677 *Lond. Gaz.* No. 1239/4 A middle sized Fox Beagle, ..white breast, and her legs whitish, with three quarter sterne. **1684** J. PETER *Siege Vienna* 204 Three quarter Cannons, of each 36 pound. **1700** T. BROWN *Acc. Journ. Exon* Wks. 1709 III. II. 101 As if he had been riding three-quarter-speed. **1766** ENTICK *London* IV. 448 Adjoining to the walls are ten three-quarter columns. **1837** *Civil Eng. & Arch. Jrnl.* I. 33/1 Secured with three-quarter inch bolts. **1867** AUG. J. E. WILSON *Vashti* xxii, A three-quarter moon was staring down at her own image.

b. *spec.* Of portraits, etc. (*a*) Originally applied to a canvas measuring 30 inches by 25 (about three-fourths of the area of a kitcat, 36 in. × 28). (*b*) Now usually applied to a portrait showing three-fourths of the figure (in full, ***three quarter(s length)***). Also of a coat, sleeve, etc.: (having) three-fourths of the normal length. (*c*) ***three-quarter-face*** (esp. in *Photogr.*), the aspect intermediate between full face and profile.

1712–13 SWIFT *Jrnl. to Stella* 27 Feb., I have a very fine picture of lady Orkney,..by sir Godfrey Kneller, three quarters length. **1831** WILLIAMS *Life & Corr. Sir T. Lawrence*, 1769–1830, I. 77 The last prices received by Sir Thomas Lawrence. For a head-size, or three-quarters, 210*l.*; for a kit-kat, 315*l.*; for a half-length, 420*l.*;..and for a full-length, 630*l.* *c* **1850** *Catalogue of Wm. Macgill, Edinb.* 10 Canvasses on Frames kept in Stock..24 by 20, head size; 30 by 25, ¾ size; 36 by 28, Kitcat,..50 by 40, half-length [etc.]. **1865** MISS BRADDON *Sir Jasper* ii, There were several sketches of the Baronet's elder daughter; now a three-quarter face..; now a profile..; now a full face. **1882** J. ASHTON *Soc. Life Reign Q. Anne* xxvii. II. 42 Wollaston, a portrait painter, who could only command five guineas for a three-quarters canvas. **1894** H. GAMLIN *G. Romney* 202 Lady Susan Murray is a beautiful three-quarter standing figure. **1911** *Queen* 4 Nov. Suppl. 14/3 A three-quarter length [coat] comes out at only 5 guineas. **1919** in C. W. Cunnington *Eng. Women's Clothing in Present Cent.* (1952) 156 The three-quarter coat is the latest rage. **1940** GRAVES & HODGE *Long Week-End* xvi. 280 Swagger coats..were of three-quarter length. **1943** P. CHEYNEY *You can always Duck* v. 85 She is wearin'..a loose three-quarter length coat. **1960** *Woman's Own* 19 Mar. 42/3 Three-quarter sleeve overblouse. **1960** *News Chron.* 4 Apr. 6/1 The collar sits well away from the face; the sleeves are definitely three-quarter. **1960** *Harper's Bazaar* Aug. 8/2 A brief tartan jacket ..which has..three-quarter length sleeves. *Ibid.* Oct. 119 A three-quarter coat in oatmeal tweed. **1972** A. PRICE *Col. Butler's Wolf* xi. 119 A reversible three-quarter length overcoat.

c. *ellipt.* Measuring or relating to three quarters (of a yard) in Cloth Measure, or three fourths of any quantity indicated by context; *spec.* of a coal seam, three quarters of a yard thick.

1708 J. C. *Compleat Collier* (1845) 16 The 3 Quarter Coal about 3 Quarters thick or more. **1838** *Civil Eng. & Arch. Jrnl.* I. 381/2 A half-inch service pipe will fill a cistern in one-third the time now taken by the three-quarter cock. **1846** MCCULLOCH *Acc. Brit. Empire* (1854) I. 75 The principal beds of coal are one of 6 feet thick, and a lower one called the three-quarter bed. **1894** HESLOP *Northumbld. Gloss.*, *Three-quarter-coal*, a seam of coal about three-quarters of a yard in thickness. *Mod.* The three-quarter chimes.

C. as *adv.* To the extent of three quarters.

a **1584** MONTGOMERIE *Cherrie & Slae* 110 That little God of Loue..With bow thrie quarteris scant. **1832** *Regul. Instr. Cavalry* III. 106 The..Troops wheel three-quarters left about. **1869** 'LEWIS CARROLL' *Phantasmagoria* 106 Prone to the dust he bent his head, And lay like one three-quarters dead.

D. Spec. Comb. and Collocations: **three-quarter back**, in *Rugby Football* (also in *Hockey*), one of two, three, or four players stationed between the half-backs and the full-backs; **three-quarter bed**, a bed intermediate in width between a single and a double bed; **three-quarter binding**, a style of bookbinding having more leather than half-binding: see quot.; **three-quarter-bred** *a.*, having three quarters of pure blood; **three-quarter cleft (clift)**, *dial.* a person three-quarters 'cracked': cf. QUARTER-CLEFT 2; **three-quarters face**, *Mil.* three quarters of a full 'face' or turn; **three-quarter fiddle**: see quot.; **three-quarter line** *Rugby Football*, the row of three-quarter backs aligned (and usu. angled back) across the field, esp. at a set-piece; **three-quarter plate (watch)**: see quot.; **three-quarter veneer** *Dentistry* = *partial veneer* s.v. PARTIAL *a.* 3 i.

1880 *Daily Tel.* 20 Dec., One of the Northern *three-quarter backs sustained an injury to his leg. **1889** H. VASSALL *Rugby Football* 10 This led to the increase in the number of three-quarter-backs, first, from one to two, with two full-backs, and then to three, with one full-back—in other words, three-quarter-back became the main line of defence against the rush of opposing forwards. **1890** CRESSWELL *Hockey* 10 The three-quarter-backs, generally two in number. **1919** L. R. BALDERSTON *Housewifery* vii. 196 *Size of Bedspreads*..80 in. × 100 in.—*three-quarter bed. **1978** *Lancashire Life* Oct. 141/2 The old four foot wide 'three-quarter' bed—known in the trade as a 'landlady's double' because seaside landladies used it to get two people into what should have been a single room—is rarely seen nowadays. **1897** *Let. to Editor*, *Three quarter binding is a very wide back and large corners. The sides may be of anything, paper, cloth [etc.]. **1902** BODKIN *Shillelagh* 32 The fast *three-quarter bred mare between the shafts. **1843** CARLETON *Traits Irish Peas.* I. 5 'A *three-quarter clift' of a fellow—half knave, half fool. **1833** *Regul. Instr. Cavalry* I. 14 The recruit..makes a *three quarters face. **1889** E. J. PAYNE in Grove *Dict. Mus.* IV. 813/1 *Violino Piccolo* (..*Dreiviertel-geige*, *Three-quarter fiddle), a violin of small size, but of the ordinary parts and proportions, differing in this respect from the pochette or kit. **1960** E. S. & W. J. HIGHAM *High Speed Rugby* vii. 58 The scrum-half's first and foremost duty is to feed the *three-quarter-line. **1976** *Eastern Even. News* (Norwich) 9 Dec. 19/8 Norfolk took an early lead when the ball was quickly fed along the three-quarter line to put Hopkins over for a try. **1884** BRITTEN *Watch & Clockm.* 199 In *three-quarter plate watches there is a piece cut out of the top plate sufficiently large to allow the balance to move in the same horizontal plane. **1924** J. F. HOVESTAD *Pract. Dental Porcelains* xii. 110 (*heading*) The partial coping or the all porcelain *three-quarter veneer crown. **1963** J. OSBORNE *Dental Mechanics* (ed. 5) xxiii. 415 Three-quarter or partial veneer crowns. Such crowns are usually employed as bridge retainers.

So **three-quartered** *a.*, †(*a*) made in three sections (*obs.*); (*b*) *Her.* of an animal as a bearing: turned so as to be nearly affronté, but showing a part of the flank.

c **1450** LOVELICH *Grail* xxxv. 535 There-Inne stoden peleris of Marbil stones..thre-qwarterid they weren Of Gold & Asure And Of Silver. *c* **1828** BERRY *Encycl. Her.* I. Gloss., *Three-quartered*, showing three-fourths of an animal; termed, also, *trian-aspect*, as an eagle, &c. in a *trian-aspect.* **1889** in ELVIN *Dict. Her.*

threes, obs. form of THRICE.

threescore (ˈθriːskɔə(r), ˌθriːˈskɔə(r)), *a.* (*sb.*) *arch.* Forms: see THREE and SCORE *sb.* [SCORE *sb.* 16.] **a.** Three times twenty; sixty. (Formerly sometimes written in Roman numerals, iij[xx].)

1388 WYCLIF *Lev.* xii. 5 Thre scoor and sixe daies. **1470–85** MALORY *Arthur* VI. viii. 194, I wil delyuer al the prysoners that I haue that is thre score and foure. **1535** COVERDALE *Ps.* lxxxix. [xc.] 10 The dayes of oure age are iij. score yeares & ten. **1599** in *Thanes of Cawdor* (Spald. Club) 218 Violentlie cuttit doun iij[xx] dussonis young growand treis. **1610** HOLLAND *Camden's Brit.* (1637) 529 Almost threescore miles in length. **1699** DRYDEN *Epist. J. Driden* 91 But we their sons, a pamper'd race of men, Are dwindled down to threescore years and ten. **1741** CHESTERF. *Lett.* (1792) I. 216 Very long ships, rowed by oars, some of forty, some of fifty, and threescore oars. **1850** N. HAWTHORNE *Scarlet Letter* 22 The brave soldier had already numbered, nearly or quite, his threescore years and ten. **1896** A. E. HOUSMAN *Shropshire Lad* 3 Now of my threescore years and ten, Twenty will not come again. **1922** JOYCE *Ulysses* 683 Evermoving from immeasurably remote eons to infinitely remote futures in comparison with which the years, threescore and ten, of allotted human life formed a parenthesis of infinitesimal brevity. **1977** *Drive* Mar.–Apr. 44/3 Cyril shed..more than threescore pounds of weight from his celebrated 28-stone frame. **1977** *Chicago Tribune Mag.* 2 Oct. 49/1 Those of us who have attained 'three score years and ten' more often now look backward with nostalgia, remembering the years when we were younger.

b. *absol.* with ellipsis of *years*, in reference to age; hence as *sb.* the age of sixty years, or *transf.* a person of this age. So ***threescore (years) and ten***, seventy years.

1605 SHAKS. *Macb.* II. iv. 1 *Old man.* Threescore and ten I can remember well. **1719** YOUNG *Revenge* II. 18 And reverend Grey Threescore is but a Voucher. **1764** GOLDSM. *Trav.* 254 The gay grandsire..Has frisk'd beneath the burden of threescore. **1822** GALT *Provost* xl, The worthy man was hale and hearty, not exceeding three score and seven. *Mod.* He has long passed the three score and ten.

†**c.** Used as ordinal numeral (*threescore and one* = sixty-first). *Obs.*

1596 DANETT tr. *Comines* (1614) 219 The King..when he died was well forward in the threescore and one yeere.

Hence †**threescorth** *a. Obs.* [-TH[2]], sixtieth.

1571 GOLDING *Calvin on Ps.* xlv. 1 The threescorthe Psalme is intytled (A Lilly). **1657** *North's Plutarch, Add. Lives* (1676) 38 Acacanius the threescorth King of the Scots.

'three-'sided (stress var.), *a.* Having three sides, trilateral (either as a plane figure or flat body with three edges, triangular; or as a solid figure or body with three lateral surfaces, trihedral); *fig.* having three parts or aspects.

1601 HOLLAND *Pliny* (1634) II. 489 In the triumph..he made a shew of three-sided tables, cub-bourds, and bourds, supported by one foot all of brasse. **1793** MARTYN *Lang. Bot.*, *Three-sided stem*,..having three plane sides. **1823** H. J. BROOKE *Introd. Crystallogr.* 115 Dodecahedrons with triangular planes, appearing as three-sided pyramids on the planes of the tetrahedron. **1878** H. H. GIBBS *Ombre* 8 One of those three-sided tables with pits in them to hold the counters. **1901** *Westm. Gaz.* 5 Feb. 10/1 The taste of Queen Victoria in books was..a three-sided taste.

threesome (ˈθriːsəm), *sb.* and *a.* (*adv.*) orig. *Sc.* Also 4–6 **thresum**, 6 **thriesum**. [f. THREE + -SOME.]

A. *sb.* **a.** Three persons together; three forming a company.

1375 BARBOUR *Bruce* III. 420 It [boat] sa litill wes, þat It Mycht our þe wattir bot thresum flyt. **1549** *Compl. Scot.* xv. 131 It is nocht possibil to gar thresum keip consel. *a* **1578** LINDESAY (Pitscottie) *Chron. Scot.* (S.T.S.) I. 275 McCleine ..eschapit and thriesum with him. **1816** SCOTT *Bl. Dwarf* viii, The rest disperse by twasome and threesome through the waste, and meet me at the Trysting Pool. **1893** STEVENSON *Catriona* xxix, We..sat down to meat, we threesome. **1926** [see FOURSOME *sb.* 2]. **1951** [see GAY *a.* 2 c]. **1959** *Times Lit. Suppl.* 5 June 333/2 The stresses and strains of this uneasy threesome are subtly conveyed. **1972** *Screw* 12 June 33/1 (Advt.), Especially well endowed & very fond of threesomes (with couples or 2 women). **1977** *Gay News* 24 Mar. 14/4 These may include threesomes in which one or both partners bring home a person who is shared in bed. **1977** *New Yorker* 8 Aug. 57/1 A number of them were looking down from the Turnberry Hotel at the Ailsa course, on which the last threesomes were finishing their rounds. **1980** *TWA Ambassador* Oct. 92/1 Robbins's first and better novel, *Another Roadside Attraction* (praised by an odd threesome: Lawrence Ferlinghetti, Graham Greene and Thomas Pynchon). **1981** M. McMullen *Other Shoe* (1982) ii. 22 Justin, why don't you squire Meg?.. Threesomes are awkward.

b. A game of golf in which one person plays against two opponents.

1901 *Rules of Golf* 5 A single player may play against two, when the match is called 'a threesome'. **1931** W. Martyn *Scarlett Murder* iv. 48, I was playing a three-some against Sir Griffith Wadham and Lord Eerrington.

B. *adj.* Chiefly *Sc.* **a.** Consisting or composed of three; performed by three together; threefold, triple.

1839 *New Monthly Mag.* LVII. 42 Any thing like a country-dance, or a threesome or foursome reel. **1872** Morris *Love is Enough* (1873) 8 To have seen Your nimble feet tread down the green In threesome dance. **1875** —— *Æneid* v. 580 Then.. they.. in threesome order slip Their cloven ranks. **1878** H. H. Gibbs *Ombre* 4 Tresillo means a threesome game. *Mod. Sc.* A threesome cluster of nuts. She does her back-hair in a threesome plait.

b. quasi-*adv. nonce-use*: cf. foursome 1 b.

1875 Morris *Æneid* vii. 639 Mail-coat threesome laid Of golden link.

Hence **'threesomeness** *nonce-wd.*, the quality of existing in threes, triplicity.

1853 *Athenæum* 15 Oct. 1216 What may be called the threesomeness of everything in the moral world.

'three-,square, *a.* Now *dial.* or *techn.* [f. three, after *four-square*; cf. *five-square, six-square*.] Having three equal sides; equilaterally triangular. Also *fig.* threefold, triple.

c **1440** *Jacob's Well* 119 Þis wose of coueytise is thre sqware. Þe firste sqware is.. desyre.. to haue.. wordly ryches. **1527** Andrew *Brunswyke's Distyll. Waters* b ij, Ye must haue x or xii fyltes.. beyng thresquare, a fote of length. **1590** Spenser *F.Q.* i. vi. 41 Catching up in hast his three-square shield And shining helmet. **1642** Fuller *Holy & Prof. St.* i. iv. 10, I intend not to range over all his life as he stands threesquare in relation, Husband, Father, Master. **1683** Moxon *Mech. Exerc., Printing* xiii. ¶2 For.. Triangular Punches, I commonly reserve my worn out three square Files. **1766** J. Bartram *Jrnl.* 9 Feb. in W. Stork *Acc. E. Florida* 63 A good sort of rush to bottom chairs with, much better than the.. bull-rush or the three-square ones. **1873** *Routledge's Yng. Gentl. Mag.* July 502/1 Take a triangular file, three-square file it is called.

†**'three-squared,** *a. Obs.* [f. as prec. + -ed.] = prec.

c **1400** Maundev. (1839) xiv. 160 Summe [diamonds] ben .vj. squared, summe iiij. squared, and summe iij. as nature schapeth hem. [*Fr.* Et totes sont quarrez et ont pointes de lour nature; et ascuns sont a vj. quarrez et ascuns a iiij. et ascuns a iij., si come nature les fourme.] **1577** *Wills & Inv. N.C.* (Surtees) I. 415 One dosen three-squarde fyles. **1585** Lupton *Thous. Notable Th.* (1675) 144 A hole made.. with a three squared stake. **1701** *Lond. Gaz.* No. 3708/4 Lost.., a Three-squared turning Seal, with 3 Stones.

'three-stringed (-strɪŋd), *a.* Having three strings: usually of a musical instrument.

1599 Sandys *Europæ Spec.* (1632) 145 The whole Realme ..hath beene scourged with a three stringed whip, Warre, Ill-governement, and Injustice. **1611** Bible *1 Sam.* xviii. 6 *margin*, Three stringed instruments. **1752** Newton *Note Milton's L'Allegro* 94 Rebeck is a three-stringed fiddle. **1843** *Penny Cycl.* XXVI. 346/1 Medals.. representing Apollo playing on a three-stringed instrument.

threete, obs. form of threat *v.*

'three-tined (-taɪnd), *a.* Having three tines or prongs, three-pronged.

1558 Phaer *Æneid* ii. E iij b, The God Neptune.. With forck thretinde the walles vprootes. **1587** Fleming *Contn. Holinshed* III. 1339/1 Neptune with his threetined mace, riding ouer waues vpon a dolphin. **1706** *Lond. Gaz.* No. 4259/3, 6 Silver three-tined Forks. **1904** *Daily News* 7 Nov. 4 A three-tined dinner fork.

'three-toed (-təʊd), *a.* Having three toes; in *Zool.* a descriptive epithet of particular species of animals.

1752 Sir J. Hill *Hist. Anim.* 562 The three-toed Armadilla. **1772** Forster in *Phil. Trans.* LXII. 388 Three-toed Woodpecker. **1879** E. P. Wright *Anim. Life* 211 The Three-toed Sloth.. is a native of Brazil, Para, and Rio Janeiro. **1906** *Westm. Gaz.* 24 Jan. 12/1 That the three-toed horse became extinct ages ago—geologically speaking.

'three-tongued (-tʌŋd), *a.* Having three tongues; also, knowing or using three languages, trilingual.

1594 Carew *Huarte's Exam. Wits* xi. (1596) 152 The vowels, and phrases of speech hold a very different signification from that which the vulgar and three-tongued men do know. **1690** C. Nesse *O. & N. Test.* I. 18 That Doeg aforesaid.. was *trilinguis*, three-tongued. **1743** Francis tr. *Hor., Odes* iii. xi. 22 From his three-tongu'd Jaws the Poison flow'd.

'three-way, *a.* **a.** Having, or connected with, three ways, roads, or channels; situated where three ways meet. Also, involving three participants. ***three-way cock, valve,*** one with an inlet and two alternative outlets. ***three-way mirror,*** one with three panels to provide a view from three different angles, and often forming part of a dressing-table suite.

1587 Fleming *Contn. Holinshed* III. 1338/2 His highnesse passing foorth still beyond the place called the Threewaieleet, came to the street named Hwiuetterstreet, that is to say, the chandellors street. **1603, 1608, 1674-91** [see leet *sb.*[3]]. **1633** Ames *Agst. Cerem.* ii. 325 To have set up Altars of devotion at every three-way-leet. **1838** *Civil Eng. & Arch. Jrnl.* I. 189/2 Five three-way cocks and their appendages. **1884** Coues *Key N. Amer. Birds* (ed. 2) 190 This curious extra-vestibular chamber, which may be named the *trivia*, or 'three-way' place. **1888** Lockwood *Dict. Mech. Engineering Terms, Three-way-cock*.. for diverting the liquid from the inlet branch into two different directions at pleasure. **1907** *Installation News* June 11/2 This necessitates a three-way distribution board. **1961** Webster s.v., A three-way profit split, a three-way play-off. **1964** *McCall's Sewing* v. 63/2 If you can arrange a three-way mirror it will be even better. **1967** *Economist* 29 Apr. 459/1 The slogan of 'three-way alliances' was coined [in China] three months ago. **1978** *Lancashire Life* Oct. 143/2 (*caption*) With a threeway mirror, concealed lighting and a matching stool it is about £154. **1979** *Tuscon* (Arizona) *Citizen* 20 Sept. 9D/1 Billie Harper won the second flight with 38, followed by a three-way tie at 41 between Ann Pearsall, Lori Emery and Mary Stewart. **1983** *Daily Tel.* 27 Oct. 21/2 A three-way merger among property groups could result in a new company with combined assets of around £700 million.

b. Of a loudspeaker: having three separate drive units for different frequency ranges.

1960 C. Brown *Introd. Hi-Fi* iv. 91 Small horn-loaded diaphragm loudspeakers are used in some two- and three-way systems of the direct radiator type (*i.e.* all units facing the listener). **1972** *N.Y. Times* 3 Nov. 10/4 (Advt.), One of the finest 3-way speaker systems available... Contains a 10" woofer, 5" direct radiating mid-range element and Sonodome ultra-tweeter.

'three-years, -year, *a.*

1. Of or pertaining to, or lasting for, three years; of the age of three years.

1665 Pepys *Diary* 7 Apr., We having already.. spent one year's share of the three-years tax. **1727** [Dorrington] *Philip Quarll* (1816) 37 They set sail for a three years voyage. **1798** Coleridge *Anc. Mar.* i. iv, The Wedding-Guest stood still, And listens like a three years child.

2. 'three-year-,old, of the age of three years; *spec.* of horses; also, of three years' standing, that has been such for three years. Also ***three years old.***

1825 Bentham *Offic. Apt. Maximized, Observ. Peel's Sp.* (1830) 10 Exclusion of all Barristers but three-year-old ones. *Ibid.* 13 Three years old Barristers. **1838** *Penny Cycl.* XII. 307/2 A three-year-old colt. **1894** *Field* 9 June 850/3 A three-year-old animal may have all the permanent incisors well up. **1910** *Westm. Gaz.* 2 Apr. 7/3 A strange story of an alleged three-year-old treaty between Russia and China.

b. *absol.* or as *sb.*; also *attrib.*

1617 in *T. Pont's Topogr. Acc. Cunningham* (Maitland Cl.) 200 Saxtein auld kye... Item, thrie thrie-yeir-aldis. **1825** Bentham *Offic. Apt. Maximized, Observ. Peel's Sp.* (1830) 18 Turn now to the three year olds [i.e. barristers]. **1856** 'Stonehenge' *Brit. Sports* ii. (ed. 2) §119 By Training the three-year-old is understood the preparation of the colt for racing as a three-year-old, in his fourth year. **1882** *Daily News* 26 Dec. 3/5 Not only in the three-year-old prizes did the fillies make their mark.

So **three-'yearling** *a.* = *three-year-old*.

1621 Ainsworth *Annot. Pentat.* (1639) 58 Take unto thee a three-yeerling heiffer and a three-yeerling she goat.

thref(e, threff, obs. ff. thrave, thrift.

threies, threin, threip, threist: see thrice, thrin, threap, thirst.

threit, -en: see threat, threte, threaten.

threitol ('θriːɪtɒl). *Chem.* [f. thre(ose + -itol.] A crystalline tetrahydroxy alcohol, $HOCH_2(CHOH)_2CH_2OH$, formed by the reduction of threose.

1935 *Jrnl. Amer. Chem. Soc.* LVII. 2262/2 Consistency also strongly urges limiting the term 'erythritol' to the natural inactive alcohol.., and using the terms '*d*-threitol' (rotating + 4·33° in water) and '*l*-threitol' (rotating − 4·4° in water) for the active tetritols derived, respectively, from the two threoses. **1948** *Biochem. Jrnl.* XLII. 330/1 The new product is apparently identical with the substance synthesized by Maquenne from natural xylose and described under the name of '*l*-erythritol'. The name was later changed to '*d*-erythritol' in accordance with the Rosanoff convention for sugars, but recently it has been thought advisable to change the name to D-threitol to relate it more closely to the tetrose threose. **1960** *Ibid.* LXXVII. 272/1 Preparations are given for L-threitol and *meso*erythritol. **1975** *Nature* 11 Dec. 519/1 In adult tenebrionid beetles.. an unusual combination of two polyhydric alcohols, sorbitol and threitol, is associated with the ability to tolerate prolonged freezing to at least − 50°C. The occurrence of threitol is of particular interest, since this compound has not previously been found in nature.

threll, var. thrill *sb.*[2] *Obs.*, obs. f. thrall *sb.*

threll multure: see thirl-multure.

thremmatology (θrɛmə'tɒlədʒɪ). *Biol.* [f. Gr. θρέμμα (-ατ-) nursling + -logy.] That part of biology which treats of the propagation or breeding of domestic animals and plants.

1888 E. R. Lankester in *Encycl. Brit.* XXIV. 802/1 The area of biological knowledge.. which relates to the breeding of animals and plants, their congenital variations, and the transmission and perpetuation of those variations.. may be called thremmatology. *Ibid.*, Darwin's introduction of thremmatology into the domain of scientific biology. **1889** *Athenæum* 12 Jan. 47/2 The second subdivision, 'Bionomics', includes.. thremmatology—a word coined for the subjects of variation, heredity, and the breeder's lore.

threne (θriːn), *sb.* Forms: 5-6 **trene,** 7 **threen,** 6- **threne.** [ad. Gr. θρῆνος funeral lament. So obs. F. *thrène* (1526 in Godef. *Compl.*).] A song of lamentation; a dirge, threnody; formerly *spec.* (in *pl.*) the Lamentations of Jeremiah (LXX θρῆνοι Ἱερεμίου, Vulgate *Threni*).

1432-50 tr. *Higden* (Rolls) III. 85 The seide Ieremy.. made also the trenes, that is to say, the lamentaciones. **1493** *Festivall* (W. de W. 1515) 7 Yᵉ paynfull deth of our sauyour ..of the whiche is made mencyon in the fyrst chapytre of Trenys. **1593** Southwell *St. Peter's Compl.* 2 My threnes an endlesse Alphabet doe finde. **1601** Shaks. *Phœnix & Turtle* 49 Whereupon it made this threne To the phœnix and the dove. **1651** Bp. H. King in *Ussher's Lett.* (1686) 567 Some of these Psalms may serve as Threnes and Dirges to lament the Present Miseries. **1811** Lamb *Guy Faux* Misc. Wks. (1871) 372 The tears and sad threnes of the matrons in universal mourning. **1960** R. Eberhart *Coll. Poems 1930-60* 14 The perfect lament, and threne of sorrow's throat.

So **threne** *v.* [cf. Gr. θρηνεῖν], to compose or sing a threne; **thre'netic, thre'netical** *adjs.* [Gr. θρηνητικός], pertaining to a threnody; mournful.

1890 *Univ. Rev.* Dec. 540 Her voice grew strangely low as she *threned. **1656** Blount *Glossogr.*, **Threnetick*.. mournful, lamentable. **1850** Mure *Hist. Lang. & Lit. Greece* III. 325 Threnetic odes are also ascribed to Sappho. **1829** Carlyle *Misc., Voltaire* (1872) II. 152 *Threnetical discourses.

†**threng,** *sb. Obs.* [variant of thring *sb.*[1], assimilated to threng *v.*] A crowd, throng; = thring *sb.*[1]

c **1275** Lay. 2229 Among þe þrenge of sipmen hii funde þeos maydenes. **13..** *K. Alis.* 2533 (Bodl. MS.) Abouten hij gonnen goo Par force smyten in to þe þrenge And duden beastes from oþere drenge. *c* **1330** *Arth. & Merl.* (Kölbing) 6099 Of Sarazins gret þreng About our Cristen made reng.

†**threng,** *v. Obs.* Pa. t. **threngde.** [Early ME. *þrengen*, wk. vb.; in form a factitive from thring *v.*:—OTeut. **þrangian* (cf. MHG. *drengen*, Ger. *drängen* to press, throng, late ON. *þrøngva, -gja*, Icel. *þrengja*, Sw. *tränga*, Da. *trænge* to press), in signification not differing from thring *v.*]

1. *trans.* To press or crush into a narrow space; to force into confinement: = thring *v.* B. 5 c.

a **1154** *O.E. Chron.* an. 1137, Sume hi diden in crucethus ðæt is in an cæste þat was scort and nareu and undep.. and þrengde þe man þær inne ðæt him bræcon alle þe limes. *c* **1380** Wyclif *Wks.* (1880) 473 Anticrist wolde faste to men godis of fortune bi coueytise, þat shulden drenge a man to helle. [But perh. this is for *drenche* = sink.]

2. *intr.* To go in a crowd or throng, press *in, out*, etc.: = thring *v.* B. 1.

c **1200** Ormin 16182 Þatt he swa swiþe mikell follc Draf all ut off þe temmple... Swa þatt teȝȝ alle þrenngdenn ut Off all þatt miccle temmple.

threnode ('θriːnəʊd). [Alteration of next, after *ode*.] = next.

1858 Kingsley *Misc., Chalk-stream Stud.* I. 167 The threnodes of a certain peevish friend who literally hates a mountain. **1876** Stedman *Victorian Poets* 99 As a threnode nothing comparable to [Arnold's *Thyrsis*] had then appeared since the *Adonais* of Shelley. **1903** *Daily Chron.* 16 June 3/2 In death the old wailing of the threnode is still raised, and sometimes Charon's penny is still put under the tongue.

threnody ('θrɛnədɪ, 'θriːn-). [ad. Gr. θρηνῳδία dirge, f. θρῆνος threne + ᾠδή song.] A song of lamentation; *spec.* a lament for the dead, a dirge.

1634 Sir T. Herbert *Trav.* 10 They repaire vnto the Sepulchre,.. vsing Thrænodies and dolorous complaints. **1647** Farindon *Serm.* 34 (L.) The most powerful eloquence is the threnody of a broken heart. **1827** Carlyle *Misc., Richter* (1872) I. 4 Next came threnodies from all the four winds. **1876** Stedman *Victorian Poets* 168 This elegiac poem [*In Memoriam*], the great threnody of our language.

So **threnodial** (θriː'nəʊdɪəl), **thre'nodian, threnodic** (-'ɒdɪk), **thre'nodical** *adjs.*, of or pertaining to a threnody, mournful; **'threnodist,** one who composes or utters a threnody; **'threnody** *v., trans.* to mourn in a threnody.

1817 Southey *Lett.* (1856) III. 81, I would.. fain be excused from any *threnodial service. **1837** —— *Doctor* cxxxiii. IV. 352 This was pretty well for a threnodial flight. But Dr. Watts went farther. **1624** Quarles *Funeral Elegies* Poems (1717) 416 If this *Threnodian story Intend her honour with thy loss of glory. **1891** *Cent. Dict.*, *Threnodic. **1881** *Nation* (N.Y.) XXXII. 188 The brief *threnodical essay published at the time of Irving's death. **1827** Carlyle *Misc., Richter* (1872) I. 4 To think of laughing over these unhappy *threnodists and panegyrists. **1832** De Quincey *Cæsars* Wks. 1862 IX. 5 Peace, then, rhetoricians, false threnodists of false liberty! **1893** G. Allen *Scallywag* III. 254 Mr. Solomons, thus *threnodied by the appointed latter-day bards,.. was buried.

‖**threnos** ('θriːnɒs). Also in Lat. form **threnus.** [a. Gr. θρῆνος, L. *thrēnus*.] = threne, threnody.

1601 Shaks. *Phœnix & Turtle* (heading), Threnos. **1840** tr. *C. O. Müller's Hist. Lit. Greece* iii. §5. 21 These singers of the threnos were at the burial of Achilles represented by the Muses themselves, who sang the lament. **1850** Mure *Hist. Lang. & Lit. Greece* III. 97 The Threnus of Homer's bards.. was probably in dactylic measure. **1903** *Speaker* 28 Feb. 539/1 A lad.. whose short life may be likened to a threnos.

ˌthrenothriˈambics. *humorous nonce-wd.* [f. Gr. θρῆνο-ς THRENE + θριαμβικ-ός triumphal (f. θρίαμβος a hymn to Bacchus).] Verses in which lamentation and triumph are combined.

1673 *S' too him Bayes* 57 In such lamentable threnothriambicks that you would think Nineve were going to be destroy'd immediately.

threo, threottene, obs. f. THREE, THIRTEEN.

threonine (ˈθriːəʊniːn). *Biochem.* [f. THREO(SE + *-n-* + -INE[5].] A natural amino-acid, α-amino-β-hydroxy-butyric acid, $C_4H_9NO_3$, considered essential for growth and for maintenance of the nitrogen equilibrium in adults.

1936 MEYER & ROSE in *Jrnl. Biol. Chem.* CXV. 727 It is proposed that henceforth natural α-amino-β-hydroxy-*n*-butyric acid be known as d(——)-threonine, inasmuch as it possesses a spatial configuration analogous to that of *d*(——)-threose. **1956** [see PLASMA 6 b]. **1974** *Nature* 19 Apr. 643/2 Eight essential amino acids—[including]..valine, threonine, phenylalanine and tryptophan—are required by human adults.

threose (ˈθriːəʊz). *Chem.* [a. G. *threose* (O. Ruff 1901, in *Ber. d. Deut. Chem. Ges.* XXXIV. 1364), f. *erythrose* ERYTHROSE by omission and transposition of letters.] A tetrose sugar, $CHO{\cdot}[CH(OH)]_2{\cdot}CH_2OH$, isolated as a hygroscopic solid and existing in two molecular configurations; it differs from erythrose in having the hydroxyl groups on the second and third carbon atoms on opposite sides of the carbon chain.

1901 *Jrnl. Chem. Soc.* LXXX. I. 449 The calcium salt [of *l*-xylonic acid]..was then oxidised with hydrogen peroxide and ferric acetate to *l*-threose. **1963** [see ERYTHROSE]. **1982** T. W. G. SOLOMONS *Fund. of Org. Chem.* xix. 709 One cyanohydrin ultimately yields D-(−)-erythrose and the other yields D-(−)-threose.

threp, threpe, obs. ff. THREAP.

threpel, -il, obs. ff. TRIPLE *v.*

threpˈsology. *rare*⁻⁰. [irreg. for **threpsiology*, f. Gr. θρέψις nutrition + -LOGY.] See quot.

1857 DUNGLISON *Dict. Med. Sc.*, *Threpsology*,..the doctrine of, or a treatise on, the nutrition of organized bodies. **1860** in MAYNE *Expos. Lex.*

threptic (ˈθrɛptɪk), *a. rare*[1]. [ad. Gr. θρεπτικ-ός able to feed, f. τρέφειν to nourish.] Of or pertaining to nutrition.

1845 MAURICE *Mor. & Met. Philos.* (1850) I. vi. §6. 199 We may define all the faculties which can exist in any living creature to be these: first, the faculty of receiving nourishment (θρεπτική); secondly, [etc.]... The threptic faculty is the lowest of these, and is present in all cases.

thresch, threser, obs. f. THRESH, TREASURE.

threschefold, threschwald, etc., obs. ff. THRESHOLD *sb.*

thresh, *v.*, the earlier and etymological form of the vb. now also written THRASH, q.v.; still frequent in the sense of beating out corn; so **thresh** *sb.*, **threshing**, etc.: see THRASH, etc.

threshal, -el, fold, etc., varr. THRESHOLD *sb.*

threshel (ˈθrɛʃ(ə)l). Now *dial.* Forms: 1 **þerscel, þyrscel**; 7–9 **threshal, -all, -el**, (7 **thressal, threshold**, 9 **-le**), 9 *dial.* **thrashel, drashel**, etc.: see *Eng. Dial. Dict.* [OE. *þerscel*, f. *þersc-an*, THRASH, THRESH *v.* + -EL[1]; cf. OHG. *driscil*, MHG., G. *drischel*.] A flail.

a **1000** *Ags. Gloss.* in Wr.-Wülcker 192/3 *Bainus*, þerscel. *c* **1000** *Ælfric's Voc.* ibid. 107/2, 141/16 *Tritorium*, þerscel. **1674** FLAVEL *Husb. Spir.* I. xix. 159 As they have threshals of different sizes, so they bestow on some grain more, on other fewer, strokes. *Ibid.* 161 He little regards whether it be bruised and battered to pieces by the threshold or no. **1685** R. DUNNING *Plain & Easie Method* 5 By his Threshall, Mattock, and the like, he now gains his Meat and Drink. **1688** R. HOLME *Armoury* III. 333/1 A Threshall or Flail [to Thrash or Thresh the Corn]. **1813** T. DAVIS *Agric. Wilts.* Gloss. s.v., A pair of threshles or drashols, or flyals, a flail. **1881** MISS JACKSON *Shropsh. Word-bk.*, *Thrashal, Thrashat*, ..a flail. **1882** JAGO *Cornw. Gloss.*, *Drashel*, a flail.

†**b.** A mediæval weapon: see quot., and cf. FLAIL *sb.*[2] and MORGENSTERN. *Obs.*

1688 R. HOLME *Armoury* III. xvi. (Roxb.) 88/1 A round Iron or Lead Ball sett on all sides with spike nayles, or sharp pointed Irons, hung in a chaine, to the end of a staffe or cudgell... Some terme it a slinged Galthrope, others Waring thressal.

thresher[1]: see THRASHER[1].

ˈ**Thresher**[2]. A member of an Irish political organization instituted in 1806, which issued manifestos signed 'Captain Thresher'.

1806 LD. PLUNKET *Sp.* 5 Dec. in Howell *State Trials* (1822) XXX. 7 For some time past the peace of the county [Sligo] has been infested by a set of persons assuming the name of 'Threshers'. **1808** *Hist.* in *Ann. Reg.* 1806. 263 Disturbances..occasioned by a banditti, who went about in the night time under the name of Threshers, committing every sort of crime and outrage. **1812** *Chron.* ibid. 31/1 The spirit of party broke out between several of the lower orders, styling themselves Threshers on the one side, and Orangemen on the other.

thresher, var. of THRASHER[2], a N. Amer. bird.

threshold (ˈθrɛʃəʊld, ˈθrɛʃhəʊld), *sb.* Forms: see below. [OE. *þerscold, -wold, þerxold, -wold, þrexold, -wold* = ON. *þreskjǫldr, -kǫldr*, nom. pl. *þreskeldir*, mod.Icel. *þröskuldr*, Norw., Sw. *tröskel*, Da. (*dør*)*tærskel*; cf. OHG. *driscûfli* neuter, MHG. *drischuvel, durschufel*, Ger. dial. *drischaufel*, etc. The first element is generally identified with THRESH *v.* (? in its original sense 'to tread, trample'), the forms of which it generally follows; but the second is doubtful, and has in English, as in other langs., undergone many popular transformations.]

1. a. The piece of timber or stone which lies below the bottom of a door, and has to be crossed in entering a house; the sill of a doorway; hence, the entrance to a house or building.

α. 1 **þresc-, þrex-, þerxold**, 5 **thresshhold**, 6 **threshould, thressald, threszsh-, tresholde**, 6–7 **thresholde**, 6– **threshold.**

c **1000** ÆLFRIC *Exod.* xii. 22 And dippað ysopan sceaft on þam blode, þe ys on þam þerxolde. —— *Deut.* vi. 9 And write þa on þinum þrescolde. *c* **1000** Ðrexold [see β]. **1513** DOUGLAS *Æneis* VI. i. 100 To the dur thressald cumin ar thai. **1530** PALSGR. 280/2 Thresholde, *seuil de luys* [*l'uis*]. **1535** COVERDALE *1 Sam.* v. 5 They..treade not vpon the threszsholde of Dagon. —— *Prov.* xxvi. 14 Like as the dore turneth aboute vpon the tresholde. **1553** BECON *Reliques of Rome* (1563) 256 b, At euery time the bishop shal come vnto yᵉ church dore & strike yᵉ threshold thereof with his Crossier staffe. **1607** SHAKS. *Cor.* IV. v. 124. **1727** GAY *Fables* xxiii. 30 The horse-shoe's nail'd (each threshold's guard). **1837** LYTTON *E. Maltrav.* I. i, A tall figure crossed the threshold.

β. 1 **þrex-, þræx-, þreox, ðærsc-, þersc-, þeorsc-, þercs-, þer(e)xwold, þrexwald, -weald, þersc-, þærsc-, þirscwald**, 2 **þreoxwold**, 4 **þrex-, thresshe-, thresh-, threswold, thers-, þreis-, thrys-, throssche-, treswald**, 5 **thrys-, threschwolde, thris-, thresche-, thryshwald**, 6 **threskwolde** (9 *dial.* **thresh-wood**).

[*c* **888** þeorscwold: see sense 2.] **971** *Blickl. Hom.* 207 Of ðæs portices dura..ðærscwolde wæs ȝesyne þæt [etc.]. *c* **1000** ÆLFRIC *Gram.* ix. (Z.) 40 *Limen*, ofersleȝe oððe þerexwold [*v.rr.* þræx-, þreox-, þerxwold, ðrexold]. *c* **1000** *Sax. Leechd.* II. 142 Ofer þa duru, & under þone þerxwold. *c* **1000** *Ags. Voc.* in Wr.-Wülcker 280/15 *Limen*, þerscwald. **11..** *Voc.* ibid. 551/32 *Limen*, ofersleie, *uel* þreoxwold. *c* **1325** *Gloss. W. de Bibbesw.* in Wright *Voc.* 170 *La lyme*, the therswald. **1362** LANGL. *P. Pl.* A. v. 201 He þrompelde atte þrexwolde [*v.rr.* þresshewold, þreschfold, throschfold] and þreuh to þe grounde. *c* **1375** *Sc. Leg. Saints* xviii. (*Egipciane*) 579 Quhen we come to þe thryswald. *Ibid.* 593, I..furth can gange to þe treswald. **1382** WYCLIF *1 Kings* xiv. 17 Whanne she wente in the threshwold of the hows, the child dyede. *c* **1386** CHAUCER *Clerk's T.* 232 (Lansd.) And as sche wolde ouer þe þresshewolde gon [*Camb.* throswald, *Petw.* thresshold, *Ellesm.*, *Heng.*, *Corp.* thresshfold, *Harl.* þreisshfold]. *c* **1400** *Ywaine & Gaw.* 3222 He come to the thriswald. **14..** *Nom.* in Wr.-Wülcker 733/8 *Hoc limen, -nis*, thryswold. *c* **1440** *Promp. Parv.* 492/2 Threschwolde, *limen.* **1444** in J. R. Boyle *Hedon* (1875) App. 184 Thryshwald. **1483** *Cath. Angl.* 385/1 A Threschewalde, *limen.* **1511** *Nottingham Rec.* III. 333 Makyng ye seid doore and leyeng of ij. threskwoldes. **1825** J. BRIGGS *Rem.* 215 (E.D.D.) Upon this thresh-wood..cross straws were laid.

γ. 4 **þreschefolde, threshfoold, þreshe-, thressh-, þresch-, threissh-, threis-, throschfold**, 5 **thresh-, thresfold(e** (9 *dial.* **thresh-fod**).

c **1374** CHAUCER *Boeth.* I. pr. i. 3 (Camb. MS.) They passeden sorwfully the thresshfold [*B.M. MS.* þreschefolde]. **1382** WYCLIF *Ezek.* ix. 3 At the threshfoold [**1388** threisfold] of the house. **1393** LANGL. *P. Pl.* C. VII. 408 He thrumbled at þe þreshefold [*v.rr.* þresshfold, þrescwolde, treshfold]. **1413** *Pilgr. Sowle* (Caxton 1483) III. ix. 56 Not by the dore but vnder the threshfold drawen oute. **14..** *Voc.* in Wr.-Wülcker 592/47 *Limen*, a thresfolde. **1828** *Craven Gloss.*, *Thresh-fod*, threshold.

δ. 6 **thressholl**, 7–8 **threshal**, 9 *dial.* **threshel, thrashel (drashel).**

1593 Thressholl [see 2 b]. **1607** CHAPMAN *Bussy d'Ambois* IV. G ij b, Ile make th' inspired threshals of his Court Sweat with the weather of my horrid steps Before I enter. *c* **1645** HOWELL *Lett.* (1688) IV. 494 He dragg'd her Body to the Threshal of the Door. **1787** in *Coll. Sc. Poems* 12 (E.D.D.) Luckie out o'er the threshal goes. **1898** MACMANUS *Bend of Road* 90 The house crammed..from the threshel to the backstone. **1900** G. WILLIAMS *Fairmner's Tint Laddies* iv. (E.D.D.), To cross the thrashel o' oor hoose.

ε. *dial.* 7 **treshwart**, 9 **threshwort, threshut**; 9 **freshwood**: cf. TH-[1] (6).

1608 *Vestry Bks.* (Surtees) 151 Pᵈ to John Lamb for mendinge of the treshwart of the portch, iiij d. **18..** BRIERLEY *Out of Work* x. (E.D.D.), Mind thou doesno' tumble o'er that threshut. **1888** W. DICKINSON *Lit. Rem.* 234 (E.D.D.) The threshwort's worn quite hollow down. **1825** J. BRIGGS *Rem.* 201 (E.D.D.) The entrance from the front door was called the freshwood. **1879** SIMMONS *Lay Folks Mass Bk.* Notes 399, I bids thee..never again set thy foot over my freshwood. **1892** HESLOP *Northumbld. Gloss.*, *Fresh-wood*, the threshold, or foot-beam of the front door.

¶**b.** (*erron.*) The upper horizontal part of a door-case; the lintel. *rare.*

[Cf. *c* **1000** in 1 α, 1 β. **1382**: see OVERTHRESHOLD.] **1821** CLARE *Vill. Minstr.* I. 11 The rural sports of May, When each cot-threshold mounts its hailing bough. **1834** HT. MARTINEAU *Demerara* iv. 52 Cassius stood, leaning his forehead against his low threshold.

2. *transf.* and *fig.* **a.** Border, limit (of a region); the line which one crosses in entering. *spec.* in an airfield: the beginning of the landing area on a runway. Also *attrib.*

c **888** K. ÆLFRED *Boeth.* xxi, Se ilca [*sc.* Godes miht] forwyrnð þære sæ þæt heo ne mot þone þeorscwold oferstæppan þære eorþan. *a* **900** tr. *Bæda's Hist.* v. vi. (1890) 398 Forðon þe he mæc..from deaðes þirscwalde wæs aceȝende. **1642** FULLER *Holy & Prof. St.* III. iv. 159 Know most of the rooms of thy native countrey before thou goest over the threshold thereof. *a* **1863** FABER *Hymn*, '*The happy Gate of Heaven*' ii, Fair are the thresholds of blue sea. **1899** *Westm. Gaz.* 2 Sept. 2/1 On what is known as 'the threshold of England', the Sussex coast. **1937** *Jrnl. R. Aeronaut. Soc.* XLI. 295 Sites..for threshold lighting and other signal apparatus required to assist the pilot. **1960** *Guide Civil Land Aerodrome Lighting* (*B.S.I.*) 15 A pilot needs to be given a clear indication of the runway threshold and the addition of wingbars, composed of green lights, is recommended to make the threshold more conspicuous in poor visibility.

b. In reference to entrance, the beginning of a state or action, outset, opening. (In quot. 1659, in reference to going out or leaving, close, end.)

c **1586** C'TESS PEMBROKE *Ps.* (1823) cxix. R. i, Right wonderfull thy testimonies be,.. Their very threshold gives men light. **1593** Q. ELIZ. *Boeth.* II. pr. iv. 28 The thressholl of thy felicitie. **1659** *Clarke Papers* (Camden) IV. 297, I.. shall be moste glad to heare that you are gott over the thresholde of your present troublesome stay in London, the country being the most proper place for [etc.]. **1834** L. RITCHIE *Wand. by Seine* 8 The youth, stepping proudly upon the threshold of manhood. **1877** FOSTER *Phys.* III. i. (1878) 389 We are..met on the very threshold of every enquiry [etc.].

c. In technical language, a lower limit.

(i) *Psychol.*: esp. in phr. ***threshold of consciousness***: see quots., and cf. LIMEN, SUBLIMINAL. In *Physiol.* and more widely: the limit below which a stimulus is not perceptible; the magnitude or intensity of a stimulus which has to be exceeded for it to produce a certain response. (ii) The magnitude or intensity that must be exceeded for a certain reaction or phenomenon to occur.

1874 SULLY *Sensation & Intuition* 47 There is a certain limit below which our several sensibilities are unable to discriminate. This boundary.. Fechner calls the 'threshold' (*die Schwelle*). **1886** GURNEY, etc. *Phantasms of Living* I. 453 A telepathic disturbance may take place below the threshold of consciousness. **1886** WARD in *Encycl. Brit.* XX. 47/2 We do not distinguish or attend separately to presentations of less than a certain assignable intensity. On attaining this intensity presentations are said to pass over the threshold of consciousness, to use Herbart's now classic phrase ['*Schwelle des Bewusstseins*' (*Psychol. als Wissenschaft* (1824) §47)]. **1902** J. M. BALDWIN *Dict. Philos. & Psychol.* II. 696/2 The least noticeable difference in sensation is called the threshold of discrimination or difference. **1919** W. D. HALLIBURTON *Handbk. Physiol.* (ed. 14) iii. 767 That strength of stimulus which just suffices to evoke a sensation is called..its absolute threshold. **1922** *Electr. Communication* I. I. 45/1 Articulation tests were made upon the..telephone system..when it was set to deliver various intensities from the threshold of audibility to very large values. **1930** *City Noise* (N.Y. Noise Abatement Commission) 34 This means decibels above the threshold of hearing. **1931** *Brit. Jrnl. Psychol.* Jan. 285 There is a definite 'colourless interval' between the 'general threshold', or the intensity which just suffices to produce a sensation of light, and the 'specific threshold', or the intensity at which colour is just noticeable. **1936** G. K. ZIPF *Psycho-Biol. of Lang.* 113 Every phoneme must also have a lower threshold below which it cannot pass without strengthening. **1938** *Ann. Reg. 1937* 346 The view [was] advanced that spontaneous mutations are mono-molecular reactions produced by thermal agitation when this over-steps the energy threshold of the chemical bonds. **1941** in M. Gowing *Britain & Atomic Energy 1939–1945* (1964) 403 From..the fact that [uranium] 238 does not give fission with slow neutrons, it is clear that the jump at 1 MeV represents the threshold of 238. The fission which takes place with neutrons of energy less than 1 MeV must therefore be ascribed to 235. **1948** P. M. MORSE *Vibration & Sound* (ed. 2) vi. 227 The upper contour is the threshold of pain, above which the sensation is more of pain than of sound (and the result is more or less damaging to the ear). **1949** KOESTLER *Insight & Outlook* xv. 207 Heightening the threshold of some sensory receptors and lowering the threshold of others. **1949** S. C. ROTHMANN *Constructive Uses Atomic Energy* 205 The Geiger threshold of a radiation counter tube is the lowest operating voltage at which the charge transferred per isolated count is substantially independent of the nature of the initial ionizing event. **1950** *Gloss. Aeronaut. Terms* (*B.S.I.*) I. 25 *Cruising threshold*, the equivalent air speed giving the lowest comfortable continuous cruising speed. **1955** J. A. WHEELER in W. Pauli *Niels Bohr* 166 A photofission threshold of 5·15 MeV..goes with a half life against spontaneous fission of the order of $10^{15 \cdot 8}$ years. **1958** *Oxford Univ. Gaz.* 27 Jan. 524/2 (*heading*) Non-random sequences in visual threshold experiments. **1959** *Sunday Times* 5 July 8/6 The absence of a lower threshold for the production of mutations by radiation. **1962** A. NISBETT *Technique Sound Studio* v. 98 At 1,000 c/s the threshold of pain is 110 dB or more above the threshold of hearing. **1963** B. FOZARD *Instrumentation Nucl. Reactors* v. 46 The scaling circuit which is used to count the pulses from the G.M. tube has some more or less well defined 'threshold', *i.e.* it accepts only those pulses which exceed a certain amplitude. **1965** *Proc. R. Soc.* B. CLXI. 338 While a climatic change in one area may have produced conditions very favourable for a new species, in another area the same climatic change may have produced conditions only just above the critical physiological thresholds for the existence of that species. **1965** W. LAMB *Posture & Gesture* iii. 44 There has been a lot of investigation of the threshold of fatigue in athletics and the type of training required to push this threshold back is well understood. **1972** J.

MOSEDALE *Football* ix. 124 Performances like Nevers' demonstrates [*sic*] the high threshold of pain common to many athletes. **1973** *Times* 19 Oct. 7/8 A GP who might only see one case of child abuse a year might not have as low a threshold of suspicion as I have. **1983** *Sci. Amer.* Jan. 98/2 Above a certain threshold, known as the critical density, the expansion [of the universe] will eventually cease and contraction will begin.

(iii) In contexts of wages and taxation, in which wage or tax increases become due or obligatory when some predetermined conditions are fulfilled (esp. above a specified point on a graduated scale). Also in more general use in contexts of work. Freq. *attrib.*

1967 L. B. ARCHER in Wills & Yearsley *Handbk. Managem. Technol.* 131 Usually there is a threshold between 'good enough' and 'not good enough' in respect of each objective, below which a design proposal would not be acceptable. **1971** *Guardian* 7 Sept. 11/2 Mr [Tom] Jackson ..argued in favour of a single threshold claim on behalf of all public employees. **1972** *Observer* 13 Aug. 10/8 Threshold cost of living agreements could make things much happier so long as the threshold is put fairly high and/or there is a big reduction in the effective basic level of wage settlements. **1974** *Ann. Reg. 1973* 14 The main features of the incomes plan [of Mr. Edward Heath] were..threshold payments of a maximum of 40p. a week if the retail price index were to rise by 7 per cent [etc.]. **1976** [see *tax threshold* s.v. TAX *sb.*[1] 7 b]. **1979** H. WILSON *Final Term* ii. 42 Viewed with hindsight the thresholds were a disastrous mistake. That does not in fact mean that Mr Heath had been wrong to introduce them in October 1973. **1980** J. BOYD-CARPENTER *Way of Life* xiii. 169 The alternative relief was to make a big increase in the level of the 'Thresholds', that is to say the point on the income scale at which people became liable to tax.

†**d.** An obstacle, stumbling-block. *Obs.*

1601 SIR W. CORNWALLIS *Ess.* iv, Makes his imagination build blockes and thresholds, in the plainest and most beaten way. **1705** HICKERINGILL *Priest-cr.* II. vii. 70, I hope it was left by chance, and not on purpose to be a Threshold, or Stumbling-block at the Church Door. *Ibid.* viii. 91.

3. *attrib.* and *Comb.* **a.**

1535 COVERDALE *2 Kings* xxii. 5 The money that is brought vnto y[e] house of y[e] Lorde (which the tresholde kepers haue gathered). *a* **1661** HOLYDAY *Juvenal* vi. (1673) 95 The hangings too, and threshold-boughs yet green. **1678** OTWAY *Friendship in F.* v. i, Let all the Doors be barr'd.., and Gunpowder under each Threshold-place. **1805** SCOTT *Last Minstr.* I. i, No living wight, save the Ladye alone, Had dared to cross the threshold stone. **1842** TENNYSON *St. Simeon Styl.* 188 His footsteps smite the threshold stairs Of life.

b. (Having a value or intensity) equal to that of a threshold (sense 2 c).

1906 J. R. MURLIN tr. *Tigerstedt's Text-bk. Human Physiol.* xvi. 455 In order that an external stimulus may produce a sensation, it must exceed a certain lower limit of strength, which is called, after Herbart, the threshold value of the stimulus. **1921** J. MILLS *Within Atom* 215 *Threshold frequency*, the minimum frequency of radiation which will produce photo-electric effects. **1926** J. S. HUXLEY *Ess. Pop. Sci.* 199 It is needful, not merely that some thyroid secretion should be circulating in the body, but that it should reach a certain definite concentration, a certain 'threshold value'. **1941** in M. Gowing *Britain & Atomic Energy 1939–45* (1964) 400 Neutrons of less than a certain threshold energy ..do not cause fission of ^{238}U. **1959** *Listener* 26 Nov. 929/1 It is possible that the radiation level has to exceed a critical or threshold value before any genetical effects arise. **1964** W. G. SMITH *Allergy & Tissue Metabolism* ii. 23 The tissue response would depend upon the number of susceptible cells..reached by a threshold concentration of histamine. **1971** J. H. SMITH *Digital Logic* iv. 69 The device is actuated when the input signal crosses a certain 'threshold' voltage. **1978** J. PAXTON *Dict. European Econ. Community* (rev. ed.) 46 Imports were kept up to minimum, or threshold, prices by means of variable import levies.

c. *Electronics.* ***threshold device, element***, etc.: a circuit element having one output and a number of inputs, each of which accepts a binary signal and multiplies it by some factor; the output is 0 or 1 depending on whether or not the sum of the resulting quantities is less than a certain threshold value; ***threshold function***, a Boolean function that can be realized by such an element; ***threshold logic, switching*** (based on such elements).

1960 *IRE Trans. Electronic Computers* IX. 122/1 Another useful logical two-state device is a threshold element. **1960** *Proc. IRE* XLVIII. 1335/3 The increasing use of threshold devices such as magnetic cores and parametrons. **1961** *IRE Trans. Electronic Computers* X. 6/1 Linearly separable switching functions..have been studied under different names, such as..linear-input logic, threshold logic, majority logic, and voting logic. *Ibid.* 798/2 Elementary threshold functions, *i.e.*, functions that can be implemented by a single threshold circuit, are first characterized for the cases of 2, 3, and 4 variables. **1962** *Proc. Internat. Federation Information Processing Congr.* 757/1 A threshold gate determines its output in two steps: a linear summation followed by a discrimination. **1964** H. C. TORNG *Introd. Logical Design of Switching Systems* viii. 133 Threshold switching devices are..extensively used in pattern recognition systems and perception-like automata. **1970** Z. KOHAVI *Switching & Finite Automata Theory* vii. 183 One of the limitations of threshold logic is its sensitivity to variations in circuit parameters. **1975** N. N. BISWAS *Introd. Logic & Switching Theory* vii. 183 In many cases where the NAND or NOR realizations may require a number of gates, the threshold logic may realize the function by only one gate. **1978** S. C. LEE *Mod. Switching Theory* iv. 117 As another simple example of a threshold function, consider $f(x_1, x_2, x_3) = x_1x_2 + x_3$.

threshold ('θrɛʃhəʊld), *v.* [f. the sb.] *trans.* To alter (an image) by reproducing it in two tones only, each part being dark or light according as the original is darker or lighter than some chosen threshold shade. Hence **'thresholding** *vbl. sb.*

1968 *Brit. Med. Bull.* XXIV. 262/2 One..comes across objects which have obviously been thresholded at too low or too high a level, resulting in incorrect segmentation. *Ibid.*, Simple thresholding (setting a limit above which everything is considered to be picture and below which everything is considered to be background) seems to work out quite well in coarse density-resolution scanners. **1976** *Physics Bull.* Sept. 381/3 Figure 2 shows the result of magnifying and electronically thresholding a small portion of a LANDSAT infrared image of the UK. **1983** *What's New in Computing* Jan. 16/2 The software modules comprise such algorithms as image thresholding, edge enhancement, [etc.].

Threskite, obs. form of TRASKITE.

thresorer, -ory, -our, obs. ff. TREASURER, TREASURY, TREASURE.

†**threst, thrast**, *sb. Obs.* [f. OE. *þrǽstan*: see next.]

1. Torment, affliction, trouble, hardship.

13.. *Cursor M.* 4283 (Cott.) For o quat pine es herder threst þen tharn þe thing men luues best. *Ibid.* 11829 Ydropsi held him sua in threst, þat him thoght his bodi suld brest. *Ibid.* 29168 þai sal..Bren in þe fier of purgatori,..Bot efter-ward þat herd threst, Sal þai be borun in to rest. **1340** *Ayenb.* 121 þe yefþe of drede is þe doreward to þe greate þreste, þet is..to þe greate þreapninge of godes dom. *Ibid.* 183 þe guode kniȝt..þet..heþ y-byine uele þrestes mid grat wil and grat honger.

2. A thrust, a sharp stroke; the stroke or dart of lightning, a thunderbolt.

13.. *E.E. Allit. P.* B. 952 þe þik þunder þrast þirled hem ofte. **13..** *Gaw. & Gr. Knt.* 1443 For þre at þe fyrst þrast he þryȝt to þe erþe. *a* **1400–50** *Alexander* 554 þe liȝt lemand late laschis fra þe heuyn, Thonere thrastis ware thra thristid þe welkyn.

†**threst, thrast**, *v. Obs.* Forms: α. 1 **þrǽstan**, 3 **præsten, þreaste**, 3–4 **þreste(n**, 4 **þrest**, 4–5 **threste**, 4–6 **threst.** β. 3 **þrasten**, 4 **þrast**, 5–6 **thrast**, *Sc.* **thraist**. *Pa. t.* α. 3 **þreaste (þærste)**, 3–4 **þreste**, 4 **threste**, 4–5 **threst**, 5–6 **þrested**. β. 3–4 **þraste** (3 **þarste**), 4–6 **thraste, thrast** (5 **tharst**). *Pa. pple.* 1 **þræst, þrǽsted**, 4–5 **þrast**, 5 **(y)threst**, 5–6 **thrast(e** (5 **threstyd**), 6 **threst.** [OE. *þrǽstan* to writhe, twist, torture, torment, constrain, representing an OTeut. type **praistjan*, not known in the other Teut. languages.

OE. *þrǽstan* had no etymological connexion with THRUST, early ME. *þrusten, þrysten, þristen*, from ON. *þrýsta* (OTeut. **þrūstjan*), nor did the original senses of the two agree. But, app. from the contiguity of the two forms *þrest*, and *þrist*, and possibly from the development in both vbs. of the notion of constraint or pressure, the OE. vb. appears to have been, by 1200, identified with the Norse vb., so that in ME. they were treated more or less as parallel forms of one and the same word, and actually appear in some cases as variant MS. readings. In ME., *thrust, thrist* was esp. northern and north midland, and *threst* predominantly southern, where it still survived in 1542. The past tense *thraste* is here placed under *threst*, to which in form it belongs; but it is possible that it was also used by some whose present tense was *thrist*, or *thrust*.]

(The OE. sense 1. *intr.* to twist, writhe, 2. *trans.* to torture, torment, plague, afflict, 3. to compress, constrain, compel, did not come down into ME.)

1. *intr.* To press (*in, out, together*, etc.); to push one's way; to crowd; = THRUST *v.* 3.

α. *c* **1205** LAY. 23372 Mine cnihtes balde scullen þræsten [*c* **1275** þreaste] bi-foren me. *a* **1225** *St. Marher.* 9 In his ihurnd heauet..þreaste smeorðrinde smoke ut. *a* **1225** *Ancr. R.* 220 (MS. C) 'Irruerunt super me' þet is, heo þresten in uppon me. *Ibid.* 314 One schipe þet haueð monie þurles, þer þet water þrest in. **13..** *Sir Beues* (A.) 4157 So harde þai þreste to gedre þo, Þat here gerþes borste ato. *c* **1386** CHAUCER *Knt.'s T.* 1754 He thurgh the thikkeste of the throng gan threste. *c* **1500** *Melusine* 289 The valyaunt geffray..smote his hors with his sporys, & thrested in to myddes of his enemys.

β. *c* **1205** LAY. 26318 Moni þusenden þrasten [*c* 1275 þreste] ut of telden. *Ibid.* 26633 þer after comen þrasten [*c* 1275 comen þreaste] þritto þusen[d] anan. *c* **1375** *Cursor M.* 19462 (Fairf.) þen sulde alle to him þrast. *c* **1380** *Sir Ferumb.* 1977 Forþ sche þraste among hem alle. *c* **1386** CHAUCER *Doctor's T.* 260 But right anon a thousand peple in thraste To saue the knyght. *a* **1400–50** *Alexander* 2939 Ʒit he threw to þe thrid & thrast inn þare-eftir. *c* **1440** *Partonope* 7053 Forth into the Reynes he tharst And aboute hym leyde on fast.

2. *trans.* To pierce, stab; to give (one) a thrust; = THRUST *v.* 5.

c **1205** LAY. 30853 He com him bæften and imong al þan þrunge þærsten him in þan ruge. **1508** FISHER *7 Penit. Ps.* xxxii. Wks. (1876) 30 Lyke as he hadde ben thraste thrugh the herte with a thorne. **1526** R. WHYTFORD *Martiloge* 138 After all she was thrast unto the herte with a swerde. **1532** —— *Werke for Househ.* G iij, One of the sowdyours made a wounde in his syde, and thraste him to the herte with a spere.

3. To push forcibly or violently; = THRUST *v.* 1, 6.

c **1275** LAY. 1898 Gemagog..þraste [*c* 1205 þudde] Corineum framward his breoste. *c* **1325** *Song of Yesterday* 69 in *E.E.P.* (1862) 135 þenne schal vr bodies in eorþe be þrast. **13..** *K. Alis.* 3326 Beste He can his launce thorugh threste [*Bodl. MS.* þrest]. **1340** *Ayenb.* 204 Hy þresten out hare eȝen. *c* **1374** CHAUCER *Troylus* II. 1106 (1155) And yn here bosom þe lettre doun he þraste. *c* **1400** *Rom. Rose* 6825 By my treget, I gadre and threste The gret tresour into my cheste. *c* **1430** *Syr Gener.* (Roxb.) 8740 The cheke in twoo he brast, And his neke on sondre thrast. **1484** CAXTON *Fables of Auian* ii, The Egle..thrested his clowes in to the tortoses bely. **1508** FISHER *7 Penit. Ps.* cii. Wks. (1876) 171 Now we be thraste downe in to a very streyght angyll. *c* **1510** MORE *Picus* Wks. 22 As a thefe betwene two theues threst. *c* **1530** L. COX *Rhet.* (1899) 61 He thrast his hande into the fyre. **1534** WHITINTON *Tullyes Offices* III. (1540) 131 In no wyse he ought to threst downe that man that proueth maystryes with hym.

4. To press, squeeze; to crush; = THRUST *v.* 4.

c **1410** *Master of Game* (MS. Digby 182) xxiv, If..þe foote and þe knees haue ythrest doune wele þe erth and ypressede þe grasse a doune,..it is a grete deere and an heuy. *a* **1450** *Tundale's Vis.* (Wagner) 1357 He thrust [*MS. A*, thrast] hem, as men dose Grapes, to wryng out the wose. **1494** FABYAN *Chron.* VII. 417 At whiche coronacion was so excedynge prease, that a knyght, called sir Iohn Bakwell, was threstyd to deth.

b. To crowd; to cram; = THRUST 3 c.

c **1400** *Destr. Troy* 4129 Two and thretty thried shippes þrast full of pepull. **1542** UDALL *Erasm. Apoph.* 49 b, [They] poure their throtes and bealies thrasting full.

c. *fig.* To oppress, vex.

1513 DOUGLAS *Æneis* I. v. 58 Sen sic thochtis the thraistis [*rime* traistis].

Hence †**thresting** *vbl. sb.*, pressing, squeezing, crushing.

1481 CAXTON *Reynard* xli. (Arb.) 111 The threstyng that he suffred in his colyons made hym so faynt. **1483** —— *Gold. Leg.* 245/2 The deken fyll [= fell]..by thympulsion and threstyng of the paynems.

threst(e, obs. ff. THIRST.

threstel, -yll, obs. ff. THROSTLE.

threstle, obs. f. TRESTLE.

threswold, obs. f. THRESHOLD *sb.*

thret, threte, obs. forms of THREAT.

†**threte**, *sb. Sc. Obs.* In 6 threit, *pl.* thretis. Origin and meaning obscure. Occurs app. only in Douglas's *Æneis*, where it is expletive, answering to nothing in the Latin. Referred in Ruddiman's *Glossary*, 1710, to THREAT *sb.*, and explained as 'a throng, crowd, haste, speed'.

Jamieson takes it in the first quot. as 'throng, crowd' (which does not suit the context); the second and third examples he renders 'in haste, eagerly', the fourth 'in pairs, in couples'. In all the passages we have perhaps strained applications of THREAT *sb.* sense 2, 'pressure, etc.' introduced for the sake of rime.

1513 DOUGLAS *Æneis* II. [x.] ix. 33 Scho..Him towart hir hes brocht, but ony threte. *Ibid.* v. ii. 117 Sum vthir..the colis hett Wndir the speitis swakkis, to roist in threit The raw spaldis ordanit for the muld meit. *Ibid.* XII. xii. 141 The rynnyng hund dois hym [the hart] assail in threte Baith with swyft raise and with his questis grete. *Ibid.* XII. ix. 78 That this Murranus the renis and the thetis Quharwyth hys stedis ʒokkit war in thretis Vndyr the quhelis hes do weltit doun.

†**threte**, *v. Obs. rare.* Pa. t. in 5 thret. [a. ON. *þrǽta* (*þrætta*) to quarrel, dispute, wrangle, Sw. *träta* Da. *trættes* refl. to quarrel, strive, contest. (See Falk & Torp s.v. *Trætte*.)] *intr.* To dispute, contend; to quarrel, wrangle.

13.. *E.E. Allit. P.* A. 560, I hyred þe for a peny a grete, Quy bygynnez þou now to þrete? *c* **1430** *This World but Vanyte* 20 in *Hymns Virgin* (1867) 83 þe kinde of childhode y dide also, Wiþ my felawis to fiȝte and þrete. *c* **1450** *St. Cuthbert* (Surtees) 7110 þai were stonyd what þis moght mene, What þai suld do þai thret þaim betwene. **1513** DOUGLAS *Æneis* VIII. Prol. 17 So thochtis thretis in thra our breistis ourthwort. [Probably belongs here.]

threten, thretne, thrett(e, etc., obs. ff. THREAT, THREATEN.

thretinde, obs. f. THREETINED.

threttene, -tende, -tethe, -ty, obs. ff. THIRTEEN, -TEENTH, THIRTIETH, -TY.

threu, obs. form of THREW, THROUGH.

threuch, threwgh, obs. ff. THROUGH *sb.*[1], tombstone, etc.

threuth, obs. form of TRUTH.

threve, obs. and dial. form of THRAVE.

threw, pa. t. of THROW *v.*

threw, obs. form of THROUGH *prep.*, TRUE.

thribble, thrible ('θrɪb(ə)l), dial. var. of TREBLE *sb.*, *a.* and *adv.*, *v.* Also *spec.* in oil drilling (see quots. 1932, 1975).

1829 J. HUNTER *Hallamshire Gloss.* 90 *Thribble*, treble. **1877** *Wide Awake* IV. 348/2 O, let the corn swell till it's three times as bulky as it was in the beginning; that's that's [*sic*] we call 'thribbling'. **1904** E. NESBIT *Phoenix & Carpet* i. 1 The man at the shop said they were worth thribble the money. **1932** *Amer. Speech* VII. 271 *Thrible*.., a *stand* of three joints of pipe. *Thrible-board*.., a platform in the derrick at the height of a *thrible*. **1975** J. BLACK *Oil* II. ii. 158 Drill pipe came in thirty-foot lengths. These were screwed into sixty- or ninety-foot segments, known to oil field workers as 'doubles' or 'thribbles'.

thricche, thrich(e, obs. forms of THRUTCH.

thrice (θraɪs), *adv.* Forms: α. 3 (*Orm.*) **þriȝess**, 3–5 **þries**, thryese, 4 **þryys**, 4–5 **thries**, 4–6 **thryes**, **-is**, 5 **threes**, **threies**, **thryess**, 6 *Sc.* **thryiss**. β. 4 **þrys**, **þriis**, **thrijs**, 4–5 **thrys**, **threys**, 4–6 **thris**, 4–7 **thrise**, **thryse**, 5 **thrisse**, 5–6 **thryss**, 7 **thryce**, 6– **thrice**. [ME. *þriȝes*, *priës*, *pryës*, f. *prië*, *pryë*, THRIE + *-s* of advb. genitive, after ME. *anes*, *ones*, ONCE: cf. *twice*.

From *c* 1600 spelt *thrice*, to indicate the long vowel and the breath sound of *s*, as in *dice*, *mice*, *nice*, *twice*, etc.]

1. Three times (in succession); on three successive occasions.

c **1200** ORMIN 1149 Ure Laferrd..Badd hise bedess þriȝess. *a* **1225** *Ancr. R.* 106 He weop himsulf þries mid his feire eien. *c* **1275** LAY. 26066 And so Arthur..bi-vrne hit þries [*c* 1205 þreie]. *a* **1300** *Cursor M.* 20973 (Cott.) Paule.. Scipbreging he suffurd thrise [*v.rr.* þries, thrijs]. *c* **1330** R. BRUNNE *Chron. Wace* (Rolls) 11340 Was þer no knyght of so hey blod..þat þer fore scholde be holde in pris, But he in dede were proued þrys. **1350–1400** *Sir Beues* (MS. E.) 4313 + 208 þryys sche ffyl doun to þe grounde. *c* **1375** *Lay Folks Mass Bk.* (MS. B.) 308 At þo ende [he] sayes sanctus thryese. *c* **1400** MAUNDEV. (Roxb.) xi. 45 þare denyed Petre oure Lord threyes. *a* **1400–50** *Alexander* 2279 þus fall þou thrisse. *c* **1400** *Brut* cxciv. 214 [He] felle adoun..and þries [**1480** CAXTON thryes] cussede þe grounde. **1425** in Entick *London* (1766) IV. 354 Threies seaven Ave Marias, with xv Pater Nosters and thre credes. *a* **1450** *Knt. de la Tour* (1906) 85 The king sent vnto her onis, tuyes, thries, and she denied not to come. **1456** SIR G. HAYE *Law Arms* (S.T.S.) 170 Israel was discomfyte twys, or thris. **1548–9** (Mar.) *Bk. Com. Prayer, Baptism*, Namyng the childe, [he] shall dyppe it in the water thryse. *a* **1550** *Freiris of Berwik* 356 in *Dunbar's Poems* (S.T.S.) 297 He turnit him abowt Weill thryiss. **1563–7** BUCHANAN *Reform. St. Andros* Wks. (1892) 16 Twyss or thryis in the ȝeir. **1611** BIBLE *Mark* xiv. 30 Before the cocke crowe twise, thou shalt deny me thrise [TIND. thryse]. **1732** ARBUTHNOT *Rules of Diet* in *Aliments*, etc. 418 A Spoonful or two of Canary Wine twice or thrice a day. **1842** BORROW *Bible in Spain* xxxiv. (Pelh. Libr.) 246 Though I left it thrice, it was of my own free will.

2. Three times as much as (in number, amount, or value). Often vaguely or hyperbolically: Many times (as much).

Usually preceding a numeral, or const. with *as*, or with comparative (now *rare* or *obs.*).

a **1300** *Cursor M.* 430 Angels..þat suld of ordres haf thris thre. **1427** in *10th Rep. Hist. MSS. Comm.* App. v. 295 Threes as much as he..shall losse. *c* **1460** *Wisdom* 649 in *Macro Plays* 56 More þan I take, spende I threys iij. **1528** in *Exch. Rolls Scotl.* XV. 666 Bot giff the personis..be vailȝeand in gudis wortht thryss the gudis at ar pundit. **1552** HULOET, Thrise as muche, *triplaris*, *e.* *c* **1600** SHAKS. *Sonnets* lvi. 14 Which..Makes Sommers welcome thrice more wish'd, more rare. **1605** *1st Pt. Ieronimo* (1901) I. i, I haue a hart thrice stronger then my years. *a* **1771** GRAY *Death Hoel* 12 Thrice two hundred warriors. **1849** MACAULAY *Hist. Eng.* iii. I. 344 A sum more than thrice as great as the whole income of the English crown in 1685. **1859** TENNYSON *Geraint & Enid* 557 With some surprise and thrice as much disdain.

†**b.** In three manners or respects. *Obs.*

1607–12 BACON *Ess., Great Place* (Arb.) 278 Men in great place, are thrice seruauntes; Servauntes of the Sovereigne, or State, Servauntes of fame, and seruauntes of businesse.

3. Combined with a pa. pple., forming an attrib. phrase or compound adj. (in senses 1 and 2).

1508 KENNEDIE *Flyting w. Dunbar* 30 Thryse scheild [? sealed] trumpir. **1600** SHAKS. *A.Y.L.* III. ii. 2 Thou thrice crowned Queene of night. **1693** J. DRYDEN in *D.'s Juvenal* xiv. (1697) 353 A Dish Of thrice-boil'd Beans. **1742** YOUNG *Nt. Th.* IV. 37 Like a thrice-told tale. **1864** PUSEY *Lect. Daniel* v. 283 A hundred millions thrice-told.

b. Similarly with any adjective, used vaguely or hyperbolically (as in 2): Very, highly, greatly, extremely (cf. L. *ter*).

1579 G. HARVEY *Letter-bk.* (Camden) 60 Howe will my right worshipfull and thrisevenerable masters of Cambridge scorne at the matter? *Ibid.* 61 Thrishonorable. **1593** SHAKS. *2 Hen. VI*, III. ii. 157 This thrice-famed Duke. **1631** WEEVER *Anc. Fun. Mon.* 536 This thrice-noble family of the Percies. **1667** MILTON *P.L.* III. 570 Thrice happy Iles. **1850** TENNYSON *In Mem.* xxxii. 13 Thrice blest whose lives are faithful prayers.

4. As quasi-*adj.* Thrice performed; threefold, triple (*rare*); in first quot. vaguely: Very great.

1470–85 MALORY *Arthur* IV. xix. 143 Ther were many knyghtes that ouermatched syr gawayne for alle the thryes myghte that he had. **1600** W. WATSON *Decacordon* (1602) 44 S. Peter..after his relapse with thrise denial and forswearing of him. **1619** DRAYTON *Heroic Ep., E. Cobham to Dk. Humphrey* Argt. 9 For which, she her thrice-Penance was assign'd. *a* **1866** NEALE *Sequences, Hymns*, etc. 21 Till the thrice Confession Blot the thrice Denial out.

thrice-cock ('θraɪskɒk). *dial.* [f. var. THRUSH[1] + COCK *sb.*[1] 9 b.] = MISSEL-THRUSH; cf. *storm-cock* s.v. STORM *sb.* 6 e.

1819 M. EDGEWORTH *Let.* 26 Jan. (1971) 160 The Thrice-Cock..is the largest kind of thrush. **1913** H. K. SWANN *Dict. Eng. & Folk-Names Brit. Birds* 236 Thrice Cock. A Midland and North of England name for the Mistle-thrush. **1965** *Jrnl. Lancs. Dial. Soc.* XIV. 9 Mistle Thrush... Thricecock: Oldham. Cf. Fieldfare.

thrid, var. THREAD, esp. the vb.; obs. f. THIRD.

thridace ('θrɪdəs). *Pharm.* Also *erron.* **thridach.** [ad. mod.L. *thridacium*, f. Gr. θρίδαξ lettuce. Cf. F. *thridace*.] The inspissated juice of lettuce, used as a sedative; = LACTUCARIUM.

1831 J. DAVIES *Manual Mat. Med.* 313 Thridace... Juice furnished during the time of fructification by the Garden Lettuce, *Lactuca sativa*. **1836** J. M. GULLY *Magendie's Formul.* (ed. 2) 164 The *lactucarium* of Dr. Duncan, and the thridach of Dr. François, are nothing more than the white, viscid juice of the garden lettuce..at the flowering time of the plant. **1857** DUNGLISON *Dict. Med. Sc.*, *Thridace*.

thridde, thriddendele, obs. ff. THIRD, THIRDENDEAL.

thride, obs. f. THIRD, THREAD.

†**thrie, thrye,** *adv.* *Obs.* Forms: α. 1 **þriwa**, **ðriȝa**, **ðriȝe**, **ðria**, 2 **þreowe**, 3 **þreie**, 3–4 **þrie**, 4–5 **þrye**, **thrie**, (4 **thry**), 5 **thrye**. β. 3 **þrien**, **þreoien**, 4 **thrien**. [OE. *þriwa*, *ðriȝa* = OFris. *thrî(i)a*, OS. *thrîuuo*, *thrîio*. Like *twiwa*, etc., not found outside the Saxon-Frisian group of WGer., and of obscure formation. They seem to have the form of genitival advbs., *twi-a*, *pri-a*, with the gap between *i* and *a* variously filled up by *w* and ȝ (again lost in ME.), and lengthened by assimilation to *prí*, THREE. See further under TWIE.] Three times; thrice.

α. *c* **950** *Lindisf. Gosp.* Mark xiv. 30 Ðria [*Rushw.* ðriȝe] mec ðu bist onsæcc. *c* **1000** *Ags. Gosp.* ibid., þriwa [*c* **1160** *Hatton Gosp.*, þreowe] wiðsæcst min. *c* **1020** *Rule St. Benet* ix. (Logeman) 38 Oðer sidon þriwa is to singanne. *c* **1205** LAY. 17432 þrie he eode abuten. *Ibid.* 26066 Arður & þe scucke biurnen hit þreie a-buten. **1297** R. GLOUC. (Rolls) 10056 þer on he smot þrie þe wrecche to gret pine. *c* **1375** *Cursor M.* 13627 (Fairf.) Quy quarto sulde I tel ȝou mare? Twy or thry I talde ȝou are. *c* **1460** *Compl. Criste* 88 in *Pol. Rel. & L. Poems* 164 The devylle me tempttyd neuer but thrye, But þou me temptyst frome day to daye. ? *a* **1500** *Chester Pl.* (Shaks. Soc.) II. 25 Or the cocke have crowen thrye Thou shalte forsake my companye.

β. *c* **1205** LAY. 14338 þenne cusseoð heo þreoien. —— 14352 þat maide..þrien hine custe. **13..** *Judas* 33 in *Rel. Ant.* I. 144 Thou wolt fursake me thrien, ar the coc him crowe.

thrie, þrie, obs. form of THREE.

thrief, -ve, thriep, obs. ff. THRAVE, THREAP.

thries, þries, obs. form of THRICE.

thrift (θrɪft), *sb.*[1] Also 3–5 **þrift(e**, (4 **þruft**, **þreft**, **þref**), 4–5 **þryft**, 4–6 **thryft(e** (**threft**), 5–6 **thrifte** (6 **thryfft**). [f. THRIVE *v.* + -T *suffix*[3] a: cf. *drift*, *gift*, *rift*, *weft*, etc.; also ON. *þrift*, occasional synonym of *þrif* thriving condition, well-doing, prosperity, which may have reinforced the word in the north of England.]

†**1. a.** The fact or condition of thriving or prospering; prosperity, success, good luck; in early use sometimes = fortune (good or bad); luck: cf. THRIVE *v.* 1. *Obs.*

c **1305** *St. James* 70 in *E.E.P.* (1862) 59 Sorewe him mote bifalle And liþer þrift vpon his heued. **13..** *Cursor M.* 4439 (Cott.) He ferd ai wit so mikel thrift þat al was don als he wald scift. **1362** LANGL. *P. Pl.* A. x. 105 And men þat Cunne mony Craftes..þruft or þeodam with hem selden is I-seye. *c* **1380** *Sir Ferumb.* 2017 Mahoun ȝyue þe euele þref. *c* **1386** CHAUCER *Reeve's T.* 129 By my thrift [*v.rr.* þreft, thryft], yet shal I blere hir eye. *c* **1412** HOCCLEVE *De Reg. Princ.* 386 Now good thrifte come vn-to þe, sone dere! *c* **1440** *Promp. Parv.* 490/1 Thedam (or thryfte), *vigencia*. **1549** COVERDALE, etc. *Erasm. Par. Phil.* 5 The entrie vnto immortall thrifte is throughe losse of transitorie thynges. *a* **1625** FLETCHER & MASSINGER *Laws of Candy* IV. i, I could wish All thrift to his affections. **1679** BUNYAN *Fear of God* Wks. (ed. Offor) I. 485 Every grace is nourished by the Word, and without it there is no thrift in the soul.

b. Means of thriving; industry, labour; profitable occupation. Now *dial.*

c **1580** LODGE *Reply Gosson's Sch. Abuse* (Hunter. Cl.) 3 You are..a man of the letter little sauoring of learning, your giddy brain made you leaue your thrift, and your abuses in London some part of your honestie. **1596** SPENSER *State Irel.* Wks. (Globe) 662/1 To fall to thrifte, as I have seene manye souldiours after the service to proove verye good husbandes. **1612** DEKKER *If it be not good* Wks. 1873 III. 270 Dread King of Ghosts, weele plye our thrift so well, Thou shalt be forc'd to enlarge thy Iayle of Hell. **1612** R. CHURTON (*title*) An Old Thrift newly Revived, wherein is declared the manner of Planting..and Husbanding Young Trees. **1721** RAMSAY *Ode to Mr. F——* 17 Poor Vulcan hard at thrift, Gets mony a sair and heavy lift. **1816** SCOTT *Antiq.* xxvi, With her distaff..and her spindle..she plied..the old fashioned Scottish thrift, according to the old fashioned Scottish manner.

c. Prosperous growth, physical thriving.

c **1230** *Hali Meid.* 37 His waxunge se lat & se slaw his þrifti [? þrift; *v.r.* þriftre]. **1615** W. LAWSON *Country Housew. Gard.* (1626) 22 Manie trees stand so thicke, that one could not thriue for the throng of his neighbours... Hence small thrift, gals, wounds. **1857–8** SEARS *Athan.* viii. 66 The outward bark..scaling off that the tree may expand with more thrift and freedom.

d. Growing-pains. *dial.*

a **1800** PEGGE *Suppl. Grose*, *Thrift*, the pain which young persons feel in growing. Lanc. **1886** *Chester Gloss.* s.v., What ails thee, pooin thi face? It's nowt bu' th' thrift that tha's getten. **1887** *S. Chesh. Gloss.*, *Thrift*, 'thriving' or growing pains.

2. a. Savings, earnings, gains, profit; acquired wealth, estate, or substance. *arch.* (Cf. FRUGALITY c.)

a **1310** in Wright *Lyric P.* xv. 47 In luthere lastes y am layn, That maketh myn thriftes thunne. **1436** *Eng. Policy* in *Pol. Poems* (Rolls) II. 174 They bere the golde owte of thys londe, And souketh the thryfte awey oute of oure honde. **1508** KENNEDIE *Flyting w. Dunbar* 443 Thou drank thy thrift, sald and wedsett thy clais. **1530** PALSGR. 280/2 Thrifte gayne, *proufit*. **1605** *Play Stucley* in Simpson *Sch. Shaks.* (1878) I. 195 He that drinks, or spends his thrift at dice. **1805** HOLCROFT *Bryan Perdue* III. 264 Our worldly thrift was more than equal to all our wants. **1893** CHR. G. ROSSETTI *Poems* (1904) 223/2 If much were mine, then manifold Would be the offering of my thrift.

†**b.** That which is saved (*of* something); savings. *Obs.*

In quot. 1387 rendering L. *nucleus*; sense intended doubtful.

1387 TREVISA *Higden* (Rolls) II. 15 þe þrift of þe fatnesse drieþ himself þeryn. **1519** HORMAN *Vulg.* 159 Mynse all the thryfte [L. *compendium*] of the fresshe: and mengle it with the spice.

3. a. Economical management, economy; sparing use or careful expenditure of means; frugality, saving; †euphemistically, parsimony, niggardliness (*obs.*).

1553 *Respublica* v. iii. 1343 As..bodylye foode is never founde to bee so pleasaunte nor so goode As whan fretting hongre and thrift hathe pincht afore. **1570** LEVINS *Manip.* 118/6 Thrift, *frugalitas, atis*. **1600** J. PORY tr. *Leo's Africa* II. 58 These people are well given to thrift and good husbandry. **1608–11** BP. HALL *Medit.* 99 So devotion is counterfaited by superstition, good thrift by niggardliness. **1784** COWPER *Task* IV. 398 With all this thrift they thrive not. **1849** LONGF. *Kavanagh* 152 The air of comfort and plenty, of neatness, thrift, and equality, visible everywhere. **1876** GREEN *Stray Stud.* 26 The true cure for pauperism lies in the growth of thrift among the poor.

b. *U.S.* A savings and loan association.

1981 *Economist* 24 Jan. 28/1 This new charter for the thrifts, as they are called, has not been welcomed by all of them. **1982** *Sunday Sun-Times* (Chicago) 12 Sept. 65 In an effort to keep the funds, banks and thrifts will fire a fusillade of advertising.

4. A name given to various plants.

†**a.** Said by Turner to have been a name for the Stone Orpine (*Sedum reflexum*). *Obs. rare.*

1538 TURNER *Libellus* s.v. *Sedum*, Sedum minus puto esse herbam quam uulgus appellat Thryft; aut Stoncrop. **1548** —— *Names of Herbes* (1881) 72 The seconde kynde is called in English thryft or stoncroppe. **1562** —— *Herbal* II. 133 The lesse Semperuiuum, that we call thrift or great stone crop, groweth in walles, rockes, mudwalles,..it hath manye stalkes comming from one root.

b. The plant *Armeria maritima* (*vulgaris*), a well-known sea-shore and alpine plant bearing rose-pink, white, or purple flowers on naked stems growing from a dense tuft of grass-like radical leaves. Also called *sea-pink*, *sea gillyflower*, *sea-grass*, and *ladies' cushion*.

1592 GREENE *Upst. Courtier* (1871) 5 The weed they so wrangled for was a little dapper flower, like a ground honeysuckle, called thrift. **1597** GERARDE *Herbal* II. clxxvii. 483 Called..in English Thrift, Sea grasse, and our Ladies Cushion. **1688** R. HOLME *Armoury* II. 64/1 Thrift..is only set in Gardens to keep up Borders. **1814** WORDSW. *Excursion* I. 722 Daisy-flowers and thrift Had..straggled O'er paths they used to deck. **1856** DELAMER *Fl. Gard.* (1861) 104 Thrift... The English name is derived from its thriftiness in towns and confined situations, though its native home is on the grassy tops of cliffs whose base is washed by the waves. **1862** BARING-GOULD *Iceland* (1863) 242 The thrift with its rose coloured flower heads was very abundant.

c. Hence extended to other species of *Armeria*: e.g. **great thrift**, *A. Cephalotes*, of the Mediterranean region; **plantain thrift**, *A. plantaginea*, found in Jersey; also to plants of allied genera or similar habit, as **lavender thrift**, *Statice Limonium*; **prickly thrift**, *Acantholimon glumaceum*, a pretty garden rock-plant.

1776–96 WITHERING *Brit. Plants* (ed. 3) II. 320 Lavender Thrift. Sea banks near Walton, Essex. **1866** *Treas. Bot.* 1147 Prickly Thrift, *Acantholimon*.

5. *attrib.* and *Comb.*, as (in sense 3) *thrift club*, *society*, etc.; (in sense 4) *thrift edging*; **thrift-box, -pot**, a box or pot in which savings are put; **thrift industry** *U.S.*, savings and loan associations as a whole; **thrift institution** *U.S.*, a savings and loan association; **thrift shop** chiefly *U.S.*, **thrift store** *U.S.*, a shop at which second-hand goods (esp. clothes) are sold, usu. in aid of charity.

1777 BRAND *Pop. Antiq.* 164 *note*, A Thrift-Box..is put up against the Wall, and every Customer puts in something. **1899** *Daily News* 5 June 4/3 Round these 'schools' have grown thrift clubs, and benevolent societies. **1786** ABERCROMBIE *Gard. Assist.* 95 Box and thrift edgings. **1902** *Daily Chron.* 27 Mar. 7/6 Unregulated shop clubs or thrift funds. **1981** *Financial Rev.* (Austral.) 1 May 18 When higher interest rates were paid, the thrift industry—building societies, savings banks, credit unions—tended to lose funds to competing institutions. **1982** *Times* 22 May 13/3 The United States House of Representatives..voted to shore up ailing thrift institutions. **1835** *Fair-Day* 82 You could break your thrift-pot..and get to the money. **1947** S. J. PERELMAN *Westward Ha!* (1949) xii. 153 A mound of shawls, brocades, bracelets, necklaces, purses, fans, and bric-a-brac resembling the contents of a thrift shop. **1976** *Eastern Even. News* (Norwich) 9 Dec. 2/5 Mums and toddlers and thrift shop, 76, Cadge Road, Community House, 2–4. **1897** *Daily News* 8 May 7/4 It [a mission] has established thrift societies [etc.]. **1972** T. ARDIES *This Suitcase* ix. 85 Someone had probably gone to thrift stores to put together his wardrobe. .. Even his socks were the wrong size.

thrift, *sb.*[2] [Origin obscure. Cf. ON. *þrífa* to grip: but connecting links are unknown.] The handle (usu. wooden) of a mill bill, which is fixed in a mortise in the thick head of the handle.

c **1900** *Circular of Bryan Corcoran Lim.*, Mill Bill in Wood Thrift..Iron Thrift, Steel Thrift. *Ibid.*, Model Mill Bill stone dressing machine..the thrift is set in a ball hinge... Like in ordinary hand dressing, the thrift is worked to give the blow. **1969** G. E. EVANS *Farm & Village* xiv. 150 The *mill-bill*—it's a kind of steel pick or bill mounted in a *thrift* or handle, made of wych-elm or some other suitable wood.

thrift, *v.* [f. THRIFT *sb.*[1]] *trans.* To save thriftily, to economize.

1869 BLACKMORE *Lorna D.* ii, Not that I ever bore much wealth, but because I had been thrifting it for this time. **1885** L. LEVI in *Pall Mall G.* 13 Jan. 6/2 The earnings of agricultural labourers..if well thrifted, leave a surplus.

thriftful (ˈθrɪftfʊl), *a. rare.* [f. THRIFT *sb.*[1] + -FUL.] Marked by frugality or careful expenditure, thrifty.

1933 V. MCNABB *Nazareth or Social Chaos* 75 If..only a country organization is naturally thriftful, it would seem that a town-organization will..end with a famine of real wealth. **1968** P. FALVURY *Poems Old & New* 130 No thriftful scrutiny was drawn When, ere creation's mighty dawn, Thou plannedst man's abode.

thriftily (ˈθrɪftɪlɪ), *adv.* Also 4–5 *Sc.* thryftly, 5–6 thriftly, 6 thriftely. [f. THRIFTY + -LY[2].]

†**1.** In a becoming or seemly manner, properly; worthily, handsomely, finely; hence, thoroughly, soundly, well. *Obs.*

c **1374** CHAUCER *Troylus* III. 162 (211) She toke here leue at hem ful þryftyly. *c* **1375** *Sc. Leg. Saints* xiii. (*Marcus*) 128 þe byschape anany did his office ful thryftly. *c* **1386** CHAUCER *Prol.* 105 A sheef of pecok arwes bright and kene Vnder his belt he bar ful thriftily. *c* **1449** PECOCK *Repr.* (Rolls) 43 If thei schulen thriftli serue to God. *a* **1586** SIDNEY *Arcadia* III. Wks. 1724 II. 704 Thou..hast sung well and thriftily. **1638** EARL STRAFFORD *Lett. & Disp.* (1739) II. 208 Nor that they will..be brought into their right Wits, till they be well and thriftily cudgelled back into them.

2. Frugally, sparingly, economically, carefully.

1581 PETTIE *Guazzo's Civ. Conv.* III. (1586) 140 It..doth him good to see his wife so thriftely giuen. **1599** HAKLUYT *Voy.* II. II. 108 That they might..husband it more thriftily. **1694** FALLE *Jersey* iii. 96 Our Kings heretofore did use to dispose of this Revenue more thriftily than they now do. **1712** STEELE *Spect.* No. 430 ¶1 A blind Beggar..with a Needle and Thread thriftily mending his Stockings. **1883** S. C. HALL *Retrospect* II. 315 They could neither order a household thriftily, nor cut out a gown.

3. Thrivingly, flourishingly; vigorously.

1865 E. BURRITT *Walk Land's End* vii. 215 Two of the largest and oldest California pines are growing most thriftily in these gardens. **1894** A. G. ROBINSON in *Amer. Missionary* Sept. 330 The seed..is growing thriftily, and..will bear a harvest.

thriftiness (ˈθrɪftɪnɪs). [f. as prec. + -NESS.] The state or quality of being thrifty.

†**1.** Thriving condition, prosperity. *Obs. rare*$^{-1}$.

c **1530** *Proper Dyaloge* in *Rede me*, etc. (Arb.) 137 They haue brought the lande to beggery And all thryftynes clene awaye swepte.

2. The quality of being frugal or saving; economy, good husbandry: cf. THRIFT *sb.*[1] 3.

1552 ELYOT *Dict.*, *Frugalitas*..thriftines. **1576** FLEMING *Panopl. Epist.* 225 A minde..contented with perseuerance, with frugalitie or thriftinesse. **1645** USSHER *Body Div.* (1647) 304 Parsimony or thriftiness; whereby we honestly keep and preserve our goods. **1782** KNOX *Ess.* lxxxvii. II. 22 The qualities distinguished by the homely titles of thriftiness and good housewifery. **1826** F. REYNOLDS in *Life & Times* II. 83 [He was] a compound of liberality and thriftiness. **1884** *Brit. Almanac & Comp.* 65 The actual increase of national thriftiness.

thriftless (ˈθrɪftlɪs), *a.* [f. THRIFT[1] + -LESS.]

†**1.** Not thriving or prosperous; unsuccessful; unfortunate. *Obs.*

c **1400** *Brut* ccxiii. 249 Longe berde hertles, peyntede Hode witles, Gay cote graceles, makeþ Englisshemen þriftles. **1467** *Songs Costume* (Percy) 56 Ye prowd galantts hertlesse, With your hygh cappis witlesse, And your schort gownys thriftlesse. *a* **1585** MONTGOMERIE *Flyting* 387 This thriftlesse [infant] is meit for vs. **1591** *Troub. Raigne K. John* (1611) 39 As they shoulder thee from out thine owne,..So heauens crosse them with a thriftless course. **1592** WARNER *Alb. Eng.* VIII. xli. (1612) 197 A thriftles Mariage with the trustles King of Spaine.

†**b.** Not flourishing (in physical condition).

1693 OWEN *Glory Chr.* II. Wks. 1852 I. 442 If men will neglect their daily food..it is no wonder if they be weak and thriftless.

2. Unprofitable, worthless, useless. Now *rare.*

1568 T. HOWELL *Arb. Amitie* (1879) 87 Pleasant sights begin to growe, among the thriftles thornes. **1601** SHAKS. *Twel. N.* II. ii. 40 What thriftlesse sighes shall poore Oliuia breath? *a* **1619** FOTHERBY *Atheom.* I. vi. §4 (1622) 47 The most thriftles and vnprofitable part of all the whole Tree. **1750** SHENSTONE *Rural Elegance* 65 E'en thriftless furze detains their wand'ring sight. **1840** CARLYLE *Heroes* v, A man must not complain of his 'element', of his 'time', or the like; it is thriftless work doing so.

3. Devoid of thrift; without frugality or economy; wasteful, improvident, spendthrift.

1576 GASCOIGNE *Philomene* 9 These thriftles birds..which spend the day, In needlesse notes. **1593** SHAKS. *Rich. II*, v. iii. 69 He shall spend mine Honour, with his Shame; As thriftlesse Sonnes, their scraping Fathers Gold. **1647** SANDERSON *Serm.* (1657) II. 291 The unjust Steward; a faithless, and a thriftless man. **1702** *Guide for Constables* 101 The thriftless poor. **1862** SIR B. BRODIE *Psychol. Inq.* II. iii. 105 The artisans in crowded cities..to a great extent indulging in intemperate and thriftless habits.

Hence ˈ**thriftlessly** *adv.*, wastefully; ˈ**thriftlessness**, wastefulness, improvidence.

1846 WORCESTER, Thriftlessly (citing LEE). Thriftlessness (citing CHALMERS). **1847** R. W. HAMILTON *Disq. Sabbath* v. (1848) 188 They cannot spare thus thriftlessly moments which claim each its duty. **1858** *Sat. Rev.* 20 Nov. 494/2 Lords P—— and C—— seem rather to have copied the thriftlessness of Esau. **1862** W. W. STORY *Roba di R.* xii. (1864) 228 The usual thriftlessness of the people, who live from hand to mouth and from day to day.

†**thriftre.** *Obs. rare*$^{-1}$. [If a genuine word, f. THRIFT (or THRIVE), with an uncertain suffix (cf. *laughter*, *slaughter*); but perh. a scribal error of some kind.] = THRIFT *sb.*[1] 1 c.

c **1230** *Hali Meid.* (Bodley MS.: E.E.T.S. ed. 2) 50 His waxunge se lat & se slaw his þriftre [*MS. Titus* þrifti].

thrifty (ˈθrɪftɪ), *a.* [f. THRIFT *sb.*[1] + -Y.]

(In many early quotations, it is not possible to fix the meaning of this adj.; two or three senses equally well suiting the context.)

1. Characterized by success or prosperity (see THRIFT *sb.*[1] 1); thriving, prosperous, well-to-do, successful, flourishing, fortunate.

c **1400** *Destr. Troy* 5454 A thousaund þro men þrifte in armys. *c* **1440** *Generydes* 1134 Now A dayis I lese all that I wanne, Where here before I was a threfty man. **1545** ELYOT s.v. *Res, Rem augere*, to waxe thryfty. **1634** FORD *Perkin Warbeck* v. iii, May he prove more thrifty In this world's just applause, not more desertful. **1697** DAMPIER *Voy.* I. xvii. 487 The Ships crew were not so thrifty in bargaining..as single persons. **1860** HOLLAND *Miss Gilbert* xxi. 371 The family generally has been getting thrifty in the world. **1865** E. BURRITT *Walk Land's End* x. 339 This is a thrifty, modern-looking town. **1876** GREEN *Stray Stud.* 27 Both had become zealous florists, and thrifty, respectable men. **1883** J. W. SHERER *At Home & in India* 24 No one was in thrifty and independent comfort

†**2. a.** Of a person: Worthy, worshipful, estimable, respectable, well-living. Cf. THRIVEN 2, THRIVING *ppl. a.* 1. *Obs.*

c **1374** CHAUCER *Troylus* I. 1081 The gentileste and ek þe most fre The þriftieste and oon þe beste knyght That yn his tyme was. *c* **1456** PECOCK *Bk. Faith* (1909) 202 Ech thrifti sad clerk in logik. **1463** *Bury Wills* (Camden) 26 Sum thrifty man of seynt Marie paryssh to be at the selyng. **1467** in *Eng. Gilds* (1870) 337, ij thrifty comyners, trewe, sufficiant, and feithfulle men. **1556** OLDE *Antichrist* 195 That we may be founde ready, like thriftye servauntes, at the Lordes commyng. **1596** DALRYMPLE tr. *Leslie's Hist. Scot.* IV. (S.T.S.) I. 235 A thryftie man, and proffitable ennimie to gluttonie and al vice.

†**b.** Of an action or concrete thing: Respectable, decent, becoming, proper, as it should be. *Obs.*

c **1386** CHAUCER *Man of Law's Prol.* 46, I kan right now no thrifty tale seyn. *c* **1386** —— *Wife's Prol.* 238, I sitte at hoom, I haue no thrifty clooth. *c* **1430** *Two Cookery-bks.* 31 Draw vppe a þrifti Mylke of Almaundys y-blaunchyd. *Ibid.* 34 Make a gode þryfty Syryppe. *c* **1449** PECOCK *Repr.* (Rolls) 160 The yuel..is pareable and kutteable awey bi good and thrifti bisynes therto sett

3. Thriving physically; growing with vigour; in good or healthy condition; flourishing.

c **1440** *Promp. Parv.* 492/2 Thryfty, *vigens.* *c* **1440** *Generydes* 280 This lady..Brought furth a sonne whiche was a threfte child. **1667** WATERHOUSE *Fire Lond.* 171 Thrifty Oaks, though fleeced of under boughs, yet if not headed, may thrive. **1707** MORTIMER *Husb.* (1721) II. 83 In many Forests and Woods, where you have one thrifty Tree, you have twenty unthrifty Ones. **1862** B. TAYLOR *Home & Abroad* Ser. II. 251 A small but thrifty specimen of the Sequoia, or California tree. **1886** C. SCOTT *Sheep-Farming* 143 A lot of lambs which..have a fresher and thriftier appearance. **1890** MARY E. WILKINS *Humble Rom., Bar Lighth.* (1891) 279 The bush really looked wonderfully thrifty, considering its many drawbacks to growth.

4. Characterized by thrift or frugality; economical, careful of expenditure, sparing, saving; provident.

1526 *Knaresborough Wills* (Surtees) I. 20, I wyll, if none of my sonnes be thryftie nor woll thryve,..the land to thuse of our ladie aulter. **1647** BOYLE in *Life* Wks. 1772 I. p. xix, Thrifty he was extremely, and very skilful in the slights of thrift. **1666** —— *Orig. Formes & Qual.* II. vii, Tis no very thrifty way of Transmutation. **1688** —— *Final Causes Nat. Things* iv. 205 Sometimes God's wisdom seems to be as it were thrifty and solicitous not to bestow on an animal..more than is necessary for the use for which 'tis designed. **1726** SWIFT *Gulliver* II. viii, I told my wife she had been too thrifty, for I found she had starved herself and her daughter. **1746** FRANCIS tr. *Hor., Sat.* II. vi. 167 Thrifty he was, and full of cares To make the most of his affairs. *a* **1768** SECKER *Serm.* (1770) III. v. 104 They who are sparing in their younger Days seldom fail to be much more thrifty in their Decline. *c* **1827** SCOTT *Verses* in Lockhart lxxiv, I've heard your knowing people say, Disown the debt you cannot pay, You'll find it far the thriftiest way. **1859** SMILES *Self-Help* ii. (1860) 35 He was honest,..thrifty and hard-working; and his trade prospered. **1872** YEATS *Growth Comm.* 3 Wealth would accumulate in the hands of the thrifty.

†**b.** Well-husbanded. *Obs. rare.*

1600 SHAKS. *A.Y.L.* II. iii. 39, I haue fiue hundred Crownes, The thriftie hire I saued vnder your Father.

†**c.** *transf.* (?) Of scanty or meagre dimensions.

1599 B. JONSON *Cynthia's Rev.* III. ii, Nor can my weak imperfect memory Now render half the forms unto my tongue, That were convoked within this thrifty room.

thriis, þriis, obs. forms of THRICE.

†**thrildom.** *Sc. Obs.* Also 4 threl-, thryldome. [f. THRILL *sb.*[2] + -DOM. Cf. THIRLDOM.] = THRALDOM.

1375 BARBOUR *Bruce* I. 265 3e may weile se..How hard A thing þat threldome Is. *Ibid.* 269 Thryldome is weill wer þan deid. *c* **1375** *Sc. Leg. Saints* xxii. 377 Fore til deliuer ws of thryldome. **1552** ABP. HAMILTON *Catech.* (1884) 38 In a house of miserable thrildome & bondage.

†ˈ**thrile,** ˈ**thrili,** *a. Obs.* [OE. *þrili*, *þrilig* = OHG. *drilîch*, MHG. *drilich*, *drilch*, mod.Ger. *drillich*, app. WGer. ad. L. *trilix*, *trilīc-em* woven with three threads, f. *trēs*, *tri-* three + *līcium* a thread of a web, a thrum. Cf. Ger. *zwillich*, TWILL.] Woven with three threads; threefold, triple; three in one.

c **725** *Corpus Gloss.* (Hessels) *Interpr.* 322 *Trilex*, ðrili. *a* **800** *Leiden Gloss.* (O.E.T.) 158 *Triplex*, drili. *a* **1000** *Ags. Glosses* in Wr.-Wülcker 279/3 *Triligium*, þrilig hrægil. *a* **1225** *St. Marher.* 11 þrumnesse þreo fald..þrile i þreo hades. *a* **1225** *Ancr. R.* 26 3if me on, almihti God, þrile ine [*printed* me] þreo hodes, þeos ilke þreo þinges.

†**thrill** (θrɪl), *sb.*[1] *Obs.* [A metathetic form of THIRL *sb.*[1]; originally northern.] A hole or aperture; *esp.* a NOSE-THIRL, nostril.

1382 Noose thrillis. *c* **1400** Nose thrilles [see NOSE-THIRL β]. *c* **1400** *Destr. Troy* 3045 Hir nose..With thrilles noght thrat, but thriftily made. *a* **1400–50** *Alexander* 4073 Hale he þam [images] fyndis..& aithire thrill stoppis. **1634** SIR T. HERBERT *Trav.* 211 Her [dodo's] bill is crooked downwards, in midst is the thrill.

Comb. **1618** BRATHWAIT *Descr. Death* xiv, Naked his scalpe, thrill-open is his Nose.

†**thrill,** *sb.*[2] *Sc. Obs.* Also 4 threll, thryll, thril. [OE. *þrǣl*, ON. *þræll*, THRALL *sb.*[1], app. became in Sc. *threll*, which was later narrowed to *thrill*. Cf. THIRL *sb.*[2] 2.] One who is bound in servitude; a thrall. *Comb.* †**thrillman,** bondman.

1375 BARBOUR *Bruce* I. 243 He þt thryll Is has nocht his, All þt he has enbandownyt Is Till hys lord. *Ibid.* 274 Schortly to say, is nane can tell þe halle condicioun off A threll. *Ibid.* III. 220. *c* **1375** *Sc. Leg. Saints* ii. (*Paulus*) 974 To..pure men, to thrillmen & to women. *Ibid.* v. (*Johannes*) 202 Riche man is thril alway to twa: þe tane, is riches. *Ibid.* l. (*Katerine*) 220 Be þe body giff þu will Gowerne þe, þu beis a thrill. *c* **1470** *Golagros & Gaw.* 435 Our doughty elderis has bene endurand Thriuandly in this thede, vnchargit as thril.

thrill (θrɪl), *sb.*[3] [f. THRILL *v.*[1]]

1. a. A subtle nervous tremor caused by intense emotion or excitement (as pleasure, fear, etc.), producing a slight shudder or tingling through the body; a penetrating influx of feeling or emotion.

a **1680** GLANVILL *Serm.* vii. (R.), Joy warms the..blood, and sends it about with a pleasant thrill through all the channels of its motion. **1799** HT. LEE *Canterb. T., Frenchm. T.* (ed. 2) I. 240 Those communications..shot cold thrills through his frame. **1852** MRS. STOWE *Uncle Tom's C.* xxii, St. Clare would feel a sudden thrill, and clasp her in his arms. **1867** SMILES *Huguenots Eng.* xi. (1880) 195 The intelligence caused a thrill of indignation to run throughout England.

b. Thrilling property (of a play, novel, narrative, speech, etc.); sensational quality; *transf.* (*slang*), a literary work having this property, a sensational story, a 'thriller'.

1886 *Westm. Rev.* Oct. 382 The sensational title of a shilling thrill. **1891** E. KINGLAKE *Australian at H.* 97 Relevancy..is apparently not a matter of so much consequence as thrill, as the man says in Mark Twain's book. **1894** MRS. H. WARD *Marcella* I. 14 Whatever had been spoken by him had grace, thrill, meaning.

c. A thrilling experience or incident.

1936 G. B. SHAW *Simpleton Unexpected Isles* I. 48 *The Clergyman*: Yes: I know I should have explained that. But she let me kiss her. *Mrs. Hyering*: That must have been a thrill, Mr Hammingtap. Life came to you that time, didn't it? **1947** *Sporting Mirror* 7 Nov. 8/1, I must add that in actual fact there was not much scientific football. But the dizzy paced thrills made up for that. **1951** R. CAMPBELL *Light on Dark Horse* ii. 37 To be driven round in these new horse-less machines was a thrill of which we never tired in those days. **1964** in Hamblett & Deverson *Generation X* 32 Going to a party and being rowdy, dancing to very loud music,..being driven in a very fast car, are all great thrills.

2. a. The vibrating or quivering of anything tangible or visible; acute tremulousness, as of a sound; a vibration, throbbing, tremor.

1817 MOORE *Lalla R., Veiled Prophet* (1854) 96 While a thrill Lives in your sapient bosoms. **1825** SCOTT *Talism.* xiv, As the thrill of a nerve, unexpectedly jarred, will awaken the sensation of agony. **1865** BARING-GOULD *Werewolves* xiv. 240 Listening to the harplike thrill of the breeze in the old grey tree-tops. **1874** LOWELL *Agassiz* I. i, The electric nerve, whose instantaneous thrill Makes next-door gossips of the antipodes. **1892** TYNDALL in *Times* 3 Feb. 5/6 The sudden ..dropping and lifting of an opaque screen over the electric light, thus producing vivid thrills upon the fog.

b. *Phys.* and *Path.* A vibratory movement, resonance, or murmur, felt or heard in auscultation.

1822–34 *Good's Study Med.* (ed. 4) I. 544 That vibratory thrill [of the pulse] which has been called wiriness. **1877** ROBERTS *Handbk. Med.* (ed. 3) II. 9 Thrill or purring tremor ..indicate the special character of a peculiar vibratory sensation conveyed to the fingers. **1879** KHORY *Princ. Med.*

56 Besides impulse we have another movement of the heart, known as thrill. **1897** *Allbutt's Syst. Med.* III. 58 He..has a well-marked pre-systolic thrill and a loud pre-systolic murmur at the cardiac apex.

3. a. *Comb.*, as ***thrill-seeker***. **b.** *attrib.* passing into *adj.*, of a crime: committed purely for the sake of the excitement experienced in carrying it out, as ***thrill hold-up, killing, murder***.

1928 *Daily Tel.* 30 Oct. 11/5 A long series of 'thrill' hold-ups [at Atlanta, Georgia]..is cleared up here with the arrest of two Oglethorpe University students. The youthful thrill-seekers are George Harsh and James Galogly, both members of good families. **1978** LaRosa & Tanenbaum *Random Factor* (1979) xi. 172 Billy Krieg died because he was part in a series of thrill killings. **1973** R. C. Dennis *Sweat of Fear* xiii. 98 The police think it was a thrill murder. Do you feel such a person can be wholly sane? **1928** Thrill-seeker [see *thrill hold-up* above]. **1967** W. & J. Breedlove *Swinging Set* xii. 146 A variety of sexual thrill-seekers.

thrill, *sb.*[4] *dial.* Corruption of thill[1].

1688 R. Holme *Armoury* III. xviii. (Roxb.) 139/1 The shafts, are the side of the thrill or thill. **1772** *Sterne's Tr. Shandy* VII. xv. Wks. V. 93 (Jod.) The thrillhorse [*edd.* 1765, 1776 thill-horse] trotting. **1886** *Cheshire Gloss.* s.v. *Cart*, Two longitudinal pieces, known as *thrill bars* or *mid thrills*, are morticed into the binders, and these support the boards which form the bottom of the cart. **1887** *S. Cheshire Gloss.* s.v. *Cart*, The shafts are also called *thrills*..; hence we speak of '*thrill-gears*'.., 'a good *thrill-hoss*'... But the simple word *thrill*, though still universally understood, is less commonly used than formerly.

thrill (θrɪl), *v.*[1] Forms: 4 thril, 4–5 **þrill(e, þrulle(ü)**, 4–6 thrille, 5 thryl(le, 5–6 thryll, 4– thrill. [A metathetic form of thirl *v.*[1]]

I. Of the action of material bodies.

†**1. a.** *trans.* To pierce, bore, penetrate; = thirl *v.*[1] 1. Also *intr.* with *through* (quot. 1387[1]).

a **1300** *Cursor M.* 11824 Þe fester thrild his bodi thurgh. *c* **1330** R. Brunne *Chron.* (1810) 30, & scharp lance þat thrilled Ihesu side. *a* **1340** Hampole *Psalter* iii. 4 Þe fors of fire of luf..þat makis his prayere to thrill heuen. **1387** Trevisa *Higden* (Rolls) I. 339 A torf..i-doo aboute a worme sleeþ hym oþer makeþ hym þrulle þoruȝ þe erþe [*terram penetrare*] for to scape a way. *Ibid.* VII. 349 A grym strook of liȝtnynge..þrulled þe wal. **1530** Palsgr. 755/2, I thrill, I perce or bore thorowe a thyng... This terme is olde and nowe lytell used. **1605** Sylvester *Du Bartas* II. iii. I. *Vocation* 115 Through Corslets, Rivets, Jacks, and Shirts of Mail His shaft shall thrill the Foes that him assail. **1634** A. Rhead *Descr. Body Man* C vj/2 A roughnesse where there is a hole, but not thrilled through. **1661** *Merry Drollery* 13 The sword..doth nimbly come to the point.., Thrilling, and drilling, And killing, and spilling.

†**b.** To break or penetrate through (an enemy's line). Also *intr.* with *through*. *Obs.*

1375 Barbour *Bruce* XVI. 430 [Thai] thrillit thame [the ynglis rout] weill neir throu-out. **1470–85** Malory *Arthur* IX. iv. 343 Thorou the thyckest prees he thrulled thorou them.

†**2.** *intr.* To penetrate or pass through, proceed (*into* or *to* a place); = thirl *v.*[1] 6. *Obs. rare.*

13.. *Cursor M.* 21098 (Edin.) Thomas..he soȝte þat estern thede, And þrillid [*v.rr.* þirled, thirlid] intil haiþinhede.

†**3. a.** *trans.* To cause (a lance, dart, or the like) to pass; to dart, hurl (a piercing weapon). *Obs.* (Perhaps sometimes including a notion of the quivering motion of the missile.)

1609 Heywood *Brit. Troy* XIII. lxx, He thrild a Iavelin at the Dardans brest. **1624** Quarles *Sion's Elegies* ii. 4 Darts, thrill'd from heaven, transfixe my bleeding hart. **1637** Heywood *Dial., Pelopæa & Alope* Wks. 1874 VI. 301 Our well-tride Nymphs,..thrild their arrowie Iavelins after him. **1646** G. Daniel *Poems* Wks. (Grosart) I. 77, I am..deeply strucke, and beare The fatall Iaveline, with me everie where; Into the Marrow thrill'd.

†**b.** To hurl, to send (persons) flying. *Obs. rare.* (Cf. thirl *v.*[3] 1, quot. 1587.)

1606 Warner *Alb. Eng.* XIV. lxxxv. (1612) 353 But leauing Romaines thrilled thence, and Brutes by Rome opprest, What hapt meane while betwixt the Picts and Scots shall be digest.

II. Of the action of non-material forces.

†**4.** *fig.* from 1: To pierce, penetrate (as a sound, or an emotion). *Obs.* (passing into 5).

a **1300** *Cursor M.* 17738 Of his ded als þe sorful ord Sal thril þin hert thoru als a suord. *c* **1375** *Sc. Leg. Saints* xxxvi. (*Baptista*) 131 Þi word thrillit myn ere. *c* **1440** *Gesta Rom.* xlv. 177 (Harl. MS.) Synne in twynkelynge of an ye þrillithe alle the erþe. **1590** Spenser *F.Q.* I. viii. 39 With percing point Of pitty deare his hart was thrilled sore. **1629** Milton *Ode Nativity, Hymn* x, Such sound..the Airy region thrilling. **1642** H. More *Song Soul* I. I. vi, Which in their sprights, may cause sweet agony, And thrill their bodies through with pleasing dart.

†**b.** *intr.* with *through*. *Obs.* (passing into 5 b).

1526 *Pilgr. Perf.* (W. de W. 1531) 258b, Many moo sorowes dyd teare & thryll thorowe her herte. **1590** Spenser *F.Q.* I. viii. 6 Eger greedinesse through every member thrild. **1592** [see 5 b].

5. a. *trans.* To affect or move with a sudden wave of emotion. Also as *pa. pple.*, extremely pleased or delighted (*colloq.*).

1605 Shaks. *Lear* IV. ii. 73 A Seruant that he bred, thrill'd with remorse, Oppos'd against the act. **1718** Pope *Iliad* XIX. 266 Greece around sat thrill'd with sacred awe. **1791** Mrs. Radcliffe *Rom. Forest* ii, A kind of pleasing dread thrilled her bosom. **1805** Wordsw. *Waggoner* II. 34 His ears are by the music thrilled. **1842** Tennyson *Sir Galahad* ii, Me mightier transports move and thrill. **1908** E. F. Benson *Climber* vii. 98 Though she would not have dreamed of doing what Elizabeth had done and looked over the letter, she could not but be thrilled with the fact that there were four pages. **1964** in Hamblett & Deverson *Generation X* 153, I adore Nureyev. When he danced on the Palladium show on telly I was thrilled to bits. **1976** A. Miller *Inside Outside* iv. 40 Naturally I was thrilled to bits and accepted with alacrity.

b. *intr.* To produce a thrill, as an emotion, or anything causing emotion; to pass with a thrill *through*.

1592 Shaks. *Rom. & Jul.* IV. iii. 15, I haue a faint cold feare thrills through my veines. *a* **1719** Addison *Milton's Style Imitated* 124 A sudden horror..Ran through each nerve, and thrill'd in ev'ry vein. **1823** Scott *Quentin D.* xii, When some peculiar feeling of hope, or perhaps of remorse, happened to thrill across his mind. **1854** J. S. C. Abbott *Napoleon* (1855) II. xx. 356 In tones which thrilled upon every heart. **1874** Green *Short Hist.* viii. §5. 513 The news of Hampden's resistance thrilled through England.

c. *intr.* (? for *pass*) To feel, or be moved by, a thrill of emotion. Often const. *at, to, with.*

1595 Shaks. *John* v. ii. 143 To thrill and shake, Euen at the crying of your Nations crow, Thinking this voyce an armed Englishman. **1596** —— *1 Hen. IV*, II. iv. 407 Art not thou horrible afraid? Doth not thy blood thrill at it? **1825** T. Hook *Sayings* Ser. II. *Passion & Princ.* x. III. 179 He..read over..the 'last words' of his adored Fanny, till the blood thrilled in his veins. **1874** Green *Short Hist.* viii. §3. 488 England was thrilling with excitement at the thought that her own hour of deadly peril might come again. **1935** *Motion Picture* Nov. 29/2 If you live within range of a national radio network, you've thrilled to their voices. **1940** J. Buchan *Memory Hold-the-Door* ii. 42 Stevenson..thrilled as we did to those antecedents—the lights and glooms of Scottish history. **1952** T. Pyles *Words & Ways Amer. Eng.* ii. 34 Generations of European children have thrilled to the novels of J. F. Cooper.

6. a. *intr.* To move tremulously or with vibration; to quiver, vibrate. (Said esp. of sound or light.)

1776 Mickle tr. *Camoens' Lusiad* IX. 396 Here..The solemn harp's melodious warblings thrill. **1816** Scott *Bl. Dwarf* iii, Exhausting his voice in shrieks and imprecations, that thrilled wildly along the waste heath. **1827–35** Willis *Absalom* 79 My pulses thrill, Like a rich harp-string. **1862** Tyndall *Mountaineer.* i. 8 Watching the lightning thrilling behind the clouds. **1878** T. Hardy *Ret. Native* IV. vi, The great valley of purple heath thrilling silently in the sun.

b. *trans.* To send forth or utter tremulously.

1647 Crashaw *Music's Duel* 57 Her supple breast thrills out Sharp airs. **1868** Farrar *Silence & V.* ii. (1875) 35 The spirit within us thrills its glad response to the noble utterance.

c. To cause to quiver; to throw into vibration.

1800 Moore *Anacreon* lviii, Sweet [are] the sighs that thrill the lyre. **1860** Farrar *Orig. Lang.* i. 12 The air is thrilled with the voice of birds. **1872** O. W. Holmes *Poet Breakf.-t.* v. (1885) 124 An earthquake thrills the planet.

† **thrill**, *v.*[2] *Sc. Obs.* [f. thrill *sb.*[2]]

1. *trans.* To make a thrall of, enthrall, enslave; = thirl *v.*[2] 1.

1456 Sir G. Haye *Law Arms* (S.T.S.) 157 It is..na to be tholit..sen he [Christ] has maid man free, he suld thrill his brother. **1536** Bellenden *Cron. Scot.* (1821) I. 73 To thrill us to maist schamefull servitude.

2. To bind or engage (lands) in thirlage: = thirl *v.*[2] 2.

1480 *Act. Dom. Conc.* (1839) 70/2 þ[t] þe said Robert..sall be na maner of way thrill þa landis bot deliuer þaim fre as said is.

† **thrill**, *v.*[3] *Obs.* [Cf. drill *v.*[2], trill *v.*] *intr.* To flow in a small stream or in drops; to trickle, percolate; to drip; = drill *v.*[2] 1.

1545 Raynold *Byrth Mankynde* 22 Water passing and thrilling through y[t] narow conduit. *Ibid.* 79 Y[e] bloud.. penetratith, thryllith, and yssuyth furth the soner. **1607** Walkington *Opt. Glass* xiii. (1664) 137 They razed his Skin with a Razor till the Bloud thrilled down. **1615** Brathwait *Strappado* (1878) 220 No streams of grace, Thrilling or trickling from thy blubber't face.

†'**thrillage.** *Sc. Obs.* Also 5 -ege. [f. thrill *sb.*[2] + -age.] Thraldom, bondage, subjection; = thirlage 1.

1375 Barbour *Bruce* I. 101 Þat he put to swylk thrillage, That þai..Suld ryn on fute, as rebaldaill. *c* **1400** *Sc. Trojan War* II. 984 They askede thame to be, As worthy, of all thrillege fre. *Ibid.* 2784 And frome all thrillege be maid fre. *c* **1470** Henry *Wallace* I. 136 He thocht ay till hald hym in thrillage.

† **thrillant**, *a. Obs. rare.* [irreg. f. thrill *v.*[1] + -ant[1].] = thrilling *ppl. a.* 1.

1590 Spenser *F.Q.* I. xi. 20 His thrillant speare. *Ibid.* II. iv. 46 One of his thrillant darts he threw. **1594** ? Greene *Selimus* 1784 Pierce my poor heart with thy thrillant steel.

thrilled (θrɪld), *ppl. a.* [f. thrill *v.*[1] + -ed[1].]

†**a.** Pierced, penetrated. *Obs.* **b.** Affected by a thrill of emotion. **c.** Caused to vibrate.

1615 Sylvester *Byrth Triumphant* IV. xxxiv, My thrilled Wound Is past all cure. **1850** Robertson *Serm.* (1872) III. 116 Incoherent utterances and thrilled sensibilities. **1900** *Daily News* 19 Feb. 2/1 When the thrilled listener has refreshed the tale-teller. **1908** *Daily Chron.* 16 July 5/6 There was no thrilled and electrified populace such as in the old Greek Games packed the amphitheatre.

†'**thrillehod, thrillihod.** *Obs.* [f. ME. *þrille-, þrilli-* for *þrile-*: see thrile and -hood.] Threefold condition; trinity.

c **1320** *Cast. Love* 9 God ffader and Sone and Holigost, ..þat O God art and þrilli-hod. *Ibid.* 129 þrilli-hod. *Ibid.* 1239 Persones þreo in þrille-hod And o God cleped in on-hod.

thriller ('θrɪlə(r)). [f. thrill *v.*[1] + -er[1].]

a. One who or that which thrills; *spec.* (*slang* or *colloq.*) a sensational play, film or story (cf. shocker[1] 1).

1889 *Pall Mall G.* 1 July 6/1 It is always painful to see clever actors..wasting their energies on a worthless play... It is seldom that we are treated to a more bald and empty production than this invertebrate 'thriller'. **1896** *Pall Mall Mag.* Nov. 380 Fullblown detectives..the sort you read of in the thrillers! **1934** C. Lambert *Music Ho!* v. 301 The opera *Wozzek* is on paper a soberly planned symphony, but in performance a 'thriller' of the most theatrical order. **1950** *Sport* 24–30 Mar. 3/2 That was in 1946 when the 'Bishops' were beaten 3–2 by Barnet in a Stamford Bridge thriller. **1968** M. Richler in R. Weaver *Canad. Short Stories* 2nd Ser. 186 'My mother made me promise that one day I would make a picture in Israel.' 'Did she specify a sexy thriller?' **1976** *New Yorker* 16 Feb. 54/3 The thriller of the afternoon occurred when Redundancy came up in the last stride to beat Summertime Promise by a nose in the Columbiana Handicap.

b. *Comb.*, as ***thriller-writer, -writing***.

1925 J. M. Robertson *Mr. Shaw & 'The Maid'* ix. 85 Villains there are in plenty, though those shaped by the thriller-writers are apt to be improbable. **1983** *Listener* 20 Jan. 23/3 The pseudonymous A. J. Quinnell belongs to the generation of good thriller-writers who specialised in South-East Asia. **1958** *Times Lit. Suppl.* 17 Jan. 33/2 It is a fair guess that thriller-writing led to his first interest in the precious stones which are the lure for so many crimes of real life.

Hence '**thrillerdom** [-dom], the world of thrillers or exciting, sensational novels; '**thrillerish** *a.* [-ish[1]], suggestive of such a novel.

1922 *John o' London's* 4 Jan. 18/2 The first three-quarters of the play were so good anyway, simply on the level of off-beat thrillerdom. **1957** *Times Lit. Suppl.* 28 June 395/1 When, in the 1930s, one of his best novels, *La Condition Humaine*, was translated under the thrillerish title of *Storm in Shanghai*, many young people must have opened it in the hope that they were going to read a thriller.

thrillful ('θrɪlfʊl), *a.* [f. thrill *sb.*[1] + -ful.] Full of thrills, thrilling.

1887 J. Ashby Sterry *Lazy Minstrel* (1892) 234 O lilt of leaves! O song of sea! O mingled thrillful harmony! **1893** E. L. Wakeman in *Columbus* (Ohio) *Dispatch* 15 June, We.. passed a thrillful hour at a genuine Whitechapel 'penny gaff'.

thrilling ('θrɪlɪŋ), *vbl. sb.* [f. thrill *v.*[1] + -ing[1].] The action of thrill *v.*[1], in various senses; an instance of this. Also *attrib.*

1526 *Pilgr. Perf.* (W. de W. 1531) 241 As though we bare the same stonges thryllynges & persyng turmentes that he suffred. **1747** Hervey *Medit.* II. 104 From the Thrillings of polluted Joy, to the Agonies of eternal Despair. **1748** Hartley *Observ. Man.* I. ii. 120 A Thrilling or Shivering may be felt to run along the Skin. **1835–6** *Todd's Cycl. Anat.* I. 241/2 On laying the finger on it [the vein], a peculiar thrilling sensation is perceptible. **1879** J. D. Long *Æneid* IX. 806 Go to the heights of Dindymus, And list the thrilling of the pipe.

thrilling ('θrɪlɪŋ), *ppl. a.* [f. as prec. + -ing[2].] That thrills, in various senses. †**1.** Penetrating, piercing. Also *fig. Obs.*

1579 Spenser *Sheph. Cal.* May 208 A thrilling throbbe from her hart did aryse [*gloss, A thrilling throb*, a percing sighe]. **1590** —— *F.Q.* I. iii. 42 He perced through his [the lion's] chaufed chest With thrilling point of deadly yron brand. **1621** G. Sandys *Ovid's Met.* VIII. (1626) 160 Æsonides then threw his thrilling lance [L. (l. 412) *Misit et Æsonides jaculum*]. **1718** Pope *Iliad* XV. 528 Through his fair neck the thrilling arrow flies.

b. Piercing or penetrating, as cold; causing shivering or shuddering.

1603 Shaks. *Meas. for M.* III. i. 123 To recide In thrilling Region of thicke-ribbed Ice. **1753** *Scots Mag.* Oct. 516/1 Attended with a thrilling coldness. **1760–72** H. Brooke *Fool of Qual.* (1809) II. 59 A thrilling sort of chillness would run through my blood. *c* **1820** S. Rogers *Italy, Campagna of Rome* 91 Regions of thrilling ice.

2. Producing a sudden wave of excitement or emotion; piercing the feelings.

1761 Gray *Odin* 24 The thrilling verse that wakes the Dead. **1821** Joanna Baillie *Metr. Leg., Columbus* xix, A thrilling, fearful joy. **1867** Lady Herbert *Cradle L.* viii. 220 Nazareth, a place of such deep and thrilling interest to every reader of the Gospel history.

3. Quivering, vibrating.

1850 Kingsley *Alt. Locke* xi, Insects..that poised themselves motionless on thrilling wings. **1871** Tyndall *Fragm. Sc.* (1879) I. ii. 78 Let us look for a moment at this thrilling medium.

Hence '**thrillingly** *adv.*; '**thrillingness.**

a **1822** Shelley *Posthum. Poems* (1824) 320 The liquid voice Of pipes, that fills the clear air thrillingly. **1825** Southey *Tale Paraguay* III. xl, So thrillingly attuned the cadence fell, That with the music..She moved herself to tears. **1847** Webster, *Thrillingness.* **1863** Cowden Clarke *Shaks. Char.* iii. 71 How thrillingly grand is all this! **1891** *Blackw. Mag.* CL. 637/2 Emotions..of unexpected thrillingness.

thrill-multure: see thirl-multure.

thrilly ('θrɪlɪ), *a.* [f. thrill *sb.*[1] + -y. Cf. *chilly.*] **a.** Affected with a thrill. **b.** Having a thrilling quality.

1893 *Illustr. Sporting & Dram. News* 25 Feb. 848/1, I felt somewhat 'thrilly' about the heart region. **1896** *Punch* 21 Mar. 133/3 Oh the feeling sweet and thrilly. **1924** R. Frost *New Hampshire* 68 A likeness to surprise the thrilly tourist.

1947 *Sun* (Baltimore) 2 Jan. 13/7 The thrilly spot was at Pasadena where the Rose Bowl job was unfolded for the fans. **1967** *Listener* 16 Feb. 239/2 It [*sc.* a story by Conan Doyle] was a chilly, thrilly piece not at all in the Holmes tradition.

thrimble, thrimmel, etc.: see THRUMBLE.

thrimlar *Sc. Obs.*: see THRUMBLER.

† **'thrimness.** *Obs.* Forms: 2 **þrimnis, þreomnes,** 2–3 **þrem-, þrim-,** (*Orm.*) **þrimmnesse,** 3 **þrum-** (ü). [Early ME. alteration of OE. *þrines, þrinnes*, THRINNESS. The change may have been due to association with OE. *þrymm* THRUM *sb.*[1], majesty, glory, and its compounds, as *þrymsetl* throne, *þrymsittende* (cf. 'seo þrynis þrymsittende', 'the Trinity sitting in glory'); but in that case we should have expected the form with *þrym* to have appeared in OE.] The Trinity. Cf. THREENESS.

a **1175** *Cott. Hom.* 219 þeos þrimnis is an god. *c* **1175** *Lamb. Hom.* 99 He scal ileafan on þa halȝa þreomnesse and on soðre annesse. *Ibid.* 101 þere halȝan þremnesse. *c* **1200** ORMIN 11177 Þatt iss an Unnseȝȝenndliȝ þrimmnesse, Faderr, & Sune, & Haliȝ Gast. *c* **1200** *Trin. Coll. Hom.* 25 þe holie þremnesse shop and biwalt alle shafte. *a* **1225** *St. Marher.* 11 þrumnesse þreo fald ant anfaldte hweðere. *a* **1240** *Sawles Warde* in *Cott. Hom.* 259 þe hali þrumnesse, feader ant sune ant hali gast.

thrimp, *v. Sc.* and *north. dial.* In 6 **thrymp;** 9 *dial.* **thrump.** [? Akin to THRUM *v.*[1]] *intr.* and *trans.* To press; to push.

1513 DOUGLAS *Æneis* XI. xii. 8 Apon thar strait born bridillis brankand fast, Now thrympand heyr, now thayr, thayr hedis can cast. **1825** JAMIESON, *Thrump*,.. to press.. as in a crowd... To push; especially applied to school-boys, when they push all before them from the one end of a form to another. *a* **1828** T. BEWICK *Howdy* (1850) 10 His hands.. thrimpt owr his Thees. *Ibid.* 13 Mouny oh them thrimped in. **1894** *Northumberl. Gloss.*, *Thrimpt*, pressed closely.

'thrimsa, thrymsa. *Hist.* [repr. OE. *þrimsa, þrymsa*, late altered form of *trim(e)sa, trym(e)sa*, genitive pl. of *trimes, trymes, *trims* (nom. pl. *trimsas, trymsas*), ad. L. *trēmis*, the third part of an aureus; also a weight, a drachma: cf. OHG. '*drimisa, trimisa* = dragma'. (Both in OE. and OHG. assimilated to *þrí, drî*, three.) The genitive pl. is frequent in OE. Laws, etc., after a numeral, and has been erroneously taken by 17th c. antiquaries, and from them by later writers, for a nominative singular.]

An erroneous name for the OE. *trimes* or *trims*, a coin (or money of account) representing the Roman *trēmis*, the value of which varied in OE. times and is uncertain; also, as a weight, a drachma.

In early times the Merovingian gold *tremis* had circulation in England, where a few are said also to have been struck in the early 7th century; but in the 10th c. the name appears to have been applied to a small silver coin of similar size; perhaps in some districts to the *sceatt*; see quots.

a **954** *Norð-leoda laga* § 1 in Schmid *Gesetze* 396 Norðleoda cynges gild is xxx þusend þrymsa [*v.r.* þrimsa]. § 3 Biscopes and ealdormannes viii þusend þrymsa. *c* **950** *Lindisf. Gosp.* Matt. xvii. 27 [Staterem, *gl.* þæt wæs feor trymes *vel* viii [*Rushw. Gosp.* scilling, *Ags. Gosp.* ænne wecg, *Hatton Gosp.* ænne penig].

1614 SELDEN *Titles Hon.* II. ii. 204 A Thrymsa was a third part of their shilling; not three shillings as some much mistake. **1706** PHILLIPS (ed. Kersey), *Thrimsa*, an old German Coin, valued at the third part of a Shilling, or Four Pence. **1720** J. JOHNSON *Canons Eng. Ch.* (Laws Ethelstan an. 926 No. 2), In Mercia the common Man's Weregild is 266 Thrymsa, this is 200 Shillings. **1754** HUME *Hist. Eng.* (1761) I. App. I. 100 His weregild.. was by law thirty thousand thrimsas, near 1,300*l.* of present money. **1860** HOOK *Lives Abps.* (1869) I. v. 243 A bishop was on the same footing as an ealdorman, reckoned at eight thousand thrymsas. **1875** JEVONS *Money* viii. 71 The *mark*, the *ora*, and the *thrimsa* were other moneys of account used by the Anglo-Saxons.

thrin, thrinne, *a.* (*sb.*) Forms: 1 **þrinna,** 3–4 **þrinne,** 3–5 **thrinne,** 4 **þrynne, þrine, thrine, threin, thriȝn,** 5 **thryn,** 4 (9 *sb.*) **thrin.** [Late OE. *þrinna*, a. early ON. *þrinn-r* (later *þrenn-r*) triple, threefold; often = three (Sw. *trenne*, Da. *trende*), prob.:—OTeut. **þrizno-z*, f. **þris* (Indo-Eur. **tris*, Skr. *tris*, Gr. τρίς) thrice, with adj. ending: cf. L. *trī-nus*, pl. *trī-nī* = *ternī*.]

† **A.** *adj.* Threefold, triple; also three kinds of, three. An adj., but sometimes best rendered by 'thrice' (cf. ON. *þrennar tylptir* 'triple twelves', i.e. 'thrice twelve'). *Obs.*

a **1012** *Laws Æthelred* III. c. 13 Ladiȝe hine mid þrinna XII [L. *cum ter* XII]; and se ȝerefa namiȝe þa lade. *c* **1200** ORMIN 1144 Her habbe icc shæwedd þrinne lac Forr þrinne kinne leode. *a* **1300** *Cursor M.* 3381 Ysmael had wijfs thrin [*v.rr.* þrinne, thre]. *c* **1300** *Havelok* 716 Hauelok.. he dide þerinne, Him and his wif, hise sones þrinne, And hise two doutres. **13..** *E.E. Allit. P.* B. 1805 Þus vpon þrynne wyses I haf yow þro schewed.

absol. *c* **1330** R. BRUNNE *Chron. Wace* (Rolls) 385 Þey departed þys land in þrynne. **13..** *Cursor M.* 9815 (Cott.) His hert aght ar atbrest in thrin [*Gött.* o thrinne]. **13..** *E.E. Allit. P.* B. 1727 Mane, Techal, Pharez, merked in þrynne.

B. *sb.* (in *pl.*) [perh. a new formation after *twins*.] Three children at a birth. ? *dial.*

1838 THOREAU *Jrnl.* 14 June (1949) I. 51 Truth, Goodness, Beauty,—those celestial thrins. **1878** *Cumbld. Gloss.*, *Thrins*, three at a birth. **1887** *Indian Med. Gaz.* 1 Sept. 246 In the case of twins and thrins about three times more than in the case of singletons.

† **'thrinfald,** *a.* (*adv.*) *Sc.* and *north. dial. Obs.* Also 4 **thrine-,** 5 **thryn-,** 6 **trin-, trene-.** [Assimilation of the earlier *thrifald*, OE. *þriefeald*, THREEFOLD, to THRIN.] = THREEFOLD *a.*; triple, treble.

In 1st quot. (Fairfax MS.) as *adv.* = THREEFOLD B. 1.

13.. *Cursor M.* 26986 (Cott.) Þis hope þan mai be thrinefald [*Fairf.* vnderstande þis hope þrinfalde]. *c* **1375** *Sc. Leg. Saints* vi. (*Thomas*) 390 God.. in substance bot ane Is, & thrinfald in-to personis. *Ibid.* xxxvi. (*Baptista*) 463 He þe thrinfald crone sal euir bruk fore his wardone. *c* **1470** HENRY *Wallace* VII. 141 The thrynfald buk is bot this brokyn land. **1513** DOUGLAS *Æneis* IV. ix. 78 The thrinfald goddes Proserpina. **1552** LYNDESAY *Monarche* 4407 Two and thretty gude papis.. Ressauit the crown of Martyrdome, Bot nocht the Thrinfald Diadame. **1570** *Satir. Poems Reform.* xxi. 19 Thay trinfauld Tratours Hes steirit vp this stryfe.

† **thring,** *sb.*[1] *Obs.* Forms: α. 3–4 **þring, þ-, thryng,** 4 **thring.** β. 3 **þrung** (ü). [f. OE. *ȝeþring* neut. press, crowd, tumult, f. *þring-an* to press, crowd. The β-forms probably belong here.]

1. A crowd, press, or throng of people.

[*a* **1000** *Andreas* 368 (Gr.) þæt hi þe eað mihton ofer yða ȝeþring drohtað adreoȝan.] *c* **1205** LAY. 12448 Heo comen to hustinge mid alle heore þringe. *Ibid.* 27524 Amidden þan þrunge [*c* **1275** þringe] þer heo þihkest weoren. *a* **1225** *Ancr. R.* 160 Engel to mon ine þrunge ne scheawude him neuer ofte. *c* **1275** *Wom. Samaria* 72 in *O.E. Misc.* 86 Monye.. vrnen vt of þe bureuh myd wel Muchel þrynge. **13..** *K. Alis.* 2533 Aboutyn heom they can go; Parforce smyten into the thrynge. **13..** *Sir Beues* (A.) 1365 Vnneþe i scapede among þat þring, For to bringe þe tiding!

2. Pressure, tightness; some kind of disease.

a **1300** *Cursor M.* 11821 (Cott.) Þe scab ouer-gas his bodi all, In his sides him held þe thring.

† **thring,** *sb.*[2] *Obs.* [app. an altered or erroneous form of *dring* (also used by Layamon), *dreng*, perh. influenced by THRING *v.*] = DRENG.

c **1205** LAY. 6725 In to þere burh senden Æfter þon hehste þringe [*c* **1275** after on eorl] þat he comen to þen kinge. *Ibid.* 31455 Þa þringes norðerne makeden hine to kinge. *Ibid.* 31740 þer weoren niȝe þusunde ðringes norðerne islaȝen. **1861** PEARSON *Early & Mid. Ages Eng.* 201 Drenghs or thrings, owing special service to ride as couriers or to keep horses or dogs, were settled on certain estates.

thring (θrɪŋ), *v. Obs.* exc. *dial.* Forms: see below. [OE. *þringan, þrang* (pl. *þrungon*), *þrungen*. Com. Teut. = OS. *thringan* (MLG., MDu., Du. *dringen*), OHG. *dringan* (MHG., Ger. *dringen*), ON. *þryngva, -gja* (pa. t. *þrǫng, þrungom*, pa. pple. *þrungenn*), cf. Goth. *þreihan* (pa. t. *þráih, þraihum*, pa. pple. *þraihans*) :—OTeut. **þriŋh(w)-: þriŋg(w)-*; cf. Lith. *trènkti* to shake, strike, *trànksmas* uproar, scrimmage, Lett. *treekt* to shatter. The Gothic *þreihan* passed into a different conjugational class: cf. THEE *v.*[1] In ON. *þryngva* was displaced by the weak *þrøngva, -gja*: cf. Sw. *tränga*, Da. *trænge*.]

A. Illustration of Forms.

1. *Inf.* and *Pres. stem.* 1–5 **þring-** (2 **dring-**), 3–5 **þryng-** (3 **þrung-**), 4–6 **thryng-** (5 **dryng-**), 4–7 (*dial.* -9) **thring.**

c **888** K. ÆLFRED *Boeth.* xvi. § 1 Ne þurfon ȝe.. him æfter þringan. *a* **1225** *Ancr. R.* 252 Dumbe bestes.. hwon heo beoð assailed.. heo þrungeð alle togederes. *a* **1250** *Owl & Night.* 796 An eiþer oþer faste þringe. *c* **1374** CHAUCER *Troylus* IV. 38 (66) He gan in thrynge. **14..** *Lybeaus Disc.* (Kaluza) 2187 (MS. C.) þyder þey gonne þrynge. *c* **1450** Drynge [see B. 2]. **1570** LEVINS *Manip.* 135/39 To Thring, *artare, stringere.* **1606** tr. *Rollock's Lect. on 1 Thess.* 30 (Jam.) How men and women did thring in. **1871** WADDELL *Ps.* ii. 9 Ye sal thring them wi' a gad o' airn.

2. *Pa. t.* α. *sing.* 1–5 **þrang,** 3–5 **thrange,** 7 (9 *dial.*) **thrung,** 4– **thrang;** *pl.* 1 **þrungon,** 2–3 **-en.**

a **800** *Andreas* 126 (Gr.) Duguð samnade, hæðne hildfrecan heapum þrungon. *c* **1000** ÆLFRIC *Hom.* II. 394 þæt folc hine þrang. *a* **1225** *Juliana* 67 þrungen euchan biuoren oðer. *c* **1375** *Cursor M.* 24359 (Fairf.) Þe nailis þat him þrange on rode. *c* **1400** *Destr. Troy* 11135 Two thawsaund full þroly, þai þrang cut of lyue. **1470–85** MALORY *Arthur* x. xli. 479 He thrange in to the thyckest prees. **1535** Thrang [see B. 5]. **1607** DEKKER *Knt.'s Conjur.* (1842) 41 In therefore they thrung, some wading vp to the knees. **1904** Thrung [see B. 5].

β. 1 **þrǫng,** 3–5 **þrong(e,** (4 *pl.* **þrongen),** 4–6 **thronge,** 4–7 **throng.**

c **893** þrong [see B. 2]. **13..** *E.E. Allit. P.* B. 1775 Þay þrongen þeder. *c* **1374** CHAUCER *Anel. & Arc.* 55 But [Mars] throng now here now there amongis hem both. *c* **1400** *Song Roland* 838 They preissid, and throng, And thrusten out. *c* **1400** þronge, *a* **1440** thronge [see B. 5]. *c* **1520** *Adam Bel*, etc. 224 in Hazl. *E.P.P.* II. 147 To the gate faste he throng. **1526** Thronge [see B. 1 b].

3. *Pa. pple.* α. 1 **þrunge,** 3 **i-þrunge,** 3–4 **thrungen** (4 **-un,** 4–5 **-yn,** 4–6 **-in(e);** 5–7 **thrung,** 6 **throung.**

a **1250** *Owl & Night.* 38 Wonne þu art to me i-þrunge. *a* **1300** *E.E. Psalter* lxxii. 21 [lxxiii. 22] And i am to noghte .. Thrungen. **1377** LANGL. *P. Pl.* B. v. 517 A thousand of men þo thrungen togyderes Criede vpward to cryst. *c* **1400** *Destr. Troy* 11723 Twenty thowsaund thristy, þrungyn togedur. **1513** Throung [see B. 5 b].

β. 4–5 **þrong-en (-un),** 5–6 **throng(e.**

1382 WYCLIF *Luke* viii. 42 The while he wente, he was throngun of the cumpeny. *c* **1400** þrongen [see B. 1 c]. *c* **1400** *Hymns Virg.* 13 Whanne þou were in þraldom þrong. **1435** Thronge [see B. 3]. *a* **1550** Throng [see B. 1 c].

γ. 5 **þryngid.**

c **1400** [see B. 5 c].

B. Signification.

† **1.** *intr.* To press, crowd, throng; to move or gather in a crowd; to assemble. Also *fig. Obs.*

a **800** [see A. 2 α]. *a* **1000** *Phœnix* 339 (Gr.) Ðonne fuȝla cynn on healfa ȝehwone heapum þringað.. þone halȝan hringe beteldað flyhte on lyfte. *a* **1175** *Cott. Hom.* 237 Of þe folce we siggeð þat hit.. elce deȝie þicce þringeð. *a* **1225** [see A. 1]. *a* **1300** *Cursor M.* 24637 (Gött.) Quen mi sun ras.. All till his graue [*Cott.* thrugh] þai thrang. ? *a* **1366** CHAUCER *Rom. Rose* 656 For there was many a brid singing, Throughout the yerde al thringing. *c* **1400** *Destr. Troy* 4770 Mony thoughtes full thro thrange in hir brest. **1513** DOUGLAS *Æneis* IV. vii. 58 The damecellis fast to thar lady thringis.

† **b.** *trans.* To crowd around or upon, to throng (a person). *Obs.*

c **1000** [see A. 2 α]. *c* **1000** *Ags. Gosp.* Mark v. 24 Him fyliȝde mycel meniȝeo and þrungon [*c* **1160** *Hatton Gosp.* þrungen] hine. —— Luke viii. 45 Þas meneȝeo þe ðringað. **1382** WYCLIF *Luke* viii. 45 Comaundour, cumpanyes thringen, and turmentyn thee. **1526** TINDALE *Mark* v. 24 And moche people folowed hym, and thronge hym.

† **c.** *trans.* To press or crowd together (persons or things). Chiefly in *pa. pple.* (which may belong to a). *Obs.*

c **1400** *Destr. Troy* 5748 With seven thowsaund þro men þrongen to-gedur. *c* **1460** *Towneley Myst.* xii. 416 It was a mery song; I dar say that he broght foure & twenty to a long .. so many he throng On a heppe. *a* **1550** *Hye Way to Spyttel Ho.* 171 in Hazl. *E.P.P.* IV. 30 Lyke as bestes togyder they be throng, Bothe lame, and seke, and hole them among.

2. *intr.* To press or push forward, as against or through a crowd, or against obstacles; to push or force one's way hastily or eagerly; to press, rush, hasten, push on. Now *dial.*

c **893** K. ÆLFRED *Oros.* v. xii. § 8 He for þære ondrædinge þæs þe swiþor on þæt weorod þrong. *c* **1205** LAY. 9421 Ouer þene wal heo clumben & binnen heo þrungen. *c* **1374** [see A. 1]. *c* **1400** *Destr. Troy* 2362 He þrong into þicke wodes, þester within. *c* **1450** *Hymns Virg.* 122 For alle the stonys grett and smale.. All they schalle togedyr drynge, And euerychon to oþer dynge. *c* **1470** HENRY *Wallace* IV. 454 Thrys apon fute he thrang throuch all the rout. **1470–85** MALORY *Arthur* VII. xxxi. 262 He thrang here & there, & so with grete payne he gat out of the prees. **1607** [see A. 2 α]. **1638** RUTHERFORD *Lett., to Lady Robertland* 4 Jan., That we may thring in, stooping low. **1823** CARLYLE *Let.* in Froude *Life* (1882) I. xi. 194, I shall just thring on here till I get desperate.

† **3. a.** *intr.* To press hard, use oppression. **b.** *trans.* To oppress, harass, distress, afflict; to repress. *Obs.*

c **1175** *Lamb. Hom.* 43 He walde anuppon his underlinges mid wohe motien and longe dringan [? ðringan]. *c* **1205** LAY. 10652 Carrais him on þrong and mid spere him of-stong. *a* **1250** [see A. 1]. *c* **1375** *Cursor M.* 11821 (Fairf.) On his [Herod's] heued he has þe skalle, þe scabbe ouer-gas his bodi alle, Fast þai be-gynne him to þringe. **1435** MISYN *Fire of Love* I. xviii. 40 Nouþer with resone it is restrenyd nor with drede it is thronge nor with dome tempyd. **1871** [see A. 1].

† **4.** *trans.* To press together, squeeze, compress; to crush, bruise. *Obs.*

13.. *Cursor M.* 900 (Cott.) Þou sal waite womman for to sting, And sco sal yiet þi hede thring. **13..** *St. Mergrete* 220 in Horstm. *Altengl. Leg.* (1881) 231 Sche set hir fot in his nek, to þe erþe sche him þrong.

5. To thrust or drive with pressure or violence; to cast, throw, or fling violently; to hurl, dash, knock; usually with prep. or advb. extension as *in, on, out, through, up.* Now *dial.*

a **1300** *E.E. Psalter* lxxvii[i]. 59 God herd.. And to noghte he thrange swythe Iraele. *c* **1330** R. BRUNNE *Chron.* (1810) 52 Þei did his iȝene out þring. *c* **1400** *Rom. Rose* 7419 In his sleve he gan to thringe A rasour sharpe & wel bitinge. *c* **1400** *Destr. Troy* 6516 Thretty of þe þroest he þronge out of lyue. *a* **1440** *Sir Eglam.* 1023 He to the erthe theme thronge. *c* **1470** HENRY *Wallace* XI. 621 About he turnd, and wp his armys thrang; On thai traytours with knychtlik fer he dang. **1483** *Cath. Angl.* 386/1 To Thrynge owte, *expremere.* **1500–20** DUNBAR *Poems* lxxii. 46 Vneiss.. he mycht sustene That crowne, on thrungin with crueltie. **1535** STEWART *Cron. Scot.* (Rolls) II. 247 Ilk ane of thame out throw him thrang a knyfe,.. Thair he la deid syne. **1557** *Peebles Burgh Rec.* (1872) 237 To thring him self throw the mercat becaus it wes thrang,.. and [he] culd na vther wayis evaid vntuichit. **1584** T. BASTARD *Chrestoleros* (1880) 97 Nature which headlong into life doth thring vs. **1904** M. HEWLETT *Queen's Quair* II. x. 321 She.. just let all go, and thrung herself face to the wall.

b. With *down*: To throw down by force, thrust or knock down, overthrow (*lit.* or *fig.*); to bring to ruin. (See also *down-things* s.v. DOWN *adv.* 36.)

c **1375** *Sc. Leg. Saints* xxvii. (*Machor*) 1141 For sperer of his maieste fra his Joy sall donne thrungine be. *c* **1475** *Rauf Coilȝear* 199 Thay threip that I thring doun of the fattest [deer]. **1513** DOUGLAS *Æneis* III. viii. 141 Doun throung vndir this mont Enchelades body.. lyis half bront. **1549** *Compl. Scot.* i. 19 The souerane consel of the diuyne sapiens .. doune thringis them fra the hie trone of their imperial dominations. **1570** *Satir. Poems Reform.* xix. 35 Idolatrie but reuth he did down thring. **1584** T. HUDSON *Du Bartas' Judith* I. in *Sylvester's Du B.* (1620) 695 The vassels of that onely King, That Thunder sends and scepters down doth thring. **1871** WADDELL *Ps.* xlvii. 3 He sal thring down the folk aneth us.

†**c.** To thrust or crush (into a confined space); to shut up, confine, bind; *fig.* to confine, restrict (quot. *c* 1374); in quot. *c* 1400, to bind tightly. *Obs.*

c **1250** *Death* 176 in *O.E. Misc.* 178 þu schal in þe putte faste beon iþrunge. *c* **1374** CHAUCER *Boeth.* II. pr. vii. 44 (Camb. MS.) Yowre glorye þat is so narwh and so streyte Ithrongen in to so lytul bowndes. *c* **1375** *Sc. Leg. Saints* xxxvi. (*Baptista*) 930 Herrod..petre gert in presone thring. *c* **1380** WYCLIF *Wks.* (1880) 319 Disciples of crist..weren not þringen in siche couentis. *c* **1400** *Song Roland* 290 His kneys coueryd with platis.., his thies thryngid with silk. *c* **1440** *Bone Flor.* 1370 They bonde the false..And in pryson caste them,..And ther yn can them thrynge.

†**6.** *intr.* To make way (*through* something) by pressure; to pierce, penetrate; to burst *out. Obs.*

a **1300** *Cursor M.* 16438 þai crond him wit thorn, þat thoru his hefd thrang. **13..** *Guy Warw.* (A.) 1509 þat gode swerd þurchim þrang, Gwichard wald abide nouȝt lang. *c* **1400** *Destr. Troy* 9641 The ledis on the land..thrappit full throly, thryngyng thurgh sheldis. *c* **1460** *Towneley Myst.* xvi. 240 My guttys will outt thryng Bot I this lad hyng.

†**b.** *trans.* To pierce. *Obs.*

c **1485** *Digby Myst.* IV. 672 Se how his hede with thornys is thronge!

Hence '**thringing** *vbl. sb.*; also '**thringer**, one who 'thrings' (*downthringer*, an overthrower).

1483 *Cath. Angl.* 385/2 A Thryngyn[g] downe, *articulus, pressura.* *a* **1572** KNOX *Hist. Ref.* Wks. 1846 I. 73 The down thringars of God his glore,..doctouris in idolatrie. *a* **1584** MONTGOMERIE *Cherrie & Slae* 935 With wringing and thringing, His hands on vther dang. **1637** RUTHERFORD *Lett., to J. Gordon* 14 Mar., There is no little thrusting and thringing to thrust in at Heaven's gates.

† '**thrinness.** *Obs.* [OE. orig. *þrines, þrynes, -nis, -nys* (in obl. case *-nesse, -nysse*) = OHG. *drinissa*, f. *þri-*, combining stem of *þré, þréo*, THREE + -NESS; later with *nn*, after THRIN, *þrinnes, þrynnys*; in ME. eventually THRIMNESS, q.v.] Threefold condition, threeness; the Trinity.

a **800** CYNEWULF *Crist* 379 Heah and haliȝ heofon-cund þrynes. **8..** *Halsuncge* in *Rituale Dunelm.* 114 Ic eow halsiȝe ..for ða haliȝan ðrinesse. *c* **900** tr. *Bæda's Eccl. Hist.* IV. xix. [xvii.] (1890) 312 We ondettað..Fæder & Sunu & Haliȝne Gast, þriȝnisse in Annisse..ond Annesse in þære þriȝnesse. **971** *Blickl. Hom.* iii. (1880) 29 Of þæm mæȝene þære Halȝan þrynesse. *Ibid.* xix. (1880) 249 On þære Halȝan þrynnysse. *c* **1000** ÆLFRIC *Hom.* I. 10 Ðeos þrynnys is an God. *Ibid.* 288 þæs mannes sawl hæfð on hire ȝecynde þære Halȝan þrynnysse anlicnysse. *a* **1300** *Athanasian Creed* in Hickes *Thesaurus* (1725) I. 233 Ðat o god inne þrinnesse And þrinness in onnesse Wurchip we þe more and lesse.

thrinter ('θrɪntə(r)), *a.* and *sb.* Now *dial.* Also 6 **trynter, thrwnter, thrwenter,** 9 **thrunter** (*Sc.* fronter, frunter). [In OE. *þri-winter*, three-winter-, three-year-; but the word may have been formed anew in 16th c., after TWINTER.]

a. *adj.* Of three winters; three years old: said of cattle and sheep. **b.** *sb.* A sheep or bovine animal of three years or winters (now applied only to sheep).

[*c* **1000** ÆLFRIC *Voc.* in Wr.-Wülcker 117/20 *Trimus, uel triennis, uel trimulus,* ðri-winter.] **1536** *Durham Acc. Rolls* (Surtees) 419, 4 Trynters, 7 Twynters,..20 Dynmontes, 23 Hogges. **1570** *Wills & Inv. N.C.* (Surtees) I. 341 Fyue thrwnter stotts at v[s] xiij[s] iiij[d]—iij thrwenter whyes at iiij[li]. **1577** in *Hist. Soc. Lanc. & Chesh.* LV-LVI. 27 Item. One other cowe... Item two thrinters. **1890** *Cornh. Mag.* Oct. 382 One of our thrunters, or three-winter-old ewes. *a* **1898** J. SHAW in R. Wallace *Country Schoolmaster* (1899) 339 'Twinters' and 'th[r]inters', sic like names for sheep.

thrip (θrɪp), *sb. slang.* Also 7 **threpps,** 8 **threps.** Short for THREEPENCE.

a **1700** B. E. *Dict. Cant. Crew, Threpps,* Three-pence. **1834** W. G. SIMMS *Guy Rivers* II. 108 Whom he rewarded with a *thrip* (the smallest silver coin known in the southern currency—the five cent issue excepted). **1887** J. C. HARRIS *Free Joe*, etc. (1888) 60 A little boy who wanted to buy a thrip's worth of candy.

thrip (θrɪp), *v. dial.* [app. echoic: cf. FLIP *v.*]

†**1.** *intr.* To make a noise with thumb and finger which resembles the whispering of 'thrip' or 'flip'; *trans.* to snap (the fingers). *Obs.*

1594 NASHE *Unfort. Trav.* 33 He with clapping his handes and thripping his fingers seemed to dance an antike. *Ibid.* 34 A fifth..thript with his finger and his thumbe.

2. *trans.* To jerk with a slight movement.

1674 N. FAIRFAX *Bulk & Selv.* 125 A Watch or a Jack, by being only wown up without thripping the balance or flyer. **1901** 'ZACK' *T. Dunstable Weir* 190 Her zot under the big fig tree, thripping her lace-bobbins in and out.

†**3.** [Prob. the same word.] To spin. *Obs. dial.* Hence † '**thripping** *vbl. sb.*

a **1652** BROME *Eng. Moor* III. i, *Q.* But where about in Norfolk wert thou bred? *P.* At Thripperstown, Sir, near the City of Norwich. *Q.* Where they live much by spinning with the Rocks? *P.* Thripping they call it, Sir. *Ibid.* IV. v, Yes, he has learn'd to thrip among the Mothers.

thrip, erron. sing. form of THRIPS.

thripell, þ-, obs. or dial. form of TRIPLE.

thripple ('θrɪp(ə)l), *sb.* Now *local.* Also 5 **þerrepyll,** 7–8 **thriple.** [Origin not ascertained: the suffix appears to be -EL or -LE, as in *handle, shovel*, etc.] A movable framework fitted upon a cart, so as to project in every direction beyond its sides, and thus to extend its carrying surface when loaded with hay, etc.; a cart-ladder, shelving.

14.. *Metr. Voc.* in Wr.-Wülcker 628/10 *Epredia,* the þerrepyllis. **1686** PLOT *Staffordsh.* 354 The Cart-ladder or thripple both before and behind being to be taken off at pleasure. **1688** R. HOLME *Armoury* III. 339/2 In an Oxe Teeame [the Cart Lathers] are termed Thriples. **1891** *Berrow's Worcester Jrnl.* 28 Mar. 7/2 His pair of thripples were new ones. He bought the thripples from defendant in exchange for some hay hauling he had done for him.

† '**thripple,** *v. Obs.* [Origin unknown: in form a dim. or freq.: see -LE 3.] *intr.* To practise small economies; to exercise mean thrift.

1583 STUBBES *Anat. Abus.* M vj b, This makes many a one to thripple and pinch, to runne into debte and daunger.

thrippling, *vbl. sb. Sc.* ? *Obs.* [app. f. RIPPLING *vbl. sb.*[1] with *thr-* for *r-*, as in *thresh, thrush*, for *rush.*] ***thrippling-comb,*** a comb-like implement for cleaning flax or hemp; = RIPPLE *sb.*[1]

1728 RAMSAY *Bob of Dunblane* i, Lend me your braw hemp heckle And I'll lend you my thrippling kame. **1874** *Mem. Alloa* 74 His winsome thrifty dame Plyin' wi' eident han' her thriplin' kaim.

‖**Thrips** (θrɪps). *Entom.* Often erron. taken as pl., with a false sing. thrip; the analogical Eng. pl. would be *thripses.* [L. *thrips* (Pliny), a. Gr. θρίψ, pl. θρῖπες a wood-worm.] **a.** The typical genus of the *Thripsidæ* or *Thripidæ*, the sole family of the order *Thysanoptera* (formerly called *Physopoda*), comprising minute insects with four fringed wings, many of which are injurious to various plants; an insect of this genus or family. **b.** Erroneously applied to any one of the *Jassidæ*, a hemipterous family of leaf-hoppers that feed on the grape-vine.

[**1658** ROWLAND *Moufet's Theat. Ins.* 1082 Those [worms] that are bred in..dry wood are called Thripes.] **1795** *Gentl. Mag.* LXV. II. 629/1 The whole genus of *thrips* is a perfectly innocent animal. **1829** J. L. KNAPP *Jrnl. Nat.* 299 The wireworm destroys the root, the thrips the germ of the wheat. **1844** DARWIN in *Life & Lett.* (1887) II. 30, I have seen a microscopic Thrips and a Cecidomya take flight from a flower..with pollen adhering to them. **1851** *B'ham & Midl. Gard. Mag.* Aug. 139 If thrip be troublesome, fine muslin bags should be fastened over the buds. **1869** *Rep. U.S. Comm. Agric.* 217 What insects are most injurious to the vine?.. Wisconsin: The thrips to a small extent. **1881** E. A. ORMEROD *Injur. Insects* (1890) 97 The attack of Corn Thrips..often does a great deal of harm very quietly. **1892** E. P. DIXON *Seed Catalogue* 3 Sufficient moisture to keep the red spider and thrip at bay.

thris, thrise, thrisse, obs. forms of THRICE.

thrissel, thristle, etc., obs. or dial. ff. THISTLE, THROSTLE.

thrist, obs. f. THIRST, THRUST.

† '**thristar.** *Sc. Obs.* [f. *thrist*, THRUST *v.* + -AR[3].] One who thrusts, a thruster.

1500–20 DUNBAR *Poems* lxiii. 47 Thrimlaris and thristaris, as thay war woid, Kokenis, and kennis na man of gude.

†**thriste,** *a. Obs.* [OE. *þríste* = OS. *thrîsti* (MLG., LG. *drîste*, whence Du. *driest*, Ger. *dreist*); not found elsewhere in Teutonic. Ultimate origin unknown: see suggestions in Kluge and Franck.] Bold, daring; audacious, presumptuous.

c **897** K. ÆLFRED *Gregory's Past. C.* Proem 23 Ðylæs..he to ðriste & to stið sie for ðy underfenge his lareowdomes. *a* **1023** WULFSTAN *Hom.* l. (Napier) 270 Ðencan þa nu, þe to þam þriste syn, þæt hiȝ god oferseoð. *c* **1175** *Lamb. Hom.* 117 Fela stuntnesse beoð..þer þe dusie mon bið þriste. *c* **1205** LAY. 25549 Næs þer nan swa þriste cniht under criste. *a* **1250** *Owl & Night.* 758 For ic can craft & ic kan lyste & þarfore ic am þus þriste.

thriste, obs. f. THIRST, THRUST, TRIST.

thrithing, -er, earlier ff. TRITHING, -ER: cf. also RIDING *sb.*

thrittene, -tende, -tethe, -ty, etc., obs. ff. THIRTEEN, -TEENTH, THIRTIETH, -TY.

† '**thrivage.** *Obs. rare*[−1]. [f. THRIVE *v.* + -AGE.] The quality or degree of thriving.

1610 W. FOLKINGHAM *Art of Survey* I. iii. 6 In Grouth, the thriuage, verdure, fruitage, prematurance, &c. of particular Vegetables are regardable.

thrive (θraɪv), *v.* Pa. t. **throve** (θrəʊv); pa. pple. **thriven** ('θrɪv(ə)n). Also pa. t. and pple. **thrived** (θraɪvd). [ME. *þrive*, first in Ormin (*þrifenn*), ad. ON. *þrífa-sk* refl., to thrive. So Sw. *trifvas*, Da. *trives* to thrive, flourish. No trace appears in English of the reflexive suffix, which must have been dropped before the word became naturalized. ON. *þrífa-sk* is in form the reflexive or passive of *þrífa*, recorded in the senses 'to clutch, grip, grasp, lay hold of with sudden effort'.

(For the sense-history Fritzner, Falk and Torp compare *taka-sk*, similarly used. The non-reflexive use may have started from the pa. pple *þrifinn*, thriven.)]

A. Illustration of Forms.

1. *Inf.* and *Pres. stem.* 3 (*Orm.*) **þrifenn,** 3–5 **þriue(n,** 4–5 **þryve,** 4–6 **thryfe, thryue** (5 **þr-, thrywe**), 5–6 **thrife, thryff(e,** 6 **thrif,** 4–7 **thriue,** 5– **thrive.**

c **1200** ORMIN 10868, & þrifenn aȝȝ & waxenn aȝȝ Inn alle gode þinge. *a* **1300** þriue [see B. I]. **13..** *Cursor M.* 12139 (Cott.) Âls mot we thriue. *c* **1375** *Sc. Leg. Saints* xxv. (*Julian*) 365 Allace! I thocht nocht fore to thryfe. **1398** þryue [see B. I]. *c* **1400** *Destr. Troy* 4832 þan thrive we þe bettur. *c* **1425** *Cast. Persev.* 548 in *Macro Plays* 93 Fast he gunne to thrywe. *c* **1460** þrywe [see B. I]. *c* **1500** *Debate Carpenter's Tools* in Halliw. *Nugæ Poet.* 14 He thouht ever fore to thryffe. **1508** DUNBAR *Tua Mariit Wemen* 488 That mai nought..thrif sa as thai wald. **1535** STEWART *Cron. Scot.* (Rolls) II. 398 We will nocht thryfe this ȝeir.

2. *Pa. t.* α. *north.* 3 **þraf,** 4 **thraf(e, thrave (-we),** 6 **thraif,** 9 **thrave** (also *arch.*).

c **1200** þraf [see B. I]. *a* **1300** Thraf, thrafe [see B. 2]. *c* **1375** *Sc. Leg. Saints* xxvii. (*Machor*) 49 He thrawe, þat wele fosterit was. *a* **1400** *Sir Perc.* 212 He wexe and wele thrafe. *a* **1578** LINDESAY (Pitscottie) *Chron. Scot.* (S.T.S.) II. 53 Fre that tyme fourtht the earle Bothewell thraif newer. *a* **1850** ROSSETTI *Dante & Circ.* I. (1874) 186 While yet my body thrave On earth. *a* **1910** T. DUNLOP in *Poets Ayrshire* 261 Brawer bairn..Never thrave.

β. 4 **þrof, -ff,** 4–5 **þroof,** 5 **þrofe, throf(e,** (6 *Sc.* **throuff**), 8– **throve.**

c **1330** R. BRUNNE *Chron. Wace* (Rolls) 1885 [The Britons] multeplyed, & wel þrof. *c* **1380** WYCLIF *Sel. Wks.* II. 411 In Cristis tyme..þroof þe Chirche. **1399** LANGL. *Rich. Redeles* III. 137 As he þat þroff neuere. **1470–85** MALORY *Arthur* VI. vii. 192 He..smote doune twelue knyghtes, and the moost party of hem neuer throfe after. **1597** in *Spalding Club Misc.* (1841) I. 179 Fra that tyme furthe, the said Janet throuff never. **1777** ROBERTSON *Hist. Amer.* I. I. 45 These throve prosperously. **1830, 1852** Throve [see B. 1, 1 b].

γ. 4 **þryued,** 7– **thrived.**

13.. *E.E. Allit. P.* C. 521 Couþe I not þole bot as þou þer þryued ful fewe. **1614, 1647, 1790** Thrived [see B. 1 b]. **1622–1883** [see B. 2 b].

3. *Pa. pple.* α. 4 **þriuen,** 4–5 **þ-, thryuen, threuen,** 5 **thryffyn, threvyn,** 4–7 **thriuen,** 6– **thriven;** 5 **y-threve, thryve,** 6–7 **thriue (þriv).**

c **1330** R. BRUNNE *Chron. Wace* (Rolls) 6546 Gentil damysels.., þat able to mennes companye were þryuen. **13..** *Cursor M.* 5641 (Gött.) Quen it [the child] was thriuen and sum del ald. *a* **1400** *Theophilus* ii. in *Eng. Studien* XXXII. 5 How wel þat he was threuen. **14..** *MS. Cantab. Ff.* ii. 38 lf. 128 (Halliwell) He ys welle y-threve. **1622** R. AYLETT in Farr *S.P. Jas. I* (1848) 202 By her when wee in life of grace haue thriue, With her we euer shall in glory liue. **1643** *Plain English* 16 The guard is thriven to an Army. **1830–3** LYELL *Princ. Geol.* III. xlii. (1868) II. 459 The ass has thriven very generally in the new world.

β. 8 **throve.**

1758 *Herald* No. 21. II. 89 How very prosperously the shoots of your planting have throve.

γ. 4 **þriuid,** 7–9 **thrived.**

13.. þriuid [see B. 4]. **1622** MABBE tr. *Aleman's Guzman d'Alf.* I. 228 How haue you thriu'd this yeare? **1654** GAYTON *Pleas. Notes* III. xii. 155 He might have thriv'd better upon the Tanzies. **1901** *Munsey's Mag.* XXV. 335 All the protected species have thrived wonderfully at Nehasane.

B. Signification.

1. *intr.* To grow or develop well and vigorously; to flourish, prosper.

a. Of persons or plants: in early quots. (esp. Ormin) simply †To grow, to increase in some respect; also †to be successful or eminent in arms or war; in quot. 1711, †to grow stout (*obs.*). Freq. const. *on.*

c **1200** ORMIN 8973 Hire sune wex & þraf I wissdom & inn elde. *Ibid.* 10868. *a* **1300** *K. Horn* 620 (MS. C.) Ne miȝte þer non þriue. *c* **1300** *Havelok* 280 þe kinges douther bigan þriue. *c* **1330** [see A. 3 α]. **1398** TREVISA *Barth. De P.R.* VIII. i. (Tollem. MS.), Ayer, by þe whiche all þinge þat haþ lyf breþeþ and þryueþ. *Ibid.* XVII. lxii. (Bodl. MS.), Fige treen þriueþ lasse in þe norþe contreies. *c* **1400** [see THRIVING *ppl. a.* 1]. *c* **1460** *Wisdom* 1021 in *Macro Plays* 69 As many roddys as myght grow or þrywe In þe space of a days Jornye. **1530** PALSGR. 756/1, I thrive, as a tree or herbe groweth and dothe well, *je vegete.* **1697** J. LEWIS *Mem. Dk. Glocester* (1789) 6 The young Prince continued there about twelve months, thriving apace. **1711** STEELE *Spect.* No. 32 ¶2 My Lady Ample..grudges herself meat and drink, for fear she should thrive by them. **1830** H. N. COLERIDGE *Grk. Poets* (1834) 357 The child throve wonderfully under this caustic treatment. *c* **1862** E. DICKINSON *Poems* (1955) II. 403 The Hemlock's nature thrives—on cold. **1886** CORBETT *Fall of Asgard* I. 50 In the clear mountain air he grew and thrived with marvellous rapidity. **1940** J. BUCHAN *Memory Hold-the-Door* iii. 84, I throve on a diet of oatmeal, mutton and strong tea.

b. *fig.* of immaterial things. Freq. const. *on.*

1613 *Will. I* in *Harl. Misc.* (Malh.) III. 163 Two great impediments that valour cannot thrive. **1614** C. BROOKE *Ghost Rich. III* Poems (1872) 106 What? wilt thou..where once Wisdome thriu'd, let Folly grow? **1647** DIGGES *Unlawf. Taking Arms* 50 Those innocent times, when Christianity thrived upon suffering. **1790** REYNOLDS *Disc.* xv. (1876) 110 The manner of Michel Angelo thrived but little with them. **1852** MISS YONGE *Cameos* (1877) II. xxii. 239 The spirit of resistance throve the more. **1907** *Edin. Rev.* Oct. 406 Thought thrives on conflict. **1972** *Sci. Amer.* Aug. 73/1 Patient rapport and cooperation thrived on specific instructions.

2. a. Of a person or community: To prosper; to increase in wealth; to be successful or fortunate;

in early use sometimes †To have (good or bad) fortune, to speed, fare, 'hap' (well or ill). Freq. const. *on*.

a **1300** *Cursor M.* 3911 (Cott.) Iacob wex riche, his childer thraf [*F.* thrafe, *T.* þroof]. ? *a* **1366** CHAUCER *Rom. Rose* 1067 Wel yvel mote they thryve and thee. *c* **1400** *Laud Troy Bk.* 16823 Ther schal but fewe—so mote I thryue!—Off hem passe away on lyue! *c* **1460** *Wisdom* 781 in *Macro Plays* 61 Ye! & ewyll be þou thryvande! **1530** PALSGR. 755/2, I thrive, I go forwarde in rychesse. **1593** SHAKS. *Rich. II*, IV. i. 78 As I intend to thriue in this new World. **1657** J. SERGEANT *Schism Dispach't* 225 Since he thriv'd best among the Gentiles. **1709** MRS. MANLEY *Secret Mem.* (1720) III. 250 He thriv'd in all his Pretences. **1883** TYNDALL in *Contemp. Rev.* XLIV. 52 Nations..and even villages thrive in proportion to the activity of their industry. **1930** G. B. SHAW *Apple Cart* p. xxv, The armament firms thrive on war; the glaziers gain by broken windows. **1961** J. HELLER *Catch-22* (1962) ix. 83 He thrived on good wit and stimulating intellectual conversation.

b. Of a thing: To be successful, turn out well.

1587 *Mirr Mag., Humber* xvii, God is iust, iniustice will not thrive. **1622** MABBE tr. *Aleman's Guzman d'Alf.* II. 240, I (kind foole) seeing the world thriu'd with me. **1640** E. DACRES tr. *Machiavel's Prince* 138 His coosenages all thriv'd well with him; for hee knew how to play this part cunningly. **1883** F. DAY *Indian Fish* 9 (Fish. Exhib. Publ.) A few years since, fisheries thrived along the Beloochistan coast.

†**3.** ? To be saved, to remain over. *Obs. rare.*

1509 *Parl. Devylles* xlv, Twelue lepes of relefe therof dyde thryue, To men and chyldren that had nede.

†**4.** *trans.* (?) To cause to thrive; to prosper. *Obs. rare*$^{-1}$.

13.. *Cursor M.* 22388 (Fairf.) þat alle þat wille him [Antichrist] sal with-stande, Salle þriuid [*other MSS.* coround, cruned, crouned] be to life lastande.

† **thrive**, *sb. Obs. rare.* [f. prec. vb. Cf. ON. *þrif* thrift.] Thriving; profit: = THRIFT *sb.*[1] 1, 2.

1592 WYRLEY *Armorie, Capitall de Buz* ii, Such one as seeks not after gainfull thriue, But firmely doth his thoughts to honor bind. **1604** *Sc. Acts Jas. VI* (1816) IV. 263/2 The Sweitnes of the thrife, Peace, wealth, and felicitie.

thriveless ('θraɪvlɪs), *a. poet.* [f. THRIVE *v.* or *sb.* + -LESS.] Not thriving; lacking prosperity or success; unsuccessful, profitless.

c **1520** *Treat. Galaunt* (1860) 16 This causeth our galauntes, by theyr nacyon Neuerthryfte and thryueles, noye euer vs so nere. **1620** QUARLES *Jonah* (1638) 25 The feeble Sailors..Forbeare their thrivelesse labours. **1635** —— *Embl.* I. xii, And thou, whose thrivelesse hands are ever strayning Earths fluent Brests, into an empty Sive. **1835** BROWNING *Paracelsus* I. 255 The dull stagnation of a soul, content, Once foiled, to leave betimes a thriveless quest.

thriven ('θrɪv(ə)n), *ppl. a.* Forms: see THRIVE *v.* A. 3. [pa. pple. of THRIVE *v.* Cf. ON. *þrifinn.*]

1. Advanced in growth, grown; grown up. Now only in comb., as ***ill-thriven*** (Sc. *ill-three'n*).

13.. *Cursor M.* 14806 (Cott.) And said, 'Fast es he throd and thriuen [*Fairf.* þis man is wele þriuen], And mikel grace ai es him giuen'. **13..** *E.E. Allit. P.* B. 298 Hym watz þe nome Noe,..He had þre þryuen sunez. *c* **1400** *Destr. Troy* 13760 The child..Wex & wele threvan in winturs a few. *a* **1400-50** *Alexander* 2709 A heuy As..A thing threuyn is & thike. **1697** DRYDEN *Virg. Georg.* III. 743 The thriven Calves in Meads their Food forsake. **1806, 1843** Ill-thriven [see ILL- B.]. **1907** *Daily Chron.* 8 May 5/7 The pretensions of a neurotic, ill-thriven youth.

†**2.** As an epithet of commendation, esp. in the alliterative phrase ***thriven and thro*** (see THRO *a.*[2]): ? Eminent, excellent, worthy, honourable, noble. Cf. THRIFTY *a.* 2. *Obs.*

13.. in Wright *Lyric P.* 23 ʒef he beth thryven ant thowen in theode. **13..** *E.E. Allit. P.* A. 1191 þe perle me prayed þat watz so þryuen. **13..** *Gaw. & Gr. Knt.* 1740 Hir þryuen face & hir þrote þrowen al naked. Hir brest bare bifore, & bihinde eke. *a* **1400-50** *Alexander* 1326 (Ashmole MS.) He laschis out a lange swerde.., Threschis doun in a thrawe many threuyn dukis. *Ibid.* 3307 Twa hundreth thousand..all of threuen kniʒtis.

3. That has thriven; successful, prosperous.

1863 HAWTHORNE *Our Old Home* (1879) 114 The careful, thrify, thriven man of property.

thriver ('θraɪvə(r)). Now *rare.* [f. THRIVE *v.* + -ER[1].] One who or that which thrives.

1573 TUSSER *Husb.* (1878) 25 Ill tithers ill thriuers most commonlie bee. ? **1601** BACON *Let. to Sir T. Lucy* Wks. 1879 II. 25/2 If my brother or myself were either thrivers, or fortunate in the queen's service. *c* **1613** MIDDLETON *No Wit like Woman's* I. iii, They're the best thrivers In turnips, hartichalks, and cabbishes. *c* **1659** *Elegy on Cleveland* 47 C.'s Wks. (1687) 278 Timists be only Thrivers: But a Brain That's freely Generous scorns Servile Gain.

thriving ('θraɪvɪŋ), *vbl. sb.* [f. THRIVE *v.* + -ING[1].] The action of the verb THRIVE, in various senses; prospering; prosperity; vigorous growth.

c **1460** *How Gd. Wif taught Dou.* 164 in Hazl. *E.P.P.* I. 191 Make the nought to riche of other mannys thinge; The bolder to spende the worse thriuing. **1530** PALSGR. 716/1, I set up a man, I am the occasyon of his thrivynge, or avauncement. **1622** E. MISSELDEN *Free Trade* 79 This their better thriuing is because euery man is at libertie to be a Merchant at his pleasure. **1707** MORTIMER *Husb.* (1721) II. 81 If a Tree begins to abate of its thriving, lop off some of the Branches. **1878** J. TODHUNTER *Alcestis* (1879) 28 'Twas when he made processions through the land, To test his people's thriving.

'**thriving**, *ppl. a.* Also 5 *n. dial.* -and(e. [f. THRIVE *v.* + -ING[2].] That thrives, in various senses.

†**1.** In alliterative use: Excelling, excellent, worthy; = THRIVEN 2, THRIFTY 2. *Obs.*

13.. *E.E. Allit. P.* B. 751 What if þretty þryuande be þrad in ʒon tounez. **13..** *Gaw. & Gr. Knt.* 1980 Fele þryuande þonkkez he þrat hom to haue. *c* **1400** *Destr. Troy* 1482 Of his sonnes... The þrid was a þro knight, þrivand in Armys. *Ibid.* 5435, 5458, etc. *Ibid.* 4103 Machaon & Polidus..triet shippes broght Two & thretty full thryuond, & þrong into prise. *c* **1470** *Golagros & Gaw.* 345 Ye ar thre in this thede, thriuand oft in thrang.

2. Growing vigorously; flourishing (physically).

c **1645** HOWELL *Lett.* (1650) II. x. 15 The dust of Martyrs were the thrivingst seeds of Christianity. **1681** FLAVEL *Meth. Grace* xxv. 438 The new creature is a thriving creature, growing from strength to strength. **1784** COWPER *Task* II. 714 Learning grew Beneath his care, a thriving vig'rous plant. **1848** DICKENS *Dombey* iii, 'How is Master Paul, Richards?' 'Quite thriving, sir, and well.'

3. Prospering, doing well in business; successful, fortunate.

1607 TOURNEUR *Rev. Trag.* IV. iv, Aske but the thriuing'st harlot in cold bloud; Shee'd giue the world to make her honour good. **1710** STEELE *Tatler* No. 200 ¶ 2, I am not fond of a Man only for being of..a Thriving Temper. **1758** JOHNSON *Idler* No. 16 ¶ 2 Ned was..considered as a thriving trader. **1849** MACAULAY *Hist. Eng.* iii. I. 375 Two great towns, which have a large and thriving trade with each other. *Ibid.* vi. II. 135 The colonists were in a thriving condition.

'**thrivingly**, *adv.* [f. prec. + -LY[2].]

†**1.** In a worthy or honourable manner; also, excellently, finely. *Obs.*

13.. *St. Erkenwolde* 47 in Horstm. *Altengl. Leg.* (1881) 267 A throghe of thykke stone, thryuandly hewene. **13..** *Gaw. & Gr. Knt.* 1080 Now I þonk yow þryuandely þurʒ alle oþer þynge. *a* **1400-50** *Alexander* 3747 Scho lengis in oure burʒe, And is oure thewis of oure thede thryfandly enfourmed. *c* **1470** [see THRILL *sb.*[2]].

2. Prosperously, successfully, flourishingly.

1745 H. WALPOLE *Lett. to Mann* (1834) II. 22 Our coalition goes on thrivingly. **1833** *Fraser's Mag.* VII. 571 May my poor silly sheep go on thrivingly. **1837** HAWTHORNE *Twice-Told T.* (1851) I. xiv. 231 Others..grow thrivingly among brick and stone.

So '**thrivingness** *rare*, thriving condition.

1818 in TODD. **1864** KINGSLEY *Let. to Mrs. K.* in *Life* (1879) II. 167 Thrivingness and improvement everywhere.

DOMI MINA
NVS TIO
ILLV MEA